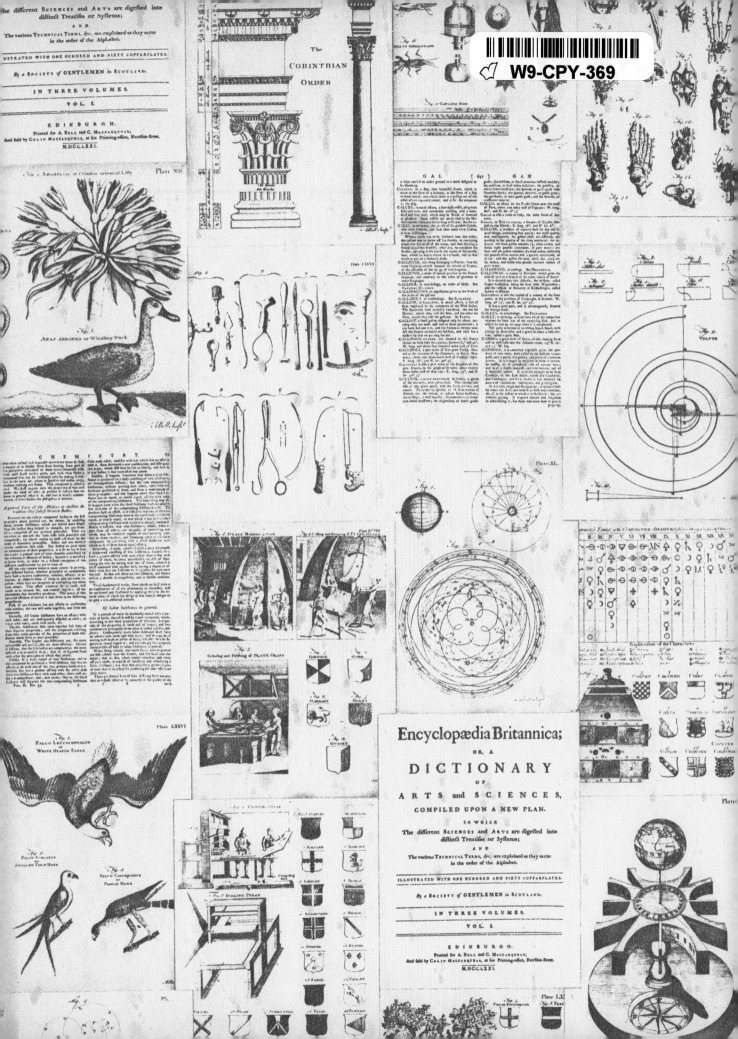

ENCYCLOPÆDIA
BRITANNICA

THE UNIVERSITY OF CHICAGO

The Encyclopædia Britannica
is published with the editorial advice of the faculties
of the University of Chicago; a committee
of members of the faculties of Oxford, Cambridge, London, and
Edinburgh universities; a committee at the University of Toronto;
and a committee drawn from members of the faculty
of the University of Tokyo

*

"LET KNOWLEDGE GROW FROM MORE TO MORE
AND THUS BE HUMAN LIFE ENRICHED"

ENCYCLOPÆDIA BRITANNICA

VOLUME

19

First Published in 1768

by A Society of Gentlemen in Scotland

ENCYCLOPÆDIA BRITANNICA, INC.

William Benton, Publisher

CHICAGO · LONDON · TORONTO · GENEVA · SYDNEY · TOKYO · MANILA

FOUNDED A.D. 1768

ENCYCLOPÆDIA BRITANNICA

Volume 19

RAZOR TO SCHURZ

RAZOR, an implement used most commonly for shaving and frequently for cutting and shaping women's hair. Razors used for other purposes, such as scraping or slicing, are common tools in the home and in industry.

Prehistoric cave drawings indicate that early shaving implements included clam shells, shark's teeth, and sharpened flints. Flints are still used by primitive tribes in certain parts of the world. Some of the razors found in Egyptian tombs of the 4th millennium B.C. are of solid gold or copper. Nobles of later Egyptian history, who wore wigs, shaved their heads as well as their faces with razors, and priests had their entire bodies shaved every third day.

Excavations of Iron Age settlements in western Europe and Britain have established that warriors were buried with their razors as well as their swords. The 1st-century-B.C. Greek historian Diodorus Siculus described the Gauls as having shaven cheeks and long moustaches. According to Livy, the razor was introduced in Rome by Lucius Tarquinius Priscus (Tarquin), 5th legendary king of Rome, in the 6th century B.C. Romans considered shaving an effeminate Greek custom, however, and it was not generally adopted by them until the middle of the 5th century B.C., when a group of Greek-Sicilian barbers came to the mainland. Barber shops then appeared in Rome but were patronized only by those who could not afford slaves; the more prosperous citizens were shaved by their valets. The general Scipio Africanus was said to have been the first Roman to indulge in a daily shave.

In Britain, Sheffield became an international centre of the cutlery industry in the 18th and 19th centuries, and steel razors, with a great variety of ornamental handles, were made by highly skilled craftsmen who hollow-ground the blades individually. It was in Sheffield that Benjamin Huntsman produced the first crucible steel in 1740. Local manufacturers at first rejected this hard steel, but after its adoption in France were forced to recognize its superiority. (*See* SHEFFIELD: *Industries.*)

Safety Razor.—A razor with a guard along one edge—the forerunner of the modern safety razor—was advertised in the Sheffield Directory for 1828. In 1880 a hoe-shaped safety razor was manufactured in the U.S. Oliver Wendell Holmes endorsed it, reporting enthusiastically that with it "one cannot cut himself." Two additional types of safety razor were soon on the market, but the

sales of all were modest. Shortly after the beginning of the 20th century, King C. Gillette patented and began to manufacture in the U.S. a safety razor with double-edged replaceable blades, which became very popular. In the early 1960s manufacturers in several countries produced stainless steel blades for safety razors that had the advantage of longer usage than the older steel blades.

Electric Razor.—Patents on electric razors were issued in the U.S. as early as 1900. The first to be successfully manufactured was the one on which Jacob Schick, a retired Army colonel, applied for a patent in 1928 and which he placed on the market in 1931. Competitive models soon appeared.

The principle of the electric razor is similar to that of the barber's hair clipper. The shearing head, driven by a miniature motor, is divided into two sections, the outer one consisting of a series of slots to grip the hairs as they rest against the skin, the inner one comprising a series of saw-edged blades. In some models the shearing head is round, in others flat, and there are variations in the number and design of the blades and in such devices as auxiliary clippers for trimming sideburns.

See BARBER; CUTLERY. (J. AY.)

RE (RA), Egyptian god of the sun, one of the most important gods in the Egyptian pantheon. He was thought to travel across the sky in his boat each day, and during the night in another boat to make his passage through the underworld, where, in order to be born again for the new day, he had to vanquish the evil deity Apophis. Originally Re was but one of many solar deities, and indeed at first was not prominent at all. Eventually, however, his worship came to pervade that of all other solar gods and also that of many of the animal-headed deities. Thus are found such syncretisms as Re-Horakhte, Amon-Re, Sebek-Re, and Min-Re, among others. In turn, aspects of other gods influence Re himself; and his falcon-headed appearance may originate from the association with Horus (*q.v.*). The influence of Re was spread by his active and powerful priesthood at On (Heliopolis; *q.v.*), which was the centre of his worship. The priesthood in turn owed its influence, or perhaps only its increase, to the fact that Re came to be the official god of the pharaohs. Beginning with the second dynasty, Re became part of the royal name (so first Nebre), and others follow at various intervals until the fourth dynasty when the name of every king after Khufu contains Re. Finally, in the fifth dynasty, every king is both the son of Re and Re himself incarnate. This is the time of the great pyramids built by Khufu, Khafre, and Menkaure, and of the great obelisk temples to Re at Heliopolis itself.

With the resurgence of Egyptian power during the 18th dynasty, Re is associated with Amon (q.v.) of Thebes as Amon-Re, a god closely connected with the rulers. Indeed the revolutionary worship of Aton during the abortive Amarna period in the 18th dynasty (see IKHNATON) may well have been influenced by the theology of Heliopolis; and, of course, Aton is the disk of the sun whose worship had previously existed under the general heading of Re worship.

Like all other important solar gods, Re was worshiped or treated primarily as a creator god. Such creation myths as are known are influenced by Egyptian syncretism and universalism, so that stories about Re are similar to those of other gods (see CREATION, MYTHS OF). Nonetheless the earliest of these, carved on the pyramid of Neferkare (sixth dynasty), represents Re as rising from the ocean of chaos on the primeval hill, creating himself and then in turn the other eight gods who form one of the enneads (groups of nine) of Egyptian gods, Shu, Tefnut, Geb, Nut, Isis, Osiris, Set (Setekh), Nephthys. See also EGYPT: History: Ancient Religion.   (J. F. O.)

RÉ, ÎLE DE, an island in the Bay of Biscay, 1½ mi. (2.4 km.) off the west coast of France opposite La Pallice and La Rochelle, and included in the *département* of Charente-Maritime. Pop. (1962) 9,484. It covers an area of 33 sq.mi. (85 sq.km.), and is aligned northwest-southeast for 18 mi. (29 km.), with a breadth of usually 2 to 3 mi. (3 to 5 km.), but on the east coast an indentation, the Fier d'Ars, nearly divides it, leaving an isthmus only 80 yd. (73 m.) across. The island is separated from the coast of Vendée to the north by the shallow water of the Pertuis Breton. It is low-lying, surrounded by limestone reefs that enclose a marshy area in the north, and is scenically uninteresting. There is a considerable amount of cultivation of early vegetables (especially asparagus) and there are extensive salt fields and oyster beds along the coast. The chief settlements are Saint-Martin-de-Ré, a port on the north coast (with fortifications by Vauban), and La Flotte, a little fishing port and bathing resort. There are ruins of the medieval abbey of Saint-Laurent.   (AR. E. S.)

REACTION KINETICS is that branch of physical science which deals with the determination and interpretation of the rates of chemical change. The subject includes the consideration of the rates both of everyday but complicated reactions such as hardboiling an egg (an example of protein coagulation) and of simpler but less commonplace reactions such as the one between hydrogen and chlorine. Rates have been measured for slow reactions (e.g., the disintegration of ordinary uranium, only half of which will decompose in 5,000,000,000 years) and for fast reactions (e.g., the combination of hydrogen and sulfate ions, which may be half complete in about a billionth of a second). An attempt is made in each case to show quantitatively the effect of changes in the experimental conditions upon the reaction velocity, and to describe in as much detail as possible the behaviour of the molecules at the moment of their reaction.

Many familiar processes involve chemical reactions which proceed at measurable rates. For example, the rusting of iron, the fermentation of sugar, the "drying" of paint, the hardening of plaster of Paris, the baking of bread and the growth of plants, all involve chemical reactions of greater or lesser complexity, and for each example there is considerable interest in the rate of reaction. In general, these familiar processes are very complex, partly because many of the materials are not single pure compounds, but mixtures. It is well known, however, that the rusting (oxidation) of iron requires both air and water, and that the reaction proceeds much more rapidly near the ocean (where salt is deposited on the iron) than it does elsewhere. The rate of rusting also depends upon the composition of the metal (pure iron and stainless steel corrode less rapidly than do cast iron and mild steel) and on temperature (corrosion is rapid in a stream of steam and air). (See CORROSION AND OXIDATION OF METALS.)

Scientists have been largely concerned with measuring the rates of reactions such as the decomposition of ozone, the oxidation of

sulfur dioxide and the nitration of hydrocarbons; they assume that an understanding of these and similar reactions of pure chemicals will eventually lead to an understanding of more complex (if more familiar) reactions.

Studies of reaction velocity have not only played a fundamental role in the growth of theoretical chemistry; the concepts developed in these studies have also been highly fruitful in industry, especially in the field of catalysis (q.v.). A case in point is the Haber process for the manufacture of ammonia (q.v.), which is based in part on studies of reaction kinetics. Both theoretical and practical research in the field of reaction kinetics was by mid-century under way in hundreds of laboratories.

A specific example of a rate study is the work on the decomposition of hydrogen iodide to form hydrogen and iodine.

$$2HI \longrightarrow H_2 + I_2 \qquad (1)$$

This reaction proceeds at a rate convenient for measurement in the neighbourhood of $320°$ C., at which temperature not only the hydrogen and hydrogen iodide but even the iodine is gaseous. (This reaction is a reversible one; however, for the moment, it is better to postpone discussion of this complication and to consider only the reaction as written.) The rate of decomposition of hydrogen iodide increases as the quantity of hydrogen iodide per unit volume is increased; quantitatively, the rate is proportional to the square of the concentration of hydrogen iodide. The rate increases by a factor of 1.9 when the temperature is increased from $320°$ C. to $330°$ C. The reaction occurs within the body of the gas, and not on the glass walls of the vessel in which the experiment is performed.

The facts just cited have been interpreted to indicate that when two molecules of hydrogen iodide collide, a chemical change occurs only if the velocity of one of them with respect to the other exceeds 2.4 km./sec. (about 5,000 m.p.h.). The average diameter (so far as collision is concerned) of these hydrogen iodide molecules can also be calculated from the kinetic data; it is of an order of magnitude (0.8×10^{-8} cm.), roughly consistent with the results of other measurements of the sizes of molecules. The effective collisions (i.e., those which lead to reaction) result in a simple interchange of atoms; here the hydrogen and iodine atoms in each of the two colliding molecules of hydrogen iodide separate; simultaneously, the two hydrogen atoms combine to form a hydrogen molecule, and the two iodine atoms combine to form an iodine molecule.

For the discussion of even the simple example of the decomposition of hydrogen iodide, it has been necessary to employ the elementary concepts of chemistry (q.v.) and of the kinetic theory of matter (q.v.). For the more detailed treatment of reaction kinetics which follows, a somewhat more extensive knowledge of these subjects is assumed. In the last sections of this article, a more sophisticated presentation is attempted.

History.—Gross differences in the rates of chemical reactions have long been recognized. By the beginning of the 19th century, several instances were known where the rate of a chemical change could be greatly increased by adding to the reacting system a small quantity of some apparently inert material. For example, it was discovered in 1796 that the dehydrogenation of alcohols proceeds much more rapidly in the presence of metals than it does in their absence. In 1836, Jöns Jacob Berzelius grouped together many reactions of this type and gave the name "catalysts" to the materials which accelerate chemical change. (The modern definition of catalysts is given below.) Although the qualitative concept of reaction rate was by that time well established, the first quantitative measurement and mathematical formulation of reaction velocity is generally credited to L. F. Wilhelmy, who, in 1850, measured the rate of "inversion" (hydrolysis) of cane sugar.

Definitions.—Chemical reactions can be classified as homogeneous or heterogeneous. Homogeneous reactions are those (like the decomposition of hydrogen iodide) which occur completely within one phase (gaseous, liquid or solid). Heterogeneous reactions are those (like the reaction between a metal and an acid) in which the reactants are components of two or more phases (solid and gas, solid and liquid, two mutually immiscible liquids, etc.) or in which one or more reactants undergo chemical change at an interface; i.e., on the surface of a solid catalyst.

Reactions may also be classified as "reversible" or "irreversible." An irreversible reaction is one in which the reactants, if mixed in the proper proportions, are almost completely converted to the reaction products; a reversible reaction is one in which appreciable quantities of all the reactants and of all the reaction products are present in the system no matter how long the reaction is allowed to proceed. The mixture eventually formed in such a reversible reaction is called the equilibrium mixture; the same equilibrium mixture may be prepared from suitable amounts of either the reactants or the reaction products. For example, the same equilibrium mixture of hydrogen, iodine and hydrogen iodide (at definite temperature and pressure) can be prepared by starting either with equivalent quantities of hydrogen and iodine or with pure hydrogen iodide. If the definition of equilibrium is that adopted in thermodynamics (q.v.), then every reaction is, in principle, reversible. There are reactions, however, where the extent of the reverse reaction is too small to be detected by any experimental means at present known; such reactions are usually regarded, for the purposes of kinetics, as irreversible.

"Order" of Reaction.—The fundamental law of reaction kinetics was developed by the Norwegian chemists C. M. Guldberg and P. Waage around 1867 (a similar formulation was made independently by Jacobus Hendricus van't Hoff). They assumed that, at constant temperature, the rate of any simple chemical reaction is proportional to the product of the concentrations of the various reacting substances. They showed in a general way that their law of chemical change is consistent with the kinetic molecular theory of matter, and that the data for many chemical reactions could be formulated quantitatively in terms of their theory. Since 1870, the concepts of Guldberg and Waage have been extended and modified, but most of reaction kinetics is still based upon their work.

Consider the simple homogeneous, irreversible reaction between two compounds, A and B (the reactants), to form C and D (the reaction products).

$$A + B \longrightarrow C + D \qquad (2)$$

An example of this sort of reaction is the saponification of ethyl acetate by alkali:

$$CH_3CO_2C_2H_5 + OH^- \longrightarrow CH_3CO_2^- + C_2H_5OH \qquad (2')$$
$$A B C D$$

Equations (2) and (2') as written represent the stoichiometry of the chemical change; i.e., the equations show the relationship between the weights of the initial reactants and those of the final products. The reaction rate may be proportional to the concentrations of the reactants which appear in the stoichiometric equation; if, however, the reaction occurs in several consecutive chemical steps, or requires a catalyst, the kinetics may be more complicated (see below) than those which could be implied from the stoichiometry.

The treatment for a simple case follows. At the beginning of the reaction, the compounds A and B are present in definite concentrations, say a_0 and b_0 moles per litre respectively[1]; the concentrations of C and D are zero. As the reaction proceeds, the concentrations of A and B decrease, whereas the concentrations of C and D increase. If the concentrations of A and B at any instant are represented by the symbols (A) and (B), then the law of Guldberg and Waage states that wherever equation (2) represents the true kinetic course of the reaction, the reaction velocity, v, is proportional to (A) and to (B). This statement in mathematical form is

$$v = k(A)(B) \qquad (3)$$

where k, the proportionality factor, is called the rate constant. Note that the rate of reaction, v, and the rate constant, k, are not the same, but are connected by an equation of the form of (3).

An equation such as (3) may accurately describe the rate of a chemical reaction. Unfortunately, however, a good experimental method for directly measuring the rate, v, of a reaction is usually not to be found. The quantities which can usually be determined experimentally are the time and the concentrations of the reactants or reaction products. An equation such as (3) can be

transformed by the methods of calculus (q.v.) into an equation expressing a relationship between these concentrations and time. Although the details of this transformation are in no way necessary for the succeeding argument, they are nevertheless presented here for the sake of continuity.

If the concentration of C at any instant is represented by x, then the rate, v, of formation of C is dx/dt, the derivative of x with respect to time; and equation (3) can be replaced by (3').

$$v = \frac{dx}{dt} = k(A)(B) = k(a_0 - x)(b_0 - x) \qquad (3')$$

The integrated form of equation (3) is

$$\log_e \frac{b_0(a_0 - x)}{a_0(b_0 - x)} = kt(a_0 - b_0) \qquad (4)[2]$$

where t is the time measured from the beginning of the reaction; the other symbols have been previously defined. In principle, it should be possible to obtain for every reaction an equation, analogous to (4), from which the concentrations of the various reactants and products at any moment may be calculated.

One method of testing experimentally whether equations (3) and (4) adequately describe the rate of any particular reaction is to measure x (the concentration of C) at several different times, t. An attempt is then made to choose a single value for the rate constant k such that all the sets of corresponding values of x and t satisfy equation (4). If this attempt is successful, the experiment is then repeated at the same temperature but with different initial concentrations (a_0 and b_0) of A and B. If and only if these new data also satisfy equation (4) with the rate constant k unchanged, the demonstration that the reaction obeys the rate equations (3) and (4) is complete. The constant, k, is thus independent of the initial concentrations of A and B; it is, however, a function of the temperature and it depends of course upon the chemical nature of the reactants A and B. Fig. 1 is a graphical representation of equation (4) for the saponification of ethyl acetate.

If the equations for various chemical reactions are treated as was equation (3) for reaction (2'), then these reactions fall into a number of different classes. A reaction the rate of which may be described by an equation of the form

$$v = k(A) \qquad (5)$$

is called a first order reaction; one described by an equation of the form

$$v = k(A)^2 \quad \text{or} \quad v = k(A)(B) \qquad (6) \text{ or } (6')$$

is called a second order reaction, etc. In general, a reaction the rate of which may be described by the equation

$$v = k(A)^m(B)^n(C)^p(D)^q \ldots \ldots \qquad (7)$$

is called a reaction of order r, where $r = m + n + p + q + \ldots \ldots$ Such a reaction is said to be of order m with respect to A, of order n with respect to B, etc. (Some reactions may be of nonintegral order; e.g., half-order. The majority of known reactions are of first or second order.)

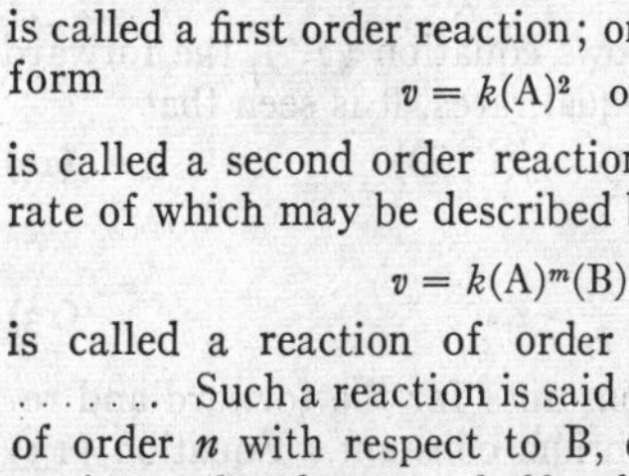

FIG. 1.—SAPONIFICATION OF 0.01M ETHYL ACETATE WITH 0.01M NaOH AT 25° C. DOTS ARE EXPERIMENTAL POINTS; LINE IS THEORETICAL FOR $k = 6.5$ Min^{-1}M^{-1}

In certain reactions, such as the inversion of cane sugar,

$$C_{12}H_{22}O_{11} + H_2O \rightarrow 2C_6H_{12}O_6 \qquad (8)$$

the rate is proportional to the concentration of some substance (in this instance, the hydronium ion of the acid) (see ACIDS AND BASES), which does not appear among either the reactants or the reaction products in the chemical equation; the reaction cited (equation [8]) is said to be catalyzed by hydronium ion H_3O^+, or hydrated hydrogen ion.

$$v = k(C_{12}H_{22}O_{11})(H_3O^+) \qquad (9)$$

If the catalyst is one of the reaction products, the reaction is said to be autocatalyzed.

Reversible Reactions.—The reactions hitherto described have been assumed to be irreversible, in the sense defined above. If the reaction between the compounds A and B, on the one hand,

---

[1] For reactions in the gas phase, the partial pressure of each gas is used as a measure of its concentration.

[2] Where $a_0 = b_0$, the corresponding equation is $\dfrac{x}{a_0(a_0 - x)} = kt$ $\qquad (4')$

and C and D, on the other, is reversible, then equation (2) must be rewritten.

$$A + B \rightleftarrows C + D \qquad (2'')$$

Wherever equation (2'') represents the true kinetic course of the reactions, the rates v_f of the "forward" and v_r of the "reverse" reactions are given by equations (10) and (10').

$$v_f = k_f(A)(B) \qquad (10)$$
$$v_r = k_r(C)(D) \qquad (10')$$

If the reaction is begun by mixing A and B (either pure or in solution), the initial concentrations of C and D are each zero; hence the rate, v_r, of the reverse reaction is also zero. However, as A and B react to form C and D, these products in turn react to regenerate A and B. The net rate at which C and D are formed is therefore the difference between v_f and v_r.

$$v = v_f - v_r = k_f(A)(B) - k_r(C)(D) \qquad (11)$$

The net rates of the forward and reverse reactions for a particular case are shown graphically in fig. 2. In the reaction in question, a mixture of the two tautomers (see TAUTOMERISM) of bromonitrocamphor is formed both from the normal (N) and from the pseudo (P) isomer.

The rate at which the equilibrium mixture is formed from pure N is shown in the upper curve; the rate at which the equilibrium mixture is formed from pure P is shown in the lower curve.

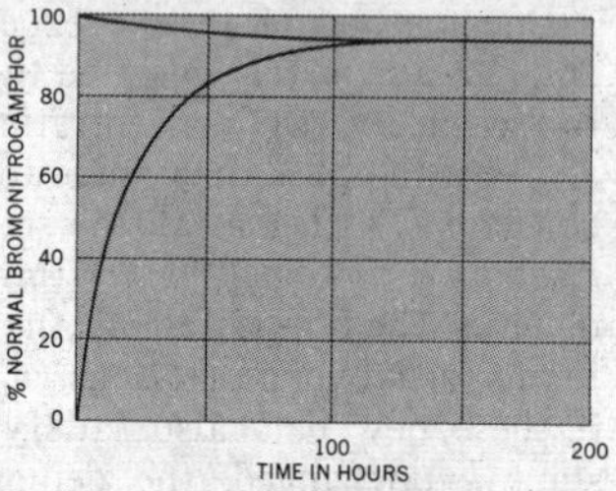

FIG. 2.—RATES AT WHICH EQUILIBRIUM IS ESTABLISHED BETWEEN THE TWO FORMS OF BROMONITROCAMPHOR

As the latter reaction proceeds, P is converted into N; hence, the forward rate decreases and the reverse rate increases. Eventually, the two rates become equal, and the net rate, v, is zero; thus, a dynamic equilibrium is achieved. This state of dynamic equilibrium is not a condition in which no reaction occurs, but is one in which the rates of the forward and reverse reactions are equal. This kinetic concept of dynamic equilibrium has been experimentally verified by the use of radioactive tracers (see ISOTOPE).

When, for a reaction which follows equation (2''), the forward and reverse reactions proceed at equal rates, it is seen that

$$v_f = v_r = k_f(A)(B) = k_r(C)(D) \qquad (12)$$

From equation (12) it follows that

$$\frac{(C)(D)}{(A)(B)} = \frac{k_f}{k_r} = K_e \qquad (13)$$

where K_e, the ratio of the rate constants for the forward and reverse reactions, is called the equilibrium constant. Equation (13) gives the relative concentrations of the compounds A, B, C, and D at equilibrium; these concentrations need not be even approximately equal, for in general the rate constants of the forward and reverse reactions differ considerably from one another.

An equation analogous to (13) but more general is obtained by a parallel treatment of a reaction (7). Although this more general expression is correct as a first approximation, it nevertheless disagrees with the precise thermodynamic definition of equilibrium. Consideration of this and similar difficulties is postponed to the sections on collision theory and on activated-complex theory.

Complex Reactions.—The reactions so far considered are of simple types; all sorts of combinations of these types are possible. For example, reactions sometimes occur in several steps.

$$A \rightarrow B \rightarrow C \qquad (14)$$

Here the rate of formation of B is proportional to the concentration of A, and the rate of formation of C is proportional to the concentration of B. Since, initially, the concentration of B is zero, the initial rate of formation of C is zero. Fig. 3 shows graphically the concentration of C at any time, t, in a system where the rate constants for the two consecutive reaction steps are of comparable magnitude. Other cases of interest are those in which one of the successive reactions is reversible, or of second order, etc. Considerable complexity is not only possible but common.

What has already been said makes it evident that the kinetic

equation for a reaction cannot be inferred from the chemical equation, which gives only the relationship between the weights of reactants which will combine with one another and the weights of the final products (i.e., the stoichiometric relations). The kinetic expression, it is true, must account for the stoichiometric findings, but it should do more than that. Usually more than one reaction path between the initial reactants and the final products is conceivable. Under favourable conditions kinetic considerations permit the selection of just one of these reaction paths, and kinetic measurements demonstrate that the path selected, and no other, is the one which the reaction takes. Under less favourable conditions, kinetic considerations are insufficient to eliminate all reaction paths but one. Even here, however, they serve to rule out many of those paths which from mere stoichiometric considerations might be considered possible.

A simple example will illustrate the ideas just expressed. A chemist might investigate an irreversible reaction, the stoichiometric expression for which is A → C. This expression means that each molecule of the reactant A is converted (eventually) into one molecule of the product C. It does not tell whether each molecule of A is converted directly into a molecule of C or whether each molecule of A is converted first into a molecule of an intermediate, B, which is in turn converted into a molecule of C. In the former instance, the proper kinetic expression for the reaction A → C may coincide with the stoichiometric expression. In the latter instance, the proper kinetic expression is A → B → C. Measurements of the extent of the reaction at various stages in its course are often sufficient to decide questions of the kind here raised. In the particular instance cited, if the reaction followed a curve of the sort shown in fig. 3, that fact would show that the kinetic expression for the reaction was A → B → C. If, on the other hand, the reaction followed a curve predicted from equation (5), and somewhat resembling the one shown in fig. 1, that fact would show that the kinetic expression for the reaction was A → C, coinciding with the stoichiometric expression. This fact alone would not rule out compound B as an intermediate, but it could be an intermediate in the reaction only under certain special circumstances (i.e., the reaction B → C would have to be very fast as compared with the reaction A → B).

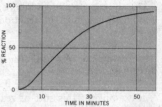

FIG. 3.—SUCCESSIVE FIRST ORDER REACTIONS, WHERE THE RATE CONSTANT OF THE SECOND IS FOUR TIMES AS GREAT AS THAT OF THE FIRST (DIAZOTIZATION OF PHENYL MERCURIC NITRATE IN 20% HNO_3 WITH 0.16M HNO_2)

If any individual reaction is to be thoroughly understood, its reaction kinetics must be investigated. The object in view is to determine by inference from the kinetic measurements whether the reaction proceeds in one or more stages, to determine the order of each reaction stage with respect to each one of the reactants, and to determine for each particular stage whether or not it is catalyzed by some substance (possibly an ion) which does not appear in the stoichiometric expression for the over-all reaction. It should, however, be stated that kinetic considerations by themselves, although they greatly aid in the treatment of the problem stated, are often insufficient for its solution in all details.

If a kinetic study shows that two molecules (of the same or of different compounds) react with one another directly, then the reaction is said to be bimolecular. In a many-stage reaction, some individual step may be bimolecular, although the over-all reaction is not of second order and may indeed (like [14]) be of no definite order. It is likewise possible for a reaction to be of the second order, but to contain no single step which is truly bimolecular. The interpretation of the reaction kinetics for any individual reaction is thus a difficult matter, and for many important reactions the conclusions are still tentative.

Application of the Kinetic Molecular Theory.—Guldberg and Waage assumed that the rate of any reaction is proportional to the product of the concentrations of the reactants (equation [7]); they interpreted this hypothesis in terms of the kinetic molecular theory. The number of collisions between the molecules of compound A and the molecules of compound B is proportional to the product (A)(B) of their concentrations; Guldberg and Waage's law amounts then to a statement that molecules react only if they collide, and that the rate at which they react is proportional to the number of collisions per second.

But although reaction between two molecules cannot occur unless these molecules collide, it does not follow that reaction must occur every time two molecules collide, even though these are molecules of substances which can react chemically one with another. For most reactions, it has been fully determined that the vast majority of collisions are "elastic"; i.e., that the molecules rebound from one another without chemical reaction. It is possible by means of the kinetic molecular theory to compute the number of collisions per second between the molecules of two compounds which are present in a solution or a gas in known concentrations. For example, the number of collisions between pairs of molecules of hydrogen iodide at a temperature of $320°$ C. and a total pressure of one atmosphere is approximately 10^{28} per cubic centimetre per second. Under the conditions stated, there are only about 10^{19} molecules of hydrogen iodide in a cubic centimetre of gas. Hence, if every collision between two molecules of hydrogen iodide led to chemical change, the reaction would be over in a small fraction of a second, almost too short a time to measure. It has been computed that in the system described, only one collision in about 10^{15} leads to chemical change.

Temperature Coefficients of Reaction Rates.—Another (and historically older) consideration leading to the conclusion that not all collisions cause reaction is based on the increase of reaction rates with increase in temperature. According to kinetic-molecular theory, the number of collisions between molecules of two compounds present at definite concentrations increases as the square root of the absolute temperature. For example, the number of collisions at $25°$ C. ($298°$ absolute) is only about 1.5% greater than the number at $15°$ C. ($288°$ absolute). But the rates of most reactions increase by a factor of two or more when the temperature is raised by $10°$ C.; as much material may react in an hour at $100°$ C. as in a year at $0°$ C. In some instances, such as the denaturation of egg albumin, the reaction rate increases one hundredfold when the temperature is raised $10°$ C.

However, the assumption that only those molecules which collide with high energy of impact react with one another not only furnishes an explanation for the high temperature coefficients of reaction rates, but also accounts for the fact that collisions effective in bringing about chemical change are usually rare. To bring out the connection between the assumption and the conclusions, it is necessary to consider the velocity of one molecule relative to another. This relative velocity is not the same for all colliding pairs, but there is a determinable probability that for any one particular pair the relative velocity will lie close to any chosen value, u, of the relative velocity. This probability is calculated from the Maxwell-Boltzmann distribution curve (see KINETIC THEORY OF MATTER) shown in fig. 4 and 5 for hydrogen iodide at $300°$ C.

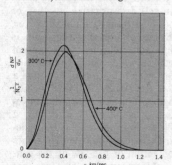

and $400°$ C. The horizontal co-ordinate represents the velocity, μ, in km./sec., of one molecule of hydrogen iodide relative to the one with which it collides; the vertical co-ordinate represents the probability that the relative velocity is μ. (More precisely, the ordinate is equal to $1/N_0^2 d$ $(N^2)/d\mu$, where N_0 is the total number of molecules under consideration, and $d(N^2)$ is the number of pairs of molecules with velocity lying between μ and $\mu +$ $d\mu$.) Fig. 5 is an enlargement of vertical scale of part of fig. 4. Fig. 4 and 5 indicate (1) that only a minute number of molecular pairs have relative velocities in excess of the 2.4 km./sec. re-

FIG. 4.—MAXWELL-BOLTZMANN DISTRIBUTION OF PAIRS OF MOLECULES OF HYDROGEN IODIDE (AT 300° C AND AT 400 C°). THE VELOCITY OF ONE MEMBER OF ANY PAIR RELATIVE TO THE OTHER MEMBER IS μ

quired for reaction (see above), and (2) that, although the average value of the relative velocity is not greatly increased by raising the temperature from $300°$ C. ($573°$ absolute) to $400°$ C. ($673°$ absolute), the number of molecular pairs with high relative velocities is increased by a large factor. Thus the assumption that reaction is limited to molecular pairs with high relative velocities at the moment of collision qualitatively explains both the fact that few collisions are "effective" in producing reaction and the fact that the rates of most chemical reactions increase sharply with increase in temperature.

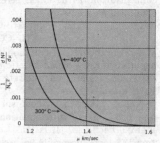

FIG. 5.—EXPANDED SCALE DRAWING OF HIGH-VELOCITY END OF FIG. 4

The complete equation (24) for the reaction rate derived from the kinetic collision theory is given in the next to last section of this article. Here it is sufficient to say that this complete equation is consistent (within experimental error) with an empirical equation (15) advanced by Svante August Arrhenius in 1889 which has proved useful.

$$\log_e \frac{k_2}{k_1} = \frac{Q}{R}\left(\frac{I}{T_1} - \frac{I}{T_2}\right) \qquad (15)$$

In equation (15) k_1 and k_2 are the rate constants at the absolute temperatures T_1 and T_2 respectively, Q is a constant called the activation energy, and R is the gas constant (1.98 cal./mole degree) ($\log_e$ refers to natural logarithms). The larger the value of Q, the more sensitive is the reaction rate to changes in temperature. Reactions with values of Q varying from less than 500 up to about 100,000 cal./mole have been discovered. Q divided by the number of molecules in a mole (Avogadro's number) is (roughly) equal to the relative kinetic energy of a molecular pair which is just sufficient to make the members of the pair react upon collision.

Reaction Mechanism.—In this section, it will be shown how reaction kinetics may be used to determine the path or mechanism of a somewhat puzzling reaction. The example chosen is the reaction in aqueous solution between acetone and bromine. Here the stoichiometric

$$CH_3COCH_3 + Br_2 \longrightarrow CH_3COCH_2Br + HBr \qquad (16)$$

expression (16) is of the same form as equation (2). In 1904, however, A. Lapworth discovered that the rate of this reaction is proportional to the concentration of the acetone and of the hydrogen bromide (one of the reaction products) but independent of the concentration of the bromine and of all other substances known to be present in the system. The kinetic equation, therefore, is

$$v = k(CH_3COCH_3)(HBr) \qquad (17)$$

These facts suggest the hypothesis that the acetone is slowly converted into some reactive intermediate by the action of the acid; this reactive intermediate then combines rapidly with bromine. The hypothesis has more recently been elaborated as follows:

$$(CH_3)_2CO + H_3O^+ \rightleftharpoons (CH_3)_2COH^+ + H_2O \text{ ("steady state"} \quad (18)$$
$$\text{rapidly reached)}$$

$$(CH_3)_2COH^+ + H_2O \longrightarrow CH_3\underset{OH}{C} = CH_2 + H_3O^+ \text{ (slow reaction) } (18')$$

$$CH_3\underset{OH}{C} = CH_2 + Br_2 \longrightarrow CH_3COCH_2Br + HBr \text{ (rapid reaction) } (18'')$$

The proposed reaction between the catalyst and the acetone results in the transformation of the acetone into a reactive intermediate (the "enolic" modification of acetone; see TAUTOMERISM), which subsequently reacts rapidly with bromine. The rate, v, of the entire reaction is equal to that for the slowest step in the process, namely reaction (18'). The kinetic equation for this step is

$$v = k'((CH_3)_2COH^+) \qquad (19)$$

The concentration of water is essentially constant and does not enter into equation (19); its concentration can be included in the rate constant, k'. The ion $(CH_3)_2COH^+$ would be in equilibrium with the acetone and acid present in the solution if it were not for the reactions (18') and (18'') which slowly but essentially irreversibly remove some of this ion.

The ion $(CH_3)_2COH^+$ is described as in pseudoequilibrium with acetone and acid, or as in a "steady state." The "steady state" concentration of the ion is given to a good approximation by the equilibrium expression

$$\frac{[(CH_3)_2COH^+]}{[(CH_3)_2CO][H_3O^+]} = K \qquad (19')$$

When the theoretical equations (19) and (19') are combined, the experimentally verified kinetic equation (17) for the bromination of acetone is obtained; the rate constant k is the product of k' and K.

Not only does the mechanism presented in equations (18), (18') and (18'') agree with equation (17), but it will further explain many other facts. It is consistent, for example, with the observation that acetone reacts with chlorine, or with iodine at the same rate as it does with bromine. This is in accord with the proposed mechanism, since equation (18'), which does not involve the halogen at all, is postulated as the rate-determining step in the halogenation.

A more detailed investigation of the reaction has revealed that it is catalyzed not only by hydronium ion but also by molecules of un-ionized acids; it is also catalyzed by bases. The catalysis by un-ionized acid molecules can be accounted for by substituting equation (18''') for equation (18')

$$(CH_3)_2COH^+ + B \longrightarrow CH_3\underset{\underset{OH}{|}}{C}=CH_2 + BH^+ \qquad (18''')$$

where B represents a molecule of any base. (The detailed mathematical analysis needed to prove the above statement, although beyond the scope of this article, is treated by L. P. Hammett in *Physical Organic Chemistry*.) Furthermore, the kinetic isotope effects (*see* below, *Reactions of Isotopes*) with deuterium and tritium strongly support the reaction scheme; in analogous but more complicated examples, the stereochemical predictions of the mechanism have been verified.

The proposed mechanism is thus consistent with a large and varied selection of quantitative kinetic evidence. This is a necessary condition, but not a sufficient one to establish the mechanism; it does, however, make the proposed mechanism quite probable.

Catalysis.—A catalyst is defined as a substance which increases the rate of a chemical reaction, but which can be recovered quantitatively and unchanged at the end of the reaction. There are many substances which (for specified reactions) approach this definition closely. Typical examples of homogeneous catalysis are the action of acids to increase the rate of hydrolysis ("inversion") of cane sugar, the action of bases to increase the rate of polymerization in the preparation of bakelite, the action of oxides of nitrogen in the chamber process for manufacturing sulfuric acid. Typical examples of heterogeneous catalysis are the action of finely divided iron to increase the rate at which nitrogen and hydrogen combine to form ammonia, the action of vanadium pentoxide to increase the rate at which sulfur dioxide and oxygen combine to form sulfur trioxide in the contact process for manufacturing sulfuric acid, and the action of finely divided nickel to increase the rate at which hydrogen combines with vegetable oils to form solid fats (*e.g.*, "Crisco"). (For a discussion of theory, manufacture and use of catalysts *see* CATALYSIS.)

Catalysts accelerate chemical reactions in various different ways. The bromination of acetone (cited above) illustrates one of the most common modes of action. Here the acid which in this case is the catalyst combines with one of the reactants (acetone) to form an intermediate chemical compound. Then, in a later step of the complex reaction, the catalyst is regenerated and so becomes available for further reaction. In this way the catalyst goes through a complete cycle, and a trace of catalyst increases the rate at which a large amount of material reacts.

It is interesting to note that a catalyst can increase the rate of a chemical reaction but cannot change its point of equilibrium. If this statement were not correct, it would be possible to construct a perpetual motion machine. Since perpetual motion is an impossibility (*see* THERMODYNAMICS), it follows that in a reversible re-

action the catalyst must accelerate both the forward and the reverse rate and in the same proportion.

Photochemical Reactions.—Reactions which take place in the presence of light but not in the dark are called photochemical reactions; their rate depends upon the amount of light absorbed. This subject is treated fully in the article on PHOTOCHEMISTRY. The principles here needed are the following: (1) Only the light which is absorbed by the system is effective in promoting chemical change; (2) radiant energy (light) is available only in units called quanta (*see* LIGHT); (3) a molecule which absorbs light and is thereby activated (*i.e.*, enters into a reaction with light) absorbs one and only one light quantum (A. Einstein). Subsequently, the activated molecule may enter into other, more complicated chemical reactions.

Chain Reactions.—Hydrogen gas reacts with chlorine at room temperature provided that the mixture is illuminated; the reaction (except under special circumstances, *see* below) does not occur in the dark. The form of the equation for the chemical reaction

$$H_2 + Cl_2 \longrightarrow 2HCl \qquad (20)$$

resembles that of the reaction for the formation of hydrogen iodide (reverse of equation 1); the kinetics of the two reactions are, however, quite different. The reaction between hydrogen and chlorine proceeds when visible light is used. Since light of this wave length is absorbed by chlorine, but not by hydrogen, it follows that chlorine is the reactant affected by the light. Measurements have shown that as many as 1,000,000 molecules of hydrogen chloride are produced for every light quantum absorbed. Evidently a very special mechanism must be postulated to account for this fact.

It has been assumed (W. Nernst, M. Bodenstein) that, as an indirect or direct result of the illumination, the molecules of Cl_2 which absorb light quanta are dissociated into chlorine atoms (21). These atoms then react as shown in equations (21') and (21'').

$$Cl_2 \longrightarrow 2Cl \qquad (21)$$
$$Cl + H_2 \longrightarrow HCl + H \qquad (21')$$
$$H + Cl_2 \longrightarrow HCl + Cl \qquad (21'')$$

Each chlorine atom obtained by the illumination reacts with a molecule of hydrogen to produce a molecule of hydrogen chloride and an atom of hydrogen (21'); the latter in turn reacts with a molecule of chlorine to produce another molecule of hydrogen chloride and to regenerate an atom of chlorine (21''). The cycle is then repeated. Reactions characterized by such cycles are called chain reactions. If there were no side reactions to destroy the intermediate hydrogen and chlorine atoms, then, in principle, one chlorine atom could convert all the hydrogen and chlorine in the system to hydrogen chloride. In fact, the chain length varies from a few units to a million, depending upon the experimental conditions. The chains are broken (or terminated) when the chlorine or hydrogen atoms are removed. There are several means of removing these reactive atoms. For example, oxygen combines with either chlorine or hydrogen atoms, and traces of oxygen are effective in decreasing the rate of the reaction in question. In this reaction then, oxygen acts as a negative catalyst, or an inhibitor, or a chain breaker. (These terms are not, however, exactly synonymous.) Another means of breaking the chain is the combination of hydrogen atoms and chlorine atoms present in the gas mixture to form hydrogen chloride. Such combination occurs on the walls of the vessel, or when a hydrogen atom and a chlorine atom, in what is called a three-body collision, collide simultaneously with some third particle (such as a chlorine molecule); interestingly, the combination does not occur when only a hydrogen and a chlorine atom collide. Such a combination independent of the wall or of any third particle would violate either the law of the conservation of momentum or the law of the conservation of energy, or both. (*See* MECHANICS.) The fact that no such combination is observed simply means that the molecular system in question obeys the laws of mechanics, as do the molecular systems in all similar reactions which have been carefully studied.

The validity of the proposed chain mechanism for the reaction between hydrogen and chlorine is supported (1) by the high photochemical yield of the reaction (*i.e.*, the large amount of hydrogen chloride produced per quantum of light absorbed), (2) by the fact that kinetic equations based upon the chain mechanism adequately describe the reaction velocity and (3) by experiments showing that the reaction can be initiated in the dark by the introduction into the reaction mixture of hydrogen or chlorine atoms from some outside source. There is good reason to believe that hydrogen atoms are produced by an electric arc discharge in hydrogen gas, and that chlorine atoms are produced in the reaction between sodium vapour and chlorine. If the products from either of these reactions are rapidly introduced into a mixture of hydrogen and chlorine, the formation of hydrogen chloride is initiated.

Reaction kinetics has provided much evidence to show that many reactions either in the gas phase or in solution proceed by chain mechanisms.

Heterogeneous Reactions.—Heterogeneous reactions include the solution of solids in solvents, and the reverse process, the crystallization of solids from solution. The reaction of metals with acids and problems of corrosion are part of the subject of heterogeneous reactions. However, by far the majority of the research on heterogeneous reactions is devoted to heterogeneous catalysis (*e.g.*, reactions between gases or liquids catalyzed by solids, etc.). For example, finely divided iron greatly accelerates the rate at which nitrogen and hydrogen unite to form ammonia. Recent studies have shown that iron adsorbs nitrogen in such a fashion as to activate it (by a reaction analogous to the formation of iron nitride); the hydrogen subsequently reacts with the adsorbed nitrogen. Although heterogeneous reactions of this sort are of considerable theoretical and practical interest (*see* ADSORPTION; CATALYSIS) the present article is devoted largely to a consideration of homogeneous reactions.

Enzymes.—Almost the earliest chemical reactions known are the fermentations by which sugar is converted to alcohol or vinegar (fermentation) or lactic acid (souring of milk). These and similar reactions occur in the presence of living organisms, such as yeasts, fungi, etc. In 1897 E. Büchner discovered that, in the fermentation of sugar, the function of the living yeast is to produce a catalyst for the reaction. He destroyed the yeast cells by grinding them with sand. The filtered juice, although it contained no living organisms, nevertheless rapidly converted sugar to alcohol. The complex organic catalysts produced by living cells are called enzymes; those so far investigated in detail have proved to be proteins or protein complexes.

The chemistry of enzymes (*q.v.*) is actively under investigation. The structure of these complex catalysts is partly known, but the mechanism of their action is incompletely understood. Part of the catalytic efficiency of enzymes arises from their ability to adsorb their specific substrates (the compounds whose reactions are accelerated) onto the enzyme molecule, and thus bring them into proximity with the catalytic groups of the protein. Possibly the cooperation of several such catalytic groups, working in concert and in intimate contact with the substrate, may account for the remarkable catalytic efficiency of enzyme systems.

Extensive investigation by a variety of methods (reaction kinetics, isotopic tracers, isolation of intermediates, spectroscopy, etc.) has shown that the fermentation of sugar is a complex process in which many enzymes take part. Similarly, enzyme systems convert starch to sugar, and sugar to alcohol; others hydrolyze proteins into a mixture of amino acids; still others (in conjunction with nucleic acids) synthesize proteins in the body. Enzymes are responsible for the conversion (by a form of combustion) of sugar to carbon dioxide and water, and for the storage, utilization and liberation of metabolic energy. The accelerating effect of some of these enzyme systems is enormous. For example, one part of beef catalase can be detected in 25,000,000 parts of water by the acceleration it produces in the decomposition of hydrogen peroxide. Since the mechanism of enzyme action is unknown, and since the kinetics of enzyme action differs considerably from the kinetics of reactions accelerated by ordinary catalysts, direct comparisons are difficult and likely to be inaccurate. As a rough first approximation, however, catalase is about 10,000 times as active a catalyst as is an equal weight of ferrous ion in catalyzing the decomposition of hydrogen peroxide, and urease is about 10,000 times as active (at 20° C. and in neutral solution) as is an equal weight of sodium hydroxide in accelerating the hydrolysis of urea. These catalysts are thus very much more effective than any so far originated by chemists.

Explosions.—Chemical explosions are rapid reactions which are strongly exothermic; that is to say, these reactions are very rapid ones which evolve large quantities of heat. The hot gases formed in the chemical reaction, or the air heated by the energy released, produce a region of high pressure near the site of the explosion. This region of high pressure travels outward through the air in the form of an explosion wave which usually causes much of the destruction resulting from the explosion. (*see* COMBUSTION; EXPLOSIVES). It is of interest to inquire what are the necessary conditions, and what are the possible mechanisms for a reaction which consumes many pounds of material in (say) 10^{-5} seconds. There are two well-known types of mechanism for explosions: the chain branching mechanism and the thermal mechanism. The latter type was suggested by van't Hoff, the former by N. N. Semenov; examples of both types have been discovered.

The theory of the chain-branching mechanism is that, during the early stages of a chain reaction, more chains are initiated per unit time than are terminated. The most spectacular example of an explosion caused by chain branching is the fission of atomic nuclei, such as occurs in atomic bombs. Here the disintegration of a particular sort of uranium, U^{235} (or of plutonium), is initiated by neutrons, but, in the disintegration, neutrons are also produced. (*See* ATOMIC ENERGY; ISOTOPE; NUCLEUS.) If exactly one neutron were produced from each disintegrating nucleus of U^{235}, a chain reaction analogous to the reaction between hydrogen and chlorine would result. In fact, however, more than one neutron is produced by each nuclear disintegration; the average number is probably about two. An equation for the atomic disintegration is

$$U + n \longrightarrow I + Y + 2n \qquad (22)$$

where U, n, I and Y are the symbols for uranium, the neutron, iodine, and yttrium, respectively. (Other elements besides iodine and yttrium are also produced in the disintegration; the principles involved are, however, the same.) The faster the reaction proceeds, the more rapidly are neutrons produced and the more rapidly does the reaction rate increase. Since the disintegration of the uranium is accompanied by a large evolution of energy, the reaction is an explosion.

The second type of explosion mechanism is the thermal one. Most chemical reactions are carried out under conditions such that the heat evolved (or absorbed) by the reaction is taken away (or supplied) by the surrounding medium. If, however, a highly exothermic reaction is carried out under conditions such that the heat is not carried away by the surroundings, the reaction mixture must become hotter. At the more elevated temperature, the rate of the reaction is much greater; the rate of heat evolution, therefore, becomes much greater also, and the reaction mixture rapidly becomes still hotter. Such a reaction must necessarily lead to an explosion. The question whether a particular exothermic reaction will lead to an explosion is thus largely a question of the conditions under which the reaction is carried out. If the reaction can be made to proceed at such a rate that the heat lost to the surroundings per unit time is small compared with the heat input caused by the chemical reaction during the same interval, a thermal explosion ensues.

Reactions of Isotopes.—In general, the reaction rates of compounds which differ only in that they contain different isotopes of the same element are identical within experimental error. When, however, one of the lighter elements is involved, this need not be the fact. A compound which contains atoms of C^{14} (radioactive carbon) may react at a rate which differs appreciably (*e.g.*, by 6%) from that of a compound identical except that it contains only normal carbon atoms. The rate of reactions of compounds containing deuterium (heavy hydrogen) frequently differs from that of the corresponding compounds of light hydrogen by factors between 5 and 8; even larger factors (and of course smaller ones) have been observed. These large differences in rate, which may occur when a bond to a hydrogen atom is formed or broken, arise from an effect (zero-point vibrational energy) predicted by quantum mechanics (*q.v.*). Although a discussion of the theory of this effect is out of place here, the phenomenon is proving a most useful tool in investigations of reaction mechanisms.

Fast Reactions.—A number of techniques have led to the determination of the rates of reactions which occur at every collision (or at nearly every collision) of the reaction partners. Since faster rates of chemical change cannot be envisioned (*i.e.*, since molecules cannot react without first colliding) these methods allow the study of reactions at one limit of the entire spectrum of possible speeds. Some of these methods depend upon advances in electronic technology; in particular, rapid-scanning oscilloscopes have permitted measurements of reactions which occur in as little as 10^{-9} seconds (M. Eigen). For example, the rate of combinations of oppositely charged ions in solution (NH_4^+ and OH^-, H_3O^+ and OH^-, H_3O^+ and $SO_4^=$) has been followed by conductometric and other techniques; the rates approach the maximum calculated for such processes in solution. Similarly, in the gas phase, rates have been measured for reactions (*e.g.*, the combination of methyl "radicals") which occur with nearly every collision.

The Collision Theory.—In the theory of reaction kinetics as so far presented, several difficulties have been noted. The present section is devoted to a discussion of these difficulties and the methods of avoiding them; a knowledge of physical chemistry on the part of the reader is assumed.

The ratio of the rates of a forward and of the corresponding reverse reactions gives an approximate expression for the equilibrium constant of the reaction in question, as shown for a special case by equation (13). In the more general case, an analogous treatment of the reaction

$$mA + nB + pC + \ldots \rightleftharpoons gR + hS + iT + \ldots \qquad (23)$$

leads to equation (24).

$$\frac{(R)^g (S)^h (T)^i \ldots}{(A)^m (B)^n (C)^p \ldots} = K_e \qquad (24)$$

The ratio of concentrations on the left side of equation (24) is obtained even if the kinetic equation for the reaction is a complex one. For example, if the reaction is catalyzed, the catalyst concentration appears in the expression for the rate of both the forward and the reverse reaction; it thus cancels out in equation (24). Careful inspection shows that other possible complexities are likewise of no effect on K_e. But equation (24) is nevertheless not precisely correct. The true equilibrium expression (*see* THERMODYNAMICS) is defined in terms of the "activities," not the concentrations, of the reactants and reaction products. Although in dilute solutions the concentration of any substance closely approaches its activity, the two functions are by no means identical. (An analogous statement applies to gases at low pressure.) It is therefore clear that the law of Guldberg and Waage, although approximately correct, is not and cannot be uniformly valid.

The difficulty noted cannot be avoided by the assumption that reaction rates are proportional to activities rather than to concentrations; this assumption has been proved false by investigations of the rates of ionic reactions. The ratio of the activity of any substance to its concentration defines its activity coefficient. The activity coefficients of ions depend upon the ionic strength of the solution in which they occur (*see* SOLUTIONS: *Solutions of Electrolytes*).

This ionic strength is a function of the concentrations and of the charges on all the ions present; in dilute solutions the activity coefficients of all ions decrease with increasing ionic strength. But the rates of reactions between two ions of like charge increase with increase of ionic strength; only for reactions between ions of opposite charge do the rates (like the activity coefficients) decrease with increasing ionic strength. Thus the rate of a reaction is not proportional to the "activities" of the reactants; it has already been shown that only as a first approximation is this rate proportional to the ionic concentrations.

The difficulty, at least insofar as ionic reactions are concerned, has been resolved by the assumption that reaction rates are proportional not to concentrations or activities, but to the number of collisions per second between the reacting ions. The number of collisions between charged particles should not be strictly proportional to the product of their concentrations. Let W be the ratio between the number of collisions among the reacting ions and the product of the ionic concentrations. Then, because of interionic effects, W should increase with increasing ionic strength for reactions between ions of like charge, and decrease with increasing ionic strength for reactions between ions of unlike charge. This predicted behaviour is in qualitative agreement with the anomaly in ionic reaction rates already cited.

J. A. Christiansen's calculation (1924) based on the theory of P. Debye and E. Hückel, accounts quantitatively for the observed rates of ionic reactions in dilute solution. Further, although the forward and reverse rates, taken separately, are not proportional to the activities of the reactants and reaction products, the expression obtained by setting equal the rates of the forward and reverse reactions (corrected to account for interionic effects) yields the thermodynamic equilibrium expression in terms of activities, not concentrations. How this happens is made clearer in the consideration (*see* below) of the activated-complex theory of reaction velocity. In general, it has been assumed that consideration of the actual number of collisions always leads to corrections for the law of Guldberg and Waage, such that the dynamic and thermodynamic equilibrium constants become equal.

It should be pointed out that interionic and other forces not only affect the change in the number of collisions with change in concentration; they also affect the actual number of collisions per unit time. Thus, in a reaction between two positively charged ions, forces of electrostatic repulsion lower the number of collisions far below that computed from the kinetic molecular theory. Furthermore, it is not true that every collision between reactant particles moving, relative to one another, with a velocity greater than the critical one, u_0, leads to chemical change. There must also be a definite orientation of the molecules with respect to one another at the moment of collision. This consideration holds especially for complex molecules, which may be capable of reacting only at one end. The collision theory is thus considerably less precise than may at first have appeared.

Application of kinetic molecular theory to a simple bimolecular reaction (*e.g.*, the decomposition of hydrogen iodide) leads to equation (25), which relates the rate constant, k, with u_0, the minimal velocity at collision, necessary for reaction.

$$k = \frac{4N^2 d^2}{c^2} \sqrt{\frac{\pi kT}{m}} \left(1 + \frac{m u_0^2}{2kT}\right) e^{-m u_0^2 / 2kT} \qquad (25)[3]$$

Here N molecules of effective diameter d and weight m are present at a concentration of c moles per litre and at an absolute temperature T. The symbol e is the base of the system of natural logarithms, and k is Boltzmann's constant, 1.38×10^{-16} ergs/degree. If the values of k are experimentally determined for a series of temperatures, the values of both u_0 (the minimal velocity of one molecule relative to another required for effective collisions) and of d (the effective diameter of the particles) can be determined. The difficulties previously discussed then appear as anomalously large or small values of d^2. That is to say, when the reacting particles attract each other, the cross sections of the molecules (proportional to d^2) which are "effective" for collisions, will be large compared to these cross sections as determined by other methods; conversely, when the particles repel one another, or when a preferred orientation is necessary for reaction, the "effective" cross section will be small. The latter condition holds (although not to a marked degree) for the hydrogen iodide reaction.

An alternative description of the reaction process may be obtained by computing a collision number on the basis of the best available estimates for molecular cross sections and by replacing equation (25) by (27), to which it is approximately equivalent.

$$k = PZe^{-Q/RT} \qquad (27)$$

---

[3] If the two molecules which react are not identical, this expression must be somewhat modified. Among other modifications, the reduced mass μ replaces m. If the masses of the two molecules in question are m_1 and m_2, then the reduced mass μ is defined by equation (26).

$$1/\mu = 1/m_1 + 1/m_2 \qquad (26)$$

Here Z is the "normal" collision factor, P is the "probability" factor defined by equation (27), and Q is the activation energy which does not differ greatly from $\frac{1}{2}Mu_0^2$, where M is the molecular weight of the substance in question. The difficulties of the collision theory are then contained in the factor P, and the problem of obtaining precise agreement between theory and experiment is reduced to that of computing P correctly.

One additional aspect of collision theory deserves attention. Some reactions (as previously stated) are of the first order. Such reactions would seem to be independent of collisions. In what way can these reactions be correlated with collision theory? Some first-order reactions probably cannot be so correlated. The disintegration of radium is strictly of the first order; the rate of the reaction depends upon changes in the radium nucleus, which are unaffected by collisions of the molecule as a whole. But in ordinary chemical, as opposed to nuclear, reactions, the energy necessary for reaction is probably acquired by the decomposing molecule through previous collisions.

The Activated-Complex Theory.—An alternative general theory of reaction kinetics is formulated in terms of the so-called "activated complex" (S. A. Arrhenius, J. N. Brönsted, N. Bjerrum, H. Eyring). In this theory, it is assumed that all the reactants are in pseudoequilibrium with an activated complex, X,

$$mA + nB + pC + \ldots \rightleftharpoons X \longrightarrow \text{products} \qquad (28)$$

which in turn decomposes to give the reaction products. The activated complex X is not a true molecule; it is merely a stage in the process by which the reactants become the reaction products. Hence, the activated complex is not in true equilibrium with the reactants. The activated-complex theory, however, is founded on the assumption that the concentration of the activated complex may be computed just as if it were a real, stable chemical compound. The rate of reaction is then the product of the concentration of X multiplied by the rate at which it decomposes. This rate can be computed by the general methods of quantum mechanics (q.v.); it is the same for all activated complexes, regardless of the materials out of which they have been formed. For a reaction such as (23), the activated-complex theory leads to equation (29)

$$v = \kappa \frac{kT}{h} K^*(A)^m(B)^n(C)^p \ldots \frac{\gamma_A{}^m \gamma_B{}^n \gamma_C{}^p}{\gamma_X} \qquad (29)$$

where k is the Boltzmann constant, h is Planck's constant, K^* is the equilibrium constant for the formation of the activated complex (its decomposition into the reaction products being disregarded), and $\gamma_A, \gamma_B, \gamma_C, \ldots \gamma_X$ are respectively the activity coefficients of the reactants and of the activated complex. The constant κ is called the transmission coefficient; it is usually nearly unity. When the activated-complex theory is used to describe a reversible reaction, a distinction must be drawn between the activated complex formed from the reactants and that formed from the reaction products. The two complexes, although structurally the same, differ with respect to the materials from which they have been formed and into which they are decomposing. Unless the distinction in question is made, the theory is self-contradictory.

Equation (29) contains γ_X, the activity coefficient for the activated complex. Although this coefficient cannot be measured (since the activated complex is not a stable entity) it can be estimated for the complexes which occur in ionic reactions. The charge on the activated complex must be the sum of the charges on the reactants; furthermore, the charge on an ion, as a first approximation, determines its activity coefficient. Equation (29) correctly predicts the rates of ionic reactions; it leads to results identical with those obtained by Christiansen. Although in particular instances the collision theory may be more convenient to apply than is the activated complex theory, or vice versa, the two always lead to the same results; they are, in essence, two different languages in which the same phenomena may be described.

At equilibrium, the rates of the forward and reverse reactions are equal. When two rate expressions analogous to (29) are used, an equation (30) is obtained from which the activity coefficient of the activated complex and the transmission coefficients have been eliminated.

$$\frac{(R)^g(S)^h(T)^i \ldots \ldots (\gamma_R)^g(\gamma_S)^h(\gamma_T)^i \ldots \ldots \ldots}{(A)^m(B)^n(C)^p \ldots \ldots (\gamma_A)^m(\gamma_B)^n(\gamma_C)^p \ldots \ldots \ldots} = K \qquad (30)$$

Here K is the true thermodynamic equilibrium constant, expressed in terms of activities (concentrations multiplied by activity coefficients).

The pseudoequilibrium constant, K^*, of equation (29) is related to the free energy of activation, ΔF^*, the heat of activation ΔH^*, and the entropy of activation ΔS^*, by equation (31).

$$-RT \log_e K^* = \Delta F^* = \Delta H^* - T \Delta S^* \qquad (31)$$

The heat of activation, ΔH^*, corresponds roughly with the energy of activation, Q, of the collision theory; the entropy of activation, ΔS^*, may be roughly related to the logarithm of the "probability" factor, P, of equation (27).

The thermodynamic concept of entropy has been interpreted, through statistical mechanics, in terms of molecular vibrations. Likewise, entropy of activation can often be interpreted in terms of the geometry and of the estimated vibrational frequencies of the activated complex.

The application of the activated-complex theory depends upon the computation of the pseudoequilibrium constant, K^*. Thus, the kinetic problem is replaced by a thermodynamic one, and all the powerful tools of thermodynamics and of statistical mechanics become immediately available for its solution. It is possible in principle (always) and in practice (occasionally) to calculate the rate of a chemical reaction without the use of any experimentally determined kinetic data. The difficulties reside principally in the selection of appropriate constants for the activated complex. For the reaction between a hydrogen atom and a hydrogen molecule (which has been investigated by the use of ortho- and parahydrogen and of deuterium), the absolute reaction rate has been computed by methods related to the activated-complex theory (E. Wigner). Modern investigations, with molecular beam techniques, seek to determine the individual vibrational and rotational quantum states of gaseous molecules and to understand in great detail the geometry and energy of the reaction process. Most reactions are, however, too complex for complete mathematical solution by methods now known.

BIBLIOGRAPHY.—H. D. Smyth, *Atomic Energy for Military Purposes* (1945); C. N. Hinshelwood, *Kinetics of Chemical Change in Gaseous Systems* (1940); S. Glasstone, K. J. Laidler and H. Eyring, *The Theory of Rate Processes* (1941); S. W. Benson, *The Foundations of Chemical Kinetics* (1960); P. D. Boyer, H. Lardy and K. Myrbäck, eds., *The Enzymes*, 2nd ed., vol. i (1959); L. Melander, *Isotope Effects on Reaction Rates* (1960); L. P. Hammett, *Physical Organic Chemistry* (1940). (F. H. Wr.)

READE, CHARLES (1814–1884), English novelist, journalist, and dramatist, worked enthusiastically for the theatre but is remembered chiefly for his novels; he was an ardent reformer, but won his greatest fame with his historical romance, *The Cloister and the Hearth* (1861). He was born on June 8, 1814, at Ipsden House, near Ipsden, Oxfordshire, and entered Magdalen College, Oxford, in 1831. He graduated in 1835, was elected Vinerian fellow in 1842, took the degree of doctor of civil law in 1847, and was vice-president of his college in 1851, but treated the position as a sinecure. Meanwhile he had studied for the bar and was called in 1843 but never practised. He made various tours in Europe and, although he kept his fellowship and his college rooms for life, lived mainly in London. He had a great interest in violins, was himself a fair performer, and, as a young man, was an active partner in a Soho violin business.

Reade spent the greatest part of his energy and money writing and staging plays. He wrote 40, including translations, adaptations, and collaborations with other authors. Like much English 19th-century drama his plays are crippled by lurid spectacle, sensational incident, crude characterization, and conventional stage morality. His greatest success in the theatre was *Drink* (1879), an emasculated version of Émile Zola's *L'Assommoir,* but the liveliest and most readable is the early *Masks and Faces* (1852), a mildly witty comedy about the 18th-century actress Peg Woffington, written in collaboration with Tom Taylor. Reade found a loyal friend in Mrs. Laura Seymour, the actress, who was his housekeeper from 1856 until her death in 1879.

Reade also wrote short stories and 14 novels which made his name and fortune. He was sensitive to injustice and inhumanity and many of his works exposed contemporary social abuses. *It Is Never Too Late to Mend* (1856) attacked conditions in prisons and *Hard Cash* (1863) exposed the ill-treatment of mental patients, especially in private asylums; *Put Yourself in His Place* (1870) dealt with the terrorist activities of trade unionists; and the melodramatic *Foul Play* (1868), written with Dion Boucicault (*q.v.*), revealed the racket in "coffin ships" and helped to sway public opinion in favour of the safety measures proposed later by Samuel Plimsoll (*q.v.*). But the very intensity of Reade's indignation against these abuses led him to exaggerate his facts, and his work was also damaged by the "stage eye" with which he regarded characters and situations, and by his naïve belief that the use of "hard facts" in a novel ensures artistic truth. He sometimes introduced into his novels people who had temporarily claimed the public's attention, such as William Austin, governor of Birmingham jail when Edward Andrews hanged himself there in 1853. Austin appears as the brutal Hawes in *It Is Never Too Late to Mend*. Unlike Mrs. Gaskell, Reade was, in fact, a "sensation" rather than a serious "social" novelist. But he amassed much information for his propaganda novels and was sincere in his attempts to do good. He often pleaded his causes in pamphlets and in magazine and newspaper columns, and made a praiseworthy attempt to establish international stage rights and copyright.

The Cloister and the Hearth, although not a propaganda novel, cost him much research. It related the adventures of the unknown father of Erasmus. Acceptance of human tragedy and ability to present it dramatically and sympathetically make this the best of Reade's novels. Next in merit comes *Griffith Gaunt* (1866) in which Reade explores a marriage relationship and the passion of jealousy, but the book is spoiled by a conventional ending.

He was a systematic writer and tried to compensate for his lack of imagination by industry. He was quarrelsome and litigious and could be malicious toward those he disliked. Yet he was capable of great generosity and would work unceasingly for a favourite cause. Like Charles Dickens a reformer, he lacked Dickens' fertile imagination and ready invention, his sense of comedy and control of language. Reade's strength as a novelist is arresting narration of exciting action; his greatest defect is reliance upon prejudices and conventions because of his inability to observe human behaviour. He died in London on April 11, 1884.

BIBLIOGRAPHY.—A. C. Swinburne, *Miscellanies* (1886); C. L. Reade and Compton Reade, *Charles Reade, a Memoir* (1887); J. Coleman, *Charles Reade as I Knew Him* (1903); W. C. Phillips, *Dickens, Reade and Collins, Sensation Novelists* (1919); M. Sadleir, *Excursions in Victorian Bibliography* (1922); M. Elwin, *Charles Reade* (1931); A. M. Turner, *The Making of "The Cloister and the Hearth"* (1938); Léone Rives, *Charles Reade, sa vie, ses romans* (1940); W. Burns, *Charles Reade: a Study in Victorian Authorship* (1961).

(S. M. SM.)

READING, RUFUS DANIEL ISAACS, 1ST MARQUESS OF (1860–1935), British lawyer and statesman, lord chief justice of England from 1913 to 1921 and viceroy of India from 1921 to 1926, was born in London on Oct. 10, 1860, the second son of Joseph Michael Isaacs, a fruit importer. He was educated at University College School, London, and in Brussels and Hanover. He served in the merchant navy for two years from the age of 16 and then worked on the London Stock Exchange without success. He turned in 1884 to the law, where he found his life's work. He qualified as a barrister in 1887 and his knowledge of city affairs helped him to build a large and rewarding practice. Entering the House of Commons in 1904 as Liberal member for Reading, from which he later took his title, he held that seat until 1913 when he was made lord chief justice (Oct. 22, 1913).

He was appointed attorney general in 1910 and two years later was given a seat in the Cabinet, the first attorney general to have received such promotion. In the same year he was involved with other ministers in a bitter party controversy which arose out of their transactions in the shares of the American Marconi Company (of which his brother, Godfrey, was managing director), shortly after the English Marconi Company had received a contract from the British government. By a party majority a select committee of the House of Commons acquitted the ministers of all charges of corruption. Reading's tenure of office as lord chief justice was marked by humanity and by the establishment of the principle that the Court of Criminal Appeal should be a real court of revision. He presided over the trial of Sir Roger Casement, the Irish patriot, who in 1916 was convicted of treason and hanged.

During World War I, his main service was to assist in securing the money Britain needed and in strengthening Anglo-American relations. He was president of the Anglo-French Loan Commission to the United States from September to October 1915, and in September 1917 he returned there for a brief period, with John Maynard (later Baron) Keynes as his economic adviser, on a mission to bring some order into Britain's war spending. From January 1918 to May 1919 he was ambassador extraordinary and high commissioner to the United States. By the time of this appointment he had been raised three stages in the peerage—Baron Reading of Erleigh (1914), Viscount Reading (1916), and earl of Reading (1917).

He resigned the office of lord chief justice in 1921 and was appointed viceroy of India at a time when that country was in a state of nationalist ferment. A dyarchy had been established by the Government of India Act of 1919 as a step toward independence, but it had not brought tranquillity (*see* INDIA-PAKISTAN, SUBCONTINENT OF: *History*). The system was rejected by the Swaraj (self-rule) movement of educated Hindu and Muslim opinion, and Mohandas K. Gandhi persuaded millions of Indians to boycott Western goods and institutions by passive resistance. They resented the humiliations suffered by their fellow countrymen elsewhere in the British Empire, and the ruthless suppression of the Amritsar Rebellion (April 1919) had driven Indians to a state of dangerous anger. Reading had only limited success in trying to gain Indian assent to British policy. He imprisoned two Muslim leaders, the brothers Mohammed and Shaukat Ali, in 1921. He sought reconciliation with Gandhi but had him prosecuted in March 1922 for incitement to civil disobedience. Some form of self-government was established in most of the provinces and there was an approach to cooperation in the central legislative council, but the constitution broke down completely in the Central Provinces and was suspended in Bengal with a return to autocratic government.

Reading tried to conciliate Muslim opinion when he cabled in February 1922 to the secretary of state for India, Edwin Samuel Montagu, suggesting that the terms of the Treaty of Sèvres (1920) should be eased for the Turks. The proposal was published by Montagu without the authority of the Cabinet, and it helped to bring Lloyd George's pro-Greek policy to an end. It also led to Montagu's resignation.

Reading's term as viceroy ended in April 1926, and on his return to England he was made a marquess (May 7, 1926), the first commoner to be so elevated since the duke of Wellington. He was secretary of state for foreign affairs (August–November 1931) in J. Ramsay MacDonald's National government. Reading died in London on Dec. 30, 1935.

See 2nd Marquess of Reading, *Rufus Isaacs, First Marquess of Reading, by His Son*, 2 vol. (1942–45). (J. F. B.)

READING, a county and parliamentary borough and the county town of Berkshire, Eng., 38 mi. (61 km.) W of London by road. Pop. (1961) 119,937. Area 14.2 sq.mi. (37 sq.km.). Reading is an important junction of railways running west from London and south from the Midlands, and the Kennet and Avon Canal, to Bath and Bristol, and the Thames afford it connections by water. It lies on the Kennet River near where it joins the Thames. All the ancient churches are restored: Greyfriars Church, formerly monastic, was completed early in the 14th century and after the dissolution of the monasteries served successively as a town hall, a workhouse, and a jail, being restored to its proper use in 1864; St. Mary's was rebuilt in 1551 from the remains of a nunnery founded by Aelfthryth in expiation of the murder of her stepson Edward the Martyr; St. Laurence's is a Perpendicular building with Norman and Early English features; St. Giles's was much damaged during the siege of 1643 by the parliamentary forces and is almost wholly rebuilt. Public gardens occupy most of the site of the Benedictine Abbey.

A University College was opened in 1892 and affiliated to Oxford; its success led to the gathering of an endowment fund and it became an independent university with a charter in 1926. Its researches into agriculture, horticulture, and dairying are of special importance. The National Institute for Research in Dairying, established in 1912, is part of the university. At the grammar school, founded in 1485 and now occupying modern buildings, Archbishop Laud (a native of Reading) was educated. There is also a bluecoat school (1656) now just outside the borough at Sonning. The municipal museum, besides an art gallery and other exhibits, includes Roman relics from Silchester (*q.v.*) and finds from the Thames.

Reading early became a place of importance. In 871 the Danes encamped there, and in 1006 it was burned by Sweyn. It consisted of only 30 houses at the time of the Domesday survey. It is thought that a fortification existed there before the Conquest, and Stephen built a masonry castle which Henry II destroyed. On the foundation of a Benedictine Abbey in 1121, the town, hitherto demesne of the crown, was granted to the Abbey by Henry I. Henry VIII converted the Abbey, whose church was among the largest in the country, into a palace and it was destroyed during the Civil War. From the 12th until the 16th century, Reading's history was that of the struggle as to rights and privileges between the Abbey and the merchants' guild. A 16th-century account of the merchants' guild shows that many trades were then carried on, but John Leland says the town "chiefly stondith by clothing." By the 17th century the trade had begun to decline; the bequest of the clothier John Kendrick (d. 1624) did little to revive it, and it was greatly injured by the Civil War. In the 18th century the chief trade was in malt.

The first town charter is that of Henry III (1253), confirmed and amplified by succeeding sovereigns. The governing charter until 1835 was that of Charles I (1639), incorporating the town under the title of the mayor, aldermen, and burgesses. The market, chiefly held on Saturday, can be traced to the reign of Henry III; four fairs granted by the charter of 1562 are still held.

Reading is an agricultural centre with famous nursery gardens. Its biggest and best-known industry is biscuit manufacture, but there is much business in printing, iron foundries, engineering works, malting, and brewing. The sale of corn, cattle, and flour is carried on extensively, and there are pottery and brick works, together with riverside boatbuilding yards. The parliamentary constituency of Reading returns one member to Parliament.

READING, a city of southeastern Pennsylvania, U.S., the seat of Berks County, is located on the Schuylkill River, 58 mi. NW of Philadelphia. Population (1960) city, 98,177 (a 10.2% decrease from 109,320 in 1950); standard metropolitan statistical area (Berks County), 275,414 (255,740 in 1950). (For comparative population figures *see* table in PENNSYLVANIA: *Population.*)

History.—In 1748 Reading was laid out and surveyed at the great ford on the Schuylkill. The plans were supervised by Thomas Penn, who insisted on the large open square, Penn Common, for market purposes, as was common in England. He named the town for the seat of Berkshire, Eng., the ancestral home of the Penns. Four years later, when Berks County was created, Reading became the county seat. It was incorporated as a borough in 1783, with a population of 2,100, and was chartered as a city in 1847.

Though there were many Germans among the first settlers they were not politically minded and control of local affairs remained in the hands of the English. As a result of the Revolutionary War, the German element in Reading and elsewhere in Pennsylvania began to assert itself and eventually elected three governors from Reading and Berks County. As early as the spring of 1775 two companies of infantry (mostly Germans) left the district for service under Gen. George Washington near Boston. Reading served as a depot for supplies and as a manufacturer of cannon and it maintained a prison camp for the Hessians captured at the Battle of Trenton. The thrifty Pennsylvania Germans hired out some of the Hessian prisoners in their charge. During the American Civil War, Reading was the first to send a military unit to defend the national capital when Abraham Lincoln called for

troops. The Ringgold light artillery, largely locally recruited, was later named the "First Defenders."

The local citizens are still proud of their predominantly Pennsylvania-German heritage, which they seek to keep alive at the widely attended annual Pennsylvania Dutch folk festival at nearby Kutztown.

Industrial Growth.—From the earliest days the making of iron and steel was important. In this area the first cold-blast furnace in America was set up and the first steel was commercially produced in Pennsylvania. At the middle of the 19th century Berks County had more iron- and steel-producing plants than any county in the U.S. The prosperity of Reading's primary iron and steel production continued until the upper Great Lakes ore replaced the use of Pennsylvania ore. Reading made the adjustment by shifting to the fabrication of iron and steel. The opening of the Schuylkill Canal to Philadelphia in 1824 (abandoned in 1922), the Union Canal to Lebanon and Middletown on the Susquehanna in 1828 (abandoned in 1880), and the building of the Philadelphia and Reading Railroad in 1838 (extended to Pottsville in 1842) greatly stimulated industrial growth, as did the building of the Pennsylvania Railroad to Reading in 1884.

An interesting feature of Reading's industrial history was the sudden mushrooming of safety-bicycle manufacturing to satisfy the fad of the 1890s. When the bicycle boom passed much hope was held out for automobile manufacturing. From 1900 to 1912 Charles E. Duryea manufactured a durable car that won a number of speed and endurance tests but did not sell well. The Reading Steamer, produced from 1900 to 1903, was a novel machine that did not catch the fancy of the buying public.

The decline of primary iron and steel manufacturing and the blasted hopes of the bicycle and the automobile business were offset by the development of the textile and hosiery industry by two German technicians, Ferdinand Thun and Henry Janssen, around 1900. Other Germans built textile and hosiery factories and gave the city a national reputation.

Reading became an important retail and wholesale trading centre. It is located in the midst of a rich agricultural, dairy, and industrial county and ranks third industrially in the state, with about 700 industrial establishments in the city and its suburbs. These include railway shops and plants producing builders' hardware, foundry products, hosiery machinery, clothing, optical goods, chemicals, dairy products, and pretzels. One of the largest full-fashioned hosiery mills in the world is located there, as are also an extensive single-unit foundry and a huge brick-burning kiln.

Skilled craftsmen form a large proportion of the population and union organizations are strong in the community, which has a tradition of unionism and socialism.

Reading was the second city in the U.S. to elect a socialist government. "Jim" Maurer was for many years nationally known as the leader of a moderate brand of socialism. (In contrast to the usual moderation, during the railroad strikes in 1877 ten men were killed and scores seriously wounded.)

The hosiery business, which once employed more than half the wage earners of Reading, has declined, but the city anticipated the slump and in the 1950s and 1960s stimulated new industries and the growth of old industries to take up the slack.

Education and Cultural Activities.—The public-school system comprises evening and summer schools in addition to the usual kindergarten through senior high school. A unique feature is the ownership by the school district of an extensive museum and art gallery, both of which are thoroughly integrated into the public school work at all levels. The butterfly collection and the collection of Carboniferous Age insects are nationally recognized. Pennsylvania State University, the University of Pennsylvania, and Temple University maintain extension centres and institutes at Reading. Albright College (Evangelical United Brethren; founded in 1856), a four-year liberal arts college, is also located there. The county historical society has a valuable collection of ancient fire-fighting equipment. Both the symphony orchestra and the Ringgold band are among the oldest in America.

Parks and Historic Sites.—Mt. Penn, to the east of the city, rises to an elevation of 1,140 ft. and is the centre of a park system of more than 2,000 ac. Penn Common (50 ac.) is still a popular recreational area in the heart of the city. The anchor of the battleship "Maine" rests there. Among the many historical landmarks in Reading and its environs are the Conrad Weiser Farm, Hopewell Village National Historic Site, and the Daniel Boone homestead. (L. A. GR.)

READING. It is difficult to discover many activities either at work or play that do not require some and often considerable reading. In general, reading is the indispensible thoroughfare of communication with an ever expanding world. This article is divided into two parts: an account of reading in the formal educational process, and an account of adult reading improvement.

What Is Reading?—There are many definitions of reading. Contrary to certain views, pronunciation of words is not reading. Many definitions centre around the notion that reading is getting meaning from the printed page. This is misleading. There are no meanings on the printed page, only symbols that stand for meanings. (*See* SEMANTICS IN LOGIC.) Printed symbols as such only stimulate recall of familiar concepts. Thus all that identification of a word or a group of words does is to stimulate arousal of earlier encountered meanings. Any new meanings come, not from the author or from the symbols as such but from manipulation of the meanings (concepts) recalled by the reader.

M. A. Tinker and C. M. McCullough in *Teaching Elementary Reading* (Appleton-Century-Crofts, New York, 1968), have defined reading as follows: "Reading involves the identification and recognition of printed or written symbols which serve as stimuli for the recall of meanings built up through past experience, and further the construction of new meanings through the reader's manipulation of relevant concepts already in his possession. The resulting meanings are organized into thought processes according to the purposes that are operating in the reader. Such an organization results in modifications of thought, and perhaps of behavior, or it may even lead to radically new behavior which takes place in the personal or social development of the individual."

History of Reading, Reading Research, and Tests.—E. B. Huey points out that wherever there has been civilization there has been reading and writing. Most, if not all, primitive people had or have some form of picture writing. Written records have been found in northern Babylonia that are more than 5,000 years old. Babylonian as well as ancient Egyptian writing advanced beyond the pictograph stage. (*See* AKKADIAN LANGUAGE; SUMERIAN LANGUAGE; HIEROGLYPHS.)

The alphabet was not invented by people of a single nation. Many alphabets were devised. The creation of an alphabet is considered one of the greatest triumphs of the human mind. The Phoenicians borrowed alphabetic characters from the Egyptians and other ancient peoples and modified them into a practical alphabet for commercial uses. Later this alphabet was used by the Greeks and in turn was adopted by the Romans. It became the basis for the present alphabet of the Western world.

Reading in ancient civilizations was done largely by the privileged classes. Even before Christianity, churchmen were the largest literate group. Reading by laymen was to a great extent delayed until after printing by movable type was invented by Gutenberg, with the help of others, in the mid-15th century. (*See* also PRINTING: *The History of Printing: The West.*) Much of the early printing was of religious materials, particularly the Bible. Before long, printing from type spread throughout Western Europe, with more and more people reading. (*See* also BOOK: *The 16th-Century Book.*)

With the development of alphabets came reading in the modern sense, and also methods of learning to read. The fact that in early times each letter was used to represent a definite sound led to learning to read by letters. The ABC method of learning to read became general among the Greeks and Romans and persisted until relatively recent times in the Western world. At first all beginning books were religious. Later, a small amount of non-religious text material appeared. The Puritans brought to America an ABC catechism. Somewhat later this was succeeded by the famous *New England Primer*. The alphabet-spelling system

of reading instruction was stressed during the colonial period as it was in Europe generally. This instruction was designed to promote religious and moral education. Reading was largely oral with great emphasis upon proper pronunciation, stress, emphasis, pauses, and gestures.

The word method was introduced by Horace Mann (*q.v.*) about 1840. All words were learned by sight. The first phonic era began about 1870 and continued until about 1920. Using this method, the pupils were kept so busy sounding out words that they became slow, laborious readers who lost sight of meanings. Disappointment with results of this extreme emphasis upon phonics led to the look-and-say method, equally unsatisfactory.

Just before 1920 the method of silent reading was launched. It was popular in the 1920s, while oral reading was neglected. Later, particularly from 1940 to the present, authorities have advocated the teaching of both oral and silent reading.

In the second half of the 20th century, many methods of teaching reading have been promoted. Among these are the linguistic, language experience, programmed, and augmented Roman alphabet methods. These may be classified under three heads: those with a code-emphasis approach (phonics); those which stress comprehension; and those which emphasize balanced reading development. Jeanne S. Chall in *Learning to Read: the Great Debate* (1967) states that a survey of research indicates a significant advantage for the code-emphasis approach in beginning reading instruction over a meaning emphasis. C. M. McCullough suggested in 1968 that best results are apt to be obtained if the teacher uses the beneficial features of each of the various methods, *i.e.*, balanced reading development. Many authorities tend toward the balanced program rather than emphasis upon phonics or meaning to the exclusion of beneficial contributions from other sources.

Reading Instruction in the 1960s.—A new idea is teaching baby to read. Glenn J. Doman's *How to Teach Your Baby to Read* (1964) excited parents and disturbed educators. He believes that children will benefit from being taught to read from the age of two years. Undoubtedly this program will delight many ambitious mothers while disappointing others. But why teach very young children to read? Is it because Mother desires it, or the child? Many believe that early childhood years are for spontaneous activity, play, use of imagination, and learning to think. It should be noted that preschool children coached in reading do not maintain their acceleration in reading during the elementary grades as well as self-taught children. The self-taught child is not forced to learn to read. He is motivated by an inner drive to learn. Although he may receive help from members of the family, he has asked for it.

Words in colour is another fad. Each of the 47 sounds in English is printed in a distinctive colour. Thus a sound is always represented by one colour. Research has shown the printing of letters of words in colour contributes nothing.

The crawling cure is another fanciful theory, put forward by C. H. Delacato. He holds that lateral dominance in the central nervous system is responsible for language ability. If a child fails to learn to read, he has not established cerebral dominance. Delacato states that dominance is established by proper childhood experiences. If a child has failed to develop his dominance to the proper level, he will tend to fail to learn to read. Guided practice in posture during sleep and in creeping and crawling can make up for the lack and the child will then learn to read. There are no valid experimental results to support these claims.

Research.—Experimental studies, beginning in the 1890s, have brought about marked changes in understanding the reading process and in the teaching of reading. After 1900, experiments increased rapidly, until more than 100 reports were appearing annually by mid-20th century. Research areas include teacher preparation and practice, sociology of reading, physiology and psychology of reading, teaching of reading, and reading of atypical learners.

Prominent among the techniques for studying reading processes are eye-movement measurement and use of reading tests. About 1900, techniques for recording eye movements were developed, particularly the photography of eye movements. Later came an electrical method of recording eye movements during reading. Both methods continue in use. The eye-movement measures are valid and reliable indicators of reading efficiency. It was discovered early that the eyes move along a line of print in quick jerks followed by pauses. These interfixation saccadic (jerky) moves are very rapid, from 10 to 17 milliseconds. They are so rapid that no vision is possible. This is easily checked: Look in a mirror at the image of the right eye and then shift your gaze to the image of the left eye. No movement of the eyes can be detected although you know it has occurred. The fixation pauses are longer, averaging about 250 milliseconds. During reading, the eyes are at rest a large part of the time, about 94%. The time for moves is about 6%. At times a backward move to the left in the line, a regression, is made to reread or to get a clearer view of words. On reaching the end of the line, the eyes swing in a backsweep to the beginning of the next line.

The patterns of these eye-movement sequences have been studied in a large variety of reading situations. A few of the findings follow: Young children make more fixation pauses per line than older children and adults; also, their pause durations are longer and more regressions are made. Eye movements of the developing child improve rapidly from the first to the end of the fourth grade and then more slowly to the eighth or ninth grade. Similarly, poor readers make many fixations and regressions of relatively long duration. The effective reader makes few fixations and regressions of short duration. These findings have led to the assumption that poor eye movements cause poor reading. So techniques for pacing eye movements have been used to improve reading efficiency. Actually, as Tinker points out, eye movements merely reflect reading efficiency, and are not causes of it. Thus when a poor reader improves, this gain is reflected by a change in the eye-movement patterns.

Eye movements have been studied in a number of special reading situations. In addition to research, eye movements have been measured in reading clinics. Actually, however, eye-movement measurement is a research tool. The clinician can dispense with the study of eye movements without loss of efficiency.

The eye-voice span is investigated by photographing eye movements during oral reading. This span is the number of words that the eyes are ahead of the voice. It varies from zero for the word-by-word reader to 6 to 8 words for the efficient reader. To be a good oral reader one must have a fairly long eye-voice span.

Another important area of eye-movement research is legibility of print. Speed of reading will tell whether one typographical arrangement is more legible than another. But only by examining the eye-movement patterns can one find out the cause of variation in speed from one arrangement to another. For instance, in reading 6-point type, fixation and regression as well as pause duration are significantly greater than for reading 10-point type. Similar analyses can be made in studying the legibility of other typographical arrangements.

Tests are used both for research in reading and for teaching purposes. There were about 200 reading tests in print in the late 1960s. A complete list of these tests is given by O. K. Buros in *Reading Tests and Reviews* (1968). Practically all are standardized tests, *i.e.*, of proven reliability and validity as measuring devices. The kinds are as follows: (1) Survey tests, such as the *Gates-MacGinitie Reading Survey*, are used primarily to ascertain a pupil's level of achievement in vocabulary knowledge, comprehension, and speed. (2) Group diagnostic tests furnish data for guidance in reading instruction and enable the teacher to discover a pupil's strengths and weaknesses in such specific skills as word perception, understanding sentences, and noting details. Some tests, such as the *Silent Reading Diagnostic Tests* (Lyons and Carnahan) and *Doren Diagnostic Reading Test*, are concerned largely with detecting difficulties in word perception. Actually there is no clear-cut division between the survey type and the diagnostic type of group tests. (3) Reading readiness tests measure those abilities and skills important in learning to read. (See *Reading Readiness* below.) (4) Informal reading tests are not standardized, and are used for day-by-day appraisals needed in individualized instruction. Some informal tests are constructed by the teacher to check daily, weekly, or monthly reading progress. Other informal tests are found in workbooks. (5) Oral reading tests are both standardized and informal. The results of these tests are especially useful for guidance in reading instruction. Errors are recorded as the child reads orally. Analysis of these errors will disclose individual needs and indicate necessary correction. (6) Individual detailed diagnostic tests, such as the *Durrell Analysis of Reading Difficulty*, are given to an individual subject by a trained examiner. These tests are used for detailed diagnosis of the more serious reading difficulties. Such areas as oral and silent reading, reversals of words, listening comprehension, word recognition and word analysis, identifying letter names, and auditory and visual discrimination are tested. (7) Speed of reading tests appear separately or as part of a survey test.

One main use of reading tests is for aid to teaching. Another is to determine what the average standing and range of scores in a particular class, school grade, or school system is. Reading tests also find wide use in research programs.

Reading Improvement a Developmental Process.—Acquisition of skill in reading is a complex, developmental process. As the student progresses, he acquires skill in word recognition, improves his vocabulary and his knowledge of concepts, and gains in ability to understand ideas. The materials read gradually become more complicated in vocabulary and concepts and in intricacy of sentence structure and language. Ever greater demands are made upon his capacity to grasp meaning and appreciate style in writing. As he moves into the middle grades, he should acquire competence in comprehension and study skills. Eventually, the proficient reader learns to do more than passively recognize and grasp meanings. In addition, he interprets, evaluates, and reflects upon these meanings. Use of reading as a tool to gain knowledge is relatively ineffective unless it is associated with thinking. Thus, the reader should be critical and use his accumulated experience and knowledge fully to comprehend whatever he may be reading.

Fundamental Aspects of Reading.—A consensus among experts as to the fundamental aspects of reading is unlikely. Certain aspects listed below, however, would probably be accepted by nearly everyone in the field of reading.

Perception of Words is fundamental to all reading. Word identification and recognition are tied in with word perception. It is desirable to define these terms: Initial inspection of a new word involves identification of its printed or written symbol in terms of its visual appearance and its sound. The meaning gained from identification may be slight or great, depending upon the experience of the reader and the amount of help available from the context in which the word occurs.

Word identification and word recognition are interrelated. As noted by Tinker and McCullough, to recognize a word means to identify it as a word previously known. Perception is involved both in identification and recognition of words. The complete perceptual act involved in reading a word is one of great complexity. For a recognized word, the meaning attached tends to be broader and the perception clearer than if the word is merely identified. Recognition of a word implies familiarity, which may have been enhanced by having met it in several contexts. And perception is basically associated with experience. Thus, the person who brings the most extensive experience to his reading gets the most from the printed page.

Concepts and Vocabulary.—Acquiring concepts and building vocabulary occur simultaneously, for the refinement and extension of word meanings automatically involve the development of concepts. That is, the concept represented by a word is the meaning that the word has come to have in general. One corrects and refines each concept through additional experiences.

Vocabulary building is achieved as one incorporates new words into his speaking and understanding. The relatively mechanical identification and recognition of words should be made secondary to the development of comprehension and use. Progress in the learning of word meanings until they become vivid and precise is a gradual process. In general, three approaches serve to enlarge one's repertory of meanings in reading: (1) varied and rich firsthand and vicarious experiences; (2) wide and extensive reading; and (3) study of words.

Comprehension and Interpretation are not synonymous, but they are closely related and interdependent. Interpretation is the thoughtful side of comprehension. Interpretation involves grasping the more profound implications and meanings, which is more than mere literal comprehension. Interpretation is required to reach conclusions or to draw inferences from what is read.

Several factors determine how easily and how much one comprehends: (1) Level of intellectual ability. The correlation between intelligence and comprehension and vocabulary knowledge is high. (2) The person whose experiences have been rich and numerous will comprehend more readily than those with more limited experience. (3) The mature reader varies his speed to fit the kind and difficulty of the material, aiding comprehension.

The more complicated aspects of comprehension are related to the study skills, which become especially important in the work type of reading such as in geography, history, psychology, and mathematics. Each kind of material has its own concepts and vocabulary, unique relationships, logic, and form of presentation. Specialized reading or study skills are needed for different subjects. The principal study skills may be briefly noted: (1) *Skimming* is a form of partial reading done rapidly to acquire specific kinds of information, such as to find a certain date, name, or other relevant fact. (2) Certain types of study material require *apprehension of relevant details*, which requires slow, analytical progress and at times some rereading. (3) *Following printed directions* is required in many activities, such as assembling a tool, making a cake, or solving a mathematical problem. (4) In reading *to generalize or draw a conclusion*, the reader exercises judgment in selecting and relating relevant material in one or more articles, then combining the findings in such a way as to draw an inference or make a generalization that may be stated in the form of a conclusion. (5) Reading often calls for *critical evaluation* of what is read. In searching for information on a specific topic one often encounters conflicting views. Reconciliation of such views demands critical evaluation. Drawing upon his whole background of experience, the reader will frequently be able to evaluate whether or not any given view seems plausible, is partly correct, or appears biased. This process should enable the competent reader to detect propaganda and evaluate it critically. (6) *Locating information* in printed sources, such as reference books, is an essential tool in the study type of reading.

Reading Readiness.—As Tinker and McCullough put it, "Reading readiness means attainment of the level of development that makes it possible for a child to learn to read in regular classroom instruction by a competent teacher." Thus a child is ready to begin to learn to read only when he has reached a certain stage of intellectual maturity, acquired fairly good emotional adjustment, attained certain favourable attitudes towards learning, and acquired considerable verbal facility in oral communication. Some children need more time than others to get ready to read. The concept of reading readiness is basic to the development of good reading ability at all levels from the kindergarten on. The program of instruction in the kindergarten is concerned to a large degree with preparing the child for reading. In fact, children who have attended kindergarten learn to read more readily than those who have not.

Several factors influence reading readiness in grade one. Intellectual development is an important determinant of reading success. The higher the mental age, the easier beginning reading is likely to be. But chronological age has little bearing on reading readiness. And when physical health is impaired the child is not ready to direct his attention consistently to learning. Physical fatigue and inability to see or hear normally are all handicaps to readiness. Auditory discrimination, the ability to distinguish between sounds in spoken words as between the vowels of *can* and *cane,* or between the initial consonants of *boat* and *coat,* is required for readiness. Also important is the ability to discriminate visually between such words as *dog* and *day, were* and *wear.* Pupils who have a rich background of general infor-

mation and are able to converse about it are apt to learn readily to read. Facility in language use is an important prerequisite for progress in reading.

Reading readiness is not limited to beginning reading. The concept of readiness implies that at each stage of reading one is prepared to read new material with understanding. Thus a student should be prepared to read with understanding each new unit or reading lesson. Preparing students for new units becomes increasingly important as the materials become more complicated in content. For each specific set of material the student must be equipped with the necessary concepts and vocabulary and the ability to handle any intricacies of the language involved.

A number of tests have been devised for appraising readiness for reading. In one or another of these tests the following are measured: (1) comprehension of spoken directions; (2) knowledge of word meanings; (3) skill in copying visual designs; (4) ability to recognize and interpret pictures; (5) auditory perception; (6) visual perception; (7) naming letters of the alphabet and the numerals; (8) recognizing words that have been taught. Other areas of appraisal for readiness include intelligence, visual efficiency, and auditory acuity. Skilled teachers, after a few weeks with a group, are able to judge reading readiness fairly well.

Reading Disability and Remedial Reading.—With the best of classroom instruction, a surprising number of pupils fail to make the progress in reading to be expected from their capacities. Disabled readers turn up at all school levels from the latter part of grade one into the university. About 15% of elementary school students are disabled readers, two to four times as many boys as girls.

Who is a disabled reader? Although different formulas are used to detect amount of retardation, a disabled reader is one whose reading is appreciably below his capacity to learn. There is not complete agreement on how much discrepancy there must be between reading grade and mental grade (capacity) before the child is classed as a disabled reader, but the following is much used: In the primary grades this discrepancy is from one-half to three-fourths of a grade. Thus a second-grade child whose mental grade is 2.7 and whose reading grade is 2.1 would be considered a disabled reader. In the intermediate grades, a difference of one to one and a half grades is used and in high school the difference is about two grades.

Reading disability prevents normal progress in learning. The need for successful achievement is fundamental in all children. When this need is thwarted, the child's feeling of inferiority tends to produce either unfortunate compensatory behaviour or a retreat into daydreaming. The antisocial compensatory behaviour, motivated largely by a desire for attention, disrupts classroom procedures. Daydreaming and other aspects of the shut-in personality can become as serious as antisocial behaviour.

Prognosis for improvement in reading of disability cases is good provided the pattern of difficulties is discovered by accurate diagnosis. Ordinarily instruction in remedial reading results in gains in reading achievement greater than one grade per year, the average for normal children. G. L. Bond and M. A. Tinker in *Reading Difficulties: Their Diagnosis and Correction* (2nd ed., 1967), cite gains of 2.0 to 3.8 grades in reading from six months of remedial instruction.

Although the diagnostic and remedial reading program is needed, emphasis should also be placed upon prevention of reading disability. Actually, many reading difficulties can be forestalled, and others can be corrected in their initial stages by the classroom teacher. Any preventive program involves at least three kinds of instructional emphasis: (1) an adequate reading readiness program; (2) satisfactory adjustment of instruction to individual differences; and (3) systematic developmental programs at all levels. If it were possible in day-to-day instruction to provide for each pupil's progress in terms of his capabilities, there would be less occasion for remedial teaching. Such an ideal educational situation cannot be achieved yet. Even with the best of contemporary teaching, a few children will be in difficulty serious enough to require diagnosis and remedial instruction beyond the capability of the classroom teacher. And with less than the best of teaching, the incidence of disability cases will increase.

Causes.—The causes of reading disability are many. The belief that such disability arose from multiple causes was generally accepted in the late 1960s. Several visual deficiencies may be contributing causes: farsightedness, binocular incoordination, fusion difficulties, and aniseikonia (unequal ocular images in the two eyes). Visual examinations are essential in diagnosing causes of reading disability. Hearing impairment can interfere with learning to read when the hearing loss is severe enough to interfere with normal auditory discrimination or when the child has high tone deafness. All reading disability cases should have a hearing test. Defects in speech that complicate word discrimination and recognition may contribute to reading disability. Also in certain cases, glandular dysfunction, particularly hypothyroidism, may contribute to reading disability. Reading disability ordinarily is accompanied by emotional involvement that adversely affects the child's social and personal adjustment. This maladjustment may be caused by constitutional factors, environmental pressures, or failure in reading. Thus, in many cases, emotional difficulties may be both cause and effect. If these difficulties are due primarily to the reading failure, they tend to disappear when the child does learn to read. Neurological factors as causes of reading disability are difficult to diagnose and apparently seldom occur.

In many instances, reading disability is due largely to educational factors. Lack of proper individualization of instruction, including lack of proper emphasis upon reading readiness, will hinder effective reading progress. One or more of the following factors may be involved in the ineffective teaching that causes reading disability: too rapid coverage of units of material; isolation of reading instruction from other school subjects; improper emphasis upon some technique or skill; treating reading as a by-product of content studies; or failure to maintain a proper balance in the growth of a large number of reading skills and abilities.

Diagnosis of reading difficulties must precede remedial treatment. An individualized approach must be adopted in diagnosing, for no two cases are exactly alike. Techniques employed for diagnosis of reading difficulties include group survey tests, group diagnostic tests, informal procedures, and detailed individual techniques. Group survey tests are used to help identify reading disability cases. Comparison of the test score with some adequate measure of learning capacity will indicate the degree to which the child is retarded in reading. Survey tests, in addition to yielding a reading grade score, are to some degree diagnostic. Some information on the individual needs of a pupil is revealed by examination of his test responses. Group diagnostic tests are analytical and provide a profile of silent reading abilities. Examination of such a profile reveals the strong and weak areas in a pupil's repertory of the abilities that are measured in the subtests.

Informal diagnosis (not standardized) is achieved by use of a carefully graded series of basic readers, ones the child has not used before. Selections of 100 to 150 words are chosen from successive books in the series. A few comprehension questions are organized for each selection. The pupil reads the selections aloud until his reading levels are determined. These levels are described in detail by Bond and Tinker in *Reading Difficulties: Their Diagnosis and Correction*. They include independent reading level, instructional reading level, frustration level, and probable capacity reading level (selection in which the child can comprehend at least 75% of the content when read aloud by the examiner). Nila B. Smith in *Graded Selections for Informal Reading Diagnosis: Grades 1 through 3* (1959) and (with Anna Harris) *Grades 4 through 6* (1963) gives selections and questions organized by grades for informal testing. Informal diagnosis is useful for preliminary determination of reading levels and to discover strengths and weaknesses. Also it can supplement detailed individual testing. Analysis of errors made in oral reading on an informal test can give the examiner a wealth of information on strengths and weaknesses of a child's reading. Such information is especially useful for dealing with moderate cases of reading disability.

For the cases of severe reading retardation, a detailed individual test should be used such as the Gates-McKillop, the Durrell, the Spache, or the Monroe diagnostic programs. For description of these tests see Bond and Tinker's *Reading Difficulties: Their Diagnosis and Correction*. A trained examiner must give these tests. An individual intelligence test, such as the Stanford-Binet or the Wechsler test, is usually included in the diagnostic program.

Remedial Procedures are based upon the diagnostic findings. A majority of difficulties, which tend to be minor or moderate, can be taken care of by the classroom teacher in her day-to-day teaching. But the more severe cases must be referred to reading specialists either in a school reading centre or a clinic.

In general, good remedial teaching approximates the regular basic program used for normal pupils but is more inclusive and more highly individualized. Significant features are its informality, its wide range of approaches, and its freedom to adapt activity to individual needs and interests. But with certain severe cases, this general method needs to be supplemented by such techniques as emphasis upon phonics, or the Fernald tracing method. For slow-learning children the program is similar but progress is much slower.

If a child fails to respond to remedial treatment, the teacher should reexamine the diagnosis, perhaps give additional tests, and revise the remedial program of teaching. With proper diagnosis, one can expect practically every disability case to make progress, some slowly, some rapidly.

Reading in Various Countries.—W. S. Gray in *The Teaching of Reading and Writing* (1956) reported studies on the nature of the reading process in various languages, using mainly the recording of eye movements. These records were made for 14 different nationalities. Thorough analysis of the records led Gray to the following conclusions: In all languages, mature readers have mastered the basic attitudes and skills needed for good oral reading and for fluent, thoughtful silent reading. The studies revealed that oculomotor behaviour, and therefore the reading process, is similar in the various languages although Arabic and Hebrew were read right-to-left and the others left-to-right.

Apparently no country devotes as much effort, in terms of professional meetings, research, development of methodology, publications, development of reading tests and of basic series with supplementary texts, as the United States. The same is true for attention paid to remedial reading and reading readiness. Great Britain and the Scandinavian countries appear to be the most progressive in teaching methods and attention to reading readiness and to remedial reading of the countries outside the United States, with the possible exception of Australia, which has programs similar to those in the United States but on a less extensive and effective level. Ireland and the Arabic-speaking countries do not have programs in reading readiness or remedial reading. In Ireland much time is devoted to the teaching of Irish to the sacrifice of adequate time for English instruction. This seems unfortunate for few make use of the Irish language after leaving school. In India, with its many languages and dialects, the teaching of reading is on a primitive level. Consequently illiteracy (*q.v.*) is widespread.

During the latter half of the 19th century and early 20th century, Germany was a leader in reading research. Soon after the beginning of the 20th century, the lead in this area was taken over by the United States under the direction of men who had done graduate work in Germany: J. M. Cattell, C. H. Judd, and G. S. Hall. Since about 1920, the United States has continued to hold the lead in all aspects of reading research.

The Mature Reader.—The ultimate goal in developing one's reading skills is to become a mature adult reader. In the general population, these expectations appear to fall short of what is hoped for. According to Gray and Rogers in *Maturity in Reading: Its Nature and Appraisal* (1956), the reading behaviour of our adult population ranges all the way from gross immaturity to a very high level of maturity. The number of highly mature readers is small. The hopeful aspects of this survey are that most adults expressed enthusiasm for reading, and the superior readers were always able, when the occasion demanded, to interpret what they read with accuracy and penetration.

Tinker and McCullough in *Teaching Elementary Reading* (1968) outlined the characteristics of the mature reader: He will be one who has mastered the essential techniques of word identification and word recognition. He will have an extensive vocabulary. His comprehension will be adequate to meet any reasonable challenge. As needed, he will be able to apply the appropriate comprehension and study skills to whatever he is reading. He will be a versatile reader; *i.e.*, he will be able to adjust his rate of reading to fit the purpose, the difficulty, and the kind of material being read. He will demand of himself that he understand what he reads. Since good reading is thoughtful reading, he will have learned to interpret, to evaluate, and to reflect upon what he reads. His reading interests will be extensive and varied. His taste will be developed and his appreciation sensitive. He realizes that his social and personal adjustment can be enhanced if in conversing he draws upon discriminating interpretations of what he has read. His ability in oral reading has reached a level that allows him to convey information and give pleasure to others. He is able to use his reading to satisfy a variety of needs as he becomes aware of them. Furthermore, he has built the foundations necessary for developing further maturity in reading.   (M. A. T.)

ADULT READING IMPROVEMENT

After World War II, an increasingly large number of adults took day and evening instruction in reading. Two types of programs evolved. One is remedial, or a basic reading program for illiterates or semiliterates; the other is developmental, or a program for those whose general reading abilities range from ninth grade through the college levels. The most popular of the latter type were the rapid reading classes for adults who could read well, but could not keep pace with the increase in knowledge. By 1963, librarians estimated that general written knowledge was doubling every 15 years.

Basic Reading.—During World War II, thousands of illiterate young men in the United States Armed Forces had to be taught to read. When they reached a fifth grade equivalent in reading, they were considered functionally literate. By the mid-1960s, however, an estimated 4,400,000 illiterates still existed. An urgent need to reduce unemployment among them and train them to fill vacant positions requiring technical skills developed. Local, state, and federally sponsored basic education programs such as the Job Corps and the Manpower Development program emerged, in addition to several industrial programs. Several million illiterate and semiliterate adults over 25 years of age returned to classrooms.

Because of the wide range of academic achievement and backgrounds of these adults, reading materials, tests, and methods had to be adjusted or redesigned to meet their needs. In comparing research that had been done on literacy programs throughout the world, W. S. Gray found adults learned to read efficiently when the materials were functional and suited to their more mature interests.

Adult Reading Interests.—The reading interests of adults at all stages of development throughout the world vary greatly. Florence Schale found most adults who enroll in reading improvement courses specify an overwhelming interest in keeping pace with instructional materials.

In the only comprehensive study of adult interests, Douglas Waples and Ralph Tyler found only two topics of common interest, international attitudes and problems, and personal hygiene. As expected, reading interests vary with age, sex, academic progress, occupation, and cultural background.

At the adolescent level, H. K. Smith and H. J. Walberg summarized and conducted research on reading interests in 1956 and 1967, respectively. Both concluded girls read more fiction than boys. Smith listed romance specifically as the first interest of girls. Walberg studied only girls and boys interested in physics. Girls in his study listed historical novels over novels (unspecified) and mysteries. Both investigators found that boys, unlike girls, preferred science, technical, and professional books first. Fiction was second with adventure and mysteries high in preference. Biography was included in both studies, although for both sexes, it was not ranked high for enjoyment. Walberg deplored the fact that 15% of science-oriented students seldom read outside of school. Most boys disliked literature, 40% rarely visited a library, and less than half kept up with their schoolwork. He observed that high school students' preoccupation with athletics, cars, and dating encouraged a tendency toward anti-intellectualism in contemporary culture.

Adult Developmental Reading.—The need for adult reading improvement programs was apparent, judging from their growth in academic and commercial establishments after 1945. A survey of college and adult developmental reading programs was conducted by Marjorie W. Geerlofs and Martin Kling in 1967. The objectives of programs in 172 institutions were ranked in the following order: comprehension, flexibility (varying rates of reading for different types of material), rate, study skills, vocabulary, and other skills. They found that many college students with poor grades needed primary emphasis on vocabulary, various levels of comprehension, and study skills; and that most adults enrolled in reading classes to increase speed. In the early 1950s a change in the highly mechanized type of speed reading course inspired by Air Force training during World War II occurred. The tachistoscope, once used to train airmen to identify enemy aircraft, was adapted to recognition of words and short sentences at rates of 1 to $\frac{1}{100}$ second. Evidence of transfer from perception of isolated groups of words to connected passages was not established. By 1967, the Geerlofs and Kling study found only 28% use of this instrument. Directional control techniques, such as paced reading films and filmstrips, were used more widely (41%) according to this study. With these devices, parts of lines and later single lines were exposed on screens at fixed rates, while a group tried to read along at increasingly faster rates. A resulting criticism was that not all people responded to visual stimuli at the same rate. Individual reading pacers, however, were used more in the 1950s. But in 1967, they had declined to 31% of 181 courses. The pacers usually have a moving bar that slides down a page at a controlled rate. The reader, of course, tries to stay ahead of it at whatever rate he sets it.

In the 1960s controversy regarding the nature of the rapid reading process arose. The Geerlofs and Kling study revealed a steady trend toward book- rather than machine-oriented reading courses. This trend began while two different methods of teaching rapid reading were developing. Until 1960, the traditional method generally consisted of giving students material, mostly fiction, to read on pacers or film at fixed rates and then checking comprehension with exercises. Most students read as fast as they could and expected to double their original rates within a range of 400 to 900 words per minute.

Because of growing needs in the 1960s, chains of speed reading courses flourished commercially. A few highlighted a predominantly vertical reading method developed by E. Wood, a radical departure from the traditional method. Students were trained to follow the tips of their fingers vertically down pages of novels. Rates began as abruptly as 5,000–10,000 words per minute until a sense of pacing was established. Eventually, a whole pattern of thought was said to "break through." Promoters of these courses advertised in the mass media; and, in the early 1960s, extremely gifted students gave public testimonials on behalf of the method.

Controversy resulted between professional and commercial reading organizations. The International Reading Association published a "code of ethics" for reading teachers. Further, they advised the public that commercial firms did not have to support their claims in the manner in which qualified reading specialists did. The public was asked to evaluate a rapid reading course based on the following questions: (1) Is a qualified reading teacher giving instruction? (2) Are standardized reading tests used? (3) Are difficult instructional as well as easy fictional materials used for practice? (4) How is comprehension measured? (5) Are there "follow-up" studies of progress after the course?

(6) Is flexibility of rates taught for different materials? (7) What are the median and average results of students?

The second departure from the traditional rapid reading method was an eclectic operant conditioning approach. In 1963, Schale developed the 2R (Reinforced Reading) Method, based on defined psychological principles of reinforced conditioning, closure, and transfer. The acronym 2R-OR-ALERT consisted of seven steps programmed to shape the behaviour of the average reader toward more efficiency. It combined both the traditional horizontal line-for-line reading method with vertical methods of skimming. Average adult students read and/or skimmed programmed instructional materials four to eight times faster with no loss of comprehension. Flexibility was also taught.

Based on copious data from eye-movement studies with average readers taught the traditional way, controversy over whether or not anyone could see a "page-at-a-glance" ensued. Theodore Roosevelt, among others, was purported to have demonstrated such ability. As early as 1908, however, E. B. Huey made available basic research on rate of reading as related to eye movements. He described the average person's eyes as moving across a line in quick hops and jumps, seeing a number of words during each pause or fixation. Depending upon the familiarity of the material, one or more words were to have been processed for meaning mentally. In experiments, he noted that the eyes made occasional regressive movements during the processing of the visual stimuli on the page. He noted that the faster a person read, the fewer fixations and regressions he made.

In 1957 H. Walton suggested the average person could accommodate clearly a total span of 1.25 inches in one fixation (glance) or 2.7 words on nontechnical materials. The average fixation rate is $\frac{1}{5}$ second. Therefore, a maximum rate at which all words can be seen acutely (for the average person) might be 810 words per minute. He also suggested it was possible, though improbable, for exceptional people to have extremely developed visual abilities.

In 1968 Schale began a scientific study of 15 gifted rapid readers. They constituted only 1% of the population studied. A case study was made of a 15-year-old Filipino girl, Maria T. Calderon. She was able to scan at a rate of one second a page on college level essays. A five-second psychological test revealed perfect recall of almost a page of small oddly designed faces dissimilar to anything in her background. She had clearly outstanding ability to recall details. Later she scanned articles with unfamiliar topics; indeed she could recall information but was unable to interpret it properly. On somewhat familiar topics, she was able to scan down the pages at astonishing rates with consistently superior comprehension. Other reading experts verified this ability.

Schale concluded that it is possible for an occasional gifted rapid reader to be discovered in courses designed for acceleration of reading. She cautioned, however, that the majority of students might become frustrated if rates are accelerated beyond their abilities. A special environment, therefore, was recommended for gifted students demonstrating extraordinary visual retentive abilities. No one method or text was claimed as essential to the development of these exceptional rapid readers.

(F. C. Sc.)

BIBLIOGRAPHY.—W. S. Gray and B. Rogers, *Maturity in Reading: Its Nature and Appraisal* (1956); Oscar Ogg, *The 26 Letters* (1961); N. B. Smith, *Reading Instruction for Today's Children* (1963), *American Reading Instruction* (1965); M. A. Tinker, *Bases for Effective Reading* (1965); C. H. Delacato, *Neurological Organization and Reading* (1966); Jeanne S. Chall, *Learning to Read: the Great Debate* (1967); M. D. Jenkinson (ed.), *Reading Instruction: an International Forum* (1967); E. B. Huey, *The Psychology and Pedagogy of Reading* (1908); C. M. McCullough, "Balanced Reading Development," in *Innovation and Change in Reading Instruction,* the 67th Yearbook of the National Society for the Study of Education, pt. ii, pp. 320–356 (1968); M. A. Tinker and C. M. McCullough, *Teaching Elementary Reading,* 3rd ed. (1968). (M. A. T.)
Marjorie W. Geerlofs and Martin Kling, "Current Practices in College and Adult Developmental Reading Programs," *Journal of Reading,* 11:517–520, 567–575 (April 1968); William S. Gray, *The Teaching of Reading and Writing,* United Nations Educational, Scientific, and Cultural Organization (1956); Hal Higdon, "Can Anyone Read 50,000 Words Per Minute?" *Northwestern Review,* 4:25–28 (winter 1969); Wayne Otto and David Ford, *Teaching Adults to Read* (1967); Florence C. Schale, "Three Approaches to Faster Reading," *Reading Improvement,* 2:69–71 (spring 1965); Douglas Waples and Ralph W. Tyler, *What People Want to Read About* (1931); Herbert J. Walberg, "Reading and Study Habits of High School Physics Students," *Journal of Reading,* 11:327–332, 383–389 (Feb. 1968). (F. C. Sc.)

REAL ESTATE: *see* REAL PROPERTY AND CONVEYANCING, LAWS OF.

REAL PROPERTY AND CONVEYANCING, LAWS OF.

The division of property into "real" and "personal," like so much in Anglo-U.S. law, can only be explained historically. In early law, property was deemed real if the courts would restore to a dispossessed owner the thing itself, the *res,* instead of merely giving compensation for its loss. All interests in land fell within this category, with the exception of leaseholds, which were at first regarded more as mere contractual rights than as interests in land (*see* LANDLORD AND TENANT). Indeed, not until late in the 13th century could a dispossessed leaseholder recover even damages against any save his lessor, and when by the end of the 15th century it was finally decided that he might recover the land itself, the classification of leaseholds as personal property had become too firmly established for it to be altered. Thus if today a testator dies leaving all his realty to R and all his personalty to P, the reason for his leasehold's passing to P instead of to R lies in a rule that ceased to exist more than four centuries ago.

This article is concerned with the law of real property and its transfer from person to person in Great Britain and the United States.

I. ENGLISH LAW

Real property is traditionally classified as either corporeal or incorporeal. A right is corporeal where it is accompanied by physical possession of land and incorporeal where it is not. Thus a fee simple in possession is corporeal, whereas a fee simple subject to a life interest is incorporeal, and so are rights over the land of another, such as easements (*e.g.,* a right of way) and profits à prendre (*e.g.,* a right to pasture cattle).

For the purposes of the common law, land includes any type of soil, even if covered by water. A plot of land is deemed to stretch indefinitely upward and to the centre of the earth downward. Buildings and other structures, and things growing in or on the land, normally pass automatically with it. The produce of any piece of land becomes the owner's by accession. Objects merely resting on the land do not form part of it; if let into the soil, however, or otherwise firmly fixed to it, or to something else which is let into it or fixed to it, they do form part of it and are called "fixtures." In certain cases persons entitled to possession of land only for a limited period, such as lessees or tenants for life, may remove, on quitting, any fixtures they have brought onto the land. In other cases they may receive from the freeholder compensation for improvements they have made; these are sometimes called "betterment," as also are works outside the property which increase its value, such as the improvement of access by the making of a public road. Statutes may oblige the landowner to contribute to the cost of such betterment works. Crops produced annually by the labour of the cultivator are termed "emblements" and constitute an exception to the rule that growing crops always pass with the land. They are personal property and so may pass separately from the land on the owner's death. On a sale, however, they pass with the soil unless specifically excluded.

Certain words have acquired a customary meaning when describing the extent of land transferred. "Messuage" means a dwellinghouse together with its outbuildings, and "curtilage" is any courtyard or garden belonging to it. "Dwellinghouse" itself may also be used with that extended meaning. "Farm" includes the farmhouse and the land held with it. "Water" gives the right to both water and fishing but not to the subsoil beneath the water. "Pool" includes both the water and its bed. Owners of land bounded by a river or by the seashore automatically acquire any gradual and imperceptible accretions to the land (alluvion) due to recession of the water.

1. Tenures and Estates.—The main distinguishing features of the English law of real property are the two doctrines of tenures and estates. The basis of these doctrines is the rule (which in theory still exists) that all land is owned by the crown and that subjects may hold land as tenants but cannot own it. There is no allodial land (*i.e.*, land that is the absolute property of the owner) in England. In days when land and its rents and profits constituted most of the tangible wealth of the country, the whole social organization was based upon tenants holding land from a lord in return for various services. However varied the services may have been originally, they became to some extent standardized, and each set of services became known as a tenure, for it showed how the land was held.

The doctrine of estates was directed to the length of time for which the land was held. Each estate could exist in land of any tenure. The two main estates were the fee simple, which endured as long as the tenant or any of his heirs survived (whether his descendants or not), and the life estate, which ended with the tenant's death. The statute *De Donis Conditionalibus* of 1285 (13 Edw. I. c.1) created a third estate, the fee tail, which endured so long as the tenant or any of his descendants lived. A variant, called a conditional fee, was an estate which would subsist until the happening of some uncertain event. Provided that the event chosen to terminate the fee was lawful and did not offend the rule against perpetuities, anything could be selected; *e.g.*, the marriage of a certain person or the destruction of a certain tree. The event could be one which might never happen, such as that members of a family should cease to be lords of a certain manor. Such an estate could be transferred, subject always to the fact that the happening of the condition would bring it to an end.

All these types of fee exemplified the central principle that what a subject could own was not the land itself but merely an estate in that land. This conception of an abstract estate rather than the corporeal land being the subject matter of ownership was a remarkable and distinctive achievement of early English legal thought which contributed greatly both to the triumphant flexibility of the English system and to its undoubted complexity. The description of that system as "an ungodly jumble," a phrase usually attributed to Oliver Cromwell, is understandable but misleading. (*See* ESTATES, ADMINISTRATION OF.)

2. Capacity to Own and Deal with Land.—With certain exceptions, any person is entitled to own and transfer land. The seven principal categories of persons whose rights are or used to be restricted are the following:

Infants.—Since 1926, infants have been unable to hold legal estates in land. Any attempt to convey a legal estate to an infant creates a settlement for the purposes of the Settled Land Act, 1925, with some person of full age entitled to exercise the powers of the tenant for life. The Infant Settlements Act, 1855, authorizes the Chancery Division of the High Court of Justice to sanction certain marriage settlements including dealings with real property made by infants.

Married Women.—Formerly, a wife needed her husband's concurrence to deal with land belonging to her; but the Married Women's Property Act, 1882, and subsequent legislation, equated her position with that of other adults. (*See* HUSBAND AND WIFE, LAWS CONCERNING: *Property and Liabilities.*)

Bankrupts.—Land belonging to a person who is adjudged bankrupt remains vested in him, but the power to deal with it is transferred to his trustee in bankruptcy or to the official receiver in bankruptcy. Public registration of bankruptcies ensures that they come to the notice of potential purchasers of land.

Corporations.—All corporations, except those created by royal charter, formerly needed a "license in mortmain" to authorize them to hold land (*see* MORTMAIN). The license was normally given automatically by the statutes authorizing incorporation, as, *e.g.*, to trading limited companies, the commonest form of corporation. In the absence of a license in mortmain, land was liable to be forfeit to the crown. The law of mortmain, and with it the necessity for licenses, was abolished by the Charities Act, 1960. A corporation, however, still must be given power to hold and deal in land by its instrument of incorporation, and without this dealings will be *ultra vires* and void. Upon the liquidation of a com-

pany for insolvency, its land remains vested in it, but the powers of the board of directors to dispose of it are exercisable only by the liquidator.

Insane Persons.—The property of persons incapable, by reason of mental disorder, of managing their affairs is administered under statutory powers. The court appoints a receiver to deal with a patient's property as directed by the court. If a mentally disordered person himself deals with his property, the transaction will, if fair, be voidable, but not void. To prevent its being enforced against him, he would have to prove that the other party knew him to be of unsound mind.

Felons.—Until the enactment of the Forfeiture Act, 1870, persons convicted of treason, murder, and other felonies forfeited their lands to the crown. They are no longer placed under this disability.

Aliens.—Aliens formerly were not allowed to hold land in England, but since 1870 nationality has been no bar to land ownership. In time of war, however, enemy aliens cannot make valid contracts and so are barred from dealing with their land for value. *See also* ALIEN.

A. HISTORY THROUGH THE 19TH CENTURY

1. Before the Conquest.—The principal features of English land law before 1066 were (1) liberty of alienation of such land as could be alienated (mainly or entirely bookland; *see* ANGLO-SAXON LAW: *Folkright and Privilege*), either *inter vivos* or by will; (2) publicity of transfer by enrollment either in the shire book or church book; (3) equal partition of the estate of a deceased person among his sons, and, in default, among his daughters; (4) cultivation mainly by serfs of various degrees, owing rents in money or labour; (5) variations by custom, tending to become uniform through the similarity of approach of local courts; (6) the *trinoda necessitas*—*i.e.*, the tenant's obligations of military service, repair of bridges, and maintenance of fortifications. The ownership of land was the basis of political privilege, conferring territorial jurisdiction on the landowner. In relation to folkland, this jurisdiction became vested in the king as ultimate arbiter, and in many cases he delegated powers to the great landowners.

2. The Formative Period.—*The Common Law.*—The main effect of the Norman Conquest upon land law was the integration of a system already largely feudal. The rule that all land was owned by the crown was firmly established, and although there might be any number of subinfeudations and so any number of mesne lords, there was always a complete chain of seigniory between the occupying tenant and the king as lord paramount. Further, tenures tended to become stereotyped. When the full effects of the Conquest had been felt, it was possible to classify tenures with some degree of exhaustiveness. The main division of tenures was into free and unfree.

The three main classes of free tenure were (1) tenures in chivalry (principally grand serjeanty and knight service); (2) tenures in socage (principally petty serjeanty, common socage, burgage, and customary socage, *i.e.*, socage subject to special customs such as gavelkind and borough English); and (3) spiritual tenures (principally frankalmoign and divine service). Grand serjeanty obliged the tenant in person to perform some honourable service for the king, while in petty serjeanty the service to the king was of a nonpersonal nature (*see* SERJEANTY). Knight service (*q.v.*) involved providing military service to the king or other lord, though by the middle of the 12th century this was usually commuted for a payment called scutage (*q.v.*). In common socage (*q.v.*), the principal service was usually agricultural in nature, such as performing so many days' plowing each year for the lord. Burgage was a variant of common socage in boroughs, and under gavelkind and borough English (*qq.v.*) the land descended on intestacy to all the sons equally and to the youngest son, respectively, instead of to the eldest son. In addition to the principal service, all these tenures were subject to a number of feudal incidents, such as relief, primer seisin, escheat and, in the case of tenures in chivalry, wardship and marriage. The spiritual tenures were appropriate to ecclesiastical corporations such as bishops or monasteries, their sole obligation being to pray for the souls of the grantor and his heirs; the number of prayers was specified for divine service and unspecified in frankalmoign ("free alms").

The two unfree tenures were villein tenure (which later was called copyhold; *q.v.*) and customary freehold. The essence of unfree tenure was that although the tenant's services were fixed as to quantity (*e.g.*, as to so many days' work per week), they were uncertain as to quality, so that the lord might set the tenant to whatever type of work he wished.

The Legislation of Edward I.—The first Statute of Mortmain, 1279 (7 Edw. I. St.2. c.13), prohibited the conveyance of land to religious bodies without licence from the crown. This avoided the lord's losing his feudal dues by the land's passing into the "dead hand" of a monastery which was never under age, never died, and could never be attainted. But the two statutes in the reign of Edward I of prime importance to the subject are *De Donis Conditionalibus*, 1285 (13 Edw. I. c.1), and *Quia Emptores*, 1290 (18 Edw. I. c.1); each is still in force, and they may with some justice be regarded as two of the main pillars of the law of real property.

Before 1285, if land was conveyed to "X and the heirs of his body," the birth of heirs of his body was treated as a condition, so that once issue had been born, X was able to convey the whole fee simple and defeat the expectations of his issue. *De Donis* provided that the land should descend to X's issue successively *secundam formam in carta doni expressam,* and on failure of heirs of the body revert to the grantor. This produced a "cut down fee" (*feodum talliatum*). By means of collusive actions known as "fines" and "recoveries," it had become possible two centuries later for a tenant in tail to "bar the entail" (*see* ENTAIL) and obtain a fee simple; but the fee tail remained to provide the foundation for the strict settlement as a means for keeping land in the family. *Quia Emptores* prohibited subinfeudation, the process whereby one tenant granted land to another to hold of the grantor as lord. Thus if after 1290 A granted land to B in fee simple, B's lord would be not A but A's lord. This prevented the growth of the feudal pyramid, but in the course of time most land came to be held from the crown and not from mesne lords.

3. The Growth of Equity.

Uses (or trusts) became fairly common during the 13th century, and early in the 15th century the chancellor began to enforce them (*see* EQUITY; TRUST). By vesting the legal estate in a number of reliable "feoffees to uses," it was possible to avoid many of the rules governing real property, especially feudal burdens such as reliefs and wardships, and the prohibitions against conveyances into mortmain, and devises; for these rules governed only the legal estate and not the equitable interests in the use. Uses were thus employed to subvert the well-settled law and defeat the feudal claims of the lord; and when the lord paramount was Henry VIII and Parliament submissive, legislation intended to destroy uses was inevitable.

4. The Statute of Uses, 1535.

This act (27 Hen. VIII. c.10) converted equitable interests in realty into corresponding legal estates: if A was seised to the use of B, the statute "executed" the use and converted B's equitable interest into a legal estate, A dropping out. This facilitated a simplification in the procedure for transferring a legal estate in land. Previously it was normally effected by "feoffment with livery of seisin"—*i.e.*, a verbal declaration of intention to convey accompanied by the giving of actual possession of the land, symbolized by handing over a twig or a clod of earth. Advantage was now taken of the concept that a vendor who had agreed to sell land was holding it to the purchaser's use. The purchaser's use was executed, vesting the legal estate in him, so that land could be transferred by "bargain and sale" (*i.e.*, a simple contract) without taking possession. As this would also have made a secret transfer possible, the Enrolment of Bargains of Lands, etc., Act, 1535 (27 Hen. VIII. c.16), required the enrollment of all bargains and sales in one of the king's courts. Early in the 17th century a means of avoiding the statute was evolved. V bargained and sold to P a lease for one year; this was outside the statute and gave P a legal lease without publicity or entry on the land. The next day V conveyed the reversion to P by a simple "release" by deed. This "lease and release" remained the normal mode of conveyance until the Real Property Act, 1845,

s.2, enabled all land to be conveyed by a simple conveyance by deed.

The Statute of Uses brought greater variety and flexibility to the legal interests in land that could be created. The rules of the common law prohibited a condition being attached to a fee which would end it and pass the land into the hands of a stranger. Upon the termination of an estate for life or of an estate tail, the land had to revert to the donor or his heirs. Equity had allowed other interests to arise by means of the creation of a use in favour of the stranger. These "conditional limitations" now became possible at law when the use was automatically executed. The Statute of Uses was also thought to have abolished the power to devise land, and the resulting outcry produced the Statute of Wills, 1540 (32 Hen. VIII. c.1), which permitted a testator to devise all socage land and two-thirds of land held in knight service. The Tenures Abolition Act, 1660 (12 Car. II. c.24), in effect made all land devisable; it converted tenures in chivalry into common socage, subject to preserving the honourable incidents of grand serjeanty.

5. Development of the Modern Law.

The Statute of Frauds, 1677 (29 Car. II. c.3), provided that certain transactions relating to land should be in writing or evidenced by writing; and in the reign of Anne, the Middlesex and Yorkshire deeds registries were established (*see* TITLE TO LAND). But perhaps the most striking feature of this period was the perfection of the settlement and resettlement as a device for keeping land in the family. The core of a marriage settlement was that the husband (H) was given a life estate, with remainder to his first and other sons successively in tail. The wife was given an annual income by means of rent charges, providing for "pin money" during H's life, and a larger sum by way of jointure after his death. All the children save the eldest son who succeeded to the land were given lump sums of money known as portions, protected by a portions term (a long lease) vested in trustees. When the eldest son attained full age, H persuaded him to join with him in barring the entail and resettling the resultant fee simple on H for life, with remainder to the son for life, and then with remainder to the son's sons successively in tail. The land was thus tied up for another generation. The common law had evolved a rule that it was not possible to create an unbarrable entail, but conveyancers circumvented this by ensuring that no person entitled under the settlement should have an entail unless he was an infant and so incapable of barring it. By these methods, great family estates could be built up by ensuring that the land passed as a whole to each eldest son in turn, and yet provision was made for the other members of the family. One disadvantage of this system was that in the absence of express provision there was no person with power to dispose of any of the land or to grant leases which would be binding after the grantor's death. Often the tenant for life was given a series of express powers, but sometimes these were defective, and in any event their presence made the settlement a document of formidable bulk.

6. The Age of Reform.

In the century after 1830 there were three main groups of statutory reforms; namely, the statutes of 1832 to 1845, the statutes of 1881 and 1882, and the statutes of 1922–25. The two main features of the legislation were (1) to eliminate anomalies and (2) to shorten documents by enacting as law those provisions which had become common form.

1832–45.—The Prescription Act, 1832, achieved a qualified success in providing greater certainty in the law governing the acquisition of easements and profits by long enjoyment, and the Real Property Limitation Act, 1833, reformed the law governing the acquisition of title to land by long possession. The Fines and Recoveries Act, 1833, substituted a simple conveyance for the dilatory and expensive methods of barring entails by fines and recoveries. The Dower Act, 1833, enabled a husband to dispose of land free from his wife's prospective claim to dower (a life interest in one-third of his land) on his death, while the Inheritance Act, 1833, reformed and clarified the law governing the descent of land to the heir on intestacy. The Wills Act, 1837, made many improvements in the law of wills, particularly as to formalities. The Real Property Act, 1845, enabled corporeal hereditaments to be transferred by grant; *i.e.*, by a deed. This brought corporeal hereditaments into line with incorporeal hereditaments, which had always been so treated. Although livery of seisin had long been superseded, the fiction of lease and release could now also be abandoned.

1881–82.—The Conveyancing Act, 1881, did much to shorten conveyances by enacting many provisions which formerly had to be set out expressly. But it was the Settled Land Act, 1882, which was the great achievement of this period. It extended some rather timid legislation of 1856 and 1867, and gave to every tenant for life of settled land wide powers of selling, leasing, and otherwise dealing with the land. On such a dealing, the interests of the various beneficiaries under the settlement were "overreached"; *i.e.*, transferred from the land to any capital money, which had to be paid to the trustees of the settlement and not the tenant for life.

B. Property Legislation of 1925

Great changes in the law were made by the Law of Property Act, 1922, most of which, however, was repealed and reenacted before it had come into force. On Jan. 1, 1926, there came into force the unrepealed portions of the act of 1922, together with the Law of Property Act, 1925, the Settled Land Act, 1925, the Trustee Act, 1925, the Administration of Estates Act, 1925, the Land Charges Act, 1925, the Land Registration Act, 1925, and the Universities and College Estates Act, 1925. These acts, often collectively called "the 1925 property legislation," were drastic, far-reaching and wholly successful in bringing the law into accord with modern needs. The main features of this legislation will be taken in turn.

1. Abolition of Unnecessary Historical Survivals.—First, all tenures were in effect converted to common socage, though the honourable incidents of grand and petty serjeanty were preserved. Copyhold was the one tenure which was still of practical importance, and the tenant was required to pay compensation for most of the incidents of any real value which were abolished. Second, the Statute of Uses was repealed. Third, a number of technical rules of no intrinsic value were repealed, such as the Rule in Shelley's Case (1581), 1 Co.Rep. 88b (which treated words which appeared to create interests in remainder in land as merely defining the extent of the prior owner's interest), the rule in *Whitby* v. *Mitchell* (1890), 44 Ch. D. 85 (which prevented a testator from leaving any property to the children or remoter issue of a person then unborn), and the doctrine of interesse termini (that a lease could not be effective until the lessee took possession of the land). Fourth, the technical and complex rules governing legal future interests in land, derived partly from feudal law and partly from the operation of the Statute of Uses, were discarded by making it possible for future interests in land to exist only in equity.

2. Assimilation of the Law of Real Property to that of Personal Property.—The difference in nature between land and chattels makes impossible any close assimilation of the differing legal rules to which they are subject. Nevertheless, some degree of approximation has been achieved. First, both realty and personalty now devolve on the same persons on an intestacy. Formerly, realty passed to the heir, whereas personalty was divided among the next of kin (*see* PERSONAL PROPERTY); the new system is in the main a modified version of the former system governing personalty. Second, the grantor's whole interest will now normally pass on a conveyance of land, even if he fails to use words of limitation which were formerly required to pass it. Third, personalty can now be entailed in the same way as realty.

3. Simplification of Conveyancing.—There has been a reduction in the number of legal estates and interests in land which can exist. The only two estates which can exist at law today are a fee simple absolute in possession and a term of years absolute (*see* LANDLORD AND TENANT; MORTGAGE); thus an entail or life interest is now necessarily equitable. In addition, only five classes of interests in land can now exist at law; the most important are rent charges, easements, and similar rights, if either perpetual or for a term of years absolute. A purchaser without notice of a right takes free from it if it is equitable, but subject to it if it is legal, so that this change effects some reduction of the risk to a

purchaser. Second, there has been an extension of the curtain principle, whereby a purchaser of land is concerned only with the legal estate, and the rights of those with equitable interests, which are kept "behind the curtain," are overreached. Third, many more interests in land now require registration as land charges if they are to bind a purchaser. Fourth, the areas in which registration of the title to land is compulsory have been extended (*see* TITLE TO LAND). Fifth, no legal estate in land may now be vested in an infant; the land is made alienable by treating it as settled land or subjecting it to a trust for sale, according to whether the infant is entitled solely or jointly with others.

4. Joint Ownership of Land.—Originally four forms of joint ownership of land were recognized by the common law: joint tenancy, tenancy in common, co-parcenary, and tenancy by entireties.

A joint tenancy is created when land is granted to two or more persons with no words indicating that they are to take separate interests. Each of the joint tenants has an equal and identical interest in the whole of the land. On the death of any joint tenant his interest automatically accrues to the survivors. Corporations could not be joint tenants until 1899, when statute altered the common-law rule. The joint tenancy can be severed by one joint tenant disposing of his interest; by agreement; and, since 1925, by notice. This converts it into a tenancy in common.

In a tenancy in common, the owners are entitled to undivided shares which need not be of equal size. On the death of a tenant in common his share does not accrue to the surviving tenants in common, but passes with the rest of his estate.

Co-parcenary was a form of joint ownership which arose when two or more persons became jointly entitled to land by descent. This arose at common law where land passed to two or more females as heirs; or, according to the custom of gavelkind, where it passed to two or more persons. Co-parceners are generally in the same position as tenants in common.

Tenancy by entireties (abolished by statute in 1882) arose when land was conveyed to or devolved upon husband and wife during the coverture in circumstances when otherwise they would have taken as joint tenants. They were together regarded as one person, and each owned the whole. Their interests could not be severed, and when one died the survivor took the whole.

Before 1926, all co-owners could be compelled to partition the land between them: co-parceners by common law; other joint owners, except copyholders, by statutes of Henry VIII; and copyholders by the Copyhold Act, 1841. Actions for partition are no longer appropriate, because the co-owners' beneficial interests are now only interests under a trust. Partitions, however, are still effected by deed where all parties are of full age.

The 1925 legislation provided that the only form of joint ownership that could subsist in a legal estate was a joint tenancy. The joint tenants hold as trustees for sale (*see* below), upon trust for the beneficial joint owners as joint tenants, tenants in common, or (exceptionally) co-parceners, as the case may be, in equity. That tenancy in common and the fast-disappearing co-parcenary can only exist as equitable interests means that a purchaser of a legal estate is not concerned with them. The equitable interests are overridden and take effect against the proceeds of sale. A purchaser has to deal with a maximum of four joint tenants instead of with an unlimited number of tenants in common with varying interests.

Party walls—*i.e.*, walls dividing properties owned by different people—constitute an important example of property in joint ownership. Previous to the legislation of 1925, when built along a boundary they would often be owned by the neighbours as tenants in common. To maintain the principle that tenancy in common could subsist only in equity, and yet to avoid the injustice of applying to party walls the *jus accrescendi* of the joint tenancy, the Law of Property Act, 1925, provided that such walls should be divided vertically, each half being in separate ownership, but with the benefit of and subject to mutual rights of support.

5. Settled Land and Trust for Sale.—The 1925 property legislation made many changes in the law governing settlements of land. During the 19th century, the trust for sale had emerged as an alternative form of providing for persons in succession. In the case of settled land, control of the land was in the tenant for life; any capital money which arose on any transaction had to be paid to the trustees of the settlement, but it was the tenant for life who had both the day-to-day control of the land and the various statutory and other powers, such as to sell, lease, or otherwise dispose of the land. In the case of a trust for sale, it was the trustees who had the control and the powers, and the main interest of any life tenant was merely to receive the income from the land. This form of settlement, sometimes called a trader's settlement, was appropriate to a row of suburban villas, whereas the rural estates of the nobility and gentry were held as settled land.

The Settled Land Act, 1925, provided that the legal estate in settled land should be vested in the tenant for life as trustee, and required every settlement to be made by two documents, the vesting instrument and the trust instrument. The vesting instrument is a short document containing the few particulars as to the trustees, the tenant for life, the powers, and the land itself, which a purchaser needs to know. The trust instrument in addition sets out all the trusts of the settlement, but it is behind the curtain and does not concern a purchaser. If there is no tenant for life, or the tenant for life is an infant, the statutory owner (usually the trustees of the settlement) takes the place of the tenant for life. The act also repeats and extends the powers conferred by the Settled Land Act, 1882, and makes the machinery of the act apply to virtually all cases where persons are entitled to land in succession, even if no life interest exists, provided the land is not held on trust for sale. When the settlement comes to an end, the trustees should execute a deed of discharge unless there is a document on the title which shows that the land is no longer settled.

No great changes have been made in trusts for sale, save that the trustees now have all the powers of a tenant for life of settled land. A power to postpone sale indefinitely is now implied in all trusts for sale, and many such trusts are created with the intention that the land shall be retained rather than sold.

C. Other 20th-Century Aspects

1. Social Control of Land.—Apart from the many reforms of the substantive law, the predominant feature of the 20th century has been the emergence and statutory recognition of the doctrine, developed piecemeal and never explicitly set forth, that under modern social conditions in an overcrowded country the right of a landowner to do as he wishes with his own must be subordinated to the public interest. Thus many important provisions have been enacted to protect tenants of dwelling houses, business premises, and agricultural land from being evicted when their tenancies expire and from suffering increases of rent. From the landowner's point of view, these provisions fetter his freedom of action. Again, even if the landowner farmed the land himself, until 1958 he was liable to dispossession for failure to attain the required standard of efficiency (see Land Tenure: Economic and Agrarian Aspects).

Yet again, under the legislation governing town and country planning, any development of land is subject to stringent control. The Town and Country Planning Act, 1947 (now replaced by an act of 1962), imposed on all land in England and Wales as from July 1, 1948, a comprehensive system of control, unrecognizable by those who drafted the first timid planning statute, the Housing, Town Planning, etc., Act, 1909. Subject to certain exceptions, no development may be carried out without the permission of the local planning authority, usually the County Council; and "development" is widely defined to include any building, engineering, mining, or other operations on land or the making of any material change in the use of land. The act also imposed a liability to pay to the state a development charge in respect of any planning permission granted, representing the increased value of the land due to the permission; but this liability, together with provisions for making some compensation to landowners for this new burden, was repealed as from Nov. 18, 1952, by the Town and Country Planning Act, 1953. Legal opinion was divided about the effect of the act of 1947 on the fee simple to land. Some even urged that a landowner no longer had a fee simple in the land, but only in the existing use in the land; others held that no alteration had

taken place in the estate in the land, and that the only change was that the fruits of ownership had become less sweet, which was nothing new in land law. This latter view had the allegiance of the great majority of practitioners, and is almost certainly also correct in theory. (See also City Planning.)

2. International Law.—In general, land is governed by the law of the country in which it is situate (*lex loci rei sitae*), and English courts will not adjudicate upon the title to foreign land. Like so many rules of the common law, however, this rule has been qualified by equity. If the proposed defendant to an action is within the jurisdiction, and he is bound by some equitable obligation, equity will assume jurisdiction even though the subject matter of the dispute is foreign land; for equity acts *in personam*. Thus in *Penn* v. *Lord Baltimore* (1750), 1 Ves.Sen. 444, a decree of specific performance was made against a defendant in England in respect of an agreement relating to the boundaries of Pennsylvania and Maryland. Again, where the defendant is within the realm, jurisdiction has been assumed over equitable rights under mortgages of foreign land. But bare questions of the title to foreign land, or damages for trespass to it, are left to the courts within whose jurisdiction the land lies.

D. Conveyancing

Conveyancing is the art or science of creating and transferring interests in property, especially in land. The two main divisions of the subject are investigation of title and drafting. Before a transaction such as a purchase or mortgage can be completed, the purchaser or mortgagee must be satisfied that the vendor or mortgagor is able to convey or mortgage the land, and for this purpose his title must be investigated; *i.e.*, his documents of title must be examined and considered, and any necessary inquiries and searches of registers must be made. Only if this investigation is satisfactory will the necessary conveyance or mortgage be drafted. Leases, settlements, and wills also occupy much of a conveyancer's time. In the work of drafting great reliance is placed on well-tried precedents to be found in the books of model forms which have been collected and published since printing became common.

1. Contract.—The practice in modern English conveyancing may best be illustrated by taking as an example the simple transaction of purchasing a house. After negotiating, the parties usually strike a bargain subject to contract. This morally commits them to the sale and purchase of the house at the agreed price, but neither is legally bound; usually the parties then proceed to the preparation of a formal contract. The vendor's solicitors first prepare and send to the purchaser's solicitors a draft contract, providing for the mode in which the transaction is to be carri[ed] through, the title which the vendor will show, and any spec[ial pro]visions such as the imposition of restrictive covenants [on the pur]chaser or the retention of easements by the vend[or].

The purchaser's solicitors then send to t[he vendor's so]written inquiries on draft contract, w[hich are mainly] with matters such as the existence [of . . .]erty, whether public (*e.g.*, b[. . .]tion) or private (*e.g.*, th[e . . .]legislation). The p[urchaser's . . .]propriate land c[harges . . .]answers to [these . . .]terms [. . .]in [. . .]th[e . . .]wha[t . . .]ticula[r . . .]These [. . .]the term[s . . .]chaser to [. . .]conclusion [. . .]property up[on . . .]opportunity f[or . . .]may be able to [. . .]purchaser.

Whether the sale is by private treaty or by auction, the contract normally requires the purchaser to pay a deposit, usually amounting to 10% of the purchase price. This may be made payable to an agent for the vendor or to a stakeholder, but in either case it is treated as a token of good faith by the purchaser and will usually be forfeit to the vendor if the purchaser defaults; otherwise, it is treated as an advance payment of part of the purchase money.

2. Abstract of Title.—Once the contract has become binding, the vendor must within the time provided by the contract deliver to the purchaser the abstract of title. This consists in part of an epitome of the various documents whereunder the vendor has become entitled to the property, and partly of a recital of events such as deaths and grants of probate affecting the title to the property. The abstract must start with a good root of title (*e.g.*, a transaction such as a sale or mortgage) and trace the devolution of the property from this root to the vendor. Unless otherwise agreed the root of title must be at least 30 years old.

The purchaser's solicitors then examine the abstract against the various documents upon which it is based, and send to the vendor's solicitors written requisitions on title. These are a series of questions seeking explanation or confirmation on any difficulties or discrepancies which have emerged from considering the abstract. With the simplification of conveyancing effected by the property legislation of 1925 and the modern growth of public and social control of land, requisitions have tended to deal less and less with the title to the land in the conveyancing sense and more and more with the existence of rights and duties adverse to the beneficial enjoyment of the land by the purchaser; it is common for requisitions to repeat most or all of the matters dealt with in the inquiries on draft contract. The vendor must deliver written replies to requisitions on title within the time stated in the contract, and the purchaser is entitled to make further requisitions on any points not satisfactorily dealt with.

3. Conveyance Form.—When the title has been examined and accepted, the purchaser's solicitors prepare a draft conveyance of the property, which is sent to the vendor's solicitors for amendment and approval. The following is a precedent of a very simple conveyance.

THIS CONVEYANCE is made the 1st day of February, 1966, BETWEEN Orlando Gibbons of No. 1 Morley Street, Dowland in the County of Tallis, Clerk (hereinafter called "the Vendor") of the one part and John Bull of No. 1 Weelkes Street Farnaby in the County of Tye, Civil Servant (hereinafter called "the Purchaser") of the other part
WHEREAS—
(1) The Vendor is the estate owner in respect of the fee simple of the property hereby assured for his own use and benefit absolutely free from incumbrances
(2) The Vendor has agreed with the Purchaser to sell to him the said property free from incumbrances for the price of £7000
NOW THIS DEED WITNESSETH that in consideration of the ... of £7000 now paid by the Purchaser to the Vendor (the receipt ...eof the Vendor hereby acknowledges) the Vendor As Beneficial ... hereby conveys to the Purchaser ALL THAT messuage or ...house with the yard gardens offices and outbuildings thereto ... known as No. 1 Byrd Street Purcell in the County of Nor- ...h premises are more particularly delineated and coloured ... plan annexed to these presents TO HOLD the same unto ... in fee simple
...SS WHEREOF the parties to these presents have here- ...ands and seals the day and year first above written.

... and DELIVERED   )
... presence   )
...k to   )   Orlando Gibbons (Seal)
)
)

... this conveyance are as follows: (1)
...ment ("This Conveyance") and date.
...s. Each person or group of persons
...pressed as being parties of a par-
...who do the conveying set out first
...ed last. Thus if the property
...ge, the parties would be the

vendor of the first part, the trustees of the settled land of the second part, the mortgagees of the third part and the purchaser of the fourth part. (3) The recitals ("Whereas—") explain how the vendor became entitled to the land (narrative recitals) and how and why the existing state of affairs is to be altered; *e.g.*, because there is an agreement to sell (introductory recitals). The modern tendency is to reduce recitals to the minimum, though the old practice of inserting elaborate recitals sometimes proved useful in later years when documents were lost or destroyed or facts had been forgotten. (4) The testatum ("Now this Deed Witnesseth") indicates the beginning of the operative part of the conveyance, while (5) the consideration and (6) the receipt clause record the payment and receipt of the purchase price. The receipt clause makes it unnecessary to have a separate receipt; and a solicitor who produces a deed containing a receipt clause executed by his client is deemed to have his client's authority to receive the money payable. (7) The operative words ("the Vendor As Beneficial Owner hereby conveys") effect the actual conveyance of the property. The words "As Beneficial Owner," however, have an important technical effect, for their use imposes upon the vendor certain covenants for title. In general, it is for the purchaser to satisfy himself before completion that the conveyance will effectually carry out the terms of the contract, and if it does not, he usually cannot after completion rely upon any provision in the contract; the contract is said to be merged in the conveyance. However, the covenants for title give him a limited measure of protection. Four covenants are normally implied: (*a*) that the vendor has power to convey the land, (*b*) that the purchaser shall have quiet enjoyment of the land, (*c*) that the land is free from any incumbrances other than those subject to which it is expressed to be conveyed, and (*d*) that the vendor will execute any further conveyance or other document needed to perfect the purchaser's title. If the property sold is leasehold, there is also implied a covenant that the lease is valid, the rent has been paid, and the covenants in the lease duly performed. These covenants are not absolute warranties, however, for the vendor's liability is normally limited to the acts of himself and of those claiming under him; he is not liable for the acts of any of his predecessors in title except those through whom he claims by an unbroken chain of gifts or marriage settlements. He is thus not liable for the acts of previous vendors, though the benefit of the covenants for title given by them runs with the land and passes to the purchaser. (8) The "parcels" describe the land conveyed, usually by reference to a plan. (9) The habendum ("to hold . . .") shows whether the purchaser takes for his own benefit or upon trust for others, and contains the words of limitation ("in fee simple") which limit, or mark out, the estate which he takes. Before the Conveyancing Act, 1881, the fee simple could normally be conveyed only by using the word "heirs"; *e.g.*, "to A and his heirs." That act introduced "in fee simple" as an alternative, and the Law of Property Act, 1925, s.60, made words of limitation unnecessary by providing that the fee simple was to pass unless a contrary intention was shown. In practice, however, it is usual to employ the words "in fee simple" to avoid doubt. If the property is being conveyed subject to any lease, mortgage, or other incumbrance, or free from some previously existing incumbrance, this is stated in the habendum. And where any special covenants or stipulations are to be entered into, or the vendor is to give the purchaser an acknowledgment of his right to the production of any deeds retained by the vendor, and an undertaking for their safe custody, this follows the habendum. (10) Finally there is the testimonium ("In Witness Whereof . . .") and the attestation clause ("Signed Sealed and Delivered . . ."); these need no explanation.

4. Completion of Transaction.—When the draft conveyance has been agreed, the transaction is ready for completion. The conveyance is engrossed, normally by having a fair copy typed on parchment substitute. This is executed by the vendor and delivered to his solicitor in escrow (*i.e.*, on condition that it is not to be effective unless the transaction is duly completed). If the purchaser is to enter into any covenants or other obligations with the vendor, a further copy will be engrossed and executed by the purchaser in escrow. A completion statement is prepared, apportioning the rates, taxes, and other outgoings up to the day fixed for completion and showing the balance of purchase money payable, and the purchaser obtains a banker's draft for the amount due. Completion normally takes place at the offices of the vendor's solicitors or, if the property is mortgaged, at the office of the mortgagee's solicitors. In return for the banker's draft the conveyance executed by the vendor is delivered to the purchaser's solicitors, with the title deeds relating to the property; the purchaser is then free to take possession of the property. He next has the conveyance stamped under the Stamp Act, 1891; with certain mitigations where the consideration does not exceed £6,000, the normal rate of duty is 1% of the purchase price. The transaction is then complete.

Where the title to land is registered at HM Land Registry (*see* TITLE TO LAND), conveyancing procedure is simplified. The abstract of title and the production of deeds tracing the devolution of title for at least 30 years is replaced by the sending from the vendor to the purchaser of a copy of the current entries on the register. Provided that the vendor is there shown as registered proprietor his title cannot be impugned. Simplified forms of document have been introduced for use in dealings with registered land. The transfer, for instance, which takes the place of the conveyance, omits all recitals, and reduces the description of its title to a reference to its title number. A dealing with registered land is not completed until recorded at HM Land Registry, for which purpose the documents have to be lodged after completion and stamping. In the case of the purchase of a property situated in an area in which registration of title has been made compulsory, but with a title as yet unregistered, the deeds must be lodged for registration at HM Land Registry within two months of completion, or the purchaser will not acquire a legal estate.

5. Leasehold Procedure.—Substantially the same procedure is followed where the property conveyed is leasehold instead of freehold, though the assignment which takes the place of the conveyance is somewhat different in form. Subject to any agreement to the contrary, the vendor need not show title to the freehold out of which the lease was created. Unless otherwise agreed, he must, where the title is not registered, commence his abstract of title with the lease, however old, and trace its devolution for at least 30 years prior to the sale. Where the title is registered, an abstract or copy of the lease together with a copy of the entries on the register suffice. The purchaser must assume, unless the contrary appears, that the lease was duly granted; and on production of the receipt for the last payment due for rent before actual completion, he must assume, unless the contrary appears, that all the provisions of the lease have been observed up to the date of actual completion. The purchaser is subject to an implied covenant to pay the rent and observe and perform the covenants and provisions of the lease and keep the vendor indemnified in these respects. On the other hand, where the transaction consists of the grant of a lease, there is normally no contract and no investigation of title; the parties negotiate the terms of the lease and not until completion is either party legally bound to the other. The same applies to mortgages and settlements, except that sometimes marriage settlements are preceded by marriage articles, which set out in brief form the main provisions of the settlement and make it possible for the drawing up of the formal settlement to be postponed until after the marriage has been solemnized.

6. Conveyancing Counsel to the Court.—These are appointed by the lord chancellor under the Supreme Court of Judicature Act, 1925, s. 217, as amended by the Administration of Justice Act, 1956, s. 14; there may be any number from three to six. They must have practised as conveyancing counsel for at least ten years, and their function is to assist the Chancery Division of the High Court in matters of conveyancing; *e.g.*, in investigating title or settling deeds. Under order 51 of the rules of the Supreme Court, business is referred to them in rotation, and the court may act on the opinion given by conveyancing counsel in any matter referred to him, though any party may require the matter to be referred for decision by the judge at chambers or in court.

See also ENGLISH LAW: *Changes in Private Law.*

(R. E. MY.; T. M. AL.)

II. UNITED STATES LAW

The law of real property of all the U.S. states except Louisiana (whose legal system was based upon the Code Napoléon) was derived principally from the common law of England, and for generations American property lawyers relied upon the standard English texts; *e.g.*, Sir William Blackstone's *Commentaries,* Sir Edward Coke's *Coke Upon Littleton,* William Cruise's *Digest of the Laws of England Respecting Real Property,* and Charles Fearne on *Contingent Remainders.* Even after James Kent's *Commentaries on American Law* and other important U.S. treatises were available, students of property in the U.S. continued to use the English textbooks of the day until those books came to be so cluttered with expositions of the English statutes of the 19th and 20th centuries that they were no longer helpful either as introductions or guides to the U.S. law.

But the U.S. law of real property, even though derived principally from the English law, is not uniform from state to state. Under the constitution of the United States, jurisdiction of land is vested primarily in the states rather than in the federal government. Conditions, both physical and social, vary greatly from state to state and problems relating to land are traditionally deemed to be peculiarly of local rather than national concern. The American Bar Association has sponsored a variety of uniform or model acts, such as the Uniform Acknowledgment Act, designed to achieve uniformity in a few isolated fields, but these have not been generally adopted and there seems to be little sentiment, even among the members of the organized bar, in favour of making the law of real property uniform throughout the country.

1. Tenure.—The colonial charters usually provided that the lands in North America were to be held of the English crown in "free and common socage," the least burdensome of the English forms of tenure. Military and copyhold tenures did not obtain a foothold in America. Indeed, so distasteful to the Americans were the notions of feudalism that the attempt to collect the rents and enforce the other obligations which were incidents of socage tenure either caused or contributed to serious incidents such as Bacon's Rebellion in Virginia in 1676 and the antirent disturbances in New York in the early years of the 19th century. Following the American Revolution, feudal tenure was either abolished by statute or, if not formally abolished, became for most purposes obsolete.

Although tenure early ceased to be an important institution of the American land law, many of the archaic rules of law which had been developed in England to further feudal policies were adopted in America and continued for many years to be vital elements of the American law of property. The history of the U.S. law consists, very largely, of the substitution of modern rules for the ancient feudal rules which should have been, but were not, abolished when feudalism became obsolete. In 1936 the American Law Institute reported in the *Restatement of the Law of Property* that the rule of law which required that a deed include the ancient formula of words of inheritance (*i.e.,* "and to his heirs") in order to transfer an interest larger than a life estate, and the equally technical rule, known as the Rule in Shelley's Case —which, when controlling, caused an estate of inheritance to be vested in a transferee who was intended to acquire only a life estate—were still a part of the U.S. common law. Fortunately, most of the states had abolished these rules and others like them before 1936, though in a few jurisdictions they had survived. In Illinois, for example, the Rule in Shelley's Case was not abolished until 1953, though it had been repealed in England by the property legislation of 1925.

2. Estates.—The English scheme of estates in land was adopted with but few changes although that system, even at the time when it was transplanted in America, included many relics of feudalism which had no relationship to conditions in America. The English classification of estates as freehold and nonfreehold was adopted with the result that leasehold interests in land (*e.g.,* a term for 99 years) were considered personal property, designated by the term "chattels real" and treated for many purposes as chattels rather than land. The term "real property" was reserved, as it had been in England, for the freehold interests in land. These included the fee simple, the fee tail, and the life estate.

Fee Simple.—The fee simple was the largest estate which could be created. Subject only to the general limitations which were imposed upon owners of property, the owner of an estate in fee simple absolute might use the land as he wished. The estate was freely transferrable and, unless conveyed or otherwise encumbered, it passed upon the death of the owner either to the beneficiary designated by the owner in his will or, in the absence of a valid gift by will, by operation of law to the owner's heirs at law. Primogeniture, though it had been recognized in some sections of America in the colonial period, was not deemed to be consistent with American ideals, and it, together with the preference of males over females, was abolished for most purposes during the period of the Revolution.

Fee Tail.—The fee tail was introduced into some or perhaps most of the American colonies at an early date and brought with it the distinguishing features that it had in England including the elaborate paraphernalia of fines and common recoveries by which the owner of such an estate might, if he wished, bar the entail and convert his estate tail into an estate fee simple. In most of the states, entails were abolished by statutes which provided either that the donee who was intended to have an estate tail should have an estate in fee simple or that the donee should acquire a life estate and that the issue of the donee should take an estate in fee simple.

By 1936 the estate tail was recognized in only half a dozen states and a simple disentailing deed had long since been substituted for the fine and the common recovery as a means of converting the estate tail into an estate in fee simple. In Iowa, Nebraska, Oregon, and South Carolina the courts had held that a conveyance to one and his bodily heirs created a fee simple conditional, the ancient common-law estate which had been abolished in England by the enactment of the statute *De Donis Conditionalibus* in 1285. In Nebraska the fee simple conditional was abolished in 1941 when the state enacted the Uniform Property Act which substituted an ordinary fee simple for the fee simple conditional.

Life Estate.—The smallest of the freehold estates was the life estate, an estate the duration of which, as the name indicates, was limited to the lifetime of a natural person. The measuring life might be either that of the owner of the estate or the life of another person than the owner, in which case it was known as an estate pur autre vie. Life estates might be created either by a conveyance which was executed for the purpose of creating such an estate or by operation of law as were the estates of dower and curtesy which were common-law incidents of a marriage relationship and entitled the surviving spouse, under certain circumstances, to life estates in some or all of the real estate which the deceased had owned at any time during the marriage.

3. Future Interests.—The complicated and largely archaic English system of future interests was adopted in colonial America with only a few alterations. The reforms which had been effected by the enactment of the Statute of Uses, 1535, were, of course, incorporated into the American law, but with few other exceptions the ancient common-law rules which had been developed to meet the needs of feudal England governed the creation of future interests in America. This branch of the law of property became, in America as it was in England, notorious for distinctions which were so technical and refined that they were difficult even for the most experienced conveyancers to apply. Consequently, the attempt to create any future interests except the simplest types would often occasion great uncertainty concerning title and serve not only to impede the development of the land out of which they had been created but also to defeat the wishes of the transferor.

The Revised Statutes of New York, 1827, abolished many of the feudal rules which encumbered this branch of the law of property. Unfortunately, the attempts of the commissioners who drafted the New York revision of 1827 to reform the law of future interests were not so successful as they should have been because they attempted to improve the relatively modern rule, known as the Rule against Perpetuities, which the English judges had developed to control the creation of the modern types of future interests which had been introduced into the law of England by the enactment of the Statute of Uses. The English Rule against Perpetuities was far from perfect, but the statutory substitute which the New York commissioners devised created more problems than it solved. Nevertheless, the New York statutes of 1827 and the Field Civil Code, which New York rejected in the mid-19th century, were copied by a number of the states, especially those in the West. But reform in the law of future interests, as in the law of real property generally, was slow, for courts and legislatures were reluctant to abandon the ancient rules.

Fortunately, future interests were not commonly created and, though now and then complicated settlements were executed, they did not become customary as they were in England, where title to much of the land in the realm was fettered by marriage settlements, a form of transfer which had been devised by the English conveyancers as a means of keeping land within the family. Thus, even though the English law of future interests was outmoded when it was received in North America, it did not seriously stifle the development of the country because, at any one time, only a very few tracts were burdened by future interests.

Though the marriage settlement was seldom used in America to keep land within a family, the various gift, estate, inheritance, and income taxes of the 20th century afforded a strong incentive to owners of substantial amounts of property to resort to various types of settlements as a means of protecting the family, not from an irresponsible member, but rather from the tax collectors. The will of Pres. Calvin Coolidge by which he left all his property to his widow was a model of brevity and simplicity, but, as conveyancers noted, even a simple form of family settlement would have reduced substantially the estate and inheritance tax liability of the Coolidge family. . The will of Sen. Robert A. Taft, executed a quarter of a century later, established a fairly elaborate family settlement; but it was drafted with such skill that the liability of the Taft family for estate and inheritance taxes was very much less than it would have been had the Coolidge will been used as a model.

4. Transfer of Title.—*Conveyances.*—By the time the American colonies were established, deeds had in England very largely supplanted the ancient feudal formalities for conveying real property. In America, the rule that title to land might be transferred by the execution of a deed was established at an early date. The form of the deed which was used might be one which had been developed by the English conveyancers or it might be one which was prescribed by an American statute. It might be either a warranty deed, which included covenants for title by which the grantor undertook to protect the grantee and his successors against defects in the title, or a quitclaim deed which was used to transfer the grantor's interest, if any, without any warranty as to title. Such deeds, whether warranty or quitclaim, operated either as a modern counterpart of a common-law conveyance by livery of seisin or as a conveyance to uses which was within the operation of the Statute of Uses. The statutes usually required that the deed, if it was to be effective for all purposes, should be signed by the grantor, witnessed and acknowledged before a notary public or other public official.

Recording Acts.—Secret conveyances, though they were usually valid as between the parties, were not enforceable against bona fide purchasers for value without notice because recording systems had been established by legislation in all of the American states. The investigation of title to lands in the U.S. was greatly simplified, not only because the records of conveyances were available for inspection by the public but also because a large portion of the land within the United States had been surveyed by the federal government under a uniform, rectangular system which was established by an act of Congress of 1796 as a part of the program to transfer the lands of the United States from public to private ownership.

Abstracts of Title.—As the years passed the public records became more and more voluminous and cumbersome. To facilitate land transfers it became customary in many localities to rely, for evidence of ownership, upon abstracts of title which summarized in convenient form the public records of the deeds and other instruments which affected the title to the particular tract which was being transferred. The abstracts of title were made either by lawyers or perhaps more frequently by specialists who were not members of the bar.

Title Insurance.—Toward the end of the 19th century the practice developed for the large title companies, which dominated the business of searching the public records in the larger urban areas, to issue insurance policies to indemnify purchasers against loss occasioned by defects in title which the examination of the title had not revealed but which were, nevertheless, enforceable against purchasers. Title guarantee policies are now commonly used in the closing of transactions relating to land.

Torrens Titles.—The determination of title to land either by the examination of the public records, or by the examination of an abstract of title, or by the procurement of a policy of title insurance was often either slow, or expensive, or both. In an effort to avoid these difficulties, about 20 states adopted the Torrens Acts, which permitted the substitution of registration of title and the issuance by public officials of certificates of title for the recording of deeds and other transactions which affected title to land; the system, however, failed to make headway. (*See* TITLE TO LAND.)

Mortgages.—Mortgages in the United States took the form either of a transfer of title to the creditor or to a trustee for the creditor subject to a provision that the transfer would be nullified if the debtor should pay the debt as he had undertaken to do. As in England, the form of the deed concealed the fact that the effect of the transaction had been revolutionized by the development by courts of equity of a right to redeem, known as the equity of redemption, which enabled the mortgagor to recover his property even though he had failed to pay the obligation at the time specified in the mortgage or trust deed. A number of states, following the lead of New York, established the rule that, whatever the form of the deed which had been executed, the mortgagor continued to own the land subject only to a lien which, though it provided a basis for a decree of foreclosure should the mortgagor default, did not entitle the mortgagee, qua mortgagee, to have possession of the land. In many jurisdictions, the decree of foreclosure directed that the land should be sold by an officer of court to the highest bidder and that the proceeds, if any, which remained after the mortgage debt and the expenses of the foreclosure had been satisfied should be paid to the mortgagor. Frequently, the mortgagor's equity to redeem the property even after he had defaulted was supplemented by a statutory right of redemption which entitled the mortgagor, if he wished, to retain the property free from the lien of the mortgage by paying, not the amount of the debt, but rather the price which had been obtained at the judicial sale.

During the depression of the 1930s, moratoria statutes were enacted in many states to shield mortgagors from the hardships occasioned by the collapse of the economy. Some extended the time within which mortgagors might redeem the security. Others protected them from personal liability upon the debts which were secured by mortgages. Under the Frazier-Lemke amendment to the Bankruptcy Act, 1935, farmers were given the opportunity to retain possession of their farms pending an arrangement in bankruptcy and permitted to wipe out the mortgage by paying, not the amount due on the debt, or the price obtained at a foreclosure sale, but, instead, the value of the property as determined by appraisers under the supervision of the bankruptcy court. (*See* also MORTGAGE; BANKRUPTCY.)

5. Rights of Enjoyment.—In the United States, as in England, the rules of law which governed the use and development of land were based upon the assumption that the owner should have the fullest possible freedom to use the land as he wished. As an owner, he was entitled to use the land as he chose without obtaining either consents from his neighbours or licences from the state. He might let the land remain unused, or, if he preferred, he might alter or destroy its substance.

Tracts of lands are not, however, independent. The development of one tract, especially if it is small, may often affect the enjoyment of other tracts. If, therefore, owners were to be secure in the privilege of using their land, the power of each must be restrained to the extent that was necessary to ensure that each would have the maximum freedom which might be attained in a civilized society. It was therefore established that, although an owner of land might leave it in its natural state even though this occasioned harm to others, he was not privileged to harm others either by using it in a careless or negligent manner, or, as it became clear in the 20th century, by using it in an ultrahazardous way even if he did so with the greatest possible care.

Nor would ownership of land justify an encroachment, even though innocent, upon the land of another, whether the encroachment was on the surface, underground, or in the air. This limitation did not mean, as some once thought, that all flight over land without the consent of the owner was unlawful. It meant, instead, that such flight at low altitudes was unlawful even though the upper boundary of the air space which must not be invaded could not be fixed as precisely as boundaries upon the surface could be marked out by a surveyor.

Moreover, the owner of land might be held accountable even though he had kept within his boundaries and his use had been neither negligent nor ultrahazardous. He was required, in addition, to refrain from any use, however carefully it might be conducted, which interfered unreasonably with the enjoyment of neighbouring lands. The difficulty inherent in this limitation upon the freedom of the owner was that it was so general that it was vague and hence extremely difficult to apply.

In some situations, the standards of reasonableness were definite. An obstruction of a vista or of the access of light and air to an adjoining tract by building close to the boundary was held not to be an unreasonable use. Some courts, apparently misled by the colourful language of Blackstone's *Commentaries*, announced that even a "spite fence," which had been built only to annoy a neighbour, was not actionable if it had been carefully constructed and did not extend beyond the boundary. This rule had been generally repudiated by the 20th century, although the Supreme Court of Pennsylvania applied it in a case decided in 1947.

On the other hand, an excavation or mining operation which, by disturbing the lateral or subjacent support, caused the soil of neighbouring land to subside was usually deemed to be unreasonable and hence actionable even though the work had been done very skilfully.

In most instances, however, the limitations imposed upon the owners of land with respect to the use and development of their tracts were extremely vague. The test of legality was the reasonableness of the particular use. The standard was that of "give and take, live and let live," and its application required the difficult adjustment of the correlative and interdependent interests of competing owners. Among the factors which were to be considered was the character of the neighbourhood. A use which might be appropriate in one locality might be unreasonable and hence unlawful in another. The application of the common-law rules thus tended to segregate uses and to impose upon landowners a crude system of zoning.

Waste.—The freedom of an owner to use his land might also be limited because his interest was not a fee simple absolute. The owner of a life estate, for example, was ordinarily accountable for waste and was not entitled to use the land in a way which would unreasonably interfere with its enjoyment by the owner who would be entitled to have possession when the life estate ended.

Easements and Restrictive Covenants.—The owner's privilege of use would also be curtailed if his estate, although a fee simple, was encumbered by a property right which entitled another person either to use the land for a limited purpose (*e.g.,* a right of way) or to require that the owner refrain from using the land in a particular way (*e.g.,* a right of access of light to a window).

Originally these restrictions were confined within narrow limits, but in the second half of the 19th century the courts decided that many types of agreements concerning the use of land should bind not only the parties to the agreement but also successors in title except bona fide purchasers who took without notice of the restriction. In the 20th century covenants were often relied upon in the development of land for residential use to assure prospective purchasers that a wide variety of uses which were thought to be undesirable would be barred from the district. Sometimes covenants were used in an attempt to keep members of a particular race from moving into an area, but enforcement of these was declared unconstitutional by the Supreme Court in the cases of *Shelley* v. *Kraemer* (1948) and *Barrows* v. *Jackson* (1953). (*See* COVENANT: *In Law.*)

6. Social Control of Land.—The freedom of an owner to use and develop his land may also be limited by the necessity of submitting to its regulation or appropriation for the public good. Under the U.S. system the powers of government agencies are restricted by the provisions of the state and federal constitutions; but subject to those limitations, private property in land is subordinated to the interests of the state.

Eminent Domain.—The owner's enjoyment of land is subject to the power of eminent domain, and his land, or an interest in it, may be taken from him so that it may be used for a project which he does not approve. The appropriation must be authorized by a statute which satisfies the various requirements of a valid act including, first, that the appropriation was for a public use and, second, that the owner was paid a just compensation for the interest which was taken from him. (*See* further EMINENT DOMAIN.)

Police Regulations.—The owner of land is also required to submit to police regulations. Even though the loss which the regulation caused an owner was large, he is not entitled, as of right, to be compensated for the sacrifice made for the benefit of the public. Thus in *Miller* v. *Schoene* (1928), 276 U.S. 272, the Supreme Court held that the Virginia landowner who was required to destroy his cedar trees to protect apple orchards in the vicinity from rust was not entitled to be reimbursed either for the value of the trees or for the depreciation in the value of his land.

In the earlier period the typical police regulations affecting the use of land were building codes and other regulations intended to protect the health and safety of those who lived in cities. At one time it was doubtful whether such regulations might be applied to existing structures, but that doubt was resolved in favour of the power by the decision of the New York Court of Appeals in the Trinity Church case (1895).

Zoning.—In the 20th century the scope of regulations imposed upon owners of land was vastly extended. In the case of *Village of Euclid* v. *Ambler Realty Co.* (1926) the Supreme Court upheld the power of the states to classify communities into zones and to impose different regulations as to use within the various zones. Planning commissions were established to formulate programs for community development, and their policies were put into effect by enactment of comprehensive zoning and subdivision ordinances regulating many aspects of the use of land in metropolitan areas.

In most instances, the courts have insisted that these regulations be justified by a showing that they are reasonably related to the protection of the health, safety, and morals of the public, and not infrequently regulations have been held to be unenforceable in particular situations because the requisite showing was not made. Frequently, regulations have been justified on the ground that they had an important relationship to the maintenance by the community of the various public services such as streets, schools, and fire protection, and sewage disposal systems. (*See* also ZONING.)

Efforts to justify land use restrictions upon purely aesthetic grounds have generally been rejected by the courts, but the fact that enforcement of such regulations would enhance the attractiveness of the locality has often been noted by judges in upholding the restrictions.

The power of the state to conserve natural resources by police regulations is widely recognized, and many statutes have been enacted to outlaw land uses that were wasteful in either the physical or the economic sense. The best examples of such legislation are the prorating and marketing schemes which were adopted in the oil-producing states during the depression of the 1930s to protect the petroleum industry from the difficulties created by the collapse of the economy.

See also references under "Real Property and Conveyancing, Laws of" in the Index.   (S. TT.)

BIBLIOGRAPHY.—*Great Britain:* W. Stubbs, *Constitutional History of England* (1896); J. Williams, *Principles of the Law of Real Property*, ed. by T. C. Williams (for the law before 1926), 23rd ed. (1920); R. E. Megarry and H. W. R. Wade, *The Law of Real Property*, 2nd ed. (1959); J. F. R. Burnett, *Elements of Conveyancing*, 8th ed. (1952); E. P. Wolstenholme and B. L. Cherry, *Conveyancing Statutes*, 12th ed. (1932); T. Key and H. W. Elphinstone, *A Compendium of Precedents in Conveyancing*, 15th ed. (1954).
United States: H. T. Tiffany, *Law of Real Property*, ed. by B. Jones, 3rd ed. (1939); American Law Institute, *Restatement of the Law of Property*, 5 vol. (1936–40), *Restatement of the Law of Torts*, vol. iv (1941); W. L. Prosser, *Handbook of the Law of Torts* (1941); R. Powell, *Law of Real Property*, 5 vol. (1949–50); A. J. Casner *et al.*, *American Law of Property* (1952).

REAPING: see FARM MACHINERY; HARVESTING MACHINERY.

RÉAUMUR, RENÉ ANTOINE FERCHAULT DE (1683–1757), French physicist and naturalist who devised the Réaumur thermometric scale, was born on Feb. 28, 1683, at La Rochelle. In 1710 he was charged with the official description of the useful arts and manufactures of France, which led him to many practical researches. He examined and reported on the auriferous rivers, the turquoise mines, the forests and the fossil beds of France; devised a method of tinning iron and investigated the chemical composition of Chinese porcelain and the chemical differences between iron and steel.

Réaumur's thermometric scale (1730) was constructed on the principle of taking the freezing point of water as 0°, and graduating the tube of the thermometer into degrees each of which was one-thousandth of the volume contained by the bulb and tube up to the zero mark. It was an accident dependent on the coefficient of expansion of the particular quality of alcohol employed which made the boiling point of water 80° R.; and mercurial thermometers the stems of which are graduated into 80 equal parts between the freezing and boiling points of water are Réaumur thermometers in name only. Réaumur wrote widely on natural history (*see* ENTOMOLOGY: *History of Entomology*), his best-known work on this subject being the *Mémoires pour servir à l'histoire des insectes*, six volumes (1734–42). He died at La Bermondière, in the old French province of Maine, on Oct. 18, 1757.

See J. H. S. Green, "De Réaumur," *Research,* vol. 10 (Oct. 1957).

REBATE. In the commercial world a rebate is a retroactive refund or credit to a buyer after he has paid the full list price for a product or for a service such as transportation. It contrasts with a discount, which is usually subtracted from the list price before the original payment. Rebating was a popular pricing weapon during the 19th century and was often used by oligopolists to preserve or extend their power over customers. Important customers were granted refunds in secret so that less influential buyers would know nothing of them. Rebating was used so universally by American and European railroad firms that published tariffs were applied only to shippers who were unsophisticated enough to pay them without bargaining for a refund. In U.S. history the rebates received by the Standard Oil Company were major factors in the company's attainment of a monopolistic position in the oil industry.

The motive for rebating among railroad firms lay in their chronically underutilized capacity. Secret rebates seemed a small price to pay for the capture of large freight orders, even though it resulted in unfair discrimination among shippers. The Interstate Commerce Act of 1887 implicitly prohibited rebates by U.S. railroads but the practice continued because of difficulties in detecting it. The growing business monopolies of the era intensified pressure for increasingly large rebates. Big firms coerced the railroads into violating the law and risking prosecution. The railroads, out of desperation, sponsored the Elkins Act of 1903, which put an end to the practice by declaring that a shipper who accepted a rebate was guilty along with the carrier who made the payment.

Rebates are not all vicious and destructive. Some are justifiable incentives that stimulate desirable action on the part of customers. Real estate firms in Europe, for example, gave rebates to buyers to encourage land improvements that would increase the value of adjoining unsold land. A partial refund of interest on a loan for repayment before the due date was once widely and correctly called a rebate but it is now popularly termed a discount. More dubious is the case of salesmen who offer secret rebates of part of their commission to customers with high sales resistance. As neither employers nor other customers are likely to discover the practice, its prevalence is unknown.

So-called deferred or exclusive patronage rebates are popular for large vendors of perishables, certain services, and consumer durable goods. To receive such a rebate the purchaser must agree to buy certain goods or services exclusively from a particular vendor for a fixed period, usually ranging from 6 to 12 months. In return for this exclusive patronage the vendor refunds a predetermined percentage of the customer's total payments. Deferred rebates can be justified on economic grounds if they are open to all customers and if production costs decline because of the stabilized sales volume of the manufacturer.

Groups of steamship lines (known as conferences) make extensive use of deferred rebates, although they were outlawed for carriage of U.S. imports and exports by the Shipping Act of 1916. The United States restricts rebating more than other industrialized nations because of its uncommonly potent antitrust statutes. *See* also SHIPPING: *Ship Operation.* (Jo. Hy.)

REBEC, a bowed stringed instrument of Middle Eastern origin, was in general use in Europe during the Middle Ages and early Renaissance, and is still commonly used in the folk music of the Balkans. The medieval rebec (the name is derived from the Arabic *rabab*) had a violin-type bridge and tailpiece, and a vaulted back like the lute, either carved from a solid block of wood or constructed from separate ribs glued together over a mold. The European instrument differed from the *rabab* in that the table or soundboard was of wood, rather than of skin. It had no soundpost, and the gut strings, two or three in number, were generally tuned in fifths. Although in western Europe a fingerboard was added at an early date, the Oriental method of "stopping" the strings with the sides of the fingernails of the left hand persisted in some countries until modern times. The medieval rebec was often held against the chest or under the chin; but when the player was sitting the instrument was sometimes held in the Oriental manner, the bottom of the instrument resting on the player's left thigh.

The medieval rebec appears to have been a treble instrument, but by the late 15th century rebecs were being made in several sizes, from treble to bass. The family of rebecs was superseded by the viols by about the middle of the 16th century; the treble rebec, however, survived in western Europe to the 18th century as an instrument for rustic music-making and, in a miniature form, as the dancing master's *pochette.* In modern times the rebec in various forms and tunings is found in the folk music of Greece, Bulgaria, and Yugoslavia, as well as in its original form in the art music of the Middle East. (M. Mw.)

REBECCA RIOTS, the name given to disturbances which occurred briefly in 1839 and with greater violence from 1842 to 1844 in southwest Wales. The rioting was directed against the charges at the tollgates on the public roads, but the attacks were symbols of a much wider disaffection, caused by agrarian distress, increased tithe charges, and the Poor Law Amendment Act of 1834. The rioters took as their motto the words in Gen. 24:60 "And they blessed Rebekah, and said to her, '. . . may your descendants possess the gate of those who hate them!' " Many of the rioters were disguised as women and were on horseback; each band was under a leader called "Rebecca," the followers being known as "her daughters." They destroyed not only the gates but also the tollhouses, the work being carried out suddenly and at night, usually without violence to the tollkeepers. Emboldened by success, the Rebeccaites in 1843 turned their attention to other grievances. The government dispatched soldiers and police to South Wales, and the disorder was quelled. An act of 1844, known as Lord Cawdor's Act, amended the turnpike trust laws in South Wales and lessened the burden of the tollgate system.

See D. Williams, *The Rebecca Riots* (1955). (R. T. J.)

REBELLION, armed resistance for political purposes by nationals of a state against the government, usually resulting in insurrection, civil war, or revolution. In law, rebellion is the act of one who engages in such resistance and is therefore subject to prosecution for treason, sedition, or rebellion. In British history, for example, supporters of the Old Pretender in 1715 and of the Young Pretender in 1745 were punished as rebels. In the U.S. Civil War the federal government regarded the Confederates as rebels although they had been recognized as belligerents by neutral states. A general amnesty after the war terminated prosecution against the leaders. In the South African war of 1899–1902 the Supreme Court of the Cape of Good Hope held that those who joined the burgher forces were liable for treason, although the burghers had been recognized as belligerents (Rex *v.* Louw, 21 C.G.H. Supreme Court Rep. 36, 1905). (*See* TREASON AND SEDITION.)

For historic rebellions *see* titles of specific rebellions. For the status of rebellion in international law *see* BELLIGERENCY. For the usual justifications for rebellion, *see* DEMOCRACY; HUMAN RIGHTS; IMPERIALISM; NATIONALISM; SELF-DETERMINATION.

(Q. W.).

REBUS. A simple rebus is the representation of a word or part of a word by a picture of a thing with a similar name. Several may be combined—in a single device, or successively—to make a phrase or sentence. Literary rebuses use letters, numbers, musical notes, or specially placed words to make sentences. Complex rebuses combine pictures and letters. As a means of communication, rebuses may convey direct meanings, especially to inform or instruct illiterate people; or they may deliberately conceal meanings to inform only the initiated or to puzzle and amuse.

An early form of rebus occurs in semiprimitive picture writings, where abstract words, difficult to portray, were represented by borrowing pictures of objects pronounced the same way. These are common in Egyptian hieroglyphs and early Chinese pictographs. Rebus pictures were used to convey names of towns on Greek and Roman coins, or names of families in medieval heraldry (in the so-called canting arms; *see* HERALDRY), and they have often been used for instructional symbols in religious art and architecture. In the Far East, especially in China and Korea, rebus symbols were commonly employed to carry auspicious wishes. Rebusmaking was long considered a specialty of Picardy, in France.

Elsewhere in Europe literary rebuses often appeared on family mottoes, personal seals, ciphers, and bookplates and ultimately in games or riddles. A familiar English rebus is the debtor's I O U, for "I owe you."

Popular in the United States after the mid-19th century were rebus picture puzzles in which the indicated addition or subtraction of letters in illustrated words produced another word or a name. Hundreds of these were devised by the puzzlemaking genius Sam Loyd. Such picture riddles have been widely used in U.S. advertising, and, beginning in the 1930s, sequences of them were presented in newspaper contests designed to attract readers. Huge prizes were offered but the final problems were so difficult that only groups of experts could solve them.

BIBLIOGRAPHY.—F. R. Hoffmann, *Grundzüge einer Geschichte des Bilderrätsels* (1869); Seikin Nozaki, *Kisshō zuan kaidai* (1928); Schuyler Cammann, *China's Dragon Robes,* pp. 100–107 (1952); William Sunners, *How to Solve Rebus Picture Puzzles* (1950).
(S. v. R. C.)

RECALL, a device, principally used in the United States, by which voters may remove a public official from office before the expiration of his regular term. Recall is based upon the principle that officials are mere agents of the popular will, and as such should be constantly subject to its control (*see* REPRESENTATION). Under the plan, if a specified percentage of the electorate are dissatisfied with an official's conduct and sign a petition for his removal, the officer must face a general election to determine the majority opinion.

Though the general principle of the recall is simple, there are many variations in its practical application. Under some plans the question of removal may be decided in one election, and the question of a successor in a subsequent election, but for economy's sake the two are often combined in one election. The vote required to remove an official is usually a simple majority of those voting. The percentage of signatures required to force an election ranges widely, the average being about 25% of those who participated in the last general election in that electoral district. An officer elected at a recall election serves out the unexpired portion of the term of the office.

The recall is, in fact, infrequently resorted to and then almost entirely for local officers. The recall found statewide application in North Dakota in 1921 when the governor, attorney general, and commissioner of agriculture were removed. At mid-20th century only a few instances of its being applied to judges were on record, all of them in minor courts. In its statewide application it becomes too cumbersome to be resorted to frequently.

Recall originated in Switzerland where it was made applicable not only to individuals but to the entire legislature. It was suggested in the U.S. Articles of Confederation and discussed in the Constitutional Convention of 1787, but its first practical application in the U.S. was in 1903 in the Los Angeles, Calif., city charter. It was soon adopted by many cities with the commission form of government as the most effective way to control the commissioners in whose hands large powers were placed. It was subsequently adopted in the following states: Oregon (1908), California (1911), Arizona, Idaho, Washington, Colorado, and Nevada (1912), Michigan (1913), Louisiana and Kansas (1914), North Dakota (1920), and Wisconsin (1926). Most of these states had many elective officers not subject to removal by the governor who were, in effect, beyond administrative control during their terms of office.

The term was also applied in the early 20th century to various proposed restraints on the judiciary. Under the slogan "recall of judicial decisions," the Progressive Party under the leadership of former Pres. Theodore Roosevelt in 1912 advocated that "when an act, passed under the police power of the State, is held unconstitutional under the State Constitution, by the courts, the people ... shall have an opportunity to vote on the question whether they desire the Act to become law, notwithstanding such decision." The 1912 proposal was not adopted, and in some states (Idaho, Louisiana, Michigan, and Washington) the recall was not made applicable to judges on the ground that the judiciary should be independent of popular passions and political pressures.

A general increase in the size of electorates, plus a greater demonstration of responsibility on the part of executives and legislative bodies alike in the second half of the 20th century, tended to diminish use of the recall. Its effectiveness is perhaps not to be measured by its use, but by the restraining influence it may exercise.

See also REFERENDUM AND INITIATIVE.

BIBLIOGRAPHY.—J. D. Barnett, *Operation of the Initiative, Referendum and Recall in Oregon* (1915); F. L. Bird and F. M. Ryan, *The Recall of Public Officers: Study of the Operation of the Recall in California* (1930); C. M. Kneier, *City Government in the United States*, pp. 398–404 (1957); W. E. Rappard, "Initiative, Referendum, and Recall in Switzerland," *Annals of the American Academy of Political and Social Science* (Sept. 1912). (W. W. CR.)

RÉCAMIER, JEANNE FRANÇOISE JULIE ADÉLAÏDE (née BERNARD) (1777–1849), Frenchwoman famous for her charm and conversation in early 19th-century literary and political circles, was born on Dec. 4, 1777, at Lyons. She was married at 15 to the rich banker Jacques Récamier (d. 1830), who was old enough to be her father. From the early days of the Consulate to almost the end of the July Monarchy her *salon* in Paris was one of the chief resorts of fashionable literary and political society. Its habitués included many former Royalists and others, such as Bernadotte (later Charles XIV of Sweden and Norway) and Gen. Jean Moreau, more or less set against the government. She was eventually exiled from Paris by Napoleon's orders. After a short stay at Lyons, she went to Rome in 1813, and later to Naples, where she was on friendly terms with Marshal Murat, then king of Naples, and his wife. Her husband had sustained heavy losses in 1805, and in her later days she lost most of the rest of her fortune; but she continued to receive visitors at the Abbaye-aux-Bois, the old Paris convent in which she took a separate suite in 1819.

Chateaubriand (*q.v.*) was a constant visitor, and, as well as continuing his liaison with her, became the centre of her *salon*, at which he read extracts from his works. Even in old age, ill health, and reduced circumstances Mme Récamier never lost her attraction. She was always renowned for her beauty, and there are well-known portraits of her by J. L. David and François Gérard. Among her admirers were Mathieu de Montmorency, Lucien Bonaparte, Prince Augustus of Prussia, Pierre Ballanche, J. J. Ampère, and Benjamin Constant, but none obtained so great an influence over her as Chateaubriand, though she suffered from his imperious temper. If she had any genuine affection, it seems to have been for Prosper de Barante, whom she met at Coppet, Mme de Staël's country house in Switzerland, which she often visited. She died in Paris on May 11, 1849.

BIBLIOGRAPHY.—*Souvenirs et Correspondances tirés des papiers de Mme Récamier,* ed. by her niece, Mme A. Lenormant, 2 vol. (1859); *Memoirs and Correspondence of Mme Récamier,* ed. and trans. by I. M. Luyster (1867); Mme A. Lenormant, *Mme Récamier, les amis de sa jeunesse et sa correspondance intime* (1872); É. Herriot, *Mme Récamier et ses amis* (1905, 1934; Eng. trans. by A. Hallard, 1906); M. Levaillant, *Chateaubriand, Mme Récamier et les Mémoires d'outre-tombe* (1936), *Une Amitié amoureuse, Mme de' Staël et Mme Récamier* (1956; Eng. trans. by M. Barnes, *The Passionate Exiles,* 1958); M. Trouncer, *Mme Récamier* (1949). See also *Lettres de Benjamin Constant à Mme Récamier, 1807–1830,* ed. by Mme A. Lenormant (1882); *Lettres de Mme de Staël à Mme Récamier,* ed. by E. Beau de Loménie (1952).

RECEIVER, in English and U.S. law, a person appointed by a court to collect and conserve assets and income, making disbursements only as authorized by the court. He may or may not be entrusted with the active carrying on of a business. Receivers were traditionally appointed by courts of chancery in Great Britain. The Judicature act of 1873, however, conferred power to appoint receivers upon all divisions of the high court. In the United States receivers may be appointed by any court of general equity jurisdiction. State statutes have contributed to the development of the law of receiverships in various types of cases.

In theory a receivership is properly only incidental to the realization of another primary objective and is not recognized as an independent object of litigation. A receiver may be appropriate whenever the court finds a need to conserve property or to distribute funds in litigation. The receiver is deemed an "arm of the court," and the property which he takes into possession is said to come into the custody of the court. Unlike a trustee in bankruptcy in the U.S., he is not deemed to take "legal title."

Typically receivers are appointed on special or general creditors' bills. A court of equity, discharging a long recognized duty to furnish an effective remedy when the remedy at law is inadequate, will entertain a special creditor's bill to reach intangible or concealed property beyond the reach of execution or other legal process and to apply the proceeds to the complainant's claim. A general creditors' bill is particularly appropriate when a creditor can show the need for appointing a receiver to avert the liquidation of a going business enterprise with threatened loss to all concerned. An ensuing general equity receivership may lead to the reorganization of a business association. The receiver may be authorized to conduct the business during the litigation in hopes of effectuating a sale of the business as a going concern. The purchaser may be a business association, frequently a new corporation in which creditors and sometimes former proprietors have interests represented by new securities distributed under a plan of reorganization which has been negotiated by the parties and approved by the court. In the last third of the 19th century, a procedure for reorganizing insolvent railroad corporations was developed in the United States, substantially without statutory authorization, under the description of the "federal equity consent receivership." Certain United States district judges became expert in resuscitating insolvent railroad corporations. A few unsecured creditors of a failing railroad, citizens of some state or states other than that in which the railroad was incorporated, would file a general creditors' bill, showing the need of conserving the liquid assets of the road. A federal court would then have jurisdiction of the proceeding by reason of diversity of citizenship of the parties. Collusive proceedings were entertained in order to keep the railroad running under the protection of a federal court. A plan of reorganization could be negotiated, approved by the court and consummated through judicial sale, typically by the issuance of securities of a new corporation with a revised capital structure. The equity receivership practice was elaborated and partly codified and reformed by sec. 77, added in 1933 to the U.S. Bankruptcy act of 1898. Initial experience with this statute led to substantial amendments in 1935. The court administers the property through an official called a trustee, but he has the powers of an equity receiver, as well as "legal title" as a statutory successor to the debtor, a concept developed with reference to trustees in strict bankruptcy.

Industrial and mercantile corporations may be reorganized under Chapter X of the Bankruptcy act. Statutory provisions for the intervention of the plans of reorganization make Chapter X proceedings elaborate and expensive affairs, transcending but still largely founded upon equity receivership practice.

In strict bankruptcy in the U.S., the receiver is merely a temporary conservator appointed when needed to serve until the trustee to liquidate the property can be elected by creditors. In England, however, permanent officials designated receivers administer bankrupt estates, but they proceed more in the tradition of bankruptcy liquidation than that of receivers in chancery. The official receiver may take charge of the affairs of a company in compulsory winding up proceedings. Creditors or stockholders may, however, nominate liquidators other than the official receiver.

(J. A. MacL.)

In English law there is a clear distinction between a receiver appointed under an instrument (such as a debenture) and a receiver appointed by order of a court. The powers of a receiver appointed under an instrument depend upon the terms of that instrument and upon the general law of agency. Receivers appointed by a court are generally appointed under section 45 of the Judicature act, 1925. A court has power to appoint a receiver whenever this appears just and convenient, and the typical reason for such appointment is the protection of property for the benefit of interested persons as, for example, pending the trial of an action. Although all divisions of the high court, besides the court of appeal, have power to appoint a receiver, the chancery division most frequently does so. An appointment is as a rule only made in the queen's bench division by way of equitable execution. Applications should be made in the probate, divorce and admiralty division when, for example, proceedings are pending to determine who shall administer a deceased person's estate, or when a wife entitled to alimony needs a receiver of her husband's interest under a settlement. Normally the court can only appoint a receiver when litigation is in process.

In English practice a named person is often made receiver on the motion for an appointment, but if there is any difficulty or dispute the matter is referred to chambers. The court or the court of appeal will not interfere with the master's discretion in appointing unless he makes a mistake in principle. *See* also BANKRUPTCY. (W. T. Ws.)

RECHABITES, a sort of religious order among the Israelites, analogous to the Nazirites (*q.v.*), with whom they shared the rule of abstinence from wine. They eschewed settled life and lived in tents, refusing to sow grain or to plant vineyards. The Rechabites represented a protest against the contemporary civilization and a reaction toward simplicity of life. Their "father," or founder, was that Jehonadab (or Jonadab), son of Rechab, who encouraged Jehu to abolish the worship of the Tyrian Baal (II Kings 10:15–27).

The "house of Rechab" fled for protection into Jerusalem at the approach of Nebuchadrezzar (Jer. 35), and Jeremiah promised them, as a reward of their adherence to the ordinance of Jehonadab, that they should never lack a man to represent them (as a priest) before Yahweh. Later Jewish tradition states that the Rechabites intermarried with the Levites.

See M. H. Pope, "Recháb," in *The Interpreter's Dictionary of the Bible*, vol. iv, pp. 14–16 (1962), with bibliography.

RECIDIVISM. The term recidivism refers to chronic criminal behaviour which results in numerous arrests and incarcerations. Studies of the yearly intake of prisons, reformatories and jails in the United States show that from one-half to two-thirds of those imprisoned have served previous sentences in the same or other institutions. Statistics from European penal institutions

come to a similar conclusion. This fact reveals two important facets of the crime problem: one is that the criminal population is made up largely of those for whom criminal behaviour has become habitual, or a way of life; the other indication is that penal institutions do little to change the basic behaviour patterns of their inmates.

Though the percentage of recidivists runs high for both felons and misdemeanants, for the latter group it is far greater. A veritable army of petty offenders appear as repeaters in courts of minor jurisdiction on charges of vagrancy, drunkenness, prostitution, disturbing the peace and other minor offenses. The short jail sentences they usually receive do nothing toward rehabilitation.

The most extensive and reliable studies of persistent criminal behaviour have been made by Sheldon and Eleanor T. Glueck in a series of research monographs of which the first was *Five Hundred Criminal Careers* (1930). These studies revealed the factors in the life situation of recidivists which differentiate them from other prisoners who make a good adjustment after their release from custody.

Among the factors that are more prevalent with the recidivists are poor family situations, broken homes, mothers working outside the home, early onset of delinquency, truancy, poor economic status and adjustment, improper use of leisure and mental deficiency or other personality disorders. Similar factors abound among those offenders who fail to succeed on probation or parole.

It is certain that longer sentences and existing penal methods are no solution to the problem of the chronic offender. Two improvements on current practice would seem to be necessary: one, the adoption of really indeterminate sentences that would enable authorities to keep recidivists in custody until their attitudes change for the better; another essential would be the equipment of penal institutions with personnel and facilities for more thoroughgoing work of rehabilitation. *See* also HABITUAL OFFENDERS; PRISON; PROBATION.

BIBLIOGRAPHY.—Sheldon Glueck and Eleanor T. Glueck, *Five Hundred Delinquent Women* (1934), *Juvenile Delinquents Grown Up* (1940), *Criminal Careers in Retrospect* (1943), *Predicting Delinquency and Crime* (1959); Ruth S. Cavan, *Criminology* (1955); Harry Elmer Barnes and Negley K. Teeters, *New Horizons in Criminology,* rev. ed. (1945); Arthur E. Wood and John B. Waite, *Crime and Its Treatment* (1941). (A. E. WD.)

RECIFE (PERNAMBUCO), a city and seaport of Brazil, capital of the state of Pernambuco. Pop. (1960) 788,569, largely Negro and mulatto.

Located at the mouth of the Capiberibe river near the easternmost point of South America, the city is comprised of four separate parts (Recife, Santo Antonio, São José and Boa Vista) which are integrated by many bridges. Because of its numerous waterways the city is often referred to as the "Venice of America."

The district of Recife occupies the southern end of the Olinda peninsula and is the principal commercial centre of the city. In addition to warehouses and terminal facilities, there are the customhouse, observatory, naval arsenal, government offices, several of the consulates and many of the more important banks, business houses and retail stores.

Santo Antonio is located on an island of the same name. Among the important institutions and public buildings in this part of the city are the government palace, the state treasury, the courthouse, the state museum, public library, several fine churches, including the city's famous church of São Francisco de Assís, the Santa Isabel theatre and many historic landmarks, including the Dutch fort of Cinco Pontas.

São José embraces a large district on the mainland and is chiefly residential. In this section of the city is Restoration square, which commemorates the end of Dutch domination.

Boa Vista, also on the mainland, is both a commercial and residential district and contains many of the educational institutions of Recife, including a normal school and schools of law, medicine, engineering, commerce and fine arts.

The hot, humid climate is mitigated somewhat by the southeast trade winds. July, the coolest month, has a mean temperature of 77°, whereas from December through March it is 82°. The total annual rainfall is 65 in., more than 80% of which falls from March through August.

The port of Recife is one of the most important of Brazil because of its proximity to Europe and its convenience for vessels passing around the east shoulder of the continent. Its harbour consists of a narrow body of water, about 2 mi. in length, which is sheltered on the east by a reef and breakwater. The latter extends about 3,600 ft. in a north and northeasterly direction from the reef—an ancient beach of firmly consolidated materials. A second breakwater (Olinda Mole), about 2,500 ft. in length, runs in a southeasterly direction from the mainland and forms the other wing of the entrance channel. The distance between the heads of these two breakwaters is about 900 ft. The northern part of the harbour is approximately 1,600 ft. in width and has been dredged to a low water depth of 32 ft. The southern part is considerably smaller and has been dredged to a depth of 25 ft. The quay is along the eastern margin of the peninsular district of Recife. The port is equipped with a modern coaling plant and grain conveyor, a sugar conveyor and more than 50 electric and steam cranes. Three sets of tracks, which connect with the Great Western of Brazil railway, serve the wharf and warehouses. There are several concrete warehouses, a cold storage warehouse, a warehouse for commodities which create a public hazard and tanks for petroleum products and alcohol. The terminal facilities are operated by a state *directoria* under the authority of the federal government. The principal imports of Recife are coal, petroleum and wheat. Exports consist largely of sugar, cotton and other agricultural products.

More than 1,600 mi. of railways serve the states of Pernambuco, Alagoas, Paraíba and Rio Grande do Norte, having outlet through Recife, and a well-developed system of surfaced roads provides additional transportation facilities. The city is served by several national and European airlines, has national and international cable connections and radio, telegraph and telephone communications.

Recife was settled in 1535, when Duarte Coelho Pereira landed there to take possession of the captaincy granted him by the Portuguese crown. The site of Coelho's capital was Olinda, but Recife remained its port and did not become an independent *villa* (town) until 1709.

Down to the close of the 18th century, when Rio de Janeiro became important, Recife was the second city of Brazil and for a time its most important port. It was captured and plundered in 1595 by the English privateer James Lancaster. It was also captured by the Dutch in 1630 and remained in their possession till 1654, during which time the island of Santo Antonio was occupied and the town greatly improved. At the end of the Dutch war the capital was removed from Olinda to Recife, where it has since remained. (R. E. P.)

RECIPROCATING ENGINE: *see* Steam; Internal-Combustion Engine.

RECIPROCITY, a term applied to special international treaties or agreements in which mutual concessions in tariff rates, quotas, or other commercial restrictions are granted. If these mutual concessions are neither intended nor expected to be generalized to other countries with which the contracting parties have commercial treaties, the agreement is frequently called a reciprocity arrangement. In addition to the commercial reciprocity treaties between pairs of countries such as those between the United States and Canada (1854), the United States and Hawaii (1875), and the United States and Cuba (1902), there are also reciprocity treaties between groups of countries. The complex of preferential tariff rates applicable to the self-governing members of the British Commonwealth embody reciprocity. The development of a full customs union, which eliminates by progressive mutual concessions all tariffs and other restrictions between participating countries, is the logical extension of reciprocity. Thus the European Economic Community, the European Free Trade Association, and the Latin-American Free Trade Area are examples of customs unions involving special concessions among the parties which are not generalized to other countries.

Membership of the General Agreement on Tariffs and Trade (GATT) runs to some extent counter to the establishment of reciprocity treaties. This is because a nation joining GATT undertakes the obligation to grant to all other members "most-favoured-nation" treatment, whereas a reciprocity treaty is an exclusive agreement between the contracting parties to make mutual trade concessions to each other. For a reciprocity treaty to be permissible for a GATT member, it would have to be extended to all GATT members and would be both difficult to implement and difficult to recognize as a "reciprocity" treaty. *See* Tariff.

(J. R. Hu.)

RECKLINGHAUSEN, FRIEDRICH DANIEL VON (1833–1910), German pathologist who contributed significantly to expanding that science, was born in Gütersloh, Westphalia, on Dec. 2, 1833. He received his degree in medicine at Berlin in 1855 and spent the next six years as assistant to Rudolf Virchow. This was the period of Germany's emergence as the centre of medical progress. Recklinghausen became professor of pathology at the University of Königsberg in 1865, accepted the chair at Würzburg the following year, and in 1872 became the first professor of pathology at the University of Strasbourg. He resigned the professorship in 1906 and died on Aug. 26, 1910.

Recklinghausen's name is perpetuated in the eponyms for two diseases he described. Multiple neurofibromatosis, a condition in which there are numerous fibrous tumours of the skin distributed along the course of the cutaneous nerves, has been called Recklinghausen's disease since his description of it in 1882. Similarly, a generalized fibrosis and cystic degeneration of the skeleton, caused by a hyperfunctioning tumour of the parathyroid gland, is known as Recklinghausen's disease of bone. The smallest lymph channels in connective tissue are known as canals of Recklinghausen.

See H. Bailey and W. J. Bishop, *Notable Names in Medicine and Surgery* (1959). (L. M. Z.; X.)

RECKLINGHAUSEN, a town of West Germany in the *Land* (state) of North Rhine-Westphalia, Federal Republic of Germany. It is on the northern edge of the Ruhr industrial region, 15½ mi. (25 km.) NE of Essen by road. Pop. (1961) 130,581. Although it is an important coal mining and industrial town, the old centre is still preserved, with St. Peter's Church (founded in 1247, mainly 16th century) and remains of fortifications. Chemicals, machinery, metals, and textiles are produced. The *Ruhrfestspiele* (festivals) are held annually in June and July. Recklinghausen was a Saxon settlement which under Charlemagne became an imperial town. From 1236 it passed under the archbishop of Cologne, its territory becoming known as the Vest Recklinghausen. From 1316 it was a Hanseatic town. After 1803 it passed to the duke of Arenberg, who from 1815 held it as a fief of Prussia.

RECLAMATION OF LAND: *see* Land Reclamation.

RECLUS, ÉLISÉE (1830–1905), French geographer and anarchist who was awarded the gold medal of the Paris Geographical society in 1892 for *La Nouvelle Géographie universelle*, was born the second son of a Protestant pastor on March 15, 1830, at Sainte-Foy-la-Grande (Gironde). He was educated at the Protestant college of Montauban and studied geography under Carl Ritter in Berlin. Having identified himself with the republicans of 1848, he was obliged to leave France after the *coup d'état* of Dec. 1851. He spent the years 1852–57 visiting the British Isles, the United States, Central America and Colombia. Returning to France, he applied himself to geography, publishing *La Terre, description des phénomènes de la vie du globe*, 2 vol. (1867–68; Eng. trans., 4 vol., 1871–73) and *Histoire d'un ruisseau* (1869). During the siege of Paris (1870–71) he participated in A. Nadar's balloon ascents. Serving in the national guard in defense of the commune, he was taken prisoner in April 1871; but his sentence of transportation for life was commuted in Jan. 1872 to one of perpetual banishment after European scientists had appealed to the government on his behalf. After a visit to Italy, he settled at Clarens, Switz.

His great work, *La Nouvelle Géographie universelle, la terre et les hommes*, 19 vol. (1875–94; Eng. trans., *The Earth and Its Inhabitants*, 1878–94), is a stupendous compilation, profusely illustrated with maps, plans and engravings and characterized by the accuracy and brilliance of exposition that give his work permanent scientific value. His *Histoire d'une montagne* was published in 1880. Though benefiting under the amnesty of 1879, Reclus had meanwhile lost none of his revolutionary enthusiasm; and in 1882 he initiated the Anti-Marriage movement, in accordance with which he allowed his two daughters to marry without civil or religious sanction. When proceedings were instituted at Lyons against the International Workingmen's association, P. A. Kropotkin (*q.v.*) and Reclus were designated as leading promoters of anarchism; but Reclus, as domiciled in Switzerland, escaped imprisonment. In 1892 he was appointed professor of comparative geography in Brussels. He died at Thourout, near Bruges, on July 4, 1905. His other works include *L'Homme et la terre*, 6 vol. (1905–08) and several anarchist pamphlets.

RECOGNITION, DIPLOMATIC. This term may refer either to the procedure by which a new state is formally accepted by other states as a member of the international community, or to the procedure by which a new government of an existing state is accepted as the legal representative of that state. The two procedures, although frequently confused, raise distinct legal questions. The recognition of a new state involves the sovereignty of the state and its independent position in relation to other states; the recognition of a new government merely involves the determination of the particular organized group that is to be accepted as having the right to speak in the name of the state, without raising any issue of the legal personality of the state.

While the term "recognition" has been applied to states already enjoying independent existence but not maintaining diplomatic relations with the western powers, as in the case of Ethiopia until its admission into the League of Nations in 1923, its more normal application is to colonies or dependencies that have declared their independence of the mother country and have proved their ability to maintain their separate existence, as in the case of the recognition by the United States of the Latin American states beginning in 1822. The provisions of the United Nations Charter concerning "the self determination of peoples" and the administration of "nonself-governing territories" support such recognitions.

On occasion, political motives have led to the recognition of a new state before it actually proved its ability to maintain its independence, as in the case of the recognition of the United States by France in 1778. Recognition by the Netherlands came in 1782 on the eve of the treaty of peace. After that treaty, the United States was in due time recognized by other states, as by Sweden, Spain and Prussia in 1783, by Portugal in 1794 and by Russia as late as 1809. Premature recognition has regularly been regarded as an offense that the mother country might resent, as Mexico resented the recognition of Texas by the United States in 1837 and Colombia, that of Panama in 1903.

During the 19th century the great powers gave collective recognition to certain new states before they had as yet won their independence by arms, as when Greece was recognized in 1827, Belgium in 1831, and Rumania, Serbia and Montenegro in 1878. Since the close of World War I recognition has frequently been given by voluntary act of the mother country or more recently by collective act of the members of the United Nations. Great Britain, for example, recognized the independence of Ireland in 1920, of Egypt in 1922, and of India and Pakistan in 1947. Recognition by other states followed promptly. Indonesia was recognized by the Netherlands as independent in 1949, and Ghana and Malaya by Great Britain in 1957, followed by their admission to the UN. Many new African nations received recognition in the early 1960s.

The "Stimson doctrine" declared by the United States secretary of state in 1932, and subsequently supported by the League of Nations, asserted that recognition should not be extended to new states or to territorial changes effected by illegal use of armed force. In accordance with this doctrine the United States and the members of the League of Nations refused to recognize the Japanese-supported state of "Manchoukuo" and the United States refused to recognize the Italian conquest of Ethiopia (1936) and the German conquest of Austria (1938).

In the case of new governments the procedure of recognition is applied only when an existing *de jure* government is overthrown by revolution and it becomes necessary for the governments of other states to decide whether the new government has the stability required to justify holding it responsible for the obligations of the state and is entitled in turn to claim the rights of the state. Recognition in such cases raises no question of the legal personality of the state or of its place in the community of nations, but merely the question whether a particular group can properly speak in the name of the state. Governments actually in power are described as *de facto* until such time as recognition by other states makes them *de jure*.

In addition to stability, the condition has frequently been put that the new government must not have been established by immoral behaviour, such as assassination, and must manifest an intention to observe the rules of international law. Such political or subjective conditions of recognition have given rise to numerous controversies and conflicting practices, the new government being recognized by some states and not by others. The United States, for example, refused to recognize the government of Gen. Victoriano Huerta established in Mexico by assassination of President Madero in 1913, and, until 1933, the Soviet government of Russia established by revolution in 1917. The U.S. also refused to recognize the Communist government of China established in 1949 and recognized by many states but continued to recognize the Nationalist government of China on the Island of Formosa. The U.S., however, promptly recognized the government of Iraq established by assassination of King Faisal II in 1958. During World War II the United States and Great Britain refused to recognize the governments of the countries occupied by the German armies and continued to recognize the refugee governments.

Efforts have been made to establish rules of international law on the subject of recognition in addition to the prohibitions of "premature recognition" and "non-recognition of the forces of aggression," but the political element of recognition has dominated and states have been unwilling to accept a collective decision applying law on a matter on which diametrically opposite points of view may be taken with respect to the conduct that may be expected of the new government.

BIBLIOGRAPHY.—J. Moore, *Digest of International Law*, ch. iii (1906); C. G. Fenwick, *International Law*, 3rd ed. rev., ch. vii, viii (1948); H. Lauterpacht, *Recognition in International Law* (1947); L. F. L. Oppenheim, *International Law*, sec. 71–75, 8th ed. (1955).

(C. G. Fᴋ.)

RECOGNIZANCE, in Anglo-American law, is an obligation entered into before some court or judicial officer (judge or magistrate) whereby the party bound (the recognizor) acknowledges that he owes (generally to the government) a stated sum of money, subject, however, to the condition that he will not owe the sum if he does (or, sometimes, does not do) a specified act. The recognizor may be required to furnish sureties. If he fails to perform the specified act, the amount stated is a debt (sometimes said to be more nearly a judgment than a debt) which may be collected in an appropriate legal proceeding.

The recognizance device serves various purposes. Its most common use is in connection with bail in criminal cases; a person arrested for a crime may generally secure his release from imprisonment pending his trial (or, sometimes, pending his appeal after trial and conviction) by filing in court a recognizance (sometimes termed a bail bond), generally with money or property posted as surety, undertaking to pay a stated amount unless the accused appears in court for further proceedings at a specified time. Where no surety is required, the accused is said to be released "upon his own recognizance." In the United States a material witness, imprisoned to ensure his presence at the trial at which his testimony is needed, may similarly secure his release by filing his recognizance, often with sureties required. In the United Kingdom a witness may not be imprisoned for this purpose. One who threatens to injure or kill others may be arrested and brought into court and released upon his recognizance (perhaps with sureties) to keep the peace. In civil litigation the recognizance of a party may be required to ensure the payment of costs (*i.e.*, amounts of money which losing parties must pay to winning parties as reimbursement for expenses of litigation).

See BAIL; CRIMINAL LAW. (A. W. St.)

RECONSTRUCTION FINANCE CORPORATION.

The Reconstruction Finance corporation in the United States was established by congress on Jan. 22, 1932, "to provide emergency financing facilities for financial institutions, to aid in financing agriculture, commerce and industry." After a few years of unprecedented depression and steady price declines, an institution was required which could pump dollars into financial institutions, railroads, etc., to enable them to meet their commitments. The RFC in turn was to obtain dollars from the federal government. In moderating the epidemic of bankruptcies in the 1930s, the RFC helped lay the groundwork of recovery. The RFC was to operate as an independent agency, not subject to political influences. Every application would be considered on its merits, not on political considerations. It was also generally assumed that loans would be made on the condition that private financing was not available and that an important public interest would be served.

In the early years Jesse Jones, chairman of the board of directors, managed the institution without much interference. But as the functions of the RFC grew, and particularly as the RFC, even in the 1930s, began to assume responsibility for disbursing huge sums of money for other government agencies, without the delays incident to the voting of funds through the appropriation committees of the congress, the agency tended to become involved in politics.

By the 1940s the situation had become precarious. The Hoover commission in 1949 noted that "direct lending by the government to persons or enterprises opens up dangerous possibilities of waste and favoritism. . . . It invites political and private pressures, or even corruption" (*Report on Federal Business Enterprises*, March 31, 1949). As early as 1948 a congressional committee (Senate Committee Report no. 974 on the RFC act) had noted that attempts to influence the business judgments of RFC by the use of political influence, even though well intended, were a constant menace to sound administration. In a report in 1951, the senate banking and currency committee (Report no. 649) complained of the increasing practice of applicants seeking direct access to the directors of the RFC through members of the Democratic national committee; and many cases of corruption were aired.

Despite this, the Democratic majority of the banking and currency committee in 1951 proposed only to correct abuses, not to destroy the RFC, for the majority emphasized the important financing contributions of the RFC in a financial market that was imperfect at best. Once the Republicans came into power in 1953, however, they provided for a quick liquidation of the RFC (RFC Liquidation act, July 30, 1953). Effective June 30, 1957, the RFC was abolished and its remaining functions transferred to the Housing and Home Finance agency, the General Services administration, the Small Business administration and the treasury department.

During 21 years and 8 months of RFC lending, more than $12,-000,000,000 was disbursed. When, in Sept. 1953, its lending authority was terminated, it had $800,000,000 outstanding in loans, securities and commitments. Aside from its peacetime activities, the RFC under legislation in 1940 and 1950 had assumed large military responsibilities; *e.g.,* purchases of strategic items, building of plant facilities. (S. E. H.)

RECONSTRUCTION PERIOD (U.S.),

RECONSTRUCTION PERIOD (U.S.), a term used in U.S. history to denote the years immediately following the American Civil War (1861–65). The reconstruction of the 11 seceded states that had made up the Confederate States of America grew out of the attempt to find acceptable solutions to peculiar political, economic, and social problems that had been raised by secession and war. The political problem was essentially a matter of restoring Southern state governments to what President Lincoln had termed their "proper relation" to the Union. The economic problem was one of adjustment to the economic revolution that was transforming a prewar agrarian nation into a postwar industrial nation. The social problem was centred around the question of the status of the newly freed slaves. As these problems involved basic questions of authority and jurisdiction, it was perhaps inevitable that any serious attempt to solve them would lead to conflict between the president, the Congress, and the individual states. The process of readjustment was further complicated by certain regional problems that were born of victory and defeat. The victorious North faced such complex problems as demobilization, conversion of wartime industry to peacetime production, and restoration of civil law in areas recently under military control. In the South, defeat and demoralization were aggravated by physical devastation, shortages of food in certain critical areas, inadequate transportation facilities, and a growing spirit of lawlessness that accompanied the paralysis of local government. (*See* UNITED STATES [OF AMERICA]: *History: Civil War and Reconstruction 1850–1876.*)

Presidential Reconstruction.—Some steps toward the reconstruction of Southern states were taken by the executive department of the government before the end of the war. First under Lincoln and later under Andrew Johnson, presidential programs of remarkable leniency were inaugurated. Lincoln's plan was put into effect during the war in areas occupied by Federal forces. In December 1863 the president issued a proclamation embodying his "ten per cent plan," which provided for the reestablishment of a state government whenever 10% of the voting population of 1860 had taken the prescribed oath of allegiance. Put into effect in Louisiana, Tennessee, Virginia, and Arkansas, the plan had slowly evolved from Lincoln's experiences with the border states and with military governments set up in occupied areas and from his own changing concept of the nation. It was, in substance, an invitation to the Southern people to reorder their political structure and take up their places in the new nation that had supplanted the old Union. Based upon the assumption that reconstruction of a state government was exclusively an executive function and that it was solely a political affair, the plan precipitated a bitter struggle between the president and the Radical wing of his own party in Congress. Once the Radicals had grasped the fact that Lincoln's program did not include social and economic reconstruction of the South, they began to challenge his control and direction of the machinery of reconstruction. Their own more stringent program was embodied in the Wade-Davis Bill passed in July 1864. Lincoln, hoping to "reanimate the states" under presidential supervision before Congress reconvened, killed the Wade-Davis Bill by means of a pocket veto. The assassination of Lincoln in April 1865 elevated Andrew Johnson of Tennessee to the presidency. Johnson, a Southern Unionist who had been elected vice-president on the Lincoln ticket in 1864, continued Lincoln's moderate program with only minor modifications. In so doing, he alienated the Radicals just as Lincoln had, and when Congress reconvened in December 1865, the Radicals were again prepared to challenge presidential control of reconstruction. On the first day of the new session the struggle was begun when the Congress, after refusing to seat the "Confederate Brigadiers" who had been elected in the South, created the Joint Committee on Reconstruction. The climax of this struggle between the executive and legislative branches of government was reached in the election of 1866 when both sides attempted to win popular support for their programs. Johnson's own intemperate outbursts against the opposition, coupled with such reactionary developments within the South as the rejection of the 14th Amendment (except by Tennessee, which was readmitted in 1866), race riots in Memphis and New Orleans, and passage of repugnant "Black Codes" (restricting the freedom of the Negroes) by Johnson-supported state governments, seriously weakened the president's position and helped the Radicals win a smashing victory in the election. With what now appeared to be a mandate from the voters in states that participated in the election, the Radicals in Congress abruptly took over control of the reconstruction process from the executive.

Congressional Reconstruction.—Congressional control of the reconstruction experiment was assured by passage of the Reconstruction Acts of March 1867 that were specifically designed to undo the work of Lincoln and Johnson. As a result of these acts, the ten remaining Southern states were divided into five military districts, each commanded by a major general of the U.S. Army. These officers were to supervise the reconstruction of the states in their respective districts until such time as a new constitution could be drawn up and approved by Congress. With the Southern states thus firmly in hand, the Radicals further strengthened their legislative hegemony by impeaching President Johnson (who escaped conviction by the margin of one vote in the Senate), badgering the Supreme Court into temporary submission, and by placing Gen. Ulysses S. Grant in the White House by the election of 1868.

Reconstruction in the South.—Under the supervision of the U.S. Army, Southern voters were registered, delegates to constitutional conventions selected, constitutions drafted, and local officials elected. Between June 1868 and July 1870 the ten remaining states were all readmitted to the Union through the processes outlined in the congressional program of Reconstruction. These newly created state governments were generally Republican in character and were governed by political coalitions of Negroes, "carpetbaggers" (Northerners who went into the South), and "scalawags" (Southerners who collaborated with the Negroes and "carpetbaggers"). Because these Republican state governments were looked upon as artificial creations that had been imposed from without, the conservative element in the South remained hostile to them. Southerners were particularly resentful of the activities of the Freedmen's Bureau, a federal agency specifically created to help the Negro adjust to his new situation, and the Union League, an organization that had originated in the North during the war and had moved into the South in the immediate postwar period where it became the most effective agency for inculcating the newly enfranchised Negro with Republican principles.

This resentment led to the formation in the South of secret terroristic organizations, the most powerful of which was the Ku Klux Klan (*q.v.*). Several other organizations such as the Knights of the White Camelia, the Palefaces, and the White Brotherhood were also employed as instruments of violence. Continual opposition from within the South led eventually to the overthrow of the congressionally sponsored state governments that had been set up once civilian rule was reestablished. Through the deliberate use of fraud, violence, and intimidation, Southern conservatives regained control of their state governments and by 1877, when Federal troops were withdrawn from Louisiana—the last Southern state to be "redeemed"—the Democratic Party had been returned to power in each Southern state.

Significance of the Reconstruction Period.—The Reconstruction era left an indelible imprint on the history of the United States. It fixed firmly on the national scene that economic revolution that had been begun during the war and was destined to make possible the remarkably rapid transformation of an essentially agrarian society into what was to become modern, industrial America. It introduced a number of worthwhile reforms into the South. Courts were reorganized, judicial procedures improved, new and improved techniques of school administration were instituted, and more feasible methods of taxation devised. Many of the state constitutions adopted during the postwar years are still in existence. It is also true that the Reconstruction experience led to an increase in sectional bitterness, to an intensification of the racial issue, and to the development of one-party politics in the South.

See also references under "Reconstruction Period (U.S.)" in the Index.

BIBLIOGRAPHY.—Paul H. Buck, *The Road to Reunion, 1865–1900* (1937); E. Merton Coulter, *The South During Reconstruction, 1865–1877* (1947); C. Vann Woodward, *Reunion and Reaction* (1951); K. M. Stampp, *The Era of Reconstruction, 1865–1877* (1965).

(O. A. S.)

RECORDER, an English judicial office originating with the creation of courts of quarter sessions for boroughs, about the 16th or 17th century. Originally one of several judges, the recorder became the sole judge of criminal cases tried before borough quarter sessions. There are three full-time, permanent recorders: one for London, who sits in the Central Criminal Court, and one each for Manchester and Liverpool. Other recorderships are part-time, honorific posts, held by eminent practising barristers.

The title has been used elsewhere to designate judges of other criminal courts and, in the United States, has been most frequently used as a title for the government official in charge of keeping records, such as a recorder of deeds.

See JUDICIARY AND COURT OFFICERS. (P. B. K.)

RECORDER, a musical instrument of the flageolet class, also described as "fipple flute" from the shape of the part which the player holds to the lips. Most modern recorders, made since the instrument's revival by Arnold Dolmetsch in 1919, follow the early 18th-century or Baroque design: the cylindrical head joint is partially plugged to direct the wind against the sharp edge below; the body tapers and its lowest part is usually made as a separate foot joint; there are seven finger holes and one thumbhole. Often the lowest two holes are each arranged as a pair of holes, one of which is left open to produce the semitone above the note made by covering both. The upper register, at the octave, is obtained by "pinching" the thumbhole; *i.e.*, flexing the thumb to make a narrow opening above the thumbnail. The larger instruments may have one or more keys, allowing holes to be pierced at points otherwise out of reach of the fingers. Recorders are made in the following sizes: sopranino in f″; descant (soprano) in c″; treble (alto) in f′; tenor in c′; bass in f; and (rarely) great

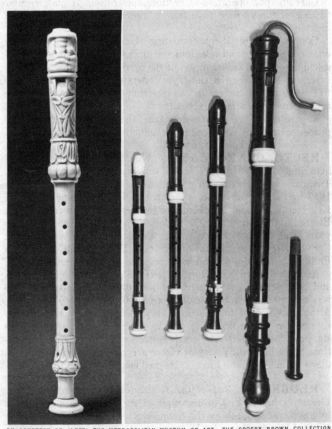

BY COURTESY OF (LEFT) THE METROPOLITAN MUSEUM OF ART, THE CROSBY BROWN COLLECTION OF MUSICAL INSTRUMENTS, 1889; (RIGHT) THE CHESTER CORPORATION

17TH- AND 18TH-CENTURY RECORDERS

(Left) French 17th-century ivory recorder. (Right) Set of recorders by P. J. Bressan, 18th century: from left to right, treble in f′, alto (voice flute) in d′, tenor in c′, and bass in f. The supporting strut, at far right, is inserted into a socket at the bottom of the bass recorder, to rest it on the floor

bass in c. (These notes refer in each case to the instrument's lowest note.) The treble and tenor recorders sound at written pitch; the sopranino and descant sound an octave higher than written; the bass, the music for which is written in the bass stave, also sounds an octave higher.

The recorder is a 14th-century improvement upon kindred instruments played earlier in the Middle Ages. The English name may derive from Old Italian *ricordo*, a keepsake. The first instructions are found in the books by Sebastian Virdung (1511) and Sylvestro Ganassi (1535), written at a time when recorder consorts were approaching the height of their popularity. The Baroque repertory, which includes many works by Handel and Bach, is almost exclusively for treble recorder (then described as "flute" or "common flute"), after which time the instrument lay obsolete until its flourishing modern revival. (A. C. BA.)

RECORDING, PHONOGRAPH: *see* PHONOGRAPH.

RECTIFIER, a device which converts one or more alternating-current waves into a unidirectional wave. It may be an electron tube (of either vacuum or gaseous type), vibrator, barrier-layer cell, or mechanical device. Although they often serve the same purposes, rotary converters and motor-generator sets are not usually classified as rectifiers.

If an alternating-current wave is applied to the diode vacuum tube, the resulting output is a succession of pulses similar in shape to the positive portions of the input wave but separated from each other by an amount of time corresponding to the negative portions of the input wave. This is termed half-wave rectification.

Two diodes may be connected in such a manner that one will conduct when the other does not. This type of operation, called full-wave rectification, results in a continuous train of pulses.

Both the half-wave and full-wave rectifier outputs may be smoothed by inserting a capacitor across the output.

Gaseous tube operation in rectifier applications is quite similar to that of the vacuum tube but the power capabilities are much greater.

Copper-oxide rectifiers, consisting of a layer of cuprous oxide on a copper disk, and selenium rectifiers, consisting of a layer of selenium on iron, are examples of the barrier-layer types. In both cases, the boundary (barrier-layer) offers relatively low resistance to the passage of current in one direction but very high resistance to current in the other direction.

Regardless of the form it may take, the rectifier's fundamental property is one of unidirectional conductivity.

See also AMPLIFIER, ELECTRONIC.   (A. L. Sv.)

RECTO, CLARO MAYO (1890–1960), Philippine statesman and unsuccessful presidential candidate, was born in Tiaong, Tayabas (now Quezon) Province, on the island of Luzon. From 1919 to 1928 he served as a member of the Philippine House of Representatives and floor leader of the minority Democrata Party. Elected to the Senate in 1931, he joined the Nacionalista Party two years later and in 1934 was chosen president of the Constitutional Convention. He served for one year on the Supreme Court of the Philippines (1935–36) and was reelected to the Senate in 1941.

After the outbreak of World War II, he stayed in the Philippines and held various government positions under the Japanese. He was returned to the Senate for six-year terms in 1949 and 1955. Although defeated for the presidency in 1957, he was highly esteemed for his brilliance as a lawyer and man of letters. He staunchly advocated "respectable independence" in foreign relations and a domestic policy of vigorous economic nationalism popularly called "Filipino First." He died Oct. 2, 1960, in Rome.
                    (C. A. B.)

REDBRIDGE, one of the 32 London boroughs constituting Greater London, Eng., forms part of its northeastern perimeter and is bounded south by the borough of Newham, south and east by Barking, northeast by Havering, north by Essex, and west by Waltham Forest. This outer London borough was established on April 1, 1965, under the London Government Act 1963 (*see* LONDON) by the amalgamation of the former boroughs of Ilford and Wanstead and Woodford, and parts of Dagenham and of the urban district of Chigwell. Area 21.8 sq.mi. (56.5 sq.km.). Pop. (1965 est.) 247,960. Redbridge returns three members of Parliament and elects three members on the Greater London Council. The Wanstead and Woodford constituency was represented (1924–64) by Sir Winston Churchill, who is commemorated by a statue (1959) on Woodford Green. Redbridge is mainly residential and within its boundaries are 730 ac. (30 ha.) of Epping Forest. Industry includes light engineering, and the manufacture of radio and electric components, photographic materials, and chemicals. The borough is served by the Central Line of the London Underground, and the Eastern Region of British Rail.

Wanstead (Wenesteda), Woodford (Wdefort), and Ilford (Ilefort) are mentioned in the Domesday Book. Ealdford is a Saxon description of Ilford, and Hyleford and Yleford are other recorded spellings probably referring to the village near the ford across the River Roding (Saxon Hyle).

In Saxon times both manors of Wanstead and Woodford were held by the king. St. Edward the Confessor gave Wanstead to the Abbey of Waltham Holy Cross; Harold II bequeathed Woodford to Westminster Abbey. Robert Dudley, earl of Leicester, entertained Queen Elizabeth I at Wanstead House (demolished in 1824) which James I gave with the manor to the duke of Buckingham. Sir Charles Bright, the telegraphic engineer, was born in Wanstead in 1832, Thomas Hood (1799–1845), the poet, lived at Lake House, and R. B. Sheridan (1751–1816) also lived in the district; William Morris (1834–1896) lived for a time at his father's home Woodford Hall (since demolished). The River Roding which flows through Woodford was crossed by the Red Bridge from which the borough derives its name.   (K. F. B. N.)

REDCAR, a municipal borough in the Cleveland parliamentary division of the North Riding of Yorkshire, Eng., on the northeast coast 8 mi. (13 km.) ENE of Middlesbrough. Pop. (1961) 31,460. Area is 8.1 sq.mi. (21.0 sq.km.). Lying midway along the continuous stretch of sand between the Tees estuary and Saltburn, it serves as residential town and holiday resort for the industrial population of south Tees-side. It was incorporated in 1922. Huge industrial developments on its western boundaries include chemical works, a steel rolling mill, and docks on the borough's frontage to the Tees River.

Kirkleatham Hall, in the lovely village of Kirkleatham, was the home of the Turner family from the 17th century until 1948 after which it was demolished.

RED CROSS, an international humanitarian agency with national affiliates in almost every country in the world, was originally established to care for the victims of battle in time of war. The scope of its program has gradually expanded to include aid to prisoners of war and other victims of hostilities and also the prevention and relief of human suffering in time of peace as well as war. The emblem of the Red Cross (the Red Crescent in the Muslim countries and the Red Lion and Sun in Iran) identifies personnel and installations entitled to protection during hostilities.

ORIGIN

The Battle of Solferino between the French and Italians and the Austrians took place on June 24, 1859. Jean Henri Dunant of Switzerland, then aged 31, was a witness of the suffering of thousands of wounded men for whom medical and nursing care was lacking. In the nearby town of Castiglione he did what he could, with the help of the local inhabitants, to organize assistance for the wounded who had been brought there. In 1862 he published "A Memory of Solferino," describing the terrible aftermath of the fighting and proposing that in every country relief societies should be formed in peacetime that would be recognized and ready to succour the wounded in time of war. The wide interest generated by his proposal led to the formation of a committee in 1863 which later became the International Committee of the Red Cross. At a meeting called by this committee in Geneva on Oct. 26–29, 1863, and attended by delegates from 14 countries, the basic principles of the Red Cross were formulated.

The first Red Cross Convention, drawn up at a diplomatic conference in Geneva the following year, committed signatory governments to care for the wounded of war, whether enemy or friend. In later years this first convention was revised and improved, and new conventions were adopted to protect victims of warfare at sea (1907), prisoners of war (1929), and civilians in time of war (1949).

THE RED CROSS MOVEMENT

The worldwide structure of the International Red Cross consists of three components: (1) the International Committee of the Red Cross (Comité International de la Croix-Rouge); (2) the League of Red Cross Societies; and (3) the national Red Cross societies. An international conference, held every four to six years, includes representatives not only of these three groups, but also of the governments that adhere to the Geneva Conventions.

International Committee of the Red Cross.—The International Committee is an independent council of 25 Swiss citizens with headquarters at Geneva. One of its functions is to accord recognition to new national Red Cross societies following inquiry concerning their structure and purpose. Its activities in wartime stem from its original concern for those wounded in battle, but have responded to modifications resulting from the changed conditions of combat. Among these developments have been visits and services to prisoners in war camps and the channeling of information about them to their families. In World War II, for example, a card index was maintained showing the location of millions of prisoners and civilian internees, thousands of visits were made to prison camps, relief supplies were provided, and letters were forwarded to the prisoners. Exchange of wounded prisoners among belligerents was also arranged.

Since direct communication among belligerent countries is blocked in wartime, the Committee acts as an intermediary not only among these governments but also among their national Red Cross societies. This role enabled it, during World War II, to make appeals to the warring nations not only in behalf of war victims but also with respect to improved implementation of the international conventions.

The dislocations and the suffering caused by war extend far beyond the cessation of hostilities. The Committee therefore concerns itself with the relief of starvation and the alleviation of distress caused by war both during and after the period of active conflict. After World War I, for example, it arranged for the repatriation of 450,000 prisoners of war. In World War II, in collaboration with the League of Red Cross Societies, it created the Joint Relief Commission which distributed food, clothing, and pharmaceuticals among civilian war victims.

From a long-range point of view the Committee's most important contribution relates to the extension and improvement of the international conventions relating to the protection and care of the victims of war. The period following World War II has been dedicated to the revision and improvement of the existing conventions and to the preparation of a new one for the protection of civilians in time of war. In 1917 and again in 1944 the International Committee was awarded the Nobel Peace Prize.

League of Red Cross Societies.—France, Great Britain, Italy, Japan, and the United States were the first members of the League of Red Cross Societies, which was established in 1919. Growth of the League has increased the number of national member societies to more than 100, with an aggregate junior and adult membership of almost 200,000,000. Each member society has a representative on the League's board of governors.

The purposes of the League are to serve as a means of communication among the national societies, to coordinate international relief work, and to protect mankind by stimulating peacetime programs for the improvement of health, the prevention of disease, and the relief of suffering. A secretariat with headquarters in Geneva carries on the work of the League, maintaining for this purpose technical departments on disaster relief, health, nursing and social service, and Junior Red Cross. Through its relief bureau, the League coordinates rescue work in catastrophes in which the scope of the disaster exceeds the resources of a national government and its relief agencies. The health bureau provides materials for health education and promotes the extension of health work by the national societies. The nursing bureau, established in 1919, was extended in 1951 to include a social service section. This bureau conducts an information service, selects and counsels candidates for Red Cross scholarships, and provides guidance to national societies in establishing Red Cross nursing schools and training programs for nurses' aides and teachers of home nursing. The Junior Red Cross bureau assists the junior sections, organized largely in elementary and secondary schools by the national societies in 75 countries throughout the world. A major objective of the junior sections is the promotion of friendship and understanding among children of different races and cultures.

From time to time the League arranges regional conferences in different sections of the world to enable national societies to exchange views concerning problems common to the countries in that area. It also maintains continuing liaison with international organizations whose programs are related to Red Cross objectives, including the World Health Organization, the International Refugee Organization, and others.

National Red Cross Societies.—Among the requirements a national society must meet to gain recognition by the International Committee are: (1) the government of its country must have adhered to the Geneva Conventions; (2) it must adopt the name and emblem of the Red Cross (except that in Muslim countries the Red Crescent and in Iran the Red Lion and Sun are used); (3) its activity must extend throughout the country and its dependencies; (4) membership must be open to all its citizens regardless of race, sex, politics, or religion; (5) it must agree to maintain contact with the other national societies and with the International Committee at Geneva, and must be guided in all its work by the spirit of the Geneva Conventions. Only one national Red Cross society is recognized in each country and, within its own territory, each is autonomous.

The first national Red Cross societies to come into existence—the Belgian, French, Italian, and Spanish (all 1864)—followed immediately on the Geneva Conference of 1863. A hundred years later more than 100 national societies were in existence. The American National Red Cross was organized in 1881 with Clara Barton, a volunteer worker on the battlefields of the Civil War, as its first president; altogether 30 societies were founded in the 19th century and an additional 7 before the outbreak of World War I. Another 26 were founded before the beginning of World War II and a further 39 after World War II. In the 1960s 22 societies were to be found in Africa (16 Red Cross, 6 Red Crescent), 23 in North and South America, 25 in Asia (18 Red Cross, 6 Red Crescent, and one Red Lion and Sun), 2 in Australasia, and 30 in Europe (29 Red Cross and one, U.S.S.R., an alliance of the Red Cross and Red Crescent).

The wartime activities of national societies have included such diverse services as providing ambulances, hospitals, and medical and nursing personnel; operating canteens for troops in transit; distributing food in occupied territories; donating comfort items to hospitalized combatants and to civilian victims of war; locating families and friends displaced by the hostilities; and conducting major programs of relief for refugees and for civilian populations impoverished by war. (A. W. M.)

Peacetime Activities.—The scope of the peacetime activities of Red Cross societies has increased enormously since the end of World War I, covering many aspects of health and welfare. Many societies have large-scale first-aid programs, including education in accident prevention, swimming and water safety, beach and highway first-aid stations, emergency ambulance services, and mountain rescue teams. A number of societies train nurses' aides, visiting housekeepers, and mothers' assistants, and maintain maternal and child welfare centres and clinics, such as those of the Iranian Red Lion and Sun and the infants' clinics of the Guatemalan Red Cross. The Indian Red Cross trains midwives. Some societies specialize in work with handicapped children; for instance, the Australian Red Cross has a service for spastic children, the British society works a great deal with the deaf and dumb, and the Swedish Red Cross runs summer camps, not only for the physically disabled but also for the mentally retarded. These services are largely carried out, under supervision, by specially trained Junior Red Cross members. School hygiene is emphasized by many societies and some operate summer colonies, preventoria, and homes for orphans and deserted children. A number of societies have services for the aged, the lonely, and the isolated, with Junior Red Cross members often visiting the blind in these categories.

Members and former members of the armed forces and their families are given financial aid, counseling, referral, and other services. Particularly in the U.S., Australian, and Philippine societies, help for former servicemen and their dependents includes assistance in establishing veterans' claims for government benefits, retraining the disabled, supplying orthopedic appliances, etc.

Maintaining hospitals, clinics, and dispensaries are the major programs of many societies, particularly in Latin-American countries; there, and in Lebanon, mobile clinics are often used for rural work. The training of nursing personnel varies from the postgraduate training provided by the French Red Cross to that conducted by the British Red Cross for voluntary auxiliary aides for civil defense. The enrollment of nurses and auxiliary personnel for ambulance, pharmaceutical, radiological, poliomyelitic, and tuberculosis work is an activity of many societies. Public health nursing services are also conducted, and the Swiss Red Cross runs a comprehensive health centre in the canton of Geneva. Health education is likewise a part of Red Cross activities, including campaigns against tuberculosis, poliomyelitis, cancer and venereal diseases, and "Health in the Home" courses, conducted by more than 50 national societies. An auxiliary service in this connection is the medical loan depot, run by some societies, including the British and Swedish, to provide equipment for those sick at home.

Procurement of blood and the maintenance of blood banks are other activities of many Red Cross societies. Outstanding examples of comprehensive blood programs are those of the U.S. and Canadian societies. Outpost work is featured by many societies, such as the visiting housekeepers for isolated areas furnished by the Australian Red Cross, which also has teams standing by in case of bush fires or floods, the first-aid posts and clinics of the South African society, and the air ambulances of the Swedish Red Cross. Among less common activities are the Belgian Red Cross "Spéléo-Secours" for emergency cave rescue work; the French Red Cross Airborne Nurses services; the Italian Red Cross special emergency ambulance service on highways; the Netherlands Red Cross hospital ship, the "J. Henri Dunant," used to give outings to the chronically ill and isolated; the Norwegian Red Cross Prison Visitors Service and home for discharged prisoners; the Swiss society's centre for Tibetan refugees in Switzerland; and the Thai Red Cross "Snake Farm" for the production of antisnakebite serum, which is sent all over the world.

See also references under "Red Cross" in the Index.

(H. Be.)

Bibliography.—Reports and publications of the International Committee of the Red Cross and the League of Red Cross Societies, especially *Handbook of the International Red Cross* (1953), *The Geneva Conventions of August 12, 1949,* 2nd rev. ed., vol. i, ii (1950), *The International Red Cross Committee in Geneva 1863–1943* (1943), *The League of Red Cross Societies, Its Foundation, Organization, Programme* (1956); annual reports of the American National Red Cross and the British Red Cross. *See* also Marcel Jounod, *Warrior without Weapons* (1951); Foster Rhea Dulles, *The American Red Cross: a History* (1950); Charles Hurd, *The Compact History of the American Red Cross* (1959); Sir James Magill, *The Red Cross, the Idea and Its Development* (1926); Jean S. Pictet, *The Sign of the Red Cross* (1952).

(A. W. M.)

REDDITCH, an urban district on the eastern boundary of Worcestershire, Eng., 19 mi. (31 km.) NE of Worcester by road. Pop. (1961) 34,151. It lies on a ridge about 500 ft. (152 m.) above sea level in a pastoral setting. In the mid-1960s Redditch was designated for development as a New Town with a population of 70,000, to relieve congestion in the Birmingham area. North of Redditch are the scanty remains of Bordesley Abbey, a 12th-century Cistercian foundation. Needles and fishing tackle are the principal industries and springs, bicycles, and motorcycles are also manufactured. Redditch is connected by rail to Birmingham (15½ mi. [25 km.]) and Alcester (8 mi. [13 km.]). It is in the Bromsgrove parliamentary division.

REDEMPTION, in religion, has both a larger association and a more limited biblical context. In the first sense it is broadly identified with salvation, atonement (*q.v.*), reconciliation, and forgiveness. It refers to the action of God within history whereby mankind has been delivered from sin and death through the life, death, and resurrection of Jesus Christ (*see* Jesus Christ). "In him we have redemption through his blood, the forgiveness of our trespasses according to the riches of his grace" (Eph. 1: 7). The biblical metaphor is that of buying back a parcel of land or of purchasing someone from slavery. In the Old Testament redemption is usually described as deliverance from material disasters, but in Ps. 130 it is promised that God "will redeem Israel from all his iniquities." Jesus' saying that "the Son of man also came not to be served but to serve, and to give his life as a ransom for many" (Mark 10:45) found its deepest expression in his crucifixion.

Emphasis has been placed on the voluntary and loving character of Christ's sacrificial act, on the costliness of this deliverance, on the representative and substitutionary activity of Christ in doing for men what they could not do for themselves, and on the needed response of men in faith, worship, and newness of life to this initiative of God in Christ.

See also references under "Redemption" in the Index.

Bibliography.—R. S. Franks, *A History of the Doctrine of the Work of Christ* (1919); Vincent Taylor, *Jesus and His Sacrifice* (1937); William Wolf, *No Cross, No Crown* (1957); R. Garrigou-Lagrange, *Our Saviour and His Love for Us* (1951).

(W. J. W.)

REDEMPTORISTS (Congregation of the Most Holy Redeemer; Congregatio Sanctissimi Redemptoris; C.SS.R.), a religious congregation founded by St. Alfonso Maria de' Liguori (*q.v.*) at Scala, Italy, Nov. 9, 1732. Benedict XIV granted papal approbation Feb. 25, 1749. Neapolitan regalism was an obstacle to the congregation, and steps were taken to settle also in the papal states. In 1785 through St. Clement Hofbauer (*q.v.*) the congregation entered the transalpine world, and eventually secured foundations throughout Europe and, during the centenary year, 1832, the United States. The congregation now is established on the five continents. The purpose of the congregation is the sanctification of the members through the imitation of Jesus Christ and the preaching of the word of God, especially to the poor, through various means, particularly parish missions. The Redemptorists also conduct parishes and foreign missions.

The congregation, composed of priests, clerical students, and lay brothers, is ruled by a superior general, who is elected for life and resides in Rome at the general mother house. He is aided by general consultors who represent geographical areas. Provincials, vice-provincials, and rectors are appointed by him. There is also an order of Redemptorist nuns, founded by St. Alfonso Liguori in 1731 and approved in 1750. *See* Orders and Congregations, Religious.

See M. de Meulemeester, *Outline History of the Redemptorists* (1956); G. Stebbing, *The Redemptorists* (1924). (A. C. Ru.)

REDFIELD, ROBERT (1897–1958), U.S. anthropologist, developed concepts that brought into a single purview preliterate tribes, folk peasantries, and complex civilizations. Born Dec. 4, 1897, in Chicago, he was associated all of his life with the University of Chicago, as student, professor, and dean. The son of a lawyer, Redfield married Margaret Park (daughter of the sociologist Robert E. Park) before graduating in law. A summer visit to Mexico turned him to anthropology. His Ph.D. dissertation (1928) reported field work in a community in Mexico; *Tepoztlan* received immediate attention as a pioneer study of the "folk" community as a way of life. After extended field work with his family in Yucatán, he showed through comparison of tribe, village, town, and city how the growth of a small isolated community into a large heterogeneous society involves social disorganization and the substitution of formal institutions for a "moral order." Later, study of the civilizations of China and India, which he visited, suggested how the intellectual-aesthetic "great tradition" alters the character of small communities and their continuing "little traditions." Peasants are seen as living in small part-societies, somewhat triballike but affected by cities and the great tradition.

Redfield died on Oct. 16, 1958, in Chicago.

Among his writings are *Tepoztlan* (1930); *Chan Kom* (1934); *The Folk Culture of Yucatan* (1941); *A Village That Chose Progress* (1950); *The Primitive World and Its Transformations* (1953); *The Little Community* (1955); *Peasant Society and Culture* (1956). His *Papers,* two volumes (1962–63), were edited by Mrs. Redfield.

See Fay-Cooper Cole and Fred Eggan, "Robert Redfield," in *American Anthropologist*, vol. lxi, no. 4 (Aug. 1959); "Robert Redfield," *National Cyclopaedia of American Biography*, vol. 44 (1962).

(S. Tx.)

REDLANDS, a city of San Bernardino County, Calif., U.S., is situated at the foot of the San Bernardino mountains, 65 mi. (105 km.) E of Los Angeles. (For comparative population figures *see* table in California: *Population.*)

The city lies at the upper end of San Bernardino valley at an elevation of 1,200 to 2,100 ft. (366 to 640 m.), surrounded by peaks more than 10,000 ft. (3,000 m.) high. While the navel orange-growing area has been its basic economy, Redlands also provides homes for military and civilian personnel who work at nearby Norton and March Air Force Bases and the local rocket company. Within easy commuting distance of Los Angeles, the nearby beaches, mountain resorts, and desert playgrounds, with a mild sunny climate, Redlands is an ideal residential town.

The University of Redlands, affiliated with the American Baptist Convention, was established in 1907. The Watchorn Lincoln memorial stands on the grounds of the public library. The San Bernardino *asistencia* (chapel), rebuilt by the historical society, represents a link with the city's Spanish heritage, and the Redlands Music Association provides weekly summer concerts in the Prosellis Bowl.

The present city was founded in 1887 by New Englanders and incorporated in 1888. While retaining "Yankee" characteristics, it is representative of all areas of the country. A council-manager system of government was adopted in 1949.

(G. B. BE.)

REDMOND, JOHN EDWARD (1856–1918), Irish nationalist leader who devoted his life to the cause of Home Rule for Ireland, was born at Ballytrent, County Wexford, on Sept. 1, 1856, the son of William Archer Redmond, M.P. for Wexford. In 1874 he entered Trinity College, Dublin, to read law, but left in 1876, when his father required his assistance in London, and he became a clerk in the House of Commons. He was called to the Irish bar in 1886 and to the English bar at Gray's Inn in 1887. Elected to Parliament for New Ross in February 1881, he created a record by taking his seat, making his maiden speech, and being suspended from the House, all within 24 hours. A fervent admirer of Charles Stewart Parnell, Redmond soon became a whip to his party. By his eloquence and practical arguments he gained for the policy of Home Rule many converts in Great Britain, and on political missions to Australia (1882) and the United States (1884) he collected large funds from Irish sympathizers.

When the Irish Nationalist Party split after the Parnell divorce scandal in November 1890, Redmond became the leader of the small minority which supported Parnell. In 1891 he was elected as a Parnellite member for Waterford, which he represented until his death. In 1900 the two sections of the Irish party were reunited and the larger section agreed to accept Redmond as leader. At first he was unable to exert a decisive pressure upon the rival English parties; only when they were equally divided could he hold the balance of power between them (*see* IRELAND: *History*). The first opportunity occurred in 1909 when the rejection of Lloyd George's radical budget by the House of Lords created a constitutional crisis. In both the elections of 1910 a Liberal ministry was returned dependent upon Irish Nationalist support, in return for which a third Home Rule Bill was introduced in April 1912.

The passage of the bill seemed assured until the Unionists in Ulster adopted new tactics by organizing an armed defiance of Parliament. Their leader, Sir Edward Carson, planned to form a provisional government in Belfast and early in 1913 enrolled an armed Ulster volunteer force. Redmond's whole life had been spent in the House of Commons and such defiance of its authority seemed to him incredible. When he discovered that a rival force of Irish volunteers were enrolling in Dublin in November 1913, he saw that there was a real danger of civil war and that the Irish volunteers, under untried leaders, might disregard constitutional methods. As a result of his efforts the movement was, in June 1914, placed under more responsible and representative leaders.

By March 1914 Redmond had reluctantly agreed that for a brief period those northeastern counties which voted against it should be excluded from Home Rule. The Ulster Unionists, however, demanded exclusion for all nine countries of Ulster. The outbreak of World War I in August 1914 imposed a sudden truce in these disputes and the Home Rule Bill was passed, though with a suspensory bill delaying its operation until the end of the war. Redmond made a dramatic speech in the House of Commons on Aug. 3 in which he declared that the Irish and English democracies had common aims and that Ireland would give full support to the Allied war effort. However, his proposal that the home defense of Ireland should be entrusted jointly to both forces of volunteers was ignored, and his efforts to recruit Irish brigades for service overseas were hampered by anti-Irish influence in the war office in London.

A split occurred among the Irish volunteers in September 1914 and the small extreme republican section actively opposed Ireland's participation in the war. The insurrection in Dublin on Easter Monday, 1916, took Redmond by surprise and shattered his whole policy. Attempts to find a settlement were made by the prime minister, H. H. Asquith, and by Lloyd George, but without success. Redmond served actively in the Irish Convention which met in Dublin to devise a new constitution in July 1917. By the beginning of 1918, however, it had almost reached deadlock. In February he went to London, where his health, which had been failing rapidly, now broke down and he resigned from the leadership of the party. After an operation he died in London on March 6, 1918, and was buried at Wexford.

BIBLIOGRAPHY.—R. B. O'Brien (ed.), *Home Rule Speeches of John Redmond* (1910); S. Gwynn, *John Redmond's Last Years* (1919); D. Gwynn, *The Life of John Redmond* (1932).   (D. G.)

REDON, ODILON (1840–1916), French painter, lithographer and etcher, who in Surrealist anthologies and exhibitions was cited along with Hieronymus Bosch, Goya, Rodolphe Bresdin, Gustave Moreau, Giorgio de Chirico, and Marc Chagall as an independent forerunner of the movement. Redon was born in Bordeaux on April 20, 1840. His aesthetic was one of the imagination rather than of visual perception. "My originality," Redon wrote, "consists in making incredible beings live according to credible laws, in placing the logic of the possible at the service of the invisible." Redon's work paralleled in imagination that of his contemporary Moreau; but the printmaker Bresdin, whom Redon met in Bordeaux, was a more immediate influence and the Symbolist poet Stéphane Mallarmé a more specific intellectual catalyst. Redon's work has itself been termed Symbolist, a connection prompted as well by his contact with the group of Symbolist painters headed by Paul Sérusier. Both painters maintained an abiding reverence for the work of Paul Gauguin.

A sharp distinction can be made, however, between Redon as a painter and Redon as a master of graphics. The oils, mostly still lifes with flowers, stress the poetics of colour. He developed a unique palette of powdery and pungent pinks, blues, yellows, or-

BY COURTESY OF THE RIJKSMUSEUM KRÖLLER MÜLLER, OTTERLO

"THE CYCLOPS" BY ODILON REDON, ABOUT 1898

chestrated to function as galaxies of vibration. The method was in fact a more dulcet form of the system of colour impact and penetration later to be known as "psychedelic." But since his colour functions with a sense of idyllic sweetness he has also been linked to the *Rose-Croix* group of Joséphin "Sâr" Péladan, with their aspirations to "musical colour" and "coloured music." Later, Pierre Bonnard, Jean Vuillard, and Henri Matisse were to acknowledge Redon's importance as a colourist. His painting embodies a crosscurrent of tendencies. It has rightly been compared to Claude Debussy's music. While Debussy and Mallarmé are also linked in Symbolist concerns, the coloration of Debussy's music—which touches Redon's own palette—was highly Impressionistic. Yet, in principle, Redon was opposed to Impressionism along with Realism as a wholly perceptual and therefore earthbound art.

In 1879 Redon turned out the first of his lithographs, collectively entitled *Dans le Rêve;* in 1882 he completed another series inspired by the works of Edgar Allan Poe, and, in 1885, he produced *Hommage à Goya.* Describing Redon's graphics as "a macabre milieu of sleepwalking presences," J. K. Huysmans, author of *À Rebours* and *Là-Bas,* summed up the lithographs as "nightmare transposed into art." It can be argued that psychologically these dark and mystical graphics have more colour (light) than even the paintings. There is an evident link to Goya in Redon's imagery of winged demons and menacing shapes. As the evocation of a dream reality the graphics also anticipate Surrealism. Redon died in Paris on July 6, 1916, before the end of World War I and just prior to the epoch of high Surrealism led by André Breton during the 1920s.

Bibliography.—André Mellério, *Odilon Redon* (1913; Eng. trans. 1968); J. Rewald, "Odilon Redon" in *Redon, Moreau, Bresdin,* catalogue, Museum of Modern Art, New York (1961); K. Berger, *Odilon Redon* (1965).   (P. W. Sc.)

REDONDA: see Antigua.

REDONDO BEACH, a resort city in Los Angeles county, Calif., U.S., is situated 19 mi. S.W. of Los Angeles on the Pacific ocean. Once seriously considered for the port of Los Angeles, Redondo Beach was developed in the 1880s with an iron pier and a narrow-gauge railroad. Though it was a commercial port for some years while San Pedro was being developed, its wide beaches and sharp palisades were tourist attractions, and promoters took advantage of its natural beauty by building fine hotels, a saltwater plunge, amusement facilities and an interurban rail line with Los Angeles. The city was incorporated in 1892 and adopted the city-manager form of municipal government in 1949. After 1945, the beach city also became a residential community for many people working in the oil refineries of Torrance, Wilmington and El Segundo. It has a public library, a symphony orchestra and a light-opera association. El Camino college (1948) and Loyola university (1911) are nearby. King harbour provides excellent boating facilities. For comparative population figures *see* table in California: *Population.*   (J. A. Sz.)

RED RIVER, a river of southeast Asia, rises in Yünnan Province, China, and flows southeastward for about 311 mi. (500 km.) across North Vietnam to the Gulf of Tongking, east of Hanoi. The Red is the principal river of North Vietnam, and the plain formed by its delta is the most extensive and one of the richest agricultural areas in the country, though frequently plagued by flooding. The reddish colour of the river is caused by the approximately 130 million metric tons of silt carried downstream each year.

RED RIVER, a river of south-central U.S., sometimes called Red River of the South to distinguish it from the Red River of the North (*q.v.*), is formed in the high plains of the Texas panhandle. It flows generally eastward into Arkansas, where it turns southeast through Louisiana to its junction with the Old River, which connects the Mississippi with the Atchafalaya River. Though the Red is considered a tributary of the Mississippi, much of its normal discharge goes directly to the Gulf by way of the Atchafalaya. The Red is 1,018 mi. long; for about half this distance it serves as the Texas–Oklahoma boundary. Among the many tributaries are the North Fork of the Red, Kiamichi, Little, and Black (Ouachita) rivers.

Early navigation of the Red above Natchitoches, La., prior to 1832 was impeded by a jam of driftwood almost 160 mi. long. Capt. Henry M. Shreve cleared this "great raft" to Oklahoma by 1837. A later raft that formed above Shreveport was cleared in 1873. After removal of these rafts navigation prospered for a time, with Alexandria and Shreveport, La., being the chief beneficiaries. Though Fulton, Ark., 455 mi. upstream, is now considered the head of navigation, vessels drawing over four feet can reach it only a few months of the year. Most of the 1,000,000-ton annual traffic is in the lower 35-mi. portion. A 9-mi. waterway project to Shreveport was inactive in the late 1960s.

In the early 1940s Denison Dam was completed on the Red 726 mi. above the mouth. This multipurpose dam forms Lake Texoma, a 223-sq.mi. lake with a storage capacity of 5,530,000 ac.ft. In the late 1960s many new reservoirs had been or were being built on tributaries of the Red in Texas, Oklahoma, Arkansas, and Louisiana as part of a comprehensive flood-control and river-development program.   (M. W. M.)

RED RIVER OF THE NORTH, a river of the northern U.S., is formed by the juncture of the Bois de Sioux River from the south and the Otter Tail River from the east at the twin cities of Wahpeton, N.D., and Breckenridge, Minn. It flows north, forming the North Dakota–Minnesota boundary, then crosses the U.S.–Canadian border and enters Lake Winnipeg 40 mi. N of Winnipeg, Man. The distance from its source to its mouth is 320 mi., but the river winds in such intricate curves over the flat plain of former glacial Lake Agassiz that the actual river mileage is 545 mi. It has cut a gorge 20 to 50 ft. deep through clay deposits throughout the greater part of its course. The principal tributaries from the west are the Assiniboine, Sheyenne, Wild Rice (of North Dakota), and Pembina rivers; from the east are the Otter Tail, Red Lake, Wild Rice (of Minnesota), and the Roseau rivers. The river drains an agricultural region famous for the production of cereal grains, potatoes, sugar beets, and livestock. Important recreation areas are found on the margins of the basin. The leading cities on the river are Winnipeg, and Fargo and Grand Forks, N.D.   (B. L. W.)

RED RIVER SETTLEMENT: see Manitoba.

RED SEA, a narrow strip of water extending south-southeast from Suez to the Strait of Bab el Mandeb in a nearly straight line, and separating the coasts of Saudi Arabia and Yemen from those of Egypt, Sudan and Ethiopia. The Red Sea was so named because of a free floating form of blue-green algae (*Trichodesmium erythraeum*) which has a red accessory pigment and occasionally gives a red colour to the surface waters. Its total length is about 1,200 mi. (1,900 km.), and its breadth varies from about 250 mi. (402 km.) in the southern half to 130 mi. (209 km.) in 27° 45′ N, where it divides into two parts, the Gulf of Suez and the Gulf of Aqaba, separated from each other by the peninsula of Sinai. Structurally, the Red Sea is part of a great rift-valley system forming one of the most marked features of the earth's crust. The rift valley of the Jordan and the Dead Sea is continued southward by the Wadi el Araba, and its submerged southern section gives the Gulf of Aqaba. This well-marked north-northeast to south-southwest line meets the north-northwest to south-southeast line, already marked in the Gulf of Suez, and together they form, to the south, the main basin of the Red Sea. The rift may be traced still farther southward among the great African lakes.

This great structural depression is probably of Tertiary age, being let down between two ancient Archean blocks—Arabia and north Africa. Secondary and Tertiary deposits appear on both flanks in Egypt and Arabia, while Archean material appears at the surface in many places on the Red Sea coast. These extensive earth movements were accompanied by much volcanic activity, traces of which are still evident. A group of volcanic islands occurs in 14° N, and on Jebel Teir, near 15°30′ N, jets of steam still appeared in the second half of the 20th century. The margin of the Red Sea itself consists, on the Arabian side, of a strip of low plain backed by ranges of barren hills of coral and sand formation, and here and there by mountains up to 6,000 ft. (1,800 m.) and more in height. The greater elevations are for the most part formed of limestones, except in the south, where they are largely volcanic. The coasts of the Gulf of Aqaba are steep, with numer-

RED SEA

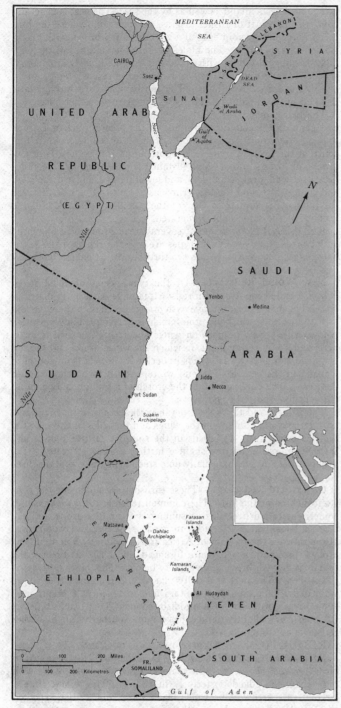

THE RED SEA

34°43′ E. Its deeper waters are separated from the deep water of the Red Sea by an entrance sill much of which is considerably less than 600 ft. below the surface. Along the mid-line of the Red Sea an irregular trough about 30 mi. broad between the 3,000-ft. depth contours extends from 27°30′ N to 17° N where it is interrupted by a transverse submarine ridge rising to within 1,200 ft. of the surface. Between 25° N and 17° N mid-channel depths occasionally exceed 7,200 ft., with a maximum of over 9,000 ft. reported near 20° N, whereas to the south the maximum depth is about 4,020 ft. and the channel shoals to about 300 ft. off Hanish Island in crossing the entrance sill which separates the deeper basin of the Red Sea from that of the Gulf of Aden. From the north end of the Red Sea to the banks of Suakin and Farasan in 20° N the 600-ft. line keeps to a belt of coral reef close inshore, but in lower latitudes the shallow coral region, 300 mi. long and 70 to 80 mi. across, extends farther and farther seaward until at 15° N, off Hodeida (Al Hudaydah), the part of the channel that is deeper than 600 ft. is only 20 mi. broad, all the rest of the area being dangerous to navigation even for small vessels. The Strait of Bab el Mandeb, the southern entrance to the Red Sea, is divided by Perim Island into two channels. The eastern channel is 1.7 mi. broad between the 30 ft. curves and has a maximum depth of 96 ft. The western channel preferred for navigation, is 1,020 ft. in mid-channel and is 10.4 mi. wide between Perim Island and the islands near the African coast.

Meteorology.—In the northern part, down to almost 19° N, the prevailing winds are north and northwest. The middle region, to 14°–16° N, has variable winds in an area of low barometric pressure, while in the southern Red Sea southeast and east winds prevail. From June to August the northwest wind blows over the entire area; in September it retreats again as far as 16° N, south of which the winds are for a time variable. In the Gulf of Suez the prevailing wind is northerly or northwesterly, but the westerly or "Egyptian" wind occurs occasionally during winter, sometimes blowing with violence, and generally accompanied by fog and clouds of dust. Strong north-northeast winds prevail in the Gulf of Aqaba during the greater part of the year; they are weakest in April and May, sometimes giving place at that season to southerly breezes. The mean monthly air temperature ranges from 71° F (22° C) at Suez to 86° (30°) at Massawa. Rainfall is light, generally less than an inch a year along the northern shores, and nowhere exceeding about ten inches. At some points a year may pass without a trace of rain. The high temperature and great relative humidity in summer make it a difficult region for active life.

Water Temperature.—The mean annual surface temperature of the waters varies from about 75° F (24° C) near the head to 80° F (27° C) in about 22° N, to 84° (29° C) in 16° N, and drops again to 82° (28° C) at the Strait of Bab el Mandeb. Temperatures in February are about 5° below and in August 5° above the annual mean. Temperature is, on the whole, higher near the Arabian than the Egyptian side. During summer the temperature decreases rapidly, dropping as much as 10° in the upper 150 ft. and then decreasing more slowly to about 70.7°, in water at depths of 600 to 1,200 ft.; this latter temperature is constant throughout the sea and the year. In winter as a consequence of increased density caused by rapid evaporation and cooling, sinking of surface water apparently occurs north of about 22° N, and the temperature changes but slightly with depth. In the southern part of the area, however, the temperature still decreases with increasing depth, but because of surface cooling the drop is less pronounced than in summer. In the Gulf of Suez temperatures are relatively low, ranging from about 64° in February to 79° in August, and decreasing quite rapidly from south to north. The waters in the Gulf of Aqaba are reportedly warmer toward the Arabian than the Sinai coast, but here as well as in the Red Sea proper temperatures will vary locally in response to wind and circulation patterns; a uniform temperature of 70.2° is observed in the deeper water.

Salinity.—The salinity of the waters is very high compared to that found in the open ocean, the surface values being highest, 41$^0/_{00}$ (per mille), in the Gulf of Suez, and decreasing to about 36.5$^0/_{00}$ near Perim Island at the southern entrance. Below a

ous coral reefs on both sides. On the African side there are, in the north, wide stretches of desert plain, which toward the south rise to elevated tablelands, and ultimately to the mountains of Ethiopia. The shores of the Red Sea are little indented; good harbours are almost wanting in the desert regions of the north, while in the south the chief inlets are near 15° N at Massawa, and at Kamaran, almost directly opposite. Coral formations are abundant; immense reefs, both barrier and fringing, skirt both coasts, often enclosing wide channels between the reef and the land.

Depths.—The mean depth of the Red Sea is approximately 1,611 ft. (491 m.) and its area and volume are approximately 169,-100 square miles (437,969 sq.km.) and 52,000 cubic miles respectively. The Gulf of Suez is shallow, with a maximum depth of about 210 ft., and outside its mouth the bottom in the Red Sea slopes rather steeply to a depth of about 4,140 ft. at 27°30′ N. The Gulf of Aqaba attains a depth of 4,200 ft. in 28°39′ N and

depth of 600 ft. the salinity ranges between $41^0/_{00}$ in the north and $40.5^0/_{00}$ in the south. South of about 20° N the salinity increases with depth, the increase being particularly rapid between 300 and 600 ft., whereas in the north, there is little change from top to bottom. In general the surface salinity is somewhat greater on the western than the eastern side. In the Gulf of Aqaba the salinity is quite uniform averaging about $40^0/_{00}$. Salinities of $50^0/_{00}$ to $55^0/_{00}$ are encountered in the Bitter Lakes section of the Suez Canal, but the prevailing current carries most of this water toward the Mediterranean.

Circulation.—The movements of the waters are of great irregularity and complexity, rendering navigation difficult and dangerous. Two features stand out with special distinctness; the exchange of water between the Red Sea and the Indian Ocean, and the tidal streams of the Gulf of Suez. During the north-northwest winds of summer surface water and a layer of highly saline bottom water flows from the Red Sea to the Gulf of Aden, and between these layers a contrary current of Indian Ocean water sets into the Red Sea. In winter surface waters enter the Red Sea from the Gulf of Aden but Red Sea water continues to discharge at depth. The water carried by the bottom current was formed and sank in the northern part of the Red Sea in winter and has a high salinity and temperature and a low concentration of dissolved oxygen. Through these characteristics it has been traced at intermediate depths in the Indian Ocean south past the equator. In the Gulfs of Suez and Aqaba, almost the only part of the Red Sea in which tidal phenomena are well developed, a sharply defined tidal circulation is found. Elsewhere, the surface movements at least are controlled by the prevailing winds, which give rise in places to complex transverse currents, and near the coast are modified by the channels enclosed by the coral reefs. During the prevalence of the north and northwest winds the surface level of the northern part is depressed by as much as two feet.

The Red Sea was important in Egyptian maritime commerce at least as early as the 2nd millennium B.C. and it had associations with India early in the 1st millennium B.C. Under the Arabs the Red Sea was an important highway of trade with connections to India, Persia and East Africa. This sea helped to keep Islam in touch with the thinkers of the East and with the glories of the ancient world during the dark ages in the West; with the revolutions in shipping and movement by sea that followed the age of discovery the Red Sea seemed to retreat into the background; but with the cutting of the Suez Canal (1869) and the shortening of the route to India, Australia and the East, the Red Sea not only recovered its former importance but became one of the greatest commercial highways in the world.

BIBLIOGRAPHY.—E. F. Thompson, "Chemical and Physical Investigations—the General Hydrography of the Red Sea. The Exchange of Water Between the Red Sea and Gulf of Aden Over the 'Sill,' " John Murray Expedition 1933–34, *Sci. Rep.*, vol. 2, no. 3, 4, pp. 83–119 (1939); *Sailing Directions Red Sea and Gulf of Aden*, U.S. Navy Hydrographic Office Publication no. 157 (1952); International Hydrographic Bureau *Special Publication No. 30* and *Series of General Bathymetric Charts of the Oceans*, plate 4 (1938).   (C. A. Bs.)

REDSHANK, the name of a snipelike bird, *Totanus totanus*, so-called from the colour of its long legs. In suitable localities it is abundant throughout the greater part of Europe and Asia, retiring southward for the winter, though a considerable number remain along the coasts of some of the more northern countries. The body of the redshank is as big as a snipe's, 11 in., but its longer neck, wings, and legs make it appear larger. Above, the general colour is grayish, freckled with black, except the lower part

ERIC HOSKING
REDSHANK (TOTANUS TOTANUS) ON NEST

of the back and a conspicuous band on each wing, which are white, and the flight-quills, which are black. The long, straight bill is reddish with a black tip.

The bird nests inland as well as by the sea. The nest is generally concealed in a tuft of rushes or grass in the swamp where the bird feeds, and contains four eggs of a warmly tinted brown with blackish spots or blotches. The males in spring have a beautiful songflight, rising and falling with quivering wings, and a striking courtship on the ground. They are very pugnacious, fights often continuing for over an hour. The redshank is very wary, and is disliked by shore gunners for giving the alarm to other species.

The black, dusky, or spotted redshank (*Tringa erythropus*) is a larger and less common bird, and in the greater part of Europe it occurs only on its passage to or from its breeding-grounds just south of the Arctic Circle. The spot chosen for the nest is nearly always in forests and at some distance from water. In breeding-dress the head, neck, shoulders, and lower parts are black, the back and rump white, and the legs crimson. At other times of the year the plumage is similar to that of the common redshank and the legs are of the same light orange-red.

REDSTART, the name of several small (four to five inches) active birds: the New World types are wood warblers of the genus *Setophaga*; Old World species are thrushes of the genus *Phoenicurus*.

New World Redstarts.—Of the two species of redstart, *S. ruticilla*, called the American redstart, is more easterly in distribution. The male is black above with orange patches on the wing and tail, and white on the belly; the female is gray-olive above, whitish below, with yellow patches on wings and tail. The bird is characterized by fluttering flight, in which the wings droop and the tail is spread frequently. It breeds in deciduous woods from southern Canada to the central U.S. and winters south to northern South America. The cuplike nest, in the crotch of a sapling, may contain three to five spotted eggs.

The painted redstart (*S. picta*) in both sexes is primarily black, with large white patches on the wings and the sides of the tail; the belly is bright red. It breeds in the southwestern highlands and into Nicaragua, wintering slightly farther south. It nests on the ground; the grassy cup, usually on a steep bank, may contain three to four speckled eggs.

Old World Redstarts.—These thrushes are noted for the constant flicking of the tail. The common redstart (*P. phoenicurus*), sometimes called firetail, is a summer visitor to Europe and the British Isles, where it resides in gardens, parks, and woodlands. It migrates to the interior of Africa for the winter. The male has a black face and throat, white forehead, and chestnut breast; the female is grayish-brown above, buffy below. The tail in both sexes is rust-red. The nest is usually placed in a hole of a tree, stone wall, or building, and may contain five to seven pale green eggs, sometimes sprinkled with reddish spots. The black redstart (*P. ochruros*), slightly darker, has a more southerly range. Other redstarts are found in Asia.

REDUCTION: *see* OXIDATION AND REDUCTION.

RED-WINGED BLACKBIRD, a common North American bird, *Agelaius phoeniceus*, the male of which is glossy black with red "epaulets" edged posteriorly in yellow. The female, like a large, dark sparrow, is brownish black above and whitish streaked with black and brown below; the wing coverts are faintly reddish. Both sexes are about eight inches long. This species, the most widely distributed member of the family Icteridae, comprises 14 subspecies breeding from Mexico to central Canada and Alaska; some subspecies are resident; others tend to move into the southern part of their range for the winter. These noisy, gregarious birds, with liquid song and shrill alarm call, often fly in flocks and nest chiefly in groups in swamp or bushland. Their diet during the breeding season consists mainly of insects; later in the year grain and other seeds are also eaten. The well-built cuplike nests, suspended on reeds or other vegetation, may contain three to five pale bluish eggs marked with dark spots or scribbles.

Related are the tricoloured blackbird (*A. tricolor*) of the West Coast, with conspicuous white margin to the epaulet; the tawny-shouldered blackbird (*A. humeralis*) of Cuba and Haiti; and the yellow-shouldered blackbird (*A. xanthomus*) of Puerto Rico.

REDWOOD: *see* SEQUOIA.

REDWOOD CITY, a city and the seat of San Mateo County,

Calif., U.S., is located about 27 mi. SE of San Francisco on the San Francisco Peninsula. Situated near the mouth of Redwood Creek, it has the southernmost deepwater port on San Francisco Bay, used since Spanish-California days when the town was on El Camino Real (historic mission trail, now a federal highway) and known as Embarcadero. Once the site of an early shipbuilding industry that served a flourishing lumber and shingle trade, the port is used mainly for the shipment of oil, cement, and salt. It was first plotted in 1854 on sections of the old Rancho de las Pulgas, largest Spanish land grant in the area, dating back to 1795. Originally named Mezesville after S. M. Mezes, its Mexican founder, the town became known by its present name because of its redwood lumber business long before it was incorporated in 1867. It has been council-manager governed since 1929.

Redwood City is a residential and industrial community. The port has always attracted some industry and the number of industrial establishments grew steadily after World War II. Some of the largest electronics firms, which have made the San Francisco Peninsula a centre of this industry, are located there. Redwood City's population increased by 81.1% from 1940 to 1960. For comparative population figures *see* table in CALIFORNIA: *Population*.   (S. B. KN.)

REED, THOMAS BRACKETT (1839–1902), speaker of the U.S. House of Representatives in the 1890s who introduced a number of important changes in the procedure of that body, was born in Portland, Me., on Oct. 18, 1839, and graduated from Bowdoin College in 1860. Admitted to the bar in 1865, he began to practise law in Portland, and was elected to the State House of Representatives in 1868 and to the Senate in 1870. In 1877 he was elected to the U.S. House of Representatives on the Republican ticket and served continuously until 1899.

Reed's knowledge of parliamentary law and his executive ability made him the leader of his party in the House, 1886–89 and speaker, 1889–91 and 1895–99. He was a "strong" speaker in his control over proceedings; developing a committee system, he made the majority of the Rules Committee consist of the speaker and the chairmen of the Ways and Means and Appropriations committees. The Reed rules, drawn by him, William McKinley, and Joseph G. Cannon (*qq.v.*), were adopted Feb. 14, 1890; they provided that every member must vote unless financially interested in a measure, that members present and not voting be counted for a quorum, and that no dilatory motions be entertained by the speaker. His dictatorial methods were bitterly attacked by the opposition, who called him "Czar" Reed. Nevertheless his rules and methods were adopted by the Democratic leadership in 1891–95 and the powers of the Rules Committee were increased. Reed's name is not associated with any particular legislation, but he exercised a powerful influence in guiding bills through Congress. He vigorously opposed free silver and advocated protective tariffs. He opposed the policies of the McKinley administration with regard to Cuba and Hawaii at the end of the Spanish-American War and as a result resigned in 1899 and began the practice of law in New York City. He died in Washington, D.C., on Dec. 7, 1902. Reed was a powerful orator with a ready wit. While opinion varied as to his conduct as speaker, he was respected and admired by Republicans and Democrats as a man of rugged honesty and intense loyalty.

See William Robinson, *Thomas B. Reed, Parliamentarian* (1930).
                                              (H. F. TT.)

REED, WALTER (1851–1902), U.S. Army bacteriologist renowned for his work on yellow fever, was born in Gloucester County, Va., on Sept. 13, 1851, and was educated at the University of Virginia and Bellevue Medical School (M.D., 1870). In 1875 he entered the Medical Corps of the U.S. Army as assistant surgeon, with rank of lieutenant. In 1893 he was promoted to surgeon, with rank of major, and was made professor of bacteriology and clinical microscopy in the newly organized Army Medical School at Washington, D.C. When the Spanish-American War began, Reed was appointed chairman of a committee to investigate the causation and mode of propagation of typhoid fever, an epidemic of which had broken out among the soldiers. The committee's *Report on the Origin and Spread of Typhoid Fever in*

U.S. Military Camps (published in 1904, after Reed's death) revealed a number of points concerning the disease not before known, and emphasized others that had been little appreciated.

In 1897 Reed and an associate proved erroneous the theory of Giuseppe Sanarelli and others that a bacillus was the specific cause of yellow fever. In 1900, when the disease broke out among U.S. troops in Cuba, Reed was made chairman of a commission to investigate its cause and method of transmission. The other members were James Carroll, Jesse W. Lazear (*q.v.*), and Aristides Agramonte. Reed's observation of many cases led him to discount the then prevalent idea that the disease was transmitted by contact with bedding, clothing, etc., of patients suffering from yellow fever, and to revive the discarded notion of Carlos Juan Finlay (*q.v.*) that the yellow fever parasite was carried only by mosquitoes. Since the disease was not acquired by animals there was no method of proof except by experiment upon human beings. By a thorough set of experiments, in which some of his co-workers sacrificed their lives, Reed proved to a skeptical world that the yellow fever parasite was carried only by the mosquito then called *Stegomyia fasciata* (later classified as *Aëdes aegypti*) and that the bite of this mosquito caused the disease only under certain conditions. Possessed of this knowledge, U.S. sanitary engineers led by Maj. William C. Gorgas (*q.v.*) eradicated yellow fever from Cuba (there was not one case in 1902), and it has since been largely eliminated from those parts of the world where scientific public health procedures are carried on. Reed returned in 1901 to Washington, where he died of appendicitis on Nov. 23, 1902. The army general hospital in Washington was named in his honour.

See H. A. Kelly, *Walter Reed and Yellow Fever* (1923).

REED, a term applied to several distinct species of large, water-loving grasses. The common or water reed, *Phragmites communis*, occurs along the margins of lakes, fens, marshes, and placid streams, not only throughout Great Britain and the United States, but widely distributed in arctic and also in temperate regions, extending into the tropics. Another very important species is *Ammophila arenaria* (also known as *Psamma arenaria*), the sea reed or marram grass, a native of the sandy shores of Europe and North Africa. Both species have been of notable geological importance, the former binding the soil and so impeding denudation, and actually converting swamp into dry land, largely by the aid of its tall (5 to 10 ft.) close-set stems. The latter species, of which the branching rootstocks may be traced 30 or even 40 ft., is of still greater importance in holding sand dunes against the sea, and for this purpose has not only been long protected by law, but has been extensively planted on the coasts of Norfolk, Eng., the Netherlands, Gascony, etc. Other reeds are *Calamagrostis* (various species), *Gynerium argenteum* (pampas grass), etc., also *Arundo donax*, the largest European grass (6 to 12 ft. high), which is abundant in Europe. Reeds have been used from the earliest times in thatching and in other branches of construction, and also for arrows, the pipes of musical instruments, etc. Reed pens are still used in the East. Plants belonging to other orders occasionally share the name, especially the bur reed (*Sparganium*) and the reed mace (*Typha*), both belonging to the family Typhaceae. The bulrushes (*Scirpus*), belonging to the family Cyperaceae, are also to be distinguished.

See also GRASSES.

REED INSTRUMENTS: *see* WIND INSTRUMENTS.

REEL, a type of dance which appears to have originated in Scotland. Early references show that reels were known throughout Scotland in the 16th century, though little is known of their precise form.

During the 17th century the Presbyterian Church in Scotland severely discouraged social dancing, and by 1700 the reel seems to have survived only in the Scottish Highlands, where Presbyterian influence was weakest. After 1700, when the church became more tolerant of dancing, reels reappeared in the Scottish Lowlands, presumably having been reintroduced from the Highlands. From about 1700 to 1770 the only specific reel mentioned in Scottish literature is the Threesome reel, but after about 1770 this was largely superseded by the Foursome reel. In both, and in most other Scottish reels, the dancers repeatedly perform a simple traveling figure alternated with elaborate steps danced in one place.

Reels of this same form also occur in England and Wales, while a different kind is known in Ireland. There is, however, no evidence to show that these English, Welsh, and Irish reels developed earlier than the late 18th century. The Eightsome reel, included at dances throughout the United Kingdom, does not conform to the usual structure. Composed about 1870, it incorporates the figures of a reel dating from about 1818.

Reel is also the name of a type of dance tune. The earlier reel tunes were simply tunes appropriate to the dances, but after about 1700 reel was used primarily for a fast dance tune in 4/4 time. These common-time reels have almost invariably an insistent semiquaver motion, particularly noticeable at the end of the phrases. *See* also STRATHSPEY; VIRGINIA REEL.   (T. M. FL.)

REESE, LIZETTE WOODWORTH (1856–1935), U.S. poet whose poetry is largely based on the rural simplicities of her childhood, was born in Baltimore County, Md., Jan. 9, 1856, and died in Baltimore, Dec. 17, 1935. She spent her childhood on the York Road, near what became the Village of Waverly, in what was then the outskirts of Baltimore. Educated privately, she began to teach in St. John's parish school in Waverly in 1873, and continued teaching in the public schools of Baltimore until her retirement in 1921.

Her lyric talent was strikingly evident even in her first book, *A Branch of May* (1887), and her reputation grew slowly. Her condensed form and sincerity of emotion broke with 19th-century conventional sentimentality and foreshadowed the tone and temper of 20th-century lyricism. The sonnet "Tears," published in 1891 in her fourth collection, *A Wayside Lute,* became deservedly well known. *Selected Poems* (1926) was followed by several other volumes of verse: *Little Henrietta* (1927), *White April* (1930), and *Pastures* (1933); and two books of reminiscences: *A Victorian Village* (1929) and *The York Road* (1931).   (LE. BN.)

REEVE, HENRY (1813–1895), English writer, an influential though inconspicuous figure in early Victorian politics, was born at Norwich, Eng., on Sept. 9, 1813, and educated at Geneva, Munich, and Paris. In 1835 he translated Alexis de Tocqueville's *Démocratie en Amérique.*

In 1837 he was nominated head of the legal department of the privy council office, a post he held for 50 years. From 1840 to 1855 he wrote leading articles for the *Times,* and practically guided its foreign policy; friendships with Lords Clarendon and Granville, and with Guizot and Thiers (*qq.v.*), and his trenchant style gave his articles weight. From 1855 he edited the *Edinburgh Review,* contributing most of the articles on foreign affairs himself. His edition of the *Memoirs* of C. C. F. Greville (*q.v.*), in three series (1874, 1885, and 1887), though carefully expurgated, gave much offense. Reeve died near Bournemouth on Oct. 21, 1895.

See J. K. Laughton, *Memoirs of . . . Henry Reeve,* 2 vol. (1898).
    (M. R. D. F.)

REEVE, a representative of higher governmental authority; in early English history the reeve's function was the effectuation of the king's fiscal rights and the maintenance of the peace, including some minor judicial duties. The title still is used in some places to designate minor government officials of various kinds.

REFERENDUM AND INITIATIVE, two methods by which the wishes of the electorate may be expressed with regard to proposed legislation. They exist in a variety of forms. The referendum may be obligatory or optional. Under the former type certain classes of actions by a legislature are required, ordinarily by constitutional provision, to be referred to a popular vote for approval or rejection. Amendments to constitutions proposed by legislatures are subject in most states of the United States, for example, to an obligatory referendum. Under the optional (or facultative) referendum a specified number of voters by petition may demand a popular vote on a law passed by a legislature. By this means actions of a legislature may be overruled.

The referendum may also be constitutional or legislative depending on the nature of the matter referred. In the United States questions subject to the obligatory referendum are mostly constitutional while those subject to the optional referendum are invariably legislative. The obligatory and optional forms are to be distinguished from the submission by legislative bodies of questions to a referendum or plebiscite, the effect of which may be determinative of the issue or only advisory to the legislature.

By the initiative a specified number of voters may invoke a popular vote on a proposed state or local law or a proposal to amend the state constitution. In its direct form a proposal supported by the requisite number of voters is submitted directly to a popular vote for decision. Under the indirect form the legislature has an opportunity to enact such a proposal. If rejected, the proposition is submitted to a popular vote, in some instances with an alternative proposal by the legislature or with a statement of its reasons for rejection.

The initiative and referendum came into common use in Switzerland in the liberal reaction after the Paris revolution of 1830. In 1831 St. Gall first adopted the facultative referendum (then and for some time after called the veto), and its example was followed by several cantons before 1848. The obligatory referendum appeared first in 1852 and 1854, but in its modern form it was first adopted in 1863 by the canton of rural Basel. The initiative was first adopted in 1845 by Vaud. Both institutions have been used freely in federal and cantonal matters.

Swiss experience with the devices of direct legislation was influential in the adoption of the initiative and the optional referendum in U.S. states and municipalities.

The United States.—The obligatory referendum on amendments to state constitutions proposed by state legislatures, first adopted by Connecticut in 1818, was in the second half of the 20th century the prevailing method for the amendment of state constitutions. In some states a referendum is obligatory on bond issues and a like rule is widespread in local government for bond issues, tax questions and related matters. Because of the detailed nature of state constitutions and the necessity for their frequent amendment, many issues not of a nature to arouse great interest among the voters are referred to them for amendment.

In U.S. usage, the terms initiative and referendum or direct legislation refer not to the obligatory referendum but to the optional referendum on legislation and to the initiation of laws or constitutional amendments by the voters (with the assumption that a popular vote or referendum on the initiated measure will follow). These devices were adopted in the U.S. under the leadership of groups hostile to machine rule, distrustful of legislatures and with a deep faith in democracy. The belief was that by granting the people a means to overrule legislative action and to initiate popular votes on legislation, abuses at the time characteristic of state legislatures might be prevented. Conservative groups were hostile to the adoption of the institution of direct legislation. The chief resort to direct legislation was in the western states, principally in California and Oregon. It did not, however, fulfill the hopes of its advocates or the fears of its opponents. In practice the referendum is used by groups that consider themselves aggrieved by an action of the legislature and feel that they might persuade a majority of the electorate to support them in their demand that the law not go into effect. The initiative tends to be used by groups which have been unable to induce the legislature to enact a desired law. The initiative and referendum proved much less important than the obligatory referendum in bringing issues to the voters. In the legislative process as a whole the initiative and referendum are comparatively unimportant insofar as the volume of legislation directly affected is concerned. The devices may be regarded, in the words of Woodrow Wilson, as a "gun behind the door" to be used when abuses arise in the legislative body. (*See* also RECALL.)

European Countries.—Formal adherence to democratic doctrines in drafting new constitutions in various European countries after World War I led to frequent provision for use of the initiative and referendum. Thus Germany's Weimar constitution of 1919 made generous provision for referenda in certain contingencies, although in fact they were little employed. The same was true of Austria. Less enthusiasm for direct democracy was felt by constitution makers after World War II, but some use of the referendum was provided for. In France the constitution originally proposed for the French republic was rejected by referendum in 1946 and its successor accepted five months later. The constitution later adopted required that any amendment must be submitted to the people unless it has obtained a two-thirds majority of the lower house of the French *parlement* or a three-fifths majority of both houses. In Italy the post-World War II constitution provided that 50,000 electors may present a proposal to the legislature, and, if 500,000 voters or five regional councils request it, a referendum must be held on the question of abrogating a law. Provision was also made for using the referendum as part of the amending process. (V. O. K.; H. G. N.; X.)

REFLECTION. When waves of any kind traveling in one medium arrive at another in which their velocity is different, part of their energy is, in general, turned back into the first medium. This is termed reflection. If the surface of separation is smooth, *i.e.,* if the irregularities in it are small compared with the wave length of the incident disturbance, the reflection is regular; if the surface is rough each facet reflects the rays incident upon it in accordance with the laws of regular reflection (*see* Optics) and the reflection, as a whole, is irregular or diffuse. Consider, for example, the reflection of light at smooth and ruffled water surfaces. From the ruffled surface rays enter the eye after reflection from suitably inclined facets distributed over a wide area on the surface and a diffuse band of light is seen, while from the smooth surface only those rays reflected at the requisite angle from a small area on the surface can reach the eye. In the first case the optical system of the eye focuses the water surface on the retina just as it does all other rough surfaces. In the latter the rays appear to come from a laterally inverted replica of the luminous source situated as far below the surface as the source itself is above, and it is this image which is then focused on the retina. The diffusion of light by matt surfaces in general is an example of the same phenomenon differing only in the number and size of the facets which scatter the light. Echoes and reverberations are caused by the reflection of sound (*see* Sound: *Reflection and Refraction of Sound*) and the fading of wireless signals (in part) by variations in the conditions under which the electromagnetic waves are reflected by the Heaviside layer in the upper atmosphere. *See* Radio: *Factors Affecting Radio Performance;* Mirror; *see* also references under "Reflection" in the Index.

REFLEX. Reflex actions consist of comparatively simple segments of behaviour in which the reactions usually occur as direct and immediate responses to particular stimuli uniquely correlated with them. Reflex actions have a widespread occurrence among complex animals. Examples of reflex activities and their neurological mechanisms are given in such articles as Animal Behaviour: *Animal Behaviour Patterns;* Psychogalvanic Reflex; Spinal Cord; Vision: *Accommodation.*

Conditioned reflexes are built-up adjustments to particular internal or external stimuli. Such conditioning processes were popularized by I. P. Pavlov (*q.v.*) and his co-workers. Pavlov, while investigating digestion, incidentally discovered that salivation occurred in dogs not only when food or acid was placed in the mouth, but also when a bell previously paired with food was sounded. What makes this a typical conditioned interaction is the observable building up of coordinate stimulus and response functions in a unique system (*see* Conditioning).

Unconditioned reflexes are exemplified by the reflex tests of the physician. When the neurologist elicits the knee jerk with his hammer stroke or the pupil-closing reflex by directing light to the eye, he is attempting to ascertain whether the organism's biological mechanisms are working properly. For this reason the stimuli may be regarded as simple energy releasers.

Development of Reflex Theory.—The notion of reflex action originally developed in a philosophical rather than scientific atmosphere. For example, René Descartes, who first elaborated the notion of reflex action, did so to distinguish between the automatic action of soulless animals and the voluntary and rational behaviour of human beings. As anatomy and physiology developed in the early 19th century, interest became centred on anatomical and physiological processes of behaviour mechanisms. Although notions of psychic or mental processes were not given up, both biologists and psychologists sought for precise biological locations of

"centres" for the production and control of actions. Actions involving mentality or consciousness were regarded as requiring brain centres, while reflex or mechanical actions were presumed to operate on the basis of isolated neural arcs located on various spinal cord levels.

Toward the end of the 19th century and the beginning of the 20th, however, the idea that animals act in parts gave way somewhat to the organismic notion that they act as units and that, therefore, the brain plays a significant part in all actions, including reflexes. In 1906 C. S. Sherrington published researches demonstrating that reflexes are very different from the traditional isolated arcs they were thought to be. Sherrington declared that the familiar diagrams of localized biological reflexes were fictitious and insisted that they must be regarded as integrated actions of the total organism, even though they are simpler than actions classified as voluntary or rational. He also suggested that the stimuli for reflex actions were not simple energy releasers but definite environmental conditions to which the organism adjusted.

With the spread of evolutionary doctrine in the 20th century, reflex theory developed rapidly. The oversimplified notions of isolated neural mechanisms, and even the organismic concept, gave way in great part to the facts of embryological development and ecological adjustment. Important here was the work of C. J. Herrick, C. M. Child, and G. E. Coghill, who showed that even simple reflexes are specialized environmental adaptations developed from original mass behaviours. The capstone of biological progress was the enlargement of the notion of reflexes to include ecologically based behaviour conditioned not only to one substitute object but to several.

Current reflex theory, then, envisages all animal behaviour, and not only reflexes, as continuous ecological evolutions. This does not in any way minimize the importance of the separate cells, tissues, and organs with their normal or pathological participation in adjustments or maladjustments to environmental circumstances. The great importance of this achievement is that both biologists and psychologists are now able to describe all varieties of behaviour, from the simplest to the most complex, without invoking any vitalistic or psychic principles.

Reflexes and Psychological Theory.—Because of the close interrelationship of psychology and biology, the development of reflex theory exerted a great influence on psychological thinking. Especially those psychologists striving for a naturalistic evolution of their science followed the development of reflex notions and were so deeply impressed with the conditioned reflex as model that reflexology became assimilated to psychology. Early behaviourists, such as Pavlov, Karl Lashley, and others, hoped to trace conditioned reflex arcs through the cortex. Evidence for brain-mediated reflexes is presented in Brain: *Physiology of the Brain.*

Later behaviourists (E. R. Guthrie, Clark Hull, E. C. Tolman, B. F. Skinner) stressed the stimulus objects and stimulating circumstances. Conditioning became synonymous with learning. In various theories they proposed principles (contiguity of response and stimulus, the manner of stimulus reinforcement, and the effect of stimulation in reducing organic needs) to explain psychological actions (*see* Learning; Behaviourism). *See* also references under "Reflex" in the Index.

Bibliography.—G. E. Coghill, *Anatomy and the Problem of Behaviour* (1929); F. Fearing, *Reflex Action* (1930, reprinted 1964); J. R. Kantor, *A Survey of the Science of Psychology* (1933); W. K. Estes, *Modern Learning Theory* (1954); E. R. Hilgard, *Theories of Learning,* 2nd ed. (1956); M. R. Fiorentino, *Reflex Testing Methods for Evaluating C.N.S. Development* (1963). (J. R. Ka.)

REFORMATION, the religious revolution which took place in the Western Church in the 16th century. It broke up medieval Christendom, giving rise to new Protestant churches and to a reformed Catholicism. The object of the Reformers was to secure amendment of errors and abuses in the medieval church, which they claimed to submit to the judgment of Holy Scripture and to the usages of the early church. Beginning as a religious movement, the revolution speedily became involved in political, social and economic pressures. As in all revolutions, there were important elements of continuity, but there was enough abrupt change, discontinuity and explosion to make the Reformation a turning point in Christian and European history.

The article which follows is divided into the following sections:

I. THE MEDIEVAL WESTERN CHURCH

Behind the façade of one western Christendom, with the pope as the spiritual head and the Holy Roman emperor as the secular arm, there had long been tension and indeed division. Heresies lingered as underground movements, while in Bohemia there had been schism and secession on a national scale (see Hussites). The unity of the empire was sapped by growing national self-consciousness and interests; in Germany political and constitutional divisions impaired the political and military effectiveness of the emperor. Despite attempted constitutional amendments under the emperor Maximilian, the very success of his policy of extending power through dynastic marriages made the government of the empire in the 16th century an almost insupportable task for his successors and prevented any consistent and coherent policies at a time when swift action was demanded. The intricate and conflicting diplomatic interests of pope, emperor and the king of France led to division and to constant war, while the decline of the crusading ideal marked the weakened opposition to the Turk hammering at the gate.

1. The Papacy.—"The Curia at the Renaissance showed a degree of secularization which the early Church would surely have denounced as anti-Christian" (J. Lortz, *Die Reformation in Deutschland*, 1939). In the 11th century St. Peter Damian had protested to Gregory VII against the tendency to pursue spiritual ends by doubtful political means. In succeeding centuries saints such as Bernard of Clairvaux, Hildegard of Bingen and Teresa of Avila, added sharp voices in similar protest. Complaints against this perversion of the gospel in terms of power politics were by no means confined to the soured polemic of the Spiritual Franciscans. The long struggle between pope and emperor, however valiantly the spiritual power championed the "crown rights of Jesus Christ in his church," deepened the political preoccupation, aggravated by the Avignon crisis and the scandal of the Great Schism (1378–1417). Thus the papacy by the end of the 15th century was committed to a network of vested interests, involving diplomatic and military adventures, as well as a whole jungle of administration and law in which was embedded an ugly element of chicanery and graft. Leo X might be a cultured patron of the arts, Julius II a more imposing politician than the bellicose ruffian depicted by Erasmus, Adrian VI a holy man, but at no point in the early 16th century had a spiritual leader arisen who could inaugurate a moral and religious renewal of the whole church.

Johann Tezel mit seinen Ablaß-Kram.

BULLA INDULGENT

O Ihr Teutschen, merkt mich recht,
Des heiligen Vater Pabsts Knecht
Bin ich, und bring euch ich, allen
Zehntausend und Neunhundert Karnen
Gnad und Ablaß eurer Sünd,

Vor euch, eure Aeltern, Weib und Kind,
Soll ein jeder, gewähret seyn,
So viel er lent ins Kästel ein,
So bald der Gülten im Becken klingt,
Im Huy d.e S.el in Himmel sich schwingt.

SATIRICAL BROADSHEET SHOWING JOHANN TETZEL AND THE INDULGENCES BROUGHT FROM THE POPE (LEO X, INSET) FOR SALE IN GERMANY

It was a legacy of the conciliar movement that the pope, who had barely escaped being dominated by the church machine, was fearful of a reforming council to which he must surrender initiative or lose control to the emperor, the curia or the episcopate (see Council). The curia itself had long been the arena of competing Italian noble families, among whom nepotism was a recognized weapon of power. The great international civil service, that fine achievement of the Avignon popes especially, had run to seed, becoming, like Charles Dickens' "Circumlocution Office" (in *Little Dorrit*), the prey of overorganization, inefficiency and venality in an age which knew too much, in any case, of "the law's delays, the insolence of office." Finance and law had come to play too big a role at the heart of the Christian world. Vast sums of money, huge debts in a great business extending from one end of Christendom to another had to be handled by bankers such as the Fuggers of Augsburg, and these financial preoccupations affected moral and spiritual issues such as those involved in the sale of indulgences. The church had come to possess immense wealth and in some countries owned an alarming proportion of the land. Much of this wealth was necessarily drained off by the papacy and the higher clergy.

The pastoral machinery of the church was concurrently distracted from the cure of souls as the higher clergy provided the administrators, councilors and officials not only of the church but of the secular kingdoms, despite the fact that a growing lay administrative class was an important fact in the pre-Reformation scene. Pluralism and nonresidence aggravated the shortcomings of the pastoral machine, while a too numerous class of poor and unlettered clergy coped badly with the duties often neglected by their superiors. The long, notorious abuse of excommunication for unworthy or trivial ends, and the grasping litigiousness of the spiritual courts, had brought ecclesiastical discipline into ill repute.

The religious orders were often relaxed and worldly, housing many who lacked any true vocation for the evangelical perfection they no longer strenuously sought. If there was not as much gross immorality as the moralists suggest, there was more than enough. At the end of the middle ages, the venality of the mendicant orders had become a byword. The result was that this over-clericalized Christian world gave rise to widespread anticlericalism in the later middle ages, among scholars and merchants and the common people, an antagonism which found expression in the writings of satirists from the time of Langland and Chaucer to Erasmus and More, which found vehement expression in the *Epistolae obscurorum virorum* ("Letters of the Obscurantists") of the Rhenish humanists (*see* REUCHLIN, JOHANN) and showed its public virulence in the crisis of Hunne's case in London, 1514–15.

It is more difficult to generalize about the religion and faith of common men. But there is plenty of evidence of widespread fear and superstition. Evidence, too, of an externalizing of religion, an emphasis on outward works and technical ecclesiastical duties, which, taken together with a doctrine of merit not clearly expounded, attracted the acid criticism of such catholic humanists as Sir Thomas More, John Colet, Desiderius Erasmus (*qq.v.*), Konrad Peutinger and Willibald Pirckheimer. The communion of saints, the sacred commerce between heaven and earth, became itself a means of clerical exploitation, and the literature of Catholic humanism bears witness to the superstitions and abuses connected with it and with the doctrine of purgatory. Witch-hunting, gross superstition, fanaticism belong as much to the social background as to the church, for the veneer of Christian civilization had always been thin in some areas of medieval Europe, but recurrent apocalyptic panic and sombre revivalism is a part of the late medieval background which is not to be ignored.

There remained, despite all this, the unfailing offices of the liturgy of the church and of its sacramental system. But it seems evident that the liturgy of the church had become overcomplicated, and the eventual reforms of the Council of Trent (*q.v.*; 1545–63) in the matter of preaching and pastoral care are the best evidence of the neglect of these things in the preceding 50 years. There is no need to overdarken this picture, for which chapter and verse could be given from Catholic writers. It was Cardinal Reginald Pole who told the second session of the Council of Trent (Jan. 1546), "We ourselves are largely responsible for the misfortune that has occurred . . . for the rise of heresy, the collapse of Christian morality, because we have failed to cultivate the field that was entrusted to us. We are like salt that has lost its savour" (H. Jedin, *History of the Council of Trent,* vol. ii, p. 26, translated by E. Graf; Thomas Nelson & Sons Ltd., 1961).

Nonetheless, it would be foolish to underestimate the positive good achieved by a creaking and groaning ecclesiastical machine. Though abuses clustered round each point of the sacramental system where it touched the cure of souls, there are abundant signs that these things did not prevent the work of divine grace.

Indeed, by the second decade of the 16th century, it was arguable that the worst was past. Not again would the papacy become what it had been as a tool of the Borgias. There had been energetic attempts to find a platform of reform in the fifth Lateran council (1512–17) and in the even more successful and reforming movement of Cardinal Francisco Jiménez de Cisneros in Spain. Though the 14th-century revival of inward religion, the *devotio moderna,* had become an ascetic and sometimes obscurantist pietism, it still inspired the valiant attempt of Jean Standonck to reform Parisian religious houses with its aid. A conflation of the *devotio moderna* with German mysticism had much to do with the reforming zeal of the German Augustinian Johann von Staupitz, who attempted a reform of his order in Germany. In fact, in this period there were many new orders, new brotherhoods and religious sodalities and, among the older orders, attempts by Observants to reform in line with the authentic intentions of their original rule. The widespread institution of preacherships in south German cities is a sign that some spiritual and secular authorities were sensitive to the need of the church at this point. The invention of printing *c.* 1440 made available a whole spate of edifying and catechetical literature of astonishing richness and diversity at the beginning of the 16th century. (*See also* PAPACY.)

2. Reformers Before the Reformation.—The older Protestant historians were wont to single out those whom they regarded as the true precursors of the Reformation, too often reading back 19th-century "principles" (*e.g.,* toleration and the right of private judgment) into the 16th century. It is easy to pick out isolated sentences in commentaries by Wycliffe, Huss, Colet, Wessel Gansfort or Lefèvre d'Étaples which suggest that they anticipated Luther's doctrine, and to forget the even more important elements they shared with their Catholic contemporaries. Of these men, perhaps John Wycliffe (*q.v.*) has most claim to be thought of as a precursor of the Reformation. In his appeal to the supreme authority of Holy Scripture there is evident, more than in the heavily Aristotelian writings of Marsilius of Padua and William Ockham, a directly biblical antidote to the canonist doctrine of the papal plenitude of power. Modern study has stressed his intricate scholasticism, how much he had in common with other students of St. Augustine in that age, and yet unlike them, but like the Reformers, he set off some kind of ecclesiastical explosion. That it was isolated, muffled, is perhaps because Wycliffe lacked two of the vital agents of the Reformation: the invention of printing and the new tools and methods of the humanists which provided a microphone and megaphone for the Reformers.

3. Humanism and the Reformation.—This is not the place to define humanism, to question whether there was in fact a Renaissance or to discuss the merits of the humanists as scholars (*see* RENAISSANCE). At least of negative importance is the fact that throughout the century before the Reformation a number of critical satirical writings had provided an acid ferment within the church, a focus for anticlerical sentiment. More positively, there was the advent of new tools and a new critical method. The return to classical antiquity, the search for better texts, was illustrated in the new edition of Aristotle which Jacques Lefèvre d'Étaples (*q.v.*) provided for his Paris students. It was when applied to sacred letters that the new technique became of catastrophic importance. There was, first, the revived study of the sacred languages, Hebrew, Greek and a renovated Latin. The lack of philological tools in the way of grammars and dictionaries limited the scope and value of humanist biblical scholarship but not the immediate effect on contemporaries. There was a new insistence on the importance of securing the best possible text, based on the best manuscript authorities, and these were to be interpreted not uncritically in terms of traditional authority but in the exact, philological, historical context.

Landmarks in this biblical humanism were the Complutensian Polyglot Bible, the work of a brilliant team of Spanish scholars at Alcalá, and the immense tour de force of Erasmus' edition of the New Testament in the original Greek (1516; revised edition, 1519), the prefaces of which were manifestoes of the new method. What had been to Lorenzo Valla or to Johann Reuchlin philological principles became of theological importance for Erasmus. The theology of Nicholas of Cusa, the thinkers of the Florentine academy, Marsilio Ficino and Pico della Mirandola had suggested a broader approach to questions of truth than had scholastic theology, and in Erasmus this became the simple, practical study of the "philosophy of Christ," the way of life set out in the Gospels and in the Epistles of St. Paul. He exhorted men to the direct study of the Scriptures, which he hoped might be made available for wayfaring men and women in their own tongue.

4. Indulgence Controversy.—The occasion of the Reformation must be clearly distinguished from the deep, underlying causes. Martin Luther (*q.v.*) claimed that, while others before him had attacked the papal morals, he had gone to the theological roots of the matter, the perversion of the doctrine of grace, the externalizing of the sacrament of penance and the consequent ensnaring of consciences in a legalism contrary to the spirit of the gospel. But the occasion was practical enough, the sale of indulgences (*see* INDULGENCE). These offered spiritual privileges on papal authority, including the commutation for money of those acts of satisfaction which formed part of the sacrament of penance. About their theory, and particularly their application to the dead, there was some of that uncertainty which J. Lortz has noted as a defect of the Roman Church before the Council of Trent, and theologians argued and moralists protested about their use and abuse. For while the wording of the indulgence excluded the notion that forgiveness might be bought, or was available to the impenitent, the language used by some sellers of indulgences was not so discreet.

The immediate cause of scandal in Germany in 1517 was the issue of an indulgence which was to pay for the rebuilding of St. Peter's, Rome. But by a secret agreement of which most Germans, including Luther, were unaware, half the proceeds of the German sales were to be diverted to meet the huge debt owed to the Fuggers by the archbishop and elector Albert of Mainz, a debt incurred by his inability to pay the fees on his accumulation of high benefices. Such a prince could not afford to be squeamish about the methods and language used by his agents, and the commissary in Germany, the Dominican Johann Tetzel, spoke in terms which were extravagant and scandalous. Luther was outraged when he learned of this from his own penitents who brandished their pardons before him. The sale of this indulgence was forbidden in Wittenberg by the elector Frederick III (*q.v.*) the Wise, who preferred that the faithful should make their offerings at his own great collection of relics, exposed on high days in the castle church. It was therefore a fateful moment when on the eve of All Saints' day Luther nailed to the door of the church 95 theses concerning indulgences, offering to dispute them "for the sake of eliciting the truth." He had on the same day written to the archbishop and to his ordinary, the bishop of Brandenburg, protesting against the language used in the handbook of instructions for indulgence sellers. Yet the theses were not extreme, and about many of them Luther himself had not made up his mind. He had preached against indulgences some months before and, though this was a public protest, it was in no sense a deliberate schismatic and revolutionary act. But here the invention of printing intervened. What might have been confined to a few copies circulating among neighbours was turned overnight into a manifesto which swiftly circulated through Germany, attracting ever-widening publicity, turning a protest about a genuine scandal into the greatest crisis in the history of the Western Church.

II. LUTHER'S REVOLT, 1517–21

1. Luther and Early Supporters.—Martin Luther, professor of theology in the University of Wittenberg, was at this time a theologian of growing repute, of some importance in the Augustinian order. He was alarmed to find that his honest protest was interpreted in terms of proud defiance and to learn that steps were being taken to secure his silence. Faced with a demand of unconditional recantation and complete submission to papal authority, Luther was forced to reconsider his whole attitude to the authority of the pope, of councils and of Holy Scripture. Two events especially stimulated him to further protest, his interview with Cardinal Cajetan (*q.v.*) at Augsburg, 1518, and his debate with Johann Eck (*q.v.*) at Leipzig in the following year. In June 1520 the papal bull *Exsurge domine* condemned 41 propositions attributed to Luther. (His excommunication followed in 1521.) Luther retorted in a fluent series of fiery writings, chief among which were his two manifestoes of 1520, *An den christlichen Adel deutscher Nation* ("An Appeal to the Christian Nobility of the German Nation") and *De captivitate Babylonica ecclesiae praeludium* ("A Prelude Concerning the Babylonish Captivity of the Church"). The first, in lucid German, summed up the rising tide of national German grievance against the exactions and tyrannies of Rome. The second, in Latin, made an even more revolutionary attack on the hierarchy and the sacramental system. By now it had become plain that there were great forces on Luther's side and that his teaching found an echo in important classes of the community, not least the knights, the peasants and the merchant burghers of the towns. The scholars were divided by the vehemence of Luther's protest, but among them too, in many lands, he won at least qualified approval, and from some wholehearted support.

With dramatic defiance which caught the imagination of Europe, Luther appeared before the young emperor, Charles V, at the imperial diet in Worms, April 1521. He refused to recant or disavow his writings, on the ground that his conscience must obey

"MARTIN LUTHER AND HIS FRIENDS." DETAIL OF A PAINTING FROM THE STUDIO OF LUCAS CRANACH THE ELDER, IN THE TOLEDO MUSEUM OF ART, TOLEDO, O. IN THE CENTRE, THE ELECTOR FREDERICK III OF SAXONY, SURROUNDED BY (LEFT TO RIGHT) LUTHER, SPALATIN, OSIANDER, BUGENHAGEN, AND MELANCHTHON

the Word of God. Under a safe conduct he was allowed to go, but the edict of Worms, passed by a rump diet after his departure, outlawed him, thus inhibiting his movements for the rest of his days and forcing caution upon the elector Frederick, his patron. The result was Luther's friendly captivity in the castle of the Wartburg. There he continued to pen influential writings, most notable of all his translation of the German Bible, a work which was deeply to influence the life and religion of Germany.

Now the far-reaching implications of the new teaching had to be faced. Theological changes, such as the restoration of communion in both kinds to the laity, the abolition of private Masses, the denunciation of celibacy of clergy and of monastic vows, had immense financial, juridical and social consequences. In Wittenberg itself some of Luther's colleagues, notably Andreas von Karlstadt (*q.v.*), wished to step up the pace of reform and go farther and faster than Luther or his gifted young colleague, Philipp Melanchthon (*q.v.*), were prepared to go. The radical party demanded the abolition of religious pictures and images and institution of a vernacular, simplified liturgy. They pushed through reforms on these lines early in 1522, when the magistracy passed the *Ordnung der Stadt Wittenberg* ("Ordinance of the City of Wittenberg"), the forerunner of innumerable civic ordinances elsewhere. At this time the imperial government at Nürnberg issued a sharp warning against any innovations involving social disorder, so that the elector Frederick and his adviser Georg Spalatin (*q.v.*) were more than ever afraid of change. In March 1522 the situation was getting out of hand, and it was redressed only by the return of Luther himself, under whose forceful preaching order was restored and a number of innovations canceled. One result was to slow down change in Wittenberg, and not until 1526 did Luther provide a vernacular liturgy (*Deutsche Messe*). Karlstadt retired to the village of Orlamünde on the Saale, where he converted his parishioners to his own brand of mystic puritanism and where he remained a troublemaker. In other parts of Thuringia, too, there was a radical ferment at work. The fiery Jakob Strauss in Eisenach inveighed against usury and tithes. More influential was the preacher in Allstedt, Thomas Müntzer (*q.v.*). In him Lutheran notions jostled alongside medieval mysticism and Hussite anticlericalism. Having failed to win the inhabitants of Prague to his new order, he returned to dominate the little town of Allstedt where his turbulent preaching and liturgical experiments became a growing scandal. He was expelled from the town in the summer of 1524 and sought new pastures in south Germany where social revolution was imminent.

2. Peasant War.—In the summer of 1524 a series of sporadic, ill-co-ordinated risings began in the Black forest, extending rapidly through Swabia and the Rhineland. The rebel demands varied, sometimes based on Catholic doctrine, elsewhere appealing to the "righteousness" advocated by Luther and Zwingli. In the main the rebels were not so much concerned with abstract justice as with the redress of specific grievances, forest and game laws, tithes and the like.

With few leaders of military ability and no planned commissariat, the peasants roamed destructively about the countryside, burning and pillaging, terrorizing the inhabitants and conscripting small towns and local gentry into their ranks. At first, in the absence of organized and armed opposition, they gained immense success, but they rarely survived a set battle. Thus the Thuringian peasants under Thomas Müntzer in May 1525 were overthrown at Frankenhausen by a coalition of the forces of the evangelical prince Philip of Hesse and the Catholic duke George of Saxony. After the rout and its bloody sequel, Müntzer was taken, tortured and, after recantation, executed. Modern Soviet historians see in him the real hero of the "People's Reformation." Yet his incitement was not to class war but to anticlericalism, and his scanty teaching about social equality is entirely subordinate in his apocalyptic theology. Many of his disillusioned disciples and followers joined the radical Anabaptist movement (*see* ANABAPTISTS).

3. Luther and German Protestantism (1525–46).—By 1525 Luther no longer dominated the already many-sided Reformation, though he remained the leader of the growingly coherent Lutheran Church. He was much criticized for his attitude during the Peasant War. Though he had for long warned civil rulers against the dangerous consequences of radical preaching in Saxony, and though he gave moderate counsel to both sides at the beginning of the rebellion, more attention was attracted by his hysterical broadsheet, *Wider die räuberischen und mörderischen Rotten der Bauern* ("Against the Murdering, Thieving Hordes of Peasants"), written at the height of rebel success but published after their collapse during bloody reprisals by the young princes. Though neither before or after 1525 could Luther be accused of undue subservience before authority, many who had rather loosely considered themselves his followers turned in disillusion to the new Anabaptists. Yet Lutheranism did not cease to be a popular movement; it continued to gain ground among all classes in the German towns and countryside. After the death of Frederick III the Wise (1525), Luther's old patron though never his disciple, the two succeeding electors, John and John Frederick, were Lutheran princes in a new sense. It was at this time, too, that Luther married a former nun, Katherine von Bora, a common-sense match which turned out marvelously well, and as the former Augustinian monastery in Wittenberg became a Protestant manse the new domesticities mark perhaps another stage in the circumscription of Luther as a Saxon Reformer.

Luther's *De servo arbitrio* (1525), in reply to the attack of Erasmus' *De libero arbitrio* (1524), was a powerful treatise on the doctrine of free will, which marks the alienation from his cause of an element in humanism which had begun by treating him with sympathy but which had been more and more alienated by the violence of his language, the boldness of his repudiation of traditional churchmanship and the failure of his reformation to produce more evident moral fruits. His treatise, also in this year, *Wider die himmlischen Propheten* ("Against the Heavenly Prophets"), was a profound exposition of the difference between his theology and that of the radicals, Karlstadt and Müntzer.

Luther's liturgical order, the *Deutsche Messe* (1526), and his catechisms (1529) became the prototype for the innumerable Lu-

theran church orders of the next half-century. His children's catechism, especially, was a work of great beauty. His translation of the Bible from the original languages into German, which was finally published in complete form in 1534, went into many editions, some of them finely illustrated, and made deep impress on the life of the German people. He encouraged his friends to write, and himself composed more than a score of fine hymns (*see* also GERMAN LITERATURE: *The Reformation;* BIBLE, TRANSLATIONS OF; HYMN).

Luther conducted a great correspondence, both in and outside Germany, dealing with problems of conscience, pastoral care and church organization. He continued to give courses of lectures, attended by students who went out into all parts of Europe as his disciples, spreading the Lutheran Reformation. In the work of Reformation he was more and more aided by his colleague Philipp Melanchthon, to whose irenical spirit he entrusted more and more ecclesiastical negotiations. Though Luther's own educational writings are important and fruitful, Melanchthon's humanistic learning and his programs and textbooks earned him the title "preceptor of Germany." Melanchthon was responsible for drafting the Augsburg Confession (*q.v.;* 1530), the foundation document of the Lutheran Church as well as of the political Schmalkaldic league. In 1527–28 a commission of lawyers and theologians began a visitation of Saxony, and this became a prototype of Lutheran administration. The Reformers had now to fill the vacuum left by canon law and Catholic discipline, and they developed the important consistorial court to deal with administrative and disciplinary problems, especially concerning marriage.

Luther himself distrusted secular influence in church affairs, and while he lived there was not much cause for complaint on this score. After his death, the way was open for more and more authority to concentrate in the hands of the secular ruler. One by one the great German cities turned to the Reformation, though after 1526 there was usually a tension between the Lutheran and Reformed types. Luther's colleague, Johann Bugenhagen, became the organizer of Lutheranism in north Germany and in Denmark. By 1529 the Lutheran cause was represented in the imperial diet by a group of princes, including the elector of Saxony, the landgrave of Hesse, the margrave of Brandenburg and the prince of Anhalt. The restoration of the Lutheran duke Ulrich to Württemberg in 1534 and, even more, the accession of ducal Saxony on the death of Luther's ancient foe, Duke George, in 1539, were signal advances. Nonetheless, the last years of Luther's life were years of growing Catholic resurgence: the long-threatened papal council became a reality, and there was a political and military coalition of Catholic powers. His aging body racked with illness, Luther continued to preach and teach and to write until his death in Feb. 1546.

III. GERMAN AND SWISS REFORMERS

1. The Emperor Charles V and the German Princes.—About the devotion of Charles V to the Catholic faith, and his hatred of the Reformers and all their works, there was never any doubt. But he had a layman's distrust of theological niceties and was prepared to make concessions for the sake of restoring unity. Circumstances forced realism upon him, and in times of emergency he was vulnerable to the advice of counselors more sympathetic than himself to the new teaching. The many preoccupations of his vast sprawling empire, in Spain, the Netherlands, Germany, Austria and Hungary, the constant menace of the Turkish invasion, his own diplomatic and military entanglement in incessant quarrels with popes and kings of France—all these intervened again and again to keep him away from Germany or to prevent him from implementing the edict of Worms against Luther and his teachings. The German princes played for their own political hands, and it was not only those who favoured the Reformers who insisted that the grievances of Germany against Roman exactions must be dealt with by a free council on German soil. In 1526 the Turks won a great victory at Mohacs. That year, under the menace of Turkish invasion, a recess of the imperial diet at Speyer left each ruler free to act as he should answer "to God and the emperor." By 1529 the emperor could take a stronger line, and the Catholic majority in the diet withdrew the earlier concessions, provoking the historic *Protestation* of the minority of evangelical princes and of 14 imperial cities, which earned them the title "Protestants."

2. Philip of Hesse.—The most energetic and politically minded of the Protestant princes was the landgrave Philip (*q.v.*) of Hesse. In Hesse the Reformation developed its own characteristics, for he enlisted the aid, first of the French Reformer Franz Lambert (*q.v.*) of Avignon, and then of Martin Bucer (*q.v.*), from Strasbourg. Reforms were canvassed at a synod at Hamburg in 1526 and promulgated at Ziegenhain in 1538. Hesse was notable for a conciliatory policy toward the Anabaptists which won many back to the church. In the vulnerable Palatinate, Philip knew the need for political alliance, and in the hope of restoring the broken eucharistic front invited Swiss and German theologians to a colloquy in his palace at Marburg in Oct. 1529, a conference which foundered on the refusal of Luther or Huldreich Zwingli to compromise their convictions (*see* MARBURG, COLLOQUY OF). Philip was one of the chief members of the Schmalkaldic league (Feb. 1531) formed to offset the coalition of Catholic princes. Though a zealous Protestant, his inability to control his passions led to the scandal of his bigamy (1540). Bucer, Melanchthon and Luther—in that order—were reluctantly driven to acquiesce in the grant of a secret dispensation for bigamy, which when it became public rendered the prince guilty of a breach of the law of the empire.

In 1530 the emperor attended in person the diet at Augsburg. While Luther, as an outlaw, had to fidget in Coburg castle, the Protestant cause was represented by Melanchthon, who drew up the Augsburg Confession for the occasion. Encouraged by hopes of reconciliation with the Catholic side, Melanchthon was prepared to draw away from the Swiss Reformers and heartily to damn the Anabaptists. Bucer presented a more radical document, the *Confessio Tetrapolitana*, on behalf of Strasbourg, Constance, Lindau and Memmingen. The Catholics replied with a vast catena of Protestant heresies, prepared by Johann Eck, with a theological *Confutatio* and with an imperial ultimatum to the Protestant princes. Nonetheless, the strength of the Protestant alliance and the need for help against the Turks forced the emperor once again to postpone action and to call a truce at Nürnberg in 1532 which gave the Reformers a critical interval in which to consolidate their gains and a valuable breathing space. Moderates on both sides of the great divide still hoped for reconciliation, and a series of conferences were held, led by Melanchthon and Bucer on the one hand and a number of Catholic theologians, some of them influenced by Erasmus, on the other. These were held at Hagenau and Regensburg (1539–41) but eventually broke down on the doctrine of the Mass.

In 1541 Philip of Hesse temporarily abandoned his allies in the Schmalkaldic league and joined the emperor's League of Nürnberg, thus seriously weakening the Protestant front. By 1546 Charles V was in a strong enough position to concentrate on disposing of the Schmalkaldic league, and with the aid of the renegade Maurice of Saxony, himself a Protestant, surprised, defeated and captured the elector, John Frederick, and Philip of Hesse at Mühlberg in 1547. In 1548 at Augsburg the victorious emperor dictated the terms of an imperial "Interim" which, though something of a compromise, resulted in the exile for conscience's sake of Martin Bucer and some hundreds of Protestant pastors. But once again the military intervention of the king of France ruined Charles V's ambitious plots, and in the next years Charles was forced to hand over German affairs to the archduke Ferdinand, abdicated his vast dominions and retired to a monastery in Spain. The peace of Augsburg (1555) recognized the stalemate between two groups of powers neither of which could immediately overthrow the other, gave recognition to the Protestants and acknowledged their legal right to secularized church property in their lands. The political divisions of Germany were now further confounded by the addition of the religious barrier, since the principle that subjects must adopt the religion of their prince (*cuius regio, eius religio*) ended the myth of German unity and substituted religious territorialism for the concept of one Holy Roman empire of the German nation, thus permanently tying religious and political affairs.

3. The Reformation in Switzerland and South Germany.

—By 1525 other patterns of Reformation were emerging, distinct in origin and ethos from that of Luther, drawing on other spiritual influences from the late middle ages, such as the *devotio moderna* and German mysticism, and developing an austere Puritanism which was critical of the "this worldliness" with which Luther opposed Catholic asceticism. Now this pattern found a more moderate setting in the Reformation in the cities of Switzerland and south Germany, in the leadership of Huldreich Zwingli (*q.v.*), Bucer and John Calvin (*q.v.*), who were the founding fathers of the emerging Reformed as distinct from the Lutheran Protestant tradition. In these oligarchic communities corporate self-consciousness was intensified by long struggle for liberties against feudal lords and by the internal movement within the complex guild structures. Here, too, the godly magistracy offered a swift and effective instrument for carrying through public reform. The situation varied very much from city to city. The presence of a bishop (Basel), a cathedral or collegiate church (Augsburg), an abbey (Sankt Gallen) or a university (Basel) slowed up the pace of reform, which was accelerated by the presence of an eminent Reformer (Zürich, Strasbourg), usually clerical but sometimes (Sankt Gallen) lay. No doubt economic interests counted, and the presence of the great Catholic banking families of Fugger and Welser held up reform in Augsburg at a time when Nürnberg had already become Lutheran.

But the story cannot be explained in terms of vested interest or of a class struggle between patricians, merchants and craft guilds. For though these considerations explain some of the facts,

BY COURTESY OF (LEFT) THE ZENTRALBIBLIOTHEK, ZÜRICH, (RIGHT) THE KUNSTMUSEUM, WINTERTHUR; PHOTOGRAPHS, SCHWEIZERISCHES INSTITUT FÜR KUNSTWISSENSCHAFT

(LEFT) HEINRICH BULLINGER, BY AN ANONYMOUS MASTER, 1521; (RIGHT) HULDREICH ZWINGLI, BY HANS ASPER, 1531

they do not account for ways in which Reformers (*e.g.*, goldsmiths) behaved against their own economic self-interest, and though in Zürich and Basel the impetus came from the craft guilds, in Constance and in Bern the patrician element was important; indeed, in Constance the main opposition to Reform came from the proletarian fishermen's guild.

Ernst Troeltsch and Max Weber, and a famous essay by R. H. Tawney, placed Protestantism in close connection with the rise of capitalism. While Luther's economic theories were medieval and backward-looking, it was asserted, Calvinism, and English Puritanism in consequence, fostered a this-worldly, forward-looking enterprise which in part provoked and certainly accompanied the new social morality of the capitalist system. The theory has been much modified by later research and criticism, and the supposed contrast between Catholic and Protestant social ethic has been shown to be less significant than had been suggested. It is true that the Reformers stressed the duty of men to labour in their calling and emphasized the virtues of thrift and industry (the "gospel of hard work" is prominent in Bucer). The work of W. K. Jordan has emphasized that Protestant religion found expression in new forms of philanthropy, in the relief of sick and poor and care for education, in ways which offset and in part replaced the medieval works of mercy.

4. Zürich and Zwingli.—Huldreich Zwingli from the Alpine

Toggenburg was a patriotic Swiss who after a few years as parish priest was appointed to the Grossmünster (cathedral) in Zürich. There in Jan. 1519 he began a ministry of prophetic preaching, expounding St. Matthew's Gospel from beginning to end and continuing with other biblical books before an audience which included most of the civic leaders, in an exposition always closely related to public affairs. An important instrument for clerical education were the "prophesyings" at which he and his clerical companions expounded the Old Testament, and one fruit of this was the Zürich Bible of 1529, the work of Zwingli and his scholarly colleagues, Conrad Pellicanus, Leo Jud and Bibliander. Though Zwingli plausibly claimed to have rediscovered the Pauline gospel of justification by faith independently of Luther, the Reformation movement in Zürich began with his protests against the Lenten fast in 1522.

The technique of the Zürich Reformation was followed in other cities. An evangelical mandate from the town council gave the new, direct scriptural preaching some kind of footing. A public disputation was held, no longer an academic exercise but rather a deliberate appeal to public opinion and official decision. There followed the promulgation of evangelical ordinances by the magistracy, regulating preaching and worship, abolishing images and the Mass, reorganizing discipline and administration.

This reform by public law was prepared for and accompanied by energetic preaching ministries in the city churches, and Zwingli and Bucer in particular were aware of the dangers of a merely outward Reformation carried through by public law. In the case of Zwingli, this appeal to the magistracy was by no means subservience or expediency but was rooted in his thought of the city as a Christian commonwealth. Zwingli prepared 67 theological articles for the first Zürich disputation (Jan. 29, 1523). His friends assembled with him in the Grossmünster behind Bibles, in Greek, Hebrew and Latin, as a sign that they would accept only Scripture, not church authority, as arbiter. Outmaneuvered, the Catholics put up no sort of fight, and the authorities declared for Zwingli. A further disputation took place in October concerning images and the Mass, but it was not until 1525 that action followed from the magistrates, and Zwingli's drastically simplified communion rite was published and authorized.

By this time a group of Zwingli's more ardent younger men had turned against him, angered by his reluctance to proceed with Reformation more swiftly than the magistrates were prepared to go; they provoked in Zürich a radical rebellion which became the Anabaptist movement. Older historians overstressed Zwingli's rationalism and humanism and overlooked his noble conception of his city as a prophetic community, where church and magistracy could work hand in hand. He prefaced his tracts with the evangelical invitation "Come unto me . . . ," for his conception of a Christian commonwealth made all life, private and public morality included, a sounding board for the gospel. Nonetheless, he was a Swiss patriot and became imbued with Zürich imperialism, evident in his dealings with Sankt Gallen and with Waldshut. Alarmed at the growing menace of Catholic power and the isolation of Zürich, Zwingli strove to build an alliance, the "Christian civic league," with the Protestant cities of Bern and Basel and with Strasbourg from without the Swiss confederation. These adventures into high politics led to the disastrous battle of Cappel against the Catholic cantons (Oct. 1531), in which Zwingli was slain. His young successor, Heinrich Bullinger (q.v.), continued the religious and theological program of Zwingli without the disastrous foreign policy, and though Zürich remained an important centre of Reform it no longer dominated the Reformation in the south.

BY COURTESY OF CARL J. BURCKHARDT, ESQ.

JOHN OECOLAMPADIUS, A CONTEMPORARY COPY OF AN ORIGINAL PORTRAIT ATTRIBUTED TO HANS HOLBEIN THE YOUNGER: FROM THE COLLECTION OF CARL J. BURCKHARDT, ESQ.

5. Basel and Oecolampadius.—Very different from the hardheaded Zwingli was his friend and colleague, the warmhearted John Oecolampadius (q.v.). He was supremely a scholar and a preacher—suited to be the leader in a university city famous for its books and its publishing houses, its rich men furnished with intellectual ability. He was of all the Reformers perhaps the most learned in the Church Fathers, and he was skilled in the Hebrew, Greek and Latin languages. In Basel there were strong Catholic forces rallying round the Münster and its chapter, and the pace of reform was slow. After assisting Erasmus with the launching of his New Testament, Oecolampadius returned to Basel in 1532 as professor of Old Testament. He outgrew an initial dilettantism and took a lead at the disputation at Baden in 1526 against Johann Eck and Johann Faber. In 1528 he attended the disputation at Bern which decided the fate of the Reformation in that city and returned determined to press for a similar success in Basel.

This second disputation took place in the winter of 1528–29, and at Easter, after growing iconoclasm and tumult, great reforming mandates were passed by the magistrates. The cathedral chapter left for the other side of the Rhine, and a number of scholars went with them, including Erasmus. Overwhelmed with grief at the death of Zwingli, Oecolampadius died only a few weeks after him. His work was carried on by Myconius (Oswald Geisshüssler). In Bern, important though it was (in subsequent decades it surpassed Basel and Zürich as a centre of reform), there was no leader of real eminence, and the clerical leader, Berchtold Haller (1492–1536), was less important than the poet-statesman Niklaus Manuel. There, too, Reformation came by civic mandate after the highly successful disputation at Basel in 1528.

6. Strasbourg and Bucer.—Strasbourg was an imperial free city, commercially important but strategically vulnerable, politically and geographically isolated from the Swiss cities. Its Reformation was launched by a group including the cathedral preacher Matthew Zell, the scholar Wolfgang Capito (q.v.), the educationalist Johannes Sturm, the statesman Jakob Sturm and above all Martin Bucer. Bucer arrived in Strasbourg, an ex-Dominican on the run, unemployed and penniless, in 1523, but soon dominated the Reformation movement in the city. He developed much of the theology of the young Luther but with his own stresses on election, on the doctrine of the church, on the need for catechetical instruction, on the importance of a doctrine of sanctification and on practical philanthropy. He was much engaged in stimulating liturgical reforms, and it has been said that "for him the Church is built round hymn-singing." Above all, as Margarethe Blaurer (sister of the Reformers Ambrosius and Thomas Blaurer) said, he was "a fanatic for unity" and spent much of his energies in attending ecclesiastical conferences in one country after another.

Although his work centred in Strasbourg, Bucer was called in to assist Reformation in Ulm, Cologne and Hesse. Strasbourg was a city of refuge for radicals and there was a considerable Anabaptist uproar with which Bucer tried to deal firmly but more tolerantly than did the Lutherans or the Swiss. After the promulgation of the Augsburg Interim in 1548 Bucer went into exile in England, where he died in 1551. Although Bucer's position mediated between the Lutherans and the Swiss, he must be regarded as one of the fathers of the Reformed Protestant tradition, though Strasbourg itself, after his departure, became dominantly Lutheran. *See also* REFORMED CHURCHES.

IV. ENGLAND

As the territorial princes of divided Germany played the role performed in the cities by the "godly magistrates," so in the politically unified kingdoms of England, Scotland, France and Scandinavia the *jus reformandi* was exercised by the "godly prince."

Much the same conditions prevailed in rather remote England as at the centre of medieval Christendom. There were notable humanists such as Thomas Linacre, William Grocyn, John Colet, John Fisher and Sir Thomas More. The case (1514–15) of Richard Hunne, a London merchant who sued a priest, was countercharged for heresy and found dead in the bishop of London's prison, revealed a ferment of anticlericalism in the capital. Pockets of sectarian heresy—simple, anticlerical, lay in leadership and roughly labeled "Lollard"—existed throughout the country, even in the north, though most strongly in the Thames valley and in East Anglia (*see* LOLLARDS). Books by Erasmus and Luther were circulating in England after 1520, and though many of these writings, with the biblical commentaries of other Reformers, were proscribed by the authorities, they were sold in secret traffic to undergraduates and doctors at Oxford and Cambridge and in some of the larger monasteries.

At Cambridge a group of scholars favouring reform were in trouble at the end of 1525, eminent among them Thomas Bilney, Hugh Latimer (*q.v.*), Robert Barnes—all eventually burned. In 1526 the exiled William Tyndale produced an English New Testament which was a work of genius. Thus, five years later than in Germany—a significant time gap never really caught up—the Reformation movement was stirring in England, particularly among the scholars, the merchants and the court.

1. Henry VIII.—Henry VIII, gifted and ruthless, was a formidable Renaissance prince. The Wars of the Roses had thinned out the nobility, saving the Reformation in England from its fate in France and Scotland where it became involved in the tussle between nobility and crown. But the fear of renewed civil war over claims to the crown remained a Tudor bogey from the 15th century and was one reason for Henry's anxiety for a male heir. This became for him a case of conscience when there was no son to his marriage with Catherine of Aragon. It called in question the validity of his marriage, as Catherine had been the wife of his deceased brother Arthur, and of the papal dispensation which had made this possible, and, once raised, the question uncovered a whole legal and theological complex of disputable arguments. Reasons of state, therefore, may be fairly added to Henry's passion for Anne Boleyn which led him to seek divorce. The king found there were limits to papal compliance, especially as Catherine was aunt of the emperor Charles V and formidable European sympathies were on her side.

The great cardinal Thomas Wolsey was an early victim of the royal impatience, and the king found a ruthless and compliant servant in Thomas Cromwell, an able administrator, and an archbishop of integrity in Thomas Cranmer, who firmly believed in the authority of the godly prince, which, with Holy Scripture, offset the papal claim to plenitude of power. The clergy were browbeaten into submission under the medieval acts of *praemunire* (*q.v.*). Henry got his divorce and married Anne. The Reformation parliament, summoned in 1529, carried through under royal direction a series of enactments which lopped off one by one the great financial, legal and administrative cables which joined the English state with western Christendom, the English church with the Roman see. An Act of Succession was passed, to which an oath of allegiance was required, and an Act of Supremacy declared Henry to be supreme head of the Church of England, the inheritor of the jurisdiction of the bishop of Rome. Henry showed his ruthless determination by executing John Fisher and Thomas More, and a noble band of obstinate Carthusians. But over the country as a whole the resistance was significantly slight.

The suppression of the monasteries (smaller houses in 1536, larger in 1539) was of major importance in the consolidation of the break with Rome. This was carried through under the oversight of Cromwell as the king's lay vicar-general on the basis of tendentious reports from his commissioners. But though the amount of scandalous immorality in the monasteries may have been exaggerated, a relaxed worldliness was evidently widespread, and most of the religious went back to the world cheerfully accepting their pensions, for the most part unlamented. The spoliation of the shrines and the sale of monastic property brought wealth to a needy and extravagant king, whose military attempts to cut a figure in Europe were as ambitious as they were unsuccessful. The sequestered monastic lands, especially, provided a strong vested interest among the new landlords, giving them a stake in the Reformation, a situation which Mary was not able to reverse. These things provoked one formidable rising, the Pilgrimage of Grace (Oct. 1536), in which political and economic motives played a part alongside religious conservatism.

Like other 16th-century rebellions, it was crushed savagely.

The danger of isolation, in view of a papal council and a combination of his enemies, led Henry to put out feelers toward the German princes of the Schmalkaldic league, and teams of English and Lutheran theologians held conversations in Germany and England in 1536, 1538 and 1540. During this decade a number of eminent Protestant preachers occupied pulpits in London and elsewhere. The appearance of Coverdale's Bible (1535) and Matthew's (1537) was followed by an authorized Great Bible (1539), through the good offices of Thomas Cromwell. An Act of Ten Articles (1536) tried to regulate preaching, and *The Institution of a Christian Man,* known as the Bishops' Book (1537), provided homiletic and catechetical material, some of which derived from Protestant documents.

Once again a great royal servant fell for the unforgivable crime of bungling a royal match, and with the execution of Cromwell in 1540 the high tide of approach to the Protestants had been reached. The Act of Six Articles (1539) affirmed Catholic doctrine with savage penalties (which were not strictly enforced) and *The Necessary Doctrine and Erudition of any Christian Man,* known as the King's Book (1543), was a more conservative compilation than the Bishops' Book, though still Augustinian in much of its theology. Nonetheless, the noble achievement of Cranmer's English litany of 1544 heralded a liturgical genius, and in the last years of the reign Cranmer went ahead with preparations for further theological and liturgical change. Although the official variations from Catholic faith were few, and England was schismatic rather than heretical, by the end of the reign of Henry VIII the Reformation had permeated all classes of society and penetrated most parts of the country, was strongly entrenched in London, among the merchants, at the universities, and in the circles about the court, not least among ladies in the entourage of Queen Catherine Parr.

2. Edward VI.—Though the death of Henry VIII enabled the Reformers to proceed with boldness, the advent of the boy king, Edward VI, and of the council of regency brought a dangerous element of instability. The tolerant rule of the duke of Somerset as protector in the first part of the reign was openly sympathetic to the Reformers, and the ambitious duke of Northumberland, though he was much more of a ruthless politician, also was committed to the Protestant side. Meanwhile, assisted by Nicholas Ridley, bishop of London, Thomas Cranmer propounded and executed a number of controversial changes. Communion was restored to the laity in both kinds and a liturgy published to this effect in 1548. The remaining shrines and images were removed. A book of homilies was published, to be a norm of preaching, in which Cranmer set forth the Protestant doctrine of justification by faith alone. Toward the end of the reign a series of 42 articles, many of them influenced by continental confessions, were put out. More important were the prayer books which prescribed a uniform liturgy for the whole land, in the vernacular, both owing much to Cranmer himself. A fine achievement was the turning of the seven Latin choir offices into the congregational English services of matins and evensong. Within the limitations of 16th-century liturgical experience and Cranmer's own wide learning, the communion services in both books were notable. The service in the first Prayer Book (1549) was noticeably more conservative than that of 1552 which put forward a view of the Eucharist more congenial to the theologians of Strasbourg and Switzerland than to the Lutherans (*see also* LITURGY, CHRISTIAN).

Cranmer had the advice and counsel of a number of eminent refugees from among the continental Reformers. Two in particular, Pietro Martire Vermigli (*q.v.;* Peter Martyr) at Oxford and Martin Bucer at Cambridge, as regius professors, were able to influence a new generation, John Jewel being a pupil of Vermigli and John Bradford and John Whitgift (*q.v.*) among those influenced by Bucer. At court the silver-tongued Hugh Latimer exercised a prophetic ministry reminiscent of that of Zwingli at Zürich, and he and his friends, called "Commonwealth men" from their concern for society, attacked the hard-faced men of the court for their covetousness and self-interest. The tension between Reformers and radicals on the continent now was reflected in England, with the infiltration of Anabaptists and the appearance of a Puritanism after the pattern of Zürich and Geneva in the persons of John Hooper and John Knox (*qq.v.*); it was conspicuous in the relation between the Stranger's church in London, which owed its rights to a royal charter and flourished independently of the impatient but helpless bishop of London.

3. Mary I.—Northumberland's desperate attempt to exclude a popish queen by putting Lady Jane Grey on the throne proved a disastrous fiasco, bringing all the council under shadow of treason, including Ridley and Cranmer. It underestimated the fund of loyalty and sympathy which Mary had won, as the daughter of the tragic Catherine of Aragon and of the great king. Herself an embittered and intransigent Catholic, she was earnest to undo the Reformation with a zeal which alarmed her uncle, Charles V, who counseled caution. England was still excommunicate, and the heresy laws had been repealed under Somerset, while the Prayer Book was still the lawful use. On one pretext or another the leading Reformers were imprisoned. Many scholars, clergy and gentlemen went into exile, some to intrigue in France, others to the centres of the Reformation in Germany and Switzerland. They took their theological differences with them, and the dissensions among the refugee congregation at Frankfurt, with a Prayer Book party led by Richard Cox and a Genevan party led by Knox, reflected a division which had been apparent under Edward VI and was to become a gulf under Elizabeth I. Mary lost sympathy by her unpopular marriage with Philip of Spain (July 1554). Nonetheless the patriotic and Protestant Wyatt's rebellion was soon crushed. The advent of Mary's royal kinsman, Cardinal Reginald Pole (*q.v.*), was the first step in the official reconciliation of England with Rome which took place solemnly on Nov. 30, 1554. The heresy laws were swiftly put back, and within a few days the trials for heresy began. Hitherto even Mary had had to use the legal instruments of royal supremacy, but now the authority of the church could be exercised by Mary and Pole in partnership.

The executions by burning were few in number compared with the pogroms on the continent. But they were compressed in time within a few months and concentrated in the southeastern counties. Although the majority of the 300-odd victims were of low estate (with a notable proportion of women), great publicity was attracted by the burning of a handful of Edwardian clergy. The execution of men of learning and high character, of Bishops Latimer and Ridley, of John Rogers, John Bradford and Rowland Taylor—above all, perhaps, the burning of an archbishop of Canterbury, Thomas Cranmer—these struck deep into the mind of England, a memory made permanent by the potent *Book of Martyrs* of John Foxe (*q.v.*). For Mary, the reign went from one disappointment to another. She gave Catholics a chance to breathe again, thus making it unlikely that Catholicism could ever be eradicated from England. But she was not able to restore the secularized lands and wealth of the church or to make more than a gesture of restoring the religious orders. There was no attempt to prevent the use of the English Bible. The failure of her marriage, her barrenness, the political disasters which ended in the loss of Calais, closed the reign in shadows which seem darker against the coming blaze of Elizabethan glory.

4. Elizabeth I.—Elizabeth I came to a throne beset by manifold and great dangers. With the country still at war with France, she proceeded in religious matters with caution which affronted the returning exiles and the Protestant old guard. She flirted with Lutheranism and with the possibility of protection under the peace of Augsburg. Though there were more contacts between the Elizabethan Church of England and the Swiss than are often supposed, they were with the godly magistracies of Zürich and Bern rather than that of Geneva, for with Genevan Calvinism Elizabeth had no sympathy at all. She pursued her own middle way, finding a great servant in William Cecil, Lord Burghley (*q.v.*), who kept the realm undiverted by the pressures of formidable court favourites and their cliques.

Throughout the reign there was tension between the queen and her house of commons; *i.e.*, between the "godly prince" and the proneness of the "godly magistrates"—increasingly Puritan in temper—to consider theological and liturgical change as within their province. In Matthew Parker (*q.v.*) Elizabeth found a scholarly and conservative archbishop of Canterbury. His consecration within the historic episcopate ensured that the Church of England, alone among the great churches of the Reformation, wittingly preserved the episcopate and the succession. But Elizabeth had no great opinion of her bishops, who in quality of mind and spirit are a poor contrast with her captains. The great leaders of the church had been disposed of in the fires of Mary's reign. After the disturbances of half a century, the clerical vocation was not attractive, and there was a long, hard struggle to improve the character and scholarship of the inferior clergy. Meanwhile medieval abuses persisted in a church which lacked the reforming benefits of the Catholic Council of Trent and which rejected the stern disciplines of Genevan Calvinism.

As was to be expected, the religious settlement was moderate. The queen was declared to be "supreme governor" of the realm—"as well in all spiritual or ecclesiastical causes as temporal." Parliament passed an Act of Uniformity which authorized the Prayer Book of 1552 with minor

BURNING OF RIDLEY AND LATIMER AT OXFORD (1555); WOODCUT. RIDLEY IS SAYING: "INTO THY HANDS, LORD"; LATIMER IS SAYING: "FATHER OF HEAVEN, RECEIVE MY SOUL." IN THE PULPIT, THE PREACHER, RICHARD SMITH, REGIUS PROFESSOR OF DIVINITY AT OXFORD, PREACHES FROM THE TEXT: "THOUGH I GIVE MY BODY TO BE BURNED, AND HAVE NOT CHARITY, IT PROFITETH ME NOTHING." LORD WILLIAMS IS SAYING: "MR. RIDLEY, I WILL REMEMBER YOUR SUITE"; CRANMER CRIES: "O LORD, STRENGTHEN THEM." FROM JOHN FOXE'S BOOK OF MARTYRS, 1563; IN THE BRITISH MUSEUM

adjustments, notably the changed words of administration in the communion service. In 1571 an abridgment of the 42 articles reached definitive form, and the Thirty-Nine Articles (*q.v.*) became the official confession of the English Reformation, remarkable for its moderation and its skilful ambiguities. Now the Church of England faced conflict from two sides. On the one hand the new Catholicism of the Counter-Reformation was of a very different temper from the seedy medievalism of Mary's reign. On the other hand a purposeful and thrusting new generation of Calvinists were determined to carry further the Reformation after the example of "the best reformed churches."

5. Catholic Recusants.—William (later Cardinal) Allen established a Catholic college for English exiles at Douai and Reims. The Reims-Douai Bible was published under his supervision. From the continent a succession of heroic and dedicated Jesuit missionaries infiltrated into the country. When in 1570 Pope Pius V in the bull *Regnans in excelsis* excommunicated Elizabeth, absolving her Catholic subjects from allegiance to her, a crisis of conscience arose for English Catholics, and a new political bedevilment entered a worsening situation. The growing severity of penal laws and the increasing number of executions (not unnaturally hailed as martyrdoms by the Catholics) accompanied the growing crisis of Protestant affairs in France and the Low Countries, while in England a succession of plots centred more and more in the figure of Mary, queen of Scots. Affairs reached a climax (1587–88) with the execution of Mary and with the great deliverance from the abortive invasion of the Spanish Armada.

6. Elizabethan Puritanism.—Puritanism (*q.v.*) was a movement "for the reform of Reformation itself" (John Milton) and for the remodeling of the church according to the Word of God. Its strength in this reign derived from a great movement in the University of Cambridge, centring in Calvinist doctrines of grace, predestination and conscience, and begetting an important Church of England Puritanism among clergy who specialized in moral theology and in pastoral care. These men were not much concerned with questions of church order, but the initial conflicts of the reign centred in the attempt to remove those clerical vestments which were despised by the radicals as remnants of popery. Now there was the more formidable attempt by a younger generation to set up the Presbyterian system within the Church of England. A new crisis developed when Thomas Cartwright, of Trinity college, Cambridge, put forward a doctrinaire Calvinism as the model for a Presbyterian Church of England, and in this was ably seconded in the writings of Walter Travers, of the Temple, London.

Archbishop Edmund Grindal (*q.v.*), who supposed that the "prophesyings" in progress among clerical groups were what he had known in exile—welcome means of clerical edification and education—had another view of the situation from the queen's agents who found in them a dangerous underground movement to set up within the church the *classis* (a meeting of clergy after the Genevan manner) and the Presbyterian system. His failure to deal energetically with the menace brought him into royal displeasure, but the queen soon found the minister she needed in a new archbishop, John Whitgift (an old antagonist of Cartwright at Cambridge). Whitgift evolved his own machinery, notably the prerogative court of high commission, some of whose methods, such as the *ex officio* oath, smacked of the inquisition and offended those of moderate Puritan sympathies, including Lord Burghley. By now Puritanism covered a wider series of movements than Calvinism. There were elements deriving in doctrine and ideal from the Anabaptists, new doctrines of the autonomy of each congregation, exercising the strict discipline of a "gathered church" and therefore not needing to tarry for the godly magistrate. There was a bitter literary war, and great stir was caused by the rough humour with which the anonymous Martin Marprelate tracts ridiculed the episcopate (*see* Marprelate Controversy). Some of the radicals were imprisoned and others driven into exile. Three of them, men of courage and high character, but perhaps with more zeal than discretion, John Penry, Henry Barrow and John Greenwood, were executed.

The literary apologetic for the Church of England did not go by default. In the earlier part of the reign John Jewel's noble *Apologia ecclesiae anglicanae* (1562) defended the church against Roman propaganda by setting it against the appeal to Scripture and the early church. The arguments of doctrinaire Calvinism were answered by Travers' fellow preacher at the Temple, Richard Hooker, whose *Laws of Ecclesiastical Polity* in sonorous and beautiful prose set forth a view of churchmanship which embraced reason and revelation, and left room for Christian liberties denied by Puritan Biblicism. At the end of the reign the apologists for the church, such as Hadrian Saravia and Richard Bancroft, stressed more and more the divine appointment of bishops against a Calvinism which found its church order in Scripture. Thus by the end of the reign of Elizabeth I the Church of England was not only established by law but was taking root in the affections of a nation, beginning to bring the first flowers of a piety based on the English Bible and the Book of Common Prayer, distinct from the spirituality either of the Counter-Reformation or of continental Protestantism. But the Catholic recusants, too, had proved their own faith and loyalty, while the diversities of Puritanism indicated that the religious tradition of the English could not be permanently confined within one national uniformity of worship, belief and discipline. (*See also* England, Church of; English History.)

7. Ireland.—England's treatment of Ireland is a black page in Reformation history. The country was conquered, and the conquerors dealt with it after the brutal fashion of that time. Few Catholics lost their lives for religion pure and simple, as apart from political revolts; but a series of unjust penal statutes were enacted, and these, although seldom enforced in their full theoretical strictness, were relaxed far too slowly in the face of advancing civilization; instead of weakening, they strengthened the attachment of the Irish to their religion. (*See also* Ireland, Church of.)

V. OTHER COUNTRIES OF EUROPE

1. Geneva and John Calvin.—The city of Geneva has special significance among the cities of the Reformation as a centre of French-speaking Switzerland, and its Reformation under its great leader John Calvin (*q.v.*) ushered in a new period of Protestant history and marked the emergence of the Reformed, as distinct from the Lutheran, tradition. In the struggle for independence from its bishop, and from the house of Savoy which was trying to extend its influence over the city, Geneva was drawn into the orbit of the thriving and aggressive city of Bern, which had been reformed in 1528 and exerted pressure on the course of events in Geneva in the following decades. The first fiery herald of the new evangel was the ebullient Guillaume Farel (*q.v.*), whose preaching made headway despite fierce opposition. In May and June 1535 public disputations were held, ending in the solemn resolution by the council, with uplifted hands, to live according to the Word of God. The initial success was swift but premature. This was the situation when John Calvin passed through the city, intending to devote his life to scholarship, for which his legal, humanist and theological studies had remarkably equipped him. He yielded to Farel's earnest conjurations to join the battle for reform and began that uneasy marriage of convenience with the city of Geneva which was to be fruitful beyond his dreams and was to persist until his death.

JOHN CALVIN, BY AN ANONYMOUS MASTER OF THE FRENCH SCHOOL, ABOUT 1550; IN THE BOYMANS-VAN BEUNINGEN MUSEUM, ROTTERDAM

Dispute with the magistrates about the disciplinary rights of the clergy and some interference from Bern led to the exile of Farel and Calvin in 1538. Calvin spent three important years as pastor of the French congregation in Strasbourg where he learned much from Bucer and his colleagues. He returned to Geneva at the request of the city, which was now prepared to accept his program, memorably enshrined in the *Ordonnances ecclésiastiques* (Nov. 20, 1541). Calvin now emerged as a great preacher and teacher. His formidable patristic learning was exceeded by his skill as a biblical expositor, and he produced a great series of commentaries on Holy Scripture. In his *Christianae religionis institutio* (*Institutes of the Christian Religion;* 1536, with revisions and additions in several editions before the definitive edition, 1559) he achieved one of the great documents of European history, a summary of biblical theology which the growing class of educated laymen as well as clergy could understand. In it he set forth the Augustinian doctrines of grace, divine sovereignty and predestination, and a good deal of Luther's teaching about salvation. But he also emphasized the importance of the visible church and of the pastoral office. Calvin found in Scripture a fourfold ministry of pastors, teachers, deacons and elders and made this the foundation of a coherent, workable system of Christian discipline. Moreover, his attitude to the state and to civil government was positive at a time when even in Germany events had brushed aside Luther's separation of the spiritual and temporal power. Here was a new shape for Protestantism, tired and slowing down in its second generation, and one which could be exported with powerful effect, more forward-looking and perhaps more democratic in temper than Lutheranism.

Thus Genevan Calvinism took into itself many elements, including the achievements of Zürich, Basel and Strasbourg. Calvin carried through liturgical reforms, and psalm singing became an important feature of Reformed worship. Reformation in the cities always included oversight of public morals, and in Calvin's last years a new austerity touched almost every aspect of civic life. Despite a persistent opposition party, and criticism of his intolerance (in the exile of the schoolmaster Sébastien Castellio for his radical tendencies and in the impeachment and execution of Michael Servetus for his anti-Trinitarian and Anabaptist views), Calvin's prestige stood high, and as a centre of reform Geneva now ranked with Luther's Wittenberg. From Geneva, trained, dedicated pastors went into France, in some ways a heroic Protestant counterpart to the Jesuit missionaries of the period. Calvin was succeeded by a theologian and administrator of great ability, Theodore Beza (*q.v.*). (*See also* REFORMED CHURCHES.)

2. Scotland.—Scotland shared the ills of the medieval church; the weakness of the crown and the entanglement with France both complicated and prolonged the struggle for Reformation, which to some extent took on the character of a national movement for independence from France. There is evidence of Lollard influence during the 15th century. Contacts with humanism and the study of Greek, Latin and Hebrew depended on students abroad, and there was no circle to compare with that of the Oxford and Cambridge humanists in England. In the 1520s Lutheran books began to circulate and in 1525 were formally prohibited by act of parliament. The first Protestant of distinction was the well-born Patrick Hamilton, a scholar who had been to Wittenberg and had been associated with Franz Lambert at Marburg. His collection of evangelical commonplaces, *Loci communes* (familiarly called "Patrick's Pleas" or "Places") were translated (1528) by the English martyr John Frith. Hamilton was burned at St. Andrews at the age of 24. The next martyr was George Wishart (*q.v.*), a learned divine who had taught at Cambridge and on the continent. When he was burned in 1546 a band of nobles avenged his death by murdering the cardinal archbishop David Beaton.

Among Wishart's associates was John Knox (*q.v.*), who was captured during the aftermath of the Beaton murder and spent some time in the French galleys. He was a man of powerful and intransigent temper, but with humour and common sense and courage. During his stay in England in the reign of Edward he was popular as a preacher in the Lollard areas and favoured by Northumberland as a goad to Cranmer. Exiled in the reign of Mary, he became minister to the English exiles at Frankfurt but quarrelled with them over the form of church service. He then went to Geneva, where he became a wholehearted Calvinist and

where he preached those sermons, the inspiring effect of which an English ambassador compared with the noise of 500 trumpets and 1,000 drums. He produced for the exiles a Genevan service book. He also wrote the indiscreet tract, *The First Blast of the Trumpet Against the Monstrous Regiment* [*i.e.*, rule] *of Women,* which successfully closed the England of Elizabeth I against him. He returned to Scotland in 1559. But though Elizabeth liked Knox little and Calvin less, it was imperative for England to offset the Franco-Scottish alliance, and armed forces were dispatched which caused the withdrawal of the French, Knox leading a great service of thanksgiving for "our confederates of England." An attempt at a moderate Counter-Reformation was launched by Archbishop John Hamilton in three national councils (1549, 1552, 1559) and produced a moderate Catholic catechism influenced by the Augsburg Interim (1548) and the theology of Johann Gropper. During critical months when the queen was absent, the Scottish parliament went ahead with reform, abolished the authority of the pope in Scotland and forbade celebration of the Mass. A confession of faith was drawn up, with Knox as principal author. This, the first Scottish Confession (1560), is the most forthright of all the Protestant confessions of the age. A Book of Discipline was also prepared, adjusting the Calvinist polity to the Scottish situation.

This direction from the centre was accompanied by the growth of many "privy kirks," while congregations met also in the houses of the gentry. In 1562 provincial synods were appointed, and in 1564 a revised form of Knox's Genevan liturgy became the official Book of Common Order (*see* LITURGY, CHRISTIAN). The extent to which the Reformation in Scotland was determined by Calvinist blueprints must not be exaggerated, and the first Scottish Reformers were by no means determined to abolish bishops. Not until 1581 was a Second Book of Discipline adopted and the principle of the equal rank of all ministers declared and established. By then Knox had passed from the scene, but the cause of Calvinism found another champion in Andrew Melville (*q.v.*) who had lived in Geneva and was devoted to the Calvinist polity. His political influence was great, but memorable too was his great work for education in Scotland, both in schools and universities. Despite the entanglements with political intrigue in high places, the Reformed church in Scotland was not, as in France, cut off from the people, and it took deep root in the common life of the whole nation. (*See* SCOTLAND, CHURCH OF; PRESBYTERIANISM.)

3. France.—Even more than in Scotland, the Reformation in France was involved in the political struggles between the crown and the nobility. The concordat of 1516 had confirmed royal authority in the church, and Francis I was a Renaissance prince more splendid and more ruthless than England's Henry VIII. During the 15th century France had produced outstanding theologians (Jean de Gerson and Pierre d'Ailly) and the Sorbonne had been the citadel of the conciliar theory which offset the canonist doctrines of the papal plenitude of power. On the eve of the Reformation there were clerics of eminence and reforming zeal—*e.g.*, Jean Standonck and Jean Vitrier, the friend of Erasmus. So strong was the humanist circle in Paris that it was said to be more important than Rome in the field of letters. Supreme among these, in the range of his interests and learning, was Jacques Lefèvre d'Étaples (*q.v.*). By reason of his biblical studies, his edition of the Psalms and his commentaries on St. Paul, he is often hailed as a reformer on the eve of the Reformation; but this is to ignore the eclectic character of his mind, to which his editions of Aristotle, of the Church Fathers, of medieval mystics and of the Hermetic writings bear witness.

As elsewhere, the writings of Luther circulated swiftly in France, and one of the first martyrs was the scholarly Louis de Berquin, who had translated many writings of Erasmus. Soon the church in France was to become a martyr church, commemorated in the martyrology of Jean Crespin (1554), who anticipated the equally potent *Book of Martyrs* of the Englishman John Foxe. Affairs went on in a series of crises. One came in 1533 when the rector of the University of Paris, Nicholas Cop, uttered a plea for toleration in his rectorial address which caused a flurry of panic. Then in Oct. 1534 Catholic opinion was alarmed and shocked when placards virulently attacking the Mass were found in the streets and in the royal palace. Many of reforming sympathies were forced to flee, some scholars taking refuge with Guillaume Briçonnet, bishop of Meaux, and later finding safety at the court of Marguerite de Valois, queen of Navarre. The poet Clément Marot was among them who, though no Lutheran, translated many Psalms, and his beautiful work was influential for French Protestant worship, alongside the translations of Theodore Beza.

A Protestant party quickly grew, supported by a number of more discreet sympathizers whom Calvin called "Nicodemites." They became known as Huguenots, and soon had eminent supporters among the nobility, such as the prince de Condé (Louis I de Bourbon), Adm. Gaspard de Coligny and Duplessis-Mornay. Individual executions began to give way to massacres, and in 1545 about 3,000 Waldensians were brutally done to death. Under Henry II the legal *parlements* took the initiative and soon the prisons were full. The year 1559 was in some ways a turning point. It saw the execution of the eminent French layman Anne de Bourg. It also saw the organization of the scattered Protestant congregations, for an important synod met in Paris and drew up a confession of faith which owed much, though by no means everything, to Calvin. For, despite Calvin's constant interest and incessant correspondence, and the scores of pastors who came to France from Geneva, the French Reformed Church managed its own life, had its own characteristics.

Now began a struggle between the Huguenots and the house of Guise. Attempts at compromise and acts of ruthlessness went on side by side. At the colloquy at Poissy in 1561 the Jesuit theologians faced in debate Theodore Beza and the aged Peter Martyr. But the massacre at Vassy in the following year showed the fierceness of Catholic opposition to reform. Then in 1570 an armistice was called and by this peace of St. Germain-en-Laye toleration was granted and an amnesty, and the Huguenots were allowed the four fortified cities of La Rochelle, Montauban, La Charité and Sognac. Worship was permitted in the homes of the nobility, but not in congregations—a move which cut off the growing movement in some measure from the common people. But in 1572 came the terrible Massacre of St. Bartholomew's day (*q.v.*) in which first Admiral Coligny and then many thousands (between 20,000 and 50,000) perished in Paris and in the rest of France.

THEODORE BEZA, BY AN ANONYMOUS MASTER OF THE FRENCH SCHOOL, 1605; IN THE ARCHIV FÜR KUNST UND GESCHICHTE, BERLIN

This by no means mortal blow only strengthened the Huguenots' resistance, ending an internal struggle about the rights of the congregations, and a democratic view of church polity which had found such formidable champions as the philosopher Petrus Ramus. A growing number of "Politiques," a section of the Catholics led by the duc d'Anjou, came to regard toleration of some kind as the only preventive against anarchy and chaos, and this policy triumphed in the Edict of Nantes (1598; *see* NANTES, EDICT OF). This made large concessions to the Huguenots, allowing them freedom of conscience and liberty of worship in many areas of France, giving them public rights both to hold public assemblies and maintain 200 fortified places and garrisons. The recognition of the Reformed Church as a powerful entity within the state was ominous, since it was obvious that if ever France found its unity under an absolute ruler, such as Louis XIV was to prove, he would not be able to tolerate such a challenge to his power. (*See* also HUGUENOTS.)

4. Holland.—In the Netherlands the struggle for Reformation was protracted by reason of severe persecutions in a land which was under the direct rule of the emperor and because the cause

of Reformation became bound up with the cause of liberation from Spain. In the 17 provinces there was a cultural and religious setting favourable to new ideas—thriving commercial towns in a land which had been the home of the late medieval *devotio moderna* and where the influence of the native Erasmus was marked. As usual, Lutheran influence came first, and two members of Luther's Augustinian order, Heinrich Voes and Johann Esch, were burned in Brussels in 1523. An imperial ordinance of great severity against the new opinions and against those who possessed forbidden heretical literature was passed in 1529, and other fierce edicts followed in 1535 and 1538. But conservative Lutheranism did not suit Dutch austerity and zeal, while Luther's emphasis on civil obedience could not please a nation restive under its foreign overlords. There was a swift development therefore of the Anabaptist movement. This, under the pressure of savage persecution and the death of thousands of humble victims, developed an apocalyptic fervour and contributed to the Anabaptist disaster at Münster where a fanatical chiliastic theocracy, under siege by both Protestant and Catholic forces, was finally destroyed with extreme atrocities in 1535. Meanwhile there was steady infiltration of Protestant literature, and of importance were the writings of the Swiss Reformer Heinrich Bullinger and a vernacular manifesto produced in Anastasius Veluanus' *Leken Wechwyser* ("Guide for the Laity"). Calvin, whose wife came from Lille, kept in sympathetic touch with the growth of a Reformed church which became the dominant form of Dutch Protestantism.

A lull in persecution (1540–45) gave the Reformed churches a chance for growth and consolidation, and the writings of Calvin were reinforced by the powerful preaching of Pierre Brully. In 1561 a confession of faith, the *Confessio Belgica* (the work of Guy de Brès) was published. The Dutch were now determined to be free from Spain, and in 1559 William I the Silent, prince of Orange, urged the states-general to press for the withdrawal of the Spaniards from the land, though not until 1573 did he become Protestant. Amid the fervour of a church struggle which was also a national revolt, violence was inevitable. Such incidents as the wrecking of the interior of Antwerp cathedral in 1566 gave excuse to Philip of Spain and his advisers for still more desperate repression under the dictatorship of the duque de Alba, which succeeded only in uniting the Dutch more closely together. In 1584 William was assassinated. Yet by 1609 the Dutch were strong enough to force upon Spain a 12-year truce which meant the establishment of the Dutch republic. Protestantism was now firmly established in the northern provinces, at the cost of a divided land, since the cause of the Reformation had been stamped out in the ten provinces of the south. In Holland, however, the strict Reformed discipline was established, in which the spirit of freedom and independence was embodied in such pronouncements as that of the synod of Emden that "no church may pretend to domination or pre-eminence over the other churches." This was the beginning of a great half-century for Holland when Dutch art and Dutch theology dominated western Protestantism.

Although strict Calvinism prevailed, it was in Holland that the formidable protest of Jacobus Arminius (*q.v.*) was made against the rigid doctrines of predestination and election. His "Remonstrant party," so-called after the Remonstrance (1610) which asserted in five points the freedom of man's will, became an important rallying place for opposition to Calvinist rigorism (*see* ARMINIANISM). But the Synod of Dort (*q.v.*) in 1619 formally declared the five articles of Calvinism, unconditional election of the predestined, atonement limited to the elect, the total depravity of man, the irresistibility of grace and the perseverance of the saints.

5. Scandinavia.—In Scandinavia, as in England, the crown determined the speed of the Reformation. The hegemony of the kings of Denmark over Norway and Iceland, and the rule of Gustavus I Vasa in Sweden and Finland, imposed the Reformation from above and carried through the secularization of church property.

Denmark.—The turbulent and ruthless Christian II was prepared to use the Reformation in his complex struggle with dissident elements in his dominion, and sought, in 1521, the not very wise advice of the Wittenbergers Martin Reinhardt and Andreas von Karlstadt. But his plans were defeated and he went into exile in 1523. His successor, Frederick I, broke with Rome and furthered Lutheran influence. In Denmark there was a bridge between humanism represented by Paul Helie and Reform represented by Christiern Pedersen (*q.v.*); both were reinforced by Hans Tausen (*q.v.*), "the Danish Luther." In 1529 Pedersen produced a Danish New Testament. A Danish confession of faith (*Confessio Hafniensis*) lacked authority and was superseded in 1536–37 when Lutheranism and the Augsburg Confession were formally adopted. The new church received its church order from Luther's colleague Johann Bugenhagen, who ordained seven superintendents for the reorganized church.

Norway and Iceland.—Norway was culturally and economically more backward than Denmark, and its Reformation was imposed from above by the Danish crown at the same time (1536–37) as that of Denmark. In Iceland after a bloody struggle reminiscent of Viking times the Reformation was imposed by Denmark. The second evangelical bishop, Gudbrandur Thórlaksson, translated the Bible (1584) into Icelandic and produced an Icelandic liturgy.

Sweden and Finland.—The Reformation in Sweden owed most to four men, the ruler Gustavus I Vasa, the archdeacon Laurentius Andreae (Lars Andersson), and the two gifted Reformers, the brothers Olaus and Laurentius Petri (*q.v.*). One feature of the Swedish Reformation, important for its future, was the preservation of the apostolic succession, in the consecration of three bishops in 1528 by royal command and without papal confirmation but using the Catholic rite. In Finland the notable Reformer was Mikael Agricola, a former Wittenberg student who wrote a Finnish catechism and translated the New Testament and much of the Old Testament into Finnish.

The religious Reformation in Scandinavia owed much to Lutheran initiative, to the work of Bugenhagen and to the labours of a number of Scandinavian Reformers who themselves had studied at Wittenberg. Thus these lands became more thoroughly Lutheran even than Germany itself, and almost complete Lutheranism has persisted there.

6. Central and Southern Europe.—In eastern Germany, Lutheranism was advanced by the conversion of the grand master of the Teutonic Knights, and in 1554 the diet of Wolmar declared Livonia to be Lutheran. In Poland a complicated political structure and a heterogeneous population with no strong central authority led to a diversity of Protestantism, including radical Anabaptists, Lutherans, Calvinists and the Unitarianism of the Socinians introduced by Faustus Socinus (*q.v.*). The Compact of Warsaw (1573) affirmed religious liberty for differing religious groups which, however, were ill equipped to meet the challenge of the Counter-Reformation formidably led by the Jesuits. In Bohemia, Lutheran influence touched the various parties in the Hussite churches, and there was Lutheran infiltration among scholars and among the nobility. In Moravia there was an Anabaptist movement, especially at the time of the refugee settlement around Nicolsburg in 1527. Political divisions in Austria made it difficult for the archduke Ferdinand to control events, and despite strong persecution a number of young men from noble houses studied in Protestant universities, while some of the gentry used Lutheranism against the Habsburg rulers. In Hungary, however, a Lutheran minority became strongly entrenched, finding its way at first into the German elements of the population and making headway in a land where the Catholic ecclesiastical structure was crumbling before Turkish invasion. But some found more congenial the second wave of Reformation with its Zwinglian and Calvinist doctrines.

Spain and Italy were to be the great centres of the Counter-Reformation, and in Spain itself a Catholic Reformation had begun under the work of Cardinal Francisco Jiménez de Cisneros (*q.v.*), which also produced the Reformed breviary of Cardinal Francisco de Quiñones, while the Complutensian Polyglot Bible was the monumental achievement of the Spanish humanists of Alcalá. There were a number of mystical groups in some ways reminiscent of the Anabaptists, but within the Catholic framework and power-

fully influenced by Erasmus. The two lay scholars Alfonso and Juan de Valdes were more evangelically inclined, and Juan exercised fruitful influence in Italy. There were groups of so-called Lutherans at Valladolid and Seville. Francisco de Enzinas (*q.v.*; called Dryander) translated the New Testament into Spanish but spent most of his career outside Spain. The most famous of Spanish Protestants was the medical scholar and anti-Trinitarian Michael Servetus.

In Italy, though there was widespread criticism and even skepticism in humanist circles, there were obvious difficulties to the spread of Protestantism in the land of the papacy. Among the many diverse cities and territories of a much-divided land, Venice and Padua offered some protection to Protestants who tended to extreme views. The great Italian preacher Bernardino Ochino (*q.v.*), vicar-general of the Capuchins, went into exile and developed radical views about the Trinity, opinions held in an even more extreme form by the lawyer Laelius Socinus. The greatest Italian Reformer was Pietro Martire Vermigli (*q.v.*), an eminent Augustinian, whose Protestantism, developed in Switzerland, England and Strasbourg, was of a Reformed, perhaps Zwinglian pattern.

VI. RADICALS, ANABAPTISTS AND SPIRITUALISTS

From the beginning of the Reformation movement a body of opinion favoured something more drastic than Luther's bold conservatism. The Puritan iconoclasm of Karlstadt and the apocalyptic violence of Müntzer found support among peasants and artisans, and the writings of both men had lingering influence after the collapse of the Peasant War in Germany. There was criticism of the biblicism of Wittenberg and its deference to secular authorities. The three laymen known as the Zwickau prophets had denounced infant baptism, influenced perhaps by its repudiation in extreme Hussite circles in Bohemia. They had attempted to set up a small community of the elect at Zwickau but in 1521 settled in Wittenberg, whence they were banished by Luther in 1522.

But though infant baptism was denounced in radical circles, it was not until 1525 that the practice of rebaptizing adults began, and it is possible to speak of an Anabaptist movement. This had its origins in Zürich, among the "Swiss brethren," a group of young intellectuals in the entourage of Zwingli, who rebelled against Zwingli's apparent subservience to the magistrates and his reluctance to proceed swiftly with thoroughgoing reform. Their leaders were Conrad Grebel (*q.v.*), of patrician family, a highly educated humanist converted to a narrow biblicism; Felix Manz, also a scholar; and the former priest Georg Blaurock. A series of debates only widened differences with Zwingli, and the sacrament of baptism became the focus of a divergence which embraced different views of the nature of the church, of Christian discipline and of civil government. The first adult baptisms took place at Zollikon outside Zürich at the end of Jan. 1525, and soon something like a mass movement was in progress, particularly strong in Sankt Gallen. The vehemence and intransigence of the leaders, the revolutionary implications of their teaching, led to their expulsion from one city after another, which simply increased the momentum of an essentially missionary movement. Soon the cities took sterner measures and most of the early Anabaptist leaders died in prison or were executed. The Schleitheim Confession (1527), drawn up under the leadership of the Anabaptist Michael Sattler, was not so much a public apologia as a document related to extremist elements within the Anabaptist camp.

In south Germany the Anabaptist movement had its own characteristics and was perhaps bedeviled by an apocalyptic strain which persisted from the time of Müntzer. It found a missionary preacher of power in Hans Hut, a disciple of Müntzer who replaced Müntzer's violent program with a dated eschatology calculated also to provoke unrest. He was rebaptized in Augsburg in 1526 by Hans Denck, in whom radical ideology was softened by Johannine theology. Denck and Hut seem to have presided at two "synods" of Anabaptists in 1527, but after some months of exile Denck withdrew from the movement. Balthasar Hübmaier was a learned theologian of ebullient spirit, who led reform in the

Black forest town of Waldshut until expelled by the Austrian troops. He wandered from city to city, adopting Anabaptist views but differing from most Anabaptists in accepting civil government and defending the use of force. In 1527 he joined the refugee stream to Nicolsburg in Moravia, where the Anabaptists found temporary asylum, and ran into a great number of south German Anabaptists encouraged by Hut to believe in the imminence of the Second Coming of Jesus Christ. There was a disputation between the two leaders, Hübmaier repudiating Hut's eschatology, which named a date for the millennium, and affirming the authority of the magistrates. Hut died in prison in the next months and Hübmaier was executed. The difference was important between the so-called *Schwertler* ("Sword") Anabaptists, who supported the use of force, and the *Stäbler* ("Stave") Anabaptists, who rejected all violence. In central Europe the radical form persisted and set up communities in which a limited communism was practised.

The apocalyptic strain continued in the visionary Messianism of Augustin Bader and Melchior Hoffman (*q.v.*). Hoffman, in jail at Strasbourg, both flattered and horrified the magistrates by announcing that their city had been chosen to inaugurate the new age. The savage persecution of this martyr church has no doubt to do with the emotional extravagances and with an ugly streak of fanaticism which began with the fratricide in Sankt Gallen, when Thomas Schugger decapitated his brother Leonard "in the Spirit," and continued until the development of polygamy at Münster. But there was also a solid core of simple fervent piety which impressed the Strasbourg Reformers Capito and Bucer, who also induced Philip of Hesse to pursue a tolerant and profitable policy. In the layman engineer, Pilgram Marpeck, the south German Anabaptists found a leader of considerable moral stature and one whose sincerity and deep biblical learning were of great importance for the development of the movement at a dangerous stage in its affairs, when it might have been unbalanced by apocalyptic visionaries.

In Holland the movement grew swiftly and here again Messianism appeared in the figure of David Joris (*q.v.*). Savage punishment led again to a refugee movement which aroused the fatal hope finding the city of refuge in Münster, Westphalia. During its siege (1534–35) the leadership passed from Jan Mathijs to the schizophrenic John of Leiden (Jan Beuckelson), whose insane brutality, added to the scandal of public polygamy, brought appalling publicity upon the movement, widely discrediting it in the eyes of all authorities, just at a time when it had thrown up a leader of noble piety and moderation in Menno Simons (*q.v.*).

The Anabaptist movement must not be oversystematized. It was a congeries of radical groups, shading off into other forms of radicalism, which included those who would give allegiance to no form of reformed Christianity. Such were Sebastian Franck (*q.v.*), the chronicler, and his friend John Campanus, author of *Contra totum post apostolos mundum* ("Against All the World From the Time of the Apostles") and the Silesian nobleman Kaspar von Schwenckfeld (*q.v.*), who developed eccentric Christological and eucharistic doctrines, about which he wrote controversial tracts and which attracted some adherents. In addition to departures from orthodox Christology, there was the development of anti-Trinitarian arguments, by Ludwig Hetzer and by the obstreperous and violent Michael Servetus (*qq.v.*), while in the writings of Bernardino Ochino (*q.v.*) are to be found the beginnings of Unitarianism.

VII. ASSESSMENT OF FUNDAMENTAL ISSUES

It is inevitable that there should be controversy about the meaning of the Reformation. It was a revolution which affected not only religion but other spheres of life. Its drastic program attacked not only generally acknowledged abuses but beliefs and practices which many Christians preferred to retain, distinguishing between needful reforms and revolutionary schism. Moreover, revolutions seldom fulfill the hopes of their makers, and the Reformation movement became caught up in political and social pressures in which religious men and their ideals were dwarfed.

Yet the Reformation cannot be understood unless it is realized that Catholics and Protestants alike believed that the gravest issues were at stake for which men must be prepared to die. Had the Reformers been asked what it was all about, they might have said that it was a conflict about the Word of God. One way and another, their creative first works centred here.

To understand the Reformation it is necessary to give full weight to the underlying theological and religious convictions which sustained it. During the 16th century basic Christian doctrines and ideas were argued, examined and redefined. It would be an oversimplification to suggest that these were at all times and everywhere the dominant causes of a revolution complex in origin and dependent on a variety of historical, political, social and economic circumstances. None the less the sequence of events which began with Luther's 95 theses and within Christendom, and ended in the separated nations and divided churches of the modern world, cannot be understood without constant reference to those religious beliefs.

The Reformation began with a crisis of conscience, embodied in the spiritual struggles of Martin Luther. Through him the doctrine of justification by faith gained priority on the Protestant theological agenda. The doctrine that salvation is a divine gift had been at the heart of the theology of St. Paul and St. Augustine and was never lost sight of in medieval theology. But the Reformers sought to safeguard this truth against a legalistic religion of works and merit, what Gilbert Burnet called a "superannuated Judaism." The doctrine of salvation "by faith alone" was intended to emphasize, once and for all, that the ground of the Christian hope is in the forgiving mercy of God, displayed to mankind in Jesus Christ and apprehended by faith.

The assertion of man's personal experience of God, as opposed to his acceptance of the authority of the church and its mediation, led inevitably to emphasis on the authority of Scripture, interpreted not by tradition but by the guidance of the Holy Spirit. Although this led to extreme Puritanism, which condemned all not expressly ordained in the Bible, and to fundamentalist belief in the Bible's literal truth and equal value, in the early Reformers, at least, it was joined with a scholarly attitude to biblical texts and to a testing of the value of its parts by the extent to which they conformed to Christ's revelation of God. The Bible was to be understood as a revelation of salvation in the light of reason and scholarship, and was seen to have supreme authority. Thus the Reformers repudiated the papal plenitude of power and set against it the authority of the Scriptures, interpreted by the Holy Spirit through the Christian church and the consciences of Christian men. Though they rejected the "traditions of men"—unscriptural infiltrations in faith and worship unsupported by, or even contrary to, the witness of the Bible—the Reformers did not reject tradition; they themselves appealed to the Church Fathers, the councils and the life of the early church.

Thus the Bible had great importance in the age of the Reformation. Vernacular Bibles existed and were printed before the time of Luther, but the innumerable editions of Luther's translation led the way in one country after another to the use of the vernacular Bible. These were the work of scholars using the humanist tools of languages and critical method. The new translations heralded a new method of exegesis and of preaching. Especially influential were the commentaries of Calvin and Bullinger, and Luther, Zwingli, Knox, Latimer were among the outstanding Christian preachers in church history. There is testimony from Catholics, such as Johann Faber, that the Reformation did indeed bring into being a new and virile form of biblical exposition, while the emphasis on the Word of God meant a reorientation of the place of preaching in the office of a minister and in the life of the worshiping congregation. One should not mention the fine, outstanding preachers without noting how concerned they were at the low level of most of the clergy in this matter; the provision of books of homilies and the long battle for an educated clergy in the England of Elizabeth I shows what a grave problem this was. (*See* also PREACHING.)

St. Paul and St. Augustine stressed the grace of God, the divine love and the divine initiative which evokes, accompanies and brings to fulfillment the human response to the calling of God. God predestined those whom he would save, in Christ, before the foundation of the world. Problems concerning this election and predestination, and concerning the fate of the nonelect, or reprobate, were a constant medieval theme, and the Reformers continued an already ancient and intricate debate. Calvin systematized the teaching of earlier Reformers like Luther and Bucer. Divine grace was contrasted with the total depravity of men since the Fall. A double predestination of elect and reprobate was affirmed. To those elect and called, all needful grace, including that of final perseverance, would unfailingly be given. It must be remembered that in practice this did not lead to a passive quietism but to the courageous independence of the Dutch patriots or the Scottish Covenanters. None the less, the dualism of the system, the uncertainty about a man's own election, brought problems of conscience which Puritan moral theology tried but on the whole failed to resolve. (*See* also PREDESTINATION.)

All the Reformers agreed that Christ's sacrifice for the sin of the world was made sufficiently, once for all, on the cross. This affected their attitude to the Eucharist and to the ministry. The medieval priest's first duty was to celebrate the sacrifice of the Mass: the new ministers and clergy were to preach the Word and to administer the sacraments, sharing with their people the only acceptable sacrifice of prayer, praise, penitence and thanksgiving. In their thought the communion of the faithful dominated the idea of sacrifice. To this end they restored to the laity communion "in both kinds" (the cup had been withheld from them during the middle ages). But if they agreed about repudiating the Mass, they were grievously divided over the nature of the divine presence in the Eucharist.

Martin Luther's belief in the real presence was a consequence not of scholastic reasoning, but of simple acceptance of the literal meaning of the words of Christ, "This is my body," which meant for him the presence of the whole Christ, God and man, with his faithful people. This meaning was challenged first by Luther's colleague Karlstadt and then by Zwingli, while Oecolampadius brought the support of his patristic learning to the alternative doctrine of a true but spiritual presence. The Strasbourg theologians supported the Swiss, the Swabians Luther, in a debate which became more and more bitter. At the conference at Marburg in Oct. 1529 the leading theologians on both sides conferred and debated but came to no agreement about the Eucharist, and the hope of a common political front was smashed on the eucharistic division. One consequence was that Bucer realized that he had misunderstood Luther to mean a local, physically circumscribed presence and henceforward was earnest in trying to reach agreement which he achieved in the Wittenberg Concord (1536). This brought the Strasbourg and Wittenberg theologians together but failed to win the Swiss. Calvin developed his own stresses in doctrine, which were of a mediating kind, and in 1549 achieved the agreement with Zürich (the *Consensus Tigurinus*) which made possible the consolidation of the Reformed, as distinct from the Lutheran churches.

The first textbook of the new theology was Philipp Melanchthon's *Loci communes rerum theologicarum* (1521), superseded by the majestic 1559 edition of the *Christianae religionis institutio* of Calvin. The martyrologies of Jean Crespin in France and John Foxe in England helped to sustain for centuries the memory of persecution. The conflict with Catholic authorities, with pope, emperor and the Council of Trent, as well as internal conflicts in the Protestant ranks, produced some important confessions of faith, of which outstanding examples are the Lutheran Augsburg Confession (1530), the First Helvetic Confession (1536), the Scots Confession (1560) and the Thirty-Nine Articles (1571) with the Anabaptist Schleitheim articles (1527). (*See* also CONFESSIONS OF FAITH, PROTESTANT.)

The Reformation produced far-reaching liturgical experiments and changes, not least those involved in the general repudiation of the Mass and the restoration of communion in both kinds to the laity. Thomas Müntzer and Thomas Cranmer both achieved a creative feat by turning the Latin medieval choir offices into ver-nacular services for the congregation. In the new rites of the Eucharist, the communion of the faithful and the commemorative aspect dominated or excluded the thought of sacrifice. Luther's German Mass (1526) was the forerunner of numerous church orders in Lutheran lands, and other notable centres of liturgical reform were Strasbourg and Geneva. Zwingli and the Anabaptists sought and in part achieved the supposed simplicity of the original apostles. The new emphasis on the priesthood of the believing congregation gave hymn- and psalm-singing an important place in Protestant worship. The Reformers themselves wrote fine hymns, and Wittenberg, Strasbourg, Constance and the Anabaptist congregations produced hymnbooks.

That the Word must be heard and understood was a principle which resulted in a stress on education. The work of Luther and Melanchthon in Germany was paralleled by the schools of Johannes Sturm in Strasbourg and Theodore Beza in Geneva. Among many catechisms, noble documents are Luther's children's catechism and the Heidelberg catechism of the Reformed Church.

Though the Reformers repudiated the papacy and a Catholic theory and rite of ordination, they did not disavow church order or a regular and ordained ministry. Differences in emphasis led to the differences in forms of church government. The Lutherans believed that every church had the right to establish its own order, in conformity only with the example of the early church as described in the Bible. No order was divinely ordained, so that some discretion could be allowed to each church to act according to external circumstances. This attitude was also, in the main, adopted by the Reformers in England, and there, as in the German states and in Scandinavia, the Reformed (Lutheran) church became also the national church. Calvinists, on the other hand, laid down an order of church government deriving its authority from its members—a spiritual democracy, in fact—imposing, however, a high degree of discipline and, although independent from the state, using secular power to enforce its rule. Their attitude to episcopacy varied. The churches of England and Sweden retained the historic episcopate within the apostolic succession, but for the most part the Reformers regarded continuity of doctrine as more important than succession of order. In some Lutheran lands and in some Reformed churches, the office of bishop was retained. For both Lutheran and Reformed churches it was essential that ministers of Word and Sacrament should be properly called and lawfully appointed. Calvin, and the Reformed churches generally, rejected the monarchical episcopate which elevates one minister above others, and returned to what was thought to be the practice of the early church as deduced from the New Testament—that of a parity of ministers, together with the office of lay elder. Among radical groups in England and on the continent of Europe there were those who stressed the autonomy of each congregation and its capacity to call and appoint its own minister. In opposition to the idea of a national church or *Volkskirche*, the Anabaptists set forward the ideal of a church of believers, kept pure from the world by strict discipline. In England there was a similar protest against the Elizabethan establishment by those who believed the church to be evoked by the Word of God and gathered out of the world into companies of believers: the living, believing, worshiping congregation was the church, and in its life there was the fullness of catholicity; it was free to exercise its own authority in accordance with the Word of God and need not tarry for any magistrate. From such separatist congregations there developed the Independent churches of the Commonwealth period and the modern Congregational Church.

Reaction against an overclericalized medieval world was bound to give prominence to the laity, who during the later middle ages had played an increasingly important role in the Christian world. This tendency continued among the Reformers, for example, the lay magistrate Vadianus (Joachim von Watt) and the lay schoolmaster and preacher Johannes Kessler, in the Swiss city of Sankt Gallen. In the kingdoms and in the cities a swift and effective instrument for Reformation was the "godly prince" and the "godly magistrate." The granting of the *jus reformandi* to the lay authority had its dangers, and the Anabaptists were not the only ones to point them out. The lay authorities on the other hand were no less apprehensive of a new Protestant clericalism in which new presbyter might be old priest writ large. Calvin, and the Reformed churches after him, sought to safeguard the right of the church to keep its own discipline. Only the Anabaptists repudiated altogether the theory of a Christian commonwealth, sometimes denying that Christians could be magistrates, sometimes contracting out of the political order to form a "pure" society with its own strict discipline.

The Reformers, Luther least of all, did not reckon with the astonishing resilience and power of recovery of the papacy, with those forces of inner renewal, which, beginning in Italy and Spain, produced the Counter-Reformation and which deserve to be considered in their own right as a Catholic Reformation (*see* ROMAN CATHOLIC CHURCH; JESUS, SOCIETY OF). Yet here, too, something was owed to the Réformation itself. It seems unlikely that anything but the immense shock of a grave disaster, a life and death crisis, could have led to the changes which the Western Church had for centuries resisted or postponed.

So far this assessment has been concerned with good religious men, some of them great men, half a dozen of them perhaps spiritual giants. But from the first there were lesser men involved with meaner motives. The ruthless egotists, the cynics, often in high places of commanding power, were able to use and exploit the movement of reform, sometimes to support political ambition, sometimes more excusably to use the wealth of the church as an escape from economic problems which were grave. The over-all picture of the age of the Reformation is therefore infinitely complex and leaves little room for romanticism. None the less, considering the needs of the church, the complexity of the task of reform, the small numbers involved (for no more than 300 Reformers are prominent in history books) there was great creative achievement. New forms of Christian proclamation and truth, new forms of worship and piety, new institutions, new philanthropies were created, above all great new communions of men and women able to endure and grow for centuries, nourished by the unexhausted inheritance received in the first works of the Protestant Reformation.

See LUTHERANISM; PRESBYTERIANISM; REFORMED CHURCHES; *see* also references under "Reformation" in the Index.

BIBLIOGRAPHY.—L. von Ranke, *History of the Reformation in Germany* (1845–47); P. Schaff, *Creeds of the Evangelical Protestant Churches* (1877); I. de la Tour, *Origines de la Réforme*, 3 vol. (1905–14); T. M. Lindsay, *History of the Reformation*, 2 vol. (1906–07); B. J. Kidd, *Documents illustrating the Continental Reformation* (1911); J. Lortz, *Die Reformation in Deutschland*, 2 vol. (1939); G. Ritter, *Die Neugestaltung Europas im 16. Jahrhundert* (1950); H. Strohl, *La Pensée de la Réforme* (1951); P. Joachimsen, "Das Zeitalter der Reformation," *Propyläen Weltgeschichte*, vol. v (1951); W. Koehler, *Dogmengeschichte der Reformation* (1951); W. Andreas, *Deutschland vor der Reformation* (1953); R. Bainton, *The Reformation of the 16th Century* (1953); H. J. Grimm, *The Reformation Era* (1954); J. T. MacNeill, *History and Character of Calvinism* (1954); G. R. Elton (ed.), *New Cambridge Modern History*, vol. ii (1958); A. Renaudet, *Préréforme et humanisme*, rev. ed. (1960); E. G. Léonard, *Histoire générale du Protestantisme*, 2 vol. (1961); G. H. Williams, *The Radical Reformation* (1963).   (E. G. Ru.)

REFORMATION DAY, the anniversary of the posting of the 95 Theses by Martin Luther on Oct. 31, 1517, thought of as the beginning of the Reformation. At first the European Lutheran territorial churches commemorated the Reformation on various days, among them the anniversary of Luther's birth (Nov. 10), his death (Feb. 18), and the presentation of the Augsburg Confession (June 25). The centennial celebrations of 1617 focused attention on Oct. 31; in the sesquicentennial year 1667 Elector John George II decreed this date as annual Reformation Day in Saxony. German Lutheran and Union territorial churches came gradually to follow this example and specify Oct. 31 or the Sunday following (or preceding). Among English-speaking Lutherans, the bodies that use the *Lutheran Liturgy* (1948) keep Oct. 31 with an octave; those using the *Service Book and Hymnal* (1958) keep Oct. 31 as Reformation Day and may keep the preceding Sunday as Reformation Sunday. The liturgical colour is red. By custom many North American Protestant churches hold services of evangelical witness on Oct. 31 or the nearest Sunday.   (A. C. Pn.)

REFORMATORY, a correctional institution for the treatment, training, and social rehabilitation of youthful offenders. Institutions designated as reformatories are of two general types: (1) residential training schools for school-age delinquents; and (2) facilities for the confinement of youthful offenders between the ages of 16 and 25 who have been convicted of criminal acts. These institutions, as their name implies, were originally intended to reform criminal youth. Now frequently referred to by the more descriptive title "correctional training schools," they represent a relatively recent development in the treatment of criminal behaviour. For a survey of philosophies and methods of crime control *see* CRIMINOLOGY: *Correction*. *See* also PRISON; CHILDREN'S COURT; JUVENILE DELINQUENCY.

HISTORY

Youthful offenders as a group were first separated from the general population of prisons and jails in the 18th century. In England, concern for the very young offender was manifested in the efforts of such organizations as the Marine Society, which was formed in 1756 to establish a school for waifs, strays, and the children of convicts; and the Philanthropic Society, which in 1788 opened a school for the children of convicts in London. These were primarily preventive efforts. Early in the 19th century, private reformatories were established under a law which enabled the crown to grant a pardon on condition that the offender place himself in the care of a charitable institution. Under this provision, Farm Colony (Stretton Colony), at Stretton in Warwickshire, was founded in 1817, and could validly claim to be the first reformatory.

Experience with institutions such as Farm Colony was favourable enough to lead to the enactment in 1854 of the first Youthful Offenders Act, which authorized the courts to commit to a reformatory offenders under the age of 16 who had been imprisoned for not less than 14 days. Such offenders would serve terms of not less than two nor more than five years. It is not clear that the regime in effect differed significantly from the repressive discipline of hard labour then prevailing in English prisons, except that some effort was made to maintain a segregation of age groups.

In the United States, experience with reformatories began in 1825 with the New York City House of Refuge, which accepted delinquent and neglected children. Similar institutions were founded in Boston and Philadelphia at about the same time. In France, an especially significant innovation was the agricultural colony of Mettray, founded in 1839. This institution received delinquent children under the age of 16, the "age of discernment" under French law, and kept them in cottages under what was referred to as a "family system."

In 1876 the first significant U.S. contribution to the reformatory movement took place with the establishment of the Elmira (N.Y.) Reformatory. This institution, which early achieved international attention by its annual reports, was historically important because (1) it was the first public reformatory institution for the specialized care of youthful offenders; and (2) it represented public acceptance of the view that, up to a certain age, every criminal might be regarded as potentially a good citizen and that it was the duty of the state to try to effect a cure. Under this principle Elmira Reformatory from the first operated under an indeterminate sentence system, by which release was determined by progress made under the program of training rather than by a judicially established sentence. The regime at Elmira provided for a system of moral, physical, and industrial training followed by parole supervision, all of which was adapted by Sir Evelyn Ruggles-Brise in the organization of the Borstal system (*q.v.*) in 1908 in England.

Early enthusiasm aroused by the reformatory movement was not followed by conspicuous success. Public apathy, uninspired administrative direction, and the lack of professional leadership combined to reduce most reformatories to a condition of bureaucratic stagnation in which, except by the age groups they confined, they were indistinguishable from adult prisons.

MODERN TRENDS

After World War II, the reformatory movement profited from an increase of interest in the behavioural sciences. New correctional training institutions began to emphasize new and varied treatment approaches, including individual and group therapy, therapeutic community plans, establishment of "bridges to the community" by participation of professional and lay persons from the community at large in institutional programs, and family case-work and counseling. The older systems, which emphasized military drill, punitive calisthenics, and "cadet officers," have fallen into disrepute, surviving only in places where community interest in correctional treatment is at a low ebb.

Types.—Modern institutions vary in every respect except their assigned task to confine and treat the youthful offender. Students of trends in these institutions have classified them in five significant patterns or types of approach to the common aim of reformation, now generally called resocialization to emphasize the goal of training the individual offender for life in society at large. These patterns are:

Disciplinary.—In the tradition of the conventional reformatory, these institutions emphasize respect for authority, good habits, and conformity to standards. Often the programs of such institutions will follow a military pattern, and there will be stress on staff domination and adherence to strict rules.

Training.—This type of institution seeks to change behaviour patterns through teaching and training. It provides gratifications and incentives to change rather than relying heavily on negative sanctions.

Mixed Goals.—While stressing obedience, this type of institution sets out to emphasize the development of individual controls. The authority of the staff is as unquestioned as in the disciplinary type of institution, but attempts are made to bring about behaviour changes through inmate-staff relationships extending to psychotherapy and other practices diverging from emphasis on strict obedience.

Individual Treatment.—A few institutions have adopted programs emphasizing gratifications and incentives, with individual counseling and psychotherapy stressed as mediums for bringing about personality change. Punishments at such institutions are few and seldom severe.

Milieu Treatment.—In institutions using milieu treatment, there is an attempt to effect change through the development of both individual and social controls. Attention is given not only to the personal problems of clients but also to their preparation for life in the community. Specialized psychiatric and casework personnel are utilized, but their attention is focused on the structure of the institutional community so that all activities are mobilized for treatment effect. Few negative sanctions and many incentives for participation are built into the system.

There is general agreement that whatever kind of program is in force, a system of aftercare is a necessity. The approach to aftercare, usually referred to as parole (*q.v.*), varies from surveillance, to perfunctory case-reporting, to sophisticated counseling relationships based on psychotherapeutic concepts. Many systems in the United States, for example, notably that of the California Youth Authority, integrate a variety of institutions with a flexible parole program designed to capitalize on institutional services.

Examples of Programs.—In the United States there are about 200 youth correctional institutions of all types administered by the 50 states, and the federal system managed by the U.S. Bureau of Prisons. Three experimental programs have received widespread attention as alternatives to lengthy and stigmatizing institutionalization. They are: the Highfields residential training centre in Hopewell, N.J.; the Pinehills project in Provo, Utah; and the Youth Authority's Community Treatment Center in Sacramento and Stockton, Calif. These progressive programs emphasize individualized treatment of short duration, aimed at inducing adherence to acceptable norms through peer-group influences as well as staff treatment. Highfields treatment is designed for groups of 20 youths living together for four months and undergoing a simple program of work and "guided group interaction." Pinehills provides nonresidential care consisting of after-school work on civic improvement projects followed by daily sessions of group counseling. California's community treatment relies on caseloads of 10, in which counselors working with individualized treatment

plans supervise youthful offenders in the community with no institutional confinement beyond a brief diagnostic study at a reception centre. All three of these programs are based on well-developed behavioural theory, and promise to reduce both the human and economic cost of correctional care.

English reformatory services have traditionally been divided between "approved schools" for the school-age delinquent, and the Borstal system for the older boy or girl. Dissatisfaction with these long-term residential services as costly and inappropriately severe for the delinquent in minor difficulties has resulted in a third variety of institution, the detention centre. These small institutions receive boys for periods of three to six months and administer a vigorous program of work and athletics. While there has been much criticism by psychiatrists and social workers of the indiscriminate nature of the detention centre approach, in which no attempt is made to diagnose, preliminary studies of their statistical success suggest that they compare well with the results achieved by Borstals and approved schools with somewhat similar boys.

Approved schools are maintained for delinquent children up to early adolescence when judged in need of long-term removal from undesirable surroundings. There are about 120 such schools with a total population of approximately 10,000. Many are maintained by private philanthropic foundations to which the government contributes a per capita rate for each child committed. Others are entirely maintained by the government. Because of the large number of these schools, it is possible to provide for specialized services through the use of strategically located schools for diagnosis and classification. Several schools have made innovations in treatment approaches, notably Aycliff, which has stressed the use of reinforcement of behaviour through incentive systems, and the Park School, in Surrey, which has used social casework methods in attempts to involve family members in the treatment programs of its residents.

The approved school model has been widely copied in Scandinavia, where systems of small residential schools have been established. At the Children's Village (Barnbyn Skå) near Stockholm, a therapeutic-community type of treatment has been pioneered under psychiatric leadership. An unusual feature of this school is its coeducational organization, despite the highly disturbed condition of most of its population. In Denmark, an unusual feature of the reformatory system is its incorporation in a larger system of child welfare schools intended for problem children whether delinquent or not. In the Netherlands, experiments have been successfully carried out in the management of residential care for delinquent boys in a vocational training institution attended also by nondelinquent day-school boys. French reformatories have continued the tradition of family cottages managed by specially trained social workers. Care is given to maintain continuity of treatment relationships so that as little interference as possible occurs in the parental relationship of house-parents to children.

In the Soviet Union, interest in the exploitation of group influences to change and maintain behaviour patterns has been continuous since the Revolution. This interest has been directed not only at the rehabilitation, or resocialization, of delinquents but also at inducting young people into the normal processes of industrial, agricultural, and community life. The leadership of Anton S. Makarenko, a gifted educator of the early postrevolutionary era, was aimed at developing a sense of community among the homeless children of that chaotic period. Observing the salutary effect on the individual of participation in the group solution of practical problems, he advocated the development of corrective labour colonies for youth in which remedial education would be combined with work projects in which all would join.

Soviet authorities minimize the incidence of delinquency in the U.S.S.R., but many residential schools have been established in which delinquent and nondelinquent children are housed and taught together. Little attention is given to aftercare, as it is known in Western countries, because of continuities which are established between schools and workers' collectives.

Summary.—The reformatory movement made significant contributions to modern penology with the introduction of indeterminate sentences and separate institutions for youthful offenders based on the premise that most youths are capable of resocialization. The early reformatories, however, did not fulfill the enthusiastic promise responsible for their establishment, and many still resemble junior prisons, with rigid discipline and little treatment. After World War II, however, more and more correctional training programs for youthful offenders were aimed at resocialization through remedial academic and vocational education, reinforced by sophisticated uses of group influences and, where indicated, psychiatric treatment. The experience of these institutions was beginning to show that for many classes of youthful offenders, long terms of confinement could be drastically shortened, if not entirely eliminated. Thus, with the development of correctional training schools, the reformatory movement had virtually abandoned the older term "reformatory," with which it began, and seemed to be on the way to abolishing the prisonlike institution it used to describe.

BIBLIOGRAPHY.—Harry E. Barnes and Negley K. Teeters, *New Horizons in Criminology* (1959) ; Herbert A. Bloch and Frank T. Flynn, *Delinquency, the Juvenile Offender in America Today* (1956) ; Lionel W. Fox, *The English Prison and Borstal Systems* (1952) ; John Gittins, *Approved School Boys* (1952) ; Howard Jones, *Crime and the Penal System,* 2nd ed. (1962) ; Sheldon Glueck, *The Problem of Delinquency* (1959) ; Anton S. Makarenko, *The Road to Life,* translated by Ivy Litvinov (1955) ; Paul W. Tappan, *Contemporary Correction* (1951), *Juvenile Delinquency* (1949), *Crime, Justice, and Correction* (1960) ; United Nations Department of Economic and Social Affairs, *Comparative Survey of Juvenile Delinquency,* part i, "North America" (1958), *The Prevention of Juvenile Delinquency in Selected European Countries* (1955), *European Exchange Plan Seminar on the Institutional Treatment of Juvenile Offenders* (1954) ; University of Michigan, School of Social Work, *The Comparative Study of Juvenile Correctional Institutions: a Research Report* (1961).   (R. A. McG. ; Jo. P. C.)

REFORMED CHURCHES are those European churches which during the Reformation undertook to reform their faith and life, as they declared, "according to the Word of God," under the leadership of such men as Huldreich Zwingli, Martin Bucer, John Oecolampadius, Guillaume Farel, John Calvin, and Heinrich Bullinger. The Evangelical (or Protestant) Reformation of the 16th century was a many-sided answer to a complex and long-standing set of problems. (*See* REFORMATION.) Consequently, it was inevitable that reform, when it came, was of several varieties. The Reformed churches represent one general type or pattern of reform which emerged in this period. The pattern first took form in Strasbourg and in Zürich, later spreading over much of Switzerland, southern Germany, France, the Netherlands, Hungary, and the British Isles, with lesser influences elsewhere. These churches are now worldwide in distribution.

Various names are used for the Reformed group of churches: Reformed, Presbyterian, and Calvinistic. The name Reformed is that most commonly used on the European continent. Originally, however, all the Reformation churches used this name (or Evangelical) to distinguish themselves from the "unreformed" or unchanged Roman Church. After the great controversy among these churches over the Lord's Supper (after 1529) the followers of Luther began to use the name Lutheran as a specific name, and the name Reformed became widely used of the other Reformation churches (including the Church of England in the 16th century). The name Presbyterian, properly, refers to the form of church polity used by the Reformed churches. Eventually, however, this term came to be used of all the Reformed churches of British background; hence these are discussed separately in the article PRESBYTERIANISM. The name Calvinistic has become almost synonymous with Reformed and Presbyterian, though John Calvin (*q.v.*) was of the second generation of leaders of these churches rather than the first. Coming after the first great reformers, he systematized, adapted, and improved upon their work. He was the greatest intellect among these early leaders and the most influential upon subsequent generations.

HISTORY
BEGINNINGS IN CHRISTIAN HUMANISM

The first phase of the development of that pattern of reformation typical of the Reformed churches occurred in the German-speaking areas of Switzerland and in southern Germany. Here, in a region deeply influenced by the newer intellectual currents of humanism, growing urban culture, and freer movements of people, trade, and ideas, the demand for reformation assumed a distinct character. The early leaders were the so-called Christian humanists, Desiderius Erasmus, Johann Reuchlin, Jacob Wimpfeling, Beatus Rhenanus, and others. Impatient of the obscurantism of the recent past, bitterly critical of the monastic orders, often anticlerical and antihierarchical, the humanists called for a return to a simple Bible-centred piety and for repudiation of emphasis on sacramentalism, institutional religion, and technical dogma. Renaissance humanism had sought to reinvigorate European intellectual life by advocating a "return to the sources"; *i.e.*, to the great classics of ancient Greece and Rome. The Christian humanists urged a return to the sources of Christianity (*i.e.*, to the Bible and to the early Church Fathers) as a means of recapturing the true nature and spirit of Christianity. Here they found a simple "philosophy of Christ" which taught that Christianity was a way of life, nurtured and furthered by education and by earnest ethical endeavour.

Almost every early Reformed leader in Switzerland and in southern Germany—Zwingli in Zürich, Oecolampadius in Basel, Bucer and Wolfgang Capito in Strasbourg, Franz Lambert in Marburg, and Farel in Bern (and elsewhere later)—had begun as a Christian humanist. However, the frank, nontraditional study of the Bible and the early Church Fathers which these men advocated made many of them dissatisfied with humanism's avoidance of serious theological issues such as the problem of sin or the nature of grace. Luther's break with the Roman faith (1517 to 1520 especially) gave to these men's thinking a new sense of direction and of urgency. Yet, as they and Luther recognized, they were not dependent upon Luther nor were they his disciples. Rather they developed a pattern of reform from their own backgrounds and studies. Their desire to "return to the sources" led them to try to restore insofar as possible the primitive patterns of church life and institutions. Like many humanists they regarded the original form of an idea or institution as the best and most ideal. Therefore, the New Testament church was the church closest to the divine plan and intention, and its pattern ought to be the standard by which all subsequent changes and developments were judged. This return to the sources led to a much more radical reform than in Lutheranism or in Anglicanism and to a sweeping away of much more of traditional Roman views and usages.

Other marked continuations of humanistic concerns were openness to cultural change and great emphasis upon ethical, political, and intellectual problems. A change, however, came in that these concerns were now dealt with more and more upon the basis of a Pauline-Augustinian view of sin, grace, etc. In general, these reformers, especially Bucer, looked for the renewal of the whole of society—religious, moral, intellectual, political—by a rebirth through divine grace which would in some measure restore the original goodness of the whole of God's creation. Concern for these aspects of human life, therefore, was not regarded as secular or nonreligious. Rather, the healing and renewal of society in general was a vital part of redemption.

SWITZERLAND

Origins.—Zürich, a city already conditioned by humanism, broke from Roman Catholicism in 1522 in a manner that was to become virtually standard for all the Swiss cities, or cantons, and that was to have far-reaching consequences. The Swiss, in general, had been loyal to the papacy, yet episcopal authority was vague in many cantons for a variety of reasons. Moreover, the Swiss had developed a remarkable federation of their cantons, within each of which a democratically elected government was in almost complete control of internal affairs. When controversy over the preaching of Zwingli and his colleagues broke out in 1522, the Council of Zürich assumed jurisdiction on the grounds that as the elected government it was the expression of the will of the people. Zwingli and his colleagues demanded a public disputation between the Roman priests and the reforming party, and that thereafter the Council, in the name of the people, should determine the theological character of the church in Zürich. Over a three-year period, 1522–25, the Council of Zürich accepted a fully Protestant church reform. Basel did likewise in 1525 under the leadership of Oecolampadius, Capito, and Farel. Bern, the most powerful of all the cantons, followed suit in 1528. Sankt Gallen, Biel, and others also made the change in the same manner.

Opposition from those cantons which remained Roman Catholic grew, and Zürich and Bern led in the formation of the Christian Civic League in defense of the Evangelical Reformation. Eventually even German cities such as Strasbourg joined, and Hesse and Württemberg showed interest. The Roman forces now joined in the Christian Union. In the two wars that followed (1529 and 1531), the Evangelical forces were finally defeated, Zwingli was killed, and the Evangelical advance was all but permanently halted. Moreover, political leadership in Swiss Protestantism passed from Zürich to Bern. Evangelical and Roman groups agreed to recognize the right of each other to exist. Heinrich Bullinger succeeded Zwingli as leader in the church at Zürich. (See also SWITZERLAND: *History;* ZWINGLI, HULDREICH.)

Meanwhile the controversy over the Lord's Supper had broken the Swiss reformers away (after 1529) from the German reformers led by Luther and had brought the Strasbourg reformers led by Bucer into the role of unsuccessful mediators (see BUCER, MARTIN). After Zwingli's death Bullinger and the other Swiss reformers came to an understanding with Bucer, and even with Philipp Melanchthon, but they could not do so with Luther. Henceforth no one theological mind dominated the Reformation of the Swiss-German Rhineland, and a great area of mutual agreement gradually arose. Bern took over and advanced the policy laid out by Zürich of forwarding the Reformation by open debate and elections. In the furtherance of this policy Bern had as agents a number of Evangelical preachers—of whom Farel was one of the leaders—who went everywhere, preaching and debating in Roman Catholic areas. So successful were their efforts that in 1532 it was possible to call a synod of 230 Evangelical preachers at Bern. Bucer was present as an adviser.

Farel turned his attention to Geneva in 1532 but found progress very slow and difficult. Only after riots and threats of force by both Catholic and Protestant cantons did Geneva finally agree to hold a public disputation in 1534. Catholic troops led by the prince-bishop besieged Geneva. Bern, by coming into the war, saved Geneva and crushed the forces of the ruling House of Savoy. This brought Geneva somewhat under Bern's tutelage, with Farel as the religious leader. He was, however, unable to get an Evangelical church life established in any real measure the first year.

Farel saved the situation by persuading John Calvin, a young French Evangelical refugee, to become his assistant. Calvin had, in addition to great theological and pastoral gifts, unusual organizing abilities. Geneva had become Evangelical for political reasons, and it wished to do as Bern, Zürich, and other Swiss cities had—that is, control and use the church. Calvin and the other Genevan pastors demanded independence for the church in religious matters and the right to criticize on religious grounds the acts of the government and the moral life of the city. The church, however, was to have no authority in civil matters. After three years Farel and Calvin were dismissed by the civil authorities because of this clash of ideas (1538). Calvin became a pastor in Strasbourg. In 1541 he returned to Geneva as pastor and teacher.

Genevan Reform.—Work was now begun on the reforming of the church in Geneva. Calvin followed many of the ideas of the older reformers, including Luther, but with some notable adaptations and additions which soon came to be characteristic in a general way of most of the Reformed churches. One of the major causes of the Reformation as a whole had been the urgent demand for moral renewal. Humanist, Lutheran, and Reformed leaders all sought this moral renewal in various ways. Zwingli and Bucer had made some slight progress in the matter, but Calvin instituted a system of church discipline more far-reaching than that of any other Protestant community. In spirit and content most of these "blue laws" were medieval, and many had been enacted before Calvin's time, but their rigorous enforcement on all persons of every class was new. This so-called Genevan theocracy was not civil rule by ministers; no minister could hold civil office in Geneva. But the ministers as interpreters of the biblical law exercised a

powerful influence on legislators, judges, and other civil officers. Moreover, Calvin had taken a doctorate in law in his youth, and in general the ministers were the best-educated men in the city. Also, excommunication from the church was regarded as a major disgrace, if not calamity. These factors gave the ministers great power in the church courts, which were composed of ministers and elders from the congregation. Yet the personal force of Calvin, Theodore Beza, and other ministers was the actual power behind this theocracy. More than ever before, the Reformed churches under Calvin's influence emphasized the ethical character of the Reformation.

The Church and Political Authority.—This emphasis led in turn to two other involvements which affected all the other Reformed churches: the problem of church and state and that of the nature of political authority. Europe had had centuries of conflict between the papacy and the various kings and emperors, a conflict that had also been a major cause of the Reformation. Since the papacy fought all aspects of the Protestant Reformation, no such movement succeeded anywhere in Europe without the aid of the civil powers. Inevitably this had meant that the civil authorities came into actual control of the church within their domains. This control was sometimes exercised paternalistically or indirectly; at other times the church was made a tool of civil policy. But, as such, the control was accepted by all the early reformers as the only alternative to control by the papacy.

Calvin sought a third possibility, a church made up of all the inhabitants of the country, a church protected by the civil government and receiving legal sanction for its basic constitutional documents from the civil authorities. This constitution, he urged, should allow the church to choose its own officers, including its pastors; to constitute its own strictly ecclesiastical courts; and to administer its own affairs under its constitution within and through its own officers and courts. This qualified separation of church and state was severely controverted in Geneva and even among other Reformed churches for a time (see ERASTUS, THOMAS). Gradually it became typical of the Reformed churches and was broadened in the direction of the ideal of a church wholly free of the state. Even the relative freedom won for the church from the state by Calvin meant that the ideals, policies, doctrines, etc., of the Reformed churches could be spread internationally with greater freedom because their acceptance in any given nation implied no negotiations with, or tie to, the Genevan government or the Swiss federation.

In the bitter social and political struggles that took place in many nations of Europe in the 16th century, as well as in the severe religious struggles between Roman and Evangelical, Lutheran and Reformed, Evangelical and Anabaptist, etc., the question of the nature of political authority over a people was debated repeatedly. Calvin adopted and greatly advanced the notions of popular sovereignty, a written fundamental law or constitution, government resting upon a contract between people and rulers, government by representatives of the people, and the right of the people to constitutional resistance if a ruler violated his contract to rule according to the constitution. The Reformed churches, the Huguenots (q.v.) especially (and the Presbyterians in England and Scotland), made these theories their major artillery against the divine-right monarchies of Europe. Men such as John Locke made them the basis of standard British and American political theory apart from their earlier religious basis.

Civil and religious authorities worked well together in Geneva for a time. However, when the church attempted to discipline members of the upper, ruling class, trouble came from the civil authorities. Also, Calvin's insistence upon making Geneva a centre for Evangelical refugees caused great resentment among the "old Genevese" party. The group in the city for whom the religious change from Catholicism to Evangelicalism had been essentially a part of the move for civic independence made common cause with those who resented the whole religious reform. In 1553 Calvin's cause seemed defeated.

Two years later the civil authorities gave up all control over the internal life of the church but still held out on the issue of the refugees. When the leaders of the opposition to Calvin were found to be in secret negotiations with the French king their whole cause collapsed. Calvin was then free to settle church affairs, found the University of Geneva, train refugee ministers for service all over Europe, and make Geneva the Evangelical centre of the continent. He held no office other than that of pastor of the church, though his influence was enormous. Gradually, leadership of the various Reformed churches passed to Geneva. Calvin died in 1564, and his successor, Theodore Beza, was the acknowledged leader of French Protestantism. Under Beza's successors Genevan leadership declined, and by the 18th century the city was dominated by the Enlightenment. German Switzerland came to greater prominence. French Reformed leadership was never again great.

Modern Switzerland.—During the Reformation most Swiss cantons had their own state churches. This pattern has never been dropped. During the 20th century most of the churches were disestablished in greater or lesser measure, without losing their character of national churches. The presbyterian form of government in general prevails in these churches. No particular creed is used by any of them, though, in general, they follow the Reformed tradition in thought and life.

Switzerland has become the international centre of world Protestantism, and the Reformed churches have contributed much to this ecumenical work. During the two world wars the Swiss churches did much to hold the Evangelical churches together. In 1948 the Swiss Reformed churches formed a federation which included roughly three-fifths of the population of Switzerland. By the 1960s this federation had nearly 3,000,000 members.

GERMANY

Strasbourg.—Matthew Zell, who had been influenced by Zwingli, began preaching Evangelical doctrine in Strasbourg as early as 1521. Soon he was joined by Wolfgang Capito from Basel, and others. Martin Bucer, who had become an Erasmian reformer, met Luther in 1518 and became an Evangelical. In 1524 he went to Strasbourg and shortly was made pastor. Subject now to influences from Zürich, Basel, and France, Bucer gradually moved away from Luther. At the Diet of Augsburg (1530) he led a small group of Germans and others who sought a middle ground between Luther's and Zwingli's groups. From then on he followed a policy of mediation first between the various reforming groups and then between the reforming groups and Rome. Melanchthon, and Calvin at times, aided him in these moves. When the Augsburg *Interim* was forced on Germany (1547–48), Strasbourg was compelled to become Roman Catholic, and the Reformed leaders were exiled. Bucer and some others went to England, still others went to Switzerland. When the *Interim* was lifted Strasbourg became exclusively Lutheran until 1789. (*See* also GERMANY: *History.*)

The course of the Reformed system in Strasbourg, therefore, was limited to the period 1521–48. However, during that period some decisive events took place. Strasbourg became the German centre of Swiss Reformation thought. All down the Rhine Valley Swiss-Strasbourg influences moved, even into the Netherlands. John Calvin found refuge in Strasbourg during 1538–41 and both made and received lasting contributions. English Puritans before, during, and after the "Marian exile" were permanently affected by the theology of the Rhineland, and Bucer eventually went to England. Without Strasbourg's role as a channel, the influence of Zürich, Basel, and Geneva upon the outside world might have been small, and the Reformed churches might have been limited to Switzerland and France.

Reformed and Lutheran.—In many ways it was the elector Frederick III of the Palatinate who gave the German Reformed Church its great opportunity. During the later years of Melanchthon's life, and for some time thereafter, grievous controversy raged among Lutherans between an ultra-Lutheran faction and a more moderate group of Melanchthon's followers. The violence of the controversy turned many minds toward Calvinism, or the Reformed views. Frederick made Heidelberg University a centre of Reformed thought, bringing to it men such as Zacharias Ursinus and Caspar Olevianus. Ursinus had been first a Melanchthonian Lutheran and had later come under Peter Martyr (Vermigli) and Farel. Frederick commissioned these men to draft a constitution for the Palatinate churches which would more nearly express the Reformed views. The Heidelberg Catechism (*q.v.*) which they drew up (1563) quickly became the catechism of all the Reformed churches. It was attacked fiercely by the ultra-Lutherans, and soon it was being asserted that those who held its views had no right to toleration under the terms laid down in the Peace of Augsburg (1555). Frederick fought the issue to a successful conclusion at the Diet of Augsburg (1566), thus gaining a clear-cut admission that the Reformed churches had the right to exist parallel to the Lutheran churches allowed by the diet of 1555.

Despite temporary or local losses the Reformed churches spread down the Rhine. The Wetterau counties became Reformed, and at Herborn a famous Reformed university was founded. Emden and Bremen also became Reformed, then Brandenburg (1613) with its capital, Berlin. Other smaller areas scattered over the German states were also brought into the Reformed church.

The Thirty Years' War brought the Reformed territories almost to ruin, and at the Peace of Prague (1635) the Reformed groups were so wholly betrayed that the war was resumed. The Peace of Westphalia (1648) explicitly recognized the Reformed churches and restored the lands of the Reformed nobles. It also recognized Switzerland's independence of the empire. The revocation of the Edict of Nantes in 1685 brought into Germany 60,000 Huguenot refugees who greatly strengthened the Reformed churches. During this same period the French ravaged the Palatinate and greatly reduced the Reformed churches, which were saved only by the intervention of Brandenburg. Yet a century of serious hardship (until 1802) was their fate.

Beginning in 1817, Prussia united, by three stages, the Reformed and Lutheran churches in its territories. The first stage was federation, the second (1830) a common liturgy, the third (1834) allowed each congregation the right of using whichever creed and liturgy it wished (Reformed or Lutheran). The territories in which the Reformed groups had their greatest strength were Brandenburg, Prussia, Pomerania, Silesia, Posen, Westphalia, and the Rhine provinces. Those provinces which joined Prussia after 1817 —Hanover, Nassau, and electoral Hesse—were not compelled to unite their churches, although Nassau had done so previously at its own order. Small local unions were made in these areas, however. Nonunion Reformed churches remained in Bremen, Lippe, Alsace-Lorraine, Lower Saxony, and elsewhere. Generally speaking the Reformed tradition was overshadowed by the Lutheran as the union continued. In 1861 Reformed leaders began to revive, but within the various union agreements, a greater appreciation for the Reformed tradition and ethic. Inner mission work among the poor and the sick also was pushed, as were foreign missions, youth work, and other social activities. A vigorous literature on the Reformed ideals began to appear.

20th Century.—World War I and the years immediately following wrought havoc in all German churches. Old cultural patterns disappeared and an industrialized, secular society emerged. The close connections of all the churches with the German state had become a hindrance, and the disestablishment which came under the Weimar Republic was in itself good. It came, however, when the churches could least afford the financial and other losses entailed. Beginning in 1918–21 a vigorous theological renewal took place in Germany. The Reformed Federation, led by August Lang, brought Karl Barth to Göttingen University, where he quickly became the leading Reformed theologian of modern times.

As the Nazi regime took over, Barth and Otto Weber, of the Reformed Federation, became leaders in the struggle of the German churches against Hitler and neopaganism. (*See* GERMAN CONFESSING CHURCH.) World War II brought serious losses to the Reformed churches. Those regions of Germany where they were strongest fell into the Russian zone of occupation. In Hesse, the Ruhr, and other regions of West Germany they recovered slowly after the war, aided by U.S. Presbyterian and Reformed churches.

The Reformed Federation in the 1960s had about 2,500,000 members. The Evangelical-Reformed Church in northwest Germany had about 230,000.

During the height of Germany's power, German Reformed

groups spread out over a large part of Europe and also into Russia. Sizable churches were established in Austria (Vienna), Yugoslavia, and Slovakia, smaller bodies among German settlers in Russia, Lithuania, and Latvia. In the territories which were alternately Polish and German in the 19th and 20th centuries there were large Reformed groups. The status of these groups deteriorated seriously after World War II.

THE NETHERLANDS

Reforming interest emerged in the Netherlands early in the Reformation era. Erasmus did much of his best work at Rotterdam. Moreover, the Brethren of the Common Life (*q.v.*) and other mystical groups had been active in the Low Countries. Erasmian and mystical types of reform were soon followed by Zwinglian and Lutheran influences. Communications, and other interests also, bound the Rhineland and the Netherlands together. Hence the Swiss-Rhineland type of reform came to predominate. The emperor Charles V instituted the Inquisition against the Reformation in the Netherlands as early as 1522. The struggle for freedom from Spain was begun by the Netherlands as a protest in demand of greater liberties, including religious, within Charles's empire. Eventually, Holland became free, and the Reformed church was established. (*See* NETHERLANDS, THE: *History.*) During this long struggle the religious situation had become clarified. The leaders in the war for freedom had been deeply influenced by French Huguenot-Calvinist political and religious thought. Lutheran and Erasmian ideas had given way to a theology blended from Rhineland, Genevan Calvinist, and French Huguenot influences, and ideas drawn from the younger Jan Laski's work. The Belgic Confession (*Confessio Belgica*), written in 1561, became the standard creed. The church was not a national church. The Netherlands comprised a federation of states with great local autonomy, and each state had its own church over which the local authorities had almost complete powers. National synods were provided for but were seldom allowed by the various states.

Arminianism.—Civic peace had scarcely been achieved before a theological revolution took place in the Dutch church. Calvinists, in their controversies with Lutherans and Catholics, had carried their philosophical development of Calvin's religious view of predestination (which he shared with Luther) to great lengths. Some Reformed thinkers began to raise objections, among them the Dutch theologian Jacobus Arminius (*q.v.*). Other issues were also involved, especially Dutch political issues. The leader of the ultra-predestinarian Calvinists in the Dutch Reformed churches was Franciscus Gomarus. To solve the issue, a synod of representatives of Reformed churches in all countries was called by the civil authorities. James I of England took special interest in the synod and sent representatives from the Church of England. The synod met at Dort in 1618–19, condemned Arminius' mild views, rejected Gomarus' extreme views, and stated in classic form the hyper-Calvinistic view which had become the badge of the Dutch Calvinists in their polemics with other theologians. The term Arminianism became a very broad designation in Europe for any deviation from any essential aspect of Calvinistic orthodoxy, whether or not connected with Arminius' followers or the original points of controversy. (*See also* ARMINIANISM; DORT, SYNOD OF.)

19th–20th Centuries.—In 1798 the Dutch Reformed Church was disestablished, but it remained partly under government control. In 1816 King William I reorganized the church and renamed it Netherlands Reformed Church. Conflict over church organization and religious orthodoxy led to a separation of some conservative elements in 1834, most of these being united in 1869 in the Christian Reformed Church. In 1886 a second exodus of conservatives from the Netherlands Reformed Church was led by Abraham Kuyper (*q.v.*). This group united with the majority of the Christian Reformed Church in 1892 to form the Reformed Churches in the Netherlands, a strongly evangelical church that remains the second largest Protestant church in the Netherlands.

In 1926 a group under Johannes Gerardus Geelkerken was expelled from this church for doctrinal reasons; they united with the Netherlands Reformed Church in 1946. A more serious schism occurred in the Reformed Churches in the Netherlands in 1944,

when a large group of zealous conservatives separated to form the Reformed Churches in the Netherlands (Freed).

Other Reformed churches, consisting of very conservative groups that did not go along with the unions of 1869 and 1892, include the Christian Reformed Churches, the Reformed Congregations, and the Old-Reformed Congregations, all with membership of less than 100,000. The Arminian group that was expelled from the Dutch Reformed Church in 1619 survives as the Remonstrant Brotherhood.

The Netherlands Reformed Church had about 3,000,000 members in the mid-1960s, the Reformed Churches in the Netherlands about 800,000.

Former Dutch Colonial Areas.—The Dutch churches followed the colonial expansion of the country. In South Africa they became the principal Christian churches. This, together with the Dutch tendency toward political parties following confessional lines, gave these churches a very great responsibility. With few exceptions, the Reformed churches in South Africa reflect the views of the Afrikaners; the post-World War II premier D. F. Malan, who led the campaign for the total segregation of the population and areas of South Africa on racial and colour lines, was an ordained Reformed minister. Most Reformed churchmen, and the Reformed churches officially, approved his policy and continued to support his successors.

Controversy over doctrinal issues divided the church in South Africa as well as in the Netherlands. Six distinct bodies in the 1960s claimed an aggregate (white) membership of approximately 1,350,000. A "mission church" for nonwhite missionary converts claimed a membership of about 150,000.

Indonesia, prior to its independence, had a Dutch church of about 300,000 adherents. The readjustments after independence seriously weakened it.

OTHER EUROPEAN COUNTRIES

France.—From the beginning, the Reformation made slow progress in France. Yet reforming movements within the Roman Catholic Church had been early in appearing. Before Luther had emerged as a Reformer French humanists had created much interest in biblical studies and had aroused a concern for a purer type of Christianity. In time Margaret of Angoulême, King Francis I's sister, became the centre of a humanistic group known as the group of Meaux, which, while it never broke with the Roman church and never became outright Evangelical, created great interest in reform. Also, members of it, such as Jacques Lefèvre d'Étaples, contributed much by their writings to biblical and theological studies which the Evangelicals could and did use. Again, several of the group—among them Nicholas Cop and Guillaume Farel—left it and became professed Evangelicals. But it was not until 1555 that any real attempt was made to organize Evangelical congregations in France.

Calvin, Farel, and Beza, all Frenchmen active in Geneva, had maintained a deep interest in the French reform movement. Hundreds of students had been sent to France from Geneva on evangelical missions. By 1560 it was estimated that there were about 300,000 Evangelicals in France and at least 49 organized congregations. In general these Reformed churches (all Protestants, Reformed and Lutheran, were called Huguenots) followed Calvin's views, yet on many critical matters they made changes. In a long series of civil wars, beginning in 1562, they alternately gained and lost.

Peace finally came when the Huguenot leader Henry of Navarre became king as Henry IV and abjured Protestantism. This satisfied the Roman Catholic faction, and Henry in 1598 promulgated the Edict of Nantes, which guaranteed the Huguenots virtual freedom of religion. (*See* NANTES, EDICT OF.) During this era of strife had occurred the greatest horror of the Reformation, the massacre of 20,000–50,000 Huguenots throughout France beginning on St. Bartholomew's Day, 1572 (*see* SAINT BARTHOLOMEW'S DAY, MASSACRE OF).

The French Reformed churches recovered in great measure from these frightful persecutions after 1598. But the Edict of Nantes was revoked by Louis XIV in 1685. Untold sufferings preceded and succeeded this act, and despite laws against emigration over a quarter of a million Huguenots fled—to Germany, Holland, England, Switzerland, and the New World. Those who remained persisted as a virtual underground movement and did not regain their full rights until the Revolution of 1789.

Since the Revolution France as a nation has been indifferent to all religions. The French Reformed churches have grown slowly under great handicaps. (*See* also HUGUENOTS.)

The Reformed Church of France in the 1960s had about 195,000 members, the Reformed Church in Alsace-Lorraine about 22,000; Evangelical Reformed churches outside the united body numbered 50 congregations.

Hungary.—The influence of the Reformation was felt early in Hungary. A synod at Erdod adopted the Augsburg Confession in 1545, and by 1567 the works of Farel and Calvin had become so well known that the Synod of Debrecen adopted the Heidelberg Catechism and the Second Helvetic Confession, thus becoming a Reformed church. Except for minor reverses the Evangelicals made progress in Hungary until 1655, when Leopold I came to the throne. The Counter-Reformation era was one of severe persecution for all Evangelicals, and not until the emperor Joseph II promulgated the Edict of Toleration in 1781 did respite come. Within the old empire the Reformed church was of two wings, the Magyar (the larger) and the German; the Magyars spread rather widely through the empire, carrying their church with them. Theologically the Reformed churches were much influenced by German scholarship. Within the empire they built up a large system of schools, elementary through university, and did much for Hungarian cultural life.

The Peace of Versailles following World War I shattered the Hungarian Reformed Church. Only half of the church remained within the new nation of Hungary; the other half was represented by minority groups in unfriendly or even hostile countries. The largest segment, 780,000 in Rumania, suffered grievously for both religious and cultural reasons. The 210,000 in Slovakia suffered less, and the small group of 40,000 in Yugoslavia led a precarious existence. World War II defeated all hopes of reuniting the Magyar people and their church.

Czechoslovakia.—The Reformed churches of Czechoslovakia are, like the nation itself, of varied origins. The Czech Reformed body is the Evangelical Church of Bohemian Brethren. The Slovak Reformed body is a wing of the Hungarian Magyar Reformed family.

John Huss's attempt at reforming the church in Bohemia ended at the stake in 1415. His followers were crushed in 1434, but underground the cause persisted. During the 16th-century reforming movement in general, the Bohemian Brethren emerged again to flourish for a brief period. In 1547 they were again suppressed, and the Jesuits were given charge of religious affairs in Bohemia. A Bohemian revolt in 1618 began the Thirty Years' War in Europe, and thereafter the House of Habsburg and the Counter-Reformation held unchallenged sway in Bohemia. Thousands of Evangelicals—nearly a quarter of the urban population and the nobility—fled the country, patriot and Evangelical leaders were executed. Not until 1781 (Joseph II's Edict of Toleration) were Evangelical groups again tolerated in Bohemia, and then only bodies holding either of the two German Protestant symbols (Augsburg or Heidelberg). The old native Bohemian church was still banned, though it remained in existence underground. Moreover, the cause of Czech independence and that of the Bohemian church became intertwined.

When the nation of Czechoslovakia was created by the Peace of Versailles, the Evangelical Church of Czech Brethren was freed, to become the leading Protestant church in the nation. Its leadership in theological education, social work, etc., was marked. During the crises preceding World War II Czech patriotism and the Bohemian Brethren again made common cause. When the German Army seized Czechoslovakia the consequences for this Reformed church were severe. Many of its leaders, Joseph Hromadka among them, had to flee. The postwar Communist government presented the church with a new crisis. It had been predominantly middle and upper class, with no great hold on the classes now influenced by

Communism. Under the leadership of Hromadka the church made great efforts to come to an understanding with the government and with the proletariat in order to overcome its previous social stratification and isolation. (*See* also BOHEMIA: *History;* HUSSITES; MORAVIAN CHURCH.)

Other Countries.—Small Reformed churches, often only a few scattered congregations, are found in Austria, Lithuania, Latvia, Poland, Belgium, the Scandinavian countries, Greece, Spain, and Portugal. The ancient Waldensian churches of Italy (*see* WALDENSES), together with their branches in Uruguay and Paraguay, have also come within the orbit of the Reformed churches, though preserving their own character.

UNITED STATES

The Reformed churches have been represented in North America largely through their English-speaking wing, the Presbyterians. However, some continental European Reformed churches have been established by immigration into the United States; none has done so in Canada or Mexico.

The Reformed Church in America.—The first Reformed church of continental European background to establish itself in North America was the Dutch Reformed Church, which during the period of Dutch sovereignty over New Netherland was the established church of the colony. When the English seized the colony they gave assurances that the Dutch Reformed Church would be allowed freedom from English control and that it would be permitted to continue under the ecclesiastical jurisdiction of the classis (Church governing body) of Amsterdam. Under this control the church grew slowly in New York, Long Island, and New Jersey. In 1679 the classis of Amsterdam allowed a colonial classis to form, but restricted its powers severely.

Early in the 18th century new movements came: colonial self-consciousness, declining interest in things Dutch, the Great Awakening revival of religion, and increasing interest in cooperation with other churches, especially the Presbyterians. The Dutch church became split into two factions, one, a colonial party, desiring greater freedom from the classis of Amsterdam, free use of the English language in worship, a local college for the training of ministers, and support of revivals in the churches; the other, a conservative Dutch party, wishing to retain Dutch authority and influence—Netherlands-trained pastors, Dutch language in worship, etc. The colonial party soon predominated. In 1770 it founded Queen's College, later Rutgers University, at New Brunswick, N.J. The two factions reunited in 1771 under a plan which left ultimate authority in Holland but gave great local autonomy. After the Revolutionary War the church became wholly independent under a new constitution drafted 1784–92; by 1820 the Dutch language had ceased to be used. The name Reformed Protestant Dutch Church was changed in 1867 to Reformed Church in America.

A large migration of Dutch people into the United States about the middle of the 19th century added greatly to the church. Most of these settled in Michigan and other midwestern areas, giving the church, therefore, two integrally related though rather distinct groups centred in New York and New Jersey and in Michigan and Iowa. The older, eastern section of the church has been much more severed from its ethnic origins and is much less conservative theologically than the newer, midwestern section.

Several attempts at union between the Reformed Church in America and other Reformed or Presbyterian bodies in the United States have been made since the early 19th century, none successfully. The church in the 1960s had about 230,000 members.

The Christian Reformed Church.—In 1822 a small group withdrew from the Reformed Protestant Dutch Church and formed the True Reformed Dutch Church. In 1857 another schism from the parent body formed the True Holland Reformed Church. Further immigrations from the Netherlands and a further schism from the parent body increased the new denominations. In 1890 they united to form the Christian Reformed Church. This church, which adheres to the Heidelberg Catechism, the Belgic Confession, and the Canons of Dort, had about 250,000 members in the 1960s.

Evangelical and Reformed Church.—This body was formed

in 1934 by the union of the (German) Reformed Church in the United States and the Evangelical (Lutheran) Synod of North America. In 1957 it entered into a merger with the Congregational Christian Churches to form the United Church of Christ; the constitution of this new body came into force in 1961. (*See* CONGREGATIONALISM: *History: United States.*)

Early in the 18th century Palatinate Germans, Reformed in confessional allegiance, began coming into the American colonies largely as refugees from the wars between France and Germany. They settled in Pennsylvania and in the Valley of Virginia for the most part. Due to the turmoil in the Palatinate their own home church could not help them, but they were aided by the Reformed Church of Holland and under Michael Schlatter, who had been sent from Holland, formed a coetus, or governing church body, in 1747. The Presbyterians also aided them in various ways. Attempts to unite them with either the Dutch Reformed Church or the Presbyterians failed, largely for cultural reasons. After the Revolutionary War, the German Reformed groups in Pennsylvania and Virginia formed a synod of the German Reformed Church in the United States (1793).

New immigrants of German Reformed persuasion came into the United States in the 19th century. Until 1863 these new groups formed separate and distinct synods only loosely allied with the older synod, but in that year a national synod of the German Reformed Church in the United States was formed. Six years later the word German was dropped from the name. From time to time efforts were made to unite this church with the (Dutch) Reformed Church in America and with the Presbyterian Church in the U.S.A.; these attempts all failed. Union with the Evangelical (Lutheran) Synod was, however, successful in 1934.

The Evangelical Synod of North America dated from 1840 and was known in its early years as the Evangelical Union of the West. It was formed under the leadership of missionaries from Lutheran and Reformed churches of Germany and Switzerland who were engaged in pioneer work in Missouri and Illinois. The original organization was strengthened by amalgamations with the German Evangelical Church Association of Ohio, which took place in 1858, the German United Evangelical Synod of the East in 1860, the Evangelical Synod of the North-West in 1872, and the United Evangelical Synod of the East, also in 1872.

At the time of merger in 1934 the Evangelical Synod of North America had 281,598 members, the Reformed Church in the United States 348,189. The union was fully achieved only in 1940–41, as the Evangelical and Reformed Church.

The union of the Evangelical and Reformed Church with the Congregational Christian Churches was the first church merger in the United States which joined denominations of extremely varied theological and ethnic backgrounds. At the time of approval of its constitution in 1961 the Evangelical and Reformed synods reported about 814,000 members in 2,726 churches; the 3,665 Congregational Christian local churches had a membership of 1,108,000.

ASPECTS OF THE REFORMED CHURCHES

For the church polity of these bodies, *see* PRESBYTERIANISM: *The Presbyterian System.*

Worship.—Though like the Presbyterians in most ways, the Reformed churches differ in that they use established liturgies. Both groups agree in their concepts of worship. The Presbyterians believe these ideals are best achieved by allowing great freedom to each congregation, whereas the Reformed churches regard an established liturgy as a valuable aid in guiding a congregation into a right service of God. All these churches regard worship as only a part of the Christian congregation's total service of God. Cultic and ritual acts, as such, have no influence upon God. They are significant only in their bearing upon the congregation as the acts become the means whereby God becomes known to the congregation as Lord, Redeemer, and Judge. In all Reformed-Presbyterian worship, therefore, there is an emphasis on the Word of God made known and interpreted through preaching and the sacraments. The appeal is to the whole of the life of the congregation, as persons and as members of a society of persons. There is no access to God which does not involve one's neighbour. The sensuous, the sym-

bolic, the nonverbal, are little emphasized in the interests of clarity, conscience, duty, and obedience. The function of worship is not the cultivation of the worshiper's religious feelings but the bringing of the sons of God more fully into the totality of the Divine purpose among all men. (*See* further PRESBYTERIANISM.)

Doctrine.—During the 16th century the various Reformed churches regarded creeds or confessions as teaching and disciplinary media. They considered it both desirable and necessary that each church body should have an adequate and contemporary creed or confession. Almost every Reformed church therefore drew up its own statement of faith. The best known of these confessions are the Second Helvetic Confession (1566) by Heinrich Bullinger, widely used in German-speaking Switzerland (*see* HELVETIC CONFESSIONS); the Genevan Catechism (1542) by Calvin (*see* CATECHISM); the Heidelberg Catechism (*q.v.*; 1563); the Belgic Confession (1561) of the Dutch church; and the Gallican Confession (1559), a revision and expansion by the Huguenots of an earlier draft by Calvin. (*See* further CONFESSIONS OF FAITH, PROTESTANT: *Reformed Churches;* PRESBYTERIANISM: *Presbyterian Thought.*)

Relations with Other Churches.—There has always been a certain ambivalence about those distinctive aspects of the Reformed churches which set them off from other Evangelical, or Protestant, bodies. The Reformed churches themselves regard nearly all of their distinctive aspects as being little more than the logical consequences of the basic Evangelical faith of any Protestant body. It has always been their policy, therefore, to define their relationship to other Evangelical churches on the basis of the Christian faith which they have in common, while insisting upon a stricter standard for their own members. Transfer of members, or of pastors, from other denominations has always been possible without any requirement of rebaptism, reordination, or other act which would call into question the former affiliation. Likewise, intercommunion (*i.e.*, freedom to receive the Lord's Supper) has always been open to members of all Evangelical bodies. Cooperative work in interdenominational enterprises has been facilitated also by this same attitude. Actual union of other bodies with Reformed bodies, however, has always raised the question of the more rigorous theological orientation in creed, polity, preaching, and social concerns.

See also references under "Reformed Churches" in the Index.

BIBLIOGRAPHY.—T. M. Lindsay, *History of the Reformation,* 2 vol. (1906–07); *Cambridge Modern History,* vol. iii–vi (1936); W. Pauck, *Heritage of the Reformation* (1950); A. Keller and G. Stewart, *Protestant Europe* (1927); *American Church History Series,* vol. viii (1895); C. E. Corwin, *Manual of the Reformed Church in America . . . 1628–1922,* 5th ed. rev. (1922); J. H. Dubbs, *Historical Manual* (1902); W. W. Sweet, *Story of Religion in America,* rev. ed. (1939); P. Schaff, *Creeds of Christendom,* 4th ed. rev., vol. iii, pp. 197–704 (1919); T. F. Torrance (ed. and trans.), *School of Faith: the Catechisms of the Reformed Church* (1959); H. L. J. Heppe, *Reformed Dogmatics,* Eng. trans. by E. Bizer (1950); W. Niesel, *Theology of Calvin,* Eng. trans. by H. Knight (1956), *The Gospel and the Churches: a Comparison of Catholicism, Orthodoxy and Protestantism,* Eng. trans. by D. Lewis (1962). (L. J. T.)

REFORMED EPISCOPAL CHURCH, a Protestant community in the United States formed as a result of a division in the Protestant Episcopal Church. The influence of the Tractarian movement (*see* OXFORD MOVEMENT) began to be felt at an early date, and the ordination in New York, July 1843, of Arthur Carey, a clergyman who denied that there was any difference in points of faith between the Anglican and the Roman churches, brought into relief the antagonism between the evangelical Protestant clergy and those who sympathized with the position of Carey. The struggle went on for a generation and with increasing bitterness. The climax was reached when George David Cummins (*q.v.*), assistant bishop of Kentucky and a leader of the evangelicals, was angrily attacked for officiating at the united communion service held at the meeting of the sixth General Conference of the Evangelical Alliance in New York, October 1873.

Cummins resigned his charge in the Episcopal Church on Nov. 11, and a month later, with seven other clergymen (*see* also CHENEY, CHARLES EDWARD) and a score of laymen, constituted the Reformed Episcopal Church. The church recognizes no "orders" of ministry; the episcopate is an office, not an order, the bishop being the chief presbyter, *primus inter pares*. It is governed by a General Council, which meets triennially. The church supports mission activities in India and Africa. Members number around 7,500. *See also* PROTESTANT EPISCOPAL CHURCH: *History: High and Low Church Divisions.*

REFORM MOVEMENT (BRITISH), a name given to the movement toward parliamentary reform in Britain which "culminated" in the passing of the "great Reform Bill" of 1832. It is difficult to date precisely its beginning, but most historians start with the rise of London radicalism in the years preceding the Middlesex election of 1768 when the House of Commons refused to allow John Wilkes, a popular hero, to take his seat. The end of the movement also is a matter of definition. Working-class radicalism, a relatively new phenomenon, associated with the rise of industry, was not satisfied with the settlement of 1832. The fight for the working-class vote antedated not only the drafting of the People's Charter in 1838 but the passing of the 1832 act, and Chartism emerged from older movements of protest. The agitation for the second Reform Bill of 1867 may also be said to be a continuation of the reform movement.

The Unreformed System.—The system of parliamentary representation which reformers attacked in the late 18th and early 19th centuries was the product of history. The 18th-century House of Commons consisted of 558 members, elected by 314 constituencies. The 245 English constituencies (40 counties, 203 boroughs, 2 universities) returned 489 members; the 24 Welsh constituencies (12 counties, 12 boroughs) and 45 Scottish constituencies (30 counties, 15 burghs) each returned one member. Ireland, with 100 members, was not represented at Westminster until the Act of Union of 1800 which abolished the separate Irish legislature.

The English franchises for the counties and boroughs differed fundamentally. The county franchise was based on the possession of freehold property, variously defined, but valued for the land tax, at 40s. per annum. In theory the county electors were able to choose their representatives freely, but in practice they were subjected to various forms of "influence." The borough franchise, by contrast, was based on no single criterion. There were six kinds of borough—household or "potwalloper" boroughs where the right of voting was held by all inhabitant householders not receiving alms or poor relief; freeman boroughs, where the right of voting was restricted to freemen, in some cases only to resident freemen; scot and lot boroughs, in which the right of voting was enjoyed by all inhabitant householders paying the poor rate; corporation boroughs, in which the right of voting was confined to members of the corporation; burgage boroughs, where the franchise was attached not to persons but to property, and could not be increased or diminished; and freeholder boroughs, where the right of voting lay with the freeholders, so that if one person owned a sufficient number of freeholds he could control the borough as easily as if the franchise were based on burgage tenure. There were only 6 freeholder boroughs and 29 burgage boroughs, but in the other types of borough there were varying sizes of electorate and varying degrees of venality. Even some of the potwalloper boroughs were controlled by patronage. "Pocket boroughs" were those where one person could usually control an election or dispense with it: "rotten boroughs" were boroughs whose existence it was difficult to justify except in terms of prescriptive right.

In the eyes of many reformers the defects of the system as a whole were more serious than particular abuses and anomalies. In the boroughs, in particular, there was a clear and increasing contrast between the distribution of electoral power and the facts of economics and geography. Large industrial cities, like Manchester and Birmingham, were unrepresented, and some of their most active and enterprising citizens lacked the vote. In Yorkshire the city of York and 13 other small boroughs with a total of 7,000 voters returned 28 members, while the county, with a population of 16,000 voters, returned only 2 members. Cornwall returned 44 members, against Lancashire's 14. The City of London, with a population of about 100,000, returned only 4 members.

Facts of this kind were put forward on a large scale for the first time on the eve of the 1768 election. An important "extraordinary number" of the *Political Register* in January 1768 complained about the limitations on the franchise, the nonrepresentation of "the monied interest" and of manufacturing towns, and the existence of rotten boroughs. "With regard to the representation," it asked, "what could blind chance have determined more unequal, irregular, and imperfect, than we see it today?" While the Wilkes case (*see* WILKES, JOHN) stirred the passions of London reformers, the Society of Supporters of the Bill of Rights was set up in 1769. This was the first of a number of societies which were to quicken the pace of politics in the late 18th and early 19th centuries by disseminating both facts and ideas and by organizing meetings and demonstrations.

War and Reform, 1775–1784.—The implications of the Wilkes case were freely discussed outside London, but it was the experience of the American Revolution which made the reform issue a major one in English politics. Two versions of "reform" became current during this period of strain and upheaval—"economical reform," centred on a reduction of the influence the government was able to exert through patronage, and "radical reform," involving a reconstruction of the electoral system. The parliamentary opposition to Lord North (prime minister from 1770 to 1782) made much of the first, and in 1779 and 1780, when the war news was alarming, there was a strong movement in the country pressing for far-reaching "economical reform." The Yorkshire Association, founded in 1779, set out, under the direction of Christopher Wyvill, to "restore the Freedom of Parliament." Middlesex also was stirred again, and radical feelings there often took more abstract form, particularly in the speeches and writings of John Jebb and Major John Cartwright, which provided the beginnings of a democratic theory of representation. Neither the Rockingham Whigs in Parliament nor the earl of Shelburne and his supporters were prepared to go as far as the most militant reformers outside Parliament. Edmund Burke, indeed, as a spokesman of the Rockingham Whigs, was opposed to organic parliamentary reform, and Shelburne, who was not opposed to it and believed in a more thorough "economical reform" than any other parliamentary politician, had more easy relations with provincial politicians like Wyvill than with the active Westminster Committee of Association and the Society for Constitutional Information which were founded in 1780.

Toward the end of the American war substantial measures of "economical reform" were carried, and motions for electoral reform won widespread parliamentary support. The Rockingham Whigs succeeded North in 1782 and passed a Civil Establishment Act in the same year. Shelburne in his short ministry of 1782–83 accomplished more substantial economic and administrative reforms. Thereafter, though there was still talk of "economical reform," parliamentary reform became the major political issue.

Pitt, The Reform Movement, and the French Revolution.—One of the youngest and most enthusiastic supporters of parliamentary reform at this time was William Pitt the Younger. In 1782, indeed, he moved for "a committee to enquire into the present state of the representation" and was defeated by only 20 votes, the best division the reformers achieved between 1780 and 1831. Even after becoming prime minister in 1783, Pitt continued to believe in reform. In 1785 he proposed *inter alia* that 36 rotten boroughs should be disfranchised and the vacant seats reallocated. Most of his own supporters were less enthusiastic than he was, and some were opposed. So too, for different reasons, were George III, North, and Charles James Fox. Leave to bring in his measure was refused, and Pitt abandoned his proposals. This was a final decision, for the French Revolution of 1789 not only effected a change in Pitt's ideas but made many erstwhile reformers join with conservatives in identifying reform with revolution.

In the first instance, however, the news of the French Revolution gave a fillip to reformers in Britain. The London Revolution Society, which had met in 1788 to celebrate the "glorious Revolution" of 1688, sent a congratulatory address to the French in 1789, and in April 1792 a group of advanced young Whigs, including Charles Grey, formed the Society of the Friends of the People. A less exclusive body, the Society for Constitutional Information, which had been suspended since 1784, sprang into life again in 1791, inspired by the London reformer Horne Tooke, and looked to the French example. More significant, however, was the growth of reform sentiment, much of it of an extreme kind, in the provinces, in places as far apart as Stockport and Norwich, Coventry and Sheffield, and above all in Scotland. Particularly after 1792, with the writings of Tom Paine as an inspiration, "Jacobin" ideas were disseminated widely and effectively. The Sheffield Society for Constitutional Information declared, for example, that it had derived "more knowledge" from the works of Paine "than from any other author or subject." The most interesting of the societies was the London Corresponding Society, formally founded by Thomas Hardy, a shoemaker, in 1792. It consisted largely of working people, had many divisions or branches, had a low entrance fee and subscription, and advocated social as well as political objectives. In an *Address to the People,* published in August 1792, they promised "taxes diminished, the necessaries of life more within the reach of the poor, youth better educated, prisons less crowded, and old age better provided for."

Although the reform movement of these years was repressed, often cruelly, after 1794, the link between political action and economic grievance was to become more important in the reform movements of the future. Years of bad harvests and unemployment had always encouraged popular disturbance. Within an industrial system they were to provide a dynamic. The Luddite movement from 1811 onward was the prelude to specifically working-class movements for parliamentary reform after 1815. There were many other important developments before 1815. Westminster's radicalism revived in 1807, when Sir Francis Burdett was elected its member. William Cobbett was converted from Toryism to radicalism and began (1802) to publish his influential weekly *Political Register.* Jeremy Bentham (*q.v.*) had developed a new theoretical defense of democracy. New organizations also had been founded, notably the Hampden Club in 1812.

Toward 1832.—The years following the end (1815) of the Napoleonic Wars were bleak and discontented, with working-class agitation culminating in 1819 in "Peterloo." Among the key figures of this period were Henry ("Orator") Hunt, the proprietors of widely read radical newspapers like *The Black Dwarf,* and a new and more searchingly critical voice, Richard Carlile of *The Republican.* Working-class protest was less effective politically, however, than the growing middle-class agitation for parliamentary reform in the late 1820s, when, particularly in Birmingham, men like Thomas Attwood associated parliamentary representation with the demand for economic reform. The Birmingham Political Union, founded in 1829, was the most important extraparliamentary body in the struggles of 1831 and 1832. The struggles centred on a Whig Reform Bill introduced by Grey in 1831 soon after the Whigs had been returned to office after years in the political wilderness. Although the bill was opposed by Tories on the grounds that it marked the beginnings of a revolution and by militant reformers on the grounds that it was far too moderate, it was passed, after two serious political crises, in June 1832.

The new act redistributed seats and changed the conditions of the franchise: 56 English boroughs lost their representation entirely; Cornwall's representation was reduced to 13; 65 seats were transferred to the counties, and 42 new English boroughs were created. The electoral qualification in the counties was extended to cover £10 copyholders, leaseholders, and tenants at will paying a rent of not less than £50, while in the boroughs a uniform £10 household qualification became the basis of the vote. The Whigs hoped that the settlement of 1832 would be "final." Within five years, however, it was clear that the country would not treat it as such. The act marked the beginning of parliamentary reform, not the end. *See also* Borough; Chartism; English History; Luddites; Parliament.

Bibliography.—E. and A. G. Porritt, *The Unreformed House of Commons,* 2 vol. (1903); Sir Lewis Namier and J. Brooke, *The House of Commons, 1754–1790,* 3 vol. (1964); G. S. Veitch, *The Genesis of Parliamentary Reform,* 2nd ed. (1964); A. Briggs, *The Age of Improvement* (1959); E. P. Thompson, *The Making of the English Working Class* (1964); J. R. M. Butler, *The Passing of the Great Reform Bill*
(1914); and N. Gash, *Politics in the Age of Peel* (1953).   (A. Bri.)

REFRACTION. When waves of any kind traveling in one medium enter another, in which their velocity is different, their direction is, in general, changed, the rays, *i.e.,* the lines perpendicular to the wave surfaces (in isotropic media) along which the energy travels, being bent or refracted at their point of incidence on the second medium. The change in direction is such that the sine of the angle formed by the incident ray and the normal to the surface of separation bears the same ratio to the sine of the angle formed by the refracted ray and this normal, as the velocity of the waves in the first medium to their velocity in the second. This ratio, known as the refractive index, may depend on the frequency of the wave vibrations. If such be the case, each frequency in the incident disturbance gives rise to a separate refracted ray—a phenomenon known as dispersion. (*See* Optics.)

Mirage (*q.v.*) is due to the refraction of light by layers of air of gradually varying temperature and density. A similar variation, due to convection currents, is responsible for the flickering appearance seen above asphalt and sand on a hot day, and also for the twinkling of the stars. The refraction of rays of light entering the earth's atmosphere from heavenly bodies is known as astronomical refraction; it has the effect of making such bodies appear higher above the horizon than they really are. *See* Light; Refractometer; Sound: *Reflection and Refraction of Sound. See* also references under "Refraction" in the Index.

REFRACTOMETER, an optical instrument for measuring refractive index. The refractive index n of a substance is equal to the speed of light V_m in that substance divided into the speed of light V_s in a standard medium: $n = V_s/V_m$. The standard medium is usually air or, in the case of gases, a standard partial vacuum. Each pure substance has a unique value of n under standard conditions of temperature, pressure, and wave length.

Refractometers are generally either of the deviation type or interference type, depending on the utilized change in light waves passing from one medium into another. These changes result from the different speeds of light in the two media and consist of: (1) a change in direction when the light strikes the boundary surface obliquely; and (2) a change in the phase of vibration of the light wave. A third, less common, type of refractometer makes use of the ratio between the intensities of light reflected and incident on an interface between two media. Sensitive photoelectric cells allow the rapid detection of small changes in refractive index by the photometric method.

A number of variables must be accurately controlled in precision refractometry. These are mainly temperature, wave length of light, and optical alignment of parts. An increase in temperature of 1° C gives, for most liquids, a decrease in n by several units in the fourth decimal. The refractive index of a colourless substance measured with red light may be as much as several units in the second decimal smaller than when measured with violet light. The most widely used monochromatic light source is the sodium lamp; unless otherwise stated, values of n refer to the average wave length of the yellow sodium spectral lines (5,893 Å). Electric-discharge tubes containing such elements as helium, hydrogen, cadmium, or mercury provide a series of well-defined wave lengths that are often used to determine optical dispersion.

Instruments designed to give fourth- or fifth-decimal accuracy require the highest quality workmanship in their optical and mechanical construction and adjustment. Reliable refractometric measurements require frequent calibrations of the instrument with known standards. The greatest accuracy is obtained by a direct comparison of the unknown with a similar known substance. The critical-angle and interference-type refractometers allow this kind of technique, known as the differential method. Easily purified liquids, such as water, serve as convenient standards of comparison; glass test plates are also used. The U.S. National Bureau of Standards has made available a series of pure hydrocarbons with refractive indices certified to the fifth decimal.

Deviation-Type Instruments.—*Optical Principles.*—Basic to all such instruments is Snell's law of refraction: $n = \sin i/\sin r$. The angle of incidence i and the angle of refraction r are the angles made with the normal (*i.e.*, perpendicular) to the boundary surface by the rays in the first and second media, respectively. The

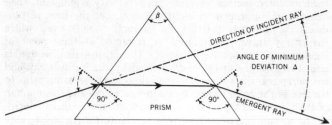

FIG. 1.—PRINCIPLE OF MINIMUM DEVIATION, USED WITH SPECTROMETER TO DETERMINE REFRACTIVE INDEX n OF PRISM: $n = \sin \frac{1}{2}(\beta + \Delta) / \sin \frac{1}{2}\beta$

angles i and r are usually found indirectly from the deviations of rays that traverse not only the sample but one or more prisms and lenses of the refractometer as well. In the spectrometer type of instrument the incident rays come from a narrow slit so that, with a proper lens system, the refracted rays can be located precisely with the aid of a telescope. The spectrometer is ordinarily used with the principle of minimum deviation, which states that the angle between incident and emergent rays (fig. 1) can be made a minimum Δ by a unique orientation of the prism. Under these conditions $i = e$, and the refractive index of the prism is $n = \sin \frac{1}{2}(\beta + \Delta)/\sin \frac{1}{2}\beta$, where β is the angle between the refracting faces of the prism (*see* SPECTROSCOPY).

Critical-angle refractometers make use of particular incident and refracted rays. The critical angle of refraction C is the greatest value of r that can be attained by any ray passing from a less to a more refracting medium (fig. 2). According to Snell's law, C corresponds to an incident ray that grazes the intersurface between the two media ($i = 90°$). All other refracted rays come closer than C to the normal direction. In critical-angle refractometers a prism of known refractive index n_p is used as the more refracting medium. A beam of nonparallel rays passes through the sample into the prism. On viewing the light refracted through the prism by means of a telescope, one finds a sharp critical boundary between a dark and a light region (fig. 2) that very precisely defines the rays having the angles $i = 90°$ and $r = C$. The refractive index of the sample is given by the equation $n = n_p \sin C$.

Abbe Refractometer.—This instrument is perhaps the most widely used critical-angle instrument. The ordinary model is

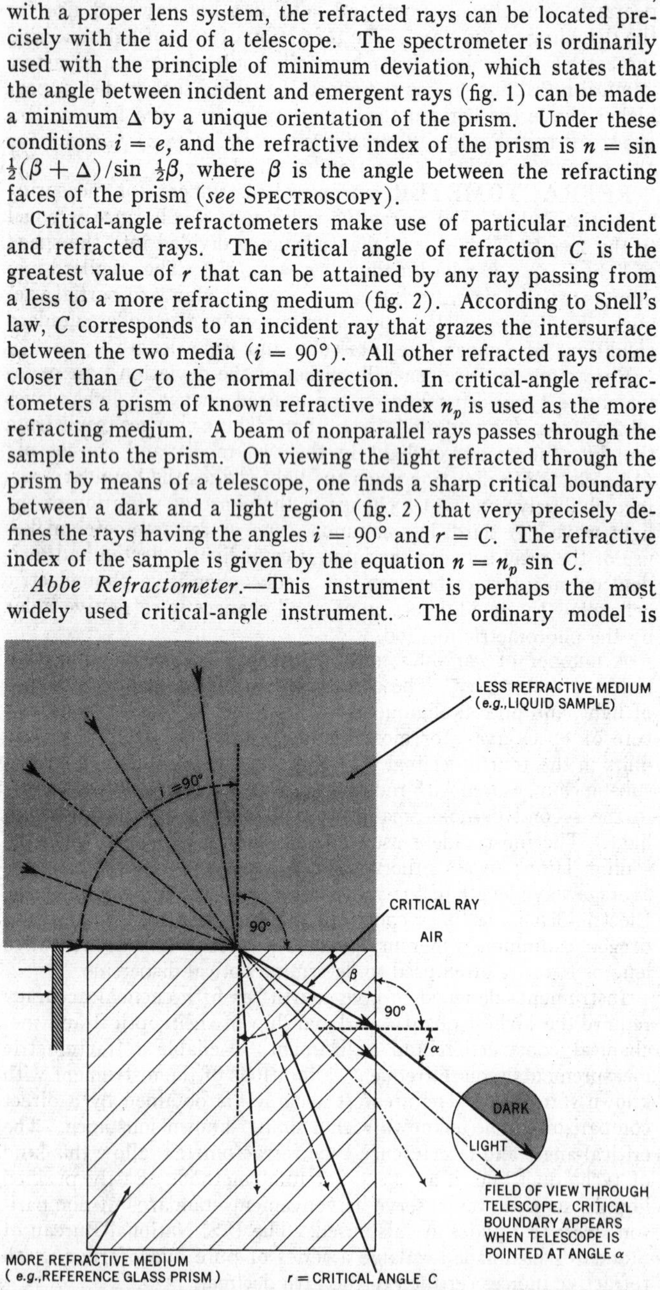

rugged, compact (about the size of a microscope) and is capable of fourth-decimal accuracy. Only a few drops of a liquid sample are required, and a determination may be completed in less than five minutes. Liquid samples are confined to a thin film between the surfaces of the refracting prism P (fig. 3), $\beta = 60°$, and an adjacent auxiliary prism P'. The latter prism serves to send light into the sample in the direction required for the critical boundary. If white light is used, the critical boundary is not sharp because of the different refraction of rays of different wave length.

Most Abbe models are provided with a pair of compensating prisms, mounted in the barrel of the telescope, which remove nearly all of the boundary colour and sharpen the boundary. The amount of rotation of one compensating prism relative to the other, required to achromatize the boundary, provides a rough measure of the dispersion of the sample. The compensating system is designed to give refractive indices corresponding to a wave length near that of the sodium lines. The prisms holding the sample can be rotated with respect to the telescope about an axis passing through the point R (fig. 3). With a solid or liquid sample

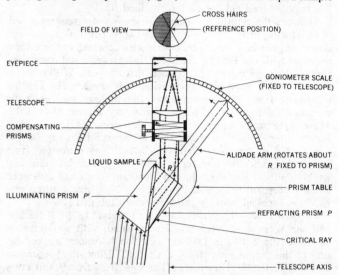

FIG. 3.—SCHEMATIC DIAGRAM OF ABBE REFRACTOMETER

on the lower face of the prism P, the critical boundary can be made to coincide with the cross hairs in the telescope by rotating the prism by means of the alidade arm and a slow-motion screw. A pointer attached to the arm indicates the degree of rotation on a circular scale attached to the telescope. The scale may read directly in terms of refractive index n or, as desired, in terms of concentration of some solute. The range of each instrument is limited by the refractive index of the prism. Usually refractive indices from 1.3 to 1.7 can be covered.

Dipping or Immersion Refractometer.—This instrument resembles the Abbe instrument without the auxiliary prism P'. The refracting P is directly immersed in liquid samples, and the critical boundary is located with respect to a movable eyepiece scale. The dipping refractometer is widely used to check the concentration of solutions. The use of interchangeable prisms gives it a greater range than the Abbe type.

Other Types.—Deviation-type instruments, such as spectrometers, cover an unlimited range of refractive indices and, when appropriately designed, can be used with ultraviolet or infrared light. The material under investigation must be in the form of an accurately shaped prism. Liquid samples are placed in a prismatic cell. Monochromatic or polychromatic light from a narrow slit is made parallel by a collimating lens before traversing the prism. For each wave length an image of the slit is located by means of a telescope mounted on a graduated circle. The many necessary careful adjustments make the spectrometer inconvenient for routine use. Its principle is employed, however, in a number of simplified image-displacement refractometers. Some of these are designed for rapid measurement of small liquid samples. The sample is made into a tiny prism by placing a drop between a

FIG. 2.—CRITICAL ANGLE OF REFRACTION. RAYS HAVING AN ANGLE OF INCIDENCE OF EXACTLY 90° APPEAR IN THE VIEWING TELESCOPE AT THE SHARP BOUNDARY BETWEEN A LIGHT AND A DARK REGION, HENCE THEIR ANGLE OF REFRACTION CAN BE MEASURED ACCURATELY

pair of glass surfaces. If an illuminated slit is viewed through such a prism, its apparent position is shifted from its true position by an amount that depends on the refractive index of the sample and the angle of the prism. The amount of image displacement can be observed on a scale mounted behind the prism. A variation of this principle is found in the Nichols refractometer, which uses a microscope to observe the image displacement. The ordinary microscope can be adapted for use as a simple refractometer of this type.

Interference-Type Instruments.—Interference refractometers are indispensable for finding the refractive indices of gases; they can also be used for liquids and some solids. The inter-

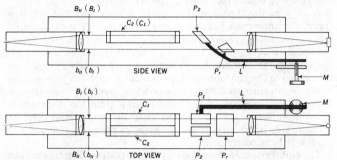

FIG. 4.—SCHEMATIC DIAGRAM OF RAYLEIGH-HABER-LÖWE INTERFERENCE REFRACTOMETER

ferometric method offers the most convenient means for determining the concentration of a substance in an extremely dilute solution.

Differences in refractive index of one part in a million may be detected easily, and still higher sensitivities have been attained. Such small differences may be of practical importance, as in the industrial analysis of air. Portable interference refractometers have been used to detect traces (0.1%) of methane (marsh gas) in coal-mine air as a means of preventing explosions.

Optical Principles.—In the interference-type refractometer a set of interference bands is produced by the superposition of two light beams originating at the same slit source. When a transparent substance having a refractive index n is placed in the path of one of the beams while the other beam travels a comparable distance in a material of index n_0, there is a displacement of the interference bands that depends on the difference $n - n_0$.

The relation between refractive index and band displacement can be understood by considering the superposition of two converging trains of wave fronts. If they originate at the same slit source, there is a series of locations along the wave fronts where the waves are in the same phase of vibration and reinforce each other to produce a maximum light intensity. At intervening places the waves will be out of phase and tend to annul each other. One then sees alternately bright and dark areas in the field of view. These interference bands usually appear as narrow vertical fringes. If one of the wave trains is slowed down somewhat by passing through a more refracting medium than the other, the locations of the maxima and minima will be displaced laterally.

A relative retardation by one wave length causes the bands to shift laterally by one fringe interval. The band displacement, in number of fringe intervals N, is consequently related to the refractive index n by the formula $n - n_0 = \lambda N/t$, where λ is the wave length of the light and t is the thickness of the interposed sample.

Rayleigh Refractometer.—The basic elements of the Rayleigh interference refractometer (fig. 4) are two achromatic lenses of long focal length, the first for obtaining parallel rays from a narrow slit source, the second for bringing together two beams, B_I and B_{II}, emerging from two broad slits in front of the first lens. The resulting interference bands are observed with the aid of a cylindrical lens focused on the focal plane of the second achromatic lens. Adjacent cells C_1 and C_2, each in the path of one of the beams B_I and B_{II}, contain the reference substance and the sample.

Commercial instruments are usually of the Rayleigh-Haber-Löwe type (fig. 4), which uses the Jamin method of determining the band displacement. B_I and B_{II} are so divided that there are actually four beams: B_I, B_{II}, b_I and b_{II}. The lower beams, b_I and b_{II}, pass through air and the lifting prism (Pr). The upper beams, B_I and B_{II}, pass through cells C_1 and C_2 and movable plate P_1 and fixed plate P_2, respectively. Instead of counting the bands the observer increases the path in the glass by tilting the plate P_1 to produce a retardation just equal to that produced by the sample in the other beam. The effective thickness of P_1 is adjusted by the tilting lever L and a graduated micrometer screw. The micrometer scale may be calibrated to read values of $n - n_0$. The screw M is turned until the central interference band is brought back into the position it had before the sample was introduced. The central band in white light can be recognized because it is the only one having a pure white colour. *See also* INTERFEROMETER; LIGHT; OPTICS.

Automatic Recording Refractometers.—Instruments of this nature show promise of wide application in science and industry as a means of detecting small changes in flowing gases and liquids. Any of the types of refractometers may be adapted to automatic recording by substituting a photoelectric cell for the human eye. The current through the cell provides a measure of the intensity of light falling on the cell at a definite location.

BIBLIOGRAPHY.—Sir R. T. Glazebrook (ed.), *Dictionary of Applied Physics*, vol. iv (1950); T. R. P. Gibb, Jr., *Optical Methods of Chemical Analysis* (1942); A. Weissberger (ed.), *Physical Methods of Organic Chemistry*, vol. i, 3rd rev. ed. (1959–60); H. Kuhn, *Reports on Progress in Physics*, ed. by A. Stickland (1951); A. C. Candler, *Modern Interferometers* (1951); S. S. Batsanov, *Refractometry and Chemical Structure* (1961); G. Boudouris, "Index of Refraction of Air . . .," *Bur. Stand. J. Res.* (Nov. 1963). (No. Br.; J. Vk.)

REFRIGERATION, the process of lowering the temperature inside an insulated enclosure by extracting heat and rejecting it to the surroundings or some other external medium of higher temperature. Since heat will not flow spontaneously from a region of low temperature to one of higher temperature, mechanical work or heat energy from an external source must be expended to move the heat from the enclosure to be refrigerated.

Refrigeration technology draws its basic knowledge from three interrelated yet distinct areas of science, namely, thermodynamics, heat transfer, and fluid flow. As refrigeration technology has advanced, improved processes and materials have made possible many consumer products and industrial applications, from kitchen refrigerators and ice-cube makers to spot-cooling of electronic devices and simulating Arctic conditions for testing and research.

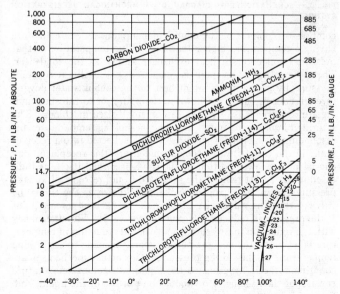

FIG. 1.—PRESSURE AND TEMPERATURE RELATIONSHIP OF VARIOUS LIQUID REFRIGERANTS

In the following sections the underlying principles of operation of major refrigeration systems (mechanical compression, absorption, and thermoelectric) are discussed, drawing on the basic sciences only to the extent necessary to achieve understanding and clarity.

In all mechanical compression and absorption refrigeration systems the working fluid used to carry away the heat from the region to be cooled is known as the refrigerant. The boiling temperature of refrigerants, like that of any other liquid, depends on the pressure at which the boiling takes place, the boiling temperature decreasing with decreasing pressure. This boiling temperature v. pressure characteristic of refrigerants can be said to constitute the main principle of operation (fig. 1). It is to be noted that, at a given pressure, the phenomena of boiling and condensation take place at the same temperature, one process being the reverse of the other.

MECHANICAL COMPRESSION REFRIGERATION SYSTEMS

The most widely used refrigeration cycle is the mechanical compression refrigeration cycle, which is schematically illustrated in fig. 2. A high-pressure refrigerant vapour is discharged from the

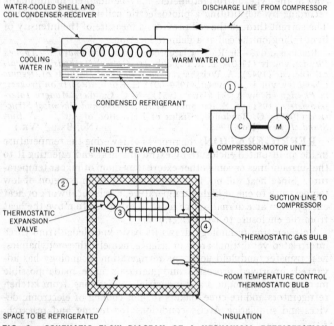

FIG. 2.—SCHEMATIC FLOW DIAGRAM OF A MECHANICAL REFRIGERATION SYSTEM

compressor (point 1 of the figure) in a superheated state (a state having a temperature higher than the boiling temperature at that pressure) and enters a heat exchanger known as the condenser. There the refrigerant vapour is condensed, essentially at constant pressure, by giving up its latent heat to the cooling water flowing through coils or tubes, as shown in the figure, or to the surrounding atmosphere, as is often the case in small-sized machines. The saturated liquid refrigerant (liquid at the boiling temperature corresponding to the condensing pressure) is collected into a receiver tank; in the case of water-cooled condensers, this receptacle may consist of the lower portion of the condenser shell itself, as indicated in fig. 2. At point 2 the saturated liquid refrigerant at high pressure enters the expansion valve, also known as the throttling valve or reducing valve. By the time the refrigerant reaches point 3, the pressure is reduced to a much lower value. Simultaneously with the reduction in pressure, an associated reduction in temperature takes place, the new temperature corresponding to the boiling temperature at this lower pressure. The actual mechanism accounting for this lowering of the liquid refrigerant temperature consists of the flashing into vapour of a portion of the liquid, and, as there exists no external source of heat, the energy for this evaporation is supplied by the liquid refrigerant itself, thus causing its temperature to drop. At point 3 the low-temperature liquid refrigerant, with a small fraction of its vapour, is admitted to a heat

exchanger known as the evaporator. Within the evaporator (which may be constructed in a variety of designs) the liquid refrigerant is evaporated by heat transferred to it from the comparatively warmer space to be refrigerated. The flow rate of the refrigerant is so adjusted by the thermostatic expansion valve that at the exit of the evaporator, at point 4 in the system, all the liquid refrigerant is in the saturated vapour state (vapour at the boiling temperature corresponding to the evaporator pressure). The vapour leaving the evaporator enters the suction side of the compressor and is compressed to a higher pressure. The work of compression raises both the pressure and temperature of the refrigerant vapour so that it is discharged in the superheated vapour state and ready to repeat the entire cycle over again.

A cycle of the type described above is known as a steady-flow thermodynamic cycle because at any one point in the cycle refrigerant conditions (i.e., flow rate, temperature, pressure, etc.) do not change with time, while heat and work are received by the refrigerant in the evaporator and compressor, respectively, and heat is rejected in the condenser. Also, this cycle operates between two levels of pressure and two corresponding levels of temperature. The high-pressure half of the cycle extends from the discharge of the compressor to the inlet of the expansion valve, and the low-pressure side extends from the discharge of the expansion valve to the inlet of the compressor.

Thermodynamic Analysis of Compression Refrigeration Cycles.—Evaluation of the performance of the various components of the refrigeration cycle discussed above requires a knowledge of some of the laws of thermodynamics that govern the interconversion of heat and work and enable the calculation of the thermal properties of substances. Extensive tables of thermodynamic properties of all commonly used refrigerants have been prepared and are available in tabular or graphical form readily usable in engineering calculations (see HEAT; THERMODYNAMICS).

From the principle of conservation of energy it can be stated that for a fluid in steady flow the summation of all its energy quantities (its total energy) entering a system (compressor, heat exchanger, etc.) must be equal to the summation of all its energy quantities leaving the system. For a unit mass flowing in and out of a system per unit time this principle can be written in symbolic form as:

$$u_1 + A(P_1v_1) + A(V_1^2/2g) + AZ_1 + {}_1Q_2$$
$$= u_2 + A(P_2v_2) + A(V_2^2/2g) + AZ_2 + A({}_1Wk_2) \qquad (1)$$

In the above relation subscripts 1 and 2 refer, respectively, to the magnitudes of the various quantities as the fluid enters and leaves the system. The magnitude of the various quantities can be expressed in any consistent set of units such as the British system of engineering units employed here, and where u = internal energy of the fluid, its value depending on the temperature and pressure of the fluid, expressed in British thermal units (BTU) per pound (one BTU is the quantity of heat required to raise the temperature of one pound of water by one degree Fahrenheit [from 63° F to 64° F]); P = pressure of the fluid, in pounds per square foot; v = specific volume of fluid, in cubic feet per pound; V = velocity of the fluid, in feet per second; Z = elevation of the inlet to the system measured from an arbitrary reference level, in feet; ${}_1Q_2$ = heat transferred to or away from the fluid from the time it enters to the time it leaves the system, in BTU per pound of fluid flowing (by convention, ${}_1Q_2$ is taken as positive if the fluid receives heat and negative if it gives up heat); ${}_1Wk_2$ = external work done by the fluid or on the fluid from the time it enters to the time it leaves the system, in foot-pounds per pound of fluid flowing (by convention, ${}_1Wk_2$ is taken as positive if it is performed by the fluid and negative if it is performed on the fluid); g = gravitational acceleration whose standard value is 32.2 ft. per square second; A = the mechanical equivalent of heat, a universal constant used to convert units of work into units of heat and vice versa ($A = \frac{1}{778}$ ft-lb. per BTU).

Examining equation (1) further, Pv, the product of the pressure times the volume, represents the magnitude of the flow work necessary to set the fluid in motion; $V^2/2g$ represents the kinetic energy caused by motion; and Z represents the potential energy of the moving fluid measured above a given arbitrary reference datum plane. In thermodynamics, because of the frequent simultaneous occurrence of the terms u and Pv, a new term called enthalpy is defined as $h = u + Pv$ (the sum of the internal energy of the fluid or body and the product of its volume multiplied by the pressure). Hence, the quantity $(u_1 + AP_1v_1)$ can be written as h_1 and $(u_2 + AP_2v_2)$ as h_2. Making these substitutions and transposing some of the terms, equation (1) can be rewritten in the form

$$h_2 - h_1 = {}_1Q_2 - A({}_1Wk_2) + A(V_1^2 - V_2^2)/2g + A(Z_1 - Z_2) \quad (2)$$

Equations (1) and (2), which are identical, are known as the general energy equations for steady flow and are used extensively in engineering calculations involving the interchange of heat and work. To simplify the analysis of refrigeration cycles it is common practice to neglect the last two terms on the right-hand side of equation (2), since their magnitude is either zero or negligible compared with the others. In fact, the difference in elevation between the inlet and outlet openings or the difference in velocity between the inlet and outlet of compressors or heat exchangers is either nil or negligible. Equation (2) can then be reduced to the form

$$(h_2 - h_1) = {}_1Q_2 - A({}_1Wk_2) \quad (3)$$

Equation (3) may be applied to any of the components that make up the refrigeration system shown in fig. 2. Considering the condenser, the refrigerant receives no external or shaft work and delivers none as it enters and leaves this equipment, and only heat is exchanged between the condensing refrigerant and the cooling water. Therefore in equation (3) the quantity ${}_1Wk_2$ is zero, and the decrease in enthalpy of the refrigerant $(h_2 - h_1)$ is equal to the heat it rejects to the cooling water, ${}_1Q_2$. The evaporator is a similar piece of equipment and again there is no work involved; therefore, the heat absorbed from the space to be refrigerated is equal to the increase of enthalpy of the evaporating refrigerant, ${}_3Q_4 = (h_4 - h_3)$. The flow through the expansion valve involves neither the exchange of heat nor work, hence, in this instance, equation (3) yields the result $h_3 - h_2 = 0$, indicating that the refrigerant undergoes no change of enthalpy. In the case of the compressor a definite amount of work, ${}_4Wk_1$, is delivered to the refrigerant vapour being compressed. While some heat, ${}_4Q_1$, is dissipated from the compressor cylinder head to the surrounding atmosphere by convection and radiation, this quantity is usually a small fraction of the total work input and may be neglected in most instances without causing serious error. Where more exact calculations are desired or, in the case of jacketed water-cooled compressors, where the heat loss from the compressor cylinder is appreciable, in applying equation (3) either the quantity ${}_4Q_1$ must be known or a different expression should be used to evaluate the work required for compression. Such an expression has the general form

$$Wk_{comp.} = [n/(n-1)]P_4v_4[1 - (P_1/P_4)^{(n-1)/n}] \quad (4)$$

where all symbols are as defined before and n is a constant which depends on the nature of the refrigerant, the type of compression (the extent of heat loss during compression), and the pressure range over which the compression takes place. Values of n are determined experimentally and are reported in reference works on refrigeration. An important observation to be made in equation (4) is the fact that the work of compression depends primarily on the pressure ratio of compression and not on the absolute values of the inlet or discharge pressures.

The Thermodynamic Diagram.—In solving refrigeration problems it is helpful to trace the processes the refrigerant undergoes on a chart of thermodynamic properties of the refrigerant, such as the pressure v. enthalpy chart shown in skeletal form in fig. 3, where the interrelationship between three of the most frequently used properties of refrigerants (pressure, enthalpy, and temperature) is graphically depicted. The properties pressure and enthalpy are chosen as the coordinates for the figure, and their variation with temperature is represented by the family of constant temperature lines $T_4, T_4', T_2', T_2, T_1, T_1'$, in order of increasing temperature. The dome A-C-B is known as the saturation dome. Points along the curve A-C represent states of dry saturated vapour and along B-C states of saturated liquid. The saturated vapour and saturated liquid curves meet at point C, which is known as the critical point. At this unique temperature and pressure the liquid and vapour phases of the refrigerant are indistinguishable and therefore possess identical properties known as the critical properties of the refrigerant. The region to the right of the saturated vapour curve A-C represents states of superheated vapour, and that to the left of the saturated liquid curve B-C represents states of subcooled (or compressed) liquid (liquid at a temperature lower than the condensation temperature corresponding to the same pressure). The region within the dome A-C-B (wet vapour region) represents states of mixtures of liquid and vapour refrigerant. The percentage by weight of vapour in the mixture at any point within the dome is obtained by taking the ratio of the horizontal distance between the saturated liquid curve and the point in question to the total distance between the two saturation curves (measured at the same pressure). For example, at point 3 (fig. 3) the percentage of vapour in the mixture is given

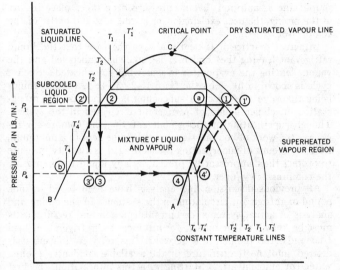

FIG. 3.—SKELETAL THERMODYNAMIC DIAGRAM ILLUSTRATING THE REFRIGERANT CYCLE FOR THE SYSTEM SHOWN IN FIG. 2 (NUMBERS CORRESPOND TO POINTS IN FIG. 2)

by the ratio of distances (b to 3)/(b to 4) or $(h_3 - h_b)/(h_4 - h_b)$. This fraction is called the quality of the wet vapour and is designated by the symbol x. On this basis, the vapour at point 4 on the saturated vapour curve would have a quality $x = 100\%$. At a given pressure or temperature, the difference in enthalpies between the saturated vapour and saturated liquid is known as the latent heat of evaporation (or condensation), representing the quantity of heat required to evaporate completely a unit mass of refrigerant from the saturated liquid state to saturated vapour state (at constant temperature and pressure). It should be noted that within the saturation dome A-C-B the constant temperature lines are horizontal and coincide with the corresponding saturation constant pressure lines.

The Thermodynamic Cycle.—The cycle of the refrigerant corresponding to the simple refrigeration system of fig. 2 is traced on the thermodynamic chart (fig. 3), with corresponding points on the flow diagram being labeled by matching numbers. Referring to fig. 3, the trace 1–2–3–4 represents this cycle. At point 1 the compressed and superheated refrigerant vapour (at temperature T_1 and pressure P_1) leaves the compressor and enters the condenser. As heat is transferred in the condenser to the cooling water the superheated vapour is cooled at constant pressure and its temperature drops from T_1 to T_2 (same as T_a). At point a the saturated vapour begins to condense, and, upon further heat transfer, condensation continues between points a and 2, the vapour giving up its latent heat of condensation until at point 2 all of the vapour is completely liquefied and is collected in the lower part of the condenser (or a receiver) as saturated liquid. At point 2 the saturated liquid refrigerant enters the expansion valve, and its pressure is reduced from P_1 (same as P_2) to P_3 ($P_3 = P_4$). As shown earlier, the enthalpy of the refrigerant entering and leaving the expansion valve is the same; i.e., $h_2 = h_3$. As a result of this pressure drop the temperature of the refrigerant is reduced to T_3 (same as T_4) at the expense of some of the liquid flashing into vapour. The fraction of the liquid flashed (the quality) is given by the ratio $x_3 = (h_3 - h_b)/(h_4 - h_3)$. At point 3 the refrigerant (mixture of liquid and vapour) enters the evaporator, and, as it absorbs heat from the refrigerated space and its contents, it continues to evaporate at constant pressure and temperature until at point 4 all of the refrigerant is completely evaporated and leaves the evaporator as saturated vapour. The dry saturated vapour enters the compressor at point 4, and by means of external work it is compressed along the path 4–1 and is discharged at point 1 to repeat the cycle. The cycle just described is known as the simple saturation ideal cycle because the refrigerant entering the expansion valve and the compressor consists of saturated liquid and saturated vapour, respectively. It is called ideal because of the simplifying assumption that no pressure drop takes place in any of the piping, the heat exchangers, or at the inlet and outlet of the compressor.

In actual practice it is nearly always the case that the liquid refrigerant leaving the condenser is somewhat subcooled and the vapour leaving the evaporator is somewhat superheated. Such a cycle is shown in fig. 3 by the trace 1′–2′–3′–4′. All other things being the same, the effect of subcooling is to increase the refrigeration effect per pound of refrigerant circulated in the system. Though superheating of the vapour entering the compressor increases the work of compression and should be kept to a minimum, a slight amount of superheating is encouraged as a safety measure to protect the compressor by preventing any liquid from entering the compressor cylinder.

All previous discussion and analysis have been based on one pound of refrigerant circulating in the system. In the design and analysis of actual systems, certain information and requirements must be known at the outset, for instance, the refrigeration load (demand), the temperature at which this refrigeration effect is desired, and the temperature of the available condenser cooling water (or ambient air). Starting with this information, the first step is to determine the condensation and evaporation temperatures and pressures for the refrigeration cycle. In practice, it is customary to assume an average temperature difference between the cooling medium and the condensing refrigerant of the order of 10° F. A similar figure is taken for the temperature difference between the evaporating refrigerant and the refrigerated medium. The smaller the temperature differential, the larger becomes the required size of the heat exchanger needed to accomplish a given heat transfer. Hence, the actual selection of temperature differentials to be used is based on both engineering and economic considerations. In general, therefore, one can write

$$T_c = (T_{c.w.})_{av.} + (\Delta T)_c \text{ and } T_e = T_r - (\Delta T)_e \qquad (5)$$

where T_c, T_e and T_r are the temperatures of the condensing and evaporating refrigerants and refrigerated medium, respectively; $(T_{c.w.})_{av.}$ is the average cooling water or air temperature; $(\Delta T)_c$ and $(\Delta T)_e$ are the design temperature differentials between the cooling water and condensing refrigerant and between the refrigerated medium and evaporating refrigerant, respectively, all temperatures being expressed in degrees Fahrenheit.

At this point the choice of a refrigerant must be made. The proper refrigerant selection is dependent primarily on the condenser and evaporator temperatures. A desirable refrigerant should not give rise to either unduly high condenser pressures or very low evaporator pressures. Some of the characteristics of refrigerants are discussed in a later section. Having decided on the refrigerant to be used and having determined the condensing and evaporating temperatures, the respective pressures are directly obtained by looking up the saturation pressures corresponding to these two temperatures. The next step in the analysis is the determination of the flow rate of refrigerant necessary to provide the desired refrigeration. Refrigeration load is commonly expressed in the unit of tons of refrigeration. In the U.S., one ton of refrigeration is equal to a cooling rate of 288,000 BTU per 24-hr. day, or 200 BTU per minute. The ton as the unit of refrigeration derives its name from the fact that to freeze one ton of water per day (one U.S. ton equals 2,000 lb.) from 32° F liquid to 32° F solid requires approximately 288,000 BTU. In Great Britain and Europe the ton of refrigeration is sometimes defined either on the basis of the long ton (2,240 lb.) or taken equal to a cooling rate of one kilocalorie per second. These units are larger than the U.S. ton by 12 and 18.8%, respectively. Referring to the cycle 1–2–3–4 of fig. 3, the refrigeration performed per pound of refrigerant is given by $(h_4 - h_3)$, in BTU per pound; hence, the required refrigerant flow rate, w, is

$$w = \text{(tons of refrigeration) } 200/(h_4 - h_3), \text{ pounds per minute}$$

The work necessary for compression is obtained from the relation

$$Wk_{comp.} = w(h_1 - h_4)/42.42, \text{ hp.}$$

where 42.42 is a conversion factor between heat units and horsepower (1 hp. = 42.42 BTU per minute).

A final quantity of interest in the analysis of refrigeration cycles is the efficiency of performance of the cycle. The efficiency of refrigeration cycles, which is known as the coefficient of performance (COP), is defined as the ratio of the refrigeration effect produced in the evaporator to the compressor work necessary to bring about this refrigeration effect. In symbolic form this may be expressed as

$$COP = w(h_4 - h_3)/w(h_1 - h_4) = (h_4 - h_3)/(h_1 - h_4)$$

The COP of all mechanical refrigeration cycles is greater than one. Since the magnitude of the COP is not directly indicative of the degree of perfection attained by an actual refrigeration system, it is often compared with the COP of an ideal cycle operating between the same condensing and evaporating temperatures. Such an ideal cycle is the Carnot cycle, named after its originator, Nicolas Sadi Carnot, the French engineer (see HEAT: Carnot: On the Motive Power of Heat). It can be shown in thermodynamics that a refrigeration system operating on the Carnot cycle requires the least amount of work per unit of refrigeration. It can further be shown that the COP of the Carnot cycle is independent of the type of refrigerant used and is fixed solely by the two temperatures at which heat is rejected and received. The COP of the Carnot cycle is defined as

$$(COP)_{Carnot} = T_e/(T_c - T_e) \qquad (6)$$

where T_e and T_c are the evaporation and condensation temperatures, respectively, expressed in degrees Rankine. Temperatures in degrees Rankine are obtained by adding 460 to Fahrenheit degrees (see THERMOMETRY).

Properties of Refrigerants.—Since the early days of mechanical refrigeration the number of available refrigerants has increased steadily as a result of the consistent efforts of chemists and physical chemists searching for new fluids possessing suitable thermal, physical, and chemical characteristics to meet demands of new applications and equipment design. The most striking example of such research is the development of the series of refrigerants known under the trade name of Freons (q.v.). With rapid advances in the understanding of the structure of matter it has become possible to synthesize almost any type of refrigerant suitable for a specific application. However, even scientific progress has not been able to produce the ideal refrigerant having simultaneously optimum thermodynamic, physical, and chemical properties. Therefore, refrigerant suitability for a specific application is determined as a result of both engineering and economic considerations, and compromises must be made among the most important factors involved in a particular situation.

ABSORPTION REFRIGERATION SYSTEMS

Absorption refrigeration systems use heat energy directly through the medium of a generator-absorber-pump circuit, which replaces the complex mechanical compressor. In some absorption refrigerators a small liquid pump constitutes the only moving part in the entire system, and in others even this is eliminated, resulting in a system with no moving parts whatsoever. Two of the most prominent types of absorption systems are discussed below.

The Ammonia-Water Absorption Refrigeration Cycle.— The most common absorption system is the two-fluid, water-ammonia (also known as aqua-ammonia) system. The operation of this system is based on the particular relationship between the temperature, pressure, and concentration of a mixture of two fluids, such as ammonia and water, while it undergoes a change of phase. When a mixture of ammonia and water boils at a given pressure, the vapour phase is much richer in ammonia (the more volatile of the two components) than the liquid phase in contact with it. Conversely, when condensing a mixture of ammonia and water vapour the condensate is poorer in ammonia than the vapour mixture in contact with it. Also, at a given pressure the boiling point temperature of the mixture decreases with increasing concentration of ammonia. This behaviour can be interpreted to mean that at low temperatures the mixture can hold more ammonia in solution than at high temperatures. Increasing the pressure on the mixture at constant temperature has the same effect. Finally, as is the case with single-component liquids, at a given concentration the boiling temperature of the mixture increases with increasing pressure. These basic behaviour characteristics of binary (two-component) mixtures will help in understanding the operation of the absorption system schematically shown in fig. 4 (*see* SOLUTIONS). Liquid ammonia (point 2) at about 85° F and 160 psi (pounds per square inch) is expanded through the expansion valve to about 22 psi and 15° F and enters the evaporator where it evaporates, absorbing heat from the space to be refrigerated. This ammonia vapour is discharged into the absorber (point 3), where it meets a shower (point 8) of weak liquor (about 30% ammonia), which absorbs the ammonia vapour into solution as it trickles down successive trays, thus forming a solution stronger in ammonia (about 38%). This strong liquor is pumped from the absorber to the top of the analyzer (point 5), being partly heated on its way as it passes through the heat exchanger. In the analyzer this

generator the part weak in ammonia gravitates to the bottom of the generator, whence it is taken to the absorber through a pressure reducer (point 7). On its way to the absorber this weak liquor is partly cooled in the heat exchanger as it heats up the strong liquor. The COP of absorption systems is much lower than that of mechanical refrigeration systems (about 0.5); however, this disadvantage is offset by the fact that they can be made to operate on inexpensive, low-grade energy. Also, the fact that they have no major moving parts makes for quiet and vibration-free operation, a feature desirable in some applications.

Electrolux Absorption Refrigeration System.—An ingenious modification of the absorption cycle shown in fig. 4 is the Electrolux absorption system, in which the refrigerant is taken around the refrigeration cycle without employing any machinery with moving parts. This system was invented in the early 1920s by two Swedish engineers, Carl Munters and Baltzar von Platen, while they were still undergraduates at the Royal Institute of Technology in Stockholm. The Electrolux system is in all respects identical to the ammonia-water absorption system with the exception that the strong-liquor pump, the expansion valve, and the pressure-reducer valve are all eliminated. In the Electrolux system the ammonia is transported from the absorber to the generator by going into solution in water, the aqua ammonia being circulated by gravity and thermal siphon effect. The functions of the expansion and pressure-reducer valves are performed by an inert atmosphere of hydrogen gas (insoluble in water or ammonia) that circulates between the evaporator and the absorber, transporting the ammonia vapour with it. Heat is supplied to the generator, forcing slugs of strong aqua-ammonia solution and its vapour into the standpipe and lifting the liquid in the same way a coffee percolator operates. As this stream discharges into the top of the generator the liquid and vapour separate, and the concentrated ammonia vapour enters the rectifier, where the concentration is increased by partial liquefaction prior to entering the condenser. The small amount of condensate formed in the rectifier returns to the top of the generator. The ammonia vapour is liquefied in the condenser and is discharged as a liquid into a flash chamber at the head of the evaporator. Hydrogen gas released in the absorber also enters the evaporator at this point, and as a result ammonia evaporates into this hydrogen, thus undergoing a drop in temperature. The evaporation of the ammonia is caused by its drop in pressure from about 180 psi in the condenser to a partial pressure of 30 psi in the evaporator. This is explained by a physical law discovered by John Dalton which states that the total pressure of a mixture of gases is equal to the sum of the pressures that each gas in the same volume and at the same temperature would exert if the other gases were absent. Therefore, when the ammonia which is liquefied at 180 psi in the condenser enters the evaporator, where the partial pressure of the hydrogen is only 150 psi, it evaporates at a rate to make up the difference between the two pressures; *i.e.*, 30 psi. The mixture of hydrogen gas and ammonia vapour leaves the evaporator and enters the absorber, where it meets a spray of weak aqua ammonia. Within the absorber the ammonia vapour is readily absorbed into solution by the weak aqua ammonia as it trickles down successive perforated trays and leaves the absorber at the bottom as strong liquor, while the inert hydrogen gas free of ammonia vapour rises up the absorber and leaves at the top to repeat its cycle. An absorber cooling jacket, in which water is circulated, is provided to remove the heat of solution generated by the absorption of ammonia vapour by the weak liquor. The strong liquor leaving the absorber proceeds to the generator, being partially heated on its way in the heat exchanger by the hot weak liquor coming from the generator on its way to the absorber. It is seen that in this system the total pressure in all its parts is the same (except for minor friction losses). While the partial pressure of the refrigerant varies from a minimum in the evaporator to a maximum in the condenser, a compensating variation in the partial pressure of the hydrogen gas enables the maintenance of the same total pressure throughout.

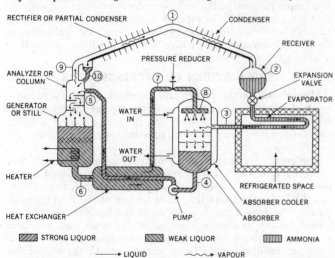

RECTIFIER OR PARTIAL CONDENSER

CONDENSER

RECEIVER

PRESSURE REDUCER

ANALYZER OR COLUMN

EXPANSION VALVE

GENERATOR OR STILL

EVAPORATOR

WATER IN

WATER OUT

HEATER

REFRIGERATED SPACE

ABSORBER COOLER

HEAT EXCHANGER

PUMP

ABSORBER

STRONG LIQUOR   WEAK LIQUOR   AMMONIA

⟶ LIQUID   ⤳ VAPOUR

FIG. 4.—SCHEMATIC FLOW DIAGRAM OF AQUA-AMMONIA ABSORPTION REFRIGERATION CYCLE

strong liquor trickles down trays against a current of vapour of ammonia and water rising from the boiling solution in the generator below it. The heater (electric, gas, or low-pressure condensing steam) boils the ammonia-water liquor, and the hot vapour (about 220° F) rises up the analyzer counterflow to the cold strong liquor. As a result of this distillation process the vapour at the top of the analyzer (point 9) reaches a concentration of about 94%. This concentration is further increased as the vapour continues its way through the rectifier, where partial condensation takes place, and the vapour is enriched to about 99.5% ammonia as it enters the condenser at about 125° F (point 1). The small amount of condensate (about 60% ammonia) formed in the rectifier flows back to the top of the analyzer (point 10). As the liquor boils in the

THERMOELECTRIC REFRIGERATION

The discovery of the phenomena of thermoelectricity dates back to 1821 when T. J. Seebeck first observed that in an electric circuit consisting of two dissimilar metals an electric current flowed in the circuit when the two junctions were maintained at different temperatures. In 1834, J. C. Peltier observed the reverse effect, namely, that if an electric current flowed across the junctions between two dissimilar metals, originally at uniform temperature, heat was either absorbed or generated at the junctions, depending on the direction of current flow and the nature of the two dissimilar metals. These cross-flow effects, namely, that an electric potential causes thermal energy to flow, and vice versa, did not receive serious consideration for heating or cooling applications because of the small magnitude of these effects in metals. In fact, until the mid-1940s the primary application of the Seebeck and Peltier effects was restricted to thermocouples as temperature measuring sensors.

The advent of semiconductor devices such as transistors stimulated research on semiconductor materials, which have much more pronounced Seebeck and Peltier effects than metals. A. F. Ioffe in the Soviet Union perhaps contributed more than anyone else to the understanding and popularization of thermoelectricity. He was among the first to realize the practical importance of semiconductors for thermoelectric cooling applications. As early as 1953, Ioffe and his associates at Leningrad built a laboratory model 0.35-cu.-ft. refrigerator that was maintained at 39° F in an environment at 80° F. From this point on, development of thermoelectric refrigerators and many other specialized cooling devices progressed rapidly, and in 1963 small-capacity household refrigeration appliances were marketed competitively in the U.S.

The effectiveness of a thermoelectric system is measured by a quantity referred to as the "Figure of Merit," Z, defined as

$$Z = \frac{(\alpha_{AB})^2}{(\sqrt{k_A \rho_A} + \sqrt{k_B \rho_B})^2} \quad (7)$$

where α_{AB} is the relative Seebeck coefficient between the two thermoelectric elements; k is the thermal conductivity; and ρ is the electrical resistivity. The subscripts A and B refer to the two materials comprising the thermoelectric couple. While results of proprietary research in a rapidly developing field are not immediately divulged, one can safely assume that actual performance is always ahead of the known state of the art. In the early 1960s, representative figures for the above quantities were: $Z = 0.003/°C$;

$\alpha = 0.0002$ v/°C; $\rho = 0.00083$ ohm-cm; $k = 0.016$ w/cm °C. Thermoelectric elements are commercially available which exhibit cooling to approximately −50° F from an ambient of 80° F with no applied heat load. This represents a temperature differential of 130° F.

Fig. 5 depicts the component counterparts and analogous functions between a mechanical vapour compression refrigeration system and a thermoelectric cooling circuit. It was indicated in the discussion of mechanical refrigeration systems that, in principle, the heating and cooling functions of the condenser and evaporator, respectively, could be interchanged by reversing the direction of refrigerant flow, but a closer examination of the mechanical equipment involved would indicate that such flow reversal would be difficult and costly. Another drawback of mechanical refrigeration systems is their drastic limitations with respect to miniaturization.

A thermoelectric circuit requires no moving parts. The conventional motor, compressor, condenser, expansion valve, evaporator, and refrigerant are replaced by one or more thermoelectric junctions and a power supply source. A simple reversal of the polarity of the power supply results in an interchange of the heating and cooling processes. Another important operational advantage is the simplicity with which the refrigeration capacity of a given unit can be modulated by simply varying the magnitude of the electric current flow through the thermoelectric junctions. The counterpart operation in the case of the mechanical refrigeration system would consist of varying the piston displacement, or the speed of the compressor, or otherwise controlling the flow of liquid refrigerant. It is also clear that a thermoelectric cooling system can be made in true miniature for special applications.

The primary disadvantage of the thermoelectric cooling system is economic. Although the situation is rapidly changing, the production of semiconductors and the fabrication processes of multiple-junction elements are expensive. This, together with high power requirements because of low thermodynamic effectiveness of the thermoelectric energy conversion, still prevents thermoelectric cooling from being competitive for major applications. However, rapid progress in the techniques of manufacturing semiconductor materials, skills in junction miniaturization, and continued research to provide cheaper and better materials will make thermoelectric refrigeration competitive with conventional methods in increasingly larger sizes.

APPLICATIONS OF REFRIGERATION

Household Refrigerators and Freezers.—With the achievement of reliability in modern, hermetic, mechanical refrigeration systems of fractional horsepower size, the main emphasis in household refrigerators was placed on improved appearance, utility, and convenience.

The greatly increased use of frozen foods resulted in the need for refrigerators with much larger and colder frozen-food storage compartments. In a variety of models the freezing compartments run the full width across the top or bottom of the food compartment. The evaporator is operated at the low temperatures required for proper food storage but at the same time maintains temperatures above freezing in the regular food storage compartment, an insulated baffle being placed beneath the evaporator. Some manufacturers provide separate cooling for the freezer and the food storage compartments with separate evaporators. In larger refrigerators an exterior two-door design was introduced, with the freezer and food storage compartments completely separated from each other. The volume of the frozen-food compartment may vary from 20 to 100% of the food storage compartment volume. Those in the latter category are normally classified as combination refrigerator-freezers.

The trend toward specialized interior designs has become a common practice. Meat storage compartments maintained at temperatures slightly above freezing, with relative humidities around 90%, special high-humidity compartments for leafy vegetables, shelves on the inner panel of the door for storage of small bottles, containers, eggs, etc., and compartments with provisions for maintaining butter at suitable spreading temperatures are common. An-

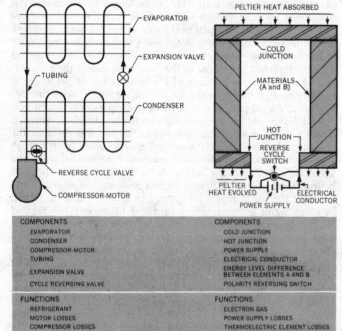

FIG. 5.—ANALOGOUS COMPONENTS AND FUNCTIONS BETWEEN (LEFT) MECHANICAL REFRIGERATION CYCLE AND (RIGHT) THERMOELECTRIC REFRIGERATION CIRCUIT

other important feature in modern household refrigerators is the rapid automatic defrosting of the evaporator. With defrosting cycles ranging from 5 to 30 min., no substantial rise occurs in the frozen-food temperature or in the normal food compartment temperature.

The use of household freezers in urban homes and on farms has constantly increased since they first assumed commercial importance in 1937. The household freezer provides a storage space at a temperature of 0° F or below and a fast-freezing zone where limited quantities of fresh food may be frozen in a reasonably short time with minimum disturbance of the stored load temperature. Modern freezer cabinets are made in two general styles, namely, the upright freezer and the chest-type freezer. Upright freezers have followed the pattern of household refrigerators, with interior locker doors that reduce air spillage and form convenient loading shelves when the main door is opened. Tests comparing chest and upright types indicate no significant difference in operating costs with a door-opening frequency of two per day. The frost accumulation in the upright type may become objectionable when more frequent door openings are necessary, but in household use this is rarely the case.

Cold-Storage Warehouses.—Cold-storage warehouses vary in capacity from 1,000,000 to 6,000,000 or more cubic feet of storage space devoted, on the average, two-thirds to freezer space and one-third to cooler space. Unless special provisions are made for quick freezing, the minimum temperatures maintained in these spaces usually are: sharp freezers, −15° to −10° F; carrying freezers, −10° to 0° F; and coolers, 30° F. The actual refrigeration capacity necessary to take care of a cold-storage warehouse is not always easy to estimate, as the load requirements vary appreciably with the nature of products stored and many other operating variables, including the size of the plant. To give an idea of the order of magnitude involved, one can say that an average cold-storage warehouse having 6,000,000 cu.ft. of storage capacity requires about 300 tons of refrigeration.

The cooling systems used in cold-storage applications come under three main classifications, namely: (1) the direct application, where the refrigerant circulates in pipe coils in the space to be cooled; (2) the indirect application, where the refrigerant cools a brine (a solution of water and calcium chloride or sodium chloride having a freezing point temperature as low as −60° F, depending on the salt concentration) in a heat exchanger, and the cold brine circulates in pipe coils in the space to be refrigerated; (3) the indirect application, where air, cooled either by a brine spray or direct expansion coils, is circulated through diffusers in the refrigerated space. Of the three methods mentioned, the brine and forced-air circulation methods are the most extensively used because of their greater flexibility and safety. It is common practice to use several refrigeration compressors to handle the total load of a cold-storage installation, a number of the units supplying refrigeration for the freezer rooms and others for the coolers, with at least one unit kept as a standby in the event of a breakdown.

Another type of installation somewhat similar to the cold-storage warehouse but much smaller in capacity and more specialized in function is the frozen-food locker plant, where foods are frozen and held in storage for families and other groups of a community.

Refrigerated Food Transportation.—*Trucks and Trailers.*—The distribution of refrigerated foods from major storage centres to retailers and even the long-distance hauling from farms and food processing centres to cities is handled to a large extent by refrigerated trucks and trailers. In the main, two types of truck bodies are constructed: those maintaining 35° to 40° F for carrying fresh meat, vegetables, and dairy products; and those maintaining about 0° F for ice cream and frozen foods. Numerous types of mechanical refrigeration systems are used in both trucks and trailers, the source of power being obtained either by a separate internal-combustion engine or from the truck engine itself, either by a crankshaft extension at the front end or by a power take-off from the transmission. Besides mechanical refrigeration, water ice and dry ice (solid carbon dioxide) are extensively used in

refrigerated transportation. These are charged in conveniently located bunkers either at the end or near the ceiling of the truck body, and air is circulated past them and through the body by means of a small blower. The use of dry ice in refrigerated transportation (truck, trailer, and rail) was steadily increasing in the 1960s despite its much higher cost per pound. Its low temperature makes it ideal for frozen-food transportation, and when it is used for fresh foods the carbon dioxide gas in the atmosphere immediately surrounding the product serves to reduce the oxygen content of the air, thus minimizing possible deterioration resulting from oxidation. Also, it inhibits the growth and development of bacteria and various molds that cause spoilage. It is often the practice to precool the interior of the truck, as well as the fresh produce, prior to or at the time of loading.

Refrigerated Railway Cars.—Despite the tremendous volume of perishables transported by trucks and trailers and their increasing competition with the railways, the main bulk of long-distance refrigerated transportation was handled by rail in the 1960s. The earliest known use of refrigeration by the railroads was in July 1851, when several tons of butter were shipped from Ogdensburg, N.Y., to Boston, Mass., in a wooden boxcar insulated with sawdust and stocked with ice. More than a century later, water ice was still more or less the universal cooling medium in refrigerated freight and express cars. The modern standard refrigerator car in the U.S. is 40 ft. long and of the end-bunker type, equipped with fans and having about 4 in. of insulation. Some cars are 50 ft. long and have 6 in. of insulation, using 30% by weight of sodium chloride salt with water ice to provide a bunker temperature of −3° F for frozen foods. The use of mechanical refrigeration on railways was still more or less in the developmental stage in the early 1960s. Considerations of high first cost and high maintenance costs were expected to delay wide-scale mechanical installations. The few mechanically refrigerated freight cars in operation were mostly equipped with Freon-12 compressors run by diesel-electric drives. Each of these cars had a refrigeration capacity of about seven tons, and they were used mainly by the frozen-food and frozen-concentrate industry.

Marine Refrigeration.—In the summer of 1880 the steamer "Strathleven" brought to England the first successfully carried refrigerated meat cargo. Early shipboard installations were equipped with dense-air machines, later being replaced by carbon dioxide and ammonia systems. In modern installations Freon refrigerants are used extensively. Design conditions and other basic principles are not greatly different in marine refrigeration from those in cold-storage warehouse practice. All equipment and installations must specify compliance with the rules and regulations of various classification societies (*e.g.*, American Bureau of Shipping, or *Lloyd's Register*, or both, etc.).

Manufacture of Water Ice.—Despite the tremendous increase in the use of fractional-horsepower mechanical refrigeration units for household and other commercial uses, the manufacture of water ice remained a major industry. The method most extensively used is the can method, using treated or untreated raw (tap) water. Galvanized steel ice cans, usually of about 320 lb. capacity, 11 × 12 in. at the top and 50 in. in depth, with an overall taper of $\frac{1}{2}$ in. in their length, are submerged in a well-insulated (10- to 12-in. granulated cork) tank in which cold brine is circulated. Tank depths are usually about 52 in. for 320-lb. ice cans, and width and length seldom exceed 40 and 120 ft. The brine is cooled by direct-expansion evaporator coils normally placed between rows of cans. The velocity of the brine flowing past the cans and the brine temperature determine the time required for freezing. Brine velocities should not exceed about 35 ft. per minute, and variations of temperature should be kept less than 1° F.

For a given brine velocity, the time required to freeze a given thickness of ice is determined first by the brine temperature. As most raw waters, treated or untreated, crack upon freezing at temperatures below 10° F, the freezing temperatures are generally somewhat above this figure. The rate of freezing drops rapidly as the ice becomes thicker. An 11 × 12-in. can holding 320 lb. of water in 12° F brine takes 24 hr. to freeze the first 280 lb. of ice and an additional 14 hr. to freeze the last 40 lb. When raw water is used to manufacture ice it is necessary to agitate the water in the cans during freezing to obtain clear ice. This is done by bubbling dry air, usually at about 15 to 18 psi gauge pressure, at the centre of each can, thus rejecting most of the dissolved minerals into the unfrozen centre core. When the water is almost frozen, the concentrated core, consisting of about three to four gallons, is sucked out and replaced with chilled fresh water to complete the freezing of the entire block. The amount of refrigeration required to manufacture ice depends on many factors, such as initial water temperature, brine temperature, insulation of brine tank, efficiency of refrigeration compressors, size of plant, etc. A good figure for a well-constructed plant of 30- to 50-ton daily ice capacity using 60° F water and 12° F brine is 1.52 tons of refrigeration per ton of ice.

Despite the large amount of ice consumption in all countries of the world, the methods for handling and processing ice have not changed significantly over the years. Only in the decade following World War II did mechanization of ice making become widespread. There was then a definite trend toward increased sales of ice in small sizes (cubed, crushed, sized, and shaved) aside from the manufacture of block ice. Installations of scoring, cubing, sizing, and packing machines for automatic vending stations expanded rapidly.

Comfort Air Conditioning.—In its strictest definition, comfort air conditioning must incorporate the following features: control of temperature, humidity, air distribution (ventilation), odour, air cleanliness, and in some instances air sterilization. All comfort air-conditioning applications are functionally similar, whether the space under consideration is that of a residential dwelling or that of a large building. In large installations, involving sometimes 1,000 or more tons of refrigeration capacity, the central system design is adapted. However, most smaller installations run in sizes from ½ ton for window air-conditioning units to 5, 10, or 25 tons for small retail shops, restaurants, etc. (*See* Air Conditioning.)

Other Applications.—The following constitutes only a partial illustrative list of the many diverse applications where refrigeration is used extensively: food processing and manufacturing of dairy products (butter, ice cream, cheese), beverages (beer, wine, and other alcoholic and carbonated beverages), bakery goods, etc.; industrial and engineering applications for liquefied storage and transportation of industrial gases (oxygen, nitrogen, hydrogen), manufacture of dry ice, synthetic and natural yarn processing and weaving in the textile industry, petroleum refining and chemical processes, metallurgical processes, engineering construction (freezing of sliding silty soils in the construction of dams, tunnels, shaft sinking, curing of large masses of poured concrete), low-temperature testing facilities, wind-tunnel cooling, etc.; industrial air conditioning for printing and paper manufacture, precision machining and assembly of metal machine parts, confectionery processing, deep-mine cooling, and preservation of valuable books, paintings, and tapestries in libraries and museums.

See Air Conditioning; Heating and Ventilation; Low-Temperature Physics; *see* also references under "Refrigeration" in the Index.

Bibliography.—American Society of Heating, Refrigerating and Air-Conditioning Engineers, *ASHRAE Guide and Data Book: Fundamentals and Equipment* (1963) and *Applications* (1964); M. W. Zemansky, *Heat and Thermodynamics,* 4th ed. (1957); R. J. Dossat, *Principles of Refrigeration* (1961); R. Wolfe, "Magnetothermoelectricity," *Scientific American* 210:70–82 (June 1964).   (Y. S. T.)

REFUGEES, persons who have fled from one place to another to escape persecution or danger, usually during time of war or political upheaval. Discrimination against particular racial, religious, or political groups has historically developed into threats to life and liberty, precipitating the flight of refugees, in many instances across national boundaries and without guarantee of asylum. Changes in national boundaries, postwar agreements, and the actions of aggressor states have also resulted in transfers or exchanges of populations, generally of minority groups, with or without the transfer of their possessions. Notable examples from early modern history are the Moors and Jews who were expelled

from Spain, the Huguenot refugees in 16th-century France, some of the early settlers in America, the Loyalists who fled to Canada during the American Revolution, and the émigrés of the French Revolution.

After a period of relative subsidence during the 19th century, the refugee problem emerged again on a vast scale in the 20th century with the rise of Communism and Fascism and the occurrence of two wars of worldwide scope. In some cases the refugee movements were only temporary. For example, although the Belgian refugees who fled from the German invaders in 1914 were numerous, they did not attempt to create a new life or to establish new homes outside their native land; their migration was only temporary, like that of the refugees who fled from the invaded provinces of France, Italy, and Rumania, and to a smaller extent from all the territories occupied by enemy troops during World War I. But in other cases, great masses of war refugees had little prospect of ever returning to their homes or of recreating their previous life there. This was the case with Jews and others who fled from Hitler's Germany and of countless thousands who were uprooted during and after World War II.

Before the 20th century, refugees attempting to escape from oppression and to found new homes did not meet with insuperable obstacles. What distinguishes the 20th-century refugees is the increasing difficulty of fleeing and, even more important, the immense difficulty, often impossibility, of gaining entrance elsewhere. The rise of modern totalitarianism, especially in Nazi Germany and Soviet Russia, brought in its train the closing of national boundaries, and the problem of getting in became as great as the problem of getting out. The result was the stateless refugee, shunted from border to border, dependent on charity and chance rather than law, a modern "man without a country."

From the Russian Revolution to World War II.—The first massive refugee movement of the 20th century was caused by the Russian Revolution of 1917. During the post-Revolutionary struggles of the Soviet government, 1,500,000 enemies of the new regime were forced into exile. Scattered throughout France, Germany, the borderlands of the Soviet Union, and parts of the Far East, these exiles hoped that the Soviet experiment would fail and that they would then be able to return to their homes. During the 1920s approximately 200,000 Armenian and 500,000 Greek refugees fled from Turkey and 100,000 Bulgarian refugees left their homes because of Bulgaria's territorial cessions to neighbouring countries after World War I.

In 1920 the League of Nations appointed Fridtjof Nansen (*q.v.*) as the first high commissioner for refugees. For the next ten years, until his death in 1930, this man was the main, almost the only, bulwark between these refugees and oblivion. Nansen's first attack upon the problem was the Nansen passport, an identity document that was recognized in lieu of a passport by 28 governments as a result of tireless prodding by the high commissioner. Even more important, Nansen constantly prodded governments to lower their immigration barriers. The twin enemies of the high commissioner were international apathy and a chronic shortage of funds. Nevertheless, the Nansen office managed to integrate close to one-third of the post-World War I refugees into over 20 European countries.

Nansen's death preceded by only three years the ascent to power of Adolf Hitler in Germany. Until 1939 the policy of the Nazi government was to rob the Jews and then to let them go. When they attempted to migrate the Jews met resistance almost everywhere and only a small minority found refuge before the policy of annihilation began in earnest in 1940. Indeed, Adolf Eichmann, speaking in his defense at the Jerusalem trial, claimed that the so-called final solution (mass execution) of European Jews had been made possible by the resistance to Jewish immigration all over the world. The well-known impotence of the Nansen office during the 1930s was part of the general decline of the League of Nations.

World War II.—The outbreak of World War II merged the tragedy of the Jewish people into the greater tragedy of worldwide military conflict. The mass movements set in motion by the expansionist policies of the Axis powers eclipsed all previous human floods in history.

While Hitler's Germany was experiencing its early successes, millions of refugees fled before the advancing Nazi armies. Following the German conquest of Poland in September 1939, 300,000 Poles sought sanctuary within the frontiers of the Soviet Union. As the blitzkrieg continued throughout 1940, and the Netherlands, Luxembourg, Belgium, and northern France were overrun, an avalanche of over 5,000,000 desperate refugees swept into southern France, only to be overtaken by the Germans in November 1942. When the Germans launched their Balkan campaign in April 1941, 300,000 refugees chose homelessness rather than life under Nazi rule. Finally, when Hitler attacked the Soviet Union in June 1941, a seemingly endless stream of fugitives from the eastern borderlands sought refuge in the vast spaces of inner Russia. It has been estimated that over 12,000,000 people were made homeless by the advancing Nazi armies.

Mass refugee movements were not limited to the European continent. Germany's Asian partner, Japan, embarked upon her own aggressive course and drove over 30,000,000 Chinese from their homes. When the Japanese conquest spread southward to Burma, the Malay states, the Philippines, and Indochina, more refugees fled from the approaching armies. By 1943, when the Axis forces had attained their greatest territorial expansion, approximately 60,000,000 human beings had been displaced from their homes throughout the world.

When the fortunes of war turned in 1943 and the Soviet armies began to push back the German invaders, the 12,000,000 displaced Russians who had sought sanctuary in the inner recesses of the Soviet Union followed in the wake of the Red Army. As Japan's expansion was checked in 1942–43, Chinese refugees began to return to their former homes. Unlike their brethren in Europe, the Chinese displaced persons had not moved over long distances, but for the most part had hidden in the neighbouring hills of the Chinese countryside and thus found it easier to return to their homes as the Japanese retreated. They returned to a gutted land and a broken economy, however, and faced as difficult a time as the European refugees.

Post-World War II Problems and Policies.—The first concerted attempt to deal with the post-World War II refugees was made through the United Nations Relief and Rehabilitation Administration (UNRRA). UNRRA was set up by 44 nations in 1943 while the sense of cooperation and urgency was still strong among the Allies. The main task of UNRRA was to be the repatriation of uprooted refugees. In this job it was largely successful but in 1945 more than 1,000,000 refugees living in almost 1,000 camps in Germany, Austria, and Italy refused to be repatriated. Mostly nationals of countries that had come under Soviet rule, they were strongly anti-Communist in outlook and were devoted to their own national states. Rather than live under Communism, they wished to settle in new homes. Because of the special problem they posed, the United Nations created a new agency to deal with them—the International Refugee Organization (IRO; q.v.).

The IRO operated between 1947 and 1952 and was the only refugee agency to deal with all aspects of the problem, including legal protection, rehabilitation, and resettlement. Within these years IRO successfully completed the greatest overseas resettlement scheme for refugees in history. It provided food, shelter, medical care, and vocational instruction in all its camps and then prodded governments to send selection missions to the camps and to relax their restrictive immigration laws. The United States, for example, passed the Displaced Persons Act in 1948; under this and later acts 395,000 refugees were admitted. When the IRO went out of existence in 1952, over 1,000,000 people had been resettled in 80 different lands.

Unfortunately, during the lifetime of IRO, the floodtide of human intolerance had not abated. For every refugee resettled by IRO, 25 new ones had been created. The partition of the Indian subcontinent in 1947 precipitated a fratricidal conflict between Hindus and Muslims which resulted in a mass migration of millions of people. The outburst of violence accompanying the creation of the state of Israel sent almost 1,000,000 Arab refugees into the Gaza Strip, Jordan, Lebanon, Syria, and Iraq. The Korean War created almost 9,000,000 refugees from both North and South Korea. The German-speaking minorities (*Volksdeutsche*) expelled from the eastern provinces as a result of the Potsdam agreement numbered close to 8,000,000. Finally, a steady influx of refugees from Communist-occupied areas to the West took place. Hence the IRO, which had aimed at a complete solution of a temporary problem, succeeded only in achieving a partial solution of a permanent problem.

After the demise of IRO, the numbers of the uprooted increased even more. The Hungarian Revolution of 1956 ended in a mass exodus of about 160,000 refugees. Refugees from mainland China added over 1,000,000 refugees to the population of the British crown colony of Hong Kong. The crushing of Tibet by the Chinese Communists created a wave of refugees from that area. In the 1960s the United States received many refugees from Cuba, where Fidel Castro had established a Communist-oriented regime. In 1965 the U.S. government agreed to provide air transportation of from 3,000 to 4,000 Cuban refugees per month. Unrest in Africa brought the refugee problem to that continent as well. When Algeria gained independence in 1962, a large number of French settlers sought refuge in France. In 1963, 150,000 persons left Angola and settled in the Republic of Congo (Léopoldville), and nearly the same number went from Rwanda to neighbouring countries. Thousands were displaced by civil strife in the Congo during 1965. The conflict in Vietnam had added approximately 1,000,000 refugees by 1966, consisting of defectors from North Vietnam who had fled to South Vietnam as well as of South Vietnamese villagers displaced as a result of the war.

The response of the world community to the refugee problem after the demise of the IRO was sporadic and divided. Two agencies were created to operate under the aegis of the United Nations. First, the Office of United Nations High Commissioner for Refugees (UNHCR) was established in 1950 to deal with the world refugee problem in general. Suffering from a chronic lack of funds, the commissioner, like his predecessor under the League, was dependent almost exclusively on voluntary contributions from governments and private sources. These funds made it possible to clear the European camps by 1960 and to give a measure of assistance to the Chinese refugees in Hong Kong. The second UN refugee organ was the United Nations Relief and Works Agency for Palestine Refugees in the Near East (UNRWA), established in 1949, which fought a valiant battle to reintegrate Arab refugees, swollen in numbers to well over 1,000,000 by 1965, in the lands surrounding Israel within the framework of general regional development. In view of the Arabs' continued insistence upon their return to Israel and the Israelis' equally adamant refusal to readmit them, no permanent solution was in sight.

Two other governmental refugee organs not under United Nations authority are worthy of note. First, the Intergovernmental Committee for European Migration (ICEM) was established in 1951 to alleviate surplus population problems in Europe. Second, the United States Escapee Program (USEP) helped Hungarian refugees to immigrate to the United States.

The services to refugees and displaced persons rendered by the two United Nations agencies and by individual governments are supplemented by those of numerous voluntary agencies. In the United States alone there were nearly 40 such agencies in the 1960s. Generally, these agencies were related to welfare organizations sponsored by various church groups or nationally organized welfare services. The Red Cross, CARE, and the United States Committee for Refugees were typical examples. Governmental bodies came to depend very heavily on such voluntary agencies.

Finally, private individuals took the initiative in working to alleviate the world refugee problem. In 1959 three young Englishmen proposed that the period July 1, 1959, through June 30, 1960, be designated as World Refugee Year (WRY). The idea caught hold and the UN General Assembly supported the proposal in a resolution passed on Dec. 5, 1958. The record of WRY was marked by both successes and failures. On the positive side, 97 countries and territories participated; financial contributions and pledges totaled over $80,000,000; resettlement opportunities for refugees were increased; and Austria, West Germany, Belgium, the Netherlands, Luxembourg, Italy, and Australia enacted measures to improve the refugees' status. On the debit side, the year made no significant difference to the Arab refugees in the Middle East and the Chinese refugees in Hong Kong. Indeed, human intolerance created new waves of displaced persons during the year. As a result, the question arose in several countries whether World Refugee Year should be extended or made a permanent institution.

One conclusion that may be drawn from the study of the refugee problem is that so long as human intolerance exists, and so long as such intolerance remains primarily within the domestic jurisdiction of states, so long will there be refugees and displaced persons. Hence the refugee will probably remain a more or less permanent phenomenon. The world community has not recognized this truth, with the result that, parading through the annals of refugee history, there has been a permanent procession of temporary agencies. Intolerance produces refugees, and indifference is the major obstacle to a solution. This indifference has been manifested in the fact that states have been financially very tight-fisted toward refugee agencies, most of which were mendicants on the international scene, moving with hat in hand from government to government before finally being starved out of existence.

It is a tragic commentary on our times that the century of the United Nations should also be the century of the homeless man. Today, the community of exiles confronts the community of nations. Human rights have become virtually identical with national rights. The twin solutions to the refugee problem would be policies of greater openness toward immigration and a concerted attack upon the problem by a permanent body, patterned on the model of the International Refugee Organization.

For current developments, see *Britannica Book of the Year.*

BIBLIOGRAPHY.—Jacques Vernant, *The Refugee in the Post-War World* (1953) ; Louise W. Holborn, *The International Refugee Organization: a Specialized Agency of the United Nations: Its History and Work, 1946–1952* (1956) ; Malcolm J. Proudfoot, *European Refugees, 1939–1952: a Study in Forced Population Movement* (1956) ; John G. Stoessinger, *The Refugee and the World Community* (1956) ; Elfan Rees, *We Strangers and Afraid,* Carnegie Endowment for International Peace for World Refugee Year (1959) ; James M. Read, *The United Nations and Refugees: Changing Concepts,* Carnegie Endowment for International Peace, no. 537 (1962) ; Joseph B. Schechtman, *The Refugee in the World* (1964).   (J. G. St.)

REFUSE DISPOSAL is the term employed in the United States and Canada for the collection and disposal of the solid wastes of a community, including garbage, rubbish and ashes. In Great Britain this type of refuse is called dry or town refuse, as differentiated from wet refuse (fecal matter) and mixed refuse (a mixture of town refuse and fecal matter).

Garbage is the waste matter resulting from the preparation and consumption of food; rubbish is all nonputrescible solid wastes, except ashes, including both combustible and noncombustible material such as paper, rags, wood, plastic and metals.

Sanitary refuse disposal is essential to community health. Refuse has been shown to be important as a breeding ground or food source for rats, flies and other potential carriers of diseases of man. It has been demonstrated to be of importance in the transmission of trichinosis of man and vesicular exanthema, foot-and-mouth disease, cholera and other diseases of swine. Rubbish has been found to be a significant factor in the incidence of building fires in the United States. Particulate matter and smoke from the burning of refuse can be a significant source of atmospheric pollution, while improper disposal has sometimes resulted in surface- and ground-water pollution. Potential nuisance factors, such as smoke and odours resulting from open dumps, are well recognized.

Refuse disposal consists of three phases: storage on the premises, collection for transport to the final disposal site and final disposal.

Quantity of Refuse.—A household of four people in an American community may be expected to produce an average of 70 lb. of refuse each week, or about 2½ lb. per capita per day. If commercial garbage and rubbish, incinerator ash and solid industrial wastes are included, over 4 lb. of refuse per capita per day may be expected from a community-wide collection system. In England about 672 lb. per capita per annum is considered average.

In U.S. and Canadian communities where the refuse has a negligible ash content, garbage has been found to comprise as little as 20%–25% of the refuse by weight, with the remainder rubbish. Garbage has a moisture content of 60%–70%. The moisture content of rubbish usually approximates 25%–35% of its over-all weight.

Premises Storage.—Most cities require that household garbage be well wrapped and stored in durable, easily cleaned containers with tight-fitting covers. Glass or metal food containers should be stored in similar receptacles. Other rubbish may be tied in easily handled bundles or so placed in boxes that it will not cause littering or fire hazard. Ashes should be stored in metal containers. In most U.S. cities household refuse containers ordinarily are not permitted to exceed 26–30 gal. in capacity.

Collection of Refuse.—Methods of collection vary. Garbage may be collected separately from the other refuse; in mixed collection, garbage and rubbish—or sometimes garbage, rubbish and ashes—are collected at one time and from a common receptacle. The trend is toward mixed collection. Separate collection is utilized when garbage is used for feeding to swine or is ground and disposed of in the sewerage system, or when cheaper methods are at hand to dispose of the less objectionable components of the refuse.

Where garbage is collected separately, it is the usual practice to collect it twice a week in the summer and once or twice a week in the winter. A few cities collect more frequently. Most make daily collections in the business sections. Most of the large cities and about half the smaller ones in the U.S. employ municipal collection, contract or private collection being used otherwise.

Collection Equipment.—There is nothing that could be called a standard type of refuse collection vehicle. In America municipal garbage-hauling vehicles are usually custom-designed. Enclosed mixed-refuse collection vehicles are equipped with mechanically or hydraulically operated packing devices to compress the voluminous refuse and thereby increase the amount the vehicle can accommodate. Many industries and other concentrated production areas use large portable containers which when full are transported to the disposal site by a vehicle equipped with a special hoist.

Disposal.—There are five methods of refuse disposal: reclamation for re-use (although this disposes only of certain components in the refuse); disposal into the sewerage system; incineration; dumping in water; and disposal on land.

Reclamation.—In its simplest form reclamation is the removal of such items as paper or heavy metals for salvage. In Great Britain this is practised in many cities in separation plants constructed for the purpose. In America reclamation is usually carried on as private enterprise, either by the individual householder or by contract arrangement at the disposal site. Metals from incinerator ash and the ash itself are often used for salvage or reclamation purposes.

Feeding waste food to pigs has long been a popular method of garbage disposal because it is relatively cheap and often can be carried on by private enterprise at a profit, thus relieving the authorities of the responsibility and expense of garbage disposal. In Great Britain and Canada it has been required for many years that garbage fed to swine be cooked to disinfect it and to prevent possible spread of disease. In the United States, vesicular exanthema, a disease of swine similar to foot-and-mouth disease and spread primarily by the practice of feeding raw garbage, became epizootic in the early 1950s. By 1960 all of the states had adopted legislation or regulations requiring the disinfection (usually by cooking) of garbage fed to pigs. Although the use of residential garbage in the U.S. for pig food has declined substantially, use of commercial garbage from hotels and restaurants is widespread.

Composting is the biochemical alteration of refuse from a noxious to an innocuous usable humus. During the first half of the 20th century a number of anaerobic and aerobic processing schemes were offered under various proprietary names. None was successfully employed in the United States on a continuing basis, primarily for economic reasons.

Composting of refuse has been successfully carried on in the

Netherlands and the Jersey Islands for many years. The method has also been used with some success in Great Britain, France, New Zealand and India.

Reduction, or the cooking of garbage to remove salvable greases and fats for industrial use and to produce tankage usable as an animal food base, was a recognized method of reclamation in the United States in the first quarter of the 20th century. The introduction of detergents, which reduced the demand for fats in soap manufacture, together with increased labour costs, made this method uneconomical, and the last municipal garbage reduction plant ceased operation in the early 1950s.

Disposal Into Sewerage System.—If garbage is ground into minute particles it can be discharged into the community sewerage system. Millions of household grinder units were installed in the United States following their introduction in the early 1930s. Little difficulty is encountered in a properly designed sewer system as a result of this practice, and household water consumption will increase only 1% to 2% with the installation of a grinder. Increases in solids handling capacities are needed at the sewage treatment plants in cities where large numbers of grinders have been placed in service, however, and for this reason some communities with already overloaded treatment plants had to forbid their use. A few cities having separate garbage collection systems used central grinding stations at which truckloads of garbage could be handled at one time.

Most newly constructed food-handling establishments in the United States, particularly hospitals and other institutions, have kitchens equipped with food waste grinders. The grinding of garbage is an important sanitation device since it eliminates the need for storage and collection of the most noisome and potentially hazardous portion of community refuse.

Incineration.—The burning of community refuse is one of the safest and most efficient methods of disposal, provided it is properly done. The special equipment and methods essential to this process are described in the article INCINERATOR.

Dumping in Water.—For many years the disposal of refuse in large bodies of water was an accepted practice. The refuse from a number of large cities was taken to sea on barges and dumped. Unfortunately, much of the lighter material found its way back to the beaches with the wind and the tides.

New York city was prohibited from continuing this practice in 1936 as the result of a ruling by the U.S. supreme court. Very few cities in North America or Europe resort to this method of refuse disposal.

Disposal on Land.—The indiscriminate dumping of refuse on land is an age-old practice still widely followed, particularly in

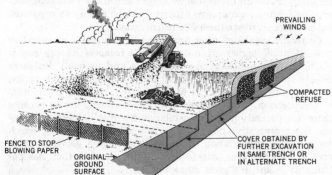

PREVAILING WINDS

COMPACTED REFUSE

FENCE TO STOP BLOWING PAPER

ORIGINAL GROUND SURFACE

COVER OBTAINED BY FURTHER EXCAVATION IN SAME TRENCH OR IN ALTERNATE TRENCH

BY COURTESY OF THE U.S. PUBLIC HEALTH SERVICE

TRENCH METHOD OF SANITARY LAND FILL USED TO DISPOSE OF REFUSE IN A FLAT LAND AREA

small communities. However, the unsightliness of dumping grounds and the unavoidable presence of flies, rats, smoke and odours led to the development of more efficient and sanitary methods.

The method of controlled tipping, known in the U.S. as sanitary land fill, was introduced in England in 1912; it makes use of the natural fermentation brought about by microorganisms in the putrescible portion of the refuse. Usually the refuse is deposited in shallow layers, compacted, and covered within 24 hours with compacted earth or other chemically inert material to form an effective seal. Mechanical equipment such as a bulldozer mounted on a heavy tractor is used to grade, compact and cover the refuse. The method often is employed to reclaim otherwise useless land and by the early 1960s was used by over 1,400 American communities. *See also* SEWAGE DISPOSAL.

BIBLIOGRAPHY.—University of California, Sanitary Engineering Research Project, *Analysis of Refuse Collection and Sanitary Landfill Disposal* (1952); Local Government Conference on Refuse Disposal Methods, *Proceedings* (1954); American Public Works Association, *Grinding as a Process in Garbage Disposal* (1937), *Refuse Collection Practice*, 2nd ed. (1958). (Lo. W.)

REGAL, a small bellows-blown keyboard instrument popular during the 16th and 17th centuries. Its sound is produced by beating reeds which have either no resonators or very short resonators. The reeds are placed immediately behind the keys and the two hand-blown bellows are placed horizontally behind the reeds. One form of the instrument, the bible regal, can be folded up when not in use and when closed resembles a large book. Several regals are mentioned in the inventories of Henry VIII's effects; in addition to the reeds some of these had a "cymbal" stop, presumably a very small mixture.

The regal's highly coloured buzzing tone made it especially suitable for accompanying brass instruments, and in this context it is specified by Claudio Monteverdi as one of the several continuo instruments in his opera *Orfeo* (1607).

The term "regal" is also used for a type of reed stop in 16th–18th-century organs. These have beating reeds and small resonators, often of peculiar shape, which give a very colourful tone; such stops were revived on the continent in the mid-20th century. The modern *vox humana* stop is, in effect, a regal. (CE. C.)

REGATTA: *see* ROWING; YACHTING; BOATING.

RÉGENCE STYLE is the designation for the French art of the period from 1715 to 1730; it did not quite coincide with the regency of Philippe d'Orléans, duc d'Orléans (1715–23), between the reigns of Louis XIV and Louis XV. The *régence* style marked the transition from the massive, serious baroque art to the more elegant, lighthearted rococo style.

The term should not be confused with the English Regency (1811–20) during the latter part of the reign of George III.

(WM. F.)

REGENERATION is the process by which organisms replace structures or organs which have been lost by accident or mutilation. This definition is not quite adequate because it does not cover two phenomena which belong undoubtedly to the category of regeneration phenomena. In some invertebrates, such as the fresh-water polyp *Hydra*, the planarian flatworm *Dugesia* and the starfish, a small fragment of the body can restore a complete, whole organism rather than merely an organ. Furthermore, many animals can restore structures lost in the normal course of life rather than by accident. The periodic molting of feathers in birds, the shedding of fur in mammals, of the exoskeleton in arthropods and of the epidermal scales in reptiles are followed by regeneration of the discarded structures. The uppermost cornified skin layers in mammals including man are constantly worn off in small bits and replaced by active, proliferating cell layers in the deeper layers of the skin. The same holds for the continuous replacement of hair, nails and claws. The teeth are replaced only once in mammals, including man, but there is a continuous succession of teeth in lower forms, such as the dogfish and shark. The antlers of deer are shed at regular intervals and then regenerated. The periodic changes in the genital tracts of female mammals during menstruation and oestrus also should be included here. All these instances in which replacements are part of the normal life functions are called physiological or repetitive regeneration, in distinction to restorative or reparative regeneration which follows injury. This article deals primarily with the latter type.

CAPACITY FOR REGENERATION

There are wide differences in the regenerative capacity of different animals. The one extreme is represented by the abovementioned invertebrates, in which a part of the body can restore a whole organism. In higher organisms, as for instance the salamanders among the vertebrates, and many crustaceans and insects, only single organs, such as limbs, can regenerate; mammals cannot restore entire organs, but they can repair damage to tissues, such as bone fractures, skin and muscle injuries and peripheral nerve loss. These phenomena of tissue repair are, of course, included under the general heading regeneration.

General Types.—Regeneration can be accomplished in two ways: (1) by outgrowth of new tissue from the wound surface or (2) by the transformation and reorganization of the remaining parts, without an outgrowth of new material.

Where new tissue is produced, a regeneration bud, or blastema, is formed at the wound surface (*see below, Regeneration Process: Blastema Formation*). It is usually cone-shaped and consists of cells of an embryonic type, which gradually form the adult structures by processes of cell differentiation and growth, much in the fashion of embryonic development. The regeneration of limbs and tails in salamanders is an example of this type of regeneration, which T. H. Morgan termed epimorphosis.

The second type of regeneration, the remodeling of old parts, is called morphallaxis (fig. 1). Very small fragments of a freshwater or marine polyp, or of a planarian, undergo a change in shape instead of growing blastemas; they break down old structures, and build in their place new ones of a smaller proportion. All regeneration processes in protozoans are of this type. Occasionally, both types of regeneration take place simultaneously, and there may be no fundamental difference between them. The term regeneration is almost universally adopted as the all-inclusive term, with "epimorphosis" and "morphallaxis" as subheadings. C. M. Child (1941) proposed "reconstitution" as the general term to cover all related phenomena. He used the term regeneration in a narrow sense, synonymously with epimorphosis, as reconstitution by outgrowth, and the term reorganization as reconstitution by internal changes.

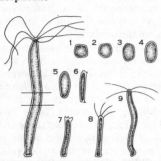

FROM E. KORSCHELT, AFTER T. H. MORGAN

FIG. 1.—REGENERATION IN THE FRESH-WATER POLYP HYDRA. THE SHORT PIECE BETWEEN THE TWO LINES (AT LEFT) REGENERATES INTO A NEW POLYP. 1 TO 9 ARE STAGES IN THE REGENERATION PROCESS

The aim of regeneration is to maintain or restore the fitness of an organism after the loss of parts. This aim is best accomplished by a replacement of precisely those structures which were lost. However, a number of cases are known in which more than, or less than, the lost part is regenerated, and other cases in which the regenerate is structurally different from the lost part. The term heteromorphosis covers all types of atypical regeneration. The term homeosis is used for those atypical regenerations in which the regenerate represents an organ different from the original. For instance, in crabs, an amputated eyestalk, under certain conditions, will be replaced by an antenna. Another type of atypical regeneration has been given special attention; namely, those instances in which the polarity of the regenerate is changed. For example, the posterior cut surface of a piece of planarian, under certain conditions, will regenerate a head instead of a tail. This type of polarity change is called polar heteromorphosis.

Theoretical Considerations.—When a regeneration blastema differentiates into the head of a planarian or into the limb of a salamander, the processes which go on in the blastema are fundamentally of the same nature as the embryonic developmental processes which created these organs originally. Although the regeneration processes are rarely exact replicas of the corresponding developmental processes, they are alike in some fundamental aspects. Both require a building material of plastic, undifferentiated, embryonic-type cells, and a set of specific organizing factors which direct and control the molding and differentiation of such building materials. In this sense, regeneration can be defined as the revival, or reactivation, of developmental potencies in or-

ganisms which have passed the embryonic stages of development.

If this point of view is adopted, then the close affinity of regeneration processes with asexual reproduction becomes evident. In fact, in some instances it is difficult to draw the line between the two. For instance, most protozoans reproduce asexually, by fission. The daughter individuals restore by regeneration those structures which they do not contain at the start of the fission. If a protozoan is cut in two by a fine instrument, the result is the same—each half regenerates the missing structures. In this instance, fission and regeneration differ primarily in the factors which set the processes in motion. Similarly, some flatworms and annelids (segmented worms) which possess high regenerative powers reproduce regularly by transverse fission or by a budding process at their posterior ends. Their regenerative potencies are placed, so to speak, in the service of reproduction. Budding is a mode of asexual reproduction particularly common among colonial forms. It is practised by coelenterates and tunicates among animals and by plants. A bud is an outgrowth on an adult organism which is an expression of the revival of growth potentialities at a localized area of the body. The parallel to regeneration is obvious. In many marine coelenterates a lateral regeneration bud can be produced easily by making a cut in the body wall. Again, the main difference between regeneration and spontaneous budding lies in the initiating stimuli.

If the ability for regeneration is considered as a residual developmental capacity which a number of organisms retain throughout adult life, it is implied that regeneration is the manifestation of a universal property of all organisms; namely, the capacity for growth and development. This point of view, now generally adopted, did not always prevail. It was seriously contested during the second half of the 19th century. Under the influence of the theory of natural selection, another theory of regeneration was strongly advocated by August Weismann and others. This theory emphasized the usefulness and adaptive value of regeneration; it stressed the point that regeneration was apparently limited to those organs and structures which are particularly in danger of being injured or mutilated by enemy attacks. It was assumed, therefore, that regeneration is not part of a basic equipment of all organisms, but is acquired secondarily as a special adaptation wherever the ability to regenerate is of crucial survival value in the struggle for existence. It was held that natural selection is instrumental in creating and improving the regenerative capacity. A just objection has been raised against this theory, namely, that in many instances inner organs regenerate which are not liable to injuries, as for instance, the crystalline lens of the amphibian eye, or the liver. For this and other reasons, Weismann's theory in its extreme form is untenable. However, its valid element, the emphasis on natural selection as a mechanism for increasing preexisting limited regenerative capacity, can be readily incorporated in the residual growth theory of regeneration.

Generally speaking, lower organisms have a better regenerative power than do higher organisms, but the regenerative capacity is distributed sporadically among animals and in many instances closely related forms differ widely in their regenerative capacity. A theory of regeneration has to explain this scattered distribution of regeneration. Natural selection cannot account for it, because there is apparently no close correlation between liability to injury and the regenerative power. The residual growth theory, which assumes that regeneration is a manifestation of a universal property of all organisms, has to account for the fact that this potentiality is lost in a great many forms.

Two prerequisites must be fulfilled if a successful regeneration is to occur: there must be available the necessary building material in the form of unspecialized cells, capable of growth and differentiation; and the necessary organizing factors must be present which direct the development of these cells. Regeneration may be prevented by the loss of either one or of both. The necessary building material may be lost in the normal course of development, during which embryonic cells undergo a differentiation into highly specialized tissues. This differentiation is undoubtedly irreversible in most instances, and the transformation of all cell materials into an irrevocably differentiated form is probably one reason for the lack of regeneration in highly organized animals. Some authors maintain that in some instances a differentiated tissue can dedifferentiate and rejuvenate under certain conditions, and thus become available as a source of regeneration material. Furthermore, in a number of invertebrates and lower chordates, certain embryonic cells remain in an undifferentiated embryonic condition and form a reservoir for regeneration and asexual reproduction (*see* below). It is obvious that regeneration is impossible in all those organisms which possess neither reserve cells nor tissues capable of de- and redifferentiation. The organizing or "field" factors for regeneration are discussed below. Their loss, in the course of embryonic development, may be an alternative cause for a lack of regenerative power. Finally, an amputation stump may be potentially capable of regenerating but be prevented from doing so either by a deficiency in one of the many subsidiary agents necessary for regenerative growth, such as hormones or nerve-produced agents, or by a block from a rapidly overgrowing skin or wound scar which prevents the outgrowth of the blastema cells. An appropriate treatment of the stump can call forth a regeneration where it would not occur under ordinary conditions.

REGENERATION IN DIFFERENT ANIMAL GROUPS

INVERTEBRATES

Protozoa.—Most Protozoa (acellular or one-celled animals) reproduce asexually by longitudinal or transverse fission, or by other modes of division. Fission requires a reorganization and new formation of structures in the daughter individuals, and this process can be considered as a physiological regeneration. The power to rebuild structures is therefore inherent in all protozoans, and it is not surprising to find that most Protozoa can regenerate parts which were lost by accident or removed in an experiment. In all instances, the presence of nuclear material is a necessary prerequisite for successful regeneration. In ciliates, which possess a macro- and a micronucleus, the former is essential; the latter is not. In forms such as *Stentor,* in which the macro-nucleus is represented by a beadlike chain, small segments of the chain are sufficient to enable a fragment to regenerate. In *Amoeba,* which has no highly specialized organelles, a non-nucleate fragment can grow and survive up to 30 days, but it cannot divide. The most highly differentiated Protozoa, the ciliates, have been the subject of extensive studies on regeneration; *Paramecium* and *Stentor* are the favourite materials. Their regenerative power is excellent. Fragments as small as $\frac{1}{64}$ of an individual can form a complete new organism. The new organelles are formed either by remodeling of the remnants of the old ones or by breakdown of the latter and rebuilding of entirely new structures. In parasitic Protozoa the regeneration capacity seems to be poor or entirely missing.

Sponges.—The regeneration of amputated parts in Porifera, or sponges, does not seem to be very extensive. However, a series of interesting experiments revealed a remarkable capacity of the sponge cells to reorganize themselves into a whole organism, following a complete breakup of their organization. Sponges were strained through bolting silk and thus completely dissociated. Following this treatment, small cell groups reunited into larger aggregates which reorganized themselves and eventually formed a typical sponge.

Coelenterates.—These occur in the forms of polyps and medusae (jellyfish). The well-known fresh-water form *Hydra* takes its name from the mythological nine-headed monster which was believed to regenerate two heads in the place of each amputated head. The regenerative power of *Hydra* is at least as startling as that of its namesake. It was on this polyp that the Swiss naturalist Abraham Trem-

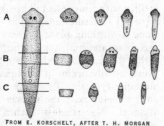

FROM E. KORSCHELT, AFTER T. H. MORGAN

FIG. 2.—REGENERATION IN THE PLANARIAN FLATWORM DUGESIA. THE THREE ROWS SHOW REGENERATION OF (A) ANTERIOR SECTION, (B) MIDSECTION AND (C) POSTERIOR SECTION OF THE ANIMAL AT THE LEFT

bley made the first planned regeneration experiments (1744), which aroused a tremendous interest and were soon followed by those of R. A. F. de Réaumur, Lazzaro Spallanzani and others. Small fragments of the body can regenerate a whole individual (*see* fig. 1). One tentacle with a small portion of the mouth region is capable of forming a new individual. The regenerative power of other hydroids differs in different species. *Tubularia* and other marine forms have been widely used for experiments on the physiology of regeneration.

The regenerative capacity of the medusae (jellyfish) is much restricted. The Anthozoa (sea anemones and corals) have a considerable regenerative capacity.

Flatworms.—This phylum, Platyhelminthes, includes the planarians, which have an exceedingly high regenerative capacity, and which have therefore been used more than any other form for regeneration experiments. A planarian (*Dugesia*) may be cut in any direction by one or more transverse, longitudinal or oblique sections, and each fragment will regenerate a whole, though smaller, individual (*see* fig. 2). Planarians possess complex structures such as eyespots, brain and pharynx. Any or all of these can be rebuilt from a fragment not containing them. Of three closely related groups of Turbellaria (free-living flatworms), distinguished mainly by differences in the shape of the intestine, only the triclads, or planarians, have a high regenerative power, and even within this group there are great differences with respect to the ability to regenerate.

FROM E. KORSCHELT

FIG. 3.—REGENERATION IN THE STARFISH. ONE ARM REGENERATES A WHOLE STARFISH (CENTRE)

The entirely parasitic flukes (Trematoda) and tapeworms (Cestoda) have not been thoroughly investigated. They seem to lack regenerative power.

Annelids.—Regeneration in the common earthworm is well known. It can regenerate many segments at the posterior part of the body, but regeneration of the anterior part is limited. Up to five segments can be completely restored, but if more are removed, fewer than the normal number are rebuilt; no regeneration takes place if 15 or more anterior segments are amputated. Some relatives of the earthworm can do better. For instance, the fresh-water worm *Criodrilus* regenerates as many as 25 anterior segments. In another fresh-water form, *Nais*, two isolated segments can regenerate a whole worm. One of the remarkable features in these annelid regenerations is the formation of gonads in the regenerated segments, although the stumps which give rise to the regenerates may not contain a trace of gonad material. The regenerative power of the more highly specialized marine polychaetes is, in general, lower than that of the earthworm and its relatives (oligochaetes). It is very low in the leeches (Hirudinea).

Echinoderms.—The arms of starfish (Asteroidea) and brittle stars (Ophiuroidea) can regenerate a whole individual in some instances, even if the amputated arm contains no trace of the central disc. Occasionally, there may be found on the seashore an odd-looking starfish with one or two normal-sized and several very short arms (*see* fig. 3); the latter are in the process of regeneration. Sea urchins can repair damage in the skeleton and restore tube feet and spines. Sea urchin and starfish larvae (plutei) have little regenerative power.

Mollusks.—Parts of the shells of snails (Gastropoda) and valves of clams and relatives (Lamellibranchia) can be replaced. Damage can be repaired at the margin, at which the shell is formed, and also in central parts. The mantle and the foot likewise can regenerate. Some snails have highly complex eyes at the tips of tentacles. The amputation of a tentacle at its base results in its regeneration, including the eye. However, the entire head of a snail cannot be regenerated. Squid, octopus and cuttlefish (Cephalopoda) can regenerate amputated arms.

Arthropods.—The body of an arthropod has many appendages such as legs, wings, antennae, stalked eyes, mandibles and tail.

These are all readily exposed to accidental damage, and most of them can be regenerated when lost. This holds particularly for the best-known and most thoroughly investigated groups, the crustaceans (crayfish, crab, lobster, etc.) and the insects. All arthropods molt periodically; that is, they shed the chitinous exoskeleton. Its replacement may be considered a type of physiological regeneration. The regenerative power of insects is high during larval and pupal stages but greatly reduced in the adult. The regeneration of structures such as wings or legs of adult insects is either limited and incomplete or entirely impossible. On the other hand, crustaceans continue to molt throughout adult stages, and they are capable of regenerating complex organs such as legs or eyes.

Sea Squirts.—High regenerative power is found in the sedentary ascidians. A small part of the body can regenerate a whole individual.

VERTEBRATES

Fishes.—In the bony fishes the regenerative capacity is limited. They can regenerate the tail fins and the other paired and unpaired fins. A few other structures are known to be capable of regeneration, such as the gill cover, parts of the gills and of the lower jaw.

Amphibians.—The tailed Amphibia, salamanders and newts (Caudata), have by far the most extensive regenerative potency of all vertebrates and have therefore been the favourite subjects for experiments on vertebrate regeneration. In particular, limb regeneration of salamanders has been analyzed in many respects, ever since it was discovered by Spallanzani in 1768. Any part of a foot or hindlimb can be regenerated; one of the remarkable features is the precision with which the missing part is restored. If the foot is amputated (fig. 4[B]), only this part is replaced; if the leg is removed at its base (fig. 4[A]), it will be replaced in its entirety. Other organs can regenerate equally well, among them the tail, parts of the snout and eyes and parts of inner organs such as lungs and gonads. The regenerative capacity of salamander larvae and of young specimens exceeds even that of full-sized specimens.

In the tailless Amphibia, frogs and toads (Salientia), the regenerative capacity is limited to larval stages. The tadpoles can readily regenerate a tail which is clipped at the tip or even near the base. The hindleg regeneration proceeds rapidly and efficiently in young tadpoles, but this capacity diminishes when the larva approaches metamorphosis. Adult frogs do not regenerate limbs, contrary to a common belief. Usually the stumps heal without regenerating. If the arm of an adult frog is amputated and the wound surface is bathed repeatedly in a saturated sodium chloride solution, the stump will proceed to form a regenerate. However, the regenerated arm is never complete and normal. It is assumed that in untreated adult frogs the thick skin closes up rapidly over the wound surface and suppresses regeneration.

Reptiles.—Vertebrates higher than Amphibia have greatly reduced regenerative potentialities. The tail of a lizard is the only highly specialized structure in reptilians which can regenerate. The animal makes occasional use of this capacity: when captured by its tail, it shakes the tail off and leaves it behind. Lizards with regenerated tails are occasionally encountered in the field. However, tail regenerates are never complete; their inner structures are atypical. Amputated limbs of lizards do not regenerate.

Birds.—The regeneration of fragments of beaks has been reported in several birds. The periodic renewal of the plumage after each molt is a type of physiological regeneration, and the growth of a feather from a feather rudiment resembles other regenerative processes.

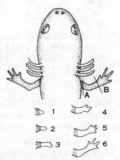

(TOP) FROM V. HAMBURGER, "MANUAL OF EXPERIMENTAL EMBRYOLOGY"; REPRODUCED BY PERMISSION OF THE UNIVERSITY OF CHICAGO PRESS

FIG. 4.—ARM REGENERATION IN A SALAMANDER. 1–6 ARE REGENERATION STAGES, FOLLOWING AMPUTATION AT A: BLASTEMA AT 1 AND 2. (SEE TEXT)

Mammals.—These present numerous instances of tissue regeneration, but very little, if any, evidence for the regeneration of complex structures. The change of hair, of teeth and of red blood cells and the regeneration of antlers in deer illustrate physiological regeneration. Reparative regeneration, following an amputation, is limited to tissues, such as bone, muscle, liver, skin and peripheral nerves. Whole organs cannot be regenerated.

GENERAL CONCEPTS

Regenerative Ability.—What general concepts can be derived from this survey? In the first place, it brings into proper relief a point which has been emphasized by students of regeneration since the early days, that there is a correlation between regeneration potentiality and level of organization; *i.e.*, lower organisms have a high regenerative power, and this power decreases with increase in complexity. Mammals, including man, pay for their high organization with an almost complete loss of regenerative capacity. The relation between regenerative power and level of organization, however, holds only in a general way and breaks down in numerous special instances. For example, some planarian species have an exceptionally high regenerative power, but closely related species have none. The same holds for Annelida. The regenerative ability of the fishes is lower than that of the more highly organized tailed amphibians. The regeneration of the crystalline lens of the eye of salamanders is perfect in one genus and absent in another. These examples could be multiplied easily. They show that factors other than the general level of organization of the animal often play a decisive role.

It has also been asserted that since regeneration is a developmental process, embryos, larvae and young animals, in general, should be more readily capable of regeneration than adult stages of the same animal. This expectation is fulfilled in many instances, but again it is not a rigid rule. It is true that salamander larvae regenerate limbs and tails more rapidly and more perfectly than adults do, and lens regeneration in some salamander species is limited to larvae; frog tadpoles can regenerate a hindlimb, but an adult frog cannot. On the other hand, sea urchin and starfish larvae do not regenerate, while the adults do. The same holds for annelids and for tunicates. Again, factors other than age determine the limitation of regenerative power in these forms. Finally, one would expect that external organs and appendages which are readily exposed to injury and loss would show a higher regenerative capacity than inner organs. This, again, holds in a general way. However, several examples have been mentioned of the regeneration of inner organs which are rarely subject to injury during the normal course of life.

Self-Amputation.—A number of animals, when attacked and caught by a leg or tail, save their lives by casting off this appendage. The organ which is sacrificed can usually be restored by regeneration. This act of self-amputation is called autotomy. Instances of autotomy are found in a number of different animal groups, such as coelenterates, mollusks, echinoderms, annelids, arthropods and others, although this means of escape is used by only a few representatives of these phyla.

The only case of autotomy in vertebrates, and perhaps the best known of all, is that of the autotomy of the tail in lizards. The facility with which the tail breaks off is astounding. This is due to a special structural adaptation. When grasped, the tail separates along a breaking plane present at the base of the tail. Several vertebrae are split across the middle. The halves are held together by cartilage which ruptures readily. The regeneration, which usually begins at the breaking plane, produces a tail that is not quite typical. It contains no vertebrae but merely a cartilaginous skeletal axis; the muscle and nerve distribution is likewise atypical. Nevertheless, such a regenerated tail can regenerate a second time.

Many crabs, insects and spiders have a similar device to facilitate autotomy, namely, a preformed breaking plane at the base of legs or antennae. The chitinous exoskeleton is soft and thin at certain levels, and the muscle arrangement expedites self-amputation. It is not always the same segment of the leg at which such a breaking plane is prepared, but the mechanism is apparently similar in all species. In the walking stick, or stick insect, all three pairs of legs are adapted for autotomy. Quite frequently, special care is taken to avoid an excessive loss of blood: the skin contracts over the wound and closes it off. A few other instances of autotomy may be mentioned: some sea anemones release a tentacle when it is strongly stimulated; starfishes cast off an arm voluntarily, and some annelids can autotomize the hindmost body segments and regenerate them subsequently.

One of the most startling instances of autotomy is the self-evisceration in sea cucumbers, which, when strongly stimulated, cast off their anterior ends, including tentacles, mouth parts and the water-vascular system, and at the same time discard through the anus the intestine and attached structures, such as gonads. The discarding of the inner organs is accomplished by strong muscle contraction. The nearly empty hull composed of skin and muscles is capable of regenerating the autotomized organs. *Thione* can accomplish this feat within a month.

There is only one step from spontaneous autotomy to spontaneous fission for the purpose of asexual reproduction. For instance, certain starfishes and certain sea cucumbers break apart at more or less regular time intervals and the fragments regenerate a whole individual. Likewise, in certain annelids and flatworms posterior parts of the body are constricted off and the fragments regenerate into new individuals. This performance has been established as a regular mode of reproduction. The close affinity of regeneration and reproduction in lower animals is thus again affirmed.

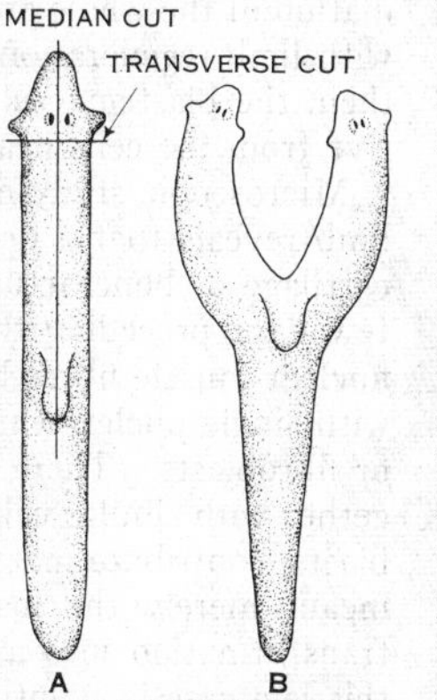

Atypical Regeneration.—A regenerate is ordinarily a replica of the original structure, but a number of cases are known in which regeneration is atypical in that either more or less than was lost is regenerated. Occasionally, the regenerate represents an organ entirely different from the one it replaces. All forms of atypical regeneration are called heteromorphosis. The last-mentioned category of heteromorphic regenerations is called homeosis.

Incomplete Regeneration.—This type of heteromorphosis is common both in naturally occurring and in experimentally induced regeneration. Regenerated tails of lizards invariably show certain structural deficiencies, such as the absence of normal vertebrae. Regenerated salamander limbs frequently have a reduced number of digits or even greater deficiencies. Those of arthropods may have a reduced number of segments. Several species of annelids can regenerate only a limited number of head segments. If more are amputated, the total segment number of the worm after completed regeneration will be subnormal. Planarians occasionally regenerate a head with two fused eyes, or only one eye, or eyeless heads, instead of the normal head with two separate eyes.

Such atypical head regenerates can be produced experimentally by exposing the regenerating animals to any one of a number of chemical agents which are known to impair developmental processes in a general, nonspecific way.

Superregeneration.—Of greatest interest among the super-regenerations are those in which a single organ is replaced by a duplicated or multiple formation. Instances of such monstrosities have been observed in practically all regenerating animal forms, as, for instance, in hydranths of *Hydra* and of its marine relatives, in heads and tails of planarians and annelids, in tails of lizards and limbs or digits of amphibians and particularly frequently in appendages of arthropods. Double claws of crabs or lobsters, double legs and antennae of beetles and of other insects have been described. Starfishes with bifurcated arms and sea cucumbers with duplicated body parts also have been observed. Triplicate appendages are commonest in arthropods and occasionally are found in other forms. They originate probably in most instances

MEDIAN CUT

TRANSVERSE CUT

A   B

FROM V. HAMBURGER, "MANUAL OF EXPERIMENTAL EMBRYOLOGY"; REPRODUCED BY PERMISSION OF THE UNIVERSITY OF CHICAGO PRESS

FIG. 5.—REGENERATION OF A DOUBLE HEAD IN A PLANARIAN (SEE TEXT). REGENERATED TISSUE IS UNSTIPPLED

in the following way: a leg, claw or antenna ruptures at a joint without breaking off completely. As a result, two wound surfaces are exposed, each of which begins to regenerate the distal parts. The two new formations, together with the persisting original structure, form the triple monstrosity. It was found that such triplicate structures follow a definite rule of symmetry relations (Bateson's rule): two adjacent components, namely, the middle one and one of the marginal components, are mirror images of each other, whereas the two marginal parts have the same symmetry pattern.

It is often difficult or impossible to decide whether double or triple monstrosities found in nature have been brought about by regeneration or whether the duplication occurred in early embryonic development. Therefore, experimental methods were devised that make it possible to study the origin of duplications by regeneration under controlled conditions. An expedient way of accomplishing this is to create a wound surface which will produce two separate blastemas instead of one. For instance, if the tail of a tadpole is amputated by two oblique cuts, in the form of an arrowhead (instead of by one transverse cut), then two blastemas and tails will grow out, each with its main axis perpendicular to the oblique, cut surface (Barfurth's rule). Multiple digits in salamander legs were produced in the same fashion, by making two oblique transections. Two-headed planarians can be obtained by making a longitudinal fission in the median plane through the anterior part of the animal, and a subsequent amputation of the two halves of the head (fig. 5[A]). Each separate anterior body half then regenerates the missing lateral parts and, in addition, a whole head at the anterior surface (fig. 5[B]). By repeating this procedure, animals with multiple heads (up to ten) have been obtained. In the same way, planarians with double tails can be produced experimentally.

Homeosis.—This category of atypical regenerations includes all those instances in which the regenerate represents a structure different in type from the original. Homeosis occurs mainly in arthropods. It is a characteristic of this phylum that most of the numerous body segments bear appendages which are of different types in different body regions (*e.g.*, antennae, mandibles, claws, thoracic legs, abdominal appendages). In homeosis, the appendage of one type substitutes for another type. A few examples may serve as illustrations: in crustaceans (crayfish, lobster, crab), a thoracic leg with claws was regenerated in place of a maxilliped; in other cases an abdominal leg was found in place of a thoracic leg. A leg may be regenerated in place of an antenna or of a mandible, and vice versa. An anterior wing of a butterfly or moth may replace a posterior wing. Of particular interest is the regeneration of an antenna in place of a stalked eye, which was observed in marine decapod crustaceans of the genus *Palinurus*, *Palaemon* and in others (fig. 6). Curt Herbst discovered that if the optic ganglion, which is located at the base of the eyestalk, is removed along with the eye, an antenna grows out, but if the optic ganglion is left intact and the eye alone is amputated, a normal eyestalk and eye regenerate. The ganglion, then, determines the quality of the regenerate.

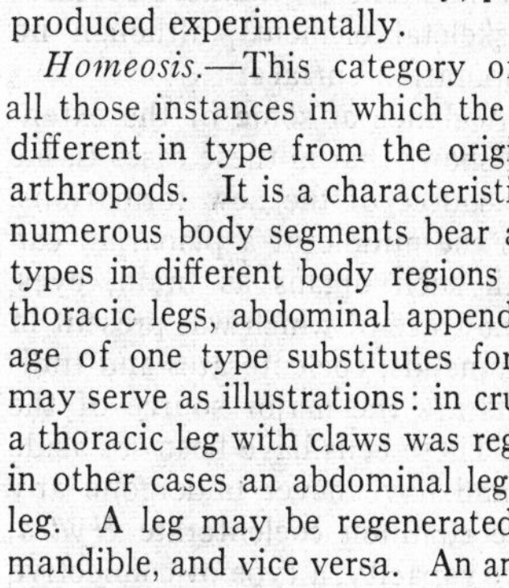

REGENERATION PROCESS
ORIGIN OF REGENERATION MATERIAL

Blastema Formation.—Regeneration, as noted above, can be performed by reorganization of the old piece (morphallaxis) or by outgrowth of new tissue at the cut surface (epimorphosis). Only the latter mode of regeneration is discussed in the following. In limb and tail regeneration of salamanders, in head and tail regeneration of planarians and in many similar instances, a regeneration bud or blastema is formed at the amputation sur-

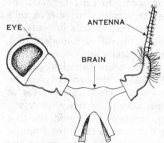

EYE   ANTENNA

BRAIN

FROM T. H. MORGAN, "REGENERATION"; REPRODUCED BY PERMISSION OF COLUMBIA UNIVERSITY PRESS

FIG. 6.—HOMEOSIS IN THE SHRIMP PALAEMON. THE EYE WITH ITS STALK WAS AMPUTATED AT THE RIGHT SIDE. AN ANTENNA REGENERATED IN ITS PLACE

face. The blastema is at first a slight elevation which grows to a cone-shaped structure and then begins to differentiate into tissues or organs. The blastema is an accumulation of cells of embryonic type, whose origin has been the topic of numerous investigations. The material that builds up the regenerate may be derived from three different sources. In several invertebrate phyla, including coelenterates, annelids and flatworms, a special type of undifferentiated cells, the so-called reserve cells or neoblasts, are stored in different parts of the body. When the need for regeneration arises they are mobilized and migrate to the site of injury. Tissue outgrowth is a second source. The differentiated tissues at the cut surface (for instance, skin or muscle) may simply grow out and each form tissue of its own kind. Finally, the blastema cells may be derived from formerly differentiated tissues of the amputation stump which have dedifferentiated and returned to an embryonic-type condition. It is conceivable that when the blastema proceeds to develop, such cells may differentiate into a type of tissue different from the one from which they were derived. For example, in salamander limb regeneration, a former muscle cell may become a bone cell, or vice versa. This transformation is referred to as metaplasia (*see below*).

Tissue Outgrowth.—This mode of regeneration is characteristic of tissue repair such as bone regeneration following a fracture, restitution of a muscle injury or liver regeneration. Peripheral nerves regenerate in this fashion, by outgrowth from the cut end. In amphibian limb regeneration, apparently only nerves and skin regenerate in this way. The skeletal elements of the regenerate do not originate from old skeletal tissue at the cut surface. This was demonstrated by an experiment in which the upper arm bone (humerus) was carefully removed and the limb then amputated across the upper arm. The regenerated forearm and digits contained all typical skeletal elements, although no bone tissue was present at the amputation surface.

Reserve Cells (Neoblasts).—A glance at some of the extensive regenerations in lower animals shows that in these cases tissue outgrowth cannot be the primary source of the new formations. For example, a narrow piece from the middle of a planarian can regenerate a new individual, with such organs as brain, eyes, pharynx and reproductive organs, no trace of which was present in the original piece. In flatworms, annelids, coelenterates and tunicates the reserve cells or neoblasts are the major source of the building material for new organs. These cells have been set aside in the embryo for this purpose, and have never undergone any specialized differentiation. In the common coelenterate *Hydra,* which is famous for its regenerative capacity, a type of connective tissue or mesenchyme cell, the so-called interstitial cell, is found scattered throughout the body; these cells migrate to a cut surface and form the chief or even exclusive source of the blastema. In some annelids the neoblasts can be identified as particularly large cells, stored in different parts of the body. However, it seems that tissue outgrowth and metaplasia also contribute to regeneration in annelids, and there is a great deal of variation in details in this group.

Different species of flatworms vary greatly in their capacity for regeneration, and a correlation seems to exist between the degree of regenerative power and the quantity of reserve cells present in the body. The role of these reserve cells in planarian regeneration was firmly established by the use of a modern tool, irradiation. It was found that reserve cells are more sensitive than ordinary body cells to X-rays and other radiation. If the whole animal is exposed to a mild dosage, the neoblasts can be destroyed without destroying the animal, which survives for at least several weeks; these individuals have no capacity for regeneration. A modification of this experiment gave evidence that reserve cells can migrate over long distances to reach the amputation surface. If the anterior part of a flatworm is irradiated and the posterior part shielded, and then the head removed by a transverse cut within the irradiated region, head regeneration occurs with a considerable delay because the reserve cells in the intact posterior region have to migrate across the irradiated band to reach the amputation surface. The wider the band, the longer the delay, but eventually a head is regenerated.

Metaplasia.—The question of whether metaplasia, as defined above, exists is of great theoretical interest: it goes to the heart of the problem of cellular differentiation. Is the process of differentiation of an embryonic cell into a highly specialized cell, such as a muscle or bone cell, reversible? Can a full-fledged muscle cell revert to an embryonic state and then, under certain conditions, differentiate in a new direction and become a bone cell? The origin of the limb-regeneration blastema in salamanders has always been in the centre of this discussion, without, however, yielding crucial evidence one way or the other. First, the question had to be settled whether the blastema cells come from the amputation stump or from more distant parts of the body, or perhaps even from formed elements of the blood. Irradiation experiments gave the answer: if part of a salamander limb is irradiated and the rest of the body shielded, and an amputation is then performed in the irradiated region, regeneration fails to occur; conversely, irradiation of the whole animal, except for the limb, does not interfere with limb regeneration. Contrary to what happens in planarians, then, the blastema cells do not come from distant parts but derive from the cells near the amputation surface.

Microscopic study of the events following the amputation of a limb reveals that a dedifferentiation of differentiated muscle and cartilage or bone actually occurs near the cut surface during the few days preceding the formation of the blastema. The multinuclear muscle fibres break up into fragments forming small cells with single nuclei, which have the appearance of embryonic cells or fibroblasts. There seems to be agreement that these cells, together with similar cells of skeletal origin and with ordinary fibroblasts, contribute materially to the blastema. If by metaplasia is meant merely the loss of highly specialized structure and the transformation into a fibroblastlike embryonic-looking cell, then this is a case in point. But this is not metaplasia in the strictest sense. The crucial question is still open: Have these cells actually lost all their biochemical and metabolic specifications? Have they reverted to a true embryonic pluripotential state which would enable them to differentiate into a cell type different from the one they represented before? A definitive answer to this question awaits new techniques.

There is, however, one clear case of true metaplasia. This is the regeneration of the crystalline lens of the salamander eye, often referred to as Wolffian lens regeneration in recognition of one of the co-discoverers and most active students of this very remarkable phenomenon. If the lens is carefully removed with fine instruments, it is replaced by a new lens that originates at the upper margin of the iris; the latter is the pigmented part of the eye, enclosing the pupil. The first change, following lens extirpation, is the disappearance of the pigment in the upper iris; that is, a process of dedifferentiation. Next, the two tissue layers that comprise the iris separate and expand at the rim where they are continuous, and form a small vesicle. This vesicle grows downward to assume the normal position of a lens; eventually it becomes detached from the iris and differentiates into a typical lens. Here may be observed directly the transformation of pigmented iris cells into lens cells. Another case of true metaplasia, the regeneration of brain tissue from epidermis in annelids, is well documented.

REGULATION

Initial Stimulus.—The regeneration process is ordinarily initiated by the injury that accompanies the loss of a part. The trauma seems to play an activating role similar to that of fertilization in the egg. The physiological and metabolic equilibrium at the wound surface is undoubtedly disturbed, and it is likely that the injured tissues produce a chemical agent or agents that set the process in motion. However, the actual loss of a part is not a necessary prerequisite for regeneration. An injury such as an incision in the stem of a coelenterate or in the body of a planarian is sufficient to initiate a new growth process. If ultraviolet irradiation is applied to the elbow region of a salamander limb, a local injury ensues, and an accessory, well-formed forearm with digits may grow out at this place. Duplications of limbs and other organs encountered occasionally in amphibians, arthropods and other groups, may have originated this way, by local injury.

In some instances not even an injury is necessary for activation of the regeneration process. The above-mentioned lens regeneration in the salamander eye is initiated simply by removal of the old lens, which can be done without injury to the upper iris, from which the regenerating lens is derived. What is the stimulus in this instance? Experiment has shown that the lens produces a chemical agent that holds the upper iris in check. If this inhibitor is removed, along with the lens, the regeneration process is set in motion. The coelenterate *Tubularia*, a marine relative of the common *Hydra*, which has been widely used for regeneration experiments, consists of stolon, stem and hydranth, the latter containing the mouth opening surrounded by two rows of tentacles (fig. 8). The stem is sheathed in a transparent coat, the perisarc. If a small area of the stem tissue is exposed to sea water by cutting a hole in the perisarc, a bud grows out at that place and forms eventually a new hydranth. In this instance, the local increase in oxygen tension serves as the activating stimulus. This experiment again illustrates the close relationship between regeneration and asexual reproduction by budding.

Regeneration Fields in Amphibians.—Once a blastema is formed, it is possible to inquire into the organizing factors that so direct the further development of the blastema that exactly the missing parts are replaced. The problems faced here are similar to those the embryologist encounters when he tries to analyze the factors that determine the origin of an embryonic organ primordium (*see* EMBRYOLOGY AND DEVELOPMENT, ANIMAL: *Experimental Embryology*). The regeneration blastema can be considered as equivalent to an organ primordium; the same types of organizing and determining factors probably are in operation in both, and the same kinds of experimental methods, such as extirpation and transplantation, are applied for their analysis. It should be stated that analysis of the regeneration process is much less advanced than that of embryonic processes.

The concept of regeneration fields has been found useful for an understanding of regeneration phenomena; the field concept also has been applied to embryonic development. The capacity for regeneration of an organ such as limb, tail or snout in salamanders is limited to a well-circumscribed area. For instance, limb regeneration after amputation can be obtained at any level down to the base, but if a still larger area, including the limb girdle, is removed, no regeneration occurs. By this type of extirpation experiment, regeneration fields for different organs have been demarcated. The fields are the units of regeneration; therefore, it is not quite correct to say that the salamander regenerates a limb; rather, the limb regeneration field restores its wholeness when it has been impaired. The field concept conveys another notion: the organizing factors for regeneration are distributed over the whole field in such a fashion that if the field district is injured at two separate points, two regenerates of the same type can be formed. In this way, duplicate limbs or tails can originate by experiment or by accidental injury. An example is an experiment mentioned above in which local irradiation at the elbow of a salamander called forth the formation of an extra limb. If a field can give rise to more than one organ, then part of a field should be able to produce a whole organ. This expectation is fulfilled in the following experiment: if the salamander hand is amputated and the forearm split lengthwise, each half of the cross section can regenerate a whole hand with four digits. The regeneration field shares this remarkable regulative property with the embryonic fields.

Determination.—Very young limb or tail blastemas apparently resemble early embryonic structures in that they are not yet irreversibly determined but show a certain plasticity. If a few-days-old blastema of a salamander forelimb is transplanted onto the stump of an amputated hindlimb, the regenerate is a hindlimb. However, if the blastema is a week old, or older, it forms a forelimb in a foreign position; that is, its fate has been determined in the meantime. Obviously, the blastema acquires gradually its specific characteristics. It must get its "instructions" from the underlying stump tissue, but the determinative mechanisms are unknown.

Organizers and Induction.—The discoveries of inductors and organizers were landmarks in experimental embryology. Transplantation experiments showed that certain embryonic areas, called inductors, produce chemical agents that stimulate the formation of an organ, such as inner ear, nose, lens, in an adjacent embryonic area. The organizer, discovered by H. Spemann in early amphibian embryos, is a complex inductor that, when transplanted to another embryo, induces in the latter not merely a single organ but a more or less complete secondary embryo. Similar phenomena were discovered in the regeneration of lower forms. If a small piece from the mouth region of a coelenterate polyp (fig. 8) is transplanted into the stem of another individual, a secondary individual grows out, composed largely of host material; the transplant contributes the organizing factors but little material. Similarly, if a piece of the head of a planarian is transplanted to the middle of the body of another planarian, a secondary individual is induced. If individuals of different colour are used in this experiment, it is possible to establish clearly the share of the graft and of the host in the new formation, and it can be seen that the graft forms only a small part of the outgrowth. Obviously, it is important to distinguish between organizing factors and building material.

Organ induction also has been demonstrated. In certain species of planarians, the brain produces a diffusible substance that induces eye regeneration. In the above-mentioned case of lens regeneration in the salamander eye from the upper iris, it is not enough to remove the lens-produced inhibitor; in addition an inductive substance, produced by the retina of the eye, must be present.

Role of the Nervous System.—The presence of nerves at the cut surface has long been recognized as a necessary prerequisite for amphibian limb regeneration. No regeneration takes place if simultaneously with limb amputation all limb nerves are transected in the region of the limb girdle. However, the nerves themselves can regenerate, and as soon as the regenerating nerves reach the amputation level a belated blastema formation begins. Limb regeneration can be prevented permanently by repeated nerve transections. If this is done in larval salamanders, not only is there no regeneration, but the amputation stump begins to regress and is eventually completely resorbed. The nerves apparently produce a trophic (nutritive) agent of unknown chemical nature that promotes the blastema formation. Once the blastema has reached a certain size, it becomes independent of the nerve influence. This trophic factor should be counted among the general, nonspecific metabolic conditions for regeneration, and not in the category of specific organizing factors, because the nerves do not determine the specific quality of the regenerate; they do not decide whether it is to be a forelimb or a hindlimb. The question of whether any special nerve fibre type, such as sensory, motor or sympathetic, is responsible for the production of this trophic agent was a matter of controversy for a long time, the issue being finally settled by M. Singer, who found that the requirement for nerves is quantitative, not qualitative; a certain minimum number must be present at the amputation surface, but the source from which they are derived is immaterial.

The nervous system also plays a role in the regeneration of certain invertebrates. For instance, head regeneration of the earthworm seems to be dependent on the presence of the ventral nerve cord at the amputation surface. Eye regeneration in some marine decapod crustaceans presents a particularly interesting case.

A normal eye regenerates if the eye and eyestalk are removed but the optic ganglion at the base of the stalk is left intact; if the latter is also removed, then an antenna is formed in the place of the eye (fig. 6; homeosis).

In other arthropods antennae and legs can regenerate in the absence of nerves.

Hormones in Regeneration.—Hormones (*q.v.*) play an important role as agents controlling a great variety of body functions. Their influence on growth and development is illustrated by the well-known cretinism, which results from deficiency of the thyroid hormone, and by the control of amphibian metamorphosis by the thyroid gland. The pituitary body (*see* PITUITARY GLAND) produces a growth hormone; its underproduction results in dwarfism and its overproduction in gigantism. Since regeneration is a special type of growth and development, similar hormonal influences on regeneration would be expected, and this is indeed the case.

The regeneration of limbs in adult newts (tailed amphibians) is inhibited when the entire pituitary is removed. This effect is exerted only on the very first phase of the regeneration process, following amputation, namely the breakdown of tissue (dedifferentiation) near the cut surface. Instead of formation of the blastema, a thick pad of skin grows over the wound and blocks further outgrowth.

Regeneration proceeds in a normal fashion if the regeneration process is allowed to get a start of five or six days before the gland is removed. It is assumed that the hormone is involved in the breakdown of proteins. Thyroid hormone has a similar effect on amphibian limb regeneration, and hormonal effects on regeneration in insects also have been reported.

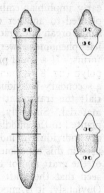

FIG. 7.—POLAR HETERO-MORPHOSIS (REVERSAL OF POLARITY) IN A PLANARIAN. AN AMPUTATED HEAD OR A SHORT POSTERIOR BODY PIECE MAY REGENERATE A HEAD WHERE A TAIL WOULD BE EXPECTED. REGENERATED TISSUE IS UNSTIPPLED

Polarity; Gradient Theory.—The familiar distinction between head, trunk and tail, or anterior and posterior end, calls attention to the axial organization, or polarity, of most animals. In the polyps of coelenterates, polarity is expressed in the formation of a tentacle-bearing hydranth with mouth opening at the apical end of the stem and a stolon at the basal end (fig. 8). One of the striking phenomena in the regeneration of lower animals is the retention of polarity even in small fragments.

A slice of a planarian taken from any part of the body regenerates a head at the anterior cut surface and a tail at the posterior cut surface. However, exceptions do occur; reversal of polarity is referred to as polar heteromorphosis (fig. 7).

How can the maintenance of polarity in regenerates be explained? Older theories that postulated specific cell types or specific morphogenetic substances for head or tail formation have been abandoned. The axial gradient theory of C. M. Child offers a more dynamic interpretation. According to this theory, polarity is the manifestation of a gradient of physiological activities along the main axis, the head end representing the highest activity and the tail end the lowest. Each section of the body or stem shares in this axial gradient. The theory assumes further that a head, or hydranth in coelenterates, regenerates at the anterior surface of an isolated piece because this is the region of relatively highest metabolic activity in the fragment; and the tail or stolon forms at the level of relatively lowest activity. In other words, the fate of a regeneration blastema is determined by its relative position in the whole gradient system.

Polar heteromorphoses, which occur predominantly in very short pieces (fig. 7), are explained by assuming that in such pieces the activity at the two surfaces is nearly equal and the differential too small to determine two different types of structures.

The nature of the physiological activity postulated by the theory has never been clearly defined, and efforts to demonstrate single gradient systems of oxygen consumption or of other general metabolic activities, consistent over a wide range of eggs, embryos and lower animals, have failed. However, there are some indirect methods that give indications of rather widespread gradients, for instance in the susceptibility of lower animals, eggs and embryos to toxic agents. In this context, gradients of regeneration capacity are of special interest. In the stem of the coelenterate *Tubularia* the rate of regeneration, measured by the amount of tissue regenerated per hour, decreases gradually from the apical to the basal regions; this is attributed to the gradient concentration of a catalyst. Likewise, if a planarian is cut in six or eight trans-

verse pieces of equal size, the quality of head regeneration is highest in the anteriormost piece and declines from there in a graded fashion.

The concept of physiological dominance is an integral part of the axial gradient theory. It is postulated that the region of highest physiological activity not only forms a head or a hydranth but at the same time suppresses head or hydranth formation at any other part of the regenerating piece. It sets itself up as a "dominant region" and thus guarantees the unity in the regenerating system. One experiment, selected from many others, may illustrate dominance. As illustrated in fig. 8, a piece of the stem of the coelenterate *Tubularia* would normally regenerate a hydranth at the apical end, at surface 1, and a stolon at surface 2. If regeneration at the apical end is prevented by a ligature, then the basal end regenerates a hydranth. In terms of the theory, the ligature has eliminated all influences of the apical region; thus, the basal end has been released from the inhibitory effect of the original dominant region and set itself up as a new dominant region. A polar heteromorphosis has thereby been produced.

Nerve Regeneration.—The great practical importance of nerve regeneration following nerve injury in man justifies a brief special consideration of this process. Only peripheral nerves can regenerate; the nerve cells, or neurons, that make up the tissue of the brain and spinal cord, and the ganglia, cannot be replaced once they are destroyed. The peripheral nerves are actually bundles of nerve fibres embedded in connective tissue. Each fibre is a delicate protoplasmic thread spun out in early development by one of the nerve cells in the central nervous system or ganglion. The fibre remains part of its cell of origin and depends on its cell body for nutriment throughout life. This fact is important for an understanding of nerve fibre regeneration. When a nerve is transected, regeneration starts from the so-called proximal stump of the fibre (that is, the part that remained connected with its cell body), whereas the disconnected, distal or peripheral stump dies off. The fibres at the proximal stump begin to sprout new threads that penetrate the gap between the two cut ends.

How do these fine processes bridge this gap? How do they find their way to the peripheral organs they are supposed to reinnervate? They obtain substantial aid from a special type of companion cells, the so-called Schwann cells. These very versatile small cells serve several important functions. They are lined up all along the nerve fibre, forming a continuous, very delicate coat around it. During development, they produce an insulating coat around the fibre, the so-called myelin sheath, which gives the nerve its white, glistening appearance. In nerve regeneration, they play a major role in reconstructing the peripheral pathway for the regenerating fibres. The peripheral parts of the nerve fibres themselves that were severed from their cell bodies break down and disappear; not so the Schwann cells that surround them. These become very active. They multiply and form long dense strands, or cords, in the peripheral nerve stump.

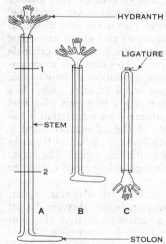

FIG. 8.—EXPERIMENTAL REVERSAL OF POLARITY IN THE MARINE POLYP TUBULARIA, ILLUSTRATING PHYSIOLOGICAL DOMINANCE. (A) PIECE 1-2 REGENERATES NORMALLY (B) A HYDRANTH AT 1 AND A STOLON AT 2. (C) IF A LIGATURE IS MADE AT 1, A HYDRANTH REGENERATES AT 2

These cords are then invaded by the newly regenerating fibres from the proximal stump and serve the outgrowing fibres as a substrate and a guide, from the cut end all the way to their destination at the periphery.

The greatest hazard for the regenerating nerve fibres is the crossing of the gap between the two cut ends of the nerve. In this they are also aided by the Schwann cells; the latter, together with fibroblasts, form between the two cut ends a bridge of parallel strands which is then used as a track by the outgrowing fibres. In this phase of nerve regeneration, the surgeon can lend a helping hand by facilitating the crossing of the gap. Particularly if the gap is wide, the two ends may be connected with sutures, or fitted together with a sleeve made of a piece of artery or other material. Growth of the regenerating nerve fibre proceeds at the rate of several millimetres per day. In man, functional recovery takes several months, the time depending, of course, on the distance between the cut end and the peripheral end organ.

See EMBRYOLOGY AND DEVELOPMENT, ANIMAL; REPRODUCTION; *see* also references under "Regeneration" in the Index.

BIBLIOGRAPHY.—T. H. Morgan, *Regeneration* (1901); C. M. Child, *Patterns and Problems of Development* (1941); A. E. Needham, *Regeneration and Wound-Healing* (1952); L. Guth, "Regeneration in the Mammalian Peripheral Nervous System," *Physiol. Rev.,* vol. xxxvi (1956); M. Singer, "The Influence of the Nerve in Regeneration of the Amphibian Extremity," *Quart. Rev. of Biol.,* vol. 27 (1952); C. S. Thornton (ed.), *Symposium on Regeneration in Vertebrates* (1959). *See* also chapters on regeneration in B. H. Willier *et al.* (eds.), *Analysis of Development* (1955); J. Brachet, *Chemical Embryology,* Eng. trans. by L. G. Barth (1950); C. H. Waddington, *Principles of Embryology* (1956); B. I. Balinsky, *An Introduction to Embryology* (1960).

(V. H.)

REGENSBURG (RATISBON), a city and episcopal see of West Germany in the *Land* (state) of Bavaria, Federal Republic of Germany. Pop. (1961) 125,047. It lies $61\frac{1}{2}$ mi. (99 km.) SE of Nürnberg by road, on the right bank of the Danube at its most northerly bend, where it is joined by the Regen. From Roman times it has been a trading centre and is now a road and rail junction and river port, the Danube being navigable there for most of the year for large barges. Goethe said of Regensburg: "Such a site was bound to attract a city." Its medieval buildings have been almost entirely preserved, the patricians' houses with their imposing towers (12th–14th centuries) being unique in Germany. The Steinerne Brücke ("stone bridge"; 1135–46) across the Danube, linking the suburb of Stadtamhof, was a medieval constructional wonder.

The Cathedral of St. Peter (1275–1530) is the most important Gothic church in Bavaria, with a beautifully proportioned interior and fine stained-glass windows (14th century). The cathedral choir (Regensburger Domspatzen) is well known. In the adjoining cloisters are two Romanesque chapels. St. Emmeram's Church is a Romanesque basilica, the interior having been remodeled in the Baroque style. The buildings of the Benedictine abbey of St. Emmeram (founded 7th century) have been since 1812 the palace of the princes of Thurn and Taxis. In the Alter Kornmarkt (Old Grain Market) are the remains of the Herzogshof, the residence of the Bavarian dukes (13th century). Nearby is the Alte Kapelle (Old Chapel), rebuilt by Henry II in 1002, with an elaborate Rococo interior. The Schottenkirche St. Jakob, founded by Irish monks, is a Romanesque basilica (12th century), the north portal having unusual Christian and pagan sculptured figures. The Dominikaner Church (13th century) is an early Gothic basilica. The town museum incorporates the Minorite Church (*c.* 1250–1350). The Town Hall (14th–15th centuries with a Baroque extension) contains the Reichssaal (*c.* 1350) with fine tapestries. The Imperial Diet was held in that building during the period from 1663 to 1806.

In the town museum is a Roman tablet commemorating the founding, in A.D. 179, of Castra Regina, a legionary camp and a main Roman stronghold; the north gate (Porta Praetoria) and parts of the walls still survive. Earlier it was a Celtic settlement (Radasbona); and the Romans first camped there in A.D. 77. In 530 Regensburg became the capital of the dukes of Bavaria. St. Boniface made it a bishopric in 739 and shortly afterward it became the capital of the Carolingians. During the 12th–13th centuries Regensburg, an imperial free city from 1245, was the most prosperous city in southern Germany. In the Thirty Years' War it was taken by the Swedes and then by the imperial troops. The French sacked and burned it in 1809 and in the following year it became part of Bavaria. The astronomer Johannes Kepler died in Regensburg in 1630. The painter Albrecht Altdorfer (d. 1538), examples of whose works are in Regensburg, was city architect and a counselor.

The city is an important industrial and commercial centre, leather, electrical, and chemical goods being the chief manufactures, and sausage is a speciality.

See F. Voggenneiter, *Die Stadt Regensburg* (1936).

REGENT, one who rules or governs, especially during the absence, minority or incapacity of the sovereign. William I of England appointed *ad hoc* administrators whenever he left for Normandy, and in the course of the 12th century it became customary for the justiciar to act as regent when the king was abroad. In 1216 the barons chose the earl of Pembroke to be *rector regis et regni* ("guide of king and kingdom") for the boy king, Henry III. By the statute of 28 Henry VIII c. 7, advance provision was made for the selection of a regent upon Henry's death to serve until the new sovereign should attain the age of 18 if a male or 16 if a female. Although it was always subsequently assumed that a regent could be appointed only by or pursuant to an act of parliament, it was not until the Regency Act, 1937, that permanent provision was made for the selection of a regent if the sovereign is under 18 or is found by a commission composed of his or her spouse, the lord chancellor, the speaker of the House of Commons, the lord chief justice and the master of the rolls to be infirm of body or mind.

At the universities of Oxford and Cambridge the term regent was applied to a resident master who presided over disputations in the schools, and Cambridge once called the upper house of the university senate Regent House. In the Scottish universities the term designated a tutor for undergraduates; in France it designated a teacher of elementary arts or sciences in a secondary school. The term was occasionally used in Europe and elsewhere to refer to the governing board of a city, and in some Muslim states for the chief of state. In Java it was the title given to a native chief through whom the Dutch colonial officials governed a residency. In the United States the term is little used except by some educational institutions, especially state universities, for a member of the governing board; *e.g.*, the regents of the University of California.

(J. A. C. G.)

REGER, (JOHANN BAPTIST JOSEPH) MAXI-MILIAN, known as MAX (1873–1916), German composer and teacher who developed the neoclassical tradition in German music inherited from Brahms, was born at Brand, Bavaria, on March 19, 1873. He studied at Weiden and in 1888 visited Bayreuth where he heard *Die Meistersinger* and *Parsifal,* but the Wagnerian influence was short-lived. From 1890 to 1893 he studied with the musicologist Hugo Riemann at Sondershausen, and at Wiesbaden where he also taught the piano, organ, and theory. From this period dates his friendship with Busoni, and also with the Leipzig organist K. Straube, who introduced Reger's organ music. He returned to Weiden in 1898. In 1901, in spite of much opposition to his traditional methods, he established himself as a composer, pianist, and teacher in Munich. In 1902 he married Elsa von Bercken (née Bagenski). In 1906, after writing many organ, piano, and chamber works, he produced his first orchestral work, the Sinfonietta, Op. 90. The following year he was appointed professor of composition at the Leipzig Conservatory and musical director at the University of Leipzig. There he wrote many choral and orchestral works, chamber music, and songs. In 1909 he went to London where he took part in performances of his chamber works. In 1911 he was appointed conductor of the court orchestra at Meiningen where he wrote his *Böcklin Suite* and one of his finest works for orchestra, the *Variations and Fugue on a Theme by Mozart.* He spent the last year of his life at Jena and died at Leipzig on May 11, 1916.

In an age of bold harmonic experiments Reger used the conventional musical language which, however, he developed in a personal way. One of the last composers to infuse life into the 19th-century style, he influenced forward-looking composers of the following generation, among them Honegger and Hindemith. His organ pieces, notably his Fantasy and Fugue on the letters of Bach's name, and his songs, some of them dedicated to the memory of Schubert and Wolf, are best known. His orchestral works include the *Suite in the Old Style* and sets of variations on themes of J. A. Hiller and Beethoven. A Reger Society was established in Germany in 1920 and in 1954 a complete edition of his works was begun at Bonn.

See E. Otto, *Max Reger: Sinnbild einer Epoche* (1957).

REGGIO DI CALABRIA, a city of southern Italy and capital of the province of the same name, is on the Strait of Messina, 338 mi. (544 km.) SSE of Naples by road. Pop. (1961) 152,071. It is an archiepiscopal and metropolitan see.

Reggio has been destroyed many times by earthquakes and by Saracen invaders. Repeatedly reconstructed, it has experienced alternately splendour and decadence. It was completely razed in an earthquake on Dec. 28, 1908, and was afterward rebuilt with wide streets and low, reinforced-concrete buildings. The cathedral was rebuilt in Romanesque-Byzantine style. The Museo Nazionale della Magna Grecia, designed by Marcello Piacentini, contains a notable collection including tablets from Locri (*q.v.*) and pictures by Antonello da Messina.

Reggio is linked with Messina, 9½ mi. (15 km.) across the strait, by steamer and train ferry. It is connected by rail northward with Naples and southward with Melito di Porto Salvo. There are air services to Rome and Palermo. Reggio is a tourist resort and seaport, and supplies the perfume and pharmaceutical industries with essences of bergamot and jasmine. Another important export product is dried pungent herbs.

The city of Rhegion (Latin Rhegium) was founded *c.* 720 B.C. by Greek colonists from Chalcis as a daughter city to Zancle (Messina). Under Anaxilas, who also ruled Zancle, it prospered, but in 387 B.C. it was captured by Dionysius I. Later it suffered under the Mamertini (mercenaries from Campania) until it fell to the Romans in 270 B.C. Throughout the Punic Wars the city was faithful to Rome, but remained a Greek city even under the empire and never became a colony. It was taken by Alaric in A.D. 410, by the Saracens in 918, and by the Normans in 1060. It was damaged during World War II.

REGGIO DI CALABRIA PROVINCE comprises the southern part of Italy's "toe." Area 1,229 sq.mi. (3,183 sq.km.). Pop. (1961) 582,409. The east and south of the province are mountainous, with the Aspromonte Range (Montalto, 6,417 ft. [1,950 m.]) near the southern extremity. In the west, where a coastal plain borders the Gulf of Gioia, fishing is carried on. Sheep and goats are raised and citrus fruit, olives, and grapes are grown. Apart from the capital the chief towns are Gioia Tauro, Palmi, and Locri, which all have some industry. (A. LA T.)

REGGIO NELL'EMILIA, capital city of the province of the same name in the region of Emilia-Romagna, north central Italy, is situated near the southern edge of the Po plain on the Crostolo River (a minor affluent of the Po) 25 mi. (40 km.) NW of Bologna on the road and rail route from Rimini to Milan. It is an episcopal see. Pop. (1961) 118,375. The Via Emilia (Roman Via Aemilia) runs through it. The cathedral (9th century) was rebuilt in the 16th century by Bartolomeo and Prospero Spani; opposite is the house where the poet Ludovico Ariosto was born in 1474. There is a modern garden-city suburb. The town is a centre for local farm produce; wine, cheese, meat products, electrical apparatus, cement, and pharmaceutical products are made.

Founded in the 2nd century B.C. by Marcus Aemilius Lepidus as Regium Lepidi, Reggio was ruled from the 15th to 18th century by the Este family and was annexed to Piedmont in 1860.

REGGIO NELL'EMILIA PROVINCE (area, 885 sq.mi. [2,291 sq.km.]; pop. [1961] 371,389) adjoins Mantova (north), Modena (east), Parma (west), and Massa-Carrara and Lucca (south). It extends from the ridge of the Etruscan Apennines, which form its southern half, to the Po River, whose valley forms its northern half. The Secchia and Enza rivers approximately delimit its eastern and western boundaries. Dairy cattle are raised; grapes are grown on the southern hillsides, and wheat on the northern plain. There are several small towns of historical interest. The ruined castle of Canossa (*q.v.*) is 12 mi. (19 km.) SW of Reggio. (M. T. A. N.)

REGICIDE means the killing, or the killer, of a king (*see* KING for ritual regicide). Christian moralists connect the act with tyrannicide, the killing of a tyrant, which some forbid absolutely but which others condone in certain circumstances. Regicide be-

came an issue with the execution of Mary Queen of Scots in 1587, the assassination of Henry III of France in 1589, and the assassination of Henry IV of France in 1610. Whereas Jean Bodin (*q.v.*) had maintained that the kings of France, England, and Spain, having no lawful superiors to judge them, could not lawfully be killed, the Spanish Jesuit Juan de Mariana (*q.v.*), in his *De rege et regis institutione* (1599), advanced some highly democratic arguments for regicide, for which the Society of Jesus was widely attacked, despite its disavowal of Mariana's theses in 1610.

In England the name regicide is given to those responsible for the sentencing and execution of Charles I (1649). At the Restoration (1660) the House of Commons first specified 84 of these "regicides" (including the two disguised executioners, whose identity was unknown). The following provisions were included in the Indemnity Act (August 1660): (1) the 4 most notable "regicides," John Bradshaw, Oliver Cromwell, Henry Ireton, and Thomas Pride, who were all dead, were excepted from indemnity (in January 1661 their bodies, except Pride's, were exhumed and hanged at Tyburn); (2) the estates of 20 other deceased "regicides" were to suffer fine or forfeiture; (3) 26 living "regicides" were totally excepted from indemnity, as were the two executioners and 4 others not numbered among the original 84; (4) 19 more living "regicides" were also excepted, with a saving clause that, if attainted, their execution must be specially authorized by Parliament. Of the remaining "regicides," 7 were debarred from office for life and 4 (of whom one was dead) were pardoned.

The trial was held in October 1660. There were 10 sentences of death executed forthwith, and 19 imprisonments (one man was later freed and two escaped). Of the 18 who had escaped arrest, 3 went to New England, the others to the continent of Europe. Of the latter, 3 were captured in Holland, taken to England, and executed (1662), and one was shot dead at Lausanne (1664).

In later French history the name regicide is given to those members of the Convention who sentenced Louis XVI (*q.v.*) to death. In the session of Jan. 16–17, 1793, there were 361 votes for death outright, 26 for death but with a preliminary debate on the expediency of postponing execution, 46 for a suspended sentence of death (*sursis*), and 288 for alternative penalties. In the final session (Jan. 19–20), there were 380 votes for death against 310 for the suspended sentence.

REGIMENT, in most armies, a body of troops headed by a colonel and organized for tactical control into companies, battalions, or squadrons. French cavalry units were called regiments as early as 1558. The word is derived from the Latin *regimen,* a rule or system of order, and describes the regiment's functions of raising, equipping, and training troops. As a regiment developed individuality, through its name or number, colours, coat of arms, distinctive uniform and insignia, and achievements in battle, it also became a central object of loyalty, pride, and *esprit de corps* of its soldiers.

In early U.S. service, as in European armies up to that time, the usual number of companies in a regiment was ten, forming a single battalion in battle. Early in the 19th century, Napoleon Bonaparte organized the regiments of the French Army into three battalions or squadrons, of which two were in the field and one was in quarters recruiting and training additional troops. Later, Edward Cardwell (afterward Viscount Cardwell) reorganized the British infantry into two-battalion regiments, each having one battalion at home and one stationed overseas. The U.S. Army adopted a three-battalion infantry regimental organization in 1901, and incorporated regiments of this type in the divisions employed in World Wars I and II and the Korean War.

Artillery batteries of the U.S. Army had been formed into regiments as early as 1821, but the organization of artillery units was changed frequently until after World War II, when the battalion organization emerged as standard practice. Similarly, the U.S. cavalry regiments in service in the western territories during the 19th century eventually gave way to separate tank battalions and reconnaissance squadrons. In the British and Commonwealth armies, comparable artillery and armoured units of battalion size are still called regiments.

In 1957 the U.S. Army, during a major reorganization of its

divisions, eliminated the infantry regiment as a tactical organization. (*See* DIVISION, MILITARY.) Concurrently, it inaugurated a Combat Arms Regimental System, in which each infantry, armour, and artillery tactical unit was identified as part of a historic regiment, carrying its name and colours and inheriting its traditions and battle honours. Thus, each regiment consisted of a varying number of separate tactical units distributed among the divisions and other organizations comprising the combat forces of the Army.

(E. SR.)

REGINA, the capital and largest city of the province of Saskatchewan, Can., is in the south central part of the province, 357 mi. (575 km.) W of Winnipeg. Founded in 1822 as Pile O' Bones and renamed Regina, it was capital of the Northwest Territories from 1882 to 1905, having been chosen because of its central location on the Canadian Pacific Railway, and was selected as capital city when Saskatchewan became a province in 1905.

At Wascana Centre the city has brought together in one park the provincial legislative building, the campus of the Regina branch of the University of Saskatchewan, a new city hall, and the Saskatchewan Museum of Natural History. The Royal Canadian Mounted Police museum and barracks is another attraction.

Regina experienced rapid physical expansion and economic development after World War II and became an important prairie manufacturing centre. It is a transportation and distribution centre for an important agricultural area. Both major Canadian railway systems serve the city. Five main highways converge on it, including the Trans-Canada Highway. It obtains abundant natural gas from provincial sources and uses local artesian and Saskatchewan River water. Regular air service is provided to most Saskatchewan cities and to the principal cities of the dominion.

Regina industry includes two large oil refineries, one cooperatively owned, and oil industry services; a steel plant and several steel fabricators; and agricultural processing plants. As headquarters for the Saskatchewan Wheat Pool, Canada's largest cooperative, it has been an important centre in the growth of the cooperative movement in Canada.

The university's branch enrolls about 3,500 students; a Jesuit college and a Lutheran college are affiliated with it. The Regina area provides a variety of sports and is a centre for waterfowl. Pop. (1961) 112,141; (1966) 131,127. (J. E. CL.)

REGIOMONTANUS: *see* MÜLLER, JOHANN (REGIOMONTANUS).

REGIONAL PLANNING, a term used by political scientists, engineers, sociologists, geographers and others to describe the process of considering systematically the functional organization of the natural and human resources of an area of the earth. Regional planning may involve extensive areas that include one or more nations or more limited areas such as drainage basins or metropolitan areas. The objectives may be general or specific. Examples of international regional planning include the European common market and the Colombo plan (*q.v.*), involving whole nations, the St. Lawrence seaway (*q.v.*) and the Nile valley and Mekong river schemes, involving parts of two or more nations. In many instances a regional plan involves the creation of a new organization for its particular purpose as, for example, the Tennessee Valley authority, the boundaries of whose area coincide with those of no general political jurisdiction but which in its operation involves the co-operation of several to their mutual advantage.

Regional planning is essentially a process of orderly and systematic anticipation of the future of a region, involving recommendations of the necessary remedial and constructive actions by public and private agencies to achieve the objectives of the plan. In one sense it is as old as society. In modern times, significant contributions to knowledge of planning principles have been made by geographers who are concerned with the nature of man's occupancy of the earth and of its regional similarities and differences; by economists whose concerns include the flows of goods, money and credit to, from, and within regions as well as theories relating to the location of economic activity; by sociologists who are concerned with the regional aspects of the organization of society and of social action; by political scientists whose concern includes the institutional means by which plans are made and effected; by psychologists, philosophers and others concerned with motivation and the setting of social goals; by engineers, architects and others concerned with the physical structures and forms involved in man's utilization of resources; and by specialists in many other fields.

Planning does not set goals or objectives within a society; it rather points out the consequences of alternative decisions relating to the utilization of resources and the organization of society in space and recommends programs of action considered most appropriate and effective in the light of the objectives which the particular society sets for itself.

The Nature of Regions.—Regions are human creations for the purpose of analysis, synthesis and planning. The extent and character of a region will depend upon the purpose or purposes for which it is created and the number of possible regions is infinite. Geographers recognize two types: homogeneous and nodal. Homogeneous regions are areas within which, for the purposes for which the region is being defined, the similarities from place to place are considered to be more significant than the differences. Such similarities may be in a single element, such as climate, soils, population density, drainage characteristics, religion or language. For multipurpose planning or comprehensive planning a combination of elements is employed in defining a region; two or more of these may exhibit coincidences in their variations or may on the other hand show no significant variations from place to place within the region. The second type of region is the nodal region, which is an area of concentration of elements or activities, such as an urban or metropolitan area or the intensively developed core of a more extensive homogeneous region.

A major difficulty in preparing and especially in effecting a regional plan is that most appropriate real units very rarely coincide with a governmental jurisdiction. Metropolitan areas such as New York, Chicago, London, Tokyo and Paris involve many municipalities and other units of local government; river basins seldom are included entirely within individual states or provinces and many of them such as the Rhine, Rio Grande, Columbia and Congo, are international. The co-ordination of capital improvement programs of a multiplicity of units of government presents a challenge to the planner. In some instances the problem can be solved by the creation of new units of government, such as the metropolitan municipality of Toronto and the various types of special-function authorities such as the Port of New York authority, the metropolitan sanitary district of Greater Chicago and the Tennessee Valley authority.

The Process of Regional Planning.—Whether the planning is for a homogeneous or a nodal region, whether comprehensive or special-purpose, and whether undertaken by a regular governmental unit, a special public agency or a private organization, it involves several steps: (1) inventory and survey of the resources or other elements relative to their character, quantity, quality, availability and distribution within and without the area; (2) analysis of the relationships among the natural and human resources of the region and of their significance; (3) making of the plan, including proposals for maximizing the effectiveness of utilization of the resources in terms of the plan objectives, and recommendations as to the staging or timing of the various proposed steps; and (4) effectuation of the plan, including the carrying out of the responsibilities of the various bodies and agencies concerned with each aspect of the regional development. The first three steps generally involve the planning agency directly; most planning agencies do not have the responsibility of effectuation but rather recommend the necessary steps to the appropriate agencies and at times may suggest the creation of new agencies for specific purposes. Inventory, analysis and the making of the plan involve the efforts of many specialists, and the professional planner is essentially a co-ordinator. Once a plan is prepared and adopted, it is essential, in most instances, that it be subjected to continuous or periodic review and revision in the light of subsequent developments. The continuity of operation of planning agencies is therefore important. The nature of the process of effectuation, of course, varies with the nature of the government and other institutional operations in the region or for the objectives of the particular plan. In some countries, as in the Soviet Union, effectuation of a plan is by a central authority with absolute powers; in democratic countries the authorities are responsible directly to the public and in many instances the plan or major elements of it may be subject to referendum. In most instances, legislative bodies within areas of appropriate jurisdiction adopt either total plans or the individual proposals contained within the plans. Educational programs and information services on the nature of planning and the objectives and content of specific plans are therefore essential aspects of planning in democratic countries. Most regional planning involves multiple purposes and the regions are demarcated in such a way as to serve the maximum number of purposes with the maximum effectiveness. The conservation movement in the United States in the early 20th century was an important incentive to regional planning; later the multipurpose development of water resources, as in the Tennessee valley and the Columbia basin, constituted an important type of regional planning. Meanwhile, the spread of cities beyond the boundaries of municipalities and the development of metropolitan areas and conurbations became important incentives for another type of regional planning, typified in the United States by the Burnham plan of Chicago, published in 1909, the Regional plan of New York city and its environs, in the 1920s, and the creation of many metropolitan planning agencies in the 1950s, and in Great Britain by the numerous regional planning schemes of the period during and shortly after World War II.

Aspects of Regional Planning.—Much of the concern of regional planning relates to two aspects of man's relations to regional resources. The first may be termed the static aspect, and it includes those features, tangible and intangible, which have fixed locations at any point in time, such as land uses, buildings, population distribution and other features of culture; the second may be termed dynamic and refers to the interchange of people, goods and ideas within and among regions and places, as expressed by transportation facilities and the flows of traffic as well as by communication. No place or region can be completely self-sufficient; each has innumerable bonds with other regions and places. The strength and relative importance of these bonds vary with the size, distance and complexity of the various regions and places and are subject to change with the existence and utilization of alternative opportunities represented by competing regions and places, the possibility of substitution of resources of other places or of other types, changes in the material or intangible cultures of the respective regions, and the competition among alternative routes and forms of transportation. Transportation makes regional specialization possible, and the planning of facilities for the handling of movement to, from, and within regions has become an important aspect of regional planning. In many regions of the world where economic development has been retarded by inadequate transportation facilities, a major concern of regional planning is the selection of appropriate forms of transportation, as between railways, highways, airways and inland and coastal waterways, and the determination of the amount and routes of transportation to be recommended. In the United States, the Federal Highway act of 1956, which provided for a new 41,000-mile interstate highway system, was a stimulus for the organization of regional planning in many areas, as was the focusing of the highway networks upon urban centres and the stimulation of peripheral expansion of population and development within and beyond metropolitan areas as a result of the increased availability of motor transportation.

Regional planning on the one hand is an extension of local planning at the municipal and county level and on the other hand is a part of national and international planning. In the United States regional planning was stimulated in the 1930s by the National Resources Planning board, which was terminated with the advent of World War II. In the second half of the 20th century, however, numerous state planning agencies were in operation, as well as a number of metropolitan and *ad hoc* regional planning agencies.

See also CITY PLANNING.

BIBLIOGRAPHY.—Benton MacKaye, *The New Exploration, A Philosophy of Regional Planning* (1928); Robert E. Dickinson, *City Region and Regionalism* (1947); *Regional Plan of New York and its Environs,* 2 vol. (1928); P. E. James and C. F. Jones, eds., *American Geography; Inventory and Prospect* (1954); various reports of National Resources committee and National Resources Planning board (1934–1942); *Annual Reports* of the Tennessee Valley authority (1934–   ); *Journal of the American Institute of Planners* (various issues); *Journal of Regional Science,* vol. I, no. 1 (Summer 1958).   (H. M. M.)

REGIUM DONUM (ROYAL BOUNTY), an annual grant formerly made from the public funds to Presbyterian ministers in Ireland and to Nonconformists in Great Britain.

In 1690 William III made a grant of £1,200 a year to Presbyterian ministers in Ulster as a reward for their services during his struggles with James II. Agitation, at first unsuccessful, against this grant on the part of certain Church of Ireland clergy, especially William King, archbishop of Dublin, led to its withdrawal toward the end of Queen Anne's reign, but George I revived and increased it (1715). Further increases were made later because the salaries of Presbyterian ministers were much lower than those of Church of Ireland clergy even in areas where Presbyterianism was in the majority. When the Church of Ireland was disestablished in 1869, the *regium donum* was discontinued.

In England during Charles II's reign Presbyterian ministers received an annual pension of £50, and in 1721 Edmund Calamy received £500 "for the use and behalf of the widows of dissenting ministers." But the *regium donum* proper began in 1723 with the annual grant of £500 (soon doubled) paid to nine Nonconformists who divided it among needy ministers and their widows, whether Presbyterian, Baptist, or Independent. Although the sums received by any one individual were small, some dissenters believed that political implications were attached to this royal charity, which they therefore subjected to various attacks almost from its inception. By the middle of the 19th century most Nonconformists had become discontented with it, and in 1851 it was discontinued.

BIBLIOGRAPHY.—J. S. Reid, *History of the Presbyterian Church in Ireland,* 3 vol., new ed. by W. D. Killen (1867); T. Rees, *Sketch of the History of the Regium Donum* (1834); R. W. Dale, *History of English Congregationalism,* pp. 524–527 (1907).

REGNARD, JEAN FRANÇOIS (1655–1709), French dramatist, one of the most successful of Molière's immediate successors. Baptized in Paris on Feb. 8, 1655, he inherited a fortune and traveled widely in his youth (he was a prisoner of the Algerian corsairs for seven months, 1678–79). He held a post in the financial administration in Paris, but from 1688 devoted himself almost entirely to the theatre, writing first for the Italian comedians, then, from 1694, for the Comédie Française. He also published accounts of his travels. Of his numerous plays, the best-known are *Le Joueur* (1696) and *Le Légataire universel* (1708), but *La Sérénade* (1694), *Le Distrait* (1697), *Démocrite* (1700), *Les Folies amoureuses* (1704), and *Les Ménechmes, ou les Jumeaux* (1705) also helped to make his reputation. He imitated both the Italians and Molière quite openly. Regnard died on his estate of Grillon, in Normandy, on Sept. 4, 1709.

There are collected editions of his works by E. Fournier, 2 vol. (1854) and by A. Michiels (1875) and selections ed. by G. d'Heylli, 2 vol. (1886).

See P. Toldo, "Études sur le théâtre de Regnard," *Revue d'histoire littéraire de la France* (1903–04); H. C. Lancaster, *History of French Dramatic Literature in the 17th Century,* part iv (1940).
(W. G. ME.)

REGNAULT, HENRI VICTOR (1810–1878), French chemist and physicist noted for his work on the properties of gases, was born on July 21, 1810, at Aix-la-Chapelle. His early life was a struggle with poverty. He worked in a textile establishment in Paris until 1829 and then entered the École Polytechnique, passing in 1832 to the École des Mines. After studying under Justus von Liebig at Giessen, Ger., he was appointed to a professorship at Lyons. In 1840 he became professor of chemistry in the École Polytechnique in succession to Gay-Lussac and was elected a member of the Académie des Sciences; in 1841 he succeeded Pierre Louis Dulong as professor of physics in the Collège de France. In 1847 he published a four-volume treatise on chemistry which was translated into many languages. In 1854 he was appointed director of the porcelain manufactory at Sèvres. His laboratory there was destroyed during the Franco-German War of 1870–71, in which also his son Henri, the painter, was killed. Regnault never recovered from the double blow, and, although he lived until Jan. 19, 1878, his scientific labours ended in 1872.

His most important contribution to organic chemistry was a series of researches, begun in 1835, on the halogen and other derivatives of unsaturated hydrocarbons. He also studied the alkaloids and organic acids, introduced a classification of the metals, and effected a comparison of the chemical composition of atmospheric air from all parts of the world. Regnault's work in physics was remarkably accurate and painstaking, and he designed standard types of apparatus for a large number of measurements. He made careful redeterminations of the specific heats of many solids, liquids, and gases. He investigated the expansion of gases by heat, and showed that, contrary to previous opinion, no two gases have precisely the same coefficient of expansion. By delicate experiments he proved that Boyle's law of elasticity of a "perfect" gas is only approximately true for real gases. In his studies of thermometry he introduced the use of an accurate air-thermometer, comparing its indications with those of a mercurial thermometer and determining the absolute expansion of mercury as a step in the process. He also devised Regnault's hygrometer (an instrument for measuring humidity). Regnault's most important work is collected in volumes 21 and 26 of the *Mémoires de l'Académie des Sciences.*

REGNAULT (Regnaud) (de Saint-Jean d'Angély), **MICHEL LOUIS ÉTIENNE,** Comte (1761–1819), French statesman and administrator who held important offices during the First Empire, was born at Saint-Fargeau (Yonne) on Nov. 3, 1761. He became an *avocat* in Paris and later a judge in the maritime provostship of Rochefort. Elected to the States-General (1789) as deputy for Saint-Jean d'Angély, he sat in the centre in the Constituent Assembly and played only a secondary role. Having opposed the Jacobins in the press (1792), he was arrested (1793) in the Terror, but escaped. Hospital administrator for the army of Italy (1796), he embarked for Egypt (1798) with Bonaparte, but stayed at Malta as civil commissioner. Regnault aided Bonaparte in the *coup d'état* of 18 Brumaire (1799) and became a member of the *conseil d'état,* presiding from 1802 over the affairs of the *Intérieur,* and helping to prepare the commercial legal code of 1807. Attorney-general in the high court (1804), registrar in charge of the imperial household, and minister of state (1807), he was created comte in 1808. Out of office during the First Restoration (1814), he was vice-president of the *conseil d'état* during the Hundred Days (1815) and was also elected to the Chamber of Representatives. He encouraged Napoleon to adopt liberal policies and persuaded him (June 1815) to abdicate for the second time. Exiled at the Second Restoration (1815), Regnault lived in the United States and then in Belgium. Authorized to return to France, he died March 11, 1819, the day after he reached Paris. (C. E. Du.)

RÉGNIER, HENRI FRANÇOIS JOSEPH DE (1864–1936), the foremost French poet of the first decade of the 20th century, was born at Honfleur on Dec. 28, 1864, of an old Norman family. Going to Paris to study law, he came under the influence of the Symbolist poets there. His first books of poems, *Lendemains* (1885), was followed by several other minor collections, eventually reprinted in two volumes, *Poèmes 1887–1892* (1895) and *Premiers poèmes* (1899). In 1896 he married the poet J. M. de Heredia's daughter Marie, herself later well known as a poet under the pseudonym Gérard d'Houville.

By this time Régnier showed a preference for themes from classical antiquity or from the Renaissance, so that while the personal quality of his approach and certain metrical licences still reflected the Symbolist influence, his subject matter came to be more like that of his Parnassian father-in-law. His most characteristic poems in this style appeared in *Les Jeux rustiques et divins* (1897), *Les Médailles d'argile* (1900), *La Cité des eaux* (1902), mainly about Versailles, *La Sandale ailée* (1906), and *Le Miroir des heures* (1910). His aristocratic manner distinguished him from his more bohemian contemporaries, and he became the favourite poet of *la belle époque.* He was elected to the Académie Française in 1911 (received 1912).

Régnier published some patriotic verse in *1914–1916* (1918), but his only major collections of poems after World War I were *Vestigia flammae* (1921) and *Flamma tenax, 1922–1928* (1928). From 1894, however, Régnier had been publishing also novels and short stories, in which he combined realism with a hedonistic attitude to morality. These include *Contes à soi-même* (1894; reprinted in *La Canne de jaspe,* 1897), *La Double Maîtresse* (1900), *La Peur de l'amour* (1907), *L'Amphisbène* (1912), *Romaine Mirmault* (1914), *La Pécheresse* (1920), *Le Divertissement provincial* (1925), and *Le Voyage d'amour* (1930). Henri de Régnier died in Paris on May 23, 1936.

RÉGNIER, MATHURIN (1573–1613), French satirist, whose acute power of observation was turned on the daily life of his time, and whose language was rooted in the speech of the people. He was born at Chartres on Dec. 21, 1573, the son of Jacques Régnier, a magistrate, and Simone, sister of the poet Philippe Desportes. Little is known of his early years except that he received the tonsure at eight and later became a secretary of Cardinal François de Joyeuse, accompanying him to Rome in 1587. After years of irksome duties and travel, on returning to France about 1605, he accepted Desportes' protection. In 1606 Desportes died and Régnier obtained a pension of 5,000 livres chargeable on one of Desportes' benefices. In 1609 he was made canon of Chartres through his friendship with the bishop, Philippe Hurault, at whose abbey of Royaumont he spent much of his time in his remaining years. He died at Rouen on Oct. 16, 1613.

His works include regular satires in alexandrine couplets, serious poems in various metres; the authenticity of the epigrams and light pieces published after his death and attributed to him is doubtful. His real greatness consists in the verve and realism of his satires, in which he depicts typical characters of the time. He recalls Horace, Juvenal, Ariosto, the Italian *bernesci* poets, and Ronsard, but his imitation is free and original. His dialogues, his narrative, and his characterization are full of life and picturesque detail, and his language is down to earth, colourful, and rich in colloquial idioms and expressions. He was an acute critic, and the famous passage in which he castigates François de Malherbe (Satire IX, *À Monsieur Rapin*) is a brilliant attack on the purist poetic theory and its conformity with precise classical and intellectual standards. His talents are fully displayed in the satiric masterpiece, *Macette,* a work that can stand comparison to Molière's *Tartuffe.*

Bibliography.—*Works: Les Premières Oeuvres de Régnier* (1608) includes the *Discours au roi* and ten satires. Editions in 1609, including 12 satires; 1612, including *Macette;* and 1613, were followed by *Les Satyres et autres oeuvres folastres du sieur Régnier* (1616), with many additions, some by other hands; and by two famous editions by Elzevir (1642, 1652). *Oeuvres,* ed. by C. Brossette (1729), contains a standard commentary on Régnier. Later editions include those by E. Courbet (1875), which follow the first editions; *Oeuvres complètes,* ed. by J. Plattard (1930), and by G. Raibaud (1958).
Studies and Bibliography: J. Vianey, *Mathurin Régnier* (1896); M. H. Cherrier, *Bibliographie de Mathurin Régnier* (1884); E. Roy, *Notes sur . . . Jean et Mathurin Régnier* (1910). J. Scherer, "Les satires posthumes de Régnier," in *Revue d'histoire littéraire* (1947); O. T. Rossettini, *Les influences anciennes et italiennes sur la satire en France au XVIe siècle* (1958). (Ra. L.)

REGNITZ, a river of south Germany and left-bank tributary of the Main. The river upstream to the confluence of the Pegnitz, 42 mi. (68 km.), is called the Regnitz; its southerly extension, 22 mi. (35 km.), is known as the Rednitz, which is formed by the confluence at Georgensmünd of the Swabian and Franconian Rezat. Its main course, from south to north, flows across a lowland of sandstones and clays. Pine forest covers most of the area. The vine is absent, but hops are important and account for the Nürnberg brewing industry. The river passes the towns of Fürth, Erlangen, and Forchheim, from which point it is navigable. It joins the Main just below Bamberg. The old and inadequate Ludwig Canal connects the Main and the Altmühl, a tributary of the Danube. A new canal was under construction in the 1960s from Bamberg, parallel to the Regnitz, through Nürnberg and thence. alongside the Ludwig Canal, to the Danube; it was due for completion in 1969. (R. E. Di.)

REGULATORY AGENCIES. Administrative regulation is a basic feature of 20th-century government that sharply distinguishes it from government in the 19th century. Formerly governmental regulation was provided for almost entirely by statutes, whose prescriptions were enforced through the traditional machinery of the courts. Such legislative regulation proved inadequate to deal with the complexities of a modern industrial economy. In its place, there developed a system of administrative regulation. Under it, the legislature provides only the broad principles of a particular regulatory scheme, leaving their detailed implementation to the agency charged with administering the law. The latter is vested with the power to prescribe regulations having the force of law, to police those subject to its authority to ensure that such regulations are not violated, and to decide cases involving alleged particular violations. The administrative agency is able to furnish the continuous supervision and expert knowledge that cannot, as a practical matter, be expected of the legislature.

United States.—The need for administrative regulation first became apparent in the United States in the railroad industry, and it was out of the attempts to deal with the railroad problem that the first modern U.S. administrative agency, the Interstate Commerce commission (ICC), was developed. Established by the Interstate Commerce act of 1887 and with its power expanded by the Hepburn act of 1906 and subsequent statutes, it is composed of 11 members appointed by the president, and confirmed by the senate, who serve for staggered terms of seven years. The commissioners may be removed only for cause and have, in practice, been able to function free from direct presidential control. This has led some to characterize them as a "headless fourth branch" of the government.

ICC is the classic example of a quasi-judicial regulatory agency. As such, it applies the broadly stated legislative policies to concrete cases by a procedure patterned upon that of the courts. The commission fixes reasonable rates and ensures that they are observed. It grants licences to those seeking to engage in interstate transportation. It exercises injunctive power over discriminatory practices. The commission also performs important nonjudicial functions. It promulgates safety and other regulations. It controls railroad financing and planning. It is the commission which gives specific form and content to the congressional policies expressed in the Interstate Commerce act as amended. Its position has been compared to that of a superboard of directors of the railroad industry. It also has extensive authority over motor carriers. (*See also* INTERSTATE COMMERCE.)

The assertion of governmental control in other economic fields led to the creation of many other regulatory agencies modeled upon the ICC, chief among these being the Federal Trade commission (FTC; 1914), Federal Power commission (FPC; 1920), Federal Communications commission (FCC; 1934), Securities and Exchange commission (SEC; 1934) and Civil Aeronautics board (CAB; 1938). (*See* COMMISSION.) In addition, regulatory powers were conferred upon the ordinary executive departments; *e.g.*, the department of agriculture under the Packers and Stockyards act, 1921, and the Agricultural Adjustment act, 1938. As traditional legal devices proved inadequate to cope with economic abuses, they were superseded by administrative controls. This was especially true of the period following the depression of the early 1930s. The New Deal program was largely carried out through administrative regulation. During the same period, a comparable development took place in the states.

Other Countries.—Administrative regulation is not a purely U.S. phenomenon. Similar problems have given rise to the creation in other countries of some analogous regulatory agencies. In England the starting point was the setting up of the Railway and Canal commission in 1888. In 1921 the Railway Rates tribunal was established to fix railroad rates. After the nationalization of British railways in 1947 the British Transport Commission (BTC) was established to assume control of Britain's railways, canals, and certain other means of transport. It was a policy-making agency, not a managing body, and was dissolved in 1962 in favour of separate boards for railways, London transport, docks, and waterways.

There is an important difference between administrative authority in the United States and that in other countries. Administrative regulation is basically of two kinds. In certain fields the normal rules of free competition are recognized to be inapplicable. In them, the state tolerates the existence of virtual monopolies, but by regulation it ensures that the monopolistic power shall not be abused. This is the usual practice regarding public utilities. In other areas, free competition governs but the state intervenes to prevent abusive practices conceived deleterious to the working of a free competitive system. Thus, the FTC was established in the United States to prevent unfair trade practices.

In other countries, there is less room for these types of administrative regulation than in the United States. In the field of public utilities the dominant theme is not regulation but operation. Toward abusive practices other governments also tend to adopt more of a hands-off policy than does the U.S. This applies in both Britain and in continental European countries, though less so in the former in view of the specific types of British regulation already mentioned, as well as the setting up in 1948 of a Monopolies and Restrictive Practices commission patterned upon the U.S. Federal Trade commission.

Abuses of Administrative Power.—Administrative regulation enables government to cope with the need to control economic power in the public interest. But at the same time it raises the basic problem of whether the regulator himself is adequately controlled; the executive and legislature are responsible to the people but the administrator has no similar responsibility. In democratic countries, he is, it is true, responsible to the law, but this "rule of law" becomes less effective under statutes delegating wholesale discretion. Under such "skeleton" legislation, the flesh and the blood (not to mention the soul) of regulation are left to the administrator. Excessive discretion opens the door to administrative arbitrariness.

The growth of administrative regulatory power was accompanied by the development of safeguards to ensure against administrative abuses. In the U.S. the emphasis is upon procedural devices and judicial review. Due process (*q.v.*) requires that, before administrative action adversely affects an individual, he be given notice and a full opportunity to be heard. Such hearings must include the essentials (though not the forms) of judicial procedure. The fundamentals of fair administrative procedure were prescribed in the Federal Administrative Procedure act, 1946, and in similar laws in many states. Those aggrieved by administrative action can obtain review in the courts. In Anglo-American countries such review is in the ordinary courts. In France and many civil-law countries there is a special administrative-court system to review the legality of administrative action. There is also legislative control. This is most fully developed under parliamentary systems; *e.g.*, in Britain, where administrative regulations are subject to direct annulment by parliament. In the United States, control by the congress did not prove effective in practice, though attempts were made to remedy the situation in the Legislative Reorganization act, 1946, by giving standing congressional committees direct responsibility over administrative agencies. This did not prove workable because of the preoccupation of such committees with other matters and their lack of adequate staffs.

BIBLIOGRAPHY.—Carlton Kemp Allen, *Law and Orders,* 2nd ed. (1956); Robert E. Cushman, *The Independent Regulatory Commissions* (1941); K. C. Davis, *Administrative Law Treatise* (1959); John Dickinson, *Administrative Justice and the Supremacy of Law in the United States* (1927); Ernest Freund, *Administrative Powers Over Persons and Property* (1928); James M. Landis, *The Administrative Process* (1938); U.S. Attorney General's Committee on Administrative Procedure, *Report* (1941); Great Britain Committee on Ministers' Powers, *Report* (1932); Committee on Administrative Tribunals and Enquiries, *Report* (1957); William A. Robson, *Justice and Administrative Law,* 3rd ed. (1951); Bernard Schwartz, *Law and the Executive in Britain* (1949), *An Introduction to American Administrative Law* (1958). (B. Sz.)

REGULUS, MARCUS ATILIUS, Roman general and consul first in 267 B.C. and again in 256 B.C. when with his colleague he defeated the Punic fleet at Ecnomus and landed an army in Africa (*see* Punic Wars). When the other consul was recalled, Regulus was left to finish the war. After a severe defeat at Adys near Carthage, the Carthaginians were inclined for peace, but the terms proposed by Regulus were so harsh that they resolved to continue the war. In 255 he was defeated and captured. According to tradition, he remained in captivity until he was sent to Rome on parole to negotiate a peace or exchange of prisoners (250); he urged the Senate to refuse both proposals and, returning to Carthage, was tortured to death. The story, insufficiently attested, was possibly invented to excuse the treatment of Carthaginian prisoners at Rome. It served to make Regulus a model of heroic endurance to the later Romans.

See E. Klebs in Pauly-Wissowa, *Real-Encyclopädie der classischen Altertumswissenschaft,* ii, 2086–92 (1896). His fate is celebrated in Horace, *Odes,* iii, 5.

REHABILITATION, MEDICAL AND VOCATIONAL.

Rehabilitation is the help and training given to a sick or handicapped person to enable him to live as full a life as his remaining abilities and degree of health will allow. The emphasis is first on the medical aspects, later on physical therapy and occupational therapy (*qq.v.*), and finally on the vocational and social aspects.

Successful rehabilitation inevitably involves not only the body but mind and spirit as well. It is the function of the rehabilitation team to support the patient and help him find satisfaction in life by understanding his physical handicap and associated psychological difficulties. In most instances the handicapped person must be retrained to walk and travel, to care for his own daily needs, to apply and remove his own prosthetic devices, to communicate orally or in writing, and eventually to find a useful place in society. Success in solving his most immediate problems goes a long way toward eliminating the patient's fear of falling out of the accepted pattern of life. Anxiety about his state and capabilities may set back a patient's chances of recovery; therefore the rehabilitation team must allay not only his own fears but also those of his family. The patient with a serious residual disability should be encouraged to accept his handicap and his consequent dependence upon others; but such encouragement should not be extended to the patient who clings to a remediable disability as an emotional excuse to justify dependence and to free himself from worries and responsibilities.

MEDICAL REHABILITATION

Physical Handicaps.—Handicaps can be inherited or they can result from accidents, disease, birth injury, or the degenerative changes of old age. In the United States it has been estimated that 88% of physical disabilities are due to disease (particularly chronic disease), 10% to accidents, and 2% to congenital malformation. A considerable proportion of persons handicapped by physical deficiency or mental subnormality are suffering from a congenital defect, either inherited or resulting from intrauterine factors or difficulties at birth.

Diseases of the joints are the most common crippling diseases. Rheumatoid arthritis and osteoarthritis both attack women more frequently than men, and elderly women most frequently. Both diseases are painful and progressive; and, even after treatment, deformity, stiffness, and limitation of movement almost invariably persist. The loss of sight, hearing, and touch also require extensive rehabilitation.

Hemiplegia (paralysis of one side) after a stroke is a major cause of disability, particularly in North America and northern Europe. For persons who survive six to eight weeks after the initial stroke, life expectancy is the same as for others of their age. Treatment starting as soon as the patient recovers consciousness prevents the stiffening of the joints on the affected side and the contractures, especially at the shoulder, which are the usual result of an attack.

Paraplegia (paralysis of the lower limbs) below a severance of the spinal cord may result from war wounds, automobile accidents, surfing and diving accidents, or disease. Training with crutches can help some paraplegics to lead noninstitutional lives; a few are able to walk in braces (splints).

Medical rehabilitation can do much to overcome spasticity (stiffness and spasms) and the sensory disorders and mental retardation in young children caused by cerebral palsy. Multiple sclerosis, attacking those between the ages of 20 and 40, is progressive and unpredictable; hence it is difficult to anticipate training ahead of the progress of the disease. Rehabilitation can produce good results in patients with chronic arthritis, pulmonary disease, epilepsy, the chronic degenerative neurologic diseases, and heart and circulatory ailments. Some babies are born deficient in limbs. Special measures are taken at the earliest opportunity to fit them with appropriate prostheses (artificial limbs) which they learn to operate by trial and error in the same way that a normal infant discovers the use of his limbs. Loss of limbs following accident or surgical operation is similarly compensated for by prosthesis. (*See* Prosthetics.)

Psychiatric Handicaps.—The psychoneurotic person may have a flawlessly functioning body and the will to become whole, but his mind is sick. He is usually isolated emotionally from his fellow man; rehabilitation is designed to break down the barriers he has erected around himself. At the mental hospital participation in social activities is part of his treatment, and toward the end of his stay weaning from the protective hospital aura takes place gradually. The patient is helped to find employment outside the hospital by day, returning there to be under psychiatric supervision in the evening and on weekends. Later still he may live at home and attend evening group sessions once or twice a week to discuss with fellow patients and with the psychiatrist the problems he encounters. An inadequate personality may need psychotherapy (*q.v.*) of a supportive kind for most of his lifetime.

Alcoholism (*q.v.*) is not wholly a psychiatric disorder, and few habitual heavy drinkers are addicts. Most can break the habit fairly easily; the addict cannot without terrible suffering, and consequently needs rehabilitation.

Treatment.—The first step in rehabilitation is to ensure that the patient is receiving adequate and appropriate medical or surgical treatment. It is particularly important to know whether his disease is (1) permanent, but nonprogressive and nonfatal; (2) fluctuating, but not immediately endangering life; or (3) steadily progressive, and, if so, the likely speed of progression, as this will affect the goal of rehabilitation.

Details of treatment depend on the nature of each patient's disability and his personality, physical condition, background, and likely future life; but group treatment is often given as well. The daily programs are made up of periods of exercises, physical and occupational therapy oriented to realistic occupations, and rest. The rehabilitation of heart and lung cases, for example, involves carefully graduated exercise, checked periodically by exercise tolerance tests. Each day the patient is encouraged to attempt one-fifth more than he did on the previous day. Few, however, achieve such uninterrupted progress; many have to mark time, repeating the previous day's prescription until it is performed with confidence before extending exertions further. Often an inexorable "upper limit" becomes apparent; the patient may then go home, having learned by experience the true extent of his limitations but confident that, provided he lives within them, all should be well. Rehabilitation centres also prescribe, fit, and (in some countries) supply aids such as hearing devices, prostheses, and invalid chairs.

Independence in Daily Life.—The patient must be taught to cope single-handedly with his daily needs, and a great deal can be done to help him to adjust to his old environment or to modify it. A hemiplegic may be helped by the provision of an electric razor and by modification of his clothing; *e.g.,* by the substitution of zippers for buttons, elastic-sided shoes for lace-ups, and clip-on bow ties for ties that must be knotted. "Lazy tongs" or spring-grip clothespins attached to the ends of rods about two feet long may enable an arthritic patient to pull stockings over feet his hands cannot reach. A banister rail fixed to the wall on the patient's "good" side will help him mount stairs, and a grip rail on each side of the lavatory seat will help him to rise from it unaided. A "nonslip" mat at the bottom of the bath and a webbing strap across its top can enable a patient to climb out by himself.

Retraining for the disabled housewife, including the provision of special kitchens and other equipment, started in the United States (1948) and spread to Great Britain (1950), where it is carried out by the occupational therapy departments of the National Health Service hospitals.

In Great Britain medical social workers (almoners) help the patient to overcome immediate domestic anxieties and will later help in reconciling him and his family to his new condition. There are hostels for patients who cannot live at home and for those who have had a serious mental illness. Social workers will help to adapt the home (e.g., by putting in ramps for a wheelchair); arrange for home nursing; and sometimes provide domestic assistance. Such assistance is part of the National Health Service, and the patient is charged, according to his means, up to a maximum.

Programs and Facilities.—In the United States, federal-state action to eliminate or reduce a handicap through medical services was first authorized by federal legislation in 1943. Care is provided through public agencies in all states, and services offered include medical and surgical treatment. Prosthetic devices are offered where the patient's condition is stable, a favourable outcome may be expected within a reasonable period of time, and financial need has been demonstrated. This approach is taken in several other countries, including Australia and Canada.

In Great Britain, medical rehabilitation facilities are provided under the national health plan in departments of physical medicine and occupational therapy at the main hospitals and in a few special centres. For the minority of patients with a multiplicity of problems some hospitals run settlement clinics. Paraplegics at the Spinal Injuries Centre, Stoke Mandeville, Buckinghamshire, are encouraged to join in modified athletic contests founded there in 1948. These games, which became international in 1952, were held in Rome in 1960 and in Tokyo in 1964, after the Olympic Games; hundreds of paraplegics from many countries competed in events such as wheelchair skiing, weight lifting, and fencing. An international sports meeting open to all disabled was held at Linz, Aus., in 1963.

Denmark gives state support to voluntary hospitals and clinics through social insurance or financial assistance to patients, and pays for the transport of outpatients to the clinics. In West Germany, where much importance is attached to sport and exercises for the disabled (including spastics), the government sponsors courses for the handicapped of all nationalities held by the German Sports Association for the Physically Handicapped, which also cooperates with the Ministry of Labour and the Ministry of the Interior. In the U.S.S.R., the Ministry of Social Welfare provides free sanatoriums, rest homes, and prostheses.

VOCATIONAL REHABILITATION

During the patient's rehabilitation, it must be decided whether he will be able to go back to his previous job. If this is impossible he may be taught new skills for a more suitable job; or he can take up some remunerative hobby pursued at home in his chair or even in his bed. The emphasis throughout is on self-help and on productive work—not entirely from financial considerations but because self-help maintains self-respect and affords an outlet for the creative drive, while productive work is more pleasurable for most people than enforced idleness.

Extent of the Problem.—Worldwide information about the number of persons who require vocational rehabilitation is meagre. In the United States it was estimated that in 1965 there were approximately 20,000,000 persons, exclusive of those in institutions, who were handicapped to some extent by chronic illness; of these, 4,000,000 were totally unable to carry out their major activity (working, keeping house, going to school). In Great Britain in 1965 there were about 655,000 persons registered with the Ministry of Labour as disabled; on any one day there were 95,000 persons who had been off work for six months or longer. A census in Canada and another in France showed that about 1% of the population aged between 16 and 64 was unable to work. If to these estimates are added the handicapped children, the chronically sick, the handicapped who are at work, and the handicapped

in retirement, a rough minimum estimate might be that the handicapped make up 5% of these populations. It is not suggested that all these people need rehabilitation, although estimates indicate that between 10 and 20% of all patients discharged from hospitals would benefit from it. The figure varies with the type of case, being highest for orthopedic, neurological, and rheumatic cases and lowest for general surgical cases.

It is important that the type and extent of training given be correlated with the level of general education and the opportunities for employment in a given locality. In less developed countries, priority should be given to the preventive medical services, the building up of the curative services, and the training of staff before ambitious rehabilitation programs are started.

ORGANIZATION OF SERVICES

The first specialized rehabilitation centres were set up toward the end of the 19th century. In the United States the Cleveland Rehabilitation Center was founded in 1889 and the Red Cross Institute for the Disabled (now the Institute for the Crippled and Disabled) followed in New York City in 1917. In Britain Dame Agnes Hunt, herself crippled from the age of ten, started the first convalescent home for cripples in 1900 and the first aftercare clinics in 1907. The problems of the disabled serviceman led to interest in expanding the rehabilitation services; during World War I, Sir Robert Jones established a series of rehabilitation departments in British military hospitals, and during World War II the Royal Air Force and the U.S. Veterans Administration, in particular, established first-class rehabilitation services. Interest was also heightened by the increase in age of the population in many parts of the world. In developed countries rehabilitation services for the handicapped prospered with an expanding consciousness of the need for social welfare work. In the 1950s there was a growth of rehabilitation and training centres with improved physical and occupational therapy; so that, for example, North America, Eastern and Western Europe, and the Middle East were all represented at an international conference on vocational rehabilitation in 1962.

In its early years vocational rehabilitation consisted largely of attempts to get around the patient's disability by specialized job training and by helping him to find work, with little emphasis on medical services. By the 1960s, however, some public and private industries had set up special workshops for their own convalescent and injured employees, often in conjunction with the local hospital service; and sheltered working conditions were provided for infectious tuberculosis patients or those with grave mental or physical difficulties.

United States.—After World War I the U.S. government and the states worked together to provide vocational rehabilitation services for persons who could be made employable. Studies show that the federal government recouped in income taxes alone ten dollars for each dollar invested in such services. This program in 1964 rehabilitated approximately 120,000 persons, whose individual earnings were increased, on the average, by $1,750 a year.

The state-federal program of vocational rehabilitation in the U.S. as authorized by the 1954 act amending the 1943 act is primarily concerned with disabled persons who can become economically independent. Its objective is to place them in gainful employment in offices, stores, and factories, in sheltered workshops, or at home. Services are also extended to persons who contribute to the national economy in other ways (e.g., homemakers). The program is organized and administered as a state-federal partnership. Federal responsibilities are discharged by the Vocational Rehabilitation Administration (VRA) of the Department of Health, Education, and Welfare. Federal grants are made to states to help pay for existing rehabilitation programs and to encourage the states to offer new services and extend coverage to new localities. VRA also conducts investigations and disseminates information on the needs and capabilities of the handicapped. Regional representatives of the department can be consulted on specialized aspects of rehabilitation, and they assist the states in interpreting their programs to the public. Actual services to the disabled are provided in all states by public agencies, each working out its individual plan with the federal office. Besides physical restoration, services include the supply of occupational tools, initial stocks of goods for small business enterprises, job placement, and follow-up. The use of public funds for services other than medical diagnosis, counseling, placement, and follow-up depends on the economic status of the client. In the 1960s, physical restoration services were received by more than half of the persons rehabilitated in the U.S., and accounted for more than 40% of the expenditure for casework.

Great Britain.—The Disabled Persons (Employment) Act (1944) is the basis of all vocational rehabilitation. Disablement resettlement officers (DROs) are employed by the Ministry of Labour and work from the local employment exchanges both to help handicapped people find work and to build contacts between employers and hospitals. Under the "quota" plan employers are required to engage a proportion of disabled drawn from the ministry's registered list. Registration is voluntary, and many disabled persons do not register; the DRO may even discourage a patient from registering if he thinks that, for him, the psychological effect of being officially categorized "disabled" may be so bad as to outweigh the practical advantage of his easier placement in a job. The direction of a patient to an occupation reserved for the disabled also may have psychological disadvantages.

Industrial rehabilitation and vocational guidance are provided at both residential and nonresidential units run by the Ministry of Labour. Other types of vocational training are given in government training centres, educational institutions, and employers' establishments. For the more seriously disabled, special residential training colleges, such as the Queen Elizabeth Training College for the Disabled at Leatherhead, Surrey (founded 1935), run by voluntary organizations with financial assistance, offer help for special categories, such as the blind. Patients who cannot leave their homes may have work brought to them. Sheltered employment in the 1960s was provided for about 6,300 by a nonprofit company, Remploy Ltd., whose directors are appointed by the Ministry of Labour and which is supported by loans and grants from the Ministry of Labour.

Other Countries.—Elsewhere in Europe arrangements are similar to those in Great Britain. In Denmark, for example, therapists, job specialists (*e.g.,* engineers), vocational guidance experts, and employment exchanges cooperate to achieve for the disabled employment conditions as near normal as possible. In the U.S.S.R. the Ministry of Social Welfare retrains the handicapped and obliges employers to give them suitable work and conditions, while special medical commissions supervise them and research institutes study their labour problems. Austria, France, Germany, Greece, and Israel have "quota" arrangements for employment of the handicapped.

In underdeveloped nations the restoration of the disabled made great strides after World War II with an increased amount of government, voluntary, and Christian-mission work and with the help of agencies of the United Nations, especially the World Health Organization (WHO) and the International Labour Organization (ILO). For example, in India, Pakistan, and a number of African and Latin-American countries the governments subsidize UN and ILO projects or run projects that receive UN and ILO help. These include training programs for physiotherapists, psychiatrists, and nurses for hospitals and clinics (many of whom are given studentships with which to qualify in Europe); prosthetic and orthopedic services; and simplified agricultural training for the rural blind.

Throughout the world the amount and kind of governmental organization vary from the highly centralized Mexican system to the cooperative relation between government and local authorities, as in Canada. France has an interministerial committee for the disabled; Japan's rehabilitation programs, for both adults and children, are administered by the Ministry of Health and Welfare. Voluntary bodies sometimes have their own cooperative organization and sometimes coordinate their efforts through national councils established by the various governments. This latter system is recommended by WHO and ILO. The Conference of World Organizations Interested in the Handicapped (CWOIH) has 30 member organizations, mostly of consultative status with the UN Economic and Social Council.

See also BLIND, TRAINING AND WELFARE OF; DEAF AND HARD OF HEARING, TRAINING AND WELFARE OF; INDUSTRIAL MEDICINE; OCCUPATIONAL THERAPY; PHYSICALLY HANDICAPPED, EDUCATION OF; PHYSICAL THERAPY; RETARDED CHILDREN; SPEECH DISORDERS.

BIBLIOGRAPHY.—W. S. Allan, *Rehabilitation: a Community Challenge* (1958); Edith Buchwald *et al., Physical Rehabilitation for Daily Living* (1952); H. H. Kessler, *Rehabilitation of the Physically Handicapped,* rev. ed. (1953); H. A. Rusk *et al., Rehabilitation Medicine* (1958), *Living with a Disability* (1953); H. A. Rusk and E. J. Taylor, *New Hope for the Handicapped* (1949); J. Garrett, "Psychological Aspects of Physical Disability," *Rehabilitation Service Series,* No. 210 (U.S. Govt. Printing Office, 1952); George H. Day, "The Tardy Convalescent," *British Medical Journal* (1960), "Spellbinding and Spellbreaking in Convalescence," *Lancet* (1962), and with M. McDowel, "Fear Banishing at Mundesley," *Nursing Times* (1963); G. G. Deaver, *Discussion on Industrial Accidents,* Bulletin No. 105 (1949); H. E. Griffiths, *The Surgeon in Industry* (1949); British Medical Assn., *The Rehabilitation and Resettlement of Disabled Persons* (1954); Ministry of Health, *Convalescent Treatment* (HMSO, 1959); J. H. Nicholson, *Help for the Handicapped* (National Council of Social Service, 1958); L. H. Lofquist, *Vocational Counseling with the Physically Handicapped* (1957); *Report of the Committee of Inquiry on the Rehabilitation, Training and the Settlement of Disabled Persons* (HMSO, 1956); *Services for the Disabled* (HMSO, 1955); M. Redkey, "Rehabilitation Centers Today," *Rehabilitation Service Series No. 490* (U.S. Government Printing Office, 1959); *Rehabilitation for World Peace,* Proceedings of the 8th World Congress of the International Society for the Rehabilitation of the Disabled, formerly the International Society for the Welfare of Cripples (1960); United Nations, *Modern Methods of Rehabilitation of the Adult Disabled* (1953); WHO, *Technical Report Series* No. 158 (1958); 7th Report of the Expert Committee on Mental Health, WHO, *Technical Report Series No. 177* (1959). (H. A. RK.; E. J. TR.; X.)

REHOBOAM, last king of the united kingdom of Israel and first king of the southern kingdom of Judah, son and successor of Solomon, began to reign *c.* 934 (or 922) B.C. The events are related in I Kings 11–14 and II Chron. 10–12. Rehoboam was not acceptable to the northern tribes, who recalled Jeroboam (*q.v.*) from his exile in Egypt and made Rehoboam's contemptuous refusal of their demands the occasion for instituting a rival kingdom under Jeroboam (I Kings 12). It is probable that this was done with the encouragement of Egypt. Sheshonk I (Shishak) of Egypt attacked the kingdom of Judah and despoiled the temple at Jerusalem of its treasures. Rehoboam's reign was marked by constant conflict with the northern kingdom of Israel. An unfavourable judgment is pronounced on him by the editor of Kings because he favoured customs connected with Baal worship. The fact that his mother was an Ammonite woman may in some measure account for this. He was succeeded after a reign of 17 years by his son Abijah (in I Kings, Abijam), of whom little is known save a victory over Jeroboam.

REHOVOT ("enlargement"), a municipal town in the Plain of Sharon, Israel, lies 13 mi. (21 km.) SSE of Tel Aviv–Jaffa. It was founded in 1890 as an agricultural village by immigrants from Tsarist Russia. Pop. (1961) 29,003. It is the centre of a flourishing region of citrus orchards and has a large packing station. Chaim Weizmann (*q.v.*), first president of Israel, had his residence there during the British mandate period; the house has been preserved under a trust, and he is buried in the garden. He made Rehovot famous by founding an institute of scientific research in 1934, which became the Weizmann Institute of Science in 1949 and is an important centre of fundamental and applied research. The Faculty of Agriculture of the Hebrew University and the state agricultural experimental station are also at Rehovot. Manufactures include plastics and pharmaceutical products. (No. B.)

REICHENAU, an island in the Untersee (western arm of Lake Constance) in the *Land* (state) of Baden-Württemberg, Federal Republic of Germany. The island is 3 mi. long and 1 mi. broad, its eastern end being connected to the mainland by a causeway 1¼ mi. long. Pop. (1961) 4,047. Fruit and flowers are grown and wine is produced. The richly endowed Benedictine abbey of Reichenau, founded in 724 and secularized in 1803, was a famous centre of the arts in the early Middle Ages. The abbey church at Mittelzell (built mainly in the 10th and 11th centuries, with a Late Gothic choir) contains the tomb of Charles III the Fat (d. 888) who retired to Reichenau after being dethroned. A school of painting flourished there *c.* 1000, the wall paintings in the Romanesque church at Oberzell being the oldest in Germany (10th century). Reichenau is a resort and centre of excursions on Lake Constance.   (A. F. A. M.)

REICHENBACH, GEORG VON (1772–1826), German astronomical instrument maker, was born at Durlach in Baden on Aug. 24, 1772. By 1796 he was engaged in the construction of a dividing engine. In 1804 he was one of the founders of an instrument-making business in Munich; and in 1809 he helped establish an optical works at Benediktbeuern which was later moved to Munich. He withdrew from both enterprises in 1814, and was instrumental in establishing a new optical business, from which he retired in 1820. He died at Munich on May 21, 1826.

Reichenbach built for F. W. Bessel in 1819 an instrument in which he introduced the meridian or transit circle, combining the transit instrument and the mural circle into one instrument. This combination had been introduced earlier, but with the exception of the transit circle constructed by Edward Troughton in 1806, had not been adopted. Reichenbach's form of instrument came into general use.   (S. C. Hr.)

REICHENBACH, a town of East Germany in the Karl-Marx-Stadt *Bezirk* (district) of the German Democratic Republic. It lies in the Vogtland, 11 mi. (18 km.) SW of Zwickau. Pop. (1962 est.) 29,359. The earliest mention of the town occurs in a document of 1212; it acquired municipal rights in 1271. Woolen manufacture was introduced in the 15th century and took the place of the mining industry which had been established earlier. Reichenbach has an important textile industry, a textile engineering school, and machinery factories. The serious destruction that occurred in World War II has for the most part been repaired.

REICHSTADT, NAPOLÉON FRANÇOIS JOSEPH CHARLES, Duke of (1811–1832), titular king of Rome from 1811 to 1814, was the Napoleon II of the French Bonapartists, who also referred to him as *le Fils de l'homme* ("the Son of the Man") and as *l'Aiglon* ("the Eaglet"). He was born in the Tuileries Palace in Paris on March 20, 1811, the only son of the emperor Napoleon I and the empress Marie Louise (*qq.v.*). As the long-desired heir to his father, he was styled king of Rome, partly because the elected heirs of the Holy Roman emperors had been styled kings of the Romans. When his father's power was collapsing (*see* Napoleonic Wars), his mother took him from threatened Paris to Blois (April 1, 1814), but his father's offer to abdicate in his favour was superseded by abdication in the name of both father and son, and Marie Louise rejected the proposal of his uncles Jérôme and Joseph (*see* Bonaparte) that he should be taken south of the Loire as the figurehead of further resistance or as a counter for bargaining with her Austrian kinsmen. He was taken instead to the court of her father, the Austrian emperor Francis I. Bonapartist plans for bringing him back to Paris during the Hundred Days (1815) came to nothing.

By the Treaty of Paris (1817) the prince was excluded from eventual succession to his mother's Italian dominions (*see* Parma and Piacenza, Duchies of). Instead he received the Austrian title of duke of Reichstadt (1818). Francis I cherished him, but foreign policy necessitated the duke's remaining under Austrian tutelage. Grieved by his father's humiliation and by revelations of his mother's later conduct, the duke dreamed persistently of some new sovereignty, especially in 1830, when revolutions overthrew Charles X's rule in France and Dutch rule in Belgium; but Metternich's hint that he might be made king of Italy was uttered only to deter the France of Louis Philippe from Italian enterprises. The military exercises that the duke passionately enjoyed were interrupted by ill health, which culminated in pulmonary tuberculosis. He died at Schönbrunn on July 22, 1832. The pathos of his existence is well brought out in Edmond Rostand's masterpiece, *L'Aiglon.*

See E. von Wertheimer, *Der Herzog von Reichstadt,* 2nd ed., 1913 (Eng. trans. of 1st ed., 1905); J. de Bourgoing, *Le Fils de Napoléon,* 2nd ed. (1950).

REICHSTEIN, TADEUSZ (1897–   ), Swiss chemist and Nobel laureate, was born at Wloclawek, Pol., on July 20, 1897. He shared with E. C. Kendall and P. S. Hench the 1950 Nobel Prize for Medicine for discovering the structure and biological effects of the suprarenal cortex hormones. He was educated at Zürich, where he obtained degrees in chemical engineering (1920) and organic chemistry (1922). He was engaged at first in industrial chemical research, but from 1930 onward he held posts in the department of organic chemistry at the Federal Institute of Technology, Zürich. In 1938 he was appointed head of the department of pharmacology and director of the Pharmacological Institute of the University of Basel, where in 1946 he became head of the organic division and director of the organic laboratories. His investigations were mainly concerned with steroids, particularly the hormones of the adrenal cortex, 26 of which he and his associates isolated. One of these hormones, isolated and described by Reichstein in 1936 and named by him "Substance Fa," proved to be identical with Kendall's "Compound E," and was later renamed cortisone (*q.v.*). Apart from these researches, Reichstein's best-known work is the synthesis of ascorbic acid (vitamin C), which he carried out independently of Sir Walter Norman Haworth and his co-workers, in 1933.   (W. J. Bp.)

REID, THOMAS (1710–1796), Scottish philosopher, was the critic of David Hume's skeptical empiricism and the first exponent of the so-called philosophy of common sense continued by the "Scottish school" (*see* Common Sense, Philosophy of). He was born on April 26, 1710, at Strachan, Kincardineshire, the son of Lewis Reid, a minister, and his wife, Margaret Gregory, who belonged to the famous family of mathematicians. (James Gregory [*q.v*] was Thomas Reid's great-uncle.) He was educated at Marischal College, Aberdeen, and after studying theology and being licensed for the ministry in 1731, remained at Marischal College as librarian from 1733 to 1736. From 1737 he held the living of New Machar, near Aberdeen, for 14 years, during which period he was aroused by his study of Hume's *Treatise of Human Nature* (1739) and began his lifelong task of examining its doctrines (*see* Hume, David). In 1751 he was elected to the chair of philosophy in King's College, Aberdeen, where he remained until in 1764 he succeeded Adam Smith as professor of moral philosophy in the University of Glasgow. During the tenure of his post at Aberdeen, he devoted himself to the problems of epistemology raised by Hume. Reid offered the preliminary results of his examination in four graduation addresses delivered to the university (*Philosophical Orations,* first edition by W. R. Humphries, 1937), which were more fully developed, with special reference to problems of perception, in his first book, *An Inquiry into the Human Mind, on the Principles of Common Sense* (1764). Further deliberation at Glasgow resulted in the *Essays on the Intellectual Powers of Man* (1785; new edition by A. D. Woozley, 1941), their scope being wider than that of the earlier work, and in the *Essays on the Active Powers of Man* (1788), in which he upheld a rationalist theory of ethics against the current subjectivism of Francis Hutcheson and Hume. His only other publications were "An Essay on Quantity" (in the *Transactions* of the Royal Society, 1748), *A Brief Account of Aristotle's Logic* (1774), and the posthumous *Statistical Account of the University of Glasgow* (1799). He died on Oct. 7, 1796, four years after the death of his wife and cousin, Elizabeth, whom he had married in 1740.

Brought up himself on the theory of ideas (the theory that ideas alone are the direct objects of the mind's awareness) and starting out as a Berkeleian (*see* Berkeley, George), Reid was shaken out of his acceptance of this orthodoxy by realizing, as he thought, the skeptical lengths to which the theory led in Hume; for it appeared to deprive us of the possibility of knowing almost all that Reid felt convinced that we do know. Finding himself unable to accept Hume's conclusions or to refute the arguments by which they were reached, he set himself to examine the premises from which the arguments started, namely the theory of ideas, and came to the conclusion (at the time bold and original) that the theory was based on no better ground than the prejudices and confusions of philosophers. Against the supposition that the immediate data of perception are ideas or in any way peculiarly mental he argued (1) that it is pure hypothesis, unsupported by evidence; and (2) that it does not perform the function for which it was introduced, since its only result is to leave all questions about the veracity of any perception in principle unanswerable. The latter objection would apply only to a representationalist theory such as Locke's; the former would apply to Berkeley and Hume as well, if Reid's interpretation of them was correct. Reid himself propounded a view of perception which might be called indirect realism. According to this, our senses provide us with immediate sensations (which are neither veridical nor nonveridical), plus a noninferential belief in the existence of corresponding material objects which cause the sensations, such a belief being liable—but not committed—to error; the function of sensation is to "suggest" the material objects. Thus Reid attempted to retain what seemed the common-sense elements in Locke's account, without the ideas and inferences from them which appeared both unjustified and fatal to it. As on many other topics, Reid's account of perception is tantalizingly incomplete and, without further explication of the notion of "suggestion," appears liable to criticisms similar to those which he had brought against Locke.

Reid rejected the orthodox representationalist theory of memory on similar grounds. In the first place, he denied the existence of the images which the theory held to be likenesses of the event or situation remembered; in effect he was protesting against being misled by the use of the noun "image" into the supposition that there was a special kind of mental entity of which it was the name. Secondly, the supposition that remembering consists of having images, related in a certain way to their originals, would preclude us from any justification of our memory beliefs. An acceptable theory of memory must be such as would entitle us (1) to claim that at least some remembering is reliable (although not infallible); and (2) to provide criteria for distinguishing correct remembering from misremembering or imagining. In general Reid was objecting, although not with entire clarity or consistency, against the "picture" model which seemed the fatal error of the theory of ideas. While all thought requires an object of thought, this does not necessitate that the object shall exist, even mentally. At times, indeed, Reid advances to a view more in accord with 20th-century thought: namely, that a concept is the meaning of the appropriate word or expression, that to have a concept is to know the meaning of the expression (e.g., to have a concept of circle is to know the meaning of the word "circle") and that to know the meaning of a word, expression, or sentence is to know how they are used.

As the founder of the philosophy named after it, Reid may appear to say disappointingly little about common sense directly, but his practice makes his principles reasonably clear. He was claiming, not that common sense is an oracle of truth (this was the view which Kant contemptuously but ignorantly attributed to him), but that there is such a thing as common-sense knowledge, as evidenced partly by the structure of language (which he held, without producing any evidence for it, to be to a high degree uniform from one natural language to another) and partly by the uniformity of our practical conduct.

The business of philosophy is not to challenge what each of us knows perfectly well to be true: for example, that there are material objects of whose existence and character we are aware by perception; that each of us is a continuing and identical person at least as far back as he can remember; that there are other persons like ourselves possessing life and intelligence; that there is some freedom of decision and of action; that expectation of the future based on experience of the past may be reasonable; and so on. To question such pieces of knowledge as these, as though they were empirical hypotheses to be tested, is to misconceive the philosopher's task, which is rather to attempt to understand more fully and clearly than is required for the unreflective, practical purposes of life the meanings of the propositions concerned. If philosophers had paid more attention to the basic facts and functions of language, they would have avoided the extravagances of skepticism and irrationalism into which they plunged. In emphasizing that the typical philosophical problem is not whether we know that something is the case, but what exactly it is that we do know when we know that something is the case, Reid was pointing the way which much British philosophy followed in the 20th century under the more immediate and more stimulating influence

of Ludwig Wittgenstein and of G. E. Moore. *See also* KNOWLEDGE, THEORY OF.

BIBLIOGRAPHY.—Thomas Reid, *Works,* ed. by Sir William Hamilton and H. C. Mansel, 2 vol. (1846–63); A. C. Fraser, *Thomas Reid* (1898); J. F. Ferrier, *Scottish Philosophy* (1856); J. McCosh, *Scottish Philosophy* (1875); O. M. Jones, *Empiricism and Intuitionism in Reid's Common Sense Philosophy* (1927). (A. D. W.)

REID, THOMAS MAYNE (later known as MAYNE REID) (1818–1883), Irish-born writer of adventure stories whose works had an important influence on juvenile fiction, was born at Ballyroney, County Down, on April 4, 1818. The son of a Presbyterian minister, he began to train for the ministry, but in 1839 sailed for New Orleans. A varied career as storekeeper, schoolmaster, actor, and trapper and trader among the Indians along the Missouri and Platte rivers provided material for the books which made him famous. In 1842 he settled as a journalist in Philadelphia where he met Edgar Allan Poe (*q.v.*), whom he later defended against the unjust accusations of his biographer, R. W. Griswold. In 1846 he volunteered to fight in the Mexican War, and on Sept. 13, 1847, sustained a severe thigh wound, which never properly healed, when leading the attack on Chapultepec castle. He was believed dead, but after some months in a hospital returned to the United States, resigned his commission, and, in 1849, sailed for Europe with a legion formed to aid the Hungarian revolutionaries, but arrived after their defeat. With *The Rifle Rangers* (1850) he began a long series of adventure stories, the best of which (including *The Scalp Hunters,* 1851; *The Boy Hunters,* 1852; *The Quadroon,* 1856) draw on his own experience. Intended to provide "pleasure and instruction," they combine vigorous action with vivid descriptions of the flora, fauna, and landscape of foreign countries. *The Child Wife* (1868) tells his own love story: in 1853 he fell in love with a 13-year-old girl and married her two years later.

After an attempt (1866) to launch a 1*d.* London evening paper, Mayne Reid returned to the United States, where he founded a boy's magazine, *Onward.* He became a U.S. citizen in 1868 but, after a severe illness, in 1870 returned to England and took up farming. He died in London on Oct. 22, 1883.

See Elizabeth Reid and Charles H. Coe, *Captain Mayne Reid* (1900).
(W. L. G. JA.)

REID, WHITELAW (1837–1912), U.S. journalist and diplomat, ambassador to Great Britain prior to World War I, was born near Xenia, O., on Oct. 27, 1837. He graduated from Miami University, Oxford, O., in 1856, and spoke frequently in behalf of John C. Frémont, the Republican candidate for the presidency in that year. In 1860 he became legislative correspondent at Columbus for several Ohio newspapers, including the *Cincinnati Gazette,* of which he was made city editor in 1861. He was war correspondent for the *Gazette* in 1861–62, serving also as volunteer aide-de-camp to Gen. Thomas A. Morris and to Gen. William S. Rosecrans in West Virginia, and was Washington correspondent of the *Gazette* in 1862–68. In 1868 he became a leading editorial writer for the *New York Tribune,* in the following year was made managing editor, and in 1872, upon the death of Horace Greeley, became the principal proprietor and editor in chief. In 1905 Reid relinquished his active editorship of the *Tribune,* but retained financial control. He served as minister to France in 1889–92, and in 1892 was the unsuccessful Republican candidate for vice-president on the ticket with Benjamin Harrison. In 1897 he was special ambassador of the United States on the occasion of Queen Victoria's jubilee; in 1902, special ambassador of the United States at the coronation of King Edward VII; and in 1905 he became ambassador to Great Britain. He died in London on Dec. 15, 1912.

His publications include *After the War* (1867); *Our New Duties* (1899); *Later Aspects of Our New Duties* (1899); *Problems of Expansion* (1900); *The Greatest Fact in Modern History* (1906); and, posthumously, *American and English Studies* (1913).

See Royal Cortissoz, *The Life of Whitelaw Reid* (1921).

REIGATE, a municipal borough (1863) of Surrey, Eng., lies 22 mi. (35 km.) SSW of London Bridge by road. The borough, largely residential, which was considerably extended in 1933, includes the town of Redhill, the village of Merstham, part of which is now a council housing estate, and the parish of Gatton. Pop.

(1961) 53,751. Cherchefelle was the Saxon village mentioned in Domesday Book, but by 1170 its name had been changed to Reigate. The town lies at the foot of the North Downs and there are remains of a Norman castle, which was a stronghold of the Warennes in the 12th–14th centuries and was destroyed c. 1648. The castle grounds (5 ac.) are laid out as a public garden. The manor of Cherchefelle was granted by William Rufus to William de Warenne, through whose family it passed in 1347 to the earls of Arundel. It was held by the Somers family from 1697 until 1922, when it was conveyed to the corporation by deed of gift. Reigate Priory, an Augustinian foundation, was rebuilt in 1779 and was purchased by the corporation and Surrey County Council in 1948. The old town hall (c. 1728, presented to the corporation in 1922) is on the site of an ancient chapel dedicated to St. Thomas Becket. In a vault below the chancel of the parish church of St. Mary Magdalene (Transitional Norman to Perpendicular) is buried Lord Howard of Effingham, who commanded the English Navy against the Spanish Armada. The Cranston Library, on the upper floor of the old vestry, was founded in 1701. The boys' grammar school was founded in 1675, but the Girls' County Grammar School is a modern foundation (1905). There are a technical college and a school of art. The artist John Linnell lived on Redstone Hill and his son-in-law Samuel Palmer, the landscape painter, died in Redhill.

REIMARUS, HERMANN SAMUEL (1694–1768), German philosopher and man of letters, a notable deist of the Enlightenment, was born in Hamburg on Dec. 22, 1694. He studied at Jena (1714) and lectured at Wittenberg and at Weimar before becoming, in 1727, professor of Hebrew and Oriental languages at the Hamburg *Gymnasium*. Married in 1728 to Johanne Friederike Fabricius, he made his own house a centre of culture and helped to found a public meetingplace for learned and artistic societies.

Reimarus used materials collected by his father-in-law, J. A. Fabricius (*q.v.*), to produce a valuable edition of Dio Cassius (1750–52). In his first noteworthy philosophical publication, *Abhandlungen von den vornehmsten Wahrheiten der natürlichen Religion* ("Treatises on the Principal Truths of Natural Religion"; 1754), he divided the essential problems into three parts—cosmological, biological-psychological, and theological—which, when related to each other, formed a unified deistic system. His *Vernunftlehre . . .* ("Doctrine of Reason"; 1756) was followed by the first version of his *Allgemeine Betrachtungen über die Triebe der Thiere* ("General Considerations on the Instincts of Animals"; 1760), which he was revising till his death: his attempt to define the unique characteristics of animal life yielded a rather complex animal psychology.

Reimarus died in Hamburg on March 1, 1768, having withheld from publication his major work, *Apologie oder Schutzschrift für die vernünftigen Verehrer Gottes* ("Apologia or Defense for the Rational Reverers of God"). G. E. Lessing (*q.v.*) aroused vehement controversy by printing fragments of this work (under the title *Wolfenbütteler Fragmente*) in his *Zur Geschichte und Litteratur*, parts iii and iv (1774 and 1777); Andreas Riem, under the pseudonym C. A. E. Schmidt, published other passages in 1787; D. W. Klose some others in 1850–52; and D. F. Strauss (*q.v.*) described the contents of the manuscript in his *H. S. Reimarus und seine Schutzschrift . . .* (1862; second edition 1877; Eng. trans., *Fragments from Reimarus*, 1879). The standpoint is that of pure naturalistic deism. Miracles and mysteries, with the exception of the Creation, are denied, and natural religion is advanced as the absolute contradiction of revealed religion: discoverable by reason, the essential truths of natural religion, namely the existence of a wise and good Creator and the immortality of the soul, can be the basis of a universal religion, whereas no revealed religion can ever be intelligible or credible to all. The fragment "Von dem Zwecke Jesu und seiner Jünger" ("On the Aim of Jesus and his Pupils") influenced some 19th-century critics.

BIBLIOGRAPHY.—C. C. Scherer, *Das Tier in der Philosophie des H. S. Reimarus* (1898); J. Engert, "Der Deismus in der Religions- und Offenbarungskritik des H. S. Reimarus," *Theologische Studien der österreichischen Leo-Gesellschaft*, 22 (1916); A. C. Lundsteen, *H. S. Reimarus und die Anfänge der Leben-Jesu Forschung* (1939).
(F. E. M.)

REIMS (RHEIMS), a city of northeastern France, lies 95 mi. (152 km.) ENE of Paris by road, in the *département* of Marne. Pop. (1962) 138,576. Reims is situated on the right bank of the Vesle River, a tributary of the Aisne, where its valley is reached by the junction canal that connects the Aisne and Marne rivers. It lies on the western margin of the chalk plain of Champagne and is overlooked from the southwest by the Montagne de Reims, the highest part of the Tertiary limestone escarpment of the Île de France. On its lower slopes, and farther south to beyond the Marne valley, are the vineyards that provide grapes for the Champagne wine industry, of which Reims and Épernay are the chief centres. The wine is prepared in vast caves.

Situated at the intersection of the main route leading north from the Rhône valley to the Low Countries with that from the Channel ports to the Rhine, Reims (Durocortorum) was the chief node of the Roman road system in northern Gaul, a much more important route focus then than Paris. It early became a centre of ecclesiastical organization and, from the 3rd century, of an archbishopric. According to tradition, the Frankish king Clovis was baptized by St. Remi (Remigius), archbishop of Reims, and from this event derived the later prerogative of archbishops to consecrate successive kings of France in Reims Cathedral. With few exceptions French monarchs from Philip Augustus to Charles X were consecrated there. The most famous of these ceremonies was that in 1429 when Charles VII was crowned in the presence of Joan of Arc.

From the advantages of its situation the great fairs of Reims developed in the 12th century, and the town received a communal charter in 1139. The woolen industry flourished in the Middle Ages, and was stimulated in the 17th century by Jean Baptiste Colbert, a native of the city, who is commemorated by a statue in the Place de Colbert. The textile industry is now represented especially by the manufacture of flannels. Engineering, glassmaking, and biscuit manufacture are also important. The city is a major junction of modern roads and railways, and its port on the Aisne-Marne Canal handles considerable traffic.

The cathedral of Notre Dame, built in the 13th century to replace an earlier building that had been burned, was one of France's greatest Gothic edifices, with an especially impressive facade. It was destroyed by German shelling in World War I, but was completely restored by 1938 and escaped damage in World War II. Reims was occupied briefly by the Germans in their offensive in September 1914, and after evacuating the city they held the surrounding heights, from which they subjected the city to intermittent bombardment during the next four years, and nearly all its buildings were destroyed. The two Romanesque towers and early Gothic facade of the church of St. Remi (11th–15th centuries) survived, however, as did the Roman triumphal arch, the Porte Mars. The Fine Arts Museum, which houses a notable collection of tapestries and paintings, occupies the buildings of an 18th-century abbey.

See also references under "Reims" in the Index.   (AR. E. S.)

REINCARNATION: *see* METEMPSYCHOSIS.

REINDEER, the name for Arctic and subarctic deer of the genus *Rangifer*, which in some parts of the northern polar lands are domesticated. Some authorities regard them as constituting a single species, *R. tarandus*, with several subspecies; others assign them to several separate species. Those native to North America are known as caribou. Reindeer were found until recently from Spitsbergen Island and Scandinavia through Finland and northern Russia to eastern Siberia. In North America two types may be distinguished on the basis of geography and habitat: the northern, or barren ground, caribou inhabit the tundra and taiga; the woodland caribou, the forest regions from Labrador and New-

CHARLES J. OTT FROM THE NATIONAL AUDUBON SOCIETY

BARREN GROUND CARIBOU BULL (RANGIFER TARANDUS)

foundland to British Columbia, formerly penetrating as far south as Maine.

Reindeer differ from all other living deer in that both sexes have antlers; those of the females are smaller and simpler than those of males. The antlers themselves are peculiar in that the brow tine of one side is directed downward over the middle of the face and is often palmated vertically. Reindeer vary greatly in size from the small domesticated races, about the size of a donkey, to much larger races of caribou. They are stockily built animals with large lateral hooves that allow the feet to spread on boggy ground or on snow. Their colour varies greatly, but in general is grayish or brownish, with lighter underparts; the coat is thick and consists of hard, brittle outer hairs covering a dense underfur.

Reindeer are strong swimmers, are always found in herds, and are famous for their seasonal migrations between summer and winter ranges. Their numbers are now greatly reduced. A single calf is usually born after a gestation of $7\frac{1}{2}$ months, but twins are not rare. The staple winter food is a lichen (*Cladonia*), popularly called reindeer moss, which the animals reach by scraping the snow away with the feet (not with the forwardly pointing brow tine as is often thought). In summer the diet also includes grasses and saplings. The main enemies of reindeer are man, wolf, lynx, and wolverine. The reindeer of the Lapps is kept as a beast of draft and burden, as stock for its meat and milk, and for its hide, used for tents, boots, and clothing. *See also* DEER, and references under "Reindeer" in the Index. (L. H. M.)

REINDEER LAKE, in northern Canada, straddles the Saskatchewan-Manitoba border in Precambrian rock terrain near the northern limit of the coniferous forest. At an altitude of 1,150 ft. (351 m.), it is 2,467 sq.mi. (6,390 sq.km.) in area, 152 mi. (245 km.) long and up to 35 mi. (56 km.) wide, irregularly shaped and island-dotted. Fed by numerous streams, it drains southward over a control dam into the Churchill River via the Reindeer. In fur trade days the lake was a transport link and two small settlements formed near its extremities. More recently, commercial and sport fishing produced a third settlement on the east shore connected by road with Lynn Lake. Man. (C. S. Br.)

REINHARDT, MAX (1873–1943), Austrian theatrical producer and director, was the most influential and productive theatre figure of his generation. Born at Baden, near Vienna, on Sept. 9, 1873, he began his stage career as an actor, mainly in Berlin at the Deutsches Theater, working under Otto Brahm. In 1903 he gave up acting to become a director. Working with the energy and speed that characterized his whole career as a director, he had, by the end of 1904, staged 42 plays. His next production, *A Midsummer Night's Dream,* put on at the beginning of 1905, made him famous far beyond Germany. At a time when Shakespearean production all over Europe was ponderously slow and shackled by convention, Reinhardt's direction of *The Dream* was inventively imaginative, swift, colourful, and joyous. The productions that followed displayed the extraordinary range of Reinhardt's tastes. During his lifetime he staged nearly 600 productions, including 22 of Shakespeare's plays, Greek drama, expressionist drama, plays by authors as different as Molière and Shaw, Ibsen and Goldoni, Goethe and Maugham, as well as many musical productions ranging from Richard Strauss to Gilbert and Sullivan.

He had no particular style of his own, no formula to which he worked. He simply sought for each play the style of direction best suited to it. Such was his versatility that he was equally at home wittily directing a light comedy in his little Kammerspiele Theater or handling the massive spectacles in his Grosses Schauspielhaus. Although these spectacular productions with their gigantic crowd scenes were a comparatively small part of Reinhardt's work, they attracted so much attention that he became mainly known outside Germany as a master showman. Among the most famous of these productions were *Oedipus Rex* in the Zirkus Schumann (1910), which he directed in London two years later at the Royal Opera House; *The Miracle* (1911), for which he converted London's huge exhibition hall, Olympia, into the interior of a cathedral; *The Oresteia* (1911) and Romain Rolland's *Danton* (1920). But probably the best known of all Reinhardt's productions was *Jedermann* ("Everyman"), adapted by Hugo von

THE BETTMANN ARCHIVE, INC.
MAX REINHARDT

Hofmannsthal from the medieval morality play; this was performed year after year at the Salzburg Festival which Reinhardt, with Hofmannsthal, founded in 1920. Staged in the square in front of the cathedral, it was one of the many open-air productions which Reinhardt directed.

Reinhardt left Germany for the United States in 1933 when Hitler came into power. He had given a season in New York (1927–28) and in 1934 he directed *A Midsummer Night's Dream* in Hollywood, making a film of the play for Warner Brothers in the same year. His final production was *The Eternal Road* at the Manhattan Opera House in New York in 1937. He had a worldwide influence on the theatre because of his technical innovations in the use of scenery and lighting and his bold and inventive use of colour and movement. He died in New York on Oct. 31, 1943. *See also* THEATRE.

BIBLIOGRAPHY.—H. Carter, *The Theatre of Max Reinhardt* (1914); E. and H. H. Stern, *Reinhardt und Seine Bühne* (1924); O. M. Sayler, *Max Reinhardt and His Theatre* (1924); H. Rothe, *Max Reinhardt 25 Jahre Deutsches Theater,* 2nd ed. (1948). (N. M.)

REINKENS, JOSEPH HUBERT (1821–1896), the first German Old Catholic bishop, was born at Burtscheid near Aachen on March 1, 1821. He was professor of church history at Breslau and became rector of that university in 1866. At the first Vatican Council (1870) Reinkens refused to support the doctrine of papal infallibility and was excommunicated in 1872. (*See* VATICAN COUNCILS.) He attended the first Old Catholic congress at Munich (1871), was elected the first German Old Catholic bishop, and was consecrated at Rotterdam (1873) by Hermann Heykamp, bishop of Deventer, the only survivor of the old Dutch Jansenist hierarchy independent of Rome since 1724. Reinkens took a leading part in the Bonn Reunion Conferences with Eastern Orthodox, Anglican, and Lutheran theologians (1874–75). In 1876 he consecrated Eduard Herzog bishop for Switzerland. In 1889 Reinkens and Herzog, with three Dutch Jansenist bishops, issued the Declaration of Utrecht, which repudiated the innovations of the Council of Trent and is still the Old Catholic doctrinal basis. Reinkens died at Bonn on Jan. 4, 1896. *See also* OLD CATHOLICS.

See Reinkens' *Life* by his nephew, J. M. Reinkens (1906); C. B. Moss, *The Old Catholic Movement* (1948). (C. B. Mo.)

REINMAR VON HAGENAU (REINMAR DER ALTE) (d. *c.* 1205), was the most notable exponent of *Minnesang* toward the end of the 12th century (*see* MINNESINGER). His birthplace was probably in Alsace but he moved early to Vienna where he became court poet of the Babenberg dukes. Among his pupils was Walther von der Vogelweide (*q.v.*), who later became his rival. Reinmar was considered by his contemporaries to be the "nightingale" of the poets of his day. In matters of form he sought purity of rhyme and smoothness of rhythm and rejected any phrase or emotion which might have offended courtly susceptibilities. The modern reader, however, may find his songs stereotyped as he sang mostly of unrequited love. The volume of songs attributed to him is considerable but modern scholarship doubts the authenticity of all but about 30 of them, assigning the rest to his pupils.

See K. von Kraus (ed.), *Des Minnesangs Frühling* (1939); F. Maurer, *Die Pseudoreimare* (1966). (W. W. Cs.)

REISKE, JOHANN JAKOB (1716–1774), German philologist, who surpassed all his predecessors in the range and quality of his knowledge of Arabic literature, was born on Dec. 25, 1716, at Zörbig in electoral Saxony. From the orphanage at Halle he passed in 1733 to the University of Leipzig, and there spent five years. He bought Arabic books, and when he had read all that was then printed he thirsted for manuscripts. He qualified as a doctor, but failed to secure any medical practice at Leipzig, and lived, as before, on ill-paid literary hack work. Although the electoral prince gave him the title of professor he was not permitted to lecture. At length in 1758 the magistrates of Leipzig rescued him from poverty by giving him the rectorate of St. Nicolai, and, though he still met with hostility in the university, he enjoyed the esteem of Frederick the Great, of Lessing, Carsten Niebuhr, and many foreign scholars. Reiske died on Aug. 14, 1774, and his manuscript remains are now in the Copenhagen library. In the *Adnotationes historicae* to his *Abulfeda Annales Moslemici,* five volumes (1789–91), Reiske collected a veritable treasure of original research; he knew the Byzantine writers as thoroughly as the Arabic authors, and was alike at home in modern works of travel in all languages and in ancient and medieval authorities. In Greek his corrections are often hasty and false, but a surprisingly large proportion of them have since received confirmation from manuscripts. He was interested too in numismatics, and his letters on Arabic coinage form the basis of that branch of study.

REITH, JOHN CHARLES WALSHAM REITH, 1st Baron, of Stonehaven (1889–   ), one of the principal architects of the modern pattern of publicly owned but independent corporations in Great Britain, was born at Stonehaven, Kincardineshire, Scot., on July 20, 1889. He was educated at Glasgow Academy, Gresham's School, Holt, Norfolk, and the Royal Technical College, Glasgow, being trained as a civil engineer. During World War I he served in 1914–15 on the western front where he was wounded, and in 1916–17 in the U.S., where he was engaged with the supply of munitions to the U.K. As general manager of the British Broadcasting Company from 1922, and director general of the corporation, as it became, from 1927 to 1938, he was responsible for the creation and development of broadcasting throughout the British Isles, and also for the inauguration of the empire short-wave broadcasting service and the first regular service of high-definition television in the world (1936). He had been knighted in 1927. It was his achievement to have established a national broadcasting service and set an exemplary standard of public responsibility and efficiency for it. In 1938 Reith became chairman of Imperial Airways and in the following year was responsible for its merger with British Airways and the creation of the British Overseas Airways Corporation, of which he became chairman. He was made a peer in 1940. In World War II, Lord Reith held ministerial and other appointments and was director of Combined Operations Material at the Admiralty, 1943–45. After the war he was responsible in 1946 for a reordering of the cable and wireless system of the Commonwealth, becoming chairman of the new Commonwealth Telecommunications Board (1946–50). He was chairman of the New Towns Committee (1946), the Hemel Hempstead Development Corporation (1947–50), and the National Film Finance Corporation (1948–51). From 1950 to 1959 he was chairman of the Colonial Development Corporation and served on other commercial and industrial boards. He was lord rector of Glasgow University, 1965–68, and lord high commissioner to the General Assembly of the Church of Scotland in 1967–68. Lord Reith published his autobiography, *Into the Wind,* in 1949, and it was followed by *Wearing Spurs* (1966), on the first year of World War I.   (G. R. M. G.)

REJUVENATION, or the restoration of youthfulness, has long been a goal of man. Although the causes of aging have been little understood, a most obvious change occurs in the reproductive capacities of men and animals. It is not unnatural, therefore, that genital powers and the genital organs have been the preoccupation of those who have sought the secret of rejuvenation. In ancient times the testicles of sacrificial animals were used to counteract sexual weakness, and records indicate that the elders and priests of ancient China and India consumed the sexual organs of wild animals to improve their vigour and acuity and thus to offset the decline of old age. Such practices have not waned during the intervening centuries, since some primitive societies still indulge in these attempts at rejuvenation.

The achievement of rejuvenation was claimed during the early 20th century by several surgeons of Europe and the U.S. who maintained that operations on the genital organs or transplanta-

tion of young testicular tissue into elderly men brought about a new feeling of well-being, physiological youthfulness and, in some instances, a renewal of sexual potency. This era stemmed from the accounts of the physiologist Charles Edouard Brown-Séquard (*q.v.*) who in 1889, at the age of 70, injected himself with testicular material from dogs and guinea pigs and claimed a renewal of vigour, mental alertness and the "enjoyment of life." Twenty-five years later Jürgen W. Harms believed that he had accomplished the same thing in senile guinea pigs and, further, that he had regenerated sexual activity by the transplantation of testicles from young, healthy animals.

The foremost names in the field of induced rejuvenation were those of the Viennese scientist Eugen Steinach who experimented mostly with rats, and Serge Voronoff, a French surgeon who combined animal and human experimentation. The Steinach operation consisted merely of ligation and severance of the male seminal duct. Voronoff transplanted young human or monkey testicular tissue into the testicular sacs of elderly men. In both procedures, the operation was regarded as increasing the secretion of the masculinizing hormones (androgens) by the testes, thereby giving new vigour to the organism (*see* Hormones). In the most dramatic cases of rejuvenation of 65- to 83-year-old men, the results claimed were long-lasting improvement in mental alertness, sense of well-being, visual acuity, muscle tone, blood pressure, hair growth, skin elasticity, libido and sexual potency.

Although loudly proclaimed, these procedures were not well founded in theory and have not withstood the tests of time and confirmation. No evidence has been discovered that aging of the body as a whole is dependent on either the activity or the failure of the sexual glands per se. These glands have their own characteristic functional life span, just as do other organs and tissues in the organism. Both the spermatozoa-forming and the hormone-secreting functions of the testes are mainly devoted to reproduction of the species and not to growth, differentiation and maintenance of the body against the ravages of old age.

Voronoff's transplantations of monkey glands in men could not possibly have persisted as active, growing tissues and could at best only have supplied a temporary exogenous source of androgenic substance. The apparent results were probably mainly responses to the sudden and temporary flood of androgen throughout the system, combined with readjustment in subjective and psychological attitudes, and improvement in nutritive and constitutional factors. It has been well recognized among clinical circles that some cases of human infertility in both men and women have responded to improved conditions of diet, rest and relaxation when previous medical therapy had been of no avail.

With the chemical identification and synthesis of the male hormone testosterone there was ample opportunity to test its capacity to induce true rejuvenation as well as to study its general physiological effects on the organism. Its administration to elderly men followed in some instances by feelings of well-being, sexual interest, improved circulation and increased muscle tone, but analogous results also have been obtained with other stimulants and strengthening methods. The effects are temporary and did not offset the slow decline of old age. Indeed, some danger is involved in such a one-sided stimulation since the organism as a whole may not be physically constituted to withstand the sudden and abnormal stress.

The systemic effects of testosterone administered to experimental animals under controlled conditions were found to include a multitude of physiological responses: modification in blood pressure, red blood cell count, muscle tone, glycogen storage, electrolyte and water retention, enzyme activity, carbohydrate and protein metabolism, oxygen and carbon dioxide exchange and brain wave pattern. Moreover, it is known that through the intricate integration of the endocrine system androgen administration has an important action on the all-powerful pituitary gland and on the adrenals as well. Obviously then, a sudden change of disturbance in the androgen balance might have profound effects throughout the system. A practical example of the effect of androgen stimulation may be found in the annals of horse racing: a run-down and over-aged horse was able, after testosterone administration, to perform well with his younger competitors. The response was temporary, however, and not devoid of some risk.

Attempts to induce the revitalization by surgical means have been confined to the male. Apparent rejuvenation, however, has been frequently described in women suffering from ovarian tumours and reproductive disorders. Misuse of the term in these instances has resulted from the effects of excessive secretion of the feminizing hormones (estrogens). Although estrogens may seem to offset some of the appearances of aging—hence their incorporation into facial creams—the rejuvenative effects are relatively superficial. As in the male, the sexual hormones may alter the background of physiological reactions and modify the structural integrity of the cells and tissues, but they have little lasting effect on the primary causes of aging and senility.

"Rejuvenescence" is the biologist's term for certain processes undergone by protozoa (single-celled animals) such as *Paramecium*. (For these processes, called conjugation and endomixis, *see* Reproduction.) Rejuvenescence, however, is analogous in the higher animals not to rejuvenation of the individual but to procreation of a new being. In man and all other creatures, life continues uninterruptedly from generation to generation through the germ plasm, the source of posterity. Thus, while the germinal elements may be considered immortal, the body seems predestined to grow old and die, and no means have been found to seriously alter this decline.

See also Gerontology and Geriatrics.

Bibliography.—Eugen Steinach, "Die Verjüngung," *Archiv für Entwicklungsmech.* (1920); Norman Haire, *Rejuvenation: the Work of Steinach, Voronoff, and Others* (1924); Serge Voronoff, *Étude sur le vieillesse et le rajeunissement par le Graffe* (1926); Charles D. Kochakian, "The Protein Anabolic Effects of Steroid Hormones," *Vitam. & Horm.* (1946); L. Landois and H. U. Rosemann, *Physiologie des Menschen* (1950); G. E. W. Wolstenholme and M. P. Cameron, *Ciba Foundation Colloquia on Aging* (1955). (D. W. Bp.)

RELAPSING FEVER (Febris Recurrens) is an infectious disease characterized by recurring febrile symptoms and caused by spirochetes that have been given a number of conflicting genus and species designations: *Borrelia* (*Treponema*) *recurrentis* (*obermeieri, duttoni,* etc.). The spirochetes are transmitted from man to man by lice of the genus *Pediculus,* and from animals to man by ticks of the genus *Ornithodoros.* The human disease is characterized by sudden onset with violent febrile symptoms, which persist for about a week in cases contracted from lice, and usually for a shorter period in the tick-transmitted disease. The attack ends by crisis with profuse sweating, followed after about a week, during which time the patient is fairly well, by a return of the febrile symptoms. Additional relapses may follow—rarely more than one or two in the louse-borne disease, but up to 12 (usually decreasing in severity) in cases contracted from ticks. The mortality is variable, ranging from nil in some tick-transmitted varieties to 6% or as high as 30% in some recorded louse-borne epidemics associated with famine conditions. The spirochetes may invade the central nervous system and cause a variety of neurological symptoms, although these usually are not severe.

Relapsing fever spirochetes were the first microscopic organisms to be associated clearly with serious human disease. Otto Obermeier observed these organisms in the blood of relapsing fever patients in 1867–68 and published his observations in 1873. The organisms are corkscrew-shaped spiral threads, which rotate rapidly in performing forward, backward, and twisting movements.

They are easily observed in dark-field microscopic preparations of the patient's blood collected during the height of a febrile attack, but disappear from the blood during the intervals between attacks. These observations, as well as the relapsing symptoms, have been related to changes in the immunological (antigenic) characteristics of the spirochetes, which cause each attack and relapse. As the patient develops immunity to the prevailing immunological type and recovers from the attack, a new (mutant) immunological type of the spirochete develops and produces the relapse. Louse-borne relapsing fever has tended to occur in extensive epidemic outbreaks when human populations live under conditions which are conducive to louse infestation. Since neither the bite nor the excreta of the louse is infectious, human infections usually result from crushing the louse on the skin while scratching.

Tick-transmitted relapsing fever does not occur in extensive epidemics. Cases usually are related to tick-infested human or animal habitats, because the ticks tend to engorge rapidly, detach, and hide about the premises while digesting their meal, mating, and laying eggs. The adult ticks may live and remain infectious for as long as five years without feeding. The spirochetes frequently invade the eggs of infected female ticks and survive in the body of the developing larvae and nymphs. Therefore, all developmental stages of the tick may transmit the infection by bite or otherwise.

Arsphenamine and related arsenical drugs have been used extensively in the treatment of relapsing fever. However, many treatment failures with these drugs have been recorded. Penicillin has proved effective in curing many cases of the disease. Other antibiotics such as aureomycin, terramycin, and related compounds also have proved to be effective therapeutic agents. Inadequate therapy commonly results in relapse after treatment, probably due to the persistence of live spirochetes in the brain, where the drug concentration does not reach curative levels. After treatment these protected spirochetes may reinvade the bloodstream and start a relapse. (V. T. S.)

RELATIVITY. Since the time of Galileo the concept of relativity, in its broadest sense, has always been present in physics. Loosely speaking, this concept can be expressed simply as a question: Do the laws of nature, and hence the physical situations described by them, always appear to be the same to different observers, even though the state of motion of the observers is not identical? It is with this question that the following discussion is concerned.

GALILEAN RELATIVITY

If we wish to describe a physical event, a system of reference is needed to specify its position. The reference system can be formed by a coordinate system in space and by clocks that are fixed to this coordinate system to indicate the time. Also, a noncommittal word is needed to describe experience. Consider the experiences as a succession of events, each of which happens at a given point in space at a given time. Mechanical experimentation has shown that there are systems of reference such that a body in them, not acted upon by external forces, moves with constant speed along a straight line, and the laws of mechanics take a very simple form; to wit, if forces are acting upon the body, the acceleration will be proportional to the acting force. Such frames of reference are called inertial. (The name originates from the way the laws were visualized. It may be assumed that an innate property, inertia, keeps the body moving on a straight line in the absence of external forces, while the acceleration arises via an interplay of the external forces and inertia.) Is there more than one inertial frame? If so, then all these inertial frames will be equivalent, since in all of them the laws of mechanics (and, hopefully, the laws of physics as well) will be the same. Make a survey of everyday experiences and it is observed immediately that such equivalent systems of reference do indeed exist. For example, consider the fact that experiments performed upon the earth, involving only observations relative to the earth, reveal nothing about the motion of the earth around the sun, not to mention the motion of the solar system through space. Similarly, observations performed in a smoothly moving railway car, without looking out the window, do not permit the decision that the car is at rest or in uniform motion. Of course, if the car proceeds with jolts it is clear that it is not at rest, or not moving with a constant velocity (*see* Mechanics).

Thus first tentatively announce this statement: if a system of reference S is inertial, and if another system S′ moves with a constant velocity relative to S, S′ will also be an inertial system of reference. However, this does not permit complete specification of the relations between the description of events in S and S′. To do this requires an answer to the following question: If in S′ an event took place at the point x' at time t', what will be the place x and time t of the same event in system S?

To fix the ideas with an example next consider a simple case. Brown is traveling in a railway train that moves with a uniform velocity of 60 mph along a straight line. This moving train is system S′; the distance x' can be measured, say, by numbering the cars. The time t' is the time shown on the clocks in each car. While Brown is walking to the dining car, he slips and breaks his leg. This is the event that will be discussed. This event happened in the first car, and x' can be specified by measuring it along the train and tracks. The time when the event happened was just two hours after the train's departure, according to the clocks in the train. This specifies t', to wit $t' = 2$ hr. Now, shifting to another frame of reference, S, the frame in which the railway stations are at rest, what are the values of x and t? Here classical mechanics makes the following assumptions: the time of the event is the same in both frames (the clock at the railway station shows the same time as the clocks in the train); lengths measured in both frames are the same. Consequently, in frame S, $t = t' = 2$ hr. In turn, x can be calculated this way: The train has traveled for two hours, and during each hour the distance covered was 60 mi.; hence, the total distance traveled is 120 mi. If distances in S are measured from the point of departure, $x = 120$ mi. Formally, this relationship between the coordinates x, y, z, t and x', y', z', t' gives the following transformation equations:

$$\begin{aligned} x &= x' + ut' \\ y &= y' \\ z &= z' \\ t &= t' \end{aligned} \qquad (1)$$

Here it has been assumed that the coordinate axes in S and S' are parallel, that their origins coincide, and that the motion takes place in the x direction; u is the velocity of the primed coordinate system S', relative to the unprimed one S. A transformation based on these assumptions bears the name Galilean transformation.

Thus the principle of special relativity takes the following form in classical mechanics: if S is an inertial system of reference, and S' is a system of reference that moves with a constant velocity relative to S, then the laws of mechanics must have the same form in S and S', provided x, y, z, t and x', y', z', t' are connected by a Galilean transformation. Briefly, it is said that the laws of Newtonian mechanics are invariant under Galilean transformations.

Of course, the next question is whether the rest of the physical laws are also invariant under this transformation. In other words, this would mean that such experiments that do not rely exclusively on the laws of mechanics should also fail in telling the observer whether he is at rest or in uniform motion, using the connections given by equations (1) between the primed and unprimed quantities. Such experiments are encountered in electrodynamics where concern is with the behaviour of the electric and magnetic fields; e.g., the propagation of light. However, it is very soon realized that such is not the case. The simplest way to see this is perhaps the following. The Galilean transformations, equations (1), give rise to a certain addition law of velocities, the relation commonly used in everyday life. For example, if a man walks along a moving train with a velocity of 2 mph relative to the train, in the direction of motion of the train, and if the train moves with a velocity of 60 mph along the tracks, then the velocity of the man relative to the tracks will be, it is said, 62 mph. If in place of the walking man there is a light signal traveling through the train, emitted from a source on the train, it would be expected that its velocity also would be different if it is measured relative to the train or relative to the tracks. However, experiments show that the speed of light is the same in all inertial systems of reference. (The early Michelson-Morley experiments will be discussed later.) Consequently, the Galilean principle of relativity applies only to mechanics, and not to electrodynamics. Putting it in another way, the Galilean principle of relativity and the constancy of the light velocity in an inertial frame of reference seem to be empirically incompatible.

SPECIAL THEORY OF RELATIVITY

The resolution of this paradox was accomplished by Albert Einstein in 1905. He clearly realized the three assumptions underlying the Galilean principle of relativity and the different roles the constancy of light velocity plays in each. The three assumptions were the following: there are inertial systems in which the laws of physics are identical; if one system is inertial, any system of reference that moves with a constant velocity relative to the

first one is also inertial; the transcription of space and time data from one inertial system to another has to be done according to the Galilean transformations as given by equations (1). The first two assumptions assert that the relative configurations of bodies determine the physical occurrences (not their configurations and motions relative to some external frame of reference), while the last indicates how observers must translate the results they have obtained in one inertial frame to get the results observed in any other inertial frame. Experiments indicate that in electrodynamics, as well as in mechanics, all phenomena depend on relative configurations and motions only. Thus the first two assumptions should be valid no matter what assumptions are made about the velocity of light. What about the third one? As has been seen in the discussion preceding equations (1), the Galilean transformations assume tacitly that the position and time of occurrence of an event are the same in all inertial frames. The question arises whether or not this assumption is sensible if the velocity of propagation of signals (light signals) is not infinite. This would question, then, in the example of the train, whether it is sensible to assume that the clock at the railway station shows the same time as those in the moving train. It can be seen that this is not a valid assumption. To show this, let us try to achieve simultaneous operation of the clocks. We could start two identical clocks, one in the railway station and one in the car when the train is at rest at the railway station. If the rate of the clock would not change when the train is set in motion we would have accomplished our task. However, we do not know this, and we either have to test this hypothesis or proceed in a different fashion. What we inevitably will do is the following: we take two identical clocks, put one on the train and leave the other one at the railway station. Now, when the train is in motion we send a signal from the station to the train, say exactly at noon. If this signal would travel with an infinite speed we simply would set the clock in the train to indicate noon, and the synchronization would be accomplished. However, if the signal travels with a finite speed we must take into account the time that is needed for the signal to reach the train. It is just this delay that is ambiguous. The conductor, knowing that the stationmaster is to send the signal at the time t later than the train was at the station, says that the distance is ut, where u is the velocity of the train, and if the signal velocity is c, the delay is $(u/c)t = \beta t$, where $\beta = u/c$. He will then expect to receive the signal at $t' = t(1 + \beta)$. The stationmaster will say that, since the train is receding during the signal's flight, the distance traveled by the signal is $u(t + \Delta t)$ and the delay time is given by $\Delta t = \beta(t + \Delta t)$ or $t' = t + \Delta t = t(1 - \beta)^{-1}$.

It will not do to let the conductor correct for his own motion, since this effectively puts him in the stationmaster's frame of reference and then there is no comparison made between clocks set up in different frames. Each must take the point of view that he is at rest and the other one is receding from him. Otherwise, one of the frames of reference would be preferred; e.g., if the conductor corrects for his own motion, this would make the stationmaster's frame preferred. The example with trains is poor in the sense that we intuitively consider the stationmaster's frame as if it were at rest and tend to correct the conductor's computation since the former is at rest relative to the earth.

The difference in the two computations is exactly that in the naïve Galilean reference the signal velocity c cannot take the same numerical value in two reference systems moving with a velocity u with respect to each other. Since both conductor and stationmaster observe, in the train and in the station, respectively, that light velocity has the same numerical value c, each computes the delay time as though the other is moving away from him. The conflict between the computations of conductor and stationmaster is resolved if each believes that the other's clock runs slow by the factor $\sqrt{1 - \beta^2} = \sqrt{(1 + \beta)(1 - \beta)}$. The conductor will then say that his clock should register $t' = t(1 + \beta)/\sqrt{1 - \beta^2} = t\sqrt{(1 + \beta)/(1 - \beta)}$, whereas the stationmaster will compute $t' = t(1 - \beta)^{-1}\sqrt{1 - \beta^2} = t\sqrt{(1 + \beta)/(1 - \beta)}$. They will still disagree about whose clock runs slow, and still disagree about the delay in the signal, but they will agree in the computation of the relation between t' and t, an agreement that is verified experimentally.

To sum up this important step, we can say that the constancy of the velocity of light in different frames, and the existence of equivalent frames, are logically compatible if we modify the transcription of space and time data from one inertial system to another. This means that we must find another set of transformations which will take the place of the Galilean transformations. Moreover, this modification is not only permissible but required, from a physical standpoint, since it is the mathematical description of the empirical procedure to set up synchronous clocks in different inertial systems of reference. It was the brilliant achievement of Einstein to realize that this modification of our space and time concepts (to achieve the logical compatibility of equivalent frames with the existence of a constant velocity of light) is required if we analyze carefully how a finite signal velocity influences the meaning of time in a system of reference, if time is defined in terms of operations such as the indications of clocks that are situated in the immediate neighbourhood of the event, moving with the same velocity as the observer.

Our next step is then to find that set of transformations which will replace the Galilean set. This will furnish us with the relations that tell us how to correlate space and time data in two different systems of reference, moving with a constant velocity relative to each other, in such a fashion that the velocity of light should be the same in both. If we try to satisfy this last condition we find the transformations to be of this form:

$$
\begin{aligned}
x &= (x' + ut')\gamma \\
y &= y' \\
z &= z' \\
t &= \left(t' + \frac{x'u}{c^2}\right)\gamma
\end{aligned}
\tag{2}
$$

where c is the speed of light, $\beta = u/c$ and $\gamma = \sqrt{1 - \beta^2}$. The relative arrangement of the coordinate systems is the same as for equations (1). These equations describe the so-called Lorentz transformations, named for Hendrik Antoon Lorentz, a Dutch physicist who investigated them before Einstein.

We have then a framework which is based on three postulates: that inertial systems of reference exist; that inertial systems differ from each other at most by the fact that they may move with a constant velocity relative to each other; and that the transcription of space and time data from one inertial system to another is done according to the Lorentz transformations, equations (2). The physical description of the external world which satisfies these conditions is called Lorentz invariant and forms the Special Theory of Relativity.

The experimental confirmation of this theory is so extensive that we can give only a few examples. First let us discuss the special implications of the Lorentz transformations. Naturally, we will expect that some interesting consequences arise from the fact that we no longer have an absolute time, the same in all frames of reference. This means that both the spatial distance between points and the duration of a process will change as we change systems of reference. For example, a metre rod, if at rest relative to us, has the length one metre. Set it in motion in the direction of its axis, measure its length again, and the new measurement will be less by a factor $\sqrt{1 - \beta^2}$. For ordinary velocities this factor is practically one; for large velocities, however, it may be much less than one. For example, if the metre rod is flying by an observer with a velocity of about 0.85 times the velocity of light ($\beta = 0.85$), the observer will measure its length to be only a half metre.

With time indications it is just the other way around. The seconds indicated by a moving clock will be longer by a fraction $1/\sqrt{1 - \beta^2}$ (longer, since this factor is larger than one). This is very dramatically confirmed by modern experiments on elementary particles. In nature we encounter elementary particles, μ mesons, which have a rather short lifetime. In principle this lifetime could be used as a time measure, and so the meson could function as a clock. Accordingly, the lifetime of a moving meson ought to be longer than the lifetime of a meson at rest. In cosmic rays the mesons move practically with the velocity of light, and thus the life of a moving meson should be much longer than that of the meson at rest. Indeed, mesons that are stopped in an absorber have a lifetime of about 1.5×10^{-6} sec. On the other hand, in cosmic radiation a meson travels a distance of about 50 km. before it decays. From this fact we find that the speed of such a meson is about $(1 - 1/5,000)$ times the velocity of light, and the lifetime of a meson in our reference frame is increased by the enormous factor of 50 (see COSMIC RAYS; PARTICLES, ELEMENTARY).

As far as electrodynamical experiments are concerned, they naturally will agree with the Special Theory of Relativity, since the latter was created just to incorporate these experiments. Consequently, the success of Maxwellian electrodynamics means automatically the success of the relativity theory as well. For historical reasons we mention the famous Michelson-Morley experiment that showed convincingly that the velocity of light is the same in all inertial systems of reference. The idea of the experiment, which is due to James Clerk Maxwell, is very simple. Suppose that the velocity of light does depend on the state of motion of the observer; then, test the consequences of this hypothesis. We send out a light signal in the direction of motion of the earth, and another signal in the opposite direction. In one case the observer travels in the same direction as the light, which, under the hypothesis, would make the observed light velocity less than if the observer had been at rest. In the other case the velocity of light as observed should be larger than the velocity observed by an observer at rest. The difference between these two velocities could be observed interferometrically. This task was performed first by A. A. Michelson (1881), and later in improved form by Michelson and E. W. Morley (1887) (see MICHELSON-MORLEY EXPERIMENT). The result was negative; no difference in the velocity of light was found. Naturally, there were attempts to explain this before establishment of the Special Theory of Relativity as discussed in ABERRATION (OF LIGHT).

In 1893 G. F. Fitzgerald, an Irish physicist, and in 1895 Lorentz proposed independently the following explanation. Suppose that the velocity of light does vary with the state of motion of the observer. But suppose as well that the linear dimension of a body in the direction of the motion contracts in the ratio $\sqrt{1 - u^2/c^2}$. Then, the observed velocity would be the same, independent of the velocity of the observer. Moreover, this supposition conformed with the theory of electrodynamics, since Lorentz showed that if matter consisted only of charged particles held together by electromagnetic forces, then, if set in motion, the relative positions of the particles would adjust themselves in such a fashion that the contraction would take place.

We know now that this contraction does not depend on the special nature of the forces which keep matter together, but is a simple consequence of the Lorentz transformations, as we have seen in the discussion of equations (2).

Let us turn now to the mechanical experiments. First, a remark. While electrodynamics was born Lorentz-invariant, though its creator, Maxwell, did not realize it, mechanics was made to be Lorentz-invariant. This happened in two steps. First, modifications were introduced in the definitions of mechanical quantities so that the Newtonian equations of motion would conform to the Special Theory of Relativity. The classical concepts of mechanics, such as inertia and force, were retained, however. Finally, with the advent of the General Theory of Relativity, even these concepts were modified or removed. In this section we will discuss the first stage of development, while the next stage will form the content of the description of the General Theory.

The reformulation of dynamics in a Lorentz-invariant form, while retaining the classical concept of force, brought some beautiful results. Classical dynamics contained three most important laws concerning the conservation of energy, momentum, and mass. These laws were essentially independent, and we would have been able (in principle) to drop one and retain the others. In the Lorentz-invariant formulation this freedom no longer exists. Here, the three conservation laws are fused into one, and the violation of one entails the violation of all. Moreover, because the conservation of energy is linked to the conservation of mass, processes are permitted which would change energy into mass, or mass into energy (if the amount of mass which disappears in a given physical event is m, there will appear an amount of energy $E = mc^2$, c being the speed of light). Indeed, the last of these processes is the one which provides us with prodigious amounts of energy in nuclear reactions (*see* ATOMIC ENERGY).

In other respects, the differences between the classical and relativistic dynamics are most pronounced in the description of fast particles. This is natural, for we know that the difference in the classical and relativistic descriptions arises from the fact that in the classical theory there is no limiting velocity. If a particle moves slowly, it cannot make any difference, as far as the result is concerned, whether we consider a limiting velocity which is very large, or actually infinite. Expressing it in another way, classical Newtonian mechanics must be a limiting case of relativistic mechanics. This limiting case can be reached from the relativistic formulation by placing the velocity of light equal to infinity, and it can be applied in cases where the actual velocities of the bodies under description are much less than that of light. (This is a good example of the growth of physical theories. Each theory describes a part of our experiences correctly. However, the conditions under which this description is correct are usually less general than was originally thought. With the arrival of new facts this is realized, and a new, more general theory is created which, though it may be based on entirely different concepts, contains the mathematical formalism of the old one as a limiting case. Thus a new physical theory does not replace the old one but generalizes it.)

There are numerous examples showing that the proper description of fast-moving particles is the relativistic one. In modern research, physicists often experiment with very fast particles, which are accelerated in machines by electromagnetic fields. In the design of these machines (cyclotrons, betatrons, etc.) the physicist uses relativistic dynamics with the same confidence that an engineer feels when he uses Newtonian mechanics to design automobiles. The successful operation of particle-accelerating machines shows how correct the relativistic description of fast particles is (*see* ACCELERATORS, PARTICLE).

The mathematical description of the Special Theory of Relativity and its content was greatly simplified by the geometrical interpretation given to it by Hermann Minkowski, a German mathematician. This interpretation had the most far-reaching significance, since geometrization provided the clues that finally enabled Einstein to generalize the theory so as to embrace gravitational forces as well. Moreover, Minkowski's interpretation suggested the proper mathematical tools, tensor calculus and differential geometry, which gave the theory great elegance.

The underlying idea is the following. Every observer must specify four data (x, y, z, t) to describe an event. The first three of these will specify the location of the event relative to a coordinate system, while the last one specifies the time relative to a clock at rest in this coordinate system. In those cases where there are only three (or two) quantities to be specified, it is quite customary to draw a graph to represent the totality of these measurements at one glance. Even if in practice we cannot draw a four-dimensional graph (plot four quantities at once), we can think about it. To facilitate our understanding we will now contemplate only situations where the position can be given by two data only. So, let us suppose that we are aboard an ocean liner and we want to have a graphical record of our journey. The simplest thing to do is to take the map and at each hour, say, put a point at the proper latitude and longitude where the boat is, and write next to it the time. It is much more revealing, however, if we make a three-dimensional model, and put the dot not on the map, but above the intersection of the proper longitude and latitude. The perpendicular distance from map to point should be proportional to the time elapsed from the departure. If we do this each hour and finally connect all these points with a thin wire, the wire will contain in a graphical form all the information about the journey.

This information shows not only the location of the boat at a given time, but much more. If the wire is straight, it tells us that the boat has traveled on a straight line with constant speed. If the wire lies in one plane (normal to the map), but describes a curve in this plane, the boat was traveling on a straight line, though the speed did change during the course, and so on.

Now if we take a particle instead of the boat and note mentally in a four-dimensional space its position (x, y, z) at time t for each instant of time, we will get a similar plot. Each point on the plot specifies an event, and the resulting curve is called the world line of the particle; it describes the history of this particle. The four-dimensional continuum in which the plotting takes place is called space-time (*q.v.*). The immense importance of this concept is as follows: suppose that several different observers, each using a different inertial system of reference, are observing the motion of a particle, and each is asked to construct a space-time diagram of the motion. According to the Special Theory of Relativity, each observer will construct exactly the same curve in space-time for the history of the particle. The different states of motion of the observers (since they use different inertial systems of reference) will manifest themselves by the fact that the coordinate axes in space-time, x, y, z, t (which localize an event in space-time relative to the inertial system of reference used by the observer), will be different for different observers. The relation between these axes is that given by equations (2); thus, we can pass from one set of axes in space-time to another set by a Lorentz transformation.

This is the great moment of geometrization. In geometry we are dealing with the description of objects and the relations among them. Such objects can be points, lines, planes, surfaces, bodies, etc. We describe them by giving the coordinates of the corresponding points relative to a coordinate system. If we change the coordinate system we change the description, but we do not change the configuration of the points we describe. In relativity theory the histories, the configurations of points describing events, are objective. Their description relative to an observer depends, however, on the coordinate system in space-time that the observer uses and the coordinate system in turn depends on the state of motion of the observer. A Lorentz transformation corresponds to a change of coordinates in space-time. As a coordinate transformation leaves the configuration of points unchanged, so a Lorentz transformation does not change the histories. Also, in a coordinate transformation the new coordinates, in general, will be given combinations of the old coordinates. In a Lorentz transformation the new space-time coordinates will be a combination of the old space-time coordinates. The mixing of space and time coordinates in a Lorentz transformation is then no more mysterious than the mixing of coordinates in an ordinary coordinate transformation. Moreover, the physical laws will now be geometrical propositions concerning world lines. In this way our geometrical intuition can come into play again, and can furnish help in the formulation of theories and problems. We will at once expect that the significant geometrical properties, such as curvature, torsion, and straightness, will also describe physically significant properties. Indeed, this is so. For example, a curved world line shows that the particle was accelerating, and thus we know that a force was acting on the particle whose history is described by this world line. The place and time of the action can be determined by locating the curved section of the world line relative to a system of reference in space-time. The magnitude of the curvature will be simply proportional to the magnitude of the force and the work done by the force. As a corollary we see that if no forces are acting on a particle its history is a straight line in space-time.

In geometry it is the distance between two points which has an intrinsic significance, while the projections of this distance upon the coordinate axes depend on the coordinate system, and vary as the coordinates change. A similar thing happens in relativity theory (*see* GEOMETRY).

The distance between events, which we will call an interval, is something absolute, represented by a line segment connecting the two events. Each observer will split this interval into a space part and a time part, relative to his own inertial system of reference; the spatial part will be the projection of the interval upon the spatial coordinates (x, y, z), while the time part will be the projection of the interval upon the time axis. This splitting into spatial and time parts will depend on the orientation of the coordinate system x, y, z, t in space-time.

For example, take as one event the Great Fire in London, and for the other event the outburst of the Nova Persei. The observer who is at rest relative to the earth (and so, relative to London) will split space-time with his coordinate axes and find that the outburst took place a century before the Great Fire and many millions of miles away from London. An observer who travels with a constant velocity relative to the earth may conclude that for him the distance and time elapsed is different. There will even be an observer with a certain velocity such that for him the two events took place simultaneously. Each observer slices up space-time into a space part and a time part, and the slicing depends on the orientation of the coordinate system. Thus, as Minkowski put it: "Space in itself and time in itself sink to mere shadows, and only a kind of union of the two retains an independent existence."

GENERAL THEORY OF RELATIVITY

The Special Theory of Relativity has not only solved problems, but has also posed some new questions. As is usual in physical theories, the advent of new viewpoints forces us to reexamine the concepts that we used freely before. With the advent of the Special Theory of Relativity these questions were abundant. In discussing the Special Theory we have learned that the histories in space-time have some permanent significance, at least as far as Lorentz transformations are concerned. Now, if the geometrical interpretation makes sense, we would think that the other, more general transformations should be also of significance. (A geometrical figure remains the same, irrespective of the coordinates we use to describe it.) At first sight the introduction of general transformations is clearly nonsensical. Such transformations in space-time correspond physically to the use of noninertial coordinate systems. Now, it is a familiar story that in noninertial systems of reference we have fictitious forces acting. Such forces are the centrifugal and Coriolis forces, which manifest themselves in rotating systems of reference. They are called fictitious because we can make them disappear by changing back into an inertial frame of reference. Consequently, we can distinguish between these frames of reference and inertial frames, and thus the simple principle of relativity cannot hold. However, our geometrical intuition insists that there must be something behind this idea. So let us analyze what happens if we observe a physical system from an accelerated system of reference. The fictitious forces we encounter have two important characteristics. First, they impart the same acceleration to every body, irrespective of its mass; second, these forces can be transformed away by the simple device of transferring ourselves to an inertial system of reference. As an example, consider what happens when we ride in a railway train. As long as the train moves in a straight line with a uniform velocity, everything inside the train behaves as if the train were at rest. Now the train makes a turn; the luggage in the train starts to slide, the water surface in a pitcher is no longer horizontal. Sitting inside the train, we conclude that a force is acting on these objects. The acceleration imparted by this force is the same for each body, and it disappears as soon as the train runs in a straight line with constant velocity. However, we can also say that, after all, the objects in the train tended to continue to travel on a straight line with a uniform velocity on account of their inertia, and only we, the observers (and our system of reference, the train), were accelerating; hence, it is natural that all objects should have the same acceleration, since after all this is just the observer's acceleration in the opposite direction. Thus, the inertia of the body is essentially what we see as a fictitious force. Also, it is obvious that if we cease to be in an accelerated frame of reference, we will see the other objects travel along straight paths with constant velocities (if they are not acted on by other forces), thereby transforming away the fictitious

forces. If we say all that, we are correct. The puzzling thing, however, is that there is another force, the gravitational force, which has these two properties. A falling apple undergoes the same acceleration as a falling cherry, though their masses differ. Also, if we fall together with the apple, it will appear to be at rest relative to us, apparently with no force acting on it (*see* FORCE; GRAVITATION: *Theories of Gravitation*).

This suggests that there must be an equivalence between noninertial systems of reference and gravitational fields, in the sense that an observer performing observations locally cannot distinguish between gravitational forces and forces which arise on account of accelerated systems of reference. Consequently, the admission of noninertial systems is necessary to construct a theory of the gravitational forces. But if accelerated systems are equivalent to gravitational forces, then gravitational forces should be in all respects similar to the fictitious forces. We have seen that these fictitious forces are essentially the manifestations of the inertia of bodies. The gravitational forces then must be similar manifestations. How could we formulate this?

We have learned in the Special Theory that the world lines of particles not acted upon by any forces are straight lines. These world lines have the important geometrical property of being as "straight" as possible. In geometry such lines are called geodesics. This we will consider as the proper characterization of inertia, and we can say that the world line of a particle subjected only to its own inertia is the straightest line in space-time; it is a geodesic. Then, if we exclude any other forces, except gravitational and other fictitious forces which should be the manifestations of the inertia of the bodies, we should be able to say the following: there are no forces acting on bodies; bodies always move freely under the influence of their own inertia. Consequently, their motion is such that their world lines are geodesics in space-time.

This space-time, of course, cannot be the space-time of the Special Theory, for there, we have just learned, the geodesics correspond to the motion of bodies which are not subjected to gravitational forces in the ordinary Newtonian usage of the word. The space-time continuum of the General Theory of Relativity must have additional properties. What are they? Again, our geometrical intuition comes to help. We know that the properties of geodesics depend on the curvature of the geometrical space. As a simple example let us take a two-dimensional space, a surface. If this surface is flat, the geodesics on it are ordinary straight lines (in the sense of Euclidean geometry); if the surface is curved, *e.g.*, if it is part of the surface of a sphere, the geodesics are not straight any longer in the classic Euclidean sense. On the surface of a sphere the geodesics are great circles, and their projections onto a plane will appear as curves. Thus, our analogy will lead us to believe that, in general, space-time will be curved, while the space-time of the Special Theory was flat. The history of a particle will be described by a geodesic in this curved space-time. If we would project this geodesic onto the flat space-time used in the Special Theory, we would get a curve which is not a geodesic in this flat space-time. The deviation from a geodesic in flat space-time will become larger as the curvature of space-time increases. However, our considerations must embrace the fact that in Newtonian mechanics gravitational forces exist only in the neighbourhood of masses. This must find its counterpart in the geometrical picture. The reasoning is very simple. If gravitational forces find their expression in the curvature of space-time, and these gravitational forces were produced by masses in the Newtonian theory, then, in the General Theory, the masses must produce the curvature of space-time. Indeed, this seems to be the solution.

The structure of the Newtonian theory of gravitation is the following. Space and time are the stage upon which physical processes are displayed. In these processes the masses are acting directly upon each other. In the General Theory of Relativity, space and time are first fused together into a continuum called space-time. The geometrical properties of this space-time determine the evolution of the physical processes in space and time. The geometrical properties of the space-time continuum in turn are determined by the masses (and physical processes) present in space and time. Thus in the latter theory we do not have anything external or uninfluenced, and the series of producers of mechanical phenomena is closed. (Observe, however, that this is not so for phenomena produced by electromagnetic and nuclear forces.)

These ideas and their mathematical formulation were finally given by Einstein in 1916. The geometrical properties of space-time are characterized by ten functions, which form the so-called metric tensor of this four-dimensional continuum. (Knowing the metric tensor, we can compute the separation of any two events in space-time.) Einstein formulated the field equations which relate these ten functions and their derivatives to ten other functions which describe the material content of space-time. These second ten functions form the so-called energy-momentum tensor, and they are the measure of the amount of energy (hence also mass) and momentum present in a specified portion of space at a given time.

The relationship mentioned has a very simple physical significance and is the mathematical expression of the idea that the curvature of space-time arises from the masses and their motion. From the metric tensor and the derivatives of its components we can form another tensor which is the measure of the curvature of space-time at a given point in space-time. Einstein's equations state essentially that the curvature of space-time at a given point in space-time is proportional to the amount of energy and momentum present at that point in space-time. Moreover, from the geometrical picture we can see that there always will be such a system of reference in which events in the immediate neighbourhood of the observer (local events) can be described according to the Special Theory. This follows from the fact that any curved space can be approximated locally by a flat space which is tangential to the curved space at that point. (For example, think of the curved space as the surface of a sphere, and the tangential flat space as the tangential plane.) Physically this corresponds to an accelerated frame of reference which has the same acceleration as caused by the gravitational forces at that point. (Thus again we can see how a more general theory embraces the special one as a limiting case.)

For any given material content, we can solve, in principle, the field equations and obtain from them the metric tensor. From the metric tensor we can compute the geodesics of space-time, which describe the history, and thereby the motion, of matter in the universe. The history of light rays can also be obtained, since they form a special class of geodesics called null geodesics. (These have no simple geometrical analogies from ordinary geometry.)

Logically, then, the theory rests in its modern form on two different postulates. First, the metric tensor shall satisfy the field equations; second, the history of a particle is given by a geodesic in space-time having the aforementioned metric tensor. Although we have seen that the second postulate played an important role in the formulation of the theory, the question arises whether we should not be able to discard it and extract all the information from the field equations only. Indeed, this proves to be the case. In a remarkable set of papers, Einstein and his co-workers attacked the problem in this fashion during the years 1938–49. Let us assume that mass points can be represented by singularities of the metric tensor. If, then, we want to have a solution for the field equations, the singularities must satisfy certain conditions. These conditions turn out to be just the equations of motion of mass points.

Now what about the experimental verification of the theory? The most basic experimental test concerns itself with the equivalence of noninertial systems of reference and gravitational fields. In principle we can associate with a body an inertial mass and a gravitational mass; the former is measured by the ratio of a nongravitational force acting on the body, to the acceleration produced; the latter is measured by the ratio of a gravitational force acting, to the acceleration produced. In principle the two masses can be different. However, experimentally they seem to have the same value. The General Theory is built on the idea that the two are the same, and indeed there is no provision in the theory to envisage their being different. Hence, if very accurate experiments should find that they differ, the whole theory must be then rejected. Experiments (1966) by a U.S. physicist, Robert Henry Dicke, show that this equality is satisfied within one part in 10^{11}. The other tests compare results obtained from the theory with experiments.

One deals with the motion of planets. We can compute the orbits of planets from the General Theory. Barring the planet Mercury, the difference between the Newtonian orbit and the relativistic one is negligibly small for practical purposes. However, for Mercury, the Newtonian theory predicted the orbit incorrectly. Since the time of Urbain Jean Joseph Leverrier, the French astronomer, it was known that there is a discrepancy between the observed motion of the Mercury perihelion and the one predicted by Newton's theory, even if we take into account the perturbations caused by the other planets. The first real success of the General Theory came when Einstein showed that this discrepancy disappears if we perform the calculations relativistically. In 1967, Dicke raised important objections to the usual interpretation of these results. He very carefully measured the shape of the sun and found it not spherical. This deviation from sphericity can alter the Newtonian gravitational field of the sun and can cause an additional precession, thereby reducing the amount to be explained as a relativistic effect. Since the theory gave the right value for the unreduced amount, it would then give too large a result to explain the new, reduced value. However, it is not yet clear whether the oblateness of the sun does give rise to a correction in the Newtonian gravitational field. (*See* MERCURY; SUN.)

Two other effects are concerned with the influence of a gravitational field on light. According to the General Theory the world lines of light rays must also be geodesics (null geodesics). Consequently the propagation of light will also be influenced by the presence of masses. For this reason light rays will be deflected from their original paths if they pass in the neighbourhood of bodies. If these bodies are very large, the effect can be observed. The most suitable large mass at our disposal is the sun. The measurements can be performed in the following fashion: First we take a photograph of a part of the sky when the sun is not in that neighbourhood. Next we take one when the sun is there. Naturally, the latter picture has to be taken during a total eclipse; otherwise, we will not see the nearby stars at all. If the sun deflects the light rays, the angular distance between two stars lying at diametrically opposite sides of the sun must be larger on the second picture than on the first one. All measurements have shown the effect to be present. The precise evaluation of the numerical magnitude, however, is very difficult on account of experimental complications. The theoretical value is 1.75 seconds of arc. The observations scatter around this value, and each observation has a probable error large enough to embrace the theoretical value. The best observations took place in 1922 and 1929.

The third experiment concerns the frequency shift of spectral lines emitted by atoms located in a gravitational field. We have already mentioned in discussing the Special Theory that atoms can be considered as clocks, since the radiation emitted by them has a periodicity, the frequency, which can be used to measure time. One of the predictions of the General Theory is that clocks in a gravitational field run slower than the same clock would run if the gravitational field were not present. Consequently, the slowing down of an atomic clock should mean the emission of light with a smaller period and thus a frequency shift in the spectral lines toward the red. All investigations have confirmed the existence of this effect. However, for atoms located on the surface of the sun, there are so many other disturbing factors which modify the effect that we hardly can attach great significance to the numerical values obtained for the red shift caused by the sun. On the other hand, measurements performed on light emitted by the companion to Sirius (Sirius B) and by one of the components of the star system in the constellation Eridanus (40 Eridani B) give the same order of magnitude as that predicted by the theory. (*See* also NEBULA: *Red Shifts and Expansion of the Universe.*) Terrestrial experiments were also performed to test the red shift. The potential differences available are now very small and only the recent methods utilizing the Mössbauer effect (*q.v.*) were accurate enough to succeed. The experiments performed in 1960 confirmed the theoretically predicted values.

Another interesting inference we can draw from the General Theory is the way gravitational disturbances are traveling. This is of great interest, since one of the chief objections to Newton's theory was the instantaneous action of gravitational forces; *i.e.,* their infinite speed of propagation. The results are the following. Moving bodies, on account of their motion, emit a weak gravitational field in the form of waves. These waves travel with the velocity of light. At a great distance from the source the waves are transverse and polarized. The energy loss of the source due to this radiation is very small, being proportional to the inverse fifth power of the velocity of light. For double stars the energy loss per year would be about 10^{-12} part of the total energy. Attention has been paid to the possibility of terrestrial detection and generation of gravitational waves. One such method would use the body of the earth itself as the detector to be set in oscillations by the waves; another method uses piezoelectric oscillators. (*See* Piezoelectricity.)

A great deal of indirect evidence is accumulating in favour of General Relativity through astrophysical observations. The General Theory makes predictions about the structure and evolution of stars; by observing stellar populations one can compare these predictions with the actual situation. At present the observations do not contradict the predictions.

In our discussion which led up to the formulation of the General Theory we have reduced the concept of gravitational force to that of inertia, eliminating the idea of force (at least the idea of gravitational force). We have done this by agreeing that the world line of a particle should be a geodesic in space-time. The action of other bodies manifests itself only by changing the geometrical properties of space-time.

However, we can now think of this in another fashion. If gravitation could have been conceived as a sort of mutual interaction of bodies (and of course we now have reduced the idea of gravitation to that of inertia) then could we perhaps conceive that inertia is actually a manifestation of a mutual action between bodies? As far as the histories of particles are concerned, we have already done that. But the inertial properties of matter find their expression also in the mass of bodies. So the question arises whether the concept of mass does not depend essentially on the existence of other bodies in the universe. Ernst Mach, an Aus-

trian physicist, first posed this problem, before the advent of relativity theory. It seems that the General Theory suggests an affirmative answer. It follows from the theory that (1) the mass of a body increases when ponderable masses approach it; (2) if neighbouring masses are accelerated there is a force acting on the body (in the same direction as the acceleration); and (3) a rotating hollow body creates a field of force inside itself, a field which acts on particles inside the hollow body. These effects are much too small (for ordinary bodies) to be observed. However, it might be possible that if the rotating masses are of cosmic magnitude, of the size of galaxies, for example, the effects could be detected. The questions raised by Mach cannot be answered from the principles of General Relativity alone, and further cosmological considerations are needed.

Until now we have discussed how individual masses influence the geometry of space-time. The result has shown that in the main the Newtonian conclusions were good approximations, though the concepts invoked were of an entirely different nature. This was connected with the smallness of the masses, distorting only a little the flatness of space-time. If this be the case, we may reasonably expect that great differences may arise if we consider problems which entail the universe as a whole, considering all the masses in the universe. In other words we may expect that the cosmological theories stemming from the General Theory of Relativity can be of an entirely different nature than the Newtonian ones. Relativistic cosmologies vary in scope and importance, and though some of them describe part of our experiences correctly, none can be singled out as the best. *See* Cosmology; Cosmogony.

UNIFIED THEORIES

The General Theory of Relativity has eliminated the concept of gravitational forces. The "guidance" of particles does not take place by a direct interaction between them, but is accomplished by the geometrical structure of space and time. Gravitational forces, in the Newtonian sense, arise only if we refuse to interpret properly the geometry of space-time.

Naturally this makes us wonder whether the other existing forces, electromagnetic and nuclear, are also merely misinterpretations of the geometry of space-time. Our aesthetic sense would be greatly pleased if these forces were found to stem from the same origin as the gravitational forces.

There were numerous attempts to endow space-time with such a geometrical structure from which the existence of the other forces would follow. However, while nature gave us a guide in the case of the gravitational forces, to wit, the similarity between fictitious and gravitational forces, we do not see any simple or suggestive relation between the gravitational forces and electromagnetic and nuclear forces. In addition to this, it is also possible that unification cannot be achieved in this fashion. We know now that the description of the microscopic properties of matter and its interaction with radiation brings entirely novel features to physics, features which are dealt with in quantum theory (*see* Quantum Mechanics). These features are not present in the General Theory; and it is quite possible that unification has to proceed via a theory that embodies the quantum aspects. (There were attempts to introduce the quantal aspects by formal manipulations in the General Theory [quantization of the gravitational field]. The non-

Outline of Hypotheses and Their Interrelationships

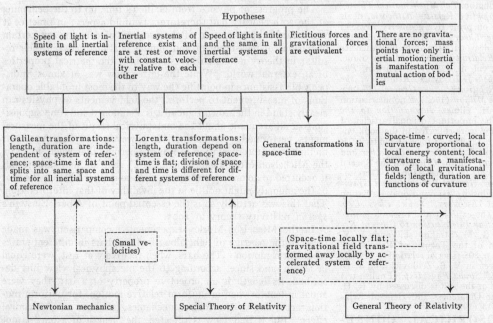

Solid arrows show how we may proceed from combinations of hypotheses (top) through their geometrical formulation to the laws of Newtonian mechanics and the Special and General theories of relativity. Dotted arrows show ways of passing from one theory to another by using the approximations shown in the dotted boxes.

linearity of the gravitational field equations makes this approach somewhat ambiguous. For weak gravitational fields the quantization is mathematically unambiguous; the results would indicate that the gravitational field has a particlelike aspect where the particles have a spin two. [Compare this with the electromagnetic field, which, upon quantization, also acquires a particlelike aspect. The particles there are called photons.])

The general trend toward constructing a unified field theory is somewhat as follows: the Riemannian geometry of four dimensions, which described the geometry of space-time in the General Theory of Relativity, has no available functions which could be used to describe other fields of forces. Consequently we have to enlarge this geometry so just the sufficient number of functions appears.

The loosening up of the geometrical structure to accommodate the additional field variables was pursued in two rather different ways. One way retained the idea of a four-dimensional continuum as the playground of physical phenomena, but used a non-Riemannian geometry in place of the Riemannian geometry which described space-time in the General Theory. The other way used a higher-dimensional continuum and projective or conformal geometries (*see* UNIFIED FIELD THEORY).

It is not easy to tell how far these attempts will prove successful. On the one hand, we cannot see clearly the conclusions which can be drawn because of the mathematical complications. On the other hand, as we have mentioned, the physical interpretation is in general far from being evident, and for this reason the interpretation and the mathematical development must proceed together. This complicates both the mathematical understanding and, thereby, the hope of experimental verification or refutation.

It is much more difficult to give a coherent and simple account of the unified theories which use higher dimensional geometries. In all these cases the additional dimensions have no physical significance and their introduction is purely formal. The additional dimensions simply enable us to obtain enough functions to describe the different kinds of fields. At some stage or another we have to eliminate, by some assumption, the explicit appearance of the variables describing the additional dimensions (but not, of course, the additional fields), since these dimensions have no physical significance.

Apart from the formal nature of these considerations the principal difficulty is that most of these theories give only a formal unification of the electromagnetic and gravitational fields, both fields remaining clearly separated, irrespective of their strength.

See also references under "Relativity" in the Index.

BIBLIOGRAPHY.—W. Pauli, *Theory of Relativity* (1958); H. Weyl, *Space—Time—Matter* (1922); A. Eddington, *The Mathematical Theory of Relativity* (1923); O. Veblen, *Projektive Relativitätstheorie,* deals only with unified field theories based on projective geometry (1933); P. G. Bergmann, *Introduction to the Theory of Relativity* (1942); E. Schrödinger, *Space-Time Structure,* deals with the affine field theories (1950); C. Moeller, *The Theory of Relativity* (1952); M. von Laue, *Die Relativitätstheorie,* vol. i (1952), vol. ii (1953); A. Einstein, *The Meaning of Relativity,* rev. ed. (1956); J. L. Synge, *Relativity: the Special Theory* (2nd ed., 1965), *Relativity: the General Theory* (1960); M. Gardner, *Relativity for the Million* (1962), a popularization that may be helpful for beginners; H. Yilmaz, *Introduction to the Theory of Relativity. . .* (1964). The important original articles of Einstein, Lorentz, Minkowski, and Weyl were collected in the book entitled *The Principle of Relativity* (1923). The history of relativity is covered by E. T. Whittaker, *A History of the Theories of Aether and Electricity,* vol. ii (1953) and G. Holton, "On the Origins of the Special Theory of Relativity," *Am. J. Phys.,* vol. 28, p. 627 (1960). Gravitational radiation is discussed in J. Weber, *General Relativity and Gravitational Waves* (1961) and V. B. Braginskii, "Gravitational Radiation and the Prospect of its Experimental Discovery," *Soviet Phys. Usp.* (English tr.), vol. 8, p. 513 (1966). The experimental research is presented in L. Witten (ed.), *Gravitation: an Introduction to Current Research* (general relativity) (1961); G. M. Strakhovskii and A. V. Uspenskii, "Experimental Verification of the Theory of Relativity," *Soviet Phys. Usp.* (English tr.), vol. 8, p. 505 (special relativity) (1966). The astrophysical implications are given in Y. B. Zeldovich and I. D. Novikov, "Relativistic Astrophysics II," *Soviet Phys. Usp.* (English tr.) vol. 8, p. 522 (1966). The oblateness of the sun is discussed by R. H. Dicke and H. M. Goldenberg, "Solar Oblateness and General Relativity," *Phys. Rev. Lett.,* vol. 18, p. 313 (1967). (N. L. B.)

RELATIVITY: PHILOSOPHICAL CONSE-QUENCES. The most important philosophical consequence of the theory of relativity is the clarification it has brought into the relations between science and philosophy. The position may be briefly summarized as follows. Up to the 17th century the subject matter of these studies formed a unity, the rudiments of that which we now call science being simply a part of a larger whole. A rift then appeared and gradually widened until, by the beginning of the 20th century, science and philosophy had become quite distinct and a person expert in one was usually very inexpert and ill-informed in the other. The effect of the relativity theory was to re-establish physics on a philosophical basis and thereby to elucidate certain bewildering implications of current research.

More particularly, the position was this. The general problem of philosophy is to give a rational account of experience with the minimum of presuppositions. Consequently it was not originally presupposed that physical experience must be regarded as an effect on our senses of an objectively existing external world having certain definite and ascertainable properties: that was a matter for discussion, and both affirmative and negative answers were given. Modern science, however, originated in the determination to ignore the metaphysical question and to accept experience as an object of study, whether or not it was "real." Thus Galileo discovered the law of falling bodies by measuring how the space covered varied with the time of fall. By carrying out certain processes of measurement he obtained results which stood in a certain relation to one another, and this relation remained true whatever metaphysical status one assigned to motion.

This became the origin and type of a large body of investigation which, by reason of its distinctive character and its rapid growth and success, came to be regarded as something other than traditional philosophy and was given the name "science." Nevertheless, it was still an attempt to give a rational account of experience with the minimum of presuppositions. Moreover, although it needed no supplement, it was in fact coupled from the beginning with a particular view of what the measurements signified. Galileo, for instance, supposed that they represented the magnitudes of certain characteristics of the external world which he regarded as possessing only mechanical properties such as size, shape, position, motion; other qualities (*e.g.,* colours, sounds, temperatures) he thought were not properties of the bodies which seemed to possess them but were contributed by the observing subject. This view was tenable in his day since he was unable to measure such things; but after the invention of thermometers, spectroscopes, etc., there remained no reason for distinguishing these so-called secondary qualities so fundamentally from motions and shapes, and they were gradually put back into the external world and included among the objectively existing properties of bodies, which science investigates.

The progress of physics from Galileo's time up to the beginning of the 20th century had therefore a twofold aspect: in practice it was a faithful prosecution of the program of carrying out certain operations of measurement and finding relations between their results; in theory it was an investigation of the metrical properties of an external world. While the latter view was of almost indispensable assistance in pointing the way to the most profitable operations of measurement to perform, the achievements of physics can clearly stand in their own right if it is abandoned and if no suppositions at all are made about the metaphysical status of the measurements performed. So instinctive, however, had this particular metaphysical interpretation of physics become that when, in 1887, the Michelson-Morley experiment (*q.v.*) gave an incredible result, it occurred to no one for nearly 20 years to inquire whether the root of the anomaly might not lie in the invalidity of that interpretation. That this was actually so is the essential point of Albert Einstein's *special* relativity theory of 1905.

In the Michelson-Morley experiment a comparison was made between the passage of light along material bars in different states of uniform motion. The bars, when relatively at rest, were equal in length, and since, according to the metaphysical view just described, its length is an objective property of a bar, they were equal in length when in uniform relative motion, for uniform motion, according to Newtonian mechanics, can have no mechanical effect. But if that view is rejected, the "length of a bar" is not an objective property but simply the result obtained when a particular operation of measurement is made. Now the operation for measuring length was well-known, but it required that the body measured must be at rest with respect to the measuring scale; it was inapplicable if the body was moving along the scale. Hence one had no right to speak of the "length" of a moving bar. This was not because the length, an objectively existing property, could not, because of practical difficulties, be ascertained. It was because one had no right to use the word until one had the result of a particular operation to which to apply it, and no such operation had been devised for a moving body.

The theory of relativity prescribed an appropriate operation, and the experiment was then satisfactorily explained. This belongs to physics, but one aspect of it has philosophical implications. The reason why the ordinary operation for measuring length was inapplicable to a moving body was that the scale readings for the two ends of the bar varied with time when the body was moving. To get a definite result, therefore, they had to be taken simultaneously. Hence one had to know how to determine that two events at different places occurred at the same time, and on analysis it appeared that this was impossible without some arbitrary stipulation. Here again, then, the idea of something existing objectively which physical measurement revealed had to be given up. It was not that, because of practical limitations, we could not determine which of a number of spatially separated events were simultaneous. There was no meaning in speaking of the simultaneity of such events until one had prescribed a process for determining it, and there was a wide degree of liberty in prescribing such a process.

Physics was thus thrown back on the unadorned description of itself as the discovery of relations between the results of chosen operations of measurement. This description adequately covered the whole of physics from Galileo's basic discoveries onward; but the metaphysical accompaniment that had provided the imagination with a model and the experimenter with a guide was now proved misleading. The philosopher must henceforth interpret physics in terms of operations and their results alone, leaving external existences out of account. But the physicist, finding a picture of an external world indispensable, began to devise a better one. In the old picture the world consisted of pieces of matter, measured essentially by their mass, moving about, without thereby becoming changed, in an infinite extension called space and an independent extension called time. According to the revised picture, matter, space and time are no longer independent but merge into a single continuum, space-time—a device made possible by the fact that, according to the definitions adopted for the length of moving bodies and the time relations of separated events, a certain combination of the space and time separations of events is independent of the state of motion which we choose to assign to any one of the bodies concerned. We can thus suppose that this combination of our measurements measures some absolute quality of events, just as we previously thought that the measurement of length indicated some absolute quality of a body. The masses of bodies, however, still change with motion; but going farther in the same direction, the *general* theory of relativity succeeds in prescribing a combination of space, time and mass measurements that is independent of motion altogether and so—for the time being, at any rate—can pose as an aspect of an external world of which physical measurements provide a quantitative description. From the philosophical point of view, however, it would be exceedingly unwise to forget, as pre-relativity physics did, that all such pictures are but an aid to investigation and have no fundamental significance whatever. It has been shown, indeed, that when the phenomenon of radiation is treated in the same manner as the phenomenon of motion, an "entropy-time" emerges which is of precisely similar character to the space-time of mechanics. Neither of these concepts is to be regarded as objective in the way that space and time were formerly thought to be.

The general effect of all this on the philosophy of science has been to emphasize the distinction between the empirical and the rational. It was the theory of relativity that chiefly inspired the Vienna circle, later known as the logical positivist school, to formulate their verification principle, according to which the meaning of any statement is determined by the empirical steps necessary to verify it. Statements that are not susceptible of empirical verifica-

tion (or falsification) are either rational (*i.e.*, tautological) or nonsensical. The absolute simultaneity of separated events is a typical example of a nonsensical concept since it is neither empirically determinable nor a rational necessity.

Precisely the same classification was made by Sir Arthur Eddington, who also was inspired primarily by the relativity theory; but whereas the logical positivists have developed their views in the direction of an analysis of language in general, without special reference to physics, Eddington undertook the detailed examination of physical theory. He was led to the conclusion that the whole scheme of physical law was rational in nature and could have been derived without any experience at all of actual events. In other words, although, as a historical fact, the laws have been derived by studying the results of measurements, they are actually so abstract that they characterize only the nature of the processes of measurement and are therefore independent of the particular results that applications of those processes have yielded.

Eddington's views on this point are not generally accepted, but it must be acknowledged that they are either not understood or misunderstood by the majority of critics—a fact for which Eddington himself is not entirely blameless. His mathematical work is not without error, and his gift for picturesque language led him at times to sacrifice rigour of expression for the sake of a vivid metaphor. He himself advanced, as the crucial argument for his view, the claim that he had derived all the dimensionless constants of physical theory from purely rational considerations; but the derivation involved such a wealth of little-known mathematical processes that a lengthy analysis was required before it could be finally appraised. One common misunderstanding, however, can here be removed: he did not claim that the whole course of physical experience could have been predicted; on the contrary, he held that none of it could. The laws of physics, he believed, were not the laws of behaviour of observed bodies but those of postulated entities. Only when observed bodies were identified with such entities were the laws applicable to them, and any lack of agreement would indicate, not a failure of the laws, but false identification.

BIBLIOGRAPHY.—P. A. Schilpp (ed.), *Albert Einstein: Philosopher-Scientist*, 2nd ed. (1952); A. S. Eddington, *The Philosophy of Physical Science* (1939); H. Dingle, *The Special Theory of Relativity*, 3rd ed. (1950). (H. D.)

RELAXATION PHENOMENA, in physics, are phenomena associated with the approach of a system to equilibrium (*see* PHASE EQUILIBRIA). If a force is suddenly applied to a system and thereafter maintained constant, some time may elapse before the system settles down to a new state of equilibrium. For instance, gas contained in a vessel contracts immediately the pressure applied to it is increased, and becomes warmer in the process; subsequently, as the gas cools to the surrounding temperature, a further slow contraction occurs. A more extreme example of relaxation is to be found in a substance like pitch, which reacts as a solid to forces of short duration, but as a liquid to prolonged stress. In such cases one may consider the system to require a certain characteristic time to stabilize itself, and to exhibit different behaviour according as the duration of the stress is much longer or much shorter than this. If the duration is comparable with the characteristic time, or if the stress is periodic with a comparable period, the failure of the system to achieve internal stability shows itself in hysteresis behaviour of the sort which commonly leads to the degradation of mechanical energy into heat. Some of these typical properties may be examined in more detail with the help of a simple electrical circuit, which serves as a useful model of a relaxing system.

The circuit is shown in fig. 1 and consists of two capacitances,

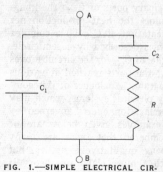

FIG. 1.—SIMPLE ELECTRICAL CIRCUIT ILLUSTRATING A RELAXING SYSTEM (SEE TEXT)

C_1 and C_2, and a resistance R. If a voltage V is applied suddenly (at time $t = 0$) across the terminals AB, the charge that flows will be as represented by the graph in fig. 2; there is an initial immediate flow of C_1V, charging up the condenser C_1, and a slower charge flow amounting in all to C_2V as current flows through R to charge the condenser C_2. This second process is described by an exponential law, the charge on C_2 being given by $C_2V (1 - e^{-t/\tau})$, in which the characteristic time τ (the so-called relaxation time) is equal to C_2R. Now consider the application of an alternating voltage across AB. If the angular frequency ω is low, so that $\omega\tau \ll 1$, the voltage will change sufficiently slowly that there is time for C_2 to receive very nearly as much charge as if the voltage were steady, and under these conditions the circuit will behave like a condenser of capacity $C_1 + C_2$. If, however, the frequency is high, so that $\omega\tau \gg 1$, there will be insufficient time for C_2 to receive any charge before a reversal of the voltage tends to remove it again and therefore C_2 will remain virtually uncharged; thus the circuit will behave like a condenser of capacitance C_1. At intermediate frequencies, when $\omega\tau \sim 1$, the effective value of the capacitance will take intermediate values and there will also be significant heat production by the currents flowing in the resistance. Fig. 3 shows on a logarithmic frequency scale the variation of the effective capacitance and the heat production per cycle; the latter varies in proportion to the frequency at low frequencies, and in inverse proportion at high frequencies. Two points may be particularly observed about the behaviour of this model. The first is that the transition is extended over a wide band of frequencies, i.e., values of $\omega\tau$ ranging between $\frac{1}{10}$ and 10; the second is that the height of the peak representing resistive losses is directly related to the difference between low- and high-frequency capacitances. This is particularly clearly shown by a graph of the (complex) effective capacitance of the circuit. If the impedance Z between A and B is used to define formally the effective capacity C_{eff} by the equation $Z = 1/i\omega C_{\text{eff}}$ the two curves in fig. 3 represent the real and imaginary parts of C_{eff}; the imaginary part is resistive and determines the heat production per cycle. In fig. 4 is shown a representation of C_{eff} on a complex diagram, where the whole variation is described by a semicircle. As the frequency is increased the value of C_{eff} for the circuit moves anticlockwise from $C_1 + C_2$ to C_1; the parts reached at various frequencies are indicated on the diagram. Analogues of this complex diagram are observed in many physical systems, which may be inferred therefrom to exhibit relaxation effects governed by a simple exponential law. The examples given below are of this type, but it should be remembered that there are many more complicated examples showing qualitatively similar, but not identical, behaviour, for which a more elaborate theory is needed.

Systems of which the above circuit is a helpful model are to be found in almost all branches of physics, but perhaps particularly in the fields of elasticity and acoustics. One of the most famous examples concerns the propagation of ultrasonic waves in gaseous carbon dioxide (CO_2). The velocity of sound in a gas is expressed by the formula $\bar{v}\sqrt{\gamma/3}$, in which $\bar{v}$ is the root mean square velocity of the molecules and γ is the ratio of the principal specific heats C_p/C_v; since $C_p - C_v$ is equal to R, the gas constant, γ may also be related to C_v by the formula $C_v = R/\gamma - 1$.

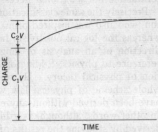

FIG. 2.—CHARGE FLOW WHEN VOLTAGE IS APPLIED TO TERMINALS AB OF FIG. 1

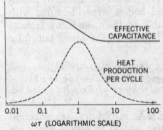

FIG. 3.—VARIATION OF EFFECTIVE CAPACITANCE AND HEAT PRODUCTION PER CYCLE

Alternating voltage across AB of fig. 1

Now it is found experimentally that sound waves of a frequency less than 2 kc. per second travel at a velocity of 268 m. per second in pure CO_2, while if the frequency is greater than 200 kc. per second the velocity is increased to 280 m. per second. Since $\bar{v}$ does not depend on the frequency this result may be interpreted to mean that the effective value of γ, or C_v, depends on the frequency. In fact the low-frequency value of C_v determined by this argument is 6.85 cal. mole^{-1} degrees^{-1} and the high-frequency value 4.95 cal. mole^{-1} degrees^{-1}. The latter value is almost precisely that predicted by the Maxwell-Boltzmann Law for a gas molecule having five degrees of freedom, and herein is an interpretation of the experiment. When a portion of the gas is alternately compressed and expanded by the passage of the wave, kinetic energy is transmitted to or extracted from the molecules by collisions—in other words, on adiabatic compression the gas is heated. This kinetic energy is taken up immediately in translational energy of the molecules, and by collision is shared almost as quickly with the rotational motions of the molecules. If enough time is allowed, ultimately some of this energy will be transmitted to the vibrational motions of the atoms constituting the molecule, but this takes much longer. The main reason is that the vibrational motions are quantized and energy can be exchanged only in units of $h\nu$, where ν is the vibrational frequency involved; in CO_2 all the quanta $h\nu$ of the various vibrations are several times higher than the mean kinetic energy of the molecules, so that only the rare collisions between exceptionally energetic molecules are effective in transferring energy. There is thus a characteristic relaxation time τ, about 10^{-5} sec. in pure CO_2 at room temperature, for imparting energy to the vibrations. If the angular frequency ω of the wave motion is such that $\omega\tau \ll 1$, the vibrational modes are able to come into thermal equilibrium with the external (translational and rotational) modes, and the value of C_v reflects about seven degrees of freedom. But if $\omega\tau \gg 1$, the vibrational modes are unable to exchange energy and C_v has a value corresponding to only the five external modes. The analogy between the internal and external modes in this example, and the capacitances C_1 and C_2 in the model analyzed above, should be obvious. At a frequency of 20 kc. per second, when $\omega\tau \sim 1$, the peak of resistive loss in the model is paralleled by a peak of attenuation of the sound wave; the energy in the sound wave is halved in a distance of only $5\frac{1}{2}$ wave lengths, or $7\frac{1}{2}$ cm. (See also CHEMISTRY: Physical Chemistry: The Maxwell-Boltzmann Law.)

Many other examples of this type of relaxation have been studied, as well as a similar type associated with structural rearrangements, particularly in liquids and solids. Detailed discussions of many will be found in the references below, but one example must suffice here, elastic relaxation of certain cubic metals containing dissolved impurities. When carbon dissolves in tantalum, the atoms occupy interstitial sites which may be said to be of three kinds, according as the nearest tantalum atom lies in the x, y or z direction, these three directions defining the cube axes of tantalum. As long as the tantalum is unstrained, there is no preference among sites, which are all equally likely to be occupied; but if the tantalum be compressed along the x-axis, the x-sites are deformed differently from the y- and z-sites, and in equilibrium the two types of site will become differently occupied by the migration of carbon atoms toward the preferred sites. The deformation resulting from a given compressional force now depends on whether enough time is given for migration to occur. In fact fig. 2 may be interpreted as a schematic graph of the deformation due to a constant force, while the curves of fig. 3 serve to represent the variation of compressibility and elastic loss with frequency when a periodic force is applied. The relaxation time

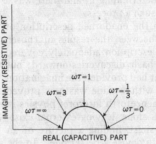

FIG. 4.—EFFECTIVE CAPACITANCE OF THE SYSTEM IN COMPLEX PLANE

Data in Fig. 3 have been replotted with $\omega\tau$ entering as a parameter

τ is related to the time taken by carbon atoms to diffuse from site to site and is highly temperature-dependent according to the law $\tau \propto e^{H/RT}$, where H is a heat of activation. Thus if the frequency is kept constant and the temperature varied, $\log(\omega\tau) = \text{constant} + H/RT$ and a plot of elastic behaviour against $1/T$ should look like fig. 3. This is shown in fig. 5, from the scale of

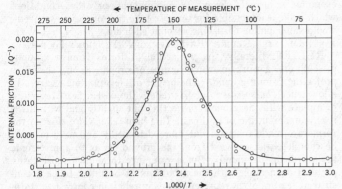

FROM T.-S. KÊ, "THE PHYSICAL REVIEW," VOL. 74 (1948)

FIG. 5.—VARIATION WITH TEMPERATURE OF ELASTIC LOSS IN TANTALUM DUE TO 0.013% DISSOLVED CARBON

which it may be immediately deduced that H for this diffusion process is 25,000 cal. per molecule. Relaxation peaks of this nature are found in many solids and are often the most sensitive way of detecting the presence of certain impurities; *e.g.*, it is possible to trace one part in a million of carbon in iron. Finally, it should be mentioned that exactly analogous phenomena are observed when sound waves pass through mixtures of substances in chemical equilibrium, when oscillatory electric fields are applied to metals and to many dielectric substances and when oscillatory magnetic fields are applied to many paramagnetic substances. Detailed study of these provides information on the rate at which equilibrium is attained and hence may suggest the mechanisms that are operative in establishing the state of equilibrium.

BIBLIOGRAPHY.—C. M. Zener, *Elasticity and Anelasticity of Metals* (1948); H. Fröhlich, *Theory of Dielectrics* (1958); C. J. Gorter, *Paramagnetic Relaxation* (1947); P. Vigoureux, *Ultrasonics* (1951); B. N. Finkel'stein (ed.), *Relaxation Phenomena in Metals and Alloys* (1963).
(A. B. PI.)

RELIC, in the strict sense, designates the mortal remains of a saint; in the broad sense, it covers also objects that have been in contact with him. The basis of Christian cult veneration of relics is the conception that reverence for the relics redounds to the honour of the saint (relative *dulia, dulia* being the reverence paid to the saint himself). While expectation of favours may accompany the devotion, it is not integral to it.

Christian Church.—The first Christian reference (Acts 19: 12) speaks of handkerchiefs carried from the body of St. Paul to heal the sick. About A.D. 156, the *Martyrdom of Polycarp* describes the bones of the Smyrna bishop as "more valuable than precious stones," yet distinguishes between the love for Polycarp and the worship of Christ. In Western Europe, an epigram of Pope Damasus (366–384) shows saints' remains in the Roman cemetery of Calixtus to have been the object of public cult. Several decades later, the protests of Vigilantius of Aquitaine against relic veneration elicited the retort in 404 of St. Jerome's *Letter CIX* ("We honour the relics of martyrs that we may adore him whose martyrs they are") and in 406 his *Treatise Against Vigilantius*.

In 356 the relics of St. Timothy and in 357 those of SS. Andrew and Luke were translated to the new imperial capital of Constantinople. Sometime before 431, Theodoret of Cyrrhus reports that a single saint's relics were often divided among many villages (*Cure of Pagan Diseases*, viii, 10). At Rome, however, in 594 Pope Gregory the Great refused to divide the relics of St. Paul, consenting only to the distribution of cloths (*brandea*) touched to the remains.

The discoveries, real or reputed, of Christ's cross at Jerusalem (probably 320–337) and of the bodies of SS. Gervasius and Protasius at Milan in 386 and of St. Stephen at Kaphar-Gamala, in Palestine, in 415 contributed to the multiplication of small relics and to an emphasis upon their miraculous possibilities. With Gregory of Tours (d. 594), this emphasis is strong; with Caesarius of Arles (d. 542), it is nil, pointing up the role played by temperament in devotion. Generally, the Middle Ages enlarged the expectation of miracles, while the flood of Oriental relics into Europe at the time of the Crusades raised serious question as to their authenticity and ethical procurement. Problems of this nature had arisen earlier: *c.* 400 St. Augustine had complained of the "hawking about of the limbs of martyrs, if indeed of martyrs." However, as medieval theology was formulated in St. Thomas Aquinas' *Summa theologica* (III, q. 25 a. 6), it hewed close to the Augustinian thesis (*City of God*, i, 13) that it is natural to cherish the remains of the saintly dead and it found sanction for such cult in God's working of miracles in the presence of relics.

The attitude of the 16th-century Reformers toward relics was uniformly negative. In 1537, the Lutheran Schmalkaldic Articles called them "useless" while in 1553 the Anglican Articles of Religion designated their adoration a "fond thing vainly invented."

Roman Catholic thought defined in 1563 at the Council of Trent and currently expressed in the *Codex juris canonici* (c. 1200, c. 1276–89) of 1917 maintains the liceity of relic veneration, requires the presence of relics in consecrated altars, and lays down rules to assure authenticity and to exclude venal practices; excommunication is the punishment for those who sell genuine relics or who manufacture or distribute false ones. Among the relics most widely venerated are the Holy Coat of Trier, of which there are two, one in the Trier Cathedral and one at the parish church at Argenteuil, both believed to be genuine garments of Christ's; Santiago de Compostela, traditionally the burial place of St. James the Apostle; and the Holy House at Loreto, near Ancona, Italy, believed to have been the house inhabited by the Virgin Mary at the time of the Annunciation and to have been miraculously moved from Nazareth to Dalmatia and thence to Loreto in the 13th century.

For the Orthodox Churches, the approbation extended to relic cult by the Eastern Fathers and the second Council of Nicaea in 787 proves normative. In practice, however, Orthodox devotion focuses upon icons rather than upon relics, though the antimension (the cloth upon which the Divine Liturgy is celebrated) always contains a relic.
(H. G. J. B.)

Other Religions.—*Islam.*—Like Christianity, Islam has had a cult of relics associated with its founder and saints. In Islam, however, the use of relics has had no official sanction; indeed, Muslim theologians have frequently denounced the veneration of relics and the related practice of visiting the tombs of saints as conflicting with the Prophet Mohammed's insistence on his own purely human, nondivine nature (Koran iii, 144) and his harsh condemnation of idolatry and the worship of anyone other than God himself (Koran iv, 48 ff., 116 ff.; etc.).

Nonetheless, veneration of relics has found a place in Muslim piety. It is no doubt partly rooted in the ancient and universally found belief that the soul-stuff of a man pervades certain parts of his body, such as his head, saliva, blood, hair, teeth, and fingernails, and that hence his spiritual powers are available to another through the possession of any of these parts, or even of his clothing and other personal belongings. Thus, the Muslim's use of relics is not for the purpose of worship, strictly speaking, but for the securing of a blessing, protection against evil, the working of a miracle, or the acquisition of magical power or spiritual grace.

The most highly valued relics are those of the Prophet, among which are hairs from his beard and head, a tooth, a prayer mat, a wine jar, the hilt of his sword, a spear and an arrow said to have been his, his staff and mantle, shoes and shirt, a stone reputedly bearing his foot imprint, and various manuscripts attributed to him.

Buddhism.—Relics have had a greater role in the life of Buddhism than in that of any other of the major non-Christian religions. Moreover, relic worship was canonically established in the religion from its earliest days. Tradition (Mahaparinibbana Sutta) states that the cremated remains of the Buddha (d. 483 B.C.) were distributed equally among eight Indian tribes in response to a demand for his relics. A stupa, or memorial mound, was built over each portion of the sacred remains, as well as over the vessel used for measuring them out and over the collected ashes of the funeral pyre. Another tradition attributes to the great Indian emperor Asoka (3rd century B.C.) the distribution of the Buddha's relics among the 84,000 monasteries he is said to have built after his conversion to Buddhism. Other sources have also recorded the existence of shrines reputedly housing relics of the Buddha or of Buddhist saints and thus serving as important centres of popular pilgrimage and devotion. The Chinese Buddhist pilgrims Fa Hsien (5th century A.D.) and Hsüan-tsang (7th century A.D.), for example, speak of several such places in India and Ceylon, and others are known to have existed in southeast Asia, Tibet, and China.

The most important of the shrines are those that claim some part of the corporeal remains of the Buddha himself. Seven bodily relics (*saririka*) in particular are said to be "the Great Relics" of the Buddha: his four canine teeth, the two collarbones, and frontal bone. Of these the teeth have received the most widespread devotion, a number of shrines having been dedicated to them throughout Asia. Other shrines reportedly have housed certain personal possessions of the Buddha, most notably his alms bowl, which, like the Holy Grail in Christianity, is associated with a romantic tradition of wanderings.

In addition to the bodily remains and personal effects of the Buddha, those of great Buddhist saints and heroes are also venerated. In Tibetan Buddhism worship is accorded the carefully preserved bodies of the deceased priest kings (see DALAI LAMA), who in their lifetimes are regarded as reincarnations of a heavenly being, the Bodhisattva Avalokitesvara.

The intention of relic worship in Buddhism, whether of the Buddha or of a saint, is primarily that of engendering faith and true piety and of acquiring spiritual merit. However, there is also the belief that the supernatural power of the Buddha and the saints continues to work through their relics and the places in which they are deposited, effecting for the worshiper miraculous and magical deeds.

Hinduism.—In Hinduism, although images of divine beings have a major place in popular devotion, the veneration of relics as found in Christianity, Islam, and Buddhism is largely absent. This is largely due to two facts: Hinduism has no historical founder, as do the other three religions, and it tends to regard the world of physical, historical existence as ultimately an illusion (*maya*). Thus, the mortal remains and earthly possessions of religious heroes or holy men are not generally regarded as having particular spiritual value.

A notable exception, however, is found in the person of Chaitanya (*q.v.*), a 16th-century saint of Bengal who is worshiped as an incarnation of the Lord Krishna. A number of statues of Krishna are especially adored in the belief that Chaitanya left the phenomenal realm by "disappearing" into one or the other of them. Moreover several items believed to have been his personal possessions are venerated as holy relics—*e.g.*, an oar, a copy of the sacred scripture the Bhagavad Gita, and a stone reputedly bearing the impress of his body made when he slept upon it one night. In addition, although not in the strictest sense relic worship, the burial places of the remains of certain other holy men (such as Ramakrishna, Mahatma Gandhi, and Sri Aurobindo) are regarded as sacred.　　　　　　　　　　　　　　　　　　　(H. P. S.)

BIBLIOGRAPHY.—*Christian:* U. Mioni, *Il culto delle reliquie nella chiesa cattolica* (1908); E. A. Dooley, *Church Law on Sacred Relics* (1931); H. Delehaye, *Les origines du culte des martyrs,* 2nd ed. (1933); A. Grabar, *Martyrium. Recherches sur le culte des reliques et l'art chrétien antique* (1943–46); H. G. J. Beck, *Pastoral Care of Souls in South-East France During the Sixth Century,* pp. 285–314 (1950); H. Fichtenau, "Zum Reliquienwesen im früheren Mittelalter," *Mitteilungen des Instituts für Österreichische Geschichtsforschung,* vol. lx, 60–89 (1952); G. Gagov, "Il culto delle reliquie nell' antichità riflesso nei due termini patrocinia e pignora," *Miscellanea franciscana,* 58, 484–512 (1958); J. Douillet, *What Is a Saint?* (1958).
Non-Christian: On relics in Islam *see* I. Goldziher, "The Cult of Saints in Islam," *Moslem World,* vol. i, no. 3, pp. 302–312 (1911); S. M. Zwemer, *Studies in Popular Islam* (1939), and "The Hairs of the Prophet," in *Ignace Goldziher Memorial Volume,* part i (1948); E. Dermenghem, *Le Culte des Saints* (1954). In Buddhism, *see* E. Conze, *Buddhism, Its Essence and Development* (1951); C. Eliot, *Hinduism*

and Buddhism, 3 vol. (1921); E. J. Thomas, *The Life of Buddha,* 3rd ed. (1952); L. A. Waddell, *The Buddhism of Tibet,* 2nd ed. (1958); also B. Rowland, *The Art and Architecture of India,* rev. ed. (1959), for discussion of the stupa. For the Chaitanya sect in Hinduism *see* M. T. Kennedy, *The Chaitanya Movement* (1925).

RELIEF, a term used colloquially to designate aid, either public or private, to persons who, because of natural disasters, wars, economic upheaval, chronic unemployment, or other conditions which make it impossible for them to take care of their own needs, would suffer undue hardships without such aid. *See* SOCIAL WELFARE; DISASTER RELIEF; PHILANTHROPY; PENSION; POOR LAW.

RELIEF, literally, the projection of forms from a ground; in sculpture, a work in which figures or ornaments are shown as projecting from a ground. The height of elevation may vary. In a low relief (*basso-rilievo* or bas-relief) the design is more or less of a piece with the ground, projecting but slightly and with little, if any, undercutting of outlines. In a high relief (*alto-rilievo*) the forms are made to stand out more detachedly and may in parts be completely disengaged from the ground, so as to approximate sculptures in the round. But a reference to and, in most cases, physical connection with the ground must be taken to be a constituent feature of all representations in relief, in contrast to statuary which is not related to any ground and can be viewed from all sides. The 19th century tendency to employ the term "bas-relief" indiscriminately for all kinds of relief, high as well as low, is unjustified linguistically and seems now to be subsiding.

Rarer forms of relief are the "sunk reliefs," especially of ancient Egypt, where the forms are carved in and beneath the surrounding ground rather than rising from it. Intaglio, likewise, is a hollow relief, but carved as a negative image like a mold instead of a positive form. Actually the most common use of intaglio is in engraved seals of precious stones or metal, designed to produce a positive imprint when pressed into a plastic material such as heated wax. However, intaglio techniques may also be used without such a purpose; *e.g.*, in the decoration of transparent materials such as glass.

Modes of representation and composition in relief are always determined by their dependence on the ground plane from which the forms emerge, or on which they are superimposed. In this important respect reliefs are more nearly related to painting than to the detached roundness of statuary. Ancient Egyptian art, which differentiated the various branches of art in the most systematic manner, from the beginning applied the same basic principles of representation to reliefs as to painting. Usually the design stands out from the ground in very low relief, however carefully modeled. Figures are shown sidewise, standing on base lines, and precisely outlined in conformity to the plane surface from which they are carved. As to their methods of representation, and regardless of their materials—wood, soft stones, hard stones or metal—they must therefore be classified with painting. Similar observations are true of other early arts, like those of Mesopotamia and the ancient near east.

High reliefs first became common in Greek art; notable examples are the Attic tomb reliefs, with individual figures or family groups shown almost in the round, of the 4th century B.C. On the whole the Greek reliefs, also, follow rather closely the development of contemporary painting. Sculptured friezes were often used in architectural decoration. A doubt may arise regarding the famous pedimental sculptures of Greek classical temples which are composed of large figures worked singly, and not physically connected with the ground, thus resembling free statues. (*See* GREEK ART; OLYMPIA; PARTHENON; etc.)

However, since these figures were placed in the pediments and consequently not seen freely but against a background wall, their compositions must in effect be regarded as a kind of high reliefs. Likewise in Roman art (*q.v.*), the pictorial character of the reliefs is undeniable. A rich field of study for the relation between ground and figures in classical reliefs can be found in the numerous sculptured sarcophagi which constitute one of the most representative achievements of Roman art during the 2nd and 3rd centuries A.D. Excellent examples of ancient relief are also available in the minor arts, both of Greece and Rome, especially in silver and ivory. (*See* SILVER AND GOLD WORK.) Moreover the rapid expansion of the classical style in and beyond the Mediterranean area after the Hellenistic period gave rise to a flowering art of relief sculpture in the far east, first of all in the religious art of India.

It appears as a natural consequence of the classical tradition that during the early middle ages, a period which generally exhibits a marked preference for painting over statuary, the emphasis in sculpture was definitely on relief work. This statement holds good of Byzantine no less than western art. Not only does a wealth of very fine reliefs appear in the minor arts, Byzantine as well as western medieval, but French Romanesque art, especially, reached a new height of relief sculpture in architectural decoration. Some of the most outstanding examples of medieval art are among the Romanesque portals ("tympana"), sculptured capitals of columns and other reliefs decorating the ecclesiastic buildings of France, England and other European countries. (See SCULPTURE; SCULPTURE TECHNIQUES.)

The Gothic period continued this tradition, often preferring a higher relief than the Romanesque, in accordance with the renewed interest in statuary typical of the later middle ages. Reliefs were much in demand also for funeral monuments of bronze or stone, a number of which include some of the finest works of the period. The latest examples of Gothic relief art are the frequent carved altars, mostly of wood, and other church furniture of the "international style" shown in churches all over western and central Europe from Spain to Poland. (See WOOD CARVING: *European and American.*)

During the Italian Renaissance period the status of relief work among the total output of art begins to change. Between painting and statuary the number of reliefs decreases, except perhaps in the minor arts. No longer are certain places traditionally reserved for decoration in relief, as was true of the medieval church buildings. On the other hand the condition of representations in relief now became subjected to new studies and experimentation with a revisory intent, as a task of art different from both painting and statuary. The first striking results of the new trend are the bronze doors which Ghiberti created for the famous baptistery of Florence. Characteristic is the free play between high and low relief, from which a strikingly illusionistic style of composition can be derived, supporting the new interest in space as a subjective, visual experience.

Donatello further exploited these experiments, adding to the interplay of high and low relief the contrasts between rough and smooth surfaces, as well as between forms shown fully modeled and others only indicated in an almost painterly, impressionistic state of incompleteness. As a result, Florentine artists after Donatello pursued for a while two rather different trends regarding the treatment of reliefs. Typical of the one are the delicate and low reliefs in marble and terra-cotta, for which Desiderio da Settignano and Mino da Fiesole became best known. The other, more contrasting trend became incorporated in the relief style of Bertoldo and later, Michelangelo.

Baroque art continued these experiments, often on a very large scale. Characteristic are large compositions—a kind of marble painting—of which the Roman churches, especially, hold many excellent specimens. These compositions, because of their large size and high relief, often approach the effect of *tableaux vivants* shown in deep boxlike frames and special, stagelike conditions of lighting. L. Bernini's "Ecstasy of Sta. Theresa," with figures carved almost fully in the round but encased in a marble altar, in the church of Sta. Maria della Vittoria, Rome, offers a most impressive example.

Neoclassic art of the early 19th century, following a more puritan attitude toward artistic principles, temporarily revived experimentation with low reliefs, relying for effect on fine surface modeling and clarity of design. The works of Antonio Canova and Bertel Thorwaldsen are typical. However, on the whole the Renaissance concept of relief prevailed. Its dramatic and impressionistic possibilities were sensed keenly and employed vigorously by subsequent sculptors of the 19th century such as F. Rude ("The Marseillaise," decorating the Arc de Triomphe in Paris) and later, most famously, Auguste Rodin ("Portal of Hell" and other

reliefs). Relief techniques came to be used in modern art, not only for representational but also for abstract compositions which exploit freely the spatial element as well as the contrasts of light and shade, in reliefs conceived as a succession of overlapping planes. The latter concept, by its nature, often leads to a greater emphasis of the pictorial qualities inherent in relief art. It is typical of this situation that modern painters not infrequently show an interest in the art of relief as did Picasso, among others, during the evolution of his Cubism. *See* SCULPTURE; SCULPTURE TECHNIQUES; *see* also references under "Relief" in the Index.

BIBLIOGRAPHY.—C. R. Post, *A History of European and American Sculpture From the Early Christian Period to the Present Day* (1921); A. Toft, *Modelling and Sculpture*, rev. ed. (1950); A. Miller, *Tradition in Sculpture* (1949). (O. J. BL.)

RELIGION (ARTICLES ON). The article that follows must be considered to represent only a selection, and that somewhat arbitrary, of the *Encyclopædia Britannica* articles on religion. It attempts a logical organization, but logic, too, is sometimes defeated, since subjects of religious or quasi-religious nature overlap one another. This article largely ignores mythology and philosophy, both of which in some aspects are related to religion.

Judaism.—The leading articles are JEWS and JUDAISM, the former concerned chiefly with the history of the Jewish people, the latter with their religion. TALMUD deals with the most important (outside the Bible) Jewish writings, APOCALYPTIC LITERATURE, TARGUM and MIDRASH with other classes of writings. Holy days are discussed in JEWISH HOLIDAYS and SABBATH; LITURGY, JEWISH and SYNAGOGUE are related. JEWISH SECTS DURING THE SECOND COMMONWEALTH is concerned with the factions (Pharisees, Sadducees, etc.) that arose in Judaism in the centuries before and the 70 years after the beginning of the Christian era and that profoundly influenced Christianity as well as later Judaism. Later divisions in Judaism are KARAISM; CABALA; and HASIDISM. Aspects of Jewish history are the concern of the articles ANTI-SEMITISM; DIASPORA; MACCABEES; MARRANO; SANHEDRIN; SCRIBES; and SEPHARDIM, ASHKENAZIM, AND ORIENTAL JEWS, among others. Articles of Jewish interest that are only indirectly related to religion are HEBREW LANGUAGE; HEBREW LITERATURE; JEWISH ART; JEWISH PHILOSOPHY; YIDDISH LANGUAGE; and YIDDISH LITERATURE.

Christianity.—The Christian religion is dealt with exhaustively, beginning with the leading articles CHRISTIANITY and JESUS CHRIST, going on to APOSTLE; CHURCH: *The Religious Community;* EARLY CHRISTIAN CHURCH; COUNCIL, which outlines the controversies within the early and medieval church; ARIANISM, HOLY SPIRIT, NESTORIUS, MONOPHYSITES, TRINITY, etc., which are concerned with these controversies; and the heretical and schismatic movements that also were related—*e.g.*, ADOPTIONISM; MONARCHIANISM; SABELLIANISM; MONTANISM; DONATISTS; PELAGIUS. The basic articles on the church in the Middle Ages are ROMAN CATHOLIC CHURCH; PAPACY; COUNCIL; MONASTICISM; and articles on the great religious orders that arose during those centuries—*e.g.*, AUGUSTINIAN HERMITS; BENEDICTINES; CARMELITES; CARTHUSIANS; CISTERCIANS; FRANCISCANS. Also significant to the medieval period are articles on such divergent bodies as BOGOMILS; CATHARI; WALDENSES.

Christian Churches.—REFORMATION is the leading article on that subject, and the history of the Reformation is also discussed in LUTHERANISM; PRESBYTERIANISM; REFORMED CHURCHES; ENGLAND, CHURCH OF; CONGREGATIONALISM; and PURITANISM. Movements for ecclesiastical change that preceded the Reformation proper are the subjects of LOLLARDS and HUSSITES; Christian humanism is discussed in RENAISSANCE. METHODISM and BAPTISTS deal with major Protestant movements that arose after the Reformation, and there are articles on all the modern Protestant churches of substantial size. Religious bodies that fall outside the main stream of the Protestant Reformation are the concern of (for example) JEHOVAH'S WITNESSES; SALVATION ARMY, THE; UNITARIANISM; LATTER-DAY SAINTS, CHURCH OF JESUS CHRIST OF.

ROMAN CATHOLIC CHURCH and PAPACY are the main articles

on Roman Catholicism. CARDINAL; CONCLAVE; and VATICAN are also dealt with at length. Disputes that arose within the Roman Catholic Church after the Reformation are the subjects of such articles as GALLICANISM; JANSENISM; MODERNISM, ROMAN CATHOLIC; and ULTRAMONTANISM. CATHOLIC ACTION is concerned with contemporary movements of importance. ORDERS AND CONGREGATIONS, RELIGIOUS provides a list of all the Roman Catholic religious orders of men, and there are separate articles on the larger orders and congregations. WOMEN'S RELIGIOUS ORDERS describes the history of the orders of women. CANONIZATION; SAINT; and CANON LAW are among the many other articles that relate chiefly to the Roman Catholic Church. MARONITES discusses these Lebanese Christians, the only Eastern body completely Catholic.

ORTHODOX EASTERN CHURCH, the main article on the church in the east, outlines the reasons behind the east-west schism and refers to other articles on this subject. BYZANTINE EMPIRE also discusses the schism. There are separate articles on national Orthodox churches (e.g., ALBANIA, ORTHODOX CHURCH OF; ORTHODOX CHURCH IN AMERICA; BULGARIAN ORTHODOX CHURCH) and on the four historic patriarchates of Constantinople, Alexandria, Antioch and Jerusalem. Subjects specifically related to the Orthodox Church are HESYCHASM; ICONOCLASTIC CONTROVERSY; and JERUSALEM, SYNOD OF.

The non-Chalcedonian ("Monophysite") Eastern churches are discussed in ANTIOCH, SYRIAN ORTHODOX PATRIARCHATE OF; ARMENIAN CHURCH; and COPTIC CHURCH. NESTORIANS describes this ancient Eastern Christian group, represented now by the Church of the East.

Writings.—The article BIBLE outlines briefly each book of the Bible and indicates the groupings into which the books fall. BIBLE, TRANSLATIONS OF is concerned with that subject, EXEGESIS AND HERMENEUTICS, BIBLICAL with interpretation. There is a separate article on each book of the Bible and standard Apocrypha, and other books are discussed in APOCRYPHA, NEW TESTAMENT and APOCRYPHA, OLD TESTAMENT. Some of the major groups of biblical books are described in, e.g., GOSPELS; PENTATEUCH; PROPHET. Early Christian writings are the subject of the articles APOLOGISTS, EARLY CHRISTIAN and APOSTOLIC FATHERS. There are articles on many subjects of interest to Old Testament studies (e.g., DEAD SEA SCROLLS; ISRAEL; ZION), archaeological sites (e.g., CARCHEMISH; ERECH; LACHISH), peoples and geographical regions (e.g., CANAAN; EDOM; KENITES), significant biblical figures (e.g., DAVID; JUDAS ISCARIOT; MOSES; PAUL, SAINT), and specific biblical topics (e.g., ARK; BEATITUDES; DECALOGUE; LORD'S PRAYER; SERMON ON THE MOUNT).

Other.—THEOLOGY, CHRISTIAN is the leading article on that subject, with major articles also on FAITH; FUNDAMENTALISM; LIBERALISM, THEOLOGICAL; MYSTICISM; NEO-ORTHODOXY; ORTHODOXY, PROTESTANT; etc. ATONEMENT; GRACE; INSPIRATION; REDEMPTION and other similar articles deal with basic elements of Christian theology. MINISTRY, CHRISTIAN; EPISCOPACY; CLERGY; HOLY ORDERS; and ORDINATION are among the articles concerned with the clergy. Other ecclesiastical offices are discussed in (among others) ACOLYTE; ARCHDEACON; DEACON; DEACONESS; DEAN. LITURGY, CHRISTIAN outlines the history and use of, and describes, Christian vestments. For priestly vestments see LITURGY, JEWISH. Besides SACRAMENT, there are several articles concerned with the sacraments individually, especially EUCHARIST and BAPTISM, CHRISTIAN.

CHURCH YEAR outlines the Christian liturgical year and provides cross references to separate articles on the important feasts and seasons. Further information about Christian worship is provided in LITURGY, CHRISTIAN; HYMN; and PREACHING. CATECHISM; CREED; and CONFESSIONS OF FAITH, PROTESTANT (along with many separate entries on catechisms and confessions) are concerned with Christian statements of belief. MISSIONS gives the history of Christian evangelistic work.

WORLD COUNCIL OF CHURCHES, THE and ECUMENICAL MOVEMENT deal with modern church reunion activities. NATIONAL COUNCIL OF CHURCHES and FREE CHURCH FEDERAL COUNCIL describe two important interdenominational co-operative bodies.

CONVOCATIONS OF CANTERBURY AND YORK; CHURCH COMMISSIONERS; and ECCLESIASTICAL LAW (ENGLISH) have to do with the government and administration of the Church of England.

Ideas of God.—These are discussed especially in DEISM, PANTHEISM and THEISM, as well as AGNOSTICISM and ATHEISM. YAHWEH is concerned with the ancient Hebrew conception of God; BRAHMA AND BRAHMAN with that of the Hindus; and ALLAH with that of the Muslims. DEVIL and SATAN deal with the concept of personified evil in religious systems. DUALISM treats of those systems that postulate the coexistence of two opposite and irreconcilable forces. (For articles on metaphysics, see PHILOSOPHY [ARTICLES ON].)

Other Religions.—The great non-Judaeo-Christian religions of the world today are dealt with in BUDDHISM; CONFUCIANISM; HINDUISM; ISLAM; TAOISM. In addition, there are articles on the major branches of these (e.g., for Islam, ISMA'ILISM, KHARIJITES, SHI'ISM, and SUFISM; for Hinduism, SHAKTISM, SHIVAISM, and VISHNUISM; for Buddhism, TIBETAN BUDDHISM and ZEN). Other religions, existing but less widespread, are the concern of BAHA'I FAITH; DRUZE; JAINISM; PARSEES; SHINTO; SIKHISM. Great religious systems of the past are discussed in BABYLONIA AND ASSYRIA: *Religion;* EGYPT: *History: Ancient Religion;* GREEK RELIGION; MANICHAEISM; MITHRAISM; MYSTERY; ROMAN RELIGION; VEDIC RELIGION; ZOROASTRIANISM; etc. GRANTH; HADITH; JATAKA; KOJIKI; KORAN; MILINDAPANHA; NIHONGI; and SANSKRIT LITERATURE (for Hinduism) are among the numerous articles on sacred scriptures. There are separate articles on the major deities of the polytheistic religions.

Among articles on subjects of concern to nearly all religions are CREATION, MYTHS OF; ESCHATOLOGY; HEAVEN; HELL; MYTH; PRAYER; FEAST AND FESTIVAL; PRIESTHOOD; SACRIFICE; SOUL.

Primitive Religion.—The basic article is RELIGION, PRIMITIVE. Among other articles concerned with aspects of religion commonly called primitive are: ANCESTOR WORSHIP; ANIMAL WORSHIP; ANIMISM; FETISHISM; HUMAN SACRIFICE; MAGIC, PRIMITIVE; PASSAGE RITES; SHAMANISM; and TOTEMISM.

More or less organized "primitive" religions are discussed in CARGO CULTS; GHOST DANCE; NATIVISTIC MOVEMENTS; PEYOTISM; SECRET SOCIETIES, PRIMITIVE; SUN DANCE; and VOODOO.

RELIGION, man's relation to that which he regards as holy. The "holy" need not be thought of as supernatural, much less as personal; and if the word "god" be defined in personal or supernatural terms, it follows that religion includes far more than the relation to God or a god. Similarly, the term "relation" to the holy may be conceived of in a variety of forms. Worship (q.v.) is probably the most basic of these, but moral conduct, right belief, and participation in religious institutions are generally also constituent elements of the religious life as practised by believers and worshipers and as commanded by religious sages and scriptures.

An outline and summary of information about religion appears in RELIGION (ARTICLES ON). Particular religions are treated in separate articles, such as BUDDHISM, CHRISTIANITY, CONFUCIANISM, HINDUISM, ISLAM, JUDAISM, and the like. RELIGION, PRIMITIVE deals with religious phenomena as they concern primitive cultures. The present article is concerned merely with the definition and description of religion as a characteristic of human life.

Man, it has been said, is incurably religious. This is an epigrammatic and slightly facetious statement of the most impressive feature of religions, viz., their wide distribution. All through human history as we know it and all through present-day societies as we know them, there appears some such relation to what is regarded as holy. To cover all these phenomena, however, the definition of religion must be so comprehensive as to become ambiguous, if not even meaningless. The very etymology of the word suggests this ambiguity. Since ancient times there has been discussion of whether "religion" comes from *relegere*, "to read again," or from *religare*, "to bind." Each successive broadening of man's physical horizon through exploration and discovery, moreover, has necessitated a redefinition of religion to include unfamiliar phenomena and to exclude features that had been part of the older definition because of a generalization based on acquaintance with too few forms of the religious life.

Thus the experience of Western men with primitive societies during the 16th and 17th centuries brought about a reconsideration of what had been thought to be the content of the natural law, the irreducible minimum of moral precepts common to all men. Western confrontations with Confucianism and with certain forms of Buddhism made it clear that theism (*q.v.*) as traditionally understood in the West is by no means a universal tenet among the world religions. During the latter part of the 19th century, therefore, students of world religions were beginning to despair of finding any universals at all. In 1917 Rudolf Otto (*q.v.*) introduced the category of "the holy" as a possible universal. Although Otto's interpretation of the category did not satisfy everyone, the category itself did gain wide acceptance as a designation for the distinctive content of religious feeling. Admittedly, Otto, who was intent upon making a case for the autonomy of religion, slighted both its communal character and its diffusion throughout a culture. Nevertheless, every religion has at least some of these elements: rituals to perform, formulas to recite, tales to narrate, objects to manipulate, places to frequent or avoid, holy days to keep, natural phenomena by which to predict the future, charismatic leaders to follow, truths to affirm, a literature to ponder, precepts to obey. Vary though they undoubtedly do in content, most of these elements are sacred to most religions, and the study of religion must consider all of them—and more.

To be religious, then, is to be related to the holy in one or more of these ways. Probably the most nearly universal among them, as suggested above, is worship, if such activities as prayer, sacrifice, contemplation, magic, and incantation are included in that term. Primitive religion is replete with instances of traditions in which there is little or no doctrine as such but many prescriptions of proper ritual. Ancient Roman official religious observance was separate from personal commitment and private morality in ways that adherents of Judaism and Christianity have found incomprehensible. If worship is obligatory, there must be a right way and a wrong way to perform it; a mistake in religious language or sacred gesture may invalidate the worship or jeopardize its effectiveness for petition, atonement, or thanksgiving. Failure to prepare adequately through fasting, etc., may profane the observance. Worship is frequently tied to specific times and locations, to holidays and festivals, seedtime and harvest, puberty and marriage, birth and death. The religious leader is commonly the functionary in worship, be he priest or shaman or medicine man (*see* PRIESTHOOD; SHAMANISM). When a religion traces its origin to a founder, he is often credited with having established and prescribed the proper forms of worship or sometimes with having purified traditional forms. The fundamental place of worship in religion is evident also in its durability: men may continue going through the motions of religion long after they have transferred their personal loyalty and trust to objects other than those of the traditional observance.

Closely associated with worship is conduct. Though it is possible to separate ritual observance from moral conduct, worship has so generally implied "being right with" the object of worship that in widely separated religions the religious man has been thought of as the one who followed a certain way of life. (In Western Christian usage, indeed, "religious" came to be synonymous with "monastic," in the sense of being bound by a vow to the observance of the way of life prescribed by a particular community.) Thus Buddhism developed its Noble Eightfold Path, Judaism its Ten Commandments, Parseeism its requirement of charitable acts. In the course of its history a religion has often been obliged to reinterpret its ancient moral commandments in the light of new experiences or unforeseen problems. Many of the most bitter controversies in the history of religions have been fought by strict constructionists who adhered to traditional prescriptions and by revisionists who sought to adapt both moral and ceremonial requirements to the changing situation. At times, interpreters of religion have virtually equated all of religion with its moral imperatives, reducing its other constituents to supports for the ethical. Eventually any such reduction has demonstrated its own inadequacy as a description of the full scope and the profound subtleties of the religious experience of individuals and communities. Even this reductionism indicates the crucial role of the moral consciousness in the determination of man's relation to what he regards as holy. (*See* also ETHICS, COMPARATIVE.)

Among scholarly interpreters of religion in the West, where the "science of religion" (German *Religionswissenschaft*) began, the Christian preoccupation with dogma (*q.v.*) has helped stimulate a concentration on comparisons between the teachings of the various religions about God, man, creation, sin, immortality, etc. An important outcome of this concentration has been the collection and translation of Oriental scriptures in such multivolume sets as *The Sacred Books of the East*, edited in 51 volumes by F. Max Müller, a pioneer in comparative philology and in the comparative study of religion. Religions that lack scriptures in the formal sense are usually endowed with mythology, in which some scholars have claimed to be able to discern a primordial form of doctrinal belief (*see* MYTH). To students of non-Western religion who have approached Oriental scriptures and myths without this theological predilection, the comparison of doctrines has often appeared to be an artificial superimposition of alien Western categories on the material and too one-sidedly cerebral account of the meaning in religious language and action. In reaction against the method of the comparative study of doctrine, historians of religion have preferred to investigate each religion on its own terms, leaving comparison to a later stage of research and reflection. Nevertheless, the practice of a religious cult or the recitation of a myth does seem to imply at least that what is being enacted or affirmed is a revelation of divine truth, whether literal or symbolic. And at some stage in the development of many religions, such implied beliefs have been brought to the level of explicit statement and critical examination and thus to the status of doctrine.

The theological, literary, and philosophical orientations of earlier generations of scholars gave way, during the 20th century, to the growing dominance of the new methods of the social sciences, especially those of anthropology, sociology, and psychology. The fundamental insights of these disciplines into the place of religion within the total life of man have significantly affected the interpretation of religious phenomena, including the interpretation underlying the present article. This shift of emphasis has rendered such ideas as Otto's definition of the autonomy of religion extremely questionable, but it has also directed attention away from the almost exclusive concern with the individual and his beliefs and experiences to the social function of religion in a family, a tribe, or a culture. William James said that religion is the "experiences of individual men in their solitude"; Émile Durkheim maintained that religion is "essentially social." The social embodiment of religion in corporate activities and institutions became the centre of interest. Religion thus became a matter of one's membership and participation in those activities and institutions, not simply in the sense of being a "joiner" but in the sense of finding one's own identity and that of one's group in the structures of the religious tradition, which hallow, celebrate, and judge the entire culture. When this social dimension is included in the definition and study of religion, the other aspects come into a new perspective and into new connections with one another; for example, myth and ritual illuminate each other when both are seen in their corporate context.

As the interest of the social sciences in religious phenomena proves, religion is too important to be left solely to interpretation by philosophers, theologians, and religionists. Several explanations of religion by thinkers in other fields are sufficiently widespread to warrant mention in even so brief an article as this. Many historians have tended to see religion as a sort of primitive science, as, for example, astrology preceded astronomy; religion is then interpreted as an attempt to explain by means of symbols what empirical scientific study describes in the nonaffective language of precise measurement. The familiar remark of Karl Marx that religion is "the opium of the people" was an expression of his observation that "religion is the sigh of the oppressed creature, the feelings of a heartless world." Sigmund Freud redefined the nature of religion in the light of his theories about human nature and development, concluding that in religion God "really is the father, clothed in the grandeur in which he once appeared to the small child. . . . [One] therefore looks back to the memory-image of the overrated father of his childhood, exalts it into a deity, and brings it into the present and into reality." Carl Jung revised Freud's theories in the direction of discovering and tracing the symbols and "archetypes" in which men, individually and collectively, find explanations for the mystery and meaning of their lives. These and other analyses of the data of religion suggest that man's relation to that which he regards as holy, as that relation is expressed in ritual, in ethics, in belief, and in institutions, continues to be a matter of interest both to those who profess a religious faith and to those who profess to have none.

See also references under "Religion" in the Index.

BIBLIOGRAPHY.—*Classic Discussions of the Nature of Religion:* William James, *The Varieties of Religious Experience,* the Gifford Lectures for 1901–02, published in 1902 and several times since; Rudolf Otto, *Das Heilige* (1917; Eng. trans., *The Idea of the Holy,* 1923). *The History of the Idea of Religion and Comparative Study of Religion:* Henri Pinard de la Boullaye, *L'Étude comparée des religions,* vol. i (1922). *Summaries of Research:* Gerardus van der Leeuw, *Religion in Essence and Manifestation* (1933; Eng. trans., 1938, reissued with additions 1963); Joachim Wach, *The Comparative Study of Religions* (1958), *Sociology of Religion* (1944); Mircea Eliade, *Patterns in Comparative Religion* (1958), *The Sacred and the Profane* (1959).

(J. J. PN.)

RELIGION, PRIMITIVE. "Primitive religion" as a descriptive and qualitative definition of the early forms of man's religious life took its place in the vocabulary of the history of religions and anthropology as a result of the work of two great scholars, Sir E. B. Tylor and Sir James Frazer. The work of both reflects the desire that motivated much of the early research into the phenomena of primitive religion: to understand the origin of religion in human history. "Origin" was understood in at least two senses: as the beginning, the first or earliest form of religion, and as the basic, elementary form of religion.

To Tylor's "minimum definition" of religion as "the belief in spiritual beings" many objections have been raised because of its incompleteness. It does not include ritual or ceremony, and Tylor's notion of "spiritual being" does not cover adequately the relationship between the spiritual and material or quasi-material realities that are prevalent in primitive religions. Frazer, in *The Golden Bough,* seems to supplement Tylor when he proposes the definition of religion as "a propitiation or conciliation of powers superior to man which are believed to direct and control the course of nature and of human life." He explains further: "Thus defined, religion consists of two elements, a theoretical and a practical, namely, a belief in powers higher than man and an attempt to propitiate or please them."

Frazer's definition seems to include religious expression as well as attitude. Nonetheless, he has some difficulty in separating religion from magic when he deals with empirical expressions, though he makes a very precise theoretical distinction between the two. By "powers" he means "conscious or personal agents." Magic practice assumes that the course of nature is determined "by the operation of immutable laws acting mechanically." On the contrary, religious belief and practice assumes that the course of nature is elastic or variable and that the conscious beings who control it can change its course for the benefit of the worshiper. Frazer believed that magic constituted a stage of development prior to the advent of religion. (*See* further MAGIC, PRIMITIVE; PRAYER.)

Frazer's difficulty in disentangling the magical from the religious points to one of the major objections to his general orientation as well as to that of Tylor. Both, by emphasizing belief as the most important element in the religious attitude, are hard put to deal with the many practices, rites, and ceremonies which, though closely related to belief, cannot be adequately understood as arising directly from it. Tylor explained these phenomena as the result of a mistaken association of ideas among primitive peoples; Frazer relegated them to the arena of magic. Their definitions of religion, therefore, are to be accepted, if at all, as definitions of type, selective designations of some features of primitive religion, but not universally applicable.

Objections have also been raised to the philosophical and historical implications in the theories of Tylor and Frazer. Their assumption that the mind of primitive man is illogical and confused, or that its operations are radically different from those of

other men, is no longer held to be true by the majority of anthropologists and historians of religion. The further assumption that present-day primitive peoples have no history has been conclusively disproved.

The argument for continued use of the term "primitive religion" thus must be made on the grounds of practicality alone—an acceptable replacement has not been found. In the article below, "primitive" will be taken to have reference to those cultures that are prior in time to the advent of the large cultural complexes called civilizations or that, though contemporary with, have not been decisively affected by "civilization."

To take account of the great mass of data in these cultures, a more comprehensive definition of religion is also needed. Such a definition is suggested by E. Crawley in *The Tree of Life,* where he points out that "neither the Greek nor the Latin language has any comprehensive term for religion, except in the one *hiera* and in the other *sacra,* words which are equivalent to 'sacred.' No other term covers the whole of religious phenomena, and . . . no other conception will comprise the whole body of religious facts." An important consequence of thus giving the study of primitive religion the wide scope of comparative hierophany is that magic no longer must be divorced from religion, since the sacred will now be found coextensive with the magico-religious. Rudolf Otto concurs with this sentiment: "*Religion is itself present at its commencement:* religion, nothing else, is at work in these early stages of mythic and daemonic experience" (*The Idea of the Holy,* Eng. trans., 2nd ed., p. 132; London: Oxford University Press, 1950). A similar judgment is expressed by Mircea Eliade when he admits that any attempt at a definition of religion must look for the evidence, and, "first and foremost, for those expressions of religion that can be seen in the 'pure state'—that is, those which are 'simple' and as close as possible to their origins." Eliade counters this proposal, however, by the recognition that "Unfortunately, evidence of this sort is nowhere to be found; neither in any society whose history we know, nor among 'primitives,' the uncivilized peoples of to-day." (From *Patterns in Comparative Religion* by Mircea Eliade, © Sheed & Ward Inc., 1958.)

MANIFESTATIONS OF THE SACRED

The manifestation of the sacred is related on the one hand to the particular cultural historical period in which it is apprehended, on the other hand to the specific phenomena through which it makes itself known. Specific religious symbols therefore tend to dominate in specific historical periods and cultural areas.

Myth and ritual constitute the general and almost universal forms of religious response. In the myth, the story of a manifestation of sacredness is related, understood to be a "true story"—*i.e.,* a story of the appearance of that reality which makes it possible for man to understand his world as real (*see* MYTH). It is therefore the basis for the world view, and it provides the pattern for man's orientation and relationship to all the other data of his experience. While a society may relate several types of myths—magical, cultic, etiological—the myth par excellence is the cosmogonic myth, the story of the first creation, which becomes the prototype for all other myths within a society. Often the myth is related to a ritual, the forms of which enable the worshiper to reenact the story. But "myth" should not be restricted to its ritual use or meaning. It is a specific type of perception and response to reality that has religious implications beyond its dramatization in ritual.

The Sacred in Nature.—G. van der Leeuw (*Religion in Essence and Manifestation*) showed that religion did not rise from a "worship of nature" but from the sacred reality in nature. The "manifestation of the sacred in nature" refers to the manner in which animals, plants, the sky, and the landscape reveal modalities of reality to man. Though these phenomena often have utilitarian meaning, this does not explain the religious veneration which is a part of the technique of dealing with them.

The oldest gods in most cultures are sky-gods. The sky expresses that which is eternal, infinite, and transcendent. When it becomes sacralized it becomes a revelation of the power of divine activity. The presence of sky-gods in most primitive religious systems led

Wilhelm Schmidt (*q.v.*) and the "Vienna school" of ethnology to infer a primitive monotheism. But though many primitive religions recognize their existence, sky-gods are, for the most part, *dei otiosi*. They seem to have retired from any direct influence on man, their places being taken by new sacred manifestations. They are called upon only in the most crucial situations and then with great fear and trembling.

Animals constitute another aspect of nature through which, apparently from very ancient times, the sacred has made itself known among primitive peoples. Evidence from prehistoric sites ranging from early Paleolithic through Neolithic times indicates a special veneration of animals. Finds of the early Paleolithic period in western Europe yield a large number of bear skeletons, suggesting that some magico-religious practices may have been involved in the hunting and eating of this animal. Johannes Maringer (*The Gods of Prehistoric Man*) thinks that some elements of an early bear cult remain in the ceremonies of modern primitive peoples of the circumpolar regions, where the bear enjoys special veneration.

Animals are the primary subject of the late Paleolithic cave art that may be found all over western Europe and eastward as far as Siberia and southward to northern Africa (*see* PRIMITIVE ART: *Prehistoric Europe*). These paintings represent animals, usually reindeer or antelope, sometimes in herds, sometimes singly, often the victims of hunters' arrows. It is possible to understand this art as part of a magico-religious complex bound up with the hunting culture. Though it is of course impossible to make any firm assertions about the thoughts of prehistoric peoples, it seems safe to say that the cave paintings probably were intended to make the game animal more accessible to the hunter and may also have expressed an identification of the hunter with the animal. In the cave of Les Trois Frères at Montesquieu Avantès (Ariège) the famous painting of the sorcerer shows a figure with a long beard, the eyes of an owl, the antlers of a stag, the ears of a wolf, the claws of a lion, and the tail of a horse—a composite of several animals that can hardly be explained except in religious terms.

Understanding of prehistoric man, knowledge of whom is entirely dependent on archaeological finds, may be supplemented at least inferentially by studying forms similar to the prehistoric among modern primitives. Among these, the phenomenon of totemism is instructive. It exhibits two primary features: (1) the existence of a human group is inextricably bound up with a particular animal (the totem); and (2) various tabus surround the totem. Totemism—and likewise, it may be inferred, the cave art of prehistoric man—represents a recognition that there is sacred power in the animal and that man's life is materially and spiritually linked with its life. (*See* further TOTEMISM.)

The Sacred in Plants.—The life of plants presents another important level of nature through which the sacred makes itself known. The Paleolithic hunting cultures, it is suggested, apprehended the sacred within a magico-religious complex emphasizing the wild animal. Man's discovery of agriculture (*see* AGRICULTURE: *World Agriculture: Origins of Agriculture*) produced a new structure of the sacred, the power of which now came to exhibit itself in the life of plants and to take the form of fertility, in plants and in the life of man. Within this religious structure the suffering god (Adonis, Attis, Osiris, as Frazer showed, but there were others as well) also appears: for if the sacred is homologized to the life of plants, then representatives of the sacred power must undergo death and resurrection.

With the domestication of animals, a new veneration of certain forms of animal life also was produced, and the bull, a symbol of fecundity, appears with the various symbols of the mother-goddess in religious rituals involving sacred marriage.

It must be emphasized that the natural phenomenon of agriculture is not responsible in itself for this new religious orientation; rather it is the religious experience apprehended within the context of the "new world" created by the advent of agriculture. This religious structure may be traced throughout the history of the world's cultures from the time of the agricultural revolution. Among modern primitives traces still remain. The cosmic duality of sky and earth, found today in Africa, America, and Oceania,

demonstrates how the old sky-gods, with the discovery of the sacred in the life of plants, took on the new religious structure involving sexuality and fertility. The earth, in the form of a mother goddess, now becomes the creator and sacred ground of all beings. This discovery, coupled with the sedentary character of life made possible by agriculture, gave rise also to the veneration of geographical places.

Sacred Representations in Man.—Man is both repelled and attracted by the manifestation of the sacred. Attracted, he wishes to participate more fully in the power revealed. In modern primitive societies a number of forms of human bearers of power, who act as mediators of the sacred to the entire community, may be catalogued, but the most pervasive are the king or chief and the medicine man or shaman.

The king or chief in primitive society holds hereditary office, his lineage usually extending back into the mythological past and his oldest ancestor usually being identified with the first man. The king represents the power that gives reality to the existence of the society, and he is therefore responsible if a catastrophe occurs, if the crops are bad. His person and all persons or objects related to him are sacred and hedged in by tabus. (*See* further KING: *Theory of the Divine King*.)

The king possesses his office not because he is a religious virtuoso but because of his lineage. The other important human representation of the sacred is based on the representative's personal religious experience. The medicine man or shaman is a manipulator of power, to which he claims direct access either through divination or through a specific type of religious experience of which only he is capable. Among Eskimos, American Indians, and Siberians, the shaman's power rivals that of the chief. (*See* further SHAMANISM; PRIESTHOOD.)

The Sacred in Community.—The avenues of sacred power issuing in kings, shamans, and medicine men are open only to the "elect." But the ordinary man in the primitive community also apprehends the sacred realities within the important events of the common life, the events called by Arnold van Gennep the transitional rites (*rites de passage*), including birth, initiation, naming, the outbreak of war, and death and burial. All these events represent periodic irruptions of sacred power within the community, and appropriate ceremonies always accompany them. With the possible exception of the ceremony accompanying the outbreak of war, all the transitional rites are initiatory—that is, they reveal to the novice a new, sometimes esoteric meaning of the sacred. Every birth is a paradigm of the birth of the first man and the sacred life given to him by the gods. In puberty rites, the mystery of sexuality is revealed; the novice assumes his role as a man and is given a name. In death and burial rites, the community prepares man for the mysteries of the afterlife. Among many primitive peoples life may almost be described as a continuous initiation. (*See* further PASSAGE RITES.)

Outside ceremonial activities, religion plays an important role in the ordering of primitive societies. Religious groups may be coterminous with natural groups, or they may be created by specific religious experience. Where the religious group is coterminous with the family, as is common in West Africa, there is usually a family cult with a member of the family as cult leader. The most prevalent form of specifically religious group in primitive culture, however, is the secret society, founded on a new, esoteric revelation of the sacred to the initiated. (*See* also SECRET SOCIETIES, PRIMITIVE.) Religion thus may be seen as one of the primary factors affecting social differentiation in primitive societies.

ASPECTS OF THE SACRED

Though in primitive religion varieties of gods, tricksters, malevolent beings, fetishes, and magico-religious practices are met with, the comprehensive reality is the reality of the sacred, the reality defined by Otto as "the holy." The religious attitude engendered by the encounter with this reality is "numinous," which may be analyzed into two dialectical feelings: the *mysterium tremendum*, the element of awe and dread; and the *mysterium fascinans*, the feeling of fascination, wonder, and attraction. (*See* also OTTO, RUDOLF.) It is possible, however, to analyze the sacred into more specific categories, outlined below.

The Sacred as Powerful.—The sacred always manifests itself as power, as seen in the notion of *mana* among the Melanesians (*see* MANA) and in similar conceptions, such as the *orenda* of the Iroquois and *wakanda* of the Sioux. Though *mana* is often understood to be impersonal—in the sense of its arbitrariness—it always manifests itself in some person or thing, endowing that person or thing with the efficacious power that resides in the sacred. This power is often identified as the "vital" or life force in all living things. Among the Melanesians *mana* may refer to influence, strength, fame, or anything regarded as extraordinary. However, men and things possess this power only because it has been given to them by more powerful beings.

The Sacred as Dangerous.—The sacred is dangerous because it is powerful. This character is expressed by the Polynesian term *tabu*, meaning that limits are set about the sacred person or object (*see* TABU). Among primitive people all ceremonial activity, the sexual life, the person of king or chief, and certain times and seasons bring into operation an elaborate set of tabus which give recognition to the sacred power manifested in these dimensions of man's existence.

The Sacred as Mystery.—The sacred is mysterious because it is the manifestation of that which is extraordinary, that which cannot be known by ordinary means. Religious knowledge is revealed by the manifestation of the sacred in a specific form to a specific person or people. The totem animal of the Australians, though commonplace in the Australian environment, is at the same time uncanny and unique. It is mysterious precisely because its relation to the totem group is more than a pragmatic economic relationship.

The Sacred as Secret.—Closely related is the notion that the sacred is secret. The literal sense of the term *churinga*, applied by the central Australians to their sacred objects and likewise used more abstractly to denote mystic power (as when a man is said to be "full of *churinga*"), is "secret." This is symptomatic of the esotericism that is a striking mark of Australian and indeed of all primitive religion, with its insistence on initiation and its strictly enforced reticence concerning traditional lore and proceedings. The religious system of a particular tribe may be based on a sacred tribal secret; more esoteric secrets are known by smaller groups within the tribe. There are secrets that are known only by men, others known only by particular groups of men, others known only by those who follow a certain occupation.

THE MEANING OF THE SACRED IN PRIMITIVE SOCIETY

The esoteric character of many of the forms and practices of primitive man has led some scholars to attribute them to a "prelogical mentality," unable to think rationally about the meaning of existence. Lucien Lévy-Bruhl, who originated this interpretation, understood primitive man to employ a "law of mystical participation": primitive man did not recognize the subject-object distinction as a basis for knowledge, but sought knowledge through identifying himself mystically with the phenomenon to be understood. Bronislaw Malinowski, on the other hand, attempted to show that primitive man is able to think rationally and that he employs different modes of thought in dealing respectively with the dimensions of life defined by magic, science, and religion. Though he affirmed the similar functioning of the human mind at all cultural levels, he finally interpreted religion as a necessary, important, but fictional dimension of culture.

Émile Durkheim, in *Elementary Forms of the Religious Life,* introduced the notion of religious symbolism as an interpretation of religious expression. The emphasis on symbolism is important, but by referring it only to the social group Durkheim fails to explain its many other meanings and referents. The religious life of primitives cannot be explained simply in terms of the social group nor by recourse to a theory of prelogical or nonrational mentality. Through the religious symbol a variety of phenomena are ordered to express the quality of ultimacy and absoluteness in the world of man. It reveals a perception of the world different from the ordinary level of experience. Primitive man, understand-

ing the sacred as the real, orients himself toward and participates in this reality through rites and ceremonies. In more highly developed religious systems the expressions are different, but the intent seems to be the same.

In religion man feels that he is in contact with ultimate reality, the power of which has created and continues to support his being. This reality is not apprehended in a general way but is mediated through specific forms and structures. The primary religious symbols of primitive societies define the "world" for the members of the society. Thus the specific symbols of the sacred refer not only to the manifestation of the sacred, or to the social group, but also to the peculiar "existential" stance man assumes in his world. Involved in the notion of the sacred in primitive societies is a complex of ideas—cosmological systems, ideas of time and space, social order, etc. Since the sacred defines the real, all important realities of life participate in the sacred. The pre-eminence of religion and religious symbolism in primitive societies confirms this observation.

See also RELIGION; MORALITY, PRIMITIVE; MYTH; MYTHOLOGY, PRIMITIVE; SOCIAL ANTHROPOLOGY: *Ritual Relations.*

BIBLIOGRAPHY.—*General Theory:* Roger Caillois, *Man and the Sacred,* Eng. trans. (1959); Mircea Eliade, *The Sacred and the Profane,* Eng. trans. (1958).

Structure of Primitive Religious Phenomena: Joseph Campbell, *The Masks of God: Primitive Mythology* (1959); Mircea Eliade, *Patterns in Comparative Religion,* Eng. trans. (1958); Jean Filliozat, *Magie et médecine* (1943); Arnold van Gennep, *The Rites of Passage,* Eng. trans. (1960); J. N. B. Hewitt, "Orenda and a Definition of Religion," *Am. Anthrop.,* n.s., pp. 33–46 (1892); E. A. Hoebel, *The Law of Primitive Man* (1954); Bronislaw Malinowski, *Magic, Science and Religion* (1948) and *Myth in Primitive Psychology* (1926); Rudolf Otto, *The Idea of the Holy,* 2nd ed. Eng. trans. (1950); G. van der Leeuw, *Religion in Essence and Manifestation* (1928); Paul Radin, *The Trickster* (1956); Franz Steiner, *Taboo* (1956); Joachim Wach, *Sociology of Religion* (1944); Hutton Webster, *Magic, a Sociological Study* (1948), *Taboo, a Sociological Study* (1942), and *Primitive Secret Societies* (1932).

Interpretations: Ernest Crawley, *The Tree of Life* (1905) and *The Mystic Rose,* 2nd ed. (1927); Émile Durkheim, *The Elementary Forms of the Religious Life,* Eng. trans. (1926); Sir James Frazer, *The Golden Bough* (1890), 1 vol. abridged ed. (1922), new ed. by Theodor Gaster, *The New Golden Bough* (1959); Lucien Lévy-Bruhl, *How Natives Think,* Eng. trans. (1926); R. R. Marett, *Faith, Hope, and Charity in Primitive Religion* (1932), *Sacraments of Simple Folk* (1933), and *The Threshold of Religion,* 2nd ed. (1909); Marcel Mauss, "Essai sur la nature et la fonction du sacrifice," *L'Année Sociologique,* ii; M. Mauss, *The Gift,* Eng. trans. (1954); Sir E. B. Tylor, *Primitive Culture,* 4th ed. (1903).

Prehistoric Religion: V. G. Childe, *The Dawn of European Civilization,* 6th ed. (1957); W. Koppers, *Primitive Man and His World Picture,* Eng. trans. (1952); Gertrude Levy, *The Gate of Horn* (1948); Johannes Maringer, *The Gods of Prehistoric Man,* Eng. trans. (1960); W. Schmidt, *The Origin and Growth of Religion,* Eng. trans. (1931).

Empirical Studies: Ruth Bunzel, "Introduction to Zuni Ceremonialism," *Annual Report of the Bureau of American Ethnology,* vol. xlvii, p. 467 ff. (1932); R. M. Berndt, *Kunapipi* (1951); R. H. Codrington, *The Melanesians* (1891); Germaine Dieterlen, *Essai sur la religion Bambara* (1951); Roland Dixon, *Oceanic Mythology* (1916); Verrier Elwin, *The Baiga* (1939) and *The Muria and Their Ghotul* (1947); Raymond Firth, *We, the Tikopia* (1936) and *The Work of the Gods in Tikopia* (1940); R. F. Fortune, *Sorcerers of Dobu* (1932); W. B. Spencer and F. J. Gillen, *The Northern Tribes of Central Australia* (1904); Marcel Griaule, *Dieu d'eau* (1948); Melville Herskovits, *Dahomey* (1938); Frederick Kaigh, *Witchcraft and Magic of Africa* (1947); W. Kinitz, "The Indians of the Western Great Lakes," *Occasional Contributions of Museum of Anthropology* (1940); A. L. Kroeber, "Handbook of the Indians of California," *Bureau of American Ethnology Bulletin 78* (1925); M. Leenhardt, *Do Kamo* (1947); Paul Radin, "The Winnebago Tribe," *Annual Report of the Bureau of American Ethnology,* vol. xxxvii, p. 35 ff. (1923); R. S. Rattray, *Ashanti* (1955) and *Religion and Art in Ashanti* (1932); Charles G. and Brenda Z. Seligman, *Pagan Tribes of the Nilotic Sudan* (1932); Placide Tempels, *Bantu Philosophy,* Eng. trans. (1959); R. W. Williamson, *Religious and Cosmic Beliefs of Central Polynesia* (1933). (CH. H. L.)

RELIGIOUS ARCHITECTURE. This article is concerned with the development of Western religious architecture in the 20th century. After a brief introductory account, the countries that have contributed most to this development are examined. For earlier Western religious architecture, *see* BYZANTINE ART AND ARCHITECTURE; ROMANESQUE ART AND ARCHITECTURE; GOTHIC ART AND ARCHITECTURE; RENAISSANCE ARCHITECTURE; BAROQUE AND POST-BAROQUE ARCHITECTURE; MODERN ARCHITECTURE. For the religious architecture of other parts of the world, *see* appropriate headings; *e.g.,* CHINESE ARCHITECTURE; IBERO-AMERICAN ARCHITECTURE; INDIAN ARCHITECTURE; ISLAMIC ARCHITECTURE. *See* also TEMPLE ARCHITECTURE.

Historical Background.—When Constantine recognized Christianity by the Edict of Milan in A.D. 313 a pattern of church architecture as such did not exist. The earliest Christians had worshiped in the houses of wealthier members or in the catacombs, which in Rome were particularly extensive. A converted house in Doura-Europus in eastern Syria is held to be the first-known Christian church, dating from 232. In both the Eastern and Western halves of the Roman Empire, however, a certain amount of uncoordinated church building took place.

As Christianity became established throughout the Roman Empire a building type for sheltering a large congregation evolved from the basilica (*q.v.*), found in Rome and Roman North Africa. This was a sizable rectangular building the interior of which was divided by two rows of columns into a large central hall with side aisles. It was easily roofed in wood. By putting the altar at one end, preferably in a niche with space for suitable circulation in front, and by locating the entrance at the opposite end, a basic church pattern was established. The basilica-inspired old St. Peter's in Rome, which Constantine built in *c.* 326 and which was substantially replaced by the present St. Peter's in the 16th century, was one of the first of these. The same plan was used later in the 4th century in Rome in S. Clemente, Sta. Maria Maggiore, St. John Lateran and St. Paul's Outside the Walls, to name only the finest extant examples. The long basilica nave was suited to church processionals and produced a stunning spatial impression as well. At the sanctuary end was a slightly raised platform, or bema, with a semicircular apse, often gloriously covered with mosaics, directly behind.

In the formative days of the Christian Church, however, plans other than the basilica were used. The circular church and baptistery, undoubtedly inspired by Greek and Roman temples and tombs, were common. S. Stefano Rotondo in Rome (*c.* 475) is the largest and best known of these. In the 6th century the Byzantines explored an even more complex geometry. SS. Sergius and Bacchus in Constantinople (523–527) is a domed octagon enclosed in a square, while its contemporary, the sublime Hagia Sophia, is square outside, domed and counterdomed within. Charlemagne's mausoleum chapel at Aachen (796–804) has 16 sides. The opulent St. Mark's in Venice, finished in 1073, has four arms of equal length, making a Greek cross. The geometry that characterized church planning until the beginning of the Romanesque had, thus, an ingenious variety.

From the fall of Rome in A.D. 476 to the Romanesque beginnings around 1000, little building of any type was done in Europe with the exception of the Byzantine work centred around Ravenna and Venice. Then came the golden age of church building in Western Europe. This began in the 11th century with the Romanesque style, reached its religious peak with the Gothic during the 12th to 15th centuries (varying in different countries), and continued in a more elegant but less spiritual form in the Renaissance of the 15th and 16th centuries. It is significant that almost all of these were adaptations of the long-armed Latin cross in plan. Indeed it is this Latin plan, largely as developed in the Middle Ages, which determined church planning, both Roman Catholic and Protestant, until modern times.

During the late Renaissance and continuing with the Baroque and Rococo periods down to the 17th and 18th centuries, however, a revolt against the rigid Latin-cross plan occurred, particularly in Italy and southern Germany where a number of extremely interesting, more centrally planned churches evolved. These churches were not only less "authoritarian"; they sought a more intimate atmosphere, and it is pertinent to note that many of these flowing geometric shapes were revived in modern German churches. But after the late 18th century and particularly during the age of architectural revivals from the 19th century onward, the familiar Latin plan again dominated church design.

20th-Century Developments.—Beginning in the early 20th century, when architects everywhere increasingly questioned the copybook styles that had stultified building for almost 200 years, a new freshness was evident. This was primarily the result of two factors: a reassessment of the basic relationship between clergy and congregation; and revolutionary new materials of steel and reinforced concrete, both of which were introduced in the mid-19th century.

The long nave of the Latin cross isolates much of the congregation from the priest or minister and the sanctuary. Not only is it difficult to hear the sermon throughout many attenuated churches —as the presence of amplifying systems testifies—it is also difficult to feel in touch with the altar and sanctuary. As church processionals largely disappeared, virtually altogether in Protestant churches, the liturgical necessity for a long nave likewise diminished. As a result a more compact planning, evolving toward a one-room ambiance and designed to bring clergy and congregation closer together, became evident. The customarily precise divisions of nave, transept, chancel, and sanctuary gave way to a more open and intimate interior. Enhanced by the overall developments of 20th-century architecture, a general simplification and unity in church architecture of all faiths evolved.

Although the changes in liturgical relationships brought obvious changes to the appearance of modern churches, even greater changes occurred through the use of new materials, such as reinforced concrete, steel, processed (*i.e.,* laminated) wood, and new forms of glass.

Concrete had been used in churches since the end of the 19th century, notably by Anatole de Baudot in his Saint-Jean de Montmartre in Paris (1894), but always as a structural means within a largely stylistic framework. It was not until 1923 that reinforced concrete was fully used and expressed in a church (Notre Dame, in Le Raincy, a suburb of Paris; Auguste and Gustave Perret, architects).

The first steel and glass church, the Stahlkirche, was built by Otto Bartning in Cologne in 1928. Modeled to a large extent after the famous 13th-century Sainte-Chapelle in Paris, this church, later destroyed, had a maximum amount of stained glass and a minimum of structure.

Industrialized or processed wood was another new material that markedly affected the structural design of 20th-century churches. New forms and uses were given to man's most venerable building material. Church architects, especially in the United States, made frequent use of prefabricated laminated wood arches which became readily available. Handsome and economical, wood has a visual and tactile warmth, plus excellent acoustic qualities, which make it well suited for religious work.

Another old material in new guise that had a stimulating role in 20th-century religious architecture is a glass technique called *Betonglas* (*i.e.,* "concrete glass") or mosaic glass. It is made from faceted bits of brilliantly coloured glass, approximately an inch thick. Instead of the various sections being supported and separated by lead dividers, as in stained glass (*q.v.*), the thick glass chunks are laid and composed, like a mosaic, on the flat, with wire reinforcing rods laced between and fine concrete poured in the interstices. When the concrete has set the panel is polished; it then forms a self-supporting, weatherproof unit ready to be raised in place. *Betonglas* has a depth and richness, a glowing quality, which is almost jewellike in its changing intensities. It became popular in France, where it first evolved in the late 1920s and early 1930s, and its use spread to much of the continent and to North and South America. One of its most impressive single installations is in Wallace Harrison's First Presbyterian Church (1958) in Stamford, Conn.

France.—France, which gave birth to the Gothic style and took it to its greatest heights, was also responsible for establishing the 19th-century Classic revival both in architecture and in art. The extraordinary archaeological discoveries of the late 18th century (particularly J. J. Winckelmann's work in Greece) and Napoleon's imperial leanings set the stage for this Neoclassical idiom. The search for ancient prototypes was far more of an architectural atavism at this time than it had been during the Renaissance. Renaissance architects sought inspiration in the glories of Greece and Rome; the Neoclassicists sought ancient models, or authentic ancient elements for new buildings. The movement was epitomized in France by Napoleon's *temple de la Gloire*, the Madeleine (1806), by Pierre Vignon.

Pleasure in the Neoclassical style in France, as elsewhere, waned, however, and toward the middle of the 19th century interest revived in the Gothic. E. E. Viollet-le-Duc was the continent's chief champion of the Gothic revival and his *Dictionnaire raisonné de l'architecture française* (1854–68), along with his many restorations, including that of Sainte-Chapelle, sparked wide enthusiasm throughout Europe. In France more neo-Gothic restoration—in some cases violation—was executed than new construction, but several prominent churches were built, such as: Sainte-Clotilde in Paris by F. C. Gau and T. Ballu (begun in 1846); Saint-Nicolas in Nantes by L. A. Piel and J. B. A. Lassus (1854–59); and Saint-Epvre in Nancy (1864–79), by M. P. Morey.

Following the Gothic revival, architectural uncertainties for almost a century resulted in a combination of styles. The most prominent Parisian example of this period is the Sacré Coeur, begun in 1875 by Paul Abadie and continued by Pierre Daumet and L. Magne. The Neoclassical and neo-Gothic had a certain "authenticity," although generally cold and lifeless, but the church architecture that followed in France and elsewhere until after World War I was almost totally undistinguished.

When the Perrets built their Notre Dame du Raincy in 1923, using reinforced concrete, they established a milestone in the rejuvenation of Christian church architecture. The roof is supported by slender concrete columns; the outside walls are pierced panels of concrete, each panel being laced with a series of geometric openings in which are set panes of coloured glass. The interior effect of this small church (it measures only 184 × 66 ft.) is one of reverent simplicity and timeless grace. It has few equals.

The effect of Notre Dame du Raincy permeated all Europe. The Perrets themselves built Sainte-Thérèse, a somewhat similar church at Montmagny (1925), and projected several others. Karl Moser in Switzerland was inspired to design his excellent St. Antonius in Basel (1926–27), and a whole school of new church architecture arose in Germany under Dominikus Böhm, Otto Bartning, and Rudolf Schwarz.

After this church renascence, however, a curious and unfortunate mediocrity characterized most French architecture, religious and secular (excluding, of course, the work of the Swiss-born Le Corbusier). After the Perrets' work at Le Raincy and Montmagny, few churches of real architectural merit were built in France until a second church-building movement was initiated after World War II. The revolution that the Perrets began in 1923 was rightly concerned with a fresh sweep in architecture; the new direction of the 1950s and '60s was primarily toward employing the finest contemporary artists in the church. As in past centuries of great church building, architect and artist worked hand in hand.

Father M. A. Couturier, O.P., was largely responsible for initiating this movement, and under his aegis a number of the greatest artists in France were invited to work on the church of Notre Dame de Toute Grâce at Assy, near Chamonix (Maurice Novarina, architect). This church was consecrated in 1950. Fernand Léger composed an enormous mosaic for the entrance, Jean Lurçat created a superb tapestry for the chancel, Georges Rouault and Henri Matisse designed the windows, while Jacques Lipchitz, Pierre Bonnard, Marc Chagall, Georges Braque, and Henri Laurens were among the other contributors. The architectural form, which is somewhat neo-Romanesque, is rather heavy and in no way equal to its art, and there is a lack of coordination in the art itself. This church, however, has had an extremely important influence throughout France and Europe. Architecture unaided by art can rarely reach the spiritual heights sought in a church because of its concern with the technical requirements of shelter.

After Assy a number of new churches were built with the active cooperation of architect and artist. One of these is Notre Dame des Pauvres at Audincourt (Doubs) (dedicated in 1951). Designed by Novarina, the building itself is simple and undistinguished, but gains distinction from the continuous band of 17 stained-glass windows by Léger and the entrance mosaic and baptistery glass by Jean Bazaine. The Léger windows are brilliant examples of contemporary thematic glass (they trace the Passion

of Christ) while the abstract glass in the baptistery, with its warm, glowing colours, is a superb statement of nonobjective art.

A small semiprivate chapel of charm is that of Notre Dame du Rosaire, at Vence near Nice (1948–51), by Matisse. Again, the church is of secondary importance architecturally, but Matisse decorated it with superb tiles and glass and continued his lovely colours and motifs in the design of the vestments themselves; thus a complete integration of the visual arts, some fixed, some in motion, was achieved. The chapel at Vence is near the interesting old church at Villefranche-sur-Mer which Jean Cocteau redecorated.

It is generally held that the greatest masterpiece of contemporary French, indeed world, religious architecture is Notre Dame du Haut at Ronchamp, Haute-Saône (1955), by Le Corbusier. This startlingly original building is thought by many to be the most important church of the past several centuries, so profound is its impact and so creative its force. Although its architecture is almost completely nonderivative, recalling little of the past, the atmosphere within is intensely and very personally religious. It is an interesting contrast to the great Gothic cathedrals which, though incomparable monuments to God, tend to humble the worshiper.

The church exterior is dominated by the enormous upturned eave of the roof which projects far over the approach or south side and on the east side well over the outdoor pulpit and altar. The massive south wall, which is 12 ft. thick at the bottom and 5 at the top, commands the approach with a series of openings of various rectangular shapes dispersed irregularly across the front. Although these windows at first appear, both from without and from within, to have been placed haphazardly, their total effect is one of careful orchestration.

The interior of the church is likewise dominated by the roof, which according to the architect was inspired by the shape of the shell of a crab; it swoops down toward the middle like the underside of a great tent. The roof is not directly attached to the supporting walls, but rests lightly on blocks atop them so that the feeling of space, flowing over and out, is intensified. Although the physical dimensions of Ronchamp are modest, a mere 84 × 40 ft., with seats for only 50 persons, it gives an impression of a very great space. This effect is intensified by the subtle relation of three chapels subsidiary to the nave and by the deeply splayed windows, only a few of which are visible from any one spot. It is necessary to move about the church to appreciate its features; they cannot be grasped from a fixed position.

Other important postwar churches in France are: Sainte-Thérèse, Hem, Roubaix (1958), by Hermann Baur, with superb *Betonglas* by Alfred Manessier; Notre Dame, Royan (1958), by Guillaume Gillet; Saint-Rémy, Baccarat (1957), by Nicolas Kazis, with remarkable windows; the extremely virile and powerful "La Tourette" Dominican friary at Éveux (near Lyons) by Le Corbusier (1960); Saint-Joseph, Le Havre (1959), a startling "tower" church, by Auguste Perret (Raymond Audigier and Jacques Poirier, associates); and the extraordinary underground basilica for 22,000 at Lourdes (1958), by Pierre Vago (Eugène Freyssinet, engineer).

Germany.—In tracing the background of contemporary German religious architecture the 19th century requires brief mention. Karl Friedrich Schinkel's St. Nicholas in Potsdam (1826–49) is the finest Neoclassic example, although obviously inspired by J. G. Soufflot's Panthéon in Paris. Sir George Gilbert Scott's St. Nicholas in Hamburg (1845–63), the nave of which was completely destroyed in World War II, was outstanding among the neo-Gothic. The Gothic revival also added a top to the ancient tower of Ulm Cathedral in 1877–90, making it the highest stone tower in the world (528 ft.).

Church architecture at the opening of the 20th century in Germany was stirring uneasily under the changing styles then prevalent. In the first years of the century several German architects, notably Theodor Fischer, made a tentative effort toward less derivative religious building, primarily by simplifying old clichés rather than attempting a genuinely fresh approach.

The first positive move was by Otto Bartning whose book *Vom neuen Kirchenbau* ("Toward a New Church Architecture") in

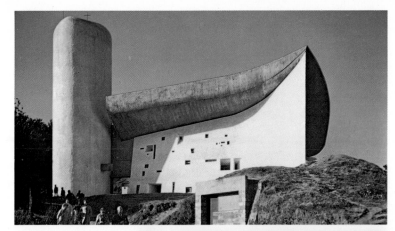

Notre Dame du Haut, Ronchamp, France; 1955. Le Corbusier, architect. (Above) The exterior walls are of concrete-reinforced stone, with a painted reinforced concrete double shell roof. (Right) Deep windows irregularly penetrate the walls of the interior

Cathedral Church of St. Michael, Coventry, Eng.; consecrated 1962. Sir Basil Spence, architect. The nave is seen through a glass wall engraved with translucent figures of angels and saints

Notre Dame des Pauvres, Audincourt, France; 1951. Maurice Novarina, architect. The windows by Fernand Léger trace the Passion of Christ

Notre Dame, Le Raincy, France; 1923. Auguste and Gustave Perret, architects. The slender concrete columns of the interior support the roof

Reformed Church, Zürich-Altstetten, Switz.; 1941. Werner Moser, architect

PLATE II

RELIGIOUS ARCHITECTURE

Vuoksenniska Church, Imatra, Fin.; 1958. Alvar Aalto, architect. To the right of the nave, and elevated in a small balcony above it, are choir and organ. The altar is marked by the three crosses of Calvary

Village church at Gravberget, Nor.; 1956. Magnus Poulsson, architect. A timber-frame construction with wood shingle roof and sides

The Chapel of Everlasting Life, one of the cemetery chapels at Gävle, Swed.; 1959. A. Engström, G. Landberg, B. Larsson, and A. Törneman, architects. A glass clerestory surrounds the chapel

Cemetery chapel, Turku, Fin.; 1941. Erik Bryggman, architect

Woods Crematorium, Stockholm, Swed.; 1940. Gunnar Asplund, architect

Matri Misericordiae at Milan-Baranzate, Italy; 1958. A. Mangiarotti and B. Morassutti, architects. Reinforced concrete columns support the roof beams of prefabricated, poststressed concrete sections. The walls are of sandwich panels

St. Maria Königin, Cologne-Marienburg, Ger.; 1954. Dominikus Böhm, architect. The great curtain of stained glass that sweeps from end to end and from floor to ceiling of the south wall was designed by Böhm and Heinz Bienefeld

St. Anna, Düren, Ger.; 1956. Rudolf Schwarz, architect. To the right of the nave is a large wall of windows of commercial glass blocks

Church of the Coronation of Our Lady, Vitoria, Spain; 1960. Miguel Fisac, architect. Small vertical windows in the stone wall at right provide general illumination for nave

Kaiser Wilhelm Memorial Church, Berlin; 1961. Egon Eiermann, architect. The windows encompass the nave, which is octagonal in shape, and suffuse it with light from all eight sides

BY COURTESY OF (BOTTOM RIGHT) LANDESBILDSTELLE BERLIN; PHOTOGRAPHS, G. E. KIDDER SMITH

PLATE IV

RELIGIOUS ARCHITECTURE

Beth Sholom Synagogue, Elkins Park, Pa.; 1958. Frank Lloyd Wright, architect. The building is a tripod of steel beams, faced with stamped aluminum, rising to an apex 100 ft. above the floor. The tripod rests securely on a vast, concrete and reinforced steel bowl

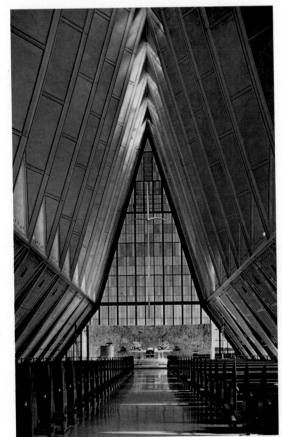

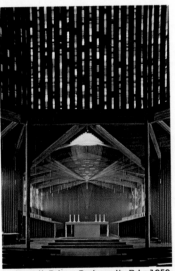

Portsmouth Priory, Portsmouth, R.I.; 1959. Pietro Belluschi, architect

Kresge Chapel, Massachusetts Institute of Technology, Cambridge; 1956. Eero Saarinen, architect

Protestant chapel in the Air Force Academy Chapel, Colorado Springs, Col.; 1961. Skidmore, Owings, and Merrill, architects. The walls and vaulted roof are formed by repetitive tetrahedrons which form 17 spires at the top of the roof. The north and south triangular walls are of tinted laminated glass

Christ Lutheran Church, Minneapolis, Minn.; 1950. Eliel and Eero Saarinen, architects

1919 was followed three years later by a model of his projected "Star Church." Although never built, it was a highly original and stimulating design which, together with the Perrets' church at Le Raincy, did much to awaken Germany to new church-building possibilities.

By 1926 several exciting new German churches had been constructed. These were Martin Weber's St. Boniface in Frankfurt am Main, and Dominikus Böhm's War Memorial Church in Neu-Ulm and his bold Catholic church at Bischofsheim. Böhm, in the latter church, took the reinforced concrete that the Perrets had confined to rigid boxlike frames and made it dramatically plastic. He built several other distinguished churches, among them St. Joseph at Hindenburg-Oberschlesien (1929) and St. Engelbert in Cologne-Riehl (1931).

Bartning, whose Protestant Steel Church for the Cologne Press Exhibition of 1928 was the great pioneer in steel, also designed two larger examples: the Round Church at Essen (1930), and the Gustav Adolf Church in Berlin-Charlottenburg (1934), later destroyed.

Rudolf Schwarz, who was to become Germany's most impressive church architect, designed a series of starkly simple but notable Catholic churches. The first was his Corpus Christi in Aachen, completed in 1930. Unquestionably one of the greatest religious architects of the 20th century, Schwarz in this, his first mature work (he was 33 at the time), showed promise of the Spartan directness and religious intensity that marked his subsequent designs.

After Hitler came to power in 1933 progressive thinking in architecture was muzzled. Schwarz, Böhm, and Bartning were largely inactive for 15 years, during which each thought deeply and maturely on the manifold problems of church building in the mid-20th century. Schwarz, probably the most profoundly religious of the three, published his *Vom Bau der Kirche* (1938) in which his architectural-religious concepts are set forth and illustrated by beautiful geometric diagrams.

When conditions finally permitted, all three set to work so actively and so successfully that Germany in a relatively few years became the leader in European religious architecture. Bartning designed a series of 48 emergency churches (*Notkirchen*), made from rubble and standardized salvaged material, while Böhm and Schwarz produced a number of new churches together with many reconstructions.

Postwar German churches are characterized by a daring, a willingness to experiment, and a directness which is very powerful. Among the most impressive examples are: St. Maria Königin, Cologne-Marienburg (1954), by Dominikus Böhm, with a lovely wall of stained glass; St. Mauritius, Saarbrücken (1956), by Albert Dietz; the very powerful Kaiser-Wilhelm-Gedächtniskirche, Berlin (1961), by Egon Eiermann; Christ Church, Bochum (1959), by Dieter Oesterlen; St. Joseph, Hasloch-am-Main (1958), by Hans Schädel; Maria Regina Martyrum, Berlin (1962), by Schädel and Friedrich Ebert; Paul Gerhardt Church, Mannheim (1960), by Gerhard Schlegel and Reinhold Kargel; and the following by Rudolf Schwarz: Holy Cross, Bottrop (1957), St. Anna, Düren (1956, one of the great churches of modern times), St. Michael, Frankfurt am Main (1954), Church of the Holy Family, Oberhausen (1958), and Maria Königin, Saarbrücken (1959).

Switzerland.—The contemporary church movement in Switzerland is, after the German and French, the most productive in Europe. Starting with Karl Moser's superb St. Antonius in Basel (1927) and continuing through the 1930s and '40s when Germany and France built little of merit, the Swiss built an impressive number of fine new churches. Having, like Germany, slightly more Protestants than Catholics, Switzerland profited from the stimulating reaction the religious architecture of each group had upon that of the other.

Following the Catholic initiative in Moser's St. Antonius, the Protestants, after a competition in 1931, launched their contemporary church building with St. Johannes in Basel (1936), by E. F. Burckhardt and Karl Egender. There followed a number of sensitively designed, handsomely detailed and constructed churches, both Protestant and Catholic.

The outstanding church in the country is the Reformed Church at Zürich-Altstetten (1941), by Werner Moser, the son of Karl Moser. Other churches of particular interest are: All Saints, Basel (1953), and Bruderklausen, Basel-Birsfelden (1959), by Hermann Baur; Reformed Church, Effretikon (1961), and Reformed Church, Oberglatt (1964), by Ernst Gisel; Liebenfels Cemetery Chapel, Baden (1957), by Edi and Ruth Lanners and Res Wahlen; and St. Francis, Basel-Riehen (1950), by Fritz Metzger.

Great Britain.—During the 19th and early 20th centuries architecture in England followed the cultural pattern of France. Neoclassicism was strong until the mid-19th century, but primarily influenced banks, clubs, and public buildings, not church architecture. The Gothic revival enjoyed a more active popularity in England than in any other European country: because of its almost continuous use in religious work, notably interrupted by Sir Christopher Wren who considered Gothic barbaric, the English Gothic revival has been referred to as the "Gothic survival." Neoclassicists and Gothicists in England fought so heatedly that their controversy was dubbed the "battle of the styles." A compromise of sorts was effected whereby most public buildings were designed in a watered-down Classical or Renaissance tradition, while most churches were Gothic.

Few churches built in England in the 19th and early 20th centuries were not inspired by the Gothic. The two most imposing examples are John Bentley's large Roman Catholic cathedral in Westminster, London (1895–1903), a curious pseudo-Byzantine edifice, and Sir Giles Gilbert Scott's enormous Liverpool cathedral, begun in 1903.

The contemporary church-building movement of the 1920s which took such an exciting hold of the continent had little effect in the British Isles. After World War II English church architecture received a decided stimulus from Basil Spence's winning design for the rebuilding of Coventry cathedral (1962). Several other progressive churches should be mentioned but they are distressingly few in number: St. Paul's, Bow Common, London (1960), by Robert Maguire, and St. Matthew, Perry Beeches, Birmingham (1963), by Maguire and Keith Murray; and Edward Mills' Methodist Church, Mitcham, Surrey (1959).

Scandinavia.—The development of architecture in Scandinavia before the 20th century followed at a discreet distance the fashions of the continent. Few buildings of international distinction were to be found. After Gunnar Asplund's Stockholm Exposition of 1930, however, Sweden, Finland, Denmark, and Norway contributed greatly to the richness and vocabulary of contemporary architectural thought. In some respects, such as land usage and housing, Scandinavia, and Sweden in particular, led the world.

The religious architecture after 1930 was also significant. Erik Bryggman's cemetery chapel in Turku, Fin. (1941), is one of the influential contemporary churches in Scandinavia, distinguished by its sensitive proportions and a wall of glass opening onto its park-like setting. Other notable Finnish churches are: the famous Vuoksenniska Church, Imatra (1958), by Alvar Aalto; Village Church, Hyvinkää (1961), by Aarne Ruusuvuori; a delightful chapel for the Technical University at Otaniemi, Helsinki (1957), by Kaija and Heikki Siren, and an unusual church by the same architects at Orivesi (1962).

In Sweden, few distinguished contemporary churches were built until the late 1950s—Ivar Tengbom's Högalid Church in Stockholm (1923) being an early exception. Sweden in the 1940s did, however, produce two of the world's most beautiful crematoria: Gunnar Asplund's Woods Crematorium in Stockholm (1940), one of the great monuments of modern architecture, and Sigurd Lewerentz' crematorium in Malmö. Some interesting churches are: St. Thomas, Vällingby, Stockholm (1960), by Peter Celsing; a superb cemetery chapel at Gävle (1959), by Engström, Landberg, Larsson, and Törneman; the highly imaginative Skarpnäck Church, Stockholm-Björkhagen (1961), by Lewerentz; the Farsta Church, Stockholm-Hökarängen (1960), by Bengt Lindroos and Hans Borgström; and the impressive Västerort Church, Vällingby, Stockholm (1956), by Carl Nyrén.

Architecture in Norway has always lagged behind that in the rest of Scandinavia. The most brilliant facet of Norway's contribution to architecture lies in its churches of the Middle Ages. From the 11th through the 13th centuries there were built, largely in the country's more remote regions, 500 to 600 stave churches. Intensely personal and highly carved and painted, these almost pagan wooden churches are unique in ecclesiastical architectural history. Only 22 were extant in modern times. The village church at Gravberget (1956), by Magnus Poulsson, is the finest recent example.

Of the 20th-century churches in Denmark, P. V. J. Klint's Grundtvig Church in Copenhagen (1913–40) is the most nationalistic in flavour (it recalls the traditionally Danish stepped gables), its facade suggesting a gigantic series of organ pipes in brick. Several more convincing recent examples—all near Copenhagen—are: St. Knud Lavard, Kongens Lyngby (1957), by Carl R. Frederiksen; Crematorium Chapel, Glostrup (1960), by Bornebusch, Brüel and Selchau; and Stengård Church, Gladsaxe (1963), by Graae and Wohlert.

Italy.—The Italians, having the most magnificent inheritance of fine churches in the world, were little disposed to construct more until the unparalleled devastation of World War II. Although several churches were built in contemporary style in Italy in the 1930s, none compared with the advanced work done by that time in Germany, Switzerland, and France. Even by the mid-1960s there were fewer fine new churches in Italy than in the northern countries, but both quantity and quality have improved steadily and the climate for progressive religious architecture is excellent. Among the impressive postwar churches are: Madonna of the Poor, Milan (1952), by Luigi Figini and Gino Pollini—brutalist but full of character; the imaginative, translucent-walled Matri Misericordiae at Milan-Baranzate (1958), by Angelo Mangiarotti and Bruno Morassutti; Sta. Maria Maggiore, Francavilla al Mare (1959), by Ludovico Quaroni; and the fantastic Church of the Autostrada, near Florence (1963), by Giovanni Michelucci.

Elsewhere in Europe.—Of the remaining countries of Europe few contributed significantly to religious architecture in the 20th century, although some good work was done in most of them. After World War I Czechoslovakia produced several advanced churches, notably St. Wenceslaus in Prague (1930), by Josef Gočár, but after 1939 little work of merit was done.

The Dutch after World War II constructed a series of good churches. Among the most successful are: Reformed Church, Aerdenhout (1958), by Karel L. Sijmons; Reformed Church, Nagele (1960), by van den Broek and Bakema; Reformed Church, Geleen (1956), by Bart van Kasteel; and St. Nicolas, Venlo (1961), by G. J. van der Grintin.

The most fantastic church of the 20th century is the Church of the Holy Family in Barcelona, Spain, by Antonio Gaudí which embodies many leading characteristics of Spanish *art nouveau*. Although begun late in the 19th century the church was never completed. Its lofty towers and facade are original and imposing; they recall a child's seaside castle of wet sand drippings. Two later and very stimulating churches—both in the small city of Vitoria—are the Church of Our Lady of the Angels (1959), by Javier Carvajal Ferrer and José García de Paredes; and the Church of the Coronation of Our Lady (1960), by Miguel Fisac.

Ibero-America.—In spite of the great growth of all Latin-American countries in the 20th century only a few significant churches have been built. The best of these are in Brazil and Mexico, the two countries that also have the richest architectural heritage from their colonial eras. One of the most provocative is Oscar Niemeyer's San Francisco in Belo Horizonte, Braz. (1943). Niemeyer's design for the cathedral for Brasília (1962), the new capital of Brazil, is startlingly handsome.

The development of contemporary architecture in Mexico was vigorous, and several churches there had influence beyond Mexico itself. One of these is Enrique de la Mora's Church of La Purísima in Monterrey (1947), constructed of intersecting paraboloids of concrete. Although details and lighting are clumsy, the structure is good. Much more successful is Felix Candela's Church of the Virgin of the Miraculous Medal in Mexico City (1954). Candela, one of the world's great experts in thin-shell warped concrete surfaces, or hyperbolic paraboloids, helped pioneer highly promising developments in reinforced concrete. Candela tended to free re-

inforced concrete from rigid boxlike shapes, rectangular beams, and flat slabs like wood and steel, and used it instead in thin, very strong curved planes, like eggshells and folded pieces of paper. The Church of the Virgin is so refined structurally that the roof is only 1½ in. thick. The aesthetic potential of concrete is enormous and Candela made bold use of it in this church, particularly on the interior. Unfortunately the finished churches are not so elegant as their structure. Others by Candela using this material are La Capilla de Nuestra Señora de la Soledad, Mexico City (1957); and San Vicente de Paul, Mexico City (1960).

United States.—The United States has an architectural heritage of some of the loveliest and most appealing small churches ever built. Outstanding among these are the 17th- and 18th-century village churches and meetinghouses, primarily Congregational and Unitarian, scattered throughout much of New England and eastern New York State. These simple white wood structures, with their tall spires, have an inherent rightness, a sense of belonging architecturally, which makes them one of the country's finest cultural contributions.

The colonists in the South brought to Virginia an established liturgy and church-building program. The program was of necessity modified somewhat by local conditions, but the 17th- and 18th-century churches of Southern colonial and Georgian inspiration reflected the Old World far more than did the churches and meetinghouses of New England. Equally reminiscent of Europe were the buildings that the Spaniards built from Florida to California. Their churches, missions, and public buildings stem in large part from Iberian models.

As the American colonies coalesced under English dominance, religious building increasingly reflected the fashions and developments of the British Isles. Sir Christopher Wren and James Gibbs inspired churches from Boston (Christ Church, 1723) to New York City (St. Paul's Chapel, 1764–66) to Charleston (St. Michael's, 1752–61). Following the Revolution a self-consciously nationalistic federal architecture arose, strongly abetted by Jefferson's enthusiasm. It evolved directly from the Classical revival then sweeping Europe, particularly France, the new nation's important friend. The general Classical revival was followed by the specific Greek revival; at mid-19th century came the Gothic revival and after that a potpourri.

Richard Upjohn's Trinity Church (1839–46), James Renwick's Grace Church (1845–6), and St. Patrick's Cathedral (1858–79), all in New York City, are among the country's outstanding Gothic revival churches. External form, however, not structural purity, was predominant. St. Patrick's vaults are not self-supporting; its flying buttresses receive no load.

U.S. architecture in most of the first half of the 20th century lagged far behind that of Europe, except in skyscraper construction. Notable buildings were built, but they were few in number and not widely accepted. After World War II, however, the U.S. produced a great many excellent structures in all categories and public acceptance of new work was widespread.

The contemporary tradition in U.S. church building has distinguished roots in Unity Temple, Oak Park, Ill., built in 1906 by Frank Lloyd Wright, and in the First Church of Christ Scientist, Berkeley, Calif. (1910), by Bernard Maybeck. Although neither constituted the architectural revolution which the Perrets' church at Le Raincy occasioned, they are unquestionably landmarks in the evolution of contemporary church architecture. Wright's other religious buildings include his chapel at Florida Southern College, Lakeland (1941), the First Unitarian Church in Madison, Wis. (1951), the striking Beth Sholom Synagogue in Elkins Park, Pa. (1958), and a circular Greek Orthodox church of dubious detail in Milwaukee (1961). His son, Lloyd Wright, built one of the country's memorable churches, the beautifully situated Wayfarer's Chapel at Palos Verdes, Calif. (1951). The design is composed basically of frames of redwood and sheets of clear glass so that the sea and surroundings become an intimate part of the service itself.

Pietro Belluschi, who went from Italy to the U.S. in 1923, designed a number of churches which are models of elegant simplicity, sympathetic scale, and carefully considered natural lighting. His Zion Lutheran, Portland, Ore. (1951), First Presbyterian,

Cottage Grove, Ore. (1951), Church of the Redeemer, Baltimore (1958), with Rogers, Taliaferro, and Lamb, and his Portsmouth Priory, Portsmouth, R.I. (1959), with Anderson, Beckwith, and Haible, greatly encouraged and enriched the U.S. church-building scene.

Eliel Saarinen and his son, Eero, both born in Finland, were among the pioneers in contemporary U.S. church design. Their Tabernacle Church of Christ in Columbus, Ind. (1942), was one of the important earlier ones built in the U.S. They collaborated even more successfully in Christ Lutheran Church in Minneapolis, Minn. (1950), which was Eliel Saarinen's last work. The younger Saarinen then designed the nonsectarian cylindrical Kresge Chapel at Massachusetts Institute of Technology in Cambridge (1956), a brilliant example of religious architecture, and several college chapels, notably at Concordia College, Fort Wayne, Ind. (1958). His last design before his death (1961) at 51 was the North Christian Church, Columbus, Ind. (1964). Louis I. Kahn's First Unitarian Church at Rochester, N.Y. (1963), quickens interest in that its nave is lit only by skylights, its walls being solid. Another university chapel of note is at the Illinois Institute of Technology, Chicago (1952), by Ludwig Mies van der Rohe.

Two striking religious buildings of large size are the Air Force Academy chapel at Colorado Springs, Colo. (1961), and the First Presbyterian Church in Stamford, Conn. (1958). The Air Force Academy chapel is of aluminum-skinned tetrahedral frames, graphically suggesting the spirit of the air age. Skidmore, Owings, and Merrill were the architects, and Gordon Bunshaft and Walter Netsch the designers. Wallace Harrison's Stamford church is powerful although overly attenuated in plan and fussy in detail. Its exterior is of canted, angular planes, resembling some great fish, with a soaring colour-drenched nave within. A dazzling flood of light fills the interior from windows that rise from the floor to the ceiling ridge. These windows are filled with 20,000 pieces of inch-thick *Betonglas,* designed by Harrison and executed by Gabriel Loire of Chartres, France.

Harrison and his partner, Max Abramovitz, also designed an interfaith centre for Brandeis University, Waltham, Mass. (1955). Instead of a single convertible building for the three faiths represented, there are three separate, individual chapels, Jewish, Protestant, and Catholic, sensitively grouped around a common pool and landscaped setting.

Synagogue architecture in the U.S. is at times of a high level. Eric Mendelsohn, who lived in the U.S. from 1941 to his death in 1953, designed several fine temples, as has Percival Goodman. Two of the handsomest synagogues in the U.S.—in addition to Wright's at Elkins Park—are the Temple Emanu-el, Dallas, Tex. (1957), by Howard R. Meyer and Max Sandfield (with W. W. Wurster, consultant), and Philip C. Johnson's elegant Kneses Tifereth Israel Synagogue in Port Chester, N.Y. (1956). This clean, geometrically precise temple is a sharp contrast to the freer, more rugged design of Wallace Harrison's First Presbyterian Church in Stamford, less than ten miles away. Though poles apart architecturally, they are among the finer religious buildings in the country.

In contrast to its magnificent accomplishments in Europe, the Catholic Church in the U.S., as in Latin America, espoused relatively traditional church forms for new building. In the first half of the 20th century there were few Catholic churches of distinctive contemporary design. Among the most notable Catholic buildings are Robert Anshen and W. S. Allen's Chapel of the Holy Cross, Sedona, Ariz. (1956), Belluschi's Portsmouth Prior Chapel already mentioned, Marcel Breuer's very impressive Benedictine Abbey of St. John in Collegeville, Minn. (1961), and his Annunciation Priory in Bismarck, N.D. (1962), and Hellmuth, Obata, and Kassabaum's St. Louis Priory Chapel (1962).

Two Protestant churches are of interest in that they illustrate the problems of the automobile age: St. Clement's Episcopal Church, Alexandria, Va. (1948), by J. H. Saunders and the former rector, Darby Betts; and the Venice-Nokomis Presbyterian Church, Venice, Fla. (1953), by Victor A. Lundy. The first, being flanked by roads with noisy traffic, is of windowless, soundproofed design, artificially lit and air conditioned. The Florida chapel is just the reverse: it is an open-air, drive-in church. Lundy has also done a fine First Unitarian Church in Westport, Conn. (1961), and the First Unitarian Congregational Church at Hartford, Conn. (1964).

See biographies of architects; *see* also references under "Religious Architecture" in the Index.

BIBLIOGRAPHY.—*Current Periodicals: Architectural Forum, Architectural Record, Progressive Architecture,* and *The Architectural Review. Postwar Books:* John Knox Shear (ed.), *Religious Buildings for Today* (1957); Edward D. Mills, *The Modern Church* (1956); Paul Thiry *et al., Churches & Temples* (1953); Anton Henze and T. Filthaut, *Contemporary Church Art,* Eng. trans. by C. Hastings (1956); Peter Blake (ed.), *An American Synagogue for Today and Tomorrow* (1954); Ernest Short, *A History of Religious Architecture,* 3rd rev. ed. (1951); Ferdinand Pfammatter, *Betonkirchen* (1948); Willy Weyres, *Neue Kirchen im Erzbistum Köln* (1957); Gherardi *et al., Dieci anni di architettura sacra in Italia* (1956); Yves Sjöberg, *Mort et résurrection de l'art sacré* (1957); Peter Hammond, *Liturgy and Architecture* (1960); R. Gieselmann and Werner Aebli, *Kirchenbau—Church Architecture* (1960); Anton Henze, *Neue kirchliche Kunst* (1958); Richard Biedrzynski, *Kirchen unserer Zeit* (1958); Otto Bartning, *Vom Raum der Kirche* (1958); Rudolf Schwarz, *Vom Bau der Kirche* (1938–47), Eng. trans. by Cynthia Harris, *The Church Incarnate* (1958); Albert Christ-Janer and Mary Mix Foley, *Modern Church Architecture* (1962); Rudolf Schwarz, *Kirchenbau* (1960); Joseph Pichard, *Les Églises nouvelles à travers le monde* (1960), Eng. trans., *Modern Church Architecture* (1962); Willy Weyres and Otto Bartning, *Kirchen—Handbuch für den Kirchenbau* (1959); A. Hoff, H. Muck, and R. Thoma, *Dominikus Böhm* (1962); G. E. Kidder Smith, *The New Churches of Europe* (1964). (G. E. K. S.)

REMAGEN, a town of West Germany in the *Land* (state) of Rhineland-Palatinate (Rheinland-Pfalz), Federal Republic of Germany, lies on the left bank of the Rhine, 19 km. (12 mi.) SSE of Bonn. Pop. (1961) 7,244. It was the old Roman fortress Rigomagus and has some Roman remains. It developed as a small medieval town and has a gate dating from the 12th century; there is now a continuous series of hotels along the Rhine waterfront. In the Allied advance to the Rhine in World War II, the 9th Armored Division of the United States 1st Army discovered on March 7, 1945, that the railway bridge at Remagen, though damaged, was usable. It promptly forced a crossing and established the first Allied bridgehead across the Rhine, which on March 25 became one of the spearheads of the Allied attack into the heart of Germany. (R. E. DI.)

REMAINDER THEOREM, a theorem of particular value in the study of polynomials and equations. If we divide

$$2x^2 + 3x + 6 \text{ by } x - 2$$

for example, the quotient is $2x + 7$ and the remainder is 20. The remainder, however, can be found by substituting 2 for x in the polynomial. This gives:

$$2 \cdot 2^2 + 3 \cdot 2 + 6 = 8 + 6 + 6 = 20$$

More generally, to find the remainder arising from dividing $f(x)$ by $x - r$, substitute r for x in $f(x)$. This evidently amounts simply to evaluating $f(x)$ for some special value (r) of x. This is conveniently done by following the plan shown at the right. This work reveals not only the remainder (20)

$$\begin{array}{r} 2 + 3 + 6 \, \underline{\lfloor 2} \\ 4 \quad 14 \\ \hline 2 + 7; \quad 20 \end{array}$$

but also the coefficients $(2 + 7)$ of the quotient $(2x + 7)$. When used for this latter purpose it is known as synthetic division. This method of dividing is very helpful in finding the roots of numerical higher equations.

See also ARITHMETIC: *Theory of Divisors;* COEFFICIENT; DIVISION; EQUATIONS, THEORY OF.

REMARQUE, ERICH MARIA (1898–   ), German novelist, was born on June 22, 1898, in Osnabrück. He achieved world fame as author of *Im Westen nichts Neues* (1929; Eng. trans. by A. W. Wheen, *All Quiet on the Western Front,* 1929), a vehement antiwar novel which, because of its sensational realism, caused a considerable controversy in Germany. Its sequel *Der Weg zurück* (1931; Eng. trans. by A. W. Wheen, *The Road Back,* 1931) describes the collapse of Germany in 1918 and the subsequent political disorders. Remarque fought in World War I and was later a teacher and journalist. He left Germany in 1932 for Switzerland, but in 1939 went to New York where he became a

U.S. citizen. After World War II he returned to Switzerland. Of his many other novels only *Arc de Triomphe* (1946; Eng. trans. by W. Sorell and Denver Lindley, 1946) was a world success.

(H. S. R.)

REMBRANDT (Rembrandt Harmensz [or Harmenszoon] van Rijn [or Ryn]) (1606–1669), the outstanding genius of the Dutch school of painting in the 17th century, was born in Leiden on July 15, 1606. His father, Harmen Gerritsz van Rijn, was a miller, while his mother, Neeltgen (Cornelia), was the daughter of a baker, Willemsz van Zuytbrouck, and they appear to have been simple, industrious and deeply pious folk, typical of the Dutch lower-middle class of this period. They originally intended him for a scholastic career and at about the age of seven he entered the Latin school in Leiden. In 1620, when not quite 14, he was enrolled in the university but he did not stay there long. In the following year his parents recognized that his talents as well as his inclinations lay in the direction of painting and he was apprenticed for three years to Jacob Isaacsz van Swanenburgh, a minor painter of architectural subjects. Rembrandt can have learned little from Swanenburgh beyond the basic elements of technique, for there is not the least trace of his first master's style in any of his work.

In 1624, having completed his apprenticeship, he went to Amsterdam for six months as a pupil of the historical painter Pieter Lastman, a far more talented artist than Swanenburgh. Lastman was a capable painter, but his somewhat theatrical style lacked any kind of profundity and he cannot have played an important part in developing that depth of human sympathy which is perhaps Rembrandt's most personal and valuable quality. However, at the more superficial level of subject matter and imagery—the visual vocabulary of Rembrandt's art—the influence of Lastman was powerful and enduring. Lastman was one of a small group of Dutch artists who had worked in Italy during the first decade of the century and were associated with the German master Adam Elsheimer (*q.v.*). The work of this group was strongly influenced by the 16th-century masters of Venice, notably Tintoretto, and in this they are quite distinct from the Dutch followers of Caravaggio, such as Gerard van Honthorst, Hendrick Terbrugghen and the other Utrecht painters, who were the principal channel of Italian influences in Holland at the time when Rembrandt was reaching maturity. Tintoretto and Caravaggio were both masters of chiaroscuro, using violent contrasts of light and shade for dramatic effect, but their methods were almost diametrically opposed, and the fact that Rembrandt's early contacts were not with the Utrecht school but with Elsheimer's followers in Amsterdam may well have been an important factor in the formation of his own chiaroscuro style. The contrast of searching light and deep shadow is one of the central elements of Rembrandt's art, and his employment of it approaches more closely to the spirit of Tintoretto—emotional, mysterious, nonnaturalistic and even arbitrary in treatment of the play of light and its source—than to the almost brutal naturalism and the quasi-scientific handling of light that characterize Caravaggio and his followers. The link with Tintoretto via Elsheimer can be traced more clearly through the works of the Pynas brothers (*e.g.*, Jan Pynas' "Raising of Lazarus," in Philadelphia) than through Lastman himself, for whom the major Venetian influence was that of Veronese. In Lastman's biblical and historical compositions the delicate daylight of Veronese takes on a cruder glare, and the cultured urbanity of Veronese's poses and gestures becomes pompous and provincial, but none the less the youthful Rembrandt found Lastman worth imitating and there are many echoes of his master in the historical pictures which he painted in Leiden between 1625–31. Examples of these are: "The Prophet Balaam" (1626; Cognacq-Jay museum, Paris) and "David Presenting the Head of Goliath to Saul" (1627?; Smidt van Gelder collection, Amsterdam), of which the latter is virtually a Lastman in miniature. Other works of these years, such as "The Tribute Money" (1629; Beit collection, London) show his growing interest in the use of expressive chiaroscuro. Rembrandt was naturally very much alive to influences other than the Italianism of the Lastman school. In addition to occasional hints borrowed from such contemporaries as Frans Hals and Adriaen Brouwer (*qq.v.*)

one can detect the persistence of the northern genre tradition of the previous century, with its love of elaborate still-life details, in such a picture as "Tobit, His Wife and the Kid" (1626; in the private collection of Baroness Bentinck von Thyssen).

So far Rembrandt has been considered only as a painter of classical and biblical themes, but already in this early period a large proportion of his work consisted of portraits and studies of single figures and he was also making his first experiments in etching, a medium in which he was later to achieve unsurpassed results. The sitters for the portrait studies were frequently members of his own family, the most frequent being himself. These are not portraits in the fashionable sense, but studies in character, expression and lighting that could be (and often were) used in his subject pictures. The borderline between portraiture, genre and historical art is often a shadowy one, as when he paints "The Artist's Mother as the Prophetess Hannah" (1631; Rijksmuseum, Amsterdam), or develops a study of an old man into "The Apostle Paul" (Museum, Nürnberg). Often his homely sitters are given an exotic look by being made to wear some piece of extravagant headgear—a colourful turban, a helmet or a curiously plumed hat —as an exercise in the rendering of textures and effects of light. Most of the pictures of this period are painted on panel, with a predominance of cool, grayish monotone in the colouring, and the technique, though vigorous, is tighter and more constrained than the broad, loose brushwork of his later years. He soon became known in Leiden, where he shared a studio with the almost equally promising Jan Lievens, and before his removal to Amsterdam he was already taking pupils, among whom the most notable was Gerard Dou. More important for his subsequent career, he had roused the interest and admiration of Constantijn Huygens, with whose remarkable family he appears to have remained in contact throughout his life.

In the latter part of 1631 Rembrandt moved from Leiden to Amsterdam, the city which by this time had risen to be the foremost mercantile and artistic centre in Holland. Since he had already received a number of commissions from patrons in Amsterdam, he no doubt felt reasonably assured of a successful future there, and in fact the next ten years were to be—in terms of material reward—the most successful period of his life. He quickly gained a lion's share of the market in middle-class portraiture, in competition with such established and competent masters as Thomas de Keyser, and was commissioned (*c.* 1633) to paint a series of scenes of the Passion for the stadholder, Frederick Henry, prince of Orange, probably through the good offices of Constantijn Huygens, who was the stadholder's secretary. In 1634 he married Saskia van Uylenburch, a relative of his landlord and business associate, the art dealer Hendrick van Uylenburch. Saskia brought a considerable property of her own as marriage portion, for her family was both wealthy and well connected, and the rise in Rembrandt's fortune and social status is fully reflected in the confident and extrovert mood of much of his work of the 1630s. In his art as in his life this was a period of growth and expansion, and the centre of both life and art was the personality of his attractive young wife. In the "Self-Portrait With the Artist's Wife" (Dresden museum) Rembrandt, jovial and resplendent in "cavalier" costume, is seated at a richly garnished table, one hand raising a drinking glass while the other clasps the waist of Saskia, who sits perched, rather demurely, on his knees. It would be foolish to regard this as a literal glimpse into their home life, but it is, in its somewhat vulgar exuberance, Rembrandt's most joyful testimony of his own pleasure in the good things of life.

Doubtless he did enjoy life, but he worked hard also, enlarging his achievement as well as his ambition in a splendid succession of portraits, historical pieces, etchings and drawings. He painted on a larger scale than in his Leiden years, with an increasing preference for canvas rather than panel. His colouring grew warmer, with brown and golden tones predominating, and his brushwork began to develop toward the unrivaled breadth and expressiveness of his fullest maturity. His first big portrait commission was in 1632 for the Surgeons' guild in Amsterdam—"The Anatomy Lesson of Professor Nicolaes Tulp" (Mauritshuis, The Hague). The official group portrait, depicting the officers of a guild, civic guard

LEFT, "NIGHT WATCH" BY REMBRANDT; RIGHT, DETAIL OF CENTRAL FIGURE. IN THE RIJKSMUSEUM, AMSTERDAM

or other corporate body, was an established and important genre in Holland (as nowhere else) and "anatomies" had already been painted by De Keyser and others, although before Rembrandt's time such pictures had tended to be somewhat rigid assemblages of individual portraits, without psychological or pictorial unity in any marked degree. Hals in his earlier groups of the Haarlem civic guards moved toward a more pictorial solution, but Rembrandt penetrates far more deeply into the human situation. Without false overemphasis his "Tulp" reveals the inherent drama of the moment, contriving at the same time to convey the humane and compassionate motives which underlie an otherwise macabre operation, and it was an important step forward in the direction of his own "Night Watch" and "Syndics." In many of his portraits of this period Rembrandt aimed at the neat and highly finished effects which characterized the work of most of his rivals, as can be seen in such pictures as the pair of oval bust-length figures (Boston Museum of Fine Arts) of an "Unknown Man" (1634) and a "Lady in a Lace Collar," or the splendid pair of full-lengths (in the private collection of Baron Robert de Rothschild) also painted in 1634, which were thought to be portraits of Maerten Daey and his first wife Machteld van Doorn, but which more probably represent Marten Soolmans and his wife Oopjen Coppit, who after the death of her husband married Maerten Daey as his second wife. Among many other fine portraits of this phase are: the undated companion pieces of "Jan Pellicorne With His Son" and of Pellicorne's wife "Susanna van Collen With Her Daughter" (Wallace collection, London); "The Shipbuilder and His Wife" (1633; Royal collection at Buckingham palace, London); "The Preacher Eleazar Swalmius" (1637; Antwerp museum); "The Mennonite Preacher Cornelis Anslo and His Wife" (1641; Berlin); "Saskia as Flora" (1634; Hermitage, Leningrad); and the "Self-Portrait" of 1640 (National gallery, London), which shows the artist at the height of his fame and prosperity. In addition Rembrandt continued to produce many studies of a more personal kind, such as heads and single figures of old men, or Jewish types in turbans or colourful robes, that could be of use in his historical paintings.

The biblical subject pictures of these early years in Amsterdam are richly varied and provide evidence that Rembrandt studied almost every contemporary current in European painting. "Christ Appearing to Mary Magdalene" (1638; Buckingham palace) and the "Visitation" (1640; Detroit Institute of Arts) continue and enrich the Elsheimer tradition. The "Sacrifice of Abraham" (1635; Hermitage) is a fully baroque design of spiraling movement. Three illustrations of the story of Samson contrast with the pictures mentioned above and with each other: "Samson Threatening his Father-in-Law" (1635; Berlin) is a straightforward scene of comedy in which the painter's own features can be recognized in the guise of the irate hero; "The Blinding of Samson" (1636; Städelsches Kunstinstitut, Frankfurt-on-Main) is a piece of savage melodrama and perhaps the most Caravaggesque of all Rembrandt's pictures; while "Samson's Wedding Feast" (1638; Dresden museum) is a sumptuous banqueting scene, in which the composed and charming figure of Saskia (Delilah) forms the central key of the composition. "The Sacrifice of Manoah" (1641; Dresden) gives a foretaste of the simplicity and the depth of feeling of Rembrandt's later religious paintings. In spite of the stylistic diversity of these works, they are all deeply impressed with the stamp of Rembrandt's individuality and humanity. Jakob Rosenberg observed that Rembrandt was never inclined to separate the human point of view from the pictorial. In this lies the peculiarly moving quality of his art, that no imitator could approach. His paintings testify to an intimate and loving knowledge of the Bible stories and he presents their characters always as samples of common humanity, not as remote and superhuman protagonists of legend or fairy tale. For Rembrandt the Bible was simple fact—and to be treated as such. The five pictures of the Passion cycle (1633–39; Ältere Pinakothek, Munich) contain all these elements of style and character. In them can be traced echoes of Tintoretto, Caravaggio, Lastman and of Rubens' great "Descent From the Cross" in Antwerp cathedral, but all are fused in the concentrated and forthright power of Rembrandt's own manner, which owes nothing crucial to any of them. All are imbued with the painter's profound compassion, and in the first of the series ("The Raising of the Cross") he painted his own troubled face among the soldiery who heave the cross into position—and who shall be forgiven because "they know not what they do."

From about 1636 onward Rembrandt produced a small number of landscapes, most of them on panel and small, or fairly small, in size. Representative examples are: "Landscape With a Stone Bridge" (1637–38; Rijksmuseum); "Landscape With an Obelisk"

(1638; Isabella Stewart Gardner museum, Boston); the comparatively large "River Landscape With Ruins on a Hill" and the tiny "Winter Landscape" (1646; both in the museum, Cassel, Ger.). These pictures strike one almost as being occasional relaxations of the artist from the hard discipline of figure painting, for they are free and spontaneous in design and technique. In general they follow the tradition of such landscape masters as Pieter Molijn, the early Jan van Goyen and Hercules Seghers, painted almost in monochrome but enlivened by spirited brushwork and dramatic tonal contrasts. Rembrandt delighted in painting an overcast or stormy sky, pierced by a single brilliant shaft of sunlight which illumines a building, a bridge or a clump of trees, producing a "spotlight" effect parallel to that of his figure and interior subjects. There is not the space here for a detailed consideration of Rembrandt's etchings, but among the more important plates of this phase are "The Raising of Lazarus" (c. 1632), "Christ Before Pilate" (1636) and "The Death of the Virgin" (1639).

The celebrated picture known as "The Night Watch" (Rijksmuseum), which was completed in 1642, may be regarded with some truth both as the culminating masterpiece of this decade of successes and as representing the transition to Rembrandt's later and less prosperous years. It might more accurately (though less succinctly) be called "The Civic Guard Under Captain Frans Banning Cocq and Lieutenant Willem van Ruytenburch," for the thorough cleaning which it received in 1946–47 proved that it was not a night scene at all, but that the crowd of figures are emerging into sunlight from the shadows of an arched gateway. It is a huge canvas, about 12 ft. high by 14½ ft. wide, and was originally even larger. Early copies show that the painting has since been cut down on all sides and especially drastically at its left edge, where two figures have been entirely lost. The composition has suffered from this curtailment, but it remains one of the supreme achievements of European art, baroque in its surging yet unified movement and its dramatic yet unified chiaroscuro, but a baroque which Rembrandt keeps under firm control by the strength of his design. "The Night Watch" also provides a foretaste of the brighter colouring that was to appear in his late style though, characteristically, it is used sparingly and effectively against a dark background. The captain's bright red sash and the lieutenant's yellow uniform provide the principal chord of colour, which is echoed in more muted tones in the reds and orange-browns of the figures on each side of them and in the paler yellow of the little girl's dress, while in the background and at the sides cooler greenish and yellowish tints predominate. To achieve the splendid unity of this complex composition Rembrandt subordinated the claims of portraiture to those of his own imaginative genius. This may well have dissatisfied some of the sitters who are placed in such deep shadow as to be almost invisible, but it is surely too much to assume, as many have done, that the decline in his popularity from about this time is directly attributable to the cool reception of this masterpiece. As a body the shooting company of Captain Banning Cocq can hardly have been displeased at acquiring a work of such evident splendour.

From 1640 onward a series of misfortunes overtook Rembrandt. In 1640 his mother died and in 1642 he suffered a still more grievous loss in the death of Saskia, a few months after the birth of their one surviving child, a son. This boy, christened Titus, was thenceforth the apple of his eye and he painted many portraits of him in childhood and as a young man. His popularity as a painter was on the wane, for patrons were turning their attention to the glossier and more readily comprehensible style of the younger generation, a style to which Rembrandt made no concessions. On the contrary, he followed undeviatingly the path of his genius toward ever broader and less "finished" effects. In 1639 he had bought a large and imposing house in the Jodenbreestraat, which contributed to his troubles for he could not really afford its upkeep, and for several years he sank deeper and deeper into financial difficulties. In 1656 he was declared bankrupt, and by 1660 the fine house and almost all of his possessions, including valuable pictures and a vast assortment of armour and other curiosities, had been sold to pay what could be paid of his

debts and he had moved into a humble lodging in a poorer quarter of the city. With him went Titus, now a youth of about 18, and Hendrickje Stoffels, who had entered his household as a servant girl in about 1645 and remained with him in his years of adversity as his mistress and loyal helper. Hendrickje and Titus formed a business partnership as dealers in works of art, with Rembrandt nominally their employee, bound to hand over to them all that he produced in return for his food and lodging. This ingenious device afforded him some protection from his creditors and permitted him at least to work unmolested as old age drew nearer. But his misfortunes were not ended. Hendrickje died in 1662, and in 1668 Titus died, only a few months after his marriage to Magdalena van Loo. Rembrandt did not long outlive his son. He died on Oct. 4, 1669, and was buried in the Westerkerk on Oct. 8. He was survived by his daughter Cornelia, born to Hendrickje Stoffels in 1654. The hardships of Rembrandt's old age have been much exaggerated by some writers, who have pictured him as almost entirely neglected after his brief period of prosperity. This was not really the case. Although no longer a successful painter in the material sense, he was far from being forgotten, as contemporary accounts fully prove. As late as 1662 he executed an important commission, the superb groups of "The Syndics." The failure of contemporary taste to accept the ultimate achievements of his late style was a fate that other great artists have endured in old age. For Rembrandt, as for them, the fulfillment of his art was more important than the applause that he might gain; his triumph was that he spurned any ignoble compromise.

It is no easy task to single out individual pictures for mention from the wealth of masterpieces which Rembrandt produced in the final phases of his career. The self-portraits, which stretch in an unbroken series from his youth to the end of his life to form an artistic autobiography of the most fascinating and moving kind, take on a more sombre and troubled look. In such examples as the half-length "Self-Portrait" of 1652 (in Vienna) and the magnificent "Self-Portrait With a Palette" (Iveagh bequest, Kenwood house, London), painted about ten years later, he analyzes his own moral and physical progress with the same objective compassion as is seen in his studies of other humble sitters, such as the "Old Man in an Armchair" (which entered the National gallery in 1957 from the duke of Devonshire's collection). Other outstanding single portraits are the "Jewish Merchant" (National gallery), the "Jan Six" (1654; in the possession of the sitter's family) and the hauntingly romantic "Polish Rider" (Frick collection, New York). Among the later portrait groups mention must be made of the superb painting of "The Board of the Clothmakers' Guild" (1662; Rijksmuseum). This group, known usually as the "Staalmeesters," or in English "The Syndics," stands supreme in its own category of Dutch group portraiture, as does "The Night Watch." Perhaps the crowning achievement of his career in portraiture was the even later "Family Group" (Herzog Anton Ulrich museum, Brunswick, Ger.). This displays all the qualities of his last manner—rich yet subdued colour harmonies, firm yet unobtrusive compositional structure, vigorous yet subtle brushwork—and is at the same time a tender expression of all that is meant by the family relationship. The same human understanding is to be found in the biblical subjects of this period. Some recall his style of about 1630, for instance "The Woman Taken in Adultery" (1644; National gallery) and the Elsheimerlike "Susanna and the Elders" (Berlin); but in the 1650s and 1660s he produced works of such unique depth of feeling that they elude comparison with any earlier master. Such are the "Peter Denying Christ" (1660; Rijksmuseum) and the profoundly moving "Return of the Prodigal Son" (Hermitage). Parallel with the development in his painted work is a similar deepening of human values in his etchings, of which the famous large plate of "Christ Healing the Sick" (the "Hundred Guilder Print"), of the 1640s, is possibly his supreme achievement in the medium. Finally, only the barest mention can be made of Rembrandt's incomparable drawings in pen or brush, or both, of which there are numerous examples in the principal collections on both sides of the Atlantic. See PAINTING: *The Netherlands: Rembrandt.* See also references under "Rembrandt" in the Index.

BIBLIOGRAPHY.—*Life:* C. Hofstede de Groot, *Die Urkunden über Rembrandt (1575–1721)* (1906); C. Vosmaer, *Rembrandt* (1868); E. Michel, *Rembrandt, sa vie, son oeuvre et son temps* (1893; Eng. trans., 1894); W. Bode, *Rembrandt und seine Zeitgenossen* (1906; Eng. trans., 1909); A. M. Hind, *Rembrandt* (1932); O. Benesch in Thieme-Becker, *Allgemeines Lexikon der bildenden künstler,* vol. xxviii (1934); J. Rosenberg, *Rembrandt,* 2 vol. (1948); S. Slive, *Rembrandt and His Critics 1630–1730* (1953).

Paintings: W. Bode and C. Hofstede de Groot, *The Complete Work of Rembrandt,* 8 vol. (1897–1906); C. Hofstede de Groot, *A Catalogue Raisonné of the works of the most eminent Dutch painters of the 17th century,* vol. vi (1916); W. R. Valentiner, *Rembrandt: Die Meisters Gemälde,* 3rd ed. (1908), and *Rembrandt, Wiedergefundene Gemälde (1910–1922),* 2nd ed. (1923); T. Borenius (ed.), *Rembrandt: Selected Paintings,* 3rd ed. (1952); A. Bredius (ed.), *The Paintings of Rembrandt* (1937).

Etchings: A. Bartsch, *Catalogue raisonné de toutes les estampes qui forment l'oeuvre de Rembrandt* (1797); A. M. Hind, *Rembrandt's Etchings,* 2 vol. (1924); L. Münz, *Rembrandt's Etchings,* 2 vol. (1952).

Drawings: C. Hofstede de Groot, *Die Handzeichnungen Rembrandts* (1906); F. Lippmann and C. Hofstede de Groot, *Original Drawings by Rembrandt Harmensz van Rijn,* 10 portfolios (1888–1911); W. R. Valentiner, *Rembrandt: Des Meisters Handzeichnungen,* 3 vol. (1925); O. Benesch (ed.), *Rembrandt: Selected Drawings* (1948).

(R. E. W. J.)

REMEMBRANCE DAY: *see* VETERANS DAY.

REMEMBRANCER, the name of certain English officials who from medieval times compiled the memoranda rolls and thus "reminded" the barons of the Exchequer of the business pending. There were at one time three clerks of the remembrance: the king's remembrancer, lord treasurer's remembrancer, and remembrancer of the firstfruits (*see* ANNATES). The latter two offices were abolished in 1833 and 1838 respectively. The king's remembrancer originally dealt with the recovery of penalties and debts due to the crown. After 1859 he was required to be a master of the Court of Exchequer. By the Judicature Act (1873) he was attached to the Supreme Court, after 1879 as a master. Since 1925 the office of king's remembrancer has been held by the senior master of the Supreme Court (Queen's Bench Division). The duties involved comprise functions connected with the selection of sheriffs, swearing in the lord mayor of London, and the Trial of the Pyx; *i.e.,* the annual examination of coins issued by the mint.

Remembrancer is also the title of an official of the corporation of the City of London, whose principal duty is to represent that body before Parliamentary commissions and at council and treasury boards. (W. T. Ws.)

REMI (REMY, REMIGIUS), **SAINT** (d. *c.* 530), bishop of Reims and friend of Clovis (*q.v.*), whom he converted to Christianity, was appointed to his see in 459. Clovis, pagan king of northern Gaul, had married Clotilda (daughter of Chilperic, Christian king of Burgundy), whose attempts to convert him he resisted. According to legend, however, during his war against the Alamanni, he promised that he would be converted if Clotilda's God would grant him the victory. He was successful, and Clotilda, therefore, summoned Remi, who with St. Vaast instructed Clovis and baptized him in 496 or 506. Later his sisters and 3,000 men of his army also were baptized. Sources for Remi's life include only scattered references in Gregory of Tours and a few letters written by Remi and some contemporary bishops. Stories such as that of the dove that brought Remi a vial of oil from heaven for the baptism of Clovis, which was kept at Reims and used at the coronation of French kings, are later legends. His feast day is Oct. 1.

See A. Van de Vyver, "La victoire contre les Alamans et la conversion de Clovis," *Revue Belge de philologie et d'histoire,* 15:859–914 (1936), 16:35–94 (1937). (J. N. G.)

REMINGTON, ELIPHALET (1793–1861), U.S. firearms manufacturer and inventor, was born at Suffield, Conn., on Oct. 28, 1793. In 1800 he traveled with his parents to the Mohawk valley, where they settled 20 mi. (32 km.) from Utica, N.Y. The elder Remington built a smithy and forge powered by a water wheel where he made horseshoes and agricultural implements. In 1816 young Remington built himself a flintlock rifle at his father's forge. It embodied no new inventions, but it was so remarkably accurate that the neighbouring sportsmen ordered similar guns from him, and within two years manufacture of sporting guns and rifle barrels became the main business of the forge. In 1828 Remington

built a sizable factory beside the Erie Canal at the present site of Ilion, N.Y., and expanded his production. He and his son Philo pioneered many improvements in arms manufacture, including the reflection method of straightening gun barrels, the lathe for cutting gunstocks, and the first successful cast-steel, drilled rifle barrel in the U.S.

In 1847 Remington supplied the U.S. Navy with its first breech-loading rifle (Jenks carbine). In 1861, at the beginning of the American Civil War, the federal government placed large orders for small arms with Remington. He died on Aug. 12, 1861 in Ilion.

The Remington Arms Company is still a large manufacturer of sporting arms and ammunition. During the American Civil War and World Wars I and II it was an important supplier of small arms and ammunition to the U.S. government.

See Alden Hatch, *Remington Arms in American History* (1956). (AL. H.)

REMINGTON, FREDERIC (1861–1909), U.S. painter, illustrator, and sculptor, noted for his realistic portrayals of the American West. He was born at Canton, N.Y., on Oct. 4, 1861, and studied at the Yale Art School and the Art Students League, New York. Thereafter he devoted himself primarily to illustrative work. He traveled widely, spending much time in the American West, and made a specialty of the subject matter for which he is best known—Indians, cowboys, soldiers, horses, and other aspects of life on the plains. He also published a number of books and articles, which served mainly as vehicles for his illustrations. During the Spanish-American War he was a war correspondent and artist. He died on Dec. 26, 1909, near Ridgefield, Conn. Remington was primarily a reporter, recording the image of the thing seen; his work is notable for its rendering of swift action and its accuracy of detail. The Remington Art Memorial, Ogdensburg, N.Y., contains a collection of his paintings, illustrations, and bronze statuettes.

See R. W. G. Vail, *Frederic Remington, Chronicler of the Vanished West* (1929); H. McCracken (ed.), *Frederic Remington's Own West* (1961).

REMIREMONT, a town of eastern France, *département* of Vosges, is situated on the left bank of the Moselle below its confluence with the Moselotte, 103 km. (64 mi.) SSE of Nancy by road. Pop. (1962) 9,020. The town is surrounded by forest-clad mountains. The abbey church, dating mainly from the 14th–15th centuries, has a crypt of the 11th century. The former palace of the abbesses (which now contains the *mairie* [town hall], the courthouse, and the public library) was rebuilt in 1752 and again in 1871. Some of the houses of the canonesses (17th and 18th centuries) remain. Remiremont is on a branch railway from Arches and Épinal. Industries include cotton spinning and weaving, embroidery, iron and copper founding, metal work, brewing, and the production of ready-made clothing. Its picturesque setting and old buildings have made it an attraction to visitors.

Remiremont (Romarici Mons) is named after St. Romaric, a companion of St. Columban of Luxeuil, who in the 7th century founded a monastery and a convent on the hills above the present town. In 910 an invasion of the Hungarians drove the nuns to Remiremont, which had grown round a villa of the Frankish kings, and in the 11th century they settled there. Enriched by the dukes of Lorraine, kings of France, and emperors of Germany, the ladies of Remiremont attained great power. The abbess was a princess of the empire and received consecration at the hands of the pope. The 50 canonesses were selected from the nobility. On Whitmonday the neighbouring parishes paid homage to the chapter in a ceremony called the "Kyrioles"; and on their accession the dukes of Lorraine, the immediate suzerains of the abbey, had to come to Remiremont to swear to continue their protection. The "War of the Escutcheons" in 1564 between the duke and the abbess ended in the duke's favour and terminated the abbess' power. The monastery and nunnery were suppressed during the Revolution.

REMONSTRANTS, those Dutch Protestants who, after the death of Jacobus Arminius, maintained the views associated with his name, and in 1610 presented to the states-general a "remonstrance" formulating their points of departure from stricter Calvinism. The Remonstrants were assailed both by personal enemies and by the political weapons of Maurice, prince of Orange, and in 1618–19 the synod of Dort expelled them and declared Remonstrant theology contrary to Scripture. The movement remains, however, and its liberal school of theology has reacted powerfully on the state church and on other Christian denominations. *See* ARMINIANISM; DORT, SYNOD OF.

REMORA, a name given generally to fishes of the family Echeneidae, which are remarkable for having the spinous dorsal fin developed into a transversely laminated sucking disc, placed on top of the head; in a more restricted sense the name refers to a particular species, *Remora remora,* other species being given common names such as sharksucker (*Echeneis naucrates*), slender suckerfish (*Phtheirichthys lineatus*), whalesucker (*Remora australis*), etc. There are about 12 species, found in all tropical and temperate seas.

Remoras attach themselves to whales, porpoises, sharks, sea turtles and large fish; they are not, however, parasitic on these animals but are merely transported by them. They detach themselves and swim when searching for food, frequently bits that fall from the mouths of their "hosts." Each plate in the sucking disc can be elevated to produce a partial vacuum when it is attached to a flat surface.

Attempts to dislodge a remora by pulling merely make the attachment more firm; the fish can be detached, however, by sliding it forward. In some parts of the tropics fishermen have used remoras with a line attached to their tails to catch larger fish and sea turtles. (C. Hu.)

REMSCHEID, a town of West Germany in the *Land* (state) of North Rhine-Westphalia (Nordrhein-Westfalen), Federal Republic of Germany, stands on a hill, 22 mi. (35 km.) NE of Cologne by road. Pop. (1961) 126,892. Situated in the heart of the Bergisches Land, Remscheid has interesting slate houses and a local museum. The neighbouring towns of Lennep and Lüttringhausen were joined to Remscheid in 1929. Lennep was the birthplace of Wilhelm Conrad Röntgen, the discoverer of X rays; and there is a Röntgen museum. Remscheid is connected to all parts of the Ruhr by railway.

The conurbation has a substantial iron industry and is the chief centre of the tool industry in Western Germany. Domestic and commercial kitchen and other equipment is made, and there is cloth manufacture.

REMSEN, IRA (1846–1927), U.S. chemist and university president, co-discoverer of saccharin, was born in New York City on Feb. 10, 1846. He was educated at the Free Academy (College of the City of New York; B.A., 1865), College of Physicians and Surgeons, Columbia University (M.D., 1867), and at the universities of Munich and Göttingen (Ph.D., 1870). At the University of Tübingen (1870–72), where he was the assistant of Rudolf Fittig, he began the investigations into pure chemistry upon which his later fame was chiefly based. He became professor of chemistry at Williams College, Williamstown, Mass. (1872), and was one of the original faculty of Johns Hopkins University, Baltimore, Md., where he was professor of chemistry 1876–1913, director of the Chemical Laboratory 1876–1908, secretary of the Academic Council 1881–1901 and president of the university 1901–13. As president of Johns Hopkins he continued to emphasize the primary function of the university as a centre of research. He was president emeritus and professor emeritus 1913–27, during which time he traveled widely and worked on government pure food commissions. Remsen brought to Johns Hopkins many of the German laboratory methods and as a teacher he had many influential students. In 1879 he founded the *American Chemical Journal,* which he edited until it merged with the *Journal of the American Chemical Society* in 1914. In the first volume he described the preparation and properties of a new sweetening compound, subsequently known as saccharin (*q.v.*), which he and a pupil discovered. A long series of studies led to the discovery and enunciation of Remsen's law, concerning the prevention of oxidation in methyl and other groups. He wrote several textbooks of chemistry. Remsen died at Carmel, Calif., on March 5, 1927.

BIBLIOGRAPHY.—B. Harrow, *Eminent Chemists of Our Time* (1920); "Impressions of Ira Remsen," *Johns Hopkins Alumni Magazine,* xvi, 215–226 (1928); "Ira Remsen," *Science,* n.s., lxvi, 243–246 (1927).

RENAISSANCE, a term commonly used in European historiography to denote, with widely different expansions and contractions of significance, a "rebirth" (Fr. *renaissance,* from Ital. *rinascenza,* more commonly *rinascimento*) or "revival" of learning or of the arts, supposed to separate the Middle Ages and the modern period. To those who interpret history in terms of modern progress, the Renaissance was the first milestone along the primrose path to be marked out subsequently by the voyages of discovery; by the Reformation; by the scientific revolution of Vesalius and Copernicus, Kepler and Galileo, Huygens and Newton; by the Industrial Revolution; by the French Revolution; by parliamentary reform in Great Britain; by the rapid exploitation of material resources in the United States; and by imperialistic expansion in Asia and Africa. Events of the 20th century, however, have done much to discourage this progressist interpretation of history, with its doctrine of steady human improvement and its emphasis on the supreme importance of European civilization and of a brief period of human activity which was limited to the inhabitants of Western Europe. At the same time the reassessment of the Middle Ages by scholars who had made real research into the documents of that period called into question many of the notions that had accumulated round the word Renaissance. In this article an attempt is made to explain the Renaissance as the "revival of learning," that is, of Latin and Greek classical literature, in Italy from the middle of the 14th century to the early years of the 16th; and to dispel some of the misconceptions long prevalent about the period.

Readers wanting to be informed on the general history of the Western world from the 14th to the 16th century are referred first to the article EUROPE: *History* and to MIDDLE AGES. For the immediate background of the Renaissance *see* ITALY: *History* and the separate articles on the states and dynasties therein mentioned. The historical sections of the articles on other European countries are also relevant.

The development of imagination and sensibility during the period can be studied in the articles on the vernacular literatures of Western Europe. Of especial importance, however, because of the period's distinction in the fine arts, are the articles PAINTING; RENAISSANCE ARCHITECTURE; RENAISSANCE ART; and SCULPTURE. It was largely on the recognition of the magnificent achievement of the period's artists and architects that the notion of the Renaissance as a miraculous age was built up; and indeed it is in the fine arts that the positive influence of the revival of antiquity first becomes discernible outside the field of scholarship. Critics of the fine arts, of vernacular literatures, and of the drama, however, use the expression Renaissance in extended senses which make it necessary to omit their subjects from this article.

Original Meaning and the Growth of Misconceptions.— The original meaning of the Italian Renaissance of the 14th and 15th centuries—for those who actually participated in it, and through subsequent centuries down to the vernacular classicism of French literature of the 17th century and of English literature of the 18th—was the revival of classical Latin and Greek literature, or, more strictly speaking, belles-lettres, by Petrarch and his followers the humanists. Petrus Ramus (*q.v.*), in an oration of 1546 attacking the Aristotelian logic of the scholastic philosophers, drew a vivid contrast between education at Paris in his own time and education 100 years before. Suppose, he said, that a master of a century ago could return now, what progress he would find, how amazed he would be! He would be as astounded as one who, rising from the depths of earth, should gaze for the first time on sun, moon, and stars. Then he could have heard no one speak save in an inept and barbarous fashion; now he would find countless persons of every age speaking and writing Latin correctly and ornately. Then no one could read Greek; now men not only read it but comprehend it thoroughly. As grammarians, orators, and poets, he used to have to put up with Alexander of Villa-Dei, Facetus and the *Graecismus;* in philosophy, with Scotists and the followers of Petrus Hispanus; in medicine, with the Arabs; in theology, with I know not what upstarts. Today he would hear

Terence, Caesar, Virgil, Cicero, Aristotle, Plato, Galen, Hippocrates, Moses and the prophets, the apostles and other true and genuine messengers of the gospel—and indeed voices in all languages!

Except for its closing allusions to vernacular translations of the Bible, this passage, though none too accurate, well expresses the original restricted significance of the Renaissance as a purifying of Latin diction and grammar, a revival of Greek and a return from medieval compilations to the old classical texts. Already before Ramus and 1546, however, this talk of a resuscitation of liberal studies had become hackneyed and had furthermore been extended to most inappropriate fields. For instance, when the astronomical Alphonsine tables, dating in fact from the second half of the 13th century, were about to be printed in 1492, an astrologer of Olmütz (Olomouc) wrote to their editor, J. L. Santritter, congratulating him on this and himself for living in such a time, when learning was being revived after long neglect. In reply Santritter agreed that all good arts were not only reviving but already in bloom, so that soon modern times would equal the golden age of ancient Rome. Yet actually the occasion of their rejoicing would seem a revival of 13th-century astronomy. Similarly, Alessandro Achillini in 1504, in the preface to a recent work on chiromancy and physiognomy, said that these subjects had remained in darkness for many years past. Similarly again, it was said that Antiochus Tibertus of Cesena, whose *Three Books of Chiromancy* were first printed in 1494, revived the magic art which had been forgotten since the time of Peter of Abano (1250–1315?); Vesalius referred to anatomy as reborn in his *Fabrica* of 1543 and was silent as to his predecessors; and Abstemius represented Pope Paul III (d. 1549) as restoring astrology after many past centuries of darkness and disrepute, barbarism and sordid squalor.

At the zenith of the Enlightenment (*q.v.*), Voltaire in the introduction to his *Siècle de Louis XIV* (1751) selected the Renaissance as the third of the great ages of mankind—to follow the period from Pericles to Alexander the Great in ancient Greece and the age of Julius Caesar and Augustus in Rome and to precede the age of Louis XIV in France and Western Europe. By the 19th century the old and limited conception of the Renaissance was regarded as wholly inadequate. The French historian Jules Michelet defined it as "the discovery of the world and of man"; and Jacob Burckhardt, in his once influential work *Die Kultur der Renaissance in Italien* (1860; Eng. trans., *The Civilization of the Renaissance in Italy*, 1878 and later editions), made this theme the subject of the fourth part, which followed immediately after its scholarly third part on "The Revival of Antiquity." To John Addington Symonds and Walter Pater the vaguest or the most potentially comprehensive uses of the term Renaissance were the most acceptable. Symonds, for example in his *Renaissance in Italy* (1875), claimed that "in many senses we are still in mid-Renaissance"; and then after an impressive catalogue of achievements in every branch of desirable activity—the arts, literature, philosophy, theology, science, government, law, exploration, and technical invention—could resume:

Yet neither any one of these answers separately, nor indeed all of them together, could offer a solution of the problem. By the term Renaissance, or new birth, is indicated a natural movement, not to be explained by this or that characteristic, but to be accepted as an effort of humanity for which at length the time had come, and on the onward progress of which we still participate. The history of the Renaissance is . . . the history of the attainment of self-conscious freedom by the human spirit manifested in the European races . . . The arts and the inventions, the knowledge and the books which suddenly became vital at the Renaissance, had long been neglected on the shores of the Dead Sea which we call the Middle Ages. It was not their discovery which caused the Renaissance. But it was the intellectual energy, the spontaneous outburst of intelligence, which enabled mankind at that moment to make use of them. The force then generated still continues, vital and expansive, in the spirit of the modern world . . . . The mystery of organic life defies analysis.

At this rate, Petrarch was soon being called the first modern man of letters, not merely the father of humanism; and Erasmus, who lived when the classical revival in Italy had already culminated, was called the first modern man. Alternatively the magical metamorphosis of medieval man or classical humanist or

scholar into *homo modernus* was postponed until Elizabethan England, which the *Boston Transcript* of Feb. 27, 1926, could describe as a "period that witnessed the birth pangs of most that is worth while in modern civilization and government." Before proceeding to contest misconceptions in detail, some account must be given both of the real progress made before the classical revival and of the revival as it really was.

The Civilization of the Middle Ages.—A chief reason for regarding the Italian Renaissance as the first milestone of modern progress was past misestimates of the preceding medieval period, which was variously stigmatized as blank or dark; disorderly, confused, and chaotic; unsanitary and dirty; primarily ecclesiastical and superstitious; in bondage as to thought; quaint, outlandish, and incomprehensible to the modern mind. By the middle of the 20th century such views had been entirely discredited by historians. The 13th century, indeed, reached a high point of civilization, to which later centuries are largely indebted for representative institutions, for municipal organization and town life, for economic development, for the first modern maps, for technical invention and scientific progress, for vernacular literature, and for Gothic art. Activity in these fields continued into the 14th century: Dante lived till 1321, Giotto till 1337; Pietro dei Crescenzi finished his important work on agriculture *c.* 1305; Lancilotto Malocello reached the Canaries in 1312; Marsilius of Padua in 1324 completed the *Defensor pacis*, Thomas Bradwardine in 1328 his work on the proportion of velocity, in which by an exponential function he applied mathematical method in physics; and in 1324 also the *Jeux floraux* of the successors of the troubadours were organized at Toulouse.

There had been occasional instances of lovers of pure Latin literature throughout the Middle Ages, notably in France; and by Petrarch's time groups of scholars in Padua and Verona were already taking an active interest in the ancient writings. It was not until the 14th century, however, that a general movement for the investigation of that literature was brought about in Italy, chiefly by Petrarch. The reasons for the delay may be explained briefly. After the breakup of the Roman Empire in the West and the Arabic conquest of most of the Mediterranean world, Arabic became the dominant language from Persia to the Spanish Peninsula. Ancient Greek works of science, medicine, and astrology were translated into it and led to further writings in Arabic in those fields; but the Arabs, who already possessed fine poetry of their own, were not interested in the translation of pure literature from the Greek. Similarly the Christian West, where Latin became the universal language of scholars, relied on what was available in Latin for its knowledge of the pure literature of the ancients. In the 12th and 13th centuries, however, the Christian West engaged itself in a great movement of translation of scientific,

MANSELL-ANDERSON

FIG. 1.—RELIEF FROM THE TOMB OF POPE SIXTUS IV, BY ANTONIO POLLAIUOLO, 1493; IN THE VATICAN

"Philosophia" is reading from Aristotle's *Metaphysics*; the book on the lectern is inscribed with the opening words of his *Physics*

medical, astrological, and alchemical works from both Greek and Arabic, and these were naturally studied and commented on in the universities that developed in the same period. In these universities Roman law was also studied, and a new living Latin was spoken, adapted to contemporary needs and environment. Though the plots of Greek story, from the Trojan War to the conquests of Alexander the Great, were utilized even in vernacular literature, they were generally derived from secondary Latin sources, and the medieval romances introduced many changes in the story and depicted the ancient heroes as feudal lords or knights. The way was therefore open for a more direct approach to ancient Greek literature and for a reappraisal even of classical Latin literature from a human and literary standpoint; namely for humanism as against the scholasticism (*q.v.*) of the medieval universities.

Petrarch.—The advent of humanism must be seen against the background of the unfortunate events that distinguished much of the 14th century from the glorious 13th. The Hundred Years' War (*q.v.*) between France and England began; the Black Death (*q.v.*) ravaged Europe; and from the Italian point of view the migration of the papacy from Rome to Avignon in 1309 was also to be deplored. Petrarch (*q.v.*), who lived from 1304 to 1374, was conscious of a great social change for the worse since his student days at Montpellier and Bologna. In Rome, he thought, all was cold and lifeless; the kingdom of Naples was ruined since the death of King Robert in 1343; the Lombard cities and likewise Pisa, Siena, Arezzo, and Perugia were in decline; even Venice, though prospering by comparison with the others, was less prosperous than it had been. The neighbourhood of Avignon, where he had himself once roamed over the hills by night, was now infested with wolves and robbers. The Netherlands and lower Germany, once so rich, were in ashes, with hardly a house left standing outside the city walls. And in Paris itself the clash of arms had replaced the sound of disputants.

BY COURTESY OF THE BIBLIOTECA NAZIONALE S. MARCO

FIG. 2.—MANUSCRIPT PAGE OF PETRARCH'S DE REMEDIIS UTRIUSQUE FORTUNAE, COMPLETED 1366, WITH PORTRAIT OF PETRARCH IN THE ILLUMINATED INITIAL. IN THE BIBLIOTECA NAZIONALE S. MARCO

It was in the midst of such catastrophic change that the Italian Renaissance was born. In his youth Petrarch had written love sonnets in Italian and been crowned poet laureate by King Robert of Naples in Rome in 1341; but in his later years he fell so much in love with classical antiquity that he deigned to write only in Latin, addressing letters to Cicero and to other ancients whom he admired, or to posterity, as well as to his living friends—who included popes and emperors, since he had traveled widely and gone on public embassies. Also, his letters, not to mention his other works in Latin prose and verse, were circulated widely to other admirers of his style and content, both of which he attempted to make classical. He thus stirred up an interest in the cultivation of classical literature primarily for its literary and human side, its personal, emotional, and rhetorical features. It was this attitude, with the activity ensuing from it, that came to be known as humanism.

Burckhardt admired Petrarch's writings for their "marvelous abundance of pictures of the inmost soul," though he recognized "much that is forced and artificial" in the poetry. On the other hand James Russell Lowell (*Among My Books*) blamed Petrarch as providing the first instance of sentimentalism—of which Lowell held the classics to have been free—and regarded him as "an intellectual voluptuary, a moral dilettante." A third estimate, by Edward Williamson (*Romanic Review*, 1959), is that the "impenetrable barrier" of Petrarch's rhetoric precludes intimacy between himself and the reader. Petrarch himself recognized that his studies and interests had changed since his youth and was glad of it; but he added that this change for the better was as nothing compared to the change for the worse in Western Europe.

The Achievement of Italian Humanism.—Petrarch's example stimulated a movement that went on through generations. Of his immediate collaborators, the most important was Giovanni Boccaccio (*q.v.*), who did much to establish the early leadership of Florence in the movement. A supremely successful seeker after Latin manuscripts, he also secured the appointment of Leonzio Pilato (d. 1367) to teach Greek there. Under the patronage of such men as Coluccio Salutati (1331–1406), chancellor of the *signoria* from 1375, and of Cosimo de' Medici (*see* MEDICI), humanism in Florence continued to prosper, and Florence profited largely from the travels undertaken in search of antiquities by such men as Poggio (*q.v.*) and Cyriacus (*q.v.*) of Ancona. The latter began life as a merchant but finally became a leading collector of ancient remains—objects of art and coins as well as manuscripts—and left several volumes of transcribed inscriptions, unfortunately destroyed by fire in 1514. Other Italian cities also played their part. Milan under the Sforza dynasty maintained Francesco Filelfo (*q.v.*) for more than 30 years. Naples, where King Alfonso I the Magnanimous (Alfonso V of Aragon) was especially benevolent to humanists, long sheltered Lorenzo Valla (*q.v.*) and Antonio Beccadelli, otherwise known as Panormita (1394–1471). After the final return of the lawful papacy (1377), Rome likewise became a humanist centre.

The humanists' efforts led to a better comprehension of classical Latin and of ancient civilization. New grammars and dictionaries were composed; classical philology and literary criticism gradually evolved; and books were written on classical history and antiquities, geography, and mythology. With regard to the pursuit of Latin manuscripts and classical inscriptions by the humanists, it should be remembered that, in the days before printing, men of learning—astrologers, physicians, or legists, for instance—were all accustomed to making copies for themselves of particularly interesting works that they encountered; and that Petrarch's copying of rare works for his own library was thus not unprecedented. Moreover, the classical manuscripts studied by the humanists were copies made at some time in the Middle Ages from earlier texts. The humanist might claim to have rescued the work from oblivion in some monastic library where no one had read it for years. But when he came to make his will he might well leave his library for safekeeping to some other monastery; otherwise the library might be dispersed on his death, as Petrarch's was. Even so, the copying of one humanist's copy by others—or even by whole workshops of scribes specially engaged for the purpose—soon led to an immense proliferation of texts in manuscript. The recording of inscriptions preserved texts that might otherwise not have survived the decay or demolition of the monuments on which they were engraved. Two Veronese epigraphers of the late 15th century did valuable work: Felice Feliciano, who made a study of the geometric construction of letterings on ancient inscriptions; and Fra Giocondo (baptized Giovanni; d. 1515), who was also celebrated as an architect and as a military engineer.

It was once held that the fall of Constantinople to the Turks in 1453 drove Greek manuscripts and scholars west and so caused the Italian Renaissance. On the contrary, it was Italian humanists who from 1393 onward took the initiative in visiting Constantinople to learn Greek and to bring Greek manuscripts back with them. Coluccio Salutati had advised Jacopo Angelo to look for lexicons, historians, and poets and, especially, for manuscripts of Homer, Plato, and Plutarch. Guarino da Verona (d. 1460), later famed as a humanist educator, returned in 1408 with more than 50 manuscripts. Giovanni Aurispa (*c.* 1375–1459) brought back 238 manuscripts, filled almost entirely with Greek works of pure literature, in 1422–23. Filelfo, after nearly seven years in the Venetian legation at Constantinople, came back in 1427 with about 40 authors. Such works were at first known chiefly through the inferior Latin translations that were made of them. Conversely, native Greeks visited the West before 1453 as Byzantine envoys or to attend church councils: both George Gemistus Pletho and

John Bessarion (*qq.v.*) first arrived in this way, at the time of the Council of Ferrara-Florence (1438–39). Some Greeks were recalled as lecturers and, like Manuel Chrysoloras (*q.v.*) at Florence in 1396, aroused interest in Greek. Others were already refugees, for the Turks had overrun much of the Balkan Peninsula before they took Constantinople. These Greeks who came to Italy usually taught their language or made translations into Latin, but they rather outlived their welcome and were not esteemed very highly. Their interests were often scholastic rather than humanistic. Bessarion defended Plato against the Aristotelianism of George of Trebizond (1395–1484); and Gemistus Pletho awakened some interest in Neoplatonism, which the Florentine Marsilio Ficino (1433–99) carried further.

Few Italians were Hellenists to the extent of doing much more than translate a single Greek work into Latin. Politian (*q.v.*), who lived till 1494, in the preface to his Latin translation of Homer, pictures the young patricians of Florence as speaking Greek so fluently that one would think oneself in the streets of ancient Athens; but this flattery may be somewhat overdrawn. In Venice the circle of Aldus Manutius (*q.v.*), founder of that Aldine press which from the 1490s produced such famous editions of the classics, tried to talk Greek, imposing the fine of a small coin for failure to do so. The first printed book in Greek was the grammar of Constantine Lascaris (1476), for which Demetrius of Crete cast the type. Original compositions in Greek by Italian humanists before 1500 were few, the chief contribution being Politian's Greek epigrams. Politian also surpassed the others in Latin diction; he was a distinguished philologist; and his *Orfeo,* a dramatic poem in the vernacular, is the seedling of Italian opera.

With the introduction of printing (*q.v.*), humanistic texts poured from the press, though it should be borne in mind that scholastic texts did so likewise at the same time. These early printed books retained many characteristics of the medieval manuscripts, including contractions and abbreviations which make them hard to read; but some incunabula, as books printed during the 15th century are called, are also beautiful works of art. Usually made from a single manuscript and very faithful to their source, the classical texts printed by the humanists are not critical editions in the modern sense involving a collation of numerous manuscripts; but modern critical editions have profited by the textual criticism of the humanists (the 15th-century manuscript of Lucretius in the Laurentian library, for instance, is of great value for the final determination of the text). The *Castigationes Plinianae* of the Venetian Ermolao Barbaro (1454–93) were still highly valued in 1875 as "of incredible erudition and singular sagacity." Barbaro moreover suggested many of the coinage problems which were

considered later in the French scholar Guillaume Budé's *De asse.*

Special Characteristics of the Italian Humanists.—Humanism made little headway at the Italian universities; even Lorenzo de' Medici gave up the attempt to develop a university in humanist Florence and returned the institution to Pisa. Humanists more often found employment as secretaries or orators for governments; and in this capacity they took their time in composing dispatches or speeches, for fear lest they might be guilty of some barbarism or defect of Latinity. In their literary style they were inclined to indulge in sententious utterances and to concern themselves with reviving a lost art of eloquence. Lorenzo Valla's *Elegantiae linguae latinae* (1444), on the niceties of the Latin language, with specific criticism of the Latin style of some of his fellow humanists, ran through 60 editions between 1471 and 1536. An effect of this preoccupation was that, as the remote classical past was recovered, the immediate medieval past was neglected and forgotten, and medieval Latin came to be regarded as barbaric. By thus substituting an artificial, bookish, and dead language for the living, spoken Latin of the Middle Ages, the humanists to some extent defeated their own purpose, and their work degenerated into antiquarian scholarship. On the other hand they aroused such enthusiasm for relics of antiquity that contemporary artists sometimes tried to pass their own work off as ancient, so as to command a higher price; and some Italian humanists were themselves guilty of literary forgeries, ascribing compositions of their own to antiquity. Thus Leonardus Dathus (Leonardo Dati), who died bishop of Massa in 1472, pretended to have discovered and translated into Latin a work by Caelius Vibenna in ancient Etruscan on the deeds of King Porsena and the Clusini; and he dedicated his translation to Pope Pius II, the former humanist Aeneas Sylvius Piccolomini. Likewise Joannes Annius of Viterbo (Giovanni Nanni; *c.* 1432–1502), who had been trained in Greek and Hebrew by Dominicans and was closely associated with popes Sixtus IV and Alexander VI, faked the lost works of the Roman historian Fabius Pictor and of the Babylonian priest Berossus.

The Italian humanists wrote on the dignity of man, on human excellence and human felicity, and on learned men from an aristocratic rather than from a democratic outlook. Cicero had used the word *humanitas* not only in the sense of human kindness but also to mean refinement of education and taste, good breeding, and mental cultivation. The humanists' concern was with their learned and noble contemporaries, not with the masses or populace. The *virtù* that they admired was an excellence transcending social considerations, an ethic ideal for the individual, not for the many.

Some of the humanists were clergymen; others were sincerely

FIG. 3.—(LEFT) A SCHOLAR OR SCRIBE AT WORK IN HIS STUDY, SURROUNDED BY MANUSCRIPTS. A MINIATURE FROM THE MANUSCRIPT OF LA VIE ET MIRACLES DE NOTRE-DAME (1456), COLLECTED BY JEAN MIÉLOT, SECRETARY TO PHILIP THE GOOD, DUKE OF BURGUNDY; SAID TO BE A PORTRAIT OF MIÉLOT HIMSELF. IN THE BIBLIOTHÈQUE NATIONALE, PARIS. (RIGHT) "PRINTING BOOKS," DRAWN BY JOHANNES STRADANUS (1536–1605) AND ENGRAVED BY P. GALLE, FROM THE NOVA REPERTA; IN THE BRITISH MUSEUM

BY COURTESY OF (RIGHT) THE TRUSTEES OF THE BRITISH MUSEUM; PHOTOGRAPH (LEFT), RADIO TIMES HULTON PICTURE LIBRARY

religious; practically all of them conformed outwardly to Catholicism. The pagan and worldly influence of classical Latin literature, however, tended to encourage a critical and skeptical attitude. This too may be illustrated by Lorenzo Valla. His *De voluptate* (1431) was a frank defense of sensual pleasure; and in 1439, while he defended freedom of the will, he attacked the Aristotelian logic of the scholastics. Whereas most humanists treated history as a mere branch of literature, Valla in 1440 employed historical and textual criticism to impugn the Donation of Constantine, which represented the first Christian emperor as surrendering the West to the pope, and to attack the legend that the Apostles' Creed had been composed independently by each apostle. His notes on the Latin text of the New Testament foreshadowed Erasmus' edition of the Greek text. A work in which Valla set spontaneous virtue above monastic vows (not printed until 1869) looked forward to the Protestant Reformation.

Valla's subversive attitude brought him occasionally into trouble with the church, but he emerged unscathed and finally received an appointment in the Roman *curia* under Nicholas V, who as Tommaso Parentucelli had himself been known as a humanist before he became pope in 1447. The scandalous *Hermaphroditus* of Beccadelli incurred ecclesiastical censure for its complaisant description of licentious practices, but the favour of secular rulers protected the author. In Rome, however, the humanist academy of Julius Pomponius Laetus (*q.v.*) was suppressed by Pope Paul II in 1468. Its assiduous resuscitation of pagan Roman customs and its enthusiasm for the ancient Roman republic gave offense; and some of its adherents, including Platina (Bartolomeo Sacchi da Piadena; 1421–81), were suspected of conspiring against the life of the pope, who had dismissed a number of humanists from the chancery in which Pius II had installed them as *abbreviatori* or clerks.

Academies or literary societies and coteries were common among the humanists. The academy founded by Beccadelli in Naples in 1442 became the Accademia Pontaniana, taking its name from that of his successor, Giovanni Pontano (*q.v.*). The Accademia Platonica, which Cosimo de' Medici founded in Florence, was the last refuge of Pico della Mirandola (*q.v.*). Among themselves, however, the humanists were strongly addicted to controversy, not only on points of scholarship but also on general issues and on matters of taste or subjective opinion. Such quarrels were conducted with extreme virulence. Poggio, for example, was involved in widely publicized disputes with Filelfo on Florentine affairs, with Guarino on the comparative merits of Scipio Africanus and Julius Caesar, and with Valla on the style of his Latin; and Valla had notable controversies of his own.

MANSELL-ANDERSON

FIG. 4.—POPE SIXTUS IV VISITING PLATINA IN THE VATICAN LIBRARY; FROM A MURAL BY THE SCHOOL OF MELOZZO DA FORLÌ IN THE OSPEDALE DI S. SPIRITO, ROME

Sixtus appointed the humanist historian Platina to organize and catalogue the Vatican's 1,200 manuscripts, accumulated for the most part by Pope Nicholas V

The Migration of Humanism to Other Countries.—Humanism spread to Germany in the last quarter of the 15th century and the first quarter of the 16th. In England, William Grocyn and Thomas Linacre (*qq.v.*) had been pupils of Politian; and both John Colet and Thomas More (*qq.v.*) were influenced in their Christianity by Italian humanism. In France, Robert Gaguin (*c.* 1425–1501), who also concerned himself with the nonclassical history of France, was the leading Latinist in the closing 15th century; and Guillaume Budé (*q.v.*) was a pioneer numismatist and Hellenist in the early 16th century. Antonio de Nebrijah took

MANSELL-ALINARI

FIG. 5.—PICO DELLA MIRANDOLA, A LATE 15TH-CENTURY PORTRAIT BY AN ANONYMOUS MASTER; IN THE UFFIZI GALLERY, FLORENCE

Italian humanism to Spain; and his pupil Juan Luis Vives (*q.v.*) has been grouped with Budé and with Erasmus as one of the triumvirs of the republic of letters in the early 16th century. In these countries the movement was associated with the universities rather than disassociated from them as in Italy; and the non-Italian humanists interested themselves in their particular national history as well as in classical history. Moreover, a man of learning could sometimes acquire the title of humanist simply by virtue of a slur or two against scholasticism to be found in his writings, or by not being a very reactionary monk or theologian. There were, however, better Greek and Hebrew scholars north of the Alps soon after 1500 than there had been in Italy in the 15th century.

Desiderius Erasmus (*q.v.*), a native of the Netherlands who visited Italy, France, England, and Switzerland and whose writings circulated widely in Spain, may be regarded as the kingpin of the movement in these lands and as the leader in what has been called the Christian Renaissance in distinction from the Italian Renaissance. If, in the 18th-century words of Alexander Pope, "the monks finished what the Goths begun," it was Erasmus who

> Stemmed the wild torrent of a barbarous age
> And drove those holy vandals off the stage.

Yet Erasmus had his blind spots. He was ignorant alike of the great writers of the 13th century and of the Greek writers and culture of the 5th and 4th centuries before Christ. He scorned modern languages and nationalism and had little interest in natural science. He hardly mentions the New World or the fine arts.

Italy's hegemony in the world of classical learning may be regarded as having been brought to an end by the sack of Rome during Clement VII's papacy by the soldiers of the constable duc de Bourbon in 1527—a by-product of the wars between Francis I of France and Charles V, Holy Roman emperor and king of Spain. Though Clement's successor, Paul III, raised the humanists Pietro Bembo (*q.v.*) and Jacopo Sadoleto (1477–1547) to the cardinalate, his pontificate was chiefly important for the opening of the Counter-Reformation at the Council of Trent. (*See* further CLASSICAL SCHOLARSHIP.)

Humanist Political and Economic Thought.—In general the humanists, from Petrarch to More and Erasmus, if they were cognizant of any alteration in political and economic conditions or in moral and social values, regarded it as for the worse. The political and economic thought of schoolmen and canonists; or of the legist Bartolus (1313–57), whom Valla criticized; or of Nicole Oresme (d. 1382); or of Wycliffe (d. 1384); or of Archbishop Antonino of Florence (d. 1459), who dared to defy the Medici by posting on the cathedral door a message written in his own hand urging the citizens to retain the secret ballot—the thought of all these surpassed that of the Italian humanists before 1500. Some credit, however, may be given to Lippo Brandolini (d. 1497) for the work of comparison between a republic and a kingdom, dealing with the relative merits of the Florentine and the Hungarian sys-

FIG. 6.—THE HUMANIST TRIUMVIRATE: (LEFT) ERASMUS, WOODCUT BY HANS HOLBEIN THE YOUNGER, 1535; IN THE ETCHING COLLECTION, ÖFFENTLICHE KUNSTSAMMLUNG, BASEL; (CENTRE) JUAN LUIS VIVES, BY JEAN JACQUES BOISSARD, FROM ICONES QUINQUAGINTA PUBLISHED IN FRANKFURT, 1597; IN THE BRITISH MUSEUM; (RIGHT) GUILLAUME BUDÉ, BY JEAN CLOUET; IN THE MUSÉE CONDÉ, CHANTILLY

tems of government (with occasional allusions to other states of Europe), which he began at the court of the Hungarian king Matthias Corvinus in the winter of 1489–90 and completed in Florence. It is in the 14th and 15th centuries that a purely economic point of view is expressed for the first time in written records, such as commercial bookkeeping and arithmetic and treatises composed by businessmen for businessmen; but these practical writings in the vernaculars had no connection with classical Latin, humanism, or the revival of antiquity.

The humanists were likely to approach political and economic problems from a literary and antiquarian angle and were lacking both in basic principles and in the logic to evolve a consistent and systematic treatise or philosophy from them. Also many of them were in the service of despots, who found them better publicists than university faculties were, and less independent. The humanists might desire the reform of social ills, but they seldom succeeded in bringing it about. Niccolò Machiavelli (*q.v.*), the greatest political thinker of the Renaissance period, was saturated with classical history and with the culture of the humanists, but he stands quite apart from them for the realism of his approach; and his *Principe* (1513), which he dedicated to the Medici pope Leo X, was not published in his lifetime.

In law such classicists as Andrea Alciati (1492–1550) and Jacques Cujas (*q.v.*) affected style and local colour more than substance.

Contemporary Technology and Science.—The fact that Valla's treatise on novelties unknown to the ancients has not survived indicates that his age was more interested in classical antiquity than in recent inventions. Of the three inventions that used to be associated with the Renaissance, namely the mariner's compass, gunpowder, and printing with movable types, only the last can still be ascribed to the period, since the other two are now known to date back at least to the 13th century. The introduction of printing into Europe, however, took place north of the Alps and cannot be shown to have had any connection with the classical revival—though insofar as judgments came later to be formed merely on the basis of what had been printed, the advantage that the humanists took of the invention served to induce a neglect of the medieval period, whose records were left in manuscript.

Italian humanism produced relatively little of scientific or philosophical importance from its investigation of the classical past: Leonardo Bruni (*q.v.*) of Arezzo said that the subtleties of arithmetic and geometry were not worthy of a cultivated mind. In any case, most available works of Greek science had already been translated into Latin before 1300. Ptolemy's *Cosmographia* or *Geography*, however, had remained untranslated among the 33 Greek manuscripts in the library of Pope Boniface VIII, probably because Arabic geographers and Latin travelers to the Far East had corrected and supplemented it on many points, and the translation of it in 1406 by the humanist Jacopo Angelo had a regrettable sequel. So great was Ptolemy's reputation as an astronomer (his *Almagest* had been translated in the 12th century, from both Greek and Arabic), and so intense was humanist devotion to classical authors, that the obsolete *Cosmographia* was often followed by navigators of the age of discovery and even more often in maps of the 16th century. At first it was hoped that new manuscripts and translations of Hippocrates and Galen would free medicine from the Arabic influence of Avicenna and others, but they made little real difference.

The preoccupation of the humanists with belles-lettres and with the fine arts was followed in the 16th century by the preoccupation of Europe with religious movements—the Reformation and the Counter-Reformation. There resulted a widespread neglect not only of the earlier scientific progress of the 13th and of the first half of the 14th century but also of the minor scientific activity that had been pursued at Venice and elsewhere concurrently with the Renaissance. Thus arose the notion that modern science originated at the earliest with Copernicus and Vesalius in the 1540s, or perhaps as late as the 17th century.

Venice, the most stably governed of the Italian states, had been a centre of scientific and technological activity that bore no relation to humanism. In 1415, after travel elsewhere, Benedetto Rinio had settled there and composed a herbal, richly illustrated by the painter Andrea Amadio, which was kept for a time at a shop in the street of the dealers in spices and which is now preserved in the library of St. Mark's

FIG. 7.—ILLUMINATED PAGE FROM DE COMPARATIONE REI PUBLICAE ET REGNI AD LAURENTIUM MEDICEM, AN UNPUBLISHED MANUSCRIPT BY LIPPO BRANDOLINI

The figures represent Matthias Corvinus, his son, and perhaps the author. In the Biblioteca Medicea-Laurenziana, Florence

—together with the rare Greek manuscripts that Bessarion left to Venice, as the safest asylum for them, under his will of 1468. Leonardo of Bertipaglia, employed by the government of Venice as lecturer on surgery at the University of Padua in the 1420s, possessed great manual dexterity and ingenuity and wrote with gusto. Sante Ardoini of Pesaro wrote his work on poisons at Venice in 1424–26, full of allusions to what he had seen or heard in Venice and to his medical practice there. Giovanni da Fontana, a citizen of Venice, wrote in 1440 and thereabouts on instruments, measurement and mechanical advance, military and hydraulic engineering, distant lands and contemporary map making. All these authors display an independence, confidence, and present experience which is in refreshing contrast to humanist studies of ancient literature and civilization. Outside the Venetian zone, Giovanni Bianchini composed his astronomical tables at Ferrara in the middle years of the 15th century, and the Florentine Paolo del Pozzo Toscanelli (1397–1482) was one of many observers of the appearance in 1456 of what later came to be known as Halley's Comet.

Nor was such activity confined to Italy. There survives, by an anonymous author and from a place unknown, a daily record of the weather from Aug. 31, 1399, to June 25, 1401, fuller than any known before, with observations in the morning, afternoon, and evening, or even through the night, and distinguishing wind aloft from wind near the ground. In 1410 the Frenchman Pierre d'Ailly wrote the *Imago mundi* used later by Columbus. Johann von

Gmunden was active at Vienna early in the 15th century in astronomy and in mathematics, in which he was followed by Georg Peurbach (Peuerbach or Purbach; 1423–61) and by Johann Müller (q.v.) of Königsberg, generally known as Regiomontanus. Nicholas of Cusa wrote on static experiments in 1440. Of all these men, in or out of Italy, only Peurbach and Regiomontanus can be closely associated with the Italian Renaissance. They had taught Latin classics at Vienna, and Bessarion turned over to them the composition of an epitome in Latin of Ptolemy's *Almagest* (this epitome was the only version of that work to be printed before the middle of the 16th century). Peurbach was astronomer-astrologer to László V of Hungary; and Regiomontanus, after his astrological selection of a favourable moment for the foundation of the University of Pressburg (Pozsony, Bratislava) had not assured that university's success, spent some time at the humanistic court of Matthias Corvinus, arranging the royal collection of Greek manuscripts.

The notebooks of Leonardo da Vinci (q.v.), who is often regarded as the example par excellence of the universal genius and all-round man of the Renaissance, have been held to forecast subsequent inventions, but they are found also to have copied a good deal from previous authors. He did important work of his own, however, on anatomy. But in any case Leonardo belongs with the artists and architects, not with the humanists.

Conclusions.—In the light of the foregoing, some of the claims made for the Renaissance in the expansive senses of the word can now be examined. If Michelet's "discovery of the world" be taken to refer to the voyages of discovery of Columbus, Vasco da Gama, and others, it should be said that these voyages had almost no relation to classical literature but were the medieval culmination of a medieval widening of the world and "dawn of modern geography" since the 13th century. Moreover, against the opening up of new continents and sea routes must be set the contraction of Europe in the face of the Turkish advance to the middle Danube, with Greece itself overrun in the process. If the phrase is taken to indicate appreciation of nature, it can be discarded because such appreciation is found to a high degree both in medieval literature and in Gothic art.

When Petrarch's ascent of Mont Ventoux is cited as the first example of a man's climbing a mountain for the sake of the view, the fact that the Parisian schoolman Jean Buridan had visited Mont Ventoux before Petrarch and had given data as to its altitude is overlooked; and Gertrud Stockmayer traces the feeling for nature in Germany back to the 10th and 11th centuries and records various ascents and descriptions of mountains from that period (*Über Naturgefühl in Deutschland im 10. und 11. Jahrhundert*, 1910).

Intensive reading of the pagan classics would undoubtedly give one a different slant on life from that given by the reading of Arabic poetry or the perusal of Christian volumes. But such acquired characteristics would scarcely be transmitted to one's posterity unless they kept up such reading. Moreover, it is to be remembered that reading of the classics was usually combined with the reading of the Bible, saints' lives, books of hours, Church Fathers, and medieval chronicles and even romances. It was not the whole story, but rather a new ingredient added to an old compound, or increased in amount over what had been previously absorbed in the grammar school.

Did the Renaissance promote a discovery of man in the sense of more marked individuality and personality, or were there more "complete men" in the 15th century than in the Middle Ages, as Burckhardt asserted? Apart from the examples of marked personality that occur continually in the period lying between antiquity and the Renaissance, individuality itself and its problems (the *haecceitas* of Duns Scotus, for instance) were frequently discussed by the medieval schoolmen, whereas not even the word is found in classical Latin. And against the claim for "completeness" may, on the one hand, be cited the many-sided men of the Middle Ages, such as Ramon Llull and, on the other, may be asked how completeness is to be reconciled with that absence of moral or social sense which so often characterized the pursuit of *virtù*, or individual excellence.

As for the first modern man or the beginning of modern ways, it should be remembered that the men before the Renaissance regularly spoke of themselves as "moderns" (*moderni*). The modern spirit has been detected in St. Francis of Assisi as well as in Petrarch and Erasmus. This modern spirit was rampant at Paris in the 12th century and was satirized by John of Salisbury in his *Entheticus* as follows:

On all sides they clamour:
Of what interest to us are the sayings or deeds of the ancients?
We are self-taught; our youth has learned for itself.
Our band does not accept the dogmas of the ancients;
We do not burden ourselves in following their utterances.
Rome may cherish the authors of Greece.
I dwell on the Petit-Pont, and am a new authority in arts.
It may have been discovered before; I boast it is mine.

Even late scholastic philosophy had its *via moderna*, the philosophy of William Ockham and his followers, as well as the *via antiqua* of the earlier 13th-century thinkers.

The period of the Renaissance, in the old sense of the term, was not one of modern progress either politically or socially, morally or materially. In most towns, walls and towers, streets and houses, were little changed even until the 19th century. Houses at Lyons which were listed in 1725 were still identified by the same signs and emblems as in the 11th and 12th centuries. If a new school were started, it would be in some abandoned hospital or half-ruined monastery rather than in a new building. Feudal castles were not dismantled till the 17th century, and the guild system was then essentially the same as it was in the 13th. In the 16th century a good cavalier on a good horse was still as superior a being as there could be in this world. There was no great improvement either in transportation or in sanitation. In fact, Francis Bacon tells us that people bathed less in his time than they used to do. Amid such static external conditions the reading of classical literature and the inspection of Italian or native masterpieces in the fine arts might well rank high. Finally, after making allowance for the introduction of printing, it must be emphasized that in many respects there was a break between the scientific activity of the 14th century and its resumption in the 16th or 17th century.

It is necessary, therefore, to reject Michelet's redefinition of the Renaissance as the discovery of the world and of man, together with all kindred attempts to assess it in vague terms and intangible conceptions such as the medieval mind and the modern mind, or the popular mind and the intelligentsia, individuality and personality, sentiment and spirit. Instead one should return to the original conception of the movement as a revival of classical Latin belles-lettres and the recovery of Greek classical belles-lettres. Since history is continuous, only a loss of records makes an apparent breach in it, but its frontier at any given moment is not a straight line; it has advanced at some points and is backward at others.

The fact that some books on the Renaissance have stretched it backward to include not only Dante and the Goliardic poets but also Ezzelino da Romano and the emperor Frederick II, while others have brought it down to Ariosto and Vesalius or even farther, is enough to show that there can no more be a sharp dividing line between medieval and Renaissance culture than between the Renaissance and the succeeding age.

See also references under "Renaissance" in the Index.

BIBLIOGRAPHY.—General works with the traditional view of the Renaissance include J. Burckhardt, *The Civilization of the Renaissance in Italy*, Eng. trans. (1878; 3rd ed. 1951); J. A. Symonds, *Renaissance in Italy*, 7 vol. (1875–88); P. Monnier, *Le Quattrocento*, 8th ed., 2 vol. (1924); J. N. Figgis, *From Gerson to Grotius, 1414–1625* (1916); F. Funck-Brentano, *La Renaissance* (1935). For the 20th-century reassessment *see* the articles by various authors in *The Civilization of the Renaissance* (1929) and in the *Journal of the History of Ideas*, vol. iv (1943), with Supplement No. 1 (1945); E. Bréhier, *La Notion de la Renaissance dans l'histoire de la philosophie* (1933); W. K. Ferguson, *The Renaissance in Historical Thought* (1948); H. Baeyens, *Begrip en Probleem van de Renaissance* (1952); P. O. Kristeller, *Studies in Renaissance Thought and Letters* (1956). For the humanist revival of antiquity *see* G. Voigt, *Die Wiederbelebung des klassischen Altertums* (1859; 3rd ed. 1893); R. Sabbadini, *Le scoperte dei codici latini e greci ne' secoli XIV e XV*, 2 vol. (1905–14); J. E. Sandys, *History of Classical Scholarship*, vol. i, 3rd ed. (1921), and vol. ii (1908); P.

Renucci, *L'Aventure de l'Humanisme européen* (1953). For special aspects *see* W. H. Woodward, *Studies in Education During the Age of the Renaissance, 1400–1600* (1906); C. Mortet, *Les Origines et les débuts de l'imprimerie . . .* (1922); A. Hyma, *The Christian Renaissance* (1924); E. Emerton, *Humanism and Tyranny* (1925); A. Haupt, *Geschichte des Renaissance in Spanien und Portugal* (1917); L. Thorndike, *Science and Thought in the Fifteenth Century* (1929) and *A History of Magic and Experimental Science*, vol. iii and iv (1934); G. Sarton, *Introduction to the History of Science*, vol. iii (1947). For the influence of humanism on Renaissance art *see* E. Panofsky, *Studies in Iconology* (1939). (L. Te.)

RENAISSANCE ARCHITECTURE. The Renaissance style of architecture originated in Florence, Italy, during the early 15th century and from there spread throughout most of the Italian peninsula; by the 16th century the new style pervaded almost all of Europe, gradually replacing the Gothic style of the middle ages. The name Renaissance (*rinascimento* in Italian) dates from the period itself, whose goal was the rebirth or re-creation of ancient classic culture. In architecture there was a revival of classic forms and ornament, such as the column and round arch, the tunnel vault and dome; but from this classic vocabulary the Renaissance architects made a completely original architecture.

This article is organized as follows:

The periods of European architecture before the Renaissance are discussed in Byzantine Art and Architecture; Romanesque Art and Architecture; and Gothic Art and Architecture. European architecture after the Renaissance is discussed in Baroque and Post-Baroque Architecture and Modern Architecture. The classic antecedents of Renaissance architecture are treated in Greek Architecture and Roman Architecture. *See* also Architecture.

I. INTRODUCTION

The Renaissance knowledge of the classic style was derived chiefly from two sources: the ruins of ancient classic buildings, particularly those in Italy, but some in France and Spain; and the treatise *De architectura* by the Roman architect Vitruvius (*q.v.*). At that time it was not realized that Vitruvius' theory was drawn to a great extent from Hellenistic Greek architectural theory, and Renaissance architects were often disturbed by the apparent discrepancies between Vitruvius and the actual Roman ruins.

The Renaissance architects considered the classic orders one of the basic elements of their architecture; the orders were organized on a system of proportions, and proportion was the essence of their theory of beauty. (*See* Order.) During the Renaissance five orders were used, the Tuscan, Doric, Ionic, Corinthian and Composite, but various ones were prevalent in the different periods of the Renaissance.

For example, the ornate, decorative quality of the Corinthian order was embraced during the early Renaissance, while the masculine simplicity and strength of the Doric was preferred during the Italian High Renaissance. Following ancient Roman architecture (*e.g.*, the Colosseum or the Theatre of Marcellus) Renaissance architects often superimposed the orders, that is, used a different order for each of the several stories of a building, commencing with the heavier, stronger Tuscan or Doric order below, then rising through the lighter, more decorative Ionic, Corinthian and Composite.

For all the Renaissance arts proportion tended to be the most important predetermining factor of beauty. The great Italian humanist and architect Leon Battista Alberti defined beauty in architecture as "a Harmony of all the Parts in whatsoever Subject it appears, fitted together with such Proportion and Connection, that nothing could be added, diminished or altered, but for the Worse" (*Ten Books on Architecture,* trans. by J. Leoni, book vi, ch. 2, 1755).

The Renaissance architect worked from a fixed unit of proportion, the module, which was usually half the diameter of the column of the order and which determined the size and location of the various parts of his elevation or plan. There was even a relationship between architectural proportions and the leading Renaissance device of perspective (*q.v.*); the Italian painter Piero della Francesca said that perspective represented objects seen from afar "in proportion according to their respective distance." In fact, it was an Italian Renaissance architect, Filippo Brunelleschi, who apparently was the first to formulate perspective. Many Renaissance architects were as concerned with perspective as the painters were, for most Renaissance architecture was meant to be seen from a fixed visual viewpoint, like a painting in perspective, and not from a moving viewpoint as were baroque and modern architecture.

In part because of the interest in proportion, architecture during the Renaissance was raised to the level of a liberal art (or a fine art). During the middle ages it was considered simply a mechanical art and the artists and architects basically craftsmen, their anonymity only occasionally dispelled by the fortunate preservation of building accounts. In the Renaissance the varying systems of proportion were dependent on a knowledge of geometry; architecture became the materialization in space of the principles of geometry and thereby an equal of geometry, which had been a liberal art during the middle ages.

Renaissance architecture was produced no longer by craftsmen but by educated men of some social standing. In Italy during the 15th and 16th centuries the architect gradually acquired this social standing through his knowledge and education which were concerned with the theory and principles of design more than with the craft of building. The Renaissance architect was, therefore, known as an individual. His life and his ideas have been preserved, and he is not merely another name in a building record.

The Renaissance was also the great moment in the history of architecture for the expression of architectural theory. Inspired by the rediscovery or reevaluation of the treatise by Vitruvius, many architects recorded their theories of architecture; some were preserved in manuscript (*e.g.*, those of the architects Francesco di Giorgio and Antonio Filarete), but most were published. Alberti's treatise, *De re aedificatoria*, modeled on Vitruvius, was written in the middle of the 15th century and published in 1485. However, it was during the last three-quarters of the 16th century, the period of Mannerism, that architectural theory flourished. The Italians Serlio, Vignola and Palladio published famous books on architecture at that time. Elsewhere, works were published by the Frenchmen Androuet du Cerceau, Delorme and Jean Bullant; the Fleming Vredeman de Vries; the German Wendel Dietterlin; and John Shute in England.

II. ITALY

Renaissance architecture commenced in Italy about 1420 and flourished until the end of the 16th century, when it was gradually superseded by the baroque style. In Italy there were three principal periods in the development of the Renaissance: (1) the early Renaissance, from the appearance of the new style early in the 15th century to the end of the century; (2) the High Renaissance, approximately the first quarter of the 16th century; and (3) Mannerism, the remaining portion of the 16th century.

The Renaissance began in Italy, where there was always a residue of classic feeling in architecture. A Gothic building such as the Loggia dei Lanzi in Florence continued to use the large round arch instead of the usual Gothic pointed arch, and preserved the simplicity and monumentality of classic architecture. The Renaissance might have been expected to appear first in the city of Rome, where there was the greatest quantity of ancient Roman ruins, but during the 14th and early 15th centuries, when the Italians were impelled to renew classicism, the political situation at Rome was very unfavourable for artistic endeavour. This was the time of a schism in the church, with the papacy located at Avignon in south France and no central power at Rome. Florence, however, under the leadership of the Medici family, was economically prosperous and politically stable.

A. Early Renaissance

In 1401 a competition was held between sculptors and goldsmiths to design a pair of doors for the old baptistery at Florence. The sculptor Lorenzo Ghiberti won, and a losing goldsmith, Filippo Brunelleschi, resolving to be the leader in one of the arts, then turned to the study of architecture. Brunelleschi spent the period between 1402 and 1418 alternately in Florence and Rome. During this time he studied mathematics intensively and formulated linear perspective, which was to become a basic element of Renaissance art. At the same time Brunelleschi investigated ancient Roman architecture and acquired the knowledge of classic architecture and ornament, which he used as a foundation for Renaissance architecture. His great opportunity came in 1418 with the competition for the completion of the *duomo,* or cathedral, of Florence. The medieval architects had intended a great dome over the crossing of the cathedral, but it had never been created, and no one knew how to accomplish it. Winning the competition, Brunelleschi began the great dome in 1420 (the finishing touches were applied in 1467, after Brunelleschi's death). The Florentine dome is really not in the Renaissance style since it was built with rib construction and a pointed arch form which were medieval. But the dome was raised on a drum, which the medieval architects had not intended; the idea of a dome being made more prominent by the added stature of a drum became characteristic of the Renaissance style. (*See* DOME.)

While he was erecting the dome, Brunelleschi produced in Florence other notable examples of the Renaissance style. The loggia of the Ospedale degli Innocenti (1419–51) was the first building in the Renaissance manner; a very graceful arcade was designed with Composite columns, and windows with classic triangular pediments were regularly spaced above each of the arches. This style was more fully exploited in the church of S. Lorenzo (1419 to *c.* 1470). Using the traditional basilica (*q.v.*) plan (*i.e.,* a long rectangle with the sanctuary at one end), the plan and elevations were organized on a system of proportions with the height of the nave, or central aisle, equal to twice its width. All the ornament is classic with Corinthian columns, pilasters and classic moldings. Brunelleschi used almost exclusively the Corinthian order with the decorative elements cut in a very crisp manner. All the moldings, door and window frames, and orders are of a soft blue-gray stone (*pietra serena*) contrasted against a light stucco wall. The ornamental features have very little projection, being rather lines on a surface. Colour was used in Florentine architecture as a contrast to stress the linear relationships rather than for over-all patternistic use as in north Italian architecture.

The traditional plan for medieval churches was the Latin cross plan, as at S. Lorenzo, with one arm of the cross longer than the others so as to form the nave or main body of the church. During the middle ages this cross plan was considered a symbolic reference to the cross of Christ.

During the Renaissance the ideal church plan tended to be centralized, that is, it was symmetrical about a central point, as is a circle, a square or a Greek cross which has four equal arms. Many Renaissance architects came to believe that the circle was the most perfect geometrical form and, therefore, most appropriate in dedication to a perfect God. Brunelleschi also worked with the central plan. In the Pazzi chapel (1430–42), set down in the medieval cloister of Sta. Croce at Florence, the plan approaches the central type. On the interior it is actually a rectangle, slightly wider than it is deep; at its rear is a square bay for the sanctuary and at the front is a porch. There are three domes, a large one over the centre of the chapel, a small one over the sanctuary and a small one over the centre of the porch on the exterior. Its plan, but not its interior space, resembles a Greek cross. On the exterior the large dome is covered by a conical roof with a lantern at the top. The porch has a horizontal en-

tablature supported by six Corinthian columns but broken in the centre by a semicircular arch which centralizes the composition, repeats the shape of the dome in the porch behind it and gives a lift to the horizontal façade. Above the columns and hiding the tunnel vault over the porch is a lovely paneled wall comparted by coupled Corinthian pilasters. The architecture is very ornate and decorative with medallions of cherub heads on the entablature and a wave pattern (the ancient strigil pattern) on the upper entablature.

Soon after the commencement of the Pazzi chapel, Brunelleschi began a true central plan church, that of Sta. Maria degli Angeli (begun 1434) at Florence, which was never completed. It was very important because it was the first central plan church of the Renaissance, the type of plan which dominates Renaissance thinking. The plan is an octagon on the interior and 16 sided on the exterior with a dome probably intended to cover the centre.

One of the outstanding examples of secular architecture was the Medici palace (1444–59) at Florence by Michelozzo (Michelozzi) di Bartolommeo, a follower of Brunelleschi. Created for Cosimo de' Medici, the great political leader and art patron of Florence, the palace had extensive additions in the 17th century. Arranged around a central court, the traditional Florentine palace plan, the Medici palace (now Medici-Riccardi palace) is a tremendous block on the exterior.

Medieval Florentine palaces were built of great rusticated blocks of stone, as if they had just been hacked out of the quarry, giving the impression of fortification, a desirable effect in that tumultuous time. With the Renaissance some fundamental changes appeared. Michelozzo crowned his palace with a massive horizontal cornice in the classic style and regularized the window and entrance openings. Even the rustication of the stonework was differentiated in each of the three stories. The ground floor has the usual heavy rustication; the second story is marked by drafted stonework with smooth blocks outlined by incised lines; and the third story has smooth ashlar stonework with no indications of the blocks. Unlike medieval patternistic rustication, the rustication of the Renaissance, while carefully distinguished between the stories, set up a logical relationship among them.

This Renaissance treatment of a palace façade was carried further in the Palazzo Rucellai (1447–51) at Florence following the design of the great humanist and architect Leon Battista Alberti. For the first time during the Renaissance Alberti applied classic orders to a palace elevation, using pilasters of the different orders superimposed on the three stories, so that there was another relationship established among the differentiated stories, from the short, strong Tuscan pilaster on the ground floor to the tall, decorative Corinthian at the top. For Alberti the beauty of architecture consisted of a harmonious relationship among the parts, with ornament, including the classic orders, being auxiliary to the proportion.

The culmination of Alberti's style is seen in two churches at Mantua. The earlier, S. Sebastiano (begun 1460, never fully completed), was built on a Greek cross plan and was intended to have in its first design an ancient temple front of six pilasters and a dominating triangular pediment. Even more important was Alberti's other church at Mantua, S. Andrea (begun 1470, completed in the 18th century). Both in plan and interior elevation this church was very influential on later architecture. The plan is a Latin cross, with one long arm for the nave flanked by side chapels, but the crossing at the eastern end was treated almost as if it were of a central plan with the nave added to it. This plan became a favourite for churches of the late 16th and early 17th century. The façade is of square proportion, with a wide bay at the centre twice the width of each of the side bays. The interior elevation was organized on this same alternating system, the so-called "rhythmic bay" which was to be popularized in the early 16th century by the architect Bramante. As a result of this system there is a close correspondence between the interior and exterior composition of S. Andrea.

From Florence the early Renaissance style spread gradually over Italy, becoming prevalent in the second half of the 15th century. In the architecture of north Italy there was a greater interest in pattern and colour. Colour was emphasized by the use of varie-gated marble inlays, as in the façade of the Church of the Certosa at Pavia (begun 1491) or in most Venetian architecture. The favourite building material of north Italy was brick with terra-cotta trim and decoration with which a pattern of light and dark was created over the entire building. On occasions when stone was used, as at the Palazzo Bevilacqua in Bologna (1479–84), the blocks were cut with facets forming a diamond pattern on the façade. This was actually a decorative treatment of rustication. Even the classic orders were affected by this decorative approach. Classic pilasters often had panels of candelabra and arabesque decoration in delicate relief on the surfaces of their shafts; the lower third of a column was often carved with relief sculpture. Florentine artists such as Filarete with his project for the Ospedale Maggiore at Milan (begun 1457) brought to Lombardy in north-ern Italy classic decoration and a slight knowledge of Renais-sance architecture.

From Lombardy the style was transferred to Venice by such Lombard architects as Pietro Lombardo and Mauro Coducci. The church of Sta. Maria dei Miracoli (1481–89) at Venice with its façade of coloured marble revetment is a typical example of Lombardo's work. The Venetian palace, such as the Palazzo Corner-Spinelli (late 15th century) and Palazzo Vendramin-Calergi (1501–09), both of which are by Coducci, with large and numerous windows, was more open than the palaces of central Italy.

At Rome in the second half of the 15th century there were sev-eral notable Renaissance palaces, principally derived from the style of Alberti, who spent extensive periods in Rome as a member of the papal court. The Palazzo Venezia (1455–91) has a rather me-dieval exterior, but set within the palace is a characteristically Renaissance court (1468–71), of which only two sides forming an angle were completed. It has been suggested without definite proof that Alberti may have furnished the design for this court; it at least reveals his influence in its full understanding of the classic style. The court consists of two stories of semicircular arches supported by piers on which are attached superimposed classic half columns, Tuscan below and Ionic above. The model for this arcade is the ancient Colosseum of Rome. The sense of mass created by the heavy piers contrasts with the lighter effect of the early Renaissance court typical of Florence, which has arches supported on columns. The Palazzo della Cancelleria (1485–1511) shows its dependence upon Alberti's style in its façade, which resembles in part his Palazzo Rucellai in Florence. The lower story simply has drafted stonework, but the two upper stories have rather flat Corinthian pilasters as well as the drafted stone. Unlike the Rucellai palace the bays composed by the pilasters alternate wide and narrow, but this alternation had been used by Alberti already in S. Andrea at Mantua. Alberti's influ-ence is also visible in the façades of the churches of S. Agostino (1479–83) and Sta. Maria del Popolo (rebuilt 1472–77) at Rome.

These examples of the early Renaissance in Rome were rapidly approaching the simplicity, monumentality and massiveness of the High Renaissance of the early 16th century. The architect Donato Bramante, who was to create this new style, was active in Lom-bardy in north Italy, but his work in Milan, as at Sta. Maria presso S. Satiro (about 1480–86), was still completely in the Lombard early Renaissance manner. However, he was in contact at this time with the great Florentine artist Leonardo da Vinci, who was active at the Milanese court. Leonardo was then considering the concept of the central plan church and filling his notebooks with sketches of such plans, which Bramante must have studied. When Bramante moved to Rome at the very end of the 15th century, his study of ancient ruins combined with the ideas of Leonardo and the growing classicism of Roman early Renaissance architec-ture resulted in the flourishing of the High Renaissance.

B. High Renaissance

High Renaissance architecture first appeared at Rome in the work of Donato Bramante at the beginning of the 16th century. The period was a very brief one, centred almost exclusively in the city of Rome; it ended with the political and religious ten-sions that shook Europe during the third decade of the century, culminating in the disastrous sack of Rome in 1527 and the siege of Florence in 1529. The High Renaissance was a period of har-mony and balance in all the arts, perhaps the most classic moment in this respect since the 5th century B.C. in Greece. It was an idealistic age in which individual characteristics or idiosyncrasies tended to be eliminated. As a result, although the architects are known as individuals, it is sometimes difficult to identify on a stylistic basis the particular architect of a High Renaissance building. The problem of attribution is further complicated by the fact that the style was confined to a small group of architects centring around Bramante in Rome.

Political and cultural leadership shifted from Florence to Rome, particularly because of a group of powerful popes who were inter-ested in developing the papacy as a secular power. The greatest of all was Julius II (1503–13), who was likewise a fabulous patron of the arts. Almost all the leading Florentine and other Italian artists were attracted to Rome. With the exception of Giulio Romano none of the important artists active in Rome at this time were Roman by birth.

Donato Bramante, the leader of this new manner, had already acquired an architectural reputation at Milan. Almost immedi-ately after his arrival in Rome in 1499, there was an amazing change in Bramante's work, as he became the exemplar of the High Renaissance style and lost his Lombard early Renaissance qualities. The Tempietto (1502), or small chapel, next to S. Pietro in Montorio typifies the new style. Erected on the sup-posed site of the martyrdom of St. Peter, the Tempietto is circular in plan with a colonnade of 16 columns surrounding a small cella. The chapel was meant to stand in the centre of a circular court which was likewise to be surrounded by a colonnade, so that the whole structure was to be self-contained and centralized. The enclosing circular court has never been erected. The ultimate in-spiration of the Tempietto was a Roman circular temple, like the temples of Vesta at Rome or Tivoli, but so many notable changes were made that the Renaissance chapel was an original creation. On the exterior it was organized in two stories, the Doric colon-nade forming the first story. Above is a semicircular dome raised high on a drum. The present large finial on the dome is of a later date and destroys some of the simplicity of the massing. Niches cut into the wall of the drum help to emphasize the solidity and strength of the whole, as does the heavy Doric order that Bramante was so fond of, in contrast to Brunelleschi who had a predilection for the ornate Corinthian. The monument is very simple, harmonious and comprehensible.

Several churches by other architects present the same qualities as the Tempietto on a larger physical scale. The church of Sta. Maria della Consolazione (1508–34) at Todi by a minor architect, Cola da Caprarola, is likewise centralized in plan, being square with a semicircular or polygonal apse opening off each side. The mass is built up of simple geometric forms, with a cube at the centre surrounded by half cylinders and capped above by the cylinder of a drum and a hemispherical dome. The Florentine architect, Antonio da Sangallo the elder, influenced by Bramante, created his church of S. Biagio at Montepulciano (1518–45) on a Greek cross plan. On the façade in the two recesses of the arms of the cross were to rise two towers, the right one never com-pleted. Otherwise the massing is similar to that of Todi with dome and drum above. All the moldings and ornamental ele-ments were carved with strong projection, so that on the interior heavy Roman arches, with deep coffers containing rosettes, define the tunnel vaults rising over the arms of the church. The sense of solid yet harmonious mass is enhanced by the travertine stone of which it is built.

Sangallo's church at Montepulciano reflects Bramante's greatest undertaking, the rebuilding of St. Peter's at Rome. Early in 1505 Pope Julius II began to consider the question of a tomb for himself appropriate to his idea of the power and nobility of his position. The sculptor Michelangelo soon presented a great project for a freestanding tomb, but such a monument required a proper setting. The Renaissance biographer Vasari claimed that the question of an appropriate location for this projected tomb brought to the pope's mind the idea of rebuilding St. Peter's, which was in very poor condition. Bramante, therefore, prepared plans for a monumental church late in 1505, and in April 1506 the foundation stone was laid. The projected church was a Greek cross in plan, with towers at the four corners and over the crossing a tremendous dome, inspired by that of the ancient Roman Pantheon but raised in this case on a drum. In elevation there was a very careful definition of all the parts of the church, so that one could visualize the plan from the composition of the elements of the elevation. At his death in 1514 Bramante had completed only the four main piers which were to support the dome, but these piers determined the manner in which later architects attempted the completion of the church.

As important as the central plan churches of this period were several notable secular buildings. At the papal palace of the Vatican next to St. Peter's, Bramante added two important features. The great Belvedere court (begun 1503) was planned to bring together the two disparate elements of the older palace attached to the church and the Belvedere villa of Innocent VIII on the hill above the palace. The new court was terraced up the hillside on three levels joined by monumental stairs. It was enclosed on the two long sides by arcaded loggias with superimposed orders. This large court was completed in the latter 16th century with some minor changes, and in 1587 the whole concept was destroyed by the building of the present Vatican library across the centre of the court. Just before his death Bramante also began a series of superimposed loggias attached to the face of the old Vatican palace looking out over the city and river. Completed by Raphael, there are two superimposed arcades with Tuscan and Ionic orders and a colonnade with Composite columns.

The largest palace of the High Renaissance is the Farnese palace (c. 1517–66) at Rome designed and commenced by a follower of Bramante, Antonio da Sangallo the younger, nephew of the older Sangallo. At Sangallo's death in 1546 Michelangelo carried the palace toward completion, making important changes in the third story. On the exterior Sangallo gave up the use of the classic orders as a means of comparting the façade into a number of equal bays; he used instead a façade more like the Florentine, but with quoins or rough cut blocks of stone at the edges of the elevation to confine the composition in a High Renaissance fashion. The façade is composed in proportions as a double square. On the interior the central square court is more classic using superimposed orders. Based on the ancient Roman Theatre of Marcellus or the Colosseum, the two first floors have an arcade supported by rectangular piers against which are set half columns. On the third story Michelangelo eliminated the arcade and used pilasters flanked by half pilasters which destroyed the High Renaissance idea of the careful separation and definition of parts.

One of the most charming buildings of the period is the Villa Farnesina (1509–21) at Rome by Bramante's finest pupil, Baldassare Peruzzi, who came from Siena. Designed for the fabulously wealthy Sienese banker Agostino Chigi, the villa was the scene of numerous fantastic banquets. A suburban villa, the Farnesina was planned in relation to the gardens around it with two small wings projecting from the central block toward the gardens. Originally there were two open loggias facing the gardens from two sides of the villa; one loggia is now completely walled in. The elevation appears as two stories comparted into equal bays by Tuscan pilasters. Other important buildings were designed by the painter Raphael, such as the Villa Madama (begun 1517) at Rome or the Palazzo Pandolfini (1516–20) at Florence.

C. Mannerism

From the third decade of the 16th century political and religious tensions erupted violently in Italy, particularly in Rome, which was sacked in 1527 by imperial troops. The school of Bramante and Raphael, which had produced the High Renaissance style, was dispersed throughout Italy as the artists fled from devastated Rome. Two years later another imperial army, with the backing of the Medici, besieged the city of Florence, imposing upon Michelangelo the difficult choice of supporting his native city or the family which had protected and patronized him. The

Medici were soon established in Florence not merely as a leading family but as the outright rulers. In such a period of insecurity, the harmonious and self-sufficient manner of the High Renaissance could not survive. It was gradually replaced by a complex style, sometimes called Mannerism, which continued until the end of the 16th century when the baroque style developed. Mannerism was antithetical to most of the principles of the High Renaissance. In place of harmony, clarity and repose it was characterized by tension, complexity and novelty. Mannerist architects were no less interested in ancient classic architecture than their predecessors; in fact, they displayed an even greater knowledge of antiquity. However they found other qualities in Roman architecture to exploit.

The change in style can be seen in the work of an architect, Baldassare Peruzzi, who was active in both periods. Unlike his High Renaissance Villa Farnesina, Peruzzi's design for the Palazzo Massimo alle Colonne (about 1535) in Rome shows indications of Mannerism. The façade of the palace was curved to fit the site on which it was erected; instead of remaining the passive form it had been in the earlier phases of Renaissance architecture, the wall surface was beginning to assert itself. The classic order is limited to the ground floor of the palace; the upper three stories have imitation drafted stonework made of brick covered with stucco, inscribed to feign stone coursing. Under these three stories in the centre of the façade is a loggia or colonnade, which seems of questionable adequacy as a support for the apparent load. The second story has classic rectangular windows crowned by Peruzzi's usual neat lintel supported on volutes, but the windows of the upper two stories are set horizontally with rather elaborate curvilinear moldings about them. There is, therefore, no longer a harmonious balance between the various stories. The architecture shows a greater emphasis on decorative qualities than on the expression of structural relationships.

In its earlier phase, until about 1550, Mannerism presented a strong reaction against the High Renaissance. In the latter half of the century the free treatment of the classic vocabulary which was typical of early Mannerism became somewhat restrained. In central Italy, because of the impact of the sack of Rome, the quantity of early Mannerist architecture was limited. A typical example is the project which Antonio da Sangallo the younger prepared for the completion of St. Peter's at Rome. A wooden model (begun 1539), still preserved in St. Peter's, reveals that Sangallo's plan is a combination of a central plan church with a large vestibule which makes the whole scheme approach a Latin cross. As a result, the exterior of the church resembles a Latin cross, but the interior space denies this by being centralized. In the same way the exterior elevation, unlike Bramante's project, does not express clearly the disposition of the interior of the church. The number of the architectural elements is increased so that the simplicity and clarity of the High Renaissance is lost. The dome of Sangallo's project has two superimposed arcades around its base and a double lantern above, so that the dome form is almost completely lost in a many-tiered, wedding-cake effect.

One of the great figures of the Mannerist period was the Florentine artist Michelangelo. He executed some extreme examples of Mannerist architecture at Florence. In his Laurentian library (1523–71) the vestibule fully illustrates his manner. Spatially it is a tall box set on end rising three stories. The large columns that line the wall of the main story are set into recesses so that a question arises as to whether the column or the wall is the supporting element. This treatment enlivens the expressive quality of the wall, for unlike its rather passive expression in the High Renaissance the wall now seems to be pressing forward between the columns. The small decorative pilasters were designed to taper toward the base in contrast to the usual classic and Renaissance pilaster. The small floor area of the vestibule is almost completely filled with the staircase leading up to the reading room. The stairs are an extreme example of the freedom of Mannerism; the function of the stairs is subordinate to their design. Commencing as three flights of stairs, the side flights at the top divert their traffic into the middle one, which was designed with curved steps so that the total effect resembles moving lava. The stairway dominates the vestibule instead of remaining a neutral, functional form. The whole atmosphere of the vestibule is that of an architectural space in tension, which contrasts with the quiet monotony of the long horizontal reading room above.

Michelangelo's later architecture in Rome was more restrained but still reveals some of the qualities of Mannerism. At the death of Sangallo in 1546, Michelangelo was commissioned to complete the great church of St. Peter's at Rome. During the next 18 years he was able to complete most of his design for the church, except the façade and great dome above. In plan he returned to a central plan church reminiscent of Bramante's idea but with fewer parts. His elevation, still visible at the rear or sides of the church, is composed of gigantic pilasters with a rather high attic story. Between the pilasters are several stories of windows or niches. Unlike the harmonious orders and openings of the High Renaissance, these are constricted by the pilasters so that a tension is created in the wall surface. Michelangelo planned a tremendous semicircular dome on a drum as the climax of the composition. Engravings of his original project suggest that this dome would have been overwhelming in relation to the rest of the design if the church had been completed in accordance with his concept. The great central dome was executed toward the end of the 16th century by Michelangelo's follower Giacomo della Porta who gave a more vertical expression to the dome by raising it about 25 ft. higher than a semicircle. This resulted in a slightly pointed profile which became the prototype for the baroque dome, whereas the semicircular dome had been typical of the Renaissance. In the early 17th century Carlo Maderno added a large nave and façade to the front of the church, converting it into a Latin cross plan and destroying the dominating quality of the dome, at least from the exterior front.

Early Mannerism in north Italy developed out of the dissolution of the school of Bramante after the death of Raphael in 1520 and the sack of Rome in 1527. Giulio Romano, the chief assistant of Raphael, became court artist and architect in the city of Mantua, while Michele Sanmicheli, a pupil of Bramante and Antonio da Sangallo the younger, returned to practise in his native town of Verona and at nearby Venice. Romano's Palazzo del Te at Mantua has a formal exterior with imitation drafted stonework and Doric pilasters, but the pilasters were not spaced in the High Renaissance manner, with an absolute regularity or an alternate rhythm of wide and narrow bays. The pilaster bays instead have a much more complex rhythm of several different widths. Mannerist tension was expressed in the court by the designing of every third triglyph of the Doric frieze to drop slightly, deliberately giving a sense of insecurity that tended to deny the structural expression of the order.

The leading early Mannerist architect in Venice was the Florentine sculptor Jacopo Sansovino, who fled to the north from Rome after the sack. Sansovino's architecture, as represented by the loggetta (1537–40) at the foot of St. Mark's campanile or by the Library of St. Mark's (Libreria Vecchia; 1536–88), is an example of the very decorative side of Mannerism. The library has two stories of arcades; the upper story is much taller than the lower. It has no basement, merely three low steps, so as to match the Gothic Palazzo Ducale opposite it. The upper entablature is extremely heavy, equaling half the height of the Ionic columns on which it rests. The decorative nature of the building is indicated by the fact that relief sculpture has been applied universally to the entablature and spandrels of the arches, with no unadorned wall surfaces.

This period of free and decorative Mannerism was followed by the more restrained, classic phase of late Mannerism seen to perfection in the architecture of one of the greatest architects of the Renaissance, Andrea Palladio. His native city, Vicenza, on the mainland not far from Venice, was almost completely rebuilt with edifices after his design; the Venetian mainland around Vicenza was profuse with his villas. The Villa Capra or Rotonda (1550–53; with later changes) near Vicenza is magnificent in its simplicity and massing. In the centre of a cubelike block (a cube is typical of most Palladian villas) is a circular hall, and on all four sides are projecting classic temple fronts as porticoes. There

is an absolute classic rigidity in the plan which when applied to domestic architecture is even more abstract than High Renaissance architecture. In Venice Palladio built several churches, all with the Latin cross plan and rather similar façades. S. Giorgio Maggiore (1566–1610) has a Roman temple front, on four giant half columns, applied to the centre of the façade; abutting the sides are two half temple fronts with smaller coupled pilasters. The resulting composition suggests the interpenetration of two complete temple fronts in a Mannerist way, since the elements of the composition are less independent than they would be in High Renaissance architecture, although the details are fully classic. Also typical of Mannerism is the way in which the interior space, instead of being classically confined, is permitted to escape through a colonnaded screen behind the sanctuary into a large choir at the rear.

Palladio's greatest fame in the history of architecture rests on his treatise, *I Quattro libri dell'architettura* (1570). The book promulgates a very classic theory of architecture; in fact, one chapter (I, xx) on the abuses in architecture decries some of the characteristics of Mannerism. In the 17th century Palladio's writings played an important role in the formulation of the French Academic theory of architecture.

In England there were at least two waves of Palladianism (*see* PALLADIO, ANDREA), one centred around Inigo Jones in the early 17th century and another around Lord Burlington in the 18th century, which later spread to America.

Late Mannerism at Rome and Florence was more varied. Pirro Ligorio's Casino of Pius IV (1558–63) at the Vatican is extremely decorative, with its façade covered with rich stucco relief and pebble mosaic ornament. In Florence the Uffizi palace (1560–74) by Giorgio Vasari and others was built about a very long, narrow court that seems to have been created by the compression of the tall side walls. It has a more dynamic spatial expression than the harmonious passive courts of the High Renaissance, which are generally square or circular. The most important architect of this period is Giacomo da Vignola, who wrote a treatise, *Regole delli cinque ordini d'architettura* (1562), devoted solely to a consideration of the architectural orders and their proportions. Like Palladio's book, Vignola's *Rules* became a textbook for later classic architecture. Of his many buildings the project for the church of Gesù (1568–75) at Rome, the central church of the Jesuit order, was very influential on the later history of architecture. The plan is a Latin cross with side chapels flanking the nave, but the eastern end is a central plan, capped by a dome. The plan was derived from Alberti's early Renaissance plan of S. Andrea at Mantua. The Gesù plan was imitated throughout Europe, but especially in Italy, during the early baroque period of the 17th century. Vignola built the church except for its façade, which was executed by Giacomo della Porta. Della Porta, inspired by Vignola's original design, created a façade concentrated toward its centre, which, like the plan, was the prototype for most early baroque façades of the late 16th and early 17th century.

III. FRANCE

The Renaissance style of architecture appeared in France at the very end of the 15th century and flourished until the end of the 16th century. As in other north European countries and Spain the new Renaissance manner did not completely oust the older Gothic style, which survived in many parts of France throughout the 16th century. French Renaissance architecture is divided into two periods: the early Renaissance, from the end of the 15th century until about 1530, and Mannerism, from about 1530 to the end of the 16th century.

A. EARLY RENAISSANCE

The many invasions of Italy from 1494 until 1525 by French armies acquainted the French kings and nobles with the charms of Renaissance art. During the reigns of Louis XII and Francis I the French possessed the city of Milan for the first 25 years of the 16th century. It was in Lombardy, therefore, that contact was made between French art and the Renaissance, and it was the

Lombard Renaissance style that appeared in France during the early Renaissance.

The new style had a certain prestige since it was imported by the nobility and aristocracy, while the middle class burghers continued to support their native Gothic style. This social difference also applied to the artists themselves. The French aristocracy imported Italian architects and artists who had been influenced by the Italian Renaissance, in which artists were considered to have a higher social level than artisans. The French builders and craftsmen who executed the designs of the Italians still belonged to the social level of medieval artisans. This created a friction between the two groups, which was, of course, furthered by the French resentment toward imported foreign artists.

With the exception of a few brief outcroppings of classicism in such centres as Marseilles and Gaillon, French early Renaissance architecture was centred in the Loire valley, since the capital of France was at Tours during the reign of Louis XII and the early part of the reign of Francis I. Most of the new architecture was secular, such as the château (q.v.), which was descended from the medieval feudal castle, combined with the idea of an Italian villa. A characteristic example is the château at Blois, where two wings in the early Renaissance manner replaced parts of the 13th-century château. The first wing, erected for Louis XII (1498–1503), is almost completely in the Flamboyant style (q.v.) and structure, with high roofs, an asymmetrical elevation, depressed arches and ogee arches. The only hint of the Renaissance is the occasional use of a bit of classic decoration, such as the egg and dart molding, mingled with the Gothic. The second wing, built by Francis I (1515–24), is more nearly in the Renaissance style. The structure remained Gothic with a high roof and dormers and the irregular spacing of the vertical windows, but all the ornament was in the classic mode, although its handling was often non-classic. Classic pilasters were used to divide the elevation into bays, but there is no consistency in the proportions of the pilasters. The most notable feature of the interior elevation of the wing of Francis I is a great octagonal open staircase, five sides of which project into the court. Within is a spiral staircase set on a continuous tunnel vault that is supported by radiating piers. On the surface of the piers are panels in low relief of arabesque decoration, of a type which is found often in Lombard Renaissance architecture. The richness of the Lombard style blends very well with Flamboyant Gothic, which had always been characterized by intricate and rich decoration. The exterior elevation of the wing of Francis I consists of a series of open loggias, the two lower ones arched, the upper one with a straight entablature, reminiscent of the famous series of loggias that had just been completed by Bramante and Raphael at the Vatican palace in Rome. However, the Italian High Renaissance concept was expressed in France in early Renaissance terms with squat pilasters, irregularly spaced bays and somewhat depressed arches.

The finest example of the early Renaissance style is the château or hunting lodge erected for Francis I at Chambord (1519–47). The Italian architect Bernabei Domenico da Cortona presumably made the basic model for the château, but the designs of Italian architects were usually executed by French builders, in this case Pierre Nepveu, often with many changes. Chambord is a tremendous structure, about 500 ft. wide, with a plan showing the gradual breakdown of the old castle plan. There is a rectangular court surrounded by walls with round towers at the corners, but on three sides of the court there are only low curtain walls. The old donjon developed into the château proper as a blocklike building with round towers at each corner. The flat passageways over the curtain walls and on top of the central block were intended to form galleries from which the ladies of the court could observe the hunt. The plan of the main block of the château reveals Italian influence in its symmetrical organization on cross-axes with a double spiral staircase at the centre. In the four corners left by the cross-axes are four identical apartments, each of which consists of three basic rooms (chamber, antechamber and cabinet); this form of apartment was from this time the favourite unit of French domestic planning. Typically for this period, the silhouette and structure remained Gothic in elevation, with strip windows,

a multiplicity of elements and a general vertical expression. However all the ornament is in the classic vocabulary of pilasters, round arches, and at times a geometric decoration of slate panels set in the cream-coloured stone.

B. MANNERISM

Commencing about 1530 Francis I imported numerous Italian artists, such as Il Rosso, Primaticcio, Serlio, Vignola and Cellini. Most of these artists were Mannerist in style, followers of Michelangelo or Raphael, so that the new period of French architecture partook of Italian Mannerism. The relations between the French and Italian artists became more strained, in part as a result of factions in the royal patronage. Francis I and his Italian daughter-in-law Catherine de Médicis favoured the imported Italians, while the son and successor of Francis I, Henry II, and the latter's mistress Diane de Poitiers supported the French artists. The style that resulted from this tension lasted until about 1590 and is sometimes known as the style of Henry II, although it actually was produced under five different kings, beginning late in the reign of Francis I.

The full influence of the new Italian style can best be seen in the château at Fontainebleau. In 1528 Francis I began to make revisions and additions to his medieval château, the exterior architecture being carried out by French builders under Gilles Le Breton, and, therefore, belonging to the French early Renaissance manner. The Italian mannerist painter, Il Rosso, after his arrival in 1530, was placed in charge of the interior decoration of the Gallery of Francis I (1535–37). The gallery is a long, narrow room covered by a wooden ceiling with rather intricate coffering. On each side of the room is a high dado of carved walnut with rich decoration above of stucco relief sculpture and painting. As Rosso was a Mannerist painter it meant that France went directly from the early Renaissance style of the Loire châteaux to Mannerism. This was natural for the French since Mannerism has affinities with the early Renaissance and late Gothic styles; it appealed to the French whose traditional native style was Gothic. Rosso, who died in 1540, was succeeded by another Italian, Primaticcio, who decorated the ballroom or gallery of Henry II (1548–56) and added the wing called the Aile de la Belle Cheminée (1568) at Fontainebleau.

The most important Italian architect to build in France was Sebastiano Serlio, a pupil of Baldassare Peruzzi, who arrived in 1541 to take Rosso's place as court architect. Serlio prepared plans for the rebuilding of the royal palace of the Louvre at Paris, but his ideas seem to have been too grandiose for Francis I. He did manage to build two châteaux, the casino of the Cardinal of Ferrara at Fontainebleau (about 1546), now destroyed, and the château of Ancy-le-Franc (about 1545–55) in Burgundy. Encountering opposition to his architecture from the French builders, Serlio devoted most of his time to an architectural treatise which he had begun in Italy. Various books of the treatise were published during his lifetime from 1537 on, but the collected work was published after his death with the title *Tutte l'opere d'architettura et prospetiva* (1584). This treatise was quite influential in spreading the Renaissance style in France, England, and the Low Countries.

The influx of Italian artists soon compelled the French architects to adopt Renaissance principles of design as well as Renaissance ornamental details. No longer content to be builders following the guild tradition, many of the French architects began to study the theory of design and often went to Italy as the source of the Renaissance style. A typical example was Jacques Androuet du Cerceau the elder, who was in Rome probably in the 1540s and was more important for his writings on architecture than for executed building. In addition to several treatises on architecture, Androuet du Cerceau published *Les plus excellents bastiments de France* (1576–79), two volumes of engravings of the most notable buildings in France in the Renaissance manner. As many of the buildings have been destroyed or changed, his book is an indispensable source for a knowledge of the architecture.

After Serlio's failure with the palace of the Louvre in Paris, a French gentleman of the court, Pierre Lescot, was ordered to

RENAISSANCE ARCHITECTURE

PLATE I

Rear of St. Peter's, Rome. Rebuilding began in 1506 from plans by Donato Bramante; architects who assisted in its construction included Michelangelo, Giacomo della Porta, and Carlo Maderno

Church of S. Lorenzo, Florence; c. 1419–c. 1470. Architect, Brunelleschi. The nave and aisles of this Latin-cross basilica are separated by Corinthian columns

Pazzi Chapel, Sta. Croce, Florence; 1430–42. Architect, Brunelleschi

The Tempietto, or small chapel, in courtyard of S. Pietro in Montorio, Rome; 1502. Architect, Donato Bramante

S. Andrea, Mantua, Italy, begun 1470 and completed in the 18th century, built on a Latin cross plan. Architect, Leon Battista Alberti

Palazzo Corner-Spinelli, Venice; late 15th century. Architect, Mauro Coducci. The façade has large, symmetrically arranged windows

PLATE II

RENAISSANCE ARCHITECTURE

Town hall, Antwerp, Belgium; 1561–65. Designed by Loys du Foys and Nicolo Scarini and executed by Cornelis de Vriendt (Floris). The building, 300 ft. (90 m.) long, rises from a sturdy rusticated basement surmounted by two stories of Doric and Ionic orders separating large mullioned windows. There is also a galleried top story

Longleat House, Wiltshire, England; 1568–c. 1580; by Sir John Thynne and Robert Smythson. A long horizontal building of three stories with the Doric order on the ground floor and Ionic and Corinthian orders above

S. Giorgio Maggiore, Venice, Italy; begun 1566 by Andrea Palladio, completed by Vincenzo Scamozzi. The church has a Roman temple front on four giant half-columns applied to the centre of the facade

Variegated marble inlay facade of the Church of the Certosa, Pavia, Italy; begun 1491

Dome of the cathedral of Florence; begun 1420 by Brunelleschi. Raised on a drum, it was added to the Gothic structure

PHOTOGRAPHS, (TOP, CENTRE LEFT) A. F. KERSTING, (BOTTOM RIGHT) HALIN—RAPHO, (BOTTOM LEFT) BRUNO STEFANI, (BOTTOM CENTRE) H. VON IRMER, INTERN. BILDARCHIV

Gallery of Francis I, château of Fontainebleau, France; 1535–37. The long narrow room, decorated by Il Rosso, shows the influence of Italian Mannerism

The palace-monastery of the Escorial, near Madrid, Spain; 1563–84, by Juan Bautista de Toledo and Juan de Herrera

The chatelet at the château of Chantilly, France; c. 1560, by Jean Bullant

The chapel at the château d'Anet, Eure-et-Loir, France; c. 1546–52, by Philibert Delorme. Built on a centralized Greek cross plan

Château of Chambord, France; 1519–47, by Pierre Nepveu. This large structure is about 500 ft. (152 m.) wide

Plate IV   RENAISSANCE ARCHITECTURE

Library of St. Mark's (Libreria Vecchia), Venice, Italy; 1536–88, by Jacopo Sansovino. With its two stories of arcades, it is an example of highly decorative Mannerism

Wollaton Hall, Nottinghamshire, England; 1580–88, by Robert Smythson. The square plan of the structure is emphasized by the corner towers; rectangular windows complement the rectangular building blocks on the exterior

The central staircase of the Laurentian Library, Florence, Italy; 1523–71, by Michelangelo. A fine example of Mannerism

The porch of the Rathaus, or town hall, Cologne, Germany; 1569–73, by Wilhelm Vernuiken. A two-storied structure with an arcade of semicircular arches and detached Corinthian columns surmounted on the second story by modified pointed arches with Composite columns. The porch was an addition to the original Gothic building, and it is the only part that survived the destruction of World War II

Villa Farnesina, Rome; 1509–21, by Baldassare Peruzzi. A two-storied structure of superimposed orders

design and build a Renaissance palace to replace the medieval castle of the Louvre. During the latter part of his reign Francis I centred the capital of France at Paris rather than in the Loire valley. Lescot in collaboration with the famous sculptor Jean Goujon designed a palace in 1546 set around a square court about 175 ft. wide. Only two sides, the west and south, of Lescot's court were built (1546–51). The execution and amplification of this design extended to the middle of the 19th century. The small section carried out under Lescot, the gallery of Francis I, reveals a thorough understanding of the principles of Italian design, but is expressed in French terms. The classic elements are used as low-relief surface decoration with little emphasis on mass.

The two leading architects of the second half of the 16th century, Philibert Delorme and Jean Bullant, studied in Rome. Delorme was trained as a builder before going to Rome and, therefore, was always interested in the constructive side of architecture as well as in the theory of design. About 1546 Delorme was commissioned by Henry II's mistress, Diane de Poitiers, to design her château at Anet. The original château (about 1546–52) formed three sides of a court closed at the front by a screen wall and entrance gateway. Much of the château has been destroyed; only the left wing of the house, the screen wall and the chapel which formed part of the right wing survive. The entrance gateway, which originally contained Cellini's "Nymph of Fontainebleau" (now in the Louvre), is very Mannerist with a complicated superstructure, a semicircular arch with raised bands cutting across the moldings, and, at the top, a bronze group of a stag which strikes the hour with his hoof as the accompanying hounds bay mechanically. The chapel at Anet has a centralized Greek cross plan with a large circle capped by a dome at the crossing. The exterior of the chapel is Mannerist with the windows cutting through the entablature and half pediments abutting the main block.

Delorme commenced in 1564 a large palace called the Tuileries, since it was situated on the site of tileworks in front of the Louvre. It was originally conceived as a very large building, but the architect was able to carry out only a very small section, which was destroyed in 1871.

Again elements of Mannerism were visible. On the first story Delorme used his own so-called French order, consisting of Ionic half columns and pilasters with decorative bands across the shafts, but this order was actually an Italian Mannerist treatment of the classic order. Delorme also wrote on architecture. His most important publication, the *Premier tome d'architecture* (1567), was based on Vitruvius and Alberti, but it is much more practical in its approach than Alberti's work, since it was largely drawn from Delorme's own practice.

Jean Bullant also wrote a book on architecture, *Reigle générale d'architecture des cinq manières de colonnes* (1564), inspired by the Italian Vignola's treatise which was issued two years previously. In fact, Bullant's architecture was rather like that of Vignola in that it was very classic in details but often Mannerist in relationships. His early and best preserved works were for Anne, duc de Montmorency and constable of France: part of the château of Ecouen (about 1555) and the chatelet (about 1560) at the château of Chantilly. The last shows many Mannerist qualities. For example, the main block of the chatelet is two stories high, but it is comparted by a series of pilasters that are higher than one story, yet not as high as the two stories. This is typical of Bullant's work; it results in the upper windows cutting through the cornice and ending as dormers in the roof. He was also very fond of penetrating the lower part of his window pediments, either with the arch of the window or with a separate little window.

The architecture of the second half of the 16th century was typically Mannerist; numerous architectural treatises appeared, as they had in Mannerist Italy. The Mannerist style died out in the early 17th century as slight hints of the baroque style blended with a renewed Classicism to form gradually the Academic style prevalent in the 17th century.

IV. SPAIN

The unification of Spain in 1492, with the final expulsion of the Moors, was accompanied by the appearance of Italian Renaissance decorative elements in Spanish architecture. There were three phases of Spanish Renaissance architecture: (1) the early Renaissance or Plateresque, from the late 15th century until about 1560; (2) a brief classic period, coexistent with the Plateresque from about 1525 to 1560; and (3) the Herreran style from 1560 until the end of the 16th century.

A. PLATERESQUE

The earliest phase of Renaissance architecture in Spain is usually called the Plateresque (from *platero,* "silversmith") because its rich ornament resembles silversmith's work. There has always been a long tradition in Spain of elaborate decoration, explained in part as an influence from Moorish art. The Moors, of course, possessed almost all of Spain during the middle ages and left this decorative heritage to the Spaniards. During the early 16th century minor north Italian sculptors and artisans, particularly from Lombardy and Genoa, were imported into Spain to execute tombs and altars for the Spanish nobles and ecclesiastics. These artisans introduced the north Italian Renaissance vocabulary of classic decoration, such as the pilaster paneled with arabesque or rinceau strips or the candelabrum shaft. Spanish architects picked up these elements and applied them to their buildings.

The Renaissance Plateresque style is purely one of architectural ornament. There was no change in structure; heavy walls were used with either Gothic ribbed vaults or intricately carved wooden ceilings, indicating Moorish influence. Many of the elements of decoration also preserved the influence of Gothic and Moorish art, such as the Flamboyant Gothic pinnacle and pierced balustrade, or coats of arms and bits of heraldry used as ornamental motifs. Richly coloured tiles created decorative patterns on the walls as in Moorish art. The richness of the classic decoration imported from north Italy blended effectively with the elements of the Moorish and Flamboyant Gothic styles to form the new Plateresque style. The luxuriance of its ornament was a fitting expression of the splendour-loving culture that Spain developed as the wealth of the Americas began to pour in during the early 16th century.

In most cases the new Plateresque decoration was confined to rich spots or panels of ornament around the portals and windows of the buildings. These ornamental areas were relieved by large expanses of bare wall, as in the façade of the Royal hospital at Santiago de Compostela (begun 1501) by Enrique de Egas, or his Hospital of Santa Cruz at Toledo (1504–14).

The greatest centre of the Plateresque style was the town of Salamanca, with buildings such as the university (about 1516–29) and the Monterey palace (1539). Perhaps the most outstanding example of the style is the Ayuntamiento, or town hall, of Seville (1534–72) by Diego de Riaño, with Lombard paneled pilasters on the ground floor and half columns completely covered with relief sculpture on the second floor. Also in the Lombard manner are the numerous medallions spotted over the wall under the windows or between the pilasters.

B. CLASSIC

Although the exuberant Plateresque style lingered in some regions until about 1560, it was soon superseded by a much more classic style, which appeared in 1526 in the palace of Charles V within the Alhambra (*q.v.*) at Granada. The palace of Charles V was the first Italian classical building in Spain, in contrast to Plateresque buildings whose classicism was limited to a few elements of Italian Renaissance decoration. Charles V as king of Spain and the Holy Roman emperor was the most powerful political figure in Europe. It was his army that invaded Italy and sacked the city of Rome in 1527 as Pope Clement VII cowered in the Castel San Angelo. As a result of his political and military power, his wealth (which was enhanced by the gold of Mexico and Peru) and his adroit diplomacy, Charles V dominated Italy, as well as Spain, the Low Countries and Austria. His palace in the Alhambra reflected the increasing contact with Italy. Designed by the Spaniard Pedro de Machuca, who had studied in Italy, the work on the palace of Charles V continued through most of the 16th century, but it has never been completed.

The palace is square in plan with a huge central circular court (100 ft. in diameter), which was intended for bullfights and tournaments. The plan is, therefore, fully Renaissance, being centralized and symmetrical; it is organized on cross-axes formed by the four entrances, one in the centre of each side. The façade shows a full understanding of the principles of Italian Renaissance design in its superimposition of orders (i.e., Ionic pilasters or half columns above Tuscan, and Corinthian above Ionic), and in the alternating rhythm of the triangular and segmental pediments above the windows of the second story. The interior court is surrounded by a colonnade with a similar superimposition of Doric and Ionic.

C. HERRERAN

The classicism of the palace of Charles V was succeeded by an extremely austere and cold style named after the greatest Spanish architect of the 16th century, Juan de Herrera. Perhaps more important than the architect was the social and cultural atmosphere in which the Herreran style developed, from about 1560 to the end of the 16th century. Charles V had been a true Renaissance prince; his only son Philip II, who came to the throne in 1556, was one of the most typical representatives of the age of Mannerism as it was manifested in Spain. Philip II was morbid and melancholic, a religious fanatic, against whose strict rule the Low Countries soon rose in revolt, beginning the difficulties that gradually dispelled Spanish political and cultural power in Europe.

The finest example of the Herreran style illustrates clearly the change in cultural atmosphere under Philip II. This is the palace-monastery of the Escorial (q.v.) (1563–84), which Philip II had built as a retreat on a rather dreary plain outside Madrid. It is a great contrast to the worldly palace of Charles V with its tournament court set in the luxurious, sensuous Alhambra. The Escorial was more than a royal palace, as it also contained provisions for a monastery and college within its great complex. A city in itself, the Escorial was planned as a tremendous rectangle (675 ft. by 525 ft.), with a large church at the centre dominating the whole. The orientation toward religion is indicative of the age of the growing Counter-Reformation, which was in part opposed to the secularism of the classic Italian Renaissance.

The Escorial was begun by the architect Juan Bautista de Toledo, who may be responsible for the planning, but the execution and architectural style was that of his assistant and successor, Herrera. Philip II himself reviewed the drawings for the palace, removing anything ornamental or ostentatious. On the exterior the architecture is very simple, a plain wall with a monotonous series of unadorned windows expressing the general monastic character of the whole. The only element of the classic Renaissance on the exterior is at the central portal with two stories of giant Doric half columns supporting a classic triangular pediment. The church, at the centre of the complex, has two bell towers and a great dome set on a drum, which surmount the whole. The austerity is enhanced by the cold, gray granite of which the Escorial was built. On the interior a similar severity of manner is indicated by the lack of decoration. Except for the classic Doric order, which is the least ornamental of the orders, there is no architectural decoration. Plain arches of stone were used under the vaults without any coffering. Occasional raised panels on the wall surface suggest where Plateresque ornament would be located normally, but instead of relief sculpture, there are only starkly smooth panels. Even the Doric order was handled severely; the pilasters on the interior show no entasis (i.e., an upward taper of the width of the pilaster to give a sense of lightness and to relieve the strict verticals). The Escorial is impressive in its size and mass and in the consistency of its austerity, but it has a forbidding quality that no other building can match. Other examples of Herrera's design are the cathedral at Valladolid (begun 1585, completed in the 18th century) and the court of the Lonja, or Exchange, of Seville (1583–98).

V. GERMANY AND THE LOW COUNTRIES

The burgeoning of Italian Renaissance architectural forms in Germany was even slower than in other north European countries.

Only by the middle of the 16th century was the Renaissance style manifestly important, generally in those regions in closest contact with Italy, such as southern Germany or the trade route along the Rhine river leading from the south to the Low Countries. The style lingered in Germany until about the middle of the 17th century. The few hints of classicism in Germany prior to the mid-16th century can be considered the early Renaissance phase. They were limited to minor architectural monuments, such as the Fugger chapel in St. Anna at Augsburg (1509–18), which was the first Renaissance building in Germany, or they consisted of bits of Renaissance decoration attached to Gothic structures. An example of the latter is the Schloss Hartenfels at Torgau (1532–44) by Konrad Krebs, which is completely medieval in structure but has occasional fragments of classic ornament, arabesque pilaster strips, candelabra and medallions applied to the surface. A great staircase in the court was somehow derived from that of the French château at Blois, indicating that the Renaissance influence was fourth hand, passing from its source in central Italy through Lombardy, and then to France and eastern Germany.

After 1550 Renaissance-style architecture in Germany often had Mannerist details derived from Italian ornamental engravings. German architecture of this period was abundant with medallions, herms (i.e., architectural elements topped by human busts) and caryatids and atlantes (i.e., human figures used as columns or pilasters). The German treatise on the five orders by Wendel Dietterlin entitled Architectura (1593) is profuse with Mannerist ornament. An architectural example is the Otto Heinrichsbau (1556–59) added to the Gothic castle at Heidelberg (burned by the French in 1689). The three tall stories presented the usual verticality of northern architecture, but there was an understanding of the classic superimposition of the orders with Corinthian above Ionic. However, there was a certain freedom in the treatment of the orders, for a Doric frieze was supported by the Ionic pilasters.

From Italian Mannerism came the rustication of the lower order, the use of herms as window mullions and the caryatids flanking the portal. Other examples of the German Renaissance are the porch of the Rathaus, or town hall, at Cologne (1569–73) by the Dutchman Wilhelm Vernuiken and the Friedrichsbau (1601–07) added to the castle at Heidelberg by Johannes Schoch.

In the Low Countries, Flanders, because of trade and finance, was in close communication with Italy from the 15th century. As a result there are slight hints of the Renaissance style in the architecture of the early 16th century, as in the palace of Marguerite of Austria, now the Palais de Justice (1507–25), at Malines completed by Rombout Keldermans.

The most important building of the Flemish Renaissance style was the Stadhuis, or town hall, at Antwerp (1561–65), designed by Loys du Foys and Nicolo Scarini and executed by Cornelis de Vriendt (Floris). It was decided to replace Antwerp's small medieval town hall with a large structure, 300 ft. long, in the new style, as a reflection of its prosperity as the leading northern port of the 16th century. As with many northern buildings there is a lack of monumentality, for its physical hugeness is not expressed in the way that it would be in an Italian building. There is a low basement with a rusticated arcade, originally used by traders during fairs. Above are two principal stories with superimposition of Doric and Ionic pilasters, between which large windows almost completely open each bay.

The advent of the baroque style early in the 17th century replaced the Renaissance in Flanders much sooner than it did in Germany. There were a few examples of the 16th century Renaissance style in the northern Low Countries, such as the town hall at Leyden (1579) and the town hall of The Hague (1565). It was during the 17th century, when Holland was independent of Spain, that architecture flourished.

VI. ENGLAND

The Renaissance style of architecture made a very timid appearance in England during the first half of the 16th century, and it was only from about 1550 that it became a positive style with local qualities. In fact, the Gothic style continued in many parts of England throughout most of the 16th century, and English Renaissance architecture was a very original fusion of the Tudor Gothic (*see* TUDOR PERIOD) and classic styles. This style flourished until the early 17th century when the architect Inigo Jones created a much more Italianate style that replaced the English Renaissance style.

During the reign of Henry VIII (1509–47) some elements of Italian Renaissance decoration were imported by England through a few minor Italian artists, such as Pietro Torrigiano who executed the tomb of Henry VII (1512–18) in Westminster abbey. At the great palace of Hampton Court, begun by Cardinal Wolsey in 1514 and continued by Henry VIII until 1540, a few bits of Italian Renaissance decoration have been added, although the structure is completely in the Tudor manner. On the gateways are several terra-cotta medallions by the Italian Giovanni da Maiano, and there is a symmetry and regularity in the plan of the palace that hints of the Renaissance. (*See* also ELIZABETHAN STYLE.)

The Renaissance style really begins in England in the middle of the 16th century in architecture built for the circle of the Lord Protector Somerset, who served as regent after Henry VIII's death. During the 16th century the patron played a much greater role in the development of English Renaissance architecture than did the architect; there were almost no professional architects who were trained as the Italians were in the theory of design and building. Most of the building was executed by mason- or carpenter-designers. A typical example of the role of the patron in introducing the Renaissance style to England is to be found in the quadrangle which John Caius added to Gonville college, now Gonville and Caius, at Cambridge (*q.v.*). Caius had spent a long time in Italy as well as elsewhere in Europe. The architecture of the new court was basically Tudor Gothic, but Caius planned three gateways in connection with the court, two of which were in the Italian style. The three gates were to mark the progress of the student through the university. At the entrance was the Gate of Humility, an unadorned doorway, now destroyed. The Gate of Virtue, opening into the new quadrangle, is a fine classic portal with Ionic pilasters, but with a Tudor Gothic many-centred arch for the opening. Finally the Gate of Honour is a separate tiny triumphal arch leading out toward the schools for the final disputation and degree. Caius probably designed these gates with the aid of the Flemish architect Theodore de Have.

There was no religious architecture created in England during the 16th century, in part because of the break of Henry VIII with Rome. It is in the great country houses of the nobility that the Renaissance style is visible. Sir John Thynne, steward to the Lord Protector Somerset, designed several notable examples. The finest of these was his own house Longleat (1568–about 1580), on which he had the assistance of the mason Robert Smythson, who was to be the leading architect of the late 16th century. Except for the symmetry of the plan, arranged around two courts, there was little new in planning at Longleat, for the Tudor house was usually organized about a court. The typical English great hall at Longleat was an element derived from the hall (*q.v.*) of the medieval castle, and retained in English architecture through the 16th century. The main entrance of the house opens directly into one end of the great hall, but a low screen at the end of the hall, topped by a musicians' gallery, forms a passageway. In elevation Longleat is a long horizontal building with a wealth of windows; it is one of the most open secular buildings in Europe of the 16th century. There is a rectangular quality about the whole exterior, which is characteristic of English architecture; it is augmented by the repeated use of the bay-window unit. There are now three stories on the exterior, with the correct classic superimposition of the Doric order on the ground floor and Ionic and Corinthian orders above, but the third story was probably added after Thynne's death in 1580, replacing a pitched roof and dormers.

Robert Smythson, who aided Sir John Thynne at Longleat, went on to design and build several notable houses, the finest being Wollaton hall (1580–88) near Nottingham. On his tomb Smythson is called "architector and surveyor," not merely a mason.

Wollaton has a magnificent site set up on a small hill overlooking a large park. The plan of the house is a square with four, square, corner towers, resembling a plan in the treatise on architecture by the Italian architect Serlio, whose book was influential in English Renaissance architecture. The great hall is in the centre of the square; it rises an extra story above the whole building. The house has a low basement story that contained the kitchens and service rooms; it is one of the first buildings to use this arrangement, which became common in the history of later English and American architecture. On the exterior the massing is that of rectangular blocks, whose rectilinear quality is further emphasized by the numerous many-mullioned rectangular windows. The decoration is completely classic with superimposed pilasters, round arched niches and classic balustrades, but it shows touches of Italian Mannerism, which came into England primarily from Flanders. The pilasters and half columns have raised bands across their middles, and the gables crowning the corner towers are decorated with Flemish strapwork (*i.e.*, bands raised in relief assuming curvilinear forms suggestive of leather straps).

Other examples of this style are Hardwick hall (1590–97) in Derbyshire, probably by Smythson; Kirby hall (about 1570–78) in Northamptonshire, perhaps by the mason Thomas Thorpe; and Montacute house (1588–1601) in Somerset.

With the possible exception of Robert Smythson, there were no important professional architects in England during the latter half of the 16th century. Once the surveyor John Thorpe was considered the most prominent architect of the period, Wollaton hall and Kirby hall being attributed to him as well as most of the other notable houses. This opinion was based on the discovery of his notebook of 280 drawings illustrating all these houses, but investigation proved that it was merely a collection of representations of all the famous buildings of the time. It is possible that Thorpe intended to prepare a book with representative examples of English architecture very much in the manner of the book prepared in France by Androuet du Cerceau. There were, however, some designs by Thorpe himself. One for his own house, presumably never built, was based in plan on his own initials I and T, and has the playful, abstract, unreal quality of Mannerism.

See JACOBEAN STYLE; *see* also references under "Renaissance Architecture" in the Index.

BIBLIOGRAPHY.—*Italy:* C. M. Stegmann and H. von Geymüller, *Die Architektur der Renaissance in Toscana*, 11 vol. (1885–1908); A. Haupt, *Palast-Architektur von Ober-Italien und Toscana vom XIII bis XVIII Jahrhundert*, 6 vol. (1886–1922); H. Willich and P. Zucker, *Die Baukunst der Renaissance in Italien bis zum Tode Michelangelos*, 2 vol. (1914–29); C. Ricci, *Architecture and Decorative Sculpture of the High and Late Renaissance in Italy* (1923); C. Terrasse, *L'Architecture lombarde de la renaissance (1450–1525)* (1926); W. J. Anderson and A. Stratton, *The Architecture of the Renaissance in Italy*, 5th ed. (1927); G. Giovannoni, *Saggi sulla architettura del rinascimento* (1935); H. Hoffmann, *Hochrenaissance-Manierismus-Frühbarock* (1938); N. Pevsner, "The Architecture of Mannerism," *The Mint*, ed. by G. Grigson, pp. 116–138 (1946); R. Zürcher, *Stilprobleme der Italienischen Baukunst des Cinquecento* (1947); R. Wittkower, *Architectural Principles in the Age of Humanism* (1950).
France: C. Martin, *La Renaissance en France* (1913–21); A. Haupt, *Baukunst der Renaissance in Frankreich und Deutschland* (1923); W. H. Ward, *The Architecture of the Renaissance in France*, 2nd ed. (1926); L. Hautecoeur, *Histoire de l'architecture classique en France: vol. i, La Renaissance* (1943); A. Blunt, *Art and Architecture in France, 1500 to 1700* (1953).
Spain: A. Byne and M. Stapley, *Spanish Architecture of the Sixteenth Century* (1917); B. Bevan, *History of Spanish Architecture* (1939); J. Camon Aznar, *La arquitectura plateresca* (1945); F. Chueca Goitia, *Arquitectura del siglo XVI, Ars Hispaniae*, vol. xi (1953).
Germany and the Low Countries: G. von Bezold, *Baukunst der Renaissance in Deutschland, Holland, Belgien und Dänemark* (1900); A. Haupt, *Baukunst der Renaissance in Frankreich und Deutschland* (1923); A. Stange, *L'Architecture des Pays-Bas méridionaux aux XVIe, XVIIe et XVIIIe siècles* (1926); G. Horst, *Die Architektur der deutschen Renaissance* (1928).
England: J. A. Gotch, *Early Renaissance Architecture in England*, 2nd ed. (1914); J. Lees-Milne, *Tudor Renaissance* (1951); M. Whiffen, *An Introduction to Elizabethan and Jacobean Architecture* (1952); M. Whinney, *Renaissance Architecture in England* (1952); J. N. Summerson, *Architecture in Britain, 1530 to 1830* (1953).   (D. R. Cn.)

RENAISSANCE ART. The period extending roughly from 1300 to 1600 was, with much fanfare, declared by Italian his-

EXAMPLES OF RENAISSANCE SCULPTURE, PAINTING, ARCHITECTURE AND MINOR ARTS

(Far left) Wing of a triptych of the Deposition showing St. John the Baptist and a donor; Flemish, late 15th century. (Top, centre left) "Prudence," sculptured plaque of enameled terra-cotta by Luca della Robbia; Florentine, 15th century. (Top, centre right) Court of the Medici-Riccardi palace, Florence, by Michelozzo di Bartolommeo; Italian, 15th century. (Bottom, centre left) "Pietà" by Michelangelo, in St. Peter's, Rome. (Bottom, centre right) Terra-cotta bust of Lorenzo de' Medici by Andrea del Verrocchio; Italian, 15th century. (Far right) "St. Paul in Prison," tapestry woven from Raphael's series, "Acts of the Apostles," in the Vatican gallery, Rome; Belgian, 16th century

torians of the time to mark the Renaissance, or rebirth, of the humanistic spirit of classical antiquity. The "barbaric and benighted" centuries that intervened were then designated the middle ages. These three centuries did indeed witness a change in the intellectual and aesthetic climate of Europe, spanning as they did the time from Thomas Aquinas to Descartes, Dante to Tasso, Chaucer to Milton, Giotto to Michelangelo, Gothic to baroque. According to these humanistic writers the Renaissance originated in Italy and spread throughout Europe whenever and wherever Italian influence was felt; the period marked a revival of classical learning in the Greco-Roman manner; and there was a sharp shift from otherworldly religiosity to worldly psychology.

To accept such assertions uncritically would be highly misleading. All of Europe was undergoing a conscious departure from the prevailing standards of the middle ages. In the north the transition was not so abrupt as in Italy, but it came about nonetheless decisively as the age of scientific discovery overcame the medieval heritage of mysticism and superstition and brought about a new attitude toward life. Through the works of such artists as Grünewald, Dürer, Cranach and Holbein men saw their environment through different eyes. If the change occurred more suddenly and explosively in Italy than elsewhere, it was perhaps because that country was closest to the Roman tradition in letters, building and crafts, all of which had never really died out, and because the Gothic, a northern style, was never particularly compatible with the sunny south and the volatile temperament of its people. Virgil and other Roman authors had continued

to be read during the middle ages, and scholarship and learning can hardly be said to have languished in medieval universities. Ionic and Corinthian capitals appear quite regularly in Romanesque and Gothic architecture, classical molding ornaments (egg-and-dart, leaf-and-tongue) are frequently found, and Gothic sculptural figures are clothed in graceful classical flowing drapery (*see* GOTHIC ART AND ARCHITECTURE).

While an increasingly secular spirit was apparent in the Renaissance, the majority of important buildings were still churches; statuary, paintings and music continued to be mainly religious in orientation.

In longer perspective, then, the Renaissance appears to be more a fermentation of ideas and a reorientation of scholarly and aesthetic thought than a rediscovery of ancient values and viewpoints. The period expressed itself in new ways, created new forms, invented new modes of representation and eventually arrived at a new understanding of the world. For convenience these tendencies can be grouped in such categories as Renaissance humanism, individualism and scientific naturalism.

Humanism.—It is a truism that every era finds what it wants in the classics. In literature and philosophy western Europe during the Renaissance veered away from a largely Roman orientation toward an inclusion of Greek studies, particularly the works of Homer and Plato. In Latin, however, humanists sought inspiration and models in the classical style of Cicero, Lucretius, Virgil and Tacitus rather than in the writings of the medieval church fathers. More broadly the humanists placed increasing emphasis on man and his values, especially the dignity of man as realized in the study of the humanities rather than scholastic theology.

In architecture, humanism resulted in the study of Vitruvius' ancient treatises and in the careful measurement and observation of the surviving ancient monuments. The consequences can be seen in Brunelleschi's Pazzi chapel in Florence, which is a model of spatial clarity, crisp contours and the elegant use of classical decorative detail. The new architecture, as exemplified in the works and writings of Alberti, Bramante and Palladio, reveals the correct yet imaginative use of the classical orders and an eye for just proportions. In design, humanism resulted in the turning away from medieval variants of such classical motives as acanthus leaves, Ionic volutes, bead-and-reel patterns toward more authentic versions based on the study of ancient examples. In painting it resulted in the study of Euclid's geometry for the mathematical laws of linear perspective, as well as the exploration of themes drawn from classical literary and mythological sources. In sculpture humanism resulted in calm classical stances, figures clothed in authentic Roman togas and the rediscovery of the expressive power of the nude as revealed in the works of Donatello and Michelangelo.

Individualism.—One manifestation of humanism was the establishment of man as the measure of all things. Such works as Pico della Mirandola's essay on the *Dignity of Man,* Machiavelli's *Prince* and Castiglione's *Courtier* emphasized the personal, political and social importance of man. Churches began to come under the direct patronage of individual families and to bear the names of their donors, as, for instance, the Scrovegni chapel in Padua, built and decorated by Giotto; the Brancacci chapel in Florence with murals by Masolino da Panicale and Masaccio; and the Church of S. Lorenzo in Florence with the Medici chapel by Michelangelo. Portraiture in painting assumed a position of major importance, and self-portraits by artists often were given considerable prominence in their religious and historical pictures. The social position of major individual artists was upgraded from that of an artisan to a place almost on a plane with that of their patrons. Leonardo da Vinci insisted that painting, sculpture and architecture were truly liberal arts, and Michelangelo took pains to point out that he worked more with his brains than his hands. Individual artists became acutely conscious of their personal fame; many achieved sufficient renown to become the subjects of biographies, such as those in Vasari's *Lives of the Most Eminent Painters, Sculptors and Architects,* and Benvenuto Cellini wrote an account of himself in his celebrated *Autobiography.*

Scientific Naturalism.—In late Gothic sculpture, manuscript illuminations and tapestry designs there was a decreasing interest in allegory and moral preachments and an awakening to the beauties and delights of nature for their own sake. Artists began thinking more in terms of aesthetic problems than religious revelations. As with the nominalistic philosophy of William Ockham, personal observation was in ascendancy over the authoritarian view of scholasticism, interest in the natural world began to override that in the supernatural, and symbolism was superseded by accurate representation. A plant, in other words, was a plant, not a symbol of the a priori universal idea of plant as it existed in the mind of God, and the rendering of particular flora and fauna was based on nature. This visual revolution opened new vistas to Renaissance artists who proceeded to investigate optics, the mathematical bases of perspective drawing, the rational proportions of the human body, all with the idea of achieving a more natural way of representing the world of appearances. This phase of the Renaissance reached a climax in the scientific studies of Antonio Pollaiuolo and Verrocchio, who dissected cadavers in order to render more accurately the bone and muscle structure of the human body in action. It was this heritage they bequeathed to Leonardo da Vinci, whose *Notebooks* give evidence of his overwhelming interest in science.

The disintegration of Renaissance art is first apparent in the work of the Mannerists of the middle and late 16th century. The term Mannerism (*see* MANNERIST ART AND ARCHITECTURE) was coined to describe the work of certain artists who departed from

accepted Renaissance ideals and emulated the manner rather than the spirit of the great masters—Leonardo, Michelangelo and Raphael. Mannerism had its origin in the psychological conflicts of the later works of the masters themselves, especially Michelangelo, who was torn between the pagan, Platonic ideal of classical beauty and the vigorous reaffirmation of traditional Christianity as exemplified in the Counter-Reformation movement.

Michelangelo's Mannerism is expressed in the twisting, turning, writhing bodies of his slave figures for Julius II's tomb and in the implausible positions of the figures atop the Medici tombs, as well as in the brooding melancholy and resignation of the late "Pietà." In his architecture it is found in the Laurentian library where the eye is led simultaneously in divergent directions, where there prevails a juxtaposition of discordant elements rather than a harmonious reconciliation of opposites and where there is a deliberate violation of the canons of proportion.

Later Mannerist artists became the first to work largely within the shadow of the giants of the immediate past. Since they could not excel their predecessors either in technique or in grandeur of expression, they could only adopt some of their vocabulary and use it to startle the spectator and produce the unexpected. Tintoretto and Caravaggio performed daring feats of foreshortening, devised surprising multiple-perspective effects, and used chiaroscuro to create dramatic spotlighting. Parmigianino's "Madonna With the Long Neck" reveals human figures with exaggerated oval faces, tapering fingers and willowy bodies. The sculptural equivalent is seen in the elegant elongation and winsome stance of Benvenuto Cellini's "Nymph of Fontainebleau," and in the airy grace and precarious balance of Giovanni da Bologna's bronze figure of "Mercury in Flight." The stage was thus set for the emergence of a new style, the baroque.

See BAROQUE ART; *see* also references under "Renaissance Art" in the Index.

BIBLIOGRAPHY.—O. Benesch, *Art of the Renaissance in Northern Europe* (1945); B. Berenson, *Italian Painters of the Renaissance* (1930); J. Burckhardt, *Civilization of the Renaissance in Italy* (1860 and subsequent editions); F. J. Mather, *Western European Painting of the Renaissance* (1939); E. Panofsky, *Studies in Iconology: Humanistic Themes in the Art of the Renaissance* (1939), *Early Netherlandish Painting* (1953); J. A. Symonds, *The Renaissance in Italy* (1875–86 and subsequent editions); F. W. Sypher, *Four Stages of Renaissance Style* (1955); H. Wölfflin, *Art of the Italian Renaissance* (1913). (WM. F.)

RENAN, ERNEST (1823–1892), French historian and philosopher whose thought anticipated both the existentialist anguish and the totalitarian messianism of the 20th century, was born on Feb. 28, 1823, at Tréguier, Côtes-du-Nord, of peasant stock. Educated at the ecclesiastical college in Tréguier, he began training for the priesthood. In 1838 he was offered a scholarship at the seminary of Saint-Nicolas-du-Chardonnet, whence he went on to that of Saint-Sulpice. There, however, he soon became involved in a crisis of faith which finally led him, reluctantly, to leave the Roman Catholic Church in 1845 because, in his view, the church's teachings were incompatible with the findings of historical criticism. But he kept a quasi-Christian faith in the hidden God, revealed to him both by Pascal's writings and by experience, as well as in himself as a kind of intellectual messiah.

1848 and Italy.—For Renan the February Revolution of 1848 was a religion in the making. Sometimes enthusiastic, sometimes critical, he participated in its messianic expectations and carried this ambiguous attitude over into *L'Avenir de la science*—a work which, in allusion to Descartes, he called his "Discourse on Method." The main theme of this work, not published till 1890, is the importance of the history of religious origins regarded as a human science having equal value to the sciences of nature. Something of an anticlerical though he now was, the French government sent him in 1849 to Italy to help classify manuscripts previously inaccessible to French scholars. In Rome, he was transformed, for a while, from an austere scholar into an artist alive to the pageantry and naïveté of popular religion.

The Second Empire.—Renan returned to Paris in 1850 to live with his sister, Henriette, on her savings and the small salary attached to his own post at the Bibliothèque Nationale. He began to make a name for himself, with his doctoral thesis *Averroès et l'Averroïsme* (1852), then with two collections of essays, *Études d'histoire religieuse* (1857) and *Essais de morale et de critique* (1859), first written for the *Revue des Deux Mondes* and the *Journal des Débats*. The *Études* inculcated into a middle-class public the insight and sensitivity of the historical, humanistic approach to religion. Many of the *Essais* denounce the materialism and intolerance of the Second Empire in the name of Renan's aristocratic ideal: the intellectuals, acting as "bastions of the spirit," must, he affirms, resist tyranny by the intellectual and spiritual refinement, that is, the humanism exemplified throughout these essays.

In 1856 Renan proposed marriage to Cornélie Scheffer, niece of the painter Ary Scheffer. When Henriette discovered that to her brother she herself was less important not only than his work but even than another woman her jealousy knew no bounds. As related by Renan with more art than truth in his tribute to her (1862), she gave way to his benevolent egoism and agreed to live with him and his wife. Yet the beginnings of his marriage were unhappy, the more so as he was still dependent on Henriette's savings.

In October 1860 Renan was entrusted with an archaeological mission to the Lebanon. The Phoenician inscriptions which he discovered were published in his *Mission de Phénicie* (1864–74). They were later included in the *Corpus inscriptionum semiticarum*, which he helped to bring out through the Académie des Inscriptions et Belles-Lettres. But archaeology was not his main interest. In April 1861, with his wife and sister, he visited the Holy Land in search of materials and inspiration for the life of Jesus which he was bent on writing. He finished a first draft of it in the Lebanon but at tragic cost, for Henriette died of malaria at Amschit on Sept. 24, 1861, while he himself fell desperately ill.

Renan had counted on his life of Jesus to secure election to the chair of Hebrew at the Collège de France. He was elected, before the book was ready, on Jan. 11, 1862. But in his opening lecture, on Feb. 21, he referred to Jesus in Bossuet's words as "an incomparable man." While this was in his eyes the highest praise one could bestow on a man, it was not enough for the clericals, who took advantage of its implied atheism and the uproar caused by the lecture to have Renan suspended. Contemptuously refusing an appointment to the Bibliothèque Impériale (June 1864), Renan decided for the next few years to live by his pen. In fact, he had to wait till 1870 before the chair was restored to him. He was thus pushed into opposition, but had already begun to frequent such dissident salons as that of Princess Mathilde (*see* BONAPARTE) and such literary notables as Flaubert, Sainte-Beuve, Taine, and the Goncourt brothers.

When the *Vie de Jésus* did appear (June 1863) it was virulently denounced by the church. While not Renan's best historical work, it can still claim the attention of 20th-century readers because it presents a "mythical" account of the making of Christianity by the popular imagination and so has a place, like his other historical works, in the literature of messianism. After a journey in Asia Minor in 1864–65 with his wife he published *Les Apôtres* (1866) and *Saint Paul* (1869), to follow the *Vie de Jésus* as parts of a series, *Histoire des origines du christianisme*. Both these volumes, largely by brilliant descriptions of how Christianity spread among the rootless proletariat of the cities of Asia Minor, illustrate his preoccupation with the question: would the intellectuals of the 19th century lead the masses toward a new enlightenment?

The Franco-German War and the Third Republic.—Renan began to interest himself increasingly in politics. In 1869, at the beginning of the "liberal" phase of the Second Empire, he stood unsuccessfully for parliament. In the same year he defended constitutional monarchy in an article, "La Monarchie constitutionnelle en France." So far he was a liberal. In the same spirit he tried during the Franco-German War of 1870–71 to work across frontiers: he corresponded with David Strauss and tried to persuade the Prussian crown prince (later German emperor as Frederick III) to stop the war. But the bitterness of France's defeat and his anger with democracy turned him authoritarian. Thus *La Réforme intellectuelle et morale* (1871) argues that France, to achieve national regeneration, must follow the example set by Prussia after

the Battle of Jena in 1806. But by taking his advice France would have become the sort of clerical monarchy which Renan soon found he did not want. He had to resign himself to the Third Republic but withdrew from public life. While he continued to travel zestfully all over Europe, visiting surviving Bonapartists such as Prince Jérôme Napoléon, his life became more and more identified with his writings. He was elected to the Académie Française in 1878.

Renan's ironical yet imaginative vision of the "festival of the universe" found expression in *L'Antéchrist* (1873; vol. iv of the *Histoire des origines*), with its satirical portrait of Nero and its apocalyptic atmosphere assuredly the most impressive of his historical narratives. The "festival of the universe" provides a visionary end to the *Dialogues philosophiques* (1876). In the first of these, however, Renan is more ironically skeptical about the hidden God than he had been. In fact, the "epicureanism" of his later years masks an anxiety about death and the hereafter. His more superficial side is illustrated in the "philosophic dramas" (collected edition 1888) which trace his acceptance of the Republic, especially *Caliban* (written 1877) and *L'Eau de Jouvence* (written 1879). In the former, the aristocracy (Prospero and Ariel) loses to democracy (Caliban) because alchemical spells (traditional sanctions) are powerless against a people infected by positivism; scientific power politics would be an effective answer, but this is out of the question because in practice it would mean a clerical monarchy. The moral of *Caliban* is therefore: rather a republic than the church.

As to the remaining volumes of the *Histoire des origines*, if Renan's "epicureanism" is hard to find in *Les Évangiles* (1877) it is present in *L'Église chrétienne* (1879), in the portrait of Hadrian; but in *Marc-Aurèle* (1882) the study of Marcus, again a self-portrait, is dominated by the author's preoccupation with death. Since 1876 Renan had been working on his memoirs, *Souvenirs d'enfance et de jeunesse* (1883), in which he reconstructs his life so as to show that he was predestined to become a *prêtre manqué* (failed priest) and that, in spite of heavy odds, his wager on the hidden God had "paid off" in terms of happiness.

In the *Souvenirs* Renan is too serene for some tastes, though his irony keeps his complacency in check. In *L'Ecclésiaste* (1882) and two articles on Amiel (1884), he is above all an ironist combating the Pharisees. On the other hand, in some of his speeches at the Académie Française, on Claude Bernard (1879) and Émile Littré (1882), he reveals his anguish in moments of doubt. Thus he manifests a baffling variety, but the moral heart of the man is to be found in one of the later dramas, *Le Prêtre de Nemi* (1885), and above all in his *Histoire du peuple d'Israël* (1887–93). For him, the history of Jewish messianism bore witness to man's capacity for faith when the odds are against him. Thus it revived his own faith. He could therefore hope that, though Judaism would disappear, the dreams of its prophets would one day come true, so that "without a compensatory Heaven justice will really exist on earth." Having exhausted himself in an effort to finish the work, he died shortly after its completion on Oct. 2, 1892.

With his leanings toward liberalism and authoritarianism in politics, faith and skepticism in religion, Renan embodied the contradictions of the middle class of his time. Politically, his influence after his death was far-reaching, on nationalists like Maurice Barrès and Charles Maurras, on republicans like Anatole France and Georges Clemenceau. He succeeded in assuaging one of the great anxieties of his time, the antagonism between science and religion, but he felt this anxiety himself.

Henriette Psichari's definitive edition of Renan's works appeared in ten volumes in 1947–61.

BIBLIOGRAPHY.—J. Pommier, *Renan, d'après des documents inédits* (1923) and *La Jeunesse cléricale d'Ernest Renan* (1933); H. Psichari, *Renan d'après lui-même* (1937) and *Renan et la guerre de '70* (1947); R. Dussaud, *L'Oeuvre scientifique d'Ernest Renan* (1951); G. La Ferla, *Renan, politico* (1953); J. Chaix-Ruy, *Ernest Renan* (1956); R. M. Chadbourne, *Ernest Renan as an Essayist* (1957); F. Millepierres, *La Vie d'Ernest Renan, sage d'Occident* (1961); H. W. Wardman, *Ernest Renan* (1964). (H. W. Wa.)

RENARD, JULES (1864–1910), French writer, best known for *Poil de Carotte* (1894; English translation, *Carrots*, 1946), a bitterly ironical account of his own childhood, in which a grim humour conceals acute sensibility. All his life, although happily married, and the father of two children, he was haunted by, and tried to hide, the misery he had suffered as a child from lack of affection.

He was born at Châlons-sur-Mayenne on Feb. 22, 1864, and educated at Nevers and in Paris. After his marriage in 1888, he devoted himself to writing. First and foremost an artist (he described himself as a *"chasseur d'images"*), he was one of the first French writers to make use of significant detail in descriptive writing. His sketches of animal life in *Histoires naturelles* (1896) are models of their kind. Although he spent most of his life in Paris, he never lost touch with his native countryside, and in *Les Philippe* (1907), and *Nos frères farouches* and *Ragotte* (both 1908), he depicted rural life with amused penetration and cruel realism. He also wrote plays, including a dramatized version of *Poil de Carotte* (1906). He was a founder member of the *Mercure de France* (1900), and was elected to the Académie Goncourt (1907). He died in Paris on May 22, 1910. His *Journal* (English translation, 1964), 17 volumes (1925–27), by F. Bernouard, is essential to a full understanding of his personality.

BIBLIOGRAPHY.—L. Guichard, *L'Oeuvre et l'âme de Jules Renard* (1935); P. Schneider (ed.), *Jules Renard par lui même* (1956); Helen B. Coulter, *The Prose Work and Technique of Jules Renard* (1935).
(Pl. C.)

RENARD THE FOX: see REYNARD THE FOX.

RENART, JEAN (fl. 1200–1222), French author of romances of adventure (*romans d'aventure*) distinguished by their stylistic originality, is associated with the village of Dammartin en Goële, near Meaux. The attribution to him of two long poems, each surviving only in a single copy, was a major literary discovery of the 1890s—an age strikingly attuned to his mood and style. Joseph Bédier drew attention to his personality in his Fribourg edition of the *Lai de l'Ombre* (1890), and the possibility of his authorship of *L'Escoufle* and *Guillaume de Dôle* was first mooted by Paul Meyer in his edition of *L'Escoufle* in 1894. Erudite stylistic analysis by A. Mussafia (1896–97), F. M. Warren (1908), and G. Charlier (1910) provided confirmation, and in 1913 Bédier discovered anagrams on the name RENART in the final lines of both romances.

L'Escoufle ("The Kite") is a picaresque novel in verse, dedicated to Baldwin VI of Hainaut, later, as Baldwin I, emperor of Constantinople. The betrothed children, Guillaume and Aelis, flee to France from their tutelage at the emperor's court; near Toul they are separated when Guillaume pursues a kite (hawk) which has stolen his mother's ring. Aelis becomes a seamstress, Guillaume an ostler and falconer. One day he tears out the heart of a kite and devours it, and this symbolic gesture leads to their reunion. *Guillaume de Dôle*, dedicated to Miles of Nanteuil, is the old tale of the calumniated bride: Guillaume's sister Lienor, on the eve of her marriage to the emperor, is slandered by the seneschal who, posing as her lover, describes a rose-shaped birthmark on her thigh (whence the poem's other title, *Le Roman de la Rose*). She appears disguised and accuses him of ravishing her: subjected to an ordeal, he sinks to the bottom of a holy water stoup, thus vindicating himself, but also invalidating his previous story! The *Lai de l'Ombre* is a brilliant *marivaudage* (i.e., a piece of elegant verse, artificial and witty in style): a knight presses a ring on his lady and when she refuses it throws it to her reflection (*ombre*) in a well in a gesture that persuades the lady to accept him.

Renart, both realistic and *précieux* (mannered in style), eschews the fey atmosphere and serious morality of his predecessor Chrétien de Troyes (*q.v.*) in favour of half-nostalgic, half-flippant portrayal of high society—the *dîner sur l'herbe* (idyllic picnic), the bathing in the spring, the exchange of girdles and rings, the tourneying and luteplaying far into the night. His colloquial syntax and blend of elegant sentiment with interspersed quips and proverbial wit convey an authentic impression of idiosyncratic poetic temperament. *See* also ROMANCE.

BIBLIOGRAPHY.—*L'Escoufle*, ed. by H. Michelant and P. Meyer (1894), and *Le Roman de la Rose ou de Guillaume de Dôle*, ed. by G. Servois with an article by G. Paris on the interpolated lyrics (1893), both for the Société des anciens textes français; the latter also

ed. by R. Lejeune-Dehousse (1936) and by F. Lecoy, in Classiques français du moyen âge (1962); *Le Lai de l'Ombre*, ed. by J. Bédier, for the Société des anciens textes français (1913), and by J. Orr (1948); *Galeran de Bretagne* (wrongly attributed to Jean Renart), ed. by L. Foulet (1925). *See* also Ch.-V. Langlois, *La Vie en France au moyen âge . . . . d'après les romans mondains du temps*, pp. 1–106, 341–357 (1924); R. Lejeune-Dehousse, *L'Oeuvre de Jean Renart* (1935); R. Bossuat, *Manuel bibliographique de la littérature française du moyen âge*, no. 1185–1219, 1224–30 (1951); *Supplément* no. 6223–27 (1955); 2nd *Supplément* no. 7301–02, 7304 (1961).
(C. A. Rn.)

RENAUD DE MONTAUBAN (or LES QUATRE FILS AYMON), the title of an old French *chanson de geste*, the theme of which long survived in chapbooks and ballads throughout Western Europe. Renaud slays Charlemagne's nephew Bertolai after a quarrel over chess. He mounts his marvelous steed, Bayard, which understands human speech, and, with his brethren, barricades himself in the rock-fortress of Montessor (at the confluence of the Semoy and the Meuse, near Sedan, still known as *La Montagne des quatre fils Aymon*). Their father Aymon helps to besiege them.

Later they hold out in Montauban as the allies of King Yon of Gascony, assisted by their cousin, the sorcerer Maugis. Finally they escape to Dortmund in Westphalia; Renaud turns to a life of religion and helps to build Cologne Cathedral, refusing any wages, and is slain by his envious fellow-workmen. His body, thrown into the Rhine, floats upstream conducted by choirs of angels, and is buried in state at Dortmund.

This story may contain elements of prehistoric myth, combined with traditions relating to Charles Martel's conflict with Eudes (Odo) of Aquitaine in 718–720 (*cf. Mainet*, another of the Charlemagne legends, *q.v.*). Such tales were rooted in the soil of Frankish Austrasia, and on to them were grafted hagiographic legends of the archdiocese of Cologne.

The French poem has more than 18,000 lines; a Middle Dutch poem of similar length (*Renout von Montalbaen*) is the ancestor of the early-17th-century German *Volksbuch*, or chapbook, version. The Spanish Reinalte or Reinaldos, of the *romancero* (*see* SPANISH LITERATURE: *Romancero*) and Lope de Vega's play, derives partly from French epic sources, partly from the numerous Italian Rinaldo poems (from the 14th century to Tasso's first epic, *Il Rinaldo*, 1562). The theme is kept alive by the ballad-singers of Naples and the puppet plays of Liège.

BIBLIOGRAPHY.—*Renaus de Montauban . . .*, ed. by H. Michelant (1862); *La chanson des quatre fils Aymon*, ed. by F. Castets (1909); *The Fours Sons of Aymon*, ed. by O. Richardson, for the Early English Text Society, Early Series, xliv-xlv (1884–85). *See* also J. Bédier, *Les Légendes épiques*, iv, pp. 189–285 (*cf.* iii, pp. 1–38), 2nd ed. (1921); M. Piron, in the *Enquêtes du Musée de la vie wallonne*, iv, pp. 181–212 (1946), vi, pp. 1–66 (1951), vii, pp. 129–192, 343–352 (1955); R. Bossuat, *Manuel bibliographique de la littérature française du moyen âge*, no. 667–682, 4059-60 (1951); *Supplément*, no. 6120 (1955); 2nd *Supplément*, no. 7193–95 (1961); L. Gautier, *Bibliographie des chansons de geste*, pp. 158–167 (1897); F. Pfaff, *Das deutsche Volksbuch von den Heymonskindern*, with bibliography of versions in all languages (1887).
(C. A. Rn.)

RENAUDOT, THÉOPHRASTE (1586?–1653), French physician, philanthropist, father of French journalism, and friend of Richelieu, was born at Loudun. He studied surgery in Paris and received the degree of doctor at Montpellier.

In 1612 Richelieu summoned him to Paris to organize a scheme of public assistance. In 1630 Renaudot, as commissary general of the poor, opened in Paris a *bureau d'adresse*—a combined labour bureau, intelligence department, exchange, and charity organization, which directed indigent sick persons to doctors prepared to give them free treatment. He established (1635) a free dispensary despite the opposition of the ultraconservative medical faculty in Paris, which refused to accept the new medicaments he proposed and restricted themselves to the old prescriptions of bloodletting and purgation. Under the protection of Richelieu, Renaudot started the first French newspaper, the *Gazette* (1631; *see* NEWSPAPER). In 1637 he was authorized to add pawnbroking to the activities of the *bureau*, and the first pawn shops were opened.

The medical faculty campaign against Renaudot, headed by Guy Patin, was prosecuted with increased vigour after the deaths of Richelieu and Louis XIII, and eventually he was denied the right to practise medicine in Paris. The *Gazette* remained to him, however, and in 1646 he was appointed by Mazarin historiographer to the king. Renaudot died on Oct. 25, 1653.

RENDERING, ARCHITECTURAL: see ARCHITECTURAL RENDERING.

RENÉ I (1409–1480), French prince who was titular king of Naples from 1435 to 1442 and duke consort of Lorraine from 1431 to 1453, but whose more permanent authority was confined to Bar, Anjou, and Provence. He was born at Angers on Jan. 16, 1409, the second son of Louis II, duc d'Anjou (*see* LOUIS, kings of Naples), and Yolande of Aragon.

On his father's death (1417), René's elder brother, Louis III, succeeded to Anjou, Maine, and Provence (*qq.v.*); but in 1419 his maternal granduncle, Duke Louis of Bar, named René as his successor (*see* BAR, COUNTS AND DUKES OF). In 1420, moreover, René married Isabella, elder daughter of Charles II (*q.v.*) of Lorraine. Sole ruler of Bar from 1430, he claimed Lorraine by right of his wife on Charles II's death (1431). Charles VII of France, husband of René's sister Mary, supported this claim, but Antony (Antoine) of Vaudémont contested it (*see* LORRAINE).

Antony defeated René at Bulgnéville (July 2, 1431), took him prisoner, and handed him over to Philip (*q.v.*) the Good, duke of Burgundy. Released on parole (May 1432), after giving his sons John (1426–70) and Louis (1427–43) as hostages, René in 1433 agreed that his elder daughter Yolande (1428–83) should marry Antony's son Ferry; but in 1434, when the Holy Roman emperor Sigismund had recognized René as duke of Lorraine (April) and when René had also inherited Anjou and Provence from Louis III (November), Philip took umbrage and, in December, summoned René back into captivity. René finally obtained his discharge on Jan. 28, 1437, promising a heavy ransom and making territorial concessions.

Meanwhile Joan II (*q.v.*) of Naples, who died in February 1435, had made René her heir (*see also* NAPLES, KINGDOM OF). After further conciliating Burgundy by the marriage of his son John, now styled duke of Calabria, to Philip's niece Mary of Bourbon (d. 1448), René in spring 1438 sailed for Naples, which his wife Isabella had been defending against his rival Alfonso V of Aragon. Besieged in Naples by Alfonso from November 1441, he abandoned the city in June 1442. In October he was back in Provence.

From the 1420s the English (*see* HUNDRED YEARS' WAR) had been occupying Maine. To recover it for his younger brother Charles, René took part in the Anglo-French negotiations begun at Tours in April 1444. These led to the marriage of his younger daughter Margaret (of Anjou; *q.v.*) to the English king Henry VI in 1445, but Maine had eventually to be won back by force of arms (1448). Meanwhile Charles VII of France had helped René to pacify Lorraine (war of Metz, 1444–45), and the long-planned marriage of Yolande and Ferry had been solemnized (summer 1445). René accompanied Charles VII on his victorious campaigns of 1449–50 against the English in Normandy. On Isabella's death (Feb. 28, 1453), her duchy of Lorraine passed to John of Calabria.

René's expedition to Lombardy (1453–54), to help Milan and Florence against the Venetians in the hope of a subsequent invasion of Naples, was frustrated by reconciliation between the Italian belligerents. In March 1454 he married Jeanne, daughter of Guy XIV de Laval (*see* LAVAL). Thereafter, apart from important measures for the economic development of Provence, which also benefited from legal reforms under him, he concerned himself more with the arts and literature in Anjou (at his residences at Ponts-de-Cé and at Chanzé, near Angers) and in Provence (at Aix, Tarascon, Marseilles, Peyrolles, and Pertuis) than with dynastic ambitions, which he left to the energetic John of Calabria. In 1466, however, he accepted the title of king of Aragon and count of Barcelona from the Catalan rebels against John II of Aragon. With Louis XI of France his relations were generally strained; and in 1476 Louis forced him to forswear any alliance with Charles the Bold of Burgundy, the French king's great opponent. René died at Aix-en-Provence, on July 10, 1480.

René has been credited with numerous paintings, often simply because they bear his arms. These works, generally in the Flemish style, were probably executed at his behest by the painters whom, together with sculptors, goldsmiths, and tapestry workers, he maintained at his courts. The "Burning Bush" triptych by Nicolas Froment, at Aix, portrays René and Jeanne de Laval.

René's writings, or works at least inspired by him (collected edition by the comte de Quatrebarbes, 1843–46), include a treatise on tournaments; an idyllic poem, *Regnault et Jehanneton* (on his courtship of Jeanne); a mystical dialogue, *Le Mortifiement de Vaine Plaisance* (edited by F. Lyna, 1926); and an allegorical romance, *Le Livre de Cuer d'amours espris,* otherwise entitled *La Conqueste de doulce Mercy* (edited by E. Winkler, three volumes, 1927).

BIBLIOGRAPHY.—R. Lecoy de La Marche, *Le Roi René,* 2 vol. (1875); J. Levron, *La Vie et les moeurs du bon roi René* (1953). *See also* P. Champion, *Le Roi René écrivain* (1925); Y. de Raulin, *Les Peintres de René d'Anjou . . .* (1938).

RENÉE OF FRANCE (1510–1575), duchess of Ferrara, a French princess notable in the history of the Protestant Reformation, was born at Blois on Oct. 25, 1510, the second daughter of Louis XII of France and Anne of Brittany. She was married in 1528 to Ercole d'Este, who became duke of Ferrara as Ercole II in 1534 (*see* ESTE, HOUSE OF). In return for renouncing her claims on Brittany, she was granted the duchy of Chartres, the countship of Gisors, and the *châtellenie* of Montargis by Francis I of France.

Renée's court at Ferrara became a meeting place for liberal thinkers and a refuge for French Protestants. The humanist Olympia Morata was brought up there; Clément Marot (*q.v.*) found shelter there in 1535; and Calvin himself visited Renée in 1536. Under Calvin's influence she ceased practising Catholicism in 1540; but Pope Paul III in 1543 granted her a brief exempting her from all ecclesiastical jurisdiction save that of the Holy Office. Her husband, however, took her children away from her and, in 1554, allowed her to be sentenced to imprisonment for heresy; but within a few days she was set free after a form of recantation.

A widow from 1559 and on bad terms with her son, Alfonso II of Ferrara, Renée returned to France in 1560 and settled at Montargis, which she made a centre of Protestant propaganda. During the Wars of Religion her château was besieged by her son-in-law, François, duc de Guise, in 1562, and she was several times harassed by Catholic troops. She died at Montargis on June 12, 1575.

BIBLIOGRAPHY.—B. Fontana, *Renata di Francia,* 3 vol. (1889–99); E. Rodocanachi, *Renée de France* (1896); D. Cantimori, "Recenti studi intorno alla Riforma in Italia," *Rivista storica italiana,* 5th series, vol. i (1936).

RENFREW, a southwestern county of Scotland, bounded on the north by the river and Firth of Clyde, on the east by Lanark county, on the south, southwest, and west by Ayr County, and on the northwest by the Firth of Clyde. Area 224.7 sq.mi. (582.0 sq.km.).

Physical Features.—The surface is low and undulating, except toward the Ayr border on the west, where the principal height is the Hill of Stake (1,711 ft. [522 m.]), and the confines of Lanark on the southeast, where a few points attain a height of 1,100 ft. (335 m.). The southwestern hills are formed of volcanic rocks, basalts, porphyrites, tuffs, and agglomerates of Calciferous Sandstone Age. Practically all the area northeast of these rocks is occupied by the Carboniferous Limestone series. Boulder clays and late-glacial silts and sands cover low-lying areas. Much of the higher land in the centre is well wooded. In the northwest Loch Thom (an artificial lake) and Gryfe reservoirs provide Greenock with water; to the southeast numerous lochs and reservoirs provide water, not only for Renfrew towns and industries, but also for parts of Ayr and Glasgow.

Apart from the Clyde (*q.v.*), the principal rivers are the White Cart, Levern, Black Cart, and Gryfe. Strathgryfe is the only large vale in the county; the scenery at its head is wild and bleak, but the lower reaches are pastureland. The wooded ravine of Glenkilloch to the south of Paisley is watered by Killoch Burn, on which are three falls.

The hills of Renfrew County are not of sufficient height to exhibit the Scottish alpine flora found on nearby highland mountains. In summer the moors are yellow with tormentil and the gaily coloured mountain pansy. In autumn the uplands are purple with ling and heath. Milkwort and bog asphodel grow abundantly.

In those parts of the county which have not been industrialized, and so remain rural in character, are found all or most of the wild animals common to Scotland, such as bats, hedgehogs, moles, and shrews; foxes, stoats, weasels, and otters; hares, squirrels, rats, mice, and voles; lizards, adders, and vipers. Rabbits are not as common as formerly. There is a great variety and abundance of bird life, particularly seabirds and moorbirds. The numerous lochs and dams are favourite haunts of duck, teal, coot, moorhen, grebe, and gull.

History.—At the time of the Roman advance from the Solway the land was peopled by the British tribe of Damnonii. Forts at Bishopton and near Greenock were built by the Romans to prevent the outflanking of the Antonine Wall, but after the Romans retired (410) the territory was overrun by Cumbrian Britons and formed part of the kingdom of Strathclyde, extending from the River Derwent in Cumberland to the Clyde. It continued so until 1124 when Strathclyde was finally united to the Scottish crown under King David. In 1314 Walter Fitzalan, high steward of Scotland, who was settled in Renfrew, married Marjory, daughter of King Robert the Bruce and mother of Robert II. In 1404 Robert III erected the barony of Renfrew and the Stuart estates into a separate county which, along with the earldom of Carrick and the barony of King's Kyle (both in Ayr), was bestowed upon his son, afterward James I. From their grant are derived the titles of earl of Carrick and baron of Renfrew, borne by the eldest son of the sovereign.

Apart from such isolated incidents as the defeat of Somerled near Renfrew in 1164, the Battle of Langside in 1568, and the capture of the 9th earl of Argyll at Inchinnan in 1685, the history of the county is scarcely separable from that of Paisley or the neighbouring county of Lanark.

The village of Elderslie between Paisley and Johnstone was the birthplace (c. 1270) of Sir William Wallace, the Scottish national hero, and the inventor James Watt was born at Greenock in 1736.

Population and Administration.—The population in 1961 was 338,872; both Gaelic and English were spoken by 1,556 persons (Gaelic only, 6 persons). The large burghs are Paisley (pop. [1961] 95,750), Greenock (74,560), and Port Glasgow (22,559). The small burghs are Johnstone (18,434), Barrhead (14,421), Gourock (9,608), and Renfrew (17,945), the only royal burgh. There are five county districts.

The county returns one member to Parliament for the eastern division and another for the western. Paisley and Greenock each return one member. Renfrew county forms a sheriffdom with Argyll and there are two resident sheriffs-substitute at Paisley and one at Greenock. (Ch. Ro.)

The Economy.—The county is one of the most highly industrialized in Scotland, and more than half the employed population is engaged in manufacturing industries.

Above about 700 ft. soils are thin and often peaty. At lower levels soils improve, especially along the lower reaches of the Black and White Cart waters, where there are extensive stretches of alluvial loam, well suited to arable cultivation. The greater part of the farmland consists of clay soils, ideal for grassland farming. This, with the urban environment, makes Renfrew primarily a dairying county, supplying milk to its own towns and to Glasgow. Even upland farms produce milk, though their main incomes may come from sheep or cattle rearing. The chief crops, grass and oats, are grown for fodder; arable farms produce potatoes, wheat, and barley as cash crops. A number of small holdings specialize in horticulture, poultry, and pig-raising. Some igneous rocks are quarried for roadstone. Forestry is insignificant, and commercial fishing, for which several of the Clyde towns and villages were once famous, has virtually ceased.

Shipbuilding and marine engineering are the chief industries in Greenock and Port Glasgow (qq.v.); there are smaller shipyards in Paisley (q.v.). The county accounts for 40% of tonnage and 25% of marine engines built on the Clyde. Renfrew burgh has the biggest general engineering works. A smaller group of engineering industries, mainly in Johnstone (q.v.), specializes in heavy machine tools; mining and office machinery are manufactured at Greenock. Motor vehicles are made at Linwood; Renfrew also has one of the few electrical cable factories in Scotland.

There are thread mills in Paisley and carpets are made at Elderslie. Woolen yarn and knitted goods are produced in Greenock and ropes at Port Glasgow. Other industries include sugar refining at Greenock and corn flour and other food products at Paisley. Within the Landward part of the county there are, in addition to the automobile factories at Linwood, paper making also at Linwood, tanning at Bridge of Weir, and tire making at Inchinnan.

See H. A. Moisley and A. G. Thain (eds.), *The County of Renfrew*, Statistical Account of Scotland, third series (1962); Land Utilisation Survey of Britain, *Land of Britain*, parts 20–23, *Renfrewshire; Lanarkshire; Dunbartonshire and Stirlingshire*, by L. D. Stamp (ed.) (1946). (H. A. M.)

RENFREW, a royal and small burgh and the county town of Renfrew County, Scot., near the south bank of the Clyde, 5½ mi. (8¾ km.) W by N of Glasgow by road. A small part of the parish of Govan is included in the burgh boundaries. Pop. (1961) 17,945. Industries include large shipbuilding works, engineering, and the manufacture of rubber and paint. The Clyde Trust has constructed a large dock and there is a ferry to Yoker. South of the town is the municipal aerodrome and civil airport. Robert III gave a charter in 1396, but it was a burgh (Renifry) at least 250 years earlier. Close to the town, on the site of Elderslie House, Somerled, lord of the Isles, was defeated and slain in 1164 by the forces of Malcolm IV, against whom he had rebelled. Robert III bestowed upon his son James (afterward James I of Scotland) the title of baron of Renfrew, still borne by the eldest son of the sovereign.

RENI, GUIDO (1575–1642), painter and engraver of the Bolognese school, the great precursor of neoclassicism, was born on Nov. 4, 1575, at Bologna. At the age of ten he entered the studio of Denis Calvaert, a Flemish painter. At 20 he was attracted by the anti-Manneristic novelty of the Carracci family and joined their "Academy of the Natural." In his early years Guido was not precocious. He trained himself by copying from Annibale Carracci, from plaster reproductions of classical pieces and from the St. Cecilia of Raphael. In 1599 he was received into the guild of painters. Between 1600 and 1601 Guido was in Rome, where a few years later he opened a studio of his own. The most important work to survive from this first period in Rome is the "Crucifixion of St. Peter" (Vatican). In 1604 Guido was in Bologna, collaborating in the painting of frescoes in the cloisters of S. Michele in Bosco. In 1607 he was back in Rome, sent for by Pope Paul V to paint the Vatican frescoes of the "Nozze Aldobrandine" and "Le Dame" (1608). He entered the service of Scipione Cardinal Borghese and painted for him the fresco "St. Andrew's Progress to the Gallows" (1608) in the chapel of S. Gregorio Magno al Celio and "The Eternal Father and the Minstrel Angels" in the chapel of Sta. Silvia. Guido surrounded himself with helpers—Lanfranco, Albani, Gessi, Antonio Carracci, Cavedone, Sementi—who were fascinated by his noble if somewhat tyrannical personality. The frescoes illustrating the stories of the Virgin in the pontifical chapel in Montecavallo (Palazzo Quirinale) date from 1610 and, though not the best known, are perhaps the most poetic of his frescoes. Following some quarrels with the pope's treasurer, Guido returned to Bologna; but, recalled to Rome by the pope himself in 1612, he finished some frescoes in the pontifical chapel of Sta. Maria Maggiore. Between 1613 and 1614 followed the celebrated fresco "Phoebus and the Hours, Preceded by Aurora" in the Borghese garden house (now Palazzo Rospigliosi). In 1614 Guido was again in Bologna and painted the fresco "The Glory of St. Domenic" in the church of the same name. From 1617 to 1621 he worked at the Mantuan court of Duke Ferdinand Gonzaga (four paintings of the "Labours of Hercules," now at the Louvre, Paris). In 1622 he went to Naples to paint the frescoes of the treasury of S. Gennaro, but, having quarreled with his patrons, he returned to Rome almost at once, leaving behind his pupils Gessi and Sementi, whom he had

CULVER SERVICE

"PHOEBUS AND THE HOURS, PRECEDED BY AURORA," FRESCO BY GUIDO RENI. IN THE PALAZZO ROSPIGLIOSI, ROME

employed the previous year for the painting of the frescoes in the Chapel of the Sacrament of Ravenna cathedral. The last documented visit to Rome is in 1627. He settled down in Bologna, where from around the year 1630 began a decade in which his art was shown to the greatest perfection, starting with the famous "Madonna With Rosary" (Bologna). He died on Aug. 18, 1642, in Bologna and is buried in S. Domenico.

Highly praised by his contemporaries and subsequently by all defenders of the Academy up to the neoclassicists, above all in France, Guido, like Raphael and the classicists, came under the condemnation of the romanticists and the epoch of Ruskin. By the middle of the 20th century art criticism had studied afresh Guido's personality, making a better appraisal of 17th-century "Academism," in a new historical perspective. In Rome, the main inspiration for Guido's art was the Raphael frescoes and the archaeological marbles, the Niobe and the Laocoön, and he stands apart from the baroque art of his day. His striving is toward a harmony of statuary, classical and elusive at the same time, in which reality is presented in idealized proportions. But since Guido works toward classicism in a period from which classical traits are absent, he remains isolated, far removed from the realistic optimism in Rome from which were to spring the baroque forms of art.

For Guido, the classical ideal becomes a feeling for beauty as the very stuff of poetry. The greatness of Guido lies in the manner in which he evokes the musical harmony of this myth of beauty, filling it with the altogether modern sentiment of nostalgia. The creative process is calm and serene, just as are the studied softness of colour and form. Guido's feeling of melancholy was, however, soon to become debased into sentimentalism and mannerized religiosity.

Other major works by Guido Reni are to be found in the galleries and churches of Bologna, Rome, Naples, Siena and Crema in Italy, in the Louvre, Paris, in the National gallery, London, at Dulwich, London, and in the Kunsthistorisches museum, Vienna.

BIBLIOGRAPHY.—G. Baglione, *Le Vite de' pittori, scultori ed architetti* (1642; new ed., 1935); G. P. Bellori, *Vite di Guido Reni* . . . (1672; new ed., 1942); C. C. Malvasia, *Felsina Pittrice. Vite de' Pittori Bolognesi* . . . (1678); G. B. Passeri, *Le Vite de' Pittori* . . . (1678; new ed., 1934); L. Lanzi, *The History of Painting in Italy* (1828); A. Bolognini Amorini, *Vita del celebre pittore Guido Reni* (1839); M. U. von Boehn, *Guido Reni* (1910); H. Voss, *Guido Reni roemische Jahre* (1923); V. Costantini, *Guido Reni* (1928); F. Malaguzzi-Valeri, *Guido Reni* (1928); O. Kurz, *Guido Reni* (1937); G. C. Cavalli and G. Gnudi, *Guido Reni* (1955).   (G. C. Cɪ.)

RENKUM, a municipality of the Netherlands, situated 2½ mi. W of Arnhem (*q.v.*) on the Utrecht road and comprising the villages of Oosterbeek (the local government centre), Renkum,

Doorwerth, Heelsum, and Wolfheze. Pop. (1960) 29,095 (mun.). Area 18.3 sq.mi. (47.4 sq.km.).

A tourist and international conference centre in beautiful surroundings, it was especially associated with the Battle of Arnhem in World War II; on the Oosterbeek village green is the Airborne memorial put up by the Dutch in memory of the British airborne forces. The Arnhem-Oosterbeek war cemetery is outside the town and Castle Doorwerth is now the Airborne Museum. Renkum is linked by road and rail with main towns. Local industries include rubber, paper, and brickmaking.

RENNELL, JAMES (1742–1830), the leading British geographer of his time, was born at Chudleigh, Devon, on Dec. 3, 1742. He served in the Royal Navy from 1756 to 1763, becoming an expert marine surveyor. Proceeding to India in 1760, Rennell in 1762 was lent to the East India Company as assistant to Alexander Dalrymple (*q.v.*) on a voyage to the Philippine Islands. He joined the company and became surveyor general in Bengal (1764) and after 1767 was surveyor general also of Bihar and Orissa. Until he left India in 1777 he was responsible for producing numerous local and provincial maps. His *Bengal Atlas* (1779) was several times reissued and was reprinted in 1911. Five editions of his *Memoir of a Map of Hindoostan* appeared between 1783 and 1793; the map itself was first published in 1782. A paper in the *Memoirs* on the Ganges and Brahmaputra rivers became a valuable source to geographers and geologists. Rennell wrote works on Herodotus, the Plain of Troy, and the expedition of Cyrus II the Great, and also a *Comparative Geography of Western Asia* (1831). As adviser to the African Association he produced papers and maps on West Africa. His work on oceanography included several papers on the English Channel and a book on ocean currents (1832). By his vast industry and wide range Rennell acquired an international reputation. He died in London on March 29, 1830, and was buried in Westminster Abbey.

BIBLIOGRAPHY.—C. R. Markham, *Major James Rennell* (1895); R. H. Phillimore, *Historical Records of the Survey of India,* vol. i (1945); J. N. L. Baker, "Major James Rennell and His Place in the History of Geography," *History of Geography* (1963).   (J. N. L. B.)

RENNER, KARL (1870–1950), Austrian statesman, first chancellor of the first republic and first president of the second, was born on Dec. 14, 1870, the son of a peasant, at Dolni-Dunajovice (Unter-Tannowitz), Moravia (Czechoslovakia). He studied law at the University of Vienna and early attached himself to the Social Democratic Party. He advocated the transformation of the Habsburg Empire into a federal democratic commonwealth based on equal political and cultural rights for all nationalities. He was elected deputy to the Austrian *Reichsrat* (parliament) in 1907 and, after the collapse of the empire, he became, on Nov. 12, 1918, the first chancellor of the Austrian Republic. He then supported the idea of a union of Austria with a democratic federal Germany. Renner was largely responsible for the decrees of the *Nationalrat* (lower chamber) which called for the dethronement of the dynasty of Habsburg-Lorraine and the banishment of all members of this house if they did not submit entirely to the laws of the republic, and he was in charge of the negotiations which led to the former emperor Charles's leaving Austria in March 1919. On May 12, 1919, Renner went to Paris as head of the Austrian delegation and, after the resignation of the foreign minister, Otto Bauer (*q.v.*), signed on Sept. 10, 1919, the Treaty of St. Germain by which Austro-German union (*Anschluss*) was prohibited.

The first coalition ministry had been succeeded in October 1919 by a second, in which Renner was again chancellor and secretary for foreign affairs. Renner, who as a Social Democrat was inimical to the nationalist Hungarian government, refused to grant demands put forward to extradite the Hungarian revolutionaries who had fled to Vienna. This brought him into conflict with the Christian Democrats and their representatives in the cabinet. The coalition dissolved on June 11; but Renner remained in charge of foreign affairs until Oct. 22, 1920. When in 1930 the Social Democrats became the stronger party, Renner was elected president of the *Nationalrat;* he resigned in 1933. After the annexation of Austria to Germany in 1938, Renner remained unmolested. In a public statement a few days before the plebiscite of April 10, 1938, he had recalled that he had already supported the *Anschluss* idea in 1918.

After the occupation of Vienna by the Soviet Army, Renner obtained approval from the Russians for the formation of an Austrian democratic government and on April 29, 1945, became chancellor of the second Austrian Republic. On Dec. 20, 1945, the newly elected *Nationalrat* nominated him president of the republic. He died at Doebling, near Vienna, on Dec. 31, 1950.

His principal works are *Grundlagen und Entwicklungsziele der Österreichisch-ungarischen Monarchie* (1904); *Österreichs Erneuerung,* three volumes (1916–17); *Die Wirtschaft als Gesamtprozess und die Sozialisierung* (1924). His memoirs (*An der Wende zweier Zeiten*) appeared in 1946.   (A. F. P.; X.)

RENNES, a town in the *département* of Ille-et-Vilaine, western France, formerly the capital of Brittany, lies at the confluence of two rivers, the Ille and the Vilaine, in the centre of a basin that opens widely on the outer reaches of Normandy, Maine, Anjou and lower Brittany. Pop. (1962) 145,013.

The town is built on a regular plan, the main axis running east and west along the canalized Vilaine. The plan originated in the reconstruction after the great seven-day fire of 1720 which destroyed the best part of the old town, but spared the magnificent house of the parliament of Brittany, the work of Salomon de Brosse, finished in 1654. It was to the credit of Jacques V Gabriel, the king's architect (whose son designed the Place de la Concorde in Paris) sent down to supervise the plans, that he achieved the harmony of the centre with the house of parliament, with a remarkable austere coherence. Also by Gabriel is the town hall, a very gracious edifice in the Louis XV style. The cathedral was partly rebuilt at the beginning of the 19th century, its most interesting element being a 15th-century gilt carved wood altarpiece of German work.

Other interesting architectural remains, all on the northern bank of the river, are the Mordelaise gate (15th century) and the cluster of 16th-century houses and 17th-century mansions in the narrow, crooked streets round the cathedral. No building of architectural value suffered from the extensive damage caused by World War II, except the interesting late Gothic church of Saint-Germain. The museum building, destroyed by enemy action in 1944, may now be considered one of the most modern provincial museums in France, the most interesting exhibit being a Nativity by Georges de La Tour (1593–1652). The recent extensions of the city, especially since 1945, have taken place mainly in the south, beyond the railway lines and yards.

Rennes, which is the seat of an archbishop, is also the seat of a prefect (an *inspecteur général* supervising the whole region of Brittany), the headquarters of the 3rd Army corps, and the centre of a university (founded in Nantes in 1461 and transferred to Rennes in 1735) with faculties of law, arts, sciences and medicine. It is also the seat of a court of appeal and a court of assize. The town, a centre of communications, is an important railway junction on the Paris–Brest line, with lines to Saint-Malo and Nantes. The French railways have extensive workshops east of the town. Rennes is a nexus of roads and road transport, where two main axes meet, Paris–Brest and Saint-Malo–Bordeaux. The large airport of Rennes–Saint-Jacques was still partly under military control in the early 1960s.

Rennes, originally an agricultural centre, was before World War II a food-producing town with a few light industries. Postwar developments have led important industrial firms to establish themselves in the town, the main example being the large Citroën automobile works. Other factories include furniture, agricultural implements, chemicals, fertilizers and printing presses.

In Celtic times, Rennes was the capital of the Redones. The Romans made it the centre of communications of the province of Armorica. It was only in the 10th century, when the count of Rennes subdued the province, that the town became pre-eminent as the seat of the dukes of Brittany, and the place of their coronation. In 1356 Bertrand du Guesclin saved the town from capture by the English under the duke of Lancaster. The parliament of Brittany, founded in 1551, held its sessions at Rennes from 1561, they having been previously shared with Nantes. Henry IV entered the city in state in May 1598. In 1675 an insurrection broke out against tobacco and stamp duties. In the repression that followed parliament was transferred to Vannes where it remained until 1689. During the French Revolutionary Wars, Rennes at first opposed the decrees of the constituent assembly: then, reconciled with the revolution, it became the headquarters of the Republican army against the army of the Vendée.   (C. F. L.)

RENNET, a milk-clotting preparation from calf stomachs, used in making junket, cheese and casein (*q.v.*).

If the fourth stomach (abomasum) of a calf is cut up and covered for several days with 10% brine and a preservative (*e.g.,* thymol), the extract so prepared will contain the enzyme rennin and will curdle many times its own volume of warm milk. This is a result of the action of the rennin upon one of the several kinds of casein present in the milk. A large fragment of the molecule is split off. Rennin is secreted by the gastric mucosa of the calf in the form of an inactive substance prorennin, which is changed into rennin by contact with dilute acid. Rennin, like pepsin, digests proteins but it differs from pepsin in requiring only a mildly acid reaction and in breaking fewer bonds in the protein molecule.

The clotting of milk does not necessarily indicate the presence of rennin since most, if not all, proteolytic enzymes including those from plants can clot milk. When sufficiently purified, rennin crystallizes as microscopic cubes, capable when re-dissolved of coagulating about 10,000,000 times their own weight of milk.

                                                        (N. J. Be.)

RENNIE, JOHN (1761–1821), Scottish civil engineer, who built or improved many canals, bridges, docks and harbours, was born at Phantassie, East Lothian, June 7, 1761. He worked under Andrew Meikle, millwright, and attended classes at Edinburgh university, though he did not graduate. His first major work was the machinery for the Albion mills, Blackfriars, London (built 1784–88, destroyed by fire 1791). Rennie greatly extended the use of iron for gears and other parts of machinery. After John Smeaton (*q.v.*) retired, Rennie carried out work on the Kennet and Avon, Rochdale, Lancaster and other canals.

From about 1800 Rennie carried out extensive drainage improvements in the Lincolnshire fens. He constructed or improved many harbours including Wick, Grimsby, Holyhead and Hull and built the London and East India docks on the Thames, and many bridges including Waterloo, Southwark and London bridges. He carried out extensive improvements to naval dockyards at Plymouth, Portsmouth, Chatham and Sheerness; he also began to build the breakwater that shelters Plymouth sound. Rennie died in London on Oct. 4, 1821, and was buried in St. Paul's cathedral.

After his death his business was divided between his sons. George, the elder, ran the mechanical engineering side and John (later Sir John) the civil, including the completion of London bridge and Plymouth breakwater.

See S. Smiles, *Lives of the Engineers* (1904).   (S. B. HN.)

RENO, a city of Nevada, U.S., the seat of Washoe county, is situated on the Truckee river, 14 mi. from the western boundary of the state, at an elevation of 4,500 ft. The city lies near the foot of the Sierra Nevada range amid magnificent and varied scenery. It has a moderate climate throughout the year.

Reno received its start in 1859 when a settler named M. C. Fuller built an inn on the south side of the Truckee river to accommodate travelers and freight teams from the Virginia City mines. When the Central Pacific railroad reached the spot in 1868, a land auction was held and homes were built almost overnight. The new town was named after Gen. Jesse Reno of Virginia, a federal officer in the American Civil War who was killed in the battle of South Mountain. Reno received a charter as an incorporated city in 1879.

Until 1900 Reno's business activity centred around its value as a distribution point. Then after several well-known people were granted divorces under the liberal state law, the town became famous as a divorce centre. (The state recognizes seven grounds for an absolute decree and requires only six weeks' residence before bringing suit.) Another attraction is the "no-waiting" period for marriages in Nevada. In an average year during the 1960s, for example, almost 20,000 marriages were performed in Washoe county compared with about 4,500 divorces granted.

Being close to the Sierra Nevada, Reno is a recreation centre during all seasons of the year. Good skiing, hunting and fishing areas are located nearby. With the full legalization of gambling in the state in 1931, the city began to attract tourists and weekend visitors to its many gambling casinos, most of which also furnish musical entertainment. The gambling combined with the fact that three federal highways run through the city account for the flourishing motel trade.

There are some small manufacturing plants in the area and Reno also continues to be an important warehousing and distribution centre because of Nevada's "Free Port" law under which merchandise originating in either the east or the west and moving in interstate commerce may be stored and assembled in transit free of taxation.

The University of Nevada is located on a beautiful 60-ac. campus overlooking the city from the north.

Immediately adjacent to Reno is the city of Sparks, founded in 1903 by the Southern Pacific Railroad company and named in honour of the state's incumbent governor at that time. For many years most of the town's residents were railroad employees. However, in the 1950s new housing developments constructed to meet the demands of people employed in Reno caused a sharp jump in population. The business district is centred along one main street which also serves as a federal highway. Gambling and the motel trade are also important businesses in Sparks.

The population of Reno in 1960 was 51,470. The Reno standard metropolitan statistical area, comprising all of Washoe county, had a population in 1960 of 84,743. For comparative population figures for both Reno and Sparks *see* table in NEVADA: *Population.*
     (D. W. Ds.)

RENOIR, PIERRE AUGUSTE (1841–1919), French painter, one of the greatest of the Impressionists, was born at Limoges on Feb. 25, 1841, the son of a tailor who moved to Paris about 1845. After working as a painter of porcelain and as a painter of fans and banners, in 1862 Renoir entered the studio of C. G. Gleyre, where he made the acquaintance of Monet, Sisley and Bazille (with whom he frequently shared a studio until 1870). In 1864 and 1865 Renoir first exhibited at the Salon, but his entries were rejected in 1866 (despite the intervention of J. B. C. Corot and C. F. Daubigny) and again in 1867. With the closure of Gleyre's studio in 1864, Renoir spent some time of each year up to 1867 working in the region of Fontainebleau, frequently in the company of one or another of his friends. Although his studies in the Louvre had been devoted largely to the French painters of

BY COURTESY OF THE PHILADELPHIA MUSEUM OF ART; TYSON COLLECTION

"BATHERS," (1884–87), BY PIERRE AUGUSTE RENOIR. IN THE C. S. TYSON COLLECTION, PHILADELPHIA MUSEUM OF ART

the 18th century, some landscapes of this period show the influence of the Barbizon school, while the influence of Courbet is more evident in the figure work (*e.g.*, "Diana," National gallery, Washington). In the years immediately following, Renoir worked in close contact with Monet both in Paris (1866–67) and at Bougival (1869), and the pictures executed (*e.g.*, "The Skaters," 1868; "La Grenouillère," 1869) represent one of the earliest stages of the concerns and techniques of Impressionism and were developed from the example set by Manet. The Salon of 1870 included, however, the "Bather," which is still reminiscent of Courbet, and the "Woman of Algiers," which gives clear evidence of Renoir's enthusiasm for Delacroix.

During the Franco-German War of 1870–71 Renoir served with a regiment of cavalry, returning to Paris during the period of the Commune in 1871. In the years immediately following, he resumed the practice of working with Monet, particularly at Argenteuil, near Paris. In these years (*c.* 1872–76) there developed, mainly by these two artists working in close collaboration, the form of painting known as Impressionism, a term usually understood to refer to a system of painting in which there is a far greater concern with the representation of light and atmosphere than with the representation of the physical characteristics of things and people. Renoir became a member of the "Société anonyme des artistes peintres, sculpteurs et graveurs," founded in 1874, and exhibited at four of the eight so-called "Impressionist" exhibitions organized by that society between 1874 and 1886. Characteristic examples of his work during the 1870s are "La Loge" ("The Box at the Theatre") 1874; "Portrait of Monet," 1875; "Paris Boulevards," 1875; "Mme. Charpentier and Her Daughters," 1878; and "Boating Party at Chatou," 1879.

During the course of 1881–82, Renoir visited Algeria, Guernsey and Italy (where he admired the work of Raphael and the wall paintings of Pompeii), and worked with Cézanne at L'Estaque. It was about this time that Renoir, in common with the majority of the Impressionists, began to modify his style. "I had gone to the end of Impressionism," he said later, "and I was coming to the conclusion that I did not know either how to paint or draw." The characteristic work of this period is the large "Bathers" (1884–87, C. S. Tyson collection, Philadelphia), which illustrates the renewed importance given to the representation of volume and structure defined principally by line, with colour (which tends to be acid) and brush strokes playing a subordinate role. A key work for the comparison of the style of the "dry period" with that of the preceding Impressionist phase is "The Umbrellas" (National gallery, London), which seems to have been painted over a number of years from about 1881–82 to 1885–86.

The work of the late 1880s is varied in character, but by the early 1890s the characteristics of the late style had begun to appear. In the late works the subject matter and the compositional devices of Impressionism are frequently used (*e.g.*, "Lunch at Berneval"), but the range of colour (usually based upon warm, earthy reds and yellows) is arbitrary and personal and the paint is applied in a manner derived from the traditional system of glazing. The most frequent theme of the late years was that of the female nude characterized by a monumentality of proportions comparable to that found in Rubens, and by considerable stylization of features. Examples of this period are "Bather With a Hat" (*c.* 1904, Vienna); "Seated Bather" (1914, Chicago); "Woman Tying Her Shoe" (*c.* 1918, Courtauld Institute of Art, London) and "Rest After Bathing" (1919, Louvre, Paris).

In his late years Renoir undertook sculpture, but since he was crippled with arthritis almost all the works were executed by assistants working under close supervision. Renoir died at Cagnes in Provence on Dec. 17, 1919.

See also PAINTING: *France: 19th Century.*

For a bibliography *see* M. Drucker, *Renoir* etc. (1955); J. Rewald, *The History of Impressionism* (1949). (R. A. Dy.)

RENOUVIER, CHARLES BERNARD (1815–1903),
French philosopher, leading exponent of the neocritical modification of Kantianism, was born at Montpellier, Jan. 1, 1815. He went to Paris in 1831 and attached himself at first to the comte de Saint-Simon and his group. He studied mathematics at the École Polytechnique (1834–36) and then devoted himself to the study of social science and philosophy.

Renouvier's first works were handbooks of philosophy, ancient (1842) and modern (1844); he contributed several articles to Pierre Leroux's *L'Encyclopédie nouvelle.* The revolution of February 1848 led him to write his *Manuel républicain de l'homme et du citoyen* (1848) and his *Gouvernement direct* (1851), the latter in collaboration with a group of democratic socialists. After the *coup d'état* of December 1851, he confined himself to philosophical and religious speculation.

Renouvier became the declared enemy of any doctrine that explained man's moral life in terms of a necessary though passing manifestation of a universal law or reality. His philosophical theories were related to three parallel themes. The first, derived from his study of Augustin Cauchy's work on the infinitesimal calculus, is the law of numbers: any real group must be finite. The second theme is liberty: free will is the root not only of moral life but also of intellectual life and no certainty is ever attainable without it. The third theme is idealistic relativism, derived from Kant and from Auguste Comte: only phenomena have any real existence and each phenomenon is relative in that it can only be apprehended as a component or a compound in relation to another given phenomenon. Renouvier claimed that all known systems of philosophy could be classified in one of two categories: (1) those maintaining the infinite, necessity, substance, the "thing in itself," historical fatalism, and pantheism; and (2) those maintaining the finite, liberty, phenomenalism, and theism. A choice had to be made between the two, but could not be determined on purely intellectual grounds. Renouvier's own option was determined by his belief that man has a moral destiny: a philosopher, he claimed, does not believe in death. He shared Leibniz' belief in the indissolubility of the monad. Thus Renouvier's universe is built around the destiny, not of humanity itself as with Comte, but of the individual. God, for him, is not a substance or an absolute, but the moral order itself, infinite only as the infinity of moral perfection.

Renouvier refused to believe in the inevitability of progress. His *Uchronie* (1876, anonymous; 2nd ed., 1901) gives an outline of the development of European society such as it might have been if Christian preaching had failed and Europe thus had had no Middle Ages. Later, his concept of the evolution of the physical world echoed Herbert Spencer's evolutionist naturalism. Renouvier died at Prades on Sept. 1, 1903.

His works include *Essais de critique générale,* four volumes (1854–64); *Science de la morale* (1869); *Esquisse d'une classification systématique des doctrines philosophiques,* two volumes (1885–86); *Philosophie analytique de l'histoire,* four volumes (1896–97); *La Nouvelle monadologie,* with L. Prat (1899); *Les Dilemmes de la métaphysique pure* (1900); *Le Personnalisme* (1903); and *Critique de la doctrine de Kant,* edited by L. Prat (1906).

BIBLIOGRAPHY.—O. Hamelin, *Le Système de Renouvier* (1927); L. Foucher, *La Jeunesse de Renouvier et sa première philosophie* (1927); G. Milhaud, *La Philosophie de Charles Renouvier* (1927); R. Verneaux, *L'Idéalisme de Renouvier* (1945).

RENT, in law, is a periodical payment due from a tenant for the use of land, buildings, or other property. It is usually payable in money but is sometimes paid in kind. If payable to the landlord, as under a lease, it is called rent service; if to any other person, it is called a rent charge. *See* FARM TENANCY; LANDLORD AND TENANT; LAND TENURE: ECONOMIC AND AGRARIAN ASPECTS.

As a term in economics, with which this article is mainly concerned, rent is differently defined. According to the British economist Alfred Marshall, rent is the income derived from the ownership of land and other free gifts of nature. He, and others after him, chose this definition for technical reasons, even though it is somewhat more restrictive than the meaning given the term in popular usage. Apart from renting land, it is of course possible to rent (in other words, to pay money for the temporary use of any property) houses, automobiles, television sets, and lawn mowers on the understanding that the rented item is to be returned to its owner in essentially the same physical condition.

The more restrictive use of the term became popular rather early among writers on economic matters. For the classical economists of the 18th and 19th centuries, society was divided into three groups: landlords, labourers, and businessmen (or the "moneyed classes"). This division reflected the socio-political structure of Great Britain at the time. The concern of economic theorists was to explain what determined the share of each class in the national product. The income received by landlords as owners of land was called rent.

It was observed that the demand for the product of land would make it profitable to extend cultivation to soils of lesser and lesser fertility, as long as the addition to the value of output would cover the costs of cultivation on the least fertile acreage cultivated. On land of greater fertility—intramarginal land—the costs of cultivation per unit of output would be below that price. This difference between cost and price could be appropriated by the owners of land, who benefited in this way from the fertility of the soil—a "free gift of nature."

Marginal land (the least fertile cultivated) earned no rent. Since, therefore, it was differences in fertility which brought about the surplus for landowners, the return to them was called differential rent. It was also observed, however, that rent emerged not only as cultivation was pushed to the "extensive margin"—to less fertile acreage—but also as it was pushed to the "intensive margin" through more intensive use of the more fertile land. As long as the additional cost of cultivation was less than the addition to the value of the product, it paid to apply more labour and capital to any given piece of land until the net value of the output of the last unit of labour and capital hired had fallen to the level of its incremental cost. The intensive margin would exist even if all land were of equal fertility, as long as land was in scarce supply. It can be called scarcity rent, therefore, to contrast it with differential rent.

However, since the return to any factor of production, not only to land, can be determined in the same way as scarcity rent, it was often asked why the return to land should be given a special name and special treatment. A justification was found in the fact that land, unlike other factors of production, cannot be reproduced. Its supply is fixed no matter what its price. Its supply price is effectively zero. By contrast, the supply of labour or capital is responsive to the price that is offered for it. With this in mind, rent was redefined as the return to any factor of production over and above its supply price.

With the supply price of land zero, the whole of its return is rent, so defined. The return to any other factor may also contain elements of rent, as long as the return stands above the next-most-lucrative employment open to the factor. For example, a singer's employment outside the opera may bring a great deal less than the opera actually pays. A large part of what the opera pays must therefore be called rent.

The opera singer's specific talent may be nonreproducible; like land, it is a "free gift of nature." A particularly effective machine also, though its supply can be increased in time by productive effort, may for a period also earn a quasi rent, until supply has caught up with demand. Where its supply is artificially restricted by a monopoly, the quasi rent may in fact continue indefinitely. All monopoly profits, it has been argued, should therefore be classified as quasi rent. Once this point has been reached in the argument, there is perhaps no logical barrier to extending the meaning of rent to cover all property returns. After all, profits and interest can persist only as long as there is no glut of capital. The possibility of producing capital would presage such a glut, one that has been staved off only by new scarcities created by technical progress.

See FACTORS OF PRODUCTION; LAND; *see* also references under "Rent" in the Index. (H. O. S.)

RENTON, a city in King County, western Washington, U.S., on the south shore of Lake Washington, is located about 12 mi. SE of Seattle. It can be reached by deepwater vessels from Puget Sound via the Ballard Locks and Lake Washington.

A large airplane plant, devoted especially to the manufacture of jet transports, is located there. Lumber, shingles, steel and clay products, railroad freight and passenger cars, logging machinery, and stokers are also produced. Coal mines near Renton, exploited since the 1860s, played an important role in the history of the Pacific northwest. Truck and poultry farming are the chief agricultural activities of the area.

The city was named for William Renton, one of the founders of a coal-mining company, and was incorporated in 1901. For comparative population figures *see* table in WASHINGTON: *Population.* (R. E. BU.)

RENWICK, JAMES (1662–1688), Scottish covenanting leader, the last of the prominent covenanting martyrs, was born at Moniaive in Dumfriesshire, on Feb. 15, 1662, the son of a weaver, Andrew Renwick. Educated at Edinburgh University, he joined that section of the Covenanters known as the Cameronians about 1681 and soon became prominent among them. (*See* COVENANTERS; CAMERONIANS.) Afterward, at their direction, he studied theology at the University of Groningen and was ordained a minister in 1683. Returning to Scotland to take up the work for which he had been trained, he became one of the field preachers and was declared a rebel by the Privy Council. He was largely responsible for the "apologetical declaration" of 1684 by which he and his followers disowned the authority of Charles II; the Privy Council replied by ordering every one to abjure this declaration on pain of death. Unlike some of his associates, Renwick refused to join the rising under the earl of Argyll in 1685; and in 1687, when the declarations of indulgence allowed some liberty of worship to the Presbyterians, he and his followers, often called Renwickites, continued to hold meetings in the fields, which were still illegal. A reward was offered for his capture, and early in 1688 he was seized in Edinburgh. Tried and found guilty of disowning the royal authority and other offenses, he refused to apply for a pardon and was hanged on Feb. 17, 1688.

BIBLIOGRAPHY.—Renwick's life by Alexander Shields, *Biographia Presbyteriana* (1827); R. Wodrow, *History of the Sufferings of the Church of Scotland* (1839); W. H. Carslaw, *Life and Letters of James Renwick* (1893); A. Smellie, *Men of the Covenant* (1904). (X.; H. WA.)

REPARATIONS. In their customary meaning reparations are a levy on a defeated nation forcing it to pay some of the war costs of the winning countries. They were levied on the Central Powers after 1918 to compensate the Allies for some of their war costs; they were meant to replace war indemnities which had been levied after earlier wars as a punitive measure as well as to compensate for economic losses. The United Nations (UN) levied reparations after World War II, principally on Germany, Italy, Japan, and Finland. In the decade following the war, the meaning of the term became more inclusive; it was applied to the payments undertaken by the Federal Republic of Germany to the state of Israel for crimes against the Jews in territory controlled by the Hitler regime and to individuals in Germany and outside it to indemnify them for their persecution. The term was also applied to the obligations of Israel to the Arab refugees who suffered

property losses after Israel's victory over the Arab states in 1948.

There are two practicable ways in which a defeated country can make reparation. It can pay over in cash or kind a portion of the goods and services it is currently producing; *i.e.,* a part of its national income. Or it can pay over in cash or kind some of its capital in the form of machines, tools, rolling stock, merchant shipping, and the like, which is a part of its national wealth. The payment of gold or other universal money is not a practicable method of paying reparations. The supposed consequence of reparations is a decrease in the income, and hence level of living, of the defeated nation, and an increase in the income of the victorious nation, the capitalized value of the increase being equal to its war costs. However, there is no warrant for these suppositions in either the economics of reparations or in historical experience with them.

Experience suggests that the smaller the reparations levy the more likely it is to be paid, and conversely that large levies are unlikely to be collected. In both World Wars I and II the failure to obtain desired reparations was unmistakable. Indeed, some of the victorious nations eventually had to make payments to the defeated in the interests of restoring economic and political stability.

Magnitude of Reparations.—The size of the defeated nation's liability cannot be determined by the war costs for which it is directly or indirectly responsible. These costs are of two kinds, economic and social. The economic cost of war is the value of civilian goods and services which must be forgone in order that resources can be used for war production, plus the capital destruction resulting from war. The social cost is the burden created by loss of life and disorder in social institutions. The loss of life has economic implications, but its cost cannot be measured because the labour value of human life is not capitalized as, for instance, the income value of equipment can be. Estimates can be made of the economic costs of war, and they are usually much in excess of the capacity of the defeated nation to make reparation. For example, after World War II the principal belligerents submitted claims of $320,000,000,000 against Germany. This sum was more than ten times the prewar national income of Germany (at constant prices) and an even greater multiple of income after the war.

Since the magnitude of reparations cannot be determined by war costs, it must be determined by the defeated nation's ability to pay, which is much less than its stated liability; and, surprisingly, the magnitude of reparations also is determined by the ability of the victorious nations to receive payments. Hence the size of reparations depends on three factors: (1) the national wealth or national income of the defeated nation; (2) the ability of either the occupying powers or the government of the defeated nation to organize the economy for the payment of reparations; and (3) the capacity of the victors to organize their economies for the productive use of reparation receipts. The first of these three factors is most important.

The political instability that usually follows a war makes it difficult to organize the defeated economy for the payment of reparations. Authority is diffuse and uncertain; there are conflicts among the victorious nations, and the populace of the defeated country is, to say the least, uncooperative, particularly in the matter of transferring its capital or income to recent enemies. Finally, the payment of reparations depends on the willingness and ability of the victorious countries to accept the new economic structure attendant upon transfers of income or capital. Here occurred the paradoxes of reparations history in the 20th century.

Following World War I, some of the Allied Powers were able to conceive of no limit to a justifiable tribute from Germany, but when payments out of income began, the Allies found the imports competing with domestically produced goods and services and thereupon took measures which prevented Germany from honouring its obligations. After World War II, the transfers of capital from Germany and Japan so threatened to dislocate the economic structure of Europe and Asia that measures were taken to reduce reparation liabilities.

METHODS OF PAYMENT

The payment of reparations in kind or cash out of income or capital constitutes an export surplus; *i.e.,* the paying nation sends out of the country more goods and services than it imports. Reparations are impossible without this surplus, and it is for practical purposes more dependent on increasing exports than on decreasing imports. The fact that reparations are possible only via an export surplus should not be obscured by the financial mechanics of reparations. The defeated nation usually compensates the private owners of capital for the export of the goods which constitute reparations, and to do this it taxes or borrows from its citizens. But reparations cannot be paid out of revenue raised internally; the revenue must be converted into income or capital for transfer to the victor nation or into the currency of that nation. After World War I, reparations were designed to be paid mainly in cash out of income. After World War II, they were meant to be paid in kind, mainly out of capital.

Payments in Kind.—If payments in kind are made out of capital, the defeated nation pays over to the victors specific assets within the defeated economy and titles to assets held abroad. After 1918, the Allies obtained the largest vessels in the German merchant marine and a small amount of additional capital. After 1945, the United Nations seized merchant vessels and industrial equipment in Germany and Japan, acquired German- and Japanese-owned assets within the victor countries and sought to obtain Axis-owned assets within neutral countries. Most of the owners of this property were compensated by revenue raised within the defeated nations, the effect being to distribute the burden of the loss among enemy nationals, whether property owners or not.

Reparations in the form of capital transfers in kind have certain, though limited, advantages. They avoid some of the more complex monetary problems of cash payments. They are adaptable to a general program of economic disarmament whereby victor nations dismantle and remove industrial equipment of actual or potential military value. Some of this equipment may be of immediate peacetime value to the victorious economies, relieving critical shortages and assisting in reconstruction. Against these advantages must be set the complex economic problems created by the transfers. It is difficult if not impossible to distinguish between industrial equipment of military value and that which can be used only to produce peacetime goods. The steel industry may be used for peaceful purposes or it may become the centre of the munitions industry. The war potential of an industry may be reduced by limiting its capacity but this also limits its peaceful uses. An even greater problem is the dislocation of economic structure which capital removals produce. Reducing plant capacity or eliminating it is a complex technical and economic undertaking. A slight error in removing too much of one kind of equipment can produce a great loss in another industry which in consequence must operate at undercapacity. Even with complete technical consistency in scaling down plant facilities there can be unnecessary losses when the reduced output is measured in monetary (*i.e.,* economic) units. The removal and transportation of capital is expensive, and if any of the labour is done by enemy nationals there is likelihood of additional expense through sabotage. Capital removals require a reallocation of resources in both the defeated and the victorious countries. During the process there is loss of income resulting from installation costs and partial unemployment. Meanwhile the defeated country may become a charge on its conquerors, requiring relief of various kinds until it can become self-supporting. These problems are present in the most ideal circumstances which can be supposed.

In the conditions likely to be present, capital reparations mean a long-term reduction in income for the victorious nations as well as for the defeated nation if, as is likely, the two trade with each other. This is probable because capital is removed from an economy where it has been used efficiently with trained labour to one where it must be used less efficiently for a considerable time. The net effect is then a lower income for all countries, victorious as well as defeated. This consequence is avoidable only by the creation of a perfect mechanism for the transfer of capital and by supposing that the recipient nations will be able to use it as ef-

ficiently as the paying nation. Such conditions are improbable. This being so, reparations are apt to produce quite the opposite of their intended effect. This was the experience after World War II.

Following World War I there was some payment of reparations in kind out of income. There were other instances of this method. Out of its annual production, a paying country exports certain commodities to its creditors or performs certain services for them. It can, for example, ship specified quantities of raw material, fuel, or manufactured goods, and it may perform transportation and labour services. It may send numbers of its workers to the victorious nation to restore areas damaged by the war and repatriate them when the work is completed. The difficulties encountered in a scheme of capital reparations are present here also but on a lesser scale. The excessive export of current output may force a reduction in plant operations within the defeated countries. The receipt of these goods and services by the victors disturbs their normal exchange pattern. After World War I, the immigration of German workers into France to restore the devastated areas caused French workers to protest that their wages were being reduced by the increased labour supply. After World War II, some British trade unions resisted the attempt of the Labour government to use German prisoners of war to relieve critical labour shortages. Similarly, some U.S. manufacturers complained that the import of Japanese goods on reparations account was driving down prices in the U.S.

Cash Payments.—Prior to World War II, reparations were more often made as cash payments than as transfers in kind. It was believed that such a method was easier to organize and more productive of a successful settlement (a viewpoint which was reversed after World War II). Cash payments can be made out of accumulated capital, in which case the paying country sells certain of its assets held either at home or abroad, converts the proceeds into the currency of the victorious nation and pays it over to the latter's government. The effect of capital transfers via cash payments need not be quite as disturbing as that of capital transfers in kind, though in practice both may produce much the same result. A conceivable advantage of the former is the greater opportunity given the paying nation to dispose of its capital at a minimum loss; it may sell it on the highest paying market and convert the receipts into the currency of the victor nation, while capital transfers in kind must be made directly to the victor nation and valued realistically at the worth to it.

After World War I, the bulk of reparations levied on Germany was to consist of cash payments out of income over a period of years. The successful execution of this plan called for an export surplus in the paying country and conversion of the surplus into the currency of the receiving nations. The effect was a reduction in the income of the paying nation and an increase in that of the recipients. Cash payments produce distinctive effects which are not present when reparation is made in kind; they arise because the debtor country must obtain the currency of the creditor nation. The nature and importance of the effects depend on the size of reparations in relation to the national income of the debtor and creditor countries, on the sensitivity of their price levels to expenditures and receipts from imports and exports, on the flexibility of their foreign exchange rates and on the money supply together with the rate at which it is spent. If any one result is more probable than others, it is a fall in the foreign value of the paying nation's currency and a concomitant rise in that of the receiving country. This in turn increases the real cost of reparations to the debtor and creates a corresponding gain to the creditor. Because its money buys less of the money of the creditor, the debtor must offer a greater quantity of exports in order to obtain a given quantity of the creditor's money. It is to be repeated that this is a probable, not an invariable, consequence.

There are two major conditions for the successful settlement of cash reparations. Payments must be within the defeated nation's ability to pay after full account is taken of their monetary effects, and payments must be acceptable to the receiving country. The latter must either increase its net imports from the paying nation or from a third nation which is in debt to the paying nation. The inherent complexities of a reparations program of any kind usually have been made more troublesome by the imposition of controls over the economies of the defeated and victorious nations. This was significant after World War II when the German and Japanese economies were closely regulated and when there was regulation in every important victorious nation except the U.S. Control over prices, the movement of goods, and labour represent a comprehensible wish to soften the rigours of reconstruction and of readjustment from war. This, however, does not alter the fact that control removes from the economy the price mechanism whereby gains and losses from alternative lines of action can be compared. This was recognized after 1945 when an effort was made to remove Japanese industrial equipment to non-industrial nations of Asia and the Pacific. As the Japanese economy was controlled, there was no realistic way of appraising the final results of the transfer, nor was there any method of measuring the usefulness of the equipment to the recipient nations, because they too controlled their economies. Eventually it was concluded that the transfers had no economic justification.

REPARATIONS AND WORLD WAR I

Germany's Liability.—Without specifying the exact amount, the Treaty of Versailles held Germany responsible for all damages to civilians and their dependents; for losses caused by the maltreatment of prisoners of war; for pensions to veterans and their dependents; and for the destruction of all nonmilitary property. Reparations in kind were to include merchant ships, coal, livestock, and many kinds of materials. The treaty provided that there should be a "ton for ton and class for class" replacement of Allied shipping by German vessels, Britain being the largest beneficiary under this head. France received most of the coal deliveries and Belgium most of the livestock. The greater part of reparations after World War I were, however, to be paid in cash. Following a series of conferences in 1920, Germany's liability was fixed tentatively at a minimum of 3,000,000,000 gold marks annually for 35 years with maximum payments not to exceed 269,000,000,000 marks. Germany immediately declared it was unable to pay even the minimum, and there followed successive reductions culminating in the decision of the London Conference of 1921, which fixed the liability at 132,000,000,000 (all figures in gold marks) to be paid in annuities, or annual installments, of 2,000,000,000 marks plus an amount equal to 26% of Germany's annual exports. Germany's default brought the occupation of the Ruhr in 1923 by French and Belgian troops in order to collect reparations by force. Dispossessed of this important area, Germany was unable to make payments and each attempt to convert marks into foreign currency drove down their value. The result was the disastrous inflation of 1923 when the mark became almost worthless.

In 1924 the Allies sponsored the Dawes Plan which stabilized the nation's internal finances by a reorganization of the Reichsbank; a transfer committee was created to supervise reparations payments. The total liability was left to later determination, but standard annuities of 2,500,000,000 marks were set subject to increase. The plan was initiated by a loan of 800,000,000 marks to Germany. The Dawes Plan worked so well that by 1929 it was believed that the stringent controls over Germany could be removed and total reparations fixed. This was done by the Young Plan, which set reparations at 121,000,000,000 marks to be paid in 59 annuities. But hardly had the Young Plan started operation than the world depression of the 1930s began, and Germany's ability to pay dwindled to the vanishing point. In 1932 the Lausanne Conference proposed to reduce reparations to the token sum of 3,000,000,000 marks, but the proposal was never ratified. Adolf Hitler came to power in 1933, and within a few years all important obligations under the treaty—political as well as economic—were repudiated.

Obstacles to Settlement.—Two circumstances were mainly responsible for the failure of reparations. One was the political instability of Germany and its refusal to accept responsibility for the war. A more fundamental circumstance was the unwillingness of the creditor nations to accept reparation payments in the only practicable way they could be made—by the transfer of goods and services. The attitude of the creditors had its origin in the notion that a nation is injured by importing more than it exports. Through the 1920s the creditor nations tried to exclude Germany from world trade and simultaneously to increase their exports to Germany (on credit, of course).

Germany's Actual Payments.—The total of reparations paid is not exactly known because of uncertainty over payments between 1918 and 1924; the value of reparations paid during this period was probably about 25,000,000,000 marks. From 1924 to 1931 Germany paid 11,100,000,000 marks, making total payments about 36,100,000,000 marks. During the postwar period, however, Germany borrowed 33,000,000,000 marks from abroad; its net payments to the rest of the world were therefore 3,100,000,000 marks. The reparations program was most successful during the period of greatest borrowing, between 1924–31, when Germany paid 11,100,000,000 marks on reparations account and borrowed 18,000,000,000 marks, the net transfer being 6,900,000,000 marks to Germany. Although reparations often were called the cause of Germany's postwar difficulties, their direct effects were actually negligible. Reparations never were a sizable proportion of any important economic magnitude, being only a small fraction of government expenditures, exports, or national income.

In 1952, the Federal Republic of Germany accepted responsibility for the external debts of Germany (except those of the Eastern zone), including the Dawes and Young Plan loans which stabilized Germany in the 1920s in order to facilitate reparation payments. But the Federal Republic did not assume the reparations debt.

REPARATIONS AND WORLD WAR II

Reparations for World War II were viewed in two distinct ways. In one they were made incidental to a program of economic disarmament and were to be paid out of capital that was: (1) of actual or potential military value; and (2) in excess of the amount permitted the defeated nations by the victorious powers. In the other view, reparations were regarded in the conventional way as payments in compensation for the costs of war and were to be made in kind out of capital and income.

The two conceptions are not wholly consistent, and the attempt to apply both of them created confusion and conflict. Removals of capital reduce the economic power of the defeated nation but they do not necessarily increase the power of the recipient nation correspondingly, so that the loss of income by the defeated nation may be (and usually is) greater than the gain to the victors. With each removal of capital, the ability to pay and receive reparations is lessened. If, on the other hand, maximum reparations are wanted by the victorious nations they cannot disarm the defeated nation of its economic power. These difficulties of the Allied reparations program were later complicated by two additional factors: the disagreement between the U.S.S.R. and U.S., which prevented the conclusion of peace treaties with the major defeated nations; and the establishment by the U.S. of the Economic Cooperation Administration (ECA) for the purpose of capital reconstruction and development in Europe and Asia.

German Reparations.—The express policy was formulated at Potsdam in 1945. Uniform control was to be established over the entire German economy and administered jointly by four powers in their zones of occupation. The purpose was to dismantle German industry so that the nation never again could engage in war. Dismantlement was to be limited by two considerations: the German standard of living was not to be less than the average living standard of other European countries excepting Britain and the U.S.S.R.; and Germany was to be left with sufficient capital to pay for its essential imports and so be self-supporting. Reparations were to be paid out of the difference between total German capital and the permissible amount. The distribution of reparations was to be made by the Inter-Allied Reparations Agency established in 1945. A "level of industry" plan was formulated to specify the kind and amount of reparations available to claimant nations. It soon was recognized that the initial claims of $320,000,000,000 could not be satisfied, and the Allies announced their satisfaction with reparations which would "compensate in some measure for the loss and suffering caused by Germany."

Shortly after the end of the war, the political disagreement between eastern and western Allies made unified control over the German economy impossible. Its division into eastern and western areas curtailed the useful exchange of agricultural for industrial products and removed the possibility of Germany's supporting itself.

The division also increased the difficulties of capital removals since there was no way of appraising their effect on the total economy. The Western powers sought to unify control over their zones in order to advance the reparations program, but here too there was disagreement over the amount of capital to be removed, France insisting on maximum removals in order to disarm Germany completely and Britain and the United States maintaining that Germany should be allowed enough industrial power to assist in the recovery of the entire economy of Western Europe. In 1947 the U.S. offered large loans to European countries if they in turn would cooperate by increasing their output and by reducing trade barriers. The conditions were accepted and the ECA (originally called the Marshall Plan) was begun. It was quickly discovered that European reconstruction would be assisted by allowing the Germans to retain the capital in their western areas (no assistance was given to the eastern area). There was then a conflict between the program for reparations and that for reconstruction. This was resolved by reducing reparations to a token amount, and by 1950 payments stopped. Moreover, West Germany had become so important by this time that the Allies made loans to it for reconstruction. In 1953 the U.S.S.R. stopped collecting reparations from East Germany and stated it would return capital goods worth 3,000,000,000 eastern deutsche marks.

After World War II, reparations from Germany probably were less than occupation costs and loans to it. The U.S.S.R. and Poland secured about a quarter of Germany's arable land and $500,000,000 in reparations out of income. Reparations in kind out of capital were extremely valuable to some of the receiving countries because of the world shortage of equipment after 1945.

Italy and Finland.—Italy's reparations debt was $100,000,-000 to the U.S.S.R. to be paid in kind out of capital and income. Against this should be set relief payments by the Western countries of a larger but unknown amount.

Finland's reparations payments were the most remarkable. By the armistice of 1944 with the U.S.S.R., its liability was set at 300,000,000 gold dollars to be paid in kind out of income, the goods to be valued at 1938 prices. Valued at 1944 prices, the liability was $800,000,000, or 15% to 17% of Finland's national income, the heaviest burden on record. (Germany's World War I liability was never more than 3.5% of its national income.) One-third of the reparations was to be paid in wood products, a traditional export of Finland, and about two-thirds in metal and engineering products, most of which Finland had never made before. The penalty for late deliveries was equal to 80% of the value of the goods. The U.S.S.R. later reduced the bill one-fourth, but the reduction was in wood products. Finland completed its payments by 1952, on schedule, and thereafter sold many of the goods to the U.S.S.R. which it earlier had paid on reparations.

Japanese Reparations.—The initial policy was identical with that for Germany and the consequences quite similar. Japan was to be disarmed of its economic power but left with enough capital to become self-supporting and to maintain a living level equal to that of other Asiatic countries. Reparations were to consist of capital in excess of the permissible amount. To this end an inventory of surplus capital was taken in 1945 and large-scale removals were planned. The Pauley report embodying the program was challenged and its conclusions were later modified, reducing Japan's liability. The major recipients were to be Asiatic countries which Japan had occupied during the war.

As in Germany, the collection of reparations was more expensive than expected and their value to the recipients less than expected. The claimant nations were unable to agree on their proper shares, which delayed execution of the program. Meanwhile, reparations capital in Japan was allowed to deteriorate, and Japan continued as a deficit economy supported mainly by the U.S. as the major occupying power. The continued deficit caused the U.S. to suspend all reparations deliveries in May 1949. To that date, total reparations paid out of assets held within Japan were 153,000,000 yen or $39,000,000 (at 1939 values). In addition, an unspecified sum was paid out of Japanese assets held in foreign countries. Offsetting total receipts from reparations was a considerably larger sum representing relief and occupation costs of the victor nations. As in Germany, occupation costs in Japan were not allocated as reparations receipts were. Some nations therefore obtained net reparations. Taken together, however, Allied reparations from Japan were also negative; net payments were made to Japan as well as to Germany. That these payments might have been still larger had no reparations whatever been collected is a moot question; it is to be noted that some of the payments were necessitated by the reparations program itself.

INDEMNITY PAYMENTS

At the close of its occupation, West Germany assumed liabilities of about $2,000,000,000 (8,000,000,000 DM) to make amends to the victims of Nazi persecution. The internal restitution law of 1953, based on the restitution principles applied by the Americans in their zone, provided $952,000,000 to indemnify persons for bodily loss, loss of liberty and property, and injury to professional careers because of racial, religious, and political persecution. It provided for paying persons who had been in concentration camps $35.70 for each month's imprisonment and for pensions to the survivors of victims. In 1953 also, West Germany agreed to pay the state of Israel $820,000,000 for the cost of resettling 500,000 Jews who to the end of 1951 had emigrated from countries formerly controlled by the Hitler government. The reparations did not cover restitution of Jewish property or claims against the government of East Germany.

After the war between Israel and the Arab states, the United Nations Conciliation Commission for Palestine estimated that $336,000,000 in land and movable property had been lost by the Arabs who became refugees from Palestine. The UN recommended Israel accept the liability and make reparation. Israel refused to accept responsibility on the ground that the losses were caused by the Arab states which started the war, but agreed to make compensation through the UN if it received a loan or other assistance. The agreement was a rare instance of a victorious country making compensation for war losses.

See also WAR DEBT; and references under "Reparations" in the Index.

BIBLIOGRAPHY.—Reparations Commission, *Reparations Papers*, no. 1–23 (1922–30); H. G. Moulton and Leo Pasvolsky, *War Debts and World Prosperity* (1932); Hans Neisser, *The Problem of Reparations* (1944); Edwin W. Pauley, *Report on Japanese Reparations to the President of the U.S.* (1946); E. Mantoux, *The Carthaginian Peace; or The Economic Consequences of Mr. Keynes* (1946); David Ginsburg, *The Future of German Reparations* (1947); Inter-Allied Reparation Agency, *Report of the Secretary General, for the Year 1947* (1948); Department of State *Bulletin* (1954). (W. D. G.)

REPERTORY THEATRE: *see* THEATRE.

REPIN, ILYA EFIMOVICH (1844–1930), Russian historical painter, was born in 1844 at Chuguyev in the department of Kharkov, the son of parents in straitened circumstances. He learned the rudiments of art under a painter of saints named Bunakov, for three years gaining his living at this humble craft. In 1863 he obtained a studentship at the Academy of Fine Arts of St. Petersburg, where he remained for six years, winning the gold medal and a traveling scholarship that enabled him to visit France and Italy. He returned to Russia after a short absence and devoted himself to episodes from Russian history. In 1894 he became professor of historical painting at the St. Petersburg Academy. He died at Kuokkala in Finland on Sept. 29, 1930.

Repin's paintings are powerfully drawn, with not a little imagination and with strong dramatic force and characterization. His chief pictures are "Procession in the Government of Kiev," "The Arrest," "Ivan the Terrible's Murder of His Son," and, his best-known painting, "The Reply of the Cossacks to Sultan Mahmoud IV."

REPLEVIN, in English common law, a suit whereby one recovered personal property (chattels personal) wrongfully taken from his possession. The plaintiff, upon giving the sheriff security that he would both prosecute the suit and return the chattels if judgment was rendered against him, obtained immediate possession of the chattels until final judgment. The judgment awarded the chattels plus damages for their wrongful withholding. The action of detinue lay for chattels wrongfully detained by one who acquired possession rightfully. In the United States, statutes broadened replevin so that it lay to recover chattels wrongfully detained, whether or not wrongfully taken. See also PERSONAL PROPERTY.   (E. M. M.)

REPNIN, ANIKITA IVANOVICH, PRINCE (1668–1726), Russian army officer, one of the collaborators of the emperor Peter the Great, grew up as Peter's playmate. He participated in the two Azov expeditions of 1695 and 1696 against the Turks and from 1700 to 1721 took an active part in many battles of the Northern War against Sweden. In the winter of 1705–06 he commanded the Russian Army besieged by Sweden in Grodno in Poland and in April 1706 succeeded in breaking through the Swedish lines and moving with his army to Brest. At the end of June 1708 he was ordered to hold Holowczyn (Golovchino) in Belorussia. The battle fought there in July was lost through the inadequacy of the precautions taken by Repnin and his tactical mistakes. As a punishment for his unworkmanlike and old-fashioned generalship Peter deprived him of his rank and his command. Reinstated in October 1708, Repnin distinguished himself at Poltava (1709) at the head of his infantry regiments. In 1724 he temporarily replaced Prince A. D. Menshikov as president of the War College. In the intrigues for the succession he first favoured Peter Alekseevich but after the emperor's death set an example to the other notables by joining the party of Catherine I (q.v.) and Menshikov, who rewarded him with the rank of field marshal. He died on July 14 (new style; 3, old style), 1726.   (L. R. LR.)

REPNIN, NIKOLAI VASILIEVICH, PRINCE (1734–1801), Russian diplomat and general who won many victories over the Turks, was born on March 22 (new style; 11, old style), 1734, a grandson of Prince A. I. Repnin (q.v.). He joined the army and, after a period of study in Germany, was sent by the emperor Peter III as ambassador to Berlin (1762). In November 1763 Catherine II transferred him to Warsaw, with instructions to form a Russian party in Poland from among its Orthodox subjects (the so-called dissidents). Although the Polish *Sejm* (Diet) flatly refused to grant concessions to the dissidents, Repnin at first refrained from violent measures. Having failed to break the opposition of the Diet, however, he finally achieved Russian aims by force (October 1767).

In 1768, Repnin went to fight the Turks. At the head of an independent command in Moldavia and Walachia, he prevented a large Turkish army from crossing the Prut (1770); distinguished himself at the actions on the Larga and Kagul rivers; and captured Izmail and Kilia. In 1771 he received the supreme command in Walachia and routed the Turks at Bucharest. A quarrel with the commander in chief, Count P. A. Rumyantsev, then induced him to send in his resignation, but in 1774 he participated in the capture of Silistra and in the negotiations which led to the Peace of Kuchuk Kainarji. In 1775–76 he was ambassador at the Porte. On the outbreak of the War of the Bavarian Succession (1778) he led 30,000 men to Breslau, and at the subsequent Congress of Teschen, where he was Russian plenipotentiary, compelled Austria to make peace with Prussia (May 13, 1779). During the second Turkish war (1787–92) Repnin was, after A. V. Suvorov, the most successful of the Russian commanders. He defeated the Turks on the Salcha River, captured the whole camp of the *seraskier* ("commander in chief") Hassan Pasha, shut him up in Izmail, and was preparing to reduce the place when he was forbidden to do so by Prince G. A. Potemkin (1789). On the retirement of Potemkin in 1791, Repnin succeeded him as commander in chief, and immediately routed the grand vizier at Machin, a victory which compelled the Turks to accept the truce of Galati (Aug. 11 [N.S.], 1791). In 1794 he was made governor-general of the newly acquired Lithuanian provinces. The emperor Paul raised him to the rank of field marshal (1796), and, in 1798, sent him on a diplomatic mission to Berlin and Vienna in order to detach Prussia

from France and unite both Austria and Prussia against the Directory. He was unsuccessful, and on his return was dismissed from the service. He died in Moscow on May 24 (N.S.; 12, O.S.), 1801.   (Lo. L.)

REPORTING. For news reporting see JOURNALISM and also NEWSPAPER: *The Newspaper Office*. For recording the course of proceedings in an open court of law see COURT REPORTING.

REPOUSSÉ, in metalwork, the term used for designs raised in relief from the reverse side. See METALWORK, DECORATIVE.

REPRESENTATION, a term with the broad general connotation of making present something or somebody that is not present; but more especially the term is used in a political meaning and pertains to modern government as a method of solving the problem of how to enable a very large number of people to participate in the shaping of legislation and governmental policy.

Representation in the broadest sense has roots which link it with the world of beliefs called magic, a world in which mysterious connections were regularly assumed to prevail between distinct persons and beings, both natural and supernatural. Without going into the historical evolution of the various meanings of "represent," "representation" and "representative," it is worth noting that the modern governmental meaning was not attached to these expressions until the 16th century, when parliamentary development began. Sir Thomas Smith, in his *De Republica Anglorum* (1583), uses the expression freely in describing parliamentary institutions.

It must be admitted, however, that a magical element remained in spite of the continuous effort to rationalize the relationship spoken of as representation. Some writers, such as Jean Jacques Rousseau, simply denied that representation of the will of the people is possible. While few would be willing to follow Rousseau, it is generally agreed that representation of the electorate in modern representative assemblies poses very real problems, because the views both of the representative and of those represented are likely to undergo change as the situation changes.

Theoretical Problems of Representation.—In large modern countries the people cannot, of course, assemble in the market place as they did in democratic Athens or Rome. If, therefore, the people are to participate in government, they must select and elect a small number from among themselves to represent them and act for them. Through the course of a long historical evolution, the methods for such elections have been rationalized. The extended 19th-century struggle for electoral reform in England was fought over this issue; rotten boroughs, patrons and other features of aristocratic nepotism were eliminated. In these reforms, Jeremy Bentham's "rational" principle of utility prevailed against Edmund Burke's earlier defense of traditional practices. Direct general elections have since that time been accepted as the most "rational" method for choosing representatives, whether they be legislative or executive. For executives are also representatives of the people. The view that this is not so is a survival of attitudes developed during the monarchical age, when progressive forces fought the crown as unrepresentative. It is important that executives be included among the people's representatives because of the paramount role the executive establishment plays in modern government. Public policy in most modern democratic governments is shaped as much by the executive as by the legislative. Since parties are usually led by the chief executive, their role in determining the pattern of representation strengthens the executive's representative position.

Somewhat different are the role and position of the courts. The thorough legal knowledge required of a good judge has stood in the way of choosing judges by election. Wherever judicial bodies have been elective, much dissatisfaction has developed. In most jurisdictions, judges are ordinarily selected on the basis of technical competence—a relatively objective standard. Elections have not seemed a "rational" method. The supreme court of the United States would certainly seem to most people less representative if it were elected by the people. The reason for this is that all representation involves ideas; for only through an idea can the making present of one thing or person by another be conceived. Another problem would arise as the result of the divisions of the electorate; minority interests might be neglected.

The deepest and most obscure aspect of representation is its ideological foundation. There has always been controversy between those who would have the representatives of the people act as delegates carrying out instructions and those who would have them be free agents acting in accordance with their best ability and understanding. The latter alternative was stated by Edmund Burke in his celebrated speech (1780) to the electors at Bristol:

Parliament is not a *congress* of ambassadors from different and hostile interests, which interests each must maintain, as an agent and advocate, against other agents and advocates; but parliament is a *deliberative* assembly of *one* nation, with *one* interest, that of the whole; where not local purposes, not local prejudices ought to guide, but the general good. . . .

Certainly, gentlemen, it ought to be the happiness and glory of a representative to live in the strictest union, the closest correspondence, and the most unreserved communication with his constituents. Their wishes ought to have great weight with him; their opinion high respect; their business unremitted attention. . . . But his unbiased opinion, his mature judgment, his enlightened conscience, he ought not to sacrifice to you, to any man, or to any set of men living. These he does not derive from your pleasure; no, nor from the law and the constitution. They are a trust from Providence, for the abuse of which he is deeply answerable.

Burke's idealistic conception accords neither with the reality of popular politics nor yet with the democratic ideal that the will of the people should prevail. The issue as to whose will is to prevail and is therefore to be taken as the will of the whole cannot be sidestepped by asserting, as Burke does, that parliament represents *one* nation, with *one* interest. While this is true in the abstract, the issue at hand is who is to say what that general interest is at a given time. For the conflict of various interests and their possible relation to a more comprehensive public interest is the real issue. Abstractly considered, a special mandate cannot be admitted, since it would make the members of representative assemblies into mandatories for special interests. But there is a great difference between a special mandate and a broad indication as to the general line of policy to be pursued.

The reason that the elected representatives of a party can be said to represent their electorate is basically that these representatives and those whom they represent are bound together by a world of ideas and beliefs that they share. Consequently, it can be assumed that any conclusion the representatives come to with regard to a new issue is likely to be the same as the conclusion the electorate would have come to had it been able to consider the new facts. But one gets lost in metaphysics of a rather shady sort when one claims that the majority represents the minority in any concrete sense. It is the majority and the minority together who represent the people as a whole and their general interest. But what about the single chief executive? All attempts to lift a chief executive above parties have proved abortive. A disastrous example is provided by the institution of the presidency under the German republican (Weimar) constitution. Such insistence upon the nonpartisan character of the chief executive is a result of the persistence of ideas prevalent during the monarchical age, when the king or the crown was supposed to be the preordained representative of all.

Dual Nature of Representation.—Historically speaking, representative assemblies developed in most European countries in the course of the later middle ages as an important part of the medieval constitutional order. Though great variations existed, the three estates were usually composed of nobility, clergy and the merchants of the cities (the burgesses). In the English parliament the higher nobility was joined with the higher clergy in "the lords spiritual and temporal," while the lower squirearchy and the burgesses together constituted the commons. This latter, the English system of two estates, proved more viable than the commoner continental system of three. The representatives of the lower estate were originally called by the crown in order to secure additional financial support over and above the feudal dues. (*See* FEUDALISM; PARLIAMENT.) Quite naturally, these representatives when gathered together proceeded to present complaints and petitions in an effort to strike a bargain. Such bargains were in favour of their own class. They represented their class as agents of the local powers and acted under instructions or mandates. But

when, after the deal was struck, the king and the two houses of parliament acted together as "the king in parliament," they were taken to represent the whole realm. This historical background shows clearly that it is not justifiable to draw the sharp distinction Burke had in mind between agents with definite instructions and representatives speaking for one nation. An elected body is both: a deliberative assembly from *one* nation with *one* interest, that of the whole, *and* a congress of ambassadors from different and hostile interests. This dualism in political representation cannot be escaped. Many political philosophers have tried to do it, but with unsatisfactory results. The fascists and Communists have, by their insistence upon a monistic view, been forced into seeking some kind of religious or inspirational sanction, deifying the state, the proletariat or the folk and their respective leaders. The dualism of representing both the whole and one or another of its parts lies deeply embedded in representative schemes.

Representation Defined.—In the light of the foregoing, it is possible to suggest a definition of political representation: Representation is the process through which the attitudes, preferences, viewpoints and desires of the entire citizenry or a part of them are, with their expressed approval, shaped into governmental action on their behalf by a smaller number among them, with binding effect upon those represented.

Some features of this difficult definition require further comment. It is necessary to speak advisedly of attitudes, preferences, viewpoints and desires, rather than of will, influence or control, because the large citizen bodies of modern times do not possess a clearly defined will in most matters of public policy, because of lack of knowledge. It is necessary to use the general expression "governmental action," rather than legislation or policy, because all kinds of governmental activity are expressive of popular reactions. Perhaps the most important part of this definition is the phrase "with their expressed approval." Since such approval can be secured only periodically, it must be in a form covering a specified period of time. Finally, it is essential for genuinely representative action that it be accepted by those represented as theirs and hence binding upon them in all its consequences—a result which flows from their expressed approval. But while periodic elections are the commonest method for demonstrating expressed approval, there are exceptions, such as in constitutionally established courts, where the expressed approval may be found in a constitution adopted by common consent; or as in a special interest represented in so-called economic councils.

SOME HISTORICAL AND CONSTITUTIONAL ASPECTS OF REPRESENTATION

Representative systems of the rationalized type are a modern growth. They certainly were not found, as Montesquieu implied, in the forests of ancient Germany. It has been shown that political representation arose as part of the medieval constitutional order. Like so many medieval institutions, this political representation drew its inspiration from the church, whose vast body of the faithful was presumably represented by the great councils in which all Christian people were believed to be present.

Reasons for the Late Appearance of Representation.—But why did representation appear so late in the history of mankind? Essentially, the answer must be that it was not needed before modern times. The great empires of Asia had been animated by religious beliefs in which the individual human being counted for little and his personal preferences for less. In classical antiquity, with its city-states, the small number of citizens made personal participation possible. Aristotle deemed this participation so vital that he opposed altogether a political framework larger than the average city-state. Such personal participation became impossible whenever such a city-state expanded beyond the local unit. Attempts to solve the problem through federal organization foundered because of the lack of an ideological base upon which a representative scheme might have been evolved. The Romans undertook to embody the citizenry of each city of their Latin federation in the Roman citizenry by using various fictions, but the system broke down when republican Rome expanded and the Romans adopted the Asiatic technique of deifying an emperor. Still, the Roman constitution unquestionably contained elements of genuine representation. These elements were crippled, however, by the ascendancy of the unrepresentative senate. By contrast, the spirit of corporate solidarity in the medieval towns, shires, monasteries and cathedrals was sufficiently developed to make the group willing to participate in the larger community through group representatives. Unless such solidarity provides a common base of ideas, true representation cannot take place.

Representation and Constitutional Government.—Except in small communities, constitutional government is impossible without a system of representation. Constitutional government is government in which the use of power is restrained by a constitution which defines the functions of various power-holders. Restraint necessarily calls for dividing governmental power. Undivided power is unrestrained power.

From a historical standpoint, the need for securing responsibility in government is the central objective in all the various schemes of representation. This is true even of completely supernatural schemes, such as that by which a king is supposed to represent God on earth. For this notion may be the most powerful restraint upon the ruler and provide an impulse for him and his officials to act justly and avoid abuse of power. Examples abound not only in the experience of Europe but in such systems as the sultanate of Turkey or the empire of China. But this scheme works only as long as the faith lasts. If the ruler becomes an unbeliever, the most arbitrary tyranny easily develops.

The division of power may take many different forms. Perhaps the two most important modern forms are the so-called separation of powers, and federalism. For both, representation is of vital importance. Distinct federal divisions of the electorate, created and maintained under a constitution, require the selection of distinct groups of representatives among whom the several functions of government may be divided. (*See* FEDERAL GOVERNMENT.) The same is true under any kind of separation of powers; it presupposes a variety of representatives for different constituencies. Looked at from this angle, these schemes for dividing "power" really amount to dividing the people in a number of different ways and then giving these several subdivisions a voice in shaping governmental action through different representatives who are kept from abusing their power by holding each other in check. Such a plan could, of course, have no practical effect unless the community were actually divided into a number of groups, parties and classes.

Not only does constitutional government depend upon representation, but representation in turn depends upon constitutionalism. For unless the community is ready to agree upon and live by a basic charter in accordance with which power is wielded, plans for representation are liable to break down, as they did in post-World War I Italy and Germany. The representative quality rests upon a belief in common ground as far as doing things is concerned, and while there is no need for agreement on fundamentals other than the constitutional mores themselves, the latter, which have sometimes been called constitutional morality, are indeed of paramount importance. Representation, it might be said, is a game in which the rules are prescribed by the constitution as approved by the people. (*See* CONSTITUTION AND CONSTITUTIONAL LAW.)

Representation and Legislation.—Ever since the 16th century, legislation has been considered the most important phase of governmental action. Legislation involves the making of rules binding upon the whole community. Such general rules, it was felt, should bear the closest possible relation to the community's general beliefs. The higher law which Sir Edward Coke and others expounded as the yardstick for evaluating parliamentary statutes was believed immutable, a precious heritage of principles upon which all legislation should be based. At this point, the Protestant idea that one cannot force men in matters of belief, now generally accepted by all Christians as well as by many other faiths, reinforced the growing idea of the necessity of consent in matters of general legislation. A specific act of government may be justified in terms of a specific emergency, but no general rule

can be considered valid unless assented to by those to whom it is to apply. Since the citizenry is too large, representation becomes essential. "No taxation without representation" is a vivid expression of this general view.

There is another aspect which suggests the use of representative assemblies as the natural agents for the purpose of making laws. A general rule presupposes that there is a series of events which have certain aspects in common. There must be a normal situation. If an event is recurrent, time elapses. Time is available, therefore, for deliberation to determine what is right and proper. Deliberative processes in turn are well suited to the relatively slow procedure of representative bodies. Nevertheless, the procedure of a well-organized representative assembly is so arranged as to result in action; namely, the adoption of a general rule. The enactment of such a general rule requires careful adjustment of conflicting viewpoints; really workable compromises need to be reached. Through argument and discussion the area of agreement is determined in the representative legislature. It symbolizes the consent which legislation presupposes, if it is to be compatible with the dignity of man's autonomy in matters of basic conviction and belief.

ELECTORAL SYSTEMS AND REPRESENTATION

In our discussion so far the electing of representatives has been spoken of as if an election were as simple a thing as throwing a stone. Actually, some of the most difficult problems of representation arise in connection with elections. Should elections be secret or public? Should limiting qualifications be required of those participating in the elections? How should the country be divided so as to make it possible for people to vote? These and related issues have all been sharply debated at one time or another, with a view to their bearing upon the central issue of making the results representative.

To the ancients, democracy meant that the whole citizenry met in the market place and decided all matters of common concern. To the modern world, democracy means that the whole citizenry regularly elects representatives, after having read about their platforms in the newspapers or listened to them in a meeting or over the radio or television. But there is a great difference between those elections in which the citizen is confronted by a clear-cut alternative between electing either A or B, and thereby supporting either party X or party Y, and elections in which he must choose among A, B, C, D, E, F and so forth and thus align himself with one of at least half a dozen parties, none of which has any chance of securing a majority.

The English and U.S. System.—The so-called two-party system has long been traditional in the United States and Great Britain. British parliamentary government rested for a long time upon a strictly traditional system of elections. It abounded with abuses of all kinds, such as rotten boroughs—unpopulated or depopulated areas which retained the right of representation in parliament. Through a series of reforms Britain eventually arrived, in 1884–85, at the single-member constituency, though the constituencies continued to lack uniformity of size and structure. Elections thereafter were decided in England by relative majority or plurality. This means that the candidate who secures the largest number of votes wins the seat. The balloting is secret, though before 1885 it was public, with much brawling and rioting. The British electoral system is thus clearly directed toward the goal of dividing each constituency, and thereby all of the United Kingdom, into two parts: the majority which is to govern and the minority which is to criticize. This situation may mean permanent minority status for a man who belongs to the wrong party in a particular constituency. As the English writer Walter Bagehot wrote in *The English Constitution* (1873), "I have myself had a vote for an agricultural county twenty years, and I am a Liberal; but two Tories have always been returned, and all my life will be returned."

The main criticism brought against this system of single-member constituencies is that the number of representatives elected is usually not proportional to the ratio of votes cast. Such is virtually certain to be the case, because in many constituencies one of the parties may predominate, as Democrats do in the southern states of the United States or Tories do in many rural constituencies in England. It may result in apathy among the voters, or in a shift to primary contests as the key political decision. It may even happen that a minority of votes secures a majority of representatives.

Gerrymandering ("Electoral Geometry").—If the desirability of a majority (plurality) system of elections be conceded, the issue of how to divide the electorate appropriately is of great importance. As long as the population shifts, periodic readjustments of the boundaries of electoral districts are necessary, if gross injustices such as rotten boroughs are to be avoided. In the United States and elsewhere this issue is a familiar one; there is a recurrent political fight over reapportionment. Even with skillful and competent handling, there are bound to be lags. Under adverse conditions, reapportionment becomes a football of party politics. Since in order to gain a seat all a party needs is a small majority of votes, it is very tempting for the party in power to redraw the political map, that is, the boundaries of districts, wards and other subdivisions, so as to distribute its voting power most effectively. The resulting shapes of electoral subdivisions are often fantastic and not even always contiguous. Because a salamanderlike sprawling district was first constructed under a governor of Massachusetts, Elbridge Gerry, in 1812, this practice is known as gerrymandering. It is easy to construct cases which illustrate how the same electorate may give a majority to opposing parties as a result of adroit electoral geometry. (*See* APPORTIONMENT, LEGISLATIVE.)

The Issue of Proportional Representation.—The nonproportionality of single-member constituencies electing representatives by pluralities as well as gerrymandering has given rise to a series of proposals for proportional representation which seek to remedy these defects. The idea first appeared in the French national convention in 1793, without practical results. It was further elaborated by a number of writers (see *Bibliography*) who invented several systems.

It is clear that proportional representation responded to a widely felt need. The underlying idea of all the various proposals was to secure a representative assembly reflecting with more or less mathematical exactness the various divisions in the electorate. Why should such divisions be reflected? "The voice of minorities should be heard," is the answer.

The most penetrating philosophical argument in support of the general idea of proportional representation was set forth by John Stuart Mill. He called it "one of the very greatest improvements yet made in the theory and practice of government. . . . In the first place, it secures a representation, in proportion to numbers, of every division of the electoral body: not two great parties alone . . . but every minority in the nation. . . . Secondly, no elector would be nominally represented by someone whom he had not chosen. Every member of the House would be the representative of an unanimous constituency." Mill stressed the strong tie, the complete identification, the weakening of localism, the higher intellectual qualification of the representatives and the avoidance of collective mediocrity. Finally, Mill saw it as a check on "the ascendancy of the numerical majority" by offering "a social support for individual resistance. . . . a rallying point for opinions and interests which the ascendant public opinion views with disfavour." In his enthusiasm, Mill called proportional representation "personal representation" which offers a refuge to the "instructed elite." No objections of real weight could be seen by Mill, though in his usual deliberate manner he examined a few which he found wanting. Yet it is obvious that his whole argument rested upon certain unexplained major premises. His is an extreme individualist argument which he reinforces by the undemocratic preoccupation with the enlightened few who might be lost in the shuffle of the ignorant mass.

But the key assumption is that there can be no representation of the whole without a representation of each of the whole's parts. What actually is the primary function of a representative assembly? Is it to represent or is it to do something else? To put the question is to answer it. The primary function is to participate in governing. In order to be able to do that, a representative assembly needs a measure of cohesion. It cannot be, as we have seen, solely a congress of ambassadors from different and hostile interests. It must be able to reach decisions.

The elusive quality of Mill's approach is made evident by the opposing view of Walter Bagehot, another eminent writer on government and a 19th-century liberal like Mill, albeit more to the right. Bagehot, in rejecting proportional representation, put the following question: What will proportional representation do to the functioning of a parliament as we know it? Bagehot was a practical man, a banker, and his great achievement in this debate was to spell out what everyone knew in practice, namely, that the function of a parliament was twofold: (1) for the majority to support the cabinet in its conduct of the government; and (2) for the minority to criticize the actions of the government. This combination of action and criticism enables a parliament to represent the people as a whole.

Bagehot considered the basic difference between election by majority and proportional representation the fact that proportional representation makes the constituency voluntary—each voter individually is able to choose his own constituency. He votes as a voluntary member of a group which has no other tie. A constituency being the group or segment of voters that is entitled to send a member to parliament or congress, this is indeed the basic point, although the language of advocates of proportional representation often obscures it. To put Bagehot's point another way, all proportional schemes suggest saying to the electorate: If a certain number among you, say 10,000, can agree upon a candidate, that candidate shall be elected. The majority system, by contrast, is based upon this approach: A certain number among you shall constitute an electoral district, and the one for whom the largest number among you vote shall be considered elected. "Under the compulsory form of constituency the votes of the minorities are thrown away. . . . Again this plan gets rid of all our difficulties as to the size of constituencies. . . . Again the admirers of a great man could make a worthy constituency for him." But central party organizations would acquire an overweening influence. "The crisis of politics would be not the election of members, but the making of the constituency. . . . The result of this would be the return of party men mainly. . . . Upon this plan, in theory voluntary, you would get together a set of members bound hard and fast with party bands and fetters infinitely tighter than any members now. . . ." These are brief bits from a memorable passage in Bagehot's *The English Constitution* which anticipated with remarkable clairvoyance some of the troubles that arose when proportional-representation schemes were actually tried. His arguments do not, of course, exhaust the problem. They are focused upon the issues which arise when the cabinet governs with the support of the majority of a parliament. They fail to take into account the problems which appear when the divisions or cleavages among the electorate have gone so far that failure to represent them adequately would undermine the belief of the people in the justice of the constitution.

Theory and practice suggest that the truth lies somewhere between the lines of argument taken by Bagehot and Mill. There are situations, such as in multinational Switzerland, where proportional representation is probably to be preferred, but then parliamentary government should be discarded or at any rate considered very difficult of operation. There are others, such as in Great Britain, where the later evolution of parliamentary government, with its increasing emphasis on executive leadership, would seem to make a majority system advisable.

The Problem of Justice.—A broader philosophical issue which deserves special consideration is the justice of a representative system. Mill, in his plea for proportional representation, laid considerable stress upon this aspect. "There is a part," he wrote in *Considerations on Representative Government*, "whose fair and equal share of influence in the representation is withheld from them; contrary to all *just* government. . . . The injustice and violation of principle are not less flagrant because those who suffer by them are a minority. . . ." Mill considers this matter of justice to the minority so obvious that he proclaims representation in proportion to numbers the first principle of democracy. What kind of justice and democracy is this? Let it be assumed for the moment that representation should be that of individuals and that it is unjust to a minority not to be "represented," or "represented adequately." If there were only one such minority, perhaps it would not be too bad, although the number of representatives who would criticize rather than help to decide would be increased. It would mean less action, rather than different action. If there were many such minorities, so that no group any longer had a majority, it might mean complete inaction for long periods. This situation arose toward the end of the Weimar republic and spelled its doom. It arose in France in the 1930s with disastrous effects, and again in the early 1950s. What then about justice for the majority? Is it not a question of competing claims? Why should the question of what is just to the minorities be given precedence over what is just to the majority? Admittedly, the majority wants some action. If such action is, through proportional representation, delayed or altogether prevented, what is the justice of that? Problems of justice are problems of adjustment between conflicting claims.

The election of representatives, therefore, always involves the paring down of some claims; justice can be achieved only through a careful balancing of these. Presumably the majority's claims are weightier than those of any minority. Representation is a broad thing: The majority participates through acting, the minority through discussion and criticism. Proportionalists fail to consider the possibility that there might not be any majority at all, in spite of the fact that the need for action, and hence the existence of a majority, may be paramount. A just government is above all a government which governs. No government which fails to do that can possibly be just.

Experience with Proportional Representation.—As contrasted with the time when Mill and Bagehot wrote, there is today a substantial body of experience with the workings of proportional representation. But the conclusions to be drawn from this experience divide the experts. On the one hand the enthusiasts for the proportional scheme contend that it is the only truly democratic method that at the same time solves the problem of gerrymandering and other forms of corruption.

On the other hand, there are scholars who have been inclined to blame proportional representation for the collapse of the Weimar republic, as well as the general tendency toward the anarchy of multiple parties and boss rule. A detailed analysis of the 20th-century experience of Belgium, the Netherlands, the Scandinavian kingdoms, Switzerland and Ireland, as well as local experience in the United States and in the British Commonwealth, makes it difficult for the detached observer to agree with either of these views. Leaving aside the rigid list system used in the German republic, and generally condemned, it would seem that all these countries achieved substantial stability and a great deal of social progress under proportional representation, whether combined with parliamentary government or not.

The systems differ from each other in many interesting details. In Belgium lists were used, but the voter could indicate personal preference for individual candidates; in the Netherlands the same was true, but there was also a national pool; in Norway and Sweden there were likewise lists in use, but the voter himself determined how the candidates on the lists were ranked. In Denmark a complicated plan of combining single-member constituencies with proportional representation by way of a transferable vote was employed. Switzerland made use of a list system which gave the voter extreme freedom in making up his list and an almost mathematical representation of views in the community was achieved; yet the resulting complex party structure in the representative assembly permitted effective action, because the Swiss did not use a parliamentary system of government. Finally, Ireland adopted the single transferable vote system long advocated by the British Proportional Representation society, with virtually every county an electoral district. A critical evaluation of the different systems may be looked for in the special works suggested in the bibliography below. Suffice it to say that these countries found proportional representation compatible with their govern-

mental tasks and settled down to a general acceptance of it. The same might be said of quite a few U.S. municipalities.

The conclusion regarding proportional representation is not simple. It all depends upon the group and class structure of the community, the constitution and pattern of the government at large, the extent to which foreign policy is vital and imposes its requirements of integration and consistency. The fact that Switzerland did well under proportional representation does not prove that the United States might do well also.

Yet proportional representation does provide an opportunity for political self-expression to minorities which are already crystallized as politically self-conscious groups. If the representative assembly is capable of integrating these conflicting groups, either by foregoing the task of "supporting" the government, as in Switzerland, or by remaining content to co-operate with a monarchical head, as in the Scandinavian countries and the Netherlands, proportional representation may work better than a majority system. In many U.S. cities the city manager has provided a neutral balance wheel which enables a city council proportionally elected to function effectively. (*See* also PROPORTIONAL REPRESENTATION.)

In the last analysis, the problem of representation under modern conditions should be seen functionally in relation to the task assigned to the representatives. Legislation is one function, executive direction and leadership another, judicial and administrative determination something else again. Any system of representation, electoral or other, which works will be acceptable to the people at large and considered just; any system which fails to do so will be rejected or will become a fatal flaw which may bring on the collapse of the entire governmental system. For technical as the problems of representation may seem, they relate to the very core of modern popular government: Unless the people can be made present in their thought, their opinions and their will, democratic government becomes impossible.

See also references under "Representation" in the Index.

BIBLIOGRAPHY.—Besides the broad philosophical discussions and some continental legal studies, there are only rather partisan analyses. The broad treatments of comparative government contain general analyses. Here might be mentioned Carl J. Friedrich, *Constitutional Government and Democracy,* ch. xiv, xv and xx (1950), and Herman Finer, *Theory and Practice of Modern Government* (1932). Special treatments are to be found in G. H. Hallett and C. G. Hoag, *Proportional Representation—the Key to Democracy* (1937), and F. A. Hermens, *Europe Between Democracy and Anarchy* (1951). An important source is still the *Report of the Royal Commission Appointed to Enquire into Electoral Systems,* Cd. 5163, and its *Minutes of Evidence,* Cd. 5162 (1910); May McKisack, *Parliamentary Representation of the English Boroughs in the Middle Ages* (1932); James Hogan, *Election and Representation* (1945); W. Konopczynski, *Liberum Veto* (1918). For American parties, *see* V. O. Key, Jr., *Politics, Parties and Pressure Groups,* 4th ed. (1958).   (C. J. FH.)

REPRIMAND, a public, formal, severe reproof or censure administered to a person at fault by his superior officer or by a body to which he belongs. The presiding officer of a legislature may reprimand a member for improper conduct in that body, in accordance with a vote of the house censuring him for a violation of its rules, such as disorderly conduct in the house or intemperate language in debate. A military officer may be punished by a reprimand administered by his superior officer or the civilian head of the military department, and in English law the most familiar use of the term is as a sentence imposed by a court-martial, as for example when a naval officer is found guilty of hazarding his ship but the court does not consider any more severe penalty is appropriate.

In ecclesiastical law, censure is a spiritual punishment which withdraws from a baptized person (lay or clerical) a privilege given him by the church, denies him the use of certain spiritual goods, or even expels him entirely from the church communion. One type of religious censure is inhibition, which is a command of a bishop or ecclesiastical judge, designed to compel obedience to his order or monition, that a clergyman shall cease performing any service of the church or other spiritual duty.

In civil law inhibition is a prohibition which the law makes or the judge ordains to an individual. Under Roman law, infamy was a censure on individuals pronounced by a competent state official; it resulted in disqualification for certain rights in public and private law. Under the common law, conviction for an infamous crime disqualified an individual from giving legal testimony in court or serving as a juror. In modern times these disqualifications have largely been abolished by statute, so that a previous conviction affects the credibility of a witness but does not impair his legal capacity to give evidence. At common law, crimes resulting in infamy were treason, felony, or any offense such as forgery or perjury which involved deceit or falsification. Infamous crimes are now defined in terms of the punishment imposed—death or imprisonment in a state penitentiary. (RT. K.)

REPRISALS are measures of self-help in violation of normal international law to remedy past injuries or to stop continuing injuries in time either of peace or of war. They have been considered permissible only if in retaliation for an injury resulting from a violation of international law, if peaceful measures for obtaining redress have been exhausted without success and if the measures adopted are no more severe than the injuries complained of. (Naulilan Incident, Portugal and Germany, Arbitral Decision, July 31, 1928; H. W. Briggs, *The Law of Nations,* p. 951 [1952].)

Formerly a private person might be given "letters of marque and reprisal" by his government permitting him to seize ships of foreign flag at sea in order to gain compensation for a claim against a person of the nationality of the vessel's flag, in case the courts of that state had "denied justice." This practice was, however, ended by the Declaration of Paris (1856), which abolished privateering. Reprisals were, therefore, permitted only by the public forces of a state. (*See* PARIS, DECLARATION OF.)

Reprisals in time of war should be preceded by a public declaration calling upon the enemy to cease its illegal behaviour; should, so far as possible, be of a type not to injure innocent enemy or neutral persons; and should be stopped as soon as the enemy discontinues its illegal behaviour. The legitimacy of naval reprisals against the enemy, but injuring neutral commerce, was a matter of controversy between the United States and Great Britain before the War of 1812 and during the period of U.S. neutrality in World War I. In spite of neutral protest, British prize courts sustained orders in council, injurious to neutral commerce, in their character of measures of reprisal. (*The Fox,* Edw. 311; *The Stigstad,* [1919] A.C. 279; *The Leonora* [1919] A.C. 974.)

Reprisals in time of peace have taken the form of territorial occupation, administration of customs, detention of vessels in port, and "pacific blockade." The United States has contended that vessels of third states cannot be seized or otherwise interfered with for breach of "pacific blockade" although they can for breach of a "war blockade." In 1902 Germany, Great Britain, and Italy changed their pacific blockade of Venezuelan ports to a war blockade in response to a protest based on this contention. In the 19th century, pacific blockades in fact often extended to vessels of third states, and a League of Nations committee held that in accord with this practice economic sanctions against a covenant-breaking state might extend to vessels of nonmember states.

After the occupation of Corfu by Italy in 1923 as a measure of reprisal against Greece, a League of Nations committee of jurists implied that the obligation of members not to "resort to war" prohibited reprisals of warlike character. The more extensive obligations, of parties to the Kellogg Pact of 1929 and the United Nations Charter, to settle disputes only by peaceful means and to refrain from use of threat or force have been held to abolish peacetime reprisals in international law unless authorized by a competent international authority. Hostile acts in "individual or collective self-defence" against "armed attack" are, however, permitted by the charter (art. 51).

In August 1964 the United States executed retaliatory attacks on North Vietnam naval installations after U.S. naval vessels were attacked in the Gulf of Tonkin. Similar retaliatory action was taken in February 1965 after attacks on a U.S. barracks at Pleiku and on other points in South Vietnam.

BIBLIOGRAPHY.—A. D. McNair, "The Legal Meaning of War and the Relations of War to Reprisals," *Grotius Society Transactions,* vol. 2 (1926); Grover Clark, "The English Practice with Regard to Reprisals by Private Persons," *American Journal of International Law,* 27:694 (1933); Quincy Wright, *A Study of War,* p. 1392 ff. (1942); Julius Stone, *Legal Controls of International Conflict,* p. 292 ff. (1954); Wesley L. Gould, *An Introduction to International Law,* p. 590 ff. (1957). (Q. W.)

REPRODUCTION, the process by which living organisms duplicate themselves. This function of animals and plants is regarded by biologists as the most fundamental characteristic of life. A distinction is commonly drawn between duplication of substance within a single individual or organism (growth) and duplication of the individual itself (reproduction); this distinction inevitably breaks down wherever there is any question of what constitutes an individual, as in colonial animals and in many plants. The distinction also loses its meaning when analysis is carried to microscopic or submicroscopic levels of living material. The present discussion will begin with reproduction as commonly observed in the individual organism, and will then proceed to smaller living units.

This article is divided into two main sections: *Essential Features* is primarily an introductory survey of the diverse ways in which organisms insure the continuity of their species; *Physiology of Reproduction* deals exclusively with animal reproduction, chiefly nonhuman. Human reproduction is treated in detail in a separate article, REPRODUCTIVE SYSTEM. The details of plant reproduction are given in PLANTS AND PLANT SCIENCE; ANGIOSPERMS; and GYMNOSPERMS. Biological aspects of sex, sex determination, and sex ratio are covered in SEX.

I. ESSENTIAL FEATURES

Centuries of observation and experiment, culminating in the celebrated researches of Louis Pasteur, served to establish that living organisms, within the scope of competent observation, come into being exclusively as products of other similar living organisms. This generalization is often referred to as biogenesis, or the genetic continuity of species. The nature of the process of inheritance (*see* HEREDITY) has been elucidated by intensive research, mainly during the 20th century, based on the pioneering studies of Mendel. It must be emphasized that what is inherited by organisms from their parent or parents is a life history: a process that may be as uneventful as the increase in size of a single bacterium or protozoon after fission, or as complicated as the succession of different larval forms and metamorphoses in certain parasites, but always eventually culminating in a form resembling the parent.

A. SEXUAL LIFE HISTORY

The mode of reproduction of new individuals in the human species furnishes a sexual-biparental life cycle that may be taken as a norm for the animal kingdom, both vertebrate and invertebrate.

1. Human Cycle.—The general aspects of the human life history may be enumerated as follows. Adults are of two mating types, or sexes: either male or female. Each mature adult contains within its body paired reproductive glands, testes or ovaries respectively, active usually on a cyclic basis. The reproductive glands produce germ cells, or gametes, sperm and egg cells respectively, which carry the hereditary pattern to the next generation.

The union of the germ cells from the two parents results in a zygote, or fertilized egg, which embarks on a series of relatively rapid progressive transformations. This period of rapid change is the portion of the life history with which the science of embryology is chiefly concerned. Briefly, the zygote divides by repeated cleavage, with little or no increase in the total mass of living material, until a hollow ball of cells (blastula) is formed. The fluid-filled blastula, or blastocyst as it is termed in mammals, passes into the uterus, or lower portion of the duct leading from the ovary to the exterior, but does not develop further unless implanted in the wall of the uterus or some equivalent site. This implantation is accomplished largely by the activity of the external cells of the blastocyst, which dissolve away the uterine lining locally. Meanwhile, the blastocyst enlarges and its internal portions undergo marked growth and cellular translocations involved in the process of gastrulation, which culminates in the production of a three-layered embryo enclosed within protective membranes. The peripheral extra-embryonic tissues, at this time, form an inextricable union with the maternal uterine wall, composing a temporary intermediary organ, the placenta, between maternal and embryonic body. Respiratory, nutritive, and excretory exchanges take place through the placenta.

The three embryonic or germ layers (ectoderm, mesoderm, entoderm), by processes of folding, local thickening, or budding, form the axis of the embryo within the protective membranes. This is, in general, a polar process, beginning at the anterior end and progressing posteriorly. During the first part of the life history of an individual, the anterior levels are always developmentally in advance of the posterior ones; the balance is not fully redressed until adult proportions are reached. The main features of the embryonic axis are first marked out: the neural tube, the notochord underlying it, and the mesodermal somites or segments lateral to these two median organs. The organ systems of the body arise by orderly local modifications of the primary germ layers.

The human body is complete as far as the organ rudiments are concerned by the sixth week after fertilization. From this time on, increase in size, in an orderly differential growth pattern, and physiological maturation of the several organs, are the major features of development. Approximately ten lunar months after fertilization, the new individual is capable of independent existence and is expelled by the maternal body. Then follow the developmental stages known as infancy, childhood, adolescence, etc., which are in effect a continuation of the intrauterine growth period at an ever-decreasing tempo. By the time the growth rate of the individual as a whole has decreased to zero (some tissues of the body never cease growing), the period of sexual maturity has been reached. The individual is now capable of being parent to a new generation, and the cycle is complete. After maturity, senescence and death complete the history of the separate individual.

2. Animal and Plant Cycles.—For an understanding of the sexual life-cycle as found in the plant and animal kingdoms, certain special aspects of the human model should be emphasized.

Parental Protection.—In man, as in practically all other mammals, the fertilized egg is retained within the female reproductive passages during the period when changes are most intensive and when, presumably, the new individual would be most susceptible to injury. In seed plants, the fertilized ovum is protected by the embryo sac, seed coverings, and ovary wall. In many animals the young are retained within the maternal body until they are fully motile and capable of getting food for themselves. In most of these cases the new individual has a preformed food supply in the yolk of the egg. There are instances, however, in which an organ of nutritive exchange (placenta in higher mammals) is formed between mother and embryo; but examples can be cited of similar organs from among cartilaginous fish, amphibians, even insects.

Physical protection may be furnished the new generation by the old in the form of external brood pouches (some degree of chemi-

cal interchange may occur even in this relatively external situation). Such devices are found particularly in certain specialized aquatic forms: the sea horse, certain crustaceans, echinoderms, etc. In other cases, parental protection takes the form of elaborate behaviour patterns involving cocoon production in earthworms, and nest building and guarding in birds and fishes. Instinctive activity of this nature is common among insects, where the digger wasps furnish a spectacular example of maternal provisioning, and the social insects afford equally striking instances of collective responsibility for the immature young.

Critical Stages.—A second noteworthy feature of the life history is the presence of what may be called critical stages. Among placental mammals the most obvious of these is the implantation period. The mammalian egg develops as far as the blastocyst stage as a free individual; until then it can be kept alive and progressing even in artificial nutrients. At this point, however, development ceases and does not resume until implantation. The occurrence of some similar developmental block, or dormant period, lasting until some threshold is passed, is a feature to be found in many life histories. Often such dormant periods assume relatively lengthy proportions, as is the case in seeds of higher plants, resting spores in some of the lower ones; insect diapause; or in parasite life histories where development is blocked until a suitable host is available.

Asexual Phases.—A third element in the direct biparental life history pattern is the interposition of an asexual phase. Occasionally, in humans, one (rarely, more) asexual reproduction is interposed in the sexual cycle; this is called true, or one-egg, twinning. In some mammals, as the armadillo, such asexual multiplication is a regular feature of the life history. Among the invertebrate phyla are many cases where the normal life history includes a stage of asexual reproduction, usually budding or fission, which in some forms constitutes the major means of replicating individuals. In certain invertebrate groups, e.g. tunicates and coelenterates, a regular alternation of generations between sexual and asexual reproduction has been established as the life history pattern. In multicellular plants alternation of generations is the rule (see below).

Larval Stages.—Among vertebrates, the amphibians in particular display a fourth variant of the life cycle. Here, typically, the development of the zygote is external and largely unprotected by the parent; the primary development leads to formation of a precociously independent larva (e.g., the tadpole stage of frogs and toads), living as an aquatic organism and looking very different from the parents. Only after considerable feeding and growing does the larva undergo a radical metamorphosis into the adult.

This life history pattern, in which a larval stage, or more than one such stage, is interposed between egg and adult, is typical of many marine invertebrates. In these cases, parental protection is minimal or nonexistent. Vast numbers of germ cells are produced and zygotes that survive the vicissitudes of the open sea develop rapidly into minute larvae, which, after feeding and growing, metamorphose into the parental form.

Among the arthropods, which are characterized by the possession of a nongrowing exoskeleton that is periodically molted, the life history can be resolved into a series of growth stages (larval or nymphal), punctuated by molts. In the higher insects (beetles, flies, butterflies, bees, etc.), certain molts are accompanied by truly radical changes, as from an active larva (a wormlike caterpillar or grub) to a quiescent pupa, and from a pupa to a winged and sexually mature adult. (*See* METAMORPHOSIS.)

In the case of parasitic flatworms (flukes and tapeworms) there are many instances of a whole series of successive larval stages in the life history, each adjusted to a separate host or to a transfer from one host to another, and frequently including asexual division cycles during the sojourn in a host. There are examples of paedogenesis, in which a larval form becomes precociously sexually mature. Regardless of the number of stages, the cycle always comes round to an adult form like that of the original parents.

Hermaphroditism.—There are many instances, both in plants and animals, where organs of both sexes occur in the same individual. The so-called perfect flower produces both male and female sex cells. In flatworms, hermaphroditism is the rule, as it is in the free-living segmented worms of freshwater and land habitat and in many mollusks. Cases can be cited from other phyla. Experimental analysis of sex differences has revealed that, among vertebrates as well as invertebrates, the gonad rudiments are, at the beginning of their development, potentially bisexual; thus hermaphroditism may be considered latent in all sexual organisms.

In most overtly hermaphroditic organisms, self-fertilization is prevented by mechanical obstruction, or, more commonly, by the difference in time of maturation of the reproductive organs, so that germ cells of only one of the sexes are liberated at any one time (usually the male precedes). In some snails and bivalve mollusks, only one type of gonad is present, the hermaphrodite gland, in the follicles of which first sperm, then eggs, are produced. The production of these two sex cells indeed may overlap, sperm and eggs developing in the same follicle. (*See* HERMAPHRODITE.)

Parthenogenesis.—Parthenogenesis, the variant of sexual reproduction in which the egg may become activated without intervention of a sperm, is found normally in various invertebrates. Rotifers and water fleas, in particular, reproduce parthenogenetically during summer or favourable seasons; they also produce "winter eggs," which require fertilization and then enter a resting phase that outlasts unfavourable conditions. Parthenogenesis differs markedly from any type of asexual reproduction, even though no fertilization occurs, in that it involves the production of an egg with all its hereditary material and cytoplasmic structure. *See* PARTHENOGENESIS.

B. ASEXUAL REPRODUCTION

1. One-Celled Organisms.—Unicellular organisms, in many of which sexual processes have never been reported, all reproduce by cell division exclusively. Sexual processes, when they occur in one-celled forms, do not strictly speaking increase the number of individuals. The primary function of fertilization in these cases is not reproduction per se, but the promotion of hereditary variation.

2. Many-Celled Plants.—In multicellular plants, asexual reproduction takes two quite different forms. One is the so-called asexual reproduction of the sporophyte generation, involving the production of spores that develop, without fertilization, into gametophyte plants. This aspect of reproduction in plants is part of a complicated sexual cycle; it is not strictly comparable to what is called asexual reproduction in animals. Plants, however, also have a strong tendency to reproduce vegetatively; these processes bear much more direct comparison to asexual reproduction in animals.

Vegetative reproduction in vascular plants (ferns, seed plants) —*i.e.*, formation of tubers, stolons, bulbs, runners, rhizomes, buds, and indeed all growth and branching of the plant axis—is traceable to meristems, or reserves of cells that have not taken on a specialized form or function, but instead have remained capable of continued cell division. The meristematic tips of stems and roots, and certain other localized reserves, may become the source of a new axis if properly stimulated. Meristems are an intrinsic part of the organization of the vascular plant body; thus relatively indefinite growth is a property of even the most highly differentiated plants. In nonvascular multicellular plants (mosses, liverworts), asexual reproduction is accomplished by localized growth centres (gemmae, etc.) in less highly differentiated tissue regions.

3. Many-Celled Animals.—Among multicellular animals, various types of asexual reproduction are common. The sessile colonial forms such as sponges, coelenterate polyps, bryozoans, and tunicates may undergo branching, stolon formation, or budding not unlike the pattern found in plants. The reserve cells that give rise to branches and buds are not localized in tissue groups as are the plant meristems, but in coelenterates, at least, they are mobile, continually being replaced. It is not known to what extent an animal cell that has assumed a specialized function in the body can revert to an undifferentiated state and partake in any sort of asexual reproduction; it is possible that in lower animals, cells other than the known reserve cells can lose their specializations and participate in forming a new individual.

Flatworms and annelids frequently reproduce by transverse fission. Regeneration in these forms, clearly parallel to asexual reproduction, definitely involves reserve cells called neoblasts, but other types of cells may also participate. When the animal is severed crosswise, whether by normal fission or by cutting, reserve cells are mobilized at the cut surface, and the missing portions of the axis are reconstituted by a new growth or blastema that develops at this surface. (*See* REGENERATION.)

Asexual reproduction in some invertebrate groups is associated with protective devices for withstanding adverse conditions. Gemmules and statoblasts, as examples, are groups of cells in a dormant state, formed presumably from reserve cells and covered with resistant capsular material. The reserves appear to be mobilized in response to critical environmental conditions; formation of these reproductive devices is usually accompanied by the death of the parent colony, much as annual plants die after dropping their seeds.

C. CELLULAR ASPECTS

Cytologists and embryologists in the last half of the 19th century established the cellular basis of reproduction by delicate and precise microscopic examination.

1. Hereditary Mechanism.—The chromosomes, stainable threadlike bodies in the nucleus, are constant in number, form, and molecular structure in the cells of an organism and in all members of a species (discounting mutations and a slight variation that may occur between sexes). In most animals and in plant sporophytes, the chromosome set is demonstrably double: in humans, 23 pairs of chromosomes is the accepted number. This double condition is called diploid. At ordinary cell division (mitosis) each single chromosome is seen to split longitudinally into two strands. At this time all the chromosomes become tightly coiled, short and thick; the nuclear membrane dissolves, the chromosomes arrange themselves midway between the poles of the spindle, a fibrous bipolar figure that appears in the cell at this time. The two daughter strands of each chromosome pass to opposite poles of this spindle; thus identical (except for genic changes) chromosome sets are consigned to each of the daughter nuclei. The cytoplasm of the cell is then divided in two, and cell division is complete.

Since all cells in an individual are descendants, through mitotic division, of one zygote, the chromosome set is constant within the organism. The maintenance of such a precise species pattern, passed intact from one generation to the next, is easily understood in organisms reproducing in asexual fashion since mitotic division is the basis of all asexual reproduction.

In sexual reproduction, the crucial event is fertilization. In this case, two cells, sperm and egg (or their equivalents), unite to form one zygote cell. The nucleus of each germ cell carries a single, or haploid, chromosome set (only one chromosome of each pair). The zygote therefore contains the diploid set. In the reproductive organs, the divisions that give rise to the haploid germ cells are characterized by a special type of nuclear behaviour termed meiosis.

The random segregation of members of each chromosome pair into separate germ cells, and the reconstitution of the pairs by fertilization, account for the phenomena of Mendelian heredity. Visible traits are determined by genes, units of submicroscopic size arranged in a fixed pattern along the length of a chromosome. When a strand splits into two, each gene is duplicated. Duplication of the genes at cell division is not always perfect; occasionally an imperfect or slightly altered copy, or mutation, arises. The altered copy will duplicate its imperfection from that time on. (*See* HEREDITY; MUTATION.)

2. Cellular Cycle in Animals.—In multicellular animals that reproduce sexually, meiosis occurs only in the specialized germ cells in the gonad. Two meiotic divisions occur while these cells are being transformed into sperms or eggs, as the case may be. In the male gonad, or testis, the germ cells enlarge slightly preliminary to meiosis. The two meiotic divisions follow in rapid succession, and the four equal-sized daughter cells generally remain together as they transform into sperm. The nucleus condenses to form the sperm head; certain cytoplasmic elements transform into the remaining elements of the sperm body, and the residual cytoplasm is cast off. In many species the transformation of cells into sperm is accomplished with the aid of nurse cells. In mammals, including humans, the germ cells, after meiosis, become enclosed within the cytoplasm of such nurse cells until they are fully transformed into sperm.

In all but a few exceptional cases four functional sperm arise from one original germ cell of the testis. The same is never true of the egg. In the female gonad, or ovary, the immature germ cells undergo a prolonged growth period before entering into meiosis; in most animals adjacent cells play a prominent role in growth, as nurse cells or the equivalent. Meiosis is not initiated until the growth period is completed. In many species (perhaps most) the egg is released from the ovary and the fertilization process initiated before the meiotic divisions are brought to completion.

Meiosis in egg formation (oögenesis) differs from that in sperm formation (spermatogenesis), not in the essential matters of chromosome segregation but in the distribution of cytoplasm. First and second meiotic divisions each result in one giant cell, the egg itself, and one abortive cell, called a polar body, containing its full share of chromosomes, but only a tiny sheath of cytoplasm. The polar bodies formed at the first and second meiotic divisions soon degenerate, leaving only a haploid set in the nucleus of the egg itself. Meiosis in egg formation thus results in only one functional gamete from each original immature germ cell, along with three abortive polar bodies.

Fertilization is a physiological reaction of great specificity. It occurs with few exceptions only between two members of the same species, and is limited temporally to a short interval of maturity in the germ cells. There are many adaptations among animals for ensuring that ripe germ cells will be available to one another at time most favourable for fertilization. Synchronism of breeding activity, under hormonal or other chemical control, is one such mechanism; internal fertilization, the production of tremendous numbers of gametes in forms with external fertilization, the motility of sperm, and the controlling action of seminal fluids surrounding the sperm, are others. The crucial process of fertilization itself is, however, dependent on the cell surface in both sperm and egg, where antigenic reactions similar to agglutination effects occur. Substances presumably released by both germ cells act on the surface of the opposite cell type; following this, the sperm is gradually engulfed by the egg surface. The sperm head then swells into a form resembling the egg nucleus and sooner or later unites with the latter to form a fully diploid zygote nucleus. The egg, continuing its surface activity, proceeds to divide. In some species spindle elements used in this division are brought in by the sperm. (The occurrence of parthenogenesis, however, indicates that the egg is capable of producing a complete mitotic apparatus unaided.)

After fertilization, the mitotic process takes over, and the zygote, in successive cell divisions, becomes subdivided into cells of proportions standard for the species. These cells progressively become more and more differentiated, partly, at least, because each cell derived its cytoplasm from a different region of the original egg cytoplasm. The different cells then react with one another in the complicated pattern of events that comprise formation of the embryo.

3. Germ Plasm Concept.—The behaviour of the chromosomal material during the life cycle gave rise, in the 19th century, to the concept of the germ plasm as stated by August Weismann. The germ plasm can be conceived as a self-reproducing, potentially immortal, entity that persists intact through the generations, and gives rise, at each generation, to a soma or body, often thought of as a transient shell or vessel for the germ plasm. Weismann originally thought the determining factors of development and reproduction to lie exclusively in the nucleus. It has been necessary to modify this view in consideration of the important role that cytoplasmic factors have been shown to play in embryonic development.

At present the concept of the germ plasm, or rather the germ line, is properly a cellular concept. The cleaving zygote is compared to a colony of cells, all derived from the original zygote by successive mitoses. Identical nuclei thus populate differing cytoplasmic regions. One such specialized cytoplasmic region, when brought into contact with one of these nuclei, interacts in such fashion that the cell retains the properties of the whole organism and thus is destined to become a potentially immortal germ cell, whereas its sister cells take on partial functions as integumentary, nervous, secretory, etc., in fulfillment of their somatic role. In support of this view it can be cited that in many animal species the prospective germ cells are recognizable very early in development, long before a gonad is present, and can be seen to migrate into the reproductive organ after it is formed. Samuel Butler's aphorism that a hen is only an egg's way of making another egg sums up the germ-line point of view.

4. Alternation of Generations in Plants.—In all plants above the most primitive, the life cycle falls clearly into a pattern of alternation of generations. The gametophyte produces germ cells, or gametes: sperm in small capsules, or antheridia; eggs singly in archegonia. The fertilized egg develops into a sporophyte, differing from the gametophyte in appearance and producing spores in spore cases, or sporangia. Spores, which develop without fertilization into gametophytes, are, in many cases, of two sorts: microspores, which become male gametophytes; and megaspores, which become female gametophytes.

The evolutionary history of plants has clearly progressed from a state in which the gametophyte generation was the prominent one, and motile sperms requiring aquatic conditions were the rule, to the most recent situation in the seed plants, in which the visible plant is the sporophyte. In seed plants the gametophytes are very reduced in size and very short-lived. The male gametophyte is the pollen grain, in which the fertilizing elements are two nuclei borne in the outgrowing pollen tube. The female gametophyte is the embryo sac, concealed in the base of the pistil.

Examination of the chromosome content of the nucleus at various stages of the life cycle has shown that meiosis invariably takes place at the time of spore formation. Spore mother cells, borne on the diploid sporophyte, generally undergo two meiotic divisions, so that four haploid cells result. In cases where the product will be a megaspore, the meiotic divisions are modified in a manner reminiscent of the formation of the animal egg and its three polar bodies. The gametophyte, in consequence of meiosis, is haploid; the germ cells it produces are therefore haploid. Thus the alternation of generations in plants is an alternation between diploid and haploid generations. Comparable chromosomal changes in animals that exhibit alternation of sexual and asexual generations have not been described.

4. Sex Among Lower Forms.—As pointed out earlier, the origin of new individuals among single-celled animals and plants always depends on cell division; *i.e.,* binary or multiple fission. This mitotic process may be modified in various ways. In fungi, particularly, nuclear division frequently occurs independently of cytoplasmic division. In protozoans, the mitotic spindle usually develops inside the nucleus before the membrane dissolves. In bacteria, where a distinct nucleus is not detectable, the occurrence of anything resembling a mitotic spindle is doubtful.

Under certain conditions, many unicellular species form germ cells that undergo fusion, or fertilization. Some species, particularly among algae, form isogametes, two types of cells that are structurally indistinguishable but physiologically complementary. Among molds, the ends of strands or hyphae may fuse to form resting zygotes, or zygospores. Many algae and protozoa however form anisogametes, two types of germ cells, one large and relatively immobile, the other small and motile. In higher algae, sperms and eggs are found. In parasitic fungi and protozoa, elaborate life cycles may be found where asexual multiplication occurs in one host and fertilization in the alternate host. The wheat rust and the malarial parasite are examples.

Among one-celled animals, the ciliated protozoa exhibit a unique sexual cycle. These forms have two sorts of nuclei: a macronucleus, or somatic nucleus, which degenerates when sexual processes occur; and one or more micronuclei, which become active when the macronucleus degenerates. Conjugation occurs between animals of suitable complementary constitution. At this time the micronuclei undergo a series of divisions that are in effect meiotic. Four daughter micronuclei are formed by the division of each original micronucleus; three of the four degenerate, much as do polar bodies in egg formation. The remaining micronucleus divides into a stationary and a migratory daughter. The migratory element from each conjugating animal crosses over to the partner, and once inside, fuses with the stationary nucleus there. This constitutes fertilization, and accomplishes the restoration of the diploid state and the introduction of new hereditary material. The conjugating animals then separate, and each undergoes a series of cell divisions, during which both macro- and micronuclei are reconstituted from the zygote nucleus. Inheritance in these animals follows exactly the course that would be anticipated from this nuclear behaviour.

D. Subcellular Aspects

Modern genetics and biochemistry have shown that the causal mechanisms of reproductive cycles lie in the intimate molecular structure of protoplasm, particularly in the chromosomes. These bodies have been shown to be composed of deoxyribonucleic acid (DNA) combined with proteins of relatively simple structure. Proposed models of DNA structure suggest that the chromosome is a highly polymerized complex with a core of nucleic acid in the form of a double helical coil. Each strand is conceived as acting as a template or pattern for a complementary helical coil, breaking away from its partner and unwinding, then assembling smaller units on its surface in an order fixed by its own structure. Thus exact duplication of chromosomal strands can be envisioned; this precision is extended to duplication of mutations in the original. Biochemical studies have verified that the synthesis of new DNA precedes the visible splitting of chromosomal strands in mitosis.

In the ciliated protozoa the nuclei themselves behave as germ cells, crossing from one cell partner to the other. Nucleic acid particles can behave similarly. Viruses evidently are composed largely if not entirely of nucleic acid and protein. Introduced into cells, viral particles interact in a variety of ways with the nucleic acid of the cell. Bacterial cells, for example, display a series of phenomena relating fertilization to virus infection. Transformation of inherited characters in bacterial strains can be performed by DNA alone. In the process known as transduction, a bacterial virus carries a foreign nucleoprotein particle into a bacterial cell, whereupon the foreign particle may alter the heredity of the host cell. In certain strains of bacteria temporary conjugation of bacterial cells and exchange of hereditary material has been observed. In all these cases the interpretation is that newly introduced DNA has altered the genetic mechanism of the bacterium.

A second type of nucleic acid, ribonucleic acid (RNA), is closely involved in protein synthesis in the cytoplasm of cells. Thus the nucleic acids are implicated not only in the continuing heredity of cells, but in the continuing reproduction of their specific proteins. Biochemists interested in the possible course of evolution of living systems believe that the appearance of self-duplicating molecules was a critical event in the history of the earth. In contrast to other types of synthetic mechanism in mixtures of organic compounds, self-duplication makes possible systems relatively stable yet plastic enough to undergo variation and evolution. The whole subject of reproduction in the contemporary organic world can be related convincingly to the peculiar molecular structure and behaviour of the nucleic acids. (D. Rk.)

II. PHYSIOLOGY OF REPRODUCTION

The large variety of forms within the animal kingdom gives rise to many variations in the processes of reproduction. In general the insects, after mating, lay fertilized eggs at a time of year, and in a place or under conditions most suitable for food supplies for their larvae, during which time the main body increments for the adult condition occur. In amphibians and fishes fertilization and development of the egg frequently occur outside the body, although in a few species the egg develops internally and birth takes place when it has developed far enough to be self-supporting. In many reptiles and in birds the fertilized eggs laid contain considerable quantities of nutrient material so that the young when hatched can lead an independent existence, although there is considerable variation in this respect. The pigeon, hatched in an early stage of development, needs to be fed from the crop gland of its mother, whereas the chick, except for warmth, is quite independent of its mother at hatching. In marsupials such as the kangaroo, the young, born at a very early stage of development, are transferred to the pouch where they obtain milk until they are able to live independently. In placental mammals, too, there is considerable variation between species in the stage of development at which the young are born: the guinea pig is in an advanced stage, fully haired, and can eat solid food at birth; the foal can follow its dam for long distances; rats and mice have to be kept warm in a nest and are dependent on the mother's milk supply for some time after birth.

While in the lower forms of life the individual animal may be bisexual, in the higher forms this is of rare occurrence, partial hermaphrodites occurring from time to time in pigs, goats, etc. In a heifer born twin to a bull calf the fetal cow's sex organs are masculinized in utero by fusion of the twin blood circulations. In birds the female always contains the rudiments of the other sex. The processes of reproduction described below are those that occur chiefly in mammals, some reference being made to birds.

A. Production of Sex Cells

1. Male.—The essential cells concerned in reproduction—the spermatozoa—are minute structures visible only under the microscope. The exact form varies with the species, but in the main each sperm consists of a head that contains the genes and a tail, which, by lashing movements, propels the sperm through the surrounding fluid.

Sperms are produced in the testis, an organ that contains long coiled tubes lined with sperm mother cells which after meiosis become sperms. (*See* Cell: *Cell Division: Meiosis.*) Sperms begin to be formed at the age of puberty; the number formed gradually increases to the prime of life and decreases in extreme old age. From the testis the sperms pass through small ducts to the epididymis, a coiled tube adjacent to the organ. They pass quickly through the first half of the epididymis and are stored in the end portion, where they mature (sperms taken directly from the testes are incapable of fertilization).

In mammals the two testes are contained in the scrotum, a sac outside the body cavity. In the fetus the paired testes are developed in the body cavity near the kidneys, a position in which they remain throughout life in the lower animals and birds. In most mammals, however, they pass down through canals in the groin and descend into the scrotum; if this descent does not happen, the individual remains sterile, as sperm production (but not the other functions of the testes; *see* below) is prevented by the higher temperatures that exist in the body cavity as compared with the scrotum. If in the ram, for example, the scrotum is enclosed in insulating material the temperature is raised and he becomes sterile in a few days; after the material is removed, fertility returns again in a month or so. There are species differences in the degree to which the scrotum is held near or away from the body and hence differences in optimum temperature for sperm production and storage. The temperature at which the sperms are formed bears a relation to their length of life in the female tract, which is of course at internal body temperature. In the bull the scrotum is very pendulous, and the sperms live in the female tract only about 30 hr.; in the stallion, on the other hand, the scrotum is held closely against the body wall, and the sperms will live about 5 days in the female tract. In birds, where the sperms are produced from testes in the body cavity, they will live in the female tract for a considerable time; in the female turkey eggs can be fertilized for up to 30 days after a single mating. In the epididymis the sperms remain fertile for a period of about 30 days but retain their motility for a longer period. Under most circumstances the power of fertility is lost before that of motility.

At mating the muscular walls of the lower epididymis contract and force the sperms along the duct (vas deferens) toward the exterior. The number of sperms driven up in this way varies with the species but in all cases of normal fertility amounts to many millions. Sperm numbers at an emission can be increased by "teasing" the male before service; this causes the epididymis to contract, forcing sperms into the lower part of the vas deferens from which they are ejaculated at mating. When, at mating, the sperms pass up the vas deferens, they are diluted with fluids produced by the accessory glands (the seminal vesicles, prostate gland, and Cowper's gland). These secretions provide a medium in which the sperms can swim; some of these secretions precede the sperm and lubricate the urethra, the common tube for both semen and urine, extending from the bladder to the penis. In some species, *e.g.*, rats, mice, and pigs, a jellylike substance prevents the sperm running out of the female tract.

For purposes of mating, the penis is rendered turgid by contraction of muscles over the veins so that the blood spaces within the organ become engorged with blood; failure of these muscles to function, for which there are various reasons, is sometimes a cause of impotency. During mating the sperms are deposited in the female tract (*see* below), but the exact position varies in different species. In the horse sperms are ejected through the cervix directly into the uterus; in cattle and sheep they are sprayed over the entrance to the cervix. Which of the two methods occurs in a species is determined by the form of the penis and of the cervix.

2. Female.—The essential cells in the female are the ova, or eggs. These are formed in the ovaries, which lie in the body cavity just below the kidneys. In mammals there is one ovary on each side, but in birds only the ovary on the left side is functional. Unlike the sperms, which are produced throughout adult life, the ova are preformed in the ovary before birth; in the newborn calf some 75,000 are present. The ova, which are microscopic in size, are nourished by surrounding cells that, as the ova ripen, increase in number and later produce a fluid that forms a vesicle, the Graafian follicle; as this fluid accumulates the follicle gradually rises and projects above the surface of the ovary. At the appropriate stimulus (see *Hormonal Control* below) the follicle ruptures and discharges the fluid and ovum into the top of the Fallopian tube, where, if mating has occurred, the egg is penetrated by a sperm and fertilization takes place. It is only in this position that fertilization can occur, so that the time during which the ovum can be fertilized is comparatively short, a matter of hours. The sperms do not attain their fertilizing power until they have been in the female tract for some hours, so that for fertility, mating should take place several hours before the eggs are shed. In most species the ovum requires about three days to pass down the thin Fallopian tube and gain entrance to the uterus, where it becomes attached and develops into an embryo. If fertilization does not occur, the egg perishes.

After the egg is shed from the ovary, the cells of the follicle, which have hitherto been nourishing the egg, enlarge and fill the space formerly occupied by the fluid that surrounded the egg. This transformed follicle is the corpus luteum, or yellow body, within the ovary, the function of which is to supply progesterone, a hormone that prepares the uterine lining for the reception of the developing egg. If the animal becomes pregnant, the corpus luteum persists for the whole, or in a few species (mare, woman) the early part of pregnancy only. If the animal is not pregnant, the corpus luteum disintegrates after a time that varies with the species (woman 14 days, cow 20 days, ewe 15 days).

The presence of an active corpus luteum in the ovary suspends the development of the remaining follicles, but development resumes as soon as the corpus luteum begins to die. Thus a cycle, the estrous cycle, is instituted in the ovaries and affects other organs of the female reproductive tract. The ripening of the follicle is associated with the period of estrus, or heat, the only time in most mammals that the female will accept the male. Estrus is followed by a quiescent period during which the corpus luteum takes control; when this body dies another estrous period begins. In women the menstrual period marks the atrophy of the corpus luteum; the uterine bleeding normally results from a withdrawal of progesterone and the consequent breakdown of tissues that were built up under the influence of the corpus luteum. Shedding of the egg occurs about 14 days after the beginning of menstruation (*q.v.*).

The changes that take place in the inner layer of the uterus during the estrous cycle bear a relation to the type of placenta that occurs in the species. In all species the uterine glands are modified under the influence of the corpus luteum (see *Pregnancy* below).

B. Hormonal Control

1. Generative System.—The functioning of the reproductive organs is controlled by hormones (chemical substances circulating in the bloodstream). The primary centre for the production of these hormones is the pituitary gland, at the base of the brain. Its close association with the nervous system (hypothalamus of the brain) is the means by which environmental conditions such as daylight hours (*see* below) can affect reproduction. The pituitary gland consists of two lobes, posterior and anterior. The former produces oxytocin, which is released into the bloodstream when the nipples are sucked; oxytocin causes contraction of the muscle cells surrounding the milk-producing cells, thus forcing the milk down into the teat. Similarly coitus or insemination stimulates a release of oxytocin, which, in this case, causes rhythmic contractions of the muscles of the female reproductive tract and drives the sperms upward to the tops of the Fallopian tubes. The anterior pituitary produces a number of hormones, among which are the three main reproductive ones: prolactin, which promotes milk secretion; follicle-stimulating hormone (FSH), which causes the follicles in the ovary to ripen; and luteinizing hormone (LH), which causes the follicles to rupture and form corpora lutea. The developing follicle generates estrogens, which give rise to the symptoms of heat, and prepare the female tract for the reception of sperm; the corpus luteum produces progesterone, which prepares the uterus for pregnancy and causes the mucus formed in the cervix (neck) of the uterus to become viscous, and so seal off the embryo from the exterior. To an extent that varies greatly from species to species, the placenta may assume the function of the ovary, and secrete both estrogens and progesterone. In some species the placenta also produces hormones of the pituitary type: in the first third of the mare's pregnancy a follicle-stimulating hormone (PMS, which stands for pregnant mare's serum, from which the hormone was first derived); in the human placenta LH activity is generated (which forms the basis for various pregnancy tests). Some placentas produce prolactin activity and so are concerned in some degree with the development of the mammary glands for milk production.

In most species the release of LH from the anterior pituitary is automatic; *i.e.*, after a sufficient buildup of estrogen by the ripening follicle. In a few species (notably rabbit and ferret) the release of LH does not occur without the additional stimulus of mating: at orgasm, the sensory nerves to the hypothalamus are stimulated, causing the release of LH. In some birds, such as the pigeon, this nerve stimulation can also be effected by "social stimuli." A female pigeon in solitary confinement does not shed its eggs, but if it can see other pigeons, or even itself in a mirror, eggs are shed.

When the end products of hormone action, or their synthetic counterparts, build up in the body, they dam further release of the primary hormones. Thus when tablets of stilbestrol (a synthetic estrogen) are implanted under the skin (as they are sometimes, to induce a sterile heifer to produce milk), the high concentration in the blood dams the secretion of FSH in the anterior pituitary; as a consequence the ovaries cease to function.

In the male the primary anterior pituitary hormones are necessary for the nutrition of the testes and production of the sperm. These primary hormones act on the interstitial cells of the testes (cells that lie between the tubules) inducing them to secrete secondary hormones (androgens), which in turn cause the development and formation of the secretions of the accessory male glands (seminal vesicles, prostate) and create the desire for, and power of, mating (sex drive).

2. Secondary Sex Characteristics.—The differences in plumage in birds, distribution of hair in man, and body conformation in cattle are the results of the action of secondary sex hormones on the parts concerned. If the testes and ovaries are removed from chicks at hatching, the adult plumage of each assumes the same neutral form. When, however, the castrated male hatchling chick is implanted with an ovary, the adult plumage is completely female; when the spayed female hatchling chick is implanted with a testis, it assumes male plumage. However, body size does not change perceptibly. Among most mammals and birds the male is larger than the female. The cock that has assumed female plumage by transplantation of ovaries remains larger in size than the hen that has assumed male plumage by the transplantation of testes. Sex differences in body size are due mainly to size-controlling genes associated with sex and only secondarily to hormones.

The secondary sexual characters begin to develop in the young animal somewhat before the time at which fertility begins. These changes can be speeded up by the injection of anterior pituitary hormones: newly hatched male chicks thus inoculated for about 12 days develop enormously enlarged combs and wattles, utter squeaky crowing sounds, and attempt to mount their young hen mates. Similar changes can be brought about by injection of the secondary male hormones.

3. Puberty.—In the young animal the reproductive organs grow at much the same rate as the body as a whole, but at the age of puberty, when the reproductive hormones come into play, the sexual organs develop at a much faster rate than the rest of the body. Rearing poultry on a high plane of nutrition lowers the age at which the first egg is laid but not to the same extent as it increases body weight, for birds on a low plane of nutrition lay their first eggs at lower body weights than those on a high plane. This is also true for reproduction in cattle and mammals generally.

In young bulls high-plane nutrition speeds up sperm production but not to the same extent as it speeds up the internal secretions of the testes. On the other hand injections of FSH in young rabbits and calves will cause the shedding of the eggs long before the normal age of puberty and before the rest of the reproductive tract has developed sufficiently to support a pregnancy. These eggs, however, can be fertilized, and if transplanted to adults (*see* below), can develop into normal young.

C. PRODUCTION OF OFFSPRING

1. Fertility.—*Female.*—This is controlled at three main stages in the process of reproduction: (1) the number of eggs shed; (2) the number of such eggs fertilized; and (3) the number of fertilized eggs that develop normally to birth.

(1) The number of eggs shed depends on the level of FSH in the bloodstream. Normally, a rabbit will shed about five eggs from each ovary, but if one or even one and a half ovaries are removed, ten eggs are still shed, showing that the number shed does not depend on the number of eggs in the ovary but on some substances (FSH) circulating in the bloodstream. In the cow and ewe, which normally produce one or two eggs, injection of PMS four days before the expected heat period will cause, according to dose, up to 30 or more eggs to be shed. Appropriate doses increase the percentage of cows and ewes producing twins. Fertilized eggs can also be taken from the tubes of one female and put into the tubes or uterus of other females at a similar stage of the estrous cycle. Such eggs can be kept alive for about three days outside the body; fertilized rabbit eggs have been sent successfully by air across the Atlantic. This method can also be used to increase the number of offspring of a female of good genetic worth: the animal becomes, in a sense, an egg-producing "machine," relieved of the burdens of bearing the young.

The number of eggs shed at each estrus is an inherited character and can be modified by nutrition and selection. Since the number of eggs shed is controlled by environmental and nutritional conditions as well as by genetics, selection for high fertility in sheep is best made by using rams from ewes that have a high lifetime average for high fertility. In young females the level of FSH in the blood is lower than in adult life so that in ewes the average number of eggs shed gradually rises to a maximum at about the fourth year.

Among many animals eggs are produced only during a specific breeding season. In some mammals (mare, cow, ewe, sow) the estrous phase may recur at rhythmic intervals during the year or during one limited breeding season; in others, like the bitch, one

estrous cycle occurs in the season. The former condition is described as polyestrous, the latter as monestrous, the quiescence between the seasons being known as the anestrum. This system probably evolved in association with the most favourable time of year for their survival, which is usually the spring. The breeding season is therefore more limited in those breeds and species that have their origin near the poles. The mechanism that determines this cycle is based on the changing ratio of daylight to darkness hours throughout the year; this ratio, or photoperiod, acts on nerves in the region of the head to stimulate or inhibit the release of FSH from the anterior pituitary gland. In species that have a short gestation period (ferret, 6 weeks), or a very long one (mare, 11 months) *lengthening* daylight hours stimulate FSH release. In species that have a medium duration of pregnancy (ewe, 5 months), release is stimulated by *shortening* daylight hours. In both cases the animals are born in the spring. Under the influence of daylight hours the release of FSH gradually rises to a peak, then falls again toward the end of the breeding season. Thus, fewer eggs are shed very early in the breeding season than at its peak, which in sheep is some six weeks after the beginning of the season. In hens the winter production of eggs can be much increased by providing artificial light, turning a short day into a long one.

The shedding of the egg is sometimes prevented by internal factors. In the mare, where LH is normally in short supply, there may not be enough to rupture the follicle. In the cow, where LH is usually abundant, persistence of the corpus luteum and consequent prevention of ovulation is not infrequent. In woman, failure of ovulation (the menopause [*q.v.*]) occurs much earlier in the span of life than in other animals.

(2) The number of eggs fertilized depends very largely on the time of mating in relation to the time the egg is shed, for, as already mentioned, both egg and sperm have a short life in the female tract. In most species the times of estrus and ovulation are well synchronized, but in the mare and sow, where ovulation occurs before the end of a prolonged estrus, or in woman, where there is no estrus, the time relations are very important. Failure of fertilization also occurs where sperm production by the male is poor (*see* below).

(3) The number of fertilized eggs that develop normally up to the time of birth is influenced by many factors. In addition to diseases that cause abortion or absorption in utero of the young, there are genetic causes of malformation or death of the embryo. The most frequent cause is, however, probably due to deficiencies in the uterine secretions, which cause early death of the fertilized egg (see *Pregnancy* below).

Male.—Except in most birds and a few mammals such as the hibernating hedgehog, the nonbreeding season for the male is not so marked as for the female, although in all species with a nonbreeding season, sperm production is at a much lower level at this time. The male breeding season, when it occurs, is called the rutting season.

There are various causes of poor sperm production in males. Fevers temporarily reduce sperm numbers. There may be genetic causes and in some cases deformed sperms are produced. Blockage of the epididymis may also prevent the emission of sperms. The number of sperms produced by the male cannot be increased above the normal level by hormone injections and when one testis is removed only half the normal number of sperms are produced. Normal males produce many more sperm than are actually required for fertilization. By collecting such sperm and using it to artificially inseminate females, it is possible to increase the number of offspring produced by a male. Bulls of good genetic worth, which normally would produce only about 50 calves a year, may now father 10,000 calves a year. Under proper conditions bull sperms have been kept fertile for many years (*see* FERTILIZATION).

2. Pregnancy.—During the early stages of pregnancy (*q.v.*) the uterine glands, under the influence of progesterone from the corpus luteum, secrete actively and prepare the uterus to receive the developing embryo. Progesterone initiates formation of the maternal part of the placenta, which is the means of transference of materials between mother and fetus. Oxygen and food pass from the mother's bloodstream to the fetal bloodstream, and waste products flow in the opposite direction, from the fetus to the mother. Blood vessels in the cord attached to the navel of the fetus carry these products between fetus and placenta. During pregnancy the uterus enlarges greatly and its muscles become strong enough to expel the fetus at birth. In the early stages the uterus is expanded by the production of fluids within the fetal membranes. This fluid environment provides space within which the fetus can develop well cushioned from the mother's movements.

There are three main stages of pregnancy, each marked by a different method of fetal nutrition. In the first, the blastocyst stage, the developing egg, lying free in the uterine cavity, is nourished from the secretions of the uterine glands. A number of fertilized eggs in all species perish at this critical stage.

In the second, or embryonic stage, the embryo, after attachment to the uterine wall, is nourished by the outer (trophoblastic) cells of the membranes, which actively absorb nourishment from the maternal tissues. These cells have priority of nourishment, so the level of the mother's nutrition has little effect on the size of the offspring at this stage. During this time the placenta increases in size; the extent to which this occurs determines the amount of nutrition the fetus will receive in the third stage. In the case of twins each placenta will be smaller than that of a single one and in large breeds the uterus and placenta will be larger than in small breeds.

In the third, or the fetal stage, the placenta ceases to grow and the trophoblast cells atrophy; nutrition is supplied at this time by diffusion between maternal and fetal bloodstreams. During this time the level of nutrition of the mother is of great importance, particularly in the case of twins or triplets, where placental area is limited. This stage in cattle and sheep comprises the last 6 to 8 weeks of pregnancy; during this period the weights of the individual twins can be greatly increased by supplementing the mother's diet (see DIET AND DIETETICS).

The duration of gestation varies greatly in different species, from 19 days in the mouse to 21 months in the Asiatic elephant. While in general the duration of gestation increases with the size of the species and with the stage of development at which the young are born, this is not invariable, for in man, with a nine-month pregnancy, the young are born in a much less advanced stage of development than in sheep, with only a five-month gestation period. In some species the implantation of the egg is delayed, increasing the duration of pregnancy. For example, in the badger fertilization occurs in August, but the egg develops only for a few days, then lies dormant, development resuming in January and birth occurring about 50 days afterward. In some bats, too, mating takes place in the autumn but young are not born until the following June; only two months are required for the development of the embryo, but ovulation and fertilization do not take place till the spring. As the time for parturition (the act of giving birth) approaches, a hormone, relaxin, takes effect and softens connective tissues; this causes relaxation of the ligaments in the pelvic region and makes the passage of the fetus easier. At the same time the cervix gradually relaxes under the influence of estrogens. This stage is marked also by a decrease in progesterone from the corpus luteum or placenta. The ratio of estrogen to progesterone increases, rendering the muscles of the uterus sensitive to secretions of oxytocin from the posterior pituitary. Oxytocin stimulates rhythmic contractions of the uterus that increase in intensity—at the same time that the vagina relaxes—eventually expelling the fetus (see BIRTH, HUMAN). After parturition the thick muscular walls of the uterus undergo involution, and normal estrous cycles are resumed again. In some species, such as the cow, normal cycles occur during lactation, but in others, such as the sow, they are not resumed until after weaning.

In the widest sense the process of reproduction is not complete until the adult form of the animal has been reproduced: this part of the process, however, is generally referred to as growth (q.v.). See EMBRYOLOGY AND DEVELOPMENT, ANIMAL; see also references under "Reproduction" in the Index.

BIBLIOGRAPHY.—F. H. A. Marshall, Physiology of Reproduction, ed. by A. S. Parkes, vol. ii (1952), vol. i, part I (1956), part II (1960); E. Allen, C. H. Danforth, and E. A. Doisy (eds.), Sex and Internal Secretions (1939), 2nd ed. by W. C. Young (1961); H. H. Cole and P. T. Cupps (eds.), Reproduction in Domestic Animals, vols. i and ii (1959); J. Hammond (ed.), Progress in the Physiology of Farm Animals, vols. i–iii (1954–57); H. Burrows, Biological Actions of Sex Hormones (1945); S. A. Asdell, Patterns of Mammalian Reproduction, 2nd ed. (1964); H. Knaus, Periodic Fertility and Sterility in Woman (1934); T. R. R. Mann, The Biochemistry of Semen (1954); E. J. Perry et al. (eds.), Artificial Insemination of Farm Animals (1947); E. S. E. Hafez (ed.), Reproduction in Farm Animals (1962); J. F. D. Frazer, The Sexual Cycles of Vertebrates (1959).   (J. Hd.)

REPRODUCTIVE SYSTEM.

The human reproductive system, which is the subject of this article, comprises the organs, glands, secretions and other elements of reproduction. Since in some parts of its course the reproductive system shares certain structures with the urinary system, the two are commonly referred to in medical practice as the genitourinary or urogenital system. Allied information will therefore be found in the article URINARY SYSTEM.

The present article deals chiefly with three main topics: (1) the anatomy and physiology of the male and female reproductive systems; (2) the diseases of these systems and their treatment; (3) the surgery of the male system. Surgery of the female system is discussed in GYNECOLOGY, which is a general discussion of disorders of the female reproductive tract. Related information appears in ENDOCRINOLOGY; FERTILITY AND FECUNDITY; HORMONES; PREGNANCY; REPRODUCTION; SEX.

The main sections of this article are as follows:

I. ANATOMY AND PHYSIOLOGY
A. MALE

The external genitalia of the male consist of the penis, the erectile copulatory organ, and the scrotum, a loose pouch of skin just beneath the base of the penis (see fig. 1). Within the scrotum are the gonads, or testes, which produce the male germ cells, called spermatozoa. The spermatozoa accumulate in a convoluted tubular organ, the epididymis, which is closely applied to the surface of the testis. From the epididymis, the germ cells pass through a muscular duct, the ductus deferens, and into the urethral canal of the penis, through which they are discharged into the female reproductive tract. Opening into the male reproductive passages are accessory glands: the seminal vesicles, prostate gland and bulbourethral (Cowper's) glands. These contribute secretions that add to the bulk of the semen and create a fluid medium favourable for transport and sustenance of the spermatozoa.

1. Penis.—The penis is made up of three cylinders of erectile tissue covered by skin and subcutaneous tissue devoid of fat. Two of these cylinders, the corpora cavernosa, are side by side, while the third, the corpus spongiosum, is underneath. The posterior ends of the two corpora cavernosa diverge at the root of the penis, becoming more and more fibrous in structure, and are attached on each side to the inner border of the pubic arch. The corpus spongiosum ends posteriorly in a bulbous enlargement that is situated between the diverging columns of the corpora cavernosa. The head of the penis is formed by a large bell-shaped expansion

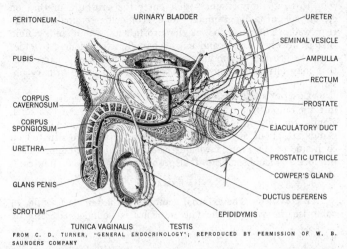

FROM C. D. TURNER, "GENERAL ENDOCRINOLOGY"; REPRODUCED BY PERMISSION OF W. B. SAUNDERS COMPANY

FIG. 1.—DIAGRAMMATIC SAGITTAL SECTION SHOWING THE RELATIONSHIP OF THE MALE REPRODUCTIVE ORGANS

of the corpus spongiosum, known as the glans. On its posterior surface are two concavities, which receive the rounded anterior ends of the corpora cavernosa. On the upper surface and sides of the penis the posterior rim of the glans projects as a well-marked ridge, the corona glandis, which is set off from the shaft by a constriction called the neck of the penis. The corpus spongiosum is traversed for its entire length by the urethra, a canal that begins at the bladder, passes downward through the prostate and pierces the urogenital diaphragm to enter the bulb of the corpus spongiosum from above. Thence it runs forward through the shaft of the penis to terminate in the external meatus, a vertical slit at the end of the glans. The penile portion of the urethra serves for passage of both urine and seminal fluid and is therefore a portion of the reproductive system that is shared with the urinary system.

The skin of the penis is thin, distensible and loosely attached to underlying structures. Near the head it forms a fold, the foreskin or prepuce, that normally covers the greater part of the glans; when this is drawn back, two folds on the undersurface of the penis are seen to unite to form a median fold, the frenulum, which is attached to the glans just below the meatus. In the depression behind the corona, the skin is reflected from the inner aspect of the prepuce onto the glans, where it forms a thin, closely adherent, transparent layer that is rich in sensory nerve endings. The prepuce is often removed surgically—a practice called circumcision (*q.v.*).

The corpora cavernosa consist of strong, fibroelastic, cylindrical sheaths; from their inner surfaces incomplete walls of connective tissue extend into the interior, dividing each corpus into a labyrinthine system of spaces or compartments. These spaces in the erectile tissue are lined with endothelium and are interposed between the arteries and the deep veins of the penis. When the penis is flaccid, the spaces in the corpora cavernosa are largely collapsed, but upon psychical or mechanical stimulation, the blood vessels supplying the penis are dilated and the influx of blood into the erectile tissue is thereby enhanced. At the same time a layer of muscle investing the posterior part of the corpora cavernosa contracts and restricts the outflow. The impounding of blood within the vascular spaces of the corpora cavernosa causes them to elongate and to become distended and stiffened, resulting in erection of the penis. The internal structure of the corpus spongiosum and glans resembles that of the corpora cavernosa, but the connective tissue trabeculae are finer and the spaces they delimit are smaller. The engorgement of this finer-meshed erectile tissue causes the enlargement of the glans and the swelling of the wall of the urethra in erection.

2. Scrotum.—The scrotum is a pouch of skin that is divided into two compartments by a wall down the middle. Each compartment contains a testis, an epididymis and a portion of the spermatic cord. The left half of the scrotum reaches a somewhat lower level than the right half. The skin contains scattered coarse hairs and well-developed sebaceous and sweat glands. The deep layers of the scrotal skin contain smooth muscle fibres forming contractive tissue, the dartos; contraction of these fibres draws up the scrotum and produces a corrugated appearance of the skin.

During development of the fetus, the scrotum arises as a pair of outpouchings of the abdominal wall called the genital swellings. The testes develop in the abdominal cavity and later descend into the genital swellings (see *Embryology* below). The vessels, nerves and ductus deferens that are drawn down with the testes constitute the spermatic cords. The two passageways in the abdominal wall through which the testes and spermatic cords enter the scrotum are called the inguinal canals. Each canal is at first widely open but eventually forms a flat-sided oblique passage in the abdominal wall about 3 cm. (1½ in.) in length. In the adult it remains a point of potential weakness in the body wall through which abdominal contents may be forced into the scrotum in the common pathological condition called inguinal hernia. In the descent of the male gonads the layers of the anterior abdominal wall are carried into the scrotum as coverings of the testes and spermatic cords. Thus the entrance to the inguinal canal, the abdominal inguinal ring, is formed by a funnel-shaped expansion of the transversalis fascia as it envelops the spermatic cord; the exit from the canal, the subcutaneous inguinal ring, is surrounded by the aponeurosis (sheet-like tendon) of the external oblique muscle.

In the scrotum, beneath the dartos, there is a thin layer of connective tissue, the external spermatic fascia, which is continuous at the subcutaneous inguinal ring with the aponeurosis of the external oblique muscle of the abdominal wall. The next deeper layer in the scrotum, the cremasteric fascia, contains bundles of muscle fibres derived from the abdominal internal oblique muscle. In fear, rage or exposure to cold, contraction of the cremasteric muscle tends to draw the testes upward toward the abdominal cavity. The next layer, the internal spermatic fascia, is relatively thin and is derived from the transversalis fascia of the abdomen. The innermost layer, the tunica vaginalis, is a double layer forming the serous investment of the testis; it is derived from the peritoneum lining the abdominal cavity. The outer, parietal layer is closely adherent to the internal spermatic fascia; the inner, visceral layer invests the testis and a portion of the epididymis.

The scrotum has a lower temperature than the body cavity, and it is believed to have a heat-regulating function. Migration of the testes to a scrotal pouch occurs only in certain mammals, and for these species it has been shown that the germinal elements of the testis produce spermatozoa only at a temperature below that of the abdominal cavity.

Testes.—The testes, or testicles, are the essential male organs of reproduction. Each is oval, about 4–5 cm. (1½–2 in.) in length and 2.5–3 cm. (1 in.) in width. The testis has a dense fibrous capsule, the tunica albuginea, from which thin walls penetrate into the interior, dividing it into about 250 compartments or lobules. Within each lobule there are from one to three highly convoluted seminiferous tubules. These join straight tubules (tubuli recti) that open into a plexus of communicating tubes, the rete testis. The spermatozoa produced in the seminiferous tubules are carried via the tubuli recti to the rete testis, and from there they pass through 15 to 20 small ducts, the efferent ductules (ductuli efferentes testis, or vasa efferentia), into the epididymis.

The microscopical seminiferous tubule has a small, irregular passage surrounded by the germinal epithelium, which is enclosed by a membrane. The germinal epithelium is composed of the germ cells in different stages of maturation (called, according to their stage of development, spermatogonia, spermatocytes, spermatids and spermatozoa) and their supporting elements, the Sertoli cells. The mature spermatozoon is a highly specialized motile cell consisting of a head, a middle piece and a long tail, or flagellum, which executes vigorous lashing movements that propel the cell forward. Spermatozoa are produced in astronomical numbers. It has been estimated that an average man discharges 400,000,000,000 sperm in his reproductive lifetime. A single ejaculate contains hundreds of millions; yet, if fertilization is achieved, only one of this enormous number enters the ovum. The condensed nucleus in the head of the fertilizing spermatozoon contains all the hereditary material contributed by the father.

The endocrine function of the testes is believed to reside in the interstitial tissue, which is located between the seminiferous tubules. The cells of this tissue produce the male sex hormone responsible for maintenance of accessory reproductive organs and development of secondary sex characteristics such as deep voice, beard, muscular build, etc.

Epididymis.—The epididymis is a firm, elongated body closely adhering to the posterior surface of the testis. At the upper pole it is enlarged to form the head, and at the lower pole there is a lesser enlargement, the tail. The entire epididymis consists of an extremely tortuous tube that is 15 to 20 ft. long when extended. Because of its great length it can accommodate a large number of spermatozoa. The cells lining this convoluted tube are believed to produce a secretion that plays a role in the nutrition of the spermatozoa.

3. Ductus Deferens.—The ductus deferens (or vas deferens) is the continuation of the tube of the epididymis. It extends from the tail of the epididymis to the posterior surface of the prostate, where it joins the duct of the seminal vesicle to form the ejaculatory duct (*see* fig. 1). The ductus deferens ascends from the epididymis to the subcutaneous inguinal ring, being joined in this part of its course by testicular arteries, veins, lymphatics and nerves to form the spermatic cord. These structures pass obliquely through the abdominal wall, via the inguinal canal. At the abdominal inguinal ring they separate, the ductus passing down the side of the pelvis and then turning inward along the back wall of the bladder to the prostate, where it meets its fellow of the opposite side. The ductus deferens has a thick muscular wall with a uniform diameter of about 3 mm. ($\frac{1}{10}$ in.) until it reaches the seminal vesicle; there it broadens out and forms the ampulla of the ductus deferens, the lumen of which has numerous outpocketings. Immediately before joining the excretory duct of the seminal vesicle, the ductus deferens again becomes round and slender.

4. Seminal Vesicles and Ejaculatory Ducts.—The seminal vesicles are two saclike appendages of the ductus deferens that are fixed to the rear surface of the bladder and lie lateral and parallel to the corresponding ductus deferens. Each vesicle is composed of a thin-walled tubular structure, 10 to 12 cm. (about 4 in.) long, folded back and forth upon itself and enclosed in a fibromuscular capsule. Arising from the main tube are numerous pouches (sacculations or diverticula). The excretory duct of the seminal vesicle on each side joins the ductus deferens to form an ejaculatory duct. The two ejaculatory ducts are narrow, have thin walls and run side by side through the prostate gland to open into the urethra. The seminal vesicles were formerly regarded as seminal receptacles for the storage of semen, but according to the modern view their function is purely glandular and they do not store semen. The principal reserves of spermatozoa are contained within the epididymis, and those that are to be delivered in any one ejaculation accumulate in the ampulla of the ductus deferens just prior to ejaculation. Here, in the secretion of the ampulla, the spermatozoa first come into contact with fructose, the principal carbohydrate substrate for their metabolism, and it is probable that sperm motility is initiated at this time. The main source of fructose is in the secretion of the seminal vesicles, which is discharged in the process of ejaculation into the prostatic urethra together with the secretion of the prostate and the spermatozoa contained in the ampulla. In man, the greater part of the volume of the ejaculate is derived from the secretion of the seminal vesicles.

5. Prostate.—The prostate is situated just below the bladder and is traversed by the urethra and the ejaculatory ducts. It is pyramidal in form, with the base upward in contact with the floor of the bladder. The vertical dimension is from 2.2 to 3 cm. (1 to $1\frac{3}{8}$ in.), the transverse diameter from 3.5 to 4 cm. ($1\frac{3}{8}$ to $1\frac{3}{4}$ in.) and the thickness from 2 to 2.5 cm. ($\frac{4}{5}$ to 1 in.). The prostate is composed of glandular tissue enclosed in a dense fibrous capsule. Microscopically it consists of 30 to 50 branching tubuloalveolar glands embedded in a tissue rich in smooth muscle fibres, which aid in discharging the prostatic fluid in ejaculation. The glands join 16 to 20 minute ducts that enter the prostatic urethra on either side of a longitudinal ridge (colliculus seminalis) in its rear wall. The secretion of the prostate is a thin, milky fluid that is weakly alkaline and has a characteristic odour. In older men, the prostate commonly undergoes a generalized enlargement that may ultimately constrict the urethra and cause urinary obstruction.

6. Cowper's Glands.—Opening into the urethra where it passes into the bulb of the corpus spongiosum are the ducts of two small glands, the bulbourethral or Cowper's glands (*see* fig. 1). The glands are about 5 mm. ($\frac{1}{5}$ in.) in diameter and are situated on each side of the urethra within the urogenital diaphragm. They produce a mucoid secretion that probably functions as a lubricant.

B. Female

1. External.—The external genitalia in the female (*see* fig. 2) comprise the vulva. The vulvar orifice is bounded laterally by

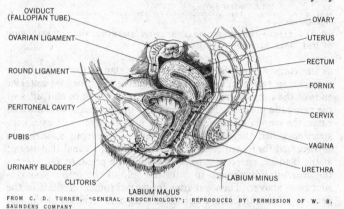

FROM C. D. TURNER, "GENERAL ENDOCRINOLOGY"; REPRODUCED BY PERMISSION OF W. B. SAUNDERS COMPANY

FIG. 2.—DIAGRAMMATIC SAGITTAL SECTION SHOWING THE ARRANGEMENT AND RELATIONSHIP OF THE FEMALE REPRODUCTIVE ORGANS

the labia majora, two prominent rounded folds of skin that correspond to the scrotum of the male. They have a sparse covering of hair and meet in the midline so that they largely conceal the other external genital structures. Between the labia majora are a pair of pendulous skin folds, the labia minora, that enclose a shallow elliptical depression called the vestibule. Toward the front the labia minora are continuous with one another, forming the prepuce, a thin fold of skin that covers the sensitive clitoris. The clitoris is a rudimentary erectile organ, the counterpart of the penis of the male. Opening into the vestibule below it are the urethra, the urinary passage from the bladder; and the vagina, the flattened fibromuscular tube that receives the penis during copulation. In virgins, the entrance of the vagina is narrowed by a circular fold of mucous membrane called the hymen.

2. Internal.—The internal reproductive organs consist of the female gonads, or ovaries, located within the body cavity and a system of tubular organs that communicate with the exterior at the vaginal orifice. Egg cells, or ova, are produced in the ovaries and are released singly at monthly intervals. Closely associated with the ovaries are the open ends of the right and left oviducts (Fallopian tubes). At the time of ovulation either of these may receive the ovum. If coitus occurs, the ovum may be fertilized by one of the spermatozoa reaching the upper part of the oviduct. The developing ovum then passes down through the oviduct to the cavity of the uterus, or womb, where it becomes implanted and is nourished until birth. The lower end of the uterus projects into the upper end of the vagina. The dilated neck of the uterus and the vagina constitute the birth canal, through which the infant emerges at the termination of pregnancy (*see* BIRTH, HUMAN).

Ovaries.—The mature ovary is a firm organ about the size of a large almond shell, with a scarred or wrinkled exterior (*see* fig. 2). Its surface is covered by a layer of low cuboidal cells forming the germinal epithelium. Near the surface are many minute egg cells that have remained dormant since birth. Each is surrounded by a layer of flattened follicle cells. An ovum and its covering layer of cells form a primordial follicle. In a young adult woman each ovary may contain as many as 200,000 of these, but the number decreases progressively throughout the reproductive period of life. From time to time, certain of the primordial follicles begin to grow. The ovum within slowly enlarges and the follicle cells multiply rapidly, giving rise to a thick cellular wall. Fluid accumulates between the follicle cells, and a central cavity gradually develops. The vesicular structure formed in this manner is called a Graafian follicle. Within it the eccentrically placed ovum and the cells immediately surrounding it form a domelike projection from the wall into the fluid-filled cavity (*see* fig. 3). Several hundred partially developed follicles of this kind may be present in an adult ovary. In each ovulatory cycle one of these continues to grow to large size and finally releases a ripe ovum. The great majority of the follicles develop only to a certain stage and then degenerate. Although their ova are thus wasted, these follicles nevertheless serve a useful purpose before their degeneration in that their cells are active in the production of female sex hormone. Of the thousands of primordial follicles present in the ovaries at birth, fewer than 400 are likely to produce mature ova during a woman's reproductive life.

Oviducts (Fallopian Tubes).—The oviduct is a sinuous tube of involuntary muscle, 10–13 cm. (4–5 in.) long, running laterally from ovary to uterus (*see* fig. 2). It is lined by an extensively folded mucous membrane. Near the ovary the open end of the oviduct is expanded into a thin-walled, funnel-shaped structure, the infundibulum. Its edges are prolonged into a number of slender, tapering processes called fimbria, some of which are attached to the ovary. The shape and position of the oviduct are changed by contractions in its muscular wall. It is particularly active at the time of ovulation, when it becomes reddened from dilatation of all its blood vessels and moves so as to bring its open fimbriated end into close apposition with the surface of the ovary, thus facilitating the passage of the ovum directly into the infundibulum. The passage of the oviduct narrows and becomes very small where it passes through the thick, muscular, uterine wall. Ciliated cells lining the oviduct maintain a constant slow movement of fluid from the body cavity toward the uterus.

Uterus.—The uterus, when not pregnant, resembles a flattened pear in size and shape, with the stem end directed downward toward the vagina (*see* fig. 2). The body of the uterus, the corpus uteri, is usually bent forward so that it lies upon the urinary bladder and is thus at an angle to the cylindrical neck, the cervix uteri. The thick wall of the uterus is composed largely of involuntary muscle. The uterine cavity is flattened from front to back and is roughly triangular in form, with the upper angles extending out

toward the openings of the oviducts, and the lower angle directed downward toward the cervix (*see* fig. 3). The lining of the corpus uteri, the endometrium, is a mucous membrane specially adapted for the reception and sustenance of the fertilized ovum. It is covered by a single layer of ciliated and secretory cells that is continuous with the lining of many simple tubular glands that extend from the surface of the endometrium down to the muscle of the uterine wall. The glands are embedded in a loose connective tissue richly supplied with blood vessels. The cervix of the uterus has a slender cavity narrowed by projecting folds of mucous membrane. Opening into it are numerous branching, mucus-secreting glands. At its lower end the cervical canal communicates with the vagina through a narrow slit, the external os.

Attachments.—The attachments of the ovaries, oviducts and uterus support them, while at the same time permitting their independent movement and allowing for enlargement of the uterus in pregnancy. The principal support for all three organs is provided by the two broad ligaments. Each of these consists of a double layer of peritoneum extending from the sides of the uterus to the lateral wall of the pelvis. The blood vessels, lymphatics and nerves reach the uterus by passing between the layers of the broad ligaments. Each ovary is suspended from the back of the broad ligament by a fold of peritoneum, the mesovarium. A small peritoneal fold also passes upward from the tubal end of the ovary to the pelvic wall. This is the infundibulopelvic ligament. Through it, blood vessels reach the ovary from above. The ovarian and uterine vessels communicate within the broad ligament, and blood can reach these organs via either route. The medial pole of the ovary is attached to the uterus by a stout band of connective tissue, the ovarian ligament. A fibrous cord, the round ligament, runs laterally from the uterus to the wall of the pelvis; from there it passes anteriorly through the abdominal wall via the inguinal canal and terminates in the skin and subcutaneous connective tissue of the labia majora. The round ligament in the female corresponds to the gubernaculum in the male, the fibrous band that attaches the lower pole of the testis to the skin of the scrotum. The cervix of the uterus is held back by the uterosacral ligaments, two folds of fascia and peritoneum that run from the back of the cervix around the rectum on either side to attach to the fascia over the anterior surface of the sacrum.

C. REPRODUCTIVE FUNCTION IN WOMAN

During childhood there are no signs of activity in the female genital organs, but at the beginning of adolescence (8 to 12 years) the ovaries are activated by the hormones of the pituitary gland (hypophysis) to begin the production of large follicles, which in turn secrete ovarian hormone. The latter is carried in the blood stream and stimulates development of all parts of the reproductive tract. In addition, the bony pelvis, breasts, hair and fat depots begin their progress toward maturity. There is a rhythmic alternation in the dominance of the hormones of the hypophysis and ovary. Eventually the hormonal tides attain a height that results in bleeding from the endometrium and the first menstrual flow occurs (*see* MENSTRUATION).

During the childbearing period of life the sequence of events in the cycle is usually as follows: at intervals of about a month, under stimulation from the hypophysis, one ovarian follicle outstrips its fellows in growth. In a few days it attains a diameter of about 1.25 cm. ($\frac{1}{2}$ in.) and protrudes from the ovary like a clear blister. Usually only one follicle at a time enters upon this final growth period, but occasionally more may develop; if the ova produced are fertilized, multiple births may result. At ovulation the ripened egg cell loosens from the wall of the large follicle and soon the wall bulges, breaks and the viscid follicular fluid wells out, carrying the ovum along with it. At this time of the cycle, the level of ovarian hormone circulating in the blood stream reaches a peak, and the oviducts and uterus are stimulated to greater activity. It has been possible to peer into the body cavity through an endoscope at such a time and see the fimbriated end of the oviduct wrapped closely about the ovary while the organs move rhythmically. The close joining of the open end of the infundibulum to the ovary facilitates the entrance of the ovum into the

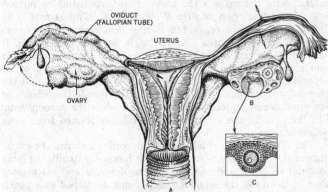

OVIDUCT (FALLOPIAN TUBE)

UTERUS

OVARY

A B C

FROM G. W. CORNER, "OURSELVES UNBORN," YALE UNIVERSITY PRESS

FIG. 3.—(A) DIAGRAM OF HUMAN OVARIES, OVIDUCTS (FALLOPIAN TUBES) AND UTERUS, AS SEEN FROM THE REAR. THE RIGHT TUBE AND UTERUS ARE DRAWN TO SHOW CANAL OF TUBE AND CAVITY OF UTERUS. DOTTED ARROWS AT LEFT INDICATE COURSE OF OVUM FROM OVARY THROUGH TUBE TO UTERUS; (B) RIPE FOLLICLE IN OVARY, WITH EGG CELL (NOT TO SCALE) IN ITS WALL; (C) ENLARGED SECTIONAL VIEW OF EGG HILLOCK OF FOLLICLE

oviduct. If spermatozoa are present, the egg may be fertilized almost as soon as it is liberated from the follicle. In any case it is swept into the oviduct by ciliary action and is slowly moved along by peristaltic contractions, reaching the uterus about the fourth day after ovulation.

In the interim, the uterine endometrium has grown thick through cell division and accumulation of interstitial fluid, and its glands have increased in length and complexity. This preliminary period of preparation of the uterus for reception of the ovum is called the follicular phase of the cycle because it is dominated by the hormone produced by the growing follicles. Ovulation is expected to occur on about the 14th day of a 28-day cycle, but it may occur as early as 7 days after the beginning of menstruation or may be delayed for 18 days or more. The period of the cycle subsequent to ovulation is called the luteal phase because it is dominated by the hormone produced by the corpus luteum, or yellow body, an organ of internal secretion that arises in the ovary from the wall of the ruptured follicle. Immediately after ovulation, while the egg is still in the oviduct, the thin wall of the collapsed follicle thickens rapidly and its cells undergo a marked change in their appearance. A meshwork of thin-walled capillary vessels develops between them, and the entire structure is transformed into a conspicuous yellow body grossly visible in the ovary at the site formerly occupied by the follicle.

The hormone secreted by the cells of the corpus luteum produces further changes in the uterus that make it a most favourable site for implantation and nourishment of the embryo. Under its influence the contractions of the uterus are slowed down; the endometrium thickens and its arteries lengthen and become more coiled; its glands grow more contorted and are distended with a secretion rich in nutrient substances. These changes take place whether the egg has been fertilized or not.

If conception does not occur, the corpus luteum remains active for only 10 to 14 days. With the decline in its hormone output, the blood flow to the uterus is reduced and the endometrium begins to shrink. Its superficial zone suffers particularly, for it is supplied by the coiled arteries, which, at this time, begin to constrict intermittently. The walls of the superficial vessels are damaged and ultimately break down, permitting blood to seep out into the surrounding tissue. The extravasated blood at first accumulates within the endometrium but finally drains into the cavity of the uterus. This marks the beginning of menstruation. The blood-soaked, degenerating tissue soon loosens and sloughs off, leaving a raw surface. The greater part of the thickness of the endometrium degenerates and is lost during menstruation, but the bases of the glands persist, and the multiplication and migration of their cells quickly restores the surface layer after menstruation is over. A period of relative inactivity may ensue before another set of ovarian follicles enter upon their final growth and release the follicular hormone that stimulates anew the growth in thickness of the endometrium.

Menstrual cycles continue more or less regularly unless interrupted by pregnancy. They are accompanied by various general bodily changes. At the middle of the cycle a sudden slight fall, followed by a rise, in the basal body temperature may be detected. Rarely abdominal pain may be experienced at the time of ovulation. The relations between hypophysis and ovary may be affected by other hormones and by the nervous system as well. Changes in climate, living conditions, infections or psychic disturbances may consequently affect the reproductive cycle. When the responses of the ovaries begin to wane at the age of 45 to 50 years, the hormonal balance is upset and changes occur in the economy of the body as a whole. These give rise to the characteristic symptoms of the menopause (q.v.), or change of life.

(D. W. Ft.)

D. Embryology

The development of the reproductive organs (see fig. 4) is closely interwoven with that of the urinary system. It is convenient to take up the development at the stage in which the genital ridge is seen on each side of the attachment of the mesentery; external to this, and forming another slight ridge of its own, is the Wolffian duct, while, a little later, the Müllerian duct is formed and lies ventral to the Wolffian. Until the fifth or sixth week the development of the genital ridge is very much the same in the two sexes and consists of cords of cells growing from the epithelium-covered surface to the mesenchyme, which forms the interior of the ridge. In these cords are some large germ cells that are distinguishable at a very early stage of development. The germinal epithelium covering the ridge, and the mesenchyme inside it, are both derived from the mesoderm, or middle layer, of the embryo.

About the fifth week of embryonic life the tunica albuginea appears in the male, from which septa grow to divide the testis into lobules, while the epithelial cords form the seminiferous tubes, though these do not gain a lumen until just before puberty. From the adjacent mesonephros, or perhaps coelomic epithelium, cords of cells grow into the attached part of the genital ridge, or testis, as it now is, and from these the rete testis is developed.

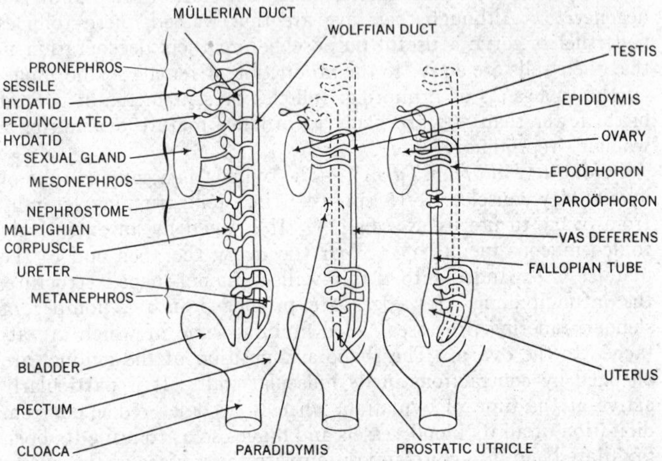

FIG. 4.—FORMATION (LEFT TO RIGHT) OF GENITOURINARY APPARATUS (SUPPRESSED PARTS ARE DOTTED); UNDIFFERENTIATED, MALE AND FEMALE

In the female the same growth of epithelial cords into the mesenchyme of the genital ridge takes place, but each one is distinguished by a bulging toward its middle; only here are the large germ cells found. Eventually this bulging part is broken up into a series of small portions, each of which contains one germ cell or ovum and gives rise to a Graafian follicle. Mesonephric cords appear as in the male; they do not enter the ovary, however, but form a transitory network (rete ovarii) in the mesovarium.

As each genital gland enlarges it remains attached to the rest of the intermediate cell mass by a constricted fold of the coelomic membrane, known as the mesorchium in the male and the mesovarium in the female. Lying dorsal to the genital ridge in the intermediate cell mass is the mesonephros, consisting of numerous tubules that open into the Wolffian duct. This at first is an important excretory organ but during development it becomes used for other purposes. In the male, as has been shown, it may form the rete testis and certainly forms the vasa efferentia and globus major of the epididymis; in addition, some of its separate tubes probably account for the aberrant ducts and the paradidymis, or organ of Giraldès. In the female the tubules of the epoöphoron represent the main part, while the paroöphoron, like the paradidymis in the male, is probably formed from some separate tubes.

The Wolffian duct, which in the early embryo carries the excretion of the mesonephros to the cloaca, forms eventually the body and tail of the epididymis, the ductus deferens and ejaculatory duct in the male, the seminal vesicle being developed as a pouch in its course. In the female this duct is largely done away with, but it remains as the collecting tube of the epoöphoron and in some mammals as the duct of Gartner, which runs down the side of the vagina to open into the vestibule.

The Müllerian duct, as it approaches the cloaca, joins its fellow of the opposite side, so that there is only one opening into the ventral cloacal wall. In the male only the lower part of it remains as the prostatic utricle, but in the female the Fallopian tubes, uterus and probably the vagina are all formed from it. In both sexes a small hydatid, or vesicle, is liable to be formed at the beginning of both the Wolffian and Müllerian ducts; in the male these hydatids are close together in front of the globus major of the epididymis and are known as the sessile and pedunculated hydatids of Morgagni. In the female there is a hydatid among the fimbriae of the Fallopian tube, which of course is Müllerian and corresponds to the sessile hydatid in the male, while another is often found at the beginning of the collecting tube of the epoöphoron and is probably formed by a blocked mesonephric tubule. This corresponds to the pedunculated hydatid of the male. The development of the vagina is peculiar. Instead of the two Müllerian ducts joining to form the lumen of its lower third, as they do in the case of the uterus and its upper two-thirds, they become obliterated, and their place is taken by two solid cords of cells, which later became canalized, while the septum between them is obliterated.

The common chamber, or cloaca, into which the alimentary, urinary and reproductive tubes open in the fetus has the urinary bladder (the remains of the allantois) opening from its ventral wall.

During development the alimentary or anal part of the cloaca is separated from the urogenital. According to F. Wood Jones, the anal part is completely shut off from the urogenital and ends in a blind pouch that grows toward the surface and meets a new ectodermal depression, the permanent anus, which is a new perforation and not a part of the original cloacal aperture. This description is in harmony with the malformations occurring in this region.

The external generative organs at first have the same appearance in the two sexes and consist of a swelling, the genital eminence, in the ventral wall of the cloaca. This in the male becomes the penis and in the female the clitoris. Throughout the generative system the male organs depart most from the undifferentiated type, and in the case of the genital eminence two folds grow together and enclose the urogenital passage, thus making the urethra perforate the penis, while in the female these two folds remain separate as the labia minora. In the male the folds sometimes fail to unite completely and then there is an opening into the urethra on the undersurface of the penis—a condition known as hypospadias.

In the undifferentiated condition the integument surrounding the genital opening is raised into a horseshoelike swelling with its convexity over the pubic symphysis and its concavity toward the anus; the lateral parts of this remain separate in the female and form the labia majora, but in the male they unite to form the scrotum. The median part forms the mons veneris, or mons pubis.

It has been shown that the testis is formed in the loin region of the embryo close to the kidney, and only in the later months of fetal life does the testis move downward into the scrotum (see *Scrotum* above). In the lower part of the genital ridge a fibromuscular cord is formed that stretches from the lower part of the testis to the bottom of the scrotum; it is known as the gubernaculum testis, and by its means the testis is directed into the scrotum. Before the testis descends, a pouch of peritoneum called the processus vaginalis passes down in front of the gubernaculum through the opening in the abdominal wall (which afterward becomes the inguinal canal) and into the scrotum; behind this the testis descends, carrying with it the mesonephros and mesonephric duct. These, as has already been pointed out, form the epididymis and ductus deferens. At the sixth month the testis lies opposite the abdominal ring, and at the eighth it reaches the bottom of the scrotum and invaginates the processus vaginalis from behind. Soon after birth the communication between that part of the processus vaginalis that now surrounds the testis and the general cavity of the peritoneum disappears, and the part that remains forms the tunica vaginalis. Sometimes the testis fails to pass beyond the inguinal canal, resulting in the condition known as cryptorchidism.

In the female the ovary undergoes a descent like that of the testis, but it is less marked since the gubernaculum becomes attached to the Müllerian duct where that duct joins its fellow to form the uterus. Thus, the ovary does not descend lower than the level of the top of the uterus, and the part of the gubernaculum running between it and the uterus remains as the ligament of the ovary, while the part running from the uterus to the labium is the round ligament. In rare cases the ovary may be drawn into the labium just as the testis is drawn into the scrotum.

See also EMBRYOLOGY AND DEVELOPMENT, ANIMAL.

(F. G. P.)

II. DISEASES AND THEIR MEDICAL TREATMENT

The male and female gonads, *i.e.*, the testes and ovaries, have a dual function: (1) they are the glands of internal secretion that determine the normal growth, development and maintenance of the physical characteristics of maleness and femaleness; and (2) they produce the gametes (*i.e.*, spermatozoa and ova), which are responsible for reproduction. Disorders of the testes and ovaries may cause subnormal, excessive or untimely secretion of hormones and may adversely affect the reproductive function, leading to sterility. Gonadal diseases are caused by abnormal sexual differentiation, congenital anomalies, deficient pituitary function, infections and tumours. Disorders of the strength or direction of the sexual impulse generally are caused not by organic diseases of the gonads but rather by environmental difficulties, usually beginning early in life.

1. Abnormal Sex Differentiation.—Sex in man is largely determined by the chromosomal constitution of somatic (body) cells. Each cell of the normal human organism contains 46 chromosomes (44 autosomes and one pair of sex chromosomes, designated as $44 + XY$ in the male and $44 + XX$ in the female). If, during development of the gametes, an X or a Y chromosome is lost, or if reduction division (meiosis) is abnormal during gametogenesis, a sperm or an ovum lacking a sex chromosome will result. An abnormal number of sex chromosomes may also result from an error of cell division in the fertilized zygote. The ensuing anomalies of chromosomal number are associated with the so-called disorders of chromosomal sex (*see* below). The effects of the chromosomal abnormalities become manifest early in fetal life. Fetal sex differentiation takes place in three successive steps: (1) gonadogenesis; (2) development of the genital ducts; and (3) development of the urogenital sinus and the external genitalia. The primordial gonad and accessory sex apparatus have bisexual potentialities. In the presence of a Y (male) chromosome, the gonad differentiates into a fetal testis, which secretes a substance or substances that in turn determine the differentiation of the embryo into a male. In the absence of a Y chromosome, as in the normal female fetus, the embryo follows its inherent tendency to become feminized.

Turner's Syndrome.—This condition can be looked upon as an example of abnormal sex differentiation. Persons with this disorder are apparent (phenotypic) females but lack the normal female chromosomal constitution. They generally have only 45 chromosomes: $(44 + X0)$; internal genitalia are female in type but the ovaries are rudimentary, consisting of ridges of connective tissue. These undifferentiated gonads produce no ova and virtually no female hormone, so that the patients remain sexually infantile and sterile. Associated features are short stature and anomalies of the cardiovascular system and the skeleton. In rare instances, other types of chromosomal complements are found. Treatment of this disease, which occurs in about one of 3,000 phenotypic females, consists of substitution therapy with female hormones (natural or synthetic estrogens). The hormones stimulate moderate growth and development of secondary sex characters; there is no way to correct the sterility.

Klinefelter's Syndrome.—Persons with this defect are phenotypic males. The disorder occurs in approximately 1 in 400 newborn males. The chromosomal abnormality consists of an excessive number, 47; the chromosomal complement is typically $44 + XXY$. Less frequently, 48 or 49 chromosomes are present, composed of $44 + XXXY$ or $44 + XXXXY$; individuals with 48 or 49 chromosomes are mentally retarded. The constant clinical features of the syndrome are infertility and small testes. These testes may secrete normal or profoundly subnormal amounts of male hormone (testosterone), resulting in normal or deficient virilization (eunuchoidism). Whether the internal secretion (*i.e.*, Leydig cell function) of the testis is normal or deficient, the gametogenic function is absent. The seminiferous tubules are small, underdeveloped or even rudimentary and generally undergo degenerative changes at puberty. Spermatozoa are not elaborated and sterility is the rule. The testicular lesion is a consequence of the chromosomal abnormality. The single Y chromosome is a sufficiently strong determinant of maleness so that the embryonic gonad differentiates into a testis and the fetus becomes more or less completely masculinized. Associated abnormalities are failure of the testes to descend into the scrotum (cryptorchidism), abnormal position of the urethra (hypospadias), excessive development of breast tissue (gynecomastia) and, rarely, mongolism and leukemia. If deficient virilization is apparent at or after the expected time of puberty, treatment with male hormone (testosterone) promotes satisfactory growth and development of secondary sex characters so that normal sexual performance becomes possible. As in Turner's syndrome the sterility cannot be corrected.

2. Congenital Anomalies.—Developmental defects of the genital system are relatively common congenital malformations. Such defects are frequently associated with malformations of the urinary tract because of the close association of the genital and urinary systems in embryogenesis. Congenital anomalies of the gonads occur infrequently. Probably the most common congenital abnormality of the gonads is cryptorchidism, or failure of the testes to descend into the scrotum. This abnormality occurs in 0.2% to 0.4% of adult males. The cause is disputed; the two most likely are mechanical abnormalities (*e.g.*, hernia) that impede the descent of a normal testis, or, more commonly, a developmental defect in the testis itself. Failure to descend may be unilateral or bilateral; the abnormally placed gonad may be in the inguinal canal (groin) or in the abdominal cavity. The chief danger arising from the misplaced testis is a very much higher incidence of cancer. Efforts should therefore be made to bring undescended testes into the scrotum; in addition to preventing the development of cancer, such action also will preclude the degeneration of spermatogenic function with resultant sterility owing to the higher temperature of an extrascrotal environment. Although ideal treatment is controversial, a reasonable practice is to attempt to stimulate growth of the testis at the age of 8 to 11. This is done by administering gonad-stimulating hormone derived from human pregnancy urine (human chorionic gonadotrophin) for a few weeks. If descent does not occur, it is then necessary to resort to surgical methods.

True hermaphroditism, or intersexuality, is an extremely rare condition characterized by varying degrees of ambisexual differentiation of the gonads and accessory sexual apparatus. The body form may be predominantly male, predominantly female or ambiguous. The chromosomal constitution is either normal male or, more commonly, normal female. In order to establish the diagnosis it is frequently necessary to explore the abdomen and locate and identify the gonads, which may consist of an ovary on one side and a testis on the other, or a gonad containing both testicular and ovarian elements (ovatestis) on one or both sides. Since such gonads tend to become cancerous, it is necessary to remove them. Sexual development is then brought about by administration of either male or female hormone. The decision whether to give testosterone or estrogen depends upon the structure of the external genitalia and the sex in which the patient has been reared. This problem is easiest to solve if the ambiguous sex is recognized early in infancy. Plastic surgical reconstruction is then done in an effort to preserve the dominant sex.

Intersexes may be further subdivided into two categories: (1) male pseudohermaphrodites when the gonads are testes, and (2) female pseudohermaphrodites when the gonads are ovaries.

In male pseudohermaphrodites (syndrome of feminizing testes) the occurrence is familial and the patients appear to be normally developed females, but the chromosomal sex is 44 + XY (normal male) and the gonads are well-developed testes located in the abdomen or elsewhere. The clinical features result from failure of the abnormal fetal testis to bring about complete masculine differentiation of the genital ducts or external genitalia. After puberty, the testis secretes estrogen in an amount comparable to that produced by adult women. Anatomically, the patients look like normal women, but the internal genital ducts are primarily male, and sexual hair is sparse. Since these gonads are apt to form cancers, they should be removed surgically, and since the disease is generally recognized at or after puberty, when female behaviour patterns have become fixed, female sexual characters are maintained by the administration of estrogenic hormones.

The two principal forms of female pseudohermaphroditism are associated with (1) congenital adrenal cortical hyperplasia and (2) exposure of the fetus to androgens from the maternal circulation.

Congenital adrenal cortical hyperplasia is the most common form of female pseudohermaphroditism and accounts for at least half the cases of ambiguous external genitalia. The disorder is genetically determined. The patients are chromosomal females (44 + XX) who resemble normal females but display varying degrees of masculinization of the external genitalia. The chemical basis of the disease is defective synthesis by the adrenal gland of its principal, life-maintaining hormones. This deficiency results in overproduction by the pituitary of adrenocorticotrophin, or ACTH, a hormone that stimulates the adrenal so that it grows to a very large size and secretes enormous quantities of androgenic (male-inducing) steroids. This process begins early in fetal life; varying degrees of masculinization of the internal and external genitalia ensue. If treatment is not started in early childhood, growth of the bones stops prematurely, resulting in short stature, failure of secondary sex characters (viz., breast growth, menstruation) to develop, and the appearance of such masculine features as deepening of the voice, increased body hair and beard growth. Effective treatment can be achieved by administration of those adrenal cortical hormones that the gland cannot synthesize (*e.g.*, hydrocortisone). These hormones suppress the pituitary so that its stimulus to adrenal production of androgenic hormones is minimized. This form of therapy occasionally permits normal female development even to the point of normal conception and pregnancy. Often, however, full development of secondary sex characters and menstruation requires the administration of estrogens.

The less common form of female pseudohermaphroditism occurs in a child when testosterone, natural or synthetic progestational hormones or synthetic estrogens are administered to the mother during the first three weeks of pregnancy; rarely, the condition is associated with the presence in the mother of a masculinizing tumour of the ovary or the adrenal. The patients are females with more or less ambiguous genitalia; no treatment with hormones is needed, and normal female development occurs at the usual age of puberty. (*See also* HERMAPHRODITE.)

3. Deficient Pituitary Function.—*Precocious and Delayed Puberty.*—Normal growth of the gonads and normal hormone secretion by the gonads are dependent upon normal function of the anterior lobe of the pituitary gland, which secretes at least two hormones that influence gonadal activity (*see* PITUITARY GLAND). Two mechanisms regulate the secretion of these pituitary hormones: (1) the influence of the brain and (2) the quantity of gonadal hormone circulating in the blood. The higher the blood level of gonadal hormone, the smaller the amount of pituitary hormone secreted. A delicate balance of these factors is required for the normal occurrence of adolescence and for the normal maintenance of the menstrual cycle. Any structural lesions (*e.g.*, tumour, inflammation) of the brain centres that influence the release of pituitary hormones will materially delay or accelerate the onset of puberty.

Delay in the onset of puberty in boys or girls may not be due to any detectable cause. The delay may result from tumours that destroy the pituitary itself, or from malnutrition or severe debilitating illnesses. Finally, delayed puberty may be caused by primary diseases of the gonads. Treatment consists of detection and removal of tumours of the brain or pituitary, or treatment of the underlying systemic disorder. In the majority of cases, where no definite cause can be found, the appropriate sex hormone or gonad-stimulating hormone is given; a short course of treatment is often followed by the onset of spontaneous pubertal development.

Precocious puberty (*i.e.*, puberty starting before the age of ten years in either sex) is caused by a great variety of disorders; in many instances, there is no discernible cause. In both sexes, precocious puberty may accompany organic lesions of the brain, *e.g.*, encephalitis, congenital defects and tumours of the basal portions of the brain or pineal body (also called the epiphysis, or pineal organ).

Congenital adrenal hyperplasia in the male, the counterpart of the major cause of female pseudohermaphroditism in girls, is the commonest cause of sexual precocity; treatment consists of pituitary-adrenal suppression by administering cortisone or related hormones. A rare cause in boys is interstitial cell tumour of the testis, usually benign and curable by surgical removal. In girls, sexual precocity may be associated with estrogen-secreting granulosa cell tumour of the ovary, or with rare tumours of the adrenal gland that may secrete estrogens (or, more commonly, androgens, resulting in virilization). Treatment consists of surgical removal of the tumours.

Pituitary-Adrenal Relationships in Adult Life.—Failure of pituitary function in the adult is most commonly the result of tumours of the gland, of vascular injury to it after a catastrophic delivery, or of severe malnutrition. Treatment consists of X-radiation of tumours, or, if that fails, surgical removal. Gonadal deficiency due to pituitary failure can be effectively treated by administration of testosterone or estrogen, but there is no treatment for the ensuing infertility.

4. Infections and Tumours of the Gonads.—Infections of the testis occasionally cause sterility. The commonest testicular infection is the acute orchitis of mumps; this is a frequent, painful complication of mumps that is followed in almost half the cases by some degree of testicular atrophy but only infrequently by sterility since the involvement of the gland is spotty. Chronic orchitis is usually painless and is a result of syphilis, tuberculosis, leprosy and certain parasitic diseases. Treatment of the infectious disease usually fails to restore the reproductive function of the gland. Infections of the ovary include mumps oöphoritis and abscesses of the ovary due to gonorrhea. The latter are effectively treated with penicillin.

Tumours of the testis comprise only 2% of all forms of cancer in the male but they are frequently malignant. Very rarely, they are benign and hormone-secreting (*e.g.*, the interstitial cell tumour); the usual forms are the so-called germinal tumours (*e.g.*, seminoma, teratoma) that occur with increased frequency in the testes of intersexes and in undescended (cryptorchid) testes. These malignant tumours may or may not be amenable to X-ray treatment.

The ovary is the site of a great variety of tumours, benign or malignant; treatment is generally surgical unless cancer is present and has spread, in which case X-radiation may be used. A few of these ovarian growths are hormone-secreting: granulosa-cell tumours secrete estrogens and are a rare cause of sexual precocity; arrhenoblastomas and adrenal cortical-like tumours secrete androgens and cause failure of menstruation and masculine changes; and ovarian struma may contain enough functioning thyroid tissue to bring about the clinical picture of hyperthyroidism. The androgen-secreting tumours must be distinguished from adrenal disease and from other virilizing disorders of the ovary (*e.g.*, polycystic ovary, or Stein-Leventhal syndrome) that are associated with failure to menstruate. Other causes of menstrual disorder are pituitary disease, primary disease of the gonads, chronic illness, starvation, emotional upset and a variety of poorly understood disturbances in hormonal balance that have been termed functional.

5. Sterility.—Involuntary failure to reproduce (infertility) occurs in 10% of married couples in most populations that have been studied. In about one-third of the sterile couples, the deficiency is in the female, in another third in the male and in the remaining third in both parties. In a small proportion of the cases no organic cause can be found. Although the progressive increase in world population is regarded as a serious threat on a global scale, the sterile man or woman is plagued by feelings of inadequacy that not only are individual but also are racial and atavistic. Man has always worshiped fertility and from the earliest times sterility has been looked upon as disgraceful: "He whose testicles are crushed or whose male member is cut off shall not enter the assembly of the Lord" (Deut. 23:1). In his diagnostic study the physician tries first to exclude primary developmental or infectious diseases of the gonads, failure of the pituitary gland and severe debilitating diseases of either partner. Next, the number and quality of the sperm are assessed. Finally, an attempt is made to determine the adequacy of the female's Fallopian tubes, the occurrence of ovulation and the presence or absence of various mechanical impediments, *e.g.*, pelvic inflammations, endometriosis and fibromyomas (fibroids) of the uterus. Treatment of the pituitary and of serious systemic disease is followed only very rarely by restoration of fertility. Deficient production of spermatozoa generally cannot be corrected by hormonal treatment. Correction of female infertility is more successful; mechanical problems can sometimes be corrected surgically and it is even possible to induce ovulation by giving human gonadotrophin. The treatment of infertile couples is said to result in pregnancy in 30%–40% of cases; many of these therapeutic successes are undoubtedly due only to the passage of time.

6. Disorders of Sexual Impulse.—Homosexuality (*q.v.*), in which the sexual drive is directed toward members of the same sex, has been observed in all societies, ancient and modern. The cause is almost never organic disease of the gonads, which are generally normal in the homosexual person, as are the secondary sexual structures. Study of body form, hormone secretion and chromosomal complement has yielded normal findings. The usual basis is emotional and usually is rooted in abnormal attachments to or repulsion from one or the other parent, or in unduly early exposure to traumatic sexual stimuli. Homosexuality also may be associated with severe mental disease (*i.e.*, psychosis) or with alcoholism.

Satyriasis and nymphomania, or excessive sexual desire in the male and female respectively, are emotional disorders. Similarly, impotence (inability of the male to perform the sexual act) and frigidity (inability of the female to achieve sexual climax, or orgasm), while characteristic of severe deficiency of gonadal function, are nearly always caused by emotional disturbances. The disorders of sexual impulse are generally resistant to psychiatric treatment and always are refractory to misguided treatment with sex hormones.   (N. P. C.)

III. SURGERY IN THE MALE

The purpose of surgery of the male reproductive system is to preserve sexual function. This is a dual objective in that potency (erections and ejaculations) and fertility (a sufficient number of normal spermatozoa) are not synonymous. Erections may be satisfactory, yet spermatozoa may not be produced or delivered. In other instances spermatozoa may be produced but erections may not be satisfactory. Procreation requires both fertility and potency.

Treatment of impotence and infertility may be the task of medicine, psychiatry or surgery. Removal of tumours of the genital organs, draining of abscesses, removal of hopelessly diseased tissue, repair of the results of trauma and correction of congenital defects are exclusively surgical procedures. When the passage of sperm is mechanically blocked, surgery may restore the channel of the vas deferens. It is perhaps strange that, except for circumcision, most operations on the male reproductive system are performed on the prostate gland, which is not essential either to potency or to fertility; when diseased it damages the urinary tract more than the reproductive system.

Some operations on the external genitalia are performed solely to improve appearance. When both testicles are absent because of disease, trauma or congenital defect, artificial testes can be implanted in the scrotum. In hermaphroditism, operations improve the mental well-being of the patient by reinforcing the appearance of the elected sex. For example, in a hermaphrodite with apparent male organs who is to be female, a large clitoris that has the appearance of a penis may be partially excised and a vagina formed. Some of these operations belong to gynecology.

1. Penis.—In operations on the penis an effort is made to preserve as much of the erectile bodies as possible in order to permit erections.

Circumcision.—This operation is performed most generally on infants shortly after birth but may be performed at any age (*see* CIRCUMCISION). Surgical objectives are to remove excess skin of the prepuce when it cannot be retracted or when it is of such length that it interferes with sexual gratification or urination. Circumcision also reduces the incidence of infection and tumour formation beneath a long foreskin. Unless infection is severe the surgery is carried out in one operation by excising the redundant skin covering the end of the penis. If there is severe infection, the surgery may be performed in two stages: first, a dorsal slit is made to drain the area and later the excess skin is removed. A contraindication to circumcision is the congenital defect in which the anterior urethra has not formed, as in hypospadias. All available skin is required in such operations to form a new urinary channel.

Amputation.—Partial amputation of the penis is indicated for cancer of the penis, a rare form of tumour. When the cancer involves the end of the organ, the line of amputation is one inch proximal to gross signs of tumour. Partial amputation does not impede the power to gain erections. Complete amputation of the penis is indicated for cancer of the penis involving a large part of the organ. A new urethral opening is formed in the perineum and the penis and neighbouring lymph glands are excised to remove structures which may be involved in possible spread of the tumour.

Repair of Lacerated Penis.—In injuries to the penis, such as fractures sustained when the penis is erect, surgery consists of evacuating blood clots and suturing the dislocated and lacerated portions into their normal position. If performed soon after the injury is sustained, this operation is usually successful.

Priapism.—Priapism is prolonged erection of the penis without sexual gratification. Blood vessels of the penis remain engorged and detumescence does not take place. Removal of retained blood by incision and drainage or evacuation with a large surgical needle is one form of treatment. Regardless of treatment, impotence is the usual result.

2. Scrotum.—Few operations are required for abnormalities of the scrotum itself. Most are performed on the scrotal contents. Aside from removal of moles or nevi, the chief indication is elephantiasis. Here the lymphatics are obstructed and the scrotum enlarges to tremendous proportions, reaching to the level of the knees or even to the feet. This condition is common in regions (*e.g.*, India) where filariasis is prevalent; in this disease, small worms obstruct the lymph vessels. Surgery consists of excising most of the mass of the greatly enlarged scrotum.

3. Spermatic Cord.—In surgery of the spermatic cord the aims are to preserve the blood supply to the testicle and the continuity of the vas deferens.

Varicocelectomy.—Dilated veins of the spermatic cord occasionally cause pain. The dilated portions are excised, leaving the arteries to the testicle intact and sufficient veins to drain the testicle.

Correction of Torsion.—When the spermatic cord becomes twisted (torsion of the spermatic cord) through overactivity of the cremaster muscle, which surrounds the cord, the condition must be corrected promptly or gangrene of the testicle results. Operation consists of untwisting the cord and fixing the testicle to the base of the scrotum. The fixation is called orchiopexy. Since torsion is likely to occur in both sides, bilateral orchiopexy is performed even though torsion affects only one side.

Bilateral Vasectomy.—To produce sterility small sections of each vas deferens are excised through small scrotal incisions. This prevents passage of spermatozoa. However, the patient may remain fertile for weeks or months following operation because of spermatozoa stored in the seminal vesicles or prostate. In some rare instances the operation is unsuccessful; the divided vas deferens may grow back together or there may be an accessory vas deferens.

Vasectomy is performed along with operations on the prostate to prevent infection in the prostate from spreading down the vas deferens and causing inflammation of the epididymis (epididymitis). Partial vasectomy may be performed to remove a tumour of the vas deferens; such tumours are rare and usually benign.

Vasovasostomy.—After the vasa have been divided it may be desired to restore fertility. This is accomplished by sewing the divided ends together (vasovasostomy).

4. Cowper's Glands.—Operation on these glands is rarely necessary. Occasionally a tumour develops and excision is required.

5. Tunics of Testicle.—Fibrous layers covering the testicle are minor structures in themselves, but they may give rise to a large swelling of the scrotum by retaining fluid as a result of infection, the entrance of blood into the sac or obscure causes. A collection of clear fluid that transmits light is called a hydrocele; fluid that contains blood and does not transmit light is a hematocele. In a hydrocelectomy, the sac is opened and the edges everted and sutured together behind the testicle. This eliminates the sac. If the wall of the sac is very thick or calcified it is excised, rather than everted.

6. Epididymis.—Since the epididymis serves only as a reservoir for spermatozoa its function is not vital.

Epididymectomy.—Excision of the epididymis is indicated for an infection (most frequently tuberculous) that is not curable with antibacterial drugs. Tumours, which are rare and usually benign, require excision.

Epididymovasostomy.—When the vas deferens is obstructed near its emergence from the epididymis, as from scar tissue following gonorrhea or from congenital defect, sperm cannot pass. In such instances corrective surgery may be performed to restore fertility, provided the testis is normal. An opening is made in the vas deferens and a new communication is formed with the epididymis to short-circuit the obstructed portion of the vas.

7. Testis.—Conservation of a portion of one testis is essential to provide the normal male hormone that gives men a deep voice, male bodily habitat and sexual function. The production of male hormone is distinct from the other function of the testis, *i.e.*, the production of spermatozoa for procreation. The two functions are carried out by different types of cells intermingled in the glandular portion of the testis. When the testis is removed it is useless to preserve the epididymis, since the testis no longer supplies sperm. The chief indication for removing one testis is malignant tumour; both testes are removed to eliminate hormone production in some cases of cancer of the prostate (*see* below).

The testis is exposed through either a scrotal incision or an incision in the inguinal region. If the latter incision is used, the testicle is drawn up by traction on the spermatic cord into the opening in the inguinal region.

Total Orchiectomy.—Removal of the entire testicle is indicated for malignant tumour; testicle tumours usually are malignant. For malignancy, orchiectomy consists of removal of the testis, epididymis and spermatic cord up to the internal inguinal ring where the spermatic cord enters the abdominal cavity. In types of malignant tumour in which X-ray treatment cannot destroy outgrowth of the tumour into the lymphatics, radical orchiectomy may be performed; in this procedure the testis, epididymis, spermatic cord and lymph chains surrounding the blood vessels of the bony pelvis and retroperitoneum are removed.

Bilateral Simple Orchiectomy.—This operation is performed in advanced cancer of the prostate. The purpose is to remove the cells that secrete male hormone, since this hormone (androgen) promotes growth of prostatic cancer. Both testes and epididymides are removed, leaving the spermatic cord, since the sole purpose is to terminate secretion of male hormone. Elimination of the hormone usually suppresses growth and causes recession of cancer of the prostate for a variable time. Other hormonal factors are involved; one is that some male hormone is secreted by glands other than the testis; *e.g.*, the adrenal.

In subcapsular orchiectomy the glandular tissue of the testis is removed, leaving the capsule of the testis and the epididymis in place for cosmetic effect. The same result is obtained by implanting an artificial (usually plastic) testis in the scrotum to replace a removed testicle.

Partial Orchiectomy.—This operation is indicated when the testis is invaded by an infection that spreads from the epididymis that requires operation, *e.g.*, some cases of tuberculous epididymitis. Tiny portions of the testis occasionally are removed for diagnosis (biopsy) in infertile males. Microscopic examination of the tissue usually gives a clue to the extent and reason for the lack of normal spermatozoa.

Orchiopexy.—This is an operation to correct cryptorchidism, a congenital defect in which the testis does not descend into the scrotum from its site of formation in the lumbar region. When, as is usual, the undescended testicle lies in the inguinal canal, it is possible to isolate the testicle, free and lengthen the spermatic cord and implant the testis in the scrotum. An undescended testis is usually associated with a potential inguinal hernia, which is repaired at the same operation.

8. Prostate.—Surgery of the prostate is performed frequently because of the relatively frequent occurrence of benign enlargement and cancer of the prostate. Prostatic enlargements are most frequent in men over 50 years of age. The enlargement obstructs the outflow of urine through the urethra, which tunnels through the gland. The purpose of this surgery is to relieve urinary obstruction but at the same time to preserve urinary control by avoiding damage to the external urinary sphincter.

Removal of the entire prostate (radical prostatectomy) is the

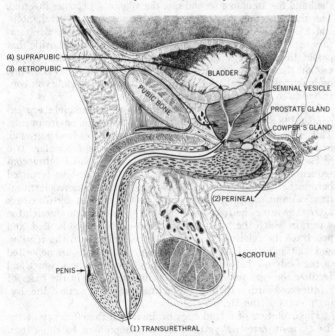

(4) SUPRAPUBIC
(3) RETROPUBIC
BLADDER
PUBIC BONE
SEMINAL VESICLE
PROSTATE GLAND
COWPER'S GLAND
(2) PERINEAL
SCROTUM
PENIS
(1) TRANSURETHRAL

FIG. 5.—VERTICAL SECTION THROUGH PELVIS, SHOWING FOUR SURGICAL APPROACHES TO BLADDER AND PROSTATE GLAND

accepted treatment for cancer if the tumour has not spread beyond the gland. Operations for removing so-called benign prostatic enlargements (conservative prostatectomy) are almost always performed for enlargements of the glands of the urethra and not the prostate. The term prostatectomy is a misnomer when used to describe the removal of the urethral glands because the prostate is not removed and remains in place after the enlarged glands are removed.

Less frequently, a portion of the prostate is removed for stones or for infection (partial prostatectomy). Removal of a thickened outlet of the bladder is sometimes erroneously called a prostatectomy; in this operation, part of the vesical neck is removed. Obstruction of the urethra at the bladder outlet is known as median bar.

Because it is located deep within the bony pelvis, the prostate is difficult to expose by surgery. One of four approaches (*see* fig. 5) is commonly employed, as follows:

Perineal.—The oldest type of incision to expose the prostate is the perineal incision. A curved incision anterior to the rectum is used to expose the posterior surface of the gland by displacing the rectum backward. This operation is suitable for both so-called conservative prostatectomy (removing enlarged periurethral glands from within the prostate) and radical perineal prostatectomy.

Radical perineal prostatectomy consists of removing the prostate for early cancer. After the entire prostate and the seminal vesicles are removed, the neck of the bladder is sewed to the cut end of the urethra.

Suprapubic.—This route provides the most direct approach to the prostate. A low abdominal incision exposes the bladder, which is then opened to gain access to the prostate. For this reason the operation is also termed transvesical prostatectomy. The approach is adaptable only to benign enlargements since the entire prostate cannot be removed through the bladder. The surgeon's finger is introduced far into the urethra, and a line of cleavage makes it possible to shell out the enlarged periurethral glands from within the prostate.

Retropubic.—This approach is likewise through a lower abdominal incision. The bladder is dissected away from behind the pubic bone and the prostate is exposed extraperitoneally. This operation is suitable for both the radical operation for cancer and for removing benign enlargements. In the former, after the prostate and seminal vesicles are removed, the divided neck of the bladder is sutured to the cut end of the urethra. In so-called conservative prostatectomy, after the anterior surface of the gland is exposed retropubically an incision is made through the capsule of the prostate and the enlarged urethral glands are enucleated from within the prostate.

Transurethral.—This approach is made through the urethra without an open surgical incision. This technique makes use of an incandescent lamp, multiple lens optics and high-frequency electrosurgical currents that are capable of making precise cuts of tissue under water. This operation is most useful for removing all types of small enlargement, either within the prostate or at the vesical neck; it is not suitable for radical removal of the entire prostate for cancer.

9. Seminal Vesicles.—Surgery on the seminal vesicles is rarely necessary. Very occasionally these glands, which lie posterior to the prostate, are the site of tumour and require excision (seminal vesiculectomy). Surgery is also occasionally indicated for an infection that is not relieved by antibacterial drugs.

See also references under "Reproductive System" in the Index.

(H. M. WE.)

BIBLIOGRAPHY.—M. Campbell (ed.), *Urology,* 2nd ed. (1963); J. P. Schaeffer (ed.), *Morris' Human Anatomy* (1953); C. M. Goss (ed.), *Gray's Anatomy of the Human Body,* 27th ed. (1959); F. H. A. Marshall, *Physiology of Reproduction* (1956); C. H. Best and N. B. Taylor, *The Physiological Basis of Medical Practice,* 7th ed. (1961); P. B. Beeson and W. McDermott (eds.), *Cecil-Loeb Textbook of Medicine,* 11th ed. (1963); C. L. Buxton and A. L. Southam, *Human Infertility* (1958); G. W. Henry, *Sex Variants* (1948); A. P. Noyes and L. C. Kolb, *Modern Clinical Psychiatry,* 6th ed. (1963); E. B. Astwood (ed.), *Clinical Endocrinology* (1960); L. Wilkins, *The Diagnosis and Treatment of Endocrine Disorders in Childhood and Adolescence,* 2nd ed. (1957); R. H. Williams (ed.), *Textbook of Endocrinology,* 3rd ed. (1962); J. Rogers, *Endocrine and Metabolic Aspects of Gynecology* (1963); W. C. Young (ed.), *Sex and Internal Secretions,* 3rd ed. (1961); R. Flocks and D. Culp, *Surgical Urology* (1954); A. I. Dodson, *Urological Surgery,* 3rd ed. (1956); H. M. Weyrauch, *Surgery of the Prostate* (1959), "The Male Reproductive System" in *Christopher's Textbook of Surgery,* 8th ed. (1964).

REPTILE, any member of the class Reptilia, including snakes, lizards, crocodiles, alligators, turtles, and the tuatara, among the living forms, and a great many extinct types such as dinosaurs, pterosaurs, and ichthyosaurs.

Intermediate between amphibians and the warm-blooded vertebrates, reptiles may be described as those air-breathing vertebrates practising internal fertilization and having a scaly body covering instead of hair or feathers.

This article deals with the following subjects:

I. EVOLUTIONARY SIGNIFICANCE

Reptiles occupy an evolutionary position between amphibians, on the one hand, and the birds and mammals on the other, the last two classes having evolved from reptilian ancestors. Reptiles first appear in the fossil record of the Carboniferous Period, over 250,000,000 years ago. By the Triassic, about 50,000,000 years later, they began to dominate the terrestrial life of the world and continued that dominance through the Mesozoic Era. Reptiles succeeded in adapting to deserts, swamps, forests, grasslands, rivers, lakes, and even the air and the seas. Coincident with the rise of mammals at the end of the Mesozoic, most of the varied reptilian groups became extinct. (*See* PALEONTOLOGY.)

1. Basic Changes.—The big evolutionary step made by reptiles was the final emancipation from life in water, for until that step was taken vertebrates could not exploit all of the earth's surface. That breakthrough required two basic changes.

The first of these changes took place in the skin. Modern amphibians have naked skins that lack horny scales, hair, or other protective devices. One small amphibian group, the caecilians, has small fishlike scales embedded in the skin, and similar scales occurred in some ancient extinct amphibians. Because of their thinness and position, these amphibian scales are no protection against desiccation, one of the principal hazards of life for all animals, vertebrate or invertebrate. This susceptibility to drying-out forced (and still forces) amphibians to remain in water or in very humid places, thus limiting their exploitation of the terrestrial environment. Reptiles evolved a different type of scale consisting of keratin (or horn) deposited in the outermost layer of the skin (fig. 1). This type of scale was in a position and of a thickness to prevent desiccation.

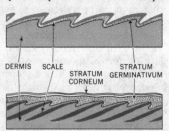

DERMIS   SCALE   STRATUM CORNEUM   STRATUM GERMINATIVUM

FIG. 1.—COMPARISON OF (TOP) REPTILIAN AND (BOTTOM) AMPHIBIAN SKINS SHOWING THE DIFFERENCE IN POSITION OF THE SCALES

The second basic change made by the reptiles was the development of what is called the amniote egg. The eggs of their evolutionary predecessors, the amphibians, are surrounded only by several layers of gelatinous material after they are laid. Sperm penetrate the gelatinous envelopes and fertilize the eggs. Embryos develop still surrounded by the gelatinous layers until the young hatch. Amphibian eggs must be laid in water or in places where the air is saturated with moisture, for the gelatinous coverings cannot protect them from desiccation. This exigency requires all amphibians to return to water for breeding and limits the kinds of environments in which the adults can live.

The embryo of a reptile soon develops a thin sac, the amnion, that envelops the embryo and becomes filled with a watery fluid (fig. 2), the entire structure serving to protect the embryo from desiccation and mechanical injury. A parchmentlike shell produced by the female parent surrounds the amnion, but between the shell and the amnion a second sac, the allantois, becomes inserted. The shell also contributes mechanical protection. The allantois, which is supplied with many fine blood vessels, serves as a respiratory organ to absorb the oxygen and emit the carbon dioxide that passes through the somewhat porous shell. All of these layers around the embryo persist in birds. Only the shell has been lost by mammals. The allantois in mammals forms the embryo's contribution to the placenta.

2. Consequences.—The development of the amniote egg expanded the possibilities of exploitation of terrestrial environments. This egg could be laid under rocks or logs, in holes in the ground, in deserts or forests, in fact, almost anywhere except in water.

The development of the reptilian egg had several other consequences. An egg that is enclosed by a shell must be fertilized before that shell is deposited, thus necessitating internal fertilization. Animals evolutionarily prior to the reptiles fertilize eggs after they leave the female's body; the sperm wriggle through the water, in which the fish and amphibian eggs have to be laid, and penetrate the gelatinous layers. But beginning with the reptiles, and continuing with the birds and mammals, sperms are deposited in the body of the female, where they move up the oviduct and fertilize the eggs prior to deposition of the shell (in the cases of reptiles and birds), thereby protecting the sperm against the drying powers of the air.

The evolution of a land egg also increased the efficiency of the life cycle of terrestrial vertebrates. An amphibian, hatching from an aquatic egg, must develop and grow in water in a larval form, the tadpole. Because the supply of yolk—the sole source of food for the developing embryo—in an amphibian's egg is small, the length of time between fertilization of the egg and hatching of the tadpole is very short. In that short interval, and with that small amount of raw material, the amphibian embryo cannot develop all the organs needed for terrestrial life; it can only develop a nervous system, with sense organs, and digestive, circulatory, and excretory systems. It has no bony skeleton or limbs, without which support and locomotion

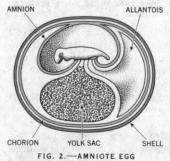

AMNION   ALLANTOIS

CHORION   YOLK SAC   SHELL

FIG. 2.—AMNIOTE EGG

on land are impossible. The tadpole differs from the adult amphibian in anatomy, behaviour, and environmental needs because of its aquatic existence; it therefore must undergo a radical and physiologically dangerous change called metamorphosis between its aquatic and terrestrial lives.

The reptile, on the other hand, does not lead a double life. From the time of fertilization onward, the history of a reptile is one of development and growth of adult structures adapted for a terrestrial life. It need not develop gills or a lateral line system, which are needed by the aquatic tadpole and which must be resorbed and reworked into other structures later. This important change in the type of development was made possible by a great increase in the amount of yolk in the reptilian egg.

The large amount of yolk also permitted the lengthening of the embryonic period, in turn allowing the development of all structures necessary for successful existence on land. When a reptile hatches, it is ready to carry out all of the activities of the adult, and in the same environment and manner. The only exception is the inability of juvenile reptiles to reproduce; the sex organs still require time to mature.

After reptiles acquired scaly protection for their skin and an egg that did not have to be laid in water, they were free to move over most of the earth's surface. That freedom set the stage for the evolution of the many varied types of reptiles and, ultimately, the evolution of birds and mammals.

II. NATURAL HISTORY

A. LOCOMOTION

1. Walking and Crawling.—The majority of reptilian orders are and have been quadrupedal. Turtles (Chelonia), lizards (Squamata), crocodiles (Crocodilia), rhynchocephalians (Rhynchocephalia), pelycosaurs (Pelycosauria), therapsids (Therapsida), and many of the ornithischian dinosaurs (Ornithischia) walked on all fours, though not all with the same gaits. Among the land vertebrates, the limbs gradually shifted from a purely lateral to a purely ventral position. In most amphibian types the limbs projected out to the side and then bent downward to the ground at the knee and elbow. With few exceptions, the quadrupedal reptiles had and have the same awkward position (fig. 3). With that orientation, the centre of gravity of the body was not in the same axis as the hands and feet, resulting in a sideways as well as a forward component of thrust when the animal walked. The typical reptile throws its body into a slight horizontal curve to progress straight forward. In mammals the limbs are directly underneath the body; the centre of gravity is in the axis of the limbs; and all of the thrust of the limbs is directed forward. The latter position and type of motion are more efficient. The lateral orientation of the limbs in amphibians and reptiles also makes it more difficult to raise the body off the ground.

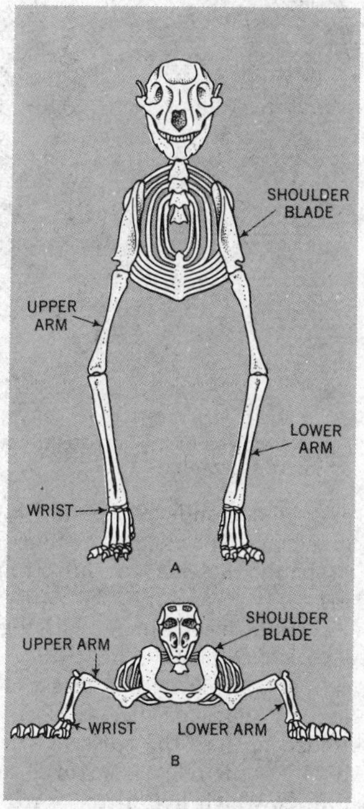

Despite the awkwardness of the orientation of their limbs, some reptiles are (and many extinct forms probably were) capable of moderate speeds. Crocodilians, for example, raise their bodies off the ground and make short, fast rushes. Short-bodied lizards are also often fast, though for short distances. Longer-bodied lizards have greater difficulty in raising their bodies, and some cannot. The last usually have short legs and proceed in a serpen-

FIG. 3.—COMPARISON OF LIMB ORIENTATION IN (A) MAMMAL AND (B) REPTILE

tine fashion, with the body, thrown in horizontal curves, doing more or less of the work depending on whether the legs are shorter or longer, respectively.

A snake (or a virtually limbless lizard) moves by pushing backward against rocks, sticks, or any relatively fixed point—a lump of earth or a small depression in uneven ground will do—with the rear surface of the horizontal curves of its body. Each joint of the body passes through the same curves, pressing against the same object and thrusting the fore part of the body forward. Even arboreal snakes use this method of locomotion, pushing against branches as they extend their bodies across gaps to new perches. On very smooth surfaces, such as glass or a wide board covered with a thick layer of fine dust, this horizontal undulatory movement, as it is called, does not work. Instead the snake remains in one place while its body executes "swimming" motions.

Heavy-bodied snakes such as pythons and certain rattlesnakes can move forward without throwing their bodies into curves. This rectilinear movement depends on the ability of snakes to stretch or contract their bodies in the longitudinal axis. By raising a part of its belly, stretching that part forward, lowering it to the ground, and repeating the process alternately with other parts of the body, a heavy snake moves forward smoothly in a straight line.

Returning to the more general type of reptilian locomotion, some modern lizards have adopted semibipedal locomotion. Unrelated lizards, such as the collared lizard (*Crotaphytus collaris*) of the United States and the frilled lizard (*Chlamydosaurus kingi*) of Australia, show the early stages of bipedalism, a phenomenon widespread among the dinosaurs and therefore important in their history. These lizards run on their long hind legs with the forward parts of their bodies at an angle of about 60° off the horizontal when they travel at top speed, which, though fast for a reptile, is still much slower than that of a running man. A long tail held off the ground acts as a counterbalance.

Presumably, bipedalism among the dinosaurs began as it did among modern lizards, as an occasional means of obtaining bursts of speed. Because the centre of gravity is in front of the hips, modern bipedal lizards must move forward continuously in order to maintain a semierect posture; they can stand still in that position only for very short periods. At the culmination of this evolutionary trend, a bipedal dinosaur probably remained semierect habitually and dropped to all fours only occasionally. This inference is based on the observations that the front limbs of these dinosaurs became very short and weak and were probably incapable of supporting much weight for any length of time. Furthermore, since the tails of bipedal dinosaurs were on the whole relatively heavier than those of the lizards, thus shifting the centre of gravity closer to the hips, it probably required less effort for the dinosaurs to remain erect. (*See* also DINOSAUR.)

The awkward sideways orientation of the limbs forces bipedal lizards to swing each leg outward as it is brought forward and to push the body sideways and forward when each leg thrusts backward against the ground. Bipedal dinosaurs eliminated this inefficient rocking motion, for during the course of evolution their hind limbs were rotated forward so that they were directly under their bodies. Thus they delivered their full force in the forward direction. So successful was this mode of locomotion that dinosaurs utilizing it dominated terrestrial life for millions of years.

2. Clinging and Climbing.—Considering the range of habitats occupied by the extinct reptilian orders, one may safely assume that some were arboreal. But animals having that mode of life are not likely to be preserved as fossils. Hence our knowledge of arboreal adaptations in reptiles is limited to those of contemporary groups.

Associated with arboreal life are groups of anatomical features mainly concerned with clinging. The commonest clinging structures in vertebrates are claws; they seem to be the only arboreal adaptations of some lizards, for example, the common iguana (*Iguana iguana*). Similar structures appear in many lizards of the family Gekkonidae, in the anoles (*Anolis*) of the family Iguanidae, and in some skinks of the family Scincidae. The pads consist of wide plates or scales under the fingers and toes. The outer layer of each plate is composed of innumerable tiny hooks formed by the free, bent tips of cells. These minute hooks catch in the slightest irregularities and enable geckos to run up apparently smooth walls and even upside down on plaster ceilings. Since the hooklike cells are bent downward and to the rear, to disengage them a gecko curls its toes upward. Thus in walking or running up a tree or wall, a gecko must curl and uncurl its toes at every step.

The giant Solomon Islands skink (*Corucia*), true chameleons (Chamaeleontidae), arboreal vipers, and pythons use prehensile tails—that is, tails capable of supporting most of the weight of the animal or used habitually for grasping—for clinging to their aerial supports. For this purpose, however, true chameleons rely mainly on a tonglike arrangement of their digits, which are united into two opposed bundles on each foot—three on the inside and two on the outside of the front foot, and two on the inside and three on the outside of the hind foot.

Although all snakes can curl their tails around objects, prehensile tails are confined to the heavy-bodied types mentioned above. Other parts of the snake's body may be used to supplement the tail in grasping branches, as when a python moves through trees, but the most important assist to the tail is the even distribution of weight of the body on each side of a branch.

At the opposite pole from the thick-bodied vipers and pythons are the excessively slender vine snakes of several genera of the family Colubridae. Any of these slender snakes is capable of extending half of its body length in a horizontal plane without support, and usually does so habitually in bridging the gap between branches. Most snakes can reach across an open space, but all except these vine snakes can extend only a short length of the body, and that portion invariably sags like a cable. The vine snakes bridge an open space like an I-beam. This ability is based partly on a reduced body weight, which follows from the body form, and partly on deepened and strengthened vertebrae.

3. Swimming.—In water, of course, neither bipedal nor quadrupedal locomotion is very effective. Aquatic reptiles, with few exceptions, use the same means of propulsion as do fishes and whales, that is, powerful beats of the tail. Crocodilians and aquatic lizards such as some monitors (Varanidae) lash their tails from side to side while the limbs are held against the body. This same method was used by the ancient mesosaurs (Mesosauria) and ichthyosaurs (Ichthyosauria). The marine ichthyosaurs, which were the reptilian counterpart of the porpoises, may have used their very short limbs for steering.

This fishlike method of swimming requires a flexible body and at least a moderately long tail. Turtles, encased in armour and having what is probably the most inflexible body among vertebrates, cannot use the common swimming technique. Instead they propel themselves by using their feet as paddles—the hind feet, which have webbed toes, in the case of fresh-water turtles, and the fore feet, which are modified into large paddles, in the case of marine turtles.

The extinct marine plesiosaurs (suborder Plesiosauria), with their short bodies and tails and their large paddlelike limbs, swam the way marine turtles do, although they may have used their hind limbs for more than just steering. Both pelvic and pectoral (shoulder) girdles were modified in the plesiosaurs into structures having small upper portions and very large lower portions. As the upper element, especially that of the pelvic girdle, has the important function of transferring the weight of the body to the limbs, it is likely that the limbs of plesiosaurs could not support the body weight on land and that the plesiosaurs never came out of water. The much-enlarged lower parts of the girdles served for the attachment of the strong musculature operating the paddles.

Most plesiosaurs had moderately long necks, and some had very long necks. By moving toward their prey (probably fishes) with the neck curved, they probably could strike suddenly forward or sideways to catch their agile prey. The heavy trunk would provide the inertia against which the head and neck could move, thus preventing a significant backward shift of the animal as the head and neck shot forward.

A contemporary group of marine reptiles, the sea snakes (Hydrophidae), show the same adaptation. Though they swim with a fishlike or, rather, an eellike undulation of the body, the sea snakes have relatively small heads, slender necks, and very heavy-bodied mid and rear sections. If a sea snake had the body proportions of an ordinary terrestrial snake, each segment of the body would have roughly the same mass. If such a snake struck at a fish with the forward third of its body, about half of the forward motion would be lost as the rear of the body (by reaction) was thrust backward. But with most of the body mass concentrated in the second half of the animal, almost all of the force of the strike is used to drive the head forward.

4. Flying.—Three groups of reptiles have experimented with flight. Thecodontia, a group of Archosauria (the so-called ruling reptiles, which included dinosaurs and crocodilians), became almost unbelievably successful at this means of locomotion, and almost overnight (as these things are measured in geological time) evolved into birds.

A second group of archosaurs, the Pterosauria, developed wings that were supported along the front margin by the arm and an extremely elongated finger (fig. 4A). The pterosaur wing was made of skin, and since it lacked both internal supports and feathers it probably lacked the flexibility or durability of a bird wing. Flight of the pterosaurs presumably amounted to soaring and gliding. What is not understood is how pterosaurs moved about when not flying and how they managed to take off if they

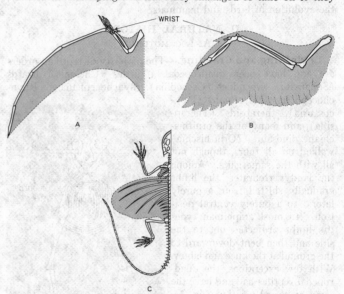

FIG. 4.—WINGS OF (A) PTEROSAUR AND (B) BIRD. (C) GLIDING MEMBRANE OF FLYING LIZARD

ever landed on level ground. Since most remains have been found in marine deposits, it is assumed that they lived along ocean shores, probably roosting on cliffs from which takeoff would have been easy.

The third experiment with flight was made by a group of modern lizards (*Draco*). The "wing" of these small lizards consists of skin supported by five or six elongated ribs between the arm and leg, as shown in fig. 4C. At rest the ribs and the wings are folded against the sides of the body. In flight the wings form broad semicircles from arm to leg on each side. These flying lizards, which live in the forested country of Southeast Asia and the East Indies, are capable only of gliding. Like flying squirrels, which they resemble in the position of the flight membrane, a flying lizard launches itself into the air and glides toward another tree, descending slowly and turning upward sharply just before lighting on the new perch. Since the arms and legs are not modified, this lizard is capable of scampering up and down tree trunks like any strictly arboreal lizard.

B. THERMAL RELATIONSHIPS

Reptiles are often described as being cold-blooded, which is not always true. Their body temperatures are not always low, but these animals have no internal mechanism for regulating body temperature and thus approximate closely the temperature of their surroundings. This condition is termed poikilothermy. Mammals and birds maintain their relatively high body temperatures at a relatively constant level by physiological means that are independent of the external environment, a condition called homoiothermy (see ANIMAL HEAT). When the body temperature of a dog or a man falls below the normal range, he begins to shiver, blood vessels in the skin contract, muscular activity generates heat, and the contraction of the superficial blood vessels, by reducing the volume of blood flow at the surface, reduces heat loss by radiation. By contrast, a reptile, when its body temperature falls below the optimum, must move to some portion of the environment having a higher temperature; in less than optimal temperatures its activity drops, its movements become sluggish, its heartbeat is slowed, and its rate of breathing drops. In short, it becomes incapable of normal activities required for growth, reproduction, and survival.

High temperatures also are hazardous for animals. Mammals and birds have some physiological means of cooling their bodies (e.g., panting and sweating, expansion of superficial blood vessels), but a reptile must move away from a spot in which the temperature is too high or perish very quickly. It may need only to move to the shady side of a bush, or it may retreat into a burrow or move into water.

By such movements reptiles seek out those portions of their environments in which they can maintain their bodies near the optimal temperatures, the level at which each species carries out its bodily functions at maximum efficiency. Characteristically, a reptile that normally is active by day moves into the morning sun and basks until its body temperature reaches the optimum. It then begins to forage for food, momentarily moving into places that are too hot or too cold but remaining most of the time in places close to the optimal temperature. As night falls the reptile seeks shelter; its body temperature falls with the temperature of the environment; and it remains inactive until temperatures rise the next morning. In certain environments having low air temperatures but strong sunlight (e.g., the Peruvian Andes at about 14,000 ft.) reptiles can raise their body temperatures 30°–40° F (17°–22° C) above the air temperature by basking.

If, because of cloudy weather, the environmental temperatures do not rise to the optimal level of a given species for several days, the reptile operates at less than maximum efficiency (if the temperatures are high enough for any activity) or remains inactive. It is this kind of physiological inefficiency that mammals and birds have overcome by internal temperature control to their great ecological advantage.

Each group of reptiles has its own characteristic thermal range. One genus of lizards, for example, may require temperatures of 85°–90° F (29°–32° C) for maximum efficiency, and another may require 75°–80° F (24°–27° C). As a result of such physiological differences, lizards of these two groups will be active at different times of the day or occupy slightly different habitats (shaded versus exposed situations), and may rarely come in contact even though they live in the same general area.

In general the normal activity temperatures of reptiles are lower than those of most mammals; however, a few sun-loving (heliothermic) lizards (e.g., the greater earless lizard, *Holbrookia texana*, of southwestern United States) have average activity temperatures above 100° F (38° C), several degrees higher than the average human body temperature. Such high temperatures are exceptional, and the majority of lizards have normal activity temperatures in the 80°–95° F (27°–35° C) range.

C. DEFENSES

1. Avoidance.—This, the commonest form of defense in the animal kingdom, is also the commonest in reptiles. At the first recognition of danger, most snakes and lizards crawl or scamper away into the undergrowth, whereas turtles and crocodilians plunge into water and sink out of sight. But should the danger arise so suddenly and so close at hand that flight may be hazardous, other expedients are adopted.

2. Noise.—Crocodiles, some lizards, turtles, and some snakes hiss loudly when confronted by an enemy. The most spectacular use of sound in warning or threatening behaviour is made by rattlesnakes. The buzzing of the tail rattle is a sound instantly recognized, even when heard for the first time by anyone who has read about these snakes. (A few snakes without rattles [e.g., the fox snake, *Elaphe vulpina*, of the United States] vibrate the ends of their tails rapidly, and if, as often happens, the tail hits dry leaves, it makes a sound deceptively like the rattle of a rattlesnake; but this use of sound is fortuitous.)

3. Change in Body Form.—Change in body form is relatively common in snakes and usually involves spreading the neck, as in cobras (family Elapidae), or the whole body, as in the harmless hognose snakes (*Heterodon*) and DeKay's snake (*Storeria dekayi*) of the United States. Some snakes inflate the forward parts of their bodies; inflation is one of the defensive actions of the large South American tree snake *Spilotes* and of the African boomslang (*Dispholidus*).

4. Posturing.—Threatening postures may be assumed by snakes at the same time that they change their body form. A cobra raises the fore part of its body and spreads its hood when endangered. The typical defensive posture of a viper is with the body coiled and the neck held in an S curve, the head poised to strike.

Some lizards flatten their bodies, puff out their throats, and turn broadside to the enemy. The helmeted iguanids (*Corythophanes*) of Central America and the chameleons of Africa, both arboreal groups, increase their apparent size in this way when approached by snakes. Other lizards face their enemies before displaying. The Australian bearded lizard (*Amphibolurus barbatus*) spreads its throat downward and outward. The Australian frilled lizard (*Chlamydosaurus kingi*) suddenly raises a wide membrane or frill, extending backward about 2½ in. from the throat. The span of the frill in *Chlamydosaurus* may be 7 in. in a lizard having a head and body length of 8 in. As this lizard spreads the frill, it opens its mouth. Many lizards and snakes open their mouths when threatened, but do not strike. A common African lizard, *Agama atricollis*, faces an enemy with head held high and its mouth open to show the brilliant orange interior.

5. Display of Colour.—Display of colour in the case of *Agama atricollis* may not be part of a threatening mechanism, but it is in the instances of certain red- or yellow-bellied snakes that turn over or curl their tails up, exposing the brightly coloured undersurface. This behaviour, known in harmless (e.g., the American ring-necked snake, *Diadophis*) as well as venomous snakes (e.g., the coral snake, *Micrurus frontalis*), is displayed only by snakes having red, orange, or yellow undersides. These colours must have some significance, as yet not fully understood, to predacious animals, for they are the common colours in insects having warning coloration. (See also COLORATION, BIOLOGICAL.)

6. Striking and Biting.—If a threatening posture does not succeed in driving off the enemy, many reptiles become more aggressive. Some snakes (e.g., DeKay's snake) strike, but with their mouths closed. Others (e.g., the hognose snakes) strike with their mouths open, but do not bite. Still others strike and bite viciously. Among the nonvenomous snakes of North America, few are as quick to bite as the water snakes (*Natrix*). The sole danger from the bites of these snakes is infection of the wound.

Most of the dangerously venomous snakes (vipers, pit vipers, and cobras) bite in self-defense. Vipers and pit vipers usually strike from a horizontally coiled posture. From this position the head can be shot forward, stab the enemy, and be as rapidly pulled back in readiness for the next strike. It is not necessary for a pit viper to lunge forward in order to inject its fangs; many a careless snake handler has been bitten by a rattlesnake that simply twisted its neck and grabbed the hand that held it. But when free the characteristic defensive strike of a viper is a quick horizontal lunge and withdrawal. From the typical raised posture a cobra sweeps its head forward and downward to bite. To strike again it raises its head and neck once more. These aggressive, defensive movements of cobras are slower than those of pit vipers. (For treatment of poisonous snakebite, see SNAKE.)

Many lizards, regardless of family and size, bite in defense.

The largest of the geckos, *Gekko gecko* of Southeast Asia, an animal 10 to 14 in. long, will bite with a bulldoglike grip if sufficiently threatened. Although small lizards have a bite effective against only the smallest predators, a large monitor lizard (*Varanus*) can inflict a painful wound with its large teeth and strong jaws. Some turtles, particularly the soft-shelled turtles (*Trionyx*), bite frequently, vigorously, and effectively.

7. Spitting.—The spitting of venom by certain African cobras, the ringhals (*Hemachatus haemachatus*) and the black-necked cobra (*Naja nigricollis*), is a purely defensive act directed against large enemies. A fine stream of venom is forced out of each fang, which, instead of having a straight canal ending in a long opening near the tip as in most cobras, has a canal that turns sharply forward to a small round opening on the front surface well away from the tip. At the moment of ejection the mouth is opened slightly, and venom is forced out of the fangs by contraction of the muscle enveloping the poison gland. At least one observer noted that a cobra hissed sharply each time it spat, suggesting that part of the propulsion of the venom comes from air forced out of the lung by the body musculature. Usually a spitting cobra raises its head and fore part of its body in the characteristic cobra defensive posture prior to spitting, but venom can be ejected from any position. The venom is aimed high and usually strikes the victim in the face. The effect on the skin is negligible. The eyes, however, may be severely damaged, and blindness can result unless the venom is washed out quickly. One explanation of the function and evolution of spitting holds that the large herbivores of Africa form a group of enemies because of their weight and sharp hooves and that it has been advantageous to these cobras to be able to warn off these herbivores at a distance (up to six feet). A similar explanation has been suggested for the evolution of the rattle of rattlesnakes.

8. Use of Tails.—A few lizards, representing different families, have in common thick tails covered by large, hard, spiny scales. Such a tail swung vigorously from side to side is an effective defense against snakes, especially when the head and body of the lizard are in a burrow or wedged between rocks.

Lizards' tails are useful in defense in another way. When captured, many lizards voluntarily shed their tails, which wriggle violently, temporarily confusing the predator and allowing the lizard to escape. Each vertebra of the tails of lizards having this capacity has a fracture line and can be split on that line when tail muscles contract violently. Simultaneous stimulation of the nerves in the severed portion keeps it twitching for a few seconds after separation. Usually the tail is broken in only one place, but a few lizards, particularly the so-called glass snakes (*Ophisaurus*), break their tails into several pieces. The stump heals quickly and a new tail is grown, though often not so long as it was originally and often with simpler scales.

Snakes, turtles, and crocodiles may have their tails bitten off by predators, but they cannot break them voluntarily or regenerate them. Some snakes use their tails in diversionary tactics by raising them and moving them slowly. Species with this habit commonly have thick, blunt, brightly coloured (often red) tails as, for example, that of the Oriental pipe snake, *Cylindrophis*. The movement and form of the tail may be said to mimic the head and thus confuse an enemy. However questionable that suggestion may be, a moving part of the body attracts more attention than an immobile part, and the predator's attention is probably drawn from the head to the less vital tail. The small African python *Calabaria* and the Oriental venomous snake *Maticora* wave their tails in the air as they move slowly away from a threat.

9. Balling.—Many snakes, harmless (*e.g.*, the North American ring-necked snakes and the African *Calabaria*) or venomous (*e.g.*, the coral snakes, *Micrurus*, and the Oriental *Maticora*), attempt to hide their heads under coils of their bodies. The body may be coiled loosely, as it is in most species with this habit, or tightly so that it forms a compact ball with the head in the centre. Balling, as the latter habit is called, is a characteristic response of *Calabaria* and another African python, *Python regius*.

The African armadillo lizard (*Cordylus cataphractus*), a species having heavy scales on its head and hard spiny scales covering its body and tail, rolls on its back and grasps its tail in its mouth. It thus presents a ring of hard spines to a would-be predator.

10. Odours.—Some reptiles use musk-secreting glands when other defensive measures fail. The water snakes (*Natrix*), the garter snakes (*Thamnophis*), the alligator lizards (*Gerrhonotus*), and the musk turtles (*Sternotherus*) emit a foul-smelling substance from anal glands.

11. Combining Elements.—All of the defensive tactics mentioned so far must be considered a series of responses, not all of which are elicited at once or during the course of each instance of danger. Not all species have the same set of tactics, but each usually has more than one response. Which tactic is used depends on the imminence of danger; enemies evoke one response when at a distance, another when they are close. The change from one response to another as the intensity of the threat increases is illustrated by the behaviour of the North American hognose snakes. If approached by a man, a hognose snake spreads its head (by spreading the hinges of its jaws) and neck and flattens its body. If the man comes closer, the snake hisses and strikes, but does not bite. Should the man tap the snake with a stick or his foot, the snake goes through a series of writhing convulsions, finally rolling over on its back as though dead, with its tongue hanging limply out of its mouth. The performance can be interrupted at any point by the removal of the threat, but as long as the danger appears to increase, each successive response is evoked.

Many reptiles also exhibit passive defenses, among which camouflage involving form and colour is common. Many arboreal snakes and lizards (*e.g.*, chameleons) are green; some of the green snakes (*e.g.*, the vine snakes of South America, *Oxybelis*, and of southern Asia, *Dryophis*) are excessively slender, resembling plants common in their habitat. Lizards of semiarid and rocky country frequently are pale in colour and blotched in pebble fashion, *e.g.*, the leopard lizard (*Crotaphytus wislizeni*) of southwestern United States.

Mimicry of dangerous species by harmless snakes is another passive defense, but one whose validity is challenged by some biologists. The venomous coral snakes (*Micrurus*) of the Western Hemisphere are ringed with bright red, yellow, and black. A series of relatively harmless snakes, such as *Erythrolamprus* and *Anilius* of South America and the scarlet king snake, *Lampropeltis doliata*, of southeastern United States, have similar colours and patterns that may confer some protection against predators.

III. FORM AND FUNCTION
A. Diet and Feeding Mechanisms

1. Diet.—With few exceptions, modern reptiles feed on some form of animal life: insects, mollusks, birds, frogs, mammals, fishes, or other reptiles. Land tortoises are vegetarians, eating leaves, grass, and in some cases even cactus. The big green iguana (*Iguana iguana*) of Central and South America, its relative the chuckwalla (*Sauromalus obesus*) of southwestern United States and northern Mexico, and the spiny-tailed agamids (*Uromastix*) of North Africa and southwestern Asia are examples of the few herbivorous lizards. The marine iguana (*Amblyrhynchus cristatus*) of the Galápagos Islands dives into the sea to pull up its seaweed food.

The majority of carnivorous reptiles have nonspecialized diets, feeding on a variety of animals. Small- to medium-sized lizards (*e.g.*, the eastern fence lizard, *Sceloporus undulatus*, of the United States and the sand lizard, *Lacerta agilis*, of England and Europe) usually eat many kinds of insects, spiders, snails, and other invertebrates. The common water snake (*Natrix sipedon*) of the United States feeds on fishes, tadpoles, frogs, salamanders, and crayfish; the coachwhip snake (*Masticophis flagellum*) feeds on rodents, birds, lizards, and snakes. Aquatic carnivorous turtles usually eat snails, earthworms, crayfish, frogs, and fishes. Crocodiles prey on fishes, frogs, turtles, birds, mammals, and even insects.

In general the smaller the reptile, the smaller its prey. This principle operates not only in comparing different species, but also within species. Newly hatched alligators feed almost exclusively on insects and only begin to prey on small vertebrates such as frogs and small fishes as they grow larger. Wading birds, turtles, muskrats, raccoons, and other mammals are attacked by older alligators. Similarly young coachwhip snakes at first eat insects and, as they grow, eat small vertebrates.

Only the very largest of living snakes—the reticulated python (*Python reticulatus*), the Indian python (*P. molurus*), and the anaconda (*Eunectes murinus*)—are capable of eating large mammals such as small pigs and deer. Among crocodiles it is the largest species—the Nile crocodile (*Crocodylus niloticus*), the East Indian saltwater crocodile (*C. porosus*), and the Orinoco crocodile (*C. intermedius*)—that are known to attack and eat men. Presumably even larger prey was devoured by the great carnivorous dinosaurs such as *Allosaurus* and *Tyrannosaurus,* which were almost certainly capable of killing the largest of their herbivorous contemporaries.

Some carnivorous reptiles specialize on one or a few types of food. The gavial (*Gavialis gangeticus*) of India, a narrow-snouted crocodilian, feeds largely on fishes caught by quick sidewise sweeps of its head. The elongate, narrow snout encounters relatively little resistance in water, permitting the rapid movements necessary to catch such agile prey. By contrast the relatively broad snouts of other crocodilians prohibit the same kind of mobility because of the resistance they generate in water.

Other carnivorous reptiles have acquired the habit of eating mollusks. The cayman lizard (*Dracaena*) of northern South America, a snail feeder, has broad, flat-crowned rear teeth for cracking hard shells. This specialization was carried to an extreme by the extinct *Placodus*, which had teeth so broad that they reached halfway across the palate.

2. Dentition.—The dentition of most reptiles shows little specialization along the tooth row. A division into distinctive bladelike incisors, tusklike canines, and flat-crowned molars, such as characterize mammals, does not occur in reptiles. Instead the entire tooth row usually consists of long conical teeth, whether snakes, crocodilians, or dinosaurs are involved or whether the reptile eats reptiles, birds, or mammals. Venomous snakes have one or several hollow or grooved fangs, but these teeth have the same shape as most snake teeth. The principal differences between species lie in the number, length, and position of the teeth. Mammalian teeth are restricted to one row in the upper jaw and one in the lower. Crocodilians among the living forms and dinosaurs among the extinct forms have but a single upper and a single lower tooth row. Snakes and many extinct reptilian groups have teeth on the palatal bones (vomer, palatine, pterygoid) and on the bones of the upper jaw (premaxilla, maxilla); only one row of teeth is present on the lower jaw.

Lizards have conical or bladelike bicuspid or tricuspid teeth. Some species have conical teeth at the front of the jaws and cusped teeth toward the rear, but the latter are not comparable to the molars of mammals in either form (they are not flat-crowned) or function (they do not grind the food). Turtles, except for the earliest extinct species, lack teeth, and have instead two horny plates, an upper and a lower, that serve to bite off chunks of food. The teeth of reptiles, less specialized in form than mammalian teeth, are also less specialized in

function. A mammal with the typical mammalian tooth row can tear or bite off pieces of food (the incisors at the front), cut it up into smaller pieces (the premolars), and finally grind it up (the molars at the rear) before swallowing. The larger carnivorous reptiles (*e.g.,* crocodilians and certain dinosaurs) are equipped only to tear off or bite off large pieces of their prey and to bolt them without chewing. Insectivorous lizards (the majority of lizards) usually crack the exoskeleton of their insect prey, which are then swallowed without being ground up. Snakes simply swallow their prey whole without any mechanical reduction.

3. Skull and Joint Structures.—Many reptiles developed joints (in addition to the hinge for the lower jaw) within the skull, permitting at least slight movement of one part relative to others. The capacity for such movement within the skull is called kinesis and enables an animal to increase the gape of the mouth. It is thus an adaptation for swallowing large objects. Apparently some of the large carnivorous theropod dinosaurs (*e.g., Allosaurus*) had a joint between the frontal and parietal bones on the roof of the skull. All reptiles of the subclass Lepidosauria (lizards, snakes, rhynchocephalians, and the extinct eosuchians) have had kinetic skulls, but they differ from the dinosaurs in having the joint on the floor of the skull at the juncture of basisphenoid and pterygoid bones (fig. 5).

The skulls of the lepidosaurians became increasingly kinetic as new groups evolved. The Rhynchocephalia (which include the living tuatara) and their antecedents, the Eosuchia, had only the basisphenoidal-pterygoidal joint. The lizards lost the lower temporal bar, thereby freeing the quadrate bone and allowing greater movement to the lower jaw, which is hinged to the quadrate. Finally, in the snakes this trend culminates in the most kinetic skull among the vertebrates—a skull having the ancestral basisphenoidal-pterygoidal joint, a highly mobile quadrate (which gives even greater mobility to the lower jaw), upper jaws capable

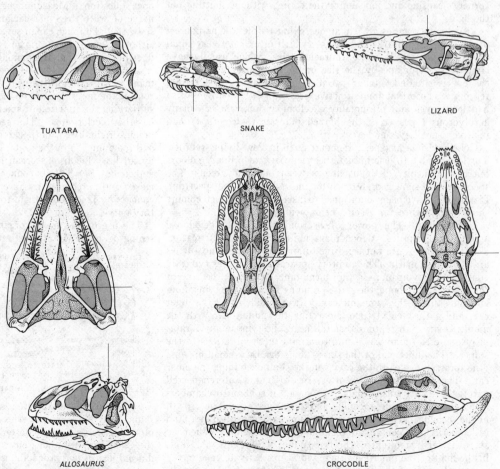

FIG. 5.—COMPARISON OF REPTILIAN SKULLS SHOWING POSITIONS (ARROWS) OF JOINTS OTHER THAN THOSE BETWEEN UPPER AND LOWER JAWS. THE TWO UPPER ROWS (LATERAL AND VENTRAL VIEWS) ARE OF LEPIDOSAURIAN REPTILES, THE BOTTOM ROW, OF ARCHOSAURS. THE CROCODILE SKULL HAS ONLY THE JOINT BETWEEN THE JAWS

of rotating on their longitudinal axes and of moving forward and backward, and often a hinge on the roof of the skull between the nasal and frontal bones that allows the snout to be raised slightly. In short, the only part of a snake's skull incapable of movement is the brain case.

B. Sense Organs

The sense organs of reptiles, as of most vertebrates, comprise organs for the detection and analysis of light, chemicals, and sound waves. Not all sense organs are equally developed in all reptiles; some species or groups of species rely heavily on sight, others on smell, and others on a combination. Some sense organs operate at a distance (e.g., the eyes), others at very close range only (e.g., taste buds).

1. Sight.—In general construction the eyes of reptiles are like those of other vertebrates. Accommodation for near vision in all living reptiles except snakes is accomplished by pressure being exerted on the lens by the surrounding muscular ring (ciliary body), which thus makes the lens more spherical. In snakes the same end is achieved by the lens being brought forward under pressure built up on the vitreous humour by contractions of muscles at the base of the iris. The pupil shape varies remarkably among living reptiles, from the round opening characteristic of all turtles and many diurnal lizards and snakes to the vertical slit of crocodilians and nocturnal snakes and the horizontal slits of a few tree snakes. Undoubtedly the most bizarre pupil shape is that of some geckos, in which the pupil contracts to form a series of pin holes, one above the other. The lower eyelid has the greater range of movement in most reptiles. In crocodilians the upper lid is more mobile. Snakes have no movable eyelids, their eyes being covered by a fixed transparent scale. The tuatara and all crocodilians have a third eyelid, the nictitating membrane, a transparent sheet that moves sideways across the eye from the inner corner, cleansing and moistening the cornea without shutting out the light.

Visual acuity varies greatly among living reptiles, being poorest in the burrowing lizards and snakes (which often have very small eyes) and greatest in active diurnal species (which usually have large eyes). Judging by the size of the skull opening in which the eye is situated, similar variation existed among the extinct reptiles. Those that hunted active prey (e.g., the ichthyosaurs) had large eyes and presumably excellent vision, whereas many herbivorous types (e.g., the horned dinosaur Triceratops) had relatively small eyes and weak vision.

Colour vision has been demonstrated in few living reptiles. Turtles are able to discriminate between pairs of primary colours but have difficulty distinguishing between blue and green. The species tested show a preference for the red end of the spectrum. Lizards that have been conditioned to discriminate between colours show a preference for green when given a choice.

2. Hearing.—The power of hearing is variously developed among living reptiles. Crocodilians and most lizards hear reasonably well, snakes are not sensitive to airborne waves, and turtles are a question mark. The auditory apparatus in reptiles typically consists of a tympanum, a thin membrane located at the rear of the head; a small bone, the stapes, running between the tympanum and the skull in the tympanic cavity (the middle ear); the inner ear; and a Eustachian tube connecting the middle ear with the mouth cavity. In reptiles that can hear, the tympanum vibrates in response to sound waves and transmits those vibrations to the stapes. The inner end of the stapes abuts against a small opening (the foramen ovale) to the cavity in the skull containing the inner ear. The inner ear consists of a series of hollow interconnected parts: the semicircular canals, the ovoidal or spheroidal chambers called the utriculus and sacculus, and the lagena, a small outgrowth of the sacculus. These tubes of the inner ear, suspended in a fluid called perilymph, contain another fluid, the endolymph. When the stapes is set in motion by the tympanum, it develops vibrations in the fluid of the inner ear; these vibrations activate cells in the lagena, the seat of the sense of hearing. The semicircular canals, as in all vertebrates, are concerned with equilibrium.

Most lizards can hear, though details of the acuity of hearing

are largely unknown. The majority have a tympanum, tympanic cavity, and Eustachian tube. The tympanum, usually exposed at the surface of the head or at the end of a short open tube, may be covered by scales or may be absent. In general the last two conditions are characteristic of lizards that lead a more or less completely subterranean life and presumably do not hear airborne sounds. The middle ear of these burrowers is usually degenerate as well, often lacking the tympanic cavity and Eustachian tube.

Snakes have neither tympanum nor Eustachian tube, and the stapes is attached to the quadrate bone on which the lower jaw swings. It is unlikely that snakes can hear airborne sounds, although they are obviously sensitive to vibrations in the ground. A loud sound above a snake does not elicit any response provided the object making the sound does not move or provided its movements are not seen by the snake. On the other hand, the same snake will raise its head slightly and flick its tongue in and out rapidly if the ground behind it is tapped or scratched. Snakes undoubtedly "hear" these vibrations by means of bone conduction. Sound waves travel more rapidly and strongly in solids than in the air and are probably transmitted to the inner ear of snakes through the lower jaw, which is normally touching the ground, thence to the quadrate bone, and finally to the stapes. Burrowing lizards presumably hear ground vibrations in the same way.

Crocodilians, all of which have an external ear consisting of a short tube closed by a strong valvular flap and ending at the tympanum, have rather keen hearing. The American alligator (Alligator mississipiensis) can hear sounds within a range of 50–4,000 cycles per second. Hearing of crocodilians is involved not only in detection of prey and enemies but also in their social behaviour, for males roar or bellow either to threaten other males or to attract females.

Although turtles have well-developed middle ears and usually large tympanums, their ability to hear airborne sounds is still an open question. Measurements of the impulses of the auditory nerve between the inner ear and the auditory centre of the brain show that the inner ear in several species of turtles is sensitive to airborne sounds in the range 50–2,000 cycles per second, but this does not prove that the animals are aware of the sounds.

3. Chemoreception.—Chemical-sensitive organs, used by many reptiles to find their prey, are located in the nose and in the roof of the mouth. Part of the lining of the nose consists of cells subserving the function of smell and corresponding to similar cells in other vertebrates. The second chemoreceptor is Jacobson's organ, originally an outpocketing of the nasal sac in amphibians and remaining so in the tuatara and crocodilians. It has been lost by turtles. Jacobson's organ (fig. 6) is best developed in lizards and snakes, in which its connection with the nasal cavity has been closed and is replaced by an opening into the mouth. The nerve connecting Jacobson's organ to the brain is a branch of the olfactory nerve.

The use of Jacobson's organ is most obvious in snakes. If a strong odour or vibration stimulates a snake, its tongue is flicked in and out rapidly. Each time it is retracted the forked tip touches the opening of Jacobson's organ in the roof of the mouth, transmitting any chemical fragments adhering to the tongue. In effect, Jacobson's organ is a supplement to taste and is a short-range chemical receptor, as contrasted to the long-range testing of the true sense of smell located in the nasal tube.

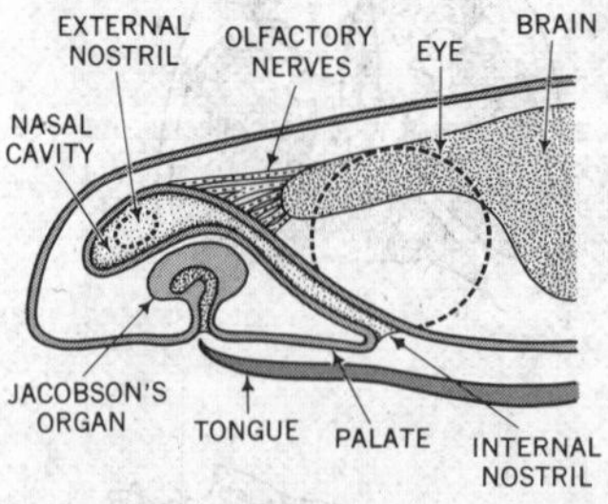

FIG. 6.—SECTION OF A SNAKE HEAD

Some snakes (notably the large vipers) and lizards (especially skinks and burrowing species of other families) rely upon the olfactory tissue and Jacobson's organ to locate food, almost to the exclusion of other senses. Other reptiles, such as certain diurnal lizards and crocodilians, appear not to use scent in searching for prey, though they may use their sense of smell for locating a mate.

Some snakes, notably pit vipers (rattlesnakes, etc.), boas, and pythons, have special heat-sensitive organs on their heads as part of their food-detecting apparatus. Just below and behind the nostril of a pit viper is the pit that gives the group its common name. The lip scales of many pythons and boas have depressions (labial pits) that are analogous to the viper's pit. The labial pits of pythons and boas are lined with skin thinner than that covering the rest of the head and supplied with dense networks of blood capillaries and nerve fibres. The facial pit of the viper is relatively deeper than the boa's labial pits and consists of two chambers separated by a thin membrane bearing a rich supply of fine blood vessels and nerves. In experiments using warm and cold covered electric light bulbs, pit vipers and pitted boas have been able to detect temperature differences of less than 1° F (0.6° C).

Since many pit vipers, pythons, and boas are nocturnal and feed largely on mammals and birds, the facial sense organs enable them to direct their strikes accurately in the dark, once their warmblooded prey arrives within range. The approach of the prey to that point is probably detected by the chemical receptors—either the nose, or Jacobson's organ, or both.

C. Internal Systems

1. Skeletal System.—The skeleton of reptiles fits the general pattern of that of all vertebrate animals. They have a bony skull, a long vertebral column that encloses the spinal nerve cord, ribs that form a bony basket around the viscera, and a framework of limbs.

Each group of reptiles developed its own particular variations on this major pattern in accord with the general adaptive trends of the group. Snakes, for example, have lost the limb bones, though a few retain vestiges of the hind limb. The limbs of several types of marine reptiles became modified into fins or flippers with obvious functional significance. In these groups, *e.g.*, the extinct ichthyosaurs and plesiosaurs, the bones of the limbs, no longer supporting the weight of the body against the pull of gravity, became much shortened. At the same time the bones that in other reptiles composed the digits multiplied in number forming a long flipper.

Groups of reptiles whose modes of life came to depend heavily on passive defense also developed specializations of the skeleton. The bony and horny shell of turtles and rows of bony plates on the back of ankylosaurs (Cretaceous dinosaurs) are cases in point.

The skulls of the several subclasses and orders vary in the ways mentioned below (see *Classification and Survey*, below). In addition to differences in openings on the side of the skull and in general shape and size, the most significant variations in reptilian skulls are those affecting movements within the skull, as mentioned above.

Reptilian skulls as a group differ from those of early amphibians, the vertebrates from which reptiles arose, in lacking an otic notch (an indentation at the rear of the skull) and several small bones at the rear of the skull roof. The skulls of modern reptiles are sharply set off from those of mammals in many ways, but the clearest differences are in the lower jaw and adjacent regions. Reptiles have a number of bones in the lower jaw, only one of which, the dentary, bears teeth. Behind the dentary a small bone, the articular, forms a joint with the quadrate bone near the rear of the skull. In mammals the lower jaw consists of a single bone, the dentary, and the articular and quadrate have become part of the chain of little bones in the middle ear. An almost complete transition between these two very different arrangements is known from fossils of mammallike reptiles (order Therapsida).

2. Nervous System.—As in all vertebrates, the nervous system of reptiles consists of a brain, a spinal nerve cord, nerves running from the brain or spinal cord, and sense organs. Reptiles have small brains compared to mammals. The most important difference between the brains of these two vertebrate groups lies in the size of the cerebral hemispheres, the principal associative centres of the brain. In mammals these hemispheres make up the bulk of the brain and, when viewed from above, almost hide the rest of the brain. In reptiles the relative and absolute size of the cerebral hemispheres is much smaller. The brain of snakes

and alligators forms less than $\frac{1}{1,500}$ of the total body weight, whereas in mammals such as squirrels and cats, the brain accounts for about $\frac{1}{100}$ of the body weight. The differences are functionally related to the much feebler mental capacities of reptiles as compared to mammals.

The extent of variation in relative brain size in reptiles and its association with mode of life has not been studied intensively, but some notion of the variation can be obtained from the fact that a stegosaur (Stegosauria), roughly the size of an elephant, had a brain case no larger than that of an eight-foot crocodile, about large enough to contain a brain the size of a big walnut.

3. Circulatory System.—Modern reptiles do not have the capacity for rapid sustained activity found in birds and mammals. It is the general notion that this lower capacity is related to dif-

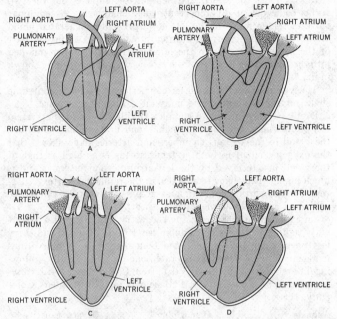

FIG. 7.—(A) LIZARD HEART; (B) SNAKE HEART; (C) CROCODILE HEART (IN EACH, STIPPLING INDICATES ENTRANCE AND EXIT OF NONAERATED BLOOD); (D) TURTLE HEART (HEAVY STIPPLING INDICATES ENTRANCE AND EXIT OF NONAERATED BLOOD; LIGHT STIPPLING INDICATES MIXED BLOOD)

ferences in the circulatory and respiratory systems. Before the origin of lungs, the vertebrate circulatory system had a single circuit: at the fish level blood flows from heart to gills, to the body, and then back to the heart. At that stage the heart consists of four chambers arranged in a linear sequence.

With the evolution of lungs in amphibians, a new and apparently more efficient circulatory system evolved. Two chambers of the heart, the atrium (or auricle) and ventricle, became increasingly important, and the beginnings of a double circulation appeared. An early stage in this evolution can be seen in amphibians today, where one of the main arteries from the heart (the pulmonary artery) goes directly to the lungs, whereas the others (the systemic arteries) carry blood to the general body. The blood is aerated in the lungs and carried back to the atrium of the heart. From the left side of the atrium, which is at least partially divided for the first time, the aerated blood is pumped into the ventricle and there mixes with the nonaerated blood from the body that was returned to the heart via the right half of the atrium. Then the cycle begins again. One of the features of the amphibian system is that the blood leaving the heart for the body is only partially aerated; part of it is the deoxygenated blood returned from the body.

As all groups of modern reptiles have a completely divided atrium (fig. 7), it is safe to assume that this was true of most, if not all, extinct reptiles. In reptiles, the ventricle for the first time becomes at least partially divided, though in various fashions in the four major living groups.

When the two atria of a lizard's heart contract, the two streams of blood (aerated blood from the lungs in the left atrium and nonaerated blood from the body in the right atrium) flow into the left chamber of the ventricle. As pressure builds up in that chamber, the nonaerated blood is forced through the gap in the partition into the right chamber of the ventricle. Then when the ventricle contracts, nonaerated blood is pumped into the pulmonary artery and thence to the lungs, while aerated blood is pumped into the systemic arteries (the aortas) and so to the body.

In snakes all three arterial trunks come out of one chamber of the ventricle, the one receiving the nonaerated blood of the right atrium. During ventricular contraction a muscular ridge forms a partition that guides the nonaerated blood into the pulmonary artery, while the aerated blood received by the other chamber of the ventricle is forced through the opening in the ventricular septum and out through the aortas.

In crocodiles the ventricular septum is complete, but the two aortas come out of different ventricular chambers. A semilunar valve at the entrance to the left aorta prevents nonaerated blood in the right ventricle from flowing into the aorta. Instead part of the aerated blood from the left ventricular chamber pumped into the right aorta flows into the left by way of an opening shown in fig. 7C.

The ventricle of the turtle is not perfectly divided, and some slight mixing of aerated and nonaerated blood takes place.

Despite the peculiar and complex circulation, a double system has been achieved by lizards, snakes, and crocodilians. Tests of the blood in the various chambers and arteries have shown that the oxygen content in both systemic aortas is as high as that of the blood just received by the left atrium from the lungs and is much higher than that of the blood in the pulmonary artery. Except for the turtles, limitation of activity in reptiles cannot be explained on the basis of imperfect heart circulation.

An explanation may lie in the chemistry of the blood. Apparently reptiles have less hemoglobin per 100 cc. of blood and carry less oxygen per 100 cc. of blood than mammals. Observations made on a few species of Temperate Zone reptiles show the following differences from mammals (data from C. L. Prosser [ed.], *Comparative Animal Physiology*, Philadelphia, W. B. Saunders Company, 1950).

Animals	Hemoglobin (per 100 cc. of blood)	Oxygen capacity (% by volume)
Reptiles	6–11 gm.	7–15
Mammals	11–17 gm.	16–29

4. Respiratory System.—The form of lungs and the methods of irrigating them may also influence activity by affecting the efficiency of respiration. In snakes the lungs are simple saclike structures having small pockets, or alveoli, in the walls. The lungs of many lizards and turtles and of all crocodilians have the surface area increased by the development of partitions that in turn have alveoli. As exchange of respiratory gases takes place across surfaces, an increase of the ratio of surface area to volume leads to an increase in respiratory efficiency. In this regard the lungs of snakes are not so effective as those of crocodilians. But the elaboration of the internal surface of lungs in reptiles is simple compared to that reached by mammalian lungs with their enormous number of very fine alveoli.

Most reptiles breathe by changing the volume of the body cavity. By contractions of the muscles moving the ribs, the volume of the body cavity is increased, creating a negative pressure, which is restored to atmospheric level by air rushing into the lungs. By contraction of body muscles, the volume of the body cavity is reduced, forcing air out of the lungs.

This system applies to all modern reptiles (and presumably the extinct ones as well) except turtles, which, because of the fusion of the ribs with the rigid shell, are unable to breathe by this means, though they use the same mechanical principle of changing pressure in the body cavity. Contraction of two flank muscles enlarges the body cavity, causing inspiration. Contraction of two other muscles, coincident with relaxation of the first two, forces the viscera upward against the lungs, causing exhalation.

The rate of respiration, like so many of the physiological activities of reptiles, is highly variable, depending in part upon the temperature and in part upon the emotional state of the animal.

5. Digestive System.—The digestive system of modern reptiles is similar in general plan to that of all higher vertebrates. It includes the mouth and its salivary glands, esophagus, stomach, and intestine, ending in a cloaca. Of the few specializations of the reptilian digestive system, the evolution of one pair of salivary glands into poison glands in the venomous snakes is outstanding.

6. Urogenital System.—During development the embryos of higher vertebrates (reptiles, birds, and mammals) use three separate sets of kidneys consecutively. They are arranged in longitudinal sequence in the body cavity. The first set, the pronephroi, are vestigial organs left over from the evolutionary past that soon degenerate and disappear without having had any function. The second set, the mesonephroi, are the functional kidneys of adult amphibians, but their only contribution to the lives of reptiles is in providing the duct (the Wolffian duct) that forms a connection between the testis and the cloaca. The operational kidneys of reptiles, birds, and mammals are the last set, the metanephroi, which have separate ducts to the cloaca. The principal function of the kidney is the removal of nitrogenous wastes resulting from the oxidation of proteins. Vertebrates eliminate three kinds of nitrogenous wastes: ammonia, urea, and uric acid. Ammonia and urea are highly soluble in water; uric acid is not. Ammonia is highly poisonous, urea slightly so, and uric acid not at all. Among reptiles the form taken by the nitrogenous wastes is closely related to the habits and habitat of the animal. Aquatic reptiles tend to excrete a large proportion of these wastes as ammonia in solution. This method, involving a great loss of body water, is no problem for an alligator, which eliminates between 40 and 75% of its nitrogenous wastes as ammonia. Terrestrial reptiles, such as most snakes and lizards, must conserve body water and convert their nitrogenous wastes to insoluble, harmless uric acid, which forms a more or less solid mass in the cloaca. In snakes and lizards these wastes are eliminated from the cloaca together with wastes from the digestive system.

Prior to the evolution of the metanephric kidney, the products of the male gonad, the testis, traveled through the same duct with the nitrogenous wastes from the kidney. But with the appearance of the metanephros, the two systems became separated. The female reproductive system never shared a common tube with the kidney. Oviducts in all female vertebrates arise as separate tubes with openings usually near, but not connected to, the ovaries. The oviducts, like the Wolffian ducts of the testes, open into the cloaca. Ovaries and testes lie in the body cavity near the kidneys.

With the evolution of the reptilian egg, internal fertilization became necessary. All modern reptiles, with the exception of the tuatara, have copulatory organs. Though these structures vary from group to group, they all include erectile tissue as an important element of the operating mechanism, and they all are protruded through the cloacal opening during copulation. Unlike the penis of turtles and crocodilians, the copulatory organ of lizards and snakes is paired, each unit being called a hemipenis. The hemipenes of lizards and snakes (fig. 8) are elongate tubular structures lying in the tail.

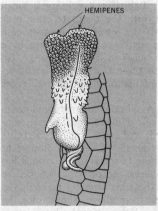

HEMIPENES

Whereas the penis of a crocodile or turtle is protruded through the cloacal opening wholly by means of a filling of blood spaces (sinuses) in the penis, protrusion of a lizard's or snake's hemipenis is begun by a pair of propulsor muscles. Completion of the erection is brought about by blood filling the sinuses in the erectile tissue. Only one hemipenis is inserted into a female, but which one is a matter of chance. Unlike the penis of mammals, the copulatory organs of reptiles do not transport sperm through a tube. The ducts from the testes, as already mentioned, empty into

FIG. 8.—UNDERSIDE OF SNAKE BODY SHOWING ERECTED HEMIPENES

Skeleton of a gaboon viper (*Bitis gabonica*), showing arrangement of vertebrae and ribs. The sharp fangs of this snake—which is poisonous—may be seen in the upper jaw

Spiny softshell turtle (*Trionyx* species) with its neck stretched out to bring its nostrils above the water. All reptiles are air breathing and have lungs

Bull snake (*Pituophis melanoleucus sayi*) with its forked tongue extended. The flicking of the tongue is a response to odour or vibration. When retracted, the tongue touches Jacobson's organ, a chemical receptor in the roof of the mouth

Close-up of the head of a sand skink (*Scincus philbyi*), showing the scaly epidermis characteristic of reptiles. The scales are composed of keratin, a hornlike tissue, which prevents drying of the skin, thus making it possible for reptiles to adapt themselves to nonaquatic life

Snapping turtle (*Chelydra serpentina*) eating a water snake (*Natrix* species). The great majority of reptiles are carnivorous, feeding on a variety of animal life

Two photos showing the egg-eating snake of Africa (*Dasypeltis scaber*) enjoying its favourite meal. The joints and hinging of the lower jaw in snakes make it possible for them to swallow objects much larger than themselves

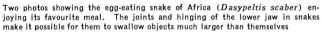

BODY STRUCTURE AND DIET OF REPTILES

BY COURTESY OF (TOP LEFT) AMERICAN MUSEUM OF NATURAL HISTORY, (CENTRE LEFT) ARABIAN AMERICAN OIL COMPANY, (BOTTOM, 2) NEW YORK ZOOLOGICAL SOCIETY; PHOTOGRAPHS, (TOP RIGHT) JOHN H. GERARD FROM NATIONAL AUDUBON SOCIETY, (SECOND RIGHT) JOHN H. GERARD, (THIRD RIGHT) LYNWOOD M. CHACE FROM NATIONAL AUDUBON SOCIETY

Small limbless reptiles, such as this wormlike lizard of the family Amphisbaenidae, move by pushing backward against a rock, twig or irregularity in the ground surface. Larger snakes move by stretching and contracting

Underside of a turtle (*Sternotherus* species), an underwater view showing the fleshy webbing between the toes, creating a paddlelike foot that the turtle uses in swimming

MEANS OF

LOCOMOTION

IN REPTILES

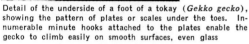

Detail of the underside of a foot of a tokay (*Gekko gecko*), showing the pattern of plates or scales under the toes. Innumerable minute hooks attached to the plates enable the gecko to climb easily on smooth surfaces, even glass

Series of three photographs showing the Arabian toad-headed agamid (*Phrynocephalus nejdensis*) burying itself in the sand, a maneuver it can accomplish quickly when frightened, by burrowing and vibrating its body

Restoration of an extinct *Iguanodon*, a Cretaceous dinosaur that walked on its hind legs, its body mass balanced by a long, thick tail. Some present-day lizards are also capable of bipedal locomotion, but only for short runs

Male green anole (*Anolis carolinensis*) with throat dewlap extended to entice female to mate. Some form of display or unusual movement is typical of reptilian courtship

Banded geckos (*Coleonyx variegatus*) mating. Internal fertilization is a major distinguishing characteristic between reptiles and amphibia

Box turtle (*Terrapene* species) laying eggs. Turtles and some crocodilians dig nests for the eggs, covering the nest and leaving it after laying is completed

Snapping turtle (*Chelydra serpentina*) hatching. Reptiles do not undergo metamorphosis; when they are born they are capable of all adult functions except reproduction

Five-lined skink (*Eumeces fasciatus*) with tail coiled around clutch of eggs. Parental care is rare among reptiles

COURTSHIP, MATING AND BIRTHS OF REPTILES

A clutch of black racer (*Coluber constrictor* subspecies) eggs hatching. Reptile clutches of eggs or broods of young vary in size from 1 to about 200, with a gestation period (for American and European species) from 2 to 3½ months

PHOTOGRAPHS, (TOP LEFT, TOP CENTRE) BERNARD GREENBERG, (TOP RIGHT, BOTTOM RIGHT) LYNWOOD M. CHACE FROM NATIONAL AUDUBON SOCIETY, (CENTRE RIGHT) HAL H. HARRISON FROM NATIONAL AUDUBON SOCIETY, (CENTRE LEFT) JACK DERMID FROM NATIONAL AUDUBON SOCIETY

PLATE IV　　　　　　　　REPTILE

Asiatic toad-headed agamid (*Phrynocephalus mystaceus*) in defense posture. The large, brightly-coloured flaps are attached to the corners of the mouth. When extended, as shown, the mouth appears much larger and wider and is thus more formidable to enemies

Australian lace monitor (*Varanus varius*), a large lizard (six feet long) with a heavy tail which can be an effective weapon when swung vigorously. The monitors also have strong jaws and large teeth

Diamondback rattlesnake (*Crotalus* species) showing the rattle which is used as a warning or threatening device. Other snakes employ noise, for example, hissing and spitting sounds, as a defense

Detail of the mouth and fangs of a water moccasin, or cottonmouth (*Agkistrodon* [*Ancistrodon*] *piscivorus*), a poisonous snake that injects its venom into its victims through a duct in the fangs

Reaction of a helmeted iguanid (*Corythophanes cristatus*) to a snake. The dewlap is extended and the body tensed to jump. This lizard will run on its hind legs when frightened

Head of an Australian thorny devil, or moloch (*Moloch horridus*), an example of passive defense through body form. Despite its appearance, the moloch is inoffensive

DEFENSE AND REACTION TO DANGER

Two male green anoles (*Anolis carolinensis*) preparing to fight. The one on the left is in a defensive position with the crest raised, dewlap extended, the dark spot behind the eye displayed and body widened and flattened

An Indian cobra (*Naja naja*) with its hood extended. Spreading or inflation of all or part of the body in defense is common among many types of reptiles

BY COURTESY OF (TOP RIGHT) AUSTRALIAN NEWS AND INFORMATION BUREAU, (SECOND LEFT) U.S. FISH & WILDLIFE SERVICE; PHOTOGRAPHS, (TOP LEFT) R. MERTENS, (SECOND RIGHT) HUGH SPENCER, (THIRD LEFT) D. DWIGHT DAVIS, (THIRD RIGHT) JOHN WARHAM, (BOTTOM LEFT) BERNARD GREENBERG, (BOTTOM RIGHT) YLLA—RAPHO GUILLUMETTE

the cloaca, and the sperm flow along a groove on the surface of the everted penis or hemipenis.

IV. REPRODUCTION AND DEVELOPMENT

1. Courtship.—Courtship in some form is such a widespread prelude to mating among modern reptiles that it must have characterized many extinct groups as well. The male of some freshwater turtles, such as the red-eared turtle (*Pseudemys scripta elegans*) of the eastern United States, when courting orients himself in the water so that he is directly in front of the female and facing her. With his forefeet close together, the male vibrates his claws against her head (this display may vary with individuals). If the female is receptive, she swims forward slowly while the male backs away. Finally the female sinks slowly down. The male then mounts her from behind, clutching her shell with all four feet. His tail is brought under hers and his penis introduced into her cloaca.

The male of some terrestrial turtles, *e.g.*, the gopher tortoises (*Gopherus*) of North America, begins courtship by extending his neck and bobbing his head up and down. The courted female may bob her head in return. The male advances and nips at the female's shell, head, and neck and then circles her as she turns away from him. As soon as the female shows signs of response, the male mounts her shell from the rear and begins a series of pumping movements that bump the rear of his shell against the ground. Finally the female extends her tail, the male moves his tail into position, and copulation begins.

Males of the smaller box turtles (*Terrapene*) also nip at the female's shell, head, and neck, and, in addition, butt against her shell. After mounting the female and clasping her shell with his rear claws, the male leans backward off her shell in order to bring his tail under hers.

Male crocodilians bellow during the mating season, but it is not known whether this sound attracts receptive females or warns other males. The American alligator, which copulates in water, grasps the female's neck with his jaws and slips the end of his body under hers to enable him to insert his penis into her cloaca. Observations on courtship and copulation of other crocodilians are almost nonexistent.

Lizards have rather elaborate courtship patterns usually involving display and posturing by the males, who often have distinctive patches of colour on their throats or low on their sides. The male bobs up and down within sight of a female by bending and straightening his legs; the bobbing usually exposes the patches of colour, which may be blue, orange, red, or black depending on the species. Males of some species, such as the green anole (*Anolis carolinensis*) of southeastern United States, have throat dewlaps that are expanded during courtship, exposing brightly coloured skin. If the female seems receptive, the male approaches and straddles her back, often gripping her back or legs with his jaws. Just before copulation his tail is bent under hers.

The courtship patterns of snakes are simpler and usually consist of the male's crawling over the back of the female and often adopting every curve her body takes. In some types, for example the water snakes, the male rubs his chin against the female's back, whereas in other species, for example, the rattlesnakes (*Crotalus*), the male frequently nudges the female with his head. Male bull snakes (*Pituophis*) grasp the female's neck with their jaws during copulation.

When the male of a king cobra (*Ophiophagus hannah*) crawls on the back of a receptive female, he flicks his tongue against her repeatedly, with his head raised a few inches above her. During this procedure the female holds her head and neck off the ground and spreads her hood. The male nudges her neck and head with his snout and finally lifts the rear of her body with his tail. Up to this point the courting pair crawl slowly forward but cease to move when the male inserts his hemipenis into the female's cloaca. The duration of copulation in one pair of captive king cobras varied from 57 to 66 min. In other snakes it has been known to last more than two hours.

2. Methods of Reproduction.—The typical reptilian mode of reproduction is oviparous—the eggs are laid shortly after fertiliza-

tion, and development of the embryos takes place largely after the eggs have been laid. This pattern characterizes crocodilians, turtles, the tuatara, most lizards and snakes, and many extinct reptiles. Fossil dinosaur eggs have been found in various parts of the world. The eggs may be deposited in a nest prepared by the female or simply laid under some convenient cover such as a rock or log.

Turtles and crocodilians invariably prepare a nest, and invariably it is the female that does the work. All turtles dig nests, scooping out a flask-shaped cavity in the ground with their hind feet. When the hole has reached the proper size, the spherical eggs, 1–1½ in. in diameter depending on the species, drop into the nest from the female's cloaca. The female scratches soil over the eggs, usually obliterating the nest site. Crocodilians either dig a nest along the bank of a river or lake, or heap together a mass of dead vegetation in which the eggs are laid. The oval eggs are usually about 2 in. long.

Most oviparous lizards merely hide their eggs under some convenient cover—under a rock, in a tree hole, or, in the case of certain house geckos, behind picture frames. A few tropical forms, *e.g.*, the tegu (*Tupinambis*) of South America, lay their eggs in termite nests. Nest construction among lizards, though appearing in such diverse families as the iguanids, skinks, and true chameleons, is not so elaborate or so rigid in pattern as among turtles. The nest consists of a small hole made by the snout or by the limbs. Soil or leaves usually are pushed on top of the eggs to hide the nest, although the entrance to the nest cavity is kept open in a few species. Snakes, like lizards, usually lay their eggs under natural, preexisting cover. The king cobra, one of the very few nest-building snakes, drags dead vegetation into a low heap by a bend in its body. The eggs are laid in a cavity at the centre. Other snakes deposit their eggs in holes they have scooped out of sand or soft earth with their snouts.

The size of eggs laid by lizards and snakes varies according to the size reached by females. The eggs of the 3- or 4-in. banded rock lizard (*Uta mearnsi*) of the western United States are about $\frac{2}{3}$ in. long, those of the 1- to 2-ft. ringneck snake (*Diadophis punctatus*) from the eastern United States are $\frac{1}{2}$ in. long. Eggs of the 10-ft. Komodo dragon lizard (*Varanus komodoensis*) and of the 20-ft. Indian python (*Python molurus*) are about $4\frac{1}{2}$ in. long.

A minority of modern and extinct reptiles are (and were) live-bearing, or viviparous. Strictly speaking, most of this minority are not truly viviparous, but ovoviviparous, because the embryos develop with their shells or shell membranes intact and are nourished wholly by the yolk. In a few modern reptiles the embryonic membranes and the tissues lining the oviducts of the females come into close contact and are modified in one of several ways to provide a temporary organ though which food and respiratory gases are exchanged. In the simplest reptilian "placenta," the most superficial layer (the epithelium) of the outer embryonic membrane and of the lining of the oviduct partially degenerates, thereby bringing the blood vessels of embryo and mother closer together. The approximation of the two bloodstreams facilitates the exchange of oxygen and carbon dioxide, this gas exchange being the only function of the organ at this stage of evolution. Several Australian snakes (*Denisonia superba* and *D. suta*) and a number of lizards—the common East Indian brown-sided skink (*Mabuya multifasciata*), the cylindrical skink (*Chalcides ocellatus*) of southern Europe and North Africa, and the Australian blue-tongued skink (*Tiliqua scincoides*), as examples—are known to have this type of organ, and presumably many ovoviviparous reptiles do.

The best-developed reptilian "placentas" consist of apposed, thickened, folded elliptical areas of the outer embryonic membrane and lining of the oviduct. The ridges of the oviductal areas are filled with blood vessels, and the epithelium between ridges is thickened and glandular. Usually eggs developing with this type of "placenta" have less yolk; food and oxygen are transmitted from mother to embryo. Several species of Australian lizards and the common European viper (*Vipera berus*) are known to provide this type of internal environment for their developing young.

The line between oviparity (egg laying) and ovoviviparity

(hatching eggs in the mother's body) is arbitrary. Females of some lizards and snakes retain the fertilized eggs in their bodies for a few days before laying them. Other species retain the eggs for most of the developmental period, hatching occurring shortly after laying. For the grass snake of England (*Natrix natrix*) the lapse of time between copulation and egg laying is usually two months; the young hatch six to ten weeks later. The interval between mating and egg laying is one month in the Texas horned lizard (*Phrynosoma cornutum*). Ovoviviparous species may be closely related to oviparous ones. For example, the horned lizards (*Phrynosoma*) of southwestern United States and Mexico are usually oviparous, but the species *P. douglassi* is ovoviviparous. The bunchgrass lizard (*Sceloporus scalaris*), an inhabitant of mountains in Arizona, is ovoviviparous, whereas most of its lowland relatives, such as the eastern fence lizard (*S. undulatus*), lay eggs.

As a final complication in this pattern, a given species may be ovoviviparous in parts of its range and oviparous elsewhere. A European lizard, *Lacerta vivipara*, living within the Arctic Circle, presumably would be unable to reproduce in the short cool summer if it laid eggs. The female by moving about the environment and remaining in the sunlight for long periods can maintain a sufficiently high body temperature to permit successful development of the embryos held within her body. In central Europe this lizard lives rather high in the mountains and retains its ovoviviparous habits in the cool climate. Farther south in the Pyrenees, where the sunlight is stronger and the summer longer, *L. vivipara* is oviparous.

Not all instances of ovoviviparity in reptiles are related to life in cooler climates. The water snakes of the southern United States and those of southern China live in similar climates, yet the American species are ovoviviparous and the Chinese species oviparous. The sea snake family, Hydrophidae, includes a group of ovoviviparous genera that never come ashore. A remarkable fossil discovery has confirmed that the extinct marine ichthyosaurs were also live-bearers. As reptilian eggs cannot develop successfully in water, a thoroughly marine reptile must either suffer through the awkwardness of coming ashore to lay its eggs, as do marine turtles, or become ovoviviparous. Live-bearing in the sea snakes and ichthyosaurs represents part of their general adaptation to a completely marine life.

3. Number of Offspring.—The number of eggs in a clutch or offspring in a brood varies from one to 200 among living reptiles; presumably similar variation occurred among the extinct types. Crocodilians lay from 20 to 70 eggs, turtles from one to 200. In turtles, more so than in crocodiles, the number varies with the species and roughly with the size attained by females of the particular species. The big marine turtles have the largest clutches (usually more than 100), the smaller land and freshwater turtles, much smaller ones. The number of eggs or young is not so closely related to the size of mature females in species of lizards and snakes. With few exceptions, lizards of the family Gekkonidae lay two eggs at a time regardless of the size of the female. Lizards of the family Scincidae have broods varying from 2 to about 30. One of the largest members of this latter family, the foot-long stump-tailed skink (*Tiliqua rugosa*) of Australia, has only two young at a time, whereas the Great Plains skink (*Eumeces obsoletus*) of the United States usually lays between 10 and 20 eggs in a clutch.

Clutch size in the five-foot bull snake (*Pituophis catenifer*) and coachwhip snake (*Masticophis flagellum*) of western United States is usually 10 or 12; in the two- to three-foot grass snake of England and Europe it is 30–40; in the giant reticulated python of Southeast Asia and the East Indies it may reach 100.

4. Parental Care.—Parental care of eggs and newborn young is not well developed or elaborated among reptiles. Female crocodilians generally remain in the vicinity of their nests and chase would-be predators from the site. In a few lizards, for example, the Great Plains skink, the female returns to the nest between feeding excursions to coil around the eggs and turn them at intervals. The male and female king cobra remain in the vicinity of the nest, and one of the parents usually is coiled above the egg cavity. Females of at least several species of pythons form nests of sorts by coiling around their eggs and thereby pulling them into a heap. They leave the eggs only to drink. Turtles and the great majority of egg-laying lizards and snakes abandon their eggs once they are laid.

5. Incubation Period.—The incubation (or gestation) period of reptilian eggs is affected by many factors to such an extent that it is difficult to assign a figure characteristic of a given species. One source of complication is the combining of oviparous and ovoviviparous habits by certain species. The eggs of the Great Plains skink or of the European grass snake may develop within the female's body for a month or more and then continue to develop for two months after laying. The fact that the female retains the eggs for varying lengths of time makes measurement of the incubation period uncertain and of doubtful significance. The eggs of wholly ovoviviparous species may be considered as incubating under special circumstances. To simplify this discussion the developmental period of the embryo, whether developing within the female's body or outside it, will be referred to as the gestation period.

In general, the gestation period lasts 60–105 days in most American and European reptiles. The eggs of the American alligator hatch about 63 days after laying, those of the small eastern fence lizards (*Sceloporus undulatus*) in about the same time. The gestation period in the common European viper lasts 60–90 days. Eggs of marine turtles hatch 30–75 days after they are laid, depending on the site.

The temperatures to which a brood is subjected will shorten or lengthen gestation according to whether the temperatures are high or low. During the course of long-range observation, the gestation period of the common garter snake (*Thamnophis sirtalis*) of the United States has varied from 87 days during the warmest year to 116 days during the coolest. Rattlesnakes in southern California have gestation periods varying from 140–295 days, depending on the species and the prevailing temperatures.

6. Growth.—Once hatched, reptiles normally grow at a much more rapid rate than is commonly supposed. Prevalent notions about the growth of reptiles are based on captive animals, which only rarely are provided the kind of environment and diet that will enable them to achieve their inherent growth rate. Giant Galapagos tortoises kept under nearly ideal conditions have been known to increase their weight from 7–13 lb. up to 179–183 lb. in nine years; shell length doubled in that period. Smaller species also grow rapidly, although the absolute magnitude of the change is of course much smaller. The box turtle of the United States has a shell about $1\frac{1}{2}$ in. long at the end of its first year; at the end of five years its length has doubled; growth is slower after that.

Under good conditions a one-year-old American alligator is about 2 ft. long and weighs about 4 lb. At the end of six years males average about 6 ft. and about 80 lb. In the following three years length will increase approximately $1\frac{1}{2}$–2 ft. and weight about 50 lb. The red diamond rattlesnake is about 12 in. long at birth, grows to about 26 in. in its first year, reaches about 34 in. by the end of its second year, and grows more slowly after that. The much smaller common garter snake is roughly $6\frac{3}{4}$ in. at birth, $14\frac{1}{2}$ in. at the end of its first year, 19 in. at the end of its third, and thereafter grows at a much diminished rate. The pattern for lizards is much the same: rapid growth early in life and slow growth afterward. The significant difference between growth in reptiles and that in mammals is that an individual reptile has the potential of growing throughout its life, whereas an individual mammal reaches a terminal size and does not grow any more, even though it subsequently lives many years in ideal conditions.

Because reptiles may continue to grow throughout their lives, the maximum size of any species is difficult to determine. As might be guessed, the maximum size of the largest snake or largest crocodile is considerably less than estimated by excitable and gullible travelers. Persistent but wholly unsubstantiated reports are heard of 40-ft. anacondas. This gigantic South American snake, granting it may be the largest living species, probably never exceeds 30 ft. The reticulated python of Southeast Asia and the East Indies has been recorded at 28 ft. and 250 lb. The rock python (*Python sebae*) of Africa reaches 25 ft. No other group of living snakes comes close to the pythons and boas in weight, although the king cobra of Asia and the East Indies comes close in length (18 ft.) and is much the longest venomous snake. The heaviest venomous snake is probably the eastern diamondback rattlesnake (*Crotalus adamanteus*), which though not exceeding 8 ft. may weigh as much as 34 lb. The largest of the common non-venomous snakes of the family Colubridae is probably the Oriental rat snake, *Zaocys carinatus* (12 ft. 3 in.).

Four living species of crocodilians grow larger than 20 ft.: the American crocodile (*Crocodylus acutus*), the Orinoco crocodile (*C. intermedius*), the saltwater crocodile (*C. porosus*), and the gavial (*Gavialis gangeticus*). The last two may approach 30 ft.

The giant among living turtles is the marine leatherback (*Dermochelys*), which reaches a total length of about nine feet and a weight of about 1,500 lb. The largest of the land turtles is a Galapagos tortoise weighing 560 lb.

The largest modern lizard is a monitor, the Komodo dragon of the East Indies, growing to a length of ten feet. Two or three other species of monitors reach six feet. The common iguana comes close to that size, but no other lizard does.

None of the living reptiles, with the possible exception of snakes, is as large as the largest extinct representative of its particular group. The 9-ft. leatherback turtle was exceeded by a 12-ft. marine turtle (*Archelon*). No modern crocodile approaches the estimated 50-ft. *Phobosuchus*. The Komodo dragon does not compare with the 20-ft. or more mosasaur *Tylosaurus*. These extinct giant relatives of living reptiles had two things in common: they lived during the Cretaceous and they were marine. None of these, however, compares with the herbivorous sauropod dinosaurs such as *Brontosaurus* (*Apatosaurus*), *Diplodocus*, and *Brachiosaurus*, the largest of which was about 80 ft. long and probably weighed close to 50 tons.

The length of time needed to reach sexual maturity varies greatly among reptiles and, though roughly related to the size usually attained by the species, is even more closely related to the climate in which the animal lives. The red diamond rattlesnakes in southern California, for example, bear their first young when three years old, whereas the northern Pacific rattlesnake (*Crotalus viridis oreganus*) bears its first litter when four years old. The much smaller common garter snake is sexually mature shortly before it is two years old.

The 5- to 6-in. long northwestern sagebrush lizard (*Sceloporus graciosus gracilis*), living in the Sierra Nevada range of California at an elevation (about 6,000 ft.) where it has, at most, six months of activity each year, requires two years or more to reach sexual maturity. Another lizard, the green anole (*Anolis carolinensis*), similar in size to the sagebrush lizard but living in the lowlands of southern United States, may reach maturity in four or five months in Florida.

Turtles mature at a slower rate. Females of the red-eared turtle of the central United States lay their first eggs when they are from three to eight years old, depending upon how long it takes them to reach a shell length of 6 in. Females of the musk turtle or stinkpot (*Sternotherus odoratus*) in Michigan require 9 to 11 years to mature, at which time their shells are 3 to 4 in. long. Presumably turtles living in the tropics and having much longer growing seasons mature more rapidly.

7. Longevity.—The maximum age, meaning the potential longevity, of modern reptiles varies greatly and can be determined only from records of captive animals. Turtles as a group seem capable of living longer than the others, and 31 species have been kept in captivity more than 20 years. Several species are said to have lived 150 years or more, but these may be cases of two individuals whose periods of captivity overlapped. It is almost a certainty, though yet to be proven, that some turtles can live more than 50 years. There is no reliable evidence for believing that the giant land tortoises live much longer than some smaller species. The crocodilians that have been kept in captivity the longest are two alligators (an *Alligator mississipiensis* and an *A. sinensis*), both of which have survived in zoos for slightly more than 50 years. Several species of pythons and boas have lived longer than 20 years, the maximum being 28 years for the anaconda. A black-lipped cobra (*Naja melanoleuca*) has been kept 29 years. Lizards seem to have an upper limit near that of snakes, though fewer species have been kept over 20 years. The record for lizards is held by a slowworm, *Anguis fragilis* (32 years), followed by the European glass snake, *Ophisaurus apodus* (25 years).

The life expectancy for most reptiles in nature remains a mystery, but it certainly is much lower than the maxima achieved in captivity and probably is related to the length of time needed to reach sexual maturity.

V. DISTRIBUTION
A. Fossil Reptiles

The geographic distribution of extinct reptiles is not and cannot be perfectly known because of lack of fossilization in some areas and destruction of fossils in others by natural geological forces. But what is known of the fossil record shows that most of the major groups, or orders, were worldwide or nearly so at some time in their individual histories. Few orders are known from South America and Australia; the absence of most major groups from these areas more likely is explained on the basis of lack of preservation or lack of discovery of fossil beds than on the basis of a genuine absence of the animals throughout such a long interval as the Mesozoic. In the following discussion the names of present-day continents are used, though it should be understood that continental outlines in the past did not always coincide with today's.

Few orders of reptiles are known from Pre-Mesozoic times (*i.e.*, Carboniferous and Permian). The stem reptiles, the Cotylosauria, have been found in Carboniferous deposits of eastern and western North America and western Europe and in Permian beds of Russia and Africa. Presumably they also lived in Asia during this interval of over 100,-

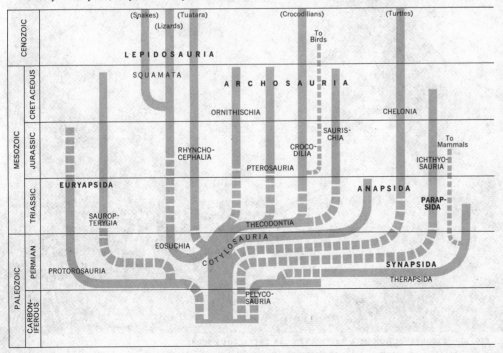

FIG. 9.—FAMILY TREE OF THE REPTILES

000,000 years, but their remains have yet to be found there. In the same period the Pelycosauria lived in North America and Europe, where their fossils are well known, and possibly in Africa and Asia. At least the related mammallike Therapsida were fossilized in Africa and Europe. The probable ancestors of turtles appeared in Africa and the first diapsids (reptiles having two-arched temporal structures) in Africa and Europe in the Permian.

By the Triassic, the earliest portion of the Mesozoic, the mammallike reptiles had spread to all of the continents except Australia. Turtles (Chelonia) were still in Africa and had spread at least to Europe. The Ichthyosauria were living in seas covering what is now western North America and western Europe and may have been much more widely distributed, considering their oceanic habitat. North America at that time was also the home of primitive diapsids (Thecodontia), of phytosaurs (suborder Phytosauria), and the earliest dinosaurs (Saurischia) and crocodiles (Crocodilia). Besides the mammallike therapsids, Eurasia and Africa in the Triassic had phytosaurs, the first Rhynchocephalia, and the early dinosaurs. The major groups of reptiles, therefore, were essentially worldwide in distribution by the Triassic.

The giant dinosaurs began their efflorescence in the Jurassic. The big carnivorous types, such as *Allosaurus*, roamed the landscapes of the major continents, presumably preying on even larger herbivorous dinosaurs (*Brontosaurus, Diplodocus,* etc.), whose remains have been found in North America, Europe, Africa, and Australia. Marine ichthyosaurs and plesiosaurs (order Sauropterygia) still swam in the shallow seas of both hemispheres. The ornithischian dinosaurs (Ornithischia), the ancestors of the duckbilled and horned dinosaurs, became widely distributed in the Jurassic. One group, the armoured stegosaurians (suborder Stegosauria), left fossils in North America, Europe, and Africa. The flying reptiles (Pterosauria) also made their appearance at least in Africa and Europe during the Jurassic.

The culmination of dinosaur evolution occurred in the Cretaceous, when every part of the world had its herbivorous ornithischian dinosaurs: the ankylosaurs (suborder Ankylosauria), medium-sized dinosaurs armoured with heavy plates and large spines, that ranged from South America to Africa; the duck-billed dinosaurs (suborder Ornithopoda) ranging from North America to Africa; and the horned dinosaurs (suborder Ceratopsia) from North America and Asia. Everywhere they were preyed upon by the big carnivorous types, which culminated in North America in the gigantic carnivore *Tyrannosaurus*. The skies over North America, Africa, and Europe (and probably Asia and South America as well) were the province of the flying reptiles (Pterosauria). Meanwhile there were inconspicuous groups that later inherited the reptilian world. Lizards (suborder Sauria) appeared in most continents and snakes (suborder Serpentes) in some places. Birds, having splintered off from reptilian ancestors in the Jurassic, became more numerous in the Cretaceous; mammals, which ultimately replaced most of the reptiles, were represented on most continents by small creatures.

Through all this evolutionary activity, the conservative turtles continued their plodding evolutionary pace, changing but little, yet lasting through it all. *See also* PALEONTOLOGY.

B. LIVING REPTILES

Though living reptiles are primarily tropical animals, many inhabit the Temperate zones. The northernmost ranges are those of the lacertid lizard (*Lacerta vivipara*) and the common viper (*Vipera berus*), both of Europe and Asia. These ovoviviparous species live north of the Arctic Circle, at least in Scandinavia. Two other lizards, the slowworm (*Anguis fragilis*) and the sand lizard (*Lacerta agilis*), and two snakes, the grass snake (*Natrix natrix*) and the smooth snake (*Coronella austriaca*), reach 60° N in Europe. Of these six northern species, all but the grass snake are

FIG. 10.—RECONSTRUCTION OF A NORTH AMERICAN CRETACEOUS SCENE

(Left) *Gorgosaurus*, a theropod dinosaur, attacking (right) *Triceratops*, an ornithischian dinosaur. (Above) *Pteranodon*, an advanced pterosaur

ovoviviparous. Across Siberia only *Lacerta vivipara* and the *Vipera berus* live north of 60°. The difference in northward distributions in Europe and Asia reflects the amelioration of the climate in western Europe effected by the warm Gulf Stream.

In North America no reptile reaches the 60th parallel. Two species of garter snakes live as far north as 55° in western Canada, and one of these species, the common garter snake (*Thamnophis sirtalis*), is the only reptile reaching 50° N in eastern Canada. As all garter snakes are ovoviviparous, seven of the eight northernmost reptiles of both land masses have this development pattern. In North America, the northern limit of turtles and lizards is about 55° N in western Canada. In Eurasia the northernmost turtle is found at 55° N.

It is only south of 40° N that reptiles become abundant. In eastern United States and eastern Asia water snakes (*Natrix*), rat snakes (*Elaphe*), racers (*Coluber*), green snakes (*Opheodrys*), northern skinks (*Eumeces*), glass "snakes" (lizards of the genus *Ophisaurus*), and soft-shelled turtles (*Trionyx*) are common elements of the faunas. One of the two living species of *Alligator* lives in southeastern United States; the other lives in China. Though both regions are characterized by many species of emydid turtles (family Emydidae), the genera to which these species belong usually are found in only one region or the other. For example, the common emydid turtles of the eastern United States are the painted turtles (*Chrysemys*), cooters and sliders (*Pseudemys*), box turtles, and map turtles (*Graptemys*). None of these genera is found in Eurasia. Lizards, aside from the northern skinks and the so-called glass snakes, of the various areas differ. Many lizards of temperate Eurasia belong to the families Agamidae and Lacertidae, which do not occur at all in the Americas. On the other hand, many lizards of North America are in the families Iguanidae and Teiidae, which do not live in Eurasia.

Oddly enough, the fauna of eastern United States is almost as distinct from that of western United States and northern Mexico (which is faunistically part of the same region) as it is from that of eastern Asia. Eastern United States has many genera and species of emydid turtles; western United States (defined by a diagonal line running southeast and northwest through Texas, then northward along the continental divide) has only four or five species. Few genera and species of iguanid lizards inhabit the eastern United States, whereas the western United States has many. Although the eastern United States has more species of water snakes, the western United States contains more garter snakes. More species of snakes appear in the eastern United States than in the western areas, where the converse is true of lizard species.

Reptiles of the North Temperate Zone include many ecological types. Aquatic groups are represented in both hemispheres by the water snakes, many emydid turtles, and the two alligators. Terrestrial groups include tortoises (*Terrapene* in North America, *Testudo* in Eurasia), ground dwelling snakes (*e.g.*, the racers, *Coluber*), and many genera of lizards. Arboreal snakes are few, the main group being the rat snakes (*Elaphe*), and arboreal lizards are almost nonexistent. Burrowing snakes are common, the worm snake (*Carphophis amoenus*) and the short-tailed snake (*Stilosoma extenuatum*) representing the blunt-headed burrowers and the bull snakes (*Pituophis*) and leaf-nosed snakes (*Phyllorhynchus*) representing the auger burrowers. Specialized burrowing lizards are few; in North America there are the legless lizard (*Anniella*), two worm lizards (family Amphisbaenidae), and the sand skink (*Neoseps*).

Southward in Central America the reptile fauna becomes richer. Besides several turtle families (snapping turtles [Chelydridae], mud and musk turtles [Kinosternidae], sliders [Emydidae], etc.) found in eastern United States, Central America has three genera of turtles (*Dermatemys, Claudius,* and *Staurotypus*) not living elsewhere. Crocodilians become more numerous in terms of species and individuals; there are no alligators, but caymans and true crocodiles occur here. The significant increase in the fauna results from the increase in lizards and snakes. The anoles, represented over most of southern United States by the one species sold at circuses as "the chameleon," have many species in Central America.

Many of the genera of iguanid lizards occurring in western United States have species in Mexico; one genus of spiny lizards (*Sceloporus*) reaches its peak of numbers of species in Mexico. South of Mexico the North American iguanid genera disappear and are replaced by tropical groups such as the black iguanas (*Ctenosaura*), the helmeted iguanids (*Corythophanes*), the casque-headed iguanids (*Laemanctus*), and the basilisks (*Basiliscus*). The lizard family Teiidae, though represented in the United States by the race-runner genus (*Cnemidophorus*), is tropical, and its real development begins in Central America with the large, conspicuous, and active ameivas (*Ameiva*) and several small secretive genera.

Among snakes, the fer-de-lance genus *Bothrops,* the coral snakes (*Micrurus*), the rear-fanged snakes such as the cat-eyed snakes (*Leptodeira*), and nonvenomous genera such as the tropical green snakes (*Thalerophis*) either appear for the first time or begin their proliferation of species in Central America.

These groups become increasingly numerous in northern South America, the heartland of the American tropics. Vine snakes (*Oxybelis* and *Imantodes*), false coral snakes (*Erythrolamprus*), slender ground snakes (*Drymobius*), and the burrowing spindle snakes (*Atractus*) have their headquarters there. Almost all of the genera of the lizard family Teiidae occur in this area. The iguanid lizards of the anole genus (*Anolis*) seem almost to have exploded in northern South America, as most of the approximately 165 species live there. Other iguanid genera, *e.g.*, the long-legged iguanids, *Polychrus*, make their appearance.

Crocodilians are still more numerous in terms of species than in Central America. In addition to the common American crocodile (*Crocodylus acutus*) and the common spectacled cayman (*Caiman sclerops*), which occur in Central America, tropical South America has the big Orinoco crocodile (*Crocodylus intermedius*), the black cayman (*Melanosuchus niger*), the smooth-fronted caymans (*Paleosuchus*), and several species of spectacled caymans (*Caiman*).

Turtles are also abundant in South America. Some of the North American groups, for example the mud turtles (*Kinosternon*) and sliders (*Pseudemys*), are represented, but the majority of species are members of genera and even families (*e.g.*, the side-necked turtles, families Pelomedusidae and Chelidae) unknown in temperate North America.

Several groups that form important, if not dominant, elements of the fauna of the Eastern Hemisphere are largely or completely absent from the American tropics: the lizard families Scincidae, Lacertidae, Chamaeleontidae, and Agamidae, and the snakes of the cobra (*Naja*) and water snake (*Natrix*) genera.

South of the tropics in the Temperate Zone of South America, the reptilian fauna diminishes rapidly. Crocodilians and turtles do not occur south of northern Argentina. One snake, an ovoviviparous pit viper, reaches almost 50° S in Argentina, and two iguanid lizards range almost to 55° S.

Apart from the genera of reptiles listed above as common to the eastern United States and eastern Asia, the Temperate Zone of Eurasia is noted for its many lizards of the families Agamidae, Lacertidae, and to lesser degrees Gekkonidae and Scincidae. These lizards are mostly terrestrial; a few are burrowers; but almost none are aquatic or arboreal. The extremely specialized burrowers among them are desert-dwelling skinks (*Ophiomorus* and *Scincus*) that literally swim through sand with the help of countersunk lower jaws and sharp snouts. Most of the snakes characteristic of this vast area are also terrestrial; the racers, common vipers, and Asian ground snakes (*Contia*) are examples. Arboreal snakes are represented almost exclusively by the rat snakes (*Elaphe*). The leaf-nosed snakes (*Lytorhynchus*) and the sand boas (*Eryx*) are the distinctive burrowing snakes of the region. Except for the Chinese alligators, temperate Eurasia lacks crocodilians. Over this vast area a few species of turtles are found, and they are about equally divided between land tortoises (*Testudo*) and freshwater genera (*Emys, Clemmys,* and *Trionyx*).

A few types characteristic of the Oriental tropics lap over into the margins of the Temperate Zone, *e.g.*, several rear-fanged snakes (*Boiga trigonata* and *Psammodynastes*), a cobra or two (*Naja*), several species of soft-shelled turtles (*Trionyx*), and some species of true chameleons (*Chamaeleo*).

In the Oriental tropics, embracing India, Ceylon, southeastern Asia, the Philippines, and most of the East Indies, the reptilian fauna is extremely rich in species and diverse types. Aquatic groups are represented by snakes of various genera (*e.g., Natrix, Enhydris, Cerberus,* etc.), several groups of lizards (*Tropidophorus* among the skinks and *Hydrosaurus* among the agamids), many emydid and soft-shelled turtles, and five species of crocodiles. The numerous terrestrial reptiles include the small kukri snakes (*Oligodon*), the big Oriental rat snakes (*Ptyas* and *Zaocys*), cobras, monitor lizards (*Varanus*), many species and genera of skinks, some geckos, and several land turtles (*Cuora, Testudo*). Specialized, blunt-headed burrowing snakes (*e.g., Calamaria*) and lizards (*e.g.,* the family Dibamidae and the skink genus *Brachymeles*) are also abundant.

But the distinctive life forms of reptiles in this great region of humid forest are arboreal. Heavy-bodied pythons and Oriental pit vipers (*Trimeresurus*); slender, green, long-headed vine snakes (*Dryophis*); slender, blunt-headed, slug-eating snakes (*Pareas*); and the widespread, thick-bodied rat snakes give some idea of the variation among arboreal snakes. Lizards of bush and tree habitats may be long legged and green (as *Calotes cristatellus*), or brown and black (*Gonyocephalus*), or short legged and gray and brown (many geckos). Some climb only with the aid of claws (*e.g.,* the monitors), a few with the help of prehensile tails (*e.g.,* the deaf agamids, *Cophotis*), and many with the help of clinging pads under the digits (*e.g.,* many geckos). The most striking arboreal reptiles of this area are the flying lizards (*Draco*) and the parachuting gecko (*Ptychozoon*), which has fully webbed digits, a fringed tail, and wide flaps of skin along its sides.

Though geographically part of the East Indies, New Guinea has a reptilian fauna more akin to that of Australia, and these two areas will be considered as one. The Australian region is the only area in the world in which venomous species of snakes outnumber the harmless species. The family Colubridae, comprising the great majority of the nonvenomous or slightly venomous snakes of the world, is poorly represented in Australia, which has only 12 species. New Guinea, being more tropical and closer to the true Oriental tropics, has 22, which is less than the number (33) living in the much smaller Temperate Zone state of Kansas. The place of the colubrids in the Australian region is taken by snakes of the cobra family. The fauna also includes a few pythons and minute blind snakes (family Typhlopidae); a variety of geckos, skinks, and agamid lizards; side-necked turtles; and three species of crocodiles.

The reptilian fauna of Africa forms two main divisions. The first of these, the fauna of the North African coast, is akin to that of central and southwestern Asia and southern Europe and is therefore partly a Temperate Zone fauna. The racers, the burrowing sand skink (*Scincus*), and the emydid turtle *Clemmys leprosa* are elements of temperate fauna in North Africa. Some species of the great tropical fauna lying south of the Sahara occur in North Africa and in Southwest Asia. Examples are the sand snakes (*Psammophis*), cobras, and the chameleons (family Chamaeleontidae). As is true of the temperate fauna of Eurasia, the North African reptiles, though representing many families, are principally terrestrial and burrowing. Many lacertid and agamid lizards scamper over rocks and sand by day to be replaced at night by small geckos. They are preyed upon by the racers (*Coluber*) and sand snakes (*Psammophis*). In addition to cobras, the venomous snakes of North Africa include the common vipers, the saw-scaled viper (*Echis carinatus*), and the horned vipers (*Cerastes*). The last two are true desert animals, the horned vipers using sidewinding locomotion like that of the sidewinder rattlesnake of the American deserts. Land tortoises (*Testudo*) are common in this semiarid land. Until the 1860s, the Nile crocodile came far down the river but has now been exterminated in southern Egypt.

The second and much larger division of the African fauna is the great tropical assemblage that ranges down to the Cape of Good Hope. In common with tropical Asia, this vast area has cobras, many skinks, and many geckos. Its fauna differs from that of Asia in the absence of pit vipers (subfamily Crotalinae), the near-absence of emydid turtles, and in the poor representation of agamid lizards. But these groups are replaced in tropical Africa by

the many true vipers (subfamily Viperinae), the side-necked turtles (family Pelomedusidae), and the lacertid lizards. Chameleons and land tortoises have their centres of development here. Four species of crocodiles, including the two dwarf crocodiles (*Osteolaemus*), occur in Africa.

In Africa are found all of the diverse reptilian types characteristic of a tropical area: aquatic turtles, crocodiles, and snakes (including *Boulengerina,* a member of the cobra family); terrestrial turtles, snakes and lizards; burrowing snakes of the blunt-headed and auger types; limbless and virtually blind burrowing lizards; and a profusion of arboreal snakes and lizards.

The large island of Madagascar off the eastern coast of Africa has a peculiar fauna that appears in part as a collection of cast-offs, groups that in Africa have not been able to meet the competition of more advanced forms. For example, there are no agamid lizards; instead their place is taken by iguanid lizards whose ancestors were undoubtedly exterminated in Africa long ago. Madagascar and its small neighbouring islets are the home of the Sanziniinae, an odd group of snakes of the family Boidae. With few exceptions the reptiles of Madagascar belong to genera found there only. The exceptions are the chameleons (genus *Chamaeleo*) found also in Africa, a side-necked turtle (*Podocnemis*) also living in South America, the land tortoises of the genus *Testudo,* so common in Africa, and several geckos that, as a group, seem better able to cross water barriers than most reptiles. *See also* ANIMALS, DISTRIBUTION OF; ZOOGEOGRAPHY.

VI. CLASSIFICATION AND SURVEY
A. CLASSIFICATION

Although the vast majority of reptiles have become extinct, living species number close to 6,000. The living and fossil forms are classified below, with living orders extended to families to show their general diversity.

The following classification may differ from arrangements given in related articles elsewhere in the encyclopaedia, particularly in regard to orders and families. These differences reflect the opinions of the various authors concerned.

Class Reptilia (reptiles)
Subclass Anapsida ("stem reptiles" and turtles)
Order Cotylosauria ("stem reptiles," extinct)
" Chelonia (turtles and tortoises)
Family Chelydridae (snapping turtles)
" Kinosternidae (musk and mud turtles)
" Dermatemydidae (Central American river turtles)
" Platysternidae (big-headed turtles)
" Emydidae (freshwater turtles)
" Testudinidae (tortoises)
" Cheloniidae (sea turtles)
" Pelomedusidae (side-necked turtles)
" Chelidae (snake-necked turtles)
" Carettochelidae (pitted-shelled turtles)
" Trionychidae (soft-shelled turtles)
" Dermochelyidae (leatherback turtles)
Subclass Synapsida (forms leading to mammals, extinct)
Order Pelycosauria (primitive mammallike reptiles, extinct)
" Therapsida (advanced mammallike reptiles, extinct)
Subclass Parapsida (marine reptiles, extinct)
Order Mesosauria (small aquatic reptiles, extinct)
" Ichthyosauria (fishlike reptiles, extinct)
Subclass Euryapsida (extinct reptiles)
Order Protorosauria (various obscure reptiles, extinct)
" Sauropterygia (marine reptiles, plesiosaurs and their relatives, extinct)
Suborder Nothosauria (primitive, chiefly marine reptiles, extinct)
" Plesiosauria (turtlelike marine reptiles, extinct)
" Placodontia (armoured turtlelike reptiles, extinct)
Subclass Lepidosauria (diapsid reptiles)
Order Eosuchia (ancestral diapsids, extinct)
" Rhynchocephalia (tuatara and fossil relatives)
" Squamata (lizards and snakes)
Suborder Sauria (lizards)
Family Gekkonidae (geckos)
" Iguanidae (iguanids)
" Agamidae (agamids)
" Chamaeleontidae (chameleons)
" Xantusiidae (night lizards)
" Scincidae (skinks)
" Dibamidae (skink relatives)
" Anelytropsidae (skink relatives)

Family Gerrhosauridae (gerrhosaurids)
"   Lacertidae (lacertids)
"   Teiidae (teiid lizards)
"   Amphisbaenidae (worm lizards)
"   Varanidae (monitors)
"   Pygopodidae (snake lizards)
"   Helodermatidae (Gila monsters)
"   Anguidae (glass snakes and alligator lizards)
"   Xenosauridae (xenosaurids)
"   Shinisauridae (Chinese crocodile lizards)
"   Anniellidae (footless lizards)
"   Cordylidae (girdle-tailed lizards)
Suborder Serpentes (snakes)
Family Typhlopidae (blind burrowing snakes)
"   Leptotyphlopidae (blind burrowing snakes)
"   Uropeltidae (burrowing snakes)
"   Aniliidae (burrowing snakes)
"   Xenopeltidae (burrowing snakes)
"   Boidae (boas and pythons)
"   Colubridae (colubrid snakes)
"   Elapidae (cobras, coral snakes, and relatives)
"   Hydrophidae (sea snakes)
"   Viperidae (vipers)
Subclass Archosauria ("ruling reptiles")
Order Thecodontia (ancestors of crocodiles and dinosaurs, extinct)
Suborder Phytosauria (phytosaurs; crocodilelike reptiles, extinct)
Order Crocodilia (crocodiles, alligators, and gavials)
Family Alligatoridae (alligators and caymans)
"   Crocodylidae (crocodiles)
"   Gavialidae (gavials)
Order Saurischia (reptilelike dinosaurs, extinct)
Suborder Theropoda (bipedal carnivorous dinosaurs, extinct)
"   Sauropoda (quadrupedal, primarily herbivorous dinosaurs, extinct)
Order Ornithischia (birdlike dinosaurs, extinct)
Suborder Ornithopoda (duck-billed dinosaurs, extinct)
"   Stegosauria (plated dinosaurs, extinct)
"   Ankylosauria (armoured dinosaurs, extinct)
"   Ceratopsia (horned dinosaurs, extinct)
Order Pterosauria (flying reptiles, extinct)

B. SURVEY

The major divisions, called subclasses, of the class Reptilia are defined by the number and position of openings in the skull behind the eye socket, or orbit, as shown in fig. 11.

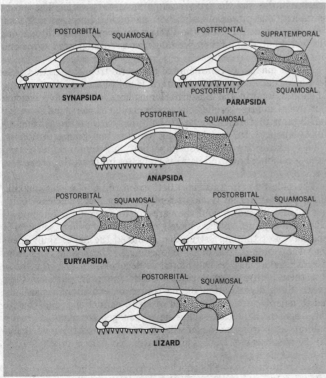

FIG. 11.—DIAGRAMMATIC REPTILIAN SKULLS

Skull differences illustrate the basis for major subdivisions of reptiles. The lizard has a modified diapsid skull

1. Anapsida.—The earliest reptiles, belonging to the subclass Anapsida, had closed skulls without any openings behind the orbit. This subclass includes two orders, the stem reptiles and the turtles.

Cotylosauria.—The order Cotylosauria, the primitive stem reptiles from which all of the other reptilian groups were derived,

FIG. 12.—RECONSTRUCTION OF DIMETRODON, A PERMIAN PELYCOSAUR

arose from amphibians in the Carboniferous and survived into the Triassic. Most of the known cotylosaurs were small or moderate (about six feet long) in size, low-slung, and stocky. Most were carnivorous but a few, judging by the teeth, were herbivorous.

Chelonia.—The turtles, order Chelonia, appeared fully developed in the Triassic and apparently arose from a small Permian reptile, *Eunotosaurus*, from Africa. With the exception of *Eunotosaurus*, all members of this order have a complete shell (formed of bone and, usually, horny scutes) that completely encloses the shoulder and pelvic girdles. From their earliest history onward they have included terrestrial and aquatic types.

Terrestrial turtles tend to have high-domed shells and stumpy feet regardless of the group to which they belong. The giant Galapagos tortoises (*Testudo*), the box turtles of North America (*Terrapene*), and the Malayan box turtle (*Cuora amboinensis*) all fit this general pattern. Aquatic turtles tend to have flatter profiles and webbed toes, a pattern found in such diverse families as the pond turtles (Emydidae), soft-shelled turtles (Trionychidae), and side-necked turtles (Pelomedusidae). The side-necked turtles represent one of the principal divisions of the order Chelonia. Most contemporary turtles pull their heads straight back into their shells by bending the neck into a vertical curve; these are the so-called cryptodire ("hidden neck") turtles. The side-necked, or pleurodire, turtles merely turn their necks to one side and press the head tightly against the fore leg or shoulder. (*See also* TURTLE.)

2. Synapsida.—The subclass Synapsida, reptiles having a single opening in the skull below the squamosal and postorbital bones, are called mammallike reptiles because of their later history. They comprise two orders.

Pelycosauria.—The order Pelycosauria ran through its life span in the late Carboniferous and Early Permian as elongated reptiles. Some pelycosaurs developed very long bony projections from the vertebrae that probably supported a membranous "sail" extending two or three feet above the back in a six-foot animal.

Therapsida.—The second group of synapsids, the order Therapsida, arose in the Permian and, after diverging into carnivorous and herbivorous forms, gradually acquired mammalian characteristics of dentition and limb orientation during the Triassic. Although they did not survive beyond that time, in the Jurassic period that followed they were replaced by several groups of mammals, all evidently derived from the Therapsida.

3. Parapsida.—The subclass Parapsida, reptiles having a single skull opening behind the eye and above the supratemporal and postfrontal bones, comprises the order Ichthyosauria and, tentatively, the order Mesosauria.

Mesosauria.—Found in deposits of the Late Carboniferous, the mesosaurs were small aquatic reptiles (about two feet long) having a deep flattened tail, short paddlelike limbs, and a long slender snout typical of fish-eating reptiles. Despite this aquatic specialization, the skeleton of mesosaurs clearly shows that the terrestrial cotylosaurs were their ancestors. Whether the mesosaurs were the ancestors of ichthyosaurs is questionable. Nevertheless the mesosaurs indicate how the ichthyosaurs could have descended from terrestrial reptiles.

Ichthyosauria.—At the time of their first appearance in the Triassic, ichthyosaurs had the essential marine characteristics of the group. Some have been preserved in such fine sediments that not merely the skeleton but the whole outline of the body has been revealed. With their short finlike limbs and fishlike tails, the ichthyosaurs looked like long-snouted porpoises. They even had a large fleshy dorsal fin, like many of today's marine mammals.

4. Euryapsida.—The subclass Euryapsida, reptiles having a skull opening above the squamosal and postorbital bones, includes other amphibious or aquatic groups, as well as some terrestrial forms.

Protorosauria.—The terrestrial forms, order Protorosauria, appeared first in the Permian and persisted through the Triassic. Some were rather nondescript, small (about one foot long), lizardlike creatures that must have lived much like many of today's lizards. One protorosaur, *Tanystropheus*, about a yard long, had a slender neck making up almost half of its total length, a short body, and normal-proportioned limbs and tail (compared to the body). The habits of this strange creature can only be guessed at.

Sauropterygia.—The protorosaurs gave rise to the order Sauropterygia, which was composed of three suborders: the aquatic Nothosauria, Plesiosauria, and Placodontia. All had the upper elements of the shoulder and pelvic girdle reduced and the ventral elements expanded—a typical aquatic modification showing deemphasis of supporting the body weight. The limbs of nothosaurs and placodonts, both of which appeared in the Triassic, could probably have been used for walking, but not the paddlelike limbs of the plesiosaurs. The placodonts had broad flat teeth in massive jaws, suggesting that they cracked mollusk shells. The plesiosaurs, found first in Jurassic deposits, were the most specialized of the subclass and probably never came ashore. Comments on their means of locomotion and probable means of getting food appear elsewhere in this article.

5. Lepidosauria.—The subclass Lepidosauria is one of two subclasses of reptiles that have what is called a diapsid skull, that is, one having two openings behind the eye, one above the squamosal and postorbital bones and one below them. It appeared first in the Late Permian and was represented then by the order Eosuchia.

Eosuchia.—The earliest diapsid was a small creature, lizardlike in general proportions and probably in habits. Several Triassic and Cretaceous reptiles, including one similar in form to crocodiles, are placed in the same order.

Rhynchocephalia.—A second group of lepidosaurians, order

FIG. 14.—RECONSTRUCTION OF ELASMOSAURUS, A CRETACEOUS PLESIOSAUR

Rhynchocephalia, arose in the Triassic and survives today as the tuatara (*Sphenodon*) of New Zealand. The rhynchocephalians or beak-heads, so-called because of a small overhang of the upper jaw, did not go much beyond the basic pattern of the earliest eosuchians. Their dentition was specialized compared to that of the more primitive eosuchians, their teeth being fused to the jaws instead of set in sockets. Never very important in the world's fauna, the rhynchocephalians died out in the Cretaceous, leaving only the tuatara in its isolated range.

Squamata.—The last of the lepidosaurians to appear, the order Squamata, comprising lizards and snakes, were the only truly successful ones in the sense that they became widespread, numerous, and important components of the natural community. Lizards, first found in Jurassic deposits, have lost the bony strut that ran underneath the lower opening in the diapsid skull. Presumably the lizards are descended from a primitive eosuchian. Except for one group, the mosasaurs (Mosasauridae), fossil lizards show no specializations not found in contemporary forms. Only one modern lizard, the Galapagos marine iguana (*Amblyrhynchus cristatus*), lives in the sea. But this shore-limited iguanid is not marine in the way the truly oceanic mosasaurs were. The mosasaurs had long powerful tails, short paddlelike limbs, short necks, and large heads. During the Cretaceous they spread throughout the world but, despite their seeming success, disappeared at the end of that period.

Lizards inhabit all continents of the world from the Arctic Circle to Tierra del Fuego in the Western Hemisphere and to the Cape of Good Hope in the Eastern Hemisphere. They have become burrowers and tree dwellers, conspicuous sun baskers, and secretive inhabitants of forest floors. In body length they range from 1½ in. to about 5 ft., and in weight from a few grams to 300 lb. Today lizards are the most important insectivorous, terrestrial (thus excluding birds and bats) vertebrates in the world. (*See* also LIZARD.)

The oldest fossilized snakes date from the Cretaceous, making them the most recent group of reptiles. Not many ancient ophidian fossils are known, and they are not important for our knowledge of the group. Snakes have gone one step farther than lizards and have lost the bony strut that bounded the upper skull opening; the result is loss of both openings. Clearly derived from lizards, snakes may be considered as degenerate lizards that have lost their limbs, external ears, eyelids, and even parts of their eyes. Such degeneration in the course of evolution has usually led to narrow specialization and often to extinction. But despite this apparent handicap, snakes have managed to invade as many habitats as lizards; moreover, they are even successful in one habitat (warm oceans) from which lizards have been driven. (*See* also SNAKE.)

6. Archosauria.—The subclass Archosauria, the second diapsid subclass, deserves the name "ruling reptiles" usually applied to it, for they dominated the land fauna of the Mesozoic, an era lasting about 140,000,000 years. All had teeth set in sockets, which dis-

FIG. 13.—RECONSTRUCTION OF STENOPTERYGIUS, A JURASSIC ICHTHYOSAUR

tinguishes them from all the diapsid lepidosaurians except the eosuchians.

Thecodontia.—Starting in the Early Triassic as the order Thecodontia, the first archosaurs were small (about one to three feet long) carnivorous reptiles without conspicuous specializations except for bipedal tendencies. In fact these generalized thecodonts had all the characteristics that should have been shown by the ancestors of the remaining groups of ruling reptiles. Though the thecodonts did not live beyond the Triassic, it would be a mistake to say that they became extinct then; rather, they evolved into the other ruling reptiles.

Crocodilia.—The order Crocodilia, one of the Triassic descendants of the thecodonts, differs very little from the theocodonts in its skeleton, which is all that is known of these early reptiles. Only the palate of the first crocodilians shows the basic aquatic specialization that they maintained virtually unchanged down to the present. The bones of the upper jaw and palate meet along the midline, forming a solid roof to the mouth and the floor of a pair of bony tubes running from the external nostrils to the rear of the mouth. The internal nostrils open behind a fleshy valve in the mouth and thus permit a crocodile to breathe while only the tip of its snout is above the surface.

Modern crocodilians have been placed in three families (or subfamilies—opinions differ): Alligatoridae, including alligators and caymans; Crocodylidae, the true crocodiles; and Gavialidae, the gavials. The last family is distinguished by an extremely long slender snout and by the separation of certain bones (nasals and premaxillaries) of the skull that meet in the other two groups. The teeth of the lower jaw fit inside those of the upper jaw in the alligators and caymans, whereas in true crocodiles the teeth of the two jaws form an interdigitating row when the jaws close. (*See* also CROCODILIA.)

Saurischia.—The order Saurischia, one of two orders of dinosaurs, also appeared in the Triassic. The more primitive dinosaurs of this order were bipedal and carnivorous and are grouped in the suborder Theropoda. They were relatively small (about 3 ft. long), and their skulls were similar to those of the thecodonts. Still in the Triassic, larger and heavier carnivorous types appeared, culminating in the Jurassic and Cretaceous in the huge bipedal *Allosaurus* (about 34 ft.) and *Tyrannosaurus* (about 47 ft.), respectively. These bipedal carnivores had short weak fore limbs and strong hind limbs and tails. (*See* also DINOSAUR.)

Along with the more usual small bipedal dinosaurs, there appeared some with relatively long front legs, rather blunt teeth, and a small head. They were the forerunners of the gigantic amphibious sauropods (suborder Sauropoda) of the Jurassic and Cretaceous. The longest of these quadrupedal herbivores, *Diplodocus,* reached 87 ft., including its slender tail. *Brontosaurus,* though shorter, was heavier and may have weighed close to 30 tons. The largest was *Brachiosaurus,* about 80 ft. long and probably weighing nearly 50 tons. These massive creatures evidently lived in marshes and swamps, their weight at least partially supported by the water.

Ornithischia.—The second order of dinosaurs, the Ornithischia, differed from the saurischians in the form of the pelvic girdle. Whereas the saurischians had the simple pubic bone and triradiate pelvis of the thecodonts, the ornithischians had a two-pronged pubic bone and, hence, a four-pronged pelvis. The saurischians were carnivorous at first and only later in their history developed into herbivorous animals. The ornithischian dinosaurs, lacking teeth at the front of the jaws, probably had horny beaks instead. These herbivorous forms made their first appearance in the Jurassic as bipedal Ornithopoda (the duck-billed dinosaurs and their relatives). Their fore limbs were only moderately shortened and never developed into grasping organs, as in the case of some saurischian dinosaurs. The early ornithopodans gave rise not only to the varied duck-billed dinosaurs but also to quadrupedal armoured (*e.g., Stegosaurus*) and horned dinosaurs (*e.g., Triceratops*).

The saurischian dinosaurs had their big evolutionary burst in the Jurassic, the ornithischians in the Cretaceous. But neither group survived into the Tertiary, the Age of Mammals. None of the varied explanations for their disappearance—change in climate, epidemics, reduction of swamps through mountain formation, egg eating by early mammals, etc.—seems adequate, and even all the explanations taken together cannot account for the total extinction of this fantastic group of animals.

Pterosauria.—The last group of archosaurs, order Pterosauria, the flying reptiles, appeared in Early Jurassic times. The first pterosaurs had long heads armed with sharp teeth, long tails, and well-developed wings, as known from some remarkably preserved fossils. Later pterosaurs had much reduced tails, larger wings, and often few or very small teeth. Like most archosaurs, the flying reptiles did not survive the Cretaceous Period.

See also references under "Reptile" in the Index.

BIBLIOGRAPHY.—A. d'A. Bellairs, *Reptiles* (1957); E. H. Colbert, *The Dinosaur Book* (1945); P. J. Darlington, *Zoogeography* (1957); J. A. Oliver, *Natural History of North American Amphibians and Reptiles* (1955); C. H. Pope, *The Reptile World* (1955); C. L. Prosser and F. A. Brown, Jr., *Comparative Animal Physiology,* 2nd ed. (1961); A. S. Romer, *Vertebrate Paleontology,* 2nd ed. (1945); K. P. Schmidt and R. F. Inger, *Living Reptiles of the World* (1957); M. A. Smith, *The British Amphibians and Reptiles* (1951). (R. F. I.)

REPTON, HUMPHRY (1752–1818), a leading English architect and landscape gardener of his time, was born in Bury St. Edmunds, Suffolk, on April 21, 1752. A financial setback soon after his marriage in 1773 caused him to retire from his mercantile business in Norwich but not until 1788 did he decide to exploit his gift for drawing and interest in landscape gardening. Lancelot ("Capability") Brown's death five years before had left no comparable genius, and Repton quickly established a wide reputation for himself as a designer. His gift for drawing led him to prepare schemes for his clients in the form of books, usually bound in red leather, containing his written proposals, illustrated by watercolour sketches, many of which had movable flaps to show the "before" and "after" effects. He claimed to have prepared about 400 of these Red Books, though less than half that number appear to have survived. Repton's landscapes were seldom as large in extent as Brown's, and tended to be more thickly planted. He advocated a gradual transition between house and grounds by means of terraces, balustrades, and steps, and took a particular interest in details such as cottages, lodges, conservatories, and "winter corridors." He was influenced by the Picturesque movement, which admired wild landscapes, though he was drawn into conflict with its leading protagonists, Richard Payne Knight and Uvedale Price, the former having attacked him in a footnote to his poem *The Landscape* (1794). He was conscious of the relation of architecture to landscape, and he collaborated for some years with John Nash. (*See* LANDSCAPE ARCHITECTURE.) He died at Hare Street, Romford, Essex, on March 24, 1818.

In addition to several essays and a short play, Repton published three major books on landscape gardening, *Sketches and Hints on Landscape Gardening* (1795), *Observations on the Theory and Practice of Landscape Gardening* (1803), and *Fragments on the Theory and Practice of Landscape Gardening* (1816).

See biographical notice in *The Landscape Gardening and Landscape Architecture of the late Humphry Repton,* ed. by J. C. Loudon (1840); Dorothy Stroud, *Humphry Repton* (1962). (D. ST.)

REPTON, a township in Derbyshire, Eng., about 8 mi. (13 km.) SW of Derby by road. Pop. (1961) 1,850. Its famous boys' school was founded in 1557 by Sir John Port; the modern buildings incorporate considerable portions (restored) of an Augustinian priory established in 1172. There was a monastery in the 7th century, the first bishop of Mercia being established there. The parish church of St. Wystan has pre-Conquest work in the chancel, and beneath is a remarkable Saxon crypt, part of the wall of which may have been included in the original monastery chapel.

REPUBLIC, a term denoting (1) a state not ruled by a monarch or emperor; (2) a state where power is not directly in the hands of or subject to complete control by the people, in contrast with a democracy (*q.v.*); (3) more loosely, any regime where government depends actually or nominally on popular will. The latter meaning is implied more generally in the adjective, "republican," than it is in the noun.

"Republic" derives from the Latin words *res publica,* "public affair" or "thing." That concept was in turn loosely equivalent to the classical Greek *ta koinonia,* "common things" or "property," a term originally applied in the early city-state to the city's treasure, the public funds, and then by analogy coming to symbolize and denote the common interests. From these root origins derive in turn the concepts of commonwealth, which was the official title of Great Britain under Oliver Cromwell's rule, the first republic in the English-speaking world, and common weal or common welfare, at that same time a widely held designation of the proper end or purpose of government.

The term republic has generally been applied by historians first to the government of ancient Rome after the expulsion of the Etruscan kings, the Tarquins, and prior to the establishment of the empire by Augustus. During that period, indeed, political institutions, constitutional arrangements and the locus of effective political power varied widely, though the regime might be generally described as one of aristocratic, or patrician, ascendancy moderated by popular, or plebeian, influence and assent. But the dual concepts which subsequently characterized the republican idea, absence of monarchy and a collective public interest and business, were present.

Some historians have also applied the term to the ancient Greek city-state. There, however, governments were normally classified by the numbers exercising power, such as monarchy, aristocracy and democracy, and their perversions, tyranny, oligarchy and ochlocracy (or, frequently, again democracy), where rule was arbitrary rather than directed by the principle of the good of the city. Nevertheless, one root idea of a republic, that of common interest and participation, was present in the contrast between Greek city-state and barbarian empires, with their irresponsible rulers and submissive mass of subjects.

In any event, republic, when applied to ancient governments, has implied some popular and collective power and the absence of hereditary or autocratic rule, as contrasted with government by kings or emperors.

The modern usage of "republic" derives from these dual ideas, absence of monarchy, and some degree of avowed concern for the common welfare of the state and for public control or participation. During the later middle ages there were established some brief-lived local republics, consequent on revolt. But it was in certain city-states of Italy during the Renaissance, of which the most celebrated are Venice and Florence (during a limited period after the expulsion and before the return of the Medici) that the republic re-emerged as a meaningful designation and form of government. Here again absence of monarchy, of an established lordly ruling family or of a self-imposed absolute ruler was the first test. In such republics a share in control of government was often confined to noble or wealthy privileged families, while the form of government tended to be by a small group, co-opted or elected on a narrow franchise, though sometimes with a titular head of state, such as the doge in Venice. On occasion, too, as a result of popular pressure or revolt, government might for a while come to rest on a broader base, and to include representatives of at least the lesser burghers and the artisans.

But republics which combined the ideas of absence of monarchy, a realm of public affairs and popular consent or participation first emerged, generally as temporary phenomena, in the 17th and 18th centuries. Cromwell's commonwealth, though it developed into rule by one man not unlike the more moderate modern dictatorships, had its genesis in antimonarchical doctrines and forces, expressed in the Great Rebellion against Charles I. During that conflict, too, the concept of the interest of the community at large in government became firmly associated with the republican idea. The Dutch republic, though it was headed by a stadholder, initially the equivalent of a modern strong president, combined opposition to monarchy (and to Catholicism) with a concept of independence not unlike the later idea of national self-determination, with implications of a common collective interest and a certain degree of public participation and control. Similar considerations also played a part in the early evolution of the Swiss republic, which after many vicissitudes became the modern federal republic of Switzerland. Here, however, the independent city-states of the Reformation, republican even when theocratic and in some cases free still earlier, provided a foundation.

The antimonarchical idea constituted a major element in both the American and the French Revolutions. The former created a lasting republic, the United States of America, while the second created a temporary republic in France but firmly established the republican idea and spread it throughout most of western Europe. In both revolutions the twin ideas of consent of the governed and the rights of man played a major part. A little later the separation of the Spanish-American colonies from Spain produced numerous republics which rested on similar ideas. During the 19th century, however, the moral significance of the republican idea declined in Europe, where monarchies continued and republics remained the exception. Constitutional government spread in the monarchies, and by the early 20th century the term "republic" no longer connoted the substance and content of political institutions and practice. "Democracy" tended to supplant "republic" in describing governments free from arbitrary and imposed authority. Democracy was widespread in Great Britain (also the British Commonwealth) and the Scandinavian countries—all monarchies. In Latin America, on the other hand, nominal republics were often dictatorships on behalf of oligarchies.

In these and other instances, the term "republic" had been stripped of its earlier appeal as the alternative to divine-right monarchy and autocracy.

After World War I, the emergence of dictatorships, which might function formally within a monarchical state (Fascism in Italy), might reject the idea of a republic without restoring monarchy (Francisco Franco's Spain), though restoring the title of empire (Hitler's third *Reich*), or might continue nominally as republics, rendered the classification of regimes into monarchies or republics practically meaningless. After World War II, moreover, the term had still less relevance. The United States of America, Franco's anti-Communist dictatorship in Spain and Joseph Stalin's Communist dictatorship in the U.S.S.R. were all nominally republics. In essence, the basic classification of governments was into constitutional governments and dictatorships, a division which corresponded in ethos to the former opposition of republic and monarchy. The term republic no longer had a manifest connection with struggles over liberty, authority and sovereignty. The adjective "republican," however, was still sometimes used with connotations equivalent to its ancient meaning in political ethics.

In the United States the term "republic" has special connotations and is frequently used with supposed historical justification to contrast with democracy and as a ground for denial that the U.S. is technically a democracy. The bases for this contrast are (1) the ancient and purist use of the term "democracy" to denote small-scale direct democracy; (2) the classical fear, which continued at least to the end of the 18th century, of such democracy as unstable and fickle; (3) the Ciceronian interpretation, which widely influenced the U.S. founding fathers, of the Roman republic as a mixed and balanced government; and (4) the revival by Montesquieu in the 18th century of the idea of democracy as direct and small scale, and his insistence that democracy was impossible in a larger state, which could be at best a representative republic. These ideas were studied and combined by a number of the founding fathers, and especially by James Madison, who used the term "republic" (1) as a technical designation for representative government as opposed to direct democracy and (2) to insist on the necessity for a system of checks and balances against the dangers of straight majoritarian decision in a legislature elected by majority on a single principle of representation. The insistence that republic is not synonymous with democracy either as direct democracy or as absolute majoritarian democracy, but rather is synonymous with constitutional democracy, is correct in the specific U.S. context, though that usage is a narrowing of the wider use of the term to denote any nonmonarchical regime. The guarantee to the states of the union of a republican form of government (in a nation whose given title deliberately excluded the designation republic) seemingly refers primarily to the more generic usage and it does not imply specific forms or checks.

See also GOVERNMENT; DEMOCRACY.

BIBLIOGRAPHY.—Thomas K. Finletter, *Can Representative Govern-*

ment *Do the Job?* (1945); Ernst Cassirer, *The Myth of the State* (1946); Robert M. MacIver, *The Web of Government* (1947); Alfred de Grazia, *Public and Republic* (1951); Scott Buchanan, *Essay in Politics* (1953).
(T. I. C.)

REPUBLIC, FUND FOR THE, a U.S. educational corporation chartered in 1952 by the state of New York "to defend and advance the principles of the Declaration of Independence and the Constitution." It was organized as an autonomous body, and the founding grant of $15,000,000 from the Ford Foundation was terminal.

In 1954 Robert M. Hutchins (*q.v.*) became president of the Fund, succeeding Sen. Clifford P. Case of New Jersey, who had resigned to run as Republican candidate for the U.S. Senate.

The Fund's concerns included restrictions and assaults upon academic freedom, due process, equal protection of the laws, and the rights of minorities; the use of censorship, boycotts, and blacklists by private groups; and the increasing exercise and acceptance of the principle of guilt by association. The Fund, in its first five years, acted as a grant-making foundation to support educational activities of civic and religious groups that opposed restrictions and infringements of civil rights and civil liberties. Among these were the Southern Regional Council, the American Friends Service Committee, the Anti-Defamation League, the National Urban League, the Legal Defense and Educational Fund of the National Association for the Advancement of Colored People, the National Council of Churches, and the interracial programs of major religious denominations and of the YMCA and YWCA.

The Fund also financed research in the areas of civil rights and civil liberties. Its largest single appropriation, $465,000, was for the preparation and publication of a definitive 15-volume study, directed by Clinton Rossiter, on Communist influence and control in the United States. Examples of the Fund's actions to bring relief to victims of civil rights and civil liberties crises were John Cogley's study of blacklisting in industry—especially the entertainment industry—and reports by Adam Yarmolinsky on the federal government's loyalty-security program and by Paul Lazarsfeld, Wagner Thielens, Jr., and David Riesman on the intimidation of teachers.

After two-thirds of the Fund's capital had been expended, its program was redirected toward clarification of the basic issues "involved in maintaining a free and just society under the strikingly new political, social, economic, and technological conditions of the second half of the twentieth century."

The Fund in 1959 established as its sole activity the Center for the Study of Democratic Institutions at Santa Barbara, Calif., for the purpose of focusing a variety of informed, frequently conflicting viewpoints on significant social, economic, political, and cultural issues in relation to democratic institutions.

The Center set up a small resident staff with permanent and special consultants. In one 12-month period, its visitors included 246 persons from 42 countries who met with the residents and consultants in their daily discussions and debate of specific issues; the resulting papers—often including dissenting comment—were published. In its first five years the Center distributed more than 5,000,000 copies of its publications to interested persons for use in classrooms and in the educational programs of business, union, and church groups. Many of the publications stimulated editorial comment and were reprinted, reviewed, and discussed in other publications; more than 75 books and hundreds of magazine articles were developed from the Center's materials or as products of Fund grants; and over 3,000 tape transcripts of Center discussion programs were made available to radio stations and to universities and adult education groups. The Center's principal contribution was to promote discussion, analysis, and argument of "those aspects of contemporary issues which are usually neglected, misunderstood, or obscured by the smoke of controversy."

REPUBLICAN PARTY (U.S.), one of the two leading political parties in the U.S. since the 1850s. The party originated in 1854 when various small group meetings, the earliest in Ripon, Wis., were held in a half dozen states. A mass meeting at Jackson, Mich., attended by former Whigs, Democrats, and Free-Soilers on July 6, 1854, adopted the name Republican. This was an appealing title not only for those who recalled Jeffersonian "republicanism," but for those who placed the national interest above sectional interests and were opposed to states' rights. The issue presented by slavery in Kansas had called this party into existence. It was from the beginning strongly nationalistic. The pronouncement that slavery was a moral, social, and political evil was coupled with denunciation of the Kansas-Nebraska legislation and the Fugitive Slave law.

An informal meeting in Pittsburgh, Pa., on Feb. 22, 1856, planned the first national convention, which assembled in Philadelphia, Pa., on June 17. Its platform denied to congress the right to recognize slavery in a territory, and held that congress had the right to abolish slavery in the territories and ought to do so. This view, no longer that of extremists, was representative of widespread sentiment in the north. John C. Frémont, who was widely known for his western exploration and in 1849 had been elected to the senate from the state of California, was the party's nominee for the presidency. He won 114 electoral votes, but was defeated in a three-cornered contest against Millard Fillmore, candidate of the American ("Know-Nothing") and Whig parties, and the cautious and conservative Democrat, James Buchanan, who was elected.

Lincoln and Civil War.—During the next four years the nation drifted toward civil war. On May 16, 1860, the Republican national convention met in Chicago, Ill., and nominated Abraham Lincoln. In a four-party contest, Lincoln led the Republicans to victory. (*See* UNITED STATES [OF AMERICA]: *History.*) The new party had rapidly displaced the Whigs in the north as the main opponent of the Democrats.

Lincoln's primary policy was the preservation of the union. The outbreak of rebellion in southern states and the secession of 11 states played havoc with existing party lines. For four years the armed conflict came to no positive conclusion. In the autumn of 1864 the president faced the necessity of going to the people at the stated election time, and did so with slight hope of a vote of endorsement. His supporters confessed their weakness. In calls for a convention and in the convention, they termed themselves the Union party. This party, with Lincoln as its nominee and a war Democrat, Andrew Johnson, as vice-presidential nominee, did defeat the Democrats who had in their national convention that year declared the war a failure. The war was continued to a successful conclusion, but the assassination of Lincoln, who died on April 15, 1865, brought a complete realignment of political forces.

Reconstruction and After.—Within a year of the end of hostilities, the Republican party had reappeared and was functioning as an organization bent upon retaining control of the government and taking a form that was to prove the most powerful yet seen in the history of parties in the United States. Throughout the following 30 years, the Republicans and the Democrats—who by the autumn of 1866 appeared as the one agency of strong opposition—fought for control of the national government, the Republicans usually winning.

The fight for improvement in the civil service, for genuine tariff revision, for a democratic land policy and for protection of the Indians persisted within the parties. Within the Republican party, insurgent groups protested in vain at the rigidity of party control. On two occasions such groups left the party, the Liberal Republicans in 1872, and the Progressives in 1912. Yet on each occasion many leaders and millions of voters remained.

In the years of chaotic reconstruction, the Republicans kept troops in the south and attempted to confer political power upon the unprepared Negro. In these years the Republican party organization was revealed as of selfish design and cowardly practice, ruled by a small and usually self-perpetuating group of politicians who made party regularity a fetish. Their list of nominees for the presidency included Generals Ulysses S. Grant, Rutherford B. Hayes, James A. Garfield and Benjamin Harrison, and Maj. William McKinley. To the support of these tickets rallied voters from the villages and country districts of the old east and of the new west, mostly men of small means attached to the traditions of their pioneering forefathers. The Republican appeal was frankly to businessmen as the 19th century ended.

The tariff was included in the Republican platform as an issue in the campaign of 1896, but as election day approached much greater prominence was given the question of the free and unlimited coinage of silver. William McKinley of Ohio was nominated by the Republicans on a gold standard platform and won the election.

Republicans in congress had in 1896 favoured recognition of the independence of the Cubans, who were in revolt against the government of Spain. The Republican party platform of that year expressed the hope that the Cubans would win their struggle for liberty and that the U.S. government would actively use its influence to restore peace and give independence to the island. In April 1898 President McKinley, responding to public opinion inflamed by the sinking of the battleship "Maine" in Havana harbour, demanded that Spain withdraw from Cuba. War came soon after, a war that for many months had seemed to members of both parties desirable and inevitable. The war nevertheless exposed issues in world relations that led to a sharp division between the two parties. A treaty of annexation of the Hawaiian Islands had been negotiated by Pres. Benjamin Harrison in 1893 and withdrawn by Pres. Grover Cleveland. The Republicans, who came to favour such annexation, argued military and commercial necessity. Despite strong Democratic opposition, in the summer of 1898 by joint resolution of congress the republic of Hawaii was annexed to the United States with territorial status.

The nation entered upon the congressional campaign of 1898 before the end of the war with Spain. The Republicans gained 8 seats in the senate, although the Democrats gained in the house by 29. The administration now called for the cession of the Philippines to the United States, and Spain was forced to yield.

Early 20th Century.—A new era in Republican party domination was dawning. Theodore Roosevelt, who in 1898 had been elected governor of New York, was supported for the vice-presidency in the campaign of 1900 by Republican party boss T. C. Platt, who was anxious to get him out of New York politics. Roosevelt had a large and enthusiastic following among the delegates from western states, and was nominated against the wishes of both McKinley and Marcus Alonzo Hanna, who, however, bowed to the will of the convention. The problem of the party managers was one of first magnitude when, in the autumn of 1901, the assassination of President McKinley brought to the presidency the independent and imaginative Roosevelt. Since the Republican party at that time did not possess a definite party program, as it had in 1897, there was both opportunity and need for a leader who could reshape its appeal and its purpose. This President Roosevelt proceeded to do.

In considering the course of action that should be his at this juncture, Roosevelt chose to direct his attention to the trusts that had become extremely powerful. The president's attack was directed not upon large business, as such, but upon business combinations that believed themselves superior to the government. The popularity of Roosevelt's position on the trusts and his aggressive action in the coal strike of 1902 brought to his support thousands who had for many years been interested in governmental control of corporations.

Roosevelt's acquisition of the widespread popular support that won him re-election in 1904 was made possible by the failure of the Democratic party to justify the expectations aroused in 1896. The party had seemed at that time to promise emancipation from the oppressions of organized wealth and millions of voters had twice supported William Jennings Bryan for these reasons. When Roosevelt professed to desire the same ends, many Democrats came to his support.

The overwhelming endorsement of Roosevelt in 1904 gave to his second administration a more personal character than had prevailed in the preceding three years. That Roosevelt subsequently brought about the nomination of William Howard Taft, who was elected in 1908, led to a widespread but erroneous belief that the Republican party organization was responsive to Roosevelt's leadership. With the overthrow in 1910 of their majority in the house of representatives, the Republicans ended 14 years of complete control of the national government. The 1910

Republican Presidential and Vice-Presidential Nominees
(Successful candidates in boldface type; unsuccessful in lightface type)

Year	Presidential nominee	Vice-Presidential nominee
1856	John C. Frémont	William L. Dayton
1860	**Abraham Lincoln**	**Hannibal Hamlin**
1864*	**Abraham Lincoln†**	**Andrew Johnson**
1868	**Ulysses S. Grant**	**Schuyler Colfax**
1872	**Ulysses S. Grant**	**Henry Wilson†**
1876	**Rutherford B. Hayes**	**William A. Wheeler**
1880	**James A. Garfield†**	**Chester A. Arthur**
1884	James G. Blaine	John A. Logan
1888	**Benjamin Harrison**	**Levi P. Morton**
1892	Benjamin Harrison	Whitelaw Reid
1896	**William McKinley**	**Garret A. Hobart†**
1900	**William McKinley†**	**Theodore Roosevelt**
1904	**Theodore Roosevelt**	**Charles W. Fairbanks**
1908	**William Howard Taft**	**James S. Sherman**
1912	William Howard Taft	James S. Sherman‡
1916	Charles Evans Hughes	Charles W. Fairbanks
1920	**Warren G. Harding†**	**Calvin Coolidge**
1924	**Calvin Coolidge**	**Charles G. Dawes**
1928	**Herbert Hoover**	**Charles Curtis**
1932	Herbert Hoover	Charles Curtis
1936	Alfred M. Landon	Frank Knox
1940	Wendell L. Willkie	Charles L. McNary
1944	Thomas E. Dewey	John W. Bricker
1948	Thomas E. Dewey	Earl Warren
1952	**Dwight D. Eisenhower**	**Richard M. Nixon**
1956	**Dwight D. Eisenhower**	**Richard M. Nixon**
1960	Richard M. Nixon	Henry Cabot Lodge
1964	Barry M. Goldwater	William E. Miller
1968	**Richard M. Nixon**	**Spiro T. Agnew**

*Officially the Union Party (*see* text).   †Died in office.   ‡Died a week before election day; his electoral votes were cast for Nicholas Murray Butler.

elections also revealed the strength of western party insurgents who henceforth opposed the national party on many issues.

In Feb. 1912, Roosevelt announced that he was willing to accept the Republican nomination, thus attempting to obtain what he seemed to have in 1908, but which he had never won in open competition—control of the party machinery. He now attempted to make the party organization responsive to the demands of the party's voters. State primary elections revealed the popularity of his candidacy, but Taft won the nomination at the party convention. Roosevelt's supporters thereupon bolted the party and organized the Progressive party (*q.v.*) with a platform calling for a change in political machinery and an aggressive program of social legislation. The Progressives nominated Roosevelt for president and Gov. Hiram W. Johnson of California for vice-president. With the Republican vote thus split, the Democratic candidate, Woodrow Wilson, was elected.

At the end of World War I the Republicans returned to power, electing Sen. Warren G. Harding of Ohio as president. When Harding died in Aug. 1923 he was succeeded by Vice-Pres. Calvin Coolidge. By this time the Republican party had become more than ever a coalition of sectional leaders and divergent economic interests. Its outstanding national figures were not regulars but insurgents such as Sen. Robert M. La Follette of Wisconsin, who led his followers out of the party in 1924. In the three-party election of that year Coolidge rode to victory on a wave of prosperity that continued until after the election of Republican Herbert Hoover in 1928. An engineer by profession, Hoover had gained widespread recognition for his service as administrator of U.S. relief abroad at the end of World War I and as secretary of commerce under Harding and Coolidge. The world-wide depression that overtook the U.S. economy in 1929, and defections by Republicans in congress, led to Hoover's defeat in 1932 by Franklin D. Roosevelt. Roosevelt's three re-elections, the succession of Harry S. Truman upon Roosevelt's death and Truman's election in 1948 kept the Republicans in a minority position for 20 years.

Since 1950.—In 1952 with the nomination of a popular World War II general, Dwight D. Eisenhower, the Republican party returned to power under the dominance of its liberal-moderate wing, as opposed to its conservative wing led by Sen. Robert A. Taft of Ohio. Eisenhower's moderate course in domestic and foreign affairs attracted much non-Republican support and in 1956 the Republicans renominated him and his vice-president, Richard M. Nixon of California. Eisenhower easily defeated the Democratic candidate, former Gov. Adlai E. Stevenson of Illinois, for the second time. The Republicans failed to win control of either house of congress and in 1958 lost more congressional seats.

In 1960 the Republicans nominated Nixon for president and Henry Cabot Lodge, U.S. ambassador to the United Nations, for vice-president. Both vigorously ran on the Eisenhower record. The campaign featured a series of joint television appearances by Nixon and Sen. John F. Kennedy of Massachusetts, the Democratic candidate. In the election, Nixon and Lodge lost in the closest popular vote in the 20th century. The defeat, followed in 1962 by failure to make substantial gains in congress, widened the breach between conservative and liberal Republicans. The conservatives came under the leadership of Sen. Barry M. Goldwater of Arizona. The liberal-moderates were divided, looking for leadership to such men as Nixon, Lodge, Gov. Nelson Rockefeller of New York, Gov. George Romney of Michigan and Gov. William Scranton of Pennsylvania.

The conservatives, with superior organization at the delegate level, dominated the 1964 national convention. The liberals and moderates were unable to unite effectively behind any one candidate, and Goldwater was nominated on the first ballot. For his running mate he chose Rep. William E. Miller of New York, the Republican national chairman, whose views were close to Goldwater's. Goldwater made no concessions to the moderates in his acceptance speech, and shortly after the convention he filled the strategic posts in the national organization with conservatives of his choice.

Some moderates, including Eisenhower, Nixon, and Scranton, eventually endorsed him, but other Republican candidates concentrated on their own campaigns, giving little or no support to the national ticket. During the campaign Goldwater and Miller denounced the trend toward centralized government under Democratic administrations and urged greater firmness in opposing Communism abroad. Their campaign strategy was based on exploiting the presumed discontent of many voters with current developments in American society, including the opposition of normally Democratic white southerners to the civil-rights policies of the Kennedy-Johnson administration.

The election on Nov. 3 was an overwhelming Democratic victory. The Republican national ticket carried only Arizona and five states of the deep south. The Johnson landslide cut across all levels of government, bringing with it large Democratic majorities in congress and in state legislatures throughout the country.

With the party's fortunes at their lowest point since 1936, Goldwater's appointees were removed from the national organization and Ray Bliss of Ohio, an astute organizer not identified with any particular faction, was named as national chairman. Bliss's announced intention was to intensify Republican appeals to urban and ethnic groups. However, the party's organizational and financial efforts continued to be splintered among a number of independent factional groups, such as the liberal Republicans for Progress and the conservative Free Society association, which Goldwater helped to found.

In the 1966 elections the party gained in national power and in prestige, capturing 8 governorships, to give it 25 out of 50; 3 new seats in the senate; and 47 additional seats in the house—still short of a majority in either house.

In 1968 Nixon made a comeback, sweeping through a first-ballot nomination over the opposition of Governor Romney, Governor Rockefeller, and Gov. Ronald Reagan of California. Nixon's running mate was Gov. Spiro T. Agnew of Maryland. They campaigned to capitalize on the electorate's dissatisfaction with an unpopular Democratic administration, especially on the issues of the Vietnam war and the rapidly worsening urban crisis on all fronts: housing, crime, education, and civil rights. The Republican nominees suffered, as did the Democratic nominees, from an attrition of their normal support by the campaign of George C. Wallace, candidate of the American Independent party, who appeared popular with conservative Republicans and with rank-and-file working class voters, traditionally Democratic voters. In the Nov. 5 election, the Republican candidates won.

See also references under "Republican Party" in the Index.

BIBLIOGRAPHY.—A. Larson, *A Republican Looks at His Party* (1956); M. Moos, *Republicans: a History of Their Party* (1956); G. H. Mayer, *The Republican Party, 1854–1964* (1964).   (E. E. R.; X.)

REQUESTS, COURT OF, in England, one of the prerogative courts, was a minor court of equity, in origin a committee of the King's Council, presided over by the lord privy seal. Its records begin in 1493. It followed the king until established at Whitehall in 1516 or 1517 by Cardinal Wolsey, and until about 1529 it was called the Court of Poor Men's Causes. A popular court because of the lesser expense involved, it dealt chiefly with matters such as title to land, covenants, annuities, forgery, and debt.

Two permanent masters of requests were appointed about 1550 and four in 1603; the link with the council was gradually forgotten. From 1590 onward a series of prohibitions from the Court of Common Pleas reduced business in the Court of Requests. It was not abolished in 1641 with the other prerogative courts, but the masters ceased to sit after 1642 and appointments made after the Restoration of Charles II (1660) were only for the purpose of assessing compensation due to royalists.

The name courts of requests was also given to inferior local courts established by special act of Parliament to deal with small debts. These courts were abolished by the County Courts Act (1846). The City of London's Court of Requests, often called the Court of Conscience, was abolished in 1847.

See I. S. Leadham, *Select Cases in the Court of Requests* (1898); J. R. Tanner, *Tudor Constitutional Documents* (1922).

RESCUE MISSION (GOSPEL MISSION), an institution designed to administer spiritual and physical succour in city slums. It originated in the city mission movement among evangelical laymen and ministers early in the 19th century. David Nasmith, a Scottish philanthropist, was instrumental in founding the Glasgow City Mission (1826) and the London City Mission (1835), both of which sought to evangelize and rehabilitate the urban poor. Beginning with home visitation and tract distribution by volunteer lay missionaries, the city mission movement expanded into Sunday school, day school, and temperance activities with paid missionaries, and eventually provided food, lodging, employment, and medical care to the destitute and sick.

In 1848 Johann Wichern, a German Sunday school worker, founded the Hamburg Society for the Inner Mission which coordinated church and charitable activities in Hamburg and later spread throughout Germany. The New York City Mission and Tract Society began home visitation in the 1830s and founded its first mission station in 1852. The work of William Booth and the Salvation Army (*q.v.*) after 1865 brought a new impetus to rescue mission endeavour.

Most rescue missions have been founded and supported denominationally or interdenominationally, but some of the most successful have been nondenominational, among them the North End Mission in Boston (1867), Jerry McAuley's Water Street Mission in New York (1872), and Col. George Clarke's Pacific Garden Mission in Chicago (1877). Although the work of rescue missions resembles that of settlement houses (*see* SOCIAL SETTLEMENTS), institutional churches, and charitable societies, it is distinguishable from these by its emphasis upon religious conversion through evangelistic preaching services.

BIBLIOGRAPHY.—John Campbell, *Memoirs of David Nasmith* (1844); John M. Weylland, *Round the Tower: the Story of the London City Mission* (1875); Martin Gerhardt, *Johann Hinrich Wichern; ein Lebensbild*, 3 vol. (1927–31); Harold Begbie, *The Life of General William Booth* (1920); Aaron I. Abell, *The Urban Impact on American Protestantism: 1865–1900* (1943); Charles Booth, *Life and Labours of the People in London*, vol. vii (1902); Samuel H. Hadley, *Down in Water Street* (1906); Kenneth S. Inglis, *Churches and the Working Class in Victorian England* (1963); Kathleen Heasman, *Evangelicals in Action: an Appraisal of Their Social Work in the Victorian Era* (1962).   (W. G. McL.)

RESEARCH, INDUSTRIAL, is research undertaken on problems related to industrial products or production methods. Traditionally it stood in contrast to fundamental or basic research carried on without regard for its immediate practical value, but with increasing government financing of research projects the contrast between industrial research and fundamental research has lessened considerably. In the middle years of the 20th century industrial research also extended its scope to include the systematic study of industrial operations, the handling of materials, and the layout of plants. As it became concerned broadly with the economic efficiency of industry it contributed to raising the level of productivity through the better use of human and material resources.

In the early days of industrial research an individual inventor would present his idea to a producing firm in the form of a model, which had then to be redesigned by the firm's engineers if it were to be made suitable for industrial production. (*See* INVENTIONS AND DISCOVERIES.) The process, while yielding good results in the long run, was slow, haphazard, and wasteful. From about the beginning of the 20th century, therefore, industrial firms began to employ men who were trained in scientific methods, most of whom were drawn from the universities. These men worked independently on individual projects, with or without assistants. But as projects became more complex they could not be completely carried through by a single researcher and had to be tackled by research teams. The increasing scale of industrial research led throughout the world to its concentration into ever bigger units, controlled by large organizations or groups of companies. The importance of its results led to increasing government interest in it; and by the 1960s many countries were supporting industrial research projects with government funds. A striking feature of modern industrial research is the degree to which countries such as the United States and the U.S.S.R., with their profound differences of ideology and of organization, have relied upon government financing.

Many problems are so vast that they have to be tackled internationally as, for example, with the union of smaller nations in joint scientific projects such as the European Atomic Energy Establishment, and even by collaboration between the United States and the U.S.S.R., as in the International Geophysical Year of 1958. This international network produces a type of organization with complex scientific instruments, libraries acting as memory stores, and elaborate communications systems. In this last field lies the greatest handicap to smooth growth. The very mass of scientific data being processed all over the world may clog the machine; the accumulated knowledge in the libraries of the world is recalled very erratically and a considerable portion is forgotten forever and has to be rediscovered. This problem was being investigated the world over in the 1960s.

There is no way of evaluating the results of research in terms of accountancy. Most good industrial research laboratories can point to some outstanding achievements over a period of years and claim rightly that if they had done nothing else they would have paid for themselves handsomely. But although this may inspire confidence it does not enable a board of a company to determine how much of its profits it should devote to research. Research expenditure in industry is frequently expressed as a proportion of annual turnover, and the proportions, as would be expected, vary greatly from industry to industry (3% is not uncommon in firms in the newer science-based industries). There is, however, no logical justification for comparing or estimating research expenditure on this basis; experience and judgment are the only guides, and boards of companies who are alive to the needs of the times endeavour to maintain a level of research which will enable them to remain competitive in world markets.   (A. G. Fo.)

UNITED STATES

In the United States, as elsewhere, research and development had, by the middle of the 20th century, gained recognition as significant factors in economic growth and national security. This had, of course, not always been the case. In the early 1900s a few large firms had organized research departments but, in the main, these had grown out of the work of private inventors like Thomas A. Edison (1847–1931), who were formally associated with particular companies. Before 1900 technological advance depended solely on the skills of individual inventors and upon the industrialists who were prepared to make use of their discoveries. The patent system was specifically referred to in the U.S. Constitution of 1789 but during the following century few industrialists realized that they could emulate early inventors and increase their profits by contributing to the research and development process.

There was, in fact, much misunderstanding between scientists and industrialists, and many businessmen strongly doubted the wisdom of operating research departments within their industrial organizations. It was only at the beginning of the 20th century that the drawing office started to evolve into the engineering department and test house, and then into the research laboratory. World War I did much to call attention to the benefits that could be gained by the systematic application of scientific methods and discoveries to industrial problems; and after the war many companies regarded research as an integral part of their business activities.

Between the World Wars.—Reliable statistics on the extent and character of industrial research in the United States are virtually nonexistent for the period before World War II, but figures compiled by the National Research Council suggest that there was a sevenfold increase in the industrial research effort during the period 1920–40. In 1920 about 300 industrial companies employed 9,300 research workers, and by 1940, 2,350 companies were employing more than 70,000 workers. The expenditures by industrial companies for research in 1940 were thought to be about $300,-000,000 a year. Industrial research was still confined mainly to the large corporations, but smaller companies were beginning to appreciate its influence on their business operations.

The number and size of industrial research laboratories grew steadily, and their importance began to rival that of government research establishments. After World War I, the government could have taken the lead in organizing the development of industrial research, as in Great Britain; but the strong desire for economy and tax reductions resulted in the government's leaving the bulk of industrial research to the large industrial corporations. Nevertheless in the Department of Commerce there was a strong link between the government and industrial research, which had grown out of the need for effective governmental control of weights and measures and of standardization in general. The secretary of commerce (1921–28), Herbert Hoover, who had begun his career as a mining engineer, was one of the few major political figures of his time who had a true appreciation of the value of science. He believed that his department should carry out scientific research and should also help to eliminate inefficiency from industrial operations. Under his guidance the National Bureau of Standards worked with industry to launch a cooperative program of simplified practices and commercial standardization; and by 1924 about 23 industrial trade associations were supporting 29 research associates, who worked alongside government scientists at the National Bureau of Standards. Hoover appreciated the dependence of industrial research on fundamental research, and he was also well aware of the paucity of American fundamental research at that time. Believing that industry should bear some responsibility for fundamental research, and in an effort to redress the balance, he was instrumental in establishing the National Research Fund in 1926. This fund was designed to allow industry to make regular and substantial contributions to a monetary pool to be used as a common source of finance for universities carrying out independent fundamental research. For a variety of reasons the fund was a failure and was discontinued in 1934; but it marked a realization that both government and industry had a responsibility for maintaining a balance between pure and applied science.

The depression years (1929–38) resulted in substantial reductions in the research activities of both government and industry. At the same time the government undertook a detailed examination of the function of research within the national economy. This led to the modern concept of research as a vital national resource, and a recognition of government responsibility for the total national research effort. As a result, from 1935 onward, the federal government played a larger and larger part in national research activities, a trend which was accelerated by the demands of World War II.

After World War II.—Many of the characteristics of wartime research effected permanent changes both in research itself and in the relations between government and industry. By 1961 the government had become the principal source of funds; but because the perpetuation of the wartime research contract system resulted in the expenditure of most of this money in industry, industry became responsible not only for research designed to improve its own products and methods, but also for a major proportion of military research. This, far from being a handicap, enabled U.S. industry to build up larger and more versatile research facilities than those of any other country.

The rapid and spectacular growth in federal research and development in the decades following World War II tended to disguise the equally significant growth in nonfederal research activity —a ten-fold increase between 1941 and the early 1960s. There is no single reason for this great expansion in privately sponsored research. In addition to the evidence provided by World War II of the value of research, there was the effect of taxation policies, and also the rapid expansion of training facilities at academic institutions, which helped to make society more research-conscious.

In 1961 the aircraft industry and the electrical industry together accounted for nearly three-fifths of the $10,900,000,000 spent on industrial research and development. This heavy concentration of activity arose because of the large numbers of government-sponsored projects in such fields as rocketry, electronics, and atomic energy. Next came the chemical and allied industries which spent $1,100,000,000, and then the transport industry with an expenditure of $896,000,000. In nearly all industries, the bulk of research and development was undertaken by firms employing more than 5,000 persons; and in several industries; *e.g.*, aircraft production and oil refining, more than nine-tenths of it was conducted by large firms. Although nearly all industrial research was financed by the government and by companies, a relatively small amount was financed from "other sources" (which spent $79,000,000 in 1961). These included commercial and nonprofit organizations providing an extensive range of specialized services for industrial firms on a contract basis.

Of the nonprofit-sponsored research institutes that have long played an important role in industrial research in the United States, the Mellon Institute, Pittsburgh, founded in 1913, is typical. It is an endowed, nonprofit, corporate body "for conducting comprehensive investigations on important problems in the fundamental and applied natural sciences, for training research workers and for providing technical information adaptable to professional, public and industrial advantage." There being no need to consider owners or shareholders the institutes have complete freedom to choose their program. They are free to pay their workers at the current market rates; and, as they are not hampered by conditions of academic tenure or by civil service regulations, they can employ staff on short-term contracts. This flexibility enables them to respond rapidly to the changing research needs of their sponsors, and thus contributes toward their effectiveness. Methods of operation are varied. First, an institute can perform a complete investigation for a sponsor, providing the same service as a central research laboratory does for its company. It is often only by recourse to an institute that a small company can afford to undertake any substantial research, which increasingly demands the facilities of a large and expensive laboratory and the combined efforts of a team of highly qualified scientists and engineers. Large firms, too, often use institutes when they do not wish to disrupt their current activities, or when they require special extra skills and facilities. Second, a sponsored research institute can provide valuable training for graduates, who will eventually be employed by the sponsor company. Third, many of the institutes can use funds of their own for investigations of their own choice. For example, by 1962 about 55% of the total contract research undertaken by the Armour Research Foundation was the result of its own efforts to build up specialized knowledge in particular areas selected by its staff. About 30% of its 650 then-current sponsored projects had stemmed from ideas generated by the staff and had been subsequently taken over by suitable sponsors.

Numerous universities, too, undertake sponsored research for industry in much the same way as the nonprofit and commercial research institutes. When research on specific problems is required, special arrangements can be made to safeguard the "rights" of the sponsor, and the results can remain secret for an agreed period. Generally, however, educational institutions prefer to accept research contracts only when the freedom of action of their workers can be maintained; and it is increasingly recognized that industry has a responsibility to support fundamental research on an unrestricted basis and that this should preferably be carried out in a university or college. This has led to the development of industrial research fellowships and industrial grant-in-aid schemes for the support of long-term basic research programs in universities, with few restrictions on the field of work, which is often selected by the universities themselves.

An interesting development took place in 1963 when the Carnegie Institute of Technology, the University of Pittsburgh, and the Mellon Institute jointly set up the MPC Corporation to enable them to collaborate on scientific and educational studies. A major aim of the corporation is to stimulate collaboration between its constituent institutions and local industry.

Another type of nonprofit research institute is the federal contract research centre, which had its origin in technological operations conducted by the Office of Scientific Research and Development (OSRD) during World War II. OSRD was empowered, among other functions, to coordinate and supplement research activities for the public good, and in this capacity it created by contract what are in effect national research laboratories to undertake projects demanding unusual equipment or special skills such as, for example, projects on radar and proximity fuses. After the termination of OSRD in 1947, responsibility for the Federal Contract Research Centres passed to a variety of other government agencies, and later on a number of other facilities of the same type were set up. By 1963 there were 60 such centres, together absorbing $1,300,000,000—or about 10% of all federal funds spent on research and development during that year. The 19 centres administered by industrial companies spent about $440,000,000 per annum in the early 1960s. The majority of these centres were concerned with large-system engineering projects in such fields as electronics, space research, and atomic energy. The Jet Propulsion Laboratory, for example, was administered by the California Institute of Technology on behalf of the National Aeronautics and Space Administration, and was concerned with the development of unmanned interplanetary spacecraft and related technology. Although administered by an educational institution, much of its work (which cost about $300,000,000 in 1962) was subcontracted to industry.

The end results of industrial research are new and improved products and processes. But it has long been realized that no one company or industry could afford to undertake all the research that might be relevant to its business. Of more and more importance has become the task of providing information to guide the wise formulation of research programs and the selection of development projects on a basis of comprehensive knowledge of the results of current and previous work elsewhere. Scientists have always realized the importance of such information; but only after about 1950 was information recognized as a vital industrial research tool, and systematic attempts to improve national and company information services date from then. Thus emerged the specialized information centre, whose task is to collect, assess, and consolidate information in a narrow field, and to disseminate it to potential users. By the middle 1960s there were more than 200 such centres operating on a national basis. The majority were financed with federal funds, but some were financed on a cooperative basis by groups of companies, and others were operated by universities and scientific societies. Large companies, too, recognized the importance of the centres, and some had established them within their research departments in much the same way as laboratory equipment. (ED. G. H.)

GREAT BRITAIN

The government role in industrial research first became important in Great Britain during World War I, which led to the setting up of the Department of Scientific and Industrial Research (DSIR) in 1916. In 1918 this department became financially responsible for the National Physical Laboratory, which had been established in 1900 by the Royal Society with a small treasury grant. The department grew steadily, and by 1939 it had a net annual expenditure of £500,000. World War II hastened its development so that by 1960 it was spending more than £8,000,000 yearly. Increasing government awareness of the importance of industrial research and the need to encourage postgraduate work in universities led to even faster expansion, so that annual expenditure by the mid-1960s was rising above £20,000,000.

The work of DSIR is carried out in 15 research establishments of its own and in more than 50 autonomous industrial research associations to which it makes grants. It also contributes to research at universities and colleges and makes awards to postgraduate students. The DSIR's own laboratories tend to concentrate on work of national importance which no one private industry can undertake; e.g., road research, water pollution research, geological survey, building research, and chemicals research.

The research association scheme, by which the government financially assists groups of firms with similar interests to carry out research in collaboration, was started in 1917. By the mid-1960s more than 50 associations had a total annual income of approximately £8,000,000 (compared with £5,000,000 in 1955); less than a quarter of this being contributed by the government with the advice of the Industrial Grants Committee of DSIR. More than 60% of industry is able to make use of associations, from the large British Iron and Steel Research Associations (BISRA, annual income, £1,000,000) to the much smaller File Research Council (annual income £12,000). Among the largest associations are those for the metal industry, electrical engineering, marine engineering, and shipbuilding.

The research associations are autonomous and are governed by councils mostly drawn from industry, but with DSIR representation. The councils are responsible for research programs on which they have the advice of committees consisting of members of industry and often of university or government scientists or trade union representatives as well. The DSIR appoints two visitors to each association; usually a scientist and an industrialist. Commonwealth and other overseas manufacturers are often members. The associations provide bulletins, technical reports, lectures, films, training classes, exhibitions, and mobile demonstration units for their member firms.

The nationalized industries have their own research organizations. The National Coal Board has three centres; the electricity supply industry and the Gas Council have each three principal laboratories.

Nuclear energy research and development is carried out by the Atomic Energy Authority (AEA; set up by the Atomic Energy Authority Act, 1954) under the minister for science. Although the AEA is free from day-to-day government control, most of its income is from public revenue. The AEA produces explosive nuclear material, carries out weapon research for the armed services, and builds the prototypes of nuclear power stations for civil use. Various government committees coordinate research on nuclear power for ships and on the health and safety aspects of work with atomic energy.

Space research is coordinated by the minister for science, with the advice of other ministers and of a steering group representing government and university scientists. This group is advised by the British National Committee on Space Research, which the Royal Society appoints, and which also represents the United Kingdom internationally in, for example, the Special Committee on Space Research (established in 1958 by the International Council of Scientific Unions). The practical work is done at universities (to which DSIR directs grants) and government research establishments. Equipment and materials also are developed by private industry. Government expenditure was estimated at more than £1,000,000 in 1963.

The dissemination of the results of research to other workers and to users in industry is difficult because of the rapid increase in the amount of information available. The time lag between the discovery of scientific or technological facts and their industrial application grows constantly. Therefore, while the traditional publication of papers is still carried on, other means of dissemination are utilized, such as the establishment by the government of technical liaison centres in industrial regions to help in channeling inquiries from industrialists to research workers. The research

associations also try many ways of improving communications between their scientific staff and industry; while firms themselves have established technical information departments within, or parallel with, their research and development departments. The need for qualified staffs to run these departments resulted in the establishment in 1958 of the Institute of Information Scientists, a qualifying body which sponsors postgraduate training and research with the help of a DSIR grant.

DSIR also supports ASLIB (the Association of Special Libraries and Information Bureaux); and has set up a National Lending Library for Science and Technology (1961). In collaboration with the National Science Foundation of the United States, this library makes available foreign works, particularly Russian and Chinese, in translation.

By 1964, scientific policy was a major item in electoral programs of political parties, and a major reconstitution of the government departments dealing with science, and probably of the DSIR also, seemed likely as a result of the implementation of the report (1963) of the committee of inquiry into the organization of civil science set up in 1962 under the chairmanship of Sir Burke Trend.

(A. G. Fo.)

U.S.S.R.

In the U.S.S.R. the organization of scientific research, including industrial research, is very different from its organization in non-Communist countries. The scientific activity itself, if the social sciences and biology are excluded (and therefore this applies virtually to the whole of industrial research), is much the same in the Soviet Union as elsewhere. Developments are taking place along similar lines in all parts of the world, although, inevitably, differences exist as to the rate of progress, which depends on resources and on the degree of priority or importance attached to various fields in various countries. The broad objectives also are similar in many ways. A comparison of the aims, in the field of scientific research, of the Communist governments with those of Western governments, for example, has revealed many similarities. But the organization of research could hardly be more different.

The Role of Scientific Research.—In the U.S.S.R. science is called upon to play a decisive role. This has been so ever since Lenin in 1918 called upon the Academy of Sciences to organize committees of specialists who would draw up a plan for the reorganization of industry on a basis of the formation of large enterprises. The aim was to make the Russian Soviet Republic largely independent of the outside world for its raw materials and industrial products. An important factor in the achievement of this aim was to be electrification.

The extent to which science is allowed to lead a life of its own independently of the needs of industry has varied. Under Stalin, there was great emphasis on the need to solve industrial problems, often short-term ones, at the expense of basic or long-term research. After Stalin's death in 1953, however, fundamental research became more acceptable officially, and although science was still considered valid only within the philosophical confines of Marxism-Leninism, the pressures on scientists to reject spheres of work (e.g., relativity theory or cybernetics) on ideological grounds were greatly lessened.

As a result of the view of science as a powerful force for the development of the economy, an important feature of Soviet industrial research is the continuing effort through exhortation and legislation to "strengthen the ties between science and production." The program adopted at the 22nd Congress of the Communist Party on Oct. 31, 1961, describing the "tasks of the Communist Party of the Soviet Union in building a communist society," began the section *Tasks in the Field of Science* with the assertion that, under the socialist system of economy, scientific and technical progress enables man to employ the riches and forces of nature most effectively in the interests of the people; and ended it with the sentence: "It is a point of honour for Soviet scientists to consolidate the advanced positions which Soviet science has won in major branches of knowledge and to take a leading place in world science in all the key fields."

Research Institutes.—It is difficult to draw a line between industrial and nonindustrial research in the U.S.S.R. All organizations engaged in civil research can be said to a greater or lesser extent to be carrying out industrial research. A number of categories of research organization can be described, however. First there is the Academy of Sciences of the U.S.S.R. in Moscow (founded by Peter I the Great in 1724), which combines the functions of a society of learned men (*cf.* Great Britain's Royal Society) with those of a large research organization. It is responsible for about 100 research institutes. It has throughout its career had practical tasks assigned to it; but for most of the time it has tended to concentrate on fundamental scientific investigation. This Academy is also the Academy of the Russian Soviet Federated Socialist Republic, in various parts of which regional branches have been established. The most important of these is in the new scientific town near Novosibirsk. Each of the other 14 republics of the U.S.S.R. has an academy of sciences, the largest and oldest being that of the Ukrainian S.S.R. (founded in 1918 and reorganized in 1919).

Industry and industrial research, including thousands of institutes, laboratories, and bureaus (some of them very small), are administered by the State Planning Commission (Gosplan, founded 1921), by more than 40 regional economic councils (*sovnarkhozi*), and by about 60 state committees some of which have all-union responsibility. The committees are in effect special ministries which secure liaison between industry and the central government and provide the technological foundation for the work of Gosplan. Some of them are responsible for progress in whole industries, such as heavy power generation, transport engineering, instrumentation, automation and control, fuel, chemicals, and food, while others, called production committees, supervise not only research and development but also individual factories and enterprises. All of these bodies are responsible to the Supreme Economic Council of the U.S.S.R. In addition to the research institutes there are thousands of research laboratories and design and planning institutes and construction bureaus. Some are large and have international renown (*e.g.*, the I. V. Kurchatov Institute of Nuclear Physics in Moscow, or the Paton Institute of Welding in Kiev); and some occupy little more than one or two rooms.

Finally, research is carried out in the universities, but this is on a relatively small scale compared with that in the remainder of the country. In the past the view has been taken that universities exist to teach, research institutes exist to do research, and industry exists to design and produce. These rather clear-cut definitions have led to some difficulty of communication. There is growing insistence on the importance of strengthening the research potential of the universities, but this is proving difficult to bring about, and there is steady pressure from both scientists and government officials to end the rigid demarcation between teaching and research activities.

Research Coordination.—The Marxist view is held to lead to the concept of science as an organism with mutually dependent parts which serves the economic needs of the country. The question is: Who is to provide the brain of the organism—or, in the words of Academician A. N. Nesmeyanov, a former president of the All-Union Academy of Sciences: "Who is to conduct the Soviet Scientific Orchestra?" The indications, about 1959, were that the All-Union Academy would undertake the task; at about that time the Academy listed the "Thirty Basic Directions of Science," resolving to concentrate its forces on these (23 of them being within the field of physical science and the remainder being concerned with history, linguistics, law, etc.). The "basic directions" concentrated attention on fairly broadly defined fields which were considered to have high economic significance; *e.g.*, the problem of controllable thermonuclear synthesis and the nature of elementary particles, in atomic physics; geophysical research; and photosynthesis, nutrition, and development of plants.

But in 1961 another state organization, the State Committee for the Co-ordination of Scientific Research, was formed and given executive powers, control over the finance of research and development, and a broad mandate to eliminate "parallelism" or duplication of effort throughout the Soviet Union.

The following years saw intense reorganization. The All-Union

Academy of Sciences shed almost one-half of its institutes, mainly those of the Technical Sciences Division, engaged on engineering problems. These were transferred to the state committees and to industry. State coordination committees were founded in all of the republics.

By the mid-1960s a division of responsibilities for coordinating research appeared to have been established between the All-Union Academy of Sciences and the All-Union State Co-ordination Committee. Broadly speaking, the academy was to be concerned with the more fundamental scientific work and was to coordinate the research programs of all the republican academies of sciences in addition to its own; the committee was to concentrate more on applied research or development. Scientific councils were set up to guide development along most or all of the "basic directions" of science, their members being drawn from the academies, the government, the universities, and industry. "Leading institutes" were appointed to lead the attack in each direction.

Important weapons in the elimination of "parallelism" and the improvement of efficiency are the information services and technical libraries. The chief scientific information centre (and the largest in the world) is the All-Union Institute of Scientific and Technical Information, VINITI. With a permanent staff of 2,500 and more than 22,000 specialists working part-time, it produces 750,000 abstracts of Russian and foreign scientific and technical papers each year.

Finance and Staffing.—The "science budget," according to Soviet sources, was approaching 5,000,000,000 roubles, or £2,000,000,000 per annum at the 1964 rate of exchange. This figure is not very meaningful, however, since productivity, the concentration of resources on specific targets, and standards of living, all have to be taken into account in assessing its real value.

The U.S.S.R. has about 400,000 "scientific workers," roughly half of whom work in research institutes and half in higher educational establishments; but the difficulties of definition preclude any precise estimate of the scientific endeavour of the country in terms of manpower. At all events it is gigantic; and planning on such a scale, especially according to the rigid Soviet specifications, presents enormous problems.

See also references under "Research, Industrial" in the Index.

(X.)

BIBLIOGRAPHY.—*United States:* Standard Oil Development Company, *The Future of Industrial Research* (1945); D. H. Killeffer, *The Genius of Industrial Research* (1948); C. C. Furnas (ed.), *Research in Industry* (1948); D. B. Hertz, *The Theory and Practice of Industrial Research* (1950); C. E. K. Mees and J. A. Leermakers, *The Organization of Industrial Scientific Research* (1950); American Council on Education: Committee on Institutional Research Policy, *Sponsored Research Policy of Colleges and Universities* (1954); A. H. Dupree, *Science in the Federal Government* (1957); G. S. Simpson, "Scientific Information Centres in the United States," *American Documentation*, 13:1 (January, 1962); National Science Foundation, *Federal Organization for Scientific Activities, 1962* (1963), *Research and Development in Industry, 1961* (1964), *Federal Funds for Research Development, and Other Scientific Activities: Fiscal Years 1962, 1963, 1964* (1964), *Research and Other Activities of Private Foundations, 1960* (1964); Mellon Institute, *Fifty-first Annual Report* (1964); E. Roberts, *The Dynamics of Industrial Research* (1964).

Great Britain: D. S. L. Cardwell, *The Organization of Science in England* (1957); C. F. Carter and B. R. Williams, *Science in Industry: Policy for Progress* (1959); D. Colley (ed.), *Industrial Research in Britain,* 5th ed. (1964); Federation of British Industries, *Industrial Research in Manufacturing Industry* (1961); K. E. B. Jay, *Nuclear Power Today and Tomorrow* (1961); J. Jewkes, D. Sawers, R. Stillerman, *The Sources of Invention* (1958); Her Majesty's Stationery Office, *Report of the Committee of Enquiry into the Organization of Civil Science,* Trend Committee Report (1963), *Report of the Committee on Management and Control of Research and Development* (1961), *Nuclear Energy in Britain* (1962); Central Office of Information, *Britain and Space Research* (1962), *Industrial Research in Britain* (1961), *Notes on Science and Technology in Britain* (1963).

U.S.S.R.: N. G. Bruevich (ed.), *220 Years of the Academy of Sciences of the U.S.S.R.,* in Russian (1945); A. Vucinich, *Soviet Academy of Sciences,* Hoover Institute (1956); *Great Soviet Encyclopaedia of the U.S.S.R.,* vol. 50, in Russian (1957); Institute for the Study of the U.S.S.R., *Biographic Directory of the U.S.S.R.* (1958); A. A. Zvorykin (ed.), *Biographical Dictionary of Workers in Science and Technology,* in Russian (1959); P. L. Horecky, *Libraries and Bibliographic Centers in the Soviet Union,* in Russian (1959); *The Statutes of the Academy of Sciences of the U.S.S.R.,* in Russian (1959); G. I.

Fedkin, *Government Organs of the U.S.S.R. Which Exercise Control over Scientific Establishments,* in Russian (1959); K. T. Galkin, *The Training of Scientists in the Soviet Union,* Eng. trans. by A. Shkarovsky (1959); H. Koch, *5000 Sowjetköpfe* (1959); K. Meyer (ed.), *Scientific Life in the U.S.S.R.,* in German (1960); Short Reference Book of Addresses, *Scientific Institutes and Educational Establishments* (1962).

(A. G. Fo.; Ed. G. H.; X.)

RESEDACEAE, the mignonette family of dicotyledonous annual and perennial herbs and shrubs. There are six genera and about 70 species.

Reseda odoraia is the fragrant mignonette (*q.v.*), a popular garden annual; *R. luteola* is dyer's rocket or weld.

RESENDE, ANDRÉ DE (*c.* 1499–1573), the father of archaeology in Portugal, became a Dominican friar but, about 1540, entered the ranks of the secular clergy and was made a canon of Évora. He traveled in Spain, France, and Belgium and corresponded with Erasmus and other leading humanists. He was also intimate with King John III of Portugal.

Resende died in Évora, Sept. 9, 1573.

Resende's main Portuguese works are *História da antiguidade da cidade de Évora* (1553) and *Vida do Infante D. Duarte* (1789). His chief Latin work is *De antiquitatibus Lusitaniae* (1593).

See Francisco Leitão Ferreira, *Notícias da Vida de André de Resende,* ed. by A. Braamcamp Freire (1916).

RESENDE, GARCIA DE (*c.* 1470–1536), Portuguese poet, chronicler, and editor, whose life centred around the Portuguese court during the period of splendour and achievement under John II, Manuel I, and John III. Born at Évora, he began to serve John II as a page at the age of ten, becoming his private secretary in 1491. He continued to enjoy royal favour under King Manuel and later under John III. In 1498 he accompanied Manuel to Castile; and in 1514 went to Rome with the admiral Tristão da Cunha, as secretary and treasurer of the famous embassy sent by the king of Portugal to offer the tribute of the East at the feet of Pope Leo X. He died at Évora on Feb. 3, 1536.

Resende's *Crónica de D. João II* (1545), though largely plagiarized from a work by Rui de Pina (*c.* 1440–*c.* 1523), contains personal anecdotes which give it special interest. Much of his work provides an invaluable insight into the social life and manners of the period. In the 300 stanzas of his *Miscelânea* he surveys with wonder and pride, and not without social criticism, some of the notable events (including the great Portuguese discoveries) of the age in which he lived. The *Cancioneiro Geral* (1516), a vast anthology edited by Resende, and containing compositions of his own, is the chief source of knowledge of late medieval Portuguese verse.

BIBLIOGRAPHY.—*Livro das obras de Garcia de Resende* (1545; 2nd ed., containing the *Miscelânea,* 1554); *Cancioneiro Geral,* ed. by A. J. Gonçalves Guimarães, 5 vol. (1910–17); *Crónica,* ed. by G. Pereira (1902); *Miscelânea,* ed. by J. Mendes dos Remédios (1917).
See also A. F. de Castilho, *Garcia de Resende: Excerptos, seguidos de uma noticia sobre sua vida e obra* . . . (1865); A. Braamcamp Freire, "Garcia de Resende," in *Critica e História, Estudos,* I (1910); J. Ruggieri, *Il Canzoniere di Resende* (1931).   (T. P. W.)

RESERVOIR. Water storage reservoirs are places where water, accumulated from the flow of streams and rivers, is retained to serve the needs of man.

Changes in weather cause the natural flow of streams and rivers to vary greatly throughout the year and from year to year. There are periods of excess flows and valley flooding following heavy rains or during the melting season of snow-fed streams, and low flows (in some cases no flow at all) in periods of dry weather and droughts. The role of water storage reservoirs generally, therefore, is to impound water in periods of higher flows so that it may be released gradually during periods of lower flows.

Simple storage reservoirs were probably created early in man's history to provide drinking water for human beings and domestic animals and water for agricultural irrigation in areas where streams intermittently ran dry. The advance of civilization and the growth of population have been accompanied by an increasing use of water, creating a need for more extensive water storage facilities. From southern Asia and northern Africa the construction of reservoirs spread to Europe and the other continents. In the 20th century water storage reservoirs in ever increasing numbers are essential to control floods and provide assured supplies

of water in large quantities for a multitude of vital uses. (*See* HYDRAULICS, APPLIED.)

On-Channel and Off-Channel Storage.—Reservoirs ordinarily are formed by the construction across river or stream valleys of dams, which vary from relatively simple earthen embankments to complex masonry structures (*see* DAM). In special situations off-channel reservoirs may be provided, making use of diversion structures and canals or pipelines to convey water from the stream or river to natural depressions or artificially created storage basins situated outside the river valley from which the water supply originates. Off-channel storage is also common in pumped storage hydroelectric power schemes; in these, during periods of low demands for electricity, the surplus electricity is used to pump water to reservoirs at a higher elevation, the stored water being released to generate electricity during periods of peak demands.

Gated and Ungated Outflow Control.—A feature common to all storage reservoirs is some form of outlet by which the rate of outflow of water may be regulated. The outlet may be pipes through the dam, tunnels through the dam abutments (valley walls), notches through the top of the dam, or canals or pipelines leading from a point along the perimeter of the reservoir. In many cases valves, or movable gates, which can be opened or closed as the need arises, are provided in the outlet passageways. Reservoirs with such controlled outlets can retain water for long periods and thus are frequently referred to as retention reservoirs. Reservoirs for practically all purposes except flood control are of this type, and most of the larger flood control reservoirs also have such controlled outlets. (*See* DAM: *Outlets from Reservoirs.*)

"Retarding" reservoirs, used to retard temporarily the discharge of water during floods, do not have valves or gates in the water outlet passageways; instead, the outlet pipes or notches are built to a size that will permit only a limited rate of flow to be discharged. Ordinarily these ungated outlet passageways are designed so that the rate of water discharge up to full reservoir level approximately equals the safe carrying capacity of the stream channel downstream from the dam. As a flood flows into such a retarding reservoir, the release of water into the stream below is automatically restricted to nondamaging rates without the necessity for any change of valve or gate openings as the flood progresses.

This feature is particularly desirable in small watershed-type flood control structures where floods may occur at any time of day or night and last only a few hours. Thus, almost all small flood control reservoirs controlling runoff from a drainage area of only a few square miles are of the uncontrolled outlet, retardation type. In some special situations, of which the Miami River Basin (Ohio) is a noteworthy case, considerably larger flood control reservoirs have been constructed with uncontrolled discharge outlets. But in most cases of large flood control reservoirs on large streams, more effective flood protection can be provided for greater distances downstream by use of controlled outlets, allowing reservoir discharges to be varied to suit the differing conditions of flood situations as they arise. In these cases, of course, floods last much longer, and there is time for river-control engineers to collect and analyze information on each flood as it progresses and to vary the rates of water discharge from each reservoir for most effective control. (*See* RIVER ENGINEERING.)

Sedimentation.—The flowing water in natural streams and rivers transports varying quantities of sedimentary materials, depending on the nature of the watershed and the physical characteristics of the watercourse. The reduction in flow velocity that results when the stream flow is impounded in a reservoir greatly reduces the sediment transport capacity, so that much sediment is deposited in the reservoir. On a stream carrying heavy loads of sediment this silting up of the storage area may severely shorten the useful life of a small reservoir. Even in larger reservoirs on larger rivers, sedimentation can be a serious problem. Removal of the deposited sediments from reservoirs is generally too costly to be practical. The usual procedure in planning a reservoir on a sediment-laden stream, therefore, is to provide a reserve of storage capacity to offset the storage depletion caused by sedimentation.

Water Losses from Reservoirs.—Water may be lost nonproductively from storage reservoirs by evaporation from the surface, by seepage into the surrounding soil or rocks, and by seepage through the dam foundations. Seepage losses ordinarily can be reduced to negligible proportions through adequate geological investigation and treatment at the time of project design and construction. Evaporation losses, however, often are of major consequence. Gross evaporation from water surfaces in the temperate and tropical climatic zones may amount to several feet a year. In humid regions this is offset by precipitation accretions directly to the water surface of reservoirs, so that the net surface water loss may be moderate or negligible. But in regions of lower rainfall the net water loss by evaporation may be substantial, amounting to five feet or more of water annually in some desert areas. In Australia, the world's driest region, evaporation exceeds rainfall over about three-quarters of the continent and is at least double the rainfall over half the country. At Broken Hill, where the average annual rainfall is about 7 in. (178 mm.), average potential evaporation loss is about 96 in. (2,438 mm.). From reservoirs in South West Africa, annual evaporation losses range from about 80 to 100 in. (2,032–2,540 mm.). In East Africa losses generally run from 48 to 96 in. (1,219–2,438 mm.) of water and may be as high as 120 in. (3,048 mm.). The highest mean annual evaporation figures recorded include those for Bulawayo, Rhodesia, 111 in. (2,819 mm.); Yuma, Ariz., 100 in. (2,540 mm.); and Hyderabad, India, 148 in. (3,759 mm.).

Evaporation losses thus can become critically important in water planning in dry regions when attempts are made to fully utilize the available natural water supply. In extreme cases, evaporation from the additional water area created by reservoirs can offset the gain in firm water supply that otherwise would be provided by the additional amount of water stored. Similarly, indiscriminate construction of great numbers of small, shallow reservoirs in a watershed may seriously deplete the total water yield of the parent stream.

Considerable success has been achieved in experimental programs for reducing evaporation losses, notably in Australia, Africa, and the U.S., by the application of a liquid, monomolecular layer of a saturated long-chain fatty alcohol such as hexadecanol on the water surface. Substantial reductions in evaporation losses from reservoirs are in prospect as practical suppression methods are developed for widespread use. In ordinary circumstances, however, evaporation losses are not critical and can be accommodated by moderate increases in storage capacities or by tolerating moderate decreases in firm water yields.

Single- and Multiple-Purpose Reservoirs.—Early development of rivers was accomplished principally by use of so-called single-purpose reservoirs, usually as isolated units; and many, especially the smaller, reservoirs are still constructed as single-purpose developments. However, aided by governmental programs for comprehensive development of river basin areas, the prevailing trend in the 20th century has been toward construction of multiple-purpose reservoirs, particularly on the larger streams and rivers.

Single-Purpose.—A single-purpose reservoir, illustrated schematically in (A) of the figure, is designed to fulfill a single function, even though other benefits may accrue. Thus, a reservoir constructed simply to supply water for irrigation is considered as a single-purpose (irrigation) reservoir, even though it might have some incidental value for other purposes. Other functions of a single-purpose reservoir may be power generation, navigation, flood control, municipal and industrial water supply, low-flow regulation, recreation, etc.

The manner in which water is stored in or withdrawn from single-purpose reservoirs varies considerably, depending on the function. Thus a flood control reservoir is normally empty except at time of flood, when sufficient excess water is impounded to prevent over-bank flooding downstream; the impounded water is released as rapidly as practicable after each flood so that full storage space will be available when the next flood occurs. In contrast, single-purpose irrigation, navigation, and water supply reservoirs

are normally kept filled, except when stored water must be drawn off to supplement deficient natural stream flows; the storage space is refilled as soon as practicable after stream flows again increase.

A variant of the latter type of operation is used for a single-purpose power reservoir where a power plant is served directly from the reservoir. The rate at which power can be generated is a function of (1) the amount of head (*i.e.*, the difference in elevation) between the level of the water in the reservoir and the level of the water downstream from the power plant and (2) the rate of water-flow through the power plant. Thus a single-purpose power reservoir is normally kept full except when deficient natural stream flows must be supplemented with stored water in order to supply the increased rate of flow necessary to generate power, but the amount of storage drawdown (*i.e.*, the decrease in storage level) in low-flow periods is restricted to a lower limit sufficient to provide the minimum head needed to operate the power turbines.

Multiple-Purpose.—Multiple-purpose (sometimes called multipurpose) storage reservoirs, designed to serve two or more principal functions, usually contain two or more zones, or layers, of storage, impounded behind a single dam. Where two (or more) functions need to be served, it is less expensive to build and maintain a high dam and a large reservoir than it is to build and maintain two smaller dams and reservoirs.

In simple cases, as illustrated schematically in (B) of the figure, a multiple-purpose reservoir may consist of two zones, or layers, of storage, each adequate to serve its own function and operated more or less independently of the other. For example, the lower zone might be provided for water supply and kept full except as drawdown is necessary to supply water in low-flow periods; and the upper zone might be provided for flood control and kept empty except during and immediately after floods. This would be termed a multiple-purpose flood control and water supply reservoir. Similar combinations of storage for flood control with storage for irrigation, navigation, or other water conservation functions are possible. Multiple-purpose designs of this type were the first generally used in the transition from single-purpose reservoirs.

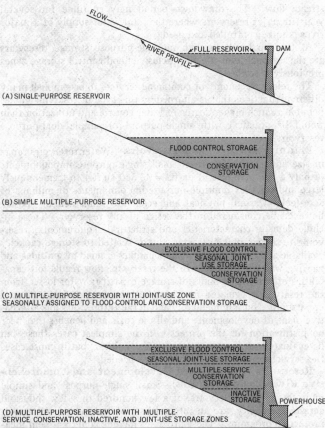

SCHEMATIC PROFILES OF SINGLE- AND MULTIPLE-PURPOSE RESERVOIRS

A seasonal joint-use storage zone, interposed between the flood control storage zone and the conservation storage zone, as illustrated schematically in (C) of the figure, can be used effectively in regions where major floods are limited to well-defined seasons or where there are consistent high-water and low-water periods at different times during the year. In many areas of the world the annual stream runoff has pronounced patterns of this sort; it is particularly evident in streams fed by the seasonal melting of high-altitude mountain snow or in regions where precipitation varies substantially from season to season, as in monsoon areas. In these situations the storage capacity in the joint-use zone is assigned to flood control and emptied of water by the beginning of the main flood season; this zone is then refilled as the flood season draws to a close and is assigned to conservation usage until the onset of the next flood season. The relative volumes of storage that can be assigned effectively in the seasonal joint-use storage zone and are needed in the exclusive flood control and conservation zones depend upon the seasonal characteristics of runoff in any given stream. In the Columbia River Basin in the northwestern U.S., for example, the flood season is so well defined that all flood control storage requirements can be served adequately by the seasonally assigned joint-use storage capacity, and no year-round exclusive flood control storage capacity is required. This is a rather exceptional situation, however.

The maximum application of the multiple-purpose, joint-use reservoir storage concept is illustrated by (D) of the figure. Lowermost in a reservoir of this type is an inactive storage zone used to provide an assured minimum water level for any of several purposes, such as power head, water diversion from the reservoir, or navigation and recreation on the lake. After its initial filling, this bottom zone ordinarily remains permanently filled.

Above the bottom storage zone is a multiple-service conservation zone that serves to augment low natural stream flows for several different uses, such as navigation, irrigation, and power generation, as well as other functions. This conservation storage zone is filled in times of above-normal natural stream flow and is drawn down as necessary to sustain the desired level of water releases from the reservoir during periods of deficient natural stream flow. The drawdown period may continue for several years in major reservoirs where the total water supply of a major river is to be controlled and used.

At the top levels in such multiple-purpose storage reservoirs are the seasonal joint-use and exclusive flood control storage zones previously described.

The relative economy of combining services to accomplish many different functions that is afforded by this type of reservoir makes possible a much higher degree of water control and utilization than would be practical with single-purpose or simple dual-purpose reservoirs.

Planning and Design of Reservoirs.—Water reservoirs range in size and complexity from small single-purpose impoundments of only a few acre-feet (1 ac-ft. = 43,560 cu.ft.) to tremendously large and complex multiple-purpose impoundments of millions of acre-feet. Certain physical and economic fundamentals should, however, be considered in the design of any reservoir. These include damsite characteristics and structural requirements; reservoir-site topographic characteristics as related to storage capacity available at various depths of impoundment; flood magnitudes and varying water inflow rates to the reservoir; flow-regulation capabilities of varying amounts of storage capacity; water losses from the reservoir; regulated flow and water usage requirements and opportunities both immediately and in the future; possible alternative plans of development; and all the costs and benefits that bear on justification for the project. In the simplest cases these can be evaluated satisfactorily by a single engineer, but in most cases the services of several specialists are needed.

Reservoirs in Watershed Development and Comprehensive River Basin Programs.—Small single-purpose and simple multiple-purpose reservoirs, of a few hundred to a few thousand acre-feet capacity, are an integral part of agricultural watershed protection programs. These programs include land treatment measures to protect the soil from wind and water erosion and to im-

prove productivity. They also include companion structural programs for water flow control, including small reservoirs specifically designed as components of individual watershed work programs. The reservoirs impound excess flows during periods of high runoff, to reduce flood damage along the small watercourses and streams in the watershed, and in many cases they provide rural water supplies and local recreation facilities.

Reservoirs of all sizes and types play vital roles in comprehensive river basin plans for control and utilization of a major basin's water resources. Under the basin planning concept, the collective effects of many reservoirs acting as a coordinated system, as well as the effects of individual reservoirs, are considered in locating and determining the size of the reservoirs and associated works. In most basin plans, single-purpose and simple multiple-purpose reservoirs are located on subtributaries and tributaries of the principal basin river. Their functions may include flood control, water impoundment and low-flow regulation, and power generation. In some basins, conditions also permit the location of large multiple-purpose reservoirs on the main river. In addition to reservoirs, basin plans include associated works, such as flood control levees and flood walls, navigation channels, pumping plants, irrigation canals or water supply pipelines, power plants and transmission lines, and other features. All of these are planned as integral or compatible elements of one overall basin program.

An outstanding example of the use of reservoirs in a comprehensive basin plan exists in the Missouri River Basin in west north-central U.S. The Missouri Basin program includes six major multiple-purpose reservoirs constructed by the U.S. Army Corps of Engineers on the main stem of the Missouri River and more than 100 major tributary reservoirs in programs of the Corps of Engineers and the U.S. Bureau of Reclamation; the total storage capacity of the reservoirs in the basin exceeds 100,000,000 ac-ft. This program provides flood control, irrigation, navigation, hydro-electric power generation, sediment retention, recreation, and other needs. A high degree of coordination is required to operate such a major program. In the Missouri River Basin this has been provided by special interagency reservoir operations coordinating committees and a special Missouri River reservoir control centre.

All the major reservoirs of the world are similarly multiple-purpose, and all, because of the immense size of the projects, have been constructed by or for government agencies. In the U.S. Lake Mead, the reservoir formed by Hoover Dam on the Colorado River, provides a total storage capacity of 31,047,000 ac-ft. (38,-296,474,000 cu.m.) for irrigation, flood and silt control, domestic and industrial water supply, and power generation. Glen Canyon Reservoir, part of the upper Colorado River Basin project, has a capacity of 28,040,000 ac-ft. (34,587,340,000 cu.m.), while Oahe Reservoir in South Dakota—a power, navigation, irrigation, and flood control project—has a capacity of 23,600,000 ac-ft. (29,110,-600,000 cu.m.). The reservoir formed by Kariba Dam on the Zambezi River between Zambia and Rhodesia in Africa has a total capacity of 130,000,000 ac-ft. (160,368,000,000 cu.m.) for power generation and flood storage. In India, the Rihand Reservoir (8,600,000 ac-ft. [10,607,900,000 cu.m.]) on the Rihand River, the Bhakra Reservoir (8,000,000 ac-ft. [9,868,000,000 cu.m.]) on the Sutlej, and the Hirakud Reservoir (6,600,000 ac-ft. [8,141,-100,000 cu.m.]) on the Mahanadi provide for power generation, irrigation, and flood and river control. Lake Eucumbene, formed by damming the River Eucumbene in New South Wales, Austr., is the key storage of the Snowy Mountains hydroelectric scheme, but its capacity of 3,600,000 ac-ft. (4,761,310,000 cu.m.) also provides water for irrigation. The reservoir behind the Volgograd Dam on the Volga River in the U.S.S.R. has a total capacity of 47,020,000 ac-ft. (58,000,000,000 cu.m.) for power generation and for flood and river control.

See also DAM; RIVER ENGINEERING.   (R. J. PD.)

RESHAT NURI GUNTEKIN (1892–1956), Turkish novelist, short-story writer and playwright, first achieved fame with his *Chalikushu* (1922), the most popular Turkish novel of the day. Born in Istanbul, he was educated in Izmir and Istanbul and, after teaching in various schools, traveled widely in Anatolia as an inspector of education. He was elected to parliament (1939) and later became Turkish delegate to UNESCO. In *Chalikushu* (Eng. trans., *The Autobiography of a Turkish Girl*, 1949) he combined a realistic description of the Anatolian scene with romance. Other novels and short stories in the same vein included *Aksham Guneshi* (1926; Eng. trans., *Afternoon Sun*, 1951). *Yeshil Gece* (1929), a penetrating study of the reactionary elements in Turkey, initiated the second phase of Guntekin's career, the writing of a series of novels dealing with the social problems brought about by radical changes in Turkish life. His style is easy and straightforward, though sometimes almost too sentimental. He died in London, Dec. 6, 1956.   (F. I.)

RESHID PASHA, MUSTAFA (1800–1858), six times Ottoman grand vizier of Turkey, was born at Istanbul on March 13, 1800. The protégé first of his uncle Ali Pasha and then of Pertev Effendi, a famous poet and statesman, Reshid was successively, during 1829–39, private secretary of the grand vizier Selim Pasha, secretary of the divan, member of a commission sent to Egypt (1833), ambassador in Paris and London, and minister of foreign affairs. During his stay in the French and British capitals he studied Western civilization and won the friendship of the principal French and British statesmen. He supported the westernization reforms of the sultan Mahmud II and after the death of Mahmud was charged by Sultan Abdul-Mejid I with the preparation of a new program of reforms. Elaborated in the form of a rescript or decree (*khatt-i sherif*), this program was proclaimed on Nov. 3, 1839, by Reshid, in the presence of the sultan, the ambassadors of the powers, and Ottoman dignitaries, at the royal court at Gulkhane. This rescript became the Magna Carta of the subjects of the Ottoman Empire, guaranteeing them equality, without distinction of race or religion, and security of life and property. Although these provisions were not completely carried out, Reshid became the symbol of westernization reform (the *tanzimat*). Between 1839 and 1858 he was twice appointed minister of foreign affairs and six times grand vizier.

With the support of Lord Stratford de Redcliffe, the British ambassador, Reshid abolished the slave trade and introduced new codes of commercial and criminal law. He also introduced regulations to end the traffic in favours and appointments. A supporter of France and Britain in his foreign policy, Reshid was grand vizier at the outbreak of the Crimean War. He died on Dec. 17, 1858. *See also* TURKEY: *History*.   (E. Z. K.)

RESIA, PASSO DI (Ger. RESCHEN SCHEIDECK), an Alpine pass 4,947 ft. (1,508 m.) high which separates the lower Engadine section of the Inn Valley in Austria from the Val Venosta, the upper Adige Valley in Italy, thus forming a watershed between the Adriatic and Black seas. The Austrian-Italian frontier is about 1 mi. N of the pass; the Italian hamlet and lake of Resia are below, at an altitude of 4,911 ft. (1,497 m.). Below Resia village is the old, abandoned refuge of San Valentino alla Muta (Sankt Valentin auf der Haid), mentioned as early as 1140. The Resia Pass road starts from Landeck in Austria, follows the Inn as far as Pfunds, then rises slowly to the Finstermünz Pass 3,100 ft. (945 m.) above the Inn gorge, and continues past the village of Nauders to the Resia Pass. The road then descends through the Italian towns of Malles and Glorenza to Merano and Bolzano, where it joins the Brenner Pass road and railway.   (G. KH.)

RESIDENCE, in general, a place of abode. In law, it is an ambiguous term frequently found in statutes. Used in such a context, residence normally bears the same meaning as domicile. *See* DOMICILE AND RESIDENCE.   (W. L. M. R.)

RESIDENTIAL ARCHITECTURE. This article deals with the evolution of structures for human habitation, particularly single-family units, from earliest times to the present, in all parts of the world. (A discussion of the factors involved in the design and construction of contemporary dwellings will be found in HOUSE DESIGN. For discussions of multifamily structures, *see* APARTMENT HOUSE and HOTELS AND INNS; for social context of residential architecture, *see* HOUSING; CITY PLANNING; and ZONING. *See also* ARCHITECTURE.) The dwelling is the oldest branch of building, dating from man's first crude solutions for his most pressing problems: protection from the elements, wild beasts and human enemies. The architecture of shelters has developed extensively since the late 19th century.

Separate dwellings developed in three principal types: in hot climates the rooms usually were open or they surrounded an open-air courtyard; in colder regions the rooms generally were placed together in a compact block to facilitate heating. The third type was informal: the rooms were strung in rows at will. Bricks appeared with the beginning of civilization in Mesopotamia. Wood was the staple residential building material; brick and stone were employed in more luxurious houses. Two distinct methods of construction developed: one used the solid load-bearing wall, originally of rock or adobe, and later of masonry or reinforced concrete; the other method employed a framework of wood or, later, metal, with a covering of reeds, bark, wooden boards or, eventually, various composite materials. After the middle of the 19th century more glass and metal were introduced into the structure and, in an uneven progress, mechanical and electrical labour-saving devices were added to the ordinary house. Technical improvement in housing (*e.g.*, safety, comfort, sanitation) was complicated, however, by social pressures and by various intellectual and artistic trends.

Public buildings and palaces, monuments on which a higher art of building design was concentrated, were emulated in private dwellings. Residential design followed the main stream of public architecture through historic periods and styles, but was always a little more inclined to place convenience before effect. In western society, from the time of the Renaissance, the house came to be thought of as a vehicle of self-expression, and attracted the attention of architects. During the 20th century, residential architecture often led other forms of design.

The evidence of housing in prehistoric and preclassical eras is scant, and to some extent historians' accounts are in conflict. Nevertheless the houses of each important era may be visualized from archaeological fragments and knowledge of the materials that were available to the builders.

Primitive.—Masonry construction may have begun when the cave dweller sought to elaborate his cave by partially closing the mouth with a wall of piled rocks, or by adding external baffle walls, as in prepueblo dwellings on river banks in parts of the U.S. southwest. Frame construction may have begun when sticks were planted in a circle, their tops bound together and the conical frame covered with thatch or leaves. Either of the two structural systems were used by prehistoric builders, according to the availability of materials. Defense was an important consideration to early village settlers. Little round cabins of stone, clay or wood were gathered within wooden palisades, rectangular huts were raised on piles above the water of lakes or sheltered bays. Roofs were pitched high on wooden frames, and thatched. Walls of thick wooden slabs were smeared over with clay to fill the crevices.

In the typical African compound each hut was made of a low circular wall of closely spaced and plastered sticks, roofed by a tall, conically framed cap of grass thatch. Huts were linked by fences. In the long houses of Borneo, which were elevated beside a river, series of one-family rooms were strung in long lines behind common verandas. The yurt of the wild nomadic Mongolian tribes was a circular house up to 20 ft. in diameter, made of felt fastened over a diagonally framed wall, its curved rafters rising to a wide smoke hole above the central fire. An exceptional example of primitive masonry and indigenous design is the Eskimo's igloo, a temporary winter home of compacted snow cut into beveled blocks and built into a dome. American natives produced several other ingenious house types. The wigwam of the Penobscot Indians of the north was a primitive cone, about ten feet wide and ten feet high, but the construction was slightly advanced. Bark paneling was held between two separate frames of wooden poles lashed together at the ends. The construction of the tipi of the nomadic Indians on the semiarid plains was similar, but decorated hides or canvas (in the 20th century) formed a paneling more flexible than bark, and made the whole structure more easily portable.

The long house of the Iroquois tribes in the northeast was a windowless, rectangular building occupied by several families, each with an open alcove of its own. It was made, as the wigwam, of big bark panels held in a double framing. The pueblo of the U.S. southwest was a multistory agglomeration of family cells in adobe or stone. The ends of the closely spaced logs that supported the adobe slab roofs projected through the walls. Each floor receded from the one below, forming irregular roof terraces, from which ladders led up and down to other cells. (*See* also INDIAN, NORTH AMERICAN.)

Between the 17th and 19th centuries European colonists often revived the crudest types of mud and stick construction. Primitive dwellings are still being built in many parts of the world. In north Australia nomadic aborigines sleep in caves or behind low bark breakwinds erected for the night. Neolithic types of lake villages are still occupied in Cambodia and New Guinea. Various rude forms of wood hut and mud cabin persist in Africa and parts of Asia. (*See* DWELLINGS, PRIMITIVE.)

Egyptian.—The great advances of Egyptian civilization did not extend to the poorer family house. It was still no more than a sleeping room and a storehouse, a low single cell open on one side. It was made of mud brick or of reeds plastered with mud and was roofed with palm leaves. However, the government did provide protection, eliminating the necessity of stockades, and the equable weather encouraged an outdoor life. Wealthier citizens built rooms behind or on either side of the central cell. The flat roof was strengthened with poles or with barrel vaults of brick and was used for eating and sleeping. Houses of leading citizens were either the block or the courtyard type, detached and sizable. A courtyard house was about 40 to 50 ft. square within a high surrounding fence. Rooms might occupy two sides of the square; the remainder was a semiroofed garden court serving as the main living area. In populous areas houses were pressed together on opposite sides of narrow streets. Often an outside staircase led to the flat roof. To the Egyptian the real home was the tomb (*q.v.*); it was the eternal habitation and the house was merely a temporary shelter. Nonetheless, the homes of the rulers were comfortable. An aristocrat's country house had a number of rooms grouped around a private courtyard. The house was set within a luxuriant formal garden enclosed by stables, storerooms and linking walls. Palaces were big, and the Pharaoh's central apartments were colourfully decorated and lavishly furnished for comfort and elegance. (*See* EGYPTIAN ARCHITECTURE.)

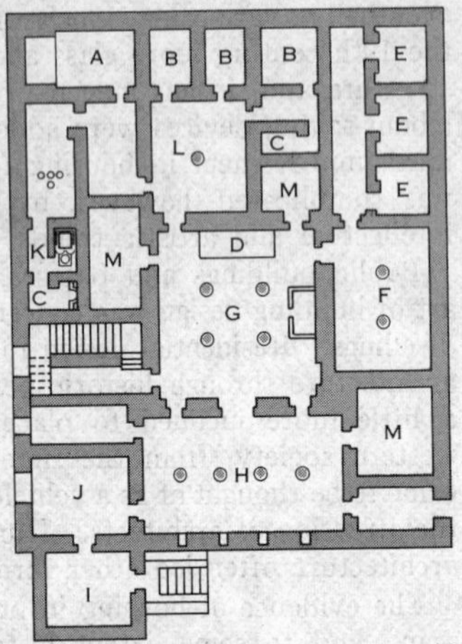

Western Asiatic.—The pattern of housing changed little in the Mesopotamian and Aegean cultures. The poor-man's house was generally a single-cell hovel. The middle classes had multiroom blocks of various sizes. The upper classes enjoyed elaborate buildings, reasonably comfortable and sanitary, with courts, gardens, loggias and colonnades developed into spatial compositions. Architecture was called upon to provide a rich visual background for the indulgent life. In Babylonia, although a somewhat more even distribution of wealth improved the standard of housing, the techniques of building did not advance beyond those of the Egyptians. For about 2000 years these techniques remained fairly constant. The poor man's cell was of mud brick, laid in the form of a tall pointed dome. Plain-faced stucco houses lined the winding, crowded, muddy city streets.

The middle-class house was built of sun-baked bricks; it was a compact block with a flat roof, which, when shaded by a light awning, was the principal living space. A rich merchant's house typically consisted of two stories, with thick brick walls, a central court

ringed by dark, narrow rectangular rooms, and a veranda with bright awnings in front. Most of the rooms were storerooms, but some were used for refuge when both roof and court became too hot. Then the walls were watered and their fine white plaster surfaces were cooled by evaporation. (*See* PRE-HELLENIC ARCHITECTURE.)

Greek.—In the golden age of classic Greece the houses of ordinary peasants were still crude cabins. A colder climate than that experienced by previous civilizations necessitated some heating. Through the brief cold winter, farm beasts shared single unpartitioned brick rooms with their owners. Smoke from a central hearth on the earth floor rose to a hole in the reed roof. Although the refinement of the monumental architecture was unsurpassed, the houses of even the illustrious Greeks were modest. Temples, theatres and public meeting places were the centres of living for men. Wives were restricted and generally segregated in rooms behind or above the men's quarters. Family life hardly existed. The thalamus, or inner chamber, was the official centre of house life. For the middle classes, three- or four-story rental tenements crowded the tortuous, earthy streets of the cities.

After the Macedonian conquest, the houses of the wealthy began to reflect some of the architectural qualities of the public monuments. The remains of a big house of Hellenistic date at Palatitza in Macedonia indicate multiple courts, long wings and ranges of rooms linked by colonnades. House exteriors became almost as formal as those of temples, and interiors were splendid with murals, statues, pottery and textiles. (*See* GREEK ARCHITECTURE.)

Roman.—The Roman house of every size and degree of wealth was centred around the atrium (*q.v.*). The atrium derived from the single cell of the primitive hut, with its smoke hole in the centre. As the room enlarged, so did the smoke hole, and columns were erected to support its edge. By the time of the empire the atrium had become a semiopen court ventilating and lighting surrounding rooms. The richer houses developed a peristyle, or court with a garden, at the back; a second story was added and the atrium was made resplendent with ornament and statues. The appearance of the reception rooms always took precedence over comfort in the family areas.

The middle-class house had a smaller atrium, sometimes roofed over, with kitchen and dining room behind and bedrooms above. The farmhouse combined barns, oil and wine presses, storerooms and the dwelling in one building around a courtyard. Poorer free men in Rome and its more crowded colonies lived in bare rooms in tall, dark insulae, or apartment blocks, some seven stories high. Augustus limited their height, in one of the world's first building regulations, to 70 ft. There are indications that they too were planned to surround a court in which the staircase rose past balconies giving access to the upper floors. On the street front the ground floor was occupied by shops. The façade above was usually of brick, pierced by rows of simple windows, a style of apartment housing that persisted into modern Italy. Sometimes the upper stories projected dangerously.

The Roman tradition lingered for many centuries. Provincial villas of the Roman style, built in the 7th century, are found in the south of France and Syria. In Britain the atrium was unsuited to the climate; it appeared only rarely, as in Bath. (*See* ROMAN ARCHITECTURE; VILLA.)

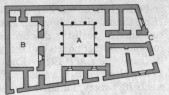

FIG. 2.—PLAN OF GREEK HOUSE, DELOS

(A) Court, (B) chief room or thalamus, (C) main entrance

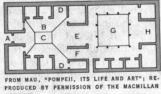

FIG. 3.—PLAN OF SMALL POMPEIIAN HOUSE

(A) Vestibulum (outer entrance court), (B) atrium (inner entrance court), (C) impluvium (skylight), (D) ala (side hall), (E) tablinum (library), (F) andron (passage), (G) peristylum (court), (H) exedra (hall)

FROM T. HAMLIN, "ARCHITECTURE THROUGH THE AGES"; REPRODUCED BY PERMISSION OF G. P. PUTNAM'S SONS, N.Y.

FIG. 1.—PLAN OF AN EGYPTIAN HOUSE AT TELL EL AMARNA

(A) Master bedroom, (B) bedroom, (C) closet, (D) dais or couch, (E) guest quarters, (F) west hall, (G) great hall, (H) north hall, (I) porch, (J) vestibule, (K) bath, (L) women's quarters, (M) storeroom

Peristyle of the House of the Vettii, Pompeii (partly rebuilt and planted)

Azay-le-Rideau, near Tours, France, chateau built during the reign of Francis I (1515—47)

Typical half-timbered farmhouse of Normandy in the 15th and 16th centuries

Palazzo Cavalli (Franchetti) on the Grand canal, Venice; 15th century

The so-called "Jew's house," Lincoln, England, a late Norman Romanesque town house of the 12th century

Villa Rotunda, near Vicenza, Italy, late 16th century; designed by Andrea Palladio, completed by V. Scamozzi

HOUSE DESIGN: ROMAN TO RENAISSANCE

Plate II   RESIDENTIAL ARCHITECTURE

Compton Wynyates, c. 1520, large manor house of Tudor England

Hôtel de Bourgtheroulde, Rouen, France, flamboyant Gothic town house, 1475

Chantrey house, Castle Donington, Eng., gabled half-timber house of the 16th century

Cabot-Endicott-Low house, Salem, Mass.; English colonial, 18th century

House in Ruhpolding, Bavaria, in the chalet style, typical of southern Germany and Switzerland from the 17th century

Great Maytham, Kent, Eng., by Sir Edwin Lutyens (1869–1944); a 20th-century re-creation of a Georgian manor house

RESIDENTIAL STYLES OF THE 15TH TO 18TH CENTURIES

"Corio Villa," 19th-century cottage of prefabricated cast iron (imported from England), Geelong, Austr.

H. G. Marquand house, Newport, R.I., about 1875, by R. M. Hunt

Villa Savoye, Poissy, France, 1928–30, by Le Corbusier (C. E. Jeanneret) and Pierre Jeanneret

Residence for the headmaster, Dartington hall, Eng. (1932–33), by William Lescaze (1896–   )

"Taliesin," home of Frank Lloyd Wright near Spring Green, Wis., 1925

19TH- AND 20TH-CENTURY HOUSES

PLATE IV

RESIDENTIAL ARCHITECTURE

House at Vastberga, Swed., by S. M. Backstrom (1903–) and L. A. Reinius (1907–)

Farnsworth house, near Plano, Ill., by Ludwig Mies van der Rohe (1886–)

House at New Canaan, Conn., by J. M. Johansen (1916–)

Home of architect George Matsumoto (1922–), Raleigh, N.C.

House of architect E. F. Catalano (1917–), near Raleigh, N.C.

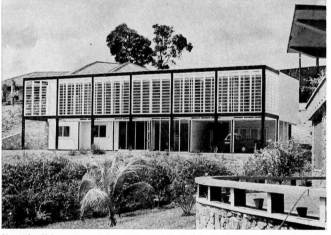

House for U.S. employees of a company at Port of Spain, Trinidad, by P. M. Bolton (1920–) and H. Barnstone (1923–)

CONTEMPORARY 20TH-CENTURY HOUSES

Medieval.—Until the 13th century the serfs of Europe lived in unrelieved squalor; sod huts partially dug out of the earth, or hovels made of low stone walls surmounted by roughly thatched roofs were typical dwellings. The early Norman castles of England were heavily fortified, dark and dirty and not intrinsically more livable than the poor man's abode. In the 13th century the manor house (*q.v.*) developed a little rugged comfort. It was centred on the hall (*q.v.*), a survival from Saxon times, to which were added buttery, pantry, larder and subsidiary compartments at one end and the solar at the other. The hall was sometimes 60 ft. by 20 ft., stone paved, with a central fireplace, small high windows, and a low dais at one end on which the family and guests took their meals. The solar was the withdrawing room and bedroom, the private family room. Walls were thick, of brick or stone and an increasing amount of half-timber work (*q.v.*). Window glass was a luxury; openings had shutters, pointed to match the Gothic arches.

The new bourgeois or middle class of the middle ages lived in houses of two or three stories packed into the narrow streets of expanding towns. Typical three-story houses of the 12th century are found at Cluny, France. In such a house a central light court cuts the narrow plan in two, with only a gallery connecting the front to the rear rooms. The front room on the ground floor is a shop, the rear a kitchen. The floor above has living rooms in the front, sleeping rooms in the rear. An attic fills the high roof space. The "Musician's house" at Reims (*c.* 1240) has a façade typical of the simple charm of the time, made notable by statues of musicians set in niches. The "Jew's house" at Lincoln is an early English town house with richly carved window arches in the Norman Romanesque manner. With their sensible plans and rudimentary plumbing these medieval town houses of northern Europe were potentially comfortable, and they changed little in 500 years. In the north of Italy town life matured earlier. Tall, sophisticated city palaces enclosed arcaded courts. The security of Venice permitted a more extroverted plan, with wider openings to the canal at the front and to the garden at the back. Walls were ornate in coloured marble and were animated by balconies, loggias and long ranges of windows, embroidered with Gothic tracery.

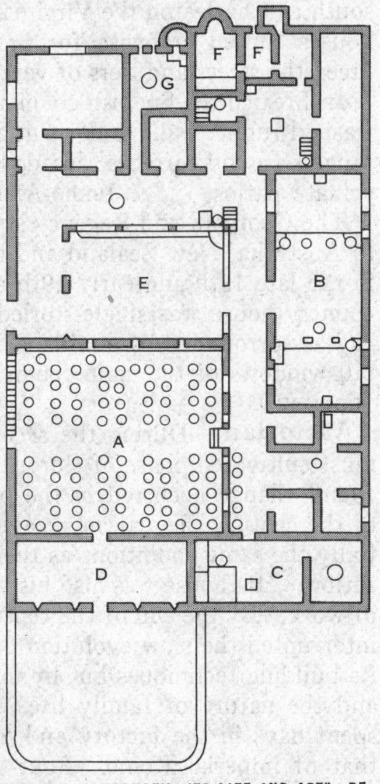

In rural areas the peasant's lot gradually improved and the farm-building complex developed, with barns, sheds and dwelling contained within a fence. Stone was usual in southern Europe, and wood in the north.

House planning, in the modern sense, began with a concern for the privacy of certain members of the household and for the accommodation of certain functions of living in English manors and the European burghers' houses. Between the 14th and 17th centuries rooms were increased in number and were more clearly differentiated. In England the great hall grew asymmetrical wings as required by function. Until the 16th century, however, circulation was tortuous, through rooms and up and down many stairs. The French château (*q.v.*) at this period was a century ahead of the English manor. With its romantic, pointed roofs and round corner turrets, its symmetry and elegance reflected in a wide decorative moat, it made a graceful transition from the grimly fortified Gothic castle to the open, formal Renaissance mansion.

The English manor's wings, growing from each end of the great hall, eventually linked to enclose a courtyard (*e.g.,* Compton Wynyates, Warwickshire, 1520). Late in the 16th century the wings opened into a U-shape, releasing the confined courtyard. At the same time the moat was abandoned (*e.g.,* Hatfield house, Hertfordshire, 1607–11). The great hall decreased in size and importance; the main passage, expanded to a wide glazed gallery, became the biggest and most pretentious room. It was graced with wood paneling, coloured window glass, black and white checked marble floor, restrained plaster ceiling and elaborate chimney pieces. The exterior, while often retaining the pointed arch and a free disposition of windows, was more composed and symmetrically balanced, gradually adopting the formalism of the Renaissance. (*See* ROMANESQUE ART AND ARCHITECTURE; GOTHIC ART AND ARCHITECTURE; CASTLE.)

Renaissance.—In Italy the architectural formality that persisted even through the middle ages grew easily into a full-blown classic revival. The master of residential architecture was Andrea Palladio (1508–80). In buildings such as the Villa Rotunda near Vicenza he adapted the temple form to domestic use without sacrificing classic symmetry, proportion, scale or ornament. The use of giant porticos resulted in precise geometric plans based on the circle and the square, which were developed into three dimensions in accordance with mathematical doctrines. The Renaissance was received enthusiastically by the French court and yielded houses of elegant conception and charming detail. The style came late to England, delayed by Henry VIII's break with Rome and the consequent anti-Italian prejudice. During the 16th century a classic quality entered via northern Europe, and the first English professional architect (John Shute) and the first architectural historian (Henry Wotton) appeared. But the English Renaissance proper began with Inigo Jones (1573–1652), self-trained artist and scholar and generally considered to be the first major English architect. He introduced the Palladian (from Andrea Palladio) style of pure form and the revived classic order (*q.v.*). The plan concept ruled the elevation and all was "masculine and unaffected," as Jones noted during his Italian travels. His monumental houses for the nobility usually consisted of a simple cubical block dominated by the pavilion, or classic loggia, with its single order of tall columns. (*See* RENAISSANCE ARCHITECTURE; TUDOR PERIOD; ELIZABETHAN STYLE; JACOBEAN STYLE.)

Baroque and Neoclassical.—England's most famous architect, Sir Christopher Wren, was mainly occupied with monumental work, but during his time the "Wrenish" style, a reserved baroque, eclipsed Palladianism. For two prosperous generations of country-house building the classic orders gave way to some originality. Still the house had a rectangular plan, rigid symmetry, a hipped roof and eave cornices broken by central pediments. Early in the 18th century the Palladian style returned, to be replaced about the middle of the century by the characteristically English neo-classical manner known as Georgian. This was an elegant, simplified, lightly ornamented style looking to Rome and Greece for inspiration, and relying for effect on harmonious proportions in the severe rectangles of the façades and the fine, regular glazing bars of the windows.

Robert Adam perfected a graceful personal style drawn from

FIG. 5.—PLAN OF CHARNEY-BASSETT, BERKSHIRE, ENG., 1270

(A) Hall, (B) chapel (upper story), (C) solar (upper story)

FIG. 4.—PLAN OF ROMAN FARMHOUSE, VILLA RUSTICA, BOSCOREALE, IT.

(A) Store for oil jars, (B) oil press, (C) wine press, (D) stable, (E) court, (F) bath, (G) kitchen

FIG. 6.—PLAN OF THE HOUSE OF JACQUES COEUR, BOURGES, FRANCE, 15TH CENTURY

(A) Main entrance, (B) court, (C) gallery, (D) secondary hall, (E) great hall, (F) kitchen, (G) bedroom

Greek and Roman precedents, plain in form but delicate in ornament, which was accused by its more robust opponents of being effeminate and paper-thin. A rich London house by Adam at 20 St. James street, a typically medium-sized house of its day and class, had seven main living and entertaining rooms on its tall ground floor, and bedrooms above. Within the narrow rectangular confines of the structure Adam shaped the music room as an oval and the dressing room as a circle. At the rear was a garden court enclosed by the stables and coach house. Smaller town houses, foregoing individuality, combined to form long façades, as in the magnificent curve of Royal Crescent at Bath. The typical house was plain red brick with simple windows, a thin cornice and a neat stringcourse above the arched, fan-lighted doorway.

Early in the 19th century the firm Georgian style divided into the Romantic movement with its exotic Gothic and eastern conceits, and the Regency style, with its plain stucco walls, curved bays and spidery shadows of delicate iron balconies.

Colonial.—Through the 17th and 18th centuries European colonists carried their local house styles to the Americas, Asia and the antipodes, changing them no more than was necessary to adapt them to new materials and changed climatic conditions. After a temporary phase of primitive shelter Early American house types appeared. In the densely forested lands of the north, clearing was an essential first task and wood the obvious choice for building. The lapped horizontal weatherboard or clapboard, hardly known in England, was used generally. The rectangular, frame house with two low stories and a high gable roof was centred on a brick chimney stack. Later a lean-to addition at the rear produced a "salt box" profile. The Cape Cod style grew from an ingenuous functional plan of four rooms on each floor clustering around fireplaces in the stack; a small stairway rose between the stack and the central front door. In Virginia, which was warmer and richer, the plan was longer and thinner and there was a chimney at each end. Brick was more common. The stair hall cut through the centre of the house and opened to front and back.

As early as 1667 Palladian books and plan publications carried more sophisticated architectural ideas across the Atlantic. Ar-

FROM B. FLETCHER, "A HISTORY OF ARCHITECTURE"; REPRODUCED BY PERMISSION OF THE ATHLONE PRESS, UNIVERSITY OF LONDON

FIG. 7.—PLAN OF OXBURGH HALL, NORFOLK, ENG., 1482

(A) Drawing room, (B) dining room, (C) great hall, (D) napery, (E) buttery, (F) kitchen, (G) bakery, (H) servants' hall, (I) breakfast room, (J) library, (K) laundry, (L) courtyard, (M) moat

chitects arrived early in the 18th century; a John James was practising in Boston in the 1730s. Soon the American Georgian style appeared, closely following the English model. In the north the style was adapted to wood construction with slender columns or flat pilasters. The rooms were tall, the plan compact. Fine moldings dressed the eaves cornice, fanlights, stairways and shuttered window trim. In the colonies at New York and Pennsylvania, German and Dutch influences were strong; in Virginia and Maryland great plantation homesteads settled in spacious lawns on river estates. These big houses were generously conceived and graciously furnished. They were characterized by the hospitable, heroic scale of a two-story portico in a single classic order. As far south as Charleston the Virginian influence was felt, but there the houses turned crabwise for protection: a formal Georgian end faced the street and tiers of veranda faced the private side garden.

In Mexico the Spanish colonial houses had plastered and pastel-washed rubble walls under sun-baked tile roofs. Rooms were arranged around terraces, arcaded courts, and fountains playing in private patios. (*See* IBERO-AMERICAN ARCHITECTURE.)

The Georgian and Regency styles were adapted in various ways to Australia, New Zealand and the islands of British colonization in the late 18th and early 19th centuries. The typical Australian country house was single-storied with a low, hipped shingle roof. It was surrounded by a wide, slim-posted veranda onto which the tall windows of the main rooms opened. (*See* COLONIAL ARCHITECTURE.)

Victorian.—During the second half of the 18th century, the most cultivated phase of European residential architecture, a profound change occurred in the poor-man's house. In the middle of the century the artisan, weaver, miller or farmer lived in essentially the same conditions as the freeman worker of earliest civilization. His house was also his workshop, and his children's place of work. By the end of the century the Industrial Revolution had interrupted the slow evolution of this house, not by transforming its building techniques but by upsetting the function of the home and the nature of family life. Most members of poor families spent days in the factory and nights in mass housing not unlike that of imperial Rome. Four- or five-story walk-up tenements gathered around the factories. They were ill-lit, poorly ventilated and the only outdoor living area they provided was on the pavement of a narrow street. The construction was brick, unencumbered with ornament or plumbing. By the middle of the 19th century, slum areas were extensive in most big cities. Room areas diminished and ingenious plans were devised to save space (*e.g.*, the New York "railroad" apartments with rooms packed four deep, only the end ones seeing daylight). Meanwhile the city was dissolving at the edges. Rail transport permitted middle-class workers to live away from their places of employment. Suburbs usually developed around the rail centres and radiated like spokes from the city. The typical Victorian suburban mansion was as elaborate as the palaces of earlier eras, but reduced in scale for a single family with servants and guests. The newly prosperous, hospitable manufacturers and merchants had no patience with cultivated tradition. Georgian and Regency taste was called mawkish and simplicity was seen as a poverty of dress unbecoming in the home of a man of substance. Ambition and acquisitiveness complicated the desire for comfort, sometimes resulting in a clutter of ornamentation unique in the world's history. The multiplying members of the lower middle class moved to the suburbs to nominally detached houses on narrow strips of land. The less successful man was able to emulate the mansion's ostentation effectively, thanks to the machinery of mass-produced moldings, pressings,

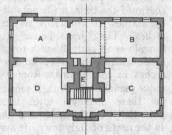

FROM A. F. BEMIS & BURCHARD, "THE EVOLVING HOUSE," VOL. I; REPRODUCED BY PERMISSION OF THE TECHNOLOGY PRESS

FIG. 9.—PLAN OF CAPE COD HOUSE WITH LARGE CENTRE CHIMNEY, AMERICAN COLONIAL

(A) Storeroom, (B) kitchen, (C) parlour, (D) bedroom, (E) chimney

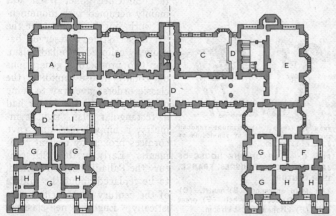

FROM B. FLETCHER, "A HISTORY OF ARCHITECTURE"; REPRODUCED BY PERMISSION OF THE ATHLONE PRESS, UNIVERSITY OF LONDON

FIG. 8.—FIRST-FLOOR PLAN OF HATFIELD HOUSE, HERTFORDSHIRE, ENG., 1607–1611

(A) Library, (B) winter dining room, (C) upper part of hall, (D) gallery, (E) King James's room, (F) state bedroom, (G) bedroom, (H) dressing room, (I) chapel

printings and castings; any desired decorative effect could be reproduced cheaply. The ordinary man began to reap some of the benefits of industry. Built-in equipment and mechanical appliance, including the fitted English bathroom, were novelties in expensive homes early in the century and gradually became commonplace toward the end of the Victorian era. The great increase in personal possessions produced a storage problem that was solved by the built-in cupboard, closet and pantry. Cellar central heating was introduced in the U.S. in the 1830s and was fairly general in mid-century American homes, as were centrally supplied water and gas. Waterborne sewerage began in Hamburg in 1843 but was not adopted by many cities until late in the century. Electricity had been proved an effective source of power by 1900. Industrial techniques did not, however, extend to the construction of the house. The promise, popularly recognized in the Crystal Palace in 1851, of a new world of mass-produced metal and glass homes, did not materialize as expected. (It had not yet arrived, but was still imminently expected, a century later.) No part of a wall or ceiling was left undecorated. During construction, handicraft ornament supplemented machine-made ornament. Graining, imitating expensive wood or marble, was often painted on plaster or plain boards, a practice about which John Ruskin (1819–1900) commented: "There is no meaner occupation for the human mind." Ruskin and William Morris (1834–1896) were among the few Englishmen who protested against commercialised design and the decline of taste. They sought a return to simple, natural ornament and an appreciation of genuine handcraft. In the U.S. the sculptor Horatio Greenough (1805–1852) called for the elimination of all ornament. These pleas had little effect. Ruskin helped to inspire the Gothic Revival, and Morris' medieval decorations helped it grow. In residential architecture the Gothic Revival usually manifested itself in tall gables with intricate fretwork ornament and pointed-arch windows, later enriched by polychromatic brickwork and ornate lead lights. It was the principal rival to a coarsened neoclassical style in the "battle of the styles," but there were many other revivals. Eclectic architects and builders raked history for embellishments and added to their houses distorted fragments of Norman castles, French châteaux, Swiss chalets, etc. The nadir of taste was reached in England about mid-century, in the U.S. after the Civil War.

Two major, separate revolts began toward the end of the 19th century. One was the *art nouveau* (*q.v.*) movement initiated in Brussels, an attempt at a new nonhistorical style in which form and ornament were to be based on nature's shapes. This produced only a popular passing fashion of superficial sinuous lines on the trimmings of a house. The other revolt slowly developed toward a rational, styleless architecture shaped to the function of the shelter by the nature of the construction, devoid of ornament. These concepts were the basis of nearly all of international modern architecture as it gradually evolved during the next half-century in the work of temperamentally diverse architects in widely separated localities. (*See* also MODERN ARCHITECTURE; ARTS AND CRAFTS MOVEMENT.)

20th Century.—The roots of 20th-century residential architecture may be traced in Morris' aim to elevate domestic taste, in the quasi-rational theories of the Frenchman E. Viollet-le-Duc (1814–1879), and in C. F. A. Voysey's big English country houses of the '90s, with their boldly composed roofs and plain white walls. Some of the most important formative steps were taken by nondomestic architects: Louis Sullivan in Chicago, Otto Wagner in Austria, Peter Behrens and Walter Gropius in Germany, Auguste Perret in France, and others. But the crystallization of the movement and a great number of the most auspicious early designs were in the residential field. Many of the best-known architects of the century, including Frank Lloyd Wright, Mies van der Rohe and Le Corbusier, first established their personal styles in houses.

A house on the Geneva water front in 1904 by Adolf Loos, exemplifying his passionate distaste for ornament, introduced the functionalist house. California houses in the early 1900s by Bernard Maybeck and Greene & Greene developed a carpenter-rationale unknown in Europe. However, the U.S. prairie houses by Wright (1867–1959) were published in Germany and injected a new enthusiasm into the European movement.

Although Holland was slow at first to accept the new movement, the vociferous *de Stijl* group appeared there in 1917. It formalized the theories of functionalism; it probably was largely responsible for the development in Europe through the 1920s and '30s of the naked white-plastered modern house in easily comprehensible cubist shapes. Plain blocks were fashionable for the first and only time; after half a century of ornamental excesses they seemed artistically satisfying, even when not accompanied by any creative idea.

In a postwar atmosphere the Bauhaus (*q.v.*) school was founded in Germany in 1919 by Walter Gropius. With its all-embracing concept of the creative simultaneity of technology and all the arts of living, it had untold influence on the development of house design throughout the world.

In France the Swiss-born architect Le Corbusier (1887–1965) contributed influential writings to the journal *L'Esprit Nouveau.* In 1930 he built his most famous house, the Villa Savoye, at Poissy; a wide white box, whose hollowness was emphasized by its open decks and by its being elevated on poles. It was one of the most vigorous expressions at that time of the new interest in negative form; *i.e.*, the composition of spaces rather than the proportioning of masses.

In Russia shortly after the revolution constructivism was a style recommended for the huge housing blocks. It was an experimental branch of modern architecture following structural methods. It soon met official reaction, and after 1930 the Soviet government adopted severe neo-Renaissance façades for its bulky apartment buildings.

The Stockholm exhibition of 1930 introduced modern architecture to Scandinavia. Sweden accepted the principles more thoroughly and naturally than any other country, and for many years the simplicity, without self-consciousness, of its houses and household wares received world-wide attention. Central urban-planning control, exceptionally high and level living standards, and a tradition of first-rate craftsmanship aided the development. Generally, 12-story elevator apartments were built near the cities, and 3-story walk-up flats and single-family houses formed satellite groups. All units were well planned and equipped to give comfort, if not privacy, and care was given to the external architectural relationships and the preservation of the best qualities of the landscape. Notwithstanding a certain monotony which developed later, Sweden thus produced the most cultivated and fully pervasive national pattern of housing in history.

Germany under Hitler called for a nationalistic style and outlawed the new architecture. Many of its leading designers left for England and later the U.S., where eventually they were responsible, with American confreres, for a revolution of taste against historic revivals. After World War II Germany returned to its earlier rational architectural principles for the design of many enormous apartment blocks. Its comparatively few single-family houses, however, tended to be designed in the traditional pattern of German country houses.

While the European functionalist phase developed through the early part of the century, most English-speaking countries persevered with architectural eclecticism. It was more restrained than in the 19th century and extremes, such as the Gothic Revival, were rare. But exotic effects continued to dress the faces of houses, such as, Italianate villa, Spanish mission and English style (outside England). At the same time more and more people wanted private, detached houses. In the 1930s some were "modernistic"; *i.e.*, ornamented with parallel grooves or streamlined curves or skyscraper profiles on the chimney tops.

During this time Frank Lloyd Wright built numerous houses of remarkable individuality, his artistic range including the wide, reposeful roofs of the Robie house, Chicago (1909), as well as the striking suspension of "Fallingwater" (1936–38) over a mountain stream in Pennsylvania. His favourite materials were wood and stone, his line horizontal, his spaces wide and subtly interrelated. He made each house an artistic idealization of free family life. In his retention of ornament and his increasing romanticism he steadily drew away from the Europeans. Not until after World

War II was his art popularly recognized in the U.S.; then it had at least superficial influence on many houses.

During this period it was often possible for the poor to possess the ancient symbol of independence, the private house. The cities' suburbs, which had been growing slowly for a century, escaped urban control. Young married people sought immediately to own a home, and the home was the centre of nearly all social contacts and entertainment. A new nomadic segment of the U.S. population rebelled and took to living in car trailers which compressed all the mechanical aids of the 20th century into the area of an Inca hut. Town housing remained comparatively stable in the U.S. The more prosperous cities proceeded slowly with slum-clearance schemes for their crowded tenement areas, usually rehousing the same number of people in taller blocks set apart on lawns. In many European and Latin-American countries, on the contrary, big new apartment blocks continued to increase the density of urban populations.

Most suburban houses were built without architects' guidance. Standard designs were repeated tirelessly with minor fashion changes and some colouring by local idioms. Mechanical equipment constantly increased and improved. Buckminster Fuller in 1927 designed a fully industrialized house hung on a central mechanized mast, and later many other proposals were made in the same vein. But society resisted radical change from the traditions of wood and brick.

Architectural character continued to be dominated by a few creative men whose well-publicized ideas carried to suburbs everywhere. Some were bent on perfecting anonymous, universal shelters in which each owner could create an environment to his taste. Most residential architects, however, still aimed to compose in spaces and textures a delightful background for the kind of life the occupants liked best.

Asiatic.—Before contact with the west and modern technology, antique rules of building in Asia descended unchanged from one generation of builders to another.

Indian.—Building rules were recorded in Sanskrit about A.D. 500 in a code determining sizes, proportions, structure and details of design down to the doors, windows and drains. The poor peasant of the plains had a single hut. The villager had a house of four huts—one each for the men, women and cattle, and one for cooking and storage—on four sides of a courtyard. The Hindu multifamily group repeated the court and its rooms for each brother. A rich-man's house extended the system again with extra stories.

In the thickly populated areas around great rivers the floors and walls were made of clay, the roofs thatched. In the arid northwest the walls were brick or stone, the flat roofs were of an

BY COURTESY OF LUDWIG MIES VAN DER ROHE

FIG. 10.—PLAN OF FARNSWORTH HOUSE (1952), PLANO, ILL., BY LUDWIG MIES VAN DER ROHE

indigenous cement. In the western Himalayas the court was omitted, the stone walls rose two floors under a slate roof. In some parts intricate carvings adorned the balconies and surrounded the door and window openings.

The English in India developed a single-story house with a shaded veranda and well-ventilated rooms. It was known in the vernacular as a bungalow, a name which later came to mean in other countries a single-story house of any design.

Chinese.—The traditional Chinese house was a single-story row of rooms linked by a narrow veranda and surrounded by a high wall. A screen directly inside the entrance gate balked devils, who cannot negotiate corners. Brick was common, and adobe faced with brick made the thicker walls. The top halves of some interior partitions were open latticework with paper panels. Windows usually had decorated paper panes. The roofs had a characteristic drooping gable, suggestive of tent origins. Houses of the rich had black ebony carvings against their brick walls and beneath their green glazed tile roofs. The plain interiors were often well decorated with fine sandalwood or teak furniture and elaborate embroideries and porcelain. (*See* CHINESE ARCHITECTURE.)

Japanese.—In Japan the traditional vernacular house was based on an order of design that western civilization first approached in the 20th century. The house was light, adjustable, unpretentious, virtually unadorned and planned on a precise mathematical concept. The standard grass floor mat, about 6 ft. by 3 ft., was the module for all planning. Whether square or oblong each room was a multiple of the mat size (*e.g.*, a four-mat room). Posts on the perimeter of the veranda and at the corners of rooms supported the hipped or gabled roof frame. The roof was tiled or thatched on top and lined on its flat underside with boards or panels of wood. Some external walls, such as those for the kitchen and privies, were permanent in bamboo, boards or plaster. But the unique feature in the traditional Japanese house is that most exterior walls and nearly all interior partitions were movable screens sliding in grooves which ran in the floor and the ceiling between structural posts. These screens permitted the rooms to open to the veranda and to each other as required, and allowed for supervision of family activities by the patriarch.

The modern Japanese adoption of U.S. fashions threatened to end the tradition, but some Japanese architects have succeeded in advancing the structural principles of the unpainted wood and paper idiom without destroying its order, flexibility or unaffected artistry. *See* JAPANESE ARCHITECTURE.

BIBLIOGRAPHY.—Albert Farwell Bemis and John Burchard, *The Evolving House* (1933); Robert Woods Kennedy, *The House and the Art of Its Design* (1953); F. R. S. Yorke, *The Modern House* (1944); John Gloag and C. T. Walker, *Home Life in History: Social Life and Manners in Britain, 200 B.C. to A.D. 1926* (1928); Reginald Turnor, *The Smaller English House, 1500–1939* (1952); S. F. Kimball, *Domestic Architecture of the American Colonies and of the Early Republic* (1922); Raymond McGrath, *20th-Century Houses* (1934); T. F. Hamlin, *Architecture, an Art for All Men* (1947); Burnham Kelly, *The Prefabrication of Houses* (1951); Bernard Rudofsky, *Behind the Picture Window* (1955). After 1900 the best contemporary descriptions of residential architecture are often found in volumes of architectural magazines: *House and Home, Progressive Architecture, Architectural Record,* etc. (U.S.); *Architectural Review* (Eng.); *Werk* (Switz.), etc. (Ro. B.)

RESINS are among the most versatile of all chemical compounds, and their industrial applications are still expanding. Natural resins range from pitch and asafetida to frankincense, myrrh, and the fossilized form known as amber. Synthetic resins are the bases of products as varied as nylon, billiard balls, and equipment for softening or desalting water.

Prior to the introduction of synthetic resins, the term resin was applied exclusively to certain sticky substances in the form of yellow or brown deposits that exude from certain trees, particularly from the pine and the fir. As knowledge grew about the nature of such natural resinous products and the means by which similar compositions could be made by known chemical reactions, a large and ever-increasing number of products have been included in the category of resins. At first these laboratory products were hesitatingly referred to as resinlike products, then as artificial resins and resin substitutes, and finally as synthetic resins. In almost every respect the natural resin can be replaced by one of the synthetic varieties in many industrial applications, especially in the molding and coating industries. By studying chemical reactions that lead to resinification, a better insight was gained concerning the chemical transformation that takes place in the natural product, and in certain instances it became possible to combine chemically the natural and the synthetic product to form a new material possessing unique properties.

At one time resins were recognized by certain well-known attributes, that is, by their transparency and amorphousness and by their brittleness and conchoidal fracture. Some synthetic resins fail to exhibit any of these characteristics; some are tough and colourless, others opaque and crystalline. There appears to be only one property common to natural and synthetic resinous products—in one stage of their existence both products are plastic.

The distinction between resins and plastics is at best arbitrary, since many of the later synthetic materials can be called both resins and plastics. Historically, it appears that the term resin was applied to those products primarily used as substitutes for the natural product in coating compositions, whereas the term plastic was used to designate those compositions that involved a molding operation in their fabrication. It is generally recognized that resins, plastics, rubbers, and fibres are part of one large group of chemical compounds, and by suitable transformations it is possible to change any one member of this group into another. (*See* Plastics.)

This article is divided into the following sections:

I. NATURAL RESINS

1. Resin Formation.—Resin formation in a tree occurs as a result of injury to the bark caused by wind, fire, lightning, or other means. Initially this secretion is fluid in nature and appears in the form of an oleoresin or as a balsam. In contact with air certain of the more volatile components evaporate, and the residue oxidizes, polymerizes, and gradually converts to a soft resinous product that is readily soluble in appropriate media. As the natural resin ages, it becomes more insoluble. When the resin flow from the tree is copious, some of the secretion passes into the ground, with the result that many fossil resins are found as buried deposits. Even in the case of the recent fossil resins, the chemical reaction leading to resinification may have proceeded for thousands of years. For example, the kauri pines are known to attain an average age of 1,000 years, and since resin can now be found in areas where the original forest has wholly disappeared, it is obvious that the resin must be extremely old, even though it is still soluble. The fossil resin, amber, is less soluble; its very existence indicates that the process and time of polymerization from the oleoresin to resin, to recent fossil resin, to fossil resin must be reckoned in geological periods.

2. Occurrence.—Resinous deposits are found in many parts of the world, and many varieties derive their names from the locality where they are collected. Certain tree emanations were utilized by the Chinese and the Japanese in their preparation of Oriental lacquers. There is reason to believe that the Incas and the Egyptians used varnishlike materials. The Carthaginians, Phoenicians, and Greeks were acquainted with resinous products, and the association between resins and varnishes can be seen in the derivation of the word varnish. This term appears to originate from Berenice, queen of Cyrene, the name the Greeks applied to amber. The term Berenice became corrupted gradually to Pheronice and then Verenice and Vernis.

3. Characteristics.—Any mucilaginous exudation of a tree is considered a gum. Shellac is a distinctive product inasmuch as it is an insect secretion. True gums, as distinct from varnish gums, are related to sugars and carbohydrates; they are soluble in water, insoluble in organic liquids, and on heating decompose without fusion. They differ from glues in that they are soluble in cold water. Varnish gums, on the other hand, are resinous materials related to terpenes and essential oils; they are soluble in oils and organic liquids, insoluble in water, and on heating generally melt, decompose, and become more readily soluble. Although the tendency has been to decry the use of the word gum for varnish resins, the term is too well established to be eradicated. Moreover, there are certain natural products that take on the properties of both gums and varnish resins. From Indian frankincense or olibanum, a water-soluble gum has been isolated as well as terpenes and a resinlike product.

Natural varnish resins, as has been noted, can be recognized by their transparency and translucency, their brittleness and conchoidal fracture, and their brown or yellow coloration. As a rule they possess no taste or smell in the solid state, but on heating they melt and often give off a distinctive odour; on burning they yield a smoky flame. Certain of these gums will dissolve directly in various organic liquids such as alcohol or turpentine. In dispersing the more insoluble resins in oils, it is necessary to preheat the resin—a process referred to as running or sweating. No generalization can be made concerning the chemical changes that occur during the running operation, but complex and deep-seated chemical rearrangements such as cracking, decarboxylation, and dehydration are involved. All of these changes are accompanied by a loss in weight; it is by such heat treatment that the resins become more readily dispersible in oil.

Solubility and hardness are the chief criteria used to classify resins, and on the basis of solubility they can be divided into spirit-soluble and oil-soluble types. Many new powerful organic solvents have been developed for the preparation of cellulose lacquers, and a number of these liquids can likewise be employed in the preparation of solutions of natural resins.

A. Spirit-Soluble Resins

1. Balsams.—Balsams are resins of a fluid character and are chiefly used in healing preparations. Certain of the more aromatic varieties have been incorporated into incense. Balsams are generally considered to be solutions of resins dispersed in benzoic or cinnamic acid esters, whereas oleoresins are considered to be solutions of resins in essential oils. However, it is difficult to draw a rigid distinction between balsams and oleoresins, although the latter are usually considered to be slightly more fluid. Canada balsam, an oleoresin derived from *Abies balsamea* and used in cementing lenses, is not a true balsam in that it does not contain benzoic acid or its ester. Certain of the true balsams are the balsam of Tolú (Colombia), the balsam of Peru, as well as the Sumatra (Indonesia) and Thailand benzoins and storax. The storax balsam is of particular interest from the standpoint of synthetic resins, since it was from this material that M. Bonaster in 1831 first isolated styrene, and doubtlessly this product arose through decarboxylation under heat of the cinnamic acid present in the balsam. Another variety of balsam is derived from the grass trees (*Xanthorrhoea*) of Australia. The most important varieties are the yellow and red types, often referred to as accroides gum. This resin contains phenolic bodies that appear to possess some medicinal values, particularly for treating infections of the mucous membranes.

2. Turpentines.—Various oleoresins (solutions of resins dispersed in essential oils) are known as turpentines. Venice turpentine is a pale green, viscous liquid which is collected from the larch (*Larix decidua*, or *europaea*). A liquid of lemonlike odour known as Strasbourg turpentine is derived from *Abies alba*, whereas Bordeaux turpentine is an oleoresin derived from the *Pinus pinaster*. The chief American varieties yielding oil of turpentine are the loblolly pine, *P. taeda*, and the slash pine, *P. caribaea*. On evaporation of the oleoresin a solid resin results, together with a volatile component (spirit of turpentine). The residue from distilling Bordeaux turpentine is known as Burgundy pitch and is used in medicinal plasters.

3. Mastic.—Mastic, a soft resin melting at about 105° C (about 221° F), is derived from the tree of the *Pistacia* genus, which grows in the islands of the Greek archipelago. When dissolved in turpentine, it is used as a varnish for the protection of paintings; when dispersed in bodied linseed oil, it is known as megilp and is used as a colour vehicle.

4. Dragon's Blood and Gamboge.—Dragon's blood is a black-brown resin in bulk, but in thin films it is transparent and of a deep crimson-red colour. The resin is found on the fruits of the rattan palm growing in the East Indies. It is soluble in alcohol and benzene, but not in ether or turpentine. The resin has been used as a varnish for violins and as a dye to colour spirit varnishes a deep red. Another resin used as a colour vehicle and in medicine is gamboge.

5. Dammar.—Dammar, one of the harder resins, is usually secured in the form of clear, pale yellow beads, melting at about 140° C (about 284° F). Various other coloured varieties are obtained from the *Agathïs alba*, which is indigenous to Malaysia and the East Indies. The resin is insoluble in alcohol but dissolves in both aliphatic and aromatic hydrocarbons. Excellent varnishes can be made from these solutions, and the resulting films have a light colour and a good lustre. The resin is also readily soluble in oils without preliminary thermal processing. This resin in combination with nitrocellulose made possible the formulation of rapid-drying lacquers.

6. Sandarac.—The cypress pine, *Callitris*, which grows in Australia, North Africa, and North America, produces the hard resin called sandarac, which is soluble in alcohol as well as in the more powerful lacquer solvents. The resin melts at 150° C (about 302° F) and is used as a spirit varnish for coating paper, leather, and metal. Although the initial film is brittle, it can be readily modified to yield elastic films by the addition of elemi, an oleoresin.

7. Lacs.—Shellac has been considered a zoochemical substance, inasmuch as it is a secretion of an insect known as *Laccifer lacca*. The term shellac has been used incorrectly to cover generically all of the lac products. Insects growing on certain of the trees of the genus *Acacia* produce a scaly substance known as stick lac. This material is ground, washed, and filtered hot, the filtrate passing onto water-cooled drums from which it is removed in the familiar flakelike form. The button lac is a lac which has been allowed to fall on a flat surface. Lac is one of the widely used resins in industry. It is also used in electric insulation, as a coating for wood and metal, and as a binding agent for molding composition. Certain varieties are incorporated into sealing waxes.

Chemically, shellac consists of a mixture of polyhydroxy acids. Two varieties have been isolated, one a hard lac and the other a softer material that appears to act as a plasticizer for the harder component. The softer portion consists primarily of uncombined acids, whereas the harder material consists of polyesters. A major portion of the hard lac was found to be a monobasic ester that could be made to undergo hydrolytic fission to aleuritic acid and lacollic lactone. Other acids which have been isolated from shellac are a tetrahydroxy acid known as kerrolic acid, as well as shellolic acid, together with a natural yellow dyestuff known as erythrolaccin. Aleuritic acid is considered to be 9,10,16-hexadecanetriol acid: $HOCH_2-(CH_2)_5-(CHOH)_2-(CH_2)_7-CO_2H$. Although the solubility of shellac is usually associated with alcohol, it is also dispersible in aqueous solutions. There appears to be some indication that on long standing alcohol may react with shellac. A white variety can be made by a bleaching process from which colourless, transparent lacquers can be made.

B. Oil-Soluble Resins

1. Rosin.—Upon distillation of the oleoresin from the long-leaf pine two materials are obtained: one a volatile component (spirit of turpentine) and the other a nonvolatile, resinous residue (rosin). The word rosin is used for this product, rather than resin because the latter is a term used generically to cover all of the compounds of this type. Depending on the source of the oil of turpentine, it is possible to have either gum turpentine and gum rosin or wood turpentine and wood rosin; the former variety originates from the turpentine secured by tapping the trees. By solvent extraction of the stumps, wood rosin is obtained, and this is generally of a darker colour. Various designations are employed to distinguish the colour of the product. The colour of French rosin is designated by the letter A, and the greater the number of A's used the paler the grade. The U.S. designation is more arbitrary, and the better classes are known as WW (water white) and WG (window glass). Rosin is a brittle resin that powders readily and becomes sticky when warm. Its specific gravity is about 1.070 to 1.080, and it dissolves in the usual organic liquids. Rosin is also known by the name of colophony or colophonium (from the Greek *kolophonios*).

At one time much of the rosin was used untreated, but the trend is to subject it to chemical processing. The chief constituent of rosin is an acid known as abietic acid, and many of the uses of rosin are dependent upon its acidic properties. Combined with alkalies or with metallic oxides, soaps are obtained. The sodium soap is water dispersible and is employed in sizing paper. Sodium abietate is mixed with other alkali soaps in the manufacture of laundry soap. The lime and zinc salts find use as so-called gloss oils in the paint industry, whereas the metallic soaps derived from lead, cobalt, and manganese are used as driers in paints and varnishes. When rosin is esterified with glycerol (glycerine), the resulting product is known as ester gum. Somewhat harder esterification products are made through a conjoint ester of rosin with glycerol and with phthalic anhydride. Partial decarboxylation of acid occurs when rosin is heated to elevated temperatures; such products are known as rosin oils.

The acids isolated from rosin include abietic acid,

CH₃ COOH
  \ /
   C   CH₂
  / \ / \
CH₂ CH CH
 | | ‖
CH₂ C   C
  \ / \ / \
  CH₂ CH CH CH₃
       | | /
 H₃C CH₂ C—CH
    \   /   \
    CH₂   CH₃

pimaric acid, CH_3 COOH

$$
\begin{array}{c}
CH_3 \quad\quad COOH \\
C \quad\quad CH_2 \\
CH_2 \quad CH \quad CH_2 \\
CH_2 \quad C \quad C-CH=CH_2 \\
CH_2 \quad CH \quad CH \\
H_3C \quad CH_2 \quad C-CH_3 \\
CH_2
\end{array}
$$

and laevopimaric acid, CH_3 COOH

$$
\begin{array}{c}
CH_3 \quad\quad COOH \\
C \quad\quad CH_2 \\
CH_2 \quad CH \quad CH_2 \\
CH_2 \quad C \quad C \\
CH_2 \quad C \quad CH \quad CH_3 \\
H_3C \quad CH_2 \quad C-CH \\
CH_2 \quad\quad CH_3
\end{array}
$$

It will be noted that certain of these acids appear to possess a system of conjugated double bonds, which may account for the ease with which rosin oxidizes when it is exposed to air. By chemically combining rosin with hydrogen it is possible to obtain a product that exhibits greater stability and is less subject to discoloration on storage. The abietic acid in rosin can be made to undergo hydrogen disproportionation leading to the so-called dehydrogenated rosin. This type of chemically modified rosin, as the sodium soap, was used extensively during World War II as the emulsifying agent in the preparation of synthetic rubber. The properties of the modified rosin were such that it could be allowed to remain in the coagulated rubber. Hydrogenation and disproportionation both cause rosin to crystallize more readily, and consequently the hydrogenation is carried only to the point where satisfactory stability can be secured without crystallization. By combining rosin chemically with certain unsaturated types of dibasic acids, such as maleic and fumaric acid, it is possible to destroy the unsaturation without inducing crystallization. It is probable that the character of the varnish made from China wood oil and the rosin derivative may reside in the chemical combination that takes place between the unsaturated components of both products.

2. Copals.—The copals form an important group of varnish resins. The word copal appears to have been derived from the Spanish or Mexican word *copalli* ("incense"). Various types of products are known—the recent varieties as well as the fossil types. Soft Manila copal is readily soluble in organic solvent liquids and in oils or, as in the case of the pontianak variety, it requires running before it can be dispersed in oil. Several varieties are employed in the varnish trade: kauri copal, melting at about 150° C (about 302° F), is derived from the New Zealand pine; Congo copal originates in the Congo; while Zanzibar (East African) copal is dug from the coast of the mainland opposite the island of Zanzibar. Some of the South American copals derived from Brazil and Colombia have attracted some attention. Copal has been esterified with glycerol in a manner similar to that employed in making ester gum. Because of the high melting point of the copal gum, it is necessary to conduct this thermal decomposition to a point much further than is customarily employed when the resin is to be dissolved in oil, and temperatures as high as 330°–340° C (about 626°–644° F) are employed. Two acids have been isolated from Congo copal; one is the dibasic congocopalic acid, $C_{36}H_{58}(COOH)_2$, and the other is the monobasic congocopalolic acid, $C_{27}H_{32}(OH)COOH$.

3. Amber.—Amber, the hardest natural resin known, finds little use in the varnish industry because of its lack of solubility. When it is incorporated in oil, so much discoloration takes place during the running operation that the resulting varnish has a poor colour. The resin is found in the so-called blue earth, in East Prussia in the Baltic region. The fact that it is derived from a variety of *Pinus* indicates that over a sufficiently long period of time under appropriate conditions an oleoresin can be converted into a heat-infusible product. Amber is used chiefly for fabricating beads and other items of jewelry. In certain respects amber can be handled in much the same manner as that used in the fabrication of cast plastics.

4. Oriental Lacquer.—Oriental lacquer is a distinct product derived from *Toxicodendron vernicifluum*, a tree indigenous to China. The manufacturing process was introduced into Japan and remained secret for centuries. A milklike emulsion secured from the tree is concentrated by evaporation to a viscous liquid resembling a bodied oil. When this is applied as a thin film, it hardens in about a day to form a tough skin. The composition is peculiar in that it will dry only in a dark, moist atmosphere; when exposed to light and warmth, the varnish remains tacky. The varnish contains a skin irritant, and this material may be the urushiol which is similar to a product isolated from the *Toxicodendron radicans* (poison ivy).

5. Cashew-Shell-Nut Oil.—Another product containing phenolic bodies is derived from the nuts of the cashew tree (*Anacardium occidentale*); the oil known as the cashew-shell-nut oil possesses materials which lead to vesicant action (blistering), but by appropriate chemical treatment the irritant is destroyed. This product has found some commercial importance in the United States.

II. SYNTHETIC RESINS

1. Characteristics and Usage.—Synthetic resins, while possessing most of the physical characteristics of natural resins, have many unique properties of their own. Chemically there is a certain degree of resemblance between the synthetic resins of phenol-formaldehyde and the natural phenolic resins found in Oriental lacquer and in accroides gum. Moreover, one can trace a certain amount of resemblance between the polyester resins known as alkyds and the polyesters found in shellac. Although it has usually been considered that the synthetic resins possess the unique characteristic of becoming insoluble and infusible on heat treatment, it is known that shellac will become insoluble on prolonged heating, and the same phenomenon has been observed with certain of the other gums.

The synthetic resins are of industrial interest not only as substitutes for natural resins in the coating industry but also because they find extensive use as adhesives, textile impregnants, binders, as agents for removing ions from water solutions, and as binders in the plastics molding industry (*see* PLASTICS).

2. Classifications.—Physically it is possible to classify synthetic resins according to their solubility. There are those resins which remain permanently soluble and those which are initially soluble but become insoluble and infusible under the action of heat. The first type is known as the thermoplastic type of synthetic resin, whereas the latter is known variously as heat hardenable, thermosetting, or thermocuring resins.

The permanently soluble or thermoplastic resins consist of molecules that are more or less linear in form. During solution in an organic medium, the solvent penetrates within the threadlike molecule; irrespective of the size of the resin molecule, solution will eventually occur. Under the influence of heat the threadlike molecules can be forced to move, and on cooling the impressed form is retained. On the other hand, the thermosetting resins consist of resinous molecules that are tied together three-dimensionally into a network pattern. In the initial stages where the network is small, the solvent can readily penetrate the interstices of the network, but after chemical combination has taken place and a large three-dimensional network is formed, the resin becomes insoluble. Since the network is tied together rigidly, the resulting molecular structure is infusible.

Two main classes may be distinguished under chemical classification: (1) the condensation resin, such as the phenol-formaldehyde or melamine-formaldehyde type, in which the molecules unite with the elimination of water; and (2) the polymerization resin, in which chemical reaction takes place through loss of unsaturation, without the evolution of any low-molecular-weight material.

A. Coating Resins

1. Phenol-Formaldehyde Resins.—The chemical combination of phenols with aldehydes was noted by many investigators in the 19th century. Among the organic chemists who had studied the reaction were C. F. Gerhardt (1853), Adolf von Baeyer (1872), and A. Michael (1883), but it was only after the advent of cheap formaldehyde in 1891 that a more extensive investigation was made toward the commercial applications of this resin. Various investigations were made by W. Kleeberg, A. Smith, and A. Luft, and certain of the methods employed resembled the technology that had proved successful with thermoplastic nitrocellulose plastics but which failed when extended to thermosetting compositions. The first successful work in this field was carried out by L. H. Baekeland. Through a study of the various stages of resinification and through the utilization of a so-called bakelizer, he was able to mold many products, many of which were used in electrical goods. Meanwhile, the possibility of employing this condensation product to replace shellac in phonograph records was considered by J. W. Aylsworth, and the manufacture of phenolic resins was started as a result of the studies of L. V. Redman.

In spite of the marked commercial success of these resins in molding, in casting, and in laminating, they were not suitable for coating compositions. While it was possible to make a phenolic varnish for laminating purposes, this varnish could be dissolved only in alcohol and could not be dispersed in cheap solvents or in drying oils. The first successful attempt to use phenol-formaldehyde resins directly as substitutes for natural resins in coating compositions was the result of the work of K. Albert of Germany. He found that by a preliminary heating or fluxing of the phenol-formaldehyde resin with rosin, it was possible to disperse the resulting mixture in drying oils. These products, when dispersed in China wood oil, possessed rapid drying characteristics and formed films possessing good durability.

In 1928 the first so-called oil-soluble phenolic resin appeared on the market. Through the use of appropriately substituted phenols and the combining of such substituted phenols with formaldehyde, it was possible to obtain a resin which was directly soluble in oil without preliminary fluxing with rosin. These oil-soluble phenolic resins found wide acceptance in the varnish field. Among the phenols useful for such purposes are phenyl phenol (I), tertiary butylphenol (II), and cyclohexylphenol (III), as well as certain

tar acids which boil in the xylenol range. The resins are incorporated into the oil by adding resin in increments at a rate at which frothing can be controlled. The temperature then is raised until satisfactory increase in viscosity occurs. The European procedure favours the addition of the resin to the pretreated oil, and, while it appears to yield lighter coloured and less viscous products, the resulting films appear to be less resistant chemically. Other combinations are known, certain of which consist in substituting an alkyd resin for a part of the drying oil. Durable finishes have been made from alkyd-phenol-formaldehyde oil combinations.

2. Alkyd Resins.—These resins are reaction products of polyhydric alcohols and polybasic acids, and various modifications can be made by adding monohydric alcohols or monobasic acids to the polyester composition. The derivation of the term alkyd becomes apparent when it is pointed out that the "cid" from acid was changed to "kyd" for the sake of euphony. J. J. Berzelius prepared glycerol tartrate in 1847; J. M. van Bemmelen prepared a resin by reacting succinic acid with glycerol in 1856; M. P. E.

Berthelot esterified glycerol and sebacic acid in 1854; while M. A. von Lourenço prepared a resin from glycerol and citric acid in 1863.

The most important dibasic acid employed in the manufacture of alkyd resins is phthalic acid (or phthalic anhydride), which is obtained by the catalytic oxidation of naphthalene. Once this synthesis was properly worked out a ready source of this valuable commodity was available at a reasonable price. While the reaction product of glycerol and phthalic anhydride is of limited utility by itself, it is upon this structural vertebra that such ingredients as natural resin acids as well as drying and nondrying varieties of vegetable fatty-oil acids can be hung. Other dibasic acids are used where specialized properties are required. Maleic acid is obtained by the vapour-phase oxidation of benzene, while its geometrical isomer, fumaric acid, is obtained either by rearrangement of the maleic acid or by fermentation processes. Succinic acid can be prepared by the reduction of maleic acid. Sebacic acid and azelaic acid are incorporated into alkyd resins where exceptional flexibility is required, and these acids are manufactured commercially by treatment of castor oil or cottonseed oil, respectively, with caustic at elevated temperatures. Adipic acid is also available by the oxidation of cyclohexanol, which in turn can be derived from phenol. Glycerol is by far the most important polyhydric alcohol used, but ethylene glycol, diethylene glycol, and pentaerythritol are used for merits of their own.

The drying-type alkyd resins first came into commercial prominence when it was demonstrated by R. H. Kienle that it was possible to form a new type of product by recombining the component parts of a drying oil, that is, the glycerol and the drying-oil acid in the presence of a saturated dibasic acid such as phthalic. Under these conditions the co-condensation of glycerol, phthalic acid (as anhydride), and a drying-oil acid yielded a high-molecular-weight, resinous condensation product in which the unsaturation of the drying-oil acid was substantially unimpaired. The result was that the resin would dry in a manner similar to the natural drying oil. Such resins in organic liquids yield solutions that resemble varnish and can be used as such. Since the resins could be dispersed in relatively cheap organic liquids, these varnish solutions found wide acceptance for coating various metals and as priming paints and enamels. They are used to finish automobiles, streetcars, and railway coaches and, because of their good chemical resistance are used as enamels for coating refrigerators and washing machines. Similar resin solutions are used in ornamental hardware; for coating metal furniture, metal signs, and farm equipment; and, because of good heat resistance, for coating radiators, smokestacks, and light reflectors. They find wide acceptance as architectural enamels, traffic paints, and as printing-ink ingredients.

These resins are often used alone, but they show excellent compatibility characteristics with a wide variety of other film-forming agents, such as nitrocellulose, natural resins, phenolic resins, and urea- and melamine-formaldehyde resins. With nitrocellulose it is possible to secure films possessing toughness, hardness, durability, as well as good gloss. It was this combination with nitrocellulose and alkyd resins which initially permitted the formulation of automotive finishes possessing an enamellike quality and excellent outdoor durability. When these resins are modified with natural resins, the melting point and hardness are increased; since such compositions release solvent very readily, they are used as rubbing and sanding vehicles. When mixed with urea-formaldehyde and melamine-formaldehyde condensation products, the alkyd resin becomes harder and more mar-resistant.

3. Polyester Resins.—While closely related to alkyd resins, the polyester materials differ from the conventional alkyd resins in that the cure is associated with a low-molecular-weight unsaturated organic liquid. The polyester resins, or anhydrous thermosetting resins, usually comprise an unsaturated alkyd resin prepared from a polyhydric alcohol with an unsaturated acid such as maleic or fumaric acid. This alkyd resin is then dispersed in an organic liquid such as monomeric styrene or with diallyl phthalate. This solution, appropriately stabilized for shipping, is treated with a peroxide catalyst just before use. The catalyzed resinous material is then employed in saturating various fibrous materials such as fabric or glass fibre. The cured composite structure of resin and glass fibre found use in such widely differing applications as plastic armour, trays, radar housings, luggage, and light-weight boats.

The term polyester resin has also been used for an entirely different type of product derived from terephthalic esters. Because of the high symmetry of this acid, the resulting polyesters are high-melting crystalline compositions and, when properly oriented, form a self-supporting film structure of high transparency and strength. The same resin, in oriented fibrous form, finds application both in England and in the United States as a textile fibre.

Still another polyester possessing unusual physical properties has been prepared by reacting phosgene with a phenolic substance commonly designated as bisphenol-A. In this instance the phenolic body serves as the dihydric alcohol to yield resins of outstanding toughness. A number of firms have promoted markets for this product, initially developed in Germany.

4. Epoxy Resins.—When bisphenol-A is reacted with epichlorohydrin, one has the basis for the preparation of a curing resin where the reaction occurs without the elimination of water. Such resins have been used not only as coating materials but as potting compositions. Currently they are being utilized as textile finishes.

5. Urea-Formaldehyde Resins.—The chemical condensation of urea and formaldehyde yields resins of great value in both the molding and coating industries. The resins are characterized by extremely light colour, and products fabricated from such materials can be made into colourless moldings. The fundamental chemical investigations of Hanns John laid the foundation for the use of this resin in the plastics industry; but insofar as coating resins are concerned, it was the observation of Kurt Ripper that proved most valuable. He found that under suitable conditions the water-soluble condensation product of urea and formaldehyde could be dispersed in organic liquids. To make the resin soluble in varnish solvents for coating use, it was first necessary to conduct the condensation of urea and formaldehyde in a solvent such as alcohol and then to remove the water of condensation as an azeotrope with the alcohol. The resin thus formed in alcoholic solution could then be diluted with aromatic solvents.

By themselves, films and coatings of the unmodified urea resins are hard and marproof and possess good colour and gloss but lack distensibility. From the standpoint of their use in enamels the resins are neutral, and consequently any type of pigment can be admixed with them. When these urea resins are blended with alkyd resins, they become flexible and adhere to metal surfaces. This combination of urea-formaldehyde resins and alkyd resins is in many ways a unique combination whereby the urea resins improve certain deficiencies of the alkyd resins, such as increasing hardness and eliminating the tendency of the oil-modified alkyd resins to wrinkle on rapid drying. The urea-formaldehyde resins under the influence of heat contribute hardness, colour, and gloss to the cured film, while the alkyd resins produce flexibility, drying ability, and adhesion to metal surfaces.

6. Melamine-Formaldehyde Resins.—Many of the excellent characteristics exhibited by the urea-formaldehyde resins in coatings are also shown by the melamine-formaldehyde resins. Melamine, or polymerized (trimerized) cyanamide, is a heterocyclic compound which reacts and cures rapidly in combination with formaldehyde. Unlike urea, which is low melting and soluble in water, melamine possesses a high melting point (354° C, or about 669° F) and dissolves very slightly in water. It is characterized by an exceptionally stable ring system of alternate carbon and nitrogen atoms—a stability reflected in the resins made from it. The melamine and formaldehyde resin can be dispersed in organic solvents by procedures similar to those employed for the urea-formaldehyde condensation product. When used in admixture with alkyd resins a much faster heat cure can be secured than when urea-formaldehyde is used. The outstanding characteristics which urea resins supply to films are further enhanced with melamine resins; these are superior in resistance to various chemical reagents, in outdoor durability, and in colour retention on exposure to both heat and light. These properties, in addition to porcelainlike appearance and resistance to abrasion, enabled such finishes to enter into automotive coatings and industrial finishes.

7. Polyethylene.—While most uses of polymerized ethylene are in moldings and self-supporting films, there are certain newer developments whereby the thermoplastic product is converted to a thermosetting variety. When the polymer is exposed to radiation, such as the γ-rays, a certain amount of hydrogen is knocked out of the system, and under appropriate conditions, depending on whether the polymer is in aerobic or anaerobic environment, the fragments will reunite to form an insoluble product. This infusible material possesses about the same electrical characteristics as the unmodified material. When this radiation is performed in the presence of polyethylene that has been milled with carbon black, an infusible, filled, molded composition is obtained.

Closely allied to polyethylene is polypropylene, but the preparation of this polymer requires wholly different catalysts from those used in the ethylene reaction.

8. Coumarone-Indene Resins.—From the light oils present in the distillation of coal tar, it is possible to secure a fraction rich in indene, coumarone, and related isomers. This mixture can be polymerized by means of sulfuric acid into resins of soft or hard consistency. These synthetic resins are among the oldest-known synthetic products and have been available from the time of the initial investigations of G. Kraemer and A. Spilker in 1890. The resins exhibit good compatibility characteristics with a wide variety of other polymeric products, both synthetic and natural, and have been used in coating concrete, in the manufacture of antifouling ship-bottom paints, as additives to paraffin wax, in admixture with bitumens, and as compounding agents in butadiene-styrene synthetic rubber.

9. Silicones.—The silicone resins are based on the silicon-oxygen skeleton rather than the carbon-oxygen chains or the carbon chain found in the conventional resins. This siloxane linkage, as the silicon-oxygen combination is called, introduces a degree of resistance to heat that is not found in those chains possessing carbon atoms exclusively. Naturally, those same reagents which can break the silicon-oxygen bridge in silicate minerals are also instrumental in causing the silicone resins to undergo cleavage; both hydrofluoric acid and strong caustic will cleave the siloxane chain in the silicone resins. Through the proper choice of ingredients, groupings can be introduced into the molecular structure whereby growth may be made to occur essentially linearly as, for example, through the introduction of saturated dialkyl-siloxy groups, or three-dimensionally through the utilization of the monoalkyl-siloxy groupings.

Various silicones can be made by changing the nature of the alkyl group, but most of the commercial production is restricted to the methyl silicones. Various polymeric structures have been made, certain of which are viscous liquids, others resinous, and even rubbery products have been produced. The liquids have found use as hydraulic oils and as instrument and transformer oils. Some of the higher-molecular-weight materials have found further application as varnishes as well as in high-temperature-resisting paints and enamels and as coatings for electrical insulation. When applied to the surfaces of glass or ceramics and baked, the silicones yield water-repellent surfaces.

10. Fluorine Resins.—Even though elementary fluorine is a relatively reactive gas, when this element is united with carbon in the form of an unsaturated monomer and then polymerized, compositions of remarkable heat and chemical resistance are formed. Compositions are commercially available where only carbon and fluorine exist in the polymer matrix, but in certain instances chlorine may replace a portion of the fluorine. Two resins that have achieved the greatest success are the tetrafluoroethylene polymer and trifluorochloroethylene derivatives. In certain instances modification has involved the use of perfluorinated propylene. While most applications are directed toward plastics, outstanding coatings and fibres have been prepared from these compositions. Because polytetrafluoroethylene possesses an extremely low coefficient of friction, it has been used in the fabrication of composite metal bearings. Even when only one surface is coated, friction is reduced. Through the use of fluorinated diolefins, heat-resistant rubber compositions have been formulated.

11. Polyamides.—By substituting diamines in place of diols and conducting the condensation with dibasic acids at elevated temperature polyamides may be secured. To insure crystallinity, symmetrically structured acids and amines are employed, such as adipic acid and hexamethylenediamine. Amino acids such as aminocaproic acid may be condensed to high-molecular-weight derivatives, or the internally dehydrated product, caprolactam, may be polymerized to similar types of polyamides. Fibres from these polyamides are known as nylon, but the same polymer can also be fabricated into sheets, coatings, and rods. It is important to select ingredients that avoid imide formation, but these imides have found applications in condensation products known as poly-imides, which are resin systems stable at elevated temperature. Polyimide-based resins are marketed as insulating varnish, wire enamel, and glass-coated fabrics. Because the polyimides possess high thermal stability and good electrical and mechanical properties, together with radiation resistance, they are desirable for use in aerospace applications. Polyimides are produced by condensing a dianhydride of an aromatic tetrabasic acid, such as pyromellitic anhydride, with an aromatic diamine. There have also been developments on the reversed type of product. These polymers are formed from aromatic tetramines and dibasic acids, the poly-benzimidazoles. When the dibasic acids are aliphatic, the heat resistance is not as outstanding as when aromatic acids are used in the condensation.

12. Polyurethanes.—These products masquerade under a variety of names, such as urethanes, isocyanate polymers, and poly-urethanes, but these names are expedient rather than accurate. While polymers can be prepared by polymerizing isocyanates, polyurethanes are not derived by polymerizing a monomeric ure-thane molecule. Commercial polyurethanes encompass a variety of oils and resins, such as castor oil, polyesters, and polyethers which have been combined chemically with di- and triisocyanates. The reaction was initially studied in Germany by Otto Bayer in 1937 in an effort to prepare a product competitive with polyamides by reacting diamines with diisocyanates. While these polyureas were used for some time in Germany, they were not accepted at first in the United States. Extensive studies were conducted during World War II in the preparation of foams, adhesives, and coatings. While isocyanates had been employed in the United States for bonding rubber to metal, the full commercial impact of the new structures was not appreciated until after the war, when the scientific teams studying German developments reported their findings. Nevertheless, commercial interest in these materials grew slowly until machinery was developed for continuous production methods in manufacturing flexible foams. Initially, polyester resins were employed as the principal complementary component, but it was the advent of less expensive polyethers derived from the polymerization of propylene oxide which boosted these products to large volume uses. Flexible foam was found to be superior to foam rubber, but now major attention is directed toward rigid formulations, particularly for insulation. The latter development has been aided by techniques for introducing gaseous fluorocarbons as an integral part of foam architecture. The presence of this fluorocarbon in the intracellular spaces insures highly effective insulation.

13. Polyethers.—The polyether component in polyurethane systems, as well as its lower homolog polyethylene oxide, is characterized by an oxygen bridge as an integral part of the polymer chain. A simple, different type of polyether may be prepared by polymerizing vinyl ethers such as methyl vinyl ether as well as other vinyl ethers derived from higher alcohols by reaction with acetylene. Polyvinyl methyl ether is produced not only as a high polymer in the atactic form but also in a stereoregular isotactic variety.

14. Acetal Resins.—Polyvinyl butyral, used in safety glass, and polyvinyl formal, used as wire enamel, both fit under the term acetal. Most frequently, however, acetal resins refer to high-molecular-weight, stable linear polymers of formaldehyde. Because of the insoluble nature of these acetal polymers, they are used most frequently as molding and extrusion compositions.

B. Resin Adhesives

1. Plywood Adhesives.—Prior to the introduction of synthetic resins for plywood construction, laminated wood was susceptible to deterioration by water and high humidity. The natural protein products such as albumin and casein could not be rendered insoluble to the same extent as later became possible with various condensation products such as phenol-formaldehyde, urea-formaldehyde, and melamine-formaldehyde resins. The new resin adhesives permit the construction of plywood in which the glue line is strong, resistant to water, and immune to attack by the action of fungi, molds, and vermin. Such plywood can be used not only for architectural and automotive purposes but also for aeronautical and marine construction. Phenolic-resin adhesives became commercially available about 1935; urea condensation products were introduced about 1937.

Two types of synthetic glues are manufactured—cold-setting and hot-setting. Certain resins are supplied in powder form requiring solution prior to use, whereas other types are already dispersed in a liquid medium. Extenders such as cereal flour and wheat flour are sometimes employed where maximum strength and waterproofness are not essential. Phenolic resins yield an especially durable bond, but the resin is coloured, and the colour may bleed through thin veneers. Such colour is also a disadvantage where the glued edges are exposed. The urea resin is characterized by a rapid cure at low temperature and is widely employed in the preparation of cold-setting adhesives. The urea resin, moreover, is colourless and will not change the colour of the wood. Melamine resins likewise possess excellent colour characteristics, and the glue line formed from them is resistant to both cold and boiling water.

Keeping pace with the development of new adhesives were new fabricating and molding techniques that allowed construction of complicated shapes, particularly in aeronautics and boat construction. Flat sheets can be "post-formed" into simple curves, but for construction of compound curved surfaces a molding procedure is preferred. This is accomplished by applying the glue of the veneers and allowing them to dry in order to permit easy handling. A mold is constructed with the exact contours needed in the finished assembly, and the coated wood veneers are placed in the mold and fastened by staples. The laminates are enclosed in a rubber bag which is evacuated in order to keep the veneers rigidly in place, and the assembly is placed in an autoclave and heated in order to render the resin insoluble and infusible. Such procedures enabled rapid construction of large aircraft parts, pontoons, and motor torpedo boats.

2. Wood Impregnation.—Wood that has been subjected to reduced atmospheric pressure to remove occluded air can be impregnated with various resin solutions dissolved in water or in alcohol. After drying, the temperature is raised, whereupon curing of the resin occurs in the interior of the wood, rendering it harder, stronger, and more resistant to water and water vapour. By adding appropriate accelerators prior to impregnation the cure can be effected at a lower temperature with less damage to the structure of the wood. Phenol formaldehyde, urea formaldehyde, and mixture of the two resins have been employed for this purpose.

3. Other Adhesive Applications.—Many other resinous and rubbery compositions, dispersed in water or dissolved in organic liquids, are used to bind metals, plastics, glass, rubber, paper, brickwork, leather, fabrics, and cork. Others are used in the manufacture of shoes, gaskets, furniture, lighting assemblies, sound insulation, and upholstery. Certain adhesives have natural or synthetic rubber as a base, whereas others contain synthetic thermoplastic and thermosetting resins. During World War II the reinforcement of starch by urea-resin adhesives in paperboard manufacture led to paper containers having a high resistance to water.

C. Resins for Textile Applications

1. Continuous Coating.—One method of separating electrical conductors is by using a covering of cotton or silk. As long as anhydrous conditions exist, such insulation is satisfactory, but in a humid atmosphere the textile absorbs water, and its insulating efficiency is markedly decreased. To overcome this disadvantage, the dried fabric is treated with a varnish subsequently cured, thereby sealing the fabric. The varnish selected is such that water-vapour transmission through the film of resin will be as small as possible. Of those resins used, the phenolic resins are the best known, although almost every type of natural and synthetic resin has been tested for this type of insulating varnish.

2. Impregnation of Fabrics.—Resins are applied to fabrics for purposes other than insulation—for instance, to improve the finish of cotton and rayon and to render them nonshrinking and crushproof. Resins have also been employed to bind pigments to the fabric, to minimize bleeding and crocking of dyes, and as mordants for dyeing cellulose fibres with wool dyes (animalized cellulose). Since no resin discoloration can be tolerated in uses of this type, the thermosetting resins having widest acceptance are the urea-formaldehyde condensation products. In numerous applications, superior results can be secured only with the melamine-formaldehyde resins. The more notable achievements of the latter resin include shrinkage control of cotton and wool, improved crease resistance of cotton and rayon, production of durable glazes on chintz, treatment of binders to prevent thread slippage, and minimized gas fading of acetate colours. Many of these effects are achieved by treating textiles with low-molecular-weight, water-soluble condensation products and then causing resin formation to occur on the fabric.

Quite different effects are obtained by using high-molecular-weight, water-insoluble thermoplastic resins which are dispersed in water. Such resins render the fabric stiff, crisp, and full, and when properly formulated such properties are not destroyed by laundering. Other thermoplastic resins impart good draping characteristics and improve the abrasion resistance of the textile, whereas still others are employed for upholstery finishing, raincoats, shower curtains, and other waterproofing applications.

Through suitable modification of resinous ingredients, particularly through the use of phosphorus or compounds of phosphorus and halogen, it has been possible to devise cotton finishes having substantial resistance to flame. This does not imply that the fabric is fireproof, but when the appropriate phosphorus compounds are combined chemically with cellulose, such materials will yield water and carbon at elevated temperatures. When the flame is removed, the charred cellulose will not propagate combustion, and there is no flaming or afterglow.

D. Resins Possessing Ionic Charges

1. Ion-Exchange Resins.—By the introduction of strong acid groupings such as carboxyl and sulfonic acid into a three-dimensional polymer, high-molecular-weight resins can be made where the resin is ionic in character and where the ion is chemically bound in the resin molecule. These ionic resins in the form of sodium salt can be used as a means of softening water whereby the calcium ions of the hard water are replaced by the sodium ions from the resin. In this respect the synthetic ion-exchange resins, generally known as cation resins, behave like the natural zeolites and, like the zeolites, the resins used under such conditions do not change the amount of dissolved salt in the water.

Condensation products can also be prepared synthetically where basic groupings such as amino- and guanido- are bound in the resin molecule, and these so-called anion resins can replace anions. It follows that a combination of the acidic and basic resins or a cation and an anion resin can completely eliminate the mineral content of water by first allowing the cation-exchange resin in the form of a free acid to react with the salt and subsequently reacting the effluent with an anion exchanger.

Once the resins become saturated with minerals, they can be regenerated chemically and used over again as often as required. The process works most expediently where the concentration of mineral matter is low, but the scavenging is so complete that the method has found favour not only in producing a so-called demineralized distilled water but in numerous industrial processes where the removal of ionic impurities is not possible by distillation. Ion-exchange resins have been used to remove mineral impurities from pharmaceutical preparations, dyestuffs, sugar, syrups, enzyme preparations, emulsions, glycols, and formaldehyde. Other industrial uses include the recovery of valuable metals and various other inorganic and organic materials from industrial wastes. The resins have also been employed as catalysts in chemical reactions, particularly in the inversion of sugar.

Water-soluble resins might most properly be designated as gums. The alternative nomenclature appears more attractive even though the definition distorts the initial distinction between resins and gums. Since the same raw materials are so closely allied with the resin industry, this terminology is useful to distinguish these synthetic products from the natural water-soluble gums. In the same way that resins may be modified, various water-dispersible functional groups may be introduced into the polymer molecule; these groups may be ionic or nonionic. By suitable adjustment a wide range of physical properties may be incorporated into the final polymer, permitting it to be more or less sensitive to accompanying ions. The carboxyl group is the preferred ionic residue, where this functional group is introduced using either acrylic and methacrylic acid or maleic anhydride. Of the nonionic residues, a much wider range of components are available, such as the alcohol group, methoxides, pyrrolidone, and amides. Considerable attention had been directed to various copolymers of acrylamide and acrylic acid. One of the newer outlets for these water-soluble colloids has been approved for removing the "chill haze" in beer. Polyvinylpyrrolidone will precipitate tannins and other complex proteins from beer and wine. The polymeric acids also have applications in a number of unusual outlets such as in soil stabilization and in drilling fluids containing mud. A number of soils are fine powders when dry and slimy muds when wet. If these soils are treated with a small concentration of these polymeric acids, the mud seems to dry up, yielding a friable soil that allows water to drain away without serious erosion. In drilling muds these polymeric acids allow the mud to retain water and prevent its loss into the pores or fissures of rocks where water loss might cause seizure of the drilling bit.

2. Resins for Treating Paper.—Another resinous ion which has attracted attention is the cationic melamine-formaldehyde resin. Unlike the ion-exchange resins, the cationic melamine resin is initially dispersible in water. The large ion is attracted toward and adheres to the cellulose fibre. It can be incorporated into paper as an acidic dispersion to a pulp suspension, and after migration to the paper fibre the resin becomes insoluble and infusible as the paper stock is dried. The resulting product is characterized by superior fold resistance and by a nonlinting behaviour when dry; when wet it does not disintegrate. Water-dispersible urea resins with ionic properties can be added to paper stock in a similar manner. While certain of these resins are anionic (i.e., they contain sulfonic acid groups and are flocculated on the fibres through the use of aluminum sulfate), others are cationic and need no flocculation agent.

3. Ionomer Resins.—This term has been coined for a family of polymers comprising covalent and ionic bonds in high-molecular-weight form. By introducing ionic components into a semicrystalline structure, the crystallinity is depressed, but the modulus of elasticity, yield point, oil resistance, and solvent resistance are notably improved. The anions are carboxyl residues to which are attached various metallic cations such as sodium, potassium, zinc, and magnesium.

E. Electrically Conductive Resins

Semiconducting organic solids fall into two major classes, molecular crystals and polymers. The classical example of a molecular crystal is anthracene, which is possibly the most extensively investigated organic semiconductor. The semiconducting characteristics of polymers are not as well established as those of the molecular crystals. Nevertheless, carbon resistors, which have been in commercial production for many years, are a type of organic semiconductor system. An electrically conductive resin has been produced that may be a forerunner of a wide spectrum of similar products. This resin was produced by combining 7,7,8,8-tetracyanoquinodimethane with a poly-N-methylvinylpyridinium derivative. This polymeric composition can be cast from organic liquids to form films where conductivity is electronic rather than ionic, and where values of 10^{-3} reciprocal ohm centimetres have been observed.

See also references under "Resins" in the Index.

BIBLIOGRAPHY.—H. W. Chatfield, *Varnish Constituents* (1944); C. Ellis, *The Chemistry of Synthetic Resins* (1935); N. Heaton, *Outlines of Paint Technology* (1928); R. Houwink, *Chemie und Technologie der Kunststoffe*, 2 vol. (1942); J. J. Mattiello (ed.), *Protective and Decorative Coatings*, vol. i–v (1941–42); R. S. Morrell *et al.* (eds.), *Synthetic Resins and Allied Plastics*, 2nd ed. (1943), *Varnishes and Their Components* (1924); J. Scheiber and K. Sändig, *Artificial Resins* (1931); P. J. Flory, *Principles of Polymer Chemistry* (1953); G. F. D'Alelio, *Fundamental Principles of Polymerization* (1952); C. E. Schildknecht, *Vinyl and Related Polymers* (1952); T. S. Carswell, *Phenoplasts* (1947); R. H. Boundy and R. F. Boyer, (eds.) *Styrene: its Polymers, Copolymers and Derivatives* (1952); J. H. Saunders and K. C. Frisch (eds.), *High Polymers*, vol. xvi, part i (1962), part ii (1964); J. J. Brophy and J. W. Buttrey, *Organic Semiconductors* (1962); R. B. Akin, *Acetal Resins* (1962); M. B. Horn, *Acrylic Resins* (1960); C. R. Martens, *Alkyd Resins* (1961); J. F. Blais, *Amino Resins* (1959); I. Skeist, *Epoxy Resins* (1958); M. A. Rudner, *Fluorocarbons* (1958); D. F. Gould, *Phenolic Resins* (1959); D. E. Floyd, *Polyamide Resins* (1958); J. R. Lawrence, *Polyester Resins* (1960); T. O. J. Kresser, *Polyethylene* (1957), *Polypropylene* (1960); W. C. Teach and G. C. Kiessling, *Polystyrene* (1960); B. A. Dumbrow, *Polyurethanes* (1957); M. W. Smith, *Vinyl Resins* (1958); E. Müller, *Methoden der Organischen Chemie*, band xiv/i (1961), band xiv/ii (1963).

(E. L. Ka.)

RESISTENCIA, a city of northeastern Argentina, capital of the province of Chaco (*q.v.*), is situated on the Barranqueras stream that connects with the Paraná River at Barranqueras, its port. Pop. (1960) 80,089. It is the administrative centre of the province and the nucleus of a zone of frontier settlement extending toward the northwest. Cotton, quebracho, leather, cattle, and lead are the main industries in the area. A railroad runs west to Metán and Rosario de la Frontera, and south to Santa Fe, 348 mi. distant.

(J. L. Tr.)

REȘIȚA, a town in the Banat *regiune* (administrative and economic region) of western Rumania, is situated in a coal basin and a metalliferous region. Pop. (1960 est.) 46,008. Reșița is an important industrial centre, smelting the iron ore from Dognecea and Ocna de Fier. In the neighbourhood, coking coal is mined at Anina, Doman, and Secu. The Reșița iron and steel works, rebuilt under the Communist regime, operate blast furnaces, steel foundries, rolling mills, and metalworking and machine-building enterprises.

RESONANCE, a term used in physics and related fields originally denoting a prolongation or increase of sound because of sympathetic vibration of some body capable of moving in the proper period. An example is the oscillation induced in a violin or piano string of a given pitch when a musical note of the same pitch is sung or played nearby. For resonance in acoustical theory and experiment, *see* SOUND; in rooms and buildings, *see* ACOUSTICS OF BUILDINGS; as a theory of hearing, *see* HEARING; in violin construction, *see* VIOLIN FAMILY. The term has been extended by analogy to the familiar selective mechanical resonance of a springboard or bridge to certain frequencies of jumping or walking; and to the selective electrical resonance of a tuned radio circuit to the radio frequency transmitted by a single radio station. At the high frequencies used in microwaves and radar (*q.v.*), the tuned circuit is actually constructed most easily in the form of a small metal cavity resonator not unlike the cavity of an acoustical resonator such as an open-mouthed bottle.

See also references under "Resonance" in the Index.

(J. R. Pt.)

RESONANCE, THEORY OF, in chemistry, is an extension of the theory of valence (*q.v.*), which contributed greatly to the understanding of the structure of molecules and the structural interpretation of the chemical and physical properties of substances. The concept of resonance has been applied in chemistry in the elucidation of the nature of the covalent bond, of the partial ionic character of bonds and of other aspects of valence. Its most important chemical applications have been to aromatic molecules, molecules containing conjugated systems of double bonds, hydrocarbon free radicals, and other molecules to which no

satisfactory single structure in terms of single bonds, double bonds and triple bonds can be assigned.

For many molecules it is possible to formulate valence-bond structures which are so reasonable and which account so satisfactorily for the properties of the substances that they are generally accepted and are used as the basis for chemical reasoning. Examples of such molecules are:

It is sometimes found, however, that a choice cannot be made between two or more conceivable structures which are expected to be about equally stable and of which no one accounts in a completely satisfactory way for the properties of the substance. The concept of quantum-mechanical resonance provided the solution to this problem; namely, the actual normal state of such a molecule can be described as corresponding not to any one of the alternative reasonable structures but rather to a combination of them, their individual contributions being determined by their nature and stability. The molecule is then said to resonate among the several valence-bond structures or to have a structure which is a resonance hybrid of these structures. The molecule is stabilized by this resonance, its energy being less than the energy which would be expected for any one of the structures among which it resonates. This stabilization is characteristic of the phenomenon of quantum-mechanical resonance, which was discovered by Werner Heisenberg in 1926 (*see* below). The physical and chemical properties of the substance and the configuration of the molecule are determined by the nature of the resonating structures; these properties are, however, not the properties averaged for the resonating structures but are instead the averaged properties as influenced also by the effects of resonance and in particular by the additional stability resulting from the resonance energy.

The aromatic substance benzene provides not only an illuminating but also the most important example of the application of the concept of the resonance of molecules among two or more valence-bond structures. The formulation of the structure of benzene as a six-membered ring of carbon atoms with attached hydrogen atoms was made by F. A. Kekulé in 1865. To make the structure compatible with the quadrivalence of carbon he introduced alternating single and double bonds in the ring, and later, in 1872, in order to account for the nonobservance of isomeric orthodisubstituted benzenes (differing in having a single bond or a double bond between the substituted carbon atoms), he introduced the idea of an oscillation between two structures:

The Kekulé structure for benzene is unsatisfactory in that the substance does not show the properties of unsaturation to be expected for a molecule containing double bonds. After a period during which the centric structure of H. E. Armstrong and Adolf von Baeyer, the diagonal structure of A. Claus and the structure of J. Thiele based on his theory of partial valence were proposed, an important advance was made in the years following 1920 in the theory of intermediate stages proposed by F. Arndt and the theory of mesomerism developed by Sir Robert Robinson, C. K. Ingold and other English and U.S. chemists. The suggestion of these investigators, induced from the facts of chemistry, was that the true state of a molecule may be intermediate between those represented by several different valence-bond structures. Complete clarification of the structure of benzene was provided by Linus Pauling (1931) through application of the theory of resonance and consideration of the effect of resonance energy. According to the quantum-mechanical discussion of the structure of benzene, the normal state of this molecule can be represented as a hybrid of the two Kekulé structures ⬡ and ⬡ and three diagonal structures of the form ⬡ ⬡ ⬡ (the *para* bond in these structures being a weak bond, almost equivalent to a free valence on each of the para carbon atoms) and other structures which make smaller contributions. The configuration of the molecule should be a suitable average of those configurations corresponding to the individual structures. Because of the resonance the six carbon-carbon bonds are equivalent, and because of the stereochemical properties of a double bond the molecule as a whole is planar; hence the benzene molecule is predicted to be a planar hexagonal molecule, in agreement with observations made by the electron diffraction, X-ray diffraction and spectroscopic methods. Moreover, each carbon-carbon bond should be intermediate in length between a single carbon-carbon bond and a double carbon-carbon bond, the lengths of which, in molecules represented by a single valence-bond structure, are 1.54 Å and 1.33 Å, respectively. The observed value in benzene, 1.39 Å, is compatible with this prediction. Moreover, the benzene molecule is predicted from the quantum-mechanical considerations to be stabilized by resonance energy to the extent of about 40 kg.cal. per mole, relative to the value expected for one of the Kekulé structures. The amount of resonance stabilization can be estimated experimentally by measurement of the heat of combustion or heat of hydrogenation of benzene and related substances. For example, the heat of hydrogenation of cyclohexene is 28.6 kg.cal. per mole; if each of the three double bonds in benzene were the same as the double bond in cyclohexene, the heat of hydrogenation of benzene would be 85.8 kg.cal. per mole, whereas in fact the observed value is 49.8, indicating that the benzene molecule is stabilized relative to a Kekulé structure by the amount of energy 36 kg.cal. per mole, in approximate agreement with the quantum-mechanical prediction. The characteristic chemical stability and non-reactivity shown by benzene, relative to simpler unsaturated substances, may be attributed to this stabilization by resonance. It is possible, moreover, by the detailed consideration of the resonating structures to explain in a reasonably satisfactory way the other striking chemical properties of benzene, such as the influence of one substituent in determining the position of attachment of further substituents to the ring.

The structures of polynuclear aromatic hydrocarbons are similar. Naphthalene, for example, can be described as resonating among the three structures ⬡⬡ , ⬡⬡ and ⬡⬡ , with small contributions from other structures analogous to the *para*-bonded structures of benzene, and the resonance energy of naphthalene is found to be about 75 kg.cal. per mole.

The stabilization of the aromatic heterocyclic molecules such as thiophene results from resonance of the most important structure

with structures such as

and

The resonance energy for thiophene is about 30 kg.cal. per mole.

The characteristic properties of substances which contain conjugated systems of double bonds can be readily accounted for by the theory of resonance. A molecule such as biphenyl, ⬡—⬡, is stabilized not only by Kekulé resonance but also by the resonance energy of conjugation, resulting from the contributions of the somewhat less stable structures of type ⬡=⬡.

For biphenyl, phenyl ethylene and butadiene the resonance energy of conjugation is about five kg.cal. per mole. There are two stereochemical effects of this conjugation: the carbon-carbon distance for the single bond involved in the conjugated system is decreased from the single-bond value, 1.54 Å, to about 1.48 Å, as the result of the contribution of the conjugated structures with a double bond in this position; and the double-bond character of this bond also finds expression in the tendency to hold the adjacent bonds in the planar configuration. These molecules are observed to be planar or nearly planar, except when planarity is prevented by the arrangement of valence bonds or by steric effects, in which case the properties of the substance show that there is interference with the conjugation.

The phenomenon of resonance can be invoked in the discussion of the colour of dyes and other organic substances. The normal state of the cation of malachite green, for example, involves resonance among all structures of the sort shown below, in which the positive charge is located on different atoms within the molecule:

The excited states of the molecule are similar resonating states involving these structures. The absorption of light by the molecule, with its transition from the normal state to an excited state, occurs with great ease; the quantum-mechanical molecule can be compared with a classical oscillator in which a positive charge is resonating through a large amplitude, from one nitrogen atom across to the other, and from this comparison it can be predicted that the molecule should show intense absorption of light of suitable wave lengths.

Resonance also provides an explanation of the properties of many inorganic substances. For example, the carbon-monoxide molecule is a far more stable molecule than would be expected from the apparent bivalence of carbon, and there was formerly discussion as to whether its structure should be written as :C=Ö:, containing a double covalent bond, or as :C≡O:, similar to the nitrogen molecule. The molecule can be assigned a hybrid structure based upon these structures, and its stability can be attributed to resonance stabilization. For carbon dioxide the structure :Ö=C=Ö: was for many years accepted without question; later, however, evidence of interatomic distances and other properties showed that this structure is in resonance with the two structures :O≡C—Ö: and :Ö—C≡O: Nitric oxide, which is surprisingly stable for a molecule containing an odd number of electrons, can be described as achieving this stability through resonance between the structures :N̈=Ö: and :N̈=Ȯ:, and may be said to have a double bond plus a three-electron bond between its two atoms. The nitrate ion, NO_3^-, resonates among the three structures

making each of the nitrogen-oxygen bonds a hybrid between a single bond and a double bond.

The general rules regarding the resonance of a molecule among alternative valence-bond structures are the following: Equivalent structures contribute equally to the normal state of the resonating molecule. The more stable structures in general make larger contributions to the normal state, and less stable structures make smaller contributions. The electronic state of the resonating molecule applies to a definite configuration of the atomic nuclei; accordingly the energy values of the individual structures to be considered in connection with the foregoing statements are those calculated for the nuclear configuration of the actual state of the molecule and not for nuclear configurations which would be the most stable for the individual structures. The strain involved in this change in configuration in some cases makes structures unimportant which otherwise might be important. All of the structures which contribute to a resonance hybrid structure must have the same number of unpaired electrons; significant resonance does not occur, for example, between a structure with no unpaired electrons (singlet state) and a structure with two unpaired electrons (triplet state).

The basis of the theory of resonance is the fundamental principle of quantum mechanics that the wave function representing a stationary state of a system can be expressed as a sum of wave functions which correspond to hypothetical structures for the system, and that, in particular, the wave function representing the normal state of a system is that sum which leads to a minimum calculated energy of the system. The concept of resonance was introduced into quantum mechanics by Werner Heisenberg in an illuminating discussion of the stationary states of the helium atom (*Z. f. Physik*, vol. 38, p. 411; vol. 39, p. 499 [1926]). Heisenberg discussed certain excited states of this two-electron atom in terms of structures in which one electron occupies an inner orbit, close to the helium nucleus, and the second electron occupies an outer orbit; and he showed that an actual stationary state can be represented by a wave function obtained by adding to or subtracting from the wave function for this structure another wave function, representing the structure in which the second electron occupies the inner orbit and the first electron the outer orbit. On the basis of analogy with the classical system of resonating coupled harmonic oscillators, he assigned the name quantum-mechanical resonance to this concept (*see* ATOM; QUANTUM MECHANICS; SPECTROSCOPY).

The special usefulness of the harmonic oscillator in the interpretation of quantum mechanics results from the fact that when this system is treated by the methods of classical mechanics and the old quantum theory, with the number ½ added to the integral values of the quantum number, many of the calculated properties of the system are the same as those given by quantum mechanics.

The simplest system illustrating resonance consists of two equivalent harmonic oscillators with a weak Hooke's law coupling between them. The potential energy for this system may be represented by the expression $2\pi^2 m v_o^2 x_1^2 + 2\pi^2 m v_o^2 x_2^2 + 4\pi^2 m \lambda x_1 x_2$, and the kinetic energy by $\frac{1}{2}mx_1^2 + \frac{1}{2}mx_2^2$, where m is the mass of each oscillator, x_1 and x_2 are the displacements of the oscillators from their positions of rest, v_o is the characteristic frequency of oscillation of each oscillator when there is no coupling ($\lambda = 0$), and λ is a parameter determining the strength of the coupling. The classical equations of motion for this system can be solved in terms of the normal co-ordinates

$$\xi = \frac{1}{\sqrt{2}}(x_1 + x_2) \text{ and } \eta = \frac{1}{\sqrt{2}}(x_1 - x_2).$$

Each of these normal co-ordinates varies harmonically with the time, t, the integrated equations of motion being $\xi = \xi_o \cos(2\pi\sqrt{v_o^2 + \lambda} \, t + \delta_\xi)$ and $\eta = \eta_o \cos(2\pi\sqrt{v_o^2 - \lambda} \, t + \delta_\eta)$ in which ξ_o, η_o, δ_ξ and δ_η are the constants of integration. It is seen that the characteristic frequencies for ξ and η, $\sqrt{v_o^2 + \lambda}$ and $\sqrt{v_o^2 - \lambda}$ respectively, differ from v_o. The co-ordinates x_1 and x_2 are then given by the equations

$$x_1 = \frac{\xi_o}{\sqrt{2}}\cos(2\pi\sqrt{v_o^2 + \lambda} \, t + \delta_\xi) + \frac{\eta_o}{\sqrt{2}}\cos(2\pi\sqrt{v_o^2 - \lambda} \, t + \delta_\eta)$$

and

$$x_2 = \frac{\xi_o}{\sqrt{2}}\cos(2\pi\sqrt{v_o^2 + \lambda} \, t + \delta_\xi) - \frac{\eta_o}{\sqrt{2}}\cos(2\pi\sqrt{v_o^2 - \lambda} \, t + \delta_\eta).$$

If η_o is zero, the two oscillators carry out, exactly together in phase, a simple harmonic motion with amplitude $\frac{\xi_o}{\sqrt{2}}$ and frequency $\sqrt{v_o^2 + \lambda}$; and if ξ_o is zero, they carry out, with phase difference π, a similar harmonic motion with amplitude $\frac{\eta_o}{\sqrt{2}}$ and frequency $\sqrt{v_o^2 - \lambda}$; but if neither η_o nor ξ_o vanishes, each of the oscillators vibrates in a complex way, the amplitude changing slowly from $\frac{\xi_o + \eta_o}{\sqrt{2}}$ to $\frac{|\xi_o - \eta_o|}{\sqrt{2}}$. This is the phenomenon described as classical resonance.

The rules of the old quantum theory with zero-point energy lead to the value $(n_\xi + \frac{1}{2}) h\sqrt{v_o^2 + \lambda} + (n_\eta + \frac{1}{2}) h\sqrt{v_o^2 - \lambda}$ for the energy of this system, and to the equations

$$\xi_o = \{(n_\xi + \tfrac{1}{2})h/2\pi^2 m\sqrt{v_o^2 + \lambda}\}^{\frac{1}{2}}$$
$$\text{and} \quad \eta_o = \{(n_\eta + \tfrac{1}{2})h/2\pi^2 m\sqrt{v_o^2 - \lambda}\}^{\frac{1}{2}}$$

for the amplitudes. Each of the quantum numbers n_ξ and n_η can assume the values 0, 1, 2, ... Since neither ξ_o nor η_o can vanish, even when the quantum number is zero, the oscillators show the phenomenon of classical resonance in every quantized state.

The stationary states of a harmonic oscillator in quantum mechanics are described by wave functions $\psi_o(x)$, $\psi_1(x)$, $\psi_2(x)$, ..., $\psi_n(x)$, ..., corresponding to the energy values $(n + \frac{1}{2})hv_o$, with integral values for the quantum number n. The wave functions $\psi_n(x)$ are the successive Hermite orthogonal functions. The system of two equivalent coupled harmonic oscillators (with the same frequency) can be treated rigorously by use of the co-ordinates ξ and η, and the correct wave functions for the system are $\psi_{n_\xi}(\xi)\psi_{n_\eta}(\eta)$, the energy values being the same as for the old quantum theory, as given above. In this discussion of the system there is no need to mention resonance. However, the system may also be treated by a perturbation method, based on the wave functions $\psi_{n'}(x_1)\psi_{n''}(x_2)$ for the unperturbed system, with no coupling between the oscillators. For the normal state of the system, with $n' = n'' = 0$, there is only one wave function. There are, however, two independent wave functions, $\psi_o(x_1)\psi_1(x_2)$ and $\psi_1(x_1)\psi_o(x_2)$, for the next energy level; these functions correspond to states in which one oscillator has small energy, $\frac{1}{2}hv_o$, and the other has larger energy, $3/2hv_o$. It is found on treating the system of coupled oscillators that these functions are not satisfactory approximations to the correct wave functions representing the two slightly different energy levels of the system, but that their normalized sum and difference, $\frac{1}{\sqrt{2}}[\psi_0(x_1)$

$\psi_1(x_2) + \psi_1(x_1)\psi_0(x_2)]$ and $\frac{1}{\sqrt{2}}[\psi_0(x_1)\psi_1(x_2) - \psi_1(x_1)\psi_0(x_2)]$, are satisfactory; the first wave function, symmetrical in the two coordinates x_1 and x_2, represents the more stable of the two states, and the second, antisymmetrical in x_1 and x_2 (changing sign when x_1 and x_2 are interchanged), represents the less stable state. Each of these states is a hybrid of the two structures represented by $\psi_0(x_1)\psi_1(x_2)$ and $\psi_1(x_1)\psi_0(x_2)$, and, from analogy with the classical system, it has become customary to describe these hybrid states as resonance hybrids. This description is applied also to other quantum-mechanical systems which are conveniently discussed by a similar perturbation method, even though there is no close classical analogue for them.

The arbitrary nature of quantum-mechanical resonance is evident from the foregoing paragraphs. The system of coupled harmonic oscillators can be treated rigorously without mentioning resonance. It is for convenience, resulting from knowledge of the unperturbed wave functions, that these functions are used in the perturbation treatment. Quantum-mechanical resonance is not a property of a system, but of a system in relation to structures which are assumed as the basis for its discussion. In chemistry the theory of resonance is used primarily as an aid in discussing the structure and properties of complex molecules in terms of simple molecules. Simple structures similar to those which have been assigned to simple molecules are assumed as the basis for the discussion of complex molecules; and often when no one of the simple structures is satisfactory, a resonance hybrid can be formulated which represents the complex molecule in a satisfying and useful way.

The arbitrariness mentioned above is not characteristic of the theory of resonance in chemistry, but is shared by it with other branches of structural theory. It is recognized now that the structures of molecules may be correctly described by the quantum-mechanical wave functions pertaining to their normal states, and that the structural formulas assigned by chemists are symbols for the wave functions. For nearly a century chemists have written the simple valence-bond formulas H — H for molecular hydrogen, Cl — Cl for molecular chlorine and H — Cl for hydrogen chloride. The dash in the formulas H — H and Cl — Cl is a symbol for wave functions describing the normal states of these diatomic molecules formed of identical atoms. The normal state of the hydrogen chloride molecule is, of course, correctly described by its wave function, and this wave function is not rigorously related to the wave functions of the hydrogen molecule and the chlorine molecule. Nevertheless, chemists have found it convenient to assign the structural formula H — Cl to the molecule with use of a dash like that used in the formulas H — H and Cl — Cl, and to describe the hydrogen chloride molecule, like the hydrogen molecule and the chlorine molecule, as involving a single valence bond. Thus the valence-bond structural theory, which has been of great value in the development of chemistry, is an arbitrary approximate representation of the wave functions that alone correctly represent the molecules. It is conceivable that a system of symbols much different from the valence-bond dashes could be developed that would correspond just as well to the wave functions, but in fact a satisfactory alternative system of this sort has not been discovered, and chemists continue to use the valence-bond theory.

The theory of resonance in chemistry has been subjected to criticism because of its arbitrariness. The critics may not have recognized that, as mentioned above, the same criticism applies to the whole of structural theory. A structural formula for a nonresonating molecule such as ethane is a rough description of the wave function in terms of wave functions involving first a hydrogen nucleus, a carbon nucleus and a pair of electrons, and second two carbon nuclei (each with its inner shell of K electrons) and a pair of electrons. In the same way the structural formula for the resonating molecule benzene is a rough description of the wave function of benzene as a sum of valence-bond wave functions similar to the one assigned to ethane; the two Kekulé structures and other structures that are hybridized in the resonance representation of the benzene molecule do not correspond separately to states of the benzene molecule, but are symbols that, taken together, provide a rough description of the wave function of the molecule in its normal state.

The theory of resonance is of value in chemistry in the discussion not only of the configuration of molecules, interatomic distances, electric dipole moments, force constants of bonds and similar molecular-structural properties, but also of thermodynamic stability (as of aromatic substances, conjugated systems, free radicals), strengths of acids and bases, existence of tautomers (see TAUTOMERISM), and chemical properties in general.

See L. Pauling, *The Nature of the Chemical Bond and the Structure of Molecules and Crystals,* 3rd ed. (1959); G. W. Wheland, *Resonance in Organic Chemistry* (1955). (L. C. P.)

RESONANCE ENERGIES, also resonance potentials, are general expressions denoting energy differences between the stationary states of atoms, molecules, and atomic nuclei. The term resonance was first applied because of the apparent analogy between acoustical or electrical resonance (*q.v.*) and the selective absorption or emission of certain light frequencies by these microscopic systems. Since the energy absorbed is proportional to the frequency, the microscopic system can only absorb or emit particular selected amounts of energy, which carry it from one stationary state of internal energy (or potential) to another; this holds whether the energy is the radiant energy in a particle of radiation or the kinetic energy of motion in a colliding particle of matter that hits the microscopic system (see ATOMIC AND MOLECULAR BEAMS; ELECTRON PARAMAGNETIC RESONANCE).

In structural chemistry, however, the "resonance energy" of a molecule has quite a different meaning. It refers to the deviation of the energy of formation of a molecule from a hypothetical ideal energy which is conceived as the sum of the energies of its parts. Here the term resonance is supposed to be drawn from a branch of quantum theory and is only distantly related to acoustical or mechanical resonance (see RESONANCE, THEORY OF). (J. R. PT.)

RESORCINOL (also called RESORCIN) is an organic chemical used in the manufacture of adhesive resins, plastics, dyes (*e.g.,* fluorescein, *q.v.*), photographic developers, explosives, cosmetics, and pharmaceuticals, and as an intermediate in the synthesis of many other organic compounds. It is used medicinally as a dehydrant, antiseptic, antiferment, and bactericide. Resorcinol was first obtained in 1864 by H. Hlasiwetz and L. Barth by the potash fusion of certain natural resins (galbanum, asafetida, etc.). Chemically it is meta-dihydroxybenzene, $C_6H_4(OH)_2$, crystallizes in colourless rhombic prisms or plates, which dissolve readily in water, alcohol, or ether, and sparingly in benzene. It melts at $110.7°$ C and boils at $281°$ C; its specific gravity is 1.2710. It has an unpleasant sweet taste, and its aqueous solution gives a deepviolet coloration with ferric chloride.

Resorcinol is manufactured in large quantities from benzene. The general procedure consists in sulfonating benzene with fuming sulfuric acid to benzenesulfonic acid and fusing the sodium salt of this acid with caustic soda.

Resorcinol-formaldehyde-type resins are used extensively as pre-dip before impregnating rayon and nylon with rubber. They are used in bonding when a cold set is necessary; *e.g.,* in bonding wooden members that are too thick to be heated.

BIBLIOGRAPHY.—*J. Industr. Engng. Chem.,* 12:857 (1920); A. Davidson, *Intermediates for Dyestuffs* (1926); *Plastics News Letter,* 5:1 (1945); *J. Amer. Chem. Soc.,* 43:348 (1921), 48:1688 (1926); *Chem. Week,* 68:43 (June 16, 1951), 70:53 (March 8, 1952); Arthur and Elizabeth Rose (eds.), *The Condensed Chemical Dictionary,* 6th ed. (1961). (C. B. Bl.)

RESPIGHI, OTTORINO (1879–1936), Italian composer, was born at Bologna on July 9, 1879, and studied at the Liceo of Bologna and later with Rimski-Korsakov in St. Petersburg and with Max Bruch in Berlin. From his foreign masters Respighi acquired a command of orchestral colour and an interest in orchestral composition. In 1913 he was appointed professor of composition at the Sta. Cecilia Academy in Rome. He was director there in 1924, but resigned in 1926, retaining a class in advanced composition. He had a talent for colourful descriptive music of a lyrical character illustrated in the series of suites, *Le Fontane di Roma* (1917), *I Pini di Roma* (1924), *Vetrate di chiesa* (1927), and *Trittico botticelliano* (1927), the last for chamber orchestra. He was also drawn to old Italian music, which he arranged with skill and taste in two sets of *Antiche danze e arie per liuto*. One of his most popular scores was his arrangement of pieces by Rossini, *La Boutique fantasque,* produced by Diaghilev's Russian Ballet in London (1919).

As a composer of opera Respighi had less success outside his own country. His best works for the theatre were *Belfagor,* a comic opera produced at Milan in 1923, and *La Fiamma* (Rome, 1934), which transfers the gloomy Norwegian tragedy of H. Wiers Jenssen (known to English-speaking audiences in John Masefield's version as *The Witch*) to Byzantine Ravenna with brilliant effect. In a different, more subdued vein are the "mystery," *Maria Egiziaca* (1932), and *Lucrezia* (completed by his wife E. Respighi, 1937), the latter showing Respighi's interest in the dramatic recitative of Claudio Monteverdi, of whose *Orfeo* he made a free transcription for La Scala, Milan, in 1935. Respighi died in Rome on April 18, 1936. His wife and pupil, Elsa Olivieri-Sangiacomo Respighi, born in Rome on March 24, 1894, was a singer and composer of operas, choral and symphonic works, and songs.

See E. O. Respighi, *Ottorino Respighi* (1954; Eng. trans. 1962); R. de Rensis, *Ottorino Respighi* (1935).   (Dy. H.)

RESPIRATION is the transfer of gases between living organisms and their environment. It goes hand in hand with metabolism (*q.v.*), a process akin to combustion, whereby foodstuffs are oxidized, just as fuel is, with the release of energy for the needs of the organism. The gaseous exchange for man is the same basically as that for a fire, oxygen being taken out of the environment and carbon dioxide released to it. Yet biological oxidations go on at temperatures hundreds of degrees lower than those of a fire, owing to the presence of enzymes (chemical catalysts) in the tissues.

This article explains the principles of respiration generally, describes various respiratory mechanisms in animals, and then considers in detail the physiology of respiration in man. For closely related information *see* RESPIRATORY SYSTEM, ANATOMY OF; RESPIRATORY SYSTEM, DISEASES OF; and references under "Respiration" in the Index. For the respiratory process in plants *see* PLANTS AND PLANT SCIENCE: *Plant Physiology: Respiration.*

Diffusion of Gases in Respiration.—Virtually every living animal, be it amoeba or whale, receives its oxygen and gets rid of the carbon dioxide produced by means of diffusion (*q.v.*). This process refers to the net movement of molecules, by virtue of their constant random activity, from regions of higher toward those of lower concentration. Transfer of substances by diffusion, however, is characteristically slow except over extremely short distances. This is illustrated by Fick's law of diffusion, which in simplified form is:

$$\frac{Q}{t} = \frac{DA(C_1 - C_2)}{h}$$

where $\frac{Q}{t}$ = quantity of substance diffusing per unit time; D is the diffusion coefficient, a constant depending on the nature of the substance diffusing, on the material it is in, and on the temperature; A = the area of the surface; $(C_1 - C_2)$ = the concentration difference across the material; and h = the thickness of the substance across which diffusion is occurring. Thus, the rate of diffusion is directly proportional to the surface area and to the concentration difference, and inversely proportional to the thickness.

Respiratory Adaptations in Evolution.—Sufficient gas exchange for an amoeba (diameter 0.5 mm., or $\frac{1}{50}$ in.) can be provided by diffusion across the surface membrane. With increasing size of spherical organisms, the mass of metabolizing tissue increases more rapidly than the surface area, a point being reached at a diameter of about 1 mm. ($\frac{1}{25}$ in.) when the diffusing area is not large enough to meet the need. As a result, there has evolved

in the majority of metazoa, or multicellular organisms, some kind of specialized respiratory system, and with it a circulatory system. These are well-suited to their function by virtue of the thin walls and large surface areas of the layers separating the circulating fluid (usually blood) from the external environment (water or air) on the one hand and from the active cells on the other.

Four chief means for respiration have appeared:

1. The first and simplest is by way of the surface membrane, mentioned above in the case of the protozoan amoeba. Diffusion across the surface layer also suffices in certain of the more primitive metazoa, both aquatic and terrestrial. Convection often aids diffusion by movement of sea water, as in sponges, and by the constant stirring of blood that occurs in animals with circulatory systems.

In some cases the skin shares the burden of respiration with specialized organs. Thus, in cold surroundings, eels and frogs can obtain most of their oxygen through the surface of the body but, when the temperature is higher, need their gills and lungs, respectively. In mammals, including man, however, the amount of oxygen received through the skin is negligible (usually less than 1%).

2. Gills represent a second chief means for respiration. Most gills are motile and are located, usually inside the body, in a moving current of water, the gas exchange being enhanced by the "countercurrent" principle, whereby the blood flows in a direction opposite to that of the water. (Purification of the blood would be much less complete were the two to go in the same direction.)

3. Third are lungs, usually aerial, though sometimes water-filled. One of the simplest forms is seen in the pulmonate land snails, in which the lung consists of a simple air sac, called a diffusion lung because there is no active ventilation.

Ventilatory lungs are those in which there is a bellows function, air being moved in and out by mechanical movements. There are positive pressure lungs, in which air is pushed into the lung while the nostrils are closed, as in frogs, contractions of abdominal muscles causing expiration. Negative pressure lungs are those in which air is pulled in by expansion of a bony thoracic cage, as in man and other mammals.

With increasing demands for energy the surface area available for diffusion becomes increased by subdivision of the lung into progressively smaller and smaller air sacs, called alveoli. Thus, the lung of an amphibian such as a frog contains a few hundred alveoli, whereas that of a man or a large animal contains hundreds of millions.

Greater efficiency per unit of diffusing surface exists in birds through improved ventilation. This is achieved by means of two unique anatomical features—a tubular diffusing system (in contrast to the dead-end alveoli of mammals) and a group of air sacs located beyond the lung. An idea of this arrangement is given in fig. 1. Airways called parabronchi lead off each main bronchus and continue through the lung into one of several pairs of air sacs, located in the neck, thorax, abdomen, and even inside the long bones. Each air sac is also connected to the bronchus by way of a mesobronchus. Diffusion of gases takes place in air capillaries, which, connecting adjacent parabronchi, are surrounded by a rich network of minute blood vessels.

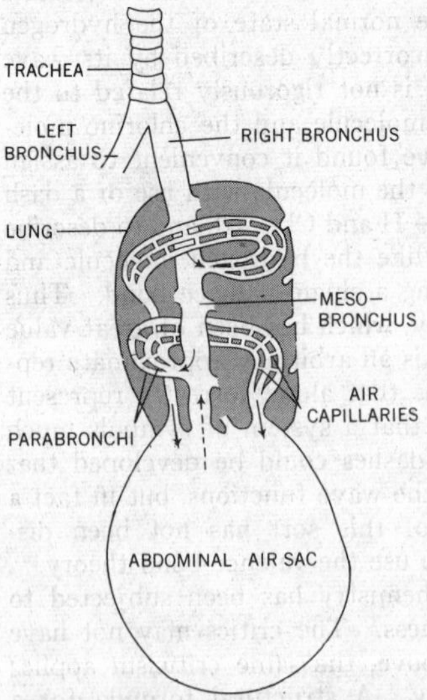

FIG. 1.—RESPIRATORY SYSTEM IN BIRDS SHOWING RIGHT LUNG AND ONE OF THE SEVERAL AIR SACS CONNECTED TO IT

Solid arrows indicate probable pathway of air flow during inspiration; dashed arrow, probable pathway during expiration

By means of rapid gas analyzers for oxygen and carbon dioxide, R. H. Shepard showed that in the chicken, inspired air passes almost solely through the parabronchial diffusing system and on into the air sacs. Air leaves the latter during expiration by way of the mesobronchus without passing back over the respiratory surfaces, as suggested by earlier investigators. The path is therefore mouth to lung to air sacs to mouth, a process requiring a valvelike action despite the absence of anatomical valves.

4. The fourth type of respiratory mechanism consists of the tracheae of insects—narrow, air-filled, branching tubes that open to the outside of the body by way of spiracles. A circulating fluid such as blood is of minor importance for breathing in these organisms, the air being piped directly to the tissues. Tracheal respiration has served the insects well, but because gases diffuse slowly along a narrow tube, it has been a factor in limiting their size. *See* INSECT: *Structure and Function: Respiration.*

VENTILATION OF THE LUNGS IN MAN

Distribution of Gas and Blood to the Lungs.—Incoming air is filtered by hairs in the nose, which remove larger dust particles, and is warmed and moistened as it passes down through the pharynx, becoming saturated with water vapour by the time it reaches the trachea (windpipe). The trachea branches into the right and left main stem bronchi, the branching continuing with the secondary bronchi, the bronchioles, and finally the respiratory bronchioles which lead into the primary lung lobule, the functional unit of the lung. The incoming air is thus distributed to the 300,-000,000 or so alveoli, where exchange of oxygen and carbon dioxide between air and blood takes place. Each alveolus, 0.1 to 0.3 mm. ($\frac{1}{250}$ to $\frac{3}{250}$ in.) in diameter, consists essentially of a bundle of capillary blood vessels suspended in air. Most of its surface is covered by these vessels, the total length of which is about 2,400 km. (1,500 mi.), spread out in order to provide 65 to 80 sq.m. (700 to 860 sq.ft.) of diffusing surface, only about 0.36 to 2.5 microns ($\frac{14}{1,000,000}$ to $\frac{1}{10,000}$ in.) in thickness in an adult man. The blood in each capillary is renewed each 0.9 second at rest and each 0.3 second or less during exercise. The total blood flow through the lung is about 5 l. ($5\frac{1}{4}$ qt.) per minute at rest and up to 20 to 27 l. (21 to $28\frac{1}{2}$ qt.) during severe exercise. About 4 l. ($4\frac{1}{4}$ qt.) of air reach the alveoli each minute during rest and as much as 100 l. (106 qt.) during exercise.

Diffusion of Oxygen and Carbon Dioxide Across the Lung.—In the closed swim bladders of physoclist fishes, a special gas gland in conjunction with a network of blood vessels is able to secrete oxygen at concentrations up to 87% and at several atmospheres' pressure. Partly because of this fact, C. Bohr and later John Scott Haldane postulated that oxygen was secreted by the lungs of human beings under certain conditions. Repeated experiments, however, have indicated that the oxygen concentration is always higher in the air of the lung than in the blood (the reverse being true for the outgoing carbon dioxide), a fact consistent with diffusion and not with secretion.

The concentration of a gas at a given temperature is expressed in terms of partial pressure, in millimetres of mercury (as indicated under *Dalton's Law of Partial Pressures and Its Application to Respiration*, below). During rest, the partial pressure of oxygen in the air of the lung is about 8 to 10 mm. higher than the average partial pressure of the blood in the capillaries of the lung. This diffusion gradient increases as the oxygen consumption goes up, reaching as high as 50 mm. during severe exercise. Even with so large a mean gradient, however, the partial pressure of oxygen in the blood leaving the lung is normally only a few millimetres less than that of the air in the lung. This is because the average partial pressure of oxygen in the pulmonary capillary lies somewhere between that of venous and arterial blood.

It is customary to speak of the diffusing capacity ($\mathrm{D_{L_{O_2}}}$) of the lung as a whole, defined as the number of millilitres of O_2 diffusing each minute, as a result of a 1-mm. diffusion gradient for O_2. At rest, $\mathrm{D_{L_{O_2}}}$ = approximately 25 (*i.e.*, 250 ml. of O_2 diffuse across the lung per minute when the diffusion gradient equals 10 mm.). During exercise, the $\mathrm{D_{L_{O_2}}}$ may rise to as high as 80, due presumably to enlargement of existing lung capillaries and the opening up of new ones. The $\mathrm{D_{L_{CO_2}}}$ is about 20 times as great as the $\mathrm{D_{L_{O_2}}}$ because CO_2 is more soluble in tissues and

blood than O_2 and therefore diffuses more readily.

Mechanics of Respiration.—Air is moved in and out of the lungs as the result of changes in the volume of the thoracic cavity, the lungs playing an entirely passive role and neither expanding nor contracting by themselves. Thus, the energy required for

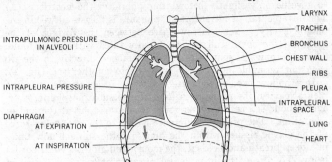

FIG. 2.—DIAGRAM OF CHEST SHOWING HOW LUNG EXPANDS AND AIR IS TAKEN IN BY DESCENT OF DIAPHRAGM

Distance of descent of the diaphragm, here exaggerated for illustrative purposes, is about 1.25 cm. (½ in.). Inspiration is aided by expansion (not shown) of chest wall. Intrapleural pressure and intrapulmonic pressure in alveoli are explained in text

breathing comes from muscles located entirely outside the lungs. These are (1) the powerful muscle known as the diaphragm, on the bottom of the cavity, and (2) numerous muscles of the thoracic and abdominal walls. The lungs are elastic sacs constantly tending to collapse. Suspended within the barrellike thoracic cage, they are prevented from doing so by the arched structure of the ribs at the sides and by the contractions of the diaphragm below.

Approximately 500 ml. (about a pint) of air is taken in with each breath as a result of two mechanical events:

1. Impulses descending the phrenic nerve, which goes solely to the diaphragm, cause the latter to contract and move downward. Since the descent averages 1.25 cm. (½ in.) and the surface area equals 250 sq.cm., about 300 ml. of air (60% of the total) is taken in by this means.

2. Contractions of several sets of muscles that originate at the spine and run forward and downward to the ribs elevate the latter during inspiration, causing an increase in the internal volume of the chest. About 200 ml. of air is taken in by this means. The expansion is due to the arrangement of the ribs, which are semicircular strips of bone, hinged posteriorly at the spine, the plane formed by their circumference inclined downward and outward. Each rib may be compared to the handle of a pail. Raising the handle increases its horizontal distance from the pail. Similarly, raising the ribs increases the antero-posterior diameter of the chest. Because the ribs are hinged obliquely to the spine, the lateral dimension of the chest is also increased, the enlargement being accommodated by the flexible rib cartilages which connect the forward ends of the ribs to the sternum (breastbone).

At the end of inspiration, with normal, quiet breathing (eupnea), the nervous activity originating in the respiratory centres of the brain ceases, and the chest collapses as a result of the elastic recoil of the lungs. However, during hyperpnea—the rapid, deep breathing seen in exercise or disease—expiration becomes active, involving various thoracic muscles, which pull the ribs down, and abdominal muscles, which push the diaphragm upward to facilitate the expulsion of air.

The mechanical factors involved in respiration have been evaluated by measuring the hydrostatic pressures in certain parts of the respiratory system, together with the volume of air breathed in or out and the rate of air flow. As a result, quantitative information is available regarding the elastic properties of the lungs, the resistance to air flow within the airways, and the mechanical work of breathing.

The significant hydrostatic pressures are: (1) Atmospheric (barometric) pressure, the reference level to which other pressures are compared, including that of the surrounding air. (2) Intrapulmonic pressure, defined as the pressure inside one of the airways of the respiratory tree. The location must be specified, because as a consequence of the resistance offered by the air passages to the flow of air there is a gradient of pressure in the direction of flow, just as in a river the level falls on approaching the sea. During inspiration, therefore, the pressure is lowest of all in the alveoli, and rises progressively at points farther upstream to a value only slightly below atmospheric in the nostrils. (3) The intrapleural, or intrathoracic, pressure is measured within the pleural cavity, a very narrow space between the surface of the lung and the chest wall; it is normally filled with lymph fluid. Thus, the lungs of mammals are not attached directly to the rib cage but resemble a sac suspended within another sac (fig. 2).

If a hollow needle is inserted between adjacent ribs into the pleural cavity, the pressure is found to be subatmospheric, averaging about −3 cm. of water (see next paragraph) at the end of expiration. The pressure difference is due to the collapsing force of the elastic tissues within the lung. If the subject now takes in a deep breath and holds it, the mouth and glottis (vocal cords) being kept open, the intrapleural pressure falls to −20 cm. of water or even lower, due to the further stretching of the pulmonary elastic tissues.

The relation of the volume of air inhaled to the change in intrapleural pressure is called the "compliance" or ease of expansion of the lung, and is expressed as litres of change in lung volume per change in pressure in centimetres of water. Values for normal subjects average 0.225 l./cm. (i.e., after inhalation of 0.225 l. of air the intrapleural pressure falls 1 cm. H_2O). The compliance decreases in illnesses in which fibrous tissue forms within the lung.

When a given volume of air is flowing, the resulting pressure

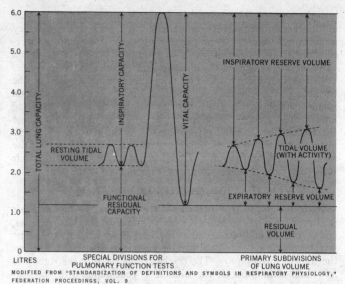

FIG. 4.—LUNG VOLUMES AS THEY APPEAR ON THE TRACING OF A SPIROMETER (VOLUME MEASURING DEVICE)

The vital capacity is the volume of a largest single breath; the tidal volume that of a normal breath. Inspiratory capacity is the volume that can be inhaled at the end of normal expiration; expiratory reserve, the volume exhaled at the end of normal expiration; and residual volume, the air remaining even after a forced expiration. The latter volume cannot be measured by a spirometer, but by an indirect method involving collection of an inert gas such as nitrogen

drop is proportional chiefly to the airway resistance, R (= pressure/flow, as in Ohm's Law for electricity), and slightly to the resistance of the tissue to deformation (viscosity). Expressed in centimetres of water per litre per second, R averages 2 cm./l./sec. for normal subjects. (This means that if air is being exhaled at the rate of one litre per second, the pressure in the alveoli will be 2 cm. H_2O higher than atmospheric.)

The dynamic events occurring during one respiratory cycle are shown in fig. 3. The highest air flow during inspiration and expiration = 0.5 l./sec. in this example. As predicted by the equation relating pressure to flow (assuming R = 2 cm./l./sec., as above), intra-alveolar pressure reaches peak values of ±1 cm. of water.

The changes in intra-alveolar pressure due to resistance to the flow of air are transmitted through the lung and hence influence intrapleural pressure in the same direction. Thus, the curve for intrapleural pressure is made up of two components, elastic and resistive.

During heavy breathing accompanying exercise, the rapid flow of air causes greater swings in intra-alveolar and intrapleural pressures. The mechanical work required to inflate and deflate the lung, equal to change in intrapleural pressure times volume of air breathed, is therefore increased. It is also increased, even to the point of exhaustion, in patients with asthma, due to the wide swings in pressure needed to overcome the increased resistance to air flow which accompanies this condition.

Lung Volumes.—The lung of a man who weighs 80 kg. (175 lb.) holds about 6 l. ($6\frac{1}{3}$ qt.) of gas; this is called the total lung capacity. This is subdivided into components as indicated in fig. 4. Measurement of vital capacity and of the other lung volumes is an important diagnostic procedure in pulmonary disease.

Dalton's Law of Partial Pressures and Its Application to Respiration.—Certain physical properties of gases in general must be considered in relation to gas exchange in the body. Whether a gas such as oxygen will combine with the hemoglobin of the blood and will diffuse from air to blood and thence to the tissues depends on the molecular concentration of the oxygen.

Chemical analysis of atmospheric air has shown that it contains the following percentages of gases, expressed as volumes of dry gas per 100 volumes of dry air: O_2, 20.95%; CO_2, 0.03%; N_2, 78.08%; argon, 0.93%; and traces of each of seven other gases. These percentages are virtually constant, not only all over the surface of the earth but up to altitudes of approximately 40,000 m. (25 mi.).

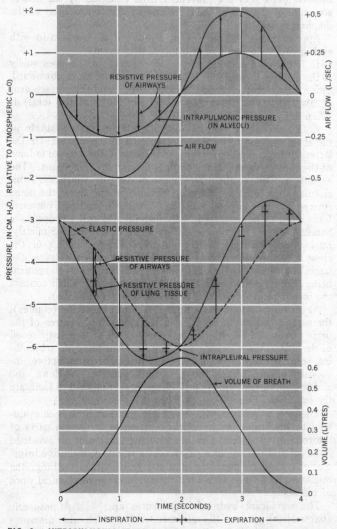

FIG. 3.—INTRAPULMONIC PRESSURE IN ALVEOLI, INTRAPLEURAL PRESSURE AND VOLUME OF AIR BREATHED, PLOTTED DURING ONE RESPIRATORY CYCLE. NUMERICAL VALUES SHOWN ARE FOR A NORMAL SUBJECT

Yet the percentage composition of a gas does not alone determine its molecular concentration. This is illustrated by the fact that a man breathing air suffers from oxygen lack at an altitude of 5,500 m. (18,000 ft.), and without an extra source of oxygen will die if he goes higher than about 7,500 m. (25,000 ft.). (*See also* Hypoxia.) The percentage of oxygen is still 20.95, but its molecular concentration is much lower than at sea level. This is because there is less atmosphere pressing down from above, hence the barometric pressure is less, and the molecules of oxygen and other gases are spread farther apart.

John Dalton (1766–1844) explained this behaviour of gases by an expression which now bears his name. According to Dalton's Law of Partial Pressures, in a mixture of gases each gas behaves as if it alone occupied the total volume of the gas mixture, and exerts a pressure, its partial pressure, independent of the other gases present. The sum of the partial pressures of the individual gases equals the total pressure of the gas mixture. At a given temperature, the partial pressure provides a measure of the molecular concentration of a gas. The partial pressure, P, of a gas, G, may be calculated by Dalton's Law as follows:

$$P_G = \frac{(\% \text{ concentration of G in dry gas})}{100} \text{ (total pressure of dry gases)}$$

If air at sea level were dried, then the partial pressures of its constituent gases would be:

$$\begin{aligned}
P_{O_2} &= 20.95/100 \times 760 = 159.2 \text{ mm. of mercury (Hg)} \\
P_{CO_2} &= 0.03/100 \times 760 = 0.2 \text{ mm. Hg} \\
P_{N_2} &= 78.08/100 \times 760 = 593.4 \text{ mm. Hg} \\
P \text{ other gases} &= 0.94/100 \times 760 = \underline{7.2 \text{ mm. Hg}}
\end{aligned}$$

Total of partial pressures = 760.0 mm. Hg = barometric pressure

However, air normally contains some water vapour, which exerts a partial pressure of its own. The air in all parts of the lungs is saturated with water vapour, the tension of which is related to the temperature, being equal to 47 mm. at 37° C (= 98.6° F, body temperature). This vapour tension must be subtracted from the barometric pressure in order to get the total pressure of the dry gases in the lung. One may then calculate the partial pressures of any dry gas, G, in the lung from Dalton's Law (percent concentration of each constituent gas being expressed always in terms of volumes of dry gas per 100 volumes of the dry gas mixture) as follows:

$$P_G = \frac{(\% \text{ concentration of G})}{100} \text{ (Bar. P. } -47)$$

The French physiologist Paul Bert pointed out in 1878 that it was the partial pressure and not the percent composition that determines the physiological effects of a gas. Dalton's Law, he indicated, explains why it is difficult to breathe at high altitudes. The barometric pressure falls, and with it the partial pressures of all the gases. Only that of oxygen affects respiration, the P_{CO_2} in atmospheric air being negligibly low and the nitrogen gas inert. At 5,500 m. (18,000 ft.) the P_{O_2} in moist air entering the lung has fallen to only 69 mm., which is not enough to oxygenate the blood adequately. Even breathing pure oxygen, the P_{O_2} has again fallen to 69 mm. at an altitude of 13,400 m. (44,000 ft.), which is close to the "ceiling" above which a man cannot go without a pressurized cabin or flying suit.

The data in the table illustrate what happens to atmospheric air as it is breathed into the lungs. In the moistened air of the trachea the P_{O_2} is (20.95/100) (760−47) = 150 mm. However, less than this tension of O_2 is available for diffusion into the blood

because the incoming air is diluted by the CO_2 leaving the alveoli, while at the same time the O_2 diffuses out of the air, further reducing the O_2 tension. Thus, there is exchanged (in almost equal quantities) O_2 for CO_2, as the incoming gas moves on down into the depths of the lung, into the alveolar ducts, the atria which open into the alveoli, and finally the alveoli themselves. The air here is called alveolar gas and is defined as gas which, in contact with the respiratory epithelium, is essentially in equilibrium with the blood leaving the lung. That is, the P_{O_2} in the gas is almost the same as in the purified blood, and similarly for the P_{CO_2}.

Thanks to the researches of Haldane, it is easy to sample alveolar gas in a normal person. The subject has only to breathe out forcefully through a long rubber tube, then the last portion of the gas exhaled is withdrawn and the percentage of carbon dioxide and oxygen present can be determined by analysis. From these data the corresponding partial pressures may be calculated by means of Dalton's Law.

As indicated in the table, the P_{O_2} of alveolar gas = 100 mm., P_{CO_2} = 40 mm. These values are remarkably constant at rest at sea level and deviate only slightly during exercise. This, as will be shown below, results from the fact that the respiratory centres in the brain seem to be set to a P_{CO_2} close to 40 mm.

Respiratory Dead Space and Alveolar Ventilation.—As indicated in the table, expired gas has a higher P_{O_2} and lower P_{CO_2} than alveolar gas, because it consists of alveolar gas mixed with atmospheric air from the respiratory dead space. This term refers to that inspired air which does not come in contact with the alveolar membranes but simply fills the air passages, including the nose, pharynx, trachea, bronchi, and bronchioles. At the beginning of expiration this atmospheric air is simply breathed out again, having taken no part in respiratory exchange. The dead space can be measured anatomically in a cadaver by filling the air passages with water, which presumably goes down to but does not enter the alveoli. The volume of the water is measured and equals, on the average, 150 ml. In living subjects, the anatomical dead space may be determined by measuring the volume of gas exhaled before the tension of carbon dioxide rises sharply. Indicating the boundary between dead space and alveolar gas, this rise is detected by a rapid-acting gas analyzer which operates on the physical principle that carbon dioxide absorbs infrared light.

The physiological dead space is more closely related to the efficiency of ventilation because it includes not only the gas in the anatomical dead space but also that ventilating alveoli with relatively poor or no blood flow. It may be calculated from the partial pressure of carbon dioxide, as determined by chemical analysis in (1) arterial blood, (2) expired gas, and (3) inspired gas (P_{CO_2} is essentially zero when breathing air), and from the tidal volume (V_T), using the following equation introduced by the Danish physiologist Christian Bohr:

$$V_D = \frac{V_T (P_{CO_2}, \text{ arterial blood} - P_{CO_2}, \text{ expired gas})}{(P_{CO_2}, \text{ arterial blood} - P_{CO_2}, \text{ inspired gas})}$$

For example, P_{CO_2} in arterial blood was 40 mm., in expired gas 28, and in inspired gas 0, and tidal volume was 600 ml. Then:

$$V_D = \frac{600 (40 - 28)}{(40 - 0)} = 180 \text{ ml.} = \text{the physiological dead space}$$

The volume of gas effectively ventilating the alveoli with each breath is equal to the difference between the tidal volume and the physiological dead space, and when multiplied by the number of breaths per minute (f) gives the alveolar ventilation, $\dot{V}_A$, expressed in litres per minute. Or, in arithmetic form, $\dot{V}_A = (V_T - V_D)$ f. It is $\dot{V}_A$, rather than the total volume of gas exhaled per minute ($\dot{V}_E$), that determines how well the air in the lungs is being renewed. With rapid, shallow breathing, $\dot{V}_E$ must be larger in order to provide a given alveolar ventilation than with slow, deep breathing. This point is illustrated if we resort to a *reductio ad absurdum*, decreasing the tidal volume to that of the dead space. Then $(V_T - V_D) = 0$, and regardless of how rapid the breathing is, alveolar ventilation is zero. Of course this situation is not compatible with life; no oxygen could reach the lung or carbon dioxide

---

Pressures of Gases in the Respiratory Tree and in the Tissues, expressed in mm. Hg.

Sample of gas	P_{O_2}	P_{CO_2}	P_{N_2}*	P_{H_2O}	Total P
Inspired	158	0.3	596	5.7	760
Tracheal	150	0.3	562.7	47	760
Expired	116	32	565	47	760
Alveolar	100	40	573	47	760
Arterial blood	95	40	573	47	755
Venous blood	40	46	573	47	706
Tissues	30	50	573	47	700

*Includes argon and the trace gases.
Modified from J. F. Fulton (ed.), *A Textbook of Physiology*, 17th ed., p. 827 (1955).

leave until the tidal volume was again increased. In the rapid, shallow panting of dogs, V_T is only slightly greater than V_D, the panting serving to move large volumes of air over the tongue to facilitate cooling by evaporation, without V_A being increased to the point where the lungs are overventilated and the blood carbon dioxide tension lowered below normal.

CARRIAGE OF OXYGEN AND CARBON DIOXIDE BY THE BLOOD

An average man at rest uses 250 ml. (more than $\frac{1}{2}$ pt.) of pure oxygen per minute and gets rid of almost as much carbon dioxide, the chief by-product of the combustion of foodstuffs. These two gases are transported in the blood largely because of the activity of hemoglobin (symbol Hb) one of the most remarkable chemical substances produced during the course of evolution. Located inside the red blood cells, hemoglobin combines reversibly with oxygen as indicated by the reaction: $Hb + O_2 \rightleftarrows HbO_2$. Over 96% of the oxygen is carried in this form, the rest being dissolved in the blood.

A much smaller fraction (about 25%) of the carbon dioxide produced is carried in direct combination, as so-called carbamino hemoglobin; most of the CO_2 is transported as the result of a series of chemical reactions dependent on the special properties of hemoglobin.

Oxygen Dissociation Curve.—As the arterial blood passes through the tissues, each 100 ml. gives up about 5 ml. of O_2; as it does so the P_{O_2} falls from 100 mm. to near 40, that of venous blood. This unloading of large quantities of oxygen as a result of a relatively small fall in P_{O_2} is one of the unique properties of hemoglobin. Without it, the oxygen could theoretically be carried in dissolved form, much as carbon dioxide is dissolved in soda water. But only 0.2 ml. of O_2 would be given up under conditions comparable with those outlined above, and 25 times more blood would have to be pumped through the body, requiring an impossibly large circulatory system.

The quantity of oxygen combining with hemoglobin at various tensions of O_2 is given by an oxygen dissociation curve (fig. 5). Each point on the curve is obtained by exposing a sample of blood to a gas containing oxygen in a glass vessel. The vessel is rotated at body temperature long enough to equalize the oxygen tensions in blood and gas. The volume of oxygen in the blood sample and the P_{O_2} of the gas are then determined by chemical analysis. For example, the hemoglobin in 100 ml. of blood was found to hold 14.8 ml. O_2 at a P_{O_2} of 40 mm. Another portion of the same blood was exposed to a gas with a P_{O_2} high enough (150 mm.) to oxygenate essentially all of the hemoglobin. The latter sample held 20 ml. O_2 per 100 ml. The oxygen saturation of the first sample was therefore 74% ($14.8/20 \times 100$). Thus, 74% of the hemoglobin molecules were combined with oxygen, the remaining 26% being reduced; i.e., without oxygen. (The term oxygen saturation refers only to the oxygen combined with hemoglobin and not to dissolved oxygen.)

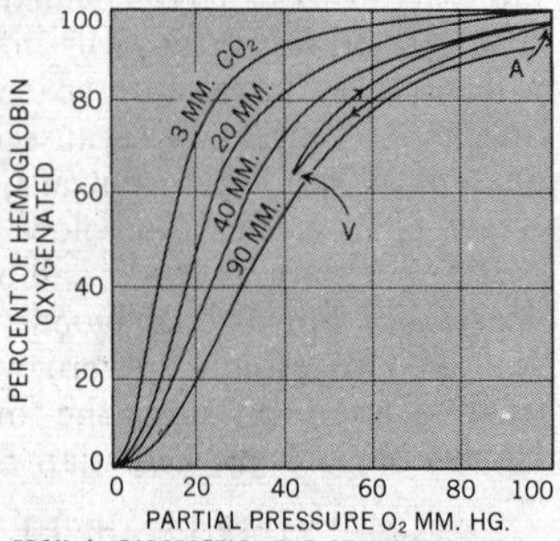

Because of the unique properties of hemoglobin, the carriage of oxygen is related to that of carbon dioxide and vice versa. Each process helps the other. This is illustrated by the fact that the position of the oxygen dissociation curve is shifted to the right by an increase in the tension of carbon dioxide (fig. 5). That is, adding CO_2 to the blood tends to drive oxygen out. This is known as the Bohr effect. It helps to deliver oxygen to the tissues. For a given fall in P_{O_2} more O_2 is released than if a dissociation curve at constant P_{CO_2} were followed. Conversely, as CO_2 is given off

FIG. 5.—OXYGEN DISSOCIATION CURVES FOR WHOLE BLOOD

FROM J. BARCROFT'S "THE RESPIRATORY FUNCTION OF THE BLOOD" (1928); REPRODUCED BY PERMISSION OF THE CAMBRIDGE UNIVERSITY PRESS

Increase in P_{CO_2} shifts curve to right, an illustration of the Bohr effect. Loop labeled A (arterial) and V (venous) shows approximate actual curve followed in the body

in the lungs, the uptake of O_2 is facilitated.

CO_2 Dissociation Curve and Carriage of CO_2.—There is a converse of the Bohr effect: adding oxygen to blood drives carbon dioxide out. This, known as the Haldane effect, may be demonstrated by means of carbon dioxide dissociation curves, determined first for oxygenated and then for reduced blood. It will be noted (fig. 6) that the latter holds considerably more CO_2 at a

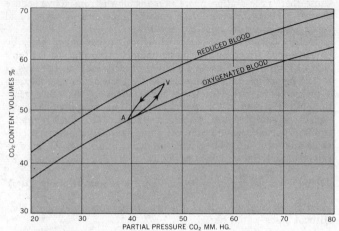

FROM J. P. PETERS AND D. D. VAN SLYKE, "QUANTITATIVE CLINICAL CHEMISTRY," VOL. 1, WILLIAMS & WILKINS CO., BALTIMORE, 1931

FIG. 6.—CARBON DIOXIDE DISSOCIATION CURVES FOR REDUCED AND OXYGENATED BLOOD

given P_{CO_2} than the former. Carriage of carbon dioxide is facilitated by the Haldane effect in much the same manner as the carriage of oxygen is facilitated by the Bohr effect. As the arterial blood gives up part of its oxygen to the tissues it is able to take up more carbon dioxide for a given increase in P_{CO_2} than if it remained fully oxygenated. This is shown in fig. 6 by the loop labeled "A" (arterial) "V" (venous), which describes the pathway followed by the blood as it goes from artery to vein.

Though the CO_2 dissociation curve makes it possible to predict the volume of CO_2 contained in blood at a given P_{CO_2}, it does not describe how carbon dioxide is carried in the blood. Actually it is carried in several ways, as follows:

1. About 10% is carried in dissolved form (as carbon dioxide is in soda water).

2. About 25% is in direct combination with hemoglobin as carbamino hemoglobin.

3. About 10% is carried as carbonic acid (H_2CO_3). This splits into hydrogen ions (H^+) and bicarbonate ions (HCO_3^-). The latter, nontoxic ions, are carried inside the red blood cell and in the plasma (the clear portion of the blood). Hydrogen ions, however, which in their active state would cause damage to tissue cells, are buffered; i.e., the ions are "soaked up" by the blood proteins including hemoglobin. A buffer solution (see HYDROGEN IONS: *Buffer Action*) resists change in acidity by combining with added hydrogen ions and essentially inactivating them. Because not all of the added acid can be removed from the solution, the acidity does rise slightly, but only a fraction of what it would were the buffer not present.

4. The remaining 55% or so of the carbon dioxide is also carried as carbonic acid, except that the hydrogen ions are buffered in a special way by the hemoglobin as the latter gives up its oxygen. This process is related to the Haldane effect, and depends on the fact that when hemoglobin gives up its oxygen it becomes less acid, and can therefore take up most of the hydrogen ions produced in the tissues without any change in acidity at all. This is known as the isohydric exchange.

Were carbon dioxide carried entirely in solution, no hemoglobin being present, the hydrogen ions produced from carbon dioxide would make the venous blood 800 times more acid than the arterial, the pH (hydrogen ion concentration, a measure of acidity) changing from 7.4 to 4.5. In actual fact the pH falls only 0.03 units, thanks to the two buffering mechanisms described.

The series of chemical reactions involved in the transport of oxygen and carbon dioxide by the blood is shown in fig. 7. Because of the participation of chloride ions in this process, it is often referred to as the chloride shift.

The sequence of events is as follows: In the tissues, foodstuffs such as carbohydrates are oxidized, the by-products of this energy-producing reaction being carbon dioxide and water. The carbon dioxide produced immediately dissolves in the water of the blood, and 10% of it will be carried in that form to the lungs. Now, dissolved carbon dioxide reacts with water to form carbonic acid: $CO_2 + H_2O \rightleftarrows H_2CO_3$. This hydration of carbon dioxide takes place very slowly in water or in plasma. For this reason most of the carbon dioxide, in the form of molecular carbon dioxide, diffuses through the plasma and into the red blood cells. In the latter there is a high concentration of the enzyme carbonic anhydrase, which catalyzes (i.e., speeds up) the hydration of carbon dioxide to carbonic acid inside the red cells. The carbonic acid ionizes slightly; that is, it splits into positively and negatively charged particles as follows: $H_2CO_3 \rightleftarrows H^+ + HCO_3^-$. The hydrogen ions are immediately taken up by the hemoglobin by the buffering mechanisms described.

A portion of the dissolved carbon dioxide combines directly with hemoglobin to form carbamino hemoglobin. In the process, a hydrogen ion must be buffered by the hemoglobin.

More and more bicarbonate ions accumulate inside the red blood cell and are carried to the lung. A somewhat greater portion is carried as bicarbonate in the plasma, having diffused out of the red cell as a result of increasing concentration.

The plasma now contains excessive negative charges in the form of bicarbonate ions. Unless there is an equal number of positive and negative charges in any solution, enormous electrostatic forces will be built up. Compensation for such inequality always occurs. In this case a number of negatively charged chloride ions, equal

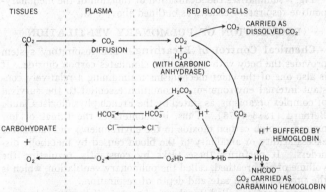

FIG. 7.—SEQUENCE OF CHEMICAL EVENTS BY WHICH CO_2 IS CARRIED BY THE BLOOD FROM TISSUES TO LUNGS. THE REVERSE PROCESSES OCCUR IN THE LUNGS AS THE BLOOD GIVES OFF CO_2 AND TAKES UP O_2

to that of the bicarbonate ions entering the plasma, are drawn by electrostatic forces into the red blood cell.

These events take place in the blood passing through the tissues. The reverse processes occur in the lungs as the blood gives off carbon dioxide and takes up oxygen.

RESPIRATORY CENTRES AND NERVOUS ORIGIN OF RESPIRATION

Since the early part of the 19th century it has been known that a small region in the medulla oblongata (the basal part of the brain) is essential to breathing and hence to life. Occupying in a man a volume no larger than that of a good-sized grape, the respiratory centres consist of motor nerve cells imbedded in a crisscrossing matrix of nerve fibres. This reticular formation, as it is called, serves to coordinate the activity of the widely spaced respiratory muscles.

Three basic experimental approaches have been used in order to analyze in anesthetized animals the respiratory function of various parts of the medulla oblongata and also of the region forward of it called the pons. These are: (1) effects of removal or local-

ized destruction of discrete areas; (2) effects of stimulation by electric shocks or injected chemical solutions; and (3) recording of action potentials, the tiny electrical impulses set up by all active nerve cells. In spite of extensive studies, in the mid-1960s it still was not entirely clear (a) how the impulses from the respiratory neurons originate, or (b) why these bursts of impulses are rhythmically interrupted every few seconds at a rate corresponding to that of breathing.

With regard to (a) it is not surprising that reflex activity has been considered. When, for example, a person steps on a nail, nerve impulses ascend to the spinal cord and stimulate motor nerve cells there so that the foot is reflexly (i.e., automatically) withdrawn. As early as 1832 the English physiologist Marshall Hall stated that the medullary respiratory centres were not spontaneously active but were merely stimulated reflexly by various sensory nerves. As evidence, he cited the familiar observations that dashing cold water in the face, bathing in the cold sea, or pinching certain nerves during an experiment on an animal all cause "an act of inspiration to be excited."

The modification of respiration by these strong stimuli is far different from the regular breathing of rest or sleep, which originates in complex nerve networks in the medulla and adjacent pons. Yet controversy still exists as to whether this rhythm persists after all incoming impulses have been cut off from the brain above, from structures sensitive to the chemical composition of the blood, and from the spinal cord below.

There is undisputed evidence that mammalian cardiac muscle cells, in particular those located in the cardiac "pacemaker," became spontaneously depolarized, thus generating, without the need for nervous activity, the periodic beat of the heart. Nerve cells in regions such as the cerebral cortex presumably can be stimulated by fluctuating potentials produced by firing of neighbouring neurons. R. Gesell suggested that truly spontaneous activity of respiratory neurons might exist, as the result of a steady current flowing in the external medium from the base of the axon (the nerve fibre) back to the cell body in sufficient strength to depolarize and thus stimulate the nerve cell respectively. (See also NERVE CONDUCTION.)

Such a mechanism has not yet been demonstrated experimentally. Even if it had been, the steady firing of respiratory motor neurons needs to be modulated so that expiration follows inspiration in a regular sequence in order to produce rhythmic respiration. Two divergent theories have been proposed and extensively evaluated. The first assumes that the medullary respiratory centres are not by themselves inherently rhythmic, but produce only a steady stream of impulses. These are said to be periodically inhibited or turned off by influences outside the medulla, much as in a steam engine the flow of steam to the moving piston is turned on and off by the valve. According to the second theory the neurons of the respiratory centres have the inherent capacity to fire in regularly repeated bursts, apart from outside influences. Such a process resembles the ticking of a watch, with the balance wheel, driven by the escapement, turning to and fro at its own natural rhythm by a "pacemaker" action.

Evidence for the first theory goes back to 1868, when the Viennese physiologists Ewald Hering and Josef Breuer discovered that inflation of the lungs with a bellows caused inspiratory activity to be inhibited, the resulting apnea, or lack of breathing, lasting for a considerable period. They found that this effect was abolished when the tenth cranial nerves (the vagi) were cut. It has since been shown that receptors in the lung are stimulated by inflation, sending impulses up the vagi which cause the inhibition. The Hering-Breuer reflexes could, as their discoverers pointed out, permit a tonic (steady) inspiratory drive to be converted into a rhythmic process. Supporting evidence was obtained in 1887 by M. Marckwald, who discovered that, if the pons is transected in its midregion, breathing remains normal as long as the vagi are intact. If they are then cut, the experimental animal takes a deep breath and holds it until he dies. But if the brain stem is initially severed higher up, leaving the entire pons intact, the animal continues to breathe even after the vagi are cut, though more slowly and deeply than before. Thus, Marckwald had obtained evidence for a second inhibitory mechanism, in addition to the vagal one, located in the rostral (forward) part of the pons. Though either mechanism could convert the tonic inspiratory drive into a rhythmic process, it was the vagal one that was considered to be involved in normal breathing.

Much evidence in support of this periodic inhibition theory has subsequently been gathered. T. Lumsden in 1923 located and named: (1) the pneumotaxic centre, located in the rostral pons, responsible for inhibiting the steady activity of (2) the apneustic centre, in the caudal (rearward) pons, responsible for sustained inspiration, which Lumsden called apneusis.

As a result of a comprehensive series of studies on the medullary-pontine respiratory complex, R. F. Pitts in the 1930s and '40s located by electrical stimulation a centre responsible for inspiratory activity in the reticular formation of the medulla, and a separate expiratory centre situated close to it. He obtained evidence that the inspiratory centre was dominant to the expiratory centre, the two being interconnected by nerve fibres so that stimulation of one caused inhibition of the other, an example of reciprocal innervation as in the spinal cord.

Confirming the existence of apneusis after midpontine section and vagotomy, Pitts like Marckwald concluded that the medullary respiratory centres were not inherently rhythmic, sustained activity of the inspiratory centre being converted to periodic breathing by the vagal stretch reflexes from the lungs and, following vagotomy, by the pneumotaxic centre. This concept of the genesis of rhythmic respiration became widely accepted during the next ten years, tending almost entirely to replace the "pacemaker" theory. In the late 1940s and early '50s, however, H. E. Hoff and C. G. Breckenridge produced evidence in favour of the latter theory. They pointed out, as had some of their predecessors, that apneusis was neither permanent nor total after midpontine section and vagotomy. Superimposed on the deep, prolonged inspirations were small, rhythmic respiratory movements capable of keeping the experimental animal alive for an hour or more. More important, when they sectioned the brain stem below the pons in order to isolate the medulla, rhythmic respiration, sometimes normal though often gasping in character, appeared. S. C. Wang concluded, in agreement with Hoff and Breckenridge, that inherent medullary rhythmicity has a role in originating the normal respiratory rhythm. However, this may be profoundly modified by the apneustic centre, located in the pons, which tends to produce sustained inspiratory activity, and by the inhibitory action of vagal afferents and of the pneumotaxic centre, in the nerve cells of which Wang recorded, by means of microelectrodes, bursts of action potentials correlated with various phases of respiration.

G. C. Salmoiraghi and B. D. Burns failed to observe such activity in the pneumotaxic centre and therefore tended to minimize its importance in the genesis of the respiratory rhythm. They and Wang agree that motor nerve cells discharging during inspiration are closely mingled with cells discharging during expiration—both groups, inspiratory and expiratory, being linked together by nerve fibres so that activity in one cell spreads rapidly to others of the same group. It is also clear, as stated previously by Pitts, that activity of the inspiratory cells tends to decrease or inhibit the activity of the expiratory cells, and vice versa—an example of reciprocal innervation (see SPINAL CORD: *Physiology*).

Salmoiraghi and Burns found that the firing of medullary respiratory motor neurons decreased to only 10% of normal when cuts were made through the brain stem in order to eliminate all afferent impulses. They concluded that activity of the respiratory centres depends on excitation from nonrespiratory sources and also from neural structures sensitive to chemical stimuli such as CO_2 in the blood. Afferent impulses initiate firing in an inspiratory neuron and the activity spreads, causing inspiration to occur and at the same time inhibiting the activity of expiratory motor neurons. The inspiratory activity dies out, and the expiratory cells take over. The system swings one way or the other, like a metronome or a "flip flop" electronic multivibrator circuit. If respiratory movements are made to stop by excessive anesthesia or by lowering blood CO_2 concentration, either inspiratory cells or expiratory cells are found to be discharging continuously; the cells

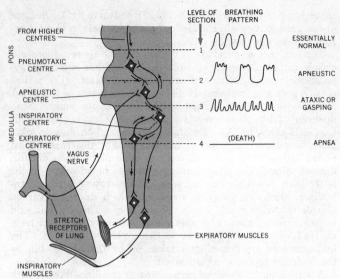

MODIFIED FROM NIMS IN J. F. FULTON (ED.), "A TEXTBOOK OF PHYSIOLOGY," 17TH ED., 1955, PHILADELPHIA, W. B. SAUNDERS COMPANY

FIG. 8.—SCHEMATIC REPRESENTATION OF THE MEDULLARY-PONTINE RESPIRATORY CENTRES INVOLVED IN RHYTHMIC BREATHING
Arrows show direction of nerve impulses involved in the periodic inhibition theory for the origin of rhythmic breathing

of both groups are never silent. Much research involving electrical stimulation, recording of action potentials and steady potentials, localized destruction, and correlated histological examination is necessary before a clear understanding of rhythmic breathing can be obtained.

Fig. 8 summarizes the localization of function of the medullary-pontine respiratory centres as outlined above.

REGULATION OF PULMONARY VENTILATION

Chemical Control of Breathing.—The respiratory system provides the body with oxygen and eliminates carbon dioxide. It is also one of the chief mechanisms maintaining a relatively constant internal environment, a condition essential to the survival of complex organisms, as stated by the French physiologist Claude Bernard (1813–1878). Thus, it counteracts the threat of low oxygen or high carbon dioxide in the environment, and minimizes excess acidity or alkalinity of the blood caused by metabolic disorders. It performs these tasks by constantly regulating the volume of air breathed, called the pulmonary ventilation, which is the product of the rate and depth of respiration.

This process is called the chemical control of breathing because it is carried out by specialized nerve cells, sensitive to the chemical composition of the blood, which vary the activity of the medullary respiratory centres. These cells are called chemoreceptors, or sometimes chemostats, because they stabilize the internal chemical environment much as a thermostat maintains a constant temperature in a room.

Though a man will die if he is deprived of oxygen for only a few minutes, his pulmonary ventilation is normally regulated by the tension of carbon dioxide in the blood rather than by that of oxygen. These facts were first discovered by Haldane and J. G. Priestley in 1905. Having developed a method for obtaining alveolar gas (which has essentially the same P_{CO_2} and P_{O_2} as arterial blood), they proceeded to analyze hundreds of samples obtained from normal subjects at various altitudes relative to sea level, and consequently at varying barometric pressures, even including that in a compressed air chamber used to treat certain respiratory disorders. In the laboratory at Oxford, at a barometric pressure (P_B) of 755 mm., the alveolar P_{CO_2} was 42.1 mm. It remained within 1.4 mm. of that figure on a mountain 1,360 m. (4,400 ft.) high (P_B = 646), at the bottom of a mine (P_B = 832), and in the compressed air chamber (P_B = 1,260). Yet the corresponding alveolar oxygen tensions varied widely, being 99 in the laboratory and 79, 115, and 203 mm., respectively, at the other locations. These simple data, from what has come to be known as a classic experiment in respiratory physiology, indicate that the pulmonary ventilation is normally regulated by the P_{CO_2} and not by the P_{O_2}.

Confirmatory evidence was obtained by adding small quantities of carbon dioxide to the inspired air. With 3% CO_2, the alveolar ventilation was doubled, the alveolar P_{CO_2} rising only 1.5 mm., indicating the extreme sensitivity of the respiratory centres to increases in P_{CO_2}. The increase in ventilation occurring when carbon dioxide is inhaled is compensatory, tending to minimize a rise in alveolar P_{CO_2}.

Haldane then reasoned that if a small rise in alveolar P_{CO_2} would double the ventilation, a corresponding fall might be expected to cause breathing to cease. This was investigated by having subjects hyperventilate (i.e., breathe deeply and rapidly), thereby reducing the alveolar P_{CO_2} from the normal value of 40, down to 15 or even 10 mm. Apnea (absence of breathing) invariably ensued, its duration, often of several minutes, being related to the degree of lowering of the P_{CO_2}. That it was due to this factor was shown by keeping the P_{CO_2} essentially normal by having the hyperventilating subject breathe air containing 5% carbon dioxide, following which no apnea occurred. Nor did it occur on quietly breathing pure oxygen, thus eliminating increased P_{O_2} as a cause of posthyperventilation apnea as had been suggested by a previous investigator, who had believed that respiration was normally regulated by the oxygen tension of the blood.

That oxygen lack is at best a poor stimulus to respiration, by no means as effective as a rise in carbon dioxide, was emphasized by Haldane. Little increase in ventilation occurs until the alveolar P_{O_2} falls from its normal value of 100 mm. down to about 70 mm., equivalent to an altitude of between 1,800 and 2,100 m. (6,000–7,000 ft.). Yet the hyperpnea cannot be accounted for in terms of CO_2, since the tension of the latter falls, by 10 mm. or more, during hypoxia. It was proposed, but never proved, that lactic acid might be the stimulus, the lack of oxygen causing its production inside the medullary respiratory centres. These centres were long known to be the site where carbon dioxide exerted its chief influence on respiration, and it was natural to expect hypoxia to act there too.

The explanation was not forthcoming until the early 1930s, when Corneille Heymans and his associates demonstrated the existence of respiratory reflexes originating from the carotid arteries in the neck. Close to where the latter branch into the internal and external carotid arteries lie, first, a set of pressoreceptors important in the regulation of blood pressure and also influencing respiration; and, second, a set of chemoreceptors sensitive to decreases in the oxygen tension of arterial blood and to a lesser extent to rises in P_{CO_2} and acidity. Similar sets of presso- and chemoreceptors are located at the arch of the aorta. The carotid and aortic bodies or glomera, as these chemoreceptors are called, consist of rounded epithelioid receptor cells, richly innervated and provided with a profuse supply of arterial blood. Impulses are generated in the receptor cells when the P_{O_2} falls sufficiently. Carried by nerves to the medullary respiratory centres, these impulses increase the activity of the centres and thus increase pulmonary ventilation.

That oxygen lack stimulates respiration almost entirely by way of the peripheral chemoreceptors has been shown by the fact that after their nerves are cut the inhalation of nitrogen almost always decreases respiration, due to depression of the medullary respiratory centres, whereas normally ventilation is more than doubled.

Though these chemoreceptors serve chiefly an emergency function, normal respiration being controlled mainly by the action of CO_2 or acid (see below) on the medullary respiratory centres, evidence for a significant degree of ventilatory drive due to O_2 even at sea level has been obtained by P. Dejours.

It is of some interest to speculate what would happen were respiration in man controlled not largely by P_{CO_2} but by P_{O_2}, as it appears to be in lizards, snakes, and fishes. Assuming the alveolar P_{O_2} to be held at 100 mm., the normal value at sea level, the pulmonary ventilation would be approximately doubled on the 1,360-m. mountain referred to by Haldane, and would be reduced to less than one third in the pressure chamber. Values for alveolar P_{CO_2} would be approximately 20 and 140 mm., respectively. Corre-

sponding acidity of arterial blood, expressed in terms of pH, would be 7.6 (alkaline) and slightly below 7 (markedly acid). Such marked deviations from the normal P_{CO_2} of 40 and pH of 7.4 would probably lead to muscular spasms, known as tetany, in the first instance and to CO_2 narcosis and anesthesia in the second.

Nature of the Chemical Stimulus to the Respiratory Centres.—After Haldane's discovery of the importance of carbon dioxide in the control of respiration, physiologists sought to find its mode of action. When, as the result of new measuring techniques, data relating rise in arterial acidity to rise in P_{CO_2} became available, H. Winterstein, and Haldane himself, came to believe that the pulmonary ventilation was regulated by the arterial hydrogen ion concentration rather than by the P_{CO_2}. This reaction theory, as it came to be called, gained further support from the fact that in metabolic acidosis, as in diabetes, respiration is increased even though the P_{CO_2} is below its normal value of 40 mm.

There were, however, experiments of a quantitative nature which cast doubt on the reaction theory. Marius Nielsen found that for a given increase in acidity produced by the acid-producing salt ammonium chloride, the hyperpnea was trifling compared to that accompanying inhalation of CO_2. Similarly, D. R. Hooker perfused the medulla of an anesthetized animal with blood kept at constant acidity, first by adding hydrochloric acid and second by adding carbon dioxide, the increases in pulmonary ventilation being 128% and 3,069%, respectively. The inference to be drawn from these and similar experiments is that carbon dioxide has a marked stimulating effect on respiration in addition to its property of increasing the acidity of the blood.

That a special property of molecular carbon dioxide did not need to be postulated was illustrated by the experiments of M. H. Jacobs in the early 1920s. The flowers of certain carnations were known to be blue in alkaline media and red in acid. Blue flowers immersed in acid solutions remained blue for long periods, but in solutions saturated with carbon dioxide and buffered to the alkaline side with sodium bicarbonate, the flowers turned red immediately. The explanation was that dissolved carbon dioxide was able to diffuse freely into the interior of the cell, rendering it acid. With the flowers in acid solution, however, the acid went in very slowly, because the cell membrane was relatively impermeable to the positively charged hydrogen ions. The same effect was observed in living sea urchin eggs. Jacobs' investigations made it clear that the acidity inside the cells of the respiratory centres might differ widely from that of the arterial blood.

On the basis of these findings, Winterstein modified his original reaction theory in order to identify the acidity inside the cells of the respiratory centres, rather than that in the blood, as the unique stimulus to respiration. Gesell pursued this idea and found evidence for disparities between the acidity of the blood and that of the cerebrospinal fluid which surrounds the central nervous system, including the medullary respiratory centres. These differences are known to be due to the blood-brain barrier, composed of the meninges covering the brain, which prevent free passage of many substances, including hydrogen ions.

In spite of numerous investigations, there remained two schools of thought regarding the "unique" chemical stimulus to the respiratory centres, if indeed there is one. The Scandinavian group, led originally by A. Krogh and later by Nielsen, advocated P_{CO_2} as the stimulus, the hyperpnea of metabolic acidosis being explained on the basis of increased sensitivity of the respiratory centres to P_{CO_2} as a result of the acidosis. On the other hand, Winterstein, Gesell, and others advocated intracellular pH.

An ingenious attempt to resolve the dilemma is provided by the multiple factor theory of J. S. Gray, according to which each chemical stimulus to respiration acts in its own right, the existing level of ventilation being the resultant of the additive effects of the known stimuli, namely P_{CO_2}, hydrogen ions (acidity) and, during hypoxia, P_{O_2}. For example, the marked response to breathing CO_2 could be due to the effect of increased P_{CO_2} plus that of the increased acidity produced by adding CO_2 to the blood. On the other hand, the much smaller response that accompanies an equal degree of acidity produced by metabolic acidosis could be due to the difference between a stimulus, increased acidity, and an

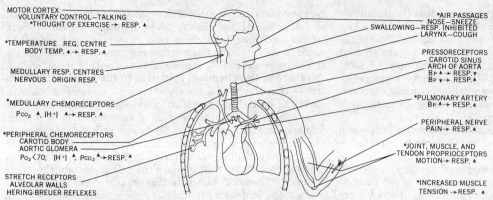

MOTOR CORTEX
VOLUNTARY CONTROL—TALKING
*THOUGHT OF EXERCISE → RESP. ▲

*TEMPERATURE REG. CENTRE
BODY TEMP. ▲→ RESP. ▲

MEDULLARY RESP. CENTRES
NERVOUS ORIGIN RESP.

*MEDULLARY CHEMORECEPTORS
PCO₂ ▲, [H⁺] ▲→ RESP. ▲

*PERIPHERAL CHEMORECEPTORS
CAROTID BODY
AORTIC GLOMERA
PO₂<70; [H⁺] ▲, PCO₂ ▲→RESP. ▲

STRETCH RECEPTORS
ALVEOLAR WALLS
HERING-BREUER REFLEXES

*AIR PASSAGES
NOSE—SNEEZE
SWALLOWING— RESP. INHIBITED
LARYNX—COUGH

PRESSORECEPTORS
CAROTID SINUS
ARCH OF AORTA
BP ▲→ RESP. ▼
BP ▼→ RESP. ▲

*PULMONARY ARTERY
BP ▲→ RESP. ▲

PERIPHERAL NERVE
PAIN → RESP. ▲

*JOINT, MUSCLE, AND
TENDON PROPRIOCEPTORS
MOTION→ RESP. ▲

*INCREASED MUSCLE
TENSION →RESP. ▲

FIG. 9.—DIAGRAM SUMMARIZING PROCESSES INVOLVED IN THE NERVOUS AND CHEMICAL CONTROL OF RESPIRATION
Asterisks indicate factors probably contributing to the increased breathing of exercise. Horizontal arrows (→) denote "leads to"; vertical arrows indicate increase (↑) or decrease (↓) in the factor referred to. BP is the symbol for blood pressure

antagonist, decreased P_{CO_2} (below normal in this condition). In other words, the addition is algebraic in this instance.

The concept of an antagonist—*i.e.*, a less than normal contribution of a respiratory stimulus—though implicit in the finding by Haldane of apnea following hyperventilation when the P_{CO_2} was only slightly reduced, is one of the keystones of Gray's theory. According to him, there is no unique stimulus, all three combining their effects.

I. R. Leusen showed (1954) that perfusion of the cerebral ventricles (cavities within the brain, filled with cerebrospinal fluid) with solutions possessing increased P_{CO_2} or acidity increased pulmonary ventilation. H. H. Loeschcke later emphasized the importance of acidity rather than P_{CO_2} in mediating the response, and R. A. Mitchell found that the acid-sensitive regions were located bilaterally on the ventrolateral surfaces of the medulla oblongata. It seems clear that these chemosensitive areas play a major role in mediating the normal respiratory response to CO_2 and possibly to "fixed" acid, *e.g.*, lactic acid, in the blood.

Regulation of Ventilation During Physical Exercise.— Haldane proposed that carbon dioxide was responsible for the increase in breathing that accompanies exercise. The experimental data, however, have not supported him. The highest ventilation produced by increasing the P_{CO_2} is about 70 l. per minute during breathing of 7.5% CO_2, the alveolar P_{CO_2} then being 60 mm., which is 20 mm. above normal. In severe exercise, not only is the ventilation considerably higher, 100 to 120 l. per minute, but, what is more striking, the P_{CO_2} is actually below its normal value of 40 mm. Hence an elevated P_{CO_2} cannot possibly explain the great increases in ventilation observed during severe exercise, and can account only partially for the hyperpnea of moderate exercise, when the P_{CO_2} is only slightly (2 to 4 mm.) above normal. Nor does the P_{O_2} fall markedly during exercise at sea level.

No known simple factor can explain the increase in ventilation occurring during exercise. Several stimuli appear to combine their effects and in such a way that the volume of air breathed increases in direct proportion to the increase in work done and the oxygen used. It is difficult to conceive of so precise a regulation without the intervention of a chemical factor which, produced as a result of the exercise, acts so as to increase the ventilation. Yet no such agent has been found. It is true that an increase in blood acidity occurs during severe exercise and could be a factor in that condition alone. An increase in sensitivity of the respiratory centres to P_{CO_2} has also been postulated. A rise in body temperature can produce such an increase, and the body temperature does rise 1° or 2° C (about 2° to 3½° F) or more during severe exercise. One investigator found an 11-l. increase in ventilation per 1° C rise in body temperature, due apparently to increase in sensitivity of the medullary respiratory centres to CO_2.

Nervous reflexes also contribute their share. Passive motion of the limbs in man or animals produces an increase in ventilation. The effect is abolished when the sciatic nerve to the leg is anesthetized by injection of procaine. The impulses responsible are known to arise in the special "position-sense" nerve endings (propriocep-

tors) located in joints and muscles, which permit an individual to tell whether a joint is extended or flexed and how much. F. F. Kao has stressed the importance of these afferent nervous impulses in the hyperpnea of exercise, induced in the lower extremities of anesthetized animals by electrical stimulation of the muscles. Breathing was not markedly reduced when the blood supply to the exercising muscles was provided entirely from another animal, but when the nerves from the limbs were cut, the hyperpnea was largely eliminated. P. Dejours has emphasized fast and slow components in the hyperpnea of exercise. Thus, immediately after the onset of muscular work, pulmonary ventilation increases abruptly, presumably as the result of the afferent nervous impulses referred to. There is then a delayed increase in breathing, possibly from chemical substances produced by the muscles. Similarly, after cessation of exercise there is a sudden, and then a gradual, decrease in ventilation.

Other nervous and chemical factors have been proposed to help account for the hyperpnea of exercise. These include afferent impulses initiated by movement of air through the smaller air passages, nerve impulses originating as the result of a rise in the blood pressure in the pulmonary artery, impulses produced by nerves sensitive to accumulation of metabolites such as lactic acid in exercising muscles, and rises in temperature of these muscles. Yet the experimental evidence for these other nervous and chemical reflexes is dubious at best. It is entirely possible that physiologists, in attempting to explain the hyperpnea of exercise, are at a stage similar to that existing before the discovery of the peripheral chemoreceptors, when many theories were proposed to account for the stimulation of ventilation by hypoxia, though none proved adequate.

Those reflexes that may contribute to the hyperpnea of exercise are marked by an asterisk in fig. 9. This diagram also gives some idea of the many other factors that influence breathing.

BIBLIOGRAPHY.—J. Barcroft, *The Respiratory Function of the Blood*, vol. i and ii (1926, 1928); P. Bard (ed.), *Medical Physiology*, 11th ed. (1961); J. H. Comroe, Jr., *et al.*, *The Lung* (1955); H. W. Davenport, *The ABC of Acid-Base Chemistry*, 4th ed. (1958); T. C. Ruch and J. F. Fulton (eds.), *Medical Physiology and Biophysics* (18th ed. of *Howell's Textbook of Physiology*) (1960); J. S. Gray, *Pulmonary Ventilation and Its Physiological Regulation* (1950); A. Krogh, *The Comparative Physiology of Respiratory Mechanisms* (1941); C. L. Prosser and F. A. Brown, Jr. (eds.), *Comparative Animal Physiology*, 2nd ed. (1961); W. O. Fenn and H. Rahn (eds.), *Handbook of Physiology*, section 3, "Respiration," vol. 1 (1964).   (J. F. Ps.)

RESPIRATORY SYSTEM, ANATOMY OF. The respiratory tract, including all the organs concerned in the act of breathing, consists of the nasal cavities, pharynx (throat), larynx, trachea, bronchi and lungs (*see* fig. 1). In ordinary breathing the nasal cavities warm, moisten and filter the inspired air (*see* OLFACTORY SYSTEM). The pharynx, which lies between the nasal cavities and mouth, above, and the larynx and esophagus, below, is a transitional zone in which the pathways of swallowing and breathing cross each other (*see* THROAT). In certain mammals in which the sense of smell is all-important, breathing through the nose is made obligatory by an interlocking of the epiglottis and the uvula of the soft palate. In man there is a gap between the two; consequently food is sometimes misdirected into the larynx and windpipe.

Larynx.—When the physician looks into the throat with a laryngoscope, he is examining the mucous surfaces of the interior of the voice box. Reflected in his mirror are the structures shown in fig. 2: a lid-shaped epiglottis that can be folded backward over the larynx; the aryepiglottic folds, backward extensions of the epiglottis that help prevent spilling of food into the larynx; the pear-shaped piriform recess, through which food is guided into the esophagus; the vallecula ("little valley"), which separates the epiglottis from the tongue; the ventricular folds or false vocal cords; and beneath them the glottis ("mouthpiece of a flute"). The latter consists of the vocal folds (or cords) and the slit between them, the rima glottidis.

The ventricular folds point downward and, when closed by action of sphincter muscles, form an exit valve that permits the

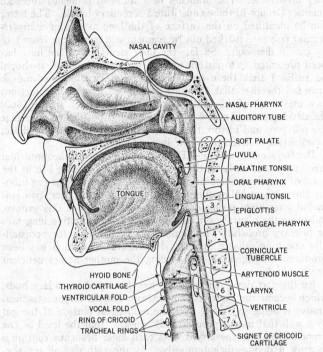

FIG. 1.—SAGITTAL SECTION OF HEAD AND NECK
Numbers indicate the cervical vertebrae

NASAL CAVITY
NASAL PHARYNX
AUDITORY TUBE
SOFT PALATE
UVULA
PALATINE TONSIL
ORAL PHARYNX
LINGUAL TONSIL
EPIGLOTTIS
LARYNGEAL PHARYNX
CORNICULATE TUBERCLE
ARYTENOID MUSCLE
LARYNX
VENTRICLE
SIGNET OF CRICOID CARTILAGE
TONGUE
HYOID BONE
THYROID CARTILAGE
VENTRICULAR FOLD
VOCAL FOLD
RING OF CRICOID
TRACHEAL RINGS

building up of abdominal pressure, as in straining at stool or in expulsion of the fetus. Coughing is produced by releasing the air explosively. Between the ventricular and vocal folds of each side is a pitlike cavity, the ventricle, which is prolonged into an appendix or saccule. In the great apes these saccules become enormous accessory organs of respiration.

The vocal folds are whiter than the ventricular folds because their areas of contact with each other are covered by stratified scalelike epithelium. These are the hard membranes that vibrate to produce sound. In breathing, they approach each other rhythmically. When closed by the surrounding muscles they form an inlet valve that prevents the entrance of air during fixation of the ribs for movements of the arms.

The physician examines the cords for evidence of inflammation, for the presence of tumours and for paralysis of muscles that regulate their action. They stretch across the interior of the voice box from the shieldlike thyroid cartilage, in front, to the vocal process of the pitcher-shaped arytenoid cartilage, behind (see fig. 1-3). The arytenoids are the key to the understanding of the movements of the cords. These cartilages slide and rotate upon the signet portion of the ringlike cricoid cartilage (see fulcrum, fig. 3), abducting or adducting the cords in response to muscles that insert upon the muscular process of each arytenoid. Tensing and loosening of the cords are produced, respectively, by the crico-thyroid muscles, which tilt the thyroid cartilage forward, and by vocal muscles within the cords that shorten the distance between thyroid and arytenoid cartilages. (For action of the laryngeal muscles in the production of sounds, see VOICE.)

Injury of the recurrent laryngeal nerves, or their more central connections, results in paralysis of all laryngeal muscles except the crico-thyroids.

Trachea.—The trachea, or windpipe, is the tube that connects the larynx and the bronchi (see fig. 4); it is from 4 to 4½ in. long and lies partly in the neck and partly in the thorax. It begins where the larynx ends, at the lower border of the sixth cervical

vertebra (see fig. 1), and divides into its two bronchi opposite the fifth thoracic vertebra. The tube is kept open by rings of cartilage, shaped like horseshoes and embedded in an external fibroelastic membrane. Behind, where the trachea rests upon the gullet, there is a layer of smooth muscle that can draw the open ends of the rings together and so diminish the calibre of the tube.

Inside there is plentiful submucous tissue containing submucous glands and much lymphoid tissue. The whole is lined internally by columnar ciliated epithelium. These cilia form one segment of a continuous field of upward stroking lashes that carry mucus and inspired material from the lungs to the larynx. At this upper level it can be coughed up.

The cervical part of the tube is not much more than an inch in length, but it can be lengthened by throwing back the head. This is the region in which tracheotomy is performed. At the bifurcation of the trachea the lowest cartilage forms a carina, or keel. In birds the bifurcation is converted into a vocal organ, the syrinx, consisting of vibrating membranes controlled by special muscles. In man, the topographic relations, at this level, are of special importance (see fig. 4). If the aorta is pathologically enlarged it may compress the esophagus, causing difficulty in swallowing; or press against the left bronchus, causing difficulty in breathing; or put traction upon the left recurrent laryngeal nerve where it curves around the arch of the aorta, thus affecting the voice.

Below the bifurcation right and left primary bronchi diverge to enter the hilum of the lung. Since the right bronchus more nearly continues the direction of the trachea than the left, foreign bodies swallowed inadvertently by children fall more commonly into the right than into the left lung.

As each primary bronchus enters the lungs it is accompanied by a large pulmonary artery, carrying venous blood to the lung, and a large pulmonary vein conveying oxygenated blood to the heart (see fig. 5). In addition there are small bronchial arteries, lymphatics and nerves.

Lungs.—These are the organs that are formed when right and left bronchial buds of the embryo push out into that portion of the body cavity that later becomes the pleural cavity (see COELOM AND SEROUS MEMBRANES). Each lung, therefore, represents the total branching of the primary bronchus plus its supporting tissue, its associated arterial and venous trees and the layer of pleura that surrounds it. Medially it is attached by a reflection of the pleura to the mediastinum, the vertical wall that divides the chest into right and left compartments.

Grossly, each lung is a somewhat conical organ having an apex, which extends into the neck; a base, which rests upon the diaphragm; and other surfaces that are costal and mediastinal. Superficially the right lung is cleft by horizontal and oblique fissures into three lobes; the left lung is cleft into two lobes. This asymmetry is characteristic of most mammals. Equally significant divisions are the bronchopulmonary segments, first recognized as such in 1932. These are polyhedral wedges of tissue separated from each other by veins and thin connective tissue membranes. They represent the zones of distribution of the larger secondary bronchi. On the right side ten such segments have been recognized. On the left the number is restricted to nine, since apical

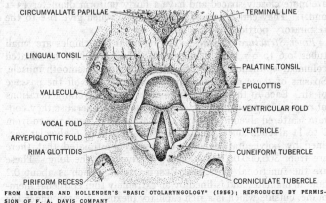

CIRCUMVALLATE PAPILLAE
TERMINAL LINE
LINGUAL TONSIL
PALATINE TONSIL
EPIGLOTTIS
VALLECULA
VENTRICULAR FOLD
VOCAL FOLD
VENTRICLE
ARYEPIGLOTTIC FOLD
CUNEIFORM TUBERCLE
RIMA GLOTTIDIS
PIRIFORM RECESS
CORNICULATE TUBERCLE

FIG. 2.—LARYNGOSCOPIC VIEW OF LARYNX

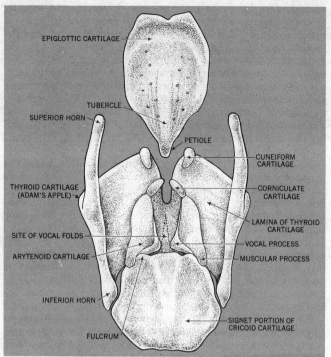

FROM MORRIS' "HUMAN ANATOMY" (1953); REPRODUCED BY PERMISSION OF BLAKISTON DIVISION, MCGRAW-HILL BOOK COMPANY, INC.

FIG. 3.—CARTILAGES OF LARYNX SEEN FROM BEHIND

and posterior segmental bronchi have developed into a single shrublike unit. Although segments are not demarcated by surface fissures they are nevertheless surgical units that can be excised individually, thus making possible the preservation of adjacent healthy tissue that formerly was sacrificed when surgeons were compelled to remove entire lobes in order to remove small lesions.

Commonly, three techniques are available for determining the site of tumours or other lesions in lobes and segments: (1) X-rays of the chest; (2) direct examination of the orifices of the segmental bronchi by means of a bronchoscope lowered into the trachea; and (3) X-rays of the bronchial tree (bronchograms) made after the tree has been filled with a radiopaque fluid.

Bronchial Divisions.—Each of the segmental bronchi divide more or less dichotomously until there are from 20 to 25 generations of branches ending in the terminal bronchioles. The first ten generations are widely spaced divisions and occupy two-thirds to three-fourths of the way to the periphery. These are secondary bronchi, lined by ciliated, pseudostratified epithelium. In their walls are cartilage plates, to keep the air passages open; mucous glands to moisten the ducts; and a mesh of smooth muscle fibres to regulate the calibre of the tubes. These tissues are supplied by bronchial arteries of aortic origin, and by nerves, and are drained by lymphatic vessels and veins. The remaining 10 to 15 generations are bronchioles. These branches have no cartilages, are more closely spaced and have a fairly uniform diameter (3–1 mm.). They end in terminal bronchioles, which give rise to the respiratory portions of the tree.

Finer Structure of Lung.—The terminal bronchioles are small tubes, 0.6 to 0.7 mm. in diameter. They are lined by ciliated columnar epithelium and completely invested by smooth muscle. Spasms of these muscles, as in asthma, can shut off the passage of air. Each of these short tubes gives rise to several generations of respiratory bronchioles (*see* fig. 6), so named because they contain scattered alveoli. Each of these bronchioles gives rise to from 2 to 11 alveolar ducts, and each of these to 5 or 6 alveolar sacs lined by polyhedral alveoli. It has been estimated that there are from 300,000,000 to 400,000,000 alveoli in the lung. These are the functional units (*see* RESPIRATION). Each is about 0.2 mm. in diameter and is lined by an extremely thin epithelial membrane, outside which is a rich capillary plexus. As seen under the electron microscope, adherent alveolar and capillary walls measure

only $\frac{1}{2500}$ mm. in thickness. It was the first sight of blood corpuscles circulating through these capillaries in 1661 that led Malpighi to exclaim, "I see with my own eyes a certain great thing" (Sir Michael Foster, *Lectures on the History of Physiology,* p. 96, Cambridge University Press, 1901).

According to W. S. Miller, all the branches of an alveolar duct form a primary lobule. Other investigators start with the respiratory bronchiole. The branches of a terminal bronchus form an acinus. Groups of these constitute a secondary lobule. The latter can be identified on the surface of the lung as one of many irregular polygons marked out by pigment and measuring from 1 to $2\frac{1}{2}$ cm. in diameter. So far, the finer structure of the lung has been presented as a pattern of arborization. However, it should be realized that these peripheral respiratory units become so crowded together that the lung appears in microscopic sections as a meshwork of thin walls separating air spaces. In the 1960s the development of a new technique made it possible to disengage the polygons and restore the treelike form, thus permitting direct examination of alveolar sacs in diseased lungs.

Development of Lungs.—The rudiment of the tracheobronchial tree appears as early as the 25th day of intra-uterine life in the form of a laryngotracheal groove on the ventral side of the tubular foregut just below the pharynx. A day or so later, two epithelial lung buds push out from the lower end of this groove, indenting the pleural cavities. These are the primitive lung sacs or primary bronchi. This period is a critical one, for occasionally one lung fails to appear. In rats, this condition has been produced experimentally by feeding the mother a diet deficient in vitamin A.

By the 31st day each bronchus has developed secondary buds, which become the lobar bronchi. Meanwhile the laryngotracheal groove is being separated from the esophageal portion of the gut by a wall that moves progressively upward from the level of the bronchial buds to the larynx. As each lobar bronchus continues to grow it divides dichotomously. By the 36th day all ten segmental buds have appeared, giving the exterior of the lung a scal-

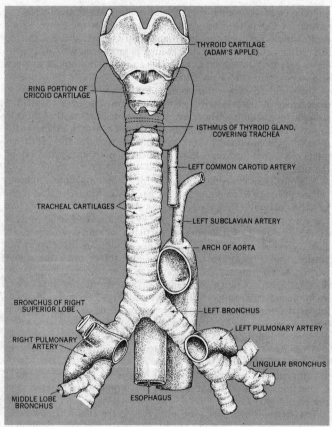

AFTER CUNNINGHAM'S "TEXT BOOK OF ANATOMY" (1951); REPRODUCED BY PERMISSION OF OXFORD UNIVERSITY PRESS

FIG. 4.—LARYNX, TRACHEA AND PRIMARY BRONCHI

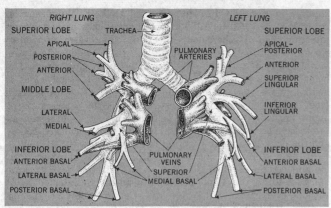

RIGHT LUNG — LEFT LUNG

SUPERIOR LOBE — TRACHEA — SUPERIOR LOBE
APICAL — APICAL-POSTERIOR
POSTERIOR — PULMONARY ARTERIES — ANTERIOR
ANTERIOR — SUPERIOR LINGULAR
MIDDLE LOBE — INFERIOR LINGULAR
LATERAL
MEDIAL
INFERIOR LOBE — PULMONARY VEINS — INFERIOR LOBE
ANTERIOR BASAL — SUPERIOR — ANTERIOR BASAL
LATERAL BASAL — MEDIAL BASAL — LATERAL BASAL
POSTERIOR BASAL — POSTERIOR BASAL

FIG. 5.—SEGMENTAL BRONCHI AND PULMONARY VESSELS

loped appearance. By the 40th day several additional generations of branchings have appeared, so that a model of the bronchial tree resembles great clusters of grapes.

This period of branching of epithelial tubes continues through the fourth month of fetal life and is known as the glandular period. About 16 to 26 generations of branching are then established. The last seven of these are lined by cuboidal epithelium. Between the fourth and sixth months— the canalicular period—capillaries protrude into the lumina of the more peripheral bronchi, pushing connective tissue fibrils ahead of them to separate the cuboidal cells. Such protrusions give rise in time to the walls of alveoli. At six months there are no alveoli as yet, but the number of capillaries protruding into the lumina is sufficient to support for several hours the life of an infant born prematurely at this age. In the alveolar period—seven months to term—vascular walls have protruded far enough into the lumina to outline shallow alveoli. From this time on the premature infant is viable.

Obviously, birth is another critical period. The first respirations expand only a limited area.

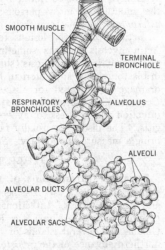

SMOOTH MUSCLE

TERMINAL BRONCHIOLE

RESPIRATORY BRONCHIOLES — ALVEOLUS

ALVEOLI

ALVEOLAR DUCTS

ALVEOLAR SACS

FIG. 6.—TERMINAL RESPIRATORY UNITS OF BRONCHIAL TREE

days, and sometimes weeks. Not infrequently portions of the lung never dilate (congenital atelectasis).

In premature infants, and those delivered by caesarean section, a hyaline membrane of unknown origin sometimes lines the alveoli, preventing respiration. Nor is it known whether aspiration of amniotic fluid before birth is a normal or abnormal occurrence. These and other problems dealing with respiration at birth await solution.

M. S. Dunnill has estimated that from birth to maturity the lung volume increases from 0.2 to 5.5 litres, that the number of alveoli increase from 24,000,000 to 296,000,000, and that the air-tissue interface (for exchange of gases) increases from 2.8 to 75 sq.m. How this is accomplished is only just beginning to be understood. At birth the only alveoli present are located in the very end branches of the tree, in tiny clusters of alveolar sacs 1 mm. in diameter. Within two months new alveoli appear along the bronchioles in a centripetal direction so that what were smooth respiratory bronchioles become transformed into alveolar ducts and what were the terminal bronchioles become transformed into respiratory bronchioles. It seems unlikely that growth is accompanied by the formation of new acini.

See also references under "Respiratory System" in the Index.

BIBLIOGRAPHY.—Sir Michael Foster, *Lectures on the History of Physiology* (1924); William Snow Miller, *The Lung*, 2nd ed. (1947); V. E. Negus, *The Comparative Anatomy and Physiology of the Larynx* (1950); James G. Wilson and Joseph Warkany, "Aortic-Arch and Cardiac Anomalies in the Offspring of Vitamin A Deficient Rats," *Amer. J. Anat.*, 85:113–156 (1949); Clayton G. Loosli and Edith L. Potter, "Pre- and Postnatal Development of the Respiratory Portion of the Human Lung," *Amer. Rev. Resp. Dis.*, vol. 80 (1959); U. Bucher and Lynne Reid, "Development of the Intrasegmental Bronchial Tree," *Thorax*, 16:207–218 (1961); H. von Hayek, *Die menschliche Lunge* (1953); Frank N. Low, "The Pulmonary Alveolar Epithelium of Laboratory Mammals and Man," *Anat. Rec.*, 117:241–263 (1953); L. J. Wells and E. A. Boyden, "The Development of the Bronchopulmonary Segments in Human Embryos of Horizons XVII to XIX," *Amer. J. Anat.*, 95:163–201 (1954); E. A. Boyden, *Segmental Anatomy of the Lungs* (1955); K. K. Pump, "The Morphology of the Finer Branches of the Bronchial Tree of the Human Lung," *Dis. Chest*, 46:379–398 (1964); M. S. Dunnill, "Postnatal Growth of the Lung," *Thorax*, 17:329–333 (1962). (E. A. Bn.)

RESPIRATORY SYSTEM, DISEASES OF. Respiratory diseases may involve the upper respiratory tract from the nose, with its accessory sinuses, through the pharynx and larynx to the lower respiratory tract, which includes the trachea, bronchi and lungs. From beginning to end the mucous membrane of the entire tract is continuous. The anatomy and physiology of the respiratory tract are described in the articles RESPIRATORY SYSTEM, ANATOMY OF and RESPIRATION. This article is concerned mainly with diseases of the lower respiratory tract. For the upper respiratory system, *see* NOSE, DISEASES OF and THROAT, DISEASES OF. The diseases affecting the lungs are approached somewhat differently in LUNG, DISEASES OF; and PLEURA, DISEASES OF deals with the disorders specifically affecting the pleura. An inflammation of the lung from any cause may be called pneumonia, hence *see* also PNEUMONIA.

Disease Barriers.—Normally, inspired air is warmed and moistened as it passes over the nasal turbinates, which act as baffles. This mechanism is interfered with when infection or allergy causes swelling of the mucous membrane. Particles in the inspired air are usually deposited in the nose, from which they are eliminated. A circle of lymphoid tissue surrounds the pharynx, acting as a barrier against the dissemination of infection. The mucous membrane of the trachea and bronchi is supplied with minute hairs, the cilia, which beat upward away from the lungs. This cleansing device raises to the pharynx inhaled foreign particles, which can then be expectorated. Toxic agents may slow or paralyze ciliary action; dehydration or infection may so thicken the secretions that the cilia cannot beat freely. Some noxious particles actually reaching the alveoli (air sacs) of the lungs are engulfed and disintegrated by special cells and then brought to the ciliary stream. Cough is a mechanism for forcible ejection of foreign matter and infected secretions.

Interference with any of these mechanisms predisposes to disease. In addition, there are local and general factors of resistance involving nutrition, hormones, previous experience with disease, chilling, unconsciousness due to anesthesia or inebriation, etc.

INFECTIONS

Infections can be grouped most easily by causative organisms.

Viral Diseases.—Great difficulty occurs in attempts to correlate respiratory diseases with their viral causes. One virus may be responsible for several different illnesses, and one disease may be caused by several different viruses. This is a field of active research, and new viruses are being discovered.

Influenza has a short incubation period and occurs in epidemics, usually of relatively minor significance but occasionally in pandemics of great severity, as in 1918 and 1957. The later world-wide influenzal outbreak was caused by a substrain of type A virus named the Asian strain because the first recognized cases occurred in the Orient. There is no effective treatment for pneumonia produced by the influenza virus. Total prevention (as for smallpox, yellow fever, and rabies) is not available, but partial control may be achieved through vaccination, provided the responsible strain has been included in the vaccine. Antibodies against one influenza virus are ineffective against another type of the same strain. One of the great medical feats of the 20th century was the world-wide cooperation that resulted in the prompt identification of the Asian strain of type A influenza virus, its incorporation into vaccines, and the use of vaccine on a mass scale so that protection was available immediately during the 1957–58 Asian influenza epidemic. Immunity from an attack of influenza is short-lived. (*See* also INFLUENZA.)

Another viral disease is pleurodynia, caused by the Coxsackie B virus. It occurs in small epidemics and is associated with severe chest pain made worse by deep breathing.

Primary atypical pneumonia is caused by more than one virus, is characterized by a normal white blood cell count (as are most viral infections) and by the presence of cold hemagglutinins, antibodies rarely present in other diseases. Like all viral diseases, it is resistant to treatment.

Rickettsial Pneumonias.—Bronchopneumonia may occur in louse-borne typhus (*q.v.*), a disease of world-wide distribution caused by *Rickettsia prowazekii*. Pneumonitis is a feature of many cases of Q fever (*q.v.*), a disease caused by *Coxiella burnetii* and first recognized in Australia. It is transmitted mostly by inhalation through occupational exposure to infected sheep, cattle, or goats, or by working with the rickettsiae in the laboratory. Many cases have been reported from California, Montana, and Texas as well as from Africa, Europe, the Middle East and Panama. The rickettsial diseases respond well to treatment with the tetracyclines or chloramphenicol.

Bacillary Infections.—The commonest bacillary infections of the nasopharynx are due to hemolytic streptococci and staphylococci, and to pneumococci.

(*See* also BACTERIA.)

Streptococcal sore throats are of great significance, since serious distant effects include kidney infections and flare-ups of rheumatic fever, with its possible sequel of rheumatic heart disease. Fortunately, excellent antibiotic treatment is available, penicillin being most effective. Early diagnosis is important, and for persons with a history of rheumatic fever prophylactic drug therapy during cold weather is desirable.

Staphylococcal infections occupy a major place among the pneumonias because of their rapid and often fatal course. The emergence of staphylococci resistant to many of the most potent antibiotics has presented a grave problem in treatment. Many staphylococcal infections are acquired in the hospital: resistant staphylococci have been cultured from throats and fingernails of hospital personnel, from air emerging from hospital laundry chutes and operating rooms, from blankets and from "clean" glasses and water bottles delivered to patients. Most hospitals have committees which not only review each case of staphylococcal infection but also draw up housekeeping procedures designed to prevent the transmission of such infections.

Pneumococcal pneumonias appear to be less common than they once were. It is not apparent whether this is due to a true reduction in prevalence or to the fact that cases are being successfully treated at home with the many antibiotics available. Friedländer's pneumonia, caused by Friedländer's bacillus, *Klebsiella pneumoniae*, remains a grave infection seen mostly in older men, frequently in alcoholics or grossly malnourished persons.

Tuberculosis.—This is a disease with a declining death rate; however, in many areas, including Eastern Europe, Asia, and the western Pacific islands, tuberculosis is still rampant. In remote or overpopulated places diagnosis is often erroneous and statistics are inadequate, so that the true magnitude of the problem is unknown.

The number of persons suffering from active tuberculosis constitutes a better measure of the problem than the number of persons dying from the disease, particularly since modern treatment is effective. Though morbidity rates are slowly diminishing in the economically advanced countries, the problem remains of considerable magnitude. For a full discussion of this disease, *see* TUBERCULOSIS.

Fungus Infections.—Certain geographic areas are endemic foci of fungus diseases, many of which affect the lungs. In the U.S., portions of the South and the whole Mississippi Valley have high rates of infection with *Histoplasma capsulatum*. A ten-year study of histoplasmin and tuberculin reactors among kindergarten children in Kansas City, Mo., reported by L. E. Wood and his co-workers in 1958, revealed a higher prevalence of histoplasma infection than of tuberculous infection. Histoplasmosis is a serious problem in these endemic areas. Its behaviour closely resembles that of tuberculosis. Amphotericin B gives promise of being effective in therapy. As with tuberculosis, some cases of histoplasmosis run a benign course. Miliary calcifications result from benign disseminated disease; their X-ray appearance remains unchanged over years. Localized epidemics of histoplasmosis have occurred in association with the soil of chicken houses, and the disease has been reported in association with bat dung.

In the western and southwestern United States, northern Mexico and certain areas of South America, infection with *Coccidioides immitis* is prevalent; nearly all residents are infected, many without ever having had symptoms. Coccidioidomycosis is contracted by inhaling chlamydospores (the *Coccidioides* reproductive organs) in dust. About half the cases exhibit respiratory symptoms. The pneumonitis which develops may clear entirely or may leave characteristic thin-walled cavities. Small cavities tend to close slowly. Larger cavities frequently give rise to expectoration of blood-stained sputum and occasionally rupture; for this reason surgical removal may be advised. The drug amphotericin B is sometimes helpful. Coccidioidomycosis may be prevented by avoiding endemic areas, particularly during dry, dusty seasons.

Less common fungus diseases of the respiratory tract include actinomycosis, due to *Actinomyces bovis*, a fungus harboured in the mouths of most persons; nocardiosis, due to *Nocardia asteroides*; and blastomycosis, due to *Blastomyces dermatitides*. In actinomycosis the lesions tend to penetrate the chest wall. Actinomycosis patients sometimes are helped by penicillin or sulfadiazine; in nocardiosis, sulfonamide therapy alone is used; in blastomycosis, amphotericin B is the drug of choice. Surgical drainage is indicated for abscesses. Cryptococcosis, caused by *Cryptococcus neoformans*, may begin with a mild respiratory infection and progress to involvement of the lungs and to meningitis. The disease is usually fatal, though amphotericin B may bring a measure of recovery. *See* also FUNGUS INFECTIONS.

OTHER DISEASES

Parasitic Infestations of the Lung.—Chronic pulmonary schistosomiasis (*q.v.*) has been reported from Egypt, Brazil and other countries. Infections with blood flukes are widely distributed in Japan, China, the Philippines, Africa, Brazil, Dutch Guiana and several islands of the West Indies. With the slow northern advance of the *Schistosoma*, the disease has come to be of interest in the United States. Exposure occurs through contact with water infested by snail hosts, through bathing, laundering, etc.

Amoebiasis occurs all over the world, mostly in the tropics and where sanitation is poor. Prevention consists of avoiding contaminated water and raw foods which may have been washed with such water. Pulmonary abscesses occur secondary to amoebic abscesses of the liver. (*See* also PARASITOLOGY.)

Allergic Diseases.—Vasomotor rhinitis (cold in the head), hay fever, and bronchial asthma are a triad of common allergic diseases of the respiratory tract.

Vasomotor rhinitis, characterized by copious watery nasal discharge, is nonseasonal, in contradistinction to hay fever, which is seasonal and caused by pollens. Hay fever is associated with sneezing, itching of the eyes and nose, outpouring of watery secretions from the eyes and nose and an abrupt onset when the causative pollen first becomes airborne. While it is not in itself serious, it is annoying, interferes with sleep and appetite as well as with the normal functions of the nasal mucosa and thus predisposes to infection. (*See* also COLD, COMMON; HAY FEVER.)

Bronchial asthma, the most serious of the allergic diseases of the respiratory tract, is characterized by sporadic attacks of wheezing due to spasm of the involuntary muscles in the bronchial walls. The wheezing is bilateral, intermittent and changeable, in contrast to the unilateral fixed wheeze of tumour, ulcer or scarring of a bronchus. Clear tenacious secretions are difficult to raise.

Allergies include a wide variety of exogenous materials such as dust and feathers, but, especially in cases in which the onset of asthma occurs in middle age, endogenous bacteria are often causative. There are usually multiple factors. The actual attack may be precipitated by an emotional upset, a sudden marked change of temperature or a respiratory infection. During an attack air hunger is acute, the spasm of the smaller bronchi exerting a ball-valve effect by which air gets in but cannot get out because the spasm increases the normal shortening and narrowing of the bronchi on expiration. The mucoid secretions may actually plug some bronchi. Occasionally the patient goes into a serious prolonged life-threatening episode called status asthmaticus. Most attacks of asthma can be successfully treated by adrenaline or adrenalinlike drugs and can be averted by avoidance of allergens, infections, rapid changes of temperature and by the achievement of emotional tranquility. While recurrent asthmatic attacks are usually not grave, they lead over the years in many cases to a state of chronic overdistention of the lung and to emphysema. (*See* also ASTHMA.)

Chronic Bronchitis and Emphysema.—Repeated attacks of acute bronchitis (*q.v.*) predispose to chronic bronchitis characterized by chronic cough productive of sputum. Such persistent productive cough tends to be associated with recurrent bouts of respiratory illness, during which fever is often present and expectoration increases. Ultimately, wheezing is heard and, in an unknown but probably significant percentage of cases, overdistention of the lungs with thinning of the alveolar walls—emphysema (*q.v.*)—develops. Shortness of breath gradually increases until the slightest physical effort is followed by great difficulty in breathing. This major crippling disease of the lungs is progressive and results in total incapacitation. Death finally occurs either from heart failure or from an acute episode of infection. Drugs relieve bronchospasm, and antibiotics produce brilliant results in combating the pneumonias from which emphysema patients suffer recurrently, but there is no cure. Criteria for early diagnosis are lacking. In the absence of definitive information as to cause, measures which prevent bronchial irritation and cough may help in prevention.

Occupational Diseases of the Lungs.—The pneumoconioses are lung diseases due to inhalation and retention in the lungs of industrial dusts, with the production of fibrosis. Silicosis (*q.v.*), the most important pneumoconiosis, occurs as a result of inhalation of fine particles of quartz. Disability is due to the emphysema associated with the progressive fibrosis. Silicotics are more susceptible to tuberculosis than are nonsilicotics. Asbestosis may develop in those exposed to inhalation of asbestos fibres. Over a protracted course, it involves the pleurae and pericardium—the coverings of the lungs and heart—and causes heart failure. Prevention of inhalation of such dusts is important, since there are no successful cures once the fibroses have actually developed. Berylliosis, an acute disease associated with extreme shortness of breath, was largely caused by the inhalation of beryllium phosphors in the manufacture of fluorescent lamps; cases even occurred in persons living in the neighbourhood of such plants. The industry has changed its manufacturing process so that fewer and fewer cases are seen. Treatment with steroid hormones is suppressive. A number of other less common pneumoconioses occur due to exposure to diatomaceous earths, finely divided tin, etc.

"Farmer's lung" is an acute pneumonitis resulting from the handling of a variety of dusty, moldy, organic materials. Repeated exposure produces recurrence. "Silo filler's disease," another uncommon disease reported among agricultural workers, is a pneumonitis apparently caused by the inhalation of certain oxides of nitrogen. Bagassosis occurs as a result of inhaling bagasse, a residue from sugar cane. (*See* also DANGEROUS OCCUPATIONS; PNEUMOCONIOSIS.)

Nonoccupational Disseminated Diseases of the Lung.—Sarcoidosis, a widespread disease which often involves the lungs, is characterized frequently by dramatic bilateral chest X-ray abnormalities in the presence of few or no respiratory symptoms. The causative agent is unknown. Most of the patients have come from the southeastern United States, and the U.S. Public Health Service has postulated a relationship to some of the pollens of pine forests in that area.

M. Bergmann and his co-workers applied the term thesaurosis to a disease they reported, implying that it resulted from the storage of macromolecules of resins used in hair spray and inhaled by the sprayer. Two cases of bilateral lung disease were found associated with the use of hair spray. Bergmann produced experimental granulomas in guinea pigs by injecting into them the residue from a well-known hair spray suspended in saline solution.

Tumours.—A dramatic rise in the incidence of lung cancer occurred after about 1930 in the United States, England and Wales, Australia, Canada, Denmark, Japan and Turkey. The rise was much more marked in men, among whom, in the United States, lung cancer became the commonest cancer. A statistical association with smoking has been pointed out by numerous British and U.S. investigators. Since lung cancer is found in urban rather than in rural areas, the possible causative role of air pollutants needs study also. As of the mid-1960s the only cure for the disease was surgical removal before distant spread could occur. Five-year survival rates reported by surgeons were less than 10%.

See CANCER; TUMOUR; LARYNGITIS; *see* also references under "Respiratory System, Diseases of" in the Index.

(K. R. B.)

RESSEL, JOSEF LUDWIG FRANZ (1793–1857), an inventor of the screw propeller for steamships, was born at Chrudim, Bohemia, June 29, 1793. He first tried a small boat fitted with a screw propeller at the bow, turned by two men (1826). Ressel obtained his Austrian patent in 1827, and a British patent, believed to have been also on his behalf, was obtained in 1828 by Charles Cummerow. Ressel tried his steamboat, the "Civetta" of 48 tons' displacement, at Trieste in 1829. The screw propeller was of copper, 5 ft. 2 in. diameter, and placed at the stern. The vessel attained a speed of six knots. Ressel died of malaria in the night of Oct. 9–10, 1857, at Laibach (now Ljubljana, Yugos.). In 1924 his native town, Chrudim, raised a monument to his memory.

See Ferdinand Thomas, *Josef Ressel, der Erfinder der Schiffsschraube* (1880). (H. P. ST.)

REST: *see* MUSICAL NOTATION: *Development of Notation.*

RESTAURANT. The word restaurant, from the French *restaurer* ("to restore"), was originally used to describe a nourishing soup. It came later to be used for taverns where this soup, with other food, was served to the public.

The first dining room to be known as a restaurant was opened in 1765 by A. Boulanger, a soup vendor in Paris. Referring to his soup as a *restaurant* ("restorative"), Boulanger inscribed on the sign above his door the Latin phrase *Venite ad me; vos qui stomacho laboratis et ego restaurabo vos* ("Come to me, you with laboured stomachs and I will restore you").

Early Inns and Taverns.—Inns and taverns have probably existed since the beginning of trade and commerce. In ancient Greece the *leschai*, primarily a local club, served meals to strangers as well as to its local members. By the 5th century B.C. there were sumptuous hostelries called *phatne* that served a local and transient clientele of traders, envoys, and government officials. Hotels had separate dining rooms in which the excellence of the food varied with the chef. Meat from sacrificial altars was served, a practice that continued in Greece and Rome until Christian times, and winecake, honey, dried figs, cheesecake, ham, and sweetbreads were among the dishes available.

In ancient Rome no man of any social standing could be seen in a tavern, although one type of establishment, the *lupanar*, flourished behind locked doors on the quietest of side streets, and men with veiled heads entered in the dark of night to dine, drink, or gamble. Nor was the reputation undeserved, for the *deversoria*, *tabernae*, *cauponae*, and *bibulae* of republican and imperial Rome were haunts of the jaded and degraded at best, and of criminal types at worst. Yet cooked delicacies and full meals were traditionally served in the *caupona* (low-class inn) and *taberna meritoria* (better-class tavern). These were long chambers having vaulted ceilings, with serving boys standing at semiattention and the proprietor sitting at a raised platform at one end. The walls were decorated with inscriptions and decorations scrawled with burned sticks. Often food was on display near the front—eggs, goose liver pâté, ham, cheese, fowl, and game—to draw customers. The fare served inside was more likely to be sluggish pea soup, chick-peas fried or in porridge, twice-cooked cabbage or raw vegetables soaked in vinegar, or boiled sheeps' heads, all highly seasoned with garlic, onions, asafetida (a gum resin of certain Oriental plants), and pungent sauces, the commonest base for which was *garum,* the juice from putrid fish entrails.

The restaurants of Roman England were the *cauponae* and the *tabernae* of Rome itself. These were followed by alehouses, run by women (alewives) and marked by a broom stuck out above the door, and in the 12th century by cookshops, from which most customers carried away cooked meats, though they could also eat them on the premises.

The English inns of the Middle Ages were sanctuaries of wayfaring strangers, cutthroats, thieves, and political malcontents. The tavern, the predecessor of the modern restaurant, originated the custom of providing a daily meal at a fixed time.

By the middle of the 16th century the dining-out habit was well established among townsmen of all classes. Most taverns offered a good dinner for 1s. or less, with wine and ales as extras. Tobacco was also sold after its introduction into England in 1565. Taverns offered companionship as well as refreshment, and some of the better houses became regular meeting places and unofficial clubhouses. Among the more famous London taverns of Tudor times were the Mermaid, frequented by Ben Jonson and his friends; the Boar's Head, associated with Shakespeare's Sir John Falstaff; and the Falcon, where actors and theatre managers of the day gathered.

Samuel Sorbière, a noted French scientist, observed on a visit to England in 1663:

the English are not very Dainty; their Tables are covered with large Dishes of Meat; they are Strangers to Bisks and Pottages; their Pastry is course and ill-baked; their Stewed Fruits cannot be eat; they scarce ever make use of Forks or Ewers, for they wash their Hands by dipping them into a Bason of Water. There is scarce a Day passes but a Tradesman goes to the Alehouse or Tavern to smoke with some of his Friends, and therefore Publick Houses are numerous here.

César de Saussure in 1725 on a visit from Switzerland observed:

in London there are a great number of coffee houses, most of which are not over clean or well furnished owing to the great number of people who resort to these places and because of the smoke, which would quickly destroy good furniture. In these coffee houses you can partake of chocolate or tea or coffee, and all sorts of liquors, served hot, also in many places you can have wine or punch or ale. What attracts enormously are the gazettes and other public papers.... Workmen habitually begin the day by going to a coffee house in order to read the latest news.

Certain "ordinaries" run by Frenchmen in London seem to have been closer to the modern idea of a restaurant than the contemporary taverns and coffeehouses. The set dinner of one or two dishes was the 18th-century equivalent of the modern *table d'hôte* restaurant meal.

In France Catherine de Médicis, with the help of Italian cooks, revolutionized cookery, and by the time Boulanger founded his restaurant, shortly before the French Revolution, Frenchmen had become discriminating, and nobles vied with each other over the excellence of their cooks. During and after the Reign of Terror, the shortage of nobility created a surplus of cooks, and to survive many of these opened their own eating places. By 1804 Paris had from 500 to 600 restaurants, and to dine in them had become the fashion.

The identity of the first public dining place in the U.S. is obscure. It is certain, however, that it was known as an inn, tavern, or ordinary, names not always interchangeable. It is probable that taverns appeared in the U.S. almost as soon as the first Dutch settlers arrived. Boston's first tavern, Cole's, opened its doors in 1634. New York's first tavern was opened in Dutch Colonial days by Governor Kieft, who stated that he was tired of entertaining strangers and travelers in his own home and thus opened a tavern to lodge and feed them. The building became New Amsterdam's (and later New York's) city hall and was used for that purpose until the present city hall was built in the 1880s.

Modern Restaurants.—*France.*—French cuisine is generally agreed to be the luxury cuisine of the world, and in the 20th

century it has been offered in many first-class restaurants and hotels around the globe, so much so that in some cities, Rio de Janeiro, for example, native cuisine is almost nonexistent in restaurants catering to an international clientele. Among the highlights of French cuisine are three varieties of steak: *chateaubriand,* or sirloin; *tournedos,* or filet mignon; and *entrecôte,* the French minute steak. French roasted and grilled meats are first-rate, as are their seafoods. The French are famous for delicate sauces for both meats and vegetables, omelets and soufflés, and stews, such as *pot-au-feu* and *bourguignonne.*

Of the European restaurants, those of France have the most individual character. Paris, the gourmet's paradise, has more than 3,000 restaurants, and of these, the old established places are still the most reliable. It is very difficult to find bad cuisine in Paris or, indeed, anywhere in France. Most provincial towns have well-known restaurants that specialize in a local dish. Southern France, particularly the Riviera, abounds in restaurants and cafés of all standards.

Italy.—Italian cuisine embodies an almost endless series of regional delicacies. The cooking of Emilia-Romagna in the north is said to be Italy's best. *Tagliatelle al ragu* (thin slices of *pasta* made with eggs and served with a magnificent ragout) is one of the region's famous dishes, along with fine seafoods and Parmesan cheese dishes. Tripe *alla Romana, gnocchi* (noodles with cheese and tomato sauce), and *saltimbocca* (veal and ham slices fried in butter with sage leaves) are typical Roman dishes. Italy's finest restaurants are found in Venice, Turin, and Rome.

Greece.—The restaurants of modern Athens—specializing in such national delicacies as *dolmadakia* (vine leaves stuffed with seasoned rice, meat, and onions), *moussaka* (eggplant and meat served with cheese and tomato), and *tyropitta* (Grecian cheesecake)—are often small, delightful, tavernlike places where native games, singing, and dancing go on with meals. The hotel dining rooms serve the best in regional and Continental dishes.

Switzerland.—Switzerland is renowned for its restaurants, where cuisine is for the greater part in the French style. The Swiss are expert organizers, meticulously clean, and provide first-class waiters.

Germany.—The large cities of Germany have good restaurants; those of the top-rate hotels are usually renowned. Most of the restaurants along the Rhine and the Moselle and, indeed, throughout the wine-producing country, tend to concentrate on local wines.

Portugal.—Portugal, with its ancient forts, castles, and monasteries converted into hotels and restaurants, offers reasonably good food with mostly French cooking. In most Portuguese restaurants the price of the meal includes a carafe of wine. The state-owned *pousadas* ("inns") are difficult to better.

England.—The late 19th-century tavern was replaced by the ornate hotel dining room and by the restaurant itself, which came to England under its French name in the 1880s. The tavern ceased to be the haunt of fashionable gentlemen, who preferred their clubs (*see* CLUB), and out of the old tavern emerged today's public house. In 1884, the first tea shop was opened near London Bridge, and ten years later a similar shop was opened by J. Lyons & Co. Ltd., in Piccadilly. These were the forerunners of vast chains of tea shops, where first teas and later more substantial meals were served. Their immediate popularity was due largely to women, who could not frequent taverns or fashionable restaurants unless escorted. The first department store restaurant was opened in Whiteley's in 1873, and the idea spread rapidly to other stores.

After 1951 restaurants of all types appeared, specializing in foods of all nations. Coffee bars flourished, though a far cry from the first English coffeehouse opened in Oxford in 1650. Espresso bars (so-called from the method of making coffee in machines originally imported from Italy), following the first of the coffee-houses, sprang up overnight, until almost every district in London boasted its coffee society centre, and the espresso bar became a national institution. The snack bar and the milk bar, which originated in the U.S., also became extremely popular, as did cafeterias.

Typical English food compares well with the delicacies of any nation. Savories like Welsh rarebit and Scotch woodcock; entrees like roast beef and Yorkshire pudding, steak and kidney pie, roast lamb and mint sauce, mixed grill and Dover sole; desserts like trifle, delicately flavoured puddings, and egg-custard pie are served.

United States.—The decades after World War I saw the decline of the exclusive restaurant. Though there are still many fashionable eating places, the largest number of restaurants have become successful by serving meals in pleasant surroundings and at popular prices. By far the preponderance of restaurants and coffee shops offer regional dishes, and if there is any one dish which might be tagged the national dish it is probably the hamburger, available from the smallest hamlet drugstore counter to the most lavishly endowed restaurant, although in the latter it might be disguised on the menu with a French pseudonym such as *bifteck haché.*

Several types of restaurants that are characteristically "American" include the cafeteria, the steak house, the seafood house, and the roadside restaurant. Perhaps the most popular foods offered are grilled dishes, prepared over a charcoal fire or under an open flame.

Many restaurants throughout the country offer the cuisine of other nations. The best known "foreign" restaurants are French, Italian, and Chinese. Most Italian restaurants are Neapolitan, or created in the style of Naples, relying heavily on tomato sauces and spices, as opposed to North Italian cuisine, which is subtler and closer to the French. Chinese restaurants are mainly Cantonese —this is true throughout the world, although it is only one of five schools of cooking in China. Within recent years there has been an outcropping of Polynesian, Japanese, and Mexican restaurants, principally in metropolitan centres. Polynesian food has enormous appeal because of its flavour and its exotic nature and presentation (*e.g.*, food served in hollowed-out pineapple or coconut shells). First-class Japanese restaurants offer a delicate cuisine. The most popular dish is beef sukiyaki, made with wafer-thin slices of beef, soy sauce, mirin (a type of wine), bean curd made of fermented soy beans, and vegetables. Much of the Mexican cuisine served in the nation's restaurants is Mexican by inspiration but American in execution. Among the most popular dishes are tamales, chili, and guacamole, a dish made with pureed avocado and chopped onion or garlic.

Recent Trends.—Restaurant owners have been beset with relatively new problems involving labour and cost control that have affected standards of service and the quality of food served, especially in the *grand luxe* establishments. Another major problem is a lack of training facilities for chefs and for the service staff, although Europe has many trade schools, and several universities in the U.S. offer catering courses. Until recent decades chefs trained in the European tradition spent months, and even years, at various stations where sauces, roasts, fish, desserts, and other items were prepared. There has been a decline in the number of those entering the cooking profession in both Europe and the U.S.

In the mid-1950s the average cost per seat of existing restaurants in the U.S. was about $500; in 1960 the per-seat cost of restaurants planned was about $3,000. With increased minimum wages for kitchen and dining room staffs, it became necessary to reduce expenditures for labour, equipment, and food. Several decades ago there was little accounting for food costs in first-rate kitchens, but cost control has become a vital factor in restaurant operation. Also, a more weight-conscious public prefers less rich foods.

Both the cafeteria and the specialty house were brought into being by rising costs. The cafeteria meets the problem by serving simple yet good food quickly to many people, using few employees. Cafeterias, long popular in the U.S., are now becoming more popular in Europe. Most French cafeterias provide wine in carafes and offer *le service quick.* The specialty house meets costs by limiting items on the menu, thus reducing the outlay for equipment and labour.

The early 1960s saw the large-scale refurbishment of hotel dining rooms and in many cases their conversion into lower-overhead specialty houses in an attempt to restore the dining room to its former preeminence and to help hotels meet the competition of motels and motor hotels, whose eating facilities are usually minimal.

BIBLIOGRAPHY.—H. Ballam and R. Lewis (eds.), *The Visitors' Book;* *England and the English as Others Have Seen Them, A.D. 1500–1950* (1950); D. B. Wyndham Lewis, *The Hooded Hawk; or, The Case of Mr. Boswell* (1946); A. L. Simon, *The Gourmet's Week-End Book* (1952); R. Postgate (ed.), *The Good Food Guide* (published biennially).

RESTIF, NICOLAS EDME (RESTIF DE LA BRETONNE) (1734–1806), French novelist, a forerunner of Balzac and Zola, rated above Rousseau by Paul Valéry, compared to Defoe by George Saintsbury, to Proust by Havelock Ellis, and to André Gide by Marc Chadourne, his biographer, is a much debated figure in the history of literature and ideas. Born at Sacy, Yonne, on Oct. 23, 1734, he later went to Paris, where he worked as a journeyman printer and where, in 1760, he married Anne (or Agnès) Lebègue.

Restif produced about 200 volumes, many of them printed by his own hand, and his writings cover a wide range of subjects with astonishing licence. He has been heralded by Chadourne as a prophet who foreshadowed the atom, the sputnik, flying men and air squadrons, the missile that shoots into interplanetary and interstellar space, bacteriology, atomic energy, the Superman, dictatorship, totalitarianism, the United States of Europe, social security, and Communism. But he has also been recognized as "the Casanova of the stews, the Rousseau of the gutter, or Balzac's caveman." His life and loves, real or fancied, have given him notoriety. He may not have been a fetishist or a pervert in the technical sense, but his vindication of incest was no mere rationalist exercise; after the age of 45 he felt compelled to convince himself that he was the father of the women he took as his mistresses. His eroticism, which is tinged with mysticism, and his emotional lucidity are revealed in his autobiography, *Monsieur Nicolas* (16 volumes, 1794–97), much of which is set in the Parisian underworld of the period. It is his portrayal of 18th-century society that has led to his being called the Zola of his age.

Gérard de Nerval (*q.v.*), who thought of himself as the reincarnation of Restif, retold in *Les Illuminés* (1852) the story of Sara, one of the most striking episodes in *Monsieur Nicolas.* But as, for instance, when dealing with the story of the actress *la belle Guéant*, Nerval, in spite of much research, failed to distinguish fact from fiction, a task which Restif's vivid imagination has rendered difficult.

As well as *Monsieur Nicolas*, Restif's works include *Le Pied de Fanchette* (1769); *Le Pornographe* (1769), a plan for regulating prostitution said to have been carried out by the Emperor Joseph II and to have inspired authorities in other continental countries; *Le Paysan perverti* (1775) and *La Paysanne pervertie* (1784), recast and republished as *Paysan-Paysanne perverti* (1784); *La Vie de mon père* (1779); *Mes Inscriptions* (a journal for 1780–87, discovered in 1887); *Les Contemporaines* (42 volumes, 1780–85; to which should be added the 23 volumes of *Les Françaises, Les Parisiennes*, 1786–91); and *Ingénue Saxancour* (1785). The first editions of most of his books have long been bibliographical curiosities for their rarity, the beautiful and curious illustrations they contain, and the quaint typographic system adopted. Just before his death (in Paris on Feb. 3, 1806), Napoleon gave Restif a place in the ministry of police. His funeral service, in Notre Dame on Feb. 5, was attended by 1,800 persons; they included Louis de Fontanes and the comtesse de Beauharnais, who had befriended him.

BIBLIOGRAPHY.—*Editions, etc.: Monsieur Nicolas*, 6 vol. (Editions Pauvert, 1959), Eng. trans. by Havelock Ellis (1930), also ed. and trans. by R. Baldick as *Monsieur Nicolas, or the Human Heart Laid Bare* (1964); *Les Contemporains*, etc., ed. by J. Assézat with useful introduction, 3 vol. (1875); Paul Lacroix, *Bibliographie et Iconographie de tous les ouvrages de Restif de la Bretonne* (1873); Gérard de Nerval, *Les Confidences de Nicolas: Restif de la Bretonne: Les Illuminés* (1852); *Sara*, with preface by Maurice Blanchot (1949).
Biography and Criticism: C. R. Dawes, *Restif de la Bretonne* (1946); A. Bégué, *État présent des études sur Rétif de la Bretonne* (1948); J. Rives Childs, *Restif de la Bretonne, témoignages et jugements. Bibliographie* (1949); Marc Chadourne, *Restif de la Bretonne ou le siècle prophétique* (1958).   (R. NI.)

RESTRICTIVE TRADE PRACTICES (REGISTRAR AND COURT). In the United Kingdom, the Restrictive Trade Practices Act, 1956, provided for the appointment of a registrar of restrictive trade practices and for the establishment of a Restrictive Practices

Court which was to be a division of the High Court (q.v.). The act rendered illegal the practice of collective resale price maintenance and provided for the reconstitution of the Monopolies Commission which would deal only with monopolies and other practices exempted from registration (sec. 7 and 8) and not to be investigated by the new court (see MONOPOLIES COMMISSION).

The registrar compiles a register of restrictive trading agreements and brings proceedings before the Restrictive Practices Court. Any two or more persons producing or supplying goods or carrying out any process of manufacture within the United Kingdom are required to register any agreements between them concerned with prices, conditions of sale, quantities of the goods to be produced or supplied, processes of manufacture, and persons to be supplied. Various exemptions from registration are made, notably in the case of agreements concerning goods supplied solely for export. The register of agreements is open to the public, except for a special section containing information relating to secret processes, etc. (sec. 11). The court consists of five judges and not more than ten other members qualified by virtue of their knowledge of industry, commerce, or public affairs. The court can sit in divisions, each consisting of at least one judge and two other members.

The registrar must refer to the court agreements on the register (the Board of Trade can give him directions regarding the order of cases to be taken). The court declares void restrictions contrary to the public interest and makes an order restraining the parties from giving effect to the agreement. Agreements are contrary to the public interest unless they pass through one of the seven "gateways" (sec. 21). These gateways are concerned with the effect that the removal of the restrictions would have on the quality of the goods to which the restrictions apply, the level of unemployment in an area, the export trade, etc. The court must also be satisfied that on balance the agreements are not unreasonable, having regard to any detriment that they cause to the public.

The 1964 Resale Prices Act gave the registrar and the court the further duty of considering those cases of resale price maintenance in which exemption was sought from the general prohibition of this practice contained in the act. In consequence the maximum number of judges was increased.

See also FAIR TRADE LAWS.

BIBLIOGRAPHY.—Restrictive Trade Practices Act, 1956 (4 & 5 Eliz. 2. Ch. 68) and Resale Prices Act, 1964 (Ch. 58); R. O. Wilberforce, A. Campbell, and N. P. M. Elles, The Law of Restrictive Trade Practices and Monopolies (1957); A. Hunter, "Competition and the Law," Manchester School (Jan. 1959); J. B. Heath, "The 1956 Restrictive Trade Practices Act: Price Agreements and the Public Interest," Manchester School (Jan. 1958); J. Lever, The Law of Restrictive Trade Agreements (1962); J. Heath, Still Not Enough Competition (1963).
(AU. SI.)

RESURRECTION: see ESCHATOLOGY; JESUS CHRIST.

RESURRECTION PLANT (Anastatica hierochuntica), a small herb of the family Cruciferae, called also rose of Jericho, native to Arabia, Iran and Egypt.

Upon the ripening of the seeds during the dry season, the leaves fall off and the branches curve inward so that the dry plant assumes a globular form. It then rolls about in the manner of a tumbleweed until the rainy season. When wet the branches unfold and it assumes for a time the appearance of a living plant.

The name is also given to two other plants. One is the mosslike Selaginella lepidophylla which also dries up into a ball and expands when wet. It is called also bird's-nest moss and is found from Texas southward to Peru. The other is the resurrection fern (Polypodium polypodioides), the commonest epiphytic fern in Florida.

RETAILING, the business activity concerned with the sale of merchandise directly to ultimate consumers; i.e., to people who buy for personal or household use rather than for reprocessing or resale. In industrialized countries most retail sales take place in fixed establishments, or stores, especially devoted to this activity. However, there is also some nonstore retailing, including mail-order and telephone business, sales by house-to-house canvassers, street peddling and sales from trucks, carts and automatic vending machines.

General discussions of retailing often include all stores and shops catering to the general public. Strictly speaking, however, personal service businesses, such as barber shops, beauty parlors and dry cleaners, are not part of the retail structure because they derive little or none of their income from the sale of merchandise. Government reports on retail trade activities usually exclude the receipts and expenditures of such establishments; in some cases, they also exclude restaurants and other establishments where food and drink are served.

Importance of Retailing.—The proportions of total national income and labour force associated with retail trade vary greatly from country to country. In general, retail trade is quantitatively most significant in nations with high material living standards, high degrees of industrialization and marked economic specialization. Because consumers in such countries look to the marketing system for practically all the goods they use, their retailers handle a larger total output than is the case in lands where most people support themselves wholly or partly through subsistence agriculture. In spite of the rise of self-service stores, discussed below, retailing has not been as susceptible as either manufacturing or agriculture to the introduction of labour-saving methods, such as mechanization. Consequently, the growth of retail trade in industrialized countries over the years has caused a significant expansion of retail employment.

U.S. retail employment increased steadily from 1870 to 1950, rising from about 5% of the work force to about 12%, exclusive of restaurant workers. A somewhat similar increase occurred in Great Britain, although shortages and government controls sharply reduced retail employment during both World Wars I and II. British retailing absorbed about 10% of the labour force in the 1960s. Elsewhere, retail employment estimates made at various dates in the 1950s ranged from 6% to 8% for western Europe and Japan to substantially under 6% in India and considerably less than 1% to 3% in most portions of tropical Africa. However, the interregional differences in retail employment probably were not as marked as these last figures suggest. Many students of African and Caribbean economic structures believe that official reports seriously underestimate the number of part-time, self-employed and unpaid family workers in such areas.

There have been relatively few attempts at analyzing total national expenditures for retail distribution. Investigators have calculated that retail margins (selling prices minus cost of goods sold) account for nearly 30% of the final value of all goods sold by retailers in the United States and Great Britain. These margins, of course, included retailers' payments to firms in other industries for such purposes as transportation, occupancy and advertising equipment and services. Cox, Fichhandler and Goodman concluded that the retailers' own services (after subtracting all such disbursements to other firms) constituted about 18% of the final value of all commodities purchased by U.S. householders. The department of commerce has credited retailing as the source of about 10% of U.S. national income.

The significance of retail development is not entirely measurable in statistical terms. Retailers, especially innovating retailers, have played an active role in helping to stimulate the production and consumption of commodities, as well as performing the more passive role of bridging the gap between producers and consumers. A National Planning association study reported that a mail-order and department store chain which entered the Mexican market in 1946 helped foster that country's industrialization through assistance to consumer goods manufacturers and helped encourage the rise of a middle class through the provision of quality merchandise at reasonable prices. Large U.S. retail organizations served much the same function, particularly from 1870 to 1920, and so did European department store, multiple shop (chain store), and co-operative organizations.

History.—As a specialized business, retailing apparently grew out of the activities of roving traders and of craftsmen who made and sold utensils and ornaments in their dwellings. The considerable development of trade in early Mesopotamian and Egyptian civilizations and in Minoan Crete suggests that retail buying and selling were very common, although nothing is known concerning the proportions of their populations that supported themselves through retailing alone. Even though their ruling classes scorned and despised all merchants, specialized shops were an important element in both Greek and Roman urban life.

After the fall of Rome, retailing declined in the western world along with the general reduction in living standards. Subsistence agriculture, homecrafts and the manorial system supplied most of the goods intended for personal consumption. The rest were distributed through periodic fairs and markets, crude shops and visits of chapmen (itinerant merchants). Later, retail stores assumed importance as living standards rose and a larger proportion of the population lived in cities and towns. However, the differences between even the most elegant shops of the early 19th century and their crude predecessors of the dark ages were largely matters of appearance and inventory. Retail organization and operating methods remained substantially unchanged, except for improvements in bookkeeping techniques, until about 1860. During the latter half of the 19th century, increasing urbanization, improved communications and increasing output of factory-made products provided fertile ground for the development of large retail organizations, including department stores, chain stores, mail-order houses and consumer co-operative societies.

The operating economies enjoyed by these large retailers at various stages of development have rested upon policies of both expansion and concentration. Savings resulted, on one hand, from spreading management and overhead costs over a wider assortment of goods, as in the case of department stores and supermarkets; over a larger number of locations, as in the case of chain stores; or over a combination of retailing, wholesaling and even manufacturing, as in the case of some chain stores and co-operative societies. On the other hand some large retailers have gained by concentrating upon popular, fast-selling merchandise, as in the case of discount houses and unit price (variety) chains; and by transferring some traditional functions of retailers to the consumer, as in the case of self-service stores.

A common pattern marks the history of each type of large-scale retailing, such as the department store. Each appeared first as a low-cost method of doing business and attracted trade largely through low prices. Each new method seemed an aggressive challenge to established ways of doing business. Conventional retailers and others reacted by bitterly attacking the new entrants as unfair competitors and as potential monopolists. This opposition abated as each new group exhausted its immediate opportunities for rapid expansion. Costs and prices rose, partially in response to competitive pressures that forced increasing investment to provide additional shopping conveniences, and gradually the share of total retail sales obtained by the new entrants stabilized or declined somewhat. Although every new type of retailing was once criticized as a threat to the independent merchants, those merchants still do the bulk of the total business in every country in which retail trade is not a government function.

Co-operatives.—Consumer co-operatives were the first of the large-scale innovations in retailing. The modern co-operative movement began in 1844 with a small grocery shop established by a group of impoverished weavers in Rochdale, Eng., although there had been many previous attempts at co-operation. It spread to Scandinavia and also to Switzerland, where a very aggressive retail chain, called Migros, was converted to consumer ownership in 1940.

The co-operative movement originally espoused two basic ideas: (1) democratic customer-owner control and participation in the work and profits of the enterprise; and (2) production for use instead of for profit, and hence, implicitly, elimination of expenses involved in attracting trade. The very growth of the movement forced some departures, in practice, from these principles. Membership control became more and more indirect, and the operations of the societies were increasingly entrusted to professional executives and staff. Adjustment to rising standards of living among the members, as well as competitive pressures, forced the co-operatives to carry larger assortments, particularly of luxuries and semi-luxuries, to advertise extensively and to build more attractive shops. The successes of British and European co-operatives seem to have resulted as much from the skills and abilities of the managers as from the fact of co-operative organization.

Department Stores.—A reorganization of the Bon Marché, a Parisian dry goods shop, created the world's first true department store (c. 1865). This example was soon followed by merchants in many U.S., British and northern European cities. The essential feature of department store organization was the delegation of responsibility and authority to subordinate executives. Each department head was made responsible for purchasing a related group of commodities and for overseeing their sale in a distinct section of the store. Thus department stores could offer much wider assortments of goods than the conventional shops in which only the owner or a few partners handled all supervisory and executive duties. Low prices, as well as large assortments, drew a large volume of trade, thereby providing reductions in operating costs that made the low prices possible. Department stores were also distinguished by the general use of fixed prices, clearly marked on the goods, instead of the bargaining process common to many smaller stores. This policy was not as rigid as is commonly assumed, however. Until 1940, for example, many U.S. department stores gave discounts to favoured classes of customers, such as teachers and clergymen. Eventually operating costs and margins increased, and much of the competitive threat these large stores had originally posed for small merchants waned. Department store margins in the U.S. rose from about 20% of selling price in 1900 to about 36% after World War II, and department stores as a group obtained only between 5 to 10% of total retail sales, both in the U.S. and in Britain.

Chain Stores.—Modern chain stores or multiples, i.e., groups of separate shops under common ownership and direction, first appeared in the U.S. and Great Britain between 1850 and 1870. However, prototypes can be found in the string of Canadian trading posts established in the early 18th century by the Hudson's Bay company, in the Mitsui apothecary shops established in Japan around 1630, and even in ancient China and Pompeii. Chain organization clearly demonstrates the operating advantages and disadvantages of large-scale retailing. The chains have benefited in the following ways: (1) from being able to purchase both merchandise and supplies in the most economical markets, often going so far as to direct the manufacture of goods to their specifications; (2) from the employment of highly skilled specialists in many executive tasks; (3) from standardization of operating methods; (4) from spreading risks over many locations; (5) from an ability to experiment in one store and apply the results to many; and (6) from economies in advertising and sales promotion. Many chains have also been able to lower prices through elimination of superfluous services. On the other hand, the chains have suffered from a lack of flexibility in adjusting to local conditions and from the increasing costs of their own bureaucratic administration. Discriminatory tax and licensing regulations, imposed particularly during the years between World Wars I and II, hampered chain store development, especially in some European countries and, to a lesser extent, in some U.S. states. Considerable concentration characterized the U.S. chain store movement after World War II, with many smaller chains being merged into larger organizations and with many chains using one large store to replace several smaller units. Chains operating ten or more establishments do from 20% to 25% of total retail business in both the U.S. and Great Britain, and are particularly important in the distribution of highly standardized commodities that consumers purchase repetitively, such as grocery products. Independent retailers in many countries countered the competition of the chains in part through the successful formation of voluntary or co-operative chains (which should be clearly distinguished from consumer co-operative stores). These are more or less loose affiliations of independent merchants, often formed under wholesaler sponsorship, to purchase merchandise jointly, to share experience and advice, and to engage in joint advertising and sales promotion. They tend to be heavily concentrated in food retailing.

Supermarkets and Self-Service.—Supermarkets, large stores selling groceries and other products through self-service methods, first gained acceptance in the U.S. during the great depression of the 1930s. Although low prices seemed to be their principal attraction at first, customers apparently liked the large assortments these stores offered and the opportunities for inspecting and selecting merchandise without the unwelcome attentions of salesclerks. The success of the early supermarkets led to the adoption of self-service techniques in all large-scale food retailing in the U.S., and also, but much less extensively, in hardware, variety and drug stores, and in some department store divisions. Self-service stores spread rapidly in Europe after 1954 and by the early 1960s they accounted for 25% of all food sales in Germany and the Netherlands.

Self-service has required the creation of open display fixtures that allow the customer to inspect and handle the merchandise. The package, rather than the salesclerk's persuasion, is the principal selling factor under self-service. This has encouraged improvements in packaging materials and design, has fostered standardization of goods, and undoubtedly has contributed to the growth of well-advertised manufacturers' brands, which the consumer will accept upon sight.

Resale Price Maintenance.—Differences in costs and in price policies among retailers handling the same commodities can lead to intensive price competition. Retailers in many countries have sought legislation that would limit such competition through licensing and tax restrictions on vigorous competitors, such as chains and co-operatives; through laws against "loss leader selling," *i.e.*, retailing some items below cost to attract trade; and through resale price maintenance, an arrangement whereby manufacturers specify the prices at which merchants must resell their products. Some manufacturers have felt that such control helps protect the reputation of their products, but small retailers, who call such arrangements "fair trade," have been the most ardent advocates of price maintenance. Such arrangements were generally considered illegal restraints of trade in the U.S. until the federal Miller-Tydings Act (1937) permitted the states to authorize price maintenance on goods moving in interstate commerce. Permissive statutes, adopted in 45 states, were generally sustained in the courts until about 1950, but during the next decade they were upheld in some jurisdictions and limited in others, in spite of additional supporting federal legislation (McGuire act, 1952). British (1956) and German (1957) acts outlawed agreements among manufacturers for collective enforcement of resale prices, but both sanctioned resale price maintenance by individual suppliers. Legislation has made resale price maintenance generally illegal in Canada, France, Sweden, Denmark and Norway, though in some of these countries provision is made for exemptions in special cases (*see* FAIR TRADE LAWS).

Discount Houses.—Discount house (*q.v.*) is a vague term that originally denoted certain relatively small retail firms in the U.S. that operated in inconspicuous locations; made either some pretense or some attempt at restricting patronage to favoured groups such as civil servants; offered limited services; and sold electrical appliances, jewelry, luggage, sporting goods and perhaps furniture for considerably less than the going price. Legalization of resale price maintenance, which was mainly enforced in more conspicuous stores, gave consumers standards for judging discount values and undoubtedly helped foster discount house growth in the later 1930s and after World War II. Increased public attention to this growth in turn contributed to the legal and economic attacks on resale price maintenance after 1950. The discount houses eventually adopted many attributes of conventional retailing, and many firms developed chains of large, low-margin, self-service general merchandise stores, provoking retaliatory competition and partial adoption of discount retailing techniques in many department stores.

Current Trends.—General long-run increases in over-all productivity and consumer living standards suggest further increases in retail sales volume, employment and services. Tendencies towards urbanization that provide highly concentrated markets are favoring large-scale retailers. Planned suburban shopping centres are also fostered by urbanization. New methods of stock control, using mechanical and electronic computers for statistical analysis of merchandise receipts, sales and requirements, are beginning to help the large firms increase turnover rates and reduce expenses. At the same time, rising standards of living and in-

creased consumer desires for luxury and convenience provide new opportunities for small retailers who can offer specialized or differentiated services. *See* CHAIN STORE; COOPERATIVES; DEPARTMENT STORE; MAIL-ORDER BUSINESS; *see* also references under "Retailing" in the Index.

BIBLIOGRAPHY.—H. Barger, *Distribution's Place in the American Economy Since 1869* (1955); W. R. Davidson and P. L. Brown, *Retailing Management*, 2nd ed. (1960); D. J. Duncan and C. F. Phillips, *Retailing*, 6th ed. (1963); J. Jefferys and D. Knee, *Retailing in Europe* (1962).   (S. C. Ho.)

RETALHULEU, a department in southwestern Guatemala on the Pacific lowland. Area 717 sq.mi.; pop. (1964) 122,829. Coffee is grown on the slopes of the highlands at the northern end of the department. In the lowlands at the base of the highlands there are plantations of sugar cane, cotton, rice, and cacao. Much land is devoted to the feeding of beef cattle. Retalhuleu, the departmental capital, is served by rail and highway. A railroad connects with the port of Champerico.   (P. E. J.)

RETARDED CHILDREN. The phrase "retarded child" means one whose rate of development has been in any way slower than average. The retardation may involve physical, mental, educational, or emotional development. With earlier psychological writers, however, the phrase, when used without further qualification, usually refers to backwardness in general intelligence. In studying mental defectives in Paris, Alfred Binet noticed that in their intellectual processes they commonly resembled children three or four years younger than themselves and inferred that their condition resulted from the fact that their rate of mental growth had been retarded from birth onward. Accordingly, he suggested that a child's level of intelligence might be measured in terms of a mental age, with the difference between mental age and chronological age indicating the severity of the retardation. However, a backwardness of (say) two years would mean very different things at the age of 5 and 15; and a baby of 12 months could not be retarded by that amount. Later investigations showed that, in point of fact, the range of individual variation increases from birth to puberty in rough proportion with chronological age. Hence, it was suggested that instead of taking the difference between the mental and chronological ages it would be better to take the quotient or ratio. Expressed as a percentage, the index so obtained is known as a mental ratio or an intelligence quotient (IQ).

Later writers use the term retarded child in a broader sense to include all those whose educational progress, from whatever cause, has been slower than that of an average child of the same chronological age. This is the definition suggested by the (British) Joint Committee on Mental Deficiency. Since the passing of the Education Act of 1944, however, the designation more frequently adopted in British official publications is "educationally subnormal." Occasionally the child's educational age is compared not with his chronological but with his mental age. In such cases an educational or achievement quotient is taken as the measure. With this interpretation a child whose tested intelligence was well above average would still be called retarded if his attainments in the chief school subjects were no more than those of the child whose intelligence was average for his age. However, the description of this group has evolved to be children with learning disabilities. There are many children who in their emotional behaviour show the impulsiveness, the lack of control, and the general modes of reaction distinctive of children several years younger: such children are often described as emotionally retarded, though here the term emotionally immature is more commonly employed. Finally, when a child's physical characteristics—height, weight, proportions, teeth, pubertal manifestations—are those of a younger child, he is sometimes described as physically retarded. There is a tendency for all types of retardation to go together.

Borderlines.—Since retardation is necessarily a matter of degree, the line between the retarded and the nonretarded must be a matter of convenience and convention. A pupil whose educational level is equivalent to that of children in the class below that which would be normal for his years needs no special treatment. Thus a child of 10, if normal, would be placed in a class containing children whose ages ranged from 9.5 to 10.5 years.

Those in the class below would range in age from 8.5 to 9.5 years. If the pupil is unable to do the work even of these younger children, then, as experience shows, he requires education in a specially organized class with those who are equally subnormal. This implies that at a chronological age of 10 the borderline should be drawn at an educational age of 8.5 or generally at an educational ratio of 85%, which is the line of demarcation usually adopted for administrative purposes.

In the case of so-called mental retardation (*i.e.*, retardation in tested intelligence) the upper borderline is similar. But a further classification is plainly desirable. The main division—between the milder cases and the more severe—is usually placed at an IQ of about 70. The figure is chosen because pupils below this level need educational provision in a special type of school. In the United Kingdom, before the Education Act of 1944, they had to be certified as mentally defective before they could be removed to such a school. The act abolished the need for certification and, provided the children are in some degree educable, for official purposes they are classed with the "merely dull or backward" as belonging to the educationally subnormal, though psychiatrists retain the older nomenclature.

In the United States children whose IQ falls below 70 are sometimes termed feebleminded.

Causes.—Educational retardation is due to a wide variety of conditions, and in most instances several factors contribute, although one usually stands out as the major cause. The commoner factors may be divided into two groups: extrinsic or environmental, and intrinsic or personal.

Among environmental causes statistical surveys show that home conditions are more significant than school conditions. Among the lower classes poverty, together with all the handicaps it brings in its train, is one of the most frequently reported. In Western countries, however, its influence has steadily diminished. The cultural conditions of the home—a low intellectual level or a lack of educative interests among the parents—appear far more important. But even in a comfortable and cultured home emotional disturbances within the family may at times so upset the child as to affect his work in the classroom. Of conditions more closely connected with the school, irregular attendance is the commonest. Almost equally frequent are inadequate organization of the classes, and inefficient or inappropriate methods of teaching.

Of conditions obtaining within the child himself, physical defects are less important than is popularly supposed; ill health forms a major factor in only about 10% of the cases. Innate inferiority of general intelligence occurs in well over three-quarters of the cases, and in about one-half it constitutes the major cause. Of more specific disabilities the most obvious are uncorrected defects in sight and hearing. More easily missed are defects in visual and auditory perception or imagery: some children are lacking in verbal facility, others in numerical ability, but by far the commonest defect is in mechanical memory. Temperamental conditions, notably emotional instability, are found among about 7%, often conjoined with motivational problems: the child is lazy and ill disciplined in the classroom and prone to petty delinquencies in his life out of school.

Education and Treatment.—The first step is to ascertain the cause of retardation. Where educational retardation is due primarily to basic weakness in general intelligence, it is to that extent irremediable, but much may be done by suitable training in a special school or institution. With milder cases, reclassification for specific subjects, individual coaching, attendance at a special centre (*e.g.*, for speech training), or transfer to a special class may be advised. In the investigation and treatment of special disabilities, assistance commonly is needed from an educational psychologist or child guidance clinic.   (Cy. B.)

Historically, scientific attempts to educate mentally retarded children began with the efforts of a French doctor, Jean Marc Gaspard Itard, during the latter part of the 18th century. In his classic book, *The Wild Boy of Aveyron* (1801), Itard related his five-year effort to train and educate an 11-year-old boy found running naked and wild in the woods of Aveyron. Later Édouard Séguin, a student of Itard's, devised an educational method using physical and sensory activities to develop mental processes. Séguin's published works (1846 and 1866) influenced Maria Montessori (*q.v.*), an Italian pediatrician who became an educator and the innovator of a unique method of training young mentally retarded children in Rome in the 1890s. Later she applied these methods to young normal children. Self-education through the use of specially designed "didactic materials" for sensorimotor training was the keynote of the system (*see also* PRE-ELEMENTARY EDUCATION: *History*).

In the United States the education of the mentally retarded was initiated in an institutional setting by Samuel Gridley Howe during the middle of the 19th century. Institutions for the training of the mentally retarded were then organized in all states. The first public-school special class was established in 1896.

Following World War II the demand for educational services for the retarded became more intense. Enrollment in special classes for the mentally retarded in the United States increased steadily from 87,000 in 1948 to an estimated 350,000 in the 1960s, but this provided education for only approximately one-third of the retarded needing such services.

In other countries there has also been a doubling and tripling of classes for mentally retarded children. A United Nations report (1960) compared programs throughout the world. This report indicated that where provisions were made, one-fifth to one-third of the retarded children were receiving special education. The others were either not in school or were in regular classes. Countries with low economic development usually had few special classes or none. Concentration of special classes in urban areas was common. In some countries, as in the Soviet Union, the problem of providing for rural children was solved by the establishment of boarding schools.

The organization of special classes follows different patterns in different localities. In the United States the pattern is, with few exceptions, to establish special classes in the regular school, with private boarding schools available for some. In some other countries special day schools enroll only retarded children. A third type of organization is the publicly operated boarding school for the retarded. This plan, as mentioned above, is appropriate for rural children. In many countries a combination of facilities is provided.

There has been a growing tendency, especially in the United States, to use the term "exceptional children" to designate those atypical children who deviate from the ordinary child in physical, social, or intellectual traits to such an extent that they require special educational provisions in special schools and classes. Mentally retarded children are usually classified educationally as either "educable" or "trainable." The educable retarded child is one whose IQ ranges between 50 and 75, and who is capable of attaining minimum literacy standards and supporting himself, partially or totally, at the adult level. The trainable retarded child is one whose IQ ranges between 30 and 50, and who is not expected to attain minimum literacy standards but who can be trained for self-help, social adjustment, and economic usefulness in the home or a sheltered environment.

The trainable mentally retarded have been providing an increasingly large proportion of those enrolled in state residential schools, while the educable are being served more and more in special day-school classes. However, community classes for the trainable are also on the increase under the auspices of health authorities, public-school systems, or social welfare departments. Programs for the educable retarded are under the auspices of educational authorities.

The cost of educating a mentally retarded child is twice that of educating an ordinary child. As a rule the education of a mentally retarded child is free when under public auspices; private boarding schools charge fees depending on the type of care and services provided.

The special education of the mentally retarded in special schools and classes is characterized by a number of features. The class size is generally limited to 10 or 15 so that more individualized instruction is possible. The curriculum is similar to that of the regular classes except that academic instruction begins at a later age with readiness experiences being extended to the age of 8 or 9, since these children are developing mentally at approximately one-half to three-fourths the rate of a normal child. These children may acquire functional literacy at about a third- to fifth-grade level by the age of 16. Materials are presented more gradually and more concretely with more repetition and practice (*see* also READING). Much emphasis is given to social adjustment, to interpersonal relations, and at older ages to occupational education.

There was a paucity of research relative to the education of the mentally retarded until after 1950, since few educational researchers were attracted to the area before that time. Since that date research programs have been initiated primarily in the U.S., in England, and in the U.S.S.R. In the U.S. the Institute for Research on Exceptional Children was organized at the University of Illinois in 1952, and later, centres were established at George Peabody College for Teachers, Nashville, Tenn., and at Syracuse University. In England research was initiated at Maudsley, Manor, and Fountain hospitals. In the U.S.S.R. research has been conducted at the Institute of Defectology in Moscow.

Research and the training of professional personnel were stimulated internationally by the interest of the Joseph P. Kennedy Jr. Foundation and in the U.S. by Pres. John F. Kennedy. Kennedy's sponsorship of federal legislation resulted in the organization and expansion of programs for the training of teachers and other professional personnel in this field and for the establishment of research centres for the mentally retarded, affiliated with universities.

See also INTELLIGENCE; PHYSICALLY HANDICAPPED, EDUCATION OF; MENTAL DEFICIENCY. (S. A. K.)

BIBLIOGRAPHY.—Ministry of Education, *Education of the Handicapped Pupil* (1956); National Society for the Study of Education, "The Education of Exceptional Children," *49th Yearbook* (1950); S. A. Kirk and G. O. Johnson, *Educating the Retarded Child* (1951); M. F. Cleugh, *The Slow Learner* (1957); C. Burt, *The Backward Child*, 4th ed. (1958); UNESCO, *Organization of Special Education for Mentally Deficient Children* (1960); S. A. Kirk, "Research in Education," in *Mental Retardation: a Review of Research,* ed. by H. A. Stevens and R. F. Heber (1964). (Cy. B.; S. A. K.)

RETFORD (officially EAST RETFORD), a market town and municipal borough in the Bassetlaw parliamentary division of Nottinghamshire, Eng., 30 mi. NNE of Nottingham by road. Pop. (1961) 17,792. Area 7.3 sq.mi. (18.9 sq.km.). Retford (Redforde in Domesday Book) owes its beginnings to its position near one of the Roman roads and on the River Idle, where there was a ford. In 1086 the archbishop of York owned a mill at Retford. It was a borough by prescription.

The earliest charter in the possession of the corporation is that of Edward II (1313), but charters were granted by Henry III (1246) and Edward I (1276). Other charters which have survived are those of Edward III (1329), Richard II (1378), Henry IV (1401), Elizabeth I (1562), and James I (1607). East Retford returned two members to parliament from 1315 to 1330 and again from 1571 to 1830. The borough was joined with the hundred of Bassetlaw and two members were returned until 1885 when the representation was reduced to one member.

The town has flourishing markets and engineering, rubber, wire, and dyeing and cleaning works, iron foundries, and paper and grain mills. Coal is mined in the vicinity.

RETHEL, ALFRED (1816–1859), one of the few exponents of monumental painting and historical subjects of 19th-century Germany, was born at Aix-la-Chapelle (Aachen) on May 15, 1816. At 13 he entered the Düsseldorf academy, which was at that time flourishing under the direction of Wilhelm von Schadow-Godenhaus. In 1836 he moved to Frankfurt (where artistic life centred around Philipp Veit) and was selected to decorate the walls of the imperial hall in the Römer palace with figures of famous men. Four years later he was commissioned to ornament the restored council house of Aix-la-Chapelle with frescoes from the life of Charlemagne, but the execution of this work was delayed for about six years. Meanwhile, Rethel occupied himself with the production of easel pictures and drawings. In 1842 he began a striking series of designs in which the weird power that animates his later art became apparent. In 1844 he visited Rome, executing

among other works his famous cycle "Hannibal Crossing the Alps." Returning to Aix in 1846, he began the Charlemagne frescoes. But he was now showing the first signs of mental derangement. Hovering between madness and sanity, he produced during this period some of his most impressive works. He died at Düsseldorf on Dec. 1, 1859.

His assistant Joseph Kehren continued Rethel's work on the half-finished series of the Charlemagne frescoes, and five of the original eight frescoes survive. Rethel is best known for his powerful series of woodcuts entitled "The Dance of Death," suggested by the Belgian insurrections of 1848, and two woodcuts, "Death as Friend" and "Death as Foe."

See K. Zoege von Manteuffel, *Alfred Rethel, Radierungen und Holzschnitte* (1929); H. Franck, *Alfred Rethel* (1937). (H. FH.)

RETIEF, PIET (1780–1838), ablest of the leaders in the Great Trek, the migration of certain South African Boers to become independent of British rule, was born in the western Cape Colony on Nov. 12, 1780. Better educated than other trekker leaders, Retief enjoyed a varied business and farming career. From 1814 he lived near the eastern frontier of the Cape Colony, where he was a field commandant and achieved some prominence by publicizing the grievances of the frontier Boers. Having decided to trek, Retief in February 1837 published his manifesto on behalf of the emigrant Boers, explaining their motives for trekking. He joined other trekkers north of the Orange River and, being the only leader acceptable to all parties, was elected governor and head commandant of the trekker community (April 1837). His immediate aims were to maintain unity among the trekkers and to lead them to Natal, in his view the trekkers' promised land. After descending the Drakensberg into Natal (October 1837) he visited the kraal of the Zulu king Dingaan to negotiate the cession of Natal to the Boers. During a second visit, on Feb. 6, 1838, Retief and his party, having obtained their treaty, were massacred by Dingaan's warriors. Their remains were found in December 1838, after the Boer victory over Dingaan at Blood River. *See* further CAPE OF GOOD HOPE: *History: British Colonization and the Great Trek;* NATAL: *History: The Voortrekkers in Natal.*

See G. S. Preller, *Piet Retief* (1920). (N. G. GA).

RETREAT, in religion, a period of withdrawal from the ordinary activities of daily life in order to meditate on the central truths of faith and to seek closer union with God through prayer and the ordering of one's life according to the divine will. Retreats are made by individuals or groups, under the guidance of a spiritual director, in premises set aside for the purpose, and in silence.

The general practice of retiring into solitude for prayer and meditation has always existed in Christianity; from the beginning, serious souls, stimulated by the example of Christ's 40 days in the desert, have found in it an effective means of regaining spiritual perspective and strength for life in a complex and demanding world. The late 16th century saw the rise of a definite movement in the Roman Catholic Church toward organized retreats for both clergy and laity. The movement has grown steadily. St. Ignatius Loyola's (*q.v.*) *Spiritual Exercises* not only gave the initial impetus to the movement but also provided a carefully worked out pattern of matter and method which has left its permanent mark on Christian spirituality. While the worldwide spread of retreats has been a movement predominantly within the Roman Catholic Church, retreats have also played a notable part in the practice of the Anglican Church since 1856.

In the 20th century the most noteworthy development has been the spread of retreats for the laity. The commonest form of these exercises is the weekend retreat of two or three days, sometimes extended to five or more days, as is customary in retreats for the clergy. (C. G. McM.)

RETZ, JEAN FRANÇOIS PAUL DE GONDI, CARDINAL DE (1613–1679), French prelate, the agitator and theoretician of the Fronde (*q.v.*), and a writer of extraordinary genius. He was born at Montmirail in September 1613, the third son of the devout Philippe Emmanuel de Gondi. Of Florentine origin, the Gondi family moved to France early in the 16th century and rapidly accumulated honours, including the duchy of Retz. To enable him to succeed his uncle, Jean François de Gondi, as archbishop of Paris, the young Jean François Paul was educated for an ecclesiastical career, much against his own will. By his duels and his love affairs he sought to demonstrate his worldliness. Politically he sympathized with the opposition to the cardinal de Richelieu (q.v.). His manuscript *La Conjuration de comte Jean Louis de Fiesque*, written c. 1632, ostensibly about the Genoese G. L. Fieschi, was a defense of revolution as a path to "glory."

In 1643 the queen regent of France, Anne (q.v.) of Austria, nominated Gondi as co-adjutor (that is, acting deputy and successor designate) to his uncle. Without reforming his private life, he set himself to raise the prestige of the archbishopric.

The article FRONDE provides an account of Gondi's role in the troubles of 1648–52. Any hopes that he had of supplanting Cardinal Mazarin (q.v.) in the royal council came to nothing; but his audacity and his political acumen made him a force with which both the government and the factious princes had to reckon. Anne reluctantly tried to buy his covert goodwill by nominating him for a cardinalate (Sept. 22, 1651); and before she could revoke the nomination his agents in Rome induced Pope Innocent X to give effect to it (Feb. 19, 1652), whereupon Gondi took the style of cardinal de Retz (or Rais). Among the Parisians, however, as his dealings with the government became obvious, he lost much of his popularity; and the government, which he had by turns defied, blackmailed, and outwitted, was waiting for revenge.

On Dec. 19, 1652, Retz was arrested and taken to Vincennes. The government now pressed him to resign his post of co-adjutor. While Pope Innocent X remonstrated on his behalf, Retz took secret measures so that his proxy was canonically installed as administrator of the diocese an hour after his uncle's death (March 21, 1654), before the government could intervene. A few days later, Retz agreed to resign. Pending the pope's assent, he was transferred to easier custody at Nantes. The pope withheld assent.

Fearing strict confinement again, Retz escaped from prison (Aug. 8, 1654). With his shoulder dislocated by a fall from a horse, he took shelter with embarrassed relatives in the Retz country before making his way in a small boat to Spain. The Spaniards conveyed him with honour to Italy, and he went on to Rome.

Innocent X died on Jan. 7, 1655. His successor, Alexander VII, did not want to quarrel forever with France about the archbishopric which Retz now reclaimed as having been extorted under duress. Retz left Italy in summer 1655 and spent a year in obscure movements along the Franco-German frontier. Later, apart from two visits to England (1660 and 1661), he was in the Netherlands. After Mazarin's death (March 1661), he at last agreed to resign Paris in exchange for the abbacy of Saint-Denis and a substantial income (Feb. 14, 1662).

Abhorred by Louis XIV, Retz spent his last years at Commercy or in his French abbeys, though he went to Rome on a diplomatic mission (1665) and for conclaves (1667, 1670, 1676). From 1675 he lived in penitence. He died in Paris on Aug. 24, 1679.

Retz's *Mémoires*, first published in 1717, constitute one of the great masterpieces of French prose. The first part is fragmentary, the manuscript having been mutilated, perhaps by way of expurgation; the second part covers the Fronde, the imprisonment, and the escape to Italy; the third part stops abruptly during Retz's dealings with Alexander. If Retz embellishes his own political activity, he gives an incomparable panorama of events and personalities. Frank about his private morals, he writes without bitterness toward enemies or vacillating colleagues, as if his vivid "portraits" of them were judgment enough. The style, uninhibited by the later rules of "classicism," fluctuates between rapid passages of narrative, marked by aristocratic wit and spontaneity, and elaborately constructed "periods" of political dialectic.

Retz's *Oeuvres*, in the best edition (1870–1920), fill 11 volumes in the series *Grands Écrivains de France*. The second of the *Pléiade* editions (1956) contains valuable appendices.

See L. Batiffol, *Biographie du cardinal de Retz* (1929); Albert-Buisson, *Le Cardinal de Retz* (1954). (J. G. R.-S.)

RETZIUS, ANDERS ADOLF (1796–1860), Swedish anthropologist and anatomist, the best-known member of a distinguished family of scientists, was born at Lund on Oct. 13, 1796.

He was the son of the chemist and naturalist ANDERS JAHAN RETZIUS (1742–1821), who was professor of natural history at the University of Lund and who later taught economics and chemistry there. The evergreen shrub *Retzia* is named for him. A brother, MAGNUS CHRISTIAN RETZIUS (1795–1871), became professor of obstetrics in the Carolinian Institute, Stockholm, and director of various lying-in hospitals there.

Anders Adolf received his medical education at the universities of Lund and Copenhagen and the Carolinian Institute, and subsequently held professorships of anatomy and physiology in Stockholm. During trips abroad he met the Czech physiologist J. E. Purkinje, Johannes Müller of Berlin, and other medical scientists with whom he collaborated. Retzius is best remembered for his pioneering work in craniometry (the measurement of skulls as a means of establishing racial characteristics). Named for him are a number of anatomical structures including the gyri of Retzius (convolutions in the brain) and the ligament of Retzius (in the ankle). He died on April 18, 1860. His brother CARL GUSTAF RETZIUS (1798–1833), a chemist, taught at the University of Lund and the Stockholm veterinary school. Anders Adolf's son, GUSTAF MAGNUS RETZIUS (1842–1919), an anatomist and anthropologist, is best known for his studies on the histology of the nervous system. (HD. ST.; X.)

REUBEN (in the Douai Version of the Bible, RUBEN), the eldest son of Jacob by his first wife, Leah (Gen. 29:32), and the eponymous ancestor of one of the 12 tribes of Israel. For reasons that are obscure it lost its position as the foremost tribe at an early period of history. The territory east of the Dead Sea which later tradition assigns to it is not clearly delimited or distinguished from the territories of Gad and Moab, into which it was probably merged quite early. *See* TWELVE TRIBES OF ISRAEL.

REUCHLIN, JOHANN (1455–1522), German humanist, second only to his younger contemporary Desiderius Erasmus. Jews and Protestants have cause to remember him, for he prevented the destruction of Jewish books and, by awakening the forces of liberalism and bringing about a decline in the power and esteem of the Dominicans, enhanced the possibility of success for the Reformation. Reuchlin was born on Feb. 22, 1455, at Pforzheim in the Black Forest. He studied at Freiburg, Paris, Basel, and again in Paris, specializing in Greek. Returning to Basel, he took his master's degree (1477) and began to lecture, teaching a more classical Latin than was then common in German schools and also explaining Aristotle in Greek. During this period he published a Latin lexicon (*Vocabularius Breviloquus*; 1st ed., 1475–76). After further study at Paris he switched from the classics and studied law at Orléans and at Poitiers, taking his degree as licentiate in 1481.

On his return to Germany Reuchlin was engaged as interpreter by Count Eberhard of Württemberg for a tour in Italy beginning in February 1482. His connection with the count became permanent, and he was given important posts at Eberhard's court in Stuttgart and also practised law in the city. Though he appears to have married at about this time, little is known of his married life. He left no children, though in later years his sister's grandson Philipp Melanchthon was almost as a son to him, till the Reformation estranged them.

In 1490 Reuchlin was again in Italy, where he saw Pico della Mirandola (q.v.), to whose cabalistic doctrines he afterward became heir. His mystico-cabalist ideas were expounded in the *De Verbo Mirifico* (1494) and in the *De Arte Cabbalistica* (1517). Interest in Cabala led him to interest in the Hebrew language, and on an embassy to Linz in 1492 he began to read Hebrew with the emperor Frederick's Jewish physician. Eberhard of Württemberg died in 1496, and Reuchlin, out of favour with his successor, went to Heidelberg as counselor to Elector Philip of the Palatinate and as tutor of the elector's sons. In this court of letters Reuchlin made translations from the Greek and wrote two Latin comedies in imitation of Terence. Philip sent him in 1498 on a mission to Rome, from which he returned laden with Hebrew books. In 1499 he was able to go back to Stuttgart, where he was given high judicial office which he held till 1512, when he retired to a small estate near the city.

For many years Reuchlin had been increasingly absorbed in Hebrew studies. In 1506 there appeared his epoch-making *De Rudimentis Hebraicis*—grammar and lexicon—mainly based on David Kimchi (*see* KIMCHI) yet by no means a mere copy of another man's teaching. This work was of the first importance in promoting the scientific study of Hebrew and hence of the Old Testament in its original language. Six years later Reuchlin published an edition of the seven penitential psalms (6, 32, 38, 51, 102, 130, and 143) in Hebrew with a Latin translation.

It was Reuchlin's work in Hebrew that led to his celebrated quarrel with the converted Jew Johann Pfefferkorn and the Dominicans of Cologne, a European *cause célèbre* that has been called the culminating point of humanism. It was the view of many of Reuchlin's contemporaries that the first step toward the conversion of the Jews must be to destroy their books, especially the Talmud. To such action Reuchlin, for reasons of scholarship, was strongly opposed. Pfefferkorn succeeded in getting from the emperor Maximilian authority to confiscate all Jewish books directed against the Christian faith, and thus armed he visited Stuttgart and asked Reuchlin's help as a jurist in putting the plan into execution. Reuchlin evaded. In 1511 Pfefferkorn circulated a gross libel (*Handspiegel wider und gegen die Juden*) declaring that Reuchlin had been bribed to favour Hebrew studies at the universities. Reuchlin retorted as warmly in the *Augenspiegel* (1511). When this was confiscated he met his foes with open defiance in a *Defensio contra Calumniatores* (1513). The universities were now appealed to for opinions, and all, even Paris, decided against Reuchlin. Formal inquisitorial processes were started against him at Mainz by the Dominican inquisitor Jakob Hochstraten on Sept. 15, 1513. Reuchlin would have been condemned and his book burned had not the archbishop of Mainz intervened with a letter declaring any judgment null and void. All Germany rejoiced over the discomfiture of the Dominicans.

Reuchlin had appealed to Pope Leo X, who referred the matter to the bishop of Speyer. The latter delegated it to two representatives, who condemned Hochstraten and imposed silence on him. But the Dominican had appealed in advance to the pope, and Reuchlin had to send his papers to Rome. His request for settlement was supported by the emperor, various electors, and 53 Swabian towns. The Cologne group published the opinions of the universities favourable to their side.

The pope entrusted the case to the learned Cardinal Grimani, who summoned Hochstraten to Rome; he arrived well supplied with gold. The pope had ordered that the court be expanded to a commission of 18 prelates. When these showed an inclination to favour Reuchlin, the Dominicans threatened to call a council in the event of an unfavourable verdict. Pfefferkorn continued his agitation.

Reuchlin, though retired from office, kept his courage and was cheered by the sympathy of enlightened men. In 1514 he published a collection of supporting letters he had received, *Epistolae clarorum virorum* ("Letters of Famous Men"). It now became a mark of intelligence to belong to the Reuchlinists; a whole liberal party seemed to spring into being against the reactionaries.

On July 2, 1516, the prelates, with only one dissenting vote, gave their verdict in favour of Reuchlin. Though Leo X, fearing the powerful Dominican order, issued a mandate quashing the entire dispute, in effect the success was still Reuchlin's.

In 1515 there had appeared a work that led all Europe to laugh at the Cologne group—the *Epistolae obscurorum virorum* ("Letters of the Obscurantists"), which mercilessly ridiculed late scholasticism as represented by the "obscurantist" Dominicans. It is believed that Crotus Rubianus was the author, though others may have contributed. So successful were the *Epistolae* that the work was continued (1517) in a further installment, perhaps by Ulrich von Hutten, and found imitation in other writings in the same vein. Interest in the matter was soon displaced, however, by the shift of public attention to Martin Luther and his clash with the church.

The Dominicans of Cologne did not cease to fume against Reuchlin. In the confused situation after the death of the emperor Maximilian (1519), the powerful knight Franz von Sickingen (who later sheltered the Reformers) threatened the Dominicans with reprisals if they did not desist. Eventually terms were reached, and Hochstraten stepped down from his office. The order appealed to Rome for a settlement of the dispute. But very soon it became convenient to blame Reuchlin for the rise of the troubles with Luther, and the Dominicans took advantage of this. Furthermore, many of Reuchlin's former supporters at Rome were dead or no longer at the papal court. The pope now (1520) issued a brief which canceled the Speyer sentence and condemned Reuchlin's book. But the humanist suffered no further persecution.

In 1519 Reuchlin went to Ingolstadt and taught there for a year as professor of Greek and Hebrew. He was then called to Tübingen, where he spent the winter of 1521–22. He died at the baths of Liebenzell on June 30, 1522.

During a great part of his life Reuchlin was the real centre of all Greek teaching as well as of all Hebrew teaching in Germany. Though his stand proved beneficial to the Protestant cause, he himself did not support Luther. He even sought to draw Melanchthon away from Luther and, when he failed, canceled the bequest of his library to his great-nephew.

BIBLIOGRAPHY.—*See* L. Geiger, *Johann Reuchlin* (1871), the standard biography; also D. F. Strauss, *Ulrich von Hutten;* S. A. Hirsch, "John Reuchlin, the Father of the Study of Hebrew Among the Christians," and "John Pfefferkorn and the Battle of Books," in his *Essays* (1905); M. Krebs (ed.), *Johannes Reuchlin 1455–1522: Festgabe seiner Vaterstadt Pforzheim zur 500. Wiederkehr seines Geburtstages* (1955); J. L. Blau, *The Christian Interpretation of the Cabala in the Renaissance* (1944). Some interesting details about Reuchlin are given in the autobiography of Conrad Pellicanus (ed. by Riggenbach, 1877). *See* also the article on Reuchlin by G. Kawerau in Herzog-Hauck, *Realenzyklopädie für Protestantische Theologie und Kirche,* 3rd ed. (1896–1913), and literature there cited.　(E. G. KR.)

RÉUNION, one of the Mascarene Islands and a French overseas *département* in the western Indian Ocean, lies 425 mi. (680 km.) E of the Malagasy Republic (Madagascar) and 90 mi. (145 km.) WSW of Mauritius. Elliptical in form, it has an area of 969 sq.mi. (2,510 sq.km.). The capital is Saint-Denis (*q.v.*).

Physical Features.—Réunion is entirely volcanic. The oldest erupted rocks belong to the type of the andesites; the newest are varieties of basalts. The main body is a volcanic mass which ceased activity in the Pliocene and is in an advanced state of dissection by short torrential rivers, the chief of which are the Rivières du Mât and des Galets, Bras de Cilaos, and Ravine Sèche. In the west-central area is a mountain massif with three summits exceeding 9,000 ft. (2,740 m.), the Piton des Neiges (10,069 ft.), Le Gros Morne (9,816 ft.), and Grand Bénard (9,501 ft.). Around them are scooped out three wide basins, the Cirque de Cilaos on the south and the Cirque de Salazie and Cirque de Mafatte on the north, draining through narrow gorges down the outer slopes. Around these amphitheatres are a series of plateaus—tablelike facets of the uneroded slopes of the former cones. In the east of the island is an area of about 200 sq.mi. in which vulcanism has been more recently active, and in the extreme east is Le Volcan, one of whose craters, Piton de la Fournaise, was inactive from 1860 until 1925, but has been active several times since then. Le Volcan, exceeding 8,600 ft., and its eastern lava slope, Grand Brûlé, are entirely enclosed within a parabolic mountain wall about 30 mi. long, the whole basin being a huge caldera refilled by recent vulcanism. The massif descends steeply on all sides, but everywhere except on the east it is bordered by a narrow coastal shelf or plain ½–3 mi. in width. The coast consists mainly of cliffs and has no natural harbours.

The climate is dominated by the southeast trade winds during April–October, when the northern and western sides are almost rainless and heavy rain falls in the south and east. Temperatures are cool, especially in the highlands, and snow falls frequently on the Piton des Neiges. In summer Réunion lies within the doldrums, and the lowlands are oppressively humid. Rain falls in all parts, and the island is liable to destructive tropical cyclones. There are appreciable climatic differences according to altitude. Above 2,500 ft. tropical conditions give way to subtropical and temperate conditions. Above 5,000 ft. the climate is cool, with average temperatures around and below 15.5° C (60° F), and with cold nights.

The lowlands formerly carried tropical rain forest, though with a palm savanna on the leeward side. Higher up is a mixed forest with much bamboo, *Casuarina* and *Terminalia*. Above 5,000 ft. a single species, the tamarind, covers a large part of the slopes. Conifers occur above 6,500 ft. and then a subalpine heath. Only about one-fifth of Réunion remains under forest.

The indigenous animal life is not rich in species, many having disappeared. Several bats, wildcats (the tenrec from Madagascar), and rats are the chief mammals. Common birds include the Bourbon flycatcher (*Tchitrea bourbonnensis*), the Mascarene bulbul, the Bourbon manioc bird (*Malacirops borbonicus*), and the introduced cardinal (*Foudia madagascariensis*). There is only one snake (*Lycodon aulicus*).

The People.—Réunion has no indigenous population. When discovered by Europeans it was uninhabited, and no trace of earlier settlement has been found. Present inhabitants include Creoles, Negroes, mulattoes, Chinese, and Indians. Most of the population is descended from slaves and is of African origin, mixed with other elements. A high proportion of the whites live in the highlands, whereas the lowland population is overwhelmingly dark-skinned. Fertility is highest in the lowlands, especially in the capital. Mortality is highest (23–30 per 1,000 in 1950) on the windward coastlands, especially in the towns, and lower in the highlands (10 per 1,000 in La Plaine des Palmistes, at 3,600 ft.). With high fertility and mortality, half the population is under 20 years of age. There is serious overpopulation, and massive emigration has long characterized Réunion. From the early 1950s the main direction of this movement was to Madagascar, where a plan of agricultural colonization by Réunionnais was started. In 1961 the population was 349,282, having doubled in less than a century, and with the elimination of malaria in 1950 the rate of increase steepened. The total includes about 7,000 Asians. Saint-Denis had a population of 65,614 (mun.) in 1961.

The Creole patois is French modified by Malagasy and Bantu pronunciation. French is the official language.

Most of the population is Roman Catholic, exceptions being small numbers of Hindus, Muslims (Indian and Arab), and Chinese. Culture is essentially European, modified by the tropics and by poverty. (HA. C. BD.)

History.—Réunion is usually said to have been discovered on Feb. 9, 1513, St. Apollonia's day, by the Portuguese navigator Pedro de Mascarenhas. The island was at first called Santa Apollonia; and the Mascarene Islands, of which Réunion forms a part (the others being Mauritius and Rodrigues), were named for the navigator. François Cauche first hoisted the French flag in 1638, followed five years later by Jacques Pronis, who again took possession of the island in the name of France. Pronis deported from Madagascar to the island 12 mutineers, who, after three years, took back idyllic descriptions of it. Occupation was decided on by Étienne de Flacourt, governor of Madagascar, who gave it the name of Île de Bourbon. In 1662 Louis Payen settled the first colonists, and two years later the Compagnie des Indes Orientales initiated a regular colonization plan. By 1717 there were about 900 free inhabitants and 1,100 Malagasy and Kaffir slaves.

Every colonist was obliged to own at least 200 coffee trees for every Negro working for him. Mocha coffee soon made the island prosperous. Bertrand François Mahé, comte de La Bourdonnais, named governor 1735, developed the fields of rice, grain, and manioc and established the first plantations of sugarcane, indigo, and cotton; sugar soon became the principal crop. In 1764 the company's activities were brought to an end, and the administration of the island was entrusted to a governor, or lieutenant general of the king, and an *intendant* ("administrator"). Spices (Molucca nutmegs and Amboina cloves) were introduced.

In 1793, with the proclamation of the Republic, Bourbon became the island of Réunion. Gen. Charles M. I. Decaen landed in 1803 and began preparations for war in that part of the Indian Ocean, but large numbers of English troops disembarked and in July 1810 the French capitulated. The island was occupied by the English until April 1815, when France again took possession. From then on, Réunion remained at peace. In 1848 the slaves (more than 60,000) were liberated.

In 1946 Réunion became an overseas *département* of France. (Ro. C.)

Administration and Social Conditions.—Réunion, as an overseas *département*, sends three deputies and two senators to the French legislature. Since 1960 the locally elected *conseil général* has had more local autonomy than comparable bodies in metropolitan *départements* have. Technical services are provided by metropolitan ministries, and French legislation and justice extend to the island. Réunion is divided into two *arrondissements*, the Windward (*du vent*) and the Leeward (*sous-le-vent*). The towns are governed by elected municipal councils.

The mass of the population is extremely poor, though wage labourers are generally better off than the peasantry. The white population of the highlands are among the poorest, depending on subsistence cultivation with few economic outlets. The coastal peasantry live almost wholly on rice, the inland on maize (corn). Commerce is largely controlled by a small number of sugar companies. Housing is very poor, with much overcrowding in the towns. There are two technical schools, an agricultural school, and a teachers' training school. Public and private health facilities include seven hospitals and about 80 dispensaries.

The Economy.—The sugar industry dominates the economy, production being concentrated on the coastal lowlands. It was very prosperous up to the mid-19th century but thereafter suffered very heavily through competition from beet sugar in France; improvement was slow. In the 1960s about a dozen big estates and associations with mills were producing the bulk of the crop. The approximately 20,000 small sugar growers are completely dependent on the companies, and their yield is poor. Most of the expansion of sugar production—from 70,000 tons in 1934 to about 248,000 metric tons in 1966—was achieved on the estates. Rum is distilled.

Besides sugar, which represents about 85% of Réunion's exports, the only other important export crops are geranium, vetiver (from which base oils for perfumes are extracted), and vanilla. The vanilla industry developed on the wettest part of the windward coast during the worst of the sugar crisis in the 1870s, but in the 1960s prices and demand were poor, and the industry was declining. Geranium and vetiver production, and to a lesser extent the perfume plants ilang-ilang and patchouli, are concentrated in the highlands, where they developed after the decline of coffee following an invasion of the coffee-leaf disease *Hemileia vastatrix* in the 1880s.

More than 90% of Réunion's exports (mainly sugar and rum) go to France. Imports are mainly manufactured goods (cotton piece goods) from France and foodstuffs (rice), principally from the Malagasy Republic. The currency is the CFA franc, equivalent to 0.02 French francs (CFA Fr. 246.85 = U.S. $1). There are two banks operating in the island.

Communications are good on the coast. A railway skirts the northern and western coasts, and a road encircles the island. Lateral roads give access to the interior, especially to the hill resorts of Cilaos and Salazie. Open roadsteads in front of the main towns (principally Saint-Pierre) were used until the artificial harbour at Pointe des Galets was completed in 1886. All overseas trade is now handled there. A regular shipping service runs to Madagascar and also to France via Suez, and there is a twice-weekly air service to Paris from Gillot airfield near Saint-Denis. Réunion is connected by telephone and telegraph with Mauritius and, via Madagascar, with France. (HA. C. BD.)

BIBLIOGRAPHY.—R. Barquissau *et al., L'Île de la Réunion* (1923); Jean Farchi, *Petite Histoire de l'île Bourbon* (1937); F. Maurette, "Les Mascareignes," *Géographie universelle,* vol. xii (1938); "Madagascar-Réunion" in *Encyclopédie maritime et coloniale,* vol. ii (1947); R. Decary *et al., L'Union française, côte des Somalis, Réunion, Inde* (1948); H. Isnard, "La Réunion," *La France de l'océan indien* (1952), and "La Réunion: problèmes démographiques, économiques et sociaux," *Revue de géographie alpine* (1953); C. A. E. L. Jacques Delmas (ed.), *La Réunion* (1955); C. Robequain, *Madagascar et les bases dispersées de l'Union Française* (1958); André Scherer, *Histoire de la Réunion* (1965), *La Réunion* (1967).

REUNION, CHURCH: *see* ECUMENICAL MOVEMENT.

REUS, a city of Tarragona province, Catalonia region, northeast Spain, is situated on the coastal plain 8 mi. (13 km.) WNW of Tarragona by road. Pop. (1960) 41,014 (mun.). In the old part of the town is the Gothic priory church of San Pedro, with its belfry 197 ft. (60 m.) high. Wide avenues surround the city; the modern Avenida de los Mártires has a large obelisk dedicated to those who fell during the civil war. There is much new building, particularly in the Barrio Fortuny on the Carretera de Salou. The city has a municipal museum which includes a prehistoric collection, and numerous educational, cultural, sporting, and recreational centres. Reus has good rail and road connections with Barcelona and Saragossa. Salou beach, a tourist centre on the Mediterranean, is 5½ mi. (9 km.) S. Dried fruit, wine, and oil are exported. Much horticultural produce is grown. Reus is first mentioned in the 13th century, and gained the status of city in the 1840s. It was the birthplace of Gen. Juan Prim (1814–70), of the painter Mariano Fortuny, and of the architect Antonio Gaudí.

REUSS, ÉDOUARD GUILLAUME EUGÈNE (1804–1891), German Protestant biblical scholar, whose works are representative of the painstaking historical scholarship of the 19th century, was born at Strasbourg on July 18, 1804. He studied philology in his native town (1819–22); theology at Göttingen under J. G. Eichhorn; and Oriental languages at Halle under Wilhelm Gesenius and afterward at Paris under the Baron de Sacy (1827–28). He taught at the Protestant Seminary at Strasbourg for 60 years, from 1828 until 1888, and died there on April 15, 1891.

Chief among Reuss's works are: *History of the Sacred Scriptures of the New Testament* (English translation, 1884), which first appeared in 1842 in German and was greatly expanded in later editions; *History of Christian Theology in the Apostolic Age*, two volumes (1852; English translation, 1872–74), a collection of lectures in French; *History of the Canon of the Holy Scriptures in the Christian Church* (1863; English translation, 1884), also in French; and his monumental *Geschichte der heiligen Schriften Alten Testaments* (1881), a veritable encyclopaedia of the history of Israel from its earliest beginning till the taking of Jerusalem by Titus. With A. W. Cunitz and J. W. Baum, and after their deaths alone, he edited the 59-volume edition of John Calvin's works (completed by P. Lobstein and A. Erichsen), which remains the standard edition.

See T. Gerold, *Edward Reuss, 1804–91* (1892).

REUSS, a German dynasty and the states ruled by it. Its lands, in Thuringia (*q.v.*), finally comprised two blocks, separated by part of Saxe-Weimar-Eisenach. The southern and larger block, or Oberland, with Schleiz and Greiz as chief towns, was bounded east by the Kingdom of Saxony, south by Bavaria, west by Saxe-Meiningen and part of Schwarzburg-Rudolstadt, northwest by an exclave of Prussian Saxony. The Unterland, round Gera, was bounded east and west by Saxe-Altenburg, north by Prussian Saxony.

The House of the *Vögte* or imperial advocates of Weida is traceable to the 12th century. All its male descendants have borne the name Henry from the early 13th century, necessitating complex numeration. Its Plauen line was subdivided in 1306 between a senior branch (extinct 1572) and a junior. The latter took the name Reuss from its head, Henry the Ruthenian (so designated, it seems, after marriage with a Ruthenian princess). It became Lutheran and split itself in 1564 into three lines, Elder Reuss, Middle Reuss (extinct 1616), and Younger Reuss.

Elder and Younger Reuss both acquired the rank of count of the Holy Roman Empire in 1673; Elder that of prince in 1778; and the Schleiz, Lobenstein, and Ebersdorf branches of Younger Reuss that of prince in 1806. Both lines entered the Confederation of the Rhine in 1807 and the German Confederation in 1815. Younger Reuss (unified under the Schleiz branch from 1848) joined the North German Confederation in 1866, Elder Reuss in 1867, and both became members of the German Empire in 1871. Elder Reuss had its capital Greiz and other possessions in the Oberland; Younger had the Unterland, with capital Gera, and half the Oberland.

The two territories, which became free states in 1918, merged themselves into a People's State of Reuss on April 4, 1919. This was absorbed into the new Thuringia on May 1, 1920. (Fᴴ. H.)

REUTER, ERNST (1889–1953), German political leader, mayor of West Berlin during 1948–53, was born at Aabenraa (Apenrade), in the then German Schleswig, on July 29, 1889. He joined the German Social Democratic Party in 1913 and in 1914 became secretary of the pacifist *Bund Neues Vaterland*. Conscripted into the army in 1915, he was captured by the Russians in the following year. After the Russian Revolution he organized German prisoners of war working at the Tula coal mines. In 1918 he was appointed commissar for the Volga German Autonomous Region, but at the end of the year returned to Germany. Becoming a Communist, he was appointed party secretary for the Berlin area but in 1922 rejoined the Social Democrats. In 1926 he was elected to the Berlin City Assembly. He became mayor of Magdeburg (1931) and was elected to the *Reichstag* (1932). Arrested by the Nazis in 1933, he was allowed to go to England in 1935. He became an adviser at the Ministry of Transport in Ankara, Turkey, and, from 1938, professor of public administration at Ankara University.

He returned to Berlin in 1946 and reorganized the Social Democratic Party. On June 24, 1947, he was elected mayor of Berlin by the city assembly, but was not approved by the Allied *Kommandatura* because of the Soviet veto. When the Social Democrats won a decisive victory in West Berlin on Dec. 5, 1948, however, Reuter was elected mayor; he was reelected in January 1951, although his party had lost its absolute majority in the assembly. A man of courage and an able administrator, Reuter's moral authority extended far beyond Berlin. He died in Berlin on Sept. 29, 1953.

REUTER, PAUL JULIUS, Baron von (originally Israel Beer Josaphat) (1816–1899), founder of the first news agency, which still bears his name, was born at Kassel, Ger., on July 21, 1816, of Jewish parentage. He became a Christian in 1844 and adopted the name of Reuter. At 13 he became a clerk in his uncle's bank at Göttingen, where he met K. F. Gauss, who was experimenting with electrotelegraphy. After a period of publishing in Berlin in the 1840s Reuter moved in 1848 to Paris, where he found a growing demand for political news. He began to translate extracts from articles and commercial news and send them to papers all over Germany, but the project collapsed. During 1850 there was a gap between the end of the new German telegraph line at Aachen and the French and Belgian lines at Brussels, and Reuter used 40 pigeons on a service between the two cities. After trying without success to start a news agency in Paris, he moved to England in 1851, later becoming a naturalized British subject. He opened his first telegraphic office near the London stock exchange, and at first his business was practically confined to commercial telegrams. He was not able to persuade the London newspapers to publish his foreign news telegrams until eventually the *Morning Advertiser* agreed to pay him £30 a month for them. Other papers, including the *Times,* fell into line, and the initial telegram of the new service was issued on Oct. 8, 1858. His first great success came early in 1859 when the agency relayed to London a full report of an important speech by Napoleon III to the French legislative chambers. Reuter then extended his service all over the world. In 1861 he laid a special cable from Cork to Crookhaven, Ire., which enabled him to circulate news of the American Civil War several hours before the mail steamers docked. In 1865 he secured concessions for a cable beneath the North Sea to Cuxhaven and another between France and the United States. He was created a baron by the duke of Saxe-Coburg-Gotha in 1871, and 20 years later Queen Victoria gave him and his heirs the privileges of this rank in England. He resigned his position as managing director of Reuter's in 1878, and died at Nice on Feb. 25, 1899.

See G. Storey, *Reuters' Century, 1851–1951* (1951).   (A. P. R.)

REUTERS: *see* News Agency.

REUTLINGEN, a town of West Germany in the *Land* (state) of Baden-Württemberg, Federal Republic of Germany, lies on the Echaz River below the Achalm in the Swabian Alps, 40 km. (25 mi.) S of Stuttgart by road. Pop. (1961) 67,407. The most Swabian of all Swabian towns, Reutlingen has half-timbered and gabled tanners' and dyers' houses and 16th-century fountains. The Tübinger Gate and the Garden Gate are remains of the fortifications. The Marienkirche is a fine example of High Gothic (begun in 1247), with a tower erected in 1494. It contains early-14th-century frescoes and an octagonal font of 1499. The economist Friedrich List was born in Reutlingen. In the attractive surroundings are several summer resorts. The chief industry is textile manufacturing and there is a textile technical school with a research institute. Reutlingen was founded by Frederick II between 1236 and 1240, and later became a free imperial city.

REVEL (Reval): *see* Tallinn.

REVELATION, BOOK OF (variously called the Revelation to John, the Revelation of St. John the Divine, and the Apocalypse of St. John the Apostle), last (and the only apocalyptic) book of the New Testament, is a symbolic presentation of the life of the church in a hostile world and a "prophecy" of the final end of all things.

Revelation is one of a group of Jewish and Christian books, called apocalypses, that describes, in elaborate symbols, the victory of God over an evil world. Such other apocalyptic books as Daniel in the Old Testament and II Esdras in the Apocrypha (IV Esdras in the Vulgate), and noncanonical books, such as Enoch and Baruch, as well as many parts of the Dead Sea scrolls from Qumran, provide an indispensable background for understanding the point of view of Revelation. (*See* also Apocalyptic Literature.)

In the apocalyptic view, the world was so decisively alienated from God that its structures of life and power (*e.g.*, structures of politics, economics, prestige, and success) could not be recovered to obedience to God but would have to fall under God's judgment and be destroyed. Though created by God, the world had come under the domination of an evil power—Satan—so that its life was demonically perverted, while human decision and responsibility also contributed to the evil situation of men. In the world, though apart from it, lived a community of believers that was despised and often persecuted by the world but that was yet supported by God in all its trials. In the near future, it was believed, God would overthrow the powers of evil ("this present age"), both in their satanic dimension which pervaded the whole physical and spiritual cosmos, and in their visible political dimension; and then God would establish a new world ("the age to come"). Such a faith is dualistic, since it views life as a struggle between two irreconcilably opposed principles—God and the demonic power of evil (*see* Dualism). But it is not an absolute dualism, for it looks toward the speedy victory of God; and it is not a dualism of body and spirit, for in it evil is a perverted form of selfhood.

Central to the apocalyptic vision is the hope for a perfect community (a "holy city"), in which men will be free to serve God and each other. The failure of the power structures of "this world" to make possible total obedience to God and true community among men is the centre of the world's opposition to God, and the reason why this world must be destroyed to make way for a better one.

The author of Revelation uses a traditional stock of symbols. In particular he draws on the Old Testament, especially Daniel, Ezekiel, and Zechariah. Some scholars think the author used a Jewish apocalypse of the 1st century A.D. as a source. Perhaps ancient astrology supplied some symbols (especially in ch. 12) that came ultimately from Near Eastern creation myths. Jewish and Christian liturgy probably suggested many elements in the book. The author's own visions may have suggested other elements, though as they stand the visions in the book are too carefully integrated with each other and too dependent on tradition to be reports of immediate religious experience.

Since many apocalyptic books present, in symbolic form, a history of the struggles of the faithful, it has often been suggested that the symbols in Revelation represent succeeding historical events. No doubt the actual historical struggles of the church with Roman persecution are reflected in the book, especially in ch. 13 and 17. Nonetheless, the repetitive nature of the images and the lack of concern for strict consistency suggest that the cosmic dimension of the struggle, the conflict of the powers of light and darkness, was more in the author's mind than an ordered series of historical incidents.

Contents.—An outline can only suggest the rich, interwoven texture of the book, which does not have mechanical symmetry but is woven together in complex patterns of threes, sevens, and other numbers. No one outline can claim to be final.

1:1–20	introduction
1:1–3	heading: a revelation of God through Christ
1:4–20	introductory letter: a vision of Christ
2:1–3:22	counsel to the church: the seven letters (varied praise, warning, threat, and promise)
2:1–7	Ephesus
2:8–11	Smyrna
2:12–17	Pergamum
2:18–29	Thyatira
3:1–6	Sardis
3:7–13	Philadelphia
3:14–22	Laodicea
4:1–16:21	the beginnings of Judgment: God's people persecuted; God through Christ protecting his people and destroying his enemies
4:1–5:14	introduction: a vision of God's world; the 24 elders and the Lamb
6:1–8:1	the first cycle of images: the Seven Seals, the first four of which (6:1–8) reveal the "four horsemen of the Apocalypse" (symbolizing the lust for conquest and its inevitable consequences of war, famine, and death; traditionally identified as War, Strife, Famine, and Pestilence) (*interlude* of the setting apart of the faithful and the reward of the faithful in heaven, 7:1–17)
8:2–11:19	the second cycle of images: the Seven Trumpets (*interlude* of the seer, 10:1–11; and the measurement of the temple, 11:1–4; and the witnesses to God's message, 11:4–14)
12:1–15:1	the third cycle of images: the Seven Visions (*interlude?* of the vision of the Lamb and his worshipers, 14:1–5)
15:2–16:21	the fourth cycle of images: the Seven Plagues
17:1–19:10	the Judgment of this world
17:1–18	a woman sitting on a beast; explanation of the seven heads and ten horns of the beast
18:1–24	doom pronounced on "Babylon"; her friends lament her
19:1–10	*interlude:* praise to God for the judgment of Babylon; proclamation of the marriage of the Lamb
19:11–22:5	the final purpose of God
19:11–16	the Word of God riding a white horse
19:17–21	the victory of Christ
20:1–3	the dragon bound for a thousand years
20:4–6	the millennium
20:7–15	the final defeat of Satan and final Judgment
21:1–22:5	the new heaven and new earth
22:6–21	conclusion
22:6–17	concluding words of prophecy: the end is near
22:18–20	warning not to tamper with the book
22:21	benediction

Main Themes.—*Endurance.*—The overarching practical theme of Revelation is a summons to resolute endurance in the face of coming persecution. Courageous loyalty, separation from the evil world, and enduring hope for God's destruction of evil and new creation of a good world are taught through the seven letters, the interludes, the dramatic struggle, and the vision of a new heaven and a new earth.

Cosmic Christ.—The vision of a struggle of cosmic dimensions is paralleled by an understanding of Christ as a preexistent, heavenly being, capable of overcoming the most pervasive demonic opposition. Of Christ's earthly life, only his death and resurrection are mentioned, but these events reveal the eternal purpose of God (1:18; 5:9).

God's Presence in an Evil World.—In Revelation, though Christ's triumph still lies in the future, faith in Christ makes it possible for the believer to span the gap between present and future and to participate, even in the midst of suffering, in the joy and peace of God's presence. The "interludes" in the action are thus not an irregularity in the plan of the book but an important means by which the author communicates his faith that the movement of time can be momentarily halted, as the believer participates, by anticipation, in the end.

Roman Empire as Manifestation of Evil.—The concrete manifestation of satanic power is the government under which the author lived, the Roman Empire. Rome is symbolized (though many details are obscure) by the beasts of ch. 13 and by the beast of ch. 17. The seven heads and ten horns (13:1; 17:3 and 9–14) represent (in a way about which there is little agreement) individual rulers of the 1st century A.D. The author's sense of the hopelessness of a constructive appeal to Rome is one reason for his view that in general the powers of evil must be destroyed rather than converted.

The Millennium.—The most controversial element in the Apocalypse is its prediction of a thousand years' rule of Christ on earth. The author looked forward to a real earthly kingdom, of Christ's, to come soon. That he presented it as temporary shows his conviction that this world, even perfected, could not adequately manifest the glory of God. (*See also* MILLENNIUM.)

The New Jerusalem.—The vision of a true community under God, as God's ultimate purpose, is powerfully presented in the symbols of Rev. 21:1–22:5. This vision, here set in an "otherworldly" framework, has also motivated forms of Christian faith which looked for a partial realization of the hope within the structures of this world.

Literary History.—The author is John (1:4); though most apocalyptic works were published under assumed names, this one does not seem to have been. The author regards himself as a prophet (1:3) but does not call himself an apostle. Strong early tradition identified him with the apostle John (*e.g.*, Justin, *c.* A.D. 155). Yet Papias (*c.* A.D. 140) seems to have reported an early martyrdom for the apostle John, and some early tradition denies the apostle's authorship. Thus while many Roman Catholic and some Protestant scholars support authorship by John the apostle, Protestant scholarship predominantly supports the view that some other John is the author. The differences in language between Revelation and the Gospel of John make it unlikely that the two books come from the same writer. Revelation was written for the churches in the neighbourhood of Ephesus in Asia Minor.

The Apocalypse is usually dated late in the reign of the Roman emperor Domitian (A.D. 81–96) and associated with his persecution of Christians. Since Domitian was the first to insist strongly on divine honours as a living emperor, and since Revelation opposes precisely this form of idolatry (ch. 13), the traditional date is the most probable. Some scholars maintain an earlier date, usually by identifying the sixth head of the beast, which appears to represent the ruling emperor, with an earlier ruler (17:10). But the author may have taken over and reinterpreted the symbolism of the seven heads from an earlier time, or he may have developed it in such a way that it applied to his own time. The symbolic number 666 (13:18) may refer to Nero (A.D. 54–68) but does not necessarily point to composition at the time of Nero or even shortly afterward, since the expectation of Nero's return seems to have been a popular belief even late in the 1st century A.D.

Interpretation.—Older interpretation either "spiritualized" Revelation, applying its symbolism to general truths of the Christian religion, or looked for a literal fulfillment of its prophecies in or shortly after the time of the interpreter himself. Either path may find in the book a source of deep spiritual life but will also lead to misunderstanding of its original meaning, which is better grasped by setting the book in the context of the whole body of apocalyptic literature. Then Revelation is seen as springing from and relating to a crisis in the life of the early church. Its symbols are not descriptions of events in later history.

Once the original setting and meaning of the book are seen, the interpreter must again confront its meaning for his own time. Some students have concluded that the book's lack of hope for "this world" gives it little relevance to the modern world. Others regard its message, originally focused on an ancient crisis, as a valid symbolic representation of the divine purpose. This sort of interpretation may stress the eternal truths of the book, thus standing close to the older spiritual interpretation, and it may emphasize Revelation as a portrayal of the climax of the "sacred history" of God's acts. Then the original situation of conflict with Rome is seen to typify a recurring situation in which the believing community will exist until the final end, when God's will shall be done. Still others would see the contemporary significance of the

Book of Revelation in the totality of its claim for obedience, holding that the pictorial vision of the future triumph is of secondary importance and that the call to remain faithful is the enduring message. *See also* BIBLE.

BIBLIOGRAPHY.—E. B. Allo, *Saint Jean: L'apocalypse,* 3rd ed. (1933); Martin Kiddle, *The Revelation of Saint John* (1940); Ronald Knox, *A New Testament Commentary,* vol. iii, pp. 191–237 (1956); Ernst Lohmeyer, *Die Offenbarung des Johannes,* 2nd ed. (1953); Martin Rist, "Revelation: Introduction and Exegesis," *The Interpreter's Bible,* vol. xii, pp. 347–551 (1957); John E. Steinmuller, *A Companion to Scripture Studies,* vol. iii, pp. 382–392 (1943).   (WI. A. B.)

REVELS, HIRAM RHOADES (1822–1901), clergyman and educator who became the first Negro to sit in the United States Congress when he was elected to fill the unexpired term of Jefferson Davis. Revels was born of free parents on Sept. 1, 1822, in Fayetteville, N.C. Since it was illegal for Negroes, whether slave or free, to obtain an education in the South, Revels traveled north, where he studied in a Quaker seminary in Liberty, Ind., and afterward attended Knox College in Galesburg, Ill. In 1845 he was ordained a minister in the African Methodist Episcopal Church and for the next several years worked among the Negroes in the Middle West and in Kentucky and Tennessee. Revels then settled in Baltimore, Md. He served there as a church pastor and principal of a Negro school, and he helped organize two volunteer Negro regiments for service in the Union Army soon after the outbreak of the Civil War.

In 1863 Revels went to St. Louis, where he founded a school for freedmen and helped organize another Negro regiment. In 1864 he moved to Mississippi and served as a chaplain to a Negro unit. In Jackson he organized several churches. In 1866 he settled in Natchez to preach to a large congregation and, despite some misgivings about entering politics, was appointed alderman by the military governor (1868) and was later elected to the state senate (1869). Although Revels was a Republican, he was anxious not to rub raw the feelings of white Southerners; hence he supported legislation that would have restored the power to vote and to hold office to disenfranchised Southerners.

Revels was elected to fill the unexpired term of Jefferson Davis in January 1870, serving in the U.S. Senate from February 1870 to March 1871. Upon leaving the Senate he became president of Alcorn Agricultural and Mechanical College, a recently opened Negro institution near Lorman, Miss. In 1873 he served for a few months as interim secretary of state in Mississippi, and, in 1874, he was dismissed from the presidency of Alcorn by Governor Ames. Revels once again returned to an active ministry in Mississippi. The following year Revels helped to overturn the Republican government of the state and defended his action in a letter to President Grant in which he claimed that too many Republican politicians put up for office in Mississippi were corrupt. He was rewarded for his anti-Republican activities by the Democratic governor, who returned him to the presidency of Alcorn in 1876. Revels continued his work of organizing and developing the institution until his retirement.

He died on Jan. 16, 1901, in Aberdeen, Miss.

REVENTLOW, CHRISTIAN DITLEV FREDERIK, COUNT (1748–1827), Danish statesman whose agrarian reforms led to the elimination of serfdom in Denmark, was born at Copenhagen on March 11, 1748. He made an extensive tour of Western Europe to study economic conditions before returning to Denmark in 1770. From 1773 he held office in government departments, and in 1775 he inherited the Christianssaede estates in Lolland, where he introduced agrarian reforms and raised his tenants' standard of living. In 1784 he became head of the *Rentekammeret* (Exchequer) which was responsible for agricultural policy. He set up a small agricultural commission to improve the condition of the crown serfs and among other things to enable them to turn their leaseholds into freeholds.

Reventlow induced Crown Prince Frederick (later Frederick VI) to appoint in August 1786 a grand agricultural commission to consider the whole of the peasantry. This resulted in a series of important reforms. The ordinance of June 8, 1787, modified the existing leaseholds, greatly to the advantage of the peasants, and that of June 20, 1788, abolished the so-called *stavnsbaand* of 1733 (the binding of farmers' sons as serfs on the estates where they were born). From 1791 to 1799 voluntary agreements between landowners and tenants considerably modified the *hoveri* system, whereby the tenant had been compelled to cultivate his lord's land as well as his own; and the *hoveri* was clearly defined and regularized by the ordinance of Dec. 6, 1799. Reventlow also started public credit banks enabling small farmers to borrow money on favourable terms.

Denmark's financial distress resulting from its involvement in the Napoleonic Wars (*see* DENMARK: *History*), and Frederick's growing personal rule, prevented Reventlow from completing his reforms. He was dismissed on Dec. 7, 1813, and retired to his estates in Lolland, where he died on Oct. 11, 1827.

BIBLIOGRAPHY.—A. F. Bergsöe, *Greve Christian Ditlev Frederik Reventlow's Virksomhed* (1837); L. T. A. Bobé, *Efterladte Papirer fra den Reventlowske Familiekreds*, 10 vol. (1895–1931); H. Jensen, *Chr. D. Reventlowske Liv og Gerning* (1938). (F. Sk.)

REVERE, PAUL (1735–1818), American patriot, craftsman and industrialist, best known for his ride on the night of April 18, 1775, to warn the Massachusetts colonists of the approach of British troops, was born in Boston, Mass., on Jan. 1, 1735. His father Apollos Rivoire (later changed to Revere) was a Huguenot refugee who had come to Boston as a child and had been apprenticed to a silversmith. This craft he taught his son Paul Revere, who became one of America's greatest artists in silver. As a boy Revere received sufficient education to enable him later to read the difficult metallurgical books of his period. When Benjamin Waterhouse was brought to Massachusetts by Harvard college to teach this and allied sciences he thought Revere the only man in America with a competent knowledge in the field. It was in metal that Revere did most of his work. But his energy and skill (and the necessity of supporting an ever growing family) turned him in many directions. He not only made silver but sold spectacles, replaced missing teeth and made surgical instruments. He cut many copper plates, mostly for anti-British propaganda. His "Boston Massacre," in spite of its many inaccuracies, is probably America's most famous print. He took an active interest in politics, was a leader of the Boston Tea Party in 1773 and influenced his fellow artisans toward independence.

With the outbreak of the American Revolution in 1775, Revere was called upon to construct a powder mill to supply the colonial troops. Later he and his sons cast hundreds of church bells, several of them of great beauty. Although he began making copper hardware for ships soon after the Revolution it was not until 1800 that, after considerable experimentation and great expense, he set up in Canton, Mass., a rolling mill for the manufacture of sheet copper. From this factory came the sheathing for many American ships, including the "Constitution," and for the dome of the Massachusetts state house. He worked closely with the inventor Robert Fulton on copper boilers for steamboats. With such ventures he became a connecting link between the medieval craftsman and the modern industrialist.

Revere's military career was undistinguished. In 1776, as a lieutenant colonel, he was in command of Boston harbour's principal defense, Castle William. In 1778 he was sent on the Rhode Island expedition, which proved as complete a failure as the Penobscot campaign a year later. In both of these futile attacks on the British the colonial sea and land forces were unable to work together. The retreat from the Penobscot region became such a scandal that most of the officers involved lost their reputations. Revere's good name was restored several years later after his continual demand for a court martial. Largely because of Longfellow's stirring ballad, he is remembered as the man on horseback who warned Middlesex county on "the 18th of April in '75" that the British troops were leaving Boston to seize military stores at Lexington and Concord. Although not good history the poem is still an impressive memorial to him. For years Revere had been the principal express rider for Boston's Committee of Safety.

By virtue of his title of colonel, his postwar ventures as an importer, the great importance of his copper mill and the fortune he had amassed, he could have referred to himself by several prouder titles than the simple goldsmith or silversmith that he seems to have preferred to his dying day. This attitude J. S. Copley emphasized in the portrait he painted of him shortly before the Revolution, seated at his work bench, in his shirt sleeves. Gilbert Stuart's portrait of him as an old man emphasizes not only his energy but the generosity and kindness that characterized him throughout his long life. Both of these portraits along with the finest collection of his silver are in the Museum of Fine Arts, Boston. The American Antiquarian society possesses the outstanding collection of his engravings.

The house he lived in or owned for about 30 years before his death on May 10, 1818, still stands in Boston's North Square.

See Esther Forbes, *Paul Revere and the World He Lived In* (1942); Clarence S. Brigham, *Paul Revere's Engravings* (1954). (E. Fo.)

REVERE, a city and resort in Suffolk County, Mass., U.S., on Massachusetts Bay, 6 mi. (10 km.) NE of Boston. It is the "Coney Island of Boston" with three miles of beach, a dog track, and nightclubs. Almost from its founding (1636) as Rumney Marsh, it was a Boston resort. Subsequently the development of residential suburbs to the north made it turn almost exclusively to its beach front with its roller coaster and numerous concessions.

Because of the extensive marshes the community developed slowly. It was successively a section of Boston, part of Chelsea (1739), and reincorporated as North Chelsea (1846). The latter changed its name in 1871 in honour of Paul Revere. It became a city in 1914. Council-manager government, adopted in 1950, was discontinued by the voters in 1964. Revere is still tied to Boston through the county government. There are large colonies of Russian, Lithuanian, and Italian immigrants and their descendants. The 19th-century Slade Spice Mill is a local point of interest.

Light industry includes electrical equipment, machine parts, chemicals, spices, and beverages. For comparative population figures *see* table in MASSACHUSETTS: *Population*. (R. C. Mo.)

REVERSING LAYER. It was formerly believed that the solar continuous spectrum originated in hot lower strata of the sun's atmosphere or photosphere and that the dark line spectrum was all produced in an overlying cooler stratum called the reversing layer, in accordance with Kirchhoff's third law of spectrum analysis. Early eclipse observations, especially that by C. A. Young in 1870, apparently substantiated this picture. Later work showed that the dark line and continuous spectra of the sun or stars were formed in essentially the same layers. Weak spectral lines are formed in the same layers as the continuous spectrum; stronger lines are produced predominantly in higher layers; whereas the centres of the strongest lines are formed in the chromosphere. Although the term has been used occasionally to indicate the upper layers of the photosphere where the strongest spectral lines are predominantly formed, it is now infrequently employed. *See also* SPECTROSCOPY. (L. H. A.)

REVIVALISM in the broadest sense applies to any instance of renewed religious fervour within a group, church or community, whether that group be Christian or non-Christian. However, in common usage it refers primarily to concerted efforts among evangelical churches to revitalize the spiritual ardour of their members and to win new adherents. Revivalism in its modern form can be attributed to that common element in Anabaptism, Puritanism, German pietism and Methodism in the 17th and 18th centuries which stressed personal religious experience (*Herzensreligion*), the priesthood of all believers and holy living, in protest against established church systems which seemed excessively sacramental, sacerdotal and secularistic. Each of these pietistic movements contributed to the revival tradition.

Protesting against the sacramentalism and ritualism of the Church of England, the Puritans who left England carried their fervour for experiential religion and devout living to the new world in 1629. Although this fervour waned toward the end of the century, Jonathan Edwards (*q.v.*) revived Puritan zeal in New England in a period of extraordinary religious excitement from 1734 to 1742. Edwards is sometimes credited with inspiring the first Great Awakening in America (*c.* 1725–50), but this widespread movement of social, theological and ecclesiastical reorientation actually had its beginnings in Europe and reached America in the 1720s through the Dutch Reformed and Presbyterian churches of New Jersey and the German immigrants in Pennsylvania. While the awakening in New Jersey and Pennsylvania was in part a process of adapting European ecclesiasticism and theology to frontier conditions, it was also closely related to the pietist movement of Philipp Jakob Spener and August Hermann Francke (*qq.v.*) in Germany and to the evangelical revival in England.

Between 1670 and 1730 Spener and Francke had revitalized Lutheranism by forming within the church devout groups of believers who emphasized personal conversion, devotional prayer, asceticism and practical Christian charity. Their influence extended throughout northern Europe, affecting the Reformed churches, the Anabaptists and the revived Moravian church under Count Nikolaus Ludwig von Zinzendorf and August Gottlieb Spangenberg. The Moravian missionaries Spangenberg and Peter Boehler in turn influenced John Wesley (*q.v.*), and his religious conversion in 1738 inaugurated the evangelical revival within the Church of England. Between 1738 and 1791 Wesley traveled throughout the British Isles preaching to large crowds and laying the foundations for what became after his death the Wesleyan Methodist Church. Wesley's preaching emphasized free will and free grace, experiential conversion, the priesthood of all believers, moral perfectionism and philanthropic reform.

His associate George Whitefield (*q.v.*), the founder of Calvinistic Methodism in England, was also influenced by German pietism, and his preaching tours of the American colonies between 1739 and 1770 had a profound effect upon the first Great Awakening in America. Whitefield was welcomed to New Jersey in 1739 by Theodore J. Frelinghuysen, the pietistic leader of the revival among the Dutch Reformed churches; by Frelinghuysen's friend Gilbert Tennent (*q.v.*), the leading revivalist among the Scotch-Irish Presbyterians; and by most of the German-speaking immigrants in the middle colonies. When he toured New England in 1740, Whitefield was also endorsed by Jonathan Edwards and other influential Congregationalists. Throughout America Whitefield's preaching aroused intense religious enthusiasm; however, his emotional mass meetings and the religious disorders aroused by itinerants who imitated his flamboyant methods produced vigorous opposition to the awakening after 1742.

While the first Great Awakening created temporary schisms within almost every denomination in the American colonies, it also stimulated the churches to a vigorous new growth; it paved the way for the separation of church and state; it broke down denominational barriers and helped to unify the colonies; it produced an energetic social and intellectual ferment among the lower classes; and it instituted that emphasis upon religious activism and lay leadership that has since characterized American Protestantism. Like pietism in Germany and Wesleyan evangelicalism in England, the first Great Awakening in America promoted missionary activity, philanthropy, charity and education. Dartmouth college and Princeton and Brown universities were direct outgrowths of this awakening.

Despite the spread of deism during the 18th century the revivalistic impulse continued strong. The evangelical revival flourished in Britain, and at the end of the century a new awakening occurred in America. This second Great Awakening (*c.* 1795–1835) was divided into three phases: The first phase (1795–1810) was associated with the frontier camp meetings conducted by James McGready, John McGree and Barton W. Stone in Kentucky and Tennessee. (*See* CAMP MEETING.) The second and more conservative phase of the awakening (1810–25) centred in the Congregational churches of New England under the leadership of Timothy Dwight, Lyman Beecher, Nathaniel W. Taylor and Asahel Nettleton. The third and final phase (1825–35) stemmed from the activities of Charles Grandison Finney (*q.v.*), who began his revivalism in small towns in western New York in the 1820s but eventually conducted revival meetings in the largest cities in the U.S. and Britain. During the second Great Awakening revivalistic theology in all denominations shifted from Calvinism to Arminianism as preachers emphasized the ability of sinners to make an immediate decision to save their own souls; theological differences almost disappeared among evangelical churches. Moreover, under Finney's aegis a rationale for carefully contrived revival techniques

evolved. After 1835 an irregular corps of professional revival experts traveled through the towns and cities of America and Britain organizing annual revival meetings at the invitation of local pastors who wanted to reinvigorate their churches. The second Great Awakening produced a great increase in church membership, made soul winning the primary function of the ministry and stimulated a host of moral and philanthropic reforms including temperance, emancipation and foreign missions. In 1857–58 the famous "prayer meeting revival" swept the cities of the United States following a financial panic. It indirectly instigated a revival in Northern Ireland and England in 1859–61 that rivaled the camp meetings in enthusiasm.

The preaching tour of the American lay evangelist Dwight L. Moody (*q.v.*) and his singing companion Ira D. Sankey through the British Isles in 1873–75 marked the beginning of a new outburst of Anglo-U.S. revivalism. And in his subsequent revival activity in the major cities of Britain and America Moody perfected the highly businesslike techniques that characterized the urban mass evangelistic campaigns of 20th-century professional revivalists such as Reuben A. Torrey (*q.v.*), J. Wilbur Chapman, Gypsy (Rodney) Smith and Billy (William A.) Sunday (*see* SUNDAY, BILLY). The interdenominationally supported revivalism of Moody and his imitators in 1875–1915 constituted in part a conscious co-operative effort by the Protestant churches to alleviate the unrest of urban industrial society by "evangelizing the masses," and in part an unconscious effort to counter the challenge to evangelical orthodoxy brought by higher criticism of the Bible and Darwin's *Origin of Species* (1859). In the first half of the 20th century most educated evangelical churchmen lost interest in revivalism because of its association with fundamentalism (*q.v.*) and turned their attention to social reform. After World War II a renewed interest in mass evangelism appeared, symbolized by the widespread support given to the "revival crusades" of the Southern Baptist evangelist Billy (William F.) Graham (*q.v.*).

Whether mass revivalism has been as helpful to the churches in the long run as its exponents claim is highly debatable, but there is no doubt about its ability to generate at least temporary religious enthusiasm. The best historical explanation for the recurrent nature of revivalism is based upon the inevitable need for theological and ecclesiastical reorientation from generation to generation and the concomitant religious excitement generated by such changes.

BIBLIOGRAPHY.—For European pietism *see* Ernst Troeltsch, *The Social Teachings of the Christian Churches*, Eng. trans. by Olive Wyon (1949); for Methodism *see* Luke Tyerman, *Life and Times of John Wesley*, 3 vol. (1870–73), and Sydney G. Dimond, *The Psychology of the Methodist Revival* (1926); for Puritanism *see* Perry G. E. Miller, *The New England Mind*, 2 vol. (1939, 1951); for the first Great Awakening *see* Joseph Tracy, *The Great Awakening* (1842); Edwin S. Gaustad, *The Great Awakening in New England* (1957), Wesley M. Gewehr, *The Great Awakening in Virginia: 1740–1790* (1930), and Charles H. Maxson, *The Great Awakening in the Middle Colonies* (1920); for the second Great Awakening *see* Catharine Cleveland, *The Great Revival in the West 1797–1805* (1916), Charles R. Keller, *The Second Great Awakening in Connecticut* (1942), Timothy L. Smith, *Revivalism and Social Reform in Mid-nineteenth Century America* (1957) and W. G. McLoughlin, *Modern Revivalism: Charles Grandison Finney to Billy Graham* (1959). (W. G. McL.)

REVUE, a light form of theatrical entertainment, originally deriving from the French street fairs of the Middle Ages, at which events of the year were passed in review in comic song and spectacle. It differs from variety in its use of pointed burlesque and satire, and from musical comedy in having no plot. Revue in its present form, dating from the early 19th century, was first developed at the Théâtre Porte-Saint-Martin in Paris by C. T. and J. H. Cogniard with their *Folies Marigny*. In the 20th century the French revue was the vehicle of such stars as Yvette Guilbert and Maurice Chevalier.

The English revue developed on one hand into a costume display and spectacle, reaching its peak in the Court Theatre productions of the 1890s; and, on the other, intimate shows such as André Charlot Revues of the 1920s in London and the provinces, the handsome shows at the Hippodrome, and especially the performances at Sir Charles Cochran's Ambassadors' Theatre. Revues of the intimate club type played an important part in keeping up the morale of Londoners during the blitz of 1940, both at the highly regarded Gate Theatre and the famous "Revuedeville" of the Windmill.

In the United States, *The Passing Show,* produced in New York in 1894 (second edition 1911), led the producer Florenz Ziegfeld in 1907 to initiate the 24 annual *Follies,* usually built around a star personality. George White and his *Scandals* put more emphasis on comedians and girls, less on spectacle for its own sake. More modest revues have been the *Music Box Revues,* the *Little Shows* of Dwight Wiman, *The Garrick Gaieties,* the Depression *Pins and Needles* of 1937, and the postwar G.I. show, *Call Me Mister. La Plume de Ma Tante* in 1959–60 returned the revue to its French origins.

See also BURLESQUE; MUSICAL COMEDY; MUSIC HALL AND VARIETY; VAUDEVILLE. (R. N. LE.; X.)

REWA, a town, district, and division of Madhya Pradesh, India. The town, formerly capital of the Rewa princely state and now the district headquarters, is situated on a Vindhyan outcrop 980 ft. (300 m.) above sea level and 70 mi. (113 km.) SSW of Allahabad. Pop. (1961) 43,065. It has no rail connection but metaled roads link it with Chhatarpur, Jabalpur, and Allahabad. There are three colleges affiliated with Saugar University.

REWA DISTRICT is roughly triangular in shape and covers an area of 2,509 sq.mi. (6,498 sq.km.) with a population (1961) of 772,602. Many of the inhabitants of the hilly tracts are Gonds and Kols. It is mostly hilly and is cultivated only in shallow depressions covered with laterite soil. Millets, maize (corn), and oilseeds are produced. More than one-third of the total area is under forests, yielding timber and lac. There are valuable coal deposits in the Umaria field.

The history of the former princely state of Rewa was a record of almost continuous warfare until it came under British guarantee in 1812. The ruling family belonged to the Baghela clan of Rajputs, a branch of the Solanki people. (M. N. K.)

REWARD is money or other compensation offered orally or in writing, either by the government or by an individual, to the public generally, or to a particular person or class of persons, for the performance of a designated service, such as the return of lost property or the apprehension of a suspected criminal. The offer expires a reasonable time after it is made, unless it stipulates otherwise. Prior to substantial compliance with the offerer's terms, it may be withdrawn at any time, even if the claimant is unaware of the withdrawal. The offer may contain such terms, provided they are lawful, as the offerer wishes to prescribe. Where a reward is lawfully offered, the first one who satisfies the prescribed conditions is entitled to it. Performance of these conditions constitutes acceptance of the offer and creates a binding contract. If several persons jointly perform the stipulated act, either by concerted action or, according to some authority, by acting independently, the reward may be equitably apportioned among them. Whether a person who is unaware of the offer at the time he performs the requested act may obtain the reward is disputed. One under a moral or official duty to perform the act usually may not claim a reward, unless he was required to perform acts beyond the scope of his duty for the reward. Police officers, therefore, ordinarily may not claim rewards for the apprehension of criminals or the recovery of stolen property, unless a statute provides to the contrary. (RT. K.)

REYKJAVÍK, the capital city of Iceland, is on the northern side of Seltjarnarnes Peninsula on the southeastern corner of Faxaflói (Faxa Bay) in the southwest of Iceland. Pop. (1965 est.) 78,000. Originally on a flat area between the harbour and the small Lake Tjörnin, the town now extends over low hills east and west of the lake. It is on the whole strikingly modern in aspect. Nearly all the houses are built of concrete; most of them are heated by natural hot water from drill holes 1,500–7,000 ft. (460–2,100 m.) deep. Among official buildings are the parliament house, the cathedral, the National Library, the university (founded in 1911), the National Museum, the National Theatre, the state hospital, and the navigation school. Bessastadir, the residence of the president, is outside the town.

Reykjavík is Iceland's main centre of commerce and the location of about half of the country's industrial establishments. The chief industries are food processing, metal and textile manufacture, and printing. Almost one-third of the fish landed in Iceland (apart from herring) is brought ashore there. There are regular shipping services to New York and the principal ports of northern and western Europe; and there are air services from Reykjavík airport (situated within the town) to the United States and many European countries. The international airport at Keflavík is 20 mi. WSW of the city.

Reykjavík ("Bay of Smokes") is situated on the place where the first settler of Iceland, the Norseman Ingólfur Arnarson, took up his abode in about 870. His farmstead derived its name from the smoke of nearby hot springs. A small village grew up there in the 18th century and was granted municipal rights in 1786. Since 1796 it has been the seat of the Icelandic bishop and since 1843 the seat of the Parliament (*althing*). It became the capital of Iceland in 1918; capital of the independent Republic of Iceland in 1944. (S. TH.)

REYMONT (REJMENT), **WLADYSLAW STANISLAW** (1867–1926), Polish novelist and writer of short stories, awarded the Nobel Prize for literature in 1924 for *Chlopi,* a novel of peasant life, was born at Kobiele Wielkie, near Lodz, in central Poland, on May 6, 1867, the son of a village organist. After failing to enter the *Gymnasium,* he became, in turn, a tailor, a wandering actor, a novice in a monastery, and a railway clerk. He began his literary career by writing short stories (published 1893). His account of a pilgrimage to the shrine of the Virgin at the monastery of Jasna Gora in Czestochowa (*Pielgrzymka do Jasnej Gory,* 1895) shows understanding of popular religious feeling. *Ziemia obiecana* (1899; English translation *The Promised Land,* 1927) describes Poles, Germans, and Jews competing ruthlessly for material "milk and honey" in the manufacturing town of Lodz. By contrast, *Chlopi,* four volumes (1902–09; English translation *The Peasants,* 1924–25), presents a panorama of Polish country life. It shows a village in every phase of the recurring cycle of the seasons, and thus, despite the realistic contemporary setting, creates an illusion of timelessness. Each of the numerous characters is endowed with unmistakable individuality. The villagers are the collective hero of this quasi-epic, often lyrical, but seldom idyllic, in tone. Reymont died in Warsaw on Dec. 5, 1926.

See J. Lorentowicz, *Ladislas Reymont, essai sur son oeuvre* (1924); W. Borowy, "Reymont," in *Slavonic Review,* vol. xvi (1937–38). (L. R. LR.)

REYNARD THE FOX, a medieval cycle of animal stories; its main heroes are Reynard the Fox and Isengrim the Wolf. Some of the stories (the wolf, or bear, fishing with his tail through a hole in the ice) are found all over the world; others (the sick lion cured by the wolf's skin) derive by oral transmission from Hellenistic sources. The cycle arose in the Lotharingian area, between Flanders and Germany, in the 10th and 11th centuries, when clerks began to forge Latin epics out of popular tales. The name "Ysengrimus" which appears as a satirical nickname at Laon in 1112 was used as the title of a poem in Latin elegiac couplets by Nivard of Ghent in 1152; some of the stories were soon recounted in French octosyllabic couplets. This early stage is attested by the High German poem *Vom Fuchs Reinhart,* by Heinrich (der Glîchezâre ?), a little masterpiece of 2,000 lines, freely adapted from an old French original.

The status of the extant French "branches" of the *Roman de Renart* (about 30 in number, nearly 40,000 lines of verse) is controversial (*see* FRENCH LITERATURE). Even those branches (II–IV, I and X) which come closest to Heinrich's material are probably elaborations of a kernel poem utilized by him. The facetious portrayal of rustic life, the camel as a papal legate speaking broken French, the animals riding on horses and recounting elaborate dreams, suggest the atmosphere of St. Louis' reign, and point forward to the still more sophisticated "Nun's Priest's Tale" of Chaucer (*q.v.*). The main literary tradition descends from these branches and the Flemish adaptations of them by Aernout and Willem (*c.* 1250). These were the sources of the Dutch and Low German prose manuscripts and chapbooks, used in their turn by Caxton and subsequent imitators down to Goethe's *Reineke Fuchs* (1794). Because of the popularity of these tales the nickname *renard* has replaced the old word *goupil* ("fox") throughout France.

BIBLIOGRAPHY.—*Texts: Ysengrimus*, ed. by E. Voigt (1884); *Das mittelhochdeutsche Gedicht vom Fuchs Reinhart*, ed. by G. Baesecke, 2nd ed. by I. Schröbler (1952). The α collection of branches of the *Roman de Renard*, ed. by E. Martin, 3 vol. and supplement (1882–87); the γ collection by D. M. Méon, 4 vol. (1826; supplement by P. Chabaille, 1835); the β collection by M. Roques, *Classiques français du moyen âge*, 5 vol. (1948–60), no. 78–79, 81, 85, 88. *Van den vos Reinaerde*, ed. by J. W. Muller, 2nd ed. (1939). *Reinke de vos* (1498), reprinted by F. Prien (1887), the 2nd ed. by A. Leitzmann (1925) contains a valuable introduction by K. Voretzsch; reprinted in the 3rd ed. by W. Steinberg (1960); Caxton's *Historye of Reynart the Foxe* (1481), ed. by H. Morley (1889), ed. by D. B. Sands (1960); a free rendering into verse by F. S. Ellis (1894); modernized with introduction and glossary by W. S. Stallybrass (1924).

Studies: Jacob Grimm, *Reinhart Fuchs* (1834); G. Paris, "Le Roman de Renard" in *Mélanges de littérature française du moyen âge*, pp. 337–423 (1912); L. Foulet, *Le Roman de Renard* (1914); R. Bossuat, *Le Roman de Renard* (1957), and *Manuel bibliographique . . .* (1951), no. 2560–2601, *Supplément* (1955), no. 6517–22 (*cf.* p. 126), *2nd Supplément* (1961), no. 7688–7702; H. R. Jauss, "Untersuchungen zur mittelalterlichen Tierdichtung," *Zeitschrift für Romanische Philologie*, Beiheft 100 (1959); J. Flinn, *Le Roman de Renart dans la littérature française et dans les littératures étrangères du moyen âge* (1961).

(C. A. Rn.)

REYNAUD, PAUL (1878–1966), French statesman, a conservative and patriotic republican, was the next to last premier of the Third Republic and an architect of the Fifth. Born at Barcelonnette, Basses-Alpes, on Oct. 15, 1878, and educated in Paris, he became a lawyer. He served in World War I on the Western Front and on a mission to Russia. In the Chamber of Deputies after the war he represented Basses-Alpes (1919–24) and then a Parisian constituency (from 1928). Between 1930 and 1932 he held successively the posts of minister of finance, of the colonies, and of justice. Out of office for the next five years, he advocated resistance to Nazi Germany and in 1935 called in vain for preparation for tank warfare, as recommended by Charles de Gaulle. As minister of justice under Édouard Daladier (from April 1938), Reynaud protested against appeasement of Germany over Czechoslovakia, but was dissuaded from resigning office (though he could still break with his parliamentary group, the Alliance Démocratique, when its leader, Pierre Flandin, sent congratulations to Hitler after the Conference of Munich). Appointed minister of finance (Nov. 1, 1938), he devalued the franc and sponsored measures of austerity to restore national solvency and to pay for better defenses.

In World War II Reynaud became premier on March 21, 1940. He strongly favoured Allied intervention in Norway, made De Gaulle undersecretary of state for war (with the rank of general), and, when France was collapsing, argued for standing by the British alliance. On June 16 he resigned, so as not to be a party to an armistice with Germany. He was arrested on Sept. 6 by the Vichy regime and spent the rest of the war in captivity.

After the liberation, Reynaud returned to politics, his vigorous physique unimpaired. As deputy for the Nord *département* (1946–62), he was an active spokesman for West European unity. He held office in two governments (1948 and 1950) and twice (1952 and 1953) tried to form cabinets of his own. Welcoming De Gaulle's accession to power, he presided in 1958 over the Consultative Committee on the drafting of the constitution of the Fifth Republic. In 1962, however, he forcefully denounced the Gaullist inauguration of an overtly presidential regime. He died in the American Hospital of Paris (Neuilly) on Sept. 21, 1966.

Reynaud's major publications are *La France a sauvé l'Europe* (1947, revised as *Au coeur de la mêlée, 1930–45*, 1951; Eng. trans., *In the Thick of the Fight, 1930–45*, 1955); and *Mémoires*, 2 vol. (1960–63).

REYNOLDS, SIR JOSHUA (1723–1792), English painter, perhaps the dominant figure in the history of British art, was born at Plympton, Devon, on July 16, 1723. He was educated at the Plympton grammar school and was well read in classical literature. Influenced by the essays of Jonathan Richardson, Reynolds aspired to become a painter, and in 1740 he was apprenticed for four years to Thomas Hudson in London. In 1743, however, he returned to Devon and began painting at Plymouth dock portraits that reveal his inexperience and that are very much in the tradition then prevailing. Returning to London for two years in 1744, he began to acquire his independent style and his knowledge of the old masters. An outstanding picture of this period is "Capt. the Hon. John Hamilton" (owned by the duke of Abercorn), which shows Reynolds' bolder style combined with a considered use of impasto.

Back in Devon in 1746 he painted his large group of the "Eliot Family," which clearly demonstrates his knowledge of the vast picture by Van Dyck at Wilton house, Wiltshire. In 1749 he sailed with his friend Augustus Keppel to Minorca, where he stayed for five months and endured the accident that permanently scarred his lip, the scar being a feature prominent in all his self-portraits. From Minorca he made his way to Rome, where he remained for over two years. There he was able to give full reign to his scholarship and to store his mind with the great masterpieces of classical and modern painting and sculpture. The impressions that he retained from this visit were to inspire his paintings and his *Discourses* for the rest of his life, for he felt that it was by allying painting with scholarship that he could best achieve his ambition of raising the status of his profession. He returned to England via Florence, Parma, Bologna and Venice, where he absorbed and noted the colour and composition of works by Titian, Tintoretto and Veronese. He was immediately seduced by Venetian colouring and, although all his life he preached the need for all young artists to study the classical forms of Michelangelo and Raphael, his own works are redolent of the light and shade of Venetian colouring.

In 1753 Reynolds settled in London, where he was to live for the rest of his life, first in St. Martin's lane and finally, after 1760, in Leicester square. From the first his success was assured, and by 1755 he was employing studio help, notably Giuseppe Marchi. The first great work from this period is "Commodore Keppel" (in the National Maritime museum, Greenwich, London). The pose is not original, being a reversal of that of the "Apollo Belvedere" statue in the Vatican, but the subject is shown striding along the seashore in a new and vital way. It could be said that with this portrait all of English portrait painting took on a new life and vigour and the tradition of Sir Godfrey Kneller was entirely destroyed. A painter could not always hope to have such a heroic sitter, but Reynolds was equally successful with the more domestic portraits of men and women. In these first years in London his knowledge of Venetian painting is very apparent; *e.g.*, the portraits of "Lord Cathcart" (owned by Lord Cathcart) and "Lord Ludlow" (at Woburn abbey, Bedfordshire). Of his domestic portraits the most enchanting is that of "Georgiana, Countess Spencer, and Her Daughter" (owned by Lord Spencer), painted in 1760, which is one of the greatest English portraits, full of tenderness and careful observation. In the 1760s he was more and more under the influence of the painters of the Bolognese school, and the pose and clothes of his sitters take on a more rigid, classical pattern, losing in consequence much of the sympathy and understanding he could have given them. It was from these portraits that he hoped to equate portrait painting with the "grand style," and they are indeed an illustration to much that he has to say in his *Discourses*. It has been suggested that the painting of "Garrick Between Tragedy and Comedy" (on loan from Lord Rothschild to King's college, Cambridge) is a parody of his own predicament, Comedy being painted in the softer and more domestic manner of Correggio and Tragedy in the classical manner of Guido Reni.

Reynolds was to realize his ambitions for his profession in a new and public way. Hitherto there had been no public exhibitions of contemporary artists in London, but in 1760 the Society of Artists was founded and the first of many successful exhibitions held. After some internal squabbles the patronage of King George III was sought and in 1768 the Royal Academy was founded. Although Reynolds' painting had found no favour at court, he was the obvious candidate for the presidency and the king confirmed his election and knighted him. Reynolds guided the policy of the academy with skill, and the pattern he set has been followed with little variation ever since. His yearly *Discourses* are some of the wisest words an older painter has offered to those beginning their careers, and they also clearly mirror many of his own thoughts and aspirations, as well as his own problems of line versus colour and public and private portraiture.

From 1769 nearly all of Reynolds' most important works appeared in the academy, and this undoubtedly influenced the rather more public manner of his portraits. In certain exhibitions he included historical pieces, such as "Ugolino" (at Knole house, Kent), which were perhaps his least successful contribution to painting. Many of his child studies are tender and even amusing, though now and again the sentiment tends to be excessive; two of the most enchanting are "Master Crewe as Henry VIII" (owned by Lord O'Neil) and "Lady Caroline Scott as Winter" (owned by the duke of Buccleuch). His most ambitious portrait commission was the "Family of the Duke of Marlborough" (at Blenheim palace, Oxfordshire), which was shown at the academy of 1778. Although not wholly successful it is a monumental group entirely suitable to the house that holds it: a conversation piece enlarged to the scale of a history piece. It may have been the arrival of Thomas Gainsborough in London in 1774 that caused Reynolds to revert to a more informal mood.

In 1781 Reynolds visited Flanders and Holland, where he studied the work of Rubens, and this seems to have affected his own style as from that time the texture of his picture surface becomes far richer. This is particularly true of his portrait of the "Duchess of Devonshire and Her Daughter" (at Chatsworth house, Derbyshire). It was this last phase of dramatic and baroque style that influenced John Hoppner and Thomas Lawrence, but they paid perhaps more attention to the painting of silks and satins and rather less to the characterization. Reynolds was never a mere society painter or flatterer and he never forgot what James Northcote called, when writing of Allan Ramsay, the "mental part" of a portrait. It has been suggested that his deafness allowed Reynolds a clearer insight into the character of his sitters, the lack of one faculty sharpening the use of his eyes. His vast learning allowed him to vary his poses and style so often that the well-known remark of Gainsborough, "Damn him, how various he is!" is entirely understandable. In 1782 Reynolds had a paralytic stroke and about the same time he was saddened by bickerings within the

Royal Academy. Seven years later his eyesight began to fail and he delivered his last *Discourse* at the academy in 1790. On Feb. 23, 1792, he died.

Reynolds preferred the company of men of letters to that of his fellow artists. Although his 14th *Discourse* is a tender and moving appreciation of Gainsborough, who stood for so much that he himself disliked in painting, it was in the company of Dr. Johnson and of Edmund Burke and Oliver Goldsmith that Reynolds was happiest. When Goldsmith died, Reynolds could not bring himself to paint for a whole day, and the moving essay he wrote on his friend showed that he could write a portrait as well as he could paint one. Reynolds and his friends were members of "The Club," which he established in 1764. He never married and his house was kept for him by his sister Frances.

Reynolds' state portraits of the king and queen were never considered a success and he seldom painted for them, but the prince of Wales patronized him extensively and there were few distinguished families or individuals who did not sit to him. Nonetheless some of his finest portraits are those of his intimate friends and of fashionable women of a questionable way of life. Unfortunately Reynolds' technique was not always entirely sound, and many of his paintings have suffered as a result. After his visit to Italy he tried to produce the effects of Tintoretto and Titian by using transparent glazes over a monochrome underpainting, but the carmine he used for his flesh tones was not permanent and even in his lifetime began to fade, causing the overpale faces of many surviving portraits. An example of this can be seen in the "Roffey Family Group" (in Birmingham art gallery, Eng.). This paleness has been increased by injudicious cleaning in certain paintings. The most interesting picture to show how Reynolds worked is the unfinished double portrait of "Burke and Lord Rockingham" (in Fitzwilliam museum, Cambridge). In the 1760s Reynolds began to use bitumen more extensively, which was detrimental to the paint surface. Of his later style the "Duchess of Devonshire and Her Daughter" is in almost matchless condition. Though a keen collector of old master drawings, he was never a draftsman and indeed few of his drawings have any merit, but there is an interesting early "Self-Portrait" drawing (owned by Lord Harcourt) and a design for "Comedy" (in the Ashmolean museum, Oxford). His ledger books from 1755 to 1789, which, with a few gaps, are preserved, make it possible to date most of his sittings with reasonable accuracy.

His work is represented in most public and private collections and he is splendidly shown in the royal collection. The National gallery, London, has, among other paintings, "Capt. Tarleton," "Lord Heathfield," "The Countess of Albemarle" and "Three Graces Adorning a Term of Hymen." Among his portraits in the National Portrait gallery, London, are those of "Johnson," "Boswell" and his own early "Self-Portrait" shading his eyes. The Wallace collection, London, has "Nelly O'Brien," "Mrs. Carnac" and "Miss Bowles." Private collections particularly rich in his work include those of the duke of Bedford, duke of Devonshire, duke of Buccleuch, earl of Harewood, George Howard, earl of Ilchester, John Wyndham and Lord Spencer. An interesting portrait of Reynolds, not by his hand but by Angelica Kauffmann, belongs to Lord Morley.

His work is not richly represented in the United States, although his great portrait of "Mrs. Siddons as the Tragic Muse" is in the Huntington library, San Marino, Calif.; and Washington and New York also have important examples.

See also references under "Reynolds, Sir Joshua" in the Index.

BIBLIOGRAPHY.—R. Fry (ed.), *Discourses Delivered to the Students of the Royal Academy by Sir Joshua Reynolds, Kt.* (1905); J. Northcote (ed.), *Memoirs of Sir Joshua Reynolds* (1813) and *Supplement* (1815); C. R. Leslie and T. Taylor, *Life and Times of Sir Joshua Reynolds*, 2 vol. (1865); A. Graves and W. V. Cronin, *A History of the Works of Sir Joshua Reynolds*, 4 vol. (1899–1901); J. Steegmann, *Sir Joshua Reynolds* (1933); E. K. Waterhouse, *Reynolds* (1941), the most fully illustrated work, and *Painting in Britain 1530–1790* (1953); Derek Hudson, *Sir Joshua Reynolds* (1958); *Catalogue* of the exhibition held at 45 Park lane, London, in 1937, with illustrated *Souvenir*; *Catalogues* of "The First Hundred Years of the Royal Academy 1769–1868" (1951), "British Portraits Exhibition" (1956), both at the R. A., and the "Reynolds Exhibition," Birmingham, Eng. (1961). (J. O. W.)

"NELLY O'BRIEN" BY SIR JOSHUA REYNOLDS, 1763

REYNOLDS, OSBORNE (1842–1912), English engineer and physicist, best known for his work in the fields of hydraulics and hydrodynamics, was born at Belfast on Aug. 23, 1842. Gaining early workshop experience and graduating at Queens' College, Cambridge, in 1867, he became in 1868 the first professor of engineering in the Owens College, Manchester. He was elected a fellow of the Royal Society in 1877 and a Royal medalist in 1888. He retired in 1905 and died at Watchet, Somerset, on Feb. 21, 1912.

Reynolds' studies of condensation and the transfer of heat between solids and fluids brought radical revision in boiler and condenser design, while his work on turbine pumps laid the foundation of their rapid development. A fundamentalist among engineers, he formulated the theory of lubrication (1886), and in his classical paper on the law of resistance in parallel channels (1883) investigated the transition from smooth, or laminar, to turbulent flow, later (1889) developing the mathematical framework which became standard in turbulence work. His name is perpetuated in the "Reynolds stress," or drag exerted between adjacent layers of fluid due to turbulent motion, and in the "Reynolds number" (*see* AERODYNAMICS), which provides a criterion for dynamic similarity and hence for correct modeling in many fluid flow experiments. He developed and exploited corresponding criteria for wave and tidal motions in rivers and estuaries, and made pioneering contributions to the concept of group velocity. Among his other work was the explanation of the radiometer and an early absolute determination of the mechanical equivalent of heat. Reynolds' *Scientific Papers* were published in three volumes (1900–03).

See A. H. Gibson, *Osborne Reynolds and His Work in Hydraulics and Hydrodynamics* (1946).   (C. H. B. P.)

REZAIYEH (formerly URMIA or URUMIA), the capital of the *ostan* (province) of Western Azerbaijan, Iran, lies on a large plain west of Lake Urmia, 75 mi. (120 km.) WSW of Tabriz. The population in 1956 was 67,605, mainly Turkish, with Kurdish, Assyrian (Nestorian), and Armenian minorities. The plain of Urmia has plenty of water for irrigation and is very fertile; cultivation, especially of fruits and tobacco, is of a high standard.

Ancient remains are scattered over the plain. The kingdom of Urartu (*q.v.*) has left some marks. During the Muslim period the region was frequently dominated by Kurdish princes. For long periods the city belonged to the Ottoman Empire. About 1900, Christians (Nestorians and Orthodox) formed 45% of the total population. In July 1918, however, there was a large-scale exodus of Christians after the retreat of the Russians. Most of the remaining Christians were massacred in the same year and the remnant of 600 transferred to Tabriz. Later, some survivors were repatriated by the Iranian government and agriculture was fully restored. Rezaiyeh is connected by main road with Tabriz via Khoi northward and with Kermanshah via Mahabad and Sanandaj southward. There is an airfield in the vicinity.   (H. Bo.)

REZANOV, NIKOLAI PETROVICH (1764–1807), Russian trader, diplomat, and administrator who was a founder and an outstanding executive of the great Russian-American Company which played a major part in the history of Alaska (*q.v.*) and of the North Pacific. He was born in St. Petersburg on April 8 (new style; March 28, old style), 1764.

Having met G. I. Shelekhov, head of the Shelekhov-Golikov Fur Company, in 1788, Rezanov became interested in that merchant's project of obtaining a monopoly of the fur trade of the Russian settlements along the northwestern coast of America. He entered into partnership with Shelekhov and, on the latter's death (1795), made himself the leading spirit of the company. Wanting privileges analogous to those granted by Great Britain to the East India Company, he had just persuaded the empress Catherine II to sign a charter for him when she died (1796). He then had to begin new negotiations with the emperor Paul, whom he finally induced (1798–99) to grant to the Russian-American Company dominion for 20 years over the American coast northward from latitude 55° and over the Aleutian and the Kuril Islands. This "trust," which crowded out the smaller enterprises, was at first a source of great revenue to Rezanov and to the other 400 shareholders (including members of the imperial family).

Rezanov did much to instigate the voyage of Adam Ivan Krusenstern on the first Russian circumnavigation of the globe (1803–06). He sailed with this expedition from Kronshtadt across the Atlantic and round Cape Horn to Kamchatka, whence in 1804 he went to Japan on an unsuccessful mission as the emperor Alexander I's ambassador. Returning to Kamchatka in 1805, he there received orders to remain in the North Pacific area as imperial inspector and plenipotentiary of the company, and to correct the abuses that were ruining the great enterprise. He traveled slowly to Sitka (Novo-Arkhangelsk, or New Archangel, centre of the company's colonial administration) by way of the islands.

At the end of a winter in Sitka, Rezanov sailed for the Spanish settlements in California to trade his wares for foodstuffs (of which the Russian colonies were seriously in need) and to arrange a treaty for the provisioning of the company's colonies twice a year from New Spain. Storms prevented his taking possession of the mouth of the Columbia River for Russia during his voyage, but he reached San Francisco early in April 1806. Though he was received with courtesy, he was told that the laws of Spain forbade the colonies to trade with foreign powers, and that the governor of all the Californias was incorruptible. Rezanov would have failed again had it not been for a love affair with the daughter of the *comandante* of San Francisco, Don José Argüello, and for his personal skill in winning the clergy over to his cause. As it was, when he sailed for Sitka six weeks later, his ship's hold was full of breadstuffs and dried meats, he had the perplexed governor's promise to forward a copy of the treaty to Spain at once, and he was affianced to the most beautiful girl in California. From Sitka he returned again to Kamchatka, whence he dispatched ships to wrest Sakhalin from the Japanese. He then started overland for St. Petersburg to obtain Alexander I's signature to the treaty. He died of fever and exhaustion in Krasnoyarsk, Siberia, on March 13 (N.S.; 1, O.S.), 1807.

Rezanov was deeply and humanely concerned for his employees and for the wretched natives who were little more than the slaves of the company. His correspondence with the company shows clearly that he wished to annex to Russia the western coast of North America, and to encourage immediate emigration from Russia on a large scale. His Californian treaty, however, was never ratified; his reforms were allowed to lapse; the fortunes of the colonies deteriorated, and his Spanish fiancée became a nun. One of the ablest and most ambitious men of his time, he was forgotten in the cemetery of a poor Siberian town.

BIBLIOGRAPHY.—H. H. Bancroft, *History of California* (1889) and *History of Alaska* (1887); P. Tikhmenev, *Istoricheskoe obozreniye obrazovaniya Rossiisko-Amerikanskoi Kompanii* (1861–63); T. C. Russell (ed.), *The Rezanov Voyage to Nueva California* (1926); A. Yarmolinsky, "A Rambling Note on the Russian Columbus," *New York Public Library Bulletin*, vol. xxxi (1927); S. B. Okun, *Rossiisko-Amerikanskaya Kompaniya* (1939).   (G. At.; X.)

REZA SHAH PAHLAVI (1878–1944), shah of Iran from 1925 to 1941, was born at Alasht, in the Savad Kuh district of the northern province of Mazanderan, on March 16, 1878. His father, who died soon after his birth, was an army officer. Entering the army as a private soldier at an early age, he rapidly obtained commissioned rank and showed such exceptional aptitude and ability that he rose at length to the command of the Persian Cossack brigade.

Persia, because of its involuntary involvement in World War I and the ineptitude of Ahmad Shah and his ministers, had been reduced to a sad plight by the beginning of 1921. In February of that year the patriotic leader and reformer Sayyid Zia ad-Din Tabatabai, in conjunction with Reza Khan and his Cossack brigade, carried out a *coup d'état* in Teheran and took over the government, Sayyid Zia becoming prime minister and Reza Khan minister of war and commander in chief. In 1923 Reza Khan became prime minister and virtual ruler of the country. At this stage of his career Reza Khan modeled himself closely on his Turkish contemporary Mustafa Kemal. There was for a time a movement in Persia in favour of abolishing the monarchy and substituting a republic, with Reza Khan as president; this idea, however, met with much opposition, particularly from the *'ulama'* (learned men or "clergy"), who were alarmed by acts of the Turkish government which they regarded as anti-Islamic. It was therefore decided to retain the monarchy but to depose Ahmad Shah (who had been absent in Europe for some time) and to place Reza Khan on the vacant throne. These steps were accordingly taken, and Reza Khan became shah on Dec. 16, 1925.

Reza Shah proceeded to carry out many reforms on Western lines, largely modeled on those of Mustafa Kemal. He ruthlessly suppressed brigandage, curbed the power of the tribes, and made the authority of the central government effective throughout the country. Though some of Reza Shah's reforms were ill-conceived and in certain cases harshly enforced, there can be no doubt that, on the whole, he contributed many benefits to his country, especially in the earlier part of his reign. His greatest achievement was the construction of the Trans-Iranian Railway, which was completed in 1938 without recourse to foreign loans. The shah likewise paid much attention to the improvement and development of the road system.

Being strongly desirous of modernizing the industries of his country, and not wishing to be beholden to either Great Britain or the U.S.S.R. for help, he sought and obtained much machinery and many technicians from Germany. When World War II broke out, the presence of about 2,000 German technicians in Persia (Iran after 1935) aroused fears in Great Britain lest these men might destroy the refinery of the Anglo-Iranian Oil Company at Abadan and put its pipeline system and oil fields out of action. After Germany's attack on the U.S.S.R. in 1941, the necessity arose for the Western allies to send military supplies across Iran to the hard-pressed Russians. When Great Britain and the U.S.S.R. asked for permission for these supplies to be sent, Reza Shah refused. The two powers then repeated their request and also demanded the expulsion of the German technicians, who, they feared, might sabotage the Trans-Iranian Railway. The shah, however, again refused, whereupon British and Soviet troops entered Iran. Reza Shah abdicated in favour of his eldest son, Mohammed Reza Pahlavi (q.v.), on Sept. 16, 1941. The former shah was then exiled first to Mauritius and later to South Africa. He died in Johannesburg on July 26, 1944. *See* also PERSIAN HISTORY: *Pahlavi Dynasty.*

See J. M. Upton, *The History of Modern Iran: an Interpretation* (1960); Mohammad Reza Pahlevi, *Mission For My Country* (1961).

(L. Lo).

RHAMNACEAE, the buckthorn family, a group of thorny shrubs, woody vines, and trees found in the warmer parts of both hemispheres. It includes 45 genera and about 550 species of dicotyledonous plants. Large genera are *Rhamnus* with about 230 species, *Zizyphus* with 100 species, and *Phylicia* with 90 species. Jujube (q.v.), or the Chinese date, native to Asia, is the fruit of *Zizyphus jujube* (*Z. vulgaris*), and the Indian jujube is the fruit of *Z. mauritiana.* The bark of various species of *Rhamnus* is utilized in the practice of medicine, cascara sagrada (q.v.) being that of the western American *R. purshiana. Ceanothus,* a genus highly developed in the western United States, is known as the California lilac. *See* also BUCKTHORN. (E. D. ML.)

RHÄTICUS (RHETICUS), a surname derived from Rhaetia (Austria), the district of his birth, by GEORG JOACHIM VON LAUCHEN (1514–1576), astronomer and mathematician who, as an associate of Nicolaus Copernicus (q.v.), was among the first to adopt and to spread his heliocentric theory. Rhäticus was born at Feldkirch on Feb. 16, 1514. In 1537 he was appointed to a chair of mathematics and astronomy at Wittenberg. He was much attracted by news of Copernicus' heliocentric theory and in 1539 he resigned his professorship and went to Frauenburg, where he studied for two years with Copernicus. Rhäticus published the first exposition of the new heliocentric views in his *De libris revolutionum . . . Nic. Copernici . . . narratio prima . . .* (1541) and for about ten years thereafter produced ephemerides based on the Copernican system. He persuaded Copernicus to complete the great *De revolutionibus orbium coelestium* and to permit him to take the manuscript to Nürnberg for publication. Because of the religious objections of Luther and others, Rhäticus left Nürnberg before *De revolutionibus* was actually published in 1543, and moved to Leipzig.

From his time at Wittenberg until his death at Kassa, Hung., on Dec. 5, 1576, Rhäticus worked on his great treatise *Opus Palatinum de triangulis,* which was published posthumously in 1596 by Valentine Otto, mathematician to the electoral prince palatine. The work contains tables of sines, cosines, tangents, etc., in intervals of ten seconds of arc and calculated to ten decimal places. Rhäticus proposed to compute similar tables to 15 decimal places, but did not live to complete the task. The table of sines on this scale was published in 1613 by B. Pitiscus (1561–1613) under the title *Thesaurus mathematicus,* Pitiscus himself completing certain of the calculations. (CN. A. R.)

RHAZES (ABU-BAKR MOHAMMED IBN ZAKARIYYA AR-RAZI) (*c.* 865–923 or 932), undoubtedly the greatest physician of the Islamic world, also a philosopher of remarkable independence of mind and a well-known alchemist, was a Persian Muslim, born in the city of Rayy (Ray) about 865. The tradition that he was an alchemist before he became thoroughly acquainted with medicine may be reliable. He became chief physician in a new hospital at Rayy and subsequently held a similar position in Baghdad for some time. As so many "intellectuals" in his day, he lived at different small courts enjoying the protection of minor rulers. He claimed to fulfill in his own time the function of a Socrates in philosophy and that of a Hippocrates in medicine. He died in his native city in 923 or 932.

The two most important medical works of Rhazes are the *Kitab al-Mansuri,* which he composed for Mansur ibn Ishak, the ruler of Rayy, and which became well known in the west in Gerard of Cremona's 12th-century Latin translation; and *Al-Hawi,* the "Comprehensive Book," in which he surveys Greek, Syrian, and early Arabic medicine in their entirety, as well as some Indian medical knowledge, adding his own considered judgment and his own medical experience throughout. Among his numerous minor medical treatises, *A Treatise On the Small Pox and Measles* is famous, having been translated into Latin and various modern languages and into Byzantine Greek.

The philosophical writings of Rhazes (*see* ARABIC PHILOSOPHY) were completely neglected for centuries: not until the 20th century did their importance come to be appreciated again. He claims to be a Platonist, and his views are everywhere at variance with the philosophy of such thinkers as al-Farabi, Avicenna, and Averroes. He was probably acquainted with Arabic translations of Democritus and followed a similar line in his own atomic theory of matter. His *Autobiography* is rather a spirited defense of the philosophical way of life as he understood it than an account of actual events (Eng. trans. by A. J. Arberry in the *Asiatic Review,* 1949). *On Spiritual Medicine* (Eng. trans. by A. J. Arberry, *The Spiritual Physick of Rhazes,* London, 1950) is a popular ethical treatise. The main alchemical work of Rhazes is the *Secret of Secrets* (German trans. by J. Ruska, 1937).

BIBLIOGRAPHY.—C. Brockelmann, *Geschichte der arabischen Literatur,* vol. i, 2nd ed., p. 267 ff. (1943); E. G. Browne, *Arabian Medicine* (1921), *passim;* L. Leclerc, *Histoire de la médecine arabe,* i, p. 337 ff. (1876); G. Sarton, *Introduction to the History of Science,* vol. i, p. 609 (1927); P. Kraus and S. Pines, "Al-Razi," *Encyclopedia of Islam,* vol. iii (1936); M. Meyerhof, "The Philosophy of the Physician Al-Razi," in *Islamic Culture,* vol. xv, p. 45 ff. (1941); S. Pines, "Razi critique de Galien," in the *Actes* of the 7th International Congress for the History of Science (1953), and *Nouvelles Études sur Abu 'l-Barakat al-Baghdadi* (1955). (R. R. WR.)

RHEA, in Greek mythology an age-old goddess, probably pre-Hellenic in origin, as her connection with Crete suggests. A daughter of Uranus and Gaea (Heaven and Earth), she married her brother Cronus (q.v.). His parents informed Cronus of a prophecy that one of his children was fated to overthrow him. Accordingly he swallowed his children Hestia, Demeter, Hera, Hades, and Poseidon soon after they were born. Rhea, however, concealed the birth of Zeus in a cave on Mt. Dictys in Crete, and the Curetes (q.v.) drowned the infant's cries by performing their war dance in armour. Cronus was given a stone wrapped in swaddling clothes, and swallowed it in the belief that it was Zeus. Subsequently Cronus was vanquished by Zeus and forced to disgorge the swallowed children.

Rhea was worshiped sporadically throughout the Greek world, often in association with Cronus or Zeus, her cult being well attested at Athens, in Arcadia, at Olympia, and especially in Crete. She was associated with fruitfulness and had affinities with Earth, with the Mother Goddess, and with Cybele (Rhea-Zeus corresponding to Cybele-Attis; *see* GREAT MOTHER OF THE GODS). No doubt her cult could be as primitive and barbaric as her myth; but it could also be spiritualized into the worship of a divine mother, whose tender care for humanity won a ready response from her children, an archetypal religious concept of extreme antiquity in the Mediterranean area.

See H. J. Rose, *A Handbook of Greek Mythology* (1958).

(D. E. W. W.)

RHEA, the American cousin of the African ostrich (*q.v.*), a giant flightless ratite bird confined to South America. The two species are the common rhea, *Rhea americana,* of open country from northeastern Brazil to central Argentina, and Darwin's rhea, *Pterocnemia pennata,* of uplands from Peru to the tip of the continent. Considerably smaller than the ostrich, about four feet tall, the rheas are further distinguished by the possession of three toes, the absence of fine plumes, and the general brownish colour of the feathers, which in Darwin's rhea are white tipped. Rheas are polygamous, and the cock bird performs the duties of incubation. Rheas frequently associate with deer or guanacos to form "mixed herds" similar to those formed by the ostrich with zebras and antelopes.

RHEDEN, a commune in the province of Gelderland, Neth., comprises the villages of Velp, Rheden, De Steeg, Ellekom, Dieren, Spankeren, and Laag Soeren, which lie along the highway from Arnhem to Zutphen, between the IJssel River and the Veluwe hills. Pop. (1964 est.) 44,083 (mun.). Velp, Rheden, Ellekom and Spankeren have 11th- and 12th-century churches. Other old buildings are the 16th-century castles of Biljoen (Velp) and Middachten (De Steeg) and the 12th-century Gelderse Tower. A striking modern building is the high school in Velp (1959). The commune is served by railways to Apeldoorn, Arnhem, and Zutphen. Manufactures include steel and concrete constructional components, enamelware, and clothing. The tourist industry is important, as much of the commune is in the Veluwezoom National Park.

RHEE, SYNGMAN (1875–1965), Korean statesman, first president of the Korean Republic, was born on April 26, 1875, in Whanghae province, Korea. He completed a traditional classical education and then entered a Methodist school, where he learned English and enough Western thought to become a confirmed Nationalist and ultimately a Christian. He joined with other Korean leaders in 1896 to form the Independence Club and served briefly as a member of the privy council. When reactionary elements destroyed the club in 1897, Rhee was arrested and imprisoned until 1904. On his release he went immediately to the United States, where he attended George Washington University (A.B. 1907), Harvard (M.A. 1908), and Princeton (Ph.D. 1910). He was the first Korean to earn a doctoral degree in an American university. While a student he made frequent but unsuccessful appeals to the United States to save his country from Japan. When he returned home in 1910 he found it impossible to hide his hostility toward Japanese rule, and after short terms as a YMCA worker and high school principal he returned to the U.S. in 1912.

For the next 30 years Rhee served as a spokesman for Korean independence, publicizing Korea's plight and trying in vain to win international support for his cause. In 1919 he was elected president of the Korean Republic in exile, holding that post for 20 years. He returned to Korea in 1945 after spending the war years in trying to secure Allied promises of Korean independence. Elected president of the Republic of Korea in 1948, he was reelected in 1952, 1956, and 1960.

As president of the ROK, Rhee's great objective was the freedom and unification of his country. He used his broad powers to remove domestic opposition to his program, and even defied the United Nations when he felt that body threatened those ends (for Rhee's participation in the Korean War *see* KOREAN WAR). He purged the national assembly and outlawed the opposition Progressive Party, whose leader was executed for treason. Rhee controlled the appointment of mayors, village headmen, and chiefs of police, but in 1956 failed to prevent the election of an opposition vice-president. Government claims that the March 1960 elections gave Rhee over 90% of the popular vote (55% in 1956) provoked student-led demonstrations resulting in heavy casualties and demands for his resignation, supported by the unanimous vote of the national assembly. Rhee resigned April 27, and left for exile in Hawaii. A caretaker government pledged new elections and the repudiation of the most widely criticized of Rhee's domestic and foreign policies. Rhee died July 19, 1965, in Honolulu. *See also* KOREA: *History.*

(F. G. WN.)

RHEGIUM: *see* REGGIO DI CALABRIA.

RHEINBERGER, JOSEPH GABRIEL VON (1839–1901), German composer and teacher whose organ sonatas are among the finest 19th-century works for that instrument, was born at Vaduz, Liechtenstein, on March 17, 1839. As a child he studied the organ in his native town and became organist at the parish church there when only seven years old. He later studied at Feldkirch and Munich, and in 1867 became professor of organ and composition at the Munich Conservatory. Among his pupils in composition were E. Humperdinck, E. Wolf-Ferrari, W. Furtwängler, and the U.S. composers G. W. Chadwick and H. W. Parker. Besides 20 organ sonatas, Rheinberger wrote 4 operas and much church music and chamber music. He received a title of nobility in 1894. He died at Munich on Nov. 25, 1901.

See H. Grace, *The Organ Works of Rheinberger* (1925).

RHEINE, a town of West Germany in the *Land* (state) of North Rhine-Westphalia (Nordrhein-Westfalen), Federal Republic of Germany, is situated on the Ems 31 mi. (50 km.) W of Osnabrück by road. Pop. (1961) 44,322. St. Dionysius' Church (1484), the main square, Bentlage Castle, the Gottesgabe Bath with its pump room, and the zoo are of interest. Rheine is a junction of eight railway lines, the chief being the Ruhr-North Sea and the Berlin-Hanover-Hook of Holland routes. Nearby is the secondary airport of Rheine-Eschendorf. Industries include cotton spinning, weaving, and the manufacture of stockings, machinery, and lime. The town suffered in the Thirty Years' War and was severely damaged in World War II, but it has been rebuilt.

RHEINHAUSEN, a town of West Germany in the *Land* (state) of North Rhine-Westphalia (Nordrhein-Westfalen), Federal Republic of Germany, lies on the left bank of the Rhine a short distance upstream from Duisburg. Pop. (1961) 68,126. The site was chosen by the Krupps for a large iron and steel plant, which started production in 1898. Rheinhausen has docks to handle imported iron ore, fuel, and limestone. The town grew up to house workers at the Krupp plant. It was formed in 1923 through the incorporation of Hochemmerich and Friemersheim and was chartered in 1934. Neither the town nor the plant suffered serious damage during World War II, and the works, which have remained in the possession of the Krupp family, have been fully restored.

(N. J. G. P.)

RHEINISCHES SCHIEFERGEBIRGE: *see* MIDDLE RHINE HIGHLANDS.

RHEINLAND PFALZ: *see* RHINELAND-PALATINATE.

RHENANUS, BEATUS (BEATUS BILDE) (1485–1546), German humanist and historian noted for his editions of Latin texts, was born in Schlettstadt (Alsace) in 1485. An intimate friend of Erasmus, he was from 1511 to 1526 one of the scholars working for Johann Froben's press at Basel. Using recently discovered Rhineland manuscripts whenever possible, he edited Tertullian (*editio princeps,* 1521) and the historians Curtius Rufus (1518), Velleius Paterculus (*editio princeps,* 1520), Procopius, Jordanes, and Agathias (1531), Tacitus (1533), and, in collaboration with Sigismund Gelenius, Livy (1535). His *Res Germanicae* (1531), a pioneer study of the early history of the Germans, was notable for the care with which it dated and handled its sources and for its discussion of social, cultural, and economic developments. But his life of Erasmus (1540) was, disappointingly, a mere panegyric. He died at Strasbourg on Aug. 28, 1546.

See A. Horawitz in *Sitzungsberichte der philos.-hist. Classe der Kaiserlichen Akademie der Wissenschaften zu Wien,* vol. 70–74 (1872–74); G. C. Knod, *Aus der Bibliothek des Beatus Rhenanus* (1889).

(R. R. Bo.)

RHENIUM, a very rare metallic element discovered by Ida and Walter Noddack in 1925. Its chemical symbol is Re; its atomic number 75; and its atomic weight 186.2. Until 1965 the annual world production of rhenium was conveniently estimated in kilograms (or pounds). The metal and its alloys have found limited application as fountain-pen points, high-temperature thermocouples, catalysts, electrical contact points, instrument-bearing points, and in electric components.

Rhenium is widely distributed in a variety of minerals but usually in concentrations below 0.1 part per 1,000,000. It occurs in concentrations as high as 10 to 20 parts per 1,000,000 in molybdenum sulfide ores, and to a lesser extent in sulfidic copper ores. It is probably present as its stable disulfide (ReS_2). The recovery of rhenium follows from the concentration of its volatile heptoxide in the flue dust during the smelting of molybdenite ore, or from its concentration with the platinum metals in the "anode sludge" during electrolytic copper refining. The extracted element is recrystallized as the sparingly soluble potassium perrhenate ($KReO_4$). This material is transposed to the ammonium salt and reduced in hydrogen to give black metal powder. The powder may be compressed and sintered in hydrogen at an elevated temperature to give sintered bars (density, 19). Cold working and annealing permit the fabrication of wire or foil.

The silvery massive metal has a density of approximately 21.0 g. per cc., melts at about 3,180° C, and is extremely hard; its wear resistance is good and it is not easily corroded. The powder slowly oxidizes in air above 150° C and rapidly at higher temperatures to form volatile Re_2O_7. This yellow, stable, and relatively nontoxic oxide is the anhydride of perrhenic acid ($HReO_4$), which results from dissolution of the metal in hydrogen peroxide or nitric acid. The metal is not soluble in hydrochloric acid, and dissolves only with difficulty in other acids. The perrhenates, the heptoxide, and perrhenic acid have been extensively studied; unlike the corresponding manganese compounds, the (VII) state of rhenium is its commonest and most stable form. Perrhenate, unlike permanganate, is only a weak oxidant, comparable in strength with ferric ion.

There is some evidence for the existence of rhenium in each of the oxidation states from (VII) through (−I). The solution chemistry of rhenium is quite complex because of the large number of possible, acid-base sensitive, disproportionation reactions. The best characterized oxides are Re_2O_7; the insoluble red trioxide (ReO_3); and the black dioxide (ReO_2). The existence of an unstable black (possibly impure) sesquioxide (Re_2O_3) is probable, and both a monoxide and a suboxide have been reported. A number of tungsten, arsenic, silicon, and other rhenium alloys are known, and the heated metal reacts more or less readily with many nonmetals such as sulfur, phosphorus, or the halogens. As does tungsten, rhenium forms numerous anhydrous halides or oxyhalides with fluorine, chlorine, or bromine, which are hydrolyzed by water. The hexafluoride (ReF_6), pentachloride ($ReCl_5$), tribromide ($ReBr_3$), and two simple iodides (ReI_3 and ReI) have been reported. The trichloride ($ReCl_3$) is a trimeric red solid which behaves as a nonelectrolyte in solution; on heating, it emits a green vapour from which metal may be deposited by thermal decomposition. Complex rhenium (IV) halides of the type K_2ReX_6 have been reported for all four of the common halogens.

There are two naturally occurring isotopes: with mass numbers 185, which is stable, and 187, which is radioactive and the more abundant; radioactive isotopes with mass numbers 182, 183, 184, and 188 have been prepared. The arrangement of electrons in the unfilled orbits (O and P) is: $5s^2$, $5p^6$, $5d^5$, $6s^2$.

BIBLIOGRAPHY.—B. S. Hopkins, *Chapters in the Chemistry of the Less Familiar Elements* (1940); J. G. F. Druce, *Rhenium* (1948); N. V. Sidgwick, *The Chemical Elements and Their Components* (1950).
(C. L. R.)

RHEOLOGY (from the Greek *rheein,* "to flow") is the science of the deformation and flow of matter. The subject traditionally excludes hydrodynamics and the classical theory of elasticity, which are not normally concerned with the properties of specific materials. Rheology is a branch of physics but, because of its concern with the composition and structure of flowing and deformed materials and with the rheological behaviour of components of living organisms, it has applications in chemistry, engineering, biology, and medicine.

Early History.—Empirical studies of flow and deformation began in very early times. In a conical water clock from an Egyptian tomb of the 16th century B.C., the sides slope at an angle which suggests a correction deliberately made to allow for changes in the viscosity of the water corresponding with variations of nighttime temperature. Early Indian philosophers attempted to explain the rheological properties of materials in terms of what would now be called their atomic and molecular constitutions. Among Greek philosophers, Heraclitus claimed that everything is in a state of flux; his dictum was *panta rhei* ("everything flows").

Quantitative Studies.—The first quantitative experiments probably were those of Robert Hooke, who in 1660 worked with coiled and suspended weights on the ends of long metal wires, measuring the extensions of the wires in terms of distances of the weights from the ground. From these experiments he derived his law *ut tensio sic vis:* "as the extension, so is the force." E. Mariotte in France independently propounded the law in 1680. Hooke's law describes the simplest type of deformation. The atoms of the metal are strained out of their positions of equilibrium in which attractive and repulsive forces are balanced, the energy being stored potentially until the load is released, when the original form is restored.

Newton suggested in the *Principia* (1687) that "the resistance which arises from the lack of slipperiness of the parts of a liquid, other things being equal, is proportional to the velocity with which the parts of the liquid are separated from one another." In this simplest type of steady flow, all the energy is dissipated as heat and the removal of the driving force does not lead to any recovery.

Static friction, requiring that a limiting force be applied before flow or sliding can take place, was studied first by Leonardo and then by G. Amontons (1663–1705), C. A. Coulomb (1736–1806), and others (*see* FRICTION). Here again, energy is dissipated as heat. This and other aspects of rheology make technical use of the terms "stress" and "strain," which are almost synonymous in ordinary English. "Stress" refers to the whole system of forces (per unit area) acting on the surface of a body and "strain" to the changes of shape and volume associated with these forces. (For precise definitions, *see* ELASTICITY.)

In the latter half of the 19th century, studies were made, mainly in Germany, on the stretching of filaments, rubber strands, and wires under constant load (creep). L. Boltzmann proposed a principle of superposition to define conditions under which the amount of creep would be independent of the conditions of stressing, whether by a single load or by intermittent loads. The experiments led to theoretical treatments involving the statistical distribution of elements in creep and in stress relaxation under constant deformation.

J. C. Maxwell proposed (1868) a treatment for certain systems having imperfect elasticity; *i.e.,* those in which the stress gradually relaxes under constant strain at a rate which, in the simplest cases, is proportional to itself. Such systems, now called elastico-viscous, may be described in terms of a viscosity (ratio of stress to rate of flow), or of an elastic modulus (ratio of stress to initial strain), or of the ratio of these quantities, known as the relaxation time. The corresponding system, called visco-elastic, in which an elastic element is damped by a viscous unit in parallel, has a ratio of viscosity to elastic modulus called the retardation time. Priority in the study of this system is generally ascribed to Lord Kelvin. In time it became apparent that many real materials are neither perfectly elastic nor viscous, nor do they obey the simple combined equations which follow from the treatments of Maxwell and Kelvin. As early as 1889, F. N. Shvedov in Russia demonstrated the need for a static frictional term to account for the flow of certain complex materials; and in 1904–06 F. T. Trouton in England, in comparing conditions in tensile and shear experiments on pitch, implicitly postulated the same requirement. (Shear is the sliding over each other of parallel planes.)

Modern Rheology.—The founding of modern rheology is generally ascribed to E. C. Bingham of Easton, Pa. His early work on paints and clays established the existence of a type of plasticity such that when an increasing shearing stress is applied to a suspension or paste, there is no appreciable flow until a well-defined critical stress ("yield-value") is reached, after which the rate of flow is proportional to the excess of stress over yield-value.

Bingham appreciated the need for cooperation among industrialists and biologists working with complex systems of flow and deformation and, in 1929, he and a group of friends defined the term rheology and started a society for its study (see below). Very soon, those who worked with bitumens, concrete, tar, soils, fibres, starch, cheese, flour doughs, and various synthetic high polymers found it convenient to describe behaviour in terms of models consisting of Hookean springs, Newtonian viscous elements ("dashpots"), and static frictional "sliders" linked in series and in parallel. It was soon realized, however, that many of the models were equivalent to one another, and that they could all be grouped into a small number of "canonical types." The organization and naming of the principal types was largely the work of M. Reiner.

Early attempts to construct models and to associate their elements directly with molecular mechanisms were not, on the whole, successful. Rheologists gradually accepted the view that models are only helps to envisage the meaning of the equations they represent. Moreover, in the late 1920s many systems were found which did not conform easily to this type of treatment. Wolfgang Ostwald and his school in Germany, and A. de Waele in England, then proposed equations according to which rates of flow are proportional to powers of the applied stress. The decision as to which type of treatment more adequately fitted the experimental data was generally settled on purely statistical grounds. It gradually became possible, especially in the field of high polymers, to relate rheological data to molecular constitution as determined by independent means. For a time there was a tendency to regard as "empirical," and in some sense inferior, any rheological treatment which did not purport to do this.

Early in the second half of the 20th century, however, the phenomenological approach was considerably extended and ceased to be regarded with distrust, partly because so many very complex modes of behaviour were discovered which were better classified phenomenologically than in terms of their molecular correlates. Another advantage of the phenomenological approach is that it often draws together systems that behave alike but whose molecular or atomic mechanisms differ greatly. Thus many interesting comparisons have been made between creep and relaxation of metals and of noncrystalline materials having different ultimate structures.

As more and more complex systems were investigated, the spring-dashpot-slider models became, very often, mere linear units within nonlinear distributions; the distribution functions (relaxation and creep functions) yielding quantities which describe the behaviour of the materials. This amounted to a return to the concepts of E. Wiechert, F. Kohlrausch, and others, 50 years earlier.

Many systems flow and deform in ways which depend not only on the applied stress but on the previous stress-and-strain history. The extreme case is that of a perfectly solid jelly with a characteristic rigidity modulus (ratio of intensity of shear stress to shear strain). This, on shearing, breaks down into a simple liquid of measurable viscosity, the jelly being re-formed on subsequent resting. This characteristic of liquefying on disturbance and solidifying at rest, reversibly and without change of temperature, was named thixotropy (Greek *thixis*, "touch") by H. Freundlich and his school; and, for a time, all less complete changes of that kind, involving merely a reversible fall in consistency on shearing, were called "false-body" changes. But, although some rheologists, notably J. Pryce-Jones, insisted on the quite distinct nature of these two phenomena, the term thixotropy was eventually used to cover both. Freundlich himself, in his later papers, used the term to include materials which do not exist as perfect solids and liquids. There are many examples: some clays, paints, inks, honey, etc. Some materials show "negative thixotropy"; *i.e.*, they increase their consistency reversibly on shearing and standing; and many

more offer an increasing resistance to shear but do not recover, or recover only slightly, on resting. At one time all such behaviour was classed as "dilatancy" but it was later generally accepted that this term should only be used where a real dilatation, or moving of component particles into a more open form of packing (as originally studied by Osborne Reynolds for wet sand), can be demonstrated. The corresponding irreversible softening processes have been called "rheodestruction" (etymologically an unfortunate term; "rheomalaxis" would be better).

Many systems show a lower apparent viscosity (ratio of shear stress to shear rate) at higher shear rates either with or without any marked yield-values. Such behaviour is distinguishable from thixotropy only in terms of the magnitude of the time of resetting. If some structure is destroyed by rapid shearing (*i.e.*, if it possesses "shear thinning") but recovers so fast that there is always experimentally a unique value for the apparent viscosity for each value of shear-rate, few rheologists would describe this behaviour as thixotropic. The attitude of most is philosophically not unreasonable: glass and pitch are liquids, even at room temperature, if measurements are made over long periods of time, but for all practical purposes they are regarded as solids.

The Tensorial Approach.—The state of stress and the strain of an elastic body are described in terms of the whole combination of forces and of changes in volume and form to which it is subjected. If a unit cube be considered, the forces and deformations on each face may be resolved into three components at right angles to one another, which, bearing in mind Newton's law of action and reaction, would seem to lead to a composite of nine vector components. Such a composite is known as a second-rank tensor (see TENSOR ANALYSIS). For reasons of symmetry, the stress and strain tensors each reduce to six independent components, and the fourth-rank elasticity tensor, which relates them to one another, reduces from $6 \times 6 = 36$ to 21 components (see fig.).

Since tensors can be treated mathematically as wholes, their use has greatly reduced the complexity of elasticity theory. Until World War II, however, most rheologists were satisfied with vectorial methods (see VECTOR ANALYSIS). Experiments usually involved tensions, compressions, or shears in a well-defined plane; measurements of displacements seldom had to be made in directions other than those in which the forces were applied. During the war, however, much work was done on systems which, when sheared in a concentric cylinder viscometer, for example, climb up the inner cylinder against the force of gravity. Such phenomena, generally called after K. Weissenberg, one of their principal investigators, show the presence of cross-stresses, and for their adequate study a tensorial treatment is advisable. The most striking Weissenberg phenomenon is shown by a sticky commercial product for catching rodents. Rubber solutions, many low polymers (intermediates in plastics manufacture), and sometimes sweetened condensed milk, also show the phenomenon.

FROM G. W. SCOTT BLAIR AND M. REINER, "AGRICULTURAL RHEOLOGY," 1957

TRACTIONS ACTING ON A CUBE

Normal components (those at right angles to the faces) are marked σ; the shear components (those across the faces), τ

The application of tensor theory to highly complex rheological systems forms an important part of rheological theory. Its most difficult applications are to relatively large deformations (often a concern of rheologists), to which the classical theory of elasticity is inapplicable; and to anisotropic materials. The latter are materials, such as wood, that show different properties according to the axis along which they are tested; many of them also change their rheological characteristics as they are strained (the strain hardening and softening shown by many plastics, mastics, and metals). A. S. Lodge has shown that the use of tensors can be avoided, but only at the cost of introducing other, more complex concepts; *e.g.*, contravariance.

High Elasticity.—The atoms of a material cannot be drawn far apart without leading to rupture of the specimen. When a coiled spring is stretched, the large extension is due to the accumulation of rotations—the turning around of the individual atoms—and not to their separation one from another. In some highly extensible elastic materials the molecules may perhaps behave like coiled springs; but it is certain that in most cases, of which rubber is typical, the elasticity is caused by quite a different mechanism. Rubber molecules consist of very long chains of carbon and hydrogen atoms, free to rotate in such a way that many different configurations are possible. When not subjected to stress, rubber has many more coiled configurations than extended ones. When a stretched rubber strand is released, molecular movements rapidly change the configurations to more probable and therefore more contracted forms. If the probability of an event is p_1 and of another event p_2, the probability of both events occurring will be p_1p_2; that is, probabilities are multiplicative. For many purposes, additive properties are preferred; therefore much use is made of the logarithms of probabilities, expressed as "entropies," which are additive (see THERMODYNAMICS). Rubber contracts because the contracted state has a higher entropy than the stretched state, not because of any storage of potential energy by the molecules.

The shift of emphasis from energy to entropy, *i.e.*, to probabilities, in the rheology of complex systems is important (see HEAT: *The Nature of Heat in Matter*). E. Schrödinger (1887–1961) pointed out that the characteristic feature of life is to delay the inevitable rise of entropy which ultimately brings death. Living systems are not "closed" in the thermodynamic sense; for open systems, a new science of "irreversible thermodynamics" is being developed (L. Onsager, 1931; I. Prigogine, 1947; A. Katchalsky and O. Kedem, 1961; S. R. de Groot, 1962). This science will be needed for rheological theory when the flow properties of living matter come to be more widely studied.

Biorheology.—In the 1830s, J. L. M. Poiseuille established the laws of flow through capillary tubes of simple fluids such as water. As a medical man he was interested in the flow properties of blood, on which E. C. Bingham also later worked. The flow of blood, even in rigid artificial capillaries, is extremely complex. The corpuscles do not flow in trajectories parallel to the capillary walls; therefore Poiseuille's Law, which states that the rate of flow at a given pressure is proportional to the fourth power of the tube radius, does not hold. Such anomalies are also known for paints, clays, etc., and are called sigma phenomena. In the case of blood, it has been shown that in a given capillary the square root of the rate of flow is linear with the square root of the applied pressure (N. Casson's equation). In such a case, what is being measured is not an invariant physical property in the classical sense, but rather a characteristic change in behaviour more like the entities observed when rheological changes are studied subjectively by experts handling industrial materials. G. W. Scott Blair named such entities "quasi-properties" and showed that they play an important part in subjective quality judgments. Their mathematical treatment starts with power-equations like those of Ostwald and De Waele (see above), and leads to the use of fractional differential coefficients and gamma functions. Similar treatments were successfully applied by A. Graham to data for creep of complex metal alloys.

The importance of rheology to medicine has been realized in many fields besides that of hematology. The properties of uterine cervical mucus reflect the levels of sex hormones; the lubricative characteristics of synovial fluids may well be related to rheumatic conditions; the consistency of bronchial mucus affects the breathing difficulties of chronic bronchitics; etc.

See also COLLOID: *Irreversible Systems: Pastes (Concentrated Suspensions)*; CRYSTALS, DISLOCATION OF; FRICTION; LUBRICATION: *Theory;* MATERIALS, STRENGTH OF; VISCOSITY.

BIBLIOGRAPHY.—A. E. Love, *A Treatise on the Mathematical Theory of Elasticity,* 4th ed. (1927); E. C. Bingham, *Fluidity and Plasticity* (1922); R. Houwink, *Elasticity, Plasticity and Structure of Matter* (1937); G. W. Scott Blair, *An Introduction to Industrial Rheology* (1938); *A Survey of General and Applied Rheology,* 2nd ed. (1949); M. Reiner, *Lectures on Theoretical Rheology,* 3rd ed. (1960), *Deformation, Strain and Flow,* 2nd ed. rev. (1960); A. Frey-Wyssling (ed.), *Deformation and Flow in Biological Systems* (1952); A. L. Copley and G. Stainsby (eds.), *Flow Properties of Blood and Other Biological Systems* (1960); G. W. Scott Blair and M. Reiner, *Agricultural Rheology* (1957); F. R. Eirich (ed.), *Rheology: Theory and Applications,* 4 vol. (1956 *et seq.*); J. M. Burgers, J. J. Hermans, and G. W. Scott Blair (eds.), *International Rheology Monographs* (1952–56); A. S. Lodge, *Elastic Liquids* (1964). (G. W. S. BR.)

RHETORIC is the name traditionally given to the use of language as an art based on a body of organized knowledge. The study of rhetoric exerted an important formative influence on European culture from ancient times to the 17th century A.D., after which it became less important. Both the nature of its influence and the reason for its decline become apparent from a study of the real character of the so-called art at various stages of its history. The techniques of rhetoric and the knowledge on which they were based were always organized to serve only some specific and limited purpose. Thus, when the purpose changed and new techniques, based on new theories, emerged, the new system was as incomplete as the old had been. The textbooks of rhetoric that men studied never covered more than a small part of the field of linguistic expression; and it was the realization of this that finally led to widespread abandonment of the effort to create an art of discourse.

Rhetoric as the Art of Oratory: Ancient Greece.—In its original form, rhetoric was the systematic study of oratory (see GREEK LITERATURE: *Early and Attic Prose: Rhetoric and Oratory*). It was, as Aristotle later pointed out, the art of persuasion. The first man to teach oratory was the Sicilian Corax (*q.v.*) during the spate of litigation which followed the establishment of democracy in Agrigentum and Syracuse in the 460s B.C. Another Sicilian, Gorgias (*q.v.*) of Leontini, introduced the new art—along with the idea that it could be taught—to Athens in 427 B.C., and rhetorical training, taught by the sophists (*q.v.*), rapidly became the favoured form of higher education.

This initial flowering of rhetoric in the 5th and 4th centuries B.C. was marked by important controversies, one of which concerned the use of stylistic devices. Gorgias had employed colourful epithets, antitheses, rhythm and rhyming terminations; the prevalence of antitheses can be clearly seen in Thucydides, both in the speeches and in the historical narrative, and the interest in argument in many of the plays of Euripides. The next generation saw a reaction, and the plain style of Lysias (*q.v.*) found many supporters. But the criteria by which each party sought to establish the superiority of its choice—clarity, impressiveness, decorum, beauty, purity of language—depended, except for the last, largely on subjective assessments, and so the problem of mannerism was posed but not solved. The outstanding teacher of the day, Isocrates (*q.v.*), and the outstanding orator, Demosthenes (*q.v.*), championed a compromise style between the plain and the mannered. But their example was not decisive, and at the close of the 4th century the long battle between the Atticists and the Asian mannerists was still to come.

Another dispute concerned the relationship between rhetoric and morality. It was recognized that scientific proof was not usually possible in oratory. Speeches were concerned with probabilities. They were often addressed to an uneducated or a potentially inattentive audience, and Gorgias had maintained that an orator therefore could argue the just and the unjust cause with equal force. Regarding rhetoric as an amoral instrument, he was attacked by critics who claimed that oratorical skill had an essentially moral character, since truth and justice provided the best opportunities for persuasion. This view, which Aristotle later endorsed, has much to be said in its favour at the theoretical level, but the fact that an orator's skill could often counterbalance the superior persuasiveness of a just cause remained uncontroverted, and Gorgias continued to find adherents as late as the Renaissance.

A third group of controversies concerned education. The popularity of the rhetorical schools put them in control of the intellectual development of Greece, and rhetoricians who were prepared to accept the consequent responsibility criticized those of their utilitarian colleagues who kept their eyes fixed on the needs of the law courts, and at the same time disagreed among themselves as to what should be added to the rhetorical course. Isocrates recommended political thought.

Plato's *Gorgias* and *Phaedrus,* and the *Antidosis* of Isocrates, deal with these controversies (for Plato's views *see* PLATO: *Gorgias*) but the best ancient Greek account of the development of the art is the *Rhetoric* of Aristotle. Aristotle limits his comments on all points to the requirements of oratory for politics, for the law courts, and for a show speech (either on a ceremonial occasion such as a public funeral or as a tour de force for rhetorical public entertainment). This, taken in conjunction with the fact that he composed a separate *Poetics,* suggests that rhetoric at this stage made no claim to be a complete "arts of discourse."

Aristotle's *Rhetoric* begins with the orator's construction of his case. First, he must assemble all the possible arguments, by examining all the "places" (*topoi,* hence "topics") where arguments can be found. Aristotle's spatial metaphor confuses rather than clarifies his meaning, but an example will show what is intended. Suppose that a political speaker is recommending some measure. He must appear to advise what is good. Happiness is universally regarded as good. So are justice, moderation, magnanimity, magnificence. These then are the speaker's "topics." If he examines each in turn, he will see which applies to the case he is handling.

When the arguments have been collected, the orator must decide which to use, and here great stress is laid on understanding the psychology of the audience. Orators must know what provokes anger, admiration, shame, and how different categories of hearers—the young, the old, the well-born—are likely to react. Syllogistic argument is rarely possible in a speech and would in any case appear too cumbersome. Rhetoric must rely on "enthymemes," incomplete syllogisms often based on probable premises ("If you, who are a bad man, admit you would not have taken a bribe, is it likely that I, a good man, would have done so?" and "Dorieus has won a race at Olympia, therefore he has won a crown" [omitting the middle term "the prize at Olympia is a crown"] are both enthymemes) and on "examples," one or more instances which lead to an inductive demonstration (*e.g.,* "Pisistratus asked for a bodyguard and so became dictator; so did Theagenes; therefore Dionysius in asking for a bodyguard is aiming at a dictatorship"). Knowledge of how an audience reacts is important because what is not strictly proof must pass as such. This is the least satisfactory section of the treatise. In stating that truth and justice provide the best arguments, Aristotle would seem to have committed himself to the opinion that the rhetorical substitutes for the syllogism had a certain validity, but he makes no systematic effort to analyze their relation to scientific proof. The work then closes with a discussion of style and the general pattern a speech should follow. Aristotle emphasizes the need for clarity, but admits that metaphors and figures of speech may be used in moderation. Considered as a whole, his survey can be seen to have many gaps which later generations were to fill (see *Traditional Rhetorical Method,* below), but its combination of practical experience with a philosophic breadth of view gave it a lasting importance.

Aristotle's generation saw the passing of the free cities with their active political life; and for the next two centuries the development of rhetoric under the Hellenistic empires was decided by the needs of the courts and the activity of the schools. It was an age of useful but unspectacular advance under the shadow of the noisy controversy between the Atticists and the Asian mannerists. The discussion of general themes, developed in the philosophy schools, proved a handy teaching device and was accepted as a regular branch of oratory. The imitation of well-known orators became a popular exercise. Hermagoras of Temnos (*c.* 150 B.C.) revolutionized the technique of constructing a case when he pointed out that there was always a key point of conflict—which might concern law, fact, or principle—and was the focus round which arguments ought to be grouped.

Rhetoric as the Art of Oratory: Rome.—The discoveries of the Hellenistic age are known through their influence on Latin oratory (*see* LATIN LITERATURE: *Rhetoric and Education*). The important achievement of Roman rhetoric was the transmission

of the Greek tradition to medieval Europe. By the 2nd century B.C. republican Rome was attracting the most adventurous of the Greek teachers. But Greek rhetorical theory was not only restated in such textbooks as the anonymous *Rhetorica ad Herennium* (86–82 B.C.) or Cicero's *De inventione*. It was also applied; and speeches were produced which equaled the best work of the Athenian orators. At the same time, the career and genius of Cicero lent the study of rhetoric a dignity it had previously lacked. In his accusation of Catiline, Cicero portrayed eloquence as wielding real power in great affairs. After his time, the aims of the rhetorical education were linked in men's minds with the urbanity and versatility he had glorified.

With the advent of the empire, political and judicial oratory gradually ceased to be important in the evolution of rhetoric, for Roman autocracy, like its Hellenistic predecessors, extinguished political debate and restricted the scope of the courts. But writers of all kinds had long been using rhetorical devices, and the interest in rhetoric was not sustained by cultivated society's interest in literature. The Greek author Dionysius of Halicarnassus (fl. *c.* 20 B.C.) commented on the orators from the point of view of a literary critic. The 1st century A.D. was still a transitional period in which oratory was brought closer to literature. Quintilian's *Institutio oratoria* (*c.* A.D. 95), in spite of certain contemporary emphases, still looked to the past, giving the most complete account that exists of the art of oratory. It is therefore convenient to take from him the account of rhetorical method that was followed in classical antiquity and continued to be used in the schools.

Traditional Rhetorical Method.—The speaker is concerned with three matters: the art of rhetoric, the speech itself, and the situation that calls it forth. The first of these has five parts: collecting the material (called invention), arranging it (disposition), putting it into words (style; Latin *elocutio*), memorizing it, and finally delivering it. The second matter, the speech itself, should be divided into five: an introduction (to gain the goodwill of the audience), a statement of the point at issue, arguments to prove it, refutation of contrary arguments (this by some authorities is included under the preceding division), and a conclusion (either a recapitulation or an appeal to the audience's emotions). The third matter, which is the situation, covers the kinds of speech: whether the discussion is general (*e.g.,* "should a man marry?") or particular (*e.g.,* "should Crassus marry?") and whether it is a show speech (called demonstrative), political (called deliberative), or legal.

To return to the five parts of the art of rhetoric, the one dealing with style (the putting of the material into words) received the most space in rhetorical handbooks and is indeed regarded by the modern reader as the chief concern of rhetoric. This is justified insofar as, of the threefold aim of rhetoric, to instruct, to move, and to delight, the thing that contributes almost exclusively to delight is style.

Quintilian and most other ancient authorities teach that the chief virtues of style are four: correctness, clarity, elegance, and appropriateness. Of these, elegance receives most space as it is the easiest to teach, including as it does all the varieties of the figures of thought and of words (or syntax). (*See* FIGURES OF SPEECH.) Among the former are rhetorical questions, impersonation (whereby the speaker invents the actual words of the persons described or even of nonhuman entities such as one's country), and vivid description (whereby an event is not merely stated to have occurred but described in full imaginative detail). Figures of words (or syntax) include antithesis, parallelism of phrases, and repetition of words. Ancient rhetoric was also much concerned with the rhythms of speech, the order of words, and the length and cohesion of sentences.

Imitation of the Past.—When Quintilian wrote, a new kind of rhetoric was beginning to appear. The Roman emperors, in order to win support for the culture their state represented, had begun to subsidize the schools, in which rhetoric provided the syllabus of secondary education. Rhetoricians thus became the high priests of an official cult of the past. The following three centuries produced a mass of historical, critical, and anecdotic writing; and they also saw a determined effort to perpetuate the language and style of the great classics. Imitation, which had hitherto played a subordinate role in rhetorical training, now became its focus, and the popular textbooks of the period, the *Progymnasmata* of Hermogenes (b. *c.* 150) of Tarsus and of Aphthonius (fl. *c.* 400), a pupil of Libanius at Antioch, make it clear that the exercises particularly studied—narrative, description, the expansion of a moral saying, prosopopoeia, and so on—were those that are found not only in oratory but in many other literary genres as well. Rhetorical study now covered a field coextensive with Greek and Latin literature; but, looked at from another point of view, its scope was narrower than before because, within this larger field, only certain writers were thought to deserve imitation.

Declamations.—The imitation of historians and poets as well as of orators played an important part in rhetorical training, and the vogue for academic declamations showed that oratory itself was admired primarily as a literary genre. Declamations were not normally concerned with contemporary life. A deliberative speech (*suasoria*) would choose a situation from the historical or legendary past: for instance, it might urge the Spartans to hold the pass of Thermopylae against the enemy, or take the part of Agamemnon and argue that he will not sacrifice his daughter Iphigenia at Aulis. Similarly, a legal speech (*controversia*) would deal with a situation that referred to some fictitious "law," such as that the man who kills a tyrant shall be rewarded; the declamation might argue that a man should receive the reward because he was the chief agent in causing the tyrant's death, even though he had not actually killed him with his own hands.

The preparation of declamations as a school exercise gave the pupil practice in getting to the heart of a problem, to the actual issue (Latin *status*) at stake, and had long been used in rhetoric. The method was to ask three questions: Did it happen (*an sit*)? What was it (*quid sit*)? Was it good or bad (*quale sit*)? Thus, in the case of tyrannicide cited above, the pupil would have to discover if the event (a killing) had taken place, how it should be defined (murder, tyrannicide, etc.), and finally, whether it was a praiseworthy or a blameworthy act. Of course in an imaginary case the answer to the first question requires not investigation of fact but plausible conjecture.

Early Middle Ages.—Christian literature adopted the imaginative approach of the imperial schools. In the Byzantine Empire, schools used the *Progymnasmata* and encouraged imitation (*see* GREEK LITERATURE: *Byzantine: Rhetoric*). In the west Augustine, who distrusted pagan models, in his *De doctrina Christiana* advised imitating the style of the Bible, though his own writings contain the stylistic devices which came naturally to him after his education in rhetoric. Cassiodorus (6th century) and Isidore of Seville (7th century) both included the traditional rhetorical scheme in their encyclopaedic treatises, counting it among the seven liberal arts as forming one of the trivium together with grammar and dialectic. Bede (d. 735) followed Augustine by showing in his short work *De schematibus ac tropis* how the Bible is not inferior to secular classical literature as a storehouse of figures of speech to imitate. Alcuin (d. 805) continued the traditional rhetorical teaching, but without excessive stress on style, in his dialogue on rhetoric and the virtues.

The disputes of the 11th century provoked a revival of judicial rhetoric which petered out when it was realized that dialectic and law provided better weapons for controversy, and a century later imitation flourished briefly at the school of Chartres. But not until 1150 was education far enough advanced for a unified rhetorical tradition to appear.

Mannerist Rhetoric in the Later Middle Ages.—The 12th century tried to build a new culture based on the theoretical knowledge at its command. In rhetoric, this knowledge was drawn principally from the *Rhetorica ad Herennium* and Cicero's *De inventione*. But the statements in these works concerning the handling of the subject matter were too closely linked with judicial oratory to be useful in an age whose main interest was in epistolary composition, and so attention centred on the sections discussing style. It was assumed that in every genre, in both prose and poetry, two sorts of writing were possible: the one plain, the

other "artistic," employing figures of thought and speech. The view that figures were a source of stylistic distinction was a commonplace of classical rhetoric, but their possible functional relation to meaning had not been adequately examined. It is not surprising therefore that the 12th century accepted them as ornamental in character and came to believe that the more figures were used, the better the style. There followed a cult of mannerism, with insistence on particular rhythmic endings, and on etymologies—often fantastic—which gave a richer colour to individual words.

The Renaissance: The Revival of Imitative Rhetoric.—The obscurity of manneristic writing provoked a reaction. Petrarch reinstated the cult of the classics and popularized their imitation. Already, as early as the 11th century, Byzantium had seen a recrudescence of the Atticism which had flourished under the late Roman Empire, and its scholars had developed the instructional techniques and compiled the grammars and lexicons required for the exact reproduction of an earlier stage of Greek. The arrival of Byzantine scholars in Italy in the 15th century meant therefore that the systematization of imitative technique spread to the west. Humanist rhetoric was born, with its dictionaries, its handbooks of Latin usage and *exempla* (adages, anecdotes, and other illustrative material), and its memorizing procedures. Ultimately, it accomplished more than its Greco-Roman and Byzantine predecessors; for its imitative purpose was linked with wider ambitions. The humanists were the first to see the literature of a people in its totality as a cultural achievement. They were not content merely to write classical Latin. Desiring to equal the cultural triumphs of antiquity, they attempted every classical genre, thus giving imitation a range it had not had before. And this was also the age when the national literatures of Europe were attaining their maturity, so that imitation was no longer limited to Latin. It was practised in the vernaculars, and with striking success.

The Renaissance: Ramism.—By 1550, the humanist tradition, embodied in the rhetorical works of Erasmus (*q.v.*), had a firm grip on education, but Latin, on which that education rested, was going out of use, and the vernaculars had absorbed all they could absorb through imitation. A new approach to rhetoric was required. As early as the end of the 15th century the Dutch humanist Rodolphus Agricola recommended that writers should develop their subjects with reference to genus, species, causes, effects, similarities, opposites, and suggested 30 such headings, analogous to the "topics" of classical rhetoric. In the 16th century Petrus Ramus (Pierre La Ramée) popularized Agricola's ideas and had an enormous influence. Ramism detached invention and disposition from rhetoric (reckoning them as part of dialectic), leaving it only with style and delivery (memory having fallen into the background). Rhetoric was thus severely limited in scope by losing all concern for content (*see* RAMUS, PETRUS).

The Decline of Rhetoric.—Ramism carried the seeds of its own destruction. The dichotomy it established between thought and the words that formulated thought provoked a search for a plain style which would represent facts without adventitious verbal ornament. Rhetoric fell into discredit. Still an important school subject in the 18th century, it followed rather than led contemporary taste as is evident from the lectures of Hugh Blair, the first professor of rhetoric and belles lettres in Edinburgh University, which mirror the period's preoccupation with sensibility and the sublime. But Adam Müller's impressive *Reden über die Beredsamkeit* (1816) and Archbishop Richard Whately's *Principles of Rhetoric* (5th edition revised; 1836) were already, in the main, works of literary history. Convinced of the supreme value of experiment, the 19th century was led eventually to condemn all traditional techniques of style and all organized rhetorical study. Jacob Burckhardt described antiquity's interest in rhetoric as a "monstrous aberration." These extreme views remained popular until the 1930s, when logical positivism drew attention to the importance of studying how language is used. I. A. Richards' *Philosophy of Rhetoric* (1941) emphasized the need for a new art of discourse and substantial attempts were later made, particularly in the United States, to develop such an art in a form suitable for teaching in schools and universities.

BIBLIOGRAPHY.—W. Kroll, *Rhetorik* (1937), reprinted with revisions in Pauly-Wissowa, *Real Encyclopädie der classischen Altertumswissenschaft,* Supplementband vii, col. 1039–1138 (1940); G. Kennedy, *The Art of Persuasion in Greece* (1963); H. I. Marrou, *Histoire de l'education dans l'antiquité,* 3rd ed. (1955; Eng. trans. 1956); D. L. Clark, *Rhetoric in Greco-Roman Education* (1937); E. Norden, *Die Antike Kunstprosa,* 5th ed. (1958); E. Curtius, *Europäische Literatur und lateinisches Mittelalter,* 3rd ed. (1961; Eng. trans. 1953); E. Faral, *Les Arts poétiques du XIIe et XIIIe siècles* (1924); K. Krumbacher, *Geschichte der byzantinischen Literatur,* 2nd ed. (1897); W. J. Ong, *Ramus: Method and the Decay of Dialogue* (1958); W. S. Howell, *Logic and Rhetoric in England 1500–1700* (1958); Cleanth Brooks and Robert Penn Warren, *Modern Rhetoric,* 2nd ed. (1958). (R. R. Bo.)

RHEUMATIC FEVER is a generalized disease commonest in children between the ages of 5 and 15 but occurring with considerable frequency in young adults. The manifestations, severity, duration and aftereffects are highly variable. In a small percentage of patients death may occur because of inflammation of the heart in the acute attack, but in a much larger number the acute attack subsides with a variable amount of cardiac damage. Recurrences are frequent in the absence of appropriate measures for the prevention of streptococcal infection.

Causative Factors.—The exact cause of rheumatic fever was still unknown in the 1960s, although a close relationship to previous streptococcus infection had been well established. This is based on the high incidence of known streptococcus infection preceding attacks of acute rheumatic fever, the presence of streptococcal antibodies (particularly antistreptolysin) in the blood of patients with the disease, and the prevention of recurrent attacks of rheumatic fever by the continued use of drugs that prevent streptococcus infection. It is generally believed that the disease results from the reaction of the body to the streptococcus rather than the direct effect of streptococcal infection.

Many authorities believe that this illness represents a hypersensitivity reaction, although direct evidence for this view is lacking.

Clinical Characteristics.—The clinical recognition of rheumatic fever is made difficult by the wide variety of symptoms. The most important evidences are those that result from inflammation of the heart, and of these the commonest are certain types of murmurs and increased heartbeat rate. It is frequently difficult to determine whether a given murmur results from active rheumatic fever or a previous attack. With more serious heart involvement there may be rapid enlargement of the heart, heart failure resulting in difficulty in breathing, evidence of inflammation of the membranes overlying the heart (pericarditis) and irregularities of the heartbeat. Additional evidence of cardiac involvement is sometimes obtained on electrocardiographic tracings. The extent and duration of cardiac inflammation is extremely variable in all age groups, but in general tends to be severer in young children than in young adults. Severe cardiac involvement may result in death in a relatively short time.

Involvement of the joints is a common manifestation. This may vary from mild aches and pains to severe swelling, redness, tenderness and limitation of motion. Characteristically several joints are involved, with migration from day to day. The joint symptoms are commoner in older patients than in young children. Joint manifestations are commonest in the early stages and never result in permanent impairment of function.

Nodules may occur beneath the skin, but rarely before the third or fourth week of disease. The presence of nodules is usually associated with involvement of the heart. A variety of skin rashes may be present in acute rheumatic fever, the most characteristic of which is erythema marginatum, which is considered highly specific for the disease by most authorities.

Chorea (*q.v.*) represents a nervous system manifestation of rheumatic fever. It is characterized by purposeless movements of the arms and legs and inability to perform coordinated movements of muscle groups. Emotional disturbances may also be present. The severity and duration of these symptoms are highly variable.

Fever occurs early in the disease in a relatively large percentage of patients, but it is not necessarily present. A wide variety of other signs and symptoms may also occur, among them nosebleeds,

weakness, abdominal pain and weight loss. Examination of the blood usually shows an increase in the rate of sedimentation of red blood cells, and frequently shows anemia and an increased number of white blood cells.

In typical cases a combination of the above symptoms makes diagnosis relatively certain. Many patients have the disease in subtler form, so that the first recognition of the previous rheumatic episode comes from the presence of structural abnormalities of the heart characteristically produced by rheumatic fever.

The length of an individual attack of acute rheumatic fever is variable and is sometimes difficult to ascertain. In certain persons symptoms may be transient, while in others the disease remains obviously active for periods of more than a year.

The degree of cardiac damage sustained during an individual attack is not related simply to the severity of the acute attack, but may be more closely related to the total duration of active disease. The interference with normal heart function, usually referred to as rheumatic heart disease, results in the main from distortion of the valve structure. Although such distortion may lead to extreme cardiac disability, patients with rheumatic heart disease may carry on relatively normal lives. The greatest threat to life is reactivation of the rheumatic process. A large percentage of people have no interference with cardiac function following recovery from acute rheumatic fever.

Pathology.—Although clinical evidences of rheumatic fever may occur in the heart, joints, skin and central nervous systems, the most characteristic pathological findings are seen in the heart. On gross examination the heart is usually dilated, and the surface may be covered by a stringy material that adheres to the membrane covering the heart (pericardium). The heart muscle is paler and softer than normal. Microscopic examination shows evidence of a peculiar type of inflammation in the connective tissue. The most characteristic microscopic lesion is the Aschoff nodule, which consists of an accumulation of large pale cells together with smaller cells surrounding degenerating connective tissue fibres. Aschoff nodules are most characteristically found in the connective tissue of various parts of the heart, but similar lesions have been identified in the connective tissue of other organs.

In later stages of the disease scar formation occurs. Such scarring results in deformity of the valves of the heart, bringing about interference with normal function. The mitral valve is most frequently involved, although the aortic valve is also commonly distorted. The tricuspid valve is rarely affected, while the pulmonary valve is almost never involved.

Treatment.—Until 1949 the usual treatment of rheumatic fever consisted of the use of salicylate drugs. There remained some difference of opinion as to whether these drugs have any specific effect on the rheumatic process. Adrenocorticotropic hormone (ACTH), cortisone and certain synthetic hormones related to cortisone have striking effects on rheumatic fever, but it is not clear whether use of these drugs prevents subsequent development of heart disease and has an advantage over salicylate treatment. Of cardinal importance in treatment is the complete eradication of any streptococcal infection, usually accomplished by large doses of penicillin.

Patients with active rheumatic fever are usually kept at bed rest for the duration of the active disease. In patients with severe cardiac failure, digitalis, mercurial diuretics, restriction of salt intake and oxygen are valuable. Adequate nutrition and good nursing care are important. The administration of prophylactic drugs (usually penicillin or sulfadiazine) has resulted in a considerable reduction in the rate of recurrences by preventing further streptococcal infection.

Surgical treatment is successfully used to relieve the narrowing of the openings of the valves of the heart. By 1958 some progress also had been made in correcting by surgical means the defect in closure of valves that occurs in rheumatic heart disease. *See* also HEART AND LUNG, SURGERY OF.

Public Health Aspects.—Rheumatic fever frequently occurs in more than one member of a family, apparently due to a hereditary susceptibility to the disease. It has been found in many parts of the world in representatives of all races. In the United

States (as measured by mortality statistics) it is commoner in the northern half of the country, the highest rates occurring in the middle Atlantic and mountain states. The observed rates cannot be correlated simply with latitude, average temperature, altitude or rainfall. The disease is not confined to any socioeconomic group, but studies indicate high mortality in low-income groups. It is difficult to estimate the true incidence because of difficulties in diagnosis and poor reporting, but there is evidence that rheumatic fever is the leading cause of death among children in the U.S.

Because of the frequently long duration of rheumatic fever, few families are able to meet the financial burden; the disease thus became an important public problem. In some large cities special hospitals are maintained for the care of children with rheumatic fever and rheumatic heart disease.

One of the earliest community attempts to meet the problem was the London County council's Rheumatism scheme, which provided for both hospital care and a follow-up program for all children with rheumatic fever. The financial difficulties in the care of rheumatic fever in Great Britain were overcome by the National Health Insurance scheme.

In the United States special programs for the care of children with rheumatic fever were developed after 1939 under the Social Security act. These programs were operated on a state basis with funds provided jointly by the states and the children's bureau of the federal department of health, education and welfare. The nature of the services and of their administration varied somewhat from state to state. The American Council on Rheumatic Fever, organized in 1944 under the American Heart association, promoted public and private programs for care, research and education. Under the National Heart act of 1948 the National Heart institute of the United States public health service began to conduct research on heart disease, including rheumatic fever. Through a program of grants-in-aid the Heart institute also supported research, training, demonstration programs and community programs for the control of rheumatic fever. Local communities also developed control programs.

See also references under "Rheumatic Fever" in the Index.

(A. Dor.)

RHEUMATISM: *see* ARTHRITIS; JOINTS AND LIGAMENTS, DISEASES AND DISABILITIES OF; RHEUMATIC FEVER.

RHEUMATOID ARTHRITIS: *see* ARTHRITIS.

RHEYDT, a town of West Germany in the *Land* (state) of North Rhine-Westphalia, Federal Republic of Germany, lies 14 mi. (22 km.) SSW of Krefeld by road. Pop. (1961) 94,004. The reconstruction of the town, heavily damaged in World War II, was rapid. The civic hall (with theatre, 1930), savings bank (1955), Schmölder Park, stadium, Bellermühle swimming pool, zoological gardens and Zoppenbroich Stud are notable. Rheydt Castle (with museum) is a Renaissance building by Pasqualini (1560–70) with charming arcades in the inner court. Each September a festival with a flower procession is held. Railways connect Rheydt with Krefeld, Düsseldorf, Cologne, Aachen and the Netherlands. Principal industries are spinning and weaving and the manufacture of cotton, woolen, silk and man-made fabrics, clothing, heavy machine tools, electrical goods (motors, generators, transformers, cables), and printing materials. Rheydt received formal civic rights in 1856. In 1929–33 it was united with Mönchengladbach to form Gladbach-Rheydt but afterward incorporated Odenkirchen and Giesenkirchen-Schelsen to form a separate town.

(H. H. M. H.)

RHIANUS (fl. *c.* 225 B.C.), Greek poet, was a Cretan and, according to the Suda lexicon, a slave who became a scholar. His only surviving works are 10 or 11 epigrams of some merit preserved in the *Greek Anthology*. He produced a recension of Homer, in which he seems to have shown good judgment, but was best known as an epic poet. His *Messeniaca* dealt with a 7th-century war between Messene and Sparta and the exploits of the Messenian hero Aristomenes, but of four other epics little more than the titles is known. All 5 extended to several books, and the *Thessalica* to 16. Evidently therefore he disregarded the call of Callimachus and Theocritus for a smaller scale in epic poetry.

See fragments and epigrams ed. by J. U. Powell, *Collectanea Alex-*

andrina (1925). *See* also W. Aly in Pauly-Wissowa, *Real-Encyclopädie der classischen Altertumswissenschaft,* 2nd series, vol. 1, col. 781–790 (1914).

(A. S. F. G.)

RHINE (Ger. RHEIN; French RHIN; Dutch RIJN; from Celtic *Renos,* Lat. *Rhenus*), a major European river. With a length of about 820 mi. (1,320 km.) and a catchment area exceeding 85,000 sq.mi. (220,150 sq.km.), it is culturally, historically, and economically the most important river in Europe.

Physically the Rhine can be divided into five distinct sections: the Alpine Rhine, High Rhine, Upper Rhine, Middle Rhine, and Lower Rhine. The Alpine Rhine has two principal headwaters: (1) the Vorderrhein, which issues from Lake Toma (7,691 ft. [2,344 m.]) near the Oberalp Pass and, following a northeasterly course, receives the Medelserrhein, the Glenner, and the Rabiusa; and (2) the Hinterrhein, which originates at 7,611 ft. (2,320 m.) in the Rheinwaldhorn glaciers west of the San Bernardino Pass and, after flowing northeastward through the Rheinwald, turns north to receive the Averserrhein and, below Thusis, the Albula. It unites with the Vorderrhein at Reichenau, Switz. After continuing for a short distance northeastward the Rhine turns north at Chur, where it receives the Plessur. Farther downstream it is joined by the Landquart and Ill on the right, and by the Tamina on the left. Forming sections of the Swiss-Liechtenstein and Swiss-Austrian border along an artificially straightened course, it flows through a delta in two separate branches into the Lake of Constance (*q.v.*). The lake receives as affluents the Bregenzer Ache, the Argen, and Schussen and, through the Aach, it receives water lost through underground drainage from the Danube where that river crosses the limestone of the Swabian Alb.

At Constance the river leaves the main lake and flows into the Untersee. Leaving this at Stein, the High Rhine follows as far as Basel a winding westerly course which for most of its length forms the Swiss-German border. Rapids, especially the Rheinfall (about 69 ft. [21 m.]) below Schaffhausen, render this section, like the Alpine Rhine, unsuitable for through navigation. The construction of a dam in 1891 made the lowest part of the High Rhine navigable below Rheinfelden, which became a port terminal in 1934. Seven further dams with hydroelectric stations have been built. The High Rhine receives as tributaries from the south the Thur, Töss, Aare (with Limmat and Reuss), and Birs; its only large tributary from the north is the Wutach.

At Basel, where the river turns sharply northward and enters the rift valley, the Upper Rhine begins and extends to the entrance to the Rhine gorge above Bingen. The broad valley is bounded westward by the Vosges and Hardt mountains and eastward by the Black Forest, Kraichgau, and Odenwald. Above Mannheim the Rhine is confined to a largely artificial bed.

The Upper Rhine flows past the ancient cities of Strasbourg, Speyer, Worms (of the *Nibelungenlied* fame), and Mainz, and the comparatively new ones of Kehl, Karlsruhe, Mannheim, Ludwigshafen, and Wiesbaden. Forming the Franco-German boundary from Basel almost to Karlsruhe, the Rhine receives as major tributaries in this stretch the Ill from the west and Kinzig from the east. Farther north the Upper Rhine is joined from the east by its most important tributaries, the Neckar and the Main.

The Middle Rhine, which extends from Bingen to below Bonn, is the most beautiful part, especially the southern stretch where the river is confined to a gorge separating the Hunsrück Mountains in the west from the Taunus Mountains in the east. At the entrance to the gorge the Rhine receives the Nahe from the west. Above Sankt Goarshausen on the right bank, the Lorelei cliff rises sheer to 433 ft. (132 m.). It was immortalized in Heinrich Heine's lyric, set to music by P. F. Silcher, commemorating a legend invented by Clemens Brentano. Above Coblenz, where the valley widens, it is joined from the east by the Lahn and at Coblenz by the Moselle (Mosel) from the west. Joining farther north, the Rivers Ahr from the west and the Sieg from the east are not navigable. The volcanic crags of the Siebengebirge and Drachenfels, opposite Bonn, are the last uplands to approach the river.

The Lower Rhine is a lowland river about 1,000 yd. (914 m.) wide, flowing slowly past ancient Cologne, fashionable Düsseldorf, and Duisburg-Ruhrort, a city of heavy industry and the leading

Rhine port. Its main tributaries thereabouts are the Erft from the west and the Ruhr and Lippe from the east. Below Emmerich the Rhine leaves Germany and after a further brief stretch in Dutch territory divides into the numerous distributaries of its delta, which mingle with those of the Meuse (Maas) and Scheldt (Schelde). The first division is into a southern branch, the Waal, and a northern, the Pannerdensche Kanaal. The Waal, which carries about two-thirds of the total flow, after skirting Nijmegen becomes known as the Merwede near Gorinchem. Below Gorinchem it sends off a branch southwestward, the Niewe Merwede, through which 55% of the combined Meuse-Rhine water reaches the sea in the Haringvliet. The Merwede itself divides at Dordrecht into the Noord (leading toward Rotterdam) and the Oude Maas, which reaches the sea through the Nieuwe Waterweg. The Pannerdensche Kanaal divides south of Arnhem into the IJssel, which takes about one-ninth of all the Rhine water into the IJsselmeer (*q.v.*), and into another branch first called Rijn, then Nederrijn and, from south of Utrecht onward, Lek. Utrecht itself lies on a distributary, the Kromme Rijn, which splits into the Vecht, leading northward, and the Oude Rijn, which reaches the sea near Leiden. In the mid-1960s weirs were constructed on the Nederrijn to increase the freshwater supply to the IJsselmeer, prevent the saltwater boundary from encroaching farther inland, and generate electricity. After being joined by the Noord, the Lek becomes the Nieuwe Maas, which below Rotterdam joins the Oude Maas, linked with the sea by an artificial channel, the Nieuwe Waterweg.

Evolution.—The ancestor of the present Rhine originated in the later Tertiary as one of the three great rivers draining the northern Alpine foredeep. This *Urrhein*, however, still lacked the High Rhine and Alpine Rhine, then part of the Danube system; it acquired them by river capture during the Quaternary.

Hydrography.—The Alpine Rhine with its steep gradient, high runoff coefficient (80% of the precipitation in its catchment area), high winter minimum, and high summer maximum, is a characteristic Alpine stream. Although variations of the regime are evened out by the Lake of Constance, which is fed by upland streams as well as by the Rhine, they are increased again by the confluence with the Aare, which on an average carries more water than the Rhine (19,800 as against 15,500 cu.ft. per sec. [561 as against 439 cu.m. per sec.]). Below this confluence, however, the tributaries from the uplands, with their spring or winter maxi-

mums, increasingly moderate the unbalance. Thus at Cologne the average deviations from mean flow are slight, and the pronounced summer maximum of the higher sections gives place to winter and summer maximums, yielding a regime favourable to navigation. Moreover, the river freezes only in exceptional winters.

The Rhine as a Waterway.—As a commercial artery, the Rhine is unrivaled among the world's rivers, historically as well as in the amount of traffic carried. The Romans maintained a Rhine fleet, and the importance of the river increased enormously with the rise of medieval trade, which relied on water transport wherever possible because of the poor roads. The rock barrier of the

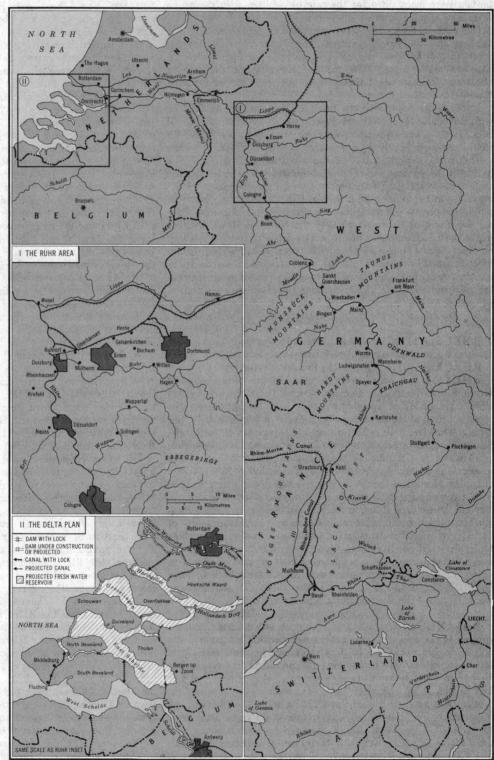

THE RHINE AND ITS TRIBUTARIES. THE RUHR AREA AND DELTA PLAN ARE SHOWN IN INSETS I AND II

gorge at Bingen divided navigation into two sections: predominantly upstream traffic by seagoing vessels to Cologne, and predominantly downstream movement of transalpine commodities from Basel to Mainz and Frankfurt am Main. After about 1500 navigation declined, because of reorientation of trade toward the Atlantic and political disintegration of the Rhineland. The rise of modern navigation began in the 19th century and its present magnitude is attributable largely to three factors: removal of political restrictions on navigation; physical improvements and canalization; and increasing industrialization of the riparian countries.

The principle of free navigation on the Rhine was agreed upon by the Congress of Vienna in 1815, and was put into effect by the Mainz Convention of 1831, which also established the Central Commission of the Rhine. This first treaty was simplified and revised in the Mannheim Convention of 1868 which, with the extension in 1918 of all privileges to ships of all countries and not merely the riverain states, remains (broadly speaking) in force.

As regards physical improvements, two sections presented serious handicaps: the rock barrier at Bingen and the southern Upper Rhine. At Bingen two navigation channels were blasted out in 1830–32; canalization of the Upper Rhine by confining it within an artificial bed and straightening its course was undertaken 1817–74. In neither case were the resulting improvements entirely satisfactory; for the passage at Bingen ships always take a pilot. Navigation on the Upper Rhine, despite the shortening of its course by 51 mi. (82 km.) and further improvements made after 1907, suffers from seasonal variations of flow and the swift current.

Canalization.—Plans exist for extending navigation through the Alpine Rhine into Switzerland by canalizing the Aare system, and a Swiss-German Convention of 1929 envisaged canalization of the High Rhine between Rheinfelden and the Lake of Constance. To improve navigation and to procure hydroelectric power, France at the Treaty of Versailles obtained the right to divert Rhine water below Basel into a canal that was to rejoin the Rhine at Strasbourg. Construction of the first section of this Grand Canal d'Alsace, designed to take vessels of 1,500 tons, was completed with the building of a dam at Kembs in 1932, and greatly improved navigation. Construction was resumed after World War II, but in the treaty of 1956 France, in return for German agreement to the canalization of the Moselle, consented to terminate the canal at Neu Breisach. The remaining four of a total of eight dams are to utilize Rhine water by the construction of canal loops only.

Below Basel the Huningue branch of the Rhine-Rhône Canal leads to Mulhouse, where it meets the main arm of that waterway, which joins the Rhine at Strasbourg. The Rhine-Rhône Canal (1810–33) is navigable by 300-ton craft and carries only moderate traffic. More important, although no larger, is the Rhine-Marne Canal (1838–53), which also joins the Rhine at Strasbourg.

The Neckar is canalized through Stuttgart as far as Plochingen and the Main as far as Bamberg, both waterways being navigable by 1,350-ton craft. A treaty signed in 1956 between the Federal Republic of Germany, France, and Luxembourg provided for canalization of the Moselle from Coblenz to Thionville (170 mi. [274 km.]) for ships of 1,500 tons; this was completed in 1964. The Lahn is canalized for 200-ton craft for 42 mi. (68 km.).

In the Ruhr region, the Ruhr itself (except for the last 7 mi.) and the Lippe are not used as waterways. Their place is taken by: (1) the Rhine-Herne Canal, completed in 1916 between Duisburg and Herne, navigable by craft of 1,350 tons, linking the Rhine through the Dortmund-Ems Canal with the German coast and through the Mittelland Canal with the waterways of central and eastern Germany and eastern Europe; and (2) the less important Wesel-Datteln-Hamm Canal (1930), parallel to the lower course of the Lippe and navigable by craft of 1,350 tons. Nearer the mouth, the Merwede Canal (enlarged 1952) past Amsterdam provides another route to the sea for ships of up to 4,300 tons.

Traffic.—The decisive factor that made the Rhine a major waterway was the rise of modern industry. This necessitated the bulk movement of coal, ore, building materials, and oil, and provided transport able to compete successfully with rail and road. The first steamship to appear on the Rhine was one which in 1817 made the voyage from London to Coblenz. Basel was first reached by steamship in 1832. From 1840 onward most transport was by tugs towing barges; development since 1945 involved mainly self-propelled units, but the introduction of push tugs portended another change. By the mid-1960s the total Rhine fleet of about 7,600,000 tons consisted of roughly 16,000 craft, of which three-quarters were on passage at any given moment. Over one-half of this fleet was Dutch, nearly one-third West German, and the remainder French, Swiss, and Belgian. Regular passenger services run between Mainz and Cologne and (in summer) between Basel and Rotterdam.

Although passenger transport is substantial, the Rhine is chiefly important for its freight traffic. This rose from about 1,500,000 tons at mid-19th century to 189,300,000 tons in 1962. More than twice as much cargo moves upstream as downstream and traffic density increases rapidly downstream, the figure for the Dutch section being about 12 times that for the southern Upper Rhine. Of the commodities transported, coal, which on the German section amounts to nearly a quarter of the total, takes first place, followed by ore, building materials, and petroleum products. Other freight includes grain, lignite, and fertilizers. Although it is only 1% of the total German Rhine traffic, there exists a genuine Rhine sea traffic which, with modern motor ships, can reach Rheinfelden. A direct Basel-London cargo service was opened in 1936. Basel is also the port of registry for the Swiss merchant fleet of about 25 ships.

The Rhine in History.—The effects of rivers on the regions through which they flow tend to alternate between trends toward unifying the regions culturally and politically and making a political boundary of the river. Of this phenomenon the Rhine is a classic example. During prehistoric times the same culture groups existed on both banks; similarly, in early historic times Teutonic tribes settled on either side of its lower and Celts alongside its upper course. Bridged and crossed by Caesar in 55 and 53 B.C., the Rhine became for the first time, along its course from the Lake of Constance to its mouth at Lugdunum Batavorum (Leiden), a political boundary—that of Roman Gaul. This did not endure for long, because before the death of Augustus the provinces of Germania Superior and Germania Inferior were carved out of Gaul, and south of Bonna (Bonn) the boundary of the Roman Empire was marked by the *limes* (Roman fortified frontier) well east of the Rhine; but it was fateful because it resulted in later claims by France, esteeming itself the successor to Gaul, to the Rhine as its natural boundary. When the Roman Empire disintegrated, the Rhine was crossed along its entire length by Teutonic tribes (A.D. 406), and the river formed the central backbone of the kingdom of the Franks and the Carolingian empire. When in 843 that empire was divided, stretches of the Rhine formed the eastern boundary of the central part, Lotharingia, until 870 when the Rhine again became the central axis of a political unit, the later Holy Roman Empire. Subsequent events shifted this axis eastward and caused political disintegration along the Rhine. The Thirty Years' War ended with the final loss to Germany of the Rhine headwaters and delta area, and a gradual advance of France toward the Rhine, which it reached under Louis XIV through his acquisition of Alsace.

The French Revolutionary Wars saw further French advances, and the Treaty of Lunéville (1801) made the Rhine, along most of its course, France's eastern boundary. But France advanced beyond the Rhine and included northwest Germany within its borders, and the Confederation of the Rhine extended French control as far as the Elbe and Neisse. The resultant upsurge of German nationalism was expressed by E. M. Arndt (*q.v.*) who, in 1813, wrote: "The Rhine is Germany's river, not its boundary." Nevertheless, the Congress of Vienna left France in possession of Alsace and thus with a Rhine frontier. Ambitions of Napoleon III to acquire further Rhenish territory strongly aroused German feelings. In 1840 Max Schneckenburger wrote his patriotic poem *Die Wacht am Rhein,* which was set to music by Karl Wilhelm in 1854 and became the rousing tune of the Prussian armies in the Franco-German War of 1870–71. One result of this war was that France lost Alsace and thus its Rhine frontier. For the subsequent history of the region *see* RHINELAND. The fortified defensive system of the Maginot Line (built 1927–36) adjoined the French bank of the Upper Rhine from the Swiss frontier to near Lauterbourg. The opposing *Westwall*, or Siegfried Line (1936–39), adjoined the German bank from the Swiss frontier to near Karlsruhe.

Events after World War II suggested that the struggle for possession of the Rhine had been superseded by a trend toward economic and even political union of the riparian states.

See also references under "Rhine" in the Index.

BIBLIOGRAPHY.—G. Whittam, *The Rhine*, "Rivers of the World Series" (1962); E. M. Yates, "The Development of the Rhine," *Publ. Inst. Brit. Geogr.*, no. 32 (1963); G. R. Crone, "Notes on the Rhine Distributaries and Land Reclamation in the Netherlands," *Geogr. J.*, vol. 104 (1944).

(K. A. S.)

RHINELAND, the historically controversial area of Western Europe lying along the Rhine (*q.v.*), east of the modern frontier between Germany on the one hand and France, Luxembourg, Belgium, and the Netherlands on the other. Apart from the strip of country from Karlsruhe southward to the Swiss frontier (west of which the Franco-German frontier is formed by the Rhine), the Rhineland extends from the northern borders of the French *départements* of Moselle and Bas-Rhin over the Saarland and the German *Land* Rhineland-Palatinate into northwestern Baden-Württemberg, western Hesse, and southwestern North Rhine-Westphalia (*qq.v.*).

Ancient History.—Julius Caesar in the 1st century B.C. thought of the Rhine as the natural frontier between the Celtic peoples of Gaul (*q.v.*) and the Germanic peoples (*q.v.*) to the east; but even in his time Germans were crossing it westward. From the 1st century A.D., under the Roman Empire, the country immediately west of the Rhine was divided between two provinces: Germania Superior, from the Alps to the vicinity of Antunnacum (Andernach), with Argentoratum (Strasbourg), Mogontiacum (Mainz), and Confluentes (Coblenz); and Germania Inferior, from Bonna (Bonn) to the Rhine estuary, with Colonia Agrippina (Cologne). Northward and westward of the former province and southward and westward of the latter, the hinterland was in the province Belgica, which included the upper and middle Moselle valley, with Augusta Treverorum (Trier). East of the Rhine, opposite Germania Superior, were the Agri Decumates (*q.v.*), a zone of defense for Gaul. From the 3rd century the Franks (*q.v.*) began gradually to occupy the Rhineland, overcoming other Germanic tribes (Chatti and Alamanni); and by the first decade of the 6th century Salian Frankish predominance was established under Clovis, founder of the Merovingian dynasty's rule over Gaul (*see* FRANCE: *History;* GERMANY: *History;* MEROVINGIANS). Under the partitions effected by the successors of Clovis the Rhineland was included in Austrasia (the eastern Frankish kingdom).

The early Carolingians (*q.v.*), whose power originated in Austrasia, made the Rhineland a base for their military and missionary penetration of Germany; and Aachen (*q.v.*) became the second city of the Frankish Empire of Charlemagne. In 843, however, the Treaty of Verdun divided the Frankish dominions between Charlemagne's grandsons: the emperor Lothair I received the Middle Kingdom (from the North Sea to Italy), Charles II the Bald the West Frankish Kingdom (France), and Louis the German the East Frankish (Germany, mainly east of the Rhine). When the Middle Kingdom was in turn divided (855), its Rhineland areas were included in Lotharingia, the kingdom of Lothair I's son Lothair.

The article LORRAINE describes the boundaries of Lotharingia; its partition between Charles the Bald and Louis the German under the Treaty of Mersen (870); the subsequent acquisition of the formerly West Frankish part by the Germans; and the formation of the duchies of Upper and Lower Lorraine (959). East of the two Lorraines, areas of the Rhineland belonged in the 10th century to the duchies of the "stem-lands," Saxony, Franconia, and Swabia (*qq.v.*). In the course of the following centuries, however, while Upper Lorraine was diminished, the other duchies were dissolved, and the Rhineland became the seat of numerous territorial principalities. These included: in the north, the electoral archbishopric of Cologne, with the secular territories of Cleves, Berg, and Jülich (*qq.v.*); in the central area, the electoral arch-

bishoprics of Trier and Mainz, and the bishoprics of Worms and of Speyer, with the electoral Palatinate, the countship of Nassau, and some dependencies of Hesse (*qq.v.*); and, in the south, the bishopric of Strasbourg, with the cities and various lordships of Alsace and the margraviate of Baden, with Breisgau (*qq.v.*).

Modern Times.—Exploiting the troubles of the Reformation in Germany, France encroached on Lorraine in the 16th century; Brandenburg acquired Cleves and Mark in 1614, forming the nucleus of the future power of Prussia (*q.v.*) in the Rhineland; and the Thirty Years' War (*q.v.*) and Peace of Westphalia gave France a foothold in Alsace. Louis XIV's wars consolidated the French position on the Alsatian Rhine (*see* DUTCH WARS; GRAND ALLIANCE, WAR OF THE; SPANISH SUCCESSION, WAR OF THE), but the farther-reaching claims that Louis made through his policy of "reunions" and his attempt to annex the Palatinate were frustrated. Ducal Lorraine was not definitively incorporated in France till 1766.

The French Revolutionary and the Napoleonic Wars (*qq.v.*) transformed the situation. The whole left bank of the Rhine from the frontier of the Batavian Republic to that of the Helvetic was ceded to France by the Treaty of Lunéville in 1801; and a radical reorganization of the right bank was effected by the *Reichsdeputationshauptschluss* of 1803 before further changes followed the establishment of the Confederation of the Rhine (1806). In 1810 the French frontier was extended from the Rhine at Wesel northeastward to the Baltic Sea at Lübeck. (*See* GERMANY: *History.*)

After Napoleon's downfall the Congress of Vienna (1814–15) limited France's frontier on the Rhine to the Alsatian zone again, opposite Grand-Ducal Baden. North of Alsace a new Palatinate was constituted for Bavaria. Northwest of the Palatinate were some little exclaves of other German states, namely Saxe-Coburg's Lichtenberg, Oldenburg's Birkenfeld, and Hesse-Homburg's Meisenheim; but north of these the whole left bank as far as Cleves, together with Jülich and Aachen in the west and Trier and Saarlouis in the south, became Prussian. This Prussian territory was united with Prussia's adjacent possessions on the right bank to form the Rhine Province (Rheinprovinz) in 1824. To the southeast of the Rhine Province lay Nassau (on the right bank) and part of Grand-Ducal Hesse (Darmstadt on the right bank, Mainz and Worms, north of the Palatinate, on the left). Prussia purchased Lichtenberg in 1834 and annexed Nassau and Meisenheim after the Seven Weeks' War of 1866. Alsace-Lorraine (*q.v.*), ceded by France after the Franco-German War of 1870–71, was organized as a condominium of the states of the new German Empire. The Rhineland became the most prosperous area of Germany, the Prussian north in particular being highly industrialized.

The 20th Century.—After World War I the Treaty of Versailles not only restored Alsace-Lorraine to France but also went some way toward satisfying France's desire for a farther barrier against the danger of German invasion. Great Britain and the United States objected on ethnic grounds to the French demand for the permanent detachment of the left bank of the Rhine from Germany; but the treaty stipulated that Allied troops should occupy it, with large right-bank bridgeheads opposite Cologne, Coblenz, and Mainz (including Wiesbaden), and at Kehl. Belgian troops were to occupy a zone from Aachen northward, British troops a zone round Cologne, U.S. troops a zone round Coblenz, and French troops a zone round Mainz. Occupation might last 15 years from Jan. 10, 1920; but if Germany fulfilled the other obligations of the treaty, in particular with regard to reparations (*q.v.*), a northern zone might be evacuated after 5 years only and a central zone after 10, before the final evacuation of the south. The German left bank, however, and a right-bank strip 50 km. deep were to be permanently demilitarized. An Inter-Allied Control Commission (set up by a separate arrangement in 1919) was to provide for the security of the occupying forces but was not to interfere with the German civil administration. It should, however, erect a customs barrier to protect the area's economy.

Great Britain and the U.S. inclined to lenience, the French and the Belgians to severity. Appealing to the largely Catholic population's anti-Prussian feeling and to fear of Communism, the French also sponsored separatist movements. J. A. Dorten's attempt to create a Rhineland state within the German Republic (1919) came to nothing, partly because the Germans resented his dealings with Gen. Charles Mangin, head of the French occupying forces, partly because the British and the Americans did not support it. In spring 1920, however, when the German government sent troops into the demilitarized Ruhr district to suppress a Communist insurrection, the French temporarily seized Frankfurt am Main, Homburg, and Darmstadt on the right bank (April–May); and in March 1921 the French, the British, and the Belgians occupied Duisburg, Ruhrort, and Düsseldorf, the so-called Sanctions districts in the Ruhr area, on the ground of German default on reparations. The U.S., however, which had not ratified the Versailles Treaty, made a separate peace with Germany in August 1921 and began withdrawing troops from the Rhineland in 1922.

The Franco-Belgian occupation of the rest of the Ruhr (q.v.) in January 1923 on the one hand precipitated the completion of the U.S. withdrawal (whereupon the Coblenz zone was taken over by the French), and on the other revived the separatist movements. A "Rhineland Republic," proclaimed at Aachen on October 21, lasted till November 2; and a separatist coup in the Palatinate led to fighting before the British induced the French to disavow it. In 1924 France agreed to the evacuation of the Ruhr and to the Dawes Plan on reparations (q.v.); but the evacuation, scheduled for January 1925, was postponed till August.

Thanks largely to the diplomacy of the German statesman Gustav Stresemann (q.v.), the Pact of Locarno (q.v.), which covered not only the Rhineland but also Eastern Europe, was signed in London on Dec. 1, 1925. With France's consent, the northern two-thirds of the Belgian and British zones were evacuated by Jan. 31, 1926. The Inter-Allied Control Commission was replaced by a commission of the League of Nations.

In response to diplomatic pressure from Germany (which had moreover to pay the occupation costs), France agreed to a reduction of troops in the Rhineland to 60,000, but still insisted on occupation pending the due payment of reparations. An interview between Stresemann and the French statesman Aristide Briand at Thoiry in September 1926 came to nothing, and Stresemann's raising the question of "war guilt" caused France to fear a German repudiation of the Versailles Treaty. By 1929, when the Young Committee met to revise the Dawes Plan, it was understood that if financial agreement could be reached, complete evacuation of the Rhineland should ensue. Great Britain and Belgium announced that they would withdraw their troops before the end of the year, and France had to be content with referring difficulties to arbitration and with postponing total evacuation only till Germany's acceptance of the Young Plan. On June 30, 1930, five years before the date fixed in 1919, the last occupying troops left the Rhineland.

The Franco-Soviet five-year treaty of mutual guarantee (May 2, 1935) was declared by Nazi Germany to be a violation of the Locarno agreement. While the French Senate was still debating ratification of the treaty, Hitler on March 7, 1936, repudiated the Rhineland clauses of Versailles and Locarno and announced that German troops had entered the demilitarized zone. Unaware that Hitler had instructed his troops to retreat if the French invaded, the French general staff refused to act unless partial mobilization were ordered, which the French cabinet refused. Only a few specialized units were sent up to the Maginot Line along the French frontier, while the other Locarno Powers and the League of Nations were invited to take cognizance of the situation. Of the Locarno Powers, Great Britain did nothing because the British public regarded the Rhineland as German territory; Belgium was too weak to act; Italy secretly approved Germany's move; only Poland and Czechoslovakia were ready to stand by France. Protracted negotiations failed to undo the German remilitarization of the Rhineland, and the passive attitude of the Western Powers foreshadowed their acquiescence to Hitler's annexation of Austria and to his demands on Czechoslovakia in 1938. Had the Western Powers reacted strongly, World War II might have been averted.

RHINELAND-PALATINATE (RHEINLAND-PFALZ), a *Land* (state) of the Federal Republic of Germany constituted in 1946 from the southern part of the Prussian Rhine province, the Bavarian Palatinate, and part of Rhine-Hesse and of Hesse-Nassau. It is bounded north by North Rhine-Westphalia (Nordrhein-Westfalen), east by Hesse and Baden-Württemberg, west by Belgium and Luxembourg, and south by Saarland and France. Area 7,657 sq.mi. (19,832 sq.km.). Pop. (1961) 3,417,116.

The northern portion covers the southwest section of the Rhine Plateau. This includes the Eifel (q.v.) and farther south the Hunsrück, which slopes northward to the Moselle (Mosel) Valley. The deeply entrenched meanders of the Moselle, extending from Trier downstream to the Rhine confluence at Coblenz, are covered with vineyards on the south-facing slopes, with woods on the steep north-facing slopes and patches of arable land on the valley floor. A closely settled lowland between Mayen and Coblenz contains volcanic materials which are used for building. East of the Rhine gorge on the lower Westerwald Plateau lies Montabaur, the centre of an old-established ceramics industry. South of the Hunsrück is lower terrain with woods, arable land, and many small villages. The Haardt, or Pfälzer Wald, is a wooded sandstone plateau whose low hills overlooking the Rhine support important vineyards and orchards. This southern portion of the *Land*, known as the Palatinate, has a number of industrial towns such as Pirmasens. Ludwigshafen dominates the Palatinate, and its chemical industry along the left bank of the Rhine employs more than 30,000 workers, many from the large villages in the Rhine plain.

The *Land* is divided into the administrative divisions of Coblenz, Trier, Montabaur, Rheinhessen, and Pfalz (Palatinate). The principal towns are Ludwigshafen, Mainz (the capital), Kaiserslautern, Trier, Coblenz, Worms, and Pirmasens (qq.v.). About 58% of the people are Roman Catholics and 41% are Protestants. According to the constitution, primary schools in Rhineland-Palatinate are confessional (or have confessional religious instruction), as are the five teachers' training colleges. Establishments for higher education include the Johannes Gutenberg University at Mainz and a technical college for administration in Speyer.

Forestry and farming are the staple occupations. Much of the farming is arable, grain crops in particular (wheat, rye, and oats) being grown, as well as potatoes and sugar beets. The warmth of the river valleys allows tobacco to be grown; but far more important are the vineyards along the Rhine and its westbank tributaries, the Moselle, Nahe, and smaller rivers. Rhineland-Palatinate contains more than two-thirds of the whole area devoted to vines in the Federal Republic and has by far the greatest wine production per acre. Although the *Land* is primarily agricultural, industry is of importance in the economy. Ludwigshafen is an important river port and its major industries include metalworking and papermaking as well as the production of chemicals. Other industries include footwear (Pirmasens) and sewing machines and bicycles (Kaiserslautern). Tourists also bring in much revenue. For history, *see* HESSE; PALATINATE; RHINELAND.

BIBLIOGRAPHY.—J. Niessen, *Geschichtlicher Handatlas der Deutschen Länder am Rhein* (1950); A. Schulte (ed.), *Tausend Jahre deutscher Geschichte und deutscher Kultur am Rhein* (1925); R. Klöpper and J. Korber, *Rheinland-Pfalz in seiner Gliederung nach zentralörtlichen Bereichen* (1957); R. E. Dickinson, *Germany: a General and Regional Geography* (1953).   (R. E. DI.)

RHINITIS: *see* NOSE, DISEASES OF.

RHINOCEROS, a large, hoofed mammal characterized by one or two horns on the face. Rhinoceroses, along with tapirs and horses, belong to the order Perissodactyla, all members of which have an odd number of toes. The family Rhinocerotidae contains five extant, and many extinct, species. Those now existing have been greatly reduced in number since the mid-19th century, and are in danger of extermination.

The animal is large, massively built, with a long, barrel-shaped body and comparatively short legs. The skin is extremely thick and tough, and the coarse hair is sparse, almost lacking in some species. The horn has a fibrous structure and is an outgrowth of the skin; it has no core of bone, though the skull is thicker at the base of the horn. The horns are used as weapons, though there can be few occasions when their use is actually required in defense —except against man—for no other animal predator is powerful enough to overcome a healthy adult rhinoceros. The rhinoceros' eyesight appears not to be acute, but its senses of hearing and smell are highly developed.

All species of rhinoceros are vegetarians; some browse on leaves and buds of shrubs or small trees, others graze on grasses and other herbage. The Asiatic species stay near water or mud holes in which to wallow; some species prefer prairie, while others stay mostly in bushland or forest. Rhinoceroses are usually solitary, but a calf may accompany its mother for a long time, even after the birth of a younger sibling. A single calf is born after a lengthy gestation (16 months in the Indian rhinoceros), and the horns are at first represented by mere thickenings of the skin. The longevity of the Indian rhinoceros is almost 50 years.

In spite of their size, rhinoceroses are generally placid, inoffensive creatures. The black rhinoceros, however, has a reputation

CAMERA PRESS—PIX FROM PUBLIX

AFRICAN BLACK RHINOCEROS (DICEROS BICORNIS)

for unprovoked attack because it may panic and charge blindly at a strange object such as a man when disturbed. The flesh of rhinoceroses is relished by some African tribes. The skin was used for making sjamboks, the whips used in the days of the ox wagons. Horns of all species are greatly prized in the Far East, where the powdered product is believed to be a powerful aphrodisiac.

In former geologic periods rhinoceroses inhabited both the Eastern and Western Hemispheres but are now restricted to tropical Africa and Asia. The Indian (*Rhinoceros unicornis*) and the Javan (*R. sondaicus*) species resemble each other in having the skin thrown into deep folds on the shoulders and thighs and round the neck and in possessing only one horn. The Indian is much the larger, standing over 6 ft. at the shoulder and reaching a length of more than 14 ft. The skin of the sides and upper limbs is studded with large rounded knobs. This species was once widely spread throughout India but is now greatly restricted to certain areas in Nepal and Assam. The Javan species, considerably smaller, has less voluminous skin folds, a much shorter horn (generally absent in the female), and the skin not decorated with knobs but divided into scalelike polygonal divisions. The ears have a hairy fringe and the tail is hairy below and at the tip. This species, once widely distributed throughout southeast Asia, is now greatly restricted.

The Sumatran rhinoceros (*Dicerorhinus sumatrensis*) is the only Asiatic species with two horns. It is rather larger than the Javan rhinoceros. There are folds of skin on the forequarters only, and the rough skin is covered very sparsely with short black hair. Its range coincides with that of the Javan rhinoceros, and, although its numbers are reduced, it has not been brought so near extermination as the Javan species.

Both species of African rhinoceros have two horns and no skin folds. The widespread black rhinoceros (*Diceros bicornis*), with a hooked prehensile upper lip, is a browser; the larger white rhinoceros (*Ceratotherium simus*), with a blunter upper lip, is a grazer. The latter species is, among land mammals, second only to the elephant in size; it is restricted to reserves in Zululand, Uganda, and the Congo.

See PERISSODACTYL; see also references under "Rhinoceros" in the Index.   (L. H. M.)

RHODE ISLAND, a North Atlantic state of the United States, belonging to the New England group, is bounded north and east by Massachusetts, south by the Atlantic ocean and west by Connecticut. Rhode Island, official name "the State of Rhode Island and Providence Plantations" (see *History*, below), is the smallest state in the union, having an extreme length, north and south, of 44 mi., an extreme width, east and west, of 35 mi. and

a total area of 1,214 sq.mi., of which 156 sq.mi. are inland water area. The capital is at Providence (*q.v.*). Rhode Island was one of the original 13 states. Its state song is "Rhode Island," the official state tree is the red maple and the official state bird is the Rhode Island Red. The origin of the name has been variously traced to a corruption of the Dutch words for "red island," a name supposedly given to the island in Narragansett bay by the Dutch navigator Adriaen Block, and to the Florentine Giovanni da Verrazano, who is said to have called it after the Island of Rhodes. The island referred to is Aquidneck on which the city of Newport stands.

PHYSICAL GEOGRAPHY

Physical Features.—Rhode Island lies between approximately 41° 9′ and 42° 3′ N. and 71° 8′ and 71° 53′ W. The region of which it is a part was at one time worn down to a gently rolling plain near sea level, but has since been uplifted and somewhat dissected by stream action. As a result the topography is characterized by low rounded hills but is nowhere mountainous. Since the uplift and stream dissection a slight depression has allowed the sea to invade the lower portions of the river valleys, forming bays such as Narragansett bay, Providence "river" and Sakonnet "river." Glaciation has disturbed the river systems.

The mean elevation for the entire state is 200 ft., the lowest portions occurring along the ocean and the shore of Narragansett bay. The upper bay region is composed of gently rolling lands, but about two-thirds of the state consists of higher ground which begins abruptly just west of Providence and rises toward the northwest where Jerimoth hill, 812 ft., is the highest point within the state. The coast line, including the shores of the bays and islands, is extensive; its western portion is only slightly indented, but its eastern portion is deeply indented by Narragansett bay, a body of water varying in width from 3 to 12 mi. and extending inland for about 28 mi. Within Narragansett bay are numerous islands characteristic of an area that has suffered comparatively recent depression, the largest being Rhode Island (or Aquidneck), Conanicut Island and Prudence Island. Of these the most important is Rhode Island, 15 mi. long and 3 mi. wide. About 10 mi. offshore and south of the central part of the state is Block Island.

The rivers are short and of no great volume, but they flow swiftly and are useful in supplying water for industry. The Providence river is really an arm of Narragansett bay, into which flow the waters of the Pawtuxet and Blackstone rivers. The latter stream has a fall of about 50 ft. at Pawtucket, and the Pawtuxet also has a number of falls along its course. Mount Hope bay is a northeastern arm of Narragansett bay and is also the estuary of the Taunton river. The Sakonnet river is a long bay separating Aquidneck or Rhode Island from the mainland on the east. The Pawcatuck river forms part of the boundary between Rhode Island and Connecticut.

Climate.—Rhode Island has a more moderate climate than that of the northern sections of New England. There are no great extremes of either heat or cold. Narragansett Pier has a mean annual temperature of 50° F. (10° C.), a mean summer temperature (for June, July and August) of 68° and a mean winter temperature (for December, January and February) of 30°. The mean annual temperature at Providence is 50.5°; the mean for the summer, 70.1°; and for the winter, 30.2°; while the highest and lowest temperatures ever recorded are respectively 102° and −17°. The mean annual precipitation is about 38.68 in.

Soil.—As in most of New England, the soil in Rhode Island is for the most part sterile. Its quality improves, generally, from west to east. Almost half of the state is covered by an acidic sandy loam derived from the weathering of the underground rocks. Because of its rocky subsoil it drains very thoroughly, and in times of drought may become too dry even for pasturage. Very little of it has been cultivated and for the most part it supports a growth of stunted woodland. The best soil is found farther east on the rolling hills of the Narragansett basin: a firm, brown glacial type. Near Warwick and across the bay in East Providence a sandy loam, while loose and porous, occurs for the most part at low enough elevations to ensure sufficient moisture, and it has proved well suited to market gardening. About 8% of the state is covered by either a thin, coarse, sandy soil supporting scrubby pine and grass or by swamp.

Vegetation.—The flora is surprisingly rich. About 60 species of trees are native to the state, among them ash, oak, birch, hickory, poplar, pine and maple. Where the long inlet of Narragansett bay moderates the climate more southerly species such as the tulip tree flourish, while northern types such as the paper birch and sugar maple are found in the northwest. The sand plains, rocks and tidal pools along the coast support a wide variety of seaweeds, ferns and mosses. The swamps have a particularly interesting flora, which includes the insectivorous sundew and pitcher plant and several kinds of orchids. Some of the most beautiful wildflowers occur in the wooded areas—among them violet, trillium, columbine, rhododendron and mountain laurel—and the meadows are often covered with daisies and wild carrots and, in the autumn, goldenrods and asters. Wild blackberries are abundant on the sandy soil in the western part of the state.

Animal Life.—A maritime state with a long and, for much of its length, protected coast line, Rhode Island boasts an extensive representation of marine invertebrates, among them the sea anemone, sea cucumber, jellyfish, several types of marine worms, crustaceans such as the barnacle, lobster and crab, and the squid, clam and oyster. The quahog, a highly-prized hard-shelled clam, is protected by law. Both the coastal waters and the inland ponds and streams contain a variety of fish. Cod, perch and alewives are common and sea bass, bluefish and swordfish are often caught off Block Island. Inland species include perch, bass, pickerel and trout. There are many types of turtles, salamanders and frogs and nearly 20 species of snakes. Rhode Island lies at the edge of the migration route for a number of types of shore birds. In the uncultivated western portions of the state the blue jay, ruffed grouse, barred and screech owls live the year around, while the catbird, flicker and robin are common during the summer. The osprey is frequently seen in the vicinity of Touisset, and pheasants are abundant, especially in Newport county. A number of small mammals inhabit the woodlands, including foxes, rabbits, woodchucks and skunks.

State Parks and Historic Sites.—Seventeen state parks, 5 major state beaches, and over 30 roadside groves, plus other recreation areas, are maintained by the division of parks and recreation of the state department of natural resources. Recreation facilities, both public and private, are liberally provided in the state, and Newport and Narragansett Pier in particular have long been noted as summer resorts.

Rhode Island's long and colourful history has left its cities and towns dotted with monuments, buildings, ancient graveyards and other points of interest which vividly recall the past. The home of Gen. Nathanael Greene of American Revolution fame is located in Coventry and the birthplace of the painter Gilbert Stuart in North Kingstown. Bishop George Berkeley, the philosopher, lived at Whitehall in Middletown during his stay in the colony. The village of Wickford contains a number of well-preserved 18th-century houses, among them the Stephen Cooper house (1728) and the John Updike house (1745). Other historic sites include the grave of Elizabeth Alden, daughter of John Alden and Priscilla Mullins, in Little Compton and Acote's hill in Gloucester which figured in Dorr's rebellion. *See also* NEWPORT; PROVIDENCE: *Historic Sites.*

HISTORY

Rhode Island was founded by refugees from Massachusetts who went there in search of religious and political freedom. The first settlements were made at Providence by Roger Williams (*q.v.*) in June 1636 and at Portsmouth on the island of Aquidneck (Rhode Island) by the Antinomians William Coddington (1601–78), John Clarke (1609–76) and Anne Hutchinson (*c.* 1600–1643) in March–April 1638. Becoming dissatisfied with conditions at Portsmouth, Coddington and Clarke moved a few miles farther south in April 1639 and established a settlement at Newport. In a similar manner Warwick was founded in Jan. 1643 by seceders from Providence under the leadership of Samuel Gorton. The union of Portsmouth and Newport, March 12, 1640, was followed by the consolidation

of all four settlements, May 19, 1647, under a patent of March 14, 1644, issued by the parliamentary board of commissioners for plantations. The particularistic sentiment was still strong, however, and in 1651 the union split into two confederations: one including the mainland towns, Providence and Warwick; and the other the island towns, Portsmouth and Newport. A reunion was effected in 1654 by Roger Williams and a charter secured from Charles II on July 8, 1663.

In the patent of 1644 the entire colony was called Providence Plantations. On March 13, 1644, the Portsmouth-Newport general court changed the name of the island from Aquidneck to the Isle of Rhodes or Rhode Island. The official designation for the province as a whole in the charter of 1663, therefore, was Rhode Island and Providence Plantations. Block Island was admitted to the colony in 1664. The charter was suspended at the beginning of Sir Edmund Andros' regime in 1686, but was restored again after the "glorious Revolution" of 1688 in England. The closing years of the 17th century were characterized by a gradual transition from agricultural to commercial activities. Newport became a centre of piracy, privateering and smuggling as well as legitimate commerce.

The passage of the Sugar act, April 5, 1764, and the steps taken by the British government to enforce the Navigation acts seriously affected Rhode Island's trade. On June 9, 1772, the "Gaspee," a British vessel sent to enforce the acts of trade and navigation, ran aground in Narragansett bay and was burned to the water's edge by a party of men from Providence. In 1776 Gen. William Howe sent a detachment of his army under Gen. Henry Clinton to seize Newport as a base of operations for reducing New England, and the city was occupied by the British on Dec. 8. To capture this British garrison, later increased to 6,000 men, a combined operation of about 10,000 men (mostly New England militia) under Maj. Gen. John Sullivan and a French fleet carrying 4,000 French regulars under Count d'Estaing, was planned in the summer of 1778. On Aug. 9 Sullivan crossed to the north end of the island of Rhode Island, but as the French were disembarking on Conanicut Island, Lord Howe arrived with the British fleet. D'Estaing hastily re-embarked his troops and sailed out to meet Howe. After two days of maneuvering the hostile fleets were dispersed by a severe storm. On the 20th D'Estaing returned to the port with his fleet badly crippled, only to announce that he should sail to Boston to refit. The American officers protested in vain, and on the 30th the Americans, learning of the approach of Lord Howe's fleet with 5,000 troops under Clinton, decided to abandon the island. The British evacuated Newport Oct. 25, 1779, and the French fleet was stationed there in 1780–81.

Rhode Island's association with the other colonies, particularly its New England neighbours, was characterized by individualistic tendencies. It had been one of the first colonies to advocate and

AERIAL VIEW OF NEWPORT HARBOUR AND RESORT AREA, SHOWING 19TH-CENTURY SUMMER MANSIONS IN FOREGROUND

to put into practice religious freedom. Throughout its early history, not only did it refuse to give up its independence by joining Massachusetts but, as noted, there was even some difficulty in keeping the colony itself united. Under the Articles of Confederation it was principally Rhode Island that defeated the proposal to authorize congress to levy an import duty of 5% to meet the debts of the central government. When the Constitutional Convention met in Philadelphia in 1787 the Rhode Island farmers and merchants, fearing that a more centralized system of government would interfere with their local privileges, refused to send delegates. Not until the federal government threatened to sever commercial relations between the United States and Rhode Island did the latter, in May 1790, ratify the new constitution, and then by only two votes.

At the end of the American Revolution, instead of providing itself with a new state constitution, Rhode Island continued to be governed under the charter of 1663. This charter and the franchise law of 1724 had established substantial equality of representation among the towns and also restricted the suffrage to freeholders and their eldest male heirs. Drastic changes were beginning to take place in the state's economy and population, however. Agriculture and commerce declined in relative importance as Rhode Island became one of the most completely industrialized among the states. The population, which had been increasing since 1800, began an accelerated expansion about 1840 and quadrupled between then and 1900. The bulk of this increase, which continued into the 20th century, was accounted for by successive waves of immigration, beginning with the Irish in the second quarter of the 19th century. The French Canadians arrived shortly after the Irish; the Italians around 1900; and numerous other national groups in the next two decades. In addition, the population shifted from approximately 20% urban and 80% rural in 1800 to nearly 90% urban in 1900.

BY COURTESY OF BROWN UNIVERSITY, PROVIDENCE

FIRST BAPTIST MEETINGHOUSE, PROVIDENCE, COMPLETED IN 1775 TO HOUSE THE BAPTIST CHURCH OF AMERICA, FOUNDED BY ROGER WILLIAMS IN 1639

Demands for a more equitable representation of the urban communities in the legislature and for an extension of the suffrage to nonproperty owners precipitated the first of a long series of struggles for constitutional reform, Dorr's rebellion of 1841–42. About 1840 Thomas W. Dorr (1805–54), a young Providence lawyer, began a systematic campaign for reform. A convention summoned without any authority from the legislature and elected on the principle of universal manhood suffrage met at Providence from Oct. 4 to Nov. 18, 1841, and drafted a document which came to be known as the People's constitution. A second convention met on the call of the legislature in Feb. 1842 and adopted the Freeman's constitution. On being submitted to popular vote (Dec. 27, 28 and 29, 1841) the former was ratified by a large majority; the latter was rejected (March 21, 22 and 23, 1842) by 676 votes. At an election held on April 18, 1842, Dorr was chosen governor. The supreme court of the state and U.S. Pres. John Tyler both refused to recognize the validity of the People's constitution, whereupon Dorr and a few of his more zealous adherents decided to organize a rebellion. They were easily repulsed in an attack upon the Providence town arsenal. Dorr, after a brief period of

exile in Connecticut, was convicted of high treason, April 26, 1844, and sentenced to life imprisonment. He was released by act of the assembly in June 1845 and restored to the rights and privileges of citizenship in May 1851.

The Freeman's constitution, modified by another convention held at Newport and East Greenwich from Sept. 12 to Nov. 5, 1842, was finally adopted by popular vote, Nov. 21–23, 1842. Only a partial concession was made to the demand for reform. The suffrage was extended to nonfreeholders, but only to those of American birth, so that naturalized citizens could vote only if they held property. The charter legislature was replaced by one comprising a senate, to which each town was to send one representative, and a house of representatives of 72 members, apportioned by population. In the lower house, however, each town was to have at least one representative and no city or town more than one-sixth of the total, and the small towns were left in a dominant position.

After the American Civil War agitation for further reform was renewed. Under the leadership of Charles E. Gorman, himself naturalized, a prolonged campaign was waged to secure the same voting rights for naturalized as for native-born citizens. The constitution was finally amended in 1888 to eliminate all property restrictions but one: only property owners were allowed to vote for members of city councils. This limitation was removed in 1928.

It was not until 1909 that further change was made in the apportionment of legislative seats. In that year an amendment to the constitution increased the number of seats in the lower house to 100 and raised the allowable limit for any one city or town to one-quarter. The status of the senate was unchanged. Providence illustrates the inequities that remained in representation. With well over one-third of the state's population in 1910 and 1920, the city was entitled to only one-quarter of the house seats and to one seat in the senate. In 1928 a further change in legislative apportionment was made as a result of which Providence was able to return five senators and Pawtucket two, with the other cities and towns continuing to send one each.

Throughout most of its history Rhode Island has tended to cast its presidential vote for the more conservative party—the Federalists, then the Whigs and, following the American Civil War, the Republicans, until Alfred E. Smith carried the state in 1928. The Democrats continued to receive the state's electoral votes from 1932 through 1948. Rhode Island returned temporarily to the Republican fold in 1952 and 1956, but voted Democratic again in 1960 and 1964 by enormous margins. National Republican allegiance was matched in its congressional representation as well as on the state level from the post-Civil War period until 1932 when it became predominantly Democratic. Beginning with the election of Gov. John H. Chafee in 1962, the G.O.P. has seen a revival of its electoral fortunes in statewide office. In 1966 Chafee was re-elected, and carried with him a Republican lieutenant governor and attorney general.

An important result of Rhode Island's adherence first to the Republican party and then to the Democratic during their periods of national ascendancy was the prominence thus given to Rhode Island's representation in the councils of the nation—a prominence at times far out of proportion to its size and population. These long periods of one-party dominance made possible the building up of seniority in congress toward positions of national leadership. U.S. Sen. Nelson W. Aldrich (served 1881–1911), backed by a highly-disciplined Republican state organization under his lieutenant, the "blind boss" Gen. Charles R. Brayton, was one of the foremost architects of American tariff policy. Aldrich was so influential nationally that he came to be referred to as the "general manager of the United States." Democratic U.S. Sen. Theodore Francis Green, who was first elected in 1936 and served continuously until his retirement in 1960, rose to the chairmanship of the powerful senate foreign relations committee.

GOVERNMENT

The Freeman's constitution of 1842, frequently amended, remains the basic law of Rhode Island. The state's first unlimited constitutional convention in 122 years was called by referendum in 1964. At the same time, the voters elected 100 delegates to the convention. Leading proposals for changes in the constitution included reapportionment of the state legislature, elimination of a $300 limit on the legislators' annual pay, extension of the governor's term from two to four years, giving the governor an item veto for the state budget, bracketing of candidates for governor and lieutenant governor on the election ballot, appointive instead of elective status for secretary of state and treasurer, and appointment of the supreme court by the governor with senate approval instead of election by the legislature. Another proposal was for the provision of a state lottery. In the meantime, a special census was taken, as of Oct. 1, 1965, to form the basis of a temporary reapportionment. The new constitutional draft was finally put to a referendum in April 1968, and resoundingly defeated by a four-to-one vote.

Throughout much of the state's history the legislature possessed most of the governmental power. The governor did not even have the veto until 1909, and until 1935 he had little control over the administrative agencies of the state government or over appointments to these agencies. The members of the state supreme court were (and remained) removable by vote of the legislature. In 1935 Democratic Governor Green, acting with the first Democratic majority in both houses of the legislature in many years, brought about a complete reorganization of the state administration. Administrative control was centralized in the hands of the governor through the consolidation of approximately 80 independent boards and commissions into 11 departments whose heads were appointed by him. This reform, for the first time, made the governorship a full-time position and gave the governor, in effect, the major responsibility for state policy.

The executive officers of the state government are the governor, lieutenant governor, secretary of state, attorney general and general treasurer, each elected for two-year terms in even-numbered years. Each of the latter three is in charge of the department of state government corresponding to his title. Eleven additional departments are responsible to the governor: executive, administration, education, social welfare, labour, public works, natural resources, health, business regulation, employment security, and state library services. Two of the original departments set up in 1935, finance and civil service, were combined in 1951 into the department of administration. The object of this merger was to bring together in one agency all the services needed to operate the other agencies of government, while at the same time keeping the total structure under the close control of the governor.

The legislative branch consists of a two-house general assembly made up of a 50-member senate, presided over by the lieutenant governor, and a 100-member house of representatives. The judicial branch is headed by a supreme court consisting of a chief justice and four associate justices, all elected by the legislature; a superior court with appellate jurisdiction and original jurisdiction in certain cases, consisting of a presiding justice and ten associate justices appointed by the governor with the consent of the senate; a family court of five judges; and 12 district courts.

Government at the local level is carried on by the 8 cities—Providence, Pawtucket, Cranston, Warwick, Woonsocket, East Providence, Newport and Central Falls—and 31 towns into which the state is divided. The state is also divided into five counties, but the Rhode Island county is not a governmental unit as such, and it is the cities and towns which provide the usual services that are the normal responsibility of local government.

Finance.—Property taxes represent the primary source of revenue for the cities and towns. The major sources of income to the state government, in addition to federal grants, are a state sales tax and taxes on motor fuel, cigarettes and corporations. The post-World War II period saw rapidly increasing state expenditures and, hence, corresponding demands for more revenue. State expenditures almost trebled in the 1960s and the enactment of a state income tax was frequently discussed.

POPULATION

The population of Rhode Island in 1790 was 68,825; in 1840, 108,830; in 1880, 276,531; in 1910, 542,610; in 1950, 791,896;

ROBERT FINKELSTEIN

BUSINESS DISTRICT OF PROVIDENCE, SHOWING THE INDUSTRIAL TRUST BUILDING AT LEFT

and in 1960, 859,488. According to a special census in 1965 it was 892,709. The population per square mile in 1960 was 812 as compared with 749 in 1950 and with 50.5 for the U.S. in 1960.

The two most important long-term trends in the state's population have been rapid urbanization and the great impact of immigration. The urban area of the state dropped from 91.6% in 1940 to 84.3% in 1950, partly because the census definition was changed to include the suburban fringe but excluded the outlying portions of several towns formerly classed as urban under a special rule. In 1960 the urban population was 742,897, or 86.4% of the total. The state contains a portion of the Providence-Pawtucket standard metropolitan statistical area. The area within Rhode Island had a population of 731,358 or 85.1% of the total population of the state in 1960.

Rhode Island: Places of 5,000 or More Population (1960 census)*

Place	Population				
	1965	1960	1950	1940	1920
Total state	892,709	859,488	791,896	713,346	607,397
Barrington†	16,390	13,826	8,246	6,231	3,897
Bristol†	15,716	14,570	12,320	11,159	11,375
Central Falls	18,677	19,858	23,550	25,248	24,174
Cranston	71,913	66,766	55,060	47,085	29,407
East Providence	44,828	41,955	35,871	32,165	21,793
Middletown†	19,562	12,675	7,382	3,379	2,094
Newport	35,901	47,049	37,564	30,532	30,255
North Providence†	21,206	18,220	13,927	12,156	7,697
Pawtucket	77,538	81,001	81,436	75,797	64,248
Providence	187,061	207,498	248,674	253,504	237,595
Wakefield-Peacedale	—	5,569	5,224	7,282‡	5,181‡
Warwick	77,637	68,504	43,028	28,757	13,481
Westerly†	15,711	14,267	8,415	11,199	9,952
West Warwick†	21,915	21,414	19,096	18,188	15,461
Woonsocket	46,678	47,080	50,211	49,303	43,496

*Populations are reported as constituted at date of each census. †Town (township) population. ‡Population of South Kingston township in which Wakefield-Peacedale is located.
Note: Dash indicates place did not exist during reported census, or data not available

As elsewhere in the United States, the post-World War II years in Rhode Island brought a movement to the suburbs. This meant a flow of population out of densely settled cities such as Providence and Central Falls to residential cities and towns nearer the fringe of the urbanized areas such as Cranston, Warwick and Barrington. For example, the population of Providence fell from 253,504 in 1940 to 248,674 in 1950 and from 207,498 in 1960 to 187,061 in 1965. Warwick's population, on the other hand, increased from 28,757 in 1940 to 43,028 in 1950 and from 68,504 in 1960 to 77,637 in 1965.

The foreign-born white population in 1880 was 73,831, or 26.7% of the total. The number of foreign born in the population reached its peak in 1910 when 178,025, or 32.8% of the total, were listed in this category. Both the number and percentage decreased from then on. In 1960, out of a total population of 859,488 the state had 539,804 inhabitants 21 years of age and older. The total population in 1960 comprised 754,216 native white, 84,667 foreign-born white and 20,605 non-white, practically all Negro. Of the foreign-born white population 12,321 were born in England, Scotland or Wales, 5,216 in Ireland, 18,438 in Italy and 18,072 in Canada (largely French Canada). There are smaller totals for Portugal, Russia, Poland and other countries.

There were 96.4 males per 100 females in 1960; 10.4% of the population was 65 years of age and older; and 57.3% of the population 14 years of age and older was in the labour force. Of the total number of employed males, 1.6% were engaged in agriculture, 8.1% in construction, 38.4% in manufacturing and 20.4% in transportation and trade.

EDUCATION

The public-school system was established in 1800, abolished in 1803 and re-established in 1828. A state board of education (provided for in a 1951 act of the general assembly) exercises policy-making power over educational programs in the state and controls the state department of education. A commissioner of education is responsible for the administration of the department's functions under the jurisdiction of the board. Each city and town has a school committee elected by the people and independent of the town or city council.

School attendance is compulsory between the ages of 7 and 16. The total public-school enrollment, as of Oct. 1967, was 166,776 and that of private and other schools 50,800.

The institutions of higher education supported by the state are the University of Rhode Island at Kingston, Rhode Island college at Providence, and Rhode Island Junior college, all administered by the board of trustees of state colleges. In Sept. 1967 the first chancellor of state colleges took office, to act as executive officer of the board and to coordinate development of the system.

The University of Rhode Island, a land-grant institution, was chartered in 1892 as Rhode Island College of Agriculture and Mechanic Arts. The name was changed to Rhode Island State college in 1909 and the institution became a university in 1951. It includes colleges of arts and sciences, agriculture, business administration, engineering, home economics and pharmacy and a school of nursing. The division of university extension is located

ROBERT FINKELSTEIN

VIEW OF BROWN UNIVERSITY CAMPUS: (LEFT) MANNING HALL, 1834; (RIGHT) UNIVERSITY HALL, 1770, THE ORIGINAL COLLEGE EDIFICE

at Providence. The university maintains a computation laboratory and the Narragansett marine laboratory. There is a graduate school of arts and sciences, a graduate school of library sciences and one of oceanography.

The Rhode Island College of Education was established in 1920 as the successor of the Rhode Island Normal school which opened in 1854; the name was changed to Rhode Island college in 1960. Rhode Island Junior college was opened in 1964. The oldest institution of higher learning in the state is Brown university at Providence, chartered in 1764 as Rhode Island college (*see* also PROVIDENCE).

Other colleges in the state are the Rhode Island School of Design (founded 1877; nonsectarian) and Providence college (1917; Roman Catholic), both at Providence, Salve Regina college (1947; Roman Catholic), for women, at Newport and Barrington college (1900; nonsectarian) at Barrington.

HEALTH AND WELFARE

As in most states, these functions are shared by the state and local governments in Rhode Island. Two state administrative departments are involved: the department of health and the department of social welfare. The functions of the former have been grouped under four general headings: (1) the recording of vital statistics, regulation of professions active in the health area, etc.; (2) personal health services, including chronic disease control, maternal and child care and programs for crippled children; (3) the provision of local health services pursuant to legislation authorizing the department of health to take over all local city and town health departments, effective in July 1966; and (4) environmental health services, such as food and drug control, the state laboratories, general sanitation, air and water pollution control.

The small size of Rhode Island has made possible a high degree of centralization of the institutions relating to welfare services. The department of social welfare's division of curative services operates an institute of mental health and general hospital at Howard which together form the Rhode Island medical centre, the Ladd school for mentally retarded children, the Zambarano memorial hospital and other related health and welfare services. The division of correctional services maintains the male and female correctional institutions, a training school for boys and one for girls. The division of community services administers programs for old-age assistance and aid to the disabled, to dependent children and the blind and general public assistance, which is handled co-operatively with local governments. The combined health and welfare services of the two departments discussed above account for one-quarter to one-third of the state's total annual expenditures.

THE ECONOMY

Agriculture.—Rhode Island ranks low in the list of agricultural states, chiefly because of its small area, density of population and the nature of its soil. As has been generally true throughout the United States, there has been a decline in farm acreage and number of farms in the state. Within 30 years from 1935 acreage declined from 380,000 to 125,000, and number of farms from 4,327 to fewer than 1,500. Nearly two-thirds of farm income represents the value of livestock and related products—dairy products, eggs, chickens and turkeys—while the remainder represents crop value. The most important crops are hay, corn, potatoes, five principal commercial vegetables, apples and peaches.

Industry.—Throughout its history Rhode Island has had to depend on sources of income other than agriculture. Before the growth of manufacturing this meant reliance chiefly on the activities of merchants and shipowners. In the period preceding the American Revolution molasses was virtually the cornerstone of the colony's economy. Rhode Island ships carried cargoes of locally produced cheese, fish, lumber and similar products to ports in the West Indies and returned laden with molasses which was exchanged for English-manufactured goods or distilled into rum, a valuable item of commerce. Some idea of the significance of rum in the prerevolutionary economy of Rhode Island can be gained from the fact that in 1764 there were more than 30 distilleries in the colony. Some of the product of this early manufacturing enterprise was bartered for slaves in Africa. The acute concern felt in Rhode Island over regulation of colonial commerce by the British government and the state's later reluctance to join the newly established government under the constitution are closely related to this early growth of a commercial and mercantile economy.

The beginnings of manufacturing activity other than shipbuilding and the production of rum may be said to date from the formation of a company at Providence in 1786 to spin cotton. A factory containing a spinning jenny of 28 spindles (the first machine of its kind to be used in the United States) was put into operation the following year. This factory also included a carding machine, and the fly shuttle was first introduced at Providence in 1788. In 1790 a factory was established at Pawtucket equipped with Arkwright machines constructed by Samuel Slater, an immigrant from England. These machines were operated by water power and they marked the beginning of the factory system in Rhode Island.

The first power loom used in the United States was set up at Peacedale in 1814. During the rest of the 19th century and into the early 20th century textile manufacturing grew to become the major employer of labour in the state. Another industry which came to occupy an important place in the state's economy was jewelry manufacture, begun in Providence in 1784 and greatly promoted ten years later by Nehemiah Dodge's invention of the process of gold filling. Rhode Island's water power was the only natural resource in the state which contributed to this growth of manufacturing enterprise.

The most important industries are textiles (including cotton and woolen worsted), metals and machinery, jewelry, apparel, rubber and plastic products and optical instruments. Textiles, however, have declined in both absolute and relative importance. For example, just before World War II there were 907,000 cotton spindles in the state; 15 years later this number had fallen to 475,000.

Trends after mid-20th century showed that manufacturing employment had declined steadily while government, construction, trade, finance and services increased. In the face of this trend, the Rhode Island Development council was created by law in 1953 to encourage industrial expansion and a number of financial inducements to new industry were provided.

Mining.—The only minerals of value produced in significant quantities in the state are sand and gravel, stone and graphite. Sand and gravel accounted for almost three fourths of the value of mineral products. With the state's population density, this extractive industry raises difficult regulatory problems.

Fisheries.—Whaling was early an established industry in Rhode Island. As late as 1846 about 50 whaling vessels sailed annually from Rhode Island ports; but by the close of the century the industry had become practically extinct. In the second half of the 20th century Rhode Island ranked third among the New England states in number of persons engaged, investment and yield of its fisheries. Almost half of the total value of fishery products was accounted for by shellfish.

Trade and Finance.—As already indicated, prior to the growth of industry, Rhode Island's economy was heavily dependent on trade and commerce with neighbouring states and overseas. Until the American Revolution, Newport was the primary centre of this activity. The British occupation of the city during the war, however, spelled the end of Newport's supremacy and Providence, at the head of Narragansett bay, rapidly overtook the former and has remained the commercial centre of Rhode Island and of adjoining areas.

During the early 19th century patterns of commerce changed. Instead of being carried on for its own sake, shipping and commercial activity became adjuncts to the burgeoning factory economy of the state. Cargoes landed at Providence were now mainly coal, cotton, lumber, cobblestones and other materials consumed directly or indirectly in manufacturing. Coal is an example: as steam supplanted water power in the mills, coal imports grew rapidly. About 200,000 tons were landed at Providence in 1856, and by 1878 the total approached 1,000,000 tons. In the 20th

THE SECOND SLATER MILL (1793) ON THE BANKS OF THE BLACKSTONE RIVER IN PAWTUCKET

century petroleum products replaced coal as a major item of seaborne commerce.

Trade in the more localized sense grew along with the population and wealth of the state. By the beginning of the 19th century wholesale and retail enterprise had become differentiated in Providence, whereas in an earlier and simpler era no such distinction was made. Retail establishments became more elaborate and numerous. The Arcade in Providence, built in 1828 to house shops fronting on a common covered thoroughfare, typified this development, and is still in use by Providence merchants. In the 20th century, in Rhode Island as elsewhere, the small shop was replaced by the chain store, the department store and the suburban shopping centre, all of which owe their existence in large part to the development of more elaborate modes of organization and to new merchandising and packaging techniques.

The year 1791, which saw the chartering of the Providence bank, was a major landmark in the history of banking in the state. Until that date the state had no such institutions largely because the state government itself, through its issue of paper currency, performed many of the functions of a private banking system. Once the federal constitution, which prohibited the states from issuing paper money, had been ratified, banks became essential. About 12 or more additional banks had been chartered by 1810, and 43 filed reports in 1825. In 1856–57, 98 reported, the largest number in Rhode Island history. Bank services during the 19th century were provided by numerous small local banks and failures were not uncommon. The first savings banks in the state came into existence in 1819.

Around the turn of the 20th century a trend toward consolidation of many of the small banks into fewer large institutions became pronounced. This trend had progressed to the point, by mid-20th century, that the state had less than ten savings banks and only a slightly larger number of commercial banks. The latter in particular developed an ever-expanding system of branches which take the place, as it were, of the numerous independent local institutions.

Transportation.—Because of its small size and the general decline of rail transportation in relative importance, Rhode Island's highway network represents by far the most important part of its transportation system. While rail mileage in the state has declined from 211 in 1920 to about 150, total highway mileage exceeds 4,000. Approximately 20% of the over-all total comprises the state highway system, the remainder being under the jurisdiction of the cities and towns. State expenditures for highway construction and reconstruction, including federal grants, more than doubled between 1955–57 and continued to rise thereafter. Included in the highway-building program is a system of limited-access divided highways linking with similar road systems in neighbouring Connecticut and Massachusetts, plus expressways to route traffic through the congested Providence metropolitan area.

Most of the state's water-borne commerce passes through the port of Providence. By far the largest proportion of the tonnage handled there is accounted for by petroleum products. Foreign commerce amounted to more than one-sixth of the total, the remainder comprising coastwise and internal shipments. Numerous sheltered harbours around Narragansett bay are used chiefly by fishing boats and pleasure craft.

Communications.—The first printing press was set up in Rhode Island in 1727 by James Franklin, brother of Benjamin Franklin. He published the first newspaper in the colony, the *Rhode Island Gazette,* in 1732. Other newspapers were started in the 18th century, including the *Newport Mercury* by James Franklin, Jr., and the first foreign-language paper printed in the state, which appeared in 1780, issued by the French who were in Newport with Count Jean Baptiste Rochambeau. The most famous and influential newspaper has long been the *Providence Journal,* which was started as a semiweekly in 1820 and appeared daily from 1829. The owners of the *Journal* began publishing the *Evening Bulletin* in 1863 in response to the demand for news of the American Civil War, and started the *Sunday Journal* in 1885. Of the newspapers published in the state, the *Journal* and *Bulletin,* have a state-wide readership. There are a half dozen other dailies in various local communities, and about a dozen weeklies.

Among the radio stations in operation, the oldest began broadcasting in June 1922, two others were established in the 1920s and the remaining dozen or so date from after World War II. This total includes both AM and FM outlets, with some stations combining both. The state's first television channel began transmitting programs from Providence in 1949.

See also references under "Rhode Island" in the Index.

BIBLIOGRAPHY.—Paul F. Gleeson, *Rhode Island: the Development of a Democracy* (1957), deals with the history, economy, government and other aspects of the state, and contains numerous bibliographical references. *See* also Peter J. Coleman, *The Transformation of Rhode Island, 1790–1860* (1963), and Erwin L. Levine, *Theodore Francis Green: the Rhode Island Years, 1906–1936* (1963). Duane Lockard, *New England State Politics* (1959), has chapters on Rhode Island. For general physical description *see:* N. S. Shaler, J. B. Woodworth and A. F. Foerste, *Geology of the Narragansett Basin* (1899); and C. T. Jackson, *Report on the Geological and Agricultural Survey of Rhode Island* (1840). For administration *see:* the *Rhode Island Manual,* issued biennially by the secretary of state; C. Carroll, *Outline of Government in Rhode Island,* in Rhode Island Educational Circulars; and the annual reports of the various state officials, boards and commissions. For general bibliographies *see:* J. R. Bartlett, *Bibliography of Rhode Island* (1864); C. S. Brigham, *List of Books Upon Rhode Island History* (1908) in Rhode Island Educational Circulars, "History Series," no. 1; H. M. Chapin, *Bibliography of Rhode Island* (1914) and *Cartography of Rhode Island* (1915). *See* also I. B. Richman, *Rhode Island: Its Making and Meaning, 1636–1683* (1902) and *Rhode Island: a Study in Separatism* (1905); T. W. Bicknell, *The History of Rhode Island and Providence Plantations* (1920); David S. Lovejoy, *Rhode Island Politics and the American Revolution* (1958); James B. Hedges, *The Browns of Providence Plantations: Colonial Years* (1952, reprinted 1968), and *The Browns of Providence Plantations: the Nineteenth Century* (1968); Jay S. Goodman, *The Democrats and Labor in Rhode Island, 1952–1962* (1967); A. M. Mowry, *The Dorr War: or the Constitutional Struggle in Rhode Island* (1901); *Records of the Colony of Rhode Island and Providence Plantations, 1636–1792* (1856–65); H. M. Chapin, *Documentary History of Rhode Island* (1916–19); C. S. Brigham, "Report on the Archives of Rhode Island" in the *Annual Report* of the American Historical Association, vol. i (1903); *Rhode Island Historical Society, Collections* (1827–1941), *Proceedings* (1872–92; 1900–06), *Publications* (1892–1900); *Rhode Island History* (1941–); *Rhode Island Historical Tracts, Series 1* (1877–84), *Series 2* (1889–96); publications of the Rhode Island Soldiers and Sailors His-

torical Society (1878–1915); A. R. Hasse, *Index of Economic Material in Documents of the States of the United States, Rhode Island 1789–1904* (1908).

Current statistics on production, employment, industry, etc., may be obtained from the pertinent state departments; the principal figures are summarized annually in the *Britannica Book of the Year.*

(E. E. Co.)

RHODES, CECIL JOHN (1853–1902), British-born South African statesman, financier, founder of the Rhodes Scholarships at Oxford, and one of the great empire builders of the late 19th

RADIO TIMES HULTON PICTURE LIBRARY
CECIL RHODES

century. The territories of Rhodesia took their name from Rhodes, and it was mainly through his efforts that the area now covered by Botswana, Southern Rhodesia, Zambia, and Malawi came under British dominion.

Rhodes was born at Bishop's Stortford, Hertfordshire, on July 5, 1853, the fifth son of the vicar there, Rev. F. W. Rhodes, and was educated at the parish school. In 1869, threatened with tuberculosis, he went to Natal to join his brother Herbert, who was attempting to grow cotton in the Umkomanzi Valley. Cecil landed at Durban in September 1870. Their first crop failed, but they made a profit on the second. In 1871 Cecil was left in charge while Herbert went to prospect at the newly discovered diamond fields

in Griqualand West. Cecil joined Herbert at the diggings that year, and they abandoned cotton farming in 1872.

On arriving at Kimberley, Cecil managed Herbert's three claims alone, while his brother settled affairs in Natal. He became seriously ill, and when Herbert returned they took a long journey to the Transvaal interior. This helped to restore Cecil's health and made a lasting impression on him, giving him his first experience of the interior and helping to mold the future pattern of his life. After their return, Herbert Rhodes left Kimberley (1873).

Oxford.—Cecil Rhodes stayed on to gain a rapid success in the diamond mines, but in spite of his growing influence he spent much of the next few years as an undergraduate at Oxford. He matriculated in 1873, and went to Oriel College. In 1874, however, a severe illness affected his heart and lungs. Given six months to live, he went back to Kimberley. He recovered and returned to Oxford in 1876. He took his B.A. degree in 1881.

Although not a hard-working student, what Rhodes read he thought over deeply. He became convinced that the Anglo-Saxon race was the highest point of evolution in fulfillment of a divine plan and that his aim must be to help secure its predominance. Hence his preoccupation with British expansion, particularly in Africa, and with making money for the power he felt was necessary if his big ideas were to be carried out.

He wrote his first will in 1877, making the colonial secretary a trustee, and leaving his fortune (yet unmade) to form a society to extend the British Empire throughout the world, to recover the U.S., to inaugurate colonial representation in the imperial Parliament at Westminster, and to found a power great enough to make wars impossible. These ideas, modified in his five later wills (the last made in 1899), remained the driving force of his life.

Kimberley and Diamonds.—Even during his Oxford career, Rhodes had been building his fortune at the diamond mines. He had formed a partnership with C. D. Rudd in 1873, and they had secured a lucrative contract to pump out the flooded Kimberley, Dutoitspan, and De Beers mines in 1874. Assisted by Alfred Beit, a brilliant financier, they began accumulating claims, particularly in De Beers Old Rush, by purchase or amalgamation with other claim holders. In 1880 Rhodes, by then the biggest claim holder in De Beers Old Rush, floated the De Beers Mining Company. By 1887 the company was sole owner of the De Beers mines, and his only significant rival for control of the diamond industry was Barney Barnato (*see* BARNATO, BARNETT), the main owner in the Kimberley Mine. Rhodes, given a £1,000,000 guarantee by Rothschilds, was victorious in the ensuing race to increase production and buy up shares. Finally Barnato acknowledged defeat in 1888 and sold his Kimberley mine for £5,338,650 to Rhodes, who formed the new De Beers Consolidated Mines, Ltd. Rhodes also acquired the Dutoitspan and Bultfontein mines in 1888 and the newly discovered Wesselton mine in 1891, thus securing control of all South African diamond production—90% of the world total. He had also invested in the newly discovered gold mines of the Transvaal after 1886 and had formed the powerful Gold Fields of South Africa Company in 1887. On his insistence the terms of incorporation of both the De Beers and Consolidated Gold Fields companies were framed to allow them to finance northward expansion.

Politics and Northward Expansion.—Meanwhile, Rhodes was advancing his political career. He entered the Cape Parliament in 1881 as member for Barkly West, a rural, predominantly Dutch constituency, which he kept throughout his career. He soon gained influence in Parliament, and from the first he was concerned with the north, already dreaming of British expansion to the great lakes. He urged vainly that the imperial government, not the weak Cape government, should be responsible for Basutoland, where war had broken out in 1880. While on a Basutoland commission he met Gen. Charles G. Gordon, who tried unsuccessfully to persuade Rhodes to leave South Africa and work with him.

His next concern was Bechuanaland, of vital importance to his aims because it commanded the route to the Zambezi River via the trading road from the Cape to the interior, known as the "Missionaries' road." The establishment of two small republics, Stellaland and Goshen, settled from the Transvaal, threatened to block this route, which had been placed outside the Transvaal boundary by the Pretoria Convention (1881). Rhodes succeeded in having a boundary commission to Bechuanaland set up in 1882, and he himself became a member. In Stellaland in 1882 he obtained an offer from a local chief to cede his territory to the Cape Colony, and also a petition from Stellalanders for Cape annexation. But he could not persuade the Cape government to take action, despite rumours that the republics might be incorporated with the Transvaal. However, both the imperial and Cape governments saw the force of Rhodes's arguments when Germany established a protectorate over Namaqualand-Damaraland (1883–84), making possible an east-west link between the Germans and the Transvaal which could block British expansion from the Cape. The London Convention (February 1884) finally excluded Stellaland and Goshen from the Transvaal, and the Cape government promised to help finance a protectorate over Bechuanaland. The imperial government sent a deputy commissioner to the area, the Rev. John Mackenzie, who tactlessly offended the Boers in Stellaland and Goshen and ignored their interests. Rhodes demanded that the Cape government, not the "imperial factor," should annex southern Bechuanaland and was sent to replace Mackenzie in July 1884. He successfully conciliated the Stellalanders, mainly by guaranteeing their land titles. But he was unable to prevent the Transvaal president, Paul Kruger, from declaring a protectorate over Goshen, enlarged by systematic raiding. Rhodes could do nothing and returned to the Cape demanding imperial intervention. Both the Cape and the imperial governments protested, Sir Charles Warren was dispatched with an expeditionary force to restore order, and Kruger withdrew. At the conference at Fourteen Streams in February 1885 Rhodes met Kruger for the first time but failed to establish a friendly contact, because the president distrusted Rhodes's aims. Kruger remained the greatest obstacle to Rhodes's dream of federation of South African states within the British Empire.

Rhodes soon quarreled with Warren and resigned his post of deputy commissioner in March 1885. But the high commissioner, Sir Hercules Robinson, sympathized with his aims, and in September 1885 southern Bechuanaland became a crown colony, and the north, up to the 22nd parallel, was declared a protectorate. It was not until 1895 that British Bechuanaland was annexed to the Cape, as Rhodes had always wished, and part of the protectorate was handed over to Rhodes's British South Africa Company.

In 1887 it seemed that Rhodes's plan for northward expansion might again be jeopardized by the Transvaal, which was negotiating with Lobengula, chief of the Matabele, who controlled Mashonaland and Matabeleland. To secure British influence there, Rhodes persuaded the high commissioner to make a treaty of friendship with Lobengula, who agreed to make treaties with other powers only with British consent (February 1888). But since neither the Cape nor the imperial government was prepared to take over the territory, Rhodes determined to do so himself. His agents obtained the Rudd concession from Lobengula, which gave Rhodes a prospecting monopoly in Mashonaland, rumoured to be rich in gold. This was the basis of the British South Africa Company's charter, granted in 1889, after Rhodes had amalgamated with rival concessionaires and had gained widespread support in England.

The company secured control of the area of present-day Southern Rhodesia by 1893, but Rhodes's dream extended beyond the Zambezi. In 1891 he made an agreement with the imperial government whereby a British protectorate was established over Nyasaland (the company contributing £10,000 annually for its upkeep, and Rhodes privately giving a further £10,000), while the rest of central Africa north of the Zambezi to Lake Tanganyika was administered by the company. A foreign office official and friend of Rhodes, Sir Harry Johnston, was both imperial commissioner and the company's administrator in Nyasaland until 1895, when the company assumed direct administration of the area of Northern Rhodesia. Despite Rhodes's efforts to secure Nyasaland also for the company—his strong pressure on Johnston amounted almost to blackmail—the British treasury took full responsibility for Nyasaland after 1894.

Prime Minister.—Rhodes became prime minister of the Cape in 1890. His main support came from J. H. Hofmeyr (*q.v.*) and the Afrikander Bond, which had been won over to Rhodes's schemes of northward expansion under the British flag partly by the Transvaal's refusal to allow a rail link with Johannesburg until 1892, and its high duties on Cape products, partly by Rhodes's express policy of conciliating Afrikaner opinion. Rhodes's frank aim was to unite English and Dutch interests. His premiership was important in the development of local politics and education, the advancement of agriculture, and the steps taken in native policy. The Franchise and Ballot Act of 1892 restricted the vote to men who could write and earn a labourer's wage, removing the abuses of the tribal African "blanket" vote. In native policy Rhodes wanted to introduce measures of local self-government and education and to replace tribal land tenure by individual tenure. His policy was applied in the controversial Glen-Grey Act of 1894. He took a personal interest in agriculture, encouraging scientific methods of farming, and developing the railways to link the rural districts to most of the large towns. Rhodes also increased the Cape Colony's territory by his annexation of Pondoland in 1894.

Until 1895 Rhodes waited patiently for economic pressure and encirclement to force the Transvaal into a South African federation, led from the Cape, but President Kruger was intransigent. In January 1895 he trebled the rates on the Transvaal section of the Cape-Johannesburg Railway, and when Cape traders attempted to transport goods by ox wagon instead, he closed the Vaal drifts (fords). This clear infringement of the London Convention stimulated protests from Rhodes and the high commissioner, and Kruger climbed down (October 1895). Kruger had also infuriated Rhodes by a speech of January 1895, when he had made very friendly references to Germany. Rhodes was at the height of his power. He was unopposed in the Cape and controlled the De Beers and Consolidated Gold Fields companies, with their huge resources, and the British South Africa Company. Frustrated by Kruger, he decided to take a short cut to federation via revolution.

Early in 1895 he became the directing spirit in a conspiracy to overthrow the Transvaal government by an *Uitlander* rising in Johannesburg supported by a force of the British South Africa Company (*q.v.*) led by his friend L. S. Jameson (*q.v.*). Rhodes arranged that his friend Sir Hercules Robinson should again be sent to South Africa as high commissioner early in 1895. He secured a strip of the Bechuanaland protectorate, ostensibly as a railway, but actually as a base for Jameson's incursion into the Transvaal. On Dec. 29, 1895, Jameson made his famous raid, despite frantic messages urging postponement and assurances that the Johannesburg rising would not take place.

The fiasco of the raid was disastrous for Rhodes. Openly implicated in the scheme, he resigned the premiership in January 1896. He lost the support of the Bond, which was horrified that Rhodes had conspired against a friendly neighbour while prime minister. He was censured by the committees of inquiry into the raid held by the Cape Parliament (1896) and the British House of Commons (1897).

The Matabele rising of March 1896 kept Rhodes from brooding on his downfall. He had temporarily lost his seat on the board of the British South Africa Company, but he went to Rhodesia as a private individual and negotiated the peace terms with the Matabele (August–October 1896). He supervised the extension of railways in Rhodesia and arranged for a rail link from Salisbury to Lake Tanganyika to further his scheme for a Cape to Cairo railway. He also concluded arrangements for a Trans-African telegraph to pass through German East Africa to Egypt. He died at Muizenberg, Cape Colony, on March 26, 1902, and was buried in the Matopo Hills, near Bulawayo, Southern Rhodesia.

Rhodes was not a great orator, but he was able to express his large ideas in popular phrases, and many of his expressions—"British dominion from the Cape to Cairo," "painting the map red," "the imperial factor," "philanthropy plus 5%"—gained common usage. He combined an almost visionary zeal for British expansion with a frank belief that money was power and that one could always deal rather than quarrel with an opponent. He gained the fervent loyalty and friendship of some of his most outstanding contemporaries, but toward the end of his career he became autocratic, imperious, and surrounded by sycophants.

Rhodes Scholarships.—In his will Rhodes provided for the maintenance at Oxford University of men from specified areas overseas. The value of each scholarship eventually rose to £900 a year, for two years in the first instance, and for a third year should the trustees so decide in individual cases.

In his will Rhodes mentioned the objects he had in view in founding the scholarships:

1. Colonial. I consider that the education of young colonists at one of the universities in the United Kingdom is of great advantage to them for giving breadth to their views, for their instruction in life and manners, and for instilling into their minds the advantage to the colonies as well as to the United Kingdom of the retention of the unity of the empire.
2. United States. I also desire to encourage and foster an appreciation of the advantages which I implicitly believe will result from the union of the English-speaking people throughout the world. . . .

He defines as follows the principles on which he wished his scholars to be selected:

My desire being that the students who shall be elected to the scholarships shall not be merely bookworms, I direct that in the election of a student to a scholarship regard shall be had to (1) his literary and scholastic attainments; (2) his fondness for and success in manly outdoor sports. . . ; (3) his qualities of manhood, truth, courage, devotion to duty, sympathy for and protection of the weak, kindliness, unselfishness and fellowship; and (4) his exhibition during school days of moral force of character and of instincts to lead and to take an interest in his schoolmates, for those latter attributes will be likely in after life to guide him to esteem the performance of public duties as his highest aim.

Subject to ratification by the eight trustees, the nomination of scholars is in the hands of local committees, which are appointed by the trustees, and on which former Rhodes scholars sit, but never preside. Candidates must be citizens of the country which they are to represent, with at least five years' domicile, and unmarried; and they must have passed their 19th and not have passed their 25th birthday by Oct. 1 of the year for which they are elected. Candidates are judged on their records and after a personal interview with the election committee. Save in certain exceptional cases, candidates are obliged to have attended a recognized degree-granting college or university for two years at least. At Oxford

the scholars are distributed, as Rhodes desired, among all the colleges of the university, as far as possible in accordance with their own wishes; but acceptance of any scholar is determined by the colleges themselves. (See also STUDENT AID.)

See SOUTH AFRICA, REPUBLIC OF: History; see also references under "Rhodes, Cecil John" in the Index.

BIBLIOGRAPHY.—"Vindex," *Cecil Rhodes, His Political Life and Speeches* (1900); Sir Lewis Michell, *The Life and Times of Cecil John Rhodes, 1853–1902*, 2 vol. (1910); P. Jourdan, *Cecil Rhodes: His Private Life* (1911); Sir J. G. McDonald, *Rhodes: a Life* (1928); W. Plomer, *Cecil Rhodes* (1933); J. E. S. Green, *Rhodes Goes North* (1936); Basil Williams, *Cecil Rhodes*, new ed. (1938); F. Aydelotte, *The Vision of Cecil Rhodes* (1946); S. G. Millin, *Rhodes*, rev. ed. (1952); E. E. Burke, *The Story of Cecil Rhodes* (1953); F. Gross, *Rhodes of Africa* (1956). See also J. van der Poel, *The Jameson Raid* (1952).
(M. F. K.)

RHODES (Gr. RODOS), the name of the most easterly island of the Aegean Sea, separated by about 10 mi. at its northernmost tip from the Turkish coast, and the name of the island's capital. The area of the island is 540 sq.mi. (1,398 sq.km.). Pop. (1961) 63,951; population of the capital 27,393. Rhodes city is the capital since 1955 of the Greek *nomos* (department) of the Dodecanese.

The island is traversed from north to south by a mountain range reaching 3,986 ft. (1,215 m.) at the highest peak, Attavyros. It commands a view of the elevated coast of Asia Minor toward the north, and of the archipelago, studded with its numerous islands, in the northwest; in the southwest Mt. Ida in Crete is sometimes visible on clear days. The rest of the island is occupied in great part by ranges of moderately high hills, on which are extensive woods of ancient pines, greatly thinned during the Turkish era.

In addition to a fine climate Rhodes has a fertile soil and produces a variety of the finest fruits and vegetables. Around the villages are extensive cultivated fields and orchards containing fig, pomegranate, and orange trees. On the sloping hills, carob trees and others grow abundantly; the vine also holds its place and produces a wine which was highly valued by the ancients, though it seems to have degenerated greatly in modern times; a strong red wine is still exported. The valleys afford rich pastures, and the plains produce a wide variety of grain.

Under Turkish rule Rhodes was a distributing centre for European manufactures to the neighbouring islands and mainland, receiving cattle, foodstuffs, and other produce in return. Under Italian rule its commercial position became uncertain and was further disturbed by World War II. But a serious attempt was later made to restore its prosperity, especially by encouraging the tourist trade.

History of the Island.—Minoan remains at Ialysos are evidence of early Cretan influence but with the collapse of Crete (c. 1400 B.C.) the island became a powerful, independent kingdom with its own distinctive Late Bronze Age culture. According to Homer the cities of Lindos (Lindus), Ialysos, and Camiros were occupied by Heraclidae (q.v.), and in historic times Rhodes was occupied by a Dorian population, coming mainly from Argos, after the Dorian invasion of Greece. Lindos, Ialysos, and Camiros belonged to the League of Six Cities (Hexapolis), by which Dorian colonists in Asia Minor protected themselves against the non-Greeks of the neighbouring mainland.

The early history of these towns records brisk commercial expansion and active colonization, illustrated by the rich tombs of Camiros. Rhodian colonies extended not only eastward along the southern coast of Asia Minor, but also to the westernmost parts of the Greek world. Examples are Phaselis in Lycia, Soli in Cilicia, Salapia on the east Italian coast, Gela in Sicily, the Lipari Islands, and Rhode in northeast Spain. In home waters the Rhodians dominated Karpathos and other islands.

The history of Rhodes during the Persian Wars is obscure, but later in the 5th century B.C. the three cities were enrolled in the Delian League and were democracies. In 412/411 the island revolted from Athens and became the headquarters of the Peloponnesian fleet. In 408/407 the inhabitants settled in the newly founded city of Rhodes, laid out on an exceptionally fine site according to a scientific plan, allegedly by the architect Hippodamus of Miletus. This town soon rose to considerable importance and attracted much commerce in the Aegean and Asia Minor that had hitherto been in Athenian hands.

In the 4th century B.C. political development was arrested by constant struggles between oligarchs and democrats, who in turn brought the city under the control of Sparta (412–395, 391–378), of Athens (395–391, 378–357), and of the Carian dynasty of Mausolus (357–340). About 340 it was conquered for the Persian king by his Rhodian admiral, Mentor. In 332 it submitted to Alexander the Great, but on his death the people expelled the Macedonian garrison and henceforth not only maintained their independence but acquired great political influence.

The expansion of trade in the Hellenistic age brought especial profit to Rhodes, whose standard of coinage and code of maritime law became widely accepted in the Mediterranean. Under modified democracy, in which the six *prytaneis* formed a powerful executive, the city long enjoyed a good administration. In foreign politics it prudently avoided the ambitious schemes of Hellenistic monarchs, but gained prestige by energetic interference against all who threatened the balance of power or the security of the seas. In 305–304 it was besieged by Demetrius, who tried to bring it into alliance with his father Antigonus Monophthalmus, and earned his nickname "Poliorcetes" ("besieger") for the ingenuity of his unsuccessful siege devices. The Rhodians commemorated their successful resistance by erecting during the 290s and 280s the famous Colossus, a bronze statue of Helios (the Sun) over 100 ft. high, which probably stood near the harbour (not astride the harbour entrance). About 225 it fell down in a severe earthquake, the damages of which all Hellenistic states contributed to repair because they could not afford to see the island ruined. In the interest of trade the Rhodians undertook campaigns in the years after 220 against Byzantium, the king of Pontus, the Cretan pirates, and Philip V of Macedonia. They supported the Romans when they made war on Philip and Antiochus III of Syria on behalf of the minor Greek states and were rewarded with grants of territory in Lycia (189 B.C.). For a time the Rhodians dominated the southern Aegean but during the Third Macedonian War a false step gave Rome the excuse to deprive them of possessions in Lycia and divert their trade to Delos (167–166). However, during the two Mithradatic Wars they remained loyal to Rome and in 88 Rhodes successfully stood a siege. The Rhodian Navy did further good service for Pompey in his campaigns against the pirates and against Julius Caesar. During the triumvirate of Antony, Octavian, and Lepidus (43), the conspirator Gaius Cassius besieged and ruthlessly plundered the people for refusing to support him and, though Rhodes continued a free town for another century, its commercial prosperity was crippled, and an extensive earthquake c. A.D. 155 ruined it. It did, however, become the capital of the later Roman province of the islands.

In the days of its greatest power Rhodes became famous as a centre of painting and sculpture; it had a school of eclectic oratory whose chief representative was Apollonius Molon, the teacher of Cicero; it was the birthplace of the Stoic philosopher Panaetius, and the home of the poet Apollonius Rhodius and the historian Poseidonius.

The sites of Lindos, Ialysos, and Camiros, which in the most ancient times were the principal towns of the island, are clearly marked, and the first of the three is still occupied by a small town with a medieval castle, both of them dating from the time of the Knights, though the castle occupies the site of the ancient acropolis, extensively excavated by the Danes and now crudely

restored. The remains of the Temple of Athena Lindia are noteworthy (rebuilt 4th century B.C.). There are few ruins of any importance on the site of either Ialysos or Camiros, but excavations at both places produced valuable and interesting results.

The history of Rhodes under the Byzantine rule is uneventful except for some temporary occupations by the Arabs (A.D. 653–658, during which the fallen Colossus was broken up and sold for scrap, and 717–718) and the gradual encroachment of Venetian traders after 1082. In the 13th century the island stood as a rule under the control of Italian adventurers, who were, however, at times compelled to acknowledge the overlordship of the emperors of Nicaea, and who failed to protect it against the depredations of Turkish corsairs.

In 1309 it was conquered by the Knights Hospitallers of St. John of Jerusalem at the instigation of the pope and the Genoese and converted into a great fortress for the protection of the southern seas against the Turks (*see* SAINT JOHN OF JERUSALEM, ORDER OF THE HOSPITAL OF). Under their mild and just rule both the native Greeks and the Italian residents were able to carry on a brisk trade. But the piratical acts of these traders, in which the Knights themselves sometimes joined, and the strategic position of the island between Constantinople and the Levant necessitated its reduction by the Ottoman sultans. A siege in 1480 by Mohammed II was repulsed with severe losses; after a second investment, during which Sultan Suleiman I is said to have lost 90,000 men out of a force of 200,000, the Knights evacuated Rhodes under an honourable capitulation (1522). The population henceforth dwindled in consequence of pestilence and emigration, and although the island recovered somewhat in the 18th century under a comparatively lenient rule, it was brought to a very low ebb as a result of the severity of its governor during the Greek revolt from the Turks.

The island was taken by the Italians from the Turks in 1912 (*see* ITALO-TURKISH WAR) and the city became capital of the administration of the Dodecanese (*q.v.*). Under the Allies' peace treaty with Italy in 1947, the island, together with the other Dodecanese islands, was awarded to Greece. The capital was under military government until 1955.

Rhodes City.—The capital, the only large town in the island, stands at its northern tip. Beside the small northern Mandrakhi port, used by small craft, lies the modern town extending westward, with the government building, the new market, national theatre, and Church of the Evangelismos (Annunciation) built in 1925 on the plan of the former Church of St. John. Beside the southern, or commercial, port rises the old walled city, its ramparts, towers, and gates being much as they were in the 15th century. The walls and defenses were built by the Knights. The

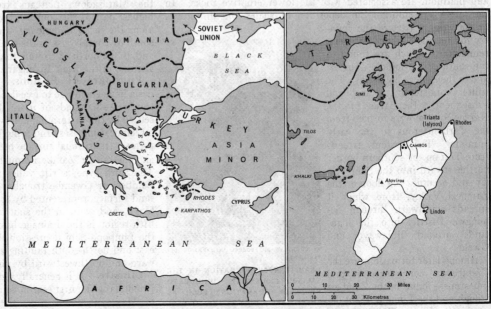

THE ISLAND OF RHODES, SHOWING ITS LOCATION IN THE AEGEAN SEA

northern area of the old city contains the Collachium, within which are the former hospital of the Knights, now a museum, and the Palace of the Grand Masters, thoroughly restored in the 20th century during the Italian period. Linking these is the Street of the Knights, in which are restored Auberges des Langues; *i.e.*, the lodges of the groups into which the Knights were divided. The 13th-century Church of the Panaghia (Virgin), and several mosques from the Turkish period, are also in the old city. About 1¼ mi. (2 km.) W of the walls is the old acropolis with excavated remains of temples of Zeus, Athena, and Apollo, and a theatre and stadium.

Rhodes is the seat of an Orthodox metropolitan and was the meeting place of Pan-Orthodox Conferences from 1961.

See also references under "Rhodes" in the Index.

BIBLIOGRAPHY.—*Inscriptions:* F. Hiller von Gaertringen, *Inscriptiones Graecae*, vol. xii, 1 (1895); A. Maiuri, *Nuova silloge epigrafica di Rodi e Cos* (1925). *Archaeology:* C. Blinkenberg *et al.*, *Lindos*, i–iii (1931–60); K. F. Kinch, *Fouilles de Vroulia* (1914); *Clara Rhodos*, i–x (1928–41); P. M. Fraser and G. E. Bean, *Rhodian Peraea and Islands* (1954). For details of modern literature before 1937, G. Fumagalli, *Bibliografia Rodia* (1937), and especially H. van Gelder, *Geschichte der alten Rhodier* (1900); *see* also A. Philippson, *Die Griechische Landschaften*, vol. iv, pp. 329–352 (1959).

RHODESIA (SOUTHERN RHODESIA), an internally self-governing British colony in southern Africa which in November 1965 made a unilateral and unconstitutional declaration of independence. Rhodesia is bounded north by Zambia, northeast and east by Portuguese East Africa (Mozambique), south by the Republic of South Africa, and southwest and west by Botswana (Bechuanaland). The total area is 150,333 sq.mi. (389,363 sq.km.). The capital is Salisbury (*q.v.*).

PHYSICAL GEOGRAPHY

Geology and Structure.—Rhodesia is landlocked and has some of the world's most ancient rock formations, known collectively as the Basement Complex, and consisting of gneisses, schists, quartzites, banded ironstones, phyllites, and crystalline limestones, together with numerous other metamorphosed sedimentary and igneous rocks, which are associated with granites and gneisses of a somewhat later period. These Basement rocks occupy large areas of Rhodesia, the schist belts containing veins and lodes of minerals including gold, silver, and many others. Overlying the Basement Complex is a system of Precambrian conglomerates, sandstones, and dolomite of which the Lomagundi System is an example. In the later Precambrian basic intrusions resulted in the formation of the great dike, the norite of the dike now forming an almost straight outcrop trending a little west of south for about 320 mi. (515 km.). Chrome ore, nickel, and platinum are associated with the lower eruptive rocks. In the latest Precambrian the deposition of shales and limestones in the western part of the country formed the Umkondo System, remnants of which are found to the south of the middle Zambezi and in the eastern highlands. The tillite, sandstones, shales, and subsequently the lavas of the Karroo System were formed from the Carboniferous to the early Jurassic. The system extends from Tuli on the southern border northeastward into the Sabi Valley and occupies the floor of the Zambezi Valley, from which it spreads southward through Sebungwe District into the highlands around Bulawayo and Gwelo.

Among later formations are the Cretaceous conglomerates and limestones, found in the Zambezi trough and the Limpopo-Sabi depression, and the Kalahari Sys-

BY COURTESY OF FEDERAL INFORMATION DEPARTMENT

GRANITE ROCK FORMATION IN THE SALISBURY DISTRICT. UNIQUE TO RHODESIA, FORMATIONS SUCH AS THESE ARE AMONG THE OLDEST KNOWN

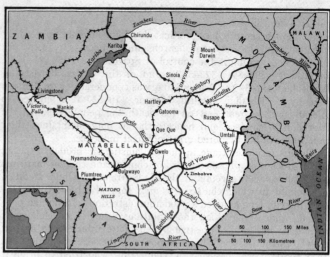

MAJOR TOWNS AND TRANSPORTATION ROUTES OF RHODESIA

tem, composed of limestone, sandstone, and loose sand, which is believed to date from the early Tertiary. Redistributed Kalahari sand and alluvium are deposits which have accumulated since Quaternary and Recent times.

Relief and Drainage.—The surface features of Rhodesia have been considerably affected by large-scale faulting. During the early Cretaceous a southwest-northeast trending fault formed the middle Zambezi trough and, in the extreme south, the Limpopo-Sabi depression was also affected by major west-east and north-south faulting. These rifting movements have broken up the plateau surface represented by the highlands. These consist of a fairly even surface, more than 4,000 ft. (1,200 m.) in altitude, in which the Plumtree-Marandellas watershed divides the middle Zambezi from the middle Limpopo drainage. A lower area of midland surface (2,000–4,000 ft.) is transitional between the highland and the lowland (below 2,000 ft.). The main mountain features in these altitudinal zones are formed by hard outcrops of the granite-gneiss, such as the Matopo Hills and the innumerable rounded *kopjes* ("hillocks") composed of ball granite or by the schist belts with their prominent ridges of quartzite and banded ironstone.

The great dike (see *Geology and Structure* above) forms a series of long, low ridges increasing in height to the north to about 1,500 ft. (450 m.) above the plateau surface in the Umvukwe Range. To the southeast of the middle Zambezi Valley the most prominent features are faulted blocks such as the Siwalila and the Matusadona plateaus trending southwest-northeast. The highest part of the country, however, is the eastern highland area, along the eastern boundary, where the Melsetter Highlands, to the south of Umtali, rise in the peak Himalaya to 7,253 ft. (2,211 m.), and, to the north of Umtali, the Inyanga Plateau attains its greatest altitude in the peak Inyangana (8,503 ft. [2,592 m.]).

Physiographic Regions.—The structure and surface of Rhodesia have given rise to five defined physiographic regions, of which the first—highlands of more than 4,000 ft. in altitude—is represented by the eastern highlands. The second region, the Sebungwe midland, comprises land lying between 2,000 and 4,000 ft., which forms a transitional surface between the highland to the southeast and the middle Zambezi trough, and also the upper Mazoe basin. The third type is rift valley which in Rhodesia is the middle Zambezi or Gwembe trough. The fourth region is the Kalahari sand surface, represented by the extremely flat Wankie-Nyamandhlovu sand plain in the southwestern part of the country. The fifth region is the drainage basin comprising the northern part of the Limpopo-Sabi depression which originated in extensive west-east and north-south faulting and has since been extended northward and northwestward by vigorous headstream erosion.

Climate.—It is generally agreed that there are three seasons in Rhodesia. The first season comprises the cool, dry winter months of May, June, and July; the second, the hot, dry months of August, September, and October; and the third, the warm months of summer rain during November–April. On the whole the considerable altitude partly compensates for the low latitude, temperatures being closely related to altitude. Thus Beitbridge (1,505 ft. [459 m.]), on the Limpopo River, has a coolest month (June) mean temperature of 60° F (15° C) and a warmest month (November) mean temperature of 80° F (27° C). To the north of the Limpopo Valley the coolest month is generally July and the warmest October. For the following stations, therefore, the July and October means are given. On the whole plateau stations have lower temperatures than valley stations: thus Bulawayo (56° and 72° F) at 4,405 ft. and Salisbury (56° and 70° F) at 4,831 ft. are considerably cooler than Beitbridge; and Inyanga (52° and 60° F) in the eastern highlands, at 5,514 ft., has still lower temperatures. Farther north, in the Zambezi trough, Chirundu, at 1,312 ft. (400 m.), has a July mean of 68° F and an October mean of 87° F, with a mean maximum for October of 100° F.

Annual rainfall is greatest on parts of the eastern highlands, where it exceeds 70 in. (1,800 mm.). Westward there is a marked decrease in the middle Zambezi trough to between 25 and 30 in. (635 and 760 mm.). The areas receiving least rainfall are in the far south where, in the Limpopo Valley, annual falls of less than 25 in. are usual.

Vegetation.—The country's climate, with its wet summers and dry winters, has produced a vegetation in which savanna, either as dense or widely dispersed tree growth, is predominant, with some grassland and swamp, and Kalahari sand in the extreme west. Between 3,500 and 5,000 ft. various species of *Brachystegia* and *Isoberlinia* are the dominant savanna. Other types include the mangwe (*Terminalia sericea*); the thorn savanna; the umgusu (*Baikiaea plurijuga*); and, in the dry, hot valleys of the Limpopo and the Zambezi rivers, the mopane woodland, with which the baobab, the knobthorn (*Acacia nigrescens*), and a species of doum palm are found in association. True forest grows in the areas of heavy rainfall on the eastern highlands. There are also found the yellowwood and cedar; and at lower levels red and brown Rhodesian mahoganies (*Khaya nyasica* and *Lovoa swynnertonia*) are common. Pure grassland occurs in the eastern highlands bordering the forests. (*See* also *Forestry* below.)

Animal Life.—Primates of Rhodesia include the vervet, the Samango monkey, the smaller and larger galagos (bush babies), and the chacma, Rhodesian, and yellow baboons. Among the carnivora are the lion, leopard, cheetah, spotted and brown hyena, aardvark, serval, civet, genet, mongoose, zorilla (striped polecat), ratel (honey badger), black-backed and side-striped jackals, hunting dog, bat-eared fox, ant bear, and scaly anteater. The elephant is found in the northwestern, northern, and northeastern parts of the country. The hippopotamus is to be seen in the larger rivers and the giraffe in the extreme west and in the southwest. Members of the Bovidae family include the eland, greater kudu, blue duiker, common and singsong waterbuck, reedbuck, impala, klipspringer, oribi, steinbok, Sharpe's grysbok, sable and roan antelopes, hartebeest, and tsessebe. Reptiles and birds abound and there is a wide variety of insects.

National Parks and Reserves.—The Wankie National Park, in northwestern Rhodesia, extends from the Bulawayo-Victoria Falls railway line to the boundary of Botswana, covering an area of more than 5,000 sq.mi. (13,000 sq.km.). It includes the Robins Game Reserve and the adjacent Khazuma Pan Reserve. Most of the animal life of Rhodesia, Zambia, and Malawi is found in this park. Other areas where game can be seen are the Robert McIlwaine National Park, near Salisbury; the Matopos National Park and the Khami ruins, both near Bulawayo; and the Zimbabwe National Park. (J. H. Wn.; X.)

HISTORY

The remains of Stone Age cultures dating back 500,000 years have been found in Rhodesia, and it is thought that the Bushmen, who still survive mostly in the Kalahari Desert of Botswana, are the last descendants of these original inhabitants of southern and central Africa. They were driven into the desert by the Bantu tribes during the long migrations from the north in the course of which the Bantu populated much of Africa from Lake Chad to

Zululand. The first Bantu are thought to have reached Rhodesia between the 5th and 10th centuries A.D. The stone ruins of Zimbabwe (*q.v.*) date mainly from about the 9th century, although the most elaborate belong to a period after the 15th century, and are of Bantu origin.

Portuguese Exploration.—The Portuguese, who arrived on the east coast of Africa at the end of the 15th century, dreamed of opening up the interior and establishing an intercoastal route to connect their eastern settlements with Angola in the west. The first European to enter Rhodesia was probably António Fernandes, who tried to cross the continent and reached the neighbourhood of Que Que. Nearly 50 years afterward the "emperor" Monomotapa (*q.v.*) was baptized by a Jesuit father, and in 1569 an abortive military expedition entered the interior in search of gold. (*See* further PORTUGUESE EAST AFRICA: *History.*)

Bantu Migration: the Arrival of Missionaries.—A second great movement of the Bantu peoples began in 1830, this time from the south. To escape from the power of the great Zulu chief Chaka (Shaka) three important tribes fled northward, one of them the Ndebele (*q.v.*; Matabele), who carved out a kingdom for themselves in Rhodesia. The Ndebele were warriors and pastoralists, in the Zulu tradition, and under their formidable chief Moselekatse (Mzilikazi) they mastered and dispossessed the weaker tribes, known collectively as Shona (Mashona), who were sedentary, peaceful tillers of the land. For more than half a century, until the coming of European rule, the Ndebele continued to enslave and plunder the Shona. During this period, however, British and Afrikaner hunters, traders, and prospectors had begun to move up from the south, and with them came the missionaries. Robert Moffat, father-in-law of David Livingstone, visited Moselekatse in 1857, and this meeting led to the establishment in 1861 of the first mission to the Ndebele by the London Missionary Society.

The British South Africa Company.—In South Africa, Cecil Rhodes (*q.v.*) formed the British South Africa Company (*q.v.*), which received its charter in October 1889. Its objects were: (1) to extend the railway from Kimberley northward to the Zambezi; (2) to encourage emigration and colonization; (3) to promote trade and commerce; and (4) to secure all mineral rights, in re-

CONICAL TOWER OF THE ELLIPTICAL TEMPLE OF THE ZIMBABWE STONE RUINS, SOUTHEAST OF FORT VICTORIA. THE RUINS AS A WHOLE ARE RADIOCARBON-DATED FROM THE 9TH CENTURY A.D.; THE TEMPLE IS OF MUCH LATER DATE

turn for guarantees of protection and security of rights to the tribal chiefs.

In 1890 a pioneer column set out from Bechuanaland and reached the site of the future capital of Rhodesia without incident on Sept. 12. There, the new arrivals settled and began to lay claim to prospecting rights. The Ndebele resented this European invasion, and in 1893 they took up arms, being defeated only after months of strenuous fighting. Lobengula fled and the company assumed administrative control of Matabeleland. In 1895 many of the pioneers were persuaded to take part in the Jameson raid into the Transvaal and were captured and sent to England for trial (*see* TRANSVAAL: *History: Jameson Raid*). In the same year the territories administered by the company, which had previously been loosely known as Zambesia, were formally named Rhodesia, by proclamation. In 1896 the Ndebele rose again. Returning from London, Rhodes went out, unarmed, to meet the Ndebele chiefs and persuaded them to make peace. The Shona had at first accepted the Europeans, but they too became rebellious and the whole country was not pacified until 1897.

Economic and Political Development.—By 1892 about 1,500 settlers from the south had arrived in Rhodesia. The railway reached Bulawayo in 1896 and the Victoria Falls in 1904. By the following year there were 12,500 settlers in the country and in 1909 gold exports were worth more than £2,500,000. Agricultural development, however, was slower, and it was not until 1907 that steps were taken to facilitate the acquisition of land. By 1911 tobacco to the annual value of nearly £35,000 was being exported and the European population had risen to 23,600.

From the earliest years the settlers had demanded representation on the Legislative Council, which in 1903 comprised seven company officials and seven elected representatives of the settlers. In 1907 the settlers were given a majority of seats. In 1914, when the 25-year term of the company's charter was due to expire, the settlers, faced with the alternative of joining the Union of South Africa, asked for the continuation of the charter pending the grant of self-government. The British government therefore extended the charter for a further ten years, with the proviso, however, that self-government could be granted earlier if the settlers showed themselves capable of administering the country unaided.

Self-Government.—Immediately after World War I the pressure for self-government was resumed and a royal commission under Lord Buxton was appointed to consider the future of the territory. As a result of the commission's report a referendum of the electors among the 34,000 Europeans in the country was held in 1922, on the choice between entry into the Union of South Africa as its fifth province and full internal self-government. In spite of the offer of generous terms by the Union prime minister, Gen. J. C. Smuts, 8,774 people voted for self-government as against 5,989 for joining the Union. On Sept. 12, 1923, the 33rd anniversary of the arrival of the pioneers at Fort Salisbury, Southern Rhodesia was annexed to the crown and became a self-governing colony. The British government retained control of external affairs and a final veto in respect of legislation directly affecting Africans.

The interwar period was one of material progress, with the development of a reasonably prosperous economy based on copper, gold, and other minerals, maize (corn), tobacco, and cattle. By 1953 Southern Rhodesia had a European population of 157,000 and an annual revenue of more than £28,000,000.

The declared policy of Sir Godfrey Huggins (later Lord Malvern), who served as prime minister of Southern Rhodesia for 20 years, was to build a society in accord with Cecil Rhodes's dictum of "equal rights for all civilized men," one in which merit and not colour should be the test of political and economic advancement. He believed that political power should not be given to the Africans until they were sufficiently experienced to know how to exercise it in friendly cooperation with the Europeans and thus to maintain the economic development built up over the years.

A second principle in which Lord Malvern and most other Europeans in Southern Rhodesia and Northern Rhodesia (later Zambia) profoundly believed was that the two countries should be joined together, both for their mutual economic benefit and to ensure the establishment of a powerful state based on British culture and traditions. Malvern failed to secure their amalgamation, but he supported the federation of Southern Rhodesia, Northern Rhodesia, and Nyasaland (later Malawi) when that solution was eventually accepted by the British government in 1953. (*See* RHODESIA AND NYASALAND, FEDERATION OF.)

Federation Period.—Constitutional development continued in Southern Rhodesia after federation. In 1957 a new electoral law was passed providing for a common roll of voters with a special roll for those with lower qualifications. At the same time there was growing political consciousness among the African population, together with increasing hostility to the idea of federation. In 1960 disturbances broke out after the arrest of some African nationalist leaders belonging to the National Democratic Party (NDP). In the following year proposals for a new constitution were strongly criticized by the NDP, which considered them insufficient to meet African demands. The NDP was subsequently banned for acts of intimidation. After that, the African nationalist movement split into two rival organizations, the Zimbabwe African People's Union (ZAPU), led by Joshua Nkomo, and the Zimbabwe African National Union (ZANU), led by Ndabaningi Sithole, both of which were later banned and their leaders placed under restriction. The situation in Southern Rhodesia began to attract the attention of the United Nations Special Committee on Colonialism, and in June 1962 the UN General Assembly passed a resolution calling for a more liberal constitution for the territory.

The election of December 1962, when the new constitution (see *Administration and Social Conditions*, below) came into force, was boycotted by the African nationalists. It resulted in the defeat of the ruling United Federal Party by the more conservative Rhodesian Front. Winston Field became prime minister. At the end of 1963 the federation was dissolved, and Southern Rhodesia reverted to its former status as a colony.

BY COURTESY OF RHODESIA HOUSE, LONDON

SALISBURY, CAPITAL OF RHODESIA

Unilateral Declaration of Independence.—The U.K. government was now faced with, on the one hand, demands by the new Rhodesian government for complete independence and, on the other, by pressure from the UN and much of the rest of the Commonwealth for a change in the constitution to suit the Africans, who wanted first majority rule and then independence. In a referendum held in November 1964 the Rhodesian Front government led by Ian Smith (prime minister from April 1964) gained the approval of the electorate for independence under the existing constitution. It further strengthened its position by an overwhelming victory in the general election of 1965.

During 1965 the possibility that the Rhodesian government would declare its independence unilaterally grew steadily stronger. While accepting the need for independence, the British government wanted an assurance that the basis upon which this would be granted would be acceptable to the people of the country as a whole. In October fruitless discussions on this issue were held between the British and Rhodesian prime ministers in London and in Salisbury.

On Nov. 11 the Rhodesian government under the leadership of Smith proclaimed the country's independence. The British government immediately declared this move to be an act of rebellion and began (with the general support of the UN) the imposition of economic sanctions.

The freezing of Rhodesian sterling balances in London, the progressive curtailment of imports from Rhodesia by other countries, and the imposition of an oil embargo in December 1965, and the cutting off of trade between Rhodesia and Britain (its best customer) in January 1966, began slowly but cumulatively to have an effect on the Rhodesian economy. Rhodesia's trade with the Republic of South Africa, however, was not affected, and landlocked Zambia had to continue to buy consumer goods from Rhodesia.

At two Commonwealth prime ministers' conferences held in Lagos and London during 1966, increasing pressure was put upon the British government to take more drastic steps to end the rebellion. In September the British government undertook that, if the illegal government had not accepted its terms for a settlement by the end of the year it would, if supported by the rest of the Commonwealth, propose to the UN the imposition of mandatory sanctions on selected commodities considered to be vital to the Rhodesian economy.

In Rhodesia itself most of the African nationalist leaders were in detention and outbreaks of violence were few. Disaffection within the University College in Salisbury resulted in arrests of students and lecturers and the deportation of eight lecturers. Security precautions were taken under regulations consolidated in March in the Emergency Powers Amendment Act, and there was censorship of news. Various measures such as import control, direction of labour, and gasoline rationing were introduced to safeguard the economy.

A meeting held in the British cruiser "Tiger" off Gibraltar during Dec. 2-4, 1966, between representatives of Britain and Rhodesia led by Harold Wilson and Ian Smith, failed to produce any immediate solution of the crisis. Britain thereupon applied to the UN Security Council for the imposition of selective mandatory sanctions against Rhodesia. These, after amendment by the African members of the council to include an embargo on imports of oil, were agreed on Dec. 16.

The effect of the sanctions was not as immediate as their supporters had hoped, and the Rhodesian government was able to carry on as before, though under increasing pressure from Europeans with more right-wing views to declare a republic and defy their opponents. In October 1968, however, Ian Smith again met Harold Wilson for talks on board the British assault ship "Fearless" off Gibraltar, but the views of the U.K. government and of the Smith regime were too far apart to admit of a compromise being easily reached.   (K. G. B.; K. I.)

POPULATION

In 1962 the total population of Rhodesia was 3,857,470, of whom 3,618,150 were Africans. The census of 1962 was the first com-
plete census of Africans ever taken in Rhodesia. In 1968 the estimated total population of Rhodesia was 4,670,300, of whom 4,410,000 were Africans and 237,000 were Europeans. The African population is believed to have increased by some 150% in the last 25 years and the European population has grown even more rapidly in the same period. Immigration was the major factor in this increase. According to the 1956 census less than one-third of the European population had been born in the country, and the majority of migrants (of predominantly British stock) had come from South Africa and the United Kingdom. Populations of the chief towns in 1968 were: Salisbury (380,000, of whom 96,000 were Europeans); Bulawayo (270,000: 54,000); Umtali (54,000); Gwelo (41,000).

The indigenous people of Rhodesia are the Bushmen, of whom there remain only a handful, and the Bantu. The Bushmen, who live along the western border of Matabeleland, are now of mixed race, having intermarried with the Bantu. The Bantu of Rhodesia, who belong to the southern section of the Bantu peoples, are generally divided into two groups, each containing a large number of smaller, tribal divisions: the Ndebele, the smaller group, occupy roughly the southeastern area of the country; and the Shona-speaking peoples the rest of the country. They are pastoral peoples who also cultivate corn (maize) and finger millet. They follow patrilineal descent and practise virilocal marriage. Before the establishment of British control some tribes, notably the Ndebele, were highly centralized chiefdoms headed by powerful chiefs. Most tribes, however, were organized into small autonomous units led by chiefs with limited secular and spiritual power. Reverence for ancestors is the basis of traditional religion. Among the Shona-speaking peoples there are spirit mediums through whom the spirits of powerful ancestors are believed to speak. A considerable number profess Christianity. Although the African population is still predominantly rural, Africans have settled in towns in increasing numbers and are adopting European modes of behaviour.

The majority of Africans speak Bantu languages, Ndebele and Shona being the main languages. English is the language of the administration and of most Europeans, though some immigrants from South Africa are Afrikaans-speaking.   (J. C. Mi.; X.)

ADMINISTRATION AND SOCIAL CONDITIONS

Constitution and Government.—Under the 1961 constitution the British sovereign is represented in Rhodesia by a governor. The Parliament comprises a Governor's Council and a single-chamber Legislative Assembly of 65 members. The Governor's Council (cabinet) consisting of the prime minister and other ministers is responsible to the Legislative Assembly, which is presided over by a speaker. The franchise is extended to voters of all races aged 21 or more registered on one of two electoral rolls, subject to certain property, income, or educational qualifications which effectively limit African participation. Fifty members of the Legislative Assembly, representing electoral districts, are elected by the more highly qualified voters of the "A" roll; the remaining 15, representing electoral districts, are elected by the voters of the "B" roll, who have lower qualifications. In 1965 there were 97,283 voters on the "A" roll, of whom 92,405 were European and 11,577 on the "B" roll, of whom 10,689 were Africans. The constitution also eliminates the reserved powers previously vested in the British government for the disallowance of laws passed by the Legislative Assembly, with the exception of matters affecting the position of the sovereign and the governor; international obligations; and undertakings given by the Rhodesian government in respect of loans under the Colonial Stock acts. Notable features of this constitution are the Declaration of Rights and the provision for a Constitutional Council. The Declaration of Rights concerns the fundamental rights and freedoms of the people of Rhodesia irrespective of race, colour, or creed, and provides for the enforcement of these rights and freedoms in the courts, with ultimately the right of appeal to the Privy Council. The main function of the Constitutional Council is to scrutinize all bills passed by the Legislative Assembly to ensure that their provisions conform to the Declaration of Rights.

Following Rhodesia's unilateral declaration of independence a new constitution was announced on Nov. 11, 1965, and approved by the Rhodesian Parliament on Feb. 18, 1966. It contained several important new provisions: it set aside the office of governor and made arrangements for the appointment of an "officer administering the government"; it removed the power of the British Parliament to legislate for Rhodesia; it repudiated the power of the British crown to issue orders in council under U.K. legislation in respect of Rhodesia; and it abolished appeals to the Privy Council. Certain provisions—including franchise qualifications, the Constitutional Council, the Declaration of Rights, and matters concerning tribal trust lands—which were previously subject to approval by the four principal races voting in separate referendums, or by the British government, could henceforth be amended by a two-thirds majority of the total membership of Parliament.

Municipal councils have been established in Salisbury, Bulawayo, Umtali, Gwelo, Gatouma, Que Que, and Fort Victoria. These are elected bodies with certain powers, including the right to levy rates, to maintain and build roads, and to provide services such as water, electricity, and transport. They are also responsible for the administration of African townships built near European residential and commercial areas. As a result of the encouragement given by the government to the development of local government among the Africans, 68 Native Councils had been established by the late 1960s.

Living Conditions.—*Employment.*—In the 1960s more than 830,000 Africans and more than 90,000 non-Africans were employed in Rhodesia. Africans were mostly employed in agriculture, forestry and fishing, and services, including domestic service. About 26,000 non-Africans were employed in services and about 24,700 in commerce. Almost 50% of the African labour force was composed of immigrants from Malawi, Zambia, and Mozambique. From 1961, however, steps were taken to restrict the employment of immigrant labour. The conditions of service of all workers except those engaged in agriculture and private domestic service are regulated by the Industrial Conciliation Act, 1959.

Housing.—Housing for Europeans and Asians is mainly the responsibility of private enterprise. Local authorities generally provide urban housing for Africans and Coloureds (people of mixed ancestry). When, in the early 1950s, the accommodation of African urban workers became a serious problem, the government began a program to house married African urban workers, in addition to housing projects carried out by local authorities.

Health and Social Welfare.—Rhodesia had six central hospitals, eight general hospitals, and a number of district and rural hospitals in the 1960s. In addition, there were several special institutions, including mental and tuberculosis hospitals.

Welfare services include the supervision of juvenile delinquents, the rehabilitation of maladjusted adults, including alcoholics, the care of the aged and physically handicapped, and the encouragement of voluntary social services. Private institutions for children and old people are supported by the government.

Education.—By the later 1960s the government claimed that about 95% of African children of school age were receiving a minimum of five years education. Most schools were run by missions which were grant-aided by the government. More than 680,-000 African children were attending primary and about 17,000 secondary schools. Approximately 33,000 European children were in government primary and 22,000 in government secondary schools. There were also about 5,000 European children at private primary and 4,000 at private secondary schools. Students of all races attended the University College at Salisbury.

Justice.—The Ministry of Law and Order, formed in September 1962, is responsible for the maintenance of law and order and for the prosecution of criminals in the courts. The High Court, established in 1898, has criminal and civil jurisdiction over all persons. Most criminal and civil litigation is conducted in magistrates' courts. There are also African courts with jurisdiction in matters which can be decided by native law and custom.

The Rhodesian police force—composed of both Africans and non-Africans—is also controlled by the Ministry of Law and Order.

Defense.—Before the unilateral declaration of independence the Rhodesian Army consisted of about 3,400 regulars and 8,400 territorials and reservists. The Air Force had a strength of about 1,000 men and nearly 100 aircraft. Since independence the size of the defense force has increased considerably.

THE ECONOMY

Of the country's 96,600,000 ac., 40,125,600 have been allocated as African trust lands, 4,276,500 ac. are available for purchase by Africans, 36,673,000 ac. are set aside for Europeans, and the rest are either unreserved or have been designated as forests or national land.

Sanctions imposed against Rhodesia after the unilateral declaration of independence had a severe effect on the country's economy, the prohibition by many countries of the import of Rhodesian tobacco being believed to have been particularly damaging. It is estimated that exports, which in the mid-1960s were valued annually at approximately £150,000,000, had been reduced by more than half by the late 1960s. Since, however, publication of statistics has been withheld the following assessment refers to the condition of the economy as it was before sanctions were imposed.

The Rhodesian economy is based primarily on agriculture, with tobacco as the main export product, but mining and an increasing number of secondary industries are assuming major importance. These are backed by the subsistence agriculture practised by the great majority of the African population. In agriculture, mining, and industry Africans are generally employed as unskilled and semiskilled labour.

Production.—*Agriculture.*—Because of the importance of agriculture every effort is made to improve farming methods wherever possible, special attention being paid to irrigation and to better land utilization in general. Rhodesia's sandy soil has proved especially suitable for the production of Virginia flue-cured tobacco, the output of which in the mid-1960s was about 300,000,000 lb. annually valued at some £33,000,000. This represented an increase in production and value of more than 100% compared with the 1950s. The increase has been chiefly due to higher yields per acre. Most crops, including tobacco, corn (maize), peanuts, and cotton, are grown in the summer. Corn is the most important grain. In many parts it is a staple of subsistence agriculture, is used in livestock feed, and has become increasingly significant as an export crop. Wheat, grown under irrigation, is the most important winter crop, and attempts are being made to evolve better strains. Other winter crops include barley, oats, peas, rye, and cabbage. Sugar production (beet) was mounting rapidly in the 1960s.

BY COURTESY OF RHODESIA HOUSE, LONDON

FARMER WATERING TOBACCO SEEDLINGS. TOBACCO IS A MAJOR CASH CROP IN RHODESIA

Under the stimulus of cooperative programs African farmers are engaged in the production of the country's chief crops. In the 1960s Africans harvested annually about 3,300,000 bags (200 lb. each) of corn (about one-third of the total production), while the production of wheat (about 15,000 bags) was much higher than the European output. Other crops grown by Africans include Turkish tobacco (which requires little capital investment and gives a high yield), tea, sugar, Arabian coffee, vegetables, and fruit.

Livestock.—In the mid-1960s the cattle population amounted to about 3,500,000, of which more than half were owned by Africans. The value of the output of the livestock industry, which developed under a stimulus of a guaranteed market with guaranteed minimum prices, was second only to tobacco.

Forestry.—Before independence was declared the control of crown forests and the establishment and maintenance of plantations were the responsibility of the Southern Rhodesian Forestry Commission, founded in 1954. Utilized forests, covering an area of about 2,000,000 ac. (800,000 ha.), yield mainly Rhodesian teak, which is used for railway ties (sleepers) and parquet flooring. The main species of trees being planted as part of afforestation projects were eucalyptus, pines, and wattle. By the 1960s the total area planted to eucalyptus exceeded 60,000 ac. (24,000 ha.) and the total area planted to pine was about 100,000 ac. (40,000 ha.).

Mining.—Rhodesia's mining industry has steadily expanded, and the industry forms an important sector of the economy. More than 30 minerals are produced, the total annual output being valued at about £32,000,000 ($90,000,000) in the mid-1960s. The most important were asbestos and gold, followed by chrome, copper, and coal. The value of production of these minerals (except gold) almost doubled between the 1950s and 1960s. World resources of asbestos are limited, and substantial capital investment has been made in efforts to obtain access to additional Rhodesian reserves of asbestos ore. Chrome of all grades is found in abundance in Rhodesia, which is the world's second biggest producer. The chief coal deposits are at Wankie, which has reserves of more than 500,000,000 tons. Production of tin is also assuming increasing importance. There are substantial reserves of high-grade iron ore.

Industries.—In value, the country's manufacturing industry makes the greatest contribution to the gross domestic product (or at least did so before the declaration of independence). Its gross output rose from about £90,000,000 in the early 1950s to more than £200,000,000 in the mid-1960s. The chief industries are iron and steel, metal products, textiles, clothing and footwear, chemicals, timber, and food processing. Most large towns contain manufacturing industries, particularly Salisbury and Bulawayo. The iron and steel industry is situated in the vicinity of Que Que (near the iron ore and limestone deposits), and heavy industries based on iron and steel are established in the town. At Umtali there are pulp, board, and wattle extract industries, drawing their raw material from the forests of exotic timber and wattle in the eastern districts of the country. Gatooma has a cotton-ginning plant, which can handle nearly 50,000,000 lb. of seed cotton in a season, and spinning mills. Bulawayo has railway workshops, a radio manufacturing industry, and a tire factory; a ferrochrome industry is found in Gwelo. The country also possesses cement factories and motor vehicle assembly plants.

Power.—Most of Rhodesia's generating requirements are met by the Kariba hydroelectric project (*see* KARIBA, LAKE). Consumption of electricity has risen rapidly and production increased from about 740,000,000 kw. in the early 1950s to more than 2,000,000,000 kw. in the mid-1960s.

An oil pipeline runs from Beira, in (Portuguese) Mozambique, to Rhodesia's only oil refinery, near Umtali.

Trade and Finance.—In the 1960s the chief Rhodesian exports were tobacco, asbestos, corn, meat and meat products, pig iron, and chrome ore. Among the chief imports were wheat, petroleum, fertilizers, cotton fabrics, and motor vehicles.

The principal sources of revenue were taxes on income and profits, customs duties, personal tax, and interest on loans, deposits, etc. Annual revenue totaled about £75,000,000 ($210,-000,000). The principal items of expenditure were service of loans, African education, police, and internal affairs. Expenditure was about £75,000,000 annually. The Reserve Bank of Rhodesia issues Rhodesia's currency. It is also empowered to control banking, deal in gold and currencies, and exercise exchange control functions.

Transport and Communications.—The Rhodesian government is responsible for about 5,200 mi. (8,400 km.) of road of which about 3,000 mi. (4,800 km.) are bituminized. There are in addition nearly 14,000 mi. under the supervision of the road councils in the European areas and about 29,000 mi. in the African areas. Both Rhodesia and Zambia are served by Rhodesia Railways (owned jointly by both countries) which are linked with South African Railways. There are nearly 1,600 mi. (2,600 km.) of single-track railway in Rhodesia, of 3 ft. 6 in. gauge. There is an international airport at Salisbury, and Bulawayo, Fort Victoria, and Kariba also have airports. The chief towns are linked by Central African Airways, and other services are operated by British United Airways and Commercial Air Services.

Communications include direct radio, cable, and telephone services to the United Kingdom, and the country has a telephone network. There are broadcasting stations at Salisbury, Bulawayo, and Gwelo.

See also references under "Rhodesia" and "Rhodesia, Southern" in the Index.

BIBLIOGRAPHY.—H. M. Hole, *The Making of Rhodesia* (1926); N. S. Kane, *The World's View: the Story of Southern Rhodesia* (1954); P. Mason, *The Birth of a Dilemma: the Conquest and Settlement of Rhodesia* (1958); W. D. Gale, *Zambezi Sunrise* (1958); C. Leys, *European Politics in Southern Rhodesia* (1959); E. Colson and M. Gluckman (eds.), *Seven Tribes of British Central Africa* (1951); J. F. Holleman, *Shona Customary Law* (1952); A. J. B. Hughes, *Kin, Caste and Nation Among the Rhodesian Ndebele* (1956); M. Gelfand, *Medicine and Magic of the Mashona* (1956), *Shona Ritual* (1959), *Shona Religion* (1962); C. H. Thompson and H. W. Woodruff, *Economic Development in Rhodesia and Nyasaland* (1955); W. V. Brelsford (ed.), *Handbook to the Federation of Rhodesia and Nyasaland* (1960); Lord Alport, *The Sudden Assignment* (1965); N. M. Shamuyarira, *Crisis in Rhodesia* (1965); James Barber, *Rhodesia: the Road to Rebellion* (1967); Theodore Bull (ed.), *Rhodesia: Crisis of Color* (1968).

(K. I.)

RHODESIA, NORTHERN: *see* ZAMBIA.

RHODESIA AND NYASALAND, FEDERATION OF, a short-lived federation of three British central African countries, Northern Rhodesia, Southern Rhodesia and Nyasaland, which came into existence in Sept. 1953 and was dissolved at the end of 1963. This article deals with the events leading up to the formation of the federation and the history of the federation itself. For all other information concerning the countries which composed the federation *see* MALAWI (the former Nyasaland; *q.v.*); RHODESIA; and ZAMBIA (the former Northern Rhodesia).

Europeans in the Rhodesias began to press for the amalgamation of the two territories during the 1930s, and after World War II Roy (later Sir Roy) Welensky in Northern Rhodesia and Sir Godfrey Huggins (Lord Malvern) in Southern Rhodesia abandoned their campaign for this union (including, by then, Nyasaland) only when the British government made it clear that it was not prepared entirely to relinquish its responsibilities for Northern Rhodesia and Nyasaland. It did, however, agree that there were forceful economic and political arguments for creating a strong state based on co-operation between Europeans and Africans. The solution was a federation of the three territories in which those matters which most directly affected the lives of the Africans, such as the administration of land, African taxation and local government, African primary and secondary education, and agriculture, were to be left with the territorial governments. The commonwealth relations office would be in charge of federal and Southern Rhodesian affairs but the colonial office would retain full responsibility for the political advancement of the peoples in the protectorates, with the ultimate aim of granting them self-government.

All these safeguards, however, did not satisfy the Africans in Northern Rhodesia and Nyasaland who still feared that eventually their destinies would be controlled by the 220,000 Europeans in Southern Rhodesia, whereas, if they stayed out of the federation, they would achieve complete national independence. There was much controversy in Britain over this issue, but the Conservative government held to the view that the proposed federation would so greatly benefit all the peoples in each territory that the Africans would in time lose their fears and give it their support. Accordingly, after the Europeans in Southern Rhodesia had, in a referendum, voted in favour of federation by a large majority, the Federation of Rhodesia and Nyasaland was formally established on Sept. 3, 1953. Lord Llewellin was appointed first governor general of the federation and its first prime minister was Lord Malvern, who, on his retirement in 1956, was succeeded by Sir Roy Welensky. The federal assembly consisted of a speaker and an elected majority. The federal government's responsibilities included external affairs, defense, immigration, external trade and fiscal matters. A special feature of the constitution was the African Affairs Board, designed to safeguard African interests.

The belief that the creation of the federation would result in great economic progress was fully justified, one remarkable achievement being the completion of the Kariba dam on the Zambezi in 1960 at the cost of about £120,000,000. There was also a marked liberalization of social policies in the Rhodesias, especially in Southern Rhodesia, where the tradition of a "white man's country" and economic competition between Europeans and Africans made this particularly difficult.

Nevertheless, with the achievement of independence by other African countries, nationalist feeling was rapidly increasing, and the opposition of Africans to the idea of federation led to the growth of nationalist political parties in all three territories and to considerable unrest.

In 1960 a comprehensive inquiry into the federal constitution was instituted by a commission under the chairmanship of Lord Monckton. Its conclusions were that African opposition to the federation had grown to the point where the latter could not survive unless it were so modified as to be made acceptable to the peoples of all the constituent territories, and that each territory should be given the right to secede. The provision about secession was strongly opposed by Sir Roy Welensky and a subsequent conference in London on the future of the federation proved abortive. It was, therefore, decided to postpone the conference until the next steps in constitutional reform in Northern Rhodesia and Nyasaland had been taken. In 1961 Nyasaland was given representative government. In April 1962 the United Federal party, under Sir Roy Welensky, was returned to power with a greatly increased majority in the federal general election, which had been boycotted by most of the other parties.

In March 1962 the British government took away from the colonial office and the commonwealth relations office all responsibility for the territories in the federation, which were thenceforth entrusted to a newly formed Central Africa office.

Toward the end of 1962 an African-dominated government took office in Northern Rhodesia and elections subsequently held in Southern Rhodesia, which were boycotted by the African parties, resulted in the defeat of the ruling United Federal party by the more conservative Rhodesian Front. In Dec. 1962 the U.K. government announced its acceptance in principle of Nyasaland's right to secede from the federation, following this in March 1963 with a declaration of any territory's right to secede. The governments of all three territories were then demanding independence and after a conference at Victoria falls in June–July, attended by representatives of the U.K., federal, Northern Rhodesian and Southern Rhodesian governments, the U.K. passed an enabling measure to start the process of dissolution of the federation. The federation officially came to an end on Dec. 31, 1963.

See also references under "Rhodesia and Nyasaland, Federation of" in the Index.   (K. G. B.)

RHODESIAN MAN: *see* Man, Evolution of: *Neanderthal Man and Neanderthaloids.*

RHODES SCHOLARSHIPS: *see* Rhodes, Cecil John; Student Aid.

RHODIUM is a chemical element which is a precious silver-white metal. It is one of the platinum metals (*q.v.*). The symbol for rhodium is Rh. Its atomic number is 45; its atomic weight,

102.905. It has a specific gravity of 12.4 and melts at 1,966° C; thus it is difficult to fuse or cast. It is fairly hard and cannot be easily worked at room temperature; but it can be forged above 800° C, a red heat.

The surface of the metal has a high reflectivity for light and is not corroded or tarnished by the atmosphere at room temperature. It is frequently electroplated onto metal objects and polished to give permanent attractive surfaces for jewelry and other decorative purposes. In particular, the black tarnish of silver is avoided by the use of rhodium plate. Rhodium also serves for the preparation of "silvered" surfaces for reflectors of searchlights and motion-picture projectors.

Rhodium added to platinum in small amounts yields alloys which are harder and lose weight at high temperatures even more slowly than does pure platinum. Therefore crucibles for heating materials in the chemical laboratory are commonly made from these alloys. In the industrial manufacture of nitric acid, gauze catalysts of the rhodium-platinum alloys are used because of their ability to withstand the flame temperature as ammonia is burned to nitric oxide.

A wire of the alloy 10% rhodium–90% platinum joined to a wire of pure platinum forms an excellent thermocouple for measuring high temperatures in an oxidizing atmosphere. The international temperature scale is defined over the region from 660° to 1,063° C by the electromotive force of this thermocouple.

The only stable isotope for rhodium has a mass number of 103, *i.e.*, Rh^{103}. Its nuclei possess a high cross section or probability for the capture of neutrons with thermal energies. The Rh^{104} formed by neutron capture is radioactive, and consists of two nuclear isomers (half-lives of 44 sec. and 4.3 min.). In nuclear physics experiments, a flux of neutrons can be conveniently and quickly measured by the determination of the amount of radioactivity induced in a thin rhodium foil, exposed for a few minutes to the neutrons. Another radioisotope, Rh^{106}, with a half-life of 30 sec., is the product of decay of Ru^{106} (*see* Ruthenium).

Rhodium always accompanies platinum in minerals, but only to a minor extent. It was first isolated from crude platinum by William Wollaston, who announced its discovery in 1804. He gave it the name rhodium in consequence of the red colour of a number of its compounds. Rhodium is almost as resistant as iridium to chemical attack by acids. The massive metal is not dissolved by hot concentrated nitric or hydrochloric acid or even by aqua regia which dissolves gold and platinum. The element dissolves in fused potassium hydrogen sulfate to yield a complex sulfate, soluble in water. Rhodium, in all well-characterized compounds, possesses the +3 oxidation state. Possibly some compounds of lower oxidation state can form, and strong oxidizing agents yield higher oxidation states of transient stability, probably +4 and +6. All its compounds are readily reduced or decomposed by heating to yield the powdered or sponge metal. Many rhodium compounds contain coordination complexes in which ammonia, water, chloride, or other groups are bonded covalently to a central rhodium ion (*see* Co-ordination Compounds). Characteristically, the groups in these complexes are replaced slowly. A series of substituted ammine compounds is analogous to familiar compounds of cobalt. A yellow hydrous rhodium hydroxide, soluble in acid or alkaline solutions, can be precipitated, but some conditions will cause a black precipitate to form. Rh_2O_3 is a gray compound, insoluble in acids. $RhCl_3$ can be prepared in a form which does not dissolve in water or acids. Other forms dissolve readily to give solutions whose colour may range from brown to yellow and in which some or all of the chloride is not precipitated by silver nitrate.   (D. S. Mn.)

RHODOCHROSITE, one of the calcite group of carbonate minerals, consisting of manganese carbonate. It is used as a source of manganese for the ferromanganese alloys consumed in steelmaking and in the preparation of other manganese chemicals. Named from the Greek meaning "rose coloured," it sometimes is known as manganese spar.

The formula for rhodochrosite is $MnCO_3$. Extensive substitution of iron and calcium, as well as lesser amounts of magnesium, may occur in place of the manganese. It crystallizes in the rhombohedral system, and occurs commonly as compact crystalline masses and incrustations rather than as single crystals. When pure it is usually some shade of pink or rose-red, with a specific gravity of 3.7 and a hardness of 3.5–4.

Rhodochrosite is found in sedimentary deposits, in mineral veins of silver, lead, copper and zinc minerals formed at moderate temperatures and in high-temperature metamorphic deposits. It is found in England, at a number of localities in Europe, in Siberia and in Argentina, Brazil and Peru.

In the United States it occurs abundantly at Butte, Mont., and is found in California, Colorado, Nevada, Utah, Arkansas, Tennessee and Maine. (D. L. G.; X.)

RHODODENDRON, of the heath family (Ericaceae), is one of the largest genera of woody plants. It comprises 800–900

ROCHE

RHODORA (RHODODENDRON CANADENSE) BLOSSOMS

species including about 70 azaleas. Azaleas, together with rhodora, were once considered as constituting a distinct genus, but are now treated as species of *Rhododendron*.

The true rhododendrons are mostly evergreen and with campanulate corollas while the azaleas are usually deciduous and with funnelform corollas. They are commonly kept distinct by gardeners but botanical characters distinguishing the two are not constant. Some azaleas are evergreen while some true rhododendrons are deciduous.

Rhododendrons are among the most popular garden plants, much planted for their beautiful showy flowers and for their ornamental foliage in the evergreen species. The species are distributed throughout the colder regions of the northern hemisphere, and also on the high mountains of southern Asia, Malaysia and New Guinea, with one in northern Australia, but none in Africa and South America. The greatest development is found in the Himalayas eastward to western and central China, in the wet monsoon zone of Asia. There are about 26 species in North America, but none extending into Mexico.

There is no wild species in Britain, although *R. ponticum* is practically naturalized in the south, but the genus is exceedingly popular for gardens and most species do extremely well there. In North America they are best cultivated along the Atlantic seaboard, in the Alleghenies and on the Pacific coast.

The rhododendrons are shrubs, rarely small trees. Some species are epiphytic. The leaves are alternately arranged, stalked and, generally, with entire margins. The flowers are large and showy, on stalks, generally several to many grouped together in terminal umbellike clusters. There is a small calyx, generally five-parted.

The corolla is red, blue, yellow or white, or of intermediate shades, rotate to campanulate or funnelform, usually slightly irregular, and five- or rarely six- to ten-lobed, occasionally divided to the base. There are five to ten stamens with anthers opening with apical pores. The ovary is 5- to 20-celled, each cell many ovuled. There is a slender style ending in an enlarged stigma. The fruit is an ovoid or elongate capsule, splitting from top into 5 to 20 valves when it becomes mature, liberating numerous minute seeds.

The species grow only in acid soils rich in humus. They thrive best in a cool, damp atmosphere and prefer "high shade." To prepare ground for cultivation, peat moss or acid leafmold, especially from oaks, or sawdust can be used to mix with loamy soil. The roots are shallow and are without root hairs but are associated with a mycorrhizal fungus. It is important to mulch the soil to keep the roots from drying out in summer as well as in winter. The evergreen rhododendrons are generally propagated by seeds or layering. Grafting is generally resorted to in only the rarer and more tender kinds.

A number of American species are highly ornamental and much planted. Among these are the coast rhododendron, *R. macrophyllum*, the state flower of Washington; the catawba rhododendron, *R. catawbiense*, of the southern Alleghenies; and the rose bay rhododendron, *R. maximum*, of eastern North America. The latter two, together with the less hardy *R. arboreum* and *R. campanulatum* from the Himalayas, *R. caucasicum* from the Caucasus, *R. ponticum* from the Mediterranean region and other species, have given rise by hybridization to numerous horticultural varieties now in general cultivation. (H. L. L.)

BIBLIOGRAPHY.—Clement G. Bowers, *Rhododendrons and Azaleas*, 2nd ed. (1960); David G. Leech, *Rhododendrons of the World* (1961); Judith M. Berrisford, *Rhododendrons and Azaleas* (1965).

RHODONITE, a member of the silicate group of minerals, consisting of manganese metasilicate. It commonly occurs as cleavable to compact masses with a rose-red colour; hence the name, from the Greek word meaning a rose. The formula is $MnSiO_3$. It crystallizes in the triclinic system and crystals often have a thick tabular habit; there are perfect cleavages parallel to the prism faces. The hardness is 5.5–6.5, and the specific gravity 3.4–3.68. Rhodonite is liable to alteration, and in certain cases forms the primary source of very important deposits of ores of manganese, mainly in the form of oxides, such as pyrolusite (*q.v.*); such oxides are a considerable part of the manganese ores of India.

Rhodonite occurs as large rough crystals with franklinite and zinc ores at Franklin, N.J. Fine-grained rhodonite of clean colour is a desirable gem and ornamental stone. The finest quality is mined near Sverdlovsk, U.S.S.R., in the Urals. Good stone occurs in Siskiyou and Plumas counties in California. Rhodonite has often been used for beads, pendants and other ornaments.

(W. F. Fg.)

RHONDDA, DAVID ALFRED THOMAS, 1ST VISCOUNT (1856–1918), British colliery owner and statesman, who was responsible for the introduction of food rationing during World War I, was born in Ysgyborwen, near Aberdare, Glamorgan, on March 26, 1856. He was the son of Samuel Thomas, a former grocer who subsequently became rich through colliery speculations. Educated at Caius College, Cambridge, Thomas joined the family coal business on his father's death (1879). In 1882 he married Sybil Margaret Haig. Liberal M.P. for Merthyr Tydfil from 1888 to 1910, and for Cardiff for a few months in 1910, he made no impact in politics, partly because of the dullness of his speeches, and from 1906 he devoted himself more and more to his coal business. His extraordinary commercial ability, his foresight, and the sympathy which he brought to bear on conditions in the mining industry made him the leading figure in industrial South Wales. His amalgamation of many mining companies, which made him very wealthy, culminated in 1913 in the formation of the huge combine, Consolidated Cambrian Ltd., which produced 6,000,000 tons of steam coal a year.

Between 1913 and 1915 he made several business visits to Canada and the United States. Returning to England in 1915, Thomas and his daughter Margaret both narrowly escaped death when the "Lusitania" was sunk on May 7. Immediately afterward Lloyd George, then minister of munitions, sent Thomas back to the United States to organize the supply of American munitions to England (July–December 1915). Created Baron Rhondda in January 1916, he took office in Lloyd George's ministry as president of the local government board in December and was appointed controller at the food ministry in June 1917. Taking stern measures to end the speculation in food, he gradually fixed prices, controlled supplies, and from February 1918 introduced the system of compulsory food rationing. Created a viscount in June, he died at Llanwern, Monmouthshire, on July 3, 1918.

By special remainder he was succeeded to the viscountcy by his only child MARGARET HAIG THOMAS (1883–1958), political journalist and a supporter of rights for women, who was born in London on June 12, 1883. She was an active suffragette before World War I and underwent a short term of imprisonment. Shortly after her marriage to Humphrey Mackworth (later 7th baronet) in 1908, she became her father's personal assistant in his colliery concerns and throughout her life remained an active business woman in the coal industry. After succeeding to the title, for many years she unsuccessfully fought for the right of women to sit in the House of Lords. She was chiefly responsible for the founding of the weekly newspaper *Time and Tide*, which she edited for the last 30 years of her life, and established as a leading weekly. She died in London on July 20, 1958. Her books include an autobiography, *This Was My World* (1933), and a biography of her father, *D. A. Thomas, Viscount Rhondda* (1921).

RHONDDA, a municipal borough (1955) of Glamorgan, south Wales, 12 mi. (19 km.) long by about 4¾ mi. (7 km.) across at its widest part, comprising two main valleys, named after their respective rivers, Rhondda Fawr and Rhondda Fach. Pop. (1961) 100,-287. Area 37.3 sq.mi. (96.6 sq.km.). The valleys are deeply incised in the coal measures of the south Wales geological basin and their lateral boundaries are formed by hills varying from 560 ft. (171 m.) near Trehafod to 1,567 ft. on the northeast of Maerdy in the Rhondda Fach and 1,742 ft. on the southwest of Treherbert in Rhonnda Fawr. The upper end of the latter valley rises to the Rhigos plateau where Craig-y-Llyn (1,969 ft. [600 m.]) is the highest point in Glamorgan. The two valleys are separated by the ridge of Cefn-y-Rhondda, which ranges from 600 ft. above Porth to 1,690 ft. There are tributary valleys where it joins the Rhigos plateau of which Cwmparc, Clydach vale and Cymmer are the chief.

Rhondda is the centre of the eastern division of the south Wales coal field. Coal exploitation there started in 1807 and so it was later than that of the northern sections of the south Wales area where coal was worked early for iron smelting. It was the realization of the steam-raising properties of the Rhondda coal and the opening of the Treherbert pits in 1855 that made the region famous.

With the great demands made for steam coal by the ever increasing railway traffic, steamship services and navies of the last half of the 19th century, Rhondda was transformed from being a purely pastoral upland region into a densely populated industrial area. No thought was given then, however, to the development of other industries which could provide alternative employment in the event of a setback in the coal-mining industry. With the rapid growth of each township provision was made for miners' libraries and institutes and numerous places of worship, and around these grew and flourished social, religious and cultural activities, particularly in music and drama, which, in turn, led to the creation of a strong community of interest and civic pride.

In 1801 the population was 542, but by 1871 it had reached 23,950; in 1881 it was 55,632 and in 1901 it was 113,735. The peak population figure was 167,900 in 1924 but during the severe industrial depression of the 1930s it fell to 121,940 by 1938. Further migration during World War II reduced the population seriously and by 1951 the figure stood at 111,389.

With the development of the coal exporting trade a number of small railway companies connected Rhondda with Cardiff, Port Talbot and Swansea but all these lines were eventually merged in the Great Western railway, and in 1947 the Western region of British railways. The slump in world demand for Welsh coal following World War I undermined the prosperity of the area and led to mass unemployment and migration. In 1934, of Rhondda's 61,460 insured men more than 47% were without work. In an attempt to relieve this critical situation two new factories were opened in the area in 1939. After World War II the policy of redistribution of industry to help depressed areas brought new industries to Rhondda, and at mid-century the area had a stable and varied industrial pattern.   (J. C. G. J.)

RHÔNE, a *département* of east-central France, formed in 1793 from the eastern portion of the *département* of Rhône-et-Loire, and chiefly comprised of the old districts of Beaujolais and Lyonnais (*q.v.*). It lies west of the Saône and Rhône rivers above and below their confluence at Lyons but also includes a small area to the east around the city. The *département* is bounded north by Saône-et-Loire, east by Ain and Isère, and southwest and west by Loire. Area, 1,104 sq.mi. (2,859 sq.km.); pop. (1962) 1,116,664.

Rhône consists largely of broken highlands, with summits about 3,000 ft. (914 m.), in the eastern part of the Massif Central and built of granite, gneiss, and schists that weather to give only poor soils. There is better farmland in the Rhône-Saône Plain, where wheat, maize (corn), sugar beet, and fodder crops are grown. The lower slopes of the hills flanking the Saône Valley in Beaujolais are an important vine-growing district, with Villefranche the local market centre. Iron pyrites are worked at Sain-Bel and Bully, but Rhône has little mineral wealth. It owes its importance and large population to Lyons (*q.v.*) and the great industrial development centred there, especially concerned with silk textiles, and now with man-made fibres also. The whole *département* comes under the domination of Lyons, and there are scattered factories and workshops in the countryside, with tentacles of more intense industrialization along the main routes. Tarare, on the road and railway from Lyons northwest to Roanne, is especially concerned with making velvet, plush, and mixed fabrics. In the extreme south, the Saint-Étienne coal field extends into the *département* along the valley of the Gier, and Givors, at its confluence with the Rhône, has heavy metallurgical and glass industries as well as textile mills. Lyons is the *préfecture*, centre of an archbishopric and of an educational division (*académie*), and has the court of appeal. Rhône is divided into two *arrondissements*, centred upon Lyons and Villefranche.   (AR. E. S.)

RHÔNE RIVER, one of the most important rivers in Europe, and the main one flowing from that continent directly into the Mediterranean. It rises at the eastern extremity of the Swiss canton of the Valais, flows through Switzerland and France, and enters the Mediterranean at the Gulf of Lions. Its total length is 505 mi. (812 km.), of which the Lake of Geneva (Lac Léman), through which it flows, claims 45 mi. (72 km.); and its total fall is 5,898 ft. (1,798 m.). Its course (excluding the Lake of Geneva, *q.v.*) falls naturally into four divisions: (1) from its source to the Lake of Geneva (105½ mi. [170 km.] and fall 4,679 ft. [1,426 m.]); (2) from Geneva to Lyons (124 mi. [200 km.] and fall 689 ft.); (3) from Lyons to Arles (200 mi. [321 km.] and fall 530 ft.); and (4) the delta, from Arles to the Mediterranean (30 mi.).

From Its Source to the Lake the Rhône is a purely Alpine river, flowing through a great glacially deepened trench, first in a synclinal structure between the Aare and Saint-Gotthard massifs, then along the front of the Pennine nappes. (*See* ALPS.) It issues as a torrent, at the height of about 5,909 ft. (1,801 km.), from the Rhône glacier at the head of the Valais. It is almost immediately joined (left) by the Mutt torrent, coming from a small glacier, and then flows past the Gletsch Hotel (where the roads from the Grimsel Pass and the Furka Pass unite). About half a mile from the glacier the river descends through a wild gorge to the more level valley, to reach the first village, Oberwald. It preserves a southwesterly direction till Martigny.

The uppermost valley of the Rhône is named Goms, its chief villages being Münster and Fiesch. The river there is swollen by mountain torrents, descending from the glaciers on either side, by the Geren (left), near Oberwald; by the Eginen (left), near Ulrichen; by the Fiesch (right), from the Fiesch glacier, at

Fiesch; by the Binna (left), near Grengiols; by the Massa (right) from the Aletsch glaciers, above Brig. At Brig the Rhône has descended 3,678 ft. (1,121 km.) from its source in 28 mi. (45 km.), and is already a considerable stream when joined (left) by the Saltine, descending from the Simplon Pass. Its course below Brig is less rapid and lies through wastes of alluvial deposits. The valley is wide and marshy, the river frequently overflowing its banks. Further mountain torrents fall into the Rhône: these are the Visp (left) from the Zermatt Valley, at Visp; at Gampel, the Lonza (right) from the Lötschen Valley; at Leuk, the Dala (right) from the Gemmi Pass; at Sierre, the Navizen (left) from the Einfisch or Anniviers Valley; at Sion, the capital of the Valais, the Borgne (left) from the Val d'Hérens; below Sion, by the Morge (right), from the Sanetsch Pass; and at Martigny by the Drance (left) from the Great St. Bernard and the Val de Bagnes. At Martigny the flat-floored trench is nearly 2 mi. (3 km.) wide, but from there the river bends sharply to the northwest toward the Lake of Geneva, its glaciated valley narrowing markedly as it cuts across the structures. Opposite Dorénaz it receives the Salanfe (left). Immediately below St. Maurice the Rhône rushes through a narrow and striking defile which commands the entrance of the Valais.

The river then enters the wide alluvial plain, formerly occupied by the southeastern arm of the Lake of Geneva. It receives at Bex the Avançon (right) flowing from the glaciers of the Diablerets Range, at Monthey the Vièze (left) from Champéry and the Val d'Illiez, and at the Aigle the Grande Eau (right), from the valley of Ormonts-dessus. It passes Port Valais, once on the lake, before emptying through a delta into the Lake of Geneva, between Villeneuve (right) and St. Gingolph (left).

The upper Rhône, being fed by glacial streams, has three times more flow in summer than in winter and is overburdened with sediment, much of which is deposited along the course, the remainder settling down in the Lake of Geneva, in the blue waters of which it is possible to follow the whiter course of the stream for some distance before it disappears. During all this portion of its course the Rhône is not navigable, but its valley forms an artery into the Alps which is followed by the railways and roads.

From Geneva to Lyons.—

About $\frac{1}{2}$ mi. below Geneva the Rhône is joined by the Arve (left) from the glaciers of the Mont Blanc Range. About 12 mi. (19 km.) S of Geneva the Rhône enters France. The river between the Lake of Geneva and its confluence with the Ain cuts transversely across the folds of the southern Jura, breaking through them in a series of zigzags by means of narrow gorges or *cluses*. After surging through the deep gorge Défilé de l'Écluse about 25 mi. (40 km.) SW of Geneva, at Bellegarde the Rhône is joined by the Valserine from the north and the river swings in a southerly direction. Below Bellegarde it flows in a steep-sided cleft providing the site for the Génissiat Dam which creates a narrow 14-mi.-long lake for hydroelectric power production. Above Seyssel the Usses (left) joins the Rhône, while just below that village the Fier (left) flows in from the Lac d'Annecy; from there the channel of the river widens and the hills diminish in height. The waters of the Lac du Bourget are linked with the Rhône by the Short Canal de Savières.

The river continues southward until joined, near Corbelin, by the Guiers (left) from the Grande Chartreuse Mountains, and from there swings around the southern spur of the Juras. The Geneva-Paris railway follows the river as far as Culoz before turning due west to Lyons. Some way below Bellegarde at Le Parc, 95 mi. (153 km.) above Lyons, the Rhône becomes officially "navigable," although down to Lyons the navigation consists almost entirely of flat-bottomed boats and rafts, the average depth being no more than one metre. The last of the *cluses* is at the Pont du

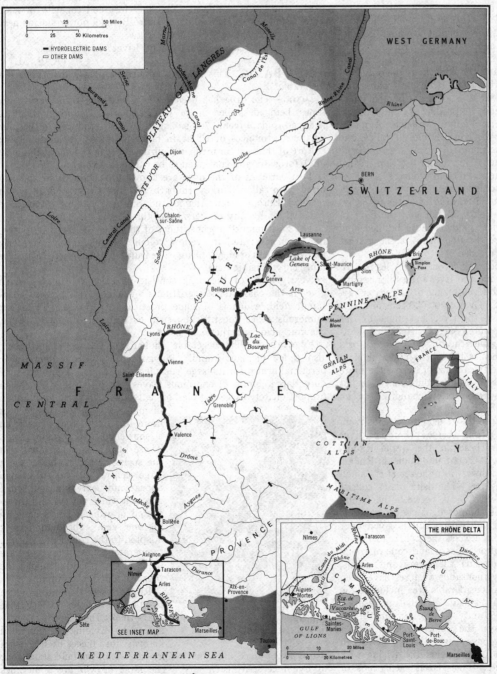

THE RHÔNE RIVER AND ITS TRIBUTARIES

Saut or Sault, just south of Lagnieu, from where the river enters the Plain of Bresse. The river there widens and before its regulation by the Canal de Jonage and the Canal de Miribel much of the surrounding countryside was liable to inundation.

About 20 mi. (32 km.) above Lyons the Rhône receives the Ain (right), which descends from the French slope of the Jura. At Lyons the Rhône makes its junction with the Saône, flowing from the north. The Saône (*q.v.*), which has received the Doubs (left), is the real continuation of the lower Rhône, both from a geographical and a commercial point of view. It is by means of canals branching off from the course of the Saône that the Rhône communicates with the basins of the Loire, Seine, Rhine, and Moselle.

From Lyons to Arles.—It is here that the Rhône becomes one of the great historical rivers of France. It was up its valley that various civilizations penetrated from the Mediterranean. This stretch of the Rhône provides a narrow north-south corridor between the abrupt eastern edge of the Massif Central and the western foothills of the French Alps. The river flows alternatively through narrow gorges and open basins, a sequence owing much to the Alpine earth movements. Rapids occur in some of the gorge sections, hampering navigation. The steepest gradient lies between the confluence of the Isère and that of the Ardèche. Most of the tributary streams in this section of the Rhône's course join it from the Alpine region to the east; the Ardèche is the only considerable affluent from the Massif Central. The left bank, followed by both road and rail, serves as a great medium of commerce by which central France sends its products to the sea, and possesses such historical cities as Vienne, Valence, Avignon, Tarascon, and Arles. It receives the Isère, Drôme, Aygues, and Durance rivers, all formed by the union of many streams from the Dauphiné Alps. Completed in 1956, a 17-mi. (27 km.) canal parallels a turbulent stretch of the river from Donzère, south of the plain of Montélimar, to Mondragon, near Pont-Saint-Esprit, easing navigation and providing an 85-ft. head of water for a hydroelectric station near Bollène. Below Mondragon the floor of the valley becomes marshy, the river channel more braided, and drainage ditches increasingly score the floodplain as the market gardening area around Avignon is reached.

The average depth of channel between Lyons and Arles is 5 ft. (1.6 m.) but the series of rapids and the river's irregular regime have not favoured the commercial development of the waterway, for upstream navigation is difficult. Over 1,000,000 tons of traffic is borne annually by this stretch of the river, but much of this traffic is local. Powerful tugs and motor barges with skilled pilotage are needed to make headway against the current. Since World War II large civil engineering schemes have been undertaken to harness the river for electricity and to canalize or bypass the more difficult sections (such as the Donzère-Mondragon Canal), so that eventually the river may offer a new route for merchandise between the Mediterranean and the North Sea.

From Arles to the Mediterranean.—The delta extends from near Arles, about 25 mi. (40 km.) from the sea where the river divides into two main branches. These are the Grand Rhône, flowing southeast to meet the sea at Port-Saint-Louis-du-Rhône, and the Petit Rhône which flows southwest into the sea at the small resort of Les Saintes-Maries-de-la-Mer. The delta plains consist of the Crau and the Camargue. The Crau, between the Grand Rhône and the Alpine foothills, is composed of coarse detritus. Much of this area is too dry for cultivation and is given over to sheep pasture. The Camargue, between the two branches of the Rhône, is the delta proper, and provides a landscape of rough pasture, marsh, lagoons, and, alongside the rivers and canals, patches of cultivated land. Many thousands of acres have been leveled for rice cultivation, while a considerable area including the large Étang de Vaccarès has been set aside as a nature reserve. The coast of the delta is nearly 50 mi. (80 km.) in length and consists of a series of sandy bays, the dunes backing onto a labyrinth of reedy marshes and lagoons. Several canals have been constructed from the vicinity of Arles, linking the Rhône with Marseilles, Port-de-Bouc, and Sète. Post-glacial oscillations of sea level, the great load of detritus brought down by the river, and

the small tidal effect in the Mediterranean account for the delta formation which is still slowly growing seaward, its shape modified by the east-west longshore drift.

The regime of the river reflects its Alpine origin and that of most of its tributaries, since it rises to a maximum with the snow melt of early summer and shows a second peak with the increasing rainfall of autumn. Freezing of the Alpine tributaries reduces considerably the winter flow. The Lake of Geneva helps to regulate and clarify the upper Rhône. Immediately below Lyons the flow is more even because of the greater winter volume of the Saône, but from the Valence Basin southward the Alpine character of the left-bank tributaries is again noticeable in the flow of the main river.

The principal commodities carried on the waterway are, southward, *vin ordinaire* for export, bauxite, and, locally, sand and gravel for construction work. Petroleum products, fertilizers, and Algerian wine provide the major northward cargoes.

By 1964 the French had harnessed one-half of the Rhône's potential hydroelectric power by means of an integrated series of works, the largest being at Génissiat (installed capacity 400,000 kw.), Montélimar, Baix, and the André-Blondel power station near Bollène (installed capacity 300,000 kw.).

See also references under "Rhône River" in the Index.

(A. B. M.)

RHUBARB. This name is applied both to a drug and to a vegetable.

Drug.—The drug has been used in medicine from very early times, being described in the Chinese herbal *Pen-king*, which is believed to date from 2700 B.C., and it is still produced in the four northern provinces of China in modern times. In England the culture of rhubarb for medicinal purposes began in 1777 at Banbury in Oxfordshire and continued to be carried on there.

Two varieties of the drug are known, viz., kiln dried and sun dried. So-called Turkey rhubarb was the Chinese drug which reached Europe from Aleppo and Smyrna, having traveled to Asia Minor by way of Persia and the Caspian.

The most important constituent of this drug, giving it its purgative properties and its yellow colour, is chrysarobin, formerly known as rhein or chrysophan. The rhubarb of commerce also contains chrysophanic acid.

Nearly 40% of the drug consists of calcium oxalate, which gives it the characteristic grittiness. There is also present rheotannic acid, which is of some practical importance. There are numerous other constituents, such as emodin, mucilage, resins, rheumic acid, aporrhetin, etc.

Vegetable.—The vegetable rhubarb (*Rheum rhaponticum*), also called pieplant (family Polygonaceae), is a hardy Asiatic perennial grown for its large, succulent leafstalks. The plant produces large clumps of enormous leaves, up to two feet across, on proportionately large petioles or leafstalks—an inch or more in

RHUBARB (RHEUM RHAPONTICUM) IN FLOWER

diameter and up to two feet or more in length—that arise from a shortened underground stem. These huge leaves arise early in the spring; later in the season a large central flower stalk may appear and bear numerous small greenish-white flowers and three-angled or winged fruits containing one seed. The plant is best adapted to the cooler parts of the temperate zones; the roots are quite hardy to cold although the tops are killed in autumn.

Rhubarb seed does not produce plants true to the variety that bears them; therefore it is propagated by dividing the perennial "crown" into pieces each consisting of a root piece and a bud. These are set in the field about four or five feet apart each way. The large crowns are sometimes moved into forcing houses in late winter for producing the leafstalks under artificial heat, and in subdued light. A greenhouse is not necessary. Only the fleshy leafstalks are eaten; they are highly acid and contain considerable amounts of oxalates. The leaves should never be eaten since they are sometimes poisonous.

(J. M. Bl.)

RHYL, an urban district of Flintshire, Wales, lies 18 mi. (28 km.) WNW of Flint by road at the mouth of the River Clwyd. Pop. (1961) 21,737. Rhyl has developed since the mid-19th century from a small fishing town to a thriving seaside resort. It is popular with family parties because of its safe, sandy beaches. On the 3½-mi. (6 km.)-long promenade is the domed pavilion with a theatre seating 1,100 persons, and the all-glass Royal Floral Hall. The town's oldest building, known as T'yn Rhyl, dates from 1608. There are two parks: the Botanical Gardens (opened 1928) and the King George V Coronation Gardens for outdoor sports (opened 1937). The main industry is tourism, but steel, rayon, and glass factories, and the coal mines are nearby. (G. H. Wi.)

RHYME (Rime), that phenomenon which occurs when two or more words with similarly sounding final syllables are so placed as to echo one another. Though normally used at the end of a line to make it chime with the end of another line, and termed "end rhyme," it can also be used in other positions, as in leonine verse (q.v.). In premature rhyme one rhyming word is at the end of the line and the other is not, thus causing the rhyme to occur ahead of expectation. Suspended rhyme occurs when the second, or rhyming, word has two rhyming syllables, one roving over to the next line; e.g., ". . . tenfold/. . . men,/Bold. . . ."

Masculine rhyme occurs when the two words end with the same vowel-consonant combination (e.g., "stand"/"land"). Feminine rhyme has two rhyming syllables (e.g., "profession"/"discretion"). Trisyllabic rhyme has three (e.g., "patinate"/"latinate"). These, all called "true rhymes," are the only varieties acceptable to purists, though poets have often been less particular. The device of para-rhyme, first identified and used systematically by Wilfred Owen (q.v.; 1893–1918), is a rhyme in which the two syllables have different vowel sounds but identical penultimate and final consonantal groupings (e.g., "grand/"grind"). Feminine para-rhyme has two forms, one in which both vowel sounds differ, and one in which only one does (e.g., "ran in"/"run on"; "blindness"/ "blandness"). Weakened, or unaccented, rhyme occurs when the relevant syllable of the rhyming word is unstressed (e.g., "bend"/ "frightened"). Because of the way in which lack of stress affects the sound, a rhyme of this kind may often be regarded as consonance, which occurs when the two words are similar only in having identical final consonants (e.g., "best"/"least").

Another form of near rhyme is assonance, in which only the vowel sounds are identical (e.g., "grow"/"home"). Many folk-poems and nursery rhymes use assonance, and French poetry of the 12th century and earlier used it rather than rhyme. The *Chanson de Roland* (see Roland, Chanson de) is a notable example of assonantal structure, as all the lines in each stanza end with the same vowel sound. Assonance continues to dominate poetic technique in the Romance languages, especially Spanish, but performs only a subsidiary function in the verse of the English-speaking world. The two main advantages of its use in English verse derive from its ability to facilitate smooth rove-overs from line to line, there being no overemphatic chime to suggest a jarring conclusiveness, and to suggest a casual ease and, even, lack of sophistication. Thus, in the earliest and best-known version of the nursery rhyme "Ding Dong Bell" we are partly persuaded of its childlike simplicity by the assonance of "in" with "Green": "Who put him in?/Little Tommy Green." In general, use of end-assonance in a poem increases its fluidity.

Subtlety is often given to a poem by occasional use of assonance and other forms of near-rhyme, as well as by unstressed rhyme, in which the two syllables are not accentuated (e.g., "ever"/ "killer"). The rather harsh effect of a masculine rhyme can also be softened by using trailing or semi-rhyme, in which one of the two words trails an additional unstressed syllable behind it (e.g., "trail"/"failure"). At the opposite end of the scale is rime riche, which, first used extensively by Victor Hugo, is commoner in French than in English poetry. It occurs when the two words

are identical in appearance, but not in meaning; thus it could occur as the consequence of manipulating the different meanings of e.g., "foil" (= "metal" and "thwart"), and "leaves" (= "foliage" and "departs").

Many traditional verse forms depend upon set rhyme patterns. The main stanza forms are ottava rima, the Spenserian stanza, rime royal (qq.v.), terza rima, the quatrain, the heroic couplet (see Couplet), and the Burns's stanza (or metre), an arrangement of six lines, with 8, 8, 8, 4, 8, and 4 syllables, rhyming *aaabab,* first found in 11th-century Provençal lyric poetry, and used in English late 14th- and early 15th-century miracle plays, but preserved only in Scotland and used with consummate skill by Robert Burns. The main poetic forms depending upon set rhyme patterns are the sonnet, villanelle, rondeau, ballade, chant royal, triolet, canzone, and sestina (qq.v.): the last two are only rhymed poems inasmuch as the repetition of the same end-words in successive stanzas produces a rhyming effect.

Rhyme seems to have developed as a combination of earlier techniques of end-consonance, end-assonance, and alliteration (see Alliterative Verse). It occurs only occasionally in classical Greek and Latin poetry, but more frequently in medieval religious Latin verse, and in songs from the 4th century A.D. onward. Periodically opposed by devotees of the ancients, such as Gabriel Harvey (q.v.; 1550?–1630), and by 20th-century advocates of so-called free verse (q.v.), it has never fallen into complete disuse.

Bibliography.—T. Campion, *Observations in the Art of English Poesie* (1602); S. Daniel, *A Defence of Rhyme* (1603); T. Hood, *The Rules of Rhyme* (1869); J. Walker (ed.), *The Rhyming Dictionary of the English Language* (n.d.); M. Boulton, *The Anatomy of Poetry* (1953); B. Deutsch, *Poetry Handbook* (1957). (R. S.)

RHYOLITE, the volcanic, mostly effusive, equivalent of granite, takes its name from the Greek word for torrent or stream because of the frequency and variety of its fluxional textures. The term liparite, from the Lipari Islands of Italy, originally proposed for the same rocks, was subsequently restricted to porphyritic varieties and is rarely used.

The glassy rhyolites include obsidian, pitchstone, perlite and pumice, though microscopic examination sometimes shows that pumices are actually ash flows and thus better designated as tuffs.

At atmospheric pressure granitic liquid above its melting point is exceedingly viscous. Cooled rapidly, as when extruded from a volcanic vent, it tends to chill to a glass rather than crystallize, as under plutonic conditions. The glassy or partly glassy rocks so formed are metastable, however, and devitrify into minutely crystalline, frequently spherulitic or felted aggregates, in periods of time that are relatively short by geological standards. Hence pre-Tertiary rhyolites which were originally true glasses almost invariably display one of the vitrophyric, stony or felsitic textures characteristic of devitrification. The glasses are also especially susceptible to hydrothermal alteration and weathering.

Most rhyolites are porphyritic, indicating that crystallization had begun prior to extrusion. Indeed, intratelluric crystallization may sometimes continue until the rock consists largely of phenocrysts at the time of extrusion, and the amount of microcrystalline matrix in the final product may then be so small as to escape detection except under the microscope. Such rocks (nevadites) are easily taken for granite in hand specimens.

In most rhyolites, however, the period of intratelluric crystallization is relatively short, so that the rock consists largely of a microcrystalline or partly glassy matrix in which are set a few per cent of phenocrysts. The matrix is sometimes micropegmatitic or granophyric.

Composition.—Except for occasional gross enrichment in silica, usually due to hydrothermal alteration, the chemical composition of rhyolite is very like that of granite (q.v.). There can be little doubt of the equivalence, and this is perhaps the strongest single reason for supposing that at least some and probably most granites are of magmatic origin.

The phenocrysts of rhyolite may include quartz, alkali-feldspar, oligoclase, biotite, amphibole or pyroxene, and the rules governing the coexistence of the different species are similar to those obtaining in granite. Thus, if an alkali-pyroxene or alkali amphibole is the principal dark mineral, oligoclase will be rare or absent and the feldspar phenocrysts will consist largely or entirely of alkali-feldspar. Rocks of this sort, for which the names comendite and pantellerite have been proposed (the latter has priority), are the volcanic equivalents of the alkali-granites.

If both oligoclase and alkali-feldspar are prominent among the phenocrysts the dominant dark silicate will be biotite, and neither amphibole nor pyroxene, if present, will be an alkaline variety. Such lavas, the quartz porphyries or "true" rhyolites of most classifications, are the volcanic equivalents of the two-feldspar granites.

Certain differences between rhyolite and granite should not be glossed over. Muscovite, a common mineral in granite, occurs very rarely and only as an alteration product in rhyolite. In most granites the alkali-feldspar is a soda-poor microcline or microcline-perthite. In most rhyolites the alkali-feldspar is sanidine, thought to be a high-temperature form, and not infrequently rich in soda.

A great excess of potassium over sodium is uncommon in granite except as a consequence of hydrothermal alteration; it is not uncommon in rhyolites, and though it sometimes seems to be produced in the same way, this is not always the case.

Occurrence.—Rhyolites are known from all parts of the earth and of all geologic ages, though the pre-Tertiary ones are ordinarily so devitrified or otherwise altered as to receive special names, viz., felsite, quartz-keratophyre, quartz-porphyry, etc. Obsidian is well developed in Yellowstone National park, Mont., and Mono craters, Calif. The classic localities for perlite are in Hungary, and pitchstone is perhaps best known from Arran, Scot. Pumice is of world-wide occurrence. Porphyritic rhyolites showing every ratio of phenocrysts to matrix abound in Colorado and Nevada. The pantellerites are spectacularly developed on the island of Pantelleria, southwest of Sicily, but are found throughout the Mediterranean, in East Africa, eastern Siberia, Indonesia and west Texas.

Plagioclase and biotite are rare or lacking as phenocrysts in these rocks and in many of them quartz phenocrysts are not common. Quartz is usually abundant in the groundmass, however, and the silica content is generally appropriate for a granite or quartz syenite. The ferromagnesians are alkali amphiboles and pyroxenes, cossyrite (evidently a titaniferous amphibole) and, occasionally, fayalite.

Fractional Crystallization Hypothesis.—It is known that granites are confined to continental areas and the association can hardly be fortuitous. Rhyolites are for the most part also confined to the continents or their immediate margins, but they are not entirely lacking elsewhere. Small quantities of rhyolite (or quartz trachyte) have been described from the Marquesas Islands, Tonga, Hawaii, Gambier, Samoa Islands, St. Helena and Ascension, all genuine oceanic islands remote from any continental land-mass. There seems no way to explain such occurrences except as residual liquids from the fractional crystallization of basalt, and they are the clearest kind of evidence that granitic magma may indeed form in this fashion. Furthermore, on the continents proper and on continental islands, there is often a close and quite possibly genetic association between basalt, andesite and rhyolite. Sardinia and the Lipari Islands in the Mediterranean offer examples of this association, as do Steens mountain and Newberry volcano in Oregon.

If the ratio of rhyolite to basalt in the oceanic islands is any criterion of the efficiency of the fractionation process, however, the derivation of the known or reasonably inferred volume of granite in the continents by this means would require an immense volume of basaltic magma. Granting that this amount of basalt was available, and that it did indeed fractionate during cooling to yield granite magma, it must yet be explained why rhyolites should be so much less abundant than granites.

The derivation of granitic and rhyolitic magma by fractional crystallization of basalt is the most reasonable working hypothesis available; it is nothing more.

For additional information respecting the special characters and the occurrences and uses of the more important rhyolites *see* OBSIDIAN; PERLITE; PITCHSTONE; PUMICE. More detailed discussion of fractional crystallization will be found in PETROLOGY: *Plutonic Complexes. See also* GEOCHEMISTRY: *Geochemistry of*

the Lithosphere: Crystallization of Magma. (F. Cs.)

RHYS, ERNEST PERCIVAL (1859–1946), English man of letters, who, as editor of Everyman's Library, a series of inexpensive editions of world classics launched in 1906, influenced the literary taste of his own and succeeding generations of readers. He was born on July 17, 1859, in London, and spent his early years in Carmarthen and Newcastle upon Tyne. Ill-health interrupted his education but he showed early promise and an innate love of books. In 1886 he settled in London as a free-lance poet and critic. He contributed to reviews and to the two volumes published by the Rhymers' Club of which he, with W. B. Yeats, was a founder-member, and was employed by various publishers as an editor. In 1891 he married Grace Little (d. 1929), who, herself a writer, encouraged his literary interests; their home in Hampstead became a meeting place for the literary men and women of the time. His association with the publisher J. M. Dent began with his editing a series of lyric poets (1894–99), and in 1904 Dent invited him to edit Everyman's Library (a title suggested by Rhys). The first volume came out in 1906, and by the time Rhys died (on May 25, 1946), of the 1,000 volumes planned, 983 had been published. Rhys's own writings included volumes of essays and poems, one of his best-known poems being "The Leaf Burners," and two volumes of reminiscences, *Everyman Remembers* (1931) and *Wales England Wed* (1940). (E. F. Bo.)

RHYTHM (Greek *rhythmos*, derived from *rhein*, "to flow") is, in its most general sense, an ordered alternation of contrasting elements. The problem of rhythm is by no means specific to music and language: there are the rhythms of nature (*see* RHYTHMS, BIOLOGICAL) and the rhythms of work; and the word is used, in a rather metaphorical sense, of painting, sculpture, and architecture.

Attempts to define rhythm in music and poetry have produced much disagreement, partly because rhythm has often been identified with one or more of its constituent but not wholly separate elements, such as accent, metre, tempo. As in the closely related subjects of verse and metre, opinions differ widely, at least among poets and linguists, on the nature and movement of rhythm. Theories requiring "periodicity" as the *sine qua non* of rhythm are opposed by theories which, with a wider conception of rhythm, include in it even nonrecurrent configurations of movement, as in prose or plainsong. Difficulties also arise from attempts to interpret the rhythms natural to one language in terms of another; *e.g.*, prosodists have tried to relate the rhythmic principles of the Germanic languages (including English) to those of classical Greek and Latin, and of Romance languages. The connection between linguistics and rhythm has not always been fully recognized.

The following analysis principally concerns rhythm in music, although comparative references are made to verse and prose. For a more detailed discussion of the linguistic and literary aspects of English rhythm, *see* METRE and VERSE; for Greek and Latin verse metres, *see* PROSODY, CLASSICAL. For dance rhythms as such, *see* DANCE and related articles.

Importance of Rhythm in Music.—Unlike a painting or a piece of sculpture, which are compositions in space, a musical work is a composition dependent upon time. Rhythm is music's pattern in time. Whatever other elements a given piece of music may or may not have (*e.g.*, patterns in pitch or timbre), rhythm is the one indispensable element of all music. For instance, rhythm can exist without melody, as in the drumbeats of primitive music, but melody cannot exist without rhythm. In music which has both harmony and melody, the rhythmic structure cannot be wholly separated from the harmonic and melodic structures, and each molds the other to an appreciable extent. Plato's observation that rhythm is "an order of movement" (*kinesis taxis*) provides a convenient starting point for an analysis of rhythm. The first task is to discover the various elements of this order.

Beat.—The unit division of musical time is called a beat. Just as we are aware of the body's steady pulse, or heartbeat, so in composing, performing, or listening to music we are instinctively aware of a periodic succession of beats. No matter whether each beat be separately sounded (as in Ex. 1) or not (as in the other examples, we feel its constant underlying presence.

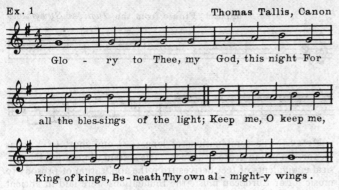

Ex. 1   Thomas Tallis, Canon

Glo - ry to Thee, my God, this night For

all the bles-sings of the light; Keep me, O keep me,

King of kings, Be-neath Thy own al - might-y wings.

For the purpose of fixing music in writing, signs are used to denote beats of varying lengths, as follows:

- o   whole note (semibreve)
- ♩   half note (minim)
- ♩   quarter note (crotchet)
- ♪   eighth note (quaver)
- ♫   sixteenth note (semiquaver)
- ♫   thirty-second note (demisemiquaver)
- ♫   sixty-fourth note (hemidemisemiquaver).

A dot placed after a note increases its length by half. Thus a crotchet equals two quavers, whereas a dotted crotchet (♩.) equals three quavers.

Tempo.—The pace of the fundamental beat is called tempo (Ital., "time"). The expressions "slow tempo" and "quick tempo" suggest the existence of a normal tempo, i.e., a tempo built on a pulse of 60 to 80 beats per minute—a range comparable with that of the heartbeat (72 per min.) or man's natural walking pace (76 to 80 paces per min.). The expression of tempo as a given number of beats to the minute resulted from the work of Johann Maelzel who, in 1816, perfected the metronome (q.v.). A piece of music in which the beat runs at 64 to the minute may thus carry the indication at the opening of the score,(♩.) = 64, together with a less precise but more suggestive verbal indication, such as *andante moderato*. In practice the slow and fast extremes of tempo are built on pulses of 32 and 128 beats to the minute; i.e., half of and double the normal 64. Modern metronomes extend to 208 beats per minute, but such beats are felt to be sub-beats of longer units in a slower tempo. The tempo of a piece of music indicated by a composer is, however, neither absolute nor final. In performance it is likely to vary, according to the performer's interpretative ideas or to such considerations as the size and reverberation of the

Ex. 2

Grazioso   Brahms, *Variations*

hall, the size of the ensemble, and, to a lesser extent, the sonority of the instruments. A change of tempo within such limits does not affect the rhythmic structure of a work.

Rubato.—The tempo of a work is never inflexibly mathematical. It is impossible to adhere in a musical manner to the metronomic beat for any length of time. In a loosely knit passage a tautening of tempo may be required; in a crowded passage a slackening may be needed. Such modifications of tempo, known as *tempo rubato*—i.e., "robbed time"—are part of the music's character. Rubato needs the framework of an inflexible beat from which it can depart and to which it must return. In fact, true rubato never passes the point where the exact basis can no longer be perceived through the inexact. Moreover, it cannot alter the rhythmic organization of the work; it is an essential part of it. Rubato, being essentially a matter of instinct, is rarely written as a direction in musical scores. Chopin, however, uses the term in his Mazurka, Op. 24, No. 2. *Tempo rubato* is illustrated in the above passage from Brahms' *Variations on a Theme of Haydn* (Ex. 2), where a pressing-on in bar four is compensated by a slackening in bar five, before the subject passes to the violins.

Time.—Music is not built on steady, unemphasized beats. The mind seeks some organizing principle, and, if a grouping of sounds is not objectively present, it imposes one of its own. Experiments show that regular and identical sounds are instinctively grouped by the mind into twos and threes, with a stress on every second or third beat. The mind thus creates, from a monotonous series, a regular succession of strong and weak beats.

In music such grouping is achieved by actual stress; i.e., by periodically making one note stronger than the others. When the stress occurs at regular intervals the beats fall into natural time-measures. Though in European music the concept of time-measures reaches back to a remote age, only since the 15th century have they been indicated by means of bar-lines.

The length of each beat in a bar may be a time-unit of short or long duration. The time-measure is indicated at the opening of a piece by a time signature; e.g., $\frac{2}{4}$, $\frac{4}{8}$, $\frac{3}{4}$, $\frac{6}{8}$. The lower numeral (always a multiple of 2) indicates the time-unit of the beat. The principle of time signature is illustrated in the following:

$\frac{4}{1}$ o   o   o   o

$\frac{4}{2}$ ♩   ♩   ♩   ♩

$\frac{4}{4}$ ♩   ♩   ♩   ♩

$\frac{4}{8}$ ♪   ♪   ♪   ♪

The two basic types of time-measure are notated by bars of two or of three beats:

$\frac{2}{4}$ ♩ ♩ : "two time" (cf. $\frac{2}{2}$ or ¢ ; see Ex. 4)

$\frac{3}{4}$ ♩ ♩ ♩ : "three time" (cf. $\frac{3}{2}$, $\frac{3}{8}$; see Ex. 3)

"Four time," or "common time," is really a species of duple time allied to "two time," as it can hardly be thought of without a subsidiary stress at the half-bar, i.e., on the third beat, thus:

$\frac{4}{4}$ ♩ ♩ ♩ ♩ : "four time" (cf. $\frac{4}{2}$; see Ex. 1)

Duple, triple, and quadruple time-measures, i.e., those in which there are two and three beats to a bar, are known as simple time. The division of each of the component beats into three produces compound time:

$\frac{6}{4}$ ♩♩♩♩♩♩ : compound duple

$\frac{9}{4}$ 𝄽 : compound triple

$\frac{12}{4}$ 𝄽 : compound quadruple

More complex times, such as the quintuple, $\frac{5}{4}$, usually fall into groups of $3 + 2$, as in "Mars" from Gustav Holst's suite *The Planets*, and the second movement of Tchaikovsky's Sixth Symphony. Rimski-Korsakov, in *Sadko*, and Stravinsky, in *Le Sacre du Printemps*, use 11 as a unit. Ravel's piano trio opens with a signature of $\frac{8}{8}$ with the internal organization $\frac{3+2+3}{8}$. Folk song and folk dance, particularly from eastern Europe, influenced composers in the use of asymmetrical time-measures, as in the "Bulgarian Rhythm" pieces in $\frac{7}{8}$ and $\frac{5}{8}$ in Bartok's *Mikrokosmos*.

Period.—The time-measures, or bars, of music are part of a larger design known as a "period." The period most commonly found in classical music is of four bars, as in Mozart's *Jupiter* Symphony. (*See* Ex. 4 below.) Periods of three or six bars, though found in the songs of the troubadours and trouvères, are less frequent in later European music. Five-bar periods are still rarer, though Brahms uses a five-bar theme (*see* Ex. 2) and certain of Henry Purcell's grounds, *e.g.*, the Chaconne in G Minor, are based on a five-bar period. Some 20th-century composers use a recurrent cycle of bars of different time-signatures.

Influence of Body Movements.—The instinct for stress accent in music is closely associated with the exertions of the body; thus for example, the rhythms of music have been much influenced (through folk music) by occupational movements such as hauling on a rope or rocking a cradle, which are reflected as strong stress accents (*see also* FOLK MUSIC: *Melodic and Rhythmic Patterns of Folk Songs*). In music as an art the influence of the dance has been paramount, and for this reason the types of musical instrument traditionally associated with the dance, *i.e.*, the drum and other percussion instruments (*q.v.*), have had an important place in music in most parts of the world. In Europe the cultivation of musical dance-forms during the Renaissance has left an important heritage, from the keyboard music of the 16th century to the suites of J. S. Bach. (*See* DANCE FORMS IN MUSIC.) Perhaps the most popular and influential dance of all has been the minuet, which originated as a French rustic dance; numerous examples are to be found in classical music. In Ex. 3, from the first minuet of Bach's orchestral Suite No. 1, the stresses are very clear.

Accent by Note-Values.—Just as the pulse of music can be periodically accented by stress ("qualitative accent"), so can it be accented by duration of the notes actually sounded ("quantitative accent"). The range of note-values in common use has been indicated above in the section *Beat*. Several or all of these values may be found in a single piece, as in Ex. 4, the first eight bars of the finale of Mozart's *Jupiter* Symphony.

Influence of Language.—The arts of language, especially poetry, have always had an important part, through vocal music, in determining note-values. In language the units of duration are the long and short vowels, whose quantities are taken to be: one long = two shorts. Consequently their musical equivalents are: long = ♩ and short = ♪ (or respectively ♩ and ♩, or any other similar relationship of note-values).

Ex. 3   J. S. Bach, Minuet 1, from Orchestral Suite No. 1

Ex. 4   Mozart, Finale from the *Jupiter Symphony*

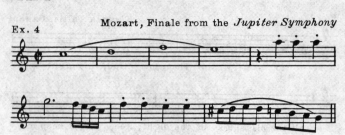

Metre.—The combinations of long ($-$) and short ($\cup$) syllables are known in prosody as feet. The system of notating the musical equivalents of feet derives from the application of prosody to music. For European music the foundations were laid in ancient Greece, where classical music and poetry were regarded as parts of a single art (*see* GREEK MUSIC [ANCIENT]). These principles were taken over by the Romans and were transmitted, by way of Latin poetry, to medieval Europe. The feet of classical poetry, and their equivalents in music, include:

	Poetry		Music	Groups of beats	Equivalent time-measures
duple	dactyl	$-\cup\cup$	♩ ♫	$2 + 2$	$\frac{2}{4}$
	anapest	$\cup\cup-$	♫ ♩	$2 + 2$	$\frac{2}{4}$
triple	trochee	$-\cup$	♩ ♪	$2 + 1$	$\frac{3}{8}$
	iamb	$\cup-$	♪ ♩	$1 + 2$	$\frac{3}{8}$
quintuple	cretic	$-\cup-$	♩ ♪ ♩	$3 + 2$	$\frac{5}{8}$

and in late antiquity St. Augustine (354–430), in *De Musica*, added more.

Until the 12th century church music was virtually limited to unadorned plainsong (*q.v.*). The early polyphonic composers found that polyphony required a rhythmical organization to keep the parts together, and for this purpose rhythmic modes (*q.v.*) were adopted. These were classified as follows:

I	$-\cup$	(trochee)	♩ ♪	
II	$\cup-$	(iamb)	♪ ♩	
III	$-\cup\cup$	(dactyl)	♩. ♪ ♩	
IV	$\cup\cup-$	(anapest)	♪ ♩ ♩.	
V	$--$	(spondee)	♩. ♩.	
VI	$\cup\cup\cup$	(tribrach)	♫♫ ♫♫	

These metres were all considered to be in triple time, though No. IV is rarely found in music, and No. V and VI, having no differentiation in note-values, are not metres at all in a musical sense (but *see* METRE). Duple metres were also in use, as in two 13th-century French motets from the Montpellier Codex, where the notation indicates a note-grouping corresponding to the dactyl in duple time, *i.e.*, $-\cup\cup$ interpreted as ♩♫.

Compared with a hypothetical flow of beats equal in stress, metre adds significance to what was merely a forward flow in time—though the continuation of a metrical pattern may itself become monotonous. Thus metre, though "rhythmic" by comparison with pulse, is not the whole of rhythm.

The 13th-century musicians often varied the rhythmic modes by combining several of them simultaneously in different parts of polyphonic composition.

Theoretically, metre appears to be without stress accent, and certainly much polyphonic music of a later period, such as the Masses of Palestrina, has an almost stressless flow. Yet despite the absence of strong and weak accents the rhythmical organization of these works is very subtle. At a later period metre and time-measure cannot be wholly separated. In their "purest" forms they may be extremes, but in music predominantly of one type, the other element is rarely wholly absent, though on an instrument such as the organ actual dynamic stress is impossible. After all, metres like the spondee ♩♩, and the dispondee, ♩♩♩♩, need an accent on the first beat to keep their identity. Notwithstanding the opposite tendencies of metrical organization and stress accent, however, some metre is very obviously subject to stress, so that metre and time-measure become very closely linked, as in the scherzo of Beethoven's Ninth Symphony, where a bar has a strong first beat, while at the same time following a metre.

The organizing influence of language has sometimes led to combinations of different metres in the same melodic line; e.g., the duet "Fear no danger to ensue," from Purcell's *Dido and Aeneas*, combines in alternation iamb and trochee (Ex. 5).

Purcell, Duet from *Dido and Aeneas*

Ex. 5

Fear no dan-ger to en-sue, the

He-ro loves as well as you.

Phrase.—Tempo, time-measure, and metre may be regarded as the essential means of assessing music's flow in time. These form, so to say, the straight line of time. But rhythm needs also the "curves" of time. Curves are achieved not only by the use of rubato, cross-accent, and other means, but also by the use of the phrase. Phrases may coincide with periods, but more often go across them, to create an organic structure. The first eight-bar period (or first two four-bar periods) of the first stanza of the song quoted in Ex. 5, for instance, comprises 24 beats divided into a group of 11 beats followed by a group of 13 beats. These groups are called phrases, and the second phrase is further subdivided into 6 and 7 beats. Though the ultimate groupings of the melody refer to the mathematical framework of periods, they do not exactly correspond with these. In the example this is because of the need to convey the shape and sense of the words; for one feature of phrase is really the observance of "breath," whether this breath be actually taken or not. In vocal music, this often means shortening the last word—and therefore the last note—of a phrase, and taking an actual breath, as at a comma or semicolon in speech. But asymmetrical phrases are not confined to vocal music, and instrumental music often displays much ingenuity in the asymmetrical use of phrase. Phrasing, however, may be entirely symmetrical, and sometimes, especially in very simple music such as a hymn tune or a folk dance, it may correspond exactly to the framework of the period.

In broad terms, the mathematical framework of music, i.e., its time, is comprised of tempo, time-measure, metre, and period; and its rhythmical life hangs on rubato, musical motif (which may already include cross-accent), and metrical variation, as well as on asymmetry and balance of phrase. Whereas the former are more or less mechanical factors, measured and rational, the latter are organically inspired and, numerically speaking, irrational—the very life of the music itself.

Prose Rhythms and Plainsong.—Rhythm is, therefore, not any one of these rational or formal features, nor is it comprised solely of a combination of these factors. Yet rhythm requires the background of a rational framework in order that it may be

fully perceived. But this framework need not embrace all the rational factors described above. Thus plainsong, as it is known in modern times, makes no use at all of measure or of regular metre, yet it is, at the same time, supremely rhythmical in conception; its "free" rhythms are felt, as it were, not as rhythms of the body but of the soul. Whereas so much music has for its framework a regular repetition of underlying accent, whether stress or durational, the framework of plainsong is irregular (nonmetrical). While omitting metre, it has developed other factors in greater degree. Its rhythm belongs to the Latin tongue and springs from the correct accentuation of each word in the Latin text and the dynamic quality already inherent in the grouping of the words. The opening phrase of the tonus simplex for the *Te Deum* (Ex. 6) illustrates these qualities.

Ex. 6

Plainsong: Tonus simplex for the Te Deum

Te Dé - um lau - dá - mus

te Dó - mi - num con - fi - té - mur.

Relationship of Rhythm and Melody.—Although, so far, music's structure in time has been examined separately from its structure in tone, no such separation is really possible. Melody and rhythm are intimately connected in the rhythmitonal structure of music. In Ex. 1, for instance, in which the music pursues a steady equal beat varied only by rubato and by the natural phrases and breaths arising from the words, it will be noticed that, whereas the melody usually moves from note to note conjunctly, the first note of each phrase takes an appreciable leap away from the last note of the previous phrase. This feature is so marked that it becomes a rhythmical factor, because of its periodic and time-organizing impression on consciousness. It is, in fact, accent by tone (or "tonal accent")—the equivalent of the "tonic accent" (i.e., the principal stress in each word) in poetry. Moreover, various styles of music tend to standardize their melodic cadences, and, with them, their time-divisions. Thus, a typical cadence of plainsong prolongs the value of the penultimate note (as in Ex. 6).

Relationship of Rhythm and Harmony.—In music employing harmony the rhythmic structure is inseparable from harmonic considerations. The time-pattern controlling the change of harmonies is called harmonic rhythm. In 17th- and 18th-century music harmony tends to limit rhythmic subtleties and flexibility of the melodic elements (as well as determining the basic type of melody), at least in regard to stress accents. It is, therefore, no accident that the polyphonic music of Indonesia and southeast Asia, like much European music, exhibits certain four-square melodic tendencies. By contrast, the music of India and the Perso-Arab world employs a melody-instrument or voice performing in a given metre which a drum offsets by playing cross-rhythms, or (in the Arab world) by playing a quite different metre; and with no harmony (a drone excepted) to impede its flow, the rhythm can reach great subtlety and complexity.

Rhythmitonal Structure and Style.—In European music the great variety of styles derives from different concepts of rhythm in its relation to melody. They include the strict rhythmic modes of the 13th century; the free oratorical speech-rhythms of the Renaissance; the almost stressless flow of Renaissance polyphony; the strong body rhythms of the Baroque Period; the rhapsodic freedom of the late Romantics; and the primitivistic rhythms of 20th-century composers, with their composite and everchanging time-signatures.

Thus, study of musical history shows a varying attitude to rhythm, sometimes closer to strict rule, sometimes to "freedom," as the temper of the times and the relative influence of poetry, dance, and folk music decree. Plato's definition as "an order of movement" might, therefore, be expanded. As a determining factor in the vitality of music, rhythm may be described as "an inspired, organic order of movement," communicating intelligibly to the senses. From the analytical viewpoint, it operates in the rational framework described, which it varies in terms of rubato, motif, and phrase. Ultimately, rhythm is the organic process of music in time; it is music's direction in time. The quality of rhythm is the quality of life, and however vitally the composer may conceive his music, he is ultimately dependent upon the performer to re-create it rhythmically (*see* EXPRESSION, MUSICAL).

See also references under "Rhythm" in the Index.

BIBLIOGRAPHY.—G. W. Cooper and L. B. Meyer, *The Rhythmic Structure of Music* (1960); E. Fogerty, *Rhythm* (1937); M. H. Glyn, *The Rhythmic Conception of Music* (1907); W. F. Jackson Knight, *St. Augustine's De Musica: a Synopsis* (1949); E. Jaques-Dalcroze, *Rhythm, Music and Education* (1921); Mathis Lussy, *A Short Treatise on Musical Rhythm,* Eng. trans. by E. Fowles (1909), and *Musical Expression,* Eng. trans. of 4th ed. by M. E. von Glehn (1885); Curt Sachs, *Rhythm and Tempo* (1953); E. Sievers, *Rhythmisch-melodische Studien* (1912); W. Thomson, *The Rhythm of Speech* (1923); C. F. Abdy Williams, *The Rhythm of Modern Music* (1909), *The Rhythm of Song* (1925), and *The Aristoxenian Theory of Musical Rhythm* (1911).   (P. C.-Ho.)

RHYTHMS, BIOLOGICAL, deep-seated rhythmic patterns of activity, exhibited by living things widely, and perhaps universally, the cycles of which are related to all the major natural geophysical periods. These rhythms, which appear to persist indefinitely—even in organisms shielded from fluctuations in all ordinary environmental factors such as light, temperature, humidity, pressure, and chemical changes—are considered to be a result of the continuous operation of a "biological clock" system.

PERIODS OF CYCLES

Daily Rhythms.—The activities of many animals and plants take place during periods of natural light, which follow a solar-day rhythm. Animals such as mice, cockroaches, and moths are active chiefly during the night; most songbirds and butterflies are active only during daylight hours. Many plants, including bean seedlings, show a daily sleep rhythm, their leaves drooping at night and becoming elevated by day; other plants display a comparable rhythmic closing of their blossoms at night. Man himself has a daily rhythm of sleep and wakefulness. All such daily changes as these simply reflect, and depend upon, innumerable interrelated supporting physical and chemical transformations within the individual organism. In the case of man, as an example, the daily alternation of sleep and wakefulness is accompanied by many substantial correlated changes, including activities of nervous and endocrine systems, and liver and kidneys. Daily variations occur in body temperature, and in pressure and composition of the blood. Such rhythmically recurring phenomena are each set to occur at the most effective time of day for the organism. Hence, concurrent 24-hour rhythmic fluctuations, set to various times of day, have been reported for numerous kinds of physiological changes in one and the same organism.

Another major environmental period involves the regular ebb and flow of the ocean tides, a cycle that subjects seashore plants and animals to a rhythmic change with typically two high and two low tides, occurring each lunar day of about 24 hours and 50 minutes duration. The ocean tides are effected chiefly by the gravitational rhythm caused by the earth's rotation relative to the moon. Some intertidal organisms such as barnacles, snails, clams, and oysters are most active when submerged by the rising tide. Others, like shorebirds and fiddler crabs, are specially adapted to feed on beaches exposed at ebb tide. Like solar-day rhythmic changes, these lunar tidal activity patterns are dependent upon numerous underlying and supporting physiological changes.

Although the ocean tides are effected chiefly by the moon, the gravitational attraction of the sun also has an influence. The sun and moon "cooperate" at new and full moons to produce the highest tides of each month, the so-called spring tides. At the moon's quarters the moon and the sun maximally oppose one another to produce the lowest high tides, or neap tides.

An interesting expression of solar and lunar rhythmicities in such animals as birds, insects, fishes, turtles, and crustaceans is evident in their sun-compass or moon-compass navigation. These animals can use the azimuthal angle of the sun or moon as a directional guide. This requires that the animals rhythmically alter their orientational angle at rates adjusted to compensate exactly for the earth's rotation relative to the sun and the moon.

An additional daily period suggested to occur in a living system is the sidereal day, of about 23 hours, 56 minutes. This is the period of the earth's rotation using stars as the reference. An explanation of bird navigation employing the stars as a compass requires that the angle of orientation of the bird gradually change with a sidereal-day period. Metabolic rate of potato plants is reported to have a sidereal-day rhythm, along with the other rhythms.

Monthly Rhythms.—The period from one new moon to the next, the synodic month, averaging 29.5 days, is the consequence of "beats" produced by periodic interference between the two closely similar rhythmic periods, the solar day and the lunar day. Among the biological activities linked to the synodic month are the reproductive cycles of some marine animals and certain plants and the human menstrual cycle. Monthly reproductive rhythms occur in the palolo worms of the Southwest Pacific, the fireworms of Bermuda, the grunion of the California coast, and a brown alga, *Dictyota.* These breeding rhythms are sufficiently precise in their relation to moon phase to enable one to predict quite accurately the times of the reproductive activity. The changing relations of the solar-day and lunar-day physical rhythms appear to time these breeding cycles, since the phase of the moon at which, for example, *Dictyota* breeds is related to the times of occurrence within the lunar day of the local high tides. The times, of course, differ from place to place.

Although little is known about the timing of the human menstrual cycle or the approximately semimonthly estrus cycles of such animals as sheep and pigs, two fundamentally different hypotheses have been offered for the timing of these cycles. One is that they are timed by fully independent periodic oscillations; the other is that the cycles are dependent for their timing on periodic interference between 24-hour and circalunadian (about a lunar day) cycles.

Yearly Rhythms.—Another major rhythmic period for living things is the year. In most parts of the world substantial seasonal changes in light and temperature are correlated with rhythmic biological phenomena predominantly related to activity, reproduction, and growth. For example, in higher plants in the northern hemisphere, growth, flowering, and seed production typically occur during the warmer months. In the oceans there are conspicuous rhythms in abundance of planktonic organisms. Also evident among many animals are annual reproductive rhythms, correlated with physiological, morphological, and behavioural changes, and extensive migrations to and from breeding grounds.

Longer Cycles.—Cycles of abundance in a variety of species in nature with periods of several years have been described. These include three- to four-year cycles of abundance of lemmings and the approximately ten-year cycles of Canadian lynx, varying hare, and ruffed grouse.

ADAPTED FROM W. ZIMMERMANN IN "TÜBINGEN NATURWISSENSCHAFTLICHE ABHANDLUNGEN"

FIG. 1.—BEAN SEEDLING LEAVES IN (LEFT) DAY AND (RIGHT) NIGHT POSITIONS, ILLUSTRATING A LIGHT-INFLUENCED CIRCADIAN RHYTHM

Cyclic changes in growth rate, displaying several period lengths of a number of years each, have been noted from studies on tree rings. These long-period cyclic variations are still controversial as to their genuinely rhythmic character and their exact period lengths.

PERSISTENCE OF CYCLES

Endogenous Rhythms.—The French astronomer J. J. D. de Mairan (1729), who observed plant sleep rhythms, was the first to report that these rhythms were somehow independent of the daily changes in environmental light. This persistence of the leaf rhythm in unvarying light and temperature was studied extensively about the turn of the century by Wilhelm Pfeffer. Since Pfeffer's time, numerous investigators have discovered comparable persistence of daily rhythmic patterns in a wide variety of animals and plants, establishing the concept of endogenous, or inherent, rhythms.

Likewise, other investigators, studying marine intertidal organisms, noted that such organisms continue to exhibit tidal rhythms when moved to the laboratory, far from immediate tidal changes. Such persistence of lunar-tidal

BY COURTESY OF FRANK A. BROWN, JR.

FIG. 2.—FIDDLER CRABS IN NIGHT (PALE) AND DAY (DARK) STATES

The colour change rhythm of one of the crabs has been reset 12 hours by a few days of inverted light cycles

rhythms in marine organisms has since been confirmed for a wide variety of species ranging from diatoms and protozoans to fishes. The most extensive studies have concerned the rhythms of activity and feeding of bivalve mollusks and crabs.

Annual rhythms have been demonstrated to occur in the absence of all known environmental cues. Seeds display an annual rhythm in their rate of germination under carefully controlled constancy of all factors known to influence them. Potato plants, carrot slices, and freshly germinated bean seedlings hermetically sealed under conditions of constant light, temperature, humidity, and pressure have a higher metabolic rate in spring and early summer than in fall.

Clearly, living organisms even when fully shielded from all natural rhythmic forces to which they are known to react still have "biological clocks" for maintaining rhythmic changes closely similar in their period lengths to the natural environmental cycles.

The timing mechanism for these "clocks" possesses some extraordinary properties. The period lengths of the persisting daily cycles are influenced relatively little by temperature changes that accelerate or depress greatly the rate of all ordinary metabolic processes within the body, or by most chemical substances. The persistent solar-day rhythm of colour change in fiddler crabs shows no change in its cycle length over a temperature range of about 20° C; the period of the lunar-tidal rhythm in activity is also unaffected by temperature. Dried seeds display an accurate annual rhythm in germination whether stored at −22° C or +45° C.

Resetting of Rhythmic Events.—Such daily rhythmic events as running activity in mice or cockroaches, skin darkening in fiddler crabs, bioluminescence in dinoflagellates, and sleep or wakefulness in man are adaptively set to occur at particular clock hours of the day. When man or other organisms are transported rapidly to a different time belt of the earth, they arrive with their rhythmic changes still set to the time of their former abode. But subjection for a few days to the physical cycles of the new time belt results in gradual resetting of the biological rhythms until they come to bear a relation to the new local time fully comparable to that of their former location. That the local light and temperature changes normally play important roles in this resetting activity is evident from the fact that without any geographical displacement whatsoever, one can reset such organismic daily rhythms to accord with light cycles of any given time belt simply

by experimentally subjecting the organism to a few 24-hour cycles of light or temperature changes as they would occur in any particular time belt.

Similarly, the lunar-tidal rhythmic events of such creatures as mussels, oysters, and crabs normally correspond with the times of the tidal changes on a particular beach. Mussels transported to another beach gradually alter their time of activity over the course of a few days to accord with the new tidal schedule. Oysters and crabs removed from their beaches to tideless laboratory containers gradually reset the time of their activities to synchronize with upper and lower transits of the moon; i.e., with the times of high lunar tides of the atmosphere. The normal setting factors for the tidal rhythms are not known.

Components of Rhythms.—The daily rhythmic changes of organisms possess two kinds of components: phase-labile and phase-stable. One of these, the phase-labile, like the majority of the examples described earlier, is capable of having the pattern of events in each cycle shifted or reset by artificial light or temperature cycles to any desired relationship to the clock hours of the day. The phase-stable rhythms are of extrinsic origin, a consequence of continuous biological response to fluctuations in subtle geophysical forces. Evidence for such origin comes from continuing correlation between day-to-day irregularities and distortions in these daily variations and the concurrent, unpredictable irregularities in the daily tides of the atmosphere, measurable as barometric pressure changes, or other rhythmic physical forces such as atmospheric temperature and high-energy radiation. Pressure and temperature are not themselves the direct agents of daily rhythms, since, as mentioned earlier, these correlations persist in organisms completely shielded from variations in the environment.

Along with the phase-labile, adaptive tidal rhythms of behaviour of marine organisms, there are also phase-stable lunar-day fluctuations of extrinsic origin. Evidence for their extrinsic nature is of two kinds. One is the strikingly parallel patterns of the lunar-day fluctuation in organisms as diverse as potatoes, seaweed, carrots, earthworms, salamanders, and mice. The other is the tendency, mentioned earlier, of oysters and crabs taken from their beaches to assume a new common setting related to the lunar atmospheric tides.

An annual organismic rhythm that persists in constant light, temperature, and pressure seems also of extrinsic origin. The day-to-day organismic correlations with solar tides of the atmosphere continue through the year, reflecting the annual variation in these tides. Such extrinsically derived annual variations are distinguished from such phase-labile annual biological rhythms as that of flowering of plants and of bird migration and reproduction, whose times of occurrence in the year may be reset to an earlier or later time by subjection to experimentally lengthened or shortened light periods. Such response to photoperiodism (q.v.) appears to play a "setting" role for phase-labile annual rhythms comparable to that of light onset and termination for phase-labile daily cycles. It appears probable that the daily rhythm normally serves the organism as the reference to enable it to measure accurately the lengths of the light and dark periods.

The rhythmic geophysical forces responsible for extrinsic biological rhythmicity have not been identified. Recent demonstrations of extraordinary organismic sensitivities to very weak magnetic, electrostatic, and electromagnetic, including gamma-ray, fields have provided theoretically possible means of regulating certain cycles.

Rhythms in Unvarying Light and Temperature.—Both the phase-stable and phase-labile daily rhythmic changes continue with an accurate aver-

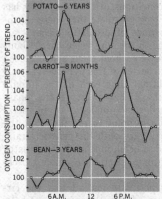

FIG. 3.—MEAN DAILY FLUCTUATION OF METABOLIC RATE OF POTATOES, CARROTS, AND BEAN SEEDS HELD IN CONSTANT LIGHT AND TEMPERATURE

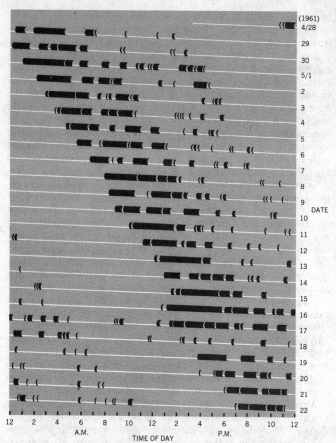

FIG. 4.—TYPICAL CIRCADIAN RHYTHM OF A HAMSTER, SHOWING SPONTANE-
OUS DAILY ACTIVITY PATTERNS

age 24-hour period as long as the organism is exposed to natural day-night changes at the same longitude. When, however, organisms are held in artificially maintained constant levels of illumination and temperature, the phase-labile rhythmic complex very commonly drifts steadily toward earlier or later hours of the day.

Consequently, rhythmic periods either shorter or longer than 24 hours are observable. The length of these latter cycles may usually be increased or decreased by changing the level of the constant illumination or temperature. These rhythms that deviate slightly from a 24-hour period have been termed circadian (about a day). Their period seldom exceeds 20 to 28 hours. The extrinsic component always retains an accurate average 24-hour period under these conditions of unvarying light and temperature.

THEORIES REGARDING RHYTHMS

Natural Oscillation.—The origin of the odd-lengthed periods observed in the controlled conditions of the laboratory has long been a controversial issue. Some postulate that these rhythmic fluctuations reflect natural periods of oscillation, characteristic of each organism, which come to the fore when the 24-hour cycles of light and temperature cease to hold them synchronized with the local day-night cycle. Advocates of this hypothesis argue that external physical cycles could not time each of the infinite variety of observed period lengths. They point to the phase lability, and a commonly observed small influence of temperature level on cycle length. They also point to the fact that the length of the circadian periods may vary with the genetic strain. In brief, the organism is postulated to be an independent oscillator whose periods have evolved by natural selection to match closely the period of the solar day.

Extrinsic Influence.—Others postulate instead that the circadian rhythms are continuously derived from the extrinsic 24-hour variations which thus serve as a temporal frame of reference. The organism is presumed to be a variable frequency transformer, depending upon the steady 24-hour rhythmic input to derive the

circadian periods through operation of the same rhythm-resetting machinery that normally adjusts the phase-labile daily patterns to a different time belt. Organisms normally employ phase-labile daily rhythms of sensitivity to light and temperature in resetting their rhythmic patterns. During a sensitive part of each daily cycle increased light or temperature will reset the cycle either backward or forward; for the remainder of the cycle relative insensitivity prevails. Under natural conditions the sensitive period becomes and remains set to fall at night.

In unchanging light and temperature the organisms' daily rhythm of sensitivity is postulated to present an illusion that the environmental light and temperature are varying, with times of day of the "illusory light changes" resembling the natural experience of organisms abruptly displaced halfway around the earth. This would be expected to activate resetting of the phase-labile sensitivity rhythm and all other associated phase-labile rhythms. Such daily resetting, termed autophasing, would be expected to continue indefinitely generating a circadian period slightly longer or shorter than 24 hours, depending on the direction of resetting. With this hypothesis the small influences of temperature and light levels and of genetic constitution on cycle length are readily interpreted, and the extraordinary drug and temperature independence of the rhythm period finds a simple, plausible explanation. This postulated dependence of the circadian rhythms upon extrinsic timing brings them into a common general explanation along with persistent lunar-day, monthly, and annual rhythms.

It has not yet been possible to design a crucial experiment to learn which of the two foregoing hypotheses of persistent rhythms is the correct one. It is possible that both kinds of mechanisms exist simultaneously in organisms.

BIBLIOGRAPHY.—"Biological Clocks," *Sympos. Quant. Biol.*, vol. 25 (1960); F. A. Brown, Jr., *Biological Clocks* (1962); E. Bünning, *The Physiological Clock* (1964); J. L. Cloudsley-Thompson, *Rhythmic Activity in Animal Physiology and Behaviour* (1961); J. E. Harker, *The Physiology of Diurnal Rhythms* (1964); Lloyd B. Keith, *Wildlife's Ten-Year Cycle* (1963); C. S. Pittendrigh and V. G. Bruce, "An Oscillator Model for Biological Clocks," *Rhythmic and Synthetic Processes in Growth*, ed. by D. Rudnick, pp. 75–109 (1957); "Rhythmic Functions in the Living System," *Ann. N.Y. Acad. Sci.*, vol. 98, pp. 753–1326 (1962); H. M. Webb and F. A. Brown, Jr., "Timing Long-Cycle Physiological Rhythms," *Physiol. Rev.*, vol. 39, pp. 127–161 (1959).
(F. A. Bn.)

RIBATEJO, a province of central Portugal, lying astride the Tagus Valley. It was formed in 1933 and is bounded west by Estremadura and east by Beira Baixa and Alto Alentejo. Area 2,807 sq.mi. (7,270 sq.km.). Pop. (1960) 478,261. There are three marked relief zones. In the west the detrital hills border the Upper Jurassic and Tertiary massifs from Alcanena (and Alenquer in Estremadura) to Vila Nova da Rainha. East of this zone and north of the Tagus are extensive rolling plateaus, less developed south of the Tagus except to the east and northeast of the Sierra de Almeirim. The third zone includes the three Quaternary terraces and the alluvial plain of the Tagus, forming a broad lowland, especially south of the river. The northern border of Ribatejo coincides neatly with the edge of the Tertiary depression and the Mesozoic limestone hills of Estremadura. To the south, the region merges almost imperceptibly into Alentejo.

On the north side of the Tagus, land use is diverse. Vineyards, olives, and cereals are found on the hill lands, and many districts (*e.g.*, Cartaxo and Torres) are famous for their wine. Along the Tagus Valley, maize (corn) and vines on the light soils, rice and wheat on the heavy lands, and wet meadows for the rearing of bulls and horses, provide a variety of intensive agriculture. South of the Tagus the landscape is less tamed; much is still unproductive or in extensive estates of cork forest. This contrast explains the density of population: 75 per sq.mi. on the north side, under 25 per sq.mi. on the south.

Along the Tagus are the chief towns: Santarém (17,276), the capital; Almeirim (8,815); and Vila Franca de Xira (14,633). An important centre in the north is the historic town of Tomar (15,118). (J. M. Ho.)

RIBBENTROP, JOACHIM VON (1893–1946), German statesman, minister for foreign affairs (1938–45) in the Nazi government, was born at Wesel on April 30, 1893, the son of an army officer. Educated at Kassel and Metz, then in Grenoble and in London, he went to Canada in 1910 as a commercial representative. Returning to Germany in 1914 he served in World War I in a Hussar regiment on the eastern front but in 1915 was attached to the German Military Mission in Turkey.

After the war he entered the wine trade and married Anna Elisabeth, the daughter of a manufacturer of sparkling wine, Otto Henkell. Having been adopted by a distant relative whose father had been knighted in 1884, he styled himself "von Ribbentrop."

On Aug. 13, 1932, at Berchtesgaden, he met Hitler for the first time and joined the National Socialist Party in the same year. As German chancellor, Hitler made Ribbentrop his chief adviser on foreign affairs and put him in charge of the so-called *Dienstelle Ribbentrop*, housed in the Wilhelmstrasse opposite the Foreign Office, to which it became a rival and duplicate organization. Having been appointed special commissioner for disarmament in 1934, Ribbentrop toured foreign capitals to prepare the way for German rearmament. As ambassador-at-large he negotiated the Anglo-German Naval Agreement of June 18, 1935. In August 1936 he was appointed ambassador to Great Britain. He had hoped to use his tenure of the embassy to develop a close Anglo-German understanding, along the lines envisaged by Hitler in *Mein Kampf;* but he failed to do so and found himself treated as a tactless parvenu. His attitude toward Britain changed as a result, and when, on Feb. 4, 1938, Hitler appointed him his minister for foreign affairs he was a convinced Anglophobe. Although he thought conflict with Britain to be inevitable in the long run, he assured his master in 1939 that he need not fear any effective British support for Poland.

He signed in Moscow the German-Soviet nonaggression agreement of Aug. 23, 1939, which contained a secret annex describing how Poland would eventually be partitioned, and he returned there to sign a second German-Soviet treaty (Sept. 28, 1939) readjusting that partition. Thereafter his importance declined.

Ribbentrop was a vain man, impressed with his own importance, always subservient to Hitler. Although he was responsible for many important acts of German foreign policy, he did not make policy, was lacking in judgment, and showed no skill as a negotiator. He made himself neither respected nor feared and survived only through the support of Hitler. He was further discredited by the complicity of some of the Foreign Office staff in the assassination plot of July 20, 1944. In April 1945 he disappeared from Berlin but on June 14 was found and arrested by the British in Hamburg. Indicted as a war criminal at the Nürnberg war crimes trial he was found guilty on four principal counts and sentenced to death. He was hanged at Nürnberg Prison on Oct. 16, 1946.

In prison he wrote his memoirs entitled *Zwischen London und Moskau,* published by his widow in 1953 (English translation, *The Ribbentrop Memoirs,* 1954).

See P. Schwarz, *This Man Ribbentrop: His Life and Times* (1943).
(W. Kp.)

RIBBLE, a river in Yorkshire and Lancashire, Eng., is formed by the confluence of the Gayle and Cam becks, which rise in limestone country on Langstrothdale Chase at heights of 1,650 and 1,850 ft. (503 and 564 m.). The river first flows almost due south between Ingleborough (2,373 ft. [723 m.]) and Pen-y-ghent (2,273 ft. [693 m.]) and, after passing the villages of Horton-in-Ribblesdale and Stainforth, reaches Settle, a local centre with a 700-year-old market charter and Giggleswick School (founded 1512) ¾ mi. away. The Ribble then passes into open country and traverses the bed of a postglacial lake, originally 4 mi. (6 km.) in length, but now drained. The preglacial course of the river is believed to have been southeastward to the River Aire, but an extensive spread of morainic material and drumlins, left by the glaciations, blocked this route, and the river now turns southwestward through an attractive 8-mile gorge at the end of which, near Bolton-by-Bowland, it meets Tosside Beck, which may have been the original main river. From this point to Preston it flows in a wide valley, mostly devoted to pastoral farming but with numerous scattered trees, passing Clitheroe, Whalley, and Ribchester. Near Whalley it is joined by its two main tributaries, the Hodder, draining much of the Bowland Forest from the north, and the Calder, which switches from the Burnley Valley to the Ribble

by a deep cut through the Pendle ridge. Thus augmented, the Ribble meanders between bluff lines, which rise 150 ft. (46 m.) high, a mile apart, on either side of the floodplain. They are largely composed of boulder clay. Preston (*q.v.*) lies on the northern side of the river at its lowest bridge point, where the Lancashire Plain is narrowed to a few miles by a westerly bulge of the Pennines and an easterly incursion of the Irish Sea, the Ribble Estuary. From Preston to the general line of the coast between Southport and Blackpool (*qq.v.*) is 12 mi. (19 km.), and most of this is infilled by extensive sandbanks and mud flats, many of which have been reclaimed by embanking for agricultural land. The shipping channel to the port of Preston makes its way through these banks and is the artificially straightened main channel of the Ribble. Its depth is maintained by dredging where necessary.
(R. K. Gr.)

RIBBON, a narrow woven fabric of varying widths made from rayon, acetate, silk, nylon, etc. It is used for trimming, military decorations, packaging, typewriter ribbon, and adornment. Some acetate and nylon ribbon has a seared rather than a woven edge.

Both single- and double-faced satin weaves are used for ribbon, the latter being lustrous on both sides. Faille, taffeta, and moire also are popular ribbon weaves. Lingerie ribbon, of which there are several types, is soft, smooth, and supported by strong, compact selvages that make it ideal for women's and children's undergarments. Grosgrain ribbon, especially popular for millinery, has a silk, acetate, or nylon warp and a cotton weft. Because of the rib construction the weft is not visible.

Typewriter ribbon is a plain weave of cotton or nylon and has the highest thread count of any fabric in general use—from 200 to 350 threads per inch.
(G. R. Co.)

RIBBON WORM, the common name for mostly aquatic invertebrate animals constituting the phylum Nemertina (Nemertea) and called also nemertines or nemerteans. All are characterized by a soft, highly extensible body, elongate and ciliated, and by a readily eversible proboscis, for which the group is sometimes called proboscis worms. "Nemertea" is from the Greek meaning "unerring" and refers to the accuracy with which the proboscis can be aimed at prey. Most species are found along seashores round the world but some are found in fresh water and on land. The blackish-brown bootlace worm (*Lineus longissimus;* fig. 1) of North Sea shores is a fragile nemertine that may reach a length of many feet, while the slender reddish *Prostoma rubrum,* of pools and streams in North America, is usually less than one inch long.

GENERAL FEATURES

Description.—Nemertines vary greatly in size and shape; some are long, flattened and ribbonlike, while others are short and threadlike; some are cylindrical, while others are broad and flat.

FIG. 1.—A HETERONEMERTINE, THE BOOTLACE WORM (LINEUS LONGISSIMUS), ON A SPONGE-COVERED ROCK ON THE SEASHORE

In nearly all forms the body may be contracted to a small fraction of the length it has in full extension. In some species of nemertines the proboscis is coiled and is longer than the body.

Many of the species are brightly coloured in life, with shades of red, orange, yellow, green, gray and brown predominating. Some have a uniform coloration, others have definite patterns or markings of contrasting colours, with rings, longitudinal lines, spots or reticulations. The physical basis of the colour patterns consists of pigment granules secreted within the epithelial cells of the integument or in the underlying connective tissue cells or both.

All nemertines are carnivorous, feeding on protozoa, turbellarians and other worms, mollusks, crustaceans and the young of all the invertebrates with which they come in contact. Some have such distensible mouths that they can devour animals of almost their own diameter. Others have small mouths and suck in only the juices of their prey. When food is not obtainable the nemertine is able to live for a long time upon the nourishment to be obtained from its own tissues. Individuals of some species may thus survive starvation for a year or more. In the meantime the body may have shrunk to $\frac{1}{20}$ or less of its former size. Some of the small forms may survive unfavourable conditions by coiling their bodies in a firm cyst of secreted mucus, to resume activity at a later time.

Habitat and Distribution.—Most of the species are marine and littoral; many of them burrow in sand or mud; others hide beneath stones or creep about among algae and other growths between tide marks or in shallow water. The members of the tribe Pelagica are strictly bathypelagic, with flattened, gelatinous bodies adapted for floating idly or swimming sluggishly far beneath the surface of the deep oceans. A few species inhabit fresh-water streams and lakes; others have migrated to the land, living in moist earth or beneath fallen logs, stones or dead foliage. Certain species live as commensals in the mantle cavities of bivalve mollusks or of tunicates, in the canals of sponges or beneath actinian sea anemones; and finally several species are parasitic on the gills and among the egg masses of crabs.

Nemertines are found along all the seacoasts of the world and off the shores to depths of hundreds of metres. Some of the species are circumpolar, extending southward along the coasts as far as Madeira, southern New England, California and Japan. A few species live in both the northern and southern hemispheres. Some are limited to the polar seas and others to the tropics. Some of the bathypelagic species live at depths of 1,000–2,000 m. or more and the population may be carried for thousands of miles by the deep ocean currents, reproducing generation after generation in their endless circuits throughout the great oceans, or the individuals may congregate in eddies among the currents.

Structure and Function.—The morphological characteristics of a nemertine are shown in fig. 2. Although there is no external indication of segmentation, most of the internal organs are arranged metramerically. The body is covered with a layer of ciliated epithelial cells, interspersed with mucous and sensory cells. The epithelium is supported on a basement layer of firm gelatinous tissue, beneath which, in the order Heteronemertina, is a thick layer of mucous glands and connective tissue, the cutis. The musculature of the body wall consists of two or more layers of circular, spiral and longitudinal muscles

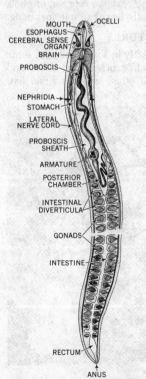

FIG. 2.—ORGAN SYSTEMS OF A HOPLONEMERTINE

MOUTH
ESOPHAGUS
CEREBRAL SENSE ORGAN
OCELLI
BRAIN
PROBOSCIS
NEPHRIDIA
STOMACH
LATERAL NERVE CORD
PROBOSCIS SHEATH
ARMATURE
POSTERIOR CHAMBER
INTESTINAL DIVERTICULA
GONADS
INTESTINE
RECTUM
ANUS

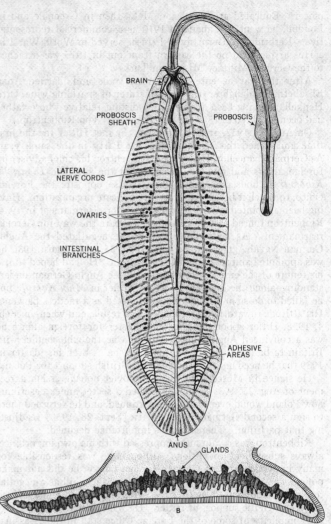

BRAIN
PROBOSCIS SHEATH
PROBOSCIS
LATERAL NERVE CORDS
OVARIES
INTESTINAL BRANCHES
ADHESIVE AREAS
A
ANUS
GLANDS
B

AFTER HIRSCH AND BRETSCHNEIDER IN L. H. HYMAN, "THE INVERTEBRATES," VOL. II; REPRODUCED BY PERMISSION OF MCGRAW-HILL BOOK CO., 1951

FIG. 3.—CROSS-SECTIONAL VIEWS OF: (A) PLOTONEMERTES, FEMALE; (B) ADHESIVE DISK SHOWING GLANDS OF MALACOBDELLA

that enable the worm to carry on rapid changes in body form. Locomotion is accomplished by creeping or gliding, by alternate elongation and contraction, by twisting spirally or, in a few species, by swimming. The proboscis is sometimes used as an aid in creeping or burrowing.

Proboscis.—The proboscis is formed by an invagination of the anterior body wall and consequently has essentially the same muscular and epithelial layers but in reverse order. In its normal position within the body it lies within the proboscis sheath, which forms a closed, saclike cavity, the rhynchocoel, filled with a corpusculated fluid. In a few species of the order Hoplonemertina the sheath is provided with paired diverticula. The anterior end of the proboscis is anchored firmly into the tissues of the head near the brain, while the posterior end commonly terminates in a long retractor muscle attached to the proboscis sheath or in some species to the musculature of the body wall in addition. The proboscis is everted through the rhynchodeum by the combined action of its own muscles and such contractions of the musculatures both of the sheath and body walls as will exert pressure on the fluid in the rhynchocoel. It is withdrawn by reducing this pressure, aided by its own musculature and by the retractor muscle, if present. In the class Anopla the tenacious mucus and paralyzing secretions of the everted proboscis aid in capturing the prey, while in the class Enopla the stylet is also used. Most of the Enopla have two or more pouches of accessory stylets which may replace the central stylet if lost or broken. In the heteronemertine *Gorgonorhynchus* the proboscis is forked.

Digestive System.—The digestive system consists of an anterior mouth, which may open either ventrally posterior to the brain or terminally in connection with the proboscis opening. In the order Bdellonemertina and some Hoplonemertina the mouth joins the rhynchodeum to form an atrium. The mouth leads to a slender esophagus and thence to a more spacious stomach. The intestine continues as a straight tube, usually with numerous paired lateral diverticula, from the stomach to the rectum, which opens at the posterior end of the body (fig. 2). Some forms have a large caecum, with caecal diverticula, which extends forward from the anterior end of the intestine, while in some of the order Paleonemertina and all of the Bdellonemertina there are no intestinal diverticula whatever (fig. 4). Digestion of the food materials is accomplished mainly by enzymes secreted into the stomach and intestine, although the fats are taken by phagocytosis directly into the cells of the lining epithelium. In these cells also the nutrients are stored in vacuoles until needed in the body metabolism.

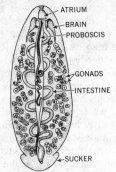

FIG. 4.—ORGAN SYSTEMS OF A BDELLONEMERTINE

Circulatory System.—The circulatory system consists typically of three longitudinal blood vessels, united at both ends of the body, and in most species with reservoirs, or lacunae, in the head and esophageal region and with numerous cross branches throughout the body.

Excretory System.—The excretory system is highly diversified. Typically there is a pair of profusely branching nephridia in close proximity with the lateral blood vessels and having one or more pairs of efferent ducts leading to the exterior of the body (fig. 2). Each of the numerous minute branches originates from a multinucleate terminal organ (metanephridium) or from a single cell (protonephridium) with long flagella that draw fluid from the surrounding parenchyma into the nephridial canal. Other cells in the walls of the canals excrete metabolized waste products. In the terrestrial nemertines (*Geonemertes*) there are several thousand separate nephridia, each with its own efferent duct. Excretory organs have not been found in any of the bathypelagic species.

Nervous System.—The central nervous system consists of a four-lobed brain, from which a pair of large lateral nerve cords extend to the posterior end of the body. Many species have in addition a dorsomedian and a ventromedian nerve with branches communicating with the lateral nerve cords. Connected with the central nervous system are one or more pairs of proboscidial nerves and numerous, often paired, peripheral nerves associated with the muscular and digestive systems, integument, ocelli and such other sense organs as may be present.

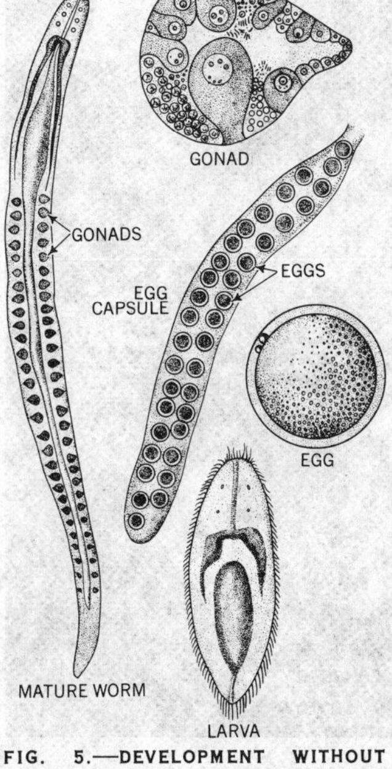

Sense Organs.—In addition to the sensory epithelium everywhere present in the integument, some of the species have other specialized sense organs, including ocelli, cerebral, lateral and frontal sense organs, cephalic grooves and pits. In a single family (Ototyphlonemertidae) there is a pair of statocysts connected with the brain. With the exception of these organs of equilibrium and the ocelli very little experimental evidence has been obtained as to the precise nature

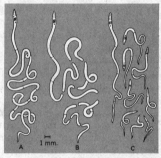

of the sense organs. Chemical senses, including the recognition of food substances, positional sense, tactile sense and a certain degree of light sense must be located in the epithelium on all parts of the body, for headless fragments respond to the corresponding stimuli.

Life Cycle.—*Reproduction and Development.*—In most nemertines the sexes are separate, although a few species are hermaphroditic. The gonads are simple sacs which usually alternate with the intestinal diverticula and may therefore be very numerous (fig. 2 and 5). In most species the sexual cells from each gonad are discharged directly into the water. Fertilization is thus external except for the few cases of viviparity in which the development of the embryo takes place within the body of the parent. In a few of the bathypelagic nemertines the spermaries have been shifted to the head, and in the parasitic *Carcinonemertes* there is a common sperm duct that opens into the rectum.

Embryonic development may be direct, leading to the formation of a larva similar to the adult, or it may be indirect, with a free-swimming, hemispherical larva of complicated pattern known as the pilidium. The young worm later develops by metamorphosis within the pilidium. Increase in length occurs by constant additions to the posterior end of the body.

Modes of Living.—Young *Carcinonemertes* species are parasites on the gills of certain crabs; as one-inch-long reddish adults, these ribbon worms feed on the egg masses of crabs and live as commensals, preying on small animals that attach to their hosts. Many commensal ribbon worms live in tunicates, sponges and bivalves and share the food drawn in by their hosts.

Regeneration.—Enemies are numerous, particularly annelids, crustaceans and fishes. Contributing to survival, however, is the tendency of most individuals with long bodies to break in fragments whenever any part of the body is seized. If only the posterior portion of the body is lost the missing parts are soon restored by regeneration.

In certain species any small fragment of the body, with or without the head, will regenerate into a minute worm of normal proportions (fig. 6). Fragmentation thus becomes a method of asexual propagation. Only a few species, however, have the capacity of restoring a missing head, but a lost or injured proboscis is promptly replaced.

FIG. 6.—ASEXUAL REPRODUCTION BY FRAGMENTATION IN LINEUS SOCIALIS

CLASSIFICATION

Approximately 600 species of Nemertina have been described. Nearly 200 of these are found along the coasts of Europe, 150 on the Pacific coast of North America and Japan, 60 on the Atlantic coast of North America and 70 are bathypelagic, floating far beneath the surface of the oceans. The phylum is conveniently divided into two classes, each of which consists of two orders.

Class Anopla.—Mouth posterior to brain; central nervous system imbedded in body wall, either between the muscular layers or external thereto; and proboscis not armed with stylets.

Order Paleonemertina.—Body musculature of two or three layers; cutis absent. Example, *Procephalothrix, Tubulanus* (fig. 7).

Order Heteronemertina.—Body musculature of three layers, to which a thin inner circular and an outer spiral layer are sometimes added; cutis well developed. Examples, *Lineus* (fig. 1), *Cerebratulus.*

Class Enopla.—Mouth anterior to brain; central nervous system situated in parenchyma internal to body musculature; and proboscis (except in Bdellonemertina) armed with one or more calcareous stylets.

Order Hoplonemertina.—Proboscis with armature; intestine straight, with paired lateral diverticula; and sucker absent.

Suborder 1. Monostylifera, with single stylet on awl-shaped basis. Examples, *Amphiporus, Prostoma* (fig. 5).

FIG. 5.—DEVELOPMENT WITHOUT METAMORPHOSIS IN A HOPLONEMERTINE (PROSTOMA RUBRUM)

Suborder 2. Polystylifera, with several stylets on curved basis.

Tribe 1. Reptantia, adapted for creeping or burrowing.

Tribe 2. Pelagica, adapted for swimming or floating in the ocean depths. Example, *Pelagonemertes*.

Order Bdellonemertina.—Proboscis without armature; intestine convoluted, slender, without diverticula; with sucker at posterior end of body; and commensal in the mantle cavity of marine bivalves. Example, *Malacobdella* (fig. 3).

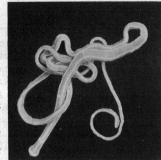

RUPERT RIEDL AND ENCYCLOPÆDIA BRITANNICA FILMS

FIG. 7.—A PALEONEMERTINE (TUBULANUS ANNULATUS)

BIBLIOGRAPHY.—W. R. Coe, "Nemerteans of the West and Northwest Coasts of North America," *Bull. Museum Comp. Zool. Harv.,* vol. xlvii (1905), "The Pelagic Nemerteans," *Mem. Mus. Comp. Zool. Harv.,* vol. xlix (1926), "Biology of the Nemerteans of the Atlantic Coast of North America," *Trans. Conn. Acad. Arts Sci.,* vol. xxxv (1943) and "Bathypelagic Nemerteans of the Pacific Ocean," *Bull. Scripps Instn. Oceanogr.,* vol. vi (1954); W. R. Coe and S. C. Ball, "Nectomertes," *J. Morph.,* vol. xxxiv (1920); B. Scharrer, "Cerebral Organ of the Nemerteans," *J. Comp. Neurol.,* vol. lxxiv (1941); P. S. Galtsoff *et al., Culture Methods for Invertebrate Animals,* pp. 162–165 (1937); R. Buchsbaum, *Animals Without Backbones,* rev. ed., ch. 14, pp. 151–155 (1948); L. H. Hyman, *The Invertebrates,* vol. ii, ch. II (1951). (W. R. Ce.; X.)

RIBE, a town of southern Jutland, Denmark, and capital of the *amt* (county) of Ribe, lies 4 mi. (6 km.) from the west coast on the north-south road and railway. Pop. (1960) 7,809. The town (one of the oldest in Denmark and first mentioned in 862) became a bishopric in 948. The cathedral dates from 1117. The Church and Monastery of St. Catharine were founded in 1228 by the Dominican Order. Many of the half-timbered houses date from the 16th and 17th centuries. Local industries include iron founding, food processing, leather working, bulb growing, and dairying. (Ro. H. T.)

RIBEIRO, BERNARDIM (*c.* 1482–1552), the father of bucolic prose and verse in Portugal, was a native of Torrão and the son of a treasurer in the household of the duke of Viseu. The details of Ribeiro's life are very uncertain. Between 1507 and 1512 he was a student in the faculty of law at the university, which was at that time in Lisbon. He later frequented the court of King Manuel where he won the friendship of the poet Sá de Miranda and perhaps fell in love with one of the court ladies, whose identity is unknown. In 1521 he probably went to Italy; it was there, perhaps, that he wrote his chivalric and pastoral romance, *Menina e Moça,* in which, it is thought, he may have related his own love story, personifying himself under the anagram of "Binmarder" and the lady under that of "Aonia."

On his return he was appointed secretary to King John III (1524). About 1540 he seems to have suffered some mental derangement and he died insane in Oct. 1552 in the hospital of Todos os Santos, Lisbon.

The *Menina e Moça* was first printed at Ferrara in 1554, together with six eclogues (including the eclogue *Crisfal* which may not be his) and some minor poems. A second edition appeared in Évora in 1557, containing a much longer version of the story but it is doubtful how much of this is Ribeiro's own work.

Modern editions are *Obras de Bernardim Ribeiro e Cristovam Falcão* by A. Braamcamp Freire, two volumes (1923); *Obras Completas de Bernardim Ribeiro* by A. Ribeiro and M. Braga, two volumes (1949–50); and *História de Menina e Moça* by D. E. Grockenberger (1947).

See A. Salgado Júnior, *A 'Menina e Moça' e o Romance Sentimental* (1940), a valuable critical study. (N. J. L.)

RIBERA, JUSEPE (JOSÉ) **DE** (LO SPAGNOLETTO) (1591–1652), Spanish painter and engraver who worked in Naples, Italy, was born at Játiva, near Valencia, but spent most of his life in Italy, where he was known as Lo Spagnoletto. Apart from his certificate of baptism (Feb. 17, 1591), there is no record of his life in Spain, though he is said by A. Palomino to have received his first training there under Francisco Ribalta. It is not known when he went to Italy but there is evidence that he worked as a young man in Parma and Rome. In 1616 he married in Naples, then under Spanish rule, where he was established during the rest of his life. In 1626 he signed as a member of the Roman Academy of St. Luke and in 1631 as a knight of the Papal Order of Christ. He died in Naples on Sept. 2, 1652.

The whole of Ribera's surviving work appears to belong to the period after he settled in Naples. His very large production comprises mainly religious compositions with a number of classical and genre subjects and a few portraits. He did much work for the Spanish viceroys, by whom many of his paintings were sent to Spain. He was also employed by the church and had numerous private patrons of various nationalities. Whether or not he first studied painting in Spain, he became in Italy one of the chief followers of Caravaggio, who formed the Neapolitan school, and he is often referred to as a Neapolitan artist.

Ribera's earliest known painting is probably the "Crucifixion" (Colegiata, Osuna), presumed to have been made for the duke of Osuna, viceroy in 1616–20. From 1621 onward there are numerous signed, dated and documented works; some of the more important are: etchings of "St. Peter" and "St. Jerome" (1621); "St. Jerome" (1626, Hermitage, Leningrad), "Drunken Silenus" (1626, Naples museum), his earliest dated paintings; "Martyrdom of St. Andrew" (1628, Budapest); "Archimedes" (1630, Prado museum, Madrid); "Portrait of a Bearded Woman" (1631, Lerma collection, Toledo); "Tityus" and "Ixion" (1632, Prado museum); "Immaculate Conception" (1635, Augustinian convent, Salamanca); "Pietà" and "Prophets" (1637–38), first commissions for the monastery of S. Martino, Naples; "Venus and Adonis" (1637, Galleria Nazionale, Rome); "Clubfooted Boy" (1642, Louvre, Paris); and "Holy Family" (1648, Metropolitan museum, New York). In 1651 he completed the "Institution of the Eucharist" (S. Martino, Naples), one of his last and most important works.

The chief elements of Ribera's style, tenebrism and naturalism, derived from Caravaggio, are used to emphasize the mental and physical suffering of penitent or martyred saints or tortured gods. Realistic detail, often horrific, is accentuated by means of coarse brush marks on thick pigment to represent wrinkles, beards, flesh wounds, etc. The influence of Bolognese and Venetian artists and probably of Velázquez, who visited Naples in 1630–31 and

ANDERSON

"THE MARTYRDOM OF ST. BARTHOLOMEW" BY RIBERA. IN THE PRADO, MADRID

1649–50, contributed to the more spacious settings, lighter tones, richer colours and more pleasing subjects which appear in Ribera's works after 1630; but he never entirely abandoned detailed realism or dramatic lighting. The objective realism of his portraits relates them to the early manner of Velázquez and to the school of Seville; while his figures of ancient philosophers in picaresque guise are typically Spanish subjects which Ribera popularized in Italy and Spain. He had many pupils and followers in Naples. In Spain his works were widely copied and imitated and were one of the chief sources of Caravaggesque naturalism. He was one of the few Spanish artists to produce numerous drawings, which were also much imitated. His etchings as well as his paintings contributed to his European fame. Like other Spanish "naturalists" he was admired and studied by 19th-century French painters.

See A. L. Mayer, *Ribera,* 2nd ed. (1923); E. du G. Trapier, *Ribera* (1952).   (E. Hs.)

RIBONUCLEIC ACID (RNA): *see* CELL; GENE: *Genes and Development;* NUCLEIC ACIDS.

RICARDO, DAVID (1772–1823), English economist who systematized and gave classical form to the rising science of economics, was born in London, April 18 or 19, 1772, of Jewish origin.

RADIO TIMES HULTON PICTURE LIBRARY

DAVID RICARDO, ENGRAVING AFTER A PORTRAIT PAINTED BY THOMAS PHILLIPS

His father, who was of Dutch birth, was a successful member of the London Stock Exchange. In 1786 Ricardo entered his father's office, where he showed much aptitude for business. After 1793, upon abandoning the Jewish faith for the Unitarian and marrying a Quaker, he was separated from his family for about eight years and was thrown upon his own resources. He continued as a member of the stock exchange, where his talents and character won him the support of an eminent banking house. He prospered immediately, and by 1815, when he prepared to retire from business, he had accumulated a large fortune. In 1819 he entered Parliament as a member for Portarlington. There he made valuable speeches on economic questions and helped bring about a change in opinion respecting freedom of trade which eventuated in the legislation of Sir Robert Peel (*q.v.*) on that subject. Ricardo died on Sept. 11, 1823, at his estate in Gloucestershire.

His first published work on an economic subject appeared in 1809, a decade after a chance reading of Adam Smith's *Wealth of Nations* had diverted his attention from geology and mineralogy, which, along with mathematics and chemistry, had begun to interest him about 1797. His tract, *The High Price of Bullion, a Proof of the Depreciation of Bank Notes* (1810), gave a fresh stimulus to the controversy respecting the resumption of cash payments and indirectly led to the appointment of a committee of the House of Commons, commonly known as the Bullion Committee, to consider the question. The report of the committee confirmed Ricardo's views and recommended the repeal of the Bank Restriction Act, but the House of Commons declared that paper had undergone no depreciation.

In 1815, when the Corn Laws were under discussion, Ricardo published his *Essay on the Influence of a Low Price of Corn on the Profits of Stock,* directed against a tract by T. R. Malthus but based upon a theory of rent already stated by Malthus and James Anderson. In this essay are set forth the essential propositions of the Ricardian system: that an increase of wages does not raise prices; that profits can be raised only by a fall in wages and diminished only by a rise in wages; and that profits, in the whole progress of society, are determined by the cost of the production of the food which is raised at the greatest expense. These ideas

were afterward incorporated in Ricardo's chief work *Principles of Political Economy and Taxation* (1817). In the field of the theory of banking and currency some of Ricardo's best work appears. His main ideas are expressed in three pamphlets: (1) *The High Price of Bullion,* in which he discusses the available means of testing the value of paper money and the power of the Bank of England to regulate the supply; (2) *Proposals for an Economical and Secure Currency* (1816), in which he elucidates the quantity theory and pronounces in favour of a monometallic standard; and (3) the *Plan for a National Bank* (1824), which was, in fact, an indictment of the methods of the existing bank, particularly in connection with its issue of paper money. In an essay on the "Funding System" (1820), written for the Supplement to the 4th, 5th, and 6th editions of the *Encyclopædia Britannica,* Ricardo urged that nations defray their expenses, whether ordinary or extraordinary, at the time when they are incurred instead of providing for them by loans.

In his *Principles of Political Economy and Taxation,* Ricardo undertook "to determine the laws which regulate" the distribution, under free competition, of the "produce of the earth" among the "three classes of the community," namely, the landlords, the farmers, and the agricultural labourers. He applied his findings more widely, however, and elaborated various other economic principles. He found that the relative domestic values of commodities are dominated, but not wholly determined in the longer run, by the quantities of labour required in their production, rent being eliminated from the costs of production. He concluded that profits vary inversely with wages which move with the cost of necessaries; and that rent tends to increase as population grows, rising as the marginal costs of cultivation rise. He supposed, following J. B. Say, that there was little tendency to unemployment, but remained apprehensive lest population grow too rapidly, depress wages to the subsistence level, and, by extending the margin of cultivation, reduce profits and check capital formation. He concluded that trade between countries was not dominated by relative costs of production, but by differences in internal price structures which reflected the comparative advantages of the trading countries and made exchange desirable. He treated monetary questions and especially tax incidence at length.

In his exposition Ricardo usually made use of apposite hypothetical examples·rather than of empirical data. While he built in part upon the work of Smith, he defined the scope of economics more narrowly than had Smith and included little explicit social philosophy. His views early won considerable support in England despite their abstract character and the many criticisms to which they were subjected. For this support Ricardo's two principal disciples were significantly responsible. J. R. McCulloch, a voluminous writer, was chosen to fill a lectureship on political economy commemorating Ricardo. James Mill, friend and political and editorial counselor to Ricardo, made of his son, John Stuart Mill, an able expounder and influential improver of the Ricardian system. Ricardo and the theories associated with his name have continued to command the critical attention of economists ever since.

His works and correspondence, in ten volumes, were edited by Piero Sraffa and M. H. Dobb for the Royal Economic Society (1951–55). *Principles of Political Economy and Taxation* appeared in several editions, including Everyman's Library. Several of the minor works were edited by J. H. Hollander.

See also references under "Ricardo, David" in the Index.

See also B. Franklin and G. Legman, *David Ricardo and Ricardian Theory* (1949); M. Blaug, *Ricardian Economics* (1958).   (J. J. S.)

RICCI, CURBASTRO GREGORIO (1853–1925), Italian mathematician, celebrated for the discovery of the absolute differential, or Ricci calculus, was born at Lugo, Romagna, on Jan. 12, 1853. From 1880 until his death on Aug. 7, 1925, he was professor at the University of Padua. His earliest work was in the fields of mathematical physics and differential equations. In 1887 appeared his first contribution to absolute differential calculus. Its origins are to be found in the differential geometry of G. F. B. Riemann, where it is necessary to study the behaviour of functions of partial derivatives in which the variables undergo transformation. First steps in the development of the appropriate technique of tensors had been taken by E. B. Christoffel, while important concepts had been introduced by E. Beltrami and R. O. S. Lipschitz. But the systematic theory is due to Ricci (1887–96); significant extensions were later contributed by his pupil T. Levi-Civita. For some time the new calculus found few applications; when, however, Einstein came to formulate his theory of general relativity, Ricci's methods proved to be the natural tool. The impulse given by Einstein has resulted in an intensive study of differential geometry based on the tensor calculus. (L. R.)

RICCI, MATTEO (1552–1610), Italian Jesuit missionary who with Michael Ruggieri opened China to evangelization, was born at Macerata in the march of Ancona on Oct. 6, 1552. After some education in his native town he went to study law at Rome (1568), where in 1571 he entered the Society of Jesus. He studied mathematics and geography under Clavius at the Roman college between 1572 and 1576, and in 1577, accompanied by others, he left for the Indies via Lisbon. He arrived in 1578 in Goa, where, after finishing his religious training, he taught in the college until 1582; he was then called to Macao to prepare himself for the task in China.

It was only after Alessandro Valignani became visitor of the Jesuit missions in the far east that the opening of China to Christianity was really taken up, although fruitless efforts had been made since Francis Xavier (q.v.). First Michael Ruggieri and then, in 1582, Ricci were summoned to Macao by Valignani for the undertaking. After various disappointments they established themselves at Ch'ao-ching, Kwangtung province, in Sept. 1583. Though never forgetting the spiritual purpose of his mission, Ricci proceeded with circumspection and contented himself with exciting the interest of the Chinese, even the more educated, with clocks, maps, European paintings and books and his own vast erudition. When in 1589 the new viceroy of Kwangtung-Kwangsi forced the missionaries to leave, Ricci obtained permission to settle elsewhere in the province in compensation for selling the mission property at a lower price. The church at Shao-chou was constructed in Chinese style and the missionaries themselves, relinquishing the costume of the despised bonzes, adopted that of the literati.

When after various misfortunes the occasion presented itself in 1595, Ricci, in the company of a high official, set out to realize his own fondest plan to establish himself in Peking. Upon arrival in Nanking, however, he found that, because of Toyotomi Hideyoshi's invasion of Korea, all foreigners were suspect and that it would be unwise to continue northward; he therefore established a new residence in Nan-ch'ang, Kiangsi province. His second chance to go to Peking came in 1597 when an official of the tribunal of rites, Kuang by name, invited Ricci to accompany him and help him compose the calendar. After waiting for two months before the gates of Peking he had to return south, again because of the Sino-Japanese conflict in Korea. He settled in Nanking until 1600 when, accompanied by two confreres, he traveled north once more. Their entrance into Peking was delayed by the intrigues of the eunuch Ma T'ang, who tried to take possession of the presents brought for the Wan-li emperor. The emperor, however, having already heard about Ricci, granted permission to enter and to offer the presents on Jan. 25, 1601. This event is recorded in the history of the Ming dynasty (Ming-shih).

They obtained a settlement with an allowance for subsistence in Peking, and from this time on to the end of his life Ricci's estimation among the Chinese increased. Besides the missionary and scientific work, from 1596 he was also superior of the mission, which in 1605 numbered 17. Ricci died on May 11, 1610, and was granted a place for burial by imperial order.

Ricci's efforts to attract and convert the Chinese intelligentsia brought him into contact with many outstanding personalities, among them Hsu Kuang-ch'i, Li Chih-tsao and Yang T'ing-yun, who became known as the "Three Pillars of the Early Catholic Church" in China and who assisted the missionaries, especially in their literary efforts. Ricci's literary efforts include about 20 works, mostly in Chinese, ranging from religious and scientific works to treatises on friendship and local memory. Probably the most famous are the "Mappamondo" and the "True Idea of God."

Ricci's "accommodation method" was the foundation of the subsequent success obtained by the Roman Catholic Church in China. The unhappy rites controversy (q.v.), however, which erupted shortly afterward, brought the mission near ruin. Probably the name of no European of past centuries is so well known in China as that of Li Ma-tou (Ricci Matteo).

Bibliography.—Louis J. Gallagher, S.J., *China in the Sixteenth Century: the Journals of Matthew Ricci* (1953); Vincent Cronin, *The Wise Man From the West* (1955); Arthur W. Hummel, *Eminent Chinese of the Ch'ing Period*, vol. i (1943), vol. ii (1944); Pasquale M. D'Elia, S.J., *Fonti Ricciane*, vol. i–iii (1942–49). (J. S. Ss.)

RICE, THOMAS DARTMOUTH (1808–1860), popularly known as "Jim Crow" Rice and regarded as the father of the American minstrel show, was born in New York City on May 20, 1808. He was an itinerant actor until his song and dance "Jim Crow," first presented in Louisville in 1828, caught the public fancy and made him one of the most popular specialty performers of his day. Although he was not the first entertainer to impersonate a Negro, Rice created a vogue for such impersonations in both the U.S. and England through a series of extremely successful tours. He wrote and appeared in *Ginger Blue, Jim Crow in London,* and a burlesque of *Othello.* These engendered the stereotypes for the skits in the popular minstrel shows which evolved in the 1840s, primarily as a result of Rice's success. Rice died in poverty at New York on Sept. 19, 1860.

See also Minstrel Show. (O. G. B.)

RICE, a well-known cereal, constitutes about one-quarter of the world's total cereal production, and is the staple food of hundreds of millions of people in Asia. Cultivated rice, *Oryza sativa,* was first mentioned in history in 2800 B.C. when a Chinese emperor proclaimed the establishment of a ceremonial ordinance for the planting of rice. Other authorities have traced the origin of rice to a plant grown in India in 3000 B.C. Rice culture gradually spread westward from southeastern Asia with the passage of time and was introduced to southern Europe in medieval times by the invading Saracens. This article briefly summarizes the botanical characteristics of rice and discusses its cultivation, preparation for the market, and production. For additional information *see* Tropical Agriculture; Grain Production and Trade; Food Supply of the World; Cereals. *See also* articles on various rice-growing countries, as China; etc.

The cultivated rice plant, an annual grass about 4 ft. tall, has numerous varieties that differ markedly in morphological characters and in physiological behaviour. It originated from wild species that are indigenous to Africa, India, and southeastern Asia. The rice plant has long, flattened leaves, about 2 ft. long and $\frac{1}{2}$ in. wide, each provided with a pointed membranous structure called a ligule, where the leaf arises from the sheath, which surrounds the culm, or stem. The spikelets are borne on a loose panicle, which is erect at blooming, but nodding as the grains develop and mature. Each spikelet contains one flower enclosed by the compressed lemma and palea. At the base of each of these organs is a small lance-shaped glume. (Lemma, palea, and glume are modified leaves, or bracts, typical of grass inflorescences.) The flower consists of six stamens and an ovary surmounted by two styles bearing a feathery stigma. The ovary, after fertilization, develops into the fruit or grain, which is enclosed by the lemma and palea, or hull. Most varieties are grown on submerged land, but others, known as upland rice, are grown on land not submerged.

Cultivation.—Rice is grown in coastal plains, tidal deltas, and river basins in tropical, semitropical, and temperate regions where fresh water is available to submerge the land. In the Orient, where most of the farms are too small for the use of farm machinery, rice is generally grown by hand labour, although animals, when available, are used in preparing the land, and after World War II small hand tractors were introduced. The rice is sown broadcast on well-prepared beds, and when the seedlings are 25 to 50 days old they are transplanted to the field by hand. Before transplanting, the fields, which are enclosed by levees, or bunds, are submerged 2 to 4 in. and the surface soil is thoroughly stirred. Two to five seedlings are placed in hills 3 to 6 in. apart in rows 8 to 12 in. apart. The land is submerged during most of the growing season, and the crop is harvested by hand. Over 90% of the world's rice is produced in Asia and the Japanese, Philippine, Indonesian, and other nearby islands; mainland China is estimated to produce slightly more than a third of the world total.

Outside of the Orient, farm machinery usually is used for preparing the land, seeding, and harvesting. The crop is grown in essentially the same manner as wheat, oats, and barley, except that the land is submerged during most of the growing season. The principal rice-producing countries outside of the Orient are Egypt, Italy, Spain, Brazil, and the United States. Rice was introduced to North America in the colony of South Carolina about 1685. By 1839 South Carolina produced 60% of the rice grown in the United States. Other rice-producing states were North Carolina and Georgia. The American Civil War and the Reconstruction period adversely affected production along the Atlantic seaboard, and the centre of production shifted to the lower Mississippi region with the introduction of machinery into southwestern Louisiana and Texas about 1885. Commercial production of rice began in Arkansas in 1905–10, and in California's Sacramento Valley in 1912. In the second half of the 20th century, many farmers broadcast seed and fertilizer by airplane on submerged land while others seeded and fertilized their fields with a grain drill.

Development of Hybrid Rice.—Most varieties of rice are classified as either *Oryza sativa indica* or *O. s. japonica* types. *Indicas*, traditionally grown in tropical areas, are tall, weak-stemmed plants, light (photoperiod) sensitive, and generally not yield-responsive to improved cultural practices, particularly to nitrogen fertilizer applications. They are relatively low yielding, producing 1 to 2 metric tons per hectare in India, Thailand, and the Philippines, as compared with average yields from *japonicas* of 4 to 6 tons per hectare in temperate zone countries. By contrast, *japonicas* are shorter-stemmed, higher yielding, and more responsive to nitrogen applications and improved cultural practices. But their direct transfer to tropical regions is frustrated by the effects of high temperatures and day length, as well as by lack of dormancy of their grains and low acceptability by tropical consumers. A third general type of rice, regarded as *indica* but resembling *japonica* and grown in subtropical areas such as Taiwan and the southern United States, is characterized by short, sturdy, erect plants, and high yield-response to nitrogen applications. These short-stemmed types are also more resistant to lodging, *i.e.*, the matting-down of plants by wind and rain, than are the longer-stemmed tropical varieties.

PANICLE OF RICE

Plant scientists, searching for higher yielding varieties that would be adaptable in cereal-short tropical regions, undertook a concentrated effort at the International Rice Research Institute at Los Baños, in the Philippines. Their goal was a plant type that would overcome the shortcomings of local, tropical varieties, such as low yields, unresponsiveness to nitrogen, long growth period, and susceptibility to lodging, and yet retain such desirable qualities as grain dormancy, resistance to local diseases, and consumer acceptability. To achieve such a plant, crosses were made between the short-statured *indicas*, particularly from Taiwan, and the taller, tropical *indicas*; *indicas* have also been successfully crossed with *japonicas*. One notable cross produced a hybrid known as IR8-288-3, which demonstrated wide adaptability in southeastern Asia, as well as yields of 6.5 to 7.5 tons of paddy (rice kernels with husks) per hectare. Maturing in 120 to 130 days, the new variety was relatively photo-period insensitive, lodging resistant, and had a high yield-response to nitrogen applications. But its susceptibility to bacterial leaf blight and blast disease, as well as its low milling quality and limited consumer acceptability in southeastern Asia, left room for additional adaptive research. Later, the development of the IR5 variety appeared to have overcome some of the problems associated with IR8's, in that the newer variety was less susceptible to leaf blight and blast disease, and had a higher consumer acceptance.

Expansion of planting of these new hybrids is expected to relieve current cereal shortages in a number of underdeveloped areas. To achieve this, growers must have available the nitrogen fertilizers and pesticides and must be willing to adopt the advanced farming methods that the successful cultivation of hybrids requires. An additional shortcoming of the hybrids, with respect to relieving food shortages, is their relatively low protein content. Plant-breeding programs have concentrated on raising yields, rather than on nutritional improvement, in response to the urgency of food shortages. Additional research may overcome this deficiency; in the meantime, protein supplementation of heavy rice diets is a more feasible alternative.

Preparation of Rice.—The kernel of rice as it leaves the thresher is enclosed by the hull, or husk, and is known as paddy or rough rice. Rough rice is used for seed and feed for livestock, but most of it is milled for human consumption by removing the hulls. Although used as a staple by millions, rice is not a complete food; and a nutritional balance cannot be obtained by eating it in larger quantities. Diets largely limited to well-milled rice result in a high incidence of malnutrition and protein-deficiency diseases, caused by inadequate amounts of some essential amino acids. Although the nutrient composition differs with the variety, protein content of husked rice is usually 8 to 9%; generally, rice compares favourably with other cereals in amino-acid content, although the low lysine content is a serious deficiency. The fat content is low, and much of it is lost in milling. The milling and polishing of rice result in considerable loss of nutrients, since proteins, fats, vitamins, and minerals are present in the germ and outer layers, and not in the starchy endosperm. The treating of rice by a variety of parboiling processes prior to milling results in high retention of thiamine, riboflavin, and niacin; the process drives some of the vitamins into the endosperm and gelatinizes the starch of the outer layers, in effect sealing them against removal by milling. Another method of restoring to milled rice the nutrient level of husked rice involves a process known as enriching—the addition of a fortified "premix" of essential nutrients before and during the milling process.

Most of the rice is milled in or near the areas in which it is produced. In modern mills, special machines are used for removing the hull from the kernel, for removing the bran layers by attrition, for polishing, for coating, and for grading. The object in milling is to remove the hull and the bran layers of the kernel with as little breakage as possible, for the most valuable product is the whole kernel.

Milled rice is sometimes coated with glucose and talc to give a high glossy finish. The by-products of milling—bran and rice polish (finely powdered bran and starch resulting from polishing)—are used as feed for livestock, and oil is processed from bran for edible and industrial uses. Broken rice is used in brewing, distilling, and manufacturing starch and rice flour. The hulls are used for fuel, packing, poultry litter, industrial grinding, and in manufacturing furfural and fertilizer. Straw is used for feed, bedding livestock, thatching roofs, and for mats, garments, packing, and broomstraws.

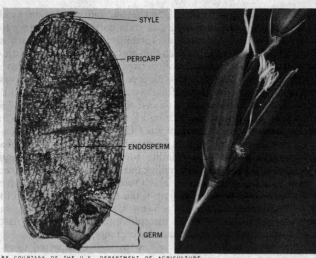

BY COURTESY OF THE U.S. DEPARTMENT OF AGRICULTURE

(LEFT) VERTICAL CROSS SECTION OF A RICE KERNEL; (RIGHT) SINGLE RICE FLORET. ANTHERS PROTRUDE NEAR THE TIP OF THE LEMMA AND PALEA. BELOW, THE CATKINLIKE STIGMA PROTRUDES BETWEEN TWO GLUMES

World Production.—In the second half of the 20th century, the world rice crop rose from an average 167,238,000 metric tons (1948–52) to 282,300,000 tons in 1968; area in this period increased from about 102,580,000 ha. to 126,243,000 ha. Yields in the same period rose from an average 1,600 kg. per ha. to 2,000 kg. per ha. Principal rice-producing countries were mainland China, India, Pakistan, Japan, Indonesia, and Thailand.

Annual rice production in the United States rose from an average 2,887,300 metric tons in 1960–65 to 4,066,400 metric tons in 1968; harvested acreage in the same period increased from 1,703,000 ac. to 2,353,400 ac., and yields rose from 3,738 lb. per ac. to 4,475 lb. per ac. Leading states were Texas, Louisiana, Arkansas, and California. *See* also references under "Rice" in the Index.

BIBLIOGRAPHY.—John Norman Efferson, *The Production and Marketing of Rice* (1952); Donald H. Grist, *Rice,* 4th ed. (1965); V. D. Wickizer and M. K. Bennett, *The Rice Economy of Monsoon Asia* (1941); U.S. Department of Agriculture, *Rice in the United States: Varieties and Production* (1966); M. F. Chandraratna, *Genetics and Breeding of Rice* (1964); H. ten Have, *Research and Breeding for Mechanical Culture of Rice in Surinam* (1967); J. J. Doyle, *The Response of Rice to Fertilizer,* UN Food and Agriculture Organization (1966); V. M. Mallaraj Urs, *Agricultural Machinery and Implements Used for Rice Cultivation in Japan* (1965); *Int. Rice Commn. Newsl.* (quarterly); *Rice Journal* (monthly); International Rice Research Institute, *International Bibliography of Rice Research* (1963). (H. R. Sh.)

RICE, WILD (*Zizania aquatica*), or Indian rice, water oats, also known locally by many other names, is an indigenous, coarse, annual grass, the grain of which has long been used as an important food by various Indian tribes and early settlers. It is commonly found on muddy bottom in fresh to brackish water along shores, streams, or in lakes and swampy places from the Atlantic coast west to the Mississippi Valley and is widely planted as food for waterfowl. This self-sowing grass, 4 to 8 ft. high, has a fruiting panicle up to 2 ft. long, the lower spreading branches of which bear male flowers whereas the upper erect branches bear female flowers. When well cooked, the slender, round, purplish black, starchy grain (nearly ¾ in. long) is delicious.

Among northern Indians "ricing" means harvesting wild rice by canoe and preparing it for winter storage. The primitive methods employed by them still yield a superior product. Unless kept in wet, cool storage, wild rice loses its viability. (T. K. J.)

RICH, EDMUND: see EDMUND, SAINT.

RICH, JOHN (1682?–1761), English theatre manager and actor, was the originator of English pantomime and founder of Covent Garden Theatre. He was a manager by inheritance, receiving a half share in Lincoln's Inn Fields Theatre from his father, Christopher Rich (d. 1714), and after running that house successfully for 18 years he founded Covent Garden Theatre (1732). At both he staged entertainments of a new type based on Italian foundations, known as pantomime, in which, from 1717 until the year before his death, he played Harlequin (*see* COMMEDIA DELL'ARTE) under his stage name of Lun. He has thus a claim to be the inventor of the harlequinade of English pantomime tradition. After Rich's death David Garrick paid tribute to the matchless expressiveness of his miming.

Rich has another special claim to be remembered. In 1727 he was offered John Gay's Newgate pastoral *The Beggar's Opera,* which Drury Lane had refused. Rich appreciated Gay's satire and produced the play on Jan. 29, 1728, at Lincoln's Inn Fields Theatre. It ran 62 performances, the longest then known, and, as was said at the time, "made Gay rich and Rich gay." (W. A. Dn.)

RICH, RICHARD RICH, 1ST BARON (*c.* 1496–1567), lord chancellor of England, was born in the parish of St. Lawrence Jewry, London. Richard, a lawyer of the Middle Temple and M.P. for Colchester (1529), held various minor offices before becoming solicitor general in 1533. He took part in the trials of Sir Thomas More and Bishop Fisher, seeking their conviction, and was one of Thomas Cromwell's agents in the dissolution of the monasteries, himself obtaining large grants of monastic property. In 1536 he was M.P. for Essex and speaker of the House of Commons. That year also he was knighted and became the first chancellor of the newly established Court of Augmentations. By August 1540 he was a privy councilor. He was one of the executors of Henry VIII's will, was created Baron Rich in February 1547, and became lord chancellor in October. In October 1549 he joined the earls of Warwick and Southampton in overthrowing the duke of Somerset, the Protector, over whose trial he presided. He resigned the lord chancellorship, on grounds of ill-health, in December 1551, at the time of the final breach between Warwick (now duke of Northumberland) and Somerset. Like other councilors, he had to subscribe Edward VI's settlement of the succession on Northumberland's daughter-in-law, Lady Jane Grey, but after Edward VI's death he soon declared for Mary Tudor, whose religious policy he now supported, although henceforward he did not take a prominent part in public affairs. A "civil servant" rather than a politician, he had never been a heroic or a very attractive figure. He died at Rochford, Essex, on June 12, 1567, and was buried in Felsted Church. (R. B. Wm.)

RICHARD I (1157–1199), king of England, nicknamed "Coeur de Lion" and "Yes and No," was the third son of Henry II and Eleanor of Aquitaine. Born on Sept. 8, 1157, he was given the duchy of Aquitaine, his mother's inheritance, at the age of 11, and was enthroned as duke at Poitiers in 1172. In 1169 he had been betrothed to Alice, second daughter of Louis VII of France and Constance of Castile. Richard possessed precocious political and military ability, quickly won fame for his knightly prowess, and quickly learned how to control the turbulent aristocracy of Poitou and Gascony. Like all Henry II's legitimate sons, he had little or no filial piety, foresight, or sense of responsibility. He joined his brothers in the great rebellion (1173–74) against Henry II, who invaded Aquitaine twice before Richard submitted and received pardon. Thereafter Richard was occupied with suppressing baronial revolts in his own duchy. It was in crushing these that he made his lifelong reputation as a brilliant soldier: in 1179 he captured the supposedly impregnable fortress of Taillebourg in Saintonge. His harshness infuriated the Gascons, who revolted in 1183 and called in the help of the "Young King" Henry and his brother Geoffrey of Brittany in an effort to drive Richard from his duchy altogether. Alarmed at the threatened disintegration of his empire, Henry II brought the feudal host of his continental lands to Richard's aid, but the younger Henry died suddenly (June 11, 1183) and the rising collapsed.

Richard was now heir to England and to Normandy and Anjou (which were regarded as inseparable), and his father wished him to yield Aquitaine to his youngest brother John. But Richard, a true southerner, would not surrender the duchy in which he had grown up; and even appealed, against Henry II, to his close friend the young king of France, Philip II (Philip Augustus). At Bonmoulins, near Mortagne (now in the Orne *département*), he did homage (Nov. 18, 1188) to Philip for all the Angevin lordships on French soil, although his father was present. In 1189 Richard openly joined forces with Philip to drive Henry into abject submission. They chased him from Le Mans to Saumur, forced him to acknowledge Richard as his heir, and at last harried him to his death (July 6, 1189).

So far Richard had proved himself as a soldier and given promise of political adroitness. Now, after his accession to Normandy (July 20) and England (Sept. 3, 1189), he was to show himself a match even for Philip of France, the ablest ruler of his time in Western Europe. Richard, however, unlike Philip, had only one ambition, to lead the crusade prompted by Saladin's capture of Jerusalem in 1187. He had no conception of planning for the future of the English monarchy. Consequently, his policy in 1189 was to put everything up for sale, to buy allies, troops, ships, and munitions, regardless of the harm which the crown might suffer in consequence. Yet he had not become king to preside over the dismemberment of the Angevin empire. He broke with Philip of France and did not neglect Angevin defenses on the continent. Open war was averted only because Philip also took the cross. Richard dipped deep into his father's treasure, sold sheriffdoms and other offices, and for 10,000 marks released the king of Scots from the vassalage forced on him after his capture by Henry II in 1174. With all this he raised a formidable fleet and army and in 1190 departed for the Holy Land, traveling via Sicily. While in Sicily he repudiated his fiancée, Philip's sister Alice:

GIRAUDON

RICHARD COEUR DE LION, TOMB EFFIGY IN THE ABBEY CHURCH OF FONTE-VRAULT, FRANCE

Richard found the Sicilians hostile and took Messina by storm (Oct. 4). To prevent the German emperor Henry VI from ruling their country, the Sicilians had elected the native Tancred of Lecce, who had imprisoned the late king's queen, Joan of England (Richard's sister), and denied her possession of her dower. By the Treaty of Messina Richard obtained for Joan her release and her dower, acknowledged Tancred as king of Sicily, declared Arthur of Brittany to be his own heir, and provided for Arthur to marry Tancred's daughter. Ominously, this treaty infuriated the Germans, who were also taking part in the Third Crusade, and it incited Richard's brother John to treachery and rebellion. Richard joined the other crusaders at Acre on June 8, 1191, having conquered Cyprus on his way there. While at Limassol, Richard married (May 12) Berengaria, daughter of Sancho VI of Navarre.

Acre fell in July 1191, and on Sept. 7 Richard's brilliant victory at Arsuf put the crusaders in possession of Joppa. Twice Richard led his forces to within a few miles of Jerusalem. But the recapture of the city, and the reconquest of the Christian feudal principalities of the Levant, which constituted the chief aim of the Third Crusade, eluded him. There were fierce quarrels between the main Western contingents, French, German, and English; more seriously there was a fundamental difference of outlook and policy between the Westerners as a whole and the resident Frankish nobility of the Latin kingdoms. The Westerners wanted spectacular victories and were ruthless and aggressive toward the Muslim. Richard, for example, allowed 2,600 prisoners to be massacred at Acre. The resident "Easterners" were half converted to an Oriental manner of living and more tolerant toward the Muslim. Richard insulted Duke Leopold of Austria by tearing down his banner and quarreled with Philip Augustus, who returned to France after the fall of Acre. Richard's candidate for the crown of Jerusalem was his vassal Guy de Lusignan, whom he supported against the German candidate Conrad of Montferrat. It was rumoured, unjustly, that Richard connived at the murder of Conrad by the Assassins. After a year's unproductive skirmishing, Richard (September 1192) made a truce for three years with Saladin which permitted the crusaders to hold Acre and a thin coastal strip and gave Christian pilgrims free access to the Holy Places.

Richard sailed home by way of the Adriatic, because of French hostility, and a storm drove his ship ashore near Venice. Because of the enmity of Leopold of Austria he disguised himself, but was discovered at Vienna in December 1192 and imprisoned in the duke's castle at Dürrenstein on the Danube. Later, he was handed over to Henry VI, who kept him at various imperial castles. It was round Richard's captivity in a castle whose identity was at first unknown in England that the famous romance of Blondel was woven in the 13th century.

Under the threat of being handed over to Philip II, Richard agreed to the harsh terms imposed by Henry VI: a colossal ransom of 150,000 marks and the surrender of his kingdom to the emperor on condition that he receive it back as a fief. The raising of the ransom money was one of the most remarkable fiscal measures of the 12th century and gives striking proof of the prosperity of England. The money was found chiefly by levying an aid of £1 on each knight's fee and imposing a general tax of one quarter of rents and movable goods. Ultimately a very high proportion of the ransom was paid, and meanwhile (February 1194) Richard was released.

He returned at once to England and was crowned for the second time on April 17, fearing that the independence of his kingship had been compromised. Within a month he went to Normandy, never to return. His last five years were spent in warfare against Philip II, interspersed with occasional truces. The king left England in the capable hands of Hubert Walter, justiciar and archbishop of Canterbury. Richard's conduct of the war showed that he had lost none of his early vigour and that he had learned something of the art of fortification while in the East: in 1196 he built the famous Château-Gaillard on the island of Andely in the Seine to guard the border between the Norman and the French Vexin, while in battles and skirmishes he was nearly always victorious. It was his characteristic impetuosity which brought him to his death at the early age of 42. The vicomte of Limoges refused to hand over a hoard of gold unearthed by a local peasant. Richard laid siege to his castle of Châluz, and in an unlucky moment was wounded. He died on April 6, 1199. He was buried in the abbey church of Fontevrault, where Henry II and Queen Eleanor are also buried, and his effigy is still preserved there.

Richard was a thoroughgoing Angevin, irresponsible and hot-tempered, possessed of tremendous energy. He was more accomplished than most of his family, a soldier of consummate ability, a skilful politician, capable of inspiring loyal service, and, last but not least in the eyes of his own age, a lyric poet of considerable power and the hero of the troubadours. But there was a cold, cruel side to his character, and in striking contrast with his father and with King John he was, there seems no doubt, a homosexual. He had no children by Queen Berengaria, with whom his relations seem to have been merely formal. As king of England, Richard brought the country great honour and prestige through his own crusading prowess, but he made no contribution to its government and recklessly commercialized royal offices and privileges. Of his reign of ten years, he spent only six months in England.

See also references under "Richard I" in the Index.

BIBLIOGRAPHY.—K. Norgate, *Richard the Lion Heart* (1924); J. H. Ramsay, *The Angevin Empire* (1903); F. M. Powicke, *The Loss of Normandy* (1913); A. L. Poole, *From Domesday Book to Magna Carta*, 2nd ed. (1955); R. C. Smail, *Crusading Warfare, 1097–1193* (1956).
(G. W. S. B.)

RICHARD II (1367–1400), king of England from 1377 to 1399, younger son of Edward the Black Prince by his cousin Joan of Kent, was born at Bordeaux on Jan. 6, 1367. Created prince of Wales on Nov. 20, 1376, he succeeded his grandfather Edward III as king on June 22, 1377. Government during his minority was in the hands of councils nominated in Parliament, and little is heard of Richard until the Peasants' Revolt of 1381, when he displayed great courage and presence of mind in pacifying the rebels in London on June 14–15. Despite this exciting taste of power, the young king was allowed little influence, and until 1386 his uncle, John of Gaunt, duke of Lancaster, remained the most powerful figure in government. The Parliament of 1381 expressed concern about Richard's education and associates, and Richard Fitzalan, earl of Arundel, and Michael de la Pole (afterward earl of

Suffolk) were appointed "to counsel and govern" the king's person. In January 1382 Richard was married to the emperor Charles IV's eldest daughter, Anne of Bohemia, to whom he became deeply devoted. His sensitive interest in literature and art was later expressed in his patronage of Chaucer, Gower, and Froissart, and in the rebuilding of Westminster Hall; but he had no taste for the warlike and chivalric pursuits so admired by his contemporaries. His Scottish expedition of 1385 proved an expensive promenade which achieved little success. By then a "court party" was beginning to form around the young king. Its nucleus was a group of chamber knights, organized by his tutor and acting chamberlain, Sir Simon Burley, but its most prominent figure was the vapid and frivolous Robert de Vere, earl of Oxford, Richard's closest friend and favourite. The courtiers soon became unpopular for their greed and extravagance. Their influence encouraged Richard to rebel against his tutelage. As early as April 1384 he had thrown off the control of Arundel, whom he hated, and had quarreled with his uncles, Lancaster and Thomas of Woodstock (afterward duke of Gloucester). He soon showed himself unduly sensitive to any criticism, and answered Archbishop William Courtenay's complaints about his household by drawing a sword and threatening to strike him down.

The first major crisis of the reign was provoked by Lancaster's leaving England in July 1386 to pursue his private dynastic ambitions in Castile. The removal of the moderating Lancastrian influence brought the royalists face to face with the hostility of Gloucester, Arundel, Thomas de Beauchamp, earl of Warwick, and other lords, who despised Richard for his indifference to war, for his dependence on a small circle of friends, and for the excessive favour shown to de Vere, who was created duke of Ireland in October 1386. When this opposition tried to make the chancellor, de la Pole, now earl of Suffolk, a scapegoat for the unpopular policies of previous years, Richard came to his defense, haughtily telling the Parliament of 1386 that he would not remove a scullion from his kitchen at their request. But parliamentary pressure was too great; Suffolk was dismissed and impeached, and a continual council was appointed with wide powers, to prolong the king's subjection to magnate control. In his resentment Richard began to recruit a bodyguard of archers from his Cheshire palatinate, and in August 1387, at Nottingham, he obtained from the judges a statement of the royal prerogative, which branded as treasonable some of the opposition's recent acts. In November 1387 Gloucester and his allies demanded the arrest of Suffolk, de Vere, and other royalists. Richard permitted their escape, and de Vere assembled an army in the northwest which marched on London, only to be dispersed by the magnates at Radcot Bridge in December 1387. Richard now had to pay the penalty for his rash defiance. His supporters were declared guilty of treason and attainted in the "Merciless Parliament" of 1388 by five lords appellant, and those who could be apprehended, including the faithful Burley, were put to death. The defenseless king had to submit to appellant control until May 3, 1389, when he declared his intention to rule freely as a monarch of full age.

Lancaster's return from Spain in November 1389 began "the period of appeasement" when the king worked in apparent harmony with Gaunt and the barons. It is unlikely, however, that Richard had forgiven his humiliations in 1387–88, and he was cautiously waiting the opportunity to avenge himself on the appellants. Grad-

RICHARD II, PORTRAIT BY AN UNKNOWN ARTIST. IN WESTMINSTER ABBEY, LONDON

ually he attracted to himself a second and stronger royalist party, including magnates like his cousin, Edward of York, earl of Rutland, and new men such as the notorious Sir John Bussy, Sir William Bagot, and Sir Henry Green. Meanwhile, his first Irish expedition (1394–95) brought him some prestige, and his prudent conciliation of France led in 1396 to a further extension of the truce of Leulinghen (1389) and his marriage to the French princess, Isabella (Queen Anne had died in 1394).

By 1397 Richard felt strong enough to attack his former enemies. After being convicted of treason in the Parliament of September 1397, Arundel was executed, Warwick banished, and Gloucester murdered in his Calais prison. In September 1398 the famous quarrel between the two younger appellants, Gaunt's son, Henry Bolingbroke, and Thomas Mowbray, duke of Norfolk, enabled the king to order their summary banishment. Richard had now embarked on a policy which some historians believe was designed to establish an arbitrary despotism. Yet many of his acts were inspired by motives of revenge; others, such as his violent resentment of any pretended affront to the crown, reflect the growing unbalance of his character in later years. He did little to create the institutions of despotism, and the suspicion that he intended to supersede Parliament cannot be proved. His obsession with the pageantry of kingship and his high view of the prerogative and the divine character of his office suggest a ruler more concerned with the outward trappings of monarchy than with the less spectacular substance of power. His final acts of folly were his confiscation of the Lancastrian estates after Gaunt died on Feb. 3, 1399, followed by his departure for Ireland at the end of May. These provided the justification and opportunity for Gaunt's heir, Henry Bolingbroke, the future Henry IV, to invade England in July.

Few of Richard's subjects were willing to defend him, and the majority approved the deposition of a king whose caprice and malice had alienated their loyalty. On his return from Ireland, Richard was tricked into surrender at Conway in August 1399, and on Sept. 30 was compelled to abdicate his throne. On Oct. 28 he was sent to Pontefract Castle, where he died in February 1400, probably of starvation, which may have been self-inflicted. Shakespeare's story of his murder by Piers Exton, a squire of Henry's, rests on no reliable authority.

See also references under "Richard II" in the Index.

BIBLIOGRAPHY.—T. F. Tout, Chapters in the Administrative History of Mediaeval England (1920–33); A. B. Steel, Richard II (1941); B. Wilkinson, Constitutional History of Medieval England, 1216–1399, vol. ii (1952); M. McKisack, The Fourteenth Century, 1307–1399 (1959); E. Curtis, Richard II in Ireland, 1394–5 and Submissions of the Irish Chiefs (1927); E. Perroy, L'Angleterre et le grand schisme d'occident (1933); M. V. Clarke, Fourteenth Century Studies (1937); V. H. Galbraith, "A New Life of Richard II," History, vol. xxvi (1942); G. Mathew, The Court of Richard II (1969).   (C. D. R.)

RICHARD III (1452–1485), king of England, youngest son of Richard, duke of York, by Cicely, daughter of Ralph Neville, 1st earl of Westmorland, was born at Fotheringhay castle on Oct. 2, 1452. At the coronation of his eldest brother Edward IV in June 1461 he was created duke of Gloucester. In contrast to his brother George, duke of Clarence, he was faithful to Edward IV and accompanied him into exile in 1470. On their return in 1471 he commanded with distinction the van at the battles of Barnet and Tewkesbury. According to Tudor historians, after the latter battle he stabbed to death in cold blood Queen Margaret's son Edward, the Lancastrian heir; but the contemporary evidence suggests that the prince was killed in battle. There is, however, strong testimony that Richard was implicated in the murder of Henry VI on the night of May 21–22, 1471, when he was certainly present in the Tower of London. For his services and fidelity he was rewarded with large grants of land and offices, and by marrying Anne (1456–85), younger daughter of Richard Neville, earl of Warwick, he secured a claim to half the vast Neville inheritance. This was resented by his brother, the duke of Clarence, who had already married the elder sister Isabel. The breach between them was never healed, but Richard does not seem to have been implicated in Clarence's death in 1478; this was a much later charge, developed in Tudor days.

Richard's share of the Neville inheritance was chiefly in the north; and in view of his proved ability and fidelity Edward IV used this as a foundation on which to build Richard's power in the north to viceregal proportions, to bring order and effective royal authority to this turbulent region. Eventually Richard was

RICHARD III, PORTRAIT BY AN UNKNOWN ARTIST

made king's lieutenant general in the north (1480) and hereditary warden of the west marches (1483). He used his powers with efficiency and wisdom to promote peace and justice and became much beloved in the north. To help him in the administration he instituted a council, which was the forerunner of the later celebrated council of the north. In 1482 he commanded a successful expedition into Scotland and recaptured Berwick-upon-Tweed.

The reputation which he had built up in the north helped him on the death of Edward IV (April 1483). His brother had named him protector during the minority of his young son, Edward V, and the old nobility and the administrators of Edward IV supported him against the upstart Woodvilles, relations of Edward IV's queen, Elizabeth. The young king had been brought up by the queen's kindred, and Richard feared that through their influence over the boy they would dominate the government and effect his destruction. Hence he arrested the king's escorts and maternal relatives, Lord Rivers and Sir Richard Grey, at Stony Stratford (April 30, 1483) and took Edward V under his own protection. Later Rivers and Grey were executed. The Woodville faction was overthrown and the queen with her younger children took sanctuary at Westminster. Loyal supporters of the young king may have become alarmed at Richard's growing power and conspired against him; at any rate on June 13 he suddenly arrested Lord Hastings, John Morton, bishop of Ely, and Lord Stanley, and beheaded Hastings the same afternoon. By now it was probably too dangerous for him not to go forward; and on June 22, a friar, Ralph Shaw, was put up at St. Paul's cross to preach against the legitimacy of Edward IV's children. On June 25 an assembly of the three estates of the realm met in London and declared that Edward's marriage was invalid on the ground of his precontract with Eleanor Butler, daughter of John Talbot, 1st earl of Shrewsbury, and that Richard was rightful king. Richard accepted the proffered crown and from the following day began his formal reign.

On July 6 Richard was crowned at Westminster and immediately afterward made a royal progress through the midlands, on which he was well received. But he could not be secure while his nephews were alive. Queen Elizabeth Woodville had been induced to give up Edward's younger brother Richard and both he and Edward were lodged in the Tower of London. There seems to be little doubt that early in August they were murdered there by their uncle's orders. Attempts have been made to clear Richard's memory (*see* EDWARD V). But the report of the princes' death was believed in England at the time and it was referred to as a definite fact before the French estates-general in Jan. 1484. Richard never produced the boys to refute the charge, and for the alternative explanations of their disappearance no evidence (as distinct from speculation) has ever been offered.

The widespread disquiet in the south of England found expression in the duke of Buckingham's rebellion (Oct. 1483). Richard was lucky, however, and the revolt collapsed. But the defection of Buckingham and his supporters reduced still further the unsure foundation of Richard's power, a base rendered even more insecure by the death of his only son, Edward, in April 1484 and of his wife in March 1485. He tried hard to live down the past and gain support by his energy and devotion to his kingly

duties. He showed zeal for trade and English interests abroad; he tried to repress disorder and promote justice; he made it easier for poor suitors to present their petitions to him and his council; he strove to make financial reforms and lessen the burden of royal demands for money. He endeavoured to win support among the clergy by his tenderness for their privileges, his building of churches, his advocacy of morality, his patronage of learning. He strove to win the approval of the people by his magnificent dress, his princely building, his care for heraldry and pageantry, his liberality, his magnanimity toward the dependents of some of his fallen opponents, his many recorded acts of kindness to petitioners in distress. Given time, he might hope, like King John, to live down the murder of a boy heir and to die as a favoured son of the church. But time was not on his side; the support of the aristocracy and the gentry had been so largely alienated that the many timeservers among his remaining adherents doubted his power to survive; and public opinion was scandalized by the rumour that Richard intended, on the death of his wife, to marry his niece, Elizabeth of York.

His rival Henry Tudor (later Henry VII) was joined in France by supporters of Edward IV, the Woodvilles, the Lancastrians and of Buckingham, and was encouraged by the French government, which was alarmed by Richard's declared intention to maintain English claims in France. On Aug. 7, 1485, Henry Tudor landed in South Wales, and, gathering support as he marched east, met Richard at Bosworth on Aug. 22. Richard had the larger forces, but the earl of Northumberland was disaffected, and the issue was decided by the treachery of Lord Stanley, Henry's stepfather, and his brother Sir William Stanley. Richard refused to flee and died fighting bravely against overwhelming odds. After the battle his bloody and naked body was carried to Leicester, trussed across a horse's back, and buried without honour in the church of the Greyfriars.

His reputation in Tudor days as a monster of unparalleled villainy was largely because of the fact that he had too little time to live down his deeds of 1483 and the fact that in Tudor England it was impolitic to vindicate his memory. As for the allegation that he was a hunchback, neither the portraits of Richard nor contemporary evidence testifies to any such deformity, though there is some indication that one shoulder was higher than the other.

See also references under "Richard III" in the Index.

BIBLIOGRAPHY.—*See* P. M. Kendall, *Richard the Third* (1955), for the most recent biography and full references to the sources; A. R. Myers, "The Character of Richard III," *History Today*, vol. iv (1954); Mortimer Levine, "Richard III—Usurper or Lawful King," *Speculum*, vol. xxxiv (1959); E. F. Jacob, *The Fifteenth Century* (1961).

(A. R. M.)

RICHARD, EARL OF CORNWALL and KING OF THE ROMANS (1209–1272), second son of John, king of England, born at Winchester (Jan. 6, 1209), was knighted and given the title "count of Poitou," and the county and tin mines of Cornwall (1225). On returning from his unsuccessful expedition to recover Poitou (March 1225–May 1227) he was created earl of Cornwall (May 30, 1227). Between 1227 and 1238 he frequently opposed his brother King Henry III, joining the barons in several crises, but never proceeding to rebellion and always making Henry pay heavily for reconciliation. He married (March 30, 1231) Isabella, daughter of William Marshal, earl of Pembroke, and widow of Gilbert de Clare, 6th earl of Gloucester; of their four children only Henry (of Almain) survived.

Richard joined Henry III's inglorious Breton expedition (1230); he took the cross (1236), and after Isabella's death (Jan. 17, 1240) led a small English force to the Holy Land (June 1240–January 1242) refortifying Ascalon and negotiating an advantageous treaty. During Henry's disastrous Poitevin campaign (1242), Richard's prompt retreat at Saintes and his persuasive diplomacy at Taillebourg saved Henry from capture. Richard married Sanchia of Provence, sister of Henry's queen (Nov. 23, 1243), abandoning his Poitevin title a few days later; his second surviving son, Edmund, was born of this marriage, which bound Richard closely to Henry's circle. As farmer of the mint he executed and financed the great recoinage of 1247–48, making £20,000 profit thereby. While acting regent of England during Henry's Gascon visit (1253–54), Richard summoned knights to represent the shires at the critical Parliament of Easter 1254. He founded and built the Cistercian Abbey of Hailes (1245–46). Reputedly the richest magnate in England, he refused Pope Innocent IV's offer of the Sicilian crown (1252–53), but accepted imperial candidature (1256), purchased four of the seven electoral votes, was elected king of the Romans and crowned at Aachen (May 17, 1257) by the archbishop of Cologne. By lavish bribery he gained recognition throughout the Rhineland, returning home in January 1259. He helped Henry to overthrow the Provisions of Oxford, but from June to October 1260 he again visited Germany, now discovering the absurdity of his hopes of the imperial crown. His third visit to Germany (June 1262–February 1263) also achieved nothing useful. He helped Henry invaluably against the rebel barons (1263–64) but was captured at Lewes (May 14, 1264) and imprisoned at Wallingford and then at Kenilworth until the overthrow of Simon de Montfort at Evesham (Aug. 4, 1265). Ably supported by his son Henry, he then worked ceaselessly to obtain the relatively moderate settlement of the *Dictum de Kenilworth* (Oct. 31, 1266). His fourth visit to Germany (August 1268–August 1269) is notable only for his third marriage, to Beatrice of Falkenburg (June 16, 1269). The murder of his son Henry at Viterbo (March 13, 1271) was a deadly blow to Richard, who died at Berkhamstead Castle on April 2, 1272.

See N. Denholm-Young, *Richard of Cornwall* (1947); H. Koch, *Richard von Cornwall, 1209–1257* (1887), continued by J. F. Baffert (1905).
(R. F. T.)

RICHARD OF ST. VICTOR (d. 1173), theologian noted for his mystical treatises, was born in Scotland or England. He entered the Abbey of St. Victor in Paris, where he was a student of Hugh of St. Victor and where he became prior in 1162. Although Richard wrote doctrinal treatises on the Trinity and exegetical studies of the Scriptures, it is for his works on mysticism, which synthesize and elaborate Victorine teachings, using extensive symbolism, that he is chiefly remembered. They reflect the influence of Neoplatonism, St. Augustine, and especially Dionysius (*q.v.*) the Areopagite. According to Richard, the soul proceeds by six successive steps from sense perception to ecstasy, using the faculties of imagination, reason, and intuition, and employing secular learning as well as divine revelation, until it is finally carried beyond itself and united with God in divine contemplation. Richard profoundly influenced medieval mysticism, as exemplified by St. Bonaventura and Jean de Gerson, and also early modern mysticism, as is evidenced by the appearance of six editions of his works between 1506 and 1650. Dante placed Richard among the greatest teachers of the church.

His collected works are published in volume cxcvi of J. P. Migne's *Patrologia latina*.
(D. D. McG.)

RICHARDS, I(VOR) A(RMSTRONG) (1893–　　　　), English critic and poet, one of the most influential modern critical theorists. Born on Feb. 26, 1893, at Sandbach, Cheshire, and educated at Clifton College, and at Magdalene College, Cambridge University, he achieved fame as a lecturer in English at Cambridge in the 1920s and the early 1930s. The English syllabus had been revised in 1926 to include social history, the history of ideas, and psychology. Richards, trained in the Moral Sciences (philosophy and psychology), was thus well equipped to introduce new and controversial ideas into criticism and the study of English literature.

His theoretical interests had already found expression in *Foundations of Aesthetics* (1921; with C. K. Ogden and James Wood). In *The Meaning of Meaning* (1923) he again collaborated with Ogden (*q.v.*) in a work whose anti-metaphysical doctrines, with the emphasis on the desirability of resolving philosophical problems through linguistic analysis, gave it much in common with logical positivism (*q.v.*). Its much discussed distinction between the "scientific" and "emotive" uses of language is elaborated in his *Science and Poetry* (1926). Meanwhile, in *The Principles of Literary Criticism* (1924), he had redefined the status of imaginative literature and the grounds for its reappraisal. Rejecting the religious assumptions of earlier critics, he proposed to measure

literary value, and value in general, in quantitative terms, by establishing formerly haphazard intuitions on a basis of scientific psychology.

In *Practical Criticism* (1929), he demonstrated the application of psychological method to criticism by discussing opinions recorded by readers (mainly university students) about poems presented to them without authors' names or dates. The book aroused great interest, especially for its suggestions of ways to encourage a more perceptive reading of poetry; and the term "practical criticism" came to be used to describe the close analytic study, at schools and universities, of short passages of verse and prose. This aspect of his work carried his influence to the U.S., in the movement known as "the New Criticism," with its insistence on the importance of "the words on the page" (*see* CRITICISM). Both its potentialities and shortcomings are anticipated in Richards' own writings. The great advantage of the method was that students were encouraged to read particular texts carefully; its drawback was that wider historical and cultural inquiries tended at first to be discouraged.

In *Coleridge on Imagination* (1934), in which he set out to consolidate Coleridge's psychological theory of poetry and to exhibit it as a forerunner of his own ideas, Richards' thought seemed to be moving toward the wider problems of language and meaning. With Ogden, he had become the leading exponent of Basic English (*q.v.*), working on it as director (1936–38) of the Orthological Institute of China. His later work in the U.S., where from 1944 till retirement in 1963 he was a professor of English at Harvard, was largely concerned with the study of language in its semantic or "semasiological" aspect. He was also interested in the adaptation of liberal education to modern life. Late in his career, Richards unexpectedly made his debut as a poet, with a published collection of poetry in 1958.

The best of his verse, however, seems witty or charming rather than imaginatively powerful. It seems likely that his work in educational and critical theory, especially that of his "English" period, may prove to be the most lastingly influential.

BIBLIOGRAPHY.—W. H. N. Hotopf, *Language, Thought and Comprehension* (1965); Stanley Edgar Hyman, *The Armed Vision* (1948); J. P. Schiller, *I. A. Richards' Theory of Literature* (1969).
(W. W. Ro.)

RICHARDS, THEODORE WILLIAM (1868–1928), U.S. chemist, received the Nobel Prize for Chemistry in 1914 for his researches on atomic weights (*q.v.*). He was born in Germantown, Pa., on Jan. 31, 1868. He graduated from Haverford College, Pa., (1885) and took advanced degrees at Harvard, where he became instructor in chemistry in 1891 and full professor in 1901.

Richards greatly improved the technique of gravimetric atomic weight determinations, introducing quartz apparatus, the bottling device, and the nephelometer (an instrument for measuring turbidity). Although the atomic weight values of Jean Servais Stas had been regarded as standard, about 1903 physicochemical measurements showed that some were not accurate. Richards and his students revised these figures, lowering, for instance, Stas's value for silver from 107.93 to 107.88. Richards' investigations of the atomic weight of lead from different sources helped to confirm the existence of isotopes. His later researches were concerned mainly with the physical properties of the solid elements, and included much original work on atomic volumes and compressibilities. He died at Cambridge, Mass., on April 2, 1928.
(R. E. O.; X.)

RICHARDSON, DOROTHY MILLER (1873–1957), English pioneer in stream-of-consciousness fiction, was born in Abingdon, Berkshire, on May 17, 1873, and passed her childhood and youth in secluded surroundings in late-Victorian England. After her schooling, which ended when, in her 17th year, her home broke up, she engaged in teaching, clerical work and journalism. In 1917 she married the artist Alan Elsden Odle (1888–1948). She commands attention for her sequence novel *Pilgrimage* (published in separate volumes—she preferred to call them chapters—as *Pointed Roofs*, 1915; *Backwater*, 1916; *Honeycomb*, 1917; *The Tunnel*, 1919; *Interim*, 1919; *Deadlock*, 1921; *Revolving Lights*, 1923; *The Trap*, 1925; *Oberland*, 1927; *Dawn's*

Left Hand, 1931; *Clear Horizon,* 1935; the last part, *Dimple Hill,* appeared under the collective title, four volumes, 1938). She died June 17, 1957, at Beckenham, Kent.

Pilgrimage is the extraordinarily sensitive story, seen cinematically through the eyes, of Miriam Henderson, an attractive, spinsterish and mystical New Woman. Unfortunately, she is more new than woman, since, for a character committed to the stream-of-consciousness technique of self-revelation, her reactions to her various experiences are selected and edited with peculiarly improper reticence; while hers is entirely a woman's consciousness, it is not nearly a woman's entire consciousness. Moreover, the author too often lavishes her surpassingly delicate perceptiveness upon dull material. Nevertheless, no student of fiction can afford to overlook *Pilgrimage,* one of the significant novels of the 20th century.

See J. C. Powys, *Dorothy M. Richardson* (1931); Caesar R. Blake, *Dorothy Richardson* (1960). (J. Pt.)

RICHARDSON, HENRY HANDEL (pseudonym of ETHEL FLORENCE LINDESAY RICHARDSON) (1870–1946), one of Australia's leading novelists, was born at East Melbourne, Victoria, on Jan. 3, 1870. From 1883 to 1887 she was a pupil at the Presbyterian Ladies' College in Melbourne. In 1888 she left Australia to study music in Leipzig, and spent the rest of her life abroad, making only one brief visit to Australia in 1912. In Leipzig she met J. G. Robertson (1867–1933), whom she married in Dublin in 1895, and who in 1903 was appointed first professor of German at London University. She abandoned the idea of becoming a concert pianist, and began writing, her first publications (in 1896) being translations of *Niels Lyhne* (as *Siren Voices*) by J. P. Jacobsen, and *Fiskerjenten* (as *The Fisher Lass*) by Bjørnstjerne Bjørnson. In Germany she began her first novel, *Maurice Guest* (1908), the story of a young English music student in Leipzig whose career and life are ruined by a tragic love affair. In it she drew extensively on her own experiences of the musical and social life of Leipzig.

In 1904 she and her husband settled in England. Her second novel, *The Getting of Wisdom* (1910), is an account of her life at boarding school in Melbourne. On completing it she began the trilogy that occupied the next 20 years of her life, *The Fortunes of Richard Mahony* (1930; *Australia Felix,* 1917; *The Way Home,* 1925; *Ultima Thule,* 1929). The central character is a portrait of her father (who had emigrated from Dublin to Australia, and who died in 1879), reconstructed with the help of his letters and diaries. The novel is a detailed and sympathetic account of his tragic life, in particular of his inability to adjust himself to his adopted country. Into it Henry Handel Richardson poured much knowledge of conditions of life in 19th-century Victoria, and many of her own memories of Australia and of her father's declining years. Her last novel, *The Young Cosima* (1939), is a reconstruction of the love affairs of Richard Wagner, Cosima Liszt, and Hans von Bülow. She also wrote a number of short stories, published as *The End of a Childhood and Other Stories* (1934), and an unfinished autobiography, *Myself When Young* (1948). She died at Fairlight, Sussex, on March 20, 1946.

BIBLIOGRAPHY.—J. G. Robertson, "The Art of Henry Handel Richardson," in *Myself When Young* (1948); N. Palmer, *Henry Handel Richardson: a Study* (1950); L. J. Gibson (Kramer), *Henry Handel Richardson and Some of Her Sources* (1954); E. Purdie and O. M. Roncoroni (eds.), *Henry Handel Richardson: Some Personal Impressions* (1958); V. Buckley, *Henry Handel Richardson* (1961); L. J. Kramer, "Henry Handel Richardson," in Geoffrey Dutton (ed.), *The Literature of Australia* (1964). (L. J. K.)

RICHARDSON, HENRY HOBSON (1838–1886), U.S. architect, was both the initiator of the Romanesque revival and a pioneer figure in the development of an indigenous, modern American style. He was born on Sept. 29, 1838, in St. James parish, La. After graduating from Harvard college in 1859, he studied architecture at the École des Beaux-Arts, Paris, returning to the United States in 1865. Shunning the neoclassical traditions in which he had been trained, Richardson experimented briefly with Victorian Gothic and then turned to the French Romanesque style epitomized in his famous Trinity church of Boston (1872–77).

The Marshall Field Wholesale building, Chicago (1887; de-

molished 1930), was the masterpiece of the bold, original style that he gradually evolved: characterized by an unornamented exterior and rows of tall, arched windows, it relied for effect upon its lines and the skillful handling of material. This style survives in his Ames-Pray building, Boston. Among his other notable works are the Pittsburgh courthouse and jail; the capitol at Albany, N.Y.; Sever hall, Harvard university; and many distinctive, shingled country houses such as Stoughton house, Cambridge, Mass. His Romanesque had an integrity and grace seldom achieved by his many imitators in the latter half of the 19th century; his modern style presaged the revolutionary work of Louis Sullivan (*q.v.*). Richardson died on April 27, 1886, in Boston.

See Henry Russell Hitchcock, *The Architecture of H. H. Richardson and His Times* (1936).

RICHARDSON, JOHN (1796–1852), Canadian novelist, whose most valuable works are autobiographical and historical, was born at Queenston, near Niagara Falls, on Oct. 4, 1796. During the War of 1812, Richardson, a gentleman volunteer, was taken prisoner at Moraviantown, where Tecumseh was killed. Released in 1815, Richardson served as a British officer in England, Barbados, and Spain. *Écarté* (1829), a novel of the salons of Paris, and *Kensington Gardens in 1830,* a satire in verse, reflect his gay life abroad. Drawing upon his experiences in Canada, he published *Tecumseh* (1828), a metrical romance, and *Wacousta* (1832), an exciting novel about the Pontiac conspiracy. Several minor books recorded Richardson's disagreement with Lieut. Gen. De Lacy Evans, his commanding officer in Spain.

Returning to Canada in 1838, he edited *The New Era* (1841–42) in Brockville and published *The Canadian Brothers* (1840), a sequel to *Wacousta; War of 1812* (1842), a historical account; and *Eight Years in Canada* (1847), an autobiography. Attracted by the American market for inexpensive editions of his works, including *The Monk Knight of St. John* (1850), *Hardscrabble* (1850), and *Wau-nan-gee* (1852), he spent his last years in New York, where he died on May 12, 1852.

See A. C. Casselman, *Richardson's War of 1812* (1902); W. R. Riddell, *John Richardson* (1923). (C. F. Kk.)

RICHARDSON, LEWIS FRY (1881–1953), British pioneer in the application of mathematics to weather forecasting, was born at Newcastle upon Tyne on Oct. 11, 1881, of an old Quaker family of tanners. He was educated at Bootham School, York, and at King's College, Cambridge. His mathematical work, marked by great originality of thought, mainly concerned the calculus of finite differences, the prediction of weather by computation, the study of diffusion, and, later, the use of mathematics to elucidate the causes of war (speculations arising from religious conviction). Richardson made major contributions to numerical methods of solving boundary-value problems in physics, and during 1913–22 applied these ideas to meteorology in a bold attempt to produce a systematic method of forecasting depending entirely on calculation. This work culminated in his classic *Weather Prediction by Numerical Process* (1922), with its scheme for "numerical" forecasting including a worked-out example. Although this example was a failure, caused partly by inadequate upper-air data and partly by the limitations of the mathematical method, the line of thought thus pioneered and the later invention of the high-speed electronic computer together made numerical forecasts practicable. In his work on diffusion Richardson was likewise ahead of his time, in that concepts that he advanced in 1926 were not fully recognized as valid until 20 years later, when they were rediscovered by others. His name is preserved in studies of convection by the "Richardson number," a fundamental quantity involving the gradients of temperature and velocity. He died at Kilmun, Argyll, on Sept. 30, 1953.

See E. Gold, *Obituary Notices of Fellows of the Royal Society,* 9 (1954); J. R. Newman (ed.), *World of Mathematics,* vol. 2 (1956). (G. Sn.)

RICHARDSON, SIR OWEN WILLANS (1879–1959), English physicist awarded the Nobel prize for physics in 1928, was one of the founders of atomic physics. He discovered the Richardson law, concerning the emission of electricity from hot bodies, on which is based the action of wireless valves; his work on valves helped to revolutionize radio communication through the development of the hard thermionic valve. Born at Dewsbury, Yorkshire, on April 26, 1879, Richardson was educated at Trinity college, Cambridge. He was professor of physics at Princeton university, 1906–13, and at King's college, London, 1914–24, Yarrow research professor of the Royal society, director of research in physics at King's college and, from 1944, emeritus professor of physics of London university. Richardson was elected fellow of the Royal society in 1913 and was knighted in 1939. He died at Alton, Hampshire, on Feb. 15, 1959. Among other standard works he wrote *The Emission of Electricity From Hot Bodies* (1916; 2nd ed., 1921).

RICHARDSON, SAMUEL (1689–1761), English writer who created the dramatic novel in English. His detailed exploration of feelings and motives introduced a new dimension into fiction, and profoundly influenced the novel's development as an intimate record of inner experience and a means of expressing a serious criticism of life.

Life.—Little is known of Richardson's early life. The son of a London joiner, or cabinetmaker, he was born in Derbyshire in 1689, but later his family returned to London. He himself says that he had only "common school learning." Being "not fond of play" he was nicknamed "Serious" and "Gravity," but was in demand as a teller of stories, which always carried "a useful moral." He also acquired a reputation as a writer of letters. At age 10 he wrote anonymously to a widow of 50, reproving her hypocrisy and malice. He was "an early favourite with all the young women of taste and reading in the neighbourhood" and was employed to write answers to their love letters.

In 1706 he was apprenticed to the London printer John Wilde. He rose steadily, becoming a freeman of the Stationers' Company in 1715, and in 1718 or 1719 setting up his own business. In 1739 he acquired the lease of part of a house at North End, Hammersmith. This became a much-loved home, and in a "grotto," or summerhouse, in the garden, he wrote his novels and voluminous letters, and entertained his admirers, including the so-called "garden of ladies"—Sarah Fielding and her sisters, Mrs. Elizabeth Carter, Hester Chapone, Susannah Highmore, daughter of Joseph Highmore (*q.v.*), Sarah Westcomb, to whom he became an "adopted" father, Charlotte Lennox, and other "bluestockings," with whom he discussed his novels before publication. This country house was also a meeting place for other friends—Aaron Hill, Dr. Johnson, Hogarth, Colley Cibber, Arthur Onslow (the speaker of the House of Commons, who in 1724 had employed him to print its *Journals*), and Edward Young, whose *Night Thoughts* he published. In 1754 he became master of the Stationers' Company, and moved from North End to Parsons Green, where he died on July 4, 1761.

In his business career, Richardson was prosperous, respectable, hardworking, thrifty, prudent, and humdrum. His outward success concealed the impact of private tragedy. He was twice married, in 1721 to Martha Wilde (d. 1731), his master's daughter, and in 1732 to Elizabeth Leake, sister of a prosperous bookseller in Bath. Of six children of his first marriage, five died in infancy, and one, a boy of four, in 1730. Another son, born in 1739, died in 1740. These and other bereavements—11 between 1729 and 1731—helped to bring on the nervous ailments of his later life. His professional success also concealed any hint that he was to write the great tragic novel of his time.

Works.—*Pamela.*—Richardson began his first novel at the age of 51. He had acquired a reputation for writing indexes, prefaces, dedications, and abstracts; and in 1739 the booksellers Charles Rivington and John Osborn asked him to compose a collection of model letters for the use of people with little formal education. He wished to make it morally instructive, as well as useful, and when it was published (January 1741), it was entitled *Letters written to and for particular Friends, on the most Important Occasions. Directing not only the requisite Style and Forms to be observed in writing "Familiar Letters"; but how to think and act justly and prudently, in the common Concerns of Human Life.* Meanwhile, in writing letters suitable for a maidservant and her father, which would warn against masters' designs on their maids' virtue, he had remembered a real-life story about a girl whose resistance had been rewarded by marriage to her master, and had hit upon the idea of telling it in a series of letters written to her parents. So arose *Pamela, or, Virtue Rewarded,* published anonymously in November 1740. It became probably the most widely read novel of the century, going through five editions in less than a year, and being translated info French, Dutch, German, Italian, and Danish by 1750. Richardson's success was embittered, however, by attacks on its morality. Opinion in Europe became deeply divided, some regarding *Pamela* "as an example for Ladies to follow .... Others ... [discovering] in it the behaviour of an hypocritical, crafty girl ... who understands the Art of bringing a man to her lure." Outstanding among the attacks were two by Henry Fielding (*q.v.*): the parody of the *Apology for the Life of Mrs. Shamela Andrews* (1741), and *Joseph Andrews* (1742). Since Richardson brought to fiction a deeply moral purpose he was considerably stung, and he was further annoyed by the unscrupulous compilation of a sequel by the hack writer John Kelly. Having tried to prevent this, Richardson began his own continuation in two volumes (published, September 1741, as *Pamela's Conduct in High Life*), which had formed no part of his original plan, and, since it sprang from no imaginative impulse, shows him at his worst and most didactic.

Pamela's real significance lies in its dramatic and exploratory use of the letter form. The heroine is created from inside; the reader is not told about her by an all-knowing narrator, or a later self, but experiences her story through her own mind as the events occur. Writing a novel in letters has its own difficulties and clumsiness, but also great advantages. Pamela is startlingly alive, her homespun language gives immediate and complex insights into her mind, and the reader's understanding of her experience develops with hers. The form is "dramatic" because the author banishes himself and creates only through his characters, by imagining himself into their minds. It is "exploratory" because the more vividly he imagines this consciousness other than his own, the more he is led to discover in it unrealized depths. This exploration is increased when one character is set in conflict with others. Even in *Pamela,* in which the letters come almost entirely from the heroine, the conflict of values between the puritan girl and her rakish master, Mr. B., allows the reader to see Pamela as clearly through his eyes as to see him through hers, and to realize that both views are inadequate. We must never make the easy mistake of confusing Richardson with his characters. Through his dramatic exploration of his heroine's character in the carefully constructed early scenes, he came to realize weaknesses in her values, which may have been his own when he began to write. This led him to isolate her to explore the implications of his discovery. He finds a kind of blindness in her purity, a pride behind her prudence, a lack of faith in God and in man behind her guarded self-reliance. Only after 40 days and nights of imprisonment and temptation, during which she nearly succumbs to the ultimate sin of suicide, does she find that double faith; only when she finds it can she find happiness, or create the possibility of a human relationship with her tormented tormentor, struggling with his barren pride.

The novel has faults. It is often crude, sometimes comically so. Many of its attitudes, to class, to sex, to the "rewards" of virtue, especially, are limited. Richardson fails to examine his hero, or to create his development from plotting seducer thoroughly enough to make his final offer of marriage convincing. Yet the novel's significance lies in the way that its insights grow in depth, humanity, and understanding. It is not a great novel, but it is the preparation for one.

Clarissa.—Richardson had completed an outline of *Clarissa: or, the History of a Young Lady* by June 1744, but the first two volumes only appeared in November 1747. They are a powerful study of bourgeois materialism and family tyranny. The acquisitiveness of the Harlowes (Clarissa's parents), their authoritarianism, pride, and cruelty, slowly enclose her in a trap from which there are only two exits: marriage to a man she despises, in obedience to their will, or elopement with the rakish Lovelace, into which she is eventually tricked. Volumes III and IV (April 1748) explore the conflict between Clarissa's absolute moral values and the unscrupulous sex-war code of Lovelace, who uses her propriety and delicacy against her in a plan to seduce her if he can, and marry her only if he must. He tricks her into a London brothel, from which she escapes, only to be brought back as the darkest phase of the novel opens. In volumes V, VI, and VII (December 1748), Lovelace, incapable of giving up the view of men and women on which his view of life is based, his heart hardened by the urgings of the prostitutes and by his own wounded pride at his failure to win Clarissa, and obsessed with the need to satisfy that pride and impose his will, rapes Clarissa while she is under the influence of drugs. She temporarily loses her reason, her appeals to her family are rejected, and she herself rejects a Lovelace now aware of what he has done. She dies: but it is a holy death which Richardson clearly sees as a mark of divine grace, releasing her from a world in which human beings torture one another and themselves.

This novel is many things. Most significantly, perhaps, it explores the two chief forces in the world from which Richardson himself sprang. It is a sombre indictment of a life lived in terms of money and power; both the bourgeois Harlowes and the aristocratic Lovelace are opposed to deeper and truer values. It is also, however, a revealing exploration of the strength and weakness of the absolute, ultimately puritan, code of ethics to which Richardson himself subscribed. In his imaginative realization of Clarissa he brings out the implications of her passivity, her vulnerability to people less scrupulous than herself, her inability to understand evil. Yet, in tragedy and dissolution, he triumphantly vindicates her integrity, the ultimate moral and religious strength of her "holy living and dying."

Formally *Clarissa* represents a great advance on *Pamela*. Though most of the narrative is carried by Clarissa's letters, Richardson uses three further points of view to explore all the implications of the events: the consciousness of her vivacious and rebellious friend, Anna Howe; that of Lovelace; and that of his reforming friend, Belford. There is thus a continuous cross-illumination and complexity of analysis; but the reader must be constantly aware of the implications of each attitude, continually building up an understanding that is fuller, deeper, and more complex than that possessed by any character in the novel. The disadvantage is the novel's great length, as events are repeated from different points of view. Yet few who have experienced its slow inevitability and the depth of its gradually unfolding meaning count it too long. There are also letters from numerous minor characters, in all of which Richardson gave rein to his belief that "styles differ, too, as much as faces, and are indicative . . . of the mind of the writer."

Sir Charles Grandison.—The History of *Sir Charles Grandison* was published in 1753–54. Fielding's *Tom Jones* had achieved great success in 1749, and though there is little evidence that Richardson really knew it, and much that, if he did, he misunderstood it, it seems likely that *Grandison* was written to show what a really good man was like in contrast to Fielding's hero. Though it shows deeply felt ideals, it has only glimpses of the imaginative genius of *Clarissa*. Its hero behaves with undeviating rectitude and benevolence, in all kinds of awkward situations, including the ultimate one of a triangular relationship with two beautiful and good women, Harriet Byron and Clementina della Porretta, both of whom merit his respect. He is used to illustrate his creator's conviction that the foundation of morality is goodness of heart, and that the truest human pleasure flows from virtue and benevolence. Both ideas, ironically, are very close to Fielding's. The novel also illustrates Richardson's longing to extend the family beyond the mere accident of blood, as his men and women develop from friendship into a deeper brotherhood and sisterhood on a basis of profound moral harmony and love—so, in real life, he offered brotherhood and fatherhood to his admirers. It also shows his liberal attitude to religious differences, and his championship of a more liberal attitude to women.

With all this, however, the novel has a deadness at the core. If we find Sir Charles priggish it is because he knows little uncertainty, he is never forced into the abysses of his being as

Pamela and Clarissa are. But good things remain. The lively description of Harriet Byron's first experiences of London are a reminder of Richardson's influence on Fanny Burney and Jane Austen. Into the mental conflicts of Harriet and Clementina the probing imagination of the author of *Clarissa* has entered, if not with the same sombre resonance, yet with life-giving and revealing power.

Influence.—Richardson had little permanent direct influence on English fiction. But his works played a part in the growth of the novel of sentiment, especially on the continent. Diderot eulogized him, Rousseau adapted him, and a whole series of German writers admired his emotional power. Yet this kind of influence misses his real strength. It was indirectly through Jane Austen—though after her epistolary juvenilia she discarded the letter-form—that the legacy of Richardson's "point-of-view" writing was transmitted to later English novelists. The modern novel, after Henry James and James Joyce, if it has not turned to Richardson himself, has been largely concerned with extending and developing the type of dramatic novel he created.

Bibliography.—The standard edition of the novels is the Shakespeare Head edition, 19 vol. (1930–31). The *Familiar Letters on Important Occasions* of 1741 were ed. by B. W. Downs (1928). There are bibliographies of the works, by W. M. Sale (1936), and of critical studies (1896–1946), by F. Cordasco (1948). Scholarly studies are: A. D. McKillop, *Samuel Richardson, Printer and Novelist* (1936); and W. M. Sale, *Samuel Richardson: Master Printer* (1950). A useful critical introduction is R. F. Brissenden, *Richardson,* "Writers and Their Work" series (1958). A selection of Richardson's letters was ed., with a memoir based on Richardson's own manuscript memoirs, by A. L. Barbauld, 6 vol. (1801); *see also Selected Letters of Samuel Richardson,* ed. by J. Carroll (1964). I. P. Watt, *The Rise of the Novel* (1957), studies Richardson in the light of 18th-century society; Morris Golden, *Richardson's Characters* (1963), studies the works more psychologically. (M. K.-We.)

RICHBOROUGH, a port on the Stour, in Kent, Eng., 15½ mi. N of Dover by road.

Richborough Castle is one of the most remarkable monuments of the Roman occupation of Britain. It marked the beginning of Watling Street and guarded the channel of the Wantsum, then separating the Isle of Thanet from the mainland. The site shows signs of occupation in the Early Iron Age but it only entered history with the invasion of Claudius in A.D. 43. A base, Rutupiae, was established there which was used throughout the occupation. The extant remains include the north wall of the Saxon Shore fort, possibly built by Carausius in the 3rd century, 460 ft. long and 22 ft. high. There is a cruciform platform of concrete, 126 ft. long and 82 ft. wide. It was probably a monument to the emperor Domitian. A subterranean passage runs under the foundations of the platform. In 1926 excavations revealed a double series of ditches surrounding the fortifications.

During World War I, to relieve the traffic in military stores through Dover, the old port was reestablished. The Stour was widened and deepened, a canal cut across a bend, and 250 ac. of marsh were reclaimed. Nearly a mile of wharfage was built and equipped. The port eventually became derelict.

RICHELIEU, ARMAND EMMANUEL DU PLESSIS, Duc de (1766–1822), French statesman, prime minister from 1815 to 1818 and from 1820 to 1821, had previously served Russia for two decades as a soldier and administrator. Born in Paris on Sept. 25, 1766, the son of Louis Antoine du Plessis, duc de Fronsac, and grandson of Louis François Armand du Plessis, duc de Richelieu and marshal of France, he was known as the comte de Chinon. After a tour of Europe (1782–85), he succeeded his grandfather at court as first gentleman of the bedchamber and became duc de Fronsac on his grandfather's death (1788). Sent on a mission to Germany and Austria in September 1790, he joined the Russian army and was at the capture of Izmail from the Turks (December 1790). Succeeding his father as duc de Richelieu (1791), he fought (1792) with the royalists under Louis Joseph de Bourbon, prince de Condé, and with the Austrians (1793–94). Visiting Russia (1795), he was appointed lieutenant colonel of the cuirassiers of St. George. In 1803 the emperor Alexander I persuaded Napoleon to remove his name from the list of proscribed persons in France. In the same year the tsar appointed Richelieu governor of Odessa, and in 1805 he also became governor general of the whole area north of the Black Sea, between the Dniester and the Kuban rivers. In a notable administration he established schools, reorganized finances, and particularly encouraged agriculture and exports.

Richelieu went to Paris (November 1814) during the First Restoration. On Napoleon's return from Elba (March 1815) he accompanied Louis XVIII as far as Lille but joined the tsar for the campaign against Napoleon. After the Second Restoration he was persuaded to become prime minister (September 1815), with control of foreign affairs. Despite the extreme difficulties of the period (*see* FRANCE: *History*), Richelieu's achievement was considerable. The Congress of Aix-la-Chapelle (1818), which he attended, marked the culmination of his work to clear France from a crippling indemnity and to obtain the withdrawal of the army of occupation. He resigned in December 1818 and toured Italy and Germany. From this time onward he suffered the unwanted attentions of Désirée, queen of Charles XIV John of Sweden, who followed him everywhere he went. After the murder of the duc de Berry, Richelieu reluctantly became prime minister again (February 1820). A moderate, caught between the attacks of the Independents and the increasingly powerful Ultras (extreme royalists), his position soon became untenable and he resigned in December 1821. He died in Paris on May 22, 1822. A statue of him was erected in Odessa in 1828.

Richelieu's marriage with Rosalie de Rochechouart had been arranged before his tour of Europe (1782–85); on his return he discovered his bride to be deformed and left her immediately after the wedding. Nevertheless, although their relations were never more than platonic, in later years he took pleasure in her company.

BIBLIOGRAPHY.—L. de Crousaz-Crétêt, *Le Duc de Richelieu en Russie et en France, 1766–1822* (1897); R. de Cisternes, *Le Duc de Richelieu, son action aux conférences d'Aix-la-Chapelle* (1898); J. Fouques-Duparc, *Le Troisième Richelieu, libérateur du territoire en 1815,* new ed. (1952); C. Cox, *Talleyrand's Successor: Armand-Emmanuel du Plessis, Duc de Richelieu* (1959); G. de Bertier de Sauvigny (ed.), *France and the European Alliance 1816–1821: the Private Correspondence between Metternich and Richelieu* (1958).

RICHELIEU, ARMAND JEAN DU PLESSIS, CARDINAL AND DUC DE

(1585–1642), French statesman, was the principal minister of Louis XIII for 18 years, during which he raised the monarchy to unprecedented heights of power both in the domestic and in the European field of affairs. For the background to this article *see* FRANCE: *History;* THIRTY YEARS' WAR.

The Rise to Power.—Richelieu was born in Paris on Sept. 9, 1585, the youngest son of François du Plessis, seigneur de Richelieu (d. 1590), and Suzanne de La Porte. His father, who belonged to the petty nobility of Poitou, had been a favourite of Henry III, on whose death he transferred his services to Henry IV. His mother came from a family of lawyers.

Nominated bishop of Luçon, in Poitou, by Henry IV late in 1606, when he was still below the canonical age, the young Armand went to Rome to obtain his dispensation from Pope Paul V and was consecrated there in April 1607. In December 1608 he arrived in

BULLOZ

ARMAND JEAN RICHELIEU. DETAIL FROM A PORTRAIT PAINTED BY PHILIPPE DE CHAMPAIGNE. IN THE MUSÉE CONDÉ, CHANTILLY, FRANCE

his little bishopric, where he remained for nearly six years. Elected by the clergy of Poitou to the Estates-General, which met in Paris in October 1614, he there attracted the attention of the queen mother, Marie de Médicis, who was continuing to govern France for her son Louis XIII (*q.v.*) after the formal termination of her regency. Richelieu was chosen to present the final address of the clergy of France, and thereafter he remained in Paris, be-

coming almoner to Louis XIII's consort, Anne of Austria, in 1615. The marshal d'Ancre, favourite of the queen mother, procured Richelieu's appointment as a secretary of state on Nov. 30, 1616.

The murder of the marshal d'Ancre (April 24, 1617) was followed by the exile of Marie de Médicis to Blois. Richelieu, no longer secretary of state, went with her, leaving Louis XIII's government under the control of Charles d'Albert de Luynes (*q.v.*). As Marie's chief adviser, he sought to ingratiate himself with the government by reporting on her actions; but his protestations of loyalty were received with skepticism, and a few weeks later, when he had retired to one of his benefices in Poitou, he received orders to remain there or in his diocese. In this retirement he composed *Les Principaux Poincts de la foi de l'église catholique* (1617), in answer to Protestant propaganda. Indiscretions by Marie and her supporters led to his being exiled to Avignon (April 1618).

When Marie de Médicis escaped from Blois to the protection of the duc d'Épernon (February 1619), the government decided that Richelieu should rejoin her to moderate her attitude. The Treaty of Angoulême (April 1619), which temporarily reconciled her with the king and allowed her to reside at Angers, was negotiated by him, and he remained with her as her chief adviser. After the futile rebellion of the following year, in which he was perforce involved, he negotiated the Peace of Angers (August 1620), which saved Marie and her faction.

The death of Luynes (December 1621) made possible a *rapprochement* between Louis XIII and Marie de Médicis, who was admitted to the king's council. Richelieu furnished her with arguments and with criticisms of other ministers. She in turn promoted his interests, and on Sept. 5, 1622, he was created cardinal by Pope Gregory XV.

On April 29, 1624, Richelieu was himself admitted to Louis XIII's council. He was recognized as one of the chief (*premier*) ministers on the disgrace of the *surintendant* of the finances, Charles de La Vieuville (Aug. 13); and in subsequent letters patent Louis XIII designated him as "principal minister in our council of state."

Relations with the King.—Louis XIII had the highest concept of the royal authority and wished to reign as a great king; and in Richelieu he saw an energetic minister who would see that his decisions were respected. Initially, Louis felt a genuine friendship for the cardinal; but after a few years this affection cooled, as Louis resented the way in which Richelieu enhanced his personal authority and exercised control over all the kingdom's affairs by dealing with them himself or by entrusting them to creatures of his own. Above all, the scrupulous king's conscience was troubled by the cardinal's foreign policy and by the misery which long war and heavy taxation imposed on the people of France. There was thus the risk that someone might supplant Richelieu, and he had always to beware of intrigues woven in the king's immediate entourage—with the complicity, moreover, of members of the royal family. His pliancy in such moments of stress was the complement of his resolute and authoritarian nature. Louis XIII, meanwhile, however much he might sometimes wish for a change, never forgot that Richelieu was the only man capable of maintaining order. He therefore never consented to schemes for dismissing the cardinal. The consequence was a *ministériat*, that is, a sustained period of government through the "principal minister."

Internal and Foreign Politics.—Richelieu's political objectives were clear from the beginning: to reduce all the king's subjects to obedience, and to raise the monarchy's international prestige to its due height. Thus he had on the one hand to struggle against the refractory nobility and against the Huguenots (*q.v.*) in France; and on the other to intervene in the Thirty Years' War in order to prevent the Habsburgs from winning supremacy throughout Europe. The imperial line of the Habsburgs was ruling Austria, the lands of the Bohemian crown, and Alsace, apart from its theoretical suzerainty over Germany, while the Spanish line ruled the whole Iberian Peninsula, the southern Netherlands, Franche-Comté, Milan, Naples, Sicily, and Sardinia, as well as the Central and South American colonies.

Order within the kingdom was a prerequisite for action abroad. Circumstances, however, did not favour the immediate application of a program of thoroughgoing reforms, and once the major war started (from 1635) new disorders ensued within the kingdom. Thus Richelieu's domestic and foreign policy must be considered together.

At the Assembly of Notables of 1626–27 Richelieu presented a program of reforms which he had planned as early as 1625. This comprised the cleansing of the financial system, measures to revive the economy and overseas trade, the destruction of the private strongholds owned by the nobility, the prohibition of dueling and blasphemy, and the reorganization both of teaching and of the Catholic Church in France. If this program was to be implemented, peace was necessary, at least temporarily; and this necessity explains the shortlived settlement with the Huguenots (February 1626) and the Treaty of Monzón with Spain on the question of the Valtellina (May).

Richelieu had also tried to reach agreement with England through the marriage of Louis XIII's sister, Henrietta Maria, to Charles I (1625). But just as the French supported the English Catholics, so did the English support the Huguenots; and the latter's main stronghold in France was the seaport of La Rochelle. Richelieu, moreover, as "grand master, head, and superintendent of the commerce and navigation of France" (from 1627), was determined to uphold the king's power at sea and to protect the coasts of France. So it was not for religious reasons but on grounds of general policy that he undertook the great enterprise of 1627–28 against La Rochelle, which had abetted an English attack on the Île de Ré and was expecting help from the English Navy. After the fall of La Rochelle, a campaign against the Huguenot rebels in Languedoc led to the Peace of Alès (1629), which put an end to the political and military privileges of French Protestantism.

Richelieu's action against the Huguenots encouraged the *parti dévot,* or pious Catholic faction, headed by the keeper of the seals, Michel de Marillac, to believe that he would favour an alliance between the Catholic Powers of Europe, but in fact he had little faith in friendship with Spain. After the reduction of La Rochelle, when the *dévots* stood for retrenchment and peace, Richelieu advocated an active foreign policy for which he was ready to sacrifice "all thought of repose, of thrift, and of adjustment within the kingdom." Consequently, while he was ruthless toward nobles who conspired or broke the law, as in the case of Henri de Talleyrand, marquis de Chalais (*see* Chevreuse, Marie de Rohan-Montbazon, Duchesse de), or François de Montmorency, comte de Boutteville (*see* Duel), he had also to use force of arms to suppress the revolts of peasants and townsmen against new taxes.

Richelieu did not entertain any impracticable designs for territorial aggrandizement, such as the pushing of the French frontier to the Rhine. He wanted, however, to occupy strategic points which would hinder the movement of the Spanish and imperial armies and make their junction more difficult—the so-called "policy of gateways." He was thus interested above all in Italy, taking advantage of the War of the Mantuan Succession (1628–31) to establish French garrisons at Pinerolo (on Savoyard territory) and at Casale (*see* Montferrat). At the Diet of Regensburg, moreover, in 1630, French diplomats worked to weaken the authority of the Holy Roman emperor Ferdinand II in Germany and to procure the dismissal of Wallenstein, who had led the imperial army to great success against the Protestant princes.

It was during this period, toward the end of the Diet of Regensburg, that Richelieu was most in danger of falling from Louis XIII's favour. Marie de Médicis had come to terms with the keeper of the seals and his brother, the marshal Louis de Marillac; and they almost succeeded in procuring the cardinal's disgrace. Richelieu discovered their intentions and tried in vain to justify himself. He finally despaired and was on the point of retiring when the king decided to uphold him as his principal minister. This crisis (Nov. 10–12, 1630) is known as the Day of Dupes. Michel de Marillac was dismissed from office, and Louis de Marillac was accused of peculation and beheaded after an iniquitous trial. The cardinal was created duc de Richelieu and a peer of France (August 1631), and obtained the rights to a personal bodyguard.

Marie de Médicis in July 1631 fled to the Spanish Netherlands to join her younger son, Gaston, duc d'Orléans (*q.v.*), who was heir presumptive to the throne in view of the king's childlessness. In 1632 the governor of Languedoc, Henri de Montmorency, put himself at the head of a revolt against taxation, and Gaston led an army to support him. Taken prisoner at Castelnaudary, Montmorency was tried and beheaded at Toulouse.

Richelieu continued to make the influence of France felt in the affairs of Europe. When Germany, devastated by ravaging armies, was ready for peace, Richelieu kept the war going because its continuance was the only means of ensuring that the House of Austria would not establish its supremacy in the Empire (*see* again Thirty Years' War). He made the Treaty of Bärwalde with Gustavus II Adolphus of Sweden (1631), began obscure negotiations with Wallenstein, and after the death of Gustavus (1632), provided French subsidies for the upkeep of the Swedish armies in Germany and for Bernhard of Saxe-Weimar. After the imperial victory at Nördlingen (1634), however, the electors John George I of Saxony and George William of Brandenburg came to terms with the emperor under the Peace of Prague (1635). Then Richelieu, whose hand was strengthened by France's alliances with the United Province of Netherlands and with several Italian princes, passed to the declaration of open war against Spain (May 1635). Hostilities in Germany were already in progress before the emperor Ferdinand II retaliated by declaring war on France (1636).

Richelieu had some unequivocally devoted collaborators: for example, Father Joseph, the chancellor Pierre Séguier (*qq.v.*), François Sublet de Noyers, Michel Le Tellier, and the comte de Chavigny (Léon Bouthillier; *see* Bouthillier). With their help he managed to obtain from different social groups things which they had had no intention of giving him—above all, money for the war. The assembly of the clergy, manipulated by subservient bishops, voted subsidies; the *bourgeoisie* bought administrative or judiciary offices, the number of which was increased; the nobility became accustomed to serving with more regularity in the army; the ordinary people submitted, for the most part, to heavier taxation; and the tax farmers, who enriched themselves in the process, always contrived to find the necessary money. The most dangerous of the popular risings was that of the *Va-nu-pieds* in Normandy (1639), which was put down with the help of foreign mercenaries. Generals who failed were liable to be punished, as in the case of the duc de La Valette (Bernard de Nogaret) after his defeat at Fuenterrabia in 1638. While the right of remonstrance of the *parlements* was restricted, extraordinary judicial commissions were instituted to force recalcitrants to obedience. Even so, there were conspiracies against Richelieu till the end: for example, that of Louis de Bourbon, comte de Soissons, in 1641, and that of Cinq-Mars (*q.v.*) in 1642.

It is difficult to say whether fear or apathy did more to subdue public opinion, or rather public opinions, into accepting the cardinal's regime. Richelieu was clever enough at whipping up enthusiasm for his policy by hiring propagandists or by granting special protection to journalists, such as Théophraste Renaudot (*q.v.*), founder of the *Gazette.* The splendour with which he surrounded himself and his accumulation of honours and enormously lucrative offices made a gross contrast with the misery of the people but did much to raise his personal prestige; he built the Palais Cardinal (later the Palais Royal) for himself in Paris, transformed his family's house at Richelieu into a magnificent château, and also bought a great suburban house at Rueil. Lastly, he did not extinguish all hope of reform in the kingdom, but simply postponed such reform till the return of peace.

Economic and Overseas Affairs.—Richelieu always encouraged profitable investments in overseas trade. He believed that France's products could compete advantageously with those of other countries and that a proper exploitation of resources should make France self-sufficient—able to export much and needing few imports. He encouraged the manufacture of tapestry and glassware, the plush and silk industries of Tours, the cloth of Normandy and Berry, the linen of Normandy and Maine.

Irked by the fact that overseas trade was at first virtually monopolized by the Dutch, Richelieu made great efforts to bring it into French hands; to French shipowners he sold well-found mer-

chant vessels which could be armed in time of war; and he granted
privileges to companies which established colonies on the American
mainland and in the West Indies. Samuel de Champlain (*q.v.*) set
up permanent French posts in Canada; and Richelieu favoured this
colony especially because he thought that the fur trade, carried
on by barter, would not involve the dispatch of any money from
France and that the conversion of the Indians to Catholicism by
French missionaries would redound to the king's glory. The companies did not all prosper, as the Breton and Norman shipowners
looked askance at monopolies. The Compagnie de Saint-Chris-
tophe, however, was successful in the Antilles, bringing artisans
and labourers to populate the islands and eventually becoming the
Compagnie des Îles d'Amérique, with exclusive rights of trading
and sovereign powers. Other companies reached the region of the
Amazon, the Cape Verde Islands, Senegal, and even Madagascar,
where Port-Dauphin was founded.

Treaties were concluded with the Barbary States and with Morocco. At first hesitant about the Mediterranean trade, which he
regarded as confined to expensive luxury goods, Richelieu became
interested in it when he saw how French wood and hemp could be
exported and exotic produce obtained for consumption in France
or for sale along the Italian coasts, payment being made in Spanish
doubloons. Wartime taxation, however, diminished the purchasing power of the French consumer, without which this trade could
not be conducted regularly or profitably; and only a small number
of capitalists were rich enough to make the prerequisite investments. The war, though it was ruinous to the country as a whole,
helped individuals to make great profits, especially men who were
already rich. Meanwhile the cardinal's interest in the navy led
to victories on the high seas and to successful operations in the
Mediterranean.

Intellectual and Cultural Interests.—From 1622 Richelieu
was provisor, that is to say, official protector, of the Sorbonne (the
chapel of which he reconstructed in the style of the churches in
Rome). In matters of teaching, he wanted to develop a spirit
of friendly rivalry between the universities and the Jesuits. He
was unwilling to see any great extension in the study of law, lest
it should increase the number of lawyers in a nation already overly
addicted to litigation. On the other hand he was glad to see the
upper classes concerning themselves with literature and the fine
arts, and he enjoyed listening to the debates of experts on aesthetic
questions. His incorporation of the Académie Française by royal
letters patent (1635) bears witness to his belief that the prestige
of the intellect would contribute to the glory of the reign. France's
achievement in the intellectual field during his regime owed very
much to his personal benevolence.

Conclusions.—Foreign affairs, his chief concern, in fact prevented Richelieu from giving effect to the far-reaching reforms
outlined in his *Testament politique;* and in any case he was gifted
more with the broad vision of statesmanship than with any talent
for administrative detail. First and last in his political thinking
was the "reason of state," which required above all that the state
should be powerful internationally. For internal affairs, so long
as circumstances did not allow any radical reorganization, empirical methods sufficed. This explains his recourse to the employment of commissioners, sometimes with the title of intendant
(*q.v.*), who were sent into the provinces to supervise local officials, to impose new taxes, and, so far as possible, to maintain
order, but who could be recalled at the king's pleasure. While the
war lasted, men counted for more than institutions, though Richelieu was well aware that the authority and the efficiency of institutions ought to be enhanced.

Richelieu's regime transformed France from a state medieval in
many respects into a more modern one, with a discipline overriding the concurrent interests of the various social elements.
When he died, worn out by overwork, in the Palais Cardinal on
Dec. 4, 1642, his death was greeted as a relief by the people; but
it made no difference to events in the long run, since Jules Mazarin
(*q.v.*) was eventually able to bring his work to completion.
Though Richelieu died before victory had been won in his war, the
king's armies were occupying important towns in the Spanish
Netherlands, had overrun Lorraine and Alsace, and, on the farther
bank of the Rhine, were in possession of Breisach, while on the
southwestern frontier Roussillon had been conquered and Catalonia, in revolt against Spanish rule, had put itself under Louis
XIII's protection. France had never before been so powerful or
so much feared in Europe.

Writings.—Richelieu's letters, diplomatic instructions, and
state papers are edited by the vicomte G. d'Avenel in eight volumes (1853–77). Of his *Mémoires*, the best edition is that by the
Société de l'Histoire de France, in ten volumes (1908–31), covering the years 1600–29; but the editions in the Petitot and Michaud-
Poujoulat collections (ten volumes [1823] and three volumes
[1837–38] respectively) supply also the text for the years 1630–
38. The *Testament politique*, which reflects Richelieu's thought
even though the authenticity of the whole is open to question
(since the manuscript is lost), first appeared in 1688 and is best
edited by L. André (1947).

See also references under "Richelieu, Armand Jean du Plessis"
in the Index.

BIBLIOGRAPHY.—G. Hanotaux and A. de Caumont, duc de La Force,
Histoire du cardinal de Richelieu, 6 vol. in 7 parts (1893–1947), gives an
authoritative survey. *See* also, for general accounts, H. Belloc, *Richelieu* (1920); M. Deloche, *Autour de la plume du cardinal de Richelieu*
(1920); L. Batiffol, *Richelieu et le roi Louis XIII* (1934), and *Autour
de Richelieu* (1937); J. Canu, *Louis XIII et Richelieu* (1944); C. V.
Wedgwood, *Richelieu and the French Monarchy* (1950); G. Pagès,
Naissance du grand siècle 1610–1661 (1949); V. L. Tapié, *La France
de Louis XIII et de Richelieu* (1952). For administration *see* R.
Mousnier, *La Vénalité des offices sous Henri IV et Louis XIII* (1945);
O. A. Ranum, *Richelieu and the Councillors of Louis XIII . . . 1635–
1642* (1963). For economic activity *see* F. C. Palm, *The Economic
Policies of Richelieu* (1922); H. Hauser, *La Pensée et l'action économiques du cardinal de Richelieu* (1944); L. Boiteux, *Richelieu: grand
maître de la navigation et du commerce de France* (1955); R. La
Bruyère, *Richelieu: 9 septembre 1585–4 décembre 1642* (1958). For
literary and ecclesiastical aspects *see* L. Batiffol, *Richelieu et Corneille*
(1936); J. Orcibal, *Jean Duvergier de Hauranne, abbé de Saint-Cyran,
et son temps* (1948); P. Blet, *Le Clergé de France et la monarchie*
(1959). For earlier works, many of them still useful, *see* the list in
E. Préclin and V. L. Tapié, *Le XVIIᵉ Siècle*, 2nd ed. (1949).
(V. L. T.)

RICHEPIN, JEAN (1849–1926), French writer in the tradition of Villon and the poets of low life. Born at Médéa, Algeria,
Feb. 4, 1849, the son of an army doctor, he left the École Normale
early and during the Franco-German War joined the *francs-
tireurs*. He worked as a sailor, an actor, and a docker before his
first book of poems, *La Chanson des gueux* (1876), won him both
instantaneous fame and a month's imprisonment for its immorality.
When Zola revolutionized the French novel by introducing Naturalism, Richepin did the same for poetry in *Les Caresses* (1877),
Les Blasphèmes (1884), and *La Mer* (1886). He wrote novels
himself: *Les Morts bizarres* (1876), *La Glu* (1881), and *Miarka*
(1883·); besides very successful plays: *Nana Sahib* (1883), in
which he acted with Sarah Bernhardt, *Le Flibustier* (1888), *Par
le glaive* (1892), *Les Truands* (1899), and *Le Chemineau* (1897;
Eng. trans. by W. Wallace, 1910), a lyric drama with music by
Xavier Leroux. To be properly appreciated he should be considered in his period, when thinkers were preoccupied with materialism and "scientism" as expounded by Ernst Haeckel and
Ludwig Büchner. *Les Blasphèmes* translates this philosophy into
verse of great power, and it has been said that Richepin's very
defiance of God was almost a tribute to him. He was director of
the Académie Française (to which he was elected in 1908) when
he died in Paris on Dec. 11, 1926.   (R. DL.)

RICHET, CHARLES (ROBERT) (1850–1935), French
physiologist, who was awarded the Nobel Prize for Medicine in
1913 for his work on anaphylaxis (hypersensitive reaction of the
body to foreign proteins; *see* ALLERGY AND ANAPHYLAXIS), was
born in Paris on Aug. 26, 1850. Richet received his medical degree in 1877, but before this he had carried out important researches on the role of conditioned reflexes in the digestive process
and had discovered that the acid of gastric juice is hydrochloric
acid. In 1881 he was appointed codirector of the *Revue Scientifique* and in 1887 became professor of physiology at the University of Paris. He worked on the physiology of respiration, on
epilepsy, on the regulation of body heat, and on the treatment
of tuberculosis by feeding with raw meat. Most important were

his researches on immunity and serum therapy. His studies of anaphylaxis (the term is Richet's) threw new light on such conditions as hay fever and asthma and on drug reactions and serum sickness, and explained mysterious cases of intoxication and sudden death.

Richet was a man of many interests. He was distinguished not only as a physiologist but also as a bacteriologist, pathologist, psychologist, and medical statistician, and he won further fame as a pioneer of aviation, an earnest worker on behalf of peace, a scientific investigator of occult phenomena, and as a poet, novelist, and playwright. He died in Paris on Dec. 4, 1935.

(W. J. Bp.; X.)

RICHFIELD, a village of Hennepin county in southeastern Minnesota, U.S., is located immediately south of Minneapolis. It experienced rapid growth after 1940, its population increasing from less than 7,000 to more than 40,000 by 1960. (For comparative population figures *see* table in MINNESOTA: *Population*.)

Originally called Harmony and Richland, it was renamed in 1858 when the early residents of the area held their first town meeting in a schoolhouse near Richfield Mills. It was incorporated as a village in 1908; in 1950 it adopted a village-manager form of government.

Although mainly a residential suburb of Minneapolis, it has several small light-industrial establishments that manufacture metal and wood products. Agriculture was once the dominant industry and, while its importance has diminished in the economy of the community, there is still significant dairying and truck farming of small vegetables, fruits and berries. (R. W. F.)

RICHLAND, a planned city and atomic-industry town in Benton County, Wash., U.S., is located near the confluence of the Yakima and Columbia rivers about 50 mi. W of Walla Walla. Once it was the home of the Wanapam, or Wanapum, Indians, a division of the Sahaptin stock. Nelson Rich, builder of a local irrigation system, laid out a town there in 1892; incorporated in 1910, its population of about 250 remained virtually static until the site became part of the 400,000-ac. reservation of the Hanford atomic energy plant.

Its population was 1,415 by 1944, grew to 13,453 the next year, and rose to 23,548 by 1960. (For comparative population figures *see* table in WASHINGTON: *Population*.)

First administered by the U.S. army corps of engineers and E. I. du Pont de Nemours & Co., the Atomic Energy Commission and the General Electric Company took over on Jan. 1, 1947. Transfer of real estate to its residents began in 1957, and in 1958 it became incorporated as a city with a council-manager form of government. (H. J. DE.)

RICHMOND, EARLS AND DUKES OF. The English title earl of Richmond appears to have been in existence for some time before it was held in accordance with any strict legal principle. Until the end of the 14th century it was usually held by counts or dukes of Brittany or by claimants to the duchy, and the honour (territory) was at first called the honour of Brittany. EUDON (d. 1079), younger brother of Alan III (d. 1040), duke of Brittany, at first disputed the ducal title with Alan and with Alan's successor Conan II (d. 1066), but was eventually satisfied with a partition of the family lands and the style of "count of Brittany." Eudon's third son ALAN I (d. 1089), the Red, accompanied William the Conqueror to England (1066) and a few years later was granted the Yorkshire lands formerly belonging to Edwin, earl of Mercia. He built a castle at Richmond. Alan died unmarried and was succeeded in turn by two of his brothers, ALAN II (d. 1093), the Black, and STEPHEN (d. 1135–36), Eudon's youngest son. Stephen also succeeded his eldest brother Geoffrey Boterel (d. 1093) or Geoffrey's son Conan (d. 1098) as count of Brittany. Stephen's second son ALAN III (d. 1146), the Black, the first to be formally styled earl of Richmond, fought for King Stephen at the Battle of Lincoln (1141). His wife Bertha was daughter and heiress of Duke Conan III, and their son CONAN (d. 1171) became duke of Brittany as Conan IV as well as earl of Richmond. He married Margaret, sister of Malcolm IV of Scotland. Conan IV left no sons and Brittany and the honour of Richmond passed to his daughter Constance (d. 1201). Her first husband GEOFFREY

(d. 1186), a son of Henry II of England, was recognized as duke of Brittany and earl of Richmond in the year of their marriage (1181). RANULF DE BLUNDEVILLE (d. 1232), earl of Chester, second husband of Constance, also assumed the style of duke of Brittany and earl of Richmond. His marriage was annulled (1199). Constance's third husband Guy de Thouars administered the honour after his wife's death, without, however, obtaining the title.

ARTHUR I (1187–1203; *q.v.*), duke of Brittany, son of Constance and Geoffrey, was styled earl of Richmond during his mother's lifetime. He disappeared in 1203 (probably murdered by his uncle, King John) and his sister Eleanor died in prison in England, unmarried, in 1241. Meanwhile Peter, count of Dreux (Pierre Mauclerc), husband of Alix (daughter of Constance and Guy), established himself as duke of Brittany. He was granted seisin of the Richmond lands by Henry III in 1219, but the grant was revoked in 1235 when he renounced his allegiance to the English king. In 1240 Henry III gave the honour of Richmond to his wife's uncle, PETER OF SAVOY (d. 1268; *q.v.*), and he was popularly styled earl of Richmond. On Peter's death any title he may have held reverted to the crown. The earldom of Richmond was then (1268) granted to JOHN I (1216–85), duke of Brittany, eldest son of Alix and Peter. John I, however, soon surrendered the earldom to his son JOHN II (1239–1305), duke of Brittany, who accompanied the future Edward I on crusade (1270–74) and fought in the Welsh wars in 1277. His eldest son Arthur II (d. 1312) succeeded him in Brittany; his second son JOHN (c. 1266–1334) fought in Edward I's Scottish wars and was granted the earldom of Richmond in 1306. He died unmarried and his nephew JOHN III (1286–1341), duke of Brittany, son of Duke Arthur II, successfully claimed the honour of Richmond and was summoned to Parliament as earl in 1335. Although on friendly terms with Edward III he fought in the French Army in the early engagements of the Hundred Years' War. He left no legitimate issue and in Brittany the succession was disputed between his half-brother JOHN (1293–1345), count of Montfort-l'Amaury, and his niece's husband Charles of Blois. John of Montfort was supported by Edward III who made him earl of Richmond. But after John's capture at Nantes (1341), Edward gave the earldom (1342) to his son JOHN OF GAUNT (1340–99), afterward duke of Lancaster (*see* LANCASTER, JOHN OF GAUNT, Duke of). Gaunt surrendered the earldom in 1372 and it was restored to JOHN IV (c. 1339–99; *q.v.*), John de Montfort's son, who was recognized as duke of Brittany in 1365. On the death of John IV the earldom was seized by the crown and was not again held by a duke of Brittany. The Richmond lands (but not the title) were granted in October 1399 to Ralph Neville (d. 1425), earl of Westmorland, and on his death passed by a reversionary grant to JOHN (1389–1435), duke of Bedford, third son of Henry IV, who had been created earl of Richmond in 1414. Bedford died without heirs and all his honours became extinct.

EDMUND TUDOR (c. 1430–56), eldest son of Owen Tudor by Queen Catherine, widow of Henry V, was created earl of Richmond by his half brother Henry VI in 1452. He married Margaret Beaufort, heiress of John Beaufort, duke of Somerset. Their son HENRY TUDOR (1457–1509) was deprived of the title and lands on the accession of Edward IV in 1461 and after 1471 was in exile in France. He returned to England in 1485, defeated Richard III at the Battle of Bosworth, and became King Henry VII. The earldom of Richmond was thus merged in the crown.

HENRY FITZROY (1519–36), illegitimate son of Henry VIII by Elizabeth Blount, was created duke of Richmond in 1525. He left no successor and the title was not granted again until the 17th century. LUDOVIC STEWART (1574–1624), duke of Lennox in the peerage of Scotland, was created earl (1613) and duke (1623) of Richmond by James I. On his death without legitimate issue, his English honours became extinct but his Scottish titles passed to his brother Esmé, who was already earl of March in the peerage of England (*see* LENNOX, EARLS AND DUKES OF; MARCH, EARLS OF). Esmé's son, JAMES STEWART (1612–55), created duke of Richmond in 1641, supported Charles I during the Civil War and was in charge of the king's funeral in 1649. His son ESMÉ (1649–60) died while still a child, and most of his dignities, including the dukedom of Richmond, passed to his cousin CHARLES STEWART (1639–72), a gentleman of the bedchamber to Charles II, whose wife Frances Teresa was a celebrated beauty at the same court. On his death without heirs the titles became extinct.

CHARLES LENNOX (1672–1723), illegitimate son of Charles II by Louise de Kéroualle, was created duke of Richmond in 1675. He was aide-de-camp to William III from 1693 to 1702 and lord of the bedchamber to George I from 1714 to 1723. His son CHARLES LENNOX (1701–50), the 2nd duke, held household appointments under George I and George II and fought at Dettingen (1743) and against the Jacobites (1745). On the death of his grandmother Louise de Kéroualle in 1734, he inherited the title of duc d'Aubigny in France. The 2nd duke's daughter, Lady Caroline, married (1744) Henry Fox, afterward Baron Holland, and became the mother of the statesman Charles James Fox. Another daughter, Lady Sarah, became, by her second husband George Napier, mother of the generals Sir Charles and Sir William Napier. Lennox' son CHARLES (1735–1806), the 3rd duke, was secretary of state for the southern department (May–July 1766) and master general of the ordnance with a seat in the cabinet (March 1782–April 1783, December 1783–February 1795). An ardent advocate of reform, he steadily opposed the war against the American colonists, favoured relief measures for Ireland, and in 1780 introduced a bill proposing annual parliaments and manhood suffrage. His "Letter . . . to lieutenant-Colonel Sharman of the Irish Volunteers," first published in 1783, became almost a manifesto of the reforming societies of the time.

The 3rd duke was succeeded by his nephew CHARLES (1764–1819), who had an army career, was a Tory M.P., and in 1818 became governor general of Canada. His son CHARLES (1791–1860) fought in the Peninsular War. As a member of the House of Lords he opposed Catholic Emancipation in the 1820s and in the 1840s opposed Sir Robert Peel's free trade policy. On succeeding in 1836 to the estates of his mother's brother George Gordon, 5th duke of Gordon, he took the name Gordon-Lennox by royal licence. His son CHARLES HENRY GORDON-LENNOX (1818–1903), 6th duke of Richmond, led the Conservative peers from 1870 to 1876, when he was created duke of Gordon. His son CHARLES HENRY (1845–1928) was succeeded in turn by his son CHARLES HENRY (1870–1935) and by his grandson FREDERICK CHARLES (1904–   ), 9th duke of Richmond.

RICHMOND, a municipal borough in the Richmond (Yorks) parliamentary division of the North Riding of Yorkshire, Eng., 45 mi. NNW of York. Pop. (1961) 5,776. It lies on the left bank of the Swale, where the valley is still narrow and steep-sided before the river emerges from the Pennines into the Vale of York.

The town is chiefly interesting because of the castle, which occupies the summit of a high cliff. The castle was founded about 1071 by Alan Rufus of Penthièvre in Brittany, who is said to have rebuilt the town on obtaining from William the Conqueror the estates of the Saxon earl Edwin, which embraced some 200 manors of Richmond and extended over nearly a third of the North Riding. This tract was called Richmondshire at that time, but the date of the creation of the shire is uncertain. William the Lion of Scotland was imprisoned in the castle in the reign of Henry II; otherwise the town owes its importance chiefly to its lords. It was a valuable possession in the Middle Ages, and was usually in royal or semiroyal hands. The whole shire reverted to the crown on the accession of Henry VII. The original castle covered an area of 5 ac., but the only portions remaining are the Norman keep, with pinnacled tower and walls 109 ft. high by 11 ft. thick, and some smaller towers.

The French name of Richmond (*Richemund*) was not traced farther back than about 1100, but it is probable that there was an earlier settlement on the site. As far as is known, the earliest charter was granted in 1145 giving the burgesses the borough of Richmond to hold for ever in fee farm at an annual rent of £29, but a charter dated 1146 shows that the burgesses enjoyed some municipal liberties at an earlier period. In 1278, a yearly fair was granted and in 1329, Edward III gave the first royal charter to the town. A charter of incorporation, under the title of aldermen and burgesses, was granted in 1576 by Queen Elizabeth I who

also allowed a market each Saturday, an animal market every fortnight, and a fair each year on the vigil of Palm Sunday. In 1668, Charles II granted a charter under the title of mayor and aldermen.

This charter, though superseded later, was restored in the reign of James II, and, until the passing of the Municipal Corporations Act of 1835, was regarded as the governing charter of the borough. Although Richmond received a summons as early as 1328, it was not represented in Parliament until 1584, from which time it usually sent two members. From 1867 to 1885 one member was sent. In 1889, Richmond became the seat of a bishop suffragan in the diocese of Ripon, but the second and last bishop died in 1921.

The church of St. Mary is transitional Norman, Decorated, and Perpendicular, and is largely restored. The Church of the Holy Trinity, in the large marketplace, is ancient and was restored to use from ruins; only the nave and a detached tower remain. A curfew bell is tolled every evening and in the mornings the 'Prentice bell. The 16th-century tower of a Franciscan abbey, founded in 1258, still stands. Close to the town are the ruins of Easby Abbey, a Premonstratensian foundation of 1152, beautifully situated by the river. The remains include a Decorated gateway, an Early English chapel, and fragments of the transepts and choir of the church, with sufficient portions of the domestic buildings to enable the complete plan to be traced. In Friar's Wynd is the Theatre Royal, a Georgian theatre (1788). In Hill House lived Frances l'Anson or Janson, "the lass of Richmond Hill," to whom her future husband, Leonard MacNally, wrote the verses of the famous song.

The free grammar school existed in 1390, and was refounded in 1567, but the present building dates from 1850.

RICHMOND, a city of Contra Costa county, Calif., U.S., is situated on the eastern shore of San Francisco bay, 16 mi. NE of San Francisco via the San Francisco-Oakland bay bridge. The Richmond-San Rafael bridge connects it with Marin county.

The city, which is in the San Francisco-Oakland standard metropolitan area, experienced a phenomenal growth during World War II, and the population grew from 23,642 in 1940 to 99,545 in 1950, but with removal of wartime public housing declined to 71,854 in 1960. (For comparative population figures *see* table in CALIFORNIA: *Population*).

Development of the area dates from 1899, when the Santa Fe railway purchased a right of way to the bay shore. In 1900 Point Richmond became the western terminal of the system, and ferry service was established to San Francisco. The construction of a large oil refinery in 1902 furthered settlement. The city is an important industrial centre, and its harbour is one of the busiest on the Pacific coast. Major industries include petroleum refining, railroad shops, food processing and the manufacture of chemicals, electronic equipment, aircraft parts and plumbing fixtures.

The city was incorporated in 1905 and adopted the council-manager form of government in 1920. Richmond civic centre includes the city hall, hall of justice, a public library and an auditorium.   (M. H. Mo.)

RICHMOND, a city of Indiana, U.S., is located 68 mi. E. of Indianapolis; the seat of Wayne county. Settled in 1806 by migrating North Carolina antislavery Quakers and German and Irish immigrants, Richmond has always been a centre of Quaker influence and organizations. The publications office and the general offices of the Five Years Meeting of Friends (Quakers) are located there, and the sessions of this group are regularly held in the city. Earlham college, a Quaker-controlled liberal arts coeducational institution founded in 1847 and noted for the large number of its graduates who have distinguished themselves in public life, is also located in Richmond, on a modern 120-ac. campus.

The Art association, civic theatre, symphony orchestra, Musical Arts society and Wayne County Historical museum are civic enterprises. Richmond also has several golf courses and city parks. Located in a prosperous agricultural area, early industries included grain threshers and steam engines, buggies and carriages, and lawn mowers; later industries were diversified and include automotive parts, school-bus bodies and cut-flower production. It was chartered as a city in 1840. For comparative population figures *see* table in INDIANA: *Population*. (WI. R.)

RICHMOND, a borough of New York city and a county of New York, U.S., the two having identical boundaries. Richmond includes all Staten Island and part or all of several smaller islands in New York harbour. It was named after the duke of Richmond, son of Charles II of England.

Indian attacks wiped out the earliest settlements. The first permanent settlement was made under Dutch authority in 1661 at Oude Dorp ("Old Town"). Three years later the British drove out the Dutch and took control. Gen. William Howe landed his forces on Staten Island in 1776, making it a base for his successful attack on Gen. George Washington's positions on Long Island and Manhattan. During the 19th century, Richmond grew more slowly than other sections of modern New York city, partly because it was cut off by water barriers and had to rely on ferries for transportation. When greater New York city was formed in 1898, Richmond county became one of its five boroughs.

Modern Richmond is linked by bridges to the mainland. It is an important shipping and manufacturing centre and an expanding residential area. In Richmond are Wagner college (Lutheran, established 1883), Notre Dame College of Staten Island, for women (Roman Catholic, established 1931), a community college, a zoo, museums, libraries, hospitals and several historic houses. There at Billopp house in 1776 Adm. Richard Howe tried to persuade representatives of the Continental congress to reconcile their differences with England. *See also* NEW YORK (CITY); STATEN ISLAND. (J. A. FR.)

RICHMOND, the capital of Virginia, U.S., and the seat of Henrico county, is located at the falls of the James river, 100 mi. S. of Washington, D.C. Its maximum elevation above sea level is 312 ft. The annual precipitation is 43 in. and the mean annual temperature is about 58° F. (about 14° C.), combining to give the city a moderate and comfortable climate. In 1960 Richmond had a population of 219,958. The standard metropolitan statistical area (SMSA), comprising the city of Richmond and Chesterfield and Henrico counties, had 408,494 inhabitants; in 1963 Hanover county was added to the SMSA resulting in an adjusted 1960 population of 436,044. For comparative population figures for the city *see* table in VIRGINIA: *Population*. Although the city lost population between 1950 and 1960, the metropolitan area made a substantial gain. Residential suburbs have grown with great speed since World War II. Despite this rapid growth, Richmond has managed to preserve a civic personality which, in its friendliness and good humour, is usually found only in much smaller communities.

History.—The first Europeans to visit the present site of Richmond were a party of 21 men led by Christopher Newport and John Smith, who sailed up the James in 1607 a short time after the founding of Jamestown. In 1637 Thomas Stegg established a trading post at the falls of the James, and in 1644, following the Indian massacre of that year, Ft. Charles was built. Indian attacks continued to harass the settlers, and in exchange for a grant of land William Byrd I undertook to maintain 50 men at Ft. Charles to protect the frontier. In 1737 William Byrd II, who had inherited a large tract of land at the falls, allowed Maj. William Mayo to lay out a town on what is now Church hill; it was incorporated by the general assembly in 1742 and in that year had a population of 250.

Richmond was the scene of the Virginia conventions of 1774 and 1775, and in 1780 was made the state capital, replacing Williamsburg. At that time the town had less than 300 buildings and when it was occupied by the British in 1781 the capitol was so humble a structure that the invaders were unable to find and destroy it. Construction of the present capitol was begun four years later.

By the beginning of the 19th century, Richmond's population had grown to 5,735, and the city was becoming a commercial and transportation centre of increasing prominence. In 1840 it was linked to Lynchburg by the James river and Kanawha canal. By 1860 there were 43 tobacco factories, several iron foundries, flour and corn mills, and establishments manufacturing carriages, tex-

tiles, nails, cutlery and paper; the census of 1860 ranked Richmond 13th among American cities in manufacturing. By that same year six railroads terminated in the city. Culturally the ante-bellum years were brightened by visits of such famous literary and stage figures as Charles Dickens, William Thackeray, Jenny Lind and Joseph Jefferson. Edgar Allan Poe edited the *Southern Literary Messenger* in Richmond from 1834 to 1837.

The coming of the American Civil War brought Richmond into a national and international prominence unparalleled in the city's history. Following the secession of Virginia in April 1861, the capital of the Confederacy was moved to Richmond from Montgomery, Ala. As the seat of government, and also because of its factories and railroads, Richmond was the major military objective of Union armies for four years.

In 1862 Gen. George B. McClellan's army of the Potomac was within hearing of the city's church bells but was driven away in the Seven Days' battle, June 26–July 2. Although threatened from time to time by cavalry raids, the city was not again closely beset until June 1864, when the siege of Richmond and Petersburg began. Finally, on April 2, 1865, Gen. U. S. Grant broke through the Confederate defenses, and the city was abandoned that same night, a large part of the business section being destroyed by fire in the course of the evacuation.

During the difficult postwar years Richmond was more fortunate than other southern cities in having an industry with a seemingly unlimited market: tobacco, especially cigarettes. With this as an economic base, rebuilding and recovery were soon under way. Flour mills and an iron foundry were revived; railroads were reconstructed; paper and chemical factories were established. By 1890 the population was 85,000, more than twice that of 1860. The depression of the 1930s once again demonstrated the value of the tobacco industry to the municipal economy, for Richmond suffered much less than many other U.S. cities.

Economic revival and growth were greatly stimulated by the advent of World War II. After the war, in 1948, the strong mayor type of government was discarded in favor of the council-manager system.

Historic Sites.—Richmond is pre-eminently a historic city, a fact in which its citizens have always taken great pride. The capitol was designed by Thomas Jefferson, after the Maison Carrée at Nîmes, France, and contains the famous Houdon statue of George Washington. St. John's church, where Patrick Henry delivered his "Liberty or Death" address, is still a place of worship. At the corner of 9th and Marshall streets stands the house designed, built and occupied by Chief Justice John Marshall. Reminders of the American Civil War period are numerous. Richmond is, in fact, perhaps the chief repository and guardian of the Confederate legend. The Confederate White House, the Valen-

BY COURTESY OF VIRGINIA CHAMBER OF COMMERCE, PHOTO BY FLOURNOY
THE STATE CAPITOL AT RICHMOND

tine museum, Battle abbey and the Virginia Historical society all contain books, paintings, relics and manuscripts from the war years. On Monument avenue stand large bronze statues portraying Jefferson Davis, Generals Lee, Jackson and Stuart and Comdr. Matthew Fontaine Maury. Remains of elaborate entrenchments that encircled the city can still be found in many places.

Commerce, Industry and Transportation.—In the economic life of the city, commerce is more significant than manufacturing. The chamber of commerce estimates that retail stores draw customers from 40 counties and 9 cities, including a population of over 1,000,000. The three leading components of this trade are general merchandise, food and automobiles. Richmond's wholesale market embraces most of the state plus the eastern half of North Carolina, with a sales volume twice that of retail trade. The most important products manufactured or processed in the Richmond area (ranked according to employment) are tobacco, chemicals, food, metals, paper products, printing, clothing, lumber and wood products. The presence of a federal reserve bank makes the city a financial centre for five states and the District of Columbia.

Richmond is the state's most important transportation centre and is served by several major railroads and airlines, as well as bus and truck lines. The Richmond-Petersburg turnpike allows north-south traffic to bypass both cities. At the Deepwater terminal on the James ocean-going vessels bring cargoes from the Gulf coast, Canada and elsewhere.

Education and Cultural Activities.—Richmond has a vigorous public-school system, which absorbs one-fourth of the municipal income, and a number of excellent private and parochial schools. Among the institutions of higher learning are the University of Richmond (Baptist, founded 1830), Medical College of Virginia (state-supported), Union Theological seminary (Presbyterian, founded 1812) and Virginia Union university (Baptist, established 1865).

The Mosque, a municipal auditorium seating over 4,500, is the scene of dramatic productions, as well as concerts by the Richmond Symphony orchestra and visiting orchestras. The state's finest collection of paintings and *objets d'art*, including the works of Rubens, Murillo and Reynolds, is exhibited by the Virginia Museum of Fine Arts. Library facilities include the Virginia State library and the Richmond Public library.

See also references under "Richmond" in the Index.

(L. H. J.)

RICHMOND RIVER, one of the main coastal streams of New South Wales, Austr., is usually associated with the Tweed and Clarence as the "Northern Rivers" region of the state. The three valleys form a sizable coastal lowland, in part floored by rich alluvial soils largely devoted to sugar cane. The region is also one of the leading dairying areas of Australia, especially on the low red-soil uplands to the north, formerly the "Big Scrub" but now largely under paspalum pasture. Maize (corn) and (more recently) millets are important crops associated with dairying, which (because of distance from the Sydney market) is for butter rather than raw milk. Bananas are also grown. The lower reaches of the rivers are navigable, the chief towns being Lismore and Grafton (q.v.).   (O. H. K. S.)

RICHMOND UPON THAMES, one of the 32 London boroughs constituting Greater London, is bounded west by the Borough of Hounslow; north by the Thames; east by the Borough of Wandsworth; and south by the Royal Borough of Kingston-upon-Thames and the Thames. This outer London borough was established on April 1, 1965, under the London Government Act 1963 by the amalgamation of the former Boroughs of Barnes and Richmond in Surrey with the Borough of Twickenham in Middlesex (*see* LONDON). Area, 22 sq.mi. (57 sq.km.). Pop. (mid-1965 est.) 181,130. The borough comprises the parliamentary constituencies of Twickenham and Richmond. It is administered by a council consisting of nine aldermen and 54 councilors, including a mayor and deputy mayor.

The area is served by the Southern Region of British Railways, with 11 stations on the line to Waterloo Station, and by the District Line of the London Underground, with two stations for the West End of London. The Chertsey arterial road traverses the

borough from east to west; the most important north to south route is the road from Kew Bridge to Kingston-upon-Thames.

The borough lies on each side of the Thames and is primarily residential in character, providing homes for about 60,000 families, most of whom depend on employment in London itself.

It has a river frontage of 12 mi. (19 km.) which extends from Hammersmith to Sunbury-on-Thames in Surrey. At its nearest point it is about seven miles from Charing Cross. It is one of the most attractive suburbs in the southwest outer London area. Outstanding features are the large number of open spaces and famous buildings. Richmond Park, Bushy Park, Barnes Common, Sheen Common, Ham Fields, Marble Hill Park, and Old Deer Park are all available to the public. There are six golf courses. Twickenham, the international home of Rugby Football, lies within the borough, and the course of the Oxford and Cambridge universities boat race follows its river boundary. The Richmond Royal Horse Show is of national importance.

Famous houses, past and present, include Hampton Court Palace (the home of Henry VIII); the former Richmond Palace (used by Queen Elizabeth I); White Lodge, Richmond Park (where the Duke of Windsor was born; later, the headquarters of the Royal Ballet); Strawberry Hill (built by Horace Walpole; later a teachers' training college); Kneller Hall (built by Sir Godfrey Kneller, the painter; later the Royal Military School of Music); Marble Hill (erected by George II for the Countess of Suffolk); Orleans House (the refuge of the exiled French royal family); York House (the home of Lord Clarendon, chancellor to Charles II); and Ham House (built in 1610 and now preserved by the National Trust). The Royal Botanic Gardens at Kew are world-famous. Kew Observatory which is still in use was built in 1768 for George III.

More modern buildings are the Star and Garter Home for ex-servicemen erected on the summit of Richmond Hill to replace another famous house of the same name, and the National Physical Laboratory and Admiralty Research Laboratory, both at Teddington. There are extensive film and television studios in the borough, but no general industry of any size.

Richmond has an important shopping area which serves most of the eastern side of the borough. Smaller shopping centres are in East Sheen, Twickenham, Teddington, Hampton, and Whitton.

The greater part of the borough is influenced by its proximity to the Thames, around which it has developed. Small riverside industries are a feature of the older parts of the area, including yards for the building and repair of small craft and marine stores and accessories. There are many clubs for enthusiasts in rowing, yachting, sailing, and fishing.

There are four cinemas in the area; one professional theatre and many amateur ones; a large ice-skating rink on the riverside; and a host of clubs and societies for the benefit of those interested in drama, the arts, and other recreational and educational pursuits. The Richmond Institute of Adult Education provides a wide program of classes and the Twickenham College of Technology offers industrial and commercial courses especially for building, printing, and allied crafts.   (W. H. Jo.)

RICHTER, HANS (1843–1916), German conductor who introduced the works of Wagner and Brahms into England, was born at Raab (Győr), Hungary, on April 4, 1843. He studied at the Vienna Conservatory and in 1867 was recommended by Wagner as conductor of the Munich opera, where he was associated with Hans von Bülow. In 1870 he introduced *Lohengrin* to Brussels and later conducted at Pest and Vienna. In 1876 he conducted the *Ring des Nibelungen* at Bayreuth and later became principal conductor of the Wagner festivals there. In 1877 he shared the conductorship of the Wagner festival in London with the composer and in 1882 gave the first London performances of *Die Meistersinger* and *Tristan und Isolde*. He was in charge in London of the annual Orchestral Festival Concerts (later known as the Richter Concerts) until 1897, when he became conductor of the Hallé Orchestra in Manchester. It was under his direction that this orchestra acquired its high reputation. He introduced to England many German works of the Romantic period, and also gave the first performances of Elgar's *Enigma Variations* (London, 1899), *Dream of Gerontius* (Birmingham, 1900), and First Symphony (Manchester,

1908). He last conducted at Bayreuth in 1912 and died there on Dec. 5, 1916. (E. Lr.)

RICHTER, JOHANN PAUL FRIEDRICH (1763–1825), usually called JEAN PAUL, the most important German humorist and, according to Stefan George, "the greatest German poetic power (although not the greatest poet)," was born in Wunsiedel, in the Fichtelgebirge, on March 21, 1763. He was the eldest of five sons of a musically gifted school teacher, who in 1765 became pastor in the village of Joditz on the Saale. There he spent an idyllic childhood, later poetically transfigured in his unfinished autobiography. In 1776 his family moved to the rather larger Schwarzenbach on the Saale where he was able to go to school more or less regularly. Eager to learn, he had access to the large library of the neighbouring pastor Erhard Friedrich Vogel, who first recognized the boy's genius. In Schwarzenbach Richter began the collection of excerpts which he continued, although in different forms, all his life, and he started to write short essays which he called "Exercises in Thinking." From 1779 to 1780 he attended the grammar school in Hof in the Vogtland, but in 1779 his father died and the family was reduced to great poverty. At Easter 1783 Richter started to study theology at the University of Leipzig, but soon gave up his studies for free-lance writing. In 1783 he found a publisher for a collection of satirical essays which he called *Grönländische Prozesse*. Soon afterward debts forced him to return to Hof, where he lived with his mother and brothers in one room, tirelessly writing witty satires, abounding in metaphors and similes, on the model of Swift and Pope, which no one would publish. It was not until 1789 that he again appeared in print, with a satirical collection, *Auswahl aus des Teufels Papieren*, which was even less successful than his first. Richter then spent several years as a private tutor in Töpen and as headmaster of a little school in Schwarzenbach (1790–94).

About 1790 the death of two intimate friends and a hallucinatory vision of his own death brought about a fundamental change in his nature, and sentiment and imagination, hitherto intentionally suppressed, broke through, bitter satire turned into sentimental humour, and Sterne replaced Swift as a model. The first product of the new period was the comic idyll *Leben des vergnügten Schulmeisterleins Maria Wuz in Auenthal*, which appeared in 1793 as an appendix to an unfinished novel in the Sterne tradition, *Die unsichtbare Loge* (English translation, *The Invisible Lodge*, 1883); as a token of admiration for Jean Jacques Rousseau, he published it under the pseudonym Jean Paul, the French form of his first two names. It was only, however, with the next work, the sentimental novel *Hesperus* (1795; English translation, 1865), that he had a decided success. He was invited by Charlotte von Kalb, the friend of Schiller and Hölderlin, to visit Weimar, where he was received warmly by Herder, and with reserve by Goethe and Schiller. Other works quickly followed, the most important *Leben des Quintus Fixlein* (1796; English translation by Thomas Carlyle, 1827) and *Ehestand, Tod und Hochzeit des Armenadvokaten Siebenkäs* (1796–97), a story of a provincial town. At the end of 1797 Richter moved to Leipzig and a year later to Weimar, where he began to write his chief work, the four-volume novel *Titan* (1800–03; English translation, 1862), in which he discusses the revolutionary ideas of the time.

During a stay in Berlin he married Caroline Mayer, the daughter of a member of the Supreme Court (1801); she bore him two daughters and one son. Richter moved with his wife to Meiningen, then, in 1803, to Coburg and, in 1804, to Bayreuth, which was his home until his death on Nov. 14, 1825. In 1804–05 he followed *Titan* with the unfinished novel *Flegeljahre* (English translation, *Walt and Vult, or the Twins*, 1846), which is at once his most "German" and his most charming work. He then published two theoretical writings, *Vorschule der Ästhetik* (1804), on poetry, and *Levana* (1807; English translation, 1848), on education. In his Bayreuth period he published several humorous works: *Des Feldpredigers Attila Schmelzle Reise nach Flätz* (1809; English translation by Carlyle, 1827), *Doktor Katzenbergers Badereise* (1809), in the manner of Tobias Smollett, and the great comic novel *Der Komet* (1820–22), which was to have been a kind of German Don Quixote but which remained a fragment. He also published several political writings inspired by the desperate situation of his country (*Friedenspredigt*, 1808; *Dämmerungen für Deutschland*, 1809; *Fastenpredigten*, 1817) as well as numerous periodical essays and reviews for the *Heidelberger Jahrbücher*, including a long one of Madame de Staël's book on Germany (1814; English translation by Carlyle, 1830). An unfinished treatise on the immortality of the soul inspired by the early death of his son was published posthumously (1827).

Longfellow called Richter "Jean Paul the Only-One" and he was indeed in many respects a unique phenomenon, hard to classify among the usual concepts of literary history. He stands between *Sturm und Drang* and *Romanticism*, but his work includes rationalist elements taken from the Enlightenment, and in certain respects it is reminiscent of Baroque writing. He united the great contrasts of humour and sentimentality, reason and imagination. His overflowing creativity often produced formlessness. He was incapable of either poetic or dramatic form, but as a prose writer he wrung from the language, to quote Stefan George, "die glühendsten Farben und die tiefsten Klänge" ("the most glowing colours and the richest music"). He had a great influence on his contemporaries, particularly on women and young men, and on later generations down to the middle of the 19th century. Then for a long time he appeared to be almost forgotten. But Ludwig Börne's prophecy that he was waiting for his public on the threshold of the 20th century was largely fulfilled.

BIBLIOGRAPHY.—A complete edition of Jean Paul's works planned by himself appeared posthumously, 65 vol. (1826–38); historical critical edition of the Preussische (now Deutsche) Akademie der Wissenschaften directed by E. Berend, in three parts, *Werke, Nachlass, Briefe* (1927 et seq.). Numerous selected works and anthologies include Stefan George, *Stundenbuch für Jean Pauls Verehrer* (1900). *See* also C. Otto and E. Förster (friend and son-in-law respectively), *Wahrheit aus Jean Pauls Leben*, 8 vol. (1826–33); R. O. Spazier (nephew), *J. P. F. Richter*, 5 vol. (1833); J. Firmery, *Jean Paul* (in French, 1886); P. Nerrlich, *Jean Paul, sein Leben und seine Werke* (1889); W. Harich, *Jean Paul* (1925); J. Alt, *Jean Paul* (1925); M. Kommerell, *Jean Paul*, 2nd ed. (1939); *Denkwürdigkeiten*, ed. by E. Förster, 4 vol. (1863); E. Berend, *Jean-Paul-Bibliographie*, 2nd ed. (1963). (ED. BE.)

RICHTHOFEN, FERDINAND PAUL WILHELM, BARON VON (1833–1905), German geographer and geologist and one of the outstanding personalities during the period of re-emergence of geographical studies in Germany, was born on May 5, 1833, at Karlsruhe in Silesia. He studied chemistry, physics, and geology at Breslau (now Wroclaw, Pol.) and then Berlin, where he also attended Carl Ritter's geographical lectures. Geological investigations in the Dolomites and Transylvania established his reputation and in 1860 he was invited to join, as its geologist, a German economic mission to the Far East. He visited Ceylon, Japan, Formosa, Celebes, Java, and the Philippines, and journeyed across the Malay Peninsula from Bangkok to Moulmein. From there he went to California where he stayed from 1863 to 1868 carrying out geological investigations, some of which led to the discovery of vast goldfields. In 1868 he went back to the Far East and in remarkable journeys penetrated into almost every part of China. In 1872 he returned to Germany and devoted the following years to the preparation of his work, *China, Ergebnisse eigener Reisen und darauf gegründeter Studien*, five volumes plus atlas (1877–1912), the last three volumes published posthumously. He was appointed professor of geography at Bonn in 1875 but deferred taking up his duties until 1879.

In 1883 Richthofen succeeded O. Peschel at Leipzig and in 1886 he took over the chair at Berlin and held this post until his sudden death on Oct. 6, 1905.

Von Richthofen's main achievements are his great work on China and his contributions toward the establishment of the science of geomorphology, and toward the development of geographical methodology. He was president of the Berlin Geographical Society and in 1899 he organized the Berlin International Geographical Congress. He also founded the Berlin Institute of Oceanology.

He was honoured by the award of the founder's medal of the Royal Geographical Society in 1878, and on his 70th birthday by the establishment of the Richthofen Foundation. In his memory a Richthofen Colloquium is held annually at Bonn and the

Richthofen Medal is awarded by the Berlin Geographical Society.

The most important of his other writings are his inaugural lecture, *Aufgaben und Methoden der heutigen Geographie* (1883); *Führer für Forschungsreisende* (1886), the first systematic treatment of geomorphology; *Triebkräfte und Richtungen der Erdkunde im neunzehnten Jahrhundert* (1903), his address on the occasion of his installation as vice-chancellor. Posthumously published were: *Tagebücher aus China,* two volumes, edited by E. Tiessen (1907); *Vorlesungen über allgemeine Siedlungs- und Verkehrsgeographie,* edited by O. Schlüter (1908).

See E. G. Ravenstein, *Geogr. J.,* 26:679–682 (1905); G. Wegener and H. v. Wissmann, *Die Grossen Deutschen,* vol. v, pp. 390–397 (1957).
(K. A. S.)

RICIMER (FLAVIUS RICIMER) (d. 472), patrician and "king-maker" in the Western Roman Empire, was the son of a chief of the Suebi and of a Visigothic princess, and early became a friend of the future emperor Majorian (*q.v.*). He defeated an attempted Vandal invasion of Sicily at Agrigentum in 456, pursuing the enemy's fleet to the neighbourhood of Corsica, where he overcame it. He was appointed master of the soldiers in that year, and defeated the emperor Avitus at Placentia (Piacenza) on Oct. 17, 456, compelling him to abdicate. On Feb. 28, 457, he was appointed patrician, and, after elevating Majorian to the Western throne, he became consul in 459. But he was soon at enmity with his protégé Majorian. When the latter returned from Gaul to Italy without an army after the disastrous failure of his campaign against the Vandals, he fell into Ricimer's hands at Dertona (Tortona) on Aug. 2, 461, and was dethroned and executed on Aug. 7. On Nov. 19 Ricimer appointed Libius Severus as Western emperor at Ravenna. A dangerous rival to his power was Marcellinus, a former officer of Aetius, who had set up something like an independent state in Dalmatia. After Avitus' death a conspiracy was formed with a view to putting this Marcellinus on the throne; but it came to nothing, and Ricimer was able to keep him at a distance. Another foe was Aegidius, a general of Majorian, but he was tied down by wars against the barbarians in Gaul and died in 464. Gaiseric and the Vandals constantly raided Italy and Sicily, and on Aug. 15, 465, Libius Severus died. The Eastern emperor Leo I appointed Anthemius (*q.v.*) as emperor of the West on April 12, 467; and in the following year both emperors launched a vast expedition against Vandal Africa. It was utterly defeated, and Anthemius soon fell under Ricimer's displeasure. In April 472 Ricimer elevated Olybrius to the throne, and laid siege to Anthemius in Rome. He completely defeated his opponent's forces outside the city, and Anthemius was beheaded on July 11, 472. But Ricimer himself died on Aug. 18 and his puppet Olybrius on Nov. 2 of that year.

Ricimer was an Arian Christian, and as a barbarian he could not hope to have himself recognized as emperor. Hence his policy of elevating puppet rulers in whose name he could act. For 16 years he held the fate of Italy in his hands, apart from the time when Majorian was on the throne (for Majorian was no puppet). He was not wholly unsuccessful in defending Italy against the Vandal fleets, and he also kept under control the barbarian mercenaries on whom his power largely rested. In addition, he defended the provinces successfully against the Ostrogoths and the Alani. He was succeeded as master of the soldiers by his nephew, the Burgundian Gundobad.

See J. B. Bury, *History of the Later Roman Empire From the Death of Theodosius I to the Death of Justinian* (A.D. 395 to A.D. 565), vol. i, ch. 10 (1923); E. Stein, *Histoire du Bas-empire,* vol. i, ch. 11 (1959).
(E. A. T.)

RICKENBACKER, EDWARD VERNON (1890–   ), U.S. airline executive, was born in Columbus, O., Oct. 8, 1890. He had little formal education but very early became interested in internal combustion engines and in engine-driven vehicles of all kinds. By the time the United States entered World War I, Rickenbacker had become famous for his reckless preoccupation with speed on the racetracks. He was one of the country's top three racing drivers and had set a world speed record of 134 m.p.h. at Daytona Beach, Fla. He went overseas as an army sergeant-driver attached to Gen. John J. Pershing's staff but quickly gravi-

tated into aviation. He proved to be a natural fighter pilot and ended the war as America's outstanding "ace," with the rank of captain. He was awarded almost every decoration attainable.

Rickenbacker returned to the automobile industry after World War I. He headed his own company, the Rickenbacker Motor Car Company, for a time and on its dissolution joined Cadillac Motor Car Company and then its associated aviation interest, General Aviation Mfg. Co. He transferred to the airline business in 1932, first with American Airways and then with North American Aviation, Inc. On Jan. 1, 1935, he began his career with Eastern Air Lines, rising from general manager to chairman of the board of directors. Except for a period during World War II when he toured many of the combat theatres as a special representative of the U.S. secretary of war, he applied his energies to build Eastern Air Lines into one of the leading air-transport systems of the world.
(S. P. J.)

RICKETS, a disease of infancy and childhood characterized by a disturbance of the normal process of calcification of bones, with resultant deformity. It most commonly occurs toward the end of the first year and during the second year of life. The disease is caused by a deficiency of vitamin D, which is found in certain foods and is synthesized in the skin under the influence of ultraviolet light (*see* VITAMINS: *Vitamin D*). Rickets is uncommon in the tropics, whose inhabitants are exposed year-round to strong sunlight; and in regions where fish is a main article of diet, as in the far north. It has become a rare disease in the United States, Canada, Western Europe, and other places where supplementary vitamin D is regularly prescribed for infants and where eggs and milk are part of most children's diet.

Factors predisposing to the development of rickets are premature birth and unusually rapid growth. Common early symptoms include restlessness and profuse sweating particularly during sleep; lack of muscle tone in the limbs and abdomen; slowness to sit, crawl, and walk; and delay in the eruption of the teeth. Softening of the bones of the skull in the first few months of life is another early sign. Enlargement of the ends of the long bones and a knobbed appearance of the ribs at their junctions with the costal cartilages, due to enlargement of the epiphyseal cartilages, are common findings. Definitive diagnosis is made by X-ray examination of the long bones, and determination of calcium and phosphorus levels in the blood.

Unless treatment is instituted early, the bones show various degrees and types of curving and deformity, the legs being more deformed than the arms so that "bow legs" or "knock knees" develop. Bending may occur in the legs before walking is begun, although with weight-bearing the bending increases. Deformity of the pelvis in the female may have the long-range effect of difficulty with childbearing. If untreated, the disease terminates in time with the hardening of the deformed bones. Complications associated with rickets include bronchitis, bronchopneumonia, gastroenteritic disturbances, muscular weakness, enlargement of the liver and spleen, and anemia. Tetany (spasms of the hands and feet, and sometimes convulsions, caused by abnormal calcium metabolism) may occur, particularly in early spring.

Rickets is treated with vitamin D in the form of concentrates, irradiated ergosterol, fish-liver oils, exposure to sunlight or ultraviolet light, or at times merely with an adequate enriched diet. The disease is observed in conjunction with, or as a complication of, other diseases such as scurvy, coeliac disease, cystinosis, paroxysmal laryngitis, and renal failure. A rare form of rickets is refractory to vitamin D therapy; the cause for this is unknown.

OSTEOMALACIA, sometimes called adult rickets, is a progressive softening of the bones due to vitamin D deficiency in later life. The spine, pelvis, and lower limbs may become deformed. Osteomalacia occurs chiefly in the Orient. It is fairly frequent among Muslim women, who customarily remain indoors much of the time and, when they do go abroad, are completely shrouded against sunlight.

BIBLIOGRAPHY.—J. Warkany, "Infantile Rickets," *Textbook of Pediatrics,* ed. by W. E. Nelson, p. 325 (1959); M. M. Eliot and E. A. Park, "Rickets," *Practice of Pediatrics,* ed. by J. Brennemann, vol. i, ch. 36 (1948); A. F. Hess, *Rickets: Including Osteomalacia and Tetany* (1929).
(B. J. G.; X.)

RICKETTS, LOUIS DAVIDSON (1859–1940), U.S. mining engineer who brought more of the world's great copper-mining properties into production than perhaps any other engineer, was born in Elkton, Md., on Dec. 19, 1859. He received the degrees of B.S. and doctor of science from Princeton University in 1881 and 1883, respectively, then spent seven years acquiring experience in western mining camps. He was given important assignments as consulting engineer and manager by the Phelps Dodge Corporation and the Anaconda Copper Mining Company chiefly in properties in which those firms were interested in Arizona and Mexico. Though he was consultant to many companies, his connection with the Inspiration Company, beginning in 1912, was perhaps his most important administrative post, as he became president of the firm. His specialty was the design and construction of copper-ore concentrators, smelters, and leaching plants.

He was president of the American Institute of Mining Engineers in 1916, and was designated Arizona's "most useful citizen" in 1915. He died on March 4, 1940. (E. H. R.)

RICKETTSIAE are microorganisms which resemble very small bacteria but which grow only within susceptible cells—not in cell-free culture media, as bacteria do. The rickettsiae are primarily parasites or symbiotes of arthropods—especially lice, fleas, mites, and ticks; from these hosts the rickettsiae may spread to man and domestic animals, causing serious disease. (*See* Q Fever; Typhus Fever; Rocky Mountain Spotted Fever and Other Spotted Fevers.)

History.—The history of the rickettsiae is intimately associated with those forms causing human disease. Epidemic typhus, one of the great plagues of mankind, was first differentiated from typhoid fever on clinical grounds in 1837. Its nature was so catastrophic that it completely dominated the field, and sporadic occurrences of other similar diseases were hardly noticed. Late in the 19th century, however, a typhuslike disease (Rocky Mountain spotted fever) was recognized in the United States and river fever (tsutsugamushi disease, or scrub typhus) was first clearly described in Japan. By 1910 association of these diseases with arthropods was being established on firm scientific grounds with the demonstration of tick transmission of spotted fever and louse transmission of typhus. Elucidation of the microbes causing these diseases began with the work of Howard Taylor Ricketts, who described the organism of spotted fever in 1906 and who, with R. M. Wilder in 1910, also described the organism of typhus fever from the blood of patients in Mexico. Confirmatory reports appeared in rapid succession, and in 1916 the typhus-fever organism was named *Rickettsia prowazekii* in honour of Ricketts and Stanislas von Prowazek, both typhus victims themselves. For a time the etiology of typhus again became clouded because of technical difficulties, isolation of spurious agents, and the discovery of nonpathogenic rickettsialike microorganisms in lice, but the relation between the louse-borne *Rickettsia prowazekii* and typhus fever was clearly settled by 1922. A louse-borne rickettsialike agent causing trench fever was discovered during World War I.

Meanwhile, productive studies continued on spotted fever in the United States; variants of spotted fever were recognized in different parts of the world; and scrub-typhus rickettsiae were isolated. In the 1920s and 1930s numerous symbiotic organisms resembling rickettsiae were found in various arthropods. The tick-transmitted agent of heartwater fever in ruminants was identified with the rickettsiae, as were several other agents from domestic animals.

A mild typhuslike disease (Brill-Zinsser disease) was first noted in 1898 in New York, later also in other eastern seaboard cities, in immigrants from typhus-afflicted areas of Europe; the disease existed under conditions precluding louse transmission. A very similar disease, for a time confused with Brill's disease, was recognized in the southern United States beginning about 1913. However, on epidemiological grounds Kenneth F. Maxcy correctly postulated in 1929 that the southern disease was harboured by rodents and transmitted by a biting arthropod. During the 1930s murine typhus, borne by rat fleas, was clearly differentiated from epidemic typhus, borne by body lice. Still, the northern cases did not seem to be explained by the distinction. Hans Zinsser then suggested that they were sporadic recrudescences of past epidemic typhus infections—a hypothesis later verified.

In the late 1930s Q fever, first recognized independently in Australia and the United States and subsequently shown to have a wide geographic distribution in man and domestic animals, yielded a new rickettsial agent, *Coxiella burnetii* (or *Rickettsia burneti*). Still another rickettsial disease, rickettsialpox, caused by *R. akari* and transmitted by mites of the house mouse, was recognized in New York City in 1946.

Morphology and Chemistry.—Rickettsiae are minute (usually under 0.5 micron in diameter), nonspore-forming, nonmotile organisms which vary in form from round to rod-shaped. They stain poorly with ordinary aniline dyes, are Gram-negative but may be seen readily under the ordinary light microscope with special stains. A cell wall from which the protoplast inside readily shrinks on drying is clearly visible under the electron microscope and, at least in typhus rickettsiae, contains an antigenic polysaccharide. Like bacteria, rickettsiae of typhus and Q fever contain both ribonucleic and deoxyribonucleic acids; purified suspensions of some, unlike small viruses, display a modest array of independent metabolic activities.

Taxonomy.—Despite a long-felt and still-growing impression among many authorities that rickettsiae are closely related to bacteria, they have been placed in a separate class (Microtatobiotes) along with the viruses. Controversy has long existed about the inclusion of numerous other pathogenic and nonpathogenic morphologically similar organisms with the rickettsiae. While there is no sound biological basis for excluding nonpathogenic rickettsialike organisms from the rickettsial group, the fact remains that the human pathogens have been subjected to the greatest study. Controversy about classification will undoubtedly persist until more adequate information is at hand on all forms to provide sound taxonomic criteria.

Biological Properties.—Most rickettsiae are peculiarly adapted to arthropods. The mite- and tick-borne forms are especially well adapted, being harmless to the vector and transmitted from one generation to the next through the egg. Spotted-fever rickettsiae from overwintering ticks must undergo a unique reactivation phenomenon to gain full virulence for mammals. The association of *R. prowazekii* with body lice, wherein the vector itself succumbs to the infection and passage through the egg does not occur, suggests less complete and possibly more recent adaptation. From the widespread occurrence of rickettsialike symbiotes in arthropods and the prominent role of arthropods in rickettsial transmission has evolved the idea that pathogenic forms may have developed originally from symbiotes accidentally introduced into the vertebrate host by biting arthropods. Man appears only as an incidental host except in epidemic typhus, and probably trench fever, where man is the only known reservoir.

Most rickettsiae pathogenic for man (except possibly *R. quin-*

Some Important Human Rickettsioses

Disease	Causative rickettsia	Main vector	Vertebrate reservoir
Typhus group			
Epidemic typhus (including Brill-Zinsser disease) .	*Rickettsia prowazekii*	body louse	man
Murine typhus (endemic typhus) .	*Rickettsia typhi (mooseri)*	rat flea	rats
Spotted fever group (selected examples)			
Rocky Mountain spotted fever .	*Rickettsia rickettsii*	ticks	probably wild rodents
Fièvre boutonneuse .	*Rickettsia conorii*	ticks	dogs, rodents (?)
Rickettsialpox .	*Rickettsia akari*	mites	mice
Scrub typhus (tsutsugamushi disease) .	*Rickettsia tsutsugamushi*	chiggerlike mites	wild rodents
Trench fever . . .	*Rickettsia quintana*	body louse	man
Q fever	*Coxiella burnetii*	occasionally tick; mainly air, dust, contact	cattle, sheep goats, bandicoots

tana) grow only within animal cells (in intact animals, embryonated eggs, or tissue cultures), where they multiply by binary fission. There is no confirmed growth in cell-free media. Optimal growth occurs at about 35° C, lower than the body temperature of most mammalian hosts. Outside cells, most rickettsiae perish quickly unless they are preserved by freezing ($-70°$ C) or lyophilization. Suspensions of some pathogenic rickettsiae exert a rapid toxic effect on the vascular systems of susceptible laboratory animals as well as a destructive (lytic) action on the red blood cells of certain animal species.

Rickettsial Diseases.—Most human rickettsial diseases resemble one another remarkably. Symptoms include abrupt onset of fever, lasting one to two weeks and accompanied by headache, varying degrees of mental clouding, prostration and, after a few days, a rash. Q fever, an outstanding exception, is generally mild, produces no rash but commonly presents lung infiltrations. All are naturally transmitted by some arthropod. Q fever, however, is more often contracted by contact with infected domestic animals (including carcasses) or by the inhalation of contaminated airborne particles.

During infection the organisms are disseminated throughout the body by the blood, although some proliferate also at the site of introduction to produce a small ulcer (eschar). Except for *R. quintana* and *C. burnetii*, rickettsiae causing human disease tend to proliferate in, and damage, the cells lining small blood vessels. Vascular damage in the skin is often associated with rash, hemorrhage, or necrosis.

The intracellular habitat is probably responsible for certain unusual features of rickettsial infections, for within some body cells rickettsiae seem to be protected from antibodies and other deleterious substances. Despite the appearance of circulating antibodies just preceding and during convalescence, some viable rickettsiae persist within lymphoid tissues for months and even years after apparent recovery from epidemic typhus, Rocky Mountain spotted fever, or scrub typhus. In most instances they persist there harmlessly, but sometimes recrudescence of the latent epidemic typhus infection at a later date gives rise to a relatively mild, recurrent, typhuslike illness (Brill-Zinsser disease). During recrudescences rickettsiae again circulate in the blood. Lice feeding upon such a patient may become infected and capable of transmitting fully virulent epidemic typhus.

See BACTERIA; *see* also references under "Rickettsiae" in the Index.

BIBLIOGRAPHY.—R. S. Breed *et al.*, *Bergey's Manual of Determinative Bacteriology*, 7th ed. (1957); American Association for the Advancement of Science, *Rickettsial Diseases of Man*, Symposium (1948); T. M. Rivers and F. L. Horsfall, Jr., *Viral and Rickettsial Infections of Man*, 3rd ed. (1959); E. A. Steinhaus, *Insect Microbiology* (1946); H. Zinsser, *Rats, Lice and History* (1935).   (Cs. L. W.)

RICKMANSWORTH, an urban district in the South West Herts parliamentary division of Hertfordshire, Eng., lies at the confluence of the Colne, the Gade, and the Chess on the borders of Buckinghamshire and Middlesex. Pop. (1961) 28,549. Area 11.9 sq.mi. (31 sq.km.). Rickmansworth is an old market town which has grown since World War I into a large residential district spreading into the river valleys and the surrounding woodland. Stretches of water meadows and woods have been acquired by the council as part of London's greenbelt. In the long High Street are some red-brick Georgian buildings including St. Joan of Arc's Convent School and Basing House, once the home of William Penn, the founder of Pennsylvania, and now the council offices. The Royal Masonic School for Girls was built in Rickmansworth in 1928–33 and Merchant Taylors' School was built (2 mi. [3 km.] E) in 1931–33. Moor Park, to the east, is an 18th-century mansion built on the site of a house once belonging to Cardinal Wolsey. It now belongs to the council and is used as a golf clubhouse; there are three golf courses in its 400 ac. (162 ha.) of parkland.

RICKOVER, HYMAN GEORGE (1900–   ), U.S. naval officer who made a major contribution to the development of nuclear propulsion for ships, was born on Jan. 27, 1900, in tsarist Russia. Taken to the United States as a child, he was reared in Chicago, Ill., and graduated from the U.S. Naval Academy in 1922. After serving at sea in various types of ships he was given command of the USS "Finch," a minesweeper, in 1937. Meanwhile he studied electrical engineering at the Navy's postgraduate school and at Columbia University, and during World War II was placed in charge of the electrical division of the Navy Department's Bureau of Ships.

After the war, Rickover went to Oak Ridge, Tenn., for instruction in nuclear physics and engineering, returning to the Bureau of Ships in September 1947. It was at this time that he began to manage the Navy's nuclear propulsion program. His driving energy was an important factor in the successful development and early delivery of the world's first nuclear-powered submarine, the USS "Nautilus," which went to sea under nuclear power in January 1955. While continuing his duties with the Navy he was placed in charge of research on reactor development for the Atomic Energy Commission. In this capacity he helped to develop the experimental nuclear plant built at Shippingport, Pa., in 1956–57 to generate electric power. Rickover was promoted to the rank of rear admiral in 1953, and to vice admiral in 1959; in the latter year he received a gold medal awarded by Congress. He became a highly controversial figure because of his single-minded insistence on the development of nuclear power and because of his public criticism of U.S. educational practices.   (J. B. HN.)

RIDDLE, a word used to describe many kinds of enigmatic questions and intentionally ambiguous statements requiring an answer. In some cultures, the term includes more than it does in Western use. African riddlers regard legal aphorisms illustrated by examples as riddles; and among Middle Eastern peoples, riddles are not differentiated from some narrative forms (*e.g.*, allegory, fable [*qq.v.*], and parable); from some proverbs; or from other kinds of enigma (the logograph, the long riddling passage properly called an enigma, the rebus [*q.v.*], and the epigram; *q.v.*).

Robert Petsch (see *Bibliography*) recognizes two main kinds of riddle: the descriptive riddle, and the shrewd or witty question. These are differentiated in subject, use of traditional formulas, and in relationship to culture.

Descriptive Riddles.—These describe an animal, person, plant, or object, in an intentionally enigmatic manner, to suggest something different from the correct answer. "What runs about all day and lies under the bed at night?" suggests "A dog" but the answer is "A shoe." The description usually consists of one general and one specific element. The general element stands first and is to be understood metaphorically. Thus, in an English rhyming riddle of ancient origin, with counterparts in France, Sweden, Denmark, Finland, Switzerland, and Germany, beginning "Humpty Dumpty sat on a wall/ Humpty Dumpty had a great fall," the name seems to describe a man. And in

> Little Nancy Etticoat
> In a white petticoat
> And a red nose:
> The longer she stands
> The shorter she grows.

a girl seems to be described. The second element, to be understood literally, appears to contradict the first. Humpty Dumpty cannot be put together again, because he is an egg; Nancy Etticoat grows shorter the longer she stands, because she is a lighted candle.

Either element may be implied. Thus, a general element is lacking in the "cow-riddle": "Two lookers, two crookers, two fly-flappers,/ Four walkers, four hang-downers, and one switchabout," but the puzzling names for eyes, horns, etc., provide the difficulty. A few simple riddles, such as the Araucanian "It is stretched out in the path"—"A snake"; and "Jumping, it moves along the path"—"A toad," seem to lack the contradictory element, but may have a puzzling quality in the original language. Riddles of this sort are characteristic of relatively primitive cultures. An apparently late development is the use of puns: *e.g.*, "Black and white and red all over"—"A newspaper," in which both "red" and "all over" are to be understood in more than one sense.

Descriptive riddles may begin with a request for solution ("Here's a hard one"), a formula ("Riddle me, riddle me ree"), or a suggestion of locality ("As I was walking over London

Bridge"), and may end with a threat, or the promise of a reward.

Traditional descriptive riddles describe familiar plants, animals, objects, natural phenomena, and parts of the body. Abstract ideas, such as love or anger, are not found as answers. Hunger and death occur occasionally, generally in riddles of literary origin. The worldwide comparison of a year with a tree, with 12 limbs, 30 branches, and 365 leaves, each black on one side and white on the other, seems to be a literary invention accepted by the "folk."

Descriptive riddles deal with appearance, not function. Thus, an egg is "A little white house without door or window," not something to eat or something from which a chicken hatches. Paradoxical riddles (e.g., "What grows bigger the more you take from it?"—"A hole." "The man who made it did not want it; the man who bought it did not use it; the man who used it did not know it"—"A coffin") are descriptions in terms of action. "Humpty Dumpty," "Little Nancy Etticoat," the worldwide "fish-riddle"—"Robbers came to our house/ And we were all in./ The house leaped out at the windows/ And we were all ta'en" (fish caught in a net)—and many other versifications are the work of folk poets. At two periods when riddles were popular in England, in the 10th century, and at the Renaissance, many riddles were versified and new ones invented. Some of the earliest Anglo-Saxon riddles are in the Exeter Book (q.v.). At the Renaissance many early riddles were given a more polished form. For example, the comparison of a bird to a snowflake, known to Herodotus, became the 17th-century

> White bird featherless
> Flew from Paradise,
> Perched upon the castle wall.
> Up came Lord John Landless (i.e., the sun)
> Took it up handless,
> And rode away horseless
> To the king's white hall.

which alludes to the legend of the wingless bird of Paradise. This is also known in Scottish, German, and Swedish versions.

Descriptive riddles are universal. They rarely occur in folktales and ballads, although in Germanic legends the winning of a bride may depend on the answer to a riddle. A rare example of a descriptive riddle in a folktale is that asked by the Sphinx, the monster that terrorized the Boeotian Thebans: "What has one voice, and walks on four legs in the morning, two at noon, and three in the evening?" The answer was given by Oedipus: "A man, who crawls on all fours in infancy, walks on two feet when grown, and leans on a staff when aged."

The origin of riddles and their place in folk culture have been much discussed. Johan Huizinga calls them evidence of the play element in folk culture (Homo Ludens, 1949). As tests of wit and ingenuity they may be used in rituals, especially of initiation.

In one kind of descriptive riddle, things characterize themselves by speaking, as in the Basque " 'Let's go, let's go!' 'Let's stay, let's stay!' 'Let's play, let's play!' "—"River," "Stone," and "Fish." Perhaps the most widespread dialogue riddle is " 'Zigzag, where are you going?' 'Bald is your crown, what do you care?' 'Hair will grow on my head/ Before the straightening of your crooked steps' " (the mown hayfield speaks to the winding brook flowing through it), found from Wales to India.

The "neck-riddle" describes something known only to the asker, and, by its proving insoluble, a condemned man may save himself. The earliest example, in the Book of Judges 14, although not involving such a serious penalty, can only be solved by someone sharing the secret. Samson offers a reward to anyone who, in seven days, solves the riddle "Out of the eater came something to eat,/ Out of the strong came something sweet" (honey made by bees that had settled in a dead lion that he had seen).

Questions.—Lacking a generic name in English, shrewd or witty questions are classed with riddles. They are of ancient origin. Those in English, German, and Scandinavian ballads (e.g., "What is whiter than milk?"—"Snow" and "What is deeper than the sea?"—"Hell") have parallels in the Sanskrit Rigveda, and may be associated with ancient rituals. A classical example, the Greek "What is the strongest of all things?"—"Love: iron is strong, but the blacksmith is stronger, and love can subdue the blacksmith,"

has been widely translated. Questions of this sort have only been reported in the higher cultures.

Shrewd questions may be classified by subject and form. Those dealing with letters of the alphabet, words, and symbols are generally statements calling for interpretation: e.g., "ICUR YY 4 me" ("I see you are too wise for me"); "What is in the middle of Paris?"—"R"; "Spell 'dry grass' with 3 letters?"—"Hay." The influence of school in such riddles (sometimes called "catch riddles") is clear. An ancient variety of the shrewd question is catechetical in character. Juvenal's scornful allusion to those who ask who was Achilles' nurse, and Suetonius' remark that grammarians ask what song the sirens sang, imply use of question and answer in instruction. Medieval collections of biblical questions (e.g., "Who died but was not born?"—"Adam") have modern parallels: e.g., "Why did Cain kill his brother?" "Because he was able."

Shrewd questions may be serious or humorous. Arithmetical questions such as "One friend said to another 'Give me a dollar, and I'll have twice as much as you.' How many dollars did they have?"—"Five and seven," are parodied in, for example, "If you had five pennies and spent two and lost three, what would you have in your pocket?"—"A hole." Questions such as "What is the difference between . . . and . . . ?" or "Why is . . . like . . . ?" usually contain puns and are probably modern. Such catch questions as these seem to be known only in European cultures.

See also MYSTERY AND DETECTIVE STORIES: *Riddle Stories;* NURSERY AND COUNTING-OUT RHYMES.

BIBLIOGRAPHY.—K. Ohlert, *Rätsel und Rätselspiele der alten Griechen,* 2nd ed. (1912); R. Petsch, *Neue Beiträge zur Kenntnis der Volksrätsel* (1899); W. Schultz, "Rätsel," in *Real-Encyclopädie der classischen Altertumswissenschaft,* vol. ix, col. 62–125 (1913); A. Taylor, *English Riddles from Oral Tradition* (1951), *Annotated Collection of Mongolian Riddles* (1954); V. E. Hull and A. Taylor, *Collection of Irish Riddles* (1955); D. V. Hart, *Riddles in Filipino Folklore: an Anthropological Analysis* (1964).   (A. Ta.)

RIDGWAY, MATTHEW BUNKER (1895–   ), U.S. army officer who, during World War II, was responsible for the planning and execution of the first major airborne assault in the history of the U.S. Army with the attack on Sicily in July 1943. He was born at Fort Monroe, Va., March 3, 1895, and graduated from the United States Military Academy in 1917. Before World War II he served in various staff positions. As commanding general of the 82nd Airborne Division, he parachuted with his troops into Normandy in 1944 and subsequently led the 18th Airborne Corps in action in the Netherlands, Belgium, and Germany.

Assuming command of the U.S. 8th Army in Korea during the Chinese Communist offensive in late 1950, Ridgway rallied the United Nations forces and initiated a counteroffensive that drove the enemy out of South Korea. (See KOREAN WAR.) Assigned in 1951 as the overall Allied commander in the Far East, succeeding Gen. Douglas MacArthur, he continued the successful defense of the Republic of Korea and assisted in the rehabilitation of Japan. In 1952 he succeeded Gen. Dwight D. Eisenhower as supreme commander, Allied forces in Europe, and in 1953 was appointed chief of staff of the U.S. Army. He retired in 1955, having reached the rank of general in 1951. Ridgway's war memoirs appeared in 1956 under the title of *Soldier.*   (W. Si.)

RIDING, a Scandinavian term for the third part of a shire or county, e.g., the ridings of Yorkshire and of Lindsey in Lincolnshire. In Iceland the third part of a *thing,* which corresponds roughly to an English county, was called *thrithjungr;* in Norway, however, the *thrithjungr* seems to have been an ecclesiastical division. To the riding were brought causes which could not be determined in the wapentake, and a matter which could not be determined in the riding was brought into the court of the shire. There is abundant evidence that riding courts were held after the Norman Conquest.

Each of the ridings of Yorkshire has its own lord lieutenant and commission of the peace and, under the Local Government Act of 1888, forms a separate administrative county. They are distinguished as the north, east, and west ridings.

RIDING: see HORSEMANSHIP AND RIDING.

RIDLEY, NICHOLAS (c. 1503–1555), English Reformer

and martyr, who made his mark as one of the best academic brains in the first generation of the English Reformation. Born about 1503, the eldest son of Christopher Ridley (younger son of a landed gentleman), possibly of Unthank Hall in Northumberland, he entered Pembroke Hall, Cambridge, in 1518, proceeding B.A. in 1522 and M.A. in 1525. After a period of study in Paris and Louvain, he returned to a university career at Cambridge. He began to show sympathies with Reformed doctrines about 1534 and became chaplain to Archbishop Thomas Cranmer in 1537. He took a leading part in the general conversion of Cambridge into that Reformist seminary which was to contribute so much to the intellectual life of English Protestantism. In 1540 he was elected master of his college, having meanwhile obtained promotion in the church (vicar of Herne in Kent, 1538). During the last years of Henry VIII, when a reaction toward Catholicism had set in, he attracted attention as a suspected heretic (1543). As soon as Edward VI's accession returned the Reformation to favour, Ridley was appointed bishop of Rochester (1547). In 1550, after the trial and condemnation of Edmund Bonner, in whose deprivation he had played a leading part, he was promoted to Bonner's see of London, which he rapidly made into the showpiece of Reformed England. Especially he caused much uproar by a campaign for the use of a plain communion table in place of the altar. On Mary's accession (1553) he was arrested. Tried at Oxford with Cranmer and Hugh Latimer, he was burned at the stake together with the latter on Oct. 16, 1555.

Ridley was rather younger than his colleagues in the period of England's move away from Rome, but his theological learning, efficiency, and stern character put him among the leaders. Apart from his martyrdom, his chief service to the Church of England lay in the fact that he contributed an element of a native tradition to the debates and decisions of Edward VI's reign, which were strongly guided by continental influences. Clear-sighted without being a fanatic, he played an important part in assisting Cranmer to lay the foundations of Anglican doctrine.

BIBLIOGRAPHY.—Ridley's *Works*, ed. by H. Christmas (1841); J. G. Ridley, *Nicholas Ridley* (1957). For Ridley's part in the Reformation *see* also C. H. E. Smyth, *Cranmer and the Reformation under Edward VI* (1926).   (G. R. E.)

RIDOLFI (DI RIDOLFO), **ROBERTO** (1531–1612), Italian-born conspirator whose name has been given to the plot (1570–71) to overthrow Elizabeth I of England, place the imprisoned Mary Stuart, queen of Scots, on the throne, and marry her to a Catholic, Thomas Howard, duke of Norfolk, was born at Florence on Nov. 18, 1531. He was trained as a merchant and banker, and settled in London about 1555 as a mercantile agent. Although employed by Elizabeth's government in financial business, his ardent Catholic beliefs led him to interfere in politics on behalf of discontented English Catholics. These activities culminated in the plot in 1570–71. Ridolfi left London in March 1571 and visited the duke of Alva, Pope Pius V, and Philip II, in order to describe his plot and to gain the necessary military and financial support. But before the scheme could mature, Ridolfi's messenger, Charles Baillie, was arrested at Dover; his confession, and the letters he was carrying, led to the capture of many of the English conspirators. Norfolk was executed in June 1572. Ridolfi, who was still abroad when the plot was discovered, returned to Florence, where he died on Feb. 18, 1612.   (T. I. R.)

RIEBEECK, JAN VAN (1619–1677), Dutch East India Company official, was the founder in 1652 of the settlement that became Cape Town and was primarily responsible for the introduction of free burghers (colonists) which inaugurated the history of white settlement in South Africa. Born at Culemborg, in Holland, on April 21, 1619, he joined the company as an assistant surgeon in April 1639 and sailed that month to Batavia. He achieved rapid promotion in the clerical service, went to Japan (1643), and in 1645 took charge of the company trading station at Tonking (Tonkin). After returning to Batavia in 1647, he left in January 1648 for Holland, where he was dismissed for having defied the ban on private trading by company officials when he was in Tonking. In 1651 he interested himself in the company's preparations for an expedition to establish a provisioning station at the

Cape for ships plying the East India route. Having previously visited the Cape, he compiled a memorandum for the company and was placed in command of the expedition (December 1651).

Riebeeck's *Journal* records the arrival in Table Bay of his ship, the "Drommedaris," on April 6, 1652. When the expedition had landed, work began on the construction of a fort and garden, while cattle and sheep were bartered from local Hottentot clans. After early setbacks caused by crop failures and Hottentot thefts of cattle, Riebeeck informed the company in 1655 that his mission would fail unless free burghers, working their own farms, were introduced. His suggestion was adopted in 1657 with the establishment of former company servants, who were granted "letters of freedom" under conditions which protected company interests. He also encouraged the importation of slaves and the exploration of the interior and fought a "war" with the Hottentots (1659–60). He enforced no colour bar, and interracial marriages were permitted, provided both parties were Christians. When he left the Cape in May 1662, after pressing throughout his stay for a transfer to the East, there were over 100 colonists proper, including the wives and children of free burghers, and the Cape, though still a financial burden, was fulfilling its function as a provisioning station. He returned to Batavia and in 1665 became secretary to the Council of India, a post he retained until his death in Batavia on Jan. 18, 1677. A translation of Riebeeck's *Journal*, edited by H. B. Thom, was published in three volumes in 1952–58. For portrait, *see* article SOUTH AFRICA, REPUBLIC OF.

See C. L. Leipoldt, *Jan van Riebeeck* (1936).   (N. G. GA.)

RIEGER, FRANTISEK LADISLAV (1818–1903), Czech political leader, a major representative of the more conservative element in the national reawakening, was born at Semily in Bohemia on Dec. 10, 1818. The son of a miller who wished him to follow the same calling, he secretly studied law with the encouragement of his mother, and at an early age was drawn into the Czech national movement. In April 1848 he headed a delegation to present the demands of the Czechs to the new Austrian government in Vienna; and in November he was one of the Czech representatives at the Kremsier (Kromeriz) Parliament (*see* AUSTRIA, EMPIRE OF). When this Parliament was dispersed (March 1849), Rieger went into exile in France, a country which was to remain of great significance to him. Returning home in 1851, he married the daughter of Frantisek Palacky (*q.v.*) in 1853. Having been refused an academic position in Prague, he brought out the *Slovnik Naucny*, 11 volumes (1850–74), the first encyclopaedia in Czech. In 1861 he founded the first important Czech newspaper, *Narodni Listy*.

In 1861 Rieger was elected to the Bohemian Diet and also to the lower house of the Austrian *Reichsrat* in Vienna; since Palacky had been nominated to the upper house, Rieger was thenceforward the political leader of the Czechs for most practical purposes. Friction with the dominant Germans caused Rieger to decide to withdraw from the *Reichsrat* in June 1863; and, except for a brief period in 1870–71, the Czechs maintained this boycott till 1879. The bitterest experience of the Czechs came in 1867, when the emperor Francis Joseph made his "Compromise" with Hungary, but refused to recognize the Czechs' claim to the same autonomous status as the Magyars. In that year Rieger went with Palacky to Moscow as part of a Pan-Slav gesture, which offended the Poles.

In 1869 Rieger had a secret audience with the French emperor Napoleon III, the news of which leaked out; in 1870 he took the lead in pro-French demonstrations. Criticism from his own people of these actions and the lack of any practical gain for the Czech nation led to the emergence of a new and more intransigent party called the Young Czechs. The younger generation regarded Rieger as too conservative and frowned on his association with the Bohemian nobility. It was increasingly felt that to boycott the *Reichsrat* left the German deputies in control at the expense of the Czechs. At last in 1879, when Eduard, Graf von Taaffe, headed a new government more favourable to the Slavs in its attitude, Rieger abandoned the policy of abstention and the Czech deputies returned to Vienna. In 1891 Rieger lost his parliamentary seat and retired from political life, after very nearly realizing a practical compromise between the Czechs and Germans of Bohemia. He was, however, frustrated to the last by opposition from the Young Czechs, who then stepped into his political inheritance. He was created a baron in 1897.

Rieger took great interest in the municipal government of Prague and was particularly concerned with the establishment of the Czech National Theatre there—the foundation stone of this was laid in 1868, though a fire caused many years' delay before the theatre was opened. Rieger was also a champion of a Czech university in Prague; it had, indeed, been tacitly agreed before the Czechs returned to the *Reichsrat* in 1879 that the Charles University should be divided into separate German and Czech institutions, and, in 1881 to Rieger's great satisfaction, the independent Czech university emerged. He died in Prague on March 3, 1903. His *Vybrane řeči* ("Selected Speeches") appeared in 1924.

(E. Wi.)

RIEL, LOUIS (1844–1885), French-Canadian political leader of discontents in western Canada, was born in St. Boniface, Red River Settlement, Oct. 22, 1844. He was educated at St. Boniface and, between 1858 and 1866, at the Sulpician Collège de Montréal, in Canada. After briefly studying law he secured employment as a clerk in St. Paul, Minn.

During 1868–69, arrangements for the transfer of the Hudson's Bay Company territories to Canada aroused the local inhabitants, largely made up of French and Scotch métis (having some Indian blood). Riel assumed leadership of these discontents, and in 1869, not only halted Canadian surveyors but organized the French métis into a politico-military party which prevented William McDougall, the governor-designate, from entering Red River. He then seized Ft. Garry (Winnipeg) and established a provisional government of which he became president. In 1870 he sent delegates to Ottawa where, in May, the Canadian Parliament adopted legislation (Manitoba Act) by which the province of Manitoba, which included Red River, was established. However, such was the emotional excitement aroused in Ontario by the execution of an Ontario Orangeman, Thomas Scott, by a métis court-martial, that the Canadian government refused to fulfill the promise of amnesty to the insurgents. When Canada sent a military expedition to Red River to maintain order, Riel and his associates fled.

Several times elected a member of the Canadian Parliament, Riel did not take his seat, and in 1875 was outlawed for five years. After spending some months in mental hospitals in Montreal and Quebec, he moved to Montana. In 1883 he became a U.S. citizen, and endeavoured to organize the American métis on behalf of the Republican Party.

Aroused by the westward expansion of Canadian settlement and encouraged by discontented whites, the métis of the Saskatchewan Valley sent for Riel in June 1884, to lead the Second Riel Rebellion. In March 1885 he formed a provisional government and solicited the support of the Indians. Following his defeat by Canadian government forces, Riel was tried for treason and executed at Regina, Nov. 16, 1885. His death increased racial and religious tensions in Canada, severely damaged the Conservative Party in Quebec, and gave rise to a French-Canadian "nationalist" movement under Honoré Mercier.

See also CANADA: *History.*

BIBLIOGRAPHY.—A. H. de Trémaudan, *Histoire de la nation métisse* (1935); G. F. G. Stanley, *The Birth of Western Canada* (1936; Canadian ed. 1961), *Louis Riel, Patriot or Rebel* (1954), *Louis Riel* (1963); J. K. Howard, *Strange Empire* (1952). (G. F. G. S.)

RIEMANN, GEORG FRIEDRICH BERNHARD (1826–1866), German mathematician, exerted a profound influence on several branches of mathematics, particularly geometry and function theory (*see* RIEMANNIAN GEOMETRY). He was born on Sept. 17, 1826, in the village of Breselenz in Hanover, the son of a Lutheran pastor. From 1846 to 1851 he studied at the universities of Göttingen and Berlin.

In 1851 he obtained his doctorate at Göttingen with his celebrated dissertation, "Foundations for a General Theory of Functions of a Complex Variable." In it he set forth an approach to function theory based on general principles and geometrical ideas rather than on formal calculation. His probationary essay for admission to the faculty in 1853 was "On the Representation of a Function by Means of a Trigonometrical Series." His trial lecture for admission to the faculty in 1854 was "On the Hypotheses Which Form the Foundation of Geometry." In this he introduced a new approach to geometry which covered ordinary Euclidean geometry, the non-Euclidean geometry of Nikolai Lobachevski, Johann Bolyai and C. F. Gauss, and other possible non-Euclidean geometries as special cases. His idea was to study the properties of a geometrical space locally rather than to insist on one overall framework for the whole space.

He became successively a *Privatdozent* (official but unpaid lecturer), assistant professor (1857), and professor (1859), succeeding P. G. L. Dirichlet (who had succeeded Gauss four years earlier). Tuberculosis began to take its toll in the early 1860s and Riemann died on July 19, 1866, at Selasca, in northern Italy.

In addition to the work mentioned above he published equally significant papers on Abelian functions, the distribution of primes, and air waves of finite amplitude. His posthumously published papers and even the fragments published in his collected works proved to be rich in new ideas. Some idea of his influence can be obtained from the impressive list of methods, theorems, and concepts that bear his name: the Riemann approach to function theory, the Riemann-Roch theorem on algebraic functions, Riemann surfaces, the Riemann mapping theorem, the Riemann integral, the Riemann-Lebesgue lemma on trigonometrical integrals, the Riemann method in the theory of trigonometrical series, Riemannian geometry, Riemann curvature, Riemann matrices in the theory of Abelian functions, the Riemann zeta function, the Riemann hypothesis, the Riemann method of solving hyperbolic partial differential equations, Riemann-Liouville integrals of fractional order and others. In fact, it has been said that he anticipated a large part of 20th-century research in geometry and analysis.

Riemann was interested in physical problems and for a time was an assistant in the Göttingen physics laboratory. His idea of defining analytic functions and geometrical spaces in terms of their local properties no doubt was motivated by physical considerations. His approach to geometry made possible the general relativity theory of Albert Einstein. Riemann also gave the first mathematical treatment of shock waves.

In view of the tremendous importance of Riemann in the history of mathematics, it is somewhat surprising that his collected works occupy only one moderately sized volume edited by R. Dedekind and H. Weber (1876; second edition, 1892; French translation, 1898; reprint of second German edition with the 1902 supplement, 1953).

See also references under "Riemann, Georg Friedrich Bernhard" in the Index.

BIBLIOGRAPHY.—For further biographical details *see* the account of his life by R. Dedekind in the German editions and in the reprint edition. For evaluations of his work *see* an article by F. Klein in the French edition and an article by H. Lewy in the reprint edition. For a popular discussion *see* E. T. Bell, *Men of Mathematics* (1937). For technical discussion *see* G. Springer, *Introduction to Riemann Surfaces* (1957); L. P. Eisenhart, *Riemannian Geometry* (1949); E. C. Titchmarsh, *The Theory of the Riemann Zeta-Function* (1951); H. Weyl, *The Concept of a Riemann Surface*, 3rd ed. (1964). (P. T. B.)

RIEMANNIAN GEOMETRY, one of a group of non-Euclidean systems that reject Euclid's postulate of parallels. Founded by G. F. B. Riemann (*q.v.*) in 1854, it is the geometry of a coordinate space $(x^1, \ldots, x^n)$ in which there is a nondegenerate quadratic differential form called the element of arc:

$$ds^2 = \sum_{1 \leq i,\, k \leq n} g_{ik}(x)dx^i dx^k$$

The geometry reduces to Euclidean geometry if the element of arc takes the special form $ds^2 = (dx^1)^2 + \ldots + (dx^n)^2$. The two-dimensional case was considered before Riemann by C. F. Gauss, as the intrinsic geometry on a surface in ordinary Euclidean space. In pure mathematics the differential form ds^2 is generally supposed to be positive definite, an assumption that is essential to many of the important consequences. In applications to general relativity, where the Riemannian space is the physical universe, ds^2 is supposed to be hyperbolic; *i.e.*, reducible to a sum of squares minus the square of a linear differential form (*see* GEOMETRY, NON-EUCLIDEAN).

Basic Properties.—The ds^2 allows the definition of the arc length of a curve $x^i = x^i(t)$ as the integral

$$s = \int_{t_0}^{t_1} \sqrt{\left| \sum_{i,k} g_{ik} \frac{dx^i}{dt} \frac{dx^k}{dt} \right|}\, dt \qquad (1)$$

Geodesics are curves that are shortest between any two of their points, sufficiently near to each other. An n-dimensional domain has a volume given by the integral $\int \sqrt{|g|}\, dx^1 \ldots dx^n$, where g is the determinant of g_{ik}.

The coordinates x^i are local coordinates in the sense that they can be subjected to a general differentiable transformation $x'^i = f^i(x^1, \ldots, x^n)$, where $i = 1, \ldots, n$ with nonvanishing Jacobian determinant (*see* DIFFERENTIAL GEOMETRY). For ds^2 to be invariant under such changes of local coordinates g_{ik} should be transformed according to the equations

$$g_{ik} = \sum_{i,l} g'_{jl} \frac{\partial x'^j}{\partial x^i} \frac{\partial x'^l}{\partial x^k} \text{ where } i, j, k, l = 1, \ldots, n \qquad (2)$$

and are therefore the components of a symmetric covariant tensor field of order two. The elements g^{jl} of the inverse matrix of the matrix (g_{ik}), which are related to g_{ik} by the equations

$$\sum_{k} g_{ik}\, g^{kl} = \delta_i^l = \begin{cases} 1, & i = l \\ 0, & i \neq l \end{cases} \text{ where } i, k, l = 1, \ldots, n \qquad (3)$$

are the components of a symmetric contravariant tensor field of order two. The fundamental tensors g_{ik} and g^{jl} can be used to derive new tensors from those given. Thus, if A^{ij}_k is a tensor field,

$$A^i_{ik} = \sum_{l} g_{lj} A^{il}_k, \quad A^{ijk} = \sum_{l} g^{kl} A^{ij}_l$$

are new tensor fields. They are said to be associated to each other, and the process is described as that of raising or lowering indices. The length of a vector A^i is

$$|A| = \sqrt{\left| \sum_{i,k} g_{ik} A^i A^k \right|}$$

The angle θ between two vectors A^i, B^j of lengths different from zero is defined by the formula

$$\cos \theta = \sum_{i,k} g_{ik} A^i B^k / |A| \cdot |B|$$

From the fundamental tensor g_{ik} E. B. Christoffel (*see* TENSOR ANALYSIS) constructed in 1869 the quantities

$$\Gamma_{ijk} = \frac{1}{2}\left(\frac{\partial g_{ij}}{\partial x^k} + \frac{\partial g_{ik}}{\partial x^j} - \frac{\partial g_{jk}}{\partial x^i} \right), \quad \Gamma^j_{ik} = \sum_{l} g^{jl} \Gamma_{ilk} \qquad (4)$$

These are not the components of a tensor, but can be used to define the covariant derivative of a tensor field, giving a tensor field of one more covariant order. In the cases of contravariant and covariant vector fields and that of a mixed tensor field of type (1,1), their covariant derivatives are respectively

$$A^i_{k} = \frac{\partial A^i}{\partial x^k} + \sum_{j} \Gamma^i_{jk} A^j$$

$$A_{i,k} = \frac{\partial A_i}{\partial x^k} - \sum_{j} \Gamma^j_{ik} A_j \qquad (5)$$

$$B^i_{j,k} = \frac{\partial B^i_{j}}{\partial x^k} + \sum_{l} (\Gamma^i_{lk} B^l_{j} - \Gamma^l_{jk} B^i_{l})$$

Similar expressions are valid for the covariant derivatives of more general tensor fields. The covariant derivative of g_{ik} vanishes identically. Conversely, Γ^i_{jk} can be characterized as the quantities that are symmetric in i,k and for which the covariant derivative of the fundamental tensor is zero. In geometrical lan-

guage Γ^i_{jk} defines a parallel displacement of vectors along curves: the vector field A^k is parallel along a curve $x^i = x^i(t)$ if

$$\frac{dA^i}{dt} + \sum_{i,k} \Gamma^i_{jk} \frac{dx^i}{dt} A^k = 0, \text{ where } i, j, k = 1, \ldots, n \qquad (6)$$

This is called the Levi-Civita parallelism. It is an affine connection in the general terminology of connections, but is one related in a special way to the Riemannian metric. Under the parallelism of Levi-Civita the scalar product of two vectors remains unchanged. A geodesic is either a curve of zero length or one along which the unit tangent vector is parallel. The former possibility does not appear in the case of a positive definite metric.

The notion of curvature arises in studying the parallel displacement of a vector around a closed curve. When the closed curve is an infinitesimal parallelogram the new position of the vector can be obtained from the initial position by an infinitesimal rotation. Analytically this association is described by the Riemann-Christoffel curvature tensor. Its expression is

$$R_i^{j}{}_{kl} = \frac{\partial \Gamma^j_{il}}{\partial x^k} - \frac{\partial \Gamma^j_{ik}}{\partial x^l} + \sum_{m} (\Gamma^m_{il}\Gamma^j_{mk} - \Gamma^m_{ik}\Gamma^j_{ml}), \quad R_{ijkl} = \sum_{m} g_{jm} R_i^{m}{}_{kl} \qquad (7)$$

The components of the curvature tensor have the following symmetry properties

$$R_{ijkl} = -R_{jikl} = -R_{ijlk}$$
$$R_{ijkl} = R_{klij} \qquad (8)$$
$$R_{ijkl} + R_{iklj} + R_{iljk} = 0$$

As a result there are $n^2(n^2 - 1)/12$ independent components; *e.g.*, 6 for a three-space, 20 for a four-space, and 1 for a two-space. In the latter case the quotient $K = -R_{1212}/g$ is a scalar and is the Gaussian curvature (*see* SPACE-TIME: *Riemann's Geometry*). If a vector is given a parallel displacement around a closed curve on a surface, it returns with its direction changed by an amount equal to $\int K d\sigma$, the Gaussian curvature of the surface integrated over the surface area bounded by the closed curve. As a consequence, the excess (over π) of the angle sum in any geodesic triangle is $\int K d\sigma$, a famous theorem due to Gauss.

In the case of three or more dimensions the curvature properties can no longer be expressed by a single magnitude, but require for their description the whole curvature tensor. The concept of Gaussian curvature is replaced by that of Riemannian curvature or sectional curvature. This is, at any point p and any plane element (two-dimensional) through p, the Gaussian curvature of the geodesic surface through p and tangent to the plane element. If the latter is spanned by the vectors A^i, B^j, the Riemannian curvature is given by the formula

$$K = -\sum_{i,j,k,l} R_{ijkl} A^i A^k B^j B^l / \sum_{i,j,k,l} (g_{ik} g_{jl} - g_{il} g_{jk}) A^i A^k B^j B^l \qquad (9)$$

In general, K will depend both on the point and on the plane element through it. In other words, with regard to curvature, the space may be nonhomogeneous as well as anisotropic. However, for $n \geq 3$, F. Schur's theorem says that if K is everywhere isotropic (*i.e.*, independent of the choice of the plane element at every point) it is constant throughout. Riemannian spaces for which the Riemannian curvature is constant for all points and all plane elements through them are said to be of constant curvature. They include the Euclidean and non-Euclidean spaces. Analytically they are characterized by the conditions

$$R_{ijkl} = -K(g_{ik}g_{jl} - g_{il}g_{jk})$$

with constant K. The curvature tensor gives by contraction the symmetric tensor $R_{ik} = \sum_{j} R_i^{j}{}_{jk}$ called the Ricci tensor. A further contraction gives the scalar invariant $R = \sum_{i} R_i^{i}$.

Potential Theory on a Riemannian Manifold.—A Riemannian manifold is a differentiable manifold with a positive definite Riemannian metric (*see* MANIFOLDS). One of the main reasons for the importance of Riemannian geometry is that such a metric exists on every manifold and can therefore be used to describe its properties. If the manifold is oriented (*i.e.*, if a covering exists such that the Jacobian determinants of overlapping local coordinate systems are everywhere positive) the orientation of the manifold defines an orientation in every tangent or cotangent space (*i.e.*, the space of covariant vectors). The Riemannian metric on the manifold gives rise to an inner product in the cotangent (or tangent) space, which defines the lengths of vectors and, more generally, the r-dimensional measures of r-vectors. To an r-vector L of the cotangent space there exists a uniquely determined $(n-r)$-vector $*L$ having the properties: 1) $*L$ is completely perpendicular to L; 2) the r-dimensional measure of L is equal to the $(n-r)$-dimensional measure of $*L$; 3) L and $*L$ span the whole oriented cotangent space. This passage from L to $*L$ is a generalization, for $n = 3$, $r = 2$, of the vector product of vectors in ordinary vector analysis (*see* VECTOR ANALYSIS). By linearity this star operator can be extended into a linear operator which maps an antisymmetric covariant tensor of order r into one of order $n - r$. If the former has the components $A_{i_1 \ldots i_r}$, the components of $*A$ are given by the formula

$$(*A)_{i_1 \ldots i_{n-r}} = \frac{1}{r!} \sqrt{g} \sum \epsilon_{i_1 \ldots i_r i_1 \ldots i_{n-r}} g^{i_1 k_1} \ldots g^{i_r k_r} A_{k_1 \ldots k_r} \quad (10)$$

In this sum $\epsilon_{i_1 \ldots i_n}$ is equal to zero if the indices are not all distinct and is otherwise equal to 1 or -1, according as $i_1, \ldots, i_n$ form an even or odd permutation of $1, \ldots, n$, while the summation is taken over all repeated indices from 1 to n. Combination with the operator of exterior differentiation gives rise to the further operators

$$\delta = (-1)^{nr + n + 1} *d*, \quad \Delta = d\delta + \delta d \quad (11)$$

When expressed in terms of exterior differential forms, the star operator converts a form of degree r into one of degree $n - r$, d increases the degree by one, δ decreases it by one, while Δ keeps the degree unchanged. The operator Δ is called the Laplace operator, generalizing the one with the same name in Euclidean space. An exterior differential form ω such that $\Delta\omega = 0$ is called harmonic.

For compact orientable Riemannian manifolds of class C^∞ the use of harmonic forms is justified by the following fundamental decomposition theorem: Every C^∞ exterior differential form can be expressed in one and only one way as a sum $\omega = \omega_1 + d\eta + \delta\zeta$ where ω_1 is harmonic. It follows that every closed form differs by a derived form from a harmonic form, and that the latter is uniquely determined. The dimension of the space of harmonic forms of degree r is the rth Betti number of the manifold. Every cohomology class (with real coefficients) contains one and only one harmonic form. These results give a hold on the study of homological properties of a manifold (*i.e.*, topological properties pertaining to homology or bounding), when certain analytical behaviour of the manifold is known. This is, for instance, the case of the manifolds of the classical Lie groups (*e.g.*, the unitary group and the rotation group) for which the Betti numbers can be determined by the use of this theorem (*see* GROUPS, CONTINUOUS).

Among the important geometrical applications of harmonic forms is the analysis of the homological properties of compact Hermitian-Kählerian manifolds. A complex manifold with the local coordinates $z^1, \ldots, z^n$ is called Hermitian, if there is given a positive definite Hermitian differential form

$$\sum_{1 \le i,k \le n} h_{ik}(z,\bar{z}) dz^i d\bar{z}^k$$

To this is associated a real-valued quadratic exterior differential form

$$\frac{i}{2} \sum_{i,k} h_{ik} dz^i \wedge d\bar{z}^k$$

If the latter is closed, the Hermitian manifold is called Kählerian. The complex projective space of n dimensions and, in particular,

the Riemann sphere in the theory of functions of one complex variable, are Kählerian manifolds. The same is true of any nonsingular algebraic variety in complex projective space. W. V. D. Hodge, the initiator of harmonic forms, gave a deep analysis of the differential forms on compact Kählerian manifolds. Instead of the real differential forms it is necessary to consider on a complex manifold complex-valued exterior differential forms. A form which can locally be written

$$\sum A_{i_1 \ldots i_p j_1 \ldots j_q} dz^{i_1} \wedge \ldots \wedge dz^{i_p} \wedge d\bar{z}^{j_1} \wedge \ldots \wedge d\bar{z}^{j_q}$$

is said to be bihomogeneous of bidegree (p,q). Let h_{pq} be the dimension of the space of complex-valued harmonic forms of bidegree (p,q). These are integers which describe the global properties of compact Kählerian manifolds. They are symmetric in p,q: $h_{pq} = h_{qp}$, and are "finer" than the Betti numbers. In fact, the rth Betti number is equal to the sum $\sum_{p + q = r} h_{pq}$

Space-forms and Symmetric Riemannian Spaces.

Riemannian manifolds of constant curvature K, on account of the very restrictive curvature property, can be described rather explicitly. Examples of such manifolds are, for $K = 0$, the Euclidean space; for $K > 0$, the sphere of radius $1/\sqrt{K}$ in Euclidean space; and, for $K < 0$, the hyperbolic space of curvature K. A Riemannian manifold is called complete if every geodesic can be extended indefinitely, where return of the point to its original position and repetition of the geodesic are allowed. The completeness assumption is to exclude those Riemannian manifolds which are open subsets of a larger one. A complete Riemannian manifold of constant curvature is called a space-form. Its universal covering manifold has the further property of being simply connected. The fundamental theorem on space-forms asserts that a complete simply connected Riemannian manifold of constant curvature is isometric to the Euclidean space, the spherical space, or the hyperbolic space mentioned above, according as the curvature is zero, positive, or negative. The problem of determination of space-forms then reduces to that of determination of discontinuous subgroups Γ of motions without fixed points in these three spaces, the space-form being a quotient space relative to Γ. The multitude of such subgroups depends very much on the sign of curvature. Roughly speaking, they are relatively few if K is positive and far more numerous if K is negative, while the case of zero curvature occupies an intermediate position. In fact, an even-dimensional space-form of positive curvature is either the spherical space or the elliptic space obtained from the former by the identification of its antipodal points. Odd-dimensional space-forms of positive curvature exist already in abundance. The question of three-dimensional Euclidean space-forms (*i.e.*, zero curvature) is related to crystallography (*q.v.*), where the discontinuous subgroups of the group of Euclidean motions are studied. Space-forms give an important source of examples of manifolds.

In applications of Riemannian geometry the condition of constant Riemannian curvature is too restrictive. A wider and more important class of Riemannian manifolds is the symmetric Riemannian spaces of E. J. Cartan (*q.v.*). These are the Riemannian spaces which locally have the property that the symmetry at every point is an isometry with the point as an isolated fixed point. This is equivalent to the property that the sectional curvature is preserved under the parallelism of Levi-Civita. Analytically it is expressed by the condition that the covariant derivative of the Riemann-Christoffel curvature tensor is zero. Symmetric Riemannian spaces include the spaces of simple Lie groups and spaces which play an important role in the theory of automorphic functions of several complex variables.

Global Problems.

Among the most important problems in Riemannian geometry are those which relate the local curvature properties with the behaviour of the manifold as a whole. Thus a theorem of O. Bonnet says that if a two-dimensional complete Riemannian manifold has a positive lower bound for its curvature, it must be compact. The Gauss-Bonnet formula then implies that its Euler characteristic is positive and hence that the manifold is homeomorphic to a sphere. The delicacy of such problems can be realized when it is observed that a two-dimensional Riemannian manifold of positive curvature need not be compact.

Global problems in Riemannian geometry can generally be classified into three categories: characteristic classes, implications of local properties of curvature, and behaviour of geodesics. The simplest result of the first category is the Gauss-Bonnet formula, expressing the Euler-Poincaré characteristic of a compact orientable Riemannian manifold M as an integral: $\chi(M) = \int I \, dV$, where dV is the volume element and the integrand I is zero when n is odd and is equal to

$$\frac{g^{-1}}{(2\pi)^{\frac{n}{2}} 2^n \left(\frac{n}{2}\right)!} \sum \epsilon_{i_1} \ldots {}_{i_n} \epsilon_{j_1} \ldots {}_{j_n} R_{i_1 i_2 j_1 j_2} \ldots R_{i_{n-1} i_n j_{n-1} j_n}$$

when n is even, the summation being over all the repeated indices from 1 to n. It follows from the formula that the Euler-Poincaré characteristic of a four-dimensional compact Riemannian manifold is positive, if the sectional curvature is positive for all plane elements or negative for all plane elements. The formula has a generalization for a domain with boundary in the manifold; as such it is a generalization of the formula for the sum of solid angles of a simplex. The Euler-Poincaré characteristic is only one of a set of invariants derived from the differentiable structure of the manifold and independent of the choice of the Riemannian metric on it. Further invariants of this kind are the Pontryagin characteristic classes introduced by L. Pontryagin in 1942. These are cohomology classes with real coefficients and can all be described in the sense of De Rham's theorem by exterior differential forms constructed explicitly from the curvature tensor.

The problems of the second category begin with a study of Riemannian manifolds whose sectional curvature keeps the same sign. If the sectional curvature is nonpositive and the manifold is complete, its universal covering manifold is homeomorphic to the Euclidean space. From this follow properties of the fundamental group of compact manifolds of negative curvature, one of which says that it is not Abelian. If the sectional curvature has a positive lower bound, Bonnet's theorem mentioned above can be generalized to n dimensions, so that the manifold is compact. S. B. Myers observed that the same conclusion remains true under the weaker hypothesis that the Ricci curvature tensor majorizes a fixed positive definite tensor. As a consequence, the fundamental group of a compact Riemannian manifold with a positive definite Ricci tensor is finite and hence its first Betti number is zero. The last conclusion was also shown by S. Bochner (1948) by applying the theorem on harmonic forms. Bochner's method also gives sufficient local conditions on curvature for the vanishing of the higher Betti numbers. J. L. Synge showed that an even-dimensional orientable Riemannian manifold with a positive lower bound for the sectional curvature is simply connected. While these results deal with the topological implications of the curvature properties of a Riemannian manifold, a more decisive theorem was demonstrated by H. E. Rauch in 1951. Rauch's theorem asserts that if the sectional curvature of a complete simply connected Riemannian manifold satisfies the inequalities $0 < hL < K \leq L$, where $h = 0.74$, then M is homeomorphic to a sphere; this value of h is not the best possible.

The behaviour of the geodesics on a Riemannian manifold has been the object of extensive study. If the manifold is of constant negative curvature, the geodesic flow is ergodic. Another problem is that of closed geodesics. They certainly exist on a complete Riemannian manifold that is not simply connected, for the shortest curve in a free homotopy class of curves nonshrinkable to a point is a closed geodesic. The famous Lusternik-Schnirelmann theorem says that on a closed surface of genus zero there are at least three closed geodesics (see CRITICAL POINTS). A geodesic segment can be assigned an index, depending on the number of conjugate points on it. This notion has been found useful in homotopy problems in topology.

General Relativity.—The space of general relativity (see RELATIVITY) is a four-dimensional Riemannian space with an indefinite metric that can be written locally as $ds^2 = \omega_1^2 + \omega_2^2 + \omega_3^2 - \omega_4^2$, where $\omega_1, \ldots, \omega_4$ are linear differential forms. The components g_{ik} of the fundamental tensor define the gravitational potential. The light rays are the null curves defined by the differential equation $ds^2 = 0$, while the trajectories of particles without the action of external force are the geodesics. In this way the geometry of the space is not a priori given, but is determined by matter. An essential restriction on the metric is given by Einstein's field equations $R_{ik} = -\mathcal{H}(T_{ik} - \frac{1}{2} g_{ik} T)$, where T_{ik} is the impulse-energy tensor, T is the contraction of T_{ik} relative to the fundamental tensor, and $\mathcal{H}$ is a constant. Many attempts have been made, some by Einstein himself in his late years, to develop a unified field theory that would include both the gravitational and the electromagnetic fields. This leads to a generalization of Riemannian geometry to more general geometric objects, such as the Weyl geometry, the Kaluza five-dimensional metric, projective relativity of O. Veblen, and so on. The results are not conclusive.

See also references under "Riemannian Geometry" in the Index.

BIBLIOGRAPHY.—Riemann's fundamental paper, "Über die Hypothesen welche der Geometrie zu Grunde liegen," can be found in his *Gesammelte Werke,* 2nd ed. (1892), later published with commentaries by H. Weyl, 3rd ed. (1923). For introduction to Riemannian geometry, see E. Cartan, *Leçons sur la géométrie des espaces de Riemann,* 2nd ed. (1946); L. P. Eisenhart, *Riemannian Geometry* (1949); O. Veblen, *Invariants of Quadratic Differential Forms* (1927); T. Levi-Civita, *Lezioni di calcolo differenziale assoluto* (1925; Eng. trans. by M. Long, 1927); C. E. Weatherburn, *Introduction to Riemannian Geometry and the Tensor Calculus* (1938); H. Weyl, *The Concept of a Riemann Surface,* 3rd ed. (1964). For generalized potential theory, see W. V. D. Hodge, *The Theory and Applications of Harmonic Integrals,* 2nd ed. (1952); G. de Rham, *Variétés différentiables* (1955). For global problems, see M. Morse, *The Calculus of Variations in the Large* (1934); K. Yano and S. Bochner, *Curvature and Betti Numbers* (1953); H. Hopf and W. Rinow, "Über den Begriff der vollständigen differentialgeometrischen Fläche," *Comment. Math. Helvet.* (1931); G. Vincent, "Les groupes linéaires finis sans points fixes," *Comment. Math. Helvet.* (1947); C. B. Allendoerfer and A. Weil, "The Gauss-Bonnet Theorem for Riemannian Polyhedra," *Trans. Amer. Math. Soc.* (1943); S. S. Chern, "A Simple Intrinsic Proof of the Gauss-Bonnet Formula for Closed Riemannian Manifolds," *Ann. Math.* (1944); L. S. Pontryagin, "Some Topological Invariants of Closed Riemannian Manifolds," *Am. Math. Soc. Transl.* (1951); S. B. Myers, "Riemannian Manifolds in the Large," *Duke Math. J.* (1935); A. Preissmann, "Quelques propriétés globales des espaces de Riemann," *Comment. Math. Helvet.* (1942); H. E. Rauch, "A Contribution to Differential Geometry in the Large," *Ann. Math.* (1951).   (S. S. Ch.)

RIENZO, COLA DI (1313–1354), the Roman tribune who tried unsuccessfully to apply his humanist ideas to practical politics, was born in Rome in 1313. After spending most of his youth at Anagni, he returned at the age of 20 to Rome, where he became a notary. In 1343 he was sent to Pope Clement VI at Avignon to plead the case of the Roman popular party. During his long stay at Avignon he was befriended by Petrarch, who was deeply impressed by his patriotic concern over the conditions in Rome.

Appointed notary of the *camera urbana* (the Roman city treasury) by Clement VI, Cola di Rienzo returned to Rome in 1344 and used his new position to press for reforms. Reviving earlier Roman hopes and inspired by his studies of Roman history and antiquities, he dreamed of restoring Rome to its past greatness. In 1347 he assumed the leadership of the popular party and, on May 20, denounced the oppressive rule of the nobles to a parliament on the Capitol, which entrusted him and the papal vicar with the government of the city. A few days later, a second parliament conferred on him dictatorial powers. He adopted the ancient title of tribune and, amid elaborate ceremonies which showed the impact of his antiquarian interests, he was dubbed knight of the Roman people on Aug. 1 and crowned tribune on Aug. 15.

Cola di Rienzo used his powers to subdue the nobility and to improve Rome's finances and administration. Not content with this, he declared all Italians to be Roman citizens (Aug. 1, 1347) and summoned Louis IV the Bavarian and Charles IV to Rome to defend their rival claims to the Holy Roman Empire. His invitation to the principal Italian cities and rulers to form a federation under Roman leadership met with scant response; and his Italian policy helped to turn the pope against him. Though in November he succeeded in repulsing an attack by the Colonna (*q.v.*), he decided to submit to the pope; and, after a rising against him, he suddenly resigned office (Dec. 15) and fled from Rome shortly afterward. Excommunicated, Cola di Rienzo spent about two years in the Abruzzi among Spiritual Franciscans, where he came under the influence of Joachim of Fiore's prophecies. In 1350 he went to Prague and, announcing an early judgment and renewal of the church, implored Charles IV to come to Italy. Imprisoned by the archbishop of Prague (Ernest of Pardubitz) as an excommunicate, he was transferred, in 1352, to Avignon; but his trial for heresy ended, in 1353, with his absolution. As Pope Innocent VI decided to use him in the papal state, Rienzo joined Cardinal Albornoz (*q.v.*) in Perugia later in 1353 and was appointed Roman senator in July 1354. His arbitrary rule, however, roused growing opposition in Rome, and on Oct. 8, 1354, he perished in a popular rising.

His letters are edited by K. Burdach and P. Piur (1912).

BIBLIOGRAPHY.—Apart from the anonymous contemporary biography (modern editions by A. M. Ghisalberti [1928] and by A. Frugoni [1957]), *see* P. Piur, *Cola di Rienzo* (1931); also K. Burdach, *Rienzo und die geistige Wandlung seiner Zeit* (1913–28). (N. R.)

RIESA, a town of East Germany in the *Bezirk* (district) of Dresden, German Democratic Republic. It is situated on the Elbe, 44 mi. (71 km.) NW of Dresden and 37 mi. (59 km.) E of Leipzig. Pop. (1962 est.) 38,235. It is the junction of the Berlin–Karl-Marx-Stadt and Leipzig–Dresden railway lines and the chief river port of northern Saxony. Riesa is an important industrial centre with steelworks, a rolling mill, match factory, tire factory, cotton mill, and oil refinery. The town grew up in the 12th century alongside a monastery founded in 1111. It received its municipal charter in 1623 but lost it shortly afterward. With the development of industry and railways in the 19th century Riesa regained its importance and was again given a municipal charter in 1859.

RIESENER, JEAN HENRI (1734–1806), French cabinetmaker, the greatest of his time, was born at Gladbeck, Ger., on July 4, 1734, the son of a courtroom usher. Coming to Paris as a young man, he began work under Jean Francois Oeben, whose widow he subsequently married, thereafter taking control of the Oeben workshop. Having qualified as a master craftsman in 1768, he embarked on a long and successful career. His first great achievement was the completion, in 1769, of the celebrated *bureau du roi* (now in the Louvre, Paris) that Oeben had begun for Louis XV; and this was followed by his supplying the contents for the king's *garde meuble* or personal furniture store. In recognition of this work he was appointed "ordinary cabinet maker to the king" (Louis XVI) in 1774; and from then onward he was the regular supplier of furniture to the queen, Marie Antoinette. He died in Paris on Jan. 6, 1806.

Riesener was a consummate craftsman. His graceful furniture is often richly finished with marquetry of exceptional delicacy and with perfectly carved bronzes. His early work naturally shows Oeben's influence in the strength and architectural quality of the design, but he gradually developed a more individual, more delicately conceived style. This was to become the pure Louis XVI style, with its rectilinear side view and harmoniously distributed ornamentation. Riesener used both European and exotic woods, with a preference for mahogany; he occasionally used lacquer and mother-of-pearl to enrich the surfaces of his works.

See Pierre Verlet, *Mobel von J. H. Riesener* (1955), for a description of many exquisite pieces of furniture now in museums or private collections in Europe and America. *See* also F. de Salverte, *Les Ébénistes français du XVIIIe siècle,* new ed. (1953). (S. Gr.)

RIETI, an ancient city of the region of Lazio, capital of the province of Rieti, central Italy, and seat of a bishopric, is situated on the Velino River among the Abruzzi Mountains 1,318 ft. (402 m.) above sea level and 53 mi. (85 km.) NNE of Rome by road. Pop. (1961) 35,748 (commune). The cathedral is 12th-century Romanesque (much rebuilt) and there are a papal palace (1283) and remains of the 13th-century walls. Rieti is linked by rail with Rome via Terni and is a road junction for Rome, Terni,

and L'Aquila. Artificial textile fibres, sugar, olive oil, fertilizers, and quarrying machinery are produced. There is an experimental wheat culture station.

The ancient city was first Sabine and then Roman. From the 6th-century Lombard dukedom of Spoleto, Rieti passed to the papal states (popes often resided there) and then to Napoleon.

RIETI PROVINCE (area 1,061 sq.mi. [2,749 sq.km.]; pop. [1961] 156,630) is bounded north by the provinces of Terni, Perugia, and Ascoli Piceno; west by Viterbo; south by Rome; east by L'Aquila and Teramo. Sheep and cattle are raised; wheat, fodder, grapes, and olives are grown. The hills are thickly wooded. Terminillo, 13 mi. (21 km.) NE of Rieti, is a holiday resort. Marble is quarried at Cottanello and there is a hydroelectric power station at Cittaducale. (MA. CA.)

RIEVAULX, a ruined Cistercian abbey, situated in the wooded, steep-walled vale of the River Rye—whence the name—$2\frac{1}{4}$ mi. ($3\frac{1}{2}$ km.) WNW of Helmsley, North Riding of Yorkshire, Eng. Of its church, 125 yd. (114 m.) long, built between the foundation in 1131 and *c.* 1230, the chancel and transept walls stand to full height, exhibiting some of the best English Gothic extant. The elaborate remains of this great monastery, the motherhouse for northern England of St. Bernard's mission and once ruled by Aelred (*see* AELRED, SAINT), have been well conserved by the Ministry of Works, custodian since 1918.

There is a small modern village. Along the brink of the eastern hill overlooking the abbey is Rievaulx Terrace, with two classical temples, built (1750–60) by Thomas Duncombe late in the progressive landscape adornment of his Duncombe Park estate.

BIBLIOGRAPHY.—*The Victoria History of the County of York,* passim, esp. the general vol. iii, pp. 149–153 (1913) and *North Riding,* vol. i, pp. 494–502 (1914); *The Chartulary of Rievaulx,* vol. lxxxiii of Surtees Society Series; Sir Charles Peers, Ministry of Works *Official Guide* (HMSO); J. McDonnell (ed.), *History of Helmsley, Rievaulx and District* . . . (1963). (C. K. C. A.)

RIFF: *see* ER RIF.

RIFIS (RIF, RIFF, RIFFI, RIFFIANS), Berber tribes occupying a part of northeastern Morocco known as *al-Rif,* an Arabic word meaning "edge of cultivated area." This country, with its mountains, rolling fields and deserts, is bordered to the west, east and north by the Uringa and Muluya rivers and 145 mi. of Mediterranean seacoast. To the south are tribal territories of Senhaja Berbers and Arabs (*see* BERBER).

The Rifis are divided into 19 tribes: 5 in the west along the coast, 7 in the centre, 5 in the east and 2 in the southeastern desert. One central tribe, of Targuist, is Arabic-speaking, as are the sections of the five western tribes. The others speak the Riffian tongue, a regionally variable Masmuda Berber language mutually incomprehensible with the neighbouring Senhaja dialects but grading in the east into Zenata. Many also speak Spanish and Arabic. The Rifis are Sunni Muslims; their material culture is characteristically Berber, based on cultivation, herding and sardine-seining. They are the fairest of Berbers; about two-thirds have light skins, a tenth have reddish or light hair, over half have light or mixed eyes, and there is a high frequency of stocky builds and square faces.

Before their loss of independence in 1926 (*see* MOROCCO: *The French and Spanish Protectorates*) they were organized by kinship and residence into graded units: the extended family (or vein); the endogamous clan (or bone); a multiclan territory (or fourth); and a group of contiguous fourths (or fifth). In 14 cases the tribe is itself a fifth; in 4 others (Gzennaya, Beni Urriaghel, Temsaman and Galiya) the tribe has five fifths. Unlike the simpler town-meeting structure of the Kabyle (*q.v.*) and Shluh, the complex Riffian system was representative. Each unit above the vein had a council of elected or appointed *imgharen* (sing., *amghar*), renowned fighters and masters of intrigue, one of whom, in time of war, became commander. When clans began to fight each other, their neighbours united to battle both sides at once, forcing a truce and collecting indemnities. Although internally at peace since their pacification by the French and Spanish in 1926 and the restoration of Moroccan sovereignty in 1956, thousands of Riffians, who fought many campaigns in elite French and Spanish regiments, maintained their reputation in the 1960s as one of the world's great warrior peoples. *See* also ABD-EL-KRIM.

BIBLIOGRAPHY.—V. Sheehan, *An American Among the Riffi* (1926); C. S. Coon, *Tribes of the Rif* (1931), *Flesh of the Wild Ox* (1932), *The Riffian* (1933); N. Barbour (ed.), *A Survey of North West Africa* (1959); D. E. Ashford, *Political Change in Morocco* (1961).
(C. S. C.)

RIFLE. In the broadest sense of the term, a rifle is any firearm with a rifled bore, *i.e.*, with shallow spiral grooves cut in the surface of the bore to impart a spin to the bullet or projectile. The term is most often applied to small-bore weapons fired from the shoulder and used either for sport or for military service. (*See* GUNS, SPORTING AND TARGET; SMALL ARMS, MILITARY.) In military language the term also denotes larger weapons with rifled bores, such as recoilless rifles and big naval guns. Though field guns, howitzers, and machine guns have rifled bores they are not normally referred to as rifles.

The practice of rifling the bore of a weapon is old, dating back at least to the 15th century. As the earliest examples of rifled guns had straight rather than spiral grooves, it is thought the purpose of the grooves may have been to receive the powder residue or fouling that was an annoying problem with all early firearms. Gunmakers soon discovered that spiral grooves caused bullets to spin and that the spinning action increased their range and improved their accuracy. The spinning principle increased in importance when spherical lead balls were replaced by elongated bullet-shaped projectiles. The latter type of bullet rotated on its longitudinal axis in the same manner that an arrow rotated due to the angle of its feathers. Over the years, gun designers experimented with a great variety of rifling forms to achieve the best results. Most military rifles of the 20th century have four grooves with a right-hand twist of one turn in something between 10 and 20 inches.

A major difficulty with early muzzle-loading rifles was the problem of loading. As the bullet had to fit tight against the grooves, it had to be rammed down the bore with a ramrod. Rifles of the muzzle-loading era could not be loaded as rapidly as smooth-bore muskets and therefore never gained wide acceptance as military arms. With the advent during the 19th century of breech-loading repeating rifles using metallic cartridges the picture changed completely; the rifle soon replaced the musket as a military weapon. The repeating rifle that held sway during World War I was succeeded during and after World War II by the semi-automatic rifle, notably the U.S. army's Garand rifle. In the 1950s improved rifles capable of both semiautomatic and full automatic fire came into common use.

See also references under "Rifle" in the Index.   (H. C. T.)

RIFT VALLEY REGION, KENYA, the largest of the seven regions of Kenya. *See* KENYA.

RIGA (Lettish RĪGA), a Baltic seaport and the capital of Latvia (the Latvian Soviet Socialist Republic, U.S.S.R.), lies on both banks of the Daugava (Western Dvina, Düna), 9 mi. (14 km.) above its mouth in the Gulf of Riga and 343 mi. (552 km.) SW of Leningrad by rail. Pop. (1959) 604,700. The centre of modern Riga is the old or inner town, bordering the right bank of the river and bounded landward by a canal, formerly part of the 17th-century Swedish fortifications (demolished 1857). This quarter, with narrow streets and churches and monuments dating from the 13th century, has preserved much of its medieval character, although during the withdrawal of Soviet troops from Riga in 1941, some of the oldest and finest buildings (*e.g.*, the Hanseatic "House of the Black Heads") were destroyed, and St. Peter's Church (begun 1209) lost its 400-ft.-high wooden tower. The Doma, or Cathedral of St. Mary (*c.* 1215), rebuilt and restored in the 16th and 19th centuries, has a notable organ; it became a museum and concert hall in 1959. The castle of the master of the Livonian Order (built 1328–40) remains largely as reconstructed by *Landmeister* Wolter von Plettenberg in 1494–1515. It served as the residence of the Swedish governors-general and as the presidential palace during Latvia's independence. On the site of the former fortifications are parks traversed by boulevards, with various public buildings, including the Latvian University (founded 1919), the Conservatory, Opera House, and National Theatre. The Vidzeme, Latgale, and Jelgava (Mitau) suburbs, respectively north- and southeast of the old town and on the left bank of the Daugava, have expanded since the mid-19th century to form the newer Riga. The resort of Rigas Jūrmala, with its broad beaches, lies southwest of the river mouth.

Riga's port (depth 23–27 ft. [7–8 m.]) has installations, including cold storage, warehouses, and a grain elevator, extending downriver to the outer ports of Vecmīlgrāvis (Mühlgraben), Bolderāja (Bolderaa), and Daugavgriva (Dünamünde). Ice-breakers are used to maintain navigation during the winter. Railway lines extend from Riga throughout the republic and to Tallinn, Kaunas, Moscow, Leningrad, and other Soviet cities. The town is an important military base and has an airport.

By the Daugava and the Gauja (Aa) went the ancient trade route of the Vikings, and from 1282 Riga was an important member of the Hanseatic League and the greatest trading centre in the Baltic. Its commercial importance declined in the 17th century although it was then the largest town in the Swedish realm. In the 19th century, after the railways were built, it was, with St. Petersburg, chief among Russian ports, and was the European centre of the timber trade. Before World War I Riga was the third-ranking industrial town in Russia, but during that war all the industry was evacuated. During the period of Latvia's independence, agriculture flourished and industry was partly renewed. After World War II factories for the production of diesel engines, turbines, transport and electrotechnical equipment, and other machinery were installed to supply the needs of the Soviet Union. Other products include paper, textiles, chemicals, glass, and cement, but the export of agricultural products has ceased. There are shipyards at Vecmīlgrāvis.

About 1190 in the camp of Livs by the Ridzene River, where Bremen merchants were already established, the monk Meinhard erected a monastery. In 1201 Bishop Albert I of Livonia removed his seat there from Ikškile (Uxküll) and obtained from Pope Innocent III extensive privileges for the city of Riga, which in 1253 became an archbishopric. At first Riga was governed by the city laws of Visby in Gotland, but later developed its own special laws. These, supplemented by the laws of Hamburg, were granted to the towns of Vidzeme, Kurzeme, and Estonia, and preserved until the Russification in 1885. In the long struggles between the archbishops and the Teutonic Order (which in 1237 absorbed the Livonian Brothers of the Sword founded by Bishop Albert in 1202), Riga often acted independently, but took part in the confederation of von Plettenberg against the attacks of the Muscovite tsar Ivan IV. In 1522 the Reformation gained ascendancy in Riga. While Vidzeme became a Polish possession in 1561, Riga remained a free city until 1581. Thereafter the Polish king Stephen Báthory promised to respect its autonomy, privileges, and the Evangelical-Lutheran religion. Gustavus II Adolphus of Sweden acted similarly on taking Riga in 1621. During the Northern War the Russian commander also accepted, in the terms of its surrender by the Swedes (1710), Riga's special position, and this was confirmed by Peter I the Great in the Treaty of Nystad in 1721. In 1812, the approach of the French being apprehended, the suburbs were burned.

During World War I Riga was occupied by German forces from Sept. 3, 1917. Following the proclamation of the Latvian Republic on Nov. 18, 1918, it became the capital of Latvia. During World War II it was first occupied by Soviet troops—being incorporated in the Soviet Union on Aug. 5, 1940—and then by the Germans until Oct. 13, 1944.   (J. A. Bo.)

RIGAUD, HYACINTHE (HYACINTHE FRANÇOIS HONORAT MATHIAS PIERRE MARTYR ANDRÉ JEAN RIGAU Y ROS) (1659–1743), was one of the most prolific as well as the most successful of French portrait painters at the court of Versailles during the end of Louis XIV's reign and the beginning of Louis XV's. He was born at Perpignan on July 18, 1659, and was trained at Montpellier before moving to Lyons and finally in 1681 to Paris. Although successful in obtaining the Grand Prix de Rome, he allowed this to lapse on the advice of Jean le Brun and devoted himself to painting portraits. By 1688, when he received his first royal commission, he already had a considerable reputation among the wealthier bourgeoisie of Paris. From 1690 onward his work, primarily for the court, consisted almost entirely of portraits. A private ambition was realized when he gained admission to the Academy as a historical painter in January 1700. He died in Paris on Dec. 29, 1743.

Rigaud excelled in the great formal portrait, and the famous portrait of 1701 of Louis XIV in robes of state (now in the Louvre) is the most distinguished example of a manner that derives primarily from Van Dyck. His more intimate manner, reserved for personal friends, reflects an interest in portraits by Rubens and Rembrandt, unusual in France at that period, and is best exemplified in the double portrait of the artist's mother, painted in 1695 in connection with the commission of a portrait bust from Antoine Coysevox, and now in the Louvre.

BIBLIOGRAPHY.—*Le Livre de raison du peintre Hyacinthe Rigaud* (ed. by J. Roman, 1924); W. Weisbach, *Französische Malerei des 17. Jahrhundert* (1932); A. Blunt, *Art and Architecture in France, 1500–1700* (1953).

RIGAUDON, a lively dance of frivolous nature in 2/2 or 4/4 time. It should properly begin (although exceptions occur) with two eighth-note upbeats on the count of 4. Most authorities believe it to be truly French, specifically a Provençal sailors' dance, deriving its name from a famous Marseilles ballet master named Rigaud who brought it to Paris around 1630. It became very popular in England as the Rigadoon. The dance itself included much running, hopping and turning; also *balancés* done with quick little jumps. The music, the melodic structure of which closely resembles that of most English hornpipes, is only occasionally found in the suite. (L. HT.)

RIGEL, the bright star at the heel of the constellation Orion (*q.v.*). It is one of the brightest stars in the sky. Its equivalent in the alphabetical series is β Orionis. Rigel is in reality—as well as apparently—one of the brightest stars known.

Rigel is a blue supergiant located at a probable distance from the sun of between 550 and 1,100 light-years. If Rigel were as close to the sun as the bright star Sirius (nine light-years), it would shine with a brilliancy similar to that of the half-moon. *See* STAR. (W. W. M.)

RIGGING, a general term denoting the whole apparatus of masts, yards, sails and cordage of a ship. (*See* also SAILS; SEAMANSHIP; SHIP; YACHT.) The word is also used to mean cordage only. Sailing vessels are classed according to their rig; *i.e.*, the arrangement of their spars, sails and cordage. Cutter, brig and ship are really convenient abbreviations for cutter-rigged, brig-rigged and ship-rigged.

Elements of Rigging.—The basis of all rigging is the mast, which may be composed of one or many pieces of wood or steel. The mast is supported against fore and aft or athwartship strains by fore and backstays and by shrouds, known as the standing rigging, because they are made fast, and not hauled upon. The bowsprit, though it does not rise from the deck but projects from the bow, is in the nature of a mast. The masts and bowsprit support

F. B. GRUNZWEIG—PHOTO RESEARCHERS, INC.

STANDING OR RUNNING RIGGING SHOWING MAINMAST, YARDS, AND JUNCTIONS WITH SHROUDS AND RATLINES

all the sails, whether they hang from yards slung across the mast; or from gaffs projecting from the mast; or, as in the case of the jibs or other triangular sails, travel on the ropes called stays, which go from the mast to the bowsprit or deck.

The bowsprit is subdivided like the masts. The bowsprit proper corresponds to the lower fore-, main- or mizzen mast. The jib boom, which is movable and projects beyond the bowsprit, corresponds to a topmast; the flying jib boom, which also is movable and projects beyond the jib boom, answers to a topgallant mast.

The ropes by which the yards, booms and sails are manipulated for trimming to the wind or for making or shortening sail are known as the running rigging. The rigging also provides the crew with the means of going aloft and for laying out on the yards to let fall or to furl the sail. The shrouds (*see* below) are utilized to form ladders, the steps of which are called ratlines. Near the heads of the lower masts are the tops—platforms on which men can stand—and in the same place on the topmasts are the crosstrees whose main function is to extend the topgallant shrouds. The yards are provided with ropes, extending from the middle to the extremities or yardarms, called footropes, which hang down about two or three feet and on which men can stand. The material of which the cordage is made varies greatly. Leather has been used, but the prevailing materials have been hemp or grass rope, chain and wire.

As the whole of the rigging is divided into standing and running, so a rope forming part of the rigging is divided into the standing part and the fall. The standing part is that which is made fast to the mast, deck or block. The fall is the loose end or part on which the crew hauls. The block is the pulley through which the rope runs. A tackle is a combination of ropes and blocks which gives increased power at the lifting or moving end, as distinct from the end being manned. If the ship in the illustration is followed from the bow to the mizzenmast, it will be seen that a succession of stays connect the masts with the hull of the ship or with one another. All pull together to resist pressure from the front. Pressure from behind is met by the backstays, which connect the topmasts and topgallant masts with the sides of the

HANK SIMONS—PHOTO RESEARCHERS, INC.

SECTION OF BOWSPRIT AND JIB BOOM SHOWING PORT AND STARBOARD CHAINS AND CHAINS RUNNING FROM DEADEYE

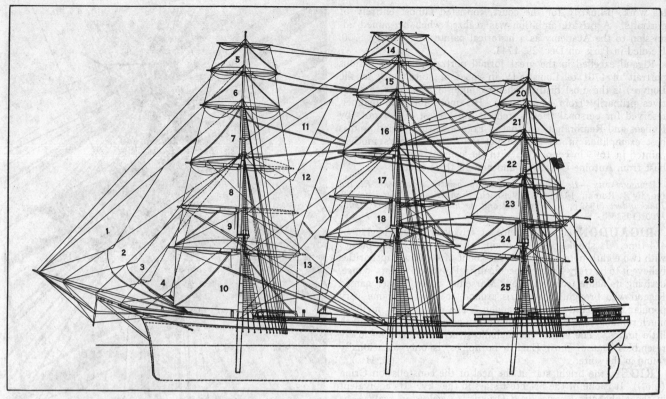

THE SPARS, SAILS AND RIGGING OF A FULL-RIGGED SHIP

1. Flying jib; 2. Outer jib; 3. Inner jib; 4. Jib; 5. Fore skysail; 6. Fore royal; 7. Fore topgallant sail; 8. Fore upper topsail; 9. Fore lower topsail; 10. Foresail; 11. Main royal staysail; 12. Main topgallant staysail; 13. Main topmast staysail; 14. Main skysail; 15. Main royal; 16. Main topgallant sail; 17. Main upper topsail; 18. Main lower topsail; 19. Mainsail; 20. Mizzen skysail; 21. Mizzen royal; 22. Mizzen topgallant sail; 23. Mizzen upper topsail; 24. Mizzen lower topsail; 25. Crossjack; 26. Spanker

vessel. Lateral pressure is met by the shrouds and breast backstays. A temporary or preventer backstay is used when great pressure is to be met. The bobstays hold down the bowsprit, which is likely to be lifted by the tug of the jibs and of the stays connecting it with the fore-topmast. If the bowsprit is lifted the fore-topmast loses part of its support.

The running rigging by which all spars are hoisted or lowered and sails spread or taken in may be divided into those which lift and lower—the lifts, jeers, halyards (haulyards)—and those which hold down the lower corners of the sails—the tacks and sheets. A long technical treatise would be required to name the many parts of standing and running rigging and their uses. All that is attempted here is to give the main lines and general principles or divisions.

The vessel dealt with here is the fully rigged ship with three masts. But the principles of others are the same. The simplest of all forms of rigging is the dipping lug, a quadrangular sail hanging from a yard and always hoisted on the side of the mast opposite to that on which the wind is blowing (the lee side). When the boat is to be tacked so as to bring the wind on the other side, the sail is lowered and rehoisted. One rope can serve as halyard to hoist the sail and as a stay when it is made fast on the side on which the wind is blowing. The difference between such a craft and the fully rigged ship is that between a simple organism and a very complex one; but it is one of degree, not of kind. The steps in the scale are innumerable. Every sea has its own type. Some in eastern waters are of extreme antiquity, and even in Europe vessels are still to be met with which differ very little if at all from ships of the Norsemen of the 9th and 10th centuries.

Types of Rigging.—When the finer degrees of variation are neglected, the types of rigging may be reduced to comparatively few, which may be classed by the shape of their sail and the number of their masts. At the bottom of the scale is such a craft as the Norse herring boat. This boat has one quadrangular sail suspended from a yard which is hung (or slung) by the middle to a single mast which is placed (or stepped) in the middle of

the boat. She is the direct representative of the ships of the Norsemen. Her one sail is a course such as is still used on the fore- and mainmasts of a fully developed ship; a topsail may be added (above the course) and then we have the beginning of a fully clothed mast. A similar craft called a Humber keel is used in the north of England.

The lug sail is an advance on the course, since it is better adapted for sailing on the wind, with the wind on the side. When the lug is not meant to be lowered, and rehoisted on the lee side, as in the dipping lug mentioned above, it is slung at a third from the end of the yard, and is called a standing lug. A good example of the lug is the junk. As the lug is a lifting sail, and does not tend to press the vessel down as the fore-and-aft sail does, it is much used by fishing vessels in the North sea.

The type of the fore-and-aft rig is the schooner. The sails on the masts have a gaff above and a boom below. These spars have a prong called the jaws, which fit to the mast and are held in place by a jaw rope on which are threaded beads called trucks. Sails of this shape are carried by fully rigged ships on the mizzenmast, and can be spread on the fore and main. They are then called trysails and are used only in bad weather when little sail can be carried, and are hoisted on the trysail mast, a small mast above the great one. The lateen sail, a triangular sail akin to the lug, is the prevailing type of the Mediterranean.

These original types, even when unmodified by mixture with any other, permit of large variations. The number of masts of a lugger may vary from one to five, and of a schooner from two to five or even seven. A small lug may be carried above the large one, and a gaff topsail may be added to the sails of a schooner. A one-masted fore-and-aft-rigged vessel may be a cutter or sloop. But the pure types also may be combined, in topsail schooners, brigantines, barkentines and barks, when the topsail, a quadrangular sail hanging from and fastened to a yard, slung by the middle, is combined with fore-and-aft sails. The lateen rig has been combined with the square rig to make such a rigging as the xebec, a three-masted vessel square rigged on the main, and lateen on the fore and mizzen. Triangular sails of the same type as the jibs can be set on the stays between the masts of a fully rigged ship, and are then known as staysails. Studding sails (pronounced "stunsails") are lateral extensions to the courses, topsails, etc., of a square-rigged ship to increase the spread of sails.

Historical Development.—The development of the rigging of ships is a very obscure subject. It was the work of centuries and of practical men who wrote no treatises. It has never been universal, yet a comparison of a four-masted junk with the figures of ships on medieval seals shows much similarity. By selecting a few leading types of successive periods it is possible to follow the growth of the fully rigged ship in its main lines in modern times.

For a time, and after the use of spritsails had been given up, the spritsail yard continued to be used to discharge the function now given to the gaffs. The changes in the mizzen have an obscure history. About the middle of the 18th century it ceased to be a pure lateen. The yard was retained, but no sail was set on the fore part of the yard. Then the yard was given up and replaced by a gaff. The resulting new sail was called the spanker. It was, however, comparatively narrow, and when a greater spread of sail was required, a studding sail (at first called a driver) was added, with a boom at its foot. At a later date "spanker" and "driver" were used as synonymous terms, and the studding sail was called a "ringtail." The studding sails are the representatives of a class of sail once more generally used.

In modern times a sail is cut of the largest size that can be carried in fine weather, and when the wind increases in strength it is reefed; *i.e.*, part is gathered up and fastened by reef points, small cords attached to the sail. Till the 17th century at least the method was often to cut the courses small, so that they could be carried in rough weather. When a greater spread of sail was required, a piece called a bonnet was added to the foot of the sail, and a further piece called a drabbler could be added to that. An example of the tenacious conservatism of the sea is seen in the retaining of this practice by the Swedish small craft called *lodjor* in the Baltic and White seas. It will be easily understood that no innovation was universally accepted at once. Jib and sprit topsail, lateen-mizzen and spanker, and so forth, would be found for long on the sea together.

The history of the development of rigging is one of adjustment. The size of the masts had to be adapted to the ship, and it was necessary to find the proper proportion between yards and masts. As the size of the medieval ship increased, the natural course was to increase the height of the mast and of the sail it carried. Even when the mast was subdivided into lower, top and topgallant, the lower mast was too long, and the strain of the sail racked the hull. Hence the constant tendency of the ships to leak. Sir Henry Manwayring, when giving the proper proportions of the masts, says that the Flemings (*i.e.*, the Dutch) made them taller than the English but were forced to make the sails less wide.

A few words may be added concerning the tops. In the earlier form of ship the top was a species of crow's-nest placed at the head of the mast to hold a lookout, or in military operations to give a place of advantage to archers and slingers. Tops appeared occasionally as mere bags attached to one side of the mast. As a general rule they were round. In the 16th century there were frequently two tops on the fore- and mainmasts, one at the head of the lower, another at the head of the topmast, where in later times there have been only the two traverse beams which make the cross-trees. The upper top dropped out by the 17th century. The form was round, and so continued until the 18th century when the quadrangular form was introduced.

Power Ships.—Steam and motor ships still carry one or more masts for supporting derricks, for lifting heavy weights in and out of the ship, for carrying wireless antennas, for providing a platform for lookout aloft, for mounting the steaming lights and for visual signaling. In the bigger ships the masts are usually hollow steel structures, occasionally with an internal ladderway, while in some merchant ships they also act as uptake ventilators. Stays are usually provided on the same principle as in sailing days, but dead-eyes have given way to bottle screws as rope has to wire. Where masts are provided with ladderways, either internally or externally on the iron structure itself, ratlines on the rigging are dispensed with. Modern battleships, battle cruisers and light cruisers in the Royal Navy usually have a tripod foremast in which the lower mast is supported by two inclined steel struts instead of rigging. This is to give the necessary rigidity for mounting the gun director and range finder (*see* GUNNERY, NAVAL).

The main mast usually carries the main derrick and is stayed on the old lines. Wooden topmasts and sometimes topgallant masts are fitted for wireless and signaling, while one or more signal yards are always carried on the foremast. In light cruisers the main mast is usually a small wooden pole. Destroyers and other light craft are fitted with a light wooden foremast and usually a short main or mizzen mast.

The upper end of the standing rigging is shackled to steel bands round the lower masthead. The lower ends are secured to the deck by bottle screws and slips, the screw being locked by a check piece which prevents its easing back; together with its slip it is covered with painted canvas.

The topmast rigging, consisting of the usual shrouds, stays and backstays, is fitted with insulators to avoid interference with radio and danger from lightning. A Jacob's ladder gives access to the masthead, while above all is a lightning conductor connected by a copper strap running down the mast to the hull of the ship. Where a masthead flashing lamp is fitted, a gallows is provided for its reception. In flagships a pole 16 ft. long is clamped to the fore topmast or fore topgallant masthead to carry the admiral's flag. Clothes lines and hammock gantlines (used for drying clothes and hammocks) are of thin flexible steel rope in warships. They lead through blocks on a shroud near the fore or main lower mastheads and are set up well forward or well aft.

Dressing lines lead from the foremast awning station over both topmasts and down to the after awning station. To these are attached flags for dressing ship.

Signal halyards, made of light white line, lead through blocks

(LEFT, CENTRE) EDWIN LEVICK, (RIGHT) MORRIS ROSENFELD

EXAMPLES OF SAILING VESSELS AND THEIR RIGGING

(Left) Yawl with Bermuda or jib-headed rig; (centre) full-rigged ship, square-rigged on all three masts; (right) staysail schooner, so called because of the staysails between the masts instead of the regular foresail

on the yards and trucks for hoisting signal flags.

BIBLIOGRAPHY.—*A Treatise on Rigging* (about 1625), Society for Nautical Research (1921); R. C. Anderson, *The Rigging of Ships— 1600–1720* (1927); H. A. Underhill, *Masting and Rigging the Clipper Ship and Ocean Carrier* (1946); W. E. Rossnagel, *Handbook of Rigging* (1950).

RIGHT ASCENSION, in astronomy, the co-ordinate on the celestial sphere analogous to longitude on the earth. It is the angle at the celestial pole reckoned eastward from the hour circle through the vernal equinox to the one through the body in question, or the arc of the celestial equator measured eastward from the vernal equinox to the foot of the object's hour circle. (An hour circle is a great circle passing through the celestial poles, perpendicular to the equator). The one through the vernal equinox, the origin for this measurement, takes the place of the Greenwich meridian in earth geography. Right ascension is expressed in time more often than in angular units, and is measured entirely around the equator, having any value from 0 hours to 24 hours, or $0°$ to $360°$ ($15°$ is equivalent to 1 hour, and $1°$ to 4 minutes of time). The common abbreviation is the Greek letter α.

(H. M. Lo.)

RIGHTS OF MAN AND OF THE CITIZEN, DECLARATION OF, one of the basic charters of human liberties, was a philosophical preamble to the French Constitution of Sept. 3, 1791, expounding the principles that inspired the French Revolution. The Constituent Assembly adopted the outline of the declaration on Aug. 4, 1789, and approved the text on Aug. 26. Louis XVI accepted it on Oct. 5, 1789, during the riots which forced him the next day to leave Versailles for Paris.

The declaration was derived from the constitutions of certain North American states, such as Virginia and New Hampshire. Its notion of the separation of powers came from Montesquieu, its doctrine of natural rights from the *Encyclopédie* and John Locke, its theory of the general will and of the sovereignty of the nation from Jean Jacques Rousseau. From Voltaire came the idea that the individual must be safeguarded against arbitrary police or judicial action and from the Physiocrats the doctrine of the inviolability of private property. The whole declaration is characteristic of 18th-century French thought, which strove, before making practical rules, to isolate and specify principles which are fundamental to man and therefore universally applicable.

The declaration, omitting any reference to God (except, in the preamble, by the non-Christian designation "Supreme Being"), to the king (although the constitution provided for the retention of the monarchy), or to tradition, the three cornerstones on which the French state had hitherto rested, announced society to be an association of "free and equal" individuals, united "for the protection of their natural rights." It recognized the sovereignty of the nation and the existence of the general will, but carefully limited the authority of the law to ensure that it should not crush the individual, who confronted the state alone (no right of association being recognized). The right to private property was strongly affirmed, both against communistic theories and against the crown's claim to dispose of subjects' property. The 17 articles comprising the declaration are as follows:

1. All men are born and remain free, and have equal rights. Social distinctions are unjustifiable except insofar as they may serve the common good.

2. The purpose of political association is to preserve the natural and inalienable rights of man, *i.e.*, liberty, private property, the inviolability of the person, and the right to resist oppression.

3. Sovereignty resides essentially in the nation as a whole; no group or individual can exercise any authority not expressly delegated to it or him.

4. Liberty is the right to do anything which does not harm others. Thus, each man's natural rights are limited only by the necessity to assure equal liberty to others. Only the law can determine what restrictions must be made.

5. The law can proscribe only those actions which harm society. Any action not forbidden by law cannot be disallowed, nor can anyone be forced to do what the law does not specifically command.

6. Law is the overt expression of the general will. All citizens have the right to participate in legislation, either in person or through their representatives. The law must be framed to operate completely impartially. Since all are equal before the law, all are equally eligible, in accordance with their abilities, for all public offices and positions.

7. No man can be indicted, arrested, or held in custody except for offenses legally defined, and according to specified procedures. Those who solicit, transmit, execute or cause to be executed arbitrary commands must be punished; but if a citizen is summoned or arrested in due legal form it is his duty to obey instantly.

8. The law must impose only penalties that are obviously necessary. No one can be punished except under the correct application of an established law which must, moreover, have existed before he committed the offense.

9. Everyone must be presumed innocent until he is pronounced guilty. If his arrest and detention are thought necessary, then no more force may be used than is necessary to secure his person.

10. No one must suffer for his opinions, even for religious opinions, provided that his advocacy of them does not endanger public order.

11. Free communication of thought and opinion is one of the most valuable rights of man; thus, every citizen may speak, write, and print his views freely, provided only that he accepts the bounds of this freedom established by law.

12. Some form of military or police force is necessary to guarantee the maintenance of the rights of man and of the citizen; thus, such a force exists for the benefit of all and not for the particular ends of those who command it.

13. To maintain the police force and to meet administrative expenses a financial levy is essential; this must be borne equally by all citizens, in accordance with their individual means.

14. All citizens have the right to decide, either personally or through their representative, the necessity of a financial levy and their free assent to it must be obtained. They can appropriate it, and decide its extent, duration, and assessment.

15. Society has the right to require of every public official an account of his administration.

16. A society in which rights are not guaranteed, and in which there is no separation of powers, has no constitution.

17. Since the right to private property is sacred and inviolable, no one can be deprived of it except in certain cases legally determined to be essential for public security; in such cases a fair indemnity must first of all be granted.

BIBLIOGRAPHY.—G. Jellinek, *The Declaration of the Rights of Man and of Citizens,* Eng. trans. by M. Ferrand (1901); Léon Blum, "La Déclaration des droits de l'homme," *Encyclopédie française*, vol. x (1935).

(CL. H.)

RIGORISM, in general, means stern attachment to a rule, as in asceticism or monasticism (*qq.v.*). In the 18th century, however, the term was applied in particular to the practice of those moral theologians who insisted on the strictest interpretation of the laws of God and of the church in cases of conscience (*see* CASUISTRY). The Jansenists, especially, were described as rigorist in their opposition to probabilism. In philosophical ethics, Kant took the term to describe a system of morality based on reason alone, without any appeal to hedonism.

RIIS, JACOB AUGUST (1849–1914), U.S. newspaper reporter and social reformer who shocked the nation's conscience in 1890 by factual description of slum conditions in his book *How the Other Half Lives.* He was born on May 3, 1849, at Ribe, Den., and emigrated to the United States at the age of 21. For the next three years he went from job to job, gaining a firsthand acquaintance with the ragged underside of city life. In 1873 the chance offer of a newspaper job started him on his life's work. Riis became a police reporter, assigned to New York City's lower East Side, where he found that in some tenements the infant death rate was one in ten. Riis employed the newly invented flashbulb technique to take photographs of the rooms and hallways of these buildings to dramatize his lectures and books.

How the Other Half Lives made Riis famous. A typical response to it was that of the future president of the United States Theodore Roosevelt, who called at the reporter's office and left his card with the message: "I have read your book, and I have come to help." The book stimulated the first significant New York legislation to curb tenement house evils. Of Riis' many other books, which dealt largely with slum problems, the most noteworthy was his autobiography, *The Making of an American* (1901). His writing foreshadowed the muckraking literature of the years 1900–14 (*see* MUCKRAKERS). His death at Barre, Mass., on May 26, 1914, helped to mark the passing of a great era of reform in American life.

See Louise Ware, *Jacob A. Riis: Police Reporter, Reformer, Useful Citizen* (1938). (S. C. L.)

RIJEKA (Italian FIUME), a port of Yugoslavia on the Gulf of Kvarner (Quarnero), 120 mi. (193 km.) WSW of Zagreb by road. Pop. (1961) 100,989. Rijeka has two parts: the old town is built on a ridge of the karst, while the newer quarters together with the harbour are crowded into the amphitheatre between the ridge and the shore. The terrain for the new section of the town was obtained by reclaiming marshland. The modern name of the city dates from the 13th century and referred to the river called Recina in Serbo-Croatian, Fiumara or Eneo in Italian. This river separates the town from the suburb of Susak.

The old town has a 3rd-century Roman triumphal arch, and was known in ancient times as Tarsatica. Captured by Charlemagne, the town long remained under the Franks; later it was held by the bishop of Pola. The counts of Duino held it from 1139 and in 1377 the Cathedral of the Assumption was founded. In the Renaissance period a Franciscan monastery 500 ft. (150 m.) high was built in the old town. Rijeka was next held by the counts of Frankopan. In 1466 it was incorporated into Austria. It was made a free port in 1723, united to Croatia in 1776, and declared a *corpus separatum* of the Hungarian crown in 1779. The French held it from 1809 to 1813 when the English took it. Restored to Austria in 1814 it passed to Hungary in 1822; it was Croatian from 1848 to 1870 and thereafter under Hungarian rule until World War I. In 1851 there were 12,598 inhabitants, over 11,000 of whom were Croats. The Croat political leaders passed a resolution there in 1905, known as Rijecka Rezolucija, an action program which included a call for the union of Dalmatia with Croatia.

Rijeka became a controversial issue after World War I. Although the secret Treaty of London (April 26, 1915) had assigned Rijeka to Yugoslavia, the Italians claimed it at the Paris Peace Conference on the principle of self-determination. Ignoring the suburb of Susak, which had 11,000 Yugoslavs and 1,500 Italians, they claimed that the rest of Rijeka had 22,488 Italians against 13,351 Yugoslavs and certain others. On Sept. 12, 1919, Gabriele D'Annunzio (*q.v.*), who had mustered a body of men at Ronchi near Trieste, occupied Rijeka and proclaimed himself the "commandant" of the "Reggenza Italiana del Carnaro." The Italian government, however, on concluding the Treaty of Rapallo (Nov. 12, 1920) with Yugoslavia, resolved to turn D'Annunzio out of Rijeka. Giovanni Giolitti, the premier, ordered the battleship "Andrea Doria" to shell D'Annunzio's palace only, predicting that the surprise would cause the "commandant" to escape at once—as indeed it did. Riccardo Zanella, who then took office, representing the Autonomist Party, as opposed to the Italian Nationalist, supported Count Carlo Sforza's solution of the problem, namely a free state of Fiume-Rijeka with an Italo-Fiuman-Yugoslav consortium for the port; and such a solution was approved by the Fiuman electorate on April 24, 1921. But when the Fascists gained power in Italy the Rapallo plan for a free state came to nothing. Pressed by Benito Mussolini, the Yugoslav government yielded and a new Italo-Yugoslav treaty, signed in Rome on Jan. 27, 1924, recognized Rijeka itself as Italian while Susak became Yugoslav. As Italy was unable to maintain three ports in the northern Adriatic (Trieste, Pula, and Rijeka-Fiume), Rijeka-Fiume's traffic declined. The port handled only 770,000 metric tons of merchandise in 1938 as compared with 2,100,000 metric tons in 1913.

In World War II, Rijeka was occupied by the Germans in September 1943. On May 3, 1945, after two weeks' fighting, the Yugoslavs occupied the town, the Germans having blown up the port installations. By the Treaty of Paris (Feb. 10, 1947) Rijeka became part of Yugoslavia. The port was rebuilt and by 1949 its sea traffic again exceeded 2,000,000 tons. (K. SM.; V. DE.)

RIJSWIJK, a town in the province of South Holland, Neth., lies on the southeastern outskirts of The Hague and is traversed by the Rotterdam highway and the Vliet River. Pop. (1960) 35,581. The Reformed Church dates from the 14th century and there are some 17th-century houses. The town is mainly residential but there are oil wells and scientific laboratories, and the fruit auction market is important. Nearby is IJpenburg airfield. Rijswijk is famous in history for the treaty signed there in 1697 ending the War of the Grand Alliance (*see* RIJSWIJK, TREATIES OF). (C. v. V.)

RIJSWIJK, TREATIES OF (1697), the agreements terminating the War of the Grand Alliance (*see* GRAND ALLIANCE, WAR OF THE). Largely because Louis XIV of France wanted peace in order to be free to exploit the question of the Spanish succession, a congress opened at Rijswijk, near The Hague, on May 9, 1697. Matters between France and the Maritime Powers (Great Britain and the United Provinces of the Netherlands) were settled quite smoothly, and the French capture of Barcelona induced Spain to participate. By treaties signed with the Dutch, with the British, and with the Spaniards in the night of Sept. 20–21, France repealed the tariff on Dutch goods and the embargo on Dutch salted herring; recognized William III of Orange as king of Great Britain and agreed to a restoration of the *status quo* in the principality of Orange and in the French and British colonies; and retroceded Catalonia, Luxembourg, and some places in the southern Netherlands to Spain. It was also arranged that the Dutch should garrison a chain of fortresses in the Spanish Netherlands (*see* BARRIER TREATY). Against the Holy Roman emperor Leopold I, however, France's attitude had stiffened, with the determination to keep Strasbourg and the rest of Alsace. Finally, on Oct. 30, on the expiry of a French ultimatum, Leopold accepted Louis XIV's offers: the lands east of the Rhine which France had annexed under the policy of "reunions" were given back to the Empire; Lorraine was restored to its duke, Leopold Joseph; the Palatinate was assigned to the House of Neuburg, with the last-minute stipulation that Catholicism was to be maintained there; and Leopold's protégé, Joseph Clement of Bavaria, was acknowledged as archbishop-elector of Cologne.

RILEY, JAMES WHITCOMB (1849–1916), U.S. poet famous for nostalgic dialect verse, was born in Greenfield, Ind., on Oct. 7, 1849. "The poet of the common people," Riley was elected to the American Academy of Arts and Letters, received the gold medal of the National Institute of Arts and Letters and was given several honorary degrees. His boyhood experience as an itinerant sign painter, entertainer and assistant to patent-medicine venders gave him the opportunity to compose songs and dramatic skits, to gain skill as an actor and to come into intimate touch with the rural folk of Indiana. His first reputation was gained by the series in Hoosier dialect ostensibly written by a farmer, "Benj. F. Johnson, of Boone," contributed to the *Indianapolis Daily Journal* and later published as *The Old Swimmin' Hole and 'Leven More Poems* (1883). Riley was briefly local editor of the *Anderson* (Ind.) *Democrat*, but his later life was spent in Indianapolis, where he died on July 22, 1916. Among Riley's numerous volumes are: *Pipes o' Pan at Zekesbury* (1888), *Old-Fashioned Roses* (1888), *The Flying Islands of the Night* (1891), *A Child-World* (1896), and *Home Folks* (1900). The best collected edition is the memorial edition of his *Complete Works*, 10 volumes (1916).

See M. Dickey, *The Youth of James Whitcomb Riley* (1919), *The Maturity of James Whitcomb Riley* (1922); J. Nolan *et al., Poet of the People* (1951); Richard Crowder, *Those Innocent Years* (1957).

RILKE, RAINER MARIA (1875–1926), the greatest of modern German poets and the most internationally read, was born in Prague on Dec. 4, 1875, the only surviving child of German-speaking and German-descended parents, who separated when he was nine years old. After a lonely and abnormal upbringing (his mother, pretending that he was the daughter who had died in infancy, dressed him as a girl) he was sent (September 1886 to June 1891) to the military schools of St. Pölten and Mährisch-Weisskirchen. Rilke suffered at these schools, where he learned little and made no friends, and from which he was finally removed on grounds of ill-health. After a year at the Commercial Academy in Linz he joined his father in Prague and enrolled as a student of law at the university, although he had already resolved to be a writer. In 1896 he left the University of Prague for that of Munich, and in October 1897 he enrolled at the University of Berlin. During these years he wrote incessantly, both in prose and verse, engaging in all kinds of literary activities, to prove, as he said later, that he could make a success of his chosen career.

THE BETTMANN ARCHIVE INC.

RAINER MARIA RILKE, PHOTOGRAPHED IN 1925

His early verse is fluent, imitative (especially of Heine), and, for the most part, evocative of vaguely "poetic" moods and attitudes. His prose tales are more objective and naturalistic, and reveal a keen eye for the individuality of people and things. Especially notable is the short, semiautobiographical *Ewald Tragy* (written *c.* 1898, published 1927–28), which evokes the stifling conventionality of the family circle in Prague. He accepted the tradition (later proved to be without foundation) that his father's family was descended from an ancient and noble one in Carinthia, and in his attempt to transform himself into the kind of person and poet he wanted to be, there is a remarkable affinity between Rilke and W. B. Yeats and his doctrine of the "anti-self." Much of the best poetry of both was largely generated by inner tensions and contradictions.

It was in Munich, in May 1897, that he met Lou Andreas-Salomé (1861–1937), a remarkable woman older than himself, to whom he became passionately attracted, who exerted a decisive influence upon him, and to whom he continued, from time to time, to turn for counsel until the end of his life. She had been born in Russia and encouraged Rilke, who had moved to Berlin, where she and her husband lived, to learn Russian and to study Russian literature. In the spring of 1899 he paid his first visit to Russia with her and her husband. Later he declared that he experienced there for the first time something like a feeling of being at home and of belonging. In the following autumn, in a sudden and unexpected fit of continuous inspiration, he wrote the first part of what eventually became *Das Stunden-Buch* (*The Book of Hours*), *Das Buch vom mönchischen Leben* (*The Book of the Monastic Life*), a series of 67 short verse meditations, supposedly those of a Russian monk, on God, nature, and human life. In these, Rilke's experience of Russia has coalesced with the scarcely less liberating experience of a long stay in Florence during the spring of 1898, when he had basked in what seemed to him the "life-enhancing" this-worldliness of Italian Renaissance art. Art as a discovery and revelation of the mystery and wonder of life, poets and painters as the true revealers and, in a sense, creators, of God—it was with this Blake-like conviction that "the whole business of man was the arts" that Rilke escaped from the sentimental and overparaded Catholicism of his mother and of his own early years. This was the characteristically modified manner in which he accepted that Nietzschean life worship and insistence on this-worldliness in which too many of his contemporaries found release; for in his conception both of life and of art and of his mission as a poet there remained always a religiousness which, however much it may differ from true religion, can be neither explained away nor identified with mere aestheticism.

From May to August 1900, he paid a second visit to Russia, this time with Lou Andreas-Salomé alone, and on his return accepted an invitation to stay with a friend in the artists' colony of Worpswede, a remote heath village near Bremen. There, in April 1901, he married the young sculptress Clara Westhoff, a pupil of Rodin's, settled down in a peasant's cottage in the neighbouring hamlet of Westerwede, and in September 1901 wrote *Das Buch*

von der Pilgerschaft (*The Book of Pilgrimage*), the second part of his *Book of Hours*, full of his memories of Russia. A daughter was born, but soon Rilke and his wife decided that they must pursue their careers separately; so they broke up their household, entrusting the child to Clara's parents. Rilke had received from a German publisher a commission to write a book on Rodin, and in August 1902 he departed for Paris to meet Rodin, for whom he already felt the reverence of a disciple.

Paris, with many long absences (in Capri, 1907; Germany, Austria, Italy, Algeria, Tunis, Egypt, 1910–11; Spain, 1912–13), remained his headquarters until the outbreak of war in 1914. His first letters are full of admiration for Rodin and terrified recoil from the miseries, cruelty, and indifference of the city. In March 1903 he escaped for a month to Viareggio, and there wrote the third and last part of his *Book of Hours, Das Buch von der Armut und vom Tode* (*The Book of Poverty and of Death*). *The Book of Hours*, eventually published in 1905, is the first of Rilke's really unneglectable books. It is also the one in which his overwhelming tendency to subjectivity, reverie, and rhapsody, which he later so successfully corrected, finds its most uninhibited expression. The poems in all three parts are essentially outpourings, with a play of imagery and a rhythmical energy by which most readers are irresistibly swept along. Rilke regarded them as improvisations; on the other hand, long after his conception of what a poem should be had become far more exacting, he often wished he could reachieve something like the inspired and exalted mood in and out of which they had been written.

In July 1902 he had published *Das Buch der Bilder* (*The Book of Images*), containing Neoromantic poems written between 1898 and 1901, with a peculiar combination of the descriptive, the evocative, and the symbolic, but still with "poetic" treatments of "poetic" subjects and moods: among the 37 added to the second edition (1906) are several which are very beautiful. But now, under the influence of Rodin and of French poets such as Baudelaire, he tried to achieve something altogether different—to work regularly, as in front of a model, like a sculptor or painter. The result was the two parts (1907, dedicated to Rodin, and 1908) of *Neue Gedichte* (*New Poems*), that astonishing combination of German "inwardness" and French elegance and objectivity. Essentially all these poems are *Dinggedichte* (poems of "things"), even when they evoke human beings. Cathedrals and statues, palaces and parks, fountains, pavilions, and staircases; dolphins, panthers, flamingos, and gazelles; hydrangeas, heliotropes, poppies, and roses; young girls and lovers, the beggars and the blind—Rilke seems to have entered into them all and to speak for them rather than of them. There is magic in the "things" presented, steeped in their own atmosphere and most of them impregnated with the sense of the past. In his interpretation of the legends of Alcestis, of Orpheus and Eurydice, in other poems in these collections, and in the contemporary requiems, he voiced that absorption with the problem of death which was a lifelong preoccupation.

Much of the subjectivity and *Angst* which he was able to keep out of *New Poems* found its way into his remarkable prose work *Die Aufzeichnungen des Malte Laurids Brigge* (*The Notebooks of Malte Laurids Brigge*), begun at Rome in 1904, continued mainly in Paris, and published in 1910. This study of the dark side of existence and the night side of the mind reveals the mental and spiritual terrors which the young Danish hero undergoes in Paris, and the agonies of fear he lived through in his childhood. It is confessional in much the same way as Goethe's *Werther;* but, unlike Goethe, Rilke could not exorcise the horrors which haunted him.

For a time he seems to have contemplated yet a third part of *New Poems*, but he came to recognize that his next task would be the writing of a kind of poetry which, in a very special sense, would have to be lived before it could be written; for he must first achieve and then communicate some vision, of what might be called the value and destiny of the individual. During a solitary sojourn at Schloss Duino on the Adriatic near Trieste, placed at his disposal by his friend and benefactress Princess Marie von Thurn und Taxis-Hohenlohe (November 1911–May 1912), a type of inspiration, different in kind from anything he had so far experienced, seized upon him and dictated the first two poems of the cycle which was finally completed in 1922 and called *Duineser Elegien* (*Duino Elegies*). During the ten years between its inception and its consummation Rilke lived in a state of suspension, waiting, working, and hoping for the miracle of Duino to recur.

When war broke out he was in Germany and, strangely uplifted by the greatness of the calamity, he composed five magnificent hymns addressed to the god of war. Hölderlin's influence is discernible in the apocalyptic quality of the style of these and one or two other poems of the period. But the rising tide of inspiration was checked by the mental suffering the war induced, aggravated by Rilke's short period of war service (November 1915–June 1916), for a few weeks in the infantry of the second reserve and then for a few months as a clerk in the war ministry in Vienna. This was a kind of sinecure, but it increased the poet's hopelessness and apathy, which were hardly lessened by the many friends he made in Munich where he spent most of the war years. In 1919 he accepted an invitation to Switzerland to give readings of his poems; there he remained until his death, undertaking short visits to Venice and Paris, but never returning to Germany or Austria.

The third Duino elegy was completed in Paris in 1913 and the fourth was written in Munich in 1915; but it was not until February 1922, during about 18 days of tumultuous inspiration, in the little Château de Muzot, at Raron near Sierre in the Swiss canton of Valais, his final refuge and home, that he was able to complete the cycle of ten. About the power of these poems there can be no doubt; how far the situations and problems they evoke are those of humanity in general, and how far those of the solitary and almost religiously dedicated poet himself can be questioned.

The completion of the *Duino Elegies* in February 1922 was both preceded and followed in the same burst of inspiration by the composition of the 55 entirely unexpected *Sonette an Orpheus* (*Sonnets to Orpheus*). In these, as in many of the other poems which Rilke wrote during the remaining four years of his life, we may perceive the emergence of something new: of a mood (the reward, perhaps, of much patient endurance of silence, terror, and perplexity) of joyful acquiescence and celebration.

Rilke died at the Château de Muzot on Dec. 29, 1926, from acute leukemia, from which he seems to have been suffering since 1923, but which was diagnosed only shortly before his death.

The international fame to which Rilke attained in his lifetime has continued to increase after his death, as the innumerable memoirs, monographs, commentaries, biographies, and translations in many European languages bear witness. His voluminous correspondence constitutes both a literary and a psychological phenomenon of absorbing interest. Some letters read like literary essays of a descriptive or reflective nature; others contain first sketches or rough drafts of poems to come; passages from letters to his wife and to Lou Andreas-Salomé were later used almost *verbatim* in *Malte Laurids Brigge;* there are confessional outpourings, and elaborate essays in self-portraiture and self-exegesis.

Rilke's poetical reputation achieved its summit with the *Duino Elegies* and the *Sonnets to Orpheus*. The mysterious philosophical undertow of the elegies and the sonnets with its doctrinal implications creates that impression of something greater than art which great works of art produce. The cosmic isolation of man facing the glorious, austere, aloof, and indifferent angels of the elegies, the tragic nature of his attempts to transcend mortality by love as he journeys irrevocably deathward, the summons received by the poet toward the end of the elegies to justify his existence by transforming the visible world into visible art—all this, expressed with visionary intensity, embodies an appeal or a message to humanity which also pervades the sonnets. Some of these practice the doctrine they preach by magically transforming objects, already half-dematerialized in *New Poems,* into sound so pure that only their vibrations seem to linger in the air.

BIBLIOGRAPHY.—*Editions, Correspondence, and Bibliographies: Sämtliche Werke,* 5 vol. (1955–); *Gesammelte Briefe,* 6 vol. (1936–39); *Briefe,* 2 vol. (1950); *Tagebücher aus der Frühzeit* (1942); *Lettres à Rodin* (1928); *Briefe an einen jungen Dichter* (1929; Eng. trans. 1934 and 1945); *Briefe an seinen Verleger,* 2 vol. (1949); *Briefe an Frau Gudi Nölke* (1953; Eng. trans., 1955). Correspondence with: *Marie von Thurn und Taxis-Hohenlohe,* 2 vol. (1951; Eng. trans., 1958); *Lou Andreas-Salomé* (1952); *André Gide* (1952); *Benvenuta* (1954; Eng. trans. 1953); *Katharina Kippenberg* (1954); *Merline* (1954); *André Gide et Émile Verhaeren* (1955). F. A. Hünich, *Rilke Bibliographie* (1935); W. Ritzer, *Rilke Bibliographie* (1951).

English Translations: M. D. Herter Norton, *Translations from the Poetry of R. M. Rilke* (1938); *Selected Works:* vol. i, *Prose,* by G. Craig Houston; vol. ii, *Poetry,* by J. B. Leishman (1954–60); John Linton, *The Notebook of Malte Laurids Brigge* (1930); J. B. Leishman, *Sonnets to Orpheus,* 2nd ed. (1946); *From the Remains of Count C. W.* (1952), *Poems 1906–26,* 2nd ed. (1959), and *New Poems* (1964); A. L. Peck, *The Book of Hours* (1961); J. B. Leishman and Stephen Spender, *Duino Elegies,* 4th ed. (1963); R. F. C. Hull, *Selected Letters of R. M. Rilke, 1902–26* (1946); M. D. Herter Norton, *Wartime Letters of R. M. Rilke, 1914–21* (1940). For translations of individual correspondences, *see* above.

Biography and Criticism: E. Jaloux, *R. M. Rilke* (1927); Lou Andreas-Salomé, *R. M. Rilke* (1928); Marie von Thurn und Taxis, *Erinnerungen an R. M. Rilke* (1932); K. Kippenberg, *R. M. Rilke* (1935, 4th ed. 1948); J. R. von Salis, *R. M. Rilkes Schweizer Jahre* (1936; Eng. trans. 1964); R. Kassner, essays in *Buch der Erinnerung* (1938), in *Umgang der Jahre* (1949), and in *Geistige Welten* (1958); W. Rose and G. Craig-Houston (eds.), *R. M. Rilke: Aspects of His Mind and Poetry* (1938); E. C. Mason, *Lebenshaltung und Symbolik bei R. M. Rilke* (1939), *Rilke und Goethe* (1958), *Rilke, Europe, and the English-Speaking World* (1961), and *Rilke* (1963); E. M. Butler, *R. M. Rilke* (1941); M. Betz, *Rilke à Paris* (1941); N. Wydenbruck, *Rilke, Man and Poet* (1949); H. W. Belmore, *Rilke's Craftmanship* (1954); I. Schnack, *Rilkes Leben und Werk im Bild* (1956); F. H. Wood, *R. M. Rilke, the Ring of Forms* (1958); H. F. Peters, *R. M. Rilke: Masks and the Man* (1960); E. Simenauer, *Rainer Marìa Rilke: Legende und Mythos* (1953). *See* also introductions, etc., to J. B. Leishman's translations listed above. (E. M. Br.; J. B. Ln.)

RIMBAUD, (JEAN NICOLAS) ARTHUR (1854–

1891), French poet and adventurer, who, although his creative life lasted only from his 15th to his 20th year, became, unbeknown to himself, one of the masters of the Symbolist movement. When he abandoned literature he became first a wanderer and eventually a trader, gunrunner, and explorer in Abyssinia. He was born at

Charleville in the Ardennes on Oct. 20, 1854, the second son of an army captain and a local farmer's daughter: his brother was a year older and there were two younger sisters. In 1860 Captain Rimbaud and his wife separated, and the children were brought up by their mother, who hoped to keep her sons from following the example of her two wastrel brothers. Arthur, who early displayed unusual intellectual ability, showed a gift for writing at the age of eight. Later he was the most brilliant pupil at the Collège de Charleville. He had a particular talent for Latin verse and in August 1870 won the first prize for a Latin poem at the Concours Académique. His first published poem had appeared in January 1870 in *La Revue pour tous,* and in April he had submitted to Théodore de Banville (*q.v.*), one of the selection committee for *Le Parnasse contemporain,* a number of poems including one entitled *Credo in Unam,* which, although derivative, showed signs of an original genius.

GIRAUDON
ARTHUR RIMBAUD, DETAIL FROM A PORTRAIT PAINTED BY FANTIN-LATOUR, 1872

The outbreak of the Franco-German War (July 1870) ended his formal education. In August he ran away to Paris, but was arrested for traveling without a ticket and spent some days in prison. His friend and schoolmaster, Georges Izambard, paid his fine and had him sent to Douai, where he spent three weeks at the house of Izambard's aunts, and where he joined the national guard. Izambard then took him home but in October he disappeared again, wandering through northern France and Belgium in the wake of the invading armies. Again he arrived at Douai, where he made fair copies of the poems composed during his two weeks of freedom, hunger, and rough living. These express an innocent joy in life and liberty, and are his first wholly original works.

His mother had him brought back by the police, but in February 1871 he sold his watch and again went to Paris, where for a fortnight he lived in great poverty. Then, in early March, he returned home on foot, a completely changed character, perhaps as a result of some shattering, yet enlightening, experience. He repudiated his early verses as false and wrote some of his most violent and blasphemous poems, expressing a disgust at life, a desire to escape into a world of innocence, and a sense of struggle between good and evil. His behaviour matched his poetic mood—he refused to work, and spent his days drinking in cafés, in conscious revolt against religion, morality, and every kind of discipline. At the same time he read books on occult philosophy, Cabalism, magic, and alchemy, and formulated his new aesthetic doctrine, expressed in two letters, to Izambard and to Paul Démeny (May 13 and 15, 1871), later called *Lettres du Voyant*. This is based on the belief that the poet must become a seer, a "*voyant*," who can penetrate infinity, and, who, by breaking down the restraints and controls which make up the conventional conception of individual personality, must become the instrument for the voice of the Eternal. But because the new visions cannot be rendered in contemporary forms, a new language must be invented, a language accessible to all the senses in one—this is the ideal of "total art" first formulated by Charles Baudelaire and adopted by the Symbolists (*q.v.*).

At the end of August 1871, on the advice of a literary friend in Charleville, Rimbaud sent to Paul Verlaine (*q.v.*) specimens of his new poetry, among them "Sonnet des voyelles," in which he attributes to each vowel a different colour—"A noir, E blanc, I rouge, U vert, O bleu." The poem has been variously interpreted, but its true beauty lies in the originality of its images. Verlaine, impressed by the brilliance of the poems, summoned Rimbaud to Paris and sent the money for his fare. In a burst of self-confidence, Rimbaud composed *Le Bateau ivre*. Although traditional in versification, it is a poem of astonishing verbal virtuosity, and of daring choice of images and metaphors, inspired by a deep emotional and spiritual experience. In this masterpiece, Rimbaud reached one of the highest peaks of his art.

Arriving in Paris in September 1871, he stayed for three months with the Verlaines, who were living with Mathilde Verlaine's parents, and met most of the well-known poets of the day, but antagonized them all—except Verlaine himself—by his arrogance, boorishness, and obscenity. Requested to leave, he lived for some weeks in destitution, and then in an attic in the house where Banville was living. Again his behaviour caused complaints and in January 1872 he moved to a room where he lived, on money subscribed by Verlaine and his friends, a life of drink and debauch, and was involved in a homosexual relationship with the older poet which gave rise to scandal. In March he returned to Charleville so that Verlaine could attempt a reconciliation with his wife, but was recalled in May by his friend who vowed he could not live without him.

During this period (September 1871–July 1872), Rimbaud composed the last of his poems in verse which show an advance in technical freedom and originality on those written earlier. This freedom is daring for that period, then at the height of the Parnassian movement (*see* PARNASSIANS). At this time he also composed the work which Verlaine called his masterpiece, *La Chasse spirituelle*, the manuscript of which disappeared when Verlaine and Rimbaud went to England. Some critics also date from this creative period the transcendental prose poems which form part of *Illuminations*.

In July 1872 Verlaine abandoned his wife and fled with Rimbaud via Belgium to London, where they lived in Soho. Rimbaud may there have composed some of *Illuminations*. He returned home for Christmas but was recalled (January 1873) by Verlaine who dramatized an illness to play on his sympathy. In April Rimbaud went to the farm at Roche, near Charleville, where his mother and sisters were staying, and began to write what he called his "Livre Païen ou Nègre" which eventually became *Une Saison en Enfer*. Verlaine was meanwhile staying at Jehonville, near Roche, and in May he persuaded Rimbaud to accompany him to London. Rimbaud's sense of guilt at yielding to an influence from which he had wished to escape caused him to treat Verlaine with sadistic cruelty, varied by remorseful kindness. Finally, at the end of June, after one of their frequent quarrels, Verlaine abandoned Rimbaud and went to Belgium. Failing, however, to effect a reconciliation with his wife, he sent for Rimbaud and begged him to return with him to London. When Rimbaud tried to leave, Verlaine shot at him, wounding him in the wrist, and threatened to do so again. Rimbaud, terrified, asked a policeman for protection; Verlaine was arrested, imprisoned, and later sentenced to two years' imprisonment. After a week in hospital Rimbaud returned to Roche. There he finished *Une Saison en Enfer*, an account of his spiritual descent into Hell, and of his failure in art and love, which acquired some of its tragic character from the events in Brussels. It was printed in Belgium and, in October 1873, he went to Brussels to collect the copies, and then to Paris to arrange for its publicity. Discouraged by its reception there, he abandoned the whole edition and, returning on foot to Charleville, it is alleged that he burned his manuscripts and papers. The bales of the book remained in the attics of the printers where they were discovered in 1901, by the Belgian bibliophile Losseau. He, out of consideration for his fellow bibliophiles, who possessed the only copies known to exist, did not make his discovery public until 1915.

In February 1874 Rimbaud returned to London with Germain Nouveau, a wild bohemian poet. There they earned a precarious living in menial employment: Rimbaud may also have been composing some of *Illuminations*. Nouveau returned to Paris in June and Rimbaud seems to have fallen ill, or to have suffered acutely from poverty, for his mother and elder sister went over to help him to find a job. At the end of July he took up a post at a coaching establishment at Reading, but went home for Christmas, never to return.

In January 1875, he went to Stuttgart to learn German—his interest then was in languages. There he was visited by Verlaine, but this, their last meeting, ended in a violent quarrel. It was probably then that Rimbaud gave Verlaine the manuscript of *Illuminations*. In May he left for Italy, crossing the Alps on foot, but, taken ill with sunstroke, was repatriated by the French consul at Leghorn. He spent the winter at home, learning Arabic, Hindustani, and Russian, and, in April 1876, set out for Russia, but, after being robbed of money and luggage in Vienna, was arrested as a beggar and again sent home. In May he went to Holland, where he enlisted in the Dutch colonial army. He arrived at Batavia on July 23, but deserted on Aug. 15 and eventually reached home at the end of December. In the spring of 1877 he went to Hamburg, and, failing to find work on a ship sailing east, he is said to have joined a circus going to Scandinavia, but returned to France in the summer. In the autumn, however, he set out for Alexandria, but, taken ill on board ship, was landed in Italy, and again returned home. There he remained, enfeebled by illness, until October 1878, when he set off for Egypt. He took a boat from Genoa to Alexandria and then went to Cyprus, where he worked as a labourer, but in June 1879, he fell ill with typhoid fever and returned home to recover.

It was during this winter of illness that he apparently decided to abandon his life of wandering and to plan for the future. Returning to Cyprus in the spring he found work as a builder's foreman but, in August, he quarreled with his employers and set out in search of work. A coffee exporter at Aden, Pierre Bardey, sent him to open a trading post at Harar, in the interior, at that time occupied by the Egyptians, but, after the Mahdi rising in the Sudan and the consequent Egyptian evacuation of Harar, the trading post was closed and he went back to Aden. From Harar, however, he had been sent by Bardey on a journey of exploration into Ogaden, the region south of Harar, where no white man had ever penetrated. His report of this journey, in the proceedings of the Société de Géographie (February 1884), aroused some interest.

After the Egyptian withdrawal from Abyssinia, the contest for power between the emperor, John IV, and Menelik, king of Shoa, gave rise to an arms race. Rimbaud, deciding to risk his savings on an expedition to sell arms to Menelik, resigned his position with Bardey (October 1885), and, in October 1886, after a series of frustrating delays, set out for the interior. He reached the capital of Shoa in February 1887, but unforeseen circumstances and the rapacity and double-dealing of Menelik robbed him of his expected profits, and he returned to Aden no better off than when he had left it, with no prospect of employment, exhausted and embittered. He spent the summer in Cairo, where an account of his journey was published in *Le Bosphore Egyptien* (August 1887), and then returned to Aden, where he sought in vain for work. In May 1888 he returned to Harar, as manager of a trading station for a firm called Tian, which, as well as exporting coffee, gum, ivory, and hides, engaged in the profitable traffic in arms and ammunition. At first Rimbaud's chief business was supplying Menelik with arms but he may also have been in some way associated with the slave trade. However, after John IV was killed (1889) and Menelik became emperor, the profits from gunrunning declined and, although Harar was the chief trading centre of the empire, and the more settled conditions encouraged commerce, Rimbaud lacked the hardheaded business sense needed for success. He lived as simply as the poorest native, spending as little as possible in order to save money so that he could one day retire and live at leisure. His meanness to himself was matched by unobtrusive generosity to others, and the little house where he lived with a native woman became the meeting place of the Europeans in Abyssinia.

His gift for languages and his humane treatment of the Abyssinians made him popular with them, and by his honesty and sincerity he even managed to win the confidence of the chiefs and of Menelik's nephew, the governor of Harar, who became his close friend. He began to wish to do "something good, something useful," and his letters to his mother reveal a longing for affection and intellectual companionship. The marriage of his servant and only close companion, Djami, made him long for a family of his own, and he planned to go home for a holiday and to look for a wife, in the spring of 1891. In February, however, he developed a tumour on his right knee, and when he left Harar, on April 7, he had to be carried by stretcher for the week's journey to the coast. At Aden, the treatment tried had no result and he was sent back to France. He landed at Marseilles in May, and was taken to the Hospital of the Immaculate Conception, where his right leg was amputated. His mother had gone to Marseilles to be with him, but, despite the growing warmth of their letters toward the end of his time at Harar, she remained unable to show her affection for him, to his great disappointment. In letters to his sister, Isabelle, he poured out his sense of frustration and despair, and when, in July, he returned to Roche, a helpless cripple, it was she who looked after him.

He still hoped to marry and return to Abyssinia, but his health grew steadily worse. At last, made wretched by his helplessness and by the gloom of a bad northern summer, in August 1891, he set out on a nightmare journey to Marseilles. His disease was diagnosed as carcinoma, and Isabelle, who had accompanied him, was told that his case was hopeless. He however still believed that he might be cured and endured agonizing treatment. Shortly before he died, Isabelle persuaded him to make his confession to a priest. This conversion seemed to bring him new peace, and to reawaken the poetic imagination of his early youth so that he became once more a *voyant,* seeing visions which, according to his sister, surpassed in depth and beauty those which had inspired *Illuminations.* He died on Nov. 10, 1891, still hoping to return to the East.

Reputation, Poetic Genius, Influence.—While Rimbaud had been in Abyssinia, he had become known as a poet in France. Verlaine had written about him in *Les Poètes maudits* (1884), and had published a selection of his poems. These had been enthusiastically received and, in 1886, unable to discover where he was, or to get an answer from him, he published prose poems under the title *Illuminations,* and further verse poems, in the Symbolist periodical *La Vogue,* as the work of "the late Arthur Rimbaud." It is not known whether Rimbaud ever saw these publications. But he certainly knew of his rising fame after the appearance of *Les Poètes maudits* for, in August 1885, he had received a letter from an old schoolmate, Paul Bourde, who told him of the vogue of his poems—especially "Sonnet des voyelles"—among avant-garde poets. Also he did preserve, for it was among his papers, a letter received in July 1890 from a review inviting him to return to France and put himself at the head of the new literary movement, but he does not seem to have answered it.

Rimbaud was an amazing phenomenon in literature. His meteoric poetic life spanned only five or six years. But in these few years he opened up a rich field for literature, and few poets have been the object of more passionate study, or have exercised greater influence on modern poetry. It is in the prose poem, in *Illuminations,* that he reached the highest peak of his originality, and this is the form best suited to his elliptical and hermetic style, allowing considerable freedom. With him the prose poem was stripped of all the anecdotal, narrative, and even descriptive content of his predecessors, and it is highly concentrated. In these poems he increased the evocative power of literature, independently of the sense conveyed, and words with him are no longer meant to bear their dictionary meaning or to express logical content, but are a form of magic charm, and are intended to evoke a state of mind— *"état d'âme,"* the Symbolists were to say. He also showed how much rich material exists for poetry in the subconscious mind, and in the half-remembered sensations of childhood. Finally, after nearly a century, his writings are still capable of expressing intensely modern revolt and recoil from the very essence of life in a so-called civilized society.

BIBLIOGRAPHY.—*Editions and Correspondence:* The first collected edition of Rimbaud's writings was that by P. Berrichon and E. Delahaye (1898); the only complete edition, including correspondence, rough notes, etc., is the Édition de la Pléiade by J. Mouquet and R. de Renéville (1946). The best annotated edition is that for the Classiques Garnier by S. Bernard (1960). His correspondence from the East was edited by P. Berrichon, in *Lettres de Jean-Arthur Rimbaud (Égypte, Arabie, Éthiopie)* (1899). Earlier letters were edited by J. M. Carré as *Lettres de la vie littéraire* (1931).

Biography and Criticism: The first complete biography was P. Berrichon, *La Vie de Jean-Arthur Rimbaud* (1897). Of many other works the most notable are: P. Verlaine, *Les Poètes maudits* (1884); M. Coulon, *Le Problème de Rimbaud* (1923); E. Delahaye, *Rimbaud l'Artiste et l'Être Moral* (1923); E. Rickword, *Rimbaud, the Boy and the Poet* (1924); R. de Renéville, *Rimbaud le voyant,* 3rd version (1947); F. Ruchon, *Jean-Arthur Rimbaud* (1929); B. Fondane, *Rimbaud le voyou* (1933); R. Étiemble and Y. Gauclère, *Rimbaud* (1936); C. Hackett, *Rimbaud l'enfant* (1948); H. de Bouillane de Lacoste, *Rimbaud et le problème des Illuminations* (1949); J. Gengoux, *La Pensée poétique de Rimbaud* (1950); R. Étiemble, *Le Mythe de Rimbaud* (1952–54); E. Noulet, *Le Premier Visage de Rimbaud* (1953); D. de Graaf, *Arthur Rimbaud* (1961); E. Starkie, *Rimbaud en Abyssinie* (1938), *Arthur Rimbaud,* 3rd version (1961); H. Matarasso and P. Petitfils, *Vie d'Arthur Rimbaud* (1962).

(E. St.)

RIME, a beautiful, white, friable, crystalline ice deposit formed by freezing of supercooled cloud- or fog-water droplets on objects exposed to the air. It occurs in two typical shapes: (1) growths of uniformly short, projecting, feathery branching crystal aggregates on all sides of a freely exposed object; and (2) asymmetrical growths of crystal aggregates in the form of long plumes or flags orientated into the direction held by the wind during the formation of the deposit. The latter type, which may reach a length of six feet, is common on exposed upper slopes of mountains in middle and high latitudes; the terms "frozen fog deposit" and "frost feathers" are often applied to the phenomenon in such places. The first type is less common and occurs chiefly in valleys from winter ground fogs with calm air. Under the microscope, rime appears to be a mosaic agglomeration of minute crystal accretions, almost amorphous, with spaces of entrapped air. Often wind-blown snowflakes become embedded in the deposit, giving it a greasy consistency when crushed between the fingers. When the temperature at formation is just below freezing, the rime becomes a denser, smoother deposit which is hard and tenacious like ordinary ice, sometimes called rough frost, or hard rime, in contradistinction to the more usual types, or soft rime. Some hydrologists and glaciologists claim that the larger part of the alimentation of the icecaps in such regions as Greenland, Norway, Iceland, and Spitsbergen is provided by rime depositing on the surfaces of the mountain snowfields. Field measurements, however, cast some doubt on the general validity of this assumption. *See* also FROST.

(R. G. SE.)

RIME (RHYME) **ROYAL,** the name given to a stanza form of seven decasyllabic (iambic) lines, rhyming *a b a b b c c*. The name is traditionally derived from use of the form in *The Kingis Quair*, attributed to James I of Scotland (1394–1437). Introduced to England by Chaucer (*c.* 1340–1400) in *Troilus and Criseyde* and *The Parliament of Fowls*, it became the favourite form for long narrative poems during the 15th and early 16th centuries.

Chaucer probably borrowed it from the French poet and musician Guillaume de Machaut (*c.* 1300–77), who may have invented it or derived it from earlier French and Provençal poets. Chaucer's skilful use of it recommended it to his followers in England and Scotland (*see* ENGLISH LITERATURE: *From Chaucer to the Renaissance: Poetry: The Chaucerian Tradition;* SCOTTISH LITERATURE: *The Makaris*). It continued to be popular in the 16th century, and, after Chaucer, one of the most successful writers of rime royal was Thomas Sackville, who used it for his *Induction* to the 1563 edition of *A Mirror for Magistrates*. Shakespeare's *Lucrece* (1594) is, perhaps, the last important poem of the period in rime royal, although Milton experimented with it, and it was used by Sir Francis Kynaston (1587–1642)—an admirer of Chaucer who translated part of *Troilus and Criseyde* into Latin rime royal—for *Leoline and Sydanis* (1642). By this time, however, it had been generally replaced by the octave. It was successfully revived by William Morris (1834–96).

RIMINI (anc. ARIMINUM), a town of Forlì province, Italy, and the seat of a bishopric, lies on the Riviera del Sole of the northern Adriatic Coast, a short distance from the foot of the Apennines where the steep Monte Titano is crowned by the republic of San Marino. Pop. (1961) 94,403 (commune). Area of commune 59 sq.mi. (152 sq.km.).

The plan of the old Roman city is apparent in the area between the Marecchia river, the Ausa torrent and the railway, where streets follow the ancient lines. The crumbling remains of 15th-century walls raised under the rule of the Malatesta family, when the town was extended, stretch along the left bank of the Marecchia. The town was divided into four quarters, known since the 18th century as Cittadella, Clodio, Pataso and Montecavallo. In the mid-19th century the suburbs of S. Giuliano, Mazzini and Marina grew up outside the walls and the first bathing stations on the coast were joined to the town by Principe Amedeo avenue. Since 1920 the town expanded farther south and the seaside suburbs of Marebello, Riva Azzurra and Miramare came into being, and many fashionable houses and hotels were built. In spite of the destruction of 90% of its houses during World War II the town recovered, and its seaside resorts stretch for nearly 10 mi. from Torre Pedrera to Miramare. The centre of the town is the Piazza Giulio Cesare, the meeting point of the old Roman roads Via Flaminia and Via Aemilia; nearby are most of the monuments.

Monuments.—The oldest monument is the arch of Augustus, erected in 27 B.C. over the south gate of the city, but not finished until A.D. 22, by Tiberius; it was dedicated to Augustus. It has a single opening and a frieze added in the middle ages. The bridge built by Augustus over the Marecchia and also completed by Tiberius (A.D. 21) had a fifth arch added in 552. There are some remains of a Roman amphitheatre. Only ruins remain of the castle built by Sigismondo Pandolfo Malatesta (see *History*, below) in 1446. Rimini's most famous building is the Malatesta temple, designed to glorify Sigismondo's love for the beautiful Isotta degli Atti. Converted from the old Gothic church of S. Francesco, the temple was designed by Leon Battista Alberti, and the decoration of the interior was mostly the work of Agostino di Duccio, who enriched it with exquisite reliefs: figures of the liberal arts, the sybils, angels with fluttering veils, shields with the Malatesta arms, the planets and the moon, dancing children holding festoons of flowers and fruit; everywhere are repeated the intertwined initials S and I. The scheme for the temple, a monument of frankly pagan character, remained unfinished on Sigismondo's death.

Churches include S. Giovanni Evangelista (1247), with painted murals of the 13th-century Romagna school; S. Giuliano (16th century), built on the site of a Benedictine abbey, which preserves an altarpiece by Paolo Veronese; the little octagonal temple of S. Antonio on the Piazza Giulio Cesare; and the church of the Servi (14th century, rebuilt in the 16th). Other buildings include the restored Palazzo dell'Arengo (1202). The Piazza Cavour has a 15th-century fountain of Giovanni da Carrara. A bronze statue of Paolo V, begun by Niccolò Cordier and finished by Sebastiani di Recanati, was later transformed into S. Gaudenzio, patron saint of the town. The picture gallery contains Dutch arras of the 16th and 17th centuries and pictures by Giovanni Bellini, Ghirlandaio and Giuliano da Rimini. The Gambalunghiana civic library (1619), badly damaged in World War II, was afterward repaired, and preserves valuable incunabula and illuminated manuscripts.

Communications and Commerce.—Rimini is an important railway junction of the lines to Brindisi in the south, Venice and Trieste in the north and Bologna and Turin in the west, and is also a road centre. It has sea links with Ancona, Ravenna, Venice and Trieste, and an airport at Miramare. The district is rich in cereals and fruit and the town is equipped with processing factories and railway repair shops. The principal occupation, however, is the tourist industry. The gently sloping beaches backed by promenades and hotels are an attractive feature, and international shows, sporting events, concerts, etc., take place.

History.—The Roman city, called Ariminum from the old name of the Marecchia, Ariminus, stood on the boundary of Aemilia and Umbria. According to Strabo it belonged to the Umbro-Etruscan civilization. It was occupied in 268 B.C. by the Romans, and a Latin colony founded there. During the Second Punic War it was a base for military and naval operations. It became a Roman municipality and was later sacked by Sulla's troops. It witnessed the decisive step taken by Julius Caesar, when he crossed the Rubicon and marched on Rome.

In A.D. 359 the town was host to the Council of Rimini, which failed to resolve the Arian dispute. Rimini passed to the Byzantines and from them to the Goths, from whom it was recaptured by Narses, and then fell to the Lombards and Franks. It was for a long time governed for the pope by dukes and counts till the end of the 10th century when the imperial power became dominant. Transformed in the 13th century into an independent commune, it was the scene of struggles between the Guelphs and Ghibellines (*q.v.*). The leaders of the Guelphs were the Malatesta family who had established themselves at Verucchio and Rimini.

In 1239 Malatesta da Verucchio was made *podestà* ("mayor") of Rimini. The struggle with the Ghibellines had a respite when his son Malatesta II married Concordia Pandolfini, daughter of the Ghibelline leader, but her death broke the truce. Malatesta II's long life was filled with struggles and misfortunes, among them the tragedy when his son Gianciotto the Lame killed his own wife, Francesca da Polenta, daughter of the lord of Ravenna, and his brother Paolo the Fair, her secret lover. This episode was immortalized by Dante (*Inferno*, v, 73 ff.) and in Silvio Pellico's tragedy *Francesca da Rimini*. In 1334 the Council of Rimini recognized the family as lords of the town and for two centuries the town's history was united with that of this family.

Sigismondo Pandolfo Malatesta (1417–68), lord of Rimini, Fano and Senigallia, was the personage to whom Rimini principally owes its renown during the Renaissance. An unscrupulous tyrant but a valiant soldier who understood the science of fortification, he was a man of letters and a patron of the arts. Both his first wife, Ginevra d'Este, daughter of Lionello, duke of Ferrara, and his second, Polissena, daughter of Francesco Sforza, later duke of Milan, died, and Sigismondo was accused of having killed them in order to marry Isotta degli Atti.

The quarrels and rivalries of Sigismondo with other rulers and the papacy led to Pope Pius II's indictment of him in 1461. Sigismondo was compelled to submit and yielded most of his territory to the pope, keeping only Rimini and a few lands. After commanding an expedition for the Venetians against the Turks in the Morea he returned to Rimini in the hope of recovering his dominions from the new pope, Paul II. Unsuccessful in this, he went to Rome with the intention of stabbing the pope; when

Paul received him in the presence of his cardinals, Sigismondo lost courage and returned to Rimini where he died on Oct. 3, 1468, appointing his wife Isotta and their son Sallustio to succeed him.

Sigismondo's illegitimate son, Roberto, had assisted him in his struggle against Pius II, and on his father's death got rid of the legitimate heirs and made himself lord of Rimini. Reconciled with the pope, Roberto became commander in chief of the papal army. His son Sigismondo failed to defend his lands against Cesare Borgia.

Following the league of Cambrai in 1508, Rimini and its lands passed to the papal states. In 1815 it was occupied by Joachim Murat, king of Naples and brother-in-law of Napoleon, whose "Rimini proclamation," promising the Italians a constitution, failed in its purpose when Murat was defeated by the Austrians at Tolentino. Rimini then returned to the papal states. The Rimini manifesto which accompanied the insurrection of Sept. 23, 1845, reflected the ideas of the moderate party and asked for political reforms in the modern sense. In 1860 Rimini was annexed to the kingdom of Italy. During World War II it suffered severe bombardment for it lay on the easiest route to the Po plains.

BIBLIOGRAPHY.—A. F. Massera, *Cronache Malatestiane* in Rer. it. Scrpt., 2nd ed., xvi; C. Tonini, *Compendio della storia di Rimini dalle origini al 1869* (1926); Cavalucci-Dupre, *Il Rinascimento* (1927); Carli-Dell'Acqua, *Storia dell'Arte,* Ist. d'Arti Grafiche, Bergamo (1955).
(M. T. A. N.)

RIMSKI-KORSAKOV, NIKOLAI ANDREEVICH

(1844–1908), one of the principal nationalist figures in Russian music of his time, was born at Tikhvin, in the Novgorod *guberniya,* on March 18 (new style; 6, old style), 1844. In 1861, when he was a student at the St. Petersburg naval school, he made the acquaintance of M. A. Balakirev (*q.v.*) and his circle, and was inspired to study music and to compose. His First Symphony was partly written during a three-year cruise in foreign waters (1862–65) and was successfully performed in St. Petersburg on his return. In 1871 he was appointed professor of composition and instrumentation at the St. Petersburg Conservatory, though he did not leave the navy till 1873; in that year his first opera, *The Maid of Pskov,* was produced in St. Petersburg. Two further operas, *May Night* (1880) and *Snow Maiden* (1882), were produced in St. Petersburg, and in 1887 and 1888 he wrote three brilliant orchestral works, the *Spanish Capriccio, Sheherazade,* and the *Russian Easter Festival Overture.* About this time he occupied a number of official positions: inspector of naval bands (1873–84), director of the Free School of Music concerts (1874–81), assistant music director of the Imperial Chapel (1883–94),

THE BETTMANN ARCHIVE INC.
NIKOLAI RIMSKI-KORSAKOV, PHOTOGRAPHED IN 1904

conductor of the Russian Symphony Concerts (1886–1900). His pupils at the conservatory at this period included some of the outstanding composers of the following generation, notably Liadov and Glazunov. He also found time to complete, orchestrate or re-orchestrate, and drastically edit the unfinished works of his friends Borodin and Mussorgsky. Without his editorial work neither the *Prince Igor* of the one nor the *Khovanshchina* of the other could ever have been staged; but his total rewriting of the completed *Boris Godunov,* however well-intentioned and brilliant in result, was misguided (*see* also MUSSORGSKY, MODEST PETROVICH).

Between 1891 and 1893 Rimski-Korsakov passed through a physical and intellectual crisis marked by an inability to compose and even a distaste for music itself. Recovering, he composed the opera *Christmas Eve* (St. Petersburg, 1895), and followed it with a series of operas produced in Moscow, including *Sadko* (1898), *The Tsar's Bride* (1899), *The Story of Tsar Saltan* (1900), and *Kashchei the Immortal* (1902). *Kitezh* was produced in St. Petersburg in 1907 and *The Golden Cockerel* was produced post-

humously in Moscow in 1909. This series of operas contains much of his finest music.

In the course of the revolutionary disturbances of 1905, Rimski-Korsakov defended the rights of the conservatory students against the reactionary director; he was in consequence dismissed and became a hero of the liberals. Demonstrations after a performance of *Kashchei* led to the imposition of a two-month ban on the performance of all his works, with the result that they became unprecedentedly popular when it was lifted. Rimski-Korsakov was later reinstated at the conservatory but took advantage of the period of retirement to complete his memoirs, *Letopis moei muzykalnoi zhizni* (new edition, 1955; English translation by J. A. Joffe, *My Musical Life,* 1942), a book of great interest and importance. In May 1907 he visited Paris to take part in Diaghilev's festival of Russian orchestral music. He had not quite completed another important book, *Principles of Orchestration* (edited by M. Steinberg; English translation by E. Agate, 1923), when he died at Lyubensk, near St. Petersburg, on June 21 (N.S.; 8, O.S.), 1908.

Rimski-Korsakov was one of the greatest masters of orchestration in the history of music. His handling of the orchestra influenced not only his pupils Stravinsky and Respighi but Debussy, Ravel and other French musicians, Gustav Holst, and many others. He was a melodist but he lacked the dramatic power and architectural sense necessary to a symphonist. His unique contribution was the half-real, half-fantastic world portrayed in the best of his operas.

BIBLIOGRAPHY.—G. Abraham, *Rimsky-Korsakov: a Short Biography* (1945); D. Kabalevski (ed.), *Rimski-Korsakov: Issledovaniya-materialy-pisma,* 2 vol. (1953, 1954); A. N. Rimski-Korsakov, *N. A. Rimski-Korsakov: Zhizn i tvorchestvo,* 5 vol. (1933–46). (G. AB.)

RINDERPEST, a disease of ruminant animals, primarily cattle, has been known also as steppe murrain, contagious bovine typhus, and cattle plague. Rinderpest was first recognized in early Christian times. Earliest records suggest that it originated in Asia or Eastern Europe, its incursions into Western Europe having followed the paths of invading armies in the periodic sweeps of barbarous tribes from the east. Rinderpest killed cattle by the thousands in Europe in the 18th and 19th centuries. The disease reached Africa in the late 19th century and, after spreading throughout the continent with disastrous effect, was eventually cleared from the southern half but remained endemic in the northern parts, its southernmost extension being in Tanganyika (Tanzania). The disease is also endemic in India and parts of southeastern Asia. It has occurred, but was quickly eradicated, in Brazil and Australia. Rinderpest has not been reported in the United States.

Characteristics.—Rinderpest is an acute, highly contagious disease characterized by an unusually rapid course and high mortality, especially in areas where it is not endemic. The causative agent is the virus *Tortor bovis.*

Signs of illness appear after an incubation period of three to five days. Early signs are depression and loss of appetite accompanied by fever, generally of 105° to 107° F (about 40° C). In the midcourse of the disease, ocular and nasal discharges and salivation with buccal ulceration and a disagreeable fetid odour are characteristic. Profuse diarrhea with progressive emaciation and dehydration occur, often with dysentery, and eventually marked straining to evacuate. In many cases an eruptive condition termed streptothricosis develops on the back and flanks. Prostration, coma, and death come usually after four to eight days.

Autopsy shows involvement of the mucous membrane of the entire alimentary tract. This is usually most marked in the mouth, where ulcers containing cheesy deposits are often found, and in the abomasum (fourth stomach), intestines, and rectum, where deep congestion and sometimes ulceration occur. In the lower bowel the congestion is often in well-defined, dark streaks referred to as zebra marking. Pneumonia frequently is seen as a complication, and often cystitis and vaginitis are present. Diagnosis is made on the clinical appearance of the disease and autopsy findings, but, since these may be similar to those found in certain other diseases, virus transmission and cross-immunity tests are necessary for confirmation.

Spread and Control of the Disease.—The virus is generalized in the animal body and is passed out in all the secretions. It gains access to the tissues of a susceptible animal via the mucous membranes, most probably those of the nostrils. In areas where the disease is endemic, wild animals play an important part in the epidemiology. Many species of wild ruminants, together with wild pigs and warthogs in such areas as Tanganyika and Uganda, are susceptible to rinderpest and form vast reservoirs of infection. These animals come into contact with domestic animals in competition for limited grazing and water. Eradication of rinderpest in these areas depends therefore on control of the disease in wild animals or elimination of their contact with domestic animals. In nonendemic areas, strict quarantine measures alone can be effective. However, it was early recognized that some form of immunization combined with quarantine was the most promising method of control under all circumstances. By mid-20th century a number of effective vaccines had been developed.

(J. A. Br.; J. K. H. W.; X.)

RINEHART, MARY ROBERTS (1876–1958), U.S. novelist and playwright best known for her mystery stories beginning with *The Man in Lower Ten* (serialized 1907) and *The Circular Staircase* (1908), her first book. Born in 1876 in Pittsburgh, Pa., she received nurse's training there and in 1896 married Stanley M. Rinehart, a physician. In 1903 the family found itself in financial difficulties as a result of a stock market crash, and Mrs. Rinehart turned to writing; her work proved to be a great popular success almost from the beginning. A long series of comic tales about the robust, redoubtable "Tish" (Miss Letitia Carberry) appeared in the *Saturday Evening Post* through many years. Of her plays (most of them written in collaboration with Avery Hopwood), the most successful was *The Bat* (1920), derived with significant changes from *The Circular Staircase*. She produced as well, always with a keen responsibility to her craft, a number of romances and several books of travel, some of the latter reflecting her experience as a correspondent during World War I. She died in New York City on Sept. 22, 1958.

Mrs. Rinehart established what has been called the "had-I-but-known" sort of mystery, and her tales make it plain that she was mistress of a form in which few other writers excelled.

(J. S. Sa.)

RING: *see* Jewelry.

RINGKÖBING (Ringkøbing), the largest Danish *amt* (county), covers a rectangular area bounded by the smooth dune and lagoon coast of western Jutland between Nissum Bredning and the southern shore of Ringköbing Fjord, and extending about 40 mi. (64 km.) inland across old morainic landscape and sandy outwash plains (*see also* Denmark: *Physical Geography*). Area 1,799 sq.mi. (4,659 sq.km.). Pop. (1960) 205,772. It is a district of rather poor mixed farming with tracts of unreclaimed heath. The principal towns, Herning (pop. [1960] 24,790) and Holstebro (18,563), lie inland. Struer, Lemvig, and Ringköbing are minor ports.

(Ha. T.)

RING TENNIS: *see* Deck Tennis.

RINGWORM: *see* Skin, Diseases of.

RIOBAMBA, a city in highland Ecuador, capital of the province of Chimborazo. Pop. (1962) 61,411. It is located at an elevation of about 9,000 ft. in the basin of Riobamba, just south of Mt. Chimborazo and about 100 mi. S of Quito. It is reached by railroad or by the Pan-American Highway from both Quito and Guayaquil. Domestic airlines serve its airport. The railroad and highway pass a short distance to the west of the city, and connection is by branch line and an all-weather road. A weekly fair held in the central plaza attracts Indian farmers from the surrounding countryside. Small-scale manufacturing industries produce cotton and woolen textiles, carpets, shoes, beer, liquor, butter, and cheese. The first constitution of Ecuador was proclaimed there in 1830.

(P. E. J.)

RÍO CARONÍ, in southeastern Venezuela, has its source in Sierra Pacaraima in the rainy Guiana highlands. Its normal volume is 1,200,000 gal. per sec. but as many as 4,000,000 gal. per

sec. have been recorded during heavy floods. The river flows approximately 400 mi. (640 km.) N to merge with the Orinoco River, 4 mi. W of San Félix and about 67 mi. E of Ciudad Bolívar. Its mouth lies in the heart of the industrial complex of Santo Tomé de Guayana (*q.v.;* Ciudad Guayana), about 300 mi. SE of Caracas. The river is navigable at its mouth and in the 1960s was well supplied with efficient equipment for loading iron ore and other products onto oceangoing vessels for export. But the Caroní's greatest value to Venezuela is as a source of hydroelectric power, the river having a potential of 10,500,000 kw. This power is well located with respect to markets for electricity—a rarity among rivers in underdeveloped tropical lands. Besides a fast-growing market at Santo Tomé, much electricity is sent by high voltage transmission line to Caracas (the metropolitan area accounted in the 1960s for about 70% of Venezuela's industrial production) as well as to the Barcelona–Puerto La Cruz district.

In the 1960s hydroelectric sites on the Caroní included Macagua, located only a few miles from the river's mouth in the heart of Santo Tomé de Guayana, with 370,000 kw. developed and a potential development of 600,000 kw.; and Guri, 75 mi. (120 km.) upstream from Macagua, with 525,000 kw. developed and an ultimate capacity of 6,000,000 kw. Additional possible sites are at Tócoma, 11 mi. (18 km.), and Caruachí, 37 mi. (60 km.) downstream from Guri. It is reported that the lower 134 mi. (215 km.) of the Caroní contain the largest hydroelectric potential in South America.

In addition to abundant cheap power, Santo Tomé de Guayana benefits from nearby minerals (iron ore, bauxite, manganese), a navigable outlet (the lower Orinoco is dredged to a depth of 34 ft. from its confluence with the Caroní to the Atlantic Ocean), proximity to abundant supplies of petroleum and natural gas (the eastern llanos region), and a population of 100,000 persons which in the 1960s was growing rapidly and drawing into the area many new primary and secondary industries.

(L. We.)

RÍO CUARTO, a town of Argentina in the province of Córdoba, 140 mi. S of the city of that name, and about 385 mi. NW of Buenos Aires. Pop. (1960) 70,505. It stands 1,440 ft. above sea level and about halfway across the great Argentine pampas, on the banks of a river of the same name. The town is built on the open plain and is surrounded with attractive suburbs. It is the commercial centre of a big district and has a large and lucrative trade. Its geographical position gives it great strategic importance, and the government maintains there a large arsenal and a garrison of the regular army. Before 1872 this region was overrun by the Ranqueles, a warlike tribe of Indians. The surrounding country belongs to the partially arid pampas region and is devoted to stock-raising agriculture. Irrigation is employed in its immediate vicinity. There are some manufacturing industries in the town, although it is primarily an agricultural centre. The San Martín and the Mitre railways pass through Río Cuarto, giving railway communication with Buenos Aires, Rosario, Tucumán, Córdoba, San Luis, Mendoza, and other cities.

The revolution which overthrew President Perón in 1955 began with an uprising at the Río Cuarto military air base. (Ge. P.)

RIO DE JANEIRO, one of Brazil's maritime states, is bounded by the Atlantic Ocean and the states of Espírito Santo, Minas Gerais, and São Paulo. Brazil's former federal district containing the city of Rio de Janeiro and fronting on the Guanabara bay forms a small enclave near the middle of the state. Area 16,568 sq.mi., pop. (1960) 3,402,728.

Historically it is closely associated with the city Rio de Janeiro. Its territory was selected by the Portuguese for some of their first settlements, and on parts of its coast the French waged their early struggles for the control of Brazil's resources. When Brazil was divided into captaincies in 1642, Rio de Janeiro was one of the original ten. The city of Rio de Janeiro was the seat of the captaincy's government and centre of its social and economic life throughout the colonial period. After independence was declared the *município* or county containing the national capital was separated from the state and made into a federal district.

The territory of the state may be divided roughly into four regions, namely: a low, narrow, and irregular coastal plain; the

Baixada Fluminense, a large basin surrounding Guanabara Bay; the rugged chain of mountains, Serra do Mar, which traverses the state longitudinally; and the large valley through which the Paraíba River flows northeastward to the Atlantic. In the northeastern part of the state this river cuts through the mountain chain and its valley then broadens out into a rich alluvial plain on which for centuries sugar plantations were the basis for the wealth of some of Brazil's most opulent families. The climate is tropical or subtropical depending on altitude.

Agriculture long was the mainstay of the state's economy, but since World War II industrialization has proceeded rapidly. The chief crops are coffee, oranges, bananas, sugarcane, rice, and corn, but many other fruits and truck crops are grown. The cattle population numbers more than 2,000,000; and the salt refineries and fisheries are among the most important in Brazil. Since 1945 the industrial belt surrounding the city of Rio de Janeiro and the iron and steel centre at Volta Redonda in the upper Paraíba Valley developed tremendously. Pig iron, steel, steel products, textiles, cement, and food products are the principal industrial products. Rio de Janeiro is a leading state in hydroelectric power production.

The major cities are: Niterói (q.v.), the state capital, on Guanabara Bay opposite the city of Rio de Janeiro (q.v.); Campos; Petrópolis (q.v.), the nation's summer capital; Duque de Caxias, Nova Iguaçu, São João de Meriti, and Nilópolis, all suburbs of Rio de Janeiro.

The state is served by road and rail networks which radiate from the great port of Rio de Janeiro. Most of the 1,663 mi. of railroads in service belongs to two systems, the Central do Brasil whose main lines connect the city of Rio de Janeiro with São Paulo and with Belo Horizonte, and the Leopoldina Railway which links Rio de Janeiro and Niterói with places to the north and east.

(T. L. Sh.)

RIO DE JANEIRO (in full, São Sebastião do Rio de Janeiro, colloquially shortened to Rio), a city and port of Brazil, capital of the republic until 1960, when Brasília (q.v.) became the capital, on the western side of Rio de Janeiro, or Guanabara Bay. It is the capital of the state of Guanabara. The city occupies about 60 sq.mi. (155 sq.km.) in the southeast angle of Guanabara State, formerly the Federal District, which was until 1960 an independent commune with an area of 524 sq.mi. (1,357 sq.km.), detached from the Province of Rio de Janeiro in 1834. The city stands in great part on an alluvial plain formed by the filling in of the western shore of the bay, which extends inland from the shoreline in a northwesterly direction between a detached group of mountains on the south known as the Serra da Carioca, and the imposing wooded heights of the Serra do Mar on the north. The spurs of the Carioca range project into this plain, in some places close up to the margin of the bay, forming picturesque valleys within the limits of the city. Some of the residential quarters follow these valleys up into the mountains and extend up their slopes and over the lower spurs, which, with the hills covered with buildings rising in the midst of the city, give the city a distinctive charm. At the entrance to the bay is Sugar Loaf Mountain (Pão de Açúcar), a conical rock rising 1,296 ft. (395 m.) above the water level and forming the terminal point of a short range between the city and the Atlantic coast. The culminating point of that part of the Carioca range which projects into and partly divides the city is the Corcovado (Hunchback), a sharp rocky peak, 2,310 ft. (704 m.) above the Botafogo Inlet, on whose narrow summit towers the imposing statue 98½ ft. (30 m.) high of Christ the Redeemer, the construction of which was completed in 1931. The Corcovado, approachable either by road or inclined railway, provides a point of vantage from which the entire capital, the bay, and its surrounding districts may be viewed. Considerably beyond the limits of the city on its southwest side is the huge isolated flat-topped rock known as the Gávea, 2,762 ft. (841 m.) high, which received its name from its resemblance to the square sail used on certain Portuguese craft. The skyline of this range of mountains, as seen by the approaching traveler several miles outside the entrance to the bay, forms the rough outline of a reclining figure called "the sleeping giant."

The entrance to the bay, between the Sugar Loaf on the west and the Pico do Papagaio (Parrot's Beak) on the east, with the Fortress of Santa Cruz on one side and the Fort of São João on the other, is about a mile wide. Although the entrance is free from obstructions, dangerous swells are produced by a deeply submerged bar whenever storms come out of the south or southwest. Almost midway in the channel is the little island and Fort of Laje, temporary site of the first Huguenot settlement in Rio de Janeiro. On the west is the semicircular Bay of Botafogo, round which are grouped the residences of one of the wealthiest suburbs; on the east, the almost landlocked Bay of Jurujuba. (See Niterói.)

The bay extends northward about 16 mi. (26 km.) from the entrance channel, opening to a maximum width of about 15 mi. near its head. The irregular shoreline was modified by the construction of sea walls, the filling in of shallow bays, and the expansion of nearby islands. Close to the shore are the substantially enlarged islands of Villegagnon (Villegaignon; occupied by the national naval academy), Cobras (occupied by fortifications, naval storehouses, hospital and dry docks, and a causeway connecting with Ilha Fiscal), and the unimproved islands of Santa Bárbara and Enxadas.

The oldest part of the city, which includes the commercial section, lies just south of São Bento, Conceição and Livramento Hills, and extends inland to the Praça da República, though the defensive works in colonial times followed a line much nearer the bay. This section was extended southward along the bay shore during the 19th century and led to the development of a string of suburbs such as Catete and Botafogo, with that of Laranjeiras behind Catete in a pretty valley of the same name. Along the Atlantic beaches, from east to west, appeared the suburbs of Leme, Copacabana, Ipanema, and Leblon, which expanded rapidly after a tunnel was cut through the stone ridge separating Copacabana from Botafogo early in this century. Just inland from Leblon, west and north of the Lagôa Rodrigo de Freitas are the districts of Gávea and Jardim Botânico. Between them is Rio's famous botanical garden, which dates from the 19th century. The major trend of later developments was northward and westward, where are to be found the suburbs of São Cristóvão, Engenho Novo, Vila Isabel, Tijuca, Andaraí, Rio Comprido, Cajú, and others, some of which are residential, while others are essentially industrial. The outlying, poorer suburbs are reached by the Central do Brasil Railway; those closer in are served by electric and diesel-powered buses. The northern and southern zones of the city are connected by a highway tunnel between Jardim Botânico and Rio Comprido. Completed in 1968, it is said to be the longest urban tunnel in the world. The population of the former Federal District, according to the census of 1960, was 3,307,163; and of the city 3,223,408. In the late 1960s the population of the greater Rio de Janeiro metropolitan area was estimated in excess of 4,207,000. Rio's citizens are known locally as *cariocas*.

Climate.—The climate of Rio de Janeiro is warm and humid, the average temperature for the year being about 74° F (23.3° C), with July, the coolest month, having an average temperature of 68.7° F (20° C). The rainfall averages about 44 in. (112 cm.) annually, with July and August being the least rainy months. Formerly the low-lying and poorly drained areas which are marginal to the bay, plus the lack of adequate sanitary facilities, created a serious health problem in Rio de Janeiro, which was, however, in no way connected with the climate. Yellow fever, the first recorded appearance of which was in December 1849, was for many years almost a regular occurrence, and the mortality from it was exceedingly high. This and other dangerous diseases disappeared as epidemics as a result of improved sanitary conditions following the notable work begun by Oswaldo Cruz, under whose direction Rio de Janeiro was made one of the most healthful of tropical cities.

Streets and Parks.—Some of the most modern streets were laid out with Spanish-American regularity, but much the greater part seems to have sprung into existence without any plan. Most of the streets of the old city are parallel and cross at right angles, but they are narrow and enclose blocks of unequal size. Each suburb is laid out independently, with straight streets where the ground permits, and crooked ones where the shoreline or mountain con-

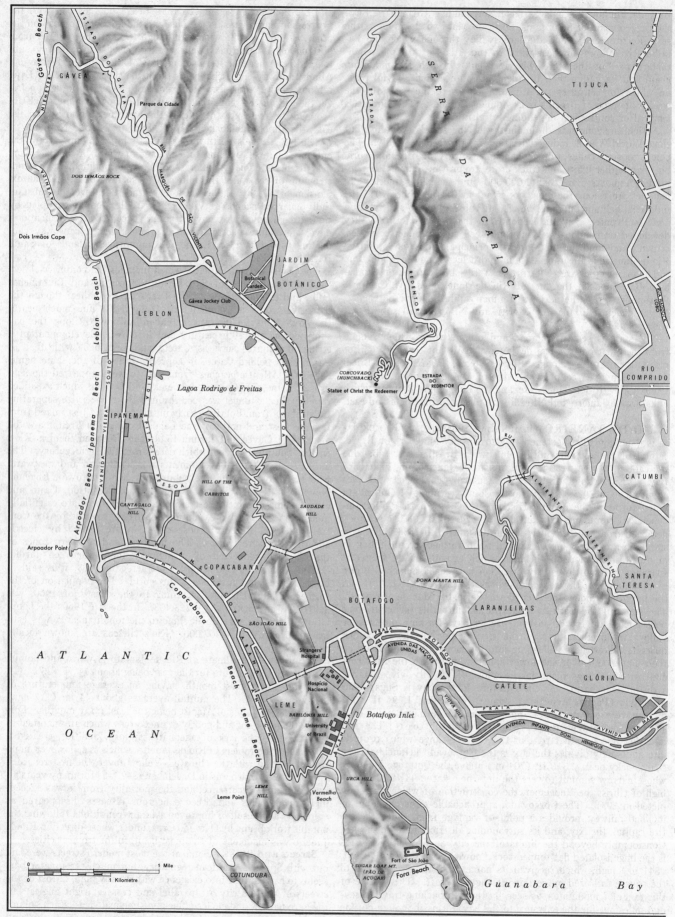

SERRA DA CARIOCA

TIJUCA

RIO COMPRIDO

CATUMBI

SANTA TERESA

GLÓRIA

CATETE

LARANJEIRAS

Gávea Beach

GÁVEA

Parque da Cidade

DOIS IRMÃOS ROCK

Dois Irmãos Cape

JARDIM BOTÂNICO

Botanical Garden

Gávea Jockey Club

LEBLON

Leblon Beach

Ipanema Beach

IPANEMA

Arpoador Beach

Arpoador Point

Lagoa Rodrigo de Freitas

HILL OF THE CABRITOS

CANTAGALO HILL

COPACABANA

SÃO JOÃO HILL

Strangers' Hospital

Hospício Nacional

LEME

BABILÔNIA HILL

University of Brazil

Copacabana Beach

Leme Beach

Leme Point

LEME HILL

CORCOVADO (HUNCHBACK)

Statue of Christ the Redeemer

ESTRADA DO REDENTOR

SAUDADE HILL

DONA MARTA HILL

BOTAFOGO

Botafogo Inlet

VIUVA HILL

PRAIA FLAMENGO

URCA HILL

Vermelha Beach

SUGAR LOAF MT. (PÃO DE AÇÚCAR)

Fort of São João

Fora Beach

COTUNDUBA

A T L A N T I C

O C E A N

Guanabara   Bay

0   1 Mile

0   1 Kilometre

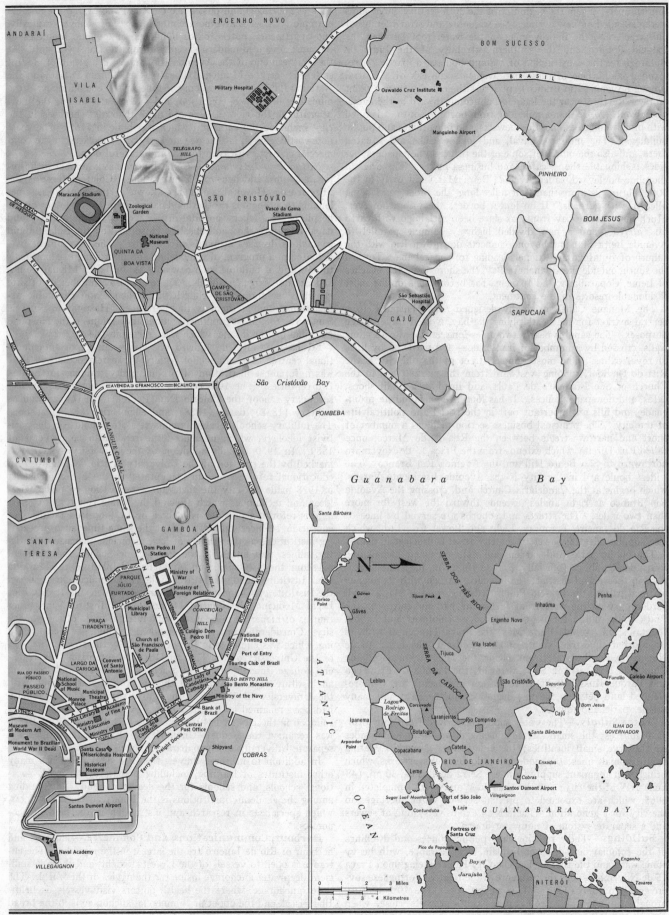

ENGENHO NOVO

BOM SUCESSO

ANDARAÍ

VILA ISABEL

BRASIL

Military Hospital

Oswaldo Cruz Institute

Manguinho Airport

PINHEIRO

TELEGRAFO HILL

BOM JESUS

Maracanã Stadium

Zoological Garden

SÃO CRISTÓVÃO

Vasco da Gama Stadium

National Museum

SAPUCAIA

QUINTA DA BOA VISTA

CAMPO DE SÃO CRISTÓVÃO

São Sebastião Hospital

PRAIA DE SÃO CRISTÓVÃO

CAJÚ

CATUMBI

São Cristóvão Bay

POMBEBA

Guanabara Bay

Santa Bárbara

GAMBÔA

Dom Pedro II Station

SANTA TERESA

Ministry of War

Ministry of Foreign Relations

PARQUE JÚLIO FURTADO

CONCEIÇÃO HILL

PRAÇA DA REPÚBLICA

Municipal Library

Colégio Dom Pedro II

National Printing Office

PRAÇA TIRADENTES

Church of São Francisco de Paula

Port of Entry

Touring Club of Brazil

RUA DO PASSEIO PÚBLICO

LARGO DA CARIOCA

Convent of Santo Antonio

Our Lady of Candelária Cathedral

SÃO BENTO HILL
São Bento Monastery

PASSEIO PÚBLICO

National School of Music

Municipal Theatre

Monroe Palace

Ministry of the Navy

Nat'l Library

Academy of Fine Arts

Bank of Brazil

Museum of Modern Art

Ministry of Education
Ministry of Finance

Central Post Office

Monument to Brazilian World War II Dead

Santa Casa (Misericórdia Hospital)

Shipyard

COBRAS

Historical Museum

Ferry and Freight Docks

Santos Dumont Airport

Naval Academy

VILLEGAIGNON

N

SERRA DOS TRÊS RIOS

Marisco Point

Gávea

Tijuca Peak

Penha

Inhaúma

Engenho Novo

ATLANTIC

Gávea

SERRA DA CARIOCA

Tijuca

Vila Isabel

Leblon

São Cristóvão

Fundão

Galeão Airport

Lagoa Rodrigo de Freitas

Corcovado

Sapucaia

Bom Jesus

Ipanema

Laranjeiras

Rio Comprido

Cajú

ILHA DO GOVERNADOR

Arpoador Point

Botafogo

Catete

Santa Bárbara

Copacabana

RIO DE JANEIRO

Enxadas

Leme

Botafogo Inlet

Cobras

Santos Dumont Airport

OCEAN

Sugar Loaf Mountain

Fort of São João

Villegaignon

Contunduba

Laje

GUANABARA BAY

Fortress of Santa Cruz

Pico do Papagaio

Bay of Jurujuba

Conceição

Engenho

NITERÓI

Tavares

0   1   2   3 Miles
0 1 2 3 4 Kilometres

PUBLIC BUILDINGS AND PARKS, AND ALSO THE TOPOGRAPHY OF THE AREA

tour compels. From the beginning of the 20th century, large sums were expended on new avenues, the widening and straightening of old streets and the improvement of the waterfront between the Passeio Público and the southern extremity of the Praia de Botafogo by the construction of a grand boulevard, partly on reclaimed land. One of these improvements consists of a central avenue (Avenida Rio Branco) cut across the old city from a point on the waterfront near the Passeio Público northward to the Saúde waterfront. More than a mile long from north to south, it is lined with brazilwood trees, mosaic sidewalks, and fine private and public buildings. The military, naval, and jockey clubs are situated there, and also the offices of some of the principal newspapers, besides fashionable shops, cafés, and business places. The original shoreline boulevard, called Avenida Beira Mar, built early in the 20th century, is more than four miles long, the wider parts being filled in with gardens. It no longer borders the water, however. Much more of the bay front has since been reclaimed with earth fill (atêrro), and a new divided highway running parallel to Avenida Beira Mar and beyond connects downtown Rio with the suburb of Botafogo and tunnels leading to Copacabana. Toward the south, outside the Guanabara Bay, the shore along the beaches of Leme, Copacabana, and Ipanema has become one of the most fashionable resorts of the continent.

The Mangue Canal, originally designed as an entrance to a central market for the boats plying the bay, is used for drainage purposes. The canal is nearly two miles long, enclosed with stone walls, crossed by a number of iron bridges and bordered by lines of royal palms. The most famous street of the old city is the Rua do Ouvidor, running westward from the marketplace to the Church of São Francisco de Paula, and lined with retail shops, cafés, and newspaper offices. It has long been a favourite promenade, and fills an important part in the social and political life of the city. The principal business section includes a number of short and narrow streets between the Rua 1° de Março, once called Rua Direita, which extends from the Praça 15 de Novembro northward to São Bento Hill and the Avenida Rio Branco. The widest boulevard in the city is the Avenida Presidente Vargas, which begins at the Candelária Church and, crossing the Avenida Rio Branco at right angles, extends toward the west for more than two miles. The streets and suburbs are served by lines of the Rio de Janeiro Tramway, Light and Power Co., Ltd., which also supplies electric power to the city from hydroelectric plants.

The public parks and gardens are numerous and include the Praça da República (officially, Parque Júlio Furtado), the largest park in the central district; the botanical garden with its avenue of royal palms: the Passeio Público (dating from 1783), a small garden once on the waterfront facing the harbour entrance; the Praça Paris, noted for its contemporary sculptures and lighted fountains, on Avenida Beira Mar; the Praça Tiradentes with its magnificent equestrian statue of Dom Pedro I; the Praça 15 de Novembro on the waterfront facing the Old City Palace; the Quinta da Boa Vista in São Cristóvão; the Parque do Flamengo and Parque Russel, built as recreation and beach areas on reclaimed land between the new highway and the bay; and many smaller parks and squares.

Water Supply.—The water supply is derived from four principal sources: the small streams flowing down the mountainsides which serve small localities; the old Carioca Aqueduct, dating from colonial times; the modern Rio do Ouro Waterworks, which bring in an abundant supply from the Serra do Tingúa, 30 mi. (48 km.) NW of the city; and the Guandú Waterworks, completed in 1965, which are expected to prevent serious water shortages in the city for a generation. There is an extensive system of sewers and a separate system of rainwater drains.

Buildings.—There remain many public edifices and dwellings of the colonial period, severely plain in appearance, with heavy stone walls and tile roofs. The Old City Palace facing upon Praça 15 de Novembro, once the residence of the fugitive Portuguese sovereign Dom John (João) VI, is an example. The 19th century brought no important modifications until near its close, when French and Italian styles began to appear, both in exterior decoration and in architectural design. The Praça do Comércio (mer-

chants' exchange) and post office on Rua 1° de Março are notable examples. After that time architectural styles changed radically, and apartments, hotels, office buildings, and public buildings of the most advanced modern design and construction were built. At the southern end of the Avenida Rio Branco is a group of elegant state edifices, the Municipal Theatre, the Monroe Palace and the National Library, and Academy of Fine Arts. The buildings of the ministries of finance, education, and war are also among the most beautiful in the city. There are more than 200 churches in the city, including the cathedral which was built in 1761. The most noteworthy church is that of Our Lady of Candelária, in the commercial district, with twin towers and graceful dome.

Hospitals and Asylums.—Rio de Janeiro has a number of hospitals, asylums, and benevolent institutions. Chief of these is the Misericórdia Hospital, popularly known as the Santa Casa, belonging to a religious brotherhood dating from 1591. Other public hospitals are a lepers' hospital in São Cristóvão, the military and naval hospitals, the São Sebastião Hospital, and the isolation and contagious diseases hospitals in Jurujuba. The government participated in a program of remodeling and improving existing institutions and of building such new ones as the Jesus, Miguel Couto, and Getúlio Vargas hospitals. There are also a number of private hospitals maintained by church brotherhoods and charitable associations; among them is the Portuguese Hospital in Rua de Santo Amaro. Most prominent among the asylums is the Hospício Nacional for the insane, which was erected in 1842–52.

Education.—Rio de Janeiro was always an important educational centre. A Jesuit school (*colégio*) transferred there in 1567 was a foremost institution of pre-university training for almost two centuries. The 19th century saw the creation of a "model" secondary school, the Colégio Dom Pedro II (1837), as well as military (1838), naval (1858), and engineering (1874) schools. The military school became famous as a stronghold for the positivist ideology, which influenced the republican coup d'état of 1889. In 1920 Brazil's adoption of the university system was marked by the creation of the University of Rio de Janeiro. An educational reform program inaugurated in the Federal District in 1928 made the city the focus for a renovation of pedagogical ideas and techniques which affected the whole country. As part of this reform, a presidential decree of 1931 created faculties of education, sciences, and letters. At the same time, such preexisting institutions as the schools of law, medicine, pharmacy, dentistry, mines, and fine arts, the Polytechnic School, the National Museum, the Geological and Mineralogical Institute, the Oswaldo Cruz Institute (medical research), the Astronomical Observatory, the Institute of Chemistry, the Botanical Garden, the Institute of Legal Medicine, the Central Meteorological Institute and other centres of higher learning were made integral parts of the university. Considerable progress was made in the field of teacher training, which was climaxed in Rio de Janeiro by the creation in 1935 of the University of the Federal District—comprising the teachers' college, schools of letters, sciences, economics and law, and an institute of arts. In 1939 this institution was merged with the University of Brazil, as the University of Rio de Janeiro had been renamed two years earlier. A Catholic university was founded in the city in 1940. After 1960 the University of Brazil was renamed the Federal University of Rio de Janeiro, and a separate University of Guanabara was opened.

In addition to its three universities, Rio de Janeiro has many other institutes of learning, including preparatory schools, vocational schools, and schools for the deaf and blind. Outstanding among the academic institutions is the Fundação Getúlio Vargas, which specializes in research and instruction in the field of economics.

Harbour, Communications, and Commerce.—The port and harbour of Rio de Janeiro are the largest in the republic. The entrance is open to vessels of the largest draught, and there is sufficient deepwater anchorage inside for the navies of the world. The lower anchorage, where the health officers visit vessels, is below Ilha Fiscal, and the upper or commercial anchorage is in the broad part of the bay above Ilha das Cobras, the national coasting vessels occupying the shallower waters near the Saúde and Gambôa

RIO DE JANEIRO

PLATE I

Statue of "Christ the Redeemer" on Corcovado mountain. In the background are Guanabara bay and Sugar Loaf mountain

Cable car to Sugar Loaf mountain from Urca hill. Copacabana beach is in the background

Sunbathing and a volleyball game on Copacabana beach

Copacabana beach, skirted by Avenida Atlântica and lined with hotels and apartment buildings

S.S. "Argentina" docked at the Touring Club of Brazil with other ships on Guanabara bay in the background

PLATE II

RIO DE JANEIRO

The Avenida Presidente Vargas, one of the city's principal thoroughfares, here seen at carnival

Praça Paris, which covers several city blocks between the business district and the Avenida Beira Mar

View looking southwest from Corcovado. In the distance are the two crests of Dois Irmãos ("Two Brothers") mountain

Vendor in Flamengo park near downtown Rio

Mosaic pavement in Floriana square. The former federal senate building is in the background

Granite ridges, some of them tunneled to provide communication, separate Rio de Janeiro into a city of narrow valleys that stretch inland

PHOTOGRAPHS, (TOP LEFT, CENTRE LEFT) FPG, (TOP RIGHT) DAVIS PRATT—RAPHO GUILLUMETTE, (CENTRE) DAVE FORBERT—IMAGE INTERNATIONAL, (BOTTOM LEFT) BAILEY—PUBLIX, (BOTTOM RIGHT) DANA BROWN—FPG

districts. The customhouse occupies a considerable part of the shoreline before the old city.

The newer port works consist of an improved waterfront for the Saúde, Gambôa, and Saco do Alferes districts, in which the shipping interests are centred, and a continuation of the seawall across the shallow São Cristóvão Bay to the Ponta do Cajú, the large reclaimed area being filled in by the removal of some small hills. The commercial quays are built in deepwater and permit mooring alongside the largest vessels. The total length of the commercial quays is about 7,500 yd. (6,858 m.). Railway and streetcar connections are provided, and both electric and hydraulic power are available. Special surtaxes are levied on imports to meet the interest and redemption charges on the loans raised for the execution of these important works.

Railway communication with the interior is maintained by the Central do Brasil and the Leopoldina lines, besides which there is a short passenger line to Corcovado Mountain about 2½ mi. long, an electric line to Tijuca, and a narrow-gauge line to the Rio do Ouro Waterworks. There is communication with Petrópolis by a branch line of the Leopoldina system, and also by a steamer to the head of the bay and thence by rail up the *serra*.

Rio de Janeiro is the seaport for a large area of the richest, most productive and most thickly settled parts of Brazil, including the states of Rio de Janeiro and Minas Gerais and a small part of eastern São Paulo. Its exports include coffee, sugar, hides, cabinet woods, tobacco and cigars, tapioca, gold, diamonds, iron ore, manganese, and sundry small products.

The city is also a distributing centre in the coasting trade, and many imported products, including jerked beef (*charque*), hay, flour and wines, appear among the coastwise exports, as well as domestic manufactures. Formerly Rio de Janeiro led all other ports in Brazil in the export of coffee, but the enormous increase in production in the State of São Paulo later gave Santos the lead.

Air travel is of increasing importance for the city's communication with other coastal cities and with the vast hinterland of Brazil, as well as with the rest of the world. Rio de Janeiro is served by two airports, Santos Dumont, built on a filled-in area of Guanabara Bay adjacent to downtown Rio, for domestic flights by propeller-driven aircraft, and Galeão, on Ilha do Governador, for domestic and international jet flights.

Manufactures.—Rio de Janeiro ranks second only to São Paulo as an industrial and manufacturing centre. In 1960 it accounted for about 5% of all industrial plants in Brazil, employed nearly 10% of the nation's industrial labour force, and provided nearly 10% of Brazil's industrial production. Output consists primarily of consumers' goods, largely but not exclusively for the domestic market. Chief among these are foodstuffs, beer and liquors, clothing of all kinds, and tobacco products. Specialized manufactures include soap, candles, perfumes, furniture, rope, matches, ink, printing type, glass, chemicals, and tires. The publishing industry is concentrated heavily in Rio de Janeiro. In addition there are plants that manufacture finished products from processed imported and domestic components, especially electronics, drugs, and sundries. Metallurgy, ranging from small repair and machine shops to railway maintenance and shipbuilding concerns, is a major industrial activity. The Central do Brasil Railway and Ishikawajima do Brasil Shipyards are two of the largest such firms in Brazil. One of the most important industrial enterprises in Rio is the Rio de Janeiro Tramway, Light and Power Co., whose generating plants are located about 50 mi. (80 km.) from the city. In the mid-1960s there were more than 5,000 industrial establishments employing about 200,000 persons. Promotion of trade in the city is largely a function of the Chamber of Commerce of Rio de Janeiro and the Federation of Brazilian Chambers of Commerce.

Government.—Until it became the State of Guanabara in 1960, the Federal District, including the city of Rio de Janeiro, was governed by a prefect, appointed by the president of the republic for a four-year term, and a municipal council of *intendentes*, elected by direct suffrage for a term of two years and composed of 50 members. In April 1960, a national law ordered the election, the following October, of a governor for the new State of Guanabara and a legislative assembly of 55 members that would meet during its first four months as a constituent body. The first governor, Carlos Lacerda, took office in December 1960 for a five-year term. The office of vice-governor, provided in the new state constitution, was filled by election in October 1962. The second governor, Francisco Negrão de Lima, was elected and installed in office in 1965. The governor is assisted by an appointed cabinet of *secretários*, each assigned to a special field of activity. These include such areas as education, public health and welfare, public works, transportation, finance, police, archives and statistics, and tourism. Under the federal constitution of 1967 the term in office of governor, vice-governor, and legislative assemblymen shall be four years, coinciding with that of the president of the republic and the national Chamber of Deputies.

History.—It has been said that the Bay of Rio de Janeiro was discovered by André Gonçalves and Amerigo Vespucci on Jan. 1, 1502, and that Gonçalves named it "River of January." More probably it was discovered in 1504 by Gonçalo Coelho. The name "Rio de Janeiro" appeared on maps only in about 1515. Another Portuguese navigator, Martim Afonso de Sousa, visited the bay in 1531, but passed on south to São Vicente, where he established a colony. The first settlement in the bay was made by an expedition of French Huguenots under the command of Nicolas Durand de Villegaignon, who established his colony on the small island that bears his name. The French called their colony La France Antarctique, and the island stronghold Fort Coligny. In 1560 the fort was captured and destroyed by a Portuguese expedition from Bahia under Gov. Mem de Sá, and in 1565 another expedition under Estácio de Sá, cousin of the governor, founded a Portuguese settlement in another part of the bay which was called São Sebastião do Rio de Janeiro, in honour of King Sebastian of Portugal. Two years later the French were decisively defeated by Mem de Sá, who moved the settlement to the hill later known as the Morro do Castelo. He laid out streets and a plaza, and encouraged construction of the first houses. The following governor built a sugar mill on the island that is still called the Ilha do Governador. Twice during the next hundred years Brazil was divided for short periods into two governorships, with Rio serving as capital of the southern jurisdiction. In 1710–11 the French made two expeditions against Rio and finally withdrew after exacting a heavy ransom.

The discovery of gold in Minas Gerais at the end of the 17th century greatly increased the importance of Rio de Janeiro. During the governorship of Gomes Freire de Andrade (1733–63) the Carioca Aqueduct, the Governor's Palace, the Convent of St. Teresa, and other architectural landmarks were built; fortifications were strengthened; urbanism and public health received attention; intellectual life was encouraged; and Brazil's first printing press was set up on a temporary basis, but was soon withdrawn. In 1763 Rio succeeded Bahia as the capital.

In 1808 the Portuguese court, under the regent John (Dom João), took refuge in Rio de Janeiro and gave a new impulse to its growth. It was thrown open to foreign commerce, foreign mercantile houses were permitted to settle there, printing was permanently established, industrial restrictions were removed and a college of medicine, a military academy, and a public library were founded. John VI, regent until 1816, returned to Portugal in 1821, and on Sept. 7, 1822, Brazil was declared independent with Dom Pedro I as its first emperor and Rio de Janeiro as its capital. In 1834 Rio became an autonomous municipality and was declared capital of the empire. In 1839 a steamship service along the coast was opened, but direct communication with Europe was delayed until 1850 and with the United States until 1865. These services added largely to the prosperity of the port. The first section of the Dom Pedro II Railway was opened in 1858, and the second or mountain section in 1864, which brought the city into closer relations with the interior. The first telegraph, connecting Rio de Janeiro with Petrópolis, was installed in 1867. During the Paraguayan War (1864–70) telegraph and cable connections were extended southward to the River Plate republics, and in 1874 cable communication with Europe was opened. The first telephones to be used in Latin America were installed to link government offices in Rio with the summer palace at Petrópolis shortly after the invention of the telephone in 1876.

During the five years following the declaration of the republic in 1889 life in Rio de Janeiro was interrupted by political disorders, particularly by a six-month blockade of the port and desultory bombardment. Under the presidency of Francisco de Paula Rodrigues Alves (1902–06), however, the problems arising from the city's narrow, congested streets and deplorable health conditions were attacked in a coordinated effort led by Lauro Müller (federal minister of industry), Pereira Passos (city prefect), and Dr. Oswaldo Cruz. The avenues, parks, and port facilities for which Rio is famed were planned, while the diseases of yellow fever, bubonic plague, and smallpox were eliminated or greatly reduced. Until 1930 Rio was the scene of a number of political outbreaks, notably the short-lived revolt of the army officers of Fort Copacabana in 1922, but none was of great importance. Under the first regime of Pres. Getúlio Vargas (1930–45) and thereafter the rapid expansion of the government bureaucracy and the congestion and overbuilding of Rio de Janeiro gave impetus to plans, dating from even before the republican period, for moving the national capital to an inland site that would enjoy a cooler climate and be a stimulant for opening up Brazil's unexploited hinterland. Pres. Juscelino Kubitschek (1956–61) resolved to effect the transfer during his administration and sanctioned a law for the construction of the new capital, Brasília, 580 mi. (935 km.) NW of Rio. The official change of capitals took place on April 21, 1960. *See* also references under "Rio de Janeiro" in the Index.   (R. M. M.; R. E. P.)

RÍO DE ORO, the name commonly used for all of Spanish Sahara (*q.v.*) on the northwestern coast of Africa, but strictly applicable only to the southern two-thirds of the territory, between Cap Blanc (Blanco) and Cape Bojador.   (R. J. H. C.)

RIO GRANDE (Rio Grande do Sul), a port in the state of Rio Grande do Sul, Braz. It is located on the western side of the Rio Grande, the name also given to the wide outlet to the Atlantic of the Lagôa dos Patos. The city is built on a low peninsula, barely 5 ft. above sea level, and about 8 mi. upstream from the mouth of the river. Pop. (1960) 83,189.

The peninsula on which Rio Grande has been built is a part of a long sand bar extending from north of Pôrto Alegre southwestward into eastern Uruguay. Cut off from the ocean by the bar are several shallow lagoons, the largest of which are Lagôa dos Patos and Lagôa Mirim. For hundreds of miles on either side of Rio Grande the ocean is bordered by a smooth, sandy beach, backed by strings of live sand dunes, in many ways similar to the coast of southern Georgia. The outlet of the lakes in back of the bar is located at the southern end of Lagôa dos Patos. Where the river enters the ocean it passes over a submerged bar which once limited passage to ships of 26 ft. draft or less. The bar was dredged and the channel is kept open so that ocean-going vessels of larger size can dock at Rio Grande or Pelotas, 20 mi. N.N.W.

Rio Grande was founded in 1737 by José da Silva Paes, who built a fort on the river near the site of the present city and called it Estreito. In 1745 the garrison and settlement were removed by Gomes Freire d'Andrade to its present site, which became a *vila* in 1751, with the name of São Pedro do Rio Grande, and a *cidade* (city) in 1807. It was the capital of the captaincy until 1763, when it was occupied by a Spanish force from Buenos Aires under the command of Don Pedro Zeballos. The seat of government was then removed to Viamão at the northern end of the Lagôa dos Patos. The city was occupied by the national forces in the ten years' war of secession, which began in 1835, and in 1894 it was unsuccessfully besieged by a small insurgent force that attempted to overthrow the government at Rio de Janeiro.

Rio Grande competes with Pelotas as the outlet for the products of Rio Grande do Sul. As the outport for Pôrto Alegre, with which it is connected by shallow-draft lake boats, Rio Grande has an advantage; but for the products of the south, Pelotas is better situated. The exports, mostly to other parts of Brazil, include jerked beef (*xarque*), hides, lard, tallow, wool, rice, wheat and fish. In the city are factories processing meat products, fish and vegetable canneries, a woolen textile mill, breweries, cigarette

manufactures and a shoe factory. The city is linked with Pelotas by rail.   (P. E. J.)

RIO GRANDE, the fifth longest North American river, forms the southwestern boundary of Texas. From its sources in the snow fields and alpine meadows of the San Juan mountains of southwestern Colorado, it flows southeast and south 175 mi. in Colorado, southerly about 470 mi. across New Mexico, and southeasterly between Texas and the Mexican states of Chihuahua, Coahuila, Nuevo León and Tamaulipas, for about 1,240 mi. to the Gulf of Mexico. The total length is approximately 1,885 mi.

It starts as a clear Rocky mountain stream, fed by springs at an elevation of more than 12,000 ft., then flows in a canyon through forests of spruce, fir and aspen, into the broad San Luis valley in Colorado, after which it cuts the Rio Grande gorge and White Rock canyon and enters the open terrain of the basin and range and Mexican highland physiographic provinces. There declining elevation, decreasing latitude and increasing aridity and temperature produce a transition from a cold steppe climate with a vegetation of piñon, juniper and sagebrush, to a hot steppe and desert climate characterized by a vegetation of mesquite, creosote bush, cactus, yucca and other desert plants. Shortly before entering the Gulf coastal plain, the Rio Grande cuts three canyons between 1,500 and 1,700 ft. in depth across the faulted area occupied by the "big bend" where the Texas side of the river is included in the Big Bend National park. In the remainder of its course the river wanders sluggishly across the coastal plain to end in a true delta in the Gulf of Mexico.

The principal tributaries are the Pecos and Devils rivers from the left bank in the United States, and from the right bank the Chama and Puerco in the United States and the Conchos, Salado, and San Juan in Mexico. The basin contains about 172,000 sq.mi. The peak of flow may occur in any month from April to October, but in the upper reaches it usually is in May or June due to melting snow and occasional thunderstorms, while the lower portion commonly has highest water in June or September due to summer rain storms. It has been estimated that the Rio Grande has an average annual yield of more than 9,000,000 ac.ft. of which about one-third reached the gulf before the building of the Falcón dam in 1953.

Irrigation has been practised in the Rio Grande basin since prehistoric times, as among the Pueblo Indians of New Mexico. Increase in population and in use of water made necessary the 1905–07 and 1944–45 water treaties between the United States and Mexico, as well as the Rio Grande compact (1939) among Colorado, New Mexico and Texas concerning the waters of the upper Rio Grande sub-basin (above Ft. Quitman, Tex.), and the Pecos river compact between New Mexico and Texas (1948) concerning the Pecos above Girvin, Tex. Essentially all of the average annual production of more than 3,000,000 ac.ft. in the upper Rio Grande (including the 60,000 ac.ft. allotted to Mexico by treaty) is consumed within this sub-basin. Not only below Ft. Quitman, but in many stretches of the river from the New Mexico-Colorado border to below Brownsville there has been no surface flow at various times. In some places the depth has varied from nearly 60 ft. to a bare trickle or nothing. The lower Rio Grande (below Ft. Quitman) is renewed by the Conchos and other Mexican rivers which produce about two-thirds of the available water. A number of large springs in the area between Hot Springs and Del Rio, Tex., including many in the bed of the river, are important and dependable producers of water. The total storage capacity of the reservoirs in the basin is more than 13,000,000 ac.ft., with a normal storage of some 5,000,000 ac.ft., chiefly in the International Falcón reservoir on the lower Rio Grande, Lago Toronto (La Boquilla) on the Conchos, Elephant Butte on the Rio Grande in New Mexico, Marte Gómez (El Azúcar) reservoir on the San Juan and Venustiano Carranza (Don Martín) on the Salado. The international Amistad dam, below the confluence of Devils river, designed for a capacity of some 5,325,000 ac.ft., was constructed in the late 1960s under terms of a U.S.-Mexico treaty. About 3,000,000 ac. are irrigated within the basin (about two-thirds of these are in the U.S.). The leading crops raised by irrigation vary from potatoes and alfalfa in Colorado to cotton, citrus fruits and vegetables in the valley of the deltaic lower Rio Grande in Texas and Tamaulipas.

After agriculture and animal husbandry, the leading industries are mining (petroleum, natural gas, coal, silver, lead, gold, potash, gypsum, etc.), and recreation (national and state parks and monuments, dude ranches, fishing and hunting, summer and winter resorts, etc.). More than 3,000,000 people live in the basin, principally in urban communities, the largest of which are Monterrey, Mex.; El Paso, Tex.; Ciudad Juárez, Mex.; Albuquerque, N.M.; Chihuahua, Mex.; Saltillo, Mex.; Nuevo Laredo, Mex.; Matamoros, Mex.; Reynosa, Mex.; and Laredo, Tex.

During the Spanish period the middle and upper portions commonly were termed the Río del Norte or Río Grande del Norte and the lower course usually was called the Río Bravo (apparently because of the turbulent flash floods). The river is officially the Rio Grande in the U.S. and the Río Bravo del Norte in Mexico. The earliest European settlements were in the Conchos basin of Chihuahua in the 16th century, but many of the Pueblo Indian settlements of New Mexico date back to before the Spanish conquest. Small steamboats were used for navigation on the lower Rio Grande up to Rio Grande City, and even to Roma when the river was high, from the 1850s until the great hurricane of 1874 swept the river clean. Since then accelerated erosion, silting and sand-bar formation have precluded navigation, and have forced the U.S. and Mexico to spend much money and time in adjusting the boundary to the numerous changes in the river channel. On Oct. 28, 1967, the United States formally returned to Mexico the Chamizal area, between El Paso and Ciudad Juárez, which a shift of the river in 1864 transferred to the left bank. In the delta region on the Mexican side a drainage canal, an extension of the Morillo drain, financed by both nations, was constructed to keep the saline water that runs off from the lower San Juan irrigation district from contaminating the Rio Grande. There has been considerable development of hydroelectricity within the basin.

On Sept. 20, 1967, Hurricane "Beulah," one of the most powerful hurricanes to hit this portion of North America, entered the Rio Grande embayment near Brownsville. It spawned scores of tornadoes and gave rise to many 20 in. and more cloudbursts which resulted in the most devastating floods ever to afflict Texas or northern Tamaulipas. The lower valley cities from Rio Grande City and Ciudad Camargo to Brownsville and Matamoros were flooded; more than 60 persons perished; and some 300,000 had to flee from the waters. The destruction of buildings, trees, crops, animals, roads, and canals was estimated at more than $1,000,000,000, of which the major part was in the lower Rio Grande drainage area of Texas, Tamaulipas, Nuevo León, and Coahuila.

BIBLIOGRAPHY.—Laura Gilpin, *The Rio Grande, River of Destiny* (1949); Paul Horgan, *Great River, The Rio Grande in North American History,* rev. ed. (1960); The Report of the President's Water Resources Policy Commission, *Ten Rivers in America's Future,* vol. 2 (1950).
(D. D. B.)

RIO GRANDE DO NORTE,

RIO GRANDE DO NORTE, a state in the northeast of Brazil, bounded by the Atlantic Ocean on the north and the east, by the state of Paraíba on the south, and by Ceará on the west. Area 20,469 sq.mi., pop. (1960) 1,157,258. The state capital is Natal; the only other town of importance is Mossoró.

Except for the coastal strip from Natal southward, which receives adequate rainfall to support a forest, the state is semiarid. The northern coast, beyond Cape São Roque, is low and sandy, but the land rises inland to some low mesas (*taboleiros*). Inland from Natal, along the southern border of the state, is the northern edge of the Borborema, a hilly upland with rounded slopes and steep margins. The Apodi, the Piranhas, and the Potengi rivers rise in the Borborema and flow northward. The first settlement was near Natal in 1599. The Dutch held this region for 25 years in the 17th century. Because of semiarid conditions the land was useful mostly for the grazing of cattle and goats, but from Natal southward some sugarcane was and still is grown. Carnauba wax is produced in the western part of the state and cotton is grown in the south. The Borborema is known to contain a number of rare minerals—including beryl, diatomite, columbite, and tantalite.
(P. E. J.)

RIO GRANDE DO SUL,

RIO GRANDE DO SUL, the southernmost state of Brazil, is bounded on the north by Santa Catarina state, on the east by the Atlantic Ocean, on the south by Uruguay, and on the west by Argentina. The Uruguay River (*q.v.*) forms the boundary on the west. Area 108,951 sq.mi., including inland waters; pop. (1960) 5,448,823.

Physical Geography.—In the north, the state occupies the southern part of the Paraná plateau. This highland, which extends from southern São Paulo state to the middle part of Rio Grande do Sul and which crosses the border into Argentina and Paraguay, is made up of a succession of outpourings of dark-coloured basaltic lava now solidified into sheets of rock known as diabase. The surface of the plateau stands between 2,000 and 3,000 ft. above sea level. Along the streams it was dissected into a rolling hilly country, but because of the resistance of the diabase its margins are everywhere marked by steep cliffs or *cuestas*. In Rio Grande do Sul the diabase cliffs cap the southern extremity of the Great Escarpment (the eastern edge of the Brazilian highland) along the Atlantic coast almost as far south as Pôrto Alegre. Just north of this city, however, the diabase cliffs turn westward and form a sharply marked descent facing to the south along the northern side of the Jacuí valley. The southern half of Rio Grande do Sul is much lower. The Jacuí River drains a lowland along the base of the plateau, flowing into the northern end of the Lagoa dos Patos near Pôrto Alegre. South of the Jacuí there are gently rolling hills, standing only some 1,000 to 1,500 ft. above sea level and extending across the border into Uruguay. West of Livramento the land forms are tabular rather than rounded, for here the diabase continues southward into western Uruguay, but at a much lower elevation than on the Paraná plateau to the north. The Uruguay River cuts through the diabase, its course frequently interrupted by rapids. All along the immediate Atlantic coast there are long sand bars and lagoons, the largest of which are Lagoa dos Patos and Lagoa Mirim.

Climate.—Rio Grande do Sul is far enough south to experience mild winters, but sometimes with freezing temperatures. At this time of the year cold air masses from the south pass by at frequent intervals, bringing heavy rains along their fronts. Occasionally colder winters bring snow to the higher elevations. In summer, the winds from the northeast prevail and there is less rain. Hot weather prevails, especially inland from the open ocean. Although the whole state has abundant rainfall, the prevailing vegetation cover is that of a tall-grass prairie. Forests occur only along the steep slopes of the Great Escarpment, along the south-facing margin of the Paraná plateau and along the deeper valleys that are cut into the plateau.

The Economy.—There are four chief agricultural regions in Rio Grande do Sul. The first is the oldest—the zone of large cattle and sheep ranches which lies south of the Jacuí River and extends almost unbroken to the borders of Uruguay and Argentina. This is the domain of the Gauchos, the herdsmen whose cattle and sheep feed on the unimproved pastures. The beef produced is lean and tough, the kind chiefly required for the manufacture of *charque* or jerked beef (sometimes called *carne seca*) which is eaten by the poorer Brazilians; it is also the beef most desired by the people of Italy who import it directly from this region. The second region from south to north is the flood plain of the Jacuí River, and of its northern tributary, the Taquarí. It supports a dense population of Brazilians of Portuguese descent. The main product is rice. The properties are large, and each owner provides his own irrigation and drainage. The river floods in winter, but there is usually enough moisture left to support the rice crop during the following summer. The better estates are equipped with pumps to raise water from the river during the summer. The Jacuí valley produces something like 25% of the Brazilian rice crop, a crop that is consumed partly in Pôrto Alegre, but chiefly in the large cities of Rio de Janeiro and São Paulo. The third agricultural region is the zone of the German colonies, located on the terraces above the Jacuí valley and on the lower slopes of the Paraná plateau. Maize, rye, and wheat are raised here, and maize is fed to hogs. Around Santa Cruz is one of Brazil's chief tobacco-growing areas. The fourth region is higher up on the plateau—the Italian colonies with their vineyards. Each of the four regions is strikingly different not only in agriculture, but also in rural landscape, kinds of roads and buildings, and in traditions of the people.

On the plateau top large tracts of land are still used for pasture, but since 1940 there has been a considerable increase of wheat farming. In the forests of the Uruguay valley there is pine to be cut for timber, and also the leaves of the Maté which are collected and roasted to prepare the beverage known as maté, or Paraguay tea, widely used through south Brazil and the neighbouring countries.

Coal of an inferior quality is mined at São Jerônimo, just south of the Jacuí River a short distance upstream from Pôrto Alegre, to which it is shipped by river barge. The coal contains so much sulfur and other impurities that special grates must be used to burn it. In Pôrto Alegre, however, the cost of bringing in better coal is so great that the local product is used to manufacture gas and to generate electricity. The principal industries of the state are concentrated at Pôrto Alegre (q.v.), the state capital, and the outports Rio Grande and Pelotas (qq.v.). Bagé, Santa Maria, Uruguaiana (qq.v.), and Livramento are important towns of the interior.

History.—The Rio Grande area, the so-called "Mission" country, was a zone of conflict between the Portuguese and Spanish. The open grasslands were entered both by Portuguese coming from São Paulo and by Spaniards from Buenos Aires, but neither group established settlements except for forts at key positions around the edge. Seven Jesuit missions were established along the Uruguay River between 1632 and 1707 and the scanty Indian population was gathered together around these places. In 1737 the Portuguese established a fort near the present site of Rio Grande, and in 1738 a large extent of territory which included the present states of Santa Catarina and Rio Grande do Sul, and a part of Uruguay, was named the captaincy of El Rei, to be administered from Rio Grande. But the Spaniards resented the proximity of Portuguese settlements to what they considered their domain and from 1763 to 1776 they occupied Rio Grande. The Portuguese moved their administration centre to the northern end of Lagoa dos Patos, first to Viamão, then to Pôrto dos Cazães which was renamed Pôrto Alegre.

When Brazil declared its independence in 1822, its territory extended southward to the shores of the Río de la Plata. But the Argentines promptly invaded and were in process of pushing the Portuguese back, when, in 1828, Great Britain succeeded in getting the warring countries to agree to the existence of an independent Uruguay. The boundary between Rio Grande do Sul and both Uruguay and Argentina was then fixed. In 1865 a Paraguayan army captured Uruguaiana and held it for a month or so. To this day the Brazilian army spends much of its time training to protect this southern frontier.

In 1822 Emperor Dom Pedro I realized that if this southern territory was to be secured for Brazil, colonies should be established there. In 1824 a small group of German peasants and craftsmen was settled at São Leopoldo (q.v.), just to the north of Pôrto Alegre. By the time of independence all the open grasslands were divided into large private properties for use as cattle and mule ranches. The Portuguese were never attracted by forested country; it was German pioneers who occupied the forests. Between 1824 and 1859 more than 20,000 Germans were settled on small farms along the lower slopes of the plateau to the west of São Leopoldo. They planted rye and potatoes, and grew maize to feed to hogs—an agricultural procedure unknown to the Portuguese. The farm products were sent to Pôrto Alegre by boat on the Jacuí River. Between 1870 and 1890 a large group of Italian pioneers came to Rio Grande do Sul, and these settled above the German settlements, along the upper slopes of the plateau, especially around the town of Caxias. The Italians introduced vineyards and made wine.

Rio Grande do Sul, because of its position on the edge of the Brazilian nation, has often tried to secede. In 1835 a war of secession broke out which lasted for ten years. The state was kept a part of Brazil less by military force than by gifts from the federal treasury. Under Dom Pedro II, who ruled Brazil until 1889, even the more remote states were made to feel contented. But in 1892, during the presidency of Floriano Peixoto, too much interference with the state government led again to insurrection in the south. The revolutionaries carried the war northward even as far as Curitiba, but were forced to surrender in 1894 because of the lack of munitions. In 1930, the revolt led by Getúlio Vargas against the domination of São Paulo started in Rio Grande do Sul.   (P. E. J.)

RIOJA, LA: see La Rioja.

RIOM, a town of central France and a subprefecture in the *département* of Puy-de-Dôme, 13 km. (8 mi.) N of Clermont-Ferrand by road. Pop. (1962) 13,473. The Ricomagus or Ricomum of the Romans, Riom was seized, with Auvergne, for the crown by Alphonse de Poitiers. Thereafter it became the capital of the provincial administration of Auvergne. The town stands on the Ambène River, on the western edge of the fertile Limagne Basin. It has a distinctive beauty; the houses, some dating from the 15th and 16th centuries, are built of gray lava. The church of Saint-Amable (Romanesque and Early Gothic, restored) dates from the 12th century; that of Notre-Dame-du-Marthuret (14th–15th centuries) has a well-known statue of the "Virgin with Bird." The Sainte-Chapelle of the 14th and 15th centuries is a relic of the palace of Jean de France, duc de Berry. The rest of the site of the palace is occupied by the law courts. The court of appeal for four *départements*, Allier, Cantal, Puy-de-Dôme, and Haute-Loire is at Riom. There, in February–April 1942, the trial of French political leaders (including Édouard Daladier, Léon Blum, and Maurice Gamelin) took place at the supreme court of justice set up by the Vichy government. The F. Mandet Museum and the small Jeanne d'Arc Museum (in the *hôtel de ville*) are of particular interest.   (P. M. Sa.)

RÍO MUNI is a river flowing into the Bight of Biafra, West Africa, just north of the Equator. It is also the name of a province of Equatorial Guinea within which the river flows, and which adjoins the republics of Cameroon and Gabon. This territory includes the estuary islets of Corisco, Elobey Chico, and Elobey Grande. *See* Equatorial Guinea.   (R. J. H. C.)

RÍO NEGRO, a province of Argentina lying within the windswept region generally referred to as Patagonia (q.v.). It was created a territory of the republic in 1884 and was raised to the status of a province in 1955. It stretches from the Atlantic coast to the Chilean frontier in the Andes. Pop. (1960) 193,292. Area 78,383 sq.mi.

The land between the Colorado and Negro rivers is similar in formation and characteristic to the "dry pampas"; but a great dam was built on the Negro River near Neuquén, making possible the irrigation of a large district and the growing of alfalfa (lucerne) for cattle fodder and the planting of extensive fruit orchards, particularly pears and apples, which have earned fame for the province. The other important occupation is sheep breeding.

South of the Negro River most of the country consists of a series of arid tablelands, but there are several chains of lakes in the forested valleys of the Andes that are held to rival Swiss scenery. The principal lake is Nahuel Huapí, which lies partly in the province of Neuquén (q.v.).

The Atlantic coastline has one deep indentation, the Gulf of San Matías, in the northern bend of which is the little port of San Antonio Oeste. The provincial capital is Viedma on the right bank of the Negro River about 20 mi. from its mouth and opposite Carmen de Patagones, a port of the province of Buenos Aires. There are numerous small settlements along the Negro River valley and on the railway that runs inland from San Antonio Oeste, but the only other town of importance is San Carlos de Bariloche, a holiday resort consisting of hotels and wooden chalets picturesquely situated among trees on the shore of Lake Nahuel Huapí. Bariloche is one of the two terminals of the railway from San Antonio. It can also be reached by road from Buenos Aires (1,200 mi.) and by air.   (Ge. P.)

RIONI, a river in the Georgian Soviet Socialist Republic, U.S.S.R., is 179 mi. (288 km.) long and drains a basin of 5,200 sq.mi. (13,500 sq.km.). It rises just south of the crest line of the main Caucasus range and cuts the southern ranges and foothills of the Caucasus in a series of deep, narrow, and highly picturesque gorges. At Kutaisi it emerges from the mountains and flows westward across the flat Rioni or Kolkhida lowland (the legendary land of the Golden Fleece) to enter the Black Sea at Poti. The Rioni receives a large number of tributaries draining the western part of the Greater and Lesser Caucasus. These rapid mountain streams bring huge quantities of silt, which are deposited in the Kolkhida lowland and have created extensive swamps, where reclamation has been in progress since World War II. The major tributaries are the Dzhodzhara and Kvirila on the left and the Tskhenis-Tskali and Tekhuri on the right. Average annual discharge at Poti is 14,550 cu.ft. per sec. The greater part of the mountain section of the river is followed by the Ossetian Military Highway across the main Caucasus to Kutaisi. There is a series of hydroelectric plants on the Rioni and its tributaries, the largest being at Kutaisi. (R. A. F.)

RÍO SAN JUAN, a department in southeastern Nicaragua, adjoining Costa Rica. Pop. (1963) 15,676; area 2,876 sq.mi. San Carlos, pop. (1963) 6,076 (mun.), departmental capital and largest town, is at the junction of Lake Nicaragua and San Juan River. Although San Juan del Norte (*q.v.*) is no longer an ocean port, small steamers use the San Juan River between Lake Nicaragua and the Caribbean. The people of the department are concentrated mostly between the central highlands and Lake Nicaragua, where they are engaged chiefly in raising livestock and growing corn, rice, beans, cassava, other vegetables, and tropical fruits. (C. F. J.)

RIOT, in general terms, is a temporary violent outbreak of civil disorder, falling short of an attempt to overthrow the government, and thereby distinguished from insurrection or rebellion. As a legal concept, riot has a more limited meaning: it is a criminal offense against public order involving a group, however small, and the use of violence, however slight. In some countries, the gravamen of the offense is the breach of peace occasioned by it. That is notably the case in the criminal law of England and of the United States. In other countries, such as those under the continental codes, the offense requires interference with or resistance to public authority.

At common law, there are three offenses which, in ascending order of seriousness, involve group breaches of the peace: unlawful assembly, rout and riot. An assembly of persons is unlawful if the participants share a common illegal purpose, regardless of whether steps are taken to effect that purpose. Rout is a kind of way station between unlawful assembly and riot: it consists of an unlawful assembly which has taken some step, short of actual violence, to put its illegal purpose into operation.

Rout becomes riot when violence is used. Riot has been judicially stated to consist of the following elements: (1) the presence of three or more persons; (2) a common unlawful purpose; (3) the execution or inception of the common purpose; (4) an intent to help one another by force if necessary against any person who may oppose them in the execution of their unlawful purpose; (5) force or violence not merely used in demolishing, but displayed in such a manner as to alarm at least one person of reasonable firmness and courage.

A person is guilty of riot if he shares the common unlawful purpose of the assembly and has the requisite intent to use force if necessary, regardless of whether he himself has used force once actual force has been used or threatened by others. The concept is obviously a broad one, capable of embracing a wide range of group conduct from a bloody clash between picketers and strikebreakers to the antics of a street-corner gang.

At common law, riot was an indictable misdemeanour, punishable by fine and imprisonment. In England the Riot act of 1714 made it a felony under certain circumstances of aggravation. The act was passed in response to the widespread rioting which attended the accession to the throne in that year of the first Hanoverian king, George I. Under its provisions, as subsequently modified, whenever an unlawful assembly of twelve or more persons (as contrasted with the three or more required for the com-

mon-law misdemeanour) fail to disperse within an hour after a magistrate has read or tried to read a proclamation, couched in language prescribed by the statute, directing them to disperse, those present cease to be merely misdemeanants and become guilty of a felony, punishable by life imprisonment. The procedure of reading the proclamation came to be known, inaccurately but inevitably, as "reading the riot act," a phrase which has enriched the language in situations far removed from its original meaning. An oddity of the law is that the proclamation must be read verbatim in the prescribed language; otherwise the prosecution fails. A conviction was quashed on this ground in 1830 because the proclamation omitted the concluding words "God save the King."

In spite of the severe penalties prescribed by the Riot act, there are several well-known instances of riots in England subsequent to 1714, including the Gordon anti-Catholic riots of 1780, the Bristol riots of 1831 and the Chartist riots of 1839.

Other provisions of English criminal law impose punishment for various harms to property committed in the course of a riotous assembly and prescribe various rights and duties arising out of the occurrence of a riot. For instance, the law imposes on magistrates the duty of assembling subjects of the realm, whether civil or military, for the purpose of quelling the riot. It is the magistrate's duty to keep the peace; if the peace is broken, honesty of intention will not avail him if he has been guilty of neglect of duty. A somewhat unsettled question is the extent of the protection afforded at common law and by the Riot act to persons acting under orders for the suppression of riots. Although, as just stated, the law of England requires everyone to aid the magistrates in the suppression of riotous assemblages, the degree of force which may be used in effecting that end depends on the nature of the riot. The use of deadly force can only be justified where lesser measures are inadequate to prevent the commission of violent felonies. These rather vague rules apply to soldiers and civilians alike. A matter of some importance is the availability of a civil remedy for persons whose property has been damaged by riot. Under the Riot Damage act of 1886, compensation is payable out of the taxes levied for police maintenance in the district where the riot occurred. Thus a form of public liability for riot damage is provided.

In the United States, laws relating to riot have in general followed the common-law view, at least to the extent of focusing upon the disturbance of the peace rather than the resistance to public authority as the gravamen of the offense. The major difference between English and U.S. law is that the typical U.S. provision on this subject imposes comparatively mild penalties.

The old common-law distinctions among unlawful assembly, rout and riot are preserved in the laws of some states. Others have created a consolidated offense. Aggravated penalties are commonly provided for failing to disperse after having been called upon by a public authority to do so; but the formal requirements of the English Riot act are not often imposed. Inciting to riot is in some states made a separately punishable offense. Some states have adopted the English view that reparation should be made out of public funds to persons whose property has been damaged or destroyed in a riot.

Canadian law is based on the common-law concepts but departs from them in several important respects. An assembly of three or more persons is unlawful not if it has an unlawful purpose but if it causes persons in the vicinity to fear that the assembly will disturb the peace tumultuously or cause others to do so. A riot is an unlawful assembly which has begun to disturb the peace tumultuously. There is no statutory offense of rout. Provision is made for reading a proclamation directing the rioters to disperse and severe penalties are provided for interfering with its reading or failing to obey its injunction to disperse.

All legal systems make some provision for dealing with conduct analogous to that covered by the Anglo-American law of riot but the formal definitions vary, as the following examples will illustrate.

Under German law, there are two separately defined offenses which are analogous to the Anglo-American concept of riot. Riot itself (*Aufruhr*) is an offense against public authority. It consists of taking part in a public riotous gathering in the course of which an official engaged in the exercise of his duties is resisted or assaulted, or in the course of which an official is subjected to force or threats to compel the commission or omission of an official act. The penalty is aggravated if the accused actually performed one of the enumerated overt acts or was a ringleader (*Rädelsführer*). Breach of the public peace (*Landfriedensbruch*) consists of several persons publicly banding together and committing jointly an act or acts of violence against persons or property. Aggravated penalties are provided, as in the case of *Aufruhr*, for ringleaders and those who have committed overt acts. In general, the penalties for *Aufruhr* are more severe than those for *Landfriedensbruch*.

French law does not separately define riot but treats it as a special case of resistance to public authority under the general heading of *rébellion*, the punishment for which varies in seriousness depending upon the number of persons involved and whether or not they are armed. The breach of peace aspect of the offense, which is central to the Anglo-American concept of riot, is not treated as a group offense in French law.   (H. L. Pr.)

RIOTS. A riot involves relatively spontaneous and temporary illegitimate group violence. While a riot may share many social and psychological factors with (and indeed grow out of, or give rise to) other forms of mass behaviour, such as panic, craze, or an expressive crowd, it differs from them in the outwardly hostile and aggressive action taken. Unlike a rebellion or insurrection, a riot usually does not involve an intent to overthrow the government. It differs from peaceful protest demonstrations and civil disobedience because it involves violence.

Riots throughout the ages have been disproportionately urban phenomena. In modern times, the social contexts in which they have occurred most frequently are factories, governmental centres, ghettos, universities, prisons, recreation centres, and colonized or occupied areas. Perhaps the most important general statement to be made about riots is that they can both reflect and cause social change and cannot be understood apart from the main sources of cleavage and social conflict in a society. Among the most important kinds of riots have been those involving political, economic, racial, religious, and nationality issues. Of lesser historical significance are revelrous crowds and the large number of instances where a specific incident such as overselling seats at a performance or inappropriate police handling of parade spectators or demonstrators leads to a riot. As a legal concept, riot is a criminal offense against public order involving a group, however small, and the use of violence, however slight (*see* also RIOT).

Riots in Europe.—Europe since the 17th century has seen much collective violence in the form of brawls between rival guilds and communes, food riots, tax rebellions, mass forest and field trespassing, attacks on châteaus, machine breaking, pogroms, political rebellions, and strikes. Some periods have been more violent than others, such as the late 17th, the latter part of the 18th, and the first half of the 19th century in Great Britain and from the middle of the 18th to the middle of the 19th century in France.

Among some of the better known riots in Great Britain were the Wilkite Riots (1760s and 1770s), against the British government's treatment of John Wilkes (*q.v.*); Gordon Riots (1780), against Catholics; Luddite Riots (1811–12; *see* below and LUDDITES); Rebecca Riots (*q.v.;* 1839; 1842–44); and the Plug Pot Riots of 1842 (*see* CHARTISM). Among important mass disturbances in France were the Grain Riots of 1775, and the violence associated with the revolutions of 1789, 1830, 1848, 1851, and 1871.

The right of resistance, or right to riot, was a part of national tradition in England, and it touched those active in the American Revolution. European riots in the 17th, 18th, and well into the 19th century were rather conservative. Rulers were seen to have obligations to their people; among the most important was providing them with a livelihood. If the ruler met his obligations, the populace was prepared to defend him. If he failed to do his duty, the populace rioted, not to overthrow him as would be the case later but to compel him to do his duty. Riots thus became quasi-institutionalized and perhaps as a result were rather patterned and restricted in their destruction. They represented a

means, understood by the people as well as their rulers, by which those with few political or economic rights might gain concessions.

The traditional rural and urban food riots illustrate this. The main thrust of food riots was a demand to buy food at a "just price." Food riots tended to be associated with periodic famines, and increases in prices and unemployment. Demonstrations would be mounted against those presumed to be profiteering through the shipment or hoarding of grain. If the authorities failed to act and impose a just price on merchants, millers, farmers, or bakers, grain and its products would be seized and sold at a lower price with the proceeds going to the owner. With technical improvements in the production and distribution of grain in the 19th century, food riots disappeared.

Artisans, as well as peasants, participated in food riots, and the artisans also were engaged in industrial disputes. Workers' demands—pursued through attacks on industrial property, workshops, mines, mills, machinery, and "pulling down" employers' houses—were common in the 18th and 19th centuries. E. J. Hobsbawm has called this "collective bargaining by riot." Violence was used by workers as a means of dealing with wage cuts and price increases or to protect their livelihood against the threat of new machinery.

Among the best known of the machine breakers were the British Luddites. Luddism occurred in a context in which war, bad harvests, and the collapse of the export trade raised prices to famine heights and seriously hurt the textile trade. Parliament had repealed paternalistic codes and imposed a laissez-faire economy on the workers. New machines and the factory system disrupted traditional ways of life. Independent artisans were displaced by unskilled factory workers operating new machines for much lower wages. Luddism of the early 19th century moved from a seemingly spontaneous demonstration of stocking workers "clamouring for work and a more liberal price" to a well-organized movement whose small disciplined bands moved swiftly at night. Attacks were selective and restrained, and frequently preceded by a letter warning the employer to change his ways or face the consequences. Machines rather than people were attacked until the authorities began attacking the Luddites. Luddism was short-lived because of increased efforts at social control.

In the mid-19th century, as the modern labour movement emerged and workers gained rights, the classical city mob tended to disappear. In its place emerged more organized demonstrations, strikes, and more sophisticated revolutionary efforts. Violence became more ideological, more associated with the political left, and concentrated more on institutions than on particular individuals. Instead of protesting some change or action that seemed to deprive them of rights they had once enjoyed, rioters came to protest the absence of new rights they felt entitled to. Workers' organizations, however, also meant greater control over potential rioters. To an important extent the amount of violence that occurred came to depend on how violent the authorities were in responding to large demonstrations.

The tolerance for, and amount of, public disorder declined as the nation-state increasingly gained a monopoly on the means of violence. This was related to new value patterns stressing national integration, new bureaucratic forms of police organization, and technical advances, such as the railway and telegraph, that greatly aided efforts at control.

Riots in the United States.—In the United States, with its diverse population, riots have involved issues of race and ethnicity to a much greater extent than in Europe, taking the form of pogroms, communal riots, and the type of uprisings characteristic of colonized or occupied countries. Lynching, a form of mob violence somewhat restricted to the United States, originated in the middle of the 18th century. (*See* LYNCHING AND LYNCH LAW.)

Among prominent examples of ethnic violence were early attacks on Indians and Quakers; anti-Mormon and anti-Catholic riots in the 1840s; occasional slave uprisings; the New York City 1863 anti-draft, anti-Negro riots; the 1871 anti-Chinese riot in California; major race riots involving whites and blacks at East St. Louis in 1917, Chicago in 1919, and Detroit in 1943; the anti-Mexican riot in Los Angeles in 1943; and anti-Negro riots at the

University of Mississippi, the burning of freedom buses, and attacks on Negroes participating in nonviolent demonstrations in the 1950s and 1960s.

Starting in 1964, racially inspired violence appeared in new form and on a scale unprecedented in American history. More than 200 American cities experienced black ghetto riots, with the largest disturbances occurring in the Watts area of Los Angeles in 1965 and in Newark, N.J., and Detroit, Mich., in 1967. By the late 1960s, approximately 200 persons, mostly Negro, were killed, 8,000 injured, and 50,000 arrested.

These riots followed a period in which black aspirations had been raised and promises to end racism and inequality went unfulfilled. A decade of nonviolent protest demonstrations had been relatively unsuccessful in changing the life situation of the average black. Earlier racial violence, such as that in East St. Louis, Chicago, and Detroit, was not restricted to ghetto areas, tended to be initiated by whites and involved white civilians attacking blacks (pogroms) or battles between white and black civilians (communal riots), with authorities often playing a passive role. In contrast, black riots of the 1960s, often growing out of a police incident, were restricted to ghetto areas and involved blacks striking out at the authorities, property, and symbols of white society, rather than at whites as individuals.

Other kinds of riots have not been lacking. During and after the Revolutionary War, riots such as those over the Stamp Act (1765–66), and accompanying Shays's Rebellion (1786) and the Whisky Insurrection (*q.v.*), tended to be political. As the country industrialized in the period from the Civil War to World War I, economic conflicts involving efforts at unionization and strikes were an important source of riots.

The 1960s saw the emergence of widespread student demonstrations, starting with the Free Speech Movement at the University of California at Berkeley in 1964. Many demonstrations ended in violence because of police provocation or a strategy of confrontation. The issues involved in student protest have been highly diverse, depending on the place and the country. A theme often present has been the demand for (or a reaction against encroachment upon) greater student power and participation in the affairs of the university or the larger society. The impersonality of the mass bureaucratic university and university traditionalism and imperviousness to change are conducive to student disorders.

In many universities there are long traditions of student activism. Historically, students have played important roles in movements of political change as in the French Revolution of 1848; the Russian Revolution; the Fascist movements in Italy, Germany, and Spain; and nationalist struggles for independence in the colonized countries of Africa and Asia. Youthful idealism, ambiguities and frustrations in the student role, lesser commitments to familial and occupational roles, and the setting of the university which gathers together large numbers of people in a common situation, help explain the ease with which students can be mobilized for demonstrations. Some of these causes also explain why youth in general seem to participate disproportionately in riots.

Communal Riots in Asia and Africa.—Outbreaks of communal rioting in countries such as India-Pakistan (1947), Ceylon (1958), and Nigeria (1966–67) followed the demise of European colonial empires. New countries were often artifacts of arbitrary colonial boundaries and did not correspond to traditional group divisions. The fragile unity that had often been present in a common anti-colonial struggle gave way to bitter conflicts. Various racial, ethnic, tribal, religious, and linguistic groups, often with long histories of hostility, fought among themselves for autonomy. The weaker group feared domination by the stronger.

The most violent examples of such communal rioting involved Hindus and Muslims during the partition of India in 1947. Approximately a half-million people died, many in hideous massacres while trying to reach safety in their new country (Pakistan for Muslims and India for Hindus). Fighting was most pronounced in areas of mixed population such as Bengal and the Punjab. Communal riots such as these, in which the lines of cleavage flow out of racial, religious, or ethnic differences and where the essential humanity of the opponent can be denied, seem to have a much more violent and macabre potential than riots involving strictly political or economic issues.

Analysis of Riots can usefully be divided into factors in the pre-, actual, and post-riot situations. The first deals with the causes that increase the likelihood of the occurrence of a riot. The second deals with the precipitating incident, the role of ideas and rumour, leadership, the nature of participants, the interaction between rioters and authorities, and the patterning of the riot. Analysis of the last considers the consequences of the violence.

The Pre-Riot Situation.—A riot can potentially occur anytime people are together in a group. Riots, however, do not occur randomly in time, place, or social setting. For example, 20th-century American race-linked riots have occurred when whites felt the segregatory status quo was threatened or when Negroes developed new equalitarian aspirations. Such riots have occurred especially during war periods, in urban areas, in summer, on weekends, and on main transportation routes. Certain conditions greatly increase the likelihood of rioting.

A group's predisposition to riot may be analyzed in light of the intensity of its grievances, the extent of opportunities to gain redress through normal channels, its cultural traditions regarding the use of violence, the extent to which its members are available for mass action, and the coercive power of the authorities to control outbreaks. To an important extent a riot is a function of these five factors. A riot is most likely to occur when a group has an intensely felt grievance, when it believes normal channels of protest are closed or ineffective, when its traditions favour violence, when it can easily come together for mass action, and when authorities are perceived as unable or unwilling to exercise strong control over violence.

An important impetus to many riots is some disruption, particularly if abrupt, of a group's traditional or anticipated way of life. When the expectations that previously guided action are no longer relevant, instrumental as well as expressive mass behaviour is made more likely. Riots have occurred disproportionately in periods of economic crisis, war, mass migration, catastrophe, and technical change, when normal routines of living are upset. When such changes are widespread they may not only engender dissatisfaction but also weaken traditional external and internal sources of control. The likelihood of violence from traditional as well as new strains may thus be increased.

Epidemics of plague in the Middle Ages greatly disrupted the European social order and gave rise to pogroms as well as dancing manias. Economic crises have been closely associated with a wide array of violent outbursts including European food and machine-breaking riots, American nativism, and Japanese peasant uprisings. The two periods in which American race riots against blacks were most prevalent were associated with large wartime northward migration and black entry into new areas of employment. The American prison riots of the early 1950s were associated with new administrative techniques that destroyed the informal inmate system of social control and reward distribution.

Riots are more likely not only when groups feel deprived of rights they once enjoyed but also when they come to feel that new rights are due them. Here the role of ideas, or what Neil Smelser (see *Bibliography*) has called a "generalized belief system," is particularly important. Such a belief system prepares people for action. It redefines an unstructured situation and fixes blame for the existing order which is considered intolerable. A better world seems possible if only some person or group of persons is destroyed, injured, removed, or restricted. Examples of well-developed generalized belief systems that have figured in riots include anticlericalism, anti-Semitism, Marxism, anarchism, Fascism, and various nationalisms. Scholars disagree as to whether riots are more likely when people have a sense of despair or hope, and when things are getting worse or improving. Each of these factors, under not very well understood conditions, has been linked to outbursts. Disorders seem especially likely when periods of gain are interrupted by periods of decline. The important cause is not so much the amount of objective deprivation but how a group evaluates its position relative to other groups and the kinds of expectations it has.

Not all riots, however, involve a generalized belief. Recreational riots or expressive rampages tend to be relatively issueless with respect to the larger society. The Saturday night brawls frequent in some lower status communities, ritualized disorders following school athletic events, Easter vacation riots of American students, and motorcycle riots have more of a playful tension-release character, with slight implications for social change. They are not much affected by the predisposing factors considered above. A pronounced weakening of authorities may also lead to relatively issueless rioting as was the case in the 1919 Boston police strike and some European riots as World War II ended.

Given a generalized belief that calls forth and explains dissatisfaction, it becomes important to ask what alternative means to violence are available. In colonized, occupied, or totalitarian countries, or highly authoritarian situations such as the American slave system, the early factory system, prisons, and many schools and universities—where there are no effective channels for the redress of grievances—violence may be seen as the only way of pressing a claim. In other situations the formal democratic process may be inoperative, either because a group is denied participation, or because its leaders are not seen as effectively representing the group. In many American cities that experienced riots in 1967, black political underrepresentation was pronounced and a feeling existed that all legitimate channels had been exhausted. Riots may also appear as a result of the closing off of previously accepted channels of protest, and disappear as new channels become available.

The likelihood of a riot is also increased to the extent that various social cleavages (e.g., racial, national, linguistic, religious, tribal, regional, generational, economic, and political status) overlap rather than cut across each other. Where this is the case, as in many colonized countries, mutually reinforcing grievances on the part of the subordinate group are likely. In the United States race and class overlap. New dissatisfactions may be buttressed by traditional hostilities. In this context riots are likely to involve group conflict over power, income, and prestige.

The Riot is usually foreshadowed by a series of events that arouse the relevant public and focus attention on the source of dissatisfaction. In this context of heightened concern, a given incident, often innocuous, may confirm previous fears, expectations, and beliefs and come to be symbolic of all a group feels is wrong. Rumours, which reflect tension more than cause it, may selectively focus the group's attention and help create a polarized and oversimplified conception of the situation. Intense feelings of self-righteousness may develop. As with other kinds of mass behaviour, some crowd members may feel a sense of solidarity and heightened emotional ties to each other. As collective excitement builds up, an agitated member of the crowd may take some violent action, setting a pattern that others then follow.

Sometimes a single event can precipitate like disorders in many places. Following the assassination of Tsar Alexander II in 1881, Russian mobs in more than 200 cities attacked Jews, although the assassin was not Jewish. Following the killing of Martin Luther King, Jr., in 1968, more than 100 American cities experienced racial disorders. Food, prison, and university riots have tended to cluster together in time, often radiating outward. Some observers see in this a pattern of conspiracy; perhaps it is more likely that it represents a response to similar conditions and the provision of a role model. There are parallels to the spread of behaviour in fads, crazes, and panics that clearly do not involve an organized system of control by a leadership group. The mass media, especially television, have greatly facilitated the process.

Early conservative theorists such as G. LeBon, E. D. Martin, and E. A. Ross emphasized the emotional character of crowd behaviour. For them the crowd evoked lurid images of destruction where the basest of human impulses were expressed. They wrote of "herd instincts," the "group mind," the "atavistic vulnerability of civilized men," "dirty people without name," and the "dangerous classes." The crowd was thought to be like-minded, destructive, irrational, fickle, and suggestible and made up of social misfits, criminals, and riffraff.

In extreme form such ideas are now generally rejected. There is great variation both within and between crowds. There are types and degrees of participation. These may change as the riot develops. Individuals may engage in the same activity for different reasons. In many riots, a small active nucleus, often made up of younger men, can be differentiated from a large body of spectators. The characteristics of rioters, the degree of selectivity in their activities, and the amount of violence depend on the specific issues and the period of history. Yet much research suggests the classical image of the crowd to be incorrect.

G. Rudé, using police and judicial records in his studies of the crowd in France and England between 1730–1848, finds that criminal and lumpen proletariat participation was slight. Riot participants were not those at the margins of society; rather they tended to be well integrated into local settings and had specific grievances. The mob consisted of the ordinary urban poor, the menu peuple—small workshop masters, shopkeepers, apprentices, craftsmen, and labourers: employed people with settled abode and without criminal conviction. Similarly, research on black riot participants in the 1960s suggests that in many ways rioters were broadly representative of Negro youth. They were not disproportionately unemployed, criminal, or recent migrants, and had a strong sense of indignation over the place of Negroes in America.

The personally disorganized, those with pronounced antisocial tendencies, criminals, and individualistic looters may take advantage of the general confusion in a riot to further their own ends. There are many historical examples of such people being drawn into a riot, unconcerned and perhaps even unaware of the broader issues. Riots clearly offer a cover for normally prohibited behaviour. Yet such people are always present, while riots occur infrequently and are very much related to broader social, political, economic, religious, and racial issues. An explanation that seeks the source of riots in the nature of man, or of certain men such as those of the lower social classes, cannot explain their variation.

The mechanisms by which people come to act differently in a crowd are not well understood. One relevant cause is interaction that leads to the emergence of new norms redefining the situation and justifying previously forbidden behaviour (e.g., "Merchants have been exploiting and stealing from the people for years so we are not looting, but taking what is rightfully ours"). An individual may feel group pressure to conform to the new norm since not to do so may label him as a coward, a fool, or an enemy. Another cause is the weakening of external control that may permit the expression of deviant tendencies present in most people. The failure of authorities to act (either because they are undermanned, in sympathy with the crowd, or afraid of provoking it further) leads people to think they will escape punishment. The crowd offers anonymity. The possible rewards may seem to greatly outweigh the negative consequences.

The importance of the leader or agitator has long been a subject of dispute and clearly depends on the particular situation. In some countries, such as those of the Middle East, street rioting has been a recognized means of conflict that leaders effectively use. It is doubtful, however, that large numbers of people can be made to riot without grievances.

Where speech-making and planned demonstrations are involved, leaders may play important early roles. Where the crowd has a clearly defined end, and cooperative action is required as in a lynching or forcing entrance into a building, a clear leadership structure may be present and even restraining. The leader may lose all control, however, as the specific purpose is carried out, and the crowd may even turn on him if he tries to restrain them. This situation led early observers to characterize the crowd as vacillating and immoral. In other, more diffuse riots involving small congeries of people behaving in roughly parallel ways, such leadership will be lacking, though some men out of extreme ideological commitment or personal disorganization may set daring examples that others follow. The extent to which a crowd is open to suggestions of leaders is limited to those consistent with its mood; suggestions that the crowd disperse are often ineffective.

A riot, as with any kind of collective behaviour, has an emergent quality to it and over time may change greatly. Its norms are more spontaneous, and this gives it an important element of unpredictability. Important to the course of a riot is the interaction between control officials and rioters. Authorities face the dilemma of under- or overreaction. To underreact may permit the riot to spread as people see they are not being censured. To overreact may create martyrs and lead to the involvement of many who had been passive spectators.

A pattern that has sometimes emerged involves the escalation of the riot to include new and more general issues or the triggering of traditional hostilities unrelated to the original issues as new participants with other concerns become involved. Hostility may move from being focused on a single object or class of objects to a wide array of objects. It may move from involving the crowd as a unit to individual or small group actions that are roughly parallel. An early period of milling and chaotic violence may give rise to more planned and focused attacks. The level of violence may escalate from verbal insults to rock throwing to gunfire as authorities increase efforts at control. The riot may end when the crowd obtains its objective or realizes it is impossible to obtain it, when some shocking event occurs, when the crowd becomes fatigued, or when superior force is brought against it.

Post-Riot Consequences.—Whatever the varied personal motives and characteristics of rioters, and the degree of instrumentality and spontaneity involved in their behaviour, the event they collectively help create often comes to have a meaning that far transcends their individual psychology and actions. The consequences of riots have been varied. Some have resulted only in brutal repression; others have been merely tolerated and had no important effects; while still others have been instrumental in directly or indirectly bringing about change.

Riots themselves often do not directly involve action rationally calculated to solve the issues which arouse the crowd. Indeed, the crowd's inability to deal with the issues it is concerned with can be an important stimulus to riotous action. Riots can heighten political consciousness and solidarity, however, and can serve as catalysts for more organized protest efforts carried out illegally or legally. They have often served as a prelude to broader movements of social upheaval.

Though he was unsympathetic, Gustave LeBon noted that crowds serve to destroy the old order in preparation for the emergence of a new one. An initial outburst may take on a symbolic meaning and give rise to new groups, heroes, and leaders. In ancient Greece and Rome the mob frequently led to the fall of governments and had important effects on the course of world history. The American, French, and Russian revolutions were preceded by riots. In the 1960s, student uprisings toppled governments in a number of countries. Where a riot does produce change, at a more general level, it may often be analyzed as part of a broader series of historical and social events conducive to both riots and the given change.

Riots can have a communications function and sensitize those with power to problems they previously were unaware of or had neglected. Grain riots often produced a reduction in prices and new efforts by local officials to assure an adequate grain supply at a just price. Negro riots in the 1960s visibly and forcefully brought racial problems to the forefront of domestic issues. American student disorders have triggered reanalysis of the nature of higher education. Where other means are lacking, riots can serve as a bargaining device by which powerless groups put forth their claims. This negative power to disrupt society and the threat of rioting have tempered the actions of many rulers.

In some riots a life cycle model—breakdown, chaotic violence and mass unrest, organized protest, social change, and the disappearance of violence—may be noted. U.S. labour violence and various nationalist movements have undergone this cycle. Probably a majority of riots, however, do not show this pattern. Sporadic violence may accompany, or never lead to, more organized efforts at change. Rioting may also inhibit social change by offering leaders an excuse for bloody repression or by channeling mass anger onto a scapegoat, such as Jews or Negroes, and away from the basic source of discontent.

Other effects may be more limited or subtle. Fear of riot generated by the Chartist disorders was an important factor in the creation of a national police force in England. Fear of revolution influenced the planning of Paris, Vienna, and Washington, D.C. Following American ghetto riots some new buildings have been constructed without street-level windows. Some psychiatrists have theorized that through striking out, individuals who feel oppressed obtain a sense of dignity and catharsis.

BIBLIOGRAPHY.—*Historical:* G. Rudé, *The Crowd in History* (1964); E. J. Hobsbawm, *Primitive Rebels* (1959); J. W. Heaton, "Mob Violence in the Late Roman Republic," *Illinois University Studies in the Social Sciences,* vol. 23 (1938–39); M. Beloff, *Public Order and Popular Disturbances 1660–1714* (1938); F. O. Darvall, *Popular Disturbances and Public Order in Regency England* (1934); F. C. Mather, *Public Order in the Age of the Chartists* (1959); E. P. Thompson, *The Making of the English Working Class* (1964); R. S. Longley, "Mob Activities in Revolutionary Massachusetts," *New England Quarterly,* vol. vi (1933); C. Tilly, "The Changing Place of Collective Violence" in M. Richter (ed.), *Social Theory and Social History* (1969); J. McCague, *The Second Rebellion: the Story of the New York City Draft Riots of 1863* (1968); G. Myers, *History of Bigotry in the United States,* rev. by H. M. Christman (1960); W. Heaps, *Riots, U.S.A. 1765–1965* (1966).
Social and Psychological Analysis: G. LeBon, *The Crowd* (1947); E. D. Martin, *The Behavior of Crowds* (1920); S. Freud, *Group Psychology and the Analysis of the Ego* (1955); H. Cantril, *The Psychology of Social Movements* (1941); R. Brown, "Mass Phenomena" in G. Lindzey (ed.), *Handbook of Social Psychology,* vol. ii (1954); R. Turner and L. Killian, *Collective Behavior* (1957); K. Lang and G. E. Lang, *Collective Dynamics* (1961); N. Smelser, *Theory of Collective Behavior* (1963); C. Couch, "Collective Behavior: an Examination of Some Stereotypes," *Social Problems,* vol. 15, no. 3, 310–322 (1968); E. Canetti, *Crowds and Power* (1966); F. Fanon, *The Wretched of the Earth* (1965); G. Marx, "Civil Disorder and the Agents of Social Control," *Journal of Social Issues* (Oct. 1969); R. Evans, *Readings in Collective Behavior* (1969).
Racial Riots: Chicago Commission on Race Relations, *The Negro in Chicago* (1922); A. M. Lee and N. D. Humphrey, *Race Riot* (1943); A. F. Raper, *The Tragedy of Lynching* (1933); T. Vittachi, *Emergency '58: the Story of the Ceylon Race Riots* (1958); E. Rudwick, *Race Riot at East St. Louis, July 2, 1919* (1966); A. Waskow, *From Race Riot to Sit-In* (1967); R. Conot, *Rivers of Blood, Years of Darkness* (1967); *Report* of the National Advisory Commission on Civil Disorders (Kerner Commission Report) (1968); *Supplemental Studies* for the National Advisory Commission on Civil Disorders (1968); J. Hersey, *The Algiers Motel Incident* (1968); L. Masotti and D. Bowen (eds.), *Riots and Rebellion: Civil Violence in the Urban Community* (1968). (G. T. MA.)

RIOUW ARCHIPELAGO AND DISTRICT forms part of Riouw (Riau) Province, Indon., and consists of more than a thousand islands between the Straits of Singapore to the north, the Berhala Straits to the south, and Borneo to the east. The population in 1961 was 278,966. The district comprises the Riouw (Indonesian, Riau) archipelago proper, consisting of the Great Karimun, Batam, and Bintan groups, the Lingga and Singkep islands, and, in the South China Sea, the Tambelan, Anambas, and Natuna islands. The administrative centre is Tandjungpinang (pop. [1957 est.] 54,629). The islands vary in height and size from rocky crags and small coral reefs to Bintan (sometimes called Riouw) and the main Natuna Island, each over 400 sq.mi. in area. Lingga and Singkep are almost as large; the former attains a height of 3,500 ft. and has the largest alluvial plain of the archipelago. Coral reefs and currents make navigation difficult.

The islands, scattered across main trade routes, were formerly pirate haunts. When the Portuguese took Malacca (1511), the expelled Malay ruler retained Johore on the peninsula and the islands at its southern tip. The sultans later allied themselves with the Dutch against the Portuguese. Their residence alternated between Johore and the Riouw archipelago, but after 1795 they resided in Lingga (Daik). The Dutch protested against Sir Thomas Stamford Raffles' occupation of Singapore (1819) because they considered it as part of the Riouw islands under their suzerainty. The people are Malay, Bugi, Chinese, and small groups of aboriginals known as Benua and Orang Laut. The Malays and Bugi live by simple agriculture and fishing, with rubber and copra as cash crops. The Chinese grow pepper and gambier, exploit the forests for timber, firewood, and charcoal (exported to Singapore), and work in the tin mines of Singkep and the bauxite mines on Bintan. (J. O. M. B.)

RIPON, FREDERICK JOHN ROBINSON, 1ST EARL OF (1782–1859), better known as VISCOUNT GODERICH, British statesman, prime minister from August 1827 to January 1828, was born in London on Nov. 1, 1782, the second son of Thomas Robinson, 2nd Baron Grantham. Educated at Harrow and Cambridge, he was private secretary (1804–06) to his kinsman, Philip Yorke, 3rd earl of Hardwicke, lord lieutenant of Ireland; undersecretary for war and the colonies (1809); a lord of the admiralty (1810–12); a lord of the treasury (1812–13); joint paymaster general (1813–17); and president of the board of trade (1818–23). During these years he owed his advancement first to the Yorke family and, after 1812, to his friend Viscount Castlereagh. As chancellor of the exchequer (1823–27) he was a great improvement on his predecessor, Nicholas Vansittart (afterward Lord Bexley), though he owed much of his success to the president of the board of trade, William Huskisson, who helped him to frame his popular budgets. In George Canning's ministry (April–August 1827) he was secretary for war and the colonies, and, with the title of Viscount Goderich, leader of the House of Lords. He succeeded Canning as prime minister, but was confessedly impotent and was dismissed in January 1828. In Earl Grey's ministry (formed November 1830) he was again secretary for war and the colonies, and later (April 1833), lord privy seal. He resigned in June 1834 and soon joined the Peelites. In Sir Robert Peel's second ministry he was president of the board of trade (September 1841–May 1843) and president of the India board (May 1843–July 1846). He was nicknamed "Prosperity Robinson" by William Cobbett for his unwarranted optimism on the eve of the 1825 economic crisis; it was also Cobbett who, scornful of his record as colonial secretary, called him "Goody Goderich." Created earl of Ripon in April 1833, he died at Putney on Jan. 28, 1859.

See L. Wolf, *Life of the First Marquess of Ripon*, 2 vol. (1921); É. Halévy, *A History of the English People in the Nineteenth Century*, trans. by E. I. Watkin, vol. ii, 2nd ed. (1949).　　(A. AL.)

RIPON, GEORGE FREDERICK SAMUEL ROBINSON, 1ST MARQUESS OF (1827–1909), British statesman, who during a career covering more than 50 years occupied many important cabinet posts and served as viceroy of India. Only son of the 1st earl of Ripon, he was born in London on Oct. 24, 1827. Under his courtesy title of Viscount Goderich he was returned to the House of Commons in 1852 as a Liberal. In January 1859 he succeeded to his father's title, and in November of the same year to that of his uncle, Earl de Grey. A few months after entering the upper house he was appointed undersecretary for war; in February 1861 undersecretary for India; and in April 1863 secretary for war, with a seat in the cabinet. In 1866 he was appointed secretary of state for India. On the formation of the Gladstone administration in December 1868, he became lord president of the council, and in 1871 chairman of the Joint High Commission on the "Alabama" claims, which arranged the Treaty of Washington. He was elevated to a marquessate in 1871. In 1874 he became a convert to Roman Catholicism.

On the return of Gladstone to power in 1880 Lord Ripon was appointed viceroy of India, the appointment exciting a storm of controversy, as the marquess was the first Roman Catholic to hold the viceregal office. He went out to reverse the Afghan policy of Lord Lytton. Kandahar was given up and the whole of Afghanistan was secured to Abdurrahman Khan (*q.v.*; *see* also AFGHANISTAN: *History*). The new viceroy promoted local self-government and in certain directions curtailed the privileges of Europeans. For the controversy over the Ilbert Bill of 1883 *see* INDIA-PAKISTAN, SUBCONTINENT OF: *History*. He became very popular among Indians.

In 1886 Lord Ripon became first lord of the admiralty in the third Gladstone ministry; and on the return of the Liberals to power in 1892 he was appointed colonial secretary. He was included in Sir Henry Campbell-Bannerman's cabinet (1905) as lord privy seal and retained this office until 1908. He died at his seat, Studley Royal, near Ripon, Yorkshire, on July 9, 1909.

See S. Gopal, *The Viceroyalty of Lord Ripon* (1953).

RIPON, a cathedral city and municipal borough in the Ripon parliamentary division of the West Riding of Yorkshire, Eng., 24 mi. N.W. of York and 27 mi. N. of Leeds by road. Pop. (1961) 10,486. It lies at the foot of Wensleydale at the confluence of the Ure and its tributaries the Laver and the Skell. The Saxon village of Ripon first comes into history in the pages of Bede who describes how Abbot Eata of Melrose founded a Celtic monastery there *c.* 651. About ten years later Wilfrid founded a Benedictine monastery and became its abbot. Soon after this he was made bishop of York and became one of the leading figures in the English church. At Ripon he built a famous church, whose crypt may still be seen under the present cathedral. Wilfrid's church and monastery were both destroyed by the Danes in the 9th century, and the monastery was never rebuilt. According to a local tradition of not very ancient date, Ripon received a charter from Alfred the Great in 886. By the time of the Norman Conquest, Ripon minster was a collegiate church with secular clergy. The archbishops of York owned large properties in the neighbourhood ("the Liberty of Ripon") and had an episcopal palace which stood on the site of the present courthouse, on the north side of the cathedral. In 1132 Archbishop Thurstan gave land in Skelldale to a band of monks from St. Mary's abbey, and escorted them from Ripon to the place where the ruins of Fountains abbey stand, 3 mi. W.

The greatest attraction for the modern visitor to Ripon is its lovely cathedral. Apart from the Saxon crypt the oldest parts are the chapter house and the Norman undercroft; the architecture of the present building belongs mainly to the Norman Transitional and Perpendicular periods. The nave (without aisles), north transept and part of the choir were built by Archbishop Roger in 1154, while the side aisles were added about 1500 when the central tower and south transept were rebuilt. The central tower is of special interest because it has two round and two pointed arches, indicating that the Perpendicular work was left unfinished. The twin towers of the west front are Early English (about 1216), and the Lady loft (now the library) dates from the 14th century. The chancel contains misericords, carved by the Ripon woodcarvers between 1489 and 1494, and also some fine canopies. The cathedral library, collected since *c.* 1608, has some exceptionally rare books and manuscripts. The 12th-century Leper chapel, within a few minutes' walk of the cathedral, contains a pre-Reformation stone altar.

Ripon has a large and beautiful market square, surrounded by a variety of houses, shops and inns of different dates. One of these buildings is a 15th-century house where Hugh Ripley, the last wakeman and the first mayor of Ripon, once lived. The name of the chief official was changed from wakeman to mayor in 1604 when James I gave the town a charter of incorporation. Another building in the square is the town hall (1798) on which these words are inscribed: "Except the Lord keep the City the Wakeman waketh but in vain." The ritual of the hornblowing, dating from before the Conquest, is of great interest. Every evening at nine o'clock curfew is rung on the cathedral bells, and the horn is blown at each corner of the market place and also outside the mayor's house. Originally this was a sign that the watch had been set and the citizens could sleep in peace. The original 9th-century Saxon horn may still be seen at the town hall.

The diocese of Ripon was re-established in 1836 by the division into two parts of the ancient diocese of York. The dioceses of Wakefield and Bradford have since been carved out of Ripon, which now includes Leeds and the country north as far as the Tees. A church training college for women teachers was founded in 1863. By the late 1960s it was greatly enlarged and was a College of Education for about 600 students.

Outside the town of Ripon is a race course which holds several meetings a year.　　(A. M. W.)

RIPPLE MARKS. The alternating parallel ridges and troughs formed on the surface of sand by waves and currents of water or air are known as ripple marks. Granular materials of little cohesion are essential for the formation of ripple marks by water waves and currents; they may be made by wind on dust as well as on sand. Under some conditions ripple marks may be made on deposits of small pebbles.

Wave-formed or oscillation ripple marks have sharp, symmetrically sloped crests and rounded troughs. Current-formed ripple marks have rounded, asymmetrically sloped crests and troughs, the upcurrent slope being the longer and more gently inclined. Ripple marks are readily preserved when the sediments on which they are formed are transformed into rocks. Fossilized current ripple marks show the directions of the forming currents.

Although most water ripple marks are formed in relatively shallow water, they may be formed at any depth at which wave and currents are able to move sand. Wave ripple marks have been reported in the Indian ocean at a depth of 617 ft., and current ripple marks may form at depths exceeding 2,000 ft.

Since deposits made over wave ripple marks have corresponding crests and troughs on their undersurfaces, and since these are readily distinguishable from the originals, a valuable method of determining bottoms and tops of overturned strata is provided. Current ripple marks are not of great value in such investigations.

See also WAVES OF THE SEA.

See W. H. Twenhofel, *Principles of Sedimentation,* 2nd ed., pp. 567–578 (1950). (W. H. TL.; X.)

RISARALDA, a department of Colombia, situated in the west central part of the nation just west of the Cauca River. Area 1,530 sq.mi. (3,962 sq.km.); pop. (1964) 437,211. It was a part of the department of Caldas (*q.v.*) until it was made a new department in 1966. Its capital city, Pereira, with a population of 147,487 (1964), was founded in 1863 on the original site of the colonial city of Cartago, and is the youngest departmental capital of Colombia. Pereira has long felt a strong and occasionally bitter rivalry with Manizales, capital of Caldas. Risaralda has a variety of terrain and climates, since its boundaries extend westward into the Cordillera Occidental of the Andes, the central section is in the Cauca Valley, and the southeastern part experiences the cold of the Cordillera Central. Its principal product is coffee, with sugarcane, beans, corn, plantains, yucca, cacao, and tobacco also being produced. Industries such as textiles were increasing in importance in the 1960s. The department is served by highways, airlines, and railroads. (T. E. N.)

RISENBURGH (VANRISEMBURGH), **BERNARD VAN,** the name of three generations of Parisian furniture makers of Dutch origin.

The eldest, BERNARD (working before 1696–1738), was established in Paris before 1700 and in 1722 became a member of the cabinetmakers' guild (*maître-ébéniste; see* WOODWORK, DECORATIVE).

His eldest son, BERNARD II (working before 1730–1763 or 1766), became one of the outstanding French furniture makers of the Louis XV period. Trained in the family workshop, he was a *maître-ébéniste* before 1730, when he set up his own establishment; his furniture is stamped with the initials B.V.R.B. He worked in a highly idiosyncratic style in wood marquetry and in lacquer veneers and was probably the first craftsman to embellish furniture with Sèvres porcelain. His work may be seen in the Louvre, Paris; the Victoria and Albert Museum, London, and the Royal Collection; but much is in U.S. and French private collections.

His son, BERNARD III (fl. *c.* 1765–1775), worked in the family workshop. The workshop was closed at his widowed mother's death (*c.* 1773–75).

See J. Baroli, "Le mystérieux B.V.R.B.," *Connaissance des Arts,* pp. 57–63 (March 1957). (F. J. B. W.)

RISTIC, JOVAN (1831–1899), Serbian statesman, twice regent of Serbia and three times prime minister, was born at Kragujevac on Jan. 16 (new style), 1831. He studied in France and at Heidelberg University. In government service, he went to Istanbul as secretary of Prince Milosh Obrenovich's deputation (1860) and was elected (1861) clerk of the *Skupstina* which passed new bills tabled by the prince of Serbia, Prince Michael Obrenovich. As diplomatic representative in Istanbul (1861–67) he secured the withdrawal of the last Turkish garrisons from Serbia. He was appointed foreign minister in November 1867, but having refused to comply with Prince Michael's wishes was dismissed in December before receiving his seal of office.

After Prince Milan Obrenovich's accession (July 2, 1868), although elected second regent, he was mainly responsible for the new constitution (1869), and prevented Serbia from falling under Austrian influence. When Prince Milan attained his majority

(Aug. 22, 1872) Ristic became foreign minister, then prime minister (April 5–Nov. 3, 1873). He was again twice foreign minister (1875, 1876–78). Against his will he was induced to conduct two wars against Turkey (1876, 1877–78). He represented Serbia at the Berlin congress (1878) which proclaimed Serbia's independence and increased its territory. Meanwhile having been acknowledged as the leader of the Liberal Party, Ristic formed his second government (Oct. 13, 1878–Oct. 26, 1880), resigning because of his failure to secure a trade agreement with Austria-Hungary. He presided over a coalition ministry (June 13–Dec. 31, 1887) till it broke up.

After King Milan's abdication (March 6, 1889), Ristic became head of the regency, the main duties of which were to enforce the new constitution (1888) and counteract the influence of the Radical government. This he dismissed (1892), replacing it with a Liberal government. When King Alexander Obrenovich dismissed the regents (April 1893) and declared himself of age, Ristic retired from politics. He died in Belgrade on Sept. 4 (N.S.), 1899. He published *Spoljašnji odnošaji Srbije novijega vremena* (three vol., 1887–1901) and *Diplomatska istorija Srbije za vreme Srpskih ratova za oslobodjenje i nezavisnost* (two vol., 1896–98).

See B. Petrovic, *Jovan Ristic* (1912). (K. St. P.)

RISTORI, ADELAIDE (1822–1906), Italian actress, was born at Cividale del Friuli, Jan. 29, 1822, the daughter of strolling players. She began her career as a child actress and at the age of 14 was cast in the title role of Silvio Pellico's *Francesca da Rimini.* She joined the Royal Sardinian Company as ingénue and advanced in two years to the position of leading lady. At 18 she attempted the title role in Schiller's *Maria Stuart.* In 1855 she went to Paris. The devotees of Mlle Rachel found that the foreign guest lacked the pure classicism for which the French star was famous, but there were other critics, the elder Dumas among them, who adored the passionate outbursts and spontaneity of the Italian temperament which broke through the general stateliness of Ristori's grand style. When she played the comic part of Mirandolina in Goldoni's *La Locandiera,* the approval of the Parisians was unanimous. She finally triumphed as a tragedienne in Alfieri's *Mirra.* She later appeared in Germany, Vienna, London, Warsaw, and Madrid. Her repertory included Racine's *Phèdre,* Legouvé's *Médée,* and Shakespeare's Lady Macbeth. She toured the United States for the first time in 1866, and her successes encouraged her return in 1867, 1875, and 1884. In 1874 the actress embarked upon a professional tour around the world. She retired from the stage in 1885 and three years later published her *Memoirs and Artistic Studies,* a volume containing analyses of her outstanding tragic roles. She died on Oct. 8, 1906, in Rome. (A. M. N.)

RITES AND CEREMONIES. Rites may conveniently be defined as traditional performances to which conventional symbolic meaning is attached by those who believe in them. A ritual is the prescribed order for performing a series of rites. This means that ritual acts are not explicable solely in terms of the practical effects they produce in some technological sense. If a rite is held by its practitioners to have practical effects, then these are deemed to be brought about by supernatural means. On the other hand the rationale of ritual acts, though commonly supernatural, is not invariably so. A graduation ceremony from an educational institution can, for example, be interpreted as a symbolic statement about the passage of students to a graduate status and it need not have any supernatural overtones. Note that this use of the term rite is distinct from that in ethology (*q.v.*) where it refers, *e.g.,* to the mating activities of species of fish, from which the elements of social prescription and symbolic significance are lacking. It also differs from the psychological usage where rite may refer to routines followed by obsessional neurotics, the elements of social prescription and conventional significance being similarly absent (*see* NEUROSES: *Obsessive-Compulsive Reaction*).

The analysis and classification of rituals has proved a difficult problem in social anthropology. At one time it was thought that a useful distinction could be made between magical rites and spells on the one hand and religious rites and prayers on the other. The historical development of this point of view is given in MAGIC, PRIMITIVE. A basic discussion of the significance of rites and ceremonies in all societies may be found under SOCIAL ANTHROPOLOGY: *Ritual Relations.*

See also references under "Rites and Ceremonies" in the Index.

RITES CONTROVERSY, a 17th–18th century argument originating in China among Roman Catholic missionaries about whether the ceremonies honouring Confucius and one's forefathers were so tainted with superstition as to be incompatible with Christian belief. The Jesuits were persuaded that they probably were not and could be tolerated within certain limits; the Dominicans and Franciscans took the opposite view and carried the issue to Rome. In 1645 the Congregation for the Propagation of the Faith, on the basis of a brief submitted by the Dominican Juan Bautista de Morales, condemned the rites. But after considering the arguments of the Jesuit Martino Martini, the same congregation in 1656 lifted the ban.

The continuing dispute involved leading universities in Europe, solicited the attention of eight popes and of the K'ang-hsi emperor, led to repeated intervention by the Congregation for the Propagation of the Faith and by the Holy Office, and occasioned two papal legations to China. By the end of the 17th century many Dominicans and Franciscans had come to share the Jesuits' opinion, but the tide in Rome was against them. In a decree of 1704, reinforced in 1715 by the bull *Ex illa die,* Clement XI banned the rites. Benedict XIV in 1742 reaffirmed the prohibition and forbade further debate.

Almost two centuries later the Holy See reexamined the question. A decree of Dec. 8, 1939, authorized Christians to take part in ceremonies honouring Confucius and to observe the ancestral rites.

BIBLIOGRAPHY.—For the origins of the controversy, *see* George H. Dunne, S.J., *Generation of Giants* (1962); for the history, Ludwig Pastor, *The History of the Popes,* Eng. tr. by Dom Ernest Graf, O.S.B., vol. xxxiii (1941); J. Brucker, "Chinois (Rites)," in *Dictionnaire de théologie catholique,* tome ii (1905); Henri Bernard-Maitre, S.J., "Chinois (Rites)," in *Dictionnaire d'histoire et de géographie ecclésiastiques,* tome xii (1953); for bibliography of polemical literature, Robert Streit, O.M.I., and Johannes Dindinger, O.M.I., *Bibliotheca Missionum,* vol. v and vii (1929, 1931); for Chinese documents (with translations), Antonio Sisto Rosso, O.F.M., *Apostolic Legations to China of the Eighteenth Century* (1948); for the decree of 1939, Streit, *op. cit.,* vol. xiv.   (G. H. DU.)

RITSCHL, ALBRECHT (1822–1889), German theologian whose views influenced a generation of Protestant historians, was born in Berlin on March 25, 1822, the son of an evangelical church superintendent and bishop of Pomerania. He studied at Bonn, Halle, Heidelberg, and Tübingen, and taught theology at the universities of Bonn, 1846–64, and Göttingen, from 1864 until his death on March 20, 1889. Among his principal works are: *Die christliche Lehre von der Rechtfertigung und Versöhnung* (three volumes, 1870–74; 3rd edition 1888–89; English translation of volume i, 1872; of volume iii, 1900); *Die Geschichte des Pietismus* (three volumes, 1880–86); *Unterricht in der christlichen Religion* (1875; 3rd edition 1886); *Theologie und Metaphysik* (1881; 2nd edition 1887).

Ritschl's youthful biblical conservatism was shaken by the Hegelianism of the Tübingen theologian Ferdinand Christian Baur (*q.v.*). In his earliest writings he agreed with Baur that Christianity is a historical development of perfectly logical pattern rather than a dogma once and for all revealed. By the time of the second edition of his work on the origin of the old catholic church (*Die Entstehung der altkatholischen Kirche,* 1857), he had abandoned this position completely. Henceforth he refused to force the results of historical research into preconceived speculative patterns. He thought that the New Testament history of Jesus Christ, viewed simply as history and not as miracle, can lead to a practical rather than speculative judgment affirming Jesus' divine mission. Ritschl's was a theology of revelation based on this unity of history and practical-moral or faith judgment. Heavily dependent on Kant, Ritschl understood religion as the triumph of the spirit (or moral agent) over man's natural origins and surroundings. He rejected for use in theology what he understood to be the impersonal generalizations of metaphysics and the natural sciences. The mystical or intuitive elements of the reli-

gious life were also completely foreign to his activist outlook: the goal of Christian life, he maintained, is work in and for the Kingdom of God. With Friedrich Schleiermacher (*q.v.*), from whose sensitive, aesthetic mode of thought he otherwise diverged, Ritschl shared the belief that for Christianity God is not known as self-existent; he is known only insofar as he conditions human trust in his self-revelation through Christ.

Ritschl's theology was representative of an era that had little feeling for the element of mystery in religion and no dread of a divine judgment. His effort to maintain a theology of revelation but to do so without the faith in miracles underlying the older dogma was bitterly attacked by both liberal and conservative critics. He claimed for theology the status of a properly self-contained and specialized technical discipline among many other such disciplines. For this and other reasons he failed to do justice to the subtle interweaving of Christianity with general human history and culture. His followers included such diverse figures as Julius Kaftan, Wilhelm Herrmann, Ferdinand Kattenbusch, Friedrich Loofs, and Adolf von Harnack.

BIBLIOGRAPHY.—O. Ritschl, *Albrecht Ritschls Leben,* 2 vol. (1896); A. E. Garvie, *The Ritschlian Theology* (1899); A. T. Swing, *The Theology of Albrecht Ritschl* (1901); J. Orr, *Ritschlianism: Expository and Critical Essays* (1903); F. Kattenbusch, *Die deutsche evangelische Theologie seit Schleiermacher* (1924); H. R. Mackintosh, *Types of Modern Theology* (1937); K. Barth, *From Rousseau to Ritschl* (1959).   (H. W. FR.)

RITSCHL, FRIEDRICH WILHELM (1806–1876), German classical scholar, known for his work on Plautus and as the founder of the "Bonn" school of classical scholarship (*q.v.*), was born at Grossvargula, near Erfurt, on April 6, 1806. After studying at Leipzig and Halle, he held professorships at Halle (1832–33) and Breslau (1833–39). As professor of Latin at Bonn (1839–65) he attracted many talented students and gave a new impulse to Latin studies in Germany. He left after an academic quarrel with his colleague, Otto Jahn, and spent the rest of his life as professor at Leipzig, where he died on Nov. 9, 1876.

Though active in Greek studies, Ritschl was primarily a Latin scholar. Inspired by the textual criticism of Richard Bentley and Gottfried Hermann, he early determined to lay the scholarly foundation for a new understanding of archaic Latin. He aimed at a new critical edition, based on new manuscript evidence, of the largest surviving body of early Latin literature, Plautus' comedies. Ritschl edited nine plays of Plautus (4 vol. 1848–54, 2nd ed. 1872–1902; with important prolegomena), and then returned to the task more congenial to him: the study of the preliminary problems that impede the progress of an editor of Plautus. The complete text of Plautus (4 vol. 1871–94) contained only one play, the *Trinummus,* prepared by Ritschl for the final edition, the rest being edited or re-edited by his pupils and collaborators. His contribution to classical studies, therefore, lies chiefly in his numerous papers on early Latin grammar and metre, and on the manuscript tradition of Plautus, collected with other studies, in his *Opuscula philologica* (5 vol. 1867–79). Ritschl was also one of the founders of modern epigraphy: with T. Mommsen he published *Priscae Latinitatis monumenta epigraphica* (1862), an edition of the earliest Latin inscriptions.

BIBLIOGRAPHY.—J. E. Sandys, *History of Classical Scholarship,* vol. 3, pp. 139–142 (1908); O. Ribbeck, *F. W. Ritschl,* 2 vol. (1879–81); L. Müller, *F. Ritschl* (1878); U. von Wilamowitz-Möllendorff, *Geschichte der Philologie* (1921).   (C. O. BR.)

RITTENHOUSE, DAVID (1732–1796), U.S. astronomer, who introduced in 1786 the use of spider lines in the focus of a transit instrument. He was born at Germantown, Pa., on April 8, 1732. First a watchmaker and mechanician, he afterward was treasurer of Pennsylvania (1777–89), and from 1792 to 1795 director of the U.S. mint (Philadelphia).

He was a fellow of the Royal Society of London, and a member, and in 1791 president, of the American Philosophical Society. His researches were published in the *Transactions of the American Philosophical Society* (1785–99). He died at Philadelphia on June 26, 1796.

RITTER, CARL (1779–1859), German geographer and, with Alexander von Humboldt, the joint founder of modern geographical science, was born at Quedlinburg on Aug. 7, 1779. As a boy at the famous school of Schnepfenthal he came under important teachers such as Christian Salzmann and Johann Guts Muths and was later influenced by J. H. Pestalozzi (*q.v.*). After two years at Halle University Ritter was from 1798 to 1815 tutor to the family of the bankers Bethmann Hollweg at Frankfurt am Main, traveling with his pupils in Germany, Switzerland, and Italy and visiting the universities of Geneva and Göttingen.

Pestalozzi's educational principles and the ideas of J. G. Herder (*q.v.*) on the relations between mankind and its environment led Ritter to geographical teaching and philosophy. He regarded natural history, human history, and geography as an inseparable complex and laid the foundations of human geography.

At Göttingen he wrote *Die Erdkunde im Verhältnis zur Natur und zur Geschichte des Menschen* (two volumes, 1817–18). In 1819 he taught history and geography at a Frankfurt high school, becoming in 1820 professor of geography at the University of Berlin, where he remained till his death. The second edition of his *Erdkunde* (1822–58) was on a larger scale, but it covered only Africa and Asia. His work is a regional geography and cultural history. In contrast to the geographical compendiums of the 18th century, and also to the so-called pure geography which sought to exclude political boundaries and human activities, Ritter's new concept paid regard to natural regions and the influence of human history in them. The earth was for Ritter an organism, its continents and countries individual units linked by the functional relations of their elements. In his devout Protestantism he saw his scientific activity as in the creator's service and the earth as a divine establishment for man's education. His teleology, later much criticized, was an amalgam of his pedagogic, historical, and geographical thought. Ritter died in Berlin on Sept. 28, 1859, a few months after Humboldt.

See also GEOGRAPHY: *Development of Geographic Concepts: Humboldt and Ritter.*

BIBLIOGRAPHY.—G. Kramer, *Carl Ritter, ein Lebensbild,* 2nd ed. (1875); W. L. Gage, *Life of Carl Ritter* (1867); H. Schmitthenner, *Studien über Carl Ritter* (1951); G. R. Crone, "Karl Ritter," in *Modern Geographers* (1951); E. Plewe *et al.,* "Carl Ritter zum Gedächtnis," *Erde, Berl.,* vol. xc, no. 2 (1959).   (C. T. T.)

RITUAL MURDER: *see* HUMAN SACRIFICE.

RIVADAVIA, BERNARDINO (1780–1845), first president of the Argentine republic, was born at Buenos Aires on May 20, 1780. His education at the College of San Carlos was interrupted by the British invasion of 1806. In 1811 he became secretary to the revolutionary triumvirate and later was made a member of that body. To secure the recognition of an independent United Provinces of La Plata, and a Spanish prince to rule it, he was sent with two other diplomats to Europe and was partly responsible for the British acceptance of the United Provinces into the family of nations. Upon his return to Buenos Aires he was appointed, under Gov. Martín Rodríguez, one of the two ministers of government (state) and used his office to introduce reforms in the civil government and courts and to found hospitals, asylums, and schools, including the University of Buenos Aires.

Politically, he was a Unitarist, or nationalist, and in time became the party leader in opposition to the Federalists. He favoured the establishment of a monarchy with Spanish leanings. In 1826 he was elected president of the United Provinces of La Plata, which, a few months later, adopted a constitution for the Argentine republic.

From the outset the presidency proved to be an unhappy office. Not only was Argentina bitterly divided over the question of federalism versus nationalism, but it was also involved in war against Brazil concerning the independence of Uruguay, then known as Banda Oriental. Handicapped by the internal dissension, Rivadavia accepted the offer of British mediation and a treaty of peace was drafted which recognized Brazilian hegemony of the disputed area. The people of Argentina refused to accept that arrangement, however, and Rivadavia was forced to continue the war.

When the provinces declined acceptance of the proposed constitution, Rivadavia resigned his office (1827). In 1834 his political enemies brought charges against him in the courts, and without having been given a hearing he was sentenced to exile within 24 hours.

He went first to Brazil, then to Cádiz, Spain, where he died on Sept. 2, 1845. His remains were repatriated in 1857 and 23 years later his birthday was decreed a national holiday.

BIBLIOGRAPHY.—There is a wealth of material in Spanish concerning Rivadavia, among which may be noted C. Correa Luna, *Rivadavia y la simulación monárquica de 1815* (1929); A. Lamas, *Rivadavia; su obra política y cultural* (1915). In English *see* Ricardo Levene, *A History of Argentina,* trans. by W. S. Robertson (1937).
      (R. G. Rr.)

RIVAROL (ANTOINE RIVAROLI), called COMTE DE (1753–1801), French writer remembered mainly for the pithy, sparkling wit of the maxims and comments of his *Carnets* and his brilliant essay, *Discours sur l'universalité de la langue française* (1784). Born at Bagnols (Gard) on June 26, 1753, he was educated by and for the church, but forsook his ecclesiastical career and in 1777 reached Paris, where his erudition, wit, and talents as a conversationalist made him welcome in polite society. Though a freethinker and critical of Louis XVI, he remained faithful to the monarchy, campaigning against the Revolution in the Royalist press and in his *Petit dictionnaire des grands hommes de la Révolution* (1790). Prudently, he emigrated in 1792, living successively in Brussels, London, Hamburg, and Berlin, where he died on April 11, 1801.

Rivarol's political writings anticipate French 19th-century traditionalism and defend the social order whose tastes he reflected in his literary work. A dispassionate, acute observer, Rivarol caustically satirized contemporary writers, more especially in his *Petit almanach de nos grands hommes* (1788).

See *Oeuvres,* ed. by M. de Lescure, 2 vol. (1880); A. Le Breton, *Rivarol* (1895).   (O. R. T.)

RIVAS, ÁNGEL DE SAAVEDRA, DUQUE DE (1791–1865), Spanish poet, dramatist, and politician, whose fame rests principally on his play *Don Álvaro* which marked the triumph of Romantic drama in Spain. Born in Córdoba, March 10, 1791, he was educated at the *Seminario de Nobles* in Madrid and later fought gallantly in the War of Independence. Retiring afterward to Seville he published a first book of verse, *Poesías* (1814), which reveals the influence of Juan Meléndez Valdés and Manuel José Quintana, and a number of tragedies on the French classical model (*Ataulfo,* 1814; *Lanuza,* 1822). After entering politics he was condemned to death in 1823 for his extreme liberal views. He fled to London and lived subsequently in Italy, Malta, and France, where he earned his living by painting. During his exile he came under that Romantic influence which, already visible in *El moro expósito* (1834), was to triumph in his *Romances históricos* (1841).

Returning to Spain after the amnesty of 1833, he presently inherited the title of duque de Rivas and on March 22, 1835, staged *Don Álvaro,* whose place in the history of the Spanish theatre is analogous to that of Victor Hugo's *Hernani* in France. His later dramas are undistinguished. In 1836 he became minister of the interior under Francisco de Istúriz and in the following year was again compelled to flee owing to his conversion to conservative opinions. Returning in 1838 he entered the senate and was subsequently ambassador in Naples and Paris. He died, while president of the Spanish Academy, on June 22, 1865.

      (D. L. Sh.)

RIVAS, a small department in southwestern Nicaragua, lying between the Pacific Ocean and Lake Nicaragua; also the departmental capital. Area of the department 830 sq.mi. (2,150 sq.km.). Pop. (1963) department 64,361; city 7,721.

Most of the people are concentrated in valleys in the central part of the department. This area is important for livestock raising and the production of cacao, corn, beans, rice, and tobacco. The Inter-American Highway crosses the department from north to south, and branch roads connect the town of Rivas with San Jorge, a port on Lake Nicaragua, and San Juan del Sur, the second-ranking Nicaraguan port on the Pacific and a popular seaside resort.   (C. F. J.)

RIVER. A river is a natural stream of water that flows in a well-defined channel, course, or riverbed between the slopes of a valley. Small natural streams that flow in a temporary channel but not in a valley are called brooks, streams, or creeks. Rainfall and melting snow cause overland flow that is collected in small streams. This flow may be supplemented by flow from ground-waters, swamps, and, in mountains, from melting glaciers. Streams flowing together form a river that in the course of its advancement receives tributaries, rises in size and importance, and discharges into the ocean, a sea, or a lake.

In permeable soil formations, water may soak from channels into the ground, or in arid climates it may evaporate, the channel then becoming a dry riverbed for a part of the year. In karstic regions (*see* KARST), the river may run underground for a certain distance, *i.e.*, become a "lost river" and reappear somewhere downstream. The area of land from which a river collects water is called the river basin, the watershed, the contributing area, or the catchment.

Rivers, as essential elements of the physical geography, are studied in hydrology and geology. As boundaries between countries, rivers are a part of political geography and are treated in international law. Because of their influence on human geography and development of cultures, rivers are studied in the history of civilization. *See* GEOLOGY: *Physical Geology: Geomorphology;* HYDROLOGY. For the use of rivers today *see* DAM; ELECTRIC POWER; IRRIGATION; LAND RECLAMATION; POLLUTION, ENVIRONMENTAL: *Water Pollution;* RESERVOIR; RIVER ENGINEERING; WATER SUPPLY AND PURIFICATION; WATER TRANSPORT, INLAND; for particular rivers, *see, e.g.,* MISSISSIPPI RIVER, DANUBE.

This article deals with the physical aspect of rivers and their role in the development of civilization as follows:

I. Description of Rivers
   1. River Characteristics
   2. Major Rivers of the World
II. Surface Waters of Continents
   1. River Basins
   2. River Channels and Valleys
   3. Water Balance in River Basins
III. Climatic Factors of River Flow
   1. Temperature
   2. Precipitation
   3. Snow and Glaciers
IV. Flow of Rivers
   1. Seasonal Variation of River Flow
   2. Geographic Types of Rivers
   3. Floods, Mean and Low Flow
V. Rivers in the History of Ancient Civilizations
   1. The Yellow River and the Chinese Civilizations
   2. The Nile and the Egyptian Civilization
   3. Sumerian Civilization in the Valley of the Tigris and Euphrates
   4. The Ganges and Indus Rivers, and the Indus Civilization
VI. Rivers in the History of the Christian Era
   1. Western Civilization
   2. Russian Orthodox Christian Civilization
   3. North American Exploration

I. DESCRIPTION OF RIVERS

1. River Characteristics.—The size of a river may be determined by its length, by the area of the river basin, or by the amount of water flowing in the river, *i.e.*, the discharge of the river, the river flow, or the runoff. As a measure of river flow, the total annual volume of water flowing in the river may be used. As a convenient substitute to the total annual volume of water, this volume divided by the number of seconds per year is used, *i.e.*, the average annual discharge in the river per second. Units of measurements of discharge are the cubic feet per second, or cubic metres per second. The length of a river, the basin area, and the magnitude of the discharge are independent characteristics of rivers. The discharge supplied from a unit of basin area, for example from one square mile, is called unit runoff and is an essential characteristic of a river basin, expressed as $q = \dfrac{Q}{A}$, where A is the basin area upstream of the place where the discharge Q is measured.

The major rivers of the world are given in Table I below, beginning with the longest river of each continent and ending with rivers approximately 1,000 mi. (1,609 km.) long. Large tributaries are included in the table arbitrarily on the basis of available infor-

mation and taking into account their important or interesting features. Some rivers in geography are named beginning from the point of confluence of two rivers. Other rivers have the name from the source, but may have tributaries longer than the river itself above the point of inflow of these tributaries; for example, the Missouri River upstream from its confluence with the Mississippi is longer than the Mississippi upstream from the same point. Likewise, the Siberian river Irtysh, a tributary to the Ob, is longer upstream from the confluence than the Ob itself. When a combined length of a river and its tributary is given, the name of the river and that of the tributary is hyphenated.

2. Major Rivers of the World.—The greatest number of the longest rivers flow in the largest continent, Asia. The longest river in Asia is the Siberian Ob-Irtysh river system and of almost the same length is the Yangtze River in China; but gauged by the size of the basin another big Siberian river system, the Yenisei-Angara with Lake Baikal, is the largest. By the abundance of water, the magnitude of the discharge, the Yangtze is the largest river in Asia and the third largest in the world. None of these three river systems, however, has a unit runoff as large as do South Asian river basins: the Mekong River generates 1.9 cu.ft. per sec. (cfs) from a square mile, and the Ganges 1.4. The smallest runoff in Asia, 0.05, is in the basin of a northern Siberian river, the Kolyma; and the next smallest, 0.2, in the Irtysh River Basin in southwestern Siberia.

TABLE I.—*Major Rivers of the World with Tributaries*

Name	Length (in mi.)*	Basin area (in sq. mi.)†	Discharge (in cu.ft. per sec.)‡	Outflow
Africa				
Nile	4,157	1,100,000	90,000	Mediterranean Sea
Congo	2,716	1,425,000	1,400,000	Atlantic Ocean
Niger	2,600	580,000	250,000	Gulf of Guinea
Zambezi	1,700	513,500	300,000	Indian Ocean
Kasai	1,338	350,000	380,000	Congo River
Orange	1,300	328,000	12,600	Atlantic Ocean
Volta	710	139,000	—	Gulf of Guinea
Limpopo	1,100	170,000	—	Indian Ocean
Asia				
Ob-Irtysh-Black Irtysh	3,461	959,500	441,000	Arctic Ocean
Yangtze	3,434	756,498	770,000	East China Sea
Yenisei-Angara	3,100	1,003,000	614,000	Arctic Ocean
Yellow	2,901	486,000	116,000	Yellow Sea
Amur-Shilka-Onon	2,700	711,600	390,000	Tatar Strait
Irtysh-Black Irtysh	2,640	616,000	106,000	Ob River
Lena	2,650	936,300	530,000	Arctic Ocean
Mekong	2,500	313,000	600,000	South China Sea
Ob	2,287	1,431,000	441,000	Arctic Ocean
Yenisei	2,566	1,003,000	614,000	Arctic Ocean
Brahmaputra	1,800	361,000	530,000	Bay of Bengal
Indus	1,800	372,000	300,000	Arabian Sea
Amur	1,770	711,600	390,000	Tatar Strait
Euphrates	1,740	295,000	—	Persian Gulf
Syr Dar'ya-Naryn	1,660	84,600	15,200	Lake Aral
Kolyma	1,600	248,700	13,000	Arctic Ocean
Ganges	1,557	188,800	490,000	Bay of Bengal
Tigris	1,181	145,000	—	Euphrates River
Australia				
Murray-Darling	3,371	414,253	14,000	Indian Ocean
Murray	1,609	414,253	14,000	Indian Ocean
Europe				
Volga	2,292	532,800	286,000	Caspian Sea
Danube	1,777	315,444	220,000	Black Sea
Ural	1,575	84,900	13,000	Caspian Sea
Dnieper	1,420	194,200	59,000	Black Sea
Don	1,224	170,850	32,000	Sea of Azov
Rhine	820	85,000	78,000	North Sea
North America				
Mississippi-Missouri	3,860	1,243,700	620,000	Gulf of Mexico
Mackenzie	2,635	682,000	450,000	Arctic Ocean
Missouri	2,466	529,400	64,000	Mississippi River
Mississippi	2,348	1,243,700	620,000	Gulf of Mexico
Yukon	1,979	334,000	216,500	Bering Sea
Rio Grande	1,885	172,000	2,700	Gulf of Mexico
St. Lawrence-Great Lakes	1,560	390,000	360,000	Gulf of St. Lawrence
Arkansas	1,450	157,900	45,200	Mississippi River
Colorado	1,440	244,000	22,660	Gulf of California
Columbia	1,214	258,000	235,000	Pacific Ocean
Ohio	976	203,900	231,000	Mississippi River
St. Lawrence	320	390,000	360,000	Gulf of St. Lawrence
South America				
Amazon	3,915	2,722,000	4,200,000	Atlantic Ocean
Paraná	2,796	1,198,000	550,000	Atlantic Ocean
Madeira	2,013	—	600,000	Amazon River
Purus	1,995	—	—	Amazon River
São Francisco	1,987	252,000	120,000	Atlantic Ocean
Tocantins	1,677	—	—	Atlantic Ocean
Paraguay	1,584	—	160,000	Paraná River
Araguaia	1,367	—	—	Tocantins River
Orinoco	1,281	350,000	600,000	Atlantic Ocean

*1 mi. = 1.609 km. †1 sq.mi. = 2.590 sq.km. ‡1 cu.ft. = 0.0283 cu.m.

Next to Asia North and South America have the greatest number of large rivers. The second longest river in the world is the Brazilian Amazon River. Its length exceeds only by a little that of the Mississippi-Missouri river system, but the basin of the Amazon is the world's largest, more than twice larger than that of the Mississippi-Missouri river system. Particularly impressive is the enormous discharge of the Amazon, over 4,000,000 cfs, more than five times that of the Yangtze and almost seven times that of the Mississippi. The unit runoff, 1.5 cfs per sq.mi. in the basin of the Amazon River, is also large compared with that of the Ganges and the Mekong. Other large South American rivers, all of which run to the Atlantic Ocean, are among the largest rivers of the world. Little information is available on these magnificent rivers; even the values reported on the Amazon River are not absolutely certain.

The North American rivers are better studied and better known. The largest is the Mississippi-Missouri river system, which by its length and the size of the basin is the third largest in the world. The unit runoff of the Mississippi River Basin is among average values, 0.5 cfs per sq.mi. The next largest in North America by the length and the size of the basin is a Canadian river, the Mackenzie, flowing to the Arctic Ocean, and next is the St. Lawrence River, remarkable because the Great Lakes are part of its basin.

The longest river in the world is the Nile in Africa. The second largest river in the world by the size of its basin and by the discharge is also an African river, the Congo. The unit runoff of the Nile is among the lowest, 0.08 cfs per sq.mi., but that of the Congo, 1.0, is a very respectable quantity.

The Volga, the largest European river by its length and by the area of its basin, is only among medium-sized rivers of the world. Its remarkable feature, however, is that it flows into a closed sea, the Caspian. The large Western European river, the Rhine, is the smallest of the large world rivers by the size of its basin and the second smallest by its length.

The Murray-Darling river system in Australia by its length is larger than the Volga, but smaller in discharge than the second largest European river, the Danube. The discharge of the Murray is small, and the unit runoff is extremely low, 0.03 cfs per sq.mi.

II. SURFACE WATERS OF CONTINENTS

1. River Basins.—River basins are separated by the divide, the lines passing by the highest points of the land relief. The rainfall water flows down on land slopes from each side of the divide in opposite directions until it reaches the streams of adjacent river basins. The world continents are divided into several large and many small basins. The main divide of the earth separates the land into two large drainage areas: the basin of the Atlantic and Arctic oceans, and the basin of the Pacific and Indian oceans (fig. 1). The world divide passes by the Andes from Cape Horn at the southern tip of South America, leaving all major South American rivers in the Atlantic Ocean Basin, then by the Rockies to the Bering Strait, separating the western river basins of North America (among them basins of the major rivers, the Colorado, the Columbia, and the Yukon rivers, which flow to the Pacific) from all other North American rivers (such as the Mississippi River, the Rio Grande, and the St. Lawrence, which flow to the Atlantic Ocean, and the Mackenzie which discharges into the Arctic Ocean). In northeast Asia the world divide, beginning at the Bering Strait, follows the Siberian mountain chains, Anadyr, Gydan, Stanovoy, and Yablonovy, down to the Gobi Desert leaving all the major Siberian rivers (Ob, Yenisei, Lena, and Kolyma) in the Arctic Ocean Basin; and the Far Eastern rivers (Amur, Yellow, and Yangtze) in the Pacific Ocean Basin. From the Gobi Desert the divide turns east and passes by the K'un-lun Shan Mountains in Tibet, by Karakoram and the Hindu Kush Mountains and the Iranian Plateau toward the Ararat Mountain, leaving to the north a large area with internal river basins and rivers, such as the Syr Dar'ya River, discharging into lakes, and leaving to the south, in the Indian Ocean Basin, the South Asian rivers: Mekong, Brahmaputra, Ganges, Indus, Tigris, and Euphrates. From the Ararat, the world divide turns again south to the Syrian Desert and the Red Sea. In Africa it follows the Red Sea and the East African coasts southward to the Cape of Good Hope leaving in the Indian Ocean Basin only two major rivers: the Zambezi and the Limpopo; and in the Atlantic Ocean Basin, the Orange River, the Congo, the Niger, and the Volta. Because it flows in the Atlantic side of the world divide, the Nile River discharging into the Mediterranean Sea belongs to the Atlantic Ocean Basin, as do European rivers which flow to seas connected to the Atlantic, except the Volga River, which, discharging into the Caspian Sea, a closed body of water, like the Syr Dar'ya, does not belong to any ocean basin. In Australia, only one large river, the Murray, flows into the Indian Ocean.

2. River Channels and Valleys.—When water from rainfall flows over the land, it creates erosion in the soil and this results in an initial stage of the formation of stream channels, which by fur-

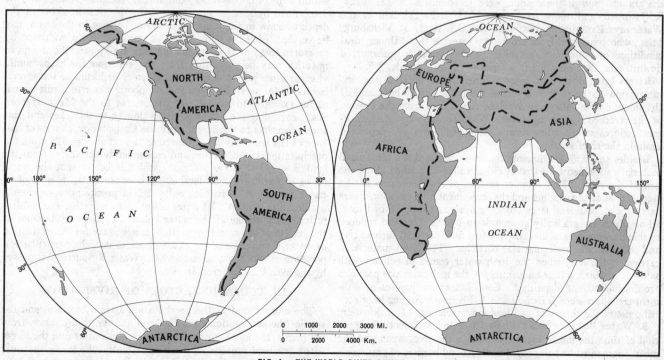

FIG. 1.—THE WORLD RIVER DIVIDE

ther erosion processes increase in size, join other stream channels, and in a later stage become river channels, located in lower portions of river valleys, depressions of the earth relief with a V- or U-shaped cross section formed in time and measured by geological epoch with longitudinal slopes steadily directed through the continents toward the sea. The slope of river channels follows the general direction of the longitudinal slope of valleys: In mountain regions steep slopes of channels cause highly turbulent flow and rivers appear as torrents; when traversing plains with gentle slopes of channels, rivers flow smoothly and the turbulence, still characterizing the current, may be noticed by an observer from the banks in the displacement of sandy particles moving in the river. The slope of channels is generally steeper at the source, milder in the middle portion of the river, and quite flat at the mouth. The decrease of slopes downstream from the source to the mouth is particularly noticeable in a river which has its source in mountains. During periods of low water a river flows in the main channel; in time of high water, the river level rises above the banks and inundates the lower parts of the valley, so that the flood discharge passes not only in the channel but on the adjacent lands of the valley. The mean velocity of water in the river channel is proportional to the square root of the slope of the surface of water. In an unobstructed channel with the surface slope parallel to the slope of the bottom the mean velocity is inversely proportional to the roughness of the channel expressed by a coefficient and increases when the depth of water increases. Formulas relating the velocity to these elements have been stated by A. Chézy and R. Manning. The outline of a river channel follows the general pattern of narrow valleys, which mostly have V-shaped cross sections, and may be highly winding; in large valleys of the plains with rather U-shaped profiles, the river is free to flow in the alluvial deposits of the valley bottom. The channel often is in a sinusoidal pattern, forming in places almost full circle, typically in the Menderes (ancient Maeander) River in Turkey, from which the word *meander* became descriptive for such rivers. The buildup of curvilinear patterns by rivers in alluvial channels was studied in the 1860s by L. Fargue by observing the Garonne River (see RIVER ENGINEERING: *Regulation of Rivers for Navigation: Removal of Shoals*). Besides meandering, a river channel as it develops may change its place in the valley or may divide in branches, thus building islands, as in the Mississippi River, or in the middle portion of the Lena River, which forms thousands of islands in its alluvial channel.

Among those who studied mutual interaction of the water and the granular soil of the channel were J. Thomson, N. Leliavsky, R. Jasmund, and, more recently in 1945, J. F. Friedkin of the Waterways Experiment Station of the U.S. Army at Vicksburg, Miss., who concluded from laboratory research that "Under ideal conditions of uniformity, an initial bend is perfectly transmitted downstream, thus resulting in a series of uniform bends."

Rivers bring down suspended sediments derived from the disintegration of the surface layers of the basin, of the hills, and of the slopes of the valleys by overland runoff, and from the erosion of the riverbed by flowing water. When the velocity of the current reduces many miles downstream, sediments are deposited again in the river channel.

Besides suspended sediments the river carries down large-sized material called bed load that is either rolled or pushed along the bed of the river. In the upper reaches of rivers because of the steep slopes of the channel and the consequent high velocity, rivers carry rocks, boulders, large stones, gravel, and sand as bed load, all of which are gradually ground down by the river and reduced to shingle, gravel, sand and silt, and to a finer material such as clay and colloidal and molecular size particles. The finest material is carried to the sea; when the fresh water comes in contact with salt water, which acts as an electrolyte, the molecular size particles are flocculated and deposited. Contributors to theories of sediment transport were J. Dupuit and A. Flament. Among later contributors to the theory of bed load movement was H. A. Einstein.

3. Water Balance in River Basins.—In a sufficiently long period of time the mean water income into the river basin and the mean outgo must be balanced if underground borders of permeable soils, which store the water infiltrated from the surface (the un-

derground catchment), coincide with basin divides. The runoff from the basin into the river, y, measured as discharge in the river channel, is the simple difference $y = x - z$ between the precipitation, x, and losses, z, by evaporation from the surface and by transpiration from plants. In high mountain basins, the melting of glaciers supplies water in addition to that coming from precipitation. The equation of water balance might be transformed to $\frac{y}{x} + \frac{z}{x} = 1$, where $\frac{y}{x}$ is the fraction of precipitation which provides the runoff, the coefficient of runoff, and $\frac{z}{x}$ is the remaining fraction, which is the loss, *i.e.*, the coefficient of evapotranspiration. In regions where precipitation is abundant the coefficient of runoff could be as high as 0.6; in arid zones it drops to zero; correspondingly the losses in precipitation are 0.4 in humid regions, 1.0 in arid, *i.e.*, in arid climates precipitation is entirely evaporated. If the groundwater is lost by subterranean passages into an adjacent basin or if it flows from another adjacent basin, the equation of water balance becomes $y + u_o = x - z + u_i$, where u_o is the outflow and u_i is the inflow of groundwaters in the basin. For a limited period of time—a year, a season, or a month—the water may be stored in the basin underground or by snow accumulation, and later be released. The equation of water balance then becomes $y + u_o = x - z + u_i \pm \Delta v$, where $+\Delta v$ is the water accumulated in the basin, and $-\Delta v$ the water released in a particular period of time. In cold climates the term $+\Delta v$ represents the water contained in the snow cover at the end of the winter. The quantities of water in the balance equation are expressed in terms of the depth of water in inches or millimetres. The amount of precipitation, x, is observed in meteorological stations, the value of runoff, y, is supplied by the magnitude of the river discharge obtained by measuring the velocity and the cross section of the channel occupied by water. By dividing the discharge expressed in cubic feet per unit of time by the area of the basin expressed in square feet, the depth of runoff, y, per unit of time, the mean for a long period is obtained. The evapotranspiration term z is most difficult to obtain. Methods of measurement of evaporation and of transpiration are extensively researched. Indirect calculation of the z term by various formulas is uncertain. The most recent method, that of C. W. Thornthweit, is more reliable than others in certain conditions.

The evaluation of the outflow u_o or of the inflow u_i of groundwater is made possible by installing a sufficient number of observation wells or boring holes; and, finally, the snow storage may be determined by a snow survey consisting in measurements of the depth of snow in the basin. The water balance in the basin may be verified using the equation if all terms of it are evaluated by measurements; or if all terms but one are known, the unknown quantity may be calculated from the equation for each month, year, or other period and for the given river basin, or for several basins, or for an entire large area supplying water to a gulf or sea, as for example, to the Gulf of Mexico, or to the Mediterranean Sea. Excluding the basins of rivers flowing to the lakes and seas without outlets to the ocean, as to the Caspian Sea, the water balance of the land may be expressed as the runoff $y = 310$ mm., the precipitation $x = 850$ mm., and consequently the losses from the land, $z = 850 - 310 = 540$ mm., which indicates that the world losses of water are considerable. Consequently the coefficient of runoff for the world is 0.36; only 36% of precipitation represents usable water, and 64% of water is lost by evaporation and transpiration. Knowledge of the water balance, particularly because of the growth of the world population, is necessary for the evaluation of water resources, and for planning water use, the particular importance of which was stressed by the Water Resources Act passed by the 89th U.S. Congress in 1965.

III. CLIMATIC FACTORS OF RIVER FLOW

The more abundant the precipitation as rain or snow, and the smaller the evaporation from the land and the transpiration from the plants, the more enriched is the land by waters and the larger is the overland runoff and, more importantly, the larger the river discharges. The climatic factors of flow are temperature, the amount of annual precipitation, the monthly distribution of precipitation, and its state, liquid or solid, as rainfall or snow. Consequently rivers are the product of climate. The relief of the land and the soils of river basins influence the character of river flow as well as the climate.

1. Temperature, because it regulates the evaporation and the duration of snow cover, is the first essential factor of flow. The temperature in some lands influences the amount of the annual flow and its monthly distribution more than precipitation does. Differences in evaporation with the same amount of precipitation may change the annual volume of river flow by a factor of three. A long period of temperatures below freezing determines the amount of snow accumulated in river basins before the spring thaw and consequently the volume of the spring flood caused by snow melting. A quick rise of temperature in spring to above freezing causes a concentration of the spring flood during a short time with high flood peak discharges, typical for such rivers of cold climates as in the rivers of the Russian Plain, Siberia, and Canada.

2. Precipitation.—The annual amount of precipitation varies from a maximum of over 3 m. (over 120 in.) in the tropics, as in Indonesia, and in mountains, such as the Alps, to a minimum below 0.1 m. (below 4 in.), as in the Sahara Desert or the deserts of Central Asia. The rainfall increases in mountains with a rate of 0.5 to 5 mm. per metre of altitude (0.06 to 0.6 in. per ft.). In the temperate belt of the Northern Hemisphere precipitation is near 1 m. in the oceanic climate on both sides of the Atlantic; it decreases to near 0.3 m. in the continental climate at the central parts of both North America and Eurasia. In the monsoonal climates of southeastern and eastern Asia, precipitation is the highest in the world, over 3 m. in Vietnam and Burma. Exceptionally high precipitation occurs in particular places in the tropics, 6 to 8 m. in Java and the Cameroon, and surprisingly high in mountains, 12 m. in the Assam (in the south oriental Himalayas). The average values in the large world basins are near 1.5 m. in the Congo; 1.2 m. in the Niger and the Yangtze; 1.1 m. in the Ohio; 0.9 m. in the Rhine; 0.8 m. in the Danube, the Mississippi, and the Nile; and only 0.5 m. and even less for the Dnieper and Volga; 0.4 m. for the Yellow, Ob, Yenisei, and Lena rivers. Besides the total amount of precipitation received by a river basin, the distribution of precipitation by months influences the total volume of river flow per year. The larger the part of the total annual precipitation during the cold season when the evaporation is reduced, the larger the part of precipitation transformed into river flow. Water supplied by precipitation in the warm season, when evaporation is high, is returned in large quantity into the atmosphere. The amount of precipitation and its seasonal distribution depends on circulation of the air masses in the atmosphere, which in turn is affected by the distribution of the land and the ocean on the earth. In the occidental parts of the oceans, such as the west coast of America and Europe, the largest amount of precipitation is in autumn and in winter, that is, the cold season; and the minimum is in spring and summer, which is favourable for river flow. The monthly maximum precipitation moves in the direction of the continent from winter to summer. The change in character of precipitation from the ocean to the centre of continents in the temperate belt may be measured by the coefficient of seasonal distribution of precipitation, C/F (proposed and used by B. S. Browzin), where C represents the average monthly precipitation in the warm season, and F that of the cold season. Coefficient C/F below 1 indicates oceanic type precipitation, as on the west coasts of England and at the mouth of the St. Lawrence River in Canada. East of Denmark and west of Lake Erie begins a continental type of precipitation with the values of C/F over 1.5; precipitation with a seasonal distribution factor between 1 and 1.5 is of a transition type from oceanic to continental. Eastward from the Ural Mountains and westward from Lake Michigan, the C/F factor is over 2, which indicates a pronounced continental type of precipitation; in eastern Siberia, in the basins of the Yenisei and Lena rivers, the same coefficient is over 3, which corresponds to ultracontinental precipitation; i.e., there is three times more precipitation in summer than in winter. The total annual amount of precipitation decreases correspondingly from

over 1 m. in Ireland to less than 0.35 m. in eastern Siberia. So not only the low total of precipitation but its unfavourable distribution contributes to a low runoff from a square mile in continental-type rivers, such as the Yenisei or Lena, as compared with oceanic-type rivers, as the Rhine, or the lower tributaries to the St. Lawrence. Due to a change in the type of precipitation, the unit runoff q changes by a factor of five in the St. Lawrence Basin, from 0.55 cfs per sq.mi. east of Lake Michigan to an exceptionally large value, 2.75 cfs per sq.mi. near the mouth of the St. Lawrence.

3. Snow and Glaciers.—Snow covers the plains in the cold climates of the temperate belt and farther to the north, and it covers mountains. The length of time plains and mountains are covered by snow, and the depth of the snow cover before spring, determines the seasonal distribution of flow in rivers of the temperate and cold belt. The relative amount of atmospheric water supplied to the rivers by rainfall and by the melting of snow may be determined by the snow coefficient, the ratio of the depth of snow water to the total depth of precipitation. The snow coefficient in the plains of the Canadian sector of the Great Lakes Basin ranges from 0.2 to 0.3; it averages 0.25 in the northern part of the Volga River Basin and in the Ob and the Yenisei, but farther east in the ultracontinental climate it drops to less than 0.2 in the basin of the Lena.

The snow coefficient is much higher in mountains; at 10,000 ft. (nearly 3,000 m.) in the Alps it is from 0.8 to 0.9, at 7,000 ft. from 0.5 to 0.6, dropping to 0.2 to 0.3 at 3,000 ft. The glaciers occupying large areas in the high mountains supply meltwaters to the rivers flowing from the mountains. At the maximum intensity of melting in the middle of summer, the flow of mountain rivers increases markedly.

IV. FLOW OF RIVERS

1. Seasonal Variation of River Flow.—Because of continuous day to day change in factors of flow, in temperatures, and in precipitation, river discharge changes daily. The daily discharge of rivers plotted against the dates of the calendar represents the hydrograph of the river for a particular year (see fig. 2). The river flow does not repeat itself identically so that the hydrograph of one year differs from another. Essential characteristics remain the same, however: the period of high discharges of rivers with large snow-water supply will always be in the spring and the period of low discharges in summer. The magnitude of the highest daily spring discharge or the highest discharge at any given time varies considerably from one year to another.

An average characteristic of river flow is the monthly discharge mean for the period of observation, Q_m. The monthly mean discharge Q_m divided by the mean annual discharge for the same period Q_y provides a monthly flow coefficient $K = \dfrac{Q_m}{Q_y}$ proposed and used by A. Coutagne, M. Pardé, and D. Sokolovski, which makes possible comparison of rivers with different magnitude of discharges but with the same climatic characteristics. The 12 monthly coefficients plotted from January to December represent a dimensionless monthly hydrograph, which is an index of seasonal flow variation. Of all elements of river hydrology (see HYDROLOGY) the seasonal

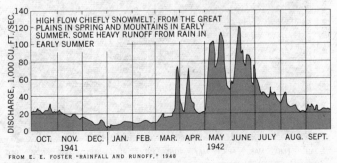

FIG. 2.—HYDROGRAPH OF DAILY DISCHARGES OF THE MISSOURI RIVER AT OMAHA, NEB., FOR THE 1942 WATER YEAR (OCTOBER 1941 TO SEPTEMBER 1942)

variation of river flow is the most astonishing, even to the least attentive observer; the seasonal variation, as represented by the graph of monthly coefficients K, shows most visibly the noncoordinate action of climatic factors and makes it possible to determine and classify the types of rivers.

2. Geographic Types of Rivers.—Types of rivers change from the subpolar to the equatorial zone, from ocean coasts to the interior of continents, and from the plains to the mountains. Depending on their geographic location and on the mean altitude of the river basin, rivers are supplied by water from different sources. In high latitudes the water is supplied primarily by melting snow, in low latitudes by rain, and in the temperate belt by a mixture gradually changing from snow to rain. If snow supplies 35–50% or more of the total yearly volume of runoff, the hydrology is of snow type. If the volume of snow water is below 35%, the hydrology is of mixed type. The type is defined as snow-pluvial if at least 15% of yearly runoff is supplied by melting snow, and as pluvial-snow if the runoff percent is below 15 but at least 5%. If less than 5% of river runoff is snow water the type is defined as pluvial. If glaciers occupy 15 to 20% of the basin area, as often occurs in the Alps, rivers are of the glacial type. A river may be of glacial type in its upper reaches and then downstream become predominantly pluvial. Consequently the seasonal variation of river flow is determined at a particular gauging station, upstream or downstream from which the seasonal distribution of flow may change. At each gauging station there is a particular hydrograph of K-coefficients. The shape of the hydrograph makes possible the determination of the source of water supply and consequently the geographic type of the river. The seasonal variation of flow may be illustrated as follows:

Snow-Type Rivers of the Plains.—In the plains of Canada, Eastern Europe, and Siberia, rivers are supplied predominantly by water from melting snow. The temperature is below the freezing point for several months; most of the precipitation is snow, which reduces winter flow. In summer, a great deal of precipitation is evaporated. The principal event is the spring high

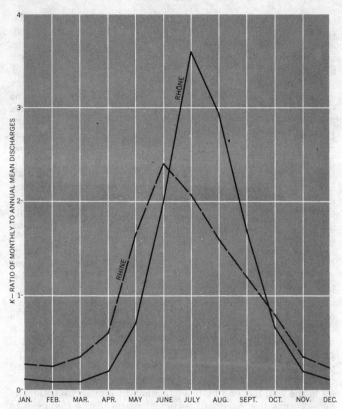

FIG. 4.—SEASONAL FLOW VARIATION IN MOUNTAIN RIVERS, THE RHINE, WITH PREDOMINANTLY SNOW WATER SUPPLY, AND THE RHÔNE, WITH PRIMARY GLACIAL WATER SUPPLY

flow lasting two or three months. Snow melting begins in large basins of the plains almost simultaneously, causing enormous daily discharges during the peak of the flood and large inundations in all rivers from the Dnieper to the Yenisei in Eurasia. The highest monthly flow coefficients are between 3 and 4 or more in these rivers (*see* fig. 3). A rise of flow is observed in autumn because of the decrease of temperature and of evaporation.

Snow-Type Rivers of Mountains.—In the Alps the season of abundant flow is the hot season when the snow melts intensively in the mountains (*see* fig. 4), the maximum flow coefficient in June being only near $2\frac{1}{2}$ as compared with 3 to 4 in snow rivers of the plains. The period of high waters is longer than in the plains; for example, in the Rhine River it is five months, from May to September. The period varies depending on the altitudes of different parts of the basin. In this type of river, after the summer maximum, the winter minimum flow begins.

Glacial-Type Rivers.—Intensive melting of glaciers begins later in summer than the melting of snow in mountains, and so the maximum of high water is one month later; in July in the Rhône River (*see* fig. 4) with its sources in the Alps as compared with the Rhine supplied by snow waters. The duration of high waters is less, four months in the Rhône as compared with five in the Rhine. The winter low flow is lower in glacial rivers than in mountain snow rivers.

Pluvial-Type Rivers in Oceanic Climate.—Because of heavy precipitation in winter, when temperatures and evaporation are both low, the flow in oceanic pluvial rivers is high, as is seen in the graph of the Seine River (*see* fig. 5). During the entire cold season beginning with the autumn, the rise of flow follows the gradual decrease of temperatures, becoming maximum with a coefficient near 2 in February and beginning to decrease in spring when the temperatures rise. The minimum of flow is consequently in the summer.

Pluvial-Type Rivers in Tropical Climate.—As opposed to oceanic pluvial rivers, tropical pluvial rivers have their maximum during the hot season, despite temperatures higher than in the oceanic climate of the temperate belt. The high flow in summer

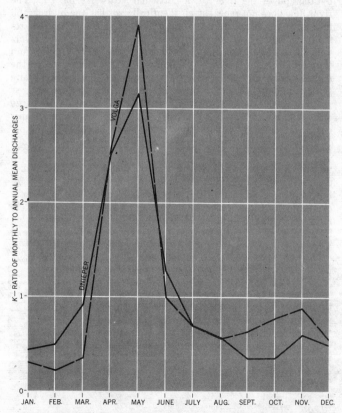

FIG. 3.—SEASONAL FLOW VARIATION IN TWO RIVERS, THE VOLGA AND THE DNIEPER, WHICH FLOW THROUGH PLAINS AND DERIVE MUCH OF THEIR WATER FROM MELTING SNOW

is due to the excessive abundance of precipitation which is not counterbalanced by evaporation; there is also a relatively dry winter. The tropical pluvial type occurs throughout monsoonal southeastern and eastern Asia with even higher flow coefficients, up to 3 and 4, than in the São Francisco River in Brazil (*see* fig. 5) where it is near to but below 2. The low flow in these rivers is considerably lower in Asia than in the São Francisco River, south of the Equator.

3. Floods, Mean and Low Flow.—Floods, the large discharges and high-water levels that exceed the capacity of the river channels, are caused by melting snow in snow-type rivers, by rainfall accompanied by the snow melt or glacial melts in mountain rivers, and by rainfall alone in any type of river. Floods cause destructive effects on human life and property and erosion in the river channel, and they may even displace the channel. Exceptional floods in rivers occur rarely, moderate floods more often; the study of frequency of the floods and of the duration of other river phenomena is done by methods of mathematical statistics. For protection from inundation by flood waters, river engineering provides dikes and dams with reservoirs. (*See* RIVER ENGINEERING: *Regulation of Rivers for Flood Protection.*)

If the fluctuation of the mean monthly flow from the lowest to the highest is near 18 times in a snow-type river such as the Volga (*see* fig. 3), or near 36 times in a glacial-type river such as the Rhône (*see* fig. 4), the fluctuation of the daily discharges measured by ratios of the highest to the lowest may be hundreds of times in some rivers.

For example, the most typical snow-type rivers of the plains, the Volga, the Dnieper, and the Don, have highly excessive ratios of high to low daily discharges. Nearly simultaneous thawing in 10 to 20 days in open portions of the basins and in less than 35 days in the forests, and thawing of enormous snow masses in the broad spaces of the Russian Plain accompanied by rainfall causes spring deluges in the Volga, Dnieper, and the Don. During one of the highest floods in the Dnieper, in May 1931, the discharge at Kiev was 812,000 cfs, as against the lowest observed flow at the same place of 7,400, corresponding to a ratio of high to low flow of 110. The Don at Kalach, near the connection of the river to the new Volga-Don Canal, discharged during one of the highest floods, in April 1917, 442,000 cfs, as against the lowest flow of the Don at this place of 1,500, with an extremely high ratio, 290,

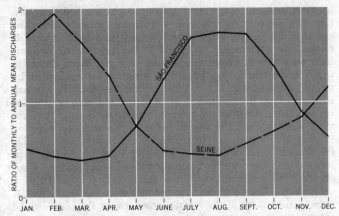

additional water is supplied by rains, the flood discharges may become enormous. The Mississippi River, which is supplied by rainfalls primarily and snow melting in the upper portions of the basin, generated in February 1932 a flood discharge at Vicksburg of 1,410,000 cfs, when the low flow at its lower reaches is near 90,000, and the ratio of high to low flow is near 16, relatively low because of the enormousness of the basin and the large tributaries draining areas of different climatic conditions that bring nonsynchronized floodwaters to the main river. Other exceptional flood discharges in North American rivers may be compared with their mean flow: the Arkansas discharged at Van Buren in May 1943, 850,000 cfs, nearly 19 times greater discharge than the mean annual discharge at its mouth. The Columbia at The Dalles in June 1894 generated a flood discharge of 1,240,000 cfs, five times more than its mean flow near the estuary. Because of technical difficulties, the flood discharges on large rivers cannot always be measured, particularly in remote places of industrially undeveloped countries; such flood discharges are estimated on the basis of more or less reliable data. From a study of the floods by Pardé, the flood discharges in some major rivers (converted to English units) are shown in Table II.

Extremely high flood discharge in the Yangtze River, caused by rainfalls of long duration over a large portion of the basin in the monsoon rainy season in August 1954, inundated several towns and the lowlands in the valley for a width of over 50 mi. (80 km.) near Hankow, including the city, and for a distance of 100 mi. (160 km.) upstream from it. Near Nanking the inundated lands stretched 40 mi. (64 km.) across from this flood.

An exceptionally high ratio, 11, of the flood discharge to the mean for a very large basin has been noted in the Yellow River. The terrible floods of the Yellow River result from rainfalls, as in the Yangtze, but are caused more directly by the situation of the river channel eroded in alluvial deposits located above the adjacent lands in the highly populated delta. The Yellow River discharged during a flood in August 1933 and again in 1942 nearly 900,000 cfs; by retrospective studies the discharge may have been 1,230,000 cfs in 1843, approaching the record Mississippi discharge of 1932 but for an area almost five times smaller.

TABLE II.—*Flood Discharges in Major Rivers*

River	Place	Flood discharge (in cu.ft. per sec.)	Approximate ratio of flood discharge to mean annual discharge
Africa			
Congo	Kinshasa	2,820,000	2
Niger	Koulikoro	420,000	1.7
Kasai	Kwamouth	880,000	2.3
Asia			
Yangtze . . .	Hankow	3,100,000	4
Yellow . . .	—	1,230,000	11
Brahmaputra . .	Gauhati	2,260,000	4.4
Indus . . .	Sukkur	2,400,000	8
Ganges . . .	Sara Bridge	2,450,000	5
South America			
Paraná . . .	Corrientes	1,650,000	3
São Francisco . .	Juazeiro	600,000	5

for a large river of the flood discharge to the low-flow discharge. The Don in its lower reaches almost yearly causes flooding across tens of miles in the lowland prairies. The Missouri, supplied by the melting of snow in the Rockies and heavily supplied on the prairies in its lower reaches by rainfall, is a river of mixed snow-pluvial character. Its high-flood discharge is 900,000 cfs and the low flow is 4,200 cfs, resulting in an extremely high ratio, 215, of high to low flow for a basin, three times larger than that of the Don.

The melting of snow in mountains occurs gradually, beginning in the spring from low altitudes at the foot of slopes and progressing higher with the advent of warmer weather, rising to the high mountain chains and to glaciers in the middle of summer. Mountain-type rivers with water gradually supplied from melting of snow as the Rhine, or by melting of snow and glaciers as the Rhône, generate only moderate floods in summer; but when

V. RIVERS IN THE HISTORY OF ANCIENT CIVILIZATIONS

River disasters caused by floods are only one aspect of the influence of rivers on the life of man. As ways of communication, rivers have beneficially influenced the life of peoples since prehistoric time. One of the oldest civilizations grew on the banks of the tumultuous and savage Yellow River, when man fighting the river achieved his first stages of cultural life. Why did the Chinese civilization grow on the banks of the horrifying Yellow River, which inundated and destroyed many settlements and killed people by the hundreds, when not too far to the south, the gentle and quiet Yangtze River, despite its occasional flooding, flowed in plains that seemed to invite man to dwell on its pleasant banks in pastoral tranquillity? Historians have asked the question: The answer may be found in the broad concept treating the causes of the genesis, birth, growth, decline, and death of ancient civilizations. According to Arnold J. Toynbee, ancient civilizations were born in environments which provided the challenge to which ancient man responded unconsciously but responded by action and achievements. If nature imposes conditions which are too severe, the civilization is not born, and man perishes or remains barbaric; if nature offers too mild, too easy an environment, man does not feel any challenge to rise or improve his existence; and likewise, in severe and too difficult conditions, his life remains stagnant and in a primitive state for centuries, or forever, until some outside domination invades his paradise. Consequently the optimum conditions are necessary for birth of a civilization. Those had been created by nature in the past glacial time, in the valleys of the world's largest rivers, the places where ancient civilizations were born.

1. The Yellow River and the Chinese Civilizations.—The genesis of Chinese civilization is found in the lower valley of the Yellow River (Huang Ho), where the challenge of nature, the marshes, bushes, and floods, capped by seasonal severe extremes of summer heat and winter cold, caused a human response, whereas the same race of people occupying the vast lands to the south and southwest of the river on the banks of the Yellow remained culturally sterile. As Toynbee puts it:

The great artery, the Yellow River, with its rapids and sandbanks, is dangerous to navigate; its innumerable branches wandered off capriciously across the low level places where there is hardly any fall. This was the country which was called the Nine Rivers, because, it was said, the Yellow River had there nine principal branches. It extended over a broad zone at the foot of the Shansi Plateau; for its course at that time was different from its present course, and it proceeded, after a long detour, to flow out into the sea along the present course of the Pei Ho in the neighbourhood of Tientsin. Adjacent land was too wet for agriculture, was covered with tall grassy vegetation broken by thickets of white elms, plums, and chestnuts. This was not real forest. The forests existed at the periphery at the hills of the mountains, in the east in the Shantung, on the west in Shansi and was the domain of the barbarians. In the earlier age of civilisation born in the Yellow River valley, dykes were built against inundation and lands protected by these produced millet, sorghum, rice and some wheat. All these lands were conquered by pioneers from the bank and from the waters. Dykes had had to be built as bulwarks against the floods, canals had had to be dug to drain the swamps and turn them into dry land. All these works were so ancient that the memory of them was lost in the fog of the legends. They were attributed to the heroes of remote antiquity. (Arnold J. Toynbee, *A Study of History,* Oxford University Press, 1948–61.)

That is Toynbee's narrative of the birth of the Chinese civilization.

Numerous reconnaissances undertaken during the 1950s demonstrated the lagging of south China behind the north. Evidence collected from over 150 sites along the lower Yangtze River showed that as late as the beginning of the 11th century to the end of the 8th century B.C., the inhabitants of the lower Yangtze Valley were centuries behind those of the north and had not advanced beyond a Chalcolithic Age. (*See* CHINA: *History: Prehistory and Archaeology: Late Neolithic of South China.*) The discovery in 1951 at Chengchow (Chenghsien) in over 20 localities of several archaeological horizons in the valley of the Yellow River led to the recognition of four Chang levels, the latest corresponding to 1300 B.C. and after. Thus, the sinologists believe that Chengchow was a large Shang settlement, indeed a walled city, whose flourishing period fell to the earlier phase of the dynasty, the period of the tenth Shang king.

2. The Nile and the Egyptian Civilization.—The oldest and greatest civilization of antiquity grew on another continent as man responded to the challenge offered to him by nature, namely the Egyptian civilization that grew on the banks of the Nile River in Africa.

When, following the Pluvial Age which corresponded in time to the Ice Age in Europe and North America, Afroasia began to dry out, the fathers of Egyptian civilization, in response to the challenge presented by the desiccation of the Afroasian steppe, mastered the valley of the Lower Nile. In *A Study of History* Toynbee says:

They took their plunge into the forbidding jungle-swamps because their former habitat in the neighbourhood was beginning to turn from a genial savannah into an inhospitable desert. The ordeal of transition to the difficult environment of the un-reclaimed river-valleys from the easy environment which the savannah had provided before desiccation set in was the dynamic event by which, in our view, the fluvial civilizations were brought to birth. We may now observe that the wilderness of the river-valleys, formidable though it was at the time when the fathers of the fluvial civilizations came to grips with it, was nevertheless not quite so formidable then as it must have been in the preceding period.

If we are right in conjecturing that the desiccation of Afrasia in the "post-pluvial" age was the challenge which impelled the fathers of the fluvial civilizations to descend into the river-valleys out of their former habitat on the surrounding savannah, then, *ex hypothesi,* the new environment which they were entering must have been tending to become easier at the same moment, and for the same reason, that the old environment which they were abandoning was becoming more difficult. For the process of desiccation which Afrasia was undergoing in this "post-pluvial" age was part and parcel of a wide-spread climatic change which was simultaneously melting the icecap in Europe, and therefore, *a fortiori,* it must have been at work ubiquitously throughout Afrasia itself—on the savannah and in the river-valleys alike.

The severity of the conditions in the swamps of the lower valley of the Nile in the glacial-pluvial age was excessive. In the post-pluvial time these conditions, while remaining severe, became milder; they came to an optimum stimulating the challenge for man to overcome the difficulties that the swamps of the Nile presented him. The ordeal to which the fathers of the Egyptian civilization exposed themselves when they plunged into these jungle swamps under the changing conditions of the climate administered a stimulus which evoked a brilliantly successful response, which is seen today in studies of the history of Egypt and in the remains of the Egyptian civilization.

The use of the Nile waters for irrigation required measurements of levels in the river. The Roda (Cairo) Nilometer constructed in the 8th century A.D. is the oldest gauge still being used for river level measurements. The maximum yearly flood levels recorded on this gauge were preserved as state documents because, according to old established routine, the annual land taxes levied from the cultivated area depended on them. Too low a level meant insufficient irrigation, while too high a level was accompanied by inundations. Thus, taxpaying capacity was a function of the river level, and this principle was reflected in a tradition of land-tax assessment, the origin of which predated the earliest recorded Egyptian history.

The history of Egypt shows that remains of Paleolithic man have been found on the gravel terraces bordering the Nile Valley; the settlements of Neolithic man were in the low desert bordering the swamps of the Nile Valley. The excavation of ancient dwellings and cemeteries of the Neolithic period disclose that period as well as changes during subsequent ages of man's development. Over a period of perhaps 4,000 years the Nile Valley swamps were gradually cleared and settled by a succession of peoples from Africa and perhaps from western Asia. A fusion of elements in time produced the civilization of ancient Egypt of the prehistoric period, when simple village communities gradually learned techniques of agriculture, domestication of animals, and manufacturing of stone and pottery vessels, and at the same time reclaimed the swamps.

Known from their tombs or epitaphs at Abydos are the names of eight kings of the 1st dynasty of the Archaic Period with its founder Mena, who supposedly united the southern and the northern kingdoms and founded Memphis as his capital.

3. Sumerian Civilization in the Valley of the Tigris and Euphrates.—At the same time that northern Africa was in the process of desiccation in the post-pluvial age, western Asia including the Tigris and Euphrates Valley was being subjected to the same uniform physical change. The reduction of the amount of humidity made the Euphratean jungle swamp, left uninhabited because of excess humidity in the preceding pluvial time, less difficult for man to reclaim. The ordeal to which the fathers of the Sumerian civilization exposed themselves when they arrived at the jungle swamps of the Tigris-Euphrates Valley under these changing conditions administered a stimulus which evoked, as in the valley of the Nile, the birth of a new great civilization. Had the same people come earlier to this valley to conquer the same jungle swamps, the severity of conditions during the pluvial age would have been repressive rather than stimulating. The necessary conditions, says Toynbee, "of 'mean' or 'optimum' severity," caused the creation of the Sumerian civilization, in the same way they had caused the birth of the Egyptian civilization.

As well as fighting the jungle swamp, the pioneers of the Sumerian civilization faced severe damages from the floods (*see* MESOPOTAMIA). Archaeologists find evidences of a particular flood of abnormal magnitude in thick layers of flood-deposited sediments of clays between the earlier and later strata with remains of human habitation on the sites of certain historical seats of the Sumerian culture. The flood caused exceptional calamity in the Tigris-Euphrates Valley. Because of its severity this flood was associated by archaeologists with the Deluge. The basin of the Tigris and Euphrates, like the basin of the Nile, offers to the historians a museum in which they can study how man transformed wilderness created by nature into prosperous early civilizations. The remains of the Sumerian civilization, dating back 5,000 to 6,000 years, are found at the confluence of the two sister rivers at the head of the Persian Gulf, which formed a common delta in times after the Sumerian period and even after the extinction of its Babylonian successor.

The oldest written language in existence, around 3100 B.C. in South Mesopotamia, was Sumerian. The first example of a temple that remained dominant throughout the ages, excavated at Tepe Gawra in the neighbourhood of Mosul, is the oldest known building whose walls were decorated with pilasters and recesses. Sumerian King Lugal-zaggisi founded the first empire, including Mesopotamia, by marching along the Tigris and Euphrates to the "upper sea," the Mediterranean. In 2400 B.C. En-Temena dug a canal from the Tigris to Lagash which still exists. Safe trade routes existed in the 19th century B.C. from Ashur along the upper Tigris and across Mesopotamia to the upper Euphrates.

4. The Ganges and Indus Rivers, and the Indus Civilization.—One of the earliest civilizations, the Indus, after the Egyptian and Mesopotamian (including Sumerian) civilizations, has been studied from vestiges found in the lower Indus River Valley, as well as over 1,000 mi. away in Simla Hills (*see* INDIA-PAKISTAN, SUBCONTINENT OF; and INDUS CIVILIZATION). The Indus civilization, which was literate, is assumed to have begun between 2500 and 1500 B.C. The existence of the Indus civilization was challenged by warlike highlanders descending from the southeastern escarpment of the Iranian Plateau upon the northwestern wing of the Indus River Valley. This resembles the pressure of the barbarians of the Shensi and the Shansi highlands upon frontiersmen of the Chinese world. The pressure on Indian frontiersmen by local highlanders was far surpassed in severity by pressure exerted by the barbarian nomads of the Eurasian steppes, who penetrated into India across the highlands of Afghanistan, invaded the Indus Valley, occupied the Indian desert beyond it and the Ganges Valley as well. The beneficial role of major world rivers in the development of ancient civilizations was handicapped in some instances, as in India, by the invasion of barbarians who followed the river valleys where the fathers of the Indus civilization had developed their dwellings.

The Indus civilization began in a similar fashion to that of Mesopotamia but evolved more rapidly and successfully than its predecessor, using particular skill to reap the advantages of the spacious and fertile valleys and controlling the formidable annual floods which fertilized the lowlands but tended to destroy dwellings. The most amply excavated Indus site is that of Mohenjo-Daro, beside the Indus River, with large blocks of buildings separated by wide streets and by narrow lanes, fortifications, and a citadel built of good baked bricks.

VI. RIVERS IN THE HISTORY OF THE CHRISTIAN ERA

1. Western Civilization.—Physical challenge in the postglacial epoch evoked Western civilization and the Russian offshoot of the Orthodox Christian civilization. In northern Europe and Russia, "the necessary conditions of mean or optimum severity were realized for the first time, when the post-glacial climatic change melted the icecap, and conjured up the north European forest in its place. It is under these new conditions of mean severity that a region which was formerly inimical to life has given hospitality to two great civilizations in the fullness of time," writes Toynbee (*op. cit.*). The post-glacial topography of this smallest continent, Europe, is cut by a network of small rivers with only two large rivers in the west: the Rhine and the Danube, and of several large rivers in the Russian plateau, among them the Dnieper, the Don, and the Volga. In the basin of these five great rivers and in a number of small rivers, two millenniums of the history of the Christian era have developed. In Western Europe in nearly eight centuries each successive dynasty that held power had its roots in the Rhine River Basin which was also the ancient continental march of the Roman Empire relegated eventually to the innermost interior of the expanding Western world. The Danube River Basin sheltered the centuries-old Danubian Habsburg monarchy.

2. Russian Orthodox Christian Civilization.—There is no better example, with the exception of that on the North American continent, of the unique role of rivers in the genesis, birth, and development of a civilization, than the Russian Orthodox Christian civilization. Transplanted from Constantinople across the Black Sea to the basin of the Dnieper, the Russian civilization was transferred in the course of the 12th century to the upper basin of the Volga, and penetrating then by the way of the Siberian rivers deeply into Asia, it reached the shores of the Pacific Ocean early in the 17th century, and completed its march onto the North American west coast. The challenge offered by nature on the Russian Plain, covered with forests and abundant with rivers, and the severity of a climate rigorous enough to stimulate the response but not detrimental enough to prevent it, met a remarkable response in the course of the second millennium A.D. by the fathers of the Russian Orthodox Christian civilization. The frontiersmen of this civilization, the Cossacks, from a single mother community on the Dnieper, reduced the nomads in the south and the east to military impotence by seizing the rivers. The rivers were formidable obstacles and were useless for transportation to the nomad horsemen, whereas the Russian peasants, lumbermen, and the horsemen Cossacks were expert river navigators. Thus it was by boat and not on horseback that they eventually won the domination of Eurasia. Descending the Dnieper, the Cossacks held the river line, maintained communication with Russian centres and cut the nomads' communication from river to river. The large tributaries, such as the Kama to the Volga and the Irtysh to the Ob, led the Cossacks from one river basin to another, where they established the parent Cossack communities as those of the Don River, of the Ural River in the 16th century, and later the Ussuri River, tributary to the Amur, in the Far East. The expedition of the legendary Cossack leader Ermak along the Chusovaya River, after crossing the Ural Mountains, led to the conquest of the Tatar in 1582 on the Irtysh River and the annexation of Siberia. In 1638 the Cossack exploration of Siberian rivers brought them to the shores of the Pacific Ocean on the Sea of Okhotsk.

3. North American Exploration.—The vast lands of the North American continent, like those in Eurasia, were explored largely by way of rivers. The bearers of Western civilization arrived from Europe on the east coast of North America and penetrated into its northern interior, first by way of the St. Lawrence River. The French seaman Jacques Cartier (*q.v.*), in a series of expeditions beginning in 1534, ascended the St. Lawrence up to Lachine Rapids, at the site where Montreal stands today. In 1603 a French geographer, Samuel de Champlain (*q.v.*), visited the Gulf of St. Lawrence and explored the St. Lawrence River again up to the island of Montreal. He then revisited the New World twice, founding in 1608 at the mouth of the St. Lawrence River the first white settlement in the north, where Quebec stands now, and in 1611 established the Mount Royal trading post, now Montreal. In 1615 Champlain ascended the Ottawa River, and, crossing the divide, reached Georgian Bay by way of the French River, and then crossed Lake Ontario. The missionary work by

Jesuit fathers and the fur trade stimulated further explorations which went along the rivers of the north. In 1671–72 Paul Denis, following the Saguenay and Rupert rivers and crossing the divide, reached James Bay. In the same year two French officers, Daumont and Greysolon, Sieur Dulhut (Duluth), reached Sault Ste. Marie and the Wisconsin River, the latter descending the St. Croix and the Mississippi. In 1673 Louis Jolliet and the Jesuit Father Jacques Marquette, both Frenchmen, followed the Fox-Wisconsin traverse from Green Bay and descended the Mississippi River, reporting the first accurate data of its course, up to the confluence with the Arkansas, and returned by the Illinois River to Lake Michigan. Nine years later, in 1682, René Robert Cavelier, Sieur de La Salle, another of the French king's noblemen, descended to the mouth of the Mississippi and claimed the whole region, which he named Louisiana, for France. In the 18th century notable expeditions were undertaken by other Frenchmen: by de la Harpe along the Red, the Arkansas, and the Canadian rivers in 1719–22; and by the Mallet brothers in 1738–39, who followed the Missouri, the Platte, and the South Platte into the higher plains and descended southwest to Taos and Santa Fe before returning to the Mississippi along the Canadian and Arkansas rivers. Between 1731 and 1744 Vérendrye with his sons explored Lake Winnipeg (which had been visited before them by Kelsey in 1690–92), and then went on to Lakes Winnipegosis and Manitoba, studying their relations to the major rivers of the region and mapping the upper Missouri.

While the French explored the hinterland from the St. Lawrence and James Bay to the Gulf of Mexico, the British and the Dutch ranged south and southeast of the Great Lakes and east of the Mississippi up to the coast. The British established Jamestown in 1607 and the Dutch occupied the Hudson River Valley following its discovery by Henry Hudson in 1609. In 1673 Needham reached the upper Tennessee and the Ohio rivers. In 1690 the colonists of Carolina reached the mouth of the Arkansas River and in 1692–94 Viele from Albany descended the Ohio.

The explorations (see NORTH AMERICA) by way of rivers in the 18th century concentrated in the northern territories of the continent after the French possessions (New France) were conquered in 1763 by Great Britain. Mackenzie (see MACKENZIE, SIR ALEXANDER) descended the Mackenzie River from Great Slave Lake to the Arctic Ocean in 1789. Four years later, in 1793, he followed the Peace River into the Rockies; traversing to the Fraser he descended to the Pacific. Consequently, at the end of the 18th century the river systems of North America except those of the far north became known in their general outline. Detailed studies of rivers are continuing up to the present, in view of their utilization.

BIBLIOGRAPHY.—E. E. Foster, *Rainfall and Runoff* (1948); M. Pardé, *Fleuves et Rivières* (1955), and *Sur la Puissance des Crues en diverses Parties du Monde* (1961); R. K. Linsley, M. A. Kohler and J. L. H. Paulhus, *Applied Hydrology* (1949), *Hydrology for Engineers* (1958); W. G. Hoyt and W. B. Langbein, *Floods* (1955); W. Wund, *Gewaesserkunde* ("Hydrology") (1953); *Journals* and *Trans. Am. Soc. Civ. Engrs.*; *J. Geophys. Res.* of the American Geophysical Union; *Water Resources Research*, journal of the American Water Resources Association; *Proceedings* of the General Assemblies of the International Association of Scientific Hydrology. (B. S. B.)

RIVERA, DIEGO (1886–1957), Mexican mural painter, was one of the leaders of the revolutionary movement in public wall painting that began in Mexico in the 1920s. He was born in Guanajuato, Gto., Mex., on Dec. 8, 1886. His politically liberal father early encouraged his son's artistic bent by providing him with a studio before he was able to read and by sending him to art classes at ten. Before 1906 Diego Rivera had studied under such Mexican masters as the romantic landscape painter José María Velasco and the French-trained classicist Santiago Rebull. He then went to Spain on a government scholarship, and at the beginning of the Madero revolution in Mexico, he made an exhibition at home of his somewhat conventional Spanish canvases. Between 1911 and 1920 he lived mostly in Paris, producing hundreds of Cubist paintings and drawings in a manner largely derived from the Spanish master Picasso—though his own work retained many easily recognizable objects.

After making a firsthand study of fresco painting in Italy,

Rivera returned to Mexico with a newly wrought classical and didactic style, graced with lyrical elements, and began to make his famous proletarian frescoes. In the early 1930s Rivera was the centre of wide political controversy in the United States. A mural he painted for the Detroit (Mich.) Institute of Fine Arts in 1932 was criticized as irreligious and his mural "Man at the Crossroads" (executed for Rockefeller Center, New York City), which included a portrait of Lenin, also was the subject of strong protests. The former was defended by Institute authorities; the latter was eventually removed and reconstituted at the Palace of Fine Arts in Mexico City.

Among Rivera's most distinguished frescoes were those painted at the National School of Agriculture, Chapingo, D.F., with its decorative studies of the nude figure, and at the Cortés Palace in Cuernavaca, with its stylized and bittersweet story of the conquest of Mexico. In Mexico City he painted the lyrically landscaped staircase connecting tall frescoed corridors in the Ministry of Education; in the National Palace he portrayed Aztec

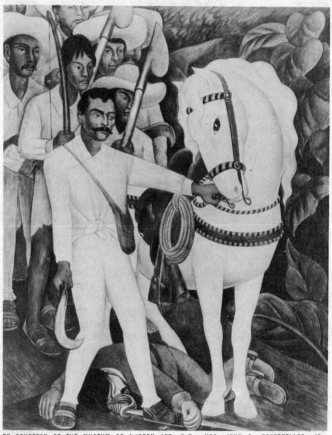

BY COURTESY OF THE MUSEUM OF MODERN ART, N.Y.; MRS. JOHN D. ROCKEFELLER, JR., PURCHASE FUND

"AGRARIAN LEADER ZAPATA" BY RIVERA IN 1931, A VARIANT OF A FRESCO IN THE CORTÉS PALACE, CUERNAVACA, MEX.; MUSEUM OF MODERN ART, N.Y.

history in archaistic forms and cold colours; and in the Social Security Hospital No. 1 he returned to his earlier lyrical style.

Rivera died Nov. 25, 1957, in Mexico City.

See also PAINTING: *Mexico and Latin America;* MURAL PAINTING: *20th Century.*

BIBLIOGRAPHY.—Diego Rivera with Bertram D. Wolfe, *Portrait of America* (1934); Bertram D. Wolfe, *Portrait of Mexico* (1937), *Diego Rivera* (1939); Laurence E. Schmeckebier, *Modern Mexican Art* (1939); MacKinley Helm, *Modern Mexican Painters* (1941). For periodical references in English and Spanish, see Bernard S. Myers, *Mexican Painting in Our Time* (1956). (MACK. H.)

RIVERA, a department in northern Uruguay on the Brazilian border; also the departmental capital. Area of the department 3,795 sq.mi. (9,829 sq.km.). Pop. (1963) department 75,826; city (1963) 41,266. Rivera has good pastureland and is noted for its sheep and cattle ranches. There is also an increasing amount of agriculture, with leading crops including rice, sweet potatoes, corn, peanuts, wheat, and fruit.

The city of Rivera is across the border from the Brazilian city of Santa Ana do Livramento, and the two enjoy an active economic and cultural interchange. (M. I. V.)

RIVER BRETHREN: *see* BRETHREN IN CHRIST.

RIVER ENGINEERING, in a broad sense, is the design and execution of works for the utilization of rivers and for the protection of adjacent lands from the action of river water. In a more narrow sense, it is the design and execution of works intended for the improvement of the navigation conditions of rivers and for flood control. The more important aspects of river engineering may be grouped under the following headings: (1) the prevention of river inundations and the mitigation of their effect; (2) the improvement of the nontidal portions of rivers for navigation by deepening the channels or by raising the water level by dams; (3) the improvement of river estuaries; and (4) works for the improvement of navigation in the tidal parts of rivers.

Other engineering works connected with the improvement and utilization of rivers are dealt with under separate headings, *i.e.*, water transport and power; water storage for supply for cities, industry, and irrigation; works related to fisheries, recreation, control of erosion, reclamation of land, and water pollution (*see* DAM; ELECTRIC POWER; IRRIGATION; LAND RECLAMATION; RESERVOIR; WATER SUPPLY AND PURIFICATION; WATER TRANSPORT, INLAND). *See* also articles on FLOOD; HYDRAULICS, APPLIED; HYDROLOGY; MECHANICS, FLUID; RIVER; TIDE; for particular rivers, *see, e.g.*, MISSISSIPPI RIVER, DANUBE.

This article dealing with physical characteristics of river channels and with river engineering projects, which vary widely in their character and object, is divided as follows:

I. PHYSICAL CHARACTERISTICS OF RIVER CHANNELS

1. River Channels.—A river channel eroded by the current depends on the flow pattern, which in turn is affected by the form of the channel. It therefore appears that the problem of the river channel contains the elements of a vicious circle.

A broader approach postulates that a process of mutual interaction exists between two mediums, water and granular soil, and that the channel formation due to such an interaction is controlled by certain general laws.

Among the authors who contributed to the discovery of these laws are L. Fargue, N. Leliavsky, R. Jasmund, G. Lacey, and E. W. Lane. One of the main laws established by Fargue in the 19th century is that the natural shape of a river channel eroded in an alluvial plain does not follow a straight line but shows a tendency to meander, and, even if it were made straight through artificial means, it would soon begin to serpentine again.

This law and others belonging to the same theory of river channels were essentially confirmed by modern experimental evidence. The experiments of J. F. Friedkin, of the Waterways Experiment Station of the U.S. Army, as reported in *A Laboratory Study of the Meandering of Alluvial Rivers* (Vicksburg, 1945), show that "meandering is essentially a natural trading process of sediments from banks to bars. . . . Under ideal conditions of uniformity,

an initial bend is perfectly transmitted downstream, thus resulting in a series of uniform bends. . . . The natural process might be likened to the oscillatory course taken by a ball which has been started down a grooved incline so that it oscillates. . . ."

The more uniform the configuration of the earth's surface, the nearer the river channel approaches the described meandering shape. Mountains and various other natural and man-made obstructions interfere with the formation of a natural river channel, causing local deviations from its ideal sinusoidal shape.

The velocity of river flow depends mainly upon the slope and the roughness of the channel. A steeper slope causes higher velocity, but a rougher channel decreases it. The slope of a river corresponds approximately to the fall of the country it traverses. Near the source, frequently in hilly regions, the slope is usually steep; but it gradually flattens out, with occasional irregularities, until, in traversing plains along the latter part of the river's course, it usually becomes quite mild. Accordingly, large rivers mostly begin as torrents with highly turbulent flow and end as gently flowing rivers.

2. Materials Carried by Currents.—In floodtime, rivers bring down a large quantity of detritus, derived mainly from the disintegration of the surface layers of the hills and slopes of the valleys by rain and from the erosion of the river bed by flowing water. Glaciers, frost, and wind also contribute to the disintegration of the earth's surface and to the supply of detritus to rivers. The power of a current to transport materials depends to a large extent on its velocity, so that torrents with a rapid fall near the sources of rivers can carry down rocks, boulders, and large stones. These are gradually ground by attrition in their onward course into shingle, gravel, sand, and silt and are carried forward by the main river toward the sea or partially strewn over flat plains during floods. The size of the materials deposited in the bed of the river becomes less as the reduction of velocity diminishes the transporting power of the current.

Since the earliest days of modern applied hydraulics (*see* HYDRAULICS, APPLIED) during the 17th century in Italy, engineering research has attempted to solve the problem of sediment transportation. Because sediment particles are generally heavier than the amount of water they displace, the Archimedes principle (*see* MECHANICS, FLUID: *Basic Relations: Buoyancy*) could not be used to explain the fact that heavy sediment was capable of being lifted and transported by flowing water. Another explanation was, consequently, required. The solution of this problem would also provide information on the means to be taken to control soil erosion and silt deposits in the channels of rivers. Twentieth-century research distinguishes, in this connection, between "bed load" on the one hand and "suspended sediment" on the other. The former is composed of the larger particles, which are either rolled or pushed along the bed of the river or which "jump," or saltate, from the crest of one ripple to another if the velocity is sufficiently great. On the other hand the smaller particles, the suspended sediment once picked up and lifted by the moving water, may remain in suspension for considerable periods of time and thus be transported over many miles. Various theories suggested to explain the phenomenon of sediment suspension include the following: (1) the belief of J. Dupuit and A. Flament that a rigid body transported by the flowing water tends always toward the region of maximum velocities, and, as the surface velocity is usually greater than the bed velocity, that a sediment particle, picked up from the bed, must of necessity rise toward the surface. (2) The conclusion of N. Leliavsky from numerous observations of velocities in rivers that the scour of a granular river channel and the lifting of its particles is due to convergent currents possessing a surplus of energy, while divergent currents have the opposite effect; *i.e.*, they cause suspended sediment to be dropped. (3) A third school of thought attributes the lifting of particles to the rising components of the crosscurrents.

II. REGULATION OF RIVERS FOR FLOOD PROTECTION

1. Mitigation of Floods and Protection from Inundations.—As the size of a river channel is generally inadequate to carry down the discharge of floods, the river overflows its banks in floodtime and inundates adjacent low-lying lands. An enlargement of a large riverbed, principally by deepening it, in order to increase its discharging capacity, is precluded by the cost and in some cases by the large deposit of sediment that would take place in the enlarged channel from the reduction in the velocity of the current when the flood begins to subside. Where, however, the depth of a smaller river has been considerably increased by dredging, the enlargement of its channel and the lowering of its low-water line facilitate the passage of the land water and consequently reduce the danger of flooding.

It is possible to restrict or prevent the inundation of some river areas by embankments, but occasionally low-lying lands are so unfavourably situated that pumping is necessary. The flow of water off mountain slopes can be retarded by planting trees on the slopes.

The most efficacious way of mitigating floods, however, is to reduce the peak of the flood by withdrawing some part of the natural discharge from the river. This withdrawal may be done either by diverting the flow in a low-lying depression or by building a dam across the valley of the river and storing behind it a part of the flood discharge. An example of diversion is the scheme of works on the Tigris and Euphrates rivers, in Iraq, part of which was completed in the early spring of 1956. The floods of these rivers have always been a major problem and have caused much damage to the town of Baghdad and the surrounding cultivated area. The Ramadi barrage and Warrar regulator were built to divert part of the flood of the Euphrates into Lake Habbaniyah, some of the water to be returned into the river during the drought season through the Dhibba outlet. In more or less the same manner, the Samarra barrage and inlet regulator were designed to divert the flood of the Tigris into the Tartar depression through a 41-mi. (66 km.) inlet canal. On the other hand contemporary river projects include flood control as a part of multi-purpose developments. The Tennessee Valley Authority (q.v.) projects furnish an example of reservoirs built for flood control and for several other purposes. Seven dams on the main Tennessee River provide a 9-ft. (3 m.) navigation channel from the mouth of the river to Knoxville, Tenn., and power stations built at these dams generate electricity. More than ten other large dams constructed on tributaries to the main river serve for flood control, power generation, and related benefits. The 726-ft. (221 m.)-high Hoover Dam on the Colorado River is another example of a multipurpose project, which includes flood control. In the United States, during the 25-year period ending in 1952, 300 projects were constructed in the interest of flood control, 77 of which were dams, while the remainder were local protection projects. The flood control project in the lower Mississippi Valley (see fig. 1) included five reservoirs, all completed by the mid-1950s. It has served its purpose well.

2. Increasing the Discharging Efficiency of a river within the limits of its bed depends on the fall and the cross section of the channel. The only way of increasing the fall is to reduce the length of the channel by substituting shorter cuts for a winding course. In the case of a large river, however, it is very difficult to maintain a straight cut because the current tends to erode the banks and form again a sinuous channel. Cuts therefore should be in the form of one or more flat curves. Nevertheless, where the available fall is exceptionally small, as in lands originally reclaimed from the sea, for example the English fen districts, straight channels have been formed for the rivers.

In the early 1930s a system of channel cutoffs was inaugurated on the lower Mississippi River. By 1941 they had demonstrated their worth by lowering river stages more than 12 ft. (4 m.) at Arkansas City, Ark., and 6 ft. (2 m.) at Vicksburg, Miss. Sixteen such cutoffs, combined with other channel shortenings, reduced the river distance from Memphis, Tenn., to Baton Rouge, La., by 170 mi. (274 km.).

3. Prediction of Floods may be interpreted in two different ways. It may refer to a definite flood, the levels and dates of which must be known beforehand in order to protect the riparian population, or it may designate the probabilities of the flood magnitudes and flood frequencies of a river, which are of fundamental importance in many design problems of flood control.

The only generally accepted solution for predicting a definite flood consists in establishing a number of gauges for recording the water levels in the upper stretches of the river itself and in all its affluents and, on the basis of observations made at these gauges, in calculating the magnitude of the flood. The probability of flood levels and their incidence can be solved by methods of mathematical statistics. Many advances have been made in applying these methods to fluvial hydrology since the early decades of the 20th century and more particularly since the beginning of the 1930s.

4. Embankments.—Earthen banks protecting inhabited river valley areas against inundations during floods are among the earliest types of engineering works. In Egypt, the left bank of the Nile, extending from Aswan to the Mediterranean, a distance of more than 600 mi. (966 km.), was begun in the time of the pharaohs, while the right bank was built somewhat later by Arab engineers. Since the very life of the country depended on these banks during floods, legend has it that some of the earlier rulers of Egypt ordered the engineer in charge of the maintenance of a bank to be thrown into any breach that occurred within his district. It has been suggested that the joint enterprise involved in building the long, tall banks necessary for the general safety must have been a strong incentive for the development of organized communal life and that it might have contributed to the rise of the great monarchies, such as those of Egypt, Mesopotamia, and China, where irrigation and hydraulic engineering were practised on a large scale.

Embankments have been adopted in other places also, where tracts of fertile alluvial land below flood level stretch for long distances away from the river. Thus the fens of Lincolnshire, Cambridgeshire, and Norfolk in England are protected from inundations by embankments along their rivers and drains; a great portion of the Netherlands is similarly protected. Along a considerable length of the Rhine are embankments built and continuously maintained by the German Federal Agency for Waterways Structures; and the plains of Lombardy are shut off from the floods of the Po by embankments along each side of the river for a distance of about 265 mi. (426 km.).

For such towns as New Orleans on the Mississippi and Szeged on the Tisza (Tisa) in Hungary, which were established below the flood level of an adjoining river, the channel of the river should be improved to facilitate the passage of floods past the town. The town also should be enclosed within embankments raised above the highest possible flood level.

A system of levee embankments was extensively developed along the Mississippi River in its alluvial valley extending from Cape Girardeau, Mo., to the Head of Passes in the delta, a distance of 1,014 mi. (1,632 km.) by river channel. The alluvial valley has a length in latitude of 600 mi. (966 km.) and ranges from 20 to 80 mi. (32 to 129 km.) in width, with a total area of 35,500 sq.mi. (91,945 sq.km.). It comprises the St. Francis, the Yazoo, the Tensas, the Lafourche, the Atchafalaya, and portions of the White and Arkansas basins, as well as the alluvial lands around Lake Pontchartrain (fig. 1).

These levees, begun by the French settlers in Louisiana in the early 18th century, were in 1735 about 3 ft. (0.9 m.) high and had been constructed from 30 mi. (48 km.) above New Orleans to 12 mi. (19 km.) below. From this beginning the system was extended until by the late 1960s it included more than 3,500 mi. of levees having an average height of 24 ft. (7 m.). The levees above Baton Rouge are roughly parallel to the river but have a width between them of from ¾ to 15 mi., thereby greatly increasing the cross-section area of the river in times of flood. Below Baton Rouge the levees follow the bends in the river but are set back from the river bank sufficiently to prevent undercutting by the current during floods. In some parts the spacing is much greater. The height of the levees had not been adequate during certain floods (before the record flood of 1927) that had a maximum rise at Vicksburg of 61.7 ft. (19 m.) above 1940 low water at that point. In 1927 the river at Vicksburg rose

3.5 ft. higher and 65.2 ft. above the low stage of 1940. The floods tend to increase in height due to the confinement of the river between levees. Breaches, or crevasses as they are termed in the United States, have occurred during extraordinary floods, but no crevasses occurred after 1928 in the lower Mississippi Valley.

The great floods of the Mississippi and its tributary rivers in April–June 1927 were particularly serious. They were due to the

extraordinary coincidence of flood conditions in all the chief tributaries of the river. Normally the eastern floods culminate between January and April, while the crests of the Missouri River floods usually enter the Mississippi in June. In 1927 the levees were breached in many places, and the floodwaters overflowed throughout the alluvial valley. An area of more than 23,000 sq.mi. was inundated, and 700,000 people were driven from their homes. Flooding was averted at New Orleans by cutting a gap in the levees at Poydras, a few miles below the city, thus permitting part of the floodwaters to take a short course of about five miles to an arm of the sea instead of following the normal course of the river through the delta.

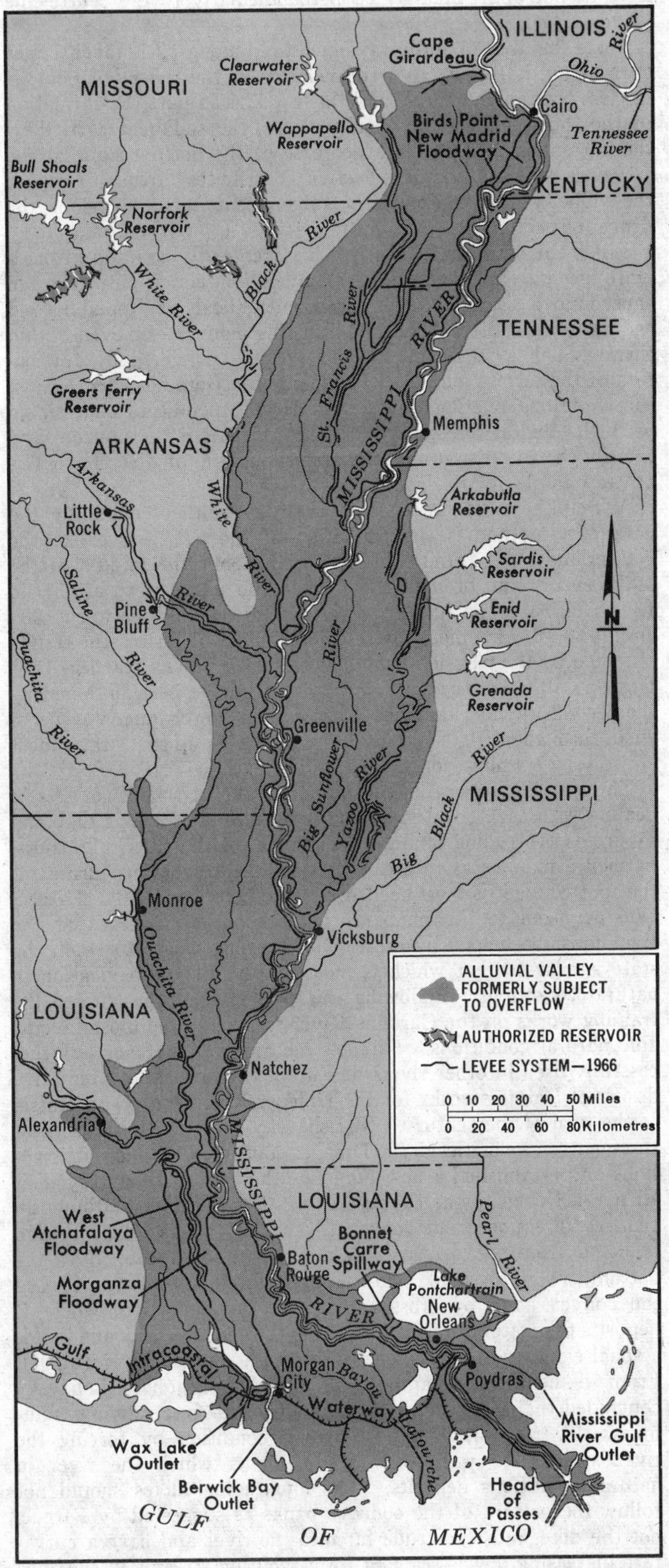

In January–February 1937, while the greatest flood of record was developing in the Ohio River, the conditions in the Mississippi River were favourable for receiving and disposing of this unprecedented discharge. The lower Mississippi was called on to carry a flood of more than 2,000,000 cu.ft. per sec. The improved levee system successfully held the water within bounds, except in backwater areas of the tributaries, which were not protected. The 1950 flood, which produced the third highest stage of record at Cairo, Ill., was safely carried to the Gulf of Mexico within the levee system and control works.

The unprecedented flood that occurred in April–May 1965 on the upper Mississippi River resulted in extensive damage to a five-state area, extending along the course of the river for more than 1,000 mi. from Minneapolis and St. Paul, Minn., to a point somewhat below Hannibal, Mo. At Muscatine, Ia., the flood crested at 24.8 ft., 8.8 ft. above flood level, and at one point, near Burlington, Ia., the river stretched 8 mi. wide. Some levees, such as that constructed in 1963 in St. Paul, withstood the flood, but most of the dikes along the river had to be bolstered with makeshift levees, many of which could not restrain the waters.

Levees and flood walls are also utilized for protection of municipal areas. After 1930 the United States especially developed many local projects of this type, designed to provide better protection for highly developed industrial and residential areas than that provided by the continuous embankment type. A good example is that for the protection of Kansas City, Kan., and Kansas City, Mo., located at the junction of the Missouri and the Kansas rivers, which provides for a combination levee and flood wall, pumping plants, construction of a river cutoff and a highway bridge across the cutoff, and alteration of 14 bridges across the Kansas River and 2 across the Missouri River.

III. REGULATION OF RIVERS FOR NAVIGATION

Because rivers form an important means of transportation, it is frequently necessary to increase the depth of the channel and thus permit larger craft to navigate the river.

Since a natural river channel constitutes a succession of deeps and shoals associated with its winding alignment, the removal or at least the deepening of the shoals is most necessary for navigation. On some rivers it is practicable to concentrate flow and fix the low-water channel by closing subsidiary low-water channels with dikes and narrowing the channel at the low stage by low-dipping cross dikes extended from the riverbanks down toward the middle of the river, sometimes pointing slightly upstream so as to direct the water flowing over them into a central channel. On some other rivers it is wise to raise the level by construction of navigation dams with locks.

1. Removal of Shoals.—There are two schools of thought concerning the removal of shoals. The first, traditional school maintains that the flow in a river is generally parallel to the banks, and therefore it suffices to constrict the channel by training works in order to cause the velocity to increase and thus to wash away the sand and silt forming the shoals. The second school postulates that the flow is not parallel to the banks and is itself the main cause of the formation of shoals and that neither the flow nor the shoals can be disregarded in designing training works. J. L. Van Ornum describes this second approach as "directing control of the current of the river."

Sinusoidal paths of rivers in alluvial plains—that is, meanders —are caused, according to some laboratory experimental evi-

FIG. 1.—MISSISSIPPI RIVER SHOWING PROTECTIVE ENGINEERING WORKS: LEVEES AND RESERVOIRS

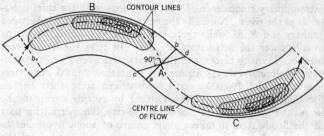

FIG. 2.—PLAN OF MEANDERS

dence, by transversal circulation in the stream observed even in rectilineal trapezoidal channels. The transversal flow in an alluvial channel washes out one bank and deposits the washed material downstream on the other, so forming S-shaped meanders, with a point of inflection, A, at their junction (fig. 2). The pattern of a meandering river may be visualized as a succession of such S-shaped elements. Beginning in 1868 L. Fargue, following his work for the improvement of the Garonne River in France for navigation and his observations and measurements of the geometric characteristics of the Garonne, formulated ideas, new for his time, regarding the behaviour of rivers flowing in alluvial channels. The six principles, or laws, formulated by Fargue dealt with relations between the shape and dimensions of the river meanders in plan and distribution of the depths in the river channel. The Fargue principles involve a three-dimensional correlation among river elements. Despite the fact that his conclusions were drawn from measurements on only one river, later observations on a multitude of other rivers confirmed the validity of the principles at least qualitatively. One of the facts established from the Garonne River investigation, known as Fargue's law, essentially states that the slope of the river channel is proportional to the curvature of the concave bank of the meander. The contour lines of the river bottom (fig. 2) show the largest positive slope at the points of maximum curvatures, at B and C, whereas the maximum depth is located downstream from the same points. Upstream from the point A the slope is negative, and at the same time the curvature approaching A becomes zero in accordance with Fargue's law. The depth of water within the limits of the curved parts of the river, at the concave side of the banks, is usually ample for the requirements of navigation. At the point of inflection A, the depth is small, ordinarily insufficient for navigation, and constitutes a technical design problem for deepening of the shoal at A.

Since the main objective in training a river is to permit navigation of deeper-draft craft, the attention of training-works designers has been concentrated on improving channels at inflection points. This aspect of training-works design is one of several problems where parallelist and nonparallelist principles are par-

ticularly in disaccord. So long as the flow is assumed to be parallel to the banks, nature's choice of the inflection point as a locus for silting and a centre for sand deposits appears rather arbitrary. On the other hand, the reason for these deposits becomes quite clear if it is realized that at the inflection point the nonparallelism between flow and banks is particularly pronounced, for the main current crosses here from one concave bank to the other, and the area of waterways measured at right angles to the flow lines is not ab (fig. 2), as the parallelist school would have it, but approximately cd perpendicularly to the centre line of flow.

Since the area of waterways measured along cd is much larger than at ab, it follows that the velocity at the inflection point is far less than in the curve, and this explains in part the formation of the shoal, for as the velocity drops, the sediment carried by the current is deposited. A decrease of the bottom slope at the approach to the point of inflection contributes farther to reduce the velocity and consequently to augment the amount of the deposited sediment.

While the traditional principle has frequently resulted in moderate general improvements of navigation conditions, it often caused much disappointment because new shoals developed beyond the limits of the reaches trained in this manner—or even within them. Such local troubles could then be remedied by application of the second method. The main objection, however, against the traditional method is the very large expenditure on training works located at the spots where they are altogether unnecessary, i.e., in the curves, where the natural depth of the channel is already ample for navigation.

A well-known instance of successful results obtained by the parallelist method is the regulation of the Waal River, in the Netherlands. The improvement began about the middle of the 19th century and brought the river to the state shown at Tiel in 1896 (fig. 3). The further works carried out in it between 1909 and 1919 afford a most interesting example of successful results obtained by the parallelist method as shown at Tiel reach in 1927 (fig. 3); although the same results might have been obtained by the second method at much lower cost. The channel was deepened, throughout its length of 53 mi., from $7\frac{1}{2}$ up to 13 ft., almost entirely by training works.

The solution advocated by the nonparallelist school consists in dealing with each shoal individually by means of a long dike and by groins protruding far into the channel of the river, like spurs, in such a manner as to create a convergent, scouring current at the spot where it is most needed, i.e., the inflection point. Fargue, who belonged to the nonparallelist school, postulated that the river must be helped by erection of training works to reach the state similar to that which is most favourable for navigation in natural conditions. Following this principle he constructed the training works on the Garonne River to imitate the most favourable natural conditions. Fargue's method was more or less successfully used in other rivers of Europe, as well as in a tentative design of training works for the Dnieper River (fig. 4) in Russia at the turn of the century. N. Leliavsky by a multitude of measurements of velocities in the Dnieper confirmed Fargue's observations and established a new fact, i.e., the flow in rivers is not at all parallel even to the concave banks, but the flow continuously changes direction from convex to concave banks. The stream reflected from the concave banks is directed downward to the bottom, scours the bank, and then is directed downstream toward the convex bank by crossing the point of inflection, where it deposits the material washed out from the concave bank and builds a shoal elongated in a diagonal direction across the river (fig. 4). From a new understanding of fluvial hydraulics, Leliavsky concluded that it is necessary to modify the river flow by training works to improve the navigation condition by forcing the river streams to wash out the sediments which the river in natural conditions deposits. The longitudinal dikes should not follow the pattern of the concave banks as suggested by Fargue, but the dikes must protrude far into the river and have a curvature increasing downstream to form scouring streams in the zone of the inflection point to wash out the shoals. The shape of longi-

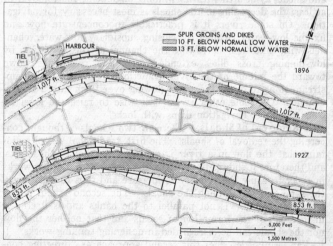

FIG. 3.—WAAL RIVER AT TIEL, NETH., IN 1896, AFTER REGULATION WORKS REDUCED THE CHANNEL WIDTH TO 1,017 FT., AND, IN 1927, AFTER REGULATION WORKS REDUCED THE CHANNEL WIDTH TO 853 FT.

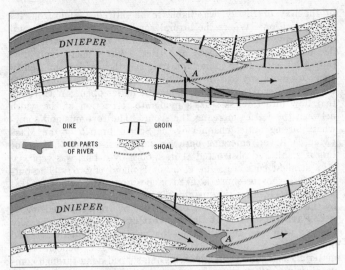

FIG. 4.—A REACH OF THE DNIEPER RIVER, IN THE U.S.S.R., WITH REGULATION TRAINING WORKS DESIGNED FOLLOWING L. FARGUE (TOP), AND THE SAME REACH SHOWING TRAINING WORKS ERECTED BY N. LELIAVSKY AT THE TURN OF THE 19TH CENTURY (BOTTOM) WITH THE OUTLINE OF THE NAVIGATION CHANNEL DEEPENED BY THE WORKS

tudinal dikes is an essential point of difference between Fargue's and Leliavsky's method. The second point of difference consists in the location of training dikes on one bank of the river at the given reach supplemented by groins, leaving the opposite bank in its natural conditions (fig. 4) instead of locating training works on both sides as suggested by Fargue. Leliavsky erected training works in many reaches of the Dnieper with relatively good results on most of them.

Where there is danger of flood, relatively low training works are used to minimize obstructions to the flow. Thus an almost free channel is left for the passage of the flood. Results of this type of construction were rather indifferent on the Rhône, somewhat better on the Rhine, and still better on the Mississippi above Cairo, Ill.

Various materials are used for the construction of dikes and groins. On the Rhône below Lyons the dikes are constructed of rubble, consolidated above low water with concrete. The dikes on the Rhine consist mostly of earthwork mounds protected by a layer of rubble or pitching on the face, with a rubble mound forming the toe exposed to the current, but occasionally fascines (bundles of wooden sticks) are employed in conjunction with the stone or simple rubble mounds. On the Waal the newer cross dikes have a core of sand protected by a mattress weighted with stone. The dams closing subsidiary channels on the Mississippi are almost always constructed of fascine mattresses weighted with stone; but whereas the regulating dikes on the upper Mississippi are usually similar in construction, a common form for dikes in the United States consists of two parallel rows of piles filled in between with brushwood or other materials not affected by water and protected at the sides from scour by an apron of fascines and stone.

2. Construction of Navigation Dams and Locks.—The modern trend in river engineering on large rivers with heavy navigation traffic is to increase the depth by raising the water level throughout the length of the river. The old Ohio River lock and navigation dam system completed in 1929 is an example of a river canalization (fig. 5). The 46 movable dams lowered at flood time provided a navigable depth of 9 ft. from the river source at Pittsburgh, Pa. Locks 110 ft. wide and 600 ft. long were built at the dam sites to allow ships and barges to pass the step between the low and high water elevations at the dams. A plan was proposed in 1958 to replace the old system with 19 new navigation structures that would include 110-by-1,200-ft. locks, larger steps, and a channel up to 12 ft. deep. The new system scheduled for completion in the 1970s would permit passage of deeper-draft vessels, reduce maintenance costs and shipping

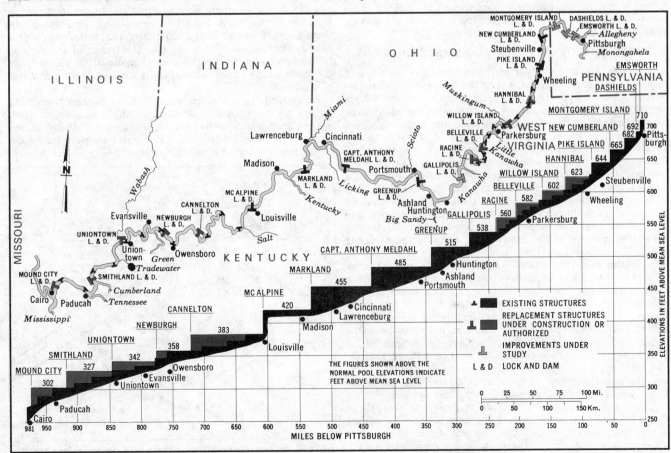

FIG. 5.—NEW AND OLD NAVIGATION DAMS AND LOCKS ON THE OHIO RIVER FROM PITTSBURGH, PA., TO CAIRO, ILL., MAP AND PROFILE

charges, speed river traffic, and ultimately further encourage industrial development throughout the Ohio River Valley.

The St. Lawrence Seaway at the time of its dedication in 1959 with its 27-ft.-deep channel and its 80-by-860-ft. locks provided the first deep inland waterway capable of accommodating the passage of about 80% of the existing oceangoing vessels from the Atlantic into the Great Lakes. The construction of dams to raise the navigable depth of the St. Lawrence also created a source of considerable hydroelectric power.

Navigation on the Volga River was also impressively improved by the construction of several large dams with twin navigation locks of about 90 by 900 ft. The system was designed to provide a channel adequate for 16-ft.-draft vessels from the Caspian Sea to Moscow when completed, and by the Volga-Don Ship Canal to the Don River and the Sea of Azov and Black Sea. The upper Volga dams and navigation locks were completed in 1942, those at Gorki and Kuibyshev in 1957, the structures at Volgograd in 1960, and the Saratov Dam was scheduled for completion in 1967. The last dam was planned for Cheboksary. Besides navigation facilities at all these sites, the power stations built were the largest in the world. The Volga River development, as well as the St. Lawrence with its power station of a capacity similar to those of the Volga, and the Tennessee River projects are typical of multipurpose, large investment projects, while those on the Ohio River are typical of predominantly navigational structures.

3. Protection of Vessels During Floods.—Vessels exposed to damage from floating débris and ice floes during high floods on large rivers, and on large reservoirs, can be sheltered in refuge ports. These are formed in a recess along the river under the protection of a solid jetty or embankment constructed parallel to the bank. There are numerous examples of such river harbours on the Danube, the Rhine, and other European and North American rivers. Many of those constructed in the vicinity of towns, as at Düsseldorf, Ger., are inland ports of considerable size. The need for refuge ports is particularly acute on the Don and Volga rivers, where internal seas have been created by building dams across the channels and valley of the rivers (*see* WATER TRANSPORT, INLAND).

IV. IMPROVEMENT OF RIVER ESTUARIES

Rivers flowing into the sea are often obstructed in different degree by drift of shingle or sand along the coast and by sedimentation of the material carried by the river itself. Rivers with a small discharge and with estuaries located on an exposed coast where the flow falls very low in dry seasons are completely closed by a continuous line of beach, any inland or tidal waters merely trickling through the obstruction; it is only on the descent of floods that the outlet is opened. In rivers that always have a fair discharge or a small freshwater flow combined with a tidal flow and ebb, the direct outlet is sometimes closed, and the flow is deflected parallel to the shore till it reaches a weak place in the line of beach, through which a new outlet is formed. Where the current keeps the outlet open, a bar is sometimes formed across the entrance by the littoral drift, reducing the navigable depth. (*See* HARBOURS; JETTY.)

1. Jetties at River Outlets.—The bar formed across the outlet of a river not heavily charged with sediment and flowing into a tideless sea can be lowered by carrying out solid jetties on each side of the outlet across the foreshore, so as to scour the bar by concentrating the issuing current over it. By combining slightly curved jetties with dredging, the depth at the entrance to the Swinemünde of the Oder River in Germany was increased from 7 to 27 ft.; the approach channels to the Parnu River, Estonia, and other rivers flowing into the Baltic were deepened by jetties; and the outlet channels of some rivers flowing into the Great Lakes were improved by permanent jetties and dredging.

In some locations, the littoral drift is powerful enough to divert the outlets of rivers from their proper position. The Yare River, Eng., for example, at one time was driven to an outlet 4 mi. south of its direct course into the sea at Yarmouth; and the outlet of the Adour River in France, because of the violent storms

of the Bay of Biscay, was liable to be shifted 18 mi. from its initial position. Where the littoral conditions are so detrimental for the river outlets, it proved practicable to fix as well as to deepen the outlet by means of jetties. Where such rivers flow into tidal seas, it is important to place the jetties sufficiently apart to avoid any loss of tidal influx, since the tidal flow assists the freshwater discharge in keeping the outlet open. With rivers that flow into tideless seas, a moderate restriction of the width between the jetties increases the scour. The tortuous and somewhat shifting outlet channel of the Scheur branch of the Maas (Meuse) River, emerging onto a sandy coast where the rise of tide is small and obstructed at its mouth by a bar, was replaced by a straight cut across the Hook of Holland (fig. 6). The outlet across the foreshore is fixed in position by fascine-mattress jetties (*see* JETTY), the maintenance of the depth at the mouth by the tidal and fresh waters being aided by frequent dredging.

2. Parallel Jetties at Deltaic Outlets.—Large rivers heavily charged with sand and silt, when the current is gradually arrested on entering a tideless or nearly tideless sea, deposit these materials as a constantly advancing fan-shaped delta through comparatively shallow diverging channels which convey the freshwater and sediment discharge into the sea. These deltaic channels deposit sediment in front of their outlets, forming bars which advance with the delta; their rate of progress seaward and the distance in front of each outlet are proportionate to the sediment load and discharge of the several channels. A channel dredged on the bar in front of an unimproved outlet of a deltaic river retains its depth for only a moderate period because of the deposit continually accumulating at the outlet.

The construction of parallel jetties, prolonging seaward the banks of an outlet channel, concentrates the scour of the issuing current on the bar at the outlet and under favourable conditions will procure and maintain an adequate depth for navigation. The requisite conditions for the success of this system are (1) a sufficient depth in the sea beyond the bar to allow for a considerable deposit of alluvium before the increased depth is interfered with; and (2) a littoral current carrying a portion of the alluvium away from the outlet. Both conditions retard the progression of the delta in front of the outlet and the inevitable formation of a new bar farther out. Thus the rate of advance of the delta in front of an outlet is proportionate to the size of the channel, and the length of the jetties required is proportionate to the discharge of the channel.

Experiments with a model, molded to the configuration of the estuary under consideration and reproducing in miniature, according to the Froude simulation law, the freshwater discharge passing through the delta into the sea, can furnish valuable indications of the respective effects and comparative merits of the different

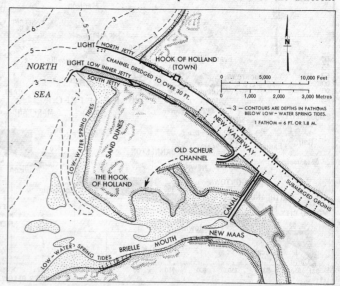

FIG. 6.—JETTY OUTLET OF THE MAAS RIVER INTO THE NORTH SEA SHOWING THE CUT FOR THE WATERWAY THROUGH THE HOOK OF HOLLAND

schemes proposed for works. For the purpose of studying the effect of the discharges of the Neva River, polluted by the wastes of the city of Leningrad, on the waters of the Neva Bay, a large scale model was built in 1967 of the delta and the bay by the State Hydrological Institute of the U.S.S.R. This study resulted in recommendations for erection of works for stimulating the self-purification of bay waters by directing the currents in the most effective way.

3. The Mississippi Delta represents one of the largest and most complicated deltas, being composed of numerous outlets and branches. In 1876–79 the South Pass outlet to the Gulf was selected for improvements by parallel jetties for reasons of economy because the Southwest Pass, which had a larger channel and a better depth over its bar, was twice as far at its bar from the shore as that of the South Pass (fig. 7). Fascine-mattress jetties, $2\frac{1}{4}$ and $1\frac{1}{2}$ mi. long, weighted with limestone and with large concrete blocks at their exposed ends, constructed slightly curved southward at their outer ends at the Gulf to direct the sediment-bearing current more directly at right angles to the westerly littoral current, increased the depth of 8 ft. over the bar in 1875 to 31 ft. The prolonged flow of the river produced by the jetties carried most of the heavier sediment into fairly deep water, so that the greatest advance of the foreshore in front of the South Pass occurred in the 70-ft. line of soundings, though the shallower soundings also advanced. Mattresses and spurs constructed to counteract shoals in the jetty channel reduced its width from 1,000 to 600 ft., and eventually the jetties were rebuilt on lines reducing the channel width to about 650 ft. While the outer channel was deflected to the east and narrowed by the alluvium carried westward by the littoral current, dredging was required to maintain the stipulated central depth of 30 ft. and the 26-ft. depth for a width of 200 ft. out to deep water. After 1901 the combination of dredging and increased discharge at the South Pass widened the channel across the bar to about 600 ft. and deepened it to a minimum of 30 ft.

In order to provide for the increasing requirements of seagoing vessels, the formation of a channel 35 ft. deep and 1,000 ft. wide through the larger Southwest Pass and its 9-ft. bar to deep water in the Gulf of Mexico was begun at the end of 1903. The discharge through this pass is rather more than three times that through the South Pass. Converging jetties, about 5,600 ft. apart at their land ends and about 3,000 ft. apart at the seaward outlet, were substituted for the parallel jetties constructed at the South Pass, and suction dredging was relied upon to maintain the channel between the jetties and across the sea bar. The amount of channel dredging was found to be excessive, and in 1916 the project was modified by limiting the channel to a width of 2,400 ft. between two parallel interior bulkheads and extending the jetties to the 30-ft. contour beyond the bar. In 1923 the width was further restricted to 1,750 ft. by building spur dikes, or groins, and by 1924 a depth of 35 ft. was secured by dredging and aided by the scour of the current. The jetties, formed of fascine mattresses weighted with stone and capped with rubble and concrete, were extended seaward from time to time. In 1956 the east jetty extended about $4\frac{3}{4}$ mi. from the shore, and the west jetty had a length of about $3\frac{3}{4}$ mi. The amount of dredging required to maintain the 35-ft.-deep channel through the pass and over the bar was reduced after the width was narrowed. By the 1960s the channel had been further deepened and maintained at the depth of 40 ft.

V. IMPROVEMENT OF TIDAL RIVERS FOR NAVIGATION

Whereas the size of tideless rivers depends wholly on their freshwater discharge, the condition of tidal rivers is due to the configuration of their outlets, the rise of tide at their mouths, the distance the tide can penetrate inland, and the space available for its reception. Accordingly, tidal rivers, even when possessing a comparatively small freshwater discharge, sometimes have much better natural navigable channels at high tide than the largest deltaic rivers, as shown by a comparison of the Thames, the Humber and the Elbe with the Danube, the Nile, and the Mississippi.

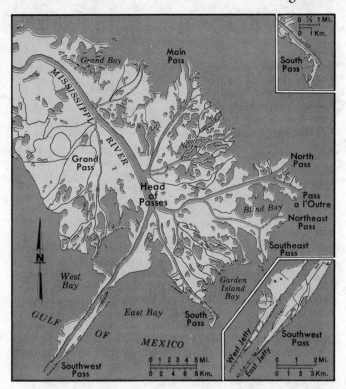

FIG. 7.—THE MISSISSIPPI RIVER DELTA SHOWING SOUTHWEST PASS JETTIES

Tidal water is, indeed, unlimited in volume; but unlike the drainage waters which must be discharged into the sea, it only flows up rivers where there is a channel and space available for its reception. The aims of all tidal river improvement should be to facilitate the flow of the flood tide up the river, to remove all obstructions from the channel so as to increase the scouring efficiency of the flood and ebb tides, and to reduce to a minimum the period of slack tide when deposit takes place.

1. Tidal Flow.—The progress of the flood tide up a river and the corresponding ebb are clearly shown by a diagram giving a series of tidal lines obtained from simultaneous observations of the water level at different points along the river. The steep form assumed by the foremost part of the flood-tide lines on some rivers indicates the existence of a bore. This is caused by sandbanks in the channel obstructing the advance of the flood tide till it has risen sufficiently in height to rush up the river as a steep, breaking wave, overcoming all obstacles and producing a sudden reversal of the flow and an abrupt rise of the water level. Such phenomena are observed on the Severn (U.K.), the Seine, the Amazon, and other rivers. Since bore indicates defects in the tidal channel, it can be reduced only by lowering the obstructions and by the regulation of the river. No tidal river of even moderate length is ever completely filled by tidal water, for the tide begins to fall at its mouth before the flood tide has produced high water at the tidal limit. Every improvement of the channel, however, expedites and increases the filling of the river, while the volume of water admitted at each tide is further augmented by the additional capacity provided by the greater efflux of the ebb, as indicated by the lowering of the low-water line.

2. Deepening Tidal Rivers by Dredging.—The improvement of tidal rivers mainly by dredging may be illustrated by the works performed on the Thames. In its natural state the minimum low-water depth in the Thames, according to a profile of the river bottom dating from 1836, was 27 ft. below Thames Haven located about 13 mi. from Nore Lightship; the depth was 17 ft. upstream of Thames Haven to Purfleet located at 32 mi. from the Nore Lightship, and the depth was 10 ft. farther upstream about up to London Bridge. After dredging, a channel 30 ft. deep at low-water ordinary spring tide was provided from the sea to King George V Dock, 37 mi. from the Nore Lightship. Farther upstream, the river was dredged to 20 ft. to about Millwall Dock and to lesser depth above it, decreasing to 14 ft. at London Bridge. Consequently the Thames was considerably deepened: on the length of about 24 mi., from the Thames Haven to King George V Dock it was dredged for 10 ft. below its natural depth and even more at the distance of near 10 mi. approaching the dock.

3. Regulation Works.—Considerable improvements in the navigable condition of tidal rivers above their outlets or estuaries can often be effected by regulation works aided by dredging. Examples of such works include those on the Nervión in Spain between Bilbao and its mouth, on the Weser in Germany from Bremen to Bremerhaven at the head of its estuary, and on the Huang-p'u Chiang in China from Shanghai to Wusung where it enters the Yangtze River estuary. These works resemble those on large rivers with only a freshwater discharge, but on tidal rivers the channel should be trained with an enlarging width seaward to facilitate the tidal influx.

To secure a good and fairly uniform depth on a tidal river, it is essential that the flood and ebb tides should follow the same course in order to combine their scouring efficiency and form a single, continuous, deep channel. In wide, winding reaches, however, the flood tide in ascending a river follows as direct a course as is practicable, and on reaching a bend the main flood-tide current, in being deflected from its straight course, hugs the concave bank. Keeping close alongside the same bank beyond the bend, it cuts into the shoal projecting from the convex bend of the bank higher up, forming a blind shoaling channel.

The average rate of enlargement of the width adopted for the trained channel of the Nervión in proportion to its length is 1 in 75 between Bilbao and its mouth; 1 in 71 for the Weser from Bremen to Bremerhaven; and about 1 in 73 for the Huang-p'u Chiang from Shanghai to its outlet. A divergence comprising between 1 in 70 and 1 in 80 for the regulated or trained channel of the lower portion of a tidal river with a fairly level bed may be expected to give satisfactory results. The divergence as originally laid down for the Seine training works, 1 in 200, was found to be too small. In rivers in which the channels are more or less in natural condition, such as the Thames, the divergence is nearly 1 in 50.

The training and dredging works carried out in the Huang-p'u Chiang after 1906 successfully deepened the alluvial channel to about 30 ft. at low water up to Shanghai, including the bar crossing in a wide reach between Gough Island and Wusung, where formerly the low-water depth was no more than 13 to 15 ft.

The general effect of deepening and regulating the tidal section of a river by dredging and the removal of obstructions is to facilitate the propagation of the flood tide up the channel and the efflux of the ebb. Consequently such works often result in lowering the low-water level and raising the high-water level in the upper part of the improved channel and sometimes above it. Thus the deepening of the River Tyne in England raised the level of mean high-water spring tides at Newcastle about 1 ft. and lowered the low water level by 2 ft. at Newcastle quay.

The average high-water level in the Thames at Chelsea increased 8 in. between 1890 and 1927, a period when dredging was carried out on a large scale in the lower reaches of the river. The maximum flood levels also increased steadily after 1874, when a tide rose 16 ft. 10 in. above ordnance datum (a horizontal plane from which water elevations and depths are measured) at Westminster, considerably higher than any previous record. This height was exceeded on several later occasions, including that of the disastrous tidal flood of Jan. 6–7, 1928, when 18 ft. 3 in. above ordnance datum was reached at London Bridge (equivalent to about 18 ft. 5 in. at Westminster).

4. Works at the Outlets and Through Estuaries of Tidal Rivers.—A tidal river flowing straight into the sea, without expanding into an estuary, is like a nontidal river, subject to the obstruction of a bar formed by the heaping-up action of the waves and drift along the coast, especially when the freshwater discharge is small. The scour of the currents is often concentrated and extended across the beach by parallel jetties for lowering the bar, as at the outlets of the Maas and the Nervión rivers.

Many tidal rivers in Europe flow through bays, estuaries, or arms of the sea before reaching the open sea, as, for instance, the Mersey through Liverpool Bay; the Liffey through Dublin Bay; the Thames, and other rivers in Great Britain; on the Continent: the Seine, the Scheldt, the Weser, the Elbe; and the Yangtze in China through their respective estuaries. These estuaries vary greatly in tidal range, the distance inland of their ports, and in facilities for navigation. Some possess a very ample depth in their outer portions, though they generally become shallow toward their upper ends. Dredging often suffices to remedy their deficiencies and to extend their deepwater channels. Thus the St. Lawrence, which possesses an ample depth from the Atlantic up to Quebec, was rendered accessible up to Montreal for large seagoing vessels by a moderate amount of dredging and farther upstream to the Great Lakes by the construction of the St. Lawrence Seaway.

Dredging was also required in parts of the Thames and Humber estuaries and on the Elbe below Hamburg to provide for the increasing draft of vessels. The Mersey bar in Liverpool Bay, about 11 mi. seaward of the actual mouth of the river, was lowered by suction dredging from a depth of about 9 ft. down to about 26 ft. below low water of equinoctial spring tides.

A remarkable improvement was effected in the navigable condition of the upper portion of the Seine estuary by training works essentially begun in 1848 and completed 100 years later, in 1948 (fig. 8). In place of a shallow, intricate channel through shifting sandbanks, whose dangers were at times intensified by a bore, a stable channel was provided down to Saint-Sauveur, rendering access as far as Rouen for vessels drawing up to about 20 ft. The channel itself, however, was originally made too narrow between Alzier and Berville and was subsequently enlarged, and large tracts of land were reclaimed in the upper estuary. The reduction in tidal capacity due to the reclamations, together with the fixing and undue restriction in width of the channel, resulted in large accretions at the back of the training walls and at the sides of the estuary beyond them, besides an extension of the sandbanks seaward.

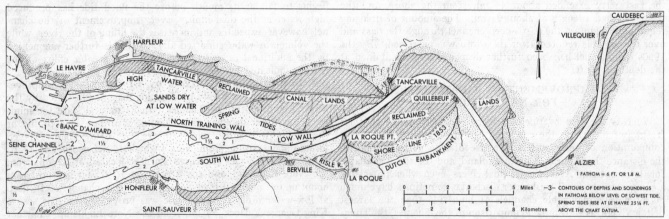

FIG. 8.—TRAINING WORKS IN THE SEINE RIVER ESTUARY

Experience has proved that training works through sandy estuaries, by stopping the wanderings of the navigable channel, produce an increase in its depth and, consequently, in the tidal scour for maintaining it. This scour, however, being concentrated in the trained channel, is withdrawn from the sides of the estuary, which in its natural condition is stirred up periodically by the wandering channel. Therefore, accretion occurs in the parts of the estuary from which the tidal scour and freshwater discharge have been permanently diverted. This accretion reduces the tidal capacity of the estuary and, producing a diminution in the tidal volume passing through the outlet, should not be raised more above low-water level than absolutely necessary to fix the channel.

Experiments with a model reproducing a river with a tidal ebb and flow of freshwater discharge, similar to a model of a nontidal river delta in which various lines of training walls can be successively inserted, can furnish valuable indications of respective effects and comparative merits of the alternate schemes proposed for works.

BIBLIOGRAPHY.—S. Leliavsky, *An Introduction to Fluvial Hydraulics* (1959), *River and Canal Hydraulics* (1965); Hunter Rouse, *Engineering Hydraulics* (1950); C. V. Davis, *Handbook of Applied Hydraulics* (1952); W. H. Hunter, *Rivers and Estuaries* (1913); J. L. Van Ornum, *The Regulation of Rivers* (1914), an excellent and comprehensive work dealing mainly with nontidal rivers; C. M. Townsend, *Hydraulic Principles Governing River and Harbour Construction* (1922), with bibliography; *Encyclopédie de génie civil*, two volumes by Vidal deal with rivers (1921–22); L. Fargue, *La Forme du lit des rivières* (1908); M. Pardé, *Fleuves et rivières* (1955). *See* River and Harbor Act, 1945 (79th U.S. Congress); Water Resources Act, 1965 (89th U.S. Congress).

The *Proceedings* of the Institution of Civil Engineers, *Transactions and Journals* of the American Society of Civil Engineers, and the International Navigation Congress. The bibliographies issued by the INC bureau (Brussels) are exhaustive.

(L. F. V.-H.; N. G. G.; S. N. L.; B. S. B.)

RIVERINA, a district occupying the central southern portion of New South Wales, Austr., bounded on the south by the Murray River and on the north by the Lachlan-Murrumbidgee from about Hillston down to the Murray confluence. The eastern boundary runs from the Lachlan above Hillston to Corowa on the Murray, but the lower slopes of the southern tableland are sometimes included in the Riverina. Except in the east, the whole district is flat, with the rivers falling only ten inches a mile in the east and four to five inches in the west. The rivers meander across vast alluvial plains, periodically flooding and forming distributaries and billabongs (lagoons); in their upper reaches in the east they offer many sites for dams. The soil is prevailingly rich. The climate is generally mild and warm but the summers are hot and dusty and rainfall is variable. Average annual temperatures range from 24° to 9.5° C (75° to 49° F), with extremes of from 47° to −6.5° C (117° to 20° F); the average annual rainfall ranges from 12 in. (30 cm.) in the northwest to 25 in. (62 cm.) in the southeast.

The greater part of the Riverina provides good natural fodder for sheep grazing and was originally a pastoral area, but improvements in farming (particularly in wheat breeds and in dry farming) and the development of water conservation projects led to great increases in cultivation. Along the southeastern slopes, with their cooler temperature and more reliable rain, much arable farming is carried on, including fruit growing and some dairying. Farther west mixed wheat and sheep farming is characteristic. The great wealth of the Riverina, however, lies in its irrigation farming, the bulk of irrigated land being along the Murray and Murrumbidgee, with a smaller area on the Lachlan. The Murrumbidgee irrigation areas consist of about 450,000 ac. served with water from Burrinjuck Dam and Berembed Weir, from which the irrigation channels lead. Leeton (pop. [1961] 5,354) and Griffith (7,696) comprise about 2,000 irrigation farms and a total population of about 26,000 people established in a once sparsely inhabited pastoral area. The farms are either horticultural (principally citrus fruits, apricots, peaches, wine grapes, and vegetables) or mixed (rice, wheat, oats, meat, and wool). The industry of the area is restricted to processing local products. There are wineries, canneries (including the largest in Australia), rice mills, and fruit-packing houses. Smaller irrigation areas are at Hay on the Murrumbidgee and Tullakool on the Murray. Larger areas on the Murray (Berriquin, Wakool, Denimein, and Denibooth) and on the Murrumbidgee (Waa Waa and Tabbita) are farmed less intensively, water being allotted on the basis of the irrigation of a portion only of each holding. The Snowy Mountains hydroelectric project was begun in 1949 to make available a much larger volume of water for irrigation.

The area of the Riverina is 26,533 sq.mi., with a population in 1966 of 95,127. The chief towns are Albury (25,212) and Wagga Wagga (25,939 [mun.]); others are Leeton, Griffith, Junee, Narrandera, and Hay. There were about 7,370 rural holdings (16,200,000 ac.) in the mid-1960s, with about 1,500,000 ac. under cultivation, and a further 1,300,000 ac. under sown pastures. The farming is intensive and the pastures support about 8,500,000 sheep, producing much of the best wool of New South Wales. The entire rice crop of Australia is grown in the Riverina. The eastern valleys have in the past yielded considerable quantities of gold, both alluvial and reef, especially at Adelong and Gundagai, but production is now negligible. In 1915 soft black subbituminous coal was discovered near Oaklands, but production was always small and after the late 1950s almost negligible. The area also produces some tin and gypsum. (R. M. Hl.)

RIVER ROUGE, a city of Michigan, U.S., in Wayne County, bordering Detroit on the southwest, is located on the Detroit and Rouge rivers. The available rail and water transport encouraged industrialization, and manufactures include paper, ships, gypsum products, and steel. Most of the residents are employed by local firms. Zug Island, a highly industrialized 400-ac. site formed by a canal dredged between the Rouge and Detroit rivers, is located in the northeast corner of the city. The concentration of industry results in favourable tax rates for homeowners and, during normal periods, a solvent municipal economy. Although a site of early French settlement, the nucleus of a town did not appear until 1817 when a toll bridge was erected over the Rouge River at River Road (Jefferson Avenue). With the advent of industrialization, River Rouge was incorporated as a village in 1899. During World War I, mainly because of the construction of the Ford Motor Company's River Rouge plant nearby, a population influx occurred which, in 1921, resulted in the incorporation of River Rouge as a city. For comparative population figures *see* table in MICHIGAN: *Population*. (E. K. R.)

RIVERS, ANTHONY WOODVILLE (WYDEVILLE), 2ND EARL (*c.* 1440–1483), brother-in-law of the English king Edward IV, was the eldest son of Sir Richard Woodville (afterward Earl Rivers) and Jacquetta of Luxembourg, widow of John duke of Bedford. He married (*c.* 1461) Elizabeth, daughter and heiress of Thomas, Lord Scales; and in 1464 the secret marriage of his sister Elizabeth to Edward IV established the Woodvilles in preeminence at court.

Yet Anthony's part in government, as opposed to his political influence, does not seem to have been very great. His reputation was rather as the leader of those young men who were fascinated by the splendours of the court of Burgundy and thought there was "never non lyek to it save kyng Artourys cort"; and his spectacular tournament in 1467 with Anthony, the Grand Bastard of Burgundy, was only one among deeds of arms which made him an international figure. The attack on the Woodvilles by the duke of Warwick in 1469 led to his father's death and his own succession to the earldom. Woodville accompanied Edward IV in his temporary exile, fought at the Battle of Barnet (April 1471) after Edward's return, and held London for him at the time of the Battle of Tewkesbury (May 1471). But these events weakened his position. A certain measure of otherworldliness seems to have overtaken him, to the king's fury; in 1471 it was reported as a result that "he may do leest with the gret mastyr." Although he commanded a force in Brittany in 1472, took part in Edward's French expedition in 1475, and was put forward as a proper candidate for the hands of Mary, duchess of Burgundy, in 1477, and of Margaret, sister of James III of Scotland, in 1479, "the stormes of fortune" had evidently been too much for his morale. By 1479 William Caxton wrote of him "it seemeth that he conceiveth wel the mutabilite and the unstablenes of this present lyf and that he desireth with a greet zele and spirituell love our goostly helpe and perpetuel salvacion" (Epilogue to *Cordyale*). To this end he had sought to campaign against the Saracens in Portugal in 1471, had gone on pilgrimage to Santiago de Compostela in 1473 and to Rome and other holy places in Italy in 1475; to this end also he began to translate from French a series of moralistic and devotional works, *The Dictes or Sayengs of the Philosophres*, the *Moral Proverbes* of Christine de Pisan and *Cordyale*, a treatise of the Four Last Things, all of which were printed by Caxton between 1477 and 1479. He also composed "diverse balades ayenst the seven dedely synnes."

Woodville had become governor to the prince of Wales in 1473; but after the death of Edward IV (April 1483), Richard, duke of Gloucester, protector of the kingdom, had him arrested on a barely possible charge of treason and he was executed without trial on June 25, 1483. Fortune's wheel had turned once more; on the eve of his execution, Rivers wrote her possibly the only poem of his that has survived.

BIBLIOGRAPHY.—W. H. Black (ed.), *Historical Illustrations of the Reign of Edward the Fourth; Comprising Memoirs of Anthony Earl Rivers* (1830); C. L. Scofield, *The Life and Reign of Edward IV*, 2 vol. (1923); *The Prologues and Epilogues of William Caxton*, ed. by W. J. B. Crotch for the Early English Text Society (1928).   (P. S. LE.)

RIVERS, RICHARD WOODVILLE (WYDEVILLE), EARL (d. 1469), father of Elizabeth Woodville, queen of Edward IV of England, was the son of Richard Woodville (d. *c.* 1441), a squire who served with distinction in the Hundred Years' War. Richard the younger also served in this conflict and won a reputation as an accomplished knight. He was outstandingly handsome and founded his fortunes by marrying, between September 1435 and March 1437, Jacquetta of Luxembourg, widow of John, duke of Bedford. In 1448 he was created Baron Rivers. A staunch supporter of Henry VI, he was in 1459 stationed at Sandwich to prevent a landing by Richard Neville, earl of Warwick, from Calais; but in January 1460 Warwick captured him in a surprise raid. He escaped in time to fight for Henry VI at Towton (March 29, 1461), but soon afterward made his peace with Edward IV. His fortunes were more than restored by the marriage of his eldest daughter Elizabeth to Edward on May 1, 1464. Through royal favour most of his five surviving sons and eight daughters were married into the noblest families, and Rivers himself was in 1467 made constable of England. This upstart family soon aroused the hatred of the old nobility, especially the Nevilles, and one of Warwick's aims in 1469 was the destruction of the Woodvilles. After the royalist defeat at Edgecote (July 1469) Rivers and his second son, Sir John Woodville, were captured at Chepstow, given up to Warwick, and beheaded at Kenilworth on Aug. 12, 1469.

See J. H. Ramsay, *Lancaster and York*, 2 vol. (1892); *The Complete Peerage*, vol. xi, ed. by G. H. White (1949).   (A. R. M.)

RIVERS, THOMAS MILTON (1888–1962), U.S. pioneer in virology (the study of viruses) and a key figure in the development of poliomyelitis vaccines, was born in Jonesboro, Ga., on Sept. 3, 1888. He graduated from Emory College, Oxford, Ga., in 1909 and the Johns Hopkins School of Medicine in 1915. At that time viruses were little understood; Rivers' interest in them was confirmed by his work as an investigator, in 1918, of a type of pneumonia then prevalent as a complication of measles. In 1922 he joined the Rockefeller Institute for Medical Research, New York City; from 1937 until his retirement in 1955 he was director of its affiliated hospital. At the institute he worked on influenza, chicken pox, and other viral infections, and campaigned for the recognition of viruses as distinct causative agents of disease. In 1938 he was named chairman of the virus research committee of the National Foundation for Infantile Paralysis (later the National Foundation–March of Dimes) and after 1955 served full time as its vice-president for medical affairs. Rivers was credited with outlining and recruiting support for the long-range research program that led to discovery of the Salk and Sabin antipolio vaccines. He died in New York City on May 12, 1962.
    (M. FI.)

RIVERS, WILLIAM HALSE RIVERS (1864–1922), English physician, psychophysiologist, and anthropologist, who helped lay the groundwork for modern kinship terminology (*q.v.*), was born on March 12, 1864, at Luton, near Chatham, Kent.

Completing his medical training at St. Bartholomew's Hospital, London, he then devoted his attention to problems of physiological psychology—notably the nature of colour vision; and his work in this field and, later, on the influence of drugs (particularly alcohol) and on mental fatigue quickly established his reputation. In 1897 he became director of the first British laboratory for experimental psychology (opened by J. Sully at University College, London); and in the same year he was appointed lecturer on the special senses at Cambridge, where, with C. S. Myers, he was the effective founder of experimental psychology in that university.

Toward the close of 1898 he joined the Cambridge expedition to the Torres Strait with A. C. Haddon, C. S. Myers, and W. McDougall. With them he administered a number of tests of sensory functions to the Melanesians, and became keenly interested in anthropological field work. In 1901–02 he made a firsthand study of the Toda (*q.v.*), a polyandrous group in southern India, and later paid several visits to Melanesia. In 1908 he was elected fellow of the Royal Society.

His two main anthropological publications—*The Todas* (1906) and his monumental *History of Melanesian Society* (two volumes, 1914)—are of enduring interest. His main contribution was his demonstration of the relation between kinship names and social organization. On the outbreak of World War I he became neurological consultant to the British Army, and for the remainder of his life he devoted himself to medical psychology. His critical discussion of Freudian theories in his *Instinct and the Unconscious* (1920) did much to encourage a sympathetic attitude toward psychoanalytic doctrines. He died on June 4, 1922.

See for biographical reviews *The Eagle*, vol. xliii, pp. 2–14 (1924); G. H. Brown, *Lives of the Fellows of the Royal College of Physicians of London, 1826–1925* (1955).   (CY. B.)

RIVERSIDE, a city of southern California, U.S., is situated on the Santa Ana River at the base of the San Bernardino range, about 55 mi. SE of Los Angeles; the seat of Riverside County. Pop. (1960) 91,922; San Bernardino-Riverside-Ontario standard metropolitan statistical area (Riverside and San Bernardino counties), 809,782. (For comparative population figures *see* table in CALIFORNIA: *Population*.)

Despite nearness to Los Angeles, the city has a strongly individual character, marked by extensive planting of palm, pepper, and orange trees. In the 1960s housebuilding was diminishing the orange groves, but these were still extensive.

Settlement in the area began in the 1870s, sponsored by Judge John W. North of Tennessee. Street names (Victoria, Prince Albert, Dufferin) commemorate the largely British and Canadian character of early immigration. The original idea of a silk-cultivating colony was replaced in 1878 by the successful propagation of the Washington navel orange tree; the parent tree still survives. Riverside was incorporated in 1883 and adopted the city-manager form of government in 1953.

The city is the location of a general campus of the University of California, including the citrus experiment station (founded 1907), a college of letters and science (1954), and a graduate school (1960). Other educational institutions include Riverside City College (Jr.) (1916), California Baptist College (1955), and Sherman Institute (1901), a school for Indians. Its unique hotel, the Mission Inn, is a show place of Spanish-style architecture.

Riverside's climate is dry and warm. Its economy, formerly based almost entirely on oranges, is diversified and includes the manufacture of aircraft motors, precision instruments, air-conditioning equipment, paints, and building materials. It remains, however, an important food distribution centre with extensive citrus-fruit and vegetable packing.   (A. C. TR.)

RIVET, a headed pin or bolt used as a permanent fastening in metal work. A head is formed on the plain end of the pin or bolt by hammering or by direct pressure. Cold riveting is practicable for small rivets of copper, brass, aluminum, iron, or steel, but the larger iron and steel rivets have to be heated in order to secure rapid and easy closing.

Machine riveting in small sizes is done either with a power press, where the ram works a snap and closes the tail with a blow, or with a rotary rivet-spinning machine, in which hard

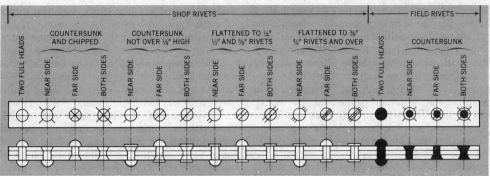

CONVENTIONAL SYMBOLS USED TO INDICATE RIVETING IN PLAN AND ELEVATION ON ALL STRUCTURAL DRAWINGS

steel rollers spin the tail quickly and noiselessly into shape. In engineering structures, machine riveting is employed whenever practicable, using portable pneumatic hammers or fixed or portable hydraulic riveters.

The various shapes of rivet heads or tails include the countersunk head, which is beaten flush into a conical recess in the plate; the cup or round head; the pan head, which has sloping sides and a flat top; the conical head, with sloped sides ending in a point; and the thin flat head. Bifurcated rivets for belts and harnesses have thin heads, but the tails are split and opened like a paper fastener. Often gas or electric welding has been substituted for riveting in the case of hollow ware and other sheet-metal products. Electric welding is an alternate method for the connection of structural members such as columns and beams in building construction. *See also* PNEUMATIC TOOLS.

RIVIERA, the Mediterranean coastland between Cannes in France and La Spezia in Italy. The French section comprises part of the Côte d'Azur (which extends farther west), while the Italian is known as the Riviera di Ponente and the Riviera di Levante, respectively west and east of Genoa. Effectively sheltered to the north by the Maritime Alps and Ligurian Apennines, the district has exceptionally mild winters (January mean 9° C; 49° F), brilliant, hot summers (July mean 24° C; 76° F) and much sunshine throughout the year. Rain usually falls only on about 60 days in the year, and on the coast itself snow is almost unknown. Many delicate plants, including the pomegranate, agave, mimosa, and some types of palm, flourish; flowers are grown out of season for export in large quantities to northern markets. The favourable climate, the grandeur of the rugged coastal scenery, and the attractions of the sea have drawn the leisured rich, especially for wintering, since before the mid-19th century.

The popularity of Cannes dates from 1834, when Lord Brougham, avoiding a cholera epidemic in Nice, stayed there instead and, returning regularly for the next 30 years, set the fashion. Modern transport has increased the influx of tourists; luxury villas and hotels are now mixed with resort facilities of a more popular kind. Monte Carlo in the tiny principality of Monaco (*q.v.*) offers additional attractions for high living. From west to east the main centres of this beaded coastal urban development are Cannes, Juan-les-Pins, Antibes, Nice, Menton, Bordighera, San Remo, Alassio, Santa Margherita, Rapallo, Sestri Levante, and Levanto. A three-tiered system of motor roads (the Corniches) runs between Nice and the Italian frontier at Menton. The highest, Grande Corniche, constructed by Napoleon I to replace the Roman road, passes the picturesque village of La Turbie, with its Roman remains, and the 10th-century Roquebrune Castle, and overlooks Monaco from a height of more than 1,400 ft. (430 m.). The lowest Corniche, built in the 18th century by a prince of Monaco, connects the coastal resorts; while the middle road, opened in 1939, was created for the tourist industry and passes by the perched village of Eze. The railway burrows through the projecting limestone headlands by numerous tunnels.

(AR. E. S.)

RIVIÈRE, JACQUES (1886–1925), French essayist, whose delicacy of perception and acute sense of responsibility had a profound influence on the writers associated with the *Nouvelle Revue française* (*N.R.F.*), was born in Bordeaux on July 15, 1886. He was secretary of the *N.R.F.* immediately before World War I and became editor in 1919. Among his friends were André Gide, Paul Claudel, Charles Péguy, and Jacques Copeau, and he was an early admirer of Marcel Proust. He himself aspired to write an analytical novel (*Aimée*, 1922; and the unfinished *Florence*, published posthumously, 1935). His personal anxieties and aspirations are best reflected in his letters to Alain-Fournier (his brother-in-law), in his correspondence with Claudel, published after his death, and in his essay *À la trace de Dieu* (1925). He was brought up a Catholic, but later an oppressive awareness of "the reality of nonbeing" prevented him from accepting the Christian faith, much as he would have liked to do so. He died in Paris, on Feb. 14, 1925, before the promise of his work had been fulfilled. His other writings include *L'Allemand* (1918), *Carnet de guerre* (1929), *Études* (1912), and *Nouvelles Études* (published posthumously, 1947).

See the commemorative number of the *Nouvelle Revue française*, vol. 24 (1925). (A. PE.)

RIYADH (AR RIYAD), the capital of Saudi Arabia, in the province of Najd (*q.v.*), lies 535 mi. (860 km.) NE of Jiddah (on the Red Sea), and 250 mi. (400 km.) SW of Ad Dammam (on the Persian Gulf) with which it has been connected by a railroad (350 mi.) since 1951. The first census, taken in 1962, gave the population of Riyadh as about 170,000, a figure considerably lower than earlier unofficial estimates but high enough to make Riyadh the largest city in the kingdom.

In 1824 Riyadh became the capital of the Saudi state, which was then confined to the region of Najd. The ruins of the former capital, Ad Dir'iyah, still tower above Wadi Hanifah 10 mi. NW of Riyadh. The discovery of oil and the resulting spread of modern means of communication have revolutionized the life of the desert kingdom. The general tendency has been toward the development of large urban communities at the expense of what was a tribal and oasis economy. Riyadh best illustrates this process. The old walled town with about 30,000 inhabitants, forming an irregular square of 600–700 yd. to the side, remained intact until the end of World War II, though a few fairly large royal dwellings made their appearance outside the perimeter toward the end of that period. By 1951 the population had grown to about 60,000. After that time the walls were torn down and many old houses destroyed to make room for modern buildings. Expansion proceeded in every direction, over uprooted date groves and past neglected and dying palms and out into the desert, to cover an area estimated at about 40 sq.mi. (104 sq.km.). The character of the population, once exclusively Najdi, has changed substantially with the influx of people from other parts of the kingdom and from other Arab countries, such as Syria, Lebanon, Egypt, and Yemen, in search of employment and commercial opportunity. Although the presence of these elements has brought about a relaxation of the old puritan way of life, some aspects survive, as may be seen in the ban on public cinemas and the discouragement of smoking in the streets of the more ancient quarters.

In the centre of old Riyadh the king's town palace, once said to represent all that is best in modern Arabian architecture, has made way for a large concrete structure of cubist affinities, providing offices for the local provincial administration. Opposite it the old Wahhabi mud-brick mosque with its low minaret disappeared in favour of a concrete mosque 200 yd. long and wide, with two tall minarets equipped with loudspeakers to relay the calls to prayer. The palace square is a busy crossroads from which broad asphalt streets, lined with shops, run east, west, south, and north into the modern suburbs of greater Riyadh. The fort of Al Mismak, not far from the square, and parts of the former royal palace complex of Al Murabba' outside the perimeter were among the few important buildings of former times still standing in the 1960s. The north road leading to the airport provides a good view of Al Murabba' and is lined with western-style buildings housing most of the ministries of the central government, hotels, hospitals, and military agencies, including the military college. The east road leads to the railroad station and on to the large military base in Al Kharj, about 50 mi. SE. After passing through new residential suburbs, the south road reaches the royal country palace on the right bank of Wadi Hanifah. Finally, westward, a broad divided highway, with gay flower beds in the centre, runs past the mansions of the princes and the rich to the royal palace of Al Nasiriyah, standing in its own vast grounds. Massive gates guard the eastern and western entrances, and tree-lined avenues crisscross the interior. The main buildings are of pink-tinted concrete in a mixture of styles ranging from pseudo-Moorish to modern European, but the general effect is not unpleasing.

More than half the buildings in Riyadh are equipped with main water or electricity or both. Water supply remains a serious problem because of the rapidly growing population, the extensive use of water for gardens and green spaces, and the steadily subsiding underground water table.

Set on high ground above Wadi Hanifah, which is waterless most of the year, Riyadh and its vicinity have almost no agriculture, and provisions must be imported from other parts of the country and from abroad. The climate is dry and invigorating, with occasional sandstorms. There is no heavy industry.

There has been extensive development in education, public health, and the social life of the community. King Sa'ud I University (now Riyadh University) was founded in the suburb of

BY COURTESY OF THE ARABIAN AMERICAN OIL COMPANY

ROOFTOP VIEW OF RIYADH SHOWING BUILDINGS IN AN OLDER SECTION OF THE CITY

New Riyadh in 1957. Various international conferences, including sessions of the Arab League, are held in the city.

Riyadh is linked with Ad Dammam via Khurays by an asphalt road, and the remaining portion of the transpeninsular highway, running to Mecca and Jiddah, is under construction. Saudi Arabian Airlines operates regular flights from Riyadh to Jiddah, Dhahran, and other centres in the kingdom, and the Riyadh airport is also used by aircraft of other countries, particularly during the season for the Mecca pilgrimage. A radio-telephone network puts Riyadh in direct touch with the outside world.

(H. St. J. B. P.; G. S. Re.)

RIZAL, a province of the Philippines, in central Luzon, northeast and south of Manila. It is named after the Philippine national hero, José Rizal. Area 791 sq.mi. (1,971 sq.km.); pop.

(1960) 1,456,362, an increase of 75% over 1939. Included within the boundaries of the province, yet politically separate, are the chartered cities, Quezon (q.v.) and Pasay; included geographically, but politically a separate province, is the city of Manila (q.v.). The eastern half of Rizal province lies in the Sierra Madre, while the remainder lies on the fertile Central Plain. The province is drained by the Marikina and the Pasig rivers; the latter drains Laguna de Bay, over half of which, including Talim Island, lies in the province. Caloocan and Malabon, provincial municipalities lying on the northern border of Manila, are industrial and residential suburbs. Malabon is also an important site of fish ponds. Parañaque (q.v.), south of Manila on the shore of Manila Bay, is a suburb famous for the production of Philippine embroidery. Pasig (pop. [1960] 62,130), the provincial capital, is an important trading centre between Manila and Laguna de Bay and is known for the manufacture of shoes. Pasay City (sometimes called Rizal City; pop. [1960] 132,673) lies between Manila and Parañaque on the shore of Manila Bay. It is a major residential suburb of Manila and is well known for the nightclubs lining the beautiful waterfront along Dewey Boulevard. Ft. William McKinley, immediately east of Pasay City, is a former U.S. Army reservation which was returned to the Philippines in 1947; it is the site of a large cemetery dedicated to the dead of World War II. (R. E. He.)

RIZAL Y MERCADO, JOSÉ (1861–1896), Filipino patriot and inspirer of Philippine nationalism, sought to prove throughout his career that Filipinos were the intellectual and moral equals of their Spanish masters; he also worked for fundamental political and social reforms. These aims pervaded his writing, most of which was done in Europe, where, with one brief interruption, he resided between 1882 and 1892. His education, centring in medicine but extending to many fields, was acquired in the Philippines and Europe. His two novels, *Noli Me Tangere* (1886) and *El Filibusterismo* (1891), vividly pictured the evils of Spanish rule in the Philippines. In 1890 he published an annotated edition of Morgas' *Sucesos de las Islas Filipinas,* hoping to show that the Philippines had its own history before Spanish rule. He also wrote articles for *La Solidaridad,* a Filipino reformist periodical published in Spain.

Rizal returned to Manila in 1892 and founded a nationalist reformist society (Liga Filipina), with the result that the Spanish exiled him to Dapitan on northwest Mindanao (1892–96). When the Philippine revolution of 1896 began, Rizal, who was on his way (via Spain) to Cuba for medical service with the Spanish Army, did not take any direct part. He was, nevertheless, arrested aboard ship and brought back to Manila to stand trial for complicity in the insurrection. A military court found him guilty, and he was shot Dec. 30, 1896. His death enhanced his already great prestige among Filipinos and stimulated national sentiment.

See Rafael Palma, *The Pride of the Malay Race,* trans. by Roman Ozaeta (1949); Frank C. Laubach, *Rizal: Man and Martyr* (1936); W. Retana, *Vida y Escritos del Doctor José Rizal* (1907).

(E. C. Cn.)

RIZE, a town on the Black Sea coast and headquarters of the *il* (province) of Rize, Turkey, lies about 45 mi. E of Trabzon. Pop. (1960) 22,181. The commercial quarters are on the narrow strip of land around a small bay and the residential quarters are scattered on the surrounding steep slopes. With its mild climate and luxuriant vegetation Rize is one of the most attractive towns of the Black Sea coast. It is the centre of the Turkish tea industry.

RIZE IL (pop. [1960] 248,930) is rugged, densely forested, and very humid. The interior is occupied by high mountains and is economically unimportant, but the coastal strip produces a large variety of agricultural products, the principal being maize (corn), the staple food, tea, and citrus. The climate is exceptionally mild and humid with January average temperature at Rize 6.6° C (44° F) and annual average precipitation 100.4 in. (255 cm.). The most important cash crop is tea, which was established there in the 1930s. The first Turkish crop of tea was taken at Rize in 1939 and the industry has been successfully expanded. (N. Tu.; E. Tu.; S. Er.)

ROADRUNNER, a slender bird, *Geococcyx californianus*, characteristic of the deserts of the United States and Mexico, that spends most of its life on the ground, running about in search of food. Averaging about 22 in. in length, about half

H. CHARLES LAUN FROM NATIONAL AUDUBON SOCIETY

ROADRUNNER (GEOCOCCYX CALIFORNIANUS)

of which is tail, this picturesque member of the cuckoo family is further distinguished by a fairly long bill, ragged brownish crest, heavily streaked brown and white upperparts, striped breast, buff belly, and white-tipped tail feathers. In flight the short wings show a white crescent.

The roadrunner runs swiftly, carrying its body in a horizontal position, and halts abruptly, raising its tail vertically. It darts about in this manner after lizards, small snakes, scorpions, small mammals, insects, ground-dwelling birds, and fruits and seeds. It kills and eats poisonous snakes, a habit that has given rise to considerable local folklore about its prowess. The saucerlike nest is built in a bush, low tree, or cactus and the four to nine white eggs are incubated for an unknown period. Probably two broods are reared annually.   (R. S. Pr.)

ROADS AND HIGHWAYS.

Though in principle the terms "roads" and "highways" are synonymous, in practice "highways" is used only for the more important thoroughfares. The term "road" is used in a narrow sense to denote routes of minor or local importance, but it also retains its broader meaning of any prepared route on land destined for the movement of goods and persons. The term "street," formerly of more general significance, now refers to roads lying within the limits of a municipality.

This article discusses the following topics:

I. HISTORY

The earliest roads developed from the paths and trails of prehistoric peoples. Land routes—well-worn trails—covering great distances existed at the dawn of recorded history. The origin of road building as a distinct art, however, had to await the rise of central governments rich and powerful enough to command large numbers of labourers and to provide technical experts.

1. Pre-Roman Times.—The early civilizations in the Tigris-Euphrates valley and in the valley of the Nile apparently met these requirements, but because they covered comparatively small areas and were confined to the river basins, they had slight need for long-distance land transportation and they developed roads only very slowly. They first built paved streets in cities, sometimes elaborately decorated with coloured tile, bricks, or marble, which served ceremonial purposes. For more utilitarian purposes the early Egyptians and Mesopotamians also built relatively short roads and even causeways to transport materials from mines and quarries to the sites where pyramids and temples were being built. The rise of ancient empires of greater territorial extent than city-states required a more elaborate system of communication and transportation. Roads were needed for trade, conquest, and, most important, for civil administration. Because of the character of the traffic and the nature of the climate and terrain at the eastern end of the Mediterranean—arid, semidesert land with few large mountain ranges—it was not essential that these roads be paved. Traffic over them consisted of pedestrians, horsemen, light war chariots, and caravans or pack trains; long-distance transport by means of wheeled vehicles remained too difficult and expensive to be commonly employed even on paved highways. The art of the road builder in such circumstances consisted mainly of clearing and leveling a track across the countryside, making occasional cuts through mountainous territory, and building firm roadbeds through marshy areas. In settled times the more powerful empires also built and maintained fortified posts or hostels along the main routes to facilitate communication and preserve order.

Tradition ascribes to the Assyrians the first such system of highways, but the evidence is vague and conflicting. By the time of the Persian expansion in the late 6th century B.C., however, several roads spanned the area east of the Mediterranean from Egypt and the Aegean Sea to the Persian Gulf and perhaps as far as the Indus River. The most famous was the so-called Royal Road described by the Greek historian Herodotus, who claimed to have traveled it himself. It connected Susa, the ancient capital of Persia, with Anatolia and the Aegean seaports, a distance of more than 1,500 mi. Royal messengers could traverse the entire course in nine days, about ten times as fast as the normal travel time of three months for such a distance. Between Babylon and Susa they averaged 100 mi. a day, a speed not surpassed in ordinary human travel until the 19th century.

2. Roman Roads.—The Romans were the greatest road builders of antiquity. Among the outstanding features of Roman roads were their straightness, solid foundations, cambered surfaces, and systematic arrangement. Lime and pozzolana (volcanic ash) cement were widely used to make concrete. The first of the great Roman roads, the Via Appia or Appian Way, was begun by the censor Appius Claudius Caecus in 312 B.C. It stretched southeast from Rome for a distance of 162 mi. Later administrators extended it to Brundisium (Brindisi), the port of embarkation for troops going to Greece and Asia Minor, and to Reggio, whence troops and traffic were ferried across to Sicily and ultimately to North Africa. By the end of the Punic Wars seven great roads led from, or to, Rome; together with their many branches and connecting roads they formed a comprehensive network, giving rise to the expression "all roads lead to Rome." (*See* Italy: *History.*)

As Roman armies expanded their conquests beyond Italy, Roman road builders followed. Indeed, in many instances the soldiers, assisted by slaves and prisoners of war, were themselves the road builders, and many of the later roads began as lines of military advance or frontiers. In 145 B.C. they began the Via Egnatia, an extension of the Appian Way across the Adriatic in Dalmatia and northern Greece; by 130 B.C. this road extended into

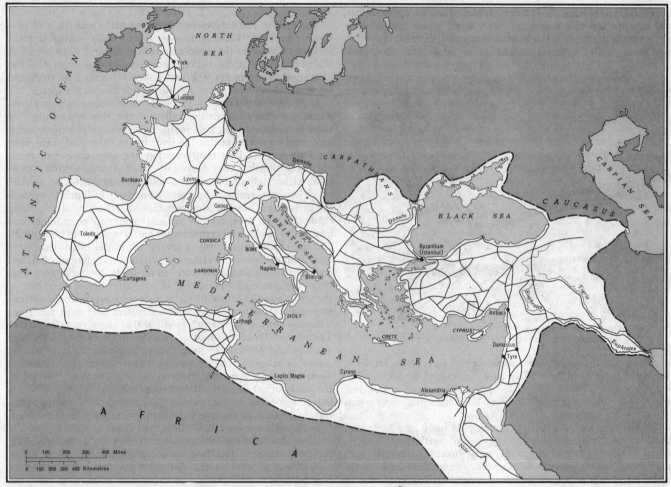

ADAPTED FROM C. DAREMBERG AND E. SAGLIO, "DICTIONNAIRE DES ANTIQUITÉS GRECQUES ET ROMAINES," VOL. 5, © LIBRAIRIE HACHETTE

EXTENT OF IMPERIAL ROMAN ROAD NETWORK

Asia Minor where it joined the former Persian Royal Road, re-built by the Romans, and linked with other roads built or rebuilt around the eastern end of the Mediterranean. After the conquest of Carthage the Romans also built in North Africa a highway system that eventually spanned the entire south shore of the Mediterranean. The road system in Roman Gaul centred on Lyons, which was reached from Italy by two principal Alpine passes. Four main roads extended from there to the Rhine, the channel ports, and Bordeaux, with a southern road down the Rhône Valley connecting with the coast road at Arles. In Britain the conquest took place in stages, and engineers designed roads accordingly: examples of originally military roads are Fosse Way and Stanegate, south of, and superseded by, Hadrian's Wall. However, the main road network came to radiate from London (see BRITAIN: *Roman Britain*). The road system of Spain differed from that of other Roman provinces: instead of radiating from a single centre such as Lyons, London, or Rome itself, the main roads followed the periphery of the peninsula; secondary roads were built later into the central plateaus.

At the height of the empire, in the 2nd century A.D., the Roman highway system consisted of more than 50,000 mi. of first-class roads. Planned for the imperial courier service and the rapid movement of troops, these were furnished with posting stations with relays of horses about every 10 mi. and with lodging places (*mansiones*) about every 25 mi. Solidly built, Roman roads took the direct line wherever possible, using piles and embankments over marshy ground and cuts and even tunnels in hilly or mountainous country. In addition, a network of lesser roads, amounting altogether to perhaps 200,000 mi., linked the smaller towns and rural areas with the main highways.

3. After the Fall of Rome.—The decline of road building in Rome coincided with the decline of Roman political power. New construction fell off markedly after A.D. 200, and by the 4th century Roman officials found it difficult even to maintain existing roads. Though laws passed in the late 4th and early 5th centuries called upon local landlords to provide maintenance (a sure sign of the decay of central authority), they had little effect. A long period of economic and technological stagnation set in, and, except in the immediate vicinity of the larger towns and cities and where bits of Roman pavement survived, the roads of the Middle Ages and early modern times were simple dirt tracks, narrow, rutted, and rough, dusty in dry weather and muddy in wet. Wheeled passenger vehicles were rarely seen on them until the 17th century. Passengers went on foot, on horseback, or in litters, according to their status; merchandise was carried by pack trains. Gradually wagons and coaches came into use, at first for the transport of goods and later for carrying passengers. It is likely that the effects of these heavy, iron-tired vehicles on the soft dirt surfaces had something to do with the deplorable state of the roads described by Daniel Defoe, Arthur Young, and other 18th-century travelers.

The latter half of the 18th and the early 19th century witnessed a brief revival in the art of road construction. The initiative came first in France where, as early as the 17th century, the great ministers of Henry IV and Louis XIV, Sully and Colbert, made determined efforts to improve the state of the French roads. These efforts achieved little, however, until the creation of the *École des Ponts et Chaussées* (School for Bridges and Roads) in 1747, the first professional engineering school in the world, following the establishment of a central administration for roads and bridges in 1716. The graduates of this school, as engineers of the state, built many miles of new and improved highways in France, but, as civil engineers, they did not succeed in raising the level of the art above that achieved by the Romans.

In Great Britain, meanwhile, the rapid growth of commerce and industry urgently required better and more extensive means of transportation. Canals received the first and major emphasis, but new and improved roadways also came into existence. In Britain, unlike France, private initiative supplied the means and the intellect, although the state cooperated by allowing canal and turnpike companies to exercise the right of eminent domain and the right to collect tolls. A number of self-taught engineers, three of whom are outstanding, contributed new ideas and techniques: John Metcalf, Thomas Telford, and J. L. McAdam. They all recognized the importance of proper drainage, and McAdam devised an inexpensive self-sealing pavement consisting of small stones, chips, or gravel that could be applied directly to the soil or subsoil of a properly drained roadbed. As a result of the economy of this method of construction it was widely copied, and such water-impervious roads today are still called "macadamized," even when the chips or stones are mixed or covered with oil or a bituminous substance.

4. Early American Roads.—The first American roads were the narrow Indian foot trails that crisscrossed the wilderness. Many of these trails followed the well-worn paths originally formed by the movements of deer, elk, or buffalo. Early American explorers and colonists used water routes whenever possible. In many cases, however, the narrow winding Indian trails offered the only course. These trails sought the high ground, which offered a dry route that was generally kept free of leaves and snow by the wind. Among the more important Indian trails were the Old Connecticut path, which traveled from the upper Hudson valley near Albany to Boston; the Iroquois trail, which followed the Mohawk Valley and terminated near Niagara Falls after crossing the area south of Lake Ontario; Nemacolin's path, which was named after a Delaware chief and led northwest from the upper Potomac to Pittsburgh; and the Warrior's path, through the Cumberland Gap and Kentucky to the falls of the Ohio River. A notable military road built by the British forces was Gen. Edward Braddock's road from Ft. Cumberland on the Potomac to the forks of the Ohio. In 1775 Daniel Boone widened the Warrior's path into the Wilderness Road. As colonists moved farther westward they followed the maps prepared by Lewis and Clark, Mackenzie, Frémont, Thompson, and others who used the Indian trails as paths to open the West.

Virginia's first highway law was passed in 1632, and in 1639 the general court of Massachusetts passed a comprehensive act which ordered each town to appoint two or three men who would be responsible for building highways "where they may be most convenient." The early roads and streets were relatively local in character and were often seas of mud or clouds of dust, depending on what the previous day's weather had been. The Conestoga wagon, which made its first appearance in Pennsylvania, was probably the most famous vehicle of this period; later models of it became known as the Western "prairie schooner."

Toward the end of the 18th century the increased demand for better roads stimulated the construction of many routes with private capital as turnpikes (toll roads). The first United States turnpike utilized existing roads to connect settlements in the Blue Ridge Mountains with Alexandria, Va. The first American macadamized road, the Lancaster turnpike, was completed in 1794. It ran between Lancaster, Pa., and Philadelphia.

As early as 1802 the federal government undertook to build a road from tidewater to the Ohio Valley; known as the Cumberland Road or National Road, it reached the Ohio at Wheeling, Va. (now W. Va.), in 1818, and by 1830 had been extended to Illinois. Meanwhile, to meet the rapidly growing demand for improved means of transportation (commonly called "internal improvements"), states, counties, and lesser units of government either built canals and roads on their own account or chartered private companies to build them. In the history of transportation the first three decades of the 19th century are known in America as the "canal and turnpike era."

The advent of steam railways later in the 1820s spelled the end of progress in road construction for almost three-quarters of a century. Turnpike companies went bankrupt and their road-

ways fell into disrepair. Road building became almost the exclusive concern of counties and municipalities. With the westward expansion of settlement and the growth of population, the mileage of roads gradually increased, reaching a total of about 2,000,000 mi. at the end of the century; but the roads were poorly constructed and maintained, and in many instances were no more than dirt tracks. Of the total mileage in the United States, less than 100 mi. were hard-surfaced with tar, asphalt, or brick; about 100,000 mi. were "improved"—that is, graded and drained, and occasionally surfaced with crushed stone or gravel. Many roads ended abruptly at state or even county lines; nothing resembling a "system" could be said to have existed at the national or even the state level. Throughout the world at the end of the 19th century the quality of roads was scarcely better than it had been 1,000 or even 2,000 years before.

II. MODERN HIGHWAYS

The first demands for better roads, both in Europe and the Western Hemisphere, came in the latter part of the 19th century from the devotees of a new invention, the bicycle. The cyclists were soon joined by the owners and users of a still newer invention, the automobile. It was for the automobile in its various forms—passenger cars, motor trucks, and buses—that modern systems of highways were built. In 1900 there were only 8,000 motor vehicles in the United States; by 1925 there were 20,000,-000; and by the mid-1960s more than 86,000,000. Western Europe and other prosperous regions of the world did not lag far behind this phenomenal rate of increase. (*See* MOTORING; TRANSPORTATION.)

1. The First Phase.—The increase in automobile traffic required more roads and better road surfaces. When oil, tar, and asphalt surfaces were introduced early in the 20th century, they served mainly as coatings to allay dust; later they were used as binders to prevent "raveling" of gravel and macadamized surfaces. These surfaces served light automobile traffic well enough, but the rise of heavy truck transportation during and after World War I led to demands for more durable pavements. Three new methods of road surfacing evolved in the 19th century, though none became common until after 1900. The first of these was concrete, which was used in cities such as London in the early 19th century, spread across Europe, and was first used in the U.S. at Bellefontaine, O., in 1893. Bituminous surfacing (asphalt), which was adopted in Paris, was used in Switzerland and France about the middle of the century and in the U.S. by the end of the 1870s. Tar macadam, used in Britain in the mid-19th century, spread in the next 25 years to the U.S. and later to Australia. In the 20th century experiments with other surfaces and road-building materials, such as brick and bituminous concrete, took place. By the 1930s most main highways were surfaced with concrete or various bituminous mixtures.

Between 1920 and 1940 all countries with any appreciable automobile traffic undertook road-building projects on a scale previously without precedent. In many instances the new highways followed existing routes so that the total increase in road mileage was less than the construction activity would indicate. The main objective was to provide hard-surface roads between major centres of population and economic activity; by the end of the 1930s the achievement of this objective was in sight when the outbreak of World War II interrupted road construction in almost all countries. With the resumption of road building after the war the major effort again went into improvement of existing highways to repair wartime damage and deterioration and to accommodate the larger volume and higher speed of postwar traffic. As a result, the first phase of the modern highway period, which seemed to be drawing to a close in the 1930s, did not actually end until about 1950.

Nations with Communist governments have not reported data on road mileage, but the totals are not believed to be impressive. Private automobiles in such countries are rare, and it is known that the Soviet Union, to take the most important case, has placed major emphasis on railways for the movement of both goods and persons, with airways supplementing them. Some other countries that have been economically undeveloped and have been almost passed over by both the railway and automobile ages are now making extensive use of airways in their efforts to modernize and catch up economically with the rest of the world.

2. Express Highways.—The outstanding development of mid-20th-century highway history was the construction of controlled-access, divided highways, frequently called superhighways or throughways in the United States, and motorways (in contrast to all-purpose roads) in Britain. These highways feature two or more traffic lanes in each direction, with opposing traffic separated by a median strip of grass or shrubs; elimination of grade crossings; controlled entries and exits; and advanced designs eliminating steep grades, sharp curves, and other hazards and inconveniences to driving. Frequently they have been constructed over completely new routes, passing near but not through large centres of population, on more or less direct lines between desired termini. Their advantages include high speed; greater safety, comfort, and convenience for drivers and passengers; and lower vehicle operating costs. Many of these new express highways, especially in the United States, are toll roads, but that is an incidental, not an essential, feature.

In 1924 Italy began construction of toll motor highways or *autostrada* that soon totaled 320 mi. in length. Although these did not attain the standards of later express highways, they did incorporate the features of limited access and elimination of grade crossings. They were built and owned by private companies and paid for by tolls and advertising. The first true express highways, the *Autobahnen*, were built in Germany. Although the idea originated and plans were formulated between 1930 and 1932, a national network, the *Reichsautobahnen*, totaling 1,310 mi. by 1942, was built by the Nazi regime for both economic and military purposes. The only other European country to undertake construction of express highways before World War II was the Netherlands. In the United States the Pennsylvania Turnpike and the Merritt Parkway in Connecticut were completed shortly before the nation's entrance into the war in 1941.

After the war the express highway movement gained momentum, slowly at first because of financial difficulties and the urgency of postwar reconstruction, then more rapidly. By 1950 eight U.S. states had toll roads that met express highway standards and totaled more than 750 mi. After that date virtually every state constructed some express highway mileage on either a toll or toll-free basis. In Great Britain the Special Roads Act of 1949 provided for a network of about 700 mi. of new express highways. By the mid-1960s nearly 300 mi. were built, the most important being the London-Birmingham motorway (1959). The Nether-

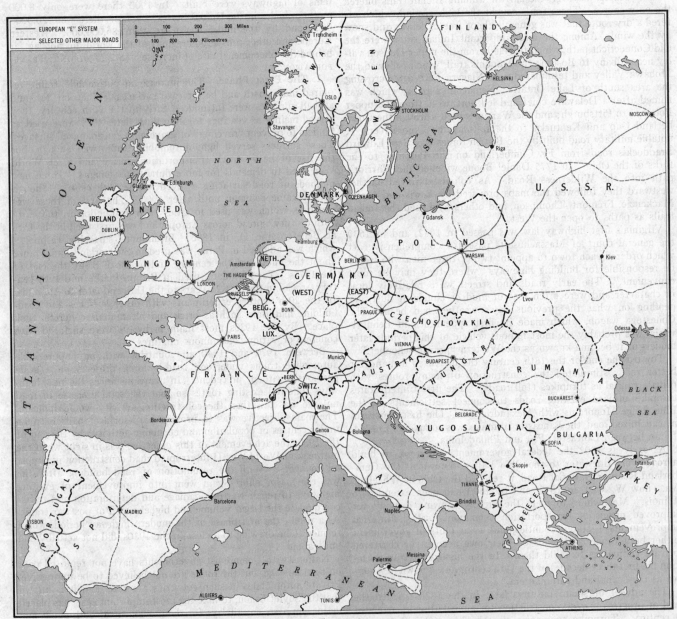

PROPOSED "E" SYSTEM OF HIGHWAYS AND OTHER MAJOR ROADS IN EUROPE

lands resumed its construction program in 1946 and by 1960 had about 300 mi. of modern express highways, giving that country one of the greatest highway densities in the world. Belgium completed the Ostend-Brussels motorway in 1958 and its share of the Antwerp-Aachen *autoroute* in 1964. Motorways were also planned to connect all principal cities and border points. France built several short express highways or *autoroutes* in the 1950s to facilitate egress from its major cities, but, with governmental policy favouring rail travel, only 200 mi. had been built and 260 mi. were under construction by the mid-1960s. West Germany resumed construction of the *Autobahnen* in 1957, with three four-year plans for federal highways. In 1964 Italy completed the *Autostrade del Sole*, stretching almost 500 mi. from Milan to Naples. By the mid-1960s the six countries of the European Economic Community, together with Britain, Austria, and Switzerland, had completed 4,270 mi., half of which was in Germany and a quarter in Italy, with plans to triple this amount by 1970.

The most ambitious of all express highway systems was the National System of Interstate Highways of the United States. Recognizing the military value of highways as well as the need for a vast program of highway improvement, Congress authorized the project in 1944 but did not appropriate special funds for it until several years later. Originally limited to 40,000 mi. (subsequently extended to 41,000 mi.), the system incorporates existing express highways built to its specifications, whether toll or free; but by far the largest part results from new construction financed mainly by the federal government. In 1956 Congress authorized $25,000,000,000 of federal funds, approximately 90% of the total estimated cost, to be expended over a 12-year period. As of the mid-1960s the 41,000-mi. project was scheduled for completion in 1972 at a revised estimated cost of $47,000,000,000, of which the federal funding would be 90%. As its symbol the interstate system employs the U.S. shield with white lettering on a red and blue background.

3. International Highways.—International highways, insofar as they are anything more than simple continuations of roads across national borders, must rest on treaties or agreements. In 1950 all European countries except Ireland, Spain, the Soviet Union, and Bulgaria signed an agreement calling for a European highway network totaling about 26,000 mi. A number of specific routes were designated, some covering existing highways, others to be built anew. The system envisaged both express highways and all-purpose roads; to qualify for inclusion in the system all roads were to be built or rebuilt to minimum specifications for each type of road. They were to be marked with the letter *E* preceding their number, with white symbols on a green background.

In 1929 delegates to the Second Pan-American Highway Congress in Rio de Janeiro worked out a general plan for a road system spanning the entire length of the Western Hemisphere. Little progress was made until World War II when, working against difficult obstacles and under great pressure, U.S. Army engineers and civilian contractors cut a primitive but usable road, the Alaska Highway, through the wilderness from Dawson Creek, B.C., to Fairbanks, Alaska. In 1946 the Canadian government assumed control of the portions of the road on its territory, in accordance with the original agreement, and the road was later made suitable for tourist traffic. Another section of the Pan-American system, the Inter-American Highway from Laredo, Tex., to Panama, also benefited from U.S. engineering and financial aid during the war, but was not completed until the early 1960s. Mexico completed the portion of the road within its borders without outside assistance. *See* PAN-AMERICAN HIGHWAY.

III. HIGHWAY ADMINISTRATION AND FINANCE

With the exception of the Roman and a few other ancient empires, the administration and finance of roads and highways have usually, until the 20th century, been the responsibility of local authorities. In English common law, for example, the responsibility for roads rested on the parish; this tradition was taken over in the United States by county and township authorities, and similar conditions prevailed elsewhere. Usually a local official such as a manorial landlord, justice of the peace, or county com-

missioner had ultimate responsibility for the upkeep of roads, although in some cases this responsibility was delegated to a special highway commissioner or overseer. Most able-bodied men were liable for labour on the highways, which was in reality a special tax called the *corvée* or road tax; it varied according to time and place from a few days to several weeks of work each year. Under such circumstances, without specialized technical competence in either labour or direction, the deplorable state of roads throughout most of recorded history is small wonder. The tendency of modern times, however, especially in the 20th century, has been to create specialized authorities responsible for greater mileages of roadways, endowed with special sources of financing, and employing specialized engineers and other technically competent personnel.

Highway systems as a whole function under a set of national and local policies applied through various administrative arrangements. In the provision and conduct of highway transportation, the roadway is generally provided and maintained by government through some designated administrative highway agency. The vehicles, though generally produced by private industry and operated by millions of individual operators who set their own origins, destinations, and schedules, are subject to limitations imposed by a government agency. These include limitations on some vehicular features (*e.g.*, size and weight), general rules concerning the conduct of the use of the vehicles (*e.g.*, vehicle codes), and various controls on the use of the roads (*e.g.*, signs, signals, markings, speed limits).

The capabilities and productivity of a highway transportation system are affected in great measure by governmental policies. In particular, the layout of the road network, the design features built into the roads, the traffic controls, and the level of maintenance have an important influence on the cost, safety, use, and convenience of the system.

The role of the modern highway agency (department, ministry, commission, or office of roads), then, is more than the performance of the technical functions of design and construction of the physical highway projects, even though these are basic functions. It is concerned also with translating policy into action, with underwriting, to the extent that it can, the effectiveness of the highway transportation effort of the economy, with how the road systems affect various aspects of community functioning, and with coordinating the road activities under its jurisdiction with those of other highway agencies in the same region.

Because of the essential nature of the design and construction functions, especially in the periods of development of new roads or appreciable improvement of the road plant, the highway agencies have tended to be basically engineering organizations. However, the staffs of modern highway agencies also may include attorneys, economists, sociologists, scientists, right-of-way land appraisers, accountants, and public information officers. In a small agency concerned only with an established and limited road system, a few engineers and skilled operating personnel may serve to maintain an effective road plant.

Generally, the world's industrialized nations have in existence fairly extensive road networks, where the major emphasis is improvement in capacity or operating effectiveness of the system. While the construction effort and expenditure may be large, the addition to the total road system mileage may be relatively small. On the other hand, in regions or nations where economic development is just beginning, the basic problem is that of providing roads where none exist. Criteria concerning what routes to build and in what priority are derived from general social and economic development policies and decisions.

1. The United States.—After the partial and temporary involvement of the state and federal governments in highway administration and finance at the beginning of the 19th century, New Jersey was the first state to participate directly in the construction of roads, beginning in 1891. It established a department employing trained engineers who acted in an advisory capacity to county officials for improvement of road construction. The highway department developed plans and specifications, and inspected and supervised the construction, but contracts were let by the counties and the roads remained subject to maintenance by the counties. As an inducement for the counties to seek state aid, funds were appropriated by the state legislature to pay one-third of the cost of road construction.

With minor modifications, the New Jersey principle of state aid was adopted by many other states. By 1900 six other states had similar laws, and by 1917 every state had some form of state aid for road construction. A major stimulus to the movement for state highway departments resulted from the 1916 act making federal funds available for highway construction under certain conditions, one of which was the existence of a state highway department to receive and disburse the funds. In time the relations between state highway departments and local officials changed, with the states taking greater and usually exclusive responsibility for certain highways, called state highways. Most states also assist counties and localities with local roads.

The federal government resumed its interest in highways (apart from military roads and national park and forest roads, which have always been a federal responsibility) in 1893 with the creation of the Office of Road Inquiry in the Department of Agriculture. Not until the Federal-Aid Highway Act of 1916, however, did Congress agree to share with the states the cost of construction of certain main roads. Under that legislation the states retain the initiative in choosing projects and carrying them out (subject to federal inspection) and also assume the costs of maintenance and policing. The federal-aid primary system, first designated in 1921, connects all principal cities, county seats, and other traffic-generating areas, and, in general, encompasses most of the nation's main roads. The Federal-Aid Highway Act of 1944 authorized the first funds for use in urban areas and created the federal-aid secondary system, designed to link feeder roads from smaller communities and farms to the primary system. Until the establishment of the Interstate System the federal government usually shared the costs of construction on a 50–50 basis, but in some cases (e.g., for unemployment relief during the depression and for the elimination of railway crossings), it did not require any matching funds. Federal contributions rose from an average of $100,000,000 to $200,000,-000 annually in the 1920s and 1930s to more than $3,000,000,000 annually in the 1960s. The mileage encompassed in the federal aid system rose from 179,000 in 1925 to 233,000 in 1945 to almost 1,000,000 in 1960.

The total road mileage in the United States in the early 1960s, including urban mileage, was approximately 3,500,000, of which more than 3,000,000 was in rural areas. Slightly more than two-thirds of the total was paved. About 650,000 mi. were under state control, and more than 2,300,000 mi. under county or local control. The federal government controlled directly about 100,-000 mi. of park, forest, and military roads.

For many years property taxes and poll taxes were the only sources of road revenues. They were collected and expended by local governments. Commutation of taxes was permitted and "working off the road tax" was a familiar off-season occupation of farmers; it also helps to account for the poor state of roads in the 19th century. Prison labour and slave labour were also used by some states for road construction and maintenance.

The first motor vehicle fees levied by the states were small and were designed merely to cover the cost of registration, but the states soon recognized them as excellent methods of collecting highway taxes from those who used the highways. By 1915 the income from registration fees reached $18,000,000 per year, and by 1917 all states had motor-vehicle registration laws. Oregon, in 1919, was the first state to levy a special tax on gasoline for highway purposes. Within ten years all states had such taxes, and by 1930 they yielded approximately $500,000,000. In a few states local government units, especially cities, also collect taxes from highway users by means of registration fees and gasoline taxes. Early in the century expenditures on highways greatly exceeded income from taxes paid by highway users, and the difference was made up from general tax funds. Since that time, highway-user taxes have accounted for a larger and larger proportion of the expenditures on highways, and in some cases highway tax money has been diverted to nonhighway uses.

The federal government also collects taxes on gasoline, lubricating oil, new motor vehicles and parts, and tires and tubes. The

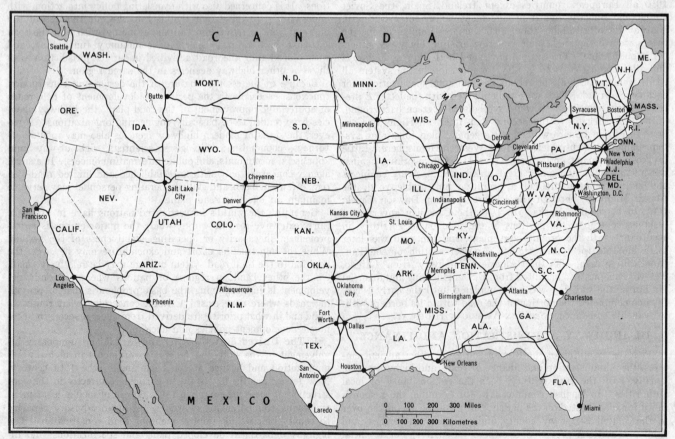

EXTENT OF PROPOSED INTERSTATE HIGHWAY SYSTEM IN THE UNITED STATES

Highway Revenue Act of 1956 established a highway trust fund into which go a group of specified (but not all) highway-related excise taxes and which became the sole source of funds for federal expenditures on the federal-aid highway systems. Thus, for the first time at the federal level, linkage was provided between highway-user imposts and highway expenditures. From the first federal grant for highways until 1952 Congress appropriated a total of $9,000,000,000 for this purpose; during the same period expenditures by all government units on streets and highways amounted to about $75,000,000,000 in terms of 1953 prices. During the early 1960s federal funds accounted for a substantially larger proportion of total highway expenditures, which for all government units was more than $12,000,000,000 annually.

2. Great Britain.—Before the Highway Act, 1835, responsibility for the repair of highways in England and Wales normally rested on the inhabitants of the parish in which the highway was situated. Roadwork was performed under the supervision of the justices of the peace in special highways sessions, through the two highway surveyors appointed annually for each parish. There were two important exceptions to parochial responsibility: certain streets in towns might be the responsibility of paving commissioners under local acts; and turnpike roads were repairable by the turnpike trustees under their private acts. The act of 1835 permitted the constitution of two other bodies which might become the authority for parochial highways, namely, elective highway boards and highway districts comprising two or more parishes. The act also provided that roads thereafter laid out should not become repairable by the inhabitants unless the procedure for their acceptance was complied with. This is the origin of the "private street."

The Highways and Locomotives (Amendment) Act, 1878, created a new class of roads called main roads, which included all roads which were no longer turnpikes after 1870 and other roads so declared by county quarter sessions; the county was made responsible for paying half the cost of maintaining these roads. Under the Local Government acts of 1888 and 1894, county councils became responsible for main roads and district councils for other roads. County borough councils became sole highway authorities in their respective areas. During the 20th century the central government assumed responsibility for certain roads that are main arteries of communication, known as trunk roads, and the Local Government Act, 1929, reallocated certain functions between local authorities. The highway authorities in 1965 were: (1) the minister of transport and civil aviation for trunk roads; (2) county borough councils for all roads in their areas other than trunk roads; (3) county councils for main roads, all roads in rural districts, and classified roads in noncounty boroughs and urban districts; and (4) noncounty borough and urban district councils for unclassified roads in their areas. The council of a noncounty borough or urban district having a population exceeding 20,000 was empowered to exercise the functions of repair and maintenance of any county road in its area. The minister could arrange with a highway authority to act as his agent in relation to any trunk road.

The Highway Act of 1959, the first consolidation measure since 1835, attempted to streamline the system by sweeping away more than 30 existing acts, some of which were 400 years old; but the committee responsible for the bill admitted that needed changes went beyond the scope of the new law and called for further legislation. Roads are designated as special roads or motorways, trunk roads, classified roads, and unclassified roads. The functions of each authority are not uniquely related to each type of road, however, and can be explained only by describing which authorities are responsible, and in what degree, for each type of road.

3. Other Countries.—After completion of the Alaska Highway during World War II, Canada built a road from the Peace River to Great Slave Lake in 1948. Two years later construction was begun on a 4,500-mi. trans-Canada highway. Work on this project continued throughout the 1950s and was nearing completion in the early 1960s.

During World War II Australia made a vigorous effort to fill some of the gaps in its road system by building roads that would connect strategic centres and thus be of military value. The 950-mi. Stuart Highway, for example, was built between Alice Springs (near the geographic centre of the continent) and the northern city of Darwin. The 875-mi. Queensland inland defense road was built to connect Ipswich in southern Queensland with Charters Towers in the north. After the war a lengthy legal battle developed between the state governments, which had large sums invested in railways, and those who advocated the construction of additional highways. Reasonable taxes and license requirements for the highway carriers were upheld by the courts in 1955, but prohibitory legislation was held unconstitutional. Most hard-surface roads in Australia are in the southern and eastern coastal regions near the cities of Melbourne, Sydney, and Brisbane.

Most nations with well-developed road systems classify their roads into two or three categories according to whether the controlling authority for each type is central, provincial, or local. France, for example, has its *routes nationales, routes départementales,* and *routes vicinales.* The tendency, however, is for the central authority to assume greater control and responsibility. In most countries motor vehicles, registrations, and fuel are taxed at much higher rates than in the United States; but the tax receipts are regarded as general revenue and do not necessarily return to the highway systems. Generally speaking, however, there is a greater awareness than in former years of the utility of a modern highway system, and more care and effort are being expended to that end in all countries.   (Ro. Ca.)

IV. MODERN PLANNING AND DESIGN

1. Classes of Roads.—The routes that form a road network or system may be classified according to their principal function. Although they serve much short-haul traffic, the primary routes, or trunk-line highways, comprise the main routes that serve especially the through and long-distance movements of traffic and that interconnect the important centres of activity of a region or nation. When built to high standards and when lateral access to them is controlled to permit movement of large volumes of traffic safely at relatively high speeds, they are variously designated as expressways, throughways, freeways, motorways, etc. Although they comprise a relatively small percentage of the total network mileage, trunk-line routes carry a relatively large percentage of the total traffic.

A second class of roads (sometimes called the secondary system, collector-distributor system, or in rural areas farm-to-market roads) collects traffic from purely local roads and streets and feeds it to the trunk-line system; conversely, these routes distribute traffic from trunk-line routes to local neighbourhoods. The secondary system also provides routes for circulation within a local area.

A third class of roads serves a purely local land-access function; *e.g.,* a neighbourhood street that does not serve through traffic and a stub-end road that serves a few farms.

Although the combined road-street-highway network of a region serves vehicular movement as a whole, the functional systems may be constructed and operated by two or more agencies. Generally, the highest and most advanced prevailing standards of planning, design, and construction are incorporated into trunk-line systems, whereas secondary systems tend to reflect more or less conventional prevailing practice in a given region. Local-access roads may include excellent residential streets or the poorest dirt track to a remote mine.

2. The Highway Planning Process.—Through the planning process, the highway transportation needs of a nation, state, or community are translated into terms of the ruling features of a road system. It may be decided, for example, that a given trunk-line system shall serve cities of over 5,000 population and shall serve the principal needs for highway movements resulting from the economic activities (agriculture, natural resources development, industry) of selected regions.

Individual routes are planned, as well as the network of roads for the whole system. Further consideration is given to the way in which the location of a given route will relate to geographical features and to community layout and functioning. For example, it may be decided that expressways shall, in general, bypass the central business districts of cities, avoid destruction of places of historic or cultural importance, and avoid splitting plots of land whose integrity must be preserved. Sometimes natural features such as stream crossings or mountain passes determine the routes.

A major endeavour in highway planning is estimating the magnitude, pattern, and other characteristics of the future traffic movements needed to serve the future economic and social activities of the area under consideration. From this estimated "demand" and through a knowledge of the performance (capacity, etc.) of types of highway facilities and components, the principal features of a route or system may be chosen. The location and arrangement of the route or routes also involve the relation of the highway, as a land user, to other land uses, since improved transportation facilities induce changes in land use. The methods of determining demand range from simple projections of traffic growth to very complex estimates of the size and distribution of future population and economic activity and the resulting pattern of movement.

3. Design Considerations.—The design process translates the outlines of the system envisioned in the planning process into a statement of the form and arrangement of the specific facilities and components to be constructed. Subject to agreed-upon design standards, the facilities are designed to meet requirements imposed by ambient physical conditions (terrain, soil conditions, climate, etc.), as well as the system requirements.

Types.—One type of design activity deals with fitting the roadway and its appurtenances into the natural and man-made terrain. This may be called locational design, for it involves route location and surveys, which are discussed more fully below.

A second type is geometrical design, which includes the dimensions, form, arrangement, and spatial interrelationships of the road elements that permit, control, or induce desired vehicular performance (*e.g.,* lane widths, clearances, and degrees of curvature). The designer must not only select pertinent forms of individual elements, but must arrange the combination and succession of elements to permit stated levels of traffic service and safe operation.

A third type of design has to do with the physical elements of the roadway; *i.e.,* devising the composition of materials, such as portland cement concrete or bituminous mixtures, and designing bridges, pavements, and other road elements. From a knowledge of the availability, properties, and costs of the materials, the design engineer must conceive and delineate the nature and composition of the roadway. The resulting assemblage of materials and structural elements must resist imposed forces and perform as specified over a chosen service life. A fourth type of design deals with devising operational subsystems such as lighting and traffic signals.

The design activities may also be considered with respect to the classes of features to be designed, including the alignment and cross-sectional features of the roadway itself, earthwork, pavements, bridges, drainage facilities, and roadside features. However, all design activities must be synthesized finally into a consistent overall design of the complete system.

Cost Considerations.—Throughout the design process, a basic consideration is cost. The criterion, however, is not necessarily the absolute minimum cost of each element, but an overall economy. For example, a stream crossing that would permit the lowest possible bridge cost may result in a circuitous routing of higher overall route and transportation costs than a more costly bridge at another location.

Cost estimates of new or improved facilities can be made after the general features of a system have been chosen and after some preliminary design. From these estimates, if a project is shown to be feasible, a financing plan can be developed and a construction program established. But to be practicable, the project must be both physically and financially feasible: physically, if it is attainable within the state of the art and if the requisite skills and materials are available for its design and construction, and financially, if the benefits to be derived from the facility exceed the costs.

Design Standards.—Design standards result in a more efficient design process and more consistent treatment. For vehicular op-

erations, consistent treatment of geometrical design features promotes greater traffic safety, and the consistent treatment of physical design features tends to induce lower overall costs of construction.

Usually in each nation, and sometimes in a region or jurisdiction, professional agencies concerned with highway development establish design standards. In the U.S., the American Association of State Highway Officials develops nationwide standards for primary highways. When accepted, these standards become the criteria for design of the federal-aid highway systems and the other roads in most of the states. For example, the minimum "design" speeds specified for the interstate highway system in rural areas are: flat terrain, 70 mph; rolling terrain, 60 mph; mountainous terrain, 50 mph; and in urban areas, 50 mph. Higher values may be used by state highway departments under appropriate conditions. Requirements dealing with gradients, curvature, transition curves, superelevation, and sight distance are dependent on design speeds; *e.g.,* the gradients shall not be steeper than 3, 4, and 5% for design speeds of 70, 60, and 50 mph, respectively, except in very rugged terrain, where gradients 2% steeper may be used.

As a basis for designing features which affect the system's capacity to handle traffic volumes, the concept of the design hourly volume is used. For the interstate system this is specified to be the peak-hour traffic that is as high as the 30th highest hourly volume of two-direction mixed traffic estimated for the year 1975. (Portions of the interstate system designed after 1963 were planned to serve traffic growth estimated for 20 years, rather than to handle 1975 traffic.) The number of lanes, the use of median strips, the use and nature of grade separations, the arrangement of elements governed by sight distance, etc., are functions of the design hourly volume. Other features may be governed by the prevailing characteristics of the vehicles and consideration of safety, such as lane widths (12 ft.), shoulder widths (ordinarily not less than 10 ft.), and width of median strips. Because direct access to the traveled roadways of the interstate system is prevented, the service to adjacent property is provided by frontage or service roads designed as part of the route.

For other types of roads and systems, the design standards used by a road agency are adapted to the needs, conditions of use, and financial resources of the jurisdiction. The nature of the terrain and the general climatic conditions may have an important effect upon the physical design characteristics (and upon the construction and maintenance costs) of roads. Roads constructed in rugged mountainous terrain are more costly than roads built to the same design standards in relatively flat terrain with good soils for support. The design (and construction) practices that evolve and are used may differ considerably among regions having markedly different climatic conditions, such as the temperate climate of Western Europe, the tropical climate of West Africa or India, or the arid and semiarid climate of some regions of the southwest United States or Australia. Since the kinds of surface soils (in or on which the roads must be built) and the kinds of construction materials locally available are conditioned in the long term by prevailing climate, both costs and ways of dealing with the problems are affected.

Plans and Specifications.—The end result of the design process is a set of plans and specifications which spells out requirements that must be met for construction. The term "plans" in this context refers to drawings—graphic representations of the nature of the facility and its components.

4. Route Location and Route Surveys.—As a part of the planning-design process, or in close conjunction with it, a series of route location studies are made, leading to the final location of the roadway and its appurtenances. The "best" route is usually the most economical route within the limits of specified grade, curvature, and other design controls. In many instances, however, especially in urban areas, there may be other considerations, such as preservation of established land uses or buildings, which may override the conventional criterion of least cost of facility or even least total transport cost.

The route location process involves a series of surveys that provide the necessary information about the terrain through which a projected route will pass. After a location has been selected, detailed design and cost estimates can be made and a basis provided for designating and acquiring land for right-of-way.

Three general stages in the route location process may be distinguished: a reconnaissance stage, a preliminary location stage, and a final location stage.

In the earlier days of road building, especially in new country, the process was largely a field operation. It was essentially design-in-the-field; the key man was the location engineer, or locator, a person with experience and skill. In some instances, after preliminary reconnaissance, with a kind of "second sight" of how the road could be fitted to the terrain, he might almost telescope the three above-mentioned stages into one operation.

Later, until about World War II, location surveys became more elaborate and detailed. From reconnaissance work came a strip map having sufficient information about topography and natural control points so that several general alternate locations could be studied and a preliminary line could be run for the selected route. This line was usually laid out with transit, tape, and level, providing distances, directions (angles), and a profile in elevation; often enough topography was mapped to give preliminary information for balancing earth-moving work in cuts and fills and for dealing with drainage problems. From these data a final location was selected and staked out; during the final location work, the curves were laid out and cross sections (profiles perpendicular to the line) were taken so that slope stakes could be set and estimates of earth-moving work could be prepared for construction purposes. Minor adjustments could also be made during the final ground location.

Since World War II, the use of aerial surveys and photogrammetric methods has revolutionized the road location process. While the three stages are still present, after key ground controls are established and aerial photographs taken, the work is largely "office oriented" until the final staking out takes place. From stereophotographs, maps of varying degrees of refinement are prepared. Small scale maps (and the photographs themselves) give information for reconnaissance not only on the shape of the ground surface but also on the nature of the terrain, the soils, the ground water conditions, and potential sources of road-making materials near the line of the road. From larger scale maps various trial alignments are studied in detail, and cross sections for earthwork computations are plotted.

The use of automatic stereoplotters and electronic data processing has greatly speeded up the process and also permitted the detailed study of a variety of locations. The use of aerial survey techniques has not only reduced the effort and increased the scope of the location process in rural areas where the natural topography is a key factor, but also has proved valuable in congested urban areas where buildings and other facilities make ground surveys extremely difficult.

After deciding the location of a facility and its appurtenances, land is acquired for right-of-way. A process of legal description, appraisal, negotiation for purchase or condemnation, and legal acquisition of title is involved. Although governments may exercise the powers of eminent domain, the procedure may vary among states and nations, depending upon their legal systems and the powers granted to the highway agency.

V. CONSTRUCTION

Most highway construction is performed by private companies under contract with the highway agency. In some jurisdictions where the amount of construction is small and ordinarily consists of minor reconstruction or replacement, the highway agency sometimes performs the work with its own forces.

The major construction operations include site clearance (e.g., removing buildings and relocating utilities), grading operations (e.g., excavating, hauling, embankment construction, shaping the roadway cross section, compacting earth in embankments and subgrades), construction of drainage structures, paving, construction of bridges and other structures, and in some instances work pertaining to roadside treatment (such as landscaping).

Construction supervision and control activities performed by the highway agencies include setting of line, grade, and cross sections; measurement of quantities used as a basis for payments to the contractor; and inspection to determine conformance to the plans and specifications with respect to dimensions, quality of materials, and location of various items (e.g., culverts, abutments).

For large complex operations some contractors may have staff engineers who design various construction processes, devices, and temporary structures and who control the highly technical aspects of work.

Work scheduling and cost control are important aspects of the construction process. In the construction of new facilities on the alignments of existing routes, particularly routes carrying appreciable traffic, traffic handling requires considerable attention. The construction of temporary roadways, detours, and operation of traffic controls to maintain safe movement and minimize traffic delay calls for special design and scheduling.

1. Earthwork.—An important part of road building has to do with earth materials. The roadway as a whole must rest on soil or rock deposits of widely ranging composition and quality. Many primitive roads are composed of soil, and some better roads use soil and rock (usually treated or processed) to make up the lower portions of the composite pavement structure. To obtain desirable alignments and grades, cuts must be made in ridges and sidehills, and depressions must be filled. A fill or embankment is an earth structure that must be designed and constructed to have stability. Appropriate earth materials are selected and processed to provide sand, gravel, or crushed stone for building the road.

During recent decades, marked advance in the applied science called soil mechanics (q.v.) has contributed much to understanding soil behaviour and the technological control of soil for use in road building. The techniques for soil testing and classification provide a means for more precise identification of acceptable soil materials. Knowledge of soil strength and the factors controlling it has laid a better basis for analyzing and regulating the stability of soil masses subject to load. The evolution of techniques for compacting soils and controlling the density of compacted soils has put the design of embankments and other road components made of soil on a scientific basis.

The continued development since the 1920s of very large earth-moving equipment has revolutionized road construction. Not only has such equipment made practicable the handling of quantities of earth that would have been considered utterly unfeasible in an earlier day, but the relative cost of earth-moving has remained approximately the same for several decades, while the costs of other items of highway construction have appreciably increased. Two factors, the crawler tractor and the rugged heavy-duty engine, have enabled the development of very efficient and versatile

REMOVAL OF LOOSE SOIL FROM A HIGHWAY SITE BY CRAWLER TRACTOR-DRAWN LOADER AND DUMP TRUCKS

construction equipment: for excavation, bulldozers (a tractor with a curved blade on the front for pushing and scraping), rippers, tractor-shovel units; scraper-carryalls; for hauling, the scraper-carryall, as well as very large heavy-duty trucks; for earth compaction, a family of compaction equipment (such as the sheepsfoot roller, heavy-duty pneumatic-tired rollers, vibratory compactors); and for grading and shaping the roadbed, various bladed graders, as well as the bulldozer. Belt loaders and belt conveyors, draglines, cranes, and heavy-duty power shovels are also used. (*See* EXCAVATION.)

2. Drainage.—There are two aspects to the problem of drainage—providing structures to care for surface water and avoiding the detrimental effects of water in the soils composing the roadbed.

Streams that cross the right-of-way are carried under the roadway by culverts (generally for smaller and intermittent streams) and bridges (for larger streams). The culvert or stream channel must be large enough to carry the flow of water at all times without damaging the roadway. The maximum runoff of storm water from the watershed that contributes to a stream is estimated, and a "design" flood flow is chosen, based on the most severe flood flow within the service life of the facility. In the case of bridges, the abutments and piers (if any) must be designed and constructed to avoid being washed out during high water.

Another phase of surface-water drainage is disposal of water falling on the roadway itself. Pavements are generally crowned or cambered (or otherwise sloped laterally) so as to carry water off to lateral ditches (or gutters), which in turn carry the flow to a stream (or a specially constructed drainage channel). Highways having an extensively paved area, particularly freeways in urban areas, present special problems in drainage.

The second major aspect of drainage concerns measures to avoid the accumulation of excessive water in the soil layers that compose the pavement structure, since the strength or supporting capacity of soil is decreased with increasing water content. Water may enter the base courses and subgrade by infiltration downward through the pavement surface (and shoulders) and by lateral inward percolation of water from alongside the roadway.

Of the three measures used to keep the roadbed from losing stability, the first is to provide and maintain as impervious a pavement surface as possible. In heavy-duty pavements, a primary purpose of joint sealing and seal coating is to prevent water infiltration. A second measure is to construct the roadbed sufficiently high above the water table—both the normal water table and the temporary fluctuating water table induced by water in the lateral ditches or standing alongside the road. A third measure is the use of roadbed soils that do not attract and hold appreciable water by capillary action. For this reason granular soils are preferred for base courses. Allied to the problem of the detrimental effect of water in the subgrade is the problem of frost heave and the roadbed's subsequent loss of stability during the spring thaw.

3. Pavements.—The primary function of a pavement as a structure is to transmit the loads imposed by vehicles to the basement soil under the roadway in such a manner that the soil mass remains stable (*i.e.*, it does not exhibit detrimental deformation or does not rupture). Moreover, the wearing surface of the pavement structure must resist the abrasive action of moving traffic and must provide acceptable riding qualities. The pavement structure and its components also must resist the deteriorating influences of temperature and moisture change and various induced chemical reactions; it must also protect the roadbed from water infiltration.

The term "pavement" is used in two senses: it refers to the top layer, which provides the rid-

ing surface, and to the layered system, comprising the wearing course, one or more base courses, and the subgrade, or natural basement soil. It is this layered system that must be dealt with in the structural design of a pavement. The action of each successive layer is to "spread the load" so that the underlying layer of weaker material can support the pressures transmitted to it from above.

Among the many types of pavement, two major categories may be distinguished: those built entirely of natural earth materials (soil, gravel, broken stone); and those in which the upper layers, at least, are made from manufactured materials such as asphaltic concrete or cement concrete and with permanent surfaces containing either bituminous materials or cement as a binder.

In the more densely populated countries of Western Europe and North America, all the main roads and most of the secondary roads have pavements with permanent surfaces. In contrast most of the roads in the developing countries of Africa and Asia have surfaces of earth or gravel.

Natural Earth Materials.—Roads made entirely from natural earth materials can be suitable for carrying light traffic up to about 300 vehicles per day. Sufficient mechanical stability to carry traffic loads is provided by gravelly or sandy soils or by crushed rock combined with a small proportion of clay or some other fine material to act as a binder. The temperate and cold regions of North America and Europe generally require gravelly or stony mixtures with very little clay binder, while in hotter, drier regions, finer sandy materials are also extensively used, along with a larger proportion of clay binder.

Such roads are usually dusty in dry weather and tend to become corrugated and develop potholes, while in wet weather they are often not sufficiently stable to carry heavy traffic. Deliquescent salts such as calcium chloride and gummy residues such as lignin-sulfonates are used to reduce dust and to help in binding the road surface in dry weather. Mineral oil and occasionally vegetable oils are also used. On all such roads regular maintenance is necessary to retain an even running surface, and the frequency and cost of this maintenance generally mounts rapidly as traffic increases.

Roads with Permanent Surfaces.—Such roads consist of layers of material laid on natural soil or a prepared subgrade, each successive layer being stronger than those below, the whole being surmounted by the running surface.

1. The subgrade is a natural soil on which the road is laid. This soil, which is either found on site or imported to form an embankment, must be compacted to improve its bearing capacity. In dry, warm regions the compacted subgrades are generally quite strong, while in wet, cool regions they may be very weak, particularly where the soils are clayey. An accurate assessment of the bearing capacity of the soil subgrade is important in considering the design of the road structure.

2. The subbase is the first layer of imported material to be laid on the natural soil. Besides its structural function, it frequently

ASPHALT FINISHER LAYING A BITUMINOUS MIXTURE

serves as a working platform on which transport vehicles and construction machinery can operate in building the road. The materials used to make subbases are frequently natural gravels, sandy soils, or broken rock. As with roads made from natural earth materials, high mechanical stability is sought by the careful selection of material and sometimes by combining different materials to produce a more stable mixture. The stability of these materials and their resistance to the weakening effects of water may be improved by an additive such as portland cement, lime, or a bituminous material.

3. For the base and surfacing, two forms of construction may be distinguished: flexible construction, in which bituminous binders are employed at least in the upper layers; and rigid construction, in which the functions of base and surfacing are combined in one material, portland cement concrete.

BY COURTESY OF PORTLAND CEMENT ASSOCIATION

CONVENTIONAL CONCRETE PAVING TRAIN USING SIX SEPARATE MACHINES THAT RIDE ON METAL SIDE FORMS DOUBLING AS RAILS

In flexible construction the lower layers of the base may be of natural gravel or crushed stone; natural materials stabilized with cement or lime also may be used. The upper layers and the surfacing are invariably made with bituminous mixtures. On very heavily traveled roads in Europe and the U.S. there is a growing tendency to employ bituminous mixtures for most or even all the layers of the base and surfacing. In contrast, on more lightly traveled roads, particularly in the warmer parts of the world, the road base may consist entirely of natural gravel, broken rock, or soil stabilized with portland cement or lime, with a surfacing that consists only of a thin bituminous treatment.

The design of the road structure can thus be a complex problem requiring considerable engineering skill to produce a road that is, on the one hand, economically feasible and, on the other, strong enough to carry the expected traffic load.

This design process involves the following principal steps: (1) traffic analysis to establish the combination of load, critical wheel load, and repetitions of load to which the pavement structure will be subjected; (2) evaluation of subgrade, subbase, and base materials to determine their load-bearing characteristics; (3) investigation of alternate combinations of base course and surface course (including types) that could meet requirements for load and durability under prevailing climatic conditions; (4) economic analysis of the several feasible designs; and (5) final selection of the optimum design.

Thus while a relatively lightly traveled road in a dry region may consist of a total thickness of 6 in. of relatively cheap base and surfacing, a heavily traveled road in a more humid region may require a total thickness of construction of 20 to 30 in., with the upper layers, at least, consisting of processed materials of relatively high cost.

Bituminous Mixtures.—Two types of materials are used in making bituminous mixtures: asphalts and tars. The tars used are the residues derived from the destructive distillation of coal. Some asphalts occur naturally (*e.g.*, Trinidad asphalt), but most of the asphalts used are residues derived from the petroleum refining process.

The combination of bituminous materials with mineral aggregates, used in a variety of maximum sizes, gradings, and shapes of particle, results in numerous types of mixtures. These are designed for various uses and are adapted to various methods of processing in the field. Mixtures are designed to meet requirements such as stability, durability, effectiveness in preventing water infiltration, wearing resistance, skid resistance, etc.

Mixtures containing the harder grades of asphalt are generally processed in a "hot-mix" plant, where the final temperature reaches about 275° F (135° C). Mixtures containing the more fluid asphalts may be road-mixed or plant-mixed at atmospheric temperatures. The mixtures are spread and rolled into place with appropriate field equipment.

The mixtures (often called asphaltic concretes) used for heavy-duty bituminous pavements are generally composed of a densely graded, high-quality aggregate combined with a hard grade of asphalt, mixed in a "hot-plant," and placed by paving machines designed to produce a uniform surface having good riding qualities.

Portland Cement Concrete Pavements.—Concrete pavements are composed of portland cement and graded mineral aggregates; these materials are mixed with water, placed, cured, and allowed to harden to produce slabs having considerable flexural strength. They are often called rigid pavements because they tend to distribute the applied loads through slab action. (*See* CEMENT.)

A concrete mixture is proportioned to give specified strength, impermeability, and durability (*see* CONCRETE). It may be mixed on site or in a central mixing plant, from which it is hauled to the construction site in special trucks. In some instances the mixing process may be carried out during hauling in specially designed "transit-mixer" trucks. When mixing is done on the job, the mixer and paving machine may move as one unit along the roadway being paved. The placement of concrete requires the use of side forms usually placed so as to pave one traffic lane at a time. The freshly deposited concrete is compacted in place, usually by vibrators operated in conjunction with the paving machine. Following placement, a process of screeding (to obtain the shape and elevation of the surface) and finishing (to obtain the desired surface texture) is carried out. The freshly placed concrete must be cured in the presence of moisture for an appropriate period to attain the desired strength.

Vehicle loads produce flexural stresses in a pavement slab that may be critical at one of three locations: near a corner, near an edge, or near the centre of the slab. Also, fluctuations in temperature and moisture content of the slab produce differential tensile and compressive stresses across its thickness that result in "curling," and variations in resistance of the supporting layers may produce warping. The slab thickness, then, depends on the magnitude and frequency of the applied loads and induced stresses over the service life of the pavements, the resistance provided by the supporting base and subgrade, and the strength of the concrete.

Because of volume changes due to temperature and moisture change, the tendency of the concrete slab to expand and contract as a whole must be controlled. In one commonly used method, transverse joints are placed at intervals (about 15 ft. for unreinforced slabs and 30 to 60 ft. for lightly reinforced slabs). Longitudinal joints are also provided between slabs in adjacent traffic lanes. Although in this type of construction a slab is essentially designed as a plain concrete slab, some reinforced steel is generally used to control and distribute cracks that will form. To avoid faulting of adjacent slabs, some plan of keeping them in alignment and of transferring the load from one slab to the next is provided; steel dowels (pins) projecting into each slab are often used as load-transfer devices. The joints are sealed with some substance (*e.g.*, asphalt) that will permit expansion and contraction but prevent water infiltration.

Some use is made of continuous reinforced concrete slabs. These slabs may be several hundred feet long between construction joints. The steel serves to carry shrinkage stresses and distribute the cracks so they remain small. Experiments have also been carried on in the use of slabs in which the reinforcing is "prestressed," that is, stressed in tension so as to induce in the concrete a state of compression. The object is to provide an initial compressive stress such that the subsequent tendency of the concrete to shrink relieves the compressive stress but does not develop sufficient tensile stress to cause cracking.

Road Surface Characteristics.—Whatever materials are used to make the running surface of the road, there are certain basic requirements in the interests of service and safety. The surface should be sufficiently plane and true to provide a safe and reasonably comfortable ride for road users. The almost universal use of machines for laying and finishing all types of surfacings makes it relatively easy to obtain high standards of riding quality both in new construction and in resurfacing projects.

A high resistance to skidding is required, particularly on high-speed roads, on the approaches to junctions, and at other places where emergency braking may be necessary. Normally all forms of road surfacing have an adequate resistance to skidding when they are clean and dry. The problem of skidding on wet roads has been intensively studied and has led both to improved tire and brake design and to a better understanding of what is required to provide road surfacing that will retain a good resistance to skidding under the polishing action of traffic. Basically a sharp "toothy" texture is required so that the tire can make effective contact with the road through a film of water. Also, on high-speed roads, a coarse, open texture is desirable to provide surface water with an easy path away from the points of contact between tire and road. For the first of these the choice of stone in the surfacing is particularly important, selecting those types that continue to present a rough surface under the abrasive action of traffic. The coarse texture required on high-speed roads is secured with bituminous materials by the design of the mixture and with concrete by finishing treatments at the time of construction.

The well-tried treatment for icy roads is the application of grit and salt. Where the hazard from icy roads is particularly high, electrical heating is sometimes employed, using metal grids built into the road surface that are automatically controlled.

FOUR-LEVEL FREEWAY INTERCHANGE IN DOWNTOWN LOS ANGELES, CALIF., USED BY APPROXIMATELY 350,000 VEHICLES PER DAY AND CONSIDERED ONE OF THE WORLD'S BUSIEST INTERSECTIONS

A further requirement for road surfacings is that their surface texture should aid visibility at night. A relatively fine surface texture is required in towns and cities where the main illumination comes from street lighting, while on the open road, where only vehicle headlights are used, a relatively coarse texture is preferred.

4. Junctions and Interchanges.—An important consideration in the satisfactory functioning of a road network is the arrangement and layout of the junctions. A poorly designed junction is an obstruction to traffic flow and a source of accidents.

The treatment of a junction depends upon the volume of traffic to be handled and the design speed to be adopted. To handle traffic as safely and expeditiously as possible at junctions of conventional roads, traffic control measures are often applied (*e.g.*, restricted speed zones, lane markings, "yield" signs, and traffic signals). Also, roadside treatment may be required to provide adequate sight distance for traffic in the intersecting legs of a junction. At the junctions of modern, high-speed freeways or motorways the grade crossing of intersecting streams of traffic is eliminated by the use of grade-separation structures, often called "interchanges." The interchanges of very high-volume freeways (approximately 100,000 vehicles per day or more) may be extremely complicated, both in geometrical layout and structurally, and as many as four levels of the roadways have been used. Such interchanges may occupy several acres of land, and acceptable landscaping is an important consideration.

5. Bridges and Other Structures.—Both tunneling and the design and construction of bridges and other structures (*e.g.*, retaining walls) are specialized fields. Many highway agencies have a special division for structural design and construction supervision of structural work. (*See* also BRIDGES; TUNNEL.)

6. Roadside Treatment.—The land between the edges of the roadway and the right-of-way boundaries is important in building and operating modern highways, and, on limited-access facilities having separated roadways, the treatment of the median area between the roadways requires attention. The control of certain features on abutting lands (such as advertising signs, structures, and natural growth that affect sight distances) involves special legal problems; on controlled access facilities, access to road-user services (fuel, food, lodging) is necessary. On modern scenic highways or on long routes in sparsely settled regions, roadside rest areas with appurtenant facilities and services are often provided.

The way roadside features are designed and constructed affects maintenance costs, safety, the convenience and comfort of the road users, and the aesthetic sense of both road users and the sur-

SAFETY FEATURES OF MODERN ROAD SURFACES
(Left) Light colour and rough texture contribute to better night visibility.
(Right) Coarse, gritty texture provides high skid resistance

rounding community. In some instances, roadside treatments are designed to shield adjacent land users from traffic noise.

VI. MAINTENANCE AND OPERATION

Maintenance, in a broad sense, refers to the activities involved in keeping the physical road plant (roadway, roadside, structures, and other appurtenances) in a state of satisfactory repair and in the operation of those facilities and services necessary to provide continuous, safe, and satisfactory traffic service. The phrase "maintenance and operation," then, includes much more than repairing pavements and cleaning ditches.

Since the quality of a highway's original design and construction influences its subsequent maintenance and cost, no fixed formula can be given for the proportion of highway expenditures that should be devoted to maintenance. In contrast with construction, where most of the work is performed by contract, most maintenance is performed by the highway agencies. Some separate items of maintenance work, however, are sometimes done by contract (*e.g.*, bridge painting).

Major physical maintenance activities include keeping the road surface and roadside area in satisfactory condition, maintaining drainage facilities, repairing storm damage, removing debris and litter, and maintaining traffic control facilities.

A substantial fraction of the maintenance effort is expended on the upkeep of the roadway surface. Gravel roads require intermittent blading and shaping and occasional resurfacing. Intermediate-type surfaced roads require patching and sealing, whereas high-type pavements require replacement or reconditioning of distressed areas and sealing. When a road surface wears too smooth, various surface treatments help to improve skid resistance.

Many devices and operational plans are employed to facilitate traffic service and induce safe vehicular operation. The design of many of these features is generally the responsibility of the traffic engineering section of a highway agency, but their operation and upkeep is usually a function of the maintenance forces.

To guide the movement of vehicles on the pavement and induce orderly flow, center line and lane markings and in some cases raised median strips and islands are used. In steep terrain and on curves where careless drivers may run off the roadway, guardrails are necessary; on dual roadways, when it is difficult to pro-

BY COURTESY OF INTERNATIONAL ROAD FEDERATION

INTERSECTION OF THE AMSTERDAM-UTRECHT HIGHWAY WITH A LOCAL ROAD WHICH BYPASSES AMSTERDAM

vide an adequate width of median separations, guardrails are also used, some of special design.

To mark roadway edges and warn of objects that restrict lateral clearance (such as culvert headwalls and minor road entrances), roadside markers of various design are employed; frequently these are of some reflecting material (*e.g.*, "cat's-eyes").

Signs perform three main functions: regulatory, warning, and informational. Speed-zone signs and stop signs are common examples of regulatory signs. Warning signs are those that call attention to hazards such as steeper grades and sharper curves than

usual on the route; on modern high-speed roads, signs that can be exhibited when needed to warn of temporary hazards, such as fog or the presence of obstructions due to maintenance or construction work, are important. Included in the informational group are route markers and signs that indicate distances and turnoffs to destinations.

For positive traffic control, especially at intersections, traffic signals are used. Some intersection traffic signals are set to operate on a fixed cycle, and some are operated in coordination with preceding and succeeding signals to promote the continuous flow of traffic. In urban networks considerable experimentation has been carried on to develop area traffic-control systems; in such systems, sensor devices feed information on changing traffic flows into a high-speed electronic computer; its output schedules the settings of signals in the network to keep the network flow at an optimum.

While costly, the provision of nighttime illumination reduces accidents. Although continuous lighting of streets and highways is feasible mainly in urban areas, sufficient illumination, especially at intersections, is especially important. On major freeways, even in rural areas, there has been increasing use of lighting at interchanges.

See also references under "Roads and Highways" in the Index.

(H. E. DA.)

BIBLIOGRAPHY.—A. C. Rose, *Public Roads of the Past*, 2 vol. (1949–52); I. D. Margary, *Roman Roads in Britain*, 2 vol. (1956–57); R. Syme, *The Story of Britain's Highways* (1952); V. Hart, *The Story of American Roads* (1950); J. Labatut and W. J. Lane (eds.), *Highways in our National Life* (1950); Poyntz Tyler (ed.), *American Highways Today* (1957); E. C. Davies (ed.), *Roads and Their Traffic* (1960); U. S. Dept. of Commerce, Bureau of Public Roads, *Highways in the United States* (1954); G. R. Stewart, *U. S. 40* (1953); The Asphalt Institute, *Asphalt Handbook* (1960); R. G. Batson, *Roads: Their Alignment, Layout and Construction* (1950); J. H. Collins and C. A. Hart, *Principles of Road Engineering* (1947); J. R. Martin and H. A. Wallace, *Design and Construction of Asphalt Pavements* (1958); C. H. Oglesby and L. I. Hewes, *Highway Engineering* (1963); Portland Cement Association, *Concrete Pavement Design* (1951); L. J. Ritter, Jr., and R. J. Paquette, *Highway Engineering* (1951); U. S. Bureau of Public Roads, *Highway Statistics* (annually); K. B. Woods (ed.), *Highway Engineering Handbook* (1960); Road Research Laboratory, *Soil Mechanics for Road Engineers* (1952), *Concrete Roads: Design and Construction* (1955), *Bituminous Materials in Road Construction* (1962).

ROANNE, a town of east-central France and headquarters of an *arrondissement* in the *département* of Loire, lies on the Loire River 55 mi. (88 km.) NW of Lyons by road. Pop. (1962) 51,-468. Of ancient remains only the castle dungeon is left. The centre of the town is the Carrefour Helvétique. The *lycée* Jean Puy occupies the former 17th-century Jesuit college. The Joseph Déchelette Museum has a fine regional archaeological collection. A bridge over the Loire leads to the suburb of Le Coteau. The town is a junction of railway lines to Paris, Saint-Étienne, and Lyons (via Tarare), and of roads to Lyons, Saint-Étienne, Vichy, and Mâcon. Its situation made Roanne an important commercial centre, and it was later industrialized. It has weaving of cotton goods, spinning of artificial silk, knitting, tanning, mechanical and construction engineering, and the manufacture of hacksaws.

Roanne was a settlement of the Segusiani, known as Rodumna; it was a centre of crossroads in Gallo-Roman times, and was mentioned in ancient geography by Ptolemy. It was made a lordship by Jacques Coeur in 1443. (G. FR.)

ROANOKE, a city of western Virginia, U.S., on the Roanoke river, 166 mi. WSW of Richmond. It was settled in 1740 but did not become important until 1882 despite its favourable location in a fertile bowl between the Blue Ridge and Allegheny mountains, easily accessible from the north, east and west. It was first called Big Lick because of its salt deposits. In 1852 it became a way station of the railroad extending across southern Virginia but in 1880 it had only 669 inhabitants. Its growth started in 1882 when a railroad from the north made a junction there with the line across southern Virginia, offering an outlet for the coal deposits of the Virginias; the town acquired huge railroad shops and offices, and in that year was renamed Roanoke. In 1884 it was chartered as a city, its population at that time being 5,000. Railroads were supplemented by various industrial activities including fabricated steel. The city grew to 21,495 by 1900. Further growth was assured by the coming of the Virginian railroad in 1908 and of a large rayon plant in 1917. Roanoke suffered a labour depression after 1957 when the Norfolk and Western Railway shifted from steam to diesel locomotives and the rayon works closed because its product was outmoded. But the city's industry was too extensive for its prosperity to be halted permanently. Its truck lines expanded and hotel accommodations were provided for tourists from the Sky Line drive and the Blue Ridge parkway. The population of the city in 1960 was 97,110; that of the standard metropolitan statistical area (Roanoke city and Roanoke county) was 158,803. (For comparative population figures *see* table in VIRGINIA: *Population*.) Roanoke has a council-manager form of government, in effect since 1918. A few miles west of the city is Salem, the county seat and home of Roanoke college (Lutheran, founded 1842), and 6 mi. N. is Hollins, a private college for women, established in 1842. (F. B. S.)

ROANOKE ISLAND, in Dare county, off the coast of North Carolina, U.S., is south of Albemarle sound between the Outer Banks and the mainland. The island, which is 12 mi. long with an average width of about 3 mi., is the site of the first attempted English settlement in America and the birthplace of the first child of English parents born in the new world (Virginia Dare, Aug. 18, 1587). In 1584 captains Philip Amadas, or Amidas, and Arthur Barlowe there claimed the North American continent for Sir Walter Raleigh under his patent from Elizabeth I. After two months exploration they returned to England with two Indians, Manteo and Wanchese, and with samples of tobacco and potatoes. Next year Sir Richard Grenville (*q.v.*) transported 108 settlers under Ralph Lane, but the whole group returned to England with Sir Francis Drake in 1586. Two weeks later Grenville arrived with supplies, leaving 15 men to hold England's claim.

In 1587 John White, artist of the Lane colony (whose 75 Indian drawings are in the British museum) and grandfather of Virginia Dare, arrived at Roanoke Island but the 15 men had vanished. He planted a new colony comprising more than 100 settlers. Later he returned to England for supplies. Upon White's return in Aug. 1590, the only trace of this lost colony was the word "Croatoan" carved on one tree and "Cro" on another tree. Numerous and romantic are the conjectures as to the colony's fate. From 1937 its gallant story has been portrayed locally each summer by the outdoor drama, *The Lost Colony*, by Paul Green. The Fort Raleigh National Historic site was established in 1941 to restore this first English implantation, based on original excavations and employing authentic restorations.

Roanoke was the scene of a Civil War action in Dec. 1862 when Federal troops under Gen. Ambrose Everett Burnside took the island from the Confederates under Col. Henry M. Shaw.

Manteo, the county seat, and Wanchese, a fishing village, are added tourist attractions. (B. P. R.)

ROANOKE RIVER, of southeastern United States, rises in the Appalachian valley in southwestern Virginia and flows southeasterly in a 410-mi. long course into Albemarle sound, on the Atlantic coast of North Carolina. It drains an area of 9,580 sq.mi.

Shortly before crossing the Virginia-North Carolina state line it is joined by the Dan river, its principal tributary. The Roanoke is navigable for small craft for 112 mi. from its mouth to Weldon, N.C., which lies just below the fall line.

Ships with a draft of up to 12 ft. can reach Plymouth, N.C., 6 mi. above the mouth. In 1829 the Weldon canal, 12 mi. long, was opened to afford a passage around the falls, but it was abandoned in 1850. (F. O. A.)

ROBBER SYNOD, an irregular ecclesiastical council held at Ephesus in A.D. 449. *See* COUNCIL: *Councils to the 9th Century: From Ephesus (431) to Chalcedon (451)*.

ROBBERY, in law, is the unlawful and forcible taking of goods or money from the person of another by violence or threatened violence. Robbery is larceny (*q.v.*) with violence. *See also* CRIME; CRIMINAL LAW.

ROBBIA, DELLA, the name of a celebrated family of Florentine sculptors, mainly associated with the production of works in enameled terra cotta. The principal members of this family were LUCA DELLA ROBBIA (*c.* 1399–1482), his nephew ANDREA (1435–1525) and two of Andrea's five sons, GIOVANNI (1469–1529?) and GIROLAMO (1488–1566).

LUCA, son of Simone di Marco della Robbia, matriculated in the guild of sculptors in 1432. He is mentioned in the preface to L. B. Alberti's *Della Pittura*, along with Filippo Brunelleschi, Masaccio, Donatello and Lorenzo Ghiberti, as one of the pioneers of Florentine Renaissance style, and he must have been an established artist by 1431, when his most important work was commissioned, the *cantoria*, or "singing gallery," over the door of the

ALINARI

PANEL OF THE "SINGING GALLERY," A BAS-RELIEF BY LUCA DELLA ROBBIA FOR THE FLORENCE CATHEDRAL, 15TH CENTURY. IN THE MUSEO DEL DUOMO, FLORENCE

north sacristy of the *duomo* ("cathedral"), on which he was engaged until 1438. The balance of evidence is that at this time he practised solely as a marble sculptor. In style Luca's marble sculptures recall the work of Nanni di Banco, to whom his early training may have been due. The *cantoria* (taken down in 1688 and now reassembled in the Museo dell'Opera del Duomo) consists of ten figurated reliefs, two at the ends of the gallery, four on the front and four beneath placed between the supporting consoles. The panels illustrate Psalm cl and show two groups of singing boys, trumpeters, choral dancers and children playing on the psaltery, cithara, organ and harp, tambourine and cymbals. Two bronze *putti* from the upper corners of the gallery are in the Musée Jacquemart-André, Paris. The architectural forms throughout are strongly influenced by Brunelleschi and the handling of the figures reveals a close study of classical originals. The panels owe their great popularity to the innocence and lack of artifice with which the children in them are portrayed.

Shortly before the completion of the *cantoria*, Luca received the commission (1437) for five reliefs of the arts and sciences for the campanile of the cathedral, in completion of the cycle begun by Andrea Pisano a century before, and in 1439 undertook work on the altars in the chapels of St. Peter and St. Paul in the cathedral. Two marble reliefs from the predella of the St. Peter altar survive in the Bargello. The most important of Luca's other works in marble are a tabernacle at Peretola, near Florence (carved for Sta. Maria Nuova in Florence in 1441–43), and the tomb of Benozzo Federighi, bishop of Fiesole (d. 1450), completed in 1459. In all these works Luca appears as an artist of strongly classical stamp, with a predilection for static figures and rectilinear compositions.

Both in the campanile reliefs (designed to blend with those of Andrea Pisano) and in the figures of the dead Christ, Virgin and St. John behind the Federighi monument, Luca's style represents a conscious reversion to the practice of the 14th century. The Federighi monument is surrounded by a strip of flat foliated decoration in enameled terra cotta. Intimately connected with these works is the bronze door of the north sacristy of the cathedral (1446–63). Undertaken in its early stages in collaboration with Michelozzo and the bronze sculptor Maso di Bartolommeo, the door consists of two wings, with heads of prophets in the frames and ten reliefs of the Virgin and Child, St. John the Baptist and the evangelists and doctors of the church. Though features of the design may be due to Michelozzo, it is likely that the whole figurated area is the work of Luca della Robbia.

The medium of polychrome enameled terra cotta appears for the first time in a dated work in the Peretola tabernacle, where it is used to set off the marble sculpture. The earliest documented work wholly executed in this medium is a lunette of the Resurrection over the door of the north sacristy of the cathedral (1442–45). According to Giorgio Vasari, the glaze with which Luca covered his terra-cotta sculptures consisted of a mixture of tin, litharge antimony and other minerals. Precedents are found in pottery and there is evidence that in the studio of Ghiberti experiments were made in carving terra-cotta sculptures with transparent glaze as a basis for gilding. In relation to sculpture, however, the technique adopted by Luca and developed by the later members of the Della Robbia workshop was a novel one. In the late 15th and 16th centuries works in this medium seem to have been regarded as an inexpensive substitute for marble sculpture, but analysis of the early commissions suggests that initially the medium was employed only in architectural contexts where marble sculpture would have been inapposite and that the function of the glaze was colouristic and not preservative. The resurrection lunette in the *duomo* was followed (1446–51) by a corresponding relief of the Ascension over the south sacristy door, in which a wider range of colour is employed.

Of the many decorative schemes for which enameled terra cotta was employed by Luca della Robbia, the most important are the roundels of Apostles in Brunelleschi's Pazzi chapel (soon after 1443); the roof of Michelozzo's chapel of the Crucifix in S. Miniato al Monte, Florence (1447–48); a lunette over the entrance of S. Domenico at Urbino (1450); two altars at Impruneta; and the ceiling of the chapel of the Cardinal of Portugal in S. Miniato al Monte (1461–66). Luca's last major work in this medium is an altarpiece in the Palazzo Vescovile at Pescia (after 1472). Many notable works by Luca della Robbia are found outside Italy. Among these may be mentioned the colossal stemma of René of Anjou and 12 roundels with the labours of the months from the Palazzo Medici in the Victoria and Albert museum, London; and the Altman and Demidoff Madonnas, respectively, in the Metropolitan museum, New York city, and the Museum of Art, Toledo, O.

After Luca's death at Florence on Feb. 20, 1482, his nephew ANDREA, who had been for many years an active member of his studio, assumed control of the Della Robbia workshop. Born on Oct. 20, 1435, Andrea appears, like his uncle, to have been trained as a marble sculptor. Neither in this medium nor in enameled terra cotta, however, was he an artist of Luca's calibre, and by the supremely high standard of Luca his work is trivial in form and deficient in sculptural quality. His best-known works are ten roundels of foundlings in swaddling clothes on the façade of the Ospedale degli Innocenti in Florence (about 1480). Andrea's interest in narrative sculpture led him to develop from the reliefs of Luca a class of large polychrome reliefs of which characteristic examples exist in Sta. Maria degli Angeli at Assisi, Sta. Maria degli Angeli at La Verna, S. Bernardino at L'Aquila, Sta. Chiara at Borgo San Seppolcro and Sta. Croce in Florence, as well as in many museums outside Italy. Between 1475 and 1522 the development of Andrea's style can be followed through a sequence of dated or documented works. Many of Andrea's smaller reliefs exist in a quantity of versions turned out from the Della Robbia studio.

Andrea della Robbia died at the age of 90 on Aug. 4, 1525, and control of the workshop passed to his son GIOVANNI (b. May 19, 1469). Giovanni's early works, of which the most remarkable are a lavabo in Sta. Maria Novella, Florence (1497), and the medallions in the Loggia di S. Paolo (1490–95), were executed in collaboration with or under the strong influence of his father, but as with age Andrea's grasp relaxed, Giovanni della Robbia evolved a coarser, more pictorial style in which the poverty of modeling and composition is accompanied by vivid, often vulgar polychromy. His most ambitious work is a frieze with representations of the works of mercy on the Ospedale del Ceppo at Pistoia (1525–29), in which he was assisted by his pupils Benedetto Buglioni (1461–1521) and Santi Buglioni (b. 1494).

Giovanni's younger brother GIROLAMO (b. March 9, 1488) was trained in Andrea's studio and collaborated with his father and brother until (about 1527–28) he moved to France, where he was employed on the terra-cotta decoration of the demolished Château de Madrid. After the death of Francis I (1547) Girolamo returned to Florence, but later (1559), on the appointment of F. Primaticcio as superintendent of the royal buildings, he resumed his work at the Château de Madrid and at Fontainebleau and was also employed on the monuments of François II and Catherine de Médicis at St. Denis. Girolamo della Robbia died in France on Aug. 4, 1566.

BIBLIOGRAPHY.—A. Marquand, *Luca della Robbia* (1914), *Andrea della Robbia*, 2 vol. (1922), *Giovanni della Robbia* (1920); M. Cruttwell, *Luca and Andrea della Robbia and Their Successors* (1902); L. Planiscig, *Luca della Robbia* (1948). (J. W. P.-H.)

ROBBINS, FREDERICK CHAPMAN (1916–), U.S. pediatrician, shared with J. F. Enders and T. H. Weller (*qq.v.*) the Nobel Prize in Physiology and Medicine in 1954 for cultivation of the poliomyelitis virus in tissue culture. Robbins was born on Aug. 25, 1916, in Auburn, Ala., and attended the University of Missouri and Harvard Medical School (M.D., 1940). After two years at the Children's Hospital, Boston, Mass., he entered the army and became chief of the virus and rickettsial section, 15th medical general laboratory, stationed in the Mediterranean theatre, where he investigated epidemics of infectious hepatitis, typhus and Q fever. Following the war, Robbins completed his hospital training in pediatrics and joined Enders and Weller in 1948 in the research laboratory of the Children's Hospital, Boston. There they devised techniques for cultivating the virus of poliomyelitis in tissue culture which made possible the development of poliomyelitis vaccine, new diagnostic methods and the isolation of many new viruses. In 1952 Robbins became director of the department of pediatrics and contagious diseases, Cleveland Metropolitan General Hospital, and professor of pediatrics at Western Reserve University School of Medicine, Cleveland, O. (J. H. DE.)

ROBBINS, JEROME (1918–), U.S. dancer and choreographer, noted for the imaginative and original use of contemporary American themes in his ballets and for the excellent dances he devised for Broadway shows. A character dancer of distinction, Robbins appeared at the Gluck Sandor-Felicia Sorel dance centre, danced in musicals, and toured with Ballet Theatre before staging his first ballet, *Fancy Free*, in 1944. His ballets include *Interplay*, *Pied Piper* and *Fanfare*, and dances for the musicals *On the Town*, *The King and I*, and *West Side Story*. Robbins is associate artistic director of the New York City Ballet.

See also BALLET: *Ballet in America After 1932*. (LN. ME.)

ROBERT OF COURTENAY (d. 1228), Latin emperor of Constantinople from 1221 to 1228, was a younger son of Peter of Courtenay (*q.v.*) and of Yolande, who, as sister of the former emperors Baldwin I and Henry, reigned in her own right in Constantinople until her death in September 1219. Their eldest son, Philip of Namur, renounced the succession in favour of Robert, a lazy and irresponsible youth, who arrived in Constantinople in 1221 and was crowned emperor on March 25. To secure his eastern frontiers he came to terms with the Greek emperor at Nicaea, Theodore I Lascaris, and was betrothed to Theodore's daughter, Eudocia. But Theodore died in 1222, and Robert fell foul of his successor, John III Vatatzes, with whom he concluded a humiliating treaty in 1225, having lost almost all the possessions of the

Latin Empire in Asia Minor. At the same time his European territories were overrun by the ruler of Epirus, Theodore Angelus, who captured Thessalonica and was crowned emperor there by 1228. Robert appealed to King Louis VIII of France; but in the end, after he had repudiated the princess Eudocia and seduced the daughter of a knight of Artois, his own barons turned against him. They broke into the palace, seized the lady, and cruelly mutilated her. Robert fled to Pope Gregory IX, but died in the Morea (Peloponnese) early in 1228 on his way back. His feeble reign marked the beginning of the end of the Latin Empire of Constantinople, which had been consolidated by his uncle, the emperor Henry.

See J. Longnon, *L'Empire latin . . .* (1949); D. M. Nicol in *Cambridge Medieval History*, vol. iv, ch. 7 (1966). (D. M. N.)

ROBERT I (c. 865–923), king of France from 922 to 923, the younger son of Robert the Strong, faithfully served his more famous brother Eudes throughout the latter's reign (888–898). He inherited from Eudes (898) all the Robertian lands between the Seine and Loire rivers, but with other magnates swore fealty to the Carolingian Charles III the Simple. Nevertheless, he was already served in his domains by viscounts, officials usually regarded as instruments of regal power. From 911 onward, Robert's role became more decisive; his defeat of the Normans at Chartres in that year paved the way for the treaty of Saint-Clair-sur-Epte, by which Charles assigned to the Normans a specific territory. But dissension between Robert and Charles became undisguised after 919, and in 922 Robert and his son-in-law Rudolph (Raoul), duke of Burgundy, headed a revolt. They elected Robert king at Reims (June 29, 922) and he was crowned by Walter, archbishop of Sens. Charles, however, gathered an army in Lorraine, and in a battle fought near Soissons on June 15, 923, Robert was killed. His son was Hugh the Great, duke of the Franks, and his grandson, Hugh Capet.

See P. Lauer, *Robert Ier et Raoul de Bourgogne, rois de France* (1910). (J. DE.)

ROBERT II LE PIEUX or THE PIOUS (c. 970–1031), king of France, the son of Hugh Capet and Adelaide of Aquitaine, was born at Orléans and educated at Reims under Gerbert of Aurillac, later Pope Silvester II. Soon after his own coronation (July 987), Hugh arranged the election and coronation (December 987) of Robert, thus facilitating his eventual succession (October 996) as sole ruler. Robert's first marriage, with Rosala (or Susanna), daughter of Berengar I, margrave of Ivrea, and widow of Count Arnulf II of Flanders, lasted less than a year. He soon became attracted to Bertha, the wife of Eudes I (d. 995), count of Blois. Although their relationship was within the forbidden degrees and Robert was godfather to one of Bertha's children, he married her in 996. For this he was anathematized by Pope Gregory V. The accession of Gerbert to the papal throne in April 999 probably modified the situation; moreover, Robert had no children by Bertha and by September 1001 the couple had separated. Within two years Robert married Constance, daughter of William, marquis of Provence, by whom he had four sons and a daughter.

On the death without issue of Henry I (Eudes-Henry), duke of Burgundy, in 1002, Robert ousted a rival claimant and by 1015 had established control throughout the duchy. In his own domain he kept good order, but was less successful in quelling his greater feudatories, failing notably to prevent Eudes II, count of Blois and Chartres, from obtaining Sancerre (1015) and Champagne (1019, 1020, or c. 1023) and thus virtually encircling Robert's territory. A patron of the Cluniacs, Robert also gave considerable support to the *treuga Dei* (truce of God) movement.

BIBLIOGRAPHY.—For the life by Helgaud, see *Helgaldi Floriacensis epitoma vitae regis Rotberti pii*, ed. by M. Bouquet, *Recueil des historiens des Gaules et de la France*, vol. x (1760). See also E. Lavisse, *Histoire de France*, vol. ii, part ii (1901); C. Pfister, *Études sur le règne de Robert le Pieux* (1885).

ROBERT (1278–1343), king of Naples from 1309, of the Angevin dynasty, was born in 1278, the third son of the future Charles II (q.v.). The War of the Sicilian Vespers embittered his youth: when his grandfather, Charles I, died (1285), his father was a prisoner of the Aragonese; and under the Treaty of Canfranc (1288), which set his father free, Robert went as a hostage to the Aragonese court. The Treaty of Anagni (1295) enabled him to return to Naples. (See further NAPLES, KINGDOM OF; SICILIAN VESPERS.)

Robert's eldest brother, Charles Martel, died in 1295, leaving his claims to the Hungarian crown to his infant son Charles Robert (see CHARLES I, of Hungary); and the next eldest brother, Louis, became a Franciscan. Robert was therefore recognized by the pope as Charles II's heir, and took the title of duke of Calabria. In 1298 he married Yolande (Violante), sister of James II of Aragon. In 1299 he was sent with an army to coerce Frederick III (q.v.) of Sicily to accept the Treaty of Anagni. His successes led to the Treaty of Caltabellotta (1302). A widower in 1303, Robert in 1304 married Sancha, daughter of James II of Majorca.

Charles II's death (May 5, 1309) made Robert king. When the German king Henry VII launched his Italian expedition (1310), the Guelphs of Tuscany looked to Robert for help, but he sought Henry's friendship instead. Even so, Henry was about to attack the Kingdom of Naples when he died (August 1313).

When the Tuscan Guelphs appealed to him again, Robert sent help, but the Neapolitans and the Florentines were routed by the Ghibellines at Montecatini (1315). In the following years, however, Pope John XXII chose him to be the papacy's instrument against the Visconti (q.v.) of Milan. Several communes, most notably Genoa (1318), put themselves under Robert's protection; but numbers of them followed Florence in discarding his tutelage during Robert's sojourn (1319–24) in his countship of Provence.

Back in Naples, Robert reasserted himself in Tuscan affairs independently of Pope John. The Florentines, defeated by Castruccio Castracani degli Antelminelli (q.v.), in 1325, turned again to Robert. They appointed his son, Charles of Calabria, *signore* of the republic for ten years, but when Louis the Bavarian (see LOUIS IV, Holy Roman emperor) appeared in Italy, Charles deserted Florence; hastening to defend Naples, he suddenly died of malaria (Nov. 9, 1328). The disconsolate Robert's influence waned throughout communal Italy.

As the Sicilians disregarded the Treaty of Caltabellotta, Robert's forces had been vainly fighting since 1314 to win the island for the Angevins. With regard to the Neapolitan succession, Robert betrothed his infant heiress Joan (q.v.) to Andrew of Hungary, hoping to neutralize the claim of the Hungarian Angevins.

Robert died on Jan. 19, 1343, and was buried in Naples in the great church of Santa Chiara (built by Queen Sancha). He left a number of discourses and some theological, moral, and political treatises, as well as an essay on the poverty of Christ, which reflects Franciscan radicalism. Petrarch and Boccaccio (q.v.) extol him as a patron of literature, jurisprudence, and the arts.

See R. Caggese, *Roberto d'Angiò e i suoi tempi*, 2 vol. (1921–30); E. G. Léonard, *Les Angevins de Naples* (1954). (E. Po.)

ROBERT I, THE BRUCE (1274–1329), king of Scotland from 1306 to 1329, was a member of the Norman family of Bruce (q.v.) which had come to Scotland in the early 12th century. It was related by marriage to the royal family, and hence the sixth Robert de Bruce (d. 1295), grandfather of the future king, claimed the throne when it was left vacant on the death of Margaret ("the maid of Norway") in 1290. As a result, however, of the English king Edward I's judicial enquiry, it was awarded to John de Balliol (q.v.).

The eighth Robert de Bruce was born on July 11, 1274. His father, the seventh Robert de Bruce (d. 1304), resigned the title of earl of Carrick in his favour in 1292; but little is known of his career until 1306. In the confused period which followed the resignation of King John in 1296, he appears at one time among the supporters of William Wallace, but was later apparently restored to Edward's confidence. There is nothing at this period to suggest that he was later to be the Scottish leader in the War of Independence.

The decisive event was his murder of John ("the Red") Comyn in the Franciscan church at Dumfries on Feb. 10, 1306. Comyn, a nephew of John de Balliol, was a possible rival for the crown, and Bruce's actions suggest that he had already decided to seize the throne. He hastened to Scone and was crowned on March 25.

The new king's position was very difficult. Edward I, whose garrisons held many of the important castles in Scotland, regarded him as a traitor, and made every effort to crush a movement which he treated as a rebellion. King Robert was twice defeated in 1306, at Methven, near Perth, on June 19, and at Dalry, near Tyndrum, Perthshire, on Aug. 11. His wife and many of his supporters were captured, and three of his brothers executed. The king himself became a fugitive, hiding on the remote island of Rathlin off the north Irish coast.

In February 1307 he returned to Ayrshire. His main supporter at first was his only surviving brother Edward, but in the next few years he attracted a number of others, notably James Douglas ("the Good") and his own nephew Thomas Randolph, whom he created earl of Moray in 1312. The king himself defeated John Comyn, earl of Buchan, and, in 1313, captured Perth, which had been in the hands of an English garrison; but much of the fighting was done by his supporters. Edward Bruce conquered Galloway; Douglas recovered his own lands in Douglasdale, and occupied the forest of Selkirk and most of the eastern borders; in 1314 Randolph captured Edinburgh. During these years the king was helped by the support of some of the leading Scottish churchmen and also by the death of Edward I in 1307 and the ineptness of his successor Edward II. The test came in 1314 when a large English army attempted to relieve the garrison of Stirling. Its defeat at Bannockburn on June 24 marked the triumph of Robert I.

Almost the whole of the rest of the reign had passed before he had forced the English government to recognize his position. Berwick was captured in 1318; and there were repeated raids into the north of England, which inflicted great damage. Eventually, after the deposition of Edward II (1327), the government of Queen Isabella and Roger Mortimer decided to make peace by the treaty of Northampton (1328) on terms which included the recognition of Robert I's title as king of Scots and the abandonment of all English claims to overlordship.

The king's main energies in these years, however, were devoted to settling the affairs of his kingdom. Until the birth of the future King David II in 1324 he had no male heir, and two statutes, in 1315 and 1318, were concerned with the succession. In addition, a parliament in 1314 decreed that any who remained in the allegiance of the English should forfeit their lands: this provided the means to reward supporters, and there are many charters regranting the lands so forfeited. Sometimes, these grants proved dangerous, for the king's chief supporters became enormously powerful. James Douglas, knighted at Bannockburn, acquired important lands in the counties of Selkirk and Roxburgh, which became the nucleus of the later power of the Douglas family on the borders. Robert I also had to restart the processes of royal government, for administration had been more or less in abeyance since 1296. By the end of the reign the system of exchequer audits was again functioning, and to this period belongs the earliest surviving roll of the register of the great seal.

In the last years of his life, Robert I suffered from ill health, and spent most of his time at Cardross, Dumbartonshire, where he died on June 7, 1329, possibly of leprosy. His body was buried in Dunfermline Abbey; but the heart was removed on his instructions and taken by Sir James Douglas on a pilgrimage to the Holy Land. Douglas was killed on the way (1330), but, according to one tradition of uncertain value, the heart was recovered and brought back to Melrose Abbey.

In later times Robert I has come to be revered as one of the heroes of Scottish national sentiment. Many legends have gathered round his name, notably the famous tale of the spider, which was first given currency by Sir Walter Scott in his *Tales of a Grandfather*, 1st series (1828), where he describes it as a tradition in the Bruce family; though the same story had been told of Sir James Douglas by David Hume of Godscroft more than two centuries before in the manuscript version of his *History of the Houses of Douglas and Angus* (*see* Sir W. Fraser, *The Douglas Book*, 1885, volume i, pages 112–113). This posthumous and uncritical veneration has often obscured Robert I's true services to his country.

See also references under "Robert I, the Bruce" in the Index.

BIBLIOGRAPHY.—The most important original authority for the life of Robert I is the *Bruce*, a poem by John Barbour (*q.v.*), probably completed in 1376. The most recent edition is by W. M. Mackenzie (1909). *The Acts of the Parliaments of Scotland*, vol. i (1844), contains the materials for his parliaments, and over 90 of his charters can be found in *The Register of the Great Seal of Scotland, A.D. 1306–1424*, vol. i (1912). Many other charters survive elsewhere and can be found in the various publications of the Scottish historical clubs. The most recent life is G. W. S. Barrow, *Robert Bruce* (1964); Sir H. Maxwell, *Robert The Bruce* (1897), is of some value. *See* also W. Croft Dickinson, *Scotland from the Earliest Times to 1603* (1961).

(BR. W.)

ROBERT II (1316–1390), king of Scotland from 1371 to 1390, first king of the Stewart dynasty, the son of Walter, hereditary steward of Scotland, and Marjorie, daughter of Robert I the Bruce, was born on March 2, 1316. He may have commanded a division at the battle of Halidon Hill, fought against the English in July 1333, and was certainly a leader of resistance the next year, becoming joint regent with John Randolph, earl of Moray, for the exiled David II. Because of irresponsible conduct he was soon deposed, but was sole regent from 1338 until the king's return from France in 1341. Escaping from the defeat at Neville's Cross (1346), he was again regent during David's captivity (1346–57). Although created earl of Strathearn (November 1357), he constantly opposed the king, raising unsuccessful rebellion (1362–63) with the earls of Douglas and March, after which he was made to renew his oath of allegiance (May 1363). He opposed David's abortive scheme for cancellation of the royal ransom in return for making a son of Edward III heir to the Scottish throne, which would have nullified his own right of succession. He was later imprisoned (1368–69) in Lochleven Castle. On David's death (Feb. 22, 1371) he succeeded to the throne by hereditary right and as laid down by parliament in 1326. Throughout his reign he made little mark on affairs. In 1384 he gave over domestic administration to his eldest son, John, earl of Carrick (afterward Robert III), and in 1388, owing to Carrick's ill health, to his next surviving son Robert, earl of Fife. His first marriage (*c.* 1348) to Elizabeth Mure was solemnized after the birth of their four sons and five daughters, whose legitimation *per subsequens matrimonium* was of doubtful validity for succession to the crown. He married secondly in 1355 Euphemia Ross, the undoubted legitimacy of whose two sons (including Walter, earl of Atholl) and two daughters was one cause of the murder (1437) of James I (Robert III's son) at Atholl's instigation. He had also at least eight illegitimate sons. He died at Dundonald in Ayrshire on April 19, 1390, and was buried at Scone. (E. W.-M. B.-M.)

ROBERT III (*c.* 1337–1406), king of Scots from 1390 to 1406, was the eldest son of Robert II and Elizabeth Mure, legitimated through their marriage after his birth. In 1362–63 he joined his father in rebellion against David II, and in 1368 was imprisoned with his father and two brothers but was created earl of Carrick the same year. They were released in 1369. Robert II became king in 1371 and in 1384, owing to old age, devolved the domestic government on Carrick, but Carrick, when lamed by a horse of Douglas of Dalkeith, was supplanted by his brother Robert, earl of Fife, in 1388. On his accession on April 19, 1390, he changed his name to Robert (III) from John, which unhappily recalled John Balliol. Fife, created duke of Albany in 1398, continued to govern throughout this reign except during the years 1399–1402 when the king's dissolute heir, David, duke of Rothesay, took his place, until he met an early death in Albany's castle of Falkland. Robert III then sent his remaining son, James (afterward James I), to France for safe upbringing; but the news of his capture by the English proved fatal to the aging king, who died at Rothesay in Bute on April 4, 1406. He was buried in Paisley Abbey. He married (*c.* 1367) Annabella Drummond (d. 1401), by whom he had three sons and four daughters.

(E. W.-M. B.-M.)

ROBERT GUISCARD (d. 1085), duke of Apulia from 1059, a ruthless adventurer whose military and political genius revolutionized the history of southern Italy, was born in Normandy, the son of a petty feudatory, Tancred of Hauteville. From the first decades of the 11th century, Normans such as he had been going to southern Italy to exploit the troubled conditions there, as Apulia was trying to free itself from the Byzantine empire while Campania was torn by the rivalry between the Lombard principalities of Capua and Salerno. Robert's eldest half brother William made his name as a leader against the Byzantine Greeks and was elected count of Apulia by his colleagues in 1042. Robert went out to join his second half brother Drogo, who in 1046 had succeeded William. Drogo, however, mistrusted the ambitious Robert and sent him to Calabria, where Normans hired by the prince of Salerno were attacking the Byzantines.

At the head of a predatory band, Robert used every resource of brigandage and deceit to carve out a dominion for himself in Calabria (hence his nickname Guiscard, "the Astute"); by 1060 he had ousted the Byzantines there. Meanwhile, he kept an eye on Apulia, the main Norman stronghold. When Pope Leo IX allied himself with the Byzantines against the Normans, Robert went to the help of his third half brother Humphrey, who had taken Drogo's place some time after the latter's assassination (1051); and he contributed substantially to the victory over Leo's army at Civitate in 1053. On Humphrey's death he seized the Apulian succession for himself (1057). Finally, under the Treaty of Melfi (August 1059), Pope Nicholas II legalized Robert's conquests, actual and future, by investing him as duke of Apulia, Calabria, and Sicily, while Robert acknowledged the papacy's feudal suzerainty over the lands in question.

To his youngest brother, Roger (*see* ROGER I), who had arrived to participate in his last Calabrian campaigns, Robert entrusted the task of conquering Sicily, helping him in the first stages (from 1060) and later sending reinforcements to him. Not satisfied with the territory assigned to him, Roger more than once took up arms against Robert, who eventually constituted Calabria and Sicily as a countship for Roger.

Robert's major achievement was the expansion of the little countship left by Humphrey into a duchy spreading from the Adriatic to the Tyrrhenian Sea. His conquest of Bari (1071) put an end to the Byzantine hold on southern Italy. In 1058, Robert married Sykelgaita (Sicelgaeta), sister of the prince of Salerno, Gisulf II, after repudiating his first wife, Alberada of Buonalbergo; but this did not prevent him from encroaching on Salernitan lands. Hostilities reached a climax with Robert's undertaking to defend the prosperous community of Amalfi against Gisulf (1073), and ended with his capture of Salerno (December 1076) and the surrender of Gisulf himself (summer 1077).

Vassals who rebelled against the new discipline of Robert's unitary state were energetically punished. His aggressions in upper Campania and in the Abruzzi, some of them against ecclesiastical lands, however, alarmed Pope Gregory VII (*q.v.*), who excommunicated him in 1074, but came to terms with him in 1080, as Robert's support was needed against the German king, Henry IV.

To forestall a Byzantine counterattack and also to avenge the deposed emperor, Michael VII Ducas (whose son Constantine had married one of Robert's daughters in an attempt at a Norman-Byzantine reconciliation), Robert in 1081 sailed with a considerable fleet across the Adriatic, seized Corfu, and besieged Dyrrachium (Durazzo; modern Durres). Though the Venetians inflicted heavy losses on his fleet, he took Dyrrachium (February 1082) and might then have marched across the Balkans had he not dutifully responded to Gregory VII's appeal for help in Rome against Henry IV. Affairs in Italy detained him throughout 1083, and in the spring of 1084 he had to march on Rome again to save Gregory, whom he took back to Salerno (his troops meanwhile had sacked Rome). Returning at last to the Adriatic operations, in which his son Bohemund was hard pressed, he took Corfu again in the winter and was besieging Cephalonia when he died, on July 17, 1085. He left Apulia to Roger, his son by Sykelgaita, preferring him to Alberada's son Bohemund.

See F. Chalandon, *Histoire de la domination normande en Italie . . .*, 2 vol. (1907); E. Pontieri, *Tra i Normanni nell'Italia meridionale*, vol. i, *La Conquista* (1948). (E. Po.)

ROBERT, the name of two dukes of Normandy.

ROBERT I (d. 1035), called the Magnificent or the Devil, was the younger son of Duke Richard II of Normandy and the father of William the Conqueror. On his father's death (1026 or 1027) he contested the duchy with his elder brother Richard III until the latter's opportune death one or two years later. A strong ruler, Robert successfully quelled his feudatories, and helped Baldwin IV, count of Flanders, to suppress a serious rebellion (1030). For support given to Henry I (*q.v.*), king of France, he received the Vexin Francais. When returning from a pilgrimage to Jerusalem, he died at Nicaea in July 1035.

ROBERT II (*c.* 1054–1134), nicknamed Curthose or Short Boots, was the eldest son of William the Conqueror. Although recognized in boyhood as his father's successor in Normandy, he twice rebelled (1077 or 1078 and *c.* 1082–83) and was in exile in Italy until he returned as duke on his father's death (September 1087). His next brother, King William II of England, invaded Normandy (1091) and Robert had to yield to him the counties of Eu and Aumale. William attacked again (1094), but peace was made so that Robert could take part in the First Crusade. He fought at Dorylaeum (July 1097), and was at the capture of Jerusalem (July 1099). His courageous leadership contributed to the victory at Ascalon (August 1099).

Robert was in Italy when his youngest brother Henry I succeeded William as king of England (August 1100). His invasion of England (1101) brought only an ignominious peace and Henry in his turn invaded Normandy (1105 and 1106). Captured at the battle of Tinchebrai (September 1106), Robert was kept prisoner for the remainder of his life, first at Wareham, Dorset, then at Devizes Castle; in 1126 he was transferred to Bristol and later to Cardiff, where he died, early in February (perhaps Feb. 3), 1134. His career, apparently one of unrelieved failure, was redeemed by his conduct on the crusade. His record in Normandy was lamentable; the administration of the duchy came virtually to a standstill and he made no sustained effort to control his turbulent vassals. His son, William Clito (*c.* 1102–28), was made count of Flanders (1127) by the French king Louis VI.

See H. Prentout, *Histoire de Guillaume le Conquérant* (1936); C. W. David, *Robert Curthose* (1920).

ROBERT THE STRONG (d. 866), count of various territories in the region of the Loire River, was ancestor of the Capetian kings of France. Details of his origin are scant and their interpretation much disputed, but by 852 he was serving the Carolingian Charles II the Bald as count in western Neustria and was *missus dominicus* in the west of the kingdom (853). But, resenting authority given on the Breton marches to Charles's son Louis (later Louis II), Robert joined the magnates' revolt (856). He was reconciled with Charles (861), becoming his most trusty warrior. When the Normans of the Loire threatened all the adjacent territory (862) and Louis was in rebellion, Robert, acting with Count Rannoux of Poitiers, fought several engagements and secured the neutrality of the Normans on the Seine. Charles sent him to Burgundy (864) to keep an eye on Girard, count of Vienne, but had to recall him to Neustria (July 865), where he won a great victory over the Normans. Granted full control in western Neustria (early 866), Robert was killed in battle against the Normans at Brissarthe (between Le Mans and Angers) in the autumn of 866 (possibly Sept. 15). His sons Eudes and Robert both became king.

See F. Lot, "Robert le fort," *Bibliothèque de l'école des chartes,* vol. lxxvi (1915). (J. DE.)

ROBERT OF GLOUCESTER (fl. 1260–1300), English chronicler known only through his connection with the work which bears his name, probably written *c.* 1300. This is a vernacular history of England, from the days of the legendary Brut to the year 1270, written in rhymed couplets. The lines are of 14 syllables, with a break after the eighth syllable. In some manuscripts the early part (up to 1135) is followed by a brief continuation by an anonymous versifier, and in these slight deviations from the version generally accepted as Robert's are also discernible. The authorities employed for the earlier part were Geoffrey of Monmouth, Henry of Huntingdon, William of Malmesbury, the English chronicles and some minor sources; Robert, in making his recension of it, also used the *Brut* of Layamon. From 1135 to 1236 Robert is still a compiler, although references to oral tradition become more frequent as he approaches his own time. From 1256 to 1270 he has the value of a contemporary authority, but he is more important to the philologist than to the historian.

Robert's chronicle was first edited by T. Hearne, 2 vol. (1724), but this text was superseded by that of W. Aldis Wright, 2 vol., Rolls series (1887). Extracts (1192–1270) were edited by F. Liebermann in *Monumenta Germaniae Historica, Scriptores,* xxviii, pp. 663–669 (1888).

BIBLIOGRAPHY.—T. D. Hardy, *Descriptive Catalogue of Materials Relating to the History of Great Britain and Ireland,* 3 vol., i, pp. 25, 68, iii, pp. 181–189, 623 (1862–71); K. Brossman, *Über die Quellen der mittelenglischen Chronik des Robert von Gloucester* (1887); W. Ellmer, *Anglia,* x, pp. 1–37, 291–322 (1888); H. Strohmeyer, *Der Styl der Reimchronik Roberts von Gloucester* (1891), "Das Verhältnis der Handschriften der Reimchronik Roberts von Gloucester," *Archiv für das Studium der neueren Sprachen,* lxxxvii, pp. 217–232 (1891).
(X.; D. WK.)

ROBERT OF JUMIÈGES (d. *c.* 1055), archbishop of Canterbury, was a Norman monk who became prior of St. Ouen and in 1037 abbot of the Benedictine abbey of Jumièges, near Rouen. He was taken to England by his friend Edward the Confessor in 1042 and made bishop of London in 1044. He became Edward's leading adviser and head of the Norman party, and was appointed archbishop of Canterbury in 1051. Although Robert was instrumental in bringing about the exile of Earl Godwin in 1051, on the native leader's return in 1052 the archbishop himself was forced to flee to the continent. Deposed and outlawed by the Witenagemot, Robert died at Jumièges, possibly in 1055. The uncanonical usurpation of the primatial see by Stigand enabled William of Normandy to champion the ecclesiastical cause and obtain papal support for his invasion of 1066. (D. D. McG.)

ROBERT THE DEVIL, legendary son of a duke of Normandy, who, at 20, uses his immense strength only for outrage and crime. His mother informs him, in explanation of his evil impulses, that he was born in answer to prayers addressed to the devil; and a hermit, to whom the pope directs him, requires him as a penance to maintain absolute silence, feign madness, take his food from the mouth of a dog and provoke ill-treatment from the common people without retaliating. Later, while the emperor's court fool, he appears as an unknown knight at the bidding of a celestial messenger and delivers Rome from Saracen attacks in three successive years; his disguise is pierced by the emperor's dumb daughter, who recovers speech to identify him, but he refuses her hand and withdraws to end his days with the hermit.

This legend is found in a late 12th-century romance, *Robert Le Diable,* ed. by E. Löseth for the Société des Anciens Textes Français (1903). Another version, in which Robert is a bandit who, in penitence, kills his accomplices, feigns madness, is recognized as son of the duke of Normandy and is married by the pope to the emperor's daughter, forms the subject of the 14th-century *Mystère de Robert le Diable* ed. by E. Fournier, 1879. For another 14th-century version, in alexandrine quatrains, *see* K. Breul, *Le dit de Robert le Diable,* in *Abhandlungen Prof. A. Tobler dargebracht* (1895). The legend, distorted, also provides the Eugène Scribe libretto for Meyerbeer's opera, *Robert le Diable* (1831).

ROBERT, HENRY MARTYN (1837–1923), the author of a notable book on parliamentary procedure, *Robert's Rules of Order,* and a U.S. army general, was born in Robertville, S.C., May 2, 1837. He graduated from the U.S. Military Academy at West Point in 1857 and was commissioned in the Corps of Engineers. He served in the Union Army as an engineer and was assigned to various posts, one being at New Bedford, Mass. It was there that, as a young lieutenant, he was called upon to preside at a church meeting in which there was much controversy. Since he knew nothing of parliamentary procedure, the meeting accomplished nothing. This experience led him to make a study of parliamentary procedure, during which he found that there was no uniformity of rules. He then undertook the task of formulating a set of rules that would represent the best of the many different procedures he had discovered.

Years later, when he had completed his work, he met with disappointment. Publishers said there was no need for such a book and that no one would believe that an army officer could know enough about parliamentary law to write one. He had to offer to give away 1,000 copies to legislators, educators, clergymen, and others, with a request for their criticisms, and to assume all financial responsibility until the publisher was completely reimbursed. Finally, on Feb. 19, 1876, his *Pocket Manual of Rules of Order* was published and became an immediate success. Critics then said that no lawyer or legislator could have written the book, for he would have been bound by precedents; General Robert had broken with precedent whenever necessary. In 1915 he published a revised and enlarged version entitled *Robert's Rules of Order Revised.* More than 2,000,000 copies were sold and it became the standard manual on the subject in the United States. Robert's other works include *Parliamentary Practice* (1921) and *Parliamentary Law* (1922). He died in Hornell, N.Y., on May 11, 1923.
(S. H. Ro.)

ROBERT, HUBERT (1733–1808), French painter, sometimes called "Robert des Ruines" because of his paintings of Roman ruins, was born in Paris on May 22, 1733. His first teacher was the sculptor Michel Ange Slodtz. He went to Rome in 1754, where he had to pay a small fee for his keep at the French academy before receiving a formal appointment. French travelers to Italy began to purchase his views of Rome. In 1759 the abbé de Saint-Non and the painter Jean Honoré Fragonard, his elder, joined him and they traveled to Tivoli and Naples. Living at the Villa d'Este, they produced a quantity of drawings in red chalk of ancient buildings in ruined parks, animated with small figures. After his 11-year stay in Italy, Robert left the country in 1765, and became a member of the Paris academy the next year.

Robert was a born decorator and his paintings looked well on the gray wainscoting then much used. His popularity was enhanced by exhibitions at the Salons from 1767 on. In addition to his Italian landscapes, he painted scenes of Ermenonville, Marly and Versailles, near Paris, and of the south of France, with ruined monuments of the Roman era. During the Revolution he was imprisoned but continued his work; the fall of Robespierre saved him from the guillotine. He worked with Fragonard on a commission for the Musée Français, then a national museum in the old palace of the Louvre. He died in Paris on April 15, 1808, entirely forgotten. He is represented by works at the Louvre, Paris, the Versailles palace and many French museums; the Metropolitan museum, New York city, the Institute of Fine Arts, Detroit, Mich., and the Art Institute of Chicago.

BIBLIOGRAPHY.—Paul Sentenac, *Hubert Robert* (1929); Tristan LeClère, *Hubert Robert* (1913); Pierre de Nolhac, *Hubert Robert* (1910).
(M. N. B.)

ROBERTS, SIR CHARLES GEORGE DOUGLAS (1860–1943), Canadian poet and prose writer, is often referred to as the father of Canadian literature. He was the first poet to express the new national feeling aroused in Canada by the Confederation of 1867, and his example and counsel inspired a whole school of late 19th-century Canadian poets.

Roberts was born near Fredericton, N.B., Jan. 10, 1860. After graduation from the University of New Brunswick in 1879, he taught school, edited the influential Toronto magazine *The Week,* and was for ten years professor of English at King's college, Windsor, N.S. In 1897 he moved to New York city where he worked as a journalist, and in 1907 he went to London. Upon his return to Canada in 1925, he was enthusiastically received on a cross-Canada lecture tour and later settled in Toronto as the acknowledged dean of Canadian letters. He was knighted by King George V in 1935. He died in Toronto on Nov. 26, 1943, and was buried in Fredericton.

Roberts was almost equally adept at prose and poetry. His prose included a pioneer *History of Canada* (1897), several novels dealing with the past and present of the maritime provinces, and many volumes of the animal stories that were his chief source of fame as a prose writer. In such books as *Earth's Enigmas* (1896), *The Kindred of the Wild* (1902) and *Neighbours Unknown* (1911) he displayed his intimate knowledge of the woods and their animal inhabitants.

Later criticism, however, tended to value Roberts' poetry rather more highly than his prose. Beginning with *Orion* (1880), he published about 12 volumes of verse, of which the best were *In*

Divers Tones (1887), *Songs of the Common Day* (1893), *The Vagrant of Time* (1927) and *The Iceberg and Other Poems* (1934). *Selected Poems,* edited by Desmond Pacey, was published in 1956. Roberts wrote of nature, love, nationalism and philosophy, but his best poems by general consent were his simple descriptive lyrics about the scenery and rural life of New Brunswick and Nova Scotia.

BIBLIOGRAPHY.—James Cappon, *Roberts and the Influences of His Time* (1905); Elsie Pomeroy, *Sir Charles G. D. Roberts: A Biography* (1943); Desmond Pacey, *Ten Canadian Poets* (1958).   (D. P.)

ROBERTS, FREDERICK SLEIGH ROBERTS, EARL (1832–1914), British field marshal famous for his achievements in Afghanistan and in the South African War, was born at Cawnpore, India, on Sept. 30, 1832, the younger son of General Sir Abraham Roberts. Commissioned in the Bengal artillery in 1851, he was appointed in 1856 to the quartermaster general's branch of the staff, with which he was to serve for the next 22 years. He first distinguished himself in the Indian Mutiny (1857–58), in which he was continuously engaged in some of the severest fighting, and was awarded the Victoria Cross. After the Umbeyla campaign on the northwest frontier (1863), he was in Abyssinia as assistant quartermaster general during the campaign of 1868, and again saw service on the northwest frontier of India in the Lushai expedition (1871–72).

In 1878 Roberts was appointed to command the Kurram field force, one of the three columns organized to operate against Afghanistan in the Second Afghan War (1878–80), and in December 1878 he skilfully forced the Peiwar Kotal, a pass leading from India into Afghanistan, and defeated the Afghan Army. The murder, in September 1879, of Sir Pierre Louis Cavagnari, British envoy to the Afghan amir Yakub Khan, led to operations against Kabul, the capital of Afghanistan, which Roberts successfully occupied in October after the complete defeat of the Afghans at Charasia, south of Kabul. However, dissatisfaction incited by the preaching of the mullahs led to a sudden attack against Kabul by the Afghan tribes in December and after heavy fighting Roberts again defeated the enemy with great loss. A new amir, Abdurrahman Khan, was installed in July 1880, and the British troops were about to be withdrawn when news was received of a reverse at Maiwand (July 27, 1880) and of the siege of the British garrison of Kandahar by a large Afghan army under Ayub Khan, Yakub Khan's brother. Within a few days Roberts, who had been perfecting the transport arrangements in his force, had begun his celebrated march from Kabul to Kandahar, where, after covering 313 mi. in 22 days, he totally defeated the Afghan Army. Roberts was already known to his colleagues as a highly competent and careful staff officer, as a brilliant tactician in command of troops, and as a commander whose care for the well-being of his men earned him their devotion. The name of "Bobs" now became a household word in Britain.

After commanding the Madras army from 1880 to 1885, Roberts became commander in chief in India in 1885, and in the following year personally supervised the task of suppressing dacoity (robbery by armed gangs) in Burma. After eight years in the highest Indian military appointment, during which time he was active in measures for improving the efficiency and well-being of the army, in particular the improvement of communications to the northern frontiers and of the standards of field training, he returned to England in 1893. He was created Baron Roberts of Kandahar in 1892 and in 1895 he became a field marshal and took command of the forces in Ireland.

The reverses in the early weeks of the South African War (1899–1902) led to Roberts' appointment to command the British forces. Within a few months his conduct of operations completely changed the course of events and, after the occupation of Pretoria on June 5, 1900, he handed over the command to Lord Kitchener and returned to England in 1901. He was created an earl and became the last commander in chief of the British Army. His long service in India had not, however, fitted him for service in the war office, the organization of which he found unfamiliar, and, apart from reforms in training methods, he did not achieve a great deal. As a result of the Esher Committee's recommendations for the reorganization of the war office in February 1904, his office was abolished when the army council was instituted.

Roberts now devoted himself to the encouragement of his fellow countrymen in rifle shooting, and to the uphill task of persuading the country that the threat of war in Europe necessitated the adoption of compulsory national service. He made many speeches in all parts of the country but, despite much influential support, was unable to induce the government to introduce the measure, which was not adopted until 1916. After the outbreak of World War I he went to France in November 1914 to visit the Indian divisions which had recently arrived. There he contracted pneumonia and died at Saint-Omer on Nov. 14, 1914. He was buried in St. Paul's Cathedral, London.

Roberts' works included *The Rise of Wellington* (1895), *Forty-One Years in India,* two volumes (1897), *A Nation in Arms* (1907), *Fallacies and Facts* (1911), and *Letters Written During the Indian Mutiny* (1924).

BIBLIOGRAPHY.—H. Hensman, *The Afghan War of 1879–80* (1881); *The Anglo-Afghan War, 1878–80,* Official Account (1881); Sir J. F. Maurice, *History of the War in South Africa 1899–1902,* 4 vol. (1906–10); Sir G. W. Forrest, *The Life of Lord Roberts* (1914); H. G. de Watteville, *Lord Roberts* (1938); D. James, *Lord Roberts* (1954).
      (R. G. TH.)

ROBERTS-AUSTEN, SIR WILLIAM CHANDLER (1843–1902), English metallurgist noted for his researches into the physical properties of metals, was born in Kennington, Surrey, March 3, 1843. At the wish of his uncle, Maj. Nathaniel L. Austen, he later adopted the name commemorated in the term austenite for the solid solution of carbon in gamma iron (*see* IRON AND STEEL INDUSTRY: *Steel Metallurgy: Slowly Cooled Steels*). Educated at the Royal School of Mines, he became private assistant to the master of the mint (1865) and chemist to the mint (1870), chemist and assayer (1882), and acting deputy master (1902). He became professor of metallurgy at the School of Mines in 1880. An outstanding teacher, he won renown for his work in the new field of physical metallurgy, much of which formed the basis of the alloys research reports of the Institution of Mechanical Engineers. He served on the treasury committee entrusted with the establishment of the National Physical Laboratory (1897) and was an original member of the war office explosives committee (1899). Among the many honours bestowed upon him was fellowship in the Royal Society (1875). He died in London on Nov. 22, 1902.   (C. W. D.)

ROBERTSON, FREDERICK WILLIAM (1816–1853), well-known and influential Anglican preacher, commonly known as Robertson of Brighton, who in his powerful and thoughtful sermons faced some of the intellectual and social problems of his day with a refreshing and unusual honesty, was born into a military family on Feb. 3, 1816, in London. In 1837 he went to Oxford to study for the ministry, having relinquished an earlier intention of entering the army. In 1840 he was ordained, and in 1842 became curate of Christ Church, Cheltenham. After brief periods as minister to the English congregation at Heidelberg and rector of St. Ebbe's, Oxford, he was appointed to Holy Trinity Chapel, Brighton (1847), where he acquired an astonishing reputation as a preacher. His convictions had been originally of a narrowly evangelical type, but they gradually broadened. Like F. D. Maurice, whom he in some ways resembled, he was wholly out of sympathy with the party controversies of his time. His early death (at Brighton on Aug. 15, 1853) was perhaps connected with the bitterness of the opposition which his preaching aroused. Not a scientific theologian, he was a man of independent and penetrating insight.

Robertson's sermons were published in five series (1855–90). *See* also S. A. Brooke (ed.), *Life and Letters of F. W. Robertson,* 2 vol. (1865).   (A. MacD. A.)

ROBERTSON, THOMAS WILLIAM (1829–1871), English playwright, who, by his realistic social comedies and his pioneer work as a producer, helped to bring about the late-19th-century revival of drama in England, was born at Newark-on-Trent, Nottinghamshire, on Jan. 9, 1829, of a theatrical family. His father became manager of the traveling repertory company on the Lincoln circuit, his mother was an actress in the company, and the youngest of his many brothers and sisters became famous as Dame Madge Kendal, the wife of W. H. Kendal (*q.v.*). After leaving school (1843), Robertson helped his father in various capacities until the company disbanded in 1848, when he moved to London and continued to act, though without much success, for another ten years. His most profitable engagement was in 1854 when he acted as prompter to Charles James Mathews and Mme Vestris (*qq.v.*) at the Lyceum Theatre, for it was their work in refining the staging of comedy that he was later to perfect.

In 1856, he married the actress Elizabeth Burton, and thereafter gradually abandoned acting for journalism. He had written for the theatre since his youth, and the first of many adaptations and translations from the French, *The Chevalier de St. George*, had been produced at the Princess's Theatre, London, in 1845. His first original play, *The Cantab*, a one-act farce, was staged at the Strand Theatre in 1861; and with *David Garrick* (based on the French *Sullivan*, by "Mélesville"), presented by E. A. Sothern at the Haymarket (1864), he established himself as a playwright. Although its characters are still recognizable theatrical types and its plot and situations are conventionally handled, in its detailed directions for sets, scenery, and costumes, and for gestures and grouping, it foreshadows his later work.

In 1865, *Society*, the first of the so-called "cup-and-saucer" comedies which made Robertson famous, was produced at the Prince of Wales's Theatre, under the management of Marie Wilton and Squire Bancroft (*q.v.*). It was followed by *Ours* (1866), *Caste* (1867), *Play* (1868), *School* (1869), and *The M.P.* (1870). In these plays Robertson the playwright and Robertson the proto-producer combined to establish a delicately conceived and convincingly executed picture of the social scene. Although the broader themes suggested by the titles are merely touched on, they give unity to his presentation of the life of his time, and his delineation of his characters as individuals rather than types, his skilful manipulation of plot, and his easy, conversational dialogue make his plays still interesting, despite their sentimentality. As a producer, his insistence on the performance as a whole, on adequate rehearsal, and on detail, was encouraged by the intimacy of the small theatre, the "ensemble" playing of the Bancrofts and their company, and the success of the plays themselves, which ensured a long enough run for the actors to settle into their parts.

Robertson's first wife died in 1865 and in 1867 he married Rosetta Feist, who was of German birth. He died in London on Feb. 3, 1871. Several of his plays long remained in the repertory, and *Caste* is still performed, but it was primarily his staging methods which proved so influential on the course of English drama.

See also DRAMA: *Modern Drama*.

BIBLIOGRAPHY.—*The Principal Dramatic Works of T. W. Robertson*, ed. with a memoir, by his son, T. W. Robertson, 2 vol. (1889); *Dame Madge Kendal, by Herself* (1933); Maynard Savin, *T. W. Robertson: His Plays and Stagecraft* (1950); Allardyce Nicoll, *A History of English Drama, 1660–1900*, vol. v (1959); G. Rowell, *Victorian Theatre* (1956). (GE. R.)

ROBERTSON, WILLIAM (1721–1793), Scottish historian and Presbyterian minister, whose writings were the earliest popular histories within their respective fields and were highly esteemed by his contemporaries. He was born at Borthwick, Midlothian, on Sept. 19, 1721. After being educated at Dalkeith grammar school and Edinburgh University, he was presented to the living of Gladsmuir, near Edinburgh, in 1743. A member of the General Assembly from 1746, he was elected moderator in 1762 and for many years his influence as leader of the "moderate" party was supreme. (*See* PRESBYTERIANISM.)

Robertson's career as historian began with the publication of *History of Scotland during the Reigns of Queen Mary and of James VI until his Accession to the Crown of England*, 2 vol. (1759), which brought immediate fame and was eulogized by, among others, David Hume and Edward Gibbon. It also gained the favour of Lord Bute, who secured Robertson's appointment as principal of Edinburgh University in 1762 and revived the office of historiographer royal for him in 1763. Robertson's next work was *History of the Reign of the Emperor Charles the Fifth*, 3 vol. (1769), and this was followed by *History of America*, 3 vol. (5th ed., 1788). Robertson's reputation has not stood the test of time.

His concern for the "dignity of history" often seems mere pomposity and his straightforward prose is often dull. He had the virtue of adhering closely to his sources, but, as a corollary, held that those early periods of history which were poorly documented deserved to be forgotten. Of his three major works, the *History of America* (in effect, Spanish America) was the most outstanding and for this Robertson would undoubtedly be more widely remembered were he not unfortunate in having been followed by W. H. Prescott.

See J. B. Black, *The Art of History* (1926); R. A. Humphreys, *William Robertson and his "History of America"* (1954).

ROBERTSON, SIR WILLIAM ROBERT (1860–1933), British field marshal and chief of the Imperial General Staff during the greater part of World War I, was born at Welbourn, Lincolnshire, on Jan. 29, 1860. After serving in the ranks of the 16th Lancers (1877–88), he was commissioned in the 3rd Dragoon Guards. He served in India in frontier operations and on the intelligence staff before returning in 1896 to England where he became the first officer from the ranks to pass through the staff college at Camberley (1897). He was on the intelligence staff during the South African War (1899–1902) and became commandant of the staff college (1910) and director of military training at the war office (1913). At the outbreak of World War I in 1914 he served as quartermaster general of the expeditionary force in France and in January 1915 was appointed as chief of General Staff to Sir John French. He became chief of the Imperial General Staff in December 1915 and supported Sir Douglas Haig in stressing the importance of the Western front in the face of continuous government attempts to disperse the British forces on other projects. These difficulties led to Robertson's transfer in February 1918 to the Eastern command in England. From 1919 to 1920 he commanded the British army of occupation on the Rhine. He was created a baronet in 1919 and a field marshal in 1920. He died in London on Feb. 12, 1933. Robertson was a man of great character, rugged, tenacious, and cautious; but, although a clear and concise writer, he was unable to express himself effectively in speech.

He wrote two books of memoirs, *From Private to Field-Marshal* (1921) and *Soldiers and Statesmen 1914–18,* two volumes (1926).

(R. G. TH.)

ROBERVAL, GILLES PERSONNE (PERSONIER) **DE** (1602–1675), French mathematician, whose most important work was done on curves, was born at Roberval, near Beauvais, on Aug. 8, 1602. In 1632 he became professor of mathematics in the Collège de France and maintained this position until his death in Paris on Oct. 27, 1675.

Roberval studied the quadrature of surfaces and the cubature of solids, which he accomplished in some of the simpler cases by developing and improving B. Cavalieri's method of indivisibles. He discovered a general method of drawing tangents, by considering a curve as described by a moving point whose motion is the resultant of several simpler motions.

He also discovered a method of deriving one curve from another, by means of which finite areas can be obtained equal to the areas between certain curves and their asymptotes. To these curves, which were also applied to effect some quadratures, Evangelista Torricelli gave the name of "Robervallian lines." Roberval was an irascible person who indulged in scientific feuds with several of his contemporaries, among them René Descartes. He invented the balance which goes by his name (*see* WEIGHING MACHINES).

His works were published in 1693 by the Abbé Gallois, in the *Recueil* of the *Mémoires de l'Académie des Sciences*.

See E. Walker, *A Study of the Traité des indivisibles of G. P. de Roberval* (1932); J. F. Scott, *A History of Mathematics* (1958). (O. OE.)

ROBES, the name generally given to a class of official dress, especially as worn by certain persons or classes on occasions of particular solemnity. The word robe (*toga*) was earliest used, in the sense of a garment, of those given by popes and princes to the members of their household or their great officers. It would be going too far to assume that, for example, peers' robes were originally the king's livery, but in most early cases where robes are mentioned, if not of cloth of gold, etc., they are of scarlet, furred. A robe is properly a long garment (*toga talaris*), and the term "robes" is now applied only in those cases where a long garment forms part of the official dress, though in ordinary usage it is taken to include all the other articles of clothing proper to the full dress in question. The term "robes," moreover, connotes a certain degree of dignity or honour in the wearer. It is proper to speak of the sovereign's robes of state, of peers' robes, of the robes of the clergy, of academical robes, judicial robes, municipal or civic robes. In the case of the official dress of the clergy a distinction must be drawn. The sacerdotal vestments are not spoken of as "robes"; a priest is not "robed" but "vested" for Mass; yet the rochet and chimere of an English bishop, even in church, are more properly referred to as robes than as vestments, and, while the cope he wears in church is a vestment rather than a robe, the scarlet habit which is part of his parliamentary full dress is a robe, not a vestment. For ecclesiastical vestments, *see* LITURGY, CHRISTIAN.

Coronation robes reflect the requirements of royal ceremonial and the sacerdotal significance of Christian kingship. The robes of the British sovereign consist of a crimson surcoat, parliamentary robe and cap of estate worn before the service. During the ceremony, the sovereign is invested with the *Colobium Sindonis,* a loose linen garment, the dalmatic or cloth of gold surcoat with girdle of the same, surmounted by the *Pallium Regale* or cloth of gold mantle and *armilla* or stole. Leaving Westminster Abbey, the purple surcoat is worn under the purple robe of estate, with the imperial state crown. Queen Elizabeth II wore these traditional robes in 1953, omitting the crimson and purple surcoats for a coronation dress, and the cap of estate. The sovereign's coronation robes are described in "The King's Coronation Ornaments," by William H. St. John Hope, in *The Ancestor,* volumes i and ii (1902), also by L. Wickham Legg (ed.), *English Coronation Records* (1901).

All countries which boast an ancient civilization have some sort of official robes, and the modern tendency has been to multiply rather than to diminish their number. In the United States few except judges of the higher courts wear robes. The scarlet judicial robes were discarded at the Revolution. Those of black silk now worn are slightly modified academical gowns. John Jay, first chief justice of the United States (1789), set the fashion by sitting in the LL.D. robe granted him by King's College (now Columbia University).

Peers' Robes.—As early as the end of the 14th century peers seem to have worn, at their creation, some kind of robe of honour. An illumination on the foundation charter of King's College, Cambridge, represents the peers in 1446 wearing gowns, mantles and hoods of scarlet, furred with miniver, the mantle opening on the right shoulder and guarded with two, three, or four bars of miniver, in the form of short stripes high up on the shoulder. The origin of these is as yet unknown, though it is highly probable that these scarlet and miniver (or ermine) robes approximate to those of the medieval doctors, after they had adopted scarlet about 1340: it is not certain precisely when the peers' velvet robe of estate was first used. During the reign of Henry VIII, references are found to the "parliament robes" of peers. By the time of James II's coronation, the baron and viscount had the velvet robes of estate. The colour of these seems to have been crimson at first, sometimes varying to purple. They consisted of a long gown or surcoat with girdle, a mantle lined with ermine, a hood and a cape of ermine, the rows being as follows: for a duke 4, a marquess 3½, an earl 3, a viscount 2½, and a baron 2.

Till late in the 18th century peers continued to attend the House of Lords in parliamentary robes, with the stars and ribands of their orders, but robes now are worn only in the House of Lords, *e.g.,* at the opening of Parliament, on occasions when the sovereign gives his (or her) assent to bills by "royal commission" (when five or six peers on the government side appear in robes and the lord chancellor also wears his peer's robe of scarlet ermine), and at the introduction of a newly created peer or peeress, when the new peer or peeress and his or her two introducers wear their parliamentary robes (over morning dress) during the ceremony of introduction only. The mover and seconder of the address no longer wear

robes, but uniforms. On all the above occasions, and when the peers as a body attend church or some other ceremony, the parliamentary robe of scarlet cloth is worn; at the present day it takes the form of a mantle opening on the right shoulder, with a collar of ermine, and guarded with rows of ermine and gold lace round the right shoulder, varying in number according to the rank of the wearer. The modern coronation robes consist of a crimson velvet surcoat and a mantle with a cape of ermine and with rows of ermine as in the parliamentary robes. The surcoat is no longer a gown, but a short sleeveless garment.

As regards peeresses' robes, the order of the earl-marshal for the regulation of these at the coronation of James II shows that by then all peeresses wore the robes of state of crimson velvet and minutely regulates all details, such as shape, powderings, length of train, and width of the fur edging of the mantle. They have changed very little up to the present day. Peeresses created for life, when introduced into the House of Lords for the first time in October 1958, wore normal parliamentary robes with a hat of tricorn pattern.

House of Commons.—The speaker of the House of Commons wears on state occasions a black damask robe with gold lace and a full-bottomed wig; in the house itself he wears a black silk robe with train and a full-bottomed wig. The clerks at the table wear barristers' gowns and wigs.

Robes of the Orders of Knighthood.—The robes of the Garter were originally of blue woolen stuff, the surcoat and hood being powdered with garters embroidered in silk and gold. The surcoat varied in colour from year to year; the hood was made of the same material as the surcoat and, when hats began to be worn, was carried hanging over the shoulder. Robes were sometimes granted to ladies in the early days. The last lady to receive the robes was Margaret, countess of Richmond, in 1488. At the present day the mantle is of dark blue velvet, of the same colour as the riband, lined with taffeta, and with the star embroidered on the left shoulder. The hood and surcoat of crimson velvet are lined with white taffeta, and with these are worn a doublet and trunk hose of white satin and a plumed hat.

The robes worn by the knights of the Bath created at the coronation of Henry IV were green with furred hoods and a white silk cord hanging from the left shoulder. The mantle at the present day is of crimson velvet lined with white over a white satin undercoat and trunk hose, and a plumed hat and white boots with red tops are worn. The mantle of the Thistle is of dark green velvet over surcoat, etc., of cloth of silver; that of St. Patrick azure, with doublet and trunk hose of white satin; that of St. Michael and St. George of Saxon blue satin lined with scarlet; and that of the Star of India of light blue satin lined with white.

Judicial and Forensic Robes.—It is frequently stated that judicial robes had their origin in the dress of ecclesiastics. But though ecclesiastics in early days frequently acted as judges and though, as Sir John Fortescue says, the serjeant's long robe was "after the fashion of a priest," judicial robes more probably arose from the ordinary civilian dress of the early 14th century. The chief argument for their ecclesiastical origin has been found in the coif, a cap of white linen or silk, tied under the chin, and described by Fortescue as "the principal or chief insignment and habit wherewith serjeants-at-law at their creation are decked," which is said to have been used by ecclesiastics to hide the tonsure when in court. More probably the coif was a headdress in common use in the 13th century, which survived as the distinguishing mark of men of law. The scarlet judicial robe trimmed with white fur (ermine or miniver) together with a hood of scarlet cloth lined with white fur undoubtedly represent the survival for specialized use of the robes of the pre-Reformation doctors in canon law (*decretorum doctor*). About 1340 the doctors in theology and in canon law adopted scarlet robes and hoods, lined with miniver, and silk linings were adopted for summer use about a century later. An ecclesiastical origin is correctly assigned to these, inasmuch as, prior to the Reformation, all the members of the two ancient universities were in holy orders, or at least belonged to one of the lower clerical grades.

About the time of Queen Elizabeth I the square cap (*pileus quadratus*), otherwise known as the cornered, black, or sentence cap (the last from the fact of its being put on by the judge when pronouncing sentence of death), began to appear. Sometimes it was worn over the coif only, sometimes over the coif and skullcap. Sometimes it had ear flaps, sometimes, as at present, not.

Toward the end of the 17th century the judges took to wearing wigs, and they have continued to wear them ever since. The wearing of wigs naturally concealed the coif and velvet skullcap, so a device had to be invented by which they could still be displayed. The expedient was hit upon of putting a round patch of white stuff, with a black spot in the middle of it, on the crown of the wig of certain of the judges, to represent the coif and skullcap. Serjeants being appointed no longer (*see* above), this round patch has now disappeared, the only trace of it left being the circular depression on the crown of the wig. Minute details of court and levee dress, judicial and legal, of the present day, will be found in *Dress Worn at Court,* issued with the authority of the lord chamberlain—also details of mourning costume.

Municipal and Civic Robes.—The word "livery," the use of which is now practically confined to the official dress of the "livery companies," the dress of menservants, etc., originally meant an allowance of food or clothing granted to certain persons. It is still used of the allowances of food made to the fellows of certain colleges. As early as the 13th century, the citizens of London used to assume a uniform dress to do honour to some great occasion, as when 600 citizens rode out to meet Queen Margaret of France, second wife of Edward I, "in one livery of red and white, with the cognizances of their misteries embroidered upon their sleeves." By the 14th century there is evidence of the adoption of liveries by the trades and fraternities, and when the livery companies were incorporated they took care to have their liveries authorized by their charters. The scarlet, violet, and black robes still worn by the mayor, aldermen, sheriffs, etc., were early in use. The provincial mayors and aldermen at quite an early date followed the fashion of London, wearing what are virtually sleeved tabards. An account of the robes of modern provincial mayors will be found in William H. St. John Hope (ed.), *Corporation Plate . . . of the cities . . . of England and Wales* (1895).

At the present day the lord mayor has several sets of robes: a special coronation robe, a crimson velvet robe of state like that of an earl, worn with the chain and jewel, *e.g.,* in the presence of the sovereign when in the city; a black robe of state trimmed with gold, which is worn with the chain and jewel, *e.g.,* at the Guildhall on lord mayor's day; the scarlet robes, which are worn, with or without the chain, on most public occasions, such as the service at St. Paul's on the first day of the Easter law term, audiences of the sovereign, the election of the lord mayor, the opening of the central criminal court, etc.; a violet gown, which is worn, *e.g.,* when the lord mayor elect is presented to the sovereign, when he is sworn in, at the election of sheriffs, etc.; and a black gown worn in church on Good Friday, etc. The aldermen wear scarlet on most occasions of ceremony, former mayors "having the Cap of Dignity attached to their gown, and being entitled to introduce a sword and mace into their badges." They also wear violet robes on certain occasions marked in the almanac of the *Alderman's Pocket-Book,* and black gowns when the lord mayor wears his. The sheriffs and recorders have scarlet, violet, and black gowns, and the members of the common council have deep mazarine blue gowns, which seem to have been first prescribed in 1761. (X.)

Academical Dress.—Like judicial robes, academical dress has been considered to be of ecclesiastical origin. The medieval scholar was, of course, a clerk and had to wear the clerkly gown and the tonsure. The ecclesiastical dress that he wore had itself probably developed out of the ordinary civilian dress at an earlier period. The robes worn in the earliest times at Oxford and Cambridge, at least in part, were monastic or ecclesiastical in origin, but the hood was certainly derived from a lay garment, at one time common to all classes and both sexes, as Herbert Norris pointed out (see *Bibliography*). This lay hood was adopted by monks, clergy, and all university students, and eventually was retained in a specialized form by the various faculties, as an academical distinction. The statutes of certain colleges required of the

scholars as early as the 14th century the tonsure and a "decent habit" suitable to a clerk; *i.e.,* a long gown, which it is stipulated in some cases must be closed in front like the Benedictine habit. Some colleges had liveries, prescribed perhaps by the founder of the college and laid down by the statutes. The differences of colour and shape in the undergraduate gowns of most of the Cambridge colleges are supposed to be a survival of this, but in fact the Cambridge college undergraduate gowns all date from the period 1805–40; *i.e.,* are late Guelphic (that is, Hanoverian) in origin and thus quite modern.

The gown was worn by all grades as befitting clerks. It is hard to determine whether there was at first any difference between the gowns of the senior nongraduates and the bachelors of arts and that of the masters and doctors and the bachelors in the superior faculties, but it seems improbable. It was frequently fur-lined, or at least trimmed with fur, but the use of the more costly furs was forbidden, especially in the period between 1350–1500, to all below the degree of master, except sons of noblemen, or those possessing a certain income, bachelors using budge (common fur or black lamb's wool); students and even doctors in theology were also, at one time, restricted to budge, lamb's wool, and to sombre habits. The robes of masters had to be flowing and reach to the ankles (*toga talaris*), and it was the masters who had the earliest distinctive dress that could be called truly academical.

The cope (*i.e.,* the *capa* or *cappa clausa,* the closed and essentially ecclesiastical cope or cape, not to be confused with the open and purely decorative cope of the clergy) probably originated in the ordinary everyday mantle of the clergy. Its wear in England was made obligatory by Archbishop Stephen Cardinal Langton, 1222, at the provincial synod held at Oseney Abbey, near Oxford. All bishops, deans, archdeacons, rural deans, priests, and all church dignitaries were ordered to wear it. This kind of cope, closed in front, was originally black; sometimes, for the sake of convenience, it had a slit in front to allow of the passage of the hands, this type of opening being the form or variation adopted by the doctors in theology and retained by them until the present day, although later on the slit was extended to the ground. Another variation was to make two side slits, one for each arm, a variation (the pallium or *chimaera*) adopted by the doctors in law and in physic and by the superior bachelors; *i.e.,* the bachelors in canon law, physic, and possibly in theology. This type is the forerunner of the convocation habit and ecclesiastico-academical chimere.

About 1330–40 doctors began to adopt scarlet for their hoods and later for their robes; at any rate by about 1500, probably long before, all doctors wore scarlet and had discarded their black *cappae clausae* for scarlet ones, the original sombre, black form being retained by the M.A.'s and B.D.'s. The wearing of robes of scarlet, violet, or murrey, and also the "sleveless cote" (*i.e.,* convocation habits and chimeres), *supertunica,* of these colours, was formally ratified by an act of 24 Henry VIII (1533, *caput* 13) entitled "an Act for the Reformation of Excess in Apparel." The cope still survives at Cambridge as the dress worn by the vice-chancellor and by regius professors of divinity, law, and medicine when presenting for degrees; it is lined with white fur.

The hood was originally worn by all scholars, as by everybody, and had evidently no academical significance. Sometimes a cap was worn also, the hood being thrown back. There were evidently hoods of two kinds for masters from about 1432, when masters and doctors were allowed to use silk in their linings during the summer months, so that there were silk-lined and miniver-lined hoods. These two types of hood survived, at least in Oxford, until as late as 1657, or even a little later, in the time of John Fell, dean of Christ Church and vice-chancellor, and Anthony à Wood, M.A., the antiquary. Eventually (from about 1674–75, in the time of George Edwards and David Loggan) the silk-lined hood was the type principally retained by masters and doctors, the miniver-lined hood being preserved as a proctorial insignia only. At a later date, at Cambridge, a distinction was made between the hoods of nonregent masters, which were lined with silk, and those of regents, which were lined with miniver. Later again, the regents wore their hoods in such a way as to show the white lining, while the nonregents wore theirs "squared," so that the white did not show. Hence the name "white hoods" and "black hoods" given to the upper and lower houses of the old senate, respectively. It is not settled when the modern colouring of hoods arose; they probably followed those of the robes of the faculties, but about these there is equal uncertainty. The Oxford proctor still wears a miniver-lined hood. The modern Oxford doctors' and B.D., and the Cambridge hoods have preserved the original shape more closely than the Oxford M.A. type, being a hood and cape combined, the cape having at Cambridge now, incorrectly, square corners: the cape, being semicircular, should be rounded.

There seem to have been in Tudor times at least three varieties of academical headdress; one, the round cap of velvet for graduates in the secular faculties, survives as part of the full dress of doctors (except doctors in theology) to the present day. The square cap was adopted at the universities, according to N. F. Robinson, after 1520, in imitation of the University of Paris. In this connection should be mentioned the term "tuft-hunting" (*i.e.*, attempting to thrust oneself into the society of one's social superiors), derived from the gold tufts or tassel worn by noblemen and fellow commoners on their college caps. Originally, in the two ancient English universities, no one wore a cap except doctors in the superior faculties of theology, canon law and physic. The type of cap they wore was a tight round skullcap type, with a little point at the crown: it was called the pileus, and was thus a cap of dignity. All other graduates and nongraduates had their hoods, which were thus a shoulder cape and a covering for the head. It appears that in Paris caps were made by sewing together four pieces of cloth, and the seams produced little raised ridges, and had a squaring effect. From this particular cap (squarish in effect), two types of cap evolved: (1) the biretta or priest's cap, simply a stiffened, rather taller pileus, made of the four pieces of cloth, and (2) the academical or doctor's cap (*pileus quadratus*), a velvet cap of dignity for doctors in theology. Doctors in the secular faculties adopted in the early Tudor period a soft round lay cap of velvet (*pileus rotundus*). Foundation choristers and scholars were permitted square caps in 1549. Between 1549 and 1580 there were frequent rulings and fresh statutes issued on the subject of caps. B.A.'s and other junior graduates were not authorized to wear caps until between 1575 and 1580, and then only "humbly and submissively in the Schools." By 1580 a cap had been established for all members of the two ancient English universities, and the restriction to doctors and senior graduates had broken down. The beautiful series of illustrations of the academical dress in the Bodleian Library at Oxford, by George Edwards and by David Loggan, 1674 and 1675, respectively, show the caps then in use.

Academical dress underwent much inquiry and some revision at the time of the Reformation, chiefly in the direction of sobriety, uniformity, and laicization, "excess of apparel" being repressed as severely as ever, but not with much more effect. There have been few far-reaching changes since the Laudian Code of 1636. Cambridge in the 20th century (1932–34) inquired into and revised its regulations as to dress, after a subcommittee of the senate had submitted three reports, and in the *Ordinances* clear rules are laid down, published in the University Reporter (Feb. 28, 1934). The Oxford regulations have not been revised since 1770, and have now fallen into chaos. Some of them are dead letters: at Oxford one hood (the pale blue B.Litt. hood of 1895) by 1940 had come to be worn for four degrees, B.C.L., B.M., B.Sc., and B.Litt. The dark blue hood, lined with white fur, proper to the B.C.L. and B.M. degrees, was no longer to be seen at Oxford. The modern robe makers sell the pale blue silk B.Litt. hood, lined with white fur, for all four degrees and for the B.Phil. In 1957–58 a new hood was invented for the B.Phil. degree. This is of the debased Oxford M.A. pattern, of dark blue ribbed rayon lined with white silk: the white silk takes the place of the white fur. It is, in fact, a freak hood. The B.Mus. hood, originally dark blue like B.C.L. and B.M., was, before World War I, of dark purple: by 1945 or so it had become a brilliant lilac.

In the absence of any official regulations, the Oxford branch of the National Federation of Merchant Tailors drew up in 1957 an illustrated catalogue of what they described as the correct colours and materials of the various robes. This catalogue is said to have been approved by Congregation and it was deposited in the Bodleian. But some of the colours are still incorrect. Congregation never appointed a subcommittee to thresh out the whole subject, as did Cambridge in 1932–34, and thus, at Oxford, the tailors have prescribed for the university.

Doctors of both universities have three sets of robes: first, the full-dress robe of scarlet cloth; second, the scarlet, murrey, or violet convocation habit and hood of scarlet (now at Cambridge a cope, at Oxford the so-called *cappa clausa*); third, the black gown or undress. The first is worn by all doctors except the doctor in music, and is accompanied by the round cap of velvet except in the case of the D.D., who continues to wear the square cap (or ecclesiastical cap) with all three forms of dress; strictly, the D.D. square cap should be soft, of black velvet and with a tuft, or plain without tuft or tassel. The Oxford D.D. also wears a cassock, sash, and scarf. The scarlet robe is of a different, somewhat more of a Tudor lay (or civic) shape than the M.A. and B.A. gowns: in fact it is a tabard. As now worn, it is faced with silk of the same colour as the hood silk lining of the faculty, except in the case of the Oxford D.D. full-dress robe, which is faced with and has bell-shaped sleeves of black velvet. The second or Cambridge cope now has gone almost out of use, but is still worn when presenting for degrees, etc., but only in Cambridge. It is sometimes worn over the black gown. There are several types of black gown, but the tufted gown of David Loggan's day has now gone out of use. The M.D. and Mus.D. black gowns at Cambridge are now made after the pattern of the LL.D. gown, with a square-ended sleeve and flap collar, trimmed with black lace, but the D.D., Sc.D., and Litt.D. wear the M.A. silk gown, the former with the scarf, the two latter with lace on the sleeve, placed horizontally for Sc.D. and vertically for Litt.D. Some doctors in divinity wear the full-sleeved gown with scarf. At Cambridge the headdress of a D.D. is the square cap, of secular doctors the velvet bonnet with gold cords. The doctors in music wear, as they have done since about 1600, a full-dress robe of white or cream damask brocaded silk, lined with pink satin at Oxford and with cherry-coloured satin at Cambridge. Formerly (1550 period) doctors in music at Cambridge wore the M.D. robes (*Cambridge Grace Book* Δ 1545).

The Oxford sleeveless commoner's gown, though still by statute *toga talaris*, now reaches little below the waist, the full-sleeved or bell-sleeved scholar's gown to the knee. The tufted silk gown of the gentleman commoner and the nobleman's gold-lace gown are not yet abolished by statute, but have fallen into disuse. The University of Oxford Act, 1854, brought in and passed by Gladstone, abolished these class distinctions at Oxford, although they lingered on until about 1869 at Christ Church, so that King Edward VII, as prince of Wales, wore a gentleman commoner's bell-shaped sleeved gown when up in 1860. Vice-chancellors have no official dress, but wear the robes of their degree. The chancellors of the older universities wear a black damask silk robe with gold lace and a black velvet square cap with gold tassel and band; those of the newer universities have had robes "created" by experts or by the robe makers, who are nowadays to a large extent the arbiters of academical dress, but based largely on Oxford and Cambridge customs. The Hull chancellor's and vice-chancellor's robes are of blue: these robes at Southampton are of black figured damask silk with gold ornamentation.

United States.—An intercollegiate commission in 1893 drafted a uniform code for academical caps, gowns, and hoods which has since been accepted by 800 or more degree-granting colleges and universities in the United States. Three types of gown and three types of hood have been devised for bachelors, masters, and doctors, respectively. The square caps remain the same except that the doctor's may be made of velvet and have a tassel of gold. The bachelor's gown is made of black worsted material and may be distinguished by its pointed sleeves of the B.A. Oxford type, though hanging only to the knee. The master's gown, made of silk, has closed bag sleeves of M.A. type (the arm coming through a slit at the elbow), which are square at the end and extend well below the knee. The doctor's gown is also made of silk, and, like a judge's robe, has full round open bell-shaped sleeves, is faced with velvet and has three bars of velvet on each sleeve.

The hoods are lined with silk of the colour or colours of the college or university granting the degree and bordered with silk or velvet of the colour that represents the department of learning in which the degree was obtained. Obviously, only a very few universities, such as Harvard, Yale, and Chicago, can have a single distinguishing colour as a hood lining (crimson, blue, and maroon, respectively); other universities and colleges have to have two colours, the second or subsidiary colour being sewn inside as a chevron; Cornell and Cincinnati have two chevrons. This system, though distinctive and advantageous in some respects, produces a rather patchy effect, but it would be impossible to distinguish the degree hoods of about 800 degree-granting colleges or universities without such a device. Colours of the faculties are: arts, white; theology, scarlet; law, purple; medicine, green; music, pink; philosophy, dark blue; science, golden yellow; letters, white; engineering, orange; economics, copper; public health, salmon pink; agriculture, maize; fine arts, brown; accountancy and commerce, drab; library science, lemon; veterinary science, gray. The velvet trimming of the doctor's gown may also be of the departmental colour or it may be black if preferred.

The U.S. system of hoods is, therefore, progressive and enables anyone conversant with the system to pick out the university (by the colour or colours in the lining), the faculty (by the border on the cowl or hood portion proper), and the grade (by the size and shape, bachelors and masters having silk hoods of Oxford M.A. shape, masters' being made considerably longer than bachelors', doctors' being of cloth [rayon or silk] of the Cambridge M.A. type but with a well-rounded cape portion). The very expensive real silk is now rarely used for hood linings, man-made fabrics having taken its place.

A few institutions, notably Harvard and Yale, retain an individual code for their hoods. At Harvard, hoods for bachelors, masters, and doctors are of the simple Oxford M.A. type, of black cloth or silk; there is no border on the outside to denote the faculty. Masters' hoods are longer than bachelors'; and doctors' are longer than masters'. All these hoods are worn back to front, the liripipe being outward instead of (correctly) inward toward the back. The faculty is indicated on the gowns by "crow's-feet."

At Yale, all hoods are made of black material and are fully lined with dark blue, those of bachelors being three feet long, masters' and doctors' four feet long; and all are edged with velvet. All are of the simple Oxford M.A. type, and are worn back to front, as at Harvard.

All the institutions are governed by the intercollegiate code devised by the Intercollegiate Bureau of Academic Costume chartered by the University of the State of New York. The bureau maintains the system, adds to it when new degrees or degree-granting corporations are established; and its "repository," the firm of Cotrell and Leonard, can supply the correct hoods, gowns, and caps for any college or university of the United States.

Continental Europe.—Academical dress, as known in the United Kingdom, the Commonwealth of Nations, and the United States, is not now worn at continental universities. During the Middle Ages some countries had an academical dress, in general of the Oxford and Cambridge pattern.

In France, academical dress was in use in the University of Paris from the 13th century; and at the end of the first third of the 14th century Pope Benedict XII (Jacques Fournier), a doctor in theology of Paris, allowed doctors in canon law to wear a red shoulder cape. During the 18th century academical dress was worn less and less; until the abolition of all the universities of France by a law of the National Convention dated Sept. 15, 1793. Today, graduates of French universities wear a black or coloured gown, a round, cylinder-shaped high cap, and a silk scarf over the left shoulder, which is said to represent the tail (*liripipium*) of the medieval hood. Their rank is indicated in ascending order by one row of white fur (*bachelier*), two rows (*licencié, i.e.,* master), or three (*docteur*). The colour of the silk scarf varies according to the university.

The Italian universities of Bologna, Padua, Rome, Pisa, Florence, Pavia, and Ferrara had academical dress in the Middle Ages.

In Spain, Salamanca, Lérida, Valladolid, Huesca, Barcelona, and Alcalá universities had academical dress; as did Palma de Mallorca (Balearic Islands).

In Portugal, academical dress was prescribed for the University of Coimbra in 1321; it consisted of a gown and hood, with the addition of a cap for graduates only.

Malta's Royal University prescribes for its graduates an academical dress resembling that in Great Britain, save that there are no hoods.

German-speaking countries, Belgium and the Netherlands, and Switzerland have used academical dress; in Switzerland, Basel and Geneva universities prescribed it.

Brussels (Belgium) and Lausanne (Switzerland) are special cases, as a large number of British physicians and surgeons hold the degree of doctor in medicine of these universities and academical dress is authorized for their use in accordance with British custom. At Brussels this consists of a full-dress robe of scarlet superfine cloth of the Cambridge and London shape, the sleeves being of the open-wing type as at Cambridge. It is lined with light blue silk, and the fronts are faced with the same blue silk to a width of four to five inches. The hood also is of scarlet superfine cloth, has a rounded cape of the full or London shape, and is fully lined with light blue silk. The cap is of black velvet, round (as for London doctors), with blue cord and side tassels.

At Lausanne (of which Commonwealth physicians and surgeons also may be doctors), a full-dress robe of scarlet superfine cloth is worn, with bell-shaped sleeves (as for Oxford doctors), faced with virgin blue watered silk; the fronts of the robe are faced with the same silk. The hood is of the full or Oxford doctors' shape with a well-rounded cape, and is lined throughout with the same virgin-blue watered silk. The cap is round, of black velvet (as for London doctors), with blue cord and tassels. The undress gown is of black silk or poplin, of the M.A. Oxford type, the armhole being bound with two rows of black silk fabric (gimp) as used at Oxford.

BIBLIOGRAPHY.—George Edwards, *Ordinum habituumque Academicorum exemplaria* (1674); David Loggan, *Oxonia illustrata* (1675); *Documents Relating to the University and Colleges of Cambridge*, 3 vol. (1852); *Statutes of the Colleges of Oxford*, 3 vol. (1853); J. Griffiths (ed.), *Laudian Code of Statutes, 1636* (1888); *Transactions of the St. Paul's Ecclesiological Society*, vol. 4 (1900), vol. 5 (1905); Charles A. H. Franklyn, "University Hoods and Robes," a set of 25 large cards, illustrated by A. V. Wheeler-Holohan (1925); "Academical Dress, a Brief Sketch from the 12th to the 20th Century, with especial reference to Doctors," *Oxford*, vol. 9, no. 2 (1947); Strickland Gibson (ed.), *Statuta antiqua univ. oxon.* (1931); Herbert Norris, *Costume and Fashion*, 3 vol. (1924–38); *Statuta Univ. Oxon.* (current); *Ordinances of the University of Cambridge* (current, and especially Feb. 28, 1934, *University Reporter*); D. R. Venables and R. E. Clifford, *Academic Dress at the University of Oxford* (1958); C. A. H. Franklyn and F. R. S. Rogers, "The Dress of the Clergy," in 6 parts, in *Parson and Parish* (Oct. 1951–April 1953); F. W. Haycraft, *The Degrees and Hoods of the World's Universities and Colleges*, 4th ed. rev. by E. W. S. Stringer (1948); W. N. Hargreaves-Mawdsley, *A History of Academical Dress in Europe* (1963); Charles A. H. Franklyn, "History of Academical Dress in Europe," *Oxford*, vol. 19, no. 1 (Dec. 1963); D. Anderson, "Academical Dress," *The Sydney University Union Recorder*, vol. 44 (March 12 and 19, 1964). (C. A. H. F.)

ROBESON, PAUL (1898–   ), U.S. Negro actor and singer, was born at Princeton, N.J., April 9, 1898. He graduated from Rutgers College, New Brunswick, N.J., with an extraordinarily distinguished scholastic and athletic record, and in 1923 completed the law course at Columbia University. His first stage appearance was in *Taboo* (1922), but he made his reputation in *All God's Chillun Got Wings* and in the title roles in *Emperor Jones* (1923) and *Black Boy* (1926). After appearing in *Show Boat* in England, he toured the U.S., Europe, and the U.S.S.R. with recitals of Negro spirituals. Robeson entered films in 1933, playing in *The Emperor Jones, Sanders of the River*, and *Show Boat*. In 1943 he appeared in a New York production of *Othello*, which established the longest Shakespearean run in the United States.

In 1950 the U.S. State Department denied him a passport after he refused to sign an affidavit stating whether he was or ever had been a member of the Communist Party. In 1958 the U.S. Supreme Court ruled that refusal to sign such an affidavit was not grounds for denial of a passport, and Robeson settled in England. He made a number of trips and concert appearances in the U.S.S.R. and other continental countries and then returned to the U.S. in 1963.   (M. S. By.; X.)

ROBESPIERRE, MAXIMILIEN FRANÇOIS MARIE ISIDORE DE (1758–1794), French revolutionary known as "the Incorruptible," a leading member of the Jacobin Club and of the Committee of Public Safety, whose name is particularly associated with the period of Terror of 1793–94. Born at Arras on May 6, 1758, he was descended from a modest bourgeois family that had settled at Carvin about 1650. His father, an advocate, fell into debt, and, after his wife died in 1764, left home and died in Munich in 1777. His orphaned children were brought up by their maternal grandparents.

Early Life at Arras.—From 1765 Maximilien attended the college of the Oratorians in Arras; then, in 1769, he obtained one of the scholarships given by the Abbey of St. Vaast for the College of Louis-le-Grand in Paris. A brilliant student, he matriculated in 1780 and took a master's degree in law in 1781. His scholarship was then transferred to his younger brother Augustin, and Maximilien registered as an advocate at the Arras bar. He rapidly made a name for himself and was appointed a judge in the Salle Épiscopale, a

BULLOZ

MAXIMILIEN ROBESPIERRE, PORTRAIT BY AN UNKNOWN ARTIST. IN THE MUSÉE CARNAVALET, PARIS

court with jurisdiction over the provostship of the diocese. As a successful advocate he was assured of a comfortable living.

Robespierre also competed for academic awards and his essay "Discours sur les peines infamantes" (1784) won him a prize offered by the Société royale des Sciences et Arts at Metz. He joined the Arras literary and musical society, known as the "Rosati," and was made president of the local *académie*. Though it was rumoured at the time that he had a fiancée, his cousin Anaïs Deshorties, he never married. Already known as the advocate of the poor, in his "Mémoire pour le sieur Dupond" he harassed the privileged classes, inveighing against royal absolutism and arbitrary justice. From the time of the notification (June 1788) that the Estates-General would be called (*see* FRANCE: *History*; FRENCH REVOLUTION), he launched his appeal for electoral reform in a pamphlet, "À la nation Artésienne, sur la nécessité de réformer les États d'Artois." On March 23, 1789, the people of Arras chose him as one of their representatives and the third estate of the bailliage elected him fifth of the eight Artois members of the Estates-General. Thus began his political career: he was not quite 31 years old.

The Constituent Assembly.—Conspicuous in the Assembly by his immaculate appearance and dress, Robespierre retained throughout his life his bourgeois customs, frugality, and his strict moral code. Despite his frail appearance (he was slight in build and only 5 ft. 3 in. tall) he was of robust health. He probably made his maiden speech on May 18, 1789, and before the end of the Assembly on Sept. 30, 1791, he had voiced his opinions more than 500 times. In spite of his weak voice, and the opposition he aroused, he was nevertheless able to command the attention of its members. Described by the comte de Mirabeau as one who "believes everything he says," he was attacked by the Royalist press, excluded from the Assembly's committees and from its presidency, and only once, on June 19, 1790, elected one of its secretaries for a short time. The people, however, always supported him.

During April 1790 Robespierre was president of the Jacobin Club, of which he had been a member since its formation (*see* JACOBINS), and in October he was appointed a judge of the Ver-

sailles district tribunal. Nevertheless, he had decided to devote himself entirely to his work in the Assembly, where the constitution of Sept. 3, 1791, was being drawn up. A disciple of Rousseau, grounded in ancient history and the works of the philosophers, he welcomed the Declaration of the Rights of Man and the Citizen (*q.v.*). He fought tenaciously for universal suffrage, for unrestricted entry to the national guard, public offices, and army commissions, and for the right to petition; he opposed the royal veto, the abuses of ministerial power, religious and racial discrimination; he defended actors, Jews, and Negro slaves, and supported the demand for the incorporation (September 1791) of the papal territory of Avignon into France. It was through his efforts on May 16 and 18, 1791, that the existing deputies were debarred from reelection to the new assembly, on the grounds that a completely new assembly would better express the sovereign will of the people.

The flight and capture at Varennes (June 20–21, 1791) of Louis XVI, for which Robespierre vainly demanded the king's trial, spurred his efforts for the completion of the constitution. He foresaw the "massacre" at the Champs de Mars (July 17), when demonstrators demanding the abdication of the king were dispersed with loss of life, and afterward, fearing arrest, he went to live with a supporter, Maurice Duplay. Robespierre prevented the dissolution of the Jacobin Club after the moderate members had seceded to form the Feuillants Club (*q.v.*). His general popularity remained immense, and after the final sitting of the Assembly, the Parisians gave Robespierre, now nicknamed "the Incorruptible," and his friend Jérôme Pétion a tremendous reception, which was repeated in Artois, where he stayed briefly in October 1791.

Jacobin Club.—Although he had excluded himself from the new Legislative Assembly, Robespierre continued his political activities, giving up the lucrative post of public prosecutor at the Paris criminal tribunal to which he had been elected on June 10, 1791. Henceforth his speeches were made to the Jacobin Club, where he was heard about 100 times up to the insurrection of Aug. 10, 1792 (*see* below). There he opposed the demand of J. P. Brissot (*q.v.*) for a European war to spread the aims of the Revolution. He denounced the secret intrigues of the court and of the Royalists, their collusion with Austria, the unpreparedness of the army, and on Feb. 10, 1792, again demanded the dismissal of aristocratic officers. He also spoke for the "patriotic" soldiers, in particular those of the Châteauville regiment, imprisoned after their mutiny at Nancy in August 1790. When Brissot's supporters stirred up opposition against him, Robespierre founded, in May 1792, a journal, *Le Défenseur de la Constitution*. This new weapon strengthened his hand; he violently attacked the marquis de Lafayette (*q.v.*), the commander of the French Army, whom he suspected of wanting to establish a military dictatorship, but failed to obtain his dismissal and arrest.

The reverses suffered by the French Army after France had declared war on Austria and Prussia in April 1792 came as no surprise to Robespierre and the threat of an invasion of France rallied the people to him. But he hesitated to call for an insurrection. "You must not fight the common enemy," he told the *fédérés* (provincial volunteers) who assembled in Paris, "except with the sword of the law." When the insurrection nevertheless broke out on Aug. 10, 1792, Robespierre, like Georges Danton and J. P. Marat (*qq.v.*), did not take part in the attack on the Tuileries Palace. That same afternoon his Paris section, the *Piques*, elected him to the Insurrectional Commune of Paris. During the election to the new assembly, the National Convention, he excused the September massacres, thereby strengthening his position with the people of Paris who, on Sept. 5, elected him the first of their members in the National Convention.

The Convention.—From the very first sittings of the Convention at the end of September, Robespierre was accused of dictatorship by the Girondins (*q.v.*), the majority group. The trial of the king, which opened in December, heightened the conflict; Robespierre intervened 11 times during the course of the debates and his speech of Dec. 3 rallied those who hesitated to take action against Louis. Meanwhile he used his new journal, *Lettres à ses commettants,* to keep the provinces informed of the course of events. The execution of the king (Jan. 21, 1793) did not, however, resolve the struggle between the Girondins and the Montagnards (as the Jacobins in the Convention were called); it was finally brought to a head only by the treason (April 1793) of Gen. Charles Dumouriez (*q.v.*), who went over to the Austrians. At the same time the scarcity of food and rising prices were creating revolutionary feeling among the people. A kind of "popular front" was formed between the Parisian sans-culottes and the Montagnards, and on May 26, 1793, Robespierre invited the people "to force their way into the Convention in revolt against the corrupt members." On May 31 he supported those petitioners who demanded in the Convention a decree indicting the leaders of the Gironde and the accomplices of Dumouriez. It was passed against 29 of the Girondins on June 2, while the debating hall in the Tuileries (to which the Convention had recently moved) was surrounded by the armed sections of Paris. The democratic constitution of 1793, finally adopted on June 24, contained several articles put forward by Robespierre, but his proposals to limit the right of private property, to proclaim the right to work for all, to introduce a graduated tax, and to create a league of nations, were rejected as being too revolutionary.

The Committee of Public Safety and the Terror.—After the fall of the Girondins, the Montagnards were left to deal with France's desperate plight. Threatened internally by the movement for federalism and by the civil war in the west (*see* VENDÉE, WARS OF THE), and on its frontiers by the anti-French coalition, the success of the Revolution depended upon the support of the entire nation. "*Une volonté une*" ("one will and one only"), Robespierre noted in his diary, and this dictatorial power characterized his view of the revolutionary government. On July 27 Robespierre became a member of the Committee of Public Safety, first set up on April 6. While many of his colleagues were away on missions, and others, such as Lazare Carnot, C. A. Prieur-Duvernois, and Jean Lindet were preoccupied with special assignments, Robespierre assumed control of the committee. He also tightened his grip on the Jacobin Club and further subjected the popular societies to his views.

One after another he denounced the "factions" that endangered the committee. In August and September he brought about the arrest of the leaders of the extreme left, the Enragés; on Sept. 4 he prevented the followers of Jacques Hébert (*q.v.*), who dominated the Commune, from taking over control of the Revolution. In his report of 5 Nivôse (Dec. 25, 1793) in the Convention he justified the collective dictatorship of the committee and the centralization of the administration, and, in order to effect mass conscription and to wage total war, he decided to intensify the Terror. "It is our weakness in dealing with traitors that ruins us," he declared, and asserted the need for a "swift, harsh and inflexible justice." But he did not advocate indiscriminate indictments, and he recalled the representatives on missions, such as J. L. Tallien, J. B. Carrier, Louis Fréron, and Paul Barras, who were disgracing the Revolution by the atrocities they authorized.

As the economic situation grew worse, Robespierre struck down the Hébertistes, who had been profiting from the distress (18 were executed on March 24, 1794), and to retain the backing of the people he supported the vote for the decrees of 8 and 13 Ventôse, year II (Feb. 26 and March 3, 1794), by which the property of suspects was to be distributed to the poor. He finally turned against the Indulgents, those who favoured peace and a lessening of the Terror, bourgeois businessmen and foreign bankers, who had given their support to Danton. After much hesitation Robespierre provided L. A. Saint-Just with the notes (a series of charges against Danton) with which he was able to secure the conviction and execution of Danton and Camille Desmoulins (16 Germinal; April 5, 1794).

Cult of the Supreme Being.—A deist, like Rousseau, Robespierre had already condemned the anti-Christian movement and the "masquerades" of the cult of Reason. He went further in his report to the Convention of 18 Floréal (May 7) affirming the existence of God and the immortality of the soul, and outlining his plan for a civic religion, the cult of the Supreme Being. Meanwhile, his popularity remained immense, as is shown by the public

ovations that he received after Henri Admiral's attempt on his life (4 Prairial; May 23). He had won over the Jacobins, the Commune, the national guard, and on 16 Prairial (June 4) the Convention elected him president by 216 out of 220 votes. In this capacity he attended the inaugural festival of the Supreme Being on 20 Prairial (June 8). But overwork and the large number of speeches he made in the Convention and at the Jacobin Club (almost 450 since the opening of the Convention) began to take their toll of his health; he became irritable and aloof. After his law of 22 Prairial (June 10), reorganizing and speeding up the work of the revolutionary tribunal, a secret opposition against him began to develop, led by the representatives on missions whom he had attacked. His authority was questioned in the Committee of Public Safety, particularly by Carnot, J. M. Collot d'Herbois, and J. N. Billaud-Varenne, and the Committee of General Security, which included many of his opponents, became even more hostile. Embittered by these attacks, and by accusations of dictatorship now brought by his colleagues, the Montagnard deputies, he stayed away from the Convention and after 10 Messidor (June 28) from the Committee of Public Safety, confining his denunciations of his enemies to the Jacobin Club. At the same time he began to lose the support of the people, whose hardships continued despite the recent French victories.

Thermidor.—On 5 Thermidor (July 23) Robespierre reappeared at the Committee of Public Safety and on 8 Thermidor at the Convention. His long final speech on that day, at first gaining applause, was later received in silence, and the parliamentary majority turned against him. Next day he was prevented from speaking at the Convention, which decreed his arrest and that of his brother Augustin and his friends Georges Couthon, Saint-Just, and Philippe Lebas. Taken to the Luxembourg prison, the warden refused to take him into custody, and Robespierre later went to the Hôtel de Ville, where armed forces assembled by the Commune were awaiting his orders. But he refused to lead the insurrection, and in the early hours of 10 Thermidor (July 28, 1794) his loyal forces began to disperse. The Convention declared him an outlaw, and when their forces attacked the Hôtel de Ville, Robespierre severely wounded himself by a pistol shot in the jaw. He was guillotined on the same evening on the Place de la Révolution (now the Place de la Concorde).

Volumes 1–9 of his complete works (including his speeches) were published between 1910 and 1961, while volume 10, the final volume, was in preparation. *See* also references under "Robespierre, Maximilien François Marie Isidore de" in the Index.

BIBLIOGRAPHY.—E. Hamel, *Histoire de Robespierre*, 3 vol. (1865–67); A. J. Paris, *La jeunesse de Robespierre* (1870); A. Mathiez, *Études robespierristes,* 2 vol. (1917–18), *Autour de Robespierre* (1925), *Robespierre terroriste* (1921); J. M. Thompson, *Robespierre*, 2 vol. (1935); P. R. Rohden, *Robespierre: Die Tragödie des politischen Ideologen* (1935); L. Jacob, *Robespierre vu par ses contemporains* (1956); G. Walter, *Robespierre*, 2 vol. (1961); J. Massin, *Robespierre* (1956); M. Bouloiseau, *Robespierre* (1957), *Le Comité de salut public* (1962); W. M. Markov (ed.), *Maximilien Robespierre* (1961). (MA. Bo.)

ROBEY, SIR GEORGE (1869–1954), English music-hall comedian known for many years as "the prime minister of mirth," was born George Edward Wade, on Sept. 20, 1869, at Herne Hill, Kent. He made his first appearance on the professional stage in 1891 and of his numerous character roles, the most famous—the collarless cleric with the red nose, the startled and heavy black eyebrows, the indignant stare, the ribald smile—was a quite early development. He solaced London in the years of World War I in *The Bing Boys Are Here*, a jovial musical comedy, and for 15 years thereafter he toured in his own revues and with his own companies. In 1932 he was Sir Charles Cochran's choice for King Menelaus in a lavish production of Offenbach's *Helen,* and three years later he was chosen to play Falstaff in *Henry IV* (Part I). Though most of the critics decided that this was an artistic error, his performance was highly intelligent and very funny.

Robey appeared in many pantomimes and films, and in countless music-hall performances. A tireless perfectionist, he worked hard up to his retirement at the age of 80, and was knighted in 1954. He died in the same year on Nov. 29 at Saltdean, Sussex.

See A. E. Wilson, *Prime Minister of Mirth* (1956). (A. H. D.)

ROBIN, a large North American thrush (*Turdus migratorius*), one of the most familiar songbirds in the eastern U.S. Its name was derived from its resemblance to another bird, the smaller European robin (*Erithacus rubecula*), called also redbreast or robin redbreast.

American Robin.—The American robin is about 10 in. long, with brick-red breast, blackish-gray upper parts and a yellow bill. It has bold white markings around the eye, under the chin and on the tips of the outer tail feathers. Females are slightly paler, and the young have spotted breasts as in other thrushes. Most robins are highly migratory, spending the winter in flocks in the southern U.S., but a few winter as far north as southern Canada. The robin is a shy woodland bird in northern forests, but elsewhere it has adjusted so completely to man that to see a robin pull an earthworm from the ground is a sight familiar to everyone.

The nest, of vegetation and trash with a firm molded inner

ALLAN D. CRUICKSHANK FROM NATIONAL AUDUBON SOCIETY

AMERICAN ROBIN (TURDUS MIGRATORIUS)

layer of mud, is built in trees, open sheds, bridges, etc. Three to five bluish-green eggs are incubated by the female for 12 days. Both parents tend the young, which fly in 14–16 days. There are two to three broods per season.

Its song consists of caroling phrases, differing in pitch, with pauses between them—a cheerful, bubbling air. There are various call notes, harsh and scolding. Earthworms, insects, berries and some grains are taken for food. The arrival of the first robins, usually males, is looked forward to in the early spring.

European Robin.—The robin of the old world is about $5\frac{1}{2}$ in. long, with brownish-orange breast and forehead, brownish-olive upper parts and a white abdomen. The young have a mottled dark brown-and-buff breast. It is a woodland bird primarily but is notably confiding toward man. Everywhere it is well known for its cocky, jaunty attitudes. It is migratory in northern Europe, but only partially so or sedentary farther south. The nest is in holes and crannies in walls, banks, trees and the like. The five to six whitish eggs are incubated 13–14 days by the female, who is fed by the male. The young fly in 12–14 days and then a second brood is reared. The bird sings almost all year, uttering high-pitched warbling phrases, and has various call notes. Food is mainly insects.

There is considerable folklore about the robin; the old-world lore that it is bad luck to kill one has been applied also to the American robin.

See David Lack, *The Life of the Robin,* rev. ed. (1947), *Robin Redbreast* (1950).   (R. S. Pr.)

ROBIN HOOD, the hero of a series of ballads the earliest of which date from the 14th century, at the latest. William Langland, in the B version of *The Vision of Piers the Plowman,* usually dated *c.* 1378, mentions "rymes of Robyn Hood," and internal evidence from the earliest ballads confirms that they must have been well known by that time. Other medieval references to Robin Hood, such as that by the Scottish chronicler John of Fordun, in the work continued by Walter Bower as *Scotichronicon* (edited by

T. Hearne, 1722, vol. iii, pp. 773–74), make it clear that the ballads already in circulation were the only evidence for his existence available to these writers. Numerous attempts have been made to prove that such a person once existed. The fabricated pedigree by the 18th-century antiquary William Stukeley can be dismissed, although it may have been the origin of the popular modern belief that Robin Hood was a contemporary of Richard I. It was not until J. M. Gutch's 1847 edition of the *Lytyll Geste of Robin Hode* that the more serious view was advanced that Robin might have been one of the disinherited followers of Simon de Montfort after the Evesham defeat of 1265. This suggestion was revived in *King Henry III and the Lord Edward* (1947), by Sir Maurice Powicke, who names a midland outlaw called Roger Godberd. Hood or Hod was not an uncommon name. A. L. Poole (in *From Domesday Book to Magna Carta,* 1951) and J. C. Holt (see *Bibliography*) favour Robert Hood or "Hobbehod," a Yorkshire fugitive mentioned in the pipe rolls of the late 1220s. Another Robert Hood was discovered by Joseph Hunter in the wardrobe accounts of Edward II. He suggested that this was an outlawed follower of Earl Thomas of Lancaster, one of the "contrariants" pardoned by Edward II during his visit to the north in 1323 (see *Critical and Historical Tract, no. iv,* 1852). J. W. Walker revived this theory (*Yorkshire Archaeological Journal,* 1944) and gave it further colour by pointing to a Hood family mentioned in the court records of the manor of Wakefield in the West Riding of Yorkshire, the area where some of the ballad episodes are located.

It is clear that the evidential basis for the various identifications of Robin Hood, distributed as they are over a century and a half, is very fragile. It is indeed more likely that the origins of the legend are to be found in the 13th rather than in the 14th century. It was in the earlier period that the sheriff was most prominent as the local representative of law and order and that there was the greatest resentment against the laws of the forest. It may be that one of the persons called Robert Hood was the man around whom the legend crystallized, but there is no reason to suppose that he took part in the events recounted in the ballads. The stories must be considered primarily as projections of the popular imagination, and the ballads, properly interpreted, are thus as important as a historical record of the medieval mind as if they were a record of actual events.

Although many of the well-known Robin Hood ballads are post-medieval, there is a core which can be certainly attributed to the medieval period. These are *Robin Hood and the Monk; Robin Hood and Guy of Gisborne; Robin Hood and the Potter;* and the *Lytyll Geste of Robin Hode,* which contain all the essential features of the legends, and from which can be deduced what popular aspirations are embodied in the life and death of the hero.

The most obvious feature of Robin Hood's life is that he was a rebel against authority, and the most striking episodes show him and his companions robbing and killing men who represented it. Their most frequent enemy is the sheriff of Nottingham, the principal local agent of the central government. Next come the wealthy ecclesiastical landowners, of whom the most vividly portrayed is the abbot of the Benedictine monastery of St. Mary's, York. The courtesy which characterizes Robin's treatment of the poor knight, of women, and of persons of humble status disappears when he and his followers are dealing with the sheriff and his agents (such as Guy of Gisborne). Then, too, the early ballads reveal the cruelty which is an inescapable aspect of medieval social relations. The sheriff is shot with arrows and beheaded, Guy of Gisborne's head is stuck on the end of a bow and the face mutilated. The monk and Much "the little page" (not to be confused with Much, the Miller's son, who figures in some of the stories) are beheaded. Robin is bled to death by the prioress of Kirklees. Her lover is slain and given to the dogs to eat.

Of Robin Hood's companions the one who appears most frequently as an actor with individuality is Little John. He is the subject of some of the most humorous episodes, as when he enters the sheriff of Nottingham's service disguised as Reynald Grenelefe. Another companion traditionally associated with Robin is Maid Marion, but this is a post-medieval tradition. By the 16th century the Robin Hood stories were frequently mimed as part of the May

Day games (*see* MAY) and Marion was associated with Robin, as is appropriate in a celebration which may have originated in a fertility cult. She was, however, almost certainly borrowed from the French pastoral couple, Robin and Marion, who figure in Adam de la Halle's *pastourelle dramatique,* the *Jeu de Robin et Marion* (*c.* 1285). She appears in none of the medieval ballads, from which women are almost entirely absent.

Although Robin Hood's main enemy was the sheriff of Nottingham, the internal evidence of the early ballads makes it clear that the action took place most frequently in south Yorkshire. The meeting of Robin with Sir Richard atte Lee was in Barnesdale between Doncaster and Wakefield. "Reynald Grenelefe" was from Holderness. The wicked abbot was from York. The nunnery of Kirklees was between Halifax and Wakefield.

The authentic Robin Hood ballads, then, are the poetic expression of popular aspirations in the north, in a turbulent era of baronial rebellions and of agrarian discontent which culminated in the Peasants' Revolt of 1381 (*q.v.*). The theme of the free, but persecuted outlaw enjoying the forbidden hunting of the forest and outwitting or killing the forces of law and order would naturally appeal to both urban and rural lower classes, free or serf, and even to unruly elements among the landed gentry.

From the 16th century onward the essential character of the legend was distorted. The chronicler Richard Grafton, in his *Abridgement of Chronicles* (1562, p. 54), suggested that Robin was a fallen nobleman, and this was taken up by the court playwrights Anthony Munday and Henry Chettle in *The Downfall of Robert, Earl of Huntingdon* and *The Death of Robert, Earl of Huntingdon* (1601) which also identified Maid Marion as Matilda Fitz Walter. Though increasing Robin's romantic appeal, this new element deprived the legend of the social bite of the earlier ballads, and the post-medieval ballads, no doubt as a result of having lost an important original impulse, also lost much vitality and poetic value.

BIBLIOGRAPHY.—F. J. Child, *The English and Scottish Popular Ballads,* vol. iii (1888); R. H. Hilton, "The Origins of Robin Hood," *Past and Present,* no. 14 (Nov. 1958); J. C. Holt, "The Ballads of Robin Hood," *ibid.,* no. 18 (Nov. 1960); W. J. Entwistle, *European Balladry* (1939); E. K. Chambers, *English Literature at the Close of the Middle Ages* (1945). (R. H. HI.)

ROBINSON, EDWARD (1794–1863), U.S. biblical scholar, considered the father of biblical geography, was born in Southington, Conn., on April 10, 1794. He graduated from Hamilton College in 1816, taught mathematics and Greek there, was instructor in Hebrew at Andover Theological Seminary, and in 1826 went to Europe to study in the major German universities, returning to the U.S. in 1830. In 1837 he became professor of biblical literature at Union Theological Seminary, New York City, and left the U.S. to explore in Palestine and Syria. His *Biblical Researches in Palestine, Mount Sinai, and Arabia Petraea,* which was published simultaneously in England, Germany, and the U.S. in 1841, immediately established his reputation. *Later Biblical Researches in Palestine and the Adjacent Regions* appeared in 1856. Robinson's plans to sum up his important topographical studies in a work on biblical geography were cut short by cataract in 1862. He died in New York City on Jan. 27, 1863. *Physical Geography of the Holy Land,* including his last work as far as he had been able to carry it, was published in 1865. All of Robinson's works were based on careful personal exploration and tempered by a thoroughly critical spirit, which was possibly at times too skeptical of local tradition. He was the author also of *Harmony of the Four Gospels in Greek* (1845) and *Harmony of the Four Gospels in English* (1846), both important in their day.

See H. B. Smith and R. D. Hitchcock, *The Life, Writings, and Character of Edward Robinson* (1863).

ROBINSON, EDWIN ARLINGTON (1869–1935), U.S. poet, known best for his narrative poems and dramatic lyrics concerning the residents of "Tilbury Town," and long narrative blank verse creations out of Arthurian and biblical materials. A descendant of the colonial poet Anne Bradstreet, Robinson was born in Head Tide, Me., on Dec. 22, 1869, and spent his boyhood and youth in Gardiner, Me., generally considered the model of "Tilbury Town." After two years at Harvard (1891–93) he moved to New York City, where he spent a few years in relative obscurity. With

the award of the Pulitzer Prize for his *Collected Poems* (1921), he became a well-known poet and a subject of both critical and popular interest. He died in New York City on April 6, 1935.

Robinson's poetry falls within two general types. In his early career (from *The Children of the Night,* 1897, which included the poems from the privately printed *The Torrent and the Night Before,* 1896, to *The Man Against the Sky,* 1916), his best poetic form was the dramatic lyric (the sonnet, the quatrain, the eightline stanza), occasionally varied (as in the title poem of *The Man Against the Sky*) by a symbolic poem of loose structure and an assertive philosophy. During these years, he perfected the poetic form for which he became so well known: the firm stanzaic structure, skilful rhyming patterns, a precise diction, combined with a dramatic instance of the human condition, usually in terms of the "Tilbury Town" pattern. Robinson is often interpreted as a "pessimist," and it is true that some of his major poems of this period treat human failures of several kinds, often culminating in suicide. In his most important philosophical expression, *The Man Against the Sky,* however, the conflict between the dark side of life and a traditional American Transcendentalism was resolved by an assertion of human value that all but removed the pessimistic grounds of its beginnings.

The second phase of Robinson's career as poet began with the publication of *Merlin* (1917); it was followed by *Lancelot* (1920), *Tristram* (1927, perhaps his most popular poem, which received the Pulitzer Prize in 1928), *Cavender's House* (1929), *Matthias at the Door* (1931), and *King Jasper* (1935). The principal distinction of these later volumes was their narrative blank verse which Robinson often managed skilfully but which was nevertheless not equal to the demands of a succession of long poems.

BIBLIOGRAPHY.—C. B. Hogan, *A Bibliography of Edwin Arlington Robinson* (1936); studies, all entitled *Edwin Arlington Robinson,* by H. Hagedorn (1938), Y. Winters (1946), E. Neff (1948), E. Barnard (1952), and E. S. Fussell (1954); C. P. Smith, *Where the Light Falls: a Portrait of Edwin Arlington Robinson* (1965). (F. J. HN.)

ROBINSON, HENRY CRABB (1775–1867), English man of letters, whose diaries provide valuable details of social and literary life in a period of intellectual and political change, was born at Bury St. Edmunds, Suffolk, on May 13, 1775. In 1796 he settled in London, where he became a lawyer, being called to the bar in 1813 and practising on the Norfolk circuit until 1828. Having inherited a small private income in 1798, in 1800 he went to Germany, and there met Goethe, Schiller, Herder, Wieland, and Mme de Staël, who acknowledged his help in collecting material for her *De l'Allemagne* (1813), and, on returning to England in 1805, he was influential in making German literature and philosophy widely known. From 1807 to 1809 he acted as foreign correspondent for *The Times,* and he later played a part in the campaign against slavery, the agitation leading to the Dissenters' Chapels Act (1844), and the founding of London University.

Crabb Robinson's interest in men, books, and affairs, and his good sense, good nature, and shrewd judgment, made him generally popular. He accompanied Wordsworth on several tours in Great Britain and abroad, and was a frequent visitor at Rydal Mount. He made notes of Coleridge's lectures, befriended William Blake, of whose last years his diaries provide the only firsthand account, and on visits to Italy (1829–31) stayed with Walter Savage Landor. His diaries, reminiscences, and letters, more than 100 volumes of which are preserved in Dr. Williams's Library, London, contain lively portraits of the literary figures of his time, and his correspondence with William and Dorothy Wordsworth is an important source of information on the poet's later life. He was famous also as a conversationalist and gave Sunday morning breakfast parties which rivaled those of Samuel Rogers (*q.v.*). He died in London on Feb. 5, 1867.

BIBLIOGRAPHY.—A selection from his diaries, etc., was ed. by T. Sadler as *The Diary, Reminiscences and Correspondence of Henry Crabb Robinson,* 3 vol. (1869; 3rd ed., 2 vol., 1872). Further selections were ed. by E. J. Morley as *Blake, Coleridge, Wordsworth, Lamb, etc.* (1922), *Correspondence of Henry Crabb Robinson with the Wordsworth Circle, 1808–66,* 2 vol. (1927), *Crabb Robinson in Germany, 1800–05* (1929), and *Henry Crabb Robinson on Books and Their Writers,* 3 vol. (1938). *See also* E. J. Morley, *The Life and Times of Henry Crabb Robinson* (1935); J. M. Baker, *Henry Crabb Robinson of Bury, Jena, "The Times," and Russell Square* (1937). (N. C. N.)

ROBINSON, HENRY WHEELER (1872–1945), English Baptist theologian and Old Testament scholar, who, in the austerity of his character and in his iron self-discipline and devotion to duty, represented the highest traditions of English Nonconformity. He was born at Northampton on Feb. 7, 1872. After three years as a clerk, he studied at Regent's Park College, London, the University of Edinburgh, Mansfield College, Oxford, and Marburg and Strasbourg universities (1890–1900). He was Baptist minister at Pitlochry, Perthshire (1900–03), and St. Michael's, Coventry (1903–06), before being appointed tutor at Rawdon Baptist College near Leeds, becoming president of the Yorkshire Baptist Association in 1918. There he wrote the valuable textbook *The Religious Ideas of the Old Testament* (1913; rev. ed. by L. H. Brockington, 1956). From 1920 to 1942 he was principal of Regent's Park College, where his teaching and administrative gifts had full scope. It was largely through his efforts that the college was transferred from London to Oxford.

Robinson's most important academic work was in Hebrew psychology (notably in his exposition of the concept of "corporate personality") and Old Testament theology. His Speaker's Lectures (Oxford), posthumously published as *Inspiration and Revelation in the Old Testament* (1946), are the prolegomena to a full-scale Old Testament theology which he did not live to write. The *Christian Doctrine of Man* (1911), *The Christian Experience of the Holy Spirit* (1928), and *Redemption and Revelation* (1942) reflect his wider theological interests. His influence on his students was deep and lasting. He died at Oxford on May 12, 1945.

See E. A. Payne, *Henry Wheeler Robinson* (1946), and list of Robinson's writings in *Studies in History and Religion, presented to Dr. H. Wheeler Robinson, M.A., on His Seventieth Birthday*, ed. by E. A. Payne (1942).   (G. W. An.)

ROBINSON, SIR HERCULES: see ROSMEAD, HERCULES GEORGE ROBERT ROBINSON, 1st Baron.

ROBINSON, JACKIE (JOHN ROOSEVELT ROBINSON) (1919–   ), was the first Negro to play major league baseball, having been signed by Branch Rickey, president of the Brooklyn Dodgers, on Oct. 23, 1945, to play on the Brooklyn farm team, the Montreal Royals of the International League. Robinson was born in Cairo, Ga., Jan. 31, 1919, and moved with his mother and four brothers and sisters to Pasadena, Calif., before he was two years old. In California he developed into an outstanding all-around athlete, at John Muir Technical High School (1933–37), Pasadena Junior College, and for three years at the University of California at Los Angeles. He excelled in track, football, basketball, and baseball. He withdrew from the university in his third year to help his mother care for the family; was drafted in 1942; went to Officer Candidate School (commissioned second lieutenant, 1943); and received a medical discharge in 1945. Then he played professional football in Hawaii and coached football in Texas before he signed to play professional baseball with the Kansas City Monarchs of the Negro National League. He helped Montreal win the "Little World Series" against the Louisville Colonels in 1946. He was brought up from the minors to play with Brooklyn in 1947. That year Brooklyn lost the World Series to the Yankees, but Robinson was voted Rookie of the Year. In 1949 he was National League Batting Champion and received the Most Valuable Player Award by vote of American sportswriters. He had a .311 lifetime batting average, his base running terrorized pitchers, and he set a major league fielding record at second base. In 1962 he was elected to baseball's Hall of Fame. After retiring from baseball in 1957, he engaged in business and politics, serving as a special assistant on community relations to Gov. Nelson Rockefeller of New York.   (J. P. Da.)

ROBINSON, JOHN (c. 1575–1625), English Nonconformist minister, "the pastor of the Pilgrim Fathers," was born about 1575 at Sturton-le-Steeple, Nottinghamshire. In 1592 he entered Corpus Christi College, Cambridge (fellow 1597), and by 1602 had taken orders, becoming a "preaching elder" at St. Andrew's, Norwich, about 1603, and in 1604 married Bridget White. His refusal to conform to the anti-Puritan canons of 1604 led to his suspension from preaching, and in 1606 or 1607 he joined the Separatist congregation at Scrooby. He went with them in 1608 to Holland.

Dissension was rife among the various Nonconformist groups (*see* PURITANISM: *Stuart Puritanism*), and in 1609 Robinson, with 100 followers, moved to Leiden. As pastor of the Leiden congregation, Robinson developed a church (growing to 300 members) described by William Bradford as of such "true piety, humble zeal and fervent love towards God and his Ways [as to come nearer than any other] to the . . . pattern of the first churches."

In 1615 Robinson entered Leiden University as a student in theology, and took part in disputations with the Arminian and Calvinist professors. By 1617 he and his followers had begun to look for a more secure and permanent abode than Leiden. In July 1620 the "Speedwell" sailed, with part of Robinson's congregation, to Plymouth, from which the "Mayflower," with 35 of the Leiden contingent aboard, left for New England in September. Robinson, prevented from following, died at Leiden on March 1, 1625, and the remnant of his church was absorbed in the Dutch Reformed Church in 1658. A memorial in the Pieterskerk at Leiden, put up in 1928, refers to his having "guided and developed the religious life of the pilgrims of the Mayflower."

Robinson's writings show his humility, piety, and growth in charity from the rigid Separatism of his early *Justification of Separation from the Church of England* . . . (1610), by way of *Of Religious Communion, Private and Public* (1614), distinguishing between personal and public religious actions; to *On the Lawfulness of hearing Ministers in the Church of England* (written about 1624; published 1634). In this, he reaffirms the necessity of withdrawal from the English "hierarchical church government and ministry and appurtenances thereof," but stresses his readiness "in all outward actions and exercises of religion . . . to express . . . Christian fellowship and communion" with all "Christian brethren." His most famous words are in his sermon of July 20, 1620, bidding those about to sail to be ready to receive what God might reveal to them, "For I am very confident the Lord hath more truth and light yet to break forth out of His holy Word."

BIBLIOGRAPHY.—*Works*, ed. by R. Ashton, 3 vol. (1851); F. J. Powicke, *J. Robinson* (1920); W. H. Burgess, *J. Robinson, Pastor of the Pilgrim Fathers* (1920); D. Plooij, *The Pilgrim Fathers from a Dutch Point of View* (1932); G. F. Nuttall, *The Holy Spirit in Puritan Faith and Experience* (1946); W. Haller, *Liberty and Reformation in the Puritan Revolution* (1955).   (D. M. Pa.)

ROBINSON, SIR ROBERT (1886–   ), British chemist who was awarded the Nobel Prize for chemistry in 1947 for his research on the alkaloids, was born at Bufford, near Chesterfield, Derbyshire, on Sept. 13, 1886, and educated at Fulneck School, Leeds, and the University of Manchester, where he obtained the degree of D.Sc. in 1910. He was professor of pure and applied organic chemistry in the University of Sydney, New South Wales (1912–15), and then occupied chairs of chemistry successively in the universities of Liverpool (1915–21), St. Andrews (1921–22), Manchester (1922–28) and at University College, London (1928–30). He was appointed to the Waynflete chair of chemistry in the University of Oxford in 1930 and retired in 1955. His researches dealt not only with the structure and synthesis of many organic bodies, but also with the theory of mesomerism (*see* RESONANCE, THEORY OF). His studies of the structure of plant pigments called anthocyanins led him to extend his investigations to another group of plant substances, the alkaloids; his work on the details of alkaloid molecular structures led to the successful production of certain antimalarial drugs. Many honours were conferred on him, including the Copley Medal of the Royal Society in 1942. He was knighted in 1939 and received the Order of Merit in 1949. He was president of the Royal Society (1945–50) and of the British Association for the Advancement of Science (1955).

    (D. McK.)

ROBINSON, "SUGAR" RAY (WALKER SMITH) (1920–   ), world welterweight boxing champion from 1946 to 1951, and five times middleweight champion (1951–55), was born in Detroit, Mich., on May 3, 1920. As a ten year old, he and other Negro boys flocked to Brewster Gym in Detroit to watch a fast-rising young amateur boxer, Joe Louis, train. His family moved to New York City when he was 12, and he attended New York public schools. He won 89 amateur fights without defeat, fighting first under his own name and then as Ray Robinson, "borrowing" the certificate of another amateur boxer by that name in order to qualify for a fight. Robinson became New York Golden Gloves featherweight champion in 1939, and intercity lightweight champion in 1940. He made his professional debut at Madison Square Garden in October 1940 in a lightweight bout against Joe Echevarria, winning that and 39 other fights before losing to Jake LaMotta on Feb. 5, 1943. He won five other fights from LaMotta. By 1951 he had won 122 out of 123 professional bouts.

Robinson abandoned the welterweight title after he had won the world middleweight championship from Jake LaMotta in Chicago on Feb. 14, 1951. He lost the title to the English Negro pugilist Randy Turpin in London, July 10, 1951, but regained it Sept. 12, 1951. Total receipts from this fight, held at the Polo Grounds in New York City, were over $992,000, the largest amount made to that time on a non-heavyweight contest.

"Sugar" Ray was long the darling of boxing fans all over the world. He was awarded the Edward J. Neil Memorial Trophy in boxing in 1950 as the fighter who had done the most for boxing during the preceding year. Robinson fought as a featherweight, lightweight, middleweight, and even tried to win the light heavyweight title, losing to Joey Maxim in 1952. After retiring from boxing in 1965, he remained active in business.   (J. P. DA.)

ROBOT, a term popularly used to describe either a mechanical or electromechanical device with humanlike actions or a person whose repetitive and mechanical actions resemble those of a machine. Derived from the Czech word *robota* ("work"), the term has long been used in many languages. In layman's terminology, robot has, to a large extent, replaced the more classical terms automaton, meaning contrivances which simulate motions of animal life (Gr. *autos,* "self," and *mao,* "seize"), and *androides,* which refers to representations of the human figure and actions.

Modern use of the word robot stems from the play *R.U.R.* (Rossum's Universal Robots), written in 1920 by the Czech author Karel Čapek, in which society was described as depending on mechanical workers called robots able to do any kind of mental or physical work. In the play the robots, having developed intelligence and a spirit of revolt, turn on their human employers and finally exterminate them.

Early Robots.—The construction of mechanical men and animals has captivated the imagination of man since antiquity. In 400 B.C., Archytas of Tarentum is said to have made a wooden pigeon that could fly, and during the Middle Ages numerous instances of the construction of automatons were recorded. The German astronomer Johann Müller (Regiomontanus) is said to have made an iron fly that would flutter around the room and return to his hand, and also to have fabricated an eagle that flew before the emperor Maximilian when he entered Nürnberg. Many curious Swiss-built toys, such as flying and singing birds, are frequently displayed in industrial exhibitions. Wolfgang von Kempelen's famous chess player for many years astonished and puzzled Europe, and during the latter part of the 19th century John Nevil Maskelyne exhibited his robots, "Psycho" (who played cards) and "Zoe" (who drew pictures), at the Egyptian Hall, London. (*See* CONJURING.) These robots were actually hoaxes, although the mechanical contrivances for concealing the real performer were exceedingly ingenious.

Modern Robots.—In the 20th century a variety of machines which, when operated by remote electrical or mechanical control, perform many of the actions of a human being have been built. The "Voder," demonstrated in 1939 at Philadelphia, Pa., had "vocal cords" of vacuum tube circuits that reproduced vowels, consonants, and monosyllables. The operator, using a keyboard and a foot pedal, produced whole sentences of human speech from the mechanism. A more directly useful remote-controlled machine has been built to perform jobs in dangerous radioactive areas. It moves about and is equipped with arms and hands that can grip various objects. The actions of the machine are controlled by an operator stationed at a console at a safe distance from the radioactive sources and the machine's entire behaviour is monitored on a television screen.

Modern developers of robots endeavour to simulate, however crudely, the sensory, locomotor, memory, and learning functions

of animals and human beings. Technological developments of the 20th century have contributed exciting possibilities in this regard. Sensors, such as light-sensitive cells, microphones, contact switches, and chemically sensitive materials, permit very rough simulation of the senses of sight, hearing, touch, and taste or smell. Vacuum tube and transistor circuits serve as an electronic nervous system to alter suitably the signals detected by the sensors and to convey these signals to data-processing or memory devices composed of relays, vacuum tubes, or magnetic-switch circuits. The data-processing and memory devices in turn send commands to motors that act as mechanical muscles. Many of these electronic devices are built into the robot animal.

A tortoise-shaped robot, named *Machina speculatrix,* is a more complex type. It is attracted by moderate light and repelled by intense light or material objects; it is thus able to navigate safely across a room despite the presence of obstacles in its path.

Perhaps the greatest challenge to robot designers is that of reproducing the higher faculties, such as learning capabilities, of animals and human beings. In one such attempt the tortoise was modified to make it responsive to a reflex-conditioning process. Patterned after the conditioned-reflex experiments of the Russian physiologist Ivan Petrovich Pavlov, this robot couples a specific stimulus (light) with an unrelated stimulus (sound) so that the latter evokes, after a conditioning period, the same response as the specific stimulus. (*See* CONDITIONING.) The robot has the basic capability of moving in response to a light. Initially it will not respond to sound alone. However, its circuits are arranged so that it can be "conditioned" to associate a sound with light. Thus, after a conditioning period during which a whistle is blown each time a light is flashed, the machine, through its electronic reflexes, is conditioned to associate sound with light and will respond thereafter to sound alone.

Theseus, the mouse, is an example of a machine that learns

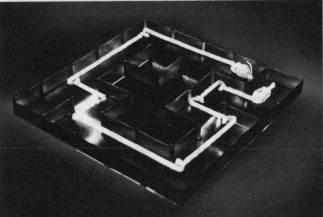

THESEUS THE MOUSE, A MACHINE THAT LEARNS

(Top) In his first try to reach his goal, Theseus wanders through the maze encountering many dead ends. (Bottom) In his second try, Theseus "remembers" the turns that led nowhere and goes directly to his objective. The light attached to his back indicates his movements during each try through use of its computer-type memory circuits. When first inserted in a maze and set in motion, the robot wanders aimlessly in and out of the corridors, encountering many dead ends en route. Eventually it finds its way to the finish point. In going through the maze the first time, the robot circuits "remember" those moves that lead nowhere. Thus, in traversing the maze the second time the robot travels directly to the finish point without making any false moves. If it is placed in the middle of the maze after having traversed it once, the robot wanders aimlessly until it recognizes the correct path and then follows it directly to the finish point.

Large-scale electronic digital computers have opened up new possibilities for simulating the learning processes of human beings. These machines are easily programmed to play games of skill such as ticktacktoe, checkers, and chess. Moreover, through their ability to recognize patterns, they analyze the playing habits of their opponents and thus improve their playing ability in successive tries. By means of this learning process, chess-playing computers have been known to defeat the person who supplied the original playing instructions to the machine.

To develop robots with increasingly complex behavioural abilities, scientists strive to achieve a better understanding of the processes of thought, along with a better understanding of the cerebral mechanisms and nervous systems of animals and human beings. Corresponding technological refinements contribute better simulations of complex behavioural functions.

See also AUTOMATION; COMPUTER.

BIBLIOGRAPHY.—W. Ross Ashby, *Design for a Brain* (1952); A. H. Bruinsma, *Practical Robot Circuits*, in "Philips' Technical Library" (1959); W. Grey Walter, "A Machine That Learns," *Sci. Amer.* (Aug. 1951).   (J. F. RE.)

ROB ROY

ROB ROY (1671–1734), the nickname of Robert Macgregor, a noted Highland outlaw whose reputation as a Scottish Robin Hood has been exaggerated and strengthened by Sir Walter Scott's novel, *Rob Roy*, and by some passages in the poems of William Wordsworth. Rob's father, Donald Macgregor, a younger brother of the chief of the Macgregor clan, received a commission from the former king James after the revolution of 1688, but Rob's politics were uncertain and his activities may as safely be ascribed to brigand tendencies as to idealistic Jacobitism. As a grazier on a farm on the Braes of Balquhidder (Perthshire), he probably also engaged in blackmail and cattle lifting, old and then still honourable Highland practices. When the penal laws against the Macgregors were reintroduced in 1693, Rob took the name of Campbell. His lands lay between those of the rival houses of Argyll and Montrose and for a time he used that rivalry for his own advantage. James Graham, 1st duke of Montrose, finally entangled him in debt and in 1712 ruined him by legal but unscrupulous means; thereafter Rob embarked upon a career of brigandage chiefly at the expense of Montrose.

Rob took little real part in the Jacobite rebellion of 1715; distrusted by both sides, he plundered each impartially in the true "cateran" tradition of the Highland brigand bands, which was an element in all the Jacobite risings. He was treated leniently after the rebellion, because of the intercession of John Campbell, 2nd duke of Argyll. But he did not mend his ways, and some of his boldest exploits against Montrose occurred at this time. He was only reconciled to him in 1722 through the influence of Argyll. Thereafter, however, he was arrested by the English, sent to London, and imprisoned in Newgate; he was pardoned in 1727 when about to be transported to Barbados. In his old age Rob became a Roman Catholic, but according to his own account for no very devout reasons. He died at Balquhidder on Dec. 28, 1734.

BIBLIOGRAPHY.—K. Macleay, *Historical Memoirs of Rob Roy* (1818); A. H. Millar, *The History of Rob Roy* (1883); J. Ramsay of Ochtertyre, *Scotland and Scotsmen in the Eighteenth Century*, vol. ii (1888).
                                                                (W. FE.)

ROBSART, AMY (1532–1560), wife of Lord Robert Dudley, afterward earl of Leicester, who has often been suspected of her murder, was the daughter of Sir John Robsart of Norfolk. She married Lord Robert on June 4, 1550. When Elizabeth I became queen in 1558, Lord Robert rose rapidly in her favour and many believed that she might marry him if he were free. His wife did not go to court with him, though he visited her and corresponded with her in the years 1558 and 1559. Early in 1560 she moved into Cumnor Place, near Oxford. There, on Sept. 8, 1560, she was found with her neck broken at the foot of the stairs. Her husband's enemies, then and later, suspected him of murder, but a coroner's jury returned a verdict of accidental death, and the latest research indicates that she may have died of a "spontaneous fracture" of the neck resulting from cancer of the breast.

BIBLIOGRAPHY.—G. Adlard, *Amye Robsart and the Earl of Leycester* (1870); W. Rye, *The Murder of Amy Robsart* (1885); E. Bekker, *Elisabeth und Leicester* (1890); I. Aird, "The Death of Amy Robsart," *English Historical Review,* vol. lxxi (1956).   (R. B. WM.)

ROC (more correctly RUKH), a gigantic fabulous bird, said to carry off elephants and other large beasts for food. It occurs in the *Thousand and One Nights* (q.v.), especially in the stories of Sindbad the Sailor (q.v.). Marco Polo (q.v.), who also refers to it in describing Madagascar and other islands off the East African coast, reports that the Great Khan "sent to those parts to enquire about these curious matters," and was brought what was claimed to be a rukh's feather, which may really have been a frond of the *Raphia* palm.

The rukh found its way into Arabic and Persian medieval scientific literature under the names of 'anqā' (Arabic) and sīmurgh ("30 birds"; Persian). (See *The Zoological Section of the "Nuzhatu-l-Qulūb" of Hamdullāh al-Mustaufī al-Qazwīnī*, edited, translated, and annotated by J. Stephens, for the Royal Asiatic Society, 1928.)

BIBLIOGRAPHY.—*The Book of the 1,000 Nights and a Night,* trans. and ed. by R. F. Burton, ed. by L. C. Smithers (1894), vol. iv, pp. 84–85, 357–360, 556, vol. x, pp. 136–137; *The Book of Ser Marco Polo,* trans. and ed. by Sir Henry Yule, 3rd ed., rev. by H. Cordier (1903), vol. ii, pp. 412–421 and 596–598; R. Wittkower, "Marco Polo and the Pictorial Tradition of the Marvels of the East," in *Oriente Poliana,* pp. 157–159 (1957).

ROCAMADOUR, a village of southwestern France, in the *département* of Lot, 40 mi. (64 km.) NNE of Cahors by road. Pop. (1962) 165. It is most strikingly situated, its buildings rising in stages up the side of a cliff on the right slope of the gorge of the Alzou. The lower town consists of a long street with five fortified gateways and a restored 15th-century town hall. Flights of steps ascend to the churches halfway up the cliff: the Chapelle Notre-Dame, containing the wooden figure of the black Madonna, a basilica (11th century), and six other chapels. On the cliff stands the 14th-century castle with a fine view over the valley. Rocamadour owes its origin, according to tradition, to St. Amadour (or Amateur), who chose the spot as a hermitage for his devotions to the Virgin Mary, and it became a place of pilgrimage in the early Middle Ages. Jacques Cartier upon landing in the New World prayed to the Virgin of Rocamadour; a chapel in Quebec records the event. Rocamadour is near the Paris-Toulouse railway (via Capdenac). It is a much visited shrine and a centre for tours by motor coach. The chief occupations are sheep breeding and the sale of truffles, nuts, and lavender.   (JE. R.)

ROCH (ROCK, ROCCO), **SAINT** (1350?–1378/79?), was venerated in France and Italy by the early part of the 15th century, but there is no authentic history of his life. According to surviving stories about him (chiefly legendary), he was born at Montpellier, Fr., about 1295, but modern scholarship favours 1345 or 1350 for the year of his birth. The stories relate that on the death of his parents in his 20th year he gave all his substance to the poor and went on a pilgrimage to Rome. During an epidemic of plague in Italy, he tended the sick at Acquapendente, Cesena, and Rome, and effected miraculous cures by prayer and simple contact. After similar ministries at Piacenza he himself fell ill. He was expelled from the town and withdrew into the forest, where he would have perished had not a dog supplied him with bread. On his return to Montpellier he was arrested as a spy and thrown into prison, where he died (traditionally 1327; more probably 1377 or 1378/79), having previously obtained from God this favour—that all plague-stricken persons invoking him be healed. His cult spread through Spain, France, Germany, Belgium, and Italy, and there is even a trace of it in England. A magnificent church was built in his honour at Venice, where his relics are still venerated. His feast day is Aug. 16.

BIBLIOGRAPHY.—G. Ceroni, *San Rocco nella vita, nel culto, nell'arte* (1927); A. Maurino, *San Rocco, confronti storici* (1936); *Analecta Bollandiana,* vol. lv, p. 193 (1937), and lxviii, pp. 343–361 (1950).
(H. DE.; X.)

ROCHA, a department of Uruguay on the Atlantic coast bordering Brazil, and also the departmental capital. The department has a population of 100,202 (1962 est.) in a territory of 4,281 sq.mi. (11,088 sq.km.). Its coastline of sand beaches increasingly attracts vacationers, as the development of Uruguayan ocean resorts continues to move eastward from Montevideo. The colonial fortress of San Miguel has been reconstructed as a historical site. Inland, Rocha is noted for its cattle and sheep ranches. Swine and poultry are also raised. The city of Rocha (pop. [1963] 19,-484) is the centre of an agricultural area producing corn, wheat, and sunflower seeds. (M. I. V.)

ROCHAMBEAU, JEAN BAPTISTE DONATIEN DE VIMEUR, COMTE DE (1725–1807), French general who commanded a French army that helped the American colonists defeat the British at Yorktown, was born at Vendôme (Loir-et-Cher) on July 1, 1725. He was educated at the local college and at the Jesuit school of Blois. Entering a cavalry regiment, he served in Germany in the War of the Austrian Succession, attaining the rank of colonel. During the Seven Years' War he distinguished himself in the Minorca expedition, fought in Germany, and in 1761 became a brigadier general and inspector of cavalry.

Rochambeau was appointed governor of Villefranche-en-Roussillon in 1776, and in 1780 was put in command of the French troops destined for America. With 5,500 soldiers he landed at Newport, R.I., on July 11 and placed himself under Washington's orders. He remained inactive almost a year, however, waiting for the rest of his force (which never came) and refusing to abandon the French fleet that was blockaded in Narragansett Bay by the British. At last, in June 1781, Rochambeau's force broke camp, joined Washington on the Hudson River, and in August made a swift descent on Virginia. Joined by the troops under Lafayette that were already there, the allies laid siege to Cornwallis in Yorktown and forced his surrender on Oct. 19.

Rochambeau's tact and ability made an excellent impression on the Americans. He remained in Virginia for another year and then embarked for France in January 1783. The king appointed him commander of Calais and later of the Alsace district. During the French Revolution he commanded the Northern Military District and was created a marshal of France in December 1791. Arrested during the Terror, he narrowly escaped the guillotine, but Napoleon subsequently pensioned him. He died at his château on May 10, 1807.

BIBLIOGRAPHY.—*Mémoires militaires, historiques et politiques* (1809); J. E. Weelen, *Rochambeau* (1934); Rochambeau's American correspondence is printed in H. Doniol, *Histoire de la participation de la France à l'établissement des États-Unis d'Amérique,* vol. v (1892).
(H. H. P.)

ROCHDALE, a county and parliamentary borough of Lancashire, Eng., 11 mi. NNE of Manchester by road. Pop. (1961) 85,787. Area 14.9 sq.mi. The town lies at the foot of a western spur of the Pennines and at the junction of the Spodden with the Roch, which latter flows through the town (the central part has been covered in). The moribund Rochdale Canal also passes through the town. The manufacture of cotton, woolen, and rayon materials are the main industries, and there are engineering, asbestos, rubber, electrical, and other works. Rochdale has an art gallery, a museum, a repertory theatre, and five parks in addition to Hollingworth Lake (117 ac.) 3½ mi. NE.

Rochdale was the birthplace of the co-operative movement, the Rochdale Pioneers' Equitable Society having been founded there in 1844. The first shop, in Toad Lane, has been restored to its original appearance. A statue of John Bright (1811–89) recalls the connection of the statesman's family with Rochdale.

Rochdale was incorporated in 1856, but the parliamentary borough has returned one member since 1832. The county borough was created in 1888 and extended in 1933.

Rochdale (Recedham, Rachedam, Rachedal) takes its name

from the river on which it stands. A Roman road passed the site, and a Saxon castle stood in Castleton. During Edward the Confessor's reign most of the land was held by Gamel the Thane, but after the Conquest the manor came into the hands of Roger de Poictou, from whom it passed to the Lacys and became merged in the duchy of Lancaster. From 1462 to 1625 the crown leased it to the Byron family. In 1625 Charles I conveyed the manor in trust, and in 1638 it was sold to Sir John Byron, afterward Baron Byron of Rochdale, whose descendants held it till 1823 when it was sold to the Deardens. Henry III (1240–41) granted to Edmund de Lacy the right to hold a weekly market on Wednesday and an annual fair on the feast of SS. Simon and Jude (Oct. 28).

ROCHEFORT, HENRI (properly VICTOR HENRI, MARQUIS DE ROCHEFORT-LUÇAY) (1831–1913), one of the most effective of French polemical writers, first for the extreme left, then for the right, was born in Paris on Jan. 31, 1831. Employed at first in the municipal administration of Paris (1851–61), he made a name as a journalist, novelist, dramatist, and author of vaudevilles, with a genius for satire. In 1868 he founded the weekly *La Lanterne,* with himself as editor. His abusive articles against the Second Empire led to the paper's suppression after its 11th issue; he himself was fined and sentenced to one year's imprisonment, but escaped to Belgium. The paper was then published in Brussels and smuggled into France, being also circulated in English, Spanish, Italian, and German editions. The violence of Rochefort's polemics involved him in four duels.

Rochefort was elected to the Corps Législatif by a Paris constituency in 1869. Arrested again, he was released when the Second Empire fell in September 1870 and became a member of the Government of National Defense. His open support of the Commune (*q.v.*) of Paris led to his resignation from the National Assembly and to his condemnation under military law. Transported to New Caledonia in 1873, he escaped after four months. The amnesty of 1880 enabled him to return to France.

After putting his powerful invective, in *L'Intransigeant,* at the service of the more extreme Radicals and Socialists, Rochefort became an outspoken supporter of Gen. Georges Boulanger (*q.v.*) and, in 1889, had to flee from France. Sentenced *in absentia* to imprisonment for his political activities, he returned to France only in 1895. The collapse of Boulangism led him to support the Socialists, but he again swung over to the right as soon as the Dreyfus affair opened in 1894 and belaboured the leaders of the Dreyfusards. He left *L'Intransigeant* in 1907, and wrote for the conservative *La Patrie.* Rochefort, who had also published an autobiography, *Les Aventures de ma vie* (5 vol., 2nd ed., 1896), died at Aix-les-Bains on June 30, 1913.

See A. Zévaès, *Henri Rochefort le pamphlétaire* (1946) and N. Roubaud, *Henri Rochefort intime* (1954).

ROCHEFORT, a town of western France, headquarters of an *arrondissement* in the *département* of Charente-Maritime, lies on the Charente River, 10 mi. (16 km.) from the sea, and 19 mi. (30 km.) SSE of La Rochelle. Pop. (1962) 26,490.

Originally Rocafortis, a fort built at the mouth of the Charente to resist the Normans, it was under the seigneurs of Rochefort in 1047. Philip the Fair acquired it early in the 14th century, and later, after the English had left Saintonge and Aunis, it was again taken over by Charles V. During the Wars of Religion it frequently changed hands. Jean Baptiste Colbert, under Louis XIV, constructed the port and arsenal there in 1665 on a grand scale. The ramparts, designed by Sebastien Vauban, have been replaced by gardens, and there is now little left of the fortifications. At the town's centre is the Place Colbert, with the Hôtel de Ville and an 18th-century monumental fountain; in the Rue Pierre Loti stands the house where Loti, the writer, was born; the Place de La Galissonnière is named after the admiral who fought Adm. John Byng at Mahón in 1756; and the Hôtel de Cheusses contains the naval museum, with ship models, figureheads, and the capstan of the old "Implacable" (built at Rochefort as the "Duguay-Trouin") which was returned to Rochefort by Britain. Also of note are the Porte du Soleil, a fine gateway to the old arsenal; the Church of St. Louis, with Corinthian columns; the Marine Hospital; and the Hôtel de la Marine, built on the site of the old citadel, and naval headquarters since the 18th century. The Hôtel Hèbre de Saint Clément (18th century) now houses the municipal library and the museum of fine arts.

Lafayette's second voyage to North America was in the "Hermione," which sailed from Rochefort on March 10, 1780. Napoleon spent his last few days on the French mainland at Rochefort before moving to the nearby Île d'Aix, where he surrendered to the British on the "Bellerophon" on July 15, 1815.

Rochefort is an important air force centre and has a mechanics' school and an aircraft construction factory. There are extensive coal and timber yards and important exports and imports of timber. Rochefort's dairies are renowned for their cheese, butter, and cream. The hot-water artesian wells, rich in iron content, are well known. The town, lying on the Nantes-Bordeaux road and railway, is the tourist centre for Charente-Maritime.

(C. C. Me.)

ROCHELLE, LA, an Atlantic seaport city of France, capital of the *département* of Charente-Maritime and seat of a bishopric, is 90 mi. (145 km.) S.E. of Nantes on the Bordeaux railway. Pop. (1962) 65,581. It stands on an inlet between the Pointe des Minîmes and the Pointe de La Pallice sheltered by the Île de Ré and the Île d'Oléron.

The medieval town has left almost no trace, but there are some 14th- and 15th-century Gothic reminders of La Rochelle's powerful and prosperous days. These include the remains of the fortified port with its three famous towers of St. Nicolas, la Chaîne and la Lanterne; the belfry and wrought ironwork of the church of St. Sauveur; the crenellated outer wall of the Hôtel de Ville; and the 14th-century tower, sole remnant of the old church of St. Barthélemy, which stands beside the 18th-century cathedral. The most important and characteristic architecture, however, is of the 16th and early 17th centuries, as seen in certain streets of arcaded houses, with gargoyles and allegorical figures carved on their facades and pedimental windows; *e.g.,* Grande-Rue des Merciers leading to the market place. The Hôtel de Ville (*c.* 1595–1606), the private dwelling known as Maison Henri-Deux, and the houses of Nicolas Venette and Jean Guiton also date from the Renaissance. The prosperity of the early 18th century was reflected in further fine buildings: the Hôtel de la Bourse (now the chamber of commerce); the former bishop's palace (now the city library and art museum); the Hôtels d'Orbigny and Fleuriau (now containing regional history, natural history and other collections). Nineteenth-century developments of the fishing port and the port of La Pallice led to an expansion of the town. A green belt (Parc Charruyer) was laid out on the west side of the town on the site of old fortifications, and promenades were built along the front. Residential districts were established there, while beyond the green belt populous working-class areas emerged, such as the large Port-Neuf zone between La Rochelle and La Pallice, which is now a modern suburb. Development continued through the 20th century and expansion was particularly rapid after 1946, when many local industries and commercial enterprises were started and numerous schools built.

There are three main road and rail routes out of La Rochelle: to Nantes via La Roche-sur-Yon; to Paris via Niort and Poitiers; to Bordeaux via Rochefort. After World War II a project was considered for a routeway to Switzerland in connection with the port extensions at La Pallice.

La Rochelle's chief importance is as a fishing port. The harbour is one of the safest on the coast, with an outer part and two inner basins. Around the basins are railway tracks, a gas-oil pipeline, refrigeration plant, ship repair yards and a slipway. Nearby stands the fish market, one of the largest and most modern in France. The fishing and trawling fleet numbers about 200 vessels. La Rochelle, however, is inaccessible to large ships. The commercial port of La Pallice, lying $3\frac{1}{2}$ mi. away, is a deep-water port constructed 1881–90 to cope with the increased size of vessels. Since then it has been several times enlarged and is equipped with a mole built out to sea and connected with the mainland by a 1,225-yd.-long causeway. It has railway sidings, a refrigeration plant, a grain silo and gasoline storage tanks, and can accommodate the largest ships. By the 1960s a project for

large deep-water docks was under way. The presence of the two ports has attracted both industry and trade to La Rochelle. There are shipbuilding yards, sawmills, chemical industries, sardine and tunny canneries, and petrol refineries. La Pallice imports coal, grain, dried fish, nitrates, pyrites, jute, petroleum, gasoline, wood pulp and phosphates. Exports include wines and cognac. La Rochelle, through La Pallice, trades regularly with South America, England, Scandinavia and the far east.

La Rochelle succeeded Châtelaillon as capital of Aunis in the 12th century. Captured by Louis VIII in 1224, the town was restored to the English in 1360. France regained it when Bertrand Du Guesclin reconquered Saintonge in 1371. Favoured first by the Plantagenets and then in the 13th century by the kings of France, La Rochelle became one of the leading French seaports until the 16th century. During the Reformation it was a centre of Protestantism and suffered several sieges. After the massacre of St. Bartholomew, La Rochelle was unsuccessfully besieged (1572–73) by the Catholic army; under Louis XIII it again supported the Huguenots. In 1628 came the famous attack by Richelieu's forces; the city, led by the mayor Jean Guiton, held out until all its ammunition and food supplies were exhausted.

The subsequent development of trade with France's American possessions in the 18th century restored La Rochelle to its former prosperity. However, when the Edict of Nantes was revoked in 1685 it was deprived of several thousand of its citizens, some of whom went to America and founded (1688) New Rochelle, N.Y. This, coupled with France's loss of Canada, and the upheavals of the Revolution followed by the wars of the First Empire led to the city's decline in commercial importance. World Wars I and II again retarded its natural growth. As a German submarine base during World War II, the town was subjected to heavy Allied bombing. Its mayor Léonce Vieljeux suffered death at German hands for his opposition to the occupying authorities.

After 1945 the fishing port re-established its activities, and by 1950 the war-damaged La Pallice was completely restored, the city as a whole regaining its standing as an important Atlantic port.

(G. Bi.)

ROCHESTER, JOHN WILMOT, 2ND EARL OF (1647–1680), English poet, wit, and courtier, whose reputation as a leader of Charles II's "merry gang" has somewhat obscured his gifts as a lyrical and satirical poet, was born at Ditchley Manor House, Oxfordshire, on April 10, 1647. He was the son of Henry Wilmot, 1st earl of Rochester, a distinguished Cavalier general, whom he succeeded in 1658. Educated at Burford grammar school and at Wadham College, Oxford, he received his M.A. in September 1661. Charles II, probably out of gratitude to the 1st earl, who had helped him to escape after the Battle of Worcester (1651), gave the young Wilmot an annual pension of £500, and appointed Sir Andrew Balfour, a Scottish physician, as his tutor. They traveled on the continent for three years, visiting France and Italy, and were back in England by Christmas, 1664. He then became a leading figure in the famous group called "the merry gang" at court. He was imprisoned for trying to abduct the beautiful heiress Elizabeth Malet in 1665. On his release he volunteered for the navy and served with distinction in the war against the Dutch. He married her on Jan. 29, 1667, and in March he was appointed a gentleman of the bedchamber to Charles II.

Rochester became known as one of the wildest debauchees at the Restoration Court; the hero of numerous escapades and the lover of various mistresses, among whom the most notable was the actress Elizabeth Barry, whom he is said to have trained for the stage himself. He was banished from the court several times but was always recalled by the king, who delighted in his conversation. In 1673 John Dryden dedicated to him his comedy *Marriage-à-la-Mode* in complimentary terms, acknowledging his help in writing it. Soon after, however, the two poets quarreled. Dryden attached himself to Rochester's enemy, Lord Mulgrave, and took offense at the outspoken criticism of his poetry in Rochester's poem, "An Allusion to Horace the 10th Satyr of the 1st Book," but there seems no foundation for the story that Rochester was responsible for the cudgeling of Dryden in Rose Alley, Covent Garden, in December 1679. Nor is it true, as has often been stated, that Rochester was always a capricious or tyrannical patron of men of letters. He befriended the young schoolmaster poet John Oldham (*q.v.*) generously, and Oldham's elegy on him shows genuine affection for the man and admiration for the poet.

In spring 1675 Rochester was appointed ranger of Woodstock Forest, and the ranger's lodge at Woodstock became his favourite place of retirement, where much of his later poetry was written. His health was declining in the late 1670s and his thoughts were turning to serious matters. His correspondence with the deist Charles Blount (dated 1679–80) shows a keen interest in philosophy and religion, further stimulated by his friendship with the Scottish priest Gilbert Burnet (*q.v.*), later bishop of Salisbury, whom he met in October 1679. In the winter of 1679–80 he entered into a series of discussions on religious subjects with Burnet, who recorded them with admirable vividness and fidelity in *Some Passages of the Life and Death of John, Earl of Rochester* (1680). In spring 1680 he became seriously ill and on June 29 experienced a religious conversion, followed by a recantation of his past life when he ordered the burning of "all his profane and lewd writings." Burnet visited him at the ranger's lodge at Woodstock on July 20, 1680, and he died there on July 26. When his son, Charles Wilmot, died a year later, the title lapsed, but was revived in 1682 for Lawrence Hyde.

Rochester was undoubtedly the most considerable poet among the Restoration wits. A few of his love songs have a passionate intensity and a crystalline purity of form that recalls the best work of Burns and Heine:

> Absent from thee I languish still,
> Then ask me not, when I return?
> The straying Fool t'will plainly kill,
> To wish all Day, all Night to Mourn.
>
> *Dear;* from thine Arms then let me flie,
> That my Fantastic Mind may prove
> The Torments it deserves to try,
> That tears my fixt Heart from my Love.

He is also one of the most original and powerful of English satirists. His "History of Insipids" is a devastating attack on the government of Charles II and his "Maim'd Debauchee" has been rightly described as "a masterpiece of heroic irony." "A Satyr Against Mankind" anticipates Swift in its scathing denunciation of rationalism and optimism and the contrast which it draws between human perfidy and folly and the instinctive wisdom of the animal world:

> Be Judge your self, I'le bring it to the test,
> Which is the basest Creature Man or Beast?
> Birds feed on Birds, Beasts on each other prey,
> But savage Man alone does Man betray.

His single dramatic work is the posthumous *Valentinian*, a remarkable attempt to rehandle a tragedy of Fletcher, which contains two of his finest lyrics. It was published, with an interesting introduction by his friend Robert Wolseley, in 1685. His letters to his wife and to his friend Henry Savile are among the best of the period and show an admirable mastery of easy, colloquial prose.

BIBLIOGRAPHY.—*Editions:* A collection, *Poems on Several Occasions by the Right Honourable the E. of R.* (1680), published shortly after Rochester's death and obviously designed for readers interested in pornography, contains, besides authentic poems, much that is not by Rochester. A facsimile edition was published with a bibliographical introduction by J. Thorpe (1950). J. Tonson published an edition of *Poems on Several Occasions* with *Valentinian* and the amusing prose skit, *Alexander Bendo's Bill* (1691). *Familiar Letters* was published in 1697. The 18th-century editions of the poems have little critical value and contain much spurious material. Modern editons are *The Collected Works of John Wilmot, Earl of Rochester*, ed. by J. Hayward (1926); *Poems by John Wilmot, Earl of Rochester*, ed. by V. de S. Pinto (1953; 2nd rev. ed. 1964); a valuable edition of *The Rochester-Savile Letters*, by J. H. Wilson (1941).
Biography: J. Prinz, *John Wilmot, Earl of Rochester* (1927); C. Williams, *Rochester* (1935); V. de S. Pinto, *Enthusiast in Wit, a Portrait of John Wilmot, Earl of Rochester, 1647–1680* (1962).

(V. DE S. P.)

ROCHESTER, LAWRENCE HYDE, EARL OF (1642–1711), English statesman who held offices under Charles II, James II, and Queen Anne, was born in March 1642, the second son of Edward Hyde, 1st earl of Clarendon. His sister Anne married James, duke of York (later James II), and Rochester therefore became uncle of Mary II and of Queen Anne.

Elected to Parliament for Newport in Cornwall (1660), Hyde sat for the University of Oxford (1661–79) and held office as master of the robes (1662–75). In 1667 he joined his brother Henry, afterward 2nd earl of Clarendon, in a vain defense at their father's impeachment, and on Clarendon's flight they shared a temporary disgrace. Hyde was sent on a diplomatic mission to Poland and Vienna in 1676 and participated in the Congress of Nijmegen in 1678. He was made first lord of the treasury and a privy councillor in 1679. He opposed the bills designed to exclude the duke of York from the succession, and was created Viscount Hyde of Kenilworth in 1681 and earl of Rochester in 1682. Although he collaborated in Charles II's subsidy negotiations with Louis XIV and furthered the Tory reaction of 1682 to 1685, Rochester was "kicked upstairs" as lord president of the council by Charles II in 1684. James II appointed him lord treasurer in 1685, but he was displaced in 1687. As a high Tory Anglican he could support only Mary's claim at the Revolution of 1688, and her husband William III did not favour him. Under Anne, Rochester held office only briefly, as lord lieutenant of Ireland (1701–03) and as lord president of the council (1710–11). In his last years he occupied himself with the publication of his father's historical works and he died in London on May 2, 1711.

The correspondence of Rochester with his brother Henry was published with notes by S. W. Singer, two volumes (1828).

See K. Feiling, *A History of the Tory Party, 1640–1714* (1924).
(H. G. Ro.)

ROCHESTER, a city and municipal and parliamentary borough of Kent, Eng., on the Medway River, 31½ mi. ESE of Hyde Park corner, London; it adjoins Chatham. Pop. (1961) 50,143. Area 5.9 sq.mi. Its situation on the Roman way from the Kentish ports to London, as well as at a Medway crossing, gave Rochester (Durobrivae; Hrofaecaestrae and Hrofi *c.* 730) an early importance. It was a walled Romano-British town, and the original bridge across the Medway (Durobrivae, an old British word probably meaning "stronghold bridge") probably dated from that period. The church of St. Andrew was founded by King Aethelberht, who also made Rochester a bishop's see. It was a royal borough in the time of William I, who built a castle there, probably on Boley Hill. Richard I granted the citizens quittance of *passagium* from crusaders in the town of Rochester in 1189. In 1227 Henry III granted them the city, a guild merchant, the right to be impleaded only within the city walls, and other liberties. These charters were confirmed by subsequent sovereigns down to Henry VI, who in 1446 incorporated the city and granted it the power of admiralty and many privileges. Charters were granted in later reigns down to Charles I, whose charter of 1629 remained the governing charter until 1835. Rochester returned two members to Parliament from Edward I's time until 1885, one from then until 1918, two from 1918 to 1950; one from then on.

The cathedral church of St. Andrew was originally founded by St. Augustine in 604, for whom Aethelberht built the church. It was partly destroyed by the Danes, but was rebuilt by Bishop Gundulph (1077–1108). Gundulph or Gundulf established Benedictine monks there. Bishop Ernulf (1115–24) completed and also renovated the church. The Norman west front was built about 1125–30, and about 1352 a low central tower was built, to which a spire was added in the next century. The ruins of Gundulph's tower stand detached from and are earlier than the church; it was built by Bishop Gundulph probably as a defensive work for the eastern boundary of the city. The library attached to the modern chapter house contains, among various relics, the *Textus Roffensis*, being records of the cathedral compiled in the time of Bishop Ernulf.

On the eminence overlooking the right bank of the river are the remains of a Norman castle, part of which was built by Bishop Gundulph at the order of William Rufus in the 11th century. The castle was besieged by King John, by Simon de Montfort in the reign of Henry III, and by the followers of Wat Tyler. It was repaired by Edward IV, but soon afterward fell into decay, although the massive keep still stands. It is a quadrangular four-storied structure, flanked by turrets, with a height of 113 ft. Remains of the 13th-century walls which once surrounded the city also exist. Charles Dickens lived at Gad's Hill, above Strood, to the northwest. At Borstal, southwest of Rochester, was a large convict prison where early experiments on the educational treatment of delinquent boys between the ages of 16 and 21 were carried out, which resulted in the Borstal system (q.v.).

Among the principal buildings in the city are the guildhall (1687), the Richard Watts' almshouses (founded in 1579), and the almshouse of St. Catherine (built 1805), which originated in 1316 as a leper's hospital. An Elizabethan mansion was acquired by the corporation for a museum as a memorial of Queen Victoria's diamond jubilee. The principal schools are the cathedral grammar school or King's School, founded in 1544, and the Sir Joseph Williamson's Mathematical School (1701), formerly for sons of freemen but now open to all. St. Bartholomew's Hospital (1708) occupies modern buildings, though the ancient chapel remains. A municipal airport has been provided by the corporation.

The Medway is navigable to Rochester Bridge and vessels drawing 26 ft. can reach it. Since the 1850s Rochester has become increasingly industrialized with cement, engineering, and other works. The towns of Rochester, Chatham, and Gillingham form one great conurbation sometimes known as the Medway Boroughs.

ROCHESTER, a city of Minnesota, U.S., in Olmsted County, home of the world-famous Mayo Clinic, is located about 80 mi. SE of Minneapolis-St. Paul in the rich diversified agricultural plains region of southeastern Minnesota. It has one of the largest poultry hatchery and breeding-farm operations in the country as well as a large dairy processing plant. The establishment of an electronic data-processing centre there has added to the growing industrial pattern of the city. The site at the confluence of three tributaries of the Zumbro River was chosen by settlers in 1854 and named for Rochester, N.Y. The city was incorporated in 1858 with a population of about 1,500.

Long famed as a health centre, Rochester houses the Mayo Foundation for Medical Education and Research, which is one of the world's largest graduate medical schools, and a branch of the University of Minnesota. There is a large privately operated hospital, and the Mayo Clinic which is actually a combination of hospitals and hotels. The clinic operates with the cooperation of the largest voluntary association of physicians, surgeons, medical technicians, and researchers in the world engaged in private practice. It was established in 1889 by William Worrall Mayo and his sons Charles Horace and William James Mayo and greatly stimulated Rochester's growth (see MAYO family).

These medical services attract patients from all over the U.S. and the world, causing a fairly constant transient population of 6,000–9,000 at any given time. (For comparative population figures see table in MINNESOTA: *Population.*) Along with excellent public education facilities, the town has five parochial schools, two schools of nursing, a school of music, and an evening community college. (J. T. LU.)

ROCHESTER, a city of northwestern New York, U.S., and seat of Monroe county, is located 70 mi. E of Buffalo and 90 mi. W of Syracuse, and is bisected by the Genesee river, which flows into Lake Ontario. The area is a prosperous manufacturing centre of quality photographic, optical and precision instruments; it is in the heart of a fruit and truck farming belt, and is gateway to the Finger Lakes resort area to the south.

History and Industrial Growth.—Rochester's first settlement dates from 1789. In 1788 Oliver Phelps obtained from the Seneca Indians land on the west side of the Genesee river to establish grist mills which would utilize the natural waterpower of the river falls. In 1789 Ebenezer ("Indian") Allen was deeded 100 ac. of this land for the construction of a sawmill and grist mill. Allen's venture was a failure, and further settlement was impeded by the malarial conditions known as Genesee fever.

Col. Nathaniel Rochester, Revolutionary War soldier and Maryland aristocrat, laid out the town in 1811 and named it Rochesterville, shortened in 1822 to Rochester. In 1812 the first dwelling unit, a log cabin, was occupied by Hamlet Scrantom and his family

and marked the beginning of permanent settlement. Rochester was incorporated as a village in 1817 and chartered as a city in 1834.

The early economy was built upon the extensive wheat production of the Genesee valley region. Rochester's cheap natural waterpower and the city's connection with the eastern section of the Erie canal in 1822 assured its economic development as a milling centre. By 1840 the city, one of the early boom towns of the "west," had 20,000 residents. By the 1860s the clothing and shoe industries, given impetus by the American Civil War and the arrival of skilled immigrants, thrived; Rochester had also become the flour milling capital of America. But by 1878 this latter industry had passed its peak and was moving westward to Minnesota. After the Civil War, Rochester was transformed from the "flour city" to the "flower city." Large nursery and seed enterprises were developed with James Vick pioneering the mail order approach to selling seeds and shrubs. Although the business aspects of horticulture declined by the beginning of the 20th century, the influence of this industry is still manifested in the city.

By the latter part of the 19th century the area was developing into a quality manufacturing centre with emphasis upon photographic, optical and precision instrument products. Notable among these was George Eastman (q.v.), who became a major film and camera manufacturer.

Two industrialists, John Jacob Bausch and Henry Lomb, who perfected better techniques for grinding lenses, established their optical company there. Other entrepreneurs built successful manufacturing firms specializing in thermometers, machine tools, check protectors, mail chutes, glass-lined enameled steel tanks and dental equipment.

Frederick Douglass, the Negro abolitionist and runaway slave, published his antislavery paper, *The North Star,* in Rochester when the community was an important terminus for the Underground Railroad (q.v.) to Canada. The area is regarded as a cradle of modern Spiritualism because of Margaret and Katharine Fox's numerous seances (the "Rochester Rappings") in the late 1840s which attracted world attention.

Population.—Rochester (pop. [1960] 318,611; [1964] 305,-849) is the central city of a standard metropolitan statistical area comprising Monroe, Livingston, Orleans, and Wayne counties with a population of 732,588. Although the city's population decreased by 4.2% between 1950 and 1960, the population of the metropolitan area increased by 20.3%. (For comparative population figures see table in NEW YORK: *Population.*) In the metropolitan area Irondequoit, Greece and Brighton are the largest suburban towns. These towns, along with Gates, Chili, Pittsford, Perinton, Henrietta, Penfield and Webster, are mainly residential, although industrial parks have been created in the last three. The fringe metropolitan area towns of Hamlin, Clarkston, Sweeden, Ogden, Riga, Wheatland, Rush and Mendon are predominantly rural in character, although limited suburbanization has occurred.

The area's earliest settlers were of northern European ancestry who migrated chiefly from New England. Prior to the Civil War, significant numbers of Irish and Germans became residents. Before World War I, large numbers of Italian immigrants arrived, and they represent the largest foreign-born group in the area.

Administration.—In 1925 Rochester adopted the city-manager form of government. The governing body, the city council, is composed of five councilmen-at-large and four district councilmen elected for four-year terms. The council selects one of its members as mayor. In the other 19 metropolitan towns the chief official, the supervisor, is elected for a two-year term.

Education, Culture and Recreation.—George Eastman's philanthropy supported or helped to establish a number of cultural and public facilities including the Eastman theatre, the city's university, the Dental dispensary and Durand-Eastman park.

The two major educational institutions are the University of Rochester (founded 1850) which includes the well-known Eastman school of music and school of medicine and dentistry, and the Rochester Institute of Technology (1829). Undergraduate collegiate education is provided by Nazareth (1924; Roman Catholic) St. John Fisher (1951; Roman Catholic) and Roberts Wesleyan

(1866) colleges, and theological education by St. Bernard's seminary and college (1893; Roman Catholic) and Colgate-Rochester Divinity school (1819; Baptist). The Rochester Philharmonic orchestra provides musical concerts during the winter season. The area has an excellent system of parks and recreational facilities including Hamlin State park on Lake Ontario, Genesee Valley park, the yacht basin in Irondequoit bay, the ski jump at Powder Mill park, and Highland park, with its floral displays, in Rochester.

BIBLIOGRAPHY.—Blake McKelvey, *Rochester: the Water-Power City, 1812–1854* (1945), *Rochester, the Flower City, 1855–1890* (1949), *Rochester: the Quest for Quality, 1890–1925* (1956), *Rochester: an Emerging Metropolis, 1925–1961* (1961); Arch Merrill, *Rochester Sketchbook* (1946). (D. J. P.)

ROCHE-SUR-YON, LA, chief town of the *département* of Vendée, western France, is situated on the right bank of the Yon, 65 km. (40 mi.) S. of Nantes by road. Pop. (1962) 22,231. The site of a 10th-century castle, it was captured by the English during the Hundred Years' War, and during the Wars of Religion in the 17th century it changed hands several times. Practically destroyed in 1794, the town was rebuilt by Napoleon in 1804 as the chief town of Vendée. It was called Napoléon-Vendée or Bourbon-Vendée, according to the ruling dynasty of the time, until the old name was restored in 1871. Little remains of the old town, but a fine Renaissance house still stands at the Place de la Vieille-Horloge. Other notable buildings include the Napoleon museum and the church of St. Louis, which contains the "Stations of the Cross" by P. J. A. Baudry, a native of the town. La Roche-sur-Yon is a prefect seat and a court of assizes, and has a tribunal of first instance. It is a railway centre, a market for horses and cattle and has an important *haras* (depot for stallions), flour mills and factories for clothing, electrical goods and plastics.

ROCKEFELLER, the name of a U.S. family founded by JOHN DAVISON ROCKEFELLER (1839–1937), industrialist, founder of the Standard Oil enterprise and of the first great American oil fortune. He was born in Richford, N.Y., on July 8, 1839, the son of a small trader. In 1853 the family settled in Cleveland, O. In 1859 Rockefeller formed a partnership with M. B. Clark in the produce and commission business. The first U.S. oil well was drilled that summer in Titusville, Pa., and in 1863 Rockefeller organized the firm of Andrews, Clark and company to enter the oil refining business as a sideline. Two years later the firm was reorganized as Rockefeller and Andrews. His brother WILLIAM ROCKEFELLER (1841–1922) joined him in the organization of William Rockefeller and company for the operation of a second refinery in Cleveland. In 1867 the two Cleveland refineries were consolidated into the partnership of Rockefeller, Andrews, Flagler and company, and three years later this firm was replaced by a joint stock company, the Standard Oil Company of Ohio, with John D. Rockefeller as president. Under his direction, this company obtained control of the oil industry by means of mergers, favourable railroad rates, rebates and other devices which at that time were not illegal. In 1882 was organized the Standard Oil trust, which controlled 95% of the oil refining business in the country and had in addition substantial interests in iron ore mines, lumber tracts, manufacturing plants, transportation and other businesses. In 1899 the supreme court of Ohio held this trust to be a violation of the Sherman Anti-Trust act, and the trust was replaced by the holding company device, Standard Oil of New Jersey, which existed until 1911 when the United States supreme court declared it also to be illegal. By this time John D. Rockefeller had retired from active business and was devoting his time to giving away a large part of his fortune. For this purpose he established charitable corporations governed by trustees and operated by officers devoted to a continuous study of opportunities for public service. It is estimated that by this means Rockefeller's benevolences mounted to more than $530,000,000. His first large benefaction was to The University of Chicago (*q.v.*), which received from him a total of $35,000,000. He died at his home in Ormond Beach, Fla., on May 23, 1937.

JOHN DAVISON ROCKEFELLER, JR. (1874–1960), the only son of John D. Rockefeller and Laura Spelman Rockefeller, was born in Cleveland, O., on Jan. 29, 1874. After graduation from Brown university in 1897, he entered his father's office, working closely with him in the business, philanthropic and civic enterprises of the family. His life was devoted primarily to philanthropic and civic activities. He was associated with his father in the creation and development of the Rockefeller Institute for Medical Research, the General Education board, the Rockefeller foundation and the Laura Spelman Rockefeller memorial. In 1923 he founded the International Education board, which operated in the fields of the natural sciences, the humanities and agriculture until it was terminated in 1937. Deeply interested in the conservation of natural resources and in preserving historic places, the younger John D. Rockefeller made many contributions for these purposes, including among them the restoration of Williamsburg, Va. His contributions from Jan. 1, 1917, to Dec. 31, 1955, amounted to about $400,000,000. He died in Tucson, Ariz., on May 11, 1960.

NELSON ALDRICH ROCKEFELLER (1908–   ), second son of John D. Rockefeller, Jr., was born at Bar Harbor, Me., on July 8, 1908. Graduated from Dartmouth College in 1930, he helped manage several family enterprises, notably Rockefeller Center in New York City. During World War II he served under Pres. Franklin D. Roosevelt as coordinator of inter-American affairs (1940–44) and as assistant secretary of state (1944–45). He was undersecretary of the Department of Health, Education, and Welfare, 1953–54, special assistant to the president, 1954–55, and chairman of the president's advisory committee on government organization, 1953–58. A collector of modern art, he became a trustee of the Museum of Modern Art in 1932, and was a founder of the Museum of Primitive Art. Entering politics as a liberal Republican, he was elected governor of New York in 1958 and reelected in 1962 and 1966. He was prominently mentioned as a candidate for the Republican presidential nomination in 1960 and in 1964 he led the unsuccessful opposition to Barry Goldwater's nomination. In 1968, after a late start, he campaigned vigorously for the nomination which went to Richard Nixon.

He married Mary Todhunter Clark in 1930. Their children were Rodman, Ann and Steven (twins), Michael (d. 1961), and Mary. They were divorced in 1962, and he married Margaretta Fitler Murphy in 1963. Their children are Nelson Aldrich and Mark Fitler.

WINTHROP ROCKEFELLER (1912–   ), fourth son of John D., Jr., was born in New York City on May 1, 1912. He attended Yale University, 1931–34, and worked in the Texas oil fields, 1934–37. In New York he helped organize the Greater New York Fund and became a leader and board member of the National Urban League, serving as a trustee, 1940–64. In 1953 he settled in Arkansas and developed the 34,000-ac. Winrock Farms, noted for its prize herd of Santa Gertrudis breeding stock, and Winrock Enterprises (manufacturing, building, land development), and the philanthropic Rockwin Fund. In 1955 he was named head of the Arkansas Industrial Development Commission. Active in building the state's Republican Party, he became Republican National Committeeman in 1961, and in 1964 campaigned unsuccessfully for the governorship. In 1966 he was elected Arkansas's first Republican governor since 1874.

A director of Rockefeller Brothers and of Rockefeller Center in New York, he became chairman of the board of Colonial Williamsburg Inc. His marriage to Barbara ("Bobo") Sears in 1948 ended in divorce in 1954; they had one son, Winthrop Paul. Rockefeller's second marriage was to Jeanette Edris, in 1956.

Others of the five sons of John D. Rockefeller, Jr., have been associated with the various Rockefeller benevolent corporations, banks, and other businesses: JOHN DAVISON ROCKEFELLER III (1906–   ), chairman of the Rockefeller Foundation and of the General Education Board; LAURANCE S. ROCKEFELLER (1910–   ), chairman of Rockefeller Brothers and a conservationist; and DAVID ROCKEFELLER (1915–   ), president of the Chase Manhattan Bank and chairman of the Chase International Investment Corporation, chairman of the board of Rockefeller Institute, of the board of trustees of the Museum of Modern Art, and trustee of the Council on Foreign Relations; author of *Unused Resources and Economic Waste* (1940).

JOHN DAVISON ROCKEFELLER IV (1938–   ), son of John D. III, worked in the Action for Appalachian Youth poverty program in West Virginia, in the mid-1960s; he was elected as a Democrat to the West Virginia House of Delegates in 1966.

See also FOUNDATIONS, PHILANTHROPIC.

BIBLIOGRAPHY.—A. Nevins, *Study in Power,* 2 vol. (1953); I. M. Tarbell, *History of the Standard Oil Company,* 2 vol. (1925); J. T. Flynn, *God's Gold* (1932); R. B. Fosdick, *The Story of the Rockefeller Foundation* (1952), *John D. Rockefeller, Jr.* (1956).   (J. R. LT.; X.)

ROCKETS AND GUIDED MISSILES.

Rockets and guided missiles are treated in a single article because almost all such devices rely on similar methods of propulsion and control. Recognition of rocket power as the key to space exploration is nearly a century old, but the state of technology did not permit the use of this propulsive technique until after World War II. Guided-missile weapon systems had their origin in unmanned, radio-controlled aircraft before World War I. Although pulse-jet, turbojet and ramjet engines have been used on many missiles, rocket power is most widely used for propulsion.

This article is divided into the following sections:

I. INTRODUCTION: ROCKETS

Rocket is the generic term for a wide variety of jet-propelled missiles, research vehicles, thrust devices and fireworks. Forward motion results from reaction to a rearward high-speed flow of hot gases generated in the rocket motor. Either solid or liquid propellants providing combustion gases, or stored high-pressure cold gas may be used.

A rocket motor, or engine, is one of the family of jet-propulsion devices which includes turbojet, pulse-jet and ramjet engines. The rocket engine is unique, however: the elements of the propulsive jet (fuel and oxidizer) are self-contained within the vehicle. The thrust produced is independent of the medium through which the vehicle travels. Other kinds of jet-propulsion engines carry their fuel only. This fuel is burned with the oxygen content of the air scooped into the engine as the vehicle flies along. Thus these other varieties of jet engines are called air-breathing and are limited to operation within the blanket of atmosphere. The upper limit of travel for air-breathing jet engines is about 90,000 ft.

Rocket power has been used for hundreds of years. Rockets can be used to hurl explosives against targets thousands of miles away, or to lift data-gathering instruments—and man—into interplanetary space for scientific research and exploration.

The recorded history of rockets dates from the 13th century,

but interest in them has risen and fallen as various other devices, such as the mortar and artillery, became competitive. Since World War II, however, rocket technology has reached such a level that it is doubtful that rockets will ever disappear again from the scene. There is no technical competitor for rocket-propulsion systems for many missions. For instance, a rocket-powered ballistic missile can be fired against targets 6,000 mi. or more away. The speed at which it travels may be as high as 15,000 m.p.h. At the same time, as the recognized power plant for space flight, the rocket is the key to space exploration. In fact, the same basic vehicle used to carry a warhead over continents can be used instead to place man or thousands of pounds of scientific instruments in satellite orbit around the Earth. Launchings of Earth satellites and of lunar and interplanetary research probes are but the prelude to an era of space exploration. Until 1955 man was a passive observer of laws of celestial mechanics. Since then he has begun to use these laws by the application of rocket power.

II. ROCKET HISTORY TO WORLD WAR II

1. Early History.—No one knows when or by whom rockets were invented. In all probability the rocket was not suddenly "invented" but evolved gradually over a long period of time, perhaps in different parts of the world at the same time. Some historians of rocketry, notably Willy Ley, trace the development of rockets to 13th-century China, a land noted in ancient times for its fireworks display. In the year A.D. 1232, when the Mongols laid siege to the city of Kai-feng Fu (K'ai-feng), capital of Honan province, the Chinese defenders used weapons that were described as "arrows of flying fire." There is no explicit statement that these arrows were rockets, but some students have concluded that they were because the record does not mention bows or other means of shooting the arrows. In the same battle, we read, the defenders dropped from the walls of the city a kind of bomb described as "heaven-shaking thunder." From these meagre references some students have concluded that the Chinese by the year 1232 had discovered gunpowder and had learned to use it to make explosive bombs as well as propulsive charges for rockets.

In the same century rockets appeared in Europe. There is indication that the first use was by the Tatars in the battle of Legnica in 1241. The Arabs used rockets on the Iberian peninsula in 1249; and in 1288 Valencia was attacked with rockets. The Italian historian L. A. Muratori writes that a lucky hit of a rocket was decisive in a battle for Chioggia in 1379.

About 1248 Roger Bacon (*q.v.*) wrote formulas for gunpowder in his *Epistola,* with great secrecy and the use of ciphers. He evidently experimented with various proportions of the three classic ingredients, saltpetre (nitre), charcoal and sulfur, raising the amount of saltpetre to 41%. The Chinese had used rather less saltpetre, which resulted in slower-burning mixtures. In Germany, a counterpart of Bacon, Albertus Magnus, was writing of powder charge formulas for rockets in his book *De mirabilis mundi.* About 1325 the first firearms were invented, utilizing a closed tube and gunpowder to propel a ball charge somewhat erratically over varying distances. Military engineers then began to invent and refine designs for guns and rockets, on a parallel basis. (*See* ARTILLERY.)

The French historian Jean Froissart (*q.v.*) suggested that rockets fired from tubes would give them better direction. In his book *Bellifortes* (1405), Konrad Kyeser von Eichstadt wrote of several designs of rockets. In Italy Joanes de Fontana conceived a number of novel war weapons based on rocket propulsion. One was a rocket-driven car designed to breach walls or gates. Another was a naval torpedo, designed to skim across water and ram its spiked nose into ships. Many other ideas were suggested in print, such as Count Reinhart von Solm's rockets with parachutes; or the count of Nassau's underwater explosive rocket. The extent to which many of these designs were reduced to working models or weapons is not known. By now rockets were used also for signaling and, especially by pirates, for setting fire to the rigging of ships at sea. They had many names, such as "flying fire" or "wild fire."

The tale of Wan-Hu, presumably legendary, is an interesting milestone in the early history of the rocket. As the story goes, about the year 1500 a Chinese, Wan-Hu, made what must have been the first attempt at rocket flight, constructing a vehicle utilizing two large kites to which were attached some sort of seat. Forty-seven rockets were attached and fired simultaneously. Wan-Hu and his contrivance simply disappeared in the loud explosion which followed!

Of considerable interest are the historical origins of rocket designs which were to be employed many years later: the staged (or step) rocket, the clustered rocket and the winged rocket. These designs evolved both from applications and requirements of fireworks and their application by ordnance masters. The Polish artillery expert Kasimir Simienowicz in 1650 published (in Latin) in Amsterdam *Artis magnae artillerae, pars prima.* Translation of this work into French in 1651, German in 1676, and English and Dutch in 1729 gave eloquent testimony of its importance.

In 1590, however, a much lesser known work of a fireworks expert revealed trade secrets in a small illustrated book, *Kunstliche und rechtschaafene Fernewerk* by Johan Schmidlap. For a long time Schmidlap was invariably accepted by historians as the earliest known originator of these concepts. In 1963 a Romanian scholar, D. Todericiu, brought to light a manuscript by Conrad Haas, an artillery officer and chief of the arsenal at Sibiu, Rom., with dated drawings and texts, identical to the Schmidlap book but preceding it by 35 years, in a manuscript archived since the 16th century. Thus Haas is apparently the earliest known person to have studied and written on these advanced rocket concepts.

By 1668 military rockets, hard-pressed by development of guns and cannons, had increased in size and performance. In that year, a German, Col. Christoph Friedrich von Geissler, designed a rocket weighing 132 lb., constructed of wood, wrapped in glue-soaked sailcloth. It carried a gunpowder charge weighing 16 lb.

Although the art of constructing rockets had now become quite widely known there was little appreciation or understanding of exactly how and why a rocket operated; *i.e.*, the physical principles involved. It was not until the last quarter of the 17th century that Isaac Newton formulated his laws of motion laying the basis for modern mechanics. Prior to this time Aristotelian theories of motion—philosophical in nature and unsupported by physical fact—had persisted for 20 centuries. Newton stated in his third law that every action is accompanied by an equal and opposite reaction. The thrust of a rocket is derived from the reaction, in the opposite direction, to the expelled jet of combustion gases.

Despite the enthusiasm of individual Europeans, the use of

rockets in military campaigns was sporadic. A revival occurred after a series of battles in India late in the 18th century. Haidar Ali, prince of Mysore, developed rockets as weapons. The rockets had metal tubes, permitting higher internal pressures. They weighed 6–12 lb. and were flight-stabilized by a 10-ft. bamboo stick. The range of these rockets was a startling 1–1½ mi. Although not individually accurate, dispersion errors of individual rockets became unimportant when large numbers were fired in mass attacks. These rockets were particularly effective against cavalry. Haidar Ali's son, Tipu Sahib, continued to develop and expand the use of rocket weapons, increasing the number of rocket gunners from 1,200 to a corps of 5,000. The British suffered heavily, particularly in battles at Seringapatam in 1792 and 1799.

2. 19th-Century Developments.—The news of the successful use of rockets in these engagements spread through Europe. A British colonel, William Congreve, began to experiment privately. Within a few years he was able to exceed the range of the Indian rockets. In 1806 British rockets caused great fires during an attack on Boulogne. The next year a massed attack, using about 25,000 rockets, burned most of Copenhagen to the ground. In the decisive battle of Leipzig (1813) Congreve rockets played an important role. Later in the same year Danzig was subjected to a series of massed rocket bombardments in three successive months. The last attack caused the surrender of the city.

In the United States, the British used their rocket corps in two important engagements during the War of 1812. One was the battle of Bladensburg (Aug. 24, 1814) when their use drove back the American troops. As a result, the British were able to capture Washington, D.C. In September the British forces attempted to capture Ft. McHenry, which guarded Baltimore harbour. They were unsuccessful but on that occasion Francis Scott Key, inspired by the sight of the night engagement, wrote the stirring words of the *Star Spangled Banner,* later adopted as the U.S. national anthem. "The rockets' red glare" and "bombs bursting in air" ever since have continued to memorialize Congreve's rockets.

Back in Europe, Captain de Boer of the Dutch army conducted some experiments and arrived at a proposal to eliminate the heavy, stabilizing guide stick and substitute three metal vanes. Despite the fact that this lighter design should have worked, it was apparently not adopted. The stick-stabilized rocket was used until William Hale's invention several decades later.

Congreve's rockets were successful for several reasons. He experimented with a number of black powder formulas and set down standard specifications. In the production of tens of thousands of rockets over two decades apparently a number of small refinements in design were made. Although none of these modifications materially improved performance, the sum total of the improvements resulted in a fairly reliable and potent weapon in the hands of a skilled rocket brigade. Congreve rockets ranged in weight from 25 to 60 lb. Some warheads were incendiary, some steel ball charges for antipersonnel use. Ranges increased to nearly three miles. They were competitive in weight and performance with the ponderous ten-inch mortar and were much more mobile. In appearance they resembled large skyrockets, the guide stick being 12–16 ft. long. Being recoilless, their launching equipment was simple and lightweight, and they could be fired from small boats. Thin copper tubes were used for initial directional guidance or, for massed bombardment, collapsible A-frames were employed. The success of Congreve's rockets caused the addition of rocket batteries to artillery units or the formation of independent rocket corps in most armies of Europe, as far east as Russia.

The next significant development in rocketry occurred about the middle of the 19th century. William Hale, a British subject, contrived a way of eliminating the dead weight of the stabilizing stick. When he placed a series of canted and curved vanes at the rear of the rocket, the exhaust gases imparted a spin to the rocket. Spin-stabilized rockets were a real improvement in performance and ease of handling. But by this time black powder rockets could no longer compete with artillery. The rocket corps of most European armies had been dissolved. Firearms and heavy field-pieces with rifled bores were outclassing rockets except on rare

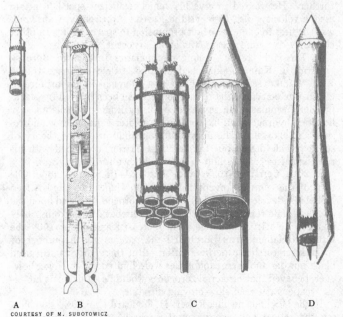

A   B   C   D

COURTESY OF M. SUBOTOWICZ

FIG. 1.—HISTORICAL EXAMPLES OF ROCKETS

(A) conventional stick-guided war rocket or fireworks skyrocket, and some early design concepts of (B) a step rocket, (C) a clustered rocket and (D) a fin-stabilized glide rocket. Drawings by Kasimir Simienowicz from *Artis magnae artillerae, pars prima* (1650)

BY COURTESY OF MITCHELL R. SHARPE

RESCUE OPERATION USING A LIFE-SAVING ROCKET, FROM A DRAWING OF THE 1870S. THE LIGHT LINE CARRIED TO THE SHIP BY THE BOXER ROCKET (CENTRE FOREGROUND) HAS BEEN REPLACED BY A HEAVIER LINE AND A BREECHES-BUOY TRANSFER IS IN OPERATION

occasions. These exceptions were usually in mountainous terrain. On such ground, rockets could move into choice firing locations while the much heavier mortars were confined to roads or flat ground. Thus we find that the Austrian rocket corps, using Hale rockets, won a long series of engagements in such terrain against Hungary and Italy. Other successful uses were by the Dutch colonial services against natives in the Celebes and by Russia in a series of engagements in the Turkestan War.

The U.S. army produced 2,000 Hale rockets for the Mexican War, but apparently they were not particularly successful. Although the *U.S. Ordnance Manual* of 1862 listed 16-lb. Hale-type rockets with a maximum range of about 1.25 mi., their use in the American Civil War is not known. There is a story that President Lincoln was interested in rocket development and was narrowly missed by an explosion in a test at the naval gun factory in Washington.

The extensive use of Congreve and Hale rockets lasted less than a century though they had appeared widely and were well known. Various applications of rocket power for other than military purposes began to appear. One of the best known was the use of a rocket to carry a lifeline to sailing ships in distress or stranded near shore. A thin line was first carried to the ship by the rocket. Then the crew would haul a heavier line out and use a breeches buoy to transfer the men, one at a time, to safety. In the 19th century hundreds of lives were saved in this way, using line-throwing mortars and rockets. Another application of rockets was in aiding lifeboats to negotiate a heavy surf. Rockets were used to throw a small grappling anchor with a light line over the surf onto the beach. By this technique, the boat could be kept straight as the occupants pulled themselves toward shore through the surf.

A line-carrying rocket designed by Colonel Boxer about 1855 achieved increased range by firing two rocket motors, one after the other, tandem fashion. This was the first known application of a concept sketched by Simienowicz 200 years earlier.

Signal flares also were carried aloft by rockets. One design of such a rocket by Congreve utilized a parachute to keep the flare visible for a longer period of time. Capt. William Scoresby hunted whales by rocket-propelled harpoon in 1821. A woodcut from an 1865 newspaper, advertising the sale of such devices, shows a seaman launching a rocket harpoon from a shoulder-held tube equipped with a circular blast shield. The launcher appears quite similar to the bazooka of World War II.

One interesting 19th-century development was the concept of a rocket-propelled torpedo. Both the U.S. army and the British navy conducted experiments with such devices in the period 1860–80 and several ingenious devices were designed. Nevertheless, none of this work led to a real weapon. One of the fundamental problems of the rocket torpedo, as pointed out by William Hale, was that as the powder in the rocket motor was consumed, the tor-

pedo grew lighter, making it difficult to hold the torpedo at constant level below the surface.

Meanwhile, there were individual enthusiasts and inventors in nearly every country. Largely unknown, and sometimes considered a dangerous nuisance, they achieved varied success and recognition. In the early 19th century Claude Ruggieri, an Italian rocket maker, staged a number of shots in Paris in which rats and mice were sent aloft by rockets and returned by parachute. Ruggieri even planned to send up a small boy, using a rocket cluster, but the police intervened.

During the 1880s and 1890s, inventors in all countries began to consider reaction propulsion. There were designs of flying devices propelled by steam jets (C. Golightly), rocket-propelled airplanes (W. von Siemens) and airships (Gen. R. Thayer, N. Petersen, S. B. Battey). There was even a helicopter design (H. F. Phillips) utilizing reaction-propelled, counterrotating blades.

Many of these concepts were ingenious and prophetic in nature, considering that at that time the only existing mechanical prime movers were the steam engine and clockwork. Steam boilers were too heavy and clockwork mechanisms too limited in power to be of value in airborne devices. It was logical, therefore, to turn to reaction jets of steam or rocket gases. Models of some of these inventions, such as Phillips' helicopter, actually flew. But technology had not advanced sufficiently for any of these aerial, reaction-powered devices to be practical, despite the fact that the principles involved in many cases were sound. What was lacking was sufficient power. But sufficient power was coming. In 1845 the German chemist Christian Friedrich Schönbein accidentally discovered guncotton (nitrocellulose). Fifteen years later Alfred Nobel was commercially producing nitroglycerin. Use was made of these and other combustible materials in firearms and artillery but it was about 50 years or so before their value was to be demonstrated for rockets. (*See* PROPELLANTS.)

The schemers and dreamers continued, however. In 1881 a Russian explosives maker, Nikolai Ivanovich Kibalchich, was arrested for his part in an assassination attempt on Tsar Alexander II. While in prison he conceived of a rocket airplane which functioned by successive explosions of compressed powder candles. Kibalchich's writings were doomed to lie in prison archives after his execution until the overthrow of the government in 1917.

About 1891 a German inventor, Herman Ganswindt, conceived of a propulsion system, similar to that of Kibalchich but employing steel cartridges loaded with dynamite. But Ganswindt went further. He wanted to give his vehicle sufficient speed to attain escape velocity; *i.e.*, to leave the Earth. Apparently, Ganswindt was the first to connect rocket propulsion to space flight. In other countries the same dream was about to occur.

In Russia in 1895 a young mathematics teacher in Borovsk (district of Kaluga) published his first article on space travel. K. E. Tsiolkovski was among the first to grasp the importance of exhaust velocity and the reason rockets had been limited by black-powder formulas. He saw that by using liquid propellants, *e.g.*, liquefied hydrogen and oxygen, much greater efficiencies would result. Tsiolkovski made important contributions to the theory of space vehicle design but the language barrier, combined with his retiring nature, caused him to be little known for many years.

3. 20th Century to World War II.—In Sweden about the turn of the century, inventor Baron von Unge interested Alfred Nobel in a device described as an "aerial torpedo." Based upon the stickless Hale rocket, it incorporated a number of design improvements. Velocity and range were increased and about 1909 the Krupp armament firm purchased the patents and a number of rockets for further experimentation. But these rockets still used black powder and their capabilities were limited. Von Unge, however, believed that his aerial torpedoes would be valuable as air-to-air weapons between slow-moving dirigibles.

In the U.S., meanwhile, Robert H. Goddard (*q.v.*) was conducting theoretical and experimental research on rocket motors at Worcester, Mass. Utilizing high-pressure steel motors with a tapered nozzle, he achieved much greater thrust and efficiency. Another of Goddard's concepts was a long-range bombardment rocket whose motor was fired in pulses. Somewhat similar to the pulsed momentum principle suggested by Kibalchich and Ganswindt, the impulses were to have derived from charges of solid fuel injected into the combustion chamber in rapid succession.

During World War I Goddard developed a number of designs of military rockets weighing 1.5 to 17 lb. to be launched from a lightweight hand launcher. By switching from black powder to double-base powder (40% nitroglycerin, 60% nitrocellulose), a far more potent propulsion charge was obtained. These rockets, forerunners of the bazooka of World War II, were proving successful under tests by the U.S. army when the armistice was signed. But Goddard's main interest as a physicist was in utilizing the new potential of rockets to reach high altitudes. His notebooks, after his death, revealed interest in a circumlunar rocket (carrying a camera to photograph the far side of the moon), in ion and nuclear rocket propulsion and in interplanetary exploration.

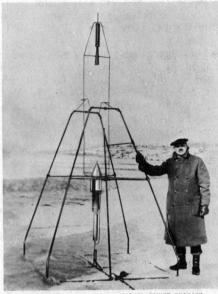

(Above) R. H. Goddard, U.S. rocket pioneer, with the liquid-propellant rocket he designed and launched in 1926. The fuel was liquid oxygen and gasoline. (Right) Aviavnito, a liquid-propellant rocket of the U.S.S.R. in 1936. The fuel was oxygen and ethyl alcohol

Using Smithsonian institution funds, Goddard continued his research. Switching from solid to liquid propellants he launched the first liquid-propellant rocket (liquid oxygen and gasoline) March 16, 1926, from a farm in nearby Auburn, Mass. The distance traveled was only 184 ft., but the significance was as great as the few feet flown by the Wright brothers at Kitty Hawk.

Later, under Guggenheim foundation funds, Goddard developed further research rockets at Roswell, N.M., in the 1930s. Although he never achieved the results he knew were possible, Goddard was a brilliant inventor. His later designs utilized both turbopumps and gyrostabilizers. Vanes were used to deflect the rocket exhaust to correct deviations from the planned flight path.

In 1919 the Smithsonian published a historic paper by Goddard entitled *A Method of Reaching Extreme Altitudes*. In it he discussed the possibility of a rocket reaching the moon with a payload of flash powder to signal its arrival to astronomers. The significance of this work, like Tsiolkovski's, was that the suggestions were made not by an exuberant inventor or enthusiast but by a thoughtful scientist with sound academic background.

World War I saw very little use of rocket weapons. Artillery development far outclassed existing rocket designs, which had changed little in the previous decades. The French, however, did successfully fire incendiary rockets from aircraft against hydrogen-filled dirigibles and barrage balloons.

Some French airplanes equipped with wing-launched rockets successfully attacked captive observation balloons. German units devised a technique for dealing with barbed wire entanglements in trench warfare: a heavy rocket was used to lob a grappling hook with a trailing line across the wire; the hook would be wound back by means of a winch, pulling down the wire.

In 1923 an obscure German mathematics teacher, Hermann Oberth, published *Die Rakete zu den Planetenräumen* ("The Rocket Into Interplanetary Space"). In this thin pamphlet was set forth, with a grasp remarkable for his time, the potentialities of rockets to achieve great velocity. Oberth pointed out that science and technology had reached a level where the realization of manned space vehicles might be achieved in several decades. A later, major work, *Wege zur Raumschiffahrt* ("Way to Space Travel"; 1929), not only set forth design concepts for immense interplanetary space vehicles utilizing clustered liquid-propellant motors but also contained a chapter on electric propulsion and the ion rocket, predating actual development work on electrostatic propulsion by 30 years.

The decade which followed was an exciting one. Germans such as Walter Hohmann, Hermann Noordung and Austrian Baron Guido von Pirquet published technical studies on rocket power and space vehicles. In France, the famous aviator and test pilot Robert Esnault-Pelterie lectured and wrote on high-altitude rockets and interplanetary flight. It was Esnault-Pelterie who coined the term astronautics. In 1929 Esnault-Pelterie and the French banker André Hirsch established an annual astronautics award for the experimenter who had done most to further space flight. In the U.S.S.R., Jakov I. Perelman and Nikolai A. Rynin were interpreting and expanding Tsiolkovski's work.

This was also the period of the promotional use of rockets—to propel cars and sleds as carried out by the German engineer, Max Valier. Although Valier was a competent designer of both solid and liquid rocket motors, such applications of rocket power tended to mislead the public by deflecting attention from high-altitude, high-speed flight.

In the period 1927–33 rocket and space flight societies were formed in Germany, Austria, the U.S.S.R., the U.S. and Great Britain. These groups provided a meeting place for discussion and experimentation and their journals became a means of disseminating information. Willy Ley, a founding member of the German space flight society, related the story of these formative years of modern rocket experimentation (*see* bibliography).

Further developments in rocket technology and its application to guided missiles during and after World War II are described in *Miscellaneous Applications of Rocket Power*, below.

III. ROCKET AND GUIDED-MISSILE SYSTEMS (WORLD WAR II AND LATER)

By World War II aircraft design, gyrostabilizing systems, rocket-engine technology, radio communications and radar had given man the tools with which to create effective short- and long-range guided missiles. Literally hundreds of designs and modifications of designs were developed by technologically capable countries. Those countries possessing nuclear bombs produced intercontinental ballistic weapons equipped with nuclear warheads, thus achieving a capability of awesome dimensions.

There is as yet no universally accepted system of classification of rockets and guided-missile systems. However, virtually all developments may be included within one of the following six categories of application: (1) surface-to-surface; (2) surface-to-air; (3) air-to-surface; (4) air-to-air; (5) space launch; (6) drones, decoys and test vehicles. Free-flight, or unguided, rockets are included in appropriate surface- or air-launch applications. Underwater missiles are included in the surface-launch category.

1. Surface-to-Surface.—*Free-Flight Rockets.*—All the rocket weapons from the 13th to the 20th century were free-flight rockets. They differ from other rockets and guided missiles in that they cannot alter trajectory in flight. Stability in flight was achieved by a long stick, fins or canted exhaust nozzles.

By the 1930s Germany had begun a program to refine rocket design. Among the innovations were double-base powder and high-explosive warheads. One of the most widely used of the German surface-launched weapons was the *Nebelwerfer*, which hurled 15-cm.- and 21-cm.-calibre rockets from six-barreled launchers. These were heavily used in Russia during World War II. The rocket-powered 15-cm. (about 6-in.) shell was about 40 in. long and weighed about 80 lb. Maximum range was more than 6,000 yd. Later, a *Wurfgerät* rocket launcher was introduced which hurled 21-cm.-calibre rockets; firing weight of each projectile was about 200 lb., and the maximum range was 2,000 yd.

Other German developments included the *Panzerfaust* and *Panzerschreck,* hand-held, tube-launched rockets. One other noteworthy rocket was the *Rheinbote*, a four-stage, solid-propellant rocket. It weighed nearly two tons, was about 40 ft. long and had an impressive range—135 mi. However, the payload of 88 lb. of high explosive could not compete with other weapons such as aircraft bombardment and the V-2. The *Rheinbote* was significant, however, in that practical recognition was made of the value of the step principle suggested by Haas more than 400 years before.

In Great Britain development of rockets was considered by the war office in 1934, and by the next year a program headed by A. D. Crow (later Sir Alwyn) was under way. Initial effort was aimed at antiaircraft weapons (see *Surface-to-Air*, below). As the war developed a 5-in. rocket, capable of projecting a 30-lb. bomb to ranges of 2–4 mi., was developed for heavy coastal bombardment prior to landings. Automatic ripple fire in successive groups reduced the chance of mutual interference between rockets. With this weapon a tremendous rate of firepower was possible. For example, a single rocket ship was able to launch 1,000 lb. per second of high explosive for nearly a full minute.

The United States did not commence active development of rockets until mid-1940. At that time, the National Defense Research committee (NDRC) authorized a program under the direction of C. N. Hickman at Indian Head, Md.; Hickman had worked with Goddard on the hand-launched rocket tests at Aberdeen in 1918. Aided by army Capt. L. A. Skinner, Hickman supervised the development of a refined design, known as the bazooka. About 20 in. long, 2.36 in. in diameter and weighing 3.5 lb., the rocket was fired from a 4.5-ft. shoulder launcher which weighed 14.5 lb. The bazooka was used extensively against tanks. Its maximum range was short (600 yd.) and it traveled slowly but it carried a particularly potent warhead weighing 1.8 lb. (*See* BAZOOKA.)

Another U.S. army development was the Calliope, a 60-tube launching projector for 4.5-in. rockets mounted on Sherman-type tanks. The launcher was mounted on the tank's gun turret, and both azimuth and elevation were controllable. Ripple fire was used to eliminate interference of rockets in salvo firing. Other launchers were developed for trucks and jeeps.

Close liaison was established between the U.S. NDRC and similar research groups in Great Britain. Advantage was taken of earlier rocket developments of the British. In this cooperative effort the U.S. developed an antisubmarine rocket-propelled weapon, known as Mousetrap, based upon a similar British design, Hedgehog.

Other conventional rockets developed in the U.S. included a 4.5-in. in barrage rocket with a range of 1,100 yd. and a 5-in. rocket of longer range. This latter rocket was extensively used in the Pacific theatre from type LSM-R launching barges against shore installations particularly just before landing operations. Firing rates of these flat-bottom boats was 500 per minute. Other U.S. rockets were used for smoke laying (3.5 in. and 4.5 in.) and demolition (7.2 in.).

Because the U.S. had great industrial capacity, unhampered by air raids, and urgent needs for its own forces as well as for allies, its production of solid-propellant rockets increased to a high rate by the end of the war. At the close, rockets of all sizes were being manufactured at the rate of 1,000,000,000 per year. Weights of different designs ranged from 3 to 1,300 lb.; diameters, 2 to 12 in.; lengths, 1 to 10 ft.; velocities, 650 to 1,500 ft. per second; maximum ranges (ground firing), 40 to 10,000 yd.; and accuracies (angular dispersion), $\frac{1}{16}°$ to 3°.

As far as is known, Russian rocket development activity during World War II was limited. Extensive use was made of barrage, ripple-fired rockets against the Germans. Both A-frame and truck-mounted launchers were used. According to Ley (see *Bibli-ography*) much of the rocket material came from the U.S. Later, however, the Russians mass-produced a 3.2 in. rocket known as *Katyusha*. From 16 to 60 *Katyushas* were fired from a boxlike launcher known as the Stalin Organ, mounted on a gun carriage.

After World War II, the impetus of advanced rocket designs of free-flight rockets continued in the U.S. but at a much slower pace. By 1950 the U.S. army had begun development of the Honest John rocket, and it became operational in 1955. As development continued on this rocket, it became a very flexible and highly mobile weapon. It could be fired from a truck-mounted, straight-rail launcher or from a helicopter-portable launcher. The Honest John is 27 ft. long, about 30 in. in diameter and weighs 4,830 lb. It has a range of more than 15 mi. and can be equipped with either a high-explosive or nuclear warhead. The rocket is both spin-stabilized and fin-stabilized. After it leaves the launcher, small rocket motors located forward of the head of the sustainer engine (but arranged tangentially to it) fire and impart a slow spin to the rocket. The four large stabilizing fins at the aft end of the rocket are set at a slight angle to maintain the spin.

In 1956 an accelerated development program began on a smaller ballistic rocket, resulting in the Little John. It was developed especially for use with airborne infantry divisions. Little John is 14.5 ft. long, 12.5 in. in diameter and weighs 760 lb. It has a range of approximately 10 mi. and can carry either a high-explosive or a nuclear warhead. Like the Honest John, it is a highly flexible, solid-propellant weapon. Unlike the larger rocket, Little John is spin-stabilized by the launching rail as it is fired; the spin is maintained by slightly offset fins.

Following World War II the U.S.S.R. produced its Frog[1] series of large, solid-propellant ballistic, free-flight rockets. The Frog-1 missile, in service since about 1957, is a single-stage spin-stabilized rocket 31 ft. long with a body diameter of about 2 ft., a bulbous nose, and six fins with a span of 3 ft. 3 in. The gases exhaust through a cluster of seven nozzles. The missile is carried on a tracked armoured vehicle and is believed to be capable of delivering either a conventional or a nuclear warhead a distance of about 15 mi.

The latest version is the Frog-5, displayed in 1965. This appears to be a much cleaner design, cylindrical in shape with four small fins and a main nozzle ringed by 12 small nozzles. It is rail-launched and carried by a new type of erector/launcher vehicle.

Between the end of World War II and the 1960s the development of smaller solid-propellant rockets spread to other countries, primarily because of the effectiveness of such weapons. Thus by the 1960s all major powers were developing and producing antitank and battlefield-support rockets.

Surface-to-Surface Guided Missiles.—The first practical surface-to-surface guided missile was based upon two sources of activity in the 1920s and 1930s. These were the theoretical work of scholars such as Tsiolkovski, Goddard, Oberth, Sänger and Esnault-Pelterie, and the experimental activity of Goddard and the amateur rocket societies. With their minds on manned interplanetary flight only, the rocket societies of Germany, U.S.S.R., U.S. and the U.K. performed an important function in proving that liquid

GERMAN V-2, A 46-FT., 14-TON MISSILE WITH A 200-MI. RANGE. FIRST FIRED IN 1944, IT CARRIED A CONVENTIONAL WARHEAD WEIGHING ONE TON

[1]In the absence of public designation of U.S.S.R. missiles the code names used by the North Atlantic Treaty organization (NATO) are used here as well as elsewhere in this article.

propellants could achieve their potential in rocket motors but that the technology required would be sophisticated and costly. The theoretical work of Tsiolkovski was largely unknown outside of the Soviet Union. Oberth was associated with amateur rocketry in Germany, but in the U.S. Goddard worked by himself.

In Germany the work of the society Verein für Raumschiffahrt attracted the attention of army Col. Walter Dornberger. In 1932 he hired young Wernher von Braun, who had been active in the experimental work of the German rocket society, and a few others and began experimenting at the artillery proving ground south of Berlin. Eventually, the vast army rocket test, development and production site at Peenemünde arose under the military leadership of Major General Dornberger and the technical direction of Von Braun. The fascinating story of the intensive development and engineering of the A-4 (popularly known as the V-2) is recorded in Dornberger's book, *V-2* (1954). The term V-2 stands for *Vergeltungswaffe zwei* ("vengeance weapon two").

The V-2 rocket was nearly 47 ft. long, had a cylindrical diameter of 5.5 ft. and weighed about 27,000 lb. at takeoff. The one-ton warhead contained 1,654 lb. of high explosive. Propellants were liquid oxygen and a 75% ethyl alcohol-water mixture. Approximately 8,400 lb. of alcohol and 10,800 lb. of oxygen were burned at a rate of 300 lb. per second. The rocket motor produced 55,000 lb. thrust for about one minute at which time the engine was shut off by an integrating gyro system. Propellant supply was by turbopump, driven by high-strength hydrogen peroxide decomposed by a catalyst. Yaw and pitch control was accomplished by two pairs of graphite-carbon vanes in the rocket exhaust. Ignition of the alcohol-liquid oxygen propellants was effected by a pyrotechnic pin wheel inserted in the motor. Estimated maximum range was about 200 mi.

The first operational V-2 was fired against Paris on Sept. 6, 1944. Two days later the first of more than 1,000 missiles was fired against London. The missile traveled on a ballistic arc trajectory reaching a maximum speed of more than 1 mi. per second and an altitude of 60 to 70 mi. Since it approached the target faster than the speed of sound, there was no warning of its approach. By the end of the war about 4,000 of these missiles had been launched from mobile bases against Allied targets. During February and March 1945, only weeks before the war ended, an average of 60 missiles was launched weekly.

Although the V-2 did not become a decisive weapon, it was nevertheless a monumental engineering achievement. Large rocket motor developments after World War II, in both the U.S. and the U.S.S.R., drew heavily upon V-2 engine design.

The only other relatively long-range, surface-to-surface guided missile to see action in World War II was the V-1 or "buzz-bomb," a development of the German air force. The V-1 has been called, from an engineering point of view, "a perfect counterpart of the naval torpedo." The analogy is striking in several ways. Once the V-1 was launched, its course could not be corrected, being determined by a preset guidance system. An accelerometer sensed deviation to the left and right of the programmed flight path and sent corrective signals to the control surface actuators. The missile's altitude was sensed and maintained in a similar manner by a barometer, and range was determined by the number of revolutions turned by a small propeller in the nose of the missile. When the requisite number of revolutions, corresponding to a linear range, had been made, a signal was sent to the aerodynamic control surface actuators to cause the V-1 to dive vertically onto the target. The average range was 150 mi. Launching ramps and a hydrogen peroxide-powered catapult boosted the V-1 to flying speed.

The V-1 used a unique pulse-jet engine that found later employment in early post-World War II Soviet and U.S. missiles. Air enters a diffuser through a series of spring-loaded flapper valves that open as the air passes through them and then close when the air is in the combustion chamber. At this point in the firing cycle, kerosene from a gas-pressurized tank is sprayed into the chamber and ignited by a spark plug. As the chamber pressure of the burning gas rises, the flapper valves close and the exhaust gases are forced through the nozzle of the motor. The warhead was a 2,200-lb. charge of high explosive set off by an impact fuze.

A final, but significant, weapon under development by the Germans during World War II, and one that spurred investigation in Great Britain, France, the Soviet Union, the United States and Switzerland, was the X-7 antitank missile. Although this missile was not developed in time for use in combat, its technology set the pattern for practically all antitank guided missiles developed during the next 20 years. The X-7 was a solid-propellant winged rocket with a shaped-charge warhead and a range of about half a mile. This missile was to have been guided in flight by means of corrective signals sent over two wires trailing from its wing tips to spoilers located on the wings, similar to the X-4 air-to-air missile. The operator visually followed the missile in flight and sent guidance correction signals by manual control.

When World War II came to a close in Aug. 1945, development and production of rockets was a massive enterprise in the United States and Great Britain. Despite a few ingenious uses of rocket

TABLE I.—*Surface-to-Surface Missiles*

Country and Service	Name	Length (ft.)	Takeoff weight (lb.)	Range (mi.)	Propulsion	Remarks
Australia, Navy	Ikara	11			Rocket, solid	Antisubmarine, homing torpedo
France, Army	Entac	2.7	27	~1	Rocket, solid	Wire guided, antitank
France, Navy	Malafon	19.7	~2,900	~11	Rocket, solid	Antisubmarine
France, Navy	SS. 11	3.9	66	~2	Rocket, solid	Wire guided, antitank
France, Army, Navy	SS. 12	6	167	>3	Rocket, solid	Spin-stabilized, infrared guidance
Germany, Army	Cobra	3.1	22.5	1	Rocket, solid	Wire guided, antitank
Great Britain, Army	Swingfire	—		>1	Rocket, solid	Wire guided, antitank
Great Britain, Army	Vigilant	3.5	31	~1	Rocket, solid	Wire guided, antitank
Japan, Army	KAM-3D	3.3	—	~1	Rocket, solid	Wire guided, antitank
Norway, Navy	Terne	6.5	265	—	Rocket, solid	Antisubmarine
Sweden, Army	Bantam	2.8	13	~1	Rocket, solid	Wire guided, antitank
Sweden, Navy	08A	18.8	—	—	Turbojet	Antiship
Switzerland, Army	Mosquito	3.7	27.5	~1	Rocket, solid	Wire guided, antitank
U.S.S.R.	Swatter	3.7	—	~1.5	Rocket, solid	Wire guided, antitank
U.S.S.R.	Serb	33	—	—	Rocket, solid	Submarine-launched ballistic missile
U.S.S.R.	Frog-5	~34	~4,500	>30	Rocket, solid	Battlefield support
U.S.S.R.	Scud	35	~10,000	~50	Rocket, solid	Battlefield support
U.S.S.R.	Skean	75	—	~2,000	Rocket, liquid	IRBM
U.S.S.R.	Sasin	80	—	~6,500	Rocket, liquid	ICBM
United States, Navy	Asroc	15	1,000	—	Rocket, solid	Rocket-boosted, acoustic-homing torpedo
United States, Army	Honest John	26	4,700	12	Rocket, solid	Battlefield support, spin stabilized
United States, Army	Lance	20	3,200	30	Rocket, liquid	Battlefield support
United States, Army	Little John	14.5	780	>10	Rocket, solid	Battlefield support
United States, Air Force	Minuteman	59.8	70,000	>7,000	Rocket, solid; 3 stages	ICBM, inertial guidance
United States, Army	Pershing	34.5	10,000	450	Rocket, solid; 2 stages	Battlefield support
United States, Navy	Polaris A-3	31	~30,000	2,875	Rocket, solid; 2 stages	Submarine launched
United States, Navy	Poseidon	—	—	>3,000	Rocket, solid; 2 stages	Submarine launched
United States, Army	Sergeant	34.5	10,000	85	Rocket, solid	Battlefield support
United States, Air Force	Titan II	103	330,000	6,500	Rocket, liquid; 2 stages	ICBM, inertial guidance
United States, Army	TOW	—	~75	>2	Rocket, solid	Wire guided, antitank

~Approximate.   >More than.

SURFACE-TO-SURFACE MISSILES

(Left) Minuteman, a U.S. solid-propellant ICBM, range 7,000 mi. (Below) Skean, a U.S.S.R. liquid-propellant IRBM, range 2,000 mi. Both Minuteman and Skean are launched from silos. (Above) Underwater launching of U.S. Polaris A-3 missile, which has a 2,875-mi. range

BY COURTESY OF (LEFT) U.S. AIR FORCE, (ABOVE) U.S. NAVY; PHOTOGRAPH, (BELOW) AVIATION WEEK AND SPACE TECHNOLOGY

power, however, the major effort was conservative and on conventional lines, adapting technical improvements to existing weapons. Nowhere was there the depth of appreciation and scope of plans for guided missiles or long-range ballistic rockets that there was in Germany. Recognition of the potential of rocket power by the Allied powers came too late in the war to catch up with German developments in rocket technology.

Appreciation of the potential importance of German technical efforts was evidenced by the speed with which technical intelligence teams followed close behind front-line troops as they moved across Germany. Intensive and intelligent work on the part of these teams resulted not only in obtaining masses of technical data, design drawings and missiles but also an opportunity for interrogation of key scientists and missile engineers. The top planning and technical staff of Peenemünde, headed by Dornberger and Von Braun, fled south in the last few days of the war in order to surrender to U.S. troops. Thus the priceless experience of the German rocket effort and the knowledge of about 150 rocket experts became available to the Allies. The Soviet troops that captured Peenemünde found mostly wreckage and had orders to destroy what was left. However, the Soviets took many German technicians to the U.S.S.R. and the exchange of technical and scientific data continued until a few years later. Thus the U.S., France, Great Britain and the U.S.S.R. all had the benefit of information on rockets and guided missiles captured in Germany.

In general, early postwar development of rockets followed most of the lines suggested by German work. Rockets were used to propel all varieties of guided missiles, competing successfully in these missions with air-breathing jet engines. Refinement of all

components of these systems and improved technology based upon extensive research programs have resulted in rocket-powered weapons of immense capabilities.

Not only did the U.S. obtain the services of top German rocket experts but also, from the underground V-2 factory at Niedersachswerfen, 300 boxcar loads of components of V-2 missiles—enough for about 100 complete vehicles. About 70 V-2s were fired during the period 1946–51 at White Sands (N.M.) proving ground. These firings provided much experience in handling and launching large rockets.

The long-range ballistic missile was not a major development in the U.S. until 1954. Until that time air-breathing subsonic missile developments such as the Snark and Navaho were counted upon by military planners to supplement and supersede long-range, strategic-bomber aircraft. These vehicles were essentially unmanned, turbojet engine-powered, high-speed aircraft equipped with warheads. A 75-mi.-range Corporal developed by the U.S. army with a mobile launcher was operational by this time as a battlefield support weapon.

In 1954 two developments put the intercontinental ballistic missile (ICBM) in a new light. One of these developments was the thermonuclear bomb with destructive power measured in megatons (millions of tons of TNT equivalent). The other was the miniaturization and refinement of inertial guidance systems so that they became sufficiently accurate to place the warhead of the ICBM close to a target 5,000 or more miles distant.

The first ICBM authorized was the Atlas, followed later by the Titan. The Atlas was a $1\frac{1}{2}$-stage vehicle. Whereas a 2-stage vehicle drops both first-stage rocket engine and tankage, the $1\frac{1}{2}$-stage vehicle drops only the rocket engine and the second stage continues to use the original tankage. The first Atlas was fired full range from the Cape Canaveral (now Cape Kennedy), Fla., missile range in Nov. 1958. The Titan was a conventional two-stage vehicle. The first successful tests of the Titan were not made until 1959. Both the Atlas and Titan burned liquid oxygen and hydrocarbon fuel (similar to kerosene).

A major logistic problem in ballistic missiles using cryogenic propellants such as liquid oxygen is the necessity for fueling just prior to launching. This weakness, which means delay in defensive, retaliatory fire, can be eliminated by the use of solid propellants or storable noncryogenic propellants. A later version of Titan used a higher-performance propellant combination of nitrogen tetroxide and hydrazine-based fuel. This propellant combination permits the missile to stand ready, fully loaded for firing.

Development of solid propellants to a level of performance near that of liquids achieved such progress by 1958 that a solid-fueled ICBM, the Minuteman, was authorized. This ICBM would be launched from underground "silos" in so-called "hard" launching sites relatively impervious to attack.

The U.S. navy became interested in long-range missiles as early as 1947 when it demonstrated that a V-2 could be launched from the deck of a ship at sea. At first the navy co-sponsored the development of the U.S. army's Jupiter intermediate range ballistic missile (IRBM), with the idea of using it aboard ships. But the problems associated with the production and storage of liquid propellants aboard ships soon turned the navy toward a quest for a solid-propellant IRBM. In Jan. 1957 the navy announced plans for a solid-propellant missile to be known as Polaris. The first test vehicle was launched in Jan. 1958, and the first underwater firing occurred in April 1960. The Polaris entered operational service aboard nuclear-powered submarines in 1961.

Ten years after World War II, the U.S. air force and army each undertook the development of an IRBM. The air force Thor and the army Jupiter both used the same liquid-propellant engine and had a range of 1,600 mi.

IRBM and ICBM developments in Great Britain and the Soviet Union paralleled U.S. efforts in the years immediately following World War II. The Soviets fired several captured V-2 missiles from their rocket proving ground at Kapustin Yar in 1946 and 1947 and presumably learned much from them.

Early Soviet surface-to-surface guided-missile developments borrowed heavily from German technology, but later Soviet weapons were clearly original designs. The Scud-A is a liquid-fueled, single-stage missile which appears to derive from the German Wasserfall surface-to-air missile. This missile and its successor, the Scud-B, are both believed to have a range of about 50 to 100 mi., and probably are guided by radio commands.

The first Soviet MRBM and IRBMs were the Shyster (650-mi. range), Sandal (1,210-mi. range), and the Skean (2,000-mi. range), all single-stage vehicles. The Shyster is basically a stretched and uprated version of the German V-2 rocket, which burns liquid oxygen and kerosene. The Sandal and Skean are powered by storable propellants, and appear to be essentially Soviet designs with much less borrowed from German technology. The Sandal was deployed to Cuba in 1962, but withdrawn after U.S.-U.S.S.R. negotiations. Later the Soviets displayed two mobile missiles encased in containers which were labelled Scamp and Scrooge. Little is known of these vehicles. They may be multi-stage solid-fueled rockets with ranges in excess of 2,500 mi.

The first Soviet ICBM is believed to be a dual-purpose vehicle used both as an ICBM and as the basic booster for much of the Soviet space program. It was displayed publicly for the first time at the 1967 Paris Air show where it was placarded as the booster for the Vostok spacecraft, but has probably been in use since the late 1950s. The vehicle is parallel-staged, with a central sustainer core to which are attached four large tapered boosters. The sustainer and boosters are powered by clusters of thrust chambers which all ignite upon launching; then midway in the powered flight the four-booster tank and engine combinations are detached while the sustainer continues burning. The propellants are liquid oxygen and a hydrocarbon, and the engines develop a total sea level thrust of about 1,000,000 lb. In 1964 the Soviets displayed the Sasin, a much smaller two-stage, tandem, liquid-fueled ICBM, that is probably more typical of modern U.S.S.R. ICBM technology than the large 2½-staged vehicle shown at Paris.

Two other three-stage Soviet vehicles which could fit in the ICBM category are Savage and Scrag. The former is solid fueled, similar to the U.S. Minuteman ICBM but somewhat larger. Each stage has four nozzles, and the stages are separated by open truss structures. The Scrag is large, 120 ft. long by about 9½ ft. in diameter. It has been described as sister to the launch vehicle used for the Vostok and Voskhod spacecraft; however, it could also deliver a large warhead on a ballistic trajectory.

In 1962 the Soviets displayed a 45-ft.-long missile, Sark, and claimed that it was a submarine-launched missile. Its very heavy construction and large size make it unlikely for operational use in submarines. It is considered to be more likely an experimental model. Two years later the smaller Serb was displayed and also credited with a submarine mission. The Serb is similar in configuration to the U.S. Polaris, and is thought to be powered by two solid-fueled stages with a range of less than 1,000 mi.

In Great Britain the British test-launched captured German V-2s at Cuxhaven and by 1955 began development of the Blue Streak

IRBM. This program was subsequently canceled before operational use.

Regardless of the country of origin, all IRBM's and ICBM's are equipped with either nuclear or thermonuclear warheads because (1) it is economically impractical to use such an expensive missile to deliver a relatively small amount of high explosive; and (2) the unavoidable inaccuracies in range and direction make essential the far-reaching effects of a nuclear explosion.

Underwater-Launched Missiles.—A small group of surface-to-surface missiles includes those launched by submarines. The torpedo is actually a guided missile and the oldest form of this weapon. Originally these weapons followed a preset guidance course of fixed depth and carried a warhead that exploded on impact. Later versions after World War II contained seeking and acoustic homing devices designed to steer the torpedo to its target, whether submerged or on the surface. By the mid-1960s the U.S. had placed in operation the Subroc missile. Launched by a submerged submarine, the Subroc breaks surface and is propelled by rocket power on a ballistic trajectory toward an enemy submarine. Reentering the water, the missile then assumes the role of a homing torpedo.

2. Surface-To-Air.—The major purpose of the class of surface-to-air weapons is to intercept and destroy enemy aircraft, particularly at altitudes beyond the effective capability of conventional antiaircraft artillery. During World War II high-altitude bombing above this range necessitated the development of rocket-powered weapons.

Free-flight Rockets.—Except in Germany, military rocket research during the period between the world wars was limited or nonexistent, but as war began to approach, rocketry assumed new importance. In Great Britain, as mentioned above, development of rockets was headed by A. D. Crow. Initial effort was aimed at achieving the equivalent destructive power of the 3-in. and later the 3.7-in. antiaircraft gun. Single, double and then multiple launchers were produced. Massed batteries of launchers fired salvos of as many as 128 rounds.

Two important innovations were developed by the British in connection with the 3-in. rocket. Both devices were directed against the German dive bombers. One was a rocket-propelled, aerial-defense system. A parachute and wire device was rocketed aloft, trailing a wire which unwound at high speed from a bobbin on the ground. Altitudes as high as 20,000 ft. were attained. Several versions of this were used, quite successfully, from ships. The other device was a type of proximity fuze utilizing a photoelectric cell and thermionic amplifier. Change in emission of light from a nearby airplane (projected on the cell by means of a lens) triggered a thyratron and the detonating train of the shell.

The only significant antiaircraft rocket development by the Germans was the *Taifun*. A slender 6-ft. liquid-propellant rocket of simple concept, the *Taifun* was designed to be launched to altitudes of 50,000 ft. Planned for mass production, the design embodied coaxial tankage of nitric acid and a mixture of organic fuels. This weapon, however, was never put into operational use.

Surface-to-Air Guided Missiles.—During World War I an attempt was made by Great Britain to substitute gyrostabilizing equipment, automatic and radio control for a human pilot in small propeller-driven aircraft. This aircraft was actually flown, but its speed, range and accuracy were marginal. The aim was a weapon to combat Germany's dirigible bombers.

During World War II Germany made efforts to produce effective surface-to-air missiles. Three of those under development were subsonic; the *Schmetterling* and *Enzian* resembled stubby mid-wing aircraft, and the *Rheintochter* had cruciform wings. All used solid-propellant boosters, or takeoff rockets, and sustainer motors, except that there was a liquid-propellant version of the *Rheintochter*. Altitude capability was about 50,000 ft. The *Wasserfall* was a superior weapon designed to operate at supersonic speeds. A single-stage missile weighing 8,400 lb. at takeoff, this weapon was powered by a 17,000-lb.-thrust motor at a velocity of 2,500 ft. per second. Maximum altitude was 60,000 ft., and the weight of the warhead was 330 lb. Propellants were nitric acid and vinyl

TABLE II.—*Surface-to-Air Missiles*

Country and Service	Name	Length (ft.)	Weight (lb.)	Range (mi.)	Propulsion
France, Navy	Masurca	28	4,080	25	Rocket, solid
France, Germany	Roland	7.9	140	>9	Rocket, solid
G.B., Air Force	Bloodhound	27.8	~4,000	~25	Rocket, solid; ramjet
G.B., Army	ET. 316	8.5	~500	~7	Rocket, solid
G.B., Navy	Seacat	4.8	~175	~4	Rocket, solid
G.B., Navy	Seaslug	19.7	~3,500	~20	Rocket, solid
G.B., Army	Thunderbird	20.8	~3,000	~15	Rocket, solid
Italy	Indigo	10.5	215	>6	Rocket, solid
U.S.S.R.	Galosh (anti-ICBM)	~67	—	—	—
U.S.S.R.	Ganef	30	—	—	Rocket, solid; ramjet
U.S.S.R.	Guideline	35	3,000	28	Rocket, solid; liquid
U.S., Army	Chaparral	9.5	~200	>10	Rocket, solid
U.S., Army	Hawk	16.5	1,300	22	Rocket, solid
U.S., Army	Nike-Zeus (anti-ICBM)	48.3	23,000	>150	Rocket, solid
U.S., Army	Redeye	4	28	~2	Rocket, solid
U.S., Navy	Standard	—	—	>30	Rocket, solid
U.S., Navy	Talos	31.2	3,000	~75	Rocket, solid; ramjet
U.S., Navy	Tartar	15	1,200	>10	Rocket, solid
U.S., Navy	Terrier (Advanced)	27	3,000	>20	Rocket, solid

isobutyl ether. All of these weapons would have had important effects upon enemy aircraft flying at 15,000 to 30,000 ft. However, none of them ever became operational. In no other country, however, had such weapons gotten beyond the planning stage. Also, the goal of launching missiles guided by radar beams had been proven technically feasible.

Following World War II the major nations continued the development and refinement of antiaircraft guided missiles. In the United States the U.S. navy initiated a research program the purpose of which was to develop a ramjet engine suitable for use in a high-performance antiaircraft missile. Ultimately, the Talos, Terrier and Tartar missiles resulted. During the same period,

TABLE III.—*Sounding Rockets*

Country	Name	Payload (lb.)	Altitude (mi.)
Argentina	Gamma-Centauro	11	28
Argentina	Orion	22	50
Australia	HAD	20	80
Australia	Long Tom	30–180	100–68
Australia	Aero High	45	130
Canada	Black Brant III	50	95
Canada	Black Brant IV	40	620
Canada	Black Brant V	150	145
France	Véronique Gl	220	162
France	Vesta	2,200	130
France	Tacite	450	125
France	Titus	720	170
France	Dauphin	220–660	80–43
France	Eridan	220–660	373–186
France	Dragon	66–440	373–155
Germany	Bölkow	6	50
G.B., Australia	Jabiru	200	180
G.B.	Skylark	150	150
G.B.	Skua	12	65
G.B.	Petrel	30	95
Japan	Lambda	6.5	1,600
Japan	S-B	5	37
Japan	LS-A	5	93
U.S.	Argo A-1	400–1,200	150–110
U.S.	Argo B-13	60	155
U.S.	Argo C-22	150–250	200–160
U.S.	Argo C-23	50–350	2,400–920
U.S.	Argo D-4	110	600
U.S.	Arcas	12	40
U.S.	Archer	40	90
U.S.	Iris	100	200
U.S.	Metroc	3	20
U.S.	Phoenix I	5–20	265–170
U.S.	Aerobee 150	150	170
U.S.	Aerobee 300	50	300
U.S.	Astrobee 200	125	200
U.S.	Astrobee 250	500–2,000	215–115
U.S.	Astrobee 1,500	50–300	1,990–840

development continued on two antiaircraft missiles that were originally designed in the latter days of the war, the Lark and the Little Joe. The former was a 14-ft.-long, liquid-propellant weapon with semiactive radar homing. Weighing 1,200 lb., it was accelerated to operational speed by two solid-propellant jato (jet-assisted-takeoff) units. It could deliver a 100-lb. warhead to a range of 38 mi. The Little Joe was an 11-ft.-long, solid-propellant missile with a range of 2.5 mi. Its payload was a 100-lb. warhead designed to counter Japanese kamikaze attacks on U.S. navy ships. Neither weapon was used in the Korean War.

The U.S. army concentrated its efforts in the field of antiaircraft weapons on the Nike group of missiles. The first of these was the Nike-Ajax, which was first test fired in 1951 and which remained deployed with the army until 1961. The missile is 21 ft. long, 12 in. in diameter and weighs 2,455 lb. With a range of 25 mi., it has a liquid-propellant engine that gives it a velocity of 1,500 m.p.h.

An advanced version of the Ajax was conceived in 1953. Known first as Nike-B, the name Nike-Hercules was later used. The Hercules is 27 ft. long, 31.5 in. in diameter and weighs 5,000 lb. It has a solid-propellant motor, can carry both nuclear and high-explosive warheads, and has a range of 75 mi. Both the Nike-Ajax and the Nike-Hercules employ radar-command guidance.

Out of the early experience of the Nike program also grew the possibility for an antimissile missile. The Nike-Zeus is a complex defensive weapon system designed to intercept incoming ICBM warheads and destroy them above the atmosphere. A further development is the Nike-X, which would use some of the components of the Nike-Zeus but would also include a phased-array radar installation with electronic scanning. The Nike-X/Zeus is designed for high altitude interception, while another version, Nike-X/

Sprint, is to operate at low altitudes.

Other significant current U.S. surface-to-air missiles include the Hawk, capable of intercepting low-flying aircraft, as is the shoulder-launched Redeye. Both have homing devices.

The U.S.S.R. has displayed six different surface-to-air missiles, Guild, Guideline, Goa, Griffon, Ganef and Galosh. Of these the Guideline has been widely deployed both in the U.S.S.R., in Warsaw Pact countries, in certain middle-east countries, as well as in Cuba, Indonesia and North Vietnam. It has been used in the last country against U.S. aircraft, with some limited success. The missile is similar in many respects to the U.S. Nike-Ajax, with a solid-fueled first stage and a liquid-fueled second stage. Later versions are believed to have a slant range of about 27.5 mi., an altitude ceiling of about 80,000 ft., and a speed at burnout of Mach 3. The Ganef is unique in its use of a ramjet for main propulsion. It has four small strap-on solid-fuel booster rockets to provide initial velocity. The Galosh, shown in 1964, is claimed to be an anti-missile missile, but little is known of it because it has been largely hidden by its 67-ft.-long by 9-ft.-diameter ribbed container, and only the four first-stage nozzles have been visible. It is speculated that an anti-missile requiring such a large container would be likely to operate at long range, presumably to intercept ICBMs beyond the atmosphere.

Atmospheric Sounding Rockets.—Despite their short lifetime atmospheric sounding rockets have become important scientific implements for several reasons. First, they are the only means of lifting scientific instruments to altitudes between 50 and 100 mi.—heights above the reach of airplanes and balloons but still within the atmosphere and thus impractical to explore with artificial satellites. Second, their size and simplicity, within limits, permit experiments, such as meteorological measurements, to be made at times and locations desired by the scientist. Third, on a weight basis, sounding rockets can lift a larger expendable power supply than artificial satellites for experiments of limited duration. Sounding rockets have investigated such phenomena as cosmic rays, solar ultraviolet radiation and X rays, auroral particles, micrometeorites and the Earth's magnetic field.

Before 1946 all upper-atmosphere research had been conducted from balloon sondes or aircraft. Beginning in 1946 various kinds of physical sensors were carried aloft in the nose cones of captured and reassembled V-2s to heights above 100 mi. In the next few years both the Aerobee and Viking sounding rockets obtained and telemetered much new scientific data. Photographs of the Earth were taken from space. Mice were carried aloft and photographed under conditions of weightlessness. Slowly the art of building these new, complex and expensive research tools developed. Attempts were made to lower costs and to achieve higher altitudes by launching rockets from high-altitude balloons (Rockoon and Project Far Side).

TABLE IV.—*Air-to-Surface Missiles*

Country and Service	Name	Length (ft.)	Weight (lb.)	Range (mi.)	Propulsion
France	AS. 12	6.2	165	4	Rocket, solid
France, Air Force, Navy	AS. 20	8.5	310	4.5	Rocket, solid
France, Air Force	AS. 30	12.6	1,150	7.5	Rocket, solid
France, G.B.	Martel	—	—	40	Rocket, solid
G.B., Air Force	Blue Steel	35	—	~250	Rocket, liquid
Sweden, Air Force	Robot Rb 04	14.6	1,000	~6	Rocket, solid
Sweden, Air Force	305 A	11.5	660	~5	Rocket, solid
U.S.S.R., Air Force	Kangaroo	~50	—	—	—
U.S.S.R., Navy	Kennel	28	—	—	—
U.S.S.R., Air Force	Kipper	~31	—	~200	—
U.S., Navy, Air Force	Bullpup A	10.5	570	7	Rocket, liquid
U.S., Navy, Air Force	Bullpup B	13.5	1,785	10	Rocket, liquid
U.S., Navy	Condor	—	—	40	Rocket, solid
U.S., Air Force	Hound Dog	42.5	9,600	>600	Turbojet
U.S., Air Force, Navy	Shrike	10	500	10	Rocket, solid

tained and telemetered much new scientific data. Photographs of the Earth were taken from space. Mice were carried aloft and photographed under conditions of weightlessness. Slowly the art of building these new, complex and expensive research tools developed. Attempts were made to lower costs and to achieve higher altitudes by launching rockets from high-altitude balloons (Rockoon and Project Far Side).

Typical of experiments performed by sounding rockets is one begun in 1954 that determined regions of intense turbulence and strong shear winds below the altitude of 60 mi. and extremely high winds above that altitude. These conditions were observed by Nike-Asp sounding rockets that released trails of sodium vapour into the atmosphere between 60 and 120 mi. above the Earth. Temperature measurements at high altitudes are made by timing the arrival of the sound of exploding grenades ejected from sounding rockets, such as Skylark and Nike-Cajun, at altitudes between 38 and 65 mi. By the mid-1960s much of the knowledge of the temperature and pressure of the atmosphere, as well as the composition of the ionosphere, was based on data from sounding-rocket experiments.

Sounding rockets range in size, performance and cost from a simple, single-stage, solid-propellant rocket such as the 77-lb. Arcas, which can lift a 12-lb. meteorological payload 37 mi., to the two-stage, solid-propellant 1,553-lb. Aerobee 300, which can lift a 35-lb. payload to 300 mi. Liquid-propellant sounding rockets are also used extensively. The French Véronique rockets proved valuable during and after the International Geophysical Year (IGY). First flight-tested in 1950 these rockets were subsequently flown at the French missile test range at Colomb Béchar, Alg. In its IGY flights the Véronique used an 8,820-lb.-thrust engine burning nitric oxide and turpentine. The rocket weighs 2,962 lb. and can lift a payload of 166 lb. to an altitude of 140 mi. The Véronique is 24 ft. long, 22 in. in diameter and is fin-stabilized. In 1967 a reusable meteorological sounding rocket was announced that could carry a 1.5 lb. payload to 5,000 ft. and be reused 20 times.

Cooperative worldwide efforts during the International Years of the Quiet Sun resulted in the 1960s in several dozen coordinated rocket soundings of the upper atmosphere, which yielded new scientific understanding of solar effects upon the earth.

3. Air-to-Surface.—*Free-Flight Rockets.*—Great Britain, Germany, the U.S.S.R., Japan and the United States all developed airborne rockets for use against surface as well as aerial targets. These were almost invariably fin-stabilized because of the effective aerodynamic forces when launched at speeds of 250 m.p.h. and more. Tube launchers were used at first, but later straight-rail or zero-length launchers, located under the wings of the airplane, were employed.

One of the most successful of the German rockets was the 2-in. in diameter R4M. The tail fins remained folded until launch, facilitating close loading arrangements. The U.S. achieved great success with a 4.5-in. rocket, three or four of which were carried

TABLE V.—*Air-to-Air Missiles*

Country and Service	Name	Length (ft.)	Weight (lb.)	Range (mi.)	Propulsion
France, Air Force	R. 511	10	400	4.5	Rocket, solid
France, Air Force	R. 530	10.8	430	11	Rocket, solid
G.B., Navy	Firestreak	10.5	300	0.75-5	Rocket, solid
G.B., Navy	Red Top	11.5	~350	7	Rocket, solid
U.S.S.R., Air Force	Atoll	~10	—	~2	Rocket, solid
U.S.S.R., Air Force	Awl	16	—	~9	Rocket, solid
U.S., Air Force	Falcon	6.5	110-120	5	Rocket, solid
U.S., Air Force	Genie	9.5	825	6	Rocket, solid
U.S., Navy	Phoenix	~11	~1,000	>10	Rocket, solid
U.S., Navy, Air Force	Sidewinder 1C	9.5	185	>2	Rocket, solid
U.S., Navy	Sparrow	12	400	>8	Rocket, solid
U.S., Air Force	Super Falcon	7	150	7	Rocket, solid

under each wing of Allied fighter planes. These rockets were highly effective against motor columns, tanks, troop and supply trains, fuel and ammunition depots, airfields and barges. The largest U.S. airborne rocket was the Tiny Tim. More than 10 ft. long and 1 ft. in diameter, it carried 150 lb. of TNT. The solid-propellant motor developed 30,000 lb. of thrust for 1 sec.

A variation on the airborne rocket was the addition of a rocket motor and fins to conventional bombs. This had the effect of flattening the ballistic trajectory, extending the range and increasing the velocity at impact, useful against concrete bunkers and hardened targets. These weapons were called glide bombs, and the Japanese had 815-lb. and 224-lb. versions. The U.S.S.R. employed 56-lb. and 220-lb. versions from the Stormovik fighter aircraft.

Air-to-Surface Guided Missiles.—Among the first air-to-surface guided missiles, developed by the Germans, was the radio-controlled, armour-piercing Fritz-X, which sank the Italian battleship "Roma" after its surrender to the Allies in 1944. Another was the Hs-293 winged bomb. More than 11 ft. long and weighing about 1,700 lb., this radio-controlled weapon destroyed a number of merchant ships in Allied convoys. Although these early versions of glide bombs required optical tracking (and, therefore, clear weather), plans were under way for television viewing of the target

by the weapon and radar spotting for nighttime and foul-weather use. The U.S. developed a controlled glide bomb called the Bat, similar to the Hs 293.

The Hs 293 was a radio-guided bomb with a rocket engine using hydrogen peroxide as a propellant. This chemical was decomposed into steam by the use of aqueous potassium permanganate as a catalyst. A crew of three, a pilot, an observer and a bombardier, were necessary to launch and direct the Hs 293 to its target. The observer's duty was to set the gyroscope that established a reference plane for the missile, and the bombardier piloted the bomb by remote control after its release from the aircraft. It was especially adaptable to targets at sea and found its greatest use there, sinking many merchant ships.

The American Bat had a much greater range—up to 20 mi. In guidance it was in advance of the Hs 293 since it employed an active radar homing device. The Bat was a glide bomb, however, having no propulsion system. It weighed 1,000 lb. and was 12 ft. long with a wing span of 10 ft. Developed primarily as a weapon for use against ships, the Bat was to be released from an airplane at an altitude of 3 to 5 mi. The bomb's velocity of 300 m.p.h. was considerably slower than the 470-m.p.h. Hs 293. Built in considerable numbers prior to the end of the war, the Bat was

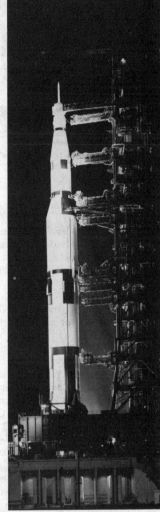

BY COURTESY OF NASA

SATURN V, VEHICLE, 365 FT. IN HEIGHT

not actually used until April 1945. Even at that late date, however, it was credited with sinking a Japanese destroyer at the maximum range of 20 mi.

After 1945 the U.S. air force explored more complex versions of the air-to-surface missile. One of these was the Rascal, a liquid-propellant missile with inertial guidance and a range of 100 mi. By the mid-1950s development turned to achieving longer ranges. This effort was aided by the advent of lighter-weight nuclear warheads. Two of the weapons developed, the United States Hound Dog and the British Blue Steel, had ranges of about 200 to 600 mi. The Skybolt, canceled in 1963, was to have had a range of 1,000 mi. The cause of the cancellation was essentially the difficulty in guidance from an aerial launch; development was stopped in favour of alternative weapons, such as the fixed-base ICBM.

The U.S.S.R. has displayed a variety of air-to-surface missiles on Bear, Badger and Blinder bomber aircraft which have been given the NATO designations of Kangaroo, Kennel, Kipper and Kitchen. All of these missiles appear to use air-breathing power plants.

The complexity and expense of air-to-surface missiles is great. Particularly difficult is the guidance problem. It was found that at extreme ranges, programmed and command systems were not feasible and that it was necessary to rely on such delicate and exacting systems as stellar guidance, usually in combination with inertial guidance.

4. Air-to-Air.—*Free-Flight Rockets.*—One of the earliest weapons concepts in this category was that of Swedish Lieut. Col. Baron von Unge. He proposed the use of his improved Hale-

HOUND DOG AIR-TO-SURFACE MISSILE FLYING AT A LOW LEVEL AFTER BEING LAUNCHED FROM A B-52

type, spin-stabilized rockets as armament for dirigibles in 1908, calling them aerial torpedos.

As might be suspected, aircraft-launched rockets can be used against aerial as well as ground targets, provided that the aerial targets are propeller-driven aircraft with a speed of 400 knots or less. Near the end of the war the German Me 262 jet fighter carried 48 such rockets. On one sortie, six Me 262s shot down fourteen B-17s during a daylight raid, without the loss of one fighter aircraft.

After World War II the U.S. fitted many aircraft with 2.75-in. Mighty Mouse and Aeromite rockets. Developed by the navy and later adopted by the air force, the AD (Skyraider), F-80 (Shooting Star), F-86D (Sabre) and F-89D (Scorpion) aircraft were equipped with launchers. Firing could be singly or in clusters. Another postwar development by the U.S. was a version of the army's 5-in., spin-stabilized rocket loaded by belt and fired from within the wing of the Skyraider.

Other countries fitted airborne rockets to aircraft for air-to-air weapons, notably Sweden (Gerda, 3 in., 15.5 lb.), Italy (2.4 in., 7.9 lb.) and Switzerland (3.15 in., 22 lb.).

Air-to-Air Guided Missiles.—As in the case of other guided missiles, Germany led in the development of the air-to-air category, although similarly, the weapon—called the X-4—never reached operational use. An ingenious design, the X-4 was 6.5 ft. long, 8.6 in. in diameter and weighed 132 lb. It had two sets of cruciform wings and fins. Two opposing wings carried pyrotechnic guide flares, and the other two carried streamlined bobbins, which trailed as much as four miles of fine copper wire. Along these wires traveled corrective directional signals which automatically imparted drag to the rear fins while the vehicle, traveling almost 600 m.p.h., spun slowly. The X-4 was powered by a nitric acid-organic fuel rocket motor and carried a 44-lb. warhead.

After World War II the first U.S. air-to-air guided missile was the Firebird. It was 10 ft. long, had a solid-propellant booster, a liquid-propellant sustainer motor, was aimed initially by radar from the launching aircraft and homed on the target, guided by an on-board radar system. First test-launched in 1947, the Firebird was considered obsolete three years later. It was replaced by more sophisticated, supersonic missiles, such as the Sparrow, Falcon and Sidewinder.

The Soviets have displayed at least four air-to-air missiles, Alkali, Ash, Atoll and Awl. The last named is the largest of the group, being over 14 ft. long and with a 9 in. body diameter. It is believed to use solid-fuel propulsion. The missile has been shown mounted on the Flipper MIG fighter aircraft. Similarly, the British developed the 14-ft. Red Dean with a range of 5 mi. which was canceled in 1957 in favour of the Firestreak and Red Top missiles, which had infrared homing guidance. Fired from a pursuit course, these missiles tracked the hot exhaust gases of the target plane and literally flew into its tail. By the late 1960s air-to-air guided missiles had achieved velocities of Mach 3 at ranges of more than 10 mi. Such improvements were necessary to keep pace with supersonic aircraft.

5. Space-Launch Vehicles.—After World War II the heritage of German rocket technology and postwar ballistic missile developments provided the technical basis to orbit an earth satellite.

Although various programs and technically feasible schemes were devised for satellite launchings before 1955, there was no national program until those of the U.S. and U.S.S.R. were announced in connection with the approaching International Geophysical Year (IGY) in 1957–59.

The U.S.S.R. launched the world's first two earth satellites, Sputnik 1 (184-lb. payload) on Oct. 4, 1957, and Sputnik 2 (1,120-lb. payload) on Nov. 3, 1957. The launch vehicles for these satellites were based upon an ICBM vehicle much larger than the U.S. Atlas ICBM.

The U.S.S.R. space-launch vehicles to accomplish these and subsequent manned missions were shrouded in secrecy until the summer of 1967 when the Vostok launch vehicle was placed on display. At that time the Soviets displayed a $2\frac{1}{2}$-stage booster utilizing five four-chambered clusters of four motors each. The four booster pods (16 engines) drop away at staging. Propellants were liquid oxygen and kerosene. Total take-off thrust was estimated at 1,000,000 lb. Purported to be the launch vehicle for 1961 manned spacecraft, this booster is a more powerful version of the original U.S.S.R. ICBM. The first application of this booster to space flight was to use the parallel-staged vehicle without upper stages to put the early Sputniks into orbit, a program which culminated in the flight of Sputnik 3, weighing 2,925 lb., on May 15, 1958.

The same vehicle with an upper stage added was also used to furnish the necessary velocity to permit a payload to escape from the earth's gravitational field, the earliest application being flights of the unmanned Luna 1, Luna 2 and Luna 3 probes to the moon in 1959. The most dramatic event of these flights was the photographing by the 614-lb. Luna 3 of the hitherto hidden face of the moon (*q.v.*). The upper stage used for lunar work was also used with the same booster to power into earth orbit the heavier payloads needed to support the Soviet manned space flight program. After some preliminary flights were made using dogs in 1960 and 1961, Maj. Yuri Gagarin became the first man in space in the 10,419-lb. Vostok 1, launched on April 12, 1961.

Soviet launches of probes to Mars and Venus used a parking-orbit technique rather than the simpler but less efficient direct-ascent trajectories of the early Luna probes. For the interplanetary flights the Vostok booster was used with a more powerful third stage to place a 14,500-lb. payload and fourth-stage combination into a low earth orbit. After less than a single orbit, the fourth stage was ignited so as to power the probe into its deep space trajectory. In addition to the Mars and Venus probes, this system has been used for Zond deep space sounders, for all lunar probes after Luna 3, and probably for the Molniya communication satellites.

The Voskhod spacecraft was somewhat heavier than the Vostoks, and to boost them the basic Vostok booster was used once more, but with a larger third stage, probably little different from the third stage of the interplanetary launch vehicle mentioned above.

In 1965 the U.S.S.R. put the first of three Proton satellites weighing 27,000 lb. into earth orbit, and claimed the launch vehicle had an "installed power" of about 60,000,000 "horsepower." While the term is technically meaningless for a rocket engine, the figure given is three times the horsepower value the Soviets announced for the Vostok booster. This suggests that the Proton satellites were powered into orbit by a new launch vehicle about three times as large as the Vostok booster, with perhaps a sea-level thrust of about 3,000,000 lb.

The U.S. launched its early small satellites with two different vehicles, the Jupiter-C and Vanguard. Jupiter-C was a modified Redstone liquid-propellant ballistic weapon of medium range to which was added additional tankage length and three upper stages of clustered solid-propellant rockets. The modification was originally designed to achieve 20,000 ft./sec. velocity to test an ablating nose cone for the Jupiter IRBM under development by

(LEFT) BY COURTESY OF NASA; (RIGHT) PHOTOGRAPH, AVIATION WEEK & SPACE TECHNOLOGY

LIQUID-PROPELLANT ROCKET MOTORS

(Left) Thrust chambers of the U.S. F-1 rocket engine, which uses liquid oxygen and kerosene. Used in clusters of five generating a total of 7,500,000 lb. of thrust, the engines were designed to power the first stage of the launch vehicle that may send three astronauts to the moon. (Right) Rocket engine cluster of the U.S.S.R.'s Vostok launch vehicle. Each unit has four rocket motors and two smaller vernier rocket motors, which are used for yaw, pitch, and roll control, except for the core power plant, which has four vernier rocket motors

the army. This was accomplished by two upper stages: one a cluster of four Baby Sergeant solid-propellant rockets and the other a single Baby Sergeant. Each Baby Sergeant developed 1,800-lb. thrust for 6.5 sec. Since the solid rockets were unguided, the upper stages were subject to course deviation induced by variation in individual motor thrust, duration of burning, and possibly off-axial thrust and non-simultaneity of ignition. These potential errors were eliminated by spinning the cluster in a tub-mount prior to launching. The re-entry vehicle tests were successful. It was obvious that by increasing the final velocity 5,000 ft./sec. to the required 25,000 ft./sec., earth satellite velocity could be obtained for a small scientific payload. This was accomplished by adding an additional cluster of Baby Sergeant rockets so that the upper stages were 11, 3 and finally one rocket carrying a payload weighing 18.1 lb. Late in 1954 the Army Ballistic Missile agency and the Office of Naval Research jointly proposed this scheme, known as Project Orbiter, to launch a satellite, but for various political reasons a newly designed Vanguard launch vehicle was selected. Failures in early attempts to launch Vanguard, however, resulted two and one-half years later in eventual approval of using the Project Orbiter approach. Thus the first U.S. satellite was launched Jan. 31, 1958, by a Jupiter-C.

By 1961 the U.S.S.R. had orbited and recovered a satellite containing dogs, a dummy-manned spacecraft, and on April 12, 1961, a spacecraft carrying Gagarin. The U.S. was well underway with the Mercury manned-spacecraft program and launched Comdr. Alan B. Shepard, Jr., U.S.N., into sub-orbital, ballistic flight (Redstone booster) on May 5, 1961, and Col. John H. Glenn, Jr., U.S.M.C., into satellite flight (Atlas booster) on Feb. 20, 1962; Glenn was recovered after three orbits.

The Vanguard launch vehicle was a three-stage booster approximately equal in length (about 72 ft.) to the Jupiter-C but much lighter in take-off weight (22,600 lb. compared to 64,000 lb.). The first-stage thrust of Vanguard was 28,000 lb. compared with Jupiter-C's 83,000 lb. Whereas the Jupiter-C burned liquid oxygen and hydrazine-base fuel, the Vanguard burned liquid oxygen and kerosene. The second stage of Vanguard developed 7,600-lb. thrust and burned nitric acid and hydrazine. Propellant supply was pressure fed. The third stage was solid propellant and developed 2,600 lb. of thrust. Vanguard launched its first satellite (3.4 lb.) into high orbit on March 17, 1958. After a few more flights the Jupiter-C was retired in 1958 and the Vanguard in 1959. By then a Jupiter IRBM (Juno II) utilizing a 165,000-lb. thrust take-off engine and the spinning rocket cluster and Thor IRBM-based launch vehicles were in use.

By the mid-1960s the U.S. National Aeronautics and Space ad-

ministration (NASA) was spending more than $5,000,000,000 a year. The U.S. had launched space probes to the moon, Venus, Mars and into solar orbit. Satellites were placed in earth orbit for communications relay, weather observation, navigation, geophysical research and photographic reconnaissance. In addition, two U.S. astronauts had spent two weeks in orbit, and others had spent time outside the spacecraft and rendezvoused with other orbiting spacecraft. By 1968 the major U.S. space effort was Project Apollo, aimed at landing two men on the moon.

The U.S. launch vehicles to accomplish these feats were based both upon military developments as well as totally new launch vehicles. The most significant military-based vehicles were those utilizing the Thor IRBM, the Atlas ICBM and the Titan II as first stages. Both the Thor and Atlas were obsolete as ballistic missiles by 1965; but because of overall reliability approaching 95%, these vehicles were heavily used as space flight launchers. The basic Thor booster burned liquid oxygen and kerosene, developing 150,000 lb. (later, 165,000 lb.) thrust at lift-off. The nuclear warhead was replaced by an adapter section which supported the second stage. Three Thor-based space-launch vehicles were used. The Thor-Able utilized the second and third Vanguard stages and sometimes a fourth, or "kick," stage. Now obsolete, it had a 300 mi. orbital capacity of about 350 lb. The Thor-Delta is an uprated version of Thor-Able capable of orbiting 500 lb. at from 300 to 500 mi. altitude. The Thor-Agena utilizes a second stage, 15,000-lb.-thrust, turbopumped, acid-hydrazine motor and is capable of doubling the Thor-Delta payload. The Agena engine is capable of multiple starts, permitting the use of "parking orbit" launch techniques. A special Thrust-Augmented Thor (TAT) version of the Thor booster uses three "strap-on" solid-propellant rockets to increase take-off thrust.

The Atlas, retired from ICBM service, continued to serve as a reliable space launcher, using an Agena as an upper stage. Orbiting capability is about 5,800 lb. to about 350-mi. orbit. The Centaur utilizes an Atlas booster and a liquid oxygen-liquid hydrogen upper stage powered by two turbopump-fed, 15,000-lb.-thrust engines. Orbiting capability of Centaur is 8,500 lb. at 350 mi. or 2,300 lb. to escape velocity. It was the first space launcher to use oxygen and hydrogen propellants recognized many years earlier by Tsiolkovski and Goddard as nearly ultimate for chemical propulsion.

The two-stage Titan II was the basic launch vehicle for the Gemini manned-spacecraft program. These two-man capsules weighed about 7,500 lb. and orbited at an average altitude of about 150 mi. By 1968 several flights had been made by the air force Titan III C. This launch vehicle is a modification of the Titan II, employing two ten-foot diameter solid-propellant booster rockets strapped to the first stage. Each booster rocket delivers about 1,000,000 lb. thrust and is segmented to permit a choice of burning time and thus payload variation. The Titan III C is designed to launch two-man, orbiting laboratories (MOL) for research purposes and for other military requirements. The orbiting capability of the Titan III C is about 25,000 lb. into low (125 mi.) earth orbit.

The Saturn series completes the U.S. family of space-launch vehicles. The Saturn I program had its beginnings in 1958 with the recognition of a need for more powerful space-launch vehicles. The U.S.S.R. had nearly a decade earlier decided to build a ballistic missile capable of carrying the early nuclear fission-type

BY COURTESY OF (LEFT) NASA, (TOP) SPACE PUBLICATIONS INC.; PHOTOGRAPHS, (RIGHT)
UPI COMPIX, (BOTTOM) AVIATION WEEK & SPACE TECHNOLOGY

SPACE-LAUNCH VEHICLES

(Left) U.S. Saturn V Apollo liquid-propellant launch vehicle. (Above) Soviet Vostok liquid-propellant launch vehicle on display. (Right) Atlas D
rocket launching U.S. astronaut L. Gordon Cooper, Jr., into orbit May 15,
1963. (Below) Scrag, a three-stage, liquid-propellant ICBM launch vehicle
on view in Moscow

warhead to intercontinental range. By the time the lighter weight thermonuclear warheads had been developed there was no longer a need for such a large ICBM but the vehicle was ideal for launching heavy payloads into space. With a lift-off thrust capability perhaps triple that of the U.S. Atlas launch vehicle, the U.S.S.R. had a significant head start on what was to become a space race. Although there was no definitive program, the U.S. in 1958 commenced a two-pronged development of larger launch vehicles. One approach was the Saturn I which utilized a cluster of eight uprated standard H-1 rocket engines used in the Thor, Jupiter and Atlas. Total thrust was 1,504,000 lb. The other approach was to commence development of the F-1, 1,500,000-lb.-thrust, single engine, also using conventional liquid oxygen and kerosene.

The Saturn program was managed by Wernher von Braun, a naturalized U.S. citizen, former technical director of Peenemünde. Saturn I performed successfully in ten out of ten launches by 1965.

In May 1961 President Kennedy committed the U.S., as a national goal, to Project Apollo, aimed at landing a man on the moon by the end of the decade. The launch vehicle, Saturn V, would launch the three-man spacecraft to lunar orbit. From this orbit two astronauts would descend to the lunar surface, remain for perhaps 24 hours and take off to rendezvous in lunar orbit, then return to earth. Saturn V required 7,500,000 lb. take-off thrust.

The Saturn V is a three-stage vehicle, composed of the S-IC, S-II and S-IVB stages. Total height is about 365 ft. and weight more than 6,000,000 lb. at take-off. It is capable of orbiting 280,000 lb. or sending about 95,000 lb. to lunar orbit.

The S-IC first stage is 138 ft. long and 33 ft. in diameter. Dry weight is 280,000 lb. and propellant tank capacity is 4,400,000 lb. Both the liquid-oxygen and kerosene tanks have baffles to reduce sloshing. Five F-1 engines are clustered to provide 7,500,000-lb. thrust. Four of the engines are mounted on a 364-in.-diameter ring and gimbaled for control purposes. The fifth engine is mounted in the centre. These five engines consume propellants

at the rate of 15 tons/sec. Burning time is 2½ min.

The S-II second stage is 81½ ft. high, has a 33-ft. diameter, and weighs 80,000 lb. empty and 1,025,000 lb. loaded with liquid oxygen and liquid hydrogen propellants. It is powered by five 200,000-lb.-thrust J-2 engines. The liquid-oxygen tank contains 93,750 gal. while the (low density) hydrogen tank contains 288,750 gal. Duration of burn is 6 min. 40 sec.

The Saturn-IVB third stage is about 60 ft. long, 22 ft. in diameter, and carries 230,000 lb. of usable liquid oxygen and liquid hydrogen propellants. It is powered by a single J-2 engine. Above the S-IVB stage is the instrument unit (IU), which contains the on-board guidance and control systems. The IU is 21.7 ft. in diameter, 3 ft. long, and weighs about 4,000 lb. Six major measuring and control systems are contained in this unit: structural, environmental control, guidance and control, measuring and telemetry, radio frequency and electrical. Signal processing, high-speed digital computations, and corrective measures are rapid and completely automatic.

During the development of the Saturn V, an interim space launch vehicle, Saturn IB, was utilized. It is a two-stage vehicle composed of an uprated S-I booster and an S-IVB second stage. The clustered booster engine performance has been increased to 200,000-lb. thrust, giving a take-off thrust of the eight engines of 1,600,000 lb. In addition, improvement in design eliminated 16,000 lb. of structural weight, bringing the dry-weight of the Saturn IB to 85,000 lb.

The purpose of the interim Saturn IB vehicle was to provide launch capability for earth orbital missions necessary for Apollo spacecraft development and astronaut training. The launcher has the capability of orbiting 36,000 lb. compared with 22,000 lb. with the S-I. The S-IB/Centaur can boost 14,000 lb. to escape velocity.

The Apollo spacecraft consists of three modules: command, service, and lunar. The command module is the spacecraft's control centre and houses the three-man crew of astronauts. It is conical in shape, 12 ft. high and 13 ft. in diameter, and weighs 10,000 lb. A launch escape system, a towerlike structure above the command module, provides power to lift the command module up and away from the Saturn launch vehicle should an emergency occur after fueling and before injection into orbit. Solid-propellant rockets provide this standby emergency power.

Below the command module is the service module. It is 12.8 ft. in diameter, 22 ft. long, and houses the propulsion system for mid-course correction, retrofire to achieve lunar orbit, and thrust to return from lunar orbit into earth trajectory. The pressure-fed rocket engine develops 22,000-lb. thrust, is ablative-cooled, and uses nitrogen tetroxide and hydrazine-type fuel.

Between the service module and Saturn V is the lunar excursion module (LEM) adapter. This unit is 29 ft. long and 21.7 ft. in diameter where it joins the S-IVB stage and tapers to 13 ft. where it joins the service module. The LEM housed in this section is designed to carry two astronauts from lunar orbit to the surface of the moon and return. It is approximately 21 ft. high and 11 ft. in diameter, weighing 30,000 lb. (earth weight). There are two engines, one with controllable thrust for descent to the surface of the moon and the other with a fixed 35,000-lb. thrust for ascent to rendezvous with the command module in lunar orbit. Both engines are pressure-fed, ablative-cooled and use the same propellants as the service module engine.

The Saturn V met with success in its first test flight in November 1967. It launched an unmanned Apollo spacecraft into a low orbit for three hours, after which the engine of the rocket's third stage was fired; this lifted that stage and the attached Apollo to an altitude of more than 11,000 mi. The second test, in April 1968, was not as successful, however. Two engines in the second stage shut down prematurely, causing the rocket to go into a different orbit than originally planned. In addition, the third-stage engine of the Saturn V failed to reignite and, therefore, did not propel that stage and the attached Apollo into deep space.

Thus, by 1968, the Saturn V was the largest space-launch vehicle in the U.S. program. Post-Apollo program planning, in fact, included studies of strap-on solid-propellant boosters similar to the Titan III design.

Aside from the U.S. and U.S.S.R. programs, three other space-launch vehicle programs exist: the European Launcher Development organization (ELDO), and those of France and Japan.

ELDO's first launcher, ELDO-A, is a three-stage vehicle. The first stage, built by Great Britain, developed from the canceled Blue Streak IRBM. Two 150,000-lb.-thrust, liquid oxygen-kerosene engines, based upon the U.S. H-1 are used. The second stage, built by France, uses a 61,700-lb.-thrust, nitrogen tetroxide-hydrazine engine. West Germany's third stage develops 5,100-lb. thrust with the same propellants as the second stage. The ELDO-A is capable of orbiting about 1,100 lb.

France, in developing ballistic missile capability, produced the Diamant-I space booster. The first stage is powered by a liquid-propellant (nitric acid-turpentine) engine which develops about 62,000 lb. of thrust. Two solid-propellant upper stages develop 32,000- and up to about 12,000-lb. thrust. Orbiting capability of the Diamant-I is about 175 lb. France became the third nation to launch satellites independently (on Nov. 26, 1965, and again on Feb. 17, 1966).

By the late 1950s Japan had embarked upon an orderly program of developing solid-propellant sounding rockets. A modest satellite launch vehicle program is under development. Utilizing solid propellant, the Mu-4 booster is four-staged and is about the size of the U.S. Minuteman.

A final class of space-launch vehicles is that in which small payloads can be launched from above the earth's surface. Both aircraft and balloons have been tried experimentally by the U.S. Potential advantages of such systems are the lower air density of high altitudes, mobility, and, in the case of aircraft, initial launch velocity. One such program was Far Side. Six attempts were made in 1957 of this four-stage solid-propellant vehicle carried to 75,000 ft. prior to launch. Payloads of 3–5 lb. were launched to altitudes of 2,000 to 4,000 mi. but orbital performance was not achieved. In the Caleb program, a four-stage solid-propellant launch vehicle was fired from an F4D airplane flying

at nearly 500 m.p.h. at an altitude of 25,000 ft. By this technique, 15-lb. payloads can be placed in earth orbit. Although a series of test firings had been made in flight, no satellite launch attempts had been made by 1968.

6. Drones, Decoys and Test Vehicles.—This category contains a variety of special-purpose vehicles closely related to guided-missile systems.

Drones.—A drone is basically a pilotless aircraft, usually under radio-command guidance and widely employed as a target for anti-aircraft weapons. Powered by propeller-driven, turbojet, ramjet or rocket engines, a large number of these maneuverable vehicles have been developed operating at velocities as high as Mach 2.

TABLE VI.—*Drones*

Country	Designation	Mission	Propulsion
Australia	Jindivik	Target	Turbojet
Belgium	Epervier	Reconnaissance	Ducted propeller
Canada	CL-89	Reconnaissance	Booster rocket, turbojet
France	CT-20	Target	Booster rocket, turbojet
France	CT-41	Target	Booster rocket, ramjet
France	R-20	Reconnaissance	Booster rocket, turbojet
Italy	P. 1/R	Reconnaissance	Booster rocket, propeller
Japan	KAQ-5	Target	Rocket, solid
U.S.	AQM-37A	Target	Rocket, liquid
U.S.	Firebee	Target	Rocket boost, turbojet
U.S.	MQM-42A	Target	Rocket boost, ramjet
U.S.	MQM-57A	Reconnaissance	Propeller
U.S.	MQM-61A	Target	Propeller
U.S.	QH-50	Antisubmarine	Helicopter, turbine
U.S.	RP-76-4	Target	Rocket, solid
U.S.	Whirlymite	Target	Helicopter, turbine

Recovery, if the drone is not destroyed, is effected by controlled landing or by parachute. Another application of drones is for military reconnaissance. Equipped with either photographic or television cameras, the drone may be shifted from radio control to present inertial guidance and flown over targets at a relatively low speed and low altitude under operationally hazardous conditions.

Decoys.—The decoy is a device designed to simulate by electromagnetic radiation an aircraft or ballistic-missile warhead. The purpose is to divert defensive antiaircraft or antimissile fire. Thus a relatively small decoy can be made to appear, by electromagnetic techniques, as large as a bomber on radar screens. Or it can emit infrared and other radiation to simulate a reentering ICBM warhead.

For military reasons, details of such devices are not released to the general public.

Test Vehicles.—The term test vehicle covers a variety of special-purpose rockets and missiles designed to produce data on components or design features that will ultimately be used in much more expensive missiles and rockets. They may be scaled-down versions of the eventual rocket or missile. For example, after World War II, many aerodynamic shapes were tested at subsonic and supersonic velocities under dynamic flight conditions by affixing them to the front of solid-propellant rockets. Data were obtained by optical tracking and telemetry. In the development of a satisfactory design for ballistic missile reentry vehicles, a five-stage rocket vehicle carried a scale model of the test shape to high altitudes; the final stage was then fired toward the earth, achieving the reentry velocity of an ICBM. In Project Fire, NASA in a similar manner achieved velocities equivalent to those of a lunar vehicle returning to earth. Another special test vehicle is the Little Joe solid-propellant booster. It was developed to launch the Mercury and (a larger version) the Apollo spacecraft to an altitude at which the parachute recovery system could be tested.

The ingenious design and use of such special-purpose vehicles built from available components can reduce costs significantly, confirm design concepts and save precious months.

7. Guidance and Control.—Most rockets require stabilization of some sort to minimize flight-path deflection caused by wind, nonuniformity of rocket structure, rocket-jet misalignment and other factors. Also, in the case of long-range ballistic missiles or satellite launchers, it is necessary for the rockets to take off vertically, programming a pitch deflection (tilt) at some predetermined altitude and velocity. The techniques used for flight control vary according to type of mission and accuracy requirements. Radio-control or inertial-guidance (stabilized-platform) systems, or both, initiate the correction and deflection signals to the vehicle.

In the case of some barrage-type rockets, launched by the thousands, dispersion errors may be accepted because of overlapping explosive effect in the target area. Aircraft rockets are often stabilized by fixed fins located at the rear of the rocket. Folding fins which open, by inertia, after firing are also used. Short-range bazooka rockets and ballistic rockets of 5-to-10-mi. range are usually fin-stabilized. Spin-stabilization is used on some rockets. In these designs, the rocket nozzle is replaced by a series of smaller nozzles, canted at an angle to impart torque as well as thrust. A unique method of wire control, based upon the German air-to-air X-4 rocket, has been used. This technique is utilized by some antitank rockets of about 1-mi. range. Fine wire is trailed from a pair of bobbins on the fins of the rocket and command signals are given by the operator observing its flight through a telescope.

If the rocket is designed to operate at high altitudes, as in the case of sounding rockets, satellite launchers and ballistic missiles of ranges greater than 100 mi., aerodynamic forces are no longer available for control because of the low density of the air. One technique, employed first by Goddard, is to place carbon or molybdenum deflection vanes within the rocket exhaust. Usually two pairs are employed for corrections about all three axes; one pair for pitch, the other for yaw and, in opposition, for roll. In flight, deviations from flight path are sensed by gyros within an automatic control (autopilot) system, and corrective signals are sent to servomotors which operate the vanes. This deflection system may be used also to program the tilt from vertical launch to ballistic flight path. Radio command may also be used to initiate the tilt program. A modification of the jet vane method is the "jetevator," a ring-shaped deflector mounted at the nozzle periphery which rotates slightly into the edge of the rocket jet as required. Gimbal mounting of the engine, permitting the motor to swivel a few degrees in any direction, is widely used for flight-path control. This system was developed for the U.S. Viking and has been used successfully on IRBM's and ICBM's. Injection of high-pressure gas in the rocket nozzle to create a local shock wave and differential pressure is a further technique of jet deflection in use. Magnetohydrodynamic (MHD) deflection of a rocket jet is another possible flight-control concept. Since a rocket jet may be highly ionized it is conceivable that a magnetic field may induce deflection of the exhaust gases without physical contact.

Roll control (*i.e.*, rotation about the long axis) is sometimes required, particularly on larger ballistic missiles. Small jets mounted transversely on the side of the missile are commonly used for this purpose.

8. Rocket and Missile Warheads.—Rocket and missile warheads are conveniently divided into three categories: (1) high-explosive; (2) nuclear (or atomic); and (3) special-purpose. The first of these is generally employed on short-range, tactical weapons. While it is possible to design such warheads to produce damage by either concussion (blast) or fragmentation, most depend upon some form of fragmentation. The efficiency of high-explosive warheads is a function of the size, number, weight and velocity of the fragments produced, and the reliability of the warhead is largely a function of its fuzing system. The spray pattern of the fragments is also important and is established by the geometry of the high-explosive charge and the arrangement of the fragments upon it. Nonfragmenting, high-explosive warheads for antitank weapons usually incorporate the shaped charge to achieve maximum penetration by concentrating the blast at one point. Nuclear warheads are used primarily, but not exclusively, on the IRBM's and ICBM's since it would be uneconomical and inefficient to use high-explosive heads on these long-range missiles. Typical of such missiles are the U.S. Thor, Titan, Atlas, Minute-

man and Polaris. Very long-range air-to-surface missiles, particularly the so-called standoff bombs, and some air-to-air missiles as well as certain short-range tactical or battlefield rockets and missiles also can employ nuclear warheads. The nuclear warheads may be either fission or fusion types; in the latter case they are called, popularly, H weapons. The power of nuclear warheads is indicated by comparing the release of energy of a certain weapon to an equivalent weight of TNT. Thus a 10-kiloton warhead or bomb has the same explosive force as 10,000 tons of TNT; a 5-megaton device has the force of 5,000,000 tons of TNT.

Special-purpose warheads can be used on a wide variety of guided missiles and large rockets. There are two types, chemical and biological. Chemical warheads include a number of different weapons categorized by the effect of their filler agent on the target. Incendiary types start fires; poison-gas types kill or incapacitate personnel. Biological warheads contain bacteria or other pathogens that attack human beings, animals or plants on a short- or long-term basis.

IV. FUNDAMENTAL PRINCIPLES OF ROCKET PROPULSION

Jet propulsion—of which the rocket is one type—is based upon reaction of a body to the rearward thrust of a jet of gas. The physical principle involved was set forth in Newton's *Principia Mathematica* published in 1687. In this work are stated three laws of motion. The third law states, in its simplest form, that for every action there is an equal and opposite reaction.

A simple example of reaction propulsion is the brief flight of a toy balloon after it has been filled with air and released. The forward motion of the balloon results from the rearward expulsion of air from the balloon. The thrust does not result, as sometimes erroneously presumed, from the jet pushing against the surrounding air. The force imparted by the jet is equivalent to the product of the mass flow of the air and the velocity of the jet. In the case of a chemical-propellant rocket, the jet is composed of the gaseous combustion products of the propellant mixture which is burned inside a thrust chamber and ejected at supersonic velocity through a nozzle. The gas velocity in a properly designed converging-diverging nozzle is sonic at the throat (most narrow) portion of the nozzle and becomes supersonic as it travels through the diverging (exhaust) end of the nozzle.

In mathematical terms, the propulsive force derives from the momentum of the gas and is expressed as

$$F = \frac{\dot{W}}{g} \times V_e \qquad (1)$$

where F represents thrust in pounds, $\dot{W}$ the propellant flow rate, in pounds per second, g the acceleration of gravity in feet per second per second and V_e the nozzle exhaust velocity in feet per second. More precisely, another term must be added.

$$F = \frac{\dot{W}}{g} \times V_e + (P_e - P_o) A_e \qquad (2)$$

where P_e is the exit pressure, P_o ambient pressure and A_e the nozzle exit area. Since P_o would be equal to zero in a perfect vacuum, it may be seen that rocket engine performance increases with altitude. Thrust ratings of upper-stage rocket engines are often given both at sea level and at operating altitudes; the latter rating is always higher. Effective exhaust velocity c may be expressed

$$c = \frac{Fg}{\dot{W}} = V_e + \frac{P_e - P_o}{\dot{W}} A_e g \qquad (3)$$

Inspection of equation (1) shows that thrust can be increased by increasing the jet velocity and/or the mass flow of propellant gases. Jet velocity is related to the heat of combustion of the particular propellants burned. This is expressed

$$V_e = \sqrt{2g J \Delta H} \qquad (4)$$

in which J is Joule's mechanical equivalent of heat (778 ft.-lb. per B.T.U.) and ΔH is the thermochemical energy of the propellant in B.T.U. per pound.

Limitations on mass flow of propellant gases arise from such design considerations as maximum temperatures and pressures feasible within permissible engine weights.

Since the kinetic energy in a rocket jet is derived from conversion of the chemical energy of combustion to directed kinetic energy, high thermochemical energy per unit weight of propellant is desired. In practice, the kinetic energy of the rocket exhaust jet may be only 40% to 70% of the theoretical heat energy from combustion of the propellant. Minor losses arise from incomplete combustion and heat lost to the thrust chamber walls. Larger efficiency losses come from unavailable thermal energy which leaves the exhaust nozzle as residual enthalpy.

An important rocket term is specific impulse, I_{sp}, which is the thrust per pound per second of propellant burned

$$I_{sp} = \frac{F}{\dot{W}} \quad \frac{\text{lb.}}{\text{lb./sec.}} \tag{5}$$

Similarly, from equation (3),

$$I_{sp} = \frac{c}{g} \quad \frac{\text{ft./sec.}}{\text{ft./sec.}^2} \tag{6}$$

Since the lb. and ft. units cancel out, I_{sp} is given in units of seconds. Specific impulse is related to the energy content of combustion in the following general equation

$$I_{sp} = \sqrt{\frac{2J}{g}(h_c - h_e)} \tag{7}$$

where h_c is the enthalpy of combustion products before expansion (B.T.U. per pound), h_e is the enthalpy of combustion products after expansion (expansion at constant entropy and chemical equilibrium maintained). Calculations performed with equation (7) are called shifting equilibrium calculations.

A more convenient expression, generally accurate to within a few per cent, assumes that specific heat of the gas is constant and utilizes ideal gas relationships; i.e., frozen composition calculation

$$I_{sp} = \sqrt{\frac{2R}{g} \cdot \frac{k}{k-1} \cdot \frac{T_c}{M} \left[1 - \left(\frac{P_e}{P_c}\right)^{\frac{k-1}{k}}\right]} \tag{8}$$

where R is the universal gas constant (foot-pounds per °R. per mole), k is the ratio of specific heats C_p/C_v, T_c is the combustion chamber temperature (°R.), M is the average molecular weight of the combustion products (pounds per mole), P_e is the pressure of the gas at the exit plane of the nozzle (pounds per square inch absolute), P_c is the combustion chamber pressure. This relationship is for a fully expanded exhaust nozzle; i.e., P_e = ambient pressure. From inspection of equation (8) it may be seen that specific impulse is increased by increased chamber pressure and combustion chamber temperature and lowering of molecular weight of exhaust gases.

As a rocket-powered vehicle moves, the weight (mass) of the vehicle continuously decreases as the propellant is consumed and disappears to the rear as exhaust jet. The velocity of a rocket vehicle may be calculated approximately

$$V = c \log_e \frac{M_i}{M_f} \tag{9}$$

where c is effective exhaust velocity, M_i is initial mass and M_f is final mass, after all propellants have been burned. The expression M_i/M_f is known as the mass ratio. The true velocity will be somewhat less in practice due to air drag and energy lost in overcoming gravity. In the design of efficient long-range rockets every effort is made to reduce structural weight to a minimum and increase to a maximum the percentage weight of the propellant. In the case of the V-2, 69% of the takeoff weight was propellants. Modern lower-stage boosters have values as high as 94%. Takeoff acceleration may vary from several g's to a few tenths of a g in large rockets taking off vertically.

The final velocity of a rocket-powered vehicle can be increased, theoretically, to any desired value by the technique of staging; i.e., setting a series of rockets one on top of the other and firing

them successively. Thus each successive stage is smaller and commences firing at a higher initial velocity. In practice, however, the complications of duplicating mechanical items, cost and reduction in reliability set a practical limit to the number of stages that are employed.

An example of the benefit of staging may be obtained from the Bumper-WAC program conducted in the U.S. in 1948–50. A WAC Corporal rocket, placed on top of the V-2, was fired after burnout of the V-2. Whereas a V-2 alone achieves a maximum altitude of about 100 mi. and a maximum velocity of 3,500 m.p.h., the Bumper-WAC sent the WAC Corporal to a velocity of 5,000 m.p.h and a peak altitude of 250 mi. Although 1,500-mi. IRBM's can achieve the necessary velocity to reach these distances with one stage (Jupiter, Thor), ICBM's are multistaged. Likewise, satellite launching vehicles that must reach speeds of at least 18,000 m.p.h. are multistaged (Thor-Delta, Saturn 1). For lunar and interplanetary flights a minimum escape velocity of 25,000 m.p.h. must be achieved.

The efficiency of a rocket-propelled vehicle increases from zero at rest to a maximum when the velocity of the jet is reached. Thus rocket systems are inefficient at low speeds.

V. ROCKET-PROPULSION SYSTEMS

A rocket-motor or thrust-chamber assembly is composed of a combustion chamber and nozzle. The injector head is considered a part of the combustion chamber in the case of a liquid-propellant motor. The term rocket engine (liquid propellant only) refers to the motor plus associated propellant and feed system, propellant lines, valves, regulators, mounting lugs, igniter, etc. A rocket power plant refers to the complete propulsion system, including propellant tankage, pressurizing system, gimbal mounting (or jetevators, vanes, etc.), tankage-level sensing devices and associated computers, etc.

The best-known rocket motors burn chemical propellants, either solid or liquid. Combustion of the propellants provides the hot gas which is exhausted in a jet through a nozzle to the rear. Other types of rocket motors employ hybrid systems (liquid propellant burned in a solid-propellant core) and air-turborockets which utilize some ram air for part of the combustion process. Two nonchemical types of rocket propulsion systems are nuclear and electrical. These systems have received serious attention only since World War II and have particular application for space flight missions.

1. Solid-Propellant Rocket Motors.—The outstanding feature of solid-propellant motors is their relative simplicity in design. All of the propellant is contained in the combustion (or thrust) chamber, usually cylindrical, to which is attached an exhaust nozzle. An electrical or pyrotechnic igniter fires the propellant charge.

Major advantages of solid rockets lie in their condition of readiness and the reliability that results from simplicity. Disadvantages arise from a somewhat lower specific impulse range at sea level (I_{sp} of 175–250 sec.) compared with liquid-propellant motors (I_{sp} of 230–270 sec.), performance variation caused by storage temperature, and heavier rocket casing to contain combustion gases at a typical 1,000 lb. per square inch (p.s.i.) pressure.

The design configuration and chemical composition of solid-propellant charges vary widely. The charge (or grain) may burn from one end only, cigarette fashion. Or, the grain may be a hollow cylinder or have a star-shaped, interior burning surface. Important parameters of solid-propellant charge design are surface area and burning rate of particular propellant mixtures.

2. Liquid-Propellant Rocket Motors.—In this class of rocket motors, the liquid combustibles are contained in tanks and fed into the thrust chamber through an injector head by a propellant supply system. Most liquid-propellant rockets use two combustibles (bipropellant system) such as liquid oxygen and kerosene. Monopropellant systems which depend upon exothermic decomposition of a substance, such as high-strength (90%–95%) hydrogen peroxide, also exist. Such systems usually have lower performance ratings but are simpler to design.

3. Combustion Chambers.—As in the case of all components of a rocket vehicle, a premium is placed on reduction of weight to

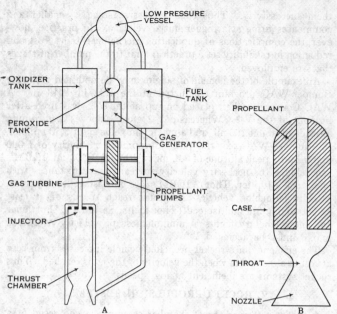

FIG. 2.—TYPICAL DESIGNS OF (A) LIQUID-PROPELLANT, REGENERATIVELY COOLED ROCKET POWER PLANT AND (B) SOLID-PROPELLANT ROCKET MOTOR

Gas pressure from the storage vessel, in a typical liquid-propellant rocket, forces high-strength hydrogen peroxide into the gas generator where a catalyst causes decomposition. Gaseous products (steam and oxygen) drive the turbine wheel which rotates centrifugal propellant pumps. Light gas pressure on propellant tanks prevents cavitation of high-performance pumps. One propellant flows directly to the rocket motor injector head; the other flows through a jacket around the combustion chamber, cooling the motor, and then through the injector. Propellants are sprayed into the combustion chamber where they burn smoothly and uniformly, exhausting in a jet through a supersonic nozzle. The solid propellant contains both the fuel and oxidizer within it. This type burns from the internal axial slot outward to the case. Early designs employed a solid-pack propulsive charge and burned cigarette-fashion from the rear toward the front end

the minimum adequate to perform the necessary function reliably. Combustion chambers are usually made of metal for strength and are cylindrical or bell-shaped in configuration. Thrust chambers for solid-propellant rockets are uncooled. Burning time is usually short and the walls of the chamber are not exposed to high temperature combustion if the grain burns outward from an interior core. In the case of liquid motors, the thrust chamber volume is designed to provide sufficient time for mixing and burning of the propellants before passing through the exhaust nozzle. Closely associated with combustion chamber design for liquid motors are cooling techniques and design criteria for combustion chambers, exhaust nozzles and injectors.

Cooling Techniques.—The wall of a combustion chamber may be uncooled if the duration of operation of the motor is a few seconds only. In such a case the metal wall acts as a heat sponge or sink, absorbing heat for a short time. At least one liquid-propellant booster rocket has been designed to operate for a few seconds with uncooled walls. But liquid rockets operate usually for longer periods of time, 2–5 seconds to 5 or more minutes. To accommodate chamber temperatures of 4,000° to 7,000° F. (2,204.5° to 3,871° C.), a number of techniques have evolved. Molded ceramic liners of low thermal conductivity and high melting point have been used, but such materials are often subject to cracking from high thermal stresses occurring at the start. Another method is film cooling wherein water or a propellant is admitted through holes in the chamber and the liquid flows along the wall and absorbs heat. The most used method is regenerative cooling. In this technique, one of the propellants flows along the outside of the nozzle and thrust chamber wall before it is injected into the motor. The heat which the propellant thus absorbs is not lost but is added to the heat of combustion in the thrust chamber. Design of the cooling flow passages is critical since it is necessary to prevent boiling of the propellant and yet obtain a lightweight structure and low pressure drop. A high pressure drop results in greater design weight and higher pressure flow systems. Because

the heat transfer rates to the walls are greatest in the narrow neck of the nozzle, the coolant flow rate is usually highest at this point.

In the early 1960s a new technique—ablative cooling—was developed, using materials similar to those employed as heat shields for reentering space vehicles. Rocket chamber liners and entire chambers were made of these materials, which absorb and dissipate large amounts of heat as they vaporize, and are lighter than comparable, regeneratively cooled systems. They are also useful when propellant flow rate may be insufficient for regenerative cooling (*e.g.*, low thrust levels) or when neither of the propellants has inherent sufficient cooling capacity to protect the rocket engine from heat damage.

Design Criteria.—In the design of combustion chambers for liquid rockets the following parameters are significant: thrust, pressure and temperature of combustion gases, average molecular weight and ratio of specific heats of products of reacting propellants, velocity of flow of propellants, ratio of chamber volume to throat area, nozzle interior contour or shape, duration of continuous operation and chemical characteristics of propellants.

In the design of exhaust nozzles the combustion gases are expanded nearly isentropically to ambient pressure. In the case of a sounding or ballistic rocket the ambient pressure decreases with altitude. For high altitude or operation in the vacuum of space the diameter of the nozzle exit becomes very large and the construction weight prohibitively high. Thus nozzle design is usually subject to compromise, and certain reductions in efficiency (nozzle losses) are accepted.

The injector head meters the propellants at a predetermined rate and mixture-ratio, and atomizes and combines the mixture within the combustion chamber so that burning takes place smoothly and completely. The pressure drop across the injector must not be too great or an excessive burden is placed upon the propellant supply system and the weight of construction increased unnecessarily. Good injector design reduces to a minimum the volume and length of a combustion chamber. A number of types of injector design have evolved. In the impinging spray type, propellant streams in pairs or clusters are injected to intersect at high velocity so that they break up into small droplets, evaporate and burn. In the showerhead type, a series of concentric rows of holes spray the propellant into the chamber. The rows of sprays may or may not impinge. Sometimes concentric slots are used to produce intersecting conical sheets of propellant sprays.

A German (*Enzian*) design utilized a splash plate within the thrust chamber on which liquid-propellant streams played. Good mixing is obtained in this design but hot spots may occur on the splash plate. Premix injectors have been tried wherein mixing is accomplished just prior to injection into the thrust chamber. Since rocket propellants by their nature are high-energy substances, this type of design is subject to explosion. Swirl-type sprays are another approach to injection configuration. Shop producibility, critical tolerances and cost enter into injector head considerations and some compromises in performances are usually accepted.

Often related to injector head dynamics is the phenomenon of oscillatory combustion instability in the combustion chamber. Often exhibiting audible effects of chugging and screaming, these high-speed pressure differentials can destroy a rocket motor in a few seconds. Because the mixture ratios of different propellants vary widely, a rocket motor is tailored for specific propellants and it is not generally possible to operate an engine efficiently on different propellants than those for which it was designed.

Valves for rocket engines offer design problems from the nature of the propellants and requirements of high reliability and precise operation. Many rocket flights have aborted because of sticking valves. Valves are usually operated by electric solenoids or are pneumatically and/or hydraulically actuated.

Design of tankage for propellants has evolved in recent years to integral systems wherein the thin wall of the tank is the skin of the rocket vehicle itself. In addition to the weight of the propellant, rocket tankage must withstand some gas pressure head for turbopump systems and several hundred pounds pressure for gas-pressurized propellant supply systems.

4. Propellant Supply Systems.—The simplest method of

forcing liquid propellants into the combustion chamber is by gas pressure. An inert gas is used, such as helium or nitrogen. Because the combustion chamber pressure is usually 300 lb. or more, the pressurizing gas must be higher to overcome frictional losses in propellant lines, valves, thrust chamber cooling jacket and injector head. This high pressure necessitates heavy tanks, affecting adversely the mass ratio of the vehicle. Gas pressurization is a simple and reliable system, however. It was used successfully in the U.S. X-1 supersonic research airplane. In this case liquid nitrogen was converted in a heat exchanger to high-pressure gas. For small vehicles helium gas at several thousand pounds pressure may be used, with operating pressure being reduced through a regulating valve. Another source of pressurizing gas is the reaction of small quantities of the propellants themselves in a special gas generator or even within the propellant tanks. In turbo-pump systems a source of high-velocity gas drives a turbine wheel which, in turn, drives centrifugal pumps between the propellant tanks and the rocket motor. High-strength hydrogen peroxide (95%-98%) is commonly decomposed by a catalyst bed within a gas generator. The decomposition products, oxygen and steam, are led through a nozzle and impinge on the turbine blades.

The propellant pumps are usually centrifugal. They may be located on opposite ends of the turbine shaft or, in cases of large pumps, driven by a gear train. A certain pressure head is necessary to prevent cavitation. This is supplied from a lightweight high-pressure storage bottle through a pressure regulator to the propellant tanks. Other turbopump-drive systems utilize a high-pressure stored gas start cycle and then bleed a portion of one of the pumped propellants to an expansion jet to drive the turbine. This turbine gas exhaust may then be burned in the combustion chamber, utilizing its thermochemical heat content.

Because of the sloshing or floating action of propellants within tanks of a maneuvering vehicle or during restart under conditions of weightlessness, "bladders," or flexible tank liners, may be used as positive expulsion devices to control the discharge of propellants from the tanks. Another technique is the use of small rockets to impart a small acceleration to the next stage at burnout. This force causes the weightless propellants to move to the end of the tank, thus making them available for ignition of the stage rocket engine. These small rockets are known as ullage rockets.

5. Ignition.—Liquid-propellant combinations which ignite spontaneously are called hypergolic. Because ignition rates may be low when propellants such as acid and aniline are sprayed into a cold thrust chamber, a slug of another more highly reactive propellant may be injected initially. Without rapid ignition the accumulation of unburned propellants may build up quickly to a point where chamber pressure limitations are exceeded when combustion does occur, resulting in an explosion. In the case of non-hypergolic propellants, such as liquid oxygen and gasoline, a source of flame, hot wire, spark or pyrotechnic (squib) igniter must be provided. The V-2 used a swastika-shaped, pyrotechnic pin wheel mounted on a light frame within the combustion chamber.

6. Ground Testing.—Many tests are required in the development of a rocket-motor design. The term static test is used to describe rocket-motor operations wherein the motor is bolted to a test stand and fired. Static test stands provide for measurements of thrust, propellant flows and a variety of significant temperatures and pressures. Control is maintained from within a reinforced-concrete bunker or blockhouse. The rocket firing is viewed by means of mirrors or periscopes or at a distance through bullet-proof glass. Closed-circuit television may also be used in the case of large motors. In liquid-motor development, so-called battleship (heavyweight)-propellant tankage is employed and gas pressure often used to force the propellants into the thrust chamber. In initial chamber-design tests water cooling provides a large safety factor over regenerative cooling. Flow measurement tests of injector heads and gas generator and turbine pump development usually proceed separately. Eventually all components are combined for system tests. When missiles are in final stages of development the entire vehicle is mounted in other test stands and fired. These are known as captive tests. The cost of rocket test facilities, with associated plumbing, tankage, propellant storage

and necessary safety provisions of reinforced concrete and large safety distances, is naturally great.

Scaling of successful rocket-motor designs is not simple. The requirements for very large thrust engines for space-flight operations can be met in two ways—manifolding (or clustering) a number of existing engines or designing one new and larger engine. The first technique is simpler. In the United States, the requirement for a rocket engine of more than 1,000,000-lb. thrust was approached by both methods. In the one case, eight 190,000-lb.-thrust engines were specified to be clustered and at the same time a single-barrel engine of 1,500,000-lb. thrust was ordered. The time for completion of the second approach was estimated to be three to four times as long but held promise of eventual higher mass ratio advantages.

7. Nuclear Rockets.—The development of reliable nuclear fission reactors has led to the possibility of utilizing nuclear energy as a source of power for rockets. In this case the energy does not derive from the heat of combustion of a chemical reaction but from fission of nuclear particles. Although the amount of energy potentially available is very much greater, the conversion to kinetic energy in a rocket exhaust jet is more complicated. Two nuclear rocket systems were under study and development in the United States in the mid-1960s. One was the rather audacious notion, suggested shortly after World War II, of obtaining impulse by a series of small nuclear explosions. In theory, these explosions behind a sturdy structure would propel it upward. The more conventional approach to a nuclear rocket is to use the heat of a fission reactor to heat a working fluid and expel the hot gas through a nozzle. Since the nuclear products are in a closed cycle, no radioactive particles are in the exhaust. The most obvious working fluid is low-molecular-weight hydrogen. The working fluid or propellant in this system would not be burned but simply heated and ejected. Some of the major problems associated with the design of a nuclear reactor are related to the design of an efficient heat exchange to transfer heat energy from the reactor to the propellant, cooling the thrust chamber walls, shutdown and restart, and nuclear radiation. The range of specific impulse (*i.e.*, pounds thrust per pound per second of propellant flow) achievable with nuclear rockets is estimated in the order of 700–1,000 sec. Chemical propellants have a limitation of about 430 sec. at sea level.

8. Electrical-Propulsion Systems.—Whereas chemical-propellant rockets are characterized by high thrust for short durations, a number of electrical systems have been proposed which would yield a low thrust over a long period of time. Specific impulses of such systems range from about 1,000 to 10,000 sec. and more. Several approaches to electrical thrust systems are under development. All such systems, because of low thrust, must be carried to a low-altitude orbit. From this orbit these devices will operate in pulsed fashion or continuously for weeks, months or even years in the case of distant interplanetary flight. Electric power to operate these thrust devices would be obtained from direct conversion of solar energy (solar batteries) or from nuclear electrical generators, as in a plasma thermocouple. Specific impulses of 1,500 to 5,000 sec. are optimum for space missions from low-altitude Earth-satellite orbit to lunar orbits. In unmanned space journeys, such as placement of communications satellites in the 24-hour, stationary orbit (22,300 mi.), additional flight time (of extra days) is not necessarily important. The advantages of using electrical propulsion of 1,500 to 5,000 sec. are, however, truly significant. Earth take-off weights may be reduced as much as one-half from the weight using chemical rocket propulsion throughout. In the particular case of a communications satellite payload, which could utilize the electrical power supply of the propulsion system, earth take-off weight might be reduced to one-third.

Among the electrical thrust devices under development is the electrothermal arc jet. This device utilizes an electric arc to heat the propellant, or working fluid, which is expelled through a rocket nozzle to the rear. Another device under development accelerates the plasma, produced by the electric arc, by means of a magnetic field. Still other electric thrust devices operate in a pulsed fashion and utilize magnetohydrodynamics (MHD) to accelerate high-temperature gases, as in the MHD shock tube.

Best known of the electrical thrust devices is the ion rocket. In this system electrostatic fields rather than electromagnetic fields are used to accelerate dust particles or positively charged ions such as metallic cesium. Specific impulse ranges of this device are estimated at 5,000 to 100,000 sec. Of even higher specific impulse is the photon rocket—wholly theoretical—wherein energy is converted to light and expelled as such. The photon rocket system, conceived and elaborated by Eugen Sänger, is not feasible to construct with currently available materials and techniques because of the extremely high temperatures required.

9. Other Systems.—One final low-thrust device for space propulsion is the so-called hydrogen heater, in which solar energy is concentrated by hemispherical reflectors onto a heat exchanger, which in turn heats hydrogen to a high temperature; the hydrogen is then accelerated through a rocket nozzle to the rear. Although the above low-thrust propulsion programs for space missions appear exotic compared to conventional rocket systems, the inherent advantages of these high-specific-impulse propulsion devices make their development desirable for interplanetary exploration.

VI. ROCKET PROPELLANTS

Rocket propellants, by the chemical process of combustion, provide the hot gases which produce reaction force (thrust) when ejected to the rear. These chemical propellants are divided classically into solid and liquid categories. Some development has been conducted on solid-liquid (hybrid) systems in which one of the propellants is liquid and injected into a solid-propellant combustion chamber. Hybrid motors of 15,000-lb. thrust and many minutes of burning time have been fired in the U.S.

In many space flight propulsion systems such as the nuclear rocket, plasma jet or hydrogen heaters, the propellant is not a combustible but serves as a working fluid, its purpose being to transform heat and other forms of energy into kinetic energy.

1. Solid Propellants.—Various formulations of black powder (gunpowder) were the only source of propellant for rockets until late in the 19th century when nitroglycerin was discovered. Saltpetre was the oxidizer in this mixture, while the sulfur and charcoal served as fuel. This exothermic reaction may be written approximately

$$2KNO_3 + S + 3C \rightarrow K_2S + 3CO_2 + N_2$$
$$+ \text{ 550 cal. per gram of mixture reacting}$$

In a rocket motor black powder yields a specific impulse (I_{sp}) of 50–70 sec., depending upon chamber pressure and formulation (typical, by weight: 75% KNO_3, 15% C and 10% S). The flame temperature of gunpowder is about 1,500°–3,000° F. (815°–1,650° C.) and the mixture burns smoothly even below combustion chamber pressures of 100 p.s.i. The volume of gas produced is about 400 times the original volume of the charge.

By shifting from potassium to sodium nitrate, 60 cal. per gram more heat is generated. Moreover, since the average molecular weight of the combustion products is reduced slightly, the exhaust jet velocity is increased.

With the advent of nitro explosives new possibilities opened up for obtaining high-temperature gases smoothly and reproducibly. Motor design changes were required to accommodate the higher combustion temperatures and pressures. Rocket propellants based upon nitrocellulose (guncotton) are known as single-base propellants. Mixtures of nitrocellulose and nitroglycerin are known as double-base propellants. These double-base mixtures are similar to smokeless powders for firearms. To improve the physical and chemical properties of double-base propellants, small amounts of additives are usually present as stabilizers. These additives prevent decomposition in storage or improve combustion characteristics and bond the propellant to the motor casing.

Double-base propellants require a minimum operating-chamber pressure of about 500 p.s.i. for smooth burning. Lower pressure results in irregular burning and oscillatory combustion. Flame temperature is in the order of 5,000° F. (2,760° C.). Heat yield is in the order of 850–1,200 cal. per gram. Specific impulse is about 180–210 sec. The volume of gases produced from double-base propellants is about 1,500 times initial propellant volume.

Solid propellants are divided into two main classes: homogeneous and composite. The term homogeneous is applied to solid-propellant mixtures in which the propellant or mixture of propellants are intimately associated in a colloidal state. Single- and double-base propellants are examples of homogeneous propellants. In composite (or heterogeneous) propellants, the substances, although finely ground, are in distinctly separate phases. An example of composite propellant is gunpowder.

Nitrocellulose or nitroglycerin is different from gunpowder with respect to the process of chemical combustion. The molecules of saltpetre (KNO_3), sulfur (S) and carbon (C) in gunpowder must be intimately mixed in order to react. Nitrocellulose contains within each molecule sufficient fuel and oxidizer for complete reaction without the addition of other substances. In this regard, nitrocellulose may be considered a monopropellant.

In World War II both single- and double-base propellants were used extensively. In an important German double-base mixture, WASAG R-61, diethylene glycol dinitrate was substituted for nitroglycerin.

In the U.S., a number of new important composite propellants were produced. One of these was the GALCIT series which was a mixture of 75% potassium perchlorate and 25% asphalt oil. Another variety was the NDRC mixtures. A typical example of these was about 46% each of ammonium picrate and sodium nitrate mixed with 8% plastic resin binder. Other composite mixtures used ammonium nitrate as oxidizer and still others utilized synthetic rubber as fuel. An important advantage of composite propellants was their ability to be cast directly in the case.

Generally speaking, a solid rocket propellant may be formulated and designed to wide performance specifications, with individual motors operating from a fraction of a second to 30 sec. or more burning time. Rocket motors 10 ft. in diameter, containing more than 100,000 lb. of propellant and developing 1,000,000 lb. of thrust, have been fired. Total impulse, *i.e.*, thrust (lb.) × time (sec.), of many million pound-seconds has been achieved in the U.S. Solid-propellant rocket systems are generally lower in performance than liquid systems but offer advantages in readiness of operation and ruggedness desired for field operations.

Programs for solid-propellant motors from 156 to 260 in. in diameter are under development in the U.S. Such motors are expected to deliver as much as 3,000,000 lb. of thrust.

Classic problems in solid-propellant production include variation in performance with temperature, development of cracks or shrinkage in storage or transit and sensitivity to moisture. Most propellants tend to have higher burning rates in warm climates. Rocket stores may vary in military field operations from −70° F. to 150° F. (−56.6° to 65.6° C.). Cracks, fissures or shrinkage increase the burning surface area so that pressure build-up on firing may reach disastrous proportions. X-ray inspections are a common specification of rocket grain manufacture. Some formulations are hygroscopic and must be stored in dry atmosphere or moisture will be absorbed and performance reduced. A new technology of rocket propellant surveillance has developed which deals with the practice and procedures of storage and periodic inspection of rocket matériel. Procedures are evolved during development of rockets so that safe and adequate provisions may be put into effect when production programs are under way. Rocket propellants are inherently high-energy, unstable substances, intimately mixed. Physical-chemical processes such as deterioration, degradation and autoignition are important, along with variations in shape, size and density resulting from temperature and humidity effects and stress relief processes resulting from aging.

2. Liquid Propellants.—Generally speaking, liquid propellants have higher specific impulse than solid propellants and are more versatile, since throttling and restart are possible. Another important advantage is that liquid engines can be checked out, fired and calibrated precisely before launch. But liquid-rocket systems are more complex and tend to be less rugged and reliable.

Rocket systems using liquid propellants fall into two general classes: monopropellant and the more common bipropellant. Monopropellants are substances which decompose when heated or upon contact with a catalyst and give off large quantities of heat.

An example is 90% hydrogen peroxide, which decomposes into water (steam) and oxygen. By mixing hydrogen peroxide with a fuel such as an alcohol, a combustion reaction also takes place, yielding more heat. Other monopropellants are nitromethane, ethylene oxide, hydrazine and propyl nitrate. Monopropellant systems are simpler but are lower in performance. Specific impulses of the above monopropellants range from 160–220 sec.

Tsiolkovski, Goddard and Oberth all independently recognized and wrote of the advantages of liquid bipropellants. In these systems one propellant is the oxidizer and the other the fuel. Common oxidizers are liquid oxygen, hydrogen peroxide, fuming nitric acid and nitrogen tetroxide. The fuels used most often have been ethyl alcohol (75% + 25% water), kerosene or gasoline, hydrazine derivatives, aniline, furfuryl alcohol and liquid hydrogen.

Although experiments have been performed on thousands of fuels and a lesser number of oxidizers, no completely ideal propellants have emerged. Each propellant has some disadvantages that must be weighed against the particular design application and mission. For example, the problems of corrosivity and toxicity of fluorine or the low density of hydrogen may be accepted to obtain their high performance in space applications. Or, the lower specific impulse of solid propellants may be accepted to obtain the advantages of readiness in antimissile defense systems.

In evaluation of liquid propellants the following properties are of engineering importance to the rocket designer: heat of reaction, average molecular weight of combustion products, stability (*e.g.*, to heat, shock), speed of reaction, ignition characteristics, density, viscosity, vapour pressure, specific heat and corrosivity. For regenerative cooling—and all large, long-burning engines are so cooled—at least one of the propellants must have sufficient stability, specific heat capacity, thermal conductivity and high saturation temperature to serve as a coolant. Despite its low temperature −297° F. (−183° C.), for example, liquid oxygen is an unsatisfactory regenerative coolant. To improve cooling ability in the V-2, the ethyl-alcohol fuel was diluted to 75% with water.

Quite apart from properties affecting rocket power plant design are the logistic and handling qualities of liquid propellants. For bulk storage and transfer of propellants, corrosivity, stability and vapour pressure are important as well as freezing point and inflammability. Toxicity is important to personnel. Cost and bulk availability are also important considerations to program planners.

By the mid-1960s achievable specific impulses of rocket motors in operational missiles had climbed to about 280 sec. In the U.S., development programs for storable oxidizers such as nitrogen tetroxide and chlorine trifluoride were under way as well as major programs for liquid hydrogen, liquid fluorine, boron hydrides, oxygen difluoride and liquid fluorine-oxygen mixtures. Fruition of these propellant programs and development of rocket motors with higher operating pressures will result in sea level specific impulses of 370 sec. or better—near the maximum for chemical-combustion rockets. In the realm of exotic propellants, considerable research effort has been applied to the study of free radicals in the hope of stabilizing these energetic metastable substances. Also, the use of liquid ozone and metal additives has been studied. *See* also PROPELLANTS.

VII. MISCELLANEOUS APPLICATIONS OF ROCKET POWER

In addition to the primary uses of rocket power—for missile propulsion, fireworks and for upper-atmosphere research and space exploration—rocket systems have been used for a wide variety of other purposes.

1. Aircraft Propulsion.—Rocket engines have been used as the prime power plant for high-speed aircraft as well as for auxiliary propulsion. Two versions of a rocket-powered airplane, the Messerschmitt Me-163B and Me-163C, appeared too late in World War II to be important militarily. But their flight speeds, 560–590 m.p.h., would have made them extremely effective against long-range bomber formations. The Austrian Eugen Sänger and his brilliant co-worker Irene Bredt (later Mrs. Sänger) headed the air force rocket test station at Trauen. It was there that the experimental work was conducted which laid the basis for the significant report, *A Rocket Drive for Long Range Rocket Bombers* by Sänger and Bredt, published by Robert Cornog (1952).

An interesting intermediate step between the guided missile and the piloted interceptor was the rocket-powered Natter, designed by Erich Bachem. This vehicle, carrying a pilot, was designed to be launched vertically toward attacking bomber formations. The Natter was designed to have a maximum horizontal flight speed of 620 m.p.h.

The concept of a rocket-powered airplane for high-speed research studies originated in the U.S. at the time the Germans were developing their Me-163 rocket-powered interceptor. After the war this work continued under air force sponsorship in co-operation with the National Advisory Committee for Aeronautics (NACA). The 6,000-lb. liquid oxygen-alcohol rocket engine was a navy bureau of aeronautics development. This engine consisted of four 1,500-lb.-thrust combustion chambers which could be fired independently or in combination.

Initial flights of the X-1 airplane were made in 1946. Because of the rapid rate of burning of the rocket propellants—almost one ton per minute, with all four motors—powered flight lasted only a few minutes. All landings were without power, gliding down to the desert floor at Edwards air force base, Calif. For the same reason, the X-1 was carried aloft and launched from a specially modified B-29 bomber. Supersonic speed was achieved for the first time in 1947. In 1948 a new altitude record was set at 70,140 ft.

Another version of this airplane, the X-1A, used a turbopump propellant supply system instead of the heavier, nitrogen pressure feed method. The X-1A reached a speed of 1,650 m.p.h. at 90,000 ft. in 1953. Meanwhile the navy in co-operation with NACA had developed another rocket research airplane. Known as the D-558 this airplane, which also carried a turbojet engine, was first to fly at Mach 2 (twice the speed of sound).

The X-2 was a rocket-powered research aircraft designed for even higher speeds. The rocket engine developed 15,000-lb. thrust—twice as much as the X-1. Mach 3.3 (2,200 m.p.h.) and 126,000 ft. altitude records were made in the X-2.

In 1958 another rocket research airplane, the X-15, was revealed to the public. The X-15 was powered by a rocket engine developing 50,000-lb. thrust and was designed to be launched above 40,000 ft. from a B-52 bomber. An altitude of 353,000 ft. and speeds greater than 4,100 m.p.h. have been achieved.

In France, the Trident fighter was powered by two 6,615-lb.-thrust rocket engines. Other fighter and interceptor aircraft (Durandal and Mirage III-A) carried liquid-propellant engines for burst speed in addition to turbojet power plants. In Great Britain an 8,000-lb.-thrust hydrogen peroxide-kerosene engine was developed which could be throttled over a wide range of thrust.

2. Jet-Assisted Takeoff.—During World War II both the U.S. and Germany developed jet-assisted-takeoff (jato) units for aircraft. Both solid and liquid propellants enabled land and seaplanes to take off with a shorter run or with increased loads, or both. Development continued after the war, particularly in the U.S. where the units were produced also for the commercial market. Jato units are sometimes designed as a fixed installation in aircraft, but otherwise are intended for parachute drop after takeoff.

3. Other Applications.—Rockets are used in the U.S. to propel supersonic sleds along a twin-rail track. These sleds serve as test beds for acceleration tests of various components such as parachutes, aircraft ejection seats and nose cones. Important aeromedical tests on men have also been performed with rocket sleds. Accelerations as high as 100 gravity (g), decelerations of 150 g and velocities up to 4,600 ft. per second are possible. Both liquid- and solid-propellant rockets are used. Braking is accomplished by a parachute or, more often, by extending a scoop beneath the sled into a trough of water between the track rails.

Buried land mines were attacked in World War II by rocket-propelled devices. One of these devices, known as the Snake, pulled a 100-ft. train of skis, linked together and carrying TNT. Another version was a U-shaped motor which dragged primacord explosive to detonate the mine field.

A unique device based upon a German development was the Wedge. This item used a powerful rocket to drive a 1-in. rod,

6 ft. long, into the ground. By pulling out the rod, inserting a length of primacord and detonating, a hole of 10–12 in. in diameter was created. Various other wartime rocket-propelled material included smoke bombs which in barrage-firing could swiftly erect a smoke screen. Antiradar rockets, used in the Allied invasion of Normandy, released metal foil strips, known as window, at peak of trajectory. These foil strips caused spurious radar reflections and appeared as swarms of aircraft on radar screens. Grapnels, even rope ladders, have been boosted over heights by rocket in commando-type operations. Recoilless rifles and mortar-fired rockets have been developed.

Solid rocket propellants have been used for turbojet engine starters, to furnish gas pressure to power small gyroscopes or electric turbogenerators for guided missiles, and to pressurize flame throwers. Firing solid-propellant charges in specially designed tools in oil wells creates high pressures which fracture the earth and increase oil production. Rocket jets have been used to drill holes through earth and rock. Rocket motors provide a high-temperature jet which is useful for materials tests as in the case of ballistic missile nose-cone development.

In the U.S. X-15 research airplane, the rocket motor is designed to accelerate the vehicle to 100 mi. altitude. In the outer reaches of the atmosphere the craft's wings and tail surfaces would be useless to orient the airplane correctly for re-entry flight on the downward side of the ballistic trajectory. Accordingly, rocket jet nozzles on the wings and fuselage are designed to rotate and correctly orient the X-15 under these conditions.

The possibility of delivering a number of men and equipment accurately and at long ranges with IRBM and ICBM vehicles has been proposed. Even rocket boost of individual soldiers for hundreds of yards has been achieved by the use of a device known as a "rocketbelt."

Rockets have been attached to automobiles, boats, gliders, iceboats, motorcycles, rail cars and even a man on skates. These experiments, which occurred mostly in the 1920s and 1930s, were more ingenious than efficient, more publicity-seeking than sound.

VIII. ROCKETS AND SPACE FLIGHT

Man's dream of traveling through space to the moon and the planets is an old one—as old as astronomy itself. Centuries before the Christian era the courses of planets and stars were plotted but there was no appreciation then of the distance to these "abodes of the gods"; no understanding of the lack of atmosphere a short distance from the Earth's surface; nor even that the world was round. However, once man had learned that the moon and planets were actual bodies, a long way off, he had an urge to visit them. Willy Ley (see *Bibliography*) traces the story of man's interest in space flight from its earliest beginnings; 17th-century authors related fantasies in which man was drawn by "wild swans" or carried aloft "on the dew" to visit the moon. As the telescope developed and Newton's laws became applied, the physical problems of space journeys became more apparent. Jules Verne's famous *De la terre à la lune* ("From the Earth to the Moon") was published in 1865. Verne shot a space ship with passengers on a flight around the moon appreciating correctly many aspects of the voyage such as weightlessness in free fall.

By 1900 the recognition of rocket propulsion as the key to space flight began to spread. Scientists such as Tsiolkovski, Goddard and Oberth wrote serious technical treatises on the potentialities of rocket-powered flight. Rocket and space flight societies focused public attention on their experimental efforts. Their dreams were great but financial support was limited and successes were few. And each society had its share of crackpots. The aim of these societies was interplanetary flight rather than improved war rockets, but the latter were to appear first, in World War II.

The German heritage of the V-2 to the postwar world made it clear that with only a small extrapolation, payloads could be accelerated to satellite velocity. The development of the ICBM by the U.S. and U.S.S.R. furnished the additional power necessary to orbit significant payloads and to probe the solar system.

Whenever a new scientific frontier has been penetrated the eventual results have been of economic benefit to mankind. It can only be hoped that in moving into this new dimension man will also learn better the art of living with his neighbours, and that the rocket, developed as a machine of war, will become a tool for peaceful research and understanding.

See SPACE EXPLORATION; *see* also references under "Rockets and Guided Missiles" in the Index.

BIBLIOGRAPHY.—*General and Historical:* F. I. Ordway, III, *Annotated Bibliography of Space Science and Technology* (1962); C. G. Philip, *U.S. Rocket Ordnance: Development and Use in World War II* (1946); R. H. Goddard, *Rockets* (1946), *Rocket Development* (1948); W. Dornberger, *V-2* (1954); M. W. Rosen, *Viking Rocket Story* (1955); T. Benecke and A. W. Quick, *History of German Guided Missile Development* (1957); R. W. Gatland, *Spacecraft and Boosters* (1964); W. Ley, *Rockets, Missiles and Space Travel* (1957); F. J. Krieger, *Behind the Sputniks: a Survey of Soviet Space Science* (1958); A. Lee (ed.), *Soviet Air and Rocket Forces* (1959); E. M. Emme, *Aeronautics and Astronautics: an American Chronology of Science and Technology in the Exploration of Space, 1915–1960* (1961); F. I. Ordway, III and R. C. Wakeford, *International Missile and Spacecraft Guide* (1960); A. Parry, *Russia's Rockets and Missiles* (1960); J. L. Chapman, *Atlas: the Story of a Missile* (1960); J. Baar and W. E. Howard, *Polaris!* (1960); A. J. Zaehringer, *Soviet Space Technology* (1961); S. E. Ellacott, *Rockets* (1961); D. K. Huzel, *Peenemünde to Canaveral* (1962); E. G. Schwiebert, *A History of the U.S. Air Force Ballistic Missiles* (1965); E. Klee and O. Merk, *The Birth of the Missile* (1965); W. von Braun and F. I. Ordway, III, *History of Rocketry and Space Travel* (1967); A. C. Clarke, *Man and Space* (1966). *Technical:* G. P. Sutton, *Rocket Propulsion Elements* (1956); L. Davis *et al., Exterior Ballistics of Rockets* (1958); A. J. Zaehringer, *Solid Propellant Rockets* (1958); H. E. Newell, Jr., *Sounding Rockets* (1959); H. S. Seifert (ed.), *Space Technology* (1959); W. R. Corliss, *Propulsion Systems for Space Flight* (1960); B. Kit and D. S. Evered, *Rocket Propellant Handbook* (1960); R. E. Wiech, Jr., and R. F. Strauss, *Fundamentals of Rocket Propulsion* (1960); A. I. Berman, *Physical Principles of Astronautics* (1961); S. S. Chin, *Missile Configuration Design* (1961); H. H. Koelle (ed.), *Handbook of Astronautical Engineering* (1961); S. S. Penner (ed.), *Advanced Propulsion Techniques* (1961); S. L. Bragg, *Rocket Engines* (1962); K. Brown and L. D. Ely (eds.), *Space Logistics Engineering* (1962); F. I. Ordway, III *et al., Basic Astronautics* (1962); F. I. Ordway, III *et al., Applied Astronautics* (1963); F. I. Ordway, III, *Advances in Space Science and Technology*, vol. 1–8 (1959–66); D. R. Samson (ed.), *Development of the Blue Streak Satellite Launcher* (1963); Ernst Stuhlinger *et al.* (eds.), *Astronautical Engineering and Science* (1963); G. Gurney (ed.), *Rocket and Missile Technology* (1964); F. R. Gantmakher and L. M. Levin, *The Flight of Uncontrolled Rockets* (1964).

(F. C. D. III)

ROCKFORD, a city of Illinois, U.S., the seat of Winnebago County, is located on the Rock River in the midst of an important industrial, agricultural, and commercial area in the north-central part of the state, 17 mi. S of the Wisconsin line and 90 mi. NW of Chicago. Founded by New Englanders in 1834, it was named for the rock-bottomed ford, the site of a stagecoach stop on the trip between Chicago and Galena. It was incorporated as a village in 1839 and as a city in 1852. Supplied with waterpower by a dam constructed in 1844, the town grew rapidly; in 1960 the population of the city was 126,706 and that of the standard metropolitan statistical area (Winnebago County) was 230,091. (For comparative population figures *see* table in ILLINOIS: *Population*.)

Rockford is a manufacturing city, its products including machine tools, hardware, furniture, farm implements, household appliances, leather goods, and paint. Camp Grant, a reception and medical-replacement centre during World Wars I and II, has been converted into the greater Rockford Airport.

Rockford College, founded in 1847 as Rockford Female Seminary, became coeducational in 1959. In 1958 the land was acquired for a new campus, the development of which was expected to extend over a 15-year period. Rockford is a city of many churches, including a Roman Catholic procathedral. The town has a symphony orchestra, an art gallery, and a little theatre, and also has many well-equipped playgrounds and parks.   (H. E. B.)

ROCKHAMPTON, a city and port on the east coast of Queensland, Austr., situated on both banks of the Fitzroy River at the head of ocean navigation 35–40 mi. (56–64 km.) from the sea. Pop. (1966) 46,052. Rockhampton, which was proclaimed a municipality in 1860, is well designed, with wide streets, many substantial buildings (including an Anglican and a Roman Catholic cathedral), and fine public parks and gardens. The city is the base of a railway system which connects such widely separated places as Longreach, Winton, Blair Athol, Callide coalfields, and Springsure, and which is being continually extended. The Great Northern line links Rockhampton with Brisbane and other coastal towns, with seaside resorts (Yeppoon and Emu Park), and with the ports of Port Alma and Gladstone, which have harbours for ocean vessels. Railway repairing and other industries are carried on in the city, and nearby are two large meat-preserving and freezing works, one of which is the largest in the southern hemisphere.

Mount Morgan, 24 mi. (39 km.) SSW, which in the 1880s became one of the richest gold mines in Australia, contributed greatly to the city's growth. The Fitzroy River and its tributaries, including the Dawson and Mackenzie, drain a basin of 58,000 sq.mi. of great diversity and economic value. The hinterland of Rockhampton thus contains extensive pastoral country extending as far west as Longreach, considerable mineral resources including coalfields (*e.g.*, Blair Athol mines and Moura coalfields), and rich agricultural and dairying lands—in particular the Dawson River irrigation area (total projected size: 170,000 ac.). The Dawson River Valley is the centre of the cotton region in Australia, which yields 75% of total production and also has 80,000 ac. of wheat which yield about 1,500,000 bu. annually. Around Rockhampton itself is fertile agricultural land noted for its tropical fruits, maize (corn), and dairy products. The climate is hot and humid with average annual temperatures from 17° to 28° C (62° to 82° F)and an annual average rainfall of 40 in. (1,000 mm.) falling within about six weeks during the summer.

ROCKINGHAM, CHARLES WATSON-WENTWORTH, 2ND MARQUESS OF (1730–1782), British statesman, prime minister from July 1765 to July 1766 and from March to July 1782 and leader of the parliamentary group known as the Rockingham Whigs, was born on May 13, 1730. He was the fifth and only surviving son of Thomas Watson-Wentworth (d. 1750), who was created marquess of Rockingham in 1746. In 1745 he ran away to serve as a volunteer under the duke of Cumberland against the Jacobite rebels. In September 1750 he was created Baron Malton and Earl Malton in the Irish peerage. Three months later he succeeded to his father's rich estates in Yorkshire, Northamptonshire, and Ireland. In 1751 he became lord of the bedchamber to George II and was appointed to judicial and military offices in Yorkshire. In 1762, after the dismissal of his friend William Cavendish, 4th duke of Devonshire, from his office of lord chamberlain, Rockingham resigned from the bedchamber in sympathy.

In July 1765 George III, failing to get the services of William Pitt, turned to Rockingham to form a ministry to replace that of George Grenville, which the king hated. From the start his cabinet was weakened by internal dissensions and Pitt refused to support it in the House of Commons. Its policy of conciliating the American colonists by repealing the Stamp Act of 1765 was wise but unpopular and parliamentary support was only obtained by coupling repeal with a Declaratory Act reaffirming Parliament's powers to pass laws for the colonies "in all cases whatsoever." In July 1766 the government collapsed and was replaced by the ministry of Pitt, who became earl of Chatham. From 1766 until 1782 Rockingham was leader of a strong parliamentary opposition, which was at times opportunist and factious, but which found a genuine cause of principle in its opposition to the war against the American colonists. From March 1782 until his death he headed a ministry which began negotiations for peace to end the American war, and legislated a program of "economical reform," mainly inspired by Edmund Burke (*q.v.*). He also gave legislative independence to the Irish Parliament by repealing the Declaratory Act (1719) and drastically amending Poynings' Law. Rockingham died on July 1, 1782, and was buried at York Minster. Many of his letters are contained in *The Correspondence of Edmund Burke,* volume ii, edited by L. S. Sutherland (1960); volume iii, edited by G. H. Guttridge (1961); volume iv, edited by J. A. Woods (1963).

BIBLIOGRAPHY.—G. H. Guttridge, *English Whiggism and the American Revolution* (1942), *The Early Career of Lord Rockingham, 1730–65* (1952); J. Brooke, *The Chatham Administration, 1766–1768* (1956); I. R. Christie, *The End of North's Ministry, 1780–1782* (1958).

(I. R. C.)

ROCK ISLAND, a city and the seat of Rock Island County, western Illinois, U.S., lies along the Mississippi River near the mouth of the Rock River and opposite the large federal island which gave the settlement its name. With Moline, East Moline, and Davenport, Iowa, it forms a complex known as the "Quad Cities." Settlers were attracted by the presence of Ft. Armstrong on the island and by the cornfields of the Fox Indians. Ft. Armstrong (now a federal arsenal) was headquarters of operations in the Black Hawk War. As settlers moved in, Rock Island (originally called Stephenson) became a transportation hub and was first incorporated in 1841. In 1854 the town was reached by the Rock Island Railroad, whose promotors built the first bridge across the Mississippi. Industry is diversified, including railroad shops and the manufacturing of footwear and farm equipment. Swedish immigrants established Augustana College and Theological Seminary in 1860. The college library contains material rich in Swedish Americana. Pop. (1960) 51,863; Davenport-Rock Island-Moline standard metropolitan statistical area (*see* DAVENPORT), 319,375. For comparative population figures *see* table in ILLINOIS: *Population.*

(D. L. A.)

ROCKNE, KNUTE KENNETH (1888–1931), U.S. football coach whose colourful personality and style of play captured the public's imagination during the "golden era" of sports in the 1920s, was born in Voss, Nor., on March 4, 1888. In 1893 his family migrated to the United States and in 1910 Rockne entered the University of Notre Dame, Notre Dame, Ind. There he became a track and football star (1911–13), assistant football coach (1914), and head coach (1918–31). Recognized as one of the game's greatest coaches, Rockne's popularity and that of his teams stemmed in large part from the loyalty of thousands of persons who had never attended college, the so-called "subway alumni," who adopted his teams as their own. In compiling his record of 105 victories, 12 defeats, and 5 ties (including five undefeated seasons), Rockne perfected such maneuvers as the "Notre Dame shift"; taught such famous players as George Gipp and the 1924 Notre Dame backfield known as the "Four Horsemen"; and was the first to substitute entire teams (which he called "shock troops") during a game, a forerunner of modern platooning. He was killed in a plane crash in Kansas on March 31, 1931. *See also* FOOTBALL: *U.S. College Football History.*   (J. D. McC.; X.)

ROCK RIVER, a nonnavigable river in the north central U.S., rises in Washington County in eastern Wisconsin and flows in a generally southwesterly direction to join the Mississippi River at Rock Island, Ill. Its 300-mi. length is shared about equally by the two states and from source to mouth it drops about 500 ft. Ten small dams on the river have a total power generating capacity of 12,545 kw. The river drains an area of 10,879 sq.mi. of good agricultural land. The bottomlands along the lower course are frequently flooded in the spring and require levee protection. Major cities along the river include Watertown, Janesville, and Beloit, Wis., and Rockford, Dixon, Sterling, and Rock Island, Ill. Its principal tributaries are the Pecatonica, Kishwaukee, and Green rivers. Near Oregon, Ill., in Lowden Memorial State Park, Lorado Taft's heroic 48-ft. statue of "Black Hawk" rises majestically above the wooded slopes of the valley.   (E. HG.)

ROCKY MOUNTAIN NATIONAL PARK, in north central Colorado, U.S., 410 sq.mi. (1,062 sq.km.) in area, was established in 1915 to preserve an outstanding section of the front range of the Rocky mountains. Located about 64 mi. N.W. of Denver, the region is famous for its high mountain peaks, broad valleys, rugged gorges, flowered meadows, alpine lakes and plunging streams, and also for its abundant wildlife, with such animals as the Rocky mountain bighorn sheep, mule deer, American wapiti, mountain lion, beaver and many species of birds inhabiting the area. A remarkable variety of plant life can be seen within the park, with more than 700 species of plants known to be present. The tundra of the high country in the park is a unique island of arctic vegetation, surrounded on all sides by plant communities of lower latitudes. Within the park are more than 100 named peaks which are over 10,000 ft. in elevation. Longs peak (14,255 ft.; 4,345 m.) is the highest summit in northern Colorado, and one of the world's most popular climbs. The pastoral landscapes of the meadows and the rolling moraines are the result of glacial deposition. There are about 300 mi. of hiking trails, and the national park service provides guided field trips. Trail Ridge road traverses the park, with about 11 mi. of the highway being above the 11,000-ft. timber line. Except for 12 mi. between Estes park and Hidden valley kept open for winter sports enthusiasts, this road is closed from about Oct. 15 to May 30. Slopes and ski runs are available for skiing in the winter months.   (C. L. Wɪ.)

ROCKY MOUNTAINS, the principal division of that vast system of highlands occupying part of the western United States, northern Mexico, western Canada and extending into northern Alaska. Standing between the great continental plains on the east and the region of elevated basins, ranges and plateaus extending from central Mexico through Nevada to northern British Columbia on the west, they constitute the backbone of the continent, as well as a major topographical feature of the entire globe. The Rocky mountain system does not include any of the Pacific border mountain system of North America (the Alaska range, Coast range, Cascade range, Sierra Nevada, Sierra Madre Occidental), from which it is separated by the basin, range and plateau province of Mexico, Nevada and British Columbia.

At the south the Rockies begin in the Sierra Madre Oriental, north of Oaxaca, Mex. North of Monterrey, Mex., the Sierra Madre Oriental is submerged in a rugged plateau region through which the Rio Grande has cut a narrow gorge at the Big Bend. North of the Mexican border, in west Texas and southern New Mexico, the mountain zone consists of a series of separate ranges and mountain basins between the Rio Grande on the west and the Pecos river on the east. In northern New Mexico the mountains become prominent again, reaching elevations above 13,000 ft. (4,000 m.). Thence they sweep northward and northwestward through the United States, Canada and across northern Alaska to the Arctic ocean near Point Hope. As a whole the mountain system is about 4,700 mi. (7,600 km.) long. The section designated as the Rocky mountains extends only 2,200 mi., 1,290 mi. of which are in the United States. Its greatest width is attained in Utah and Colorado, where the system of ranges is 350 mi. across. In Colorado there are 55 summits surpassing 14,000 ft., Mt. Elbert (14,431 ft.) being the highest of the system outside of Mexico. Colorado contains more than 250 mountains between 13,000 and 14,000 ft. Northwest of Colorado breadth and elevation diminish until at the Canadian boundary the ranges are less than 100 mi. wide, with few elevations exceeding 9,500 ft. In Canada, for 450 mi., the system forms the boundary between British Columbia and Alberta. From Colorado almost to the Peace river in British Columbia, the Rockies carry the watershed of the continent (the continental divide). But this does not mean that they present a continuous chain of great peaks. On the contrary, the zone of uplift is rather a vast complex of separate ranges, interrupted at places by wide gaps of lofty rolling plateaus and intermontane basins or parks. In the Yukon territory of Canada, the system is a broken highland zone between the upper Yukon river on the southwest and the Mackenzie river on the east and northeast. At about 67° N. latitude the system swings westward across the border into Alaska and continues in a southwesterly arc to the Arctic ocean south of Point Hope. In Alaska the system is designated the Brooks range and contains the highest, most rugged mountain zone north of the Arctic circle, reaching heights a little over 9,000 ft.

Geology.—The Rocky mountain system is one of the younger systems of the world, although very old rocks are found at the core of many of the ranges. The major uplift of the system occurred in Late Cretaceous and Early Tertiary time, in what is called the Laramide revolution, about 70,000,000 years ago. However, the portion of the continent now occupied by the Rocky mountains had undergone a number of vicissitudes prior to its final uplift. Though individual ranges vary somewhat in their story, a generalized geologic history of the system includes the following events: the oldest rocks in the system were laid down as sediments in a shallow sea in Precambrian time—1,000,000,000 to 2,000,000,000 years ago. About 1,000,000,000 years ago this thick accumulation of shales, sandstones and limestones was compressed,

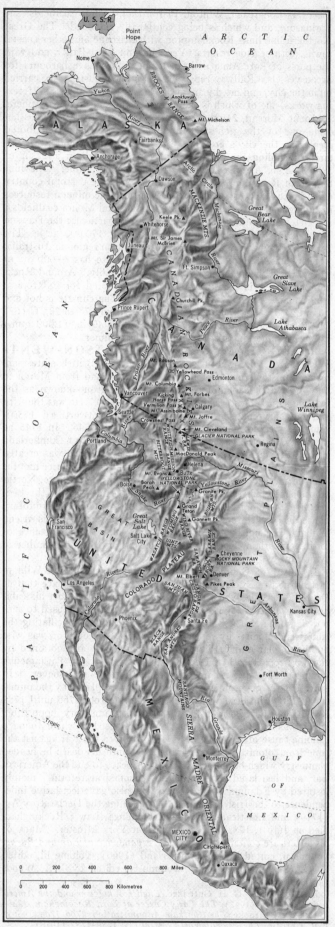

PRINCIPAL RANGES AND PEAKS OF THE ROCKY MOUNTAINS

folded and contorted by mighty forces within the earth's crust and uparched into an ancestral mountain system. The sedimentary rocks were altered by the heat and pressure into metamorphic rocks such as schist, slate, gneiss and marble. During the upheaval great masses of molten material were injected or melted their way upward into the core of the uplift. When it cooled, this material became granite. The processes of erosion now began to wear down this ancient mountain system. Rain fell; streams ate valleys into the surface; mud, silt and sand were carried out of the highlands into the adjacent water bodies. Gradually the uplift was carved into a rugged mountain system and then slowly reduced to a vast low-level plain, called a peneplain. Eventually the region again sank below the level of an encroaching shallow sea.

Throughout most of the two succeeding geologic eras, the Paleozoic and Mesozoic, the site fluctuated between low-lying swamp ground and shallow seas. In these seas were deposited a great depth of sedimentary material. Silt, mud and pebbles were carried down from highlands on the west. This material eventually consolidated into shales and conglomerates. Limey material was precipitated from sea water to form limestone. Sand accumulated along the shore and in river estuaries to form sandstones. The skeletons and shells of a complex assemblage of life forms were left in the sediments as fossils. These run a wide range from simple shells to dinosaurs. The depth of the sediments laid down during these times is very great. In some localities the total thickness from top to bottom is more than 10 mi. The greatest extent of sea occurred near the end of this episode, when a Cretaceous water body extended from the Gulf of Mexico to the Arctic ocean, and from the Mississippi to the Nevada plateaus. This vast continental trough with its great accumulation of sedimentary rocks is called the Rocky Mountain geosyncline.

Then at the end of the Cretaceous period, the bottom of the geosyncline began to arch upward. Great compressive forces from the west thrust folds and blocks of the thick sedimentary rocks upward and eastward along a zone from southern Mexico to western Alaska. Accompanying the uplift and folding was the breaking of great sheets and plates of rock, which were pushed eastward along nearly horizontal or gently dipping fractures (thrust faults) like cards in a deck pushed one over another. Displacement along some of these thrust planes is measured in tens of miles. Weakening of the earth's crust permitted molten material from below to break through in volcanic upheavals at numerous points, pouring forth lava and ash. Other steep angled faults were formed along the eastern margins of the emerging ranges. This vast upheaval was the Laramide revolution, taking its name from the Laramie range of Wyoming; it lasted through several million years.

During the upheaval and after its close, the processes of wind and water erosion ate away at the uplift, carving it first into a magnificent group of mountain ranges and eventually wearing it down again to a low peneplain. Then only several million years ago the peneplain was again uplifted as a broad highland plateau. The process of dissection was begun anew. By now many of the canyons and valleys were cutting down through the great masses of sedimentary beds to expose the old metamorphic and granite rocks which had comprised the ancestral Rockies over a billion years earlier. About 1,000,000 years ago the Pleistocene ice age capped all of the higher ranges with glaciers. These crept outward through the valleys, scouring them into their typical U-shaped profile and fretting the highlands with cirques and serrated ridges. The present-day configuration of most of the higher ranges can be traced to glacial scouring. Greatly diminished glaciers still are found in the high mountains from the Wind River range of central Wyoming northward.

Divisions.—The Rocky mountain system can be divided conveniently into six divisions. From south to north these are: (1) the Sierra Madre Oriental of eastern Mexico; (2) the southern Rocky mountains of New Mexico, Colorado and Utah; (3) the middle Rocky mountains of Wyoming; (4) the northern Rocky mountains of Montana and Idaho; (5) The Canadian Rockies of British Columbia, Alberta and Yukon territory; (6) The Brooks range of Alaska. There are natural gaps or low passes in the crest of the system between all of these divisions except one. The Rio Grande and Pecos uplands divide the Sierra Madre Oriental from the southern Rockies. The Wyoming basin (Great Divide basin) lies between the southern and middle Rockies. The Yellowstone plateau separates the middle Rockies from the northern Rockies. There is no natural break between the northern Rockies and the Canadian Rockies. The Yukon-Porcupine-Mackenzie lowland separates the Canadian Rockies from the Brooks range.

Sierra Madre Oriental.—The Sierra Madre Oriental serves as the eastern rim of the central plateau of Mexico from a point just north of Oaxaca to north of Monterrey, a distance of about 700 mi. (*See* MEXICO.) On the east it falls away abruptly to the gulf coastal lowland. Westward it descends gently onto the dissected central plateau. At the north the range is relatively low—5,000 to 7,000 ft. At the south, however, the range is met from the west by the primary east-west volcanic axis of the central plateau. At this junction stands Mexico's highest peak, the magnificent volcanic cone of Orizaba or Citlaltépetl (18,701 ft.). Nearby is Cofre de Perote or Nauhcampatépetl (14,045 ft.).

Southern Rockies.—In the Rockies of Colorado, the most magnificent groups are probably the Sawatch range (96 mi. by 32 mi.) and the Sangre de Cristo range (220 mi. long) in the central part of the state. In the southwestern corner the Elk, San Miguel (with the spectacular Lizard Head, 13,113 ft.), Needle and San Juan groups, form a wild and rugged mass of peaks.

The Wasatch mountains of central Utah, overlooking the great basin for 100 mi., present abrupt ranges. Associated with the Wasatch mountains is the Uinta group (96 mi. by 40 mi.), of which Kings peak (13,498 ft.) is loftiest.

Central Rockies.—The ranges just mentioned connect with the main axis of elevation of the Rockies in the region of Yellowstone park through a belt of rather indefinite uplands running north and south along the western boundary of Wyoming. There are the Crawford mountains, the Wyoming range, the Gros Ventre mountains, the Snake River range and the Teton range. The Teton range presents perhaps the most splendid spectacle of all the Rocky mountain ranges. It is 40 mi. long and 10 mi. wide, rugged and precipitous. Granite spires rise abruptly 6,000 to 7,000 ft. above the flats of Jackson's Hole. The principal peaks are the Three Tetons (Grand Teton, 13,766 ft.) and Mt. Moran (12,800 ft.) at the northerly extremity. Reverting to the continental divide of the western part of Wyoming, the important uplift of the Wind River range is next in order, northwest of Great Divide basin. It is about 100 mi. long; the core is more than 13,000 ft. in elevation and sends out long lateral ridges between which remarkable canyons occur. Its most prominent summits are Fremont peak (13,-730 ft.) ascended in 1842 by John C. Fremont; Gannett peak (13,785 ft.), the highest in Wyoming, and Chimney Rock (13,340 ft.). Numerous small glaciers are on the northeast slopes. The largest, Dinwoody, covers several square miles.

Northeast of the Wind river range, across the Bighorn basin, lie the Bighorn mountains, a prodigious offshoot of the main range toward the great plains, 146 mi. long and 40 to 50 mi. wide. The axis averages 12,000 ft. in elevation, rising about 9,000 ft. above the neighbouring prairies. A few of the peaks surpass 13,000 ft. and bear small glaciers in their rugged amphitheatres. The highest is Cloud peak (13,165 ft.).

Northern Rockies.—Between the northern boundary of Yellowstone park and the Yellowstone river, the Beartooth and neighbouring ranges display what are probably the principal mountain masses of this division. In the vicinity of Mt. Cowen (11,206 ft.) and Emigrant peak (10,921 ft.) the relief becomes as great as 6,400 ft., and Granite peak (12,799 ft.), the highest mountain in Montana, is situated there, as are Grasshopper glacier and other small ice bodies. The Beartooth range has a score of summits of 12,000 ft. or more.

The continental divide, however, leaves Yellowstone park in a northwesterly direction. At the 114th meridian it swings off abruptly to the northeast through the Butte and Helena districts. Beyond this swing, the western axis of elevation continues northwestward as the Bitterroot mountains to within 125 mi. of the Canadian border along the boundary between Idaho and Montana. The average elevation is between 7,000 and 8,000 ft. The highest peaks occur on projecting lateral spurs—Scott peak (11,393 ft.), El Capitan (9,936 ft.) and St. Mary (9,335 ft.). This 125-mi. interval is filled by the Coeur d'Alene (6,000 ft.) and Cabinet ranges, the latter culminating in Snowshoe peak (8,712 ft.). West of the Bitterroots in central Idaho lies a labyrinth of peaks and ridges (11,000 to 12,000 ft.); Borah Peak (12,662 ft.) is the highest point in that state.

In the region of Butte and Helena, Mont., the continental divide is generally featureless, the passes around Butte averaging 6,000 ft. or less. The Anaconda range contains Mt. Haggin (10,598 ft.) and Mt. Evans (10,635 ft.). Beyond Helena, the divide veers to the north-northwest and follows the Lewis range, which is so wild and rugged that no roads for vehicles cross it for 200 mi. Opposite the Lewis range, the westerly margin of the Rockies is defined by the Whitefish range (west of the north fork of Flathead river) and the Mission range (60 mi. long, southeast of Flathead lake). The latter culminates in the glacier-bearing McDonald Peak (10,-300 ft.). Between the Mission and Lewis ranges is the Swan range (Mt. Holland, 9,272 ft.). The principal continental pass there is Marias pass (5,215 ft.), crossed by the Great Northern railroad. The finest scenery in this quarter is within Glacier National park (*q.v.*), with 20 peaks between 9,000 and 10,000 ft. and six between 10,000 and 10,438 ft. Mt. Cleveland is the loftiest summit. The park contains about 40 glaciers and several large ones (from 2 to 5 sq.mi. apiece), besides a myriad of attractive lakes.

Canadian Rockies.—In Canada the axis of the Rockies is continuous for 1,000 mi. It is simpler, straighter and more sharply defined. Prominent passes of the divide are: Crowsnest pass (Canadian Pacific railway), 4,453 ft.; Vermilion pass (motor road), 5,376 ft.; Kicking Horse pass (Canadian Pacific railway), 5,320 ft., and Yellowhead pass (Canadian National railway), 3,717 ft. Proceeding northwesterly from the U.S. boundary, there are no glaciers for 100 mi., the peaks being mostly below 9,000 ft. A little farther on is Mt. Joffre (11,316 ft.), the first real glacier-hung peak. From there to beyond Mt. Robson (12,972 ft., the highest of all) the system is continuously alpine for about 285 mi. The Canadian Pacific railway crosses the chain 200 mi. from the boundary near the famous Lake Louise. Halfway between this and Mt. Joffre stands the handsome Mt. Assiniboine (11,870 ft.). In the 150-mi. gap between the Canadian Pacific and the Canadian National railways at Jasper, are situated Mt. Forbes (11,902 ft.) and Mt. Columbia (12,294 ft.), the fifth and second in rank in the Canadian Rockies respectively. In these mountains about 50 peaks surpass 11,000 ft. Glaciers and snow fields abound, and with the neighbouring groups just mentioned there is presented the best sweep of truly alpine territory to be found in North America outside of Alaska. The northwesterly 500 mi. of the range are imperfectly known, although the mountains are lower.

The Brooks Range.—Across northern Alaska, the Brooks range serves as a watershed between the Yukon river drainage and that of the Arctic ocean. It includes, from east to west, such separate mountain groups as the Davidson, Romanzof, Franklin, Philip Smith, Endicott, Schwatka, Baird and De Long mountains. The highest peak is Mt. Michelson (9,239 ft.) in the Romanzof mountains near the east end of the range. To the west the range crest lowers to 3,000–4,000 ft. Anaktuvuk pass (2,200 ft.) lies near the centre of the range. Almost the entire range is devoid of trees, being north of timberline. *See* also the articles on the states and provinces in which the Rocky mountains lie and on the national parks found in the Rocky mountains.

See also references under "Rocky Mountains" in the Index.

See W. W. Atwood, *The Rocky Mountains* (1945); N. M. Fenneman, *Physiography of Western United States* (1931). (T. M. G.)

ROCKY MOUNTAIN SPOTTED FEVER AND OTHER SPOTTED FEVERS.

Rocky mountain spotted fever is a typhuslike disease (*see* TYPHUS FEVER), first described in the Rocky mountain section of the U.S., caused by a specific microorganism (*Rickettsia rickettsii*) and transmitted to man by ticks. It is identical with a disease known as São Paulo fever in Brazil and with the spotted fever of Colombia. A closely related disease, but distinct etiologically, is *fièvre boutonneuse* caused by *R. conorii,* transmitted by ticks and occurring in the countries bordering on the Mediterranean sea and scattered localities of eastern and southern Africa.

History and Distribution.—Rocky mountain spotted fever was known along the Snake river in Idaho as early as 1873, but its first clinical description in a medical journal was given by E. E. Maxey in 1899. It was characteristically a disease of the open range and was noted to occur most frequently among hunters, trappers, fishermen, cattlemen and sheepherders. Up to 1930, it was thought to be confined to 11 states of the northwest, although one case was reported in Indiana. In connection with field investigations of endemic typhus in the southeastern U.S., it was noted that some cases in rural districts in the more northern states and among urban dwellers vacationing in the country were severe and did not exactly correspond to the clinical picture of endemic typhus. A high proportion of these patients had histories of tick bites within a short time preceding their illness. In 1931 L. F. Badger, R. E. Dyer and A. S. Rumreich recovered the causative agent from three patients who were residents of northern Virginia, and proved that it was identical with that of Rocky mountain spotted fever. After that time, the disease was shown to be widely distributed in the U.S., present in two provinces of western Canada, in two states of Brazil and in Colombia.

Discovery of the microbe of Rocky mountain spotted fever, by H. T. Ricketts in 1906, led to the understanding of other rickettsiae-caused diseases. (*See* RICKETTSIAE.)

Epidemiology.—The predominance of the disease in the western U.S. among persons exposed to the open range, and the seasonal limitations to late spring and early summer months, were explained when the vector (carrier) species was identified as a wood tick, *Dermacentor andersoni.* It is widely distributed in the adult form upon large mammals, particularly cattle and sheep, in the western range country of the Pacific coast states, Nebraska, North and South Dakota and Nevada, and from New Mexico and Arizona on the south to Alberta, Saskatchewan and British Columbia on the north. Adult ticks live two to four years or more. Engorged females deposit their eggs in the soil. The winter is passed in the adult, nymphal or egg stage. Larvae, or seed ticks, emerge in the late spring and seek a blood meal on small animals. If successful, they molt to the nymphal stage, which may not become active until the following spring.

Many small animals, especially rodents, are susceptible to infection with the rickettsiae of Rocky mountain spotted fever and after having been bitten by an infected tick develop an inapparent form of the disease. While the microorganisms are in the peripheral circulation, these animals serve as a source of infection for uninfected larval, nymphal or adult ticks which chance to feed upon them. The rickettsiae pass through the stage-to-stage development in the tick and are carried to successive generations in decreasing numbers by transovarial passage. The infection is thus maintained in nature by the alternation of the small animal and tick hosts. Among the rodent hosts should be mentioned particularly the jack and the cottontail rabbits. The rabbit tick *Haemaphysalis leporis-palustris,* although it does not attack man, is one of the vectors in maintaining continuous passage in small animals.

The occurrence of the human disease in the eastern and southern U.S. was explained when it was discovered that the common dog tick, *Dermacentor variabilis,* which attacks man also acts as a vector. Dogs and field mice are involved in maintaining the reservoir of infection. In the southwestern U.S. human cases were also traced to the lone star tick *Amblyomma americanum.* In Brazil the common vector is *Amblyomma cajennense.* Many other tick species were found to be experimentally infectable but were epidemiologically unimportant.

Clinical and Pathological Features.—The clinical course of the disease is essentially similar to that described for typhus fever (*q.v.*). In severe cases of spotted fever the rash tends to be more hemorrhagic and to be accentuated on the extremities, particularly about the wrists and ankles. Occasionally, a lesion may be detected at the site of the tick bite, but a typical primary eschar is lacking. Nervous and mental symptoms are common; restlessness, insomnia, disorientation and delirium are frequent manifestations of involvement of the central nervous system. Prostration may be marked from the beginning, merging into coma with death possible as early as the sixth or seventh day. Convalescence is apt to be slow and may be complicated by visual disturbances, deafness and mental confusion. Although recovery may be delayed, it is usually complete. The case-fatality rates, as in typhus, vary directly with age. The crude rate for reported cases in the U.S. is about 18%.

The underlying pathology is essentially the same as that of typhus fever. The microorganism (*R. rickettsii*) proliferates in the endothelial cells lining the smaller blood vessels, causing damage to the vessel walls with hemorrhage, infiltration with round cells and thrombosis. Lesions are widely distributed in the tissues of the body but are characteristically common in the central nervous system and skin. Occasionally, there may be large areas of subcutaneous hemorrhage, particularly in the scrotum. Diagnosis is confirmed by blood tests. The Weil-Felix reaction becomes positive with *Bacillus proteus* X 19 and usually with X 2 and negative with *B. proteus* X K during the second week of the illness. The complement-fixation test becomes positive about the same time. The microorganisms may be recovered and identified following inoculation of guinea pigs with blood obtained from a patient early in the course of the illness. Reports in the 1950s indicated that early institution of treatment with antibiotics—chloramphenicol (chloromycetin) and aureomycin—greatly shortens the disease and decreases the risk of death.

Prevention.—Prevention depends primarily upon exercise of personal care in protection against tick bites. Persons exposed to known infected areas should frequently examine the clothing and body for ticks. Usually the tick does not become attached to its host immediately but crawls about for several hours. The chance of receiving infection from the bite of a tick is directly proportional to the length of time that the tick has fed. Ticks should be removed from the person or from a pet with a small forceps or with a piece of paper. The skin area involved should be swabbed with an antiseptic and the forceps disinfected with heat or chemicals. Hands should be washed with soap and water after such an operation.

There is a satisfactory vaccination procedure against Rocky mountain spotted fever; it should be administered in the spring or early summer before the beginning of the tick season, and should be repeated annually as the maximum degree of protection conferred is for less than a year. The degree of immunity afforded is relative, but the chance for subsequent infection is lessened and the risk of death is greatly reduced.

Fièvre Boutonneuse (Fièvre Exanthématique).—A. Connor and A. Bruch in 1910 described a mild typhuslike fever which they believed to be an endemic disease of Tunisia, north Africa, and proposed the name boutonneuse fever. It was subsequently observed to occur in Marseilles, France, and still later was discovered to have a wide geographic distribution. It was reported from most of the Mediterranean countries and the Crimea. Available evidence suggests that the diseases described as Kenya typhus and South African tick-bite fever are probably identical with boutonneuse fever, although conveyed by a different species of tick. One review indicated the widespread distribution of this human tick-borne rickettsiosis in Africa.

Primarily, the vector was found to be a brown dog tick, *Rhipicephalus sanguineus;* subsequently, other ticks were incriminated. The microorganism is *Rickettsia conorii.* The reservoir probably exists in nature in the lower animals, but the dog is apparently an important source of infection. The course of the disease is somewhat similar to Rocky mountain spotted fever, but it is milder. The case fatality rate is less than 3%. A primary lesion, called a *tache noire* ("black spot") is frequently found. It is somewhat similar in appearance to the primary eschar characteristically seen in tsutsugamushi disease. It is, of course, located at the site of the infecting tick bite and, therefore, may be found on any part of the body, but usually on a part covered by clothing. The Weil-Felix reaction with X 19 strain of *B. proteus* becomes positive late in the disease. Experimental evidence suggested that both chloramphenicol (chloromycetin) and aureomycin

would be highly effective in the treatment of boutonneuse fever. Prevention depends upon protection from tick bites as outlined above.

See M. C. Pincoffs, E. J. Guy, L. M. Lister, T. E. Woodward and J. E. Smadel, "The Treatment of Rocky Mountain Spotted Fever with Chloromycetin," *Ann. Int. Med.,* 29:656 (1948); W. H. Price, "The Epidemiology of Rocky Mountain Spotted Fever," *Am. J. Hyg.,* 60:292 (1954). (K. F. M.)

ROCOCO ART is a term which stands for trends in Baroque art that developed in France under Italian influence around 1720 and lasted until about 1770. Contemporaries called the style "modern," "style of the century," and *"genre pittoresque."* The term rococo was coined toward the end of the 18th century and originally had a derogatory connotation; it may have originated in the words *rocaille* and *coquille* ("rocks" and "shells"), which were common rococo motifs.

In France the style was applied primarily to the creation of secular buildings and furnishings for the court, the aristocracy, and the *bourgeoisie.* This vast sphere of influence was possible because the style was exceptionally adaptable and because it was widely popularized by quantities of ornamental engravings published in Paris and copied and paraphrased in Augsburg. Rococo ornament was characterized by arrangements of C- and S-curves prominent amid fanciful tracery, scrollwork, and other motifs derived from classical, Chinese, and even Gothic sources, as well as from nature. The design might be shaped in symmetric or asymmetric fashion, but it always was balanced and closely related to the overall pattern.

While the French creation caught the fancy of all of Europe, a unique development took place in south Germany, Switzerland, and Austria which must not be gauged by the Paris yardstick. In marked difference from its development in France, the German rococo was essentially placed in the service of the church. It is characterized by the unity of its effect; in a rococo church of this period, all media are fused and so tightly knit that it seems neither possible nor even important to unravel the contributions made by the various artists—architect, sculptor, painter.

Rococo trends dominated the 18th century, though others of less vigour persisted. All of them withered in the last quarter of the century when neoclassicism began to gain general recognition. *See* Baroque Art; Baroque and Post-Baroque Architecture; *see* also references under "Rococo Art" in the Index.

Bibliography.—Sidney Fiske Kimball, *Creation of the Rococo* (1943); Rudolf Stamm (ed.), *Die Kunstformen des Barockzeitalters* (1956); catalogue of the exhibition held under the auspices of the Europe council in Munich (1958); Wylie Sypher, *Four Stages of Renaissance Style* (1955). (Hs. H.)

ROCROI, a fortress town of northeastern France, *département* of Ardennes, on the Belgian frontier, lies 18 mi. (29 km.) NNW of Charleville-Mézières by road. Pop. (1962) 1,542. It was heavily fortified in the 16th and 17th centuries. Nearby the Spanish were defeated by the Great Condé (Louis II de Bourbon) in 1643 (*see* Thirty Years' War), but Rocroi was captured in 1658, only to be returned to France a year later by the Treaty of the Pyrenees. The fortifications by Vauban still encase the town in the form of a pentagon, and have great interest as an example of military architecture of the period before the development of modern artillery.

(Ar. E. S.)

ROD, ÉDOUARD (1857–1910), French-Swiss writer of psychological novels and pioneer of comparative criticism, was born at Nyon, Switzerland, on March 29, 1857. After his first novels written in Émile Zola's manner, the best of which was *Palmyre Veulard* (1881), Rod soon evolved his own highly sensitive, introverted psychological art, frequently depicting frail, tragic characters in such novels as *La Course à la mort* (1885), *Le Sens de la vie* (1889), *Nouvelles romandes* (1890), *La Vie privée de Michel Teissier* (1893; English translation, *The Private Life of an Eminent Politician,* 1893), and *Le Silence* (1894). Although often a prey to pessimism and despondency, Rod insisted more and more on duty, conscience, and renunciation as decisive elements of life. As a critic he was a forerunner of modern comparative literary study, his chief works being *De la littérature comparée* (1886) and *Reflets d'Amérique* (1905). He died at Grasse, France, on Jan. 29, 1910.

See C. Beuchat, *Édouard Rod et le cosmopolitisme* (1930); C. Delhorbe, *Édouard Rod d'après des documents inédits* (1939). (A. Bx.)

RODBERTUS, JOHANN KARL (1805–1875), German economist, author of a conservative interpretation of social reform and a strong supporter of monarchy and economic nationalism, was born at Greifswald on Aug. 12, 1805, the son of a university professor. Educated in law at Prussian universities, Rodbertus acquired in 1836 the landed estate of Jagetzow in Pomerania. Until his death, on Dec. 6, 1875, he carried on economic studies as well as historical studies and participated in Prussian politics.

The substance of his social-economic reasoning is a principle of government regulation of wages so that they might rise in proportion to increases in national productivity. Unlike Malthus and Ricardo—who believed that wages rise naturally in conformance with rising conceptions of a conventional standard of living—Rodbertus maintained that wage earners, when left to their own devices, cannot earn more than a bare minimum of physical existence. All increases of national productivity therefore accrue to the owners of property. Since property owners constitute a minority of the population, crises of underconsumption and retarded production occur while yet a majority of the population is not prosperous: "thus society pays dearly because labour is hired too cheaply."

Rodbertus, unlike Marx, did not call into question the entire complex of the political and economic institutions of capitalism, but in entrusting the government with legislating the conditions of wage payments, he furnished a conservative basis of state intervention; thus in his time he won support for social legislation in circles inaccessible to socialist agitation or fearful of it.

See H. Dietzel, *Karl Rodbertus: Darstellung seines Lebens und seiner Lehre* (1886); E. C. K. Gonner, *Social Philosophy of Rodbertus* (1899). (G. W. Z.)

RODENT, any member of the order Rodentia, characterized by teeth and jaws uniquely adapted to gnawing. The largest order of mammals, both in number of individuals and in number of described species, it includes squirrels, beavers, mice, rats, lemmings, jerboas, porcupines, chinchillas, and capybaras. They occur naturally in most parts of the world, being abundant and diversified in all continents except Australia, and in all continental islands. Members of the family Muridae invaded Australia from New Guinea during the Late Pliocene and Pleistocene, but have not yet spread beyond the northeastern part of the continent. The Norway and related rats (*Rattus*) and the house mouse (*Mus*) have accompanied man in his travels, and are found almost anywhere humans are.

GENERAL FEATURES

Most rodents are small to medium sized. The pygmy mice are among the smallest of mammals, while the capybara may become as large as a black bear, reaching a length of 4 ft. and a weight of 100 lb. Rodents occupy a wide variety of ecologic niches, most being terrestrial quadrupeds: some, such as pocket gophers and mole rats, have become modified for burrowing either with their forelimbs or with their incisor teeth; some, such as squirrels, are arboreal; others, such as flying squirrels, have developed skin folds that permit them to glide from one tree to another; a number, including jerboas, jumping mice, and kangaroo rats, have enlarged hind legs and have become bipedal leapers; and a few, such as beavers, muskrats, coypus, and the Australian water rats, have made adaptations toward an aquatic habitat (fig. 1).

Because of their small size and great reproductive capacity, rodents are among the few groups of mammals that successfully survive in a human-dominated environment. It is estimated that most U.S. cities contain nearly as many rats as humans, and house mice may be almost as abundant. Norway rats cause extensive damage to stored and processed human food supplies, and some rodents cause extensive damage to growing crops. The American muskrat, introduced into Europe, is a cause of great concern, especially in the Netherlands, because of its habit of making burrows in dikes. A number of rodents act as intermediate hosts for human diseases or for the parasites that carry such diseases. The brown or Norway rat is the chief carrier of fleas that can transmit bubonic plague. Tularemia can also be transmitted by rodents.

Rodents are an important food source for primitive people because of their abundance and relative ease of capture, but relatively few except squirrels are eaten by civilized people. Beavers, squirrels, muskrats, chinchillas, and coypus produce valuable furs. Beaver skins were one of the chief ingredients in the fur trade that was responsible in large part for opening the western United States.

Rodents, in general, are herbivorous, but many of them eat animal food to the extent that it is available, including insects, young birds, eggs, and even carrion.

CHARACTERISTIC STRUCTURES

Dentition.—Rodent dentition is characterized by a single pair of upper and lower chisellike incisors, which grow throughout the life of the animal. Since the enamel is limited to the anterior face of the tooth, wear removes the softer dentine faster than the enamel, thus preserving a sharp cutting edge. The growth of the incisors, measured in millimetres per week in most forms that have been studied, reaches one centimetre per week in the burrowing pocket gophers or geomyids. The constant rubbing of the upper incisors against the lower wears them away as fast as they grow.

Behind the incisors, there is a large gap, or diastema, in front

BY COURTESY OF (BOTTOM RIGHT) THE NEW YORK ZOOLOGICAL SOCIETY; PHOTOGRAPHS, (TOP LEFT) ZOOLOGICAL SOCIETY OF LONDON; (TOP RIGHT) WILLIS PETERSON; (BOTTOM LEFT) ERNEST P. WALKER

FIG. 1.—REPRESENTATIVE TYPES OF RODENTS, BASED ON BODY FORM AND HABIT

(Top left) Quadrupedal, viscacha; (top right) leaping, kangaroo rat; (bottom left) burrowing, tuco tuco; (bottom right) arboreal, South American tree porcupine (*Coendou*)

of the cheek teeth. The latter include a maximum of two upper and one lower premolars, and three upper and three lower molars on each side. The minimum is two pairs of molars above and below. The teeth show many different patterns, ranging from very simple in the squirrels to very complex in forms like the capybara; they also range from low crowned and rooted to very high crowned and rootless (fig. 2).

Jaw Muscles.—The lower jaw is capable of anteroposterior movement at the point of articulation with the skull, which permits the cheek teeth to be used in chewing food, with the incisors disengaged, when the jaw is at the rear of the articulation; or the incisors to be used in gnawing, with the cheek teeth disengaged, when the jaw is moved forward (fig. 3).

Living rodents, with one exception (*Aplodontia*, the sewellel, or mountain beaver, of the Pacific Northwest), have evolved highly specialized jaw muscles, related to the use of the incisors in gnawing. The most important of these is the masseter, which is used to pull the lower jaw forward in gnawing. During the evolution of the rodents, the masseter has spread forward from its primitive point of origin on the cheek bone or zygomatic arch (as in *Aplodontia*), expanding either onto the snout in front of the bone; through the orbit, out the infraorbital foramen, and onto the snout; or by a combination of the two (fig. 4). J. F. Brandt, in 1855, divided what are now included in the rodents into three subdivisions on this basis, calling them the Sciuromorpha (squirrel-like), Hystricomorpha (porcupinelike), and Myomorpha (mouse-like). T. Tullberg, in 1899, noted that rodents could be divided into two groups, which he called the Sciurognathi (squirrel-jawed) and Hystricognathi (porcupine-jawed), on the basis of whether the angle of the jaw arises in the plane of the incisor or lateral to it. He then used Brandt's terms for subordinate units.

Digestive Tract.—Many rodents have cheek pouches, used for storing food to be transported to the nest or storage area. Usually these pouches open into the mouth, but in the New World Heteromyidae (pocket mice) and Geomyidae (pocket gophers), there are fur-lined pouches, opening outside the mouth, which reach back almost to the shoulders and which have a capacity about equal to the volume of the head. Rodents usually have a large alimentary pouch, or caecum (sometimes larger in capacity than the stomach), where digestion of plant tissues takes place.

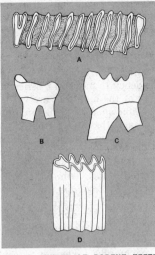

FIG. 2.—TYPES OF RODENT TEETH

(A) Surface view of a left upper molar of a capybara. This is the most complicated tooth among extant rodents (stippled areas are cement). (B, C, D) Side views of lower teeth: (B) low-crowned tooth of *Paramys* from cheek side; (C) molar, five-crested type, of *Theridomys*, from tongue side; (D) right molar, ever-growing type, of *Microtus*

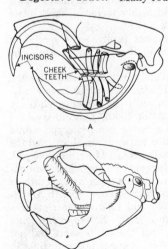

FIG. 3.—SKULLS OF RODENTS

(A) Teeth superimposed on outline of skull and jaws of a genus of pocket gophers (*Pappogeomys*); (B) incisors and relationships of upper and lower teeth of beaver (*Castor*), when lower jaw is shifted forward to the gnawing position

CLASSIFICATION AND SURVEY

Formerly the order was believed to include two major types of mammals: the Simplicidentata, with a single pair of upper incisors; and the Duplicidentata, with two pairs of upper incisors.

The Duplicidentata (rabbits and hares) are now separated by all American and most European specialists as a separate order, the Lagomorpha (*see* LAGOMORPH).

Difficulties in classification arise because the rodents, while being so abundant and successful an order, are limited in the possible directions of evolution by the initial acquisition of the gnawing adaptation. As a result, there has been a great deal of parallel evolution within the order, and relationships of different forms (and, hence, a true phylogenetic classification) are difficult to determine. All currently used classifications are merely attempts to reach a closer approximation to the correct phylogenetic arrangement. A. E. Wood's modified classification (1959) is used here, suborders being used for part of the order, whereas those rodents that cannot be shown to belong to suborders are left independent. In this article the order Rodentia is divided into four groups, three suborders—Protrogomorpha, Caviomorpha, and Myomorpha—and an independent category that comprises several families of uncertain subordinal affinities.

PRIMITIVE RODENTS (PROTROGOMORPHA)

The rodents of this suborder had the masseter muscle in its primitive position on the ventral surface of the zygomatic bone (fig. 4A). According to Wood's interpretation, this group includes the ancestral stock of the order. The infraorbital foramen is small or of medium size, and has no relationship to the masseter. The angle of the jaw may be incipiently sciurognathous, incipiently hystricognathous, or indeterminate. The cheek teeth may have cusps; if the cusps are united into crests, there are never more than four crests per tooth. The teeth are usually low crowned. Postorbital processes are normally absent. The tibia and fibula bones of the lower leg are not fused.

Ischyromyoidea.—The superfamily represents the initial (Eocene) radiation of the rodents. The premolar formula is $\frac{2}{1}$; *i.e.*, there are two premolars on either side of the upper jaw and one on either side of the lower jaw. These rodents are known from North America, Europe, and probably North Africa and Mongolia, from the Late Paleocene to the Late Oligocene.

Paramyidae.—This was a particularly abundant family in the Eocene of North America, and included all the known Paleocene rodents. In Wood's opinion, it was directly or indirectly ancestral to all other rodents. Paramyids ranged in size from animals the size of a house mouse to those as large as a beaver. The cheek teeth were cusped and low crowned. The skull somewhat resembled that of a marmot.

Sciuravidae, a family comprising small rodents derived from the paramyids, were abundant in the Middle Eocene of North America, and are represented in Mongolia. They appeared in the Early Eocene, and lasted till the end of that period. The teeth were four crested but generally low crowned and always rooted. This family may have been ancestral to the Myomorpha.

Protoptychidae, a poorly known family from the Late Eocene, was characterized by an inflated tympanic bulla, of the sort associated in living rodents with bipedal leaping locomotion. Skeletons have been discovered in Wyoming.

Cylindrodontidae, a family that occurred in the Late Eocene and Oligocene of North America and the Oligocene of Mongolia, contained burrowing forms with high-crowned to ever-growing cheek teeth, based on a four-crested pattern.

Ischyromyidae.—This family, known from the Oligocene of North America, had teeth that were four crested and low crowned.

Aplodontoidea.—A specialized superfamily of the Protrogomorpha, with high-crowned to ever-growing cheek teeth.

Aplodontidae.—This family has as its sole existing representative the sewellel, or mountain beaver (*Aplodontia rufa*), of the mountains of Oregon, Washington, and British Columbia. It is about the size of a marmot, with a short tail, small rounded ears, and small eyes. *Aplodontia* is a burrowing animal, living in damp woods. Other representatives of the family are known from the Tertiary of western North America, where the group was apparently rare but persistent. Side lines are known as fossils from Mongolia and Europe.

Mylagaulidae, a strange family of North American Miocene and

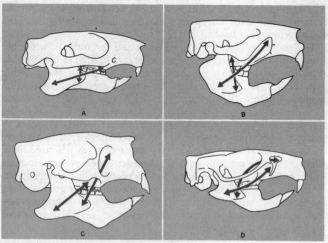

FIG. 4.—SKULLS OF THE FOUR BASIC TYPES OF RODENTS, SHOWING POSITION OF BRANCHES OF THE MASSETER MUSCLE

(A) Protrogomorphous, with masseter limited to zygoma; (B) sciuromorphous, with anterior branch of masseter shifting upward and forward on snout; (C) hystricomorphous, with deep branch of masseter shifting upward and forward through enlarged infraorbital foramen; (D) myomorphous, combining (B) and (C)

Pliocene forms, comprised burrowing members. Paired horns, present on the snouts of some individuals and absent on others, were perhaps a sexual characteristic.

CAVYLIKE RODENTS (CAVIOMORPHA)

This suborder is characterized by an enlarged infraorbital foramen through which a branch of the masseter muscle passes to attach to the side of the snout (fig. 4C). This arrangement results in a much more anteroposterior direction for the pull of the masseter, and increases the efficiency of this muscle for gnawing. The jaw angle arises lateral to the socket of the lower incisors. The Caviomorpha are exclusively South American, except for geologically recent immigrants to North America; they have a cheektooth pattern based on four cross crests in both upper and lower teeth. Ancestral members of all four currently recognized caviomorph superfamilies are present in the Early Oligocene, when the group is first known. The tibia and fibula have generally been fused since the Middle Miocene. The premolars are reduced to $\frac{1}{1}$.

Octodontoidea.—This superfamily is the central stock of the Caviomorpha. The cheek teeth, though primitive and four crested, progressively develop an E-shaped pattern by the reduction of one of the crests.

Octodontidae, of southern distribution, contains a number of rodents that have secondarily simplified bilobed cheek teeth: Ctenomyinae includes the burrowing tuco tucos (*Ctenomys*); Octodontinae contains ratlike or mouselike forms with tufted tails, chiefly found in the southern Andes. *Spalacopus* and *Aconaemys* of the latter group are burrowers; they resemble *Ctenomys* but have cheek teeth with a figure-eight rather than a kidneylike pattern.

Echimyidae contains many rodents of ratlike appearance, with rooted cheek teeth and usually coarse or spiny hair. The cheek teeth have a distorted E pattern. In the Echimyinae the cheek teeth are narrow, whereas in the Dactylomyinae they are broad, with four crests. The fur is soft and the third and fourth digits are usually elongated in the Dactylomyinae.

Capromyidae includes two groups. The hutias (*Capromys*) of the Greater Antilles and northern South America are coarsehaired, robust rodents, with ever growing cheek teeth of the E pattern. The coypu, or nutria (*Myocastor*), is a large guinea piglike rodent with soft fur, found from Brazil to Argentina and Chile, and introduced into both Europe and the United States.

Abrocomidae.—This family has only a single genus, *Abrocoma*, characterized by a ratlike appearance, short hairy tail, and inflated auditory bullae, a blisterlike bone that encloses the middle ear. The cheek teeth are ever-growing, the upper ones having a distorted figure-eight pattern and the lowers being E-shaped. *Abrocoma* lives in the Andes.

Chinchilloidea.—In this superfamily the cheek teeth are evergrowing, consisting of closely appressed, transverse plates. The skull has large auditory bullae and an inflated mastoid area, reflecting enlargements of the brain associated with a rather general tendency to move in a series of kangaroolike jumps. The lateral toes of the hind foot are vestigial or lost.

Chinchillidae.—This family is known from the plains of Argentina and the Andes from Ecuador south. Chinchillas are softfurred rodents, about the size of a large squirrel. They have been nearly exterminated in South America by fur hunters, but there is an extensive program of chinchilla raising being carried on in the United States. Almost equally soft furred are the rabbit-eared species of *Lagidium*, found from Peru and Chile to southern Argentina. The larger viscachas (*Lagostomus*) of the Argentine pampas are the size of a hare, with large head and robust body. They live in colonies and are nocturnal.

Cavioidea.—This superfamily is the most successful of the Caviomorpha. There is a deep groove on the side of the jaw for the attachment of the deep portion of the masseter muscle. The cheek teeth are high crowned or ever-growing.

Caviidae includes the guinea pigs and cavies. The cheek teeth are ever-growing and prismatic, often being heart shaped in cross section. The clavicle is absent, and the lateral toes of the hind foot are lost. The tail is short or absent. *Cavia* includes a number of species, of which the best known is the guinea pig, which was domesticated by the Incas in Peru. *Kerodon* of Brazil has toes that end in blunt nails, almost resembling hooves. *Dolichotis*, restricted to Argentina, is rather rabbitlike, especially *D. patagonica*, the mara.

Hydrochoeridae, a Miocene derivative of the Caviidae, is characterized by large size and highly complex cheek teeth. *Hydrochoerus*, the semiaquatic capybara, is the only living genus. It is found from Panama to Paraguay, and is the largest living rodent. Pleistocene relatives of *Hydrochoerus*, as much as 10% larger, are known from both North and South America.

Dinomyidae.—This family consists of a single living species with a broad, flat skull and molars made up of four transverse plates. They are found in Peru.

Dasyproctidae includes the agoutis of tropical America. They are the size of large rabbits, with a short tail, and three toes on the hind foot. These active runners are locally prized for food.

Cuniculidae.—The Cuniculidae includes the paca, a large rodent with five-toed feet. The cheek teeth are lobed. The most striking peculiarity is in the enormous and highly furrowed cheek plate developed from the zygomatic arch.

Heptaxodontidae.—This is an extinct family, some species of which exceeded the capybaras in size; they are known from the Pleistocene of the West Indies.

Erethizontoidea.—This superfamily includes a single family, the Erethizontidae, or New World porcupines, which have a relatively primitive cheek-tooth pattern and fairly low-crowned teeth. Four crests form the main part of the tooth, a subsidiary fifth crest, present in some forms, having arisen as a neomorph within the family. The skeleton is modified for an arboreal life, and the first toe of the hind foot is functionally replaced by a movable pad. *Erethizon*, the North American porcupine, a Late Pliocene immigrant from South America, has extended its range as far north as Alaska and Labrador, and is one of the best-known North American rodents. *Coendou*, from South and Central America, is a smaller animal, with a long prehensile tail. *Echinoprocta*, from Colombia, is like *Coendou* except that the tail is short and not prehensile. The South American *Chaetomys* is rather distinct in having simple cheek teeth, well-developed postorbital processes on the skull, and spines restricted to the head and forelimbs. The tail is long and scaly.

MOUSELIKE RODENTS (MYOMORPHA)

This suborder may be defined as small sciurognathous rodents, with cheek teeth primarily cusped and low crowned; the premolars are reduced to $\frac{1}{1}$ or $\frac{1}{0}$, or may be absent. Locomotion is by scampering, climbing, burrowing, or leaping, the last being very common. The masseter muscle has grown forward along the snout, either in front of the zygoma or both in front of it and through the infraorbital foramen (fig. 4D).

Muroidea.—This is the typical superfamily forming the basis of the Myomorpha. A branch of the masseter passes in front of the eye, onto the snout, compressing the ventral part of the infraorbital foramen into a slit, while another part of the masseter passes into the orbit, through the dorsal part of the infraorbital foramen and out onto the snout. The premolars have all been lost, and the cheek teeth are reduced to the molars $\frac{3}{3}$, except in the Hydromyinae where they are $\frac{2}{2}$. The cardiac part of the stomach is lined by a cornified layer; the colon forms a spiral loop.

Cricetidae.—This large family has the cusps of the molars arranged in two rows, generally alternating, so that worn teeth show a pattern of zigzag crests. Cricetids first appeared in the Oligocene of Europe and western North America. They are only slightly more primitive than some of the living forms, and are probably derivable from Eocene sciuravids like *Pauromys*.

The subfamily Cricetodontinae are primitive members of the family, appearing in the Lower Oligocene of Europe and North America. The cusps are the dominant parts of the tooth pattern, although there are five transverse ridges, subsidiary to the cusps. These ridges have become dominant in the other subfamilies, which originated from the Cricetodontinae during the Miocene or Pliocene.

The subfamily Cricetinae includes a wide variety of common rat- and mouselike rodents of the Northern Hemisphere, as well as some that have spread farther south. The hamsters, including *Cricetus* and relatives, are heavy-bodied, short-tailed burrowing rodents of Europe and Asia. *Peromyscus*, the white-footed or deer mouse, is an abundant American member from Alaska to Panama. Other cricetines include the pack rats (*Neotoma*); harvest mice (*Reithrodontomys*), with grooved incisors; the grasshopper mouse (*Onychomys*), which feeds largely on insects and other small animals; and rice rats (*Oryzomys*), found from Patagonia to New Jersey. There are a large number of tropical American genera.

The subfamily Nesomyinae, from Madagascar, includes forms descended from ancestors that accidentally reached the island, probably in the Pliocene. Some are burrowers, others scamperers. Some authors consider that they are sufficiently distinct to be recognized as a separate family. *Lophiomys*, the maned rat of eastern Asia, is given subfamily rank because of its peculiar skull. The temporal fossa, on the top rear of the skull, is completely roofed over by bone, the surface of which is granulated. No such condition is found in any other rodent. The teeth are typically cricetid. The tail is bushy, and the feet, with a partly opposable first digit, are specialized for arboreal life.

The subfamily Gerbillinae consists of the gerbils, jumping rodents with the broad brain case and inflated mastoid and auditory bulla that usually go with a leaping habit. The cheek teeth are prismatic, with transverse crests. The upper incisors are usually grooved. Gerbils are widespread in the deserts of Africa and the steppes of southern Asia, *Gerbillus*, *Tatera*, and *Meriones* being found throughout the range of the subfamily, with others having a more limited distribution. Several genera use the tail for the storage of fat.

The subfamily Microtinae is so very distinct from the other cricetids that it is often considered to be a distinct family, Microtidae. It includes the lemmings (*Lemmus* and allies), typically holarctic or northern rodents, though they extend as far south as Guatemala and Burma. The cheek teeth are high crowned and prismatic, rarely with roots, and the crown has a complex zigzag pattern. The skull is angular, marked with ridges for the attachment of muscles. In general, microtines are heavy-bodied, short-tailed animals, more or less modified for burrowing. The largest microtine is the muskrat (*Ondatra*), a valuable fur-bearing animal in North America. It has been introduced into Europe. The muskrat is semiaquatic, with a long, dorso-ventrally flattened tail

and partially webbed hind feet. Its relationships to the other microtines are traceable through *Neofiber*, the round-tailed muskrat of Florida, and *Arvicola*, the Eurasian water vole. Such genera as *Clethrionomys*, the red-backed vole of northern areas; *Phenacomys*, the red tree mouse of North America; and *Ellobius*, a burrowing vole of southern and central Asia, are primitive in having rooted cheek teeth. The microtines are one of the latest important groups of mammals to have developed. They originated in the Pliocene from the Cricetinae, through *Mimomys*, first described as a fossil and later discovered still living in the mountains of central Europe. *Mimomys* was also present in North America during the Pliocene.

Muridae.—This family, of southeast Asiatic origin, is now widespread throughout the world. The only New World forms are the semidomesticated *Rattus* (house, Norway, roof, black, or wharf rats) and *Mus* (house mouse). The upper molars have three rows of cusps, which generally unite to form cross crests. The family is especially abundant in the East Indies, which probably is the approximate area of its origin from the Cricetidae during the Miocene.

The subfamily Murinae contains the true rats and mice, with about 400 recognized species. *Rattus* is abundant and diverse in southeast Asia and the East Indies. The bandicoot rats, *Nesokia* and *Bandicota*, are burrowers, found from Egypt to China and Malaysia. *Cricetomys*, the African giant rat, may measure 30 in. in total length. The spiny mice, *Acomys*, of East Africa, southwest Asia, Cyprus, and Crete, are almost as spiny as hedgehogs. Various unrelated genera have become arboreal, developing common adaptations. A number of genera of shrew rats (*Mycteromys*, *Echiothrix*, *Melasmothrix*), with long, narrow heads and shrewlike appearance, are found in the East Indies. The Philippine shrew rat (*Rhynchomys*), with minute cheek teeth and short, weak incisors, perhaps feeds on insects and worms. Bushy-tailed rats (*Phloeomys* and *Crateromys*) occur in the northern Philippines. Some members of the subfamily reached Australia, apparently in the Pleistocene, and have begun a rapid diversification, bipedal leaping locomotion being the most notable development.

The water rat subfamily, Hydromyinae, ranges in Australia, New Guinea, and the Philippines. These rodents apparently evolved from the Murinae in New Guinea. Normally there are only two of the usual three molars, which have broad, basined crowns. The infraorbital foramen is wide. The feet are large, and the hair is dense and waterproof, both adaptations to life in the water.

The subfamily Dendromurinae, the African tree mice, is characterized by an arboreal life and a reduced number of cusps in the molars. The first digits are opposable, and the claws are frequently modified into nails. Another African group, the Otomyinae or swamp rats, also belongs in the Muridae.

Geomyoidea.—This superfamily includes the two New World families of the pocket gophers (Geomyidae) and the pocket mice and kangaroo rats (Heteromyidae). These two families are certainly closely related. The Eomyidae, an extinct family best known from the Late Eocene and Oligocene of Europe and the United States, is referred to this superfamily on the basis of similarities in skull structure, especially in the base of the skull. External fur-lined cheek pouches are present in the two living families. There is a single pair of upper and of lower premolars, except in the most primitive eomyids, where there is a second pair of upper premolars.

Geomyidae.—The pocket gopher family includes stout-bodied, short-tailed burrowing forms with massive, uninflated skulls. Members of the living subfamily, Geomyinae, have small eyes and ears and large claws on the forefeet. They are found in western North America, Central America, and northern South America. The cheek teeth are reduced to simple, ever-growing prisms; unworn teeth, however, show the ancestral pattern.

The subfamily Entoptychinae, abundant in the Miocene of western United States and Florida, developed into a dominant group of rodents at the expense of the Cricetidae. The general structure was similar to that of the geomyines, but the skulls were less angular and the tooth structure was intermediate between that of the geomyines and the heteromyids. Usually the teeth are lower crowned than in the geomyines.

Heteromyidae, like the Geomyidae, is characterized by external fur-lined cheek pouches. Some forms are leaping (*e.g.*, kangaroo rats), whereas others are mouselike and scampering (*e.g.*, pocket mice). The subfamily Perognathinae, or pocket mice, appeared in the Oligocene and became commoner in later deposits of western United States. The cheek teeth are rooted and show the primitive pattern for the family. The four cusps of the lower premolar unite in the middle of the tooth to form an X pattern. Heteromyinae, the subfamily of spiny pocket mice, separated from the perognathines during the Oligocene; its members were very abundant in western United States and Florida during the Miocene, though they are now restricted to Middle America and northern South America. They are identified by the presence of spiny hairs among the fur, and by differences in the tooth patterns, especially in that the lower premolar develops a series of cusps surrounding a central basin. The subfamily Dipodomyinae, the kangaroo rats, originated in western United States in the later Tertiary. The most striking feature of these rodents is the elongation of the hind limbs for leaping, with which is associated a great inflation of the auditory bullae and adjacent parts of the skull, and a widening of the entire posterior part of the skull. The teeth are high crowned and, when worn, show great similarities to those of the geomyids.

Eomyidae.—This fossil family is known mostly from teeth and jaws, together with a few skulls. Eomyids probably had a scampering mode of locomotion. The teeth are cricetidlike, but there are always premolars (absent in the cricetids), as well as differences in detail of pattern. The skull is similar to that of geomyids and heteromyids, to which they are probably related. The Eomyinae is a fossil subfamily, known from Late Eocene and Oligocene of Europe and North America, and Pliocene of western United States; it was abundant in mouse-sized forms. The subfamily Yoderimyinae, of the Late Eocene or Early Oligocene of Wyoming and Texas, is rare and poorly known.

Dipodoidea.—This is a superfamily of jumping rodents, including the jerboas and jumping mice. The infraorbital foramen is large, intermediate in size between the myomorphous and hystricomorphous conditions. The cheek teeth are $\frac{4}{3}$, the first upper one (the only premolar) being very small.

Zapodidae.—The most primitive living members are in the subfamily Sicistinae, including the Eurasian *Sicista*, or birch mouse, a tree-living and seed-eating animal. The Zapodinae, or jumping mice, of North America and east Asia contains species that have developed leaping locomotion but show no inflation of the auditory bulla (which may support the contention of those who believe that the inflation of the bulla is a desert adaptation rather than a leaping one, since the jumping mice inhabit non-desert areas). Fossils are known since the Early Miocene.

Dipodidae.—The jerboas are one of the most successful families of leaping rodents, and one of the most highly specialized for this mode of locomotion. The hind legs are long and the three middle metatarsal bones are usually fused, the lateral toes being lost. The hind feet are long. The bullae and mastoids are inflated. Jerboas are found in desert and steppe areas of northern Africa, eastern Europe, and Asia. They probably evolved from early zapodids.

Gliroidea.—This is an exclusively Old World superfamily of small rodents. The infraorbital foramen is sciuromorphous. The cheek teeth are usually $\frac{4}{4}$ (though the premolars may be lost), and have a very distinctive pattern. They probably were derived, via the European Eocene-Oligocene *Gliravus*, from protrogomorphs like the sciuravids or small paramyids.

Gliridae, the dormouse family, comprises arboreal forms with bushy tails. In general appearance, they are intermediate in most features between squirrels and mice. The edible dormouse, *Glis*, ranges across southern Europe into Asia Minor. *Muscardinus*, the common dormouse, about the size of a house mouse, is found from England to the Mediterranean and Asia Minor. Various other genera exist in Eurasia and Africa. The African species are sometimes separated as the subfamily Graphiurinae, with less developed crests on the cheek teeth and a primitive attachment

of the lateral branch of the masseter muscle. The dormice found in southeastern Asia, including India and China, are generally separated as the subfamily Platacanthomyinae, though some authors consider them to be a distinct family. *Typhlomys*, a Chinese member of this group, is unique because it is a burrower with greatly reduced eyes.

Seleviniidae.—This family has been established for the peculiar central Asian *Selevinia*, an aberrant dormouse that has evolved into a leaping form, with a long, jerboalike tail, inflated auditory bullae, and short front legs. The molars have large central basins, and are reduced in size.

Spalacoidea.—The Old World mole rats and bamboo rats are another group of related families, presumably also related to the same stock as the others here included in the Myomorpha. They are burrowers.

Spalacidae, including *Spalax*, the blind mole rat of southern Europe, Egypt, and western Asia, is a family of highly developed burrowers similar in body form to the pocket gophers.

Rhizomyidae is the bamboo rat family of India, China, and the Malay region. It includes the east African mole rat (*Tachyoryctes*); one of the smaller members of the family, it is about eight inches long.

INDEPENDENT MEMBERS

The remaining 13 families of rodents, recognizably distinct from the types already mentioned, cannot be placed in any of the existing suborders with certainty.

Sciuroidea.—This superfamily contains only the single family Sciuridae, the squirrels.

Sciuridae.—Some authors consider this family to represent the most primitive type of rodent. There seems to be little justification for this view except in the pattern of the cheek teeth, which are very primitive, though they are more evolved than in the least specialized members of the Paramyidae. Post-orbital processes of the frontal are always present. The small infraorbital foramen is compressed by the sciuromorphous masseter muscle. The premolars are usually $\frac{2}{1}$. The family is represented everywhere except in polar areas and in Australia and the oceanic islands.

Sciurinae is the subfamily of tree and ground squirrels. The typical squirrels of Eurasia and America (*Sciurus*) include the American gray and the European red squirrels, both of which have been widely introduced outside their native ranges. The North American red squirrel (*Tamiasciurus*) is a smaller form. The pygmy squirrels (*Microsciurus*) of Central and South America are but little larger than mice. The tree squirrels of Africa and India are large, including *Ratufa* of the Indo-Malaysian area and *Funambulus*, the palm squirrel of India. There has been extensive diversification of the squirrels in Africa. Another subgroup includes the Oriental *Callosciurus* and related forms, some of which have become ground living, especially in the East Indies. One, *Rhinosciurus*, has slender incisors and is largely insectivorous.

The spiny squirrels of Africa include *Xerus* and its relatives. They are largely ground-living species, found all over Africa south of the Sahara. The cheek teeth are much more complicated than in other squirrels, as a result of which S. Schaub (1958) considers that they belong in a distinct family.

The ground squirrels of North America and Eurasia may be recognized as a distinct subdivision of the Sciurinae, the tribe Marmotini. Chipmunks (*Tamias* and *Eutamias*) are well-known small, striped rodents with cheek pouches; they are good climbers. *Tamias* is found in eastern North America; *Eutamias* in western North America and eastern Asia. The spermophiles, susliks, or ground squirrels (*Citellus*) are found from Hungary through Asia and in western North America, south to Mexico. They are primarily plains dwellers. The tail is short and flattened. The related prairie dog (*Cynomys*), of western North America, lives in colonies. The marmots or woodchucks (*Marmota*), found from the Alps across Asia and throughout North America as far south as Alabama and New Mexico, are the largest of the squirrel family.

The flying squirrels, subfamily Petauristinae, are found throughout the forested parts of the Northern Hemisphere. The fore and hind limbs are connected by a broad skin fold, supported by a cartilaginous spur from the wrist. Using this fold, they glide from tree to tree. The largest forms (*Petaurista* and *Eupetaurus* of southeast Asia and the East Indies) reach a head and body length of two feet. The European *Sciuropterus* and the American *Glaucomys* are much smaller. Several other genera are found in Malaysia.

Castoroidea.—In this superfamily the masseter muscle is similar in its attachments and divisions to that in the Sciuridae, but there are no postorbital processes and the cheek teeth are very different. In modern forms, the teeth have complex patterns and are ever-growing, although the earliest known forms (from the Oligocene) have low crowns and a tooth pattern that, while still complex, is derivable from a four-cusped ancestral pattern.

Castoridae.—This family of burrowing rodents, abundant during much of the Tertiary, is now reduced to two species of a single genus, *Castor,* comprising the European and American beavers. The latter is a semiaquatic rodent that builds dams, thus impounding ponds. *Castoroides* of North America and *Trogontherium* of Europe and Asia were large Pleistocene forms, the size of a black bear. In all castorids, the premolars are reduced to $\frac{1}{1}$.

Eutypomyidae.—This was an aberrant North American Late Eocene to Miocene family characterized by two upper premolars and an exceedingly complicated pattern in the cheek teeth. The foot structure was peculiar; the exact adaptations of the group are uncertain. They apparently were related to the beavers.

Theridomyoidea.—This very abundant superfamily of the European Eocene and Oligocene was typically hystricomorphous in infraorbital foramen but sciurognathous in jaw structure. American authors have usually considered them to be highly aberrant and specialized, whereas many European authors allocate them to a central position in rodent evolution.

Pseudosciuridae, a European Eocene and Oligocene family with low-crowned teeth. The earliest forms are close to the Paramyidae; later ones lead directly into the Theridomyidae.

Theridomyidae.—This family is known from the Middle Eocene to the Oligocene of Europe. Early species had low-crowned cheek teeth with five crests; later species had high-crowned or even ever-growing cheek teeth.

Hystricoidea.—There is a single family that can be referred to here, the Hystricidae or Old World porcupines. They differ from the New World porcupines (Erethizontidae) in dwelling on the ground. *Hystrix* includes large rodents, two feet or more in length, with short tails and peculiar inflated snouts; they range over southern Europe, Asia, and Africa. *Atherurus,* widespread in Africa and southern Asia, is about the size of a large rat. Other genera are also small. The family is a classic example of a hystricomorphous and hystricognathous rodent group.

Thryonomyoidea.—This superfamily comprises two very distinctive living African rodents that are hystricomorphous and hystricognathous. The group frequently was considered to have special relationships with the caviomorphs; their similarities are now thought to be due to parallel evolution. These two families have been shown to be descended from the Phiomyidae.

Thryonomyidae.—The African cane rats (*Thryonomys*) are about 15 to 18 in. long, not counting the tail. The incisors are broad and powerful, the cheek teeth, $\frac{4}{4}$, are high crowned and rapidly lose their pattern. Many of the hairs are modified into spines. The milk premolars are retained throughout life.

Petromuridae.—The rock rat (*Petromus*) of southwest Africa is about eight inches long. The structure of the skull suggests closer relationships with the Thryonomyidae than with any other rodents. The milk premolars are retained throughout life.

Phiomyidae.—This family appears in the Oligocene of Egypt and was very abundant and diverse in the Miocene of Africa. The Oligocene forms show the initial stages in the retention of the milk teeth. The Miocene forms developed superficial similarities to many rodents from other parts of the world.

Bathyergoidea.—A single family, the Bathyergidae, or South African mole rats, belongs here. They are hystricognathous, but not hystricomorphous. *Bathyergus* burrows with its large claws, and has normal rodent incisors. All other members of the family burrow with their incisors as well. The incisors have been modified so that they extend out in front of the mouth; as a result, the bases of the upper incisors extend back into the palate, or even into the pterygoid bones of the skull, instead of ending in front of the cheek teeth as in all other rodents. The bathyergids are the most specialized burrowers among the rodents, never coming to the surface of their own free will.

Families of Uncertain Relationships.—The three remaining families of rodents all have a hystricomorphous masseter muscle and a sciurognathous jaw angle, but other features suggest no close relationships among them.

Anomaluridae.—This is a family of arboreal rodents with gliding membranes similar to those of the flying squirrels. Cheek teeth are $\frac{4}{4}$ and are high crowned. One genus, *Zenkerella,* does not possess the flying membrane. The family is from Africa south of the Sahara, and few fossils are known.

Ctenodactylidae, also African rodents, are found in general north of the Sahara. They are about the size of a gray squirrel. The cheek teeth are prismatic and ever growing. Related fossils are known from the Oligocene of Mongolia and the Miocene of India and North Africa.

Pedetidae.—This family includes *Pedetes,* the springhaas or jumping hare of eastern and southern Africa, the largest bipedal jumping rodent, standing about 18 in. high, two to three times the size of any other leaping rodent. The front legs are small, and the tail is long and bushy. The cheek teeth, $\frac{4}{4}$, are very high crowned. Related forms, from the Miocene of Africa, are even more specialized than the extant genus.

See separate articles on various rodents and references under "Rodent" in the Index; *see also* MAMMAL.

BIBLIOGRAPHY.—J. R. Ellerman, *The Families and Genera of Living Rodents,* vol. 1 and 2 (1940); S. Schaub, "Simplicidentata" in *Traité de Paléontologie,* tome VI, 2:659–818 (1958); A. R. Shadle, "Porcupine Spine Penetration," *J. Mammal.,* 28:180–181 (1947); A. E. Wood, "A Revised Classification of the Rodents," *J. Mammal.,* 36:165–187 (1955), "Are There Rodent Suborders?," *Systematic Zoology,* 7:169–173 (1959); A. E. Wood and B. Patterson, "The Rodents of the Deseadan Oligocene of Patagonia and the Beginnings of South American Rodent Evolution," *Bull. Mus. Comp. Zool. Harv.,* 120:281–428 (1959).

(A. E. Wo.)

RODEO, a series of cowboy contests deriving from the days of the early cattle industry of the southwestern plains of the United States when men, forced to spend months and even years on the range, would gather together in the "cowtowns" at the end of the trails and vie for the unofficial title of best bucking horse rider, roper, etc., the contests being accompanied by heavy betting. As the cowboy was curtailed in scope by the railroads and fencing, the contests became regular, formal programs of entertainment.

Many western towns and areas claim the distinction of being the first place to hold a rodeo in the United States, among them Cheyenne, Wyo., in 1872 and Winfield, Kan., in 1882, but at best such early contests were merely exhibitions of riding and roping skill and not the highly organized shows that modern rodeo became. Denver, Colo., is traditionally accepted as the birthplace of paid spectator rodeo, October 1887.

Formerly, as now, various titles were given to these shows, such as stampede, frontier day, roundup, or fiesta. The word rodeo, which is of Spanish origin, did not come into general use until the 1920s. Originally an outdoor sport, rodeo moved indoors in 1917 at the Stockyards Coliseum in Fort Worth, Tex., thus becoming a year-round sport with a season extending from the second week in January until the end of December.

Both professional and amateur rodeo programs are built around the five standard events: saddle bronc riding, bareback riding, calf roping, bull riding, and steer wrestling. Other events such as team roping, steer roping, steer decorating, wild cow milking, and barrel and a variety of other races are added as facilities and funds permit. The specialty numbers, such as trick riding, fancy roping, and the dog, horse, and steer acts (known as contract acts) are held simultaneously or spaced in the program to permit officials to prepare chutes, equipment, etc., for following contests. Integral parts of every rodeo are the queen and clown, the latter serving a useful purpose in distracting the attention of the contest animals while the dismounted or thrown rider has a chance to leave the arena. Other features such as mounted quadrilles and allied western classes may be presented, and often a popular motion-picture or television star entertains.

Organized on Nov. 1, 1936, and originally called the Cowboy's Turtle Association, the Rodeo Cowboy's Association (RCA) raised the standards of rodeo. The RCA represents the contestants' interests and regulates their personal behaviour and the types of shows to be entered, provides insurance for contestants, and establishes a system of fines and black lists to regulate managers' and contestants' activities. In 1929 the Rodeo Association of America, an organization of rodeo managers and producers, was founded to standardize events, rules, judging, and arena conditions and to work out common problems pertaining to the production of professional rodeos. In 1946 the group was renamed the International Rodeo Association (IRA). In 1959 the IRA was renamed International Rodeo Management, Inc. (IRMI). The RCA established its own point award system, naming an all-around champion and champions in the five standard events, team roping, and steer roping each year.

Rodeo contestants originally were the working cowhands of the West; today they come from all parts of the country. This highly specialized field demands a great degree of skill and stamina of the professional contestants, who may compete in as many as 80 rodeos during the year; participation does not guarantee a living, since events to be remunerative must be won, and the contestant is continually faced with the hazards of accidents and injury.

Rodeo stock is valuable, and the horses and bulls are well cared for to the point of being pampered. Good bucking horses are not from wild herds or killers but are usually halterbroken and gentle until mounted. They are encouraged in their dislike of being mounted and further annoyed by the flank strap, which is placed around the hind quarters; any foreign object on the rear of a horse has a tendency to make him buck.

After the end of World War II, rodeo became an important amateur sport among small saddle clubs, high schools, colleges, and even prisons in the United States. This resulted in formation of the National High School and National Intercollegiate Rodeo Association and the American Junior Rodeo Association. Rodeo spread to other parts of the world, becoming especially popular in Canada and Australia.   (L. Sr.; E. W. Co.)

RODERIC (Ruadri; Rory O'Connor) (d. 1198), king of Connaught and the last high king of Ireland. He succeeded his father Turloch O'Connor as king of Connaught in 1156 but did not wrest Turloch's title of high king from Muirchertach O'Lochlainn of Ulster until ten years later, when O'Lochlainn fell in battle. He then attacked Dermot Mac Murrough (*q.v.*), king of Leinster, and divided his territory. Dermot's quest for help from England (1166) brought about the Anglo-Norman invasion of Ireland. Roderic's attempt to defend Dublin (1170) was unsuccessful, and after besieging the city (June–September 1171) he was routed by a Norman sortie and retreated to Connaught. Gradually all the Irish except Roderic and the northern rulers submitted to Henry II. Roderic sent envoys to England who concluded the Treaty of Windsor (1175) by the terms of which Roderic became Henry's vassal for Connaught and was recognized as overking of territory unconquered by the Normans; he was to pay an annual tribute of hides. There is no record that he did so, and Henry continued to grant to Anglo-Norman adventurers land nominally under Roderic's rule. Milo de Cogan, constable of Dublin, invaded Connaught in 1177; Roderic defeated him at Tuam, capturing and blinding his own son Murchad who had aided the enemy. From about 1186 Roderic was opposed by members of his own family and was for a time expelled from his kingdom. In 1191 he retired to a monastery and died at the Abbey of Cong to the north of Lough Corrib in 1198.   (A. Gw.)

RODEZ, a town of southern France, and *préfecture* of the *département* of Aveyron, is situated 75 mi. (121 km.) NE of Toulouse on a defensive site at the confluence of the Auterne and Aveyron rivers, near the western margin of the Causses between the limestone Causse du Comtal to the north and the crystalline plateau of Lévezou to the south. Pop. (1962) 20,438. Roman Ruthena was the centre of the tribal area of the Rutheni, and later Rodez was the chief town of the district of Rouergue and the seat of a bishopric from 401. The duality of its development in the Middle Ages, with twin towns, the episcopal *Cité* and the feudal *Bourg*, each with a separate wall, has been imprinted in the town plan. Two distinct nuclei are evident: the *Place de la Cité* with the cathedral, and the *Place du Bourg*. The Cathedral of Notre Dame is a fine Gothic structure dating from the 13th to the 16th centuries. It has a great rose window in its main façade and a tower that rises to 290 ft. (88 m.). Nearby is the episcopal palace. Near the *Place du Bourg*, in what was the count's town, is the Romanesque Church of St. Amans. There are several fine old houses. Rodez is the administrative and service centre for the surrounding district, and its old-established woolen industry survives. It is a tourist centre of growing importance.   (Ar. E. S.)

RODGERS, RICHARD (1902–), one of the most successful composers of popular music of his time, was born in Hammels Station, Long Island, N.Y., on June 28, 1902. He began to write songs in his early youth and between 1919 and 1923 studied at Columbia University and the Institute of Musical Art, N.Y. In 1918 he met Lorenz Hart, who became his librettist. Among the products of their collaboration, which lasted until Hart's death in 1943, were the musical comedies *A Connecticut Yankee* (1927), after Mark Twain; *On Your Toes* (1936); *Babes in Arms* (1937); *I Married an Angel* (1938); *The Boys from Syracuse* (1938), after Shakespeare's play *A Comedy of Errors; Pal Joey* (1940); and *By Jupiter* (1942).

Later he was associated with the younger Oscar Hammerstein, who wrote the texts for their productions until his death in 1960. Their first musical comedy, *Oklahoma!* (1943), was an immediate success, and was awarded the Pulitzer Prize. *Carousel* (1945) and *Allegro* (1947) were somewhat less successful, but *South Pacific* (1949) became widely popular and was awarded the Pulitzer Prize in 1950. There followed *The King and I* (1951), remarkable for its exotic character; *Me and Juliet* (1953); *Pipe Dream* (1955); *The Flower Drum Song* (1958); and *The Sound of Music* (1959). Rodgers also wrote the music for the documentary film *Victory at Sea* (1952), for which he was awarded the Distinguished Public Service Award by the U.S. Navy.

See D. Ewen, *Richard Rodgers* (1957).   (N. Sy.)

RODIN, (FRANÇOIS) AUGUSTE (RENÉ) (1840–1917), French sculptor, was born in Paris on Nov. 12, 1840. From 1854 to 1857 he was a pupil at the Petite École de dessin (later renamed École des Arts Decoratifs); then, having been refused admission to the École des Beaux-Arts, he began to earn his living

BY COURTESY OF THE METROPOLITAN MUSEUM OF ART, GIFT OF THOMAS F. RYAN, 1910

"THE THINKER" BY AUGUSTE RODIN. IN THE METROPOLITAN MUSEUM OF ART, NEW YORK

as an ornament maker and became an assistant to the sculptor A. E. Carrier-Belleuse. His "Man With a Broken Nose" (1864), which was rejected by the Salon, early revealed his ability. In 1871 he was in Brussels, working for Carrier-Belleuse on the "Caryatides" of the new Bourse and also undertaking a certain amount of work on his own account. In 1875 he visited Florence and Rome, where he was much impressed by the works of Donatello and Michelangelo.

Rodin's plaster maquette of "The Bronze Age," exhibited in the Salon of 1877, attracted considerable attention; the modeling, indeed, was so fine as to give rise to the accusation of its having been cast from a living man. In 1880, however, when he exhibited his "John the Baptist Preaching" and the final bronze of "The Bronze Age," Rodin silenced his critics and established his position in the world of sculpture. Thenceforward, he was to receive commission after commission; and the first of them was from the French government, which ordered a door for the Musée des Arts Decoratifs, with a series of bas-reliefs representing scenes from Dante's *Divine Comedy*.

Rodin worked on this commission for the rest of his life. His original idea was to divide the door into panels, as Ghiberti had divided his "Gate of Paradise" for the baptistery in Florence. One panel was to represent Paolo and Francesca; another was to show Ugolino devouring his children; and the upper part of the door was to contain a seated figure of Dante himself (eventually entitled "The Thinker"). However, his old friend Alphonse Legros then invited Rodin to London (1881–82), and there Rodin made a close study of the illustrations of Dante by John Flaxman and William Blake; thereafter, he abandoned architectural considerations entirely and no longer followed Dante's text. The project underwent many changes, and Rodin's studio was filled with works begun as components of the door and then set aside. The plaster maquette of "The Gate of Hell" (1917), which was finally cast in bronze in 1938, constitutes the last version of the project that Rodin left, but there is no doubt that he would have worked still longer on it had he lived. He died at Meudon on Nov. 17, 1917.

"The Gate of Hell" does, in fact, show Ugolino, Paolo and Francesca among swirling processions of damned souls; and "The Thinker" occupies the lintel. However, a number of other works which are now quite separate from "The Gate" were originally conceived also as subsidiary themes for it. These include "Adam" (1880), "Eve" (1881), "The Fair Armouress" (François Villon's *Belle Heaulmière*, 1885) and "The Prodigal Son" (1889). Even "The Kiss" (1886), often regarded as Rodin's masterpiece, was originally conceived to form part of "The Gate" as a figure of Faith.

Other sculptures commissioned from Rodin were "The Burghers of Calais," "Victor Hugo" and "Balzac." The first of these, which was not set up in Calais until 1896, is based on Jean Froissart's account of the famous incident and shows the burghers going barefoot, with nooses round their necks, to deliver the keys of Calais to the king of England. (There is a replica of this on the embankment at Westminster.)

The "Victor Hugo" was commissioned by the state for the Panthéon in 1889, but the first maquette (1890), which showed the poet seated with the upper part of his body naked, proved to be unacceptable. Rodin eventually produced a standing version, which was set up in the garden of the Palais Royal in 1909 but withdrawn afterward. The "Balzac" was commissioned by the Société des Gens de Lettres in 1891. The maquette, sent to the Salon in 1898, consisted of a block nearly ten feet high, with the subject's head emerging from the folds of a voluminous dressing gown. This provoked an indignant outcry, but the bronze cast of it was eventually set up on the Boulevard Raspail in 1939. Meanwhile, Rodin was producing other sculptures, including "Thought" (1886) and a series of portrait busts. The latter may be counted among his finest achievements; they comprise "Dalou" (1883), "Victor Hugo" (1883), "Rochefort" (1884), "W. E. Henley" (1884), "Octave Mirbeau" (1889), "Puvis de Chavannes" (1891), "Gustave Geffroy" (1905), "Clemenceau" (1911) and "Pope Benedict XV" (1915).

In 1900, Rodin's reputation stood so high that he could envisage a special exhibition of his work as a feature of the Paris universal exhibition. Altogether 168 examples were assembled, and an unprecedented success was achieved. The sculptor received the homage of Europe. Among Rodin's later works, mention must be made of the series of "Hands," in which hands are made to exemplify some literary or moral idea. This theme may perhaps be traced back to 1898, when he produced "The Hand of God" as an image of creativity. "The Hand of the Devil," holding a woman, appeared in 1903; "The Secret," or "Prayer," in 1910 and "The Hand Coming Out of the Tomb" in 1910 also. At the same time, Rodin turned toward literature; his conversations on art were collected by Paul Gsell and published as *L'Art* in 1910 (Eng. trans.,

Art, 1912); and his book, *Les Cathédrales de France*, appeared in 1914.

From 1908, Rodin was living in the former Hôtel Biron, where the state had provided accommodation for a number of artists and writers. There, Rainer Maria Rilke, a close friend of Rodin's, suggested that they should establish themselves together, and Rodin thereupon offered to bequeath all the works of his own that remained in his possession, all his collections and his villa at Meudon to the French state, on condition that he be allowed to spend the rest of his life in the Hôtel Biron and that on his death the building be converted into a Rodin museum. The hotel and the villa now constitute the two sections of the Musée Rodin, which contains most of Rodin's sculpture, his drawings, some paintings, his library and his art collections.

Numerous replicas of Rodin's sculptures can be seen in museums outside France. The Rodin museum in Philadelphia, inaugurated in 1929, is an architectural copy of the villa at Meudon.

BIBLIOGRAPHY.—Gustave Geffroy, *La Vie artistique* (1892–1903); Judith Cladel, *Auguste Rodin, the Man and His Art* (1908; Eng. trans., 1917), *Rodin, sa vie glorieuse et inconnue* (1936); R. M. Rilke, *Auguste Rodin* (1913), *Briefe an Auguste Rodin* (1928); M. Tirel, *Rodin intime* (1923; Eng. trans., *Last Years of Rodin*, 1925); L. Bénédite, *Rodin* (1926); A. M. Ludovici, *Personal Reminiscences of Auguste Rodin* (1927); L. E. E. Riotor, *Rodin* (1927); C. Aveline, *Rodin, l'homme et l'oeuvre* (1937); *Catalogue du Musée Rodin*, 5th ed. (1944); J. Gantner, *Rodin and Michelangelo* (1953); C. Goldscheider, "Influence de la gravure anglaise sur le projet primitif de 'La Porte de l'Enfer,'" *Bull. Soc. Art Français* (1950), "Rodin et le monument de Victor Hugo," *Bull. Soc. Art Français* (1957). (P. Ln.)

RODNEY, GEORGE BRYDGES RODNEY, Baron (1718–1792), English admiral, who won several important naval battles against French, Spanish, and Dutch forces, was born in Feb. 1718. He was sent to Harrow, being appointed, on leaving, by warrant dated June 21, 1732, a volunteer on board the "Sunderland." While serving on the Mediterranean station he was made lieutenant (1739) on the "Dolphin." In 1742 he attained the rank of post captain, having been appointed to the "Plymouth." After serving in home waters, he obtained command of the "Eagle" (60 guns), and in this ship took part in Admiral Hawke's victory off Ushant (Oct. 14, 1747) over the French fleet. In 1749 he was appointed governor and commander in chief of Newfoundland, with the rank of commodore, and two years later was elected to Parliament for Saltash.

During the Seven Years' War (*q.v.*) Rodney rendered important services. In 1757 he had a share in the expedition against Rochefort, commanding the "Dublin" (74 guns). Next year, in the same ship, he served under Boscawen at the taking of Louisburg (Cape Breton). In 1759 and again in 1760 he inflicted great loss on the French transports collected on the Normandy coast for an attack on Great Britain. Elected M.P. for Penryn in 1761, he was in October of that year appointed commander in chief of the Leeward Islands station, and within the first three months of 1762 had reduced the important island of Martinique, while both St. Lucia and Grenada had surrendered to his squadron. At the peace of 1763 Admiral Rodney returned home, having been during his absence made vice admiral of the blue and having received the thanks of both houses of parliament. In 1764 Rodney was created a baronet. From 1765 to 1770 he was governor of Greenwich hospital. In 1771 he was appointed rear admiral of Great Britain, and in 1778 admiral of the white. From 1771 to 1774 he held the Jamaica command, and during a period of quiet was active in improving the naval yards on his station. Election expenses and losses at play in fashionable circles had shattered his fortune; he could not secure payment of the salary as rear admiral of Great Britain; and he lived for some time in Paris until the generosity of a friend enabled him to meet his debts.

Sir George was appointed once more commander in chief of the Leeward Islands late in 1779. His orders were to relieve Gibraltar on his way to the West Indies. He captured a Spanish convoy off Cape Finisterre on Jan. 8, 1780, and eight days later defeated the Spanish admiral Don Juan de Langara off Cape St. Vincent, taking or destroying seven ships. On April 17 an action, which, as a result of the carelessness of some of Rodney's captains, was indecisive, was fought off Martinique with the French admiral

Guichen. Rodney, acting under orders, captured the valuable Dutch island of St. Eustatius on Feb. 3, 1781. It had been a great entrepôt of neutral trade, and was full of booty, which Rodney confiscated. As large quantities belonged to English merchants, he was entangled in a series of costly lawsuits.

After a few months in England, recruiting his health and defending himself in parliament, Rodney returned to his command in Feb. 1782, and a running engagement with the French fleet on April 9 led up to his crowning victory off Dominica, when with 36 sail of the line he defeated the comte de Grasse, who had 34 sail (April 12). The French inferiority in numbers was counterbalanced by the greater size and superior sailing qualities of their ships, yet five were taken and one sunk after 11 hours' fighting. This important battle for Jamaica was a blow to French naval prestige, and it enabled Rodney to write: "Within two little years I have taken two Spanish, one French, and one Dutch admiral."

On his return to England Rodney received a barony and a pension of £2,000 a year. From this time he led a quiet country life till his death (May 24, 1792), in London.

Rodney was unquestionably an able officer, but he was also vain, selfish and unscrupulous, both in seeking prize money and in using his position to push the fortunes of his family. He made his son a post captain at 15, for example. He was accused by his second-in-command, Samuel Hood, of sacrificing the interest of the service to his own profit, and of showing want of energy in pursuit of the French after his victory off Dominica on April 12, 1782, but it must be remembered that he was then old and racked by disease.

RODÓ, JOSÉ ENRIQUE (1872–1917), Uruguayan philosopher, essayist, and educator, hailed by Spanish-Americans as their philosopher par excellence, was born in Montevideo on July 15, 1872. Patterns of life and human conduct were his primary concern; respect for freedom, tolerance, and justice guided his career.

Ariel (1900), his most extensive essay, written in a typical, majestic prose style, defines Rodó's moral credo, a cult of beauty and truth, a yearning for growth and inner harmony, a quest for a fuller life for individuals and the community. Próspero, the venerable teacher in *Ariel,* cautions his young listeners (as did Rodó throughout his life: as university professor in 1898, as journalist, as director of the National Library, and, in 1902 and 1908, as member of the Chamber of Deputies) not to be impressed by material triumph but to use their own spiritual, moral, and intellectual resources to strive for a well-rounded life. Individual self-scrutiny must result in enlightened action for the good of the group.

Continuing his probing of human behaviour and the development of character in *Motivos de Proteo* (1909), he set down his message in one sentence: "Reformarse es vivir" (to reform oneself is to live). *El Mirador de Próspero* (1913), a series of essays on political and cultural themes (among them are fine tributes to Bolívar, Juan María Gutiérrez, and Juan Montalvo), sums up his philosophy.

Despite his affinities with classical and French culture, and his cosmopolitan spirit, devotion to America and its people pervades his writings. Like Bolívar a century before him, he envisaged Spanish America as a cultural entity. Rodó died at Palermo, Italy, on May 1, 1917, on one of his rare journeys abroad.

BIBLIOGRAPHY.—H. D. Barbagelata, Introduction to Rodó's *Cinco Ensayos* (1915); Havelock Ellis, Introduction to *The Motives of Proteus* (1929); I. Goldberg, *Studies in Spanish-American Literature* (1920); M. Henríquez Ureña, *Breve Historia del Modernismo* (1954); V. Pérez Petit, *Rodó, Su vida, Su obra* (no date).   (K. L. L.)

RODRIGUES, an island dependency of the self-governing British colony of Mauritius, which lies 365 mi. W in the western Indian Ocean. Rodrigues is 9½ mi. (15 km.) from east to west and a maximum of 4½ mi. (7 km.) from north to south. Area 40 sq.mi. (104 sq.km.).

With Mauritius and Réunion, Rodrigues lies on a submarine ridge trending northeast–southwest.. Like the other Mascarene Islands it is wholly volcanic in origin, being composed of a central ridge of doleritic lava reaching 1,290 ft., partly surrounded by a raised coral reef, studded with islets and separated from the land by a shallow lagoon of varying width. There are two passages through the reef; the northern, leading to Port Mathurin, is normally used.

The climate is dominated by the southeast trades from April to October and from November to March by the belt of converging air known as the doldrums. In summer it is oppressively hot and humid, but in the winter can be quite bracing. In summer, tropical cyclones frequently pass over or close to the island; Rodrigues experiences many more of these than does Mauritius.

The island was initially covered with dense forest, but only a few areas of bush remain. The greater part is now grass-covered from the effect of goats, cattle, and cultivation aided by burning.

Of the endemic mammalian fauna of Rodrigues, the sole survivor is the fruit-eating bat (*Pteropus rodericensis*). The giant land tortoise, now surviving only on the Aldabra Islands (Seychelles), has only recently become extinct. Thirteen species of endemic birds are known, and the caves of the limestone platform have yielded many skeletons of the now extinct solitaire (*Pezophaps solitaria*). The fauna is now dominated by introduced species, including deer, pigs, rabbits, rats, goats, and cattle among the mammals; guinea fowl are numerous. An important feature is the absence of malaria, which never reached the island. Other diseases common in Mauritius are also absent.

The population in 1962 was 18,335, giving a density of 458 per square mile. With an annual death rate of about 8 per thousand and a birth rate around 40, population increase is rapid. The majority of the people are of African origin, though few are unmixed. Most of the lighter-skinned people are in Port Mathurin. The black montagnards of the interior are descended from slaves introduced in the final reoccupation of the island after 1810. Except for a few Indians and Chinese, almost the whole population is Creole-speaking and Roman Catholic. Port Mathurin, with 671 inhabitants, is the only town. Rural settlement is scattered with a concentration on the northern side, and the small village of Gabriel lies in the centre of the island.

Rodrigues or Diego Ruy's Island was discovered by the Portuguese in 1645. In 1690 the Dutch government sent a body of French Huguenots to the Island of Bourbon (later Réunion), but they, finding the French in possession, proceeded to Rodrigues where eight of them landed in 1691. The colonists left the island in 1693 and made their way to Mauritius. From the Dutch the island passed to the French, who colonized it from Mauritius. Large estates were cultivated and the islanders enjoyed considerable prosperity. In 1809–10 Rodrigues was seized by the British, in whose possession it remained. The abolition of slavery proved disastrous to prosperity, and by 1843 the number of inhabitants declined to about 250. The population has since grown steadily, mainly by natural increase. There has been no large-scale immigration from India (as in Mauritius), as the sugar industry has never become established on Rodrigues and there have been no plantations to act as importers of labour. On balance Rodrigues has for decades been a net exporter of people.

Rodrigues is administered by a magistrate and civil commissioner from Mauritius, advised by a council of 17 islanders set up by the Mauritius government. There is a small police force and the health and agriculture departments have resident officers. The three small hospitals have 70 beds in all. Living standards are low and housing extremely poor. Most houses are built of wood and fibre and have only one room. Though there is little starvation, nutrition is generally inadequate and the plight of many old people is extreme. The island has two government and four aided primary schools.

A small export of salted fish, beans, onions, lemons, and livestock, entirely to Mauritius, is the only cash economy. Rodrigues depends almost entirely on subsistence cultivation of maize (corn) on peasant holdings; the crop is liable to severe fluctuations through cyclone damage in summer and drought loss in winter. Beans are an important dietary supplement and some fruit and vegetables are grown. Most families keep a few cattle or goats pastured on the grass slopes of the central ridge. There is already severe pressure of population on land, with less than half an acre of arable land per head. Soil erosion is widespread and serious, but anti-erosion work is actively pursued.

Fishing within the reef is important, though primitive in organization. The bulk of the catch is, however, salted and sold through Chinese traders to Mauritius. Trade depends on the irregular visits of vessels from Mauritius, when peasants bring their surplus crops and livestock to the port. Production is on a joint family basis; there is no larger-scale organization for production, mutual aid, marketing, or storage. Labour migration has long been an important source of livelihood. Rodriguans work in Mauritius and in its lesser dependencies such as Diego Garcia.

Transport depends on human and animal porterage, and on small vessels operating within the reef. There are no roads outside Port Mathurin. Rodrigues has a cable station on the route between Durban, S.Af., and Perth, Austr. (HA. C. BD.)

See A. J. Bertuchi, *The Island of Rodrigues* (1923); H.M.S.O., *Colonial Report: Mauritius* (annually).

RODRÍGUEZ FRANCIA, JOSÉ GASPAR: see FRANCIA, JOSÉ GASPAR RODRÍGUEZ.

ROE, later changed by deed poll to VERDON-ROE, the name of two English brothers who were aviation pioneers.

SIR (EDWIN) ALLIOTT VERDON-ROE (1877–1958), British aircraft designer, the first Englishman to construct and fly his own airplane. He was born at Patricroft, near Manchester, Eng., on April 26, 1877, and educated at St. Paul's School, London. He went to British Columbia at the age of 14, but returned a year later and served a five-year apprenticeship at the Lancashire and Yorkshire Railway's locomotive shops. He then spent two years at sea, after which he entered the motor industry. On June 8, 1908, he flew a distance of 75 ft. in a biplane of his own design with a 24 hp.-Antoinette engine, nearly a year before the first officially recognized flight in England (by J. T. C. Moore-Brabazon, later Lord Brabazon of Tara, in 1909). He founded the aviation firm of A. V. Roe and Co., Ltd., with his brother, Humphrey, in 1910. Avro aircraft were used with great success in World War I and Avro 504N airplanes were the standard training aircraft for the Royal Air Force for a long period between World Wars I and II. Verdon-Roe later turned his attention to the design of flying boats, founding Saunders-Roe, Ltd., of Cowes, Isle of Wight. Knighted in 1929, he died on Jan. 4, 1958.

HUMPHREY VERDON-ROE (1878–1949) was born at Patricroft, near Manchester, Eng., on April 18, 1878. Commissioned in the Manchester regiment, he served in the South African War, retiring from the army soon afterward. He joined the firm of Everard and Co., webbing manufacturers in Manchester, and when his elder brother, Alliott, founded the firm of A. V. Roe and Co., he cooperated with him. He was not a pilot, but flew much as a passenger and in 1917 joined the Royal Flying Corps as an observer. In 1918, he married Marie Carmichael Stopes and with her founded the first birth control clinic at Holloway, London, in 1921. He died in London on July 25, 1949. (D. CR.)

ROE, SIR THOMAS (c. 1581–1644), English diplomat and author, was born at Low Leyton, near Wanstead in Essex, and was educated at Magdalen College, Oxford. Through family influence he was appointed esquire of the body to Queen Elizabeth I, and in 1605 he was knighted by James I. His career as a diplomat began in 1615 when, at the request of the English East India Company, he was sent as ambassador to the court of Jahangir, the Mughal (Mogul) emperor of Delhi. During the four years of his mission he greatly advanced the interests of the company. As ambassador to the Ottoman Empire at Istanbul from 1621 to 1628, Roe obtained increased privileges for the English merchants trading in the Levant. In 1624 he negotiated a treaty with Algiers, then subject to Istanbul, which resulted in the liberation of several hundred English prisoners who had been captured by the Barbary pirates. He also mediated a peace treaty between Poland and the Ottoman Empire.

Roe returned to England early in 1629 and in September helped to negotiate the truce of Altmark between Gustavus II Adolphus of Sweden and Sigismund III of Poland, which left Gustavus Adolphus free to intervene on the Protestant side in the Thirty Years' War. Gustavus Adolphus sent him a gift of £2,000, but from the English government Roe received little financial reward for these services. Finally, in 1637, after six years spent in retirement, he was appointed chancellor of the Order of the Garter and in 1638 was given an annual pension of £1,200. Roe was the English representative at conferences held at Hamburg (1638), Ratisbon (1641), and Vienna (1642), where attempts were made to end the Thirty Years' War. Meanwhile, in 1640 he was made a privy councilor and was elected a member of the Long Parliament for the University of Oxford. He participated actively in the commercial debates but after his return from Vienna his health began to fail. In July 1643 he gained the permission of the House of Commons to retire to Bath, where he died in November 1644.

Roe's journal of the mission to the Mughal, several times reprinted, was reedited with an introduction by W. Foster for the Hakluyt Society under the title *Embassy of Sir T. Roe to the Court of the Great Mogul,* two volumes (1899). Of his correspondence, *The Negotiations of Sir T. Roe in His Embassy to the Ottoman Porte (1621–28),* volume i was published in 1740, but the work was not completed and letters relating to Roe's mission to Gustavus II Adolphus (1629–30) were edited by S. R. Gardiner for the Camden Society miscellany, volume vii (1847). Several of his parliamentary speeches, dealing with trade, currency, and financial questions, were also published. (R. C. JO.)

ROEBLING, JOHN AUGUSTUS (1806–1869), U.S. civil engineer, designer of many great suspension bridges, among which the Brooklyn Bridge is the most famous, was born at Mühlhausen, Prussia, on June 12, 1806. Soon after his graduation from the polytechnic school at Berlin he moved to the United States, and in 1831 began to practise his profession in western Pennsylvania. He established near Pittsburgh, Pa., a wire rope factory, and in May 1845 completed his first important structure, a suspended aqueduct across the Allegheny River. This was followed by the Monongahela suspension bridge at Pittsburgh and several suspended aqueducts on the Delaware and Hudson Canal. Moving his wire factory to Trenton, N.J., he began in 1851 the erection at Niagara Falls of a long-span wire suspension bridge with double roadway, for railway and vehicular use (*see* BRIDGES), which was completed in 1855. Because of the novelty of its design, the most eminent engineers regarded this bridge as foredoomed to failure; but, with its complete success, demonstrated by long use, the number of suspension bridges rapidly multiplied, the use of wire ropes instead of chain cables becoming virtually universal.

The completion, in 1867, of the still more remarkable suspension bridge over the Ohio River at Cincinnati, O., with a clear span of 1,057 ft., added to Roebling's reputation, and his design for the great bridge spanning the East River between Manhattan and Brooklyn, New York City, was accepted. While personally engaged in laying out the towers for the bridge, Roebling received an accidental injury, which resulted in his death, at Brooklyn, from tetanus, on July 22, 1869. The bridge was completed under the direction of his son, Washington Augustus Roebling (1837–1926).

See H. Schuyler, *The Roeblings: a Century of Engineers, Bridgebuilders and Industrialists* (1931); D. B. Steinman, *The Builders of the Bridge* (1945).

ROEMER, OLE (OLAUS) (1644–1710), Danish astronomer who discovered that light travels at a finite speed, was born at Aarhus, Jutland, on Sept. 25, 1644. In 1662 he became the pupil and amanuensis of Erasmus Bartholinus at Copenhagen, and in 1671 he assisted Jean Picard in determining the position of Tycho Brahe's observatory (Uraniborg, on the island of Hven). Roemer went to Paris with Picard in 1672 and spent nine years on observations at the new Royal Observatory and at hydraulic works at Versailles and Marly-la-Machine. After a scientific mission to England (1679), on which he met Sir Isaac Newton, Edmund Halley, and John Flamsteed, Roemer returned to Copenhagen in 1681 as royal mathematician and professor of astronomy in the university. He also held several public offices, including that of mayor in 1705. He died at Copenhagen on Sept. 23, 1710.

Roemer discovered the finite velocity of light, which was suggested to him by his observations on the eclipses of Jupiter's moons. The first noteworthy transit instrument was erected at his house in 1690. He also set up at the university observatory an instrument with altitude and azimuth circles, and an equatorial telescope, and built and equipped the "Tusculan" observatory at Vridlösemagle, near Copenhagen. The great fire of Oct. 21, 1728, destroyed his manuscripts except those discussed by J. G. Galle in *O. Roemeri triduum observationum astronomicarum a. 1706 . . . institutarum* (1845).

See A. Nielsen, *Ole Rømer* (1944); E. Stromgren, *Ole Rømer som Astronom* (1944).

ROENTGEN, DAVID (1743–1807), German cabinetmaker to Queen Marie Antoinette, was born at Herenhag on Aug. 11, 1743, and died at Wiesbaden on Feb. 12, 1807. He was the eldest son of Abraham Roentgen, who in 1750 moved to Neuwied, on the Rhine near Coblenz, where he produced furniture of outstanding quality, often decorated with inlay work of ivory and other material, much of it for the courts of German princes. David Roentgen learned his trade in his father's workshop and succeeded to the business in 1772, his father continuing as a partner until 1784. His father's firm having already achieved renown in Germany, the son won European reputation after he had displayed his furniture in Paris in 1779 and secured King Louis XVI, Queen Marie Antoinette and other members of the French court as customers. Roentgen was appointed cabinetmaker to the queen and in 1780 was granted admission as master (*maître ébéniste*) to the trade corporation of Paris cabinetmakers, a fact which made it possible for him to keep in Paris a stock of the furniture manufactured at Neuwied. In this fashion he was able to compete with such great French cabinetmakers of the period as Jean Henri Riesener and others. King Frederick the Great of Prussia and Empress Catherine II of Russia were also customers of Roentgen. The latter, after Roentgen's first visit to St. Petersburg in 1783, bought great quantities of his furniture. When in 1795 the French Revolutionary armies threatened to cross the Rhine, Roentgen evacuated his establishment and moved his stock of furniture farther inland. While he never succeeded in starting production again, former apprentices of his whom he had helped to establish in Berlin (David Hacker) and in Brunswick (Christian Härder) were successful in their enterprises.

Roentgen had begun his career by continuing and developing the style of furniture his father had introduced. His so-called French style is characterized by furniture of curved outline sometimes decorated with rich carvings. His "English" cabinetwork is based on elements dating from the early years of George III and occasionally influenced by Thomas Chippendale. Both types of furniture are frequently decorated with rich inlay work of outstanding charm and elegance made up of a variety of woods, some tinted and composed to form figural and floral compositions, often in the *chinoiserie* manner. Between 1775 and 1780 Roentgen's previous style is altogether abandoned and rigid, classical forms are introduced, the effect of which is often based on the contrast of mahogany with rich bronze appliqués. The Roentgen workshop indulged in mechanical devices which made appear or disappear drawers and mirrors by pressing on hidden releases. Peter Kinzing was the mechanical genius who invented many of these tricks and provided clockworks. Furniture by Roentgen is in most large museums in Europe, at the Metropolitan Museum of Art in New York and at the Art Institute of Chicago.

See Hans Huth, *Abraham und David Röntgen und ihre Neuwieder Werkstatt* (1938). (Hs. H.)

ROENTGEN, WILHELM CONRAD: see RÖNTGEN, WILHELM CONRAD.

ROERMOND, a town and seat of a bishopric in the province of Limburg, Netherlands, lies on the right bank of the Maas at the confluence of the Roer, 28 mi. (45 km.) NNE of Maastricht by rail. Pop. (1960) 25,728. Within the limits of the old fortifications (now replaced by boulevards) the medieval street pattern has remained intact. Among noteworthy buildings are the Late Romanesque minster (restored), and the early-15th-century Church (cathedral from 1661) of St. Christopher. Chemicals, electrical equipment, paper, clothing, and cigars are manufactured; there is also a large egg-packing station. A prosperous centre of the cloth trade in the 14th and 15th centuries, Roermond was a domain of the counts and dukes of Gelderland until 1543. Subsequently it was under Spanish, Austrian, French, and Belgian

domination. During World War II it was heavily damaged.

(P. J. Bu.)

ROESELARE (Fr. ROULERS), a town of West Flanders, Belg., on the Mandel River, 25 mi. (40 km.) SSE of Ostend. Pop. (1961) 35,645. It was rebuilt after World War I. Surviving historic buildings are: the Late Gothic Church of St. Michael (1497–1504), with a notable early-17th-century carved pulpit; the late-15th-century Grey Sisters' House; and the town hall and Seminary church, both of the 18th century. Roeselare is an educational centre. It has rail and road connections with neighbouring towns, and the canal to the Lys River (1872) has encouraged industrial and commercial expansion. In the Middle Ages it was a centre of the linen trade. It is the birthplace of the composer Adriaan Willaert (*q.v.*) and of the Flemish poet Albrecht Rodenbach (1856–80); the poets Guido Gezelle (*q.v.*) and Hugo Verriest (1840–1922) lived there. (G. J. D.)

ROGALAND, a *fylke* (county) of southwestern Norway. Area 3,531 sq.mi. Pop. (1960) 229,555. The district of Jaeren, south of the open Boknfjord, is a shelf of lowland richly covered by morainic drift; eastward the land rises to a rather barren upland; in the southeast valuable deposits of ferrotitanium ores are mined. North of Bokn the lowland continues over Karmøy, the most densely populated island in Norway. In its inner (eastern and northern) parts Bokn is split in long narrow branches penetrating far inland between precipitous walls. Beyond the heads of the fjords the mountains reach 3,000–5,000 ft. (900–1,500 m.). Jaeren is the most important dairy-farming district in Norway. Canning of fish, pottery, shipbuilding, and shipping are the predominant industries. Stavanger (*q.v.*) and Haugesund are the largest towns; traffic between them is maintained by fast hydrofoils as well as by conventional ferries. Sola International Airport is 9 mi. (14 km.) SW of Stavanger, which is connected by rail with Oslo. (L. H. Hg.)

ROGATION DAYS, in the Christian Church, comprise the Major Rogation (*litania maior*) on April 25 and the Minor Rogations (*litaniae minores*), the three days before Ascension Day. They are days of prayer and fasting, for the benefit of the crops. *See* PROCESSION; LITANY.

ROGER I (d. 1101), count of Sicily from 1072, was born in Normandy, the last son of the second marriage of Tancred of Hauteville. He was thus the youngest brother of Robert (*q.v.*) Guiscard, whom he went to join in southern Italy in 1057. By courageous efforts he did much to help Robert's conquest of Calabria from the Byzantines; and when this was complete (1060) the brothers turned their attention to Sicily, where discord between various Muslim rulers offered them an opportunity to combine their own interests with the service of Catholic Christianity.

Having taken Messina in 1061, Robert went back to his duchy of Apulia to fight the Byzantines. Left in command in Sicily, Roger was in no hurry to pursue the enterprise, as his army was inadequate against the strong positions of the Muslims, who moreover were being reinforced from Tunis. Even so, he won victories at Cerami (1063) and at Misilmeri (1068) over superior forces before help sent by Robert enabled him to capture Palermo in 1072. Meanwhile he had no intention of being merely Robert's tool: to assert himself, he more than once went into armed rebellion against Robert. The latter met his demands on each occasion: in 1062 he agreed to a regime of condominium in Calabria, every city and castle there being owned jointly by the brothers; and in 1072 he granted Roger the title of count of Calabria and Sicily, though he reserved to himself Palermo, half of Messina, and half of Val Demone, as well as the feudal suzerainty over the countship.

After Robert's death (1085), Roger took Syracuse in 1086 and completed the conquest of Sicily by the capture of Noto in 1091 (a few months after receiving the submission of Malta and Gozo). When the feeble Duke Roger of Apulia, Robert's son, was faced by rebellion, Roger of Sicily gave him decisive support, in return for which the duke renounced to him the Sicilian territories formerly reserved by Robert. The foremost ruler in Norman Italy, Roger assumed the title grand count of Sicily and Calabria. To establish Catholicism in Sicily, Roger himself created ecclesiastical dioceses. The bishops whom he appointed came nearly all from north of the Alps. Pope Urban II in 1099 nominated him apostolic legate in Sicily, thus recognizing his control over the church there. Yet Roger was wholly tolerant toward his Muslim and Greek Orthodox subjects. The Muslims in the cities formed an autonomous community and continued to prosper as manufacturers and as merchants; and the main bulk of Roger's infantry was recruited from the Muslim serfs of the countryside.

Roger died on June 22, 1101, and was buried in the Abbey of La Trinità, at Mileto in Calabria, which he had founded.

BIBLIOGRAPHY.—E. Caspar, *Roger II und die Gründung der norman-nisch-sicilischen Monarchie* (1904); F. Chalandon, *Histoire de la domination normande en Italie et en Sicile,* 2 vol. (1907); E. Pontieri, *Tra i Normanni nell'Italia meridionale,* 2nd ed. (1964). (E. Po.)

ROGER II (1095–1154), king of Sicily from 1130, was a son of Count Roger I (*q.v.*) by his third wife, Adelaide. His father died in 1101, his elder brother Simon in 1105, leaving the countship of Sicily and Calabria to the child Roger. His mother was regent for him till 1112, but went to marry Baldwin I of Jerusalem in 1113.

Roger, who combined a keenly realistic intelligence with the typically Norman spirit of adventure, inherited his predecessors' idea of Sicily as the potential nucleus of a great Mediterranean empire. His first expedition against Mahdia, the stronghold of the Zirids of Tunisia, was unsuccessful (1123), and for some years afterward he was preoccupied with the Italian mainland. When William, duke of Apulia, died childless (1127), Roger, as William's first cousin once removed, persuaded the people of Salerno, capital of the duchy, to cede their city to him, and had himself crowned duke there. Since this destroyed the balance which the papacy had contrived to maintain between the Norman states in southern Italy, Pope Honorius II mustered a league of cities and barons in rebellion against Roger; but Roger defeated the Pope's forces and obtained investiture as duke from him (Aug. 23, 1128).

Honorius II's death (1130) was followed by a schism of the papacy. Roger supported the antipope Anacletus II against Innocent II. By a bull signed at Avellino on Sept. 27, 1130, Anacletus invested Roger with the kingdom of Sicily, Calabria, and Apulia, the principality of Capua, the honour (fief) of Naples, and the protectorate over Benevento, in return for acknowledgment of the Holy See's feudal suzerainty and payment of annual tribute. On Christmas Day, 1130, at Palermo, Roger was crowned king of a kingdom, most of which was yet to be won.

Pope Innocent II, the Holy Roman emperor Lothair II, the Byzantine emperor John II Comnenus, the French king Louis VI, the Venetians, and the Pisans formed a coalition to check Roger's growing power, while within the new kingdom cities and feudatories, in particular Robert of Capua, rose against him. Nine years of warfare ensued, but Lothair's march across the Abruzzi to Bari and the Pisans' naval attack on Salerno both came to nothing (1137), and Roger was finally free to concentrate his efforts against Innocent II, whom Anacletus II's death (1138) had made more dangerous. Taken captive (July 22, 1139), Innocent made peace and recognized Roger as king by the Treaty of Mignano (July 25). Roger then made his kingdom a reality by subduing Capua and Naples. (*See also* NAPLES, KINGDOM OF; SICILY: *History.*)

Meanwhile Roger had not forgotten his designs on North Africa and on the Aegean coastlands. His admiral, George of Antioch, built him a magnificent fleet, and between 1135 and 1148 the island of Djerba and places on the Tunisian and Tripolitanian coasts were seized. Expeditions into Byzantine territory led to the conquest of Corfu and threatened Constantinople, though Venice and the German king Conrad III gave help to the Byzantines.

Though he organized his state feudally, Roger's royal authority was extraordinarily effective. His augmentation of his prerogatives as apostolic legate led to conflict with the Holy See. In public administration his supreme organ, the Magna Curia, exercised an all-pervasive influence down to the lowest levels through a well-articulated bureaucracy. All the ethnic elements of the kingdom were admitted to a role in the administration, for which the only qualifications required were efficiency and loyalty: Arabs were active in the financial offices, Italians and Greeks in the judiciary, Frenchmen and Normans in the feudal structure. An enlightened eclectic, Roger put his kingdom on the road to racial and cultural integration. His concern for the welfare of the community as a whole, overriding personal privilege and even his own royal advantage, was exceptional among contemporary rulers. He was also a generous patron of science, literature, and art, still commemorated by Palermo's examples of Islamic, Byzantine, Romanesque, and Composite architecture. He died in Palermo on Feb. 26, 1154, and was entombed in the cathedral.

BIBLIOGRAPHY.—E. Caspar, *Roger II . . . und die Gründung der nor-mannisch-sicilischen Monarchie* (1904); various authors, *Il Regno normanno* (1932); P. Grierson and J. Ward Perkins (eds.), *Studies in Italian History Presented to Miss C. M. Jamison,* being vol. 24 of the *Papers* of the British School at Rome (1957). (E. Po.)

ROGER OF WENDOVER (d. 1236), English chronicler, whose *Flores historiarum* is the fullest narrative source for the reign of Henry III, was probably a native of Wendover, Buckinghamshire. He became a monk of St. Albans, Hertfordshire, and later prior of the cell at Belvoir, Leicestershire, but was found guilty of wasting the endowments and deposed. His latter years were passed at St. Albans where he died on May 6, 1236. He was the first of the important chroniclers who worked in the scriptorium there. The *Flores historiarum,* which begins at the Creation and extends to 1235, becomes of fully original value from the beginning of Henry III's reign and contains the sinister, savage portrait of King John, later exaggerated by Matthew Paris in his *Chronica majora,* which incorporated and continued the *Flores historiarum.*

The *Flores historiarum* survives in Douce Manuscript 207 (*c.* 1300; Bodleian Library, Oxford) and Cotton Manuscript Otho B v (*c.* 1350; British Museum, London). Matthew Paris' *Chronica majora* was edited by H. R. Luard, seven volumes, Rolls Series (1872–80). H. O. Coxe edited the *Flores,* 447 and after, five volumes, English Historical Society (1841–44), and H. G. Hewlett, 1154 and after, three volumes, Rolls Series (1886–89).

BIBLIOGRAPHY.—Prefaces to F. Madden, *Matthei Parisiensis Historia Anglorum,* i, Rolls Series (1866), and H. R. Luard's ed.; F. Liebermann, *Monumenta Germaniae Historica, Scriptores,* xxviii, pp. 3–30 (1888); V. H. Galbraith, *Roger Wendover and Matthew Paris* (1944). (R. V.)

ROGERS, HENRY DARWIN (1808–1866), U.S. geologist and foremost structural geologist of his time, was born at Philadelphia, Aug. 1, 1808, one of four brothers, all of whom achieved fame as scientists. At 21 he became professor of chemistry and natural philosophy at Dickinson College, Carlisle, Pa. Three years later he went to Europe for advanced studies. In 1835 he became professor of geology and mineralogy in the University of Pennsylvania, and also undertook a geological survey of New Jersey. In 1836 he became state geologist of Pennsylvania. In 1842 he and his brother, WILLIAM BARTON ROGERS (1804–1882), state geologist of Virginia, jointly published their views on the Appalachian Mountains. Though their understanding of mountain-building processes was imperfect, in view of concepts then current, their observations of geologic features peculiarly distinctive of the Appalachians have stood the test of time remarkably well. H. D. Rogers' investigations culminated in his final two-volume *Report on Pennsylvania* (1858), in which he included a general account of the geology of the United States and of the coalfields of North America and Great Britain. In 1857 Rogers became regius professor of natural history in the University of Glasgow, Scot., the first American to be so honoured. He died at Glasgow, May 29, 1866. (F. M. Fl.)

ROGERS, JOHN (*c.* 1500–1555), English Reformer, editor of Matthew's Bible and first Protestant martyr of Mary I's reign, was born at Aston, near Birmingham, and educated at Pembroke Hall, Cambridge (B.A., 1526). Six years later he was rector of Holy Trinity, Queenhithe, London, and in 1534 went to Antwerp as chaplain to the English merchants. There he met William Tyndale (*q.v.*), under whose influence he abandoned the Roman Catholic faith, and married an Antwerp lady. After Tyndale's death Rogers carried on with the English version of the Old Testament on which Tyndale had been working. He used it as far as II Chronicles, employing Miles Coverdale's translation (1535) for the remainder and for the Apocrypha. Tyndale's New Testament had been published in 1526. The complete Bible was put out under the pseudonym of Thomas Matthew in 1537; it was printed in Antwerp and Richard Grafton bought the sheets and got permission to sell the edition (1,500 copies) in England. Rogers had little to do with the translation, but he contributed some valuable prefaces and notes. His work was largely used by those who prepared the Great Bible (1539), out of which in turn came the Bishop's Bible (1568) and the Authorized Version of 1611. (*See* BIBLE, TRANSLATIONS OF: *English.*)

After taking charge of a Protestant congregation in Wittenberg for several years, Rogers in 1548 returned to England, where he published a translation of Philipp Melanchthon's *Considerations of the Augsburg Interim.* In 1550 he was presented to the crown livings of St. Margaret Moyses and St. Sepulchre in London, and in 1551 was made a prebendary of St. Paul's Cathedral, where the dean and chapter soon appointed him divinity lecturer.

On the accession of Mary, Rogers preached at St. Paul's Cross commending the "true doctrine taught in King Edward's days" and warning his hearers against "pestilent Popery, idolatry, and superstition." Ten days later (Aug. 16, 1553), he was summoned before the council and told to stay within his own house. In January 1554 the bishop of London sent him to Newgate, where he was imprisoned for a year. On Jan. 22, 1555, Rogers, with ten others, was brought before the council in Southwark and examined. On the 28th and 29th he came before the commission appointed by Reginald Cardinal Pole and was sentenced to death for heretically denying the Christian character of the Roman Catholic Church and the real presence in the sacrament. He was burned on Feb. 4, 1555, at Smithfield.

See H. H. Hutson and H. R. Willoughby, *Decisive Data on Thomas Matthew Problems* (1938).

ROGERS, JOHN (1829–1904), U.S. sculptor, creator of a popular series of small groups illustrating literary, historical, and humorous subjects, the so-called "Rogers groups," was born in Salem, Mass., Oct. 30, 1829. He was largely self-taught although he did work for a brief time in the studio of the English sculptor Benjamin Spence in Rome. In 1859 he settled in New York. Eight thousand copies of his most popular group, "Coming to the Parson," were sold, and it is estimated that the total number of groups sold came to about 80,000. Rogers also made portrait busts; the equestrian statue of Gen. John F. Reynolds in Philadelphia, Pa., and the statue of Pres. Abraham Lincoln in Manchester, N.H. The small plaster "Rogers groups" were reproduced from bronze master models. A large collection of these bronzes was acquired by the New York Historical Society, New York City, which also has the Rogers family portraits and papers. He died in New Canaan, Conn., July 26, 1904.　　　(A. T. G.)

ROGERS, SAMUEL (1763–1855), English poet, best remembered for the witty conversation at his breakfast and dinner parties, and as a friend of greater poets, was born at Newington Green, near London, on July 30, 1763. His father had set up as a banker with money derived from a glass factory, and his mother came of a Dissenting family notable for its piety. When he was 17 he published an essay in the *Gentleman's Magazine.* His first volume of poetry attracted little attention, but the success of *The Pleasures of Memory* (1792) made him a celebrity. He had little originality or imaginative power, but he often succeeded in concealing this by the easy harmony of his verse and the carefulness of his expression. On his father's death (1793) he became principal owner of the banking firm. In 1803 he moved to 22, St. James's Place, London, and there he remained for the next half-century, a leading figure in London society. He was an amusing, though unkind, conversationalist—he claimed that his voice was so weak that no one would have listened to him if he had not said unkind things—and he used his knowledge and wealth to form a collection of paintings and other *objets d'art* that made his apartments a Mecca for anyone ambitious of being considered a man of taste. His breakfast and dinner parties were famous for the witty conversation of the carefully selected guests, recorded by Alexander Dyce and published as *Recollections of the Table-Talk of Samuel Rogers* (1856; edited by M. Bishop, 1952). In spite

of his sharp tongue he was a kindly man, and many writers had reason to think of him with gratitude: he reconciled Thomas Moore with Francis Jeffrey and with Byron, aided the dramatist Sheridan during the last months of his life, and did a great deal to secure a pension for Henry Cary, the translator of Dante. Most important of all, it was he who secured for Wordsworth the position of distributor of stamps for Westmorland (1813).

Rogers once wrote that his "constant wish" in life had been "to live with those who were eminent." In this he was extraordinarily successful, and the length of his life gave him unusual opportunities. As a boy he once set out to visit Dr. Johnson, but modesty prevented him from knocking on the great man's door. It is remarkable to reflect that that boy lived on until the year which saw the publication of Anthony Trollope's *The Warden* and Robert Browning's *Men and Women.* His friends included Charles James Fox, Edmund Burke, Richard Porson, Sir Walter Scott, Byron (who had an exaggeratedly high opinion of his merits as a poet), and the duke of Wellington. Having attained eminence during a lean period for poetry and lived through a period of genius, he naturally became timid about publication, but two of his poems which deserve mention are *Human Life* (1819) and *Italy,* which attracted little attention on its first publication in 1822 but scored a marked success when it reappeared with illustrations by J. M. W. Turner and Thomas Stothard eight years later. On the death of Wordsworth in 1850 Rogers refused the laureateship. His poetry strikes the modern reader as Regency album verse, but Rogers remains important because of the greater men with whom he associated. He died on Dec. 18, 1855.

BIBLIOGRAPHY.—*Poetical Works,* ed. by E. Bell (1875); P. W. Clayden, *The Early Life of Samuel Rogers* (1887), *Rogers and His Contemporaries,* 2 vol. (1889); *The Italian Journal of Samuel Rogers,* ed. by J. R. Hale (1956); *Samuel Rogers and William Gilpin,* ed. by C. P. Barbier (1959).　　　(I. J.)

ROGERS, WILL (WILLIAM PENN ADAIR ROGERS) (1879–1935), U.S. humorist and motion-picture actor, writer of a newspaper column famous for its homespun humour and for its good-natured but extremely sharp criticism of contemporary men and affairs, was born Nov. 4, 1879, at Oologah, Indian Territory (now Oklahoma). Utilizing the rope twirling and lassoing he learned on his father's ranch, he began a career as a rope-throwing cowboy in steer-roping contests, Wild West shows, and vaudeville. In 1915, appearing in Ziegfeld's *Midnight Frolic* in New York, he introduced a humorous political commentary into his act. This developed into a newspaper column, syndicated weekly in 1922 and daily in 1926. Rogers also wrote a series of books in a similar vein, including *The Cowboy Philosopher on Prohibition* (1919), *Illiterate Digest* (1924), and *There's Not a Bathing Suit in Russia* (1927). Rogers was equally successful as a motion-picture actor. His films included *A Connecticut Yankee* (1931), *State Fair* (1933), and *David Harum* (1934). With the pilot Wiley Post he was killed in a plane crash in Alaska on Aug. 15, 1935.

(M. S. By.)

ROGERS, WILLIAM (1819–1896), English educational reformer, known as "Hang-theology Rogers" because of his proposals that doctrinal training be left to parents and clergy, was born in London on Nov. 24, 1819, and died there on Jan. 19, 1896. He was ordained in 1843, and in 1845 was appointed to the curacy of St. Thomas', Charterhouse, where he remained for 18 years, throwing himself passionately into the work of education of his poor and often criminal parishioners. He began by establishing a school for ragamuffins in a blacksmith's abandoned shed, and he gradually extended its scope until schools were provided throughout the parish. In 1863 he became rector of St. Botolph's, Bishopsgate, and at Bishopsgate Rogers tackled the problem of intermediate, or higher elementary, education. He advocated secular education and to the cry against "godless education" replied, "Hang theology; let us begin," earning his lasting nickname. Rogers reconstructed Edward Alleyn's charity at Dulwich and founded the Bishopsgate Institute.

ROGET, PETER MARK (1779–1869), English physician and philologist, remembered for his *Thesaurus of English Words and Phrases,* a comprehensive classified list of synonyms or verbal equivalents which is popularly supposed, in its author's own phrase, "to facilitate the expression of ideas and to assist in literary composition." This work, published in 1852 and since then seldom, if ever, out of print, was the product of Roget's retirement from active medical practice. Though begun in his 61st and finished in his 73rd year, the *Thesaurus* was based on a methodical system of verbal classification which he had set out for his own use in a manuscript notebook in 1805.

The son of John Roget (d. 1783), a Genevan refugee who was pastor of the French Protestant church in Threadneedle Street, London, Roget was born in Soho, London, on Jan. 18, 1779. His mother, from whom he is reputed to have inherited his systematizing tendency, was a sister of Sir Samuel Romilly, the advocate and law reformer. Roget studied medicine at Edinburgh, and in 1805 was appointed physician to the infirmary at Manchester, where he helped to found the medical school. From 1808 to 1840 he practised in London, also lecturing and writing on many scientific topics. In 1815 his invention of a slide rule brought him a fellowship of the Royal Society, of which, in 1827, he became secretary. He also played a part in the founding of London University.

For some time before his death (at West Malvern, Worcestershire, on Sept. 12, 1869), Roget had been working on an enlarged edition of the *Thesaurus*, which was completed and published by his son in 1879. Later editions were revised by Roget's grandson; and editions in Everyman's Library (1952), as a paperback (1953), and in dictionary form (1961), attested the work's continued popularity. (OL. S.)

ROGIER, CHARLES LATOUR (1800–1885), one of the architects of Belgian independence and the foremost Liberal statesman in the first four decades of the new kingdom. He was born at Saint-Quentin, in northern France, on Aug. 17, 1800, of Belgian immigrants. His family later moved to Liège, and he began practice as a barrister. In 1824 he was one of the founders of the journal *Mathieu Laensbergh* (afterward renamed *Le Politique*), which soon became known for its Belgian patriotism and its criticisms of the Dutch administration, Belgium being at that time part of the unitary kingdom of the Netherlands (*see* BELGIUM: *History*).

When insurrection broke out in Brussels in August 1830, Rogier mustered 150 Liégeois and marched with them to support it. Recognized at once as a leader of the revolutionary movement, he was chosen to be president of the administrative commission formed on Sept. 24. On Sept. 25 this commission was transformed into a provisional government, of which Rogier remained one of the principal members. Representing this government, he went in October to Antwerp, where the Dutch still held the citadel: he arranged the armistice there and reorganized the administration of the town.

Deputy for Liège in the National Congress, Rogier insisted on the proclamation of Belgian independence and on the establishment of a hereditary monarchy. When a regency for the vacant throne was inaugurated the provisional government resigned (Feb. 24, 1831). At first Rogier wanted the crown to be offered to the duc de Nemours (Louis Charles Philippe Raphaël d'Orléans), son of Louis Philippe, king of the French; but when Louis Philippe declined this offer for his son, Rogier transferred his vote to Leopold of Saxe-Coburg, who was elected king as Leopold I (*q.v.*).

After being governor of Antwerp from June 1831, Rogier became minister of the interior on Oct. 20, 1832. In this capacity, he carried, against strong opposition, the law for the construction of railways; but disagreement within the cabinet led to his resignation on Aug. 1, 1834, whereupon he resumed the governorship of Antwerp. For a year from April 1840 he was minister of public works, education, and the fine arts.

The growing antagonism between the Catholic or Clerical and the Liberal parties in Belgium kept Rogier out of office from 1841 to 1847, when on Aug. 12 he formed a Liberal government. In this government he was not only prime minister but also minister of the interior. His policy did much to save Belgium from the revolutionary convulsions which shook Europe in 1848. In the summer of 1852 he resigned, but was persuaded by the king to resume office till Oct. 31.

On Nov. 8, 1857, Rogier took office again as prime minister

and minister of the interior. He exchanged the latter portfolio for that of foreign affairs in October 1861 and achieved a major international success in 1863, when his envoy Auguste Lambermont (*q.v.*) negotiated the agreement with the Netherlands freeing Antwerp's commerce from liability to tolls on the Scheldt River. On Dec. 30, 1867, he retired from office, being succeeded in January 1868 by his former minister of finance, H. J. W. Frère-Orban (*q.v.*).

Rogier was active in public affairs throughout the 1870s. He died, a nationally honoured figure, at Saint-Josse-ten-Noode, Brussels, on May 27, 1885.

See E. Discailles, *Charles Rogier*, 4 vol. (1893–95).

ROHAN, a family of great distinction in French history. Of Breton origin, it is said to be descended from a junior member of the original sovereign House of Brittany, and its later claims to princely rank in France were based on this supposition. Its traditional motto, *Roi ne puis, duc ne daigne, Rohan suis* ("King I cannot be, duke I disdain, Rohan I am"), fell out of use as Rohans acquired duchies.

Alain I, a younger son of a viscount of Porhoët, is recorded as having his seat at Rohan in the 1120s. His descendants, on whose viscounty of Rohan the lordship of Guéméné (Guémenée, Guimené, etc.) was feudally dependent, increased their possessions by marrying heiresses: by the end of the Middle Ages Corlay, Rochefort, Léon, Porhoët, and Montauban (-en-Bretagne) were in their hands. By 1470, three of their wives had come from the sovereign dynasty of Brittany, one from that of Navarre.

The direct male line of the viscounts died out with Jacques de Rohan (1478–1527), and his brother Charles (1480–1540), bishop of Quimper. Their sisters Anne (d. 1529) and Marie (d. *c.* 1542) had been married respectively to Pierre II de Rohan-Gié, seigneur de Frontenay, and Louis IV de Rohan-Guéméné, both of whom were descendants of Charles I, seigneur de Guéméné (d. 1438), a younger son of the viscount Jean I (d. 1396). Louis IV's branch of the family was genealogically senior, but Pierre II's branch acquired the preponderant part of the viscounts' inheritance.

Rohan-Gié and Rohan-Chabot.—Charles I de Guéméné's grandson Pierre I de Rohan, seigneur de Gié (1451–1513), was appointed a marshal of France in 1475. He campaigned in the Low Countries and in Italy and became the rival of the cardinal Georges d'Amboise (*q.v.*) in King Louis XII's government. He was married, in 1503, to Marguerite d'Armagnac, through whom he advanced claims to the title of duc de Nemours. When Louis XII fell ill, however, in 1503, the marshal de Gié took measures to prevent the queen of France, Anne (*q.v.*) of Brittany, from retiring to Brittany, lest she should separate Brittany from France if Louis XII died. Anne and the cardinal d'Amboise, on Louis XII's recovery, misrepresented the marshal's actions as criminal. He was brought to trial (1504–06). Acquitted of the graver charges, he was found guilty of lesser ones and sentenced to five years' exile from court. He never returned to public life.

Pierre II, the marshal's son, was the father of René I (d. 1552), who in 1534 married Isabelle d'Albret, daughter of Catherine de Foix-Grailly, queen of Navarre (*see* ALBRET). Their son René II (1550–86) was a military leader of the Huguenots in the Wars of Religion and the husband of Catherine de Parthenay, heiress of the lordship of Soubise, who herself, as vicomtesse de Rohan, was a heroine of the Huguenots till her death (1630). René II's sister Françoise, demoiselle de La Garnache, had a child by Jacques de Savoie, duc de Nemours, but he broke his promise to marry her: in the consequent outcry, the Huguenot princes took her side, while the House of Guise took his. She was finally compensated in 1579 with the title of duchesse de Loudun for her lifetime.

René II's son Henry (1579–1638) was created duc de Rohan and a peer of France in 1603. He was married to Marguerite de Béthune, daughter of the duc de Sully, in 1605. Having led the Huguenots in revolt against the government of Marie de Médicis in 1615–16, he became their foremost general in the civil wars of the 1620s, campaigning with considerable success in Languedoc. Having twice made shortlived treaties with King Louis XIII's government (1623 and 1626), he took up arms again in 1627, during the War of La Rochelle, and fought on in Languedoc till the

Peace of Alais (1629). After a long stay in Venice, he returned to France in 1635 and was given command of the army sent across Switzerland to intervene against the Habsburgs' forces in the Valtellina. Militarily victorious, he failed to win the population to a pro-French policy and was driven out in 1637. After a stay in Geneva, he joined Bernhard (q.v.) of Saxe-Weimar in Germany. Mortally wounded with Bernhard's troops in battle at Rheinfelden, he died on April 13, 1638. He had published a masterpiece of military theory, *Le Parfaict Capitaine* (1636; Eng. trans., *The Complete Captain*, 1640), and left several autobiographical writings. His brother Benjamin, seigneur de Soubise (1583–1642) was also prominent as a Huguenot rebel in the 1620s. He led expeditions from England against the west coast of France and died in London a respected exile. His sister Anne de Rohan (1584–1646) was notable for a few poems.

In 1645 the first duc's daughter Marguerite (1617–84) took as her husband a poor nobleman, Henry Chabot (1616–55). The French crown erected a new peerage-duchy of Rohan for him, with the proviso that his children should be Catholics; and it was stipulated that they should bear the name and arms of Rohan. The proviso on religion, together with Chabot's poverty, infuriated the dowager duchesse, Marguerite de Béthune, who thereupon produced from obscurity a young man, Tancrède, and implausibly put him forward as her late husband's son and heir; but Tancrède was killed in 1649, fighting for the Fronde. The right of Chabot's descendants to the name of Rohan was confirmed by Louis XIV in 1704, after an attempt by the other Rohans to deprive them of it. Their title of duc de Rohan (-Chabot) survives in the 20th century.

Rohan-Guémené.—Louis II, seigneur de Guémené (d. 1508), was the marshal de Gié's elder brother. His grandson Louis IV (d. 1527) inherited Montbazon, in Touraine, through his mother. Louis IV's grandson Louis VI (d. 1611) obtained the title of prince de Guémené, but this merely decorated his fief, without conferring princely rank on the House of Rohan (*see* PRINCE for the distinctions involved). His son Louis VII (d. 1589) was created duc de Montbazon in 1588. This peerage was recreated in 1594 for his brother Hercule (1568–1654). Hercule was the father, by his first marriage, of the celebrated duchesse de Chevreuse (q.v.) and was the husband, by his second, of that duchesse de Montbazon (Marie d'Avaugour; d. 1657) who quarrelled with the duchesse de Longueville (q.v.) and was famous during the Fronde as the mistress of the duc de Beaufort (q.v.). Hercule's son Louis VIII (1598–1667), married his first cousin Anne de Rohan (d. 1685), who, as the princesse de Guémené till her husband became duc de Montbazon in 1654, was also active in the intrigues of the Fronde. It was she who began gradually to secure for the House of Rohan privileges analogous to those of foreign princes.

Anne de Rohan-Chabot (d. 1709), Henry Chabot's daughter, was married in 1663 to Hercule's son by his second marriage, François de Rohan-Montbazon (1631–1712), to whom the title of prince de Soubise was granted in 1667. This princesse de Soubise exploited her influence as one of King Louis XIV's mistresses to advance her husband's family, with such success that the ensuing decades of its princely aggrandizement became known to the envious French nobility as "the Age of the Rohans." Her son Hercule Mériadec (1669–1749) was created duc de Rohan-Rohan in 1714. Another son of hers, Armand Gaston Maximilien (1674–1749) became bishop of Strasbourg in 1704 and cardinal de Rohan in 1712. The latter's grandnephew, Armand (1717–56) became cardinal de Soubise in 1747 and bishop of Strasbourg in 1749. This pair must not be confused with their successors, Louis Constantin (1697–1779), bishop of Strasbourg from 1756 and cardinal from 1761, and Louis René Édouard (1734–1803), cardinal de Rohan from 1778 and bishop of Strasbourg from 1779 to 1801, who both were descendants of Louis VIII. (For Louis René Édouard *see* DIAMOND NECKLACE, AFFAIR OF THE.)

Louis VIII's younger son, Louis, chevalier de Rohan, led a dissipated life and finally committed high treason for money by plotting to deliver Quillebeuf to the Dutch. For this he was beheaded in Paris in 1674.

Charles de Rohan, prince de Soubise (1715–87), a great-grandson of the first prince, fought in the Seven Years' War. Better at

flattering King Louis XV's mistresses than at soldiering, he was defeated by Frederick the Great in the Battle of Rossbach (1757) but had some success later, for which he was appointed a marshal of France (1758). He also became a minister of state.

Jules Hercule Mériadec (1726–88), duc de Montbazon, of the fourth generation from Louis VIII, married Louise Henriette de La Tour d'Auvergne; and their son Henri Louis (1745–1801) married Victoire, daughter of the marshal de Soubise. Thus the latter's son Charles Alain Gabriel, duc de Montbazon (1764–1836), inherited on the one hand the title to Bouillon (q.v.), on the other the Soubise or Rohan-Rohan titles. In 1808, moreover, the House of Rohan (-Guémené) had been granted Austrian domicile and the Austrian title of prince (*Fürst*). In 1846, the accumulated titles passed to the branch of Rohan-Rochefort-Montauban, descendants of Jules Hercule Mériadec's uncle Charles (1693–1766).

(J. G. R.-S.)

RÖHM, ERNST (1887–1934), German army officer, and chief organizer of Hitler's Nazi *Sturmabteilungen* (storm troops) after World War I, was born in Munich on Nov. 28, 1887. He joined the army in 1906. During World War I he was wounded three times and rose to the rank of major. After the war he remained on the staff of the army district command in Munich until he resigned his commission on Sept. 26, 1923. He took part in founding, before Hitler, the National Socialist German Workers' Party. He helped Hitler to win the support of the army in Bavaria, and provided him with the services of his own strong-arm squads. In October 1921 these became the *Sturmabteilungen* (the brown-shirted SA). Röhm took a prominent part in the Munich *Putsch* on Nov. 8–9, 1923, was arrested and sentenced to a short term of imprisonment. Hitler wanted the SA to remain subordinate to the party, while Röhm wanted it to be on equal terms with the party, and eventually either to absorb or to replace the regular *Wehrmacht*. Röhm resigned the leadership of the SA in 1925 and went to Bolivia. At the end of 1930 Hitler persuaded him to return to reorganize the SA. For the next three years Röhm provided an organized but disreputable body of men to give the Nazis force. When Hitler became chancellor Röhm deplored his delay in continuing the revolution. For a time Hitler compromised, and brought Röhm into his cabinet. Hitler then reduced the SA to the status of a subordinate body unable to rival his own power or to make trouble with the *Wehrmacht*. He carried out the purge of June 30, 1934, on the pretext that Röhm and the SA were preparing a *Putsch*. Unsuspecting, Röhm was taken by Hitler personally from his hotel at Bad Wiessee, outside Munich, and was shot without trial at Munich-Stadelheim. His memoirs were published under the title *Die Geschichte eines Hochverräter* (2nd ed., 1934). (W. Kp.; X.)

ROHTAK, a town and district in the Ambala division of Hariana State, India. The town, headquarters of the district, lies 44 mi. (71 km.) NW of Delhi by rail. Pop. (1961) 88,193. It is of great antiquity and is said to have been founded by Raja Rohtas of the Ponwar Rajputs. Some fine pieces of sculpture of the Buddhist period have been recovered from Khokra Kot, an ancient mound near the town. The old town of Rohtak was surrounded by a wall with 11 gates, the remains of which can still be seen. There are five colleges affiliated to Panjab University. The town is a grain centre and has a large sugar mill. Viewed from the hills to the south, with its white Dini mosque (1140) in the centre and fort to the east, Rohtak is picturesque.

ROHTAK DISTRICT, in the Jumna-Sutlej Divide, is mostly a level plain, with a few hills—outliers of the Aravalli Range—and sand dunes in the south, and an area of inland drainage in the southeast which turns marshy during the rainy season. Area 2,330 sq.mi. (6,035 sq.km.). Pop. (1961) 1,420,391. Annual rainfall averages about 19 in. (482 mm.), mostly falling in July–September. More than three-quarters of the total area is under cultivation, and nearly half of this is irrigated by the Rohtak and the Butana branches of the Western Jumna Canal and wells, the remainder depending upon uncertain rainfall. The principal crops are wheat, millets, gram, barley, sugarcane, and cotton. The district's towns and local trading centres include Sonepat (pop. [1961] 45,882), Bahadurgarh (14,982), and Jhajjar (14,234). (O. P. B.)

ROJAS, AGUSTÍN DE (1572–c. 1635), Spanish actor and author whose most important work, *El viaje entretenido* (1603), gives a valuable account of the Spanish theatre in the 16th century and the life of its actors. Born at Madrid in 1572, at 14 he ran away to Seville, and led an adventurous life as a soldier, serving in France, where he was taken prisoner. He returned to Spain through an exchange of prisoners, and eventually became an actor in various touring companies. After his marriage (at Valladolid in 1603), he settled down as a public functionary, being clerk to the council of Zamora in 1607 and public notary to the episcopal audience there in 1611. The precise date and place of his death are not known.

El viaje entretenido, an autobiographical novel in dialogue, of a picaresque type, contains much detailed and lively information about the life of a traveling actor. Among Rojas' other works are the play *El natural desdichado,* and 40 *loas* or laudatory dramatic prologues, which, in their varied treatment of their subject matter, provided a model for later writers in the genre.

See G. I. Dale, article on *El natural Desdichado,* in the *Hispanic Review,* ii (1934); H. A. Rennert, *The Spanish Stage in the Time of Lope de Vega* (1909; new ed. 1964). (L. J. CL.)

ROJAS PINILLA, GUSTAVO (1900–   ), former dictator of Colombia, was born March 12, 1900, at Tunja. A professional soldier, he was graduated from the Colombian Military Academy in 1920. While on inactive status (1924–1933), he earned a civil engineering degree in the United States. After 1933 he rose rapidly in the army to the rank of lieutenant general, represented Colombia at a number of international conferences, and was a member of the Inter-American Defense Board (1951–1952). Rojas' political interests date from his suppression of the April 1948 riots in Cali. Increasingly identified with the Conservative opposition to the administration of Pres. Laureano Gómez, Rojas seized control of the government on June 13, 1953, after Gómez had resolved to remove him as commander of the armed forces. Rojas promised peace, justice, and liberty to end violence in rural areas. However, his corrupt authoritarian administration converted nationwide popularity into united national hostility. On May 10, 1957, he appointed a military junta to govern in his place and left the country. Impeached after returning in October 1958, he lost his civil rights in April 1959. Nevertheless, he reentered politics and in 1962 won 2.5% of the votes cast for president.

Disillusionment with National Front progress and disintegration of the leftist faction of the Liberal Party made Rojas' Acción Nacional Popular (ANAPO) the leading lower sectors' protest group. It won 18% of the congressional election vote in 1964 and roughly 28% of the presidential election votes in 1966. A high Colombian court in 1967 ruled that Rojas could not be deprived of his civil rights. Rojas and the ANAPO were the significant political threat to the government of Colombia. (R. L. GE.)

ROKITANSKY, KARL, FREIHERR VON (1804–1878), Austrian pioneer in the science of pathology, was born at Königgrätz, Bohemia, on Feb. 19, 1804. He studied medicine at Prague and at Vienna, where he was appointed professor extraordinary of pathological anatomy in 1834. He became president of the Vienna Academy of Sciences in 1869 and was named freiherr in 1874. He was active in the Austrian legislature, becoming speaker of the House. He died in Vienna, July 23, 1878.

Rokitansky performed more than 30,000 autopsies. The differentiation of lobar and lobular pneumonia is based on his findings, as are the pathology of acute dilatation of the stomach, acute yellow atrophy of the liver (Rokitansky's disease), and the pulmonary complications of typhoid fever. He elucidated the micropathology of emphysema, a lung disease, and is credited with the first description of spondylolisthesis, or dissolution of a vertebra. His *Handbuch der pathologischen Anatomie* (1842–46, English translation 1849–52) was an important work.

ROKYCANA, JAN (Czech JAN Z ROKYCAN) (c. 1390–1471), third of the chief religious leaders of the Hussites (q.v.), was the son of a poor smith of Rokycany near Plzen, in Bohemia. He went to Prague probably in 1410, becoming there the close assistant of Jakoubek (Jacobellus) of Stribro and finally his successor as organizer of the Hussite Church. Like Jan (John) Huss a powerful preacher, Rokycana became in 1423 minister of the largest church in Prague and soon chief of the clergy of the Prague party, as well as, from 1432, of that of the "Orphans" (moderate Taborites). In the peace negotiations with the Council of Basel he was in 1433 speaker for the large Hussite delegation. In 1435 he was elected by the Diet to the archbishopric of the Hussite Church and in 1436 signed in its name the peace treaty with the council. The following year the emperor Sigismund drove Rokycana out of Prague, and the ensuing reaction prevented his return until 1448. After that the leader of the undaunted Hussites, George of Podebrady, helped him to achieve general recognition.

George's election as king in 1458 meant immense success for Rokycana and the Hussites, but for the papacy it was a challenge to war. (See BOHEMIA.) In 1462 Pius II revoked the peace of 1436, and his successor declared a crusade in 1467 against the Hussites. Nonetheless both Rokycana and the king died in 1471 (Rokycana in Prague on Feb. 22; George a month later) unconquered and in the justified belief that their work was saved permanently; theirs was the first great national church which the papacy was unable to conquer, and within 50 years it became the ideal of the churches of the Reformation.

See F. M. Bartoš, *Literárni činnost Mistra Jana Rokycany . . .* (1928). (F. M. BA.)

ROLAND (DE LA PLATIÈRE), JEAN MARIE (1734–1793), French statesman of the Revolution, an author and industrial scientist who, largely through his wife's ambition and influence, was minister of the interior for two short periods in the years 1792 to 1793. He was born at Thizy, near Roanne in the Lyonnais, on Feb. 18, 1734.

On Feb. 4, 1780, Roland married Marie Jeanne (Manon) Phlipon (1754–93). Clear-headed and forceful, she exercised a commanding influence over him. In 1789 both the Rolands rapturously welcomed the Revolution. During a business visit to Paris (February–September 1791) Roland regularly attended the Jacobin Club and became closely connected with the future Girondins (q.v.). Meanwhile his wife's intense patriotism, intelligence, and charm took revolutionary society by storm. The couple moved permanently to Paris in December 1791 and on March 23, 1792, Roland, thanks to his friendship with Brissot, was appointed minister of the interior in a government formed under Girondin influence. He proved a good administrator, but when Louis XVI vetoed decrees to establish a camp of national guards outside Paris and to deport nonjuring clergy, Roland, in a letter drafted by his wife, called upon the king (June 10, 1792) to give way. Louis therefore dismissed Roland and other Girondin ministers on June 13. However, in the provisional government which was appointed after the attack on the Tuileries (Aug. 10, 1792; see FRANCE: *History*) and the overthrow of the monarchy, Roland was again minister of the interior. His wife now directed his work even more closely, making him the instrument of her opposition to Robespierre and Danton. Meanwhile Roland took an open part in the struggle between the Girondins and the Montagnards (the Mountain). His neglect to have the king's private papers, found in the Tuileries on Nov. 20, inventoried before witnesses, inevitably caused him to be accused of favouring the king. He resigned on Jan. 23, 1793, two days after Louis' execution.

At the outbreak (May 31) of the Paris insurrection which led to the fall of the Girondins, Mme Roland was arrested. Imprisoned in the Conciergerie, she wrote her memoirs, *Appel à l'impartiale postérité.* She was guillotined on Nov. 8, 1793. When Roland, who had escaped, heard of her death he killed himself at Bourg-Beaudouin, near Rouen, on Nov. 15.

See the numerous works on Mme Roland, notably M. Clemenceau Jacquemaire, *Life of Madame Roland,* Eng. trans. by L. Vail (1930). (A. So.)

ROLAND, CHANSON DE, a 4,000-line Old French epic, the subject being set in the context of Charlemagne's wars against the Saracens; in its extant form it dates from c. 1100. It is probably the oldest and certainly the finest of the *chansons de geste* (q.v.), and ranks as one of the great masterpieces of literature. Against a background which in many respects epitomizes the spirit of the First Crusade (*see* CRUSADES), its Norman-sounding author, Turold (if, as seems probable, the explicit of the oldest manuscript [*c.* 1130–40?] in the Bodleian Library, Oxford, is to be interpreted as comprising the author's signature), tells a heroic tale that has made the name Roncevaux (*Roncesvalles;* the scene of the battle between the French and the Saracens) as immortal as that of Thermopylae, and Roland, its hero, the paragon of the unyielding warrior, victorious in defeat. But, much more, Turold has placed in the foreground the human conflict between Roland and Oliver which, as well as illustrating the contrast between *fortitudo et sapientia* (valour and wisdom), is also a conflict between divergent conceptions of feudal loyalty and honour: Roland, heroic and noble, but his judgment clouded by his foolhardy insistence on, and preoccupation with, personal honour and renown; Oliver, no less heroic, but perceiving when the dictates of prudence must, in the common weal, prevail; Ganelon, the traitor, no less noble and of great courage, loyal to the emperor according to his own lights, but bent only on his feud against Roland.

The Story of the "Chanson."—After conquering all Spain save Saragossa alone, Charlemagne, about to return to France, accepts overtures from the Saracen king Marsilion, despite the opposition of his nephew Roland, and sends Ganelon, Roland's stepfather, to Saragossa to negotiate peace terms. Ganelon, incensed against Roland, who had proposed him for the perilous task, conspires with the pagans to achieve the destruction of his stepson, and on his return ensures that the emperor, despite his misgivings, appoints Roland to command the rear-guard. Perceiving the overwhelming Saracen hordes, Oliver, Roland's companion in arms, counsels prudence in the face of the battle-eager jubilation of Roland, urging him to sound his horn to recall Charlemagne. But on Roland's proud refusal, the hopeless battle of Roncevaux is joined, and soon the French, despite the massacre they inflict, are reduced to a handful. Then, in a brief and poignant scene of great beauty and dramatic power, it is Oliver who, echoing Roland's earlier words, rejects his companion's proposal to sound his horn, for now it is too late. Archbishop Turpin settles the quarrel: let the horn be sounded, that Charlemagne may avenge their death. Roland at last blows a great blast on his horn that carries full 30 leagues to Charlemagne, but such is his effort that he bursts his temple. The battle continues, but, despite their prowesses, the French are overcome; Oliver, so blinded by his wounds that he strikes Roland in error, dies. Again Roland sounds his horn, but now weakly. The Saracens, hearing Charlemagne's trumpets in reply, flee after a final attempt to kill Roland. Turpin, after blessing the bodies of his comrades in arms, also dies. Roland, whom no pagan hand has been able to touch, is alone on the battlefield, and, knowing that death is close, attempts to destroy his sword Durendal by thrice striking it against a rock, lest it fall into enemy hands; but the blade, piercing the rock, remains unharmed, and Roland, composing himself to die in the attitude of contrition (*i.e.*, in prosternation), places it with his horn beneath him; in this position he dies, and the archangels receive his soul. As the emperor arrives on the battlefield, God halts the sun in its path that he may wreak his vengeance on the fleeing army.

The news of the Saracens' defeat has been carried by Marsilion to Saragossa, where the emir Baligant, earlier summoned to help repel Charlemagne, has assembled an even vaster army. Here follows a long account, which some critics, albeit on debatable grounds, hold to be apocryphal to the original poem, of the preparations of the two armies and the great battle they lead up to, ending in Baligant's defeat by Charlemagne and the capture of Saragossa. The emperor at last returns to Aix-la-Chapelle, on the way placing Roland's oliphant on the altar of Saint-Seurin-de-Bordeaux, and burying Roland, Oliver, and Turpin at Saint-Romain-de-Blaye. At Aix he announces the news of Roland's death to *la belle Aude,* Roland's promised bride and Oliver's sister, who on hearing it falls dead at Charlemagne's feet. Here begins the trial of Ganelon, charged with treason against the emperor; Ganelon's defense is that his action was directed not against Charles but against Roland whom he had defied in due form, and the barons recommend his acquittal. Thereupon, one of the emperor's knights, Thierry, argues otherwise, and a judicial combat

is arranged between himself and Ganelon's champion, Pinabel, who is defeated. Ganelon is hanged and quartered, and thus is Charlemagne's justice achieved.

The Poem's Style.—The composition of the poem is firm and coherent, the style direct, sober, and, on occasion, stark, with no trace of ornamentation, and, despite the somewhat conventional ring of certain of the battle scenes, little visible literary device. The character drawing in particular is most striking, the most successful passages being those in which the author depicts, without comment or explanation, clashes of personality, among them those between Roland and Ganelon, Ganelon and Marsilion, Ganelon and Charlemagne, and, above all, Roland and Oliver. In these scenes, the underlying conflicting feudal concepts are vividly expressed in terms of human drama that has something of the inevitability of Greek tragedy. As opposed to the long account of the battle in which the emperor overcomes Baligant, and which somewhat suggests a set piece, the description of the earlier battle scenes is clearly subordinated to the roles of Roland and Oliver, and, to a lesser extent, of Turpin, leading in a crescendo of pathos to the death of each. This pathos is echoed in the lament pronounced by Charlemagne over the body of his nephew, and in the brief scene leading to the death of Aude. The language throughout is sure, and terse in its economy of expression. Although the *Roland* is one of the earliest monuments of French literature, and Turold its first great poet, there is nothing that does not suggest a well-established literary and linguistic medium.

Influence of the "Roland."—The success and development of the genre clearly owes much to Turold. Apart from more general considerations, many later authors appear to make a point of establishing a link between their narratives and the events of Roncevaux. Some go much farther and exploit and embellish the theme. Thus, earlier adventures are attributed to Roland and Oliver in the *chansons de geste Girart de Roussillon* (12th century), *Aspremont* (late 12th century), *Otinel* and *Anseïs de Carthage* (both *c.* 1200 ?) among others. Nor was the success of the *Roland* confined to northern France; a Provencal *Ronsasvals* and *Rollan a Saragossa* (? late 12th century) have survived. In Spain, in addition to the 13th-century fragment of *Roncesvalles*, the *Poema de mio Cid* (*see* SPANISH LITERATURE: *The Rise of Heroic Poetry*) itself owes much in conception, content, and form to the French *chansons de geste,* and an unmistakable echo of the Roland theme is found in the romance, *La Fuga del rey Marsín;* the discovery of the so-called *Nota emilianense,* a barbarous dog-Latin text inserted in a manuscript from the monastery of San Millán de la Cogolla, is evidence that French epic heroes, including Roland, Oliver, and Turpin as well as Guillaume, Bertrand, and Ogier, were early known in northern Spain, although the dating of this text as early as *c.* 1075 is not, on paleographic grounds, entirely conclusive. Italy offers not only the 13th- and 14th-century Franco-Italian manuscripts of the *Roland* itself, but also the Franco-Italian poems which exploit it—*Berte e Milone* (13th century), *Entree en Espagne* and *Prise de Pampelune* (14th century)—as well as Matteo Boiardo's *Orlando Innamorato* (publ. 1495) and Ariosto's *Orlando Furioso* (final version, 1532); in Sicily, the place names Capo d'Orlando and Capo d'Oliviere (Capo Calavà) testify to the early penetration of Rolandian themes to southern Italy, doubtless through the Normans. The German Konrad ("Pfaffe Konrad") translated an early version as the *Ruolantes Liet* (*c.* 1175), which was itself exploited by subsequent German writers, and the 13th-century compiler of the Norse *Karlamagnús-saga* translated a version of the *Roland* perhaps earlier than that of the Oxford manuscript (*see* ICELANDIC LITERATURE: *Romances*). In England, the decline of Anglo-Norman (the language of the earliest extant manuscript) led to a 15th-century adaptation, *Rowlandes Song,* and there exists a 14th-century Welsh prose narrative, *Campeu Charlyamen,* which includes an account of Roncevaux.

The *Historia Karoli Magni et Rotholandi* (*c.* 1150 ?)—the so-called *Pseudo-Turpin* (*see* TURPIN; CHARLEMAGNE LEGENDS) which constituted the fourth book of the *Liber sancti Jacobi,* composed in the interests of Santiago de Compostela (*q.v.*)—and the *Carmen de prodicione Guenonis* (*c.* 1200) are manifest derivatives of the *Roland*, while from as early as the beginning of the 12th century allusions by Latin writers to events and characters of the *Roland* became frequent; Radulfus Tortarius (1063–1108?) in his *Epistola ad Bernardum* refers to Roland's sword; Raoul (Radulf) de Caen, writing between 1112 and 1118 (*Gesta Tancredi*) exclaims: *Rollandum dicas Oliveriumque renatos!* ("Roland and Oliver come to life!"); William of Malmesbury relates in a celebrated passage of his *Gesta regum Anglorum* (*c.* 1125) how a *jongleur* accompanied the Norman troops at Hastings declaiming of Roland; and Orderic Vitalis, in his *Historia ecclesiastica* (written *c.* 1123–31), couples Roland with Achilles.

The earliest examples of the impact of the Rolandian theme on medieval artists can be seen in the representation of scenes from the *Chanson* in the 13th-century Charlemagne window at Chartres cathedral, which shows Roland alone on the battlefield, sounding the horn and striking the rock with his sword, and also, in other scenes, with Turpin, Baudouin (Balduinus), and Ganelon. There are also statues, perhaps of Roland and Oliver, on the 12th-century porch of Verona cathedral, and until its destruction (between 1215 and 1220) there existed at Brindisi a mosaic (1178), in the pavement of the cathedral nave, depicting a battle scene in which were identified Roland, Oliver, and Turpin.

Historical Basis.—As recounted by contemporary chroniclers, the historical facts are somewhat different from the account given in the *Roland*. In the early summer of 778, Charlemagne, after receiving overtures from dissident Moorish leaders, led two vast armies, which converged on Saragossa with a view to occupying the town. The plot, however, miscarried, and on Aug. 15 he recrossed the Pyrenees into France, by a route not clearly defined. There (Arabic sources tend to suggest, in addition, a military reverse closer to Saragossa) his army was ambushed by Wascones (more probably Gascons than Basques), who, after inflicting heavy casualties and pillaging the baggage train, made off before any action against them could be organized.

To attempt to identify other early references to the *Roland* of Turold is to reopen the extremely complex problem of the origins of the poem and of the genre (*see* CHANSONS DE GESTE). The traditionalist interpretation of the evidence postulates the existence of an unbroken tradition of poems, very different from Turold's if only in that they excluded Oliver, reaching back to those composed under the immediate impact of Roncevaux. Joseph Bédier's individualist theory denies this continuity: ". . . if the legend of Roland may from an early date have vegetated obscurely in the churches of Roncevaux, it took shape in poetic form only in the 11th century." A. Pauphilet carried this argument further, answering Bédier's *"Au commencement était la route"* ("In the beginning was the pilgrim road") with *"Au commencement était le poète"* ("In the beginning was the poet"). It is generally agreed that there must have existed a *Chanson de Roland*, probably not fundamentally different in essentials from the recension contained in the conserved versions, about the middle of the 11th century, and that this bears the imprint of poetic creation in such essential aspects as the figure of Oliver and the presence of Turpin and Ganelon.

Although there is unequivocal proof, numismatic and diplomatic, of a Rodlandus or Rotholandus in the entourage of Charlemagne, the only historical evidence of a Roland among the fallen at Roncevaux is contained in the *Vita Caroli Magni* by Eginhard (Einhard, *q.v.*), which, briefly commenting on the defeat, lists among the dead Eggihardus, the royal seneschal; Anshelmus, count palatine; and *Hruodlandus Britannici limitis praefectus* ("Roland, prefect of the march of Brittany"). But the manuscript tradition of Eginhard is such that the authenticity of the four essential words is uncertain. The evidence of the intervening centuries is assembled and discussed in great detail by R. Menéndez Pidal in his important, but debatable, restatement of the traditionalist theory (see *Bibliography* below).

BIBLIOGRAPHY.—*Text: See* especially *La Chanson de Roland publiée d'après le ms. d'Oxford et traduite par J. Bédier* (1921), and the complementary *La Chanson de Roland commentée par J. Bédier* (1927); *Les Textes de la Chanson de Roland, édités par R. Mortier*, 10 vol. (1940–44). Among English translations *see* D. L. Sayers, *The Song of Roland*, Penguin Books (1957).

General Studies include J. Bédier, *Les Légendes épiques*, vol. iii (1912; 3rd ed. 1929); E. Faral, *La Chanson de Roland, étude et analyse* (1934); M. Delbouille, *Sur la genèse de la Chanson de Roland* (1954); P. Le Gentil, *La Chanson de Roland* (1955); and the comprehensive work, with very detailed references, by R. Menéndez Pidal, *La Chanson de Roland y el neotradicionalismo* (1959), French trans. by I. Cluzel, *La Chanson de Roland et la tradition épique des Francs* (1960), *cf.* review by F. Lecoy, *Romania*, lxxxiv, pp. 88–133 (1963).

For complete bibliography of editions and critical studies, *see* R. Bossuat, *Manuel bibliographique de la littérature française du moyen âge* (1951), *Suppléments* (1955 and 1961); for subsequent publications *see* the annual *Bulletin bibliographique de la Société Rencesvals* (1958 et seq.). (D. McMI.)

ROLAND HOLST-VAN DER SCHALK, HENRIETTE GOVERDINE ANNA (1869–1952), Dutch poet who also played an active part in political life, as a socialist. A lawyer's daughter, she was born at Noordwijk on Dec. 24, 1869. In 1896 she married the painter (later professor) Richard Nicolas Roland Holst (1868–1938), himself a talented prose writer. Her early poetry expresses the desire to understand life rather than a desire for beauty. Gradually influenced by William Morris' writings, she became a socialist. Her volumes of poetry *De nieuwe geboort* ("The New Birth," 1902) and *Opwaartsche wegen* ("Upward Ways," 1907) reflect her political ideals, but contain no proletarian poetry. In her drama *Thomas More* (1912), dedicated to the German socialist leader Karl Kautsky, she depicted the last days of the great humanist, whom she regarded as having anticipated her own ideals for mankind. She soon became internationally famous in left-wing circles. She took part in the Zimmerwald Conference (1915), and at first eulogized the Russian Revolution, but, after visiting Russia in 1925, she expressed her disappointment in Soviet Communism in her poems in *Heldensage* ("Heroic Saga," 1927). Her later work is religious and socialist in character. She withdrew from practical politics but remained loyal to her ideals, and her pacifist and anticolonial ideas attracted much attention. Apart from poetry and drama she wrote essays on art and politics, as well as biographies of such figures as Jean Jacques Rousseau (1912), Tolstoi (1930), Herman Gorter (1933), Romain Rolland (1946), and Gandhi (1947). She died in Amsterdam on Nov. 22, 1952.

See K. F. Proost, *Henriëtte Roland Holst* (1937); J. P. van Praag, *Henriëtte Roland Holst* (1946). (GD. W. Hs.)

ROLFE, FREDERICK WILLIAM (1860–1913), English author and eccentric, generally known by his pseudonym BARON CORVO, provides the curious example of an artist rescued from obscurity by his biographer. Twenty-one years after Rolfe's death A. J. A. Symons (1900–41), intrigued by the eccentricity, misery, and scandal of his private life, built up on these foundations his colourful biographical fantasy *The Quest for Corvo* (1934), the publication of which marked the beginning of Rolfe's fame. Neglected by his own and the succeeding generation, the intrinsic merit of Rolfe's writing was nonetheless always recognized by discerning critics and for incisiveness of expression he has few rivals in English prose. And in spite of failing to interest the common reader he had an important influence on contemporary writers, notably Henry Harland, R. H. Benson, Shane Leslie, and perhaps Ronald Firbank.

Born in London on July 22, 1860, Rolfe was the oldest of six children of a piano manufacturer. He left school at 14 and became successively a pupil teacher, an unattached student at Oxford, and a schoolmaster. Reared as a Protestant, Rolfe had from boyhood been drawn to religion, and his plans for a career in the church were laid in adolescence. In 1886 he became a Roman Catholic. There followed two unsuccessful attempts to become a priest, but the independence and perversity which were to mark and embitter his life finally led to his dismissal from the Scots College in Rome. This painful episode was to cause him lifelong frustration and to deepen the shadow of loneliness and persecution.

He now began a life unusual in its richness of incident and variety of adventure. For eight years he wandered about, turning his hand to painting, photography, tutoring, inventing, and journalism. In 1898, disclaiming all literary ambition—his faith unshaken in his vocation to the priesthood—Rolfe became a professional writer. During the next decade he published a collection of short stories based on Italian folk tales entitled *In His Own Image* (1901; the first six of which had appeared in the *Yellow Book* under the title *Stories Toto Told Me*), a historical work, *Chronicles of the House of Borgia* (1901), a translation of the *Rubáiyát* of Omar Khayyam (1903), and two novels, *Hadrian the Seventh* (1904), an autobiographical fantasy, with which his name is chiefly identified, and *Don Tarquinio* (1905). Some of his works appeared after his death, notably *The Desire and Pursuit of the Whole* (1934), *Hubert's Arthur* (1935), *Nicholas Crabbe* (1958), and *Don Renato* (1963). Rolfe was a prolific letter writer and he engaged in long and violent correspondence with his enemies. An edition of his collected letters in ten volumes began publication in 1959.

Going to Venice for a short holiday in 1908 Rolfe stayed for the rest of his life. He found there, sailing his boat for days and nights on the lagoon, his happiest moments, and also suffered appalling privations. Short periods of extravagant living at the expense of friends and well-wishers and, more rarely, on money from his writings, alternated with periods of near-starvation. As in England, he was involved in many quarrels. For months he was homeless, sometimes living in an open boat. Yet he contrived to write his masterpiece *The Desire and Pursuit of the Whole*. All that is best and worst in Rolfe can be learned from this account of his years in Venice. Gifted at many points—Rolfe excelled as a swimmer, sculler, musician, photographer, painter, and scribe—in his books and letters he came near to self-expression, albeit neither to success nor satisfaction. For Rolfe was a man obsessed and his works bear the impression of the energy with which he carefully sought but never found the way out of his self-imposed martyrdom. Worn out, he died in Venice on Oct. 25, 1913.

BIBLIOGRAPHY.—A. J. A. Symons, *The Quest for Corvo* (1934); Cecil Woolf, *A Bibliography of Frederick Rolfe*, 2nd ed. (1965); *New Quests for Corvo: a Collection of Essays by Various Hands*, ed. by Woolf and Brocard Sewell (1965). (C. Wo.)

ROLLAND, ROMAIN (1866–1944), French novelist, dramatist, essayist, and Nobel prizewinner (1915), was born at Clamecy (Nièvre) on Jan. 29, 1866. In 1892 he married Clotilde Bréal, whom he divorced in 1901. In 1895 he received a doctorate and became lecturer in history of art, first at the École Normale Supérieure, then, in 1904, at the Sorbonne, where he introduced the study of the history of music. He resigned in 1912 to devote his time to writing.

At the outbreak of World War I he was in Switzerland, and remained there, helping the Red Cross and publishing a famous series of articles, collected in *Au-dessus de la mêlée* (1915), urging France and Germany to respect truth and humanity throughout their fight. These aroused a storm of protest in both countries; the posthumous publication of his *Journal des années de guerre*, 1914–1919 (1952) has made possible a more dispassionate assessment of his attitude toward war. In 1922 he settled with his father and sister at Villeneuve (Vaud), where he remained until 1938, and where he was visited by friends from all over the world. In 1934 he married a young Russian widow and in 1937 he bought a house at Vézelay, in his native countryside, where he settled at the outbreak of World War II. He died there on Dec. 30, 1944.

At first Rolland wrote plays inspired by historical events: *Les Tragédies de la foi* (1913) contains *Saint-Louis* (1897), *Aërt* (1898), and *Le Triomphe de la raison* (1899), while *Le Théâtre de la Révolution* (1909) brings together *Les Loups* (1898; English translation *The Wolves*, 1937), *Danton* (1900; English translation 1918), and *Le Quatorze juillet* (1902; English translation 1928). His ideas on drama were expressed in articles collected in *Le Théâtre du peuple* (1903; English translation, *The People's Theatre*, 1918). In these plays, he aims at illustrating *"la vérité morale"* (*i.e.*, some general moral truth) rather than at exact historical accuracy. The heroes of his *Tragédies de la foi* are meant to embody a religious, national, or rationalist ideal. In his plays on the Revolution, he treats the problems of all periods disturbed by civil strife: the ends and means of political action, and the need to combine justice to the individual with the preservation of public order. *Les Loups* is an outstanding dramatic presentation of the Dreyfus affair (*see* DREYFUS, ALFRED). There followed *Le Temps viendra*

(1903), inspired by the South African War; *Le Jeu de l'amour et de la mort* (1925), his most successful play; *Pâques-Fleuries* (1926), the prologue to his *Théâtre de la Révolution;* and *Les Léonides* (1928), its epilogue. To it he added *Robespierre* (1939).

His passion for the heroic also found expression in a series of *Vies des hommes illustres: François Millet,* published in English (1902); the brilliant *Vie de Beethoven* (1903; English translation 1907), first published in the *Cahiers de la Quinzaine*, edited by Charles Péguy, to whom he devoted his last work, *Péguy* (1944); *Vie de Michel-Ange* (1905; English translation 1912); and the *Vie de Tolstoi* (1911; English translation). Meanwhile, his studies in musicology were continued by his *Haendel* (1910) and by his great study of *Beethoven, les grandes époques créatrices*, seven volumes (1928–49).

These trends, added to his earlier project of writing a *Bildungsroman* (*i.e.*, a psychological novel), led him to create a hero of musical genius and German birth, "Jean-Christophe Krafft," whose life story he recounted in 17 numbers of the *Cahiers de la Quinzaine* (1904–12, definitive edition, five volumes 1931–34; one volume 1948). This outstanding novel-cycle introduced to France the *roman-fleuve* (or novel-sequence). In his preface Rolland explains that *Jean-Christophe* resembles a flowing river, developing and changing even when it seems most passive. The fame of this work throughout Europe, and the publication of *Au-dessus de la mêlée*, won him the Nobel Prize for Literature for 1915.

Jean-Christophe, an epic in conception and style, rich in poetic feeling, presents the successive crises confronting a creative artist who, even at moments of deep depression, is inspired by love of life. Translated into about 30 languages (English translation 1910–13; 1961–), it has induced young people everywhere to think about life and its problems, and has given them, through the very failure of its heroes, courage to live nobly. To Rolland, the development in it of the friendship between a young German and a young Frenchman symbolized that "harmony of opposites" which man should strive to establish first within himself, then between individuals and, finally, between nations.

After this major work, Rolland relaxed in writing a burlesque fantasy, *Colas Breugnon*, also glorifying life, but in the manner of Rabelais or of Voltaire's *Candide*. It was not published until 1919, in the same year as his allegorical play *Liluli*, a satire against war. *Pierre et Luce* and *Clérambault*, two novels published in 1920, continued to expound his views on war and national egoism. These views gained him sympathy among pacifists, although he must not be regarded as being one himself. Nor was he a Communist, although he followed the progress of Russia after 1917 sympathetically. Rolland entered with unusual understanding into the views of others, but regarded the claims of truth as paramount. His residence in neutral Switzerland and his writings gave him a unique position as a leading spirit of the "left," through his correspondence with Albert Schweitzer, Einstein, Gorki, George Bernard Shaw, Bertrand Russell, Rabindranath Tagore, and others—published in the *Cahiers Romain Rolland* (1948–).

At the end of World War I, he turned to Asia, especially to India, seeking to interpret its mystical philosophy to the West, and following sympathetically its struggle toward emancipation, in *Mahatma Gandhi* (1924), *Vie de Ramakrishna* (1929), and *Vie de Vivekananda et l'Évangile universel*, two volumes (1930; *see* also *Inde, Journal* for 1915–43; 1951). His part in founding the international review, *Europe* (1923), his participation in left-wing congresses and manifestos, his visit in 1935 to the U.S.S.R., have led to his, again wrongly, being identified with the Communist party. He remained, however, "one against all." But he was the declared enemy of the Fascist regimes of Mussolini and Hitler, in 1933 refusing the Goethe Medal and in 1939 accepting the war as inevitable. These feelings inspired the companion-piece to *Jean-Christophe, L'Âme enchantée* (seven volumes, 1922–33; one volume, 1951), which tells the life-story of a young, independent Frenchwoman, Annette Rivière, during and after World War I. Although less well known than *Jean-Christophe*, this novel-cycle has great spiritual strength, and concludes by exposing the cruel effects of political sectarianism. Its author was not only a courageous and clear-sighted thinker, he was also a poet of sensuous imagery. Admirers of Paul Valéry and André Gide criticized his fluid, unaffected type of prose, capable of reaching a wide range of readers. His work was appreciated by Alain, however, and Gide, who was unsympathetic to *Jean-Christophe,* nevertheless recognized, in his *Journal* for 1917, that this *"livre barbare,"* as he called it, was one of the most topical works written in France in his generation.

Le Voyage intérieur (written 1926; publ. 1942) is a revealing and poetic self-portrait. The posthumous publication of Rolland's *Mémoires* (1956), and of part of his private journals, have made it possible to understand and to value more correctly the nature of his work and of his personality, and to recognize in him a man and a writer of exceptional integrity, with high critical and moral standards.

BIBLIOGRAPHY.—P.-J. Jouve, *Romain Rolland vivant* (1920); S. Zweig, *Romain Rolland: der Mann und das Werk* (1921); R. A. Wilson, *The Pre-War Biographies of Romain Rolland* (1939); J.-B. Barrère, *Romain Rolland par lui-même* (1955); J. Robichez, *Romain Rolland, l'homme et l'oeuvre* (1961); R. Cheval, *Romain Rolland, l'Allemagne et la guerre* (1963). (J.-B. BA.)

ROLLE, RICHARD, OF HAMPOLE (*c.* 1300–1349), early English mystic and author of mystical and ascetic tracts. The *Officium et Miracula,* prepared after his death by Cistercians of Yorkshire in anticipation of his canonization (which was never effected), provides the most certain information about his life: many apparently autobiographical passages in his own writings are cloudily expressed. Rolle was born *c.* 1300 at Thornton, Yorkshire, and was sent to the University of Oxford by Thomas Neville, archdeacon of Durham, but, dissatisfied with the subjects of study and the disputatiousness, left without a degree. There is no evidence that he ever went to the Sorbonne, or took priest's orders. Against the wishes of his family, Rolle established himself as a hermit on the estate of John Dalton of Pickering, but later moved to other hermitages, and probably always led a wandering life, rousing some opposition but winning much admiration. He kept in touch with a number of religious communities in the north and seems to have become spiritual adviser to the nuns at Hampole, in south Yorkshire, before his death there on Sept. 29, 1349. His influence and reputation lived to the Reformation.

It is often difficult to distinguish his writings from those of his many followers. *The Pricke of Conscience,* formerly ascribed to him, has been denied him by 20th-century scholars. Among the genuine works is a number of scriptural commentaries of which that on the Psalms is the most important. Two distinct versions exist: one in Latin, the other written in English at the request of Margaret Kirkby, a recluse at Anderby, Yorkshire. His range of reading is wide: he draws on Gregory, Anselm, Bernard, Peter Lombard, the Victorines, Bonaventura; his knowledge of the Bible is profound. Among his Latin treatises, *Melos Amoris* is something of an *apologia* offered to his detractors. *Incendium Amoris* most comprehensively presents his doctrine which, though in the main conforming with the usual mystical theology of the late middle ages, has some emphases and terms of its own. Throughout his diffuse and repetitive writings the life of contemplation and solitude is exalted. Strict physical self-control is urged, but spiritual progress consists in the development of love of God. This life of love is consummated in mystical union, which is considered to be self-authenticating. Rolle's method is essentially a concentration and directing of the affections toward the person of Christ, with a resulting experience of intense joy. In *Melos,* ch. ix, and *Incendium,* ch. xv, he provides notable accounts of rapture, which he invariably refers to in terms of *calor, dulcor, canor* ("fire, sweetness and song"). The terms suggest the quasi-physical accompaniment of his own mystical experiences.

His English writings on similar themes, handled more simply, include *Ego dormio* for a nun at Yedingham, Yorkshire, the *Commandment of Love to God* for a Hampole nun and the *Form of Perfect Living,* for Margaret Kirkby again. Rolle's literary importance lies in these contributions to the vernacular stream of devotional prose for women readers. His English prose style is much commended: it is lively, persuasive, highly figured. The verse ascribed to him has more fervour than grace. Although he had mastered scholastic style, his Latin prose is usually fantastically rhetorical, exhibiting a curious syntax, a rich, obscure vocabulary and heavy alliteration and assonance.

BIBLIOGRAPHY.—C. Horstmann's edition of his works, in *Yorkshire Writers,* 2 vol. (1895–96), provided the basis of later study. H. E. Allen, "Writings Ascribed to Richard Rolle, Hermit of Hampole, and Materials for his Biography," *Publications of the Modern Language Association of America* (1927), established the canon. Editions are: *English Writings of Richard Rolle, Hermit of Hampole,* ed. by H. E. Allen (1931); *Incendium Amoris,* ed. by M. Deanesly (1915); *Melos Amoris,* ed. by E. J. F. Arnould (1957); *Officium de Sancto Ricardo de Hampole,* ed. by G. G. Perry, Early English Text society, rev. ed. (1921). *See also* F. M. Comper, *The Life of Richard Rolle* (1928); for Rolle's literary position, R. W. Chambers, *On the Continuity of English Prose* (1932). There is a full bibliography in J. E. Wells, *A Manual of the Writings in Middle English, 1050–1400* (1916) and *Supplements* (1919–35).

(G. SD.)

ROLLER, one of several old world birds, especially the common roller (*Coracias garrulus*), so called from its way of occasionally rolling in its flight, after the fashion of a tumbler pigeon. It is widely though not numerously spread over Europe and western Asia in summer, breeding as far north as the middle of Sweden, but retiring to winter in Africa. It is seen almost every year as a straggler in the British Isles. Except the back, scapulars and tertials, which are bright reddish-brown, the plumage of both sexes is blue (of various shades, from pale turquoise to dark ultramarine) tinted in parts with green. The bird is purely insectivorous.

Coracias forms the type of the family Coraciidae, allied to the bee eaters (Meropidae) and kingfishers (*q.v.*) (Alcedinidae), in the order Coraciiformes. There are 16 species, found throughout Europe, Asia and Africa. The oriental roller or dollarbird (*Eurystomus orientalis*) ranges from southern Siberia to Australia.

ROLLI, PAOLO ANTONIO (1687–1765), Italian poet and librettist who played a leading part in the italianization of taste in 18th-century London, was born in Rome on June 13, 1687, the son of an architect. As a young man he studied with Gian Vincenzo Gravina; and in 1715 he went to England as the protégé of Lord Thomas Pembroke. Soon after his arrival Rolli was appointed Italian master to the royal household; and during a sojourn lasting for some 30 years (1715–44) he wrote many cantatas and operatic libretti. Rolli is best remembered as the author of innumerable *endecasillabi,* odes, and *canzonette* in which he aspired to recapture the rhythms of Catullus and the lighthearted charm of Anacreon. His other works include a translation of *Paradise Lost* (1735), *Marziale in Albion,* and editions of the Italian classics. Rolli died at Todi on March 20, 1765. (D. M. WE.)

ROLLS, CHARLES STEWART (1877–1910), English pioneer motorist, aviator, and automobile manufacturer, technical managing director of Rolls-Royce Ltd., was born in London on Aug. 27, 1877, the third son of Lord Llangattock. He was educated at Eton and at Trinity College, Cambridge, graduating in mechanical and applied sciences. Rolls owned and drove a car prior to the Locomotives on Highways Act of 1896, commonly called the "Emancipation" act, and in the early days he drove George V and Queen Mary when they were prince and princess of Wales. He drove his own 12 hp. Panhard car in the Thousand Miles Trial of 1900 and took part in many of the early long-distance European classic races. In 1902 he started in business as a motor dealer, and in 1906 his firm merged with the company of Sir Frederick Henry Royce to form Rolls-Royce Ltd. Rolls was the first man to fly across the English Channel and back nonstop, in 1910, but on July 12 of that year he was killed in a flying accident at Bournemouth, Hampshire.

See L. Meynell, *Rolls: Man of Speed* (1953). (ST. J. C. N.)

RÖLVAAG, OLE EDVART (1876–1931), Norwegian-American novelist and educator, noted for his realistic portrayals of Norwegian settlers on the Dakota prairies and the clash of transplanted with native cultures in the U.S. He was born April 22, 1876, on the island of Dönna, Norway, emigrated to the U.S. in 1896, and was naturalized in 1908. Educated at St. Olaf College, Northfield, Minn., and the University of Oslo, Norway, he spent most of his life at St. Olaf as a teacher of Norwegian language and literature and the history of Norwegian immigration. He wrote in Norwegian, the language in which his works were originally published, and worked closely with the translators on the English versions. He died in Northfield on Nov. 5, 1931.

With literary antecedents reaching back to the Norse sagas and nearer influence from Henrik Ibsen, Jonas Lie, and Knut Hamsun, Rölvaag gave epic sweep to his picture of pioneering, but also deplored its cost in human values. A founder of the Norwegian-American Historical Association, he tirelessly urged immigrants to retain their customs, their speech, and their church, believing that American society would be the richer. *Giants in the Earth* (1927), his masterpiece, represented the positive joys of pioneering in the character Per Hansa, the negative griefs in his wife Beret. *Peder Victorious* (1929) and *Their Fathers' God* (1931) continued the story to the second generation in Per Hansa's son. *The Boat of Longing* (1933), which dealt with the newcomer in the city, and *Pure Gold* (1930), with immigrants whose search for money brought spiritual bankruptcy, were Rölvaag's only other novels translated into English.

See Theodore Jorgenson and Nora O. Solum, *Ole Edvart Rölvaag: a Biography* (1939).
(C. E. Bo.)

ROMA, in ancient Roman religion, the city of Rome personified and later worshiped as Dea Roma. She was first revered simply as the genius or guiding spirit of the city and from this came to be worshiped as a goddess. Like emperor worship, the worship of Roma flowered first in the provinces. She had temples in Asia Minor as early as the 2nd century B.C. (Tacitus, Annals, iv, 56), often in association with other deities (*e.g.,* Tyche, Greek goddess of fortune; *cf.* Fortuna). From the time of Augustus the worship of Roma and the emperor in association became widespread outside Rome, but it was not until the time of Hadrian that Roma was recognized officially with the construction of a temple of Venus and Roma on the Velia. Her representations are numerous. Her head, symbolic of the Roman state, appears continuously on republican coins. In the empire she is a goddess with the symbols of war, victory, and plenty.

BIBLIOGRAPHY.—Franz Altheim, *History of Roman Religion* (1938); Platner-Ashby, "Venus et Roma," *Topographical Dictionary.*
(R. B. Ld.)

ROMAINS, JULES (originally LOUIS HENRI JEAN FARIGOULE) (1885–   ), French poet, dramatist, and novelist, a founder of the literary movement known as *Unanimisme* and author of two works that have achieved international fame, the satire *Knock* and the novel-cycle *Les Hommes de bonne volonté* (*Men of Good Will*). He was born at La Chapuze, Saint-Julien Chapteuil, in the Cévennes, on Aug. 26, 1885. The son of a schoolmaster in Paris, in 1906 he entered the École Normale Supérieure, where he took degrees in both science and philosophy. After teaching philosophy, in 1919 he decided to devote his time to writing and to travel, both privately and as a delegate to international congresses of writers. He became president of the International Federation of P.E.N. Clubs in 1936. In 1940, when the German Army occupied France, he took refuge in the United States, and lived there and in Mexico until the end of the war. Soon after his return to France in 1946, he was elected to the Académie Française. In 1953 he legally adopted the name Jules Romains, which he had used as a pseudonym except for a scientific work, *La Vision extra-rétinienne et le sens paroptique* (1920).

Before World War I, Romains was known mainly as a poet, and as founder, with Georges Chennevière, of *Unanimisme*, a movement which combined belief in universal brotherhood with the psychological concept of group consciousness, and emphasized the transcendent power of collective emotion and the life of the human group as a whole. His first important book of poems, *La Vie unanime* (1908), was published by the Abbaye, a community of writers and artists led by Georges Duhamel (*q.v.*), Charles Vildrac, Henri Martin-Barzun, and others, at Créteil, near Paris, with which Romains was closely connected. Later volumes of verse include *Odes et prières* (1913), *Chants des dix années 1914–1924* (1928; including *Europe*, written during World War I, which expressed both his despair at the defeat of internationalism and his faith in its reemergence), and *L'Homme blanc* (1937). The *unanimiste* theories of prosody are discussed in *Petit Traité de*

versification (1923), written with Chennevière. Romains' first plays, *L'Armée dans la ville* (1911) and *Crome-deyre-le-Vieil* (1920), produced by Jacques Copeau (*q.v.*) at the Théâtre du Vieux-Colombier, were *unanimiste* verse-dramas as also were the tragedies *Le Dictateur* (1926; performed 1928) and *Jean de Maufranc* (1926; published 1927).

Entirely different in conception and style were such farcical comedies as *Donogoo-Tonka* (1920), *Monsieur le Trouhadec saisi par la débauche* (1923), and, above all, *Knock, ou le Triomphe de la médecine* (1924; English translation, *Dr. Knock,* by H. Granville-Barker, 1925), in which Romains gave free rein to his gift for satire. *Knock,* a satire on the power of medicine to impose on human credulity, is a masterpiece of irony, wit, and comic invention. Acted and produced by Louis Jouvet (*q.v.*), it established Romains as a comic dramatist and gained a lasting place in the international repertory.

As a novelist Romains showed both the preoccupations that inspired his poetry and the qualities of invention that distinguished his plays. *Le Bourg régénéré,* "*conte de la vie unanime*" (1906), his first published prose work, describes how a village gains a sense of community. *Mort de quelqu'un* (1910) describes the reactions of a group of people to the death of an insignificant member of society, and traces his brief influence on their collective consciousness. *Les Copains* (1913) evokes both the bond which unites seven friends in their determination to shock society, and that which holds together the communities victimized by their practical jokes. A farcical tale, told with Rabelaisian gusto and truculence, it is one of Romains' most successful works. In the trilogy *Psyché* (1922–29), a study of erotic love, *unanimiste* theory is carried, not entirely successfully, to mystical heights: Romains is himself too much of a rationalist to enter fully into mystical experience.

His masterpiece, however, is the vast cyclic epic *Les Hommes de bonne volonté* (27 volumes, 1932–46; English translation, 14 volumes, 1933–46). This attempt to re-create the spirit of a whole era of French society—Oct. 6, 1908, to Oct. 7, 1933—resembles Balzac's *La Comédie humaine* in its ambition and scope. There is no central figure or family to provide a focus for the narrative as in the epic-cycles of Émile Zola and Roger Martin du Gard (*qq.v.*), and the stage is crowded with a huge cast of characters, some drawn from life, but most of them imaginary, and all typical of their period. The action presents successively great historical events (as in *Verdun*), intimate domestic scenes (as in *Éros de Paris,* 1932), and crimes or mysteries treated in the manner of a detective story (as in *Crime de Quinette,* 1932). Romains in turn probes into the souls of his characters, or presents an objective record of their everyday life. The best sections, magnificent portrayals of collective life and emotion—the frescoes of Paris on an autumn day (Oct. 6) in 1908 with which the series opens; during the victory parade after World War I; and on Oct. 7, 1933, in the last volume—exemplify the *unanimiste* method at its best, and are both moving and artistically satisfying. The two volumes which stand at the centre of the whole work, *Prélude à Verdun* (1937) and *Verdun* (1938), are remarkable pictures of the soul of a world at war.

It may be asked, "Who are the men of good will?" Romains makes it clear that they are the good, decent, humane people, men and women with a sense of humour and a respect for other people's ideas, who, though often unheeded, often themselves groping in the dark, yet strive for freedom, rejecting "foolishness, violence, collective crimes from which proceed all the ills of the world."

Volumes 19 to 24 of *Les Hommes de bonne volonté* were published in the United States and Mexico; the last three volumes appeared after Romains' return to France. He continued to write poems, short stories, novels, and essays, and in 1958 published the autobiographical *Souvenirs et confidences d'un écrivain,* but it was generally considered that his outstanding contribution to literature had been made in *Knock* and in the central volumes especially of *Les Hommes de bonne volonté.*

BIBLIOGRAPHY.—A. Cuisenier, *J. Romains et l'Unanimisme* (1935), *L'Art de J. Romains* (1949), and *J. Romains et les Hommes de Bonne*

Volonté (1954); A. Figueras, *J. Romains* (1952); M. Berry, *J. Romains, sa vie, son oeuvre* (1953) and *J. Romains* (1959); P. J. Norrish, *Drama of the Group* (1958). (P. E. B.)

ROMAN, a town in Moldavia, northeastern Rumania, is situated at the confluence of the Moldova and Siret rivers, in the *regiune* (administrative and economic region) of Bacău. Pop. (1963 est.) 34,731. Founded by the ruling prince of Moldavia, Roman is first mentioned in documents dated 1392. The voivode Alexander the Good made it a bishopric, the seat of which was in 1467 burned down by Matthias Hunyadi, who himself was later defeated in the vicinity by Alexander's grandson Stephen the Great. Under the Communist regime, Roman became an important industrial centre, with a tube-rolling mill and food-processing and chemical factories.

ROMAN ARCHITECTURE refers to the architecture of the community of ancient Rome on the Tiber, as well as to that of the empire that spread from Britain to Mesopotamia, from the 5th century before Christ to the 4th century after Christ. Roman architecture was almost as complex as the Roman empire itself; it was influenced by a multitude of geographic, climatic, political, economic, social and cultural factors. The cohesive factor through all the differences was the Roman character, which possessed the talent and felt the necessity to organize in large and complex terms, politically or architecturally or otherwise.

(For a discussion of the architecture of classical Greece, from which many of the elements of Roman architecture were derived, *see* GREEK ARCHITECTURE. The impact of Roman architecture on succeeding cultures is discussed in BYZANTINE ART AND ARCHITECTURE and ROMANESQUE ART AND ARCHITECTURE. *See* also ARCHITECTURE and ROME: *The Ancient City.*)

Our knowledge of Roman architecture derives primarily from extant remains scattered throughout the area of the empire. Some are well preserved, others are known only in fragments and by theoretical restoration. Another source of information is the vast store of records, including dedicatory and other inscriptions on public works. Especially important is the book on architecture by Vitruvius (*q.v.*), who lived about the time of Christ. His book *De Architectura* is a handbook for Roman architects and covers almost every aspect of architecture, but it is limited, since it was based on Greek models and was written at the beginning of the more creative phase of Roman architecture, in the period of the empire.

HISTORY

Roman monumental architecture emerged around the 6th century B.C. as an Italic style, closely related to that of the Etruscans (*q.v.*). The Capitoline temple in Rome, built about this time, resembled Etruscan buildings at Signia, Orvieto, Veii and elsewhere, in resting on a podium with a triple cella, the broad low Etruscan porch and characteristic terra-cotta adornment. The Capitolium at the Roman foundation of Cosa, in the 3rd century, was similarly conceived. The forms, plastic and spatial, had evolved locally in a tradition of wood and terra cotta, though even at this time there was a slight Greek influence.

From about 200 B.C. to about A.D. 50, the rise of republican Rome and the increasing contacts with Greece resulted in a Greek influence strong enough to control the plastic forms and even to modify the spatial effects. A temple at Gabii, perhaps of the 3rd century, and the temple of Apollo at Pompeii of around 120 B.C., had approximately the Greek single-cella peripteral plan; the latter retained the Italic podium and open porch, and had pronounced modifications of the Greek Ionic order. Buildings like the temple under S. Nicola in Carcere (*c.* 31 B.C.), the round building by the Tiber (*c.* 31 B.C.), the Temple of Fortuna Virilis (*c.* 40 B.C.), all in Rome, show the height of the hellenizing movement. But the slightly later Augustan temples of Concord, Castor and Pollux in the Roman forum, and Mars Ultor in the Forum of Augustus had a native freedom of arrangement of the limited spaces, and highly elaborated moldings, particularly in the entablature, where new forms, mostly floral, were lavishly displayed in finely worked, full masses, and consoles became increasingly important.

During this period the more peculiarly Roman concepts developed chiefly in secular architecture. The Stabian baths at Pompeii, perhaps as early as 120 B.C., were already composed in vaulted spaces, though quite compactly and with little of the later freedom and spaciousness. In some buildings, like the Carcer and Tullianum of about 100 B.C. and the Tabularium, about 78 B.C., arches and concrete were basic, though hellenizing orders were used for ornament. The small theatre at Pompeii was built about 75 B.C. with the Roman interior forms already established but with no monumental exterior. The Theatre of Marcellus (*c.* 11–10 B.C.), however, had the high external façade with orders and arches blended, which became standard. The basilica, even of the 1st century, was experimental.

The beginning of Roman influence outside Italy is evidenced by theatres and amphitheatres at Arles and Nîmes, perhaps as early as 30 B.C.; by the Maison Carrée at Nîmes about 16 B.C.; and by small buildings in Greece and Syria, about the turn of the century.

Around the middle of the 1st century A.D. there was a surge of development of spatial composition. The orders and other ornament inherited from Greece were increasingly modified and elaborated in nonfunctional perspective effects, and other kinds of ornament and spatial configurations gained importance. Of course many buildings like the Colosseum (A.D. 75–82) preserved a more conservative character, but with the baths and palaces of Nero began the series of imperial compositions of grand, elaborate spaces. The movement came to a climax under Trajan and Hadrian (*c.* 98–138): in the Forum of Trajan and the great complex at Baalbek; the Pantheon; the villa of Hadrian at Tivoli, with its intricate composition of enclosed spaces and interrelated buildings and of interior and exterior vistas.

Through the 2nd and 3rd centuries countless buildings were erected in cities and towns all over the empire, in part under imperial patronage, in part by local enterprise. The provincial buildings had great individuality, but the more ambitious usually followed the influence of the capital. The forms evolved by about A.D. 140 were followed conventionally for the next 50 years—and longer—but from about A.D. 200 to the age of Constantine, there was a growing trend toward increased majesty and less emphasis on material substance. Even before the end of the 2nd century deep cutting with sharply contrasting light and shadow had begun to detract from the impression of the solid forms in carved ornament; in the arches of Septimius Severus (*c.* A.D. 200) light and shadow alone formed the design, not the masses of the forms of the motifs. Especially in Africa illogical composition of the elements of entablatures robbed them of structural significance. In the palace of Diocletian (*c.* A.D. 300) extensive use of arched colonnades, free and blind—even, as at the main gate, on consoles—emphasized the movement rather than the mass. The sheer faces of some wall surfaces, like those of the towers flanking the gates, became, with a minimum of structural articulation, austere geometric forms. Experimentation and elaboration in vaulting, as in the Temple of Minerva Medica (*c.* A.D. 260), was toward making the supports lighter structurally and aesthetically. Compared to the Baths of Caracalla (*c.* A.D. 215), the Basilica of Maxentius (*c.* A.D. 310–320) was more simple and concentrated, increasing its sense of elemental vastness and permanence, whereas in contrast to the Pantheon its shape and ornament is less tangible.

Finally, evolving into the early Christian art to come, the Constantinian mausoleum of Sta. Costanza, with its dome resting on a drum supported on arches on a circle of pairs of slender columns, and its ambulatory vaults smooth and sheathed with mosaic, already was striving to suggest the independence of roof and space from material support.

BUILDING TECHNIQUES

Building Materials.—The material employed around Rome in the earliest buildings was tuff, a volcanic rock of varying hardnesses, some soft enough to be worked with bronze tools. Later other harder volcanic stones were used such as peperino and the stone from the Alban hills. Under the later republic and the empire the most important stone for building was travertine, a limestone quarried mainly at Tibur (Tivoli). An example of the use of travertine is the exterior of the Colosseum. The use made by the Romans of marble was mainly decorative. It was applied in slabs to brick and concrete walls, and set in cement. It was used for pavements either in slabs cut and arranged in patterns, or as mosaic. Under the empire a great demand arose for coloured marbles and such stones as porphyry, granite and alabaster, which were imported from various parts of the empire. The abundant use of these marbles is well illustrated by the remains of the Flavian palace on the Palatine and of Hadrian's villa at Tivoli.

Unburned bricks faced with stucco were used especially for private houses under the republic. Of these, naturally, very few remain. Under the empire kiln-baked bricks and tiles were the most common facing for concrete. They were never used to build a whole wall in the modern manner but merely as a protective skin. These bricks or tiles were almost always used in triangular shapes. Large tiles about two feet square called bipedales were employed as bonding courses. (*See also* BRICKWORK.)

The use of stucco over unbaked brick and over coarse stone was prevalent from the earliest times in Greece, Sicily and Italy. It served as a protection against the weather and also as a finish. Later it was used over brick and concrete. It was often made of lime, sand and fine marble dust and some would take a high polish or fine molding. Thus it became the usual ground for decoration especially in the interiors of houses. Examples of its use abound at Pompeii, and at Rome in the House of Livia, in Nero's Golden house and others. Another material the use of which was mainly decorative is bronze. Doors, grilles, panels of ceilings, etc., were made of it.

For their concrete the Romans used pozzolana, of which there are extensive beds at Pozzuoli, near Naples, and also around Rome. It is a fine chocolate-red volcanic earth, which when mixed with lime forms an excellent natural hydraulic cement that will set well even under water. With this cement was mixed an aggregate of broken tuff, travertine, brick or even marble, pumice stone being used in vaults after the 1st century A.D. to lighten the weight. It was used in all the great imperial buildings (*e.g.,* Pantheon, Baths of Caracalla and Basilica of Maxentius). The new forms of architecture that were developed by the use of this material spread all over the Roman empire, although in the provinces other, often weaker, kinds of concrete were used.

Construction.—Walls were built of ordinary masonry or of concrete (faced or unfaced). While there are several examples of early stone walling without courses (cyclopean and polygonal) especially in some towns (*e.g.,* Norba, Praeneste, near Rome), most of the stone walls existing were built of squared blocks laid in regular courses as headers and stretchers (*opus quadratum*). The blocks of stone in these walls are fairly large, 2 ft. by 4 ft. or more, and were often held together by iron cramps fixed in lead.

Concrete walls, except below ground, were always faced. They are divided into types according to the kind of facing used. (1) *Opus quadratum, i.e.,* ordinary stone walling, was used as a facing for concrete, especially for important public buildings under the earlier empire (*e.g.,* exterior of the Colosseum). (2) *Opus incertum* was the most common facing for ordinary concrete walls of the 2nd and 1st centuries B.C. The face of the concrete was studded with three-inch to four-inch irregularly shaped pieces of stone, usually tuff. (3) *Opus reticulatum* came into vogue in the 1st century B.C. and remained until the time of Hadrian. The construction was like that of *opus incertum* but the pieces of stone were pyramid shaped with square bases set diagonally and wedged into the concrete walls. (4) Brick- and tile-faced concrete (so called *opus testaceum*) was by far the most common material for walling under the empire. Triangular tiles were used with their points turned into the concrete and their long sides showing, thus giving the appearance of a wall built of thin bricks. Bonding courses of bipedales were employed at intervals of two or three feet. (5) Mixed brick and stone facing (called *opus mixtum*) was popular under the later empire and especially under Diocletian.

Other kinds of supports included columns and piers. Columns were usually of stone and often monolithic; occasionally small columns were of brick covered with stucco. Piers, too, were often of stone, but those serving as primary support for large vaults were usually of concrete.

Columns and piers both bore horizontal architraves or, from the 2nd century B.C. (later for columns), arches. These occurred in gates, bridges and aqueducts as well as colonnades and doors and other openings. Not only round but segmental and flat arches were used freely. The discovery of concrete enormously facilitated the spread of arch construction. Concrete arches were faced with stone or tile voussoirs.

The vaults used by the Romans were simple geometrical forms: the barrel vault, the intersecting (groined) barrel vault and the segmental vault. By the 1st century B.C. extensive systems of barrel vaulting were employed (*e.g.,* in the substructions of the Tabularium in Rome, the Temple of Hercules at Tivoli and others). When set the concrete vault exerted no thrust. The surfaces of the vaults were tile faced or covered with stucco. A fine example of Roman vaulting is the Basilica of Maxentius. (*See also* ARCH AND VAULT.)

The construction of the dome (*q.v.*) naturally follows that of the vault. Here again the fact that the concrete dome was a dead weight without thrust simplified the problem. Tie ribs of brick were used and sometimes relieving arches, as in the case of the Pantheon where the facing bricks were laid horizontally. At the crown of the dome was a brick ring. Characteristic of imperial Roman design was the elaboration of complex forms of domes to fit multilobed ground plans.

Most monumental buildings were erected for public use and the income, if any, from rents or fees went to the public treasury. Many of these, however, were built by wealthy individuals and given to the community in a form of voluntary but well-recognized income tax. Construction was done by state agencies or private contractors, employing slave or free labour. Techniques and crafts were highly developed, though machines were simple and powered by men or animals.

Design.—The pervasive Roman predilection was for spatial composition, for organization of lines and surfaces and masses and volumes in space. In this the Romans differed from their predecessors in the ancient Mediterranean world, and however freely they used the elements of earlier styles, in Rome or in the provinces, they recast them according to their own taste.

Their most conspicuous inheritance was the order (*q.v.*). The columns and their associated motifs of superstructure were taken directly from Greek tradition, with little alteration of major form, although the Romans did use them with little attention to their internal logic. There were five orders of Roman architecture: Tuscan, Doric, Ionic, Corinthian and Composite. Tuscan and Composite were modifications of Doric and Corinthian respectively. In general the proportion of the Roman order was slenderer than that of the corresponding Greek order and there was a tendency toward greater elaboration. Columns were often unfluted, but the faces of the entablature, left plain in Greek work, were covered with decoration.

The Doric order almost invariably had a base molding that was probably taken from the Etruscan Doric or Tuscan column. Examples of Roman Doric are to be found in the Tabularium (78 B.C.) and in the lowest order of the Colosseum (A.D. 79) where it was used in conjunction with the arch. The Temple of Hercules at Cori (*c.* 80 B.C.) is one of the few known Roman Doric temples.

The Ionic order was used in some temples and public buildings and the number of isolated capitals found suggests that it had a certain vogue in private homes. Notable examples of this order are the Temple of Fortuna Virilis, the second orders of the Theatre of Marcellus and the Colosseum, Trajan's forum at Rome and various buildings at Pompeii.

The Corinthian order was by far the most popular with the Roman builder. It was popular for its richness and for the ease with which it could be used in any position resulting from the identity of the four faces of the capital. The columns removed (by Sulla) from the temple of Zeus Olympios at Athens were the model, but the whole order became progressively elaborated in detail and showed a tendency toward sharp contrasts of light and

(Right) Temple of Fortuna Virilis; 1st century B.C. A pseudoperipteral temple with fluted Ionic columns. (Left) Temple of Portunus; 1st century B.C. A circular temple, Corinthian columns. Both in the Forum Boarium, Rome

Colonnaded portico of Corinthian columns at the north side of the forum at Timgad, Alg.; 2nd century A.D. The Arch of Trajan is in the background

Detail of the great basilica of Maxentius, Rome, renamed after Constantine who finished it about A.D. 313. In construction and plan it followed the great halls of the Roman baths

Temple known as the Maison Carrée, Nimes, France. The best preserved example of a Roman temple, dating from about 16 B.C.

Temple of Venus, Baalbek, Lebanon; 3rd century A.D. It is surrounded by Corinthian columns

General view of the Roman Forum, looking toward the Colosseum. In left foreground, the remains of the columns of Saturn's Temple. The three columns at right are the remains of the Temple of Castor and Pollux with the Arch of Titus behind it

PLATE II

ROMAN ARCHITECTURE

The atrium of the House of Sallust, Pompeii, Italy; 1st century B.C.

Ruins of a wall of the Colosseum, Rome, showing the construction of the galleries behind the seats. 1st century A.D.

Vaults of the Baths of Caracalla, Rome; early 3rd century A.D., one of the most impressive examples of Roman concrete construction

Arch of Tiberius at Orange, France; 1st century A.D. Corinthian three-quarter columns flank the central opening and the outer angles of this richly decorated arch

Amphitheatre at Arles, France; 1st and 2nd centuries A.D.

Bridge across the Tagus River, Alcántara, Spain; 2nd century A.D.

shadow. Examples of this order are seen at the temples of Mars Ultor and of Castor and Pollux (the latter is one of the most beautiful examples in Roman architecture) in Rome, the Temple of Vesta at Tivoli, Agrippa's portico to the Pantheon and the third order of the Colosseum.

The Composite capital is really a Corinthian capital with the tendril at the corner replaced by an Ionic volute. Examples of this capital are to be found on the triumphal arches of Titus and Septimius Severus and the Baths of Diocletian. (*See also* CAPITAL.)

Although these forms were taken bodily from Greek architecture their real use in Roman design was wholly different. In Roman work columns came to carry arches as well as architraves, permitting more varied linear patterns, wider intercolumniations and greater freedom in articulating spatial forms. Moreover, columns were used not only as primary supports but also as detached columns and pilasters, together with other projecting elements and recessed niches of all kinds, so as to modulate the sheer face of wall or pier into a composition of mass and volume in depth, supplementing the larger forms of the main volumes. Realistic or fanciful architectural compositions were even painted on some walls to give an illusion of the same effect. So, too, carved moldings, cornices, etc., were designed with deep interplay of mass and volume.

In terms of primary architectural forms, Roman design from its first emergence from the Italic and Etruscan traditions favoured temples with spacious porches, like the Temple of Apollo at Pompeii. The very elevation of the podium poses the temple in the surrounding volume, with external spatial relationships established by the special approach and enclosing colonnades. In imperial architecture the design of the temple precinct, forum, thermae, etc., was normally conceived as a complex of variously formed spaces related to variously formed masses; even landscaping was incorporated, as, conspicuously, at Tivoli and Praeneste. Interiors of smaller houses as well as of grand structures were designed in terms of vistas through variously shaped rooms of varying qualities of illumination. There was a powerful, even rigid final dominant of axial symmetry, but against this was exploited richly every kind of spatial form in some highly developed system of organization.

TYPES OF BUILDING

Temples.—The Roman temples differed in many important respects from those of the Greeks. For the comparatively low stylobate with its three steps all round, the Romans substituted a high platform or podium with a flight of steps on the entrance façade. Greek temples were isolated from other buildings and almost always faced east and west; those of the Romans were turned to all points of the compass, their orientation being governed by their relation to other buildings. This resulted in an increased emphasis on the entrance façade, with an increased depth to the portico. The cella was wider and the colonnade that surrounded the Greek temple was often reduced to a row of engaged columns or pilasters along the cella walls, except on the entrance front. In some cases the cella was vaulted in concrete and might have an apsidal end (*e.g.*, the so-called Baths of Diana at Nîmes and especially the double Temple of Venus in Rome). The best preserved example of a Roman temple now existing is that known as the Maison Carrée at Nîmes. Among the most important temples of which remains exist are those of Fortuna Virilis, Mars Ultor, Castor and Pollux, Concord and Antoninus and Faustina in Rome; in Italy, the Temple of Minerva at Assisi and the temples at Pompeii; and in Syria, the temples of Bacchus at Baalbek and of the Sun at Palmyra.

Among the most important circular temples are those of Vesta and Mater Matuta in Rome, Vesta at Tivoli, Rome and Augustus on the Acropolis at Athens, and Venus at Baalbek, which has detached Corinthian columns joined to the cella walls by a segmental architrave. The greatest circular temple and in many respects the most important Roman building is the Pantheon (*q.v.*). It consists of a rotunda about 142 ft. (43 m.) in diameter surrounded by concrete walls 20 ft. (6 m.) thick, in which are alter-

nate circular and rectangular niches. Light is admitted through a central opening about 28 ft. (9 m.) across, at the crown of the dome. In front is a portico which originally belonged to a temple built by Agrippa, re-erected when the rotunda was built under Hadrian, A.D. 120–124. The rotunda and the dome are among the finest examples of Roman concrete work. The construction is strengthened by immense relieving arches and piers of brick set above one another in the thickness of the walls. The interior was lined with precious marbles, the coffers of the dome were decorated with bronze rosettes and the dome itself was covered externally with bronze plates. (*See also* TEMPLE ARCHITECTURE.)

Tombs.—The large Roman tomb consisted of an earth mound or tumulus surrounded by a ring of masonry rising usually to a considerable height. Few of the type now exist, the most notable being the tomb of Cecilia Metella on the Via Appia and the mausoleum of Hadrian, now the castle of St. Angelo. The smaller tombs, in particular those of the columbarium (*q.v.*) type are usually underground, though there is sometimes an upper story (often in the shape of a small temple *in antis*) built of brick, from which steps lead down to the tomb proper. There is a line of such tombs just outside Rome along the Via Appia and also along the Via Latina and such a cemetery has been found under the church of St. Peter in Rome. Examples of Roman funeral monuments of various kinds exist along the Street of Tombs at Pompeii and in the provinces (*e.g.*, at Palmyra, Jerusalem and Petra).

Forums and Markets.—A principal focus of Roman life anywhere was the forum. This was a place or space in which important business might be conducted. In a small community most business would be conducted in a forum, though gradually special buildings were built on the periphery for particular activities, civic, commercial, religious. Characteristically such a forum was lined in part with small one-room shops built in long, low buildings, sometimes with colonnades.

A city might have more than one forum, for special reasons. Conspicuous examples are the imperial forums in Rome itself, of which the Forum of Trajan is the most developed example. It consisted of a colonnaded square with great hemicycles on the sides and the tremendous Ulpian basilica lying across one end; beyond the basilica was a library with the commemorative Column of Trajan in the central court, and beyond this a (slightly later) temple in another colonnaded square. (*See also* GOVERNMENTAL ARCHITECTURE.)

Architecturally and functionally distinct from the forum, though superficially similar, is the *macellum*. This was not a square, but a market building consisting of shops around a colonnaded court. Great warehouses, called *horrea*, were another kind of market building.

Basilicas.—The basilica (*q.v.*) was a large covered hall for the holding of courts of justice and for banking and other commercial transactions. On the forum at Rome are the Basilica Julia on the south side and the Basilica Aemilia on the north side, both of which had a central hall and side aisles. The Basilica Ulpia in Trajan's forum was similar in plan but had at either end semicircular halls which served as law courts. The fourth and greatest of the basilicas was that begun by Maxentius and finished by Constantine, *c.* A.D. 313. This huge building covered 7,000 sq.yd. and followed in construction and plan the great hall of the Roman baths. The vaults over the bays on the north side are still to be seen overhanging without support, a striking testimony to the marvelous cohesion and enduring strength of Roman concrete. The basilica at Pompeii is an example of the simpler type general in the provinces.

Baths.—By the end of the republic, baths (*balneae*) had become a recognized feature of Roman life. Under the empire their numbers increased until at the beginning of the 4th century A.D. they numbered 1,000 in Rome alone. They were of the type of the Turkish bath with rooms at different temperatures. Remains of these ordinary establishments are common throughout the empire. The Stabian baths at Pompeii are the best preserved.

The imperial thermae were more than baths. They were immense establishments of great magnificence with facilities for every gymnastic exercise, with halls to which resorted philosophers, poets and rhetoricians and those who wished to hear them. The earliest of these thermae were those built by Agrippa c. 21 B.C. Others were built by Nero, Titus, Trajan, Caracalla, Diocletian and Constantine. The best preserved are the Baths of Caracalla, which covered an area about 1,000 ft. square, and those of Diocletian with accommodation for 3,200 bathers. Parts of the latter are now occupied by the church of Sta. Maria degli Angeli and by the Museo delle Terme. The remains of these two great establishments are among the most impressive examples of Roman concrete construction. (*See* also BATH.)

Theatres, Amphitheatres, Circuses.—The Roman theatres differed in several respects from the Greek. The auditorium was not excavated and the walls surrounding stage and seating were continuous, the entrance to the orchestra being by vaulted passages. As the chorus played no part in the Roman theatre the orchestra or dancing space became part of the auditorium. The façade behind the stage was elaborately adorned with architectural fantasies.

The only theatre in Rome of which any remains exist is that of Marcellus built by Augustus (c. 11–10 B.C.) but there are numerous examples throughout the Roman empire especially in Asia Minor. The theatre at Orange, France, is the best preserved example. Others of importance are those at Taormina in Sicily; Pompeii and Ostia in Italy; at Termessus, Alinda, Aizani, Aspendus in Asia Minor; the Odeon of Herodes Atticus at Athens. The Odeon of Agrippa in Athens was a good example of a completely enclosed music hall.

The largest and most important amphitheatre (*q.v.*) of Rome was the Colosseum built by the emperors Vespasian, Titus and Domitian in c. A.D. 72–80 on the site of Nero's lake. It is a huge ellipse about 620 ft. by 513 ft. covering six acres and shows remarkable skill in planning. It had seating accommodation for about 45,000 to 50,000 spectators, and its 80 entrances were so arranged that the whole building could be cleared in an incredibly short time. The whole is built of concrete, the exterior being faced with travertine and the interior with precious marbles that have long since disappeared. Other important amphitheatres are those at Capua, Pompeii, Pozzuoli, Verona, in Italy; Pola, in Yugoslavia; and Arles and Nîmes, in France.

The circus (*q.v.*) was essentially a racecourse, lined, ideally, with tiers of seats along each side and curving around one end, with the opposite end squared off and provided with arrangements for chariots to enter and draw up for the start. Down the middle ran a barrier, on which judges and referees might perform their functions. Since it was the largest facility for watching some function the circus was used for other spectacles than racing, such as, traditionally, for the burning of the Christians by Nero.

Streets, Arches, Gateways.—Characteristic of Roman towns were colonnaded avenues for main lines of traffic; even secondary streets were sometimes lined with colonnades for protection from weather. Such avenues were sometimes adorned with ornamental arches. Often these served simply to dramatize or punctuate the implied movement of the avenue. A triumphal arch (*q.v.*) was sometimes erected to commemorate an important event or campaign, often isolated rather than spanning a roadway. The triumphal arches of Septimius Severus at Rome and of Trajan at Ancona are accessible only by flights of steps and the archways themselves are too narrow for ordinary use. The triumphal arch was usually decorated with columns and bas-reliefs of the chief events it commemorated and was frequently surmounted by a group of sculpture. The most important of these arches are the Arch of Titus (c. A.D. 81) commemorating the capture of Jerusalem, the arches of Septimius Severus and Constantine in Rome and Trajan's arches at Benevento and Ancona. There are several other triumphal arches in the provinces, notably those of Tiberius at Orange, of Augustus at Susa and Caracalla at Tebessa. Others exist at Reims, Pola, Timgad and Maktar.

The monumental city gate while sometimes serving a commemorative purpose differs from the arch in being part of the defenses of the city. Of these gates one of the most famous and best preserved is the Porta Nigra at Trier. (*See* also MONUMENTS AND MEMORIALS.)

Bridges and Aqueducts.—The bridges (*q.v.*) and aqueducts (*q.v.*) of the Romans rank among their greatest monuments. They knew the principle of siphon conduits, but the conduit elevated to grade on arches or even tiers of arches was often cheaper for them and always more spectacular. The most famous examples of Roman aqueducts are the Pont du Gard at Nîmes, the aqueducts at Tarragona and Segovia in Spain, and those which crossed the Campagna bringing water to Rome.

There are not many of the larger Roman bridges now remaining. The best preserved is that built by Augustus and Tiberius at Rimini. The finest is that across the Tagus at Alcantara in Spain.

Domestic Architecture.—Private houses, even palaces, were usually of the style that emphasized interior courts and gardens rather than external façade; this tradition was even maintained so far as possible in northern Europe and Britain, where elaborate arrangements for heating had to be added. In the native Mediterranean climate, however, construction tended to be light and open rather than compact and imposing.

Even the palaces of the Caesars in Rome consisted essentially of series of gardens and, considering their purpose, relatively unmonumental buildings, spread somewhat casually over the Palatine hill. Augustus himself bought and enlarged the house known as the House of Livia which still exists. Tiberius built a palace on the northwest side of the hill. Another palace was built on the southeast corner of the hill by Claudius or Nero. The central space was covered by the palace of the Flavians, Domitian with his architect Rabirius being responsible for a magnificent suite of state apartments and for the sunken garden called the *hippodromus*. Hadrian extended the palace toward the forum. Septimius Severus raised a huge structure overlooking the Circus Maximus, partly on top of Hadrian's work and partly on an artificial platform supported on arches, finishing it with his Septizonium. Of the famous Golden House of Nero on the site now covered by the Baths of Titus, the Colosseum and the Basilica of Maxentius, very little remains.

The villa of Hadrian at Tivoli, begun about A.D. 123, was another sumptuous imperial residence with parks and gardens on a large scale. There are remains of great brick and concrete structures and the unevenness of the site necessitated large terraces and flights of steps. All the buildings are Roman in style and method of construction, though with Greek names.

The palace of Diocletian at Spalato (Split), to which he retired on his abdication in A.D. 305, combined a palace with a fortress and was truly monumental. It consisted of an immense rectangle surrounded on three sides with walls guarded by towers and on the fourth, to the south, protected by the sea. The palace itself was on the south side with a great gallery 520 ft. long with 51 windows overlooking the sea.

The word villa pertains to an estate, complete with house, grounds and subsidiary buildings. There are very few remains of Roman villas; our chief authority is Pliny, who gave a detailed description of his Laurentine villa. Hadrian's villa at Tivoli, an imperial residence, cannot be treated as typical.

In Roman architecture there were two types of houses, the *domus* and the *insula*. The *domus* consisted of suites of rooms grouped round a central hall or atrium, to which were often added further suites at the rear grouped round a colonnaded court or peristyle. The atrium, a rectangular room with an opening in the roof to the sky, and its adjoining rooms, was the peculiarly Roman element; the peristyle, or patio garden, was Greek or oriental. There were few windows on the street, light being obtained from the atrium or peristyle. The *domus,* as exemplified at Pompeii and Herculaneum (*qq.v.*) has long been regarded as the typical Roman house. In Rome itself, however, very few remains of the *domus* have come to light, the chief examples being the House of the Vestal Virgins on the forum and that of Livia on the Palatine.

From Latin writers it has long been known that there were in Rome great blocks of flats or tenements to which the term *insulae* was applied. Excavations at Ostia (*q.v.*) have revealed the design of these blocks. Planned on three or four floors with strict regard to economy of space they depended on light from the exterior, as well as from a central court. Independent apartments had separate entrances with direct access to the street. Since Ostia was a typical town of the 1st and 2nd centuries A.D. and was almost a suburb of Rome itself, it is supposed that *insulae* at Rome would present similar features. The street front of either *domus* or *insula* might be lined with shops. (*See* also RESIDENTIAL ARCHITECTURE.)

Town Planning.—Vitruvius clearly indicated that the Romans were keenly aware of the fundamentals of town planning, *i.e.*, the location of the city and its parts in terms of necessities, climate, functions and the like. When a new town was established such considerations were energetically examined.

A characteristic Roman plan, either inherited from early Italic towns or developed in the discipline of army camp engineering, was used. The over-all plan was square, with main avenues bisecting the sides and intersecting at the centre. The rest of the streets were in checkerboard grid.

At or near the centre was the forum; theatres, baths and other structures were located according to the site.

Long-established communities, which had developed by accretion rather than by plan, were often gradually brought, under Roman influence, within some approximation of this scheme, sometimes with considerable subtlety. Often, however, as in Rome itself, the scale and topography prevented the achievement of any fully logical order. In general, colonnades lined the important streets; water was conveyed to spectacular ornamental fountains or to practical neighbourhood basins from reservoirs fed by aqueducts (in some climates cisterns were necessary); many large sewers collected waste water from the street if not from private homes; also building codes were devised and enforced.

The layout of a whole town can be most easily seen in some of the towns in north Africa (*e.g.*, Timgad, Tebessa, Thuburbo Maius), where there has been little or no subsequent building to modify the original lines of the plan. (*See* also CITY PLANNING.)

See also references under "Roman Architecture" in the Index.

BIBLIOGRAPHY.—A. Désgodetz, *Les Édifices antiques de Rome* (1682; new enl. ed., 1843); J. Fergusson, *A History of Architecture*, 3 vol. (1865; 2nd and 3rd ed., by R. P. Spiers, 1892); A. Choisy, *L'Art de bâtir chez les Romains* (1872); Sir B. Fletcher, *A History of Architecture on the Comparative Method* (1896; 8th ed., rev. and enl., 1928); J. Durm, *Die Baukunst der Etrusker und der Römer* (1905); G. T. Rivoira, *Architettura romana* (1917; Eng. trans. by G. McN. Rushforth, 1925); W. J. Anderson and R. P. Spiers, *The Architecture of Ancient Rome* (1927); D. S. Robertson, *Handbook of Greek and Roman Architecture*, with valuable bibliography (1929; 2nd ed., 1945); E. Nash, *Roman Towns* (1944); D. M. Robathan, *The Monuments of Ancient Rome* (1950). (H. C. BR.; M. BRA.; R. L. SN.)

ROMAN ART. There are at least five different ways in which Roman art can be defined: (1) The term might be restricted to works produced in or near Rome itself, which reflect specifically the national life and traditions of the city or the exploits of its citizens and rulers. (2) "Roman art" and "art in Rome" might be treated as convertible terms, including all imported works which mirror the effect of foreign contacts and ever-widening horizons on thought and taste in the metropolis. (3) The phrase might be extended to cover works of art that were made in, or imported into, Italy as united under Roman hegemony. (4) The phrase might be stretched to denote all works of art produced in, or brought into, the predominantly Latin-speaking countries of the western Roman empire. (5) "Roman art" may mean nothing less than the artistic output of the entire world dominated by ancient Rome. The art of the Greek-speaking provinces may justly be described as "east Roman," where existing Hellenistic traditions not merely survived conquest by Rome but gained fresh vigour and scope through incorporation into its system. It is in this fifth and widest sense that the term "Roman art" will be used in this article.

As regards chronology, "Roman" is taken as covering a period extending to *c.* A.D. 500; in respect of content, the word includes works of Jewish and Christian subject matter, indistinguishable in style from their pagan contemporaries and often borrowing some of their motives.

This article is divided into the following main sections:

I. INTRODUCTION

The Romans themselves did not, it seems, have an innate and spontaneous capacity for art. Such works of art as were made in, or imported into, Rome during the periods of the monarchy and the early republic were produced almost certainly by Greek and Hellenized Etruscan artists, or by their imitators from the cities of central Latium; while throughout the later republican and the imperial epochs all the leading masters at least and many of the lesser craftsmen had Greek names and were Greek, or at any rate Greek-speaking, by extraction. References in ancient literature and the signatures of artists preserved in inscriptions leave no doubt on this point. According to tradition, the earliest image of a god made in Rome dated from the 6th century B.C. period of Etruscan domination and was the work of Vulca of Veii. The magnificent terra-cotta statue of Apollo found at Veii may give some notion of its character, while the celebrated bronze figure of the wolf in the Conservatori museum, Rome, is generally assigned to the same Veientine school. In the 5th, 4th and 3rd centuries, when Etruscan influence on Rome was declining and Rome's dominion was spreading through the Italian peninsula, contacts with Greek art were no longer chiefly mediated via Etruria, but were made directly through Campania and Magna Graecia; the paintings and the "idealizing" statues of gods and worthies that are mentioned in literature as executed in the capital during this period were clearly the works of visiting or immigrant Greek artists. The plundering of Syracuse and Tarentum at the end of the 3rd century marked the beginning of that flow of Greek art treasures into Rome which continued for several centuries and played a leading role in the aesthetic education of the citizens.

It was therefore to Greek artists that the Romans turned when, in the course of the 3rd century, they first apparently became aware of the potentialities of works of art for the visual expression of their own political, social and religious life and history. Greeks designed the dies for the silver coinage that Rome inaugurated in 269 to circulate through Italy, with types that displayed an ever-increasing richness and variety of style and content, particularly during the later 2nd and 1st centuries B.C., until the close of the republican epoch. Six documentary paintings depicting events from Roman history between 264 and 168 are known from literary sources. These events were, for the most part, military victories; the pictures themselves were ephemeral affairs shown at triumphs and on other public occasions to the Roman populace; and the artists who produced them were very probably Greeks, since in 168 L. Aemilius Paulus, the victor at Pydna, employed Metrodorus, a painter from Athens, to execute the topical pictures exhibited in Rome for his Macedonian triumph, and Demetrius, an Alexandrian "place painter," was in Rome in 164. The fragment of a historical wall painting with scenes from the Samnite wars, found in a family tomb on the Esquiline, probably dating from the 3rd century B.C. (in the Conservatori museum), may give some idea of the nature of these early triumphal pictures. Literature shows that by the middle of the 2nd century B.C. the Roman forum was thronged with honorific statues of Roman magistrates which, although none of them has survived, may be assumed to have been carved or cast by Greeks, since no native Roman school of sculptors of that time is known. And it is significant that the earliest account of Roman realistic portraits of private individuals is that contained in Polybius' description of the ancestral *imagines* ("masks") displayed and worn at patrician funerals—a description written about the middle of the 2nd century B.C., when the tide of Greek artistic influences was sweeping into Rome and Italy from countries east of the Adriatic, where a highly realistic late-Hellenistic portrait art, that sometimes depicted Roman or Italian subjects, had already blossomed.

The first appearance of the three art forms that expressed the Roman spirit most eloquently can be traced back to the Hellenistic age. These forms are realistic or veristic portraiture, in which every line, crease and wrinkle, and even blemishes were ruthlessly chronicled; the continuous, or "film," style in narrative art of all types; and the three-dimensional rendering of atmosphere, depth and perspective in relief work and painting. Of these three art forms there is no evidence in the early art of pre-Hellenistic central Italy, and it would be safe to guess that if Rome had not met them in the homelands of Greek art it would never have evolved them in its great art of imperial times. But Rome's own contributions to art, if of a different order, were vitally important. Its historical aims and achievements furnished late-Hellenistic artists with a new setting and centre, new subjects, new stimuli, a new purpose and a new dignity. Rome provided the external circumstances that enabled the sculptors, painters and other craftsmen to exploit on a much more extensive scale than before artistic movements initiated in the Hellenistic world, and Rome became a great new patron of art and a great new wellspring of inspiration and ideas. Thus Roman art is the child of the marriage of two traditions—one, the Hellenistic art tradition and the sculptural branch of that tradition in particular, the other, the political, social, religious and psychological tradition of Rome.

II. SCULPTURE

1. Last Century of the Republic.—The ancestral *imagines,* or funerary masks, made of wax or terra cotta, had become extremely individualized and realistic by the middle of the 2nd century B.C. The source of this realism is in the impact on Rome of late-Hellenistic veristic iconography; although this use of masks was rooted in ancient Roman social and religious practice, there is no basis for the statement that the Romans and Etruscans had, from early times, been in the habit of producing death masks proper, cast directly from the features of the dead. It was undoubtedly their funerary customs that predisposed the Romans to a taste for portraits. But it was not until c. 100 B.C. that realistic portraiture, as an art in its own right, appeared in Rome as a sudden flowering, and to that time belong the first beginnings of the highly realistic and veristic heads, busts and statues of contemporary Romans, in marble, stone or bronze, that have actually survived. The coin portraits of public men, whose names and dates are recorded, greatly assist in determining the chronological sequence of the large-scale likenesses, the earliest of which can be attributed to the period of Sulla. The veristic style reached its climax in the stark, dry, linear iconographic manner of c. 75–65 B.C., which expressed to perfection current notions of the traditional Roman virtues; of this manner the marble head of an elderly veiled man in the Vatican is an outstanding illustration. After that, an admiration for the earlier phases of Greek art came into fashion in the west, and verism was toned down at the higher social levels by a revival of mid-Hellenistic pathos and even by a classicizing trend that was to stamp itself upon Augustan portraits. Meantime, in sepulchral custom, the ancestral bust had become an alternative to the ancestral mask, a development exemplified in a togate marble statue of a man carrying two such busts in the Museo Capitolino Nuovo; while the portrait busts and figures on the numerous stone and marble grave *stelai,* characteristic of the late-republican epoch, proclaim the persistence of veris-

tic tastes in middle-class and humbler circles. Furthermore, there are some 1st-century B.C. portraits which suggest that the making of death masks proper (a sophisticated and essentially nonprimitive idea) was occasionally practised at this time. None of the vividly veristic Etruscan portraits, such as the bronze orator (*Arringatore*) at Florence and the terra-cotta married pair on the lid of a well-known ash chest at Volterra, is earlier than c. 100 B.C.; works of that type must be reckoned as provincial imitations of the new metropolitan, 1st-century B.C. portrait style.

There are no narrative reliefs from Rome that can confidently be assigned to a pre-1st-century B.C. period. The only definitely dated 2nd-century B.C. relief depicting an episode from contemporary Roman history, the frieze with the battle of Pydna on L. Aemilius Paulus' victory monument at Delphi, was worked in 168 in Greece. The most familiar republican example of this form of art as practised in the west is the frieze decoration, partly in the Louvre, Paris, and partly at Munich, from the so-called "Altar of Ahenobarbus," which has been shown to have no sure connection either with an altar or with any of the Ahenobarbi. The Louvre section gives a matter-of-fact and accurate representation of the Roman census ceremonies, while the Munich section depicts a marine procession of Neptune and Amphitrite with their train. Assuming that the two scenes belonged to the same monument, as the identity of their dimensions and material suggests, the most attractive theory of them is that they adorned the temple of the nymphs in the Campus Martius, when it was restored after its burning by Clodius in 57 B.C. That temple was the *archivium* of the census, while the nymphs were equated with the nereids and associated with Neptune; this would be an early and striking instance of that juxtaposition of Hellenistic and Roman motives, of human and divine persons and of mythology and history which was to characterize imperial state reliefs throughout their development. Fragments of a marble frieze, presenting successive scenes from Roman legendary history, were recovered from the Basilica Aemilia in the Roman forum and reconstructed before World War II. The subjects include the building of a city, probably of Rome itself, the rape of the Sabine women and the punishment of Tarpeia, and although there is no evidence for determining its date with certainty, the frieze could have been carved for the basilica's rebuilding between 54 and 34 B.C. Funerary narrative sculpture of the late republic is exemplified in the monument of the Julii at St. Rémy (Glanum), France. The base of this structure carries four great reliefs with battle and hunt scenes that allude, not only to the mundane prowess of the family, but also to the "other-worldly" victory of the souls of the departed over death and evil, since figures of the deceased, accompanied by personifications of death and victory, merge into one of the battle scenes. It is possible that these highly pictorial reliefs were partly based on lost Hellenistic monumental paintings. Southern Gaul had direct connections with Greek lands east of the Adriatic.

2. Augustan Age.—The hallmark of the portraits of Augustus is a naturalistic classicism. The rendering of his features and of the forking of his hair above the brow is individual. But the emperor is consistently idealized and never shown as elderly or aging. The marble statue from Livia's villa at Prima Porta (in the Vatican), which presents him as addressing, as it were, the whole empire, is the work of a fine Greek artist who, while adopting the pose and proportions of a classical Hellenic statue, understood completely what Augustus meant to Rome. On the ornate cuirass the princeps' aims and achievements are recorded symbolically in a series of figure groups, among which that of the restoration of the Roman standards by a Parthian to Mars occupies the central place. A marble portrait statue found on the Via Labicana represents the emperor as heavily draped, veiled and in the act of sacrificing as Pontifex Maximus; while a bronze head from Meroe in the Sudan (in the British museum, London), the work of a Greco-Egyptian portraitist, depicts him as a Hellenistic king. Of the female portraits of the period, one of the most charming is the green basalt head (in the Louvre) of the emperor's sister, Octavia, with the hair dressed in a puff above the brow and gathered into a bun behind—a popular coiffure in early Augustan times. The noblest, in many respects, of all the Roman public monuments that were adorned with sculpture is the Ara Pacis Augustae, founded in 13 B.C. and dedicated four years later. It stood in the Campus Martius and has been restored, with different orientation, not far from its original site; and in the harmonious blending, on its reliefs of Luna marble, of contemporary history, legend and personification, of figure scenes and decorative floral motives, it set a standard of distinction which no later work outrivalled. The altar proper was contained within a walled enclosure, measuring about 11½ by 10½ m., with entrances on east and west. On the upper part of the external faces of the south and north precinct walls ran a frieze representing the actual procession of Augustus and members of his family, of lictors, priests, magistrates and of the Roman people on the altar's foundation day (July 4, 13 B.C.) to its chosen site, where sacrifice was offered in thanksgiving for the emperor's recent return to Rome from the provinces. On either side of the western entrance were Augustus' prototype Aeneas sacrificing on his "home-coming" to the promised land of Italy and, since Augustus was also hailed as Rome's second founder, the suckling of the twins, Romulus and Remus, by the she-wolf. The eastern entrance was flanked by the personification of Italia with children on her knees, and by that of Roma. On the exterior of the walls, beneath all these figure scenes, was a magnificent dado filled with a naturalistic pattern of acanthus, vine and ivy, perhaps the translation into marble of a gorgeous carpet or tapestry used in the ceremony; while the swags of fruit and flowers that decked the interior faces of the precinct walls may represent real swags that were hung on the temporary wooden altar erected for the foundation sacrifice. The procession was continued in a much smaller frieze on the inner altar, from which figures of the vestal virgins and of the sacrificial victims and their attendants have been preserved. Delightful studies of imperial and other children and such homely incidents as conversations between persons taking part in the procession introduce an element of intimacy, informality and even humour into this solemn act of public worship. The Ara Pacis in fact sums up all that was best in the new Augustan order—peace, serenity, dignity without pompousness, moderation and absence of ostentation, love of children and delight in nature. The style of the altar's floral decoration strongly suggests that the sculptors who carved it were Greeks from Pergamum.

3. Julio-Claudian Period.—The somewhat cold, precise and academic portraits of Tiberius and Gaius show little further development, but it was probably from her son's principate that the finest of Livia's monumental portraits date. A seated statue of the empress, found at Paestum with a seated figure of Tiberius (in Madrid), shows her with hair simply waved from a central parting, an aquiline nose and the smooth brow and rounded cheeks of quite a young woman, although she was 72 when her son succeeded. The likeness of Antonia, Augustus' niece, is known from posthumous portraits dating from the reign of Claudius. These show her with a coiffure even simpler than Livia's and sometimes wearing the *tutulus* ("woolen fillet") appropriate to her office of priestess of Divus Augustus, as in the case of her colossal portrait head, the so-called "Juno Ludovisi," in the Roman National museum. Portraits of Agrippina I, of Agrippina II, who again occasionally wears the *tutulus* as priestess of Divus Claudius, and of the latter's rival Messallina display more elaborate hair styles. In Claudius' portraits fine, plastic modeling is combined with a realistic rendering of the subject's angular nose, sagging cheeks, clumsy neck and double chin; while those of Nero reveal an exuberant, idealizing treatment that matches his philhellenic interests. Of historical sculpture of this period relatively little has survived. Fragments of processional and sacrificial scenes, somewhat reminiscent of the Ara Pacis carvings (walled up in the Villa Medici on the Pincio) may have come from the Ara Pietatis Augustae which Claudius dedicated in A.D. 43. The "Jupiter-Column" set up in Nero's honour at Mainz (Mogontiacum) in Roman Germany, with figures of gods and personifications carved in relief on its base and shaft, is the only existing public monument which can be connected with that bizarre ruler.

4. Flavian Period.—In Vespasian's portraits something of the old, dry, relentless verism returned. This can be observed in his striking likeness on one of the two historical reliefs that were unearthed in Rome near the Palazzo della Cancelleria just before World War II. A similarly sketchy and impressionistic handling of the hair is found on Titus' portraits, whereas Domitian affected a more pictorial hairdo in imitation of the coiffure introduced by Nero. Still more picturesque are the female hair styles of the time, which display piles of corkscrew ringlets or of tight, round curls. The Cancelleria reliefs date from the close of Domitian's reign and depict respectively Vespasian's *adventus* and reception in Rome in A.D. 70 and Domitian's *profectio,* under the aegis of Mars, Minerva and Virtus, for one of his northern wars. They are worked in a two-dimensional, academic, classicizing style that is in marked contrast with the vivid, three-dimensional rendering of space and depth with brilliant interplay of light and shade on the panels of the arch of Titus in the Roman forum. Those familiar reliefs, which present two excerpts from Titus' Jewish triumph, were carved in the early 80s. The late-Domitianic classicizing manner appears again in the frieze of the Forum Transitorium, which Nerva completed. This conflict of relief styles within the Flavian period is but one illustration of the ceaseless, unpredictable ebb and flow of different aesthetic principles throughout the history of imperial art.

5. Age of Trajan.—In portraits of Trajan the deepening of the bust, already seen in the later Flavian period, was carried a stage further; there is a new fluidity in the molding of the face; in the hair, which is plastered down across the brow, there is a partial revival of the late republican linear style. Aesthetically, one of the finest known likenesses of the emperor is a marble head in the Ostia museum; while on his monumental column there is a series of less idealized and probably more faithful renderings of his features. The coiffures of Trajanic ladies are, if anything, even more elaborate and extravagant than those of their Flavian predecessors.

The reliefs of Trajan's column, illustrating the two Dacian wars of 101–102 and 105–106 and winding up the shaft in a spiral band of Parian marble, one metre wide, is generally recognized to be the classic example of the continuous method of narration in Roman art. The scenes develop like a film, merging into one another and interlocking without any lines of demarcation between them, apart from an occasional tree that serves to punctuate the flowing text; while Trajan appears again and again in different situations, activities and costumes. A statuesque figure of Victory separates the histories of the two wars. There are 23 spirals and about 2,500 figures. But a high level of technical accomplishment is maintained throughout, and the interest and excitement of the theme never flag. Since the figures of men and animals had to be distinguished from a distance, they are inevitably overlarge in proportion to their landscape and architectural settings; and in order to avoid awkward empty spaces along the upper edges of the band and to preserve an allover, even, tapestrylike effect, the background figures in the scenes are reared in bird's-eye-view perspective above the heads of those in the foreground. These carvings must be visualized as once brightly painted, with weapons and horse trappings added in metal. The sources of the scenes were probably wartime sketches made by army draftsmen at the front, but the fusing together of those isolated pictures into a single scroll was the work of a single master artist, perhaps Apollodorus of Damascus, who designed the whole complex of Trajan's forum, basilica and column. The interior of the shaft contains a spiral staircase and the column, dedicated in 113, was intended primarily as a lookout post for viewing Trajan's architectural achievements—his forum and its adjacent markets, to accommodate which he sliced away the slope of the Quirinal hill; secondly, as a war memorial, when the relief bands were added and an eagle was to top the capital; and thirdly, as Trajan's future tomb, crowned by his statue (which was replaced by that of St. Peter) and containing the funerary chamber for his and his consort's ash urns.

To the last years of Trajan's reign or to the early years of that of his successor should be attributed the four horizontal panels that adorn the main passageway and the attic ends of the arch of

Constantine. If fitted together they would form a continuous frieze of three main scenes which are, from left to right, an imperial *adventus*, a battle and the presentation to the emperor of prisoners and the severed heads of captives by Roman soldiers. The fact that the enemy is clearly Dacian, that the Roman soldiers are all clean-shaven and that the lictors on the left wear the Trajanic hair style, combined with the close resemblances between this frieze and that of the column, leaves no room for doubt that these sculptures were made between *c.* 115 and 120, perhaps for the temple of Divus Trajanus and Diva Plotina which was erected by Hadrian just to the north of the column. The presence on this frieze of chain-mail corselets, never seen on Trajan's column, seems to indicate that that type of armour, so common under the Antonines, first came into use in late-Trajanic or early-Hadrianic times. These reliefs depict, not realistic fighting, as do those of the column, but a kind of ideal or dramatized warfare, with the emperor himself participating in the mêlée and the soldiers wearing plumed and richly embossed parade helmets; the scenes melt into one another with total disregard of spatial and temporal logic. A third example of Trajanic monumental sculpture is the relief decoration of the arch at Beneventum, spanning the new Via Trajana and completely covered on passageway, pylons and attics with pictorial slabs, the subjects of which are arranged to carry out a carefully balanced and nicely calculated order of ideas. Those on the side facing the city and on one wall of the passageway present themes from Trajan's policy and work for Rome and Italy; those on the side toward the country and on the other wall of the passageway allude to his achievements abroad. With two exceptions, where a pair of scenes forms a single picture, each panel is a self-contained unit, and these reliefs already show something of the classicizing, two-dimensional character of Hadrianic work. Indeed, it seems likely that, although the arch itself was either decreed or dedicated in 114–115, some of the panels in which Hadrian is given a peculiar prominence were not carved until the early years of the latter's principate. The frieze of the great, circular Tropaeum Trajani, set up in the Dobruja (Rumania) to commemorate the Dacian victories, contains a series of metopes carved with figure scenes in an unbelievably naïve, flat and linear style that betrays the hands of army artists of provincial origin.

6. Age of Hadrian.—In the iconography of the age of Hadrian, certain Hellenizing features, the wearing of a short Greek beard by the males and the adoption by the females of a simple, classicizing coiffure, are harmonized with new experiments. The depth of the bust increases, there is greater plasticity in the modeling of the face, the men's curly hair and beards are pictorially treated and the irises and pupils of the eyes are marked in. Many marble portraits of the emperor survive from all over the empire, but his likenesses in bronze only one is extant—the colossal head recovered from the river Thames in London, torn from a statue erected in the Roman city and probably the work of a good Gaulish sculptor. The portrait statues of Hadrian's Bithynian favourite, Antinous, reveal a conscious return in the pose and proportions of the body to classical Greek standards, combined with a new emotionalism and sensuousness in the rendering of the head. The exquisite relief in Rome of Antinous-Silvanus is signed in Greek by Antonianus of Aphrodisias in Asia Minor.

The monumental reliefs of Hadrian's day cannot vie with those of his predecessor's. The most interesting and perhaps the earliest of them are the two familiar horizontal slabs once exposed in the Roman forum but later transported to the shelter of the *curia*. Both carry on one side similar figures of the victims for the Suovetaurilia sacrifice and different historical scenes on the other side, in the one case, Hadrian doling out the *alimenta* ("poor relief") to Roman citizens in the presence of a statuary group of Trajan and Italia with children, in the other case, the burning of debt registers. At one end of each of these scenes is carved a figure on a base of Marsyas, whose statue in the forum may once have been in part enclosed by the panels. In the background of both historical pictures are carved in low relief various buildings in the Roman forum that can be identified. The two scenes display the characteristically Hadrianic two-dimensional style, as

do also three large panels in the Conservatori museum, with the emperor's head restored and depicting an imperial *adventus*, an *adlocutio* and an apotheosis respectively—somewhat rigid, academic works. The eight medallions gracing the arch of Constantine give pleasantly composed and lively, if Hellenizing, pictures of sacrifice and hunting, in some of which can be recognized Antinous accompanying the emperor, whose portraits have been recut as likenesses of Constantine the Great and of his colleague Licinius. Finally, the historical reliefs found at Ephesus (now in Vienna)—one of the very few examples of provincial state reliefs that have survived—may be claimed as late-Hadrianic (not as of the period of Marcus Aurelius, to which many critics have assigned them). The most important of these Ephesian carvings shows a group of four imperial personages, who can be identified as Hadrian, his heir Antoninus Pius and the latter's adopted sons, Marcus Aurelius and Lucius Verus. The panels would, then, date from between Pius' adoption by Hadrian in Feb. 138 and the latter's death in the July of that year. Pius had been a popular proconsul of Asia, and the unorthodox representation of him in this relief as Hadrian's equal and colleague, unthinkable in Rome, could have passed muster on a provincial monument. The most imposing of the other panels of the series carries an imperial apotheosis—Divus Trajanus in full military costume mounting the chariot of the sun-god for his journey heavenward. Some fragmentary battle scenes may be excerpts from Trajan's Dacian or eastern wars, reflecting glory on his adopted son, Hadrian, and succeeding generations. In Rome and Italy during the second quarter of the 2nd century inhumation began to supersede cremation as a method of disposing of the dead, and Hadrian's reign saw the beginnings of the long line of carved sarcophagi that constituted the most significant class of minor sculptures down to the close of the ancient Greco-Roman world.

7. Antonine and Severan Periods.—Portraits of Antonine imperial persons, of which the bronze equestrian figure of Marcus Aurelius on the Capitol and the great marble bust of Commodus-Hercules in the Conservatori museum are perhaps the most arresting examples, display a treatment of hair and beard, deeply undercut and drilled, that grew ever more pictorial and baroque as the 2nd century advanced. This produced an impression of nervous restlessness that contrasts with the still, satin smoothness of the facial surfaces, particularly in the iconography of Commodus. To all this picturesqueness Septimius Severus added yet another ornamental touch—the dangling, corkscrew forelocks of his patron deity, Sarapis. The female hair styles of the time are characterized, first by a coronal of plaits on top (Faustina I), next by rippling side waves and a small, neat bun at the nape of the neck (Faustina II, Lucilla) and then by stiff, artificial, "permanent" waving at the sides and a flat, spreading "pad" of hair behind (Crispina, Julia Domna).

Of the state reliefs of this epoch the earliest are on the base (in the Vatican) of the lost column set up in honour of Antoninus Pius and Faustina I. The front bears a dignified, classicizing scene of apotheosis: a powerfully built winged figure lifts the emperor and empress aloft, while two personifications, Roma and Campus Martius, witness their departure. On each side is a *decursio*, or military parade, in which the riders farthest from the spectator appear, not behind the foot soldiers, but high above their heads —a remarkable instance of the bird's-eye-view perspective carried to its logical conclusions. All the figures in these side scenes are disposed on projecting ledges, a device employed again about 20 years later on Marcus Aurelius' column. Eleven rectangular sculptured panels, similar to those on Trajan's arch at Beneventum but displaying greater crowding of figures, livelier movement and a pronounced effect of atmosphere and depth, depict official occasions and ceremonies in the career of Marcus. Three are in the Conservatori museum, the other eight are on the attics of the arch of Constantine; and these two sets of panels represent two separate series, carved for two distinct triumphal arches. The contrast between the reliefs of Marcus' column, put up under Commodus, and those of its Trajanic predecessor measures the change of mood that the Roman world experienced during the course of the 2nd century. The diminished proportions

ROMAN ART

PLATE I

Woman of the Flavian period (last half of 1st century A.D.); marble. Capitoline museum, Rome

Constantine I (288?–337); marble. Conservatori museum, Rome

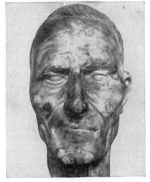

Portrait in death-mask style of 1st century B.C.; marble. Archaeological museum, Turin

Augustus as *Pontifex Maximus;* head of a marble statue. National museum, Rome

Trajan (53–117); marble. Ostia museum

Vespasian (9–79); from a marble Domitianic relief. Vatican museum, Rome

Hadrian (76–138); bronze found in the Thames river, London. British museum

Augustus; bronze found at Meroe, Sudan. British museum

An emperor of the 4th or 5th century A.D.; bronze. Near Church of S. Sepolcro, Barletta

Trajan Decius; marble, about 249–53. Capitoline museum, Rome

Agrippina the Younger (16–59); marble. Ny Carlsberg Glyptotek, Copenhagen

Head of a priest; marble, about 75–65 B.C. Vatican museum, Rome

Commodus (161–192) represented as Hercules; marble. Conservatori museum, Rome

PORTRAITS IN MARBLE AND BRONZE

Plate II   ROMAN ART

Scene showing the *profectio* (setting out) of Domitian (51–96); found near the Palazzo della Cancelleria, Rome. Vatican museum

Marble-columned sarcophagus of the middle of the 2nd century. Town hall, Melfi, Italy

Relief depicting the rain-god from the column of Marcus Aurelius, Rome

Portraits in relief of Septimius Severus and his wife Julia Domna making sacrifice. Porta Argentariorum, Rome

Grave monument of the Gessii family, 2nd half of the 1st century B.C. Museum of Fine Arts, Boston

Section of a marble frieze of the middle of the 1st century B.C. showing sacrificial ceremonies. The Louvre, Paris

MARBLE RELIEFS

BY COURTESY OF (TOP) ARCHIVES OF PHOTOGRAPHY, VATICAN MUSEUM, (CENTRE LEFT) DEUTSCHES ARCHAEOLOGISCHES INSTITUT ROM, (SECOND ROW RIGHT) A.B.A. COMUNE ROME, (THIRD ROW RIGHT) MUSEUM OF FINE ARTS, BOSTON; PHOTOGRAPHS, (BOTTOM LEFT, BOTTOM RIGHT) ALINARI

Hadrian and his heirs. Found at Ephesus. In the Kunsthistorisches museum, Vienna

Section of Trajan's column, Rome, showing the Dacian war

Part of a relief from the *Ara Pacis Augustae* (altar of peace) showing the sacrifice of Aeneas. National museum, Rome

Relief of the 1st century B.C. from the Basilica Aemilia in the Forum Romanum, showing the building of a city. Forum museum, Rome

The triumphal entry of Septimius Severus and his sons into Leptis Magna. From the Severan arch, Leptis Magna, Tripolitania (Lebda, Libya)

Antinoüs (d. 130) shown as Silvanus; found near the site of Lanuvium (near Rome). Istituto dei Fondi Rustici, Rome

Relief showing (left) the triumphal entry of Trajan into Rome, (right) a battle with the Dacians. From the Arch of Constantine, Rome

MARBLE RELIEFS

PLATE IV ROMAN ART

Gnostic painting of the early 3rd century A.D. showing a scene from the *Odyssey*. Hypogeum of the Aurelii, Viale Manzoni, Rome

Family portrait-group of the 4th century; painted on glass. Civic museum, Brescia

Portrait of Septimius Severus and his family; painted on wood. Staatliche museum, Berlin

Section of a landscape painting showing scenes from the *Odyssey*; 1st century B.C. Vatican library

Painted frieze of the 1st century B.C. showing the Bacchic initiation of a bride. Villa of the Mysteries, Pompeii

PAINTING

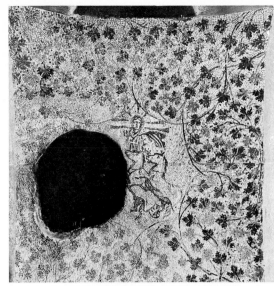

Vault mosaic depicting Christus-Helios; middle of the 3rd century. Tomb of the Julii, Vatican necropolis

Fountain niche of the late 2nd or early 3rd century A.D. from Ostia, showing the god Silvanus; glass-paste mosaic. Lateran museum, Rome

Section of a floor mosaic showing scenes from the *Aeneid*. Originally from the baths of a Roman villa at Low Ham, Somerset, Eng. In the Taunton museum, Somerset

Wall mosaic of the 4th century in polychrome marble intarsia (*opus sectile*) from the basilica of Junius on the Esquiline. Palazzo del Drago, Rome

Floor mosaic of the 4th century showing the hunting and transport of wild beasts for the arena. Roman villa near Piazza Armerina, Sicily

MOSAICS

PLATE VI

ROMAN ART

Gold patera (shallow bowl) of the early 3rd century A.D. found at Rennes, Fr. Bibliothèque Nationale, Paris

Sardonyx cameo portrait of Claudius (10 B.C.–A.D. 54). Royal collection, Windsor castle

Bronze face mask from a sports helmet of the 2nd or 3rd century A.D., found at Straubing, Bavaria. In the Straubing museum

Castor ware pot from Colchester, Eng. Colchester and Essex museum

Silver Bacchic dish (4th century A.D.), found at Suffolk. British museum

Stucco relief of the 2nd century A.D. depicting *Terra Mater*. Tomb of the Valerii, Vatican necropolis

Silver scyphus (goblet), probably of the Augustan period, found at Hoby, Denmark. National museum, Copenhagen

Silver statuettes of Roma and Constantinopolis, 4th century A.D. British museum

Ivory diptych with a double portrait of Honorius, 5th century. Cathedral treasury, Aosta, Italy

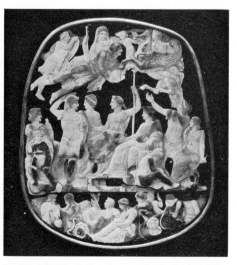

Le Grand Camée de France, a sardonyx showing Divus Augustus above and Tiberius enthroned as Jupiter below. Bibliothèque Nationale, Paris

METALWORK AND MINOR ARTS

of the squat, doll-like figures, their herding together in closely packed, undifferentiated masses, their angular, agitated gestures and the stress laid throughout on the horror and tragedy of war, suggest that the empire is facing an unknown future with diminished security and that man is at the mercy of some unaccountable power, of which the awe-inspiring winged, dripping figure, brooding above the famous rainstorm episode, represents the supreme embodiment. Again, in the imperial *adlocutiones* that punctuate this frieze, where the emperor stands in a strictly frontal pose high above the heads of his audiences, can be seen the first attempts at externalizing in art the concept of the ruler as a transcendental being. The content of these spiral bands is Marcus' northern wars of 173–175 and 177–180.

The spirit of the times is reflected no less vividly in the carved sarcophagi, with their crowded compositions, seething movement, brilliant highlights and deep wells of shadow. Their themes—familiar myths, battles, hunts, marriages, etc.—allude allegorically to death and the destiny of the soul hereafter. Meanwhile, the classicizing, statuesque tradition is maintained in the late 2nd- and early 3rd-century columned sarcophagi, originating in the workshops of Asia Minor but freely imported into, and sometimes imitated in, Rome and Italy. On such pieces single figures, or small groups of figures, occupy the niches between the colonnettes. Among the most impressive examples is the great sarcophagus at Melfi, in Apulia, Italy, with a couch-shaped lid, on which the figure of a girl lies prostrate in the sleep of death.

The novel features that have been noted in the reliefs of the Marcus column were worked out more completely in those of the official monuments set up in Septimius Severus' honour, both in Rome and abroad. The three-way arch that stands at the northern end of the Roman forum was erected in 203 to commemorate both the emperor's Parthian victories and his *decennalia* (the conclusion of his first ten years of rule). Large-scale flying Victories and groups of Roman soldiers and Parthian captives occupy respectively the spandrels above the central passage and the column bases on both faces of the arch; while above both the side passages on either face are scenes from the campaigns. There are masses of small, crowded figures, arranged in superimposed registers in laterally spreading pictures, which in the extensive use of bird's-eye-view perspective recall the spiral bands of the Trajan and Marcus columns. They, too, were doubtless based on military artists' sketches and may represent permanent versions of the public paintings of the eastern wars which, so Herodian says, Septimius exhibited in Rome. The small but richly ornamented Porta Argentariorum, dedicated in the Velabrum in 204 to Septimius and his family by the bankers and wholesale cattle dealers of the capital, carries two major sculptured panels, one of which shows Septimius and his Syrian wife, Julia Domna, sacrificing at a tripod. This composition is strictly two-dimensional and the figures are arranged in stiff, hieratic, frontal poses. They express no interest in the rite which they profess to be performing, but gaze out into the distance as though in search of the spectators' homage. The figure of Septimius' younger son Geta which was once in the group, was removed after his murder by his elder brother Caracalla who now appears alone in the second major panel, from which the figures of his wife Plautilla and of her father Plautianus were likewise obliterated at the time of their disgrace and deaths. But of all Septimius' state reliefs the most interesting are those found fallen from the four-way arch set up in his birthplace, Leptis (Lepcis) Magna in Tripolitania, to commemorate his visit to that city c. 203. On the attics were four long, friezelike scenes, of which the most impressive depicts the triumphal entry into the town of the frontally-posed emperor and his sons. The other attic panels, one of which portrays the proclamation of Caracalla as his father's colleague (*dextrarum iunctio*) in the presence of Julia Domna and representatives of Leptis, and most of the minor panels from the inner faces of the piers, refer to ceremonies held at Leptis on the same occasion. But one pier carried a great vertical picture of the siege of an oriental city, with the defenders at the top and the attackers climbing up, as it were, from below in mounting series—a magnificent example of the bird's-eye viewpoint. Flying Victories filled the spandrels

and on the outer faces of the piers were groups of strangely elongated captives and flat pilasters carved from head to foot with peopled vines scrolls, deeply undercut and drilled—a very distinctive type of design, which recurs on the pilasters that are grouped on either side of the apses of the Severan basilica at Leptis. The handsome inhabited floral scrolls, on pilasters, and the heads carved on brackets, that adorned the Hadrianic baths at Aphrodisias in Caria, are so remarkably similar to the scrolls from the arch and basilica and to the heads from the Severan forum at Leptis, that there can be little doubt that sculptors from Asia Minor were imported to carve these great Severan buildings in the African emperor's native city.

8. Third and Fourth Centuries.—A new tension between naturalism and schematization marks the history of late-antique portraiture. In likenesses of Alexander Severus (222–235) the facial planes are simplified, while all the tumbling curls of the 2nd-century baroque have been banished in favour of a skullcap treatment of the hair and sheathlike rendering of the beard. Toward the middle of the 3rd century, under Philip the Arabian (244–249) and Decius (249–251), this clipped technique in hair and beard is combined with a return to something of the old, ruthless realism in the depicting of facial furrows, creases and wrinkles. For a time Gallienus (253–268) reinstated the baroque curls and emotional expression, but in the later decades of the century the schematic handling of hair, beards and features reappears. Finally, in the clean-shaven heads of Constantine the Great and his successors of the 4th and early 5th centuries the conception of a portrait as an architectonic structure comes to stay and the naturalistic, representational art of the Greco-Roman world is exchanged for the hieratic, transcendental style that was the hallmark of Byzantine and medieval iconography. The hair is combed forward on the brow in rigid, striated locks, and the eyes are unnaturally enlarged and isolated from the other features as the channels through which the soul communicates with a higher power. The face is now so formalized that the identification of any given portrait becomes a problem. The colossal bronze emperor at Barletta, for example, has been given the names of several different rulers of the late 4th and early 5th centuries. Throughout these centuries the favourite female coiffure shows a plait or twisted coil of hair carried across the back and top of the head from neck to crown, while under Constantine there was a brief revival of the two Faustinas' styles.

Throughout the 3rd and 4th centuries carved sarcophagi carry on the story of relief work. Aesthetically, the most notable 3rd-century example is the allover tapestrylike battle piece (in the Ludovisi collection in the Roman National museum) probably made for Decius' son Hostilian. One of the main interests of this field of art, as regards content, lies in the Christian sarcophagi, which are in style and in technique indistinguishable from their pagan counterparts. During the 3rd century their themes are still allusive and symbolic, but with the peace of the church under Constantine Biblical subjects of a very varied range are openly depicted. Of 3rd-century state reliefs in Rome virtually nothing has survived. The narrow historical friezes that were carved *de novo* for the arch of Constantine, completed for his *decennalia* celebrations in 315, show dwarfish, dumpy, niggling figures. Both these reliefs and those of the slightly earlier arch of Galerius at Salonika look as though they had been worked by artists whose experience had been confined to the production of small-scale sculptures. The last examples of Roman carving are the reliefs on the base of the obelisk of Theodosius in the Hippodrome at Constantinople, where the emperor and members of his court, ranged in rigid, hieratic poses, watch the shows. No original portions are extant of the spiral relief bands that entwined the columns of Theodosius and Arcadius in Constantinople, in imitation of the Roman prototypes.

III. PAINTING AND MOSAICS

1. Wall Painting.—Evidence for painting in Rome and Latium before the 1st century B.C. is virtually confined to the fragment, described above, of a historical tomb painting from the Esquiline, to the literary accounts of triumphal pictures, already mentioned and to the record by ancient writers of the names of three painters each of whom worked in a temple—Fabius Pictor in the temple of Salus in Rome at the end of the 4th century; Pacuvius, the dramatist and a native of Brundisium, in the temple of Hercules in the Forum Boarium in Rome during the first half of the 2nd century; and Lycon, an Asiatic Greek, in the temple of Juno at Ardea in the late 3rd or early 2nd century. Of the nature of the work of these three artists no idea can be formed.

At Pompeii during the 2nd century B.C. the interior walls of private houses were decorated in the so-called "masonry" or "incrustation" style; *i.e.*, by the imitation in painted stucco of veneers of *crustae* ("slabs") of coloured marbles. But in the second half of the 1st century B.C. there suddenly appeared in Rome and in the Campanian cities a brilliant series of domestic mural paintings of the so-called "second style," the aim of which was to deny the walls as solid surfaces confining the room space. This was sometimes done by covering the whole area of the walls with elaborate landscapes, in which depth, atmosphere and light are rendered in a highly pictorial, illusionistic manner. Such are the famous Odyssey paintings, found in a Roman house on the Esquiline (now in the Vatican), consisting of a continuous flow of episodes that unfold, filmlike, beyond a colonnade of pilasters, with vertical, bird's-eye-view perspective and the human figures strictly subordinated to their settings. At other times there appears the representation of a great park or garden, filled with trees, shrubs, flowers and birds, with no pilasters in the foreground to interrupt the prospect and with no human figures to distract attention, as in the case of the room from Livia's villa at Prima Porta (transferred to the Roman National museum). The paintings in this style are so highly developed that it seems unlikely that they suddenly sprang into being at this time in Rome and Italy without any Hellenistic precursors. Nevertheless, no late-Hellenistic paintings at all like them have come to light in Greek lands, and they constitute what is perhaps the most original and interesting western Roman-age contribution to ancient art. Possibly Hellenistic painted stage sets were, in part at least, their models; Vitruvius mentions three types of back scenes, tragic, comic and satyric, which seem to be reflected in the paintings from a room in the Villa of Fannius Synistor (or of L. Herennius Florus) at Boscoreale near Pompeii. Again, the triumphal "place paintings" may have played a certain role in this development.

The celebrated frieze of life-size figures, depicting the Dionysiac initiation rites and prenuptial ordeals of a bride, in the so-called *triclinium* of the Villa of the Mysteries (or Villa Item) outside the Herculaneum gate of Pompeii, also belongs to the "second style." There, the walls are denied by the device of substituting for them a narrow stage on which the ritual is carried out before a drop scene of continuous painted panels. But the commonest "second-style" paintings are known as architectural and show a threefold horizontal division of the wall into dado, central area and cornice, combined with a triple vertical scheme of design which consists of a large central panel (in the main, intermediate horizontal area), framed by flanking columns and a pediment, and of two smaller panels on either side. The central panel, and often the lateral panels as well, are views seen through windows that break through the walls and link the spectator with the world outside, as in the house of Augustus on the Palatine. In the "third style," which covers most of the Augustan period, the central panel picture on a wall is no longer thought of as a scene through a window, but as a real picture hung on or inserted into a screen, or woven into a tapestry, which partially conceals an architectural vista behind it. The columns, entablatures, etc., are completely unreal and so complicated that this form of the "second style" is sometimes dubbed "ornate." The "fourth style," which runs from the close of the Augustan age to the destruction of the Campanian cities in A.D. 79, is less homogeneous than its predecessors and exhibits three main variants—first, a soberer, more realistic architectural design, but still with a central screen or tapestry partly covering a retreating vista; second, an architectural setout that imitates a *scaena* ("stage background"); and third, a method (sometimes known as "intricate") by which the whole surface of the wall is covered with a flat, white, neutral ground that is painted with an all-over, lattice-like pattern of fantastic architectural elements, arabesques, grotesques, small figure motifs or small panels containing pictures. This third type of "fourth-style" painting came into vogue at Pompeii between the earthquake of A.D. 63 and the catastrophe of 79, and one of its most impressive exponents is the Golden House of Nero in Rome.

The subjects of the panel pictures of the "second," "third" and "fourth" styles are for the most part drawn from Greek mythology. Some of them recall the literary descriptions of famous classical Greek and Hellenistic paintings or show motifs which suggest that their originals were painted on the Greek mainland or in Asia Minor. It is certain that many masterpieces of Greek painting did make their way to Rome as the booty of Roman generals of republican days, and wall painters could have studied them at first hand. But often these artists must have had to rely only on sketches of the celebrated pictures, and it is not known how faithfully the Roman and Campanian murals reproduce the prototypes. Other panel pictures present scenes from contemporary religious ritual, while a few show themes from Roman legend. Frequently, in the case of the Greek mythological subjects and of those taken from rustic religious cult, the artist had produced landscape with figures, as in the Odyssey frescoes, not figures with landscape, as on Trajan's column. These late-republican and early-imperial set pieces are competently executed, remarkably vivid and extremely naturalistic. But, with a few exceptions, they reveal that the principles of a single vanishing point, on which all receding lines converge, and of unified lighting from a single source of illumination, either were not understood by the Roman-age painters, or did not interest them.

The flat, uniform background of the last phase of the "fourth style" remained a constant feature of mural painting in houses, tombs, temples and other religious shrines throughout the 2nd, 3rd and 4th centuries. The decoration which stands out against that ground takes the form of latticelike, allover floral, etc., patterns, as in many pagan tombs; of small groups of figures, or of figure panels, spread out at intervals across the field, as in the Christian catacombs of Rome; of a mixture of large human figures and extensive scenes with small-scale figures, as in the early 3rd-century Hypogeum of the Aurelii on the Viale Manzoni in Rome, the interesting painted content of which is Gnostic or crypto-Christian; of large scenes with relatively big figures, such as the group of marine deities in the 2nd-century Roman house under the church of SS. John and Paul on the Caelian, the late 2nd- or the early 3rd-century leopard hunt on the south wall of the *frigidarium* of the hunting baths at Leptis Magna, or the early 3rd-century Biblical scenes from the Christian baptistery at Dura-Europos (Doura-Europus; *q.v.*) on the Euphrates. The walls of the main assembly room of the early 3rd-century synagogue in the last-mentioned city display an exceptional series of great self-contained figure panels, arranged side by side in superimposed registers with no intervening tracts of empty background between them.

In the case of Roman tombs the cross- or barrel-vaulted ceilings, where preserved, carry out normally the painted decoration of the walls, showing either a latticelike scheme of small ornamental motives or a series of small, spaced-out, figured panel pictures. At Trier in 1945–46 were found the remains of a flat, coffered ceiling with panels of painted plaster from an early 4th-century imperial hall that was destroyed to make room for the first Christian basilica built on the site of the present cathedral. Large portions of eight painted panels are preserved. Four depict female busts, three of them nimbed, which may be either personifications or portraits of members of the royal family; while the other four show pairs of dancing or sporting cupids. As the skillful modeling and lively naturalism of these figures show, Roman painting could maintain a high level of achievement in late-antique times.

2. Floor Mosaics.—Few categories of works of Roman art show more surviving examples than that of mosaic pavements. *Opus tessellatum*, made of *tesserae* ("cubes") regularly disposed in geometric designs, and *opus sectile*, in which the floor consists of a polychrome intarsia of marble fragments, larger than *tesserae* and generally forming abstract or stylized floral patterns, cannot be discussed in detail here. But *opus vermiculatum*, where figure pictures and naturalistic floral compositions are produced by small and subtly shaped *tesserae,* is almost a branch of painting, in which stone or marble or, in later times, glass paste replace the liquid medium. This type of work appeared in Italy during the 2nd century B.C. and was directly inspired by such late-Hellenistic mosaics as those unearthed in the royal palace of the Attalids at Pergamum and in private houses on the island of Delos, and from Italy it spread rapidly through the empire. Sometimes these floor mosaics are large, self-contained, panel pictures, of which an early example, of the late 2nd, or early 1st, century B.C., is the well-known Alexander mosaic (in Naples) from the House of the Faun at Pompeii. It depicts the battle of Issus and probably represents fairly faithfully a late 4th-century monumental painting. This was the work of a master mosaicist, as were also many of the small mosaic pictures or *emblemata,* which were often mounted on marble or terra-cotta trays and transported, at first from east Mediterranean workshops to Italy, and later from Greek and Italian centres of production to the provinces, where they were inserted into surrounds of geometric patterns laid by inferior local craftsmen. The master mosaicists themselves often traveled far afield to execute *emblemata* or large designs on the spot, as their signatures testify. The subjects of mosaic pictures cover an extensive range—Greek myths (the most popular), Roman legends, Nilotic and other landscapes, scenes from natural history, portraits of famous characters, personifications, topics inspired by the games and shows, by the hunting field, by rural life and by religious ritual, and naturalistic running scrolls of acanthus, vine and ivy. A most remarkable discovery is that of the pavements in the 4th-century country villa near Piazza Armerina, Sicily. These form the largest continuous area of Roman mosaic floors known and include a vast scene, in a corridor 70 yd. long, of the hunting, capturing and transport of wild birds and beasts for display in the arena. The most important and the richest dated series of floor mosaics, running from the early 2nd to the 6th century, is that unearthed, mainly in private houses, at Antioch-on-the-Orontes in Syria. The floor mosaics of the 4th-century Christian basilica at Aquileia display an interesting mixture of Christian, pagan and neutral themes.

3. Wall and Vault Mosaics.

—Wall and vault mosaics that have survived are relatively rare. The earliest and best-preserved examples are those adorning fountains in the courtyards of houses at Pompeii and Herculaneum. These show brilliant polychrome designs, with a lavish use of glass-paste *tesserae* and borders of natural shells. But in the House of Neptune and Amphitrite at Herculaneum most of one wall of the internal courtyard has been turned into a species of *nymphaeum,* with a central rounded niche flanked by two rectangular niches and the whole facade overlaid by an exquisite glass-paste mosaic depicting naturalistic vine sprays, hunting scenes and festoons of fruit and foliage. A curved fountain niche of late 2nd- or early 3rd-century date, found in a Mithraeum at Ostia (in the Lateran museum), bears a glass-paste mosaic figure of Silvanus, nimbed and equipped with pruning knife and dog, seen against a blue background. From Pompeii and Herculaneum there are a few mosaic panel pictures, mythological in content, that were set on walls; while part of a wall panel representing a harbour, found on the Quirinal, is in the Conservatori museum.

The number of pre-5th-century vault mosaics known to have survived has considerably increased. At Ostia the semidome and arch soffit of a large niche in the House of the Seven Sages are faced with polychrome mosaic worked in delicate and naturalistic plant designs. Somewhat fragmentary, but still impressive, mosaic figures—a nymph suckling a kid, a triton and a crocodile in a Nilotic landscape—appear in the semidome of the east plunge in the *frigidarium* of the hunting baths at Leptis Magna. In the mausoleum of the Julii in the necropolis beneath St. Peter's, Rome, are the earliest Christian vault and wall mosaics known, dating from about the middle of the 3rd century and worked in glass-paste *tesserae.* Their subjects are the divine angler, Jonah and the whale, the Good Shepherd and Christus-Helios in his chariot, with a great, spreading vine linking together the four pictures. All these are comparatively new finds, and there is quite a number of lesser fragments of vault mosaics that cannot be described here. The familiar mosaic decoration on the vault of the circular ambulatory in the church of Sta. Costanza in Rome contains a curious mixture of subjects disposed in large, rectangular panels; these mosaics, held by most scholars to be an instance of the early Christian use of pagan or neutral art motifs, have been regarded by some as belonging to a late 3rd- or early 4th-century pagan shrine or mausoleum later converted from its original use to Christian purposes. The 4th-century Christian mosaic from the apse of old St. Peter's in Rome, and the 5th-century Christian wall and vault mosaics at Ravenna and in the church of Sta. Maria Maggiore in Rome, while ranking as Roman, cannot be described here.

Finally, mention must be made of figured wall panels of brightly coloured *opus sectile,* such as that with a beast fight in the Ostia museum and those showing beast fights, Hylas and the nymphs and the decorative group of horsemen and a frontal chariot, which came from the 4th-century basilica of Junius Bassus on the Esquiline (in the Palazzo del Drago at the Quattro Fontane).

4. Painted Portraits.

—Roman portrait painting comes but a short way behind portrait sculpture in excellence of execution and in its superbly realistic style. One of the earliest extant examples of this art is the group of Terentius Neo and his wife, from Pompeii (in the Naples museum). Both figures recall the celebrated mummy portraits from the Fayum in Egypt, painted in encaustic, the technique by which the colours were mixed with liquid wax and fixed by heat, and ranging in date from the Flavian period to the 3rd century. A circular portrait group of frontal figures painted on wood, probably in Egypt (now in Berlin), shows Septimius Severus, Julia Domna, Caracalla and Geta, the elder (so it seems) of the two boys having been subsequently washed out. Particularly attractive are the portraits of the gold-glass medallions which, in the exquisite refinement of their treatment, may be compared to modern miniatures. The medallion at Brescia, dating from the 3rd century and carrying the portrait group of a mother with her boy and girl, is a veritable masterpiece; while some of the portraits of Christians in the same medium and found, for the most part, in the catacombs, continue the traditions of Roman veristic iconography.

5. Book Illustration.

—That book illustration existed in the late-Hellenistic world can be inferred from some of the so-called Megarian bowls, imitations in clay of gold or silver vessels and ranging from the 3rd century B.C. to the 1st century A.D. These often bear on their exteriors scenes in relief from literary texts which are sometimes accompanied by Greek quotations. They must, in part at least, have served as models for the Roman age artists, and this art is heard of in Rome comparatively early— the 700 pictures, for example, illustrating Varro's 15 books of *Imagines* and a portrait of Virgil prefixed to an edition of his poems. The miniatures in the famous codex of the *Iliad* in the Ambrosiana library, Milan, were probably painted at the end of the 5th or beginning of the 6th century, but reflect pictures of the 3rd, 2nd and even 1st century; as do also those of the codex of Virgil in the Vatican (No. 3225), written *c.* 400. The miniatures in the second great Virgilian illustrated codex in the Vatican (No. 3867 "Romanus"), written *c.* 500, are still Roman in spirit, if less classical in style; the tenacious influence of Graeco-Roman painting can be clearly traced in the illustrations to such early Byzantine books as the Vienna Dioscurides (written in 512), the Vienna Genesis (6th century) and the Joshua Roll (10th century). A most remarkable, if aesthetically crude, mid-4th-century mosaic pavement, found in a Romano-British villa at Low Ham, Somerset, and showing scenes from the first and fourth books of the *Aeneid,* undoubtedly reflects the illustrations in some Virgilian codex.

IV. STUCCO WORK

Of the minor forms of sculpture none is more attractive than the art of modeling, in relief or in the round, in fine, white stucco. Decorative stucco work was cheaper and easier to produce than carving in stone or marble, soft and delicate in texture and equally elegant whether left white or gaily painted. It was used at all levels of society, in public as well as in private buildings. In domestic architecture it was a useful alternative or accessory to painting; here it is sufficient to recall such examples as the pure white and exquisite vault decoration, showing ritual scenes with small-scale figures, of the late-republican or early-imperial house near the Villa Farnesina in Trastevere (in the Roman National museum); the handsome pairs of large white griffins, framed in acanthus scrolls against a vivid red ground, in the late republican House of the Griffins on the Palatine; and the frieze depicting the story of the *Iliad,* in white figures on a bright blue background, in the House of the Cryptoporticus or Homeric house at Pompeii. For the use of this technique in palaces the figure work in Domitian's villa at Castel Gandolfo in the Alban hills can be cited; it can be found on public buildings, in the Stabian and forum baths and in the temple of Isis at Pompeii; while the most lovely and extensive stucco relief work in a semiprivate shrine is that in the underground basilica near the Porta Maggiore, Rome, where the scenes all allude to the world beyond the grave, to the soul's journey to it and to its preparation for it in this life. Some of the best surviving stuccoes are in tombs—in the tomb of the Innocentii and the tomb of the Axe under the church of S. Sebastiano on the Via Appia; in the tomb of the Valerii and the tomb of the Pancratii on the Via Latina, in the latter of which stucco work is most attractively combined with painting in the flat; and in the tomb of the Valerii under St. Peter's, Rome, where the interior walls of both the main and subsidiary chambers are almost completely covered with recesses, niches and lunettes containing stucco figures. The whole effect is most impressive, and the Vatican tomb of the Valerii must be reckoned as a *locus classicus* for the study of this delightful and all too scantily represented branch of Roman art.

V. MINOR ARTS

1. Decorated Metalwork.—The Roman taste for costly silverware, with figured or floral relief decoration, is attested by the elder Pliny and by the numerous surviving pieces. Among the earliest-known examples in a Roman context is the *cantharus* ("goblet") with myrtle sprays, discovered at Alesia in one of Julius Caesar's siege trenches of 52 B.C. The treasure from Boscoreale containing 108 pieces (of which 102 are in the Louvre) and that of 118 pieces, which had been packed away in a strongroom in the House of Menander at Pompeii (now in the Naples museum), obviously antedate the disaster of A.D. 79. The former treasure contains two *scyphi* ("cups," in the Rothschild collection in Paris) with scenes from contemporary Augustan history. The latter comprises not only cylindrical cups and *canthari* of the early-imperial period, but also late-Hellenistic *scyphi,* perhaps dating from as early as the late 2nd century B.C., one pair being signed by Apelles. Probably belonging to the Augustan period are a number of the pieces in the two treasures found respectively at Berthouville, Normandy (in the Bibliothèque Nationale, Paris), and at Hildesheim, Germany (in Berlin), although the former hoard includes some objects that may well be later, while the latter also contains some earlier Hellenistic works; to the Augustan epoch should again probably be attributed the two *scyphi* that came to light at Hoby, near Copenhagen, signed by Cheirosophos and depicting the ransoming of Hector and the story of Philoctetes. A round *patera* ("dish") from Aquileia (in Vienna) portrays a Julio-Claudian emperor as the "new Triptolemus." Of the British museum silver pieces found in France, the Chatuzanges and Chaourse treasures probably date from the 2nd century A.D.; whereas the Seasons bucket (*situla*) from Tourdan, near Vienne, often described as Augustan, and the treasure from Caubiac, near Toulouse, display the superficially naturalistic classicism combined with a certain clumsiness and faultiness in drawing that is the hallmark of 4th- and 5th-century Roman decorated metalwork. It is, indeed, to this late-antique period that some of the most spectacular and interesting extant silver pieces and hoards belong. As regards the single pieces, special mention should be made of the silver-gilt *patera* found at Parabiago, Italy (in the Antiquities department, Milan), with scenes relating to the cult of Cybele and Attis; of the rectangular *lanx* ("dish") recovered from the river Tyne and in the duke of Northumberland's collection, which depicts Apollo, Artemis, Leto, Athena, etc., on the island of Delos, where Julian the Apostate sacrificed in 363; of the *missorium*

("circular dish") at Madrid, portraying Theodosius enthroned in the midst of his court; and of the silver-gilt *missorium* discovered at Cesena, Italy, the central medallion of which shows a group of persons picnicking *al fresco,* above, and a groom leading out a horse from its stable, below. Of the late hoards, four are in the British museum. These are the Esquiline treasure, which includes the bridal casket presented to a Christian lady, Proiecta, on the occasion of her marriage to Secundinus, and four statuettes of city-personifications; the Carthage treasure, partly Christian; the cache of pieces from Coleraine, Ireland; and the Mildenhall treasure from Suffolk, also containing some Christian objects, but of which the most outstanding items are pagan—the great Oceanus dish, nearly two feet in diameter, and the two smaller dishes with Bacchic figures, completely classical in style and virtually free from the late-antique designer's usual defects of draftsmanship. The hoard from Traprain Law, Scotland, comprising both pagan and Christian pieces, is in the National Museum of Antiquities, Edinburgh. Where precisely the Roman silversmiths' workshops were located is not known, but the great Mediterranean cities—Rome, Alexandria, Antioch and Ephesus—and also some of the leading Gaulish cities were certainly centres of this art and the master craftsmen often traveled in the service of their patrons.

An outstanding recent find of late Roman silver is the treasure buried about the middle of the 4th century in the late Roman fort of Kaiseraugst on the Rhine in Switzerland and brought to light in 1961. Its most spectacular items are three figured dishes: one rectangular; one round; and one octagonal, with scenes from Achilles' life round the flange and his discovery among Lycomedes' daughters in the central roundel.

Decorated bronze objects of the Roman age include vessels of various types, mounts for chariots, horse harness and domestic furniture and also brooches, which in the northwestern areas of the empire were often inlaid with polychrome enamel. Of particular interest are the pieces of decorated bronze armour used by gladiators, legionaries on parade and, above all, the auxiliary horsemen of the Roman army when taking part in the sports or tournaments described by the Hadrianic writer Arrian. Examples of the face-mask-visor helmets worn by horsemen on those occasions are especially impressive and have come to light in many regions of the empire, notably in Britain, Germany, the Danubian countries and northern Syria. Remarkable finds were made at Straubing, Bavaria, in 1950.

2. Ivories and Wood Carving.—Ivory was a popular material for minor sculpture. It was worked in the round and in relief and in such forms as small portraits, figurines, caskets, such as that at Brescia (5th-century) and furniture ornaments, of which the carved plaques composing the "Cathedra of Maximianus" at Ravenna (probably 5th-century) provide a notable instance. The consular and other diptychs (*see* DIPTYCH) are one of the most distinctive types of ivory relief work in the 4th and 5th centuries. Among them are such masterpieces that kept alive the traditions of Hellenistic carving as the diptych of the Symmachi and Nicomachi (of which one leaf is in the Victoria and Albert museum, London, the other in the Cluny museum, Paris) and some outstandingly fine examples of late antique portraiture, for instance, the Probus diptych at Aosta with the double portrait of Honorius, the Felix diptych in Paris (dated 428) and that of Boethius, consul in 487, at Brescia. Of wood carving one example must suffice— the panels with Biblical scenes on the 5th-century door of the church of Sta. Sabina on the Aventine.

3. Gems, Cameos, etc.—Many types of carving in precious stones were practised by Roman-age craftsmen, and it is to them that the credit goes for the majority of the *intaglios* which have survived from ancient times. The widespread taste for *intaglios* is witnessed to by the large numbers of existing glass-paste imitations reproducing their subjects, which include portraits of both imperial and private persons, and a large variety of divine and mythological groups and figures, personifications, animals, etc. Many bear the signatures of Greek artists. But the most impressive series of Roman gems consists of the great cameos, cut in different stones and representing imperial persons. Among the earliest of these pieces are the Blacas cameo of onyx in the British museum, portraying Augustus in the guise of Jupiter with aegis; the Gemma Augustea, a sardonyx in Vienna and the Grand Camée de France, a sardonyx in the Bibliothèque Nationale, which were probably carved under Gaius and respectively present the apotheosis of Augustus and of Tiberius, the latter with Divus Augustus also; and the sardonyx cameo of Claudius with Jupiter's aegis in the royal collection at Windsor castle. Late antique examples of the craft are the rectangular sardonyx in the city library at Trier, portraying Constantine I and members of his house, and the onyx in the Rothschild collection in Paris with busts of Honorius and Maria.

Other varieties of carving in precious stones are represented by the miniature head of a girl in the British museum, wearing the hair style of Messallina and Agrippina II, which is cut in *plasma* (root-of-emerald); the onyx vase at Brunswick, possibly of the 1st century, depicting an emperor and empress as Triptolemus and Demeter; and the late antique Rubens vase in the Walters Art gallery, Baltimore, carved in honey-coloured agate and decorated on the front and back with a naturalistic vine and with the head of a Pan, cupped in acanthus, on either shoulder.

4. Figured Glass.—Closely akin to cameos and vessels cut in precious stones are their substitutes in opaque "cameo glass," worked in two layers, with the designs standing out in white against a dark-blue or bright-blue background. To this class belong the Blue vase from Pompeii (in the Naples museum), with vintaging Cupids; the Auldjo vase (in the British museum), with an exquisitely naturalistic vine; and the celebrated Portland vase, also in the British museum, the scenes on which depict myths relating to the afterlife—Peleus and Thetis and perhaps Helen and Achilles on the Blessed Isles. Similar imitations of carving in precious stones are the late antique *diatreta* ("cage cups"), the decoration of which is cut back from the outer surface of the mold-cast blank. This "openwork" ornamentation sometimes represents the crisscross meshes of a net, while on other vessels it consists of an elaborate figure scene, the design in either case being very deeply undercut and, for the most part, only connected with the background by short shanks of glass. Of the figured examples the most spectacular surviving specimens are the dark-blue *situla* with a hunting scene in the treasury of St. Mark's, Venice, and the dull-green cup presenting the story of Lycurgus (the Rothschild vase in the British museum). Of the other types of glass with figured decoration, the molded cups with gladiatorial and circus scenes are characteristic of the early imperial period, while the 4th-century glass-worker's craft is represented by vessels with cut or incised designs, the subjects of which are chariot races, hunting and Bacchic scenes and, in the case of the Christian pieces, episodes from the Old and New Testaments. Among the most important centres of glass production under the empire were Syria, Alexandria and the Cologne region.

5. Figured Pottery.—The figured terra-cotta tablewares (*terra sigillata*—a term often incorrectly stretched to cover plain wares) were cheaper versions of the costly decorated silverwares. During the last century of the republic and in the early decades of the 1st century of the empire, Arretium (Arezzo) was the most flourishing centre of the manufacture of a fine type of red-gloss pottery. As the signatures on the pots reveal, the Italian firms often employed Greek and oriental craftsmen, and the mythological and floral themes of the vessels' molded ornamentation owe much to the inspiration of Hellenistic art. From shortly before the middle of the 1st century A.D. onward, the markets enjoyed by the Italian fabrics were captured by the products of potteries now established in southern, central and eastern Gaul. These manufactured cheaper, more mass-produced and aesthetically inferior red-gloss and black-gloss wares, popularly known as "Samian," some varieties of which continued into the 4th century. The decoration of the Gaulish pots was, for the most part, molded; but some vessels carry applied motifs made in individual molds; while others show designs incised to counterfeit cut glass. Yet another type of ornament was carried out in the *en barbotine* technique, by which relief work was produced by trailing liquid clay across the surface of the pot. As regards the content of the decoration, themes from daily life were added to the traditional subjects based on Greco-Roman mythology and on natural history; and it is the *en bar-*

botine hunt cups, of which the leading centre of production was at Castor, Northamptonshire, that are the highlight of the native Romano-British potter's craft. A late-antique class of red-gloss pottery, known as late A ware, with scenes in relief from Greek mythology and from the Roman spectacles and shows, was manufactured in some southern Mediterranean area, probably in Egypt.

6. Coins and Medallions.—Last, a brief allusion must be made to the die-sinker's art, closely linked with that of the gem engraver. The imperial portraits displayed on coins throughout the period of the empire, and on medallions from the early 2nd century onward, provide a continuous iconographic series that can rank with the best works of the portrait sculptors. Many of the reverse designs, beginning with those of the late republic, show figure scenes and single figures treated with the utmost delicacy and finish. Especially noteworthy for their pictorial character are the reverse types of the large 2nd-century bronze medallions, with themes from Greek mythology, Roman legend and contemporary Roman history. The reverse designs of some of the late 3rd- and 4th-century gold and silver presentation pieces illustrate most conspicuously the high standards of craftsmanship to which the late antique could still attain. For interest of content few medallions can rival the large gold multiple, found at Arras, which Constantius Chlorus struck in 296 to commemorate his entry into London after defeating the usurping "British emperor" Carausius. *See* also references under "Roman Art" in the Index.

BIBLIOGRAPHY.—*General Art.*—Otto J. Brendel, "Prolegomena to a Book on Roman Art," *Memoirs of the American Academy in Rome,* xxi (1953); Franz Valery Marie Cumont, *Recherches sur le symbolisme funéraire des Romains* (1942); Antonio Frova, *L'arte di Roma e del mondo romano* (1961); André Grabar, *The Beginnings of Christian Art* (1967), *Byzantium: from the Death of Theodosius to the Rise of Islam* (1967); Per Gustaf Hamberg, *Studies in Roman Imperial Art* (1945); Heinz Kähler, *The Art of Rome and Her Empire* (1963); D. Levi, "L'arte romana," *Annuario della Scuola Archeologica di Atene,* xxiv–xxvi (1946–48); Inez Scott Ryberg, *Rites of the State Religion in Roman Art* (1955); Helmut Schoppa, *Die Kunst der Römerzeit in Gallien, Germanien und Britannien* (1957); Jocelyn M. C. Toynbee, *The Hadrianic School* (1934), *The Art of the Romans* (1965); Jocelyn M. C. Toynbee and John Bryan Ward-Perkins, *The Shrine of St. Peter and the Vatican Excavations* (1956); O. Vessberg, *Studien zur Kunstgeschichte der römischen Republik* (1941); Wolfgang Friedrich Volbach, *Early Christian Art* (1961).

General Sculpture.—Eugénie Sellers Strong, *La scultura romana da Augusto a Costantino,* 2 vol. (1923–26); Donald Emrys Strong, *Roman Imperial Sculpture: an Introduction to the Commemorative and Decorative Sculpture of the Roman Empire Down to the Death of Constantine* (1961).

Portraits.—Ludwig Goldscheider (ed.), *Roman Portraits* (1940); Annie Nicolette Zadoks (Josephus Jitta), *Ancestral Portraiture in Rome and the Art of the Last Century of the Republic* (1932); R. West, *Römische Porträtplastik,* i (1933), ii (1941); Max Wegner *et al., Das römische Herrscherbild II, 1: Die Flavier* (1966); W. H. Gross, *Ibid. II, 2: Bildnisse Trajans* (1940); Max Wegner, *Ibid. II, 3: Hadrian, Plotina, Marciana, Matidia, Sabina* (1956), *Ibid. II, 4: Die Herrscherbildnisse in antoninischer Zeit* (1939); Hans Peter L'Orange, *Apotheosis in Ancient Portraiture* (1947); Richard Delbrueck, *Spätantike Kaiser porträts* (1933).

Historical Reliefs.—Giuseppe Moretti, *L'Ara Pacis Augustae* (1938); Jocelyn M. C. Toynbee, *The Ara Pacis Reconsidered* (1953), *The Flavian Reliefs from the Palazzo della Cancelleria* (1957); Filippo Magi, *I rilievi flavi del Palazzo della Cancelleria* (1945); Karl Lehmann-Hartleben, *Die Traianssäule* (1926); I. A. Richmond, "Trajan's Army on Trajan's Column," *Papers of the British School at Rome,* xiii (1935); P. Romanelli, *La colonna traiana* (1942); Franz Josef Hassel, *Der Trajansbogen in Benevent* (1966); Inez S. Ryberg, *Panel Reliefs of Marcus Aurelius* (1967); P. Romanelli, *La colonna antonina* (1942); Giovanni Becatti, *Colonna di Marco Aurelio* (1957); Richard Brilliant, *The Arch of Septimius Severus in the Roman Forum* (1967); Denys E. L. Haynes and P. E. D. Hirst, *Porta Argentariorum* (1939); John B. Ward-Perkins, "Severan Art and Architecture at Lepcis Magna," *Journal of Roman Studies,* xxxviii (1948); K. F. Kinch, *L'arc de triomphe de Salonique* (1890); Antonio Giuliano, *Arco di Costantino* (1955).

Sarcophagi.—Carl Robert *et al., Die antiken Sarkophagreliefs* (1890–); R. Turcan, *Les sarcophages romaines à représentations dionysiaques* (1966); George M. A. Hanfmann, *The Season Sarcophagus in Dumbarton Oaks,* 2 vol. (1952); Josef Wilpert, *I sarcofagi cristiani antichi,* 5 vol. (1929–36); Friedrich Gerke, *Die christlichen Sarkophage der vorkonstantinischer Zeit* (1940).

Painting and Mosaics.—A. Rumpf, "Malerei und Zeichnung," *Handbuch der Archäologie,* Sechste Lieferung (1953); Ludwig Curtius, *Die Wandmalerei Pompejis* (1929); Amedeo Maiuri, *La Villa dei*

Misteri, 2 vol. (1930), *Roman Painting* (1953); Christopher Mounsey Dawson, "Romano-Campanian Mythological Landscape Painting," *Yale Classical Studies,* ix (1944); F. Wirth, *Römische Wandmalerei* (1934); Josef Wilpert, *Die Malereien der Katakomben Roms* (1903); Hans P. L'Orange and P. J. Nordhagen, *Mosaics from Antiquity to the Early Middle Ages* (1966); Doro Levi, *Antioch Mosaic Pavements,* 2 vol. (1947); J. A. Blanchet *et al., Inventaire des mosaïques de la Gaule et de l'Afrique* (1909–15); Henri Stern, *Recueil général des mosaïques de la Gaule* (1957–); Klaus Parlasca, *Die römischen Mosaiken in Deutschland* (1959); Victorine von Gonzenbach, *Die römischen Mosaiken der Schweiz* (1961); Ranuccio Bianchi Bandinelli, *Hellenistic-Byzantine Miniatures of the Iliad* (1956).

Stuccowork.—E. L. Wadsworth, "Stucco Reliefs of the First and Second Centuries Still Extant in Rome," *Memoirs of the American Academy in Rome,* iv (1924); G. Bendinelli, "Il monumento sotterraneo di Porta Maggiore in Roma," *Monumenti Antichi,* xxxi (1926).

Metalwork.—Donald E. Strong, *Greek and Roman Gold and Silver Plate* (1966) (full bibliographies of all the silver treasures of the Roman period); J. Keim and H. Klumbach, *Der römische Schatzfund von Straubing* (1951).

Ivories and Wood Carving.—Joseph Natanson, *Early Christian Ivories* (1953); Richard Delbrueck, *Die Consulardiptychen und verwandte Denkmäler* (1929); J. Wiegand, *Das altchristliche Hauptportal an der Kirche der hl. Sabina* (1900); F. Darsy, "Les portes de Sainte-Sabine," *Rivista di Archeologia Cristiana,* xxxvii (1961).

Gems, Cameos.—Adolf Furtwängler, *Die antiken Gemmen,* 3 vol. (1900).

Glass.—A. Kisa, *Das Glas im Altertum,* 3 vol. (1908).

Pottery.—Robert Jesse Charleston, *Roman Pottery* (1955).

Coins and Medallions.—Edward Allen Sydenham, *The Coinage of the Roman Republic* (rev. ed., 1952); Harold Mattingly, *Roman Coins from the Earliest Times to the Fall of the Western Empire,* 2nd rev. ed. (1960); Jocelyn M. C. Toynbee, *Roman Medallions* (1944).

(J. M. C. T.)

ROMAN CATHOLIC CHURCH. The word *ecclesia* appears in the New Testament 106 times: twice in its ordinary Greek sense of the assembly of the city-state of Ephesus, once of the community of the Israelites at Sinai, and on all other occasions of the society or Church of Christ, whose members were first called Christians at Antioch. St. Paul uses the word both of local societies, "churches" of Judaea, Asia, Galatia, Macedonia, the Thessalonians or in Philemon's house (as he speaks of "them of Laodicea"), and also of the "whole Church of God." In Matt. 16:18, Christ answers St. Peter's confession, "thou art Christ, the Son of the living God," by saying, "thou art Peter; and upon this rock I will build my church." In Matt. 18:15–20, he defines what may be called ecclesiastical jurisdiction:

If thy brother shall offend against thee . . . tell the church. And if he will not hear the church, let him be to thee as the heathen and publican; . . . whatsoever you shall bind upon earth, shall be bound also in heaven: and whatsoever you shall loose upon earth, shall be loosed also in heaven. Again I say to you, that if two of you shall consent upon earth, concerning anything whatsoever they shall ask, it shall be done to them by my Father who is in Heaven. For where there are two or three gathered together in my name, there am I in the midst of them.

In tracing the origin of the church back to the apostles, Roman Catholic theologians also cite as the most mature and conscious definition of the apostolic church the following passage in the Epistles to the Ephesians and Colossians: ". . . the Kingdom of the Son of his love, in whom we have redemption through his blood, the remission of sins; Who is the image of the invisible God, the firstborn of every creature: For in him were all things created in heaven and on earth . . . all things were created by him and in him. And he is before all, and by him all things endure. And he is the head of the body, the church" (Col. 1:13–18). "To re-establish all things in Christ . . . and he hath subjected all things under his feet, and hath made him head over all the church, which is his body, and the fulness of him who fills all in all" (Eph. 1:10, 22–23).

This organic unity of Christ, "the fullness of the godhead bodily," with the church "which is his body" is the essence of Catholic ecclesiology. In Christ, according to Roman Catholic doctrine, the godhead assumed human nature: the nature of man is united in Christ with the nature of God, and the church is therefore the divine organism. But the nature of man implies a historical and instituted existence on earth. "By the very fact of being a body," said Leo XIII, "the church is visible." Its existence, institution, and operation are therefore sacramental. It is

the mystery of the incarnate godhead perpetually realized and available in all time and for all the purpose of the divine incarnation. There can be but one such church and, as it is historical and instituted on earth, there can be but one church visible on earth.

As it is divine as well as human, it contains and consummates the whole divine creation, "the church triumphant, the church suffering and the church militant, and is the fullness (*pleroma*) of him that filleth all in all." Hence it is holy and catholic. Its institution is simultaneously divine and human.

Historically and therefore upon the authority of its divine founder, Roman Catholic theologians assert, this church is the church of his apostles. It is apostolic and its apostolicity is its perpetual attribute. Within the compass of its sacramental purpose it is infallible, in the sphere of faith (*i.e.,* man's apprehension of God) and in the sphere of morals (*i.e.,* man's essential relation with God and man).

This infallible authority, Catholic theologians point out, is not to be confounded in any sense with "power": it is the infallible authority of knowledge which is of the essence of the union of man with God—knowledge not achieved as in the natural sciences externally by observation, hypothesis and experiment, but inherent and essential as God knows himself and his creatures and the nature of the unity which he wills and accomplishes. The effectual operation of this entire sacrament, the vital activity of the divine organism, is known as grace.

Grace (*q.v.*) is the universal operation of the church. It is the initiation, process, and fulfillment of the divine activity of redemption by which God unites his creatures organically with himself and endows them thus with his own vitality. This universal grace or sacrament is effectually realized and defined in seven sacraments, acts of God in and through the divine organism by which the divine life is bestowed and the organic union is accomplished and sustained (*see* SACRAMENT). In the Eucharist (*q.v.*) "under the appearances of bread and wine, Jesus Christ Himself is contained, offered and received." It is the whole act of redemption, the sacrifice—that is, the making holy—of the whole universe in the person of Christ,

the most divine gift emanating from the depth of the heart of the Redeemer "with desire desiring" this wonderful union with men which was especially designed to spread everywhere the life-giving fruit of His redemptive work (Leo XIII, encyclical *Mirae caritatis,* 1902).

Baptism is the initial reception of the human being into the body of Christ. Confirmation given to members of an age to recognize and will their membership is the sacrament of moral maturity. Marriage is the sacrament which sustains in Christ human generation and family life. Penance restores the union with God when it has been injured or broken by sin. Holy Order creates and sustains the whole institution of priesthood and episcopacy by which the divine organism lives and functions on earth. Thus the penitent confesses his sin to Christ, who hears, judges, and absolves him by means of the human priest, and the sacrifice of Calvary is contemporary with all times as the same sacrifice is offered by the same High Priest employing successive generations of men ordained by Christ for that purpose. The passage or expectation of death is sanctified by the sacrament of extreme unction.

Thus the whole earthly life of every human being is organized in the body of Christ, and the whole organization of the church exists to realize that divine-human community. The history of the church cannot be understood unless its nature and function as the divine-human organism, wholly divine and wholly human and indissolubly one, is first recognized.

St. Luke ends his account of St. Paul's apostolate at Rome with the words "this salvation of God is sent to the Gentiles" (Acts 28:28). St. Paul himself explains the significance of that climax in the Epistle to the Galatians. As a Jew turning to the gentiles he must claim that the old dispensation has been superseded and that to be "in Christ" (a phrase repeated six times in this epistle and constantly used thereafter by St. Paul) is to belong to "the Jerusalem that is above" in which "there can be neither Jew nor Greek."

It was only by the act of God that the sanctities and exclusions of the old law could be at once fulfilled and superseded, and hence the same authority which united Jew and gentile realized the purpose of history. "And if you be Christ's, then are you the seed of Abraham, heirs according to the promise" (Gal. 3:29). In the Epistle to the Ephesians, written probably from Rome, this doctrine of divine consummation becomes explicit, "the dispensation of the fulness [*pleroma*] of times, to re-establish all things in Christ. . . . For he is our peace, who hath made both one, and breaking down the middle wall of partition . . . that he might make the two in himself into one new man, making peace, and might reconcile both to God in one body by the cross. . . . Now therefore you are no more strangers and foreigners; but you are fellow-citizens with the saints, and the domestics of God. Built upon the foundation of the apostles and prophets, Jesus Christ himself being the chief corner stone: In whom all the building, being framed together, groweth up into an holy temple in the Lord."

(T. S. GY.)

This article on the Roman Catholic Church is organized as follows:

I. ORGANIZATION

In Roman Catholic theology the organization of the church—what might be called its constitutional law, or its juridical constitution—is partly of divine institution, partly of its own disposition. That is to say, some elements were established by Christ himself, and others the church, once constituted as a visible, complete human society, has added by its own law. The first, in Catholic doctrine, cannot be changed; they are derived not from principles of political philosophy but from revelation and are taught by the church rather than enacted by it. Indeed, it is not always expressly stated in the law, nor always a matter of theological agreement, whether a particular principle is to be ascribed to divine or ecclesiastical determination. The exposition of this question is presented below under two main divisions: basic constitutional principles, and the actual distribution of functions in the church.

A. BASIC PRINCIPLES

Five principles of ecclesiastical organization may be regarded as basic: (1) the threefold function or power of the priestly office of the church and its ministers; (2) the establishment of a distinct order, the clergy, as the subject of ministerial and jurisdictional authority; (3) the hierarchical disposition of this order; (4) the hierarchical mode of conferring authority in the church; (5) the active participation of all members of the church in the realization of its total mission in the world.

1. Function of the Church.—In discussing the organization of the church, it is not possible simply to equate organization and government. Catholic doctrine asserts that the church was instituted by Christ as a visible society in which, and through the instrumentality of which, men are to be united to him and through him receive redemption and sanctification. It follows that the church has the same mission and hence the same authority as Christ himself, the office of sanctification, of teaching, and of ruling, corresponding to his threefold title of priest, prophet, and king. In the church these are referred to as the powers of *orders* and of *jurisdiction* (the latter including the function of teaching as well as of legislation, judgment, and administration). But this division is concerned only with the immediate object of ecclesiastical activity. All the church's teaching and all its law-making are ordained toward the single end of sanctification and salvation of souls, and apart from it would have no meaning or finality. Hence the "organization" of the Roman Catholic Church necessarily includes the method of disposition of its cult, doctrine, and discipline, partly because they are inseparably related in purpose and in operation, partly because the three powers are commonly united in the same subject of authority.

2. The Clergy.—The threefold function of the priestly office, according to Catholic doctrine, resides in a distinct order, the clergy. The Code of Canon Law states: "Though not all forms of the clergy are divinely instituted, it is of divine establishment that there be in the Church a *clergy* distinct from the *laity* . . ." (can. 107); and "It is the institution of orders which, by establishment of Christ, distinguishes the clergy from the laity with a view to the government of the faithful and the ministry of divine worship" (can. 948). The significance of this is that as Christ chose to apply the fruits of redemption through the instrumentality of a society, the church, so he determined also that in this society the function of teaching, directing, and sanctifying in his name and person was to be vested in a distinct group, exclusively dedicated to the service of God and the sanctification of men, in the manner of the priestly and Levitical orders of the Old Testament.

The constitution of a distinct order to fill the office of ministry and government in the church does not imply that the clergy are a superior class (or caste) and the laity inferior, or that membership in the church is more complete or more perfect in the clergy than in the laity. The right of teaching, directing, and sanctifying the community is exercised by the clergy not in their own name or authority but in the name and place of Christ. By themselves and in themselves the clergy are also of the faithful.

3. Hierarchy.—The powers of orders and jurisdiction are conferred not indivisibly but in various degrees or grades, referred to as the hierarchical (*hiera*, "sacred"; *arche*, "rule") constitution of the clergy. Since both the power of orders and the power of jurisdiction exist in hierarchical form, however, a further distinction is necessary. From the point of view of orders, it is, according to Catholic doctrine, of divine institution that there be bishops, priests, and other ministers, including at least the diaconate; the further distribution of ministerial functions in the offices of subdeacon and the minor orders is attributed to ecclesiastical institution. From the point of view of jurisdiction, it is, according to Catholic theology, of divine institution that there be a supreme pontiff and an episcopate; the exercise of jurisdiction by the Roman curia, by vicars and prefects apostolic, by pastors, and by certain institutes of religious is of ecclesiastical origin.

4. Conferring Authority.—The constitution of the church is hierarchical not only in the derived sense (that the powers of ministry and government exist in unequal grades) but also in the original sense that these powers come down, in a special way, from God, rather than up, as it were, from the people. Unlike civil society, in the church neither the power of orders nor of jurisdiction ever resides in the faithful as a whole, to be conferred by them on certain subjects.

The power of orders is received by ordination (*see* HOLY ORDERS; ORDINATION). From the original meaning, of a disposition of things according to some norm, the term "order" has come to signify the rights and powers so disposed and also the rank or state of those possessing them. A man is constituted in the different grades of the hierarchy of orders by a rite signifying incorporation into a state in which a certain participation of the priestly office is enjoyed.

In jurisdiction, a distinction is made between the supreme pontificate and other grades of authority. The pope's jurisdiction is received immediately from God, upon his election and acceptance. Hence in the election of a pope the electors do not confer jurisdiction, they merely supply the condition of selecting a person. But the mode of selecting him is not determined by divine law; the form of papal election is a matter of canon law, and it has changed from time to time (*see* CONCLAVE). Since the electors do not confer the authority, neither can they revoke it, or limit it, or determine it, or require that consent be obtained for its exercise.

In every other grade besides the pope's, jurisdiction is dependent upon what is called a "canonical mission," the assignment of some jurisdictional function together with the designation of the subjects in whose regard it is to be exercised. Episcopal consecration itself is considered to confer the total priesthood, with the title of authority both of orders and of government in the church; but the use of the latter is dependent upon a further act of the Roman pontiff. This may be the assignment of a specified territory or diocese. Or the canonical mission may consist in the convocation of the whole episcopal college to deliberate in general council upon certain specified matters of doctrine or discipline. In this way the legal principle of the dependence of all nonpapal jurisdiction upon a canonical mission is compatible with the thesis

that episcopal jurisdiction itself is conferred by divine right in the act of episcopal consecration.

Since the mode of providing the canonical mission is a matter of ecclesiastical law, it has varied in the course of history. In earlier times the bishop was always consecrated for a particular see, with the consent of the bishops of the province and of the metropolitan, communion with Rome being supposed; thus the canonical mission was inseparable from consecration and the distinction between the bishop's powers of orders and of jurisdiction did not arise.

5. The Laity.—As stated above, 'the organization of the Roman Catholic Church cannot be equated with the forms and modes of its government. The laity, who do not participate directly in the government of the church, are as truly component of the people of God as are the clergy; in addition, they are not merely subjects but have their own active role in the prosecution of the church's total mission, the salvation and sanctification of the world. The detailed exposition of this activity pertains more to the next section, *Division of Functions*.

B. DIVISION OF FUNCTIONS

Authority in the church resides in the Roman pontiff, in the bishops, and in other grades of ecclesiastical institution. Some grades of the hierarchy have authority with respect to the whole church, others with respect to a part of it, the basis of the division being a title either of territorial nature, or of juridical rite, or of religious profession.

1. The Roman Pontiff.—It was defined by the first Vatican Council, and is stated in the Code of Canon Law, that the pope has full and supreme authority over the whole church, both in teaching matters of faith and morals and in enacting matters of discipline and government (*see* POPE).

In designating the acts of the pope the older terms "bull" and "brief" (*see* DIPLOMATIC: *Papal Chancery*), which refer to the external form of documents, are less significant than the terms which indicate something of their internal content. Many forms are used, principally the apostolic constitution, the encyclical, the *motu proprio*, and the allocution. (*a*) The apostolic constitution is a very solemn document that may contain a dogmatic definition, the establishment of a new diocese, the enactment of a new law, etc. (*b*) The encyclical is the form most commonly employed for magisterial or pastoral matters: to teach moral principles (social action, Christian marriage, education, etc.), to elaborate matters of dogma (on the Mystical Body, the priesthood, the Sacred Heart, biblical studies, the liturgy, virginity, precarious trends in philosophy and theology), or to request prayers for the missions, the persecuted, or some similar cause of general concern. (*c*) The *motu proprio* is usually juridical, containing either new law or an abrogation of old law, or a dispensation from a law, etc. Technically the words signify that the enactment proceeds from the pope's own initiative; in practice they indicate that, whatever its origin, the pope takes a special interest in the provision and wishes to emphasize his personal sponsorship of it. (*d*) At one time allocutions were formal addresses delivered by the pope to select groups of cardinals on the occasion of consistories. Under later popes allocutions given not only to groups of cardinals or bishops but also to audiences of the laity—congresses of doctors, scientists, educators, nurses, labour unions, groups of youth organizations, etc.—became a vehicle for the exercise of the ordinary teaching authority of the pope and gave rise to many important declarations in matters of medical, conjugal, and social morality.

2. The Episcopal College.—Properly speaking, the episcopal college, as a subject of supreme authority over the universal church, is not adequately distinct from the Roman pontiff. The pope is a member of the college, and its head. Thus the plenitude of authority in the church resides in the episcopal college, under and with the pope, the bishop of Rome. The total college of bishops is conceived as the continuation of the total apostolic college, with the pope as successor to Peter and the other bishops as successors to the other apostles. By episcopal consecration the bishop becomes a member of the college with a responsibility and authority toward the whole church, not merely toward his own particular flock (*see* above, *Conferring Authority*).

One form in which the episcopal college as a whole has functioned from ancient times is the ecumenical council (*see* COUNCIL). It is the traditional teaching that the council has full and supreme authority in the church, including the power both of teaching and of government. As a subject of supreme authority, however, the council is not adequately distinct from the pope. He is a member of the council, indeed its head, in such wise that its existence and activity depend upon his convoking it, determining the agenda, presiding, and confirming its acts. Yet the acts of the council are the acts of the whole college of bishops; they are not the acts of the pope alone, with the other bishops merely advising. The pope, on the other hand, has by himself the same supreme authority as the college of bishops. While he does not act in affairs of greater moment without attention to the judgment of the bishops throughout the world, there are no matters reserved to a council which the pope himself has not the authority to decide or to enact.

Another form of implementation of the principle of collegiality is found in the Synod of Bishops established by Pope Paul VI, Sept. 14, 1965. Although the institution itself is permanent, it is not continuously active, but only when convoked in "general," "extraordinary," or "special" sessions, together with the pope, to provide information and counsel, and in particular cases to make deliberative decisions, upon matters of doctrine or discipline proposed in advance. To a large extent the membership of the sessions is determined by the election of representatives from the various national conferences of bishops throughout the world, on a scale proportionate to the membership of the conferences.

To a lesser degree the principle of the collegial authority of the bishops is also realized in the councils and conferences of the bishops of a province or nation, in which they exercise their providence not over their own special flock alone but over that larger portion of the church which they collectively govern (*see* below, *Local Councils and Conferences*).

3. The Roman Curia.—The pope is aided by a staff of cardinals, the Roman Curia ("court"), which acts as the judicial and executive organs of the papal office. The pontiff and the Curia together comprise the Holy See or Apostolic See; the term "see" (*sedes*), which originally signified a chair (a "seat" of authority; *cf. cathedra*, "throne"), has thus come to designate the authority itself, or the community governed, or the central government. Though the pope does not have sole responsibility for the church, he does have the responsibility for ordinary government, and the Roman Curia expedites his judicial and executive functions.

From very early times there is evidence of a special staff of advisers to the popes. Obviously the need for such a staff grew as centralization increased. At first the pope depended for consultation in matters of doctrine or discipline upon the Roman synods, composed of the bishops of the province of Rome, and, in the intervals, upon convocations of the Roman clergy, or *presbyterium*. The priests of the principal churches of Rome, the deacons of the seven regions of the city, and the bishops of the suburban dioceses around Rome, who were especially called into consultation, became the "cardinal" priests, deacons, and bishops (from *cardo*, "hinge" or "turning point"). From the 11th century prominent men were called to Rome from other countries and made cardinals, and from the 12th men were appointed cardinals of the Roman church while remaining in their own countries. (*See* further CARDINAL.) By the 12th century the college of cardinals had succeeded the Roman presbytery as the senate of the pope.

The cardinals usually met to advise the pope in the form of consistories, without distinction of departments or functions (*see* CONSISTORY). For particular matters, temporary commissions or congregations of cardinals would be appointed. But from early times, too, more permanent administrative organs were established. The Apostolic Chancery, for letters and records, existed in the 4th century; and the Datary, for the authentication of documents, appears in the 11th. In the 13th century the *auditorium* of the Rota, first constituted to prepare cases for the judgment of the pope, became itself a tribunal, and about the same time the function of the cardinal penitentiary, for absolutions or dispensations reserved

to the Holy See, was given departmental form. In the 16th century several new bodies were created: the Congregation of the Inquisition (1542); the Congregation of the Council, for the interpretation of the acts of the Council of Trent (1564); the Congregation of the Index (1571). The Curia's basic structure—offices, tribunals, and congregations—was gradually taking form.

The first systematic organization of the Curia was made by Sixtus V in 1588. He established 15 congregations, the principal departments, specifying their form and functions in a way that has remained substantially unchanged. Later some were dropped or combined, and others were added. Thus, for example, Sixtus' congregation for the fleet of the papal states became obsolete, while the following were created as new needs arose: the Congregation for the Propagation of the Faith (*de Propaganda Fide*, 1622) to moderate expanding missionary activity; the Congregation of Indulgences (1669), a function later transferred to the Sacred Penitentiary; the Congregation for Extraordinary Affairs (1814); the Congregation for the Eastern Churches, originally created as a section of *Propaganda* (1862); etc.

Principally to eliminate confusion of competence, with several congregations having jurisdiction in the same matter, and to reserve the judicial function more exclusively to the tribunals, a second thorough revision of the Curia was made by Pius X in 1908. With minor modifications this revision was incorporated in 1917 into the Code of Canon Law (can. 242, ff.). In this reform the tripartite structure of the Curia was formally established: congregations (12), tribunals (3), and offices (5).

In the period immediately before and after the second Vatican Council (1963–65), several new organizations were created by the Holy See (*e.g.*, the Secretariate for Promoting Christian Unity; the Council of the Laity), and the volume of work was immensely increased as a result of new modes of communication. The desirability of modernization was expressed by the council itself, particularly with reference to the various organs' number, nomenclature, competence, and coordination of functions, in the Decree on the Pastoral Office of Bishops (1965). Accordingly, a new constitution was issued by Pope Paul VI on Aug. 15, 1967. While retaining the basic structure of congregations, tribunals, and offices, the revision of Pope Paul added the title of secretariate, giving special status and function to the Secretariate of State, and suppressed several less active offices and congregations.

Secretariate of State, or Papal Secretariate.—This is perhaps the most distinctive contribution of Pope Paul's reform. Its function is to assist the pope in the care of the whole church and in his communication with the rest of the Curia. In addition to carrying out any papal commissions, the cardinal secretary of state convokes periodically the heads of all the other departments of the Curia with a view to coordinating their work and for general consultation. He is thus the pope's closest personal collaborator and executive assistant. Related to this secretariate, and under the same cardinal, is a Council for Public Ecclesiastical Affairs, analogous to the foreign ministry of civil governments.

Offices.—In general the offices are charged with the secretarial and material aspects of the activities of the Holy See. Besides the ancient Apostolic Chancery, the Treasury, the Administration of the Property of the Holy See, and the Prefecture of the Apostolic Palace, there are two additions of Pope Paul VI: the Prefecture of Finance and the Bureau of Statistics.

Tribunals.—The tribunals exercise judicial authority. The Sacred Penitentiary has competence in matters of a private nature. The Sacred Roman Rota serves as the Holy See's court for causes appealed from local tribunals or admitted to it in the first instance. The Supreme Apostolic Signatura judges special cases assigned by the pope, reviews hearings appealed from the Rota on the basis of procedure, decides the question of competence in matters related to more than one congregation, and takes cognizance of issues arising from administrative acts (*e.g.*, of the bishops) or from decisions of the other curial organs.

Secretariates.—The constitution of 1967 formally incorporated into the Curia the previously established secretariates (for Promoting Christian Unity, for Non-Christians, and for Non-Believers) and, analogous to these, the Council of the Laity and the Commission for Studies on Peace and Justice, both founded in 1967.

Congregations.—The great bulk of curial work is done by the congregations, all of which are juridically equal: the Congregation for the Doctrine of the Faith (formerly the Holy Office), with responsibility for matters of faith and morals and for disciplinary matters with which doctrinal issues are closely connected; the Congregation for Bishops (formerly Consistorial Congregation), concerned with the establishment and government of dioceses, the appointment of bishops, and the agenda of the episcopal conferences and local councils (*see* below); the Congregation for the Clergy (formerly Congregation of the Council; *see* above), concerned with the life and pastoral ministry of the clergy and with questions of general ecclesiastical discipline; the Congregation for the Eastern Churches, with authority over all matters involving members of the Eastern Rites individually or collectively; the Congregation for the Evangelization of the World (or Propagation of the Faith), with similar authority over the affairs of mission territories; the Congregation for Catholic Education (formerly Congregation for Seminaries and Universities), to supervise the academic formation of the clergy and the establishment and administration of Catholic schools; and the remaining congregations, whose functions are sufficiently described by their titles: the Congregations for the Discipline of the Sacraments; of Sacred Rites; and of Religious and Secular Institutes.

In the reform of Paul VI, the membership of the congregations, formerly restricted to cardinals, was extended to include in each congregation seven diocesan bishops from various parts of the world, chosen by the pope from recommendations of the conferences of bishops, for terms of five years. These are to be present at plenary sessions of their congregations, to be held at least once a year, in matters of greater moment and decisions of policy.

Though every cardinal is assigned to one or more congregations, the ordinary day-to-day business is necessarily conducted by those resident in Rome. Each congregation is headed by a cardinal prefect (the pope is no longer prefect of any congregation), a secretary, and other officials. To provide a more international representation and flexibility of approach, the officials are to be selected from various countries, and the members and secretaries of the congregations are assigned terms of five years (which, however, may be continued), with all appointments requiring confirmation within three months of a new pope's accession. To each congregation are also assigned, as consultors, clerical or lay experts in Rome or elsewhere, for one or two terms of five years.

The Curia is not a legislative body; its functions are executive and judicial. The congregations issue decrees or instructions with a view to the implementation of general church law; reply to questions of interpretation proposed by bishops or other members of the church; grant permissions, faculties, dispensations, or confirmations in matters reserved to the Holy See; and supervise the conduct of government at the diocesan or regional level. By reason of its special competence in matters of faith and morals, the Doctrinal Congregation also imparts guidance and directives pertaining to the magisterial order. Even within the range of its competence, however, the Curia does little without referral to the pope. Before undertaking any extraordinary project his approval is required; and all but the most ordinary business, or that for which special authority has been given, must be confirmed by him.

4. Local Ordinaries.—The pope and the episcopal college have authority over the whole church. But the Code of Canon Law states: "The bishops are the successors of the Apostles, and by divine disposition they are placed in charge of particular churches which they govern with ordinary power under the authority of the Roman Pontiff" (can. 329). Although the bishop of a diocese is the most familiar territorial head, the territorial divisions are more varied in nature and juridical constitution than this would suggest. In terms of the hierarchy not of orders but of jurisdiction, the expression "local ordinary" designates a certain level of governing authority, whether the superior of the territory is the bishop of a diocese or the vicar of a vicariate apostolic in mission countries, or the prelate or abbot in charge of a prelature or abbacy *nullius* (distinct from any diocese). The same term is applied to a vicar general, who enjoys practically the same jurisdic-

tion as the proper superior, and to the person temporarily in charge of a territory because of the incumbent's incapacity, demise, or transfer.

The authority of the local ordinary, like that of the church itself and of the pope and episcopal college, includes both teaching and government. Of the authority to teach in matters of faith and morals, the Code of Canon Law states: "Although the bishops are not endowed with infallibility in their teaching when acting individually or even when gathered in particular councils, yet they are, under the authority of the Roman Pontiff, truly teachers and masters with respect to the faithful committed to their care." Of the bishops' authority to govern in matters of discipline, the code states: "They have the right and duty to govern their diocese, in spiritual matters and in temporal, with legislative, judicial, and coactive power, to be exercised according to the norms of the sacred canons" (can. 335, sec. 1); this principle is extended to other local ordinaries in other canons. Judicial jurisdiction is exercised by the tribunal which should be established in every ecclesiastical territory, with the *officialis* usually taking the ordinary's place as judge. Executive jurisdiction is exercised in various administrative or coactive acts, as the issuing of dispensations, regulations, or penalties. Legislative jurisdiction is exercised in the enactment of diocesan statutes or in the issuance of precepts applying to some temporary or local need.

The ordinary, of course, cannot enact contrarily to the laws of the universal church, permitting what it prohibits or prohibiting what it positively permits. In certain specified matters his power is further restricted by the necessity to obtain the consent of the cathedral chapter (where this institution exists; *see* CATHEDRAL) or of the diocesan consultors; but for the most part his dependence upon his advisers is limited to consultation. In the exercise of his legislative function he may act with representative members of his clergy and laity, sometimes in a diocesan synod (which should be held at stated intervals); but even in the synodal procedure the ordinary himself is the sole legislator. It was urged by the second Vatican Council (1965) that an advisory pastoral council be established in each diocese, with the participation of chosen clergy, religious, and laity.

The diocese is divided into parishes, presided over by pastors. It is normally upon the pastor and his assistants that the faithful depend for the ordinary ministrations of the Holy Sacrifice, the sacraments, the preaching of the Word of God, catechetical instruction, blessings, and other sacramentals. The pastor's jurisdiction is concerned chiefly with the personal spiritual welfare of the individual rather than with affairs in the public interest, though in certain emergency situations he is empowered to act in matters usually reserved to the local ordinary.

5. Local Councils and Conferences.—Besides the division into dioceses or analogous territories, each under its local ordinary, groups of such territories are formed into ecclesiastical provinces, corresponding so far as feasible with political divisions. The ordinary of the principal see is called the "metropolitan," the other bishops or ordinaries his "suffragans." The metropolitan is not juridically superior to his suffragans and does not have ordinary jurisdiction over them or over the province as a whole, though he is given by the law certain rights of vigilance and of extraordinarily supplying for deficiencies in their administration. (*See* also METROPOLITAN.) The patriarchs of the Eastern churches are not comparable to the Latin metropolitans; they do have direct and ordinary jurisdiction over the whole territory of the patriarchate and over the bishops and metropolitans of its subordinate divisions. Although the metropolitan is, ideally, an archbishop with an archdiocese, the title of archbishop is sometimes conferred as a personal distinction, and the rank of archdiocese may attach to a territory which is not the principal see of a province. Periodically all the ordinaries of a province should be assembled in the form of a provincial council under the presidency of the metropolitan.

Periodically, too, though at no specified intervals, the ordinaries of all the provinces of a nation or comparable area may gather in what is called plenary council (as the three plenary councils held at Baltimore for the whole of the United States in

1852, 1866, and 1884). For these the consent of the Holy See is required, and the latter is represented by a legate who convokes the council and presides. The acts of a plenary council must be confirmed by the Holy See. Unlike the diocesan synod, where the bishop is the sole legislator, the plenary and provincial councils are themselves legislative bodies. Their laws are valid for the whole territory involved, and the ordinaries can dispense only for a just cause and in particular cases.

Similar to the local councils, but on a less solemn scale and more adapted to the managing of contemporary and changing situations, are the episcopal conferences, composed of all the bishops of a country and commonly held annually. These were given official canonical status by decree of the second Vatican Council in 1965. For the most part the function of the conferences is consultative; *i.e.*, their resolutions, etc., do not have binding force unless they are accepted and enacted by the individual local ordinaries. In specific matters, however, determined by law or particular mandate of the pope, their decisions have the force of law throughout the territory, if they are enacted by a two-thirds majority and confirmed by the Holy See. The elected chairman of each conference is an *ex officio* member of the "extraordinary" and "special" sessions of the Synod of Bishops of the universal church.

6. Distinction of Rites.—The principles outlined above are valid both for the church of the West and for that of the East, though the terminology employed (*e.g.*, "ordinary" rather than "hierarch") is that of Western law and tradition. There is, however, another division, on the bases of liturgy and discipline, not only of a territorial nature but of jurisdiction itself, between the Eastern churches or rites in communion with Rome (*see* below, *The Catholic Eastern Rites*) and the Western or Latin rite. The primal basis of the distinction of Eastern and Western churches was the division of the Roman Empire into eastern and western parts under Diocletian in the 3rd century. In the 10th century and following, all of the Eastern churches were separated from Rome at one time or another; in the process of reunion (on the part of those that were reunited) they were reestablished hierarchically, retaining, however, their own liturgy and the discipline they had carried on from earlier times or had established by provincial synods. In 1949, however, a unified code of law for all the Uniate Eastern churches began to appear, being promulgated as the separate sections were completed. (*See* CANON LAW: *Eastern Churches*.)

In general the organization of the Eastern churches, in its larger outlines, is the same as that of the Latin rite, except for the jurisdiction of the patriarchs. But whereas the territorial division of dioceses, etc., in the Latin rite is exclusive, in the sense that only one ordinary has jurisdiction over a territory, the jurisdiction of the Eastern hierarchs may be cumulative; *i.e.*, within the same general territory more than one superior may have jurisdiction, with respect to the subjects of his own rite. Outside the territories of the patriarchates, the faithful of the Eastern rites are generally served by the Latin clergy; though in some areas, where they are more numerous, they may have their own clergy and churches and even their own hierarchy. Conversely, in regions predominantly Oriental the faithful of the Latin rite are generally served by the Eastern clergy and hierarchy. But even under the ministry of the clergy of another rite, the faithful retain their own proper rite and, so far as possible, its own specific discipline.

The principle for determining the rite to which a Catholic belongs is that a person is ascribed to that rite in the ceremonies of which he is baptized. In the case of children, this should be the rite of the parents, or of the father (if the parents are of mixed rite), or of the Catholic parent (if they are of mixed religion). Once ascribed legitimately to one rite, a person cannot change to another by his own volition or by the sole fact of following the liturgy and practice of the other for any length of time, but solely by indult from the Holy See. This is not readily given, as it is desirable to maintain the integrity and vitality of the various rites. Converts, however, are allowed to choose the rite they prefer; a wife may, at her own choice, change to her husband's rite at the time of marriage or later; and children under the legal age of puberty are automatically transferred if a change of rite is legiti-mately obtained by their parents or, in a case of mixed rite, by their father.

7. States of Perfection.—From very early times there has existed a special state, canonically recognized and regulated, composed of those who dedicate themselves to the pursuit of Christian perfection through the exercise of the evangelical "counsels" of poverty, chastity, and obedience, to which they bind themselves by public profession of vows. The canonical development of the state of perfection has seen many variations; but at least from the 6th century it was considered to include two essential elements: living in community and professing the three public vows (*see* MONASTICISM; VOW).

From the 17th century in fact, and since 1918 in the law itself, similar recognition has been extended to the "societies of common life," which, while living in common, do not make profession of the three counsels in the form of public vows accepted by the church. As of 1947, moreover, by enactment of Pius XII, "secular institutes," composed of clerics or lay people who bind themselves to the three evangelical counsels but do not live in common, have also acquired the dignity of a canonical state of perfection (*see* SECULAR INSTITUTE).

Members of these organizations are said to be in a state of perfection not in the sense that they have achieved perfection or possess it in a greater degree than others but simply because they have adopted a way of life that is conducive to the pursuit of perfection and have bound themselves to strive for their own sanctification and that of the world.

Each of these societies has the authority necessary for the direction of its members toward the ends, personal and collective, of the institute. For various reasons, especially the supraterritorial character of the larger institutes, it has been the practice, since at least the 11th century, to confer upon clerical orders a power of jurisdiction comparable to that of the local ordinaries, for the government of their own internal affairs and specific ministries; they are to this extent subject immediately to the Roman pontiff rather than to the ordinary of the territory. The major superiors of these institutes are also entitled ordinaries. This privilege, known as exemption, is limited by many provisions of the law in which the religious are subjected to the jurisdiction of the local ordinary—generally speaking, in all matters concerned with pastoral care.

8. The Laity.—A more satisfying recognition and formulation of the status and function of the laity in the church was one of the principal aims of the second Vatican Council. The church was founded for the purpose of spreading the Kingdom of Christ throughout the earth, to enable all men to share in his saving redemption, and that through them the whole world might enter into a relationship with Christ. All who are incorporated into the church form one body, and every member has a responsibility for the fulfillment of the church's total mission in the world. The laity, therefore, have not only their own personal vocation to sanctity and perfection in their state of life, but also a commission to participate actively in the threefold office of Christ and of the church. They do this by the offering of spiritual sacrifice, by bearing witness in their lives to the values of the gospel message, and by striving for the more perfect realization of Christ's redemptive mission.

The redemptive mission of Christ includes the salvation of men and the renewal of the temporal order. The laity participate in both. They assist the hierarchy in its office by advising ecclesiastical superiors in matters of their special competence, by teaching and catechetical instruction, by aiding in the organization and promotion of concerted efforts toward various religious objectives, etc. But their more specific apostolate is the endeavour to infuse a Christian spirit into the mentality, customs, laws, and structures of the community of men. By their example, by the spoken and written word, and by cooperative activity they are to be the leaven by which the world is permeated with the spirit of the gospel, created goods are perfected and directed more effectively to the ends for which they were made, and the order of truth, justice, love, and freedom is realized on earth.

(J. J. RE.)

C. The Catholic Eastern Rites

In this article, the word "rite" signifies not merely liturgical ceremonies but the whole discipline and organization of particular churches. The Catholic Eastern rites are those which have reestablished union (hence Eastern rite Catholics are often called Uniates) or canonical communion with the Roman Apostolic See, and thus with the Roman Catholic Church. In this union they accept the Catholic faith, they keep the seven sacraments, and they recognize the pope of Rome as supreme head of the church. But they retain all other characteristics, such as liturgy, spirituality, sacred art, and especially organization, proper to themselves. (*See above, Division of Functions: Distinction of Rites.*) Catholics of Eastern rites are estimated to number about 10,500,000, including around 800,000 in the United States.

The special status of the Catholic churches of Eastern rite was guaranteed on union with Rome and was approved again by the decree *De ecclesiis catholicis orientalibus* of the second Vatican Council, promulgated on Nov. 21, 1964. Their organization is based on the special Oriental canon law of the period both of the undivided church and of their separation. In 1929 the Holy See undertook the codification of the Oriental canon law. The section *De personis*, which deals with the organization of the Catholic Eastern rites, was published in 1957 (*see* Canon Law: *Eastern Churches*).

1. Organization.—The supreme head of the Eastern rite churches is the pope. The central organ of the Holy See for them is the Congregation for the Eastern Churches. The prefect of this congregation is the pope himself, and a cardinal pro-prefect performs the ordinary functions of chairman. The congregation is competent for the Oriental churches in all matters (except certain specified cases) and has exclusive jurisdiction in specified countries in Eastern Europe and the Middle East. The individual Catholic Eastern churches are organized differently according to their historical, ethnic, and political situation, the number of their faithful, the degree of their evolution, etc. The following organizational units are found:

Patriarchates.—These comprise a certain number of dioceses of a single rite, under the jurisdiction of a patriarch. The patriarchs, according to the Eastern canon law, have special rights and privileges; in the general hierarchy they rank after the cardinals and before all other bishops. In the 1960s there were six Catholic Eastern patriarchates.

Major Archiepiscopates.—Next to the patriarchs are major archbishops, who also govern a certain number of dioceses of their rite but whose territory has not yet been erected into a patriarchate. The only major archiepiscopate in the 1960s was Leopolis (Lvov, in the Ukrainian S.S.R.) of the Ukrainians, established in 1963.

Metropolitanates.—These correspond to an ecclesiastical province independent of the patriarchates and major archiepiscopates, and comprise a certain number of dioceses. One of them is the metropolis, and its archbishop, the metropolitan, is head of the whole metropolitanate. There are seven Catholic Eastern metropolitanates.

Eparchies.—These correspond to the Latin dioceses. Although they are usually subject to one of the above-mentioned higher organizations, six of them are immediately subject to the Holy See and two to a Latin metropolitan see (Hajdudorog in Hungary and Krizevci in Yugoslavia).

Exarchies.—These correspond to vicariates, and their bishops govern not by ordinary jurisdiction but by delegated authority. In the 1960s there were 12 apostolic exarchies (with authority delegated by the pope) and a few patriarchal exarchies or vicariates.

Apostolic Administrations.—These are territories whose administration the Holy See, for certain reasons, has assumed, entrusting them to the care of a neighbouring bishop or of a special bishop called apostolic administrator. This kind of organization is intended to be transitory, and in the 1960s there were only two.

Exarchical Monasteries.—These are exempt from the jurisdiction of a local bishop and subject immediately to the Holy See or to a patriarch. Grottaferrata, near Rome, was the only such monastery in the 1960s.

Ordinariates.—These, the lowest organizational units, are found either at an early stage of development, such as a mission, or in areas with a small number of faithful. Usually the head is not a bishop. Besides these, from 1950 onward four pluri-ritual ordinariates were instituted for the Eastern Catholics of some western countries (Argentina, Austria, Brazil, France).

2. Eastern Rite Churches.—The Catholic Eastern churches, grouped according to rites, are as follows:

Alexandrine (Alexandrian) Rite.—(*a*) Copts. In 1739 the Coptic bishop Athanasius joined the Catholic Church. In 1895 Pope Leo XIII reestablished the Alexandrine patriarchate for the Catholic Copts in Egypt, with the patriarchal residence in Cairo and two suffragan sees at Hermopolis Major (Al Minya) and Thebes (Sohag). In 1947 a fourth diocese, Lycopolis (Asyut), was erected. Catholic Copts number about 90,000.

(*b*) Ethiopians.—The faithful were won by the apostolate of Latin missionaries—Lazarists from 1839 and Capuchins from 1846. The first ecclesiastical organization was an ordinariate, erected in 1930 and entrusted to the care of an Ethiopian bishop, consecrated in Rome. In 1951 it was divided into two apostolic exarchies. Finally in 1961 the Ethiopian Catholic Church was organized into a metropolitanate, with Addis Ababa as its metropolis, Adigrat and Asmara (in Eritrea) being suffragan sees. The number of the faithful is about 60,000.

Antiochene (Antiochian) Rite.—(*a*) Syrians. In 1656 Andrew Akidjan, a Syrian Catholic priest, was elected bishop of Aleppo and in 1662 patriarch of all Syrians. However, the continuous series of the Syrian Catholic patriarchs of Antioch did not begin till 1782, when the Catholic bishop of the same city, Michael Giarweh, was again elected patriarch. The patriarchs resided successively in Deir al Zapharan, Sharfeh, Aleppo, Mardin (in Turkey), and finally in Beirut. There are four patriarchal vicariates or exarchies (in Lebanon, Turkey, Jordan, and Egypt), five archdioceses (Aleppo, Baghdad, Damascus, Homs, and Mosul), and one diocese (Hassake). The patriarch I. G. Tappouni (elected 1929) became the first Syrian cardinal in 1935. The faithful number about 80,000.

(*b*) Maronites. The Maronites of Lebanon are the only Eastern church which is completely Catholic (*see* Maronites). The patriarch was for many centuries the only hierarch, helped by several auxiliary bishops who resided with him. Dioceses were first formed in 1736. The patriarch resides in Bkirki and governs the diocese of Gibail-Batrun. There are further two archdioceses (Aleppo and Beirut), nine dioceses (Baalbek, Cyprus [residence in Antelias, Lebanon], Damascus, Byblos, Cairo, Saïda [Sidon], Sarba, Tripolis in Lebanon, and Tyre), and one apostolic administration (Laodicea) entrusted to the archbishop of Aleppo. The number of the faithful in the patriarchate is about 470,000 and there are about 380,000 in North and South America.

(*c*) Malankarese. In 1930 a group of the former Indian Jacobites in Kerala, South India, under the leadership of Mar Ivanios, returned to the Roman Catholic Church. In 1932 Pope Pius XI erected for them a metropolitanate, with Trivandrum as the metropolis and Tiruvalla as a suffragan see. These number about 125,000.

Chaldean Rite.—(*a*) Chaldeans. The Chaldeans of Iraq returned to the Catholic Church from Nestorianism (*see* Nestorians). The first union was realized in 1552, when the elected patriarch John Sulaqa went to Rome and made his profession of the Catholic faith. Other unions were realized in 1672, 1771, and 1778. For all Catholic Chaldeans there exists since 1830 the patriarchate of Babylonia. The patriarchal residence was at first in the monastery Rabban Hormizd, then in Mosul, and finally in Baghdad. Besides the patriarchal diocese of Baghdad, there are four archdioceses (Basra, Kirkuk, Sehnah—residence at Teheran—and Urmia, to which is united the diocese of Salmas) and seven dioceses (Aleppo, Alqosh, Amadiyah, Aqra, Beirut, Mosul, and Zakhu). There are about 190,000 Chaldean Uniates.

(*b*) Malabarese. The Malabarese are the Christians of St. Thomas in Kerala, South India (*see* Malabar Christians). For many centuries they were in close contact with the Nestorian patriarchate in Mesopotamia. They took up relations with Rome on their own initiative after the Portuguese arrived in India. In 1887 Pope Leo XIII erected for them two apostolic vicariates and in 1896 a third. In the same year there were appointed the first three Malabarese bishops. There are two metropolitanates: the archdiocese of Ernakulam (1923), with Kothamangalam, Tellicherry, and Trichur as suffragan sees; and the archdiocese of Changanacherry (1956), with Kottayam and Palai as suffragan sees. Besides these in Kerala, there is in central India the ordinariate of Chanda (1962), which is a mission of the Malabarese rite. The faithful number about 1,500,000.

Armenian Rite.—The Armenian Catholic patriarchate originated in 1740, when the Armenian bishop of Aleppo, Abraham Ardzivian, already a Catholic, was elected patriarch of Sis in Cilicia (Turkey). In 1911 the Armenian church was divided into 19 dioceses, but during the persecution of the Armenians in Turkey (1915–18) several dioceses were abolished and the faithful left for other countries. In 1928 the hierarchical organization was revised and new episcopal sees were successively erected. The Armenian patriarch of Cilicia resides in Beirut (Lebanon) and personally administers that diocese. There exist further three archdioceses (Aleppo, Baghdad, and Istanbul), three dioceses (Alexandria, Isfahan, and Kamichlie [in Syria]), one apostolic exarchy (Paris, France), and two ordinariates (Athens and Gherla [in Rumania]). There are fewer than 100,000 faithful of the Armenian rite.

Byzantine Rite.—(*a*) Albanians. A small group of about 400 Albanians of Byzantine rite already existed in 1939 when the Holy See erected an apostolic administration for them. After 1945 this group was dispersed.

(*b*) Belorussians. In the 17th–18th centuries there were several million Belorussians of the Byzantine rite belonging to the Kiev metropolitanate. But after the annexation of their territory to Russia, the union was persecuted and finally abolished in 1839. After 1918 in Belorussia, which was then under Poland, several thousands of former Eastern Catholics returned to the Catholic Church and an apostolic visitor was appointed for them. After 1945 this group was dispersed. A few, however, emigrated to the West, and in 1960 they were given a bishop residing in London.

(*c*) Bulgarians. The small group of Bulgarians, heirs of the union of 1859, grew to about 80,000 but was later reduced to about 5,000. There is one apostolic exarchy in Sofia.

(*d*) Greeks. This small group of 2,550 originated in Constantinople and in Thrace about 1882. After 1920 a part of them settled in Greece. There are two apostolic exarchies, at Istanbul and Athens.

(*e*) Hungarians. These are heirs of the Union of Uzhgorod (1646). There is one diocese, Hajdudorog (1912, residence in Nyiregyhaza), and one apostolic exarchy, Miskolc (1923), both governed by the same bishop. There are about 250,000 faithful.

(*f*) Italo-Albanians or Italo-Greeks. These are heirs of the Albanians who emigrated to south Italy after the Turks seized Albania in the 15th century. All of them gradually and without any special juridical act were united with the Catholic Church. Part of them lost their Byzantine rite. Those who preserved it are organized in two dioceses, Lungro (in Calabria) and Piana degli Albanesi (in Sicily). To this rite the exarchical monastery of Grottaferrata near Rome also belongs. The faithful number about 70,000.

(*g*) Melkites (Melchites). The union of the Melkites in the patriarchate of Antioch originated in 1724 with the election of a Catholic patriarch, Cyril VI. He was followed by several bishops and about a third of the faithful. There were also some small accessions in the patriarchates of Alexandria and Jerusalem. There is only one Catholic Melkite patriarch, who bears the title of Antioch, Alexandria, and Jerusalem and governs all three patriarchates. In each he has his own diocese (Damascus, Jerusalem, Alexandria) and is helped by a patriarchal vicar. There are seven archdioceses (Aleppo, Beirut, Bozrah [Bosra], Homs, Laodicea, Tyre, and Petra–Philadelphia [residence at Amman]) and six dioceses (Acre [residence at Haifa], Baalbek, Baniyas, Saïda [Sidon], Tripolis in Lebanon, and Zahleh-Furzol). The number of the faithful in the three patriarchates totals about 250,-000 and there are about 150,000 abroad.

(*h*) Rumanians. They were united with the Roman Catholic Church in 1698, when a union in Transylvania was stipulated by the bishop of Alba Iulia and the majority of the clergy. In 1930 a metropolitanate was erected with Făgăraş–Alba Iulia as the metropolitan see and Cluj–Gherla, Lugoj, Maramureş, and Oradea as suffragan sees. The union was officially suppressed by the government in 1948, at which time there were more than 1,500,000 faithful.

(*i*) Russians. About 1900 a small group of Russians joined the Catholic Church, preserving their Byzantine rite. In 1917 an exarchy was instituted for them, which was dispersed a few years later under the Communists. In emigration there is one Russian Catholic bishop, with residence in Rome.

(*j*) Ruthenians or Carpatho-Russians. The union effected in Uzhgorod in 1646 was the beginning of the general return of the Ruthenians to the Catholic Church. They had one diocese in Mukachevo (residence Uzhgorod), which was suppressed by the Soviet authorities in 1949. The number of the faithful in 1944 was 462,000. A considerable number of Ruthenians emigrated after 1880 to the United States, where they have two dioceses: Pittsburgh, Pa., and Passaic, N.J. The number of the faithful in the two U.S. dioceses is about 315,000.

(*k*) Slovaks. A minority of Slovaks belonged to the Byzantine rite between the Union of Uzhgorod (1646) and its abolition in Czechoslovakia by the government in 1950. They had one diocese, Presov. Many of them emigrated to North America, and in 1964 they were given a bishop as apostolic visitor, residing in Toronto, Ont.

(*l*) Ukrainians or Galician Ruthenians. These are numerically the largest Eastern Catholic church. They are heirs of the Unions of Brest-Litovsk (1596) and of Galicia (1700). After the partition of Poland, the part of this church that was assigned to Russia was eliminated in 1839 and in 1875. The part assigned to Austria was organized in 1807 into a metropolitanate, which in 1944 comprised the metropolitan see of Galich (Halicz) and Lvov (Lviv) and the suffragan sees of Przemysl, Stanislav (Ivano-Frankovsk), and Lemkyvcina. In 1946, after the occupation of the territory by the Soviet Union, this church was officially suppressed and the bishops imprisoned. In 1963 the Holy See elevated the metropolitan (later Cardinal) Josif Slipyj to the rank of a major archbishop. A great number of Ukrainians emigrated to both Americas and elsewhere. Their organization is as follows: the metropolitanate of Canada, with the sees of Winnipeg (metropolitan see), Edmonton, Saskatoon, and Toronto; the metropolitanate of the United States, with the archieparchy of Philadelphia, Pa., and the eparchies of Stamford, Conn., and St. Nicholas of Chicago. There are also the following apostolic exarchies: Australia (Melbourne), Brazil (Curitiba), France (Paris), England (London), and Germany (Munich). In the Ukraine the faithful number about 3,500,000; elsewhere there are about 750,000, including 280,000 in the three U.S. sees.

(*m*) Yugoslavs. The only Catholic diocese of the Byzantine rite in Yugoslavia, that of Krizevci in Croatia, contains faithful of different nationalities and heirs of different unions beginning in 1611. Their number is about 60,000. (M. Lo.)

II. THE CHURCH IN EUROPE

A. First Centuries

1. Preeminence of Rome.—Early in the history of the Christian church it came to be recognized that the human institution that is the fullness of the godhead bodily was to be governed on earth by a sacramental sovereign as agent or representative, the apostle or "vicar" of Christ. That this vicar of Christ should be the bishop of Rome belongs to the "logic of history." If, in "the fullness of time, God sent forth his son born of a woman," he selected the Roman Empire as the historical circumstance of that incarnation. The city of Rome was not merely the metropolis of humanity but the seat of an actual and formative sovereignty beyond comparison more effective and significant than that of any other imperial city. There if anywhere the City of God must encounter the "fullness of manhood bodily." (*See* EARLY CHRISTIAN CHURCH: *Organization.*)

Within a generation of the death of the apostles, Roman legions had destroyed the Temple at Jerusalem. Less than a century later the tradition of St. Peter's presence in Rome was, as Louis Duchesne stated, "precise and universal." Duchesne further declared that Dionysius of Corinth in Greece, Irenaeus in Gaul, Clement and Origen in Alexandria and Tertullian in Africa all referred to it, that in Rome itself Caius, about 200, pointed out the tomb of the apostles, that by the 3rd century popes built on their title of successors of St. Peter and that their right to this title is nowhere denied. Clement (c. 97) thinks it natural for the church in Rome to address a letter of advice to the church in Corinth upon the outbreak of schism. Ignatius of Antioch, late in the 1st century A.D., apostrophizes the Roman Church with a series of titles such as he addresses to no other. It is above all "a church presiding in charity, maintaining the law of Christ, and bearer of the Father's name."

2. Persecution.—The city of the Caesars and the Senate and people of Rome was the seat of the apostles; it was also the city of martyrs and heretics. Persecution and heresy contributed to the mature self-consciousness of the church. The offense of Christianity as defined by Trajan (c. 112) was of the nature of treason —otherwise harmless. The greatest persecutions, those under Decius (250–253), Valerian (257–260), and Diocletian (303–311), were virtual acts of war against "a sovereignty within a sovereignty" which seemed to threaten the empire. The danger would have been as real as it seemed but for the peculiar combination of faith and morals which enabled Christians to "dwell on earth as citizens of heaven" (*Epistle to Diognetus,* 2nd or 3rd century). They could thus pray for the emperor's welfare while they denied his divine title (Cyprian). Origen's confidence that Christ is stronger than the emperor, the army, and the Senate and people of Rome was inevitably and essentially Christian. The organic unity of the church was vigorous and visible in ceaseless missionary activity at every level of society and in every province. Christians nursed the sick, visited the prisoners, found employment for the idle, and cared for the poor, orphans, widows, and slaves.

All this, inspired and confirmed by a naïve sense of divine presence, omnipotence, and justice, gave the church not only authority over the whole life of its rapidly multiplying membership but an independence of imperial sanctions. The martyrs made explicit what the Christian faith had always implied, a totally new conception of the majesty of the human being as such and of human institutions. Constantine may have been a mystic, but he was certainly a political realist. Paganism died of its unreality. Julian's attempt to revive it in revolt against a corrupt and heretical Christianity (361–362) was no more than an adventure of sentiment and ideology.

3. Establishment of Orthodoxy.—Meanwhile the church defined its faith and established an orthodoxy. Definition is not, in the Catholic view, identical with the faith, but it is the means by which the faith becomes incarnate and available in the world and, as such, is implied in and authorized by the incarnation of God. It is thus conditioned by the "fullness of time" and is given to the church by the same authority that created the church, when and as the purpose of redemption and the existence of the church require it. So given it is infallible and final; but it is also the conclusion of a stage in the history of the church on earth, and its enunciation is prepared by a period of questions and uncertain or inadequate or controversial answers. The New Testament, whose canon was fixed c. 120, and the formulary known as the Apostles' Creed, used for the instruction of catechumens at the beginning of the 3rd century, both reveal the doubts and questions which assailed the primitive Christian. (*See* BIBLE: *Canon and Text: Canon of the New Testament;* CREED.)

The Gospels and the Acts were historical documents; the creed is a catalogue of facts. As against the Jews, the apostolic church proclaimed an eschatology which was no longer a promise but a present reality. As against the Docetism and Gnosticism (*qq.v.*) which represent the perennial reluctance to accept the faith as a fact, the New Testament and the creeds emphasized the event and the institution. Gnostic theories—those of Cerinthus, Valentinus, Basilides, Carpocrates, and others—were not and did not

claim to be histories. They were cosmological myths and speculations, ingenious and sometimes profound metaphysical guesses, against which the primitive church affirmed the supernatural history and, in doing so, realized its own divinely appointed form and existence. Fact implied revelation; revelation implied authority and tradition; and all implied the presence on earth of God in the person of Christ and in the Holy Spirit who informed the Holy Catholic Church. Irenaeus (c. 186) finds the authority in "the tradition of the great and ancient church known to all men which was founded and constituted by the most glorious apostles Peter and Paul: by its traditions and its faith announced to all men and descended through the succession of its bishops to us, we confound all those who gather where they ought not" (*Adversus haereses,* iii, 381).

Irenaeus, who wrote against the Valentinians, gave also an account of all the principal heresies down to his time. Justin Martyr wrote, besides his *Apologia,* a work against all heresies which is lost. Hippolytus in his *Refutation of All Heresies* attacked 32 heresies. Epiphanius in the 4th century catalogued 80 heresies in the *Panarion.*

B. From Constantine to Charlemagne

Conversion of the emperor brought into the church all the problems of the empire. Of these the most urgent was the pagan habit of toleration expressed in the so-called Edict of Milan (313), issued in the name of Licinius and Constantine, that "everyone may have licence to worship whatever he pleases." (*See* CONSTANTINE.) Such toleration came to the Christians as relief, but imperial protection raised the old question of Christ and Caesar in a new, subtle, and dangerous form. It not only threatened to confound the church with imperial administration but exposed the faith to the speculative ingenuity and dispute endemic in the Greco-Roman world.

These two secular problems coalesced to make theology the subject of party strife. The teaching of Arius, according to whom the *Logos* was a creature not divine but free, mutable, and adopted as Son of God in prevision of his merits, revived the ancient reluctance of the philosophical pagan to accept the incarnation as a fact and relieved the Arian of the revelation and authority which faith in the supreme mystery demanded and presupposed. It was a rationalization not apostolic or holy or catholic, and the Christians who adopted it ceased to be Christian.

At the Council of Nicaea (325) the word *homoousios* ("consubstantial"), accepted to affirm the deity of Christ against the Arians, was probably suggested by Roman legates. Eusebius, bishop of Nicomedia, who, like Arius, had learned his theology from Lucian of Antioch, used the heresy of Arius as an occasion of intrigue. Without disputing the decrees of the Council of Nicaea he devised an imperial formula to comprehend Arians and Catholics and gained the support of Constantine and of his successor, Constantius (337–361), for a policy which seemed to promise imperial peace and actually promoted ecclesiastical dissension. This policy not only raised Arian bishops to most of the Eastern sees but meant also constant secret interference by bishops in the jurisdiction of their brother bishops, the employment of imperial prefects and police in the enforcement of partisan decrees, and the habit of using theological formulas not to define the faith but as instruments of ecclesiastical diplomacy. Thus by the carefully packed Council of Tyre (335) Athanasius, bishop of Alexandria, was deposed on frivolous charges and an Arian raised, with the aid of imperial police, to the see. At Antioch in 341 an assembly of 100 bishops issued an ambiguous formulary denying that they were followers of Arius but evading the Nicene Creed. Finally, in 359, imperial pressure enforced a similar evasion on the whole episcopate, both Western and Eastern, at the councils of Ariminum and Seleucia. In 360 the formula was accepted which "with a little complaisance Athanasius and Aetius might have repeated together"; and in 361 Constantius was succeeded by Julian, and Arian victory by pagan reaction.

Rome and the West remained comparatively free from the heresy and policy of the East. No longer head of the empire, Rome was still head of the church; the decline from its imperial status emphasized its ecclesiastical independence. The bishop's residence was established on the Caelian Hill in the ancient house of the Laterani, owned by Fausta, Constantine's wife; and there Pope Miltiades held a council in 313. A basilica was raised, the existing Church of the Lateran. Athanasius, exiled from Alexandria, visited Rome. His news of Anthony, Pachomius, and the desert fathers kindled among wealthy Romans an interest in ascetic and monastic life which bore fruit in the next generation (see MONASTICISM); and in 340, before Pope Julius I and a council of 50 Western bishops, he was acquitted of the charges which had led to his deposition at the Council of Tyre. The Eastern bishops, who had asked to be invited to this council in Rome, nevertheless declined the invitation when it came. To their ultimatum requiring him to choose between Athanasius and themselves, Pope Julius replied that it was natural to hear complaints of bishops who said that they had been unjustly deposed; that in the absence of accusers he had examined the only available evidence, which they had themselves supplied at the Council of Tyre; and that he was concerned not with trifling stories but with the unity of the church.

(For the problems of this period of history, see further ARIUS; ARIANISM; ATHANASIUS, SAINT; COUNCIL; CONSTANTINE.)

1. Eastern Schisms.—Roman theology had not generated the controversial and speculative subtleties which divided the East. A schism left by persecution, between those who had endured and those who compromised with the pagans, had occasioned some disorder which was soon overcome. A greater schism, that of the Donatists (q.v.), rent the diocese of Carthage. To the historian its main interest lies in its effect upon Augustine, who during 16 years of controversy matured his conception of the Catholic Church. He was baptized by Ambrose in 387. Two years earlier Jerome had retired to Bethlehem to complete his translation of the Bible (Vulgate).

Ambrose, born at Trier about 340, son of the prefect of Gaul, became governor of Aemilia-Liguria (capital at Milan) in 370 and, on the death of the Arian bishop of Milan, Auxentius, in 374, was appointed bishop. (See AMBROSE, SAINT.) One of the best of Roman governors thus became one of the greatest of Christian bishops. His most significant task was to resist the inclination of the empire to control the church. Ambrose's friend Theodosius in 379 was made coemperor by the emperor Gratian, and in 380 was baptized a Catholic. In 381 he summoned a council to Constantinople (the second general council). Ambrose at the same time presided over a council at Aquileia.

Both councils condemned Arianism; Theodosius decreed that "all beliefs contrary to the faith clearly taught by the pontiff Damasus and by Peter, bishop of Alexandria, were heresy." The council also declared that "the bishop of Constantinople shall have the pre-eminence of honour after the bishop of Rome, for this city is the new Rome," thus founding ecclesiastical dignity on imperial status. Rome rejected this principle. In 383 Theodosius convoked a meeting of Catholic and Arian leaders, and upon its failure issued another edict, never strictly enforced, forbidding heretical worship, public and private.

The murder of Gratian (383) and the advance of Maximus through Gaul and Italy called Theodosius to the West, where, after the defeat and death of Maximus, he resided for nearly three years at Milan. The emperor Valentinian II also lived there, likewise under the personal influence of Ambrose. The bishop proclaimed and maintained the principle that "the emperor is within the church, not over the church."

Pope Leo (q.v.) was called upon to state once more and in uncompromising terms the fact in which and by which the Catholic Church exists. The Nestorian and Monophysite doctrines of the nature of Christ, both forms of the perennial desire to evade the central Christian dogma, had to be put down. The pope's definition, acclaimed by the Council of Chalcedon as "the voice of Peter," was an uncompromising statement:

Following, then, in the footsteps of the holy fathers, we all teach in harmony that the Son and our Lord Jesus Christ are one and the same, one and the same perfect in godhead, the same perfect in human nature, true God and true man, the same made of a rational soul and body, consubstantial with the Father according to His godhead, consubstantial with us according to His human nature, made in all things like us without sin: according to His godhead begotten of His Father before all ages; the same in these last days for us and for our salvation born according to human nature of the Virgin Mary, the Mother of God; one and the same to be acknowledged as Christ the Son, the Lord, the only begotten, in two natures not removed by reason of their union, but rather the characteristics of each preserved united together in one person and subsistence, not divided nor shared among two persons but one and the same: Son, Only-begotten, God, Word, Lord, Jesus, Christ, as the prophets before had said of Him, as He Himself taught us and as the creed of the fathers has handed down to us.

In that statement, there is obviously no attempt to placate human reason and no appeal to human experience. Words are used to command a rational submission of faith to a fact which transcends reason. It is the voice of original authority, not a resultant explanation; foundation, not superstructure—"the stone which the Lord laid as a foundation." Man is whole, is perfectly and eternally human in Christ who is Very God. Nothing can violate the distinction between God and Man. The incarnation does not violate but transcends it, and it is thus not an evolution but the consummate act of transcendent godhead which the church announces and embodies. It purports to be a statement of the atonement and sacrifice in which human nature is restored to perfect unity with divine or absolute being. It is announced and accepted as fact by the Roman bishop, "the voice of Peter," at the Council of Chalcedon. Thus by the 5th century the church is fully conscious of itself as the issue of that supernatural union, wholly human, wholly divine. From that position there could be no retreat.

(For these controversies, see further NESTORIUS; MONOPHYSITES; CYRIL, SAINT [OF ALEXANDRIA]; JESUS CHRIST: The Dogma of Christ in the Ancient Councils; COUNCIL.)

2. Fall of the Roman Empire.—The fall of the Western Empire (476) completed the isolation of the Roman see. Arianism, expelled from the empire, had been established meanwhile among the Goths of the Danube by Ulfilas (q.v.), appointed their bishop by the Arian Bishop Eusebius of Nicomedia. Ulfilas taught a Gothic Christianity in the Gothic language, inventing an alphabet and translating the Scriptures. Untrammeled by orthodoxy, this faith needed no apostolic see and was adopted by Goths, Suebi, Burgundians, Vandals, and Lombards as a kind of national religion. (See GERMANIC PEOPLES: Conversion to Christianity.)

Gradually the West had been subdued by conquest and infiltration to the barbarian peoples: Africa to the Vandals, Spain to the Suebi and Visigoths, Gaul to the Visigoths and Burgundians. The Avars wasted Pannonia, the Slovenes Styria, Carinthia, and Carniola. The Croats and Serbs established themselves south of the Sava. Italy was defended by a barbarian army under Odoacer until his defeat and death in 493 at the hands of Theodoric the Ostrogoth, who, though an Arian, ruled Italy from Ravenna with ability and tolerance, with the advice of the Catholics Boethius (480–524) and Cassiodorus (c. 490–c. 585). After Theodoric's death (526) Italy was conquered by the armies of the Catholic emperor Justinian, under Belisarius and, later, Narses, and until the 8th century was officially a province of the Byzantine Empire under the exarch of Ravenna.

The Lombards conquered northern Italy and established themselves at Pavia (572). At once subject to repeated attacks from the Franks and extending their own conquests in Italy, the Lombards, unlike the Goths, had neither genius nor opportunity for peace. Thus when Gregory (q.v.) I the Great became pope in 590 he succeeded to what might be described as "the grave of the deceased Roman Empire." He had been praetor and then monk and had lived several years in Constantinople as the ambassador of Pelagius II seeking imperial aid against the Lombards. As Roman and as pope, he saw the world as a whole. Lawyer and judge by training, monk, bishop, and apostle by vocation, he realized the creative and redemptive possibilities of the papacy and of the Catholic Church at the moment when outside it and apart from its supernatural certainty all civilization in the west was dead beyond hope of resurrection.

(For details of the history of this period, see ROMAN HISTORY, to 476, and thereafter ITALY: History and ROME: History. See also separate articles on the barbarian peoples.)

3. Episcopacy and Monasticism.—During the next six centuries the function of the church was to create Christendom, and its chief instruments in this work were episcopacy and monasticism. During Gregory's pontificate the Arian rulers of the Lombards in Italy and of the Visigoths in Spain were baptized Catholics. In 597 his mission landed in Kent under Augustine of Canterbury. A century earlier (496 or, more likely, 506) Clovis (*q.v.*) with 3,000 Franks had been baptized by St. Remi, bishop of Reims, and was exhorted by Avitus, bishop of Vienne, to spread the faith among the barbarians "corrupted by heretical doctrines." Even as a pagan Clovis had respected the property, person, and advice of bishops, and he owed his conversion partly to the prudence which recognized in them the virtual rulers of Gaul. He broke the power of the Visigoths at Vouillé near Poitiers and extended his dominion to the Pyrenees, everywhere requiring Arians to become orthodox and restoring their churches after they had been reconsecrated.

In the 5th century the monk St. Severinus, a friend of Odoacer, established the authority of personal sanctity over the peoples of the upper Danube. During the 7th, 8th, and 9th centuries the Croats were Christianized by Roman missionaries; the Bavarians of Upper Austria by St. Rupert of Worms, who founded a see and a monastery at Salzburg (*c.* 700) that Charlemagne made an archbishopric (798); Moravia by the Greek monks Cyril and Methodius; and Bohemia by its prince, whom St. Methodius baptized (871). Prague became a see in 973. The Magyars, who had withstood a succession of missions from East and West, were at length converted under Stephen I, who established the metropolitan see of Esztergom (Gran) and founded the monastery of Pannonhalma near Gyorszentmarton (Martinsberg) with five other houses.

Monasticism was the Christian equivalent of the imperial army, the means by which the church subdued and enlisted, colonized, and administered the new peoples and revived or defended the old. The first great leader of Western monasticism, St. Martin of Tours, was a Pannonian, born of pagan parents and bred a soldier; he secured his discharge in order to renounce the world. Under St. Hilary of Poitiers, himself a convert, Martin established a monastery at Ligugé and another at Marmoutier on the banks of the Loire. As monk and bishop of Tours he devoted himself to an ascetic discipline and to the conversion of pagans. Other monastic communities gathered at Marseilles (St. Victor) and on the isle of Lérins (St. Honoratus or Honoré) whence another St. Hilary was appointed bishop of Arles (429). About 480 was born St. Benedict of Nursia, whose *Regula monachorum* or "Rule for Monks" became the pattern of all Western monasticism. (*See* BENEDICT, SAINT: *Rule of St. Benedict.*) "For thee, therefore, whosoever thou be, my words are intended who, giving up thy own will, dost take the all-powerful and excellent arms of obedience to fight under the Lord Christ, the true King." In that conception of service and society lay the seeds of the rivalry between natural and supernatural sovereignty which appeared full-grown in the 11th and 12th centuries.

The Rule established a discipline and constitution and regulated a liturgical society with impersonal precision. It represented the religious as the *Institutes* of Justinian (*see* ROMAN LAW) represented the civil society. The Rule required self-surrender rather than self-abnegation. Based on long monastic experience and devotion to the person of Christ (who is to be seen and served in the abbot and in all the brethren, in strangers who visit the monastery and in all its life and work), it was the perfect instrument for creating centres of Christian society, above all in rural and pagan territory, and for reforming the religious communities of the West. Thus a rational economy, moral training, and education in the arts of peace developed about the altars of the church and were available to transform the secular barbarity of war and heroic solitude into Christian civilization.

4. The Rise of Temporal Power.—In the civilized East the Christological discussion continued. The pope, though a subject of the (Byzantine) emperor, was head of the church, and the East, always divided in faith, had always been uncertain in ecclesiastical submission. The churches of Egypt and Syria, strongholds of Monophysite theology and jealous for the dignity of Alexandria, had refused the decision of the Council of Chalcedon. The emperor Zeno tried an accommodation, the Henoticon (482). The emperor Justinian, a Macedonian Catholic, in the controversy of the "Three Chapters" (*see* PAPACY: *The First Six Centuries: The Affair of the "Three Chapters"*), forced the aged Pope Vigilius to attend the fifth general council at Constantinople (553) and to assent to the condemnation of Theodore of Mopsuestia, Theodoret of Cyrrhus, and Ibas of Edessa, three writers who had been accused and acquitted of Nestorian heresy at Chalcedon. The emperor Heraclius tried the formula known as Monothelitism (*see* MONOTHELITES) which ascribed one "active energy" to the Saviour, translated by the Latin bishop as "one will"; and Pope Honorius, mistaking the question, professed himself willing to assent. Pope Martin I refused this concession and was exiled by the emperor Constans II to the Crimea. The sixth general council (680–681) vindicated Martin, condemned Monothelitism, and criticized Honorius. Nevertheless, in 692 the council *in Trullo* (Quinisext) was deliberately anti-Roman, and Pope Sergius, arrested at the orders of Justinian II, was saved only by force from the imperial officer. Finally the emperor Leo III the Isaurian (717–740) had initiated his campaign of iconoclasm, the most unpopular and unnecessary of reforms, enforced by persecution and confirmed by the Council of Hieria in 754. The schism endured until 843. (*See* also ICONOCLASTIC CONTROVERSY.)

But the emperor, if he was willing to force the Roman bishop to submit in matters of doctrine, was quite unable to defend his Roman subjects from their enemies in the flesh. It was out of long Roman experience that Pope Zacharias, in reply to Pepin's question, answered that the king should be he who really has power to rule. (*See* PAPACY: *The Medieval Papacy* [590–1304]: *The Carolingians and the States of the Church.*) Neither Roman nor Byzantine sovereignty had been bound by a doctrine of legitimacy: the prince was the guardian of law and peace. In Rome the bishop and the people were bound together by ties of faith, history, and administration. The walls, defenses, aqueducts, food, hospitals, finance, justice, and religion were in the bishop's charge.

Not only the city but the West as a whole was in need of defense. In 711 Spain and Sardinia had fallen to the Arabs. Sicily was frequently raided by Saracens, who exacted tribute from Syracuse. In 732 Charles Martel (*q.v.*) broke the Muslim invasion of France, saved Aquitaine, and established his title as defender of Christendom. Thus, when, in 751, the Lombard Aistulf seized Ravenna, threatened Rome, and meditated the conquest of Italy, Pope Stephen II (III), having appealed in vain for help to the emperor, turned to Pepin the Short. He journeyed into Francia, prevailed upon Pepin to help him, and, returning to Italy with the army of the Franks, received Ravenna from Pepin, who destroyed the Lombard forces (756). Charlemagne completed the conquest by capturing Pavia (773–774).

(This pivotal period of European history is discussed at length in CAROLINGIANS; LOMBARDS; FRANKS; PEPIN; CHARLEMAGNE; FRANCE: *History.*)

Thus the pope became a sovereign prince. His "temporal power" was the consequence of an inevitable severance of West from East, of the barbarian and Muslim invasions, and of his apostolic function to maintain the faith as against the heresies and schisms which were endemic in the eastern imperial system and to evangelize the pagans of the West.

Charlemagne, after 800, was not only Augustus but "crowned of God, great and peace-bringing emperor who rules the Roman Empire and who by the grace of God is king of the Franks and Lombards." For 30 years he made holy war on the pagan Saxons, and when he died in 814 his empire, extending from the Elbe to the Pyrenees, from the English sea to the Tiber, was united in so far as it was Christian. His school under Alcuin of York was the cultural centre of this empire.

Louis I the Pious, crowned at Reims by Stephen IV (V) (816), cooperated with Pope Paschal I in his desire to convert the Danes. The archbishop of Reims, the bishop of Cambrai, and a mission of monks under Ansgar spread the faith about the mouth of the Elbe. (*See* ANSGAR, SAINT.) In 826 the Danish prince Harald with many hundred followers was baptized at Mainz. Meanwhile, St. Benedict of Aniane, having reformed the monasteries of Aquitaine, was brought to advise Louis on the moral reform of the kingdom and was established in a monastery at Aachen. Under his influence the Rule of St. Benedict was imposed on all monastic houses in the Frankish kingdom.

C. The Formation of Western Christendom

At the death of Louis the Pious (840) the natural divisions of the empire and local needs, attachments, and traditions were reasserted. The idea of empire, derived from Rome, taught by Alcuin of York, and realized by the genius of Charlemagne, receded. Beginning in the 8th century, the invasion of the Normans intensified the confusion of dynastic war. (*See* VIKING; NORMANS.) Based in Flanders, they ravaged Saxony, the Rhineland, and France, burned Cologne, Rouen, Paris, and Aachen, captured Trier, besieged Orléans, seized Bordeaux, and advanced on Toulouse. They sacked the monasteries and completed the destruction of towns and communes surviving from Roman times. The Edict of Mersen (847) commanding every man to serve a lord only defined the actual situation; feudal organization was partly, if not mostly, a defense against the anarchy the Normans left behind. (*See* FEUDALISM.) Early in the 10th century they settled in Normandy. Two centuries of war thus isolated and established the church in the West as the one continuous, unifying, and civilizing institution and, as it were, defined its double function of evangelizing and civilizing mankind.

This isolation of the West was emphasized by the schism of Photius in Constantinople during the pontificate of Nicholas I. The elevation of Photius (*q.v.*), a layman, to the patriarchate and the deposition of Ignatius, his predecessor, were uncanonical. On the other hand, the interference of the Roman legates in the newly founded Bulgarian Church was perhaps unlawful. The *Filioque* question (the double procession of the Holy Ghost) was used mainly as an occasion, though the theological difference between East and West is implied in the dispute. (*See* HOLY SPIRIT: *Procession of the Holy Spirit*.) As always, the West was more simply and uncompromisingly Trinitarian and laid greater emphasis on the incarnation with its consequent exaltation of the church. Nicholas (*q.v.*) I, a canonist and political realist, advanced from the traditional Gelasian doctrine of "two swords"—that is, of the divine origin and independence of both the spiritual and the temporal power—to that which foreshadowed the doctrine of the primacy of the spiritual power, successfully advanced by Hildebrand (Gregory VII). To the emperor Michael III Nicholas wrote that, whereas the emperor needed the pope in religion, the pope had no need of the emperor in temporal matters. At the same time he demanded obedience from the Frankish king Lothair and even quashed a judgment of the great archbishop Hincmar of Reims and declared that what the pope decides all must observe. For a century, however, the Roman see, lacking temporal protection, suffered from its temporal status. The Roman nobles, the house of Spoleto, the counts of Tusculum, and the kings of Germany made and unmade popes in a succession down to John XII, deposed by Otto the Great in 963.

Weakness at the centre encouraged and exaggerated the centrifugal tendencies revealed in the wide, half-civilized rural areas that were exposed to waves of pagan and barbarian invasion. The urban organization of the church in the Roman Empire was not suited to this scattered and insecure continent. The church needed an imperial idea and the cooperation of temporal powers. During the 10th century the house of Saxony laid the foundations of the medieval empire, Cluny revived monasticism, and the canon law was gradually developed; and these three factors, together with intensified theological controversy, prepared the great reform of the 11th century, which was initiated by a reformed papacy.

1. Foundation of the Medieval Empire.—Otto I (*q.v.*) the Great, occupied during the first 25 years of his reign in uniting the German peoples and defending them against Hungarians, Slavs, and Normans, was crowned emperor in 962 by Pope John XII in Rome and thereafter was employed in restoring order in Italy. He founded a metropolitan see at Magdeburg, whose first

archbishop, Adalbert, monk of Trier and abbot of Weissenburg, had been missionary to the Russians. Bishoprics were founded also at Oldenburg and Havelberg (946), at Prague (976), at Olomouc (Olmütz; for Moravia) and at Odense (for Denmark; 980). In 936 St. Unni of Bremen undertook a mission to Scandinavia, where he died. The second bishop of Prague, St. Adalbert (Voytech), who baptized St. Stephen of Hungary, left his see in defiance of papal and imperial injunction to preach the gospel to the Prussians, by whom he was martyred in 997. The frontier churches of Bohemia, Hungary, and Poland looked to Rome rather than to Germany; and Pope Gregory V, cousin and chaplain of Otto III, revived the missionary tradition of the Holy See but fell a victim of city faction prompted by local nobles.

At his death in 999, Otto III appointed the Frenchman Gerbert of Aurillac (Silvester II). Silvester dreamed of an empire independent of the German kings which should embody a world faith and a world culture. But like other learned men he underestimated local ties and traditions, and like other Frenchmen he failed to realize the needs of German administration. Simony (*q.v.*) he counted the greatest evil in the church. But it was much more than the "sin of Simon Magus": in France it was, indeed, a corruption which was the result of generations of insecurity strengthening the hands of unscrupulous lords; in Germany it was rooted in Teutonic and feudal custom and continued by social and economic necessity.

The spread of Christianity among remote and barbarous peoples implied local autonomy and the adaptation of ancient pagan administrative custom. Churches were built, maintained, and possessed by chieftains. The mission church was virtually autonomous; its priest was the vassal and servant, often the kinsman, of the local landowner and protected by the local saint. The Holy See itself was constantly subject to imperial interference and protection, and the great reformer Leo IX, though elected at Rome, was Henry III's nominee. At every level—parochial, episcopal, papal—the question awaited decision whether the church was in effect a holy, catholic, and supernatural institution appointing its own bishops and priests upon its own authority or (in the language of a later age) part of the body politic.

The system evolved by nature was subject to natural corruption. The emperor Conrad II and King Philip I of France made a traffic of bishoprics. But deeper than these abuses was the question, presupposed in all movements of reform, of the true function of Christian priest and bishop. Councils repeatedly forbade lay interference in parochial benefices (Ingelheim, 948; Augsburg, 952; Seligenstadt, 1023; Bourges, 1031). Linked with this question was that of clerical celibacy, since a married clergy was tied by natural duties and interests to worldly affairs. (*See* CELIBACY.) Marriage implied inheritance and tended to absorb the clergy in local and feudal tenancies and obligations. But there was also the question of sexual morality and the traditional attitude of the church to virginity. Celibacy was admired by Tertullian, recommended by Eusebius, required by Cyril of Jerusalem, and said to be the general practice by Jerome. Celibacy was a tribute to the supernatural and sacramental vocation and as such was bound up with the supernatural and sacramental body which the confusion and expansion of the 9th and 10th centuries tended to obscure.

2. Revival of Monasticism.—Monks were the exemplars and instruments of the supernatural society. It was their business to live in "the course of these declining times" as in and for the "solid estate of eternity." Monasticism (*q.v.*) was in essence a lay movement, and the multiplication of monasteries and the constant succession of monastic reforms was evidence of the hold of the Catholic faith on the lay population. In 910 William I the Pious, count of Auvergne and duke of Aquitaine, founded Cluny (*see* BENEDICTINES: *Monastic Centuries*). Odo of Cluny reformed Fleury and then, invited to Rome by Alberic, reformed the monasteries in and about the city and Monte Cassino. The reform spread through northern Italy and France. Cluny became the head of an order whose 300 houses, subject to the abbot of Cluny and exempt from all other authority but that of the pope, were organized in ten provinces extending from Spain to Poland. Cluny, "a spiritual field where earth and heaven meet" (Peter

Damian), trained Urban II and Paschal II. It not only revived liturgical discipline and the Benedictine rule but realized on a world scale the practical order and common prudence of Benedictine monasticism. At the same time, Gerard of Brogne in Flanders and Dunstan of Glastonbury in England initiated monastic reform. In Italy St. Romuald founded the order of Camaldoli (c. 1012; see CAMALDOLESE). In Normandy Herluin founded Bec (c. 1040), which under Lanfranc and St. Anselm became one of the great schools of Europe. There Pope Alexander II, Ivo of Chartres, and Theobald of Canterbury received their training. The last wave of monastic reformation produced the Carthusian order founded by St. Bruno (1084) and the Cistercian founded by Robert of Molesme (1098), Alberic, and Stephen Harding. St. Bernard entered Cîteaux in 1112 or 1113 and with 12 monks founded Clairvaux in 1115. He was the "greatest of the monks" and one of the greatest preachers of the Middle Ages. (See CARTHUSIANS; CISTERCIANS; BERNARD, SAINT.)

3. Development of Canon Law.—In the West canon law developed later and more slowly than in the East. In 774 Charlemagne received from Pope Adrian I a collection of canons and decretals accepted at the Council of Aachen (802) by the Frankish church. Under the see of Toledo the Spanish church possessed a larger collection, including canons of Greek, African, Gallic, and Spanish councils and papal decretals. In the 9th century also appeared the collection of "false decretals" (see DECRETALS, FALSE). This collection, containing both real and spurious decretals, circulated in Spain, Italy, France, and even England but was not much used in Rome till the 11th century. Collections made by Burchard of Worms and Ivo of Chartres prepared the way for Gratian (q.v.), a Camaldolese monk of Bologna, who in 1139–c. 1150 produced the *Decretum*, a systematic treatise (*Concordia discordantium canonum*). During the 12th and 13th centuries five compilations were added. Gregory IX added the decretals of popes since the *Decretum* which were compiled by the Dominican Raymond of Peñafort. Later decretals were collected by Boniface VIII (1298) and Clement V (1314), and the *Extravagantes* (decretals not included in previous compilations) brought the law down to Sixtus IV (1484). These together formed the *Corpus juris canonici* ("body of canon law"), of which a definitive edition was issued by Gregory XIII in 1582. (See further CANON LAW.)

4. Theological Controversy.—St. Augustine of Hippo developed his doctrine of the church against the Donatists (q.v.) and his doctrine of grace against Pelagius (q.v.), but both doctrines were already full-grown, and the fundamental reason for his exposition lay in the need of the man Augustine, a sinner in need of grace and the citizen of a dying civilization in need of the City of God. In other words, the power and permanence of Augustinian theology was the result of his factual presentation of man as man in relation to his Maker and Saviour. The West, untroubled by the complicated disputes and theological parties of the East, developed its theology in simple and universal terms, not as a theory so much as a faith. At the Second Council of Orange (529) the Semi-Pelagians were condemned. (See SEMI-PELAGIANISM.)

The question of predestination and depravity was raised in the 9th century by Gottschalk (q.v.), a monk of Fulda, whose doctrine of a double predestination was condemned by Rabanus Maurus of Mainz and Hincmar of Reims. But the doctrine of grace developed more surely and continuously as the doctrine of the Eucharist, and here also the church insisted on the reality of the sacrifice. For Ambrose it is Christ himself who offers the sacrifice and changes the elements into his body and blood. For Augustine the church presents itself as a whole and living sacrifice. Gregory says that the daily offering of Christ's body and blood avail for salvation and that by this means "the lowest things are united to the highest, things earthly are joined to things divine and the visible and invisible become one."

In the 9th century Paschasius Radbertus (q.v.), monk and abbot of Corbie, wrote a treatise *De corpore et sanguine Domini,* which in 844 he presented to Charles the Bald, emphasizing the fact of the real change into the body and blood of Christ and equating the daily sacrifice with daily redemption. Another monk of Corbie,

Ratramnus (q.v.), at the same time described the sacrifice as "spiritual" and discussed the relation of "figure" and "truth" in a work afterward attributed to Johannes Scotus Erigena and condemned during the Berengarian controversy at Vercelli in 1050. Berengar (q.v.), *scholasticus* and archdeacon of Tours, outlined his doctrine in a letter to Lanfranc, and Lanfranc set forth the orthodox doctrine in his book *De corpore et sanguine Domini.*

The Christology of the Western Church was settled at Chalcedon. The Adoptionist heresy of Felix, bishop of Urgel, and Elipandus of Toledo was repeatedly condemned and was answered by Alcuin of York, who said that the Sonship of Christ is not of nature but of person: the divine and human natures are united in the person of the Son. (See ADOPTIONISM.) During these centuries the West developed the devotion to the Virgin Mary defined at the Council of Ephesus (431) and at Constantinople (553). The devotion to the Mother of God became articulate and instituted as the doctrine of the incarnation was defined. The same uncompromising refusal to adapt the central mysteries of the faith or to modify them in the interests of rationalization appears through all the centuries of Christological dispute and social chaos. The sacrifice is a real sacrifice, the Saviour really present, the incarnation the real fullness of the godhead bodily, the church the really divine-human community, and its head the real and effective sovereign, vicar of Christ.

5. Papal Reform.—This realism, the mark of Christian orthodoxy, is the heart of the work of St. Anselm (q.v.). His use of the ontological argument is thus the opposite in emphasis of the Cartesian: its essence is the emphasis on existence. His *Cur Deus homo* starts from divine justice, and his argument presupposes its absoluteness. Faith is the foundation of reason.

Leo IX.—The same unyielding realism of faith was expressed in the papal reform initiated in the 11th century by Leo IX: "The head of the entire discipline of the church is in that place where Peter, the summit and cardinal member of the apostles, waits for the blessed resurrection of his flesh in the last day."

Leo IX had learned administrative method in the imperial service and his episcopal duty in a poor diocese. During the first two years of his pontificate he held 12 councils. He traveled to Reims, to Mainz, and as far as Hungary, organized the papal chancery to sustain a large correspondence, employed highly able legates, and created a college of cardinals. He dreamed of the reunion of East and West. He brought to Rome young Hildebrand (later Gregory VII), who had known the city's disorders as a boy and who devoted the remaining years of his life to the reform. Stephen IX (X) (Frederick of Lorraine) was already dying when he left Monte Cassino for the chair of Peter, but in his few months he consecrated the monk St. Peter Damian cardinal bishop of Ostia, secured the cooperation of cardinals and Roman burghers to ensure the canonical and independent election of his successor, and enjoined upon them to await the return of Cardinal Hildebrand, then in Germany. Stephen was no sooner buried than the Roman nobles proved his wisdom by electing an antipope whom the cardinals excommunicated, appointing the Burgundian bishop of Florence, Nicholas II. At his death (1061) the struggle came to a head between the reforming cardinals and the bishops of Lombardy led by Milan. The cardinals elected Anselm of Lucca, Lanfranc's pupil at Bec, as Pope Alexander II. But it was only after bloodshed and an appeal to the German court at Augsburg, and even then at the risk of his life, that Alexander began his pontificate. (See further PAPACY.) Nevertheless, the reform was already visibly changing the relations between church and state.

Gregory VII.—Gregory VII, who as monk, deacon, cardinal, and pope served this cause for 40 years, was perhaps alone in his vision of all its meaning as, after 1072 (when Peter Damian and Adalbert of Bremen died), he was the sole survivor of Leo IX's circle of reformers. For him the battle was no longer limited to simony and celibacy. Likened by his contemporaries to the prophet Elijah, he was disinterestedly certain that the pope is the voice and speaks with the authority of Peter and claimed absolute authority over the souls of Christians without misgiving and without arrogance. As legate he had seen the church in France and Germany with the eyes of central authority. The arch-chancellor of the empire, who was also archbishop of Mainz, complained that Pope Alexander II had dealt directly with his suffragans of Prague and Olomouc instead of dealing through their archbishop. Liemar of Bremen refused to act at the orders of papal legates without consulting the German episcopate. Secular clergy revolted against a decree of celibacy. Only the Saxon bishops supported the pope, and that because they were opposed to the emperor. In 1075 Gregory revealed his determination: by the *Dictatus papae* he declared (renewing an earlier and never enforced decree) that no prelate might receive an abbey or see at the hands of a lay lord and asserted his power to depose any bishop or lord who might defy him.

Henry IV, the German king, having subdued the Saxons, was free to attack the pope. In 1076, at a council of German bishops held at Worms, he declared Gregory deposed, and the north Italian bishops declared their agreement. Gregory then deposed and excommunicated the German and Lombard bishops who had signed Henry's letter, declared Henry deposed and excommunicated and his subjects absolved of their allegiance. The effect of this open clash was Henry's defeat and isolation, which he saved from complete disaster by submitting to Gregory at Canossa (1077). There he did penance and awaited absolution, which Gregory gave in duty as a priest. The absolution disconcerted the papal party in Germany which had elected Rudolph of Swabia king in Henry's place. But now Gregory, who was not a partisan, remained neutral. Three years of civil war ended with the victory and death of Rudolph and the excommunication of Henry, who marched on Rome and was crowned by Guibert of Ravenna (the antipope Clement III). Gregory "having loved justice and hated iniquity therefore died in exile" at Salerno in 1085. In France, his campaign against simony and clerical marriage had been more successful. In England, Lanfranc carried out his policy but with a characteristic independence.

Crusades and University of Paris.—Urban II, after the brief pontificate of Victor III, inherited Gregory's exile and carried on his work. A monk of Cluny and a canonist, he had been employed as legate in Germany to organize the papal party. More firmly than Gregory he maintained the opposition to lay investiture and required free and lawful election of bishops. Deprived at first of his centre at Rome, he held a number of councils. At Clermont (1095) he forbade clergy to do homage to laymen and proclaimed the first Crusade (*see* CRUSADES), which, apart from its particular occasion and important results, inspired the first great movement of popular preaching. Urban employed permanent legates, encouraged appeals to Rome, graded the hierarchy and confirmed the privileges of monastic houses.

At the same time the emergence of an international school at Paris recovered scientific theology for Western Christendom. Guillaume de Champeaux established the reputation of the cathedral school. Peter Abelard, who had studied under Guillaume, made it the most famous school in Europe and, using the *Organon* of Aristotle, laid the foundation of its tradition as a school of logic and philosophy. (*See* also PARIS, UNIVERSITY OF.) By the middle of the 13th century the schoolmen of Paris had access to original translations from the Greek of nearly all Aristotle's extant works. Forbidden by the legate Robert de Courçon in 1215 and again in 1231, the physical and metaphysical works of Aristotle, together with the commentaries of Averroës, were nevertheless read and studied. (*See* SCHOLASTICISM.)

6. Heresy and Inquisition.—At the fourth Lateran Council (1215) Innocent III published a definition of the faith which, after affirming the doctrine of the Trinity, the incarnation, and the judgment, says:

There is moreover one universal Church of the faithful, outside which no man at all is saved, in which the same Jesus Christ is both the priest and the sacrifice, whose body and blood are truly contained in the sacrament of the altar under the species of bread and wine, the bread being transubstantiated into the body and the wine into the blood by the divine power, in order that, to accomplish the mystery of unity, we ourselves may receive of His that which He received of ours. And this thing, the sacrament to wit, no one can make (*conficere*) but a priest, who has been duly ordained, according to the keys of the Church, which Jesus Christ Himself granted to the apostles and their successors.

But the sacrament of baptism, which is consecrated in water at the invocation of God and of the undivided Trinity, that is of the Father, and of the Son and Holy Spirit, being duly conferred in the form of the Church by any person, whether upon children or adults, is profitable to salvation. And if anyone, after receiving baptism, has fallen into sin, he can always be restored (*reparari*) by true penitence.

Not only virgins and the continent, but also married persons, deserve, by right faith and good works pleasing God, to come to eternal blessedness (cited by Alexander Hamilton Thompson, *Cambridge Medieval History,* vol. vi, p. 635).

The last article of the definition quoted above refers to the Catharist or Albigensian heresy, which in the 12th and 13th centuries threatened large areas of Hungary, Germany, Italy, and France. (*See* CATHARI.) In Languedoc the Crusades inaugurated by Innocent III against the heresy were eagerly supported by the French nobility (1209–44). At the same time the Inquisition was organized. Proposed at the Council of Verona (1184) and established early in the 13th century, this court was designed to combine judicial procedure with propaganda. Under Gregory IX it was organized with specialist judges and advisers. Its activity varied with time and place. In an age whose most important industry was definition, in which social discipline and civilized living had still to be won, there could be no question of indifference. The enemies of faith were the enemies of man. (*See* INQUISITION.)

7. The Pattern of Catholic Humanism.—The 13th century was the age of an apostolate at every level of human life. The leaders of the movement were friars, orders initiated by laity (St. Francis) and the lower ranks of clergy (St. Dominic) under the immediate protection of the pope. In 1210 Innocent III sanctioned the Franciscan rule. In 1216 his successor, Honorius III, took under his government and protection "the order of Master Dominic and Friars Preachers." (*See* FRANCISCANS; DOMINICANS.) The Swabian Albertus Magnus, regent master of the learned order of Dominicans in Paris, "strove to make Aristotle intelligible to the Latins." His pupil Thomas Aquinas is still the "common doctor," the greatest teacher of the Roman Catholic Church. Leo XIII in the encyclical *Aeterni Patris* (1879) required bishops "to restore the wisdom of St. Thomas and to spread it as far as possible for the safety and glory of the Catholic faith, for the good of society and for the increase of all sciences." It was the work not only of St. Thomas but of the 13th century as a whole to synthesize those three purposes. (*See* THOMISM.)

In Paris, the metropolis of theological and philosophical controversy, and at the moment of the full recovery of Aristotelian method, St. Thomas (*see* AQUINAS, SAINT THOMAS) represents the arrival of scientific intelligence and the discovery by Christendom of the nature of man. His work is the first clear articulation of the full human confidence in human nature which in patristic and conciliar definitions, as in the earlier scholasticism of St. Anselm and in the preaching of St. Bernard, was still overshadowed by theological, controversial, and ecclesiastical purpose. St. Thomas realized what neither pagan philosophy nor Christian theology had as yet clearly discerned, the naturalism of supernature, the divine right of man.

8. Papal Authority.—Whether the claim of Nicholas I, Gregory VII, and Innocent III to an effective sovereignty of Christendom was theoretically sound or not, the civilization of the West did in fact cohere in the church which cohered in the papacy. The papal victory of the 11th century, the development of law, theology, and ecclesiastical order, had made the Holy See the centre of a judicial and administrative system not only more efficient than any other government but the basis of all government. It was the final court of appeal in international dealing, the source and standard of ministerial and judicial competence. The pope's authority was also popular and moral. Innocent III, feudal suzerain of a large part of Europe, exercised also as head of the church a direct and real authority over its chief administrative officers, the bishops, and over the real religion of its people. He and his successors created the universities which trained public servants and presided over an international court in which every sovereign in Europe was prepared to plead.

9. The Church and the Nations.—But the church, inherent in the social structure, also reacted to the national, social, and cultural revolution of the 13th and 14th centuries. Frederick II (*q.v.*) was the first secular sovereign of the modern kind. He ignored without resenting the papal excommunication and was equally prepared to hand Germany over to the church (by the *privilegium in favorem principum ecclesiasticorum* of 1220), to make friends with the sultan (1229), and to crown himself king in Jerusalem, which he had sworn to protect. His greatest achievement, the Constitutions of Melfi (1231), drawn up in defiance of the pope, established an enlightened despotism in the Sicilian kingdom. His University of Naples, too, was a despotism governed by a royal chancellor.

France enjoyed peace and consolidation under Louis IX, who valued his throne as a means of making Christians. The military adventures of the English Edward III and Henry V, picturesque rather than political, served, as did the wars of Burgundy and Armagnac, to confirm the French nationality which Louis XI (1461–83) centralized in the throne. By the 14th century the vernaculars of Italy, France, Spain, Germany, and England were mature, their legal systems organized. They were aware of commercial rivalries and of national ambitions. Feudalism was dying. The Italian cities of Venice, Florence, and Milan were independent powers. The age of the Crusades was passing; that of national states had arrived.

The Holy See reflected this revolution. It became the centre of Italian politics and international diplomacy, subject to international intrigue. Its judicial business was extended. From increasingly secular states it demanded increasing revenues. Nicholas III was a political realist; he accepted the situation in which every cardinal was the agent of a political interest, and he exalted his own family, the Orsini. His successor, Martin IV, a Frenchman, was the creature of Charles of Anjou. Honorius IV (Savelli) raised his family against the Orsini. Nicholas IV (who relied on the Colonna) balanced the other two. Then the cardinals sought to remedy the corruption and forced a hermit, Peter of Morrone, unacquainted with the world, into the chair of Peter; Celestine V survived five months, was persuaded to abdicate, and died in prison. His incompetence was less disastrous than the ability and ambition of his successor. When Boniface VIII (Caetani), pursuing the logic of contemporary politics and Roman law to an extreme, forbade clergy to pay taxes to the secular government (*Clericis laicos,* 1296), Philip IV the Fair forbade the export of money from France. When Boniface claimed Scotland as a fief of the pope, Edward I annexed it to England. Both kings relied on their national assemblies, Edward I on the Parliament of Lincoln, Philip the Fair on the Estates-General. Finally French troops seized and imprisoned the pope, who died in 1303. (*See* further BONIFACE: *Boniface VIII.*) His successor, Benedict XI, denounced the outrage and died in a few weeks—of poison, it was said.

The next election took more than ten months, and the next pope, Clement V, archbishop of Bordeaux, transferred his court to Avignon in 1309. The "Babylonish captivity" had begun (*see* PAPACY: *The Papacy in Avignon*). Perhaps the most dramatic as it was the most shameful sign of the changed time was the suppression by Philip IV and Clement V of the Knights Templars, whose real offense was that with the decline of the Crusades they had taken to banking, a form of usury which evoked the resentment of their noble debtors and the greed of the king. The "Great Schism" which started in 1378 with the election of Robert of Geneva as Clement VII in opposition to the reigning Urban VI was the final tribute of the papacy to national rivalry. (*See* PAPACY: *The Great Schism, 1378–1417.*) Nations bargained with one side or the other.

The doctrine which accompanied, explained, and defended the new order was nominalism, which denied the reality of universals and declared it an "error to believe that there is something in reality besides the singular entity." (*See* NOMINALISM; OCKHAM, WILLIAM.) Thus there is no such thing as the nature of man which could be defined and must be obeyed and which might be united to the divine nature in the person of Christ; there were only individual men, and the definition of human right and duty was promulgated and enforced by the prince. Nature and supernature, reason and revelation thus parted company. Natural sci-

ence, whether legal, empirical, or mathematical, could thus be rid of metaphysical assumptions and set free to handle facts and concepts each on its own terms. The prince was the source of rights and obligations and, in the words of John Wycliffe (*De officio regis,* 1379), was above human laws. The doctrine was expounded by those Franciscans who supported Louis the Bavarian in his claim to the empire as Louis IV. Marsilius of Padua and John of Jandun in the treatise *Defensor pacis* ("The Defender of Peace"; 1324) affirmed the authority of the civil power; the papacy was a human institution which had usurped temporal power (*see* MARSILIUS: *Defensor Pacis*).

Wycliffe's opinions, condemned in England, found a home at Prague and a more attractive apostle in John Huss (*q.v.*), whose preaching kindled the national imagination. Huss proclaimed the doctrine of Germany for the Germans, France for the French, Bohemia for the Bohemians. The Council of Constance which condemned him (he was burned at the stake in 1415) adopted the "nations" principle as the basis of voting and thereby defeated John XXIII's Italian majority. The conciliar movement (Pisa, 1409; Constance, 1414–18; Basel, 1431–37; *see* COUNCIL) represents an attempt to establish a parliament of Christendom or perhaps a league of nations. The decree *Frequens* of the Council of Constance declared that councils ought to be held every five years. At Basel the intention was even more explicit to make the pope the constitutional sovereign or nominal head of a Christendom whose national sovereigns were absolute.

The assembled doctors were not in a position to admit what was clear to the governments represented, that their authority was without foundation.

D. REFORM AND DEFINITION

Meanwhile the humanism of the Renaissance (*q.v.*) and a wide and increasing practice of mysticism intensified individual religion and magnified the individual person. At length the revolution broke. It is symbolized in three events. In 1517 Martin Luther nailed his theses on the door of the church at Wittenberg. (*See* REFORMATION.) In 1534 the Act of Supremacy proclaimed Henry VIII supreme head on earth of the Church of England, which he described as "part of the body politic"; as a result of this, in 1535 John Fisher, Thomas More, and the London Carthusians were martyred. In 1543 was published the treatise *De revolutionibus orbium coelestium* of Nicolaus Copernicus.

All three events in their several kinds were acts of revolt and signs of exodus into the unknown from the given and created world which Christianity presupposed. "It is not necessary," said Copernicus, "that hypotheses should be true or even probable. It suffices that they lead to calculations which agree with observations." "By reformation," said Luther, "I do not mean the reform of this human teaching and spirituality; I mean its complete and absolute abrogation." "The true significance of the Copernican revolution consisted not so much in displacing the world's centre from the earth to the sun as in implicitly denying that the world has a centre at all" (R. G. Collingwood, *The Idea of Nature* [Oxford, 1945]).

In like manner the princes denied the organic unity of Christendom. The doctrine *Cujus regio, ejus religio,* "Let the religion of each state follow that of its prince" (first announced at the Diet of Speyer, 1526) was adopted throughout Germany by the Diet of Augsburg (1555) and then throughout Europe, Catholic and Protestant. In 1572 Catherine de Médicis answered the English protest against the St. Bartholomew massacre by proposing that Elizabeth I use the same method with Catholics. In 1593 Henry of Navarre "bought Paris with a Mass." The supreme artist in this secular statecraft was Cardinal Richelieu.

1. The Counter-Reformation.—Reform of the church began under Leo X, who came to the throne in 1513. In Italy the Theatines were founded (1524) to reform parochial clergy. About 1525 Matteo da Bascio founded the Capuchins, and in 1530 the Barnabites were founded by St. Anthony Zaccaria. Paul III began the Counter-Reformation by appointing reformers—Giampietro Carafa, Gasparo Contarini, Jacopo Sadoleto, Reginald Pole—to the sacred college. In 1536 they served with five others on a commission which urged the need for reform and did not spare the abuses. In 1534 St. Ignatius of Loyola and six others initiated the Society of Jesus (*q.v.*). In 1542, by the bull *Licet initio,* Paul III established the papal Inquisition under Carafa's influence to supervise the whole church (*see* INQUISITION: *Roman Inquisition*). Pius IV and Pius V enlarged its powers, and Sixtus V reorganized it as one of the Roman congregations. In 1545 a general council met at Trent, which was postponed indefinitely in 1547. It reassembled (1551–52) under Julius III and met again, finally, in 1563. (*See* COUNCIL: *Councils of the Western Church: Council of Trent* [*1545–63*]; TRENT, COUNCIL OF.)

Trent was nothing that Constance had been, everything that Constance was not. Constance had seen the triumph of nationalism; Trent ignored it. Constance made no definition of the faith; Trent made nothing else. Constance had deposed the pope; Trent left everything in his hands. Convoked at the will of Paul III and interrupted by war, Trent made no pretense of gathering or expressing the will of Europe. It reformed the church and accepted the world. It recovered the centre which the movement and confusion of powers had displaced and obscured. Its answer to the theology of the Reformation was an affirmation of the divine-human unity: "In justification a person receives infused through Jesus Christ the remission of his sins, faith, hope and charity. For faith, unless there is added to it hope and charity, does not perfectly unite a person with Christ; nor does it make him a living member of His body; whence it is most truly said that faith without works is dead and unprofitable."

The works were not lacking. The Counter-Reformation inaugurated above all an age of sanctity: the cardinal archbishop of Milan, St. Charles Borromeo; the Florentine priest St. Philip Neri, whose Oratory founded in 1564 in Rome transformed the city; St. Francis of Sales, the most lovable of the doctors of the church, whose devout humanism and humane devotion influenced not only the Catholics of his century but Catholic and Protestant Christianity thereafter; St. Teresa of Ávila; St. John of the Cross, the greatest of the mystics; and St. Vincent de Paul.

2. Establishment of the Jesuits.—Nothing like the apostolate of the Jesuits had yet dawned on the Christian imagination. Within two years of the society's foundation, St. Francis Xavier under the patronage of John III of Portugal established a mission at Goa, on the west coast of India, and during his ten remaining years of life made thousands of converts in India, Malacca, Amboina, the Moluccas, and Ceylon; he founded a mission in Japan and was on the point of entering China when he died. At the same time Alfonso Salmerón was sent to Ireland with orders from Paul III "to be all things to all men, constant in good deeds, and to win souls by kindness."

In 1542 the Jesuits were established in Bavaria. They were invited to Salzburg, to Mainz, and to Osnabrück. Having carried the Counter-Reformation down the Danube and the Rhine, they were called to assist at Trent. They invaded Poland in 1570, England in 1580, Switzerland in 1586. In 1609 they took over the government of Paraguay and turned it into a perfect, almost too perfect, model of Christian social organization. In 1611 they arrived in Canada. Their Roman college, founded in 1551, was the mother of the greatest educational enterprise Christendom had ever known.

Placed under the direct command of the pope, the Jesuits were the natural foes of national autocracy. At Trent they supported a doctrine of episcopal jurisdiction which placed national bishops under the see of Rome, as against jurisdiction by divine right, which would have established their national independence. Hence they stood opposed to the Gallican ambition represented by the Paris Parliament, the university, and the Bourbons. Confessors of popes and princes, they were exponents of the "rights of man"; Juan de Mariana's treatise *De rege et regis institutione* ("On Kings and Royal Institution," 1599), dedicated to the future Philip III of Spain, lays its stress not on the legitimacy but on the justice of the king. It offended public opinion above all in France by defending tyrannicide. (*See* further JESUS, SOCIETY OF.)

3. National Independence.—The splendour of French culture in the 17th century was the fruit of Catholic humanism and national self-consciousness. Gallicanism was another consequence of the union of church and nation. The relations of the French church with the Holy See were defined by the concordat of 1516. The same principles of Gallican independence were affirmed in Bossuet's Four Articles (*see* BOSSUET, JACQUES BÉNIGNE) in 1682 and spread in the 18th century to the rest of Catholic Europe. The Jansenists, whose doctrines were condemned in 1713 by Clement XI in the bull *Unigenitus,* joined the Gallican cause against the Ultramontane influence of the Jesuits. In 1763, when the French Jesuits were being suppressed, Febronius (Johann Nikolaus von Hontheim; *q.v.*), auxiliary bishop of Trier and pupil of the Jansenist canonist Z. B. van Espen of Louvain, published his treatise *De statu ecclesiae et legitima potestate Romani Pontificis* maintaining the subordination of the pope to general councils and the independence of bishops. Condemned in 1764, the book circulated throughout Catholic Europe. In 1769 the ecclesiastical electors jointly protested against "papal usurpation." Joseph II, who became Holy Roman emperor on the death of Maria Theresa in 1780, carried out a Febronian policy in the Habsburg empire. In 1773 Clement XIV was forced by the governments of Portugal, France, Spain, and Naples to suppress the Society of Jesus. By 1793 the French monarchy was dead, the aristocracy abolished, and an egalitarian republic was preparing to establish the rights of man starting from the year I. The *Constitution civile du clergé* ("Civil Constitution of the Clergy"; 1790) was a Gallican measure (*see* FRANCE: *History: the Revolution and the Fall of the Monarchy* [*1789–92*]: *Civil Constitution of the Clergy*). The concordat of 1801 restored the terms of 1516.

See further GALLICANISM; ULTRAMONTANISM; JANSENISM.

E. THE CHURCH AFTER 1815

Napoleon passed like a storm and left Europe in ruins. Industrial revolution and economic determinism created a new absolute of natural necessity. The philosophers of reconstruction, idealist or utilitarian, were alike determinist (*see* DETERMINISM). J. G. Fichte deified the state; G. W. F. Hegel identified God with history; T. R. Malthus and David Ricardo regarded man as the slave of natural forces. Determinism was presupposed in theories of *laissez faire* and of the absolute state, materialism loudly proclaimed by the apostles of revolution and unconsciously generated by the preoccupations of scientific industry and efficiency. Such were the elements and climate of liberalism (*see* LIBERALISM).

1. The Catholic Revival.—The return of Pius VII from Fontainebleau, where he had been imprisoned by Napoleon, to Rome in 1814 was a triumph. Whole towns came out to do him honour; kneeling crowds lined the roads. It was a spontaneous gesture and expressed a piety deeper and older than the policies and theories which were transforming European government. In 1848, when Europe was in revolution, Pius IX at Gaeta was visited by a priest, Jean Baptiste Muard, who had begged his way from Subiaco whither he had walked a few months earlier from Pontigny, his purpose to ask the pope's approval (willingly bestowed) on the foundation of a religious house. Then he walked back to France, and in the forest near Sens, built a hut with chapel, kitchen, and dormitory where, with two companions, he lived in extreme poverty according to the Benedictine rule. Four years later he died. The community, which had become the mother of seven others in France, Palestine, and America, was driven from France in 1882, took over the ruins of Buckfast, Eng., and erected one of the most renowned of modern abbeys.

Muard was a child of peasants reared in poverty. So was John Bosco, whose work among the youth of Turin, begun in 1841, elicited the respect and won the support of the government, and who founded the Salesian order which was approved in 1874. So was Jean Baptiste Vianney, who became the *curé* of Ars in 1818, and so was Giuseppe Sarto, who became Pope Pius X. In the fall of the monarchies, the decay of aristocracies, and the advance of secularism among the intellectuals, the revival of the church sprang from the devotion, the family life, and the personal sanctity of the poor. Theirs was the mind which Pius IX, an indifferent politician and a great bishop, represented and understood. Poverty, chastity, and obedience, the ancient prescription for the Christian life, were also the condition of social vitality and the answer of the Catholic people to the proletarian or capitalist theories of the secularist doctrinaires. They presuppose a universal humanity. But except as functions of a dismembered humanity, the politics and economics of power were meaningless, while for deity they substituted a religion of individual, national, and class emancipation and enlargement.

In 1848 this ancient adversary of the church appeared in Rome and demanded a liberal pope to lead a nationalist cause, Catholic Italy against Catholic Austria. The pope fled to Gaeta. The movement carried on these secularist assumptions mastered European politics, and the pope became the prisoner of the Vatican. In 1854 he defined the Immaculate Conception. Another statement of the same faith, sorely needed in the age of Nietzsche, appeared in the constitution *Dei Filius* (1870) of the first Vatican Council, which reaffirmed the principles of St. Thomas Aquinas on the relation between faith and reason (*see* VATICAN COUNCILS: *First Vatican Council: Decree "Dei Filius"*). At the moment of Bismarck's victory the pope defined the dogma of papal infallibility (*see* INFALLIBILITY). Together with the dogma of the Immaculate Conception and *Dei Filius*, it defined the structure of Catholic humanity against the drift and skepticism of progress and power condemned in the Syllabus of 1864. (*See also* PIUS: *Pius IX.*) Forty years later Pius X began his pontificate, "taking courage in Him who strengtheneth us to proclaim that we have no other aim but that of restoring all things in Christ, so that Christ may be all in all" (*E Supremi apostolatus*, 1903).

2. The War of Ideologies.—The word Ultramontane belongs to an age of territorial dominion. With the loss of the papal states it passed into history. The war of ideologies began. In 1872 Bismarck launched his *Kulturkampf* or "cultural struggle" (*see* GERMANY: *History: The German Empire, 1866–71 and 1871–1918: Bismarck's Liberal Period and the Kulturkampf;* BISMARCK, OTTO: *The Kulturkampf*). In 1873 the May Laws inaugurated a policy of nationalization. The Catholic Bureau in the Ministry of Education was abolished, schools placed under state inspectors and seminaries under state control, and, as the war proceeded, many of the bishops were imprisoned. The radical Rudolf Virchow invented the name *Kulturkampf* to mark the real conflict not between church and state but between two civilizations fundamentally opposed. Resisted not only by Catholics and the centre but by the court, the conservatives, and the Lutherans, the policy failed.

By 1887 the *Kulturkampf* was over in Germany. It was beginning in France. The Italian governments of left and right, unable to cope with economic distress, suffered continual disorder, and the forces of communism and socialism increased. Leo XIII, who succeeded Pius IX in 1878, issued a series of encyclicals on social and political questions which were accepted through the whole church as a classical statement of its principles.

(T. S. GY.; X.)

F. 20TH CENTURY

1. To World War I.—In France at the beginning of the 20th century the church was still experiencing a period of hostility between church and state, though Leo XIII had made overtures to the Third Republic in his ruling that Catholics (for the most part monarchists) should accept the Republican constitution. Anticlerical legislation, such as the suppression of most of the religious houses ("Expulsion of the Congregations") and the removal of schools from their care, culminated in the separation of church and state in 1905. Church property was declared to belong to the state, though its use for religious services was tolerated, and freedom of worship was allowed. An unexpected consequence of the separation was that the government could no longer veto nominations for the episcopate. The Dreyfus affair, which was finally concluded in 1906, showed the depth of the cleavage between Frenchmen, with the Catholics mostly in the conservative traditional camp (*see* DREYFUS, ALFRED; FRANCE: *History: The Third Republic to 1914: Dreyfus Case* [1894–1906] and *Church and Army*). Anticlericalism declined during World War I, when priests, called up for military service, demonstrated their courage and patriotism; the army had long been a traditional

career for sons of many Catholic families, but their advancement before 1914 was very slow.

In Italy relations between church and state improved under Pius X, whose encyclical of 1905 permitted Catholics to vote in national elections. A controversy between the Spanish government and the Vatican, about the authorization of new religious orders, continued until 1912. The character of the government-nominated episcopate was repressive in Spanish Catholicism, and there was little intellectual life among the laity. In Portugal, after the unstable monarchy was ousted in 1911, the church was disestablished, the religious orders banished, and religion removed from the primary school curriculum.

2. Interwar Period.—*Russia.*—The new Communist government in Russia after the Revolution of 1917 worked against any religious influence. Its hostility came to a head in the trial of I. B. Cieplak, auxiliary bishop of Mogilev, and I. B. Budwiekicz, vicar general, both of whom were condemned on charges of plotting against the state. Budwiekicz was executed in 1923, but the bishop was later released. Catholics had always been a resented and suspected minority in this Orthodox country, and their numbers were still further reduced after Lithuania (1918) and eastern Poland (1921) had been detached from Russia.

France.—French Catholics were active in progressive political movements after World War I, though few were elected to the Chamber of Deputies. A vigorous Catholic intellectual life was inspired by Charles Péguy and Léon Bloy, whose works continued to be influential; by Jacques Maritain and Étienne Gilson, the expositors of Neo-Thomism; and by the novelists Georges Bernanos and François Mauriac. The *Action française* movement of Charles Maurras and Léon Daudet (*qq.v.*) was formally condemned by Pius XI in 1926 because it subordinated religion to politics and reduced Catholicism to a useful adjunct in the armoury of national solidarity. During the Spanish Civil War (1936–39), French Monarchists and conservative Catholics instinctively sided with the Spanish Nationalists, while the Catholics of the left, in competition with the Communists for the support of the French proletariat, were unhappy about the alignment, some even supporting the Republican government.

Germany and Austria.—In Germany, under the liberal constitution of the Weimar Republic (which rested on a coalition that included the Centre, Catholic, Party), Catholicism flourished, with a wide range of newspapers and publications; so did the Communist and the National Socialist movements. Indeed, in Bavaria the National Socialists (Nazis) went largely unchecked because the Bavarian government, dominated by the Catholic Bavarian People's Party, was opposed to the Weimar government. Catholicism, however, was not of first importance in politics, though a Catholic, Heinrich Brüning, was chancellor of the republic in 1930–32, just before Hitler came to power, and the votes of Centre Party deputies in the *Reichstag* helped to give him full powers in March 1933. In that year (1933) the Vatican signed a concordat with Hitler which seemed to promise the church all the essentials of independence, even in matters of education. But Hitler merely wanted the Catholics quiescent until his government was secure. The concordat did not save the church from Nazi interference, and by early 1937 Pope Pius XI's encyclical *Mit brennender Sorge* ("With Burning Anxiety") detailed the ways in which the concordat had not been kept. (*See also* PIUS.) Meanwhile various German bishops had condemned Nazi racial ideas and forbidden Catholics to join the Nazi Party. The prohibition was not closely observed, many Catholics regarding it as an unwarrantable intrusion by the church authorities into political life and preferring the Nazis to the Communists.

In 1938 Hitler took over Austria, where after the dismemberment of the Austro-Hungarian Empire at the end of World War I the Christian Socialist Party (relying on the Catholic peasants) had been in the majority. After the four-day civil war in 1934, the Catholic prime minister Engelbert Dollfuss transformed the parliamentary constitution into an authoritarian, one-party ("Patriotic Front") government influenced in its social framework by the encyclical *Quadragesimo anno* (1931), and a concordat was signed with the Vatican. Under this new regime the Nazis continued to infiltrate until the *Anschluss* in 1938, after which Austrian Catholics were faced with difficulties similar to those troubling German Catholics.

When World War II began in 1939, German Catholics, supported by the hierarchy, hastened to demonstrate their patriotism. And as the war began to go badly for Germany it became increasingly difficult for them to express any criticism. Although some individuals resisted Hitler's racial atrocities, no very explicit condemnation of them came either from the hierarchy or from Pius XII, who decided against placing German Catholics in the position of traitors to their country.

Italy.—Mussolini, after he came to power in 1922, began conversations with the newly elected Pius XI, from which issued the Lateran Treaty and the concordat of 1929. By the former the political neutrality of the papacy was assured, and by the latter the church was established in Italy. The pope at long last acquiesced in the seizure of Rome and the papal states in return for the acknowledgment of his sovereignty over the small area of the newly created Vatican City State within Rome and for payment in compensation for the property seized. Church and state were soon at loggerheads over education, which Mussolini claimed as the prerogative of the state. In 1931 the encyclical *Non abbiamo bisogno* protested against the educational pretensions of Fascism.

On the whole, however, the new relationship between church and state found widespread acceptance at first, because it ended the anticlerical feeling the parliamentary regime had fostered. Mussolini's invasion of Ethiopia led to a rallying of patriotic sentiment in which the Italian clergy, including a number of bishops, took part. The regime and the Vatican were also drawn together when the Italian government sent help to the Nationalists in the Spanish Civil War. But relations rapidly deteriorated after Mussolini concluded the Axis pact with Germany, and Pius XI was on the verge of a denunciation when he died early in 1939. In spite of efforts by Pius XII to keep Italy neutral, Mussolini declared war on France and Great Britain in June 1940. Thereafter the Vatican remained neutral, as the terms of the Lateran Treaty continued to operate, and much humanitarian work was done there for war victims, including Jews.

Spain.—The fall of the Spanish monarchy was followed by the violent anticlericalism of the Second Republic (1931–36). The Jesuits were expelled, religious schools were ordered to close, many churches were burned, and Pedro Cardinal Segura y Sáenz, archbishop of Toledo and primate of Spain, was expelled from the country. The Catholics organized a broadly based Christian Democratic Party (CEDA), led by José Gil Robles, which won the elections of 1933 but was unable to control the situation. In 1936 the Popular Front won a substantial majority, chaos increased, and the civil war (1936–39) broke out within a few months. The Catholics led by the hierarchy were on the Nationalist side, although theirs was an uneasy partnership with the Falangists; on the other hand, the Basque nationalists, Catholic and separatist, supported the republic to the end. More than 7,000 priests and religious were murdered, mostly by anarchists, in the Republican zone.

Portugal.—An army *coup* of 1926 followed the reelection of the left-wing government in 1925. By 1928 a Catholic professor of economics, António de Oliveira Salazar, was in virtual control and remained so. With the church his relations were defined by the concordat of 1940, which separated church and state.

Ireland.—In Ireland the tension between Catholic and Protestant had outlived emancipation, being exacerbated by the political conflict over home rule between the mainly Catholic Nationalists and the Unionists of Ulster, nearly all of whom were Protestant. The peace settlement of 1921 divided the island into two parts, one with a Protestant, one with a Catholic minority. Sporadic violence by the Irish Republican Army was condemned by the hierarchy, but as the Irish republican government disowned such actions the condemnation caused no conflict, and church-state relations were and continued to be so harmonious as to render a concordat unnecessary.

The interreligious strife of Ireland adversely affected Catholic-Protestant relations in Britain in areas of massive Irish immigration, such as Liverpool and Glasgow. Though the proportion of Catholics in Britain of Irish descent was very high, the most conspicuous Catholic figures were often converts, as G. K. Chesterton, R. A. Knox, and Eric Gill. Politically there were no more battles for the church as a whole in Britain, only for individuals.

3. After World War II.—After the end of World War II the church in Europe was faced with the Communist threat and with the increasingly secular and materialist attitude that permeated society.

Eastern Europe.—In those countries of Eastern Europe where Communist governments were in power, the church was subjected to interference in its normal activities and to imprisonment, deportation, or execution of some of its leading clergy and members of religious orders. In the Soviet Union the Catholic Byzantine rite churches were abolished entirely, their members being given the choice of joining either the Latin rite Catholics or the appropriate Orthodox Eastern Church.

In Yugoslavia Archbishop (later Cardinal) Alojzije Stepinac was imprisoned (1946) on charges of forcibly converting Orthodox Serbs to Roman Catholicism and collaborating with the Germans during World War II; in Czechoslovakia Archbishop (later Cardinal) Josef Beran was confined for his protests against state interference with church affairs; and in Hungary József Cardinal Mindszenty was imprisoned in 1949 on a charge of treason. As communications worsened between the West and the Communist countries of Eastern Europe, some bishops in the latter found it advisable to sign national agreements with their governments, against the advice of the Vatican. The clergy were under constant pressure to support the government without question.

Catholics are in the majority in Poland, where, since the country was for so long under Russian Orthodox or Prussian Lutheran rule, there is a strong national feeling in favour of the church. After emerging from Nazi persecution the Polish church after World War II was much discriminated against by the Communist authorities, who used the weapon of excessive taxation of colleges and seminaries. The bishops under Archbishop Stefan Wyszynski of Gniezno and Warsaw, who himself suffered imprisonment, did not submit in silence, but by tenacious protests managed to obtain some alleviation in 1950, when a *modus vivendi* between church and state was agreed on. After further troubles a new agreement was reached in 1956, and Wyszynski was permitted to go to Rome to receive the red hat in 1957 (he had been elevated to cardinal in 1953).

In the later 1950s there was some relaxation of pressure in Communist Europe. Concessions were made in certain publicized areas, though concurrently legislation was often introduced that obstructed the practice of religion without being obviously directed against the church. Many bishops from behind the "iron curtain," including those from the German Democratic Republic, were permitted to attend the second Vatican Council in the 1960s.

Western Europe.—After World War II Catholics in France founded the Mouvement Républicain Populaire, parallel to the Christian Democratic Party in other countries. Never strong enough to form a government, it joined coalitions with other parties, generally the Socialists. French Catholics, notably Robert Schuman, were prominent in the United Europe Movement, which was supported by the Catholic political parties in the six countries forming the European Economic Community.

A new departure in France, begun toward the end of the war, was the worker-priest movement, whereby, in an attempt to bring the church to the secularized industrial population, certain priests went to work full-time in secular posts and share the lives of working people. Unfortunately some of the worker-priests so closely identified themselves with their lay colleagues that they joined in a Communist demonstration in Paris in 1952. This led to stricter control and then to discontinuation of the worker-priest movement. There was much discontent in France among a great many Catholics who did not agree with this decision. In 1957 the *Mission ouvrière* ("Working Mission") was founded, to consist of priests and lay workers. The question of worker-priests was raised again under Pope John XXIII, who had had personal knowledge of French affairs. In October 1965 it was announced that, by agreement with the Holy See, the French bishops had authorized resumption of the movement.

The division of Germany left Catholics only slightly less numerous than Protestants in the Federal Republic of Germany, and both joined to form the Christian Democratic Party which governed the country when self-rule was achieved after World War II. The realization that the anti-Christian Nazi government had come to power so easily partly because Christian opposition to it had been divided led Catholics and Protestants to work together in the social and political sphere. German Catholics, including priests and theologians, were anxious for reform within the church which would make it easier to heal the breach with the Lutherans. German bishops and consultors thus became the leading exponents of change at the second Vatican Council, endeavouring to stress their common heritage with the Lutherans especially by using German instead of Latin, by presenting the Mass in terms of Holy Communion and the altar as the Lord's table, and above all by emphasizing the preeminent place of Scripture.

In postwar Austria the majority party was again Catholic, now called the Austrian People's Party instead of Christian Socialists. After the occupation of the country came to an end in 1955, Austria passed a law of perpetual neutrality. In 1957 the question of a new concordat was raised, but in the following year the Vatican decided that the 1934 concordat should stand.

In Italy the strongest political party after the war was the Christian Democratic, the successor of the short-lived Popular Party formed just after World War I by the priest Luigi Sturzo. Its outstanding statesman, Alcide De Gasperi, was prime minister during 1945-53. His party was unified in its opposition to Communism. The Communists had been strengthened by their activities in the resistance movement during the war, and the Italian Communist Party was the largest in Western Europe. The church had interposed the Italian Catholic Action as a lay activity between the Holy See and the Christian Democrat Party, and there were many occasions when the government acted in a way neither approved nor understood by the Vatican, as for instance in the latitude allowed to the Communists to attack the church. Communists in Italy, for tactical reasons, maintained that they were not opposed to the religion of the people but concerned only with their material betterment.

Catholic Action in 1959 was made dependent on the bishops instead of directly on the Holy See and began to be less concerned with anti-Communism, though the ban on Catholic cooperation with Communists continued. This caused friction especially in Sicily, where coalition of the Social Democrats with leftist elements was censured by the church. In 1963 there was some increase in the Communist Party's role after the publication of the encyclical *Pacem in terris*, though there was no relaxation of the Catholic ban on cooperation with Communists.

In Spain a new concordat was made (1953) by which Catholicism remained the established church of the country. The previous right of the Spanish crown to choose the bishops was modified in favour of an arrangement whereby the papal nuncio in consultation with the government was to submit six names to the pope who would return three of them, one of which was to be accepted by the head of state. Freedom of worship was guaranteed to all, though the small Protestant minority had to worship in buildings which did not resemble churches from the outside. This and other limitations on their freedom of action, such as the prohibition of Protestant processions and of the distribution of Protestant publications, were justified by the government on grounds of public order. Following the papacy of John XXIII, however, conditions for the Protestant minority improved.

Many members of the Spanish government belong to Opus Dei, a "secular institute" whose members live in the world, practising their professions but handing over most of their earnings to Opus Dei. The influence of Opus Dei members (to be found outside Spain as well) in Spanish public life has been variously estimated; it probably was less than the wholesale infiltration attributed to it by some nonmembers.

The impression sometimes given to outsiders of the monolithic solidarity of the church behind Salazar and Franco was altered by reports in the 1960s of arrest and deportation of priests for supporting the rebels in Angola, of episcopal and lay support for miners on illegal strike in Asturias, and of the protest of the abbot of Montserrat against the general lack of freedom, especially the Castilian overshadowing of Catalan culture; on this last point, it was notable that provision was made in the vernacular liturgy for the use of Catalan, Basque, and Galician in appropriate areas.

During the 20th century the number of Catholics in Great Britain increased steadily, chiefly by immigration from Ireland. The great preoccupation of church authorities in England and Wales continued to be educational. Although the government pays the salaries and running costs, Catholics must provide one-quarter of the initial costs of all new schools. Catholics share in the expansion of university education in Great Britain. During World War II and after the pontificate of Pope John XXIII a new spirit of ecumenism led to closer and better relations with other Christian bodies. In 1964 some of the long-standing prohibitions, which had become ingrained habits since penal times, against attending or taking part in Protestant services were lifted at the discretion of the hierarchy. After the disappearance of the Irish Nationalist members of Parliament, Catholics seldom had more than 25 members, with slight preponderance on the Labour side. But they became more prominent in local government and in the trade-union movement, in which they played a leading part in combating Communist influence.

See also ANTICLERICALISM; CHRISTIAN SOCIALISM; and *History* sections of articles on the various European countries.

(J. D. W.; X.)

III. THE CHURCH IN THE AMERICAS, AFRICA, AND THE ORIENT

A. SPANISH AMERICA

Colonial Spanish America showed a curious intermingling of the spiritual and the political, and as a result it is difficult to mark the limits of the activity and influence of the church. In Spain the church had been a unifying factor in the development of national life. In Spanish America it had an even greater influence because after the accession of Queen Isabella I (1474) the crown, preoccupied with consolidating its power in Spain, was unable to assume the cultural and educational responsibilities which the New World presented. With royal consent and encouragement, the church assumed those responsibilities.

1. The Spanish State and the Church.—Relations between the state and church were governed by royal patronage, a long-standing custom in Europe extended to the New World (*patronato real indiano,* "royal patronage of the Indies") by a series of papal bulls. In 1493 Pope Alexander VI granted Queen Isabella title to the new lands on condition that the crown christianize the Indies. To aid in this work he transferred to the crown jurisdiction in the ecclesiastical government of the Indies. In 1501 the crown of Castile was granted the right to collect and administer all church taxes in the Indies on condition that it defray all church expenses. In 1508 Pope Julius II issued the bull *Universalis ecclesiae*, which listed the royal rights and prerogatives in detail. (*See* also LATIN AMERICA: *The Colonial Period.*) Papal attempts to curb or revoke the *patronato real indiano* were unsuccessful during the colonial period. Its main features were:

a. Control of church offices. For the higher church offices, such as bishoprics, the king nominated a candidate who was generally confirmed in office by the pope. When Rome rejected the nomination, the king usually submitted another name without delay; if he did not, the see remained vacant and its rents flowed into the royal treasury. Lower ecclesiastical offices (cathedral canon, parish priest, and even at times the sacristan) were ordinarily filled by the local royal representative from a list of three names presented by the bishop concerned.

b. Control of church personnel. This meant that no clergyman could go to or return from the Americas, even on official business, without royal permission. Bishops could not travel outside their dioceses without express permission of the crown, nor could they resign without prior royal consent. The crown determined which religious orders could found convents in America—Franciscans, Dominicans, Mercedarians, and Augustinians, in that order—and which of their members could be sent there. When the Mercedarians aroused royal dissatisfaction by their support of rebellious movements in Central America and Peru, Philip II ordered their suppression, and the Jesuits were named in their place; Jesuits went to Peru in 1567 and to Mexico in 1572.

c. Control of church communications. More serious than the control over church personnel was that exercised over church communications. In 1538 Charles I ordered that thereafter no communication, except of conscience matters, could pass between the pope and church officials in the Spanish Indies without the approval (*pase*) of the Council of the Indies. The royal apologist Antonio Joaquín Rivadeneira maintains that only six papal bulls were denied the *pase* in two centuries. However, many more papal documents, though not bulls, were refused admittance to the colonies.

d. Control of church finances. Finally, the crown accepted financial responsibility for the church in the Indies on condition that it collect and administer church taxes. This ensured almost complete control; obviously any church effort that had to rely on royal funds was subject to the royal will. The royal treasury was not equal to the task it had assumed. Gradually the religious orders and bishops began to accept bequests and other forms of wealth as supplementary income. The growing affluence of the church brought the reduction or elimination of royal contributions. Then the crown began to look for ways to divert church monies into the royal treasury. One way was the levy (*donativo*). Theoretically this was a voluntary gift, but the crown usually determined how much it would be pleased to accept. Thus, in California, Junípero Serra in 1783 paid more than 100 pesos as the donation of Carmel Mission to the crown for prosecution of the Spanish war against the English. After 1617 the king reserved almost a third of the tithes for the royal treasury instead of using them all for church purposes. In 1798 a tax of 15% was placed on ecclesiastical property. In 1804 most of the capital of the pious foundations of Mexico, 10,656,000 pesos, was gathered into the royal treasury. Thus, by the end of the colonial period the church was contributing more to the crown than the crown was contributing to the church. However, the crown continued to support, as best it could, the vast mission enterprise on the same basis as at the beginning of colonization. (*See* also INDIES, LAWS OF THE.)

2. Early History.—The church arrived in the Americas on the second voyage of Columbus, in the persons of Bernardo Buil, vicar apostolic, and several Franciscans, sent primarily to minister to the Spaniards rather than as missionaries. Stress on the conversion of the natives eventually brought a division of labour; the religious orders concentrated on work among the Indians, while the diocesan clergy for a long time ministered chiefly to the Spaniards.

Earlier estimates of the native population in America in the 16th century place the total under Spanish jurisdiction at about 15,000,000, but more recent studies seem to indicate 30,000,000 as more nearly accurate. The eloquence of the chroniclers of the conquest tends to persuade the reader that the majority of those Indians lived in Aztec and Inca cities of relative splendour and magnificence, so that all the Spanish clergy had to do was transform the pagan temples into churches and begin the work of conversion. This is not true. Many, perhaps most, Indians were more or less nomads. Even the sedentary inhabitants of the great empires lived for the most part in crude huts scattered amid the arroyos and *quebradas* near their fields. This dispersion of the Indians was a very real obstacle to the work of conversion. The relative success of some experimental Indian settlements (or reductions) in Hispaniola and Cuba caused the adoption, after the conquest of Mexico in 1521, of the policy of settling Indians into pueblos of at least 400 families. With the sedentary tribes this was not difficult, but with the nomads, who knew nothing of community living, the friar had to instruct in selecting a town site, laying out streets, erecting houses and community buildings, bring-

ing in water, electing town officials, and planting and cultivating crops.

The friars were never more than a handful among the millions of Indians, and it was impossible even to think of individual instruction. A solution was found in the protracted catechumenate, a system that permitted baptism of the Indian after he had been instructed in the essential articles of the faith, on condition that the instruction be perfected by enforced attendance at doctrinal classes several times a week until the neophyte was completely instructed.

In the first decades the friars were aided in their work by laymen, called *encomenderos,* who, in exchange for a share of the Indian tribute, were to care for the technical and cultural instruction of their wards and to defend the priests against violence. Priests working among the Indians were called *doctrineros* and the cooperative system was known as the *encomienda-doctrina.* By 1574 this agency had founded some 9,000 Indian pueblos with a total population of about 6,000,000. Each pueblo had its church or chapel; a large proportion also had schools for the instruction of the sons of the principal families; many had hospitals which served also as hospices for travelers. Admission to these institutions was free, since the charges were already included in each Indian's tax. (*See* also MEXICO: *History: Colonial Period;* NEW LAWS.)

In 1573 Philip II forbade the expansion of the *encomienda,* and a new system had to be developed for the assimilation of the Indian into colonial society. This came to be known in Spanish as *la misión,* a term unknown in Spanish law before 1573. In the mission the Indian was to be kept in involuntary isolation from Europeans under the direct care of a priest and the protection of mercenary soldiers. Some of the older religious orders, notably the Augustinians and Dominicans, unable to adapt themselves to the new system, gradually dropped out of frontier Indian work. The Franciscans, after a period of hesitation, adopted it. The Jesuits, recently arrived in Spanish America, took to it enthusiastically and in the 17th century founded many flourishing missions, the most famous the Paraguayan reductions (*reducciones; see* PARAGUAY: *History).*

3. Social and Intellectual Developments.—There were byproducts of the major effort of the church to convert the Indians. Native languages were mastered. The customs and culture of the peoples were recorded by Bernardino de Sahagún, Antonio de la Calancha, Motolinia (Toribio de Benavente), Diego Durán. Missionaries were explorers, geographers, and cartographers as well. The Franciscan Juan de Zumárraga arranged for a press in Mexico in 1539 primarily to print books for the instruction of the Indians. By 1810 printing establishments were found in 25 Spanish-American cities. Special schools were begun for the Indians, some technical, as the Colegio de San José of Pedro de Gante in Mexico City or that of Quiroga at Pátzcuaro, others true senior colleges intended for the training of Indian leaders, as that of Santa Cruz de Tlaltelolco (1536) or San Andrés in Quito (1554).

In the 16th century church schools also offered the only elementary education to the young European or creole (Spaniard born in America). By the 17th century this burden was shared by the city councils, but secondary education remained a near monopoly of the church throughout the colonial period. This was especially true after the arrival of the Jesuits, who found the creoles almost abandoned by the older orders in favour of the Indians. Even before the Jesuits came, the church had begun a series of universities: Santo Domingo (1538), Lima, and Mexico (1553). There were 25 universities and 56 colleges at the end of the colonial period.

4. Spaniard and Spanish American.—Spain gave to America some of its noblest men: St. Alfonso Toribio of Lima, St. Francisco Solano of Argentina and Peru, St. Peter Claver of Cartagena, St. Luis Beltrán of Colombia. The gift found a worthy response among the peoples of America: St. Philip of Jesus (mestizo), St. Rose of Lima (creole), St. Anna Paredes of Quito (creole), and St. Martín de Porres (mulatto). In view of this response it is difficult to understand the refusal of the Spanish clergy to share freely not only the leadership of the church but even the priesthood itself with Spanish Americans. By the end of the colonial period there were ten archbishoprics and 38 bishoprics in Spanish America. Of the 171 bishops and archbishops of New Spain (Mexico), 130 were Spaniards, 32 were Mexicans, and 9 others were from other Spanish-American areas. Only one archbishop of Mexico had been born in that country. Of the 535 bishops and archbishops in the rest of Spanish America, a mere 64 were American-born. Only one archbishop of Lima was a Spanish American, Fernando Arias de Ugarte, native of what is now Colombia.

More serious was the denial of the priesthood to persons of Indian or Negro blood. Since a large proportion of the people of Spanish America were of either Indian or Negro parentage, this law automatically prevented development of one bond between the people and the church and removed an incentive to better their religious understanding and practice. It also placed a strain upon the relatively few in the population who were eligible for the priesthood. Fortunately this law was frequently no better observed than were numerous other royal decrees, and there were in fact many mestizo and Indian priests. But the prohibition remained, and since Spanish America never supplied the number of priests it needed the deficit had to be made up from Spain. About 11,000 priests and friars left Spain for the Americas and the Philippines during the 17th century; the number was only slightly smaller in the 18th century. Such departures created enormous problems in Spain, where no bishop and no provincial was willing to lose a good priest, and perhaps even greater problems of adjustment in the Americas.

The predominance of Spaniards among the bishops and the large proportion of Spanish priests and friars, many in preferred positions, did not help to identify the church with its people. Despite this, in the independence movements all of the colonies except Cuba and Puerto Rico received help from clergymen. Miguel Hidalgo and José Morelos are famous Mexican patriot-priests. Sixteen of the 29 who signed the declaration of independence for Argentina in 1816 were clergymen. In Peru, of the 51 members of the constituent assembly of 1822, 26 were priests and the president was Francisco Javier Luna Pizarro, later archbishop of Lima. How significant these examples were among the clergy at large is not clear, since few studies exist of priests who opposed independence. Such studies have been made for the bishops, and these reveal that the prelates were about equally divided for and against independence.

5. 19th Century.—After the achievement of independence, a readjustment had to be made in the balance of power between the new states and the church. In most of these countries the church occupied a position of suffocating superiority in organization, security of tenure, and trained and loyal personnel. The state was often merely a name, with no fixed limits, no national consciousness, few resources, and few trained administrators. In many areas the readjustment was hostile.

Some ill feeling arose from the traditional friendship of Rome with the Spanish monarchy. In accord with this policy, Pius VII solemnly condemned the Spanish-American patriots as rebels in 1816, and Leo XII in 1824, at the request of the Spanish crown, renewed the condemnation. Repeated friendly overtures by Simón Bolívar and by the governments of Argentina, Chile, and Mexico were rebuffed. More serious was the harm done to the church by the lack of influence of the Holy See at a time when the anarchy of the war years had occasioned numerous abuses and alert leadership was required to set them right. Governmental policies were being formed in areas of vital concern to the church, and it was imperative that vigorous church leaders share in their formation. Yet many sees, some the most important in the Americas, were vacant through death, exile, or desertion. Archbishop Pedro Ponte of Mexico City abandoned his people and returned to Madrid in 1822, whence he issued excommunications until his death in 1839. Independent Mexico did not get its first archbishop till 1840, by which time the trend of national development had been quite clearly determined. For many years Rome could not even fill vacant sees, since it did not recognize the new governments. In 1829 there was only one bishop (of Arequipa, in Peru) along the entire western coast of South America. This stagnation

of church leadership offered an opportunity to those who wished to organize public life on a secular basis, and the spiritual resources inherited from the colonial church were in large measure frittered away.   (A. S. Tr.)

6. 20th Century.—A deepening crisis confronted the church in the 20th century. The general absence of priestly vocations, coupled with the population explosion after World War II, aggravated clerical scarcities in a region where 90% of the 250,000,000 inhabitants (including Brazil) are Catholic. Despite an influx of over 18,000 European clergy, mainly Spanish, and over 3,000 U.S. missionaries after 1945, each priest in Spanish America served an average of 5,600 in the late 1960s. Reflecting this problem, a 1958 Latin-American bishops' report estimated that Sunday observance was limited to 13% of the Catholic laity. The lack of personnel prevented the diminution of huge parishes, averaging 383 sq.mi. with more than 15,000 members, and the dissuasion of the rural population from its practices of folk Catholicism. The great growth of Protestantism was facilitated by priestly shortages. With less than 635,000 faithful in 1937, Protestants numbered almost 10,000,000 (Brazil included) in the late 1960s.

Aligned with oligarchical structures and wary of reformers determined to emulate the 1910 Mexican revolution, which brought intense anti-clericalism, the church alienated much of Spanish American society in the first half of the century by assuming an apathetic posture concerning social questions. Activists, such as Msgr. Miguel de Andrea, who organized trade unions among Argentine workers in the 1920s, received scant encouragement from their bishops. The arrival in Latin America of several thousand Spanish priests, who fled their strife-torn nation in the 1930s, enhanced political and social conservatism among the clergy.

Despite the prevailing cautious attitude of the hierarchy, a progressive element seeking clerical identification with reform expectations gained substantial influence in the church after 1950. Bishop Manuel Larraín Errázuriz of Chile (1900–66), the foremost progressive spokesman, urged a positive church role in the socioeconomic transformation of Latin America to avert violent upheavals and the strengthening of Marxist-oriented movements. The effects of his admonitions were evidenced by increased clerical dissociation from authoritarian regimes during the 1950s. In Venezuela, Colombia, Cuba, and to a lesser degree Argentina during the Perón era, bishops criticized dictatorships which flouted constitutional procedures and ignored pressing social needs. A commitment to reform was seen in the proliferation of diverse programs throughout Spanish America, ranging from the radio schools of Msgr. José Salcedo, intended to eradicate illiteracy in the Colombian hinterland, to the distribution of ecclesiastical lands among the Chilean peasantry. The Latin-American Bishops' Council (CELAM), established in 1956, served as an information agency and coordinator for the church's widespread socio-religious projects. Another organization, the Catholic Inter-American Cooperation Program (CICOP), created in 1963, fostered greater hemispheric involvement in meeting the grave problem of the Latin-American church.

Efforts to promote peaceful change were challenged in the 1960s by dissenters who demanded direct clerical participation in revolution. Camilo Torres, a Colombian priest, was killed in 1966 after joining guerrillas in the highlands. Msgr. Ivan Illich, director of the Center for Inter-Cultural Formation in Cuernavaca, Mex., articulated the aspirations of this element in scathing denunciations of traditional church activities, such as the operation of private schools, which he claimed perpetuated oligarchies. He condemned U.S. Catholic financial aid to the church, which reached $15,000,000 annually by the late 1960s, as neo-Yankee imperialism. Summoned before the Congregation for the Doctrine of the Faith in mid-1968, he refused to answer charges concerning his controversial views. Subsequently, the Congregation prohibited Catholic religious from participating in the activities of the Cuernavaca centre, and Illich was granted temporary lay status. Massive protests against the papal ban on birth control attended the 1968 visit of Pope Paul VI to the 39th International Eucharistic Congress in Bogotá, further demonstrating increased clerical dissension concerning the role of the church in reform.   (J. A. Ga.)

B. Brazil

1. Early History.—En route to India, Pedro Álvares Cabral landed in Brazil in 1500 and claimed the land for his king. The superior of the 16 Franciscan missionaries aboard, Father Henry of Coimbra, celebrated Mass near Bahia (Salvador) on April 26, 1500, the date Brazilians regard as marking the foundation of the church in their country.

Portugal was concentrating its men and resources on the trade with India, then only recently opened by Vasco da Gama, and for a long time Brazil had to take second place in church as well as state affairs. Relations between church and state in Portugal and Portuguese America were similar to those in Spain and Spanish America. Through papal grant (the *padroado*) the king was in fact the head of the church. As a result, if royal interest in Brazil lagged, church interests were not vigorously pressed.

During the decades after the initial contact some Portuguese diocesan priests and small groups of Franciscans arrived in Brazil, but their influence was negligible. More important was the arrival in 1549, with the first royal governor general, of a group of Jesuits under Manuel da Nóbrega. They opened the first schools in the cities and, especially after the arrival of José de Anchieta in 1553, began their work among the Indians. In 1557 the Jesuits began their first Indian *aldeia*, a settlement similar to the Spanish mission. (*See also* BRAZIL: *History: Early Period: Royal Control.*)

The first bishop was appointed in 1551, with his see at Bahia. That see became an archbishopric in 1667, with suffragan sees in Rio de Janeiro and Olinda. By the end of the colonial period there were also bishops in São Luis, Belem, and São Paulo.

2. Religious Orders.—The Jesuits were the most influential force in early Brazil. However, Franciscans established elementary schools in the cities and worked among the Indians, especially in the north. The Benedictines arrived in 1584 and exerted a strong influence on culture, especially in the south, through their schools; by the end of the colonial period they had 30 foundations. The Carmelites arrived in 1589.

In general the Jesuits held almost a monopoly of work with Indians in the south. In the north in 1750 there were about 60,000 Indians in 63 *aldeias*, of which 19 were administered by the Jesuits, 15 by the Carmelites, 26 by the Franciscans, and 3 by the Mercedarians. The French scientist C. M. de La Condamine, who visited some of them in 1743, was startled by their prosperity. This work among the Indians was the glory of the church in Brazil. Little is known of any organized effort among the great number of Negro slaves. Nor did the church found any university or similar institution of higher learning in colonial Brazil.

In 1759 the marquês de Pombal, the Portuguese prime minister, expelled the Jesuits from Portugal and its possessions. In Brazil they then had 9 *colegios*, 5 seminaries, 36 missions, 25 residences, and 5 other houses. Certainly work among the Indians suffered substantially from the expulsion, but more serious for the church was the effect on the seminaries, to the faculties of which Pombal appointed professors of his own liking. Henceforth the clergy were to be more obedient to the state than to the church.

3. 19th Century.—Brazil became independent without any severe struggle in 1822 when the son of the Portuguese king declared for independence and became the emperor Pedro I. During his reign and that of his son, Pedro II, the Brazilian clergy adopted the liberalism introduced by the Portuguese court, some of them even joining the Masonic lodges, centres of liberal culture and humanitarianism, though the Holy See had repeatedly forbidden such participation. The Brazilian church was drifting toward not merely tolerance but religious indifference. The break came in 1872 when the bishop of Rio de Janeiro suspended a priest who refused to give up his Masonic affiliations. The bishops of Belem and Olinda, in sympathy, issued an interdict against those religious lay brotherhoods (*irmandades*) which refused to expel members who were Masons. Pedro II declared the interdict invalid and without effect, and the bishops, refusing to yield, were imprisoned as rebels. The attendant controversy separated the secularist elements from those who desired a strong spiritual leadership of the church. In the separation the church lost heavily. After the establishment of the republic in 1889, the new government disestablished the church, and though the bishops protested the action, the general public was apathetic. (A. S. Tr.)

4. 20th Century.—Claiming a nominal affiliation of 72,000,000 in the 1960s, the largest membership in the world, the Roman Catholic Church in Brazil encountered monumental problems in seeking an extension of its influence. In a nation where the priesthood is scorned and the population, which had reached 85,000,000 (1967), increases by about 3% annually, clerical scarcities became critical. Fewer than 12,000 priests, 60% of them foreigners, were engaged in apostolates ranging from missions among forest Indians to the operation of universities. The church had been unable to contain the persistent growth of spiritualism (*q.v.*), which, in variant forms, enjoyed adherence among 30% of the population. In addition, Protestantism thrived during the 20th century. With an active ministry exceeding 9,000, Protestants numbered 5,000,000 in 1968.

Committing itself to involvement in socioeconomic reform, the church adopted the Emergency Plan of the Brazilian Bishops in 1962 and established the Center of Religious Studies and Social Research to recommend projects. Dissatisfied with the cautious attitude of the hierarchy regarding social questions, Archbishop Helder Câmara of Recife, a spokesman of the vocal Catholic New Left in Brazil, urged direct participation in revolution. This position, which sought an accommodation with Communist elements, aroused substantial dissensions within the church. (J. A. Ga.)

C. North America

1. Early Missions to the Indians.—In colonial North America the church of Spain launched the first and not the smallest missionary effort: priests accompanied the Spanish conquistadors who first explored parts of the present United States. After several early attempts at evangelization had ended in bloody failure, the church, with the foundation of St. Augustine in Florida in 1565, began its continuing presence. In subsequent years Franciscan friars laboured among the Indians of present-day Florida, Georgia, and Alabama, an area that eventually contained 26,000 Catholic aborigines, served by 35 mission stations. This work, carried on for a century and a half, ended when the English and their Indian allies destroyed the mission during Queen Anne's War (the American aspect of the general European War of the Spanish Succession).

Far to the west, other Spanish ventures proved more lasting. In 1598 Franciscans began the evangelization of New Mexico, and by 1630 they were ministering to 30,000 Indian converts. Jesuits began the evangelization of Arizona in 1691. In 1769 Franciscans moved into California and created a series of 21 missions along the coast; by 1820 they had reported the baptism of over 50,000 aborigines (*see* CALIFORNIA: *History: Missions*). By the time the United States seized these lands in the Mexican War, the missions and the Indians were dying out, but a remnant survived to become part of the American church.

With the establishment of Quebec in 1608 the church began its existence under the flag of France. Priests accompanied the pioneers and started missions among the Indians of Acadia (Nova Scotia) and the St. Lawrence Valley. Jesuits set up stations among the Hurons on the Great Lakes. The first North American saints were the Jesuit martyrs Isaac Jogues, Jean de Brébeuf, and their companions, murdered by the Iroquois in their war of extermination against the Hurons.

In 1659 the church received its first bishop, François de Montmorency Laval (*q.v.*), who organized parochial life in Quebec and left on it the enduring mark of his own zeal and austerity. Missionary activity resumed after 1660 and continued for a century. Though the Indians of eastern Canada became Catholic, the history of the missions within what became the United States is that of a handful of zealous priests labouring with only moderate success among a sparse aboriginal population. While the Indians of Maine were converted, missions among the Iroquois, a confederation usually hostile to the French, were abandoned after the French defeat by England in the War of the Spanish Succession (1713). In the Old Northwest, several stations were maintained along the Great Lakes and others were founded in southern Illinois. When France occupied lower Louisiana after 1699, the church entered that area; but Indian wars ended the hopes of converting the aborigines.

When in 1763 France surrendered its empire in North America, the church had a few thousand adherents in the Mississippi Valley; their influence on the later American church was small. In Canada, however, some 65,000 Catholics preserved their devotion to their ancestral church, and from these developed the later church in Canada.

2. 17th–18th-Century Catholic Immigration.—The strongest Roman Catholic Church in the western hemisphere developed not from Catholic Spain or France but from Protestant England. The American church grew from that small group of English Catholics who under the leadership of the Calvert family in 1634 planted the colony of Maryland as a place of refuge from the harsh anti-Catholic laws of England. It was the first English colony founded, whether from principle or expediency, on religious toleration. While in the 17th century the English were expanding along the Atlantic coast, the church existed only in southern Maryland, where priests were permanently stationed. Jesuits came with the first settlers and served continuously down to the American Revolution. They were few in number—at times only one or two, and until the 18th century never more than five or six.

Under the Stuart Restoration the colonies, pushed by England or guided by such proprietors as William Penn, extended religious toleration even to Catholics. Yet anti-Catholic sentiment flourished as vigorously in the colonies as in the British Isles, and after the revolution of 1688 put William and Mary on the English throne colonial Catholics were the targets of discriminatory laws. Royal governors were ordered to exclude them from the general toleration, and every colonial legislature enacted anti-Catholic measures. The largest number and the severest of these laws were passed in Maryland.

In this atmosphere the church suffered some defections, yet it survived and even expanded its field of operations into southeastern Pennsylvania, where Catholics were present among the many German and Irish immigrants. When at the request of their English colleagues German Jesuits arrived after 1740 to minister to their countrymen, the number of priests reached 20. In 1775 they served a small minority of 25,000 Catholics.

3. Revolutionary War and After.—By the Treaty of Paris (1763) the British Empire had guaranteed to the Canadians the right to practise their religion. By the Quebec Act (1774) Parliament not only sanctioned this right but granted to the Catholic clergy their accustomed rights and dues. (*See* also CANADA: *History: Canada as Quebec.*) Nor were the usual anti-Catholic oaths imposed on Canada; Catholics could vote and hold office. The act was greeted by the Americans with rage, as much for the toleration extended to the Catholic Church as for the extension of the boundaries of Quebec to the Ohio and the Mississippi. Consequently, when the question of independence arose, Bishop Jean Briand and his clergy opted for London rather than Boston, rejected the embassy of Benjamin Franklin and Father John Carroll (1776), and, while the English Protestant colonies revolted, kept French Catholic Canada loyal to the British Empire. To reward and preserve this loyalty Parliament by the Constitutional Act of 1791 created a special government for the province of Quebec, called Lower Canada. Though royal officials hindered the work of the church, it grew rapidly by natural increase.

With the onset of the Revolution, Catholics in the colonies south of Canada began to venture into public life. Catholic officers and men served in Washington's army and in the rebel navy. Others held office in the new state governments and sat in the Continental Congress. A Catholic signed the Declaration of Independence, and two participated in the Constitutional Convention of 1787. The Revolution gave impetus to the forces making for religious freedom, and the church profited; with satisfaction Catholics saw state anti-Catholic laws revoked and religious liberty proclaimed in the new nation.

First Bishop.—In the year the new United States installed its first president, the Roman Catholic Church chose its first United States bishop. (The colonial antipathy to prelacy had previously made establishment of a bishopric impolitic.) In 1784 the Holy See had appointed John Carroll (*q.v.*) superior of the mission in America. In 1789 his priests elected him their bishop and selected Baltimore as his see; in 1808 suffragan dioceses were created in Boston, New York, Philadelphia, and Bardstown on the frontier in Kentucky.

Trusteeism.—The American church was unaccustomed to bishops. When the laity formed a new congregation, often before there was a priest to serve them, the property of the parish was held in trust by laymen elected for the purpose. Often the trustees sought to extend their control from material to spiritual matters. During the first half of the 19th century the church was plagued by outbursts of trusteeism, recalcitrant trustees and rebellious priests rejecting the authority of the bishops and the church suffering the consequences of interdict, excommunication, schism. In time all the quarrels were patched up, and by 1860 the trustee problem had died out. In most such disputes ethnic antagonisms played a part. Trusteeism thus was an early manifestation of a major problem the church faced throughout the century: how to merge into a single church the multitudes of immigrants of varied races, nationalities, and tongues pouring into the United States.

4. 19th-Century Immigration and Anti-Catholicism.—The church changed radically in the first half of the 19th century. In 1800 it was a small and inconspicuous denomination of fewer than 50,000 members, served by about 50 priests, and led by a single bishop, son of an old American family. By 1860 it had become the largest single church in America; bishops administered 43 dioceses served by 2,250 priests and with a membership of more than 3,000,000. The hierarchy, meeting in council in Baltimore eight times between 1829 and 1852, had produced notable spokesmen, most prominent among them John England of Charleston and John Hughes of New York. A Catholic press had appeared; Catholic schools were increasing in number. Canvassed by visitors from America, the church in Europe sent over a constant stream of priests and religious to reinforce the American clergy. Financial subsidies came from the French Society for the Propagation of the Faith and other lay organizations. The main contribution of the European church, however, was immigrants by the scores and hundreds of thousands.

While the newcomers were from all the countries of Europe, the large majority were Irish and German. Most, from choice or necessity, remained in the towns of the northeast, where they were highly visible and to many native Americans highly unwelcome. They were poor, uneducated, alien; they were blamed for the slums into which they were crowded and for the intemperance and crime which the slums produced; the power of their votes was feared and their complaints about the common schools (*see* below) were resented. After 1830 the ancient anti-Catholic bias revived and, fed by press and pulpit, grew strong. The result was violence: the 1840s and 1850s were marked by unpunished outbursts of riot and arson. In the field of politics the anti-Catholic movement achieved notable successes. The American or Know-Nothing Party won control of many cities and states and in the election of 1856 presented a presidential candidate who received 871,000 votes. But before the rising threat of secession and civil war the anti-Catholic movement subsided. (*See* KNOW-NOTHING PARTY.)

Nativism, however, was not finished. In the 1880s, now more a rural than an urban movement, it flared up again in the American Protective Association. Violence was no longer condoned, however, and the bigots were attacked by the urban press and the liberal Protestant pulpit. These tendencies became more pronounced when, after World War I, the Ku Klux Klan (*q.v.*) waged its campaign against Negro, Jew, Catholic, and alien alike. Anti-Catholic bias was present in the presidential campaign of 1928; its relative ineffectiveness in the election of 1960 suggests that as a factor in national life nativism has lost its force.

Reaction to recurring nativist attacks produced in U.S. Catholics what has been termed a "siege" or "ghetto" mentality. Accused of disloyalty to their country because of subservience to a foreign potentate, Catholics were prone to respond with ardent protestations of devotion to the United States. Only with the weakening of nativism has this defensive attitude been relaxed.

5. Growth of a National Church.—Before the Civil War Catholics, save for mavericks like Orestes Brownson (*see* BROWNSON, ORESTES AUGUSTUS), played little part in the mainstream of American life. On the defensive against nativist assaults, they learned to be suspicious of reformers; an enthusiastic abolitionist was often an equally enthusiastic religious bigot. Though there were Catholic slaves and masters in Maryland and Louisiana, the church took no stand on the institution of slavery, and during the war Catholics followed their sections; chaplains and nursing nuns served both Confederate and Union forces. When the bishops met in the second Plenary Council of Baltimore (Oct. 7–21, 1866), they considered the problem of the freedmen but did not devise a national policy on the question; they had more pressing problems to consider.

The main problem was to keep the immigrants in the church of their fathers. The tide of immigration rose after the war, and the numbers of Catholics doubled and tripled. By 1900 the church membership figure had passed 10,000,000, the number of priests had risen to 12,000 and the number of dioceses to 82. And the problem of nationalities had become even more complicated. While Irish and Germans continued to arrive, increasing numbers of Catholics came from southern and eastern Europe, others entered from Quebec, and Spanish-speaking Catholics moved north into the country. Roman Catholics of Eastern rites appeared among the immigrants.

Although the problem was immense, a solution was achieved, not without stress and not without loss. To minister to the newcomers in their own tongues, hundreds of churches were opened not as territorial but as national parishes. Catholics of the Oriental rites received their own churches and eventually their own bishops. In 1916 languages other than English were used in over 5,750 churches.

The immigrants, strangers in a strange land, wished to preserve their church as they had known it in Europe, and they wanted their own priests, independent of the American bishops. Had this tendency—called Cahenslyism after Peter Cahensly, a German worker for immigrants—prevailed, the American church would have been split into a dozen national bodies. With the support of Rome, the United States hierarchy opposed the movement, and with the passing of the years and the absorption of the immigrants it died out. The Polish National Catholic Church represents the only permanent schism suffered by the American church.

In meeting the problem two tendencies developed among the U.S. bishops. A liberal group headed by John Ireland (*q.v.*), archbishop of St. Paul, wished to force the rapid Americanization of the immigrants and the integration of the church into American society. A conservative group, led by Michael Corrigan of New York and Bernard McQuaid of Rochester, wished to delay the process. The debate was at times acrimonious and public; and it was seized upon by conservative priests in France to accuse the American church of a novel heresy: "Americanism." In 1899 Pope Leo XIII intervened and quieted the disputants. (*See* also AMERICANISM CONTROVERSY.)

6. French and English Canada.—The Catholic tendency to feel isolated and defensive was even more pronounced in Canada than in the United States. French-speaking Catholics felt uneasy when Canada was reunited by the Act of Union of 1840, though they were appeased by an act of 1851 guaranteeing all religions complete equality. When English-speaking Catholics migrated to Canada after 1820, they did not merge with the French; an English-language church rose in the Maritime Provinces and in the West. The church in Quebec flourished, but some French felt they were being overwhelmed by the tremendous majority of Anglo-Saxon Protestants in North America. Consequently they turned, led by the "beavers," to a defense of their own culture. Maintenance of French-Canadian culture, which includes membership in the Catholic Church, continued to present problems in Canada in the second half of the 20th century. (*See* also CANADA: *History*.)

7. The Church and the Labour Movement.—Directing a church composed largely of workingmen and their families, the U.S. bishops were concerned about trade-union movements. Recognizing in the days of rampant capitalism the need for secrecy in labour organization, the bishops in the council of 1866 specifically exempted trade unions from the general condemnation of secret, oath-bound societies, an exemption repeated in the third Plenary Council of Baltimore (Nov. 9–Dec. 7, 1884). They did not promulgate in their dioceses the condemnation of the Knights of Labor secured by Archbishop Elzéar Taschereau of Quebec in 1884 from the Roman Congregation of the Holy Office, and James Cardinal Gibbons (*q.v.*), archbishop of Baltimore, intervened in Rome in 1887 to have the decree suspended.

In later labour unions Catholic membership bulked large; it has been suggested that Catholic leadership played an important part in preserving American unions from radical domination. In the Great Depression of the 1930s scores of Catholic labour schools were opened, and organizations were formed to exert Catholic influence on labour, best known among these being the Association of Catholic Trade Unionists (ACTU, founded 1937) and the Young Christian Workers (*see* CATHOLIC ACTION). The latter group exists also in Canada, where alone were Catholic trade unions attempted; these unions came together in 1951 in the Confédération des Travailleurs Catholiques du Canada (CTCC).

8. 20th-Century Status.—In the 20th century the church in North America continued to grow. The Canadian census of 1901 showed that 2,229,600, or 41.7% of a population of 5,371,315, considered themselves Catholic; the census of 1961 indicated that 45.7% were Catholic (8,342,826 out of a total of 18,238,247). Two-thirds were French-speaking and almost 80% were concentrated in the provinces of Quebec and Ontario. The Canadian church at that time had 4,750 parishes served by more than 14,000 priests; it was divided into 59 dioceses and eight vicariates apostolic.

Comparable statistics show an equally impressive growth in the United States. The census of 1900 reported a U.S. population of 75,994,575, of whom 10,774,989 or 14% were Catholic. In 1960, when the population totaled 179,323,175, Catholics had increased to 42,104,900, or 23.5%. In the 140 U.S. dioceses during the 1960s over 54,000 priests served some 17,000 parishes.

The increasing strength of the Canadian and U.S. churches was recognized when in 1908 they were removed from the list of missionary territories under the jurisdiction of the Roman Congregation of the Propagation of the Faith. Apostolic delegations had been opened in the United States in 1893, in Canada in 1899. In 1909 the bishops of Canada met in their first plenary council. During World War I the U.S. bishops met in the National Catholic War Council, which after the war continued as the National Catholic Welfare Council and after 1923 as the National Catholic Welfare Conference (NCWC). Acting as a central agency organizing and coordinating efforts to carry on the church's social mission, the NCWC affects many aspects of Catholic life, as indicated by the names of its departments: executive, education, press, immigration, social action, legal, youth, and lay organizations. The Canadian church set up an organization similar to the NCWC in 1948.

An indication of the increasing importance within the universal church of the churches of North America was manifest at the first session of the Second Vatican Council in 1962. The U.S. church ranked second among the hierarchies of the various national churches, exceeded only by the Italian church, and the Canadian church ranked fifth in the number of council fathers.

The constant growth of church membership has produced among U.S. Catholics a preoccupation with brick and mortar. To serve the immigrant masses in the crowded cities of the late 19th century, commodious churches and schools had to be constructed. In the mass migration to the suburbs after World War II were large numbers of Catholics who were advanced in wealth and social standing beyond their immigrant forebears but who necessarily continued their tradition of building large edifices for worship and education.

The concern for material building, however, apparently did not preclude a growing appreciation of the spiritual values of religion.

Through the 1950s, vocations to the contemplative orders grew; the laity crowded the houses of retreat; lay men and women formed study clubs and enrolled in formal courses of theology; and organizations were created (*e.g.*, the Christian Family Movement, the Cana Conferences) to bring the faith to bear on the problems of modern life.

After Vatican Council II.—In the modernization initiated by the Second Vatican Council, the church in North America entered a period of rapid change unmatched in its history. To the man in the street an obvious symbol of the change was the new appearance of Catholic nuns, who replaced their antiquated costumes with more modern dress. The traditional Latin of the Mass yielded to English and the rubrics were simplified. Experimental liturgies, including the use of dancing and popular music, were tried. While conservatives lamented these and other changes, most Catholics apparently welcomed the liturgical innovations.

A new openness to other Christians was manifest in the ecumenical movement. Catholic, Protestant, and Orthodox dignitaries attended services in one another's churches. Catholic theologians engaged in dialogue with their Protestant counterparts. Catholic students enrolled in Protestant seminaries, and Catholic seminaries confederated with Protestant institutions. Joint action occurred in fields not obviously ecumenical. Priests and nuns marched and demonstrated with their Protestant brethren in support of drives for civil rights, and joined clergymen of all faiths to express their dissent from the war in Vietnam.

Within the Catholic Church, novel organizations, designed to facilitate communications among bishops, priests, and laity, and to make authority more responsive to the needs of the lower clergy and laymen, appeared. While a proposed trade union for priests received little support, practically all dioceses witnessed the creation of priests' senates or unions; in 1968 delegates from these organizations formed a national federation of priests. National councils of religious orders were established. Diocesan pastoral councils, including both clergy and laity, were organized; on the local level, parish councils and parochial school boards began to appear.

The movement toward modernization led to the questioning, not only of older methods in the conduct of church affairs but of all aspects of the church, not excluding traditional teachings even in the fields of faith and morals. Observers spoke of a crisis of authority. A notable example occurred in 1968 when in his encyclical *Humanae Vitae* Pope Paul VI reaffirmed the condemnation of artificial birth control. In an unprecedented *démarche*, large numbers of Catholic theologians joined together to express their open dissent. Traditional standards of the priesthood and the religious orders were challenged. Priests publicly discussed the necessity for clerical celibacy, and some abandoned their profession to marry. Members of religious orders questioned the relevance of their societies to modern life, and some nuns sought and received dispensations from their vows. One consequence was a decline in applications for admission to seminaries and novitiates.

As the 1960s drew to a close, it was clear that the Roman Catholic Church in North America had entered an extremely critical period.

9. Education.—In North America the Catholic Church maintains a larger number of schools, of all grades from elementary through university, than in any other area of the world. The first schools appeared in the colonial period, though in a sense the early missions to the Indians were educational institutions, and it appears that the Franciscans conducted a secondary school in Florida as early as 1606. In Quebec the Jesuits opened elementary schools in 1625 and founded their college in 1635. In 1639 Ursuline nuns in Quebec started a school for girls, and in 1727 they opened their girls' school in New Orleans. Bishop Laval initiated his seminary for the training of priests in 1663.

In the British colonies, a few Catholic schools were attempted, though, banned by English law, they avoided public notice. There is evidence that schools conducted by Jesuits or laymen existed briefly in Maryland after 1640. In 1775, however, no Catholic school was open in the 13 colonies.

With the emergence of the church after the Revolution, Catholic schools began to appear. St. Mary's parish in Philadelphia had an elementary school in 1782; in 1791 the first seminary, St. Mary's in Baltimore, opened, and the first student entered what is now Georgetown University; in 1799 Visitation Academy in Georgetown began as the first secondary school for girls.

Universities and Colleges.—As the American church expanded, so did its schools. About 100 Catholic colleges were opened before the Civil War, and though many of these soon closed, most major Catholic universities now in existence are numbered among the 32 that originated before 1860. While nuns conducted hundreds of academies for girls, the first Catholic women's college was not attempted until 1896; by 1955, 140 were educating more than 50,000 young women.

Colleges for men continued to increase after 1865. Many of these followed the pattern of other United States colleges, seeking university status by the addition of graduate and professional schools. In the 1960s the number of Catholic colleges and universities in the United States rose from 250 to more than 300 and enrollment from 300,000 students, both men and women, to more than 384,000.

These schools were affected by changes in the 1960s. Colleges co-opted laymen to their boards of trustees, hitherto the preserve of priests and religious, placed the laity in the highest administrative posts, and added non-Catholic clergymen to their departments of theology. Catholics questioned the right of the church to conduct higher schools, and in one instance (Webster College, Mo.), the college was withdrawn from hierarchical control.

In British Canada many colonial schools continued their existence. In 19th-century Quebec there were established two dozen classical colleges, patterned more on European than on American models. These were designed to prepare students for entrance into a university.

The first Canadian Catholic university was inaugurated in Quebec in 1853; a half dozen others were founded later. In the mid-20th century, the tendency in Canada was to open Catholic colleges affiliated with non-Catholic universities rather than to establish new Catholic universities.

Elementary and Secondary Schools.—The church's greatest efforts have been expended on elementary education, and this area has been and continues to be the focus of controversy in both the United States and Canada.

In Lower Canada after 1791 the church conducted large numbers of primary schools staffed chiefly by women religious and supported by the public treasury. When Canada was reunited in 1840, the Catholics, fearful for their French language and their faith, demanded that these schools be continued. The united government thereupon provided that churches might obtain tax funds to support their schools. In Quebec and Ontario both Catholic and Protestant churches maintained schools. When in the 1850s the Catholic schools in Ontario were attacked, the Protestants of Quebec came to their support. Eventually the dual system of church schools was accepted and extended into secondary education.

When in 1867 the British North America Act created the Dominion of Canada, this organic law stipulated, largely to quiet the fears of Quebec Protestants, that church schools must be maintained as they existed at the time of confederation. The dual system in Quebec and Ontario continued. In the Maritime Provinces, where no separate schools existed, a *modus vivendi* was gradually reached; Catholic children were assigned to schools taught by Catholic teachers. Of the western provinces, Alberta and Saskatchewan entered the dominion with separate religious schools. So too did Manitoba, but in 1891 it ended public maintenance of church schools. There and in British Columbia, which did not support denominational schools, Catholic dissatisfaction was occasionally manifest.

In the dominion the church conducts around 6,600 elementary and secondary schools with an enrollment of nearly 1,000,000. A large proportion of the 47,000 Canadian sisters are engaged in education; their colleagues include priests, brothers, and an increasing proportion of lay men and women. (*See* also CANADA: *Administration and Social Conditions: Education.*)

In the United States after 1825, when the public school system began to be extended, there were only a handful of Catholic elementary schools. But the Catholic population soon learned to regard with suspicion the common schools, which reflected the majority society they served and thus were Protestant-oriented in a period of intense nativism. Protests against anti-Catholic textbooks and teachers proved ineffective; objections to the forced use of the King James version by Catholic pupils were interpreted as attacks on the Bible. A decisive contest occurred in New York after Gov. William Seward proposed that the state revert to its earlier practice of allotting tax funds to denominational schools. When in 1841 Bishop Hughes sought to obtain such funds, the public debate ended in the rejection of the Catholic request. In subsequent years state after state enacted laws or constitutional provisions forbidding the grant of public funds to denominational institutions.

Catholics shared the common American belief of the time that religious instruction was an essential part of education. Since the common schools could not teach the Catholic religion, and indeed often imperiled it, the church turned to the construction of parochial schools. Gradually the objective of a desk in a Catholic school for every Catholic child was evolved, and this policy was formally adopted by the third Plenary Council of Baltimore in 1884. At the time, 2,532 of 6,613 parishes maintained parochial schools. The objective was never attained; so great are the difficulties, it appears likely it never will be.

In the 1890s the intrachurch "school controversy" broke out, again representing opposing views of a "liberal" wing led by Archbishop Ireland and a "conservative" wing. Archbishop Ireland advocated what became known as the Faribault plan: in essence, public schools staffed by Catholic teachers and imparting religious instruction outside school hours. Conservatives, regarding the plan as an attack on the parochial schools, strengthened their commitment to them.

In the 20th century, parochial schools continued to expand. The 3,800 elementary schools with 900,000 pupils of 1900 mounted in 1920 to 5,852 schools with 1,701,213 pupils, in 1940 to 7,597 schools with 2,108,892 pupils, and in 1960 to 10,372 schools with 4,285,896 pupils. The Catholic educational system reflected also the increasing U.S. interest in secondary schools. In 1900 there were about 260 Catholic schools with around 35,000 students; by 1920 this number had mounted to 1,552 with 129,848 students, and in 1940 to 2,361 with an enrollment of 480,483. In the next 20 years, though the number of Catholic high schools increased only to 2,433, the enrollment almost doubled, to 844,299. Schools and colleges are served by the National Catholic Educational Association, formed in 1904.

To serve children without places in Catholic schools, religious instruction classes, staffed by religious or by lay members of the Confraternity of Christian Doctrine (an organization founded for this purpose), have an enrollment of over 5,000,000. Students in non-Catholic colleges and universities are served by Newman clubs.

The problems of Catholic education, like those of American education in general, have grown with growing enrollments. Recruitment of teachers remains a serious problem. Religious orders of men and women provide a large part of the personnel, the majority of some 12,000 brothers and over 175,000 sisters in the United States being engaged in education. Lay men and women, too, have always taught in Catholic schools, and their number sharply increased with the tremendous growth of the schools after World War II.

The problem of finance is perennial, and in the 1950s it approached the critical stage. The constantly rising expenditures required to maintain schools and to construct new buildings forced a search for solutions to the problem. Various expedients have been tried: to stop new construction; to drop some classes; to have parochial school students attend part time at local public schools (the "shared time" plan). The very presence of the Catholic Church in education has been questioned; suggestions have been made that the church withdraw from either elementary or secondary education.

With the introduction of the question of federal aid to education, the controversy over denominational education became in the 1950s and '60s as lively as it had been in the 1840s. Since many Catholics believe that the parochial schools serve a public as well as a religious function, they contend that they are paying a double tax to support the public schools. They have sought, at times successfully, to procure from state or local government such benefits as free health services, textbooks, and bus transportation for parochial as well as public school pupils. Opponents of these measures have viewed them as breaching the wall of separation between church and state and have contested them in the courts. The common Catholic contention that the federal government should not exclude Catholic school pupils from any national measures to support general education has raised a question of high constitutional import. (*See* also PAROCHIAL EDUCATION, U.S.)

10. Hospitals.—The sisterhoods, besides their identification with schools, are also known for their care of the sick, the aged, and the orphaned. The first hospital in North America, the Hôtel Dieu, was established in 1639 in Quebec by Augustinian nuns, and by the 1960s Catholic hospitals in Canada numbered 780 with over 22,000 beds; homes for the aged and orphans totaled 420 with 75,000 inmates.

Similar works were undertaken in the United States soon after the establishment in the early 19th century of the first sisterhoods. In 1814 Sisters of Charity opened the first Catholic orphanage, in Philadelphia, and in 1828 they initiated the first Catholic hospital, in St. Louis. Since then the number of orphanages has mounted to nearly 275, taking care of over 25,000 children; homes for the aged total 335 and serve more than 33,000 persons. General and special hospitals in the United States under Catholic direction number around 950, serving over 14,000,000 patients annually; these hospitals also conduct nearly 350 nurses' training schools with an annual enrollment of 35,000.

11. Home and Foreign Missions.—*Domestic.*—Themselves the products of missions, and missionary territories until 1908, the churches of North America have manifested an increasing interest in propagating the faith. Missions to the American Indians, disrupted by war and revolution after 1754, were resumed at the earliest practicable moment; the Council of Baltimore of 1833 called the attention of the faithful to the needs of Indians and Negroes. In the 1840s an abortive attempt was made to plant a mission in Africa. In the United States, missions to the Indians were pushed through the Rocky Mountains to the West Coast, and, in Canada, north to the Arctic. These missions are still maintained: in Canada, served by a staff of 1,200, half the aborigines are Catholic; in the United States, a third of the Indians profess the faith.

Since the 19th-century American church was an immigrant church, it had little contact with Negroes, a situation that has changed increasingly since 1865. Notable work has been done by religious orders, especially by societies created for the field, as the Society of St. Joseph and the Sisters of the Blessed Sacrament, founded by Mother Katherine Drexel. With the migrations from the South to the North during and after World War I, the church came into closer contact with Negroes, and the efforts of the Catholic interracial councils and the strong stand of Catholic bishops against segregation in Catholic institutions may be considered at least partly responsible for the fact that in the years after 1940 the number of Negro Catholics tripled to about 800,000 in the mid-1960s.

Efforts are increasingly made to acquaint non-Catholic Americans with the church: the Knights of Columbus finance a continuing advertising campaign in secular magazines and newspapers; correspondence schools in Catholic doctrine serve scores of thousands of inquirers; Catholic information centres are widely maintained. Since 1905 the Catholic Church Extension Society has assisted struggling parishes in non-Catholic areas, and such societies as the Glenmary Home Missioners (founded 1939) have risen to supply priests for these churches. After 1946 the number of converts was never less than 100,000 a year, until after 1960 the annual total of converts fell off sharply.

Foreign.—Until the 20th century the U.S. church, continually short of personnel, could send few to foreign missions. Itself the recipient of substantial financial aid from European mission societies, it began to repay its debt after the Civil War by increasing contributions to the Society for the Propagation of the Faith. With the church in Europe devastated by depression and two world wars, the American church emerged in the second half of the 20th century as the chief source of financial support for Roman Catholic foreign missions.

The formal entrance of the American church into foreign missions can be dated in 1893, when overseas mission territories were first assigned to U.S. religious orders. Increasing interest led to the establishment in 1911 of the Catholic Foreign Mission Society of America, the Maryknoll Fathers. Canadian and U.S. priests, brothers, and sisters work in missions in Asia, Africa, and Latin America. (*See also* MISSIONS: *Later Roman Catholic Missions.*) The Canadian church maintains a foreign missionary staff of over 2,700. The U.S. interest in foreign missions can be shown by the increase in overseas personnel, from 2,230 in 1940 to 9,300 in the mid-1960s. Of this number, 550 were lay missionaries. The laity entered the mission field under the auspices of a number of organizations, notably the Papal Volunteers for Latin America (PAVLA).

12. Press.—In the 13 British colonies Roman Catholics desired to avoid attention; no Catholic work was ever printed. After the Revolution, however, Catholic pamphlets and books began to appear, and by the early 19th century Irish newspapers (as the *Hibernian Chronicle*, 1810), containing items of Catholic interest, were published. The first distinctly Catholic periodical, the weekly *U.S. Catholic Miscellany*, came out in Charleston in 1822 and continued to 1861. The first Council of Baltimore in 1829 urged the creation of a Catholic press, and in the 1830s a number of diocesan newspapers were founded. In the 1840s still other periodicals rose to answer the attacks of the nativist press. A Catholic foreign-language press appeared before the Civil War and increased notably with the new immigration after 1880. By 1900 Catholic periodicals were being published in a dozen languages, including Sioux. To the newspapers were added popular monthlies and serious quarterlies, as Isaac Hecker's *Catholic World* (1865) and Orestes Brownson's *Brownson's Quarterly* (1844).

The 20th century witnessed the proliferation of Catholic periodicals. Practically all dioceses have their own newspapers or are served by the *Register* (1905) or *Our Sunday Visitor* (1912) chains.

A Catholic press association set up in 1908 has been since 1919 a service of the National Catholic Welfare Conference. There are Catholic periodicals for all tastes and types, from children to serious scholars. In 1940 about 350 periodicals circulated to some 8,000,000 subscribers; in the mid-1960s the numbers had risen to 498 and 28,000,000. Widely read journals of opinion, such as the Jesuit-edited *America* and the lay-edited *Commonweal*, were joined by other lay-edited periodicals, notably the liberal *National Catholic Reporter* and the conservative *Triumph*.

(F. X. C.)

D. AFRICA AND THE ORIENT

The Roman Catholic Church reached Asia, Oceania, and Africa comparatively late. It should, however, be remembered that Christianity began in the Middle East. From its starting point in Palestine it rapidly spread to Asia Minor, North Africa, and the other Middle-Eastern countries of the Roman Empire. The Persian empire and Armenia were evangelized in the 3rd century, Arabia and Ethiopia in the 4th century, and parts of India by the 6th century. Already in the 5th century Nestorianism and Monophysitism had detached large bodies of Christians in the Middle East from communion with Rome, and the 7th-century Arab conquests obliterated Christianity in North Africa. From 1054, the year of the formal schism between Rome and the Orthodox Eastern Church, the Roman Catholic Church was present in the Middle East only in the Maronite community in Lebanon. The period

of the Crusades (11th–13th centuries) witnessed the creation of a Latin empire in Constantinople (1204–61) and an attempt to establish a Latin church there. The principal result of these unfortunate events was consolidation of the antagonism dividing the two halves of Christendom.

1. Later Middle Ages.—The new Roman Catholic missions outside the western and Mediterranean areas date from the 13th century. The recently founded mendicant orders—Franciscan and Dominican—were the principal agents of this new type of mission and, with no political support and very limited material resources, the friars traveled throughout Asia. One of them, Giovanni di Monte Corvino (*q.v.*), established the church at Peking between 1294 and 1328. But the fruits of his mission were lost in the downfall of the Mongolian empire. On the other hand, the difficult traveling conditions, the fact that Islam had encircled Europe, and the internal crisis that the church was going through at that time made it impossible for this missionary endeavour to receive the support necessary for continuity.

2. 16th and 17th Centuries.—In this period further great efforts were made with more durable results. In the Middle East, several Eastern rite Christian communities of varying size were reunited with Rome, and gradually the foundations were established of a new Roman Catholic hierarchy which continued to develop.

However, the major missionary endeavour of the 16th century was accomplished in the Far East. Two Catholic maritime powers, Spain and Portugal, were establishing sea routes to the farthest countries, creating commercial outlets wherever they went and imposing political domination in certain regions. In 1493 Pope Alexander VI officially recognized the spheres of influence of these two countries (*see* TORDESILLAS, TREATY OF) and accorded to their kings a right of patronage over the missions established (*see* above, *Spanish America: The Spanish State and the Church*). The expansion of the church was favoured by this agreement, which facilitated transport and the establishment of missions. The Spanish Philippines and the Portuguese territories of Goa in India (diocese in 1533) and Macao in China (diocese in 1575) became almost entirely Catholic. The foundation of the Society of Jesus in 1534 supplied the missions with new manpower.

Oceania, the coastal areas of central and southern Africa, and Madagascar received some rapid and superficial evangelization. The Catholic kingdom of São Salvador do Congo (Angola) was a short-lived and only partially successful undertaking which was ruined by the negligence and the commercial intrigues of the Portuguese. In 1541 a Portuguese colonial archdiocese was erected at Funchal (Madeira), having jurisdiction over the whole of West Africa; this was replaced in 1532 by the archdiocese of São Tiago (Cape Verde Islands), while East Africa was attached to the archdiocese of Goa in India.

At that period, the adoption of Christianity by an Eastern country usually meant the adoption of Hispano-Portuguese customs also, a fact which did much damage to the later spread of Catholicism in Asia. Two notable exceptions to this rule were the missions in India of Roberto de Nobili (1604) and in China of Matteo Ricci (*q.v.*; 1582–1610), both of whom respected the civilization and culture of the country they evangelized; but their policy was not continued.

The inherent defects of the patronage system became more and more apparent. Missionary work was often impeded by the temporal interest of the European power to which it was bound, and in the 17th century Rome endeavoured to liberate the missions from this inefficient and cumbersome tutelage. In 1622 Pope Gregory XV founded the Sacred Congregation of the Propagation of the Faith (*Propaganda Fide*), to coordinate from Rome all the Catholic missions throughout the world. This congregation provided the missions with a purely ecclesiastical organization, unified their methods, and guided them toward the establishment of local churches.

By 1627 the Propaganda Fide College was established in Rome for the training of priests from the mission countries. One of the first students of the college, Matteo de Castro, an Indian brahmin, was made a bishop in 1635 and named vicar apostolic in 1637. This was a new departure: instead of resident bishops whose nomination was subject to the patronage agreements, Rome designated as vicars apostolic bishops directly delegated by the Holy See. This system extricated the missions from the bonds of patronage and permitted a greater development. Conversions increased in China, Ceylon, and especially in the Indochinese peninsula. This development was largely due to the increased personnel that the newly·founded (1663) Société des Missions Étrangères de Paris placed at the exclusive disposal of the Congregation of the Propagation of the Faith.

The instructions from *Propaganda Fide* also aimed at renewing mission methods. Particularly noteworthy is the famous instruction of 1659 to the first vicars apostolic in the Far East: the missions must have no political association, must respect local customs and cultures, and must aim at rapid formation of an indigenous clergy and episcopacy.

In the meantime, non-Catholic powers, notably England and Holland, soon to be followed by all the Western powers, were disputing the Spanish and Portuguese rights to world supremacy. In Japan, persecution of Christians, which began early in the 17th century, drove out all the missionaries and destroyed or drove underground the Catholic communities even before the country formally adopted its policy of excluding all westerners (*see* JAPAN: *History: The Tokugawa Period*). In Ceylon, which had become a Dutch possession, to be a Catholic was considered equivalent to political loyalty to Portugal.

In China, Adam Schall and after him Ferdinand Verbiest with their fellow Jesuits gained the respect of the emperor through the high standard of their scientific work. Some religious toleration was thus acquired within the Chinese empire. Unfortunately, however, the "quarrel of the rites" arose between the protagonists of two different mission theories (*see* RITES CONTROVERSY), lasted more than a century, and caused considerable harm to the church, especially in China and India. However, at the end of the 17th century the prospects in Asia as a whole were good. (*See* also MISSIONS: *Early History: Roman Catholic Advance, 1500–1750.*)

3. 18th Century.—The hopes held out by the 17th century were not fulfilled in the 18th. Bloody persecutions in Asia, together with various difficulties in Europe, slowed the missionary effort and endangered the results already achieved. The political rule of the marquês de Pombal ruined the Portuguese missions. The suppression of the Society of Jesus in 1773, the French Revolution in 1789, the Napoleonic era, and the new conflicting ideas at work in Europe dried up the wellsprings from which missionary vocations had come. For the Catholic missions, the 18th century was a period of crisis.

4. 19th Century.—In the course of the 19th century the missions were carried on with renewed vigour. Missionary personnel was considerably increased not only by the contribution of the older religious orders but also by the foundation of numerous religious orders dedicated especially to the missionary apostolate. This renewal made it possible to reap the harvest so painfully prepared during the preceding centuries in Asia and, at the same time, to undertake systematic evangelization in Oceania and Africa.

Oceania.—Thus, in 1825, the Picpus Fathers were given the responsibility for Oceania; in 1836 they were joined by the Marists, who assumed responsibility for central Oceania and New Zealand. In Australia, Catholicism was introduced especially through the Irish immigrants. Unfortunately, the colonial rivalry between France and Great Britain was paralleled by conflict between Catholic and Protestant missionary movements, which complicated the work of evangelization in Oceania.

Southern Africa.—In Africa south of the Sahara, which had by then been thoroughly explored, missionary work was systematically organized also. The first stage was the creation, by Gregory XVI in 1841, of the vicariate of the "Two Guineas," which extended from Senegal to the Cape of Good Hope and gave rise to all the West African missions; it was entrusted in 1845 to the Holy Ghost Fathers. In 1846 the apostolic vicariate of Central Africa was set up, and the evangelization of East Africa was begun in 1878 by the Jesuits and the Society of Missionaries of Africa (White Fathers), founded in 1868 by Charles Cardinal Lavigerie. At the

close of the 19th century there were 500,000 Catholics in Africa south of the Sahara, administered by 61 ecclesiastical territories.

Far East.—In Asia, the renewal became apparent only toward the middle of the 19th century. After 250 years during which the church was banned, Japan opened its doors once again to missionaries in 1858, and a few years later (1865), in Nagasaki, groups of Japanese revealed that they had remained faithful to the Catholic faith into which their ancestors had been baptized in the 17th century. Freedom of religion was proclaimed in 1889, and in 1891 Leo XIII established the normal ecclesiastical hierarchy with an archbishop at Tokyo and three episcopal sees at Nagasaki, Osaka, and Hakodate. At that time Japanese Catholics numbered 50,000. In Korea there were frequent persecutions until 1881, when the missionaries returned to that country. Freedom of religion was proclaimed in 1884, but persecution had left only about 10,000 Catholics. In China also, a decree published in 1811 launched a persecution which lasted until 1844. At that date, the protection of the missions was assured by the French, whose example was shortly afterward followed by other Western powers having political and commercial interests in China. The ambiguous situation in which the missions were thereby placed permitted the church to enjoy some measure of progress, but at the same time it compromised it in the eyes of the Chinese. At the end of the 19th century there were more than 800,000 Catholics in China, but the antiforeign Boxer Rebellion of 1900 led to a general massacre of Chinese Christians and of the missionaries. (*See also* CHINA: *History.*)

Southeast Asia and India.—In Vietnam, from 1802 to 1825, Christianity was relatively free, thanks to the emperor Gia-Long, and 316,000 were baptized. But Gia-Long's successor, Minh-Mang, closed the country to missionaries and instituted a persecution which, except for a few brief intervals, lasted from 1833 to 1862 and counted at least 90,000 victims. French rule, established in 1883, secured religious peace, and at the end of the 19th century Vietnamese Catholics numbered more than 700,000. (*See also* VIETNAM: *History.*)

Progress in neighbouring countries was much slower. In Thailand the mission, which had been halted by persecution lasting throughout the 18th century, was resumed in 1826 and freedom of religion was proclaimed in 1856. Organized missionary work was not begun in Cambodia till 1850 and in Laos not till 1899.

In India, abolition of the Portuguese "patronage" system in favour of the apostolic vicariates established by *Propaganda Fide* brought about a considerable revival from 1832. In 1884 an apostolic delegate was named to represent the Holy See in India and Ceylon, where the normal hierarchy was established in 1886, comprising seven ecclesiastical provinces. In 1896 three Indian bishops were named for the Syro-Malabar communities. In Chota Nagpur, the social action of the Jesuit Constant Lievens set in motion a mass movement of conversions, and the numbers of Catholics rose from 16,000 to 60,000 (in 1920 there were 170,000 and in 1960 there were 500,000 in this area).

In Burma, in the first half of the 19th century, the missions did no more than survive, owing to the Anglo-Burmese wars; from 1856 they began to develop slowly. In Indonesia, any form of proselytism was forbidden by the Dutch until 1807, when freedom of religion was established in Holland. An apostolic prefecture was then established for Java, and in 1826 the prefecture was extended to include the whole of the Indonesian archipelago. However, the mission was confined almost exclusively to European residents and was severely restricted by the civil authorities. Catholic missions became established only in the second half of the 19th century.

The Arab World.—The Ottoman Empire was beginning to disintegrate, and the European powers, under the pretext of defending Christian minorities, were beginning to establish a footing, thus causing reprisals against the Christians. On the other hand, under the millet system of dealing with non-Muslim religious communities prevailing in the Muslim states (*see* RAYAH), Roman Catholics of the Eastern rite were subject to the authority of the Orthodox patriarchs. After a long struggle the Melkite Catholics achieved emancipation from this tutelage in 1848, the Chaldaeans in 1861, the Syrians in 1866, and the Egyptian Copts in 1898. From 1830, Latin missionaries were sent from Europe to the Middle East, where they opened schools and seminaries. The intention of the pope was not that they should establish the Western (Latin) church but that they should give fraternal help to the Eastern rite Catholics. But the multiplicity of Latin religious establishments and the restoration in 1847 of the Latin patriarchate of Jerusalem (created at the time of the Crusades and fallen into disuse in the 13th century) led, little by little, to the establishment of the Latin church side by side with the Eastern rite churches. On the other hand, the numbers of Eastern rite Christians in union with Rome continued to grow, and their patriarchates were reestablished (see above, The Catholic Eastern Rites). And finally the Roman Catholic Church found a footing once again in Ethiopia with the arrival of the Lazarists of Justin de Jacobis in 1839 and the Capuchins with Guglielmo Cardinal Massaia in 1846. As for the Maghreb regions of North Africa, the Roman Catholic Church was established there from 1830 but remained confined almost exclusively to the European immigrant population.

5. 20th Century.—The ecclesiastical structures established in the previous century in Asia and Africa now took on the character of local churches, and the Roman Catholic Church strove to break its identification with the political and cultural supremacy of the West by the vigorous affirmation of its "supranationality."

Development of Indigenous Clergy.—The missionary encyclicals *Maximum illud* of Benedict XV in 1919 and *Rerum ecclesiae* of Pius XI in 1926 placed great emphasis on the importance and the urgency of the need for more Asian and African clergy. In spite of the remarkable effort in the 19th century, the essential aim of the missions to enable the church to take root in the different countries and to take on a local character had been somewhat neglected. Realization of the pope's instructions was facilitated by the establishment of regional seminaries, which made available better training to the clergy through grouping of existing facilities. Due to these efforts, the local clergy of the mission countries grew from 4,516 in 1923 to 5,624 in 1929, to 6,406 in 1939, and to 11,139 in 1949; of these totals, the majority was in Asia.

The consecration of Asian and African bishops is a truer indication of the development of the church than is the increase in the number of priests. The first Chinese bishop, Gregory Lo Wantsao (known as Bishop Lopez), had been consecrated at Canton in 1685, but this was an isolated instance. In the 20th century, the Indian Jesuit Francis Roche was named bishop of Tuticorin, a newly created diocese of the Latin church which was handed over to the Indian clergy on June 12, 1923. However, the Eastern rite Malabarese church already had Indian vicars apostolic, and in 1923 a regular ecclesiastical province was created, with Ernakulam as the metropolitan see. In China the impetus was given by the apostolic delegation established by Rome in 1922. The first delegate, Archbishop Celso Constantini, selected the first six Chinese bishops and conducted them to Rome, where they were consecrated by Pius XI in 1926. From the year 1926 there was a great increase in the consecration of native bishops in the majority of Asian countries, and from 1939 in the majority of African countries.

In 1939, 52 ecclesiastical territories were administered by national Asian and African bishops and clergy; 27 of these were in China, 14 in India, 3 in Japan, 3 in Vietnam, and 1 each in Ceylon, Korea, Ethiopia, Madagascar, and Uganda. The war years retarded the movement, but after 1946 it took on considerable impetus again. By the 1960s the hierarchy of the Roman Catholic Church in Africa and the East had to a considerable extent passed out of the hands of the West. In Oceania, however, there were as yet few local clergy.

The number of Catholics in Africa and the East was estimated in the early 1960s at 50,000,000. The strongholds in the Far East were the Philippines and Vietnam and, to a lesser degree, South Korea, Ceylon, and southern India. In Oceania, the major centres were Melanesia and Micronesia; in the Middle East, Lebanon; in Africa, Uganda, Rwanda, Burundi, the Congo (Léopold-ville), Cameroon, Basutoland, and the Malagasy Republic.

6. Accommodation to Traditional Cultures.—The number of the faithful and the nationality of their bishops are not the only factors necessary if the church is to be at home in the different countries. The period of cultural ascendancy of the West led to some neglect of the church's tradition of adaptation to the cultures of the people evangelized, and this tradition had to be renewed in the 20th century. Pius XII, in his encyclicals *Summi pontificatus* (1939) and *Evangelii praecones* (1951), brought this question back as one of the principal objects of attention in missionary theory. Some concrete steps taken by Rome opened the way for this adaptation: the revision of the question of Japanese and Chinese rites (1939); a Christian adaptation of the *matanga* rites in the Congo (1938); new rules concerning the Malabar rite in India (1940); and greater flexibility in general of the regulations governing ceremonies (1961).

A similar turn was taken in liturgy and catechetics. Increasingly the use of the vernacular in liturgical ceremonies and of local melodies as sacred music was being permitted; the adaptation of certain ceremonies to ancient local customs was sometimes authorized, and various experiments and studies were undertaken with a view to integrating Christian worship and way of life with the particular genius of each nation while at the same time preserving the essential truths of Christianity.

To prepare a Christian laity to assume responsibility for certain apostolic duties is also one of the major cares of the church. With the encouragement of the Permanent Committee for the Apostolate of the Laity, a congress in Kisubi (Uganda) was organized in 1953 for Africa and another in Manila (Philippines) for Asia in 1955. The traditional monastic missionary bodies were joined by lay people working through various lay missionary movements, Catholic international organizations, and similar bodies. This new accession of manpower permitted wider and more adequate action in fields not directly the concern of priests or religious.

(JE. F. B.)

IV. THE LIFE OF THE CHURCH IN THE 20TH CENTURY

The most important single factor in the internal development of the church in the 20th century was the action of St. Pius X in fostering (by two decrees, of 1905 and 1910) frequent reception of Holy Communion. Not only did these decrees mark the final overthrow of Jansenism, but they set up a sort of chain reaction: those who had been admitted to communion at an early age became, as they grew up, more assiduous in attending Mass and thus more anxious, eventually, to have the Mass made more intelligible to themselves, whatever their level of culture. Hence the liturgical revival was turned into a popular movement culminating in the Constitution on the Sacred Liturgy passed at the second session of Vatican Council II (see LITURGY, CHRISTIAN).

The international eucharistic congresses (the 38th of which, at Bombay, was attended by Pope Paul VI in 1964) were begun by Marie Tamisier, who succeeded in persuading French Catholics to hold the first congress at Lille in 1881. The congresses grew in size and scope after the one at Rome in 1905; the London congress (1908) was opened by a papal legate, whose entry into the country was at that time illegal. Cologne, Montreal, and Madrid saw the next meetings, and after the interruption of the series by World War I there were large gatherings at Chicago (1926), Sydney (1928), Dublin (1932), Buenos Aires (1935), and Budapest (1938). After World War II there were congresses at Barcelona (1952), Rio de Janeiro (1955), Munich (1960), and Bombay (1964). Discussions about the sacrament take place at these congresses, but their manifestation of the corporate life of the church is of far greater moment than any fruit of their deliberations.

When Cardinal J. H. Newman was asked what he would do if he became pope, he replied that he would set up commissions to deal with biblical questions and the early history of the church. Leo XIII set up the Biblical Commission (Oct. 30, 1902), but was too late to avert the crisis of Modernism, which left the church intellectually numbed; between the Modernists, who wanted to treat the Scriptures like any other book, and some of the theologians, who said that Scripture was altogether divine, there did not seem to be a middle way. (*See* further MODERNISM, ROMAN CATHOLIC.) A few theologians knew that there was, and in 1943 they were upheld by Pius XII, who in his encyclical on the Scriptures (*Divino afflante Spiritu*) put forward a parallel between the Incarnate Word of God and the written Word of God; heresy in each case lay at the two extremes, when the divine and human elements were held too far apart or were fused beyond recognition. The humanity of the inspired writer has to be seen, even though God is guiding him, just as the humanity of Christ was not swallowed up by the godhead. When this middle way was reached, the church was able to give full scope to biblical studies with beneficial results to theology and devotion.

The holding of a council had been suggested to Pius X in 1912 as a means of meeting the Modernist crisis. After the solution of the Roman question by the Lateran Treaty (1929) the matter was raised again, for the liberty of the church has always been a prerequisite to a council and now it seemed assured. Pius XI, who had done so much to promote missionary expansion and to reassert that the church was not to be identified with the Latin rite, might have given more permanence to his reforms through such a council, but the turbulence of the 1930s denied him the opportunity. It was left for John XXIII to seize the chance in 1962 and thus to stimulate theological activity to a degree beyond anything witnessed before in the 20th century. (*See* VATICAN COUNCILS: *Second Vatican Council*.)

It was soon after 1850 that Newman remarked on two signs of the times, the spreading over the face of the earth of the English language and of the Irish race. These factors changed the aspect of the missionary activity of the church in the 20th century. What had been in the 19th century so largely a French or Belgian affair (and almost confined to the Levant, North Africa, India, and China) was now in large measure entrusted to men who spoke English. The setting up of the Maynooth (Irish) mission to China in 1916 and the expansion in the missionary work of the Jesuit order (which had 1,600 men at work in mission lands in 1920 and 7,000 in the 1960s) are signs of this development. They are confirmed by the number of training centres set up in England, Ireland, and the United States by Dutch, French, and Italian missionary societies. In the growth of missionary work by nuns similar changes can be seen.

On March 19, 1904, Pius X began the codification of canon law (*q.v.*) that was completed under Benedict XV in 1917.

The conversion of an Episcopalian group, the Friars of the Atonement (Graymoor, N.Y.), in 1909 led to the widespread adoption of an annual church-unity octave of prayer for reunion (Jan. 18–25). (*See* ECUMENICAL MOVEMENT.) Emphasis in this movement shifted gradually from Anglicanism to the Orthodox Churches, and in 1964 the second Vatican Council decreed that limited intercommunion between Catholics and Eastern Orthodox was tolerable. As the council was ending (December 1965) the Eastern and Western anathemas of 1054 were withdrawn by a papal mission and by the patriarch of Constantinople. In March 1966 the pope and the archbishop of Canterbury, meeting formally in the Vatican, pledged themselves jointly to work for the reunion of the churches. In July 1967 Pope Paul VI visited the patriarch in Istanbul.

The second Vatican Council's dogmatic decree on the nature of the church emphasized the laity's share in the prophetic office of the church by witnessing in their lives to the gospel.

National episcopal conferences existed at the first Vatican Council in 1870. During the long sessions of the second they built up many links; a European conference was formed before the end of the council, and much mutual help was arranged. The council's decree on religious liberty came, during the debate, to be a charter for Catholics behind the "iron curtain." During the council the principle of collegiality, recognized for the hierarchy, was extended to diocesan and parochial levels, and the working out of this began slowly. Episcopal conferences were empowered to allow the permanent office of deacon to men already married, while those young men who accepted the same office were to remain single. (J. H. Cn.)

For allied subjects, *see* further CANON LAW; CARDINAL; CONCLAVE; COUNCIL; LITURGY, CHRISTIAN; MINISTRY, CHRISTIAN; MONASTICISM; ORDERS AND CONGREGATIONS, RELIGIOUS; PAPACY; PAPAL STATES; SACRAMENT; SAINT; VATICAN; WOMEN'S RELIGIOUS ORDERS. *See* also separate articles on the major religious orders; on church feasts; on matters related to dogma and theology (*e.g.*, IMMACULATE CONCEPTION; INFALLIBILITY; TRANSUBSTANTIATION); on councils (*e.g.*, VATICAN COUNCILS); on liturgy and devotions (*e.g.*, ROSARY). *See* also references under "Roman Catholic Church" in the Index. (X.)

BIBLIOGRAPHY.—*Organization:* Pope Pius XII, Encyclical on the Mystical Body of Christ (1943), *Catholic Mind*, 41:1–44 (Nov. 1943), Encyclical on the Sacred Liturgy (1947), *ibid.*, 46:321–388 (June 1948); W. Bertrams, *The Papacy, the Episcopacy, and Collegiality*, Eng. trans. (1964); P. van Lierde, *The Holy See at Work*, Eng. trans. (1962); V. Pospishil, *Code of Oriental Canon Law, the Law on Persons* (1960); A. Cicognani, *Canon Law* (1934); T. Bouscaren, A. Ellis, and F. Korth, *Canon Law*, 4th ed. (1963); J. Abbo and J. Hannan, *The Sacred Canons*, 2nd rev. ed. (1960); E. J. de Smedt, *The Priesthood of the Faithful*, Eng. trans. (1962); W. M. Abbott (ed.), *The Documents of Vatican II* (1966). (J. J. RE.)

Catholic Eastern Rites: D. Attwater, *The Christian Churches of the East*, vol. 1, *The Churches in Communion with Rome* (1961); R. Etteldorf, *The Catholic Church in the Middle East* (1959); R. Janin, *Les Églises orientales et les rites orientaux*, 4th ed. (1955); A. A. King, *The Rites of Eastern Christendom*, 2 vol. (1947–48); *Oriente Cattolico* (1962); M. Lacko, "Churches of Eastern Rite in North America," in *Unitas*, vol. 16, pp. 89–115 (1964). (M. Lo.)

The Church in Europe: Cambridge Ancient History, vol. xii (1939); Cambridge Medieval History (1936); Cambridge Modern History, vol. i–v and relevant chapters thereafter, with bibliographies (1928); J. P. Migne, *Patrologiae Latinae cursus completus*, 217 vol. (1844–55), *Patrologiae Graecae cursus completus*, 247 vol. (1856–66); G. D. Mansi, *Sacrorum conciliorum nova et amplissima collectio*, 31 vol. (1758–98); *Corpus juris canonici; Liber pontificalis;* J. B. Lightfoot, *Apostolic Fathers*, 2nd ed. (1889); L. M. O. Duchesne, *Histoire ancienne de l'église chrétienne*, 4 vol. (1905–25), Eng. trans., *Early History of the Christian Church*, 3 vol. (1909–24); A. von Harnack, *History of Dogma*, 2 vol., Eng. trans. (1901); H. M. Gwatkin, *Early Church History to A.D. 313*, 2 vol., 2nd ed. (1909); B. J. Kidd, *History of the Church to A.D. 461*, 3 vol. (1922); F. H. Dudden, *Gregory the Great, His Place in History and Thought*, 2 vol. (1905); Bede, *Ecclesiastical History of the English People* (1935); W. R. W. Stephens and William Hunt (eds.), *History of the English Church*, 8 vol. (1899–1916); L. von Pastor, *History of the Popes from the Close of the Middle Ages*, 14 vol., Eng. trans. (1915); H. K. Mann, *Lives of the Popes in the Early Middle Ages*, 18 vol. (1925–32); P. Hughes, *History of the Church*, vol. i–ii, rev. ed. (1949), vol. iii (1947); E. H. Gilson, *The Spirit of Mediaeval Philosophy*, Eng. trans. (1936); G. de Lagarde, *La Naissance de l'esprit laïque au declin du moyen âge*, 4 vol. (1934); H. Bremond, *L'Histoire littéraire du sentiment religieux en France*, 11 vol. (1916–33); C. A. Ste.-Beuve, *Port-Royal*, 7 vol. (1922); R. A. Knox, *Enthusiasm* (1950); W. H. Jervis, *The Gallican Church* (1892). (T. S. Gy.)

20th-Century Europe: W. Gurian and M. A. Fitzsimons (eds.), *The Catholic Church in World Affairs* (1954); E. E. Y. Hales, *The Catholic Church in the Modern World* (1958); *The Persecution of the Catholic Church in the Third Reich: Facts and Documents* (1940); G. Levy, *The Catholic Church in Modern Germany* (1964); A. Dansette, *Destin du catholicisme français 1926–1956* (1957); D. A. Binchy, *Church and State in Fascist Italy* (1941); E. I. Watkin, *Roman Catholicism in England from the Reformation to 1950*, ch. 6 (1957). (J. D. W.)

Spanish America and Brazil: History of Religion in the New World (1958); R. H. Fitzgibbon (ed.), *The Constitutions of the Americas, as of January 1, 1948* (1948); *Basic Ecclesiastical Statistics for Latin America, 1958* (1958); W. J. Coleman, *Latin-American Catholicism, a Self-Evaluation* (1958); J. L. Mecham, *Church and State in Latin America*, rev. ed. (1966); R. Pattee, *El Catolicismo contemporaneo en Hispano-America* (1951); P. F. Camargo, *Historia eclesiastica do Brasil* (1955); J. J. Considine (ed.), *The Church in the New Latin America* (1964); F. Houtart and E. Pin, *The Church and the Latin American Revolution* (1965). (A. S. TR.)

North America: J. T. Ellis, *A Guide to American Catholic History* (1959), a select bibliography; many more works are listed in E. R. Vollmar, *The Catholic Church in America*, 2nd ed. (1964). Statistical information for the years to 1920 is in G. Shaughnessy, *Has the Immigrant Kept the Faith?* (1925); for more recent statistics, consult the *Official Catholic Directory* (annual, 1833–   ); for Canada, *see* Dominic of Saint-Denis, *Catholic Church in Canada: Historical and Statistical Summary*, 6th ed. (1956). On the Canadian Church, *see* also Goyau, *Les Origines religieuses du Canada* (1934); L. Groulx, *Histoire du Canada français depuis la découverte*, 3 vol. (1950–52); M. Wade, *The French Canadians, 1760–1945* (1955); H. H. Walsh, *The Christian Church in Canada* (1956). A brief survey of the American church is J. T. Ellis, *American Catholicism* (1956). The classic work on the church to 1866 is J. D. G. Shea, *History of the Catholic Church in the United States*, 4 vol. (1886–92). *See* also W. Clancy et al., *Catholicism in America* (1954); L. J. Putz (ed.), *The Catholic Church, U.S.A.*

(1956); T. T. McAvoy (ed.), *Roman Catholicism and the American Way of Life* (1960); T. Maynard, *The Story of American Catholicism*, 2 vol. (1960); J. T. Ellis (ed.), *Documents of American Catholic History*, rev. ed., 2 vol. (1967); J. T. Ellis, *Catholics in Colonial America* (1965); F. X. Curran, *Catholics in Colonial Law* (1963); B. Y. Landis, *The Roman Catholic Church in the United States* (1966); E. Wakin and J. F. Scheur, *The De-Romanization of the American Catholic Church* (1966); T. F. Donovan, *The Status of the Church in American Civil Law and Canon Law* (1966); J. Colaianni, *The Catholic Left* (1968). (F. X. C.)

Africa and the Orient: J. Schmidlin, *Katholische Missionsgeschichte* (1924); E. E. F. Descamps, *Histoire générale comparée des missions* (1932); A. Olichon, *Les Missions* (1936); R. Janin, *Églises orientales et rites orientaux* (1955); T. Ohm, *Wichtige Daten der Missions-geschichte* (1956); A. Mulders, *Missiegeschiedenis* (1957); S. Delacroix, *Histoire universelle des missions catholiques*, 4 vol. (1956–); K. S. Latourette, *Christianity in a Revolutionary Age*, 5 vol. (1958–62). (JE. F. B.)

Roman Catholic Faith: C. C. Martindale, *The Faith of the Roman Church* (1927); K. Adam, *The Spirit of Catholicism*, Eng. trans. (1929); R. A. Knox, *The Belief of Catholics* (1927); P. Hughes, *The Faith in Practice* (1938); T. Corbishley, *Roman Catholicism*, vol. 51 in Hutchinson's University Library (1950); W. Burghardt and W. F. Lynch, *The Idea of Catholicism* (1960); H. de Lubac, *Catholicism* (1950); S. Bullough, *Roman Catholicism* (1963); L. Bouyer, *Rite and Man* (1963).

Encyclopaedias: The Catholic Encyclopedia, 15 vol. (1907–12); A. Vacant, E. Mangenot, and E. Amann (eds.), *Dictionnaire de théologie catholique*, 15 vol. (1903–50); J. Hofer and K. Rahner (eds.), *Lexikon für Theologie und Kirche*, 10 vol. (1930–38; 2nd ed., 1957–); P. Paschini *et al.* (eds.), *Enciclopedia cattolica*, 12 vol. (1949–54); H. Daniel-Rops (ed.), *The 20th-century Encyclopedia of Catholicism*, Eng. trans. (1958–); *Catholic Dictionary of Theology* (1962–).

Official: The list of dioceses and prelates is given in the *Annuario Pontificio* (annually); for statistics, see *Bilan du Monde* (1958–). Church legislation is published in *Acta apostolicae sedis* (from 1909; called *Acta sanctae sedis*, 1865–1909).

ROMANCE, the name of a literary genre, difficult to define in formal terms, which originated in medieval France in the period between 1130 and 1150 (*see* FRENCH LITERATURE: *Chansons de Geste and Romances*).

The characteristic feature of early French literature is its inclination toward the wonderful, the improbable, the exaggerated, and the wholly ideal. This characteristic to some extent reflects the type of literary culture that had emerged as the culture of late classical antiquity, itself strained and rhetorical, and marked by a taste for the marvelous and the miraculous, passed into that of the so-called Dark Ages. The only type of medieval literary production exempt from these romanticizing tendencies was the family and historical prose saga developed in Iceland at the end of the 12th and in the early 13th century (*see* ICELANDIC LITERATURE: *The Sagas: Icelanders', or Family, Sagas*).

At the beginning of the 12th century, narrative literature in France was of two types, both in verse: stories of the saints; and the epics, or *chansons de geste* (*q.v.*). But, however productive of wonder such stories as that of the 5th-century St. Alexis, who left his wife on his wedding night, fled abroad and lived as a beggar, then returned, still in the guise of a beggar, to his father's house, where he lived unrecognized until at the point of death; or however marvelous the adventures of St. Brendan (*q.v.*), as he voyaged among strange islands on his way to the Earthly Paradise, the works in which these were narrated had a didactic purpose. The extravagant asceticism of Alexis, for instance, was described to inculcate contempt of the world and its vain delights, not merely to entertain. Similarly, the greatest of the French *chansons de geste, the Chanson de Roland* (*see* ROLAND, CHANSON DE), although "romantic" in the sense that it recounts, as well as religious miracles, fantastic feats of arms, and introduces a love interest, has not only a serious moral purpose (to represent warfare against Islam as a holy task), but also discusses, with high seriousness, the ethics of the blood feud and the consequences of baronial pride and recklessness. In many epics written later in the 12th century, however, there is a tendency to abandon serious treatment of such subjects in favour of narrative interest, to stress the feats and adventures of the hero, and to trace his career from childhood, a common pattern being for him to flee abroad from persecuting relatives, to achieve adventures, and then to return to claim his inheritance. These stories are rather "romanticized epics" than "romances" proper, but they would never have been written if it

had not been for the rise of romance. Romance, as a separate genre, is distinguished from epic and religious narrative by the fact that it recounts fictions for their own sake, for the delight and wonder they evoke, and not for any religious, political, didactic, or moral purpose.

Origins.—The romances of love, chivalry (*romans courtois*), and adventure (*romans d'aventure*) that arose in 12th-century France have their analogues elsewhere, notably in the novels of love and adventure developed by Greek writers from the beginning of the 1st century B.C. (*see* GREEK LITERATURE: *Hellenistic and Greco-Roman Periods: Prose: The Novel*). Some of the themes in these reappeared in the Middle Ages, but direct connection can be proved only in the case of the 3rd- or 4th-century Latin romance of Apollonius of Tyre (*q.v.*). The considerable debt of 12th-century romance to classical antiquity was contracted in a sphere other than that of subject matter. Romance, at the outset, was the creation of professional writers who had been educated in the study of Latin and in the medieval *trivium*—grammar, rhetoric, and logic—and who, writing for the amusement of aristocratic patrons, produced works primarily intended as entertainment. Like the idea of courtly love (*q.v.*) with which it is so intimately associated, romance seems to have been a by-product of the refined and leisured life that was growing up in the entourage of kings and the higher nobility in the 12th century. Thus, Benoît de Sainte Maure (*q.v.;* author of the *Roman de Troie*), Wace (*q.v.*), and Thomas (author of the courtly version of the *Tristan* romance: *see* TRISTAN; ANGLO-NORMAN LITERATURE) all apparently worked for the English court in the early years of the reign of Henry II (1154–89) and his wife Eleanor of Aquitaine (*q.v.*); and Chrétien de Troyes (*q.v.*) had as patrons Marie, countess of Champagne (Eleanor's daughter by her first marriage, to Louis VII of France), and the powerful count of Flanders, Philip of Alsace.

Historical writing in the vernacular gave free scope to the spirit of romance: when approached without didactic purpose, history could be treated as a storehouse of picturesque events and romantic happenings in places and at times remote from the present. The term *romanz*, originally meaning the "vernacular" as opposed to Latin, became used, in the period after about 1140, for vernacular translations or adaptations of Latin works the content of which was historical or pseudo-historical. Thus, Wace's translation (1155) of Geoffrey of Monmouth's *Historia regum Britanniae* was known as *Li Romanz de Brut;* and the anonymous adaptation, of about the same date, of Virgil's *Aeneid*, as *Li Romanz d'Éneas*. As will be seen, it is with these and similar works—the story of Alexander the Great and the tales of Thebes and Troy—that romance, both as a name and as a literary genre, begins its evolution.

Narrative Technique.—Chivalric exploits recounted for their own sake, adventures that befall on a journey or a quest, romantic love—these are the staple themes of romance. Yet more important than the subject matter or the "uncommitted" character of romance writing is the development of a special technique of narration. Formally, romance is distinguished from epic by being written in rhyming octosyllabic couplets—whereas epic is written in assonanced stanzas (*laisses*), and has a balladlike structure. Yet it is not merely this change in metrical pattern that led W. P. Ker, in his *Epic and Romance* (1897), to describe the rise of romance as "a genuine revolution from which all later forms of narrative are in some degree derived" and "as something as momentous and as far-reaching as that to which the name Renaissance is generally applied." Romance introduced an entirely new relationship between what is known as the "thematic" and the "fictional" modes. The epic poet had been content to tell a story; he was concerned with statement, not with motivation, and his characters could act without explicitly justifying their actions. Thus, in the *Chanson de Roland*, the hero's decision to fight against odds and let the rearguard of Charlemagne's army be destroyed rather than to call Charlemagne back is neither explained nor discussed, as if the poet takes it for granted that the reader knows why things happened as they did. Romance, on the other hand, reflects the realization that no story, however simple, can speak for itself, and that almost anything the characters do requires explanation. Trained in the 12th-century cathedral schools where poetry was studied with grammar and rhetoric (*q.v.*), romance writers discovered in the practice of these disciplines a new technique which enabled them to elucidate and elaborate their material. Hence the characteristic innovation for which they are responsible: the introduction of a commentary on the meaning of events, either directly by the author or through speeches attributed to the characters. It was thus the literary training of its authors that gave medieval romance its own peculiar texture. This it was that lay behind the method of amplification, resulting in the expansion and elaboration of simple statements; and that was responsible for the systematic use of digression, and, above all, for the technique whereby actions, motives, states of mind are commented on, debated, scrutinized, and dissected. In medieval romance can be recognized the beginning of the analytical method to which the modern novel owes its existence (*see* NOVEL).

History.—*Alexander Romance.*—In tracing the evolution of romance, one must begin with the Alexander romance (*see* ALEXANDER ROMANCES). This, in style and form an epic rather than a romance, relates the fictional biography of Alexander the Great, as established by the pseudo-Callisthenes and transmitted to the Middle Ages through Latin intermediaries, of which the 9th-century *Epitome* of the *Res gestae Alexandri Macedonis* of Julius Valerius is the most important. The *Roman d'Alexandre,* begun by Albéric de Briançon, to which several authors contributed, and which grew up piecemeal over more than half a century from the mid-12th century onward, was put into its final shape *c.* 1175 by Alexandre de Bernai. Much of it deals with wars and battles, treated in the style of the *chansons de geste,* but it is noteworthy for its introduction of fantastic elements, and especially for the marvels of India described in the third *branche,* composed by Lambert le Tort. It was mainly to these exotic and marvelous features (the springs of rejuvenation, the flower-maidens growing in a forest, the *cynocephali,* the magic ship drawn by griffons in which Alexander travels through the air) that the *Roman d'Alexandre* owed its popularity.

Romans d'antiquité.—The *romans d'antiquité: Thèbes,* an adaptation of Statius' *Thebaïs; Éneas,* adapted from Virgil's *Aeneid;* and *Troie,* a retelling by Benoît de Sainte Maure of the tale of Troy as it had been transmitted to the Middle Ages by Dares Phrygius and Dictys Cretensis (*qq.v.*), were all composed in the period 1150–65. The fact that they medievalize the classical world, in that they show the warriors of antiquity behaving very much like medieval knights, is the least important, though to modern readers the most obvious, thing about them. More noteworthy is their technique, which reflects the influence of contemporary rhetoric in the elaborate set descriptions (of, for example, tents, garments, buildings, as well as of human beings) with which the works are studded; and in the introduction of long passages in which the characters indulge in internal debate or self-examination, generally in connection with affairs of the heart. Eulogistic description of human handiwork results in the action's being set in lavish surroundings, resplendent with gold, silver, marble, fine textiles, and precious stones, and adorned with astonishing works of architecture and quaint technological marvels, which recall the Seven Wonders of the World and the reputed glories of Byzantium. *Troie* and *Éneas* have a strong love interest, based on Ovid's conception of love as a restless malady, and exhibiting the doubts, hesitations, and self-torment of young lovers, as in the Achilles-Polyxena story in *Troie* and the Éneas-Lavinie story in *Éneas. Troie* also gives us a story of the faithless Briséïs who abandoned Troilus for Diomedes, which, as expanded by Boccaccio (*q.v.*) in his *Filostrato* (*c.* 1338), formed the basis for Chaucer's *Troilus and Criseyde* and for Shakespeare's *Troilus and Cressida.* (*See* also TROY, LEGEND OF.)

Arthurian Romances.—With Geoffrey of Monmouth's *Historia regum Britanniae* (1137), adapted into French verse in Wace's *Brut* (1155), a new world of the imagination, that of Britain and the court of King Arthur, as marvelous as the world of classical antiquity and almost as remote, was opened up to writers of romance. The Breton *lais* of Marie de France (*q.v.*), composed between 1154 and 1183, and probably before 1170, are set in this "Breton" world, although only one (*Lanval*) brings in King Arthur. Marie's plots are not derived from Geoffrey of Monmouth but exploit folktale material, especially stories of mortals in love with beings from fairyland. The love element is kept in the foreground and elaborated in a lavishly sentimental fashion. Thus, *Lanval* is the story of a love affair between a knight, Lanval, and a fairy: the fairy imposes on him a vow of silence which he breaks when Arthur's queen makes lascivious advances to him; he is put on trial and rescued at the last moment by the fairy, who carries him away to fairyland. The Breton *lais* became a recognized literary type, differing from romances only by being on a smaller scale.

The lost *Tristan* romance, written probably *c.* 1155, is known only through the fragmentary late 12th-century versions of Thomas and Béroul, and through foreign adaptations. The love portrayed in this tale—the unlawful love between Tristan and Isolt, wife of Mark, king of Cornwall—is a tragic and all-absorbing passion induced by a magic potion, and the work was clearly very different from the usual courtly romance, in which love is treated in an idyllic, gently sentimental, and somewhat intellectual manner. The version of Thomas, unlike that of Béroul, softens and sentimentalizes the story, and by rhetorical amplification and analysis of action and motive, brings it nearer to the usual pattern of courtly romance. (*See* also TRISTAN.)

Although the *Éracle* (after 1164) and *Ille et Galeron* (after 1167), of Gautier d'Arras (*q.v.*), are good examples of early courtly romance, Chrétien de Troyes (*q.v.*) is by far the most outstanding writer in this kind, and the impact on later literature of its analytic and reflective method would have been less decisive had it not been handled by so accomplished a writer. Chrétien, whose four great romances, *Erec et Énide, Cligès, Le Chevalier de la charrette* (*Lancelot*), and *Yvain* (*Le Chevalier au lion*), were written, in this order, probably between 1165 and 1176, is limited to no one style or subject. He can tell with equal zeal the story of a marriage between a lord and a poor girl (*Erec*); the love story of a young knight and the wife of the emperor of Byzantium (*Cligès*); the tale of how Lancelot, the devoted and humble lover of the imperious Guinevere, the wife of his overlord, King Arthur, rescues his mistress from captivity in the land of Gorre (*Lancelot*); and the adventures of a knight who marries the widow of a man he has killed in single combat and who undertakes a series of adventures in which he is helped by a grateful lion (*Yvain*). What matters primarily to him is not the plot but the thematic pattern he imposes on it and the significance (*sen,* to use his own term) which he succeeds in conveying either through individual scenes fully interpreted by the characters in long monologues, or through the work as a whole, as in *Lancelot,* where the emphasis is on the theme of courtly love of the most sophisticated kind. (*See* also LANCELOT.) Chrétien's stories are set in Arthur's fabulous realm, and the names of some of his characters can be traced to Geoffrey of Monmouth's pseudo-history; but the reader is not expected to take the setting too seriously. Arthur (*q.v.*) is presented as ruler of a fanciful "never-never land," the scene of strange marvels and adventures; and the characters' behaviour is judged less according to the peculiar ethics of fairyland or of fictitious chronicles than according to the code of courtly love; it is intended to exemplify either obedience to, or an occasional infringement of, some courtly rule. (*See* also COURTLY LOVE; ARTHURIAN LEGEND.)

Chrétien had a faithful disciple in Raoul de Houdenc whose *Meraugis de Portsleguez* (*c.* 1300–10) reflects Chrétien's taste for love casuistry, rhetorical adornment, and fantastic adventure, but lacks his genius. The other Arthurian verse-romances of the period 1170–1250 are adventure romances (*romans d'aventure*) exploiting the element of the strange, the supernatural, and the magical in Chrétien and in Arthurian tradition. A number of them (*e.g., La Mule sans Frein, c.* 1200; and *L'âtre périlleux, c.* 1250) have Gawain (*q.v.*) as hero; the *Beaus Desconeus* (*c.* 1190) of Renaut de Beaujeu is a complicated adventure romance, the main episode of which relates how the hero breaks the spell binding Esmarée, who has been transformed into a serpent, by kissing her on the lips. He finally marries her.

Other Themes.—Many romances, although varied in their setting, are built round the theme of separation and reunion. The Latin romance of Apollonius of Tyre (*q.v.*) may be responsible for the popularity of the theme in the Middle Ages, although the legend of St. Eustace (the Roman general under Trajan who was miraculously converted to Christianity, lost his property, saw his wife and children carried off, worked as a journeyman, but was finally restored to his former position and reunited with his family) was also influential. There are versions of Apollonius in Old English, Spanish, and Italian, and a fragmentary version in 12th-century French. Its central theme is preserved in Shakespeare's *Pericles:* and the French epic *Jourdain de Blaives* (*c.* 1200), in which the hero loses and recovers his foster parents, his wife, and his daughter, is a free imitation of it. On the other hand, *Guillaume d'Angleterre,* reputedly by Chrétien de Troyes, in which the hero abandons his throne, loses his wife and twin children, only to be finally reunited with his family and restored to his kingdom, is a clear imitation of the Eustace legend.

Another common narrative pattern is that of the persecuted child, who escapes to another country, where he falls in love with, and marries, the king's daughter, and after many adventures, regains his lost inheritance. This is the theme of the French epic *Beuve d'Hantone* (*Bevis of Southampton*), of which there are four early 13th-century versions; and, with variations, of two Anglo-Norman works, the *Lai d'Haveloc* (*c.* 1150) and the romance of *Horn* (*c.* 1180). The *Protesilaus* (*c.* 1180) of Hue de Rotelande, another Anglo-Norman writer, is on similar lines, except that the scene is set in classical antiquity and Protesilaus is driven from his country as a result of a quarrel with his brother. *Huon de Bordeaux* (*q.v.; c.* 1220), technically an epic written in dodecasyllabic *laisses,* is a variant of this theme.

A number of romances are entirely love romances built round the theme of the separation and reunion of two young people. The enormously popular *Floire et Blanchefleur* (before 1170; *see* AUCASSIN AND NICOLETTE), which was translated into Middle High German, Middle Dutch, Norse, and English, is a gracious and tender story in which the heroine is sold to merchants who take her away to Babylon, where she is put in the sultan's harem. She is rescued by the hero, Floire, who manages to enter the harem hidden in a basket of flowers. A second, cruder version of the romance (before 1200) was adapted by Boccaccio in his *Filocolo* (*c.* 1336). In *L'Escoufle* (*c.* 1200) by Jean Renart (*q.v.*), Guillaume and Aelis flee away together and are separated when the hero goes in pursuit of a kite that has seized the ring Aelis has given him. In *Guillaume de Palerne* (*c.* 1200), the theme is the successful flight of two lovers: the hero, the son of the king of Apulia, is carried away as a child by a werewolf and later flees with the daughter of the emperor of Rome: the werewolf helps them in their flight, and the hero becomes king of Apulia and later emperor of Rome, while the werewolf, who proves to be the son of the king of Spain, marries the hero's sister. *Partonopeus de Blois* (*q.v.;* last quarter of the 12th century) resembles the Amor and Psyche story in *The Golden Ass* of Apuleius (*q.v.*), although there is probably no direct connection. In *Galeran de Bretagne* (early 13th century), Galeran loves Fresne, a foundling brought up in a convent; the correspondence between the two is discovered and Fresne is sent away, but appears in Galeran's land just in time to prevent him from marrying Fleurie, her twin sister.

The essentially courtly theme of a knight who undertakes adventures to prove to his lady that he is worthy of her love is represented by the *Ipomedon* (1174–90) of Hue de Rotelande; and by the mid-13th-century Anglo-Norman *Gui de Warewic,* although this has a second, clerical part, in which Gui renounces his wife and turns hermit. (*See also* GUY OF WARWICK.)

Another group of romances exploit the "Cymbeline" theme: a man has a wager with another that he will seduce the latter's wife or sweetheart and bring him proof that he has done so, but the proof is obtained by deceit and the lady's chastity is ultimately vindicated. *Le Comte de Poitiers* (*c.* 1180) is the earliest of this group, but *Guillaume de Dôle* (*c.* 1200) by Jean Renart is the most noteworthy: here, the villain misrepresents himself as an emissary of the emperor, goes to Dôle, learns of a birthmark like a rose on the lady's thigh, and uses the knowledge to slander her chastity. The *Roman de la Violette* (after 1225), by Gerbert de Montreuil, in which the birthmark is a violet, is a close imitation of *Guillaume de Dôle.*

La Manekine (*c.* 1270), of Philippe de Rémi de Beaumanoir (*q.v.*), is based on the so-called "Constance" theme (later exemplified in Chaucer's *Man of Law's Tale*), in which the heroine is the object of unnatural love on the part of her own father and flees to a foreign land where she marries the ruler, but during the latter's absence is banished because her stepmother accuses her of giving birth to monstrous offspring, and after many adventures is reunited with her husband. The theme recurs in the *Contesse d'Anjou* (1316), by Jean Maillart. *Athis and Prophilias* (late 12th century) is built on the theme of the "two faithful friends": Athis gives his newly wed bride to Prophilias, who is dying of love for her; later Prophilias repays the debt by confessing to a murder he has not committed but of which Athis is accused; Prophilias is acquitted and Athis marries his sister Gaieté. (*See also* AMIS ET AMILES.)

Very few of the verse romances are stories of adultery, although the two most celebrated love stories of the Middle Ages—the *Tristan* legend (*see* TRISTAN) and the story of Lancelot and Guinevere (*qq.v.*)—are of this type. The only other significant examples are the *Chastelaine de Vergi* (mid-13th century), in which the heroine dies of grief because her lover reveals their secret (and adulterous) love to the duke of Burgundy, who tells it to his wife; and the *Chastelain de Couci* (late 13th century) in which the hero, dying on a crusade, orders his heart to be sent to his lady after his death: the jealous husband obtains the heart, serves it up to the lady, and she, resolving that no other meat shall profane her lips, dies of starvation and so rejoins her lover. The theme was treated in German in the late 13th century by Konrad von Würzburg (*q.v.*), in his *Herzmaere.* The long Provençal romance *Flamenca* (? 1234) treats the theme of the gay young lover and the lighthearted wife who outwit the fantastically jealous husband in an amusing way (*see* PROVENÇAL LITERATURE).

The romances are normally set in remote times and places, although the setting in most cases amounts to little more than the lavish use of exotic personal and geographical names. Often there is a confused jumble, as in Hue de Rotelande's *Protesilaus,* in which the characters have Greek names, the action takes place in Burgundy, Crete, Calabria, and Apulia, and Theseus is described as "king of Denmark." The "sea-coast of Bohemia" in Shakespeare's *Twelfth Night* has its medieval antecedents.

One theme remains. The last, unfinished, romance of Chrétien de Troyes, *Perceval* (or *Le Conte del Graal; c.* 1180), introduces the Grail story into European literature. The key episode is that where Perceval sees the Grail vessel, the consecrated Host from which the Grail king's father had been sustained. What Chrétien's intentions were in introducing a deeply religious motif into a story of fantastic adventure it is hard to say, but the work had important consequences for the development of romance. A Burgundian knight, Robert de Borron, produced at the turn of the century a poem dealing with the origins of the Grail, the *Joseph d'Arimathie,* to which he appended an unfinished sequel, the *Merlin* (*see also* MERLIN). Robert's apparent aim was to connect the Grail (interpreted as the vessel of the Last Supper) with the coming of a redeemer, or interpreter, in the days of King Arthur. This notion of a predestined Grail hero appearing during Arthur's reign became, in the first quarter of the 13th century, the subject of the prose "Didot" *Perceval* and the prose *Perlesvaus.* (*See* also PERCEVAL; GRAIL, THE HOLY.)

The Development of Prose Romance.—These two works mark the beginnings of the Arthurian prose romance. Prose thereafter became the leading romance form. The first of the great prose romances, the "Vulgate Cycle," or the *Lancelot-Grail,* was in existence by *c.* 1230.

The "Vulgate Cycle" intertwines the themes of romantic love, of the advent of the Grail knight Galahad (turned into an analogue of the Redeemer), and of the downfall of Arthur's kingdom. The "pseudo-Borron" Grail romance (*c.* 1240) centres the story upon the "adventures of Logres," which include the striking of the Dolorous Stroke by the unlucky knight Balain and the healing of the maimed Grail king by Galahad. The marvelous adventures in this romance have a strange and uncanny quality, and, like some others on the Grail theme (e.g., the *Perlesvaus*), the work offers a curious mingling of religion and romance. The plot imitates the story of the Fall and Redemption: whether this means that it is a religious allegory or whether the religious theme is used to give a pious and edifying character to a purely fanciful production is difficult to say.

No such problem arises in connection with the prose romance of Tristan (*Tristan de Léonois*). Based on the 12th-century verse romances of Tristan, it relates the story of the star-crossed lovers of Cornwall, but this basic theme is overlaid by chivalric episodes in which Tristan proves his valour; the "interlacing" structure of the earlier romances is loosened, accounts of tournaments are intercalated to satisfy a contemporary interest in this pastime, digressions are frequent, and some of these form short autonomous tales connected only tenuously with the main romance. The work was enormously influential in the later Middle Ages: an early off-shoot (before 1250) was the romance of *Palamède*, which exists in several versions and deals with Palamède, the Saracen who was Tristan's rival in love, and the older generation of King Arthur's knights. A collection of rambling adventures, it fore-shadows the inconsequent and trivial "romances of chivalry" of a later period.

The vogue of these later romances, from the 14th century onward, when the narrative poems of the early period were no longer read, is a little difficult to explain; the development of private collections of books and the taste for handsome illuminated and well-written volumes may have had something to do with it. The Renaissance by no means put an end to the popularity of the prose romances. The prose *Tristan* circulated as a printed book and abridged modernized versions were produced. (*See also* TRISTAN.)

Adaptations of French Romances.—The French verse romances were early adapted into German: the *Éneas* by Heinrich von Veldeke between 1175 and 1186; the *Tristan* by Eilhart von Oberge, c. 1170; the *Erec* and *Yvain* by Hartmann von Aue between 1190 and 1210; the courtly Thomas version of *Tristan* by Gottfried von Strassburg, c. 1210; and the *Conte del Graal* (as *Parzival*) by Wolfram von Eschenbach between c. 1200 and 1210. Later in the century, the courtly romance had its final flowering in German in the work of Rudolf von Ems and Konrad von Würzburg, who wrote a long *Trojanerkrieg*, a romance of the Swan Knight (*Der Schwanritter; see* LOHENGRIN), and several shorter romances on native themes. (*See also* GERMAN LITERATURE: *Middle High German Period;* and articles on writers mentioned above.)

A great number of French romances were adapted into English, sometimes very freely, between the 13th and 15th centuries. The English verse romances have a wide range of subject matter: *Otuel* (after 1300), *Roland and Vernagu* (1330–40), and *Sir Firumbras* (c. 1380) are based on late epics of the Charlemagne cycle (*see* CHARLEMAGNE LEGENDS); Arthurian romances are represented by *Ywain and Gawain* (early 14th century), and *Sir Percyvelle of Galles* (late 14th century), adaptations of Chrétien's *Yvain* and *Perceval* respectively; by the alliterative *Morte Arthure* of the Thornton manuscript (second half of the 14th century), an outstanding work that tells the story of Arthur's campaign against the Romans; by the stanzaic *Le Morte Arthur* (end of the 14th century), which recounts the last battle with Mordred and Arthur's death; and by the alliterative *Joseph of Arimathie* (first half of the 14th century), a translation of part of the French *Estoire del Graal*.

The large number of romances with Gawain as hero, mostly crude in style and not clearly traceable to French sources, is a feature of the English Arthurian tradition. The greatest Middle English romance, *Sir Gawain and the Green Knight* (c. 1370), belongs to this category: the subject (the beheading game) is bizarre, but the execution is superb, combining fantasy and great descriptive power; the tone is elegant and sophisticated and the poet's purpose is to exemplify true courtesy and the integrity of perfect knighthood. The Thomas version of the *Tristan* poem is adapted in *Sir Tristrem* (c. 1330), a tail-rhyme romance with an unusual metrical form. Thomas Chestre's the *Beaus Desconeus* (second quarter of the 14th century) is a translation of the involved "adventure romance" of the same name by Renaut de Beaujeu. *Floris and Blauncheflur* (c. 1250) translates the French romance. The Breton *lai* is represented by Thomas Chestre's *Sir Launfal* (early 14th century), which expands Marie de France's *Lanval* into a romance; and by *Sir Orfeo*, which retells the Orpheus and Eurydice story in a medieval setting: the source was probably a lost French *lai*. The Anglo-Norman biographical romances of Bevis, Horn, and Guy of Warwick reappear in *Beues of Hamtoun* (c. 1300), *King Horn* (c. 1225), *Horn Childe and Maiden Rimnild* (1330–40), and *Guy of Warwick* (after 1300). The two romances on the "Eustace" theme, *Sir Isumbras* and *Sir Eglamour of Artois*, both from the second half of the 14th century, have no ascertainable French source, and seem to have enjoyed great popularity. *Emaré*, of roughly the same date, is an adaptation of the "Constance" theme. The alliterative *William of Palerne* (c. 1350) is based on a French original; and there are three 14th-century versions of the French *Ipomedon* and two 15th-century versions of *Parthenope of Blois*. The *Tale of Gamelyn* (c. 1350) is based on native material: the hero, persecuted by his brother, eventually turns outlaw, procures the hanging of the sheriff, and makes his peace with society. *Athelston* (c. 1350) is a story, of native origin, of a king who begins by acting unjustly to one of his barons, is launched on a career of violence, and is finally excommunicated. (*See also* ENGLISH LITERATURE: *Early Middle English Period;* and *Poetry: The Alliterative Tradition.*)

The French romances appeared in Norway in prose translations in the reign of Haakon IV (*q.v.;* 1217–63), when the country was brought by royal policy into the mainstream of western European culture. The *Tristrams Saga* (1226), a translation of the Thomas version of the *Tristan*, was undertaken for the king by Brother Robert, who also translated the *lais* of Marie de France (the *Strengleikar*). Other romances translated in this period were the *Yvain* of Chrétien de Troyes, also at the instigation of the king, and the *Erec* and the *Perceval;* and *Floire et Blanchefleur*. A translation of Geoffrey of Monmouth's *Historia*, the *Breta Sögur*, seems somewhat earlier than Haakon's reign, and there is also a "Troy book" (the *Trójumanna Saga: see* ICELANDIC LITERATURE: *Translations from Latin*). This imported romantic literature also began to influence the form and content of native stories, and from the 14th century European tales of very varied provenance were introduced into Scandinavia. Between 1300 and 1312 there were verse translations in Swedish of *Yvain* (*Herra Iwan*) and of *Floire et Blanchefleur*.

In Italy the French prose *Tristan* and the *Palamède* were influential, and are represented by such vernacular prose compilations as the *Tavola ritonda* and the *Tristano riccardiano*. The 13th century in Italy is, however, distinguished by *remaniements* and compilations of French epic material belonging to the Guillaume d'Orange (*q.v.*) and Charlemagne cycles (*see* CHARLEMAGNE LEGENDS), but this epic material is assimilated to the other great bodies of medieval French narrative fiction, and it is infused with the spirit of Arthurian prose romance. In the 15th century the great poems of Matteo Boiardo and Ludovico Ariosto (*qq.v.*) —*Orlando innamorato* and *Orlando furioso*—are based on this fusion. To quote A. Viscardi (in *Arthurian Literature in the Middle Ages*, p. 428) "they chose the geography and the personages of the Carolingian epic, but the adventures and idealism are those of Arthurian romance."

The serious themes of the Holy Grail and the death of Arthur left no mark in Italy, and it was thus the prose *Tristan* tradition that shaped the romantic idealism of Boiardo and Ariosto: extraordinary adventures, enchantments, marvels of the stock Arthurian type, the rescue of distressed ladies, brilliant feats of arms, the whole recounted lightly and with sophisticated humour. (*See also* ITALIAN LITERATURE.)

In the Iberian peninsula romance found its inspiration in the prose *Tristan*, the *Palamède*, and the pseudo-Borron romance, all of which were translated. In Spain, however, the most significant development was the appearance of a native prose romance, *Amadís de Gaula* (*q.v.*), a biographical romance which, while modeling the hero's career in its main outlines on that of Lancelot, adopts a non-Arthurian setting and freely invents its episodic content. In the form given to it by Garci Rodríguez de Montalvo (1508) it enjoyed considerable vogue and was followed by several continuations; *e.g.*, *Esplandian* (1510), of which the hero is Amadís' son; *Liduarte de Grécia* (1514) and *Amadís de Grécia* (1530), dealing with Esplandian's son and grandson respectively; and by imitations, among which are the Palmerin romances, the first of which was *Palmerin de Oliva* (1511), and the most celebrated, *Palmerin de Inglaterra*, first published in Portuguese (1544). All these works enjoyed international fame. One consequence, however, of the 16th-century revival of pastoral poetry on the classical model was the appearance of *Diana* (*c.* 1559) by Jorge Montemayor (*q.v.*), the first true pastoral romance. (*See* also PASTORAL.) It was in England, however, on the eve of the Tudor age, that late Arthurian prose romance found its great representative. For the English-speaking world "Arthurian romance" attains its definitive form in the works of Sir Thomas Malory (*q.v.*), published by William Caxton in 1485 under the title of *Le Morte Darthur*.

Post-Medieval Developments.—At the beginning of the 17th century, compendious sentimental romances with an adventurous, pastoral, or pseudo-historical colouring, based on the 16th-century Spanish romances, were popular throughout western Europe. In France, such representatives of the genre as *L'Astrée* (1607–27) of Honoré d'Urfé, *Artamène, ou le Grand Cyrus* (1649–53) of Madeleine de Scudéry, and the romances of Gauthier de Costes, seigneur de La Calprenède, were popular among the *précieux* society of the *salons*. (*See* also URFÉ, HONORÉ D'; SCUDÉRY, GEORGES AND MADELEINE DE; LA CALPRENÈDE, GAUTIER DE COSTES, SEIGNEUR DE.) However, the neoclassical literary doctrines, with their demand for psychological realism and their insistence on the *vraisemblable*, and the cult of such grand genres as tragedy, comedy, oratory, and religious apologetic, were fatal to the continued success of romance. But, before disappearing, the romances lent the French form of their name to such productions as *Le Roman bourgeois* (1666) by Antoine Furetière, and *Le Romant comique* (1651–57) by Paul Scarron, which preserved something of the outward appearance of romance, although nothing of its spirit; and so ultimately to the genre of narrative fiction that has succeeded them in modern times. In 17th-century France romance was no longer a "noble" genre.

In England, however, the greatest literary figure in the post-Restoration period was John Milton, and, for Milton, born at the beginning of the 17th century, "romance" was still an honoured term, and Edmund Spenser was its high priest. Thus, while we find Robert Boyle inveighing (in his *Occasional Discourses*, 1666) against the gentlemen whose libraries contained nothing more substantial than "romances"—evidently of the Spanish or French variety—Milton in *Paradise Lost* could still invoke "what resounds in Fable or Romance of Uther's son."

In the early 18th century, romance was discredited as being chimerical or unreasonable, but a revival of interest in the form soon set in. The Gothic romances, of which the *Castle of Otranto* (published December 1764; dated 1765) by Horace Walpole was the first, are, perhaps, less important for the history of the form than is the development of a serious antiquarian interest in the past. According to Richard Hurd (*q.v.*), in his *Letters on Chivalry and Romance* (1762), romance is not truth, but represents the free play of the imagination: a sort of delightful holiday from common sense. Hurd's justification of romance is one to which Ariosto and Chrétien de Troyes would willingly have subscribed. Hurd thus sets out an ideal of romance that is consonant with the ideas of the 18th century, but also with those of the Middle Ages. It is an ideal that, in Germany, inspired C. M. Wieland's *Oberon* (*c.* 1780), but which the later Romantic school found inadequate (*see* ROMANTICISM).

In England Hurd's principle was faithfully observed by Sir Walter Scott. Romance as understood by Scott and his contemporaries was primarily a narrative form which afforded the storyteller the opportunity of achieving suspense in the midst of complex situations. But Scott himself combined the "desire to make fables" ("*die Lust zu fabulieren*," in Goethe's phrase) with an attitude to the world essentially inspired by robust common sense. After the verse romances of distinctly "Gothic" inspiration, which established his popularity, he turned to the writing of prose romances which took the reader into an imaginative world peopled by rather colourless 19th-century young lovers, and by such unforgettable figures of romance as Rob Roy's wife, Redgauntlet, and Balfour of Burley.

But in the best novels of Scott there is at least one character who, however quaint or eccentric, embodies the sober rationalism of 18th-century Whiggism, and whose presence puts the "romantic" characters sternly into place. Scott perhaps embodies the truth of the saying: "romance is the recreation of the practical man." It is also the compensating factor in the antiquary's makeup. Jonathan Oldbuck, in *The Antiquary*, pedantic scholar and excellent man of business though he is, is only one half of a real antiquary. Scott, himself a real antiquary, not only engaged in studies of early texts, but made them pleasant and enjoyable reading, and spread their popularity far beyond the English-speaking world.

BIBLIOGRAPHY.—Among older works may be mentioned Richard Hurd's *Letters on Chivalry and Romance* (1762) and Sir Walter Scott's "Essay on Romance," in the Supplement to the *Encyclopædia Britannica* (1815–24). Modern works include W. P. Ker, *Epic and Romance* (1897; 2nd ed. 1931), and *Romance*, English Association Pamphlet, 10 (1909, reprinted 1913); George Saintsbury, *The Flourishing of Romance and the Rise of Allegory* (1897); E. Faral, *Recherches sur les sources latines des contes et romans courtois du moyen âge* (1913); J. E. Wells, *A Manual of the Writings in Middle English, 1050–1400* (1916, and supplements); H. Thomas, *Spanish and Portuguese Romances of Chivalry* (1920); H. G. Leach, *Angevin Britain and Scandinavia* (1921); Laura A. Hibbard, *Medieval Romance in England* (1924); Sarah F. Barrow, *Medieval Society Romances* (1924); Logan Pearsall Smith, *Four Words: Romantic, Originality, Creative, Genius*, Tract No. 17, The Society for Pure English (1924); R. S. Loomis (ed.), *Arthurian Literature in the Middle Ages: a Collaborative History* (1959); A. Johnston, *Enchanted Ground: the Study of Medieval Romance in the 18th Century* (1964). (E. VR.; F. WH.)

ROMANCE LANGUAGES, or Romanic languages (RL), derive their name from *Roman*(*ic*)—that is, "Latin" because they are modern continuations of Latin. To call them daughter languages of Latin is merely metaphoric, since no descent or new creation is involved. Neo-Latin is a satisfactory term, but the Romance languages are so different from ancient Latin that entirely new names are justified. Enumerating and classifying the many dialects of the RL requires determination of the extent to which idioms called by the same name must be similar or may differ. The "discovery" of a new Romance language such as Franco-Provençal merely expresses the scholar's conviction that a type of speech appears sufficiently distinct from others so as to deserve a name of its own. The problem of classification is simplified if language is defined as a standard literary form of speech as opposed to the numerous unwritten or uncodified dialects. In this sense, the following RL may be enumerated: (1) Italian, (2) Rumanian, (3) French, (4) Provençal, (5) Spanish, (6) Portuguese, (7) Catalan, (8) Raeto- (Rhaeto-) Romance and (9) Sardinian. Italian, with the exception of dialects north of the Apennines, and Rumanian are often classified as Eastern, the rest as Western Romance languages. Raeto-Romance and Sardinian have no single standard literary languages, Catalan is endeavouring to retain or revive one, and Provençal no longer has one. Other enumerations of RL are therefore possible, depending on the manner of counting and classifying.

In common usage, terms like French, Italian or Spanish refer to the standard languages as taught in schools. Dialects subsumed under each may well be as different from one another as are the standard languages from one another; hence, speaking of Italian or French dialects often reflects national or geographic rather than linguistic criteria.

Spoken Latin.—One generally says that the RL do not continue Classical Latin (CL) but Vulgar Latin (VL). The latter term is better avoided in this context because it is variously defined and mainly because it almost invariably refers to some kind of late, postclassical or unclassical, "bad" *written* Latin, whereas the RL are derived from the *spoken* idioms of the Latin-speaking world (the Romania). CL, like any other classical or standard language, had its roots in spoken language, but with grammatical codification came some measure of petrifaction. The continuous change in spoken Latin (SL), like all cultural change, was in part a consequence of passing time but it was more significantly conditioned by the cultural history of the speakers.

As Latin spread over former non-Latin-speaking areas (the earliest Latin was spoken only in Rome and its surroundings), the natives transferred some of their linguistic habits to the new language (the influence of the linguistic substratum), and immigration, more or less intense or durable, by speakers of foreign languages brought new linguistic traits which speakers of Latin then acquired (the superstratum). The history of Italy and Romania, including such recent events as the Latinization of the Americas, serves therefore as a background and base for their linguistic history.

Since not all regions of the Romania were Romanized at the same time, they were not all exposed to the same kind of Latin; indeed the new world learned Neo-Latin, *i.e.*, French, Spanish and Portuguese. Nor were they Romanized by the same Latin dialect: one district may have learned its Latin primarily from middle-class or lower-class veterans and farmers, another from upper-class administrators, officers and merchants. Some districts were soon provided with schools and learned Latin from grammarians, others learned it merely by ear in daily intercourse.

Considering all these historic and cultural causes for linguistic variety, one cannot but believe that the entire Romania spoke throughout its history many Latin and Neo-Latin (Romance) dialects, and that the uniformity of Latin is no more than an illusion due to the identification of "Latin" with standard written CL, a view which is conducive to misunderstanding. It is true that apart from good CL there existed also all over the Romania a less classical common speech, something of an international language or *koine,* which became more un-Ciceronian with the passage of time and the political and cultural breakdown that accompanied the decline and fall of the Roman empire. But not all persons spoke this progressively worsening (from a classical viewpoint) common Latin, and it is certainly not the basis of the Romance languages. This *koine* is, however, the predominant idiom of texts coming from all over the empire. Being frequently identified as VL, it has given rise to the view that linguistic uniformity prevailed throughout the Romania until the 8th or 9th century, which suddenly, cataclysmically and catastrophically, disintegrated into the numerous Romance dialects. Linguistic development does not generally occur in this way: there is no reason to assume it did in this instance.

What are the linguist's sources of real spoken Latin, not only for postclassical and Proto-Romance (PR), but also for classical and preclassical times? Latin began to be codified in the mid-2nd century B.C. under Greek influence and with the influx of Greek literature and Greek teachers of grammar. The earlier preclassical texts available, literary and epigraphic (and they are far from abundant), represent fairly well the spoken language, much better than do later texts. With the establishment of a standard language, its use by "good" writers, and grammatical instruction for the youth of the upper classes, went a rejection of all substandard colloquial and popular usage. Henceforth no one wanted to commit the (social) error of using "bad" Latin, and deviations encountered in the extant records are mainly inadvertent. During the classical period and for some time thereafter, when fair public education was accessible to many people, such lapses tended to be few in comparison with their number in subsequent centuries, which experienced a general decline in literary standards and a relaxation of the requirements for grammatical correctness. Dialect literature and "realistic" writing are lacking in the literary records—if they ever existed. Plautus' preclassical comedies, Petronius' 1st-century novel *Satyricon* and Apuleius' 2nd-century novel *The Golden Ass* are the only examples available. Hence most information comes from the less inhibited inscriptional evidence, especially the *graffiti* (scratchings on walls), from gram-

marians quoting and chastizing "bad" language, from collections of "errors" such as the *Appendix Probi* (probably of the 3rd century A.D.), from glosses (interlinear or marginal explanations of difficult words in a manuscript), and, of course, from the RL themselves.

Proto-Romance.—Owing to the poor documentation and the overpowering influence that CL exerted on all writing, it is not surprising that one cannot detect genuine local Latin dialects as forerunners of the Romance dialects, apart from a few, often inconclusive forms. But it would be shortsighted to deny their existence, just because the evidence is lacking, in an area so large and of such pre-Latin linguistic variety as the Romania, particularly since the Roman state attached no importance to the linguistic acculturation of its possessions. The absence anywhere in the Romania of dialectal texts that one could call PR rather than Latin before the 9th century, when they appear with some suddenness and differ in appearance from the Latin texts of the same localities, is due to the absence of any incentive to use what was obviously bad Latin in writing. But once it was realized that the spoken vernaculars were not really just depraved Latin but languages in their own right, and that it was useless to try to communicate in Latin either in writing or speaking with persons who knew no Latin, then these bad, rustic, vulgar dialects were eventually thought worthy of being recorded for certain purposes. All higher literary and scientific endeavour, however, remained for centuries to come the province of the prestige language, Latin. The history of the Romance dialects is the history of the linguistic emancipation of the Romania.

For a time, varying in length in the various regions, all dialects were of equal prestige, and the earlier Romance documents transmit fuller information on dialectal varieties than has since been available. But with the formation of national states, of cultural and intellectual centres, often coinciding with the residence of the monarch and the political capital, certain local dialects augmented their prestige and usefulness at the expense of others. The ultimate consequence was the elevation of such dialects, often just one for each nation, to the dignity of a written standard language such as CL had once been, and the relegation of the other dialects to patois of lesser importance. Thus French is essentially the language of Paris, Italian that of Florence and Spanish that of Madrid. (For details, *see* the articles on the separate languages.) The time when and the speed with which a new standard language was formed and acquired currency depend on the accompanying cultural conditions and events.

In the future, any one of the standard RL may share the fate of CL by becoming petrified and estranged from common use to such an extent as to wither away. This evolution, however, is counteracted, first, by the tendency observable during the past several centuries, and likely to continue at a mounting rate, of the acquisition of the standard language by an increasing number of persons thanks to growing literacy, improved communications and the retreat of the nonstandard dialects; and second, by the awareness on the part of modern grammarians that attempts to keep a language "pure" and immutable are merely conducive to its mummification.

This article deals mainly with those historic changes of SL which are more or less common to all Romance dialects and pertain to a stage of development called PR. (For the changes which specifically lead to their current distinctions, *see* articles on the separate languages.)

It is customary, and, in view of the scanty documentation, virtually inevitable, to compare PR with CL, rather than preceding stages of SL. But such comparison should not imply a linear development from CL to Romance. The chronological sequence (no matter how poorly attested in parts) is not Old Latin → Classical Latin → "Vulgar Latin" → Proto-Romance, but rather Old (spoken) Latin → Spoken Latin of the classical period → late spoken Latin → Proto-Romance.

Phonology.—The most important phenomenon in the vowels concerns the change from phonemic quantity to phonemic quality. Where at one time the relative length of the vowels was significant, so that two forms might be distinguished from one another solely by vocalic quantity, in PR only vocalic quality is distinctive. Since spelling was neither immediately nor consistently affected by this change, it is impossible to say when it began to operate. But it seems certain that its inception precedes the appearance of Romance documents not by decades but by centuries; its earliest traces can in fact be discerned in inscriptions of Rome's republican era. In general, long vowels become close ($u\bar{e}rum > u\varrho rum$) and short vowels open ($b\check{e}ne > b\varrho ne$). (On the pronunciation of Latin spellings, see LATIN LANGUAGE.) Where, then, earlier Latin distinguishes two e-like sounds by their quantity, late SL and PR distinguish them by their quality. It may be assumed that already during the period of phonemic quantity, length was accompanied by closeness and shortness by openness of pronunciation, and that there eventually occurred a shift of distinction from one to the other of the vowel characteristics. Some diphthongs became monophthongized. The following schema illustrates the evolution of the stressed vowels.

Early Latin: ă ā ĕ ae ē oe ĭ ī ŏ au ō ŭ ū eu ui

Late Latin: a ę ẹ ị ǫ au ọ ụ eu ui

Note that the qualitatively similar vowels, ē-ĭ and ō-ŭ, once their quantity ceases to be distinctive, coincide and have henceforth the same development in Romance, with the exception of dialects of southern Italy, Sardinia and some others. Following nasals, palatals or consonant clusters may produce various divergent developments in the different dialects.

The vowels not bearing the main stress develop somewhat differently. It is well to distinguish between final position (*murŬm*), secondary stress position (*pŎtestátem*) and unstressed position (initial, *mArítus, Altárem;* pretonic, *potEstátem;* posttonic, *pópUlum*). Among these, the pretonic and posttonic (which occur necessarily in words of more than two syllables—otherwise pretonic is impossible and posttonic is final) are weakest and tend to be syncopated early, whereas the secondary stress vowel is strongest and most likely to preserve its vowel in the original quality. The *a* is, among all vowels in these positions, the most stable. The place of the stress in PR is almost invariably the same as in earlier Latin.

While the history of the vowels is only secondarily determined by their phonetic surroundings and their stress, the consonants change primarily as a result of their surroundings (except *h* which disappears completely). Hence consonants that are different in terms of place of articulation (labial, dental, velar) often undergo changes of the same type in terms of kind of articulation (palatalization, lengthening, fricatization, loss, lenition) according to their position in the word (initial, medial, final) and their surroundings (intervocalic, in clusters, before *r* and *l*, before yod). The developments are too varied to be schematized briefly. They will be found in detail in the articles on the separate RL.

Morphology and Syntax.—In the noun, the most important change is from a three-gender and six-case to a two-gender and one-case (*i.e.,* "no case") declension. In some Romance dialects there are remnants of the cases (Rumanian, Old French, Old Provençal) in the noun, and in all dialects of the cases and of the neuter gender in the pronoun. Case and gender reductions are tied up with the phonemic changes which eliminate the final consonants, especially *s* and *m*, which are of crucial importance in the Latin inflection, and with the blurring of distinctions among final vowels, which are essential for recognizing gender and case. In the modern RL the noun gender is formally expressed by the article (formerly a Latin demonstrative pronoun) and the adjective, which must "agree" with the noun they modify. The function of the cases is fulfilled either by a more rigid word-order (*le père aime le fils:* subject-verb-object; *cf.* Latin *pater amat filium, filium amat pater, amat pater filium,* etc., all meaning the same) or by prepositional phrases (*filio: au fils; filii: del figlio*). The Romance constructions are neither more "logical" or "natural," nor less efficient than the corresponding Latin ones. They are merely different.

In the verb, the RL dropped a number of forms (future perfect, except Rumanian, Spanish and Portuguese, but with new mean-ings; imperfect subjunctive, except in Sardinian; pluperfect, except in Spanish, Portuguese; perfect subjunctive); they created a number of new compound tense forms (mainly of the past, indicative and subjunctive); they replaced the future by a new composition of infinitive plus *habere,* less frequently *uelle* (Rum.) or *debere* (Sard.)—*cf.* Eng. "I will," "I shall"—which has, however, now lost all appearance of compoundness in most dialects (*amare habeo > j'aimerai, amerò,* etc.).

This type of replacement of Latin simple (synthetic) by Romance compounded (analytic) locutions pervades the entire morphology. It shows itself also in the substitution of prepositional phrases for case-forms; in the entire reformation of the passive voice (participle plus form of *esse; amatur: il est aimé*), which causes the disappearance of deponent verbs; the use of *plus* or *magis* in the comparison of adjectives instead of suffixes (*grandis, grandior: grand, plus grand, mas grande;* the retained Latin comparatives are few: *melius > mieux, meglio; peius > pis; minus > moins*); the formation of the Romance adverb with *mente* (*clare: clara mente > chiaramente*).

The number of subjunctive forms is reduced, or else they are employed for other purposes. The elaborate *consecutio temporum,* the rule on the sequence of tenses, is abolished. In general, the use of subjunctives is strongly reduced, a development which still continues, especially in colloquial use. Almost all Romance dialects have so-called conditionals, which are employed for expressing conditions contrary to fact and in the main clause of conditional constructions, with the *if*-clause following various rules (*s'il pouvait, il le ferait; se potesse, lo farebbe*).

Vocabulary.—Most areas of the Romania had been thoroughly Latinized in vocabulary so that relatively few pre-Latin (Celtic, Oscan, Umbrian, Etruscan, Greek) words were retained. Similarly, linguistic superstrata in the Romania (Germanic, Arabic, Slavonic), while leaving stronger traces than the substrata, account for a small percentage of Romance vocabulary. The number depends on the political and cultural history of each region: it is greater in Rumania where the superstratum is Slavonic, for example, than in Italy where it is Germanic. The later a word is borrowed into the RL, the fewer historic changes it undergoes. This is especially true of "learned" words of Latin and Greek origin which were taken into the languages during the Renaissance and subsequent centuries, down to the present when scientists coin many of their terms from Latin or Greek roots. Any foreign word becomes, after a while, a less foreign loanword, and old enough loanwords may appear so native that they are often recognized as not such only when linguistically analyzed.

See also separate articles on the various Romance languages, and references under "Romance Languages" in the Index.

BIBLIOGRAPHY.—W. D. Elcock, *The Romance Languages* (1960); C. H. Grandgent, *An Introduction to Vulgar Latin* (1908); I. Iordan and J. Orr, *An Introduction to Romance Linguistics* (1937); A. Kuhn, *Die romanischen Sprachen* (1951); W. Meyer-Lübke, *Grammatik der romanischen Sprachen* (1890–1902; also French trans.) *Romanisches etymologisches Wörterbuch* (1935); S. Pop, *La dialectologie I: Dialectologie romane* (1950); E. Pulgram, "Spoken and Written Latin," *Language,* vol. xxvi, pp. 458–466 (1950); C. Tagliavini, *Le origini delle lingue neolatine* (1952); W. von Wartburg, *Die Ausgliederung der romanischen Sprachräume* (1950; also Span. trans.). (E. PM.)

ROMAN DE LA ROSE, one of the most popular French poems of the later Middle Ages; a work of over 21,000 lines surviving in more than 300 manuscripts. Nothing is known of the author of the first 4,058 lines except his name, Guillaume de Lorris (a village near Orléans). This part of the poem, composed about 1240 or slightly earlier, is a charming account, in allegorical form, of the wooing of a maiden, symbolized by a rosebud, within the bounds of a garden representing courtly society. The lover himself is not allegorized, and some of the other characters only faultily (*e.g.,* Amis, who is simply a guide and companion, rather than the representative of friendship), but most of the actors are personifications of various aspects of the loved one's mind, especially Bel-Accueil (that which inclines her to favour the lover) and Dangier (its opposite: Aloofness). On the outside of the garden are figures portraying all that is excluded from courtly life (Vilanie, Avarice, Envie, etc.). The lover is admitted into the garden, whose Lord is Deduit (Pleasure—since courtly life is one of pleasure), by Oiseuse (Indolence—courtly life is not for busy people), is wounded by the arrows of Amor (Biauté, Simplece, Cortoisie, etc.), and receives detailed instruction in the symptoms of love and the correct behaviour of a courtly lover. Bel-Accueil leads him to the rosebush, but he is prevented from picking the rose by Dangier, Male Bouche (Calumny), and Honte (Shame, *i.e.*, Modesty). Jalousie imprisons Bel-Accueil in a tower in the middle of the garden. Opinions differ about the intended end to the story—the lover appears to be overcoming the obstacles in his path, but the strict rules of courtly love would forbid his succeeding in obtaining his desire.

A 78-line anonymous termination exists, of small literary value, but no satisfactory conclusion was written until about 1280, when Jean de Meun (*q.v.*) seized upon the plot of Guillaume de Lorris as a means of conveying a vast mass of encyclopaedic information and opinions on every topic likely to interest his contemporaries. The allegory was for him of little importance, ·although the lover does eventually obtain the rose, and the story is frequently held up for thousands of lines while the characters discourse at length— the so-called Confession of Nature (one of the most important characters in the second part, frequently acting as a mouthpiece for Jean's own views) lasts from verse 16,729 to verse 19,400, and touches no point relevant to the original theme. Nevertheless it was these digressions that secured the poem its fame and success, for, unlike Guillaume de Lorris, Jean de Meun was writing in them for a taste that was gaining ground and not for one that was dying. His views were often bitterly contested, but they never failed to hold the attention of the age. *See also* COURTLY LOVE.

BIBLIOGRAPHY.—The great edition by E. Langlois, for the Société des Anciens Textes Français (1914–24), replaced all others. *See also* Langlois' *Origines et sources du Roman de la Rose* (1890) and *Les MSS du Roman de la Rose* (1911); G. Paré, *Le Roman de la Rose et la scolastique courtoise* (1941); Alan M. F. Gunn, *The Mirror of Love* (1952); C. S. Lewis, *Allegory of Love* (1936).

A Middle English version, of which the first 1,705 lines are by Geoffrey Chaucer (*q.v.*), covers all Guillaume de Lorris and 3,000 lines of Jean de Meun. There are translations into modern English by F. S. Ellis (1900) and into modern French by A. Mary (1928 and 1949).
(G. ME.)

ROMAN-DUTCH LAW, the system of law which existed in the Netherlands province of Holland from the 15th to the 19th century. This system, introduced by the Dutch into their colonies, was retained in those that passed to the British crown at the end of the 18th and the beginning of the 19th century; *i.e.*, the maritime districts of Ceylon, the Cape of Good Hope, and the settlements on the coast of South America now comprised in British Guiana. In a secondary sense, therefore, Roman-Dutch law is the original common law of these countries. In Ceylon it was extended to the Kandyan provinces (annexed by Britain in 1815); while in South Africa it was carried, with the expanding range of white settlement during the 19th century, into the Republics of the Transvaal and the Orange Free State and into the British colony of Natal.

Today, Roman-Dutch law is in force throughout the Republic of South Africa and the mandated territory of South West Africa; in Lesotho (formerly Basutoland); in the self-governing colony of Southern Rhodesia; and in the protectorates of Swaziland and Bechuanaland. In Ceylon it is present to a lesser degree and in British Guiana it was from 1917 largely superseded by the common law of England. Reservation is made in favour of indigenous law and custom, so far as these are recognized; moreover the general law of these countries has in many respects departed from its original type.

Development of Roman-Dutch Law in the Netherlands.— In the 15th and 16th centuries the Roman law, as interpreted by the glossators and postglossators (*see* GLOSSATORS, LEGAL), was "received" in the province of Holland (as it was sooner or later in the Netherlands generally, as well as in Germany), although general and local customs held their ground. These were based ultimately on Germanic tribal law—Frankish, Frisian, Saxon— afforced by privileges and by-laws (*keuren*) (*see* GERMANIC LAWS, EARLY), and were themselves affected by an earlier infiltration of Roman law. Hence resulted the mixed system, for which Simon van Leeuwen in 1652 invented the term "Roman-Dutch law,"

which remained in force in the Netherlands until superseded in 1809 by the Code Napoléon, which in its turn in 1838 gave place to the Dutch civil code now in effect. The old law was abrogated in the Dutch colonies also.

There is, however, a third element in the Roman-Dutch system, namely the legislative acts of the Burgundian and Spanish periods, the chief of which were passed during the 16th century. The large quantity of legislation in the 17th and 18th centuries had little effect upon the general character of the legal system. Roman-Dutch law can also be studied in collections of decided cases and of opinions (commonly termed *consultatien* or *advijsen*) and in a rich juristic literature.

Systematization of the Law.—The first attempt to reduce the Roman-Dutch civil law to system was made by Hugo Grotius (*q.v.*) in his *Introduction to the Jurisprudence of Holland*, written while he was in prison in 1619–20 and published in 1631 (English translation 1926–36). This short treatise, a masterpiece of condensed exposition, remains a legal classic. Next after Grotius comes Johannes Voet, professor at Utrecht and Leiden, whose *Commentary on the Pandects* (1698–1704; English translation 1955–58) is still used more than any work of the old law. Another 17th-century work of high merit and authority is Simon van Groenewegen van der Made's *Treatise on Roman Laws Abrogated and not in Force in Holland* . . . (1649; English translation of part of the work, 1908), in which the author goes through the Roman *Corpus juris* by book and title and considers how far it has been received or disused in Holland. (*See* ROMAN LAW.)

Toward the end of the 18th century Dionysius Godefridus van der Keessel, professor at Leiden, lectured on the *jus hodiernum* ("law of today"), of which he published a summary in *Select Theses on the Laws of Holland and Zeeland* . . . (1800; English translation 1855). The lectures, commonly known as the *Dictata*, still circulate in manuscript copies and have been cited in judgments of the South African courts. A younger contemporary of Van der Keessel, Joannes van der Linden, wrote a popular textbook, *Legal, Practical and Mercantile Manual* (1806; Eng. trans. of 2nd ed., 1922).

Survival and Growth Abroad of Roman-Dutch Law.— The law of the province of Holland was followed in the colonial empire, to which the Roman-Dutch system of law was extended. It was supplemented by local ordinances of the governors in council and, in the East Indies, by laws of the governors-general established at Batavia (Jakarta), in Java. The ultimate legislative authority in the colonies was vested in the states-general.

After the colonies passed to the British crown the old law underwent profound modifications, owing partly to changed social and economic conditions and partly to the incursion of rules and institutions derived from English law (*q.v.*).

The influence of English law (which was operative even during the period of the Transvaal and Orange Free State republics) has been most marked in criminal law and procedure, civil procedure, evidence, and constitutional law; and particularly in the commercial field of companies, bills of exchange, maritime law, and insurance. The law of tort or delict has also been considerably affected by English doctrines. On the other hand, the law relating to property, persons, succession, and, to a lesser extent, contract still preserve their predominantly Roman-Dutch character. It is, for example, settled for both South Africa and Ceylon that "consideration" is not necessary for the validity of a contract.

The South Africa Act, 1909, provided for the continuance of all laws in force in the several colonies at the establishment of the Union until repealed by the Union Parliament or by the provincial councils within the sphere assigned to them. But thereafter, the Union Parliament and the appellate division of the Supreme Court of South Africa were active in consolidating, amending, and explaining the law, and in making it more uniform. Many rules of the old law were pronounced obsolete by disuse.

In many departments of Roman-Dutch law the texts of the *Corpus juris* are still cited as authoritative, and the approach to them is still through the writings of Grotius, Van Leeuwen, Voet, Groenewegen, Van der Keessel, Van der Linden, and the rest.

Suggestions for codification have been put forward, but the

weight of professional and academic opinion is adverse. *See* also South Africa, Republic of.

Bibliography.—R. W. Lee, *Introduction to Roman-Dutch Law,* 5th ed. (1953); Sir A. F. S. Maasdorp, *The Institutes of Cape Law (Institutes of South African Law),* 7th and 8th ed. (1948, 1958); G. Wille, *Principles of South African Law,* 5th ed. (1961); R. W. Lee *et al.* (eds.), *The South African Law of Obligations* (1950), *The South African Law of Property, Family Relations and Succession* (1954); Sir J. W. Wessels, *History of the Roman-Dutch Law* (1908); H. R. Hahlo and L. Kahn, *South Africa: Its Laws and Constitution* (1961); J. C. W. Pereira, *The Laws of Ceylon,* 2nd ed. (1913); Sir L. C. Dalton, *The Civil Law of British Guiana . . .* (1921).

Textbooks: F. G. Gardiner and C. W. H. Lansdown, *South African Criminal Law and Procedure,* 6th ed., 2 vol. (1957); H. G. Mackeurtan, *The Sale of Goods in South Africa,* 3rd ed., by G. N. Holmes (1949); R. G. MacKerron, *The Law of Delict . . .,* 6th ed. (1965); Sir J. W. Wessels, *The Law of Contract in South Africa,* 2nd ed., by A. A. Roberts, 2 vol. (1951); J. C. de Wet and J. P. Yeats, *Kontraktereg,* 3rd ed. (1964); J. C. de Wet and H. L. Swanepoel, *Strafreg,* 2nd ed. (1960); H. R. Hahlo, *The Law of Husband and Wife,* 2nd ed. (1963); D. V. Cowen, *The Law of Negotiable Instruments in South Africa,* 3rd ed. (1955); G. Wille, *Landlord and Tenant in South Africa,* 5th ed. (1956); L. H. Hoffmann, *South African Law of Evidence* (1963).

See also the *Cape Law Journal;* the *South African Law Journal* (1887–   ); *Annual Survey of South African Law; Acta Juridica.*

(R. W. L.; D. V. Cn.)

ROMANESQUE ART AND ARCHITECTURE.

Romanesque is the name given to the architectural and artistic style current in Europe from about the 10th century until the advent of Gothic. The Norman, the style of the round arch in northern Europe, can be identified with the Romanesque.

I. INTRODUCTION

Romanesque is a less familiar term than classical, Gothic, or Renaissance because of the historical circumstances under which it entered artistic terminology. The classical and the Renaissance were clearly defined by men who considered their canons inevitable and who thought of the medieval styles as fanciful (if not objectionable) aberrations. Blinded by the fashionable canon, a critic of 1750 wrote: "The Goths and Vandals, having demolished the Greek and Roman architecture, introduced in its stead a certain fantastical and licentious manner of building, which we have since called modern or Gothic, full of fret and lamentable imagery." Half a century later the Gothic was understood as having a noble canon of its own, but its background was still veiled—considered to be the work of untutored barbarians, whose vigour, interpreted as crudity, repelled those who cared for the arts. Romanesque did not even have a name until 1818, when the term *roman* (Romanesque, *romanico, romanisch*) was coined by Auguste Le Prévost. The corresponding term is "romance" for the languages based on Latin; in each case the underlying elements came from Rome. Actually the name Romanesque itself is the simplest, most practical definition of the style. It is Roman, with differences—the differences being conditioned by a complex historical background, that brings about a marvelous richness of expression, varied from region to region, with a truly noble lucidity in the finest creations.

Serious study of the Middle Ages was under way by 1800. Under the historians Louis Adolphe Thiers and François Guizot, ministers of King Louis Philippe (1830–48), the French undertook an impressive series of historical activities, which embraced inventories, collection and publication of archives, development of libraries and museums, and classification and maintenance of historic buildings. This program inspired efforts all over Europe, and Romanesque studies in all the arts have benefited immensely.

It was found, for instance, that despite all losses and the fact that Romanesque churches began to be replaced in another style as early as 1140, well over 2,000 examples still exist in whole or in part within France. This would support an estimate that fully 25,000 Romanesque churches were built in all of Europe. Yet these were only the more impressive buildings. Considerable numbers of wooden churches are known of; but for a few survivors, they have vanished entirely. In many areas small cells were built as oratories. Within the narrow confines of Celtic Britain, for example, 200 of these small cells have been traced, as well as 118 characteristic round towers. There were, in addition to many hundreds of Romanesque churches, fully 10,000 castles in Germany alone, occupying sites that were in many cases chosen and first built upon in Romanesque times. There must have been an equal number of Romanesque castles elsewhere in Europe—if not more. Although no account is taken of the ordinary domestic constructions, the statistics just quoted will convey an idea of the amplitude of the Romanesque building program.

The Romanesque period was no less complex in its art than in its history, though it had a unifying theme in monasticism. To compensate for the loss of stable central governments, there was a strong movement to found monasteries from about 650 to 1200. Such brotherhoods, who lived the ideal Christian life as it was understood at the time, were islands of civilization in a very much disturbed world. The most effective of these institutions were in the great triangle of Frankish territory between the Loire, the coast to the north, and the Rhine.

It was the penetrating intelligence of Charlemagne (742–814) that perceived the strengths and focused the energies of the great triangle, with the result that a significant proportion of all the medieval conceptions in government, philosophy, and art issued from this area. In the world of art this means that there the problems of Romanesque art were earlier recognized and understood than anywhere else; there the classical, the Byzantine, and the Northern could engender a creative spark, could be melded into new creations and transmitted to the more conservative, classic-minded southerly regions.

In the great triangle nearly 100 monasteries had been founded in the 7th century alone and the number was doubled by the year 750. Charlemagne and his son Louis the Pious wisely systematized this movement, and used it in building the new state. The intellectuals whom the emperor gathered about him at his capital, Aachen (Aix-la-Chapelle), made impressive progress in the revival of learning, writing, bookmaking, painting, the minor arts, and architecture. At his command these men created the cathedral and monastic schools able to survive the darkest period of marauding Norse, Hungarians, and Muslims. Charlemagne's ideals were not forgotten. From the schools came lay and ecclesiastical administrators who set up the medieval hierarchies of power and ultimately the new intellectual and scholarly ambient.

Records of lost buildings show how much of the later architectural development was envisaged in Charlemagne's time. As a basis for monastic unity he chose the Rule of St. Benedict. An excellent recension was made by Benedict of Aniane (d. 821). On his estate at Aniane this later Benedict, with Charlemagne's encouragement, built a monastery where all the arts were brought into play (782) and later constructed a model monastery at

Cornelimünster (Inden, near Aachen). Meanwhile a monastic holy city had been built at Centula (Saint-Riquier, near Abbeville), where the monastic church of 799 was the centre of all, with its cloister and chapels. Around this the wards and various guild quarters of the city were laid out in regular fashion; at some distance there were seven satellite villages bound to the monastery by periodical ceremonial visits in the form of processions. For better exploitation of the imperial estates everywhere, a type of villa was evolved; with the passage of time and the retreat of the gentry to their castles, many of these became ecclesiastical possessions—then priories, or even monasteries, as in the case of Cluny (910). By 820 the typical monastic layout had been fully studied (Inden and St. Gall; a plan supposedly drawn at Reichenau). This latter site, the *Insula Felix* in Lake Constance, was a stopping-place for the imperial journeys, and it developed

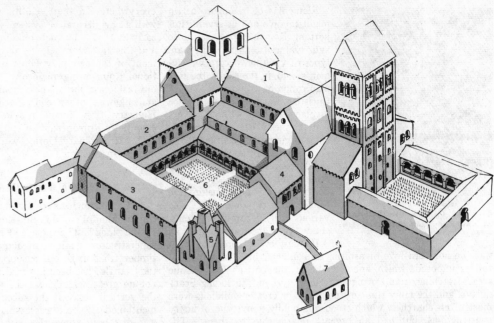

FROM K. J. CONANT, "CAROLINGIAN AND ROMANESQUE ARCHITECTURE"; REPRODUCED BY PERMISSION OF PENGUIN BOOKS, BALTIMORE
MONASTERY AT MITTELZELL, ONE OF THREE IMPORTANT MONASTERIES ON THE ISLAND OF REICHENAU, LAKE CONSTANCE; FOUNDED IN THE 8TH CENTURY, RESTORATION DRAWING AS OF c. 1050

(1) Church, (2) Dormitory, (3) Refectory, (4) Monastery gate, (5) Kitchen, (6) Cloister, (7) Chapel of St. Pirminius

as a powerful monastic and missionary centre—one of the many that enlarged the boundaries of Christendom as Charlemagne's dominions expanded to the north and east.

In the Middle Ages the population of Europe had diminished by half since Roman times. Communication and transport, either by land or by sea, might be difficult or hazardous, and this tended naturally to divide the country into neighbourhoods. Under these conditions, a great monastery, like a city, could serve a considerable surrounding area as an administrative, intellectual, and spiritual centre; and as a workshop, garner, and refuge. With increasing prosperity the monastic building complexes were progressively better organized, better built, and more impressive. They showed the way for cathedral and domestic architecture. The great patrons of the age were the abbots, though not to the exclusion of the bishops and magnates.

The Romans had not solved the problem of the highly articulated fireproof basilican church—a problem that became pressing with the frequent conflagrations in timber-built towns and, not less, the incendiarism which was a lamentable consequence of endemic local war and the incursions of organized marauders. By A.D. 1000 the monastic builders had begun to solve this problem by vaulting. Moreover, they had improved upon the Roman attempts at systematic plans for the monasteries themselves, which might accommodate 1,000 persons—monks, brethren, craftsmen, servants, slaves, and guests—with provision for their multiple activities, and also suitable storage facilities.

The solution, well exemplified in the St. Gall plan of 820, was a quadrangular court, the cloister, provided with arcaded walks or "alleys," and placed beside the nave of the church. Typically the east walk had an entrance into the church near the sanctuary, and the community, entering processionally, would turn into their choir enclosure in the nave, while the celebrants would occupy their posts in the sanctuary. Important rooms bordered the east walk: the chapter house, where the community met as a corporation; the parlour, where speaking was allowed, for the transaction of business; and the camera or workroom. The walk parallel to the church gave access to the calefactory (in early times often the only warmed room, for fellowship), the refectory, the pantries, and the kitchens. The cellars stretched along the west walk between the kitchens and a porter's lodge adjoining the church. The door at the porter's lodge was the principal entrance to the cloister. The scriptorium and library

were typically in the walk beside the church; the dormitory was usually located directly above the buildings of the east walk.

This solution of the plan problem was very flexible, for in a large monastery there would be several cloisters or courts with suitable independent arrangements for archives, administration, guests, wayfarers, servants, artisans, shops, and folds; special quarters were provided by such courts for retired or sick monks, and for novices. Special chapels were provided, where necessary, in these subsidiary parts of the establishment.

The several cloisters or courts of a large monastery carried on the tradition of the greater Germanic households of the pagan time; they too were composed of "proliferating quadrangles." The basic unit, as has been learned from excavation, was a wide, framed, compartmented longhouse with a steep thatch roof. By Charlemagne's time longhouses were sometimes adapted as churches.

Though Rome could no longer present fresh models for universal emulation, or exercise unifying control, its architectural monuments were still numerous in many regions and could not be ignored. The Roman heritage is particularly apparent in conservative southern regions, where Roman massiveness and horizontality persist, and are perceptible to some degree even in the Gothic architecture of the area. In the regions where the Roman population had been large, commonplace buildings continued for a long time to be built much as before, with increasing emphasis—especially in the north—on timber construction in small or utilitarian structures. The wet northern climate called for steeper roofs, particularly where thatch was used. New importance accrued to the fact that the various regions had differing materials and aesthetic ideals. The artists had a wider choice among sources of inspiration than the Romans, but the choices that were made by responsible architects varied from region to region. This explains the origin of "schools" of Romanesque—families of designs inspired by successful buildings in a local context. These were usually churches, often of novel design, and situated at the centre of an important region which, in modern parlance, gives its name to the school.

The forward-looking Romanesque artists were aware of, and could synthesize, ideas and practices from Rome, Byzantium, the Muslim world, Scandinavia, and the barbarian regions. The number of options was fairly large, offering a great many possibilities of variety; moreover, the importance given to features of one kind or another varied from one school to the next.

ASTURIAN CHURCH OF STA. MARIA AT NARANCO NEAR OVIEDO, SPAIN; c. 848

Elements of Roman origin might involve one or several important Roman types of fabric and materials, types of plan, types of vaulting, decorative elements, and, in the south, the Roman canon of proportion. Early Christian works offered a choice of plans, with or without towers and porches. Elements of Oriental origin might be structural or decorative, and they might be derived from Iberian, African, or Asiatic examples. From the north came not only imaginative timber construction, but also various lively decorative systems, and verve in their application.

Perhaps even more important was the northern love of aspiring and intersecting forms, powerfully composed, which affected almost the entire Romanesque area, stretching from Portugal to the Holy Land, including Scandinavia and the Holy Roman Empire. The greater buildings were most often churches, which stood out boldly above the ordinary constructions, but had an organic relationship to them. The resulting silhouette, so much in contrast with placid classic design, quite transformed man's idea of what a city or church group should look like, either from within or from a distance as an ensemble. This dynamic mode was bequeathed to Gothic, Renaissance, and modern times. It probably began with the staged lantern towers and porches of 5th-century churches in France, and it was systematized in great designs that engaged the personal attention of the emperor Charlemagne and his son Louis the Pious.

It is thus evident that a movement toward Romanesque architecture started early in the medieval period. The same was true of painting, manuscript illumination, and the minor arts. Because of the abundance of material, and the long period of time, it has become customary to consider that Romanesque existed as an established style as early as 950; before this time the various geographical and other groups in this development are called proto-Romanesque, or pre-Romanesque. The 6th-, 7th-, and 8th-century styles of Ravenna and Milan merge without a break into the Lombard style of the Romanesque period, and for this reason may be called pre-Romanesque. At the end of the 8th century, royal architects in the tiny, remote Spanish kingdom of the Asturias worked out an interesting pre-Romanesque style in which so many of the problems of the Romanesque are solved (though on a small scale) that this style merits the name of proto-Romanesque. Flourishing for 150 years, it ultimately ceased when French Romanesque came to Spain. In Germany, Carolingian Romanesque (790–950) is really Frankish pre-Romanesque, which developed into the Rhenish Romanesque school (950–1250). (See EARLY CHRISTIAN ARCHITECTURE; BYZANTINE ART AND ARCHITECTURE.)

After 950 the excellent construction, the grand scale, the assured design, the increasingly capable use of masonry vaulting, and the increasingly rich and appropriate use of foliate and figural sculpture showed that the initial period was over and that a noble new style had come into existence (fully, by 1050). The greatest works in the Romanesque style date from the period 1075 to 1125, so to speak the classic age of Romanesque; after this, in some regions, Romanesque entered a florid "Baroque" phase, which lasted a generation and then was revivified as Gothic.

The coming eclipse of Romanesque may first be sensed in new structural developments that began about 1090. Sophisticated but unsatisfactory attempts to vault the great basilican naves safely, with elements of Roman, Byzantine, or Oriental origin, impelled progressive Romanesque engineers, from about 1090 onward, to invent a new type of ribbed groin-vaulted unit bay, using pointed arches to distribute thrust and improve the shape of the geometrical surfaces. Fifty years of experimentation produced vaulting that was light, strong, open, versatile, and applicable everywhere—in short, Gothic vaulting. A whole new aesthetic, with a new decorative system—the Gothic—was being evolved as early as 1145. The new buildings were very different acoustically, and this fact may help to account for the concomitant development of the new polyphonic music that supplemented the traditional Romanesque plainsong. Romanesque architecture became old-fashioned, but its heavy forms pleased the Cistercian monks, and likewise other conservative patrons in Germany, Poland, Hungary, Italy, Spain, and Portugal. Thus buildings that were essentially Romanesque in spirit continued to be built even when such extraordinary Gothic works as the Amiens Cathedral were under construction (1220–69). See GOTHIC ART AND ARCHITECTURE.

II. PRELUDE TO ROMANESQUE IN THE NORTH

1. Constructions in Wood: The Norse Churches.—Northern construction of wood in pre-Romanesque times is well represented by the "long hall" or palace at Lojsta on the Isle of Gotland. The superstructure (tall triangular frames bay by bay, stiffened by timbers that mark out a supporting square in the lower half of the triangle) has been inferred from the continuous exterior banks (of no great height) and the lines of flat stones that supported the vertical posts of the successive squares of the bracing (just mentioned). There was a smoke hole above the hearth. Lojsta was first built about the year 1000. This type of construction, originating on the Continent, spread throughout Scandinavia. It has been traced by excavation in Greenland (Gardar) and in the mid-1960s in Newfoundland (La Baie aux Meadows, near Cape

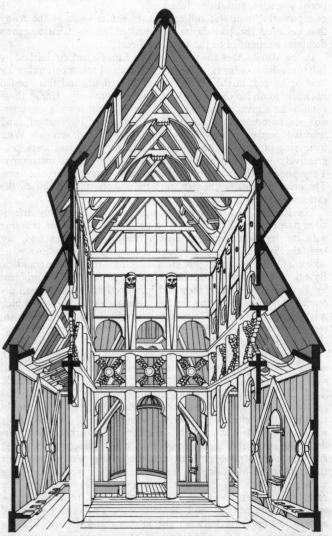

CHURCH AT BORGUND, NORWAY; c. 1150

Race), and actual modern examples of the traditional mode exist in Iceland (Viðimýri). Fine medieval examples had the timbers richly carved and painted.

By the time churches were being built, the sloping exterior bank of a longhouse was often replaced by vertical timbers and plank walls. In the more ambitious buildings there might be four files of interior supports, instead of two, under the steep two-slope roof. The churches were distinguished by having the aisles carried entirely around the central space, which projected above them in order to permit small windows. The sanctuary was a small shedlike projection with a pinnacle, and the belfry took the form of a small shed perched on the roof, with a pinnacle above it. An exterior porch with a pent roof might be wrapped around the nave (as at Borgund in Norway, c. 1150). These churches are called stave (wooden plank) churches or, more properly, mast churches, because of the novel way in which the inner middle part is supported by masts on its periphery; the masts themselves are supported on a stout chassis whose timbers extend outward to sustain the aisles and porches. It is probable that this formula was achieved by the year 1000, when Christianity began to dominate in Scandinavia. The churches are extraordinarily picturesque, in contrast with the longhouses or palaces near which they were often placed as palace chapels—their special form being suggested, perhaps, by reliquaries or manuscript drawings of churches. The elaborate examples possessed wonderfully energetic carvings, in particular the panels of interlaced "lacertine" or lizard-like creatures (as at Urnes in Norway, c. 1100). They were replaced by simple Romanesque buildings of English and German inspiration, when the congregations outgrew the mast churches, which are necessarily rather small.

When towns and cities came to be built, improved versions of the longhouses, with several stories, were placed side by side. A reminiscence of this persists in the many-gabled street frontages not only in Scandinavia but also in the Netherlands and along the south Baltic littoral. These regions are heavily timbered. In Russia walls were built of horizontal timbers sometimes as much as three feet square in cross section. In Scandinavia the ancestors of the American frontier log cabin were built in this way. In the Germanic area, however, half-timber and palisade construction were preferred. A solitary survivor of the latter type is the old part of the Saxon church (1013) at Greenstead, Sussex, Eng. While this work appears to be rather rough, the individual vertical members are carefully joined by splines, the Germans being quite capable of finished joinery where it was appropriate.

2. Carolingian Architecture.—As with the First Romanesque, there has been a great loss of important Carolingian monuments. There are, however, considerable remains at the first settled capital of the Frankish court, Aachen. The imperial palace has disappeared; the impressive atrium of the Palatine chapel, with two-story porticoes, and the twin basilicas, which flanked the chevet, have been destroyed; while the chapel itself, an octagonal design by Odo of Metz (792–805), has been overwhelmed by later additions and modern decorations. A rarity in the north, it is entirely vaulted, the middle part being buttressed by aisles on two levels. The throne was at the west, on axis at the upper level, and behind it there was an opening from which the emperor could address as many as 7,000 people assembled in the atrium. From this upper level a gallery 400 ft. in length led to the *Aula Regia* of the palace, 150 ft. in length—the impressive throne room of the imperial power. Theodulph, bishop of Orléans, was a member of the court circle, and was inspired to build himself (on a much smaller scale) a palace and a somewhat similar chapel at Germigny-des-Prés (c. 806, now replaced by a modern copy).

The construction of great Carolingian basilicas, as at Fulda in Germany (790) and Centula in France (799), was very encouraging, and the models thus created served architecture well for centuries. Fulda had an apse at each end, and this special arrangement was widely accepted. Equally, the Saviour chapel above the vestibule at Centula, with its tall spire, stair towers, and choir galleries, initiated the so-called westwork, which in its boldly composed aspiring forms presented a monumental facade enormously pleasing to northern taste. During 814–847 the build-

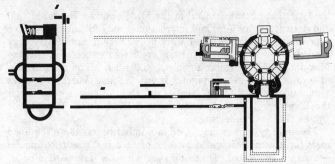

FROM K. J. CONANT, "CAROLINGIAN AND ROMANESQUE ARCHITECTURE;" REPRODUCED BY PERMISSION OF PENGUIN BOOKS, BALTIMORE

(ABOVE) PALACE AND PALATINE CHAPEL, AACHEN, GERMANY; BY ODO OF METZ; 792–805. (BELOW) SAINT-RIQUIER, CENTULA, FRANCE; 799

ers at Saint-Philibert-de-Grandlieu near Nantes worked effectively, by adding chapels to the apse, toward the pilgrimage-church ambulatory plan that was achieved at Saint-Martin of Tours in 918. Subsidiary chapels in the cloister at Centula also signaled the acceptance of simpler types: the rotunda with apses, and the shed type of church, with an oblong shedlike nave and a similar, smaller oblong sanctuary. Hundreds if not thousands of this latter type of church were built, throughout the Romanesque centuries and afterward.

By the greatest of good fortune, a large plan of a monastic group, drawn about 820 for a high ecclesiastic, has been preserved at St. Gall. While never built, this plan admirably presents the thoughtful and orderly architectural planning of the period that affected monastic building for centuries. Many of the subsidiary buildings shown on the plan were obviously intended to be constructed in half-timber, and careful study of them has yielded a great deal of information about the utilitarian structures of the age, including stove heat for the important rooms. A duct carried hot air from a furnace to the calefactory and the dormitory adjoining the cloister. The water supply and the drainage for the nearby bath and latrine are indicated, and may be inferred for other buildings. It should be noted in passing that the "Ten Books on Architecture" (*De architectura*) of Vitruvius were known and used in Carolingian times.

III. THE FIRST ROMANESQUE

The name "First Romanesque" is given to an architectural style that early developed in the Byzantine exarchate of Ravenna in Italy and in the valley of the Po. It was worked out by the Lombards, who conquered almost all of Italy beginning in 568. They might have created an Italian national state, but they destroyed Monte Cassino and threatened the pope, which brought about Frankish intervention (755–756). The Lombards had governmental cadres at Pavia, their capital, which aided the Franks—Charlemagne particularly—in organizing the medieval empire. The Lombards promulgated the earliest-known medieval building regulation, in the Code of 644. This recognized a guild system of the type that became general in the Middle Ages. Repeated ruin and destruction by local and international wars in Lombardy have wiped out the guilds' earliest work in the region, but clearly they carried on from the Early Christian architecture there. S. Lorenzo Maggiore in Milan (built about A.D. 400 when Milan was the Roman capital) is a case in point. It was the first church to possess a monumental two-tower facade, and this formula spread under the Lombards to a wide area, where it lived on in Romanesque and in Gothic architecture.

The guild system as developed in Lombardy was the disciplined basis for itinerant groups of masons, often called *maestri comacini* —a name connected, some suppose, with the Lombard city of Como. These men used a new type of wall work, employing bricks or small, roughly cut stones resembling bricks as facing, with narrower joints than those of contemporary Byzantine work. The cores were rough stone in a "mortar bath." The mortar was uniformly excellent. Naves were usually wooden-roofed but the *maestri* built excellent vaults in the Roman tradition. They often covered their walls, and always their vaulting, with good stucco. Because of the times, their buildings were often small and so have been replaced by more ambitious structures at important sites, but many still exist in surprisingly good condition after nearly 1,000 years. Thus it is possible to trace their work from Lombardy across Liguria to Catalonia and up the river valleys to eastern France, Switzerland, and Germany. Only in Switzerland, Burgundy, and Catalonia is the style now well represented, but it underlies the progressive later Romanesque in a much larger area.

The Lombards adopted the shallow exterior wall arches that are common in late Roman building and reduced them to decorative pilaster strips and eaves arcading—an attractive type of wall modeling taken over by the mature Romanesque style, where it was widely and effectively used. Crypts are frequent, and these are regularly groin-vaulted on a quadrille of supports, a scheme that was transmitted to later Romanesque building, together with the simple rib systems marking off the bays.

The end of the First Romanesque style came when greater resources and the development of local skills made it possible to build larger structures, and to employ cut stone, first for wall membering, then for ashlar walls, and finally for vaulting.

IV. EARLY ROMANESQUE

1. France.—A century (950–1050) that was of utmost importance in the history of Romanesque architecture is very poorly represented by existing buildings. The greatest structures— churches, of course—recaptured the grandeur of Roman scale, but

CATALONIAN CHURCH OF THE MONASTERY OF STA. MARIA, RIPOLL, SPAIN; NAVE, LATE 10TH CENTURY, TRANSEPT, c. 1020

NAVE, CHURCH OF ST. MICHAEL, HILDESHEIM, GERMANY; 1001–33

the buildings were rather barn-like. Many have been destroyed and others have been remodeled because of changes in taste, improvements in design and construction, and developments in decoration. The wooden roofing of these buildings has entailed a heavy toll from disasters—conflagrations, wartime destruction.

The French undertook to solve the vaulting problem; a half century was required (between Saint-Bénigne, Dijon, 1001–18, and the rebuilding of the transept at Saint-Martin, Tours, c. 1050). Saint-Martin's was a very large building, even by later standards, but by no means unique (*cf.* Orléans Cathedral, Saint-Remi at Reims, and Chartres Cathedral). At Chartres the structure of 1020–46 was nearly as large as the present cathedral, which was built upon its huge and well-constructed crypt after a spectacular fire in 1194.

The interest of this period chiefly resides in the developments of the sanctuary plan—the apse, the ambulatory, and the radiating chapels in particular. This can be followed at Clermont Cathedral, where the crypt of 946, the lower story of an archaic example, still exists. Over this a Romanesque version was built at ground level about 1080, and the latter was succeeded in turn by the present magnificent Gothic ensemble after 1248.

An ambulatory was a practical necessity in churches of pilgrimage, for the venerated relics were under the high altar; a passageway around the apse, with a view, through arches, of the shrine, made it possible to channel the visitors becomingly, and arrange radiating chapels on the periphery for lesser devotions. Other churches that did not need the passageway, had the sanctuary and the apsidioles placed with parallel axes, and accessible directly from the transept. Where the depth of the chapels is progressively smaller toward the transept ends, the apses are said to be in echelon (ladderwise). The scheme was widely used by the Benedictine monasteries from the 10th century onward, and was adopted with modifications by the Cistercians in the 12th century. There can be no doubt of the evident French skill in composition; moreover, this skill was increasingly applied to all aspects of architecture and decoration. In Burgundy, type plans for monasteries were composed, and proved their worth in all Western Europe (Cluny, 1043; Cîteaux, 12th and 13th centuries).

2. The Empire.—Better organized and prosperous under the Saxon dynasty (919–1024) and its Franconian successors, Germany had a spectacular revival of all the arts: church architecture, castle building, ivory carving, manuscript illumination, metalwork, and to some extent architectural sculpture. The style takes its name, Ottonian, from three emperors, Otto I (962–973), Otto II (973–983), and Otto III (996–1002). Byzantine influence came in with the empress Theophano (983–991), wife (972) of Otto II, and to her is credited an impulse to renew the arts through contacts with the Eastern capital.

The Ottonian church buildings, like their French contemporaries, have been rebuilt—with the difference that the newer German buildings, largely of very solid 12th- and 13th-century construction, have maintained the rather clumsy composition and blocky silhouette of their predecessors. The pilaster strips and arcading of the First Romanesque style were accepted from Italy and Burgundy, but the vaulting, when it was achieved, went far beyond First Romanesque models. The church of St. Gertrude (c. 1046) at Nivelles (Nyfels), Belgium, as rebuilt after war damage, shows very well what these immense but simple wooden-roofed naves were like. It also has a fine vaulted sanctuary. Bishop Bernward's church of St. Michael at Hildesheim, Ger. (1001–33), has been well restored to its original form. It has the characteristic scheme

Nave of S. Miniato, Florence; c. 1070

BEGINNINGS OF THE ROMANESQUE STYLE

Symbol of St. Matthew, Book of Durrow, School of Iona (?), Irish; second half of the 7th century. In Trinity College Library, Dublin

The Story of Adam and Eve, Bible of Charles the Bald, School of Reims, Carolingian; c. 870. In St. Paul's Outside the Walls, Rome

Front cover of the Lindau Codex, Reims; c. 870. In the Pierpont Morgan Library, New York

Bronze spiral column depicting the life of Christ; 1015. In the Cathedral of Hildesheim, Germany

The emperor Henry III and his wife in adoration of the Virgin, Codex Aureus of Speyer, School of Echternach, Ottonian; 1046. In the Escorial, Madrid

PLATE II

ROMANESQUE ART AND ARCHITECTURE

Christ in Majesty, apse fresco from S. Clemente Tahull, by the Master of Tahull; c. 1123. In the Museum of Catalan Art, Barcelona, Spain

MATURE ROMANESQUE STYLE

West façade, Notre-Dame-la-Grande, Poitiers, France; c. 1135

Christ on the Cross honoured as the King of Kings. Polychromed wood, Spanish; 11th–12th centuries. In the Museum of Catalan Art, Barcelona, Spain

Angel locking the damned in hell, Psalter of Henry of Blois, School of Winchester, mid-12th century. In the British Museum, London

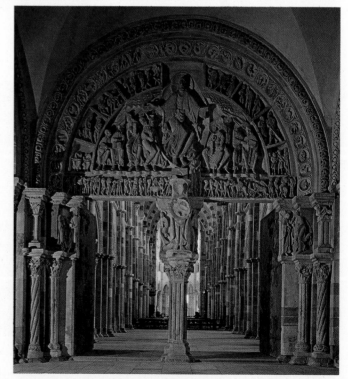

Main portal and nave, La Madeleine, Vézelay, France; 1104–32

of an apse at each end, and transepts with tall stair towers. The bishop knew Rome well, but the monumental bronze doors and Paschal candlestick that he commissioned are unmistakably German rather than Roman or Byzantine. So also is the remarkable vaulted chapel of St. Bartholomew at Paderborn, with sculptured capitals (1017), though it is reportedly the work of Greek (or perhaps Greco-Italian) builders.

In Germany very considerable effort went into exploring possible variations (usually simple) in the plans. Thus there is great variety in the size, height, and placing of the transepts; the Carolingian westwork form was imaginatively treated; arcades interrupted by piers were used—as at St. Cyriakus, Gernrode (961 and later), interesting for its galleries and for early architectural carvings in stone and in stucco.

The Ottonian style was influential in neighbouring regions to the east and south; St. George in Prague and the medieval buildings at Esztergom in Hungary are examples, though later in date. In England the period was still one of pronounced localism with a German flavour. There was a notable revival of Benedictinism from about 958, due to contacts with the reform movement on the Continent. There are a few attractive examples of ecclesiastical building; St. Lawrence at Bradford-on-Avon, Wiltshire (c. 975), and Earls Barton tower, Northamptonshire, among others. Typical "long and short" stone quoining and decorative masonry elements suggested perhaps by wood framing, are features to be noted. But the Scandinavians ravaged England in the late 10th and early 11th centuries and took over in 1066 as Normans. The local style was eclipsed by Norman work after 1045.

In the Empire, Italian contacts encouraged the spread of the Lombard First Romanesque, but otherwise there is little sign of influence. At the time Rome was afflicted by malaria and local war; the south had to deal with imperial troops, Byzantines, Muslims, and (later) Normans. When the revival came in Italy, the Lombard cities led the way, and their work at that time inspired a large area just as the First Romanesque had done.

Tuscany, which had had an effective ducal government throughout the Middle Ages, began early in the 11th century to build churches in which the Ancient imprint is strong; the so-called proto-Renaissance. The very classic octagonal baptistery of Florence is erroneously claimed for the 5th century; it probably had its present character, but not its attica or its vault, when it was dedicated in 1059. S. Miniato dates from c. 1000–1090.

V. MATURE ROMANESQUE

The coming-of-age of Romanesque architecture was signalized by the construction of five magnificent churches on the international pilgrimage routes leading from mid-France to the reputed tomb of St. James at Santiago de Compostela in Spain. These are: Saint-Martin at Tours (a huge old wooden-roofed basilica that was rebuilt on the new model beginning about 1050), Sainte-Foi at Conques (c. 1052–1130), Saint-Martial at Limoges (c. 1062–95), Saint-Sernin at Toulouse (1077 or 1082–1118), and the new church at Santiago itself (c. 1078–1211). This was a real family of buildings; each one had a splendid apse with ambulatory and radiating chapels, a transept and nave with aisles and galleries, an imposing tower system, and beautiful sculptures. Each one was entirely vaulted, typically, with barrel vaults over the nave,

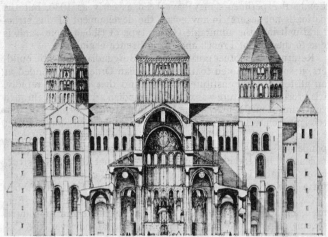

BY COURTESY OF THE MEDIAEVAL ACADEMY OF AMERICA

CLUNY III. TRANSVERSE SECTION OF THE NAVE; 1088–1130 AND LATER. DRAWING BY KENNETH J. CONANT

quadrant vaults over the galleries (visible through charming paired triforium arches), and groin-vaulted aisles. A little later, at the Cluniac priory of Saint-Étienne, Nevers, such a church was boldly built with clerestory windows under the high vault.

1. Burgundy.—Since the monasteries had done so much to create the new Europe now bursting into architectural flower, it is appropriate that there are two families of churches that express the greatness of Burgundian federative monasticism: Cluny and Cîteaux. Cluny ultimately had about 1,400 dependencies under centralized rule, of which about 200 were important establishments. The Cistercians had a ramified system that ultimately included 742 monasteries and about 900 nunneries.

It was Cluny that after an impressive rebuilding of the monastery buildings (1077–85) undertook the *Maior Ecclesia*, or Cluny III (1088–1130 and later; 615 ft. long; barrel vaults of the nave 32 ft. wide and 96 ft. high to the crown, over a clerestory). It was the largest monastic church, the largest Romanesque church, and the largest French church (demolished 1798–1824). It had many features that prepared the way for Gothic: tall proportions, grouped piers, pointed arches, specialized wall and vault construction. It had a very elaborate and sophisticated modular system and characteristic carvings of great beauty in the apse (where one of the first medieval sculptural allegories was placed by 1095) and at the portals of the nave (where the first really grand ensemble of monumental carved and painted west portals was placed, about 1108). Cluny III inspired only a few great buildings (including, however, Paray-le-Monial, La Charité-sur-Loire, and Autun Cathedral) because of its special, advanced character and the fact that the design was so soon attacked in an unfortunate Cistercian polemic (1124). It may be that certain of the architects at Cluny itself considered the design too bold, for they built at the priory of Vézelay (1104–32) a groin-vaulted nave nearly as wide, but only two-thirds as high as that of Cluny III. In the narthex at Vézelay (dedicated in 1132) there was one groin vault that had ribs, and buttresses resembling flying buttresses were concealed under roofs of the galleries. A pair of towers flanking a carved portal were planned for the facade.

Thus, between these features of Vézelay and the pointed arches composed in tall proportions at Cluny III, the "ingredients" of the Gothic style were here to hand in Burgundy by 1135, awaiting the creative Gothic spark of Saint-Denis (near Paris). The rich portals of Saint-Denis show the influence of the great Burgundian carvings. But account must be taken of another episode—the development of consistent ribbed vaulting in the Norman dominions. It is considered probable that the high-ranking Lombard ecclesiastics who undertook the reform and development of the Norman church brought with them some knowledge of ribbed vault construction, which then passed to England. The cathedral abbey church of Durham (1093–1133) was a very early demonstration of the dramatic potentialities of this type of construction.

A. F. KERSTING

WESTERN TOWER OF EARLS BARTON CHURCH, NORTHAMPTONSHIRE, ENGLAND; c. 935

Lombard experiments may have been as early as 1080, but the dating is not secure; in any event, the development of this structural unit into the admirable Gothic type of ribbed groin vault is due to the skill of French and Anglo-French engineers.

Returning to another great family of Burgundian monastic builders, it should be noted that the Cistercian Order was founded as an austere reform institute in 1098, and that it spread rapidly. Cistercian architecture was really Burgundian architecture, through conformism made international, but in a stunted form. The Cistercian architects were commanded to build well, but without bravura of any kind. They accepted the pointed arch, but built ponderously with it in a style which may be called "half-Gothic," because it has the general appearance, but not the special structural characteristics, of Gothic. Cistercian constructions were for a long time massive, like the Romanesque. Fontenay Abbey (1139 and later) represented the personal preference of St. Bernard, and it is almost Roman, with its very simple and substantial scheme of pointed barrel vaulting. In general, however, the Cistercian churches came more and more to approximate Gothic designs. In the ground floors of their monastery buildings they early introduced the idea of using ribbed groin vaulting in repetitive square bays (a Gothic scheme). To the east, the south, the west, and the northwest of Europe, the first buildings resembling Gothic were erected by the Cistercians: Pontigny, 1140–1210 (Burgundy); Alcobaça, 1158–1223 (Portugal); Poblet, 1180–96 (Catalonia); Fossanova, 1187–1208 (Italy); Maulbronn 1146–78 (Germany); Fountains 1135–50 (England); Vreta, 1162 (Sweden); Kercz, 1202 (Hungary); and Beirut, c. 1150 (Lebanon) give an idea of the power and extension of their effort.

The Cistercian establishments were located in remote places, but the husbandry of the communities was superb, and benefited the whole of Europe. Their monasteries were so uniform in conception that a monk coming from a Cistercian house anywhere would, in half an hour, feel quite at home in one of these monasteries anywhere else. The basic plan was traditional, but the western court (where visitors were usually dealt with) was reduced to a mere corridor. The Cistercians did not encourage visitors; they were not provided with space in guesthouses within the enclosures, or even in the churches. Cistercian refectories were regularly placed at right angles opposite the church, rather than parallel as in earlier plans. The monks chose well-watered sites, and used waterpower. Ideally the brotherhoods were able to supply all their own needs.

A. F. KERSTING

NAVE ELEVATION AND SOUTH AISLE OF THE CATHEDRAL ABBEY CHURCH OF DURHAM, ENGLAND; 1093–1133

2. Normandy.—Another great architectural family was Norman: Rouen Cathedral (c. 1037–63), followed by Westminster Abbey (1049?–65) and the splendid abbeys built in Caen by Duke William and his duchess Matilda. She built Sainte-Trinité, beginning in 1062, and was buried as queen in its sanctuary (1083). William's church, Saint-Étienne, was begun in 1067 and dedicated in 1081. The Norman series was continued in England by the foundation and endowment of magnificent Benedictine abbeys after the Conquest, as royal policy—to gain the favour of the church, to improve the exploitation of the land, and to pacify the country. Many of the church buildings still exist, and they are very impressive indeed. Typically they have, or have had, long wooden-roofed naves with vaulted aisles and wooden-roofed galleries, embellished, stage by stage, with bold, rich interior arcading. The churches have spacious transepts and deep sanctuaries, the apses being arranged in echelon or with ambulatories. It gives one a sense of the builders' means to know that a very large part of

the beautiful white limestone used in facing the walls was transported across the Channel from the famous quarries of Caen. Though the walls and piers are beautiful, the mortar was not good, and only great thickness made the masonry strong. The Norman parish churches that survive are neither numerous nor striking. Among the more ambitious naves originally roofed in wood, but now closed with Gothic vaults, are those of the cathedrals at Winchester (1079), Gloucester (1087), and Norwich (1089). Peterborough Cathedral (1118) still possesses its old ceiling, painted in lozenge-shaped panels. In many of the churches a large number of additions have been made in the Gothic style without impairing the dignity of the Norman construction. But Durham Cathedral, with its Romanesque ribbed-groin high vault (1093–1133), remains by far the finest "statement" of the Norman style.

3. Aquitaine, Languedoc, and Auvergne.—Long united to the English crown after 1152, Aquitaine has a quite separate church architecture. To achieve free interior space, masonry domes of special construction were used, often four in line, as at Saint-Étienne-de-la-Cité, Périgueux (c. 1100–50) and the Cathedral of Angoulême (1105–28 and later), with a richly sculptured facade. The cruciform Saint-Front, Périgueux, before and after 1120, was an exceptional building, spoiled by modern restoration.

In Poitou, elaborately arcaded facades formed somewhat illogical frontispieces for spacious "three-naved" churches with windowed aisles almost as tall as the central windowless naves. There are beautiful paintings (e.g., at Saint-Savin-sur-Gartempe). This region has several fine Romanesque castles, in the usual form (as at Loches, about 1100) of a great square tower, the donjon or keep, with guard and residential rooms on several levels, and appropriate outworks.

The churches of Languedoc have bold massing and beautiful sculpture, the tradition of which goes back to the formative period (Saint-Genis-des-Fontaines, 1020). Saint-Sernin at Toulouse (about 1080 to 1200), in the Pilgrimage style, has beautiful carvings, and many churches in the region are related to it.

In Auvergne a long tradition (Clermont Cathedral, 946) developed, more or less in the manner of the pilgrimage churches. The high "lantern transepts" are characteristic (e.g., Notre Dame du Port at Clermont-Ferrand, 1150). The cathedral of Le Puy en Velay (11th and 12th centuries), with zebra work in the masonry and a file of domes, represents reflex influence from Spain; Muslim motifs were brought in via the pilgrimage road. Such influence is perceptible also in Burgundy, and perhaps in the west of France.

4. Iberia.—The pre-Romanesque types of building in the peninsula were insufficient to satisfy the needs and ambitions of the Spaniards as the Christian states increased in population by immigration, and expanded southward by the reconquest in Romanesque times. The architecture clearly testifies to the great influx of men and ideas, particularly from Burgundy, Poitou, and Languedoc (as at Santiago Cathedral). Cistercian half-Gothic became important (e.g., Poblet, 1180–96). Catalonia long remained faithful to the Lombard style. Everywhere there are Muslim reminiscences, sometimes obvious, sometimes very subtle.

The walls of Avila (1090 and later) are among the finest of Romanesque military constructions. Loarre in Aragon, with its beautiful chapel, is perhaps the finest Romanesque castle. The Exchange at Lérida (after 1200) still has its medieval facade, with a characteristic upper window arcade. Bragança in Portugal has a municipal hall of c. 1200, also with a clerestory arcade.

5. Provence.—Turning eastward to Provence, the old *Provincia Romana,* one finds that here Romanesque architecture is most Roman in feeling: grand, simple, spacious bulks were built, usually in fine ashlar masonry, as at Avignon Cathedral (about 1140–1200), and often with fine sculpture, as at the cathedral of Arles (1150 and later) and Saint-Gilles-du-Gard (1116 and later, to about 1170). Some of the portals, especially, seem very Roman.

6. Île de France.—Paris, in the Île de France, was becoming the intellectual centre of Europe in the 12th century, and this shows in the architecture. The proto-Gothic "ingredients" that were to be seen in Burgundy and Normandy were dynamically improved by the use of lighter, cleverer cut-stone work, in the crea-

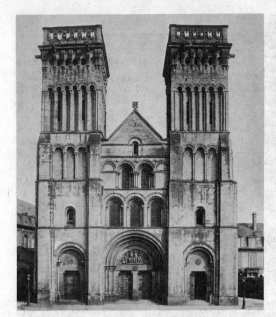

(TOP LEFT, BOTTOM LEFT) ND—GIRAUDON, (ABOVE) LAUROS—GIRAUDON, (BELOW) JEAN ROUBIER

(TOP LEFT) FACADE OF SAINTE-TRINITÉ, CAEN, FRANCE; BEGUN 1062. (BOTTOM LEFT) CHEVET (EAST END) OF SAINT-SERNIN, TOULOUSE, FRANCE; c. 1080–1200. (ABOVE) NAVE OF THE CATHEDRAL OF ANGOULÊME, FRANCE; 1105–28 AND LATER. (BELOW) INTERIOR OF SAINT-SAVIN-SUR-GARTEMPE, FRANCE; CHOIR, c. 1060–75; NAVE, c. 1095–1115

main streets would follow contour lines, and radials would make the necessary connections from level to level.

At Cluny a conflagration in 1159 destroyed a large part of the town, which had grown up on two sides of the abbey and had received a charter from Abbot Hugh in 1090. The rebuilding after the fire may serve as an example of 12th-century practice. The monastery decided to rebuild, accepting the old street lines, which were orderly rather than regular. A triangular *place* developed near each end and in the middle of the town, as a natural result of the position of the highways of access; a fortified gate was provided at the entrance of each. Many of the new streets were quite narrow, and bordered with houses of standard design, between party walls. The Romanesque and Gothic bastides (newly planted, systematic towns) must have been similar in many ways. Abbey architects designed the typical Cluny houses, which have open arched shops on the ground floor, with a court and service rooms beyond, at the back of the plot. A lateral stairway gives access to the spacious main room on the upper floor, lighted by charming window arcades. Minor rooms at the back and a loft complete these buildings. (At Saint-Gilles-du-Gard there is a Romanesque house of three stories; the Gothic houses later on often have three, and the town houses more.) The abbey of Cluny was obliged to build (1179 ff.) a substantial girdle wall because of local brigandage, and this was extended on two sides, in more or less rounded form, to include the town. Country houses had quarters for animals on the ground floor, and exterior stairways to the main rooms. The manors, because of the times, had to be like small fortresses.

tion of the first consciously Gothic design at Saint-Denis. This style attracted the attention of the bishops of the entire royal domain near Paris, and quickly superseded the undistinguished local Romanesque of the Île de France. The cities underwent a spectacular growth at this time in commerce and civic life. The new Gothic style flourished in them and became symbolic because of this.

7. Urbanism and Fortification.—We are not well informed with regard to urbanism in Romanesque times. Centula appears to have been regular; the plan of St. Gall monastery is likewise regular. Possessing the treatise of Vitruvius and the shells of ancient Roman cities, the architects could not forget the *cardo* and *decumanus* of the traditional plan, which was resurrected in somewhat modified form by the Gothic urbanists who built Aigues-Mortes (1248, 1272), towns like Montpazier (13th century), and the newly founded cities called bastides (11th to 14th centuries). Much irregularity was introduced into older cities by encroachments, and in consequence of the ruin caused by conflagrations and wars.

As early as the 9th century the monastic plans tended to be rounded, the purpose being to enclose a maximum area within a protective wall or palisade. Rounded plans resulted naturally when the towns, for safety, took to the hills; within a wall the

Knowledge of sophisticated Byzantine and Muslim fortifications, gained by bitter experience in Crusader times, introduced many newer ideas into the very simple tradition of Roman fortification, constant theretofore in the West. Military engineers are mentioned as such in English documents from 1157. A masterpiece of their effort is Château-Gaillard (1196) near Les Andelys in Normandy, built by Richard Coeur de Lion after his return from the Holy Land. It contains the germ of the great Gothic castles which were required when war in the West became national in scope.

VI. THE HOLY ROMAN EMPIRE

1. Germany and the Low Countries.—By contrast with the fresh activity in France, the imperial lands, which had done so much to further the development of Romanesque architecture, remained conservative. The period of the mature Romanesque was prosperous in Germany; new buildings were larger and more numerous, but technically less interesting. The embellishment and vaulting of the cathedrals in the Rhine country date from this time: Mainz (1036–1137), Speyer (1030–65, remade c. 1082–

1137), and Worms (12th and 13th centuries). A prime example is the abbey church of Maria Laach (1130–56). Elsewhere, there is a spectacular church design with five towers at Tournai (c. 1110–1200), and there are ponderous but handsome palaces with fine upper rooms at Goslar (c. 1050, rebuilt after 1132) and Eisenach (the Wartburg, 12th century).

2. Italy.—Lombardy was an area in which the First Romanesque style was transformed into the High Romanesque, particularly because of the development of ribbed groin vaulting. Decorative arcading was used, in enriched form. Brick was widely employed in later work. Romanesque forms continued in use long after the coming of Cistercian half-Gothic. The Lombard cities built tremendous cathedrals, simple in plan, during the 12th century; examples are Modena (1099–1221), Parma (1117–32), and Cremona (1129–1342). Parma and Cremona have large freestanding baptisteries, unusual at the time. Among other

BY COURTESY OF (LEFT) IRISH TOURIST BOARD; PHOTOGRAPH, (ABOVE) BULLOZ

(LEFT) THE CROSS OF MUIREDACH AT CLONMACNOISE, IRELAND; 923. HEIGHT: 17 FT. 8 IN. (ABOVE) "ADORATION OF THE MAGI," FRAGMENT FROM THE RATCHIS ALTAR, CIVIDALE, ITALY; c. 745

churches, S. Ambrogio in Milan and S. Michele in Pavia are notable. A very handsome type of belfry tower was brought to perfection by the Lombards. Impressive town halls were built with Romanesque inspiration, but at Gothic dates. Turbulence in the city streets caused the construction of private fortifications in the form of tall tower houses. San Gimignano has preserved a fine group of 12 or so—but Bologna had 180; at Florence there were 150, and Lucca "rose like a forest."

Tuscany retained strong Early Christian traditions, exemplified in the octagonal Baptistery of Florence (restored in 1059) and the common use of basilican church forms. In the High Romanesque, marble was used extensively, often in panels and zebra work (for example, the cathedral group at Pisa, 1063–1283).

Central Italy was still more conservative; the Early Christian style survived there with little change except degeneration. The region about Monte Cassino was more inventive; the famous abbey built the typical church of the region, basilican in form (1066–71). It is believed that Muslim pointed arches entered the European church building tradition there (in the porches), from which they spread to Cluny, and from Cluny to the Île de France and Gothic. A school of painters developed, under Byzantine influence, which was drawn on by the Cluniacs in their work.

3. Norman Italy and Sicily.—Buildings basically Lombard, Tuscan, Muslim, Byzantine, or Early Christian were built as the realm became prosperous. Nuances of design, and a strange mingling of influences, give them strong local feeling. Examples are S. Nicola, Bari (1087), where St. Nicholas is buried; the cathedral of Monreale (1174), with wonderful mosaics and a poetic,

MARBURG—ART REFERENCE BUREAU

SPEYER CATHEDRAL FROM THE NORTHEAST, GERMANY; 1030–65. REMADE c. 1082–1137

half-Oriental cloister (1172–89); and S. Cataldo at Palermo (1160), a former synagogue in the Muslim domed style. These Sicilian buildings are actually more exotic than the structures built by the Crusaders in Palestine (1099–1244).

4. Palestine.—The Crusaders built extensively in the Latin kingdom of Jerusalem. The buildings are south French or Burgundian Romanesque, or Burgundian half-Gothic in style (e.g., new constructions at the Church of the Holy Sepulchre, 1099–1147; the cathedral of Tortosa or Tartūs, late 12th century). Many remarkable castles were built before and after 1200, incorporating Byzantine and Muslim innovations in military architecture, as at the Krak des Chevaliers or at Margat "whose bastions seemed to sustain the sky; only eagles and vultures could approach its battlements"—striking witness, in so remote a place, to Romanesque faith and power.

VII. ROMANESQUE SCULPTURE

Roman statuary and relief carving were transformed, under Oriental influence, into the Byzantine style, which had an increasing influence on sculpture in the West—particularly in beautiful ivory carvings, which inspired works of similar character in Western Europe. Freestanding church sculpture was given up in Byzantium after the iconoclastic controversy (716–842).

1. Early Stone Carving.—There is probably a Byzantine background for the Northumbrian high crosses in stone with carved panels (Bewcastle, 670; Ruthwell, c. 690; later in Mercia and the south of England). Impressive carved roods, large reliefs set in the church walls, are believed to date from about the year 1000.

In Ireland richly sculptured wheel crosses were carved in the 8th century and later as, for example, the cross of Muiredach (923) at Clonmacnoise. This work shows a Celtic component in details based on spirals, and a Germanic component in interlace work, as in the beautiful contemporary Irish manuscripts.

Early Lombard carvings also have very imaginative interlace work in flat panels. The Lombard sculptors were skilled in creating savage monsters, often shown devouring one another, but they were not very successful in figure sculpture (as witness the Ratchis altar at Cividale del Friuli, c. 745—though this was painted and gilded). Similar work is to be seen in the Asturias (northwestern Spain, occupied in the 7th century by the Suevi or Swabians). At Naranco, not far from the capital (Oviedo), there are interesting flat placques in a former palace hall, and at nearby Linio the door jambs were inspired by an ivory panel.

2. Sculpture in Stucco and Wood.—Less well known in the history of Western sculpture, and equally (with ivories) a bearer of Byzantine influence is medieval stucco—so very much more beautiful than the cheap material that now has that name. The Muslims over a long period of time developed the full possibilities of ornamental stucco, and traces can be found of their influence, along with that of the Byzantines. Both influences appear in the Lombard church of Sta. Maria in Valle at Cividale del Friuli, with its very beautiful frieze of dignified freestanding female figures (762–776). Carolingian stuccoes existed at Centula and Germigny-des-Prés. The fine reliefs in stucco on the sarcophagus of Agilbert (d. *c.* 685) at Jouarre near Paris seem more native, and this is the case with the baldacchino of S. Ambrogio in Milan (in part Carolingian), and with the stucco altar frontals of Catalonia (preserved examples from *c.* 1080); also in the case of German works like the tympanum of a portal at St. Godehard, Hildesheim (12th century). The destruction of stucco sculptures, with the passage of time, has been understandably great.

(TOP LEFT) ALINARI, (TOP RIGHT) J. ALLAN CASH—RAPHO GUILLUMETTE, (BOTTOM LEFT) ANDERSON—ALINARI, (BOTTOM RIGHT) AUTHENTICATED NEWS

ITALIAN ROMANESQUE ARCHITECTURE

(Top left) Interior of S. Ambrogio, Milan; 9th century. (Top right) Piazza del Duomo with the Baptistery, Cathedral, and Leaning Tower, Pisa; c. 1350. (Bottom left) Cathedral of Monreale, Sicily; 1174. (Bottom right) Sta. Maria, Pomposa, near Ferrara; 11th century

Wood as a sculptural material was far more important in the Middle Ages than one might suppose. The Scandinavian palace-builders and the superb shipwrights who introduced a new era in maritime navigation loved and richly employed wood carvings. The wonderful carved panels of interlaced animals, the freestanding human and animal heads, and the intricate pattern work that came to light in the excavation of the Oseberg ship (the grave of Queen Aasa, d. 850) are unsurpassed in energy and grace. The extraordinary authority and skill of the carvers implies an artistic tradition of centuries.

Some early wooden furniture still exists: thrones, choir stalls, chairs, and so forth. Manuscript paintings occasionally show pieces that are quite plausible as joinery. The furniture is often ornamented with arcading like that of a building.

A great deal of medieval statuary was made in wood—in particular, cult statues provided with recesses for relics, and sheathed in precious metals. Almost all have been stripped (for the melting pot) but the cores remain, and they are beautiful pieces of three-dimensional statuary. Other figures exist that were simply painted, and this applies to certain large figures in wood that were formerly parts of Deposition groups. For at least a thousand years there has been at Lucca a wooden figure of the crucified Saviour, the "Christ who reigns from a tree," now represented by an 11th–12th-century carving. An object of pilgrimage, it was widely copied in the Middle Ages. "Rood beams" in the churches, spanning the openings into the sanctuaries, carried monumental statues of St. Mary, St. John, and the crucified Saviour, all in wood.

3. Work in Ivory and Bronze.—Byzantine ivories, sublime in sentiment and elegance, set a standard for all carvings, and the best of similar works in the West—used particularly in gorgeous book covers—approach or equal the originals. Iconographic types were transmitted in this way, and also by manuscripts. Important ateliers of ivory carvers existed at Mainz, Essen, Trier, Metz, Liège, Saint-Denis, Reims, Winchester, and, in Spain, at León.

Ivories and bronzework in the Western empire seem to have absorbed a great deal of the finest artistic energy that might otherwise have been directed to figure sculpture in stone (always a starveling in medieval Germany). Bronze calls for sculptural skills similar to those required for stone, since a full-scale, three-dimensional model must be made. This may be in wax or plaster: in the latter case, there is a relation to stuccowork. Sculpture in bronze was also to a certain extent dependent on Byzantium in the early period; the Lombards produced such works. In the 10th and 11th centuries it became very important in Germany (Hildesheim) and the Low Countries (Liège). Indeed, Saxon panels for bronze doors became an article of export (Gnesen, Novgorod, and Verona). Great losses of such sculptures have been suffered from melting down; bronze was a very valuable material in the Middle Ages—when there was, in fact, a metal famine. Nevertheless, fine examples still represent the 11th and the 12th centuries.

Among the notable productions in bronze were light-wheels for the churches (suspended by chains, they represented the Heavenly Jerusalem with its walls and towers), crosses, crucifixes with beautiful figures, elaborate censers, and candlesticks. Some of the great seven-branch candlesticks measured as much as 15 ft. or 18 ft. in height, with a profusion of figures and leafage. Bishop Bernward of Hildesheim commissioned a bronze spiral column depicting the life of Christ (1015), and also the famous bronze doors of St. Michael's (1015), now in the cathedral. Many of the figures, admirable in action, are in very high relief. It is believed that some of their energy is due to influence from manuscripts of the school of Reims, now best represented by the famous Utrecht Psalter (c. 832), which was widely known, and rightly much admired. Gothic art was already forecast in the advanced style of the font of St. Bartholomew, Liège (c. 1107–16). Southern Italy possesses a notable series of bronze doors, beginning with actual Byzantine valves at Monte Cassino (1066), and continuing with Italian works leading to the culmination at the cathedral of Benevento (c. 1200).

4. Capitals and Portals.—In Romanesque times the architects and carvers went far beyond the patterns of ancient works in the embellishment of buildings with sculpture. Irrepressible medieval fancy enriched the capitals, the columns, the moldings, the portals, and the facades—beginning about the year 1000, when the enlarged scale of the buildings required it.

There is a continuous tradition from antiquity for sculptured capitals in stone. In Carolingian times they were inspired by the ancient Corinthian and Composite orders; subsequently many variants were used, called Corinthianesque. Sometimes the upper half of the block was left square, as in Muslim practice. Cubical capitals are taken out of a cubical block by cutting down the corners, leaving the top square, the sides semicircular or triangular, and the bottom circular, as required by the columnar shaft. Ornament is lacking in many cases, and in the 10th century it was often crude. Leafage and pattern work persisted, but figural representation could not be ignored; beginning about the year 1000 it had a real interest (Saint-Bénigne, Dijon, 1001–18; Saint-Germain-des-Prés, Paris, '1005; St. Bartholomew, Paderborn, 1017; Saint-Hilaire, Poitiers, 1045–50; and others in increasing numbers, in all parts of the Continent, as time went on). The culmination of a quite splendid development came in the beautiful allegorical capitals of the ambulatory of the abbey church of Cluny (c. 1093), where there was a masterful use of human, foliate, and abstract forms. These capitals are forerunners of the 12th-century style; the reason seems to be that here an appropriate and special effort produced a remarkable synthesis, in stone, of the progress that had been achieved by the most inspired sculptors in ivory, wood, stucco, bronze, and gold. The art-loving Cluniacs and others, as patrons, furthered the development of such sculpture, and in the 12th century it flourished luxuriantly, especially in the monastic churches of France and Spain, and the cathedrals of Italy. It is perhaps because of long discipline in making structural stone capitals that the Romanesque sculptors never lost their feeling for structure; the Romanesque is perhaps the most felicitous of sculpture that is primarily architectural.

Thus it would seem that there were always artists capable of carrying out freestanding sculpture, including stone sculpture. Their number was not great, and they were doubtless itinerant, like the bell founders of the age. Their carvings showed the individual stonecutter's fancy, until, toward the end of the 11th century, the architects and patrons began to envisage serious sculptural programs suggested by manuscripts, stucco panels, and goldsmiths' work.

The process may actually be seen in the development of church portals; as time went on they became more and more elaborate, with recessed columns and arches, where the original openings were plain. The oldest preserved example of the series, at Saint-Genis-des-Fontaines in French Catalonia, has a decorated lintel of 1020 (Christ in glory with angels and apostles) which looks like an altar frontal or a reliquary translated into stone under the influence of the Muslim stuccowork of nearby Spain. The subject continued to be used on the portals, and an unmistakable spirituality entered in before the end of the century, facilitated by the use of the semicircular tympanum under the discharging arch of the structural portal as a field for a relief carving of the glorified Christ. This occurred first at the Cluniac priory of Charlieu in Burgundy, shortly before 1094. Before long other apocalyptic elements were introduced into the ensembles. It seems likely that the miniatures of a famous Great Bible produced in the scriptorium at Cluny shortly after 1100 (and now lost) may underlie the design of three impressive portals with apocalyptic imagery, created not long afterward in the Cluniac ambient—at Cluny itself (c. 1108) and at the priories of Vézelay (c. 1118) and Moissac (c. 1120–25). At Autun Cathedral, coniuncta of Cluny, a tremendous "Last Judgment" was set forth (c. 1130–35). Gislebertus, the sculptor of Autun, had worked with the masters at Cluny and Vézelay. In his own work there is an extraordinary otherworldliness, communicated by vibrant postures, by elongation, and by changes of relief and scale. This freedom was present in Romanesque sculpture all along, as it was developing, and here the freedom serves a sublime aesthetic purpose, in a great masterpiece representing an event beyond human experience. Before he carved the portals, Gislebertus had created (for another portal, c. 1125) the "Eve of Autun," perhaps the most accomplished of all individual Romanesque sculptures. The popular appeal of the "Last Judgment" probably accounts for the choice of this subject at Autun and at Conques (a pilgrimage church, c. 1124; at this latter place the polychromy survives). The more spiritual conception is exemplified, perhaps about 1118, at Perrecy-les-Forges, a priory of the great monastery of Fleury (Saint-Benoît-sur-Loire).

5. Development from the End of the 11th Century.—As is shown by the career of Gislebertus at Cluny, Vézelay, and Autun, the master sculptors trained companions to assist them, to carry on their tradition, and to spread their influence.

From about 1070 onward the sculptors in many regions carved (along with a considerable number of portals) a splendid profusion of individual capitals for the churches that were rising everywhere, and for the cloisters (Moissac, Toulouse, and many other sites in southern France and Spain). With some French collaboration, Spanish sculpture flourished at this time. There is a trace of Muslim influence in the carvings of the cloister of Santo Domingo de Silos (near Burgos), one of the most poetic (c. 1096).

The 12th-century production of sculptured decorative elements was very considerable, especially in the monasteries, but there it encountered the blind opposition of Bernard of Clairvaux, who denounced it as luxurious in a polemical letter (to William of Saint-Thierry, 1124). St. Bernard's influence among the Cistercians was such that ornament of this sort, really the birthright

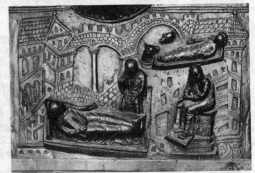

(LEFT) ALINARI, (CENTRE) ARCHIV FÜR KUNST UND GESCHICHTE, BERLIN, (RIGHT) MARBURG—ART REFERENCE BUREAU

BRONZE SCULPTURE

(Left) Detail of the panels from the main door, Cathedral of Benevento, Italy; c. 1200. (Centre) Head of Christ, detail of a Crucifixion, Abbey Church, Werden an der Ruhr, Germany; 11th century. (Right) "The Nativity," detail from the doors of the Church of St. Michael, Hildesheim, Germany; 1015

(LEFT, BELOW) GIRAUDON, (CENTRE, RIGHT) JEAN ROUBIER

FRENCH ROMANESQUE CAPITALS

(Left) Figure from a series of personifications from the abbey church of Cluny; 12th century. (Centre) Acrobat motif from the church of Anzy-le-Duc, Saône-et-Loire; 11th century. (Right) Leafage and pattern work in the cloisters at Moissac; c. 1100. (Below) Angel appearing to the Magi, from Autun Cathedral; c. 1120–30

of Burgundian Romanesque churches, was summarily banned from the designs (Burgundian in character) that the Cistercian Order built in hundreds of examples all over Western Europe.

Fortunately this blight interfered but little with other developments. In western France the church facades were enriched like ivory caskets on a large scale with arcading, borders, and figures. Oddly enough the tympana of the main arcades were left blank (Notre-Dame-la-Grande, Poitiers, c. 1135). At Angoulême after 1125 a large area in the middle of the cathedral facade was devoted to the Second Coming of the Saviour. Great works were also carried out in Provence (Saint-Gilles-du-Gard, 1142 and later).

The Italian sculptor Benedetto Antelami, who worked at the Baptistery of Parma (1178), was inspired by Saint-Gilles. An earlier man, Guglielmo, who worked after 1099 at Modena and Cremona, was inspired, at least, from Languedoc. He carved an Arthurian relief at Modena, and has been credited with the invention there of the typical Lombard Romanesque portal, with its hood sustained by freestanding columns carried on the backs of animals, usually lions; this device was used on portals in the south of Italy where Lombard influence was strong. In the south classicism was strong, as evidenced by still extant neo-Roman figures made for the emperor Frederick II (1247?). Nicola d'Apulia (Niccolò Pisano, q.v.) was trained in this tradition, and he introduced it in the famous pulpit (1259) of the Baptistery of Pisa Cathedral (1153–1278). Here, in Tuscany, the architecture was already classicizing at this time.

VIII. ROMANESQUE PAINTING

1. Manuscripts.—In Roman times the scriptoria, sometimes working almost on a factory basis, supplied a flourishing book trade. The books were typically in the shape of rolls (rotuli) or scrolls (*volumina*) made up of joined sheets of parchment, which might extend to a length of 30 ft. For reference or for notes, smaller sheets, usually of paper, were assembled. With the bar-

barian invasions and the distress of the cities, the book trade almost vanished, and its functions, like so much else, were taken over by the monasteries. The Rule of St. Benedict (529) required the monks to read, and this implied manuscript production.

It was the monks, in Carolingian and Romanesque times, who perfected the bound book (codex) as it is known today. The codices, invented in the 2nd century A.D., were infinitely more convenient than rolls as service books, and must soon have been accepted in the church. Ancient books had illustrations (in each roll, typically, an author portrait), and the illustrated scroll survived into Romanesque times as the Exultet Roll that was read at Eastertide from the pulpit—with the peculiarity that the illustrations were upside down, so that they might be appreciated in the choir as the readings continued and the scroll was payed out.

In the 9th century, both East and West laboured valiantly to make up for the losses of the preceding age by copying, and thus multiplying, the preserved ancient texts, except those of Christian heretics (which were destroyed). In the East, Constantinople, especially under the learned patriarch Photius (q.v.), was the centre; in the West a considerable number of enlightened monasteries did their full share, producing not only texts but gorgeously bound and beautifully illustrated books in large numbers. Mention should be made of Kells, Winchester, Saint-Bertin, Stavelot, Aachen, Fulda, Trier, Arras, Saint-Denis, Tours, Cîteaux, Reichenau, Bobbio, and Monte Cassino. It is symptomatic, for instance, that all modern texts of the important architectural handbook of Vitruvius, a Roman, go back to a single copy of Carolingian date.

For the work of copying, in both East and West, the late Roman round capitals (uncials), beautiful as they were, were given up in favour of minuscules, which are much easier to write. Moreover, spacing was now introduced between individual words, which made them much easier to read. Capitals were retained, as the name implies, for headings and for emphasis, and they were cleverly composed to mark the divisioning of the book, in letters of appropriate size and style. When the Slavonic alphabet was created, it was based largely on Greek capital letters, and this is the chief reason why the Russian characters differ from those of Latin script. In both East and West the medieval book hands have survived with slight modification as present-day printing type. The ease with which the new letters could be written encouraged the development of clever ligatures that further increased speed; this kind of writing is the cursive used today (except where the victims of progressive education, taught a "book hand," have developed mystifying ligatures of their own). We rarely think of our debt to the Romanesque period in writing, reading, and bookmaking.

New medieval techniques made possible a thin whitened parchment in fairly large sheets that could be inscribed on both sides,

BY COURTESY OF THE BIBLIOTHEQUE MUNICIPALE, ÉPERNAY

"ST. LUKE," GOSPEL BOOK OF EBBO, SCHOOL OF REIMS: 816–35. IN THE MUNICIPAL LIBRARY, ÉPERNAY, FRANCE

and these sheets were folded into gatherings or signatures which were sewn together, just as they are in present-day book manufacture. In formal compositions the medieval scribes employed pictures inspired ultimately by Byzantine illustrative material, and they discovered workmanlike methods by which the suitable

(LEFT, RIGHT) GIRAUDON, (CENTRE, BELOW) JEAN ROUBIER

FRENCH ROMANESQUE SCULPTURE

(Left) Detail from the main portal, Church of Saint-Trophime, Arles; 12th century.   (Centre) Detail from the Royal Portal, Chartres Cathedral; 1145–60.   (Right) Relief of the prophet Isaiah, fragment of the original portal, Sainte-Marie, Souillac; 1130–40.   (Below) Eve of Autun by Gislebertus, fragment of a lintel from the side portal, Saint-Lazarus, Autun; c. 1125.   In the Musée Rolin, Autun

gold and colours could be applied. The unquenchable fancy of the scribes was joyously deployed when they could make lively and unconventional initials and incidental decorative details,. which often involved acrobatic human figures and impossible yet entirely credible monsters, coiled and spouting heads from their tails, or devouring each other with horrifying gusto. They disport with human kind in the "inhabited scrolls" which were frequently used as borders. The integration of text with illustration, and indeed the ornamental use of lettering, went far beyond anything achieved in antiquity.

In the marvelously convoluted ornaments of the Irish manuscripts (8th century and later), one senses the gallant energy that sent the insular missionaries toward the Continent where, as in England, the characteristic spiral and plaited motifs of their style affected local scriptoria. At Winchester, the Saxon capital of England, and at Canterbury, the ecclesiastical capital, famous scriptoria developed in the 10th century. Great Winchester pages often have involved floral borders, but the scenes and the figures are always noble, and their fine quality made them influential on the Continent.

The finest books were considered to be a part of the church treasure; more commonplace items were kept in an armarium between the cloister walk which contained the scriptorium, and the door which the monks used in passing from the cloister to the church. At Cluny each monk was required to read at least one book a year. There was an attempt to make the libraries inclusive; the abbot of Cluny once requested the loan of a book for copying, because the Cluny manuscript, lent to a priory, had been eaten by a bear. An ordinary monastic library in the Romanesque period would contain several hundred books, and the total book production, therefore, must have run to hundreds of thousands in the Romanesque period alone.

A fairly representative sample of manuscripts has survived, despite enormous losses in medieval and modern times and a fantastic dispersion. A Latin translation of Plato, now at Valenciennes, for instance, was once bought from a pirate, and the various fragments of Livy's *History of Rome* were found respectively in Mainz, Bamberg, Switzerland, and on a reused parchment at the Vatican. By devoted study, paleographers have identified the scriptoria of great numbers of manuscripts, and from this work have drawn interesting conclusions regarding intellectual history.

At Aachen, the imperial capital, the manuscripts have a becoming magnificence from the 9th century on, including (among other things) impressive portraits of the emperors. Fulda, Reichenau, and Liège had notable scriptoria. In France, at Saint-Denis, Tours, and Reims, great schools and great scriptoria were active from Carolingian times. Reims, which produced the dynamic Utrecht Psalter, immensely furthered the art of drawing. Elsewhere the designs had tended (even when strongly charged with emotion) to be somewhat static in character; the drawings of the school of Reims surge with life and emotion, and convey a sense of panorama and space that is extraordinary.

The Burgundian experience has been unfortunate. For example, the 12th-century catalog of Cluny listed over 1,800 titles—many, of course, quite simple manuscripts. But the library was pillaged during the Wars of Religion of the 16th century and the Revolution of 1789. When the manuscripts were taken to the Bibliothèque Nationale in Paris (1882), less than 50 of the 1,800 remained. At Cîteaux, under English auspices, a very gifted scriptorium functioned from 1099 and did beautiful decorative work, but this effort was throttled by the ascetic St. Bernard in 1124, stunting this happy side of monastic life throughout the Order for centuries. *See* ILLUMINATED MANUSCRIPTS.

(ABOVE) ALINARI, (ABOVE RIGHT) ARCHIVO MAS, BARCELONA, (BELOW) JEAN ROUBIER

(ABOVE) "THE CRUCIFIXION," FRESCO IN STA. MARIA ANTIQUA, ROME; 8TH CENTURY. (ABOVE RIGHT) "ANNUNCIATION TO THE SHEPHERDS," DETAIL OF FRESCO IN THE VAULT OF THE PANTEÓN DE LOS REYES, S. ISIDORO, LEÓN, SPAIN; 12TH CENTURY. (BELOW) NOAH'S ARK FRESCO, NAVE OF SAINT-SAVIN-SUR-GARTEMPE, FRANCE; 12TH CENTURY

2. Wall Paintings.

—Christians have been familiar with wall decorations in their places of worship almost from the beginning, for synagogues of the time had narrative frescoes (as at Doura-Europos), and churches inherited the tradition. Roman Christians who worshipped in houses must have seen decorations of the Pompeian style, and such decorations appear, differentiated by Christian symbolism, in the Catacombs. Monumental compositions were developed after the Peace of the Church (313) and carried out in mosaic. For more modest edifices fresco was often used—increasingly as time went on—and the fact that preliminary fresco sketches actually underlie the mosaics facilitated this process, since the monumental character of the great mosaics depended on monumental designs handled, as underpainting, in fresco. (Parenthetically, mosaic was used in the Carolingian era, but there are remains only at Germigny-des-Prés, an Ark of the Covenant, 804. The quite splendid mosaic vesture of the Sicilian churches, Cefalù and Monreale, is in fact the work of Byzantines, in their own style.)

In fresco, there are several technical processes. True fresco is painted freely on areas of fresh plaster. The colours are earthen (chalk white, ochre, browns, copper blues, and reds) and they become integral with the plaster. Other methods, including fresco secco, are applied to dry wall surfaces (remoistened in the case of distemper), using a binder or adhesive: size, white of egg, or glue. In wax painting (encaustic), pigments in powdered form are mixed with wax and applied with a hot spatula. The famous frescoes at Berzé-la-Ville near Cluny (c. 1105) show these techniques combined: basic drawings are in sanguine on wet plaster, overlaid by colour with a glue binder, and enriched by more lustrous colours laid on with wax. Romanesque paintings were ordinarily much simpler than these, which clearly look back to Byzantine models.

It was quite usual from the 4th century onward to have imposing designs in church apses; the nave walls might have portrait medallions or narrative scenes. In Carolingian times narrative cycles were developed for the palaces as well. This was the case at Ingelheim (c. 814), destroyed but well reported. The church had scenes from the Old Testament; on the other side, there were corresponding scenes from the New. The Great Hall had scenes from secular history, including the deeds of Cyrus, Hannibal, and Alexander the Great, balanced by the moderns—at that date Theodoric, Charles Martel, and Charlemagne himself. There are no remains of these secular cycles, but a very considerable amount of church painting of all sorts still exists. Account must be taken also of church sculptures (even external works) which were polychromed. The most striking remains of Carolingian wall paintings are in the crypt of St. Germain at Auxerre (c. 859).

The paintings may conveniently be grouped by countries. Italy has beautiful examples in Sta. Maria Antiqua, Rome, and Castelseprio (8th century). There is a very complete ensemble at S. Angelo in Formis, a priory of Monte Cassino (c. 1075), which shows direct Byzantine influences. In the north at Civate and Galliano (11th century) and Bergusio (12th century) there are notable works.

Spain has remarkable examples in several traditions—San Baudelio de Berlanga, half-Muslim (11th century). In Catalonia a very powerful local school is now largely represented by examples gathered in the Museo de la Ciudadela in Barcelona. The Panteón de los Reyes at León has very handsome 12th-century frescoes on the vault.

The French examples lie in a zone that runs across middle France. At the two poles are Berzé-la-Ville, very Byzantine, and Saint-Savin-sur-Gartempe, with splendid scenes, tawny in colour, grand in scale, displayed on a remarkable barrel vault, held high over the nave pavement by stout round columns marbled in contrasting colours. In a nearby region there is a group of small painted churches of great appeal—Tavant and others of high merit. Examples are to be found in England (Canterbury, Winchester),

ALINARI

"THE DESCENT FROM THE CROSS" BY BENEDETTO ANTELAMI, RELIEF ON THE PULPIT, CATHEDRAL OF PARMA, ITALY; 1178

ROMANESQUE MINOR ARTS

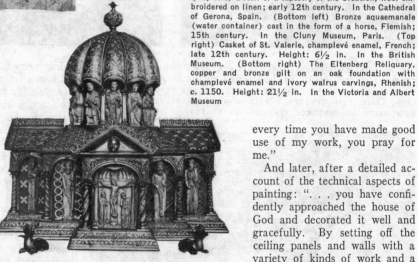

(Top left) Detail of a tapestry of the Creation, wool embroidered on linen; early 12th century. In the Cathedral of Gerona, Spain. (Bottom left) Bronze aquaemanale (water container) cast in the form of a horse, Flemish; 15th century. In the Cluny Museum, Paris. (Top right) Casket of St. Valerie, champlevé enamel, French; late 12th century. Height: 6½ in. In the British Museum. (Bottom right) The Eltenberg Reliquary, copper and bronze gilt on an oak foundation with champlevé enamel and ivory walrus carvings, Rhenish; c. 1150. Height: 21½ in. In the Victoria and Albert Museum

Scandinavia, Hungary, and Czechoslovakia (a few late examples).

In Germany, the church of St. George in the former abbey of Oberzell on the Isle of Reichenau has a notable cycle of narrative frescoes dated about 1000 in the Carolingian nave. Other frescoes exist in Germany at Regensburg (Holy Cross chapel) and Salzburg (Nonnberg, 12th century), and elsewhere. Switzerland has a fairly complete example of a Carolingian painted church (under a Gothic vault) at Müstair (Moûtier-en-Grisons); the small chapel of Mals (Malles) nearby has a Carolingian chevet with paintings and stuccoes.

All of these paintings have certain glyptic values, but they respect the mural values of the walls and the overarching vaults. The Romanesque painter, like the Romanesque sculptor, rightly wished his art to participate in the architectonic expression of the building.

IX. MINOR ARTS

We have the privilege of visiting a Romanesque painted church in the company of a first-class 12th-century craftsman. In his well-ordered, inclusive, and practical book *On Divers Arts* (trans. by J. G. Hawthorne and C. S. Smith, The University of Chicago Press [1963]) "Theophilus" (*q.v.;* Roger of Helmarshausen, a Benedictine monk) gives, by way of preface, an excellent idea of the scope of these arts, as they flourished in his time: ". . . you will find here whatever kinds of the different pigments Byzantium possesses and their mixtures; whatever Russia has learned in the working of enamels and variegation with niello; whatever Arab lands adorn with repoussé or casting or openwork; whatever decoration Italy applies to a variety of vessels in gold or by the carving of gems and ivories; whatever France loves in the costly variegation of windows; and whatever skillful Germany applauds in the fine workings of gold, silver, copper and iron, and in wood and precious stones . . . . You will repay your instructor for his pains if

every time you have made good use of my work, you pray for me."

And later, after a detailed account of the technical aspects of painting: ". . . you have confidently approached the house of God and decorated it well and gracefully. By setting off the ceiling panels and walls with a variety of kinds of work and a variety of pigments, you have shown the beholders something of the likeness of the paradise of God . . . to praise God the Creator in this creation and to proclaim Him marvellous in His works."

But this, for Roger, was far from a finished church. Remembering that he was a monk, it is interesting to have him say: ". . . Henceforth be fired with greater ingenuity: with all the striving of your mind hasten to complete whatever is still lacking in the house of the Lord and without which the divine mysteries and the administering of the offices cannot continue. These are chalices, candlesticks, censers, cruets, ewers, caskets for holy relics, crosses, missal covers. . . ." The lavish use of semiprecious stones on missal covers, reliquaries, and altar frontals should be noted.

In general, Romanesque works were based ultimately in large part on the Byzantine tradition. St. Bernard objected, in the case of monks, to the splendour which the Byzantines and the Westerners both loved. In Western thought, gorgeous cult objects at the altar and rich decorative adjuncts fulfilled a deeply felt need. In the early period, the churches were often small, dark, and austere, yet the faithful wished the divine service, despite these limitations, to be "a courtly honoring of the Highest Lord and Ruler . . . provided with such a palace as no king on earth could possess."

Even at a later time, when the churches were larger and more elaborate, considerable portions of the monastic liturgy continued to be performed at night, so that the traditional focus on splendid objects and fittings at the altar continued unchanged. During the Christmas ceremonies at Cluny about 1050 (for instance), 463 liturgically arranged candles were lighted, casting their glow on the altar with its frontals of gold, its baldacchino of niello, its sacramental dove, cross, candles, icons and reliquaries, together with gorgeously mounted service books, surrounding candlestands, tapestries, paintings, and other ornaments. One who sees such things even in well-arranged exhibits in museums can hardly realize their impact in the ambient, both architectural and religious, for which they were made.

Goldsmiths, enamelers, and glaziers had a shop in Cluny in 1043, perhaps in 1014, and the same thing would be true of many monastic centres. Often manuscripts, ivories, and gold- and silversmiths' work are traceable to the atelier of a great monastery over a long period of time. Saint-Denis, Reims, Liège, Mainz, Essen, Cologne, Aachen, Trier, Helmarshausen, Paderborn, Hildesheim, and in Italy, Milan are all distinguished; fine work was done also in pre-Conquest England, as well as in the region that is now Belgium and Lorraine, and in Spain at León. The most spectacular pieces are the covers of the Lindau codex, with semiprecious stones and filigree work (Reims, *c.* 870), the Wolvinus altar at S. Ambrogio in Milan (*c.* 835), and the golden altar of Basel (Mainz, *c.* 1010). Enamels were made at Stavelot, Maastricht, Liège, and Cologne; the most elaborate of all being the Klosterneuberg altarpiece by Nicholas of Verdun (1181). The importance of Limoges for enamels developed in this later period.

Silver was used as a base for silver-gilt objects of all kinds, and in niello work (the early baldacchino of Cluny II, *c.* 1030). Copper was used for ancillary purposes, except in the case of vessels of various types.

Among the metals, iron was in short supply, but the smithies were busy nevertheless. A myriad of small fittings, locks, keys, handles, clasps, knobs, nails, and so forth were hammered out individually, and often exhibit excellent craftsmanship. Steel was used for items of personal armour, and most notably for swords (Toledo blades). The iron hinges for the great door valves of the portals were regularly anchored by beautiful branching designs, and lively imagination as well as sensitive craftsmanship went into iron grillwork.

Very remarkable embroideries were made in Romanesque times. The most famous, at Bayeux, miscalled a "tapestry," is 20 in. high and 231 ft. long. It was executed in England about 1070 as a record of the Norman Conquest, and was designed to make the circuit of Bayeux Cathedral, whose bishop Odo commissioned it. The embroidery was displayed from July 1 to July 14 annually, for a long period (*see* BAYEUX TAPESTRY). English embroidery was internationally famous. Other pieces, from ecclesiastical indumentaria, have come down to us. Rich hangings for the palace halls and churches are known from texts and from painted imitations on wall dadoes. One design of about 1100 deserves mention —the antependium of the high altar of the cathedral of Gerona, with the Creation and a cosmology represented in striking colours. *See* also BYZANTINE ART AND ARCHITECTURE and GOTHIC ART AND ARCHITECTURE.

BIBLIOGRAPHY.—*Architecture, General:* D. Bullough, *The Age of Charlemagne* (1966); H. Busch and B. Lohse (eds.), *Romanesque Europe* (1960); A. W. Clapham, *Romanesque Architecture in Western Europe* (1936); K. J. Conant, *Carolingian and Romanesque Architecture* (1959, 2nd ed., 1966); J. Evans (ed.), *The Flowering of the Middle Ages* (1966); M. Eschapasse, *L'Architecture bénédictine en Europe* (1963); P. Frankl, *Der frühmittelalterliche und romanishche Baukunst* (1926); R. Oursel, *Living Architecture: Romanesque,* trans. by K. M. Leake (1967); A. K. Porter, *Medieval Architecture: Its Origins and Development* (1909); H. Saalman, *Medieval Architecture* (1962); H. Stolper, *Bauen in Holz* (1937); C. Ward, *Medieval Church Vaulting* (1915).
England: A. W. Clapham, *English Romanesque Architecture Before the Conquest* (1930), *English Romanesque Architecture After the Conquest* (1934); G. Webb, *Architecture in Britain: the Middle Ages* (1956).
France: M. Aubert, *L'Architecture cistercienne en France,* 2nd ed. (1947), *L'Art roman en France* (1961); J. Evans, *Art in Mediæval France, 987–1498* (1948), *Monastic Life at Cluny, 910–1157* (1931), *Romanesque Architecture of the Order of Cluny* (1938); A. Gardner, *An Introduction to French Church Architecture* (1938); R. de Lasteyrie, *L'Architecture religieuse en France à l'époque romane,* 2nd ed. (1929); C. Oursel, *L'Art roman de Bourgogne, Études d'Histoire et d'Archéologie* (1928); E. Viollet-le-Duc, *Dictionnaire raisonné de l'Architecture française du XIᵉ au XVIᵉ siècle* (1858–68).
Germany: E. Gall, *Dome und Klosterkirchen am Rhein* (1956); L. Grodecki, *L'Architecture ottonienne* (1958); E. Hempel, *Geschichte der deutschen Baukunst* (1949); O. Völkers, *Deutsche Hausfibel* (1937).
Italy: H. Decker, *L'Art roman en Italie* (1958); C. Ricci, *Romanesque Architecture in Italy* (1925); G. T. Rivoira, *Lombardic Architecture: Its Origin, Development, and Derivatives,* 2nd ed. (1933). *Levant:* T. S. R. Boase, *Castles and Churches of the Crusading Kingdom* (1967); H. R. Fedden, *Crusader Castles* (1950).
Scandinavia: E. Alnæs *et al., Norwegian Architecture Throughout the Ages* (1950); G. Boëthius, *Hallar, Tempel och Stavkyrkor* (1931); C. Curman *et al.* (eds.), *Sveriges Kyrkor,* official series (n.d.); E. Lundberg, *Byggnadskonsten i Sverige under Medeltiden, 1000–1400* (1940).
Spain: Ars Hispaniae (Plus Ultra series), vol. iii by M. Gomez (1951), vol. v by J. Gudiol Ricart and J. A. Gaya Nuño (1948), vol. vi by W. W. S. Cook and J. Gudiol Ricart (1950); V. Lampérez y Romea, *Historia de la arquitectura cristiana española en la edad media,* 2nd ed. (1930).
Painting: J. Ainaud de Lasarte and A. Held, *Romanesque Painting* (1964); E. W. Anthony, *Romanesque Frescoes* (1951); A. Grabar and C. Nordenfalk, *La Peinture romane* (1958); C. Oursel, *Miniatures cisterciennes* (1960).
Sculpture: M. Aubert, *La Sculpture française au moyen-âge* (1947); H. Beenken, *Romanische Skulptur in Deutschland* (1924); D. Grivot and G. Zarnecki, *Gislebertus, Sculptor of Autun* (1961); A. K. Porter, *Romanesque Sculpture of the Pilgrimage Roads* (1923).
Minor Arts: J. Evans, *Dress in Mediæval France* (1952); J. G. Hawthorne and C. S. Smith (eds.), *On Divers Arts: the Treatise of Theophilus* (1963); H. Schwarzenski, *Monuments of Romanesque Art* (1953); F. M. Stenton, (gen. ed.), *The Bayeux Tapestry* (1965).   (K. J. C.)

ROMAN HISTORY. This article, covering the history of Rome and the Roman Empire from the beginning to A.D. 476, is divided as follows:

I. THE MONARCHY AND THE REPUBLIC

A. THE BEGINNINGS OF ROME

1. The Formation of Roman Historiography.—The first Roman historians (Q. Fabius Pictor, Cincius Alimentus) lived in the late 3rd century B.C. and wrote in Greek. A Roman historiography in Latin developed later, in the 2nd and 1st centuries B.C. (beginning with M. Porcius Cato the Censor). Only short fragments of these early historians are preserved, and it is not known exactly how they proceeded to collect information about the past of Rome. Some idea of their method can, however, be formed from the sections of Diodorus Siculus' *Bibliotheca* that deal with Roman history, and from the surviving books of Livy and Dionysius of Halicarnassus. Diodorus (1st century B.C.) probably used Roman historians of the 2nd century; whereas Livy and Dionysius, who lived under Augustus, seem to have relied mainly on Roman historians of the 1st century B.C. For events earlier than the First Punic War Roman historians were able to draw on: (1) a pontifical chronicle (*Annales pontificum*) which apparently concentrated on events with religious implications (such as famines and eclipses); (2) traditions of individual aristocratic families (including inscriptions, written funeral speeches, oral recollections); (3) official lists of magistrates which certainly existed from about 509 B.C. onward; (4) other documents, such as religious calendars, texts of treaties, laws (*e.g.*, the Twelve Tables).

The Romans seem to have had primitive epic poems and banquet songs in honour of great men; but Cato alluded to the banquet songs as a feature which had disappeared from Rome long before his time (2nd century B.C.). They are unlikely to have contributed much to the Roman historical tradition, though authoritative modern historians (B. G. Niebuhr, G. De Sanctis) have held the opposite view. Roman events were certainly mentioned in Etruscan and Greek historical books. It is not known whether the Romans of the republican period made use of Etruscan historical books (the emperor Claudius seems to have done so), but they read what the Greeks wrote about Rome. The references to Rome which they found in Greek historians of the 5th and 4th centuries (such as Hellanicus and Theopompus) were, however, confined to the origins of Rome or to a few events of international importance of later times—for instance the occupation of Rome by the Gauls. The first Greek historian who wrote extensively about Rome, Timaeus of Tauromenium, lived only one generation before Fabius Pictor and was chiefly concerned with Pyrrhus' war, with which he was contemporary.

On the basis of the scanty evidence available it was difficult to write the history of Rome before the First Punic War. Critical skill in questions of authenticity and interpretation and scholarly detachment were needed to use it properly. Neither was to be expected. The majority of the Roman historians (at least in the 2nd and 1st centuries B.C.) were no scholars; they belonged to the senatorial class and were directly involved in political struggles. It is therefore not surprising that they wrote the history of the first five centuries of their city in an uncritical manner and that even their accounts of later events were often distorted for partisan purposes.

The ancient tales about early Rome were accepted at their face value until the Dutchman J. Perizonius (1685) and the Frenchman L. de Beaufort (1738) questioned them. More systematic criticism of the ancient literary tradition about Rome had to wait until the 19th century, and B. G. Niebuhr can be regarded as its founder. Later T. Mommsen concentrated his critical genius on the study of the Roman constitution, which in his view had been better served by ancient tradition than had the recording of military events and political struggles. In the 20th century linguistic research and archaeological excavations gave prominence to the problems concerning the place of Rome in the complex civilization of ancient Italy: the relations between Rome and Etruria and Rome and Greece (often through Etruria) have been thoroughly examined. Linguistics, archaeology, and the history of religion provide an ever-increasing amount of evidence independent of the literary tradition. The history of Rome which has thus emerged is very different from that written by Diodorus, Livy, and Dionysius. Yet this does not entitle us to disregard the ancient literary tradition. However distorted and naïve it may appear, it contains a great deal that is sound. Even for the monarchical period it has preserved some important facts. For the republican period it has provided a good chronological framework and a substantially reliable outline of the political and military developments.

2. Literary Tradition.—According to the tradition found in Livy, Dionysius of Halicarnassus, and other Augustan writers, Rome was founded by Romulus about 750 B.C. Romulus was a descendant of the Trojan Aeneas who had founded Lavinium. Aeneas' son in his turn had founded Alba. After a long series of Alban kings lasting for 300 years, Numitor was deposed by his

CAPITOLINE WOLF

Bronze sculpture from the Capitol, dating from about 500 B.C. The twin figures of Romulus and Remus were added during the Renaissance. In the Palazzo dei Conservatori, Rome

brother Amulius. Numitor's daughter, Rhea Silvia, was raped by the god Mars and bore him the twins Romulus and Remus. Romulus killed his brother Remus and later shared his power with Titus Tatius, king of the Sabines. He divided the Romans into three tribes and 30 *curiae*. After his death or ascension to heaven the Romans elected the Sabine Numa Pompilius, who introduced some of the fundamental Roman religious institutions. The third king (not counting Titus Tatius) was Tullus Hostilius, a good warrior who destroyed Alba Longa; the fourth was Ancus Marcius, who established a colony at Ostia. The fifth king, Tarquinius (Tarquin), was different from his predecessors; he had an Etruscan name but was really the son of the Corinthian Demaratus and an Etruscan woman. He fought Sabines and Latins, drained the Forum, and was altogether a tyrant in the grand style. He was followed by a Roman, Servius Tullius, who introduced coinage, divided the citizens into five classes according to wealth (*see below*), created the *comitia centuriata* and the local tribes, and surrounded the city with a wall. The seventh and last king was another Tarquinius, a son or grandson of the first. He undertook big public works, built the Cloaca Maxima (main drain; also attributed to the elder Tarquin), humiliated the Latins, made himself unpopular by tyrannical acts, and was finally thrown out by an aristocratic conspiracy in 510 B.C. The plotters set up a republican government presided over by two annual magistrates. They had to defend Rome against the Etruscans led by Lars Porsena of Clusium; and they inaugurated the Temple of Jupiter Capitolinus built by the Tarquinii.

In general outline this tradition is to be found in the earliest historian of Rome, Fabius Pictor. Some of its elements certainly go back much further. For instance, the legend about a wolf feeding Romulus and Remus was already officially accepted by 296 B.C. when the Ogulnii set up their statue celebrating the fact. On other points the early historians exercised their discretion —or their fantasy. For instance, Fabius Pictor thought that Romulus was the grandson of Numitor, but his contemporary, the poet Naevius, wrote that Romulus was the grandson of Aeneas (thus brushing aside the 12 Alban kings between Aeneas and Romulus). Even the date of the foundation of Rome remained long uncertain. Timaeus put it in 814 B.C. (and made it contemporary with the foundation of Rome's rival Carthage), Fabius Pictor chose 748, Cincius Alimentus 729–728. The so-called traditional date of 753 was made authoritative by the great antiquarian Varro in the late 1st century B.C. Even when the republican historians seem to agree among themselves they are not above suspicion. For instance, the emperor Claudius discovered a king of Rome called Mastarna whom the previous Roman historians had ignored. Rightly or wrongly, he identified Mastarna with Servius Tullius.

The same Mastarna appears in a historical scene painted in an Etruscan tomb at Vulci (variously dated 4th–2nd centuries B.C.) and has something to do with the killing of a "Roman Tarquin." Similarly, Pliny the Elder (*Natural History*, xxxiv, 139) and Tacitus (*Histories*, iii, 72) learned somewhere that Porsena had compelled Rome to surrender. This fact was conveniently ignored by earlier Roman historians.

3. Linguistic Evidence.—The inhabitants of Rome spoke the Indo-European language known as Latin. The evidence for Latin's being spoken in Rome is not earlier than the 6th century B.C., to which belong the Duenos vase and (at least according to some authorities) the *lapis niger* of the Forum with their mysterious inscriptions. It is improbable that Etruscan was at any time the language of the majority of the inhabitants of Rome. As far as is known, laws, treaties, and other official texts were always written in Latin; more particularly, the Twelve Tables composed in the middle of the 5th century were in Latin. But three 6th-century vases with Etruscan words have been found in Rome, one on the Capitol, another on the Palatine, and the third at S. Omobono; the Etruscan influence in the 6th century is thus linguistically confirmed. Even about 400 B.C. the area in which Latin was spoken was narrow: it covered about 50 sq.mi. The Romans had neighbours beyond the Tiber who spoke Etruscan, others in the direction of the Anio who spoke Sabine dialects; Volscan was spoken along the coastal plain between Latium and Campania. Words borrowed from Etruscan are few in the Latin language (almost entirely personal names and technical words). Sabine influences are more conspicuous and perhaps to be found even in domestic terms such as *lupus, bos, scrofa, popina, rufus* ("wolf," "ox," "sow," "cookshop," "red-haired"). Greek words appear early in Latin: the word *poena* ("penalty") was already to be found in the Twelve Tables. Some Greek words—especially names of mythical figures—may have come to Rome through Etruscan (*e.g.*, Hercules, Proserpina) and confirm the part played by the Etruscans as mediators between the Greek and the Roman civilization in the archaic period. (*See also* LATIN LANGUAGE; ETRUSCAN LANGUAGE; ITALIC DIALECTS.)

4. Evidence from Religious Customs.—Evidence from religious ceremonies may reflect the progressive extension of the Roman territory. Since the Luperci in the festival of the Lupercalia (*q.v.*) used to run around the Palatine, this may be evidence for the Palatine's being the earliest settlement called Rome (doubts have been expressed by A. Kirsopp Michels in *Transactions of the American Philological Association*, lxxxiv, pp. 35–59, [1953]; *cf.* however K. Latte, *Römische Religionsgeschichte*, p. 84, note 4 [1960]). Another stage of the urban development may be represented by the festival of the Septimontium, which included the three parts of the Palatine (Cermalus, Palatium, Velia), the Caelius, and the three parts of the Esquiline (Oppius, Cispius, and Fagutal); but here too there are difficulties in the interpretation of the relevant texts (Festus, p. 458; 476). Finally the festival of the Argei (Varro, *De lingua latina*, v, 45) has been taken to represent a further stage in which Rome was divided into four regions but did not yet include the Capitol and the Aventine. What is certain is that the traditional sacred boundary of Rome (the *pomerium*) did not include the Aventine until the times of the emperor Claudius. On the other hand, the religious calendar which was still in use in the age of Caesar provides evidence for the archaic culture of Rome. Its earliest part can be proved to go back to the 6th century B.C.; it does not contain any trace of the cult of Jupiter Capitolinus which was established in 509 B.C.

5. Archaeological Evidence.—There is some archaeological evidence that the Roman hills were inhabited in the second millennium B.C., but so far there is no proof of continuity between these early settlements and the 8th-century villages which can reasonably be taken as the components of early Rome. The archaeological evidence which has a direct bearing on the origins and early development of Rome is conveniently collected in the first three volumes of E. Gjerstad, *Early Rome* (1953–60). The most important facts are summarized here:

a. Tombs on the Esquiline, Forum (Via Sacra), Quirinal, and Palatine provide some essential archaeological data. The tombs on the Esquiline are numerically the most important. They are of the *fossa* (trench) type, and the burial rite seems to have been almost exclusively that of inhumation. They stretch from the 8th to the early 6th century B.C. The tombs on the Via Sacra go from the 8th to the early 6th century; they include both cremation and inhumation, but cremation prevails in the early tombs. On the Quirinal the earliest tombs (8th century) are of the *pozzo* (pit) type for cremation; in the 7th century *fossa*-type tombs for inhumation appear. The most important archaic tomb of the Palatine (discovered in 1954) is a cremation one, apparently of the 8th century.

b. Among the archaic buildings which have been explored the following deserve special mention: (1) remains of huts have been found on the Palatine near the Scalae Caci (late 8th century?) and beneath the atrium of the Domus Augustana (8th–7th century); (2) the Regia building in the Forum has been shown to go back at least to the 6th century (excavations are in progress), and the archaic finds from the area of the Temple of Vesta go back to about 550 B.C. or a little earlier; (3) the sacred area in the Forum Boarium in the region of the present church of S. Omobono contains, among others, two temples forming an architectural unit belonging to the 6th or early 5th century; (4) a votive deposit on the Capitoline Hill includes 6th-century materials; (5) votive deposits on the Quirinal (Church of Sta. Maria della Vittoria, Villino Hüffer) include late 8th-century materials and incidentally produced the Duenos vase which is dated to about 525 B.C.

c. Stratigraphic exploration of the Comitium and of the Forum seem to show that: (1) the Forum began to be occupied by huts in the 7th century; (2) about 575 a market place was laid out—the first real Forum Romanum; (3) the graveling of the open area later occupied by the Comitium was more or less contemporary with the construction of the first pebble floor of the Forum; (4) the votive deposit beneath the sacred place known as the *lapis niger* (so-called tomb of Romulus) goes back to the early 6th century.

d. Archaic architectural terra-cottas found on the Palatine and the Forum, on the Capitoline, and on the Esquiline represent armed horsemen, chariot races, banquet scenes, and gods, and are similar to those found in Veii and Velletri. They certainly belonged to sacred or public buildings and confirm the literary tradition that Etruscan and Greek artists worked in Rome in the late 6th and early 5th centuries.

e. The remains of the city wall traditionally connected with Servius Tullius (the "Grotta Oscura wall") have been proved to belong to the 4th century, but there are remains of earlier fortifications probably belonging to the 5th century.

6. The Development of Early Rome as Understood by Modern Research.—Certain archaeologists have produced revolutionary chronologies of early Rome on the basis of the archaeological evidence. For instance, Gjerstad has maintained that Rome was founded about 575 B.C., when the Roman Forum was laid out, as a unification of earlier villages; and that monarchy ended about 450 B.C. H. Müller Karpe (*Vom Anfang Roms* [1960]) put the origins of Rome in the 10th century and connected them with an emigration from Greek territories. On the other hand the French philologist G. Dumézil has made a bold attempt to relate Roman institutions to primitive Indo-European institutions. Such theories have so far found few supporters. The combination of literary and nonliterary evidence seems to suggest that Rome began to develop in the 8th century as a small community on the Palatine which soon absorbed other communities in neighbouring hills; a fusion of Latins and Sabines is mentioned in the tradition about Romulus. The origin of the name Rome is unknown, and it is not known why the Roman citizens were also called Quirites.

Rome was certainly governed by kings in early times. Later on in the republican period the patrician senator who acted as head of state when both consuls were dead was called *interrex* ("interim king")—a clear survival from the monarchic period. The kings were surrounded by an advisory body of *patres* or senators (first 100, then 300); and the citizens were divided into three tribes (Titii, Ramnes, Luceres) and 30 *curiae*. The 30 *curiae* were the voting units of a popular assembly called *comitia curiata* which—according to the most plausible interpretation of the evidence—conferred power (*imperium*) on the kings and later on the consuls. Kingship does not seem to have been hereditary in Rome.

The senators naturally belonged to wealthy leading groups or *gentes*. Each aristocratic *gens*, comprising one or more families, had its own customs and cults. From early times the senatorial families appear to have monopolized those priestly functions (of pontiffs, *augures, flamines,* and *fetiales*) which were not performed by the king himself. In Rome there was never a priestly caste separated from the ruling aristocracy. The highly respected priestesses of Vesta were also provided by the ruling families. Service in the cavalry distinguished the members of the aristocracy: the numbers of the centuries of knights went up by steps from 3 to 18, perhaps as early as the monarchic period. It is far from certain that a clear-cut distinction between patricians and plebeians existed already during the monarchy. Traditionally, the father in each family (*paterfamilias*) had absolute power of life and death over wife, children, and slaves. Wives were much respected and had considerable freedom of movement, the authority of the husband being counterbalanced to a certain extent by that of the father.

With the possible exception of Romulus, all the kings mentioned by tradition must have existed. Tradition is probably also correct in connecting the capture and destruction of Alba Longa with the name of King Tullus Hostilius. The oldest Roman religious and political ties seem to have been with those other Latin communities which gathered together for festivals at the shrine of Jupiter Latiaris on Monte Cavo and in other sanctuaries. The precise political structure of the early Latin League (or Leagues) is unknown: there may already have been regulations enabling the members of one Latin community to buy, sell, and marry in other Latin communities (what Roman law called *jus commercii et connubii*). The destruction of Alba gave Rome considerable prestige among the Latins, and later Servius Tullius seems to have tried to establish a Latin federal sanctuary in Rome by building a temple of Diana on the Aventine.

Tradition puts the Etruscan king Tarquinius I (or Priscus) about 600 B.C. This is in agreement with the general expansion of the Etruscans to the south in the 6th century when they founded settlements in Campania and established close contact with the Greek colonists of Italy. The profound transformation in the civic centre of Rome about that time is to be connected with this Etruscan influence. As a consequence the successor of Tarquinius I, Servius Tullius (himself apparently not an Etruscan), was able to reorganize the Roman constitution on lines reminiscent of Solon. He created the *comitia centuriata* in which citizens were divided according to their ability to provide themselves with weapons and therefore according to wealth. (*See* also COMITIA: *Comitia Centuriata.*) In this assembly the greatest number of voting units went to the wealthiest section of the infantry. A change in the art of war at this stage must be assumed which increased the importance of the infantry in comparison with the cavalry. It is probable that this change was due to the introduction (perhaps via Etruria) of Greek hoplite tactics. The traditional figures for the Servian classification are, with some variations, as follows (the *centuria* being the voting unit):

18 centuries of knights (*equites*)
80 centuries of the first class (census of 100,000 *asses*)
20 "   "   " second " ("   " 75,000 ")
20 "   "   " third " ("   " 50,000 ")
20 "   "   " fourth " ("   " 25,000 ")
30 "   "   " fifth " ("   " 12,500 ")
 2 centuries of engineers and artisans are ranked with the first class.
 3 centuries of musicians, supernumeraries, and proletarians are below the fifth class.

Not all the details of this scheme can go back to Servius Tullius. The very classification by coinage (*as*) cannot be as early as the 6th century, when Rome did not yet know of coinage. There appears to be no cogent reason for denying, however, that Servius Tullius created the *comitia centuriata*. He is also said to have introduced new local tribes in order to have a better fiscal organiza-

tion and to be able to absorb into citizenship the numerous aliens attracted by the prosperity of Rome. The local tribes were perhaps originally 20 and grew up to 35 (in 241 B.C.). The three tribes of old and the curiate assembly did not disappear: the curiate assembly retained the formal right of conferring *imperium*. But both old tribes and *curiae* slowly ceased to be important.

Tradition seems again to be borne out when it gives an Etruscan successor to Servius Tullius. Tarquinius II is said to have reigned from about 534 to 510 B.C. Indeed it is known that about 535 the competition between Etruscans and Greeks in Latium and Campania became acute. The Etruscans and their Carthaginian allies defeated the Greek Phocaeans at sea off Alalia (Corsica) and controlled the seas near Rome. But about 524 the Etruscans were routed on land by Aristodemus of Cumae. Only a few years later the Cumaeans found themselves in the position of helping the Latins of Aricia—a centre of the Latin League—in a struggle against Etruscan bands. It is not surprising that Tarquinius and his Etruscans lost control of Rome while other Etruscan groups were in retreat both in Campania and Latium. The tradition is almost certainly correct also in presenting Rome as being faced with the hostility of the other Latins after the fall of Tarquinius. The young republic had to fight both against King Porsena of Clusium, who tried to reestablish Etruscan rule at Rome, and against the Latin cities, which wanted freedom. Finally the Etruscan menace was warded off (the details are uncertain), and the Latins were resoundingly defeated at Lake Regillus (about 499 B.C.). By the time the Etruscan king was compelled to leave Rome the territory of the Roman state seems to have extended over about 350 sq.mi. The Temple of Jupiter Capitolinus, which was inaugurated in the first year of the republic, was paradoxically the greatest monument of Etruscan rule in Rome.

Evidence of the prosperity and expansion of the Roman state under the Tarquinians is provided by the first treaty between Rome and Carthage, if the date of 508 B.C. attributed to it by Polybius (iii, 22) is accepted. Roman annalistic tradition, as preserved by Diodorus and Livy, does not know of any treaty between Rome and Carthage before 348 B.C., but much can be said in favour of the Polybian date. The treaty shows that under the kings Rome was in control of Ardea, Antium (Anzio), Circeii, and Terracina, and had been in a position to speak on behalf of all Latium. The treaty seems to have been an attempt of the new revolutionary government to maintain good relations with Carthage—the ally of the Etruscans—and to receive support in its claim over the rest of Latium. The influence of Carthage on Etruscan cities about 500 B.C. seems to be confirmed by inscriptions discovered in the territory of Caere in 1964; they contain dedications by a sovereign of Caere to a Punic goddess in both the Phoenician and the Etruscan languages (*Archeologia Classica*, xvi, pp. 49–117 [1964]).

7. The Young Republic.—*Constitutional Changes.*—As has been shown, the creation of the republic meant that a certain number of families took over the military command, the judicial power, and the priestly functions of the kings. The rape and suicide of Lucretia (*q.v.*) may well have been the occasion for the revolt. The name of Lucius Junius Brutus (*see* BRUTUS) as the head of the successful conspiracy can hardly be a later invention. The *pontifex maximus* (*see* PONTIFEX) was given the palace of the king, the Regia; and an elective magistrate, the so-called *rex sacrorum* or *rex sacrificulus* ("king of sacrifices"), performed the sacrifices for which a *rex* seemed to be necessary (*cf.* the *basileus*, "king" archon in Athens). But the main constitutional reform was the creation of two *praetores* (later known as consuls) to rule the state collegially for one year (*see* PRAETOR). The consuls were elected by the *comitia centuriata* and formally confirmed by the *comitia curiata*. At least as from the second part of the 5th century they were assisted by two *quaestores* who managed the state treasury (*aerarium; see* QUAESTOR). In an emergency one of the two consuls was empowered to appoint a *dictator* who thus became the supreme head of state for not longer than six months. The dictator (or *magister populi*) in his turn appointed a commander of the cavalry (*magister equitum*) as his subordinate. The other magistrates remained in office but obeyed the dictator. The institution of the dictator confirms that the infantry had become

PEOPLES OF ANCIENT ITALY

the strongest part of the Roman army. Indeed it is probable that the original Roman legion of 60 centuries was divided into two legions (each of 60 centuries, but each century reduced to 60 men) when the king was replaced by two consuls. The first dictator was appointed about 500 B.C. Later, about 443, a *censor* (*q.v.*) was introduced whose duty it was to take the census; he was elected in the *comitia centuriata* for a period of not more than 18 months at intervals of four to five years. The position of censor did not imply any military power (*imperium*) but soon commanded great prestige and developed into a general supervision of Roman life; the censor could remove a man from the Senate for misconduct.

The question has been asked whether these Roman institutions imitated preexisting Etruscan, Osco-Umbrian, or Latin institutions. Present knowledge is not sufficient to provide a clear answer to this question. Yearly magistrates were certainly common in Etruscan and other Italian communities, but the details of their powers and functions are uncertain. In many cases the probability of Roman influence on other cities must be reckoned with, rather than vice versa.

Military Decline.—The consequences of the political revolution that had happened in Rome soon became apparent. For perhaps half a century Roman military power declined. The territory shrank. Class struggles became fierce, and the general economic difficulties resulted in few public buildings and temples being built (the Temple of the Castores dedicated in 484 seems to have been the last important one of the early republic). Contacts with the Greek world, either directly or via Etruria, were less frequent throughout the 5th century. The Latin League, though defeated at Lake Regillus, did not return to the previous condition of subordination to Rome. Rome had to be content with a treaty (the so-called *foedus Cassianum*, negotiated by Spurius Cassius *c.* 493 B.C.), according to which Rome and the Latins became allies on equal terms and probably alternated in the command of joint military expeditions. A similar treaty was also concluded with the league of the Hernici. Both treaties were made necessary by the pressure of the Aequi and Volsci (*qq.v.*) and of certain Sabine tribes. The legend of Coriolanus preserves the memory of the attacks of the Volsci on Rome about 490 (*see* CORIOLANUS, GAIUS MARCIUS). The better-founded story of Cincinnatus relates to wars against the Aequi about 458 (*see* CINCINNATUS, LUCIUS

QUINCTIUS). Military colonies established by the Romans (jointly with the Latins) at Signia, Velitrae (Velletri), and Norba were not always able to hold their own against the Volsci; Velitrae at least was captured by them.

Patricians and Plebeians.—Internally the new aristocratic leaders reinforced their ranks by attracting at least one powerful *gens* from abroad: the Sabine *gens Claudia* (*c.* 505 B.C.). But as soon as their power was consolidated they raised a sharp barrier between themselves and the other Romans. All that is known seems to point to the conclusion that a clear distinction between patricians and plebeians first developed in the early 5th century. It resulted in the almost complete exclusion of the plebeians from the magistracies. The plebeians were not equally excluded from the Senate, but the patrician senators, who must have been in the majority, organized themselves into a privileged group and arrogated to themselves the right to ratify the decision of the *comitia* (*auctoritas patrum*, where *patres* = patrician senators).

At the same time the continuous wars and the loss of trade worsened the conditions of the poorest plebeians. The rich patricians who had less opportunity to buy slaves from abroad took advantage of the existing right to enslave the debtors. Other plebeians were reduced to the condition of followers (*clientes*) of the patricians; they gave service and obedience in exchange for protection. Communal land (*ager publicus*) was rented by patricians at a nominal price and annexed to their estates. There is evidence of famines and of import of grain from Sicily.

The rich plebeians who were excluded from power and the poor plebeians who were in danger of enslavement united in the struggle against the patricians. Disorders followed. In 486 Spurius Cassius, one of the most eminent men of the time, was killed when he tried to help the plebeians. After his disappearance there was a period of seven years in which one of the members of the *gens Fabia* was invariably a consul. The virtual control of the state by the Fabii was ended only by the Battle of the Cremera River, in which the Fabii and their clients, waging a war against the Etruscans, met disaster.

The plebeians organized themselves into action against the patricians and resorted to strikes or secessions (the first of which happened in 494). They elected leaders called *tribuni plebis* (*see* TRIBUNE) in an assembly of which the voting units were the local tribes (*concilia* or *comitia plebis*). The *tribuni* were ten in 449 B.C., but had probably been two and then five in earlier years. They were assisted by two *aediles* (*see* AEDILE) who kept the archives of the plebs in the Temple of Ceres on the Aventine. The plebs became a state within the state. The *tribuni* asserted their right to veto any act performed by a regular magistrate (*intercessio*). The plebeians took an oath to uphold their inviolability (*sacrosanctitas*). The patricians were obliged to recognize the existence of the plebeian institutions (*Lex Publilia* of 471). This only made more pressing the plebeian claim that the deliberations in the *concilia plebis* (*plebiscita*) should have legal force. The plebeians also wanted the whole of the laws of the state to be codified in writing in order to break the exclusive patrician knowledge of them.

Many times the "conflict of the orders" seemed near a solution, but in fact it lasted for two centuries. Its most important early stage is represented by the decemviral legislation of 451–450. In 451 the Roman constitution was suspended, and the patricians were entrusted with the preparation of a code of laws. They prepared ten tables of laws, and a new college of *decemviri* (*q.v.*) which included some plebeians was appointed in 450 and prepared two further tables. According to tradition, the last two tables were particularly unfavourable to the plebeians insofar as they codified the prohibition of marriage between patricians and plebeians. The second decemvirate was dominated by Appius Claudius and retained office until Virginia (alleged to have been a plebeian) was killed by her father to save her from Appius Claudius' lust.

The decemviral legislation must have represented an uneasy compromise between patricians and plebeians. The plebeians obtained the codification of the laws and managed to be admitted to the decemvirate, but they had to accept the permanent separation of the orders. It is not known whether the decemvirate was envisaged as a provisional magistracy or as a permanent institution to replace both the consulate and the tribunate. At all events the regime came to a premature end, and the old magistracies were re-established.

Somehow patricians and plebeians had learned to work together, and the lesson was not forgotten. A tribal assembly of the plebeian type but also including the patricians (*comitia tributa*) acquired increasing importance. It was used for routine legislation, for the election of the quaestors and of the officers of the army (*tribuni militum*), and later for other magistrates. In 449 a *Lex Valeria Horatia* seems to have given legal force to the *plebiscita*, but the details are obscure and controversial; and later, in 339 and 287, other laws were passed for the same purpose. Marriage between patricians and plebeians was allowed in 445, and in the same year it was decided that *tribuni militum,* enjoying the authority of consuls, might be elected in certain years from both patricians and plebeians. The details are again very obscure, but the main facts are not in dispute. From 444 to 367 the Romans were led in some years by two consuls, in other years by a variable number (three to six, perhaps even eight or nine) of *tribuni militum*. Plebeians appear among the *tribuni,* but only seldom—much less often than might be expected.

B. ROME, 449–264 B.C.

1. The State of the Sources and Their Reliability for the Period.—Dionysius of Halicarnassus' account is available down to 443, Diodorus' to 302–301. Livy's first decade goes as far as 293. There is also valuable information in Zonaras' epitome of Dio Cassius, in Velleius Paterculus (especially about colonies), Appian, and other sources. The existing fragments of the Twelve Tables represent contemporary evidence for the social structure of Rome, and the consular Fasti (lists of consuls) provide information about the governing class. If present evidence were invariably unambiguous and trustworthy, we should have enough to write a satisfactory history of this period. Unfortunately, neither Livy nor the other literary sources can be taken at face value: a classical example is provided by the conflicting information about the Battle of the Allia in which the Romans were defeated by the Gauls c. 390. The fragments of the Twelve Tables raise more problems than they solve, and even the Fasti, though undoubtedly reliable, are difficult to interpret. It has already been mentioned how difficult it is to interpret satisfactorily the curious fact that in certain years (continuously between 391 and 367) a number of *tribuni militum* replaced the praetors-consuls as heads of the state. Another difficulty is that it is not known how the relations between Rome and the Latin League developed—and more particularly to what extent the most ancient "Latin" colonies can be described as Roman foundations (for one view *see* E. T. Salmon, "Rome and the Latins," *Phoenix,* vii, 93 ff., 123 ff. [1953]). Indeed we have only the vaguest notion of the federal organization of the Latins.

A third obstacle is our ignorance about the structure of private ownership in early Rome. Mommsen's theory that originally collective ownership prevailed did not survive R. von Pöhlmann's trenchant criticisms (*Geschichte der sozialen Fragen und des Sozialismus in der antiken Welt,* ii, 3rd ed., pp. 327 ff. [1925]). This, however, does not dispose of all the difficulties. The *curiae* may have been founded upon some communal ownership. A word like *mancipatio* to indicate transfer of property may imply that sale was originally limited to movable objects which can be seized (*manu capere*). The word *heredium,* "hereditary estate," was used in the Twelve Tables to indicate the orchard, not the fields—which may imply that only the orchard was private property. Yet the balance of the evidence would suggest that even during the monarchy private property was unrestricted. The differentiation between patricians and plebeians can hardly be explained unless there was private ownership of the land. (*See also* ROMAN LAW: *The Law of Property and Possession.*)

2. The Course of Events, 449–366 B.C.—The decemviral laws reduced the tension between patricians and plebeians and reinforced Rome. The Battle of the Algidus Pass (dated June 17 or 18, 431), in which the dictator A. Postumius Tubertus defeated the Aequi, must be accepted as historical. The Volsci and the Aequi

slowly retreated. Colonies settled by the Romans, either alone or jointly with the Latins, garrisoned the reconquered or newly acquired territories. Colonies at Ardea (442), Velitrae (404), and Circeii (393) are reported; and Fidenae was occupied in 425. The steady progress of Rome and its increasing superiority over the Latin allies became evident with the victory of Rome over the Etruscan Veii. Veii had been the traditional rival of Rome; it had supported Fidenae; and the breastplate of Lars Tolumnius, the prince of Veii who had been killed by (consul?) A. Cornelius Cossus in a battle for Fidenae, was still to be seen in the Temple of Jupiter Feretrius in the time of Augustus (Livy, iv, 20). Roman tradition made the siege of Veii a ten-year affair like the siege of Troy, but the name of the Roman dictator who conquered the city in 396, M. Furius Camillus, is authentic. Veii was destroyed. Four new tribes were established in the territory thus annexed (Stellatina, Tromentina, Sabatina, and Arniensis). The occupation of Capena and apparently of Falerii followed. The territory of the Roman state was almost doubled in size. To judge from the scanty evidence, the earlier practice of having joint military expeditions of Rome and the Latin League under the alternate command of Roman and Latin generals was by then obsolete. Pay was introduced for the Roman soldiers.

Irruption of the Gauls.—Neither the Romans nor the Latins appear to have sensed the importance of simultaneous developments in northern and in southern Italy. About 400 B.C. the greater part of the Po Valley was occupied by Celtic tribes which the Romans called Galli (*see* CELT). One of the tribes, the Insubres, established its centre in Mediolanum (Milan), others moved south to find room beyond the Apennines. In the south of Italy the Sabellian peoples pressed forward and steadily reduced the area of Greek and Etruscan influence. Capua and Cumae had fallen into their hands by about 420 (dates uncertain). On the Tyrrhenian (west) coast north of the Laus River only Naples (Neapolis) and Elea (Velia) remained Greek. Other tribes of the same Sabellian group, the Lucanians (*see* LUCANIA), were helped by Dionysius I of Syracuse to defeat a league of Greek cities of southern Italy, while still other Sabellians (known as Samnites; *q.v.*) spread their power south and west of Latium. These changes ultimately affected the whole Italian peninsula. They meant the superimposition of more primitive tribal organizations on the city-states of Etruria and Magna Graecia, though the superior civilization of the conquered nations slowly imprinted itself on the conquerors.

About 390 (the conventional date) a horde of Celtic Senones (*q.v.*) marched through Etruria and tried to occupy Clusium; then (tradition does not convincingly state the reasons) it proceeded toward Rome. Near the little stream of Allia—either on the right bank of the Tiber, as Diodorus says, or more probably on the left bank—the Roman legions were wiped out. Once the army was defeated, the city walls, if they existed at all, were not strong enough to prevent occupation. The event was registered also by Greek historians. Roman tradition is almost unanimous in maintaining that the Capitol was never occupied by the Gauls, but there is a faint voice of dissent in the poet Silius Italicus (O. Skutsch, "The Fall of the Capitol," *Journal of Roman Studies,* xliii, pp. 77–78 [1953]).

External Relations.—The Gauls had come to plunder rather than to stay, and they left after having exacted ransom. The Romans, under the leadership of Camillus, reorganized their army, rebuilt the city, and built the wall which later generations thought to be Servius Tullius' work. The Etruscan Caere distinguished itself by its readiness to support the rebuilding of Rome. It has been suggested that in 386 Rome and Caere entered into some agreement which enabled the citizens of Caere to become Roman citizens and vice versa (M. Sordi, *I rapporti romano-ceriti* [1960]).

There are other signs that Rome entered into closer relations with Etruscan cities and with Carthage. Without the collaboration of their fleets it is difficult to see how Rome could even have attempted to establish what turned out to be unsuccessful settlements in Sardinia and Corsica (Diodorus, xv, 27, 4; Theophrastus, *Historia Plantarum,* v, 8, 2). Furthermore it is known from Livy (ix, 36) that in the 4th century young Roman aristocrats were sent to Caere to complete their education and to learn Etruscan. The friendship with Carthage, which probably goes back to the beginning of the republic, remained a constant element of Roman policy until about 270, even when the relations between Rome and the Etruscan cities (traditionally the friends of Carthage against the Greeks) took a turn for the worse.

The Greek Massilia (Marseilles) also showed interest in the recovery of Rome. It is not known when Rome and Massilia first became friends. The picture of the early relations between the two cities is not clear (if it were, we should be in a better position to understand the early penetration of Greek art and religion into Rome). But when Camillus occupied Veii, Rome placed a golden bowl in the treasury of the Massiliotes at Delphi as an offering to Apollo. Tradition adds that Massilia helped Rome to pay the ransom to the Gauls.

All these friendships, however, did not compensate for the serious deterioration in relations between Rome and its immediate Latin neighbours. Restoration of Roman hegemony in Latium was the main concern of the Romans in the 30 years after the sack of Rome. Even if Polybius is not strictly correct when he says (ii, 18, 6) that in these 30 years the Gauls refrained from attacking Rome, the Romans were not seriously troubled by them. They reestablished their supremacy in Latium by a system of Latin colonies: Satricum (?) in 385; Sutrium and Nepete, 383; Setia, 382. The new Latin colonies were made up of Roman citizens who were prepared to forfeit their citizenship in return for land in the new settlements. The settlers must have been proletarians and, as such, not liable to ordinary military service in the Roman army. In 381 Tusculum seems to have received Roman citizenship. In 358 both Hernici and Latins were compelled to renew their old alliance with Rome. The new treaty changed the terms of Spurius Cassius' treaty on some points. Antium was deprived of part of its territory which was turned into two tribes (Pomptina and Poblilia).

Patricians and Plebeians.—The need to put the Roman state in order after the Gallic disaster must also have influenced the relations between patricians and plebeians. The plebeians pressed their claims and found supporters among the patricians. One of their champions was Marcus Manlius Capitolinus, who organized an unsuccessful *coup d'état* about 385. After years of struggle Camillus, who had been elected dictator for the fifth time in 367, was compelled to accept the main plebeian requests. *Concordia* became the watchword of the new political situation. According to the proposals of the tribunes of the plebs Gaius Licinius and L. Sextius, two consuls or praetors were again to be the regular supreme magistrates each year, and one of them was to be a plebeian. Furthermore a limit was put on the amount of public land to be held by any individual; tradition mentions 500 *iugera* (300 ac.) as the maximum, but this probably reflects a later situation. The conditions of debtors were improved. At the same time new magistrates were created. The two praetors or consuls were given a *minor collega*, called praetor like themselves, who was made chiefly responsible for civil jurisdiction, though he could also command an army. The third praetor was below his colleagues (*minor*) in so far as they could veto his decisions. Ultimately the name praetor was confined to him, and consul became the exclusive name for the supreme magistrate. Two "curule aediles" were created to collaborate with the "plebeian aediles" in the supervision of streets, markets, public works, games, etc. Patricians and plebeians alternated annually as curule aediles, while the plebeian aediles remained plebeian. The third praetorship was not open to the plebeians until 337. There was a plebeian dictator in 356 and a plebeian censor in 351. The legislation of 367–366, however, was not accepted without further resistance, as shown by the fact that the election of a plebeian to the consulship became regular only from 320. The mysterious *Leges Genuciae* of 342 and the *Leges Publiliae* of 339 seem to have further advanced the pacification of the two orders. One of the *Leges Publiliae* apparently abolished, or reduced to a formality, the consent of the patrician senators (*auctoritas patrum*) to the deliberations of the *comitia centuriata*. Another *Lex Publilia* reinforced the validity of the *plebiscita* as binding on both orders.

3. Military Expansion and Internal Consolidation, 366–338 B.C.

—Internal concord did not come too soon. In 359 Tarquinii declared war against Rome and was followed by Falerii and Caere. The Volsci and the Hernici too attacked Rome, and the Gauls reappeared in strength. Rome had to turn to the Samnites for help and fought for life. The Etruscans were quickly defeated. In a complex settlement Caere agreed to a 100-year truce and apparently was incorporated in the Roman state as a *civitas sine suffragio* (353), which meant that the citizens of Caere became citizens of Rome without being allowed to vote in the *comitia*. This new type of half-citizenship was later used by the Romans when they wished to extend their territory without increasing the size of their political assemblies. In 351 Tarquinii and Falerii agreed to a 40-year truce. The Gauls were at length compelled to cease their attacks, and the Carthaginians, with whom a new treaty was signed in 348, helped to ward off Greek privateers from the shores of Latium.

What happened next is most obscure. The Samnites unexpectedly appear as enemies of Rome in a war that lasted from 343 to 341. The reality of this war can hardly be denied, notwithstanding Diodorus' silence. Livy suggests that Rome fought the Samnites in order to defend the Campanians. Then there was a reversal of alliances in 341. Latins, Volscians, Sidicini, and Campanians turned against Samnites and Romans. Romans and Samnites defeated their enemies at Trifanum near Suessa Aurunca. The Campanians made a separate peace (340). Apparently, their aristocracy (the "knights") had been pro-Roman during the war and now received Roman citizenship as a reward; the details are controversial. Two years later the son of the great Camillus, L. Furius, and his colleague Gaius Maenius ended the war by resounding victories over Volscians and Latins. Antium was occupied and a Roman colony placed in it to guard the port. The Latin League was dissolved, though the ancient common worship on the Alban Mount continued.

The individual Latin cities were variously treated. Tusculum, which had rebelled, Lanuvium, Aricia, Nomentum, and Pedum were granted full citizenship. Their city administration was reformed and represented perhaps the beginnings of the Roman municipal system. Seven Latin colonies (Sutrium, Nepete, Norba, Ardea, Signia, Setia, Circeii) and other places (Praeneste, Tibur, Laurentum) remained allies, but Praeneste and Tibur lost some territory. According to one of the possible interpretations of Livy, viii, 14, the rest of the Latins were left free but were forbidden to have special ties of trade (*commercium*) and intermarriage (*connubium*) with each other, though not with the Romans. Velitrae was singled out for severe treatment. The anti-Roman leaders were driven out and their lands distributed among Romans. Two new tribes (Maecia and Scaptia) were created on conquered territory (332). The people of Fundi, Formiae, Capua, Cumae, and Suessula were granted *civitas sine suffragio* and preserved a considerable amount of autonomy. The Romans made useful investments in Campania, and the two aristocracies frequently intermarried. Campanian art, and especially Campanian popular comedies, reached Rome.

Roman Society.—This was the period in which Roman society began to take the shape that was to remain characteristic until the time of the Gracchi. It was a society in which a mixed aristocracy of patricians and plebeians controlled the state by filling the magistracies and the seats of the Senate (300 life members). The senators, though chosen by the censors, were by now increasingly former magistrates. Conflicts between Senate and magistrates were reduced to a minimum by the common background, and the collective experience of the senators was bound to have an overwhelming influence on the conduct of state affairs. The tribunes of the plebs and the plebeian aediles were recognized as *de facto* magistrates and were chosen from the upper strata of the plebs. Families which could boast of a consul were the *nobiles*. Senators who had no senator among their ancestors were *homines novi*, "new men"; they were always few. Intermarriages and political alliances counterbalanced the natural rivalries between aristocratic families.

Land was the basis of wealth, but we must beware of transferring to earlier times the picture of Roman agriculture contained in Cato's *De agri cultura* (2nd century B.C.). Trade was actually discouraged in senatorial families, but it was not difficult for them to trade through agents. Slaves, no doubt, existed both on the country estates and in the city houses of the rich. A tax on manumissions was introduced in 357. A vast amount of land, mainly taken from enemies, had become the property of the Roman state (*ager publicus*) and was rented by private citizens; members of the aristocracy were naturally in the best position to rent large portions. Membership of the rural tribes, which increased from 16 to 31 in number between 509 and 241, was restricted to landholders. Proletarians and freedmen (the latter even if landholders) were confined to the four urban tribes. An attempt by the patrician senator Appius Claudius to open the rural tribes to proletarians and freedmen was successful in 312 but defeated in 304. Thus landed gentry kept control of the *comitia tributa* and of the *concilia* (*comitia*) *plebis* where the tribes were the voting units. After 304 removal from a rural to an urban tribe became a punishment.

The relations between the poor and the wealthy were dictated by the obligations of clientship. These obligations were particularly strict in the case of freedmen. The laws affecting debtors were severe, even cruel. Information about rates of interest is uncertain (*cf.* Tacitus, *Annals*, vi, 16), but usury was practised. The Twelve Tables recognized the position of debtors as *nexi* or bondsmen of the creditors; but the *nexum* was abolished by a *Lex Poetilia* in 326. On the other hand the upper class took its obligations toward the state (and its own clients) seriously and developed an ethical code of its own.

The traditions of the leading families (*mos maiorum*) counted for much and were closely connected with the notions of authority, gravity, valour (*virtus*), dignity, glory, trust (*fides*). *Otium* (literally "leisure"), including intellectual activities, was opposed to *negotium*, public service. Some of these abstract notions, such as *fides, concordia, bona mens,* were worshiped as goddesses as early as the 4th and 3rd centuries B.C. Aristocratic families displayed the images and the list of magistracies of their ancestors in the halls of their houses, and any funeral was the occasion for an elaborate display of ancestral glories. The ceremony of the triumph for victorious generals was deemed to be the highest honour and had religious overtones. Pride in family connections contributed to the importance of married women. The Roman *matronae* were proud both of their own ancestry and of their husbands' positions. Their code of behaviour was strict, but they moved about in relative freedom. A married daughter could, according to the form of her marriage, either remain under the power (*manus*) of her father or pass into the power of her husband. Sons remained in the power of their father as long as the father was alive, and this power included the right to kill and to sell. (*See* further ROMAN LAW: *The Law of Persons.*)

The majority of the rules of the Twelve Tables remained in force. The original bronze had probably disappeared when the Gauls burned Rome about 390. But their text was known and studied at school as late as Cicero's day; only fragments of it have survived. The code as a whole was of a secular character and well suited to a community of peasant proprietors with little commerce and writing. It presupposed a patriarchal family in which the *paterfamilias* made a testament and manumitted slaves. It forbade the trial of citizens on a capital charge by any assembly or tribunal other than the *comitia centuriata*. The nature and limits of the jurisdiction of the *comitia centuriata* are, however, a doubtful matter. It has been suggested that in the relatively primitive conditions of the 5th century ordinary murders were left to private vengeance, and only political crimes were tried by the *comitia* (see W. Kunkel, *Untersuchungen zur Entwicklung des römischen Kriminalverfahrens* [1962]).

Religion.—The religion of the aristocratic upper class gradually shifted from agrarian and family cults to a centralized worship of state gods. Old cult associations, such as the *sodales Titii* or even the *Fratres Arvales* (*see* ARVAL BROTHERS), lost their importance and were not revived until the time of Augustus. But the cult of the Capitoline triad (Jupiter, Juno, and Minerva) and that of Vesta became central. Mars was made the chief military god, indeed the father of the founder Romulus. Some old Roman cults were hellenized (as is probably the case with the goddess Ceres), and the cult of Apollo was imported from Greece. State cults are never conspicuous for mythology, and the Roman cults were very poor in myths. The colleges of the pontiffs, augurs, *fetiales,* and Vestal Virgins became more important than the archaic priests called *flamines* and the *rex sacrorum*. The priestly colleges were in practice reserved for the aristocracy even when they were thrown open to the plebeians in 300 (*Lex Ogulnia*). In the 4th century a new body of ten men (*decemviri sacris faciundis*) took charge of the consultation of Sibylline oracles and other ceremonies, mainly of Greek origin. (*See* also ROMAN RELIGION.)

Army.—The Roman army excluded the proletarians from the legions but was ready to use allies as auxiliaries. Indeed the policy of the Romans toward the conquered nations was increasingly determined by the desire to use them as allies in future wars. In the 4th century the ordinary Roman levy included four legions of about 4,000 men each. Each legion was now divided into 30 *manipuli* disposed in three lines, *hastati, principes,* and *triarii,* supported by lightly armed soldiers (*velites*) and 300 knights. Mass tactics, of the type which was common to Greeks and Etruscans, were replaced by more mobile and elastic maneuvering—to which the example of the Samnites may have contributed something.

Altogether Roman society reached a considerable degree of stability and self-confidence. Stability had been obtained by a skilful and imaginative exploitation of military victories, with their opportunities for colonization, individual distribution of land, booty; it depended on constant warfare for its further preservation. Self-confidence was reflected in the readiness to extend Roman citizenship and in other remarkable developments of juridical thought. The creation of the praetor was the starting point for progressively bold interpretations and modifications of existing legal practices. The praetor was advised by a committee of legal experts (*jurisconsulti*) who slowly replaced the pontiffs as authorized interpreters of the law.

4. The Samnite Wars.—Such, in broad outline, was the Roman society which now found itself involved in new wars as a result of the expansion in the south. Naples was compelled to become an ally of Rome in 326 during a war between Naples and Capua. Latin colonies were placed at Cales and Fregellae, a Roman colony was settled at Tarracina (Anxur); alliances were concluded with Fabrateria and Frusino, and *civitas sine suffragio* was granted to Acerrae and to the conquered and half-destroyed Privernum. At least some of these events combined to persuade the Samnites to start a war against the Romans in 326. The Romans allied themselves with the Apulians. Details of the ensuing struggles are uncertain. But at the Battle of the Caudine Forks near Beneventum a Roman army surrendered and admitted defeat by passing under a "yoke" of spears (321). Peace was made and perhaps kept for some years (though tradition says otherwise). Rome took advantage of the interval to consolidate its badly shaken rule in Campania. *Praefecti* (*see* PREFECT) were sent to Capua and Cumae in 318. Two new tribes (Falerna and Oufentina) were created, one on land north of Capua, the other on land taken from Privernum.

Hostilities with the Samnites apparently were not resumed till 316. The following year the dictator Q. Fabius Rullianus suffered defeat at Lautulae near Tarracina. But in 314 the Romans won a victory at Tarracina which stopped the rebellion of Capua and restored Roman prestige. A Latin colony was planted at Luceria. Swiftly the system of Roman alliances and colonies was reinforced and extended. Other Latin colonies were planted at Suessa Aurunca, in the island of Pontia, at Saticula, and at Interamna. Calatia and Nola were captured and made allies. The first of the great Roman roads, the Via Appia, joined Rome with Capua; and a modest fleet was put under the control of two newly created magistrates, the *duoviri navales* (311).

By the time many of the Etruscan cities finally decided to throw in their lot with the Samnites against the Romans in 310, the Romans were in a position to retaliate effectively. The consul Q. Fabius Rullianus brought his soldiers into the heart of Etruria through the Monti Cimini. Cortona, Perusia, and Arretium made treaties with Rome. Volsinii was conquered, and Tarquinii was compelled into another 40-year alliance (308). But the Aequi, Marsi, and Paeligni became actively hostile. The Samnites attacked again in 307, and the Hernici rebelled in 306. Anagnia, the chief city of the Hernici, was taken by the Romans and incorporated as *civitas sine suffragio.* So was Frusino, after having been deprived of part of its territory. Then the Romans crushed Marsi, Aequi, and Paeligni. In 304 the Samnites concluded a peace which left them free within their frontiers. Latin colonies were planted at Alba Fucens, Carsioli, and Sora to control Aequi, Paeligni, and Hernici. Arpinum and Trebula were given half-citizenship.

Colonization.—While the enemies of Rome had clearly been unable to coordinate their efforts, Rome was remarkably consistent in its methods of fighting and ruling. Citizen colonies were rare before the First Punic War: Ostia (perhaps a settlement of the monarchic period which was reinforced after 350), Antium (338), Tarracina (329), Minturnae (295), Sinuessa (295), Castrum Novum (c. 289?), Sena Gallica (about 283), and possibly Pyrgi. They were all small (the standard figure is 300 colonists, each of whom was given two *iugera* of land) and placed by the sea in order to safeguard the coast against attack—perhaps more effectively than a permanent fleet. The colonists were men liable to military service who were given a special discharge to fulfil their duties as colonists. The Latin colonies were normally inland (in this period Circeii, 393; Paestum and Cosa, 273; Ariminum, 268, are the exceptions); they blocked the routes to and from enemy territories. The assignation of land to the Latin colonists was generous, and Latin allies as well as Roman proletarians were eligible. Rome was on the way to becoming not only the most important power of Italy but also the most civilized and best organized.

The Greeks of Italy were declining. Various attempts to inject new blood into them (expedition of Archidamus of Sparta c. 338, of Alexander the Molossian c. 330, of Cleonymus of Sparta in 303) were of little avail. The more serious effort by Agathocles to establish a strong Greek state with its centre in Syracuse came to an end with his death in 289. Livy mentions a treaty between Carthage and Rome in 306 which may have given a free hand to the Romans in the peninsula and to the Carthaginians in Sicily. About 303 the Romans formed an alliance with the Lucanians which perhaps contributed to Cleonymus' departure from Italy.

Rome was consolidating its progress (Latin colony at Narnia near the Umbrians in 299; creation of the new tribes Aniensis and Teretina in the same year) when a new Gallic invasion provided its enemies with an unexpected opportunity. Samnites and Etruscans officially or unofficially became the allies of the Gauls, and the Umbrians and the Sabines also took part in the struggle against Rome. The Romans answered by ruthlessly destroying and occupying the Samnite villages. Then in 295 they routed a joint army of Gauls and Samnites at Sentinum in Umbria. One of the consuls, P. Decius Mus, ritually sacrificed himself (*devotio*) for the victory of his country—not the first of his family to do so.

The war continued. Though there were further serious setbacks for the Romans, Rome was no longer in danger. In 291 the Romans planted a large Latin colony at Venusia in Apulia. The war was ended by Manius Curius Dentatus in 290. The Samnites renewed their old alliance with the Romans and remained independent for a while. The whole Sabine territory was annexed to the Roman state. There was a large confiscation of land for the benefit of Roman citizens; the Sabines who survived were given *civitas sine suffragio* which was transformed into full citizenship in 268. A Latin colony was planted at Hadria.

Coinage.—In 289 the triumvirs of the mint were created. This is the first certain evidence for the existence of coinage in Rome and may be connected with the introduction of the *aes signatum,* rectangular bronze bars, bearing types on each side, of fairly constant weight. The so-called *aes grave,* cast bronze coins, is perhaps contemporary, but its chronology is doubtful. Very soon Rome's involvement in the Pyrrhic War led to the production of two silver issues (signed ROMANO) suitable for use in southern Italy. Roman silver coinage proper started in 269 and introduced bimetallism into the Roman economy (cf. R. Thomsen, *Early Roman Coinage,* i–iii [1957–61]).

Social Developments.—Great political leaders emerged in this period of reform. Almost all of them—whether they came from the patriciate or the plebs—tried to reduce the powers of the patricians and of the Senate and to improve the lot of the poorer citizens. Q. Publilius Philo, four times consul (first in 339), was the propounder of the *Leges Publiliae.* Appius Claudius Caecus, the censor of 312, who tried to eliminate the aristocratic control of the rural tribes, was also the enterprising builder of the great road and of the aqueduct which preserves his name. Manius Curius Dentatus was behind the conquest and colonization of the Sabine territory. A client of Appius Claudius, Gnaeus Flavius, a freedman's son, became a curule aedile in 304 and worked to spread the knowledge of legal formalities among ordinary citizens.

There was by now a large zone of agreement between the patricians and the plebeian upper class. Yet the right of any Roman to be judged by the *comitia centuriata* on capital charges (*provocatio*) and the complete parity of the *plebiscita* with the *leges* remained vital issues for all the plebeians. It would indeed have been impossible for the wealthy plebeians to make a stand against the poorer plebeians on such issues. About 286 the plebs organized its last secession and finally obtained full legal status for its *plebiscita* (*Lex Hortensia*).

The aristocrats of both orders, however (now reinforced by the aristocrats of the Latin cities and of Campania), were agreed in preferring indirect control of conquered enemies to occupation of enemy territory. The poorer peasants, on the other hand, were more interested in conquests which would result in their obtaining land. For that reason they favoured expansion toward the north. Their land hunger was an important factor in that development. New attacks of the Gauls made such expansion imperative. In 284 the Senones defeated the Romans near Arretium and provoked new unrest among Etruscans, Samnites, and Lucanians. The Romans marched into the *ager Gallicus.* A Roman colony was planted in Sena above Ancona. In 283 the consul P. Cornelius Dolabella routed Galli, Boii, and Etruscans near Lake Vadimo, south of Volsinii, a victory which was repeated in the following year. Rome made peace with the Gauls on easy terms and strengthened its influence in Etruria by giving support to the local aristocracies (for instance of Arretium) against the lower classes.

5. Pyrrhus and the Roman Unification of Central and Southern Italy.—In 282 the Romans helped Thurii against the Lucanians and offended the Tarentines by sending their ships into the waters of Tarentum despite old agreements to the contrary. The Tarentines had been suspicious of Rome since the days of Cleonymus. Now they asked for the help of Pyrrhus (*q.v.*), king of Epirus. Pyrrhus' expedition (25,000 soldiers and 20 elephants) was in line with previous attempts by Greek chieftains to seek in Italy the power they were unable to obtain in Greece. But his forces were greater, and his enemy, Rome, was in a different class from the southern tribes met by his predecessors. The Roman legions, confronted with the Macedonian phalanx and with ele-

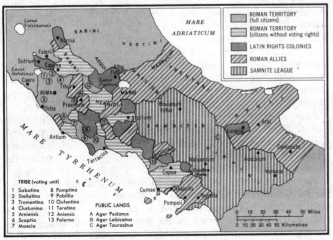

CENTRAL ITALY, ABOUT 300 B.C.

phants, were defeated twice, at Heraclea (280), and, less seriously, at Ausculum (279).

Yet offers of peace by Pyrrhus were refused. Appius Claudius was the leader of the war party. As long as the allies remained faithful to the Romans, time was working in their favour. Their manpower was far greater than that of Pyrrhus. Shortage of men and money soon persuaded Pyrrhus to proceed to Sicily, where the Greeks needed help. This move inevitably reinforced the old friendship between Rome and Carthage. Rome, if somewhat reluctantly, entered into an alliance with Carthage and used Carthaginian ships to transport soldiers. When Pyrrhus came back from Sicily, where he had achieved nothing, he found Rome stronger and his own allies weaker. In 275 he was beaten by the Romans at Malventum (Maluentum; later Beneventum) and conceded defeat by sailing back to Greece. The garrison he left at Tarentum surrendered in 272.

Consequences of Victory.—This victory was the occasion for the reorganization and consolidation of Roman rule in central and southern Italy. The Samnite League was broken up. A Latin colony was settled at Beneventum. The Lucanians were deprived of Paestum, where a Latin colony was planted. A Roman garrison was placed in Tarentum. The allies, old and new, were required to provide either soldiers or ships; and there were confiscations of land even outside the territories used for settling colonies. In Etruria a Latin colony was established at Cosa. When the serfs of the Etruscan Volsinii rebelled about 264, their masters called in Roman help. Rome destroyed the city and resettled the Volsinian aristocrats in a new place (perhaps Orvieto). Thus the Romans demonstrated again that they were prepared to protect the upper classes, at a price.

In 268 a Latin colony was sent to Ariminum in the *ager Gallicus*, and special privileges were granted to the settlers which became the basis of the so-called *jus Ariminensium* (A. Bernardi, *Studia Ghisleriana*, i, pp. 237–259 [1948]). In the same year the greater part of the Picentes, after a rebellion, was incorporated in the Roman state with *civitas sine suffragio*, and a Latin colony was settled among them at Firmum (264). Rome now had five colonies on the Adriatic coast.

The victory over Pyrrhus made a great impression on the Hellenistic world. The Ptolemaic government of Egypt (not to speak of the city of Apollonia in Illyria) sought friendly relations with Rome. As the *Alexandra* by Lycophron shows (it was probably written about 270, but the date is controversial), the Greeks realized that a new great state was rising in the west. About 264 the historian Timaeus wrote a special book on the war between Rome and Pyrrhus. Even the poet Callimachus had something to say about Roman virtues.

The Confederacy.—In terms of manpower and military organization the Roman confederation was formidable. It extended from Ariminum and Pisa to the Strait of Messina. Its core was the Roman *Res publica* which included (*a*) full citizens enrolled in the tribes, (*b*) half-citizens or *cives sine suffragio*. Full citizens lived either in Rome or in *municipia* and *coloniae*. Both *municipia* and *coloniae* eventually achieved a form of self-government with annual magistrates. The half-citizens normally enjoyed rights of trade and marriage with the full citizens but were neither electors in Rome nor eligible for Roman magistracies. They had local self-government, when not deprived of it as a punishment. Half-citizenship gradually came to be considered a transitional stage toward full citizenship.

Outside the Roman state proper, there were the allies (*socii*) who were divided into two main groups. (*a*) The Latin allies gave their quota to the Roman army and could become Roman citizens by migrating to Rome. They had rights of intermarriage and trade with the Romans, but initially not among themselves. About 264 far the greater part of the Latin allies was concentrated in the Latin colonies; probably the majority of their citizens were either former Roman citizens who had given up their citizenship to become colonists, or their descendants. (*b*) The other allies (*civitates liberae*) were tied to Rome by more or less favourable treaties. They had to provide a fixed maximum of soldiers, commanded by Roman officers, or a fixed number of ships. They were

allowed considerable autonomy in internal affairs and did not pay direct taxes to Rome. Unification of coinage, measures, and language developed slowly and apparently without much compulsion. The religious laws of Iguvium, some of which may have been written as late as the beginning of the 1st century B.C., are in the Umbrian language (*see* IGUVINE TABLES). Etruscan was still written (and spoken) at the end of the 1st century B.C.

Not all the territory controlled by the Romans was made up of cities. The tribal system remained important both in the north and in the south, in fact almost everywhere outside Latium, Etruria, Campania, and the coastal strip of Greek colonies. But directly or indirectly the Roman hegemony resulted in an increase in urban centres—not only *municipia* and *coloniae*, but marketplaces (*fora, conciliabula*). The Roman confederation included about 50,000 sq.mi., 10,000 of which were Roman territory and 5,000 Latin cities. The adult male Roman citizens (if that is the meaning of the formula *qui arma ferre possunt*, "those capable of bearing arms") numbered roughly 292,000 in 264. According to the famous list reported by Polybius (ii, 24; *cf.* F. W. Walbank, *A Historical Commentary on Polybius*, pp. 196 ff. [1957] for the difficulties of the text), in 225 the allies were required to provide Rome with a maximum of about 375,000 soldiers (and the *formula* did not include Italian Greeks and Bruttians).

The Roman system of ruling Italy was unusual in the ancient world in that it was not founded upon tributes or enslavement and was not justified in terms of racial or religious beliefs. It was basically a system of military obligations. The greater part of Italy was committed to participation whenever Rome had to defend itself or chose to attack. With a military force of that magnitude, the Romans were in a position to proceed indefinitely with their conquests, the more so because the Roman proletarians wanted land. They were an aggressive power, and Sicily became the next theatre for their ambitions. This ultimately led to the destruction of Carthage and to the extension of Roman military activities to Spain, to the Balkan Peninsula, and to Asia Minor. The roots of Roman imperialism are in the organization of the Italian Confederacy. (A. D. Mo.)

C. ROME AND THE MEDITERRANEAN STATES, 264–133 B.C.

1. Rome and the West, 264–201 B.C.—Before the 3rd century B.C., as before the first half of the 19th century A.D., Italy was "only a geographical expression"; the succeeding years in both periods witnessed the rapid growth of a united nation. The full development of the Italian Confederacy and the expulsion of Pyrrhus from Italy had demonstrated to the more civilized peoples of the Mediterranean world that a new power had arisen which would probably become involved in their affairs before much time had passed.

In particular the Greeks in the West, together with the Carthaginians who dominated the western end of the Mediterranean, soon became conscious of this fact. As early as 273 Ptolemy II of Egypt had established diplomatic relations and perhaps formal friendship (*amicitia;* not a treaty, a *foedus*) with Rome, the head of this powerful military and imperial state that was emerging. By the 4th century Greek writers, as Theopompus, Aristotle, and Theophrastus, knew of Rome's existence. Although Hieronymus of Cardia may have been the first Greek to sketch lightly the early history of Rome, Timaeus (who died after 264 B.C.) has rightly been called "the first historian of Rome"; he is the first known Greek writer to have appreciated the significance of Rome's rise to power.

First Punic War.—Carthage had long enjoyed treaties with Rome; the earliest known, which probably dated from the first year of the Roman republic as Polybius believed (508/507 by his reckoning), may well have renewed previously contacts made with Etruscan Rome.

Such agreements to limit the spheres of interest of the two parties would readily be renewed by Rome, which in the 5th and 4th centuries had no great interest in what went on outside Italy and had no objection to the merchants of Carthage dominating the western Mediterranean. But when Rome enrolled some of the Greek cities of south Italy as "naval allies," a new situation was created, since these cities had trading interests such as the farmers of Latium had not enjoyed. Further, the Greek cities in Sicily, especially Syracuse, were being hard pressed by the Carthaginians in the west and centre of the island, while the Syracusans under King Hieron II were also challenged by some Italian mercenaries, who had seized Messana (Messina) c. 288 and were plundering northeastern Sicily. When these men, who called themselves Mamertines, were threatened by Hieron, the Carthaginians were unwilling to see Messana and control of the Sicilian Straits fall into his hands; they therefore put a Punic garrison into the town. The Mamertines, however, had appealed for help to the Romans, who themselves happened recently (270) to have expelled some other mercenaries from Rhegium (Reggio) in the toe of Italy.

Thus Rome and Carthage were brought face to face across the straits, and a crisis was precipitated by the appeal by Messana. Although some senators hesitated, the Roman people decided to accept the alliance, which would mean war with Carthage. Probably neither side deliberately planned war, but each was eager to deny to the other control of the straits. Yet if war had been avoided at this point, it would probably have come some time. Rome and Carthage were so different in race, culture, and religion, with different moral and material interests, that they would tend toward a clash when once the minor states lying between them had been either eliminated or assimilated. A balance of power, such as the Hellenistic monarchies in the east, with longer diplomatic experience and a common culture, tried to maintain, was more difficult to achieve in the west.

The military history of the war that followed (264–241) is treated in the article PUNIC WARS. Here it is sufficient to note that when the Romans, with Hieron, had occupied eastern Sicily and captured Agrigentum, they were faced with a decision that fundamentally affected their future history. If they decided to try to drive the Carthaginians completely out of Sicily, they would have to smash the Punic navy, and since they had virtually no ships of their own, they would have to build a fleet. However, they were practical as well as determined, and before long they had over 100 ships ready; even more surprising was the success that attended this fleet when it first went into action off Mylae (Milazzo) and defeated an enemy who had centuries of seafaring experience behind him (260).

After this victory the Romans in 256 boldly sent an expeditionary force to Africa to attack Carthage itself, but this daring adventure under Regulus ended in failure. The war dragged on in Sicily, where the Carthaginians were gradually confined to their western fortresses of Drepana (Trapani) and Lilybaeum (Marsala); when their fleet was finally defeated off the Aegadian (Aegates) Islands in 241, they capitulated. By the terms of the settlement they agreed to evacuate Sicily as well as to pay Rome an indemnity, but they remained an independent power.

The discipline of the citizen-militia of Rome, supported by the loyalty of the allies, had defeated an enemy whose armies consisted largely of mercenaries and subject peoples, officered by Carthaginians whom the home government sometimes regarded with suspicion. The struggle was, in the view of the historian Polybius, "the longest, most continuous and most severely contested war known to us in history."

First Two Roman Provinces.—The Romans thus found that they had Sicily on their hands. While leaving Hieron in control of his kingdom in the east end of the island, they made the rest into a *provincia,* which strictly meant the sphere in which a magistrate exercised his *imperium.* At first the administration was entrusted to a quaestor, but from c. 227 B.C., when the number of praetors was raised to four, a praetor was sent out each year as the governor to administer the island, which had to pay an annual tax to Rome in the form of a tithe on harvested crops. Thus when they acquired their first overseas province the Romans did not build up the nucleus of a new civil service: they used existing magistrates as administrators and farmed out the right to collect the taxes to the highest bidder in the province.

Meanwhile Carthage had crushed a desperate revolt of mercenaries in Africa in a struggle known as the Truceless War, but some others in Sardinia asked Rome for help. At first this was refused (239), but in the following year Rome decided to intervene and seized Sardinia; in reply to Carthaginian protests Rome threatened to renew the war, and so Carthage accepted the loss of the island. This unprincipled act embittered relations between the two powers just when they appeared to be improving. Rome's motive seems to have sprung from a passing fit of apprehension that if Sardinia remained in Punic control it might provide a base for an attack upon Italy if the Carthaginians ever turned to a war of revenge. In the event, such a war was made much more probable by Rome's aggressive folly. It took the Romans a few years to gain control of the mountainous interior, but in 227 Sardinia, together with the island of Corsica, was constituted as Rome's second province.

Expansion into Cisalpine Gaul.—But more serious trouble flared up nearer home. In 236 the northern frontier of Italy had been threatened by Gallic tribes, and ten years later a crisis arose when the Boii swept down into Italy and reached Etruria. Men remembered how Gallic tribes had sacked Rome in 390. After gaining a success near Clusium the Gauls began to retire with their booty northward along the coast of Etruria with a Roman consular army following behind.

Suddenly at Telamon they found their way barred by another Roman army which had been recalled from Sardinia and had landed north of them. The Romans won a decisive victory (225) and followed it up by deciding to reduce the northern plain of Italy, which they called Cisalpine Gaul (*see* GAUL, CISALPINE), in order to secure a peaceful frontier. The Boii were conquered by 224 and the Insubres, north of the Po, by 222. The consuls of 221 and 220 then carried through the reduction of the native tribes of Istria and thus secured the northeastern frontier toward the Julian Alps.

The way was now open for the spread of Roman culture in Cisalpine Gaul. This was hastened by the construction of the Via Flaminia from Rome to Ariminum (Rimini) in 220 by Gaius Flaminius (he had defeated the Insubres in 223), and by settling Latin colonies at Placentia (Piacenza) and Cremona in 218. Flaminius was also noted for his earlier quarrel with the Senate: as tribune in 232 he had carried a measure through the plebeian assembly, despite senatorial opposition, to distribute some land in north Italy (*ager Gallicus*) in allotments to poor Roman citizens. About this time also the Roman nobility had to allow a reform of the voting arrangements in the *comitia centuriata,* whereby more middle-class citizens would get a chance to exercise their vote. Shortly before this, in 241, two new tribes (Velina and Quirina) were created in Sabine and Picentine territory, thus bringing the total number of tribes to 35; thereafter the tribal system was always kept at this figure. Shortly afterward, in 218, Q. Claudius carried a measure which in effect forbade senators to engage in overseas trade. The Senate, however, despite the existence of some opposition, maintained control of policy, both domestic and foreign.

In Illyria and the Adriatic.—The attention of the Romans was also demanded in the Adriatic. The fact that under Queen Teuta the Illyrians had extended their kingdom southward to Acarnania would worry Rome less than the increasing scale on which they were practising piracy. In 229 Rome sent a force across the Adriatic and swiftly reduced them (228). In order to check future trouble and protect the Greek cities (as Dyrrachium and Apollonia) against the Illyrians, Rome established a small coastal strip north of Epirus as a protectorate; this was not a province, but Rome had declared an interest in this area and a desire that shipping should be unmolested. Envoys were sent to various parts of Greece, including Athens and Corinth, to explain Rome's conduct. Since the Greeks benefited no less than Italian merchants from the suppression of piracy, the Romans were well received; they were admitted by Corinth to the Isthmian Games and were thereby recognized as members of the Hellenic world.

Thus Rome came into official contact with Greece for the first time, but no similar diplomatic approach was made to the kingdom of Macedonia, which was probably annoyed by Roman intervention in the Balkans—though without real cause, since the slowness with which Rome started the war and the terms imposed after it suggest that Rome was not deliberately cultivating an aggressive eastern policy. In 220 the Illyrians violated their treaty with Rome and thus provoked Roman intervention for a second time. In a whirlwind campaign the consuls of 219 reduced Illyria but made little change in the settlement, even though Illyria now enjoyed the support of Philip V, who had come to the throne of Macedonia in 221. They were in a hurry because of events in Spain.

Second Punic War.—During these years the Carthaginians had been busy building up an empire in Spain which would help to compensate for the loss of Sicily, Sardinia, and Corsica. The foundations of this dominion were laid by Hamilcar Barca (*q.v.*), who had shown great military ability as commander in Sicily during the last stages of the First Punic War. In 237 he crossed to Spain, with his nine-year-old son Hannibal, who had been made to swear eternal hatred to Rome. He quickly occupied southern and eastern Spain and managed to fob off a Roman protest, which no doubt had originated from Rome's ally Massilia, which disliked seeing the Punic frontier creeping so far north. When Hamilcar died in 229/228, he was succeeded by his son-in-law Hasdrubal, who established a new base at Carthago Nova (Cartagena). In 226/225 Hasdrubal made a treaty with the Romans, by which he agreed not to cross the Ebro River with an armed force, while the Romans possibly assured him that they would not interfere with his conquests south of the river.

A hundred miles south of the Ebro was an Iberian seaport, Saguntum, with which Rome at some point had made an alliance. If this was negotiated before the Ebro treaty, then presumably the alliance was virtually annulled by the agreement; if Rome accepted the alliance after 226, it infringed the spirit and perhaps the letter of the treaty. Thus when Hannibal, who succeeded Hasdrubal in 221, decided to regard the conquest of Spain as only preliminary to an attack upon Italy, he could use Saguntum to provoke Rome to action. In 219, therefore, when he was ready to challenge Rome, he attacked Saguntum. Disregarding Roman protests, he finally took it after an eight-month siege. This rendered a rupture with Rome inevitable, while it set his own hands free for further advance.

Even if he had not technically broken any agreement with Rome, Hannibal had deliberately provoked an incident which he knew would lead to war. For some time Barcid policy in Spain had been essentially defensive *vis à vis* Rome, but now Hannibal, ever mindful of Rome's previous seizure of Sardinia, moved to the offensive, and Rome accepted the challenge. Apart from the unprovoked seizure of Sardinia, Rome's policy after the First Punic War had not been deliberately aggressive; the Gallic wars were defensive in spirit, and the Illyrian campaigns were a necessary piece of police work. Rather, without pursuing deep-laid plans, Rome dealt with each situation as it arose. If Hannibal chose to question Roman interference in Spain, Rome was willing to face the consequences.

For details of the war that followed (218–201), *see* the articles Punic Wars; Hannibal; Scipio; Fabius; etc. Hannibal's decision to leave his base in Spain, cross the Alps, and invade northern Italy was crowned with success, and culminated in a series of victories at Trebbia, Trasimene, and Cannae (*see* Trebbia; Trasimeno, Lago; Cannae). However, although he won over much of southern Italy, including Capua, he failed to break Rome's determination to fight on, and he failed to undermine the loyalty to Rome of the Latin cities and central Italy. Hence he had to cast his strategic net more widely. But this attempt too failed. His ally, Philip of Macedonia, achieved little; the revolt of Syracuse from Rome was soon crushed; the defeat of the Scipios in Spain failed to result in the expulsion of the Romans from the peninsula; Hannibal's movements and strength in Italy were checked by Fabius' strategy; the breakthrough to Italy by his brother Hasdrubal was foiled at the Metaurus. And finally Rome produced a military genius in Scipio Africanus, who drove the Carthaginians from Spain, persuaded his reluctant countrymen to allow him to invade Africa, won such success there that Hannibal was recalled

from Italy to save Carthage, and finally defeated Hannibal at Zama.

By the terms of the peace Carthage was left as an independent state but had to give up everything outside an area roughly equivalent to that of modern Tunisia, to surrender the fleet, and to pay an indemnity over a period of 50 years. The Numidian prince Masinissa, whose cavalry had rendered Scipio invaluable service at Zama, was rewarded with an increase of territory. As Rome's ally, he stood watch over his neighbour Carthage, which by the treaty with Rome was forbidden to make war on anyone in Africa without the permission of Rome (and any war at all outside Africa).

Among the numerous factors that gave Rome the victory none was greater than the moral forces of a united people who were ready for any sacrifices in their will to conquer. These forces were soon to be blunted by ambition and avarice at home and by the contagious corruption of the eastern world into which Rome was quickly drawn. The effects of the war on Rome and Italy, on the constitution, on economic and social life, on religion and thought were profound, and it proved to be a turning point not only for them but for the history of the whole ancient world. After it no power arose which could endanger the existence of Rome. The Hellenistic monarchies of the east still flourished, but at Rome's touch they collapsed like a house of cards. German and other barbarian tribes in the north could threaten, and the emergent Parthian empire beyond the Euphrates might at times appear menacing, but for centuries such dangers were held at arms' length. Thus Rome became mistress of the fortunes of the civilized world and gradually introduced into that world a unity, unknown since the time of Alexander the Great, which was to last for five hundred years.

2. Rome and the West, 201–133 B.C.—*The Spanish Provinces.*—With the power of Carthage broken, Rome was faced by no other organized state in the west, but only by the native peoples of Spain, southern Gaul, Liguria, and the approaches of the Alps. The Romans had certainly not fought the Hannibalic War to gain Spain, but by ejecting the Carthaginians from the peninsula they found themselves in possession of the lower Ebro Valley, the east coast, and the rich Baetis (Guadalquivir) Valley. Beyond this area were the highland tribes of the interior. That the Romans finished by conquering them does not necessarily mean that they started with that intention. The need to preserve order on the borders of the more civilized south, whose rich resources Rome now began to exploit, may at least in part account for the long series of wars waged in Spain. For a few years after Scipio's conquest Spain was administered on a provisional basis, but in 197 the machinery of government was adapted by raising the number of praetors to six, and two provinces were established, Hither and Farther Spain (Hispania Citerior and Ulterior), each to be administered annually by a praetor.

Tribute was imposed in the form of a fixed tax (*stipendium*) to be paid in natural products or bullion. This later led to much extortion by unscrupulous Roman governors, unlike the fairer tithe system used in the province of Sicily, to which the former dominions of Hieron were added after his death. Sicily enjoyed peace and prosperity for many years until a slave war broke out in 135. Roman policy in Spain provoked a vast insurrection in 197 which started in the south and spread northward over the central highlands; it was checked, but not stamped out, by Cato in 195. The main resistance was in Celtiberia; it was undermined by the campaigns and wise settlement of Tiberius Sempronius Gracchus (father of the tribune of 133) in 179. Following the example of Scipio, who had left a settlement of his veterans at Italica near Seville in 206, Gracchus founded Graccuris on the upper Ebro, while later (in 168 or 151) Corduba was established in the south as another centre of Roman civilization.

In 154 war flared up farther west when the Lusitanians raided Roman territory; thanks to the brilliant guerrilla tactics of their leader, Viriathus, resistance was maintained until 139. In 138 D. Junius Brutus subdued Portugal up to the Douro and fortified Olisipo (Lisbon); a brief campaign farther north temporarily overawed the Callaici. Meantime the Celtiberians had made a second unsuccessful bid for independence (153–151) and yet a third in 143. This last war, which centred on their capital, Numantia, dragged on for ten years and was marked, like many of these Spanish campaigns, by increasing Roman treachery and lack of military discipline.

At length a competent soldier was sent out, Scipio Aemilianus (the grandson, by adoption, of Scipio Africanus, the conqueror of Hannibal); he disciplined his troops, besieged Numantia (traces of his camps and walls of circumvallation survive, as do many other camps from these Spanish campaigns), and finally reduced the city by starvation; it surrendered in 133. Rome's control of Spain, apart from the Astures and Cantabri in the extreme northwest, was now complete, and the land quickly became one of the most prosperous and romanized parts of the Roman empire.

North Italy and the Balkans.—The Gallic tribes of the Po Valley, who had given Hannibal some support, attacked Placentia in 200 or 199. This led the Romans to tighten their grip on Cisalpine Gaul. By 191 the Boii, who had been supported by the Insubres and Cenomani, were defeated and many withdrew northward to settle in Bohemia. A Latin colony was established at Bononia (Bologna) in 189 and Roman colonies at Parma and Mutina (Modena) in 183, while the road system was extended by the Via Aemilia (built by Aemilius Lepidus, consul in 187; its name survives in the modern district of Emilia).

The Romans then dealt with the tribes on either side of Cisalpine Gaul. In the west Ligurian tribes held the mountains as far as southeastern France. In 201 Rome renewed earlier control of the ports of Luna (Spezia) and Genoa, but intermittent fighting with the Ligurians continued until 180; Luca probably received a Latin colony in 180 and Luna a Roman settlement in 177. After more disturbances in the 170s, the Romans in 154 pushed back the more westerly Oxybian Ligurians who raided the Massiliote ports of Antipolis (Antibes) and Nicaea (Nice); thereby they helped to secure their own communications with Spain.

East of Cisalpine Gaul lived the Veneti, who were loyal to Rome, and beyond them the Istrians at the head of the Adriatic. After founding a Latin colony at Aquileia (181), the Romans reduced the Istrians (178–177). Brief campaigns (157–155) against the Dalmatae and in Pannonia strengthened Roman control in the Adriatic. Thus Rome had asserted its authority from the Ligurians near Marseilles, round the sweep of the Alps to Istria, and thence down the western coast of the Balkans. Behind this shield Cisalpine Gaul could flourish.

Third Punic War.—Only one potential danger remained in the west, at least in the eyes of some Romans, and that was the reviving power of Carthage. Economic recovery from the Hannibalic War had been surprisingly speedy, but Carthage was constantly harassed by the aggressive pressure of Masinissa, who built up Numidia into a powerful state. Goaded beyond endurance, the Carthaginians at last resisted him by force, thereby infringing their treaty of 201 with Rome. Cato was eager to seize the opportunity to destroy Carthage completely; other Romans advocated a more moderate policy, but the war party got the upper hand. It is unlikely that commercial interests affected the decision to any extent: hatred of their old enemy, combined perhaps with a passing mood of nervousness (such as affected the Roman attitude to Sardinia nearly a century earlier), led the Romans to declare war in 149. The Carthaginians surrendered and handed over quantities of war equipment, but when they learned of Rome's terms (the city must be destroyed, although the inhabitants could live anywhere beyond ten miles from the coast), they decided to fight on. The siege and destruction of Carthage in 146 in this Third Punic War are discussed in the article PUNIC WARS. Rome had acted perhaps with strict legality but certainly with great deceit in this final overthrow of its old enemy. The city was left in ruins, and most of the land that Carthage had controlled at the beginning of the war was organized as a new Roman province named Africa. Scipio Aemilianus, who had conducted the siege in its critical phase, returned to Rome and received, as his grandfather before him, the *cognomen* of Africanus. In the west Rome now had no possible rival.

3. Rome and the East, 200–188 B.C.—*Philip V.*—Rome's early contact with Greek cities during the First Illyrian War had been friendly (*see above*), but when Hannibal made an alliance with Philip V of Macedonia Rome had been forced to send an army to Greece to forestall a possible attack by Philip on Italy (214). Helped by Philip's unpopularity in Greece, the Romans made an alliance with the Aetolian League, which was soon joined by many other Greek states; the war dragged on until 205 when they negotiated terms with Philip in the Peace of Phoenice. The result of the war was that Rome had been drawn into formal relations with some Greek states and that many senators were resentful toward Philip or even suspicious of his ambition. But scarcely was the Hannibalic War over when the balance of power in the Hellenistic world was upset by the aggressions of Philip and Antiochus III, king of Syria. (*See also* ANTIOCHUS; MACEDONIA, KINGDOM OF.) These two monarchs took the opportunity offered by the accession of a child to the throne of Egypt to form a secret pact to seize Egypt's overseas possessions; they started in 202, and the complaints of many of Philip's victims were voiced on their behalf at Rome by an Aetolian embassy. The Senate, however, would not involve Rome in these affairs and rebuffed the ambassadors. Philip thereupon occupied the Cyclades and invaded the mainland of Ionia, clashing in naval engagements with the fleets of Rhodes and of Attalus of Pergamum, who appealed to Rome before the end of 201. The Senate then suddenly changed its mind and proposed that the Roman people, who alone could constitutionally declare war, should do so (March 200); but the people were war-weary and refused. The Senate thereupon sent an ultimatum to Philip, who was besieging Abydos, while one of his generals attacked Attica and thereby caused Athens also to appeal to Rome for help. At last in July the Senate persuaded the people to declare war on Philip, and an expeditionary force was sent to Greece.

Roman motives in undertaking this fresh war have been variously interpreted, since Rome was under no legal obligation to intervene; the appellant peoples were only "friends" (*amici*) and not treaty-bound allies (*socii*). Aggressive imperialism is not a probable cause; Rome was exhausted and in fact took no territory after the war was won. Since many Romans were at this time falling under the spell of Greek culture, it has been suggested that their policy was philhellenic, but an appreciation of earlier Greek achievements need not have led to sympathy for contemporary Greeks. Even if such sentiments contributed, a more basic explanation is still needed. Fear of Philip cannot have been strong, even if the desire to punish him for his past conduct was. The most probable explanation, and one that would account for the Senate's very unexpected change of policy, is that the Senate suddenly learned about the secret pact between the two monarchs. With Antiochus behind Philip the threat to Greece was serious, and Greece could be used as a hostile base. Rome was thus probably actuated by a defensive, rather than an aggressive, form of imperialism.

The war itself was quickly won. In 199 Rome gained the support of the Aetolians. In 198 T. Quinctius Flamininus (*q.v.*), having failed to persuade Philip to accept terms, drove him from the west to Tempe, overran Thessaly and central Greece, gained the support of the Achaean League, and in the following year decisively defeated him at Cynoscephalae (*q.v.*). Rome wisely allowed Philip to retain his kingdom of Macedonia but not his conquests nor his fleet. To have smashed Macedonia completely would have removed a barrier which protected Greece from the wilder tribes to the north and might also have encouraged Antiochus to intervene.

Amid scenes of great enthusiasm Flamininus proclaimed to the Greeks assembled at the Isthmian Games at Corinth in 196 that they were to be free, without garrisons (Philip had kept three in Greece) and without tribute, and to be governed by their own laws. Thus the Romans made clear that they had no intention of adding the administration of Greece to their responsibilities, and by 194 the Roman armies had left the country. They had, however, proclaimed their interest: all Greeks in Europe and Asia (where in fact Rome had no legal right to interfere) were to be free and autonomous. In a sense Rome thus extended a protectorate over the Greeks. A friendly Greece might seem the best guarantee against a revival of Macedonian power or any threat from Antiochus.

Antiochus III.—Meantime Antiochus, who had conquered Coele-Syria and Palestine (202–198), overran Asia Minor and crossing over to Europe established himself in Thrace, on which he had hereditary claims (196). In long diplomatic exchanges with Rome, whose fears were increased by the knowledge that Hannibal had sought refuge with Antiochus, misunderstandings prevented a settlement. In 192 Antiochus responded to the appeals of the Aetolians and sent a moderate force to Greece. He wanted the Romans to recognize him as an equal power and therefore was ready, if necessary, for a limited struggle; he did not accept Hannibal's alleged advice to invade Italy. Rome responded quickly. A force was again sent to Greece, and a single battle, at Thermopylae, was sufficient to drive Antiochus out of Greece (191). The Romans then decided for the first time to set foot in Asia, partly in the interests of their allies, Pergamum and Rhodes, and the Greek cities in Asia Minor. After the defeat of Antiochus' navy L. Scipio, the consul of 190, accompanied by his famous brother, Publius Africanus, led the legions of Rome into Asia. Again at one blow Antiochus was defeated, at Magnesia. The king was allowed by the subsequent Peace of Apamea to retain his throne, but he had to withdraw beyond the Taurus Mountains into Syria itself. Besides a heavy indemnity and the surrender of his fleet, he was forbidden to wage war in Europe or the Aegean. The terms in fact led to the rapid decline of Syria.

The Romans themselves had no intention of annexing territory in Asia, any more than in Greece. A great part of the land ceded by Antiochus was divided between Pergamum (where Eumenes II had succeeded Attalus) and Rhodes: Pergamum received Phrygia, Mysia, and Lydia, while the continental possessions of Rhodes were quadrupled by the gift of Caria and Lycia. Of the Greek cities on the western coast, those that had been subject to Antiochus were to be free, but those that had been tributary to Pergamum and those that had opposed Rome during the war were to pay tribute to Pergamum, though individual exceptions were made. Pergamum would act as a wedge between Syria and Macedonia, and at the same time would limit the ambition of the border states, Bithynia, Pontus, Cappadocia, and Galatia. The Galatians had in fact just been taught a sharp lesson by Manlius Vulso (189). They had been a constant menace to the Greek and native communities in Asia Minor, and so Manlius was sent to reduce them to submission. Unfortunately this useful piece of police work was spoiled by his cruelty and rapacity. Meantime his colleague Fulvius Nobilior had reduced the Aetolians, who had started fighting against Philip. Thus both Greece and Asia Minor were pacified, and the Romans, who had overthrown the two great Hellenistic monarchs in little more than a decade, withdrew, leaving not a single soldier behind. The Hellenistic world was left free to enjoy or abuse its liberty.

4. Greece, Macedonia, and the Hellenistic States, 188–146 B.C.

Greece and Macedonia.—Greece had been left free, but it certainly did not remain free from interstate quarrels and rivalries, which included a long struggle between Sparta and the Achaean League (189–181). Aggrieved parties tended to appeal to Rome, but Rome refused to go beyond diplomatic action and was often slow in enforcing its decisions. Under the strain of a bombardment of appeals from Greece the philhellenic protectorate policy of the Scipios and Flamininus began to weaken, especially as the political position of these men in Rome was undermined by the attacks of Cato, who wished Rome to wash its hands of Greek affairs. Thus Roman policy toward Greece hardened: the Senate began to support the pro-Roman at the expense of the nationalist patriotic parties, with less investigation into the rights or wrongs of a quarrel.

Meantime Philip of Macedonia, who had remained loyal to Rome during the war with Antiochus, was building up the power and resources of his kingdom to such an extent as to provoke Roman suspicions of his intentions. His son Perseus, who succeeded him in 179, soon decided to break with the Romans, who were forced to undertake military intervention in Greece once

again in the Third Macedonian War (171–168/167). After three years of indecisive campaigns the Romans sent out an efficient commander, L. Aemilius Paulus, who finally defeated Perseus at Pydna (for the campaign see PYDNA, BATTLE OF). The settlement followed traditional Roman policy: freedom for Greece and Macedonia and no annexation of territory. Rome, however, could not allow the Macedonian monarchy to continue, since it had proved a threat to peace. Macedonia was therefore divided into four autonomous republics, which were to be separate political and economic units. They were to pay to Rome half what they had paid to their king in direct tax, as a substitute for a war indemnity. From Rome's point of view this might appear a generous settlement, but it did violence to the Macedonians' sense of nationhood.

Illyria also was divided into three districts. More brutal was Rome's treatment of Epirus and Greece. Epirus was systematically plundered (167). In Aetolia 500 Macedonian sympathizers were put to death, and 1,000 Achaeans were deported to Italy, among them the statesman and historian Polybius. Thus the Romans showed that they still preferred diplomacy to war, but the continued bickerings of the Greeks were undermining Rome's philhellenic policy and they had become more ruthless in their handling of the Greeks.

Hellenistic States and Provinces of Asia and Macedonia.—There was a similar hardening of Roman policy toward the Hellenistic states, details of which cannot be given here. Rhodes was punished for what the Senate regarded as too independent an attitude; it was deprived of its mainland possessions, while its commerce received a blow by Rome's encouragement of Delos as a competitor. Rome itself later paid the penalty through the increase of piracy which the Rhodian navy had hitherto helped to check. Rome's other friend, the kingdom of Pergamum, also became increasingly dependent upon Rome's favour until the death of Attalus III in 133; he bequeathed his kingdom to Rome, and the Romans accepted the legacy, converting Pergamum into the Roman province of Asia. Similarly the monarchies of Syria and Egypt, both of which were weakened by constant dynastic troubles, received short shrift from Rome when they tried to resume their mutual quarrels. Diplomatic pressure alone enabled Rome to keep them weak.

Rome's settlement of Greece was upset when a pretender, named Andriscus, tried to reestablish the Macedonian monarchy in 149. The next year a Roman army under Caecilius Metellus arrived and quickly ended Andriscus' career. Rome now finally reversed the policy of leaving Greece free and ungarrisoned: Macedonia was declared a Roman province. Trouble also flared up farther south, where Achaea tried to coerce Sparta, which appealed to Rome. Anti-Roman demonstrations in Corinth, where senatorial ambassadors were mobbed, led to quick reprisals. Rome's patience at last broke. An army under Metellus swept down from Macedonia and sacked Corinth (146), whose artistic treasures were shipped to Rome. Details of the settlement are obscure. The Achaean and all hostile leagues were temporarily dissolved, and timocracies (property-based oligarchies) replaced democracies in those cities that had been reduced in the war, but Greece was not made into a Roman province until a century later; the governor of Macedonia could supervise and maintain order there if necessary. There is little evidence that Roman policy was influenced by commercial, rather than by political motives. For over 50 years Greece had been left free to settle its own affairs, but had failed to maintain peace and order; these were now guaranteed by Rome in a settlement which did not necessarily bring prosperity or happiness.

Provincial Administration.—Thus Rome was now dominant in the eastern and western Mediterranean. In the west there were five provinces (Sicily, Corsica and Sardinia, the two Spains, and Africa) which had come into Roman possession as the result of the long struggles with Carthage, and to many parts of these regions Rome brought a higher type of civilization and government than they had known before. In the east Rome had been much slower to extend direct rule (to Macedonia in 146 and Asia in 133). Here an older and more advanced civilization flourished, and although Roman governors might bring order, the east remained Greek and not Roman in language, customs, and thought.

The conditions of administration of each province were defined in a charter (*lex provinciae*) which was granted when the province was formed; it could be supplemented with detailed regulations by the governor's edict. At first he was normally a praetor, but increasing use was made of promagistrates. In the provinces a few communities (*civitates foederatae* and *liberae*) enjoyed special privileges, such as greater autonomy and relief from taxation, but the majority were under direct control and subject to taxation, normally a fixed sum (but a tithe in Sicily and Asia). In theory the system was fair enough and at first worked well: thus Polybius in a well-known passage paid tribute to the incorruptibility of the average Roman governor, whom he contrasts with corrupt Greek statesmen. But in his day abuses were beginning to creep in, although the establishment in 149 of a permanent court in Rome to try cases of extortion at least testifies to a desire to maintain high standards.

Italian Allies.—Here too may be mentioned a gradual deterioration of Rome's relations with the allies in Italy during the first half of the 2nd century. The Senate did not deliberately seek to undermine their internal independence, but Roman control gradually overshadowed the local authorities until finally they became part of the machinery worked by the central government. Thus Rome tended to intervene when a matter, such as the Bacchanalian "conspiracy" in 186 (*see* BACCHANALIA), affected the interests of Italy as a whole; and on occasion Roman magistrates acted arrogantly in allied cities. In particular, the more privileged Latin allies were treated with less generosity than earlier, and they began to feel that the overseas empire was being exploited in the interests of Rome rather than of Italy.

5. Political, Social, and Economic Developments, 200–133 B.C.—*Constitution.*—In his classic description of the Roman constitution Polybius concluded that it contained three nicely balanced principles: monarchy represented by the consuls, aristocracy by the Senate, and democracy by the people. In practice, however, the Senate had gained general control: in effect it *was* the government. It controlled the chief military commands, finance, and foreign policy; it set up judicial commissions of inquiry and it supplied the jury for the first permanent court (*quaestio perpetua*) in 149. Only occasionally did the sovereign people intervene, as when Flaminius carried a bill of which the Senate disapproved in 232. So also in general it controlled the magistrates, together with the tribunes, who gained the right to convoke the Senate and became in effect magistrates of the people (*populus*) rather than officers of the plebs; increasingly they acted in the interests of the Senate.

The Senate itself had gained great prestige by its conduct of the Hannibalic War, but war conditions had caused constitutional breakdowns. Thus, the need for continuity of command led to the irregular election of men to a second consulship within ten years, while Scipio had been invested by the people with a proconsular command when he was a *privatus*, not holding any magistracy. Such irregular commands might have encouraged ambitious soldiers to challenge the central government; to guard against such a potential threat a *Lex Villia Annalis* in 180 regulated the order in which magistracies must be held (*cursus honorum*) and made sure that no one could reach the consulship before he was 34; soon afterward (in 150?) the minimum age was raised to 42.

Rome was in practice an oligarchy; the magistrates and people were controlled by the Senate, the stronghold of the nobility. These nobles were now a mixed body of patricians and plebeians, drawn from a limited number of families and as exclusive as the old patriciate had been; ten families supplied half the 200-odd consuls between 233 and 133. *Nobilitas* was confined to members of those families which had held the consulship; the extremely few men outside this closed circle who did succeed in winning the consulship automatically ennobled their families (Cato was the outstanding example of these *novi homines* ["new men"]). It was this inner circle of nobles that in practice controlled the Senate, and they were enabled to exercise their power through patronage. Most of the nobles had numerous clients (*clientes*) whose personal, economic, social, legal, or political interests they fostered. Political relations were essentially personal, and through patronage

the nobles influenced the elections, which gave them control of the Senate, where the influence of the higher magistrates was paramount. The nobility tended to split into groups, based on families or *gentes*, which often formed political alliances (*amicitiae*), sometimes strengthened by intermarriage. These groups did not develop into political parties in the modern sense, but contended in keen rivalry with one another for the higher magistracies.

Optimates and Populares.—Such struggles may have become slightly less fierce by 133 when the nobility is found divided into Optimates and Populares. These political catchwords have sometimes wrongly been equated with "conservatives" and "democrats." The Optimates were the dominant group in the Senate. They blocked the wishes of the others, who were thus forced to seek tribunician support for their measures in the tribal assembly and hence were labeled Populares, "demagogues," by their opponents. The two groups differed therefore chiefly in their methods: the Optimates tried to uphold the oligarchy, the Populares sought popular support against the dominant oligarchy, either in the interests of the people themselves or in furtherance of their own personal ambitions. Finally, it is well to remember that the Senate's authority was based on custom and consent rather than upon law. It had no legal control over the people or magistrates: it gave, but could not enforce, advice. Until 133 B.C. any challenge to its authority was little more than a pinprick, but thereafter more deadly blows were struck, first by Populares and later by the army commanders from the provinces.

Influence of Greek and Oriental Culture.—The social, economic, and intellectual background of the Roman nobility, and indeed of Roman society as a whole, was changing rapidly, chiefly through the impact of the Greek world upon Roman thought and the *mos maiorum* ("ancestral custom"). Private tutors and teachers in schools taught the Greek language and literature, so that by 133 most educated Romans were bilingual. National consciousness, and not least an interest in Rome's legendary Trojan origin, fostered the development of Latin literature. Livius Andronicus (a Greek from Tarentum) translated the *Odyssey* into Latin; stimulated by Greek examples, Naevius and Ennius created an epic poetry. Plautus, Terence, and others produced Greek comedies in Roman form; dramatists, as Ennius, adapted Greek tragedies for the Roman stage. The satirist Lucilius developed a new literary *genre*. Roman senators, as Fabius Pictor, wrote histories of Rome in Greek, partly to justify Roman policy to the Greek world; and Cato soon followed with history written in Latin. (*See* LATIN LITERATURE.) Greek architecture influenced the construction of public buildings and private houses in 2nd-century Rome, while Greek statues and painting were increasingly admired.

Changes in religion and thought were equally profound. Greek and eastern cults, as of Phrygian Cybele (Magna Mater) and the Greek wine-god Dionysus (Bacchus), became popular in Italy. Greek philosophy, especially Stoicism and Epicureanism, although resisted at first by the old-fashioned Romans like Cato who feared it would undermine the *mos maiorum*, was increasingly studied in Rome. At first men like Scipio Africanus and Flamininus had encouraged the spread of Greek ideas and ways, while later Scipio Aemilianus gathered around himself a circle of intellectuals who included Laelius, Panaetius, Polybius, Terence, and Lucilius (*qq.v.*) They tried to blend together the best elements of Greek and Roman life.

A more material import from the east was the wealth that derived from war booty, profitable administration, and trade. In consequence many Romans enjoyed more luxurious lives, and sumptuary laws did little to check the growing extravagance. A contemporary, Calpurnius Piso (consul later, in 133), dated the overthrow of Roman modesty to the year 154. A healthy family life, the very basis of early Roman society, declined. There was greater freedom of divorce, an increasing disinclination to marry, greater emancipation of women, together with a demand for more public festivals, games, and gladiatorial shows; and above all, slavery increased.

Growth of the Equestrian Order.—The uniting of so much of the Mediterranean world under one hand naturally stimulated commerce and thus increased the importance of the business classes, who were known as the equestrian order. This comprised the original 18 *centuriae* of *equites* (younger nobles who served originally as cavalry) and a wider group of men whose property qualification would have entitled them to this status. Socially some of these men might come from the same class as the senators, but politically there was a great gulf. The *equites* were excluded from the Senate and a public career; instead they turned to business, as individuals and in companies, and became bankers, moneylenders, and traders. They also received contracts from the censors for carrying out some public works and collecting certain taxes, and they took over the operation of mines in Spain and Macedonia. They also helped to supply the Roman armies with equipment. Thus a new and important element was emerging in Roman society, which undertook many of the duties that the state itself failed to perform through the creation of an official machinery. There was some friction between them and the Senate, but this did not become serious until later.

Land System.—The wealth which these businessmen helped to create had many repercussions besides the social effects already noted and made the lot of the small farmer in Italy much harder. Men coming back to Italy, enriched by the wars or by trade, invested their capital in land, which now became an object of speculation. Landowners often ceased to be farmers and entrusted their estates to bailiffs to be run for profit. At the same time the wars increased the number of slaves, and servile labour began to oust free on the bigger estates in many parts of Italy. Thus peasant husbandry gave place to large estates (*latifundia*) worked by slaves and devoted to pasturage. Mixed farming on a moderate scale was still profitable, but the small farmer was hard pressed, and many abandoned their land to larger proprietors and drifted to Rome and other cities where they were often unemployed. This decline is reflected in the census figures, which rose until 164 B.C. and then regularly fell. The process was accelerated by the way in which the state disposed of the land that it had acquired in Italy, the *ager publicus populi Romani*. The less fertile parts had been let to squatters (*possessores*), who paid a nominal rent, but this was not enforced strictly since the state created no adequate machinery to collect it, and men came to regard the land as their own. The amount of such land that any individual might hold was limited (to 500 *iugera* or about 300 ac. in the 2nd century, and probably as early as 367). But in practice this limitation had been widely disregarded, not least because many senators, as large landowners, would benefit. The system, however, involved the possibility that, if the plight of the small farmers got very bad and they could find a leader to champion their cause, a demand might be made to enforce the law strictly and redistribute some of this "public land." Scipio's friend Laelius made such a proposal, but dropped it when he found the strength of the opposition. It was left to Tiberius Gracchus to tackle the problem in 133.

D. THE FALL OF THE REPUBLIC, 133–31 B.C.

1. The Challenge of the Gracchi.—The first serious challenge to the senatorial government came from Tiberius Sempronius Gracchus (*q.v.*), tribune in 133. When he proposed an agrarian bill, under which the "public land" held in excess of the legal limit should be taken back by the state for distribution, he had the support of several leading senators, but the constitutional methods that he adopted soon lost him this backing. Despairing of winning full senatorial support, Tiberius took his measure straight to the *concilium plebis*, where a fellow tribune, M. Octavius, vetoed it in the interests of the Senate. He then took the extreme step of getting the people to vote for the deposition of Octavius. He was thus able to carry his measure, and a commission of three men with judicial powers was set up to carry out the redistribution of the land. This was to be divided into small allotments for Roman citizens in economic difficulties. Whether Tiberius' primary concern was to cope with the unemployment problem in the cities or, as is more likely, to try to reestablish the small farmers in Italy (the yeomen on whom the army had depended) may remain uncertain, but these are really only two aspects of the same basic problem.

In order to give his settlers a start Tiberius proposed to divert to this purpose some of the legacy of Attalus of Pergamum, who had just died and left his kingdom to Rome (*see* above). The Senate strongly resented this interference in financial and foreign affairs, which had been their preserve. When Gracchus decided on the unusual step of standing for a second tribunate, disturbances broke out at the elections, and some senators resorted to force and clubbed or stoned to death Gracchus and 300 of his followers. Thus after nearly 400 years blood was again shed in Rome in civil strife. There is no doubt that Tiberius was a sincere reformer, but his methods had antagonized the Senate. His appeal to the sovereign people was legitimate, but it would be unwise to suggest that the urban mob which attended the *concilium* was sufficiently responsible and experienced to offer an alternative body to the Senate or that a prolonged tribunate might not smack of demagogy. Neither of these potential aspects was probably uppermost in Tiberius' mind, but they might well have been the ultimate consequence of such action as he took.

The Senate allowed the land commission to continue its work, but difficulties arose, especially where the interests of the Latin and Italian allies who had rented public land were concerned. Scipio Aemilianus took some action to help, but he died in 129. The allies became increasingly discontented, and their cause was taken up by M. Fulvius Flaccus, who in 125 boldly proposed that all allies who wished should receive Roman citizenship and the others should be given the right of appeal against Roman magistrates. This statesmanlike proposal failed, and Fregellae revolted but was quickly reduced; a widespread allied revolt was averted for another 35 years. The cause of the allies, however, was championed by Gaius Gracchus (tribune in 123 and reelected 122), but he could not hope to tackle this thorny question until he had built up firm political support. This he did on a much wider basis than his brother had (*see* GRACCHUS, GAIUS SEMPRONIUS).

Gaius won popular support by continuing his brother's agrarian work, by a law to provide grain at less than the market price, and by proposing to found some colonies in southern Italy and even at Carthage (Junonia). He gained the support of the *equites* by making them, instead of the senators, the jurymen to deal with cases arising from extortion in the provinces, and by giving them the right to bid for collecting the taxes of the new province of Asia. The Senate tried to thwart him by putting up another tribune, M. Livius Drusus (*q.v.*), to outbid him in popular favour with some specious proposals. Finally, Gaius proposed that the Latins should receive full enfranchisement and that the rest of the allies should get Latin rights (*see* LATIN RIGHTS). In this he failed, and he also failed to secure reelection to a third tribunate. Some disturbances ensued and the Senate for the first time passed "the last decree" (*senatus consultum ultimum*), which urged the consuls to defend the state by virtue of their *imperium*. The consul L. Opimius took to arms: Gaius, Flaccus, and many followers were killed, and others were executed without trial. Although Opimius was later prosecuted, he was acquitted.

The Senate, ruthless on this front, was more conciliatory toward the land commission, which was allowed to continue its work until 119. The whole question was wound up in 111, when all grants of land, which had been made alienable in 121, were made the private property of their occupiers, and the system of *possessio* was abolished. Thus the work of the Gracchi resulted in the setting up of many small farmers and some colonists, even though economic difficulties remained. The allies were more embittered, the *equites* more conscious of their political powers, and the people more ready to support a Popularis. Above all, the weakness of the Senate was revealed, and so the Gracchi, however unwillingly, precipitated the revolution that within a century overthrew the republic.

2. Marius, 119–100 B.C.—The rise of Marius to a political career was helped by the Caecilii Metelli, who dominated the Roman political scene for a decade (119–109). In 123 Q. Metellus crushed piracy in the Balearic Islands, where two colonies of Romans were established at Palma and Pollentia in Majorca. This helped to secure the sea route to Spain, but Rome was also concerned about the land route through southern Gaul. At the re-

ALINARI

(LEFT) MARIUS; (RIGHT) SULLA. IN THE VATICAN MUSEUMS

quest of Massilia in 125 Rome had sent a force against the Saluvii, Ligurians, and Vocontii. This provoked the hostility of the Allobroges and Arverni farther north; after they were defeated in 121, the Senate decided to annex southern Gaul (Provence) as a province (Gallia Transalpina or, later, Narbonensis; *see* GAUL). In 118 a proposal to establish a Roman colony at Narbo (Narbonne) led to a clash between the Senate and *equites,* since both strategic and economic interests were involved; the *equites* got their way, thus emphasizing their increasing political influence. A serious threat to the security of the frontiers arose when the Cimbri and Teutones, Germanic tribes, started moving in the search for fresh homes and defeated a Roman army at Noreia (113); for the moment, however, they turned westward through Switzerland. The need to guard the frontiers of Macedonia led to much fighting against the Thracian Scordisci and Taurisci, in which various Metelli and their political ally M. Aemilius Scaurus (*q.v.*) took a leading part (between 119 and 107).

At home the Metelli soon found that their "client" Marius (*q.v.*) would not accept their patronage for long; as tribune in 119 he took an independent line. He came of a good municipal family from near Arpinum, and thus, not being of senatorial descent, he had little chance of winning high office, but the traditional portrait of him as a rough uneducated soldier is scarcely true. He certainly had soldierly qualities and determination, and he knew how to use men for his own advantage. After managing to reach the praetorship in 115, he probably devoted some time to business interests and contacts with the *equites;* he also married into the noble family of the Julii. This no doubt helped his political advancement, because his aim was less to challenge the power of the Senate than to win an influential place within it: the *novus homo* wanted the consulship and recognition.

His chance came in the Jugurthine War. When Micipsa, king of Numidia, died in 118, his nephew Jugurtha (*q.v.*) quickly murdered Micipsa's two sons and seized the throne. The further murder of many Italian merchants in Cirta (Constantine, Algeria) angered the people and *equites* in Rome who demanded action. In 112 war was declared upon Jugurtha. Charges of senatorial inefficiency or corruption in the conduct of its initial stages were investigated by a special court set up at the instigation of a tribune, Mamilius, and the Senate sent out a competent soldier, Q. Metellus. His campaigns (109–108), although successful, did not lead to Jugurtha's capture or defeat, and the friends of Marius, who was himself serving on Metellus' staff, began to agitate in Rome on his behalf.

Thus with popular and equestrian support Marius won the consulship of 107. Two important developments followed. First, the people, disregarding the Senate's traditional right to assign the provincial commands, rejected its decision to prolong Metellus' command and appointed Marius to succeed him. Second, in order to secure an adequate and loyal army Marius set aside the rule that it should be recruited exclusively from the five property classes, and enrolled volunteers from those who lacked the necessary property qualifications (*capite censi* or *proletarii*). With this force Marius wore down Jugurtha's strength (107–105), and finally his quaestor, L. Cornelius Sulla, secured the handing over of Jugurtha by his former ally, Bocchus of Mauretania.

A more serious danger now threatened: Roman armies had been defeated in the Garonne Valley and at Arausio (Orange) in the Rhône Valley, and the Cimbri and Teutones were moving on northern Italy. Marius was elected irregularly to a second consulship for 104 and entrusted by the people with the northern command. As the enemy were slow to advance, he had time to train his army in those new methods and organization that gave the legions their predominance for the next two or three centuries. Elected to the consulship each year until 100, he defeated the Teutones at Aquae Sextiae (102) and the Cimbri at Vercellae (101); he returned to Rome a popular hero and the leader of a devoted army.

Meantime Saturninus, who was tribune in 103 and again in 100, carried some popular measures in the interests of Marius, the people, and the *equites* against the Optimates: a grain bill, a measure to provide land for Marius' veterans in Africa and elsewhere, and the establishment of a court to try cases of treason (*quaestio de maiestate*) which was aimed particularly at senatorial generals who had lately been disgraced. Trouble flared up during Marius' sixth consulship (100) when Saturninus was helped by some of Marius' veterans to get his measures carried, and when a rival candidate of his ally Glaucia, who was standing illegally for the consulship of 99, was killed (Saturninus himself had secured a third tribunate for 99). When the Senate passed the *senatus consultum ultimum,* Marius deserted his allies and rallied to the side of law and order. Saturninus and Glaucia, who had seized the Capitol, were lynched. Marius, who was not prepared to go further and use the army to gain power, was discredited. The authority of the nobility had triumphed over the turbulent demagogues, who might claim to be following the tradition of the Gracchi but in fact were actuated merely by personal ambition, and over a *novus homo* who had become an army commander. Future generals were to show greater political insight than Marius but less sense of responsibility and loyalty to the Senate and constitution.

3. The Social War and Sulla's Dictatorship.—The extreme actions of the Populares caused the senatorial and equestrian orders to move closer together, but any such *concordia ordinum* during the 90s was weakened by scandals in the lawcourts, such as the condemnation by an equestrian jury of P. Rutilius Rufus, who had protected the provincials of Asia from the exactions of the equestrian tax gatherers (92). More serious still was the selfish attitude of Senate and people toward the Italian question. The consuls of 95 tactlessly removed from the citizen list some allies who were wrongly registered, and the allies' cause was taken up by the younger M. Livius Drusus (*q.v.*), tribune in 91, who was an aristocrat enlightened enough to try to tackle some of the urgent problems of the day. He gained popular support by measures to provide allotments, colonies, and cheap grain, and then turned to the problem of the lawcourts which had so embittered relations between the two orders. He probably proposed that the courts should be shared between them; it is uncertain whether he also wished to add 300 *equites* to the Senate. This compromise pleased few, and when he was known to be supporting allied claims to citizenship he also lost favour with the Roman people, who were not willing to share their privileges. The Senate then declared his legislation invalid on technical grounds, and when soon afterward he was murdered the allies (*socii*) turned to war (hence called the Social War). Denied Roman franchise, they fought for independence.

The Social War.—The peoples of the hills of central Italy formed the heart of the uprising, the Marsi in the north and the Samnites in the south. Neither the Latin colonies nor Etruria and Umbria joined in. The Italians established their headquarters at Corfinium, which they renamed Italia, created a senate and officers, and issued a special coinage; soon they had 100,000 men in the field. In 90 Roman armies were defeated in the northern sector, although Marius, who had not been given the command, managed to retrieve the situation, while in the south the Italians were equally successful and burst into southern Campania. Only by political concession could Rome hope to check the revolt: by a *Lex Julia* Roman citizenship was granted to all Italians who had remained loyal and probably also to all who were ready to lay down their arms. In 89 both consuls served in the north, where Pompeius Strabo inflicted a decisive defeat on the forces that were trying to break through to Umbria and Etruria; he then captured Asculum, where the revolt had started. In the south, with Sulla in command (Marius had been passed by), the Romans also gained successes.

The back of the revolt was now broken, although some resistance continued among the Samnites for a short time. Further legislation helped: a *Lex Plautia Papiria* in 89 supplemented the *Lex Julia*, a law (*Lex Calpurnia?*) regulated the municipal organization of the communities that now entered the Roman state, while a *Lex Pompeia* of Strabo dealt with Cisalpine Gaul (probably granting citizenship to all Latin colonies, not only to the Cispadanes south of the Po, and Latin rights to the rest, not merely to the Transpadanes). But even so the newly enfranchised citizens still had a grievance: through the way they were enrolled in the tribes they were not given equal voting rights with the old citizens. Thus, at a terrible cost in human lives in a life-and-death struggle, the political unification of Italy was achieved, and Romans and Italians, hitherto linked by alliance, could now learn to become a single nation.

Civil Struggles, 88–82, and the First Mithradatic War.—There were still a few troubles abroad. In Sicily a slave war (104–101) lasted no longer than the earlier one led by Eunus (135–132), while attempts by M. Antonius to check piracy in the eastern Mediterranean (102–100) were ineffective. More serious was the threat from Mithradates (*q.v.*) VI, king of Pontus, who had profited by Rome's absorption in the Social War to invade Bithynia and Cappadocia in alliance with Tigranes of Armenia. Diplomatic pressure by Rome led him to withdraw, but in 88 he swept through the province of Asia, promising freedom to the Greek cities and massacring 80,000 Italian businessmen and their families. He then accepted an invitation from Athens to invade Greece, where a Pontic force arrived before the end of the year.

This critical position led to political differences in Rome, where a tribune of 88, P. Sulpicius Rufus (*q.v.*), was trying to secure a fair deal for the Italians and their proper distribution in the tribes. In order to gain wider support Sulpicius was prepared to seek it from the people, the *equites,* and an embittered Marius. He therefore proposed that the command against Mithradates should be transferred to Marius from Sulla (consul in 88), to whom it had already been assigned. Disturbances in Rome forced Sulla to flee; he joined his army in Campania, where he learned that Sulpicius' measures had been passed. He then took a momentous decision: he appealed to his troops and led six legions against Rome, which he captured in street fighting since Marius and Sulpicius had no troops. The latter were declared outlaws. Marius escaped, but Sulpicius, a tribune in office, was killed and his legislation was annulled.

Sulla rushed some measures through the *comitia* in order to strengthen the Senate and then crossed to Greece, where he defeated the armies of Mithradates at Chaeronea and Orchomenos (86). Meantime L. Cornelius Cinna (*q.v.*), a consul of 87, tried to reintroduce Sulpicius' measure for the new citizens, but was driven from Rome by his colleague Gnaeus Octavius and declared a public enemy. He then raised forces and was joined by Marius, who returned from his refuge in Africa; together they captured Rome and declared themselves consuls for 86. Marius gratified his thirst for revenge by a terrible massacre, but luckily he died near the beginning of his seventh consulship, leaving Cinna in control for the next three years. Cinna, who was reelected consul each year, showed considerable moderation, and in particular saw to it that at last the new citizens were fairly distributed

throughout the 35 tribes. But he had also had Sulla declared an outlaw, thereby ensuring and emphasizing that Sulla and his army stood against the republic.

Neither L. Valerius Flaccus, Cinna's consular colleague in 86, who was sent against Mithradates, nor Gaius Flavius Fimbria, who murdered Flaccus and succeeded to his command, moved against Sulla, who reached terms with Mithradates by the Peace of Dardanus (85). The king was to withdraw to Pontus and pay an indemnity, while Sulla imposed a severe settlement on Asia which crushed the province financially. He then prepared to return to Italy; Cinna, who tried to save Italy from further fighting, was unable to persuade his troops to cross to Greece and was killed by them (84). Rome was left in the hands of his colleague Gnaeus Carbo. When Sulla finally landed at Brundisium (83) he was joined by several younger men, among them M. Licinius Crassus and Strabo's son Gnaeus Pompeius (Pompey), who raised three legions in Picenum for Sulla. In a brief civil war (83–82) Sulla beat down all opposition and after the Battle of the Colline Gate at Rome itself, where he defeated Carbo and his Samnite allies, he was master of the city. Q. Sertorius had withdrawn to Spain to fight on, but the "Marians" who fled to Sicily and Africa were defeated by Pompey, whom Sulla sent against them. Massacres and proscriptions followed. Sulla confiscated the estates of individual opponents and the land of Italian cities that had taken the other side; he needed the land for his veterans and settled about 120,000 men in over ten colonies in Italy. By a vote of the *comitia centuriata* Sulla then became dictator for redrafting the constitution.

Sulla's Dictatorship.—Though Sulla's early career had not followed an orthodox Optimate pattern and he was not the fervent champion of the Senate that he has sometimes been called, he now probably realized that peace and order could be restored only if the Senate regained something of its old authority. The purpose of the reforms that he introduced was therefore probably to support the Senate and the Optimates against the Populares. He added 300 equestrians to the Senate and secured its future membership by making the quaestorship the automatic qualification. He managed to do without the censorship and controlled the other magistracies by means of the *cursus honorum;* in particular, he clipped the wings of the tribunate, making the office a dead end. He checked equestrian influence in the provinces by restoring the lawcourts in Rome to the senators. To check provincial governors he developed the law of treason (*maiestas*). He raised the number of praetors to eight and arranged that provincial governorships should normally be held by promagistrates after their year of office in Rome. His most enduring reform was his reorganization and development of the permanent courts in Rome to cover the chief crimes.

Having completed his arrangements Sulla resigned his dictatorship (79) and retired into private life, though death soon cut this short. He had given the senatorial nobility another chance, and though he must have known the weaknesses of his settlement (especially the potential threat of an ambitious and ruthless army commander) he may well have thought that it would function if sufficient men of good will tried to work it. That would be the responsibility of the younger generation, including many of his own officers. In the event, two of them, Pompey and Crassus, destroyed his work within ten years.

4. The Rise of Pompey.—The reinforced senatorial government was challenged even before Sulla's death by M. Aemilius Lepidus (*q.v.*), consul in 78, who produced a Popularis program that included the restoration of full powers to the tribunate. Availing himself of the social and economic discontent arising from quarrels between Sulla's colonists and the farmers they had dispossessed, Lepidus led a counterrevolution. After the passing of the *senatus consultum ultimum* his forces were crushed with the help of Pompey, to whom the Senate unwisely granted special *imperium* (77). Pompey then demanded that he should be sent to deal with Sertorius, who was still resisting the senatorial forces under Q. Metellus in Spain (*see* SERTORIUS, QUINTUS). The Senate capitulated and granted the young man proconsular *imperium* as the colleague of Metellus. After some early setbacks

Pompey ultimately defeated Sertorius, who claimed to be fighting not against Rome but against Sulla's illegal government (73).

Meantime Nicomedes IV of Bithynia died and bequeathed his kingdom to Rome. The Senate's acceptance, which changed the balance of power in Asia Minor, provoked Mithradates to invade Bithynia; he was driven out by Lucullus (q.v.) in 74–73 at the beginning of what proved to be a long struggle. In the eastern Mediterranean the well-organized fleets of the pirates, which were said to amount to 1,000 ships, were becoming more menacing, and M. Antonius (praetor in 74) was given a special proconsular command to deal with them. As part of this drive against the pirates, Cyrene, which had been bequeathed to Rome on the death of its ruler more than 20 years earlier, was declared a Roman province in 74. In Italy itself a slave rising, led by Spartacus (q.v.), reached menacing proportions, with the defeat of even consular armies, until it was crushed by Crassus (73–71). Pompey, on his way back from Spain, intercepted some of the slaves who were trying to escape and claimed his share of credit for Crassus' achievement.

Thus both Pompey and Crassus approached Rome with their armies. Both wanted the consulship for 70, though Pompey had not held any of the qualifying offices. But the Senate was discredited by its weak administration of recent years, combined with some scandals in the courts, and was in no way able to resist the demand of the two successful generals. Thus Pompey and Crassus, both old supporters of Sulla, gained office and proceeded to abolish most of what remained of his constitution. The tribunes regained all their former powers, the censorship was revived, and the courts were transferred from senators to a mixed panel of senators, *equites*, and *tribuni aerarii* (the next wealthiest class). The year 70 was also marked by Cicero's prosecution of Verres (q.v.). This had the effect of exposing corruption in the provinces, while Cicero's success made him Rome's leading advocate. At the end of the year neither Pompey nor Crassus took a proconsular command but both retired into private life, which for Crassus largely meant moneymaking.

Further opportunities soon came to Pompey. The pirate menace had become so great that exceptional measures had to be taken, and a tribune named Gabinius, now freed from the shackles that Sulla had imposed on the office, proposed that Pompey be given a great command in the Mediterranean and around its coasts, for three years, with considerable forces to crush the pirates. Pompey with great efficiency carried out the task in three months and thus put an end to a long-standing scandal of Rome's administration.

Meanwhile Lucullus had successfully driven Mithradates from his kingdom of Pontus and then invaded Armenia, where Mithradates had taken refuge with his son-in-law Tigranes. After defeating Tigranes near his capital, Tigranocerta (69), Lucullus then defeated the two kings in battle (68). But his men were getting restless, and his political opponents in Rome, especially the *equites*, were agitating for his recall. In 66, therefore, another tribune, Manilius, carried a measure, which was supported by Cicero, to give the Mithradatic command to Pompey. With much larger forces than Lucullus had commanded, Pompey advanced against Mithradates, who in the meantime had recovered his kingdom, and defeated him at Nicopolis (66) and forced the surrender of Tigranes. Before long Mithradates killed himself (63). His career had shown that the Hellenistic world, which he had failed to free from Rome, must come under one rule and that Rome's political horizon must now reach to the Euphrates.

Meanwhile Pompey had marched through the Caucasus area and then southward, where he reestablished order in Syria and Palestine and captured Jerusalem (64–63). He then resettled the nearer east. The chief change was Rome's annexation of Syria as a province, with the enlargement of Bithynia and Cilicia. Behind this line of Roman provinces, with outposts at Crete and (later in 58) at Cyprus, the various client-kingdoms in Asia Minor were reorganized; here Pompey, like another Alexander, encouraged city life, founding or restoring many cities with Greek institutions. His reorganization of the east gave reasonable security against the Parthian empire beyond the Euphrates; it also vastly enriched the Roman treasury and enhanced the personal prestige

and following of Pompeius Magnus.

5. Pompey and Caesar.—In Rome Crassus, supported by Julius Caesar, intrigued to build up his political power against the return of Pompey. Caesar (q.v.), a noble who drew close to the Populares, had supported Pompey in 67 and gained the aedileship for 65, doubtless with the help of Crassus' wealth. After an abortive minor "conspiracy" by Catiline (q.v.), a bankrupt noble, at the beginning of 65, Crassus sought power in Spain, Transpadane Gaul (between the Po and the Alps), and Egypt. As censor he wished to grant full citizenship to the Transpadanes but was thwarted by his Optimate colleague Catulus. A proposal that Egypt (where the claim of Ptolemy XII Auletes to the throne was questioned) should be annexed was also defeated by the Optimates, supported by Cicero, who was protecting Pompey's interests in Rome. At the end of 64 a tribune, P. Servilius Rullus, was put up to propose an agrarian bill which would have placed large powers in the hands of a commission at a time when Pompey on his return would need land for his veterans. This too was defeated, thanks to the oratory of Cicero.

Cicero had beaten Catiline at the consular elections for 63 with Optimate support; as a *novus homo* of equestrian stock and a supporter of Pompey, Cicero was not an ideal candidate from the Optimate point of view, but he was at least preferable to Catiline. When Catiline failed once again at the elections of 63 to gain position by constitutional methods, he turned to revolutionary means, and planned a general uprising in Italy and a revolution in Rome. After the Senate had passed the *senatus consultum ultimum,* the plot was unmasked by Cicero, who arrested the leading conspirators in Rome and had them executed out of hand, thus preventing a *coup d'état;* Catiline, who had joined an army which he was raising in Etruria, was killed in the field in January 62. Catiline's threat of violence had united senatorial, equestrian, and Italian opinion on Cicero's side, and he began to hope to make this agreement (*concordia ordinum*) permanent. But without sufficient family connections and not being an army commander, he lacked an adequate *clientela* to build up a political party, and he depended too much on the goodwill of the Optimates. Further, hopes of a *concordia* were weakened by the scandal of the Clodius affair (*see* CLODIUS, PUBLIUS).

When Pompey returned to Italy at the end of 62 he disbanded his troops amid general relief, but Cicero, who had hoped that Pompey would play a leading part in his plans for *concordia*, did not find him very helpful. Pompey naturally expected widespread recognition of his achievements and was nonplussed when the Senate, led by Cato (q.v.), refused to ratify his eastern settlement at once and did not provide land for his veterans. Meantime,

ALINARI

(LEFT) POMPEY, IN THE PALAZZO SPADA, ROME; (RIGHT) JULIUS CAESAR, IN THE CAPITOLINE MUSEUM, ROME

Caesar, who had become *pontifex maximus* (63) and praetor (62), had campaigned in western Spain. He now wanted a triumph and to stand for the consulship of 59, but he was blocked by the Senate, which also alienated Crassus by refusing to adjust a contract for the taxes of Asia.

Repulsed by the more conservative senators, these three men made a private compact (*amicitia*), the so-called first triumvirate, to promote their mutual interests. Thus, with the help of Crassus' money, Pompey's potential military strength, and Caesar's prestige, the three men got their way. Cicero recognized this agreement, which was strengthened by Pompey's marriage to Caesar's daughter Julia, as a turning point and the ultimate origin of the civil war of 49. He felt that he had lost freedom of speech and *auctoritas* and that henceforth the state was at the mercy of dynasts (*principes*), who strove for personal *potentia* and *diguitas*. When Caesar became consul (59) he secured the ratification of Pompey's eastern settlement and, with the help of Pompey's veterans, carried a land bill for them, together with a rebate for Crassus. He himself was given a provincial command by a *Lex Vatinia:* Cisalpine Gaul and Illyricum, to which Transalpine Gaul was added, for five years. In 58 he started that series of campaigns which added all Gaul to the empire (*see* CAESAR, GAIUS JULIUS).

During his absence his interests in Rome were upheld in 58 by the tribune P. Clodius, who gained popularity by a measure to distribute free grain (for the first time; this was a very different measure from the cheap grain sold by Gaius Gracchus; Clodius, rather than Gracchus, should be charged with the demoralization of the urban plebs). Clodius also secured the outlawing of Cicero for his execution of the Catilinarian conspirators without a trial, and sent Cato off on a mission to Cyprus. He then attacked Pompey, who was forced to turn for protection to Milo. Milo organized a rival gang to oppose the rowdies who supported Clodius, and gradually order broke down in the city; mob rule threatened. Pompey secured Cicero's return in 57.

The triumvirate seemed to be breaking up, but the three men met at Luca in 56 and agreed to continue their cooperation. Pompey and Crassus became consuls for 55, and Caesar's Gallic command was prolonged for another five years. Pompey, after his consulship, was to govern Spain (which he did through deputies, *legati,* while remaining in Italy himself). Crassus obtained Syria, where he launched a campaign against the Parthians which ended with defeat and his death at Carrhae (*q.v.*) in 53. Thus a link between Caesar and Pompey was broken; another had snapped when Julia died in 54. Disorders in Rome culminated in the murder of Clodius by Milo (52), when Pompey became sole consul to secure order.

In a rapidly deteriorating situation Pompey and Caesar drifted further apart. Caesar feared that if he came to Rome as a private citizen he would be attacked by his enemies. He therefore sought a prolongation of his Gallic command until he could step straight into a second consulship (in 49 or 48). The Optimates opposed this and Pompey did nothing to help Caesar, who relied for help in Rome on Curio (tribune in 50). The extremists in the Senate, who tried to use Pompey to crush Caesar, refused to accept a vote of the Senate that both men should give up their commands and disarm. When finally they asked Pompey to save the republic, he decided to accept the call. The Senate expelled Marcus Antonius and another tribune and passed the *senatus consultum ultimum.*

When the tribunes fled to Caesar in north Italy, he crossed the Rubicon, thereby invading Italy and precipitating a civil war that was fought in the last resort for personal power and honour rather than in defense of a free republic: few could believe that this still survived or that the Optimates could justly claim to represent it.

6. Caesar's Dictatorship and the Second Triumvirate.— Now that the die was cast, Caesar compensated for his relative weakness (his main troops were still in Gaul) by speed of movement. This, combined with the obstinate lack of cooperation by L. Domitius Ahenobarbus (who had been appointed to succeed Caesar in Gaul), forced Pompey to evacuate Italy within two months and to withdraw to Greece. Since Pompey had forces in Spain (his province), Caesar struck at these first, defeating the main army at Ilerda (*q.v.*), securing the whole peninsula, and capturing Massilia on his return to Italy. His cause was less successful in Africa, where he sent Curio to eject its Pompeian governor; Curio was defeated and Africa remained Pompeian for over two years. Back in Rome Caesar was made dictator, but as soon as he was elected to his second consulship for 48 he resigned the dictatorship after 11 days. He then crossed to Greece, where after a setback at Dyrrachium he finally defeated Pompey at Pharsalus (*q.v.*) in 48. Pompey fled to Egypt, where he was murdered on landing. Caesar followed and spent the winter in Alexandria with Cleopatra (*q.v.*), who after the death of her brother Ptolemy XIII became queen of Egypt. After a swift campaign against Pharnaces, the son of Mithradates, which ended in victory at Zela (47), Caesar returned to Italy and Rome, where there had been disturbances and no consuls had been elected for 47.

During his absence Caesar had been made dictator again, probably for a year from October 48, and his master of the horse, Mark Antony (Marcus Antonius; *see* ANTONIUS), was trying to maintain order. Caesar, who was elected to his third consulship for 46, carried some economic measures, pardoned many Pompeians who submitted, and then left for Africa, where in 46 he defeated the Pompeians at Thapsus (*q.v.*). The subsequent suicide of Cato symbolized the death of republican hopes. Before Caesar returned to Rome to celebrate a fourfold triumph, he had already been appointed dictator for ten years and *praefectus moribus* with censorial powers; later he was elected consul for 45. Meanwhile two of Pompey's sons had been organizing resistance in Spain, and Caesar was forced to go there before the end of 46. After defeating them at Munda (45), he returned to Rome where he remained until his death. He was elected to his fifth consulship for 44, with Antony as colleague, and finally, about mid-February of 44, he was made dictator for life; a month later came the Ides of March.

Caesar's Achievements.—During his brief periods in Rome Caesar had carried out an immense amount of legislation: measures to relieve debt, to reform the calendar, to suppress all political clubs, to improve the city (*e.g.,* a new Forum) and help Italy (*e.g.,* draining the Pomptine Marshes), to enfranchise Transpadane Gaul, to settle his veterans and poor citizens in new colonies (especially overseas, in Gaul, Spain, and Africa and, for commercial purposes, at Carthage and Corinth), to improve the taxation of the provinces, to grant Roman citizenship widely to provincials, and to give Latin status to communities where the native element predominated. He planned to safeguard the frontiers of the empire by campaigns against the Dacians and, to avenge Crassus, against the Parthians; he was about to start on the latter when he was murdered.

At home his power rested constitutionally upon the dictatorship; his other offices were secondary. Although he increased the number of praetors and quaestors, he overshadowed the magistrates and controlled the administration either personally or by means of his master of the horse, *praefecti,* and even private agents. He increased the Senate to 900 members, rewarding those who had helped him to victory; many of the new senators were knights, men of substance, especially from Italian towns; the number of centurions, freedmen, and provincials (who included a few notables from Gaul) was small. If the Senate retained its prestige, it lost its powers of initiative, since its majority owed all to Caesar.

There is no doubt that his conduct became more autocratic in the last months of his life when more and more honours were heaped upon him, and that therefore he became increasingly obnoxious to many of the older nobility. He traced his own ancestry to Venus Genetrix and on public occasions wore a laurel wreath and triumphal robe, but though Antony became his priest (*flamen*) the evidence that he sought worship rather than honour is highly suspect. Some have thought that he wished to become a Roman *rex,* reviving the monarchy of five centuries earlier, despite the Roman hatred of the word *rex.* Others, with even less probability, have believed that he wanted to become a Hellenistic king (*basileus*) with all the trappings of oriental ruler cult. Others again have argued that he had not decided to destroy the form of the republic and that he would not have reached any final decision until he had returned from his Parthian expedition.

His intentions may well not have been fully formulated, and they are certainly veiled from us, but he must have realized that some form of autocratic control was necessary. Since some of his contemporaries also realized and resented this, Gaius Cassius, M. Brutus, and at least 60 others formed a conspiracy to remove the "tyrant," although the Senate had taken an oath to protect his person. They struck on the Ides (15th) of March, and Caesar fell at the foot of Pompey's statue.

Civil War.—The result of Caesar's assassination was 13 years of civil war. The surviving heads of state were the consul Antony and the master of the horse, M. Aemilius Lepidus. By decisive action while the Senate hesitated, they gained control of the situation; and on Cicero's proposal the assassins were granted an amnesty and the office of dictator was abolished. But Antony's position was soon challenged by Gaius Octavius, Caesar's adopted son and heir (conventionally known from 44 to 27 as Octavian), who came from Greece to claim his position, trusting to gain the support of Caesar's veterans. During the winter of 44/43 Cicero tried to revive the old republican constitution and boldly denounced Antony's ambitions in a series of speeches, the *Philippics*. In 43 he was so far successful that war was declared on Antony, who was defeated by the republicans and Octavian. But Octavian himself then marched on Rome and demanded the consulship.

ANDERSON—ART REFERENCE BUREAU

CICERO, PORTRAIT BUST IN MARBLE. IN THE CAPITOLINE MUSEUM, ROME

Thereafter he met Antony and Lepidus, and the three formed the "second triumvirate," this time a formal commission, confirmed by a *Lex Titia*. They then proceeded to eliminate the republicans by a ghastly proscription in Rome (the victims included Cicero) and by force of arms in Greece; Brutus and Cassius, who had been mustering forces in the east, were defeated at Philippi (*q.v.*) in 42. Antony's next task was to see to the east and deal with the Parthians, while Octavian remained in the west to check Sextus Pompeius (*q.v.*) and to get land for their veterans; Lepidus was virtually ignored.

Octavian first had to eliminate opposition from Antony's brother Lucius and wife Fulvia, who were compelled to capitulate at Perusia (41), leaving Octavian master of Italy. A breach with Antony was avoided by the Treaty of Brundisium (40), and the reconciliation was strengthened by Antony's marriage (Fulvia had died) to Octavia, sister of Octavian. After temporarily recognizing Sextus Pompeius, who had gained control of Corsica, Sardinia, and Sicily (Treaty of Misenum, 39), Octavian turned against him. After a meeting with Antony at Tarentum (37), where the triumvirate was renewed for five more years, Octavian with the help of his friend Agrippa defeated Sextus in a naval campaign and then overthrew Lepidus, whose occupation of Sicily he refused to recognize. Thus Octavian had restored order by land and sea and was master of the west (36).

In the east, where the Parthians had invaded Syria, Antony was slow to act, but his generals were successful: Ventidius defeated the Parthians (39–38), and Sosius installed Herod the Great in Jerusalem. But Antony had met Cleopatra at Tarsus in 41 and had spent the winter of 41/40 with her at Alexandria; in 37 he sent his wife, Octavia, back to Italy and may have married Cleopatra according to Egyptian, but not Roman, form. At last in 36 he invaded Parthia, but with disastrous results, though in 34 he temporarily annexed Armenia. Back in Alexandria he proclaimed the Donations of Alexandria by which Cleopatra and her children received grants of lands and titles in the east. The children were Caesarion, whom Antony recognized as the legitimate son of Caesar (thereby making Octavian a usurper), and Alexander Helios, Ptolemy Philadelphus, and Cleopatra Selene, whose father was Antony himself.

Meantime Octavian was protecting Italy's northeastern frontier by campaigns in Illyricum (35–33). The break with Antony could not be long delayed, especially when he formally divorced Octavia in 32. A general swearing of allegiance (*coniuratio*) to Octavian took place in Italy and the west; the Senate annulled Antony's triumviral powers and declared war on Cleopatra. As consul in 31 Octavian mustered large land and naval forces in Greece. The final clash came by sea at Actium (September 31). Cleopatra fled to Egypt, followed by Antony; after they had committed suicide (30), Octavian annexed Egypt and settled the east. He was now undisputed master of a war-weary world.

Despite civil wars, misgovernment, corruption, the ambitions of rival dynasts (*principes*), and the collapse of the republican constitution, the Roman world still offered a foundation on which a new system could be built. Further, the political unification of Italy was reflected in the greater unity of Italian civilization. The whole of this period, and especially the Ciceronian age, showed a steady advance in oratory, art, and letters, and a greater synthesis of Greek and Roman traditions. If Cicero was the dominant literary figure, there were also Lucretius and Catullus, Caesar, Varro, and Sallust. Political instability had not undermined all creative production, nor had the civil wars destroyed the economic prosperity of Italy, supported as it was by the resources of the provinces.

II. THE EMPIRE

A. The Principate, 27 B.C.–A.D. 284

1. The Establishment of the Principate.—Octavian, the heir of Caesar, had led a faction to victory in a civil war. With the elimination of all his rivals, he could now identify his faction with the state. "By the common consent of all men I received the absolute control of affairs": in these words he proclaimed his universal sovereignty and the moral basis on which he alleged it rested. His triumviral powers may legally have terminated at the end of 33, but he held the consulship every year from 31 onward, and as long as he enjoyed the loyal support of the armies his position was unchallengeable.

But with peace reestablished, how was he to act? If he followed the example of Sulla and retired into private life, the renewal of civil war was almost certain. If, however, he openly tried to retain autocratic power, he would so offend the nobility and the traditions of 500 years that he would court the same fate as Julius Caesar. In order to safeguard internal peace and to ward off external attack by the barbarian tribes beyond the empire, he alone must retain a unified military command, otherwise history might be repeated and the central government be challenged by provincial commanders. But such authority, if retained, must be masked in republican forms if it was to endure. Octavian thus had to seek a compromise. This he reached by a careful process of testing and responding to public opinion, of trial and error, and so he ultimately found a secure basis on which to establish a principate which lasted for about 200 years.

His first task was to restore confidence and to ease the transition from war to peace. While he was still in the east he was granted various honours; if these included, and he accepted, an offer of tribunician power, he made little use of it before 23. More noticeable was his continued use of *Imperator* as a *praenomen* in place of Gaius, which he had adopted in 38; it connoted an exceptional claim to authority (*see* EMPEROR) but lacked any constitutional significance. At the beginning of 29 the Senate confirmed all his official actions (*acta*); by August he had returned to Rome, where he celebrated his triumph and marked the formal end of the civil wars by closing the Temple of Janus. He reduced his 60 legions ultimately to 28 and settled the veterans in colonies in Italy and the provinces. In 28 he held his sixth consulship, with his friend and helper Agrippa, and both consuls remained in Rome throughout the year for the first time for 20 years. By virtue of a grant of *censoria potestas* Octavian reduced the number of senators from 1,000 to 800 (later to 600) and held a census. By edict he retrospectively annulled any illegal actions taken during the civil wars.

Stability was returning and he was ready for a more general settlement, hastened on perhaps by the implications of the military achievements of M. Licinius Crassus, the proconsul of Macedonia, and by the ambitions of Gaius Cornelius Gallus, his prefect of Egypt. Thus in January 27 B.C., at a meeting of the Senate, he formally renounced all his powers and provinces and put them at the free disposal of the Senate and Roman people, but he at once agreed to administer a large *provincia,* comprising Spain, Gaul, and Syria, for ten years. Whether he received a special grant of proconsular *imperium* for this purpose, or acted through the consulship which he held each year until 23, is uncertain; the view that his *imperium* was (at this stage) greater (*maius*) than that of governors in the senatorial provinces is improbable. Despite the title *Augustus* and many other honours which he received, despite widespread oaths of personal allegiance to him, he might claim that the "restoration of the republic" was secured by the fact that his powers derived from the Senate and Roman people and were limited in time. Others might regard the settlement as a recognition by law of a personal supremacy.

In 23 important changes were made in the formal basis of the authority of Augustus. He abandoned the consulship; his long tenure of it had been unpopular with the nobles and perhaps burdensome to himself, especially in view of critical illnesses in 25 and 23. By way of compensation the Senate increased his *imperium* in two respects: it was not to lapse when he entered Rome, and it was made *maius imperium proconsulare*—that is, greater than that of any other proconsular governor, so that, if he required, Augustus could intervene in any senatorial province. This gave him ultimate control of the armies and provinces, but now that he had ceased to be the chief magistrate in Rome he needed further authority in civilian affairs. This he found in tribunician power (*tribunicia potestas*). He had been offered this previously (indeed he received tribunician sacrosanctity as early as 36), but if he had accepted the offer, he certainly made little use of this power until 23. The tribunate had a long popular history in the city, and so Augustus kept his military powers as veiled as possible and advertised his tribunician power. From 23 B.C. he numbered the years of his principate from this power, which Tacitus later described as "a term to express his supreme position." It gave him such rights as presenting legislation to the people and exercising a veto (*intercessio*). He received also the right to bring forward the first motion at any meeting of the Senate, a body which he could himself summon and consult. These powers, although originating from the Senate, were perhaps sanctioned by the people in a *lex de imperio,* such as that later passed on behalf of the emperor Vespasian, which has survived.

Proconsular *imperium* and tribunician power were the two foundations on which the authority of Augustus and his successors rested. He refused some further powers, such as the offer of a dictatorship and consulship for life in 22, but in 19 he accepted an official seat between the consuls, together with an escort of 12 lictors, and possibly some other specific rights enjoyed by a consul. When Lepidus died in 12 B.C. Augustus became *pontifex maximus,* and in 2 B.C. he was acclaimed as the "father of his country" (*pater patriae*); throughout his lifetime his pronconsular *imperium* was regularly renewed for five or ten years at a time.

Such was the ingenious compromise by which room was found for the master of the legions within the narrow limits of the old Roman constitution. Augustus could say with truth that he had accepted no office which was "contrary to the usage of our ancestors," and that it was only in *auctoritas* (prestige) that he took precedence of his colleagues. Yet the compromise was unreal, and its significance was ambiguous. It was an arrangement avowedly exceptional and temporary, yet few could suppose that in effect it would be other than permanent. The powers voted to Augustus were voted only to him; they were thus made coextensive in time with his life, and there was no provision for hereditary or any other form of succession. Thus Augustus had to devise various expedients to bridge the gap which would be caused by his death.

He had in fact developed a political position which was capable of transference, and dynastic succession was an obvious solution. But Augustus had no son, only a daughter, Julia, whom he married successively to his nephew Marcellus, his friend Agrippa, and his stepson Tiberius. But his two grandsons, born to Julia and Agrippa, died, so that he ultimately was forced to adopt Tiberius, who was granted tribunician power in A.D. 4 and proconsular *imperium* in 13. Thus when Augustus died in 14 Tiberius was virtually a co-regent, and was marked out as the man upon whom the remaining powers of the principate would naturally be bestowed. Not the least of Augustus' achievements was this somewhat makeshift arrangement for the transference of power in a way that averted the renewal of civil war. But in contrast to the maxim that "the king never dies," it has been well said that in law, though not in practice, the Roman principate died with the death of the *princeps.*

Thus Augustus did not seek to become a Roman king, a *rex,* and still less a Hellenistic monarch, a *basileus.* His private life was comparatively simple and his household moderate. But in Egypt he was the successor of the god-king pharaoh and in Syria of the Seleucid monarchs who had developed a ruler cult of the living king. Further, it was nearly 200 years since a Roman had first been hailed by grateful Greeks as divine, and many Romans thereafter had received divine honours in the east. Augustus tried to canalize this attitude by allowing Greek cities in Asia Minor to dedicate temples to "Rome and Augustus." Such cults were expressions of loyalty and were maintained by federations (*koina*), groups of cities which sent delegates to a joint assembly; a similar *concilium* was even introduced into the west for the three Gallic provinces at Lugdunum (Lyons).

In Rome and Italy, however, where Augustus fostered the revival of old Roman religious cults and practices and where he had championed the traditions of the west against the religious beliefs of the east which were reflected in the challenge of Antony and Cleopatra, Augustus deprecated any worship of himself. Since 42 B.C. and the posthumous consecration of Julius Caesar, he had been the "son of a god" (*Divi filius*), but he would countenance no more than worship of his Genius, the spirit which promoted his family and fortunes; and he linked this with the Lares Compitales (spirits that guarded crossroads). For this cult he allowed the establishment of *seviri Augustales,* freedmen in the cities of Italy. But all this, though technically not far from deification, was conceived as an expression of loyalty to Augustus and the new order, and Augustus frowned upon any suggestion of real worship of himself in Rome or Italy. Only after his death did Augustus become *Divus,* an honour which came to be reserved for those emperors whose principates had won general approval.

2. Administration by Princeps and Senate.—Although the Augustan system is not now generally regarded, with Mommsen, as a "dyarchy," a joint rule of *princeps* and Senate, Augustus clearly shared the administration with the Senate while at the same time retaining the undivided control of the army which was the ultimate sanction of his power. The *princeps* could legislate in various ways (*e.g.,* by edict), while the resolutions of the Senate (*senatus consulta*) gradually gained the force of law. In jurisdiction both *princeps* and Senate received the authority to act as high courts in cases of sufficient gravity, with no right of appeal from the verdict of one court to the other. Further, since Augustus was granted the right to reverse capital sentences passed by magistrates, "appeal (*appellatio*) to Caesar" gradually replaced the republican process of "appeal (*provocatio*) to the people."

In financial matters the republican *aerarium* remained the chief treasury; when it was in difficulties Augustus made large grants to it from his private funds (*patrimonium*). Although an imperial treasury or *fiscus* (apart from his patrimony) was probably not centralized in Rome until the reign of Claudius (if then), Augustus exercised a general financial oversight, as seen in his regular publication of a balance sheet of the empire (*rationes imperii*).

The general administration of Rome and Italy remained the primary concern of the Senate and the ordinary magistrates, who were also responsible for all those provinces which the emperor himself did not administer; these senatorial or "public" provinces were in the main those where it was not necessary to station legionary forces. In yet another way the influence of the Senate was soon increased: Augustus' successor, Tiberius, transferred the election of magistrates to it from the *comitia*. Augustus himself did not go so far, but a *Lex Valeria Cornelia* in A.D. 5 probably established a panel of senators and *equites* who by a complicated voting system (*destinatio*) recommended candidates for the consulship and praetorship; the *comitia centuriata* thereafter probably merely ratified the choice. Augustus himself seems to have made only sparing use of the powers of nominating and commending candidates which were exercised by later emperors. Thus in all spheres, except the military, the Senate retained some of its traditional activities and even gained some new duties. Its cooperation in running the empire was essential to the success of Augustus' hopes for peace and stability.

In order to make the Senate more efficient, Augustus designed a standing senatorial committee to prepare business for the main body; this council, however, was not maintained either by himself or his successors in its original form. But efficiency depended no less on personnel than on machinery, and Augustus determined to make the senators more worthy and responsible. This he did by controlling entry into the Senate, which was normally recruited from members of the senatorial order, men of senatorial birth. In addition to birth, he made a period of military service, a property qualification, and above all personal integrity indispensable prerequisites for entry. He could also grant to young *equites*, suitably qualified, the possibility of membership of the Senate. Further, senators alone would not suffice in the vast task of administering the empire, so he turned to the equestrian order and made membership of it dependent on personal character as well as on a property qualification and military service. By using members of this order in the public service, he secured their loyalty to the state and helped to heal the breach that had long divided them from the Senate.

Augustus' insistence on the moral qualities of public servants reflects his general concern to raise standards of conduct. Wealth, derived from foreign conquests and provincial exploitation, combined with the demoralizing influences of years of civil war, had corrupted Roman society, particularly those classes which would provide the leaders. And so Augustus tried not only to infuse some fresh blood from Italy into the older Roman oligarchy, but also to reform the heart of Roman society itself by a body of legislation designed to promote respect for marriage and the family by punishing adultery and encouraging the birth rate. He also tried to stem the increasing intermixing of foreign elements with the Italian citizen body by laws which put a check upon manumission. In an attempt to revive pride in older Roman ways and in the city as the heart of the empire, Augustus not only restored old temples and buildings and beautified the capital city but also improved its public services: the water and food supplies were secured, the danger of fire was reduced by the creation of seven cohorts of *vigiles* (the watch), and public order became the responsibility of three urban cohorts under the command of the prefect of the city. Further, Augustus revived many traditional cults and ceremonies. Under his patronage Virgil, Horace, and Livy recalled the earlier virtues of Rome and the Italian countryside, its destiny and imperial responsibilities, while the peace and prosperity of the new era were splendidly depicted on the Ara Pacis Augustae in the Campus Martius. The Greco-Roman culture of the Mediterranean world was now becoming one, and Augustus fixed the centre of gravity of the empire in Italy and the west.

3. The Civil Service and Army.—*Civil Administration.*—The authority of Augustus and the stability of the new regime would have been speedily undermined if he had failed to enjoy the support of the civilian administrators and the officer class. The former were drawn from the reorganized senatorial and equestrian orders, and for them Augustus provided an attractive career in which efficiency was rewarded with promotion in accordance with a well-established pattern. Members of the senatorial order who were properly qualified and had held a minor magistracy (the vigintivirate), if elected quaestors, entered the Senate, and then the more able could ascend the higher rungs of a senatorial career. After

holding either the aedileship or the tribunate of the plebs, they could stand for one of the (normally) 12 praetorships if they had reached the age of 30. Since the regular age for holding the consulship was 42, an interval followed during which many "praetorian" posts were open. A man might become the commander (*legatus*) of a legion, serve as *legatus* on the staff of a provincial governor, become the governor of a lesser imperial province (*legatus Augusti pro praetore*), or proconsul of a senatorial province (such governors received this title, whether or not they had yet held the consulship itself).

Those who then gained the consulship could look forward to the governorship of a more important imperial province, a curatorship in Rome (*e.g., operum publicorum,* responsible for public buildings), the prefecture of the city, or the governorship of one of the important senatorial provinces of Africa or Asia. A good career in administrative posts was also opened up for suitably qualified members of the equestrian order, after their preliminary military service. Augustus used them as financial agents (*procuratores*) in his provinces (their traditional business interests made them well suited in this sphere), and also as governors (*procuratores,* though at first some may have been called *praefecti*) of the less important imperial provinces (*e.g., Judaea*). Thereafter the most successful might look forward to one of the great prefectures: of the fleet (*classis*), the watch (*vigiles*), the grain supply (*annona*), Egypt, or the praetorian guard.

Thus Augustus laid the foundations of a civil service. These men were not amateurs, like the magistrates of the republic, but became professionals who served for long periods and received a salary. The greater number were the servants of the emperor, appointed by and responsible to him, and not many of those who were appointed by the Senate to serve in senatorial provinces and posts would be likely to secure appointment without his approval. Thus an efficient system was developed which avoided many of the weaknesses that had marred the administration of the late republic; misgovernment and corruption were reduced, although not totally banished. This achievement of Augustus, though unspectacular, was among his great gifts to the Roman world. By supplementing with new machinery what he could salvage from the republican system, he avoided too sharp a break with the past and created a means to hold the empire together and to promote its prosperity.

Military Organization.—Good civil administration, however, was little use if the security of the empire was threatened by attack from beyond its frontiers. A professional army was needed for defense, but its loyalty to the central government must be ensured at the same time. Since the challenge of provincial governors, backed by their armies, had been one of the main causes of the collapse of the republic, Augustus had to create a standing army whose loyalty he could count upon and which was large enough to guard the frontiers. None knew better than he the dangers inherent in the older army system when he set his hand to creating from the armies of the triumviral period a professional force which would remain loyal to state and *princeps*. First, he established a privileged corps, the praetorian guard of nine cohorts stationed in various parts of Italy. At the end of the civil war more than 60 legions were under arms; of these he discharged over half (providing land for them) and retained 28 legions. These became permanent units, each with its number and title, with adequate pay, good prospects of promotion (there were 60 centurions in each legion), and a pension in the form of money or land after 20 years' service. This pension was provided ultimately by the state and not by the emperor, who created a special fund (*aerarium militare*) for this purpose and maintained it from the revenue from a sales tax and death duties. The legionaries were recruited from Roman citizens, and therefore primarily from Italy and the western provinces.

The second main branch of the army comprised the *auxilia,* which were kept separate from the legions although coming under the command of the legionary legates. They were raised from non-citizens in the less romanized (that is, the imperial) provinces, and as a reward for 25 years' service they received citizenship on discharge. Thus Augustus made much more use of the manpower of the provinces for defense than had been the practice during the republic. In all, the *auxilia* probably numbered around 150,000 men, and the total of the legions was about the same, so a regular army of about 300,000 men was established, and its units were stationed in the provinces where they were most needed.

In relation to the length of frontiers to be guarded, this force was only just adequate, and wars often involved moving troops from one front to another. Under the immediate successors of Augustus the normal distribution was three legions in Spain, eight on the Rhine, seven on the Danube, four in Syria, two in Egypt, and one in Africa. In peacetime also they played a useful role, building roads, bridges, aqueducts, and canals, and spreading Roman ways of life to the more distant parts of the empire. (*See* also ARMY: *Ancient Armies: Rome.*)

Augustus also maintained a small regular naval force with bases at Misenum, Ravenna, Forum Julii (Fréjus), Alexandria, and probably Seleucia in Syria. These ships kept down piracy and enabled troops and supplies to be moved throughout the Mediterranean with speed and safety.

As long as Augustus could count on the loyalty of the commanders, this military reorganization would guarantee the maintenance of the *pax Romana* within the empire and guard it from external attack, provided that adequate frontiers could be established.

4. Frontiers and Provinces.—*Eastern Frontier.*—Now that one man controlled the military forces of the state and very largely determined its foreign policy, it became possible to regard the problems of the empire as a whole and to design plans to secure really effective frontiers. One danger spot was in the east, where the Parthians still held the Roman standards captured from Crassus and Antony. Augustus showed appreciation of this threat by his own presence in the east (in 30–29 and again in 22–19) and by the commands in the east granted to his friend and helper Agrippa in 23–21 and in 17–13. To the three Roman provinces in Asia Minor (Asia, Bithynia, and Cilicia) Augustus added Galatia when its king was killed in 25 B.C. The key state in the east, however, was the native kingdom of Armenia, which might prove to be a bone of contention between Rome and Parthia. Augustus decided, if possible, to avoid war, and by a show of force persuaded the Parthians to return the Roman standards in 20 B.C. and to acquiesce in a Roman nominee on the throne of Armenia. This diplomatic triumph Augustus regarded as one of the great achievements of his principate; it was confirmed by further negotiations in A.D. 1, and so the two great empires could continue to live at peace, with the Euphrates limiting their spheres of interest. Roman military defense of the east was based on the forces in Syria.

To its south lay the client kingdom of Herod the Great in Judaea, but after his death (4 B.C.) and ten years of oppressive rule by his son Archelaus, Judaea was made into a small imperial province. A Roman expedition into Arabia in 25–24, designed to promote trade and further commerce with India, met with ill success and was not followed up.

Northern Frontier.—The relative security in the east gained by agreement with Parthia allowed Augustus to undertake thoroughgoing measures to safeguard the other frontier where danger lay, the northern. Since the mass of barbarian tribes beyond the Rhine and Danube might threaten the security of Italy and the Balkans, Augustus planned by widespread conquest to advance Roman control as far as the Danube. This was achieved in a series of campaigns, in which his stepson Tiberius played a leading part: Raetia and Noricum (16–15 B.C.) and, farther east, Pannonia (13–8) and Moesia were added to the Roman Empire. When in 12 B.C. Augustus ordered an advance over the Rhine as far as the Elbe, he was apparently contemplating the permanent occupation of western Germany and a frontier along the Elbe and Danube to replace that of the Rhine and Danube which had just been gained. In order to complete this scheme it was necessary to reduce the Marcomanni in Bohemia, but before a converging attack of no fewer than 12 legions could be completed, news came of a great revolt in Pannonia and Illyricum (A.D. 6–9). No sooner was this crushed than Arminius, the chief of the Cherusci in Germany, annihilated three Roman legions under Varus in the Teutoburg

Forest in western Germany. Although the immediate situation was retrieved, Augustus, now old and disheartened, abandoned his policy of conquest east of the Rhine and reverted to this river as the permanent frontier, on which no fewer than eight legions were stationed in six camps between Holland and Switzerland. The line of the Danube was guarded by seven legions.

Africa, Spain, and Gaul.—Elsewhere in the empire there was reorganization, but this involved relatively little fighting. Egypt, where Augustus was the successor of the Ptolemies, was administered for him by a prefect of equestrian rank, and the complicated bureaucratic and monopolistic administration of the Ptolemies was adapted to the new needs; Alexandria remained a centre of commerce and culture, and the peasants of Egypt toiled to produce grain and wealth for their new master. The southern frontier was secure after a punitive raid into Ethiopia (Nubia). Another granary of Rome was the old province of Africa which now, with Numidia, became Africa Proconsularis, a senatorial province with a former consul as its proconsular governor. With Carthage restored as a Roman colony, Roman civilization continued to spread through an area already permeated with Berber and Punic influences; minor campaigns on its desert frontiers thrust raiding tribesmen back.

In Spain the Astures and Cantabri in the northwest had never really submitted to Roman authority. Augustus himself in 26 B.C. led a campaign which was ended by the more ruthless methods of Agrippa in 19. Settlement followed the conquest: hill tribes were moved down to more open valleys, new towns were developed in the northwest, and veterans were settled at Emerita (Mérida) and Caesaraugusta (Saragossa). Spain was divided into three provinces: the more civilized Baetica was handed over to senatorial administration, while Augustus became responsible for Lusitania and Tarraconensis (Hither Spain, or Hispania Citerior).

Gaul too was reorganized. Narbonensis (Gallia Narbonensis), which had been a province for nearly a century, was entrusted to the Senate, while the rest of Gaul was divided into three districts, the *Tres Galliae:* Aquitania, Lugdunensis, and Belgica. Like Spain, it flourished; tribal organization began to merge into municipal, road construction promoted commerce, and a provincial *concilium* at Lugdunum (as one at Tarraco in Spain) loyally fostered the worship of *Roma et Augustus*. Trade across the English Channel increased, but despite rumours that he would invade Britain, Augustus decided to leave the island outside the Roman Empire.

Provincial Administration.—The provinces, exhausted by long periods of civil war and maladministration during the late republic, now enjoyed peace and more equitable government from the professional salaried officials of the reformed senatorial and equestrian orders. (*See* also PROVINCE, ROMAN: *The Principate.*) In order to spread the financial burdens more fairly, Augustus surveyed the resources of the empire by means of periodical censuses which revealed the extent and ownership of land and other wealth. These returns provided the basis for fair taxation. Direct taxes were levied on all occupiers of land (*tributum soli*) and on other forms of property (*tributum capitis;* this was a poll tax in backward areas, like Egypt). Italy and a few towns that enjoyed the *Jus Italicum* were alone exempted from the land tax which all provincials, including Roman citizens, had to pay; some privileged towns were exempt from the *tributum capitis*. Indirect taxes were levied on manumission, on the sale of slaves, and on inheritances, together with some customs and harbour dues. These taxes were still collected by *publicani*, but the latter were now strictly controlled. The direct taxes in the imperial provinces were collected by an imperial procurator of equestrian rank who was largely independent of the governor, while in the senatorial provinces the quaestor was responsible for finance, although *publicani* continued to act as middlemen in some of them. In general the revenue from the taxes was only just adequate to meet the normal expenditure on the army and its pensions, on the civil service, and on public works; when it proved insufficient Augustus used some of his great personal wealth to help, a precedent which not all his successors wished or were able to follow.

Development of Urban Life.—Augustus followed the republican tradition of working through the existing provincial communities, whether cities or tribes. Without an adequate basis of local self-government the administrative system imposed by Rome on the provinces would have collapsed. The officials had to rely on the cooperation of the provincials. Where no cities with organized magistrates and councils existed, Rome made use of the tribal system (as in Gaul, and later in Britain), but the tribes (*civitates*) often quickly borrowed the titles used in Roman cities and had their own *duoviri* and senate (the *ordo*). Rome encouraged, without enforcing, city life, and towns served as centres to large areas which were attached ("attributed") to them for administrative purposes; municipal privileges would be extended to this territory when it became more civilized. The settlement of colonies of veterans in the provinces helped to spread urbanization; at least 40 were established by Augustus, the majority in the peaceful areas in the west.

The status of the provincial cities varied considerably. The most privileged were the colonies, settlements of Roman citizens, and next to them the *municipia,* existing cities which were granted Roman citizenship. Next came the "Latin" cities, whose status was between that of citizen and non-citizen towns; their local magistrates became Roman citizens. These Latin rights (*see* LATIN RIGHTS) were generally granted to cities before they were raised to the status of *municipia*. Lastly were the "stipendiary" cities, which formed the majority in most provinces.

The internal constitutions of all these various cities naturally varied, but even those without Roman citizenship tended to copy the institutions of republican Rome, with popular assemblies, senates, and magistrates, while the older Greek cities in the eastern part of the empire had enjoyed well-developed constitutions for centuries. In general the propertied classes controlled the local senates, and it was they who provided the magistrates, who in accord with Roman tradition were collegial, annual, and unpaid. Many of these men were extremely generous to their towns, providing baths, theatres, and other amenities. Thus local patriotism fostered a healthy municipal life, which was secured by the degree of civic liberty that the Romans wisely accorded to the provinces and by the increasing spread of Roman citizenship.

TABLE I.—*Roman Emperors, 27 B.C.-A.D. 180**

Reign dates	Name	Reign dates	Name
27 B.C.–A.D. 14 .	Augustus	81–96 . .	Domitian
14–37 . . .	Tiberius	96–98 . .	Nerva
37–41 . . .	Gaius (Caligula)	98–117 . .	Trajan
41–54 . . .	Claudius I	117–138 . .	Hadrian
54–68 . . .	Nero	138–161 . .	Antoninus Pius
68–69 . . .	Galba	161–169 . .	Marcus Aurelius and
69 . . .	Otho		Lucius Verus
69 . . .	Vitellius	169–177 . .	Marcus Aurelius
69–79 . . .	Vespasian	*175* . .	*Avidius Cassius (East)*
79–81 . . .	Titus	177–180 . .	Marcus Aurelius and
			Commodus

*Usurpers in italics.

Economy.—Economic life continued in much the same way as during the republic: Augustus initiated no fresh economic policy, no state controls or monopolies. Private competition was allowed to continue freely between all who engaged in industry or trade. The main difference was rather the changed conditions resulting from peace and political unity. Prosperity increased. With Italy in the lead, each province developed its natural resources with increasing specialization of production. This led to greater expansion of trade between all parts of the empire (and beyond, as to India) and to a rise in the standard of living, especially in the cities, where the middle classes enjoyed a prosperous life.

Summary of Augustus' Achievements.—All this was the result of the long years of constructive work which was achieved by Augustus and his helpers, after he had abandoned the role of a revolutionary faction leader and had become both the sole master of the Roman world and at the same time a responsible statesman. He had reached a delicately balanced *modus vivendi* with the Senate and republican traditions; he had created an improved administrative system; he had developed a consistent frontier policy to replace the somewhat haphazard development during the republic and had counseled his successors to keep the empire within the boundaries he had established; he had created a standing army to hold these frontiers against barbarian attacks; he had tried to

ALINARI
TIBERIUS. IN THE VATICAN MUSEUM

stem the decline in standards of behaviour in public and even private life, to make Rome a worthy capital of the new empire, to integrate Italian with Roman interests, and to centre the new order on a united Italy whose municipal life offered an exemplar to the provinces; and with the securing of peace he made possible the romanization of western Europe.

In an edict he once expressed the hope that he might be allowed to set the state on a firm and secure basis and as a result be regarded as the "author of the best possible government" (*optimi status auctor*), and that at death he might carry with him the hope that the foundations that he had laid for the *Respublica* would remain unshaken. In many aspects his hopes were fulfilled, but he failed to include within the *optimus status* one essential component, real and unfettered liberty.

5. The Julio-Claudian Emperors.—*Tiberius.*—The official account that Augustus himself gave of his achievements (*Res Gestae*) was set up at his death in A.D. 14 on his family mausoleum in Rome (a copy from Asia is preserved, the *Monumentum Ancyranum; see* ANCYRANUM, MONUMENTUM). But his achievements might well have been in vain if his authority had not been peacefully handed on to a successor. The transference of power was accomplished smoothly, not least because his stepson Tiberius, whom he had adopted and made a virtual co-regent with himself, was a soldier of great distinction and therefore the more easily commanded the loyalty of the legions. During his principate (14–37), however, Tiberius found it increasingly difficult to cooperate smoothly with the Senate despite a sincere desire to do so. The senatorial administration came to depend even more upon the will of the *princeps,* although the Senate now entirely replaced the people in the election of magistrates and its judicial activities increased.

Tiberius suffered from dynastic difficulties. The death of his nephew Germanicus, whom he was wrongly suspected of having poisoned, increased his unpopularity, while his son Drusus was murdered through the intrigues of Sejanus. The career of the latter, who stationed the praetorian guard at Rome (23), demonstrated the potential power of the praetorian prefect and the vulnerability of Tiberius, who trusted him until his final plot for supreme power was unmasked in 31. Betrayed and suspicious, Tiberius was less inclined to check the abuse of the law of treason (*maiestas*) which Augustus had extended to protect the person of the *princeps;* professional informers (*delatores*) increased and treason trials multiplied, but the portrait that has come down to us from Tacitus, of Tiberius as a sinister tyrant whose rule ended in a reign of terror, is unduly coloured by Tacitus' own bitter experiences under Domitian. Even Tacitus admitted that the civil government during the first nine years of Tiberius' reign was good; it deteriorated during the last few years, but although he refused to enter Rome again, he still devoted care to public affairs (as during a financial crisis in 33).

His provincial administration also was good. In general he accepted the precept of Augustus not to extend the frontiers, although he did annex Cappadocia. In the north Germanicus was allowed to restore Roman prestige in Germany by campaigns beyond the Rhine (14–16) but not to annex territory east of the river (*see* GERMANICUS CAESAR). Disturbances in Africa, Gaul, and Thrace were crushed, but Judaea was restless under Pilate's administration (26–36), which was marred by other errors besides the crucifixion of Jesus Christ. Tiberius, however, usually chose

REGIONS, TOWNS, AND MAJOR ROADS IN ROMAN ITALY, ABOUT A.D. 14

good governors and was harsh to those who fell short. When disasters occurred he could be generous, as after an earthquake in 17 in Asia, which showed its gratitude by erecting at Smyrna a temple to Tiberius, his mother Livia, and the Senate. But Tiberius deprecated the spread of emperor worship and refused a similar request from Spain; he remarked that he was satisfied to be human and to occupy the first place (*principem*) among men. With this he had to be content even after death, since he was not granted those divine honours which he himself had secured for *Divus Augustus*.

Caligula.—The chief advantage of the principate of Gaius (Caligula, Germanicus' son; 37–41) was its brevity. Although it started hopefully, he quickly developed into a megalomaniac and tyrant, imitating Oriental ideas of absolute monarchy, encouraging delation, humiliating the Senate, increasing taxation, and spending recklessly. His military operations in Germany and his abortive threat to Britain did little to enhance his reputation, while his folly in provoking rebellion in Mauretania and in outraging Jewish sentiment in both Judaea and Alexandria was stopped only by his timely murder in 41. His conduct had subjected the Augustan system to a severe strain and emphasized the autocratic tendencies latent in the principate.

Claudius I.—Gaius' uncle Claudius, who reigned from 41 to 54, was accepted reluctantly by the Senate when he was thrust on it by the praetorian guard; senatorial hopes of a revival of the republic were exposed as unrealistic. Claudius reacted sharply from Gaius' autocracy and tried sincerely to cooperate with a Senate that despised him on personal grounds. He wished to rule well, and in many ways he succeeded, although his achievements have been denigrated by a contemptuous or hostile tradition. His sense and knowledge of history impressed him with Rome's ability to introduce change without destroying essential traditions. Hence his thoughts turned to the more creative period of Augustus and even of Julius Caesar rather than to the more conformist years of Tiberius. The needs of a growing empire required a more centralized administration, so he built up the civil service in Rome by establishing special imperial departments under freedmen to deal with official correspondence, with petitions, accounts, judicial cases, and literary matters. These new imperial freedmen, who gained great power and wealth, were an offense to the senatorial aristocracy, a support to the emperor, and a means to greater efficiency in administration. Although he may not have established an imperial *fiscus* in Rome alongside the senatorial *aerarium,* he certainly tightened his control over finance. Desire for efficiency and a partiality for jurisdiction led him to improve the judicial system, but his hearing of many criminal cases privately *intra cubiculum* was unpopular and allowed his wives and freedmen to intrigue more freely. His revival of the censorship, which he held in 47–48, also gave offense to the Senate.

In foreign policy he abandoned Augustus' precept and followed his example, showing a preference for direct Roman rule in place of the use of client-kings. No fewer than five provinces were added: the two Mauretanias (*c.* 42), southern Britain (43), Lycia (43), and Thrace (46). Claudius also thought that now that Latin culture was being assimilated more widely, the time had come to extend Roman citizenship to those who had reached an adequate degree of romanization. Less careful of the privileges of Rome and Italy, he tried to improve the status of the provinces, especially in the west, by generous grants of Roman citizenship and municipal rights to individuals or communities; he also founded many colonies. Further, he admitted leading provincials, especially from Gallia Narbonensis, to the Senate. Augustus had made this body more representative of *tota Italia;* now Claudius was prepared to open it to worthy representatives of the provinces. This well-intentioned policy, however, contained the seeds of danger; the further undermining of the old governing class might lead to greater centralization of power in the hands of one man. So too the new bureaus were the seeds from which grew the gigantic bureaucratic machine which over two centuries later began to throttle the free life of the whole Roman world; but that was a development that Claudius could scarcely have foreseen.

In his domestic life he was less happy. Through the intrigues of his last wife, Agrippina, who probably poisoned him in 54, he was succeeded not by his own son Britannicus but by her son of a former marriage, Nero, a lad of not yet 17.

Nero.—The new principate (54–68) started well, since Nero was guided by his tutor Seneca and the praetorian prefect Burrus, but his reconciliation with the Senate did not last long and he gradually scandalized the aristocracy. Throwing off all controls, Nero murdered Britannicus (55), his mother, Agrippina (59), and his wife, Octavia (62), and forced Seneca into retirement. Instigated by the prefect Tigellinus, the successor to Burrus who may have died a natural death, Nero indulged his artistic passions with extravagance and excess. His unpopularity was increased by this conduct, by his reliance on Greek and Oriental freedmen, by his use of the treason law and his plundering of the rich, by the fire that ruined half of Rome in 64, by the Golden House that he built over the ruins, and by his excessive cruelty to the Christians, whom he tried to blame for the fire.

Disorders soon followed in the provinces. A more aggressive policy in the east led to a clash with Parthia and a great military defeat at Rhandeia (62), although the Armenian question was then settled through a display of Roman might by Corbulo, and the Armenian king came to Rome to receive his crown from the hands of Nero. A revolt in Britain, led by Boudicca (*see* BOADICEA), was successfully crushed (60–61), but a widespread rebellion blazed through Judaea (66–70), while provincial governors rose against Nero in the west: Vindex in Gaul and Galba in Spain. Nero had made the fatal mistake of not getting to know his armies. At home aristocrats, Stoics, army chiefs, and countless individuals

ANDERSON—ART REFERENCE BUREAU

NERO. IN THE MUSEO NAZIONALE, ROME

opposed and hated him. One conspiracy, led by Gaius Piso in 65, was betrayed and crushed. Finally the praetorian guard deserted their emperor. Nero fled from Rome and committed suicide. Thus the Julio-Claudian dynasty crashed amid rebellion and civil war, but the work of Augustus, Tiberius, and Claudius survived the disaster.

6. The Flavian Emperors.—Nero had no son, and no member of the Julian or Claudian families survived to claim the succession and maintain the link with Augustus. In the absence of a claimant at Rome, as the famous epigram of Tacitus emphasized, "a secret was revealed that an emperor could be made elsewhere than at Rome." It was not the Senate but the wishes of the armies in the provinces that settled the matter, although the armies recognized that their nominees were still pretenders until they were approved by the Senate. While all the armies had remained loyal to an heir of Augustus their separation on the various frontier provinces had proved beneficial by making any concerted action against the central authority more difficult. But now their geographical separation emphasized their differences of interest, and each army group wished to put forward the claims of its own commander.

Galba, Otho, Vitellius.—The movement started when Gaius Julius Vindex, a romanized Gaul and governor of Gallia Lugdunensis, revolted against Nero, probably desiring a better emperor rather than a restoration of republican authority or a nationalistic breakaway by Gaul. He was soon defeated by the legate of Upper Germany, Verginius Rufus, whose victorious troops offered him the empire. Verginius declined but finally gave his support to Galba, the governor of Hispania Tarraconensis, who had renounced his loyalty to Nero and secured the support of Otho, the governor of Lusitania. By October 68 Galba had reached Rome, where he was accepted by the Senate and the praetorian guard. But a series of tactless actions quickly alienated sympathy, and news soon reached him of the disaffection of the armies on the Rhine, which were proclaiming their leader Vitellius as emperor. Galba in vain hastily adopted as co-regent a certain Piso Licinianus, but this merely infuriated Otho, who was thus passed over. He won the support of the praetorian guard, which killed Galba, and Otho became emperor for three months (69). The armies of Vitellius boldly invaded Italy, where Otho managed to hold the line of the Po until he was defeated near Cremona; then, to spare his fellow countrymen from further fighting, he committed suicide in April. Vitellius soon exposed his personal incompetence and weakness as emperor, and the armies in the east, refusing to accept the choice of the Rhine armies, put forward a candidate of their own, T. Flavius Vespasianus, who was in command of the forces reducing the Jewish revolt.

Vespasian.—Vespasian's future was assured when the armies on the Danube, which had favoured Otho, now declared for Vespasian. While Vespasian himself was organizing supplies in Alexandria and his supporter Mucianus, the governor of Syria, was advancing slowly toward Europe, Antonius Primus swooped down on northern Italy from Pannonia and, at another battle near Cremona, defeated the Vitellians. By December the Danubian troops had captured Rome and killed Vitellius. On Dec. 22 all the imperial powers, including unlimited rights of "commending" candidates for magistracies, were voted *en bloc* to Vespasian by the Senate and ratified by the people in a *Lex de imperio Vespasiani*, of which a partial copy survives. He himself did not reach Rome for over six months. It remained to be seen whether he would succeed in the daunting task of stamping out civil war, winning the allegiance of all the armies, reestablishing orderly civil government, and above all of re-creating a widespread faith in Rome's future.

One of the first tasks of Vespasian (whose principate lasted from 69 to 79) was to quell two rebellions. Recent events in the west had given an impetus to the Jewish War, which Vespasian handed over to his elder son Titus. In 70 Titus besieged, captured, and destroyed Jerusalem; Judaea was made a province, and a Roman legion was stationed there. Even more serious was a rising of the Batavians of the lower Rhine district, led by Civilis, which started before the death of Vitellius. Civilis was soon joined by Classicus, a leader of the Gallic Treveri who hoped to form a new independent Gallic empire. The rebels smashed Roman power on the Rhine, destroying all but two of the Roman camps; that of Vetera held out during a bitter siege until 70. However, divergence of aims weakened the insurgents; eight legions were sent against them and the rebellion collapsed. Vespasian realized that the revolt had been facilitated by Roman troops quartered in the north who had been recruited locally. Henceforth auxiliary troops had to serve on frontiers far from their native homes; they were also to be less homogeneous and have Roman officers in place of native chiefs. The non-Italian element in the legions was increased by greater recruitment from the western provinces. Vespasian avoided Nero's mistake of neglecting the army, and he secured its loyalty; further, he reconciled it to the principate as such, even when this was no longer held by members of the Julio-Claudian family. More than a century passed before a *princeps* had serious trouble with the army. To secure the loyalty of the praetorian guard, Vespasian made his son Titus its prefect.

The fact that he had two sons was an inestimable advantage: he might hope to found a dynasty and thus minimize the threat of renewed civil war when he died. He therefore kept them in the public eye, sharing his powers and offices with Titus, who with his brother Domitian received the titles of *princeps iuventutis* and *Caesar*.

With the Senate Vespasian took a strong line. Although only 30 of the old republican families were still represented in it and a few provincials had come in under Claudius, he decided to make it more representative of the provinces. To do this he held the censorship, with Titus, in 73 (and perhaps annually thereafter), and he drew his new senators from the municipal towns of Italy and the west, although the east and Africa were not neglected (the first African reached the consulship in 80). He thereby infused a much healthier element into the Senate, and a new aristocracy of service arose. This was in line with Vespasian's own character; he was a hard-working, shrewd countryman from Sabine country, not a Roman aristocrat. But if the Senate now provided better administrators (there is only one recorded trial for provincial misgovernment in his reign), any claim it had tried to maintain to be a partner of the emperor disappeared; Vespasian might treat it with courtesy, but not on equal terms.

In finance he was faced with a treasury drained by extravagance and war; he therefore increased taxation (*e.g.*, he diverted to Jupiter the annual contribution that pious Jews had paid to the Temple at Jerusalem) and practised economy, introducing a simpler court life. Yet he spent where necessary, as with the building of the Flavian Amphitheatre, which we call the Colosseum. Much of his work antagonized the older nobility, but open opposition came only from republicans such as Helvidius Priscus, Stoics, and Cynics; Vespasian therefore banished itinerant philosophers. When he died in 79 he was deified and was succeeded without trouble by Titus.

Titus and Domitian.—Titus' brief but popular reign (79–81) was marked by lavish generosity and by the destruction of Pompeii and its neighbourhood through the eruption of Vesuvius in 79. His brother Domitian (81–96), who had been kept somewhat in the background, developed the tendencies to autocracy which had begun to show under Vespasian: he would be master of Senate, people, and army. He held the consulship frequently, assumed the title of *censor perpetuus* (from 85), entered the Senate in triumphal robes and exposed it as his servant, gave the *equites* more influence at the expense of both freedmen and senators, welcomed, although he did not demand, the form of address of *dominus et deus* ("master and god"), and probably made oaths by his Genius and sacrifice to his image a test of loyalty, which led to clashes with Jews and Christians. His costly buildings, games, and shows, and an increase in army pay, all required money, which he obtained by efficient administration and partly by confiscations (although the latter may primarily have been aimed at weakening aristocratic opposition). After the unsuccessful rebellion of Saturninus, governor of Upper Germany, in 89, Domitian was alarmed and allowed his fears and cruelty free rein. A period of terror followed, in which delation and treason trials flourished. Some senators, as Frontinus and Agricola (*qq.v.*), found safety in retirement from public life, and few senators could breathe freely until the tyrant was assassinated in 96.

DETAILS OF RELIEFS FROM THE ARCH OF TITUS, ERECTED IN THE FORUM A.D. 81

(Top) Titus standing in a *quadriga* (four-horsed chariot), led by Roma, while Victory crowns him; (bottom) triumphal parade in Rome of Jewish vessels (a seven-branched candlestick, table for the shewbread, and the sacred trumpets) removed after the sack of Jerusalem (A.D. 70)

VESPASIAN. IN THE NY CARLSBERG GLYPTOTEK, COPENHAGEN

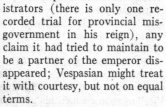

Foreign Policy under the Flavians.—The foreign policy of the three Flavian emperors was directed less to extending the empire than to strengthening its frontiers. In the east, where the province of Cappadocia was flanked by the client states of Lesser Armenia and Commagene, Vespasian made a radical change: Cappadocia and Lesser Armenia were put under the administration of the governor of Galatia, and Commagene was added to Syria in the south, whose governor was now relieved of the supervision of Judaea, which had become a separate province. This reorganization, with legionary troops stationed in camps on the Euphrates, and with the two major provinces of Galatia and Syria now facing Parthia, secured peace in the east for nearly half a century.

On the Rhine frontier the Flavians decided to annex some territory east of the river and guard this with forts and troops. In 74 Vespasian annexed the Agri Decumates in the Black Forest area, thereby eliminating the awkward angle between the sources of the Rhine and Danube. He also penetrated up the lower Neckar Valley, and later Domitian defeated the Chatti and encircled the Taunus Mountains (83–84). After the revolt of Saturninus in 89 this new frontier was consolidated by establishing Upper and Lower Germany as two "provinces" with some kind of civil as well as military organization. Farther east the Dacians who lived north of the Danube (in modern Rumania) crossed the river and invaded Moesia in 85. After an initial defeat the Romans won a victory at Tapae in 88; Domitian came to terms with Decebalus, the Dacian king, and agreed to pay him an annual subsidy. Domitian did not regard this as a great achievement.

In Britain also there was further advance. Petillius Cerialis moved north to Eburacum (York) and reduced the Brigantes (71–74), while his successor, Frontinus, conquered the Silures in southern Wales (c. 74–77). Gnaeus Julius Agricola then overran north Wales and northwestern Britain, and penetrated into Scotland. After his victory at Mons Graupius he was recalled by Domitian (84); his conquests in the north were held for some years, but the frontier was then drawn back to the line of the Solway and Tyne; to hold the north would have involved maintaining in Britain a permanent garrison of four instead of three legions.

Thus Rome and the empire owed much to the Flavians. Like Augustus, Vespasian had to restore peace and order at home and abroad after civil war; both men succeeded in establishing stable government. If the relations between emperor and Senate deteriorated and the former edged a little nearer to autocracy, at least all men had been given renewed confidence in Rome's *aeternitas* (if Vespasian had failed, the 3rd-century breakdown might have occurred two centuries earlier) and they began to look for their well-being to the *providentia* of the emperor. A firm foundation had been provided for the prosperity which was to reach its climax in the days of the Antonines.

7. The "Five Good Emperors."—*Nerva.*

—Domitian left no heir, and the threat of renewed civil war was heavy, but his murderers had been careful first to choose as a candidate an elderly jurist and senator, M. Cocceius Nerva, who was remotely linked through his mother to the Julio-Claudians. The crux was whether the army would acquiesce in a nominee of the Senate. In fact, after some early murmurings, it did, and the principate was saved; well might the coin types proclaim *Roma Renascens* ("Rome reborn"). To the Senate Nerva naturally showed deference and he tried to uphold constitutional practice; thus Pliny could speak of the restoration of constitutional government (*libertas restituta*), and Tacitus of the blending of such government and the principate, which had formerly been incompatible. Nerva tried to gain goodwill by various acts of generosity and by damning the memory of the tyrant Domitian. One of the most important measures attributed to him was an alimentary scheme (*alimenta*) to help the small farmers of Italy, to relieve poverty, and to stimulate the birth rate. But he had two weak spots: he had no son to succeed him, and his lack of military experience made the support of the army uncertain. He therefore adopted an heir who would commend himself to the army and keep the praetorians in hand (they had forced Nerva to allow the execution of the murderers of Domitian). He chose wisely in making M. Ulpius Traianus his

heir and co-regent, since Trajan was a distinguished soldier and governor of Upper Germany. This move was highly significant in two respects. First, Trajan was of Spanish descent; the choice was the logical conclusion of the liberal policy that Claudius and Vespasian had advocated for the provincials. Second, the principle of adoption was now used in place of dynastic succession; the principate was opened to talent, and the result was the so-called five good emperors.

Trajan.—When Nerva died at the beginning of 98, Trajan succeeded without a hitch to an empire which owed much to Nerva despite the brevity of his reign. He had averted the recurrence of civil war and established better relations between Senate and *princeps*. These were maintained and enhanced by Trajan (98–117) through his tactful and attractive personality. His power was no less than that of Domitian, but he used it differently. Both Pliny in his *Panegyricus* and Dio Chrysostom in his discourse *On Kingship* depicted Trajan as the first servant of the state, unchallenged, but a leader rather than a lord, *princeps*, not *dominus*. Trajan avoided honours, held the consulship seldom, treated the Senate with respect, punctiliously consulting it and reporting to it, and recognizing the moral influence that it exerted, while he mixed with individual senators as their social equal. Although he did not add to the Senate's power, he banished the atmosphere of suspicion and conspiracy which was Domitian's legacy, and he bequeathed to his successors a tradition of mutual respect between *princeps* and Senate.

This is the more remarkable since he did not hesitate to intervene in the senatorial sphere in the interest of efficiency. Thus he improved public works in Italy (*e.g.*, the Via Traiana), insisted that senators should invest one-third of their capital in Italian land, and sent out officials named *curatores* to take over the financial administration in some cities in Italy (and in the provinces). When he found that the senatorial province of Bithynia was in financial difficulties he temporarily took it over and sent out as governor the younger Pliny, whose correspondence with the emperor throws much light not only on conditions in Bithynia (*e.g.*, the position of the Christians there) but on imperial administration in general. This well-meaning interference marked a beginning of the paternalism which was increasingly shown by the central government. Trajan's concern for Italy is also indicated by his development of the alimentary system. In administration he made further use of *equites* in place of freedmen. He spent lavishly on public buildings (as his Forum and Column), especially when gold began to reach Rome from the mines of

conquered Dacia, and he made many distributions of money (*congiaria*) during his reign. Thus he gained the support of the people and Senate. He was no less popular with the army.

Near the beginning of his reign Trajan determined to annex Dacia. This was an important change in imperial policy. As Claudius earlier had felt that the time had come to advance Augustus' frontiers, so Trajan apparently judged the time ripe for further expansion after the very moderate changes since Claudius' time. Also he may have regarded Domitian's peace terms with Dacia as unworthy of Rome, and thought that the Danube frontier would be more secure if a bastion of Roman territory was thrust

TRAJAN, MARBLE BUST FOUND IN THE ROMAN CAMPAGNA. IN THE BRITISH MUSEUM

into the land north of the river where it would separate and check the barbarian tribes. The conquest was completed in two campaigns (101–102 and 105–106). Decebalus committed suicide, Dacia was annexed as an imperial province, and its capital, Sarmizegethusa, was made a colony, Ulpia Traiana. The impact of Rome was such that a Latin language (Rumanian) is still spoken in this

MANSELL—ALINARI

DETAIL FROM TRAJAN'S COLUMN, ROME
Roman soldiers defend their garrison from an assault by Dacian forces

the annihilation of one of the legions he constructed the Wall for 73 mi. from Tyne to Solway.

The only serious war resulted from Hadrian's determination to reconstruct Jerusalem as Aelia Capitolina in 131, and other anti-Jewish measures. These provoked the bitter revolt led by Bar-Cochba (*q.v.*), which caused widespread devastation and heavy casualties before it was crushed in 135. Thereafter Jews were forbidden to get within sight of Jerusalem (Aelia), and Judaea, renamed Syria Palaestina, was garrisoned by two legions.

But peace depended above all on maintaining the spirit of the army. By intensive training and frequent inspections Hadrian tried to improve its fighting qualities. He extended local recruiting so that even many of the legionary officers ceased to be Italians (only the praetorians remained predominantly Italian), and many of the differences between the legions and *auxilia* disappeared. In the higher commands he did not exclude senators but he employed more *equites*.

Hadrian's outward relations with the Senate were cordial enough, but he recognized its increasing inefficiency and narrowness of view and therefore he tended to gather more power into his own hands; relations became more strained at the end of his reign. In particular his creation of four consular judges in Italy violated the Senate's traditional sphere. Further he impinged on senatorial administrative duties by his reorganization of the imperial council, in which lawyers and *equites* predominated. He substituted *equites* for freedmen in the imperial household and bureaus and built up the civil service on the basis of the equestrian order; by making military service no longer obligatory, he created a purely civil equestrian career with a hierarchy of grades and honorary titles (as *vir egregius, perfectissimus,* and *eminentissimus;* senators became *clarissimi*). Hadrian's legal work was outstanding, in particular the codification of the *edictum perpetuum*, the law interpreted

area. One legion was stationed in the province. With three on the lower Danube, two in Upper Moesia, and four in Pannonia, ten legions now held the Danube front.

Trajan also determined on advance in the east. On the death of Agrippa II, Transjordania had been added to Syria (probably in 93), and in 105–106 Arabia Petraea or Nabataea was quietly annexed as an imperial province. The southward movement of Caucasian tribes, as the Alans, together with Parthian interference in Armenia, might have provoked a limited Roman intervention, but Trajan's aims went further: Parthia was to be challenged. He advanced swiftly over the Euphrates and captured Ctesiphon, the Parthian capital, adding Armenia, Mesopotamia, and Assyria as new Roman provinces (114–115). But the Parthians counterattacked in Armenia and a great Jewish revolt spread from Cyrene to Egypt, Cyprus, and Asia. These movements were crushed, but Trajan was reluctantly forced to decide to return to Italy, leaving Hadrian in charge in the east. However, when he reached Cilicia he died (117).

This blunt soldier was later regarded as the most clement of all the emperors, while the title of *Optimus* ("best"), used unofficially since 100 but modestly declined by Trajan until 114, might then seem to have been won by his services to all sections of the Roman world. Whether or not he adopted Hadrian on his deathbed, as his widow Plotina asserted, is of less importance than the fact that he indubitably intended Hadrian to succeed him.

Hadrian.—Hadrian, who came of a senatorial family in Spain, was Trajan's second cousin and nearest relative. His earlier military career and experience made him the obvious choice. He was accepted by the army and by the Senate, to which he wrote apologizing that he had not been able to consult it about his adoption. His interest in the empire was keen and personal, as his two long tours of the provinces showed (121–125 and 128–134), but he believed that Trajan's expansive policy imposed too great a strain on the resources and perhaps the manpower of the empire. Hence he abandoned Assyria, Mesopotamia, and Armenia, though retaining Dacia, and strengthened Rome's ties with vassal kings around the frontiers. The frontiers themselves were to be delimited and further fortified. In particular he erected fortifications on the Rhine-Danube frontier, and in Britain, where after

BERNARD G. SILBERSTEIN—RAPHO GUILLUMETTE

HADRIAN'S VILLA AT TIVOLI

by the praetor's edict. He also created a new form of Latin rights, *Latium maius*, which gave Roman citizenship to all the local senators (*decuriones*) of the towns which received this right. At the same time more members of the Senate in Rome were recruited from the provincial nobility both in the east and west; senators who looked back to the old traditions of Rome may have despised Hadrian's love of things Greek.

Since Hadrian had no children, an illness in 136 prompted the adoption of L. Aelius Verus. After the latter's death in 138 Hadrian adopted Antoninus Pius, a man of 51 and a respected senator. He also looked to the future, making Antoninus in turn adopt two sons, Marcus (later Marcus Aurelius), who was Antoninus' own wife's nephew, and L. Aelius, the son of Verus.

Antoninus Pius.—Unlike his predecessors, Antoninus did not leave Italy during his principate (138–161) and by living the life of a country gentleman he directed attention to Italy away from the more cosmopolitan ideas of Hadrian. He thus worked well with the Senate, even abolishing the consular judges of Italy, though in fact he gave it no fresh powers and maintained the centralizing policy of his predecessor. Abroad he tried to strengthen the *limes* (*q.v.*) in Britain and in Germany by building a second wall in Britain (from the Forth to the Clyde in Scotland) and also in Germany. There were minor disturbances in Britain, Dacia, North Africa, and Judaea, while Antoninus installed vassal kings to rule the Quadi on the Danube, the Lazi in Colchis, and the Armenians; this was accomplished without serious trouble with Parthia. In 147 he celebrated the 900th anniversary of Rome in an age when men could speak of the *felicitas saeculi* ("happiness of the age") with real feeling, and Aelius Aristides could deliver a eulogy of Roman rule. But there was a touch of autumnal chill in the warm air of the Indian summer.

Marcus Aurelius.—As soon as Antoninus died his successor, Marcus Aurelius, asked the Senate that his "brother" Lucius Verus be given tribunician and proconsular power and the title of *Augustus;* he thus received a colleague and the principate was made collegiate. It is anomalous that Marcus, who was a Stoic philosopher and not a soldier by inclination, had to spend no less than 16 of the 19 years of his rule (161–180) in warfare. The frontiers were threatened in east and north. When the Parthians seized Armenia and defeated two Roman armies, Marcus sent out Verus (162), but it was Avidius Cassius who invaded Mesopotamia, captured Ctesiphon, and ended the war (166). Unfortunately Verus' troops brought back with them a virulent plague which probably left a permanent mark on the strength of the empire which it ravaged (165–166). At this moment German tribes (the Marcomanni and Quadi) broke over the Danube and even attacked north Italy, while the Jazyges attacked Dacia. After the tide had been stemmed (and Verus had died, in 169), Marcus planned to annex extensive territories north of the Danube in central Europe. In a series of campaigns (169–175) he defeated the three tribes and was on the point of creating new provinces of Marcomannia and Sarmatia when news came of the rebellion of Avidius Cassius, who had been left in supreme command in the east (he had quelled a revolt in Egypt in 172).

Avidius was soon murdered, but in 177 Marcus had to return to the front to repel further attacks of the Marcomanni and Quadi, leaving his son Commodus in Rome with the title of *Augustus* and the authority of a coregent. Marcus' campaigns went

MARCUS AURELIUS IN A QUADRIGA (FOUR-HORSED CHARIOT) ENTERING ROME IN TRIUMPH; FROM A RELIEF IN THE PALAZZO DEI CONSERVATORI, ROME

COMMODUS, AS THE GOD MITHRA; BRONZE AND GILT, INLAID WITH SILVER. IN THE VICTORIA AND ALBERT MUSEUM

well and he would soon have annexed his enemies' territory, but he died suddenly, and Commodus promptly renounced his father's policy of annexation. It soon became clear that Marcus' rejection of "the choice of the best" and his return to a dynastic policy without regard to the personal qualifications of a son and heir were not without grave dangers to the empire, whose economic and social life had already suffered severe blows from war and plague.

At home Marcus showed goodwill to the Senate, though bureaucracy increased, and circuit judges (now named *juridici*) were revived for Italy. Despite all his devotion to duty and his care for jurisdiction and finance, he lacked the constructive imagination to infuse fresh life into a reasonably contented but wearying world. It is, however, scarcely fair to blame him for his failure: the "self-sufficiency" of the Stoic philosopher was a limiting ideal, while the growing and relentless pressure of the barbarians upon the frontiers claimed too much of his energy; only in the intervals of his campaigns could he turn to his *Meditations*.

8. The Empire in the 2nd Century.—It is natural to speak of the Antonine "monarchy." In appearance, and to a very considerable degree in fact, the principate retained the civilian basis that Augustus had created for it, but in practice the charismatic and autocratic aspects of the ruler were increasing, and, despite the great gifts of the five "good" emperors in humane and effective government, there was a strong progression toward the dominate or autocracy. True, the Senate, as representing the state, remained the one legitimate source which bestowed on an emperor all his powers, but the Senate's hands were already tied, occasionally by the praetorians in Rome (as with Claudius) or by the frontier legions (as in 69), but normally by the ruler's own choice of a successor, whom usually he had raised to collegiality and had adopted as his son if he had no son of his own.

The ruler's powers, which for Augustus had comprised an accumulation of separate grants, retained an apparent diversity (even though conferred in a block grant), so that an emperor might act in his role as censor or *pontifex maximus,* but in practice the *imperium,* which Augustus had tried to keep in the background, became the decisive element, by which he commanded the armies and controlled the revenues; personal names and titles, as *Imperator Caesar Augustus,* became signs of power. Less the recipient of various powers, he now exercised a general *imperium* as head of the state: he controlled the composition of the senatorial and equestrian orders, he granted Roman citizenship, together with political, social, and economic benefits, and he watched over men's moral and religious activities. In the interest of efficiency he had built up a civil service dependent upon himself, with increasing bureaucratic control from the time of Hadrian. Hence greater centralization and paternalism of government. He relied more and more upon the "friends of Caesar," the *consilium principis,* and on the help of the prefect of the city and the praetorian prefect; and by the imperial constitutions he had taken over the legislative functions of the *comitia,* which died a natural death (the last law passed by it was in A.D. 98). Little wonder therefore that throughout the empire men began to regard the emperor as benefactor and saviour: benefactor as securing the prosperity of the empire, saviour as guarding it against the barbarians beyond.

The increasing military needs, however, tended only to emphasize the emperor's military power and paved the way for the ultimate triumph of the military over the civil authority. The *princeps* was still very far from being a military dictator, yet he was an "emperor." However, if the people had no voice in the direction of affairs, at least the emperor was expected to rule in the interests of the governed, and thanks to the personal qualities of the emperors from Nerva to Marcus Aurelius they did rule with a full sense of their duties and responsibilities. By careful economy and a modest court the emperors could be liberal in public expenditure, with *alimenta* and *congiaria,* planning public works and endowing education, although the *fiscus* began to feel the strain under Marcus Aurelius.

Political Life.—The nature of the relations of *princeps* and Senate was still the final touchstone of the worthiness of an emperor. The Senate still enjoyed great prestige, though it recovered nothing of its earlier powers as an instrument of government. Augustus might appear as its servant, Marcus Aurelius was clearly its master. There was no serious senatorial opposition to principate or *princeps* after the Flavian period. In composition too it was very different from the Senate of the late republic. A few, but very few, men of the older republican nobility survived to reach the consulship in the Julio-Claudian period, but most of these families had fallen into obscurity or extinction. Augustus had reinforced the Senate with the "flower of Italy," wealthy men of the equestrian class from all parts of the peninsula. Gradually the civilized regions of the west began to supply a small number of senators, and after Claudius provincial senators became more common, at first mainly from Italian families abroad, but after Nero some descendants of native provincials.

The increase in senators from both west and east, men whose main wealth was in the provinces, made the Senate more representative of the empire as a whole, but it also meant that the real interests of many senators no longer lay in Italy (hence Trajan's measure that some of their property should be invested in Italian land). Emperors tried to strengthen the patriciate as a social elite; they used their right to grant this status chiefly to elevate men of Italian rather than provincial origin. There was much greater social mobility than earlier; families could rise in two or three generations even from freedmen status to high society. This was all the more necessary since many senatorial families, both Italian and provincial, failed to perpetuate themselves and had constantly to be reinforced by fresh blood. The new families, although providing good administrators, failed also to stimulate the Senate to creative activity; it realized too clearly its dependence on the emperor's goodwill and guidance. But membership was still highly coveted, and the social gulf between senators and the upper middle class became ever wider.

Nevertheless the Senate was still more than a mere social class; it played an active, though not a controlling, part in legislation and jurisdiction as well as in administration. It looked with favour at the decreasing use of imperial freedmen, but askance at the increasing activities of the equestrian order. On the other hand friction between the two orders was lessened by the clear demarcation of their spheres of duty, while they were drawn closer together by two circumstances: the knights were socially much closer to the senators than to the rest of the population, and it was from the equestrian order that the emperors normally chose the new senators.

In both the equestrian order and the army tendencies were developing which were to increase the significance of each group in the following century. The army, which still effectively held the frontiers, was becoming less mobile and predominantly provincial. While the praetorian guard and the urban cohorts retained a Latin tradition, the bulk of the provincial soldiers, although good fighters, were only superficially touched by Roman political ideas or Greco-Roman culture, while the higher officers, as a result of the widening gap between military and civil careers, had little experience in civil government even though the majority may still have been of Italian stock.

Social and Economic Life.—Although many of the difficulties of the 3rd century were foreshadowed before the end of the Antonine age, Edward Gibbon's famous words, that the human race was never happier than in this period, may well be true, at any rate until his day. Urbanization reached its widest extent in the provinces, where the governing aristocracies were often public-spirited men who spent generously to endow and maintain their own cities. The municipalities flourished as never before, although on occasion the financial strain of compulsory contributions imposed on the local magistrates and senators proved too heavy, and the Roman central government was forced to limit their liberties in order to support their finances or to maintain public order. The care which the emperors exercised in the provinces is attested in Trajan's correspondence with Pliny and by Hadrian's tireless tours, while these emperors' own provincial origin naturally inclined them to generosity in granting Roman citizenship, and so prepared the way for the final act when Caracalla in 212 granted citizenship to all communities within the empire.

With peace predominant throughout Mediterranean lands and with the extension of the road system and the improvement of communications, the empire reached its peak of economic development. In agriculture and industry the provinces began to outpace Italy. There were few improvements in industrial technology or organization, but some new sources of raw materials were obtained, and commerce by land and sea flourished as never before, bursting the bounds of the empire to reach Scandinavia, overland to China, and through the Indian Ocean to the east. This increasing prosperity was reflected in the growth of cities, while other new towns grew out of *canabae,* the settlements of traders around the military camps. The new buildings in Rome, such as the Colosseum, Trajan's Forum, and the Pantheon, found their counterparts in the fora, theatres, amphitheatres, baths, aqueducts, and bridges which increasingly adorned the chief cities in the provinces. Roman sculpture, which reflected many of Rome's imperial achievements, kept pace with architecture, and imperial ideals often reflected the artistic traditions of the provinces.

In contrast with the creative genius of certain epochs, some would speak of the "intellectual stagnation" of this period, yet schools and libraries showed the interest of state and private benefactors in education. Literature entered upon its Silver Age with the work of Tacitus, Suetonius, Quintilian, Pliny, Fronto, and Apuleius, of Martial and Juvenal, although admittedly the output began to decline as time advanced. There was a revival of Greek letters, Christian apologists developed a new branch of literature, and Roman jurisprudence reached its maturity. In all spheres, and especially in the religious, provincial influences spread, and the western stamp which Augustus had set upon the empire gradually became less clear-cut. Christianity, despite intermittent persecution, had taken root in Italy, Africa, and Gaul, and was developing an organization which ultimately could challenge the imperial regime.

Rome had imposed no uniformity of culture but had allowed the provincials to retain their varied customs and institutions, al-

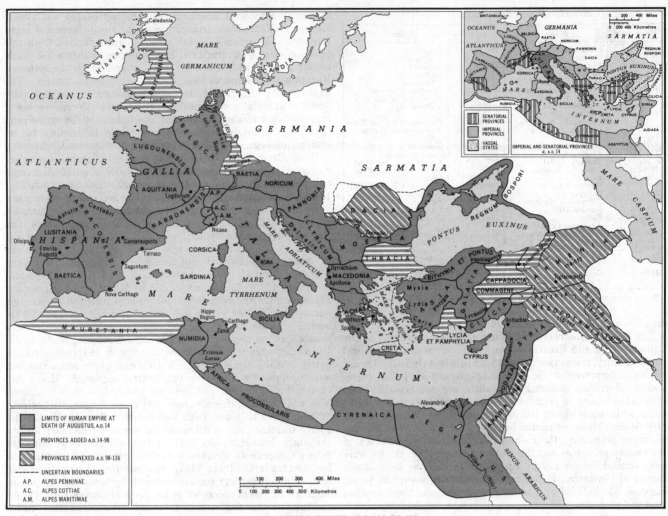

THE ROMAN EMPIRE, A.D. 14 TO 116

Map legend:

LIMITS OF ROMAN EMPIRE AT DEATH OF AUGUSTUS, A.D. 14
PROVINCES ADDED A.D. 14–98
PROVINCES ANNEXED A.D. 98–116
UNCERTAIN BOUNDARIES
A.P. ALPES PENNINAE
A.C. ALPES COTTIAE
A.M. ALPES MARITIMAE

Inset legend:
SENATORIAL PROVINCES
IMPERIAL PROVINCES
VASSAL STATES
IMPERIAL AND SENATORIAL PROVINCES c. A.D. 14

though naturally romanization had spread widely, not least by means of the armies on the frontiers. The predominantly Latin culture of the west was complementary to the Hellenism of the east. But despite diversity there was a bond of unity, and all men looked to the emperor as to a universal Providence by whose unremitting care the *pax Romana* was preserved.

There was of course another side to the picture. Many grave problems, as the social evils of slavery and the pauperization of urban populations (increased under Marcus by plague and famines) or the possibility of a wise policy of decentralization and provincial representation, were not tackled. Further, the culture of the empire meant less to the toiling masses in the provinces than to the middle and upper classes, for whose benefit the empire chiefly existed, while many future unhealthy changes were already foreshadowed. Nevertheless, the barriers between Rome and the provinces had fallen, Italy had lost its privileged position, and in an age of greater goodwill and humanity, the stability of the empire and the *Aeternitas Populi Romani* must have appeared unshaken and unshakable. (H. H. SD.)

From this point, political history is covered in detail in the articles on individual emperors (*see* tables); further information is also given in articles on individual provinces (*see* table in PROVINCE, ROMAN). This article deals henceforward chiefly with the social and economic development of the Roman Empire.

9. The Empire, A.D. 180–284.—Marcus Aurelius died in 180. Half a century later, the elderly senator and historian Dio Cassius commented that with his death "the age of gold turned to rusty iron." Like most ancient and many modern writers, Dio Cassius blames the personal character of Marcus' successors. But the rust had set in earlier. Marcus had been continuously at war longer than any of his predecessors. His Parthian campaign

achieved a sensational victory, but the victorious armies brought the plague back. He was decisively beaten, beyond the Danube, by the Germans, who devastated the Balkans, some forces reaching Italy, where no armed enemy had penetrated for 250 years. When the frontiers were recovered and Marcus determined to annex Bohemia and Moravia, his initial victories were thwarted by the revolt of Avidius Cassius.

When Cassius was dead and his supporters stilled, Marcus resumed the offensive but died in March 180. The accession speech of the young prince Commodus, certainly composed by the general Pompeianus, proclaimed the goal of continuing the war until Roman arms reached the Ocean.

But the ambition of the generals was wrecked by the numerous internal tensions bred of the long war. Two among them are immediately apparent: social discontent, and the diverging interests of the Latin West and Greek East. The long war had produced very many deserters, who, a few years after Marcus' death, were strong enough to seize a number of towns in southern Gaul, with the help of poor townsmen. A full-scale army was required to subdue them. Beaten in the field, they infiltrated Rome, where the audacious plot of their leader Maternus to seize the imperial throne was checked by treachery. It was the first internal social rising recorded since the days of the Republic, and it was soon followed by others. Twenty years later a bandit leader, Bulla Felix, with a force of runaway slaves, deserters, and bankrupts, terrorized southern Italy for two years, while from the later years of Marcus onward the lawyers emphasize the difficulty of telling a slave from a freeman and fulminate in vain against landlords, short of labour on their estates, who accept and shelter strangers without inquiry into their origins. The social discontent continued throughout the 3rd century, gaining strength from the

TABLE II.—*Roman Emperors, A.D. 180–285**

Reign dates	Name	Reign dates	Name
180–192	Commodus	251–253	Gallus and
193	Pertinax		Volusian
193	Didius Julianus	*253*	*Aemilian*
193–198	Septimius Severus	253–260	Valerian and
193–194	*Pescennius Niger (East)*		Gallienus
196–197	*Clodius Albinus (Britain)*	*c. 258*	*Ingenuus (Pannonia)*
198–209	Septimius Severus	*258 or*	*Regalianus (Moesia or*
	and Caracalla	*260*	*Pannonia)*
209–211	Septimius Severus,	*c. 258–*	
	Caracalla, and Geta	*268*	*Postumus (Gaul and West)*
211–212	Caracalla and Geta	*260*	*Macrianus and Quietus*
212–217	Caracalla		*(East)*
217–218	Macrinus	260–268	Gallienus
218–222	Elagabalus	*268*	*Aureolus (Milan)*
c. 222	*Uranius (Syria)*	*268*	*Laelian (Gaul and West)*
222–235	Alexander Severus	*268*	*Marius (Gaul and West)*
235–238	Maximin	268–270	Claudius II
238	Gordian I and II	*268–270*	*Victorinus (Gaul and West)*
238	Balbinus and	270	Quintillus
	Pupienus Maximus	270–275	Aurelian
238–244	Gordian III	*270–274*	*Tetricus (Gaul and West)*
244–249	Philip	*271–272*	*Zenobia and Vaballathus*
?	*Iotapianus (Alexandria)*		*(Palmyra)*
248–249	*Pacatianus (Danube)*	275–276	Tacitus
249–251	Decius	276	Florian
? –253	*Uranius (Syria)*	276–282	Probus
251	Decius and Herennius	282–283	Carus
	Etruscus	*283–284*	*Numerian (East)*
251	Gallus and	*283–285*	*Carinus (West)*
	Hostilian	284–285	*Diocletian (East)*

*Rival emperors in italics.

divisions among men of wealth and power.

The long war sharpened the inherent mutual suspicions of the Latin-speaking and Greek-speaking provinces; for, until the end of the century, the Senate remained overwhelmingly Latin, the far wealthier provinces of the east being proportionately ill represented. Surviving sources are too slight and too heavily biased toward the Senate to permit more than a few hints of the degree and articulateness of this feeling, but as early as 180 a contemporary African Latin inscription had described the revolt of Cassius as *motus orientalis*, "the rising of the east." The resources of the eastern provinces and the social cohesion of the empire were alike squandered on a vain attempt to subdue the unprofitable forests of Germany. It was not many months before the young emperor was induced to dismiss Pompeianus, end the Danubian war, and place his confidence in a Bithynian Greek, Saoterus.

The reaction was violent; Pompeianus' son tried and failed to murder Commodus, but the aristocracy succeeded in murdering Saoterus and in placing the Italian prefect Perennis at the head of affairs. The emperor was a great deal more interested in sport than in politics and acquiesced when a *Putsch*, initiated by the officers of the army of Britain, whose morale had recently been smashed by a disastrous defeat, removed Perennis. The next prefect, an easterner, was destroyed in a city riot organized by a rival, who fell soon after. The urban plebs and the guards came again to exercise a political influence denied them for many years under the stable empire. The chaos ended in civil war, and the victor, Septimius Severus (193–211), strove with temporary success to restore the old stability, while his wife, Julia Domna, patronized the syncretist philosophers who sought to show that Oriental, Greek, and Latin religion, philosophy, and myth were but variant expressions of a single universal truth. Severus' two sons were bitter enemies, each attracting opposing factions throughout the empire. Seeking to avert the risk of civil war, the imperial council discussed a proposal that one brother should rule the eastern provinces, with a Senate of all Greek-speaking senators, while the other ruled the west with a Latin Senate. The proposal was rejected and a simpler solution found in the murder of the younger brother. But the proposal anticipated the later division of the empire, whose causes were already present.

The senatorial writers of the 4th century saw the period between the Severan emperors and Diocletian as a uniform half-century of military anarchy, a concept that has left a deep imprint on modern writers. But this harsh schematic presentation is much too simple; the only valid sharp and sudden break with the past lies in the disasters that overtook the Roman world about the year 260. Before then, evolution was jagged and complex, determined by the uneven effect of long-term and slow-growing changes. Under the early emperors, the population had consisted

of a small number of Roman citizens, mostly Italian, and almost all from the Latin Mediterranean west, who ruled alien non-Roman subjects. The outlook of the Latin senators derived from this tradition, but two centuries of ever-widening franchise had made it long out of date, when, in 212, Caracalla abruptly bestowed Roman citizenship on all freeborn inhabitants of the empire. The legal equality of Syrian, Briton, and Italian scarcely became fully accepted in social and political practice till the 4th century, but it expressed and accelerated changes unwelcome to the aristocratic tradition; the established aristocracy fought tenaciously for its ancient privilege.

When Caracalla and his effeminate cousin Elagabalus were removed, the throne passed in 222 to a docile child, Alexander Severus, in whose name the empire was governed by a council of 16 senators, elected by the Senate to advise and control his mother. Their rule was precarious in Rome, where people and guards, in all else mutually hostile, united in dislike of the government, and they faced several provincial revolts. Their authority was destroyed by a military disaster in Persia, directly caused by the cowardice and incompetence of the emperor and his mother. When Alexander soon after bought peace from the Rhineland Germans, the angry troops killed him in 235 and proclaimed Maximinus (Maximin) the first professional soldier emperor. But the senators were not yet beaten, and in 238 they successfully organized a rebellion of Italy, which defeated and killed Maximin. But the Senate was too tied to tradition to exploit success; tradition enjoined that when the Senate chose an emperor, it should select the oldest available noble, preferably childless, whose senile function was to appoint a successor the Senate welcomed. Galba had chosen ill, Nerva well, and Pertinax had had no time to choose. Now the Senate chose colleagues, and chose former city prefects, Maximus and Balbinus, both well hated in Rome. People and guards dictated their own choice, the younger Gordian (Gordian III, then about 13 years old), and then made away with the Senate's emperors. Successive prefects struggled to control the boy, and the last of them, Philip, an *eques* from Arabia, succeeded him. Philip faced four successive revolts by senatorial army commanders, the last of which, led by Decius in 249, succeeded. Decius and his successor Gallus both belonged to the aristocracy, and a large influence fell to Valerian, a veteran of the Italian rebellion of 238, who ultimately succeeded Gallus in 253.

Valerian recognized that it was no longer possible for one emperor to control the whole empire, and appointed his son Gallienus to rule the west while he went to the east. But he was too late. Successive rebellions had demoralized the Danubian legions, which were scarcely in shape to withstand their old enemies and now faced the formidable new confederation of the Gothic empire. The frontier crumbled, and the Goths wasted northern Asia Minor and much of Greece. Before the emperors could intervene, Valerian was taken prisoner by the Persians.

Gallienus' energy recovered the Balkans and secured Italy. But the Rhineland, with Gaul, Spain, and Britain, and the eastern provinces acknowledged independent regional rulers, whom Gallienus could not even attempt to subdue. Gallienus drew the moral of the disaster; the frontiers had been demoralized by senatorial commanders who rebelled, so he forbade senators to command armies. It was the sharpest possible break with immemorial Roman tradition, and with few exceptions (most, perhaps all, under Aurelian) the new rule was permanently applied. Gallienus also raised a mobile cavalry reserve, henceforth the elite of the army. In his later years he faced a catastrophic inflation and renewed invasions, which culminated in the physical destruction of much of central Gaul.

Gallienus' edict did not end revolts. It was too late: now non-senators might also become emperors, and Gallienus was replaced by his own equestrian cavalry commanders, Claudius and Aurelian, who reduced the separate emperors of east and west to obedience. These men, and their successors, were professional equestrian officers, whose rule rested on a military crisis but gave no greater guarantee of stability than the rule of senatorial emperors. The murder of Aurelian gave the Senate a last belated and unexpected chance, for the army council, disillusioned at the small authority of military emperors, asked the Senate to choose a successor. After six months' debate, it chose again the oldest available child-less senator, the feeble Tacitus. He had no opportunity to designate a successor, and no one again troubled to ask the Senate to choose an emperor. The able praetorian prefect Probus took charge, and after him Carus, who seems to have died a natural death. There seemed no inherent reason why the army's next choice, Diocletian, should last longer than his predecessors, save that he had the wisdom to follow Valerian's example and appoint a loyal colleague to rule the west while he campaigned in the east. But the Roman world was weary of perpetual change and repeated disaster; though Diocletian faced as many rebel emperors in his first few years as any of his predecessors, none of the rebels found sufficient support to succeed.

In the crisis of Gallienus' reign, almost all the Roman world except central and southern Italy was overrun by barbarians. It is remarkable that the empire had strength to survive another century and a half. Recovery was achieved, partly because the barbarians came only to raid and were not yet familiar enough with Roman ways to settle within the frontiers, partly because the centuries of orderly Roman life were still recent and gave the empire a confident toughness strong enough to offset the shock of disaster and enable individual generals and emperors to repair the worst of the damage. But the disasters altogether killed the old financial and administrative system of the empire, destroyed the ancient authority of the Senate save in the eyes of its own members, and effaced the old preeminence of Italy. Diocletian's 20 years gave him the opportunity to consolidate and systematize the many military and administrative changes the crisis entailed, to organize them around a new centralized and unifying monarchy.

The disruptive crisis and the new unity had destroyed the force of old religions and philosophies; throughout the century, successive rulers strove to achieve a unity of ideas, grouped around a syncretist philosophy, neo-Platonism, or the worship of the unconquered Sun. Its common experience was that all older cults and philosophies were willing to sink themselves in each successive fashionable compromise, except the Christians. Decius, Valerian, and Diocletian therefore persecuted the Christians as enemies of the state, of Roman unity. Under Diocletian's successors the failure alike of the artificial world religions and of the persecutions forged Christianity into the unifying religion that the new empire needed. (X.)

B. The Dominate, a.d. 284–476

1. Diocletian and Constantine.—When Diocletian was proclaimed emperor on Nov. 20, 284, the barbarians had been repelled and the territorial integrity of the empire restored, but much remained to be done to repair the disorder and instability created by the anarchy of the preceding generation. Above all the constant military revolutions had to be checked and political stability restored. This Diocletian achieved, reigning for more than 20 years before he abdicated on May 1, 305. His success was mainly due to his sharing the government of the empire with loyal colleagues. In 285 he made Maximian Caesar and in 286 Augustus to rule the west, and in 293 he created two Caesars, Constantius and Galerius, to assist Maximian and himself. The four emperors were able to maintain close touch with all the armies and hold their loyalty; there were in fact only two rebellions, that of Carausius and Allectus in Britain (286–296) and that of Domitius Domitianus in Egypt (296–297). Diocletian also attempted to enhance the dignity of the imperial office by adopting Persian court ceremo-

ALINARI

DIOCLETIAN. IN THE CAPITOLINE MUSEUM, ROME

nial. Like his immediate predecessors, he claimed a quasi-divinity, styling himself Jovius, vice-gerent on earth of Jupiter Optimus Maximus. Maximian was styled Herculius, a title which emphasized his subordination to Diocletian.

Diocletian greatly increased the size of the army, perhaps doubling its numbers, and strengthened the fortifications of the frontiers. He made no great change in its organization. Each emperor had a small mobile field army (*comitatus*), but the bulk of the forces were as hitherto stationed on the frontiers. In some frontier provinces he separated the military command from the civil administration, appointing a *dux* in addition to a *praeses*. He increased administrative efficiency by subdividing the larger provinces and grouping them in 12 larger circumscriptions called dioceses, governed by *vicarii* (see below).

Diocletian attempted to reform the coinage, issuing good gold and silver coins. He continued, however, to issue silver-washed copper *nummi* in vast profusion, and prices (including those of gold and silver) continued to rise. He endeavoured to fix prices and wages by edict in 301, but goods vanished from the market, and prices had to be allowed to take their course. Despite this failure he placed the imperial finances on a sound footing by organizing on a systematic basis the requisitions in kind (*indictiones*) on which the government had come to depend for feeding and clothing the army and the civil service and for providing labour and materials for public works. The *indictiones* were now no longer levied sporadically, when and where required, but became universal and regular. To provide a basis for them, censuses of the land and the agricultural population were held throughout the empire. Land was assessed, according to its use and quality,

TABLE III.—*Roman Emperors, 285–476**

West†		East†	
Reign dates	Name	Reign dates	Name
286–305	Maximian (*Caesar from 293: Constantius I*)	285–305	Diocletian (*Caesar from 293: Galerius*)
286–293	*Carausius (Britain)*		
293–296	*Allectus (Britain)*	*296–297*	*Domitius Domitianus (Egypt)*
305–306	Constantius (*Caesar: Severus*)	305–308	Galerius (*Caesar: Maximinus*)
306–307	Severus (*Caesar: Constantine I*)		
306–308	*Maximian and Maxentius (Italy)*		
308–313	Licinius and Constantine	308–311	Galerius and Maximinus
308–312	*Maxentius (Italy)*		
308–311	*Alexander (Africa)*		
		311–313	Maximinus
313–324	Constantine	313–324	Licinius
	324–337 Constantine		
337–340	Constantine II and Constans	337–350	Constantius II
340–350	Constans		
	350–361 Constantius II		
350	*Magnentius (Caesar, 355–361: Julian)*		(*Caesar 351–354: Gallus*)
	361–363 Julian		
	363–364 Jovian		
364–367	Valentinian I	364–378	Valens
		365–366	*Procopius (Constantinople)*
367–375	Valentinian and Gratian		
375–383	Gratian and Valentinian II	379–383	Theodosius I
383–392	Valentinian II	383–394	Theodosius and Arcadius
383–388	*Magnus Maximus and Victor (Britain, Gaul, Spain)*		
392–394	*Eugenius (Gaul, Italy, Spain)*		
393–395	Theodosius and Honorius	393–402	Arcadius
395–421	Honorius		
407–411	*Constantine (Britain, Gaul, Spain)*	402–408	Arcadius and Theodosius II
409–411	*Maximus (Spain)*	408–450	Theodosius II
421	Honorius and Constantius III		
421–423	Honorius		
423–425	*John*		
425–455	Valentinian III	450–457	Marcian
455	Petronius Maximus		
455–456	Avitus		
457–461	Majorian	457–473	Leo I
461–465	Libius Severus		
467–472	Anthemius		
472	Olybrius		
473–474	Glycerius	473–474	Leo I and II
		474	Leo II
474–480	Nepos	474–491	Zeno
475–476	*Romulus Augustulus*	475–476	*Basiliscus (Constantinople)*

*Usurpers in italics.

†The terms West and East are used for convenience here, not to denote a split in the empire.

in fiscal units (*juga*) of equal value, and the population (and also animals) in units styled *capita*. Each year the praetorian prefects drew up a budget of all the goods required, and worked out the amount due from each *jugum* or *caput*.

For the greater part of his reign Diocletian continued the policy of tacit toleration of the Christians which his predecessors had followed since Gallienus. Toward the end of his reign, probably under the influence of his Caesar Galerius, he instituted a severe persecution, which began on Feb. 23, 303.

On May 1, 305, Diocletian abdicated, and on the same day Maximian did the same in the west. The two Caesars were proclaimed Augusti and two new Caesars were appointed, Severus for the west and Maximinus for the east. Diocletian no doubt hoped that he had solved the problem of the succession, but things did not work out according to plan. Constantius, the western Augustus, died at York, and on July 25, 306, his troops proclaimed his son Constantine his successor as Augustus. Later in the same year Maxentius, the son of Maximian, headed a revolt at Rome against Severus, whom Galerius had declared Constantius' successor, and Maximian himself resumed the purple in his son's support. Severus was defeated and killed, and Galerius himself was forced to withdraw when he invaded Italy. In 308 Galerius called Diocletian and Maximian to a conference at Carnuntum. Maximian was persuaded to resign once more, and Licinius was proclaimed Augustus of the west; Constantine and Maximinus were recognized as Caesars. Both, however, insisted on the title of Augustus, and Maxentius remained unsubdued in Italy. There were therefore now six Augusti.

In 311 Galerius died, and Licinius occupied his European provinces, Maximinus Asia Minor. Next year Constantine conquered Maxentius, thus becoming Augustus of all the west. In 313 Maximinus attacked Licinius, who defeated him and thus became Augustus of all the east. Galerius and Maximinus had been active persecutors of the Christians. Constantine, believing that he owed his victory over Maxentius to the aid of the Christian god, whose monogram (✸) he had inscribed on his soldiers' shields at the decisive Battle of the Milvian Bridge, became a Christian and granted money and privileges to the church. Under his persuasion Licinius proclaimed toleration in his dominions. Constantine soon quarreled with Licinius and in 314–315 conquered from him the dioceses of Pannonia and Moesia. The final struggle came ten years later. Licinius began to persecute the Christians, and Constantine in 324 decisively defeated him, thus becoming sole Augustus.

To celebrate his victory he rebuilt Byzantium on a magnificent scale and renamed it Constantinople. Constantinople was from the first a Christian city, furnished with many churches. It became Constantine's normal residence and was perhaps from the beginning styled the New Rome, though it lacked Rome's constitutional prerogatives.

Constantine made a major military reform in greatly increasing the size of the field army (*comitatenses*) and reducing the frontier army (*limitanei*) to a secondary role. The field army was led by commanders in chief of the cavalry and the infantry (*magister equitum* and *peditum*), and the frontier troops by zone commanders (*duces*). The praetorian prefects, vicars, and provincial governors thus lost all military power. Constantine also initiated a sound gold and silver currency; his gold coin, the *solidus*, maintained its weight and purity into the Middle Ages. He obtained the necessary bullion partly by a tax in gold and silver levied on merchants and craftsmen but mainly by the confiscation of the temple treasures in 331.

Constantine considered it his duty to heal dissensions in the church, which he feared might provoke God's wrath against the empire and more particularly against himself, to whom God had entrusted its government. Immediately after his conversion he was faced with the Donatist controversy in Africa, and on his conquest of the east with the Arian controversy (*see* Donatists; Arius). To settle the former he summoned councils of bishops at Rome and at Arles, and finally confirmed their judgment himself. To solve the latter he convoked in 325 an ecumenical council at Nicaea, at which he himself presided (*see* Council), and an-

ALINARI

OVERSIZED HEAD OF CONSTANTINE ADORNING A FAÇADE IN ROME. BELOW, AN ALLEGORICAL STATUE REPRESENTING ONE PROVINCE OF THE EMPIRE

other great council at Jerusalem in 335. He executed the decrees of these councils, persecuting those whom they condemned as heretics. He built many magnificent churches, notably at Rome, Constantinople, Antioch, and Jerusalem, and granted many legal and fiscal privileges to the churches and the clergy. Paganism he at first tolerated, but in 331 he confiscated the treasures and lands of the temples, and he seems to have banned sacrifices in the last years of his reign.

The reigns of Diocletian and Constantine gave the empire a new lease of life, but the vast increase of the army and civil service placed a heavy strain on the manpower of the empire, already depleted by the wars, famines, and plagues of the 3rd century. The maintenance of the larger army and civil service, the great program of public works—frontier fortresses, arms and clothing factories, churches, and Constantinople—and Constantine's lavish benefactions to the church placed an even heavier strain on its resources. Manpower shortages developed, and the rate of taxation on agriculture rose so high that marginal land began to fall out of cultivation, while the decurions of the cities, on whom lay the collection of the taxes, found their task increasingly difficult. The response of the government to these difficulties was to attempt to tie to their tasks various classes whose functions were vital to the empire's needs, and to extend this tie to their children; since most classes were in practice hereditary, this was a natural solution. Sons of soldiers and veterans were obliged to join the army, sons of civil servants to enter their father's office. Decurions were forbidden to resign from the councils of their cities, and their sons, who inherited their property, had to accept membership. Above all, in order to make sure that the poll tax was paid and that the land was cultivated and furnished the requisite foodstuffs for the indiction, the agricultural population was hereditarily bound to the places where it was registered in the census. Similar rules applied to miners and to the shippers who transported government cargoes. These rules were difficult to enforce and were frequently disobeyed and evaded. Ambitious men could always escape from their hereditary status, and many men of humble origin rose to high positions in the state service. But the government did achieve its object, to maintain an army adequate to repel increasing barbarian pressure.

Constantine's conversion had momentous consequences for the future of the church and of Christianity. From being a poor society, living under precarious toleration, the church became a wealthy and privileged body. Christianity, which had been confined to a small minority of mainly humble folk, on gaining official favour attracted many converts, especially from the upper classes; numbers grew, if the quality of the recruits declined. At the same time the church acquired a master, for Constantine, being convinced that he was God's servant, did not hesitate to intervene in ecclesiastical affairs.

2. The Reorganized Empire.—Diocletian approximately doubled the number of provinces, dividing some into five or six; he also partitioned Italy into provinces. The provinces were grouped in 12 large circumscriptions called dioceses, in each of which a deputy of the praetorian prefects (*vicarius*) supervised the governors and served as a link between them and the central government. In each diocese there were also representatives of the two finance ministries (*magistri rei privatae* and *rationales rei summae*). Completing a process which had begun in the 3rd century, Diocletian almost eliminated senators from the provincial administration; Asia and Africa still had their proconsuls, the Italian provinces (and Sicily and Achaea) were governed by *correctores*, who might be senators, all the rest by equestrian *praesides*. The governor was now responsible for all branches of administration, except in the provinces where the military command was held by a *dux*. Constantine completed the separation of civil administration and military command, and from his reign they were combined only in Isauria. He also admitted senators to provincial government on a larger scale, substituting senatorial *consulares* for equestrian *praesides* in a number of provinces.

Each governor was assisted by a judicial assessor, usually a barrister, of his own choice, and was served by a staff (*officium*) of about one hundred clerks and messengers. His main duties were to collect the revenue and administer justice. The average term of office was short, about a year, and the standard of official morality was low, extortion and corruption being widespread. This was partly because governorships were much sought after and were often virtually purchased by large bribes to the emperor's chief ministers and advisers, and those appointed were forced to supplement their official salaries by illicit means to recoup themselves.

(A. H. M. J.)

3. The Empire, A.D. 337–476.—For the internal politics of the period and the various usurpations *see* the articles on the individual emperors. The financial and military reforms of Diocletian and Constantine proved to be of permanent value, and the state as organized by them was little altered by their successors. The administration of the empire, too, as refashioned by Diocletian and Constantine, continued to function and develop throughout the rest of the period of the later empire.

Emperors.—After the death of Theodosius I in 395 the empire was never again ruled for any significant length of time by a single emperor. From 395 to 480 it was ruled by two or more colleagues, one in the east and one or more in the west, all with equal rights. When an emperor had sons he usually appointed his eldest son as co-Augustus, as Valentinian and Theodosius appointed respectively Gratian and Arcadius. This son was expected to become his successor, and normally he did in fact succeed. But if the emperor had no son, then the army appointed his successor (as was done, *e.g.*, on the death of Julian), and the appointment was then announced to the Senate. In the 5th century the duty of crowning the eastern emperor was given to the patriarch of Constantinople.

In theory, and in many ways in practice too, the empire remained a single unit even when ruled by a plurality of emperors; and, although it is convenient sometimes to refer to the "Western Empire" and the "Eastern Empire," this must not be taken to imply that there were two empires. Laws were published over the names of all the legitimate emperors; when the ruler of one

part of the empire died, his power automatically passed to his surviving colleague until a successor was appointed; and each emperor named one of the two consuls for each year.

Senates.—As for the Senate, Constantius II elevated the Senate of Constantinople to an equal level with that at Rome, so that there were henceforth two Senates in the empire other than the local, municipal senates. Membership was hereditary; and the sons of senators entered the Senate when they had held the quaestorship or, after the end of the 4th century, the praetorship. Senators were divided into three classes, the *illustres*, the *spectabiles*, and the *clarissimi*. The most important offices in the state gave their holders one or other of these ranks and so brought them entry to the Senate. Moreover, the late emperors showed much generosity in conferring the rank of *clarissimus* on favoured individuals. It has been calculated, in fact, that in the 5th century there were about 2,000 senators in the western empire; the number in the east may have been smaller. The wealth of these senators was derived from the landed estates they owned, and in some cases it reached fantastic dimensions. An early 5th-century historian cites some western senators as having an annual income of 1,000 or 1,500 or even 4,000 lb. of gold, together with an income in kind of one-third of these amounts. Symmachus (*q.v.*) spent 2,000 lb. of gold on the occasion of his son's holding the praetorship. The younger St. Melania, the daughter and granddaughter of senators, owned estates in Gaul, Italy, Spain, Sicily, Africa, and possibly in other provinces, too. When she died *c.* 440 she manumitted in her will 8,000 slaves. It was not unusual for the estates of wealthier senators to be distributed thus through several provinces; the loss of any one province to the barbarians thus would not necessarily bankrupt them. The growth of the large senatorial estates, however, had advanced much farther in the west than in the east, and it would appear that these vast fortunes, common enough in the west, were distinctly rare by comparison in the east.

Local Government.—The members of the local town councils, the *curiales* or decurions, as they were called, were the object of close attention on the part of the emperors. In addition to the ordinary duties of local government, they were in this period responsible for the collection of the land tax in the locality in which they lived. If there was any deficiency in the amount due to the central government, the curials were collectively obliged to make it up out of their own pockets. As the empire declined, their position became desperate; their efforts to escape from their obligations by joining the army, the civil service, the church, etc., were so continuous that in 336 Constantine had made the curial office hereditary. No fewer than 192 laws had been enacted regulating the position of the curials by the time Theodosius II published his law code in 438. Valentinian I established a new office, that of the *defensor* in the municipal towns, in an attempt to protect the poor from oppression. The *defensores* were not successful, even when Theodosius I transferred the duty of appointing them from the praetorian prefect to the curials. Local government offices, which in the early empire had been posts of honour, were in this period heavy and sometimes intolerable burdens to those who held them.

Economy.—The principle of compelling sons to follow their fathers' careers was also enforced by the government in the case of certain trades and professions, particularly those responsible for ensuring the food supply of Rome and Constantinople—the shippers who transported the grain from Africa and Egypt, and the bakers who made this grain into bread. But during the 4th century the members of all trade guilds were tied to their jobs by law; and in the state factories the workers were actually branded, to make recapture easy if they should flee from their occupations. The economy of the later empire was essentially one of private enterprise, for most industrial and commercial property was still privately owned. But this private enterprise was controlled by the state with a rigour for which it would be difficult to find a parallel in any other period of history.

It would be a mistake to suppose that all the agricultural land outside the walls of the cities was given over to the great estates of the senators and the emperors and to the smaller estates of the curials. There were also many small farms belonging to free peasant proprietors, to humble city dwellers, and to peasants who leased them in a great variety of ways. Nor were all landworkers *coloni* (peasants bound to the soil) or slaves. The labourers in the fields were now, it is thought, less often slaves than they had been in the earliest days of the empire. But agricultural slavery certainly existed still, and, even though the cessation of the great wars of aggression had reduced the intake of slaves, a slave trade still flourished on the frontiers of the empire, where slaves were apt to be cheaper than they were in the interior. But the characteristic form of labour, at any rate on the large estates, was the *colonus*, first mentioned in a law of 332 and referred to in a law of 364 as being hereditarily bound to the soil.

There was a severe shortage of agricultural labour in the later empire, and indeed very large areas of land were left uncultivated because there was no one available to cultivate them. The practice of tying peasants to the soil seems to have had a fiscal origin; but landlords found it useful, for tenants were hard to find and, once found, they could now be prevented from moving on to places where they might hope to better themselves. Dozens of laws were enacted relating to the restoration of fugitive *coloni* to their masters. Even so, the tying of the *colonus* to the land was not carried through in all parts of the empire simultaneously; it was introduced into Palestine, for example, only during the reign of Theodosius I and it does not appear at all in Egypt until the 5th century.

The condition of the agricultural workers was in general very harsh, and in Gaul and Spain extensive and prolonged revolts broke out, particularly in the 5th century. Even in 284–285 there had been a rebellion in Gaul of the "rustics," who had given themselves the name of *Bagaudae*. This name is used frequently by 5th-century authors to denote the rebellious peasants of Spain, the French Alps, and particularly Armorica (approximately Brittany), this last place being the main centre of revolt. But shortly after the middle of the 5th century these rebellions died down and are not heard of later in the west, though they continued in the Danubian provinces. While the *Bagaudae* continued to operate, many farm workers fled to join them from parts of Gaul which were not directly the scene of revolt. Many others fled in the 5th century to the Visigothic kingdom in the southwest of the country, where they found the conditions of life less harsh than in the Roman provinces. Others, too (particularly in the provinces south of the lower Danube), when a barbarian raid took place, were likely either to join the barbarians or to take advantage of the confusion caused by the raid to flee from the occupations to which the law bound them.

Barbarian Invasions.—The barbarian invasions were among the most momentous phenomena of the later empire. The eastern frontier was seriously disturbed until the year 363 when, following on the failure of Julian's great expedition into the Persian Empire, Jovian made a disgraceful peace with the Persians, surrendering to them much Roman territory and some Roman cities of great strategical importance. But thereafter the eastern frontier of the Roman Empire was comparatively peaceful, as the Persians were fully occupied by the attacks of the Hephthalite Huns on their northern frontier. The raids of the Saracens, the tribes of the upper Nile Valley, and the Moors were of minor importance.

On the other hand, the European provinces of the Roman Empire were subjected not only to innumerable small raids and plundering forays by land and sea but also to three major waves of attack by the Germanic peoples of the north. The first of these major assaults came in 376, when the Visigoths, fleeing before the Huns, were permitted to cross the lower Danube. After their victory at Adrianople (378), where they killed the emperor Valens, they settled in Moesia in 382 as federates (allies under a treaty, *foedus*, to defend the frontiers). But in 395 they left Moesia and wandered westward. In 410 they captured Rome itself and in 418 they were again settled by the Roman authorities as federates, this time on the western seaboard of France between the mouths of the Garonne and the Loire. In 443 the Burgundians were settled by Aetius as federates in Savoy, and in 456 they extended their power over most of the Rhône Valley. In the middle of the 5th century, then, the greater part of Gaul south of the Loire was occupied by Visigothic and Burgundian federates.

The second great intrusion of barbarians began on Dec. 31, 406, when the Vandals, the Suebi (Sueves), and the non-Germanic Alani crossed the middle Rhine, ravaged Gaul for three years, and then settled in Spain from 409 to 429. In the latter year those of the Vandals and Alani who still survived crossed into Africa and in 435 were recognized as federates by the government at Ravenna. But in 439, after they had captured Carthage, they became an independent state, the first free German state to be set up in the Mediterranean area of the Roman Empire. The second such state was that of the Visigoths in southwestern Gaul, for their king Euric threw off the overlordship of the Roman government in 475.

The last of the major barbarian invasions followed on the collapse of the empire of Attila (*q.v.*) and his sons in 455. Several Germanic peoples now made for the Roman frontier, and being hungry and landless begged to be admitted to the provinces as federates. The Ostrogoths were thereupon settled by the eastern Romans in Pannonia, and other less important peoples elsewhere. Fragments of several peoples also descended into Italy, where in 476 they deposed Romulus Augustulus and established Odoacer (*q.v.*) as their king. These peoples, too, were recognized as federates, and Odoacer, though in effect king of Italy, admitted the overlordship of the eastern Roman emperor. (*See* also separate articles on the various barbarian peoples.)

The position, then, in 476 was that North Africa and southwestern Gaul were in the hands of German kings who were politically independent of the Romans. Southeastern Gaul and Italy were ruled by German kings who acknowledged themselves subjects of the emperor at Constantinople. The position in northern Gaul is exceedingly obscure, for sources of information about that region can scarcely be said to exist. Little is known of Spain; much of it was presumably still in Roman hands, but the northwest of the peninsula was occupied by the Suebi, who had entered Spain with the Vandals and Alani in 409. They may have been independent. The provinces along the upper Danube were under heavy pressure from the barbarians, especially the Alamanni. Britain had stood outside these movements, and it was still controlled by the Roman administration in 409. But in that year the emperor Honorius wrote to the cities in the island bidding them look to their own defense against the barbarians. Italy, in that and the following year, was invaded by Alaric (*q.v.*), and no troops could be spared for the defense of the island. For many years thereafter nothing is heard of Britain; but there is no evidence that the Romans formally "withdrew" from the island, and presumably the Roman administration continued to function, at any rate in some parts of the country, for some time. But by 476 Roman rule had long since passed away.

In all the German states of the continent, both those of the federates and those which were independent, life continued as it did in the provinces which were still directly ruled by the emperors of the east and of the west. A somewhat exceptional case was Africa, where the Vandals expropriated many of the large Roman estates and continued to exploit them with the existing labour force and with the existing agricultural methods. The Roman population continued to be subject to Roman law in all the kingdoms alike; and this law continued to be administered by a Roman civil service, which also collected the taxes and which even in the independent states was recruited from Romans. The essential difference was that the armed forces were now composed of Germans only, and Romans were excluded from military service.

Except in Africa tension between the Germans and the Romans was slight; but it certainly existed, and the two peoples were everywhere divided by religion, the Romans being Catholics and the Germans remaining Arians everywhere throughout this period. Intermarriage between Romans and barbarians had been made a capital offense by Valentinian I, and his law remained in force both in the empire and in the kingdoms, though a few cases are known where it was broken with impunity.

The numbers of the Germans who settled in the provinces cannot be calculated even approximately; it is known that the Vandals who crossed from Spain to Africa in 429 numbered 80,000. It cannot reasonably be doubted, however, that the new settlers amounted to no more than a small percentage of the population as a whole. In all, it can scarcely be said that the 5th century marked a decisive break in the history of continental Europe or Africa in any sense except a political one. Roman laws, institutions, literature, and even the Roman administrative machine continued to flourish throughout the west. In Britain, on the other hand, the years following 409 formed a break which was both decisive and complete.

(E. A. T.)

BIBLIOGRAPHY.—*Sources: Republican Period:* The formation of Roman historiography and the sources for Roman history before 264 B.C. are described above; the material which the sources provide for the subsequent history of Rome is essentially more reliable. The early annalists, such as L. Calpurnius Piso Frugi (consul in 133 B.C.), were well informed about contemporary events, whatever their knowledge of Rome's earlier history. The collection and publication (c. 123 B.C.) of the *Annales Maximi* in 80 books by Mucius Scaevola made much early material available in a definitive form which was used by later annalists. At the same time the Greek statesman Polybius wrote an accurate "universal" history because he saw that Rome's conquest of the Mediterranean world made such treatment possible for the first time. Whereas only a few fragments survive of most of the early writers, there are large portions of Polybius' work, which started with the First Punic War. His work was continued by Poseidonius. During this period monographs (as that of Coelius Antipater on the Hannibalic War) and autobiographies (as those by Aemilius Scaurus, Rutilius Rufus, and later Sulla) appeared. In the Sullan age the annalistic tradition was carried on by diffuse and rhetorical writers such as Claudius Quadrigarius and Valerius Antias (both of whom were used by Livy). Sempronius Asellio wrote a history (*res gestae*), not in annalistic form (*annales*), probably from 146 to 91 B.C., where the story was taken up by Sisenna who probably took it down to 78, where Sallust's *Historiae* started; Sallust also wrote two valuable monographs. The excellent *Commentaries* of Julius Caesar and the exceedingly important correspondence of Cicero, as well as many of his speeches, survive. In the Ciceronian period much valuable antiquarian work was done by such men as Varro, Pomponius Atticus, and others which aided later writers to correct the mistakes of their predecessors.

In the Augustan age the materials accumulated by previous generations were worked up by compilers whose works are in some cases preserved. The work by Livy covered the history of Rome from its foundation to 9 B.C. in 142 books; of these only 35 are preserved in their entirety, while the contents of the rest are known in outline from an epitome (*periochae*) and from the compendia of Florus and later authors. Diodorus Siculus followed the earlier annalists in the sections of his *Universal History* (down to Caesar) which dealt with Roman affairs; Dionysius of Halicarnassus, in his *Roman Antiquities* (7 B.C.), treated early Roman history in a more ambitious and rhetorical style, with greater fullness than Livy, whose work he seems to have used. Universal histories were also written in the Augustan age by Pompeius Trogus, whose work is known from the epitome of Justin (2nd century A.D.), and Juba, the learned king of Mauretania. Strabo, whose *Geography* is extant, was the author of a continuation of Polybius' history (to 27 B.C.). The learning of the time was enshrined in the encyclopaedia of Verrius Flaccus, of which part of Festus' abridgment (2nd century A.D.) remains, together with an epitome of Festus by Paulus Diaconus (of the time of Charlemagne). An official list of the consuls and other chief magistrates of the republic was inscribed on the arch of Augustus in the Forum, together with a similar list of *triumphatores;* the former of these is known as the *Fasti Capitolini* (A. Degrassi, *Inscriptions Italiae,* xiii, 1 [1947]), since the fragments which have been recovered are preserved in the Palace of the Conservatori on the Capitol.

Among writers of the imperial period who dealt with republican history the most important are Velleius Paterculus, whose compendium of Roman history was published in A.D. 30; Plutarch (c. A.D. 45–125), in whose biographies much contemporary material was worked up; Appian, who wrote under the Antonines and described the wars of the republic under geographical headings (partly preserved) and the civil wars in five books; and Dio Cassius (*see below*), of whose history only that portion which deals with events from 69 B.C. onward is extant.

The evidence of inscriptions and coins begins to be of value during the last 150 years of the republic. A series of laws and *senatus consulta* (beginning with the *senatus consultum de Bacchanalibus,* 186 B.C.) throws light on constitutional questions, while many of the coins struck from about 150 B.C. onward bear types illustrative of the traditions preserved by the families to which the masters of the mint (*triumviri monetales*) belonged.

Sources: Imperial Period: The memoirs of Augustus as well as those of his contemporaries (Messalla, Agrippa, Maecenas, etc.) and successors (Tiberius, Agrippina the younger, etc.) have perished, but the *Res gestae divi Augusti* inscribed on the walls of his temple at Ancyra survive, together with fragments of copies at Apollonia and Antioch, both in Pisidia (ed. by T. Mommsen [1883] and J. Gagé, 2nd ed. [1950]). Aufidius Bassus wrote the history of the civil wars and early empire, perhaps to A.D. 49, and this was continued by Pliny the elder

in 31 books, probably to the accession of Vespasian. These works and others were used by Cornelius Tacitus, whose *Annals* (properly called *ab excessu divi Augusti*) and *Histories* carried the story of the empire down to A.D. 96. Pliny's correspondence with Trajan about the affairs of Bithynia, which he administered in A.D. 111–113, is of great historical value. Suetonius, who was for some time secretary of state to Hadrian, wrote biographies of the emperors from Julius Caesar to Domitian. Arrian, a Bithynian Greek, wrote on Rome's policy and wars in the east. Appian dealt with the wars waged under the early empire in the closing books of his work, which have not been preserved.

Dio Cassius wrote a history of Rome to the death of Elagabalus in 80 books; only epitomes and excerpts remain of the portion dealing with events from A.D. 46 onward, except for parts of the 78th and 79th books, in which Dio's narrative of contemporary events is especially valuable. Herodian, a Syrian, wrote a history of the emperors from Commodus to Gordian III, which as the work of a contemporary is not without value. The *Historia Augusta,* upon which it is necessary to rely for the history of the 3rd century A.D., consists of a series of lives of the emperors (including most of the pretenders to that title) from Hadrian to Carinus, professedly written by six authors, under Diocletian and Constantine. It is now generally believed that (at least in its present form) it is a compilation of mixed value made perhaps in the latter half of the 4th century. The fragments of Dexippus, an Athenian who successfully defended his native town against the Goths, throw much light on the barbarian invasions of the 3rd century.

The most important historian of the 4th century was Ammianus Marcellinus, a native of Antioch and an officer in the imperial guard, who continued the work of Tacitus (in Latin) to the death of Valens; the last 18 books of his history, covering the years A.D. 353–378, remain. Two compendia of imperial history pass under the name of Aurelius Victor, the *Caesares,* or lives of the emperors from Augustus to Julian, and the *Epitome de Caesaribus* (not by the same author) which goes down to Theodosius I. Similar works are the *Breviarium* of Eutropius (secretary of state under Valens) and the still briefer epitome of Festus. The writings of the emperor Julian and of the rhetoricians Libanius, Themistius, and Eunapius—the last-named continued the history of Dexippus to A.D. 404—are of great value for the latter part of the 4th century A.D. They wrote as pagans, while the Christian version of events is given by the three orthodox historians, Socrates, Sozomen, and Theodoret, and the Arian Philostorgius, all of whom wrote in the 5th century. An imperial official, Zosimus, writing in the latter half of that century, gave a sketch of imperial history to A.D. 410; the latter part is valuable, being based on contemporary writings. The bishops Synesius and Palladius, who lived under Arcadius and Theodosius II, furnish valuable information as to their own times; while the fragments of Priscus tell much of Attila and the invasions of the Huns.

Mention must also be made of the poets and letter writers of the 4th and 5th centuries—Ausonius, Claudian, Symmachus, Paulinus of Nola, Sidonius Apollinaris, Prudentius, Merobaudes, and others—from whose writings much historical information is derived. Cassiodorus, the minister of Theodoric, wrote a history of the Goths, transmitted in the *Historia Gothorum* of Jordanes (c. A.D. 550), which gives an account of the earlier barbarian invasions. Several chronological works were compiled in the 4th and 5th centuries. It will suffice to name the *Chronology* of Eusebius (to A.D. 324), translated by Jerome and carried down to A.D. 378, and the *Chronography of A.D. 354,* an illustrated calendar containing miscellaneous information.

The codes of law, especially the *Codex Theodosianus* (A.D. 438) and the code of Justinian, as well as the army list of the early 5th century, known as the *Notitia Dignitatum,* possess great historical value. Inscriptions of the empire are of incalculable importance as showing the working of the imperial system in its details; the coins also throw much light on the dark places of history in the lack of other authorities. Papyri are not only instructive as to legal, economic, and administrative history but also contribute to general knowledge of events. *See* especially L. Mitteis and U. Wilcken, *Grundzüge und Chrestomathie der Papyruskunde,* 4 vol. (1912), and bibliography in M. Rostovtzeff, *Social and Economic History of the Roman Empire,* 2nd ed. (1957). *The Journal of Egyptian Archaeology* gives an annual bibliography of this subject.

Modern Works: General Histories: The Cambridge Ancient History, ed. by S. A. Cook, F. E. Adcock, M. P. Charlesworth, and (vol. xii) N. H. Baynes; vol. vii–xii (1928–39) cover the history of Rome to A.D. 324; M. Cary (ed.), *Methuen's History of the Greek and Roman World,* vol. iv, *A History of the Roman World from 753 to 146 B.C.,* by H. H. Scullard (3rd ed., 1962), vol. v, *146–30 B.C.,* by F. B. Marsh (3rd ed., 1963), vol. vi, *30 B.C.–A.D. 138,* by E. T. Salmon (4th ed., 1963), vol. vii, *A.D. 138–337,* by H. M. D. Parker (2nd ed., 1958); M. Cary, *A History of Rome down to the Reign of Constantine* (2nd ed., 1954) is the best one-volume history; M. Rostovtzeff, *A History of the Ancient World,* vol. ii, *Rome* (1927); A. E. R. Boak, *A History of Rome to 565 A.D.,* 5th ed. (1964); G. Glotz (ed.), *Histoire ancienne,* part iii, *Histoire romaine,* 4 vol. (1926–47); A. Piganiol, *Histoire de Rome,* 3rd ed. (1949); L. Pareti, *Storia di Roma,* 6 vol. (1952–61); A. Heuss, *Römische Geschichte* (1960).

Modern Works: Early Rome and Italy: J. Whatmough, *The Foundations of Roman Italy* (1937); E. Gjerstad, *Early Rome,* vol. i–iii

(1953–60; three more volumes in preparation), collects the archaeological evidence; recent literature and theories are discussed by A. Momigliano in *Journal of Roman Studies,* vol. liii, pp. 95–121 (1963); P. de Francisci, *Primordia Civitatis* (1959); R. Bloch, *The Origins of Rome* (1960).

Modern Works: The Republic: T. Mommsen, *The History of Rome,* Eng. trans. by W. P. Dickens, rev. ed., 5 vol. (1908–13); W. E. Heitland, *The Roman Republic,* 3 vol. (1909); T. Frank, *Roman Imperialism* (1914). The most authoritative work (down to 133 B.C.) is G. De Sanctis, *Storia dei Romani,* vol. i–iv (1907–64). *See also* K. J. Beloch, *Römische Geschichte bis zum Beginn der punischen Kriege* (1926); F. Münzer, *Römische Adelsparteien und Adelsfamilien* (1920); M. Holleaux, *Rome, la Grèce et les monarchies hellénistiques au IIIe siècle avant J.-C.* (273–205) (1921); G. Colin, *Rome et la Grèce de 200 à 146 avant Jésus-Christ* (1905); H. H. Scullard, *Roman Politics, 220–150 B.C.* (1951); E. Badian, *Foreign Clientelae* (264–70 B.C.) (1958); A. H. J. Greenidge, *A History of Rome, B.C. 133–104* (1904); A. H. J. Greenidge and A. M. Clay, *Sources for Roman History, 133–70 B.C.,* 2nd ed. by E. W. Gray (1960); T. Rice Holmes, *The Roman Republic,* 3 vol. (1923), deals with 70–44 B.C.; H. H. Scullard, *From the Gracchi to Nero,* 2nd ed. (1963), covers late republic and early empire. For the period of transition from republic to empire, *see* especially F. B. Marsh, *The Founding of the Roman Empire,* 2nd ed. (1927); Sir Ronald Syme, *The Roman Revolution* (1939); T. Rice Holmes, *The Architect of the Roman Empire,* 2 vol. (1928–31). M. Gelzer, *Die Nobilität der römischen Republik* (1912; reprinted in *Kleine Schriften,* vol. i, 17 ff. [1962]), interpreted the nature of Roman politics and society as a nexus of personal relations and obligations. The prosopographical approach was developed further by F. Münzer, while P. Fraccaro (*see Opuscula,* 3 vol. [1956–57]), following in the tradition of Mommsen, illuminated many aspects of republican politics and constitutional practice.

Modern Works: The Empire: Two introductory books are M. P. Charlesworth, *The Roman Empire* (1951); A. Passerini, *Linee di storia romana in età imperiale* (1949). *See also* H. Dessau, *Geschichte der römischen Kaiserzeit,* 3 vol. (1924–30); E. Gibbon, *The Decline and Fall of the Roman Empire,* ed. J. B. Bury, 7 vol. (1896–1900); E. Stein, *Histoire du Bas-Empire,* ed. J.-R. Palanque, 2 vol. (1959, 1949); A. H. M. Jones, *The Later Roman Empire, 284–602,* 3 vol. (1964); J. B. Bury, *History of the Later Roman Empire (A.D. 395 to A.D. 565),* 2 vol. (1923), *The Invasion of Europe by the Barbarians* (1928); F. Lot, *The End of the Ancient World, and the Beginnings of the Middle Ages* (1931); O. Seeck, *Geschichte des Untergangs der antiken Welt,* 6 vol. (1895–1921); H. M. Gwatkin and J. P. Whitney (eds.), *The Cambridge Medieval History,* vol. i and ii (1911–13). For the provinces, *see* T. Mommsen, *The Provinces of the Roman Empire from Caesar to Diocletian,* 2 vol., Eng. trans. (reprinted 1909); V. Chapot, *The Roman World* (1928); J. S. Reid, *The Municipalities of the Roman Empire* (1913); F. F. Abbott and A. C. Johnson, *Municipal Administration in the Roman Empire* (1926); A. H. M. Jones, *The Cities of the Eastern Roman Provinces* (1937), *The Greek City from Alexander to Justinian* (1940); G. H. Stevenson, *Roman Provincial Administration till the Age of the Antonines* (1939).

Modern Works: Constitutional: T. Mommsen, *Römisches Staatsrecht,* 3 vol. (1881–87), and *Römisches Strafrecht* (1889), are still fundamental; A. H. J. Greenidge, *Roman Public Life* (1901); L. Homo, *Roman Political Institutions from City to State,* Eng. trans. (1929); E. Meyer, *Römischer Staat und Staatsgedanke,* 2nd ed. (1961); G. W. Botsford, *The Roman Assemblies* (1909); L. R. Taylor, *The Voting Districts of the Roman Republic* (1960); A. N. Sherwin-White, *The Roman Citizenship* (1939); T. R. S. Broughton and M. L. Patterson, *The Magistrates of the Roman Republic,* 2 vol. and supplement (1951–60); A. Degrassi, *I Fasti consolari dell'Impero Romano* (1952); M. Hammond, *The Augustan Principate* (1933), *The Antonine Monarchy* (1959); F. de Martino, *Storia della costituzione romana,* 4 vol. (1958–62).

Modern Works: Economic and Social: T. Frank (ed.), *An Economic Survey of Ancient Rome,* 5 vol. (1933–40), covers Italy and the provinces. *See also* T. Frank, *An Economic History of Rome,* 2nd ed. (1927); M. Rostovtzeff, *The Social and Economic History of the Roman Empire,* 2nd ed., 2 vol. (1957); M. P. Charlesworth, *Trade-Routes and Commerce of the Roman Empire,* 2nd ed. (1926); Sir John Clapham *et al.* (eds.), *The Cambridge Economic History of Europe,* vol. i and ii (1941–52); M. Grant, *The World of Rome* (1960); W. Warde Fowler, *Social Life at Rome in the Age of Cicero* (1915); J. Carcopino, *Daily Life in Ancient Rome . . . at the Height of the Empire,* Eng. trans. by E. O. Lorimer (1940); S. Dill, *Roman Society from Nero to Marcus Aurelius,* 2nd ed. (1905), and *Roman Society in the Last Century of the Western Empire,* 2nd ed. (1899); A. Momigliano (ed.), *The Conflict between Paganism and Christianity in the Fourth Century* (1963); C. G. Starr, *Civilization and the Caesars* (1954).

Modern Works: Military: J. Kromayer and G. Veith, *Heerwesen und Kriegführung der Griechen und Römer* (1928), *Antike Schlachtfelder,* 4 vol. (1903–31), *Schlachtenatlas zur antiken Kriegsgeschichte* (1922–26); H. M. D. Parker, *The Roman Legions,* 2nd ed. (1958); P. Couissin, *Les Armes romaines* (1926); C. G. Starr, *The Roman Imperial Navy,* 2nd ed. (1961). (H. H. SD.)

ROMANIA, a name used by the Byzantines to describe the territory under their control, and, more particularly, by the Western powers to describe the Latin empire of Constantinople (1204–61). The name is derived from "Rome," the Byzantine Empire being the successor to the Roman Empire. Romania is also a variant for Rumania (*q.v.*).

ROMAN LAW. The term "Roman law" denotes first of all the law of the city of Rome and of the Roman Empire: in the West, the law in force at any period from the foundation of the city (traditional date 753 B.C.) until the fall of the Western empire in the 5th century A.D.; and in the East, the law of the Eastern empire, until it too fell with the capture of Constantinople by the Turks in 1453. The law even of the later Eastern empire remained wholly Roman in character.

But "Roman law" does not mean merely the law of those political societies to which the name Roman may in some sense be applied; for the legal institutions evolved by the Romans have had not merely influence on the law of other peoples but in many cases actual application, in times long after the disappearance of the Roman Empire as a political entity and even in countries that were never subject to Roman rule. To take the most striking example, in a large part of Germany until the adoption of a common code for the whole empire in 1900 the Roman law was in force as "subsidiary law"; *i.e.,* it was applied unless excluded by contrary local provisions. This law, however, which was in force in parts of Europe long after the fall of the Roman Empire, was not the Roman law in its original form. Its basis was indeed always the *Corpus juris civilis*—*i.e.,* the codifying legislation of the emperor Justinian I (*see* below)—but from the 11th century this legislation was interpreted, developed, and adapted to later conditions by generations of jurists and received additions from non-Roman sources. All the forms it assumed in different countries and at different epochs can be included under "Roman law." In England the term "civil law" often denotes Roman accessions, in contrast to native "common law."

Roman law is important not only as the system once in force in many places but also as an influence on the development of law in general. Even today, the legal systems of Western civilization (with some exceptions, especially the Scandinavian) fall into two groups, in one of which the main elements are of Roman origin; the other is English. To the English group belong England, nearly all the United States of America, and most British territories; to the Roman group belong the rest. Nearly all the nations of continental Europe have legal codes that are Roman in structure, fundamental categories, and general method of thought. Within the British territories, Scotland has a system largely derived from the Roman; Quebec has a system of French law built largely with Roman materials; and Ceylon has a system known as "Roman-Dutch," based on Roman law as developed by Dutch jurists. English law itself, though owing less to Roman law than does any other system, has at different times and in different ways received considerable accessions from Roman sources (*see* ENGLISH LAW).

This article is confined to the history of private law within the Empire up to the death of Justinian. It is outlined as follows:

I. Historical Conspectus
    1. Mid-Republican Period (450–150 B.C.)
    2. Late Republican Period
    3. Early Empire and Classical Period
    4. Postclassical Period
II. Sources of the Law
    A. Jus Non Scriptum or Custom
    B. Jus Scriptum
      1. Leges and Plebiscita
      2. Senatus Consulta
      3. Edicta Magistratuum
      4. Responsa Prudentium
      5. Constitutiones Principum
      6. Earlier Collections of Constitutions
    C. The Law of Justinian
      1. Codex Constitutionum
      2. Digest (Pandects)
      3. Institutes
      4. Revised Codex
      5. Novels
      6. Corpus Juris Civilis

I. HISTORICAL CONSPECTUS

The period of the Roman monarchy (753–510 B.C. according to tradition) and the republic up to the passing of the Twelve Tables (451–450) may be called the period of conjecture in regard to law. The only evidence is unreliable tradition and inference from later institutions.

1. Mid-Republican Period (450–150 B.C.).—Apart from fragments of the Twelve Tables and from the historians, who are chiefly of use for constitutional law, the evidence, when it comes to detail, is not a great deal better than it is for the previous period. The history of law, like the rest of Roman history, suffers from the destruction of records when Rome was burned by the Gauls in or about 387 B.C. Few professedly legal works were written, and none has survived. However, some laws are known, as are certain legal institutions and the names of some famous lawyers. The period is preeminently one of the *jus civile*, as opposed both to the *jus honorarium*, or magisterial law, and to the *jus gentium*, in the sense explained below.

2. Late Republican Period.—For the last century and a half of the republic the evidence is better. A few quotations from legal writers of the time survive in Justinian's *Digest*; Cicero's works contain numerous references to legal matters, and there is other nonlegal literature from which information on law can be deduced, as well as the text of a few laws in inscriptions. In this period magisterial edict comes to be the chief reforming factor in Roman law; it is the period of the earlier *jus honorarium*. The *jus gentium*, too, began to be important; it was probably through the edicts that much of the *jus gentium* found its way into the law as administered between citizens.

Jus gentium has two meanings, one practical, the other theoretical. In the practical sense it means that part of the Roman law which the Romans applied both to themselves and to foreigners. *Jus civile*, as opposed to it, means that part which they applied only to themselves. Roman law, like other ancient systems, adopted originally the principle of personality; *i.e.*, that the law of the state applied only to its citizens. The foreigner was strictly rightless, and unless protected by some treaty between his state and Rome could be seized, like an ownerless piece of property, by any Roman. But from early times there were treaties with foreign states guaranteeing mutual protection. Even where there was no treaty, the increasing commercial interests of Rome made it necessary for it to protect, by some form of justice, the foreigners who came within its borders. A magistrate charged with the administration of such justice could not simply apply Roman law, because that was the privilege of citizens; even had there not been this difficulty, foreigners, especially those coming from Greek cities and used to a more developed and freer system, would probably have objected to the cumbrous formalism which characterized the early *jus civile*.

The law which the magistrates applied probably consisted of three elements: (1) an already existing "law merchant" used by the Mediterranean traders; (2) those institutions of the Roman law which, after being purged of their formalistic elements, could be applied universally to any litigant in a Roman court, whether Roman or foreigner; (3) in the last resort, the magistrates' own sense of what was fair and just. This system of *jus gentium* was also adopted when Rome began to have provinces and provincial governors administered justice to the *peregrini* (foreigners). This word came to mean not so much persons living under another government (of which, with the expansion of Roman power, there came to be fewer and fewer) as Roman subjects who were not citizens. In general, disputes between members of the same (subject) state were settled by that state's own courts according to its own law, while disputes between provincials of different states or between provincials and Romans were resolved by the governor's court applying *jus gentium*. The law thus developed in its turn reacted on the law as administered between Romans, especially by way of making it less formal, with the result that to a considerable extent the two systems were identical, particularly in the law of contract. When a Roman lawyer says that the contract of sale is *juris gentium*, he means that it is formed in the same way and has the same legal results whether the parties to it are citizens or not. This is the practical sense of *jus gentium*; because of the universality of its application, the idea is linked with a theoretical sense, that of a law common to all peoples and dictated by nature, which the Romans took from Greek philosophy.

Aristotle had divided law into the natural (*physikon*) and the man-made (*nomikon*), and had asserted that the natural part was in force everywhere. This conception was in tune with the Stoic ideal of a life "according to nature," which became a commonplace borrowed by the Roman jurists, who, like other educated Romans, were much under the influence of the Stoic system. In their works this theoretical law of nature, "common to all mankind," then becomes identified with the practical law which the Romans administered to all free men, irrespective of citizenship, simply on the basis of their freedom. Moreover, the law of nature became an ideal which helped to introduce notions of moderation and reasonableness into the stricter rules of the older law.

3. Early Empire and Classical Period.—The change from republic to empire did not make any immediate difference to private law, except that by bringing peace after a century of turmoil it was favourable to legal progress. Legal literature, too, increased in volume, and a number of quotations from authors of the 1st century survive in the *Digest*. This age merges into the classical period, which is generally taken to include the 2nd and early 3rd centuries A.D. and is thus considerably later than the classical period of Latin literature. It falls roughly into two divisions, an earlier one covered by the reigns of Hadrian (A.D. 117–138) and the Antonine emperors (death of Commodus, A.D. 192) and a later one under the Severi (accession of Septimius Severus, A.D. 193; death of Alexander Severus, A.D. 235). The work of the earlier period was more creative, while the later represents the working out of existing principles over the whole field of law. The *Digest* has quotations from all the authors of the classical age, but those taken from three writers of the later period—Papinian (d. A.D. 212), Julius Paulus, Ulpian (*c.* A.D. 170–228)—alone comprise over half the work.

4. Postclassical Period.—With the era of confusion that followed the murder of Alexander Severus, there came a rather sudden decline in the value of the legal work done; nor did the restoration of order by Diocletian revive legal literature. The law, of course, did not stand still. New ideas were introduced, especially from Greek sources, through the establishment of the Eastern empire, with its capital at Constantinople, and through the growth of Christianity. The great social and political changes of the sinking empire had repercussions on private law. But not until just before Justinian's time was there something of an intellectual revival in legal matters.

II. SOURCES OF THE LAW

The Romans themselves divided their law into *jus scriptum* (written law) and *jus non scriptum* (unwritten law). By "unwritten law" they meant custom; by "written law" not only that derived from legislation but, literally, that which was based on any source in writing. The list of written sources comprises *leges, plebiscita, senatus consulta, edicta magistratuum, responsa prudentium,* and *constitutiones principum.* This list is repeated in Justinian's *Institutes,* though from the close of the classical period the only source of new law (apart from custom) had been the emperor's constitutions.

A. Jus Non Scriptum or Custom

Custom (*mos maiorum, consuetudo*) was recognized by the Romans not only as having been the original source of their law but as a source from which new law could spring. The theory given by the jurists is that the people, by adopting a custom, show tacitly what they wish to be law, just as they might do expressly by voting in the assembly. In the developed law it would seem, however, that custom as an independent source was not very fruitful and that it exercised its influence rather through the medium of juristic opinion and the practice of the courts.

B. Jus Scriptum

1. Leges and Plebiscita.—*Lex* is properly an enactment of one of the assemblies of the whole Roman people, the *comitia centuriata, tributa,* or *curiata* (see COMITIA). The first of these is the oldest; it lost all real political function before reliable history began, though for certain formal purposes it lived on into classical times. The validity of *plebiscita* (*i.e.,* resolutions of the purely plebeian assembly) was one of the chief matters of contention between the patricians and the plebeians. The struggle between these orders ended about 286 B.C., when, by the *lex Hortensia, plebiscita* were given the force of *leges.* Thereafter enactments which were strictly *plebiscita* were often loosely called *leges.*

Roman assemblies, like those of the Greek city-states, were primary; *i.e.,* the citizen came and voted himself and did not send a delegate. But their power was restricted by the rule that only a magistrate could put a proposal before them and by the absence of any opportunity for amendment or debate. The only function of the people was to answer "yes" or "no" to the magistrate's "asking" (*rogatio*), and constitutional practice further required that the magistrate should consult the senate before putting a proposal to the assembly. In the later republic bills were hardly ever rejected; the real power lay with the senate and the magistrates.

The historians have a good deal to say of *leges* passed in the time of the kings (*leges regiae*), but legislation at so early a date is unlikely. What they took for laws were probably statements of ancient custom from pontifical sources. Of greater importance are the Twelve Tables, said to have been passed in 451–450 B.C., about 60 years after the expulsion of·the kings. The accounts given by the historians (*see* ROMAN HISTORY: *The Monarchy and the Republic*) are inconsistent and mainly mythical, but tradition is no doubt right in representing this event as an incident in the struggle of the plebeians for political equality. The motive was a desire to obtain a written and public code which patrician magistrates could not alter at their will against plebeian litigants. What weight should be given to that part of the story which tells of a preliminary embassy sent to Athens to study the laws of Solon has been much debated. That the embassy itself is legendary can hardly be doubted.

Evidence of Greek influence appears in only a small part of the code (*e.g.,* Tab. VII. 2-D. 10.1.13). In the main the materials of the code were taken from native customary sources. The most authoritative modern opinion is that, in spite of all skepticism as to details, the Twelve Tables were an enacted code of law and that tradition is not far wrong in dating them to about 450 B.C.

The text of the code has not survived, a remarkable fact, for copies (probably in more or less modernized language) must have been abundant in Cicero's time if, as he says, it was still customary in his youth for boys to learn it by heart. Only a few "fragments" are extant, collected from allusions and quotations in the works of such authors as Cicero.

When Augustus established the empire, the assemblies did not at once cease to function, but their assent to any proposal was a mere formal ratification of the emperor's wishes. The last *lex* known to have been passed was a *lex agraria* under Nerva (A.D. 96–98).

2. Senatus Consulta.—A resolution of the senate originally had only advisory effect. It could be translated into enforceable policy through the machinery of a magistrate's edict or through the senate's influence upon a magistrate's proposal for legislation by a popular assembly. The senate acquired legislative power in early imperial times, though this was never conferred on it by any imperial enactment. The resolution of the senate preceding the placing of a bill before the people had always been practically decisive, and with the decay of the *comitia* the people's assent evidently came to be regarded as a formality which might be omitted. Actually, the senate nearly always legislated at the instigation of the emperor, latterly, indeed, simply embodying his *oratio* or proposal in a resolution, and not long after the classical period the emperors ceased to legislate through the senate.

3. Edicta Magistratuum.—An edict was a proclamation, originally no doubt oral, later in writing; any superior magistrate might find it necessary to issue such edicts regarding matters within his competence. A peculiarity of Roman law, however, was that the magistrates entrusted with jurisdiction made particular use of this power and that their edicts became one of the most important sources of law. Originally the duty of *jurisdictio,* which meant supervising the administration of justice rather than actually deciding cases, had presumably lain with the king, from whom it descended to the consuls (see CONSUL). With the growth of business it became impossible for the consuls to discharge this duty in addition to their other functions, and in 367 B.C. a new magistrate, the *praetor* (*q.v.*), was appointed for the purpose. About the year 242 B.C. the increase of foreigners at Rome made it necessary to separate the conduct of suits in which they were concerned from those to which citizens alone were parties, and a second praetor, *praetor peregrinus,* was appointed to deal with cases in which a foreigner was involved. The original praetor, now confined to suits between citizens, came to bear the title *urbanus.*

At Rome the curule aediles (see AEDILE) issued important edicts; their duties included the supervision of the marketplace. In the provinces supreme judicial power lay with the governors, and quaestors (see QUAESTOR) carried out functions analogous to those of the aediles.

The law derived from the edicts of all these magistrates was called *jus honorarium,* as opposed to *jus civile* in the sense of law based on legislation or custom; but owing to the preeminent position of the praetors, the phrase is often used simply as equivalent to *jus praetorium.* The praetor was not a legislator and could not make law directly as could the sovereign people, but the Roman system of procedure gave him great power over the provision or refusal of remedies as well as over the form which remedies were to take. Thus the edict which he issued at the beginning of his term of office, setting out what he intended to do, was a document of the greatest importance. In it he could say, for instance, "If one man makes such and such an allegation against another, *I will give an action,*" even though the circumstances alleged would not give any right at civil law. In this way, by means of fictions, by modifications of existing civil-law actions, and even by granting new actions based upon facts alleged by the plaintiff, the praetor used the machinery of the edict to expand the substantive law through his control over procedure. The edict called *perpetuum* (continuous) because it was intended to announce the principles which the praetor would follow throughout his year of office, ceased to be valid when that term expired; but it became the practice for each succeeding praetor to take over and reissue as his own much of his predecessor's edict. By the end of the republic, the part thus carried on from year to year (*tralaticium*) must have been considerable, for jurists were just beginning to write commentaries on the edict, a practice which would not have been worthwhile if the greater part of it had been liable to annual alteration.

The change from republic to empire did not immediately make any difference, and the praetors continued to issue their edicts (though it is doubtful whether they ever made changes without imperial or senatorial authority); but in the long run their wide powers were inconsistent with the emperor's supremacy. In or about A.D. 131 Hadrian therefore instructed the famous jurist Salvius Julianus to revise and settle the praetorian and aedilitian edicts. The changes in substance were not far-reaching, but the revised edict was henceforward made unalterable except by the emperor himself. This revised edict was called *edictum perpetuum*.

The relationship between *jus civile* and *jus honorarium* has often been compared with that existing in England between common law and equity. In both cases may be seen, as Sir Henry Maine put it (*Ancient Law*, p. 25 [1861]), a "body of rules existing by the side of the original civil law, founded on distinct principles, and claiming incidentally to supersede the civil law in virtue of a superior sanctity inherent in these principles"; and in both cases the resulting duality enormously complicated the law. But in detail the comparison no longer holds.

4. Responsa Prudentium.—The force attributed to professional opinions of a certain type was another feature of the Roman system, and one which contributed much to its success; for it was the "learned lawyers" (*prudentes*) who really molded the law into a coherent system.

Originally, law was considered the special province of the *pontifices* (see PONTIFEX), who seem to have regarded it as a mystery to be exploited in the interests of their order. Their monopoly was, however, broken from about 300 B.C. The legend is that, in 304 B.C., G. Flavius, a clerk of Appius Claudius Caecus, stole from his master and made public a list of *legis actiones* (i.e., forms of words which had to be followed exactly in the conduct of lawsuits), thereafter known as the *jus Flavianum*. It is more probable that the publication was encouraged by Appius Claudius, and that it coincided with the opening of the pontificate, and therefore of the function of interpreting the *legis actiones*, to plebeians. The first known legal treatise, called the "cradle of the law" by Lucius Pomponius, is the *Tripertita* of Sextus Aelius Paetus Catus (consul 198 B.C.) which contained the text of the Twelve Tables, the *interpretatio* put upon it by the jurists, and the *legis actiones*. Probably the last part was identical with the *jus Aelianum*, which, according to Pomponius, was a collection of *legis actiones* like the earlier *jus Flavianum*.

From about 300 B.C. onward there arose a class of men who made the study of the law their special interest. These *juris consulti* or *juris prudentes* were not professional lawyers in the modern sense but men of rank who sought by giving free legal advice to obtain popularity and advancement in a public career. The *responsa* (answers) which they delivered to those who consulted them were of greater weight than are modern "opinions of counsel" because the person who actually decided a case under the Roman system of procedure was not, as now, a trained lawyer, but a lay *judex*, who did not, like jurymen, have a judge to direct him on points of law. Augustus empowered certain jurists to give *responsa* with the emperor's authority, and this practice led, perhaps gradually, to the view that the *judex* was bound to abide by the prevalent opinion of jurists who had received this *jus respondendi*. Gaius mentions a rescript of Hadrian which laid down that *responsa* were binding if they agreed, and that if they disagreed, the *judex* could decide for himself which to follow. The practice of conferring the *jus respondendi* lapsed at least as early as A.D. 200.

The "law of citations," an imperial enactment of 426, ultimately laid down that only the works of five jurists—Papinian (*q.v.*), Paulus, Gaius (*q.v.*), Ulpian (*q.v.*), and Modestinus (c. A.D. 250) —might be cited and, subject to some provisos which are obscure, the works of authors quoted by these five. If the authorities cited disagreed, the majority was to be followed; if numbers were equal, the side on which Papinian stood was to prevail; if he was silent, the *judex* might please himself.

Of the long succession of jurists, mention is here confined to the two "schools," the Sabinians (or Cassians) and the Proculians, into which they were divided in the early empire—though according to one view there had been a similar division in the late republic. Marcus Antistius Labeo (*q.v.*), one of the greatest figures in the history of jurisprudence, was the founder of the Proculians (named after his pupil Sempronius Proculus); Capito was founder of the Sabinians (so called after Masurius Sabinus, who was given the *jus respondendi* by the emperor Tiberius). What principle, if any, divided these schools is unknown, though a number of controversies on particular points are preserved, especially in Gaius' *Institutes*. Probably there were teaching establishments or societies of some sort in connection with the "schools," for Pomponius gives a list of "heads." The division seems not to have survived the Antonine age; Gaius, a Sabinian, is the last jurist known to have belonged to either school.

5. Constitutiones Principum.—Neither Augustus nor his immediate successors expressly assumed legislative power, yet Gaius, about A.D. 160, wrote, "there has never been any doubt that what the emperor lays down has the force of law." Ulpian, indeed, refers the validity of constitutions to the so-called *lex regia*, passed at the beginning of each emperor's reign; and there is in the only surviving example of such a *lex* (the *lex de imperio Vespasiani*, line 17 *et seq.*) a clause conferring such wide powers on the emperor that legislation might be deemed to be included. But this was not the original meaning of the clause; the emperor's legislative power grew gradually. The chief forms of imperial legislation were: (1) *Edicta* (i.e., proclamations) which the emperor, like other magistrates, might issue; but whereas the other magistrates were confined to their own spheres, that of the emperor was unlimited. (2) *Mandata*, or instructions to subordinates, especially provincial governors. (3) *Rescripta*, written answers to officials or others who consulted the emperor, in particular on a point of law; the rescript lays down the point of law applicable, and, since the emperor is supreme, the rule may be new. (4) *Decreta*, or decisions of the emperor sitting as a judge; here too the emperor may lay down a new rule.

6. Earlier Collections of Constitutions.—Long before Justinian's time (*see* below), the growth of legal literature, especially of imperial constitutions, created a need for reference works. A beginning was made, almost certainly in Diocletian's day, by a collection of constitutions known as the *codex Gregorianus*, which was followed by the *codex Hermogenianus*, perhaps also dating in its original form from Diocletian. Both collections were unofficial, but their compilers must have had access to the imperial archives. Whereas the *Gregorianus* contained constitutions from Hadrian to Diocletian, those of the *Hermogenianus* were almost exclusively of Diocletian's time; later constitutions attributed to it probably were added in subsequent editions. The *Hermogenianus* was clearly intended to supplement the *Gregorianus*. Unlike these two, the *codex Theodosianus* was an official work compiled by a commission appointed under Theodosius II and Valentinian III; it had the force of law from Jan. 1, 439. Constitutions from the time of Constantine the Great (reigned 306–337) onward were, with very few exceptions, not to be valid unless contained in the *Theodosianus*. For the earlier imperial legislation the older *codices* still had to serve. Nearly the whole of the *codex Theodosianus* has been preserved, whereas only fragments of the others remain. Theodosius had also planned a collection which would include juristic literature as well as imperial legislation, but this was never realized until Justinian took up the idea again.

C. THE LAW OF JUSTINIAN

The emperor Justinian I (reigned A.D. 527–565), remembered chiefly as a legislator and as a codifier of laws, found the law of the Roman Empire in a state of great confusion. It consisted of two masses, which were usually distinguished as old law (*jus vetus*) and new law (*jus novum*).

The old law comprised: (1) all such of the statutes (*leges*) passed under the republic and early empire as had not become obsolete; (2) the decrees of the senate (*senatus consulta*) passed at the end of the republic and during the first two centuries of the empire; (3) the writings of the jurists, and more particularly of those to whom the right of declaring the law with authority (*jus respondendi*) had been committed by the emperors. As these jurists, in their commentaries upon the *leges, senatus consulta,* and edicts of the magistrates, had practically incorporated all that was of importance in those documents, the books of the jurists substantially include (1) and (2). These writings were very numerous. Many had become exceedingly scarce or had been altogether lost. Some were of doubtful authenticity. They were so costly that even the public libraries had no complete collection. Moreover, they contained many inconsistencies.

The new law, which consisted of the ordinances of the emperors promulgated during the middle and later empires (*edicta, rescripta, mandata, decreta,* usually called by the general name of *constitutiones*), was in a condition not much better. These ordinances or constitutions were extremely numerous. No complete collection existed, for the earlier codices did not include all the constitutions; others had to be obtained separately, and many of them were probably inaccessible to a private person. In this branch of the law too there existed some uncertainty (although less formidable than that of the *jus vetus*), for there were constitutions which practically, if not formally, repealed or superseded others without expressly mentioning them. It was thus necessary to collect into a reasonable corpus so much of the law, both new and old, as was regarded as binding and to purge away its contradictions and inconsistencies.

1. Codex Constitutionum.—Immediately after his accession, Justinian appointed a commission to deal with the imperial constitutions. The commissioners, ten in number, were directed to go through all the constitutions of which copies existed, to select such as were of practical value, to cut these down by retrenching all unnecessary matter, and to get rid of contradictions by omitting one or the other of the conflicting passages. The remaining materials were to be arranged in order of date and gathered into one volume. The commissioners completed their task in 14 months, distributing the constitutions which they "retained" into ten books, in general conformity with the order of the Perpetual Edict enacted by Hadrian. The bulk of the statute law was thus immensely reduced, its obscurities and internal discrepancies in great measure were removed, and its provisions were adapted, by the abrogation of what was obsolete, to the circumstances of Justinian's own time. This *Codex constitutionum* was formally promulgated in 529, all imperial ordinances not included in it being repealed.

2. Digest (Pandects).—The success of this first experiment encouraged the emperor to attempt the more difficult enterprise of simplifying and digesting the writings of the jurists. Before entering on this he took the preliminary step of settling the more important of the legal questions on which the older jurists had been divided in opinion. This was accomplished by a series of constitutions known as the "Fifty Decisions" (*Quinquaginta decisiones*), along with which were published other ordinances amending the law.

Then, in December 530, a new commission was appointed, consisting of 16 eminent lawyers, under the presidency of the jurist Tribonian (*q.v.*), who had served on the previous commission. They were to procure and peruse all the writings of all the authorized jurists; to extract from these writings whatever was of the most permanent and substantial value, with power to change the expressions of the author wherever conciseness or clearness would be thereby promoted, or wherever such a change was needed in order to adapt his language to the condition of the law as it stood in Justinian's time; to avoid repetitions and contradictions by giving only one statement of the law upon each point; to insert nothing at variance with any provision contained in the *Codex constitutionum;* and to distribute the results of their labours into 50 books, subdividing each book into titles, and following the order of the Perpetual Edict.

The commissioners presented their selection of extracts to the emperor in 533, and he published it as an imperial statute on Dec. 16 of that year, with two prefatory constitutions (those known as *Omnem reipublicae* and *Dedit nobis*). It is the Latin volume which is now called the *Digest* (*Digesta*) or *Pandects* (*q.v.*). The extracts comprised in it are 9,123 in number, taken from 39 authors,

and are of greatly varying length, mostly only a few lines long. The chief disadvantage of the *Digest* is its highly unscientific arrangement. The order of the Perpetual Edict, which appears to have been taken as a sort of model for the general scheme of books and titles, was doubtless convenient to the Roman lawyers from their familiarity with it, but was in itself rather accidental and historical than logical. A modern jurist has shown that the disposition of the extracts inside each title results from the way in which the committees of the commissioners worked through the books they had to peruse.

In enacting the *Digest* as a law book, Justinian repealed all the other law contained in the treatises of the jurists (the *jus vetus*) and directed that those treatises should never be cited in future even by way of illustration; at the same time he abrogated all the older statutes which had formed a part of the *jus vetus*. But he went too far, and indeed attempted what was impossible, when he forbade all commentaries upon the *Digest*.

3. Institutes.—The *Codex* and the *Digest* held the gist of Justinian's work; but Tribonian decided that an elementary outline was needed to replace the now obsolete *Institutes* of Gaius. Thus were published, shortly before the *Digest*, the *Institutes of Justinian*, a work which still owes much to Gaius, both in matter and style.

4. Revised Codex.—In the four and a half years which elapsed between the publication of the *Codex* and that of the *Digest*, many important changes had been made in the law, notably by the publication of the "Fifty Decisions." Accordingly, another commission was appointed, consisting of Tribonian and four other coadjutors, full power being given them not only to incorporate the new constitutions with the *Codex* and make in it the requisite changes but also to revise the *Codex* generally. This work was completed in a few months; and in November 534 the revised *Codex* (*Codex repetitae praelectionis*) was promulgated with the force of law, prefaced by a constitution (*Cordi nobis*) which sets forth its history and declares it to be alone authoritative.

It is this revised *Codex*, divided into 12 books, which has come down to the modern world. The constitutions contained in it number 4,652, the earliest dating from Hadrian, the latest being of course Justinian's own. A few thus belong to the period to which the greater part of the *Digest* belongs; *i.e.*, the so-called classical period of Roman law down to the time of Alexander Severus (234). But the great majority are later and belong to one or other of the four great eras of imperial legislation, the eras of Diocletian, of Constantine, of Theodosius II, and of Justinian himself. Although this *Codex* is said to have the same general order as that of the *Digest*, viz., the order of the Perpetual Edict, there are considerable differences of arrangement between the two. The *Codex* was of the utmost practical importance to the lawyers of that time, and retains much value, historical as well as legal; but its contents are far less interesting and scientifically admirable than the extracts preserved in the *Digest*.

5. Novels.—Between 534 and 565 Justinian issued a great number of ordinances, dealing with all sorts of subjects and seriously altering the law on many points, the majority appearing before the death of Tribonian (*c.* 545). These ordinances are called, by way of distinction, new constitutions, *Novellae constitutiones post codicem,* and called in English the *Novels*. Although the emperor had stated in publishing the *Codex* that all further statutes (if any) would be officially collected, this promise does not seem to have been redeemed. The three extant collections of the *Novels* are apparently private collections, nor is it even known how many such constitutions were promulgated. One of the three contains 168 (together with 13 edicts), but some of these are by the emperors Justin II, nephew of Justinian, and Tiberius II. Another, the so-called *Epitome of Julian,* contains 125 *Novels* in Latin; and the third, the *Liber authenticarum* or *vulgata versio,* has 134, also in Latin. This last was the collection first known and chiefly used in the West during the Middle Ages. Of its 134 statutes, only 97 have been written on by the *glossatores* or medieval commentators; these therefore alone have been received as binding in those countries which recognize and obey the Roman law, according to the maxim *Quicquid non agnoscit glossa, nec* *agnoscit curia* ("whatever the gloss does not recognize, the court does not recognize"). And whereas Justinian's constitutions contained in the *Codex* were all issued in Latin, the rest of the book being in that tongue, the *Novels* were nearly all published in Greek, Latin translations being of course made for the use of the western provinces. They may be found printed in any edition of the *Corpus juris civilis.*

6. Corpus Juris Civilis.—The *Corpus juris* consists of the four books described above: (1) *Codex constitutionum;* (2) *Digesta* or *Pandectae;* (3) *Institutiones;* (4) *Novellae.*

Strictly speaking, Justinian did not codify the Roman law. Codification is the reduction of the whole preexisting body of law to a new form and the restating of it in a series of propositions, scientifically ordered, which may or may not contain some new substance but which are at any rate new in form. Justinian did not codify; he consolidated. He gave to posterity not one code but two digests or collections of extracts, which are new only to the extent that they are arranged in a new order and that here and there their words have been modified in order to bring one extract into harmony with some other. Except for this, the matter is old in expression as well as in substance.

Thus regarded, Justinian's work may appear to entitle him and Tribonian to much less credit than they have usually received for it. But the reduction of the huge confused mass of preexisting law into these two collections was an immense benefit to the empire. The work took seven years; the infinitely more difficult task of codification might well have been left unfinished at Tribonian's death, or even at Justinian's own, and have been abandoned by his successor. The extracts preserved in the *Digest* contain the opinions of the greatest legal luminaries, mostly in their own admirably concise language, while the extracts making up the *Codex* afford valuable historical evidence on the administration and social condition of the later empire. To merge on scientific principles the entire law of the empire into one whole was beyond the intellectual powers of Justinian's contemporaries.

The chief defect of the *Digest* is its arrangement, a matter about which the Roman lawyers cared very little. There are some repetitions and some inconsistencies, but not more than may fairly be allowed for in a compilation of such magnitude executed so rapidly. Tribonian has been blamed for the insertions the compilers made in the sentences of the old jurists (the so-called *Emblemata Triboniani*); but it was a part of Justinian's plan that such insertions should be made, so as to adapt those sentences to the law as settled in the emperor's time. On Justinian's own laws, contained in the *Codex* and in his *Novels,* a less favourable judgment must be pronounced. Both, but especially the latter, are diffuse and often lax in expression, prolix, and pompous.

The *Corpus juris* of Justinian, with a few additions from the ordinances of succeeding emperors, continued to be the chief lawbook of the Roman world. In the 9th century a new system was prepared by the emperor Leo VI the Wise, which is known as the *Basilica.* It is written in Greek and consists of parts of the *Codex* and of the *Digest,* joined and often altered in expression, together with some matter from the *Novels* and imperial ordinances posterior to Justinian. In the western provinces, the law as settled by Justinian held its ground; but copies of the *Corpus juris* were rare, nor did the study of it revive until the end of the 11th century. See GLOSSATORS, LEGAL.

III. THE LAW OF PERSONS
A. SLAVERY

"The main distinction in the law of persons," says Gaius, "is that all men are either free or slaves." The slave was in principle a human chattel who could be owned and dealt with like any other piece of property. As such, he was not only at the mercy of his owner but rightless and (apart from criminal law) dutiless. But if the slave was in law a thing he was in fact a man, and this modified the principle. In particular, a slave might be manumitted, to become in most cases not only free but a citizen. In fact, during the republican era any manumitted slave of a Roman citizen automatically became a citizen, irrespective of the slave's ethnic origin. Exceptions developed in the early years of the empire.

B. CITIZENSHIP

This was important for the purposes of private law because certain parts of private law applied only to citizens (*jus civile*). The general rule was that, if the status of the parents differed, the child followed that of the father (if the union was one recognized as marriage by Roman law); otherwise that of its mother. The great extension of the citizenship by Caracalla in A.D. 212 reduced the importance of this part of the law.

C. FAMILY

1. Patria Potestas.—The chief characteristic of the Roman family is the *patria potestas* which the father exercised over his children and over his more remote descendants in the male line, whatever their age might be, as well as over those brought into the family by adoption—a very common practice at Rome. This meant originally not only that he had control over the persons of his children, amounting even to a right to inflict capital punishment, but that he alone had any rights in private law. Thus any acquisitions made by a child under power became the property of the father. The father might indeed allow a child (as he might a slave) certain property (*peculium*) to treat as his own, but in the eye of the law it continued to belong to the father. In classical times there were already modifications of the system; the father's power of life and death had shrunk to that of light chastisement, and the son could bind his father by contract with a third party within the same strict limits as applied to slaves and their masters. Sons too could keep as their own what they earned as soldiers (*peculium castrense*) and even make wills of it. In Justinian's day the position as regards property had changed considerably; what the father gave to the son still remained in law the father's property, but the rules of *peculium castrense* had been extended to many sorts of professional earnings (*peculium quasi castrense*), and in other acquisitions (*e.g.,* property inherited from the mother) the father's rights were reduced to a life interest (usufruct). At all times *patria potestas* ceased normally only with the death of the father; but the father might voluntarily free the child by *emancipation,* and a daughter ceased to be under her father's *potestas* if she came under the *manus* of her husband.

2. Marriage.—There were two types of marriage known to the law, one with *manus* and one without, but the *manus* type was rare already in the late republic and had disappeared long before Justinian's day. *Manus* was the autocratic power of the husband over the wife, corresponding to *patria potestas* over the sons, and it might result in any of three ways: (*a*) by *confarreatio,* a religious ceremony confined to patricians; (*b*) by *coemptio,* a type of *mancipatio* (*see* below), purely secular and originally the Roman form of marriage by purchase; (*c*) by *usus*—if a woman lived with a man as his wife for a year, he acquired *manus* over her by a kind of prescription. The Twelve Tables had already provided that *usus* might be prevented if the woman absented herself for three nights during the year (*usurpatio trinoctii*); *usus* was obsolete by classical times.

It may be that at one time marriage with *manus* was the only form of union recognized as marriage at all, but by the time of the Twelve Tables this was no longer so, since the *usurpatio trinoctii,* though it prevented *manus,* left the marriage subsisting, so that it was possible to be married without *manus.*

Marriage without *manus* was by far the more common in all properly attested periods. It was formed (provided the parties were above the age of puberty and, if under *potestas,* had their fathers' consent) simply by the beginning of conjugal life with the intention of being married, and this was normally evidenced by the bringing of the bride to the bridegroom's house. It was, however, legally independent of all attendant ceremonies, if any, and of consummation. The wife remained under her father's *potestas* if he were still alive; if he were dead, she continued (so long as guardianship of women continued) to have the same guardian as before marriage. Both spouses had to be citizens, or if one was not, he or she must have *conubium* (the right, sometimes also given to non-Romans, of contracting a Roman marriage). The chief importance of this was that if a Roman contracted a union with a foreign woman, the children would not be in his *potestas* unless she had *conubium*.

In marriage without *manus* the property of the spouses remained distinct, and even gifts between husband and wife were invalid. But usually a dowry was given to the husband on the marriage by the woman or her father. This originally became the indefeasible property of the husband, but by classical times the wife could recover it if the marriage ended by divorce or by the husband's death; by Justinian's legislation it always had to be returned to the wife or her heirs.

Divorce was always possible at the instance of the husband in cases of marriage with *manus*; in marriage without *manus* it was free to either party to put an end to the relationship at will. A letter of *repudium* was usual, but any manifestation of intention to end the relationship made clear to the other party and accompanied by actual parting was all that was legally necessary. The Christian emperors imposed penalties on those who divorced without good reason, but the power of the parties to end the marriage by their own act was not taken away.

Concubinatus was recognized in the empire as a sort of morganatic marriage, differing from marriage only by the different intentions of the parties, and excluding marriage, for a man could not have both a wife and a concubine. Constantine first enacted that the children of such unions might be legitimated by the subsequent marriage of their parents, a rule which the medieval civil law extended to all illegitimate children.

3. Guardianship.—*Of Children.*—Persons under the age of puberty (14 for males, 12 for females) needed *tutores* if they were not under *patria potestas*. Such tutors could be appointed under the will of the *pater familias*; failing such appointment the guardianship went to the nearest agnates (*see below, Intestate Succession*) until Justinian gave it to the next of kin whether agnatic or cognatic; if there were no qualified relations the magistrates made an appointment.

Of Women.—Originally all women not under *patria potestas* or *manus* needed *tutores*, who were appointed in the same way as those for children. In classical times this *perpetua tutela mulierum* was little more than a burdensome technicality, and it disappeared from Justinian's law.

Of Lunatics and Spendthrifts.—Originally such persons were placed under the *cura* of their agnates; later, magistrates appointed curators.

Of Minors.—Originally children were considered adult at the age of puberty; but, by a long development, it became usual for those above puberty and under 25 to have *curatores* who were always magisterially appointed. (H. F. J.; Rl. P.)

D. Corporations

Surviving sources of the Roman law of corporations are extremely scanty. Moreover, in most matters corporations were regarded as pertaining to public rather than private law, so that juristic discussion of the topic was minimal.

The Romans did not develop a generalized concept of juristic personality in the sense of an entity susceptible of rights and duties. They had no terms for a corporation or a legal person. But they did endow certain aggregations of persons as such with particular powers and capacities, and the underlying legal notion hovers between corporate powers, as understood in modern law, and powers enjoyed collectively by a group of individuals. The source of such powers, however, was always an act of state.

Four types of corporation may be distinguished:

1. *Municipia* (*i.e.*, the citizen body, originally of the conquered cities, and later of other local communities), whose corporateness was recognized in such matters as the power to acquire things *inter vivos*, and to contract. In imperial times, they are accorded the power to manumit slaves, take legacies, and finally—though this became general only in postclassical law—to be instituted heir.

2. The *populus Romanus*, which could acquire property, make contracts, and be appointed heir. Such property included property of the treasury (*aerarium*) and was thought of as *res publicae*. The *fiscus*, which in postclassical times superseded the *aerarium*, vested in the emperor as a personification of the state, somewhat like the English corporation sole.

3. *Collegia*, private associations with specialized functions, like craft or trade guilds, burial societies, and societies dedicated to special religious worship. These seem to have carried on their affairs and to have held property corporately in republican times and were apparently numerous. The emperors, viewing the *collegia* with some suspicion, enacted from the beginning that no *collegium* might be founded without state authority, and such rights as the manumission of slaves and the taking of legacies were closely regulated. Unfortunately, the basic law of classical times, the *Lex Julia de Collegiis*, has not survived.

4. Charitable funds. Postclassical law saw the development of corporations *ad pias causas*; property might be donated or willed—normally, but not necessarily, to a church—for some charitable use. It seems that the church would then have the duty to supervise the fund. Imperial legislation controlled the disposition of such funds so that their alienation in excess of powers was void. Ownership is thought in such cases to have vested in the administrators for the time being. Some scholars contend that the fund itself was the owner, as in the *Stiftung* of German law. Such a view, however, seems excessively abstract for Roman thought; further, it offends the rule that corporate powers can exist only if conceded by the state.

It is much controverted whether partnerships which contracted with the state for purposes such as tax collecting (the *societas vectigalis*), mining, or quarrying might rank as corporations, but the textual material is too slender to yield a conclusive answer. The commercial corporation characteristic of modern times does not figure in Roman law. (M. A. Mr.)

IV. THE LAW OF PROPERTY AND POSSESSION

The most striking thing to a lawyer accustomed to the complexities of Anglo-U.S. real property law is the absence of any fundamental distinction among the Romans between the treatment of land and the treatment of movables. In Roman law as known today, both can be owned absolutely by individuals, though there may have been a time at Rome as elsewhere when land was subject to communal ownership of some sort. This conception of absolute ownership (*dominium*) also is characteristically Roman, as opposed to the relative idea of ownership as the better right to possession which underlies the Germanic systems; although this also, originally, underlay that of Rome. This can be seen by comparing the form of a *vindicatio* (the claim of an owner out of possession) under the *legis actio* system of procedure with that which it later assumed under the formulary system. In the earlier system the plaintiff first makes his assertion of ownership ("I say that this thing is mine") and then the defendant makes a similar assertion. Finally, the thing goes to the one whose assertion is based on the better right. Under the later formulary system there is no assertion by the defendant at all; the *judex* is instructed to condemn the defendant if it appears to him that the thing belongs to the plaintiff, otherwise to absolve the defendant. Hence, unless the plaintiff makes good his title absolutely, the defendant, though he may have no title at all, remains in possession.

Much property jurisprudence comes under the heading "methods of acquiring ownership." These were divided into two classes according as they fell under the *jus civile* or the *jus gentium*.

A. Methods of the Jus Civile

1. Mancipatio.—This was a ceremonial conveyance needing for its accomplishment the presence of the transferor and transferee, five witnesses (Roman citizens of full age), a pair of scales, a man to hold them (*libripens*), and an ingot of copper. The transferee grasped the thing and said: "I assert that this thing is mine by Quiritarian law; and be it bought to me with this piece of copper and these copper scales." He then struck the scales with the ingot, which he handed to the transferor "by way of price." Clearly this was, as Gaius says, a "symbolical sale," and the relic of a real sale. Originally, when money was unknown, the price in uncoined copper had been really weighed out to the vendor. When this became unnecessary there was still a pretense of weighing, but the price was paid separately, and the form could be used as a conveyance where it was not intended that a price should be paid at all;

e.g., because the transferor was making a gift to the transferee.

2. In Jure Cessio.—This was a conveyance in the form of a lawsuit. The transferee claims before the magistrate that the thing is his, and the transferor, who is the defendant, admits the claim. The magistrate then adjudges the thing to the transferee. The sham-lawsuit theory is not acceptable to all scholars, principally because the judgment of ownership was valid against any possible private claimant, not merely against the defendant as in a true lawsuit.

3. Usucapio.—According to the Twelve Tables, two years' continuous possession gave title in the case of land, one year in the case of movables. In the developed law, possession must have begun in good faith, the thing must not have been stolen (even though the possessor himself is quite innocent of the theft) or occupied by violence (this applies especially to land, which could not be stolen), and the possession must have had a justifiable beginning (*justus titulus*). *Usucapio*, being an institution of the *jus civile*, was possible only to citizens, but Justinian fused it with a similar institution (*praescriptio longi temporis*) which had grown up in the provinces. Under his system, possession for 3 years was required for movables, 10 or 20 years for land.

B. METHODS OF THE JUS GENTIUM

1. Occupatio.—Ownerless things, provided they are capable of private ownership (not, *e.g.*, *res sacrae*, such as temples), became the property of the first person to take possession of them. This applies, *e.g.*, to wild animals and to islands arising in the sea. In some views, it also applies to abandoned articles.

2. Accessio.—If an accessory thing belonging to *A* was joined to a principal one belonging to *B*, the ownership in the whole went to *B*; *e.g.*, if *A*'s purple be used to dye *B*'s cloth, the dyed cloth belongs wholly to *B*. By far the most important application of this rule is expressed by the maxim *superficies solo cedit; i.e.*, whatever is built on land becomes part of the land and cannot be separately owned.

3. Specificatio.—If *A* made a thing out of material belonging to *B*, the Proculian school held that ownership went to *A*, the Sabinian school that it remained in *B*. Justinian adopted a "middle opinion," according to which *B* retained ownership if reconversion to the original condition was possible (a bronze vase can be melted down); *A* obtained ownership if it was not (wine cannot be reconverted into grapes).

4. Thesauri Inventio.—The final rule on treasure trove was that if it were found by a man on his own land, it went to him; if on that of another, half went to the finder, half to the landowner.

5. Traditio.—This was simple delivery of possession with the intention of passing ownership, and was the method of conveyance of the *jus gentium*. It sufficed to pass full Quiritarian ownership of *res nec mancipi*, but not of *res mancipi* (land in Italy, slaves, beasts of draft and burden, and certain rustic servitudes) for which either *mancipatio* or *in jure cessio* was necessary. If therefore *A* sold and merely delivered a slave to *B*, *A* remained at civil law owner of the slave until *usucapio* had taken place. The praetor, however, devised methods of protecting *B*'s possession in such a way that *A*'s title became valueless, and *B* was said to have the thing *in bonis*. From this phrase later writers coined the expression "bonitarian" ownership; the term "praetorian ownership" also has been applied, in recognition of the role of the praetor in developing the concept. Before Justinian's day *mancipatio* and *in jure cessio* had become obsolete, and Justinian took the final step of abolishing the theoretical distinction between Quiritarian and "bonitarian" ownership.

C. FORMS OF PROPERTY IN LAND OTHER THAN OWNERSHIP

The ordinary leaseholder according to Roman law had no protection beyond a contractual right against his landlord, and he could not assign his tenancy, but there were two kinds of tenure which, under the praetorian system, obtained for the tenant protection against third parties as well, and became assignable. These were *superficies* and *emphyteusis*, the former resulting from building leases granted for a long term or in perpetuity, the latter from similar agricultural leases. Both appear to have first originated in grants by the state or by municipalities. Under *emphyteusis* the grantee did not become owner though he enjoyed a *jus in re aliena* hardly distinguishable from ownership.

1. Servitudes.—Praedial servitudes (*i.e.*, easements or *profits à prendre*) were divided into two categories, rustic and urban, according as they served the need of agricultural land or of buildings. Thus rights of way and of water are usually classed as rustic, while rights to light, to view, or to support were urban. Praedial servitudes could only be appurtenant; *i.e.*, they could not exist except as additional advantages attached to the ownership of a piece of land (the "dominant tenement").

The law of Justinian's day brought under the heading of servitudes also the rights of *usufructus* and *usus*. Usufruct was the right to use and take the fruits (*e.g.*, crops) of a thing and corresponds to the modern life interest. *Usus* was a more restricted right, likewise not extending beyond the life of the holder but merely to the use of a thing; thus the usuary of a house could live in it himself but could not let it, as that would be equivalent to taking the fruits.

2. Possession.—Since ownership was absolute, it was sharply distinguished from possession, which the civil law did not protect as such. One of the most important parts of the praetorian system was constituted by the *interdicta* (special types of remedy), which protected an existing possession irrespective of its rightfulness. Anyone wishing to interfere with it must bring an action and prove his title. If he interfered on his own authority, the praetor would see that the original state of affairs was restored.

D. OBLIGATIONS

Obligations were classified by the jurists into two main categories, according as they arose from delict (tort) or contract; those left over were placed by the Byzantines under the headings of quasi-contract and quasi-delict. Quasi-contractual remedies are of peculiar importance because they mark the recognition, in defined spheres, of obligations founded on the principle of unjust enrichment, one of the major contributions of Roman law to legal thought.

1. Delict.—The Twelve Tables already show the law in a state of transition from the system of private vengeance to that in which the state insists on the acceptance of compensation instead of vengeance by the person wronged and fixes its amount. Thus in the case of assault (*injuria*), if one man broke another's limb, talion was still permitted (*i.e.*, the person wronged could inflict the same injury as he had received); but in other cases there were fixed money penalties (*e.g.*, 25 *asses* for a blow). Theft involved a penalty of twice the value of the thing stolen, unless the thief was caught in the act (*furtum manifestum*), in which case he was flogged and "adjudged" to the person wronged.

In classical times, praetorian reforms had substituted a fourfold penalty in the case of *furtum manifestum*, and penalties for *injuria* (which now included defamation and insulting behaviour) were assessed in each case by the court. The law of damage to property was regulated by a statute (*lex Aquilia*) dating from the republic but later than the Twelve Tables; it was much extended by interpretation and by the praetor. Praetorian actions also lay for a number of new delicts of varying importance.

2. Contract.—At the time of the Twelve Tables a law of contract hardly existed. However, there was an institution called *nexum*, of which little can be said with certainty except that it was a kind of loan so oppressive in character that it might result in the debtor's complete subjection to the creditor. It was obsolete long before classical times. The contracts of classical law were divided into four classes: literal, verbal, real, and consensual. The literal contract was a type of fictitious loan formed by an entry in the creditor's account book; it was comparatively unimportant, and obsolete in Justinian's day. The verbal contract or *stipulatio* was of great importance, for it provided a form in which any agreement (provided it was lawful and possible) might be made binding by the simple method of reducing it to question and answer; *e.g.*, "Do you promise to pay me ten thousand sesterces?" "I promise." Originally it was absolutely necessary that the words should be spoken, but it may be said (technicalities apart) that by

Justinian's day a written memorandum of such a contract would be binding, even though in fact there had been no speaking at all.

If an agreement was not clothed in the form of a stipulation, it must, to be valid, fall, according to its content, under one of the types of real or consensual contracts. A real contract is one which needs for its conclusion (in addition to the consent of the parties) that some thing should be transferred from one party to the other and that the obligation arising should be for the return of the thing transferred. The real contracts are *mutuum* (loan, *e.g.*, of money), *commodatum* (loan, *e.g.*, of a horse), deposit, and pledge. Consensual contracts need no element for their formation except agreement—whether expressed in words or otherwise—between the parties, and though there were only four such known to the law, these were the most important in ordinary life—*emptio venditio* (sale), *locatio conductio* (hire of things or services and also giving out of jobs to be done), *societas* (partnership), and *mandatum* (acting upon instructions). In Justinian's day there was a further principle that in any case of reciprocal agreement, *e.g.*, an agreement for exchange (which was not sale), if one party had performed, he could bring an action to enforce performance by the other ("innominate contract"). Apart from the foregoing contracts, a few specific agreements were recognized as enforceable. But the general recognition of all serious agreements as binding was never achieved by the Romans.

E. Succession at Death

1. Testamentary Succession.—That wills existed already at the time of the Twelve Tables is certain, and it is highly probable that the form used was still that mentioned by Gaius as the oldest; *i.e.*, the will made publicly in the assembly of the *curiae* (*testamentum comitiis calatis*), with the will made before the people drawn up for battle (*testamentum in procinctu*) as a variant. It may be, however, that the mancipatory will (*testamentum per aes et libram*) had already been invented. This began as an expedient for effecting the purposes of a will in an emergency, when the other forms were impossible, and consisted in the use of mancipation to convey the estate of the dying man to a kind of trustee (*familiae emptor*), who then distributed it in accordance with the testator's instructions. By the end of the republic the older forms had disappeared, mancipation had become a mere formality, and the testator's instructions, now contained in a written document, constituted a true will, operative only at death and revocable at any time during the testator's lifetime by the making of a new will. In postclassical times the mancipation had ceased to be necessary, and the commonest form of will was the *testamentum tripertitum*, needing for its completion the seals of seven witnesses and the signatures of the witnesses and testator.

The first requirement of any Roman will of historical times was the appointment of one or more *heredes*. A *heres* is a universal successor; *i.e.*, he takes over the rights and duties of the deceased (in so far as they are transmissible at all) as a whole. On acceptance, the heir becomes owner where the deceased was owner, creditor where he was creditor, and debtor where he was debtor, even though the assets be insufficient to pay the debts. It was thus possible for an inheritance to be *damnosa*; *i.e.*, to involve the heir in loss. Until Justinian's day this consequence could be avoided only by not accepting the inheritance, but Justinian made one of his most famous reforms by introducing the *beneficium inventarii*, which meant that the heir who, within a certain time after the acceptance, made an inventory of the deceased's assets need not pay out more than he had received. In addition to appointing an heir, the testator might also leave legacies; *i.e.*, particular gifts which are a burden on the heir. Freedom of testation was, however, not complete, a man being obliged to leave a certain proportion of his property to his children and in some cases to ascendants and brothers and sisters.

2. Intestate Succession.—For intestate succession a purely agnatic system (one which counts relationship only through males) was superseded by a cognatic system (in which relationship is traced through males or females). The agents in this change were first the praetors and, later, imperial legislation.

By the Twelve Tables those first entitled were the *sui heredes*

of the deceased; *i.e.*, those who were in his *potestas* or *manus* when he died and became free from power at his death. Failing these, the nearest agnatic relation (or relations, if there were several of the same degree) succeeded, and, if there were no agnates, the members of the *gens* (clan) of the deceased. Praetorian reforms placed emancipated children on an equality with *sui heredes* and gave to the nearest cognates or, failing them, to the surviving spouse (in marriage without *manus*) rights of succession in the absence of agnates; gentile succession became obsolete probably in the 1st century A.D. Even under this system a woman would not succeed to a child of hers if any agnate (*e.g.*, a paternal uncle) were alive, nor a child to its mother if there were any agnate of hers. Both these cases were dealt with before the end of the classical period, the former by the *Senatus consultum Tertullianum* (under Hadrian), which gave certain rights of succession to mothers who had the *jus liberorum* (*i.e.*, had borne three children), and the latter by the *Senatus consultum Orfitianum* of A.D. 178, which gave to children the first right to succeed to their mothers. Later emperors made many changes, but it was not until Justinian's day that the cognatic system prevailed. *Novel* 118, completed by *Novel* 127, introduced a new system, laying down that descendants had the first claim, and failing these, a composite class consisting of ascendants, brothers and sisters of full blood, and children of deceased brothers and sisters. Next came brothers and sisters of the half blood and finally the nearest cognate or cognates.

Husband and wife were not mentioned, but their old (praetorian) rights were kept alive in the absence of any of the above categories. Justinian also gave to the poor widow a right to one quarter of her husband's estate unless there were more than three children, in which case she shared equally with them. If, however, the heirs were her own children by the deceased, she only received the usufruct (life interest) in what she took.

F. Procedure

The earliest form of procedure known to have existed is that of the *legis actiones;* this was superseded by the formulary system which, in its turn, gave way to *cognitio extraordinaria*. Characteristic of both the earlier systems is the division into two stages, a preliminary one before the jurisdictional magistrate (*in jure*) and the actual trial before the *judex*. The object of the first stage is to arrive at an issue, which under the *legis actio* system has to be achieved by the speaking of set forms of words by the parties and, sometimes at least, by the magistrate. Thus in a *vindicatio* each party, when making his assertion of ownership, grasps the thing in dispute and lays a wand on it, after which the magistrate intervenes and says, "Let go, both of you." So formal was the procedure that a plaintiff who made the slightest mistake lost his case. For this the formulary system provided a remedy. It superseded the older system, so Gaius says, as a result of the *lex Aebutia* (date much disputed, perhaps between 149 and 126 B.C.), and two *leges Juliae* (of Augustus). Between the *lex Aebutia* and the *leges Juliae* both systems were in use.

Under the new procedure the issue was formulated in written instructions (*formula*) to the *judex,* couched in the form of an alternative, *e.g.*, "If it appears that the defendant owes the plaintiff 10,000 sesterces the *judex* is to condemn the defendant to pay the plaintiff 10,000 sesterces; if it does not so appear, he is to absolve him." A draft of the *formula* was probably prepared for the plaintiff before he came into court, but there could be no trial until it was accepted by the defendant; for there was always a contractual element about a lawsuit under both older systems. Pressure could, however, be exercised by the magistrate on a defendant who refused to accept a *formula* of which the magistrate approved, just as a plaintiff could be forced to alter a *formula* of which the magistrate disapproved, by the magistrate's refusal otherwise to give his order to the *judex* to decide the case.

The process by which the *cognitio extraordinaria* superseded the formulary system was gradual, and was accomplished in the provinces earlier than in Rome. Under the new system the magistrate used his administrative powers, always large, for the purpose of settling disputes. He could command, and thus if one man brought a complaint against another before him, he could investigate the matter and give the order he thought fit. As imperially appointed officers, who had *no jurisdictio* in the old sense, superseded republican magistrates, this administrative process became more common. The result is that the old contractual element in procedure disappears, as well as the old division into two stages. Justice is now imposed from above by the state, not, as originally, left to a kind of voluntary arbitration supervised by the state.

See also references under "Roman Law" in the Index.

BIBLIOGRAPHY.—*Modern textbooks:* J. K. B. M. Nicholas, *An Introduction to Roman Law* (1962); W. W. Buckland, *A Text-Book of Roman Law from Augustus to Justinian,* 3rd ed. (1964); F. Schulz, *Classical Roman Law* (1951); P. F. Girard, *Manuel élémentaire de droit romain,* 7th ed. (1924); M. Kaser, *Das römische Privatrecht* (1955); R. Sohm, *Institutionen des römischen Rechts,* 17th ed. (1926; Eng. trans. of 12th ed. by J. C. Ledlie, *The Institutes of Roman Law,* 1907). *Sources and history:* H. F. Jolowicz, *Historical Introduction to the Study of Roman Law,* 2nd ed. (1952); H. J. Wolff, *Roman Law* (1951); L. Wenger, *Die Quellen des römischen Rechts* (1953). For modern collections of the Twelve Tables *see* Bruns' *Fontes iuris Romani antiqui,* 7th ed. (1919); Girard's *Textes du droit Romain,* 5th ed. (1923); Riccobono's *Fontes iuris Romani anteiustiniani.* The best edition of Justinian's *Digest* is that of T. Mommsen (1868–70), of the *Codex* that of P. Krüger (1875–77). For full references to modern literature, *see* A. Berger, *Encyclopedic Dictionary of Roman Law* (1953). (H. F. J.; RL. P.)

ROMANO, GIULIO (GIULIO PIPPI, originally GIULIO DI PIETRO DI FILIPPO DE' GIANUZZI) (?1499–1546), painter, architect, principal heir of Raphael and one of the founders of Mannerism. (See MANNERIST ART AND ARCHITECTURE.) As his name implies, Giulio was born in Rome, but the exact date is unknown. According to the archives of Mantua, where he died, he was 47 at his death on Nov. 1, 1546, so that he was presumably born in 1498/99. G. Vasari, however, says that he was 54 at his death (which he dates correctly), thus making his birth fall in 1491/92. The earlier birth date, which is not usually accepted, would make Giulio less precocious. He certainly went to Raphael as a child apprentice and had become so important in the workshop by Raphael's death in 1520 that Vasari names him with G. Penni as Raphael's chief heir; he became his principal artistic executor. Among the works of Raphael which Vasari specifically records as having been worked on by Giulio are the frescoes in the Sala dell'Incendio in the Vatican, completed in 1517, and many of the frescoes, from Raphael's designs, in the *logge,* certainly finished by June 16, 1519. He also worked on such oil paintings as the "Joanna of Aragon" and the "St. Margaret" for the king of France (*c.* 1518, now in the Louvre, Paris). His almost proverbial facility is testified to by his works, as well as by Vasari.

In the period between Raphael's death on April 6, 1520, and Oct. 1524, when Giulio went to Mantua, it is clear that he and Penni finished a number of works left incomplete at Raphael's death. The most important such commission was the Sala di Costantino, the last and largest of the Vatican rooms, which had hardly been begun by Raphael. After some intrigue, Giulio and Penni secured the contract, completing the frescoes on Sept. 5, 1524. The two certainly finished the "Coronation of the Virgin" (now in the Vatican) for the nuns of Monteluce, Giulio painting the upper part and Penni the lower. They may also have put the finishing touches to the "Transfiguration." Giulio also painted some original works during these years, including the "Madonna and Saints," now in Sta. Maria dell' Anima, Rome; the "Stoning of St. Stephen" (1523; S. Stefano, Genoa); and the Naples "Madonna." He also undertook some of the decorative painting at the Villa Madama, begun under Raphael's general direction in 1516, and at the Villa Farnesina. The Roman palaces of the Cicciaporci and Maccarani families, closely based on the palace of Raphael by Bramante, are also by him.

Giulio left Rome in Oct. 1524 for Mantua, apparently at the request of Federigo Gonzaga, marquis of Mantua. Very soon, there was a great scandal over some obscene engravings which Marcantonio Raimondi (*q.v.*) had made from Giulio's drawings; Raimondi was imprisoned, but Giulio was by then safe in Mantua. Much the most important of all his works is the Palazzo del Te, on the outskirts of Mantua, begun in 1525 or 1526 and built and decorated entirely by him and his pupils. This palace is one of the first and greatest examples of Mannerist architecture, being

almost a parody of the serene classicism of Bramante while retaining the forms of Roman antiquity. The building consists of a square block around a central court, with a splendid garden opening off at right angles to the main axis—in itself characteristic of the way in which all the elements are slightly different from what would be expected. There is a series of splendid staterooms, mostly decorated in the rich but elegant Roman manner invented by Raphael on the basis of the recently rediscovered Golden House of Nero. The principal rooms are the Sala di Psiche, with erotic frescoes of the loves of the gods; the Sala dei Cavalli, with life-size portraits of some of the Gonzaga horses; and the fantastic Sala dei Giganti. This is one of the showpieces of Mannerist decoration and consists of a room, roughly square, which is painted from floor to ceiling with a continuous scene of the giants attempting to storm Olympus and being repulsed by the gods. On the ceiling, Jupiter hurls his thunderbolts, and the spectator is made to feel that he, like the giants, is crushed by the mountains which topple on to him, writhing in the burning wreckage. Even the fireplace was incorporated into the decoration, and the flames had a part to play. This room was completed by 1534, with much help from Rinaldo Mantovano, Giulio's principal assistant. The colour is very crude; the subject is all too suited to virtuosity and tends to bring out the streak of cruelty and obscenity which runs just below the surface in much of Giulio's painting.

In Mantua itself he did a great deal of work (including the Sala di Troia) in the huge Reggia dei Gonzaga. He also built for himself a very Mannerist version of the house of Raphael (1544–46) and began the rebuilding of the cathedral (1543 onward). The decorations of the Sala di Troia are particularly noteworthy in that they look forward to the illusionistic ceiling decorations of the baroque; but this was probably inspired by the presence in Mantua of the Camera degli Sposi by Andrea Mantegna, who must have inspired Giulio to further audacities of illusionism, as well as confirming his taste for antique motives. *See* also RENAISSANCE ARCHITECTURE: *Italy: Mannerism.*

BIBLIOGRAPHY.—G. Vasari, *Vite . . . ,* Eng. trans. by De Vere, vi (1913); C. d'Arco, *Storia della Vita,* etc. (1842); E. H. Gombrich in Vienna *Jahrbuch,* new series, viii, p. 79 ff. (1934), ix, p. 121 ff. (1935); F. Hartt, *Giulio Romano* (1958). (P. J. MY.)

ROMANOS, SAINT (called MELODOS) (fl. 6th century A.D.), Byzantine hymnographer and greatest master of the *kontakion* (*q.v.*), was born at Emesa (Homs) in Syria. After officiating as deacon at Berytus (Beirut), he went to Constantinople during the reign of the emperor Anastasius I (491–518). Legend relates that when asleep one Christmas eve he was commanded by the Virgin to eat a scroll, and on awaking after doing so he recited his famous Christmas *kontakion.* About 80 of his *kontakia* are extant but none of the music accompanying them survives. This literary form reached its full development in Romanos' *kontakia,* with their elaborate metrical system and vigorous dialogues, but they often contain too many rhetorical devices for modern taste. Romanos borrows heavily from earlier Greek sermons and other sources, though it is not certain whether he also depends on Ephraem Syrus. His most famous *kontakia* are perhaps those on Christmas, Easter, and the Passion. His feast day is Oct. 1.

A complete edition of Romanos' *kontakia,* edited by P. Maas and C. A. Trypanis, was published in 1963. G. Cammelli edited selections, with an Italian translation, in 1930.

See H. G. Beck, *Kirche und theologische Literatur im byzantinischen Reich* (1959); K. Krumbacher, *Geschichte der byzantinischen Literatur,* 2nd ed. (1897). For further bibliography, *see* KONTAKION. (CE. A. T.)

ROMANOV, the name of the dynasty that ruled Russia from 1613 to the March Revolution of 1917.

The ancestor of the Romanovs was Andrei Ivanovich Kobyla, or Kambila, who is recorded as a boyar (*q.v.*) in Moscow during the reign of the grand prince Ivan I Kalita, of the House of Rurik, in the middle of the 14th century. This Kobyla is sometimes said to have been the son of the Old Prussian or Lithuanian prince Glanda, who had come to Russia as a refugee and taken the name Ivan on receiving Christian baptism. One of Kobyla's many sons, Fedor Andreevich, was known as Koshka ("the Cat"), and his descend-

TABLE I.—*The Romanov Dynasty to 1762*

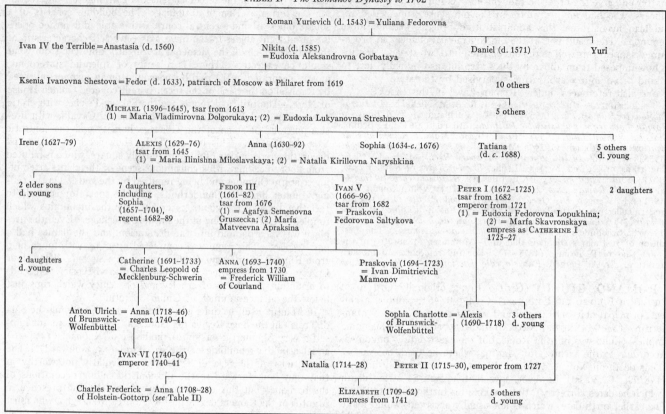

ants received the surname of Koshkin. These Koshkins were soon divided among many branches: for instance, the Zakharievs, descending from one of Fedor's grandsons, Zakhari; and the Yurievs, descending from one of Zakhari's sons, Yuri. Thus one of Yuri's sons, Roman (d. 1543), gave the surname Romanov to his own descendants.

Roman's daughter Anastasia was the first wife of the tsar Ivan IV the Terrible, who married her in 1547. Her brother Nikita was president of the council of regency that Ivan IV appointed for his son by her, Fedor I, the last tsar of the House of Rurik; but on Nikita's death control of the regency passed to Boris Godunov. Boris, who became tsar himself on Fedor I's death (1598), forced Fedor Nikitich Romanov to become a monk, whereupon the latter took the name Philaret (*q.v.*). The Romanov boyars, however, were active during the movements against Boris and against the tsar Vasili Shuiski, and the period known in Russian history as the "Time of Troubles" ended with the election of Philaret's son Michael as tsar in 1613.

The article RUSSIAN HISTORY provides the background to what has been indicated above and then a survey of the subsequent regime of the Romanovs. Tables I and II of the present article show the genealogy of the tsars and (from 1721) of the emperors and empresses of the dynasty, all of whom are also treated in separate biographical articles. A few words may here be added on the dynasty in general.

In the first place, accession to the Russian throne, which had been governed by a form of collateral succession under the House of Rurik, was a precarious matter from the end of the 16th century to the end of the 18th. The ruler might try to designate his successor without regard to primogeniture, and even if primogeniture were observed, a weak successor might soon be set aside if a stronger member of his kin, male or female, could organize a *coup d'état*. This state of affairs gave rise to the 18th-century saying that the Russian throne was "not hereditary or elective, but occupative."

Thus in the 1680s the accession of the half brothers Ivan V and Peter I led to grave disorders, from which Peter emerged victorious; but Peter, having put his own son Alexis to death in 1718,

left the succession to his wife, Catherine I, who was a Romanov only by right of marriage. On Catherine I's death, however, in 1727, the throne reverted to Peter I's grandson Peter II. When the latter died (1730), Ivan V's second surviving daughter Anna became empress. On Anna's death (1740), her elder sister's daughter Anna Leopoldovna, whose father belonged to the House of Mecklenburg, assumed the regency for her son Ivan VI, of the House of Brunswick-Wolfenbüttel; but in 1741 this Ivan VI was deposed in favour of Elizabeth, daughter of Peter I and Catherine I. With Elizabeth the Romanovs of the male line died out in 1762, but the name was conserved by the branch of the House of Holstein-Gottorp which then mounted the Russian throne in the person of Elizabeth's nephew Peter III. From 1762 to 1796 Peter III's widow, a German princess of the House of Anhalt-Zerbst, ruled as Catherine II, but with Paul I, Peter III's son, a Romanov of Holstein-Gottorp became emperor again. Thereafter primogeniture usually obtained. Even so, in 1825, Alexander I was succeeded, not by his eldest surviving brother, Constantine (who had secretly renounced his rights), but by the next brother, Nicholas I; and in 1917 Nicholas II abdicated the throne, not in favour of his son, the sickly Alexis, but in favour of his brother Michael, who, however, did not assume the succession.

In the course of the Russian Revolution the Bolsheviks killed the emperor Nicholas, his consort, all his children (unless one believes the claimant to Anastasia's identity, who appeared in 1928), his brother Michael, and other members of the dynasty between July 1918 and February 1919. The grand duke Cyril, in exile, proclaimed himself warden of the throne, as head of the House of Romanov, in 1922 and emperor in 1924.

By an imperial ruling of 1886, applicable to the offspring of marriages made in conformity with the laws of the House of Romanov as a sovereign dynasty, the sons, daughters, brothers, and sisters of emperors, and also the grandchildren of emperors in the male line, were to bear the title of grand duke or grand duchess (properly grand prince or grand princess; *see* GRAND DUKE), with the predicate "Imperial Highness"; great-grandchildren of emperors in the male line, and also the first-born son of each such great-grandson, were to be princes or princesses with the predicate

TABLE II.—*The House of Romanov-Holstein-Gottorp*

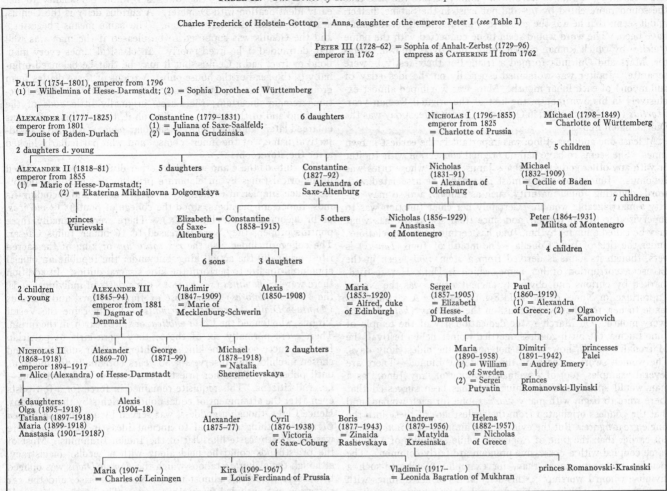

"Highness"; and other descendants in the male line were to be princes or princesses with the predicate "Serenity."

From the 19th century onward morganatic marriages by Romanov males were increasingly frequent. In such cases a princely title, with a new name, was often accorded to the morganatic wife and her issue. Apart from the Yurievski and Palei princely titles created by the emperors in 1880 and 1915 (*see* Table II), the grand duke Cyril in 1935 accorded not only the Romanovski-Krasinski and Romanovski-Ilyinski princely titles (indicated in the same Table), but also a Romanovski-Brasov princely title for Natalia Sheremetievskaya, widow of his first cousin Michael, as well as Romanovski-Kutuzov and Romanovski-Strelinski princely titles for the wives and issue of more remote cousins (great-grandsons of the emperor Nicholas I through the latter's sons Michael and Constantine respectively). These titles must not be confused with the Russian title of Prince Romanovski granted in 1852 to Nicolas, duke of Leuchtenberg, son of the emperor Nicholas I's daughter Maria by her marriage to Maximilien de Beauharnais (*see* BEAUHARNAIS).

ROMAN RELIGION. The religion of ancient Rome, from the earliest known times to the final suppression of paganism, may be conveniently divided into four periods: (1) native; (2) Italian (including Etruscan); (3) Greek, passing into Greco-Roman; and (4) oriental. These divisions emphasize the principal influence at each stage, without implying that no other influences existed.

Native.—The earliest Romans were a small community of peasant farmers, probably held together in a loose organization with a king at its head. Under him would be the heads (*patres*) of families or clans, with their retainers (*clientes*). Even in its earliest days the community probably engaged in a certain amount of trade in addition to farming and stock raising, since Rome lies advantageously on the principal natural highway of central Italy, which is the Tiber, and on the border between the Etruscan cities northward and the towns of the Latin league farther south. According to tradition the people were of mixed stock, with some Latin and some Sabine highland blood; various linguistic and other facts tend to confirm this. Threatened by powerful neighbours, they were of necessity warlike.

Like many peoples at a comparable or even at a lower stage of culture, the Romans had developed a few "high gods" by the earliest known period of their history. The names of some of their deities can be recovered, chiefly from surviving festival calendars. None of these was composed earlier than the 1st century B.C., and by that late date many of the oldest feast days and religious seasons had lost their former prominence; but the calendars nevertheless record the gods' names in large letters. Chief among them comes Jupiter (in Latin, Iuppiter), whose name is etymologically equivalent to the Greek Zeus and the Sanskrit Dyaus. It must therefore have come down from immemorial antiquity in the Indo-European family, along with the Latin language. The name Jupiter includes also the stock title *pater*; i.e., head of the house, hence, person in authority. (Neither *pater* nor its correlative *mater* had originally any physiological meaning.) Like Zeus and Dyaus, Jupiter was a sky- and weather-god, obviously important to farmers. With him were early associated two other gods, Mars and Quirinus. Mars was a deity of great importance, widely worshiped in Italy, but of doubtful origins—his name is of highly uncertain etymology. His functions were very wide, and included the protection of his worshipers, their cattle and other possessions against all manner of evils, such as disease or the devastation of their property. These evils included the perils of war, and Mars was consequently a warlike god. Quirinus, whose name is plainly adjectival, was much less important. He is said to have been Sabine, despite the fact that the sound represented by *qu-* did not exist in the Sabine dialect, and it seems that he was the god of the *quirium*, whatever that may have been. The word would seem to be connected with the name *Quirites* by which Roman citizens were collectively known. Jupiter, Mars and Quirinus formed a triad, but their festivals were separate. Jupiter was worshiped especially on the ides (day of full moon) of each lunar month. Mars was worshiped almost exclusively in his own month, the first of the original Roman year, *Martius* (*i.e.*, March), and in October. Quirinus' feast day was the Quirinalia on Feb. 17.

At least one goddess, Juno, was important in the earliest-known times. She seems to have had no original connection with Jupiter or with any other god save perhaps Janus, one of whose titles was Iunonius. Juno's name may most reasonably be associated with words denoting young maturity, such as *iuuenis*, and so may signify a marriageable woman. Certainly her chief function was to supervise the life of women, and since their sexual life has what may be called a lunar rhythm, Juno has certain lunar associations, under the title of Iuno Couella. The month of June (*Iunius*) is hers, though its name is derived from a stem, *iuni-*, seen in the Etruscan corruption of her name, which is Uni. Her festival, marked by curious and obviously ancient ritual, was the Nonae Caprotinae, or Nones of the Wild Fig, on July 7. A sacrifice was made to her, together with Janus, on the first day (*kalendae*) of every month. On March 1, the dedication day of the temple of Juno Lucina, the birth-goddess, married women held a festival, the Matronalia. This, however, is not one of the oldest holy days. The women swore an oath by this goddess, "Eiuno." There are several examples, too, of a woman speaking of "my Juno," as a man would speak of his "Genius." It has been suggested that there were to begin with many *iunones*, one for each woman, and that the goddess originated from the coalescence of these into the single great figure. But the evidence for an individual *iuno* is late, not earlier than the time of Augustus; while examples of a divine name coupled with a possessive pronoun are fairly common. The locution means no more than, for example: "Such-and-such a divinity, whom I worship"; "this deity in his or her dealings with me." Juno was widely worshiped outside Rome, being sometimes the chief deity of a state, and as such on occasion having warlike functions. Thus at Lanuvium, Juno Sospita Mater Regina was represented clad in a goatskin and bearing a spear and shield.

But the most characteristic deities of this period were vague figures of limited and sharply defined functions. Like the greater gods, they were regarded as possessing superhuman power, known as *numen* from at least the 2nd century B.C. This they could be induced to employ for the benefit of their worshipers if rightly approached. Beyond this, Roman curiosity did not go; the gods have no myths, do not form married pairs (though a masculine and a feminine name are often conjoined) and have no offspring. To name them correctly and to worship them with the proper words and gestures were supremely important; hence there grew up in time elaborate lists of liturgical formulas, the *indigitamenta* (*indigitare* means to address a deity with the appropriate titles, etc.). These are complicated by the intrusion into surviving documents of a host of names of godlings presiding over the most minute details of human life and activity. Some of the names were apparently invented for special occasions, others are due to false etymologies. These numerous godlings appear to be the result of priestly elaboration at a comparatively late period; but it seems true that some such *di minuti* did exist. Thus Janus, who was on his way to develop into a god of beginnings (hence the name, January, of the first month in the reformed calendar and the sacrifice to Janus on all kalends), is almost certain to have been nothing more originally than the personification of an *ianus* or gateway, to pass through which is an act often of magico-religious significance. Vesta, the hearth-goddess, is the sacred hearth itself, the recipient of some cult in every household. Terra or Tellus Mater, the earth-goddess, probably was the holder of that *numen* which was necessary to make the Roman territory productive; certainly she was not goddess of the whole earth. The name of Ceres, the grain-goddess, may have been an adjective, "produc-

tive," applied to Terra; she owes her whole personality to her early identification with Demeter. A curious deity is the Genius, a sort of divine double of a man. The name means "begetter," and the Genius was supposed to be pleased if the man was well fed, defrauded if he lived poorly. In classical times every man, bond or free, had a Genius, but it may be that he belonged originally to the head of the house only. Various of these deities form groups. Such are the Indigetes and the Novensides, whose functions remain uncertain; the Lares, originally little gods of the farmland and of the houses standing on it, though their office was enlarged later; and the Penates (singular *penas*), who have an adjectival name, "of the inner rooms," and who particularly looked after the storeroom.

The cults of these and numerous other divinities were regulated in historical times by an elaborate priesthood, which was doubtless much simpler in earlier days. At its head, and including its most important members, stood the college of pontiffs (*pontifices*, or bridgebuilders; *see* PONTIFEX). There were originally three pontiffs proper; they were increased to 16 under Julius Caesar. The college included also the *rex sacrorum* or king of the sacred rites, originally the actual king, but under the republic an official appointed for life to perform the king's sacral duties. In addition there were 15 *flamines* (*see* FLAMEN) or priests of individual gods, the 3 chief (*maiores*) being those of Jupiter, Mars, and Quirinus (*flamines Dialis, Martialis, Quirinalis*). Lastly came the Vestal Virgins, who tended the *Vesta publica*, or state hearth, in the forum. There were normally six of these; they were girls of patrician families, successors of the king's daughters or their substitutes, and chosen in childhood to serve for 30 years (originally for five; *i.e.*, until puberty). All other priests were men, at first patricians— *i.e.*, full citizens. This requisite remained in force for a few posts even after the attainment of equal political rights by the plebeians. Hence Ceres, though a goddess, was served by a man (the *flamen Cerialis*), a thing abnormal to ancient ideas in general. There was no priestly caste like that of the Indian Brahmins. Most of the priesthoods could be held along with a secular magistracy, although the elaborate taboos which the *flamen Dialis* was obliged to observe made this almost impossible in his case, and the *rex sacrorum* was excluded from other posts. The head of the whole body was the chief pontiff (*pontifex maximus*), who exercised disciplinary functions and formally appointed each new vestal and *flamen Dialis*. Outside their purely sacral duties, the priesthood had advisory (not executive) powers.

Outside the college of pontiffs stood the augurs (*q.v.; augere*, "to increase"). The derivation of their name implies that they had once been officiants in fertility rites; they were now specialists in divination, particularly from the behaviour of birds. They did not themselves conduct the *auspicia* or taking of omens to ascertain whether the gods favoured a proposed action, for that was the business of every magistrate and could be done even by private citizens on occasion; the augurs were there to advise and direct as needed. There were also several minor bodies. The *Salii* (dancers) performed ceremonial dances, in archaic war equipment, in honour of Mars and Quirinus; the *Luperci* ran naked, save for a girdle of goatskin, around the boundary of the original Palatine settlement every year on Feb. 15 (the Lupercalia; *q.v.*), striking everyone whom they met with thongs of goatskin. They were popularly known as he-goats (*creppi*). Yet other bodies included the Arval Brothers (*q.v.*), who were concerned with agricultural ceremonial of a very archaic type.

It is clear that not all these rites were of the same date. For instance, very ancient custom decreed that the *flamen Dialis* might not touch iron, his hair and nails being cut with a bronze implement. There is evidence that the customs of the vestals were less ancient; their goddess had her seat in the forum, outside the oldest settlement, and they regularly used an iron tool in the preparation of the salt needed for their ritual. The antiquity of some of the rites is evidenced by their not being directed to any deity. The performance of the *Luperci*, in particular, seems to have been purely magical; they drew a kind of magic circle around the Palatine, to keep good influences in and bad ones out. The evidence for the connection of the Lupercalia with a god or goddess is of the feeblest, and is probably the result of ancient speculation. Another piece of magic was the annual ceremonial of the *Argei* (*q.v.*), in which 27 puppets were thrown from the oldest bridge (*Pons sublicius*) into the Tiber. Here may be recognized a primitive function of the "bridgebuilders" (*pontifices*); the river-god, who may feel insulted at the building of a bridge over his stream, is soothed by a pretense that many persons fall from it and are drowned. The reason for the exact number 27 is unknown.

Italian and Etruscan.—The Etruscan dynasty of the Tarquins (latter half of the 6th century B.C.) brought innovations to Rome, although it does not appear that the spirit of the local religion was much influenced. Cult statues were introduced, the worship having previously been conducted without images. Temples of Etruscan type began to appear; at any rate one such temple, that on the Capitol, was planned and nearly completed toward the end of the dynasty. (In Latin the word *templum* does not mean a temple in the accepted modern sense, but a piece of ground set apart and consecrated. This might or might not contain a "holy house"—*aedes sacra*—for the god or his emblem to reside in.) Elaborate funeral rites, such as remained in use for prominent people in historical times, appear also to be Etruscan. The Etruscans made known to the Romans a complicated method of divination by taking omens from the entrails, especially the liver, of a sacrificial victim. The practitioners of this rite (*haruspices; q.v.*) never became Roman priests, however; they remained foreign or foreign-trained experts, consulted on occasion. Etruscan also was a system of divination from lightning, and a reform of the calendar. The primitive Roman calendar had consisted of only ten lunar months, a gap intervening between December ("tenth month") and March. This calendar was now replaced by one of 12 months, obviously meant to begin with January, since that month is named from the festival of Janus occurring in it, presumably at first called Ianuar. The fall of the Tarquins seems to have prevented the full use of the reformed calendar, however, for the year continued to begin with March for several centuries. (Two month-names, *Iunius* and *Aprilis*, witness to the Etruscan influence behind the reform. *Aprilis* cannot be derived, as was anciently supposed by some, from *aperire*, so as to mean "month of opening," but comes from the name of the goddess Aphrodite, corrupted into some such form as *Apru*.) The 12 lunations of the new calendar were about $11\frac{1}{2}$ days short of a solar year. An extra month, called Mercedonius or Intercalaris, was therefore inserted at intervals to make up the difference, but so clumsily that the calendar lost touch more and more with the seasons until Julius Caesar's reform.

During this period (*i.e.*, the end of the regal epoch and the earlier part of the republican), importations of deities from other than purely Etruscan sources took place. The Capitoline cult gave Jupiter as partners Juno and Minerva, the latter not originally a Roman goddess. The grouping is most readily explained by Greek influence coming through Etruria, for the two goddesses were early identified with Hera and Athena, respectively the wife and the daughter of Zeus. Venus, Fortuna and Diana came in during this period from native Italian sources. Very early in the republic, Castor and Pollux were given a temple in the forum, in consequence, according to tradition, of their aid to the Romans at the battle of Lake Regillus (499? B.C.) against the Latin league. (The form Pollux is the Latin corruption of the Greek Polydeuces.) Even among the earliest-known deities are some whose names yield no discoverable Latin etymology, and certain of them are probably Etruscan. Examples are Volcanus, god of destructive fire, at first volcanic fire; Saturnus or Saeturnus, a deity of very uncertain original functions; and Volturnus, apparently a river-god, probably of the Tiber. Almost certainly a very old importation was Hercules. This form of his name is an Italian corruption of the Greek Herakles. His altar stood in the cattle market (*Forum boarium*) near the Palatine, whose traditional boundary swung out to enclose the market. A widely recognized deity, such as Hercules had become, was needed to keep the peace in a market where strangers were dealt with.

Greek (Greco-Roman).—As Rome expanded, its relations with the Greek communities of southern Italy and, later, with Greece itself and with the empires of Alexander's successors became more frequent. As a result, Greek cults made their appearance, being sometimes new importations, sometimes modifications of existing worships brought about by identification of Greek with Roman or other Italian deities. A new importation was the cult of Apollo, which steadily grew in importance; he had no generally accepted Italian equivalent. The oracles of the Sibyl of Cumae, supposedly inspired by him, were acquired at an early date, according to tradition by the elder or the younger Tarquin. They were thereafter consulted on occasion by a new priestly college, the *duouiri sacris faciundis*, whose numbers were gradually increased from the original 2 to 15 or even more. In the hands of these priests lay the general management of all worship conducted otherwise than in native fashion (*i.e.*, worship by the *Graecus ritus*), and their importance grew as more foreign cults made their way into the city. Such cults did not as a rule invade the inner circle of Roman worship, for this lay inside the sacral boundary (*pomerium*) of the city; but they often spread into the inhabited quarters, which rapidly grew beyond the traditional limits. Apollo himself, in his capacity as a divine physician, soon followed the oracles of his inspired prophetess. His first Roman temple is said to have been vowed in 433 B.C. "for the public health," which presumably means on the occasion of a plague; he appears, however, to have had some sort of sacred place (*Apollinar*) earlier than this. Evidence of the latter species of cult is the temple (on the Aventine and thus outside the *pomerium*) of Ceres, Liber and Libera, a triad copied from the Eleusinian worship of Demeter, Kore and Iacchus. Iacchus was commonly identified with Dionysus and hence with Liber, the Italian wine-god and associate of Jupiter. The Aventine temple became the central sanctuary of the Roman plebs. It was dated 493 B.C., having been vowed three years earlier; its style was Etruscan, but its decorations were Greek. With Greek cults came Greek art, at least in the form of statues of deities, and Greek mythology also. This the Romans accepted eagerly and apparently at a fairly early date—for, despite their intense national pride, they were remarkably ready to learn from foreign sources anything that struck them as important.

The Romans also developed a Greek attitude toward their own early history. It was hardly respectable for any important place not to have a founder with high, preferably divine, connections, and for a barbarian city to be thought something better than barbarous it was well for it to produce some evidence of Greek or, failing that, Trojan origins. As a result of this tendency there grew up various highly artificial legends concerning the foundation of Rome, which finally took their most familiar shape in the tale of Romulus and Remus, sons of Mars and descendants of Aeneas of Troy. The sequel of this particular legend stated that Romulus was transformed into the god Quirinus, this despite the fact that native Roman feeling drew a very sharp line between men and gods. Roman cult had nothing corresponding to Greek hero worship. This embellishment, however, is not known to have been current before the age of Cicero. A landmark in the hellenization of Rome is the *lectisternium*, a sort of banquet at which the gods were guests, which was held in 217 B.C. Such a banquet in itself was nothing new, but the old manner was to have the gods invisibly present, their attendance at the couches (*puluinaria*) prepared for them being denoted merely by bunches of herbs known as "gods' heads" (*capita deorum*). On this occasion, however, moved by their ill success in the early battles against Hannibal, the Romans resorted to a number of measures intended to secure divine favour. At the *lectisternium* of 217 the gods were represented by their statues and paired in a manner wholly Greek—Jupiter with Juno, Neptunus the water-god with Minerva, Mars with Venus, Apollo with Diana, Volcanus with Vesta, Mercurius, the traders' god, with Ceres. These, in fact, were Zeus with his consort Hera; Poseidon with Athena (a union of the two most characteristic Athenian cults); Ares with his love Aphrodite; Apollo and his sister Artemis; the two powers of fire, Hephaestus and Hestia; and the two deities most concerned with trade, for grain was a very important article of commerce. Together, therefore, the figures at the *lectisternium* made up the typical and popular Greek group of the 12 gods.

Greek myths seem to have had a remarkable effect on a people formerly piously incurious about the gods' character and activities except insofar as these concerned their worshipers. This effect was felt at a time when serious belief in the gods was at least greatly weakened among the Greeks themselves, and when they had a tendency to explain the traditional tales away or to use them merely as literary ornaments with the divine characters strongly humanized. The Romans, however, do not seem to have been greatly scandalized either by such plays as Plautus' *Amphitruo*, in which Jupiter and Mercurius appear as comic figures, or by Ennius' introduction of Euhemerus (*q.v.*), according to whom the gods were not gods at all, but deified kings and other notabilities. Such manifestations marked a stage toward the weakening of the traditional reverent attitude, and this by the last century of the republic had led to widespread indifference or skepticism. Yet, through their native conservatism, the Romans kept up all or most of the traditional observances, even when they had ceased to have any meaning or were at best a subject for learned speculation.

The age of Augustus saw a revival of the old cults, fostered and sponsored by his government and reinforced by new splendour of temples. An addition was the development of the worship of the emperor's patron, Apollo. His great temple on the Palatine became the centre of what might not unjustly be called a rival system to that headed by the Capitolian triad. Whatever Augustus' own beliefs may have been, and however much he may have regarded his religious revival as a useful political instrument, it was the beginning of something resembling an age of faith.

Oriental.—Although the Roman and the Greco-Roman modes of worship were as a rule decent and originally expressed genuine religious feeling, neither was exciting. Moreover, they were state or family cults concerned with this world, little attention being paid to aspirations for a future life. A dead Roman was thought to join the company of the Good People (*Manes*, a word that has no singular). As a member of a family or of a clan he would be one of the *di parentes*—again, no singular form of this description is known until at earliest the latter part of the 2nd century B.C.—and as such he would share in the respectful attentions of the surviving kin. But little hope was entertained of any effective survival for him, though it was trusted that the memory of a distinguished person would be long kept alive.

During the later years of the republic, however, and still more under the empire, a strong but mostly inarticulate demand for some kind of personal religion was growing. There grew up, chiefly in the east, sundry cults that promised their votaries the personal favour of deities, or even divine rank, if certain conditions were fulfilled. These usually included some form of initiation. The orient first obtained a foothold in Rome in 204 B.C., when by advice of the Sibylline oracles the Great Mother of the Gods (*q.v.; Mater deum magna Idaea*) was imported from Pessinus in Asia Minor and in 191 B.C. given a temple on the Palatine, in the heart of Rome itself. Her rites, carried out by eunuch-priests, shocked Roman sentiment, and citizens were long forbidden to take part in them; but the goddess was treated with respect, especially as she was associated with Troy and with the legendary ancestry of the Roman people. In 186 B.C. came the affair of the Bacchanalia (*q.v.*). A cult of Dionysus was introduced into Italy, comprising rites of initiation and nightly ceremonies that had something of the wildness of the god's original Thracian or Thraco-Phrygian worship. They were alleged to be attended by all manner of sexual and other crimes. Scenting a conspiracy against law and order, the senate took severe and effective measures to suppress the movement, but it was the precursor of numerous Dionysiac mysteries, apparently harmless enough, and varying from serious religious associations to dining and drinking clubs nominally under the patronage of the god. These last characterized the early empire especially. The older mysteries, especially the Eleusinian, retained their prestige and drew many Roman initiates, who seem to have read into them whatever philosophical doctrines they found attractive; but the most marked tendencies of the age were definitely toward the east, to Asia or to Egypt.

Astrology gained ground rapidly from about the age of Augustus, and its rigid determinism dismayed many, who sought refuge in anything that would enlist the power of the gods in their favour. (The gods were supposed to live beyond the stars, and so to be free from their centripetal influence.) Some people used elaborate magical practices of a kind supposed to bring the practitioner into contact with deities, and particularly those of theurgy (*theourgia*), a term literally meaning "god-working." But the most characteristic feature of this age (the last century B.C. to the end of paganism) was the multiplying of mystery cults. These generally had for their central feature the adventures, often including death, of a god with whom the initiates were brought into contact, being even perhaps identified with him, so that they passed through some simulacrum of his sufferings and shared his triumph. There were three principal mysteries. First came those of Isis, which although ultimately of genuine Egyptian origin, had been considerably hellenized in passing to the west. Their language was Greek, and they contained several elements not really Egyptian. Then there were the mysteries of Attis, which were an offshoot of the cult of the Great Mother. Attis, the goddess' young favourite, who had died and been at least partly revived, was their central figure. Lastly came the mysteries of Mithra (*see* MITHRAISM). They were in some ways the most important of all, and were originally Persian. The worship was for men only, and was popular especially in the army. It centred on the mythical career of Mithra, was divided into grades vaguely reminiscent of those of freemasonry, and carried with it a high and stern morality. It was for a while a formidable rival to Christianity.

Solar worship was very characteristic of the later imperial epoch. Certain Syrian cults, either originally solar or later held to be so, were partly responsible for this. Perhaps more important, however, was the conception that to the emperor corresponded the greatest of the visible heavenly bodies. The emperor was lord on earth, with power now grown absolute and having many features of that of an oriental despot, while the sun was lord in the sky. There was even a kind of solar monotheism, for a strong tendency existed to explain all other gods as equivalent to the sun. On occasion, the sun cult provided a sort of bridge to or compromise with Christianity, through the identification of the sun-god with the Sun of Righteousness (Mal. iv, 2).

Such was the religious world within which Christianity grew up, and over which it finally triumphed. Constantine the Great recognized Christianity (313) and Theodosius I in 391 and 393 forbade all pagan cult, public or private.

See also under names of individual deities, festivals, etc.; and references under "Roman Religion" in the Index.

BIBLIOGRAPHY.—*Standard work:* G. Wissowa, *Religion und Kultus der Römer*, 2nd ed. (1912). *Good English works:* W. Warde Fowler, *Roman Festivals of the Period of the Republic* (1908), *Religious Experience of the Roman People* (1911), *Roman Ideas of Deity* (1914); Sir W. R. Halliday, *Lectures on the History of Roman Religion* (1922), *Pagan Background of Early Christianity* (1925); C. Bailey, *Phases in the Religion of Ancient Rome* (1932). *Short account:* H. J. Rose, *Ancient Roman Religion* (1949). *Early Italian religion:* H. J. Rose, *Primitive Culture in Italy* (1926). *Etruria:* K. O. Müller and W. Deecke, *Die Etrusker*, 2 vol. (1877); G. Dennis, *Cities and Cemeteries of Etruria*, 2 vol. (1883); C. O. Thulin, *Die etruskische Disciplin* (1906). *Augustan revival and after:* G. Boissier, *La Religion romaine d'Auguste aux Antonins*, 2 vol. (1874), *La Fin du paganisme*, 2 vol. (1891). *Oriental religions:* F. Cumont, *Les Religions orientales dans le paganisme romain* (1929). *Mysteries of Dionysus:* M. P. Nilsson, *The Dionysiac Mysteries of the Hellenistic and Roman Age* (1957).

(H. J. R.)

ROMANS, EPISTLE TO THE, the first and probably the most influential in the collection of letters by Paul the apostle in the New Testament. The epistle is addressed to the Christian congregation in Rome, a city Paul is intending to visit for the first time; he is thus introducing himself to a congregation he does not yet know personally. This is especially necessary as he intends to go on from Rome to Spain and hopes to be helped in this enterprise by the Roman Christians (Rom. 15:23–24). As he therefore has to tell the Romans who he is and what he stands for, he gives in this letter a fuller and more systematic account of his ideas and purpose than he does in any of his others. First and foremost, however, it is a genuine letter, written only for its first readers in Rome. This combination of personal address with general arguments makes the interpretation of the epistle at the same time both attractive and difficult.

Contents.—The Epistle to the Romans may be outlined as follows:

1:1–7	greeting
1:8–17	Paul's plans to preach the gospel in Rome
1:18–4:25	believers are saved by faith, not by obedience to the Law, just as Abraham was
5:1–6:23	believers thus reconciled to God are freed from sin
7:1–8:34	having passed from the power of the Law they should now live in the spirit of God
8:35–39	nothing can separate them from the love of God
9:1–10:21	the Jews, who do not believe in Christ, seem to have been rejected by God
11:1–36	but God's purpose for them too is salvation in the end; after all, the gentiles have been saved
12:1–13:14	moral exhortations
14:1–15:13	how to deal with the scruples of the "weaker brethren"
15:14–33	Paul's plans to visit Jerusalem and Rome
16:1–23	recommendation of Phoebe, and various personal greetings
16:25–27	doxology

The sentence of greeting at the beginning (1:1–7), which is much longer than in Paul's other epistles, shows that the purpose of the letter is to stress Paul's apostleship and to detail the content of the gospel he has to preach. And in the introduction he at once mentions his intention of visiting Rome and preaching the gospel there too (1:8–15). In so doing he formulates the essence of this gospel: "in it the righteousness of God is revealed through faith for faith" (1:17), thus announcing the theme that is treated in the main part of the epistle (1:18–11:36). As no man, whether Jew or gentile, can on his own be righteous before God (1:18–3:20), it is good news to proclaim that God has now revealed his righteousness by the death of Jesus Christ, which atoned for men's sins so that those who believe may be saved without performing the works of the Law (3:21–31).

This new dispensation of God's grace is in reality an old one, for Abraham too was saved by faith (ch. 4). Paul goes on to show that God's saving action in Christ has already reconciled the believer who has been declared righteous by faith, so that he can be as sure of final salvation as man has been certain of death since the fall of Adam (ch. 5). But as Paul knows that this message can lead people to licentious behaviour he passionately avers that every believer who has been baptized and has died in this way with Christ has been given a new life and should therefore not continue to sin; Paul is clear that for the believer, too, "the wages of sin is death" (ch. 6). The believer, who has been freed from bondage to the Law and is therefore no longer compelled to sin, can by the help of the Spirit of God given to him do God's will and be confident that nothing whatever "will be able to separate us from the love of God in Christ Jesus our Lord" (ch. 7–8). The hymn at the end of this argument (8:35–39) shows that Paul feels he has brought to a conclusion the theme stated in the introduction (1:16–17).

One problem, however, remains: Why did the Jews, God's chosen people since Abraham, fail to believe the gospel that proclaims God's power for salvation "to every one who has faith, to the Jew first and also to the Greek" (1:16)? Paul—who, as a Jew, is personally concerned—tries to show that there is a secret purpose of God in this failure of the Jews. Certainly God, as God, has the right to reject even his chosen people, and certainly the Jews should have been able to believe that they had no exclusive rights to salvation, for the Old Testament itself teaches that God's message is for all men (ch. 9–10). God, however, certainly has not rejected his chosen people, but by the extension of faith to the gentiles he intends to incite the Jews also to believe in the new dispensation: "a hardening has come upon part of Israel, until the full number of the Gentiles come in, and so all Israel will be saved" (11:1–32). The idea of this universal saving intention of God induces Paul to end the whole argument with a hymn of praise to God's unsearchable ways (11:33–36).

Yet Paul does not limit himself to a demonstration of God's saving act and purpose but goes on to show how this salvation affects the everyday life of the Christian. The last five chapters of the epistle, composed of general exhortations combined with the special instruction to live in subordination to secular authority, are throughout inspired by the duty of presenting one's body to God as a living sacrifice and by the urgency of a belief that the end of the world is imminent (ch. 12–13). It is uncertain whether any of these exhortations arise from knowledge of life in the Roman congregation, but the advice which follows about dealing with the "weak" members (*i.e.*, the vegetarians) is undoubtedly directed to a specific situation (ch. 14–15). The epistle continues with information about Paul's plans to go via Jerusalem and Rome to Spain and his fears of the "unbelievers in Judea" (15:14–33). Then the letter ends with a recommendation of the deaconess Phoebe of Cenchreae, with greetings to numerous people, with a somewhat unexpected warning against "those who create dissensions," and finally with greetings from some of Paul's friends, including "Tertius, the writer of this letter" (16:1–23; *i.e.*, the amanuensis). The concluding doxology (16:25–27) is longer and more elaborate than those in Paul's other epistles.

Purpose of the Epistle.—Why did Paul write this unusually long letter to a congregation he did not himself found? It is clear from the introduction, the final chapter, and the exposition of his leading ideas in the main part of the letter that he wants to introduce himself to the Christians of Rome. But he does not merely explain, he also defends the Christian gospel from the misunderstanding that everyone can be righteous by performing "the works of the Law" (3:20). (In so doing, however, he is not attacking any opponents in the Roman congregation.) He insists again and again that the Jew as such is not in an advantageous position before God, but, like the Greek, will be asked only for faith and good deeds (1:16–17; 2:9–10). Yet at the same time Paul warns the Christian converts from paganism not to despise the Jews who do not believe in Christ and not to forget that the Jewish people is the root from which the church has grown. He insists further that the Jewish Law is holy, though it does not lead to life, and that the Christian too is to fulfill the just requirements of the Law, for submission to the gospel of Christ must not lead to a life of sin (7:12; 8:4; 6:1, 12).

It is clear, however, that this polemic is not directed against actual Jewish-Christian opponents (as in Galatians and possibly II Corinthians), for Paul never warns the Roman Christians not to submit themselves to the Law. His words are intended to minimize the attraction of this particular error and to guard against a temptation to which every Christian is prone. But apart from this there seems to be a practical motive for Paul's defense of the Law and his polemic against antinomian consequences drawn from the gospel of grace. (*See* ANTINOMIANISM.) Paul probably knew of an antinomian tendency in the Roman church, composed as it was chiefly of converts from paganism, and he was certainly aware of the tension between scrupulous Christians who, possibly influenced by some form of pagan asceticism, wished to abstain from meat, and those who are convinced, like Paul himself, that a Christian may eat anything. This knowledge that Paul has of the difficulties and dangers threatening the Roman church motivate his writing to them, for he feels bound, as the "apostle to the Gentiles" (11:13), to help and advise all gentile Christians, including those who do not owe their faith to his own mission work.

Date and Place of Origin.—The date and place of origin of the Epistle to the Romans cannot be precisely determined. Paul thinks he has finished his work in the eastern Mediterranean area and intends to go to Rome and Spain, after bringing the collection of the Greek Christian congregations to the poor of the church of Jerusalem (15:23–26). This corresponds to the situation at the end of his so-called third missionary journey (Acts 20), and there is thus general agreement that Paul wrote the Epistle to the Romans at this period of his life, in the spring of A.D. 57.

The question where the epistle was written is more difficult. As Paul spent some time in Corinth at the end of his third so-called missionary journey (Acts 20:2 ff.) and as he recommends the deaconess Phoebe of Cenchreae, the harbour of Corinth (Rom. 16:1), it is a plausible suggestion that the epistle was written in Corinth. No convincing evidence can be brought against this theory, which is therefore generally accepted. It could, however, have been written elsewhere, for instance at Philippi, as T. M. Taylor proposes, on Paul's way to Jerusalem some months later.

Authenticity.—It is generally agreed among scholars that the first 15 chapters of the Epistle to the Romans were written by the apostle Paul. The language is Pauline, and the central ideas correspond so closely in detail to those of the other Pauline Epistles, especially Galatians, that no doubt on this point is possible. Further, the sequence of the long argument (ch. 1–11), followed by a paraenetic section (12–15:13) and then Paul's personal plans concluding the epistle (15:14–33), corresponds to I Thessalonians, Philippians, and Colossians. The final chapter, however, must be discussed separately.

The Doxology.—Not all manuscripts place the doxology at the end of ch. 16. In the oldest (3rd century) papyrus of the Pauline Epistles it comes after the end of ch. 15. In most of the oldest manuscripts, it appears at the end of ch. 16 (but the Codex Alexandrinus and a 9th-century manuscript insert it after ch. 14 as well). Many later manuscripts place it after ch. 4, whereas one important manuscript of the 9th century leaves it out altogether. The canon of the heretic Marcion omits both it and the whole of ch. 15 and 16. These variants in the manuscript tradition cannot be satisfactorily explained if the doxology originally stood at the end of the letter.

Further, the doxology states that the mystery of the gospel has been kept secret since eternal ages and mentions Christian prophetic writings—both notions being incompatible with Pauline theology but in full agreement with Marcionite ideas (*see* MAR-CION; MARCIONITES). It therefore looks as if the doxology had been coined in Marcionite circles and then attached to the Pauline epistle. If this hypothesis is true, as seems likely, the doxology was not written by Paul nor was it part of the Epistle to the Romans as accepted in the oldest collection of the Pauline Epistles. The grace (16:24: "The grace of our Lord Jesus Christ be with you all") is missing in the best manuscripts and consequently in many modern translations. It must have been added originally to a copy of the epistle that did not yet have the doxology.

The Rest of Chapter 16.—Neither content nor manuscript tradition has led scholars to doubt the authenticity of the rest of ch. 16, but many have accepted the hypothesis that it originally formed a separate letter (addressed probably to the church at Ephesus) which was combined with the Epistle to the Romans when the first collection of the Pauline Epistles was made. The following arguments are usually brought forward to support this theory: (1) Paul does not send greetings to so many people in any other letter. (2) As he knows many of them personally they must have moved from the east to Rome: Aquila and Prisca lived in Ephesus after leaving Corinth with Paul (Acts 18:18–19; I Cor. 16:19), yet they are now in Rome (Rom. 16:3), while Epaenetus, "the first convert in Asia for Christ," who might also be assumed to be in Ephesus, is now also in Rome (Rom. 16:5). (3) The unexpected attack on those who create dissensions and scandals, who do not serve Christ but their bellies, fits in much better with the strictures that Paul made against the Galatians and Corinthians, when he wrote to them from Ephesus, than with the situation in Rome, since the rest of the epistle gives no indication that such heretics are to be found there.

These arguments, however, are not convincing. The great number of greetings is explained by the fact that Paul wants to show friendliness to the congregation of a place he has not yet visited, and a parallel is to be found in Col. 4:10–17. There was always a strong migration from the east to the capital; Prisca and Aquila were Roman Jews driven out when the emperor Claudius ordered all Jews to leave Rome (Acts 18:2), but they could have returned after Claudius' death (A.D. 54). The attack in Rom. 16:17–20 could be equally appropriate for the Roman congregation, as one need not suppose that such heretics were at this stage of any real influence in that Roman church.

Further, the suggestion sometimes advanced that this chapter was originally a separate letter, composed chiefly of greetings and a warning, has no evidence in its support and is intrinsically improbable. Neither the theory that this chapter was added to Rom. 1–15 nor T. W. Manson's conjecture that Rom. 1–15 was addressed to the Romans and then, with the addition of ch. 16, to the Ephesians is convincing enough to explain the other difficulties: why the end of the original letter to the Romans was lost and why a letter to the Romans was sent to the Ephesians without changing the address. The most plausible solution is to take the disputed ch. 16 as the original conclusion to Paul's epistle to the Romans.

Influence.—As the Epistle to the Romans provides the fullest and least polemical statement of Paul's message, it is fundamental for the understanding not only of his theology but also of New Testament teaching in general. The interpretation of this epistle was central to the controversies between Augustine and Pelagius, between Luther and Erasmus, and between Karl Barth and Adolf von Harnack. From the early church up to the 20th century, leading theologians—Origen, John Chrysostom, Augustine, Cyril of Alexandria, Pelagius, Theodoret of Cyrrhus, Thomas Aquinas, the Reformers, Karl Barth, Emil Brunner, and A. Nygren—have written commentaries on it. Luther discovered afresh the primitive gospel message while lecturing on Romans (1515–16), John Wesley found certainty of personal salvation through listening to Luther's preface to Romans, and Barth, by a fresh and subjective interpretation of Romans, initiated a new orientation of Protestant theology in Europe. Roman Catholics and Protestants have come closer to each other than formerly in the interpretation of the New Testament, but it is precisely in the Epistle to the Romans that the remaining differences are most clearly apparent. For this epistle gives the most detailed as well as the most difficult statement on the central problems of Christian theology, such as salvation by faith, the importance of the works of the believer for salvation, and the meaning of baptism, election by God, and the work of the Holy Spirit. *See also* BIBLE; PAUL, SAINT.

BIBLIOGRAPHY.—Greek text ed. by E. Nestle and K. Aland in *Novum Testamentum Graece*, 25th ed. (1963). Eng. trans. with commentary by W. Sanday and A. C. Headlam, 5th ed. (1902), in *International Critical Commentary*; by C. H. Dodd (1932) in *Moffatt New Testament Commentary*; by C. K. Barrett (1957) in *Black's New Testament Commentaries*; and by G. R. Cragg and John Knox in *Interpreter's Bible*, vol. 9 (1954); commentary by A. Nygren (1952), by F. J. Leenhardt (1961), and by A. Theissen in *A Catholic Commentary on Holy Scripture* (1953). French trans. with commentary by M. J. Lagrange, 3rd ed. (1922), in *Études bibliques*; German trans. with commentary by H. Lietzmann, 4th ed. (1933), in *Handbuch zum Neuen Testament*; by O. Michel, 12th ed. (1963), in *Meyers Kommentar*; and by O. Kuss (1957–   ); commentary by E. Gaugler (1945–52).

See also W. Lütgert, *Der Römerbrief als historisches Problem* (1913); J. H. Ropes, "The Epistle to the Romans and Jewish Christianity," *Studies in Early Christianity*, pp. 353–365, ed. by S. J. Case (1928); T. M. Taylor, "The Place of Origin of Romans," *Journal of Biblical Literature*, 67:281–295 (1948); T. W. Manson, "St. Paul's Letter to the Romans, and Others," *Bulletin of the John Rylands Library*, 31: 224–240 (1948); P. Bonnard, "Où en est l'interprétation de l'épître aux Romains?" *Revue de théologie et de philosophie*, 3rd series, 1:225–243 (1951); K. H. Schelkle, *Paulus, Lehrer der Väter; die altkirchliche Auslegung von Römer 1–11* (1956); W. Schmithals, "Die Irrlehrer von Römer 16, 17–20," *Studia theologica*, 13:51–69 (Lund, 1959); D. Guthrie, *New Testament Introduction: The Pauline Epistles* (1961).

(W. G. KÜ.)

ROMANSH: *see* RAETO-ROMANCE DIALECTS.

ROMANTICISM, a term loosely used in both a historical and an aesthetic sense to designate the numerous changes in literature and the arts during a period of more than 100 years (roughly, 1760–1870), in reaction against neo-Classicism (but not necessarily the classicism of Greece and Rome), or against what is variously called the Age of Reason, the Augustan Age, the Enlightenment, and 18th-century materialism.

Historical.—Major changes in the arts (unless begun by one person of genius) are usually related to some social upheaval, or to changes in the philosophical concept of man which may precede, accompany, or follow it. Thus, historians often identify the rise of Romanticism with the Industrial Revolution, or with the American War of Independence and the French Revolution, both of which produced significant Declarations of the Rights of Man. Attention must first be given, however, to pre-Romanticism, which anticipated these events. This term refers (among other things) to the so-called Rousseauistic stream of sensibility which accompanied the declining neo-Classicism of the 18th century, already weakened by the quarrel between the Ancients and the Moderns (*see* ANCIENS ET DES MODERNES, QUERELLE DES). Rousseau's assertion of man's natural goodness, social equality, and the social contract, together with the sentimental idealism of his *La Nouvelle Héloïse* and the vague religiosity and "natural religion" of the *Rêveries* and the "Vicaire Savoyard," and the portrait of a split personality in the *Confessions,* disturbed orthodox religion and political, moral, and mental philosophy. His largely anarchistic influence was accompanied, accidentally, by the constructive but equally liberating impact of the so-called Shakespearean explosion beginning in the 1760s with Jean François Ducis, Pierre Letourneur, Herder, and the *Sturm und Drang* movement.

Other influential, though minor, pre-Romantic figures were Edward Young, James Thomson, James Macpherson, Salomon Gessner, and J. G. Hamann, all of whom developed in poetry that picturesque element which in landscape gardening and painting was being explored by William Gilpin, David Cox, Ramond de Carbonnières, Giambattista Piranesi, George Morland, Hubert Robert, and William Shenstone, a landscape gardener, poet, and arbiter of taste. Pre-Romanticism in the novel is represented by Samuel Richardson, Marivaux, the abbé Prévost, Rousseau, Diderot, Horace Walpole, Beckford, Bernardin de St.-Pierre, Goethe's *Werther* (1774), and the marquis de Sade. Other important precursors were Thomas Paine, Niemcewicz, Alfieri, and Burns; but the great hinges between neo-Classicism and Romanticism were Goethe, André Chénier, Blake, Schiller, Coleridge, Wordsworth, and Chateaubriand.

Romanticism proper was, as Mme de Staël suggested in *De la Littérature* (1800) and *De l'Allemagne* (1810, 1813), largely of northern origin, but nobody followed her in setting "Nordic" literatures above those of Greece and Rome. The French Revolution, by shaking feudalism throughout Europe, hastened the decline of patronage and resulted in the liberty, poverty, and Bohemianism of the artist. It started the elaboration of theories of Utopian Socialism from Babeuf to Marx, at the same time stimulating Feminism (Condorcet, Mary Wollstonecraft Godwin, Olympe de Gouges, Jeremy Bentham). Liberating the message of de Sade, it strengthened a complex erotic literature running from the Gothic or Black novel (the *roman noir*) to Surrealism. However, the influence of the French Revolution was not felt immediately in all the arts, nor at the same time in all countries: France itself had what has been called "a revolutionary literature but not a literary revolution." But the generation of Chateaubriand, Goethe, Blake, Coleridge, and Wordsworth was profoundly disturbed by it.

The second phase of Romanticism was stimulated by the Napoleonic Wars. Napoleon's legend contributed to the image of the Romantic hero: even in real life many writers (Chateaubriand, Byron, Lamartine, Vigny, Musset, Hugo, Pushkin) adopted the attitude of Olympians or fallen angels, a pose which lasted down to Oscar Wilde and D'Annunzio. But the most important result of the Revolutionary and Napoleonic Wars together was the quickening of nationalism, marked by a return to local origins: the collection and imitation of folklore, folk dance, and music, and of medieval and Renaissance works. This passed beyond a revival of themes and forms into a rebirth of the use of inhibited languages (Tuscan, Flemish, Erse, Welsh, Breton, Provençal, Czech, Magyar) in literature. National scholarship prepared the way for imaginative writing: the historical fictions in prose and verse by Scott, Southey, Hugo, Mickiewicz, Niemcewicz, Pushkin, and Manzoni were the flowering of a scholarly trend begun 30 years earlier. Long-neglected writers and works—Dante, Chaucer, Villon, Chrétien de Troyes, Sir Thomas Malory, the *chansons de geste,* the *Nibelungenlied,* the *Mabinogion,* the *Pléiade,* Spenser—were restored to honour. Scholarship also underlay the ballad poetry produced in Britain, Germany, Hungary, Poland, Rumania, Belgium, Bulgaria, and elsewhere.

But the medieval revival had undesirable side effects, tainting poetry, painting, and architecture with bogus archaism or anachronism throughout the 19th century. Perhaps the most important result of the folk revival was the stress laid on the supernatural. The folk supernatural of romance and balladry branched off into gratuitous hair-raising in, for instance, Mary Shelley's *Frankenstein* (1818), C. R. Maturin's *Melmoth the Wanderer* (1820),

and the work of Charles Nodier, Achim von Arnim, and Edgar Allan Poe; and into metaphysics with Goethe's *Faust* and the work of Novalis, Hölderlin, E. T. A. Hoffmann, and Gérard de Nerval. A splintering, too, is seen in Scott's influence. The Waverley Novels began to appear in 1814, but it was long before imitation came from Manzoni, Hugo, Balzac, Dumas, Jacob van Lennep, Bernhard Severin Ingemann, Angel de Rivas, and Mariano Larra. After this the Waverley Novels were adapted first as plays and later as operas. Scott's manner also influenced the writing of history (Carlyle, Michelet, Lamartine, Vincenzo Cuoco), before the positivist reaction set in, and was the source of "romanced" biography from Vigny (*Stello,* 1832), Carlyle, Théophile Gautier (*Les Grotesques,* 1834–36), to the mid-20th century.

A third Romantic wave may be dated from about 1830, with the changes of political regime in Greece, Belgium, and France; the Polish and Italian risings; and the English Reform Bill (1832). This third movement mainly consolidated the tendencies already referred to; but it also saw the beginning of Romantic Realism in the theatre and the novel and a closer identification between Romanticism and political liberalism and socialism. Romanticism gradually declined after 1848 into frantic protest or sheer lassitude, finding no alternative "classical" stand, except in the French Parnasse, but rather the aestheticism of the Pre-Raphaelites and "art for art's sake," sentimental Naturalism, or a final neo-Romantic expression in such European movements as Symbolism, Impressionism, Futurism, Imagism, etc.

Historically, therefore, Romanticism can be seen to be neither a school nor a movement but rather a period of restless experiment (except in local cases such as the short-lived Cénacle, in France; *see* FRENCH LITERATURE: *The Second Period: 1815–1848*). But the spirit of the age was so strong that certain literatures which then took shape (those of the United States, Czechoslovakia, Belgium, Provence, and Ireland, for instance) have remained basically "Romantic." Some important writers (*e.g.,* Jane Austen, Leopardi) remained aloof from the Romantic influence. Historically Romanticism represents no single tendency but rather the simultaneous pressure of many different, often conflicting, principles and aspirations in a stage of European history which is not yet over. One serious historical and critical difficulty is that in most European countries several generations were involved. The term would be historically questionable if we accepted, for instance, Sir Herbert Grierson's three "Romantic ages" (Plato, etc.; 12th- and 13th-century "romance"; modern Romanticism; *see Bibliography*).

Aesthetic.—Aesthetic objections to the use of Romanticism as a critical term are even stronger. In the arts there is no common Romantic style to be compared with, for example, Heinrich Wölfflin's definition of a Classical and a Baroque style (*see* BAROQUE ART). Is there, in fact, any common denominator between the poets, musicians, painters, and novelists of the time, apart from secondary characteristics deriving from the historical moment? Local and personal variations of Romanticism were so great (and often so extreme) that no critical theory can be based on the word. Goethe set the example of pejorative definition by identifying Classicism with health and Romanticism with sickness, but most "Romantics" did not know what they were: Hugo identified Romanticism with liberalism and revolt; Delacroix with a metaphysical interpretation of the world; Blake with "Imagination, the Divine Vision"; Berlioz with heroicism and expressionism; Gautier with youth; Nerval and Hölderlin with Dream; Musset with the *mal du siècle,* or disenchantment; Herder with Magic; Schlegel with yearning or nostalgia (*Sehnsucht*); Baudelaire with "a manner of feeling"; Coleridge with Imagination and Wordsworth with Illumination, or intuition (though the last two were not thinking specifically of Romanticism). The dichotomy of the *Lyrical Ballads,* straining at once toward both a popular common-speech poetry and the supernatural and a calculated poetic diction, is typical of the Romantic dilemma: Romantic art was weakened by a striving toward a superhuman totality beyond any individual's powers and resulted, paradoxically, in excessive fragmentation.

Hegel, in describing what he called Symbolic, Classical, and Romantic forms of art, appears (according to his dialectic) to confer the highest status on the third (as Synthesis) and to associate Romanticism with Transcendental Idealism by stressing the Inwardness (*Innerlichkeit*) of Romantic art: "The world of Inwardness celebrates its triumph over the outer world." This helps to pinpoint the essential subjectiveness of Romantic art, with its emphasis on the inspired or privileged visionary or seer; autoanalysis and introspection; the self-display of the Byronic stream; the revelation theories which abounded from Novalis to Rimbaud, Mallarmé, and Rilke; the extraordinary value given to Dream, particularly by German and French writers, leading to an overvaluation of the unconscious and the irrational. Generally speaking the writers and artists of the Romantic period—*i.e.*, the 19th century—took subjectivism to the point of almost ridiculous personal vanity, which they undermined by what Irving Babbitt called "romantic irony" or self-denigration. This could only come of uncertainty about the nature of man, religion, and art. The Germans from Herder onward emphasized feeling and imagination in arbitrary opposition to logic and reason; but such thinking was possible only because the age was dominated by a faculty psychology related even to psychophysiological types by J. C. Lavater, or to "bumps" (*i.e.*, phrenology), by Franz Joseph Gall. Thus Shelley could assert, naïvely, that "Poetry is not subject to the control of the active powers of the mind, and its birth and recurrence have in no way connection with the consciousness or will." This is contradicted, however, by the fact that works of any length (*e.g.*, Goethe's *Faust*, Wordsworth's *The Prelude*) are not casual effusions or visitations (like Coleridge's *Kubla Khan*) but involve a complex mental and physical effort, sometimes over a period of years. Coleridge's failure to finish *Kubla Khan* was not a failure of will, reason, or imagination, but a failure to accept the Classical creative technique, by which inspiration is prolonged by invention (*i.e.*, sustained imitation of a given intuitive experience).

This Romantic suspicion of will, reason, knowledge, and tradition is also reflected in F. W. Schelling, whose notion that "essence always outgrows form" led to Sir Herbert Read's theory of "organic form," this being exalted as Romantic, while geometrical, abstract, or "mechanical" form would be either Classical, or worthless, or both. This does not mean that the Romantics did not use traditional forms, revolutionizing them, erasing distinctions between the genres, reviving archaic forms and creating new ones, such as the prose poem or the Wagnerian opera. But, organic or not, such anarchic experiment with forms does not constitute a *Style*: it would be more satisfactory to invent the term "Romantic Mannerism" to describe this breakdown of the old rhetoric and the absence of a new one, for the most significant break with neo-Classicism was the rejection of the idea of decorum.

Among other fallacious definitions of Romanticism might be mentioned the efforts of Pierre Lasserre (in his *Le Romantisme français* . . . , 1907, a defense of Classicism against Romanticism) and Babbitt to identify it with decadence; Lascelles Abercrombie's dissociation of it from Realism (as if Balzac, Dickens, and Stendhal, for example, existed in some other literary world); and T. E. Hulme's scorn of it as "spilt religion." Hulme, T. S. Eliot, Benedetto Croce, Charles Maurras, and others, in associating Romanticism with a collapse of religious belief, overlooked the coincidence of the Romantic revival with the upsurge of Methodism and Unitarianism (*qq.v.*), or its first manifestations in France (before its liberal phase) as being both monarchist and Catholic. It is dangerous to isolate the term from its historical context, as Melchiori has done, or to oversimplify as do Brunetière and Grierson in seeing it only as the absence of something else (refusal of the classical synthesis, etc.); or, like Valéry, to regard it only as a disorder which precedes classical order. Mario Praz has identified it with such erotic abnormalities as sadism, masochism, algolagnia (though these have always been present in the arts), but has ignored the Romantic age's aspiration toward truth and beauty and other forms of idealism. He asserts

there is such a thing as a Romantic Movement and Classicism is only an aspect of it. . . . There is no opposite pole to 'romantic,' merely because 'romantic' indicates a certain state of sensibility which, simply, is different from any other, and not comparable either by co-ordination or by contrast.

The answer to this may be seen in the historical survey above, which shows that much more than a special "state of sensibility" was involved. In the arts it is not possible to deal with states of sensibility alone: the critic, like the artist, is always challenged by the limitations or frontiers of language or plastic means of expression and by the facts of the historical process. Croce, while exaggerating in defining Romanticism as feeling and Classicism as representation, was perhaps right in saying that each term is only a half-truth. Having said that a work is Romantic (other than historically) it still remains to name, in further terms, all the qualities which are supposedly included under that expression. While the term Romanticism may be legitimately used in a historical context, though even then only with numerous qualifications, it is no more satisfactory in criticism or aesthetics than Classical, Baroque, or Symbolist, although they, also, may be used for historical convenience.

See articles on the literatures of Europe, also AMERICAN LITERATURE; and the articles POETRY; NOVEL; DRAMA: *Modern Drama;* HISTORY: *Historiography* and *Philosophy of History;* PAINTING; LANDSCAPE PAINTING; NINETEENTH-CENTURY ART; BAROQUE AND POST-BAROQUE ARCHITECTURE; LANDSCAPE ARCHITECTURE; AESTHETICS, HISTORY OF; CRITICISM; also articles on most of the people mentioned and on particular movements and theories: SYMBOLISTS, THE; IMAGISM; IMPRESSIONISM; PARNASSIANS; etc. For medieval romance, and its connections with Romanticism, *see* ROMANCE; *see* also references under "Romanticism" in the Index.

BIBLIOGRAPHY.—*See* the bibliographies to the articles mentioned above; also Hegel's *Philosophy of Fine Art* (introduction), ed. by B. Bosanquet (1886; new ed. 1905); B. Croce, *Problemi di estetica* . . . (1910), *The Essence of Aesthetic* (1921); I. Babbitt, *Rousseau and Romanticism* (1919), *The New Laokoon* (1910); W. R. Worringer, *Abstraktion und Einfühlung: ein Beitrag zur Stilpsychologie* (1908; new ed. 1948; Eng. trans. *Abstraction and Empathy: a Contribution to the Psychology of Style*, 1953); F. Strich, *Deutsche Klassik und Romantik oder Vollendung und Unendlichkeit* (1922); A. O. Lovejoy, "On the Discrimination of Romanticisms," *Publications of the Modern Language Association*, no. 39 (June 1924); Sir Herbert Grierson, "Classical and Romantic," in *The Background of English Literature* (1925; reissue 1963); L. Reynaud, *Le Romantisme. Ses origines Anglo-Germaniques* (1926); Sir Kenneth Clark, *The Gothic Revival* (1928; new ed. 1962); R. Ullmann and H. Gotthard, *Geschichte des Begriffs "Romantisch" in Deutschland* (1927); H. Focillon, *La Vie des formes* (1934; new ed. 1939; Eng. trans. *The Life of Forms in Art*, 1942); L. Abercrombie, *Romanticism* (1927; new ed. 1963); F. L. Lucas, *The Decline and Fall of the Romantic Ideal* (1936; reissued 1962); T. E. Hulme, *Speculations* (1936); M. Praz, *The Romantic Agony*, 2nd ed. (1951); F. Baldensperger, "*Romantique—analogues et équivalents,*" in *Harvard Studies*, XIV (1937); A. Beguin, *L'Âme romantique et le rêve*, 2 vol. (1937; new ed. 1946); F. C. Gill, *The Romantic Movement and Methodism* (1937); D. M. Foerster, *The Psychological Basis of Literary Periods* (1940); J. Barzun, *Romanticism and the Modern Ego* (1943); D. G. James, *The Romantic Comedy* (1948); Sir Maurice Bowra, *The Romantic Imagination* (1949); M. Abrams, *The Mirror and the Lamp: Romantic Theory and the Critical Tradition* (1953); Sir Herbert Read, *The True Voice of Feeling* (1953); G. Melchiori, *The Tightrope Walkers* (1956); F. Kermode, *Romantic Image* (1957); A. Rodway, *The Romantic Conflict* (1963); C. P. Barbier, *William Gilpin: His Drawings, Teaching, and Theory of the Picturesque* (1963); E. de Keyser, *Romanticism in Europe: 1700–89* (1965).   (F. Sc.)

ROMANTIC PAINTING AND SCULPTURE reflects a climate of feeling in Western culture so abundant and diverse in its forms of expression as to defy any concise elucidation. A question of personal approach, romantic attitudes have been present at all times, but the period that has earned the title of "Romantic" and that stretches roughly from the last decades of the 18th century until the middle of the 19th century saw an unprecedented flow of works whose prime impulse and effect derives from individual rather than collective reactions. Its chronological development began in Northern Europe with a rejection of prevailing standards of excellence based on the classical ideal that perfection could and should be sought and attained in art.

The writers and poets of the later 18th century gave initial expression to Romantic ideas, and painters, while prompted by similar experiences, acquired fundamental inspiration from the literature of the period. The literary emphasis in painting did not lend itself to transposition into three dimensions and perhaps on this account, together with a continued dependence on

"Raft of the Medusa" by Théodore Géricault; 1818. 193 x 281 in. In the Louvre, Paris

"Burning of the Houses of Parliament" by J. M. W. Turner ; c. 1835. 36¼ x 48½ in. In the Philadelphia Museum of Art

CONTEMPORARY AND HISTORICAL EVENTS IN ROMANTIC PAINTING

"Fur Traders Descending the Missouri" by George Caleb Bingham; c. 1845. 29¼ x 36¼ in. In the Metropolitan Museum of Art, New York

"The Death of Sardanapalus" by Delacroix; 1827. 31⅞ x 39¼ in. In the Louvre, Paris

Plate II

ROMANTIC PAINTING AND SCULPTURE

"Weymouth Bay" by John Constable; 1816. 21 x 29½ in. In the
National Gallery, London

"Kindred Spirits" by Asher B. Durand; 1849. 44¼ x 36¼ in. In the
New York Public Library

**ATTITUDES TOWARD
NATURE IN ROMANTIC
PAINTING**

"The Cross and the Cathedral in the Mountains" by Caspar
David Friedrich; *c.* 1811. 45 x 38 in. In the Kunstmuseum,
Düsseldorf

"Souvenir de Mortefontaine" by Camille Corot; 1864.
25¼ x 34½ in. In the Louvre, Paris

SPIRIT AND EMOTION IN EARLY ENGLISH ROMANTICISM

(Left) "The Nightmare" by Henry Fuseli; 1781. 29½ x 25¼ in. In the Goethe Museum, Frankfurt. (Above) "Pity" by William Blake; c. 1795. In the Tate Gallery, London

ture's multifarious and ever-changing aspects and found at once solace and stimulation in her pathos and destructive energy. An almost reverential affection, animated by the belief that the Divine Mind was imminent in nature, engendered at times a Christian on Theistic naturalism. The artist was seen as the interpreter of hidden mysteries to which end imaginative insight must combine with absolute fidelity and sincerity. In England and Germany especially the moral implications inherent in an appreciation of natural or artistic beauty outweighed for many painters and poets any aesthetic considerations. Everywhere a state of heightened awareness bred interest in the more elusive, transitory phenomena, and artists devoted themselves to an accurate study of light and atmosphere and their effects on local colour. Concern to preserve the spontaneity of the immediate impression brought about a revolution in painterly technique, with the rapid notation of the sketch carried into the final conception. Whether emphasizing expressive or visual considerations the landscape paintings of the period illuminate appearances with a dazzling play of luminous colour.

A widespread curiosity in the external world and a spirit of scientific inquiry led many artists to explore the minutiae of the natural world. Technological advance also excited artistic interest, and the humanitarian sympathy and generosity so vital to the Romantic spirit gradually effected a reconciliation between art and life. The political and social upheavals of the 19th century involved many artists of the period in revolutionary movements and stimulated a solicitude toward the helpless and downtrodden that found most passionate and powerful expression in the works executed during and immediately after the French Revolution of 1848. Drawing on their experience of the visual world and an ever-expanding range of technical resources, the realists of the mid-century, though not wanting in sensibility and involvement with their subject, were gradually abandoning the subjective and imaginative approach that distinguished the previous generation.

1. England.—In the late 1760s and 1770s a circle of British artists in Rome had already begun to look outside academic precepts: James Barry (1741–1806), the brothers John (1744–69) and Alexander (1736–85) Runciman, John Brown (1752–87),

classical antecedents, Romantic sculpture never flourished independently. In more important ways, however, an awareness of the subtle interrelationships of the various arts became increasingly apparent. Delacroix and Runge explored the implications of musical analogies for painting, and everywhere writers, artists, and composers could be found in intimate association.

Romantic critics unanimously agreed that all the arts held in common a belief that experience of profound inner emotion was the mainspring for creation and appreciation of great art. "Romanticism" wrote Baudelaire, "is precisely situated neither in choice of subjects nor in exact truth, but in mode of feeling." "Good taste" became anathema, and the power of the individual will was pitted against the demands of society. The artist asserted the right to evolve his own criteria of beauty and in so doing encouraged a new concept of artistic genius. The genius was one who refused to conform, who remained defiantly independent of society, and whose chief virtues were novelty and sincerity. Napoleon's mastery over his own fate and denial of accepted norms of behaviour captivated the Romantic generation, for it exalted the rough over the smooth, the primitive over the sophisticated. At an extreme this led to bizarre and extravagant projects where the determination to shock, excite, and involve strikes a melodramatic, almost hysterical note which fails to convince by its very lack of restraint.

As in the literature of the period, tragic themes predominated, and interest turned sharply from classical history and mythology to medieval subjects. A lasting enchantment with the Middle Ages set in, and the strong nationalist tendencies of Romanticism disposed artists to the history and folklore of their own countries. Frequently at odds with the present, they sought themes that were distant in time or place, and the imagination fastened on the remote past or exotic, unfamiliar places. Accounts of foreign travel aroused renewed interest, and the favourite authors of the period were Dante, Shakespeare, Byron, Goethe, "Ossian," and Walter Scott. A passion for medieval sagas and romances stimulated a closer study of medieval culture from which certain artists derived a Christian ideal of simplicity and moral integrity to sustain them in the uneasy spiritual climate of the 19th century. (*See* also GOTHIC REVIVAL.)

Any artistic movement which exalts to such a degree the validity of individual experience is in danger of indulging a maudlin self-consciousness and of disguising lack of talent beneath a cloak of feeling. Romantic art cannot be absolved of such charges, but at the same time it is notable how many artists, both good and bad, carried their artistic convictions into their own lives.

One of the most salient features of Romantic sensibility was a keen perception of the beauties of the natural world, entailing an imaginative and emotional experience of profound personal significance. Artists learned to identify subjective feelings with na-

"EXPERIMENT WITH THE AIR PUMP." BY JOSEPH WRIGHT; 1767–68. 72½ IN. X 96 IN. IN THE TATE GALLERY, LONDON

ATTITUDES TOWARD NATURE IN ENGLISH ROMANTIC PAINTING

(Left) "Coming From Evening Church" by Samuel Palmer; 1830. 11⅞ x 7⅞ in. In the Tate Gallery, London. (Centre) "Sadak in Search of the Waters of Oblivion" by John Martin; 1812. 30 x 25 in. In the Southampton Art Gallery, Eng. (Right) "Castle Eden Dean" by John Sell Cotman; c. 1803. 16⅝ x 14¾ in. In the National Gallery of Scotland, Edinburgh. (Bottom) "Lion Attacking a Horse" by George Stubbs; 1770. 40⅛ x 50¼ in. In the Yale University Art Gallery, New Haven, Conn.

George Romney (1734–1802), and the Swiss-born Henry Fuseli (1741–1825) favoured themes, whether literary, historical, or purely imaginary, determined by a taste for the pathetic, bizarre, and extravagantly heroic. Mutually influential and highly eclectic, they combined, especially in their drawings, the linear tensions of Italian Mannerism with bold contrasts of light and shade. Though never in Rome, John Hamilton Mortimer (1740–79) has much in common with this group, all participants in a move to found a national school of narrative painting. Fuseli's affiliations with *Sturm und Drang* writers (*see* GERMAN LITERATURE) predisposed him toward the "primitive," heroic stories of Homer and Dante, a partiality shared by John Flaxman (1755–1826), though endorsed in an entirely different form. The two-dimensional linear abstraction of Flaxman's drawings, implying rejection of Renaissance perspective, seen for instance in the expressive purity of "Penelope's Dream" (1792–93), had important repercussions throughout Europe. The simplicity and refinement of his reinterpretation of classical sculpture is seen in the "Monument to Dr. Joseph Warton" (1804) where traditional formulas are given contemporary significance.

William Blake (1757–1827)—painter, poet, prophet—absorbed and outstripped the Fuseli circle, evolving new images for a unique private cosmology, rejecting oils in favour of tempera and watercolour, and depicting, as in "Pity" (*c.* 1795), a shadowless world of soaring, supernatural beings. His passionate rejection of rationalism and materialism, his scorn for both Sir Joshua Reynolds and the Dutch naturalists, stemmed from a conviction that "poetic genius" could alone perceive the infinite, so essential to the artist since "painting, as well as poetry and music, exists and exults in immortal thoughts." The spiritual, symbolical expression of Blake's complex sympathies, his ability to recognize God in a single blade of grass, inspired Samuel Palmer (1805–

81), who with his friend Edward Calvert (1799–1883) extracted from nature a visionary world of exquisite, though short-lived, intensity.

Empiricism and acceptance of the irrational, however, were not mutually exclusive, and each profoundly affected attitudes to nature. Susceptible to the ideas of Blake and other radical theorists and animated by a growing spirit of inquiry into natural phenomena, painters slowly abandoned the picturesque desire to compose and became willing to be moved, awestruck, and terrified by nature unadorned. Early artists of the sublime, such as Alexander Cozens (1717–86) or Francis Towne (1740–1816), worked largely in watercolours and solved the problem of scale by abstraction—a use of broad areas of colour to suggest the vast scope of natural forces, an approach continued and developed by Thomas Girtin (1775–1802) and John Sell Cotman (1782–1842).

By the early 19th century John Varley (1778–1842) echoed current practice when he told his pupils John Linnell (1792–1882), William Mulready (1786–1863), and William Henry Hunt (1790–1864): "Go to nature for everything." But already developments were being overtaken by the achievements of the two outstanding English landscape painters, John Constable (1776–1837) and J. M. W. Turner (1775–1851). Both artists, while admiring Claude and Poussin, understood that personal feeling was the mainspring of artistic activity, and both felt an almost mystical sympathy for the natural world. They made atmosphere palpable and painted everything from clouds to lichens with astonishing technical diversity. Constable considered himself before all else a "natural" painter and sought to capture "light—dews—breezes—bloom—and freshness" with scientific precision and deepest affection. For Constable light clarified and enlivened, and his nostalgia for the Suffolk countryside is personal and explicit. With Turner light increasingly diffused the objects illuminated, and a more literary expression satisfied his concept of the sublime, drawing him to mountain grandeur, raging seas, storms, and conflagrations. Their technical innovations were better understood in France than in England; and John Ruskin's (1819–1900) passionate defense of Turner, by an emphasis on absolute fidelity to nature, helped deflect their successors on a very different course.

An eager investigation of the material world is reflected in "Experiment with the Air Pump" (1767–68) by Joseph Wright of Derby (1734–97) and in "The Green Monkey" (1798) by George Stubbs (1724–1806), whose exhaustive anatomical studies and accurate delineations of animals herald similar preoccupations from Thomas Bewick's (1753–1828) bird studies to the drawings of Sir Edwin Landseer (1802–73) and Ruskin's reverent and closely observed renderings of naturalistic detail. Stubbs's empathy for the animal world reemerges in the work of James Ward (1769–1859), together with an exultation in the power of nature, shared by Philippe de Loutherbourg (1740–1812). Curiosity extended also to geographical exploration, and the picturesque views of Paul Sandby (1725–1809) and nostalgic recollections of Italy by Richard Wilson (1714–82) or John Robert Cozens (1752–97) were superseded by a demand for information about distant places. Following William Hodges (1744–97), who accompanied Capt. James Cook's second voyage, such artists as Richard Parkes Bonington (1802–28), Samuel Prout (1783–1852), John Frederick Lewis (1805–76), and Edward Lear (1812–88) traveled widely, recording scenes of historic or exotic interest.

In portraiture increased attention to psychological implications and creation of a particular mood found most eloquent and elegant expression in the work of Sir Thomas Lawrence (1769–1830), who combined in such portraits as those of Richard Payne Knight (1794) and Pope Pius VII (1819) brilliant freedom of handling with subtle evocation of character.

History painting too was ultimately affected by the empirical state of mind; Bonington's "Henry III and the English Ambassador" (1827–28), while testifying to a sustained delight in the medieval world, already betrays commensurate interest in period detail and the finer points of human insight. The authentic, domestic treatment of biblical themes in the hands of William Dyce (1806–64) and the Pre-Raphaelites contrasts sharply with the earlier apocalyptic fantasies of John Martin (1789–1854) and Francis Danby (1793–1861). Inspired by Sir David Wilkie's (1785–1841) mellow, unassuming representation of Scottish country life, Mulready turned to modern genre, adopting a brilliant palette that distinguishes English painting for the next half-century. Accurate and sympathetic observation characterizes Victorian narrative painting from the panoramic activity of William Powell Frith's (1819–1909) "Derby Day" (1858) to such intimate glimpses of reality as "The Travelling Companions" (1862) by Augustus Egg (1816–63). Often a vehicle for social or moral comment, a sentimental tendency is redeemed in the work of Sir Luke Fildes (1843–1927) and Frank Holl (1845–88) by a genuine regard for the sufferings of the poor. In the 1850s the Pre-Raphaelites gave most generous expression to the painting of contemporary life with such memorable images as "The Blind Girl" (1856) by Sir John Everett Millais (1829–96) or "The Stonebreaker" (1857–58) by John Brett (1830–1902).

The Pre-Raphaelite movement, echoing that of the Nazarenes in Germany, reiterated many earlier Romantic ideals. Literary inspiration and a passion for the Middle Ages were tempered for

BY COURTESY OF BIRMINGHAM CITY ART GALLERY, ENG.

PRE-RAPHAELITE MORALISM

"The Blind Girl" by John Everett Millais; 1856. In the Birmingham City Art Gallery, Eng.

the Pre-Raphaelites by a moral outlook that recoiled from sophistication and virtuosity and demanded rigorous studies from natural life. These painters handled literary, historical, biblical, and contemporary themes with the same sincerity and fidelity that yielded the sparkling precision of Pre-Raphaelite landscape. Together with Ford Madox Brown (1821–93) they sustain the devotion to colour and light in painting that underlies the finest endeavours of English Romanticism. (*See* PRE-RAPHAELITE BROTHERHOOD.)

2. Germany.—In Germany also there was a reaction against classicism and the academies, and as elsewhere it involved all aspects of the arts. Again, as elsewhere, theory preceded practice: *Herzensergiessungen eines kunstliebenden Klosterbruders* ("Effusions of an Art-Loving Monk") by Wilhelm H. Wackenroder (1773–1798), published by Ludwig Tieck (1773–1853) in 1797, had an immediate and widespread influence: Wackenroder advocated a Christian art closely related to the art of the early German masters and provided the artist with a new role as interpreter of divine inspiration through his own feelings. In *Phantasien über die Kunst, für Freunde der Kunst* ("Fantasies on Art for Friends of Art"; 1799) Tieck used Wackenroder as a basis for developing his own ideas on the interrelationship between poetry and music, and *Franz Sternbalds Wanderungen* ("The Wandering of Franz Sternbald"; 1798), the culmination of a decade of *Sturm und Drang* novels, became, together with the "Effusions" and "Fantasies," a kind of breviary for the German Romantics.

P. O. Runge (1777–1810) was introduced by Tieck to his circle in Dresden. Reared on 17th-century German mysticism, Runge was susceptible to the ideas of Tieck and Wackenroder and formed a close association with Caspar David Friedrich (1774–1840). Like Friedrich he was fascinated by the potential symbolic and allegorical power of landscape, which he used as a vehicle for religious expression. Like Friedrich's too, his vision of nature was pantheistic, and in his portraits his aim was to capture the soul of the individual as part of the universal soul of nature. "The Artist's Parents and Children" (1806) reflects not only his constant search for truth but also his admiration for the early German masters, through whose work he was made aware of the expressive power of line and colour. His interest in the German past, including folklore and fairy tales, was reflected in a bizarre fairylike quality in much of his work (*e.g.*, "Night"; 1803), and it was this quality that was taken up and popularized by his two most important followers, Moritz von Schwind (1804–71) and L. A. Richter (1803–84), in whose hands the intensity of the first generation declined into popular genre and the comfortable Biedermeier Romanticism (*see* BIEDERMEIER STYLE).

Runge in turn introduced to the Dresden circle Friedrich, who became the greatest of the German Romantic landscape painters.

BY COURTESY OF THE STÄDELSCHES KUNSTINSTITUT, FRANKFURT

"THE ENTRY OF THE EMPEROR RUDOLF OF HABSBURG INTO BASEL IN 1273" BY FRANZ PFORR; *c.* 1809. 35½ X 46⅝ IN. IN THE STÄDELSCHES KUNSTINSTITUT, FRANKFURT

A deeply religious man, his vision demanded complete subjection to the spirit of God in nature, and in suggesting through landscape the eternal presence of the Creator, he intended to induce in the beholder a state of religious awe. Among his pupils was C. G. Carus (1789–1869), a physician, philosopher, and self-taught painter, whose chief contribution was as theorist: *Briefe über Landschaftsmalerei* (nine "Letters on Landscape Painting"; 1831) elucidates and expands the ideas of Friedrich adding Carus' own more scientific approach to natural phenomena. Also influenced by Friedrich were E. F. Oehme (1797–1855), a landscape painter, and G. F. Kersting (1785–1847), who captured in his stark interiors something of the master's aura of silent worship. Two other pupils afterward abandoned the tragic landscapes: the Norwegian Johann C. C. Dahl (1788–1857) to revert to his naturalist inclinations and Karl Blechen (1798–1840) to join and stimulate the Romantic realists.

Whereas Runge, Friedrich, and their progeny adopted a highly personal interpretation of Tieck and Wackenroder, others extracted a program of communal activity. A number of young painters in Vienna founded in 1809 a group they called the Brotherhood of St. Luke. Founder members were J. F. Overbeck (1789–1869), their leader; Franz Pforr (1788–1812), Josef Wintergerst (1783–1867), Josef Sutter (1781–1866), and G. L. Vogel (1788–1879). In 1810 they moved to Rome, where they were soon joined by Peter von Cornelius (1783–1867), Julius Schnorr von Carolsfeld (1794–1872), F. W. Olivier (1791–1859), the brothers Philipp (1793–1877) and Johann (1790–1854) Veit, Wilhelm von Schadow-Godenhaus (1788–1862), J. E. Scheffer von Leonardshoff (1795–1822), and Joseph von Führich (1800–76). Their semi-monastic existence occasioned the nickname "Nazarenes" (*see* ART, SOCIETIES OF: *Nineteenth and Twentieth Centuries*).

In general their highest aspirations—toward monumental history painting—produced the least successful results, and they came closest to realizing their intentions on a small scale in highly finished watercolours and drawings, as in Overbeck's "The Raising of Jairus' Daughter" (1814). Only J. A. Koch (1768–1839) and Cornelius, who were both older and more experienced than their associates, achieved great vigour in their history paintings, combining medievalizing tendencies with the powerful classicism of the German painter A. J. Carstens (1754–98), as seen in Cornelius' "The Recognition of Joseph by His Brethren" (1815–16). Even Overbeck, an articulate leader and a lucid draftsman, could not escape, in his "Joseph Being Sold by His Brethren" (1816–17), a self-conscious naivete common to many of the Nazarenes, seen also in Pforr's "The Entry of the Emperor Rudolf of Habsburg into Basel in 1273" (*c.* 1809) or in Schnorr's "The Procession of the Three Magi" (1819). Alfred Rethel (1816–59), a late arrival, however, escapes this in his haunting "King David

GIRAUDON

"LES PESTIFÉRÉS DE JAFFA" BY ANTOINE JEAN GROS; 1804. 209 X 283 IN. IN THE LOUVRE

with his Harp" (*c.* 1831). Not long afterward there was a move toward the more dramatic, though no less nostalgic, approach of von Schadow and his pupil K. F. Lessing (1808–80).

Portraiture required less self-consciousness than history painting, and there are a number of highly sensitive portraits, mainly of their friends, by Overbeck, Schnorr, Scheffer von Leonardshoff, and Carl Philipp Fohr ("Portrait of Wilhelm von Schadow"; 1818). The Nazarenes' greatest contribution, however, was to landscape painting: inspired by the heroic landscapes of Koch—*e.g.,* "The Bernese Oberland" (1817), by the German "primitives," and by their own concept of truth to nature, they renounced the conventional Italianate solution and turned instead to memories of Germany and German painting and to the countryside around them. As the movement gathered momentum the possibilities for development expanded, and the Nazarene landscape was valuable to later painters of Biedermeier, of naturalistic landscape, of Romantic realism and secular history painting.

3. France.—One of the manifold repercussions of the French Revolution was the stimulation of artistic interest in the depiction of contemporary events. Led by J. L. David (1748–1825), many artists sought to represent authentically the crucial moments of their own time. Napoleon enthusiastically endorsed this awareness of modern heroism and demanded pictorial celebration of the glorious achievements of the empire. David recorded the ceremonies of the imperial court with scrupulous precision. Napoleon's potent hold on the artistic imagination is well illustrated by Baron Antoine Jean Gros's (1771–1835) "Les Pestiférés de Jaffa" (1804), where he is endowed with godlike authority and the humanitarian sensibility of the true Romantic hero. At the same time other artists, Baron François Gérard (1770–1837), Girodet de Roucy-Trioson (1767–1824), and J. A. D. Ingres (1780–1867), readily responded to the emperor's admiration for Macpherson's "Ossian" stories. With the fall of Napoleon the modern subject presented a really decisive challenge that few were disposed to consider. Théodore Géricault (1791–1824), whose work realizes so abundantly the implications of earlier interpretations of actual events, was separated from his immediate predecessors both by temperament and by the sincerity of his approach. Individual suffering rather than collective drama is vividly portrayed in the "Raft of the Medusa" (1819), Géricault's masterpiece, whose strenuous forms acknowledge a new appraisal of the 17th-century school of Caravaggio. His studies of the poor, aged, and insane, more realistically observed, have a sympathetic intensity unmatched before the generation of H. Daumier and G. Courbet.

The wildness and fatality of the animal world inspired many artists of the 19th century and provided themes for several sculptors of the period. In his bronze groups of fighting animals A. L. Barye (1795–1875) compresses the elemental energy of nature that explodes into violent life in the Lion Hunts of Eugène

BY COURTESY OF THE MUSEUM FERDINANDEUM, INNSBRUCK

"BERNESE OBERLAND" BY J. A. KOCH; 1817. IN THE MUSEUM FERDINANDEUM, INNSBRUCK, AUSTRIA

Delacroix (1798–1863). The paintings of Delacroix frequently disrupted the salons of the 1820s and '30s with their tumultuous colour and emotive energy. To many young men of that generation France appeared after 1815 to settle into a bourgeois respectability bitterly resented by those who regretted the lost exhilaration of republican and imperial times. In consequence the art of the period often assumed a melancholic and introverted temper where discontent expressed itself in historicist and exotic themes or in an impassioned interpretation of the humble outcasts of society. Delacroix has justly been acclaimed the leader of the "Romantic School" in France. His fertile imagination, embracing a novel range of literary and historical themes and fastening with characteristic melancholy on moments of death, defeat, and suffering, together with his prodigious technical resources exemplify the most obtrusive aspects of Romanticism during this period. His vigorous handling of paint and exploitation of expert knowledge of colour values both descriptively and expressively were invaluable to the later development of French painting. The "Massacre at Chios" (1824) transposes contemporary events into a realm of tragic fiction soon established unrestrainedly with such melodramatic works as the "Death of Sardanapalus" (1827), a riot of brilliant colour and ebullient forms.

Delacroix's Moroccan paintings released a flood of North African subjects, although in the hands of lesser artists such as Eugène Fromentin (1820–76), Ary Scheffer (1795–1858), and Eugène Devéria (1805–65) the treatment tends to become anecdotal. A. G. Decamps (1803–60), whose small canvases have a delicate, jewellike quality, provided the most refreshing variations on the theme. But Delacroix was not the first to handle Oriental subjects; Ingres had already done so with a reticence that belies the sensuous delight in "The Bather" (1808) and in "Odalisque" (1814). Ingres began his career in the historicist genre with episodes from medieval French history painted in a style of linear purity that parallels the methods of Flaxman and Blake in England and the Nazarenes in Germany. Under the spell of Raphael he returned to the academic fold, but his portraits always retained that trenchant simplicity and lucid insight that make him such a memorable exponent of lyric realism. The career of Ingres and in a converse sense that of Paul Delaroche (1797–1856) well illustrate the impropriety of too readily distinguishing between academic and Romantic artists. Delaroche, perhaps the most popular representative of the "Romantic School," specialized in sentimental histrionics with royal protagonists of which "The Children of Edward" (1831) is a typical maudlin example executed with a flatness that lacks either linear or colouristic inspiration. In comparison the work of Théodore Chassériau (1819–56) is animated by powerful emotional overtones that imply close kinship with Delacroix. "The Cossack Girl Finding the Body of Mazeppa" (1851) reveals a similarly expressive use of paint together with a poignantly suggestive imagery, both characteristic of his regrettably slender *oeuvre*. At the end of the century Gustave Moreau (1826–98) and Odilon Redon (1840–1916) transformed these features, together with others present in the work of Louis Boulanger (1806–67), into whimsical, haunting fantasies that delighted the Symbolist poets.

Inspiration for French Romantic sculpture stemmed largely from literary and pictorial sources and some of the most original sculptors, Géricault, Honoré Daumier (1808–79), and Constantin Meunier (1831–1905), were primarily painters. Literary antecedents are apparent in the work of Antonin Moine (1796–1849) and Jehan du Seigneur (1808–66) and are epitomized by the latter's "Roland Furieux" (1831), a bronze rendering of the "style troubadour." Dependence on painting encouraged a frequent resort to relief rather than free-standing sculpture and even led to such bizarre essays as a relief of the "Raft of the Medusa," modeled by Antoine Etex (1808–88) for Géricault's tomb. One of the few sculptors, with Barye, to realize the plastic potential of the medium was Auguste Préault (1809–79) who attempts to convey a destructive energy in his "Massacre" relief (1834) through concentration of interlocking forms.

As the influence of the socialist ideas of Fourier and Proudhon were felt in the 1830s and 1840s statuettes of the humble pariahs of society made their appearance. P. A. Graillon (1809–72) popularized this kind of figure while a more satirical note was struck by J. P. Danton (1800–69). Meunier and Jules Dalou (1838–1902) approached peasant life with greater gravity, but Daumier, more than any other artist, made the outcast his own. Daumier, whose spiritual ideal was embodied by the wandering, melancholy Don Quixote, transfigures the hounded and homeless in his reliefs of "Refugees" (c. 1850), and in numerous drawings and paintings expresses the patient resignation and misery of the oppressed. Moreover, his penetrating regard for the weaknesses and vices of the oppressor often excited the displeasure of official authority that had long been convinced, not without good reason, that Romanticism was identified with political liberalism. A strain of poetic realism in the 1840s, essentially Romantic in approach, gathered sudden momentum with the Revolution and short-lived Republic of 1848, confirming the establishment's direst suspicions. Jean François Millet (1814–75) and Gustave Courbet (1819–77) turned to peasant life and invested it with timeless monumentality. Courbet's "Stonebreakers" (1850) and Millet's harrowing "Quarriers" (1847–49) are powerfully expressive of a passionate personal concern for the poor. Courbet, a vehement and liberating force in the art of the period, created a sombre monument to his own village community in "The Burial at Ornans" (1850) while Millet elicited an epic grandeur from the humble scenes of rural life. A new approach to the familiar and unsophisticated, found in the novels of George Sand and other writers of the period, is reflected in the landscape painting of the 1830s and 1840s; for although French Romanticism produced no Turner, it generated a flourishing school of naturalist painters associated with the Barbizon School in the forest of Fontainebleau. This period saw the recognition of the charm of the spontaneous sketch over the finished study; painters set up their easels in the open air and scrutinized the scene before them with fresh enjoyment and sympathy. A direct approach to nature and an interest in transitory moments, especially the changing effects of light, were features common to Romantic landscape painters throughout Europe and America. Paul Huet (1803–69), a friend of Delacroix and Bonington and closely associated with the "Romantic School," represented dramatic,

NINETEENTH-CENTURY SOCIAL CONSCIOUSNESS

(Left) "The Sower" by Jean François Millet; c. 1850. 40 x 32½ in. In the Museum of Fine Arts, Boston. (Right) "The Third-Class Carriage" by Honoré Daumier; c. 1862. 25¾ x 35½ in. In the Metropolitan Museum of Art, New York

BY COURTESY OF (TOP) COLLECTION OF THE BOATMEN'S NATIONAL BANK, ST. LOUIS, (ABOVE LEFT) NEW YORK STATE HISTORICAL ASSOCIATION, COOPERSTOWN, N.Y., (ABOVE RIGHT) THE DETROIT INSTITUTE OF ARTS, (RIGHT) CINCINNATI ART MUSEUM

HISTORIC, NARRATIVE, AND GENRE PAINTING

(Top) "Caravan En Route" by A. J. Miller; 1810–74. In The Boatmen's National Bank, St. Louis. (Above left) "Eel Spearing at Setauket" by William S. Mount; 1845. 28½ x 35¾ in. In Fenimore House, Cooperstown, N.Y. (Above right) "Watson and the Shark" by John Singleton Copley; 1778. 36 x 30½ in. In the Detroit Institute of Arts. (Right) "The Sortie of the British Garrison from Gibraltar" by John Trumbull; 1789. 20 x 30 in. In the Cincinnati Art Museum

The freedom and freshness of Constable's handling is echoed in Daubigny's flickering treatment of sunset and light over water. An empirical approach combined with a poetic insight into nature was characteristic of N. V. Diaz de la Peña (1808–76) and Constant Troyon (1810–65). In a similar way the work of Camille Corot (1796–1875), despite the restrained classicism of his style, is enlivened by an instinctive feeling for naturalistic landscape. For while they laid the foundation for the painterly revolution of the Impressionists, the Barbizon painters always retained the generous appreciation of natural beauty and emotional involvement with their subject that everywhere distinguishes the Romantic temperament.

4. United States.—American Romantic painters drew to a large extent on currents in late 18th-century European art and literature, especially those of England, but the absence of an indigenous artistic tradition permitted a much more intuitive development. At the same time their work, like that of the early French Romantics, is closely associated with the new spirit fostered by a national revolution. The American Revolution, by reinforcing the democratic ideal, inspired a unique brand of Romantic realism that was a strong force in American painting from the late 18th century onward and that anticipated the emergence in Europe by a whole generation. Benjamin West (1738–1820) and John Singleton Copley (1738–1815) developed a sturdy style of narrative painting with dramatic subjects taken from contemporary life, and while they painted their most significant work in England, it was on American rather than English artists that it made most impact. John Trumbull (1756–1843), emulating Copley's robust interpretation of contemporary events, undertook a series of 12 scenes from the American Revolution, where careful studies of the principal participants were incorporated in colourful, Baroque compositions, which at their best, as "The Sortie of the British Garrison from Gibraltar" (1789), if somewhat theatrical, nevertheless carry great conviction. In 1784 one of the most candid portraitists of the period, C. W. Peale (1741–1827), completed a similarly ambitious project to paint the leading figures of the Revolution. A more limited enthusiasm for precise naturalistic study informs the work of Alexander Wilson (1766–1813), whose devoted love of birds emerges in the freshness and simplicity of the plates to his *American Ornithology* (9 vol.; 1808–14). His achievement has been obscured by his greater successor, J. J. Audubon (1785–1851), who combined scientific exactitude with a delight in his specimens that transforms his watercolour drawings of birds into works of rare and delicate beauty.

At the beginning of the Romantic period artists still ac-

stormy scenes of solitude; yet though scarcely a naturalist, he was deeply impressed by the works of Constable, several of which he copied and which inspired him to adopt a broken style of brush-work with dabs of bright pigment. The changed attitude to landscape is fittingly expressed in the words of the most controversial representative of the new school who believed "Our art can only attain pathos through sincerity." Théodore Rousseau (1812–67) attempted to render nature as he found it, though his melancholic temperament is inevitably reflected in the desolate panoramas and gloomy sunsets in which he expressed an almost pantheistic feeling for the natural world. At the same time his close attention to detail and painstaking accuracy in the delineation of plants and grasses betray that scientific concern that was shared by many Romantic artists. A similar penetration informed his studies of light, and both he and Charles Daubigny (1817–78) repeated virtually the same subjects under different weather conditions in order to capture the ephemeral effects of light and atmosphere.

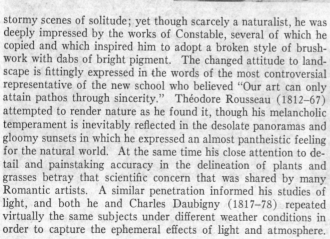

knowledged a debt to English painting, but this grew less and less perceptible as the 19th century progressed. The portrait of "Colonel Thomas Handasyd Perkins" (1831–32) by Thomas Sully (1783–1872), the leading exponent of a new portraiture of mood, bears references to Thomas Lawrence in the delicately brushed surface, strong contrasts of light and dark, and exquisite elegance of pose. Although Samuel F. B. Morse (1791–1872), S. L. Waldo (1783–1861), William Page (1811–85), and others practised a similar emotive style, the portraits of the 19th century generally endorsed the native tradition of solid characterization.

The career of the landscape painter Washington Allston (1779–1843) reflects the development of American painting. Absorbed by German and English Romantic poetry and, like Poe, susceptible to disquieting and gruesome tales, he began on a note of high drama. Intimately involved in international literary and artistic circles in Rome, his early landscapes stimulated the friendship of Coleridge. His impetuous and brooding temperament now found expression in an ideal interpretation of nature in the darker, more destructive moods dear to Turner. "The Deluge" (1804) is a typical macabre invention with bodies swept ashore in a raging tempest to the lurking mercies of wolves and serpents. On his return to America, however, his work assumed a quieter, more musing aspect. "The Flight of Florimell" (1819) illustrates this later style.

An uncomplicated love for their own natural scenery emerges in the work of a succession of landscape painters who frequently strike this contemplative, lyrical note. Thomas Cole (1801–48) reverently recorded scenes in the valley of the Hudson River that echo the loneliness and mystery of the North American forests. With his generous humanitarian sympathies Asher B. Durand (1796–1886) gave a serene and artless account of nature. His feeling for space and finely diffused light renders "Kindred Spirits" (1849) a touching tribute to the friendship of Cole with the poet Bryant. An interest in light and atmosphere was shared by George Brown (1814–99), FitzHugh Lane (1804–65), Frederick E. Church (1826–1900), and George Harvey (c. 1800–78); all followed Durand and painted in the open. Simplicity and reticence distinguish the landscapes of Thomas Doughty (1793–1856), who was content to paint the Hudson River Valley as he knew and loved it. The details of country life that fill the stories of Washington Irving are portrayed with like affection by William Sidney Mount (1807–68), who invests "Eel Spearing at Setauket" (1845) with a timeless significance transcending the anecdotal. George Caleb Bingham (1811–79) approached the American frontier in a similar spirit, devoid of the passionate concern that motivated many contemporary French artists. Solemn and severe in style and glowing with colour, his striking "Fur Traders Descending the Missouri" (c. 1845) captures the silence and solitary grandeur of frontier life. The wildness of the frontier caught the imagination of many 19th-century artists: George

BY COURTESY OF THE BOSTON ATHENAEUM

"COLONEL THOMAS HANDASYD PERKINS" BY THOMAS SULLY; 1831–32. 94 X 58 IN. IN THE MUSEUM OF FINE ARTS, BOSTON

BY COURTESY OF THE DETROIT INSTITUTE OF ARTS

"THE FLIGHT OF FLORIMELL" BY WASHINGTON ALLSTON; 1819. 36 X 28 IN.

Catlin (1796–1872), Seth Eastman (1808–75), J. M. Stanley (1814–72), A. J. Miller (1810–74), and Karl Bodmer (1809–93) all discovered a picturesque drama and excitement in Indian life. The Romantic period witnessed the emergence of a truly national school of painting in America where the events and scenery of the New World provided a constant source of stimulation for artists content to distill their own poetry from the world around them.

BIBLIOGRAPHY.—*General.*—M. Praz, *The Romantic Agony* (1933); E. P. Richardson, *The Way of Western Art, 1776–1914* (1939); Arts Council of Great Britain, *The Romantic Movement* (1959); F. Novotny, *Painting and Sculpture in Europe, 1780–1880* (1960); M. Brion, *Romantic Art* (1960); F. Antal, *Classicism and Romanticism* (1966). *England.*—J. Ruskin, *Modern Painters*, 5 vol. (1843–60); R. Todd, *Tracks in the Snow* (1946); G. Grigson, *The Harp of Aeolus* (1948); A. Blunt, *The Art of William Blake* (1959); T. S. R. Boase, *English Art 1800–1870* (1959); G. Reynolds, *Constable the Natural Painter* (1965); L. Gowing, *Turner: Imagination and Reality,* Museum of Modern Art, New York (1966); R. Rosenblum, *Transformations in Late 18th-Century Art* (1967); F. Cummings *et al., Romantic Art in Britain: Paintings and Drawings, 1760–1860* (1968).
Germany.—M. von Boehn, *Biedermeier: Deutchland von 1815–1847* (1911); W. Wolfradt, *Caspar David Friedrich und die Landschaft der Romantik* (1924); F. Landsberger, *Die Kunst der Goëthezeit* (1931); R. Benz and A. von Schneider, *Die Kunst der deutschen Romantik* (1939); A. von Schneider, *Deutsche Romantiker—Zeichnungen* (1942); B. Dörries, *Zeichnungen der Frühromantik* (1950); P. F. Schmidt, *Philipp Otto Runge: Sein Leben und sein Werk* (1956); K. Andrews, *The Nazarenes* (1964).
France.—E. Delacroix, *Journal,* 3 vol. ed. by André Joubin (1950); C. Baudelaire, *Curiosités esthétiques* (1868), *L'Art romantique* (1869); Luc-Benoist, *Le Sculpture romantique* (1928); M. W. Brown, *The Painting of the French Revolution* (1938); L. Rudrauf, *Eugène Delacroix et le problème du romantisme artistique* (1942); R. L. Herbert, *Barbizon Revisited* (1962); L. Johnson, *Delacroix* (1963); W. F. Friedlander, *David to Delacroix* (1964).
United States.—J. T. Soby and D. C. Miller, *Romantic Painting in America* (1944); E. P. Richardson, *American Romantic Painting* (1944), *The World of the Romantic Artist: a Survey of American Culture from 1800–1875* (1945); F. A. Sweet, *The Hudson River School and the Early American Landscape Tradition* (1945); J. I. H. Baur, *American Painting in the 19th Century* (1953); J. T. Flexner, *The Light of Distant Skies, 1760–1835* (1954). (S. E. B.)

ROMANUS, the name of four Byzantine emperors: ROMANUS I LECAPENUS (*c.* 870–948); ROMANUS II (938–963); ROMANUS III ARGYRUS (*c.* 968–1034); and ROMANUS IV DIOGENES (d. 1072). *See* BYZANTINE EMPIRE. It was also the name of a pope (d. 897).

ROMANY LANGUAGE, the language of the gypsies, is one of the Indo-Aryan languages (*q.v.*), a fact which constitutes the strongest proof that the gypsies originally came from India. Romany is not only derived from the same original source as the other Aryan languages of India, but must for many centuries after the Vedic age have shared their development within or near the borders of India, for in general it shows the phonetic and grammatical changes which the Indian languages as a whole reached not long before the beginning of the Christian era.

Dialectal Position.—The dialect group in which Romany had its origin is a question that has been widely discussed. One school holds that it belongs to the northwestern and especially to the Dardic, which comprises certain dialects of the Hindu Kush and also includes the more important Kashmiri. These languages, in some respects more conservative than those of areas farther in India, have kept certain features of the old Sanskrit sound system unchanged; *e.g.,* the preservation of two or more sibilants ($ś, ṣ, s$) or of an r preceded by a consonant. The Romany dialects also show some of these peculiarities, but the preservation by descendants of characteristics that existed in the parent language is not proof that they have any specially close relationship other than common origin. The existence of the same early innovations in both is proffered by those who hold that Romany originally belonged to a more central group of dialects of which a typical modern representative in India is Hindi. It is with these that it shares its earliest sound changes. Romany does not however share other later innovations of the central group which had set in or were setting in at the time of Aśoka (*c.* 250 B.C.). They must, therefore, have severed their relations with this group before that date. The word *rom,* "gypsy man," southeast European *rom,* Armenian Ry. *lom,* Palestinian Ry. *dōm,* is the same word as the Skt. *ḍomba,* "a low caste of dancers and singers," from whom the *Ḍōms* of India derive their name. It is probable that wandering tribes, perhaps of the same character as some criminal tribes of modern India and speaking a central dialect, made their way to the northwest (probably western Punjab or Peshawar district) before the middle of the 3rd century B.C. There, among speakers of the northwestern dialect group, they stayed until some time before the 9th century A.D. they left India in a migration which spread them all over western Asia, Europe and even America.

Dialects.—It is not known whether the gypsies left India in one or several separate migrations or whether there were even marked dialectal variations in the language they spoke. But presently there are at least three distinct groups of dialects, Asiatic, Armenian and European. One of the most noticeable differences lies in the treatment of the original voiced aspirates of Sanskrit. The Asiatic dialects have either preserved these or, losing the aspiration, have reduced them to simple voiced sounds; the European and Armenian dialects on the other hand have changed them to surd aspirates: Skt. *bh, dh, gh* became Asiatic *b,d,g*, but Armenian and European *ph,th,kh* (*p',t',k'*). Thus Skt. *bhrátā* "brother," *dhūmáh* "smoke," *ghṛtám* "melted butter" are in Eur. Ry. *p'ral,- t'uv,k'il* and in Pal. Ry. *bar, dif, gir*.

There is considerable dialectal variation even within a single group such as the European Romany group, dating probably from the time of separation within Europe itself. These dialects differ according to locality and the degree to which they have been influenced by surrounding languages. In this respect they may vary from the comparatively pure Indian idiom of, for example, some of the Balkan gypsies or even the gypsies of Wales, to mere jargons consisting of a framework of the local language, *e.g.*, English, in which a portion of the vocabulary is replaced by Romany words.

Phonology.—The vowel system rests on Sanskrit. As in all Middle Indian dialects, Skt. *ai* and *au* have become *ē* and *ō; e.g.*, Arm. Ry. *tel* "oil" from *tailám; mol* "price" from *maulyam*. In the European dialect, Skt. *a* in an open syllable appears as *e* but in an originally closed syllable as *a*, which is also the representative of Skt. *ā: merel* "dies," *rak'el* "keeps," *manuš* "man," from *márate, rákṣati, mānuṣáḥ*.

In the consonant system, the chief innovation is the change of the voiced aspirates already mentioned. Of the surd aspirates, *ph* appears to remain (*p'al* "board" from Skt. *phálaḥ*); *ch* loses its aspiration in west European Romany (W. Eur. *čin-* "to cut," S.E. Eur. *č'in-* from Skt. *chinná-*); *kh* perhaps becomes a spirant χ (χ*anro* "sword" from Skt. *khaṇḍakaḥ*). Intervocalic consonants, as in all other descendants of Sanskrit, are weakened. The gutturals and palatals disappear altogether; the cerebrals remain as *r* (S.E. Eur. *ṛ*), the labials partly as *v*, the dentals as *l* in the European and Armenian dialects and as *r* in the Asiatic.

Sanskrit	Romany	Sanskrit	Romany
yūkā "louse"	.*ǰuv* id.	*āgataḥ* "came"	*alo* id.
sūcī "needle"	*suv* id.	*vijanati* "bears young"	*benel* id.
kīṭaḥ "insect"	*kiri* "ant"	*bidālaḥ* "cat"	*blári* (Syr.) id.
sthāpáyati "places"	*t'ovel* id.	*pibati* "drinks"	*piel* id.
yuvatiḥ "young woman"	*ǰuvel* id.	*hṛdayam* "heart"	*yilo* id.
	ǰuār (Syr.)		*hri* (Syr.)

Assimilation of consonant groups has occurred generally, with the exception of *r* preceded by a stop and of sibilants followed by dental or cerebral stops, except in the Armenian dialect.

Sanskrit	Romany
dugdhám "milk"	*t'ud* (from *duddham*), Arm. *lut'*.
bhrátā "brother"	*p'ral* id., Arm. *p'al*, Syr. *bar*.
hástaḥ "hand"	*vast*, Syr. *ḥāst*, Arm. *at'*.

Grammar.—In grammar too the main structure of the better preserved dialects rests upon its Sanskrit original. The declension of the noun is based on two cases, a direct (descended from the Sanskrit nominative and accusative) and an oblique (descended from the Sanskrit genitive) to which various postpositions can be added.

	Sanskrit	Prakrit	Romany
Sing. nom.	*cōráh* (-*ó*)	*cōrō*	} *čor*
acc.	*cōrám*	*cōraṁ*	
gen.	*cōrásya*	*cōrassa* (-*asa*)	*čores*
Pl. nom.	*cōráh*	*cōrā*	*čor*
gen.	*cōráṇām*	*cōraṇaṁ*	*čoren*

The verb is built up of the old present stem, of which the indicative, the imperative and the participle still survive, and of the past participle, which alone or combined with auxiliaries forms past tenses.

		Sanskrit	Romany
Present indicative:	Sing.	*rákṣāmi*	*rak'av*
		rákṣasi	*rak'es*
		rákṣati	*rak'el*
	Pl.	*rákṣāmas*	*rak'as*
		rákṣatha	*rak'en*
		rákṣanti	*rak'en*

The opposition between present stem and past participle, though in most cases the latter has been remodeled on the former, still survives in a few verbs:

Skt. *márate* "dies" : *mṛtáḥ* "dead" = Ry. *merel* : *mulo*.
" *yáti* "goes" : *gatáḥ* "gone" = " *ǰal* : *gelo*.

Romany has preserved the Sanskrit numerals 1 to 6, 10, 20 and 100 but 7, 8, 9 and higher numbers are borrowed—by Asiatic generally from Persian, by European from Greek—or are formed by various methods of addition or multiplication from existing numerals.

Vocabulary.—The borrowing of vocabulary has been extensive. The first examples can be dated back to the time when, leaving the central group of dialects in India, the gypsies sojourned among the speakers of the northwestern group. Indeed, the borrowed words of a Romany dialect disclose the itinerary of its migrations. When in the dialect of the gypsies of Wales there are borrowed words from Persian, Armenian, Greek, Rumanian, Bulgarian, Serbian, Czech, German, French and English, it may be assumed that at some time or other the ancestors of this particular group passed through the countries where these languages were spoken. The form in which the words appear may give some clue as to the date when they were borrowed. The most numerous source for the European dialects is Greek, a fact which accords with the long stay the gypsies appear to have made in the Eastern empire. *See* also GYPSY.

BIBLIOGRAPHY.—G. F. Black, *A Gypsy Bibliography* (1913); *Journal of the Gypsy Lore Society* (from 1888); J. Sampson, *The Dialect of the Gypsies of Wales* (1925), invaluable for the study of any gypsy dialect; R. L. Turner, *Position of Romani in Indo-Aryan* (1927); R. A. S. Macalister, *Language of the Nawar* (1914); F. N. Finck, *Sprache der armenischen Zigeuner* (1907); A. G. Paspati, *Les Tchinghianés de l'empire ottoman* (1870); R. von Sowa, *Die Mundart der slovakischen Zigeuner* (1887), *Wörterbuch des Dialekts der deutschen Zigeuner* (1898); B. C. Smart and H. J. Crofton, *The Dialect of the English Gypsies* (1875); F. Miklosich, *Mundarten der Zigeuner Europas* (1872–80); Albert Thomas Sinclair, "An American Romani Vocabulary," comp. and ed. by George F. Black, *New York Pub. Lib. Bull.*, vol. xix., pp. 727–738 (1915); Serboianu C. J. Popp, *Les Tsiganes, histoire, ethnographie, linguistique, grammaire, dictionnaire* (1930); Izydor Kopernicki, *Textes tsiganes* (1930); Eduard Hrkal, *Einführung in die mitteleuropäische Zigeuner-Sprache* (1940); Ragnvald Iversen, *Secret Languages in Norway* (1944–45); Brian S. Vesey-FitzGerald, *Gypsies of Britain* (1946); Dora Esther Yates, *My Gypsy Days: Recollections of a Romani Rawnie* (1953); Jules Bloch, *Les Tsiganes* (1953); Jan Kochanowski, *Gypsy Studies*, pts. I, II (1963); S. A. Wolf, *Grosses Wörterbuch der Zigeunersprache* (1960); R. L. Turner, *A Comparative Dictionary of the Indo-Aryan Languages* (1966).

(R. L. T.; ET. B.)

ROME (ROMA), a province of Italy, in the Lazio region. Area 2,066 sq.mi. (5,352 sq.km.). Pop. (1961) 2,842,268. The city of Rome represents nearly four-fifths of its population. The heart of the province is the lower valley of the Tiber; the Sabatini Mountains (north), the Sabini Mountains (east), and the Alban Hills (southeast) separate it from the provinces of Viterbo, Rieti, Frosinone, and Latina. Around the city is the Campagna di Roma, an undulating plain, much reclaimed from marsh in the 20th century. The province includes Lago di Bracciano in the north and Lago di Albano in the Alban Hills to the south. Notable places are Tivoli (*q.v.*), Velletri, Marino, Grottaferrata (with its castle-like monastery and fine wines), Albano Laziale (Roman camp), and Castel Gandolfo (the pope's summer residence and the Vatican Observatory). Rome is the focal point of transport in the Italian Peninsula, and the province is thus connected by rail and road with all parts of the country. The Leonardo da Vinci airport at

Fiumicino handles much of Italy's air traffic. Civitavecchia and Anzio are the principal fishing ports. Market gardening and dairying are important in the reclamation district of Maccarese on the lower Tiber and around Tivoli, and fruit and vines are grown in the Alban Hills. Industry is confined mainly to the city of Rome, its suburbs, and Civitavecchia. (G. Kн.)

ROME, capital city of the Italian Republic and of the province of Rome (*q.v.*). The seat of the Italian government, it is one of the great cultural centres of the world and, as the seat of the pope (in the Vatican City), it is also the administrative and spiritual capital of the Roman Catholic Church. Rome is on the Tiber (Tevere) River in central Italy, 15 mi. (24 km.) from the Tyrrhenian Sea, and is surrounded by the undulating plain of the Campagna di Roma (*q.v.*). Pop. (1961 census) 2,188,160; (1964 est.) 2,429,594. The Tiber flows through the city from north to south, the Seven Hills (the Capitoline, the Quirinal, the Viminal, the Esquiline, the Caelian, the Aventine, and the Palatine) being on the left bank of the river. The earliest settlement was on the Palatine, and from there the city spread until the Seven Hills were enclosed. On the right bank of the river are the Vatican City and the hills Monte Mario and Monte Gianicolo (Janiculum). The Tiber is unsuitable for navigation except for small vessels.

Proximity to the sea has influenced the climate, summer temperatures being high with little humidity and winter temperatures seldom falling as low as −3.8° C (25° F). The wettest season is the autumn, and the annual rainfall averages 33 in. (838 mm.).
(X.)

This article is divided into the following sections and subsections:

I. ARCHITECTURE AND ART
A. The Ancient City

1. Topography.—The location of Rome resembles that of the City of London in that it occupies the last point on the River Tiber at which higher ground approaches the water's edge on both banks,

offering, in conjunction with the Tiber island, an ideal crossing point. By classical times the growth of the delta and the progressive deterioration of the river's navigability had already led to the establishment of a river-mouth port, Ostia (*q.v.*), and most of the traffic between Ostia and Rome was by barge. But during the critical earliest centuries of the city's growth the Tiber was still the major traffic artery of central Italy, and it was Rome's location at the intersection of this and of the principal land route from Etruria to Latium and Campania that made it the natural political and economic centre of the whole region. The subsequent establishment of a network of main roads, and in modern times of railways, radiating from the same point perpetuated a situation first established by the logic of geography.

The detailed topography of the city from its first foundation until quite modern times has been largely determined by the character and disposition of the hills and valleys upon which it was established. Geologically the whole of the Campagna, the countryside of which Rome is the centre, is the product of the volcanic action which resulted in the hills and craters of the Bracciano Range (the Monti Sabatini) 20 mi. (32 km.) to the northwest, and those of the Alban Hills 15 mi. (24 km.) to the southeast. The ash and other debris from these eruptions built up a series of mainly horizontal and gently sloping stratified deposits, up to 100 ft. (30 m.) deep near Rome and far deeper nearer the Alban Hills. These deposits, bedded on the underlying Pliocene clay, comprise a variety of brownish tufas (cemented ash), ashes and cinders, cappellaccio or friable gray tufa, and temporary weathered surfaces, interrupted here and there by the hardened streams of lava that flowed from the craters from time to time.

Contrary to long-established belief, this volcanic activity took place long before historic times, the only record of prior human settlement being at Torrimpietra, near the coast 12 mi. (19 km.) to the west, where a Paleolithic (Acheulean and Mousterian) working floor was excavated in 1953–58 beneath the tufas characteristic of the latest eruptions of the Monti Sabatini series. Geologically speaking, however, the Roman Campagna is very recent and still in a state of very active erosion. In particular, the edges of the higher ground bordering the Tiber and its main tributaries are seamed with shallow, steep-sided, lateral valleys delimiting tongues of undulating higher ground that were ideally suited for primitive settlement. These projecting ridges, rising 60–80 ft. (18–24 m.) above the riverside plains, constitute the traditional "hills" of Rome, of which the highest point within the walls, at Porta Pia, is 128 ft. (39 m.) above sea level, compared with 39 ft. (12 m.) at the Forum.

The difference in level between the various quarters that came to be comprised within the city boundaries, though superficially much altered by human activity, have remained at all periods a cardinal factor in the city's topography. The initial settlement took place on the hills nearest the river, gradually spreading down into and draining the adjoining valleys. In the later Republic two large new areas were made available: the higher ground at some distance from the river by the building of high-level aqueducts; and the Campus Martius, the stretch of low-lying ground within the bend of the river, as a result of drainage and the embankment of the river itself.

At its maximum extent in the 3rd century A.D. the city came to occupy the whole area within the Aurelian Walls, an area of 4 sq.mi. (10 sq.km.) with a population variously calculated at 800,-000 to 1,200,000. In the early Middle Ages the destruction of the aqueducts made the higher ground once more virtually uninhabitable, and with the steady dwindling of the population to a mere 35,000 in the later Middle Ages the medieval town came to be concentrated almost entirely on the riverside plains in and around the Campus Martius and across the river in Trastevere. It was not until the reactivation of the Acqua Felice, the first of the new high-level aqueducts, by Pope Sixtus V in 1586–89 that the city was once more able to expand upward and outward toward its ancient limits. The process was still far from complete by 1870, when there were still large areas of parkland, vineyards, and market gardens within the circuit of the Walls of Aurelian.

2. The First Settlements.—The Roman Campagna was one of

the last areas of central Italy to be settled. There are substantial traces of Neolithic and Bronze Age settlements along the coast, in the Sabine and Volscian hills, and here and there along the Tiber Valley, but penetration into the forests that covered the rest of the countryside seems to have been local and sporadic. Then about 1000 B.C. there was an extensive and complex movement of many small but related groups of peoples, affecting the whole western coastal area of central Italy, with repercussions as far afield as Lucania (Sala Consilina), the Aeolian Islands, and Sicily (Morgantina). The precise affiliations of this movement are disputed, but it was certainly related to the broader movement of the Late Bronze Age Urnfield peoples of the Danube Basin and central Europe, and it incorporated elements of the Bronze Age populations of central Italy. The upshot was the establishment of the settlements from which the historic peoples of southern Etruria and Latium were derived: to the north of the river the Villanovans, who established the cultural and political framework within which the historical Etruscan civilization developed; and closely related to, but distinct from them, a group of peoples who spoke Latin, a branch of the Indo-European family of languages, and who settled predominantly south of the river.

The later traditions which attributed the foundation of Rome to refugees from Alba Longa, united with elements drawn from the Sabine peoples, is now known to be substantially founded on fact. Already in the Bronze Age there had been a small riverside settlement, perhaps on the Aventine, the remains of which have been found in deposits of earth that were used later to raise the level of the adjoining Forum Boarium. In the Early Iron Age, probably toward the middle of the 8th century, this settlement was superseded or absorbed by immigrant groups of shepherd farmers, who took possession of the hills overlooking the river crossing and the Forum Valley (notably the Palatine, though not at this early date the Capitoline). Excavation has revealed their huts on the Palatine and an important, predominantly cremation cemetery at the east end of the Forum, the utensils and pottery in both cases attesting a close relationship with the contemporary or slightly earlier settlements on the Alban Hills. Once established, they were soon joined by the peoples whose remains have been found on the Esquiline and Quirinal ridges. Though closely related, the latter buried their dead and their affinities are with the older settlements of the Sabine Hills.

There is much still to be learned about the stages by which the several communities, consisting at first probably of a loose grouping of small villages, each retaining a certain independence within the larger unit, gradually coalesced into a closer association. The processes of urbanization were greatly hastened by the Etruscan domination of the city in the 6th century B.C. To this or to the immediately preceding period belong the drainage and first paving of the Forum Valley (about 575 B.C.) to serve as a common centre for the adjoining village communities; the introduction of the building methods already established in Etruria; the extensive importation of luxury goods, including Corinthian and, later, Attic pottery; the spread of settlement down into the valleys and over the adjoining uplands; and, shortly before 500 B.C., the building on the Capitoline of a large state temple to Jupiter, Juno, and Minerva.

The so-called Servian Wall, a rampart and wall enclosing the Palatine, Capitoline, Quirinal, Viminal, and Aventine, and most of the Esquiline and Caelian hills, is substantially a later monument, dating almost certainly from 378 B.C. With the possible exception, however, of the southern hills (Caelian, Aventine) for which evidence is lacking, the greater part of the area within it had already been occupied before the Etruscan kings were expelled, an event which took place traditionally in 509 B.C. (or, as one school of archaeologists believes, 25 to 30 years later); and there is reason to believe that across the northern hills the Servian Wall was built into an earlier rampart, of early Republican or even late regal date. By then the essential framework within which the centre of Rome was to develop had already been established.

3. Building Methods and Materials.—The buildings of the earliest settlements were simple huts (*capanne*) of wickerwork plastered with clay upon a timber framework, as represented in the hut urns of the Forum cemetery; and as late as the end of the Republic the normal materials for domestic use were timber and mud brick. Monumental architecture in more durable materials was first introduced by the Etruscans in the 6th century B.C. The local volcanic tufa lent itself to quarrying in large squared blocks, which for many centuries remained the normal building practice for the walls of temples and other public buildings. The softer tufas were regularly faced with stucco, to weatherproof them. Columns, architraves, and roofs were of timber, the exposed surfaces of which were faced with brightly painted revetments of molded terra cotta. It is these architectural terra cottas that constitute the principal direct sources for knowledge of Roman monumental architecture in this early, etruscanizing phase.

Before the Gallic fire of c. 390 B.C. practically the only building stone in use was the soft gray tufa called cappellaccio, quarried at the foot of the Capitol. The capture of Veii in 396 B.C. made available the more uniformly textured yellowish-gray tufa of Grotta Oscura, 6 mi. (10 km.) N of the city near the Tiber, which remained the most popular building material for the next two centuries. Though more durable than cappellaccio, it was still far from satisfactory and accordingly, during the 3rd century, the stronger, dark-gray tufa (*lapis Albanus, peperino*) of the Alban Hills began to come into use, followed soon afterward by the similar though rather coarser Gabine stone from the quarries beside the Gabine Lake, a volcanic crater 12 mi. (19 km.) E of Rome. These were better-quality stones and their introduction made it possible increasingly to substitute stone for the traditional timber of columns and architraves; but they were also expensive to transport and were normally used in conjunction with softer local tufas, the latter being relegated to positions of secondary structural importance. Under the late Republic and early Empire such differential uses of materials were normal.

During this period the tufa in common use was the cheap, durable, brown stone from the Anio Valley just above Rome, which was discovered in time to be used for the building of the Aqua Marcia (144 B.C.). Together with travertine and marble, it is the building stone most widely represented in the surviving monuments. Travertine, the splendid silvery-gray stone of the Colosseum, the Farnese Palace, St. Peter's, and countless other Roman monuments, is a limestone of recent origin. Soft and easily worked when first exposed, it soon hardens on exposure. The quarries at Bagni di Tivoli, which are still worked, are on level ground and escaped attention until the latter part of the 2nd century B.C.; but thereafter for nearly two centuries travertine was used in Rome in very large quantities both for its strength and for its handsome appearance.

The other materials that made their appearance under the late Republic were marble and concrete. Marble, first imported as a luxury material from Greece soon after 150 B.C., was important also at first as the medium for the introduction of a whole new set of building styles and practices, based on Hellenistic rather than Etruscan models. Then, with the opening up of the quarries at Carrara about 40 B.C., it became the fine building material par excellence of Augustan Rome, a position which—supplemented by the ever-increasing importation of marbles, porphyries, and granites from Greece, Egypt, and Africa—it retained throughout antiquity.

Less showy, but of even greater architectural and structural importance, was Roman concrete, which makes a first tentative appearance in the form of random mortared rubblework during the 3rd century B.C. and was already used for substantial vaulted buildings in the 2nd century (e.g., the Porticus Aemilia, 193 B.C.) but which was not finally perfected until Augustan times. It was essentially a hydraulic cement, used normally with an aggregate of tufa, tile, or whatever other material was available, and it derived its unique strength from the properties of the dark volcanic ash (pozzolana) of the Roman subsoil, which was employed as a substitute for sand. Used at first as an inert fill for ramparts and platforms, it proved to be cheap, easy to handle, and very strong. The development of concrete barrel vaulting in place of the traditional flat timber roof opened up important new constructional fields. Together with the perfection of the material and the realization that it could be used to create architectural forms that were no longer restricted by the limitations of the traditional building materials, it paved the way for the revolution in architectural thinking which is Rome's great original contribution to the history of classical art. The key monuments of this revolution, which falls between A.D. 65 and about 135, are all in or near Rome: Nero's Golden House, Domitian's Palace, the Pantheon, Hadrian's Villa near Tivoli. It was in these buildings that the concept of architecture as the organization of interior space first found conscious expression, an event which can fairly be claimed as changing the whole subsequent history of European architecture.

Roman concrete was normally used in conjunction with other materials, at first stone and then, from Augustan times onward, increasingly brick and tile. It is important to realize, however, that although these secondary materials served a purpose during construction, helping to contain the concrete core while it was drying out, and also gave a decorous finish to the completed building, the essential structure was that of the concrete itself. Brick was never used in classical Rome as a material in its own right. The brickyards lay just outside Rome in the Tiber Valley and beyond the Vatican Hill, and many of them came in time to be organized for very large-scale production. The stamped trademarks of the individual yards are a valuable aid to the chronology of the buildings in which they were used.

4. Town Walls.—On both the Palatine and the Capitoline hills there are traces of defensive walling that may date from the 6th century B.C., and in the 5th century there was probably an earthen rampart and ditch across the exposed northeastern flank of the Quirinal and Esquiline promontories. The first continuous defensive wall, incorporating parts of these earlier fortifications, was the so-called Servian Wall, built in the early 4th century B.C. after the Gallic disaster, a representative stretch of which, denuded of its earthwork, can be seen just outside the modern railway station. By the 3rd century B.C. the area it enclosed (about 800 ac. [325 ha.]) was proving inadequate for the city's growing needs; but although the formal city limits (pomerium) were extended on numerous occasions, Rome for many centuries felt no need of fresh defenses. The great wall of brick-faced concrete which was Rome's defense throughout the Middle Ages, and which as late as 1870 had to be assaulted and breached by Raffaele Cadorna's troops, was begun by Aurelian in A.D. 270. Nearly 10 mi. (16 km.) long and enclosing an area of about 4 sq.mi. (10 sq.km.), it marks the approximate maximum extension of the classical city. The principal gateways were rebuilt by Honorius and Arcadius in A.D. 401–403.

5. Aqueducts.—The first aqueduct was built in 312 B.C. by Appius Claudius. It was 7 mi. (11 km.) in length and ran underground. The first of the high-level aqueducts, the Aqua Marcia, followed in 144 B.C., bringing an abundance of excellent water from the Sabine Hills, 44 mi. (71 km.) away. In order to serve the higher ground within the city it was raised on arches where it crossed the plain outside the walls, an example that was followed by later builders, among whom Augustus, Agrippa, Claudius, and Trajan were outstanding. Within the city there was elaborate provision for distributing the water in conduits and lead piping to individual quarters and buildings on a scale unequaled until the present century. (*See* further AQUEDUCT.)

6. The Forum.—Nowhere in Rome has human activity done more to alter the natural contours of the landscape than in the area of the Forum. It is not merely that the modern ground level has risen by as much as 50 ft. (15 m.) in the valley bottom. In laying out the Via dei Fori Imperiali, Mussolini was only completing the work of Vespasian and of Trajan in cutting away the saddles of higher ground which once linked the Quirinal and the Esquiline with the Capitoline and Palatine hills respectively. The drainage of this whole area passed, and still passes, through the narrow gap between the Capitoline and the Palatine, and when the adjoining hills were first settled the open space just above the gap was a marshy valley, around the edges of which accumulated the rubbish and building debris from the settlements on the higher ground. Along the western edge of it, flanking the southern extremity of the Esquiline and the western slopes of the Velia, the saddle between the Esquiline and the Palatine, there grew up the extensive cemetery which, together with the excavated hut sites on the Palatine, is the principal source of detailed information about the earliest stages of the city's history. Three monuments of the classical period preserved memories of the same pre-urban period: the Lacus Curtius, on the site of an open pool in the centre, and the Lacus Servilius and the Lacus Juturnae, marking the sites of springs at the foot of the Capitoline and Palatine hills respectively. The former disappeared during the early Empire, but the latter survived and was restored in 1953 to the form which it bore in Augustan times.

The line of the Cloaca Maxima, running obliquely across the later Forum, marks the approximate line of the original valley-bottom stream. Although little of the surviving structure is as early as the traditional 6th-century date of the Cloaca, the original canalization of the stream must have taken place when the valley between the early communities on the several hills was first laid out to serve as a meeting place common to all of them. Stratigraphic excavations near the centre of the later paved area and again near the east end date this event about 575 B.C.

The topography of the successive phases of the Republican Forum has been the subject of much learned controversy. With the exception of a few venerable monuments, few of the remains now visible are earlier than the time of Caesar and Augustus, when the Forum paving reached the level to which it has now once more been excavated; and although many of the Imperial buildings perpetuate the names and approximate positions of earlier monuments, not all of these by any means are on the exact sites of their predecessors. Trial excavations in depth undertaken since World War II have done much to clarify the chronology but have yielded little detailed information about the buildings themselves. There remain a great many points upon which, in the present state of knowledge, one can only speculate.

In its broad outlines the development is clear enough. From the outset the Forum served a multiplicity of purposes—market, place of political assembly, lawcourt, a setting for parades and spectacles, the natural location for temples and public buildings of all sorts. Many of these aspects came in time to be housed elsewhere, but many others, particularly those with religious connotations, remained to shape the later development. Among the later buildings of which the origins date back to the early days of the Republic were the temples of Castor and Pollux, Janus, Saturn, and Vesta; the Regia, the office of the *pontifex maximus;* and the group of buildings at the northwestern corner of the Forum, associated with the Curia and the Comitium.

The central area, itself a formally consecrated monument, was an open space, roughly trapezoidal in shape, measuring about 125 by 70 ft. (38 by 21 m.). On it converged a number of streets. The Via Sacra, which crossed the area longitudinally, entered near the northeastern corner beside the Regia through an arch (the Fornix Fabianus), leaving it at the southwestern corner under the name of the Clivus Capitolinus, which led up to the Temple of

AQUA ALEXANDRIANA, BUILT ABOUT A.D. 226

Jupiter and the citadel. Descending the valley from the Quirinal and the Viminal by the Argiletum, one entered near the Temple of Janus, beside the Curia. The Clivus Argentarius, from the Campus Martius, entered at the northwestern corner. Of the two streets leading up the valley from the Forum Boarium, the Vicus Jugarius entered at the southwestern corner, beside the Temple of Saturn, and the Vicus Tuscus near the southeastern corner, between the Temple of Castor and Pollux and the Basilica Julia. Along the south and north sides were two rows of shops, the Tabernae Veteres and Novae respectively, and to a late Republican date there were still private houses near enough to overlook the central space.

The first large civil buildings were the great Republican basilicas, open columnar halls designed to serve as covered extensions of the main open space, the sanctity of which was preserved by building them alongside. The first was the Basilica Porcia (184 B.C.), west of the Comitium; it was burned in 52 B.C. and never rebuilt. The Basilica Aemilia followed in 179 B.C. behind the Tabernae Novae, and opposite it nine years later the Basilica Sempronia, behind the Tabernae Veteres, on the site later occupied by the Basilica Julia. With the construction of the two latter, and the addition in 78 B.C. of the Tabularium at the west end, up against the steep slopes of the Capitoline, the haphazard layout of the Forum began to assume a certain monumental character. It was Caesar, however, who completed the process. Hitherto the Comitium, the political assembly, had been a virtually independent open space opening off the northwest corner of the main Forum and separated from it by the Rostra, the orator's tribunal, which stood between the two, facing northward across the Comitium toward the Curia. Caesar moved the Rostra to the centre of the west side of the main Forum, facing axially down it; and the Curia, burned together with the Basilica Porcia in the riots following Clodius' funeral, he brought forward to the position adjoining the main square which it was to occupy thereafter throughout antiquity. With the construction shortly after his death of the Temple of Divus Julius facing axially down the Forum from the opposite end, the essential layout of the Forum as we see it today was complete.

The description that follows describes the monuments in clockwise order, starting from the northwest corner. For convenience in reading, the names of major structures are italicized at the beginning of a description.

The *Carcer* or *Tullianum* ("Mamertine Prison") took the place, as death chamber, of the old quarry caverns beneath the northeast corner of the Capitoline. The original structure, a truncated cone of Alban stone entered only by a trapdoor in the roof, dates from the 3rd century B.C.; the existing travertine facade, the last of a series of additions and modifications, dates from the time of Tiberius. This is the chamber where noted prisoners like Jugurtha, the Catilinarian conspirators, and Vercingetorix were kept before execution.

Below it, on the lowest slopes of the hillside and stretching out into the open valley, lay the political centre of early Rome, the Comitium. The stretch of pavement now visible between the Curia and the Arch of Severus is only a part of the original area, which until the time of Caesar extended farther to the north. In and beneath it can be seen a number of venerable remains, including those of the *Republican Rostra* and of the group of structures associated with the much-discussed inscribed archaic stele. The Rostra, the scene of Rome's early legislative struggles, took its name from the iron rams (*rostra*) taken as trophies from the warships of Antium (338 B.C.) and fastened on the back of the platform, facing the Forum. The stele, already damaged when buried, bears the lower part of a boustrophedon inscription in lettering which can hardly be later than about 500 B.C. The language is a very archaic Latin, and, although the content of the text is controversial, it was certainly religious in character, stipulating certain duties of the priestly *rex*, perhaps in connection with the prevention of evil omens. The adjoining remains include a tapering drum, which may have carried a statue, and the lower part of a double base with Tuscan moldings, said by Varro to have supported two lions and possibly funerary in character. Being sacred, the group was carefully buried and marked by a slab of black Greek marble,

the *lapis niger,* when Sulla rebuilt the Rostra and repaved the whole area.

Of the other buildings associated with the Republican Comitium only the *Curia* (Senate House) is now visible, and that in the position to which it was moved by Caesar. The present building is the work of Diocletian after the fire of A.D. 284. The evidence of coins suggests that, except for the omission of a low portico in front, it repeats closely the design of its predecessors, a gabled building with a single large door and three windows above it. The bronze door is a replica of the Diocletianic door, now in the Church of St. John Lateran. The bare brick of the facade was faced with marble and with stucco imitating masonry. Inside can be seen the handsome (partly restored) marble intarsia floor and the steps for the wooden stools of the senators and the two consuls and the base for the altar of Victory, the building's presiding divinity. Also housed here for safety are the *Anaglypha Traiani,* two marble reliefs showing the buildings of the Forum as they were about A.D. 100. The Curia survived the Middle Ages as a church, dedicated to S. Adriano in A.D. 630, and it was restored to its original form and level in 1938. The adjoining Church of SS. Luca e Martina similarly incorporates remains of the Secretarium Senatus, the senatorial archives.

East of the Curia, across the Argiletum, lay the *Basilica Aemilia*. The scanty surviving remains are those of the Augustan rebuilding, after the fire of 14 B.C., modified and enriched as to its upper story in A.D. 22. The shops along the facade replaced the former Tabernae Novae, and there were galleries facing both inward on to the central hall and outward on to the Forum. One of the first buildings in Rome to make lavish use of imported coloured marble, it was ranked by Pliny as one of the three finest buildings of the capital. The date of the marble frieze from the lower of the two classical orders of the interior, portraying scenes from the legendary history of early Rome, is controversial; it is most likely that it was reincorporated in the Augustan structure from one of its predecessors, perhaps that of 34 B.C. The foundations exposed near the west end are those of the Republican basilica.

East of the basilica stands the temple dedicated in A.D. 141 to *Faustina*, deified wife of Antoninus Pius, and after his death to *Antoninus* himself. It was preserved through the Middle Ages as the Church of S. Lorenzo in Miranda, the door of which marks the height (39 ft. [12 m.]) above the classical pavement to which the ground level within the Forum had risen since classical times by the 17th century. Opposite it stood the Regia, one of the earliest buildings of Rome. By tradition the residence of Numa Pompilius, it became the office of the *pontifex maximus,* who succeeded to the priestly duties of the monarchy. It occupied an elongated triangular site between the two branches of the Via Sacra, which forked at this point, the two branches passing along the northern and the southern edges respectively of the Forum. The left-hand branch is certainly a very ancient feature, and the early foundations of the Regia were aligned upon it. Like the adjoining buildings it suffered badly at the hands of medieval lime burners and Renaissance marble robbers. The scanty remains are chiefly those of the building of 36 B.C., one of the earliest monuments in Rome to be built of marble from the newly opened quarries near Carrara.

Across the street lay the *Domus Publica*, the official residence of the *pontifex*, and beside and to the west of it the Atrium Vestae, the House of the Vestal Virgins, whose task it was to tend the sacred flame in the *Temple of Vesta*. The circular form of the temple, which stood just west of the Atrium Vestae, was traditional, deriving originally from that of a timber hut, but although the cult was of great antiquity, the flame symbolizing the well-being of the city, the only remains now visible are of much later date. The foundations and podium are from the reconstruction of the building in marble undertaken by Augustus in 14–12 B.C., as portrayed in a relief now in the Uffizi in Florence. The partially restored superstructure is the work of Julia Domna, wife of Septimius Severus, after the fire of A.D. 191. The cult was one of the last pagan cults to be suppressed, by Theodosius in 394. The well-preserved remains of the *Atrium Vestae*, consisting of a spacious central courtyard surrounded by two stories of marble porticoes from which suites of rooms opened off, date from after the fire of A.D. 64, with additions and alterations by Trajan, Hadrian, and Septimius Severus. Around the courtyard are the bases of statues in honour of distinguished Vestals. The building now visible follows the Neronian alignment, but here and there can be seen remains of the earlier, smaller buildings, aligned on the Via Sacra, including (near the northeast corner) those of the Caesarian Domus Publica, which Augustus handed over to the Vestals in 12 B.C., when he transferred his residence to the Palatine.

After passing the Temple of Vesta the Via Sacra entered the Forum between, on the left, the Temple of Castor and Pollux and on the right, closing the eastern end of the paved area, the Temple of the Deified Caesar (Divus Julius). Between the two stood the *Arch of Augustus*. Originally a single arch built in 29 B.C. to commemorate the victory of Actium, it was enlarged to form a triple arch in 19 B.C., after the recovery of the standards captured by the Parthians from Crassus. On the walls of the arches were inscribed the *Fasti consulares,* the official lists of eponymous magistrates since the foundation of the Republic, the surviving fragments of which are now in the Conservatori Museum.

The *Temple of Castor and Pollux* dates back to 484 B.C., commemorating the divine intervention of the twins at the Battle of Lake Regillus (*see* CASTOR AND POLLUX). Parts of the original podium, in blocks of cappellaccio, and of its replacement in concrete faced with tufa are preserved within the surviving structure, which is that dedicated by Tiberius in A.D. 6. The core of the latter was of concrete faced with travertine and tufa, the outer facing and the superstructure, including the three standing columns (since the Middle Ages one of the landmarks of the Forum area), of Carrara marble. Castor and Pollux were the patron deities of the Roman knights, and the temple not only became their official meeting place and an unofficial centre of the city's commercial interests, but also it came to include in the basements safe deposits and a bureau of weights and measures.

Of the *Temple of the Deified Caesar,* dedicated in 29 B.C., all that remains is part of the concrete core and the partly reconstructed front of the podium. Of the temple itself, which was a lofty Ionic building, only a few fragments are preserved. A semicircular recess in the centre of the facade marks the position either of the marble column erected immediately after Caesar's death to mark the spot where his body was cremated or else of the altar that accompanied it.

The very large brick structure behind the Temple of Castor and

Pollux, long thought to be the Temple of Augustus, is in fact the *Vestibule* or official entrance to the Flavian Palace on the Palatine. It comprises the vestibule proper, a large chamber decorated with niches and once vaulted, a series of guardrooms, and a broad ramp zigzagging up to the plateau above. The site of the guardroom was converted in the early Middle Ages into the Church of Sta. Maria Antiqua, remarkable for its series of wall paintings dating from the 7th, 8th, and 9th centuries. Beyond the Vestibule, along the Vicus Tuscus, is a warehouse, the Horrea Agrippiana, and across the street, as yet unexcavated, lay the Temple of Augustus.

The whole of the south side of the Forum was occupied by the *Basilica Julia,* begun by Caesar in 54 B.C. on the site of the Tabernae Veteres and the Basilica Sempronia. It was destroyed by fire soon

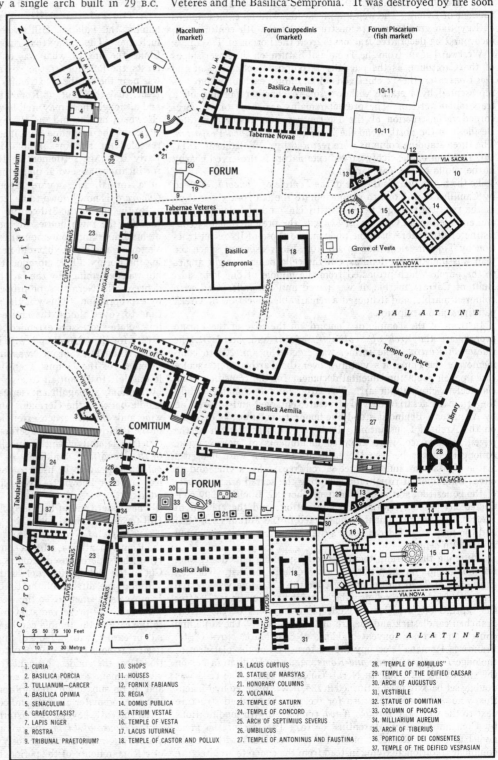

1. CURIA
2. BASILICA PORCIA
3. TULLIANUM—CARCER
4. BASILICA OPIMIA
5. SENACULUM
6. GRAECOSTASIS?
7. LAPIS NIGER
8. ROSTRA
9. TRIBUNAL PRAETORIUM?
10. SHOPS
11. HOUSES
12. FORNIX FABIANUS
13. REGIA
14. DOMUS PUBLICA
15. ATRIUM VESTAE
16. TEMPLE OF VESTA
17. LACUS IUTURNAE
18. TEMPLE OF CASTOR AND POLLUX
19. LACUS CURTIUS
20. STATUE OF MARSYAS
21. HONORARY COLUMNS
22. VOLCANAL
23. TEMPLE OF SATURN
24. TEMPLE OF CONCORD
25. ARCH OF SEPTIMIUS SEVERUS
26. UMBILICUS
27. TEMPLE OF ANTONINUS AND FAUSTINA
28. "TEMPLE OF ROMULUS"
29. TEMPLE OF THE DEIFIED CAESAR
30. ARCH OF AUGUSTUS
31. VESTIBULE
32. STATUE OF DOMITIAN
33. COLUMN OF PHOCAS
34. MILLIARIUM AUREUM
35. ARCH OF TIBERIUS
36. PORTICO OF DEI CONSENTES
37. TEMPLE OF THE DEIFIED VESPASIAN

THE FORUM ROMANUM: (TOP) THE REPUBLICAN PERIOD; (BOTTOM) THE IMPERIAL PERIOD

after, and again in A.D. 284. The scanty surviving remains follow substantially the lines of the building dedicated by Augustus in A.D. 12. It consisted of a lofty central hall surrounded by two stories of ambulatory galleries and was subdivided internally by curtains or partitions for use as a lawcourt. Along the back can be seen the row of shops and offices that replaced the old Tabernae. Immediately to the west of the basilica, across the Vicus Jugarius, lay the *Temple of Saturn*. One of the oldest temples in Rome (traditionally 497 B.C.), from its proximity to the Senate House it came to be used for the storage of state money, the vaults serving as the Aerarium, or state treasury. The surviving podium and a few fragments of the marble superstructure date from its rebuilding *c.* 30–22 B.C. by Munatius Plancus, the founder of Lyons. The well-known facade, with its eight columns of Egyptian granite, is a reconstruction of the 4th century A.D., incorporating decorative fragments from the Forum of Trajan.

Westward again from the Temple of Saturn, on the lower slopes of the Capitoline, is the partially recomposed colonnade of the *Dei Consentes,* the 12 chief gods of Olympus, each of whom was represented by a statue within a square chamber opening off a trapezoidal portico. The present remains are those of an unrecorded reconstruction of the 1st century A.D., restored in 367. Beside it to the north stood the *Temple of the Deified Vespasian*. The three standing columns were restored by G. Valadier in 1811, and a section of the richly carved entablature is preserved nearby in the vaults of the Tabularium.

To the north again is the site of the *Temple of Concord*. Vowed by Camillus in 367 B.C. to commemorate the temporary cessation of the political struggle between patricians and plebeians, rebuilt and enlarged by L. Opimius in 121 B.C., the present remains, consisting of little more than the podium, are those of its reconstruction by Tiberius, dedicated in A.D. 10. For reasons of space the plan was unusual, the long axis of the cella being at right angles to the porch, which projected from the middle of one long side. Built of Carrara marble, it was paved and its walls faced with coloured marble, and it housed a remarkable collection of Greek paintings and sculpture.

In front of the Temple of Concord, on the edge of the Forum proper, are the *Arch of Septimius Severus* and, beside it, the *Caesarian Rostra*. The former was erected in A.D. 203 to commemorate the emperor's victories over the Parthians; its sculptured panels are a fundamental document for the transition from classical to late antique art. The latter is of two main periods, the original Caesarian curved structure, enlarged and squared off by Augustus. Behind it stood five honorary columns, as depicted on the Arch of Constantine. In front, down the length of the paved open space, were crowded monuments of every period. Among them can be seen the enclosure in which were housed a statue of Marsyas and the three sacred trees, a fig, a vine, and an olive; a number of ritual pits delimiting the sacred area; the site of the equestrian statue of Domitian, where G. Boni in 1899 conducted his pioneer stratigraphic excavation; and the column of Phocas, the last monument to be erected in the Forum (A.D. 608) and the first to be cleared when systematic excavation was begun in the 19th century.

Adjoining the Forum, though strictly speaking outside it, were the monuments on the Velia, the low saddle to the east. The elegant *Arch of Titus* on the crest astride the Via Sacra was erected after his death. The reliefs, which depict his triumph in 71 after the capture of Jerusalem, include representations of the seven-branched candlestick and the ark of the covenant. The adjoining church and former convent buildings of Sta. Maria Nova ("Sta. Francesca Romana") occupy the western part of the platform of the huge *Temple of Venus and Rome*, begun by Hadrian in 121 on the site of the vestibule to Nero's Golden House. The cella was double, set back to back. Burned in 284, it was restored by Maxentius, who was responsible also for the gigantic vaulted structure next to the west, the *Basilica Nova*, completed with modifications by Constantine after Maxentius' death. The last of the great civil basilicas of Rome, it marked a decisive break with the old columnar tradition, deriving instead from the concrete architecture of the great Imperial bath buildings. The three standing arches,

together with three identical arches facing them, buttressed a grandiose central hall, 265 ft. long by 78 ft. wide (81 by 24 m.) and 108 ft. (33 m.) from the pavement to the crown of the vault. It fell probably in the earthquake of 847.

Maxentius also built the small circular building next to the west (so-called *Temple of Romulus*), the projecting wings and reentrant forecourt of which illustrate the Baroque character of much of this late Imperial architecture. In the 6th century it became the vestibule for the Church of SS. Cosmas and Damian. The bronze doorway is original. The confused medley of foundations that occupies the western slopes of the Velia in front of these buildings include all that remains of Nero's grandiose monumentalization of the approach to his palace from the Forum.

7. The Palatine Hill.—Tradition and archaeology agree in naming the Palatine Hill as the site of the earliest settlement in Rome. The valley that runs up from the Arch of Titus continues the line of what was once a saddle between two distinct crests, the Palatium to the east and the Germalus to the west. It was near the southern extremity of the Germalus, overlooking the river, that the "hut of Romulus" stood in later classical times; and although there may well have been other groups of early huts elsewhere on the hill, as there certainly were on the adjoining slopes of the Esquiline Hill, it is here that excavation has in fact revealed the remains of huts dating from the earliest phase of Early Iron Age settlement in Rome. There are traces of early fortifications at several points on the Germalus, but the tradition of a formal, four-square layout of the primitive city, *Roma Quadrata,* is now known to be late and mistaken.

By the end of the 3rd century B.C. the hill was a favoured location for the town houses of the wealthy, and Cicero and many of his important contemporaries owned houses along the Clivus Victoriae, the street that ran near the crest of the hill, overlooking the Forum. The subsequent architectural development of the hill was determined by the fact that Augustus established his residence on the Germalus, on property acquired through his wife and by expropriation. This was the nucleus of a palace which came in time to cover almost the entire Palatine Hill. Tiberius and his immediate successors extended it over the whole of the Germalus except for the western end, with its venerable monuments. Nero's work, though extensive, was incidental to his more grandiose schemes for the Domus Transitoria and the Golden House, and it was left to Domitian to give the palace an architectural unity by building a magnificent series of state apartments across the saddle between the Germalus and the Palatium, with a domestic wing and sunken garden extending over most of the western end of the Palatium. Later emperors, notably Septimius Severus, were concerned mainly with the embellishment and southward extension of the Domitianic building. As early as Augustus' day the word *palatium* began to be used to designate the imperial palace. The last emperor known to have repaired and occupied it was Theodoric.

The western end of the Germalus is the only part of the Palatine Hill to have retained something of its pre-Imperial physiognomy. The *Temple of Cybele,* the first of the Oriental divinities to join the Roman pantheon, offers a convenient reference point for identifying the superimposed remains of seven centuries of habitation. Cut in the bedrock in front of the temple steps are the postholes and drainage ditches of the timber-and-daub huts of the original Iron Age settlement. To the west of this, on the edge of the Hill, there is a well-preserved stretch of the archaic fortifications, and to the east of the temple can be seen a cistern of the 5th century B.C. or earlier, with a vault of fine corbeled masonry. The temple itself was built in 204–191 B.C. to house an image (nonrepresentational) of the goddess brought from Pessinus in Phrygia; the surviving remains are those of a reconstruction undertaken in 110 B.C. and of its subsequent restoration by Augustus in the traditional manner and materials, tufa and concrete with a facing of stucco.

To the east, beyond the cistern, are the well-preserved remains of the *House of Livia*, the private residence of Augustus. Built about 50 B.C. and never seriously modified, it offers a vivid picture of a Roman house of the period, including an outstanding series of wall paintings of the so-called second style. Beyond it to the southeast are the remains of other contemporary houses with paintings, preserved by their incorporation within the substructures of the buildings added by Augustus to this nucleus. The central feature of these was the great *Temple of Apollo,* erected in 28 B.C., a large and elaborate building of Luna marble facing on to an open space framed by porticoes of Numidian marble and a pair of libraries, one Greek and one Latin. Of this, one of the richest and most lavishly adorned buildings of its day, hardly anything has survived except foundations, still only partly excavated. The visible remains of the libraries date from their reconstruction by Domitian after the fire of A.D. 64.

The rest of the Germalus was occupied by the rectangular platform of the *Domus Tiberiana,* most of it still covered by the Farnese Gardens. Built by Tiberius, it was gradually extended northward by his successors, linking up with and dominating the Forum. Caligula added a wing at the foot of the hill behind the Temple of Castor and Pollux to serve as a formal entrance to the palace; only scanty traces of this survived the grandiose remodeling of the area by Domitian, to whom are due the present Vestibule and guardrooms (now Sta. Maria Antiqua) and the great zigzag ramp up to the hilltop. The arched platform thrown out across the Clivus Victoriae, now such a prominent and picturesque feature of the Forum landscape, is the work of Trajan and Hadrian. A large covered corridor (cryptoporticus) marking the eastern limit of the Tiberian building was added by Nero.

Immediately to the southeast of the Domus Tiberiana, terraced high above the saddle between the Germalus and the Palatium, are the impressive ruins of the official wing of Domitian's palace, the *Domus Augustiana.* The facade, which faced north, opened into a basilica, used when the emperor sat in judgment, a large ceremonial audience hall, and a smaller room which may have been associated with the imperial cult. Beyond this suite lay a spacious peristyle garden with a central fountain, off the far end of which opened a state banqueting hall, flanked by two fountain courtyards. The official wing constituted the west wing of the Flavian Palace. Corresponding to it on the east side was an elongated circus-shaped sunken garden, suitable for the holding of parades or displays, and between the two, set back from the north frontage beyond a pair of colonnaded courtyard gardens, lay the domestic wing. This was built at a lower level, the surviving remains being those of the two main floors and a mezzanine floor grouped around a square, two-storied, porticoed courtyard with an elaborate central fountain. The rear facade opened on to the Circus Maximus, with the imperial box as its central feature.

The whole palace, the work of the architect Rabirius, is a landmark in the history of Roman concrete architecture. The barrel vault over the basilica was of unprecedented size, and throughout the building curvilinear walls and vaults display a new and significant interest in the properties of interior space. Other notable features are the Baroque fountains, the lavish use of imported marbles, and the central heating of the banqueting hall. The bath building beyond the sunken garden and the lofty, arched substructures at the southeast end of the hill, overlooking the Circus Maximus, were added by Septimius Severus, who was responsible also for the Septizodium (demolished in 1588), a three-tiered columnar structure resembling the stage building of a Roman theatre, erected as a decorative screen opposite the end of the Via Appia.

Incorporated within the foundation platform of the official wing are the well-preserved remains of a number of the buildings that previously stood on the open ground of the saddle between the Germalus and the Palatium. The "House of the Griffins" is a residence of the time of Cicero, noteworthy for its stuccoes, architectural wall paintings, and pavements. A painted hall adjoining it, with Egyptian motifs, is probably part of a building devoted to the cult of Isis established by Caligula; it was destroyed by Nero to make way for a circular building, perhaps a fish pool. Also Neronian, destroyed in the fire of A.D. 64, is a richly decorated nymphaeum beneath the Domitianic banqueting hall.

The northern spur of the Palatium occupied by the churches of S. Bonaventura and S. Sebastiano is still largely unexcavated. The terrace overlooking the Arch of Titus carried a large temple which is only partly explored. Originally dedicated to Augustus and the other deified Caesars, the present structure is that of Elagabalus' Temple of the Sun, rededicated by his successor, Alexander Severus, to Jupiter the Avenger.

8. The Capitoline Hill.—Though not apparently part of the original Iron Age settlement, the Capitoline Hill at a very early date was incorporated to serve as the fortress and chief sanctuary of the archaic city. It comprised two distinct heights: that on the north housed the citadel (arx) and a temple of Juno Moneta, the site of the early mint; that on the south was an area sacred to Jupiter, with a wooded asylum on the depression that lay between the two. The remains of the Arx lie concealed beneath the Church of Sta. Maria in Aracoeli and the Victor Emmanuel Monument.

In the area sacred to Jupiter the last of the kings built a magnificent temple in honour of Jupiter, Juno, and Minerva, known officially as the *Temple of Jupiter Optimus Maximus.* Dedicated in 509 B.C., it was—as the remains of the platform now exposed beneath and behind the Palazzo dei Conservatori confirm—in its day the largest temple in central Italy. The platform, measuring 203 by 174 ft. (62 by 53 m.), was built of blocks of cappellaccio. There were probably three rows of six columns each across the facade and six columns and a pilaster on either flank, and there were three cellas, one for each divinity of the triad. The walls and columns of the original building were of tufa faced with stucco, and the low, overhanging timber roof was faced with brightly painted terra cottas in the Etruscan manner. A terra cotta quadriga of Jupiter by Vulca of Veii which stood on the crest was a work of the same school as that which produced the Apollo group from Veii now in the Villa Giulia Museum. The original temple stood until it was burned in 83 B.C. Rebuilt, and twice again burned and rebuilt, each time following the same plan though with new materials and proportions, it reached its final form under Domitian, whose richly decorated marble structure with gilded tiles and gold-plated doors stood intact until the end of pagan antiquity. It was in this temple that victorious generals deposited their laurel crowns after driving in triumph up the Clivus Capitolinus, the paved way that winds up from the Forum.

The *Capitoline Palace,* which today dominates the Forum from the eastern edge of the hill, incorporates the impressive remains of the facade of the *Tabularium.* Built in 78 B.C. across the saddle between the two crests to serve as a fireproof repository for the state records, it is one of the outstanding early examples both of concrete vaulting and of the use of the arch in association with traditional classical orders. In the vaults beneath the southeast angle of the present building can be seen the substantial remains of the Temple of Veiovis, dating from the late 2nd century B.C.

9. The Imperial Fora.—*Forum Iulium.*—By the end of the Republic the old Forum Romanum had already become impossibly cramped, and the century and a half from Caesar to Trajan saw the gradual development on all the level ground to the north of it of a series of new, secondary civic centres. This whole area was cleared by Mussolini during the 1930s, and large stretches of the classical structures are now exposed on either side of the modern Via dei Fori Imperiali. The first of the new fora, planned by Caesar as early as 54 B.C. and financed in part out of Gallic booty, was completed after his death. It consisted essentially of an elongated rectangular enclosure with porticoes down the two long sides and, projecting from one of the short sides, a temple dedicated to the "ancestress" of the Julian family, Venus Genetrix. The surviving marble detail of the temple dates from a reconstruction by Trajan in A.D. 112, and the flanking porticoes were rebuilt in late antiquity; but the vaulted shops that open off the south portico are a fine example of Caesarian masonry.

Forum Augustum.—The Forum of Augustus lay immediately to the north of that of Caesar, which it resembled in plan, with the addition of a pair of semicircular courtyards opening off the two lateral porticoes. The temple, vowed at Philippi in 42 B.C. and dedicated to Mars Ultor ("the Avenger"), was not completed until 2 B.C. With its lavish use of Italian and imported marbles and fine craftsmanship, the work in part of Attic sculptors, it represents the culmination of the great Augustan building program.

Fora of Vespasian and Nerva.—Vespasian's Forum, more correctly known as the Templum Pacis (Precinct of Peace), was situated near the foot of the Via Cavour. Nothing of it is now visible. It was an almost square, cloisterlike precinct, the temple proper standing in the middle of the east portico, and the central area being planted with trees. It had a fine library, its collections including the treasures from the Temple in Jerusalem. It was separated from the fora of Caesar and of Augustus by a space 180 ft. (55 m.) wide through which ran the Argiletum, the main street from the Forum Romanum to the crowded tenement area of the Subura. This space was given monumental form by Domitian, who created therein the *Forum Transitorium*, completed and dedicated after his death by Nerva. The surviving stretch of the eastern flanking colonnade and its sculptured frieze have long been one of the most familiar monuments of ancient Rome, but of the Temple of Minerva, still largely standing in the 17th century, excavation has revealed only the shattered core of the podium.

Forum Traiani.—The last and most elaborate of the Imperial fora extended westward from the Forum of Augustus between the Capitoline and Quirinal hills, the lower slopes of which were cut back to make room for it. A triumphal arch led into the Forum proper, an open space nearly 400 ft. (122 m.) long and 280 ft. (85 m.) wide with flanking porticoes, beyond which were a pair of monumental hemicycles. Across the west end stood the *Basilica Ulpia*, a vast columnar hall, 390 ft. (119 m.) long, with two ambulatory colonnades and a large apse at either end. To the west again a pair of libraries flanked a small, two-storied courtyard in which stood the *Column of Trajan*. This column, which has survived intact and is one of the outstanding masterpieces of Roman relief sculpture, stands 125 ft. high together with its base, within which the emperor was buried; the shaft is covered with reliefs arranged in a spiral band representing the events of his two campaigns in Dacia. Nothing now remains of the great Temple of Trajan which Hadrian erected west of the column. To the north of the basilica and the northern hemicycle of the Forum, terraced up the steep slopes of the Quirinal Hill, are the remarkably preserved remains of *Trajan's Market,* an ingeniously planned complex of concrete structures incorporating a covered market hall with shops accessible at three distinct levels.

10. The Forum Boarium, Circus Flaminius, and Campus Martius.—*Forum Boarium.*—The original river crossing lay at or near the Tiber island, opposite the Palatine and Capitoline hills. Here were the early cattle market (Forum Boarium) and vegetable market (Forum Holitorium) around which there came in time to be grouped a number of small temples. Two of these, tradttionally but incorrectly known as the *temples of Vesta* and *of Fortuna Virilis* (the true dedications are disputed), are still standing, having been rededicated as churches early in the Middle Ages. The former, an elegant circular building, lacks only the steps and entablature; built of Pentelic marble, it is a product of the imported hellenizing taste of the early 1st century B.C. The latter, a nicely proportioned rectangular Ionic building, may be a few decades later. It is constructed of tufa reinforced at all points of special stress with travertine, and the whole was once faced with stucco.

The remains of three more temples, one Doric and built of travertine and the other two Ionic and built of tufa, are incorporated into the Church of S. Nicola in Carcere. Dedicated to *Juno Sospita, Spes,* and possibly *Janus,* and dating originally from the 3rd or early 2nd centuries B.C., the present buildings are probably Augustan, as restored after the fire of 31 B.C. with a liberal reuse of earlier materials. A sacred area exposed beneath and beside the Church of S. Omobono is almost certainly that of the twin *temples of Fortuna* and *Mater Matuta,* rebuilt by Camillus after the conquest of Veii and again in 212 B.C. after a fire in the previous year. From the deeper levels of the excavation came important architectural terra cottas of Etruscan and Latian type and, redeposited here from some nearby site, numerous Bronze Age sherds. The remains of the very ancient circular *Temple of Hercules Victor* were destroyed by Sixtus IV (1471–84). It stood behind the Church of Sta. Maria in Cosmedin, the body of which incorporates the columns of the offices of the grain commissioners.

Other surviving monuments in the Forum Boarium are a late (Constantinian?) four-way arch (Janus Quadrifrons) which stands over the Cloaca Maxima and a small arch erected to Septimius Severus by the silversmiths of Rome. Extensive riverside wharves, offices, and warehouses were uncovered and destroyed when the Via del Mare (now Via del Teatro di Marcello) was built in the 1930s, and a short distance downstream, beyond the Aventine, can still be seen part of the *Porticus Aemilia,* a unique example of vaulted warehouses of the 2nd century B.C. Nearby is the site of the marble yards and behind it Monte Testaccio, an artificial hill 150 ft. (46 m.) high, composed entirely of broken fragments of the jars used for transporting grain, wine, and oil to the capital.

Proceeding northward up the Via del Teatro di Marcello one passes the handsome travertine facade of the *Theatre of Marcellus,* built by Augustus and named after his nephew and heir, who died in 23 B.C. It owes its preservation to having been turned by the Savelli family into a fortress, later converted into the Palazzo Orsini, which still occupies the interior. Immediately beyond it are the re-erected marble columns of the *Temple of Apollo.* A temple of this dedication had stood here or hereabout since 431 B.C., but the visible remains are entirely those of the Augustan restoration of about 20 B.C., which is notable for the virtuosity of its ornament, the work of Greek craftsmen.

Circus Flaminius.—Beyond this point, occupying the lowlying ground in the bend of the river, lay the districts of the Cir-

ALINARI

RUINS OF THE BASILICA ULPIA, IN THE FORUM OF TRAJAN, WITH TRAJAN'S COLUMN. IN THE BACKGROUND, THE CHURCHES OF (LEFT) SANTA MARIA DI LORETO, BEGUN ABOUT 1507, AND (RIGHT) SS. NOME DI MARIA. 1738

cus Flaminius and the Campus Martius. The former area took its name from the stadium that was built in 220 B.C. on the site later occupied by the medieval ghetto. The principal Roman buildings still visible are the entrance to the *Porticus Octaviae* and the temples of the Largo Argentina. The former, a porticoed enclosure with a public library, was built by Augustus' sister, Octavia, replacing an earlier building, the Porticus Metelli of 146 B.C. Within it stood temples of Jupiter and of Juno. The entrance is a Severan restoration (A.D. 203). The sacred area of the *Largo Argentina*, excavated between 1926 and 1929, consists

ROBERT BRIGHT—RAPHO GUILLUMETTE

THE THEATRE OF MARCELLUS, COMPLETED IN 13 B.C. BY AUGUSTUS

of a group of four small temples, three rectangular and one circular, which in their present form date from the 2nd and 1st centuries B.C. and which survived with only minor alterations throughout the Imperial period. The dedications are not known. Behind them, to the west, lay the *Theatre of Pompey*, the first permanent theatre in Rome (55 B.C.), considerable remains of which survive incorporated in the houses to the east of the Campo dei Fiori. Scanty traces of the Augustan *Theatre of Balbus* (13 B.C.) have been identified beneath the Palazzo Mattei di Paganica.

Campus Martius.—The Campus Martius, though public property from a very early date, was still open and in places swampy ground right down to the time of Augustus, when it was drained and laid out as a new monumental quarter by Agrippa (d. 12 B.C.). Though few of the actual Agrippan buildings survived the fire of A.D. 80, the quarter retained its monumental character throughout antiquity. In the Middle Ages, when the inhabited centre of the city shifted to the lower ground by the river, most of the Roman buildings were destroyed. The principal surviving monument is the *Pantheon,* which owes its preservation to its rededication as a church in A.D. 609. Nothing remains of Agrippa's building except the dedication, the present structure being entirely the work of Hadrian. The pedimental porch, with its bronze roof beams and gilded bronze tiles (removed in 1625 to provide bronze for Bernini's canopy in St. Peter's) and its gigantic columns of Egyptian granite weighing about 60 tons, is grandiose but conventional. On the other hand the body of the building, an enormous circular space lit solely by the light that floods in through the oculus at the centre of the dome, was revolutionary in design, possibly the first of the great buildings of antiquity to be designed exclusively as an interior. It was also a remarkable feat of engineering, the dome (141 ft. [43 m.] in diameter) being the largest ever built until modern times. Two things made this possible—the magnificent quality of the mortar used in the concrete and the very careful selection and grading of the aggregate, which ranges from basalt in the foundations and lower part of the drum, through brick and tufa, to the lightest of pumice toward the centre of the vault. The brickwork outer facing of the drum is divided into three zones, the uppermost of which corresponds with the lower part of the dome and helps to contain the thrust. Contrary to common belief it is only in this lowest part of the dome that there is any use of brick ribbing. The interior, with its rich marbling and uniform lighting, conveys better than any other surviving monument the sense of colour, light, and space which was the architectural objective of these great Roman concrete interiors.

Adjoining the Pantheon were *Agrippa's Baths,* the first of the great public bath buildings of Rome. Surviving buildings in the Campus Martius include the shattered drum of the *Mausoleum of Augustus* and, re-erected beside it, the *Ara Pacis* (13–9 B.C.), which stood beside the Via Flaminia at the corner of the modern Via in Lucina. The *Column of Marcus Aurelius* (dedicated A.D. 193) stands in the Piazza Colonna; it was modeled on Trajan's column and depicts the emperor's Danubian campaigns. Much of the

Temple of Hadrian can be seen incorporated into the Borsa, the stock exchange, and on the opposite bank of the Tiber is the *Mausoleum of Hadrian,* converted in the Middle Ages into the fortress of Castel S. Angelo. Much of the Egyptian sculpture in the Vatican and other museums and several of the smaller Egyptian obelisks come from the destroyed *sanctuary of Isis and Sarapis* near the Collegio Romano, and the obelisk now in the Piazza di Montecitorio was the pointer of the monumental sundial erected by Augustus near the Ara Pacis. The Piazza Navona preserves the shape and much of the structure of the *Circus of Domitian.* Wholly or partly surviving Roman bridges are the Pons Fabricius (62 B.C.), the Pons Aelius, now Ponte S. Angelo (A.D. 134), the fragmentary Pons Aemilius, or Ponte Rotto (179–142 B.C.), and some distance upstream the Pons Milvius (109 B.C.).

11. The Aventine, Quirinal, Esquiline, and Caelian Hills. —The line of the Servian Wall shows that by the 4th century B.C. the city had come to include almost the whole of the Aventine Hill and large parts of the Quirinal, Esquiline, and Caelian hills. The building of the first high-level aqueduct in the 2nd century B.C. (Aqua Marcia, 144 B.C.) made possible the development also of the higher ground beyond, later enclosed by the Walls of Aurelian. Within the first of these areas lay the most populous quarters of the Republican city and several of its most venerable shrines. The outer periphery was largely occupied by the parks and ornamental gardens of the wealthy, which by the end of the Republican period extended in an almost unbroken ring around the city, very much in the manner of the "villas" of 18th-century Rome. During the Empire many of these properties passed to the emperors and were used for the building of large monuments for which there was now little room in the crowded city centre.

Most of the Republican monuments, including the great Temple of Diana on the Aventine, were rebuilt or swept away in the successive fires that devastated the old quarters. The great fire of A.D. 64 was made by Nero the occasion for expropriating an area of over 200 ac. (81 ha.) in the heart of the city for the construction of the *Golden House.* He had already planned and begun an earlier palace, the Domus Transitoria, which was to link the existing buildings on the Palatine with the gardens of Maecenas and other Imperial properties on the Esquiline and adjoining hills. To these he now added a large part of the Caelian and Oppian hills and the valley between them and the Palatine, extending to the Servian Wall in one direction and to the high ground followed by the modern Via Lanza in the other. This whole area he laid out as parkland with porticoes, pavilions, and fountains, the centrepiece being an artificial lake on the site later occupied by the Colosseum. At the east end of the Forum the slopes of the Velia were remodeled to form a grandiose colonnaded approach and vestibule, within which stood a colossal gilded bronze statue of Nero, 120 ft. (37 m.) high. The domestic wing stood on the slopes of the Oppian Hill, facing south across the lake. Sadly little has survived of the sumptuous paintings and stuccoes which inspired the "grotesque" style of Raphael and his followers (so called from the "grotte" or caverns which were all that was then visible). But the building itself, which has since been excavated, is important as representing the first recorded monumental expression of the new architectural ideas that were to transform the face of Roman architecture under Domitian, Trajan, and Hadrian.

The expropriations involved in the creation of the Golden House were deeply resented, and Nero's successors hastened to put large parts of it to public use. The domestic wing owes its preservation to its incorporation within the foundations of the *Baths of Trajan,* the ruins of which are now laid out as a public garden (Parco Oppio). The *Temple of Claudius,* partly dismantled by Nero, was completed by Vespasian; part of the arcaded facade of the platform can be seen beside the Church of SS. Giovanni e Paolo. The vestibule was swept away by Hadrian to make way for his great double Temple of Venus and Rome, and the lake was drained and its place taken by the *Colosseum.* This gigantic amphitheatre, more correctly known as the Amphitheatrum Flavium, measured 615 by 415 ft. (187 by 126 m.) externally. Begun by Vespasian and inaugurated by Titus in A.D. 80, it was used for hunts, sham battles, and gladiatorial shows, and the arena could be flooded for naval displays. The facade consists of three superimposed series of 80 arches and an attic story, rising to a total height of 160 ft. (49 m.). Together with the rest of the main structural framework of the building, the facade is of travertine, the secondary walls being of tufa, and the vaulting of the arcades and the inner bowl of concrete. All that survives of Hadrian's *Temple of Venus and Rome* is the platform, the surviving superstructure being the work of Maxentius. It was decastyle and almost certainly the largest temple in the city. Nearby stands the fine *Arch of Constantine*. Erected hastily to celebrate Constantine's victory over Maxentius in A.D. 312, it incorporates sculpture from many earlier buildings, including part of a battle frieze and figures of prisoners from the Forum of Trajan, a series of Hadrianic roundels, and a set of eight panels from a monument of Marcus Aurelius.

Parts of Caracalla's great *Temple of Sarapis,* which occupied the site of the Colonna Gardens and the Gregorian University on the edge of the Quirinal Hill, were still standing until demolished about 1630. Of Aurelian's *Temple of the Sun,* near the Piazza S. Silvestro, nothing is now visible. Generally speaking, however, few of the main public sanctuaries lay outside the ancient centre and the Campus Martius. There were, on the other hand, many private cult buildings, notably of the cult of Mithra, of which the two finest examples now visible lie beneath the churches of S. Clemente and Sta. Prisca respectively. A sanctuary dedicated to the Syrian gods was excavated in 1908 on the Janiculum, and another to the Syrian Jupiter Dolichenus (A.D. 138) in 1935 on the Aventine. A remarkable subterranean basilica found in 1917 just outside the Porta Maggiore had been suppressed, dismantled, and filled in soon after its construction in the mid-1st century A.D. Its splendidly preserved stuccoes show it to have belonged to a neo-Pythagorean sect.

Of the many private houses of the wealthy found when the higher ground of the city was being developed in the Renaissance and again in the decades following 1870, very little has survived. Exceptions are the *Palace of the Gardens of Sallust* and the so-called *Temple of Minerva Medica,* in reality a 3rd-century domed pavilion of the gardens of the emperor Gallienus (A.D. 253–268). Of the several barrack buildings, the outer wall of the camp of the Praetorian Guard, established by Tiberius, is still largely intact, incorporated into the Walls of Aurelian. When the Praetorians were disbanded and reorganized by Septimius Severus their place as the emperor's household troops was taken by the Equites Singulares, parts of whose camp, including the commandant's house, are preserved beneath the Church of St. John Lateran.

The most impressive remains of the outlying quarters are those of the great baths, which played such an important part in the daily life of Romans of all classes. The *Baths of Caracalla* covered an area of over 6 ac. (2.4 ha.) at the foot of the Aventine. The plan, derived with modifications from that of Trajan's baths, consists of the baths proper, surrounded by a garden, which is in turn enclosed by a rectangular outer precinct containing suites of lecture halls, libraries, clubrooms, and other social facilities, as well as the vast cisterns that served the baths. The bath building is a huge, rectangular concrete structure which still stands in many places to vault height. Across the shorter axis lay the swimming pool (*natatio*), cold hall (*frigidarium*), warm room (*tepidarium*), and main hot room (*caldarium*), and symmet-

ALINARI

TOMB OF CAECILIA METELLA, ALONG THE VIA APPIA, BUILT ABOUT 20 B.C. WREATHS OF FLOWERS AND OX SKULLS DECORATE THE MARBLE FRIEZE BELOW THE CORNICE

rically disposed to right and left were the changing rooms, gymnasia, smaller heated rooms, service rooms, etc.

The plan, with its ingenious heating installations and arrangements for water supply and drainage, is one that was repeated many times both in Rome and the provinces. In Rome it appears again in the *Baths of Diocletian,* the great central hall of which, as finally converted by L. Vanvitelli into the Church of Sta. Maria degli Angeli, gives an excellent idea of the architectural intentions of these huge enclosed spaces before they were stripped of the marbles and mosaics that gave them light and colour. (*See also* BATH.)

12. Cemeteries.—Beyond the city limits, beside every road leading out of Rome, lay tombs and funerary monuments of every size. The best known of these cemeteries is that which extends for miles beside the Via Appia, which includes such familiar monuments as the tomb of Caecilia Metella, the drumlike mass of which served in the Middle Ages as a fortress of the Caetani family; the Mausoleum and Circus of Maxentius (A.D. 306–312); and the family tomb of the Scipios, as well as several of the earliest Christian catacombs (*q.v.*). The cemetery beneath St. Peter's (*see* PETER, SAINT) illustrates a type of middle-class mausoleum, faced with brick, which was very common in the 2nd and 3rd centuries A.D. Other well-preserved examples, with fine stuccoes and paintings, are those beside the Via Latina. To the same category of Imperial mausoleums as the tomb of Maxentius belong those of the Gordians beside the Via Praenestina and that of Helena, mother of Constantine ("Tor Pignattara"), beside the Via Casilina. Among the more eccentric tombs are the early Augustan Pyramid of Cestius, beside the Porta S. Paolo, and the slightly earlier tomb of the baker Eurysaces outside the Porta Maggiore.

B. MEDIEVAL ROME

With the transfer of the effective capital of the Empire from Rome to Constantinople, the great program of civil building came to an abrupt end. Apart from ecclesiastical architecture, the 1,100 years that followed Constantine were for the city of Rome a period of slow but steady decline, punctuated by fire, earthquake, and, particularly after the Edict of Theodosius in 391, the destruction of ancient buildings for their materials. As the population dwindled (estimated at 30,000–35,000 between the 10th and the 14th centuries) and as the aqueducts fell into disrepair, increasingly large areas of the higher ground within the city walls were abandoned, until by the later Middle Ages the population was concentrated very largely in the well-watered lower ground on either side of the river, in the Campus Martius, near the Vatican, and in Trastevere. Despite the laying out of new streets and quarters in the late 15th and early 16th centuries, it was not until the pontificate of Sixtus V (1585–90) that Rome began seriously once more to expand, and as late as 1870 the distribution of population still reflected the medieval rather than the classical pattern.

In contrast to most of western Europe, the lowest point of Rome's fortunes fell late rather than early within the Middle Ages, during the anarchy of the 10th and early 11th centuries and again at the time of the Avignon schism in the 14th century. Theodoric is the last ruler recorded as having systematically restored the classical monuments, although many were seen and recorded, still substantially intact, by the early pilgrims from the north several centuries later. After the 9th century the destruction was rapid. Of the buildings that have survived, many, such as the Pantheon, the Senate House (S. Adriano), and the temples of the Forum Boarium, owe their survival to their consecration as churches; others, such as the Colosseum, the Theatre of Marcellus, and the Mausoleum of Hadrian (Castel S. Angelo), remain because they were converted into the private fortresses of the warring nobility. The rest fell into ruin and were ruthlessly quarried by the builders of the Middle Ages and the Renaissance.

1. Ecclesiastical Architecture.—*Early Christian.*—It was only in the field of ecclesiastical building that there was almost continuous activity throughout the Middle Ages. The pattern was firmly established by Constantine immediately after the Edict of Milan in 313. Before this date there was no monumental Christian architecture. The meeting places of the early Christian community had been private houses, many of which were subsequently converted into churches, a notable surviving example being that beneath the early 5th-century church of SS. Giovanni e Paolo. Of more immediate importance, however, than these modest urban *tituli*, the equivalent of the later parish churches, were a number of monumental new foundations on the periphery of the city. A few, such as the new cathedral church and papal residence of St. John Lateran, lay just inside the walls, but the majority were martyr shrines, established outside the city limits over the burial places of the early martyrs. In course of time, as large new churches were founded in the heart of the city (Sta. Maria Maggiore, *c.* 432, is one of the earliest) and as outlying buildings were abandoned because of the increasing insecurity of the countryside, these distinctions became blurred. But in the 4th century, during the early, formative years of Christian architecture, it was the cathedral church of Rome and the great martyr shrines which established the models that were to be followed by ecclesiastical builders in the West for many centuries to come. Many of them, such as St. Paul's Outside the Walls, S. Lorenzo al Verano (S. Lorenzo Outside the Walls), and S. Sebastiano, survived to become important features of the medieval and post-medieval urban redevelopment of Rome itself. The outstanding example of this was Constantine's great Church of St. Peter in the Vatican; the proximity of the fortress of Castel S. Angelo led to the Vatican's becoming the preferred residence of the pope; and so it and St. Peter's usurped much of the position and prestige that would otherwise have belonged to the cathedral church and the Lateran Palace.

The Lateran Palace was presented by Constantine to Pope Miltiades, and beside it, over the remains of the Severan barracks of the Equites Singulares, Constantine built the first of the great Christian basilicas, the cathedral church now known as St. John Lateran. The plan was that of a five-aisled basilica, 320 by 170 ft. (98 by 52 m.) internally, with a single western apse and two transept-like chapels projecting slightly from the western ends of the two outer aisles. The baptistery, originally an adapted part of the palace bath suite, dates from 432–440, with mosaics and intarsias of the 5th and 7th centuries. The cloister (1222–30) is a fine example of Cosmati work. The interior of the church was entirely transformed (1646–50) by Borromini.

The basilica of St. Paul's Outside the Walls (390 by 195 ft. [119 by 59 m.]) was begun in 386, replacing a smaller Constantinian church. As at St. Peter's, the latter had been built over a cemetery of the 1st–3rd centuries A.D., within which was the traditional burial place of the apostle. Faithfully restored after a fire in 1823, it is the outstanding surviving example of 4th-century basilical architecture, with a single eastern apse, a lofty transept, and five majestic nave aisles. Noteworthy later additions are the cloister (about 1200), the 12th-century Easter candlestick, and Arnolfo di Cambio's altar canopy (1285).

A controversial group of early 4th-century basilicas in the shape of a classical circus, with an apse the full width of the three-aisled nave (S. Sebastiano, S. Lorenzo al Verano, S. Agnese Outside the Walls, Tor Pignattara), appears to have originated as communal burial places associated with martyr shrines. The two last-named incorporated Imperial mausoleums, of which that later dedicated to Sta. Costanza marks an important stage in the development of a centrally planned Christian architecture and contains a superb series of contemporary vault mosaics, largely pagan in character. The porphyry sarcophagi from Sta. Costanza and Tor Pignattara are now in the Vatican Museum. The Church of Sta. Pudenziana preserves its original 4th-century apse mosaic, much restored.

5th–9th Centuries.—The surviving churches of the period from the 5th to 8th centuries are very varied in character and inspiration. An important early 5th-century group is predominantly Roman in inspiration. It includes SS. Giovanni e Paolo (about 400, replacing and in part incorporating an earlier house church), S. Vitale (416), and Sta. Sabina (about 430), with its original carved wooden doors. It includes also the foundations of Sixtus III (432–440): Sta. Maria Maggiore, the first great church of the Virgin in Rome, founded immediately after the Council of Ephesus and containing a magnificent series of contemporary mosaics; S. Pietro in Vincoli;

S. Lorenzo in Lucina; and the Lateran baptistery. The great circular church of S. Stefano Rotondo (468–483) probably reflects the influence of the Church of the Holy Sepulchre (Anastasis) in Jerusalem.

Greek influence is apparent in the earlier church of S. Clemente (before 532), the chancel screens of which, now in the upper church, are Constantinopolitan work; in the galleried naves of S. Agnese (625–638) and of the earlier Church of S. Lorenzo al Verano (579–590), and in the remarkable 7th-century paintings of Sta. Maria Antiqua, the work of Greek refugees from the iconoclastic movement. Other good mosaics of the period are those of SS. Cosma e Damiano (526–530), Sta. Sabina, S. Lorenzo al Verano, and S. Agnese. (*See* also EARLY CHRISTIAN ARCHITECTURE.)

The years immediately before and the half-century after Charlemagne's consecration in St. Peter's on Christmas Day, 800, were a period of great building activity, much of it deliberately based on Early Christian models. This archaizing tendency is already felt in the buildings of Pope Adrian I (772–795), parts of which survive in Sta. Maria in Cosmedin and in S. Giovanni a Porta Latina, and of Leo III (795–816) in S. Stefano degli Abissini and SS. Nereo e Achilleo. It is unusually clear in Sta. Prassede, where the transept, the anular crypt, the horizontal architrave, and the quadrangular atrium are all patently copied from St. Peter's. Sta. Prassede, which contains a magnificent cycle of contemporary mosaics in the church itself and in the annexed chapel of S. Zeno, was the work of Paschal I (817–824), who also built Sta. Maria in Domnica and rebuilt Sta. Cecilia. To the next 30 years belong S. Giorgio in Velabro and the apse of S. Marco (both 827–844), the exterior of S. Martino ai Monti (844–847), the nucleus of SS. Quattro Coronati (847–855), including the entrance tower, and probably Sta. Maria Nova (Sta. Francesca Romana), replacing Sta. Maria Antiqua which had been destroyed by earthquake in 847. Other well-preserved mosaics of the period are in S. Marco, Sta. Maria in Domnica, and SS. Nereo e Achilleo.

Romanesque.—The two centuries that followed were a period of weakness and dissension that saw little except the essential maintenance of existing buildings; an exception is S. Bartolomeo all'Isola, built shortly before 1000 by the emperor Otto III. The reestablishment of papal authority by Gregory VII (1073–85) was followed by a great deal of building and rebuilding. Good early examples of Romanesque architecture in Rome are Sta. Prisca and S. Saba, both *c.* 1100; S. Clemente, rebuilt after the Norman sack of 1084; and S. Crisogono, 1122. To the 12th century belongs most of what is now seen in SS. Quattro Coronati and Sta. Maria in Cosmedin and, a notable example of the classicizing tendencies at work, Sta. Maria in Trastevere; to the 13th, the nave of S. Lorenzo al Verano, the apse and the transept of Sta. Maria Maggiore, and the main structure of Sta. Maria in Aracoeli, a Franciscan church of about 1250. Many of these Romanesque churches had slender brick campaniles, those of Sta. Maria in Cosmedin and Sta. Francesca Romana being typical of the 40 or so that survive and of many others now destroyed.

Another characteristic feature is the carved and inlaid decoration carried out by the Roman marble workers often known as the Cosmati (*q.v.*), the name of one of the most active of several families of traditional craftsmen. They specialized in mosaic pavements and intarsia, using porphyries and marbles robbed from classical buildings (and in their later work glass paste) and frequently copying classical motifs. Architecturally notable examples of Cosmati work are the porch of S. Lorenzo al Verano and the cloisters of S. Cosimato, St. John Lateran, St. Paul's Outside the Walls, and SS. Quattro Coronati. There are innumerable fine pavements (*e.g.*, Sta. Maria in Aracoeli, S. Clemente, Sta. Maria in Cosmedin) and fittings such as pulpits, choir screens, bishop's thrones, and Easter candlesticks (*e.g.*, S. Clemente, S. Lorenzo al Verano, SS. Nereo e Achilleo). There are good Romanesque mosaics in Sta. Maria in Trastevere (apse, 1140; panels by P. Cavallini, about 1300), S. Clemente (12th century), Sta. Francesca Romana (1160), and Sta. Maria Maggiore (apse, 1295). Paintings of the period include S. Giovanni a Porta Latina (consecrated 1191), the chapel of S. Silvestro in SS. Quattro Coronati (13th century), and the magnificent remains of a "Last Judgment" by Cavallini (c. 1293) in Sta. Cecilia.

End of the Middle Ages.—The century of the Great Schism saw no new building in Rome, and the only Gothic church, Sta. Maria sopra Minerva, begun by the Dominicans in 1280, was not completed until the 15th century. The plan is closely modeled on that of Sta. Maria Novella in Florence. It is only in such features as tombs, tabernacles, and altar canopies that the influence of Italian Gothic is strong, introduced from Tuscany by artists such as Arnolfo di Cambio, creator of the tomb of Boniface VIII in the Vatican Grottoes, and of the altar canopy in St. Paul's Outside the Walls.

2. Secular Architecture.—Of the secular architecture of medieval Rome, the only substantial remains are those of a number of tower fortresses, notably the Torre delle Milizie, the Tor dei Conti, and the so-called Casa di Crescenzio. Nothing remains of the medieval Senator's Palace, the building of which soon after 1143 on the site of the ancient Tabularium established the Capitoline Hill thereafter as the seat of municipal government. The great steps of Sta. Maria in Aracoeli were built in 1348 as a thank offering after a plague.

(J. B. W.-P.)

C. Renaissance and Modern Rome

1. Early and High Renaissance.—By the early 15th century, artistic patronage in Rome had reached a very low ebb, owing to the prolonged struggles over papal elections during the Schism and to the deserted state of the city during the exile in Avignon. After the return of the papacy to Rome with Martin V (1417–31) a start was made with the restoration of some of the main churches; fresco cycles for the Lateran were commissioned from Gentile da Fabriano and Pisanello (both works have now disappeared), and Masolino was commissioned by Cardinal Branda Castiglione to decorate a chapel in S. Clemente with frescoes. Eugenius IV (1431–47) commissioned from Filarete the great bronze doors of St. Peter's (1433–45).

During the reign of the humanist pope Nicholas V the walls of the city—the old Roman Aurelian Wall on which the greatly shrunken city, now reduced to a few small congested centres amid vineyards and vast tracts of abandoned wilderness, still relied for defense—were repaired, and a start was made on clearing blocked roads, restoring the 40 pilgrimage churches, and renewing fountains (in particular what is now the Trevi Fountain, fed by the Acqua Vergine, the only aque-

duct to survive the destructions of the Goths). Fra Angelico painted two chapels in the Vatican, one of which is now lost; the other was Nicholas' private chapel. Alberti was concerned in a large project for rebuilding, probably in the Borgo. Nicholas also brought Bernardo Rossellino to Rome to build a new choir onto the Early Christian basilica of St. Peter's, the uncompleted parts of which later had considerable bearing on the plans for the new basilica drawn up by Bramante at the beginning of the 16th century. The three-story Benediction Loggia added to the front of old St. Peter's during the pontificate of Pius II (the humanist

(ABOVE) ALINARI; (LEFT) URSULA MAHONEY—NANCY PALMER PHOTO AGENCY; (BELOW) FROM "ITALY BUILDS" BY G. E. KIDDER SMITH

THE CAMPIDOGLIO, DESIGNED BY MICHELANGELO AND BUILT ON THE CAPITOLINE HILL

(Above) Monumental ramp leading to the Palazzo Senatorio (centre), the Capitoline Museum (left) and the Palazzo dei Conservatori (right). (Left) 2nd-century bronze statue of Marcus Aurelius in the centre of the piazza. (Below) Stairway leading to a triple-arched colonnade behind the Palazzo dei Conservatori; erected in the 16th century by Giacomo da Vignola to complete Michelangelo's plan

Aeneas Silvius Piccolomini) may have been by Alberti, and is the first Renaissance use of superimposed arcades of the type of the Theatre of Marcellus or the Colosseum (the loggia is lost, but drawings of it survive).

The Palazzo Venezia, which incorporates the Early Christian basilica of S. Marco, was begun in 1455 by Cardinal Pietro Barbo, and enlarged from 1465, after his election as Paul II, when it was used as a papal residence. The large loggia of superimposed arcades in the courtyard, built during his pontificate, is the first domestic use of the antique prototype used in the Benediction Loggia. This grim, fortresslike palace, with its huge tower, was much altered from the 18th century onward, particularly during the years when it served as Mussolini's headquarters.

The Cancelleria, originally built as a residence by Cardinal Raffaello Riario, was begun possibly as early as the 1480s, which rules out any attribution to Bramante, who did not arrive in Rome until after 1499. In painting, the major works of the latter part of the 15th century were the fresco cycles of the "Lives of Moses and Christ" on the upper part of the walls of the Sistine Chapel in the Vatican (built by Sixtus IV, during 1473–84), commissioned in 1481 from Florentine and Umbrian masters of whom the chief were Cosimo Roselli, Botticelli, Ghirlandajo, and Perugino. Perugino had the major part, but only one of his works there survives, the limpid and harmonious "Charge to St. Peter," the others having been destroyed in 1536 to make room for Michelangelo's "Last Judgment."

Between 1492 and 1495, Pinturicchio decorated for Alexander VI the six rooms of the Appartamento Borgia, but despite their charm and their highly involved symbolism and imagery they form but a slight prelude to the grand and significant works created in the rooms above—the "Stanze"—during the pontificate of Julius II. Bramante's designs for the new St. Peter's, the Vatican Palace, and the Belvedere courtyard, Raphael's "Stanze," Michelangelo's Sistine ceiling, and his abortive projects for the Julius Tomb were all created for this magnificent and imperious patron.

The superb intellectual and artistic high-water mark of High Renaissance was reached with Bramante's tiny Tempietto in the courtyard of S. Pietro in Montorio (1502), on the traditional site of the martyrdom of St. Peter, and his cloister in Sta. Maria della Pace (1504); with Michelangelo's "Pietà" now in St. Peter's (1498–99); and with a handful of works by Raphael, such as the decorations in the Villa Farnesina (c. 1518), the tapestries for the Sistine Chapel (1515–16; in the Pinacoteca Vaticana), and the Chigi Chapel (1516) in Sta. Maria del Popolo. The period broke up with the dearth of patronage, the dispersal of artists after the disastrous sack of Rome in 1527, the evolution of Mannerism, and the concentration of all artistic interest in the work and personality of Michelangelo, who dominated all the arts until his death in 1564 and for another quarter-century thereafter. (*See also* RENAISSANCE ARCHITECTURE.)

2. Late Renaissance.—Baldassare Peruzzi, who created one of the first purely illusionistic painted decorations in Rome in the Farnesina (1509–21), built the Palazzo Massimo alle Colonne (1535); while the principal architectural works, St. Peter's and the Farnese Palace, were in the hands of Antonio da Sangallo the younger until his death in 1546, when he was succeeded by Michelangelo (*q.v.*). In the Vatican, the "Last Judgment" in the Sistine Chapel (1536–41) and the two frescoes in the Cappella Paolina (1542–50), both executed for Paul III (Farnese), were Michelangelo's last works in painting. From Jan. 1, 1547, when he was appointed to direct the works at St. Peter's, Michelangelo returned to Bramante's idea of the central plan, from which his successors had departed under pressure from the clergy who desired a long-nave church for liturgical reasons. The dome, designed as a hemisphere, was built after Michelangelo's death in a more conical form by his pupil Giacomo della Porta, and Domenico Fontana, and his central plan was eventually frustrated by Maderno's addition of a long nave to his unfinished east end (the orientation of St. Peter's reverses the normal). His other architectural works include the upper story and entrance of the Palazzo Farnese and the redesigning of the Capitol, which involved a reconstruction of the Palazzo Senatorio and the building of the two palaces (Palazzo dei Conservatori and Palazzo Capitolino) flanking it.

To Giacomo da Vignola is due the introduction of the oval plan at S. Andrea in the Via Flaminia (completed 1554) and Sta. Anna dei Palafrenieri (*c.* 1572), both extremely influential for the development of this form during the Baroque period. B. Ammanati, with G. Vasari and Vignola, built the Villa Giulia for Julius III (1550–55; now the Etruscan Museum), with its contrast between interior and exterior facades and its delightful sunken water garden, or nymphaeum. Vignola began the mother church of the Jesuit order, the Gesù, in 1568 (finished after his death by Giacomo della Porta), returning to the long-nave form with deep side chapels instead of aisles, but its projected simplicity and bareness was later overlaid by an exuberant illusionistic decoration in fresco and stucco by Baciccio (1683). Vignola's *oeuvre* was dominated by his desire to return to the simplicity and clarity of Bramante and by his veneration for the antique, expressed in his book, *Regola delli cinque ordini d'architettura* (1562), which was of vital importance outside, as well as inside, Italy.

The end of the century, which saw this extinction of the wayward individualism of Mannerism in favour of an academic strictness of canon, also saw the development of a parallel movement in painting, given final form in the frescoes of the Farnese Gallery (1597–1604) by Annibale Carracci. This sole competitor in Rome in size and splendour to the "Stanze," the Sistine ceiling, and the Farnesina decorations—and owing a good deal to the last two—blends brilliant illusionism with a return to the clarity and firmness of the High Renaissance, a renewed consciousness of the antique, and a robust sense of humour. Its vigour extinguished the debilitated survivals of Mannerism, such as the Cavaliere d'Arpino's feeble mosaic decorations in the dome of St. Peter's, and encouraged the flights of illusionistic fantasy of G. Lanfranco's dome of S. Andrea della Valle (1621–25) and apse of S. Carlo ai Catinari.

Parallel with the Carracci's revival of lucidity and simplicity came Caravaggio's revolt of naturalism. His stormy career (1573–1610) matches his strong effects of light and shadow, unidealized models, uncomplicated imagery, and direct technical methods in oil painting, all of which are present in his Contarelli Chapel paintings in S. Luigi dei Francesi (1597–c. 1603) and his Cerasi Chapel in Sta. Maria del Popolo (1600–01); but his influence was felt more in northern Europe and Naples than in Rome itself.

The transformation of a still largely medieval city into modern Rome began with the vast building program started by Sixtus V (1585–90). With his architect Domenico Fontana, he laid the basis of the modern street plan by driving new streets through the city, the chief of which were those from the Vatican to the Lateran, and to Sta. Maria Maggiore, and the Via Felice from the Lateran via Sta. Maria Maggiore to the Piazza del Popolo, across the Quirinal Hill. Sixtus also laid out new squares in front of Sta. Maria Maggiore and the Lateran; rebuilt the palace there, at the Quirinal, and the Vatican; restored the aqueduct of the Acqua Felice to bring water to the higher parts of the city and rebuilt many fountains; raised the obelisks in front of St. Peter's, the Lateran, Sta. Maria Maggiore, and Sta. Maria del Popolo; placed the antique statues of the Dioscuri in front of the Quirinal Palace; built the Vatican Library; and completed the dome of St. Peter's. Fortunately, his project to convert the Colosseum into a wool factory, to provide honest employment for the prostitutes of Rome, came to nothing.

3. Baroque.—The Baroque, that characteristic and predominantly Roman style, opens with C. Maderno's imaginative, vigorous, and lucid facade for Sta. Susanna (finished 1603) and with his completion of St. Peter's, to which he added the long nave and a rather consciously imposing facade. He also began the Barberini Palace (now the National Gallery) in 1628 but was succeeded in this, on his death in 1629, by Bernini, who then had Borromini as an assistant.

This brought the two major exponents of High Baroque on to the architectural scene at virtually the same moment, although Bernini as a sculptor had already achieved great fame through his statues for Cardinal Scipione Borghese (now in the Borghese Gallery), in which he established the principles governing the new

HENRI CARTIER-BRESSON—MAGNUM

CHRISTMAS FAIR ON THE PIAZZA NAVONA. ON THE RIGHT, THE CHURCH OF
S. AGNESE DESIGNED BY BORROMINI, 1652, AND, FACING IT, BERNINI'S
"FOUNTAIN OF THE RIVERS"

style and demonstrated his legendary technical accomplishment.
For his great patron, the Barberini pope Urban VIII, he created
in St. Peter's the Baldacchino (1624–33), the Loggie and the
niches under the dome (1629 onward) with their gigantic statues
(of the figures, only the "Longinus" is by Bernini himself, the
others being by F. Duquesnoy, F. Mochi, and A. Bolgi), and the
tomb of Urban in one of the apse niches. He also completed Maderno's exterior with the vast colonnaded piazza (1656–67). It was
also Bernini who rebuilt the Scala Regia as a new grand entrance
to the Vatican, placing his statue of the "Vision of Constantine"
at the point of intersection of church and palace, and made the
tomb of Alexander VII (1671–78).

Bernini's "Ecstasy of St. Theresa" in the Cornaro Chapel in Sta.
Maria della Vittoria (1645–52) is the most complete exposition of
Baroque grand decoration, using coloured and white marble, gilded
bronze, and the light itself, filtered through a yellow-paned window,
to create an overwhelming emotional impact. Similar use of light
and mixed media characterize his "Cathedra Petri" in the apse of
St. Peter's. Through his fountains—the "Triton" near the Barberini Palace, the "Fountain of the Rivers," and "Fountain of the
Moor," in the Piazza Navona, are his most celebrated—his poignant "Angels of the Passion" for the Ponte S. Angelo, and his
amusing elephant-borne obelisk behind the Pantheon, he contributed as much to the splendour of the city as to its amenity and
significance.

Borromini's architecture, more subtle, delicate, less dependent
on decoration, makes its impact through its interplay of architectural forms and its deliberate counterpoint of void and solid, con-

cave and convex curves, and involved interlockings of different
spatial rhythms. His first church, S. Carlo alle Quattro Fontane,
begun in 1634, the facade of which was his last work before his
suicide in 1667, established him as a master of flowing line and
profound sensibility. S. Ivo della Sapienza (begun 1642) shows
him creating entirely novel virtuoso effects on a star-shaped ground
plan of great complexity and daring. In S. Agnese in Piazza
Navona, the Propaganda Fide College, the Oratory of St. Philip
Neri, and S. Andrea delle Fratte, he enriched architecture with new
forms, using only the most restrained decoration.

The counterpart to Bernini in painting was Pietro da Cortona,
whose vast, congested, and rather harshly coloured "Allegory of
Divine Providence" decorates the ceiling of the *salone* of the Barberini Palace. In architecture, his works are of a more restrained
magnificence—SS. Luca e Martina (1635–50) contrasts in its simple Greek cross ground plan with Borromini's more complex spatial
rhythms, and in the purity of its plain stone with Bernini's lavish
use of colour. The extreme of illusionistic decoration was reached
in Baciccio's ceiling and apse of the Gesù and in Andrea Pozzo's
vertiginous perspective fantasies in S. Ignazio (1691–94).

A classical reaction to Bernini's exuberance of style existed in
A. Sacchi and C. Maratti, but it found its principal exponents not
in Italians but in the expatriate Frenchmen Poussin and Claude.
In sculpture, Bernini's rival A. Algardi worked in a barely more
restrained style, and the Fleming Duquesnoy pursued a purely personal style influenced as much by his friend Rubens as by contemporary Italian sculpture.

Before the Neoclassical reaction against Bernini's spectacular
art finally seized the Baroque, the subdued Roman version of
Rococo had a brief day. It is displayed in the church of Sta. Maria
Maddalena finished by G. Sardi in 1735, in the portions of the
Palazzo Doria built by G. Valvassori (*c.* 1734), and in the Spanish
Steps by Francesco de Sanctis (1725). The grand and rather ex-
hibitionist set piece of Late Baroque can be seen in A. Galilei's
Lateran facade (1732–36), F. Fuga's facade of Sta. Maria Mag-
giore (1741–43), D. Gregorini and P. Passalacqua's gigantic facade
for Sta. Croce in Gerusalemme (1743), and N. Salvi's Trevi Foun-
tain (completed in 1762). (*See* also BAROQUE AND POST-BAROQUE
ARCHITECTURE; BAROQUE ART.)

4. Neoclassicism.—Neoclassicism was born of the ideas emanating from Winckelmann's thesis of the supremacy of classical,
and above all Greek, art and was translated into painting by A. R.
Mengs, in his "Parnassus" (Villa Albani-Torlonia, 1761). In its
frigid mixture of motives derived from the antique, Raphael, and
the 17th-century Bolognese, it reflects the new ideals which were
to spread all over Europe and extinguish Baroque and Rococo alike.

Other factors were G. B. Piranesi's Sta. Maria del Priorato
(1765), which revived stricter classical forms in architecture,
though combined with imaginatively rich decorative detail based
on antique trophies, and the cult of ruins. The traditions of *veduta*
painting, established by G. P. Pannini's views of selected antique
and modern monuments, painted chiefly for foreign visitors on the
Grand Tour, were continued and considerably extended by Piranesi's stupendous series of huge etchings of Roman ruins, views,
and antique fragments. The publication of the discoveries at Pompeii and Herculaneum stimulated excitement and interest and particularly influenced the important contingent of northern artists in
Rome—Mengs, Thorvaldsen, Vien, David, Clérisseau, Adam, Flaxman; even the principal Italian sculptor, Canova, was a Venetian.
His "Pauline Borghese" (1808; Borghese Gallery) shows to what
extent his pure sense of form agreed with the Romantic concepts
of antiquity pervading Neoclassicism and provides an interesting
contrast to Piranesi's entirely Romantic vision. In architecture
G. Valadier's town planning schemes—for instance, the Pincian
Steps at the Piazza del Popolo—are decked out in classical forms;
these imitative trends culminate in the dead historicism of G. Sac-
coni's Victor Emmanuel Monument (1884), in the agitated and
overloaded eclecticism of G. Calderini's Ministry of Justice (1888–
1910), and in the dry evocation of antique-cum-Baroque in G.
Koch's Piazza dell'Esedra (now Piazza della Repubblica; 1888),
saved by the exuberance of M. Rutelli's *art nouveau* Fountain of
the Naiads (1901).

5. 20th Century.—The 20th century produced two conflicting movements: the pompous, pseudo-antique of Mussolini's era, such as the Foro Mussolini sports centre (now renamed Italico) by E. del Debbio (1933), or B. Lapadula's Palace of Italian Civilization intended for the World's Fair planned for 1942; and the amazing postwar development of which the finest example is the main railway station, the Stazione Termini. This was begun in 1937 as a typically Fascist piece of theatrical display, but, abandoned unfinished in 1942, was completed by E. Montuori and L. Calini and saved architecturally in 1952 by a brilliant facade which displays a feeling for movement, proportion, inventiveness, and a fine grasp of the structural possibilities of modern methods of building.

Rome has grown enormously since 1945, and it is rapidly swamping the rather inhospitable surrounding countryside. Much of its mushroom growth of huge apartment buildings, in both private and public ownership, is of a monotonous and distressing vulgarity, insensitiveness, and shoddiness. Some of the newer blocks, however, combine the finest modern structural methods, imaginative use of form and detail, and respect for the grandeur of the setting.

The architectural treasures in the Vatican are described at greater length in the article VATICAN.   (L. M. Mu.)

II. ADMINISTRATION, COMMUNICATIONS, INDUSTRIES, AND CULTURE

1. Administration.—An elected council of 80 members chooses a mayor and 14 committee members, with 4 reserves, from among its members. The council is deliberative, the committee

ALINARI

RAILWAY TERMINUS IN THE PIAZZA DEI CINQUECENTO CONTRASTS WITH THE REMAINS OF 4TH-CENTURY-B.C. SERVIAN WALL ABUTTING THE BUILDING

executive. The mayor, besides being head of the city administration, is a government officer responsible for such matters as the publication of laws, regulations, and government announcements and the registration of civil status and population statistics. The territory of the Roman communal administration covers an area of 582 sq.mi. (150,738 ha.). It can impose taxes and bylaws on all residents and has the responsibility for providing local amenities such as city police, health and hygiene services, street lighting, road maintenance, and certain aspects of public assistance.

2. Communications.—Public transport is in the hands of two large public utilities, Azienda Tramvie e Autobus del Comune (ATAC) and Società Tramvie e Ferrovie Elettriche di Roma (STEFER), the first providing urban and suburban services, the second long-distance services. The two operate more than 2,500 vehicles including streetcars, trolley buses, buses, and railway cars. There are about 620 mi. (1,000 km.) of roads. In 1955 services started on a state-built metropolitan railway linking Rome's central station with Lido di Roma (Ostia-Lido). In the 1960s additional metropolitan lines to neighbouring towns were being added. Rome also has more than 300 bus routes operated by private companies, which help to serve the residential suburbs. There are six railway stations besides that of Vatican City. The central station is the Roma Termini, from which 12 main and numerous secondary lines go to all parts of the country. About 6 mi. (10 km.) distant from Campidoglio, the heart of Rome, runs the wide ring road which links together nearly all the ancient roads and other main roads.

Rome's special geographical position has been favourable to the development of air traffic, which is centred on Leonardo da Vinci International Airport at Fiumicino, at the mouth of the Tiber, opened in 1960.

3. Industries.—Rome cannot be called an industrial city, though it has a substantial amount of medium and light industry. Building takes first place in the number of employees; other industries include metallurgical works (foundries, ironwork, machinery), electrical apparatus, woodworking, printing, soft furnishings, clothing (including several *haute couture* houses), chemicals, and food processing. But the occupations most typical of Rome are hotel keeping and motion-picture production. There are more than a dozen film production studios and several dubbing studios, including some of the best of their kind in the world; and also many workshops for photographic development and associated processes.

(V. Ra.)

CAMERA PRESS—PIX FROM PUBLIX

(CENTRE) THE CHURCH OF SS. LUCA E MARTINA. THE UPPER CHURCH WAS BUILT FROM 1640 ONWARD, OVER A CRYPT WHICH WAS A RESTORATION, BEGUN IN 1634, OF A 7TH-CENTURY CHURCH ERECTED ON THE REMAINS OF THE SECRETARIUM SENATUS; (RIGHT) THE ARCH OF SEPTIMIUS SEVERUS IN THE ROMAN FORUM, ERECTED IN A.D. 203 IN HONOUR OF THE EMPEROR AND HIS SONS CARACALLA AND GETA TO COMMEMORATE THEIR VICTORIES OVER THE PARTHIANS

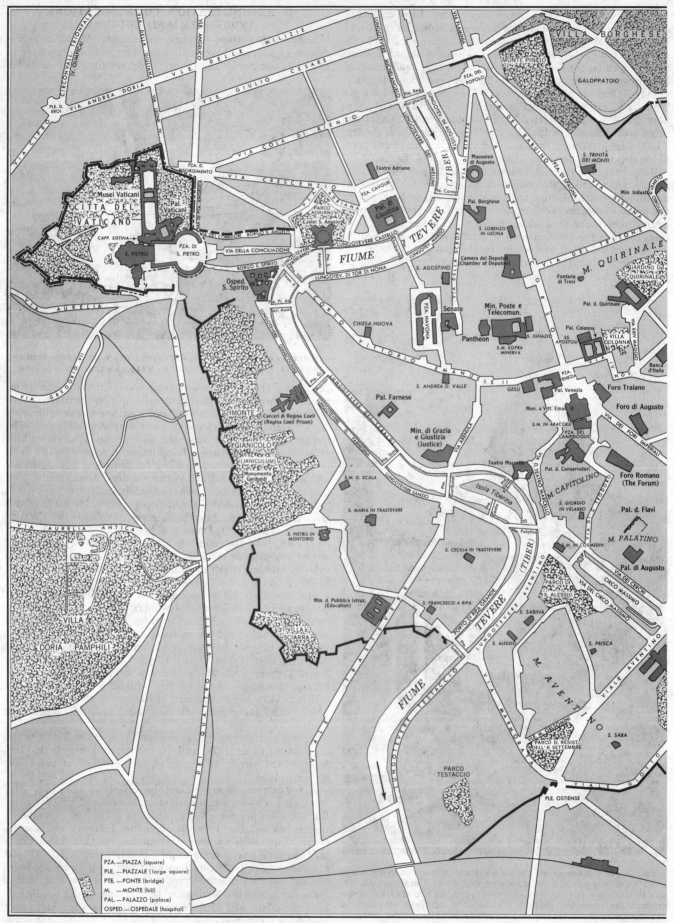

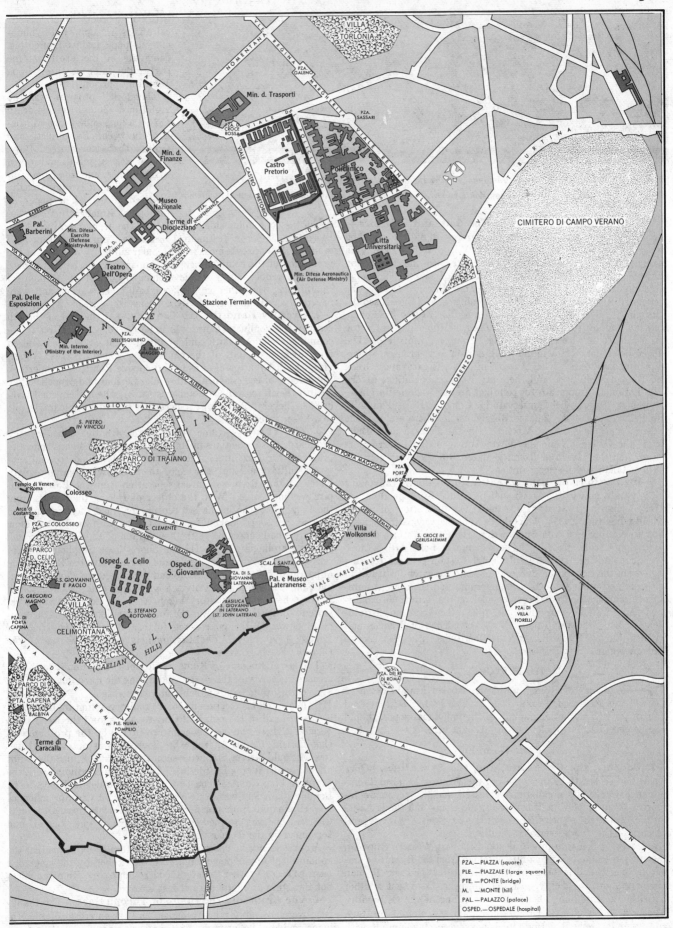

BUILDINGS, AND THE EXTANT PORTIONS OF THE ANCIENT CITY WALL

PICTORIAL PARADE

ESPOSIZIONE UNIVERSALE DI ROMA, ON THE OUTSKIRTS OF ROME

A modern complex of government buildings, sports arenas, theatres, exhibition halls, churches, and apartment buildings in a setting of parks, fountains, and piazzas

4. Public Gardens and Parks, Museums, and Galleries.— Among Rome's open spaces are the gardens of villas, including those of the Villa Doria Pamphili, the Villa Borghese, the Villa Medici, and the Villa Sciarra. There are also the Janiculum, Quirinal, and Pincio gardens and a number of parks. The many museums include historical, scientific, and military, such as the Museo del Risorgimento, the Museo Geologico, and the Museo dei Bersaglieri. The Museo Capitolino and the Museo Nazionale Romano contain sculpture. The Museo di Roma illustrates the history of Rome with casts, paintings, drawings, prints, etc. The Museo del Palazzo di Venezia exhibits paintings, bronzes, silverware, and tapestries. The Museo Torlonia has excavated Greek and Roman sculptures, and there are Etruscan paintings at the Villa Torlonia. Important for paintings are the Gallerie Borghese, Capitolina (Palazzo dei Conservatori), Colonna, Doria Pamphili, and Pallavicini (in the Palazzo Rospigliosi). There are also the Galleria Nazionale d'Arte Moderna (in the Palazzo delle Belle Arti); the Galleria Nazionale d'Arte Antica, in the Palazzo Barberini; and the Museo di Roma (Palazzo Braschi) with contemporary Italian and foreign paintings.

5. Institutions of Higher Education.—Rome University (now a state university) was founded in 1303 by Pope Boniface VIII. Other institutions include the Istituto Superiore di Sanità (Health Institute, 1935), which has a veterinary department; the Istituto Nazionale di Alta Matematica; the Conservatorio di Musica Santa Cecilia (1570); the Accademia di Belle Arti e Liceo Artistico; and the Istituto Centrale del Restauro, where training is given in the restoration of works of art. Research institutes in scientific and other subjects are numerous; and there are a number of national schools and centres, such as the Accademia Americana (American Academy in Rome, 1894), the Accademia Britannica (British School at Rome, 1901), Accademia di Francia, and Spanish, Slovak, Swedish, and other institutes. *See also* GRAND PRIX DE ROME. (X.)

III. HISTORY

For the history of Rome and of the Roman Empire down to A.D. 476, *see* ROMAN HISTORY. The articles ITALY: *History,* and PAPACY, as well as the biographies of the individual popes, should also be consulted to supplement the account here.

A. FROM 476 TO 1309

1. Odoacer, the Ostrogoths, and the Byzantines.—Once Rome had ceased to be the capital of the Western Empire, its importance waned, its population decreased, and its economic resources shrank. New political forces, the clergy and the lay aristocracy, emerged as the two poles of the city's history for several centuries—the two universal institutions.

Odoacer (*q.v.*), who in 476 deposed the last Western emperor, the usurper Romulus Augustulus, obtained from the Byzantine emperor Zeno the title of patrician. He also wooed the Roman aristocrats and the clergy. In 489, however, Zeno sent another barbarian against him, Theodoric (*q.v.*), king of the Ostrogoths. Theodoric defeated Odoacer (493), established himself in Italy, and lived for several periods in Rome, concerning himself with the local administration, with the restoration of buildings, and

with public order. In ecclesiastical affairs he supported Symmachus as pope against Laurentius, candidate of the pro-Byzantine party; but later he threw Pope John I into prison.

Theodoric's program was too ambitious. Soon after his death (526), a long and savage war began between Byzantines and Goths that devastated Italy. Rome was besieged and taken several times, suffering from famine and being, it is said, actually deserted in 547. The popes, as bishops of Rome, intervened between the contending sides and assisted the needy, and in 554 the Byzantine emperor Justinian I issued a "pragmatic sanction" granting the papacy a measure of secular authority in Italy for the protection of the common people. Apparently the Roman Senate had been reduced to a simple municipal council of no political significance; the other civil offices had fallen vacant and were progressively being replaced by ecclesiastical ones.

2. Gregory I and the 7th Century.—At the end of the 6th century the dominant figure was Pope Gregory I the Great, who combined religious faith and practical ability. He reorganized the patrimonial lands of the church (*see* PAPAL STATES), supervised the distribution of alms in and outside Rome, and undertook the defense of ecclesiastical and secular persons and property alike against the attacks of the Lombards (*q.v.*), who had invaded Italy in 568. Several of Gregory's successors played a comparable role to a lesser extent.

3. The Franks.—Rome stood in the frontier zone between Lombards and Byzantines in Italy. Though the Romans generally preferred the Byzantines, the latter not only failed to send adequate military aid but also were theologically at variance with Rome, so that Rome's eventual separation from the Eastern Empire was inevitable. With the object of freeing themselves from the Lombards, who in the 8th century resumed their advance on Rome, the popes looked for help to the Franks. After Pope Zacharias had consented to the assumption of the Frankish crown by the Carolingian Pepin III the Short, Pope Stephen II (III) crossed the Alps to anoint Pepin and to grant him the Roman title of patrician (754). This gesture had the immediate effect of bringing Frankish armies into Italy to save Rome; and the Donation of Pepin, whereby the territory taken from the Lombards was "restored" to the Holy See, was the foundation document of the temporal power of the popes (*see* further PAPACY: *The Medieval Papacy [590–1304]: The Carolingians and the States of the Church;* PAPAL STATES).

The lay aristocracy of Rome would not easily submit to the increased authority of the clergy, and during the third quarter of the 8th century there were violent internal struggles. Pope Stephen III (IV) owed his election in 768 to military action by the *primicerius* or head of the notaries, Christophorus, and the latter's son Sergius. These two were overthrown in 770 by the pro-Lombard chamberlain, Paulus Afiarta, who, however, was put to death before he could deliver Stephen's successor, Adrian I, into the hands of the Lombard king Desiderius. Adrian's understanding with the Frankish king Charlemagne (*q.v.*) restored order in Rome. The Lombard kingdom was destroyed in 774, and Byzantine influence was eliminated from northern Italy. On Christmas Day, 800, Charlemagne was crowned emperor in Rome by Pope Leo III and acclaimed by the Roman people.

A consequence of this revival of a Western Empire was that the appointment of the popes came to be controlled by the emperor's *missus* (legate) rather than by the clergy or by the Roman nobles; but this state of affairs did not last long.

4. The Arabs and the House of Theophylact.—The Frankish sovereigns rapidly lost prestige, and the interests of the Romans could not be ignored. Riots and some double papal elections occurred, but some degree of unanimity was reestablished in the face of an external danger—the Arab invasions. The Arabs plundered the outskirts of Rome (including St. Peter's) in 846, and their fleet was defeated off Ostia in 849. By constructing a protective wall round St. Peter's, Pope Leo IV formed the suburb known as the Leonine City, nucleus of the later Vatican State. Even so, factional conflict broke out again, and the notable efforts of Pope John VIII against the continuing Arab menace were brought to an end by his assassination in 882.

There followed a sombre period which severer historians have described as "the Iron Age of the Papacy" or "the Pornocracy" ("Whores' Regime") but which nevertheless saw the emergence of a freer civic life in Rome, with a more plentiful array of personalities engaged in it, conscious moreover both of Rome's traditions and of the most pressing economic problems. The course of political events must be briefly illustrated. Two dukes of Spoleto, Guy (d. 894) and his son Lambert, had made themselves kings of Italy (Lombardy) and had obtained the imperial title from Popes Stephen V (VI) and Formosus in 891 and 892 respectively. The dukes put such pressure on Rome that Formosus appealed to the Eastern Frankish king Arnulf, whom Formosus in 896 crowned as emperor. But when Formosus was dead and Arnulf had returned to Germany, the next pope, Stephen VI (VII), again under pressure from the resentful Lambert, had Formosus disinterred and subjected to trial, after which the corpse was thrown into the Tiber.

The first decades of the 10th century were marked by the rise to power of Theophylact, senator of the Romans. Theophylact accumulated civic offices and, together with his wife Theodora and his daughter Marozia (the persons referred to in the term "pornocracy"), came to exercise a true dictatorship, placing nominees of his own on the papal throne and undertaking the defense of Rome against Saracen assaults (his protégé Pope John X distinguished himself in a notable victory on the Garigliano River in 915). Marozia, however, made a false move when she took Hugh of Provence, king of Italy, as her third husband, since this union threatened to deprive Rome of its individual liberty. Alberic, Marozia's son by an earlier union, led a rising in the city, himself assumed the title of "prince of all the Romans," and governed the state from 932 or 933 till his death in 954. Alberic maintained good relations with Byzantium and with neighbouring lords and thought of summoning Cluniac monks to reform the life of the church; but his son, who became pope as John XII in 955 (as Alberic had intended), proved incapable of completing the reconciliation of ecclesiastical and civil authority in Rome. The period of comparative independence ended with the coming of the German king Otto I (q.v.), of the Saxon dynasty, who was crowned emperor in 962.

5. The Saxon Emperors and the Crescentii.—Otto I was determined to make his presence felt in Rome, but Leo VIII, whom he installed as pope in the place of the deposed John, was not accepted by the Romans, who chose Benedict V instead. Otto, however, took Benedict prisoner after a siege of Rome in 964, and other revolts were put down. Otto I's successors and the popes whom they protected, however, had to face the resistance of the Roman family of the Crescentii (q.v.). One Crescentius, who had rebelled against Pope Gregory V in 996, was besieged in Castel S. Angelo by Otto III in 998 and finally beheaded with great publicity. Otto's own project of a *renovatio imperii* or renewal of the Roman Empire, involving not only a close understanding with the papacy (for which he selected the learned Silvester II) but also the construction of a great palace on the Aventine and the appointment of numerous functionaries with high-sounding imperial titles, met with scant response from the Romans themselves. His premature death (1002) was followed by a resurgence of the Crescentii in the person of John (II) Crescentius, who virtually ruled Rome for a decade.

6. The Tusculans.—The Roman tradition was next carried on by another local family, that of the counts of Tusculum. Related to the house of Theophylact and possessing extensive lands around Frascati and the abbey of Grottaferrata (which they founded), these counts dominated Rome from 1012 to 1045. Three popes (the brothers Benedict VIII and John XIX and their nephew Benedict IX) were members of the family, which moreover held all the principal secular posts, with titles such as "consul and duke of the Romans" and "count of the sacred palace." Occasionally a German king came to Rome to be crowned emperor, but Roman affairs remained in the hands of the citizens, as represented by the Tusculans and other nobles.

7. The 11th-Century Reform.—Breakup of the Tusculan system came as a result of the Hildebrandine or Gregorian reform of the church, so named from its initiator, Hildebrand, the future Pope Gregory (q.v.) VII. Under Pope Nicholas II, who as a partisan of Hildebrand was determined to free the papacy from its scandalous subjection to control by laymen, the Lateran Council of 1059 resolved that the election of the pope was to rest with the body of cardinals, incumbents of the oldest and most important Roman churches (see CARDINAL); that the Roman people should simply acclaim the pope elected; and that "due honour" (an empty formula) should be paid to the emperor in the matter. The reaction of the Roman nobility, struck to the core in its interests, was long and violent, but finally ineffective, though numerous antipopes were put forward with the support, moreover, of the emperors, whose interests had been no less prejudiced than the nobility's by the reform. The reformers were upheld by new families such as the Frangipane and the Pierleoni, who later became great nobles themselves but who first appeared as representatives of a new class, closely tied to the fortunes of the reformed church and depending more on financial resources than on landed property.

The contest between Nicholas II's successor, Alexander II, and the antipope Honorius II led first to disputations between them at assemblies of the citizens in the Circus Maximus, then to savage street fighting. When both were dead, Hildebrand himself became pope (1073). Violence began again in 1075 when a nobleman, Cencius, assaulted the pope at Mass in Sta. Maria Maggiore and abducted him; but a popular rising set the pope free. Gregory's quarrel with the emperor Henry IV over the universal matter of investiture (see INVESTITURE CONTROVERSY) had more damaging consequences: Henry sponsored the antipope Clement III (1080), advanced twice to the walls of Rome (1081 and 1082), then besieged and took the Leonine City (1083), except for Castel S. Angelo, Gregory's last stronghold. Finally, in 1084, Henry entered Rome, where the citizens, bought over by him, let him appoint new officials. Gregory could only appeal to the papacy's vassals in southern Italy, the Normans, who, led by Robert Guiscard, soon came to his help. But the Norman sack of Rome (1084) so infuriated the citizens that Gregory had to flee with his deliverers; he died at Salerno in 1085.

Disputes between Gregorians and anti-Gregorians dragged on until the third decade of the 12th century. Pope Urban II (1088–99), who enjoyed great prestige in western Europe, was weak in his own house. Pope Paschal II's attempt at agreement with the emperor Henry V in 1111 was disowned by the Romans and by his fellow churchmen, with the result that fighting between Germans and Romans and civil disorders continued till Calixtus II came to terms with Henry over investiture in 1122.

8. The Movement for Civic Independence.—Meanwhile new families, the Corsi, the Barunci, the Buccapecora, and the Sant' Eustachio, were emerging in Rome beside the Frangipane and the Pierleoni. Their appearance was symptomatic of a hitherto unprecedented socio-political expansion analogous to that which was giving rise to communes in Tuscany and in northern Italy during this very period (see COMMUNE [MEDIEVAL]), but external as well as internal conditions inhibited the growth of a communal movement in Rome. The reformed papacy became dissociated from the civic life of Rome, not only because the distinction between ecclesiastical and civic offices was henceforth sharper but also because there were many foreigners in the Curia, and the clergy was developing a certain prejudice against the Romans, to which a quantity of anti-Roman propaganda gave expression in the 12th century.

The papal schism of 1130–38 originated less from ecclesiastical differences than from a persistent antagonism between the Frangipane and the Pierleoni: the Frangipane supported Pope Innocent II, whom the emperor Lothair II also backed; the Pierleoni supported the antipopes Anacletus II (one of their family) and Victor IV, with the backing of the Norman Roger II of Sicily.

There followed a *coup d'état* in 1143, the so-called *renovatio senatus* or "renewal of the Senate," whereby the Romans sought to free themselves from ecclesiastical control and to establish a civic regime of their own. Ever recalling their classical past, they gave the title of senator to their new communal councilors, who were, however, of humble social status and were concerned less with politics than with ordinary administration. This movement, which Pope Eugenius III tried in vain to suppress in 1145, was not at first "anticlerical" in the modern sense, as the Romans remained devoutly Catholic. But a touch of heresy came when Arnold (*q.v.*) of Brescia arrived preaching ecclesiastical poverty and detachment from temporal interests. Arnold also tried to create an "equestrian order" in Rome, so as to organize the industrial and financial bourgeoisie in the guise of the ancient equites and thus to consolidate the citizens' newly won independence; but the whole enterprise collapsed. The German king Frederick I Barbarossa, of the Hohenstaufen dynasty, who gave consistent support to the popes against the Romans till 1159, came to Rome in 1155 to be crowned emperor by Adrian IV (an Englishman), whereupon Arnold was taken prisoner and put to death. The Romans, though they received Frederick with hostility, came to see that they could not detach themselves from the Curia, however alien and oppressive it might be, without incurring interdicts (which checked the influx of pilgrims and damaged their economy) or provoking foreign attacks. Frederick I's breach with Pope Alexander III in 1159 gave some precarious hope of a reconciliation between the emperor and the Romans; but they had rallied to Alexander's cause by 1167, when Frederick routed their troops at Monte Porzio and captured the Leonine City. Then a sudden plague in his camp made Frederick withdraw.

Frederick and Alexander finally made peace in 1177; Pope Clement III, himself a Roman, came to terms with the citizens in 1188, making financial concessions in return for the virtual extinction of communal independence. The senator Benedetto Carushomo, who headed a largely popular revolt in 1191, was deposed and imprisoned. During the pontificate of the great Innocent III various new agreements, concluded between 1198 and 1205, strengthened the church's hold: the prefect of Rome became a papal official; numerous landed properties passed under ecclesiastical control; and the pope assumed the right of nominating the senator.

9. The 13th Century.—The strife between the popes and the Hohenstaufen emperor Frederick II (*q.v.*), which went on intermittently between 1227 and 1250, had its repercussions on Rome. The revolt of Luca Savelli (a nephew of a previous pope, Honorius III) in 1234 in defense of the people's rights—or rather of the middle classes' interest in having the roads free for commerce and in being able to dispose of large sums of money—strengthened the emperor's hand in his negotiations with Pope Gregory (*q.v.*) IX; and Frederick sought to incite further revolts by addressing manifestos full of classical references to the Romans. In 1240, however, the Romans were dissuaded by Gregory from admitting Frederick to the city. On Gregory's death (August 1241) the senator Matteo Rosso Orsini held the cardinals in conclave, under conditions amounting to siege, to make them elect a pope of his choice, and, when Celestine IV also died (November), Frederick likewise tried coercion; but Sinibaldo Fieschi, who became pope as Innocent IV in 1243, freed himself from such pressures by escaping from Italy to denounce Frederick at the Council of Lyons.

The various interests, allegiances, and antipathies of the great Roman families are an integral part of the city's history. Members of the Orsini (*q.v.*) and Savelli have been mentioned incidentally above. Other families that came to the fore at this time were the Annibaldi, the Capocci, and, above all, the Colonna (*q.v.*).

Brancaleone degli Andalò, a Bolognese, whose installation as senator in the Capitol was the result of a sudden rising in 1252, initiated a general reform of the Roman guilds (*reformatio artium*) and promoted certain measures against the power of the Curia; but the socially advanced character of his program led to a reaction, and he was overthrown in 1255. By this time, however, the papacy was engaged in its final dispute with the Hohenstaufen dynasty over the kingdom of Sicily, a crucial episode in the duel between Guelphs and Ghibellines (*see* SICILY; NAPLES, KINGDOM OF; GUELPHS AND GHIBELLINES). Attempts to win the Romans' support were made by both sides: by the Hohenstaufen Manfred (*q.v.*), who took advantage of Brancaleone's momentary return to power in 1257–58; and by Charles of Anjou, the French prince who was recognized as senator of Rome by Pope Urban IV in 1263 and who actually assumed the senatorial functions in 1265, just before he was invested with the Sicilian kingdom, as Charles I (*q.v.*), under Pope Clement IV. Having won his kingdom from Manfred (1266), Charles resigned the senatorship, which the papacy had been reluctant to see in the hands of a foreign potentate. After some disturbances, however, the office came, in 1267, to another foreigner, the Castilian infante Henry. This Henry soon declared himself for the Hohenstaufen Conradin (*q.v.*), who arrived from Germany to attack Charles' kingdom and was rapturously received by the Romans. Charles defeated Conradin and took the senatorship again (1268), holding it for ten years, dominating the papacy, and enriching himself by taxation.

Pope Nicholas III, an Orsini, took the senatorship from Charles in 1278 and decided that it should be vested in the pope as a private person (in fact he appointed deputies), believing that this change would resolve the dualism between the ecclesiastical and the secular regimes in Rome. His successor, however, was a Frenchman, Martin IV, who not only packed the Curia with his fellow countrymen but also undid Nicholas III's reform by granting the senatorship to Charles of Anjou again (1281–84). A further cause of lasting detriment to church and city alike was the antagonism between the Colonna and the Orsini. Each of these families, now indisputably the foremost in Rome, had its own train of satellites irreconcilably hostile to the other side.

The energetic and inflexible Boniface VIII, who became pope in 1294, made trouble for himself by trying to aggrandize his own family, the Caetani (*q.v.*) of Anagni, at the expense of the Colonna, against whom he launched excommunication and war. Less unfortunate for Rome was Boniface's proclamation of the first Jubilee, or Holy Year (1300): by offering indulgences to the faithful who visited the Roman basilicas and performed certain acts of charity in the course of that year, he attracted hordes of pilgrims and raised

VIEW OF ROME AT THE END OF THE 15TH CENTURY. WOODCUT FROM H. SCHEDEL, LIBER CRONICORUM, NÜRNBERG, 1493.. IN THE BRITISH MUSEUM

Sheep grazing across an ancient road on the outskirts of Rome. This road, and an elaborate network of others like it, once linked the capital with the rest of the empire

Ruins of Hadrian's Villa, about 15 mi. E of Rome; in the background is the town of Tivoli

ANCIENT ROME AND ENVIRONS

The Roman Forum, once the heart of ancient Rome, looking toward the Colosseum

PLATE II

ROME

Rome, looking northeast from the top of Gianicolo Hill. The belt of trees lines the bank of the Tiber; in the background may be seen the elaborate white top of the monument of Victor Emmanuel II

RENAISSANCE AND MODERN ROME

The Piazza del Popolo, looking west from the Pincio Hill; in the left background is the dome of St. Peter's

Aerial view of St. Peter's Basilica and the Piazza San Pietro; at right may be seen a portion of the Vatican

The Scala di Spagna (Spanish Steps), completed in 1725, leading from the Piazza di Spagna to the Church of the Trinity at the top. John Keats died in the house at right in 1821

PHOTOGRAPHS, (TOP) JOHN ROSS—PHOTO RESEARCHERS, INC., (BOTTOM LEFT) LOUIS RENAULT—PHOTO RESEARCHERS, INC., (CENTRE RIGHT, BOTTOM RIGHT) FRED BOND—PIX FROM PUBLIX

great sums of money, at the same time promoting the restoration of churches and monuments.

The Jubilee of 1300 marks the end of an era in Rome's history. In 1303 the aged Boniface, whom the Colonna and the French king Philip IV's emissary Guillaume de Nogaret surprised and humiliated at Anagni, returned to Rome to die nearly insane. In 1305 a conclave at Perugia elected an Aquitanian archbishop to the papacy as Clement V; and Clement, who did not even set foot in Italy as pope, took up residence at Avignon in 1309. The city of Rome, abandoned to its own economically inadequate resources and to factional strife, slumped into insignificance in the field of international politics. Little remained for the Romans save literary and artistic reminiscences of their ancient greatness.

(PA. B.)

B. FROM THE 14TH CENTURY TO THE PRESENT

1. The Close of the Middle Ages.—The city of Rome which was deserted by the popes in the early 14th century was already somewhat neglected. The 13th-century popes had spent relatively little time there, and the vitality of a community which had no commercial *raison d'être* suffered accordingly. The Roman walls surrounded a number of virtually distinct centres of population— at the Lateran, in the vicinity of St. Peter's, and between these two the civic centre on the Capitol. Gardens, copses, and wasteland separated them and extended over the Seven Hills. The nobility (Caetani, Orsini, Colonna, and others), with fortified residences inside the walls and extensive estates outside, constituted a continuous threat to both the precarious commune and the civil magistracy of the pope.

The French popes, established at Avignon from 1309 to 1377, neither abandoned their material interests in Italy nor maintained them successfully. The city was subjected to violent tensions. At the start of the 14th century the arrangement was reestablished whereby the commune accepted papal suzerainty, the pope nominating a senator. But this system did not operate easily in the absence of a pope. The permanent pressure of the nobility and of the kings of Naples turned every unusual situation into a political crisis: there were upheavals when the emperor Henry VII arrived to be crowned in 1312 and when his successor Louis IV came in 1328. The most dramatic of these episodes was the rise to power as "tribune" of Cola di Rienzo (q.v.).

Cola di Rienzo had evoked the glories of ancient Rome, partly perhaps because his imagination had been excited at the crowning of Petrarch (q.v.) as poet laureate on the Capitol in 1341. From this point onward there is a steady development of the notion of Rome as a capital city, in which Petrarch's writings played a decisive part. Though it was far from easy for Italians elsewhere to accept with equanimity anything savouring of Roman political ascendancy, the cultural influence of ancient Rome in both its Republican and Imperial phases continued to be felt throughout the peninsula. Elsewhere, in Florence especially, it was Republican memories which stirred men to regard their Roman heritage in a new light; in Rome itself, home of the autocratic popes, it was inevitable that the Rome of the Caesars predominated as an inspiration.

The return of the pope from Avignon in 1377 did not immediately release such sentiments. The year 1378 witnessed the beginning of the Great Schism which was to last until it was ended by the Council of Constance in 1417. This effectively deprived Rome of its significance. Indeed, during the schism any enemy of the papacy could legitimize revolt by alliance with a rival pope or by adherence to conciliar principles. These years were particularly chaotic for the city, and more than once it was at the mercy of the king of Naples. Martin V, a member of the Colonna family, elected undisputed pope at Constance, began the reestablishment of order, but his efforts were imperiled by the impolitic behaviour of Eugenius IV, who estranged the Colonna, so alienated the populace that he was forced to flee the city, and at the same time was at odds with the Council meeting at Basel (*see* PAPACY: *The Renaissance Papacy*).

These years, however, mark a turning point. The papal court spent much time at Florence, where its members became soaked in the new artistic, moral, and literary values summarized in the term Renaissance. And it was at Florence that union was negotiated with the Orthodox Greeks, a move which, though short-lived, gave Eugenius a prestige which few of his predecessors during the last century and a half had enjoyed. Subsequent popes were in fact less powerful as leaders of the church. But they were masters of Rome and imbued with a desire to enhance its standing as a cultural centre.

From the pontificate of Nicholas V (1447–55), and rapidly in and after the pontificate of Sixtus IV (1471–84), Rome began to acquire its Renaissance shape. The 14th century had seen little new construction. Now the old houses and murky corridors were swept away to make room for rational building. Great thoroughfares were constructed and palaces were raised, many of which still survive; and plans were made to rebuild the basilica of St. Peter's, though two centuries were to elapse before the work was completed. Scholars and artists were drawn from other centres, notably Florence, to decorate the new buildings and especially the papal residence at the Vatican. Rome by the end of the 15th century had become the main cultural focus in Italy. (DE. H.)

2. The 16th and 17th Centuries.—The French invasions of Italy after 1494 gave the papacy an opportunity to strengthen its hold over Rome and the papal states. Alexander VI made an alliance with Louis XII of France in 1498, and the pope's son, Cesare Borgia (q.v.), ruthlessly imposed his own and his father's authority. The capture and division of the kingdom of Naples by France and Spain in 1501 enabled Alexander to crush the house of Colonna, which had supported Frederick of Naples, and to destroy their castles. The same fate befell the Orsini in 1503, after two members of the house had been murdered by Cesare at Senigallia and Cardinal Orsini had died in prison in Rome. The defeat of Francis I of France by the emperor Charles V at Pavia in 1525, however, led to fear in Rome of the growing imperial power in Italy, and in 1526 Pope Clement VII formed the League of Cognac against the emperor. In 1527 an unpaid and mutinous army of Germans and Spaniards under Charles, duc de Bourbon, marched on Rome and on May 6 forced an entry into the city, Bourbon being killed in the assault. Clement fled to Castel S. Angelo, and for the next eight days Rome was ruthlessly sacked. The imperial troops withdrew in the summer, when plague broke out, but returned in September to sack the city a second time.

The destruction, which brought to an end the cultural influence of Renaissance Rome, was followed by the repressive governments of the Counter-Reformation popes. In 1542 Paul III established the Inquisition in Rome. Although the use of torture and the burning of heretics by Paul IV led in 1559 to a riot in which the palace of the Inquisition was sacked and a statue of the pope thrown into the Tiber, the power and authority of the papacy in Rome increased during this period. Sixtus V, by his reorganization of the papal finances, was able to begin the extensive reconstruction of the city around the Viminal, Esquiline, and Quirinal hills, and on his death in 1590 Rome was one of the wealthiest cities in Europe.

The nepotist popes of the 17th century used this wealth for the aggrandizement of their families. Under Urban VIII the family feuds and street brawls of the days before the Counter-Reformation returned to Rome; corruption and bribery became widespread under Innocent X, and the dignity of the papal authority sank even lower under the Chigi pope, Alexander VII (for the establishment of his ancestors in Rome, *see* CHIGI-ALBANI). In 1662 the Chigi faction, supporters of Spanish influence in Italy, incited the pope's Corsican guards to attack the French ambassador. Threatened with war by Louis XIV, Alexander was forced to make a humble apology for the incident and to erect a monument to commemorate his submission.

3. The 18th Century, the Revolution, and Napoleon I.— By the Treaty of Utrecht in 1713, Austria replaced Spain as the dominant power in Italy. But although in the first half of the 18th century military forces moved across the papal states in the course of the dynastic wars in Italy, Rome itself remained unmolested. The city enjoyed an era of peace under the paternalistic government of the popes until the wars of the French Revolution.

The Roman mob's fatal violence against the diplomat Nicolas de Bassville (*q.v.*) in 1793 infuriated the French government and in 1797 Napoleon Bonaparte advanced on Rome. At the Peace of Tolentino (February 1797) Pius VI was able to save the city only at the price of losing a large part of the papal states.

Rome's independence, however, did not survive for long. In a riot provoked by the Republican minority in the city in December 1797, the French general Léonard Duphot was killed by papal guards; in February 1798 Gen. Louis Berthier occupied Rome. The pope was forced into exile, and the Roman Republic was set up under an executive of seven consuls. Hostility toward the Republic increased as churches were pillaged and Rome was drained of its art treasures. In November 1798 Ferdinand IV of Naples (afterward Ferdinand I of the Two Sicilies) reentered the war against Napoleon. The Neapolitan army led by Gen. Karl von Mack marched into Rome on Nov. 28, but the French returned in December after Gen. J. E. Championnet's victory over Mack at Civita Castellana. The reestablished Republic lasted only until 1799, when the Austrian-Russian campaign swept the French out of Italy.

Napoleon's second conquest of Italy took place in 1800. Pius VII was allowed to retain Rome and the papal territory as laid down in the Treaty of Tolentino; on his refusal to take part in Napoleon's continental blockade in 1807, however, French troops under Gen. Sextius Miollis again occupied Rome on Feb. 2, 1808. In May 1809 Napoleon announced the annexation of Rome and the papal states to the French Empire. Pius replied with a bull of excommunication, which on June 11 was posted on the doors of the three great basilicas of Rome; in July he was arrested and exiled. Rome now became the second city of the Empire, and on the birth of Napoleon's son (later known as Napoleon II) in 1811 Napoleon named him king of Rome. The introduction of the Code Napoléon and subsequent reforms were received with little favour by the Roman population, still strongly influenced by the clergy, and the return (May 1814) of Pius VII, following Napoleon's fall, was greeted with popular acclaim.

4. Rome and Italy, from 1815.—The Congress of Vienna in 1815 formally restored Rome to the pope. The period of repression and reactionary government that followed was brought to an end by the liberal reforms of Pius (*q.v.*) IX. Greater freedom was given to the press, an advisory council of state was set up, and a civil guard was formed. On March 14, 1848, Pius granted a constitution. But on the outbreak of revolutions throughout Europe in that month, Pius became unable to control the extremists in Rome, and when his chief minister, Pellegrino Rossi, was assas-

sinated (November 1848), Pius fled to Gaeta. A constituent assembly, convoked in Rome in December, proclaimed the Roman Republic on Feb. 9, 1849. Meanwhile Giuseppe Garibaldi (*q.v.*) had arrived with his legion, to be joined in March by Giuseppe Mazzini (*q.v.*). The assembly thereupon appointed Mazzini, Aurelio Saffi, and Carlo Armellini as triumvirs with absolute authority. A French army under Gen. Charles Nicolas Oudinot, sent by Napoleon III to restore Pius, was repulsed by Garibaldi from the Janiculan Hill on April 30, but after a heroic defense Garibaldi was forced to abandon the city at the end of June. Pius returned in April 1850, opposed to liberal reform and protected by a French garrison. (*See* also ITALIAN INDEPENDENCE, WARS OF.)

The decision of Cavour (*q.v.*) to occupy the papal states on behalf of Piedmont in September 1860 deliberately excluded Rome and its surrounding district. The Italian Parliament at Turin declared Rome to be the capital but failed to persuade Pius to renounce his temporal power; and when the kingdom of Italy was proclaimed in March 1861, Rome remained outside. The "Roman Question" lingered on. Garibaldi tried to solve the problem by revolutionary methods and made two unsuccessful marches on the city in 1862 and 1867. The final withdrawal of the French garrison in August 1870 during the Franco-German War, and Napoleon III's defeat at Sedan (Sept. 1), removed the last obstacle to union. On Sept. 20 Italian troops under Gen. Raffaele Cadorna forced a breach in the Porta Pia and seized Rome. A plebiscite in October voted for union with Italy; nevertheless Pius refused to accept the occupation and the government's proposed settlement, the Law of Guarantees (1871), and chose to remain a "prisoner" within the Vatican.

In 1871 Rome became the capital of Italy and the king took up residence in the Quirinale Palace. From that time the population of Rome grew rapidly and there was much speculative building, interrupted by the financial crisis of 1887. New town-planning schemes led to the building of such main roads as the Via Nazionale and Corso Vittorio Emanuele.

It was at a congress in Rome in 1921 that the Fascist movement organized itself as a party, and in the following year the "march on Rome" (Oct. 28) brought Benito Mussolini to power. Rome figured largely in his plans, being the capital of both modern Italy and the Roman Empire; new roads, buildings, and suburbs were constructed, and several archaeological sites were cleared.

The Roman Question was finally solved by the Lateran Treaty and Concordat of 1929 between Pius XI and Mussolini's government. The treaty accepted the existence within Rome of a Vatican City State, under the sovereignty of the pope, and the concordat regulated the relations between the church and the Italian state.

In August 1943, following the bombing of the city by U.S. aircraft, the Italian government declared Rome an open city. Thus, on its liberation by the Allies in June 1944, it had suffered little damage in comparison with other Italian cities.

With the establishment of the Republic in 1948 the Quirinale became the official residence of the president. The Lateran pacts remained the basis of church-state relations, and pilgrims formed a large part of the annual influx of visitors to Rome, particularly during the Holy Year of 1950. Other attractions included the 17th Olympic Games, held in August–September 1960.

See also entries under "Rome" in the Index. (X.)

BIBLIOGRAPHY.—*Topography and Buildings:* R. Valentini and G. Zucchetti, *Codice topografico della città di Roma,* 4 vol. (1940–53); F. Castagnoli *et al., Topografia e urbanistica di Roma* (1958). *Ancient City:* S. B. Platner and T. Ashby, *A Topographical Dictionary of Ancient Rome* (1929); E. Nash, *Pictorial Dictionary of Ancient Rome,* 2 vol. (1961–62). *Churches:* M. Armellini, *Le chiese di Roma dal secolo IV al XIX,* rev. ed. by C. Cecchelli, 2 vol. (1942); R. Krautheimer *et al., Corpus basilicarum christianarum Romae* (1937–).
History: For ancient history *see* ROMAN HISTORY: *Bibliography. Medieval:* F. Gregorovius, *Geschichte der Stadt Rom im Mittelalter,* 4th ed., 8 vol. (1886–96), reissued ed. by W. Kampf, 3 vol. (1953–57); Eng. trans. by A. Hamilton, 13 vol. (1900–06); O. Bertolini, *Roma di fronte a Bisanzio e ai Longobardi* (1941); P. Brezzi, *Roma e l'impero medioevale (774–1252)* (1947); E. Duprè Theseider, *Roma dal comune di popolo alla signoria pontificia (1252–1377)* (1952). *Renaissance:* P. Paschini, *Roma nel Rinascimento* (1940); P. Pecchiai, *Roma nel Cinquecento* (1948). *See* also general histories of Italy and the papacy.
(DE. H.; X.)

FELICI

THE SIGNING OF THE LATERAN TREATY BY BENITO MUSSOLINI (LEFT FRONT) AND PIETRO CARDINAL GASPARRI (RIGHT), 1929

ROME, a city of Georgia, U.S., the seat of Floyd county, is located at the confluence of the Etowah and Oostanaula rivers, 70 mi. N.W. of Atlanta.

Founded in 1834 at the southern gateway of Georgia's valley region, it was an important connecting link between the middle Georgia cotton belt and Tennessee, serving as a clearinghouse for corn, wheat and livestock from the north and cotton from the Coosa river valley which begins just west of the city. The surrounding agricultural area, once devoted primarily to cotton, later became diversified, with livestock and poultry of leading importance. Considerable forest land, two-thirds of which is in pine, provides saw timber and pulpwood. Mining is of some importance, including bauxite, shales and limestones. Textile products have long been a major segment of the city's economy but other manufactured products include paper, furniture, agricultural implements, boats, cotton gins, casket shells, aluminum products and stoves.

The city has a council-manager form of government, in effect since 1919. Near Rome is Berry college, a private liberal arts college founded in 1903, whose students all participate in a work experience program on the campus; in the city is Shorter college, a coeducational liberal arts institution chartered in 1873 and affiliated with the Baptist Church, and Darlington, a private preparatory school for boys. For comparative population figures *see* table in GEORGIA: *Population.* (Js. C. B.)

ROME, a city of Oneida county, east-central New York, U.S., 15 mi. N.W. of Utica (*q.v.*) on the Mohawk river, Wood creek, the State Barge canal and the thruway. With a 1960 population of 51,646 it is the second city of the Utica-Rome standard metropolitan statistical area, comprising Herkimer and Oneida counties (pop. 330,771).

Highlights of its history revolve around colonial and Revolutionary War events. Several forts were built by the British to protect the settlement in 1755, but the most famous was Ft. Stanwix built in 1758 by the general whose name it bore. It was the scene of an important treaty (1768) between Sir William Johnson and Indians of the Six Nations in which lands of western Pennsylvania, Kentucky and West Virginia were surrendered to the crown. The fort was dismantled thereafter and rebuilt in 1776 by order of Gen. Philip Schuyler, for whom it was named (causing the original Ft. Schuyler to be renamed Old Ft. Schuyler, before becoming Utica), but the name Stanwix continued in popular usage. The fame of the fort arose from its role in the battle of Oriskany (*q.v.*), 6 mi. E., on Aug. 6, 1777, when the British advance into the Mohawk valley was stopped. According to local tradition the "Stars and Stripes" (with no stars) was raised in battle there for the first time (*see* FLAG: *Flags of the United States*).

The first earth was turned there for the Erie canal in 1817. Rome later achieved industrial importance as the "copper city" through the manufacture of wire, brass, cable and other products. Metals and machinery industries (vacuum cleaners, radiators, air-conditioning equipment) have since developed. After World War II, Griffiss air force base, with thousands of civilian and military personnel, fundamentally changed the economic and social life of Rome. The township of Rome was organized in 1796, receiving its name "from the heroic defense of the republic made here." The village of Rome was incorporated in 1819, and in 1870 it was chartered as a city. Rome tried city-manager government (1954–58) but returned to the mayor-council system. For comparative population figures *see* table in NEW YORK: *Population.* (V. C. C.)

ROMILLY, SIR SAMUEL (1757–1818), English law reformer whose chief efforts were devoted to the reform of English criminal law and procedure, was born in London March 1, 1757; he was the second son of Peter Romilly, an English tradesman of Huguenot stock. In the years that followed his call to the bar in 1783, he rose in his profession to become the outstanding chancery advocate in England. He early became identified with the liberal movement of his time. He gave assistance and sympathetic support to the early leaders of the French revolution and became associated with Jeremy Bentham (*q.v.*) and the circle of English law reformers. In 1806 he became solicitor-general in the Ministry of All the Talents and entered the house of commons where he attacked the savage penal laws of the period which indiscriminately authorized the sentence of death in a host of minor felonies. Romilly's program for mitigation of the law was founded on utilitarian assumptions similar to those expressed in the writings of Bentham and Cesare Beccaria (*q.v.*). However, his efforts were obstructed by the conservative reaction in parliament to the French revolution and its aftermath, perhaps best exemplified by the attitudes of Lord Ellenborough in the house of lords, and his immediate successes were not impressive. In 1808 he managed to achieve repeal of an Elizabethan statute that imposed capital punishment on theft from the person. He likewise secured elimination of the punishment of transportation for stealing from bleaching-grounds and the death penalty for soldiers and sailors found begging without a permit. Though frustrated in his larger efforts, Romilly, through his writings and speeches, eventually produced a profound effect and contributed importantly to the reforms that were carried out in the years following his death. Distracted by the death of his wife, he committed suicide on Nov. 2, 1818, in London. His *Memoirs,* with a selection from his correspondence, appeared in three volumes in 1840; a two-volume edition of *The Speeches of Sir Samuel Romilly in the House of Commons* was published in 1820.

See also "Life and Work of Sir Samuel Romilly" by Sir W. J. Collins, in *Trans. of the Huguenot Society* (1908); C. Phillipson, *Three Criminal Law Reformers* (1923). (F. A. A.)

ROMMEL, ERWIN (1891–1944), German army officer, outstanding field commander and desert-warfare tactician in World War II, was born at Heidenheim, near Ulm, on Nov. 15, 1891. He entered the army as a cadet in 1910 and distinguished himself in World War I. After serving mostly as infantry regimental officer and instructor between World Wars I and II, Rommel took command of Hitler's bodyguard battalion in 1939. He commanded the 7th panzer division, which led the rapid advance to the channel in May 1940. In Feb. 1941 he became German commander in Libya and pushed British forces back into Egypt.

Known as the "Desert Fox," he was highly respected by both sides. Despite reinforcements, he was compelled by logistic difficulties and superior British strength to withdraw to Tunisia, whence he was evacuated. As field marshal, Rommel commanded army group B in France, under Gerd von Rundstedt; wounded in an air raid on July 17, 1944, he was sent home to recover.

Rommel had become increasingly disillusioned with Hitler's highhanded conduct of the war and the atrocities ordered by Hitler's headquarters. He therefore did not oppose the conspiracy to remove Hitler, although favouring arrest rather than assassination. He would have been proclaimed chief of state if the assassination attempt against Hitler of July 20, 1944, had succeeded; the investigation of the plot revealed this. On Oct. 14, 1944, Rommel was taken from his home and forced to swallow poison.

Rommel wrote *Infanterie greift an* (1937) and *Krieg ohne Hass* (1950), published in English as *The Rommel Papers* (1953).

See Lutz Koch, *Die Wandlung eines grossen Soldaten* (1950); Desmond Young, *Rommel,* in English (1950). (P. N. T.)

ROMNEY, GEORGE (1734–1802), English history and portrait painter, next in importance after Reynolds and Gainsborough during the latter half of the 18th century, was born at Dalton-in-Furness, Lancashire, on Dec. 15, 1734, the son of a cabinetmaker. After working in his father's studio, in 1755 he became the pupil for two years of an itinerant portrait and genre painter, Christopher Steele, at Kendal, Westmorland. Romney's early work is a harder and provincial variant on the style of Joseph Highmore and much less accomplished than Steele's. Having married and set up as a portrait painter, he toured the northern counties, producing likenesses for a few guineas each. A series of about 20 figure compositions were exhibited in Kendal and afterward sold by lottery.

In 1762, having saved about £100, he left a portion of this sum for his wife and children and went to London, never returning, except for brief visits, until he came in 1798, a broken-down and aged man, to die. He quickly gained notice when in 1763 he won an award from the Society of Arts for a "Death of Wolfe." It was judged worthy of the second prize but, after a recommendation from Sir Joshua Reynolds in favour of J. H. Mortimer's "Edward the Confessor," Romney had to be content with a donation of £50. This incident led to a subsequent coldness between him and the president and thereafter he held aloof from the Academy. However, Romney was an ambitious yet nervous and introspective character, shunning society and the company of his fellow artists.

He paid his first visit to Paris in 1764, where he was befriended by Joseph Vernet and, significantly, admired the work of Nicolas Le Sueur; Romney had not yet seen Raphael, and Le Sueur's use of the antique would have strongly appealed to him. In all his portraits Romney avoids any suggestion of the positive characteristics or sensibilities of the sitter and, although himself unsociable, ironically his great success with society sitters depended largely upon just this ability for dispassionate flattery.

Line rather than colour dominates; it is the flowing rhythms and easy poses of Roman classical sculpture which underlie the smooth papery patterns of his compositions. Among the works exhibited at the Society of Artists from 1763 to 1772 (this is the only period that he did exhibit publicly) are the "Sir George and Lady Warren and Their Daughter" (1769) and "Mrs. Yates as The Tragic Muse" (1771), in which the figures are abnormally elongated and trapped out in pretentious classical poses. He kept his fees low and soon acquired a large clientele, rivaling in popularity Reynolds, whose near neighbour he had become in Great Newport street. A more intimate portrait group is the "Peter and James Romney" of 1766; and the "Mr. and Mrs. William Lindow" (1772, Tate gallery, London) is one of this period's maturest works.

BY COURTESY OF THE SECRETARY OF STATE FOR COMMONWEALTH RELATIONS

DETAIL FROM A PORTRAIT OF WARREN HASTINGS BY GEORGE ROMNEY, 1795. IN THE INDIA OFFICE LIBRARY

Romney spent more than two years in Italy, leaving for Rome with the miniature painter Ozias Humphrey in 1773. He studied chiefly the Stanze figures by Raphael, although several months were spent studying Titian in Venice and Correggio at Parma. He returned to London in 1775 and settled in Cavendish square. The months abroad had matured his art and a new gracefulness appears in portraits such as "Mrs. Carwardine and Son" (1775, Lord Hillingdon collection); the bland, handsome "Earl Grey" (1784, Eton college); and the conscious elegance of the large full-length "Sir Christopher and Lady Sykes" (1786, Sledmere, Yorkshire). His best years are 1775–85, although the seeds of decline were sown at the time of his meeting with Emma Hart (later Lady Hamilton) about 1781–82 and his acquaintance with the poet William Hayley. Lady Hamilton exercised a morbid fascination over Romney and she became for him a means of escape into an imaginary, ideal world. His "divine Emma" appears in over 50 paintings, in the roles of Cassandra, Circe, Calypso, a Bacchante, a Magdalene or Joan of Arc. John Flaxman, his friend in later years, attests that Romney disliked the drudgery of face painting and longed to do ideal subjects, but little remains of these except a large collection of drawings for ambitious history pieces (mainly in the Fitzwilliam museum, Cambridge) and a few unattractive compositions for John Boydell's Shakespeare gallery of 1787 onward.

Although Romney's fashionable portraits fell off in the last years of his career, his own unhappiness had given him an insight into a mature character, and the "Warren Hastings" (1795, former India office) is a grave and noble work. For Romney it was a swan song. In 1797 he moved to a large studio in Hampstead with the fine collection of casts from the antique which Flaxman had gathered for him in Italy. But he soon retired to Kendal, where he died on Nov. 15, 1802.

BIBLIOGRAPHY.—W. Hayley, *The Life of George Romney* (1809); J. Romney, *Memoirs of the Life and Work of George Romney* (1830); T. H. Ward and W. Roberts, *Romney*, etc., 2 vol., with catalogue (1904); Anne Crookshank, "The Drawings of George Romney," *Burlington Magazine* (Feb. 1957).   (D. L. FR.)

ROMNEY, HENRY SIDNEY (SYDNEY), EARL OF (1641–1704), English statesman who played a leading part in the Revolution of 1688, was born in Paris in 1641, the fourth son of Robert, 2nd earl of Leicester. He was at the English court after the Restoration of Charles II and in 1665 was appointed groom of the bedchamber to James, duke of York, and master of horse to his duchess; Charles II made him master of the robes in 1675. He was elected to the Parliament of March 1679 which introduced the first bill to exclude the duke of York (later James II) from the succession, and he became closely associated with the group, led by his nephew Robert Spencer, 2nd earl of Sunderland, and Sir William Temple, which supported the claims of Princess Mary and her husband William of Orange against those of the duke of Monmouth. Sidney was sent in June 1679 as envoy to The Hague where he took the opportunity to further his friends' policy of a close alliance between Holland and England; with Sunderland he tried at various times to persuade William to go to England. Charles II's final triumph over the exclusionists and the disgrace of Sunderland in 1681 led to Sidney's dismissal.

William, now his firm friend, offered him the command of the British regiments in Dutch service, but Charles II only allowed him to accept a colonelcy. He resigned in 1684 and returned to England where he was reappointed master of the robes, a post he held until the Revolution of 1688. Dissatisfied with James II's policy, however, he visited William of Orange in 1686 and then spent six months in Italy; his activities and political aims at this period are not clear. He returned to Holland in March 1687 and in December was sent to England to rally William's supporters among the nobility. His *pourparlers* led to the famous Invitation to William (June 30, 1688), which he signed and may have drafted, and which caused him to be described as "the great wheel on which the Revolution rolled." He returned to Holland in August 1688 and in late October sailed with William's expedition to Torbay. William appointed him colonel of the first regiment of foot guards in 1689 and created him Viscount Sidney of Sheppey.

Sidney remained high in King William's favour but did not prove to have the qualities of an administrator or statesman. He was given the secretaryship of state for the northern department in December 1690, but resigned in March 1692 and was sent as lord lieutenant to Ireland. In the difficult circumstances which followed the Treaty of Limerick (1691) (*see* IRELAND: *History*) Sidney was unable to control the fiercely Protestant Parliament of 1692, and on his recall in 1693 was appointed master general of the ordnance. He was created earl of Romney on May 14, 1694. He succeeded William Bentinck, 1st earl of Portland, as groom of the stole in 1700 and was lord warden of the Cinque Ports from 1691 to 1702. On Queen Anne's accession (1702) he was dismissed from all his offices. He died in London, unmarried, on April 8, 1704. His diary of the times of Charles II was published in 2 volumes (1843).   (J. P. K.)

ROMNEY (Kent, England): *see* NEW ROMNEY.

ROMSEY, a market town and municipal borough of Hampshire, Eng., lies 9 mi. (14 km.) NW of Southampton by road. Pop. (1961) 6,350. Situated on the River Test, famed for its salmon fishing, Romsey is dominated by its massive 12th-century Norman abbey church, which replaced a wooden church founded by King Edward the Elder for Benedictine nuns in 907. It still possesses a pre-Conquest crucifix, and a rood of probably 11th-century date built into an outside wall of the south transept. After the abbey was dissolved in 1539 the parishioners of Romsey bought the abbey church for £100, thus saving it from destruction.

King John's house, east of the abbey church, was used as a hunting lodge by King John in 1210 and is now a museum. Romsey obtained its first charter from James I in 1607, the year he visited Broadlands. This house, originally a Tudor building, was practically rebuilt in 1733 when the 1st Viscount Palmerston was in residence. The gardens were laid out under the direction of "Capability" Brown. It became the home of Earl Mountbatten, the town's high steward. Princess Elizabeth (later Queen Elizabeth II) and Prince Philip spent part of their honeymoon there.

Romsey also has a memorial park, a sports centre, and a swimming pool. Embley House, 2 mi. (3 km.) W, now a college, was once the home of Florence Nightingale. The town's chief industries are brewing and market gardening, and in the early 1960s factories for carpets, plastic boats, and light engineering works were erected. (K. C. E. H.; R. J. Wa.)

ROMUALD, SAINT (c. 950–1027), founder of the Camaldolese Benedictines (Hermits), was born at Ravenna of the ducal family (Onesti). After witnessing his father kill a relative in a duel, he retired to the monastery of St. Apollinaris near Ravenna and later took the habit. Romuald's life throughout was marked by great austerity. In 975 he went to Catalonia, and seems to have been greatly impressed by the vigorous life in the monasteries. In 996 he was appointed abbot of St. Apollinaris, but left after three years and for the next 30 years wandered through Tuscany, the Romagna and southern France reforming old or founding new monasteries. The most important was Camaldoli, near Arezzo, in Tuscany, which he founded about 1012 and which became the mother house of the new order. The order combined cenobitic and eremitical elements, though Romuald's own aim seems to have been only for a more austere following of the Benedictine rule than currently obtained. He attempted to go to Hungary, but was prevented by illness; however, a monastery founded there for him and St. Bruno of Querfurt, by Otto III, was important for missions to the Slavs and Prussians. Romuald stayed for many years in solitude on Mt. Sitria, but in 1026 returned to Val di Castro, where he died, alone in his cell, on June 19, 1027. His chief feast is Feb. 7, since on that date in 1481 his relics were taken to Fabriano. See also CAMALDOLESE.

See H. Thurston and D. Attwater (eds.), *Butler's Lives of the Saints*, p. 266 ff. (1957). (Fs. P. C.)

ROMULO, CARLOS PENA (1901–) Philippine general, government official and diplomat, was born Jan. 14, 1901, in Camiling, Tarlac Province, on the island of Luzon. After he received an A.B. degree from the University of the Philippines in 1918 the Philippine government sponsored his graduate study at Columbia University in New York City where he earned an M.A. degree. After his return to the Philippines in 1921 Romulo was appointed assistant professor of English at the University of the Philippines; later he became head of the English department. In 1931 he was made editor-in-chief of the TVT Publications, consisting of three newspapers, one in English, one in Spanish, and one in Tagalog. In 1937 he became publisher of another chain of newspapers.

In 1941 Romulo embarked on a tour of countries near the Philippines and reported his evaluation of the military situation there. His predictions, which proved to be accurate, won for him a Pulitzer Prize for journalism in 1942. When Japan attacked the Philippines in 1941, he became an aide-de-camp to U.S. Gen. Douglas MacArthur on Corregidor Island and his broadcasts became widely known as the "Voice of Freedom." After Japan captured Corregidor, he went with General MacArthur to Australia and then joined the Philippine Commonwealth government of Pres. Manuel Quezon in Washington, D.C., as secretary of information. Romulo went ashore with General MacArthur at Leyte in 1944, and participated with the U.S. forces in the liberation of Manila in 1945. He served as resident commissioner of the Philippines to the United States, 1944–46, and attended the San Francisco Conference of the United Nations in 1945. After 1946 Romulo served as chief of the Philippine delegation to the Far East Commission in Washington, D.C., as chief of the Philippine mission to the United Nations. In 1948 he served as president of the United Nations Conference on Freedom of Information in

Geneva, Switz. He was president of the General Assembly of the UN 1949–50 and in 1950 became secretary of foreign affairs of the Philippines. He represented the Philippines in the signing of the mutual defense treaty with the U.S. and the Treaty of Peace with Japan in 1951. In December 1951 he was named ambassador to the U.S. No longer satisfied with the politics of the incumbent Liberal Party, in 1953 he decided to run for the presidency of the Philippines on a third-party ticket, but he withdrew to become campaign manager for the successful Nacionalista Party candidate, Ramón Magsaysay.

Romulo continued as ambassador in Washington but he represented his country at the Bandung Conference of Asian and African nations in 1955. When the Philippines was elected to a seat on the United Nations Security Council in 1956, Romulo served as member of the Council and during the month of January 1957 was its chairman. He was appointed president of the University of the Philippines in 1962, and Pres. Ferdinand Marcos named him secretary of education in 1965.

See C. Romulo, *I Walked with Heroes* (1961). (C. A. B.)

ROMULUS AND REMUS, the legendary founders of Rome. Traditionally they were the sons of Rhea Silvia (Ilia), daughter of Numitor, king of Alba Longa. Numitor had been deposed by his younger brother Amulius and his daughter made a Vestal Virgin to prevent offspring contenders. When Rhea gave birth to twins, claiming Mars as their father, Amulius ordered them thrown into the Tiber. The trough in which they were placed came to ground at the site of the future Rome near the *ficus ruminalis*, a sacred fig tree of historical times. There a she-wolf and a woodpecker (both sacred to Mars) suckled and fed them. Later they were found and brought up by the herdsman Faustulus and his wife Acca Larentia. They became leaders of a band of adventurous youths and eventually, recognized as the grandsons of Numitor, they killed Amulius and restored their grandfather to the throne. Later they founded the city of Rome. Romulus surrounded the city with a wall, but Remus in contempt jumped over it and Romulus slew him with the words "thus perish any other who leaps over my walls." Thus Romulus ruled supreme and the city was named for him. Romulus added to the population of the new city by offering asylum to fugitives and exiles. Because of a shortage of women, he invited the neighbouring Sabines to a festival and carried off their women. The intermarriage of Roman and Sabine was followed, after some hostility, with a political union under Romulus and Titus Tatius (q.v.), king of the Sabines. Titus Tatius' early death left Romulus in complete control. After a long rule he one day mysteriously disappeared in a storm. He was believed to have been changed into a god and was worshiped as Quirinus (q.v.) by the Roman people.

This legend, probably originating in the 4th century B.C. and set down in coherent form by the early annalists at the end of the 3rd century B.C., is of course artificial and shows a strong Greek influence. Rationalizations of various aspects of the story have been made in both ancient and modern times. The theme of exposed children is a familiar one in Greek legend and literature. The name Romulus (and perhaps also Remus) is derived from Rome and is consonant with the Greek practice of seeking an eponymous hero who of course is inevitably deified. The story is well adapted to the topography of ancient Rome, but the places mentioned are clearly introduced to account for sacred areas of historical time. The *ficus ruminalis* ("the suckling fig"?) and the nearby Lupercal ("wolf's den"?) may have themselves suggested the suckling by the she-wolf. Livy gives an interesting rationalizing version: that Larentia, because of her loose morals, had got the nickname "she-wolf" among the shepherds. The story of the asylum was clearly invented to explain the name of the depression between the Arx and the Capitol. The rape of the Sabine women explains the custom of simulated capture in the Roman marriage ceremony as well as the historical admixture of Sabine elements in the Roman population.

The importance of Mars in the legend is an obvious attempt of Romans to connect their origins with this principal Italian deity, and it is perhaps no coincidence that Romulus is apotheosized into Quirinus, a god related to Mars. On earth Romulus, a warlike king, was founder of many of the Roman military and political institutions.

BIBLIOGRAPHY.—J. Carter in Roscher's *Lexikon*, s.v.; E. Pais, *Ancient Legends of Roman History* (1906); Hugh Last in *Cambridge Ancient History*, vol. vii, pp. 363 ff., 370 ff.   (R. B. LD.)

ROMULUS AUGUSTULUS, commonly known as the last of the Western Roman emperors (475–476), was in fact a usurper and was not recognized by the Eastern emperor. He was named after his grandfather, a certain count Romulus, and was the son of the patrician Orestes who had had considerable influence with Attila and had lived at the Huns' headquarters. Romulus' original name was Romulus Augustus, the latter being turned into a diminutive because he was still a child when his father elevated him to the throne at Ravenna on Oct. 31, 475, after driving out Julius Nepos (*q.v.*). For about 12 months Orestes ruled Italy in his son's name, but eventually his troops mutinied and found a leader in Odoacer (*q.v.*). Orestes was put to death at Ravenna on Aug. 28, 476. Odoacer, however, spared Romulus on account of his youth, gave him a pension, and sent him to live with his relatives in Campania. His subsequent fate is unknown.   (E. A. T.)

RONCESVALLES (Fr. RONCEVAUX), a village of Navarre province, northern Spain, lies at 3,220 ft. (981 m.) in the Pyrenees, within 5 mi. (8 km.) of the French frontier and 26 mi. (42 km.) from Pamplona. Pop. (1960) 99, with less than a dozen inhabited houses. Above the village is the Puerto de Ibañeta, or Pass of Roncesvalles (3,648 ft. [1,112 m.]), the traditional site of the ambush and defeat of Charlemagne's army (778; *see* CHARLEMAGNE). According to legend (*see* ROLAND, CHANSON DE), it was there that Roland, Oliver, and Archbishop Turpin, with the greater part of the French Army, were killed. A similar fate was avoided (810) by Louis I, "the Pious," or "*le Débonnaire*," then king of Aquitaine, who forced the wives and children of the local inhabitants to go with his army through the pass. At the summit of the pass are the remains of an early chapel of San Salvador (called Charlemagne's chapel) and the Charlemagne monument (1934). In the village is an Augustinian abbey, founded about 1130 by Sancho de la Rosa, bishop of Pamplona, and the king of Navarre, for the use of pilgrims, especially those en route to Compostela, many of whom are buried there. The main church was built by Sancho VII, "the Strong," of Navarre (*c.* 1230), and contains the tombs of Sancho and his wife, Clémence. A 13th-century statue of the Virgin of Sorrows (wood, covered with gold) stands in the centre of the altarpiece. Roncesvalles is the scene of a procession of penitent pilgrims, each carrying a heavy cross and wearing a black hood, on the Wednesday before Whitsunday.

RONDEAU, one of several related medieval verse and musical forms that were originally covered by the Old French term *rondel* (*rondellus*). Besides the rondeau, they include the virelai and the ballade (*qq.v.*); all three are characterized by the use of a refrain (a term here used in the sense of a repeated line or lines within a strophe, or throughout a poem of linked strophes). For the rondeau as a musical form *see* TROUVÈRES: *Musical Forms; see also* RONDO.

The rondeau developed in France, where a common 13th-century form follows the rhyme scheme *ABaAabAB* (the capital letters indicate the text of the refrain, shown in the examples by italics). This form was used by Adam de la Halle (*c.* 1250–1306; *q.v.*; the first to call it a *rondel*):

> *Amours et ma dame aussi,*
> *Jointe mains vous proi merchi.*
>
> *Votres grant biauté marvi,*
> *Amours et ma dame aussi.*
>
> Si n'avès pité de mi;
> Votres grant bonté marvi.
> *Amours et ma dame aussi,*
> *Jointes mains vous proi merchi.*

This has been translated as:

"Love and my lady too, with clasped hands I beseech your pity! It was to my misfortune that I beheld your very great beauty, Love and my lady too. If you do not take pity on me, then it was to my misfortune that I beheld your very great merit. Love and my lady too, with clasped hands I beseech your pity!"

This kind of rondeau is one of three types recognized by Eustache Deschamps (*q.v.*) as verse forms governed by regular rules in his *Art de dictier* (1392), the first French treatise on versification. He calls it the *rondel sangle* ("simple"). Deschamps' second type (no name is given), apparently peculiar to the 14th century, is of 13 lines. His third type, which he calls the *rondel double* (later called the *rondel redoublé*, or *parfait*), is of 16 lines; it reached its height with Guillaume de Machaut (*c.* 1300–77; *q.v.*), as is shown by the following eight-line example:

> *Blanche com lys, plus que rose vermeille,*
> *Resplendissant com rubis d'Oriant,*
> En remirant vo biauté non pareille,
> *Blanche com lys, plus que rose vermeille,*
> Suy si ravis que mes cuers toudis veille
> Afin que serve a loy de fin amant,
> *Blanche com lys, plus que rose vermeille,*
> *Resplendissant com rubis d'Oriant.*

translated as:

> *White as the lily, redder than rose,*
> *Shining with rubies from the East,*
> Thy matchless beauty I disclose,
> *White as the lily, redder than rose,*
> My charmèd heart do I dispose
> That I as lover serve at least
> *White as the lily, redder than rose,*
> *Shining with rubies from the East.*

The poets of the late 14th and 15th centuries introduced variations into the 16-line *rondel double*. Some rondeaux by Christine de Pisan (1364–*c.* 1430; *q.v.*), for example, have up to eight lines in the first strophe; make less use of the refrain; and have lines of unequal length. During this period, rondeaux with strophes of more than four lines became known as *rondeaux doubles*, and those with 16 lines (Desportes' *rondels doubles*) were renamed *rondeaux quatrains*. Charles d'Orléans (1394–1465; *q.v.*) excelled in composing this type of rondeau, and of many well-known examples the following is typical:

> "Le Printemps"
> *Le temps a laissié son manteau*
> *De vent, de froidure et de pluye,*
> *Et s'est vestu de brouderie*
> *De souleil luisant, cler et beau.*
>
> Il n'y a beste, ne oyseau,
> Qu'en son jargon ne chant ou crye:
> *Le temps [a laissié son manteau*
> *De vent, de froidure et de pluye.]*
>
> Rivière, fontaine et ruisseau
> Portent, en livrée jolie,
> Goultes d'argent d'orfavrie
> Chascun s'habille de nouveau:
> *Le temps [a laissié son manteau*
> *De vent, de froidure et de pluye,*
> *Et s'est vestu de brouderie,*
> *De souleil luisant, cler et beau.]*

translated, without the last two lines of the refrain, as:

> "Spring"
> *Time has lost her wintry gear*
> *Of wind, and cold, and rain,*
> And is attired again
> In radiant sunlight, bright and clear.
>
> All birds and beasts, both far and near
> Do sing and shout amain:
> *Time has lost her wintry gear*
> *Of wind, and cold, and rain.*
>
> Rivers, fountains, streams appear
> In all their raiment gay,
> And sparkle on their way,
> And silverly shine forth again:
> *Time has lost her wintry gear*
> *Of wind, and cold, and rain.*

The loss of the last lines of the refrain probably derives from the copyists' habit of giving only the first words of a refrain when it was repeated: this was called the *rentrement*. That this is the case in the original manuscript of "Le Printemps" is shown above by square brackets. Perhaps as a result of this copyists' convention, poets themselves reduced the refrain, substituting two *rentrements* for six refrain lines, and thus producing a 12-line rondeau from the 16-line *rondeau quatrain*. A similar use of two *rentrements* for the eight lines of the refrain of a 21-line type of rondeau (rhyming *aabba aabAAB aabbaAABBA*) created the 15-line rondeau (rhyming *aabba aabR aabbaR: R = rentrement; i.e.,* refrain). This, the standard type in the 16th century, is exemplified by Clément Marot (*q.v.*). It was revived by the early 17th-century *précieux*—writers opposed to the restrictions imposed by the academies, chief among them being Vincent Voiture (*q.v.; see also* FRENCH LITERATURE: *The 17th Century*).

Again rejected by the classical poets and critics of the late 17th and 18th centuries, the rondeau and similar forms only reappeared with the advent of Romanticism. Rondeaux were first written in the 19th century, in irregular form (*ababa* for *aabba*), *c.* 1830, by Alfred de Musset; then in regular form by Théodore de Banville (*q.v.*), who, as well as writing rondeaux of the standard 15-line type, revived the 16-line *rondeau quatrain;* his most important collection was *Rondels* (1874). These forms were used by the Parnassians and early Symbolists (*qq.v.*), and the poet and musician Maurice Rollinat (1846–1903) wrote more than 100 rondeaux. Few 20th-century poets, however, have used the forms.

The rondeau, introduced in Germany (where it was called *Rundum,* or *Ringelgedicht*) in the late 16th century by Johann Fischart for satirical verse, was used early in the 17th by poets of the Heidelberg school (*see* GERMAN LITERATURE: *The 17th Century*), especially Georg Rudolf Weckherlin (1584–1653). It was reintroduced in the 18th century by Johann Nikolaus Götz (1721–81) who wrote occasional verse trivial in theme but of interest for its use of foreign verse forms.

The rondeau was introduced to England in the 14th century by Chaucer, whose early love lyrics—"ballades, roundels and virelays"—were influenced by Machaut. An example is the "triple roundel," "Merciles Beautè," the first part of which, "Captivity" (the other two being "Rejection" and "Escape"), is as follows:

> *Your eyen two wol slee me sodenly,*
> *I may the beautè of them not sustene,*
> So woundeth hit through-out my hertë kene
> And but your word wol helen hastily
> My hertës wounde, whyl that hit is grene,
> *Your eyen two wol slee me sodenly,*
> *I may the beautè of them not sustene.*
>
> Upon my trouthe I sey yow feithfully,
> That ye bene of my lyf and deeth the queene
> For with my deeth the trouthë shal be sene.
> *Your eyen two wol slee me sodenly,*
> *I may the beautè of them not sustene,*
> So woundeth hit through-out my hertë kene.

Here Chaucer uses the French 14th-century 13-line form, to produce a lyric combining neatness of versification with expression of real, if formalized, feeling.

After Chaucer's time the rondeau lapsed, as Italian influence gained ground. In the late 19th century, however, it became briefly fashionable under *fin de siècle* French influence. Swinburne in his *A Century of Roundels* (1883) invented an 11-line rondeau (rhyming *abaR bab abaR*) by rhyming the shortened refrain at the beginning of the first line with the second line, and omitting the refrain after the second strophe. More regular rondeaux were written by Austin Dobson, Edmund Gosse, W. E. Henley, and Robert Bridges, and translations of French rondeaux were made by Henley, Andrew Lang, and Longfellow. Few rondeaux of this period were of great intrinsic merit, however. Almost the only correct example of a regular form is Austin Dobson's "In After Days," which uses refrain and recurring rhyme scheme with something of its intended effect:

> *In after days* when grasses high
> O'ertop the stone where I shall lie,
> Though ill or well the world adjust
> My slender claim to honour'd dust,
> I shall not question nor reply.

> I shall not see the morning sky;
> I shall not hear the night-wind sigh;
> I shall be mute, as all men must
> *In after days!*

> But yet, now living, fain would I
> That someone then should testify,
> Saying—"He held his pen in trust
> To Art, not serving shame or lust."
> Will none?—Then let my memory die
> *In after days!*

BIBLIOGRAPHY.—L. E. Kastner, *A History of French Versification* (1903); G. Saintsbury, *A History of English Prosody,* 3 vol. (1906–10); G. Reese, *Music in the Middle Ages* (1940), and *Music in the Renaissance* (1954), which include many rondeaux with musical settings, and full bibliographies.

RONDO (RONDEAU), in music, an instrumental form derived from a medieval verse form, the rondeau (*q.v.*), and developed in the 18th century as a solo piece or as a finale of the sonata and symphonic forms. In the 13th-century songs of the trouvères and in the polyphonic music of the 14th and 15th centuries the structure of the rondeau consisted of two sections A and B, which constituted the music for both the refrain and the *additamenta,* usually taking the form A B a A a b A B. In the harpsichord rondeaux of Couperin, Rameau, and others the refrain alternated with episodes according to the scheme A B A C A D, etc. The refrain, and also the episodes, were 8 or 16 bars in length, and each episode gravitated around a different key, such as the dominant or the relative minor. The symphonic rondo of the 18th century was not essentially different from these earlier forms. The number of episodes was reduced and their alternation with the refrain was conceived in such a way that the form had a three-part (ternary) character. A common form was A B A C A B A. A highly developed form of the rondo is the finale of Mozart's Piano Concerto in A major (K. 488). This is a movement in nine sections in which the episodes are boldly worked out and contrasted. Sometimes in the 19th-century rondo the refrain was inclined to be repeated mechanically, as in Beethoven's Sonata in E minor, Op. 90, where it is heard no less than eight times in its original form. Weber, Chopin, Mendelssohn, and Saint-Saëns are among the composers who developed the rondo in the 19th century. In the 20th century several works of Olivier Messiaen, notably the *Turângalila* Symphony, are built on the principle of the rondo.

RONDÔNIA, a federal territory in the central-west region of Brazil, bounded north by Amazonas, east by Mato Grosso, west by Bolivia and south by Bolivia and Mato Grosso. Pop. (1960) 70,783; area 93,839 sq.mi. (243,043 sq.km.). The territory, established in 1943 as Guaporé, was renamed Rondônia in 1956 after Marshal Candido Mariano Rondon, Brazil's famous explorer. The area was important during the Amazon rubber boom, but declined after the collapse of the industry, in 1912.

The Madeira-Mamoré Railroad, operational between Pôrto Velho and Guajará Mirim, was built there in connection with the rubber industry. Rubber exports still provide the territory with a large part of its income. Brazil nuts are also an important export commodity. Mineral resources include diamonds, mercury, gold, bauxite, gypsum and quartz. The population is composed largely of Indians and mestizos.

Pôrto Velho (pop. [1960] 19,387) is the territorial capital, terminus of the Madeira-Mamoré Railroad and entrepôt for the Bolivian trade. River transportation on the Madeira, Mamoré, Guaporé (*qq.v.*) and their affluents is supplemented by air service from Pôrto Velho, Guajará and Príncipe da Beira. (J. L. TR.)

RONSARD, PIERRE DE (1524–1585), French poet, chief of the Pléiade (*see* FRENCH LITERATURE), was born Sept. 11 (?), 1524, at the Château de la Possonnière (Loir-et-Cher). His father Louis de Ronsard, a member of the Vendômois nobility, held a court appointment. Ronsard spent his youth in his native province, which was often to inspire his poetry. In 1536 his father placed him as page first to the dauphin, later to Prince Charles. He accompanied Princess Madeleine to Scotland after her marriage to James V in 1537. Returning in 1538, he was sent to Flanders, again to Scotland (where his ship was wrecked in the very last stage of the voyage) and to England. Early in 1540 he resumed his education at the Écurie Royale and from May to August accompanied the diplomat Lazare de Baïf on a mission to Haguenau. In the autumn, a severe illness followed by a long convalescence at La Possonnière left Ronsard partially deaf and forced him to abandon all thought of a military or diplomatic career. In 1543 he received the tonsure, which enabled him to qualify for ecclesiastical benefices without being ordained priest.

Encouraged by Jacques Peletier, Ronsard then turned to poetry, which, he tells us, had always attracted him. His father died in 1544 and Ronsard went to Paris. He studied with Antoine de Baïf, the diplomat's son, under the famous Hellenist Jean Daurat (Dorat). Daurat's brilliant lectures at the Collège de Coqueret inspired Ronsard and Baïf with a passion for Greek poetry and a desire to revolutionize French poetry. They were joined at Coqueret by others, including Belleau and Du Bellay, who in 1549 published the manifesto of the new *brigade* of poets, the *Défense et illustration de la langue française*, preaching judicious imitation of the ancients and Italians and cultivation of their genres. Ronsard's contributions to this manifesto are erudite, full of mythological lore and arrogantly addressed to a learned élite. His *Odes* (1550, 4 books) are inspired by Pindar and Horace; his *Amours* (1552), decasyllabic sonnets of great lyrical intensity celebrating a young court beauty, Cassandre Salviati, imitate the manner of Petrarch. They were set to music by Pierre Certon, Claude Goudimel, Marc-Antoine Muret and Clément Janequin.

The *Odes* brought Ronsard fame and provoked the raillery and enmity of Mellin de Saint-Gelais, then the favourite court poet. He was defended by Princess Marguerite, sister of Henry II, and her chancellor Michel de L'Hôpital. Ronsard expressed his triumph, his gratitude and his lofty conception of poetry in the Pindaric *Ode à Michel de L'Hôpital* (1552). Then he turned to less pretentious models—the Greek Anthology, the Anacreontea, Catullus—and wrote simpler poems. The *Folastries* (1553), *Bocage* (1554), *Mélanges* (1554, title page 1555), the sonnets and odes written for new editions of the *Amours* and *Odes,* all show a lighter mood. Next Ronsard, in love with Marie, a simple country girl, published the *Continuation des amours* (1555) and the *Nouvelle Continuation* (1556), sonnets and songs no longer chastely Petrarchan but playful and epicurean in tone, with a charming background of country sights and sounds. The lofty *Hymnes* in alexandrines (1555–56) show a return to the erudite manner. Modeled on Callimachus, Theocritus and others, they contain fine epic descriptions and religious or philosophical meditations. Many of Ronsard's hymns and odes are of an official or laudatory character. He was in the favour of Henry II, who made him counselor and almoner (1559). His collected *Oeuvres* appeared in 1560.

With the deaths of Henry II in 1559 and Francis II in 1560 France entered the dangerous period of the religious wars. Ronsard, intensely loyal and patriotic, used his pen in the cause of the monarchy, the established religion and national unity. His *Institution pour l'adolescence du Roi Charles IX* (1562) shows him unafraid to preach duty and morality to the young king. His polemical *Discours des misères de ce temps, Remonstrance au peuple de France* (1562) and *Réponse aux injures et calomnies* (1563) show him aware of the political and religious problems and critical of abuses in the church. Patriotic indignation, vigorous satire and invective against the Protestants alternate with passages of imaginative poetry or sincere self-revelation. Ronsard appears here, as always, versatile and original. In 1565 the *Elegies, mascarades et bergerie* show Ronsard producing official poems and verses for court entertainments. He enjoyed the friendship of Charles IX, a passable poet, and exchanged poems with him. He went on experimenting, correcting, adding new poems for his editions of 1567, 1571, 1572–73, 1578 and 1584. Ronsard's most ambitious work, his epic *La Franciade* (1572), tracing in decasyllabic couplets the founding of the French nation by the Trojan hero Francus, had little success and only four books appeared.

Ronsard had been undisputed "prince of poets and poet of princes" for many years but a new poet, Desportes, became the favourite of Henry III. Ronsard, stung into competition, published many new poems in the 1578 edition: *Diverses amours,* the exquisite sonnets and elegies *Sur la mort de Marie* and the *Sonnets*

pour Hélène (H. de Surgères), a learned and virtuous lady-in-waiting of 20. Some are erudite or precious in the Italianate style that was again fashionable; others, harmonious, intimate and sincere, show a new maturity.

The poet's last years were tormented by arthritis and recurrent fevers; he usually avoided the court and lived at his priories of Croixval (Vendômois) and Saint-Cosme (near Tours). He gave his time to his religious duties, gardening and the tireless revision of his poems. In Paris he often stayed with Jean Galland at the Collège de Boncourt. Ronsard remained a poet to the last. The moving sonnets which he dictated to a monk a few hours before his death (*Derniers vers,* 1586) show his splendid gifts still unimpaired. He died at Saint-Cosme, Dec. 27–28, 1585.

Claude Binet in his *Life of Ronsard* (1586) gives an attractive picture of the poet—tall, athletic, distinguished, soldierly; in conversation charming, frank and sincere. "His life and his writings bore an indefinable stamp of nobility and in all his actions shone forth the characteristics of a true French gentleman." Ronsard was the greatest poet of the French Renaissance. He had a European reputation; Elizabeth I and Mary Stuart sent him gifts; he was imitated in England. He deeply influenced his contemporaries, Du Bartas, A. d'Aubigné, R. Garnier.

Ronsard held a noble conception, deriving from Pindar and Plato, of the poet's mission as the recipient of divine inspiration and the interpreter of higher truths to mankind; he believed that the poet should be morally worthy of this divine gift of genius. He also believed that the poet should work unceasingly to attain perfection. Innumerable variants (no poet has left more) testify eloquently to his labours. He had made a meticulous study of the poetic technique of the Ancients and of the problems of French verse, which he enriched with new lyrical forms. He developed the alexandrine, making it capable of the finest effects. Though deaf, Ronsard greatly loved music and harmony was for him an essential quality of poetry; his sense of rhythm is extremely subtle. His theories appear in *Abrégé de l'art poétique* (1565) and in the prefaces to the *Franciade* (1572; 2nd pref. 1586; title page 1587). Ronsard's work is immensely varied in subject, form and style. Only Victor Hugo can be compared with him for fertility of invention. He writes freely of his own emotions; his best lyrics have the quality of universality. His chief fault, in modern eyes, is an over-lavish adornment of his poems with the Greek mythology he loved. He has fine descriptive powers and, like the Elizabethans, uses magnificent imagery to express his feeling for the majesty of the universe, the power of the cosmic forces, the beauty of Nature and her impact on man's emotions. He meditated on man: his diversity, his greatness, his ambitions, his passions, his destiny of inevitable defeat by decay and death. Death is a subject on which Ronsard always writes well, whether in an epicurean mood or in a Christian spirit.

In the 17th century the development of a new poetic ideal demanding clarity, refinement and restraint put Ronsard's richly imaged poetry out of fashion. Malherbe and Boileau condemned his poetry and he was forgotten until the 19th century, when the appreciation of Sainte-Beuve and others reinstated him. In the 20th century a vast amount of research once more revealed his greatness and his reputation continues to grow. The general public, however, appreciates him most as a simple lyric poet, the poet of nature, love and fleeting time.

BIBLIOGRAPHY.—Critical ed. by P. Laumonier (1914–); other eds. by P. Laumonier (1914–19; text of 1587), H. Vaganay (1923–24; text of 1578) and G. Cohen (1938; text of 1584). *See also* P. Laumonier, *Ronsard, poète lyrique* (1909), *Tableau chronologique des oeuvres de Ronsard* (1911), critical ed. of C. Binet, *Vie de Ronsard* (1910); H. Chamard, *Histoire de la Pléiade* (1939–40); P. de Nolhac, *Ronsard et l'humanisme* (1921); P. Champion, *Ronsard et son temps* (1925); M. Raymond, *L'influence de Ronsard 1550–85* (1927); R. Lebègue, *Ronsard, l'homme et l'oeuvre* (1950); F. Desonay, *Ronsard, poète de l'amour,* 3 vol. (1952–59); A. Tilley, articles (1934–46) in *Modern Language Review;* M. Bishop, *Ronsard, Prince of Poets* (1940); D. B. Wyndham Lewis, *Ronsard* (1944); I. Silver, "Ronsard Studies, 1936–50," *Bibliothèque d'Humanisme et Renaissance,* xii (1950) and "Ronsard in European Literature," xvi (1954). (M. G. M.)

RÖNTGEN (ROENTGEN), **WILHELM CONRAD** (1845–1923), German physicist, received the first Nobel Prize for physics in 1901 for his discovery of X rays. Born at Lennep on March 27, 1845, he received his early education in the Netherlands, and then went to study at Zürich. He then became assistant to August Kundt at Würzburg and afterward at Strasbourg, becoming *Privatdozent* at Strasbourg in 1874. He was next professor of mathematics and physics at Hohenheim (1875), extraordinary professor at Strasbourg (1876), ordinary professor of physics and director of the Physical Institute at Giessen (1879), and professor at Würzburg (1885) and Munich (1900). At Würzburg in 1895 he made the discovery for which his name is chiefly known, Röntgen rays or X rays. Experimenting with a highly exhausted vacuum tube on the conduction of electricity through gases, he observed the fluorescence of a barium platinocyanide screen that happened to be near. Further investigation showed that this radiation passed through various substances that are opaque to ordinary light, and also affected photographic plates. Its behaviour being curious, particularly in reflection and refraction, he doubted that it was to be looked upon as ordinary transversely vibrating light, and guessed that it was due to longitudinal vibrations in the "ether." In view of its uncertain nature, he called it X radiation. For this discovery he received the Rumford Medal of the Royal Society in 1896, jointly with Philipp Lenard, who had already shown (as had Heinrich Hertz) that a portion of the cathode rays could pass through a thin film of a metal such as aluminum. Röntgen also conducted research in other areas, including elasticity, capillarity, ratio of specific heats of gases, conduction of heat in crystals, absorption of heat by different gases, piezoelectricity, and electromagnetic rotation of polarized light. He died at Munich on Feb. 10, 1923. *See also* X Rays.

See O. Glasser, *Dr. W. C. Röntgen* (1945); R. S. Bowen, *They Found the Unknown* (1963).

ROODEPOORT, a town of the Transvaal, S.Af., lies on the western Witwatersrand about 12 mi. (19 km.) W of Johannesburg at 5,725 ft. (1,745 m.) above sea level. Pop. (1960) 95,211, comprising 40,908 Europeans, 51,398 Bantu, 1,718 Coloureds, and 1,187 Asians. The history of the town is closely linked with the development of the Witwatersrand gold fields. Roodepoort was established as a gold mining camp in 1886 and the progress of the gold mining industry stimulated its growth, and led to the formation of other townships nearby. In 1902 a health board was set up covering Roodepoort, Maraisburg, Florida, Delarey, Hamberg, and Greymont, and in 1904 the area was proclaimed a municipality. Roodepoort, which is largely a residential area, contains separate townships (about 50 in all) for Europeans, Bantu, Coloureds, and Asians. The town has 21 primary, 7 secondary schools, and 1 technical school, and there are more than 80 public parks and a large variety of sporting facilities. The artificial lake at Florida (a popular resort) provides opportunities for yachting, boating, swimming, and fishing. The nearest main centre of communications is Johannesburg, with which the town is linked by road and rail. The economy of the town was formerly dependent upon the gold fields lying along its southern perimeter, but its manufacturing industries, which include iron and steel, wool textiles, and cement and wood processing, are now more important.

The surrender of L. S. Jameson took place in 1896 just outside the town's present boundaries, and a memorial at Doornkop marks the spot where several of the Jameson raiders fell in their last engagement. (H. Ze.)

ROOF, a cover or shelter of the uppermost part of a building that serves mainly as protection against inclement weather. While this article deals primarily with roof construction, related aspects, such as roof design, can be found in ARCHITECTURE; ARCHITECTURAL ENGINEERING; HOUSE DESIGN; INDUSTRIAL ARCHITECTURE; and RESIDENTIAL ARCHITECTURE.

FORMS OF ROOFS

The principal factors determining the form of the roof are structural or aesthetic. Roofs may have flat, pitched, vaulted, domical or warped surfaces. They may be supported on walls, columns, piers or they may extend directly to their foundations.

WOODEN ROOFS

The flat roof is the simplest, least distinguished of roof forms. It is a cover adaptable to rectilinear plan arrangements over large areas. When it is applied to dwellings a light frame construction is appropriate. This type of construction consists of beams, called joists, laid horizontally and supporting a structural cover of boarding on which a membrane type of roofing is applied. The joists have nominal widths of 2 in. and nominal depths ranging from 6 in. to 12 in. in multiples of 2 in. (Nominal dimensions refer to the sawn timber before being finished or sized.)

The joists span from wall to wall and are spaced 16 in. to 18 in. on centres. When the joists are used on long spans, 16 ft. to 18 ft., they require lateral support at intervals of 6 ft. to 8 ft. This lateral support in the form of X bracing is called bridging. Flat roofs of timber construction are found appropriate for industrial plants, but due to the risk of fire they are constructed by using heavy timber beams, spaced 6 ft. to 8 ft. on centres, supporting a plank roof cover. This type of roof is classified as a mill or slow burning construction. Although this type of framing introduces limitations in planning arrangements due to interior column supports (at intervals of 16 ft. to 18 ft.), it is found to be economical and suitable for some industrial operations. Variations of the flat roof construction, in which the plane of the roof has a decided slope, are called lean-to and shed roofs. The supporting sloping beams are called rafters and have the same proportions and dimensions as the joists in the light frame construction. These roofs have the advantage of permitting the use of unit types of roof covering when the slope is sufficiently steep.

The widespread use of the double-sloped or gable (*q.v.*) roof is attributable to tradition, as well as a certain amount of standardization. The principal elements of this type of roof are pairs of

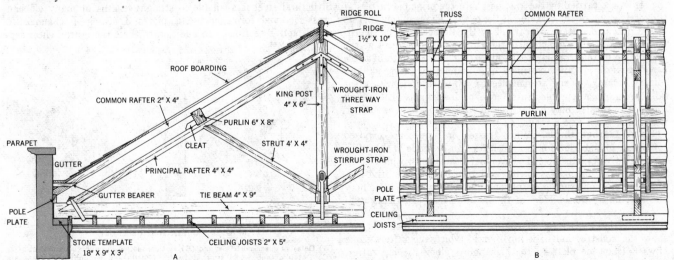

FIG. 1.—KING-POST ROOF TRUSS

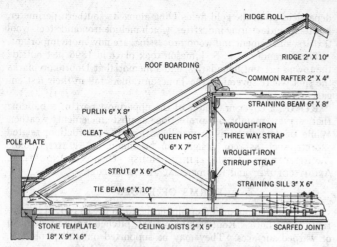

FIG. 2.—QUEEN-POST ROOF TRUSS

rafters meeting at their highest points at a horizontal ridge beam (fig. 1 [A]) that acts as a tie and stiffener. The elements are resolved into a stable framework when the sloping surfaces are boarded in. The lower ends of the rafters rest on a plate which is securely attached to the supporting walls. The weight of the structure and its covering, in addition to the snow and wind forces, bring a considerable thrust to the walls. The magnitude of these thrusts varies with the slope of the rafters, becoming larger as the slopes are reduced. To avoid the thrusts on the walls, a horizontal tie may be introduced for each pair or each alternate pair of rafters. If the ceiling joists rest on the plate or are reasonably close to the elevation of the plate, they may be secured to the walls or rafters and act as ties. If it is impracticable for reasons of headroom (clear height) to place the ties at or near the elevation of the plate, it is possible to reduce the thrust by tying the rafters at an intermediate elevation above the plate with horizontal beams attached to pairs of rafters. These ties, known as collar beams, with pairs of rafters form A frames. This type of roof structure may be used for relatively large spans, ranging up to 26 ft., without the need of intermediate supports for the rafters. When tie beams also serve as ceiling joists they may require intermediate supports on the longer spans. Support may be provided by means of a tie or hanger attached at mid-span of the rafter, or at the ridge, and secured to the ceiling joist.

When the roof span is very large (30 ft. or more), intermediate supports are required in order to avoid the necessity of excessively heavy rafters. These supports are provided by purlins which in turn are carried by roof trusses (see TRUSS). (See fig. 1 and 2.) The trusses are spaced at intervals of 10 ft. to 12 ft. and provide support for the purlins at the intersection of the axis lines of the struts and principal rafters. The vertical components of force in the struts are carried by the king post into the principal rafters at the intersection of the axis line at the peak. The resulting thrusts in the principal rafters are carried by the tie beam. The queen-post truss is similar in action to the king-post truss except at the connection of the straining beam and straining sill. Both of these early truss forms are assembled in a manner requiring skill in joinery (see fig. 3) and are inefficient even when done with great skill. A more acceptable truss form for long spans is the Fink type (fig. 7) which may be built up of rafter stock and assembled with bolts. (See also CARPENTRY.)

Open Timber Roofs.—When trusses or frames are exposed to view, a justification for less efficiency can be made in the interest of fine workmanship. The hammer-beam truss, which is essentially an A frame, was developed into a highly decorative element of roof construction displaying fine workmanship in joinery and carving by the builders of the middle ages. (See HAMMER-BEAM ROOF.)

The section and elevation (fig. 4) with the roof plan (fig. 5), show the construction of a hip roof in which the rafters slope upward from the plate to the high points along the hip rafter. The hip roof, having no gable ends, has the effect of making the

building appear lower, and transmits the thrusts through the hip rafters to corners where the plates, acting as ties, can more readily resist outward forces.

The Mansard Roof.—The mansard roof (q.v.) (fig. 6), though rarely used in present-day construction, was once a common form in Europe and the U.S. Its form was primarily a device for providing additional usable area without the necessity of adding a full story. With the cornice line at the base of the upper floor, it gave the appearance of a lower building. Remnants of its influence in the U.S. survived in the practice of using shingles for the upper story of dwellings and clapboards for the lower story. The device of lowering the cornice line to the lower chord of deep trusses and introducing a strip of sloping roof at the exterior walls may well be due to the influence of the mansard roof. (See also GAMBREL ROOF.)

Long-Span Timber Roofs.—In the early years of the 20th century the use of timber trusses and frames was generally limited to spans of 50 ft. to 60 ft. This limitation was largely due to the difficulties in joining the various parts with any real assurance of developing the predicted strengths, together with uncertainties about the behaviour and strength of the timbers. The uncertainties of joining since have been reduced with the use of split ring connectors, which in effect have the advantages of larger diameter bolts without reducing the cross-sectional areas of the timbers appreciably.

By mid-20th century the elements of the trusses could be made up of narrow stock which permitted a more accurate selection. The elements are then assembled with ring connectors.

Long-span trusses of the bowstring type, using a laminated curve member, may be employed for spans up to 200 ft., while the Pratt, Howe, Warren and Fink trusses (fig. 7) are acceptable for spans of 100 ft. Frames can be assembled from laminations $1\frac{5}{8}$ in. or less in thickness, which permits an accurate selection and arrangement of the laminates for high strengths. The improvements in glues have made the use of laminated arches and frames reliable for long-span structures. Arches and frames have been constructed for spans up to 100 ft.

Laminated frames have become increasingly acceptable for spans of 40 to 60 ft. in buildings where it would be normally undesirable to expose the structure of the roof. Since the laminated frame is a continuous formed member, proportioned in its various parts to resist the forces to which it is subjected, without any visual indication of the joining, its appearance does not conflict with other interior finished surfaces.

STEEL ROOFS

Steel as a material for roof structures has many desirable characteristics. It is strong and stiff, it can be prefabricated in a shop and erected rapidly on the site. The manufacture of steel is controlled so as to produce a uniform quality. Steel permits joining by means of rivets or welding without appreciable loss in strength. Structural steel is available in straight lengths of many efficient cross-sectional forms, including plates, I beams, [channels, L angles and T sections. In addition to these there are lighter sec-

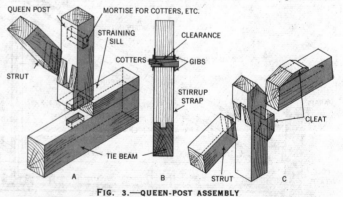

FIG. 3.—QUEEN-POST ASSEMBLY

(A) Detail of queen-post truss and (B) vertical section through queen post at base. (C) Detail of queen-post truss at head. (Purlin and wrought-iron straps are omitted for clearness)

tions formed or assembled into joists and trusses.

For flat roofs requiring noncombustible materials the open-truss steel joist supporting a steel deck and protected by a plastered ceiling is appropriate. The steel joists are available in depths varying by multiples of 2 in. from 8 in. to 20 in. and may be spaced up to 3 ft. on centres on spans ranging from 16 ft. to 36 ft. Other types of structural roof covers or decks may include wood plank or various types of composite materials consisting of a cementing agent, usually portland cement, and a light aggregate having such desirable properties as insulation, resistance to fire, holding power for nails or fasteners and strength. The decking materials are usually precast into sizes consistent with their structural capacities and attached to their supports with clips or fasteners.

Industrial buildings requiring large areas of unobstructed space are usually built with steel roof trusses supporting purlins that carry the structural roof cover. For flat roofs the chord members (top and bottom) are parallel (see fig. 7) except for long spans where the top chord is sloped slightly from the mid-span to the ends in order to facilitate draining of the roof surface. The bottom chord may also be slightly higher at mid-span (cambered) so that the deflected truss does not have the appearance of sagging. The parallel chord trusses are usually designed with depths equal to $\frac{1}{10}$ to $\frac{1}{12}$ of their span and with lateral bracing for the top and bottom chords. For aesthetic as well as economic reasons a sloping margin of roof may be introduced at the outer walls, thus reducing the height of the wall and the apparent height of the building.

For some buildings with moderate spans pitched roofs may be desirable. In principle the structure of the roof using steel trusses is the same as that for timber construction. Thus with the introduction of purlins the span of the rafters or structural roof covering is reduced. For roofs of this type it is often desirable to use a noncombustible structural cover in the form of nailable precast slabs, spanning from purlin to purlin, to which the unit type of covering may be applied. The Fink truss is well adapted to the pitched roof for relatively short spans; it may be used economically for spans of about 40 ft. up to 100 ft. For long spans, a considerable volume of the building is taken by the trusses and their bracing members. Although this volume may be used for ducts, pipelines and other services in industrial plants, it has a more limited use for auditoriums, field houses or gymnasiums, where long-span trusses are required. For these buildings steel arches or rigid frames, which require less depth, are more desirable. Frames and arches may be fabricated from the available standard elements, in the form of plate angles and T sections. Both the frame and the arch introduce thrusts at the foundation which may be taken by tie rods concealed in the floor structure or by buttresses. The purlins and structural cover are similar in arrangement to the flat or pitched roof.

Arches and frames are equally well adapted to short spans. Because of their greater strength and their ability to be incorporated with concrete, they are used for roof structures where the minimum of structural presence is desired.

Concrete Roofs

The use of concrete as a structural material had its beginning in the era of the Roman empire. The cementing material was a mixture of hydrated lime and volcanic ash, known today as a slag or puzzolan cement. With this cementing material a mortar was made having the characteristics of portland cement mortar. The dome of the Pantheon (*q.v.*) in Rome, having a diameter of about 142 ft., was constructed during the 1st century using cement mortar and masonry. The masonry material was laid with large joints of cement mortar to the extent of approximating a concrete dome. True hydraulic cement, having the ability to set under water, was made during the mid-18th century by an English engineer, during his researches in connection with the building of the third Eddystone lighthouse. The introduction of reinforcing steel and the advances in the technology of concrete since the mid-19th century have resulted in its increasing use as a structural material for roofs.

Concrete, being plastic, may be formed into various shapes hav-

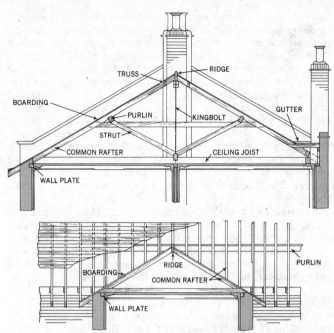

FIG. 4.—SECTION AND ELEVATION OF A ROOF FOR A DOMESTIC BUILDING

ing flat or curved surfaces. It has an inherent characteristic of continuity when reinforced with steel which eliminates most of the problems of joining and permits the construction of monolithic structures. At first reinforced concrete was used in forms that were modeled after masonry structures, but during the latter part of the 19th century the more familiar forms developed in wood and steel were followed. For roof structures, concrete is rarely used without reinforcing steel. An interesting example of concrete vaulting and domical roofing without metal reinforcement is the Roman Catholic cathedral at Westminster, London, a remarkable building designed by J. F. Bentley and constructed between 1895 and 1903.

Present-day practice tends toward the use of lighter roof structure using thin-shell forms reinforced with steel rods where tension may occur and relying on the capacities of the concrete to resist compression. Structures of thin-shell construction appeared in the 1930s in the form of semispherical domes having diameters up to 80 ft. with shell thicknesses of 3 in. The domes were supported on columns on their periphery.

In more recent years other forms have been built, including cylindrical or barrel shells, spanning in the direction of their long axis. They have cross sections in the form of segments of thin-walled cylinders with stiffening edge beams. Thus they are similar in appearance to vaults with edge beams at the springing line. When placed adjacent to one another and supported on columns along the edge beams, they can provide large unobstructed areas.

Unique roof structures using cables as the supports for the roof were constructed during the 1940s and 1950s. A stadium built in Montevideo, Urug., of this type is cylindrical with a diameter of 310 ft. The cables are arranged radially with outer ends attached to a circular ring at the top of the outer wall 85 ft. high; the inner ends are attached to a steel ring at the centre. The roof itself is of precast concrete slabs (2 in. thick) attached to the cables.

COVERING MATERIALS FOR ROOFS

Roof covers may be classified in two general groups depending upon the manner in which they seal off the entrance of water. One group consists of waterproof membrane, or built-up roofing; the other group of a unit type of waterproof material arranged in a manner so as to avoid direct passage of water through the joints. The membrane or built-up roofing is commonly applied to decks having slopes 2 in. or less per foot and single curved surfaces with varying slopes. The unit type is used on roofs having slopes of 6 in. or greater per foot.

For intermediate slopes, a wide selvage type of roll roofing may be used, or a built-up roof may be adapted. Built-up roofing is made up of several layers or plies of tarred felt, laid in coal-tar pitch so that one layer of felt is never in contact with another. Over the entire roof surface a uniform coating of pitch is poured and a covering of gravel or slag is sprinkled before the pitch has set. When the roof is to be used as a terrace or promenade, the built-up roofing is laid without gravel or slag, but with additional plies on which the tile or terrace flooring is set in a 1 in. mortar bed. Expansion joints filled with some elastic cement are usually installed in the tiled surface. Such roofs, either covered with tile, slag or gravel, are watertight, do not crack under extreme heat or cold and have become common for the better class of flat roof coverings. If adequately flashed at intersections with walls and parapets, they require a minimum of slope, sufficient only to drain the surface.

Corrugated Sheets.—Corrugated iron or steel is supplied either black, galvanized or with protective coatings. It is especially suited for the roofs of storage buildings and buildings of a temporary or semipermanent character. Being to a large extent self-supporting, it may have a specially designed roof framework of light construction. If, as is usually the case, the sheets are laid with the corrugations running with the slope of the roof, they can be fixed directly on purlins spaced at full or half lengths of the sheets according to the stiffness of the sheets. In pure air the zinc coating of the galvanized sheets is durable for many years, but in large cities and manufacturing towns its life is short unless protected by painting. In such districts it has been found that sheets manufactured with protective coatings applied on iron or steel are more serviceable. In such districts it has been found that plain sheets, well coated with paint, will last longer than those galvanized, for the latter are attacked by corrosive influences through minute flaws in the zinc coating developed in the proc-

ess of corrugation, in transit or from a defect in the coating.

For roofing purposes the sheets are supplied in several thicknesses ranging from no. 16 to no. 22 standard wire gauge. No. 16 is for exceptionally strong work. No. 18 and no. 20 are used for standard work and no. 22 for temporary buildings. The sheets when laid should lap one full corrugation at their sides and from 3 in. to 6 in. at the ends. Riveting is the best method of connecting the sheets, although galvanized bolts, which are not as satisfactory, are frequently employed. The joints should be along the crowns of the corrugations to avoid leakage. Holes can be punched during the erection of the roof. For attachment to timber framework, galvanized screws or nails with domed washers are used. Fixing to a steel framework is effected by galvanized hook bolts which clip the purlins and pass through the sheet. Sheets formed with V crimps, spaced about 15 in. on centres with the portion between being flat, give a better effect in some positions than the $1\frac{1}{4}$ in. to $2\frac{1}{2}$ in. corrugated sheets.

Aluminum.—In addition to the surface-protected iron and steel corrugated sheets, there are available in many areas aluminum sheets and rolls. As a light material having insulation value this corrugated material is well adapted to general use. It should be applied to a structural roof cover in a manner similar to that used for laying corrugated iron and steel sheets, using aluminum nails with screw shanks.

Composition.—A widely accepted corrugated sheet manufactured under various trade names consists of a formed sheet using portland cement and asbestos fibre compressed under great pressure into a monolithic unlaminated sheet having good strength characteristic and durability. It resists corrosion and has a high resistance to acid fumes and to exposure to extreme weather conditions. It may be used as the structural cover for flat roofs and the complete cover for pitched roofs having slopes greater than

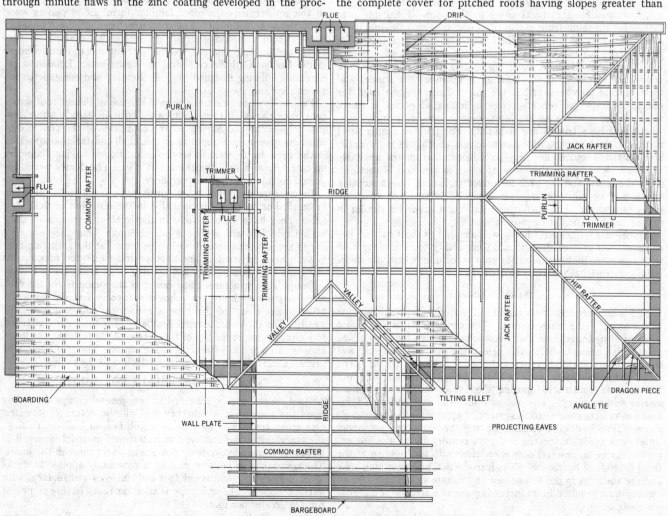

FIG. 5.—PLAN OF A ROOF SHOWING THE DETAILS OF CONSTRUCTION

2 in. per foot. The distance between supports may be 54 in., and the method of fixing is similar to that used for metal corrugated

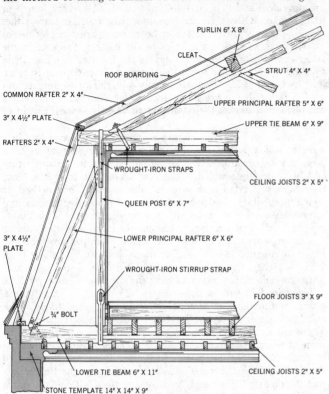

FIG. 6.—MANSARD ROOF TRUSS

Labels in figure: PURLIN 6" X 8"; CLEAT; ROOF BOARDING; STRUT 4" X 4"; COMMON RAFTER 2" X 4"; UPPER PRINCIPAL RAFTER 5" X 6"; 3" X 4½" PLATE; UPPER TIE BEAM 6" X 9"; RAFTERS 2" X 4"; WROUGHT-IRON STRAPS; CEILING JOISTS 2" X 5"; QUEEN POST 6" X 7"; 3" X 4½" PLATE; LOWER PRINCIPAL RAFTER 6" X 6"; WROUGHT-IRON STIRRUP STRAP; FLOOR JOISTS 3" X 9"; ¾" BOLT; LOWER TIE BEAM 6" X 11"; CEILING JOISTS 2" X 5"; STONE TEMPLATE 14" X 14" X 9"

sheets. The sheets are manufactured in 42 in. width, ranging in length from 3 ft. to 11 ft.

Zinc.—Zinc in sheets is a material largely used as a roof covering and, if care is taken to select metal of good quality, is strong and durable as well as light and relatively inexpensive. Zinc is stronger weight for weight than lead, slate, tile or glass, but weaker than copper, wrought iron or steel, although with the exception of the latter two it is not so durable under normal roofing conditions. It is not liable to easy breakages as are slates, tiles and glass. It is usually supplied in flat sheets, and may be had in corrugated form. When exposed to air a thin coating of oxide is formed on the surface which protects the metal beneath from further change and obviates the necessity of painting. In laying the sheets, the use of solder and nails should be avoided entirely except for fixing clips and tacks which do not interfere with the free expansion and contraction of the sheets. Zinc expands and contracts freely with changes in temperature; sheets laid with soldered seams or fixed with nails are liable to buckle, thus causing the zinc to become brittle and after repeated buckling to break away.

Zinc sheets are usually 7 ft. or 8 ft. long by 3 ft. wide, weighing from 11½ oz. to 25 oz. per square foot. The thickness varies from 25 to 19 standard wire gauge. A dependable method of laying zinc on flat roofs is with the aid of wood rolls, about 2 in. by 2 in. in section, splayed at the sides, spaced 2 ft. 8 in. apart and fixed to the roof boarding with zinc nails.

The sheets of zinc are laid between the rolls with sides bent up 1½ in. or 2 in. against them, and held firmly in position by clips of zinc attached to the rolls. A cap of the same metal is slipped over each roll; tacks about 3 in. long, which are soldered inside the cap, hook it under the same clips that anchor the sheet.

Drips of about 2½ in. are made in the slope at intervals of 6 ft. or 7 ft., i.e., the length of the sheet, and care must be taken at these points to keep the work waterproof. The lower sheet is bent up to the face of the drip and under the projecting portion of the upper sheet, which is finished with a rolled edge to turn the water. The end of the roll has a specially folded cap which also finishes with a curved or beaded water check, and this, in conjunction with the saddle piece of the wood roll beneath, forms a

weatherproof joint (fig. 8). The fall between the drips is usually about 1½ in. deep, but where necessary it may be less, the least permissible fall or slope being about 1 in 80. Felt laid beneath the zinc has the effect of lengthening the life of the roof and should always be used, as the edges of the boarding upon which it is laid are, when warped, apt to cut the sheets. It also forms a cushion protecting the zinc if there is traffic across the roof.

Lead.—Sheet lead forms a much heavier roof covering than other sheet metals, but it lasts a great deal longer and more easily withstands the attacks of impure air. Lead must be laid on a close boarding, for its great ductility prevents it from spanning even the smallest spaces without bending and giving away. This characteristic of the metal, however, conduces largely to its usefulness and enables it to be dressed and bossed into awkward corners without the necessity of jointing. The coefficient of expansion for lead is nearly as great as that for zinc and much higher than for iron; precautions to allow free expansion and contraction must be taken when laying the lead covering. The manner of laying is with rolls and drips as in the case of zinc, the details of the work differing somewhat to suit the character of the material (see fig. 9); the use of nails and solder should be avoided as far as possible. Contact with iron sets up corrosion in lead and when nails are necessary they should be copper; screws should be brass. Lead is supplied in rolls of 25 ft. to 35 ft. long and up to 7 ft. 6 in. wide. That in general use varies from $\frac{1}{14}$ in. to $\frac{1}{7}$ in. in thickness. The weights most suitable for employment in roofing are 7 or 8 lb. per square foot for flats and gutters, 6 lb. for ridges and hips and 5 lb. for flashings.

Copper.—As a roof cover, copper is lighter, stronger and more durable than either zinc or lead. It expands and contracts less than these metals, and although not so strong as wrought iron or steel it is much more durable. From a structural point of view these qualities enable it to be classed as the best available metal for roof covering, although its heat-conducting properties require it to be well insulated by layers of felt and other nonconducting materials placed beneath the metal. On exposure to the air, copper develops a feature of great beauty in the coating of green carbonate which forms upon its surface and protects it from further decomposition. Perhaps the chief disadvantage in the use of copper has been its first cost, but account must be taken of the almost imperishable nature of the metal and of the less substantial framework that its light weight requires for support. Copper roofing should be laid in a similar manner to zinc, with wood rolls at intervals of 2 ft. 4 in. It is, however, often laid with welted seams. The general stock sizes of sheets are from 4 ft. to 8 ft. long and 2 ft. to 3 ft. wide. The thickness almost invariably used is known as 24 standard wire gauge and weighs 16 oz. per square foot. Thinner material would suffice, but with the increased cost of rolling, little would be gained by adopting the thinner gauge.

Slate.—Slate is a strong and very impermeable material, it is easy to split into thin plates suitable to laying, and its cost is comparatively low; these qualities have made it the most generally used of all materials for roof covering for many years.

Slates are cut to many different sizes varying in length from 10 in. to 36 in. and in widths from 5 in. to 24 in. There are perhaps 30 or more recognized sizes, each distinguished by a different name. In common practice those generally used are "large ladies," 16 in. by 8 in.; "countesses," 20 in. by 10 in.; and "duchesses," 24 in. by 12 in. Generally speaking, the rule governing the use of the different sizes is that the steeper the pitch the smaller the slate, and vice versa. Buildings in very exposed positions naturally require steeply pitched roofs, if they are to be covered and rendered weathertight by small lapped units of covering. Slates may be fixed by nailing at the head or at about the middle. The latter method is the stronger, as the levering effect of the wind cannot attain so great a strength.

The nails used in slating are important and the durability of work depends on good selection. They should have large flat heads. The most satisfactory are those made of a composition of copper and zinc, but others of copper, zinc, galvanized iron and plain iron are used. Those of copper are most durable but are soft and expensive. Zinc nails are soft and not very durable;

they will last for about 20 years. Iron nails even if galvanized are only employed in cheap and temporary work; they may be pre-

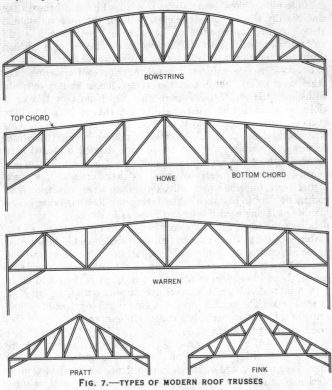

FIG. 7.—TYPES OF MODERN ROOF TRUSSES

served by being heated and plunged in boiled linseed oil. The pitch of a roof intended for slating should not incline less than 25° from the horizontal; for smaller sizes 30° is a safer angle. Modern slate roofs are frequently laid with varying courses and varying thicknesses, usually with the heavier slate from $\frac{3}{4}$ in. to $1\frac{1}{2}$ in. thick at the eaves, with thinner and smaller slate in the upper part of the roof. Marked variation of colour is often sought by combining green and purple slate, or fading and unfading slate.

Tile.—Tiles for roofing purposes are made from clay and baked in a kiln like bricks. The clay from which they are made is, however, of a specially tenacious nature and prepared with great care so as to obtain a strong and nonporous covering. Tiles are obtainable in many colours, some having beautiful effect when fixed and improve with age. They comprise tints from yellowish red, red and brown to dark blue. As with brick, the quality depends to a large extent upon the burning; underburned tiles are weak and porous and liable to early decay, while overburning, though improving durability, will cause warping and variations in colour. Variation in colour is now deliberately obtained, and artistic effects are secured by sand facing, artificial rustication and by burning to metallic surfaces. The usual shape is the "plain tile," but they are made in other shapes for lighter weight and ornamental effect. There are also several patented forms on the market for which the makers claim special advantages. The ordinary tiles are slightly curved in the direction of their length to enable them to lie closely

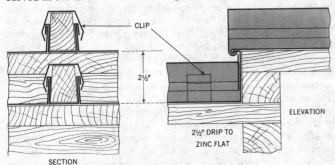

FIG. 8.—DETAILS OF ZINC FLATS

at their lower edges. Some of them have small nibs at the head by which they are hung upon the battens without nails. Nail holes are provided, and it is advisable to nail at least every fourth or fifth course. Others are made without the nibs, and are either fixed by nailing to the battens or boarding or are hung by means of oak kegs wedged in the holes to the battens, the kegs in the latter case acting in the same way as the mentioned nibs. Plain tiles are of rectangular form; the standard dimensions are $10\frac{1}{2}$ in. long by $6\frac{1}{2}$ in. wide. They are usually $\frac{1}{2}$ in. thick and weigh about $2\frac{1}{2}$ lb. each. There are many forms of ornamental tiles, which are plain tiles having their tails cut to various shapes instead of molded square.

There are also on the market many patented forms of tiles, some of which possess considerable merit. Curved pantiles have been in widespread use over a long period of time. Pantiles are laid on a principle which is different from that for plain tiles; they merely overlap each other at the edges. This method of laying necessitates bedding in mortar and pointing, inside and sometimes outside as well, with mortar or cement. This pointing plays an important part in keeping the interior of the building free from penetration of wind and water. Pantiles are generally made to measure $13\frac{1}{2}$ in. long by $9\frac{1}{2}$ in. wide and weighing from 5 lb. to $5\frac{1}{2}$ lb. each. Molded on the head of each tile is a small projecting nib which serves to hang the tile to the batten or lath.

They are laid with a lap of $3\frac{1}{2}$ in., $2\frac{1}{2}$ in. or $1\frac{1}{2}$ in., giving a gauge (and margin) of 10 in., 11 in. and 12 in., respectively. The side lap is generally $1\frac{1}{2}$ in., leaving a width of 8 in. exposed face. There are many other forms based upon the shape of the pantile, some of which are patented and claim to have advantages that the original form does not possess. Among them are "corrugated tiles" of the ordinary shape or with angular flutes, the Italian pattern "double roll tiles" and "interlocking tiles." Poole's bonding roll tiles are a development of the Italian pattern tile. French and Belgian tiles of the "Marseilles" pattern are economical and therefore popular for housing schemes and cheap building.

There are other forms of roof covers that were once in common use but no longer meet the requirements set up by regulations and ordinances of most communities. Because of the risk of fire,

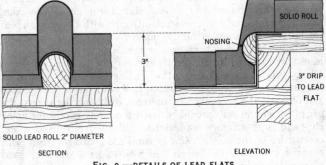

FIG. 9.—DETAILS OF LEAD FLATS

shingles of wood and other combustible materials have been replaced with asphalt and asbestos cement units. These coverings are available in many colours and textures as individual units or strips and sheets. The quality of the materials has been improved and the techniques of applying them developed to such a point that they have practically replaced the older types of roof coverings. The colours and textures of the older roofing, such as wood, slate and tile have been reproduced with limited success in the newer materials, but for the most part their acceptance has been the result of their own inherent characteristics.

Insulation has become an integral part of the roof assembly of most buildings; it is available in types adapted to various conditions of the roof structures. For the purpose of reducing the conductivity of the roof assembly a low density material composed of vegetable fibres, cork, glass fibres or mineral wool is formed into "rigid" units, semirigid units (batts) or flexible strips. The insulation for flat roofs having precast units or concrete structural covers is usually in the form of a rigid insulation board on which the built-up roofing is applied. For other types of structural roof coverings, the insulation is usually a flexible type or it consists of batts applied below the structural roof cover. The reflective type of insulation in the form of a metallic foil mounted on strong paper backing is applied as an air space boundary below structural cover. The function of the vapour seal is to prevent the warm moist air of the interior from reaching the colder areas of the roof assembly and should therefore be located below the insulating material. The vapour seal is an asphalt membrane on sheathing paper or it may be an integral part of the paper surfaced with the reflective insulation.

See also references under "Roof" in the Index.

BIBLIOGRAPHY.—C. G. Ramsey and H. R. Sleeper, *Architectural Graphic Standards,* 5th ed. (1956); Timber Engineering Company, *Timber Design and Construction Handbook* (1956); P. D. Close, *Building Insulation,* 4th ed. (1951); T. Crane, *Architectural Construction,* 2nd ed. (1956); J. Wilson and S. Werner, *Simplified Roof Framing,* 2nd ed. (1948); A. Pugin, *Ornamental Gables* (1854); W. Durbahn, *Fundamentals of Carpentry,* vol. ii (1956).   (E. N. G.)

ROOK, the most abundant Eurasian bird of the crow family. This highly social species, *Corvus frugilegus,* lives in colonies, or rookeries, that may contain more than 1,000 nests and may be more than 100 years old. The rook resembles the crow closely but has a purplish gloss to its black plumage, in the adult a face partially bare of feathers, shaggy feathered thighs, and a bill more slender, more pointed and grayer than that of the crow.

Among the variety of calls in this gregarious species (often, apparently, with rather specific meanings) the commonest is *kaaa.* The nests, in large trees or on the walls of large old buildings, are soundly constructed of twigs and earth and are used year

ERIC HOSKING
ROOK (CORVUS FRUGILEGUS)

after year. The three to five light greenish eggs, thickly speckled with gray and brown, as with crows, are laid in April. Incubation is about three weeks, and the young require a month or more in the nest before the feathers have grown sufficiently to permit flight. Rooks are economically important since they consume great numbers of insects. After the nesting period, the rooks of several colonies may band together to feed, coming into a favourite site swiftly and in zigzag fashion. In Great Britain rooks are non-migratory but over most of Europe they are migratory.

(W. J. BE.)

ROON, ALBRECHT THEODOR EMIL, GRAF VON (1803–1879), Prussian army officer who with Bismarck and Moltke brought the German Empire into being, and made Germany the leading power on the continent of Europe. As war minister in the 1860s, he reorganized the Prussian Army, thus contributing to its victories of 1866 and 1870–71. Roon was born at Pleushagen, near Kolberg (Kolobrzeg), on April 30, 1803. His family was of Flemish origin, and had settled in Pomerania. His father, an officer in the Prussian Army, died during the French occupation, and he was brought up mainly by his maternal grandmother. He became a cadet in 1816 and entered the military school in Berlin in 1818. He was commissioned in 1821 and spent the years 1824–27 at the Berlin War Academy. In 1832, after a short period of regimental duty, he joined the headquarters of the army corps at Krefeld. It was there that he first realized the inefficiency of the Prussian Army. In the same year, when only 29, he published the three-volume *Grundzüge der Erd-, Völker- und Staatenkunde* (3rd ed., 1847–55; "Principles of Physical, National and Political Geography"), which was widely read in Prussia and abroad. It is likely that it was at about this time that his ideas on remodeling the army germinated.

During the revolutionary disturbances of 1848 he served for a time under Crown Prince William (who became king as William I in 1861, and emperor of Germany in 1871) in suppressing the insurrection in Baden. This may be said to have been the beginning of his rise to the highest posts in the Prussian military hierarchy.

By 1856 he was a major general, and by 1859 a lieutenant general and member of a commission to reorganize the army. Supported by Gen. Baron Edwin von Manteuffel, chief of the royal military cabinet, and by Gen. Helmuth von Moltke (*q.v.*), chief of the general staff, Roon shaped his plans for reform, and eventually got them adopted. His aim was an extension of the system of service started by Gen. Gerhard von Scharnhorst (*q.v.*). He envisaged a "nation-in-arms," with a three-year period of full-time service. This was unpopular both with the man in the street and with the more conservative members of the general staff. Until the Franco-German War of 1870–71 proved the effectiveness of his system, Roon was the most hated man in Prussia.

Toward the end of 1859 Roon became minister of war, and in 1861 also minister of marine. For the next few years he was engaged in creating the military machine which Moltke, as chief of staff, was planning to use (*see also* PRUSSIA: *The Kingdom from 1815*). The quick victory over Austria in 1866 showed the worth of the remodeled Prussian Army; it also exposed certain weaknesses which Roon was largely able to rectify by 1870.

During the Franco-German War, Roon spent much time in attendance on the emperor. He was made a count in 1871 and in December succeeded Bismarck as head of the Prussian ministry, but resigned in the following year because of ill-health. He was made a field marshal in January 1873. He died in Berlin on Feb. 23, 1879.

Roon was a man of massive build and aggressive appearance. He was a practical military administrator rather than a fighting soldier and liked to be known by his nickname of "the king's sergeant." He was also known as "ruffian Roon" by his political opponents.

BIBLIOGRAPHY.—*Denkwürdigkeiten aus dem Leben des . . . Grafen v. Roon,* ed. by his son, 2 vol. (1892; new ed., 3 vol., 1905); R. Hübner, *Albrecht von Roon* (1933); H. M. Elster, *Graf Albrecht von Roon* (1938).   (C. N. B.)

ROORKEE, a municipal town in the Saharanpur district of Uttar Pradesh, India, lies 42 mi. (68 km.) SSW of Dehra Dun by road. Pop. (1961) 45,801 including the cantonment. There are two colleges affiliated to Agra University, and the town is the seat of Roorkee University which was originally founded in 1847 as the Thomason Civil Engineering College. The university was inaugurated in 1949 to provide for the teaching of all branches of engineering. The town is an important centre for the manufacture of surveying instruments and drawing equipment. It is the headquarters of the Ganges Canal workshops and also contains the Central Building Research Institute and an institute of irrigation research. It is well served by rail and road. (S. S. BH.)

ROOSENDAAL EN NISPEN, a town in the province of North Brabant, Neth., 15 mi. (24 km.) WSW of Breda by rail, at an important junction on the Rotterdam-Antwerp line. Pop. (1960) 38,355 (mun.). It is an industrial centre with comprehensive recreational facilities, whose growth has been encouraged by good communications. Chief products are fluorescent lighting components, hose fittings and assemblies, machinery for the paper and graphic industries, biscuits, sugar, cigars, brushes, and furniture. Its early development began when in 1268 the inhabitants of surrounding hamlets, including Nispen, were granted permission to build a church at Roosendaal. Peat-digging, mainly by the monks of Tongerlo (Belg.), gave the place its first prosperity.

(F. DE C.)

ROOSEVELT, (ANNA) ELEANOR (1884–1962), wife of Pres. Franklin D. Roosevelt (*q.v.*) and a distinguished author, lecturer, and diplomat, was born on Oct. 11, 1884, in New York City, the daughter of Elliott Roosevelt (brother of Pres. Theodore Roosevelt) and Anna Hall Roosevelt. After the death of her parents she was cared for by her grandmother and sent to school in England. On March 17, 1905, when she married Franklin D. Roosevelt, a distant cousin, she was given away by her uncle, President Roosevelt. During her husband's public career, both in Albany and in Washington, Mrs. Roosevelt developed and later pursued an active interest in educational, sociological, and political affairs. She provided help and inspiration for her husband after 1921 in his struggle with the crippling effects of poliomyelitis.

When he became president of the United States in 1933 she created a new role in the White House for the first lady of the land. Her advocacy of liberal causes and her precedent-breaking activities made her a controversial figure throughout the next 12 years.

In 1945, after President Roosevelt's death, Pres. Harry S. Truman appointed Mrs. Roosevelt a delegate to the United Nations, where she served as chairman of a commission to draft the Universal Declaration of Human Rights, which was finally accepted by the UN in December 1948 (see HUMAN RIGHTS). She spent the next two years working on a proposed covenant that would bind all member nations to carry out the declaration. She resigned from the UN delegation in 1952 when a new administration came into office in Washington.

Mrs. Roosevelt was an indefatigable traveler. She circled the world several times, visited scores of countries, and met with most of the world leaders. In addition to lecturing extensively, both in the United States and abroad, often on behalf of the American Association for the United Nations, she wrote "My Day," a syndicated newspaper column, for many years. She was the author of numerous books and magazine articles and was the recipient of many awards and honorary degrees. For years she consistently led public opinion polls as the most admired woman in the world. She died at her home in New York City on Nov. 7, 1962.

See her autobiographical works, *This Is My Story* (1937) and *On My Own* (1958). (A. E. ST.)

ROOSEVELT, FRANKLIN DELANO (1882–1945), served as 32nd president of the United States during the New Deal era and World War II, from March 1933 until his death in April 1945. To counter the great depression of the 1930s he helped formulate domestic policies that brought about substantial and lasting changes in the relationship of the U.S. government to the nation's economy. After the Japanese attack upon Pearl Harbor on Dec. 7, 1941, he led the United States and its allies in their struggle against the Axis powers; at the time of his death he was helping to establish the United Nations. He was the only president to be re-elected three times.

Early Life.—Roosevelt was born at Hyde Park, N.Y., Jan. 30, 1882, the only son of James and Sara Delano Roosevelt. James Roosevelt, a gentleman then in his fifties who had been an investor in railroads, coal lands and several speculative enterprises, was for some years vice-president of the Delaware and Hudson railroad, but was most deeply interested in his country estate. Sara Delano Roosevelt, only half the age of her husband, came from a wealthy family of New York and New England merchant shippers and developers of coal lands. The total wealth of the Roosevelt family was small compared with some of the huge fortunes of the day, but it placed them in the millionaire category and enabled the Roosevelts to live in unostentatious and genteel luxury, dividing their time between the Hudson river valley and European watering places. Young Franklin from the time he was three was taken to Europe for part of almost every year. He was taught privately at home and trained in French and German. Both in his education and in his recreation with members of a close social circle, he was reared to be a gentleman, maintaining his social position and being responsible toward those less fortunate.

At 14, Roosevelt, a rather shy youth, entered Groton school, modeled after the great public schools of England, where Rector Endicott Peabody trained rich young men to exercise Christian stewardship through public service. Roosevelt failed to make many friends at Groton and did not excel at sports, upon which there was much emphasis. But he did heed Peabody's exhortations, especially when they were reinforced by his glamorous distant relative, Theodore Roosevelt, a fifth cousin.

After he entered Harvard in 1900, Roosevelt was more successful in making friends and gaining the respect of his classmates. He threw himself with vigour into extracurricular activities, and in his senior year was chief editor (president) of the college newspaper, the *Harvard Crimson*. His strenuous extracurricular and social life left him relatively little time for his studies, in which his record was undistinguished. He was exposed to courses in economics in which classical laissez-faire doctrine was moderated by the new progressive faith in government regulation. These had a

minor effect upon him compared with the direct influence of the vigorous, progressive president, Theodore Roosevelt, for whom he voted in 1904. During his final year at Harvard, young Roosevelt became engaged to President Roosevelt's niece, (Anna) Eleanor Roosevelt (*q.v.*), who was then active in settlement work in New York city. She helped open Roosevelt's eyes to the deplorable living conditions of the underprivileged in the slums. They were married on March 17, 1905.

New York social life interested Roosevelt more than his studies at Columbia university school of law. Nevertheless he survived into the spring of the third year despite a high failure rate among his classmates. But as soon as he passed the New York bar examinations he dropped his courses and did not bother to take his LL.B. degree. This indifference to the legal profession carried over into Roosevelt's years as a clerk with the distinguished Wall Street firm of Carter, Ledyard and Milburn, defense counsel in several spectacular antitrust cases.

Early Political Activities.—His admiration for Theodore Roosevelt, who continued to urge young men of substance to enter public service, led him toward politics. His opportunity came in 1910 when the Democratic leaders of Dutchess county, N.Y., persuaded him to undertake an apparently futile campaign for the state senate. Roosevelt, whose branch of the family had always been Democrats, hesitated only long enough to make sure his distinguished relative would not speak against him. He campaigned so strenuously that, with the aid of a Republican schism and his famous name, he won the election. Within a few days after he took his seat at Albany, Roosevelt, not quite 29, won state-wide and even some national attention by leading a small group of Democratic insurgents who refused to vote for the nominee of the New York city organization, Tammany Hall, for U.S. senator—William F. Sheehan, a Buffalo traction magnate. For three months Roosevelt helped hold the insurgents firm until Tammany switched to another candidate, James A. O'Gorman.

In this controversy he had acted basically as a conservative, clean-government Democrat in the Cleveland tradition, but had won the "insurgent" label popular among farmers because of the midwestern agrarian revolt bearing that name. Further, his struggle identified him with the fight for the direct election of U.S. senators and for the destruction of city bosses. In the ensuing two years in the New York senate, Roosevelt was the foremost champion of the upstate farmers, and in the process of fighting for legislation for them he became converted to the full program of progressive reform. From the New York city legislators whom he had earlier scorned and continued to fight, he learned much of the give-and-take of politics. Among them were James Walker, later mayor of New York city; Robert F. Wagner, who became a leading U.S. senator; and Alfred E. Smith, later governor of New York state. As he learned from men like these, Roosevelt gradually abandoned the patrician airs and superior attitude he had brought to the state senate.

Before the end of 1911, Roosevelt supported the presidential boom for Governor Woodrow Wilson of New Jersey, the leading Democratic progressive. An attack of typhoid fever kept him from participating in the campaign, but even without making a single public appearance he was re-elected to the New York state senate. This was because of the publicity an Albany newspaperman, Louis McHenry Howe, spread through the district. Howe, a wizened little man with a sharp tongue and clever pen, saw in the tall, handsome young Roosevelt a politician who could go far. Beginning with the campaign of 1912, he served Roosevelt the rest of his life with a jealous loyalty.

Assistant Secretary of the Navy.—For his work on behalf of Wilson, Roosevelt was rewarded in March 1913 with an appointment as assistant secretary of the navy under Josephus Daniels, a North Carolina newspaper editor. He loved the sea and naval traditions and knew more about them than his superior, who in a careful way was trying to bring progressive reforms to the peacetime navy. Roosevelt was frequently impatient with his superior, and tended to undercut him in minor ways. Nevertheless, Roosevelt himself, with mixed success, tried to bring reforms to the navy yards, which were under his jurisdiction, meanwhile learning with marked success to negotiate with labour unions among the civilian employees. After war broke out in Europe, Roosevelt became a vehement advocate of preparedness and chafed under the deliberate policies of Secretary Daniels and President Wilson. During the war, he built a reputation as an effective administrator. In the summer of 1918 he made an extended tour of naval bases overseas. During much of his seven years as assistant secretary he had been less than loyal to Daniels, but in the end he came to appreciate his superior's skill in dealing with southern congressmen and his solid worth as an administrator.

Paralytic Attack and After.—At the Democratic convention in 1920, Roosevelt was nominated for vice-president. He campaigned vigorously with the presidential nominee, James M. Cox, on behalf of U.S. entrance into the League of Nations. After his defeat in the Republican landslide, he became a vice-president of the Fidelity and Deposit Company of Maryland, a bonding company, entered into numerous business schemes, some of a speculative nature, and remained active in Democratic politics. Suddenly, in Aug. 1921, while on vacation at Campobello Island, N.B., Roosevelt was severely stricken with poliomyelitis. He suffered intensely and for some time was almost completely paralyzed, but he refused to give way to depression and began gaily predicting (as he did for some years) that soon he would regain the use of his legs. His mother wished him to retire to Hyde Park, but his wife and his secretary, Louis Howe, felt it was essential to maintenance of his morale for him to remain active in his career and in politics. They won in the struggle over his future. Within two weeks after he was stricken with polio, Roosevelt was writing political letters. Since he could not himself attend political gatherings, Mrs. Roosevelt attended for him, acting as his eyes and ears (a service she frequently performed for him during the rest of his life). Under the tutelage of Howe, she overcame her shyness and became an effective political worker and speaker. Since for the time being he could not run for office, Roosevelt was able to function effectively as a sort of premature "elder statesman" trying to promote unity among the urban and rural wings of the Democratic party. Himself a rural Democrat, he nominated Gov. "Al" Smith of New York, the favourite of the city faction, at the 1924 and 1928 Democratic conventions.

After Smith received the presidential nomination in 1928, he urged Roosevelt to run for governor of New York in order to strengthen the ticket. Roosevelt was reluctant: he still could not walk without braces and assistance. In the years since 1921 he had worked incessantly to try to regain the use of his legs—with a doctor in Massachusetts, for several winters swimming in warm Florida waters and, beginning in the fall of 1924, in the mineralized water at Warm Springs, Ga. Wishing to share with others the beneficent effect of the warm water and a systematic program of therapy, Roosevelt in 1927 established the Warm Springs foundation, a nonprofit institution for the care of polio victims. He wished to develop Warm Springs further and to continue with his treatments in the hope of regaining full use of his legs; also, 1928 was not a propitious year to run on the Democratic ticket.

Governor of New York.—Nevertheless, Roosevelt succumbed to strong persuasion and accepted the nomination for governor of New York. It was a critical gamble. When he began campaigning by automobile, he demonstrated to his critics that he had retained his youthful buoyance and vitality; he also showed that during the years of struggle to recover from polio he had matured into a more serious and humane person. Opponents raised the question of his health against him but his vigorous campaigning effectively disposed of the issue. In the election, Smith was defeated nationally in the Hoover landslide and failed to carry New York state, but Roosevelt won by 25,000 votes.

When he succeeded Smith, who had been one of the most popular and successful governors in the history of New York, Roosevelt decided he must establish his own type of administration. He did not keep Smith's closest adviser, Belle Moskowitz, nor did he depend upon Smith for advice. Smith, already stung by his defeat for the presidency, was hurt and alienated. Whereas Smith had built his reputation on administrative reform, Roosevelt concentrated upon a program to give tax relief to farmers and to pro-

vide cheaper public utilities for consumers. He succeeded in wresting from the Republican legislature approval for a power authority, which took initial steps toward the development of the enormous resources of the St. Lawrence river. The appeal of this program in upstate New York, coupled with the effects of the deepening depression, led to Roosevelt's re-election in 1930 by the overwhelming plurality of 725,000 votes.

During his first term as governor, Roosevelt's policies, except on the power issue, were scarcely further to the left than those of Pres. Herbert Hoover in Washington. But during Roosevelt's second administration, as the depression became more catastrophic in its effects, he acted vigorously to mobilize the machinery of the state government to aid the economy. In the fall of 1931 he obtained legislation establishing the Temporary Emergency Relief administration, the first of the state relief agencies. Throughout his four years, he was successful in most of his bouts with the Republican legislature, sharpening skills that would be vital if he were to become president. And increasingly, beginning with some slight speculation in Nov. 1928, he was being talked as the most likely Democratic nominee in 1932. After his spectacular victory in 1930, he was so conspicuous a target for the Republicans and for rival Democratic aspirants that he had no choice but to begin immediately and quietly to obtain support for the convention. Since it took a two-thirds vote in the Democratic convention to nominate, it was relatively easy to stop a leading contender. While Howe conducted an intensive letter-writing campaign from New York city, James A. Farley, a leader in the New York state Democratic organization, conducted skilful negotiations with Democratic leaders throughout the country. It soon became apparent that Roosevelt's strongest opposition would come from urban and conservative eastern Democrats who were still loyal to Smith; his strongest support was in the south and the west.

Progressives and intellectuals found Roosevelt's over-all program attractive, but many feared he was weak because he sidestepped Republican challenges to use his gubernatorial powers to oust corrupt Democratic officials in New York city. The opposition became stronger when the Texas favourite son, John Nance Garner, speaker of the house of representatives, won the California primary. At the 1932 convention, Roosevelt had a majority of the delegates but could be blocked by a combination of the Smith and Garner forces. On the third ballot, Garner prevented a deadlock by allowing his delegates to be thrown to Roosevelt. In return, Garner was nominated for the vice-presidency.

Election of 1932.—In the campaign of 1932 the depression was the only issue of consequence. Prohibition, which had split the Democratic party into the wet urban and dry rural factions through the 1920s, was no longer vital; the platform pledged repeal. Roosevelt, displaying smiling confidence, campaigned throughout the country, outlining in general terms a program for recovery and reform that came to be known as the "New Deal" (*q.v.*). In a series of careful addresses prepared by a team of speech writers popularly called the "brain trust," he promised aid to farmers, public development of electric power, a balanced budget and government policing of irresponsible economic power. He declared in his most notable speech in San Francisco: "Private economic power is . . . a public trust as well." It was a program appealing to millions who were nominally Republicans, especially western progressives. In response, President Hoover, campaigning for re-election, outlined his own program for remedying the depression, and he likened Roosevelt's inconsistencies on the tariff to a chameleon on plaid. It was Hoover's personal unpopularity more than Roosevelt's persuasiveness that led to the heavy Democratic victory in Nov. 1932. Roosevelt received 22,822,000 popular votes to 15,762,000 for Hoover. The electoral vote was 472 to 59. The Democrats also won substantial majorities in both houses of congress.

Inauguration as President.—Since the 20th amendment to the federal constitution had not yet gone into effect, Roosevelt did not take office until March 4, 1933. During the intervening months President Hoover sought his co-operation in stemming the deepening economic crisis that culminated in the closing of banks in several states during Feb. 1933. But Roosevelt refused either

BROWN BROTHERS

PRESIDENT-ELECT ROOSEVELT (SEATED RIGHT) READING RETURNS, ELECTION NIGHT, NOV. 9, 1932. SEATED AT LEFT IS CAMPAIGN MANAGER JAMES A. FARLEY, STANDING IS LOUIS M. HOWE

to accept responsibility without the accompanying power or to subscribe to Hoover's proposals for reassuring business; Hoover himself granted that his proposals would mean "the abandonment of 90 per cent of the so-called new deal."

Thus it was at a time of acute economic crisis and despair that Roosevelt, whose policies were still relatively unknown and untested, came to the presidency. Most of the nation's banks were closed, industrial production was down to 56% of the 1929 level, 13,000,000 or more persons were unemployed and farmers were in desperate straits. Roosevelt, during the months since his election, had been planning wide-ranging measures to meet the crisis. He chose a cabinet which reflected his desire to hold the support of Republican progressives who had campaigned for him and maintain a balance among the political and economic forces in the nation. The cabinet included three Republicans—Secretary of Agriculture Henry A. Wallace, Secretary of the Interior Harold L. Ickes and Secretary of the Treasury William Woodin. For the first time in history the cabinet included a woman, Secretary of Labour Frances Perkins. The other members were Democrats representing both the liberal and conservative forces in the party, some coming from the south and west and others from the east.

In his inaugural address Roosevelt promised prompt, decisive action and somehow conveyed to the nation some of his own unshakable self-confidence. "This great Nation will endure as it has endured, will revive and will prosper," he asserted, ". . . the only thing we have to fear is fear itself." For the moment, people of all shades of political views were Roosevelt's to command, and he acted swiftly to obtain enactment of the most sweeping peacetime legislative program in U.S. history.

The Hundred Days.—The prelude was the enactment of several conservative measures to inspire confidence among businessmen and bankers. First, Roosevelt ended depositors' runs on banks by closing all banks until congress, meeting in special session on March 9, could pass a cautious measure allowing those in a sound condition to reopen. In the ensuing two years, the Reconstruction Finance corporation (RFC), established in the Hoover administration, bolstered banks with loans and purchases of bank stock totaling $2,000,000,000. Most weak banks had been

eliminated and few survivors failed thereafter. Banking reform came later through the Glass-Steagall act of June 1933, designed to curb speculation by banks and to establish, with Roosevelt's reluctant approval, the Federal Deposit Insurance corporation (FDIC) guaranteeing deposits. The Banking act of 1935 reorganized and increased the powers of the Federal Reserve system. In March 1933, Roosevelt redeemed two campaign pledges by introducing a program of drastic government economy and proposing legislation to legalize beer of 3.2% alcoholic content. By Dec. 1933 the 21st amendment had been ratified, repealing the 18th (prohibition) amendment (*see* PROHIBITION).

The initial measures of the new administration helped to restore confidence in the economy but did little to bring real recovery. It was only after their enactment that Roosevelt sent to congress a series of messages and draft bills proposing the program that comprised the early New Deal. This program, proposed and enacted in approximately the first 100 days of the new administration, represented Roosevelt's effort as president to provide for all the diverse economic groups in the nation. He intended through these laws to bring quick recovery and to eliminate some of the causes of depressions.

The main emphasis in the early days of the New Deal was on recovery but some attention was also given to reform. First of all, federal funds were appropriated for the relief of human suffering. Congress established the Federal Emergency Relief administration (FERA) and appropriated approximately $500,000,000 for its operation. Roosevelt appointed as its administrator Harry Hopkins, who granted funds to state relief agencies for direct relief. Congress also established a Civilian Conservation corps (CCC) which at its peak employed 500,000 young men in reforestation and flood-control work. Mortgage relief aided other millions of persons. Roosevelt consolidated existing farm credit agencies into the Farm Credit administration (FCA), which in two years refinanced one-fifth of the nation's farm mortgages. The Frazier-Lemke Farm Bankruptcy act enabled farmers who had lost their property to regain it. A sixth of the nation's homeowners, threatened by mortgage foreclosure, were aided by the Home Owners' Loan corporation (HOLC) established in June 1933. Congress in 1934 established the Federal Housing administration (FHA) to insure mortgages on new construction and home repairs. The key loan agency of the New Deal was the previously established RFC, whose powers were broadened so that it could make loans to small enterprises as well as to large. Under the sound management of Jesse Jones, it loaned $15,000,000,000 between 1932 and 1941, and most of this total was ultimately repaid. These relief agencies poured so much money into the economy that they did stimulate recovery. At the time, Roosevelt did not envisage public spending as their primary role; he hoped to be able to cut back their activities in order to balance the budget.

Recovery Measures.—The key recovery measures of the New Deal were two acts: one to restore farm prosperity and the other to stimulate business enterprise. The first act established the Agricultural Adjustment administration (AAA), whose objective was to raise farm prices and increase the proportion of the national income going to farmers. It was administered by Wallace, who was later to become a highly controversial figure in politics. Through the "domestic allotment" scheme favoured by the major farm organizations, growers of seven basic commodities (wheat, cotton, corn, hogs, rice, tobacco, and milk and dairy products) would receive subsidies in return for reducing production. The subsidies were to be paid from a processing tax on the commodities. Through the original

BY COURTESY OF THE KANSAS CITY STAR; PHOTOGRAPH, HISTORICAL PICTURES SERVICE

"LOOKS AS IF THE NEW LEADERSHIP WAS REALLY GOING TO LEAD"

A contemporary comment on the flurry of governmental activity during the first hundred days of the Roosevelt administration

law of 1933 and subsequent farm legislation, plus the effects of years of drought, production fell and farm income gradually improved. But it did not reach even the inadequate level of 1929 until 1941.

The demand of businessmen for government stabilization resulted in passage of the National Industrial Recovery act (NIRA) of 1933. It was a two-pronged program. One side was a $3,300,-000,000 appropriation for public works. Had this money been poured into the economy rapidly it would probably have done much to bring recovery, but Roosevelt, not grasping this possibility, appointed Ickes as head of the Public Works administration (PWA) and approved his slow and cautious selection of projects. The other side was a National Recovery administration (NRA) to administer codes of fair practice within given industries. While the codes were being negotiated by industrial committees, Roosevelt and the administrator of the act, Hugh Johnson, called upon the nation to accept an interim blanket code establishing for workers a 35- or 40-hour week, minimum pay of 30 or 40 cents an hour and a prohibition of child labour. The codes, as they were slowly negotiated, were designed to stabilize production and raise prices in industries such as bituminous coal and textiles and to protect labour and consumers. The consumers received scant protection. Labour received guarantees on wages and hours, and also, through sec. 7a of the act, the right to bargain collectively. During the summer of 1933 there was a quick flurry of recovery as manufacturers produced goods in anticipation of sale at higher prices under the codes; the boom collapsed by fall, for prices had risen faster than purchasing power. By Feb. 1934 code-making was over, but far too many—557 basic codes and 208 supplementary ones—had come into existence, containing innumerable provisions difficult to enforce. The business community, which had demanded the NRA at the outset, by 1935 was becoming disillusioned with it and blaming its ineffectiveness on Roosevelt. In May 1935 the supreme court of the U.S. in the Schechter decision invalidated the code system. Despite its shortcomings, the NRA had brought significant aid to several highly competitive industries like textiles and important reforms that were subsequently re-enacted in other legislation: federal wages-and-hours regulation, collective bargaining guarantees and abolition of child labour in interstate commerce.

In the fall of 1933, with recovery still beyond grasp, Roosevelt had already turned to other expedients for bolstering the economy. He experimented with "managed currency," driving down the gold content of the dollar, and tripling the price of silver through large purchases. These efforts brought little increase of prices at home but they improved the position of the United States in foreign trade by making dollars cheaper abroad. Also, silver producers received a continuing subsidy through the Silver Purchase act of 1934. In Jan. 1934 Roosevelt stabilized the gold content of the dollar at 59.06% of its earlier value. The resort to managed currency created a significant precedent even though it did little to bring recovery at the time.

Altogether, Roosevelt's program by the fall of 1934 was bringing a limited degree of recovery, but it was alienating conservatives, including many businessmen. They contended that much of the Roosevelt program was unconstitutional, that it created uncertainties for business which hampered recovery and that the lowering of the gold content of the dollar had deprived holders of government obligations of their just return. At the same time, many of the underprivileged who were still in serious difficulties felt that the New Deal had not gone far enough. They were ready to listen to demagogic leaders offering still more. In the election of 1934, they voted overwhelmingly for Democratic candidates for congress, adding to the already top-heavy New Deal majorities. But in the 1936 presidential election they might vote for a third-party candidate to the left of Roosevelt.

Reform Measures.—In order to meet the threat to his political coalition from the left, Roosevelt in his annual message to congress in Jan. 1935 put the emphasis upon reform. This was less a sharp shift from a first to a second New Deal than it was a hurry to enact a number of reform measures which Roosevelt had long been planning. In the first days of the New Deal, in the spring of

1933, congress had created the Tennessee Valley authority (TVA), to provide flood control, cheap hydroelectric power and regional planning for an impoverished region. Also, two laws had been passed to protect investors: the "Truth in Securities" act of 1933 and an act establishing the regulatory Securities and Exchange commission (SEC) in 1934. The additional legislation of 1935 did much to undermine the appeal of demagogues to the needy. This was especially true of the Social Security act of 1935, which included not only unemployment insurance as had been originally proposed but also old-age insurance. In some respects it was the most significant and far-reaching of the New Deal measures. For workers still unemployed, congress created the Works Progress administration (WPA) to provide them with work relief to stem the erosion of their skills and self-respect. Between 1935 and 1941 the WPA employed an average of 2,100,000 workers and by the end of 1935 was already bringing a marked measure of recovery through pouring billions of dollars into the economy. For workers who were employed, the Wagner act (National Labor Relations act) of 1935, only belatedly accepted by Roosevelt, strengthened the government guarantees of collective bargaining and created a National Labor Relations board (NLRB) to adjudicate labour disputes. The Holding Company act of 1935 eliminated all but two strata of holding companies above operating public utility companies. A new 1935 tax measure, labeled by its opponents the "soak the rich" tax, raised the levies on people of large incomes and on big corporations, and became a significant factor in redistributing American income.

These measures effectively undercut the left-wing opposition to Roosevelt but they further alienated conservatives. When he ran for re-election in 1936, it was with the firm support of farmers, labourers and the underprivileged; the epithets which the extreme right hurled at him merely helped to unify his following. The Republican nominee, Gov. Alfred M. Landon of Kansas, was a moderate who promised greater efficiency rather than destruction of the New Deal program; he could do little to stem the Roosevelt tide. Roosevelt received 27,752,000 popular votes to 16,680,000 for Landon, and carried every state except Maine and Vermont.

Second Term.—The only hope of the conservatives to thwart the New Deal was that the supreme court would invalidate its key measures. Following the Schechter decision ending the NRA codes in 1935, the court in 1936 ruled against the AAA processing taxes, thus forcing the administration to base crop restriction payments upon soil conservation instead. Cases challenging the Social Security act and the Wagner act were pending before the court. Roosevelt, in beginning his second term with a massive mandate, was determined to remove this threat to the New Deal program. He reasoned that the measures were well within the scope of the constitution and that it was the reasoning of the justices that was old-fashioned and at fault. Consequently, early in 1937 after an inaugural dedicating his second administration to reform on behalf of the underprivileged third of the nation, he proposed the reorganization of the supreme court, including the appointment of as many as six new justices. The proposal, labeled by its opponents as a "court-packing" scheme, touched off a vehement debate in which many of Roosevelt's previous supporters in and out of congress expressed their opposition. While the debate was continuing, in the spring of 1937, the supreme court handed down decisions upholding both the Wagner act and the Social Security act. With the need for the court plan dissolving, its enemies managed by summer to bring about its defeat. This was a severe political blow for Roosevelt, even though the new decisions by the court opened the way for almost unlimited government regulation of the economy.

Roosevelt's prestige suffered still further in the summer of 1937 as much of the public blamed him for the labour difficulties that grew out of the great organizing drives in the steel, automobile and other mass-production industries. (*See* AMERICAN FEDERATION OF LABOR-CONGRESS OF INDUSTRIAL ORGANIZATIONS.) Operating under the protection of the Wagner act, the unions engaged in strikes which often reached their climax in violence. Roosevelt himself preferred paternalistic government aid to all workers, such as the wages and hours guarantees of the Fair Labor

Standards act of 1938. But while union membership jumped to about 9,500,000 by 1941, most middle-class people returned to the Republican party. A sharp economic recession in the fall of 1937 added to Roosevelt's troubles. There had been a substantial degree of recovery by 1937, but Roosevelt, wishing to balance the budget, had curtailed government spending so drastically that he had sent the economy plummeting back toward 1932 levels. Businessmen blamed the New Deal spending policies; Roosevelt blamed the businessmen and inaugurated an antimonopoly program. But in Oct. 1937 massive government spending began again, and by June 1938 the crisis was past.

Adding to Roosevelt's troubles, many of the conservative southern Democrats heading key congressional committees, from 1937 on, were openly opposing the New Deal. In 1938 Roosevelt tried unsuccessfully to defeat several of them in the primaries, and was inveighed against as a dictator trying to conduct a "purge." Democrats won the November elections, but the Republicans gained 80 seats in the house and 7 in the senate. Republicans and conservative Democrats by coalescing could thwart the president.

Nevertheless, the second Roosevelt administration saw the passage of some notable reform legislation, less spectacular than that of the first four years but extending and improving the earlier legislation and moving into some new fields. These years also saw the development of soil conservation to stem erosion and the large-scale construction of public works, including public housing and clearance of slums. Many of the New Deal innovations, such as social security, the agricultural program, the TVA and the SEC, became accepted as permanent functions of the federal government. Clearly, the government was expected thereafter to play a much larger part in U.S. economic life.

Foreign Policy.—By 1939, foreign policy was overshadowing domestic policy as it became clear that war threatened in Europe. Even before Roosevelt took office he had endorsed the Hoover administration's refusal to recognize Japanese conquests in Manchuria. From the outset of his administration, he was deeply involved in foreign policy questions. Most of these centred around the depression. In the early summer of 1933 he refused to support international currency stabilization at the London Economic conference, but by 1934 he had stabilized the dollar and had begun helping France and Great Britain to keep their currencies from being undermined by dictator nations. In Nov. 1933 Roosevelt recognized the government of Soviet Russia in the mistaken hope that he could thus promote trade. Greater opportunities seemed to exist in negotiating reciprocal trade agreements with numerous nations, a program which began in 1935, and in fostering more cordial relations with Latin-American nations. In his inaugural

ACME PHOTO
PRESIDENT FRANKLIN D. ROOSEVELT DURING HIS SECOND TERM

address Roosevelt had pledged himself to the "policy of the good neighbor." Secretary of State Cordell Hull interpreted this to mean that the United States would not unilaterally intervene in Latin-American nations. Gradually, as European war became imminent, the Good Neighbor policy led to collective security and mutual defense agreements.

In the early New Deal years, Roosevelt was not only pursuing programs of economic nationalism but, like most of the American people, was also intent upon keeping the United States out of any impending war. Consequently he supported a series of neutrality laws, beginning with the Neutrality act of Aug. 1935. Roosevelt desired legislation that would enable him to withhold war supplies from an aggressor but sell them to the victim; congress, however, insisted upon a mandatory embargo against both. In Aug. 1936, a month after the outbreak of the Spanish Civil War, Roosevelt declared, "We are not isolationists except in so far as we seek to isolate ourselves completely from war. . . . I hate war."

In 1937 Roosevelt moved toward a new policy when Japan began a new major thrust into northern China. Until then, he had been relatively conciliatory toward Japan, except that he had supported vigorously legislation to strengthen the U.S. navy. In Oct. 1937, speaking in Chicago, Roosevelt proposed that peace-loving nations make concerted efforts to quarantine aggressors. He seemed to be thinking of nothing more drastic than breaking off diplomatic relations, but the proposal created so much national alarm that during ensuing months he was slow to develop a collective security position. He quickly accepted Japanese apologies when the U.S. gunboat "Panay" was sunk on the Yangtze river in Dec. 1937. Gradually relations between the United States and Japan worsened, but the rapid domination of Europe by Adolf Hitler of Germany was more threatening.

The Outbreak of War.—When World War II began with Germany's invasion of Poland in Sept. 1939, Roosevelt called congress into special session to revise the Neutrality act to permit belligerents to buy arms on a "cash and carry" basis. Through the quiet winter of 1939–40 this aid to Great Britain and France seemed adequate, and Roosevelt pressed congress for only moderate increases in armaments appropriations. With Hitler's sudden invasion of Denmark, Norway and the Low Countries, and the fall of France in the spring and early summer of 1940, Roosevelt and congress turned to defense preparations and "all aid short of war" to Great Britain. Roosevelt, convinced that a victory by Germany and Italy would be disastrous to the United States, even gave Great Britain 50 over-age destroyers in exchange for eight western-hemisphere bases. Isolationists, who feared that these moves would involve the United States in war, debated hotly with those who felt that national self-interest demanded aid to Britain. To strengthen the defense effort and to give his administration a bipartisan colouring, Roosevelt in June 1940 appointed two prominent Republicans to his cabinet—Henry L. Stimson as secretary of war and Frank Knox as secretary of the navy. For the presidential campaign of 1940 the Republicans nominated Wendell Willkie, who heartily agreed with Roosevelt's foreign policy. Nevertheless, as both candidates pledged they would keep the nation out of foreign war, isolationists tended to support Willkie, and many of those favouring strong measures against Hitler swung toward Roosevelt. By a closer margin than before, 27,244,000 to 22,305,000 and 449 electoral votes to 82, Roosevelt was elected to an unprecedented third term.

Third Term.—Through 1941 the nation moved gradually closer toward actual belligerency with Germany. After a bitter debate in congress, Roosevelt in March 1941 obtained the Lend-Lease act, enabling the United States to finance aid to Great Britain and its allies. In June 1941 Hitler launched a huge surprise attack against the U.S.S.R., and in September, Roosevelt extended lend-lease to the Soviet Union. Preventing submarines from sinking goods en route to Europe gradually involved more drastic protection by the U.S. navy; by the fall of 1941 the United States was engaged in an undeclared war against German submarines in the Atlantic. Meanwhile, in August on a battleship off the Newfoundland coast, Roosevelt met with Prime Minister Winston Churchill of Great Britain, and signed a joint press release proclaiming an Atlantic

Charter (q.v.) to provide national self-determination, greater economic opportunities, freedom from fear and want, freedom of the seas, and disarmament.

Yet it was in the Pacific that war came to the United States. Japan, bound in a treaty of alliance with Germany and Italy, the so-called Axis, quickly capitalized upon Hitler's victories in Europe to extend its empire in east Asia. Roosevelt, viewing these moves as part of Axis world aggression, began to deny Japan supplies essential to its war-making. Japan was regarded as a relatively mediocre power; the danger that it could launch a damaging retaliatory attack seemed light. Throughout 1941 the United States negotiated with Japan, but

WIDE WORLD

PRESIDENT ROOSEVELT ASKING CONGRESS TO DECLARE WAR ON JAPAN, DEC. 8, 1941

the proposals of each side to the other were unsatisfactory. Roosevelt did not want war with Japan in the fall of 1941, but he miscalculated in thinking the Japanese were bluffing. By the end of November, he knew that Japanese fleet units and transports were at sea and that war was imminent; an attack in southeast Asia and perhaps on the Philippines seemed likely. To Roosevelt's angered surprise, the Japanese on Dec. 7, 1941, struck Pearl Harbor, Hawaii. (See PEARL HARBOR ATTACK.)

As millions of Americans listened to their radios, Roosevelt on Dec. 8, 1941, told congress, "Yesterday, December 7, 1941—a date which will live in infamy—the United States of America was suddenly and deliberately attacked by the naval and air forces of the Empire of Japan." Congress voted a war resolution within four hours; on Dec. 11, Germany and Italy declared war on the United States.

As a war leader, Roosevelt made concessions to the conservatives in congress in order to obtain support in prosecuting the war. Several New Deal agencies were abolished. At a press conference, Roosevelt asserted that "Dr. Win the War" had taken the place of "Dr. New Deal." But apparently this was to be only for the duration of the war, and meanwhile Roosevelt fought resourcefully although not always successfully against inflationary pressures. One of the immediate problems after Pearl Harbor was to build up massive production for war. Since 1939, Roosevelt had been experimenting with various defense agencies to mobilize the economy. Conservatives wished to take some of the control of these agencies out of the president's hand, but he firmly refused to allow it. The lines of authority in the agencies sometimes overlapped, and their powers were not always clearly defined, but in the end a workable organization evolved. Key among these were the War Production board (WPB) established in Jan. 1942 and the Office of War Mobilization (OWM) in May 1943. At the time of Pearl Harbor, U.S. war production was already nearly as great as that of Germany and Japan combined; by 1944 it was double the total of all Axis nations. (See MOBILIZATION, ECONOMIC.)

Relations With Allies.—During the war, Roosevelt concentrated upon problems of strategy, negotiations with the nation's allies and the planning of the peace. At the outset, he took the lead in establishing a grand alliance among all countries fighting the Axis. On Jan. 1, 1942, the United States and its allies signed a Declaration of the United Nations, reiterating the war aims of the Atlantic Charter. Twenty-six nations signed immediately, and 20 more before the end of the war. In the realm of strategy, Roosevelt depended heavily upon the advice of his top military leaders, the Joint Chiefs of Staff. As early as 1940, the United States had decided that in case it were involved in global war, it would concentrate upon Germany, which had greater war production and was a greater military threat. Roosevelt stood by this decision but did not allow it to interfere with vigorous prosecution of the war against Japan.

Upon Roosevelt personally there fell heavy responsibility for the maintenance of effective working relations with the nation's allies. With Great Britain this was easy. Roosevelt met with Churchill in a number of wartime conferences at which differences were settled amicably. Debate at the earlier conferences centred upon the question of a landing in France, which the British succeeded in postponing repeatedly until at length the great Normandy invasion was launched in June 1944. Meanwhile the United States had followed the British lead in invading North Africa in Nov. 1942, Sicily in July 1943 and Italy in Sept. 1943. At one of the most significant of the meetings, at Casablanca, Mor., in Jan. 1943, Roosevelt, after previous consultation with Churchill, proclaimed the doctrine of unconditional surrender of the Axis. What he seemed to want was to avoid differences of opinion among the United Nations and German misunderstanding later, of the sort that had made trouble at the time of the 1918 Armistice. The unconditional surrender doctrine left the United Nations free to lay down whatever peace terms they wished. These were not extremely harsh, though Nazi propagandists warned that they were; nor is there any tangible evidence that the doctrine in any way lengthened the war. (See WORLD WAR II CONFERENCES, ALLIED.)

Relations with the Soviet Union posed an exceedingly difficult problem for Roosevelt. Throughout the war the U.S.S.R. accepted large quantities of lend-lease supplies but seldom divulged its military plans or acted in co-ordination with its western allies. Roosevelt, feeling that the maintenance of peace after the war depended upon friendly relations with the Soviet Union, hoped to win Joseph Stalin's confidence. Outwardly, Roosevelt seemed to get along well with Stalin when at last he and Churchill met with the Soviet leader at Teheran in Nov. 1943. In their optimism, Roosevelt and Churchill seemed not to see realistically that the sort of peace being foreshadowed at Teheran would leave the U.S.S.R. dominant on the continent of Europe. Meanwhile, the Axis had been suffering serious defeats in both Europe and the Pacific. By Feb. 1945, when the Big Three met again at Yalta in the Crimea, the war seemed almost over in Europe, although Americans were still on the defensive in the Ardennes forest. As for Japan, the U.S. expectation was for a last-ditch defense that might require another 18 months or more of fighting. The main Japanese armies remained intact on the Asiatic mainland. Work in developing an atomic bomb was well advanced, but its power (if it worked) was expected to be only a fraction of what it actually turned out to be. Consequently, Roosevelt and his military advisers were eager to obtain Soviet aid in the far east, and in return for Stalin's promise to enter the war against Japan, Roosevelt and Churchill offered concessions in the far east. As for eastern Europe, earlier decisions were ratified, and plans were made for the establishment of democratic governments. Had the arrangements for eastern Europe been followed by Stalin in the manner expected by Roosevelt and Churchill, there would have been little room for criticism of this part of the Yalta agreements. But the understandings were not precise enough and immediately began to receive entirely different interpretations in the U.S.S.R. By mid-March, false Soviet accusations against the United States led Roosevelt to send a sharp telegram to Stalin.

Roosevelt's increasing hope during the war was that the establishment of an effective international organization, in which both the United States and the U.S.S.R. would co-operate, could maintain the peace in years to come. He planned to attend a conference of 50 nations at San Francisco to draft a United Nations charter, opening April 25, 1945. But since Jan. 1944 his health had been declining. His political opponents had tried to make much of this during the campaign of 1944 when he ran for a fourth term against Gov. Thomas E. Dewey of New York. But a final burst of vigour on Roosevelt's part seemed to refute the rumours. Roosevelt won by 25,602,000 to 22,006,000 in popular votes, and 432 to 99 in electoral votes. But by the time Roosevelt returned from Yalta to address congress, he was in such failing physical condition that he had to deliver his speech sitting. He went to Warm Springs, Ga., for a rest, and there on April 12, 1945, died of a massive cerebral hemorrhage.

U.S. ARMY FROM A.P.

PRESIDENT ROOSEVELT (CENTRE) AT THE YALTA CONFERENCE, FEB. 1945. PRIME MINISTER WINSTON CHURCHILL IS SEATED AT LEFT, PREMIER JOSEPH STALIN AT RIGHT. BEHIND THE PRESIDENT STANDS ADMIRAL WILLIAM D. LEAHY, ROOSEVELT'S CHIEF OF STAFF

Evaluation.—During his years as president, Roosevelt had relatively little time for personal life. He continued his interest in his lands at Hyde Park, where he experimented with the planting of trees, and served as vestryman of St. James Episcopal church. His zest for sailing and his enjoyment in collecting stamps and naval books and prints continued unabated. His family life was circumscribed by the tight schedule and incessant publicity imposed upon him as president, and at times this must have been a handicap to Mrs. Roosevelt and their children. Of these there were five: Anna Eleanor (Mrs. James Halsted; 1906–), James (1907–), Elliott (1910–), Franklin D., Jr. (1914–), and John A. (1916–). As a public figure, he was, at the same time, one of the most loved and most hated men in U.S. history. Opponents ascribed to him shallowness, incompetence, trickiness and dictatorial ambitions. His supporters hailed him as the saviour of his nation's economy and the defender of democracy not only in the United States but throughout the world. As a political leader, it was generally conceded, he was unexcelled in winning and holding popular support and in retaining, in his administration, leaders of diverse views. Many experts have expressed the opinion that, despite occasional confusion and overlapping authority, his administration was unusually effective. He brought even more than this to the office: in 1932 he stated what remained his view through peace and war, "The Presidency . . . is pre-eminently a place of moral leadership."

See UNITED STATES (OF AMERICA): *History; see* also references under "Roosevelt, Franklin Delano" in the Index.

BIBLIOGRAPHY.—S. I. Rosenman (ed.), *The Public Papers and Addresses of Franklin D. Roosevelt*, 13 vol. (1938–50); E. K. Lindley, *Half Way With Roosevelt* (1937); B. M. Rauch, *History of the New Deal* (1944); Frances Perkins, *The Roosevelt I Knew* (1947); R. E. Sherwood, *Roosevelt and Hopkins* (1948); D. W. Brogan, *The Era of Franklin D. Roosevelt* (1951); Frank Freidel, *Franklin D. Roosevelt*, 3 vol. (1952 et seq.); A. M. Schlesinger, *The Age of Roosevelt*, 3 vol. (1957–62); E. E. Robinson, *The Roosevelt Leadership 1933–45* (1955); D. Schary, *Sunrise at Campobello* (1958); W. E. Leuchtenburg, *Franklin D. Roosevelt and the New Deal, 1932–1940* (1963).

(FK. F.)

ROOSEVELT, THEODORE (1858–1919), 26th president of the United States, was born in New York City on Oct. 27, 1858. His father, of an old New York Dutch family, was a man of some wealth and importance in civic affairs; his mother, Martha Bulloch of Georgia, was of Scotch-Irish and Huguenot descent. To overcome the physical weakness and ill-health of his early life, young Roosevelt became an earnest devotee of physical culture. By the time of late adolescence, through sports and outdoor living, he had developed a rugged physique and a love of the strenuous life that he never lost. Meanwhile his family, through private

tutoring and travel, had provided him with an excellent education. Roosevelt was one of the few presidents of the United States who was endowed with an encompassing intellectual curiosity and with a real sympathy for and an enjoyment of literature and the arts. After graduating from Harvard College in 1880, he married Alice Hathaway Lee of Boston and in the same year entered Columbia University Law School. But historical writing and politics soon enticed him away from a legal career.

EARLY CAREER

Roosevelt's lifelong desire for public acclaim, combined with the corrupt state of New York public life, led him to join a local Republican Reform Club. In 1881 he was elected to the New York Assembly where during the next three years he became the leader of a small group of "blue-stocking" opponents of the corruption and boss rule that typified both party machines. So successful was his legislative career that in 1884 he was his party's candidate for speaker of the Assembly and chairman of the New York delegation to the Republican national convention. Denouncing the leading Republican candidate, James G. Blaine, as an inveterate practitioner of the kind of politics he had been warring against in New York, Roosevelt vigorously supported Sen. George F. Edmunds at Chicago. But upon Blaine's nomination, Roosevelt, unlike many of his fellow reformers, supported Blaine and thus won a reputation for party loyalty. The death of his young wife in February 1884, and his defeat at Chicago, left him disconsolate and he retreated to the Dakota territory, where he lived the life of a gentleman rancher and sportsman and also continued his historical writing.

In 1886 politics called him back to New York where the Republicans nominated him as their candidate for mayor in a lively campaign against the liberal Democrat Abram S. Hewitt and the single-taxer Henry George, who was supported by labour and radical groups. Despite the divided opposition, Roosevelt ran third; for the next three years he kept out of politics and contented himself with his own personal affairs. He married Edith Kermit Carow and built a home at Sagamore Hill, near Oyster Bay, Long Island, where he was to live for the rest of his life.

Roosevelt found some balm for his three successive political defeats in his appointment by President Harrison as a member of the U.S. Civil Service Commission, a position he held from 1889 to 1895, when he accepted the presidency of the Board of Police Commissioners in New York City. Without quite alienating the professional politicians, Roosevelt added to his reputation as a reformer in both offices and was in a good position to claim some reward from the new administration of William McKinley, whose candidacy in 1896 Roosevelt had vigorously supported. It came in the form of his appointment as assistant secretary of the navy.

In this position Roosevelt distinguished himself by becoming a leading member of the jingo group in the Republican Party; he called for war with Spain and occasionally embarrassed his superiors with precipitate and unauthorized actions to strengthen the Navy. At the start of the Spanish-American War in April 1898 Roosevelt hurriedly resigned from his position to join his friend Leonard Wood (*q.v.*) in organizing the 1st U.S. Volunteer Cavalry, known as the "Rough Riders," and soon became their commander. Roosevelt's leadership of the cavalry regiment was nothing if not spectacular. His disdain for Army red tape and his impetuous charge up Kettle Hill during the battle for San Juan Hill did not endear him to his military superiors. But his colourful exploits, reports of which were widely circulated at home, made him something of a national hero.

Governor of New York.—As reentry into politics by the returning hero was almost inevitable, Thomas C. Platt, the Republican boss of New York, bowed to seeming necessity. Platt distrusted Roosevelt as "a perfect bull in a china shop," but he also needed a vote-winning, "respectable" candidate to remove the taint of fraud adhering to the incumbent administration. Two weeks after he was mustered out of the service Roosevelt was nominated for governor of New York and in November he was elected, by a very small majority, for a two-year term.

Before obtaining the nomination Roosevelt had met with Platt and promised that he would not upset the hold of the machine on the party, a promise that was seriously to limit his actions. Nevertheless, his record in office was a good one. In most instances his appointments were superior, and his removal of the superintendent of insurance, one of Platt's supporters, on grounds of fraud, indicated that his promise had limits. Over Platt's opposition and from a reluctant legislature Roosevelt also secured one measure that taxed corporation franchises and a second that established a civil service system. During his two years' administration he so irritated the regular Republican organization that Platt contrived to bring about his nomination for vice-president in 1900 to remove him from New York state politics. Roosevelt accepted the nomination in part because he was outmaneuvered and in part because his renomination and election as governor could not be taken as at all assured.

ROOSEVELT AS PRESIDENT

All of Roosevelt's dreary expectations for the vice-presidency were fulfilled. Bored beyond measure in a position of idleness, he talked about returning to the study of the law or of becoming a university professor. Then on Sept. 14, 1901, President McKinley died in Buffalo, N.Y., after being shot by an assassin, and Roosevelt became president.

Although Roosevelt's first public announcement indicated there was to be no change from McKinley's policies, it was soon apparent that the new president would not follow the same course as his predecessor. Roosevelt was worried. He knew that Bryan's defeat in 1896 and the Spanish-American War had not quieted western demands for further control of trusts, for the regulation of railroads, and for a reduction in the tariff, and he was aware that the price of inactivity might be a catastrophe for the party in 1904 and defeat for himself. But he was also acutely aware that both the Senate and the House were tightly controlled by conservative Republicans who were bitterly opposed to western demands for reform. His answer to this perplexing situation was to ask for relatively little controversial legislation and to use his executive power to the full in appeasing the rising discontent.

The Anti-Trust Campaign.—For 12 years the Sherman Anti-Trust Act of 1890, originally passed to control the power of growing industrial and financial monopoly, had been virtually ignored by both government and industry. Then on Feb. 18, 1902, Roosevelt reinvigorated the statute and launched a campaign to restore competition in the business and financial world. On that date, without prior consultation with the private interests involved, the president, through his attorney-general, Philander C. Knox, brought suit against the giant railroad complex, the Northern Securities Company. Since this holding company had been put together by J. P. Morgan, John D. Rockefeller, Edward H. Harriman, and James J. Hill, the government was attacking the very citadel of U.S. finance capitalism and corporate business. On March 14, 1904, the attack was successfully brought home when the Supreme Court reaffirmed a decree of a federal circuit court ordering the dissolution of the Northern Securities Company.

For the next seven years of his administration Roosevelt vigorously used the Sherman Act against some of the nation's greatest industrial organizations. The U.S. Steel Corporation, the Standard Oil Company, and more than 30 other industrial combinations were summarily ordered into court. But almost from the first days of his administration Roosevelt realized that breaking up big business concerns was not alone the answer to the industrial problem. Growth in size, he contended, was an inevitable part of industrial evolution and, in fact, was socially desirable. What was wrong was the use of these great organizations against the public interest. Trusts that served the public interest were good; those that did not were bad. Far more basic was his demand for government regulation of industry. Roosevelt was the first U.S. president who envisioned the federal government as an umpire upholding the public interest in the conflicts among big business, big labour, and the consumer.

Regulation of Business.—In 1902 the president asked Congress to establish a federal Bureau of Corporations with power to inspect the books of private businesses and to give publicity to its findings when it found evidence of action against the public interest. Even this small step on the way to regulation was fought by the conservatives in Congress. To get even a part of his legislation enacted the president had to agree with the Republican leader of the Senate, Nelson W. Aldrich, that he would not ask for any more measures regulating business during his first term. The president nevertheless continued to talk of the need for federal regulation, and twice during his second term he recommended measures to Congress that would have required all firms engaged in interstate commerce to obtain a license from the federal government and would have required such firms to make annual reports of sales and profits.

Since passage of the Interstate Commerce Act of 1887 even conservatives had accepted the idea that railroads were public utilities that came within the sphere of federal regulation. But, because of judicial interpretations and executive inactivity, little control had actually been exercised. Presidential pressure and persuasion were essential if anything was to be accomplished. Without Roosevelt's sustained support it is doubtful that the Hepburn Act of 1906, which gave the Interstate Commerce Commission power to fix railroad rates and to forbid discrimination between shippers, would have been passed. The president was also instrumental in securing the passage of a Pure Food and Drugs Act (1906), which forbade the making of adulterated foods, drugs, and medicines, and a measure requiring federal inspection of meat products shipped across state boundaries.

Labour.—In 1902 Roosevelt successfully interposed federal authority in a major labour dispute. Under the leadership of John Mitchell, the anthracite coal miners' union struck for higher wages, and when the operators refused even to talk with the unions the country was faced with a coal famine with winter just a few weeks away. As real suffering visited eastern cities the president, in the name of the public, demanded arbitration. When the operators at a White House conference stubbornly refused to arbitrate or even to talk with the union leaders, the president threatened to use the Army to mine coal. Faced with this threat the owners gave way and in subsequent negotiations the miners were awarded a small increase in pay and better working conditions. Throughout the rest of his administration Roosevelt welcomed union leaders to the White House. He had no sympathy for union violence, however, and some of his actions were bitterly criticized by labour as being anti-union. Roosevelt accepted big unions as he accepted big business; on balance, he felt that unions contributed to the general welfare. He opposed the closed shop and contended that the workshop should be open to both union and non-union men without "illegal interference" from either capital or labour. At all times he believed the rights of the general public as represented by government were superior to the rights of either organized capital or organized labour.

One of the lasting achievements of Roosevelt's first term was the creation by Congress in 1903 of a Department of Commerce and Labor, with its secretary a member of the president's cabinet.

Conservation.—When asked after his retirement which of his achievements he considered most important to the national welfare, Roosevelt unhesitatingly named his conservation policies. Throughout the first century of the nation's history the government had operated under a policy of rapid and cheap disposal of public lands to private interests, the theory being that this quick exploitation of natural resources would most rapidly contribute to the nation's growth and strength. But in the latter years of the 19th century a group of conservationists led by Gifford Pinchot of Pennsylvania began to argue that this policy had led to waste and the growth of monopoly. They direfully predicted that its continuation would mean that the nation would eventually face a famine, that its forests would be depleted, and that its mineral resources would be exhausted. Responding to such arguments, Congress empowered the president to convert public lands into national forests. Under the three preceding administrations only about 40,000,000 ac. had been so treated. Within seven years Roosevelt, inspired by Pinchot and James R. Garfield, had raised that figure to 194,000,000 ac., and had included not only forests but mineral and coal lands and waterpower sites as well.

Roosevelt's conservation policy soon aroused strong opposition. Throughout the West in particular, where most of the national domain lay, it was claimed that the national development was being obstructed by a group of effete, college-educated theorists. Congress, reacting to the demands of its constituents, again and again sought to limit the presidential power to create national reserves. But Roosevelt persisted even to the point of creating forest ranger stations around valuable power and mineral sites, even though some such sites lacked trees or even brush. In 1908 he called a White House conference on conservation that focused public attention on the subject. Soon thereafter the National Conservation Commission was created to make a systematic study of the nation's resources. Perhaps none of Roosevelt's actions encountered sharper criticism or enjoyed more widespread popularity than his efforts to preserve a portion of the national wealth for future generations.

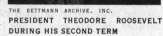

THE BETTMANN ARCHIVE, INC.
PRESIDENT THEODORE ROOSEVELT DURING HIS SECOND TERM

The president's conservation policy was finally rounded out by the Reclamation Act of 1902. Inspired by Congressman (later Senator) Francis G. Newlands of Nevada and cordially supported by the president, the act provided for setting aside almost all the receipts from public land sales in the West to pay for irrigation projects in arid regions. The program, inaugurated by the construction of the great Roosevelt Dam in Arizona, continued after Roosevelt left office and was responsible for much of the later development of the inter-mountain and Pacific coast states.

1904 Reelection.—Both Roosevelt and his policies were given a vote of confidence in the election of 1904. Seeking to divorce itself from its heritage of William Jennings Bryan and Populism, the Democratic Party nominated a conservative, Judge Alton B. Parker of New York. In a rather listless campaign the president and his running mate, Charles W. Fairbanks of Indiana, scored a smashing victory, rolling up 7,600,000 popular votes to their opponents' 5,080,000; the electoral vote was 336 to 140. Surprised and elated by the results, Roosevelt promised that he would consider his seven presidential years as constituting two full terms and that he would not seek reelection in 1908, a promise that he was later to regret.

Foreign Policy.—Something of an international social-Darwinist, Roosevelt believed that the strong and virile nations survived while the weak and placid disappeared or were conquered. He also sensed that the relatively peaceful Victorian period was giving way to an age in which naked force was likely to become the principal international arbiter. Almost every year during his two administrations he asked for larger naval appropriations, and often, to induce Congress to grant him new ships, he exaggerated the seriousness of international incidents. Through one means and another the U.S. Navy by the end of his term had been built into one of the major sea forces of the world. At the same time Roosevelt encouraged the secretary of war, Elihu Root (q.v.), to continue his reform of the U.S. Army. Occasionally he intervened in the established practices of both armed services to promote able young officers over the heads of their elders.

In the world power struggle, Roosevelt agreed with his two eminent secretaries of state, John Hay (q.v.) and Elihu Root, that Germany constituted the chief menace to the United States. Although Britain's strength was imposing, the international aims of the British were so close to those of the United States that he did not expect any serious trouble from Great Britain. Germany, Roosevelt believed, was the only nation whose international ambitions and power constituted a major threat to the United States. Both Roosevelt and Root believed that the most probable geographical point of that danger was in the Caribbean and Latin America. This attitude helps to explain Roosevelt's strong-armed intervention in Caribbean affairs and his extension of the Monroe Doctrine (q.v.).

Twice during the Roosevelt years the U.S. government feared German intervention in Venezuela because of the latter country's unpaid international debt, and twice the U.S. government acted with some vigour to secure a peaceful settlement that would protect Venezuela's territorial integrity. But whether Roosevelt actually threatened to use the Navy against German forces, as many years later he recalled doing, is still a moot question. In the Dominican Republic in 1903 the chaotic finances of the government threatened European intervention. What troubled the United States was that the European claims were valid and there seemed to be no way to bring about payment by the corrupt Caribbean dictators other than through the use of force. U.S. officials were quite aware that in other parts of the world the armed forces that were used to collect debts had a disturbing habit of becoming permanent guests. To solve the problem, Roosevelt and Root issued a policy statement in 1904 that in effect denied to any non-American country the right to intervene in Latin-American affairs, but also assured world creditors that the United States would police the area and become responsible for assuring that these governments would abide by their international obligations. There would be no interference, the president wrote, with Latin-American nations that kept the peace and met their international obligations. But "brutal wrongdoing, or an impotence which results in a general loosening of the ties of civilized society, may finally require intervention by some civilized nation, and in the Western Hemisphere the United States cannot ignore this duty. . . ." The so-called Roosevelt corollary to the Monroe Doctrine denied other governments the right to intervene in Latin America but sanctioned such intervention by the U.S. in the role of international policeman. Quickly applying practice to principle, Roosevelt forced the Dominican Republic in 1905 to accept the appointment of an economic adviser responsible to the U.S. Department of State.

Panama Canal.—The rapidly growing sensitivity of the United States to Latin-American affairs was in part due to the acquisition of the Panama Canal Zone in 1903 and the construction thereafter of the interocean canal. Roosevelt's part in the acquisition of the Canal Zone was spectacular. Impatient with the long-drawn-out negotiations with Colombia over the purchase of the zone, the president gave comfort and indirect encouragement to a revolutionary junta in New York led by two representatives of the old French Panama Company, Philippe Bunau-Varilla and William N. Cromwell, who planned a Panamanian revolution. The impatient president had already written a message to Congress, which was never sent, advising the taking of Panama "without any further parley with Colombia." But on Nov. 3 the planned outbreak occurred while a U.S. warship that had conveniently put

THE BETTMANN ARCHIVE, INC.
PRESIDENT ROOSEVELT (SEATED) RUNNING A STEAM SHOVEL DURING HIS VISIT TO THE PANAMA CANAL CONSTRUCTION SITE. THIS TRIP MARKED THE FIRST TIME A U.S. PRESIDENT HAD LEFT U.S. SOIL

into Colón the preceding evening prevented Colombian troops from interfering. Within hours the United States recognized the new government, and in a matter of days the treaty ceding the Canal Zone was negotiated with Bunau-Varilla, who now turned up in Washington as Panama's first representative. Construction of the canal was promptly started, and in 1914 the new waterway was opened to world shipping. (*See* PANAMA CANAL.)

Ever since the settlement of the Pacific Coast, American interest in the Pacific area had been growing. With the acquisition of parts of Samoa, Hawaii, Guam, Midway, and the Philippines during the late 19th century the area became a major concern of the Washington government. The Pacific position of the United States, Roosevelt said in 1902, "is such as to insure our peaceful domination of its waters." From such a supposition Roosevelt's intervention in the peace negotiations following the Russo-Japanese War of 1904 was logical. The president's skilful diplomacy in bringing Russia and Japan together at the Portsmouth Conference won him the Nobel Peace Prize; he also attempted to construct a balance of power between Russia and Japan in the Pacific, so that neither country would be able to imperil America's fast-growing interests there. In later years Roosevelt's East Asia policy was threatened by the rise of Japanese power and by the inclusion of both Russia and Japan in the system of world-girdling alliances forming in Europe. Meanwhile the president approached a variety of very thorny problems with Japan with extreme caution. The trouble over the anti-Japanese attitude on the West Coast was settled temporarily by the Gentlemen's Agreement of 1907 (by which Japan promised not to issue passports to labourers wishing to migrate to the United States) and the tacit recognition by the United States of the Japanese seizure of Korea. But by the end of his term Roosevelt was distinctly worried about future relations with Japan. It was typical of Roosevelt that he chose to send a part of the U.S. fleet on a world cruise (December 1907–February 1909) to demonstrate the nation's naval power.

By 1907, if not before, Roosevelt was acutely aware of the danger that a major war might break out in Europe. By that time also the president, as well as most of his chief advisers, had come to the conclusion that the long-term interests of the United States lay in preserving British hegemony in the non-European world. This conclusion came in part from a realistic appraisal of the world situation and in part from the increasingly friendly state of Anglo-American relations. Great Britain had been more than friendly to the United States during the Spanish-American War and had been generous in the Hay-Pauncefote treaties that cleared the way for the United States to dig the Panama Canal. In the controversy with Canada over the Alaskan-Canadian border the vote of the British representative on the arbitration commission had favoured the U.S. position on most vital issues. Against this background Roosevelt projected the United States into the 1906 Algeciras Conference (*q.v.*), which was called to prevent the outbreak of a European war over Morocco. The president had, in fact, been at the centre of the delicate negotiations that preceded the calling of the conference. The U.S. representative at the Algeciras meeting was instructed to do nothing that would imperil the existing Franco-British understanding, the continuation of which, the Department of State felt, was favourable "for the peace of the world and, therefore, the best interests of the United States. . . ." Roosevelt's European policy modified the long tradition of U.S. isolation and cemented further the rapidly growing British-American friendship that was to become so important in world politics during the next 50 years.

Last Years as President.—Roosevelt's last years as president were anything but calm. From the early days of his administration, when he invited the Negro leader and educator Booker T. Washington to lunch at the White House, he seemed to court personal controversy. He continued to preach and practise "the strenuous life." His crusade against "race suicide" (occasioned by his alarm at the falling birthrate), his public quarrels with popular naturalists, and his order to the government printers to use a system of simplified spelling all developed into national arguments. After the financial panic of 1907, which businessmen and conservatives attributed to Roosevelt's attacks on large industry

and finance, these controversies became more serious in tone. The president's rather high-handed disciplining of a Negro regiment for its part in a riot at Brownsville, Tex., and his quarrel with Congress over increased appropriations for the Secret Service—during which he implied that the opposing congressmen might have something to hide—led to a bitter controversy. But most of the opposition to Roosevelt came from a growing conflict between the conservatives and the progressives within the Republican Party. During his last two years Roosevelt veered sharply to the left in his social and economic thinking, a direction which a good many western and reform-minded Republicans enthusiastically adopted. By 1908 a small but vigorous minority of his party was already in opposition to the leadership of Nelson W. Aldrich in the Senate and Joseph G. Cannon in the House. Roosevelt sided with the progressives against the Old Guard, and by the time of his retirement the party was so split that future trouble was inevitable.

A good part of the reason for the president's inclination toward reform came from his belief that the country was rapidly heading in a radical direction and that the party was due for defeat if it did not move in the same direction. He even felt that unless his successor broadened the policies he had enunciated during his two terms the country might swing toward socialism. Consequently, during his last years he carefully evaluated his chief lieutenants and eventually settled on William Howard Taft as a worthy successor. Taft had loyally and ably served the administration in a variety of tasks, and, next to Elihu Root, whom Roosevelt considered to be too closely tied to Wall Street, was his most trusted adviser. Late in 1907 Roosevelt let it be known that he considered Taft to be the man for the presidency, and for the next year he concentrated his efforts on securing Taft's nomination and election. Thus, when he left office in March 1909, both he and the country were confident that while the pilot was changed the course was to remain the same.

UNDERWOOD AND UNDERWOOD

PRESIDENT ROOSEVELT WITH THE RUSSIAN AND JAPANESE ENVOYS TO THE PORTSMOUTH PEACE CONFERENCE. AT LEFT ARE COUNT WITTE AND BARON ROSEN, AT RIGHT IS MARQUIS KOMURA JUTARŌ. PHOTOGRAPHED AT OYSTER BAY, N.Y., AUG. 5, 1905

THE LATER YEARS

After leaving the White House, Roosevelt took a ten-month hunting trip through central and northern Africa. Roosevelt was an ardent amateur naturalist; the extent of his interest in wildlife can be measured by the 80-page typewritten letter he wrote to Sir Edward Grey on the birds of England that he saw while on a walking tour. After coming out of the African jungle, Roosevelt made a grand tour of Europe during which he visited the crowned heads and chief ministers of most of the major powers.

Return to Politics.—During his stay in Europe Roosevelt received many letters from home that kept him informed of the growing schism in the Republican Party. Soon after returning to New York, where he received a tumultuous welcome on June 18, 1910, he plunged into politics. By that time Taft, while trying to carry out Roosevelt's policies, had allied himself with the party's conservative leadership. The progressives, who included a number of Roosevelt's very close personal and political friends, were in outright rebellion against Taft and the conservatives. The immediate occasion for Roosevelt's reentrance into politics was a struggle between Gov. Charles Evans Hughes and the machine politicians of New York. Roosevelt tried to help Hughes and was defeated in part because of Hughes' own withdrawal from the battle and in part because of President Taft's wavering support. Elsewhere in the country the former president attempted to bring the two wings of the party together by making a speaking tour in which he supported both the regulars and the progressives. During the western part of this tour he delivered his most famous political address on the subject of "The New Nationalism." The central doctrines of the speech departed radically from traditional Republican theory; they called for a great increase of federal power for the purpose of regulating interstate industry more closely, and a sweeping program of social reform designed to put human rights above the rights of property. Attacking the courts as well as the reactionary politicians, both of whom had been instrumental in blocking such reforms in the past, Roosevelt concluded that the community, acting through the federal government, should have the power to regulate property "to whatever degree the public welfare may require. . . ." Despite all of his efforts, Roosevelt was not able to pacify the quarreling factions of the party nor to save it from defeat in the congressional elections of 1910. For the first time in 16 years the Democrats gained control of the House of Representatives and looked forward with growing confidence to the presidential election of 1912.

After the 1910 defeat the Republican progressives organized to nominate Robert M. LaFollette of Wisconsin in 1912, but their heart was really with Roosevelt. As a result, increasing pressure was brought upon the former president to run again. Since March 4, 1909, the once glowing friendship between Taft and Roosevelt had steadily cooled, and in October 1910, when the Taft administration brought an antitrust suit against the United States Steel Corporation for a merger which Roosevelt had tacitly approved, the former president was enraged. Soon Roosevelt intimated to friends that he would run, and, roughly shoving LaFollette aside, he formally entered into a contest for delegates against the man he had placed in office. One of the bitterest campaigns for nomination in the country's history followed.

Progressive Party of 1912.—The contest for the Republican nomination was not settled until the Chicago convention in June 1912. Roosevelt had won most of the delegates selected by direct primaries but Taft had control of the Republican machine, and in the first contest over the choice of the officers of the convention it was evident that the machine was determined to nominate Taft. During the course of the stormy convention Taft was nominated and most of the Roosevelt delegates withdrew and, with Roosevelt's approval, formed the Progressive Party (q.v.). On Aug. 7, 1912, the Progressives met in convention and nominated Roosevelt for president and Gov. Hiram Johnson of California for vice-president. The program of the party fully incorporated Roosevelt's "New Nationalism." After Roosevelt remarked to a reporter who had inquired about his health that he felt "like a bull moose," the party came to be known popularly as the Bull Moose Party. Roosevelt waged a vigorous campaign, during the course of which he was shot by an insane man in Milwaukee while on his way to make a speech. He went ahead with his address, telling the crowd that he had a bullet in his body but assuring them that, "It takes more than that to kill a Bull Moose." In spite of Roosevelt's efforts, the Democrats, united under Woodrow Wilson, were victorious over their divided opponents. Roosevelt's only solace was in beating Taft. The popular vote stood 6,293,454 for Wilson, 4,119,538 for Roosevelt, 3,484,980 for Taft; in the electoral vote, Wilson received 435, Roosevelt 88, Taft 8.

World War I Era.—For the two years following the 1912 defeat Roosevelt rarely appeared before the public. He was involved in a lively libel suit against a Michigan editor in May 1913; he won the suit and during the following autumn led an expedition into the Brazilian jungle, where he contracted a fever and almost died. By the congressional elections of 1914 the Progressive Party was almost swept into oblivion, and Roosevelt pessimistically believed that his days as a public figure were over. But the outbreak of World War I in August 1914 provided issues on which Roosevelt again made the nation's headlines. When Germany invaded Belgium, Roosevelt wrote that the United States "had not the smallest responsibility" for the plight of that unhappy country. But within a few weeks he became an ardent champion of the Franco-British cause, and after the sinking of the "Lusitania" in May 1915 he was talking about the "unforgivable treachery" of Germany.

Roosevelt had already criticized Wilson's policy toward Mexico as being born of a "mollycoddle spirit." For the president's crusade for a neutral attitude toward the war in Europe he had nothing but imperious scorn. Through numerous speeches and the monthly issues of the *Metropolitan Magazine* he advocated military preparedness and a positive policy of aid to the Allies that would unquestionably have led to war with Germany at an early date. Toward people who disagreed with him, Roosevelt showed his old spirit of impatience. He attacked the pacifists and the "peace at any price men" as more destructive of the national welfare than "all the crooks in business and politics combined." Citizens of German origin (German-Americans) who were opposed to entering the war were labeled "hyphenates." But his sharpest attacks were on Wilson whom, by January 1916, he was accusing of "dishonorable conduct."

During the elections of 1916 Roosevelt had one overriding aim, the defeat of Woodrow Wilson. He would have liked the Republican nomination himself and actually contrived to obtain it by killing off his own Progressive Party, much to the chagrin of many of his reforming followers. When Charles Evans Hughes was made the Republican nominee Roosevelt actively supported him and campaigned vigorously throughout the eastern states on his behalf. In the very close election of 1916 the Republican Party was defeated, and once more Roosevelt felt that his days of public usefulness were over. When the nation declared war on Germany in 1917, however, Roosevelt immediately attempted to raise a volunteer division of infantry and cavalry, which he hoped to lead to France. The most he could do for his country, he wrote, was to die in a "reasonably honorable fashion at the head of my division." Once again his cherished hopes were to be bitterly disappointed. On the advice of Gen. John J. Pershing, who had been selected to lead the American Expeditionary Force, the administration refused to accept his offer. Roosevelt spent the rest of the war speaking and writing in a patriotic vein and occasionally indulging in Republican politics with wistful hopes for the 1920 election. Although he had long supported the idea of some sort of international organization to keep the peace, he was vigorous in his criticism of Woodrow Wilson's League of Nations. Had he lived, he would undoubtedly have been one of the leaders of the fight against the Treaty of Versailles and the League. By 1919 the years of inordinate activity had taken their toll. The fever Roosevelt had caught in Brazil returned in 1918, and twice during that year he was hospitalized. Meanwhile the death of his son Quentin on the field of battle in France had sapped his spirit. Early in 1919 he was still trying to convince his friends that the Republican Party would nominate him in 1920. Suddenly, and without warning, he died in his sleep on Jan. 6, 1919.

See also UNITED STATES (OF AMERICA): *History.*

BY COURTESY OF THE DES MOINES REGISTER; PHOTOGRAPH, HISTORICAL PICTURES SERVICE

"THE LONG LONG TRAIL"

A cartoon tribute to Roosevelt by Jay N. ("Ding") Darling which appeared on Jan. 7, 1919, the day after the president's death

Publications.—Roosevelt wrote over 2,000 published works, including magazine articles and a profusion of books on history, politics, travel, and natural history. In addition, his letters, to be found in the Library of Congress (with copies at Harvard University), number over 150,000. They are among the most readable of all presidential letters. Roosevelt was interested in almost every facet of American life, and his correspondence is brim full of comments and allusions ranging far beyond politics. The two best collections of his works are the Memorial edition, 24 vol. (1923–26), and the National edition, 20 vol. (1926). Over 6,000 of the more important of his personal letters appear in Elting E. Morison (ed.), *The Letters of Theodore Roosevelt,* 8 vol. (1951–53).

Among Roosevelt's more important works on politics are: *New Nationalism* (1910); *Progressive Principles* (1913); and *America and the World War* (1915). His historical studies include *The Winning of the West*, 4 vol. (1889–96); *The Naval War of 1812* (1882); and *Life of Oliver Cromwell* (1900). The most widely read of his many books on natural history is *African Game Trails* (1910). *History as Literature* (1913) affords another view of this many-sided man, and *Theodore Roosevelt's Letters to His Children* reveals a tender love for and preoccupation with his offspring.

BIBLIOGRAPHY.—Henry F. Pringle, *Theodore Roosevelt: a Biography* (1931); John M. Blum, *The Republican Roosevelt* (1954); George E. Mowry, *Theodore Roosevelt and the Progressive Movement* (1946) and *The Era of Theodore Roosevelt* (1958); Carleton Putnam, *Theodore Roosevelt: a Biography, The Formative Years, 1858–1886* (1958); Howard K. Beale, *Theodore Roosevelt and the Rise of America to World Power* (1956). Among the still useful older works are J. B. Bishop, *Theodore Roosevelt and His Time Shown in His Own Letters* (1920); William R. Thayer, *Theodore Roosevelt* (1919); and Lawrence F. Abbott, *Impressions of Theodore Roosevelt* (1920). (G. E. Mo.)

ROOT, ELIHU (1845–1937), U.S. lawyer, political leader, diplomatist, and cabinet member who developed important government policies in the areas of colonial administration, organization of the armed forces, Latin-American relations, and the conduct of diplomacy, was born Feb. 15, 1845, in Clinton, N.Y. In 1864 he graduated from Hamilton College where his father was professor of mathematics. Receiving a law degree from the New York University Law School in 1867, he was admitted to the bar and formed a law firm with John H. Strahan. Root's practice was mainly concerned with banking, railroads, wills, estates, and cases involving municipal government. He generally represented large corporate interests and was drawn into close contact with conservative Republicans but was nevertheless associated with the reform element of the party. Following 1886 he developed a close friendship with Theodore Roosevelt and served him as legal adviser during Roosevelt's mayoralty and during his term as police commissioner of New York City. As governor of the state, Roosevelt continued to draw ideas from Root, especially on trusts and franchise taxes. In 1894, and again in 1915, Root served prominently in conventions that revised the New York state constitution.

Root accepted the post of secretary of war in President McKinley's cabinet in 1899 largely because of his interest in working out governmental arrangements for the former Spanish areas, a task which fell under the War Department. His recommendation of lower tariffs to aid Puerto Rico, combined with his apprehension that a centralized government would be necessary to forestall local anarchy, resulted in passage of the Foraker Act of 1900 to provide for civil government in Puerto Rico. His selection of Gen. Leonard Wood (*q.v.*) as military governor of Cuba led to a model regime of physical, medical, and educational progress for that island. At the same time, Root insisted that the Cubans safeguard U.S. interests and incorporate the Platt Amendment (*q.v.*) in their new constitution.

In the Philippines, Root was confronted with Aguinaldo's revolt and a demoralized American Army. He succeeded in tripling the size of the latter and within two years had established U.S. authority in the islands. He then wrote the instructions for an American governing commission that was sent to the Philippines in 1900 under William Howard Taft. These instructions were, in reality, a constitution, a judicial code, and a system of laws; they were reaffirmed by Congress in the Organic Act of 1902. With their emphasis upon individual liberties and the development of local institutions, they were, both in form and substance, a model for colonial administration.

Root's accomplishments in military reform were outstanding. Taking office at a time when entrenched bureaucracy and lack of planning crippled efficiency, he persuaded Congress to transform the state National Guards into the organized militia of the U.S., established the principle of rotation from staff to line, and created the Army War College. He also introduced the principle of a general staff.

Leaving the cabinet in 1903, Root returned again as secretary of state in 1905 under Theodore Roosevelt and remained until 1909. He made a tour of South America in 1906 that was notable for arousing hitherto absent goodwill. He persuaded Latin-American states to participate in the Second Hague Peace Conference and cooperated with Mexico in mediating troubles in Central America. The "dollar diplomacy" approach was refreshingly absent in all such contacts. He allayed Japanese antagonisms raised by San Francisco school segregationists in the crisis of 1907 and negotiated the Gentlemen's Agreement by which Japan undertook to control emigration to the United States. The Root-Takahira agreement of 1908 further reestablished understanding between the two nations, although it was later criticized as conceding too much to Japanese expansionists. Root also concluded treaties of arbitration with most European nations. Later, as chief counsel for the U.S. before The Hague Tribunal, he settled the extended controversy over the North Atlantic coast fisheries with the British. Canadian relations also improved under his tactful leadership. For his contribution to peace and general world harmony, he was awarded the Nobel Peace Prize in 1912.

Root's administration of the Department of State saw important progress in taking the consular service out of politics and establishing it as a career service on a merit basis. More important, he produced a new realistic view toward diplomacy based on a frank acknowledgment that isolation could no longer be the cornerstone of American foreign policy, a view which he later sought to implement through his work on the Permanent Court of Arbitration and as president of the Carnegie Endowment for International Peace.

From 1909 to 1915, as a Republican senator from New York, Root sided with the Taft wing of the party, presiding over the national convention of 1912 that nominated Taft. After the Democratic victory in the election, he rejected President Wilson and his program, opposing the Underwood Tariff (largely because of its income tax provisions), the Federal Reserve Act, the Federal Trade Commission Act, and the Clayton Anti-Trust Act. He also opposed Wilson's neutrality policy but supported him as wartime leader; he served as head of a futile mission to Russia in 1917 for the purpose of encouraging the faltering Kerenski government to carry on the war. In the postwar fight over the League of Nations, Root was a leading Republican supporter of that organization, advocating that the treaty be accepted with minor reservations. He supported Harding in 1920, urging his election as the best path to entering the League with appropriate safeguards, and later accepted appointment to the League's commission of jurists, which framed the statute for the Permanent Court of International Justice (1920–21).

Root was appointed by President Harding as one of four U.S. delegates to the International Conference on the Limitation of Armaments that met at Washington in November 1921. He sponsored a treaty to govern the operation of submarines in future wars and the curtailment of noxious gases in warfare, and had a hand in drafting the Nine-Power Treaty on China, reiterating the Open Door Policy and guaranteeing its independence and territorial integrity. (*See* WASHINGTON, TREATIES OF.) In 1929 he accepted appointment as a member of the commission to revise the World Court statute, taking the occasion to devise a formula to facilitate U.S. entry. The commission's report, although accepted by the League Council, was later rejected by the U.S. Senate.

Throughout his last years Root was active in matters affecting the bar and continued his work with various Carnegie benefactions both in the area of peace programs and in advancement of pure science. He died Feb. 7, 1937, in New York City.

BIBLIOGRAPHY.—*See* collected speeches and papers of E. Root, ed. by Robert Bacon and James Brown Scott, 8 vol. (1916–25); Philip C. Jessup, *Elihu Root*, 2 vol. (1938); Richard W. Leopold, *Elihu Root and the Conservative Tradition* (1954). (P. L. Mu.)

ROOT, JOHN WELLBORN (1850–1891), a pioneer in the "Chicago School" of modern architecture, was born in Lumpkin, Ga., on Jan. 10, 1850. His early schooling was interrupted when Union troops captured the town during the Civil War in 1864, and Root was sent to Liverpool, Eng., with a business associate of his father and placed in a school at Claremont. On his return to the United States in 1866 after a year at Oxford he entered New York University, graduating in 1869 with a degree in civil engineering.

Root began his professional career in Chicago as a draftsman in the firm of Carter, Drake, and Wight. There he met Daniel H. Burnham (*q.v.*), with whom he formed a partnership in 1873. At first they suffered financial reverses but the partnership was a creative one and it eventually prospered. Their first commissions were mainly residences. In 1880 they began a productive decade of commercial work distinguished by three extremely influential buildings, the Montauk (1882), the Rookery (1884–86), and the Monadnock (1889–91), all in Chicago. The last marked a decisive break with traditional styles of architecture, relying on pure functional and geometric form for its aesthetic character. Root served on the architectural staff of the World's Columbian Exposition (1893) and wrote many papers on the philosophy of the new architectural movement in Chicago. His prolific genius was cut short by death from pneumonia on Jan. 15, 1891.

BIBLIOGRAPHY.—Carl W. Condit, *The Rise of the Skyscraper* (1952), *The Chicago School of Architecture* (1964); Harriet Monroe, *John Wellborn Root* (1896); Frank Randall, *History of the Development of Building Construction in Chicago* (1949). (C. W. Co.)

ROOT, in popular usage, is that part of a plant normally underground. Botanically, its application is more restricted, for many plants develop subterranean structures that are in reality specialized stems (corms, tubers, rhizomes; *see* STEM). The root is distinguished from such underground stems by lacking leaf scars

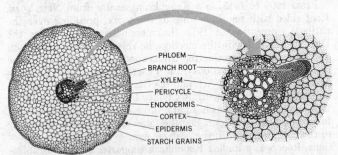

FROM "BIOLOGICAL SCIENCE; AN INQUIRY INTO LIFE" BY PERMISSION OF THE BIOLOGICAL SCIENCES CURRICULUM STUDY

ENLARGED CROSS SECTION OF A BUTTERCUP ROOT, WITH THE VASCULAR CORE AND A YOUNG BRANCH ROOT FURTHER ENLARGED AT THE RIGHT

and buds and by having its growing tip protected by a root cap. The root functions primarily as an absorptive and anchoring organ. Root branches originate irregularly along the root axis and are produced by internal tissue (pericycle and cambium), unlike stem branches, which arise from buds. The vascular tissue (xylem and phloem) is contained within a central cylinder, not in peripheral bundles or bands as in the stem. For details on root and stem structure *see* PLANTS AND PLANT SCIENCE: *Anatomy of Plants*.

Occurrence.—Not all plants have true roots; they are lacking in algae, fungi, mosses, and liverworts, although some of these lower plants develop organs (rhizoids) that perform some of the functions of roots. Phylogenetically, the root is associated with the evolution of the sporophytic generation in the higher land plants. True roots occur only in ferns and seed plants.

Parasitic plants as the mistletoe, broomrape, dodder, and *Rafflesia*, send rootlike processes (haustoria) into the body of the host plant. In the coralroot orchid (*Corallorhiza*) a stem structure, the shortly branched underground rhizome, performs all the functions of a true root, which is absent. In some aquatic plants, the root acts merely as an anchor, or it may be flattened and contain chloroplasts for the manufacture of food; in others it is altogether absent, as in the free-floating aquatic fern *Salvinia* and in the bladderworts. The epiphyte Spanish moss is rootless.

General Features.—The primary function of the root is absorption of water and inorganic salts in solution and the conduction of these to the stem, but it also affords anchorage and support and frequently serves for storage of reserve foods. In some instances it may function in vegetative (asexual) reproduction and in special cases (some aerial and aquatic roots) may carry on photosynthesis—a function usually carried out in the leaves. The root usually develops root hairs, slender unicellular out-

growths formed by the lateral extension of cells of the outer layer (epidermis). These serve to increase the absorbing surface of the root and bring it into intimate relationship with the soil particles. The older root hairs generally die—rarely some are persistent—so that the active zone of root hairs usually lies just back of the apex of the root.

When the seed germinates, the primary root or radicle is the first organ to appear. It grows downward through the soil, anchoring the seedling and establishing contact with the soil. Secondary roots, which often repeat the form and structure of the main root, are developed in regular succession from above downward (acropetal), and because they originate in a definite position in the interior of the root (generally opposite the xylem masses) they develop in longitudinal rows and must penetrate the overlying tissue of the parent root. True forking (dichotomy) occurs in the Lycopsida (club mosses and allies) but not in higher plants.

Types of Roots.—In addition to the main root and its acropetal outgrowths are adventitious roots, which may arise on any part of a plant. They are especially numerous on underground stems, such as the underside of rhizomes, and also develop from stems under favourable conditions such as moisture and absence of light; a young shoot or a cutting placed in moist soil may quickly form adventitious roots. This ability of many plants to develop adventitious roots from stems is widely used in horticulture as a means of vegetative propagation to ensure the production of plants that resemble the parent stock. It is also a rapid method of propagation in the case of slow-growing woody plants. Adventitious roots may also arise from leaves under similar conditions—for instance, from begonia or African violet leaves planted on the surface of the soil.

The form of a root depends on its shape and mode of branching. When the central axis goes deep into the ground in a tapering manner without dividing, a taproot is produced. This kind of root is sometimes short and becomes swollen by storage of foodstuffs, as in the conical root of carrot, the fusiform or spindle-shaped root of radish or the napiform root of turnip. In some forest trees the first root protruded continues to elongate and forms a long primary root axis from which secondary axes arise. In many plants, especially monocotyledons, the primary axis soon dies and the secondary axes take its place. When the descending axis is very short, and at once divides into thin, nearly equal fibrils, the root is called fibrous, as in many grasses; when the fibrils are thick and succulent, the root is fasciculated, as in the sweet potato and dahlia. Some so-called roots are formed of a stem and root combined, as in *Orchis*, where the tuber consists of a fleshy, swollen root bearing at the apex a stem-bud. As in the stem, growth in length occurs only for a short distance behind the apex, but in long-lived roots increase in diameter occurs continually in a

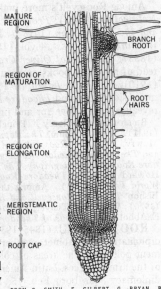

FROM G. SMITH, E. GILBERT, G. BRYAN, R. EVANS, J. STAUFFER, "A TEXTBOOK OF GENERAL BOTANY"; REPRODUCED BY PERMISSION OF THE MACMILLAN CO.

LENGTHWISE SECTION OF APICAL PORTION OF A ROOT

BY COURTESY OF THE UNITED STATES DEPARTMENT OF AGRICULTURE

STORAGE ROOT OF TURNIP, AN ENLARGED TAPROOT

similar manner to growth in thickness in the stem.

Roots are not invariably underground. In some cases where they arise from the stem they pass for some distance through the air before reaching the soil. Such roots are called aerial. They are seen well in corn (maize), screw pine, and banyan, where they eventually assist in supporting the stem and branches. In the mangrove they often form the entire support of the stem, which has decayed at its lower part. In tree ferns they form a dense coating around and completely conceal the stem; such is also the case in some palms.

In epiphytes, or plants growing in the air, attached to the trunks of trees, such as orchids of warm climates, the aerial roots produced do not reach the soil; they continue aerial and greenish and they possess stomata. Delicate hairs are often seen on these epiphytic roots, as well as a peculiar spongy investment formed by the cells of the epidermis that have lost their succulent contents and are filled with air. This layer, the velamen, serves to absorb the moisture contained in the air, on which the plant is partially dependent for its water supply. Some leafless epiphytic orchids, such as species of *Angraecum*, depend entirely upon their aerial roots for nourishment; these perform the functions of both leaves and roots. A respiratory or aerating function is performed by roots of bald cypress and certain mangroves growing in swampy soil or water and sending up pneumatophores, vertical roots provided with aerating passages.

See PLANT PROPAGATION; STEM: *Types of Stems; see* also references under "Root" in the Index. (H. E. HD.; X.)

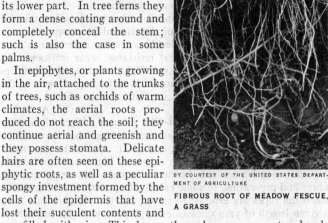

BY COURTESY OF THE UNITED STATES DEPARTMENT OF AGRICULTURE

FIBROUS ROOT OF MEADOW FESCUE, A GRASS

ROOT. Arab writers of the 9th century spoke of one of the equal factors of a number as a root, and their medieval translators used the Latin *radix* ("root") for the same concept. The adjective is "radical."

If a is a positive real number and n is a positive integer, there exists a unique positive real number x such that $x^n = a$. This number is called the (principal) nth root of a, and is written $\sqrt[n]{a}$. The integer n is called the index of the root. For $n = 2$, the root is called the square root and is written $\sqrt{a}$. The root $\sqrt[3]{a}$ is called the cube root of a. If a is negative and n is odd, the unique negative nth root of a is termed principal.

The practical determination of square and higher roots of positive numbers is discussed in the article on ARITHMETIC.

If a specific integer (whole number) has a rational nth root, *i.e.*, one which can be written as a common fraction, then this root must be an integer. Thus 5 has no rational square root since $2^2 < 5$ while $3^2 > 5$.

There are exactly n complex numbers which satisfy the equation $x^n = 1$, called the complex nth roots of unity. If a regular polygon of n sides is inscribed in a unit circle with centre at the origin so that one vertex lies on the positive half of the x-axis, the radii to the vertices are the vectors representing the n complex nth roots of unity. If the root whose vector makes the smallest positive angle with the positive direction of the x-axis is denoted by ω, then $\omega, \omega^2, \omega^3, \ldots \omega^n = 1$ constitute all of the nth roots of unity. Thus $\omega = -\frac{1}{2} + \frac{1}{2}\sqrt{-3}$, $\omega^2 = -\frac{1}{2} - \frac{1}{2}\sqrt{-3}$, $\omega^3 = 1$ are the cube roots of unity.

Any root ϵ which has the property that $\epsilon, \epsilon^2, \ldots \epsilon^n = 1$ give all of the nth roots of unity is called primitive.

Evidently the problem of finding the nth roots of unity is equivalent to the problem of inscribing a regular polygon of n sides in a circle. For every integer n, the nth roots of unity can be determined in terms of the rational numbers by means of rational operations and radicals; but they can be constructed by ruler and compasses (*i.e.*, determined in terms of the rational operations and square roots) only if n is a product of distinct prime numbers of the form $2^h + 1$, or 2^k times such a product, or is of the form 2^k.

If a is a complex number not 0, the equation $x^n = a$ has exactly n roots. (*See* COMPLEX NUMBERS.) All of the nth roots of a are the products of any one of these roots by the nth roots of unity.

The term root has been carried over from the equation $x^n = a$ to all polynomial equations. Thus a solution of the equation

$$f(x) = a_0x^n + a_1x^{n-1} + \ldots + a_{n-1}x + a_n = 0, \; a_0 \neq 0$$

is called a root of the equation. If the coefficients lie in the complex field, an equation of the nth degree has exactly n not necessarily distinct complex roots. If the coefficients are real and n is odd, there is a real root. But an equation does not always have a root in its coefficient field. Thus $x^2 - 5 = 0$ has no rational root (*see* FIELDS; POLYNOMIAL).

If $f(x) = 0$ is an equation with coefficients in a field F, there exists a unique field F^* obtained by adjoining to F all of the roots of $f(x) = 0$. This field is called the root field of $f(x) = 0$. In F^* the polynomial $f(x)$ can be factored into linear factors. (*See* EQUATIONS, THEORY OF.)

A rigorous proof of the existence of the root field F^* can be made along the following lines. Let $f_1(x)$ be a factor of $f(x)$ which is irreducible in F. The set of all polynomials in x with coefficients in F, taken modulo $f_1(x)$, constitutes a field F' containing F in which $f_1(x)$ has a linear factor. A continuation of this process leads to the root field F^*.

BIBLIOGRAPHY.—On the Greek theory, *see* Sir T. L. Heath, *A History of Greek Mathematics* (1921), *A Manual of Greek Mathematics* (1931, reprinted 1963); on the general history, L. E. Dickson, *History of the Theory of Numbers* (1920–23); on the algebraic theory, G. Chrystal, *Algebra*, 2nd ed. (1889); on the history of terms and methods, D. E. Smith, *History of Mathematics,* especially vol. 2 (1923–25, reprinted 1964). (C. C. M.)

ROPE. Rope is made of natural or man-made fibres and of metallic wires. Only fibre rope will be discussed in this article. For a discussion of wire rope *see* WIRE: *Wire Rope.*

"Cordage" is a term applied generally to ropes, yarns, cords, twines and cables. Fibre rope is cordage of stranded construction, *i.e.*, fibres are laid parallel and twisted together to make a yarn; two or more of these yarns are then twisted together, forming the strand; and three or more of these strands are next twisted together, laying the rope. Three or more ropes laid together make a cable-laid rope, sometimes referred to as hawser-laid. The smallest fibre ropes are approximately $\frac{1}{2}$ in. in circumference, or $\frac{3}{16}$ in. in diameter; similar products of smaller dimensions are not rope in the usual sense of the word.

Two or more yarns twisted together are twine; certain types of twine are sometimes referred to as cord. Single yarns are known as yarns, with the exception of binder twine, which is a single-yarn product. Braided yarns, such as sash cords, are sometimes referred to as rope. (X.)

Early History of Ropemaking.—Rope is already represented in use in southwest Asia (Elam) in the chalcolithic period (4th millennium B.C.), but this was probably made of plaited thongs, a type that has persisted down to modern times in some cultures. Probably almost, if not quite, as ancient is rope made of bark fibre, represented in more evolved forms by the coir (*q.v.*) types of southeast Asia; the most primitive coir technique consists of rolling the fibres together with the palm of the hand on the bare thigh.

Cord must have been used very early, probably in the Upper Paleolithic period at least, to attach tools to handles; and the same need for rope implies its common currency in the 4th millennium, when numerous bone handles are sometimes found with the blade or point missing. In the middle of the 3rd millennium

B.C., patterns impressed with spun cords are the definitive feature of a southeastern European pottery; and by the middle of the 2nd millennium heavy rope must have been a commonplace in the east Mediterranean, given the development there of shipping and hence ships, which even when propelled by oars require rope equipment. Moreover, at about this same time a number of terms for "rope" are found in Akkadian; examples of papyrus rope of about this period have been found in Egyptian tombs. Late in the millennium heavy cables are reproduced in bronze as handles of vessels in China, where the technique had probably been conveyed by the bronze casters, most likely from the eastern Asia Minor-Adharbayjan region, and heavy cable moldings appear about the same time on pottery from Luristan, whose bronze art can be traced to the same source.

When Xerxes (480 B.C.) built the bridge of boats across the Hellespont the Phoenicians constructed one line with cables of white flax and the Egyptians in the other line used ropes made of papyrus. In India in the 4th century B.C. ropemaking was so specialized that one class of experts made ropes just for horses, another for elephants; and in China, in the Han period if not earlier, the emperor's carriage in time of mourning was equipped with silk ropes. The craft was carried, along with various textile and other techniques such as pottery making and metallurgy, into the early American cultures. (P. An.)

Ropemaking had been going on for centuries with little change up to the time of the introduction of machinery about the middle of the 19th century. In the early days all the yarn was spun by hand. The hemp, which was the most widely used ropemaking material at that time, was first hackled by combing it straight over a board studded with sharp steel teeth. A bunch, or head, of this hackled hemp was placed around the waist of the spinner, who attached a few fibres to a hook on a spinning wheel and, as the hook was revolved by hand, walked backward away from the wheel, feeding the fibre from the supply around his waist while preserving the uniformity and proper size of the yarn. Several yarns were then twisted together by use of a hand wheel and several hooks to form the strand; and three or more strands were next twisted together to lay the rope.

The term "ropewalk" came from the long low buildings used and the walking back and forth of the spinners and ropemakers. In the early days every community of any size, especially the seaports, had its ropewalk. These walks were often 900 ft. or more in length and many were in the open air. The crude methods of ropemaking of centuries ago are still used in some parts of the world.

Raw Materials.—In the United States and Europe soft fibres, principally hemp and flax (qq.v.), were used for rope until the second quarter of the 19th century. Hemp is still used for tarred hemp rope and fittings for marine purposes and flax is used for making twine and other light cordage. Abacá fibre (q.v.), commonly referred to as Manila hemp because it was once grown commercially almost exclusively in the Philippine Islands and was exported principally from the port of Manila, has established itself as the best material for ropemaking where strength and durability are the prime requirements. Henequen (see AGAVE), next in importance as a rope fibre, comes from Yucatan and Cuba.

Sisals also are important rope fibres; they come principally from east Africa, Indonesia and Haiti (see SISAL FIBRE). Jute and cotton are used to a limited extent in the manufacture of ropes of stranded construction. Cotton is used to a greater extent in the manufacture of braided cords. (See also FIBRE.)

(J. S. McD.)

The introduction of man-made fibres exerted great changes in the use, life and care of rope. Nylon, Dacron, glass, saran, polyethylene and polypropylene ropes came into commercial use during and after World War II. The basic advantages of such fibres over natural fibres are higher strength and immunity to deterioration (rot, mildew, abrasion, etc.) on both land and sea. This latter characteristic eliminates the need for the protective treatments commonly used on ropes made of natural fibre. Their greater strength permits the use of smaller ropes within reasonable limits, thus providing greater ease of handling.

The life of a rope made of man-made fibre is generally estimated to be three or four times that of the natural-fibre rope, although the different types of man-made fibres display differing qualities, including those of elasticity, heat resistance, wear resistance, dielectric properties and resistance to light. Outstanding qualities in these properties led to new applications for rope as well as the substitution of synthetic ropes for natural-fibre ropes.

(W. A. Sc.)

Manufacturing Processes.—The primary object of twisting fibres together in a rope is to arrange them so that they will be held together by friction when a strain is applied to the whole. Hard twisting (i.e., arranging a relatively high number of twists per unit length) has the further advantage of compacting the fibres and preventing, to some extent, the penetration of moisture when the ropes are exposed to water; but the yield of rope from a given length of yarn diminishes in proportion to the increase of twist.

The ropemaking process is essentially the same, no matter what kind of fibre is used. The process divides itself into five operations. First, selection of fibre; second, preparing the sliver; third, spinning the yarn; fourth, forming the strands; fifth, laying the strands into rope. With cable-laid ropes there is another operation, i.e., laying the strands, which are in fact completed ropes, into the finished cable.

At the start of the manufacturing process using natural fibres, the bales of fibre are opened and the bundles of fibre are shaken out. The fibre is put through several processes of combing and straightening. These operations are, in general, all of the same kind. The fibre is carried along slowly on a series of bars connected by endless chains, the bars being studded in the manner of a comb with sharp steel pins that stand upright as the fibre passes along with them. A similar set of combs, moving very much faster, pulls the fibre rapidly away from the first set, combing it out at the same time. A lubricant is sprayed on the fibre as it enters the first machine.

The fibre is delivered from the machine in a heavy, continuous stream, or sliver, that is coiled by hand or machine into a receptacle, or on the floor. Several of these slivers are then fed into a similar machine, and the kinks and unevenness are further removed by a repetition of the same process. This preparation,

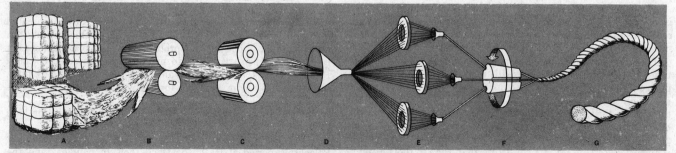

PROCESSES THROUGH WHICH FIBRE PASSES IN THE MANUFACTURE OF ROPE: TANGLES ARE SHAKEN OUT OF THE RAW FIBRES (A) AND THE FIBRES ARE LUBRICATED (B). AFTER SEVERAL COMBINGS THE FIBRES ARE COMPRESSED INTO SLIVER (C) AND TWISTED INTO YARN (D). FURTHER COMBINATION AND TWISTING IN THE OPPOSITE DIRECTION (E) RESULTS IN STRANDS OF ROPE WHICH CAN BE TWISTED ONCE MORE, AGAIN REVERSING THE DIRECTION OF TWIST (F) TO PRODUCE CABLE (G)

or combing, is repeated from 8 to 12 times on five different machines, each operation combing the fibre and producing a smaller and more even sliver until finally it comes out of the finisher in a continuous stream. The thoroughness with which these operations are carried out—the care taken in preparing the fibre—is largely responsible for the uniformity and excellence of the finished product. The object in preparing the sliver is to eliminate all dirt and foreign matter and to lay the fine, threadlike strands parallel with one another so that they can be spun together more easily.

As the sliver enters the spinning machine it is taken from the rollers by another series of fine combs. From the combs it passes through a funnel-shaped tube and is then wound about a little capstan. It is between the tube and the capstan that the yarn comes into being. The friction on the revolving capstans draws the yarn through the machine. From the capstans it is automatically wound on a large spool, or bobbin, about 12 in. long. The capstans and the bobbin whirl very fast, and the combination of this whirling motion and the drawing forward of the revolving capstans spins the heretofore parallel fibres into what is known as a yarn. For different sizes of yarn and for yarns designed for various purposes, a varying number of twists per foot are imparted to the yarn. This yarn is the first merchantable product of the cordage mill and may be sold in this form or used to make other cordage products.

A rope is usually formed of three or four strands, each strand composed of a number of yarns laid parallel and twisted together slightly. The making of these strands is called forming. As the strand is twisted it is wound on a large reel and appears as a smooth, round strand composed of a number of individual yarns. This strand is known as the ready. The yarn has a tendency to untwist; to overcome this tendency the twist of the ready is made in the opposite direction. The result is that the tendency of the yarn to untwist in one direction and the tendency of the ready to untwist in the other direction balance each other.

The ropemaking operation is called laying. In laying the rope, three or four reels containing the readies, or strands, are put on the laying machine, and the strands are led through a "block," wound around the capstan and reeled on the finishing end of the laying machine. In laying there is a different twisting problem, for the ready is neutral—that is, it has no tendency to untwist—and if the readies were twisted together without altering this neutral condition the rope would continually untwist. So an extra twist is added to the ready as it is passed into the machine, this twist being computed so that it will be just sufficient to counteract the tendency of the three strands to untwist when they are formed into a rope. Good rope is neutral; if cut in 5-ft. to 10-ft. lengths and laid on the ground, it will not untwist of its own accord.

Cable-laid rope consists of three completed ropes; i.e., nine of the simple strands that form an ordinary rope. The same method of balancing the twisted strands is used, an additional twist or foreturn being given to the three-strand ropes just before they are laid so that their tendency to untwist in one direction counterbalances the tendency of the cable to untwist in the opposite direction.

Uses and Care.—The uses of rope are many and varied. The marine and fishing industries consume more than half of the rope produced. Cable-laid rope is also used extensively in the drilling of oil, water and gas wells. Ropes are used in the transmission of motive power. Rope is used for hoisting, hauling, rigging, wrapping, towing and many other purposes, and in building and engineering projects. In the home it has many applications.

The useful life of rope depends on its quality and on the care and treatment it receives. To give best service, it must be made of high-grade raw material, selected with a thorough knowledge of what the rope is to do. It must be so made that every strand will be of even tension. Natural-fibre ropes must be treated with a lubricant that will preserve as well as lubricate. Three general sources of damage can shorten the life of rope: first, mechanical injury, such as bending over too sharp a pulley; second, damage from chemicals, such as acids; and third, damage from climatic or other conditions of storage, such as moisture or dry rot. It should be stored in a cool dry place in which air is permitted to circulate.

(J. S. McD.)

There are many varieties of cord and twine. The fishing industry uses many different types for lines and nets, while the variety of cord and twine for other industrial and for household purposes is almost unlimited. All yarn from long vegetable fibre is more or less rough as it leaves the spinning frame, even after two or more threads have been twisted together. It is therefore necessary, for many uses, to impart a polish to the cord or twine. Special machines are used for this purpose. Bobbins of yarn are placed in a bank or creel, and the ends are collected and passed under a roller that is immersed in hot starch. The yarns become saturated with this starch, but, as they emerge from the starch box, the superfluous starch is removed by passing the yarns between two rollers. The yarns now pass over a series of drying cylinders and polishing rollers and are finally rewound by the same machine onto other bobbins. This machine is termed a bobbin-to-bobbin polishing machine. In some cases the hot drying cylinders are replaced by a system of hot-air drying. The finished yarns are now made up by machinery into hanks, balls or cheeses.

BIBLIOGRAPHY.—Samuel E. Morison, *Ropemakers of Plymouth: a History of the Plymouth Cordage Company, 1824–1949* (1950); David Himmelfarb, *Technology of Cordage Fibres and Rope* (1957); *Davison's Cordage, Twine and Duck Trade* (1960).

ROPEWAYS AND CABLEWAYS. Aerial ropeways, called in the United States "aerial tramways," and cableways are often grouped together because their cars travel along steel wire ropes supported above the ground and pulled by hauling ropes. The main differences between ropeways and cableways are: (1) ropeways ensure continuous transport of many individual loads of up to 5 tons each, giving a capacity of up to 500 tons per hour from station to station, whereas cableways collect and deliver one single load, up to 200 tons, anywhere along the span; (2) a ropeway can be of any length and a cableway is usually in one span and therefore of limited length. An aerial ropeway can be compared to a belt conveyor; a cableway can be visualized as an overhead crane, fixed or traveling, in which the cross-traveling carriage runs on tensioned steel wire ropes instead of on a rigid horizontal girder.

Early ropeways consisted of a fixed carrying fibre rope attached to tree trunks; along this rope people or loads could slide in a sling. Such simple installations are still in use in many undeveloped mountainous countries. It was the invention of the steel wire rope (*see* WIRE) which made possible the rapid development of aerial ropeways and cableways during the second half of the 19th century.

Ropeways.—Aerial ropeways transport passengers and goods in carriers which are hauled along horizontal or inclined suspended steel wire ropes. These ropes connect two terminal stations in a straight line and are supported along the line by intermediate trestles. Two main systems have been evolved: bicable and monocable. The bicable ropeway (sometimes called tricable) in fact incorporates three ropes—two stationary carrying ropes (also called track ropes) and one endless hauling rope. The two carrying ropes are parallel to each other and are held under tension above ground level by floating counterweights. These ropes are placed one on each side of the ropeway centre line; one side is used for loaded traffic, goods, or passengers; the other side for the returning empty cars (though many ropeways carry passengers and goods in both directions). The continuous hauling rope passes around a return sheave at each end of the line, one of which sheaves forms part of the driving gear and the other part of the tension gear. Tension is necessary both to keep the rope clear of the ground and to prevent it from slipping on the driving sheave. Brakes are incorporated between the motor and the driving sheave to ensure that the line is brought to a halt when required.

Bicable ropeways can be further subdivided into "fixed-clip" (the carrier is attached by means of its hanger permanently to the hauling rope) and "detachable grip" (the carrier is connected by means of its hanger to the carriage which is mounted on the sta-

BY COURTESY OF BRITISH ROPEWAY ENGINEERING CO. LTD.

AERIAL CABLEWAY CONSTRUCTED IN 1951 TO CARRY OVER THE TIGRIS RIVER, IRAQ, VEHICLES OF 28 TONS GROSS WEIGHT

tionary track rope and is provided with a gripping device and wheels). The gripping device locks the car automatically to the running-hauling rope when a car is leaving a station and unlocks it when a car enters a station.

The monocable ropeway uses only one single endless carrying-hauling rope comparable to the bicable hauling rope though of larger diameter because of its dual role. The simplicity of the monocable detachable grip carriage and the fact that the ropes weigh much less than those of a bicable installation means that a monocable is easier to erect and costs about 40% less than a bicable. On the other hand a bicable negotiates steeper gradients and longer spans. A monocable can also be of fixed-clip type.

A detachable grip monocable ropeway can transport individual loads of one ton, giving a 200-tons-per-hour output. The line speed can reach more than 600 ft. (182.8 m.) per minute. A detachable grip bicable ropeway can transport up to 500 tons per hour and single loads may reach 5 tons. Both monocable and bicable ropeways can be constructed as twin lines, allowing the output to be doubled. Fixed clip ropeways give lower outputs.

If the distance is great, the ropeway is divided into straight line sections, each with its own driving and tension gear. Each section may be up to 6 mi. (9.65 km.) long, but this varies according to ground profile and line capacity.

Passenger ropeways do not differ fundamentally from industrial ropeways except for extra safety precautions. They may be bicable or monocable. Large cabin ropeways, holding up to 120 passengers are of the to-and-fro bicable type, each with two carrying ropes and two hauling ropes. Regulations require that additional (emergency) motors or engines are installed which must be promptly coupled if the main power supply fails. Cabin lifts, chair lifts, and similar installations such as ski tows and ski lifts are usually of the monocable system.

An aerial ropeway can span valleys without intermediate supports and pass over roads, railways, rivers, and other natural obstacles; it can negotiate steep gradients and join two stations in a straight line; operation is unaffected by fog, floods, snow, frost; it can be in use day and night and be efficiently run by the minimum of unskilled labour; construction, maintenance, and transport costs are low.

Modern Ropeway Achievements.—The first long monocable ropeway (in operation since 1919) was constructed in La Dorada, Colombia. Its 15 sections total 46 mi. (74 km.). Notable bicable ropeways connect: Massus and Asmara, Eritrea, 45 mi. (72.42 km.); and Kristineberg and Boliden, Swed., 60 mi. (96.5 km.) in 8 sections (constructed during World War II). The longest heavy-type monocable ropeway is the COMILOG ropeway, starting in Gabon and finishing in the Republic of Congo. Its 10 sections, which total 48 mi. (77.24 km.) and run through equatorial forest, were inaugurated in 1962. In India two complexes (costing about £7,000,000) with several ropeways were constructed in 1966-

67 to reclaim sand from rivers for backfilling disused coal mines.

Outstanding passenger ropeways are: the Mürren-Schildhorn ropeway in Switzerland, opened in 1966, whose 4 sections total 21,760 ft. (6,632 m.) and whose upper terminal is 9,740 ft. (2,969 m.) above sea level; the Aiguille du Midi (Chamonix, France) ropeway, constructed in 1953, whose upper terminal at 12,500 ft. (3,802 m.) above sea level is more than 9,000 ft. (2,750 m.) higher than the lower one; the Mérida (Venez.) to-and-fro passenger ropeway built in 1959, which is 7.8 mi. (12.5 km.) long, in 4 sections, with one of its spans approximately 10,000 ft. (3,-000 m.), an upper terminal at 15,600 ft. (4,755 m.) above sea level, and a cabin capacity of 39 passengers.

The longest to-and-fro passenger ropeway in the United States is the Sandia Peak aerial tram in New Mexico, completed in 1966. Its length is 14,185 ft. (4,323 m.), its upper terminal 10,378 ft. (3,163 m.) above sea level, and maximum span 7,760 ft. (2,365 m.). Each of the two cabins can carry 60 passengers and the trip takes 10 min. at a speed of 1,950 ft. (594 m.) per min.

Cableways.—In the simplest form a cableway consists of two fixed structural steel towers supporting one or more carrying (or track) ropes. On these ropes the cross-traverse carriage runs forward and backward over the span, motion being obtained by an endless rope tensioned at one end by a counterweight, and driven at the other. The carriage from which the load is suspended by means of a hook and pulley blocks is permanently attached to this cross-traverse rope. The same rope or another hoisting rope causes the load carried by the carriage to be lowered or lifted as required. The ropes are so reeved that all operations are controlled from a cabin usually fixed to the head tower; *i.e.*, the tower incorporating at its base the driving machinery and controls for moving both the cross-traverse and hoisting ropes (*i.e.*, the carriage and the hook load). The heavier the hook load, the larger must be the carrying rope diameter, thus increasing the weight and the sag. This, in turn, calls for higher terminal towers, the height being dictated by the purpose of the cableway. To serve a wider ground area a traveling cableway is used. This may be of two types: with both towers traveling parallel on rails, or with one tower fixed and the other moving along a circular rail.

Cableways may be for materials or passengers. As with aerial ropeways, passenger cableways do not differ in principle from those for industrial purposes except for greater safety precautions.

BY COURTESY OF APPLEVAGE, PARIS

PASSENGER ROPEWAY AT MÉRIDA, VENEZ., BUILT IN 1959, IS 7.8 MI. (12.5 KM.) LONG AND HAS AN UPPER TERMINAL AT 15,600 FT. (4,755 M.) ABOVE SEA LEVEL

Industrial applications include concrete and steel placing for bridge and dam construction, loading and unloading of ships, work in quarry and stockyard, forest industry, and cross-river transport for both passengers and merchandise.

Cableway Achievements.—Notable examples include: a cableway transporting 20-ton blocks of marble at Carrara, Italy; the 150-ton cableway at Hoover Dam, U.S., having a span of 1,256 ft. (382 m.) and using six supporting ropes for the carriages to run on; and the Tigris ropeway transporter constructed in Iraq in 1951, designed to carry across the River Tigris vehicles of 42-ft. (12.8 m.) overall length and 28-tons gross weight. The terminal to terminal length of the transporter is 1,650 ft. (503 m.), including two approach spans of 400 ft. (122 m.). Four carrying ropes 6¼ in. (158.75 mm.) in circumference are used, which terminate at a concrete anchorage block of approximately 400-tons weight.

BIBLIOGRAPHY.—G. von Hanfstengel, *Die Förderung von Massengütern,* vol. ii (1921); P. Stephan, *Die Drahtseilbahnen,* 4th ed. (1926); F. E. Dean, *Famous Cableways of the World* (1958); *International Ropeway Review* (1959–); *Internationale Seilbahn Rundschau;* E. Czitary, *Seilschwebebahnen,* 2nd ed. (1962); Z. Schneigert, *Aerial Ropeways and Funicular Railways,* trans. from Polish, ed. by Z. Frenkiel (1966). (Z. F.)

ROPS, FÉLICIEN (1833–1898), Belgian painter and graphic artist, who ranks as a modern master in printmaking, was born at Namur, July 10, 1833. Rops spent his childhood in Namur, later going to Brussels. In 1856 he composed for friends at the university the *Almanach crocodilien,* his first work. He brought out two *Salons illustrés* and collaborated on the *Crocodile,* a students' magazine. This attracted the attention of publishers and he designed frontispieces for P. A. Poulet-Malassis and Gay. In 1859–60 he contributed some of his finest lithographs to the satirical journal, *Uylenspiegel.* About 1860 he went to Paris and worked in the studio of H. A. Jacquemart but returned to Brussels and founded the short-lived International Society of Etchers. In 1865 he produced his famous "Buveuse d'absinthe" (Absinthe drinker) and in 1871, "Dame au Pantin." After 1874 Rops resided in Paris, devoting himself principally to illustrating books. Among his notable book illustrations are *Légendes flamandes* by C. de Coster, *Jeune France* by Théophile Gautier, *Les Diaboliques* by Barbey d'Aurevilly, *Zadig* by Voltaire and the poems of Stéphane Mallarmé. Many have frontispieces which exhibit his fertile and powerful imagination. He published *Cent croquis pour réjouir les honnêtes gens* ("One hundred sketches to delight solid citizens"). Rops joined the Art Society of the "XX," formed at Brussels in 1884, as their revolutionary views were in harmony with the independence of his spirit. He died at Essonnes, France, on Aug. 22, 1898.

After Rops's death, the Libre Esthétique, which had succeeded the "XX," arranged a retrospective exhibition (1899) of his paintings and drawings. M. Exsteens, in his definitive catalogue of the prints of Rops, lists 1,193 subjects. It is unfortunate that these survive more for their so-called licentiousness and their free choice of subject than for any other reason, because his work as a printmaker is most important, both for its brilliance of technique and its originality of content. His handling of dry point marks him as one of the masters of the medium; he was one of the first modern etchers to revive the neglected medium of softground etching and employ it to great effect. Although Rops was a friend of Charles Baudelaire, the poet, Rops's work has a spiritual counterpart in literature in the diabolical dandyism of Barbey d'Aurevilly more than in the *Fleurs du mal.*

See E. Ramiro, *Félicien Rops* (1905), the best monograph on the artist, and M. Exsteens, *L'Oeuvre gravé et lithographié de Félicien Rops,* 4 vol. (1928), a complete descriptive catalogue of all of Rops's prints with illustrations of each work. (H. Es.)

ROQUE: *see* CROQUET AND ROQUE.

RORAIMA, one of four federal territories in Brazil. Formerly a part of the state of Amazonas, it was created by decree in 1943 and until 1962 was named Rio Branco. Area 88,843 sq.mi. Pop. (1960) 29,489. Located in the northernmost part of Brazil, it is bounded on the northeast by Guyana, on the south by Amazonas, and on the northwest and north by Venezuela. It is drained from north to south by the Rio Branco, a tributary of the Rio Negro.

Much of the territory is covered with rain forest or selva, but around Boa Vista, pop. (1960) 10,180, the chief city and capital, there are extensive woodland savannas which extend across the border into Guyana (the Rupununi savanna). Along the Venezuelan border there are high tablelands, covered partly with forest, partly with savanna. At the border of Roraima, Guyana, and Venezuela is the plateaulike Mt. Roraima. Roraima is scantily inhabited, especially along its borders. The savannas are used for cattle ranching, and some gold and diamonds are found in the streams. (P. E. J.)

RORSCHACH, HERMANN (1884–1922), Swiss psychiatrist, who devised the ink-blot test known by his name and widely used in diagnosis of psychopathologic conditions, was born in Zürich, Nov. 8, 1884. The test involves ten symmetrical ink blots. Earlier investigators had used ink blots as free association stimuli but had generally limited themselves to studying the thematic content. Rorschach's approach involved systematically analyzing the patient's attention to wholes or details of the blot figures, colour, and shading, apparent movement in human form percepts, and other factors. Thus he hoped to detect psychologic processes or structure of the personality and reported differential patterns for several clinical disorders. The test has been criticized by experimentalists because of serious doubts concerning its accuracy (validity) in diagnosis and prognosis. It has proved to be very popular, however, and is used in many countries. Rorschach looked on his work as experiment in perception and emphasized an empirical statistical orientation. (*See* PSYCHOLOGICAL TESTS AND MEASUREMENTS.) His best-known work is *Psychodiagnostics,* 5th ed. (1951). His complete works were published in German in 1965. Rorschach died at Herisau, Switz., on April 2, 1922.

BIBLIOGRAPHY.—C. Windle, "Psychological Tests in Psychopathological Prognosis," *Psychol. Bull.,* vol. 49 (Sept. 1952); C. A. Larson, "Hermann Rorschach and the Ink-blot Test," *Sci. Dig.,* vol. 44 (Oct. 1958); S. J. Beck, *Rorschach's Test,* vol. 1 (1961). (S. J. BK.)

ROSA, SALVATOR (1615–1673), Italian painter, etcher, poet, actor, and musician, remembered for his wild or "sublime" landscapes and his romantic personality, was born in Arenella, near Naples, either on June 20 or July 21, 1615 (contemporary sources differ). He studied in Naples, coming under the influence of Jusepe Ribera, and was for a time in the studio of the battle painter Aniello Falcone. Encouraged by G. Lanfranco, he went to Rome in 1635 to study, but contracted malaria and returned to Naples, where he painted numerous battle pictures and developed his peculiarly characteristic style of landscape—savage scenes peopled with shepherds, seamen, or, especially, soldiers—the whole being infused with a poetic or romantic quality. A painting of "Tityus Tortured by the Vulture" established his reputation in Rome, and he was already famous when he returned there in 1639.

In Rome he was rash enough to satirize Bernini during the Carnival of 1639 and made a powerful enemy. For some years thereafter Florence was more comfortable for him than Rome. In Florence he enjoyed the patronage of Cardinal Giancarlo de' Medici. His own house became the centre of a literary and artistic circle (Accademia dei Percossi), where dramas were performed and Rosa's flamboyant personality found expression in acting. In 1649 he finally settled in Rome, where he remained until his death on March 15, 1673.

In Rome Rosa, who regarded his landscape paintings more as recreation than as "high art," set up as a religious and history painter, but while this aspect of his painting now seems rather dreary and academic, the landscapes have assumed increasing significance. Their "sublime" qualities (although imposed on a compositional formula as classical as that of either Claude or Poussin) were contrasted with the serene classicism of the other two artists and were particularly influential in 18th-century England. From the very outset of the Romantic era, their pseudo-Romanticism—combined with the legend of the brilliant but erratic genius and rebel against society that had grown up around Rosa's own personality—fulfilled the 19th-century ideal of what a romantic artist should be. In 1660 Rosa began etching and completed a number of successful plates. His satires were printed in 1710.

BIBLIOGRAPHY.—E. W. Manwaring, *Italian Landscape in 18th Century England* (1925); R. Wittkower, *Art and Architecture in Italy 1600–1750* (1958); L. Salerno, *Salvator Rosa* (1963).

ROSACEAE, a large cosmopolitan family of seed-bearing dicotyledonous plants belonging to the order Rosales and containing about 100 genera with more than 2,000 species.

Habit of Growth.—The plants vary widely in habit of growth. Many are herbaceous, growing erect, as *Geum,* or with slender creeping stem, as in species of *Potentilla,* sometimes sending out long runners, as in strawberry; others are shrubby, as raspberry, often associated with a scrambling habit, as in the brambles and roses, while apple, cherry, pear, plum and other fruit trees represent the arborescent habit. Vegetative propagation takes place by means of runners, which root at the apex and form a new plant, as in strawberry; by suckers springing from the base of the shoot

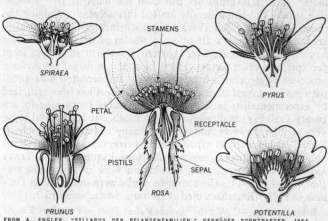

FROM A. ENGLER, "SYLLABUS DER PFLANZENFAMILIEN," GEBRÜDER BORNTRAEGER, 1964
FIG. 1.—FLOWERS OF ROSACEAE

and rising to form new leafy shoots after running for some distance beneath the soil, as in raspberry; or by shoots produced from the roots, as in cherry or plum. The scrambling of the brambles and roses is effected by means of prickles on the branches and leafstalks.

Distribution.—In North America, Rosaceae are represented by about 40 genera, the largest being *Crataegus* (hawthorn) with about 70 or more species, *Rubus* (bramble) with 100 or more species, *Potentilla* (cinquefoil, five finger) with about 100 species, *Prunus* (plum, cherry, etc.) with 30 species, and *Rosa* with 90 species. *Potentilla* is the most generally distributed genus in the United States.

The family is characteristically typical of temperate and sub-temperate regions, but some genera, such as *Rubus*, are of world-wide distribution. The strictly tropical groups are mostly trees and shrubs in such genera as *Chrysobalanus, Hirtella, Coupeia, Parinarium*, etc.

Leaf Arrangement.—The leaves, which are arranged alternately, are simple, as in apple, cherry, etc., but more often compound, with leaflets palmately arranged, as in strawberry and species of *Potentilla*, or pinnately arranged, as in the brambles, roses, mountain ash, etc. In warm climates the leaves are often leathery and evergreen. The leaves are stipulate, the stipules being sometimes small and short-lived, as in *Pyrus, Malus* and *Prunus* (cherry, plum, etc.), or more important structures adnate to the base of the leafstalk, as in roses, brambles, etc.

Flowers.—The flowers, which are regular, generally bisexual and often showy, are sometimes borne singly, as in some species of rose, or of the cloudberry (*Rubus chamaemorus*), or few or more together in a corymbose manner, as in some roses, hawthorn and others. The inflorescence in agrimony is a raceme, in *Poterium* a dense-flowered spike, in *Spiraea*, a number of cymes arranged in a corymb. The parts of the flowers are arranged on a pentamerous plan, with generally considerable increase in the number of stamens and carpels.

The shape of the thalamus, or floral receptacle, and the relative position and number of the stamens and pistils (each consisting of a stigma, style, and ovary) and the character of the fruit, vary widely and form distinguishing features of the different subfamilies, six of which may be recognized. (*See* FLOWER.)

Subfamilies.—*Subfamily I.—Spiraeoideae* is characterized by a flat or slightly concave receptacle on which the carpels, frequently two to five in number, form a central whorl; each ovary contains several ovules, and the fruit is a follicle except in *Holodiscus*. The plants are generally shrubs with simple or compound leaves and racemes or panicles of numerous small white, rose or purple flowers. This subfamily is nearly allied to Saxifragaceae, chiefly north temperate in distribution. The largest genus is *Spiraea*, with numerous species cultivated in gardens.

Subfamily II.—Rosoideae, the largest subfamily, with 40 genera and more than 1,000 species, is characterized by the receptacle being convex and swollen, as in strawberry, or cup-shaped, as in rose, and bearing numerous carpels, each of which contains one

or two ovules, while the fruit is one-seeded and indehiscent. The genera are grouped in tribes according to the form of the receptacle and of the fruit. The Potentilleae bear the carpels on a large, rounded or convex outgrowth of the receptacle. In the large genus *Rubus* the ripe ovaries form drupels upon the dry receptacles; the genus is almost cosmopolitan, but the majority of species occur in the forest region of the north temperate zone and in the mountains of tropical America. *R. fruticosus* is blackberry, *R. idaeus*, raspberry and *R. chamaemorus*, cloudberry. In the flower of *Potentilla, Fragaria* (strawberry) and a few allied genera an epicalyx is formed by stipular structures arising at the base of the sepals.

The fruits consist of numerous dry achenes, borne in *Fragaria* on the much-enlarged succulent torus, which in the other genera is dry. In *Geum* (avens) and in *Dryas* (an arctic and alpine genus) the style is persistent in the fruit, forming a feathery appendage (*Dryas*) or a barbed awn (avens), either of which is of service in distributing the fruit. The Potentilleae are chiefly north temperate, arctic and alpine plants.

The Roseae comprise the large genus *Rosa* (with possibly 200 species) characterized by a more or less urn-shaped torus enclosing the numerous carpels which form dry one-seeded fruits enveloped in the bright-coloured fleshy torus. The plants are shrubs bearing prickles on the stems and leaves; many species have a scrambling habit resembling the brambles. The species of *Rosa*, like those of *Rubus*, are extremely variable, and a great number of subspecies, varieties and forms have been described. Petals are often wanting, as in *Alchemilla* (lady's mantle) and *Poterium*, and the flowers are often unisexual and frequently wind-pollinated, as in salad burnet (*Sanguisorba minor*), where the small flowers are crowded in heads, the upper pistillate, with protruding feathery stigmas, and the lower staminate (or bisexual), with exserted stamens. *Agrimonia* (agrimony) has a long spike of small honey-less flowers with yellow petals; in the fruit the torus becomes hard and crowned by hooked bristles, which ensure the distribution of the enclosed achenes.

Subfamily III.—Pomoideae is characterized by a deep cup-shaped receptacle with the inner wall of which the two to five carpels are united; the carpels are also united with each other, and each contains generally two ovules. The fruit is made up of the large fleshy receptacle surrounding the ripe ovaries, the endocarp of which is leathery or stony and contains one seed. The plants are shrubs or trees with simple or pinnately compound leaves and white or rose-coloured often showy flowers. The genera are distributed through the north temperate zone, extending southward in the new world to the Andes of Peru and Chile.

While some botanists still continue to include the pears and the apple and even the mountain ash in *Pyrus* as a collective genus, most now recognize three genera, *Malus* to take the apples, a genus of about 25 species, the common apple being *Malus pumila*, formerly known as *Pyrus malus; Pyrus* to take the pears, a genus of about 20 species, the common pear being *Pyrus communis;* and *Sorbus*, a genus of about 80 species to take the rowan or mountain

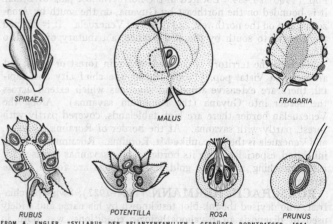

FROM A. ENGLER, "SYLLABUS DER PFLANZENFAMILIEN," GEBRÜDER BORNTRAEGER, 1964
FIG. 2.—FRUITS OF ROSACEAE

ash (*S. aucuparia*), wild service (*S. torminalis*), American mountain ash (*S. americana*) and white beam (*S. aria*). *Mespilus* (medlar), with a single species, and *Cotoneaster*, with about 50 species, are also included. All these genera are confined to the north temperate zone.

Subfamily IV.—*Neuradoideae* contains only three genera of small annual herbs of African and Indian deserts. The flowers are yellow, and the five to ten carpels are united together and with the base of the cup-shaped torus, which enlarges to form a dry covering round the one-seeded fruits.

Subfamily V.—*Prunoideae* is characterized by a free solitary carpel with a terminal style and two pendulous ovules, and the fruit a one-seeded drupe. The torus forms a cup from the edge of which spring the other parts of the flower. The plants are deciduous or evergreen trees or shrubs with simple leaves, often with small caducous stipules, and racemes or umbels of generally showy, white or pink flowers. There are six genera, the chief of which is *Prunus*, to which belong the plum (*Prunus communis*), with several well-marked subspecies—sloe or blackthorn (*P. spinosa*), bullace (*P. insititia*), wild plum (*P. domestica*), the almond (*P. amygdalus*) with the nearly allied peach (*P. persica*), cherry (*P. cerasus*), birdcherry (*P. padus*) and cherry laurel (*P. laurocerasus*). The subfamily is distributed through the north temperate zone, passing into the tropics.

Subfamily VI.—*Chrysobalanoideae* resembles the last in having a single free carpel and the fruit a drupe, but differs in having the style basal, not terminal, and the ovules ascending, not pendulous; the flowers are frequently zygomorphic. The genera are tropical evergreen trees or shrubs, the great majority being South American. *See also* STRAWBERRY; APPLE; CHERRY; PLUM.

(G. N. J.)

ROSARIO, the principal city and river port of the province of Santa Fé and the second largest city of Argentina. Pop. (1960) 671,852. Situated on the west bank of the Paraná River, 186 mi. (299 km.) NW of Buenos Aires by rail, it is accessible to ocean-going vessels of 26-ft. (8-m.) draft. The city is built 70 ft. (21 m.) above the Paraná floodplain and is laid out in a rectilinear plan with wide streets and spacious parks. Although founded in 1725 by Francisco Godoy, Rosario grew so slowly that it remained a small village until the mid-19th century. In 1856 Gen. Justo José de Urquiza (*q.v.*) made it the port of the interior provinces as a rival to Buenos Aires, and gave preferential duties on the cargoes of vessels first breaking bulk at Rosario. Increasing centralization of shipping at Buenos Aires in the 20th century retarded the growth of Rosario, although the port is well equipped with modern dock facilities and is the terminus of several shipping lines.

Principal exports include wheat, flour, hay, linseed, maize (corn), sugar, rum, cattle, hides, meat, wool, and quebracho extract, indicative of the great agricultural region of north central Argentina which Rosario serves. Its industrial structure is similarly based on the processing of a great variety of these products. Grain elevators and petroleum storage tanks are evidence of its collecting and distributing functions. There are few communication links east of the Paraná, but to the west a network of railways and roads provides easy contact with all parts of Argentina. The city's modern airport is a junction for internal services.

In addition to its great industrial, commercial, and administrative buildings, Rosario has a Renaissance-style cathedral, part of the Litoral University, and several theatres and museums.

(G. J. B.)

ROSARY (Lat. *rosarium*, "a rose garden"), a Christian devotion which in the Western Church consists of recitation of Pater Nosters, Ave Marias, and Gloria Patris while counting them on a closed string of 165 beads (chaplet) divided into 15 decades (sets) of one large bead for the Pater and Gloria and ten small beads for the Aves. The Eastern rosary (*kombologion, chotki, matanie*) is almost a purely monastic devotion. The *kombologion* (chaplet) used among the Eastern Christians of Greece and Turkey has 100 beads of the same size. The Russian Orthodox *vertitza* (string), *chotki* (chaplet), or *lievstoka* (ladder) is made of 103 beads, separated into irregular sections by four large beads and so joined together that the lines of the beads run parallel, thus suggesting the name "ladder." In the Rumanian church the chaplet is called *matanie* ("reverence") because the monk makes a profound bow at the beginning and end of each prayer counted on the beads.

The practice of counting repeated prayers is pre-Christian and was adopted in the 3rd century by Eastern Christian monks. In the West a recognizable form of the rosary emerged possibly as early as the 9th century and certainly in the 10th. In medieval England the devotion was known as the Paternoster, and Paternoster Row in London was named after craftsmen who produced strings of prayer beads. The *Livre des métiers* of Stephan Boyleau supplies full information about four guilds of *paternotriers* in Paris in 1268. The devotion received its definitive Western form *c.* 1470–75 through the preaching of the Dominican Alan de Rupe and his associates, who organized rosary confraternities at Douai and Cologne. The Roman Catholic Church calls the devotion the Rosary of the Blessed Virgin Mary. Pope Leo X in 1520 gave it pontifical approbation. In 1572 Pope Pius V established the feast of Our Lady of Victory to commemorate the victory of Christians over Turkish forces at Lepanto, Oct. 7, 1571. In 1573 Pope Gregory XIII renamed the feast Our Lady of the Rosary and in 1716, after another defeat of the Turks, by Prince Eugene in Hungary, Pope Clement XI directed its observance throughout Christendom every Oct. 7.

BIBLIOGRAPHY.—M. Gorce, O.P., *Le Rosaire et ses antécédents historiques* (1931); M. B. Kennedy, *The Complete Rosary* (1949); F. M. Willam, *Die Geschichte und Gebetsschule des Rosenkranzes* (1948); *Acta Sanctorum,* "De S. Dominico Confessore," vol. xxxv, pp. 432–437 (1733). (H. J. RY.)

ROSAS, JUAN MANUEL DE (1793–1877), tyrant of Buenos Aires and noted political figure in Argentine history, was born March 30, 1793, in Buenos Aires. His parents were Léon Ortiz de Rozas and Agustina López de Osornio, both of noble Spanish descent, and together they held perhaps the greatest family wealth in Buenos Aires province, consisting mainly of *estancias* (cattle ranches). Rosas received a primary education in the city of Buenos Aires, but as a young man preferred to spend his time on the family ranches where he became a complete *gaucho* (cowboy). He himself gradually acquired land south of the Salado river in Buenos Aires province, stocked it with cattle, and organized about him a force of *gauchos* trained with an iron discipline to which he was the first to subject himself.

On March 16, 1813, he married Encarnación Ezcurra y Arguibel. Then, after turning back to his parents all the properties he had administered for them, he established the large *estancia* of Los Cerrillos and a meat-salting plant in partnership with a friend.

His fame as a trainer of men brought him in 1815 the title of *oficial de milicias* and in 1820 he was made a colonel of cavalry. Col. Manuel Dorrego, Federalist leader and governor of the province of Buenos Aires, later made Rosas *comandante de la campaña*, and when Dorrego was overthrown and executed in 1828 by Juan Lavalle, Rosas took over the Federalist party command, defeated Lavalle, the leader of the *unitarios* (Centralists), and in Dec. 1829 had himself elected governor of Buenos Aires. During his three-year term Rosas gave the province the first peace it had known in many years, using bribery, political maneuvers and force to bring malcontents into line. A servile legislature made him brigadier-general and gave him the title of "Restorer of the Laws." He refused to be re-elected in 1832 and instead went south to fight the Indians, freeing white captives and capturing much-desired lands for himself and his followers.

Renewed political agitation, instigated and abetted by his followers (including his wife), brought disorder and confusion again to the province and an urgent demand for Rosas' return to power. But this time he refused to serve as governor unless granted complete dictatorial power, which the legislature gratefully gave him. In March 1835 he became dictator of Buenos Aires, a position he held until 1852. Other provincial governments permitted him to run their military and foreign affairs and usually did his bidding. Rosas refused to call a constitutional convention. His Argentine confederation (as he called it) continued under his domination as leader of the Federalist party, while the *unitarios* were pursued until captured or harried out of the land.

He quashed several revolutions that broke out against his tyranny. Killings of Rosas' opponents by his henchmen became the order of the day. By 1840 few dared oppose him.

Rosas' policies embroiled him also in foreign conflicts, including wars with neighbouring countries and with England and France. Finally a coalition of Brazilians, Uruguayans, French troops and native Argentines under the leadership of Justo José de Urquiza overthrew him in the battle of Caseros (Feb. 3, 1852). Rosas fled to England and retired to a farm near Southampton, where he died on March 14, 1877.

Much has been written on the Rosas regime, including some comparisons with the later Perón regime. Rosas has his modern admirers in Argentina, but in general Argentine historians have been critical of his rule, pointing out at the same time that he was perhaps indispensable in his day to bring law and order to an Argentina sunk in political anarchy following the winning of independence from Spain.   (F. L. Hn.)

ROSCELIN (*c.* 1050–*c.* 1125), in Latin called Roscellinus Compendiensis, French philosopher and theologian, famous as an extreme nominalist, was born at Compiègne (Compendium). Having studied at Soissons and at Reims, he taught at Compiègne, at Loches (where he had Abelard as his pupil), at Besançon and at Tours. His only extant work seems to be a violent and vulgar letter to Abelard on the Trinity; the little that is known of his doctrines is otherwise derived from St. Anselm's and from Abelard's works and from the anonymous *De generibus et speciebus*. According to Roscelin, universals are nothing more than verbal expressions (in Anselm's words, *flatus vocis*); Roscelin was, therefore, considered as the originator of extreme nominalism (*q.v.*). Again, no one thing can be divided into parts; every "part" is a whole in itself, and the division of "wholes" into "parts" is possible only in words, not in reality. Not even a syllogism is a unity; each proposition in it has a value in its own right without forming a whole with the others. Roscelin's doctrine of the Trinity, as consisting of three essences or substances—a doctrine inappropriately called "tritheism"—is partly based on the accepted Boëthian definition of *persona* as *substantia rationalis;* if God were one substance, all three persons would have been incarnated. It is not clear how this doctrine is connected with Roscelin's nominalism, nor how and whether he retracted it after his condemnation at the council of Soissons (1092).

See Roscelin's letter to Abelard, first edited by J. A. Schmeller in the *Abhandlungen* of the Royal Bavarian academy, vol. iii (1849–50); for a later edition *see* F. Picavet, *Roscelin, philosophe et théologien, d'après la légende et d'après l'histoire*, 2nd ed. (1911), the best documented work on Roscelin.   (L. M.-Po.)

ROSCIUS GALLUS, QUINTUS (d. 62 B.C.), a Roman actor, so famous that "Roscius" was long an honorary epithet for any successful actor, was born at Solonium, near Lanuvium. He studied the delivery of distinguished advocates in the Forum, and won praise especially in comedy. Cicero took lessons from him, and the dictator Sulla presented him with a gold ring, the badge of the equestrian order—a remarkable distinction for an actor in Rome, where the profession was held in contempt. Roscius amassed a fortune by his acting; he also trained young actors, and wrote a comparison of acting and oratory. At an unknown date, perhaps in 77 B.C., he was sued by Gaius Fannius Chaerea for payment of 50,000 sesterces and was defended by Cicero in a famous speech, *Pro Roscio Comoedo*.

ROSCOMMON, WENTWORTH DILLON, 4th Earl of (*c.* 1633–1685), English poet and critic, described by Pope as the only moral writer of Charles II's time, was born in Ireland about 1633, son of Sir James Dillon, 3rd earl of Roscommon, and nephew of the earl of Strafford, then lord deputy of Ireland. He was educated privately at Strafford's house in Yorkshire and, after his uncle's impeachment (1641), at the Protestant university of Caen in Normandy: he then toured Europe. Succeeding to the earldom in 1649, he returned to England in 1660, had his estates restored to him and soon won favour at Charles II's court. It is said that he became an immoderate gambler. After passing some time in Ireland he returned to London in 1662. He planned, together with Dryden and others, to form an academy on the continental model, which was to fix and refine the language and

translate classical works into English. The design came to nothing, but Roscommon translated *Ars Poetica* into English blank verse in 1680. In his *Essay on Translated Verse* (1684) he was the first critic to praise *Paradise Lost* publicly. Dryden spoke highly of the *Essay*, though Johnson thought it unimportant, and considered Roscommon "elegant but not great." His writings, though they have merit, might not have been so highly commended as they were in his own time had he been of inferior rank. Both Oxford and Cambridge conferred doctorates on him. He died in Westminster, Jan. 17, 1685.

ROSCOMMON (Ros Comáin), a county in the province of Connaught, Republic of Ireland, covers 951 sq.mi. (2,463 sq.km.). It consists mainly of the country between the Shannon River and its major tributary, the Suck, but a few miles south of Castlerea the boundary swings westward from this river through a thickly settled farmed lowland, and then eastward again along the Curlew Hills to Lough Allen, in the course of the Shannon. Only at Athlone is the Shannon boundary avoided, for the whole town on both banks is counted as part of County Westmeath (*q.v.*). Athlone is the main point of entry to the county: north of it lies Lough Ree, and a few miles upstream the Shannon has two other lakes, Bofin and Boderg. Along most of its course there are extensive water meadows, liable to flood but in dry periods giving excellent pasture known as callows. Similar meadows are widespread throughout the county.

In the area between the Shannon and the Suck the landscape is a mixture of limestone surfaces 200–400 ft. (60–120 m.) high with frequent outcrops of rock, and depressions varying from peat bogs to the natural pastures mentioned above. There are also some eskers (sand and gravel ridges) now extensively quarried for road metal and building, especially the one running west from Athlone. Within this area the farmers keep sheep and cattle, with oats, hay, and potatoes as the main crops, though wheat and some turnips and mangels (beets) are also grown. Sheep do very well on the limestone pastures, and at Roscommon town there are annual wool sales and heavy sales of lambs and sheep at the fairs.

A few miles north of Roscommon the Carboniferous Limestones are covered with drifts, with a fine series of eskers, some running north-south and others east-west. About three-quarters of the area is farmland and the rest peat bog. Drainage work on some of the bogs is being carried out for the production of milled peat. To the east of Boyle there are rich limestone grasslands known as the "Plains of Boyle" and famed as cattle pastures. Small farms of 25–30 ac. (10–12 ha.) are most usual, with a concentration on cattle rather than sheep. To the northeast of Roscommon there is a ridge, the Slieve Bawn, rising to 800 ft. (244 m.), formed of Devonian Sandstones; the Curlew Hills, on the northwestern boundary of the county, are of similar structure and altitude.

The northwest of Roscommon was MacDermott country and part of the south was in O'Kelly occupation. The native Irish interests generally prevailed, and the Anglo-Norman families on adjacent territories became Irish in their language and customs in the later Middle Ages. By the "Composition of Connaught" of 1585 a large number of the lords and chieftains of that province were given tenure at English law in their territories. Although the Composition was not given parliamentary endorsement, it governed procedure with respect to landed property there for many years. Later, since Connaught and Clare were left by Cromwell to Irish proprietors, this part of Ireland retained its Irish social pattern longer than any other, though it underwent the effects of the penal laws, the land acts, and other social changes which affected the country generally.

The population of the county was 56,228 in 1966. A county council meets in Roscommon town (pop. [1966] 1,659) and there is a county manager. There is no urban district in the county. Boyle (*q.v.*) is administered by town commissioners. Roscommon town was once similarly administered but the functions of its former commissioners have been transferred to the county council. The county sends four members to the *dáil*.

There is very little industry in County Roscommon, but the towns, and some villages, have a strong retail trade and monthly fairs. The county is almost completely dependent on agriculture although at Arigna, in the northeast, where iron and coal were once mined, coal mining has been resumed. The coal supplies electric power to the area. Emigration continues steadily; the population declined by 6% from 1946 to 1951, by 6% again from 1951 to 1956, and 7% from 1956 to 1961. (T. W. Fr.; Hu. S.)

ROSCOMMON (Ros Comáin), a market town and the capital of County Roscommon, Republic of Ireland, lies 90 mi. (145 km.) NW of Dublin in flat rich pasture land. Pop. (1961) 1,600. The name derives from Ros, a "gentle height," and Coman, its patron saint and first bishop of the see of Roscommon, which maintained its diocesan status until 1152 when it became part of the diocese of Elphin. Coman's monastery and school were established in the 7th century on the site of the present Anglican Church and the disused graveyard behind it. It figures prominently in several of the old Irish annals. In the monastery the Cross of Cong (so called because it was discovered in an oak chest in Cong, County Mayo) was made in c. 1123 to enshrine a portion of the True Cross which had been presented to King Tordelbach (Turlough) O'Connor (*Annals of Tighernagh*). During the 19th century the Cross of Cong was procured for the National Museum, Dublin.

A Dominican abbey, the ruins of which remain, was founded by Felim O'Connor, king of Connaught, in 1253. The founder's tomb, with eight gallowglasses at the base, still stands under an arch in the chancel. The abbey, then partially ruined, was finally vacated in 1795. Northwest of the town are the extensive ruins of a Norman castle, built in 1269 by the justiciar of Ireland, Sir Robert de Ufford. Similar in plan to the castles of Conway, Beaumaris, and Harlech (*qq.v.*), it changed hands several times in the Irish wars and was finally dismantled by Cromwell's army in 1652. Roscommon's modern Roman Catholic Church (1903–25) is noted for its mosaics and stained-glass windows.

A royal charter of 1282 gave to the prior of St. Coman's Abbey the right to hold a weekly market on Saturday. This market continues to the present day. Roscommon's monthly fairs are well-known throughout agricultural Ireland and a cooperative livestock mart has been in operation since 1959. An Irish mosaic factory was opened in 1959 and one for making and repairing textile machinery in 1962. The town is on the main railway line from Dublin to Westport. (C. J. F.)

ROSE, SAINT, of Lima (1586–1617), the first person born in the New World to be canonized by the Roman Catholic Church, was born at Lima, Peru, on April 20, 1586, to Caspar de Flores and his wife, María del Oliva. Named Isabel at baptism, the child from her earliest days was called Rose. A financially unhappy venture in mining brought poverty to the family, forcing the girl to make early use of her skill as a seamstress to help support her brothers and sisters. Drawn to penitential practices and a life of virginity, she was opposed by her mother, who wished her to marry. The struggle between them lasted the better part of ten years, during which time Rose made a perpetual vow of virginity to strengthen her purpose. In 1606 her mother relented and allowed the girl to become a Dominican tertiary, living in seclusion in a hut in the family garden. Ridiculed and persecuted by friends and enemies, she continued a life of severe austerity, yielding only to the extent of leaving her hermitage for the last three years of her life. On Aug. 24, 1617, she died at the age of 31. Her funeral was an occasion of public honour, a belated recognition of her sanctity. In 1667 Pope Clement IX proclaimed her blessed, and four years later his successor, Clement X, issued the bull of canonization, proclaiming her at the same time patron saint of South America. St. Rose's feast is celebrated on Aug. 30.

See Latin biography by Leonard Hansen in *Acta Sanctorum,* August, vol. v; Sheila Kaye-Smith, *Quartet in Heaven* (1952).

ROSE, any of the wild or cultivated flowering shrubs of *Rosa,* a genus of between 100–200 species, about 80% of which are native to Asia, 15% to America, and the remainder chiefly natives of Europe and northwest Africa.

The rose gives its name to the botanical family Rosaceae, of which it may be considered the type, and to the order Rosales. Roses, even from widely separated regions, hybridize readily, giving rise to types that overlap the parental forms, and thus make it difficult to determine basic species. They are distributed primarily in the temperate part of the Northern Hemisphere, but some are found above the Arctic Circle and a few at the higher elevations in the tropics.

The rose flower has been closely associated with the culture of many civilizations. Not only is it a favourite flower, but it also serves as a symbol of perfection, elegance, romance, and love. The Greek poetess Sappho in her "Ode to the Rose" called it "the queen of flowers." No other flower is so universally known; the name is easily recognized in most languages of Latin or Germanic origin. The flower appears frequently in embroidery, painting, architecture, music, and literature and figures prominently in legends, customs, heraldry, and religion.

History.—The spread of the rose throughout Western Europe owes much to the advance of Islam. As the Arabs moved from Persia, which they conquered in the 7th century, the flowers of the Middle East, including the rose, followed them, eventually to Spain in the West (8th century on) and to India in the East (10th century). No doubt many roses were brought to Britain during the Roman invasion, but it is impossible to say with certainty whether *R. canina,* the common dog rose, which is a native of the east Mediterranean, is also a native of Britain. Roses were also brought to Britain from the East during the Crusades (11th century on).

Uses and Importance.—Roses have been used in medicines, and during and since World War II rose fruits, or hips, have been utilized as a source of vitamin C, largely from *R. rugosa.* Rose petals can be used in cookery, particularly in crystallized form for confections, and extracts containing the essential oil, which gives the fragrance, are used for flavouring desserts or for scent in cosmetics and perfume. Many acres are devoted to rose production for garden and greenhouse culture in the leading countries of the world. The great variation in habit of growth makes them useful in almost any landscape situation. In India, Iran, the Balkans, and France, large quantities of blooms are grown for the production of the fragrant attar of roses (*q.v.*), used in perfumes.

Roses are prized chiefly for their blossoms, which range from white through various tones of yellow and pink to dark crimson and maroon. Many varieties have been bred with beautiful blends of colour. The form of the rose bloom varies from the delicate primitive charm of the wild roses to the fully double, high-centred, sculptured blooms of the modern hybrids. Size ranges from the tiny miniatures not more than one-half inch in diameter to exhibition flowers seven inches or more across. Few persons fail to enjoy the delightful fragrance of most roses, which varies according to the variety and climatic conditions. While the typical rose odour is that produced by the damask and similar roses, the scent of other kinds may suggest spices, fruits, hay, other flowers, or, as in the case of the tea rose, fresh green tea leaves. Many species and varieties have brilliantly coloured hips during the autumn and winter.

Plant Characteristics.—Roses are erect, climbing, or trailing shrubs, never true trees (though grafted sorts called standards, with a main stem, resemble small trees). Their stems are generally more or less copiously armed with prickles of various shapes and sizes called thorns. The leaves, invariably alternate and provided with stipules that are often aromatic glandular, are composed of pinnately arranged leaflets, varying in number from 1 to 11 or more, the odd leaflet always being at the apex, the others in pairs. The flowers are solitary or in loose clusters produced at the ends of the shoots. The flower stalk expands into a fleshy vase- or urn-shaped hypanthium, called the receptacle, receptacular tube, or hip, which ultimately will contain the numerous seeds (achenes).

From the edge of the hypanthium proceed five sepals, often more or less compound like the leaves and overlapping in the bud. Within the circle of sepals are five petals, generally broad or roundish in outline. The numerous stamens originate slightly above the sepals and petals; each has a slender filament and a small two-celled anther. The stamens are arranged in several concentric whorls. In many rose varieties stamens become petaloid, giving rise to the full double flowers so much admired by gardeners. The carpels are numerous, covered with hairs. Each is provided with a long style and buttonlike stigma. The carpels are concealed within the hypanthium, and only the stigmas as a rule protrude from its mouth. Each carpel contains one ovule. The ovules contain the female gametes or sex cells, and the anthers contain the male gametes in the pollen grains. The hips, which follow the flowers, are eaten by birds, thus the seeds contained in the hips are readily dispersed.

Under natural circumstances rose flowers do not secrete nectar, the attraction for insects being provided by the colour and perfume and the abundance of pollen for food. The stigmas and anthers come to maturity at the same time; consequently, while cross-pollination by insects is common, self-fertilization can occur.

Species.—Roses grow wild in various countries of the Northern Hemisphere. Of the more than 100 species not more than nine have been concerned in the breeding of garden roses. Probably the oldest of these is the French rose (*R. gallica*), a small shrub, three to four feet high, bearing single deep pink to crimson flowers. A native of southwest Europe, it was known in the 12th century B.C. and about 500 years later was used as the emblem of the Medes and Persians. In its form *R. gallica officinalis*, it was the red rose of Lancaster. *R. moschata*, the musk rose, a native of the Himalayas, is a tall-growing shrub bearing clusters of single, white roses. In its cultivated double form it spread rapidly westward across Greece and Italy to France and ultimately reached England in the second half of the 16th century. *R. gigantea* and *R. multiflora*, natives of eastern Asia, are also tall shrubs with long trailing branches. *R. wichuraiana*, the memorial rose, also a native of east Asia, has a prostrate habit with creeping branches and single white flowers, 1½–2 in. in diameter, in clusters. Another rose that has played an important part in the development of modern roses is *R. chinensis*, a double form of *R. gigantea* and cultivated largely in China (*R. chinensis* is synonymous with *R. indica* and is known both as the China rose and the Bengal rose). It is a low-growing bush, the double flowers of which vary much in colour, red, pink, and yellow varieties being known. Some of its varieties have strong fragrance (*e.g.*, *R. chinensis fragrans*, usually known as *R. odorata*), and all, but notably *R. chinensis semperflorens*, the Chinese monthly rose, have the property of perpetual flowering.

By crossings of these early species the various types of modern garden roses have been developed. *R. gallica* × *R. canina* produced *R. alba*, the white rose of York, while complex hybrids of *R. gallica*, *R. moschata*, and possibly also *R. canina* and *R. phoenicia* (a native of the east Mediterranean) produced the *centifolias* (cabbage roses), which in turn mutated to produce the small, close-petaled moss roses so beloved during the Victorian era.

A class of roses known as the damask roses (*R. damascena*) resulted by crossing *R. gallica* and *R. moschata*. *R. damascena* was, and still is, used in large quantities in the making of attar of roses.

Other important and epoch-making rose crosses were:

R. chinensis × *R. moschata* = the noisette roses; 1802 at Charleston, W.Va. These were treasured varieties till 1890.

Noisette roses × hybrid chinas = tea roses, which were in great favour from 1830 to 1900.

R. damascena × hybrid chinas = Bourbon roses, popular from 1817 to 1870. These were delicate roses that flourished in the open in warm climates only. They were first grown in the Ile de Bourbon in the Indian Ocean.

R. chinensis × *R. gallica* × *R. damascena* = the Portland rose, a much hardier type than the Bourbons.

Bourbons × Portland = hybrid perpetuals. These were strong growing varieties, some with a strong fragrance, but were not so perpetual in their flowering period as their name implies. They were the popular garden rose from 1840 to 1900, but few are grown today, although in Britain forms such as "General Jacqueminot," "Ulrich Brunner," "Mrs. John Laing," "Reine des Violettes," and "Baron Girod de L'Ain" are still to be found in the gardens of the connoisseurs.

Hybrid perpetuals × tea roses = hybrid tea, a variety which

has held sway as a garden rose since 1867 with the introduction of "La France."

R. foetida introduced yellow into the hybrid tea roses from 1900 onward and enriched the colour range by shades from pale yellow to orange.

R. multiflora × hybrid chinas, and later crossed with other cultivated varieties, produced two classes of roses: first, a class of hybrid polyantha climbers such as "Paul's Scarlet Climber" and "Chaplin's Pink"; and second, seedlings of *R. multiflora* × hybrid chinas resulting in the dwarf everblooming poly pompons; *e.g.*, "Pâquerette" and "Mignonette," which became the ancestors of "Orleans rose," "Miss Edith Cavell," and "Coral Cluster."

Poly pompons × hybrid teas = hybrid polyanthas, the first of which was "Else Poulsen" (1924). This was followed by others named after the members of the family of the raiser, Danish rose breeder Svend Poulsen.

Subsequent crossings of the hybrid polyanthas with more complex hybrid teas, hybrid perpetuals, and hybrid musks have rendered the name hybrid polyantha a misnomer. This new class, which includes a wide range of roses in great variety of colours, is best known as floribundas, the tall and more shrublike varieties of which are known in America as grandifloras and in Britain as floribunda hybrid tea type or floribunda shrubs.

R. wichuraiana × tea and hybrid tea roses produced the glossy leaved ramblers; *e.g.*, "Alberic Barbier," "Albertine," and "American Pillar." These roses are often made to climb by tying them to supports rather than letting them trail down banks as is their natural habit; if budded on tall stems, they make attractive weeping standards.

R. spinosissima, the Scotch rose, a low bush densely provided with slender prickles and producing white, pale pink, or yellow flowers, depending on where it is grown, was used between the years 1937–1950 by the German hybridist W. Kordes to produce such fine roses as "Frühlingsgold," "Frühlingsmorgen," and "Frühlingsanfang." In America, *R. spinosissima* was used to produce "Golden Wings," a vigorous shrub with recurrent large single blooms of a sulfur-yellow colour.

The ramblers previously mentioned were exclusively summer flowering. In 1952 *R. kordesii* arose in cultivation as a result of spontaneous chromosome doubling in a *R. rugosa* × *R. wichuraiana* hybrid "Max Graf." By crossing this new species with the large flowered rambler "Golden Glow," the first of a race of repeat-flowering climbers, "Köln am Rhein," was produced. These are known as Kordesii climbers.

The numerous roses native to North America belong to about 35 species. The smooth rose (*R. blanda*), usually lacking prickles and having flowers about three inches broad, occurs abundantly from Newfoundland to Saskatchewan and southward to New Jersey and Missouri. The prickly rose (*R. acicularis*), with spiny stems, leaves composed of five to nine leaflets, and solitary flowers two and one-half inches broad, ranges from Quebec to Alaska and south to Colorado. The pasture rose (*R. virginiana*), from one half to six feet high, with few or solitary flowers two to three inches across, sometimes double, occurs from Newfoundland to Wisconsin and south to Georgia. This is the commonest wild rose of the eastern states and Canada. The prairie rose (*R. setigera*), a large shrub with a tendency to climb and with leaves usually composed of three leaflets, bears rose-pink flowers that turn white with age. This handsome rose, which grows wild from Ontario to Wisconsin and south to Florida and Texas, has become naturalized eastward to New England. The California rose (*R. californica*), a sparsely prickly shrub three to nine feet high, flowering nearly the year round, sometimes forms thickets along streams.

The following are interesting species (or hybrids) not previously mentioned and often grown as shrubs. *R. eglanteria*, the eglantine or sweetbrier, is a stiff, erect, branching bush with pink-tinged white blooms and sweet-smelling foliage. The large-fruited apple rose, *R. pomifera*, is prized for its large scarlet hips, which may be one inch or more in diameter. *R. arvensis*, the parent of the Ayrshire rose, is a very thorny shrub with more or less decumbent or creeping branches. *R. rubrifolia* is an unusual shrub because of its reddish glaucous stems and gray foliage. The cinnamon rose, *R. cinnamomea*, is a hardy old garden species common along fences and roadsides; it has double, fragrant blooms in shades of red, two inches or more across.

R. rugosa is a remarkable species because of its bold rugose foliage, its large red, pink, or white flowers, and its conspicuous fruits. *R. moyesii* is an attractive ten-foot shrub with two and one-half inch deep-red flowers. *R. hugonis* is a handsome, hardy shrub producing an abundance of light-yellow flowers in early spring. The Macartney rose (*R. bracteata*), introduced into England from China, is a stout evergreen shrub producing drooping shoots 10 to 20 ft. long. The Cherokee rose (*R. laevigata*) is a rampant plant that climbs over fences and trees; it is widely planted in the southern United States, where it has run wild and appears to be indigenous. The Lady Banks rose (*R. banksiae*) is a high-climbing evergreen with few or no prickles and smooth slender twigs; the flowers are about one inch across, single or double, white or yellow, somewhat fragrant, and borne in umbellike clusters.

The number of cultivated clones, or horticultural forms, is very large, more than 100 being introduced into commerce each year. To facilitate grouping clones with similar characteristics, a complicated horticultural classification has evolved that is often inconsistent. In some cases it is based upon origin from wild species, in others upon habit of growth or manner of flowering. There is considerable overlapping and mergence of classes as the result of extensive interbreeding.

Among bush roses, the main classes include hybrid perpetuals, teas, hybrid teas, polyanthas, hybrid polyanthas, and floribundas. Climbing roses are classed as ramblers, large-flowered climbers, everblooming hardy climbers, climbing forms of hybrid teas, floribundas and other bush types, and trailing varieties. A comprehensive list is given in J. H. McFarland's *Modern Roses V* (1958), which includes 7,562 names. The list, however, represents only a small proportion of the roses hybridized and named during the preceding 250 years.

Propagation.—Roses are propagated by seeds, cutting, layering, grafting, and budding. Most rose seed requires a stratification treatment (cold storage in a moist medium) to hasten germination. Commercially, rose plants are produced largely by budding the desired clone onto an understock. In Europe, forms of *R. canina* and, particularly on light soils, *R. multiflora simplex* are used extensively; in the U.S., forms of *R. multiflora* are commonly used, although in some areas "Gloire des Rosomanes" (Ragged Robin), "Dr. Huey," and forms of *R. odorata* are employed. Tree, or standard, roses are budded from two to six feet above ground level on a tall, straight cane of the understock. For this purpose, forms of *R. canina, R. multiflora,* and *R. rugosa* are commonly used. Plants for greenhouse culture are usually budded on Manetti roses (*R. noisettiana manetti*), but *R. canina* may be used as well. For half-standards, *R. rugosa* is a good stock.

Cultivation.—It is important to select a proper location for the rose garden. In moderate or cool climates, full sun is desirable. Where summers are hot, shade during part of the day, particularly in the afternoon, is beneficial. Good drainage is essential; if the site has a tendency to become waterlogged, a tile drainage system should be installed or the beds should be raised well above the surrounding ground level. Roses should be planted away from trees or shrubs whose roots may invade the bed and compete for water and nutrients. Protection from strong winds should also be provided. Incorporating well-rotted manure, leaf mold, compost, peat moss, or similar organic substances is recommended to lighten densely compacted soil. Ideally the soil should be slightly acidic (pH 5.5–6.5). Lime can be applied to overly acid soil; alkaline soil may be acidified with ferrous sulfate or powdered sulfur.

Most roses are set out as dormant bare-rooted plants in the spring or autumn depending upon the climate and condition of soil. Mounding soil around the base of the plants after planting helps protect the stems from drying out until the roots are well established. Bushes with developed root systems, for planting at other seasons, are available in containers.

Roses respond well to annual topdressing with rotted manure or periodic applications of liquid manure or inorganic fertilizers. Watering the beds immediately after fertilizer is applied is recommended. Thorough watering is essential; this means soaking the soil to a depth of six to eight inches. Damping the surface is useless, in fact harmful, as it tends to stimulate surface roots, which soon dry out.

Cultivating the beds, to eliminate weeds, and keeping the surface loose and well aerated is recommended, but cultivation should not be so deep as to destroy roots. A better practice is mulching with grass clippings, peat moss, buckwheat hulls, ground corncobs, or rice hulls, layers of which conserve moisture, keep down soil temperature, and discourage weeds.

Pruning keeps the plants in vigorous condition and improves their quality and appearance. The different classes and even different varieties in the same class may respond to different pruning treatment, but in general the practice for bush roses involves cutting out all dead or injured wood in the spring, removing weak, twiggy growth, and cutting back the strong canes to a moderate height to give a well-balanced appearance. Ramblers that bloom only once during the season are best pruned immediately after flowering. Withered blooms should be removed promptly from everblooming climbers so that new flowering shoots will be stimulated to grow.

Where the temperature normally goes below 5° F (−15° C), protection during the winter is necessary. This is accomplished by mounding soil around the base of the plants before the surface freezes and later, after a heavy freeze, covering the mounds with evergreen boughs, marsh hay, straw, or other coarse insulating material to prevent alternate thawing and freezing. Where climbing roses are likely to freeze, their canes may be released from their supports, laid on the ground, and covered with soil; in the spring the canes are again tied back on the supports.

PHOTOGRAPHS: L. W. BROWNELL (LEFT), J. C. ALLEN & SON (RIGHT)

COMMON WILD ROSE (ROSA HUMILIS) AND DOMESTIC GARDEN ROSE

Diseases and Pests.—Roses are infected by a number of diseases, most of them caused by fungi. Powdery mildew is widespread wherever roses are grown and is observed as a grayish-white moldlike growth on the surface of young leaves, stems, and buds. Copper and sulfur fungicides are effective as controls when applied either as a spray or dust.

Black spot may occur in humid climates, if certain precautions of culture are not taken. Shortly after conspicuous black spots appear on them, the leaves drop. Heavy dews following hot days favour the development of the spores. If the surface of the leaf remains wet for a period of about six hours, the spores can germinate and cause infection unless the surface of the leaf is protected by a thin film of fungicide. Fixed or insoluble copper fungicides, finely powdered, or wettable sulfur are standard control chemicals. There are also a number of patented organic fungicides, such as Ferbam and Captan, that are highly effective if applications are timely and thorough. Spraying early is essential. Removing infected leaves as soon as a spot is detected and keeping all fallen leaves removed from the surface of the bed is recommended.

Rust appears on both cultivated and wild roses in the spring, bursting through the bark in the form of masses of orange powder consisting of the spores of the fungus. In early summer the spores infect the leaves and produce on them small orange dots and, later, groups of spores, mainly black, that can survive the winter. It is important that all affected leaves be destroyed in the autumn and the bush be sprayed with a copper, sulfur, or Ferbam fungicide in the spring to prevent infection of leaves by spores carried from stems on which they may have wintered.

Other diseases that are sometimes troublesome are canker, crown or root gall, and anthracnose.

Among the number of insects that may prove troublesome, aphids are common but are easily controlled by nicotine spray or dust or many other insecticides. Various caterpillars, sawfly larvae, and similar insects feed on the leaves and young shoots. These pests are easily controlled by stomach poisons such as arsenate of lead or DDT. Red spider mites, which multiply in great numbers, largely on the undersides of the leaves, are difficult to see and may cause extensive damage before being discovered. Materials such as Malathion, Aramite, and Ovatran are available for their control. Other insect pests are thrips, earwigs, midge, and scale insects, all of which can be reasonably well-controlled by the newer insecticides.

BIBLIOGRAPHY.—George M. Taylor, *The Book of the Rose* (1949) and (ed.), *Pearson's Encyclopaedia of Roses* (1948); Bertram Park, *Roses* (1949) and *The World of Roses* (1962); A. S. Thomas, *Better Roses,* 2nd ed. (1960); N. P. Harvey, *The Rose in Britain* (1951); J. Horace McFarland, *Modern Roses V,* ed. by C. E. Meikle and Roy E. Shepherd (1958); Jean Gordon, *Pageant of the Rose* (1953); Cynthia Westcott, *Anyone Can Grow Roses,* 2nd ed. (1954); Roy E. Shepherd, *History of the Rose* (1954); R. C. Allen, *Roses for Every Garden* (1948); A. Norman, *Successful Rose Growing* (1953); G. S. Thomas, *Shrub Roses of Today* (1962); F. Fairbrother, *Roses,* 5th ed. (1965) and *Roses* (1962); G. Edwards, *Roses for Enjoyment* (1962); H. Edland (ed.), *Pocket Encyclopaedia of Roses in Colour* (1963). See also publications of the Royal National Rose Society of Great Britain, the American Rose Society, and the Australian and New Zealand rose societies.   (R. C. AL.; F. FA.)

ROSEBERY, ARCHIBALD PHILIP PRIMROSE, 5TH EARL OF (1847–1929), British statesman, prime minister from March 1894 to June 1895, orator and racehorse owner, was born in London on May 7, 1847. His father, Archibald Primrose, son of the 4th earl, died before Archibald was four; so as heir to the earldom he bore the title of Lord Dalmeny at Eton, where Arthur James Balfour and Lord Randolph Churchill were among his contemporaries, and where he developed his brilliance of speech and manner. He went down from Christ Church, Oxford, without a degree at Easter 1869, rather than abandon, as the college authorities required, the small racing stud he had already formed. In 1868 he succeeded to the earldom and to large estates in Scotland, including the great house at Dalmeny near Edinburgh. To this and to Rosebery, a shooting lodge in Peeblesshire, he soon added The Durdans, a large country house near Epsom; in 1878 he married Hannah, orphan daughter of Baron Meyer de Rothschild, who brought him the Buckinghamshire palace of Mentmore; he had a town house in Berkeley Square, and in 1897 he bought a

villa on the Bay of Naples. These details may help to give a key to this fastidious character, for whom nothing but the best was ever good enough. Another key may be found in the remark of a woman who knew him well: "It is a curiously cold, impassive face, but surely his smile is the most irradiating that has ever been seen. He is absolutely transformed by it."

While still an undergraduate he refused in 1867 the offer of a safe Conservative seat at Darlington and his political principles, as they developed, turned gradually toward the Liberal interest. But his Liberalism was always Whiggish and lukewarm and was tinged with a keen regard for British grandeur and a strong sense of imperial destiny; it was accompanied also by a full sense of his own importance. In politics he was in fact a prickly subordinate, a difficult colleague, and an almost impossible superior. Indeed, though he rose to be prime minister at the age of 46 and died at the age of 82, his temperament was such that his ministerial career filled less than seven years, and his premiership was unusually brief.

Office under Gladstone.—Rosebery never sat in the House of Commons, but he had some direct experience of constituency life, for it was at his suggestion, with his help, and as his guest, that Gladstone fought the Midlothian campaigns of 1879 and 1880 which regained power for the Liberal Party (*see* GLADSTONE, WILLIAM EWART). Rosebery was at first too sensitive, and then too ill, to take any office at the beginning of Gladstone's second administration (1880–85). However, from 1881 to 1883 he served as undersecretary at the home office, with special charge of Scottish affairs, and his insistence that Scotland should be given more careful and more special treatment by the civil service led to the formation of the modern Scottish office in 1885. But he was often in need of careful and special treatment himself; he was a constant trial to the prime minister, and the mediation of Edward Walter Hamilton, an old school friend who was Gladstone's private secretary, was often needed to keep Rosebery pulling in harness. He resigned in June 1883 when attacked in Parliament on a minor matter and went on a journey round the world. However, at the moment of the Khartoum disaster in 1885 he placed himself again at Gladstone's disposal, and entered the cabinet for a few months (March–June) as lord privy seal. He stood by Gladstone when the Liberal Party split over Home Rule for Ireland and at Queen Victoria's suggestion he became foreign secretary in the short government of February–July 1886. He had little time to do more than get to know his staff, and to set out the doctrine that British foreign policy continues much the same irrespective of the party in power.

During the following six years spent in opposition by the Liberal Party he took some part in London local government. In January 1889 he was elected chairman of the newly formed London County Council, and held that post till July 1890. He held it again for a few months early in 1892; but meanwhile he had been stricken by a private calamity from which he never altogether recovered. His devoted wife, who had borne him two sons and two daughters, had participated in all his interests; suddenly, in October 1890, she caught typhoid fever, and died six weeks later. Rosebery was desolated. Her fortune of £800,000 was no consolation for the loss of her presence, her advice, and her love. He never remarried.

He would have preferred to mope alone; but family and friends insisted that he labour on at politics. He tried hard to avoid office in Gladstone's last government (1892–94), and was forced back to the Foreign Office much against his will. His ideas about the conduct of foreign and imperial policy diverged sharply from those of Gladstone, and the usual "committee of two" (prime minister and foreign secretary) that directs British affairs abroad failed to operate. The quarrel went so far that for 18 months from the autumn of 1892 important dispatches went abroad with the queen's sanction, but without that of the prime minister. Rosebery immediately disagreed with Gladstone about the proper policy to follow in Uganda, where the British East Africa Company was in financial difficulties. He succeeded in deferring the withdrawal of British control favoured by Gladstone, Sir William Harcourt, and the more radical half of the cabinet, and was eventually able to bring the territory under a British protectorate (1894). He devoted energy and temper in 1893 to a dispute with France about the boundaries of French and British spheres of influence in Siam, and secured an arrangement reasonably advantageous from the Siamese and the British point of view. The much more important problem of the shift in the European balance of power, brought about by the conclusion of the Franco-Russian alliance of 1894, seems to have eluded his attention. He continued the marquess of Salisbury's policy of secret collaboration with the Triple Alliance (Germany, Austria-Hungary, and Italy). However, he repudiated Salisbury's second Mediterranean agreement (December 1887) with Austria-Hungary and Italy, which created Britain's obligation to support them in maintaining the independence of Turkey, saying he had not seen the actual document, which was kept in his permanent secretary's safe. Oddly enough, Rosebery got on better with his colleagues and showed more skill in diplomacy over home affairs than foreign; under his chairmanship a troublesome conflict between coal miners and coal owners was brought to a compromise in November 1893.

Prime Minister.—In the dispute over the increase in the naval estimates (December 1893), which Gladstone opposed and which finally drove him from office, Rosebery took a leading part against the prime minister. Had she asked his advice, Gladstone would have recommended Lord Spencer to the queen as his successor, and public opinion favoured Harcourt, but on her own initiative Victoria sent for Rosebery, who reconstructed the Liberal cabinet with few changes in March 1894. His government lasted for 16 months. It achieved practically nothing; partly because the House of Lords sedulously rejected every Liberal measure except the budget, as a matter of Conservative principle, so that no legislation could be passed; and partly because Rosebery's colleagues were known to be bitterly divided. These divisions cut so deep that Rosebery and Harcourt, his chancellor of the exchequer and leader of the Commons, are said hardly to have spoken to each other directly for more than six months. Although such ludicrous discord did not originate by any fault of Rosebery's, he lacked the qualities to resolve it. When his government was accidentally defeated in the Commons on a minor war office vote in June 1895, he seized the excuse to resign. The subsequent election, which returned a large Conservative majority, seemed to show that the electorate had little use for Gladstonian Liberals without Gladstone.

Though the time during which he was prime minister was politically unrewarding and personally agonizing for Rosebery it did include a notable feat; his racing stable, long nourished, not only won the Derby of 1894 with Ladas but won it again in the following year with Sir Visto. This achievement, nevertheless, was harmful to Rosebery's standing with the dour Nonconformists who formed the backbone of his party in the country, and it confirmed them in their suspicion that he was a playboy. (Rosebery did once more own a Derby winner, Cicero, in 1905, but by that time he was set markedly apart from his former colleagues, though still far apart from his former opponents.)

Gradual Retirement from Politics.—He resigned the leadership of the Liberal Party in October 1896, because he thought the aged Gladstone's protests at the Armenian massacres inexpedient, and was both too fond of him and too keenly aware of Gladstone's standing in the Liberal Party to care to lead against the retired titan's published views. Sharper differences with the Liberals followed during the South African War (1899–1902). Rosebery was a leading Liberal Imperialist, and gave much offense to radicals in his own party and to the left of it, particularly by a speech at Chesterfield in December 1901 that referred to "fly-blown phylacteries" of the Liberal Party. His efforts to stimulate Liberal imperialism had considerable effects, though principally among Conservatives; the main body of the Liberal Party paid him little attention. His final separation from the party came with his Bodmin speech, a few weeks before the Liberals came back to power in December 1905; in it Rosebery declared himself no longer a supporter of Home Rule. While the new government was introducing a program of social legislation (*see* ENGLISH HISTORY: *Edwardian England*), Rosebery was yachting in the Mediterranean, or adjusting the affairs of distressed jockeys, or writing some of his excellent historical essays. A note of his found after his death makes clear what he thought his position was.

The secret of my life, which seems to me sufficiently obvious, is that I always detested politics. I had been landed in them accidentally by the Midlothian Election, which was nothing but a chivalrous adventure. When I found myself in this evil-smelling bog I was always trying to extricate myself. That is the secret of what people used to call my lost opportunities, and so forth. If you will look over my life you will see that it is quite obvious. But nothing is so obvious as the thing which one does not wish to see.

Rosebery made a brief reappearance in politics in September 1909, to attack Lloyd George's budget as rapacious and socialistic; and another at the end of 1910, when he brought forward proposals he had often pressed before, intended to make the House of Lords a strong second chamber. Membership was to consist of lords of Parliament, who were to be chosen from the body of hereditary peers by the peers themselves, and from others outside the House. Although carried in the Lords, the scheme was unacceptable to the Commons majority, which desired a weaker second chamber, not a stronger one. Rosebery voted for the Parliament bill in August 1911, sooner than see the lords swamped by a mass creation of new peers, but he registered a protest against it in the journals of the House. This was his last act in party politics.

It was by no means his last act in public. He was much more than a witty and graceful speaker; he was one of the most accomplished orators of his day, and if people could not hear him on party politics, they would hear him with pleasure on anything else. As a principal Scottish dignitary, Rosebery played a substantial part in mobilizing the Scots for World War I and in sustaining their efforts. Dalmeny was turned into a hospital, and in circumstances of deep distress (his younger son Neil and two nephews were killed in action), he devoted himself unreservedly to stimulating the will to fight. In November 1918, a few days before the war ended, overexertion brought on a stroke, which left him partly crippled for the rest of his life, though for many years his intellect remained clear and his conversation fascinating. He died at The Durdans on May 21, 1929, and was succeeded as 6th earl by his elder son Albert. Rosebery wrote four books, *Pitt* (1891), *Napoleon: the Last Phase* (1900), *Lord Randolph Churchill* (1906), and *Chatham* (1910). A collection of his essays and speeches, *Miscellanies, Literary and Historical,* edited by John Buchan, was published in two volumes in 1921.

See Lord Crewe, *Lord Rosebery,* 2 vol. (1931); R. R. James, *Rosebery* (1963); P. Stansky, *Ambitions and Strategies* (1964).

(M. R. D. F.)

ROSECRANS, WILLIAM STARKE (1819–1898), Union officer during the American Civil War, was born in Kingston, O., Sept. 6, 1819, and graduated from West Point in 1842. After 12 years as a regular army officer he resigned to enter business in Ohio until the Civil War brought him back to military service. He served under Gen. George B. McClellan and Gen. John Pope and succeeded each when they moved east to larger commands. During 1862 he led the Union forces to victory in the battles of Iuka and Corinth, after which he moved on to Nashville to the command of the Army of the Cumberland. He fought the bloody and indecisive battle of Stone (or Stones) River (Murfreesboro) Dec. 31, 1862–Jan. 2, 1863. His aggressive spirit had pleased his Washington superiors, who were looking always for a fighting general, but now he began to show other qualities: an excess of caution and hesitancy, a disposition to worry and to argue with his superiors. Finally, on June 23, 1863, after six months of delay in the face of official pressure to take the offensive, he pushed Gen. Braxton Bragg into Chattanooga, then maneuvered him out of the city without a battle. Here his customary caution deserted him and he followed Bragg who turned upon him at Chickamauga (*q.v.*), Sept. 19–20. An ill-advised move opened a gap in his lines and allowed the Confederates to pour through and drive him and a part of his army back into Chattanooga (*q.v.*). Only the stand of Gen. George Thomas on the Union left averted complete disaster. Gen. U. S. Grant, now charged with the defense of Chattanooga, removed Rosecrans, ending any important role for him in the war.

Rosecrans resigned his army commission in 1867. He served

for two years as minister to Mexico (1868–69) and later engaged in mining operations in Mexico and California. He served in congress, 1881–85, from California, and afterward became register of the treasury. He retired to California in 1893 and died there on March 11, 1898. (C. W. Te.)

ROSEGGER, PETER (1843–1918), Austrian novelist and poet, was born at Alpl, near Krieglach in Styria (Şteiermark), on July 31, 1843. The son of a peasant, he became a traveling tailor. His many novels paint a picture of the landscape and customs of his homeland, and he achieved wide fame, notably with *Waldheimat* (1877; English translation, *The Forest Farm*, 1912) and *Die Schriften des Waldschulmeisters* (1875; English translation, *The Forest Schoolmaster*, 1901). His religious and autobiographical writings (*Der Gottsucher*, 1883; English translation, *The God-Seeker*, 1901; *Mein Weltleben*, 1898) were also popular. His dialect stories were collected in four volumes (1894–96) and his *Gesammelte Werke* (40 volumes) appeared in 1914–16. He died at Krieglach on June 26, 1918.

BIBLIOGRAPHY.—A. Schlossar, *P. Rosegger* (1921); O. Janda, *P. Rosegger. Das Leben in seinen Briefen,* 2nd ed. (1948); R. Latzke, *Der junge Rosegger* (1943), *Der ältere und der jüngere Rosegger* (1953). (W. D. Wi.)

ROSE HILL, Mauritius: *see* BEAU BASSIN-ROSE HILL.

ROSELLE and **ROSELLE PARK,** boroughs in Union County, N.J., U.S., adjoining Elizabeth on the west, are suburban residential communities of the New York metropolitan area and also have factories whose products include rugs, toys, restaurant equipment, surgical supplies, and leather goods. Roselle, incorporated in 1894, is the site of the birthplace of Abraham Clark, one of the New Jersey signers of the Declaration of Independence. Thomas A. Edison's experiments there made Roselle the first community to be completely lighted by electricity.

Roselle Park, once named North Roselle, was incorporated in 1901. Guglielmo Marconi, inventor of the wireless, established a plant there in 1913 which during World War I was a leader in the manufacture of communications equipment. KDY, a pioneer commercial radiobroadcasting station, was located there in 1921.

For comparative population figures *see* table in NEW JERSEY: *Population.* (E. R. D.)

ROSEMARY (*Rosmarinus officinalis*), a low shrub of the mint family (Labiatae) whose leaves are used as seasoning. The only representative of the genus is a native of the Mediterranean region. It has evergreen linear leaves, dark green above, white beneath, and with margins rolled back onto the under face. The flowers are in small axillary clusters. Each has a two-lipped calyx, from which projects a bluish two-lipped corolla enclosing two stamens. The fruit consists of four smooth nutlets. Rosemary was highly esteemed by the ancients for its aromatic quality and medicinal uses. In modern times it is valued mainly for its perfume; the oil is obtained by distillation. Rosemary plays an important part in literature and folklore, being an emblem of remembrance. It is widely grown in gardens in the warmer parts of the U.S. and in Great Britain, where an old garden legend reads "where rosemary thrives the mistress is master." (N. Tr.)

ROSENBACH, ABRAHAM SIMON WOLF (1876–1952), U.S. book and manuscript collector and dealer, who combined solid scholarship and exceptional business acumen, was born in Philadelphia, Pa., on July 22, 1876. He attended the University of Pennsylvania (B.S. 1898; Ph.D. 1901) where as a freshman he bought for $3.60 a first edition of Dr. Johnson's prologue at the reopening of Drury Lane Theatre in 1747 for which he later refused $5,000. From 1895 to 1901 he was a teaching fellow in the English department, and before 1903 he joined his brother Philip, a book dealer, in launching the Rosenbach Company. Upon the death in 1903 of their uncle, Moses Polock, whose bookshop Rosenbach had haunted since his childhood, the brothers acquired a substantial collection of his books and were soon in a position to buy entire libraries, expanding their business into what may well have been the most lucrative book concern in the world. Among his clients were Henry E. Huntington, founder of the library bearing his name at San Marino, Calif., and J. Pierpont Morgan, founder of the library bearing his name in New York City. In

1947, Rosenbach bought a copy of *The Bay Psalm Book* for $151,-000, then a record price. A shrewd bibliophile, Rosenbach came to be the most formidable bidder of his time at auctions in the U.S. and Europe. The total of his purchases was estimated as exceeding $75,000,000. In addition to a wealth of English literature and Americana, Rosenbach acquired a magnificent collection of children's books that he later presented to the Philadelphia Free Library; he bought 8 Gutenberg Bibles and more than 30 Shakespeare first folios. He published a great many bibliographical and literary articles; his checklist *Early American Children's Books* (1933) is a standard reference. In 1930 he established the Rosenbach Fellowship in Bibliography at the University of Pennsylvania, and upon his death in Philadelphia on July 1, 1952, willed his estate to the Rosenbach Foundation, established in 1950 to foster interest in books, paintings, and *objets d'art.*

His other works include *Books and Bidders* (1927), *The Unpublished Memoirs* (1917) and *A Book Hunter's Holiday* (1936).

See E. Wolf and J. F. Fleming, *Rosenbach* (1960).

ROSENBERG, ALFRED (1893–1946), the ideologist of German National Socialism, was born on Jan. 12, 1893, in Reval (Tallinn) in Estonia (then part of Russia), the son of a German shoemaker. He went to Moscow to train as an architect, but left after the Revolution. In 1919 he went to Munich, taking with him the *Protocols of the Learned Elders of Zion,* a spurious 19th-century work claiming to expound a Jewish conspiracy to achieve world domination. In Munich he joined Hitler, Ernst Röhm, and Rudolf Hess in the nascent Nazi Party. In 1921 he became editor of the party newspaper *Völkischer Beobachter.* He propounded anti-Semitic and anti-Bolshevik views, drawing on the *Protocols* for his inspiration. He also expounded the ideas of H. S. Chamberlain (*q.v.*). In November 1923 he participated with Hitler in the Munich *Putsch.* When Hitler was imprisoned he placed the leadership of the party in Rosenberg's hands, knowing him to be weak and incompetent as an organizer, and thus unlikely to establish a position of power.

In *Der Zukunftsweg einer deutschen Aussenpolitik* (1927) Rosenberg advocated a ruthless drive eastward; *i.e.,* the conquest of Poland and Russia. In *Der Mythus des 20. Jahrhunderts* he laboriously claimed to reveal the origins of a Nordic race, deriving its character from the pure, cold, semi-Arctic continent, now disappeared, which was its homeland. The Germans, as the representatives of this pure Nordic race, were entitled to dominate Europe. The enemies of the Nordic race were shown as "Russian Tatars" and "Semites," the latter being a racial force far wider than modern Jewry, embracing the Latin peoples, and including in its scope Christianity, particularly the Catholic Church.

Hitler probably never read the *Mythus* but his contact with Rosenberg had a great effect on him, providing a *Weltanschauung* which gave a confused order and direction to his own prejudices, hatreds, and ambitions. In 1931 he put Rosenberg in charge of the foreign policy office of the Nazi Party, but he was given no ministerial office when Hitler came to power, and had no impact on foreign affairs, which were governed by traditional German diplomacy and Nazi policy. Although Hitler made him in 1934 "spiritual supervisor" of the party, he was unable to hold his own against Josef Goebbels (*q.v.*) in the field of propaganda. At the beginning of World War II he enjoyed a brief moment of glory when he brought the Norwegian Fascist, Vidkun Quisling (*q.v.*), into contact with Adm. Erich Raeder and through him with Hitler; but Hitler relied on armed force rather than on Quisling's offer of a *coup d'état* for the subjugation of Norway. After the fall of France, Rosenberg was given charge of an *Einsatzstab* responsible for the acquisition and transport to Germany of any works of art which appeared valuable to him.

In March 1941 Hitler asked Rosenberg to prepare a plan for the German administration of European Russia. On April 25 Rosenberg submitted a scheme proposing the partition of the European area of the U.S.S.R. into four *Reichskommissariate:* Ostland (including the three Baltic states) and Belorussia, Ukraine, Moscow, and Caucasus. On July 17 a *Reichsministerium* for the occupied eastern territories was formed with Rosenberg as minister, but his authority was crushed by the powers given to Heinrich Himmler and Hermann Göring (*qq.v.*) who were placed in charge, respectively, of the security organization and the economic agencies. Against these formidable rivals he proved totally ineffective. His ineffectiveness did not, however, save him from arrest at the end of the war. He was brought to trial in Nürnberg, found guilty on all of four counts, and hanged on Oct. 16, 1946. His writings and speeches were collected under the title *Blut und Ehre,* four volumes (1934–41).

See A. Dallin, *German Rule in Russia, 1941–1945* (1957).

(W. Kp.)

ROSENBUSCH, KARL HEINRICH FERDINAND (Harry Rosenbusch) (1836–1914), German geologist who laid the foundations of the science of microscopic petrography, was born on June 24, 1836, at Einbeck, Hanover. He studied philosophy at Göttingen, and later science at Freiburg and Heidelberg, obtaining his doctorate at the former university with a dissertation on the nephelinite of the Katzenbuckel Mountain, north Baden, in 1868.

The study of the optical properties of minerals was in its infancy, and the researches of Rosenbusch were fundamental. These are enshrined in his monumental work *Mikroskopische Physiographie der Mineralien und Gesteine,* vol. i, *Die petrographisch wichtigen Mineralien* (1873) and its companion volume on the igneous rocks (1877), both classic contributions to mineralogy and petrography.

Rosenbusch was appointed professor (extraordinary) of petrography at Strassburg (Strasbourg) in 1873 and ordinary professor of mineralogy at Heidelberg in 1878, retiring in 1908. From 1888 to 1907 he also acted as director of the geological survey of Baden. At Heidelberg his laboratory became the resort of students from many countries, attracted no less by his personal qualities than by his genius and encyclopaedic knowledge. Rosenbusch died in Heidelberg on Jan. 20, 1914.

(C. E. T.)

ROSENHEIM, a town of West Germany in the *Land* (state) of Bavaria (Bayern), Federal Republic of Germany. It lies 1,470 ft. (448 m.) above sea level at the confluence of the Mangfall and Inn rivers, 40 mi. (65 km.) SE of Munich by the main railway line to Salzburg, Aus., and 4 km. N of the Munich–Salzburg *Autobahn.* Pop. (1961) 31,611. It was an important trading town on the route from Italy to northern Europe since medieval times, and the Italian architectural influence is reflected in the town's many flat-roofed buildings. There is a technical school for the locally important timber industry. Other industries include a saltworks and the manufacture of folding canoes, tents, and other sports equipment. Rosenheim is a *Kreisstadt* (district town) and the seat of an *Amtsgericht* (district court).

ROSENWALD, JULIUS (1862–1932), U.S. merchant and philanthropist, who exercised a creative influence on philanthropy throughout the world. Opposed to perpetual endowments, Rosenwald inspired others by the example of his own gifts and frequently made his offers of donations in such form that they had to be matched by other gifts before they were received.

Born in Springfield, Ill., on Aug. 12, 1862, Rosenwald entered the clothing business in New York at the age of 16. In 1885, together with his brother Morris and his cousin Julius Weil, he established the clothing firm of Rosenwald & Weil in Chicago. In 1897 he became vice-president of Sears, Roebuck & Company, which grew to be the world's largest mail-order house and chain of retail stores. In 1910 he succeeded Richard W. Sears as President, a position he held until 1925, when he became chairman of the board. Rosenwald, with A. H. Loeb, treasurer of the company, was instrumental in establishing an outstanding employees' savings and profit-sharing pension fund (*see* Profit Sharing). In December 1921 he pledged from his personal fortune the sum of $21,000,000 to safeguard the interests of the company during the critical period of business readjustment after World War I.

Having amassed a large personal fortune, Rosenwald engaged in large-scale charitable and philanthropic activities. He was active in Jewish charities in Chicago and during the war donated $1,000,000 to the Jewish War Relief Fund. After the war he pledged $6,000,000 to the Joint Distribution Committee to settle the Jews of Russia in agricultural colonies. He also contributed $100,000 in 1920 for the relief of German children.

In the early 1900s Rosenwald became actively interested in the welfare of the Negro, and in 1917 he established the Julius Rosenwald Fund (with the provision that the fund be expended within 25 years of his death) to better the condition of Negroes through education. The fund, along with local tax funds and private gifts, contributed to the construction of more than 5,000 schools for Negroes in 15 Southern states. Rosenwald contributed large sums to the YMCA in an endeavour to erect buildings for Negroes in 21 cities of the U.S. He also served as a trustee of Tuskegee Institute, a normal school for Negroes.

Rosenwald donated more than $4,000,000 to the University of Chicago and gave approximately $6,600,000 to establish the Museum of Science and Industry in Chicago. He also founded dental infirmaries in the Chicago public schools. Rosenwald's gifts during his lifetime exceeded $22,000,000, exclusive of the Rosenwald Fund, which had assets worth $40,000,000 in 1928.

Rosenwald was deeply interested in the improvement of municipal and national government and was an active participant in the civic affairs of Chicago, for many years serving as chairman of the Bureau of Public Efficiency. He died in Chicago on Jan. 6, 1932.

(M. R. W.; X.)

ROSENZWEIG, FRANZ (1886–1929), German-Jewish religious philosopher, whose life and writings made a deep impression on German Jewry between World Wars I and II. Lasting contributions to the study of German philosophy are his *Das älteste Systemprogramm des deutschen Idealismus* (1917) and *Hegel und der Staat,* two volumes (1920).

Born at Kassel on Dec. 25, 1886, the son of an assimilated Jewish family, he first studied medicine, then turned to history and philosophy, and later to jurisprudence. After contemplating conversion to Christianity, he decided, in 1913, to remain a Jew and to devote his life to the study and reinterpretation of Judaism. On active service in the German Army during World War I, he conducted a correspondence on Jewish and Christian theology with Eugen Rosenstock (published in *Briefe,* edited by Edith Rosenzweig, 1935) and started to write his magnum opus, *Der Stern der Erlösung* (1921; 3rd ed. 1954; "The Star of Redemption"). Although steeped in idealist thought, especially that of Schelling, he broke with its fundamentally monistic outlook and replaced it by an existential philosophy of the relationship between God, man, and the world. In 1919 he opened in Frankfurt am Main a Jewish Lehrhaus (Adult Study Centre), which was on a high academic level and inspired by a sense of religious commitment. It became the model of similar institutes throughout Germany. Afflicted in 1921 by a progressive paralysis which by 1923 had robbed him of all ability to speak, write, or move, he nevertheless managed, with the help of his wife and by using a specially fitted typewriter, to produce several important essays (collected in *Kleinere Schriften,* 1937), an annotated version of 92 poems of Judah Halevi (1927), and, with Martin Buber, a new German translation of part of the Bible (1925–38), all of which reveal his intellectual clarity and the depth of his religious insight. He died at Frankfurt on Dec. 9, 1929.

See N. N. Glatzer, *F. Rosenzweig: His Life and Thought* (1953; 2nd rev. ed. 1962), which contains a selected bibliography on pp. 377–382.

(A. An.)

ROSES, WARS OF THE, was the name given many years afterward to a series of dynastic civil wars in England, which occurred between 1455 and 1487. The name derives from the white and red roses which were respectively the badges (*i.e.,* emblems given by great lords to distinguish their retainers) of the house of York and (after 1485) of the house of Lancaster (*qq.v.*), between whom the wars were fought. The main contenders were the Lancastrian king Henry VI (d. 1471), whose cause was forcefully prosecuted by his wife Queen Margaret; Henry's first opponent Richard, duke of York (d. 1460), who, descended from Lionel of Antwerp, the third (but second surviving) son of Edward III, had a better hereditary claim to the throne (though passing twice through a woman) than Henry VI himself; York's son Edward, whose success brought him to the throne as King Edward IV (d. 1483); Edward's brother Richard III (d. 1485); and Henry

Tudor, earl of Richmond (later Henry VII), who, descended from the Beauforts, the illegitimate issue of John of Gaunt, ancestor of the Lancastrian line, claimed to be the heir of the house of Lancaster. But what made the war possible and gave it its distinctive character was the power and rivalry of the great lords, most notable among whom was Richard Neville, earl of Warwick (d. 1471), called since the 16th century "the Kingmaker."

Thus the title of the wars, although not contemporary and in a way inappropriate (since the red rose appeared only after their end in the reign of Henry VII, who created the badge in contrast to the white rose of York), is, in a deeper sense, peculiarly apt, because the rose, as one of the badges given by magnates to their retainers, symbolizes the ascendancy of the great lords of the period. The crown itself (held sometimes by the house of Lancaster and sometimes by the house of York), although surrounded, particularly at the beginning of the conflict, with an aura of divinity, appeared with regard to the resources at its disposal as little more powerful than individual magnates. Apart from the not very efficient militia, it possessed an "affinity" (i.e., a vast throng of indentured adherents, comprising not only soldiers and retainers but also lawyers, clerks, knights, and other clients) of the same kind as that of the magnates who, moreover, held strongholds not markedly inferior to those of the crown. As it happened, however, strongholds played little part in the wars, except for the sieges of Northumberland castles in 1462 and 1464. England, which in the 14th century had been in the forefront of military development, was now lagging behind. Cannon rarely appeared, and the small arms used for the first time in English history at the second Battle of St. Albans (1461) proved ineffective. The weapons of the war were, in the main, the traditional bows, lances, swords, and daggers.

Although it was the power of the magnates that made the civil wars possible, the Yorkists might never have come to challenge Lancastrian supremacy but for the course of political events. Mystical reverence for an anointed king was so considerable that it took the combined effects, in Henry VI's reign, of a long and factious minority followed by the rule of a kindly but weak king, and the startling disasters in France, to shake the authority of the Lancastrian house (see ENGLISH HISTORY: *VII. Lancaster and York*; HENRY VI). Even when the war began, reverence for the king delayed a Yorkist claim to the crown for five years. This development of the war into a dynastic struggle was then greatly facilitated by the peculiar conjunction in the person of Richard, duke of York, of lordship of vast estates, kinship with an extremely powerful group of nobles, the Nevilles, and a strong hereditary claim to the throne.

The first battle of the Wars of the Roses took place at St. Albans in 1455, because York had become convinced that Queen Margaret and the chief minister, Edmund Beaufort, duke of Somerset, were scheming to destroy him. As in many of the battles of the war, the site was determined by the desire to capture or defend London. The encounter ended in less than an hour with the death of Somerset and the capture of the king. This ensured for a while the ascendancy of the Yorkists; but neither side trusted the other and each maneuvered to gather overwhelming forces. The war broke out again in 1459, when the Lancastrians tried at Blore Heath in Staffordshire to stop Richard Neville, earl of Salisbury, from bringing reinforcements from Yorkshire to join York's forces at Ludlow. The Yorkists won a hard-fought battle (Sept. 23, 1459) and marched on to Ludlow. Thither Henry VI himself soon came; and such was still the reluctance to fight against the king that after a skirmish at Ludford Bridge (Oct. 12) the Yorkist forces melted away and the leaders fled, York to Ireland, and his eldest son Edward, with his uncle Salisbury and his cousin the earl of Warwick, to Calais, of which Warwick was captain. Warwick with his fleet commanded the Channel; and, having the initiative, he landed with Salisbury and Edward at Sandwich on June 26, 1460, and advanced to Northampton to meet Henry VI and his army. There the Yorkists won a complete victory in half an hour and the king was captured (July 10, 1460). York now returned from Ireland and claimed the throne; and a compromise was made by which Henry was to remain king, but Richard was to succeed him. This meant the disinheritance of Henry's son, Prince Edward, and as Queen Margaret lived for him, she stirred up opposition in the country to the uttermost. York therefore had to go to Yorkshire to deal with Lancastrian defiance there; and just outside his castle near Wakefield he was surprised and killed (Dec. 30, 1460).

Lancastrian vindictiveness after the battle steeled the hearts of the surviving Yorkists. On Feb. 2, 1461, York's heir Edward defeated a Lancastrian concentration at Mortimer's Cross. Then, with the speed which helped to make him the best general of the war, he marched to London. He was just in time. After the Lancastrian success at Wakefield, Margaret had gathered a large force and advanced down the Great North Road to capture London; after crossing the River Trent she allowed unlimited pillage. Warwick advanced from London to oppose her at St. Albans; there, on Feb. 17, 1461, he was defeated and the way to London lay open. But while Margaret hesitated and parleyed with the Londoners, young Edward arrived (Feb. 26). The cruelties of Wakefield, the misdeeds of Margaret's army, and her alliances with the national enemies, the Scots and French, removed the last hesitations of the Yorkists and the Londoners, and Edward was hailed as king in Westminster Hall on March 4. Margaret and Henry retreated hastily to the north. Edward and Warwick sped after them and caught up with them at Towton, near Tadcaster in Yorkshire. There, in the bloodiest battle of the war, the Lancastrians suffered a crushing defeat (March 29, 1461). Henry, Margaret, and their son had to flee to Scotland. Margaret tried to organize resistance in Northumberland; but the last opposition of the Lancastrians was, for the time being, ended with the defeat of the Lancastrian armies at Hedgeley Moor and Hexham (April 25 and May 15, 1464), the surrender of the castles of Alnwick, Dunstanburgh, and Bamburgh (June–July 1464), and the capture of Henry VI (July 1465).

The revival of the war was occasioned by the growing rift between Edward IV (q.v.) and Warwick after the king's marriage (1464). After risings in the north in the summer of 1469 the forces of Warwick and Edward's rebellious brother George, duke of Clarence, defeated those of the king at Edgecote in Northamptonshire (July 25–26). The king was then captured at Olney near Kenilworth, but the reverence for the king's person which had formerly helped Henry VI now came to the rescue of Edward IV and in less than three months he had to be released. In March 1470 he received certain proof that Warwick and Clarence had stirred up a revolt in Lincolnshire; and after defeating the rebels at Losecoat Field near Stamford (March 12, 1470), he summoned Warwick and Clarence to account. They fled to France, where in their plight they accepted aid from Louis XI on his terms—reconciliation with their bitter foe, Queen Margaret. With French aid Warwick and Clarence landed in Devon on Sept. 13, 1470. Edward IV, ever too trustful in his youth, was nearly surprised by Warwick's brother, John Neville, marquess of Montagu, in whom he had always confided. He had to flee to Holland with his brother Richard, earl of Gloucester (afterward Richard III), and a few other faithful supporters; but in March 1471 he returned with Burgundian help. By his personal charm, soothing lies, and speed, he gathered forces, outmaneuvered Warwick, and gained possession of London (April 11). To defend the capital he met Warwick's forces at Barnet, where he won a complete victory (April 14, 1471); Warwick and Montagu were slain on the field. That very day Margaret and her son landed at Weymouth. On hearing the news of Barnet she wished to return to France, but her friends persuaded her that this might be her last chance, and that in Wales they might find both safety and support. It therefore became a race as to whether she or Edward could reach the Severn first; and with the advantages of interior lines and a talent for speed Edward caught up with the Lancastrians at Tewkesbury. There Margaret's force was destroyed (May 4, 1471), her son was killed, and she was captured. In the same month a Lancastrian attack on London was warded off and Henry VI was murdered; thereafter Edward IV was safe for the rest of his life.

Richard III's usurpation of the throne (1483) gave the Lancastrians an unexpected opportunity; for after the failure of the duke of Buckingham's rebellion in October 1483, discontented Yorkists turned to the last hope of the Lancastrians, Henry Tudor. As Richard had tried to maintain English claims against France, Henry received help from the French; and with both French and English troops, about 2,000 strong, he landed in Milford Haven, probably at Mill Bay, in August 1485. Marching toward London by a roundabout route, through Shrewsbury and Lichfield, and gathering reinforcements as he went, he was met by Richard at Bosworth in Leicestershire. Richard had the larger forces, but he was fatally weakened by the treachery of the earl of Northumberland and of Lord Stanley and his brother Sir William Stanley. Fighting manfully, he was slain and his crown was picked up and offered to Henry of Richmond (Aug. 22). In 1487 an army equipped by Edward IV's sister Margaret of Burgundy and headed by Richard's nephew and heir, John de la Pole, earl of Lincoln, and by Viscount Lovell, invaded England in support of the pretender Lambert Simnel. They advanced to Stoke in Nottinghamshire before they were met by Henry's forces; the subsequent battle (June 16) bore, in its manifestations of timidity and disloyalty in the royalist ranks, much resemblance to the Battle of Bosworth. The royalist forces were, however, victorious; and although Henry was not secure from Yorkist plots for more than a decade, this turned out to be the last battle of the war.

The war resulted in a big increase in the power of the crown. The ranks of the nobility whose power had become such a menace to the crown were thinned by battle, executions, and attainders. The monarchy's crippling lack of resources was largely remedied by the acquisition of the vast estates of the houses of York and Neville, and by the confiscations and resumptions of lands, in spite of exemptions and restitutions of property to pardoned opponents. And in the coming century the vivid memory of the brutalities, disorders, and impoverishment of the civil war was to be a potent aid to the monarchy; for men would now submit to strong government, and even arbitrary oppression at times, rather than court by rebellion a revival of the Wars of the Roses. *See* also references under "Roses, Wars of The" in the Index.

BIBLIOGRAPHY.—J. H. Ramsay, *Lancaster and York,* vol. ii (1892); A. H. Burne, *The Battlefields of England,* 2nd ed. (1951), *More Battlefields of England* (1952); C. W. C. Oman, *The Art of War in the Middle Ages,* rev. ed. (1953); J. Fortescue, *The Governance of England,* ed. by C. Plummer (1885); K. B. McFarlane, "Bastard Feudalism," *Bulletin of the Institute of Historical Research,* vol. xx, for 1945 (1947); C. A. J. Armstrong, "Politics and the Battle of St. Albans, 1455," *Bulletin of the Institute of Historical Research,* vol. xxxiii (1960); E. F. Jacob, *The Fifteenth Century, 1399–1485* (1961); S. B. Chrimes, "The Landing Place of Henry of Richmond, 1485," *The Welsh History Review,* vol. ii (1964). (A. R. M.)

ROSETTA STONE, an ancient Egyptian stone bearing inscriptions, the deciphering of which led to the understanding of hieroglyphics. It is an irregularly shaped stone of black basalt, 3 ft. 9 in. (114 cm.) long and 2 ft. 4½ in. (71 cm.) wide, broken in antiquity, which is now in the British Museum, London. It was found near the town of Rosetta, or Rashid, on the left bank of a branch of the Nile in the western delta, about 30 mi. (48 km.) from Alexandria.

The modern town was founded by the Arab conquerors of Egypt in the 9th century A.D., when Alexandria was suffering a commercial eclipse, but after the discovery of the sea route to India, Rosetta gradually declined in importance. The inhabitants of Rosetta include many Greeks as well as Egyptians. Pop. (1960s) about 25,000.

The Rosetta stone was found in August 1799 by a Frenchman, whose name is given variously as Bouchard or Boussard, during the execution of repairs to the fort of St. Julien, and passed into British hands with the French surrender of Egypt (1801). The inscription records the commemoration of the accession of Ptolemy V Epiphanes to the throne of Egypt in the year 197–196 B.C., in the ninth year of his reign. The decree summarizes the benefactions conferred by Ptolemy upon the priesthood and appears to have been written by the priests of Memphis after a general assembly of religious leaders. The inscription is in two languages and three scripts (hieroglyphics, demotic, and Greek) and gave the key to the translation of Egyptian hieroglyphics hitherto undeciphered.

The decipherment of the hieroglyphic inscription was largely

THE ROSETTA STONE WITH HIEROGLYPHICS IN THE TOP SECTION, DEMOTIC CHARACTERS NEXT, AND GREEK AT THE BOTTOM

the work of Thomas Young and Jean François Champollion (*qq.v.*). Young discovered that the royal names were written within ovals known as cartouches, and he worked out that foreign names, those of Ptolemy and Cleopatra, would probably be written in phonetic values which could be compared to the original group. Out of the total of 13 signs in this name he attributed the correct value to six and partially right value to three. He also discovered in 1814 the way in which the hieroglyphic signs were to be read, by examining the direction in which the birds and animals in this pictorial script faced. His main contribution to Egyptian philology was published in the *Encyclopædia Britannica* of 1824.

In 1821–22 Champollion, starting where Young had left off, published memoirs on the decipherment of hieratic and hieroglyphic and went on to establish a whole list of signs with their Greek equivalents. He was the first Egyptologist to realize that some of the signs were alphabetic, some syllabic, and some determinatives, standing for the whole idea or object previously expressed. He also established that the hieroglyphic text was the translation of the Greek, not the reverse as had been thought. The work of these two men established the basis for the translation of all future hieroglyphic texts. *See* also HIEROGLYPHS: *Decipherment.* (M. V. S.-W.)

ROSETTE, an ornament, usually circular, oval or polygonal, formed by a series of petals or leaves radiating from the centre and symmetrically placed. The form undoubtedly originated as an attempt to represent, systematically, the corolla of an open flower. Egyptian rosettes were thus, probably, representations of the open lotus. In Assyrian ornament and in the Persian work based upon it rosettes are one of the commonest ornaments and are used, by continuous repetition, to form decorative bands. Although common in archaic pottery of the Greek islands, they were little used in the developed art of Greece itself. The Romans, on the other hand, used the form lavishly and gave it great richness by employing the complex acanthus leaf as the basic radiating form. It was used not only at the centre of each face of the

Corinthian capital, but also to decorate the little panels between the modillions or the scrolled brackets of the Corinthian order and as a decoration for the centre of the coffers or sunk panels of a coffered vault or ceiling. The rosette almost went out of use in the medieval period except as it sometimes occurred as an individual flower in Gothic naturalistic ornament. In the Perpendicular period in England, the popularity of the heraldic Tudor rose gave a new importance to the rosette idea, and rosettes were frequently employed, repeated at regular intervals, to decorate hollow moldings.

Renaissance rosettes in design are based upon those of Rome, but were used even more lavishly, because of the immense development of wooden coffered and paneled ceilings.

In metalwork the idea of the rosette was probably developed independently, because of the ease with which little drops of metal could be soldered or fastened in a circle, to a basic utensil. Such rosettes, formed either of a simple circle of nearly hemispherical shape, or of one large hemisphere surrounded by several smaller ones, are favourite late Bronze and early Iron age decorations in the metalwork of the Celts, Scandinavians and the people of northern Europe generally. (T. F. H.)

ROSE WINDOW (Wheel Window), in architecture, is a term applied to any decorated circular window. Undecorated circular windows are found in certain imperial Roman structures, used especially in the upper portions of rooms or pierced through vaults, as in the tomb of the time of Hadrian known as the Casale dei Pazzi, near Rome, but structural decoration of such forms was apparently not attempted until the Byzantine and Romanesque periods.

One of the earliest decorated circular windows extant is that of the Italian Romanesque church of S. Maria in Pomposa, possibly as early as the 10th century, in which the decoration consists of a pierced marble slab of great richness, with a design of interlaces and birds purely Byzantine. In French Romanesque work circular windows also appear, but in the earlier work, such as the late 11th-century apse of S. Sernin at Toulouse, they are undecorated, like those of the Roman empire. Meanwhile, in Mohammedan work, the cusped circle had been a common form, usually, however, not as a window, but as the outer boundary of a sunk hemisphere, as in the mosque of Ibn Touloun at Cairo, Egy. (876–878).

The crusaders probably saw many examples of such forms; in any case it is only after the earlier crusades and especially toward the middle of the 12th century that the idea of making a rich decorative motive out of a round window appeared. From then on the simple rose window became more and more common, and was, in fact, a distinguishing characteristic of many transitional and early Gothic cathedrals. It was particularly used at the west end of the nave and the ends of the transepts. An exceptional early use is the round window which lighted the triforium roof space from the nave in the original form of Notre Dame at Paris (before 1177). In the west front of Laon cathedral (completed prior to 1200) there is an enormous rose window with 12 semicircles around the edge and the central foiled and cusped circle separated from the apexes of these semicircles by a considerable distance, the connection between being made by little radiating colonnettes like spokes. This window is remarkably advanced for its date, as the filling, like that of the Paris triforium, is essentially bar tracery. The rose window of the west front of Chartres cathedral (1194–1212) consists, on the other hand, of plate tracery, the circle being filled with a thin plate of stone, through which are pierced many small foiled or cusped holes.

A similar form of plate tracery within a circle is used to cap the twin windows of the clerestory bays.

The introduction of developed bar tracery gave a compelling impetus to rose window design. The general scheme consisted of a series of radiating forms, each of which was tipped by a pointed arch at the outside of the circle. The bars between these forms were joined at the centre by a pierced circle of stone and the forms themselves frequently treated like little traceried windows with subsidiary, subdividing bars, archs and foiled circles. The most beautiful examples of this type are those of the west front of Reims cathedral (end of the 13th century) and the transepts of

The rose window (1350), 30 ft. in diameter, above the west portal of St. Lorenzkirche, Nürnberg, Germany

Reims, Amiens and Notre Dame at Paris (all of the last half of the 13th century). The introduction of the wavy lines of Flamboyant tracery completely changed the character of French rose windows, but they continued basically radiating in design. The radiating elements consisted of an intricate network of wavy, double curved bars, creating all sorts of interesting circles and flame shapes and, incidentally, furnishing a diagonal bracing to the whole composition which added materially to its structural strength. The rose at the end of the transept at Beauvais (early 16th century) is characteristic.

The influence of the French rose windows was widespread from an early period. Variations of the form appear in a multitude of late Italian Romanesque churches, as in the widely varying type in the late 12th century west front of S. Pietro in Toscanella, and the more normal example in S. Zeno at Verona (late 12th century). In England the rose window has never been so popular as in France. Those in the transepts of Westminster abbey are more characteristically French than English. The most typically English examples are in the transepts of Lincoln cathedral; that on the north from the Early English period is a remarkably delicate example of plate tracery; that on the south from the Curvilinear period of the early 14th century is striking because it is not radiating in design, and therefore completely at odds with the French prototypes.

See also Tracery. (T. F. H.)

ROSEWOOD, the name given to several distinct kinds of ornamental timber, products of various tropical trees native to Brazil, Honduras, Jamaica, Africa and India. The most important commercially are the Brazilian rosewood, principally *Dalbergia nigra*, a leguminous tree of large dimensions, called *cabiúna* and jacaranda by the Brazilians—and the Honduras rosewood, *D. stevensoni.* The term jacaranda is also applied to several species of *Machaerium*, also trees of the family Leguminosae; some of the rosewood of commerce is drawn from these sources.

Rosewood earlier was exported in large quantities from Rio de Janeiro, Bahia, Jamaica and Honduras. The heartwood attains large dimensions, but as it begins to decay before the tree arrives at maturity it is always faulty and hollow in the centre; therefore, squared logs or planks of rosewood are never seen, the wood being imported in half-round flitches 10 to 20 ft. in length and from 5 to 12 in. in their thickest part. Rosewood, a deep ruddy-brown to purplish-brown in colour, richly streaked and grained with black resinous layers, takes a fine polish, but because of its resinous nature is somewhat difficult to work. The wood, once much in demand by cabinetmakers and piano makers, is still used to fashion xylophone bars, but waning supplies now restrict its use in the U.S. to the making of carpenters' spirit levels, plane handles and brush backs. (N. Tr.)

ROSH HA-SHANA: see Jewish Holidays.

ROSICRUCIANISM. There are Rosicrucian societies, fraternities, orders, fellowships or lodges in most countries of the modern world. Some of them are very active; others are obscure and highly secret; some seem to be primarily religious in their emphasis, and some categorically deny that Rosicrucianism is a religion, holding rather that it is a philosophy, making use of the most modern scientific methods and techniques, as well as the methods of the occultist, the mystic and the seer, in the quest for truth.

But, while Rosicrucianism is sectarian in character and the various branches are sometimes bitterly critical of each other, they do have common features, the central one being the purported possession of certain secret wisdom handed down from ancient times, through a secret brotherhood, an esoteric wisdom that can only be imparted to the initiated.

Their teachings so far as known seem to combine something of Egyptian Hermetism, Christian Gnosticism, Jewish cabalism, alchemy and a variety of other occult beliefs and practices. While alchemy seems to have been prominent in the movement, modern Rosicrucians affirm that their language must be taken symbolically rather than literally and that they have no interest in such things as the transmutation of metals.

Whether all Rosicrucian organizations can trace their origins back to the main historic stream of Rosicrucianism is a matter of grave doubt. But after all, what is the true Rosicrucianism?

The earliest extant writing which unequivocally mentions a Rosicrucian order appeared in the early 17th century. But even here the actual existence of such an order cannot be affirmed absolutely. Indeed, not a few scholars believe rather that the order had its rise from the publication of this document and that it was written with this definite purpose in mind.

The document was the famous *Fama Fraternitatis*, first published in 1614 but probably circulated in manuscript form somewhat earlier than this. Seven editions appeared during the years 1614–17. It recounts the journey of the reputed founder of the movement, Christian Rosenkreuz, to Damascus, Damcar in Arabia, Egypt and Fès, where he was well received and came into possession of much secret wisdom. He returned finally to Germany, where he chose three others to whom he imparted this wisdom and thus founded the order. Later the number was increased to eight who separated, each going to a separate country.

One of the six articles of agreement they adopted was that the fraternity should remain secret for 100 years. At the end of 120 years the secret burial place and the perfectly preserved body of the founder were discovered by one of the then members of the order, along with certain documents and symbols held in very high esteem by Rosicrucians. The sacred vault was re-covered, the members of the order dispersed, and no one knows its location. The *Fama* ends with an invitation to "some few" to join the fraternity.

According to the *Confessio,* which is bound up with the *Fama* in some of the editions, Christian Rosenkreuz was born in 1378 and lived 106 years, or until 1484. His tomb was then hidden for 120 years, making its discovery fall in 1604. If this is a true account of the founding of the order, it must have come into being sometime in the 15th century.

Some regard the story as a statement of fact and hold Christian Rosenkreuz to have been the founder of the order. More generally it is held to be a mythical explanation of the order and Christian Rosenkreuz not a real person at all, but a symbolic character. R. Swinburne Clymer saw in the travels of Christian Rosenkreuz in the *Fama* an obvious parallel to the travels of Paracelsus, whom he regarded as the real founder of the movement.

H. Spencer Lewis held that it marks only a revival of the order which began in remote antiquity in Egypt, where the great Ikhnaton made significant contributions to it. He listed numerous persons of antiquity, including Solomon, Jesus, Plato, Philo, Plotinus and others, as well as movements such as the Essenes of Jesus' day, the young Christian movement itself and later movements such as Jewish cabalism, as related to the ancient order. These he identified as truly Rosicrucian because he was able to find among their reported teachings ideas which he regarded as Rosicrucian. His conclusions do not seem convincing to objective students. There can be no doubt that there were in ancient times persons whose outlook and thought were similar to that of the Rosicrucians. That there was a continuing order in existence previous to the 15th century or even the 17th is impossible to prove beyond question, on the basis of any sources available to non-Rosicrucian research.

With the publication of the *Fama,* international interest in the order was aroused and it was not long before there were Rosicrucian orders in several European countries. Michael Maier, a learned alchemist, became its chief exponent in Germany. Robert Fludd is thought to have introduced it into England. Thomas Vaughan translated the *Fama* into English in 1652, and though he knew of no existing order in England at that time he remarked that he was not unacquainted with Rosicrucian doctrine and had no doubt concerning the existence of the order.

That it is not always possible to prove the existence of the order in a given country at any particular moment does not disturb the Rosicrucians, for it seems to be recognized that there occur periods when the order is deliberately "in sleep." H. Spencer Lewis reduced these periods to a definite rhythm of 108 years of activity followed by 108 years of silence, in a given country. It was in accordance with this cyclic theory, he said, that he was led at the proper time to seek out the leaders of the order in France in the early years of the 20th century and under their authority to inaugurate a new cycle of activity in the United States in 1915, under the name Ancient Mystical Order Rosae Crucis, usually abbreviated to A.M.O.R.C. It became affiliated with the Fédération Universelle des Ordres et Sociétés Initiatiques, established in Europe in 1934.

R. Swinburne Clymer, head of a rival U.S. order with headquarters at Quakertown, Pa., who as early as 1902 published *The Rosicrucians: Their Teachings,* spoke of the periods of silence, but these were determined by specific conditions rather than by the passage of time. His organization, traced through a definite line of Rosicrucian adepts in the U.S. from revolutionary times, with Paschal Beverly Randolph and Freeman B. Dowd as his more immediate predecessors, is known as the Fraternitas Rosae Crucis. Its foreign affiliation was with La Fédération Universelle des Ordres, Sociétés et Fraternités des Initiés.

Rosicrucianism and Freemasonry have not a little in common. Indeed, there is a degree in masonry known as the Rose Croix degree. Likewise, the *Societas Rosicruciana in Anglia* and its affiliates are held to be more masonic than Rosicrucian.

The symbol of Rosicrucianism is a combination of the cross and the rose, from which the order takes its name. The origin of the symbol is variously given, but there seems to be no one explanation which is completely satisfactory.

Bibliography.—Eugenius Philalethes (Thomas Vaughan) (tr.), *The Fame and Confession of the Fraternity of R: C: . . . ,* originally printed in London in 1652 (1923); A. E. Waite, *Real History of the Rosicrucians* (1887); A. E. Waite, *The Brotherhood of the Rosy Cross* (1924); Hargrave Jennings, *The Rosicrucians, Their Rites and Mysteries* (1887); J. F. Sachse, *The German Pietists of Pennsylvania;* Will Erich Peuckert, *Die Rosenkreuzer; Zur Geschichte einer Reformation* (1928); H. Spencer Lewis, *Rosicrucian Questions and Answers With Complete History of the Rosicrucian Order,* 3rd ed. (1941); R. Swinburne Clymer, *The Book of Rosicruciae,* 3 vol. (1946–48).

(C. S. B.)

ROSIN (Colophony), the resinous constituent of the oleoresin exuded by various species of pine, known in commerce as crude turpentine. The separation of the oleoresin into the essential oil spirit of turpentine and common rosin is effected by distillation in large stills. Rosin (a later variant of "resin," *q.v.*), varies in colour, according to the age of the tree from which the turpentine is drawn and the amount of heat applied in distillation, from an opaque almost pitchy black substance through grades of brown and yellow to an almost perfectly transparent colourless glassy mass. The commercial grades are numerous, ranging by letters from A, the darkest, to N, extra pale, and X, most pale, W (window glass) and WW (water white) varieties, the latter having about three times the value of the common qualities.

Rosin is a brittle and friable resin, with a faint pinelike odour; the melting point varies with different specimens, some being semifluid at the temperature of boiling water, while others do not melt till 220° F. or 250° F. It is soluble in alcohol, ether, benzene and chloroform. In addition to its extensive use in soapmaking, rosin is largely employed in making inferior varnishes, sealing wax, various cements and as a sizing agent in the manufacture of paper. It is also used for preparing shoemakers' wax, as a flux for soldering metals, for pitching lager beer casks, for rosining the bows of musical instruments, etc. In pharmacy it forms an ingredient in several plasters and ointments.

The chief region of rosin production is the south Atlantic and eastern gulf states of the United States. American rosin is obtained from the turpentine of the swamp pine, *Pinus palustris*, and of the loblolly pine, *P. taeda*. The main source of supply in Europe is the "landes" of the *départements* of Gironde and Landes in France, where the cluster pine, *P. pinaster*, is extensively cultivated.

In the north of Europe rosin is obtained from the Scotch fir, *P. sylvestris*, and throughout European countries local supplies are obtained from other species of pine.

See also TURPENTINE.

ROSKILDE, a town of Denmark on the island of Sjælland (Zealand), in the *amt* of København (county of Copenhagen). It lies at the head of the Roskilde Fjord, 30 km. (19 mi.) W of Copenhagen by road and rail. Pop. (1960) 31,928. Throughout the Middle Ages it was Denmark's most important episcopal seat, and often a royal residence. The town is dominated by its partly Romanesque, partly Gothic cathedral of red brick with verdigris-green copper roof and slender spires. Built on the site of three earlier churches (the first founded c. 960 in Viking times by Harald Blaatand or Bluetooth, first Christian king of Denmark), it was begun c. 1170 under the direction of Archbishop Absalon (*q.v.*). It is the royal mausoleum, in which lie buried 37 kings and queens of Denmark, including 15 in unbroken succession from the Reformation to the mid-20th century. Roskilde is the largest railway junction and traffic centre on Sjælland. Proximity to Copenhagen has encouraged suburban development. There are tanneries, distilleries, and bacon factories, as well as a meat research institute. On Risö Island (6 km. N) is the Danish atomic research station. (A. Fg.)

ROSMEAD, HERCULES GEORGE ROBERT ROBINSON, 1ST BARON (1824–1897), British colonial governor, high commissioner in South Africa, 1880–89 and 1895–97, was born on Dec. 19, 1824, the son of Adm. Hercules Robinson. After a brief army career he occupied certain civil service posts connected with the administration of Ireland, being especially concerned with relief measures during the famine of 1848. Robinson's first colonial appointment was as president of Montserrat in the West Indies in 1854. In the following year he was promoted to be lieutenant governor of St. Kitts, where he introduced and organized the immigration of coolie labour from India. He was knighted in 1859, and, after administering Hong Kong between 1859 and 1865, was appointed governor of Ceylon. There he was called upon to handle a serious financial and constitutional crisis and his vigorous promotion of public works, more especially road building and irrigation projects, did much to placate the colonial inhabitants. In 1872 he was made governor of the self-governing colony of New South Wales and was employed from 1874 to 1875 on special service in connection with the cession of the Fiji Islands to Great Britain.

After a brief term as governor of New Zealand (1879–80), he went to South Africa in January 1881 as governor of the Cape Colony and as high commissioner in South Africa. His arrival coincided with the war between the Transvaal and Great Britain

(see TRANSVAAL: *History*). The Pretoria Convention of August 1881 did not remove the grievances of the Transvaal Boers, and when a Boer deputation went to England in 1883 to obtain a revision of the terms, Robinson was summoned to London for the deliberations which led to the London Convention of February 1884. Robinson was sympathetic to the fears of Cecil John Rhodes, who had entered Cape politics in 1881, that British expansion into Bechuanaland, the road to the north, might be blocked by cooperation between the Transvaal Boers and the Germans who had established a protectorate over South West Africa in 1884. Following the dispatch of an expeditionary force under Sir Charles Warren to Bechuanaland, Britain annexed the territory in 1885.

When Robinson discovered early in 1887 that the Transvaal Boers were attempting to gain special privileges from Lobengula, the chief of the Matabele, in his territory north of the Limpopo River (now Rhodesia), he sent the Rev. J. S. Moffat to Matabeleland as British resident. Though Robinson refused to commit the British government more definitely in this region, he gave his blessing to the Moffat treaty (February 1888), which gave Britain a virtual option on Matabeleland, and to the Rudd mineral concession, which became the basis of the operations of Rhodes's British South Africa Company chartered in 1889.

Robinson resigned in 1889 and left the Cape for England in May. His last public utterance on this occasion, in which he declared that there was "no permanent place in South Africa for direct imperial rule," reveals him as a much less fervent imperialist than his successor Sir Henry (later Baron) Loch. Robinson was called out of retirement by Lord Rosebery's government in May 1895 to resume his previous post in South Africa. To Rhodes, now prime minister of the Cape, a pliant Robinson, over 70 years old and in ill health, was far more acceptable than Loch had been. Interest in his second term of office centred in the fact that Robinson was high commissioner at the time of L. S. Jameson's raid (December 1895). Immediately he was informed of Jameson's rash invasion of the Transvaal, Robinson tried to check the raiders by telegraph. He subsequently declared that he had no foreknowledge of the plans for the raid, but modern historical research does not support this claim, and it was perhaps fortunate for him that medical opinion as to the state of his health prevented his subsequent examination on this question in England, where he went on leave in May 1896. He was raised to the peerage as Baron Rosmead in August. After returning to the Cape for a brief period, he finally left South Africa in April 1897 and died in London on Oct. 28, 1897. (L. M. Y.)

ROSMINI-SERBATI, ANTONIO (1797–1855), Italian priest and philosopher, the founder of the Institute of Charity, was born at Rovereto on March 24, 1797. He studied theology at the University of Padua and was ordained priest in 1821. Through his friendship with Niccolo Tommasseo and Alessandro Manzoni and a lifelong concern to reconcile his deep Catholic faith with modern political and scientific thought, Rosmini exerted a considerable influence on the Italian Risorgimento. His dissatisfaction with the spiritual and educational state of the church of his time led him, in 1828, to found the Institute of Charity at Monte Calvario, Domodossola, which was approved by Pope Gregory XVI in 1839. Modeled on the Jesuit rule, it aims at the perfection of its members through the exercise of charity in any form or field, combined with absolute devotion to the church and to one's superiors in the society.

Rosmini's *Nuovo saggio sull' origine delle idee* (Eng. trans., *New Essay on the Origin of Ideas*, 3 vol., 1883) and *Massime di perfezione* (Eng. trans., *Maxims of Christian Perfection*, 1889, 1949), which contain the essence of his philosophical and religious thought, were published in Rome in 1830; later works were *Teodicea* (1845; Eng. trans., *Theodicy*, 3 vol., 1912) and *Psicologia* (1850; Eng. trans., *Psychology*, 3 vol., 1884–88). The centre of his philosophical system, which he developed also in education and in law, is ideal being, which is not an idea like other ideas but a reflection of God in man, appertaining in eternal truth, the indispensable means of acquiring, through the senses, all other knowledge. Ideal being is the supreme criterion of truth and certainty in logic and the basis of the concept of the dignity of the human person in law and politics. The synthetic character of Rosmini's system of human knowledge has made its assimilation difficult and led, falsely, to charges of "ontologism" and "pantheism."

Rosmini welcomed the Italian national movement, but was strongly critical of its anticlerical and anti-Catholic tendencies. Looking to the papacy for spiritual and political leadership, he published, in 1848, *Delle cinque piaghe della santa Chiesa* (Eng. trans., *Of the Five Wounds of the Holy Church*, 1883) and *La Costituzione secondo la giustizia sociale.* Both works were placed on the Index in 1849. As the Piedmontese government's special envoy in 1848–49, Rosmini was commissioned to negotiate a concordat with Pope Pius IX (*see* his narrative *Della missione a Roma . . . negli anni 1848–49*, 1881); and when the Roman revolution broke out and Pius had to escape to Gaeta, Rosmini, whose counsels he wished to reward with the cardinal's hat, accompanied him into exile. But Rosmini's influence declined under the impact of the Austrian victories in Italy and the pope's rejection of liberal reforms. Compelled by polemics and attacks on Rosmini's doctrines, Pius ordered an examination of all his works. Rosmini at once declared his submission and retired to Stresa where he died, broken in health, on July 1, 1855.

Before his death Rosmini learned that his works had been proclaimed free from censure by the Congregation of the Index (decree *Dimittantur*, 1854); Leo XIII's decree *Post obitum* in 1887 declared 40 propositions from his books to be "not seemingly consonant with Catholic truth"; but this mild form of censure was later regarded as not having theological significance (*see* U. Honan, *Il Decreto Post Obitum*, Domodossola, 1949).

The Institute of Charity was established in England by Father Luigi Gentili in 1835 and contributed through its missionary activities to the Catholic revival there. By the middle of the 20th century there were Rosminian foundations in Europe, the British Isles, the U.S. and Africa.

BIBLIOGRAPHY.—*Edizione Nazionale* of Rosmini's works (1934–) was planned to comprise 100 vol. *See* also his *Letters chiefly on Religious Subjects*, Eng. trans. (1901); G. B. Pagani, *The Life of Antonio Rosmini-Serbati*, Eng. trans. (1907); C. R. Leetham, *Rosmini, Priest, Philosopher, Patriot* (1957); and the periodical *Rivista Rosminiana* (Domodossola). (R. J. H.)

ROSS, EDWARD ALSWORTH (1866–1951), U.S. sociologist and a prolific writer whose flair for popular presentation did much to stimulate interest in problems of social research, was born Dec. 12, 1866, in Virden, Ill. After studying at Coe College, Cedar Rapids, Ia., the University of Berlin, and Johns Hopkins.University, Baltimore, Md. (Ph.D., 1891), he taught economics for brief periods at Indiana, Cornell, and Stanford universities. At the last-named institution, beginning in 1895, he centred his attention on sociology. Resigning from Stanford in 1900 in a dispute concerning academic freedom, he spent a few years at the University of Nebraska, Lincoln, before joining the faculty of the University of Wisconsin, Madison, where he taught sociology for 30 years.

Ross died on July 22, 1951, in Madison.

He was an early major systematizer of sociology; one of his principal contributions lay in creating a comprehensive body of theory. His best-known work, *Social Control* (1901), was long regarded as a classic, and his *Social Psychology* (1908) was one of the first American works written specifically on that discipline.

Among his other works are *Foundations of Sociology* (1905); *Sin and Society* (1907); *Russia in Upheaval* (1918); *World Drift* (1928); *New-Age Sociology* (1940).

See also SOCIOLOGY: *19th-Century Influences.*

(P. B. G.)

ROSS, HAROLD WALLACE (1892–1951), a revolutionary figure in U.S. journalism, founder and first editor of *The New Yorker*, was born in Aspen, Colo., Nov. 6, 1892. He quit high school to become a reporter, and in World War I edited *Stars and Stripes*, the serviceman's newspaper, in France. When he launched *The New Yorker* in 1925 he quickly toppled many conventional literary forms in his quest for ways to capture the contemporary scene in the magazine's pages.

Young new writers and artists, attracted by the rich odour of innovation, were drawn to the magazine. Under Ross's guidance, satire and parody flourished, reporting became lighthearted and searching, humour was allowed to infect everything, biography achieved bold strokes in the "Profiles," the short story enjoyed a reprieve from the heavy burden of plot, and social cartooning became less diagrammatic and more vigorous. In *The New Yorker*, the unknown writer was on equal footing with the established one; the editor sought good writing, not great names. Restless, noisy, consumed by curiosity, driven by a passion for clarity and perfection, Ross spent himself recklessly on each succeeding issue, and with unabating discontent.

Ross died in Boston on Dec. 6, 1951, having to a notable extent changed the face of journalism in his time. (E. B. W.)

ROSS, SIR JAMES CLARK (1800–1862), British rear admiral and polar explorer, who carried out important arctic and antarctic magnetic surveys, was born in London on April 15, 1800. He entered the Royal Navy in 1812, accompanying his uncle, Capt. (later Sir) John Ross (*q.v.*), on his first arctic voyage in 1818. Between 1819 and 1827 he accompanied Sir W. E. Parry on his four arctic expeditions, and from 1829 to 1833 again accompanied his uncle, reaching the north magnetic pole in 1831. From 1835–38 he worked on the magnetic survey of Great Britain, except from Dec. 1835 to Aug. 1836 when he searched for some missing arctic whaling ships (*see* "Polar Record," no. 40, 1950). He commanded H.M.S. "Erebus" and "Terror" during the antarctic expedition of 1839–43, sailing to Hobart and thence to the antarctic. The ships penetrated the pack ice from Jan. 5 to 10, 1841, in long. 174° E., reaching open water and discovering the Ross sea. The expedition's main object was to conduct magnetic observations in the antarctic and to reach the south magnetic pole. The ships sailed south toward the position assigned by K. F. Gauss to the pole, meanwhile discovering Victoria Land. Progress further south was barred by the Ross ice shelf, along which the ships coasted to long. 167° W. Unable to find suitable winter quarters, Ross returned to Hobart. In Nov. 1841 he sailed south to the barrier from New Zealand, reaching lat. 70° 10′ S. in 161° 27′ W., probably also sighting Edward VII peninsula. The ships wintered in the Falkland Islands and returned south to chart part of Graham coast. They sailed east along the edge of the Weddell sea ice and south to lat. 71° 30′ S., long. 14° 51′ W. On the way home Ross tried unsuccessfully to rediscover Bouvetøya (lat. 54° 26′ S., long. 3° 24′ E.). His *Voyage of discovery . . . in the Southern and Antarctic Regions* appeared in 1847. He was elected a fellow of the Royal society in 1848. From 1848 to 1849 he searched for Sir John Franklin in H.M.S. "Enterprise" and "Investigator."

He died at Aylesbury on April 3, 1862.

See also ANTARCTICA; ARCTIC, THE. (A. M. Ss.)

ROSS, SIR JOHN (1777–1856), Scottish rear admiral and arctic explorer, whose second arctic expedition in search of a northwest passage made important contributions to oceanography, was born on June 24, 1777, at Balsarroch near Stranraer, Wigtownshire, Scot. He entered the Royal Navy in 1786 and fought in the French Revolutionary and Napoleonic wars, during which he captained the Swedish fleet. In 1818 he made his first arctic expedition on which he failed to discover much that was new; but in 1829–33 he made a second, surveying Boothia peninsula, King William Land and the Gulf of Boothia, and achieved important results. In 1850 he undertook a third voyage in unsuccessful search of Sir John Franklin and in 1851 he became a rear admiral. Ross died in London on Aug. 30, 1856.

His publications include *A Voyage of Discovery . . . for the Purpose of Exploring Baffin's Bay . . .* (1819); *Narrative of a Second Voyage in Search of a North-West Passage* (1835); *Memoirs and Correspondence of Admiral Lord de Saumerez* (1838).

ROSS, JOHN (Indian name KOOWESKOOWE or COOWESCOOWE) (1790–1866), famed chief of the Cherokee Indians, the ablest leader of his people for almost 40 crucial years, was born near Lookout Mountain, Tenn., on Oct. 3, 1790. Ross's blue eyes and brown hair indicated that his Cherokee strain was small. His father, a Scottish trader, employed a tutor and later sent Ross to an academy at Kingston, Tenn. In 1813 he married a full-blooded Cherokee woman named Quatie. Some years after her death he married Mary Bryan Stapler, a white woman of Quaker faith.

During the early part of the 19th century there developed considerable pressure to open the Indian lands in Georgia to white settlement (*see* GEORGIA: *History*) and Ross became leader of the Cherokees opposed to westward removal. From 1819 to 1826 he served as president of the National Council of the Cherokees. His leadership was strengthened when, in 1823, he exposed machinations of federal commissioners who attempted to bribe him into approving Cherokee land sales. In 1828 he became head chief of the eastern Cherokees under a new constitution he had helped write. His valorous defense of Cherokee freedom and property from land-hungry Georgians utilized every means short of war and included several appeals to the federal government. After all efforts had failed, in 1838–39 Ross led his people to their new home in what is now Oklahoma. There he helped write the constitution of 1839, uniting the eastern and western Cherokees under one government, and was chosen chief of the united tribe. He held this office until his death on Aug. 1, 1866, in Washington, D.C., where he had gone to assist in making the Cherokee treaty of 1866.

See Chapman J. Milling, *Red Carolinians* (1940), which includes an authoritative account of the Cherokee removal and Ross's leadership; with bibliography.   (W. R. J.)

ROSS, SIR RONALD (1857–1932), British bacteriologist and Nobel laureate, noted for his investigations of malaria, was born at Almora, India, on May 13, 1857. He studied medicine at St. Bartholomew's Hospital, London, and in 1881 entered the Indian Medical Service. In 1892 he began a series of investigations on the subject of malaria (*q.v.*), in 1895 undertook to verify experimentally the theory that the microorganisms of this disease are spread by mosquitoes and in 1897–98 investigated the life history of the parasites. In 1899 he retired from the Indian medical service, and, after a journey to West Africa in 1899 for the study of malaria-bearing mosquitoes, devoted himself to research and teaching, joining the Liverpool School of Tropical Medicine as lecturer and subsequently becoming professor of tropical medicine at the University of Liverpool. In 1913 he became physician for tropical diseases at King's College Hospital, London, and later director in chief of the Ross Institute and Hospital for Tropical Diseases. During World War I Ross was war office consultant in malaria and after the war acted as consultant in malaria for the ministry of pensions. In 1902 he received the Nobel Prize for Medicine; in 1911 he was created knight commander of the Bath; and in 1918 a knight commander of St. Michael and St. George. He received the royal medal of the Royal Society, of which he was a fellow, in 1901. He died Sept. 16, 1932.

Ross was editor of *Science Progress,* and the author of *The Prevention of Malaria* (1910); *Philosophies* (1910); *Psychologies* (1919); *The Revels of Orsera,* a romance (1920); and *Memoirs* (1923), as well as mathematical and medical works.

See *British Medical Journal,* 2:609 (1932).

ROSS AND CROMARTY, a northern county of Scotland, and the third largest, with an area of 3,089.5 sq.mi., spans the entire width of the country from the North Sea to the Atlantic and includes the island of Lewis with numerous small offshore islets, mainly uninhabited. The boundary with Sutherland on the north is formed mainly by the Oykell River; the boundary with Inverness in the south is formed by a mountain rampart which separates the Conon drainage from that of the Great Glen and Beauly Firth. The county fans out from the productive Moray Firth lowlands in the east, segmented by the Dornoch, Cromarty, and Beauly firths, westward through mountain country of increasing grandeur to the long Atlantic coastline, indented by a dozen or more sea lochs and bays.

Physical Features.—The bulk of the county comprises the northwestern Highlands, a dissected plateau with recognizable surfaces at 1,000 (305 m.), 2,000, and 3,000 ft., and many peaks above 3,000 ft., more isolated in the west by the greater erosion attendant on higher precipitation. The east-west watershed is

never more than 15 mi. from the west coast, so streams are short and turbulent and glens are narrow in contrast to the wider straths (Conon, Bran) opening to the east. Rock structure is closely related to landscape. The oldest rocks are the Lewisian gneiss, the remnants of an ancient Archean land surface, which form low hummocky expanses of bare rock in Lewis itself and on the mainland between Loch Maree and Little Loch Broom; overlying these and east of them are the massive Torridonian sandstones sweeping northeastward from Loch Carron to Enard Bay in a 10 to 15 mi. (6 to 9 km.) belt and perhaps best represented in the Applecross Peninsula. The stepped hill slopes are sometimes dramatically capped with glittering outliers of Cambrian quartzite. A narrow belt of limestone separates the Torridonian rocks from the Moine schists which make up the bulk of the centre of the highland area where the topography is less rugged. In turn they are overlapped by rocks of Old Red Sandstone age about 15 mi. from the east coast. In general these give lower country, but it varies according to lithology; thus resistant breccias form the Mulbuie Hills in the Black Isle (actually the peninsula between Cromarty and Beauly firths).

The southwest-northeast Caledonian trend predominates throughout the county and is particularly noticeable in the coastline from Tarbat Ness to Inverness; the Alpine orogeny, however, created right-angled lines of weakness, some filled with Tertiary basaltic dikes, many subsequently etched out by ice and rivers. Glaciation, in addition, scoured soil from large areas, carved U-shaped valleys with stepped profiles, and dumped moraine on the low ground; outwash material forms a notable area of alternating gravelly ridges and ill-drained lowland between Beauly and Dingwall. Postglacial uplift has resulted in river terraces and, more importantly in this area, raised beaches at 15, 25, and 50 ft. around the eastern firths and the more sheltered western lochs (especially Loch Broom); they have their maximum extent on the northern shore of Cromarty Firth.

There is a clear distinction between the moist equable climate of the west and the drier more extreme climate of the east: Stornoway has a mean annual range of 15° F (8.3° C), Strathpeffer 19° F (10.6° C). Relief affects rainfall which reaches 90 in. (2,300 mm.) annually in the western mountains and drops below 25 in. around the Moray Firth; in addition there are wide local variations in temperature and rainfall, even from one glen to another. Snow lies less than five days in the west; from 10 to 20 in. falls in the east, and up to 100 in. in the mountains.

Glacial scouring, hard rock, and excessive rainfall have produced poor acid soils over much of the area; drainage is the main problem in making use of the boulder clay and alluvial soils in the valleys. Lighter soils develop from the Old Red Sandstone rocks, and the raised beaches give warm dry soils of considerable value in barley growing.

A large area (10,507 ac.) southwest of Loch Maree forms the Beinn Eighe National Nature Reserve. Inverpolly National Nature Reserve (created 1961), near the northwest coast, covers 26,827 ac. of wild country with ancient woodlands and the striking mountain of Stack Polly (2,009 ft.). The small reserve (202 ac.) of Rassal Ashwood is near Kinlochewe.

The estate of Kintail, which belongs to the National Trust, includes the Five Sisters, five peaks that overlook Glenshiel to the south. The trust also owns an adjoining estate in which are the spectacular Falls of Glomach and the gardens at Inverewe. Kyle of Lochalsh is the end of one branch of the "Road to the Isles," and it is also known as the "Gateway to Skye."

(A. M. LE.; A. T. A. L.)

History and Antiquities.—During the first five centuries A.D., and for long afterward, the land was occupied by Gaelic Picts, who in the 6th and 7th centuries were converted to Christianity by followers of St. Columba. Throughout the next three centuries the natives were continually harassed by Norse pirates, of whose presence tokens have survived in several place-names such as Dingwall and Tain. At that time the county formed part of the great province of Moray. The rule of the Celtic *mormaors,* or earls, ceased in the 12th century, consequent on the plantation of the district with settlers from other parts (including a body of Flemings) by order of David I, who was anxious to break the power of the Celts; at this time the bounds of the principality of Moravia were contracted and the earldom of Ross arose. At first Ross proper included only the territory adjoining Moray and Dornoch firths. The first earl was Malcolm MacHeth, who received the title from Malcolm IV. After his rebellion in 1179 chronic insurrection ensued, which was quelled by Alexander II, who bestowed the earldom on Farquhar Macintaggart, then abbot of Applecross, and in that capacity lord of the western district. William, 4th earl, was present with his clan at the Battle of Bannockburn (1314). Almost a century later (1412) the Castle of Dingwall, the chief seat on the mainland of Donald, lord of the Isles, was captured after the disastrous fight at Harlaw in Aberdeen County, which Donald had provoked when his claim to the earldom was rejected. The earldom reverted to the crown in 1424, but James I soon afterward restored it to the heiress of the line, the mother of Alexander MacDonald, 3rd lord of the Isles, who then became 11th earl. In consequence of the treason of John MacDonald, 4th and last lord of the Isles and 12th earl of Ross, however, the earldom was again vested in the crown (1476). Five years later James III bestowed it on his second son, James Stewart, whom he also created duke of Ross in 1488. By the 16th century the whole area of the county was occupied by different clans: the Rosses, Munroes, Macleods, Macdonalds, and Mackenzies. The county of Ross was constituted in 1661, and Cromarty in 1685 and 1698, both being consolidated into the present county in 1889. Apart from occasional conflicts between rival clans, the only battles in the shire were those of Invercarron (1650), when Montrose was crushed by Col. Archibald Strachan, and Glenshiel (1719), when the Jacobites, under the earl of Seaforth and aided by Spaniards, were defeated near Bridge of Shiel by Gen. Joseph Wightman.

Stone circles, cairns, and forts are found in the eastern district. A vitrified fort crowns the hill of Knockfarrel and there is a circular dun near the village of Lochcarron. Some examples of sculptured stones occur, the finest being at Shandwick. Among old castles are those of Lochslin in the parish of Fearn, said to date from the 13th century, which, though ruinous, possesses two square towers in good preservation; Balone, in the parish of Tarbat, once a stronghold of the earls of Ross; the remains of Dingwall Castle, their original seat; and the 13th-century Eilean Donan Castle in Loch Alsh, which was blown up by English warships during the abortive Jacobite rising in 1719 but restored in 1932.

Population and Administration.—The population at the 1966 census was 56,570. There were 476 persons who spoke Gaelic only and 21,581 speaking Gaelic and English. Of the six small burghs the chief are Stornoway (pop. [1966] 5,290), Dingwall (3,780), Invergordon (2,280), and Tain (1,710). Ullapool is a fishing port near the mouth of Loch Broom. There are 12 county districts and the county with Inverness returns three members to Parliament representing Inverness, Ross and Cromarty, and the Western Isles. Dingwall, Fortrose (qq.v.), and Tain are royal burghs, and Dingwall is the county town. Ross and Cromarty with Inverness, Moray, and Nairn form a sheriffdom, and there are resident sheriffs-substitute at Dingwall and Stornoway (q.v.), the former also sitting at Tain.

There are academies at Dingwall, Fortrose, Tain, and Invergordon.

The Economy.—Ross embraces wider extremes of farming types than any other county in Scotland. On the fertile soils along the east coast there are large and productive farms used for rotational cropping and the rearing and fattening of livestock, some of the Shorthorn herds being world famous. Heavy yields of cereals and potatoes are obtained, and the cattle and sheep are of outstanding quality. At the other extreme are the crofts of Lewis, where the climate, type of soil, and size of units are factors unfavourable to progressive agriculture. Between these extremes are the less intensive arable and stock raising farms on the poorer and higher land bordering the hills. In the county, the greater part of which is comprised of hills, large-scale sheep farming is practised. Poultry and pig keeping are mainly sidelines on mixed arable farms, there being relatively few dairy holdings. Dingwall is the principal agricultural market. Because of the unfavourable nature of most of the surface in the centre, the west, and in the islands, offering opportunity only for patchwork tillage, and because of the crofting organization of the land, the small holdings average only about 18 ac.

The natural woodlands were mostly destroyed long ago but pockets still exist and are being protected by the Nature Conservancy in the Loch Maree area. Large-scale afforestation has been undertaken mainly in the Black Isle, among the eastern foothills, and in a few more sheltered western glens.

Herring fishing is practised in the Minch and the fishing boats make much use of Stornoway, Ullapool, and Gairloch. White-fishing is active on a smaller scale, while lobster fishing is practised along the coasts and notably in Bernera, Lewis. Salmon fishing in the bays and river mouths is important.

The main industry is the making of Harris tweed in Lewis, employing hundreds of millworkers in Stornoway and many more handweavers throughout the island. Apart from distilleries near Tain, Alness, and Muir of Ord, most other employment is in ancillary work and services for agriculture. Much temporary employment after 1948 was provided through projects of the North of Scotland Hydro-Electric Board in the Conon Basin. *See also* LEWIS-AND-HARRIS; MAREE, LOCH. (W. D. R.)

ROSSBY, CARL-GUSTAF ARVID (1898–1957), Swedish-American meteorologist, whose studies, particularly in atmospheric circulation, had much to do with the rapid growth of the science. Born on Dec. 28, 1898, in Stockholm and educated there, his principal published works appeared after he moved to the United States in 1925. Working first in Washington, D.C., and later as professor and head of the country's first department of meteorology at the Massachusetts Institute of Technology, Cambridge, he made important contributions to the understanding of thermodynamics of air masses and atmospheric turbulence, including ocean-air boundary problems.

In the late 1930s Rossby turned his attention to the general circulation of the atmosphere, continuing this work after becoming professor and chairman of the department of meteorology at the University of Chicago. He identified the long waves in the upper westerlies, now often called "Rossby waves," and developed the theory for their movement. He is credited with having identified the so-called "jet stream" and with having developed the principal theories for its behaviour. He also worked on models for numerical weather prediction. Two nondimensional quantities useful in rotating-fluid mechanics bear his name: the Rossby number and the thermal Rossby number. A Rossby parameter is also known in meteorology and oceanography.

After 1948 Rossby was mainly identified with the Institute of Meteorology which he founded in connection with the University of Stockholm. From 1954 until his death on Aug. 19, 1957, in Stockholm, he introduced and led worldwide studies of atmospheric chemistry and radioactivity. (H. R. B.)

ROSSE, WILLIAM PARSONS, 3RD EARL OF (1800–1867), Irish astronomer and constructor of the largest telescope that had yet been made, was born at York on June 17, 1800. In 1818 he entered Trinity College, Dublin, and proceeded to Magdalen College, Oxford, in 1821, when he was also elected to the House of Commons as Lord Oxmantown. He resigned this seat in 1834, but after his father's death he served as one of the Irish representative peers in the House of Lords. President of the British Association for the Advancement of Science in 1843 and of the Royal Society from 1849 to 1854, of which he was awarded the Royal Medal in 1851, Rosse became chancellor of the University of Dublin in 1862. He died at Monkstown, County Dublin, on Oct. 31, 1867.

Although William Herschel (q.v.) had pioneered in the construction of reflecting telescopes on a large scale, he never published his methods of casting and polishing specula, and so Lord Rosse was unaided in formulating his own methods. His speculum metal was composed of four atoms of copper (126.4 parts) and one of tin (58.9 parts), a brilliant alloy. Chiefly because of the brittleness of this material, Lord Rosse's first larger specula were composed of a number of thin plates of speculum metal (16 for a 3-ft. mirror) soldered to the back of a strong but light framework made of a brass (2.75 of copper to 1 of zinc), which had the same expansion as the speculum metal. In Brewster's *Edinburgh Journal of Science* for 1828 Lord Rosse described his machine for polishing the speculum. In September 1839, a 3-ft. speculum was finished and mounted, but, though the definition of the images was good, its skeleton form allowed the speculum to follow atmospheric changes of temperature too quickly; therefore Lord Rosse decided to cast a solid 3-ft. speculum. Hitherto a great difficulty in casting specula was the fact that they generally cracked while cooling. Rosse experimented, ingeniously overcame this difficulty, and successfully cast a solid 3-ft. speculum in 1840. In 1842 he began a speculum of 6-ft. diameter, and in 1845 this great reflector was mounted and ready for work. Astronomers used this speculum from 1848 to 1878 and discovered many previously unknown features in nebulae, especially the similarity of "annular" and "planetary" nebulae and the remarkable "spiral" configuration in many of the nebulae. A special study was made of the nebula of Orion, and the resulting large drawing gives an extremely good representation of this complicated object.

ROSSELLINO (ROSSELLINI), the name of a family of stone-cutters from Settignano, near Florence, of whom two of five brothers, BERNARDO, an architect and sculptor, and ANTONIO, a sculptor, are the most important.

BERNARDO ROSSELLINO (1409–64), notable early Renaissance architect and sculptor, was born at Settignano in 1409. His earliest recorded work, the upper part of the façade of the Misericordia at Arezzo (1433–35), in which a lunette with the Madonna of Mercy is set between elegant pilasters, reveals the strong influence of Filippo Brunelleschi, as does his masterpiece, the historian Leonardo Bruni's tomb (1445–50) in Sta. Croce in Florence. The Bruni monument has the form of a triumphal arch set against the wall, with the effigy resting on a classical sarcophagus and a relief of the Virgin and Child and two figures of angels above. It inaugurated a new type of sepulchral monument, which assumed great popularity and was imitated by Desiderio da Settignano and other artists. Notable alike for its architectural and sculptural qualities, this tomb ranks with the greatest achievements of Renaissance sculpture. In a tabernacle carved by Bernardo Rossellino in S. Egidio in Florence (1449–50), for which the bronze door was cast by Lorenzo Ghiberti, the influence of Brunelleschi is also dominant. His work as a figure sculptor can also be studied in two figures of the Annunciatory Angel and Virgin Annunciate in the museum at Empoli (1444–47) and the tomb of the Beata Villana delle Botte in Sta. Maria Novella in Florence (after 1451). Much of the effect of the Bruni monument is due to the extraordinarily skillful carving of the decorative ornament. Other examples of Bernardo's use of decorative carving occur in a doorway in the Palazzo Pubblico at Siena (1447) and the tomb of Orlando de' Medici in SS. Annunziata in Florence (1456). Throughout his life Bernardo Rossellino also practised as an architect, executing the Palazzo Ruccellai in Florence and the cathedral and episcopal palace at Pienza (after 1461). Between 1451 and 1453 he was employed in Rome by Pope Nicholas V on the building of St. Peter's, the restoration of S. Stefano Rotondo and other works. Bernardo became superintending architect of the *duomo* in Florence in 1461, and died in Florence on Sept. 23, 1464.

ANTONIO ROSSELLINO (1427–79), sculptor, the youngest brother, born in 1427 at Settignano. His earliest authenticated work is a signed bust of the doctor Giovanni Chellini (1456; Victoria and Albert museum, London). This and a considerably later bust of the historian Matteo Palmieri (1468; Museo Nazionale, Florence) show him to have been a portrait sculptor of unusual incisiveness. About 1456 he executed a marble statue of St. Sebastian in the museum at Empoli, in which the style (like that of the portrait busts) is strongly influenced by the antique. Antonio Rossellino's most important and extended work is the chapel of the cardinal prince of Portugal in S. Miniato al Monte outside Florence for which he assumed responsibility after the death of its architect Antonio Manetti (1460), designing the pavement and episcopal throne and the tomb of the cardinal. The effigy of the cardinal

rests on a reproduction of a Roman porphyry sarcophagus and is accompanied by two seated children, two kneeling angels and a circular relief of the Virgin and Child, which are some of the most distinguished marble sculptures of their time. A variant of this tomb commissioned for Mary of Aragon, duchess of Amalfi, in Sta. Anna dei Lombardi, Naples, was unfinished at Antonio's death in 1479 and was completed by Benedetto da Maiano. Also for the Piccolomini chapel in the same church he executed an altarpiece of the "Adoration of the Shepherds," in which an attempt is made to invest marble relief with the properties of a painted altarpiece. A circular relief of the "Nativity," carved in the same style, is in the Museo Nazionale, Florence. In this and in Antonio Rossellino's last work, the Nori Madonna in Sta. Croce (before 1478), some deterioration from the high standard of the tomb of the cardinal of Portugal is evident. Antonio's marble reliefs of the Virgin and Child with angels, of which the finest is in the Metropolitan museum in New York, show him at his most felicitous, and enjoyed great popularity in the 15th century.

See L. Planiscig, *Bernardo und Antonio Rossellino* (1942); L. Heydenreich, "Pius II als Bauherr von Pienza" in *Zeitschrift für Kunstgeschichte,* vi, pp. 105–146 (1937). (J. W. P.-H.)

ROSSETTI, CHRISTINA GEORGINA (1830–1894), the most distinguished of English women poets both in range and quality. She excelled in works of fantasy, in verse for children, and was supreme in her religious poetry. The youngest child of Gabriele Rossetti (*q.v.*), she was born in London on Dec. 5, 1830. In 1847 her grandfather, Gaetano Polidori, printed on his private press a volume of her *Verses,* in which signs of poetic talent are already visible. In 1850, as Ellen Alleyne, she contributed seven poems to the Pre-Raphaelite journal, *The Germ.*

In 1853, when the family was in financial difficulties, Christina helped her mother to keep a school at Frome, Somerset. It did not prosper, and in 1854 they returned to London, where her father died. In straitened circumstances, she entered on her life work of companionship to her beloved mother, devotion to her religion, and the writing of her poetry. A firm High Church Anglican, she had from religious scruples broken her engagement to the artist James Collinson, an original member of the Pre-Raphaelite Brotherhood (*q.v.*) who had become a Roman Catholic, and for similar reasons she later rejected Charles Bagot Cayley, translator of Dante; but a warm friendship remained between them. The resigned passionate sadness of unhappy love is a dominant note in her poetry. In 1862 she published *Goblin Market and Other Poems,* and in 1866 *The Prince's Progress and Other Poems,* both with frontispiece and decoration by Dante Gabriel. These, which contain most of her finest work, established her among the poets of her age.

With help from her brother William Michael the family visited France in 1861, and in 1865 she paid her only visit to Italy, commemorated in the moving sonnet "Italia Io Ti Saluto." The stories in her first prose work, *Commonplace and Other Short Stories* (1870), are of no great merit: her prose is less remarkable than her verse. *Sing-Song: a Nursery Rhyme Book* (1872, enlarged 1893), with charming illustrations by Arthur Hughes, takes a high place among children's poetry of the century.

In 1871 she was stricken by Graves' disease, which marred her looks and left her life in danger. She accepted her affliction with courage and resignation, sustained by religious faith. She published a collection of poems in 1875 (enlarged, 1890), and *A Pageant and Other Poems* in 1881. But after her illness she gave herself mainly to devotional prose writings. *Annus Domini* (1874), a book of prayers, was followed by religious meditations on the Benedicite, *Seek and Find* (1879). *Time Flies* (1885), a reading diary of mixed verse and prose, is the most personal of these writings. After *The Face of the Deep* (1892), a bulky commentary on the Apocalypse, she wrote little.

After William Michael's marriage in 1874, Christina and her mother moved from his house to Bloomsbury in 1876. Mrs. Rossetti died in 1886, and Christina spent her last years in retirement there. Her name was mentioned as a possible successor to Tennyson as poet laureate. Cancer developed in 1891, and she died on Dec. 29, 1894, and was buried in the family grave in Highgate Cemetery. *New Poems* (1896), published by her brother, contains unprinted and previously uncollected poems.

Christina Rossetti takes foremost place among English women poets. A brilliant cartoon by Max Beerbohm in his book of cartoons of *Rossetti and His Circle* (1922) overstresses the quiet aspect of her personality. There were other aspects which she shared with Dante Gabriel. Beneath the humility, the devotion, the quiet saintlike life, lay a passionate sensuous temperament, a keen intelligence, and a detached observant humour. It is her greatness as an artist that, never straining beyond the limits of her sympathy and experience, she succeeded in uniting the two seemingly contradictory sides of her nature. There is a vein of the sentimental and the didactic in her weaker work: at her best her note is strong, personal, and unforced, with a metrical cadence unmistakably her own. In the words written by Edmund Gosse, a friend of her later years, for the 10th edition of the *Encyclopædia Britannica*:

In the purity and solidity of her finest lyrics, the glow and music in which she robes her moods of melancholy reverie, her extraordinary mixture of austerity with sweetness and of sanctity of tone with sensuousness of colour, Christina Rossetti . . . may challenge comparison with the most admirable of our poets. The union of fixed religious faith with a hold upon physical beauty and the richer parts of nature has been pointed to as the most original feature of her poetry.

BIBLIOGRAPHY.—*Poetical Works . . .*, *with Memoirs and Notes* (1904), and *The Family Letters of Christina Georgina Rossetti* (1908), both ed. by W. M. Rossetti; *The Rossetti-Macmillan Letters*, ed. by L. M. Packer (1963). *See also* E. Gosse, *Critical Kit-Kats* (1896); D. M. Stuart, *Christina Rossetti*, "English Men of Letters, New Series" (1930); M. Zaturenska, *Christina Rossetti: a Portrait with Background* (1949); L. M. Packer, *Christina Rossetti* (1963). *See also* bibliographies to ROSSETTI, DANTE GABRIEL and ROSSETTI, GABRIELE PASQUALE GIUSEPPE. (J. BN.)

ROSSETTI, DANTE GABRIEL

ROSSETTI, DANTE GABRIEL (baptized GABRIEL CHARLES DANTE) (1828–1882), English poet and painter, a leader of the Pre-Raphaelites, and acknowledged as their inspiration by the poets of the aesthetic movement of the 1880s and '90s, was born in London, on May 12, 1828. He was the eldest son of Gabriele Rossetti (*q.v.*) and Maria Francesca Polidori. His elder sister, Maria Francesca (1827–76), entered an Anglican sisterhood in 1873; his younger brother and sister were W. M. and Christina Rossetti (*qq.v.*).

Gabriel, who early decided to be a painter, read widely, enjoying especially the romantic and supernatural in art and literature, and began to write poems and plays. After going to King's College School (1837–41) and to a drawing school in Bloomsbury, in December 1845 he entered the Antique School at the Royal Academy. Bored with its academic method of teaching, and with the technicalities of his profession, he spent his spare time in writing poetry, and, as well as verse translations from Italian, wrote the first versions of "The Blessed Damozel," "My Sister's Sleep," "Jenny," and "A Last Confession."

The Pre-Raphaelite Brotherhood.—In 1848 Rossetti left the Academy and began to study painting with Ford Madox Brown (*q.v.*). After a time, finding Brown an exacting master, and tiring of the discipline of still-life painting, he left to join William Holman Hunt and Hunt's friend John Everett Millais in the formation of the Pre-Raphaelite Brotherhood (*q.v.*). The three young artists sought to recapture the spirit of the primitive Italian painters as revealed to them in Lasinio's engravings of the 14th-century frescoes in the Campo Santo, Pisa. Rossetti, with his enthusiasm and intelligence, was the natural leader, and it was he who later inspired William Morris and Edward Burne-Jones (*qq.v.*) to become associated with the Brotherhood.

The strictly Pre-Raphaelite period of their activity was brief, but its influence was important. After an uncompleted attempt to decorate the Oxford Union Society's new debating hall in 1857, and after Rossetti's marriage to Elizabeth Siddal in 1860, the artists went their different ways. Already, in 1853, on hearing of Millais' election as Associate of the Royal Academy, Rossetti had remarked, "So now the whole Round Table is dissolved." Only Holman Hunt remained true to the Pre-Raphaelite ideal.

Rossetti exhibited his first painting, "The Girlhood of Mary Virgin," in 1849 at the Free Exhibition at Hyde Park Corner,

London, following it with the "Ecce Ancilla Domini" (or "Annunciation") in 1850; in both his sister Christina is the central figure. In 1850, Rossetti made his first appearance as a poet, contributing "The Blessed Damozel," six sonnets, and four lyrics to *The Germ*, the Brotherhood's periodical. His first volume of poetry, *The Early Italian Poets Together with Dante's 'Vita Nuova'* (1861), consists of translations from Dante and his predecessors.

After Walter Deverell in 1850 had discovered Elizabeth Siddal working in a milliner's shop in Leicester Square, London, she posed for him, and for Hunt, and Millais used her in his famous picture of the drowning Ophelia—said to be a close likeness. But it was Rossetti who claimed her as his own. Her frail delicate features, her slight figure, and her mass of gold-red hair pervade all his early paintings. After a long engagement, troubled by misunderstandings and irritations caused by Lizzie's nervous ill health, they were at last married in May 1860 when waning passion had spent itself. They lived at Chatham Place, Blackfriars, where Rossetti had his studio, and there he had made many informal drawings of her—"drawer after drawer of wonderful and lovely Guggums" (her pet name), as Madox Brown described them. These drawings are among his most sensitive work. Dogged by ill health, and after the birth of a stillborn child in May 1861, she died in February 1862 from an overdose of laudanum, whether accidental or self-administered is not known. She was buried in Highgate Cemetery

"ECCE ANCILLA DOMINI" BY DANTE GABRIEL ROSSETTI, 1850. IN THE TATE GALLERY, LONDON

and Rossetti, in his grief and sense of guilt, laid the manuscript of his poems (the only complete copy) in her coffin. He paid his farewell tribute in a last idealized portrait, the "Beata Beatrix."

Chelsea.—In October 1862 he moved to 16, Cheyne Walk, Chelsea, henceforth his home, where he worked with energy, and with the company of younger friends, including Swinburne (q.v.), with whom he shared the house for a time, George Meredith (q.v.), and the painter Simeon Solomon. In the pictures of this middle period the intensity of his early vision weakens, and a languorous, sensuous mood replaces it. Fanny Cornforth (later Hughes) was now his favourite model. An uneducated woman, but of a golden voluptuous beauty, she acted to her own advantage at Cheyne Walk as housekeeper, as model, and as mistress. She became more demanding and less honest as time went on, but Rossetti retained affection for his "Dear Elephant" to the end of his life. In another mood Janey Morris, the wife of William Morris, is the inspiration and subject again and again of the later brooding, dreamlike pictures. In 1869 he consented to the recovery of the manuscript from Lizzie's grave. *Poems* (1870) contains, with more recent work, the poems from *The Germ*, and *The House of Life* sonnet-sequence, later enlarged.

Last Years.—An unwarranted attack by Robert Buchanan (q.v.) in the *Contemporary Review* (October 1871), entitled "The Fleshly School of Poetry," greatly distressed Rossetti. He replied with "The Stealthy School of Criticism" in the *Athenaeum* (December 1871), but the episode aggravated his tendency to melancholic depression, and the increasing use of chloral and whisky to combat insomnia led to a breakdown in health. During 1872–74 he was mainly at Kelmscott, sharing the tenancy with Morris. In his later years, Rossetti withdrew more and more into himself in a state of nervous melancholy. His painting became repetitive and less sure, but his literary powers did not fail. *Ballads and Sonnets* (1881) contains some of his best poetry, including the completed *House of Life* (in which the presence of Janey Morris is now felt), and the historical ballads "The White Ship" and "The King's Tragedy." He died on April 9, 1882, at Birchington-on-Sea, Kent, and was buried there. A memorial window by his friend, Frederick Shields, was placed in the church, and a cross designed by Madox Brown marks his grave. His work as an artist, including self-portraits, is well represented in all the major collections of Pre-Raphaelite painting—notably in the Tate Gallery, London; the Ashmolean Museum, Oxford; the Birmingham City Art Gallery; and the Walker Art Gallery, Liverpool.

Assessment of His Genius as Artist and Poet.—Rossetti, through his exploration of new themes and his break with academic convention, remains an important figure in the history of 19th-century English art. But his enduring worth probably lies as much in his poetry as in his painting. His best work as an artist consists of the early drawings in pen and pencil and watercolour. The portrait drawings of his mother and sister, of Elizabeth Siddal, and of Jane Burden (Mrs. Morris) are penetrating studies, firm in draftsmanship. The glowing watercolours, based on themes from Dante and Sir Thomas Malory's *Morte Darthur*, are harmonious in composition and charged with an intense and fresh poetic vision.

These qualities are less evident in his later, more sensuous, paintings. In them the mood is monotonously languid, and there is a cloying accumulation of symbolic detail. As a painter in oils he never acquired the sheer technique or feeling for pigment which marks the masters of this medium. He relies rather on colour and rhythm of design. The later pictures, with their evocative Latin titles, date, while his early Pre-Raphaelite work has a timeless poetic quality. In later years he was too ready to repeat a success and, helped by studio assistants, painted replicas of many of his popular subjects. Examples of his later work are "Proserpina" (1877; Tate Gallery, one of his many studies of Mrs. Morris), and the large "Dante's Dream" (1871; Walker Art Gallery).

Rossetti's poetry has a range and variety which his painting lacks, and he is not to be thought of only as the writer of such poems as "The Blessed Damozel." His craftsmanship gives evidence of the fundamental brainwork which he looked for in all great poetry. He is a thinker as well as a painter in words, and

is a poet of speculative vision as well as sensuous passion.

In his poetry the Pre-Raphaelite love of detail is subdued by the intensity of emotion, and is employed to evoke a mood—thereby achieving an effect it often misses in Pre-Raphaelite painting, where detail is too often used for its own sake. It is by means of tiny and seemingly trivial touches that time is suspended in "My Sister's Sleep," and the very silence of the sick room is heard. "The Wood Spurge" and the lyric "I have been here before" show his mastery of similar effects. The timeless moment is again caught with exquisite skill in his sonnet for "A Venetian Pastoral by Giorgione in the Louvre"—the most successful of his highly original attempts to translate well-known paintings into verse. "The Stream's Secret," haunted by the ghost of his dead wife, evokes pity and regret by the power of its verbal music.

His skill as translator is seen in the *Early Italian Poets* . . . (revised as *Dante and His Circle*, 1874), and in his version of Villon's "The Ballad of Dead Ladies" (1870).

Rossetti is a natural master of the sonnet (q.v.). His finest achievement is *The House of Life* (edited by P. F. Baum, 1928), a sonnet-sequence unique in the intensity of its evocation of the mysteries of physical and spiritual love. Here, as he claimed against his detractors, "the passionate and just delights of the body are declared to be as naught if not ennobled by the concurrence of the soul at all times." Magnificent memorable lines are created with simplicity of diction: e.g.,

> Oh! clasp we to our hearts for deathless dower,
> This close-companioned inarticulate hour
> When two-fold silence was the song of love.
> ("Silent Noon," *House of Life*, sonnet XIX.)

There are other less subjective aspects of Rossetti's poetic art. "The Last Confession," a tragic episode set against a background of the Italian Risorgimento, is a powerful dramatic monologue which can bear comparison with Browning when he writes on a similar subject. With his feeling for things medieval Rossetti caught the spirit of the ballad. Few modern supernatural ballads are less artificial than "Sister Helen" and "Eden Bower"; and among re-creations of the historical ballad "The White Ship" and "The King's Tragedy" are outstanding. One of his earliest poems shows the power of his historical imagination. The sight of the great Assyrian winged bulls in the British Museum evoked in the "Burden of Nineveh" (1850) a meditation on the unpredictable course of civilization, rich in word-music, profound in thought, and far-ranging in imaginative vision.

BIBLIOGRAPHY.—*Editions, Correspondence, etc.: Collected Works* . . ., 2 vol. (1886–90, 1897, 1901), *The Works*, authoritative text (1911), *D. G. Rossetti: His Family Letters, with a Memoir*, 2 vol. (1895), *Ruskin, Rossetti, Preraphaelitism: Papers 1854–62* (1899), *Preraphaelite Diaries and Letters* (1900), and *Rossetti Papers, 1862–70* (1903), all ed. by W. M. Rossetti; W. M. Rossetti, *A Bibliography of the Works of D. G. Rossetti* (1905); *Letters of D. G. Rossetti to William Allingham, 1854–70*, ed. by G. B. Hill (1897); *Three Rossettis: Unpublished Letters to and from D. G., Christina, William*, ed. by J. C. Troxell (1937); *Rossetti's Letters to Fanny Cornforth*, ed. by P. F. Baum (1940); *The Rossetti-Macmillan Letters*, ed. by L. M. Packer (1963); *Letters of D. G. Rossetti*, 4 vol., ed. by O. Doughty and R. Wahl (vol. i, 1965).

Biography and Criticism.—T. Hall Caine, *Recollections of D. G. Rossetti* (1882; 2nd rev. ed. 1928); W. Holman Hunt, *Pre-Raphaelitism and the Pre-Raphaelite Brotherhood*, 2 vol. (1905); Lady G. Burne-Jones, *Memorials of Sir Edward Burne-Jones*, 2 vol. (1904); H. Treffry Dunne, *Recollections of D. G. Rossetti and His Circle* (1904); H. C. Marillier, *D. G. Rossetti* (1899; 2nd ed. 1901); A. C. Benson, *Rossetti*, "English Men of Letters Series" (1906); E. Waugh, *Rossetti: His Life and Works* (1928); V. Hunt, *The Wife of Rossetti* (1932); W. Gaunt, *The Pre-Raphaelite Tragedy* (1942); O. Doughty, *D. G. Rossetti: A Victorian Romantic* (1949); H. Rossetti-Angeli, *Rossetti, His Friends and His Enemies* (1949), and *Pre-Raphaelite Twilight: the Story of Charles Augustus Howell* (1954); G. Pedrick, *Life with Rossetti* (1964); R. G. Grills, *Portrait of Rossetti* (1964). *See* also bibliographies to CHRISTINA GEORGINA and GABRIELE PASQUALE GIUSEPPE ROSSETTI, and to PRE-RAPHAELITE BROTHERHOOD. (J. BN.)

ROSSETTI, GABRIELE PASQUALE GIUSEPPE (1783–1854), Italian poet, patriot, and scholar, known for his esoteric interpretation of Dante, and as the father of Dante Gabriel, Christina Georgina, and William Michael Rossetti (qq.v.), was born at Vasto, southern Italy, on Feb. 28, 1783. In 1804 his poems and drawings attracted the patronage of the king of Naples' majordomo, who sent him to Naples University. After the king's downfall (1806), he got work as librettist to the Teatro San Carlo and as subcurator at the museum. In 1809 he became a Freemason and joined the *Carbonari,* and during the revolution of 1820 was regarded as the poet of the movement.

Forced into hiding (1821), he escaped to Malta and (1824) to England, where he taught Italian and began a commentary on the *Divina Commedia,* of which only two volumes were published (1825; dated 1826). In 1826 he married Maria Francesca (1800–86), daughter of Gaetano Polidori (1764–1853), an Italian teacher who had settled in London in 1789. Her brother had in 1816 accompanied Byron into exile as his physician, but after a quarrel returned to London and in 1821 committed suicide.

Moderate prosperity and many friends—including the Dante scholar Charles (later Sir Charles) Lyell—made the Rossetti home happy. As well as teaching, Gabriele was immersed in the researches which were to become a monomania. In *Sullo spirito antipapale che produsse la Reforma* (1831) he claimed that the *Divina Commedia* was written in the code language (*gergo*) of a humanistic secret society, opposed to political and ecclesiastical tyranny. The work's antipapal character led to his appointment (although nominally a Roman Catholic) as professor of Italian at King's College, London, founded by Anglicans opposed to Catholic emancipation. He continued his researches and his poetry, publishing *Iddio e l'uomo, Salterio* (1833), poems written mainly in Malta; *Il mistero dell'amor platonico nel medio evo,* five volumes (1840), relating his theory of a medieval secret society to the Eastern mystery religions and to Manichaeism and applying it to other medieval poetry; *La Beatrice di Dante* (1842; complete ed. 1935), which interpreted Beatrice as the symbol of Dante's soul; the autobiographical poem, *Il Veggente in solitudine* (1846); *Versi* (1847); and *L'Arpa evangelica* (1853; dated 1852), lyrics expressing faith in brotherly love.

In 1842–43 ill health forced Gabriele to give up private teaching, and in 1843 he lost the sight of one eye. In 1847 he resigned from King's College. In 1850 Mrs. Rossetti opened a school at Camden Town, and in 1853 she and Christina started a school at Frome, Somerset. In March 1854 they returned to live with William Michael in London, and there, on April 26, Gabriele died.

As a poet, Rossetti was a conventional "Arcadian," showing signs of his early experience as an *improvisatore* and occasional poet. Although he was a Dante scholar of considerable gifts, his interpretations are unacceptable. But his insistence, in his commentary (his most scholarly work), that the *Commedia* must be understood allegorically, is important; and he was a pioneer in the understanding of its structure. He was not alone in interpreting parts of the *Inferno* politically, and even his application to medieval literature of Masonic ritual was developed from ideas suggested by Lyell. His poetry was long admired in Italy, and in England his personality helped to win support for his native country.

BIBLIOGRAPHY.—*A Versified Autobiography,* trans. of *Il Veggente,* with additions, by W. M. Rossetti (1901); *La vita mia* (1910), and *Opere inedite e rare,* 3 vol. (1929–31), both ed. by D. Ciampoli; E. R. Vincent, *Gabriele Rossetti in England* (1936).

ROSSETTI, WILLIAM MICHAEL (1829–1919), English man of letters, an original member of the Pre-Raphaelite Brotherhood (*q.v.*), from whose preservation and editing of Pre-Raphaelite letters, papers, and journals is derived our most authentic knowledge of the movement, was born in London on Sept. 25, 1829. Of a different temperament from his more famous brother and sister, he entered the Excise (later Inland Revenue) Office in 1845, becoming senior assistant secretary before retiring in 1894.

His literary activities were varied. As well as editing his brother's and sister's works, and publishing *D. G. Rossetti: a Memoir with Family Letters* (1895), he wrote art criticisms for the *Spectator* (reprinted as *Fine Art, Chiefly Contemporary,* 1867). An early admirer of Blake, he edited his *Poetical Works* (1874). He edited Shelley (1870; rev. 1878), and was an active member of the Shelley Society. He introduced Walt Whitman to Britain with a selection of his poems (1868). His Pre-Raphaelite papers include *Preraphaelite Letters and Diaries* (1900), and *Ruskin, Rossetti, Preraphaelitism. Papers 1854–62* (1899). Following

the family tradition of Dante studies, he made a blank verse translation of the *Inferno* (1865), and a study of *Dante and His Convito* (1910). In 1891 he gave the Taylorian lecture at Oxford on Leopardi. His parallel texts of Chaucer's *Troylus and Criseyde* and Boccaccio's *Filostrato* (1875, 1883) remain a valuable aid to the Chaucer student.

In 1874 he married Emma Lucy (1843–94), the daughter of Ford Madox Brown (*q.v.*). He died in London on Feb. 5, 1919.

William Michael has been overshadowed by his brother and sister. Of high integrity, he was a devoted and self-denying son and brother, and the mainstay of his family. His critical work is worthy, and his literary interests were often in advance of his time. He strikingly exemplifies the civil servant and man of letters, in an age which allowed its public servants leisure to combine scholarly devotion to literature with fulfillment of their official duties.

For bibliography, *see* ROSSETTI, DANTE GABRIEL; ROSSETTI, GABRIELE PASQUALE GIUSEPPE. (J. BN.)

ROSSINI, GIOACCHINO ANTONIO (1792–1868), the principal 19th-century Italian opera composer before Verdi, was born at Pesaro on Feb. 29, 1792. His father was a town trumpeter and a horn-player in theatres; his mother was a singer. As a child Rossini studied singing and the piano at Bologna while his parents performed in theatres in the district. He was engaged to sing as a treble in churches and theatres, and he also played the horn. In

BY COURTESY OF GEORGE EASTMAN HOUSE

GIOACCHINO ROSSINI, PHOTOGRAPHED ABOUT 1868

1807 he entered the conservatory at Bologna, but over the following years his knowledge of instrumentation was gained from independent study of the quartets and symphonies of Haydn and Mozart, rather than from his teachers. He became known as *il tedeschino* ("the little German") because of his devotion to Mozart. At age 16 he won a prize at the Bologna conservatory for his cantata *Il pianto d'armonia per la morte d'Orfeo.* His first opera, *La cambiale di matrimonio,* was performed at Venice when he was 18. Between 1810 and 1813 he produced several operas with varying success at Bologna, Rome, Venice, and Milan. *Tancredi* (Venice, 1813), based on Tasso's *Gerusalemme liberatà* and Voltaire's *Tancrède,* was his first world success. This was preceded in the same year by *Il Signor Bruschino,* the overture of which later became well known, and was followed, also in the same year, by *L'italiana in Algeri,* and in 1814 by *Il turco in Italia.* Rossini continued to write operas for Venice and Milan during the next few years, but without repeating the success of *Tancredi.*

From 1815 to 1823 he was engaged to write two operas a year for Domenico Barbaja, the principal impresario of the time, who managed the theatres at Naples and Milan and the Italian opera at Vienna. Audiences greatly liked *Elisabetta, regina d'Inghilterra* (Naples, 1815), in which a leading part was taken by Barbaja's mistress, the Spanish soprano Isabella Colbran, whom Rossini married in 1822. In *Almaviva, ossia La precauzione inutile* (Rome, 1816), the libretto by Cesare Sterbini, was a version of Beaumarchais' *Barbier de Séville*—also the source for the libretto of Giovanni Paisiello's *Barbiere,* an opera which had enjoyed European popularity for more than a quarter of a century. Rossini conducted the work himself. On the first night the opera was hissed. A more favourable reception greeted the second performance, and before long it was realized that Rossini had created in this work a masterpiece of musical comedy, with the result that the title of *Barbiere di Siviglia* ("The Barber of Seville") passed inevitably to his opera.

It is eminent among Rossini's best works, which are remarkable for their light, captivating rhythms, their pictorial effects, particularly the long crescendo passages in their overtures, and their spontaneous melodies.

Rossini produced numerous operas during the years of his association with Barbaja. Of these, *Otello* (1816) is notable for its contrast with the treatment of the same subject by Verdi at a similar point in his development. In deference to the taste of the day the story was made to end happily. The comic opera *Cenerentola*, based on the Cinderella story, was produced at Rome in 1817, *Mosè in Egitto* ("Moses in Egypt") at Naples in 1818, and *Zelmira* at Naples in 1822. Rossini conducted his own works in Vienna in 1822 and in London the following year. In 1824 he was appointed musical director of the Théâtre Italien in Paris, and was later composer to the king and held the title of *inspecteur-général du chant en France*. At the Opéra he produced French versions of several of his earlier Italian works. *Le Comte Ory* was produced there in 1828, and the production there of *Guillaume Tell* in 1829 brought his career as a composer of operas to a close. The music of this final operatic work is largely free from the conventions discovered and used by him in his earlier works, and it therefore marks an important transitional stage in operatic development.

Apart from brief stays in Bologna and Madrid, Rossini remained in Paris until 1836. From 1836 to 1848 he lived in Bologna where he was president of the Liceo Musicale, and taught singing. In 1837 he separated from his wife and in 1845 married Olympe Pélissier. In 1848 he moved to Florence, and in 1855 returned to Paris. His comparative silence from 1832 onward makes his biography appear almost like the narrative of two lives—the life of swift triumph, and the long life of seclusion. Between 1832 and 1839 he wrote a *Stabat Mater;* its success compared favourably with the success of his operas. Among other compositions of his later years were the *Petite Messe solennelle* (1864) and a collection of piano pieces, songs, and instrumental works issued under the title *Péchés de vieillesse* ("Sins of Old Age"). Rossini died at Passy, near Paris, on Nov. 13, 1868.

BIBLIOGRAPHY.—Stendhal, *Vie de Rossini* (1824; Eng. trans. by R. N. Coe, 1956); F. Toye, *Rossini* (1934); F. Bonavia, *Rossini* (1941); L. Rognoni, *Rossini* (1956).

ROSSLYN, ALEXANDER WEDDERBURN, 1ST EARL OF (1733–1805), who, as Lord Loughborough, was successively chief justice of the common pleas and lord chancellor of Great Britain, was born in Edinburgh on Feb. 13, 1733, the eldest son of Peter Wedderburn, a lord of session under the title of Lord Chesterhall. Educated at Edinburgh University, he entered the Inner Temple in 1753. In deference to his father's wishes he qualified as an advocate in Edinburgh in 1754 and practised there for three years. He was called to the bar at the Inner Temple in November 1757 and in 1763 became a king's counsel.

His countrymen, the earl of Bute and William Murray (later Earl Mansfield), were useful to him; through the influence of Bute, then first minister, he was elected to Parliament in 1761. Wedderburn frequently changed his political allegiance. He resigned his seat in March 1769, in support of John Wilkes in the Middlesex elections dispute, thereby winning enormous popularity in the country. In January 1770 he received the pocket borough of Bishop's Castle, Shropshire, from the Whig Baron Clive. His new associates, however, distrusted him and with reason; in January 1771 he deserted to the ministry of Lord North and was made solicitor general. Throughout the American Revolution (1775–81) he savagely attacked the colonies and in June 1778 he was made attorney general. He became chief justice of the Court of Common Pleas in June 1780 and was created Baron Loughborough.

In the coalition ministry of Charles James Fox and Lord North (April–December 1783) he was first commissioner of the great seal. During the first eight years of William Pitt's ministry, he remained a supporter of Fox in the belief that there would be a reaction in his favour; but in 1792 he deserted him and in January 1793 was appointed lord chancellor in Pitt's cabinet. After Pitt's resignation in 1801, Henry Addington (later Viscount Sidmouth), the new prime minister, dismissed Loughborough, who received the consolation of the earldom of Rosslyn. He died at his country house in Stoke Poges, Buckinghamshire, on Jan. 2, 1805, and was buried in St. Paul's Cathedral, London.

On the bench his judgments were remarkable for their perspicuity, particularly in appeal cases to the House of Lords, but his knowledge of the English common law was rudimentary and he made little attempt to reform the abuses of the court of chancery.

See Lord J. Campbell, *Lives of the Lord Chancellors,* vol. vii and viii, 4th ed. (1857). (G. H. J.)

ROSSO, GIOVANNI BATTISTA DI JACOPO (1495–1540), called Rosso FIORENTINO, Italian painter and decorator, and one of the leaders of the Fontainebleau School, was born in Florence in 1495. He may have received his early training in the studio of Andrea del Sarto, alongside his contemporary, Jacopo da Pontormo; the earliest works of these two young painters combined suggestions from Michelangelo and from northern Gothic engravings in a novel Mannerist style, characterized by its highly charged emotionalism (*see* MANNERIST ART AND ARCHITECTURE). Rosso's most remarkable paintings from this period are the "Assumption" (1517; fresco at SS. Annunziata, Florence), the "Deposition" (1521; Pinacoteca, Volterra), and "Moses Defending the Daughters of Jethro" (*c.* 1523; Uffizi, Florence). At the end of 1523 he moved to Rome. Fleeing from the sack of the city in 1527, he worked briefly in several central Italian towns. In 1530, on the invitation of Francis I, he went to France (by way of Venice) and remained in the royal service there until his death in Paris on Nov. 14, 1540. His principal surviving work is the decoration of the Galerie François I at the palace of Fontainebleau (*c.* 1533–40) where, in collaboration with Francesco Primaticcio, he developed an ornamental style whose influence was felt throughout northern Europe. His numerous designs for engravings also exercised a wide influence on decorative arts in Italy and northern Europe.

See Kurt Kusenberg, *Le Rosso* (1931); Paola Barocchi, *Il Rosso Fiorentino* (1950). (D. KG.)

ROSSO, MEDARDO (1858–1928), Italian sculptor, after World War II the object of much study by younger sculptors, who are interested in his sensitive modeling and elusive shapes. Of all 19th-century sculpture, the wax and plaster figures of Rosso are closest in intent to Impressionist painting because their modeling is dictated by immediate sensations of light and movement. Rosso wished his figures to be closely related to their physical environment. A sensitive and introspective portraitist, he was also socially aware and produced poignant images of illness and everyday situations, such as "Sick Child" (1895) and "Impression of an Omnibus" (1883–84). The elusiveness of his forms, which Rosso felt caught the quality of movement in life, was a shocking departure from academic art. Rosso was born June 20, 1858, at Turin and died March 31, 1928, at Milan. His influence extended through the Italian Futurists to Rodin and Brancusi, and in the second half of the 20th century was spreading still further.

See Carola Giedion-Welcker, *Contemporary Sculpture,* 3rd ed. (1961). (A. E. EL.)

ROSS-ON-WYE, a market town and urban district in Herefordshire, Eng., lies 15 mi. SSE of Hereford by road. Pop. (1961) 5,641. It is characterized by narrow streets and ancient buildings, and its pillared market house (1670) is still the scene of activity on market days. Dominating the town is the parish Church of St. Mary, built in the Decorated and Perpendicular styles. The philanthropist John Kyrle (1637–1724), known as the "Man of Ross" and eulogized by Alexander Pope in his third *Moral Epistle,* did much to benefit the town and is buried in the church. Known as "the Gateway of the Wye," the town is a tourist centre famous for its panoramic views, especially that of the horseshoe bend of the Wye from the Prospect, adjoining the churchyard. It is also the centre of a highly productive agricultural district.

ROSTAND, EDMOND (1868–1918), French dramatist, known especially as the author of *Cyrano de Bergerac,* was born at Marseilles, April 1, 1868. *Les Romanesques* (1894; English translation, *The Romanticks,* performed 1955), a fantasy in the manner of Musset, on the Romeo and Juliet theme, was Rostand's first success. This was followed by *La Princesse lointaine* (1895), in which the action symbolizes the idea that an illusion or an unattained ideal is superior to real life, and then *La Samaritaine* (1897), which dealt controversially with a biblical theme. Sarah Bernhardt acted in both plays. Rostand's next venture, *Cyrano de Bergerac* (1897; Eng. trans., 2nd ed., 1953), caused the greatest stir in the French theatre since Hugo's *Hernani.* It is a highly romantic "heroic comedy." Its hero is the 17th-century philosopher, swordsman, and man of letters, Savinien de Cyrano (*q.v.*), but the connection between its plot and Cyrano's life is remote. Well-constructed and written in eloquent verse, *Cyrano* reestablished the prestige of the alexandrine on the stage for a whole decade. It represents a revolt against all the most important trends of the time—naturalism, symbolism, and Ibsenism—and is a belated manifestation of romanticism. *L'Aiglon* (1900; Eng. trans. 1934), which followed, is a historical play concerning Napoleon I's son, the duke of Reichstadt; the duke was played by Sarah Bernhardt. *L'Aiglon* is inferior to *Cyrano* but contains some brilliant scenes and well-known pieces of rhetoric. In 1910 came the long-awaited but unsuccessful *Chantecler* (Eng. trans. 1913) in which animal characters depict the poet's own unhappy plight. Rostand's last play, *La Dernière Nuit de Don Juan,* with a prologue left incomplete at his death (in Paris, Dec. 2, 1918), was produced posthumously in 1922. He had been elected to the Académie Française in 1901.

See G. Haraszti, *Rostand* (1913); J. Suberville, *Le Théâtre d'E. Rostand* (1921). (D. Ks.)

ROSTOCK, a Baltic town and seaport of East Germany, capital of Rostock *Bezirk* (district) of the German Democratic Republic. It lies on the left bank of the Warnow estuary, 8 mi. (13 km.) SSE of Warnemünde, its outport, and 140 mi. (225 km.) NNW of Berlin by rail. The *Stadtkreis* (urban district), which includes Gehlsdorf and heathland on the right bank of the estuary as well as Warnemünde, has an area of 68 sq.mi. Pop. (1962 est.) 166,456. A train-ferry connects Warnemünde with Gedser (Denmark).

The town centre has been extensively reconstructed following heavy air raid damage during World War II. The Lange Strasse has been rebuilt in the characteristic North German style. Outstanding examples of Gothic brick buildings are the Marienkirche (1398–1472, with an astronomical clock), the Nikolaikirche (early 14th century), and the Petrikirche (early 15th century). The University of Rostock (1419) was at one time a stronghold of Lutheranism. The Rathaus in the Neuer Markt is a 15th-century structure with a Baroque facade (1727). Part of the old town walls and gates survive (the Steintor, 1575; the Kröpeliner Tor, 14th century; and the Petritor).

Rostock is the chief port of the German Democratic Republic. Its population grew considerably after 1945 and a new residential district at Reutershagen arose. Shipyards (the Neptune Wharf in Rostock and the Warnow Wharf in Warnemünde were built after 1945) and fisheries are the main industries. Diesel motors, machinery, chemical products, and matches are also manufactured.

In the 12th century Rostock was a Wendish settlement. It received its municipal charter in 1218. During the 13th century the middle town and the new town developed separately from the old town. In the 14th century Rostock became a member of the Hanseatic League. In 1323 it became part of Mecklenburg and in 1352 it passed to the dukes of Schwerin. Later it was the common possession of Schwerin and Güstrow until it finally passed to Schwerin in 1695 when the Güstrow line became extinct.

Rostock *Bezirk* was created in 1952 and comprises northern Mecklenburg and Vorpommern (Western or Hither Pomerania) along the Baltic Coast between Travemünde on the west and Ahlbeck on the east. There are 11 *Landkreisen* and 3 *Stadtkreisen* (Wismar, Rostock, and Stralsund). Along the coast cliffs alternate with sand dunes. The island of Poel and the inlet of Salzhaff lie off the western coast. On the eastern coast is the peninsula of Fischland–Darss–Zingst, the islands of Rügen and Hiddensee off Stralsund, and the greater part of the island of Usedom (Uznam). The western part of the *Bezirk* is very fertile, rye, oats, and sugar beets being grown. Cattle breeding is widespread and fishing is important off the coast. The chief ports are Wismar, Rostock, Stralsund, and Sassnitz, the latter having a train-ferry to Trelleborg, Sweden. Industry, mainly located in the towns, consists of shipbuilding, woodworking, sugar manufacture, machinery, and food industries. There are tourist resorts on the coast.

(Be. R.)

ROSTOPCHIN, FEDOR VASILIEVICH, Count (1763–1826), Russian army officer and statesman, one of the closest favourites of Emperor Paul I and military governor of Moscow during the French invasion of Russia, was born at Livny, Orel Province, on March 23 (new style; 12, old style), 1763. He was of an ancient noble family of Tatar origin. He joined the army in 1785 and traveled in Western Europe (1786–88). A few days after his accession to the throne (Nov. 17 [N.S.; 6, O.S.], 1796), Paul appointed Rostopchin a major general and his personal adjutant general. In 1798 he became foreign minister and in 1799 he was made a count. Despite all these favours, he was aware of Paul's weak character and whimsical ideas and always advised him in accord with what he considered to be Russia's true national interest. On March 4 (N.S.; Feb. 20, O.S.), 1801, shortly before Paul's assassination, he was disgraced for opposing the alliance with France. He retired to his estate at Voronovo near Moscow. In 1810 Emperor Alexander I restored him to favour, and in May 1812 appointed him commander and military governor of Moscow. .

Rostopchin is alleged to have instigated the burning of Moscow on the first night after the entry of the French (Sept. 14 [N.S.], 1812); it is certain that the prisons were opened on his orders, and that he took no action to stop the outbreak. He defended himself in a pamphlet printed in Paris in 1823, *La Vérité sur l'incendie de Moscou,* but he later made serious admissions. Shortly after the Congress of Vienna, to which he had accompanied Emperor Alexander, he again fell into disgrace. He returned to Russia in 1825 and died in Moscow on Jan. 30 (N.S.; 18, O.S.), 1826. His *Mémoires écrits en dix minutes* were published in St. Petersburg (1853) and his *Oeuvres inédites* in Paris (1894).

See Marquis A. de Ségur, *Vie du Comte Rostopchine* (1873); M. de La Fuye, *Rostoptchine: Européen ou Slave?* (1937).

ROSTOV, an *oblast* (province) of the Russian Soviet Federated Socialist Republic, U.S.S.R., was formed in 1937. Area 38,919 sq.mi. (100,800 sq.km.). Pop. (1959) 3,311,747. It lies athwart the lower Don and includes the lowest part of the Northern Donets Basin and most of the Manych Basin. In the west are the low hills of the Donets ridge, but for the most part the *oblast* is low, rolling plain, cut by the broad floodplains of the rivers, especially the Don. In the east, part of the huge Tsimlyanski reservoir, formed in 1951, is included. The climate is continental and dry. January temperatures average 18° to 22° F (−7.7° to −5.5° C) and July temperatures 71° to 74° F (21°–23° C). Rainfall is about 16 in. (400 mm.) a year. The whole *oblast* lies within the steppe zone, with good chernozem soils, and much of the natural grass vegetation has been plowed up. Along the Don are floodplain meadows and marsh areas, with occasional groves of trees.

Of the 1959 population, 57% (1,898,801) were urban, living in 18 towns and 29 urban districts. Many of the towns are large, notably the major ports of Rostov-on-Don (pop. 599,542) and Taganrog (202,062), the coal-mining centres of Shakhty (196,-190), Novoshakhtinsk (103,566), Kamensk-Shakhtinski (57,525) (*qq.v.*), and Gukovo (52,969), together with the Don towns of Novocherkassk (*q.v.*; 95,453) and Bataysk (52,242). The northern part of the *oblast* represents the eastern end of the Donets Basin (Donbass) coalfield and is particularly rich in anthracite. This area from 1954 to 1957 formed the separate Kamensk *oblast*. Heavy industry based on the coal is found in the ports and mining towns. The flow of freight through the *oblast* is heavy, by the Don waterway leading to the Volga and by the railway, and the gas and oil pipelines through Rostov, between the Caucasus and central U.S.S.R. Agriculture is also important, chiefly for wheat, barley, sunflowers, maize (corn), and melons. Along the lower Don vineyards and market gardening based on irrigation are important. (R. A. F.)

ROSTOV-ON-DON (Rostov-na-Donu), a town and *oblast* centre of the Russian Soviet Federated Socialist Republic, U.S.S.R., stands on the right bank of the lower Don, 30 mi. (48 km.) above its mouth. Pop. (1959) 599,542. It was founded in 1749 as the customs post of Temernika, when the river mouth was still in Turkish hands. In 1761 the fortress of St. Dmitri was built and the town developed around it, acquiring town status in 1797.

The population rose from 3,000 in 1809 to 119,476 in 1897. The opening of the Volga-Don Canal in 1952 markedly increased the volume of trade. The town is linked to the sea by a dredged channel. It is well served by railways and lies on the Moscow-Baku road; there is also an airport. Rostov is the largest producer of agricultural machinery in the U.S.S.R. Other manufacturing products include self-propelled barges, ball-bearings, electrical and heating equipment, wire, and machinery for road-making and for the clothing and food-processing industries. There are ship and locomotive repair yards. Other local industries include the production of chemicals, clothing and footwear, glass, tobacco, and champagne. There are also flour-milling and food-processing plants. Rostov State University was founded in 1917 and there are eight other institutes of higher education. (R. A. F.)

ROSTOVTZEFF, MICHAEL IVANOVITCH (1870–1952), U.S.-Russian archaeologist, philologist, and historian, who has been called the greatest and most influential ancient history scholar of the first half of the 20th century. He was the first to use the archaeological remains of Greeks and Romans as a source for cultural history (*The Social and Economic History of the Roman Empire*, 1926, 2nd ed. 1957; *The Social and Economic History of the Hellenistic World*, 1941, 2nd ed. 1953). Born Nov. 10, 1870, near Kiev, Rostovtzeff studied at the universities of Kiev and St. Petersburg, and became familiar with the antiquities of southern Russia. He traveled to study the ruins of Pompeii; investigations of Roman lead tesserae led him into economics and social life, and the study of papyri and inscriptions resulted in work on serfdom in antiquity. Rostovtzeff's works include *Ancient Decorative Painting in South Russia* (1913); *Iranians and Greeks in South Russia* (1922); *A History of the Ancient World* (1926–28); *The Animal Style in South Russia and China* (1929). In 1918 Rostovtzeff went to the U.S., teaching at the University of Wisconsin (1920–25), and at Yale University (1925–44, professor emeritus thereafter). He directed the excavation of a Hellenistic city on the Euphrates River (*Dura-Europos and Its Art*, 1938). He died Oct. 20, 1952, in New Haven, Conn.

See C. B. Welles, "Michael Ivanovitch Rostovtzeff," *Russian Review*, vol. 12 (April 1953); J. T. Lambie (ed.), *Architects and Craftsmen in History* (1956). (C. B. Ws.)

ROSTOV YAROSLAVSKI (ROSTOV-VELIKI), a town in Yaroslavl *oblast* of the Russian Soviet Federated Socialist Republic, U.S.S.R., stands on the northwest shore of Lake Nero on the road and railway from Moscow to Yaroslavl. Pop. (1959) 29,230. Rostov is one of the very earliest Russian towns. By the 11th century it became the seat of a bishopric. The Uspenski Cathedral was burned in 1211; its successor of 1230 still survives. Rostov derived wealth and power from its position on a main route which ran from the Moscow region to the Volga at Yaroslavl and on to the fur-providing forests of the north. In 1408 it was largely destroyed by fire. The *kreml* (citadel) on the lake shore and several 17th-century churches survive. Also of the 17th century is the Belaya Palata (White Pavilion), built to receive the tsar. The Terem, or palace of the princes, is earlier (15th century). Modern Rostov is a small, local centre, with linen and starch-making industries, but the old, traditional handicraft of enamel on metal, for which Rostov was famous, is still maintained. (R. A. F.)

ROSWELL, a city of southeastern New Mexico, U.S., about 170 mi. SE of Albuquerque, is the hub for a trade area on a radius of approximately 100 mi. Nourished by an artesian basin, the city with its thousands of trees gives the appearance of an oasis in the semiarid ranching plains. It lies at an altitude of 3,570 ft. The Pecos River flows 12 mi. to the east.

Roswell began as a trading post founded in 1871 by Van C. Smith. It was incorporated in 1891. Initially a cattle town, Roswell developed agricultural production first in orchards and alfalfa, later in cotton. Its subsequent growth can be attributed to the establishment of Walker Air Force Base in 1941, and to the location of district offices by major oil companies during the decade of the 1950s. Roswell is the seat of Chaves County and the home of the New Mexico Military Institute. The Roswell Museum and Art Center has been called a model for museums in small cities. Its major exhibits include a collection of the paintings of Peter Hurd, who was born in Roswell in 1904; the Witter Bynner collection of Chinese art; and the Robert H. Goddard rocket exhibit, commemorating and illustrating Goddard's pioneer work (much of it carried out at Roswell, 1930–41).

For comparative population figures *see* table in NEW MEXICO: *Population.* (PL. HN.)

ROSYTH, a town and naval base in Fife, Scot., lies on the northern shore of the Firth of Forth, 3 mi. SE of Dunfermline. Construction of the naval base was started in 1909 but was still far from complete on the outbreak of World War I, and it was not until 1916 that the first warship was dry-docked. Among the many vessels repaired between 1916 and 1918 were the capital ships of the Grand Fleet after the Battle of Jutland. After the Armistice the number of men employed was gradually reduced and in 1925 the dockyard was placed on a care and maintenance basis until 1938. During this period the dry docks were leased to a ship-breaking firm. Among the ships broken up were the scuttled German warships salvaged at Scapa Flow. The dockyard was partially reopened by the Admiralty in 1938, and on the outbreak of World War II the labour force was rapidly expanded and more than 1,000 houses were built for skilled workers transferred from the royal dockyards in England. During the war more than 3,000 warships were repaired or dry-docked. In 1963 it was announced that Rosyth would be the refitting base for nuclear-powered submarines.

Rosyth Castle, a 16th-century tower with a dovecote, is mentioned in Sir Walter Scott's *The Abbot*.

ROTARY CLUB: *see* SERVICE CLUB.

ROTATION OF CROPS refers to the repeated growing of different crops in a specified order, on the same fields, in contrast to a one-crop system or to haphazard crop successions. Well-planned cropping practices provide the basis for a smooth-running and effective farm organization. Long before the Christian era crop growers were aware of the influences of crops on each other and of the usefulness of cropping associations. Wherever food crops are produced some kind of rotation cropping appears to be practised. In central Africa the natives use a 36-year rotation. After cutting and burning a 35-year growth of woody shrubs and trees, one crop of finger millet is produced. In the food-producing regions of the world various rotations of much shorter length are widely used. Some of them are designed for the highest immediate returns without much regard for the continuing usefulness of the basic resources. Others are planned for high continuing returns with protected resources. The underlying principles for planning effective cropping systems began to emerge in the mid-years of the 19th century. The subject remains a fruitful field in agronomic research.

The oldest American rotation experiment (begun in Illinois in 1876) reveals a yield decline of 60% by mid-20th century for corn in continuous culture. When corn and oats were alternated the yield of corn declined but at a slower rate. When corn was alternated with oats and clover the yield of corn remained constant. If all crops are accounted for, as in corn-equivalent yields, the yield for a 12-year period at mid-20th century was 20.8 bu. an acre for continuous corn. When corn and oats, a low-profit crop, shared an acre equally the total yield was 22.9 bu. Where corn, oats and clover shared an acre equally, the total yield for corn and oats on two-thirds of the acre was 29.5 bu. and that for all three crops on the acre was 35.5 bu. Competing crops provided each other with advantages, and when a complementary crop was added and removed from the land the benefits were greater. If the clover crop had functioned as a rest crop rather than a hay crop its complementary effects would, no doubt, have been much greater, as other experiments have indicated.

Rotation Ratios.—Early experiments, such as those at the Rothamsted Experimental station (*q.v.*), in England, pointed to the usefulness of selecting rotation crops from three classifications: cultivated row, close-growing grains and sod-forming or rest crops. Such a classification provides a ratio basis for balancing crops in the interest of continuing soil protection and production economy. It is sufficiently flexible for adjusting crops to many situations, for making changes when needed and for including go-between crops as cover and green manures. A simple rotation would be one crop from each group with a 1:1:1 ratio. The first number in a rotation ratio refers to cultivated row crops, the second to close-growing grains and the third to sod-forming or rest crops. Such a ratio signifies the need for three fields and years to produce each crop annually. This requirement would be satisfied with a rotation of corn, oats and clover or of potatoes, wheat and clover-timothy. If green manure or cover crops were desired, three crops could be produced in a 2:1":0 rotation of corn, soybeans and oats (sweet clover). The mark " following a number means that, after a small-grain crop is harvested, a cover crop is on the land for the remainder of the year and until the following spring. Thus a green-manure crop can be grown in rotation without taking the land out of production for a year. Such a rotation could affect soil protection and production economy in a different manner than the 1:1:1 types of rotations. Rotations for any number of fields and crop relationships can be described in this manner. In general most rotations are confined to time limits of eight years or less.

Effects on Production and Soil.—In the interest of high crop incomes some farmers use a 3:0:0 type of rotation such as corn, corn and soybeans that requires annual plowing, seedbed preparation and cultivation. If continued too long such a rotation will bring about unfavourable changes in the soil as sizable reductions in organic matter and nitrogen, development of less desirable physical conditions, accelerated loss of soil and water by surface runoff and lowered nutrient-supplying powers. These changes are often accompanied with greater damage to crops from insects, diseases and weeds. The end results are declining yields, loss of crop quality and reduced incomes. Since World War II rotations of this type have been supplemented with the heavy use of fertilizer with the idea of offsetting the unfavourable effects of such rotations. Whether such a program can be continued satisfactorily will need to be judged in the light of sufficient experience.

In the interest of maximum soil protection with effective production economy, other farmers use 2:1:1 types of rotations as corn, soybeans, wheat and alfalfa for use on four fields. Additional advantages can be provided by doubling this rotation to 2(2:1":1) for use on four fields over an eight-year period as (1) corn, (2) soybeans, (3) wheat or oats (sweet clover), (4) corn, (5) soybeans, (6) wheat or oats, (7) alfalfa and (8) alfalfa, with a moderate use of fertilizer as needed. Such rotations are increasingly effective over long-time periods but may not produce as much cash income in the beginning years as the 3:0:0 type of cropping.

Rotation planning consists essentially in fitting soils and crops together in such ways as to be suitable and desirable for livestock, grain, truck-garden and other types of farming. The acreage devoted to sod-forming and rest crops should be expanded at the expense of row crops on soils of increasing slopes and declining fertility. This will provide better vegetative covering to protect sloping land from excessive erosion and supply organic matter for improving soil productivity on both sloping and level lands. With lessening slope and increasing fertility the row crops may be expanded, but this should not be done with too much reduction in the sod-forming and rest crops. The differing effects of crops on soils and on each other and in reactions to insect pests, diseases and weeds require carefully planned sequences. Competitive and complementary relations can produce advantageous interactions.

Use of Legumes.—Rotation planning should also include a consideration of crop-handling practices. Sufficient legume residues should be returned to the soil either directly or indirectly in animal manure to supply all or much of the nitrogen required by the rotation. The nonlegume residues (stover straws) should be associated with the legume residues to obtain the greatest benefits from the legumes. Experiments show that association increases the yields of succeeding crops more than the combined yields of the two types of residues when used separately. These benefits cannot be secured if these residues are destroyed or removed from the land.

Broadly speaking, cropping systems should be planned around the use of deep-rooting legumes. If too little use is made of them, productivity will decline; if too much land is devoted to them,

wastes may occur and other useful crops will be displaced. Rotations depending wholly on green-manure legumes should be confined to the more level and fertile lands. It is desirable to include legumes alone or in mixtures with nonlegume sod-forming crops as a regular crop in many field rotations. In general this should occur about once in each four-year period. Short rotations are not likely to provide the best crop balances and long rotations on a larger number of fields may introduce complications. With a moderate number of fields, additional flexibility can be provided by split cropping on some fields.

Regional Differences.—The usefulness of individual field crops is affected by regional differences in climate and soil. A major crop in one region may have little or no value in another. In each region, however, there are usually row, grain and sod or rest crops that can be brought together into effective cropping systems. The individual crops may vary much from region to region, but the rotation ratios will be somewhat similar among the regions. Some of the rotation ratios used in practice in differing regions are: 2:0:0; 0:2:0; 0:0:1; 2:1":0; 1:1:1; 1:1:2; 1:2":1; 2:1:1; 2(2:1":1); 2:2:1; 2:1:2; and 1:1:3 or 4.

In addition to the many beneficial effects on soils and crops, well-planned crop rotations also provide the business aspects of farming with advantages. Labour, power and equipment can be handled with more efficiency; weather and market risks can be reduced; livestock requirements can be met more easily; and the farm can be a more effective year-round enterprise.

See also SOIL: *Soil Productivity.*   (F. C. BR.)

ROTE: *see* CRWTH; HARP.

ROTH, WALTER RUDOLF VON (1821–1895), German philologist, a noted Sanskrit scholar, was born at Stuttgart on April 3, 1821. He was a student and later a professor at Tübingen University. His profound studies of the Vedas brought about and clarified Western understanding of these difficult religious texts. In 1846 he published *Zur Literatur und Geschichte des Weda*, a pioneer work based on manuscript materials. He edited the Atharvaveda (1856) in collaboration with his American pupil, William Dwight Whitney. In the great Sanskrit lexicon published in St. Petersburg from 1852 to 1875 by Otto von Böhtlingk and Roth, the Vedic portion is his. He died at Tübingen on June 23, 1895.
                                                              (M. B. E.)

ROTHAMSTED EXPERIMENTAL STATION, at Harpenden in Hertfordshire, Eng., founded in 1843, is the oldest agricultural research station in the world. John Bennet Lawes (*q.v.;* 1814–1900), the founder, started to experiment at Rothamsted soon after coming down from Oxford in 1834. By 1842 he had discovered and patented a process for making a soluble phosphatic fertilizer (superphosphate) and initiated the fertilizer industry by opening a factory to produce it commercially. He considered 1843 to be the date of the station's foundation because it was then that he invited Joseph Henry Gilbert (1817–1901), a chemist, to work with him and started the long collaboration that lasted more than a half a century until Lawes's death; also, that year was the first year of the Broadbalk experiment on manuring of wheat, which still continues. It was one of a series designed to find the nutritional requirements of important crops, in which the same crop was grown year after year on the same land, with different plots getting different treatments but each plot getting the same one each year.

Other experiments conformed more to agricultural practice, with different crops grown in rotation. The crops, soils, manures and drainage water were analyzed and balance sheets produced to show the fate of what was added to the soil: whether it remained there, was removed in the crop or was lost. The general pattern of treatments was similar in most experiments: no manure; minerals only (minerals was the term used for the constituents of plant ash); nitrogen only; nitrogen and minerals; farmyard manure. The pattern was partly set by a controversy with the German chemist J. von Liebig, who thought plants could get all the nitrogen they need from the air. The Rothamsted experiments soon showed that Liebig was wrong and firmly established that nitrogenous manures greatly increase yields. The old experiments now provide soils unique in the information they carry about how plant nutrients increase and decrease with different treatments.

Lawes and Gilbert are known most for their work on the manuring of crops, but they studied such problems as the purification of sewage, the advantages and disadvantages of ensiling compared with haymaking and animal nutrition. The last established the value of different components in fodder, showed how the composition of animals changes during growth and fattening and destroyed the belief that animal fat came only from vegetable fat.

A converted barn served as the first laboratory, but the practical value of the work was soon recognized and grateful farmers subscribed to a Lawes Testimonial fund, which was used to build a laboratory in 1855. This served until the numbers of staff began to increase early in the 20th century. Until then the only new appointment was a second chemist, R. Warington, who started the study of soil microorganisms and showed that ammonia is converted to nitrate in soil by their activities. Until 1904, when the Society for Extending the Rothamsted Experiments was instituted, the work was paid for wholly by Lawes, at first directly and after 1889 by the income from the fund with which he endowed the Lawes Agricultural trust, the committee of which forms the governing body of the station. Public money was first provided in 1911, after which government grants were made annually and the work is now mostly financed by grants from the Agricultural Research council. The range of problems studied steadily increased and extended to all those affecting soil fertility and the growth of healthy crops. Rothamsted is the headquarters for the soil survey of England and Wales; it also houses the Commonwealth Bureau of Soils.

In 1934 money raised by public subscription allowed the Lawes Agricultural trust to buy the Manor house (now a residential hostel for workers at Rothamsted), the home farm and other parts of the estate. Of the 600 ac., about half are suitable for experiments and carry approximately 3,000 plots each year.

Many experiments are also made at the Woburn Experimental station in Bedfordshire, started by the Royal Agricultural Society of England in 1876, and joined to Rothamsted in 1926; the different soil there allows experiments on crops for which Rothamsted farm is unsuitable. Workers at the Broom's Barn Experimental station, near Bury St. Edmunds, Suffolk, study the manuring and the pests and diseases of sugar beet. (F. C. Bn.)

ROTHE, RICHARD (1799–1867), German Lutheran theologian, one of the most daring and original of the theologians in the tradition of German idealism, was born at Posen on Jan. 28, 1799. He studied at Heidelberg and Berlin and was a professor at Heidelberg for the major portion of his career. He died on Aug. 20, 1867.

Rothe owed much to the theology and ethics of Friedrich Schleiermacher, to the romanticism of Novalis, and to the piety of August Tholuck, but he soon went his own way. He is remembered most for his monograph of 1837 on the origins of the church and of its polity (*Die Anfänge der christlichen Kirche und ihrer Verfassung*) and for his massive work on Christian ethics (*Theologische Ethik*, three volumes, 1845–48; 2nd edition, containing his own revisions but published posthumously in five volumes, 1869–71). In both books he developed his thesis that the Kingdom of God, "the new community that proceeds from the Redeemer, must begin under the form of the Church," but that the church itself is destined to wither away in favour of the Christian state, which is to be both a religious and a moral society. Underlying this interpretation of the Kingdom of God was a profoundly evolutionary view of the historical process, whereby God, in his freedom, produced matter, out of which, in succession, mechanical nature, chemical nature, vegetative nature, and animal nature were evolved. Finally the human soul emerged from the animal nature to make man what he is. The coming of sin was both a disruption of the divinely planned evolutionary history of man and, because it brought the Redeemer, a divinely willed means for the consummation of that history. The goal of history was the elevation of man, and indeed of a "spiritualized" creation, to the level of the personal life of God.

His principal works remain untranslated, but his most charming book, *Stille Stunden* (*Still Hours*), gathered from his devotional writings in 1872, was translated into English by Jane T. Stoddard and published with an introductory essay on his life and thought by J. Macpherson in 1886.

BIBLIOGRAPHY.—H. J. Birkner, *Spekulation und Heilsgeschichte: Die Geschichtsauffassung Richard Rothes* (1959); Ernst Troeltsch, *Richard Rothe* (1899); Emanuel Hirsch, *Geschichte der neueren evangelischen Theologie*, vol. v, pp. 166–170, 395–410 (1960); Karl Barth, *Die protestantische Theologie im 19. Jahrhundert*, pp. 544–552 (1947).

(J. J. Pn.)

ROTHENBURG OB DER TAUBER, a town of West Germany in the *Land* (state) of Bavaria (Bayern), Federal Republic of Germany, is 53 mi. (85 km.) W of Nürnberg by rail. Pop. (1961) 11,134. It stands above the deep-cut, winding valley of the Tauber and is encircled by medieval, many-towered walls. The town hall has a 13th-century Gothic part and a Renaissance part (1572–78) with a Baroque arcade (1681). In it every Whitsuntide is performed a play—*Der Meistertrunk*—commemorating the siege of Rothenburg by J. T. Tilly, general of the Catholic League in the Thirty Years' War, in 1631. The church of St. Jakob (1373–1528) has a wooden altar by T. Riemenschneider (d. 1531). Rothenburg lies on the scenic route known as the "romantic road," leading from Würzburg to the Bavarian Alps. It has manufactures of baby carriages, soap, agricultural machinery, and clothing and textiles. There are also sandstone and limestone quarries. First named early in the 9th century as Rotinbure, it became a free imperial city in 1274 and attained its zenith under burgomaster Heinrich Toppler (1373–1408). (H.-J. Wi.)

ROTHENSTEIN, SIR WILLIAM (1872–1945), English artist known for portrait drawings of his contemporaries which by their fine draftsmanship and realism convey a vivid sense of character. He was born at Bradford, Yorkshire, on Jan. 29, 1872, son of Moritz Rothenstein, a German-Jewish immigrant who became a prosperous textile industrialist, and was educated at Bradford Grammar School. He studied for a year at the Slade School, London, under Alphonse Legros. At the age of 17 he went to Paris to the Académie Julian. In Paris he was encouraged by Degas, Pissarro, Toulouse-Lautrec, and Whistler. On his return to England he became prominent in the literary and artistic life of the 1890s. His friends included Wilde, Beardsley, Beerbohm, and Sargent. He married the actress Alice Knewstub (Alice Kingsley) and through her met many of the Pre-Raphaelites. From 1920 to 1935 he served as principal of the Royal College of Art, London, where he was influential in securing for students greater artistic freedom. He was an official British war artist in World Wars I and II and was knighted in 1931. His portraits (many in the National Portrait Gallery, London) include T. E. Lawrence, Joseph Conrad, W. B. Yeats, Walter de la Mare, and E. M. Forster. There is a self-portrait in the Metropolitan Museum of Art, New York City. He died on Feb. 14, 1945, near Stroud, Gloucestershire.

His writings include *Oxford Characters* (1893); *Life of Goya* (1900); and memoirs, *Men and Memories* (3 vol., 1931–39).

His son, Sir John Rothenstein (1901–), author of books on painting and a two-volume autobiography, *Summer's Lease* (1965), covering 1901–38, and *Brave Day, Hideous Night* (1966), covering 1938–65, was director of the Tate Gallery, London (1938 to 1964). Another son, Michael Rothenstein (1908–), became a painter.

See Robert Speaight, *William Rothenstein: the Portrait of an Artist in His Time* (1962).

ROTHERHAM, a county and parliamentary borough in the West Riding of Yorkshire, Eng., 6 mi. (10 km.) NE of Sheffield. Pop. (1961) 85,478. Area 14.5 sq.mi. It lies at the confluence of the Don and the Rother, which affords a notable north-south route on the east side of the Pennine upland. Rotherham is connected by the Don Canal with Goole and the Humber and is a railway and road junction. There are Bronze and Iron Age barrows, and remains of a Roman fort and settlement in the vicinity. Rotherham was taken by the Royalists in 1643, but after the Battle of Marston Moor it was surrendered to a detachment of parliamentary forces. Its industrial prosperity may be said to have begun when ironworks were established at Masborough on the opposite bank of the Don in 1746. It was incorporated in 1871 and became a county borough in 1902. A museum and art gallery was opened in 1893 and a technical college, art school, and a central public library in 1931. On Old Rotherham Bridge is a 15th-century chapel. The parish church of All Saints is 15th-century Perpendicular. In the mid-1950s there were four large parks and other open spaces covering about 500 ac. The principal industries are steel, iron, brass, glass, coal and its by-products, general engineering, brewing, and corn milling.

Wentworth Woodhouse, 4 mi. NW, is an 18th-century mansion partly inhabited by Earl Fitzwilliam and partly used as a training college for teachers.

ROTHERMERE, HAROLD SIDNEY HARMS-WORTH, 1st Viscount (1868–1940), British newspaper-owner, brother of Lord Northcliffe (*q.v.*), and the commercial brain behind the development of his publishing empire. He was born at Hampstead, April 26, 1868, the second son of Alfred Harmsworth. Largely under his mother's influence, he left the civil service in 1888 to become financial manager of his brother's magazine, *Answers,* which he saved from collapse. Thereafter he was the business genius in all of his brother's enterprises, balancing Northcliffe's enthusiastic creative exuberance with hardheaded financial realism sometimes bordering on cheeseparing, which, although it infuriated Northcliffe, ensured the stability essential to success.

Whereas Northcliffe was interested in newspapers for themselves, Rothermere was interested in them as a means of making money. To this end he brought ruthlessness and shrewd judgment. He quickly saw how much newspapers would benefit from controlling their own newsprint supplies, and founded the huge Anglo-Newfoundland Development corporation in 1906. He was created a baronet in 1910, and raised to the peerage in 1914. After a brief period as air minister in World War I, he received a viscountcy in 1919. Although he failed to secure control of the *Times* on Northcliffe's death (1922), he acquired his brother's majority interest in the other Northcliffe papers on favourable terms and began a series of operations which first gave him control of Sir Edward Hulton's Manchester newspaper properties (most of which he later resold at a profit) and then involved him in a bitter conflict, over the acquisition of a chain of provincial evening newspapers, with the Berry brothers (later Lord Camrose and Lord Kemsley) to whom, however, he sold the Northcliffe periodical interests, Amalgamated Press, for £8,000,000.

His journalistic judgment was less shrewd than his business sense. Under him the *Daily Mail* lost its lead and he nearly ruined the *Daily Mirror* before he sold it in 1931. His support for the British Union of Fascists and his attacks on all forms of public expenditure alienated readers and advertisers, and his attempt in 1929 to dictate terms to Stanley Baldwin (including the right to approve ministerial appointments before they were made) in return for his newspapers' support, brought a crushing rejoinder. His attempt to force Baldwin's hand by means of the United Empire party campaign, at first in conjunction with Lord Beaverbrook and then on his own, failed completely. Only abroad did he achieve the political acclaim he felt he deserved, when in 1927 his advocacy of a review of the treaty of Trianon brought an offer of the crown of Hungary. This he had the good sense not to accept.

Although ruthless in business and without his brother's personal magnetism, he was generous and both his personal and public benefactions were considerable. At the outbreak of World War II he accepted a mission to Canada, where his interests gave him great influence. But his health broke and he died, Nov. 26, 1940, at Hamilton, Bermuda. (E. F. Ws.)

ROTHES, EARLS OF. George Leslie (*c.* 1417–1489/90), the son of Sir Norman Leslie of Rothes in Moray and of Ballinbreich in Fife, was created earl of Rothes between 1457 and 1458. His grandson William Leslie (d. 1513), the 3rd earl, was killed at the Battle of Flodden and his great-grandson George Leslie (d. 1558), the 4th earl, was accused of complicity in the murder (1546) of Cardinal Beaton, but was acquitted at his trial in 1547. In 1558 he was one of the Scottish commissioners in Paris who witnessed the marriage of Mary Stuart and Francis, dauphin of France (afterward Francis II).

His son Andrew Leslie (d. 1611), the 5th earl, took an active part with the lords of the congregation, first against the queen mother, Mary of Lorraine, the regent of Scotland, and afterward against Mary Stuart, opposing her marriage to Lord Darnley (1565) and helping to plan the murder of her secretary David Rizzio (1566). He later changed his allegiance and fought for Mary at Langside in 1568. He continued to occupy a position of some prominence in Scottish affairs until his death. His grandson John Leslie (*c.* 1600–1641), the 6th earl, a strong opponent of episcopacy, in 1637 led the opposition to the introduction in Scotland of a new liturgy based on the English prayer book, and in the following year signed the National Covenant to defend the Presbyterian religion. His son John Leslie (*c.* 1630–1681), the 7th earl, fought for Charles II at the Battle of Worcester in 1651. At the Restoration in 1660 he was appointed lord president of the council for Scotland and became lord high treasurer for Scotland (1663) and keeper of the privy seal (1664). Deprived of all his offices in April 1667 through the influence of John Maitland (later duke of Lauderdale), he was consoled in October by being appointed lord chancellor of Scotland for life. He was created duke of Rothes in 1680, but on his death without male heirs, the dukedom became extinct. The earldom continued through his daughter Margaret Leslie (d. 1700). John Leslie (*c.* 1698–1767), the 10th earl, made the Army his career, fought at Dettingen (1743), and was commander in chief in Ireland (1758–67). From him is descended the 20th earl, Malcolm George Dyer Edwardes Leslie (1902–). (T. I.)

ROTHESAY, a royal burgh and the chief town of the county and island of Bute, Scot. Pop. (1966) 6,650. Lying on Rothesay Bay, on the eastern coast, it is a holiday town and conference centre, with a promenade 4 mi. (6.4 km.) long and a pavilion (1938). It is linked to the mainland by passenger and car ferries to Wemyss Bay (Renfrew) and Colintraive (Argyll). The sheltered bay affords excellent anchorage and is the headquarters of a submarine squadron. In the centre of the town are the ruins of a castle, originally erected *c.* 1098 either by Magnus Barfot, king of Norway, or by the Scots as a defense against the Norwegians. It is said to have been demolished by Robert Bruce, and the ruins today appear to be of 14th-century date. The village which grew up round the castle was made a royal burgh by Robert III, who in 1398 created his eldest son David duke of Rothesay, a title that became the highest Scottish title of the heir apparent to the throne of the United Kingdom. During the Commonwealth, Rothesay Castle was garrisoned by the parliamentarians. It was burned by the followers of Argyll in 1685 and remained neglected until the rubbish was cleared away by the second marquess of Bute in 1816. It was repaired by the third marquess and is now maintained by the Scottish National Trust. Although agriculture is the chief industry, the manufacture of fine tweed cloth is becoming increasingly important. There are cruises from Rothesay to the Kyles of Bute, around Arran, and to Campbeltown and Inveraray. The town is under the jurisdiction of a provost and council.

ROTHSCHILD, the name of a great European Jewish banking family, the name being derived from a red (*rot*) shield on the house in which the family lived in the ghetto of Frankfurt am Main, Ger., during the early part of its history.

Mayer Anselm Rothschild (1743–1812), the founder of the house, was born Feb. 23, 1743. He established moneylending branches in Europe and England, with his sons acting as branch managers. Anselm Mayer Rothschild (1773–1855), his eldest son, born June 12, 1773, remained with his father and took over the Frankfurt house. Solomon Rothschild (1774–1855), the second son, born Sept. 9, 1774, settled in Vienna; Nathan Mayer Rothschild (1777–1836) settled in London, Karl Rothschild (1788–1855) in Naples, and Jacob or James Rothschild (1792–1868), born May 15, 1792, in Paris. The founder laid down two maxims for the conduct of the banking operations of his family: conduct all operations in common, and set definite limits to each operation and never aim at exorbitant profits.

The Naples house was discontinued after the annexation of Naples by Italy in 1860.

Nathan Mayer, in London, came to be regarded as the financial genius of the family. The political events of the Napoleonic Wars gave the House of Rothschild its historic eminence. During that period, the Rothschilds raised £100,000,000 for the European governments. Anselm Mayer, the eldest brother, became a member of the Prussian Privy Council of Commerce, and in 1820 Bavarian consul and court banker; Solomon, who settled in Vienna, was on terms of intimacy with Metternich; and Jacob, of Paris, negotiated loans for the Bourbons. Mayer's sons received the right to use "von" before their names and were made Austrian barons in 1812. The family controlled European finance for many years.

The important London house, after Nathan Mayer's death in 1836, was managed by his son LIONEL ROTHSCHILD (1808–1879), born Nov. 22, 1808, who became the first Jewish member of Parliament, in which he served from 1858 to 1874. His son NATHAN MAYER ROTHSCHILD (1840–1915) was born Nov. 8, 1840, inherited a baronetcy from his uncle ANTHONY DE ROTHSCHILD (1810–1876) and was made a peer in 1885, the first Jew to be raised to the British peerage. Nathan's son succeeded to the title (see ROTHSCHILD, LIONEL WALTER ROTHSCHILD, 2nd Baron), and in his turn was succeeded by his nephew, NATHANIEL MAYER VICTOR ROTHSCHILD (1910–), a grandson of the 1st baron, who was chairman of the Agricultural Research Council (1948–58).

The head of the London family has been considered the lay head of British Jewry. The Balfour Declaration of Nov. 2, 1917, stating that the British government viewed with favour "the establishment of a national home for the Jewish people" in Palestine, was addressed to Lord Rothschild. EDMUND JAMES ROTHSCHILD (1845–1934), of the French branch of the family, invested more than 70,000,000 gold francs in helping to establish Jewish communities in Palestine.

Besides Lionel and Lionel Walter, three more Rothschilds have entered British politics. LIONEL NATHAN ROTHSCHILD (1882–1942) was a member of the House of Commons, 1910–23. JAMES ARMAND ROTHSCHILD (1878–) entered the House of Commons in 1929. MAURICE ROTHSCHILD (1881–) was a member of the French senate.

Other eminent members of the French branch of the family have been EDOUARD ROTHSCHILD (1868–1949), who was president of the Chemins de Fer du Nord, and HENRI ROTHSCHILD (1872–1947), physician and playwright.

Two great-great grandsons of Mayer Anselm continued the British house of N. M. Rothschild and Sons: LIONEL DE ROTHSCHILD (1882–), born Jan. 25, 1882, and ANTHONY GUSTAV DE ROTHSCHILD (1887–1961).

BIBLIOGRAPHY.—No adequate history of the Rothschilds exists, but the following may be consulted: E. C. Corti, *The Rise of the House of Rothschild* (1928); C. Roth, *The Magnificent Rothschilds* (1939); F. Morton, *The Rothschilds, a Family Portrait* (1962).   (J. R. Lt.)

ROTHSCHILD, LIONEL WALTER ROTHSCHILD,

2ND BARON (1868–1937), British zoologist who founded the Tring Museum of Natural History, eldest son of Nathan Mayer, 1st Baron Rothschild, was born on Feb. 8, 1868, in London. In 1917 his Zionist sympathies and preeminent position in the Anglo-Jewish community caused the British foreign secretary Lord Balfour to address to him the letter (known as the Balfour Declaration) declaring the British government's interest in establishing a Jewish national home in Palestine (see ZIONISM). Rothschild was a trustee of the British Museum (1899–1937), a member of Parliament (1899–1910), a fellow of the Royal Society (1911), and president of the zoological section of the British Association (1932). The museum he founded (subsequently presented to the British Museum) included the largest and most valuable collection of natural historical specimens ever assembled by one man, containing the largest collection of butterflies and moths in the world (more than 2,000,000 specimens and many thousands of types), and also a unique library of over 30,000 volumes. His collection of 280,000 bird skins is now in the American Museum of Natural History in New York City. He published alone or in collaboration with his museum staff over 800 papers and monographs dealing with zoological and botanical subjects. Lord Rothschild died on Aug. 27, 1937, at Tring, West Hertford, Eng.

See *Novitates Zoologicae,* vol. xli, pp. 1–41 (1938–39), which includes a list of Lord Rothschild's works.   (M. L. Rd.)

ROTHWELL, an urban district in the Normanton parliamentary division of the West Riding of Yorkshire, Eng., about 4 mi. SE of Leeds. Pop. (1961) 25,360. Area 16.7 sq.mi. Soon after the Conquest, Rothwell was a dependency of the castle of Pontefract, and a baronial residence, of which there are slight remains, was erected there. Coal, stone, sand, clay, and gravel are obtained and the town has copper tube, rope, chemical, and engineering factories. Rhubarb is produced on a large scale indoors. Methley urban and Hunslet rural districts were added to Rothwell in 1937.

Rothwell in Northamptonshire is a small manufacturing town 4 mi. NW of Kettering.

ROTIFERA (ROTATORIA), well-defined group of aquatic animals of microscopic size, noteworthy for the diversity of their forms, the vivacity and variety of their movements and the complexity of their structural development. They are often called wheel animalcules because in some species the ciliated bands on the head beat in a manner suggestive of the rotation of a wheel or wheels (see *Corona,* below). In length they range from .05 to 2 mm., but most are between 0.1 and 0.4 mm. In general rotifers are symmetrical in structure, although some are highly asymmetrical.

General Features.—The body, which is covered with a thin, flexible cuticle overlying a syncytial epidermis, is, in many species, weakly differentiated into several regions: head, neck, trunk and foot. These regions are separated from each other by folds (often a separate neck is not present). The foot may be divided into sections by folds. The sections, often called segments or joints, do not, however, reflect true metamerism.

The foot, an extension of the body posterior or ventral to the anus, bears at its end two conical toes, and contains within two pedal or cement glands which secrete a sticky material through ducts that open at the tips or near the base of the toes. The tail is the fold or prolongation dorsal or anterior to the anus.

At the head end is a flattened ciliated area, the corona, with a mouth near the ventral or posterior edge.

Corona.—Food is collected and swimming is brought about by the action of numerous cilia on an area close to or encircling the mouth, or on fringing lobes protrusible from the mouth. The whole area, including the mouth itself, as seen when the cilia are active, is called the corona. There are many varieties of this organ, differing widely in the arrangement of the cilia and in the presence of accessory structures.

The basic corona type can be regarded as a ciliated band around the head. The corona, prolonged posteriorly on the ventral side, encloses a bare apical area. Some rotifers have tufts of elongated cilia at the sides of the mouth or buccal area. Other species have lateral ciliated ridges, auricles, projecting from the head, the ciliation either being continuous with the buccal area, or limited to the edges. Auricles may be introvertable, in which case they are extended only when the animal is swimming.

Other coronal variations involve reduction of the ciliated band to a very narrow strip and reduction of the ciliation posterior to the mouth. Many actively swimming rotifers have the corona

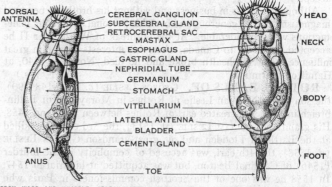

FIG. 1.—ANATOMY OF A REPRESENTATIVE ROTIFER SHOWING (LEFT) LATERAL AND (RIGHT) DORSAL VIEWS, GREATLY ENLARGED

reduced to a thin strip of cilia surrounding the head and enclosing a large apical area. A snoutlike projection or rostrum may be developed from the apical area.

In many species the cilia on the anterior and posterior margins of the ciliated areas are elongated. The anterior line of larger cilia is the trochus, the posterior line is the cingulum. The edges of the corona may be elaborated into lobes. The bdelloids (order Bdelloida), the extreme development of this type, have the dorsal margin so deeply indented toward the ventral side that it has cut through, breaking the trochus into two circles; these are the "rotating wheels" seen in many bdelloids.

The corona of members of the family Collothecidae represents a great modification. The anterior part of the body is drawn out into a wide bowl, the margin of which is usually lobed and covered with very long generally nonvibratile bristles (setae). Within the bowl is a ventral shelflike membrane, usually ciliated. There may be vibratile cilia inside the bowl and, in some species, on the margin as well; however, most do not have coronal cilia. Some adult collothecids lack coronal cilia, except for a small area at the bottom of the bowl.

Foot.—The foot may be highly developed, rudimentary or even absent as in many open-water (planktonic) species. There is often only one toe, representing a fusion of two. The toes of some rotifers are long, unequal, slender filaments, with the cement glands opening at the base. Other species lack these filaments and have a ciliated cup at the end of the foot. In the sessile species the foot usually ends in a stalk attachment or peduncle. The foot, in some species, may be withdrawn into the body.

Body Wall.—In many rotifers the cuticle is thin and pliable; in others it may be thickened in places, forming relatively stiff plates which together form the lorica. Often the anterior and posterior margins of a lorica have prominent spines, and a few rotifers have spines on the dorsal surface. Some animals have fairly flexible plates, difficult to differentiate from the connecting areas of cuticle. In some rotifers the lorica is simple and consists merely of a general thickening of the cuticle of the body, forming a boxlike structure devoid of obvious differentiation within the different regions. More commonly, however, the lorica consists of an arched dorsal plate and a flat ventral plate fused together at their edges. In such cases the anterior part of the flat plate may be connected with the arched plate by a pliable cuticular membrane which stretches to accommodate the head when it is retracted. Some have the dorsal and ventral plates joined together by lateral strips of thin cuticle folded inward, forming deep grooves along the sides; others have a dorsal groove.

Other modifications of the body wall are movable bristles and paddles, quite different from the spiny extensions of the lorica. They may be long slender filaments, flat paddles or hollow outgrowths of the body furnished with spines and powered by large muscles.

Digestive Tract.—From the mouth a ciliated gullet leads to the mastax. The cuticular lining of the pharynx is thickened, forming the trophi or jaws. Following posteriorly from the mastax, the rest of the digestive tract consists of an esophagus, a thick-walled cellular stomach and a relatively thin-walled, syncytial intestine, the posterior portion of which is differentiated as a cloaca.

The anus opens on the dorsal surface; however, in genera in which the foot projects from the ventral surface, the anus opens posterior to the foot.

Trophi.—The trophi are very characteristic features of the rotifers, and are found in no other group of animals. There are several major variations of trophi structure associated with food and feeding methods. Some types serve a simple grinding function. Others may be thrust from the mouth to grasp prey. Still others are used for sucking out the contents of organisms.

Usually, rotifer trophi consist of seven separate pieces arranged in three sections. An unpaired median ventral fulcrum is attached to a pair of rami (sing. ramus) which move in opposition to each other like a pair of pliers. Altogether, these three sections are the incus. The rami are pulled away from each other by muscles attached to the fulcrum and to the outer part of the bases of

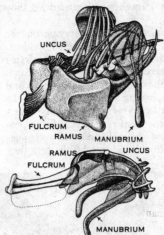

FIG. 2.—MAJOR PARTS OF TWO TYPES OF ROTIFER TROPHI

the rami. Lying adjacent to each ramus is a structure, the malleus, which consists of two pieces, a toothed uncus and a manubrium; these two pieces, hinged together, move in a plane at right angles to the rami.

In addition to these standard parts, there may be others: subunci, rods connecting each ramus to its corresponding uncus; an epipharynx, one or more rods in the wall of the gullet and serving to support the mouth. Other supporting members may be developed elsewhere.

The Muscular System.—The muscular system is composed of a group of longitudinal and circular bands in the body wall, a network of muscle in the viscera, and a few muscles between the viscera and body wall. In some rotifers some of the more powerful muscles are conspicuously cross striped or striated.

Nervous System and Sense Organs.—The chief part of the nervous system consists of a large cerebral ganglion and smaller ganglia associated with the mastax and foot. Numerous nerves lead to muscles and sense organs.

There are three conspicuous touch (tactile) sense organs on the body: two lateral antennae located toward the posterior end, and a dorsal antenna on the midline of the head. The dorsal antenna represents the fusion of two antennae and receives two nerves; a few rotifers actually possess two dorsal antennae lying close together. The corona may support stiff cirri (apparently derived from cilia), which are said to serve a tactile function. The foot sometimes has a tactile bristle on the dorsal surface just anterior to the toes.

Excretion.—The excretory system consists of a pair of convoluted tubes (protonephridia) which begin with special end cells called flame bulbs. Most commonly the tubes lead to a bladder from which a duct leads directly to the distensible cloaca; but in some species the protonephridia empty into the cloaca.

Secretion.—In most rotifers the gastric glands are attached to the anterior part of the stomach. In addition, there may be accessory glands elsewhere along the digestive tract.

The adhesive secretion of the cement glands in the foot is used for attachment, for leechlike creeping (alternate attachment of sticky foot and head end) and in the construction of tubes in some sessile forms. In sessile species there may be no distinct cement glands, the secretion being produced by swellings of the epidermis.

In the head are located prominent glands of unknown function: an unpaired glandular retrocerebral sac having a long forked duct opening on the apical region of the corona; and a pair of subcerebral glands lying beside the duct of the retrocerebral sac and the ducts leading to the apical area. The sac and glands together compose the retrocerebral organ. Rotifers may have either sac or glands; both, or neither. In some species the ducts are degenerate.

Reproduction.—The reproductive system is of taxonomic importance; the division of the group into classes is made on the basis of the number of ovaries and the development of males. Most rotifers have one ovary, but the bdelloids and seisonids have two. In the former the female reproductive system lies ventral to the digestive tract. The ovary (vitellogermarium) consists of a small germarium that supplies nuclei to eggs, and a massive yolk-gland (vitellarium). An oviduct leads from the ovary to the cloaca.

The rotifers ordinarily found are amictic females; *i.e.*, they reproduce parthenogenetically by diploid eggs (see PARTHENO-GENESIS). The eggs may be released free in the water, may be laid on plants or other surfaces; in most planktonic species the eggs may be attached to the lorica of the mother and carried till they hatch.

Some rotifers bear living young, the mother carrying one or more developing embryos within the greatly enlarged oviduct. Under adverse environmental conditions, special females, (mictic) may lay haploid eggs which then become males. When such haploid eggs are fertilized, however, they are called resting eggs and give rise to females. Resting eggs, having a thicker shell than the parthenogenetic ones, are resistant to drying, and generally take a longer time to hatch. There are reports of resting eggs being produced parthenogenetically, however. Mictic and amictic females usually look alike; they can be distinguished only by the eggs they produce. In a few species, though, there are observable differences between them.

Males, undescribed for most species, have been found in many species of the order Monogononta. Males are apparently absent among the bdelloids, but the seisonids regularly produce them. In a few genera the males look like miniatures of the females, except for the reproductive system. In most genera, however, there is great morphological difference between the sexes (sexual dimorphism); e.g., the males lack a digestive system and bear no resemblance to the females. The occurrence of males, where they are known, is restricted to short periods, though they may become very abundant while they are present. The male reproductive system of members of the Monogononta usually consists of a testis and a ciliated sperm duct with glands. The tip of the duct is capable of being turned outward (eversible) and may be lined with thickened cuticle, forming a penis.

Ecology and Distribution.—Rotifers have a distribution that is usually regarded as potentially cosmopolitan. Many species, since they are so easily dispersed, are, in fact, nearly world-wide in their distribution. The occurrence of most species in a given locality seems to be mostly the result of specific environmental features of that locality, not by its geographical location. Nevertheless, some species show a distinctly limited range: a few, some very common, are found only in North America; others have been reported only from Europe; a number of species are restricted to warmer climates or at least tropical and subtropical locations, while others are not found in the tropics. In general, the fauna of high altitudes and high latitudes is composed of relatively few species of wide distribution.

Rotifers are plentiful in most bodies of freshwater, especially ponds and bogs. Some are restricted to sea water or saline or alkaline lakes, and are tolerant of wide variations in salinity. A few bdelloids live only in places intermittently wet, such as among the parts of land-growing mosses and liverworts. Most species live along the shore (littoral zone) swimming much of the time in close contact with plants and other surfaces. The planktonic species occur in greatest numbers in open water. Some live within the cells of water plants. A few are commensal, living in the gill-chambers of fresh-water crabs and crayfish or attached to the outside of certain aquatic worms (Oligochaetes). The adults of sessile species live attached to the leaves and stems of water plants; their larvae are free-swimming.

While they live mostly in wa-

DETAIL OF ROTIFERA GROUP IN ½ IN. OF POND-BOTTOM WATER

At upper left is main stem of a bladderwort (*Utricularia vulgaris*), a water plant, showing at centre bottom bladder (utricle) about size of a pin head in the living plant. At bladder's lower right margin is trap door, with remains of captured rotifers visible inside. Stem is covered with tiny algae. At centre right is a spherical colony of rotifers (*Conochilus hippocrepis*). Above it is *Notommata copeus* with auricles extended. At left centre is crescent-shaped desmid (*Closterium*), an alga

ters of moderate temperature (10° to 20° C.), some have been found in hot springs, and others are restricted to arctic and antarctic waters. Some are capable of withstanding freezing or drying for extended periods.

The duration of their individual lives has been little studied; however, some species are known to live a few days only, while others survive more than a month.

Systematic Affinities.—Much uncertainty and dissension has been expressed about the relationships of rotifers. In some works they are regarded as one of a group of related minor phyla, but in a widely used classification (that of Libbie H. Hyman) they are a class of the phylum Aschelminthes, which includes also the following groups: Gastrotricha, Kinorhyncha (Echinodera), Priapulida, Nematoda and Nematomorpha (Gordioidea).

The following is a working classification:

CLASS ROTIFERA

Order 1. Seisonaceae (Seisonidea).—Slender with long necks, living on the marine crustacean Nebalia; sexes of equal size and like form; two ovaries. Example, *Seison.*

Order 2. Bdelloidea.—Bottom-dwelling (benthonic) rotifers with jointed cuticle; both ends retractile into the trunk; corona of two trochal discs, set on pedicels; two ovaries; mastax ramate; males lacking. Examples, *Philodina, Rotaria, Habrotrocha.*

Order 3. Monogononta.—Sessile or free-swimming rotifers; one ovary, males more or less reduced in size and structure.

Suborder 1. Ploima.—Free-swimming rotifers, with undivided terminal or ventral corona, not consisting of trochal and cingular circlets; foot with usually two toes; one ovary; mastax various. Examples, *Notommata, Proales, Synchaeta, Trichocerca, Euchlanis, Brachionus, Lecane, Asplanchna.*

Suborder 2. Flosculariacea.—Sessile or swimming rotifers with more or less lobed corona of trochal and cingular circlets; toes lacking; mastax malleoramate; one ovary. Examples, *Floscularia, Conochilus, Limnias, Hexarthra, Filinia, Trochosphaera.*

Suborder 3. Collothecacea.—Mostly sessile rotifers with large funnel-like corona, often lobed, lacking a ciliary border in most forms; mastax uncinate; toes lacking. Examples, *Collotheca, Stephanoceros, Cupelopagis.*   (W. T. E.)

Bibliography.—W. T. Edmondson, "Rotifera," Ward and Whipple, *Fresh-Water Biology,* ed. by W. T. Edmondson, 2nd ed. (1959); Libbie H. Hyman, *The Invertebrates,* vol. iii (1951); P. de Beauchamp, "Morphologie et variations de l'appareil rotateur dans la serie des rotifères," *Arch. Zool. Exp. Gén.,* 36 (1907) and "Recherches sur les rotifères: les formations tégumentaires et l'appareil digestif," *Arch. Zool. Exp. Gén.,* 40 (1909); H. K. Harring, "Synopsis of the Rotatoria," *Bull. U.S. Natl. Mus.,* no. 71 (1913); H. K. Harring and F. J. Myers, "The Rotifer Fauna of Wisconsin," *Trans. Wis. Acad. Sci. Arts Lett.,* 20, 21, 22, 23 (1922–1928); L. M. Hickernell, "A Study of Desiccation in the Rotifer *Philodina roseola,*" *Biol. Bull.,* 32 (1917); C. T. Hudson and P. H. Gosse, *The Rotifera or Wheelanimalcules* (1886–1889); A. Remane, "Rotatoria" in H. G. Bronn (ed.), *Klassen und Ordnungen des Tier-Reichs,* Band IV, Abt. I, Buch 1 (1929); C. Wesenberg-Lund, "Contributions to the Biology of the Rotifera, I and II," *Danske Vidensk. Selsk. Skrifter, Natur. Math. Afd.,* 8, R. 4, Bind 4 (1923) and 9, R. 2, Bind 1 (1930); "Rotatoria" in W. Kükenthal and T. Krumbach (eds.), *Handb. Zool., Berl.,* Band 2, Heft 1.

ROTOGRAVURE: *see* Gravure.

ROTOR SHIP, a vessel utilizing revolving cylinders, called rotors, for auxiliary power. Anton Flettner, the German engineer who invented the rotor ship, originally intended to construct ships with metal sails. In 1922, however, experiments at the University of Göttingen, Ger., with revolving cylinders indicated that the pressure exerted upon a cylinder revolving in an air current was considerably greater than had been supposed. When disks of larger diameter than the cylinders were provided at the ends, moreover, it was found possible to increase the wind effect to 9 or 10 times the amount of effect in normal sail. To achieve this effect the revolving speed of the cylinders had to be about 3 to 4½ times as great as the speed of the wind.

Though an ordinary sailing vessel is required to take down all canvas in a hurricane, it was claimed that the rotor ship could continue sailing.

Tests were made with a three-masted schooner, the "Buckau," which had a displacement of 960 tons and was fitted with an auxiliary motor of about 200 hp. The canvas rig of the vessel was dismantled, and in place of the fore and third masts two very strong masts were erected. The new masts were shorter, being 42 ft. in height. They were provided with bearings at the upper and lower ends to allow for the free rotation of the cylinders, which were placed over the masts. The cylinders were fitted at either end with disks of greater diameter than the cylinders that were built as part of them. The cylinders were rotated by means of motors, which could drive the towers at a speed of 125 rpm.

Circumferential speed was approximately 60 ft. per second, and the power required to rotate the towers was about 9 hp. By altering the circumferential speed of one or another of the cylinders, it was said, the pressure exerted by the wind could be correspondingly changed and so alter the vessel's course.

Sea tests were claimed to be successful, but little was heard of the subject thereafter.   (F. J. D.; X.)

ROTORUA, a city of Rotorua County, North Island, N.Z., lies about 150 mi. SE of Auckland by road at 938 ft. (286 m.) above sea level. Pop. (1961) 19,360. Situated at the southwestern end of Lake Rotorua in the heart of the thermal belt of North Island, the city grew up between two Maori villages: Ohinemutu, on the shore of Lake Rotorua, and Whakarewarewa, which is the centre of a remarkable array of hot springs, boiling mudpools, and spouting geysers. Rotorua was made a municipality in 1922 and received city status in 1963. Its bathhouse with its curative mineral waters and the adjacent gardens were formerly the main attraction for visitors, and there is a government sanatorium on the lake shore. Now the tennis courts, bowling greens, and swimming pools, and the yachting, bathing, and fishing facilities of the lake are equally important. However, the city's recent growth in population and its economic expansion owe more to forestry, farming, and administration than to tourism. In the late 1920s exotic conifers were planted on much of the volcanic plateau of North Island. The work was largely centred in Rotorua, and Whakarewarewa is the site of the Forest Research Institute and the Forestry Training School.

In 1939 the New Zealand forest service established at Waipa, near Rotorua, the country's first large-scale sawmill to be built on the modern Swedish pattern. Others were set up in the area after World War II by private enterprise. Since the 1930s, when the cobalt deficiency of the pumice soils of the region around Rotorua was discovered, the task of reclamation and development for dairying has been undertaken by the Department of Lands and Maori Affairs operating from Rotorua.   (K. B. C.)

ROTROU, JEAN DE (1609–1650), French dramatist, called by Voltaire the founder of French drama, was born at Dreux in June 1609. More is known of his family than of his own life. He was educated in Paris, wrote his first extant play (*L'Hypocondriaque,* publ. 1628) before he was 20, and a few years later emerged as protected by Richelieu and earning an assured income as writer for the chief established theatre of the capital, the Hôtel de Bourgogne. Rotrou returned to Dreux at the age of 30, married, served for a time as a magistrate, and died of the plague (June 28, 1650). He seems to have been a man of retiring disposition, conciliatory, and unselfish.

His 35 extant plays show the evolution of public taste in drama and the increasing attraction of the theatre for the rising middle class. Nearly half are tragicomedies, by which was meant a serious play involving peril but not death; the title was in one or two later altered to "*tragédie.*" For Rotrou, with Corneille, whom he admired, and one or two more, invented French Classical tragedy. He saw that this new form of social pleasure, both spectacular and declamatory, might achieve emotional effects more powerful and delicate than rough prose drama. With a generous admixture of incident and reversal of fortune he allied discussion of moral issues and portrayal of character under strain. He did much to refine the instrument he had invented, by concentration, omitting extraneous incident, and intensifying psychological motivation. His characters are faced with choices: the king's son in *Cosroès* (1648), between power and loyalty; the king in *Venceslas* first condemns his son to execution, and then abdicates in his favour. Racine gratefully borrowed from his study of *Antigone* (1638), and the starkest scene in *Britannicus* is reworked from Rotrou's *Belissaire* (1644). His sense for comedy was no less keen: in *Les Sosies* (1636 or 1637) he discovered the delicious comic situation which Molière was to perfect in *Amphitryon*.

Rotrou is a writer of power. He uses the alexandrine with great effect for resonant expression of stress and violence. He has the rhetoric, the concentration, the formal structure of the Classical manner, together with a Baroque sense of surprise, contrast, tension, and illusion. The last is most powerfully shown in *Le Veritable Saint-Genest* (1647), showing an actor whose professional martyr's role turns into personal conviction.

BIBLIOGRAPHY.—H. C. Lancaster, *History of French Dramatic Literature in the 17th Century*, Pt. 1, vol. 1 (1929) lists the plays and revises the dating given by other authorities, with detailed references. There are modern editions of *Venceslas* (by T. F. Crane, 1907); *Saint-Genest* (T. F. Crane, 1907; and, with excellent introduction, by R. W. Ladborough, 1954), and *Cosroès* (by J. Scherer, Societé des Textes Français Modernes, 1950). *See also* A. Adam, *Histoire de littérature française au 17ᵉ siècle*, I (1949). (W. G. Me.)

ROTTERDAM, the second largest city of the Netherlands, is situated in the province of South Holland, about 19 mi. (30 km.) from the North Sea on both banks of the Nieuwe Maas (a northern distributary of the Rhine). By 1964, on the basis of total tonnage of cargo handled, it ranked as the largest port in the world. It is connected with the North Sea by a wide canal called the New Waterway. Pop. (1964 est.) 731,525 (mun.).

Rotterdam takes its name from the Rotte, a river which in former times flowed through the marshland of South Holland into the Nieuwe Maas. A strong dike was built on the north bank of the Nieuwe Maas in about 1240, shutting off the Rotte by a system of locks. A small colony that settled on this dam was granted certain charters in 1299 and 1328. In 1340 Count William IV of Holland bestowed city rights on Rotterdam and gave the citizens the concession to dig an open canal to the Schie, another right-bank tributary of the Nieuwe Maas. This great privilege gave Rotterdam a link with the more important towns of Delft and Leiden and with The Hague which was on its way to becoming the centre of government, while the Rotte only led to the still sparsely populated marshland. Its favourable position between the great market town of Dordrecht and the other Dutch towns was a reason for the city's rise to prosperity. Its thriving growth was stemmed when in 1488 Frans van Brederode, leader of the nobles in revolt against the sovereign, Maximilian of Austria, gained possession of Rotterdam and used it as a base from which he conducted his military campaigns and pillaged the surrounding countryside.

In 1563 a large part of the town was destroyed by fire and in April 1572 it was occupied and plundered by Spanish troops. When the Spaniards withdrew, Rotterdam ranged itself on the side of the prince of Orange. In the ensuing peace it enjoyed a period of great prosperity. From the southern Netherlands, where Philip II's authority had been restored, many people fled north for rea-

sons of faith, and a number of merchants and artisans, mainly from Antwerp, settled in Rotterdam. The city council was then much under the influence of Johan van Oldenbarnevelt, who later played an important part in the government of his country and subsequently died on the scaffold. Under his auspices, in the last quarter of the 16th century, an ambitious plan was laid for the enlargement of the town. In the river in front of Rotterdam mud flats had formed; harbours were dug out of these, and the soil thus obtained was used to heighten the remaining ground; quays were constructed and houses built. The scale of this plan was so immense that the city was provided with sufficient possibilities of expansion for the next two and a half centuries.

In the 17th and 18th centuries Rotterdam increased steadily in importance. Trade was principally centred on France and England, but there was also shipping to Indonesia and America. The Court of the Fellowship of the Merchant Adventurers had been at Rotterdam since 1635; it was transferred to Dordrecht in 1656, but this circumstance had no detrimental effect on trade relations with England. After the revocation of the Edict of Nantes (1685) many French Protestants came to Rotterdam, where they contributed largely to the city's prosperity. The years of French domination (1795–1813) were lean years for Rotterdam, and it was long before prosperity returned.

In the 19th century there was also a shift of trade; transit trade grew more important and it needed time for the port to adapt itself to the new situation. After 1850 Rotterdam grew rapidly, chiefly as a result of the German unification in 1870 and the industrialization of the Rhineland in general and of the Ruhr area in particular. With the expansion of the town, a vast network of harbours was made, stretching along the New Waterway (planned by Pieter Caland) and in open communication with the sea; and this made Rotterdam one of the best equipped ports in the world. World War I and the economic depression of the 1930s were severely felt in Rotterdam.

In World War II the city and port suffered tremendously. On May 14, 1940, the German *Luftwaffe* destroyed practically the entire city centre and an extensive part of the east district. About 900 people were killed (though much higher figures were given at the time, owing to the confusion) and approximately 78,000 were rendered homeless. Of public buildings, only the city hall (1920), the main post office (1923), the stock exchange, the famous Boymans Museum, and some minor buildings escaped destruction. More than one-third of the total length of quayside for seagoing vessels and about 40% of the port's equipment were destroyed by the Germans in the autumn of 1944.

Apart from some 18th-century houses, Rotterdam possesses only two buildings of historical interest: the 15th-century St. Laurens Church and the Schielandshuis. The former was very badly damaged in the bombing but by the early 1960s was almost completely restored, and the tombs of the famous admirals Cortenaer, Witte de With, and Van Brakel were reinstated. Since 1959 services

THE HARBOUR AT ROTTERDAM, ONE OF THE LARGEST IN THE WORLD

have been held regularly in the church. The Schielandshuis, built in 1662–65 by Jacob Lois, was the meeting place for the dike-reeve (*dijkgraaf*) and his fellow reeves (*hoogheemraden*) of Schieland, where they deliberated upon everything concerning the dikes of that part of Holland. It now houses the Historical Museum. Also of historical interest is Hendrik de Keyser's beautiful statue of Erasmus, the great Rotterdam humanist, which was placed on the Grote Markt in 1622. It was spared by the fire of May 1940 and removed to a place of safety. After the war it was erected again on the van Hogendorpsplein in the neighbourhood of the Schielandshuis. Because of the construction of an underground railway, the statue had to be moved again and found its final place at a site near St. Laurens Church. The Boymans Museum, rehoused in 1935, acquired the famous Van Beuningen collection in 1958 and has since borne the official name Boymans-Van Beuningen Museum. It houses old and modern paintings of the Netherlands ranging from Van Eyck to Van Gogh; and also contemporary paintings, sculptures, drawings, prints, ceramics, glass, pewter, silver, lace, and furniture. Other important museums are the Maritime Museum and the Ethnological Museum. The municipal library is famous for its unique collection of Erasmiana. The Netherlands School of Economics (founded in 1913 by private initiative) is also in Rotterdam.

Immediately after the bombing of the city centre the area was cleared for rebuilding. To facilitate central replanning the entire devastated area was expropriated and the city architect, W. G. Witteveen, was commissioned to prepare a plan, some parts of which were carried out during the occupation. However, in 1946, it was superseded by a more radical plan, drawn up under C. van Traa, director of town planning and reconstruction. By the mid-1960s the greater part of this plan had been completed. Meanwhile the city was expanding outward by the construction of housing and industrial estates. Particularly noteworthy of the new buildings are the Central Railway Station (1957); the Wholesalers' Building (1952), accommodating the business premises of over 200 wholesalers; the Building Centre (1948–55), an international research and information centre for building and interior decoration; the Lijnbaan shopping promenade (1953–55), which consists of about 75 shops and is open only to pedestrians; the Bijenkorf department store (1955–57), the only building designed by a foreign architect (Marcel Breuer); the Dijkzigt City Hospital (1961). A controversial memorial monument of the May 1940 bombing (by Ossip Zadkine) was inaugurated in 1953 and, four years later, two monuments were unveiled, one in memory of the fallen (by Mari Andriessen) and one to honour the merchant navy for its wartime service (by F. Carasso).

The restoration of the port facilities was completed in 1949. The number of ships that entered and the amount of goods handled before the war (1938) were surpassed in 1952 and 1954 respectively. In the early 1960s, of the total trade of Rotterdam about one-third was transit trade. Almost half the cargo moving through Rotterdam-Europoort was oil, and the port is linked with Godorf, near Cologne, by oil pipeline. The harbour basins and port facilities are continuously being extended. The Botlek plan, comprising 3,336 ac. of industrial sites and harbour basins, had practically been realized by the mid-1960s. The Europoort plan, comprising 3,830 ac. of industrial sites and harbour basins, opposite the Hook of Holland, begun in 1958, was one-third complete by that time. In connection with these developments the world's first school for training dockers was opened in Rotterdam.

In May 1940 Waalhaven airport, the first civil aerodrome in Europe, was destroyed. In 1953 the heliport of the city centre (daily connections with Antwerp, Brussels, and other places) was opened. The new Rotterdam airport, north of the city, was opened in 1956. After World War II Rotterdam aimed even more than before at broadening, and thus strengthening, its economic basis by sponsoring new enterprises. Its industries include the largest oil refineries in Europe, several shipbuilding yards, engineering works, automobile-assembling plants, the processing and manufacture of coffee, tea, cocoa, tobacco, margarine, clothes, paper, railway material, and all kinds of chemical products. There are also breweries and distilleries.

BIBLIOGRAPHY.—J. Schraver (ed.), *Rotterdam, the Gateway to Europe* (1948); Hans Reinhardt, *The Story of Rotterdam* (1955); J. W. de Boer and C. Oorthuys, *Rotterdam; the Dynamics of a City,* 2nd ed. (1963).   (W. A. H. C.; H. Rt.)

ROUAULT, GEORGES (1871–1958), French painter and engraver, perhaps the greatest religious painter since Rembrandt, was born in Paris on May 27, 1871, the son of a cabinetmaker, in working-class surroundings. He was taught to appreciate art by his grandfather Champdavoine, an admirer of Daumier, whose work was to influence Rouault decisively. Apprenticed to a glazier from 1885 to 1890, Rouault worked on the restoration of the stained-glass windows of Chartres cathedral; and these awakened his feeling for decorative and architectural values and for the monumental use of colour and line. Gustave Moreau, under whom

BY COURTESY OF MUSÉE D'ART MODERNE, PARIS

"LA SAINTE FACE," 1933, BY GEORGES ROUAULT

he studied at the École des Beaux-Arts in 1892, introduced Rouault to the work of Leonardo da Vinci and of Rembrandt, but during 1898–1902, influenced by Toulouse-Lautrec and Cézanne, Rouault developed a new style, producing water colours of sober tints (blues predominating) with strong tones and emphatic forms. Hideous prostitutes, terrifying judges, repulsive millionaires, pitiful poor people, and tragic clowns (these as the symbol of the anguish of mankind) portray "the dereliction of man without God." Rouault was converted to Roman Catholicism (*c.* 1895) and later became the friend of J. K. Huysmans and Léon Bloy.

From 1906 to 1910 Rouault took an interest in pottery; and from 1917 onward he practised engraving (some of his later masterpieces were to be in this medium). In oils he began to build up colour, solidity, and tension in his compositions of the story of the Passion of Christ. From 1914 to about 1935 he pursued this hieratic style. From 1935 to about 1948, Rouault's painting became more serene and was characterized by the appearance of graceful feminine figures. He now produced small canvases on which the paint was applied thickly and with the glowing lustre of enamel. Tranquillity gave place in 1948 to an impulse of joy. Using greens and yellows (both new to his palette) so thickly as to give the appearance almost of relief, Rouault infused his works, particularly his landscapes, with universal significance and religious grandeur. Such a reawakening in an artist approaching 80 was exceptional. After this swan song he painted little more, but waited quietly for his death in Paris on Feb. 13, 1958.

Rouault stood apart from his contemporaries. Evoking form by a new use of colour and outline whose very flatness becomes monumental, he drew inspiration from French medieval masters, uniting religious and popular traditions, divorced since the Renaissance. To secular art he brought back craftsmanship and the sense of congruity between the sublime and the grotesque. To religious art he restored its concern with both human life and the transcendental. *See also* PAINTING: *Fauvism.*

BIBLIOGRAPHY.—J. T. Soby, *Georges Rouault* (1945); L. Venturi, *Rouault* (1948); B. Dorival, *Cinq Études sur Georges Rouault* (1956).   (B. DL.)

ROUBAIX, a manufacturing town in the Nord *département* of France, 6½ mi. NE of Lille, lies on the Roubaix Canal which links the lower Deule with the Scheldt by way of the Marcq and the Espierre. Pop. (1962) 112,567. It unites with Tourcoing (*q.v.*) to form a large industrial centre. The town's more important buildings and institutions include Saint-Martin Church, dating from 1471 and restored in 1849; Notre Dame Church (1846); the Hotel de Ville (1911) containing a collection of paintings by J. J. Weerts; the Chamber of Commerce (opened 1908); the National Higher School of the Textile Arts and Industries, with attached museum containing paintings, sculptures, and fabrics; the attractive Barbieux public park; the municipal sports centre and open-air school for boys and girls, and the swimming baths.

Roubaix has been called the Manchester of France, and has a universal reputation and market for its textiles. More than 200 establishments are engaged in the production of woolen, cotton, and other fabrics, including spinning, wool combing, dyeing, and weaving. There are also rubber and plastic factories. The town has a lively trade and is the centre of a network of road services.

The prosperity of Roubaix had its origin in the charter granted in 1469 by Charles the Bold, duke of Burgundy, to Peter, lord of Roubaix and a descendant of the royal house of England. This charter permitted the citizens to dress all in wool. In the 18th century the town suffered from the jealousy of Lille, of which it was a dependency, and it was not until the 19th century that its industries acquired importance. During World War I it was occupied by the Germans, and manufacture came to a standstill. As the cotton spinning plants were mostly spared, its industry was restarted in 1919 with government aid and bank credits. It was again occupied by the Germans in 1940. After World War II the employers' and workers' associations formed cooperative organizations for professional guidance, health measures, and housing. A bold housing policy assisted the construction after 1949 of more than 12,000 dwellings.

ROUBILLAC (Roubiliac), **LOUIS FRANÇOIS** (1705?–1762), probably the greatest sculptor at work in England during the 18th century, was born of French parentage at Lyons, probably in 1705. He was apprenticed to B. Permoser and later became assistant to Nicolas Coustou. He came to London about 1732 and was employed by Thomas Carter the elder. His first independent commission was the statue of Handel for Vauxhall Gardens in 1737, and a year later he set up for himself in St. Martin's Lane. In 1746 he carved the monument of the duke of Argyll in Westminster Abbey, one of his greatest works, though his more dramatic monument of Lady Elizabeth Nightingale in the same building is better known. Other works by him in the Abbey include the monuments of Field-Marshal Wade, Admiral Warren, and Handel. Outside London his most important monuments are those of Miss Myddleton at Wrexham, Denbighshire, Viscount Shannon at Walton-on-Thames, Surrey, and the duchess of Montagu at Warkton, Northamptonshire.

Roubillac's busts are unsurpassed, for he had the seeing eye as well as the skilled hand, and examples can be seen at Windsor Castle, Wilton House, Wiltshire, Trinity College, Cambridge, and the National Portrait Gallery, London. Statues by Roubillac include Sir Thomas Molyneux in Armagh Cathedral, Lord President Forbes in the Advocates Library, Edinburgh, and Sir Isaac Newton at Trinity College, Cambridge. G. Vertue, who knew Roubillac well, rightly described his works as "curious and excellent, with great skill and variety, picturesque, so light and easy, as painting." Roubillac died on Jan. 11, 1762, and was buried in the graveyard at St. Martin-in-the-Fields, London.

See K. A. Esdaile, *The Life and Works of Louis François Roubiliac* (1929); Rupert Gunnis (comp.), *Dictionary of British Sculptors 1660–1851* (1953). (R. Gs.)

ROUEN, a city of France, capital of the *département* of Seine-Maritime and the ancient capital of the province of Normandy, lies on the Seine 75 mi. (121 km.) NW of Paris by road. Pop. (1962) 118,775. Rouen is an important industrial and commercial centre, and also one of the most interesting artistic centres in Europe. Its numerous churches, ancient monuments, and old houses have given it the title of "Ville Musée." The old city lies on the north bank of the river in a natural amphitheatre formed by the hills which border the Seine valley. It is surrounded by the suburbs of Martainville, Saint-Hilaire, Beauvoisine, Bouvreuil, and Cauchoise; 2½ mi. E is the industrial town of Darnétal; and on the opposite bank of the Seine is Saint-Sever, which before its almost complete destruction in World War II was an important industrial district. In the mid-1960s it was being rebuilt as a residential suburb of Rouen. Sotteville (pop. 32,998) and Petit Quevilly (pop. 21,065) are nearby industrial suburbs. Also part of Rouen is the Île Lacroix, in the Seine.

Monuments.—In the centre of the old town is the Cathedral of Notre-Dame, one of the finest Gothic churches in France. Most of it was built in the first half of the 13th century, on the site of an earlier cathedral burned in 1200, but work was not completed until 1544. The cathedral was badly damaged by Allied bombardment during World War II, and reopened in 1956 after restoration. The western facade (1509–30) is intricately decorated, with a great central doorway. The portals of the transept are each flanked by two towers, and the central tower (495 ft. [151 m.], the tallest church tower in France) over the transept has a famous carillon. In 1934 there were found, beneath the floor of the choir, the substructure of the crypt of the Romanesque building consecrated in 1063. The Lady Chapel (enlarged 1302–20) is the most interesting feature of the interior, with the tomb (1518–42) of the two cardinals d'Amboise, archbishops of Rouen, a masterpiece of Renaissance workmanship. Behind the cathedral is the archbishop's palace, dating from the 15th and 18th centuries.

The former abbey church of Saint-Ouen, on the south side of the Place du Général-de-Gaulle, was founded in 1318 on the site of a Romanesque church. The present church, an outstanding example of late Gothic, was built mainly during 1318–39 and the western facade in the mid-19th century. The tower over the transept (1490–1515) has an octagonal lantern (the Tour couronnée or "Crown of Normandy") flanked by four turrets. The stained-glass windows are of the 14th–16th centuries. The graceful effect of the interior is created by the delicately slender soaring shafts and absence of nonstructural ornamentation. The south transeptal entrance, or Portail des Marmousets, has reliefs on the tympanum representing the Assumption of the Virgin Mary, surmounted by a magnificent rose window.

The Church of Saint-Maclou, behind the cathedral (begun 1434; consecrated 1521), is a rich example of the Flamboyant style. The lofty spire of the tower was added in 1868. The church was damaged in 1944. It has an elaborate portal with biblical scenes carved on the wooden doors, probably by Jean Goujon. The former charnel house of the church, dating from 1533, is one of the few relics of this kind remaining in France. The 16th-century Church of Saint-Vincent, near the Seine, was destroyed by bombing in 1944. Its finest stained glass is in the Musée Le Secq des Tournelles, which contains a unique collection of ironwork. There is fine stained glass also in the churches of Saint-Patrice and Saint-Godard.

The most important secular building in Rouen is the Palais de Justice, once the seat of the exchequer and later of the *parlement* of Normandy. It was severely damaged during World War II and was not completely restored by the 1960s. The building is in late Gothic style. South of the Palais de Justice is the Gros Horloge, a belfry built in 1389, adjoining which is a great gateway (1527) with a clock. The Tour de Jeanne d'Arc is all that remains of a castle built by Philip Augustus (probably in 1205), in which Joan of Arc was imprisoned. In the Place du Vieux Marché, Joan was burned at the stake in 1431. There are some interesting old mansions, including the Hôtel de Bourgthéroulde (1486–1531).

Of the museums in Rouen the Musée des Beaux-Arts, adjacent to the municipal library, is one of the most important provincial art galleries in France, with a fine ceramic collection. The Musée d'Antiquités contains religious sculptures and works of art, and Egyptian and Greek antiquities. The Musée d'Histoire Naturelle, one of the most complete of its kind, also contains a remarkable prehistory section. The University of Rouen was founded on June 9, 1964, and opened on Oct. 1, 1964.

Rouen is an important centre for trade in wines, spirits, grain, and cattle. Coal, grain, vegetables, fruit, wine, timber, and petroleum are leading imports. Besides its manufactures, it exports petroleum products, kaolin, sugar, cereals, and flour. The principal industries of Rouen and its district are the spinning and weaving of cotton, notably the manufacture of *rouenneries* and *indiennes*, the printing and dyeing of the manufactured material and the spinning of other fibres. There are also locomotive repair shops and shipyards; facilities for the manufacture of clothing, chemicals, fertilizers, soap, machinery, and newsprint; and distilleries and petroleum refineries. The port of Rouen, the chief river port of France, comprises the marine docks, extending for 8,000 m. (8,750 yd.) to La Bouille, and the river dock, extending for 1,000 m. (1,094 yd.) and including a timber, a petroleum, and a repairing dock. The Seine is tidal beyond Rouen. The port is accessible for ships drawing 16½ ft. (5 m.) up to 27 ft. (8.2 m.) of water.

History.—Ratuma or Ratumacos, the Celtic name of Rouen, was modified by the Romans into Rotomagus and by medieval Latin writers into Rodomum, of which the present name is a corruption. Under Julius Caesar and the early Roman emperors the town was the capital of the Veliocassi, and it was not important until it became the centre of Lugdunensis Secunda at the end of the 3rd century. It was taken by the Normans in 841 and again in 876. In 912 it became the capital of the duchy of Normandy, which from 1066 to 1204 and from 1418 to 1449 was an English possession. In 1203 it was the scene of the murder of Arthur of Brittany at the hands of King John of England, the last duke of Normandy. Ostensibly to avenge the crime, Philip Augustus invaded Normandy and entered Rouen after a siege of 80 days. The prosperity of the town grew and a pact between its merchants and those of Paris, relating to the navigation of the Seine, was followed by treaties with London, the Hanseatic towns, Flanders, and Champagne. In 1302 the seat of the exchequer or sovereign court, afterward the *parlement*, of Normandy was fixed at Rouen. A stubborn resistance was offered to Henry V of England, who after a long siege occupied the town in 1419; the French recaptured it in 1449. In the late 15th and early 16th century Rouen was a centre of art and culture but it suffered severely in the Wars of Religion and was sacked by the Protestants in 1562. After the revocation of the Edict of Nantes in 1685 it lost more than half its population, and the textile industry did not recover until the 18th century.

During World War II, Rouen was severely damaged in 1940 and 1944, nearly half the city being destroyed, but large-scale reconstruction was undertaken and Rouen remains one of the most interesting cities in northern France.

See also references under "Rouen" in the Index. (G. Ry.)

ROUGE: *see* Cosmetics and Cosmetology.

ROUGET DE LISLE, CLAUDE JOSEPH (1760–1836), French writer, author of "La Marseillaise." He was born, May 10, 1760, at Lons-le-Saunier, Jura, entered the army, and became a captain of engineers. While stationed in Strasbourg he composed both words and music of the "Chant de guerre pour l'armée du Rhin" on the night of April 25, 1792, after an official dinner at which his host had suggested he should write a war song. The song was adopted by the Provençal volunteers prominent in the storming of the Tuileries and thereafter, as the "Hymne des Marseillais," became the anthem of revolutionary France. Rouget de Lisle, a moderate republican, was relieved of his commission and imprisoned for a year during the Terror but was freed after the counterrevolution. Though granted his former rank in the army in 1795 and later promised promotion, he resigned his commission in 1796. Louis Philippe awarded him a small pension in 1830. He died in Choisy-le-Roi, Seine et Oise, on June 27, 1836. He published *Essais en vers et prose* in 1797, composed the settings for *50 Chants français* (1825), and wrote numerous songs.

See J. Tiersot, *Histoire de la Marseillaise* (1915).

ROUGH CAST, in architecture, a term used in the United States for the rougher textures of a stucco surface, obtained either by throwing on the finished coat in unequal masses or by sprinkling over the finished surface, while still wet, a coating of coloured pebbles, tile or brick fragments, marble chips, etc. In England the term is used for any stucco or mortar combined with gravel and sand, employed as the finishing coat of covering plaster over a rough structure of masonry and frequently decorated by the addition of coloured pebbles or small pieces of glass.

ROUHER, EUGÈNE (1814–1884), French statesman, highly influential as a conservative minister under the Second Empire and a leader of the Bonapartist party under the Third Republic, was born on Nov. 30, 1814, at Riom, Puy-de-Dôme. Trained as a lawyer in Paris, he practised at the bar in Riom until he was elected to Parliament in 1848. He made his mark as a vigorous

conservative, demanding the suppression of socialism and its "baneful theories," and insisting on the need for "order" and "strong government." He enlisted in the cause of Louis Napoleon (*see* NAPOLEON III), in whom he saw a "saviour of society" against the revolutionary menace; and in October 1849 Louis Napoleon, as president of the Second Republic, appointed him minister of justice. In this post, as head of the government prosecution office, Rouher was energetic in suppressing left-wing opposition. After the *coup d'état* of December 1851, he was responsible for drawing up the constitution which gave France 18 years of despotism, reinforced by the proclamation of the Second Empire in December 1852.

After a period as vice-president of the Conseil d'État, Rouher was, on Feb. 3, 1855, made minister of agriculture, public works, and commerce, in which office he worked to promote the economic prosperity for which this period is famous. He believed that social progress could best be obtained by the government's establishing political "order" and giving private enterprise a free hand to expand in the economic field. He was thus Napoleon III's principal instrument in introducing free trade into France in 1860.

On Oct. 18, 1863, Rouher became minister of state, that is, premier. His capacity for work, his command of detail, and his vigour as the government's spokesman in Parliament won him great influence: he was nicknamed "the vice-emperor." Hostile to the movement for liberal concessions, he did much to postpone its success; when it triumphed, he was overthrown and retired to the post of president of the senate (July 1869).

The fall of the Second Empire gave Rouher a new political role. He was the principal organizer of the Bonapartist party after 1870, and served as member of Parliament from 1872 to 1882. He owed his leadership of the party largely to the confidence placed in him by the former empress Eugénie (*q.v.*), who approved of his conservative views. The result of their combined policy was that Bonapartism tended more and more toward a narrow conservatism which demanded a regime based on a popular vote but offered the people no prospect of real power or liberty, and so became virtually indistinguishable from the program of the other monarchist pretenders. Rouher died in Paris, on Feb. 3, 1884.

See R. Schnerb, *Rouher et le Second Empire* (1949). (T. Ze.)

ROULERS, Belgium: *see* ROESELARE.

ROULETTE, a gambling game of French origin, is universally played in the gambling casinos of Europe and North and South America, but is especially identified with the gaming rooms at Monte Carlo. It is not very old as games go, dating probably from the late 18th to the early 19th century. In the U.S. its popularity as a heavy-bet game has been superseded by other games, notably craps (*see* DICE). Roulette is a banking game, and all bets must be placed against the bank (proprietor of the game); as a rule it is very fairly conducted. As many players may bet as can get near the table.

Equipment for roulette consists of a large oblong table, in the centre of which is mounted a compartmented wheel, and at either end of which there is a red and black layout, usually enameled on green cloth. Small portable wheels of relatively low price are available for home use. The original French terminology of roulette has been replaced in English-speaking countries by equivalent English terms, and both will be used in this description.

The game begins when the *tourneur,* one of the croupiers in attendance who represents the house, calls, "Make your bets, gentlemen" (*Faites vos jeux, messieurs*), whereupon players place their bets on the layout to indicate the number, or classification of number, they hope will win. The *tourneur* then spins the wheel in one direction and in contrarotation spins a small ivory

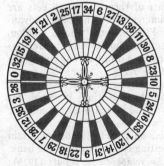

EUROPEAN ROULETTE WHEEL WITH 37 COMPARTMENTS
Numbers above the white panels are red, other numbers are black, except zero, which is green

ROULETTE CLOTH OR LAYOUT, EUROPEAN STYLE

ball which, when it slows down sufficiently, falls into one of the numbered compartments, and thus designates the winning number. When it appears to the *tourneur* that the ball will soon come to rest, he calls, "The betting is closed" (*Rien ne va plus*). No bet may be placed thereafter.

When the ball rests, the *tourneur* announces the winning number and whether it is red or black, odd or even, low (1 to 18) or high (19 to 36). The bank pays winning bets at the established rates (*see* below) and collects all losing bets, which a croupier gathers in with a rake.

For a winning bet on red (*rouge*), black (*noir*), high (*passe*), low (*manque*), even (*pair*) or odd (*impair*), the bank pays "even money"—the amount of the bet. For a winning bet on the dozen (1 to 12, 13 to 24 or 25 to 36) in which the number falls, the bank pays 2 to 1; these bets are indicated on the layout as 12p, 12m and 12d (respectively, *première*, *milieu* and *dernière douzaine*). Likewise, the bank pays 2 to 1 for a winning bet on the column in which the number lies.

Other bets, and the rate of payment when they win, are: (1) on a single number (*en plein*), 35 to 1; (2) on two numbers (*à cheval*), if either wins, 17 to 1. Such a bet is placed on the line between the two numbers. A bet may be made *à cheval* on two adjacent columns, or two adjacent dozens, and pays $\frac{1}{2}$ to 1. (3) On three numbers (*transversale pleine*), if any wins, 11 to 1. A bet on 4, 5 or 6 would be indicated by placing a coin on the line between 4 and *passe*, or between 6 and *manque*. (4) On four numbers (*en carré*), if any wins, 8 to 1. A bet on the point of intersection between 14, 15, 17 and 18 would be a bet on those four numbers. (5) On six numbers (*transversale six*), if any wins, 5 to 1. A bet on the point of intersection between 15, 18 and *impair* would be a bet on 13, 14, 15, 16, 17 and 18.

The zero may be placed *à cheval* with any adjoining number; or *en carré* (but called *quatre premiers*) with 1, 2 and 3; or in combination with 1 and 2, or with 2 and 3.

The advantage of the bank arises when the zero shows. Only bets on the zero *en plein* or in combination with 1, 2 and 3 are paid; all other bets are collected. Thus the bank should win one part in 37, or 2.7%, of all bets made against it.

At Monte Carlo, and in a few other casinos, this advantage is reduced by almost one-half in the case of the even-money bets. When the zero occurs, the player who placed such a bet may let the bank take half his bet (*partager*) or may have the bet put "in prison," to be decided on the next coup; whereon if the player wins he may withdraw his bet but is not paid in any case.

In distinction to this practice, many American gambling houses have roulette wheels with 38 compartments including both a zero and a double zero (00) and if either of them occurs all bets are taken except those involving the winning zero. The bank's advantage is thus increased to 5.26%. Finally, some wheels (seldom seen except in the smaller U.S. gambling houses and in Mexico) have 0,00 and an eagle (equivalent to a third zero), giving the bank an advantage of 3 parts in 39, or 7.7%.

There is little possibility of the exercise of skill in roulette, though a certain judgment is advisable in betting; it would, for example, be unwise to place a bet on red and also on the number 17, which is black, for if one bet wins the other must lose.

Many books have been published on roulette; most maintain that in the long run no system of betting can win against the bank.

BIBLIOGRAPHY.—Emanuel Lasker, *Encyclopaedia of Games* (1929); A. J. Lewis, *Card and Table Games,* ed. by Prof. Hoffman (1903); Albert H. Morehead, Richard L. Frey and Geoffrey Mott-Smith, *The New Complete Hoyle* (1956); "Trumps" (William Brisbane Dick), *The American Hoyle* (1890); John Scarne, *Complete Guide to Gambling* (1961).

(A. H. Md.; P. Fr.)

ROUMANIA: *see* RUMANIA.

ROUND: *see* CATCH.

ROUNDERS, an old English game which has never become a seriously competitive sport, although it may be an ancestor of baseball (*see* BASEBALL: *History of Baseball*). The earliest written reference to rounders was made in *A Little Pretty Pocket-Book* (1744), in which a woodcut also shows the children's sport of "baseball," and a letter of Nov. 8, 1748, of Mary Lepell, Lady Hervey, refers to the prince of Wales' family's "diverting themselves at Baseball." *The Boy's Own Book* (2nd edition, 1828) gives rounders a chapter and notes that in London the game is called "feeder." In 1889 the National Rounders Association of Liverpool and the Scottish Rounders Association were formed. The National Rounders Association was formed in 1943.

A hard ball, weighing $2\frac{1}{2}$ to 3 oz. and measuring $7\frac{1}{2}$ in. in circumference, and a round wooden "stick," measuring not more than $6\frac{3}{4}$ in. round the thickest part, not more than 18 in. in length and not weighing more than 13 oz., are used. The playing field is marked in the form of an open irregular pentagon (*see* diagram). The bowler must deliver the ball below the head but above the knee of the batsman and over the batting square. The batsman must strike at a good ball and attempt to run a "rounder" (even if he misses the ball or fails to strike at it) in a counterclockwise direction round the first, second, and third posts and so home to the fourth post, though he may stay at any of the first three. Three consecutive bad balls secure half a rounder for the batsman. He is out if the ball is caught on the fly; if the base (post) to which he is running is touched with the ball; or if while running he is touched with the ball by a fielder. As in cricket, the ball may be hit in any direction; but if it goes behind the batting square, the batter may run only to first post until the ball has been thrown back past the square. Nine players constitute a side, and two innings with 9 "outs" apiece are played in each match. The usual, but not compulsory, disposition for a fielding side is the bowler, the backstop (catcher), a base man on each of the four bases, and three deep fielders. There are two umpires. The game is played in Great Britain among younger schoolchildren, and some business houses and youth clubs have regular matches.

(N. D. McW.)

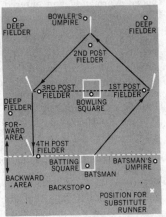

DIAGRAM OF THE PLAYING FIELD FOR ROUNDERS, SHOWING POSITIONS OF PLAYERS

ROUNDHEAD, a term applied to the adherents of the parliamentary party in England during the Civil War (1642–51). Some of the Puritans wore the hair closely cropped round the head, and there was thus an obvious contrast between them and the men of fashion with their long ringlets. "Roundhead" appears to have been first used as a term of derision toward the end of 1641 when the debates in Parliament on the Bishops Exclusion bill were causing riots at Westminster. John Rushworth, *Historical Collections,* part 3, vol. 1, p. 463 (1692), claims the word was first used on Dec. 27, 1641, by a disbanded officer named David Hide, who during a riot is reported to have drawn his sword and said he would "cut the Throat of those Round headed Dogs that bawled against Bishops." Richard Baxter (*Reliquiae Baxterianae,* 1696) ascribes the origin of the term to a remark made by Queen Henrietta Maria at the trial of the earl of Strafford (March–April 1641); referring to John Pym, she asked who the round-headed man was. The name was still in use at the Revolution of 1688.

ROUND TABLE, the celebrated table of King Arthur (*q.v.*). The first mention of the Round Table is in the *Roman de Brut* by Wace (*q.v.*), in which Arthur has a round table made at which none of his barons can claim precedence over the others. According to Wace, the Bretons told many stories about this table. In

Layamon's expanded version of this romance, the *Brut* (*c.* 1200), there is a violent quarrel among the knights, apparently because there are numerous tables and all want to be served at the most honourable. A Cornish carpenter then makes Arthur a table at which more than 1,600 men can sit and which Arthur can nevertheless carry about with him. Early Welsh literature knows nothing of Arthur's Round Table and in the absence of evidence it is idle to speculate about the source of the accounts in Wace and Layamon, especially where so simple a *motif* is concerned. Layamon's extended narrative has been widely regarded as a reflection of Celtic (*i.e.,* Irish) stories of feasts in which quarrels about precedence arise, but the details of the brawl could just as well have been suggested by Germanic heroic poetry.

The literary importance of the Round Table lies in the fact that in the French romances it provides the knights of Arthur's court with a name and a collective personality. The idea of a fellowship of the Round Table is still inconspicuous in the Arthurian romances of Chrétien de Troyes (*q.v.*), and it is only in the prose romances of the 13th century that the fellowship becomes comparable to, and indeed in many ways the prototype of, the great orders of chivalry founded in the later Middle Ages. This conception culminates in the *Morte Darthur* of Sir Thomas Malory (*q.v.*), for whom the notion of chivalry is inseparable from that of a great military brotherhood established in the household of a great prince.

In the peculiar Messianic Grail poem of Robert de Borron, *Joseph d'Arimathie* (*c.* 1200?), Joseph is commanded to make a table in commemoration of the Last Supper and to leave one place empty to symbolize the seat of Judas. This seat cannot be occupied without peril except by the destined Grail-hero. In his *Merlin,* Robert relates that Merlin constructed a table for Uther Pendragon modeled on Joseph's Grail table, with a place left vacant in the same way. When, in the 13th century, in the group of prose romances covering all the Arthurian stories and known as the "Vulgate cycle and the post-Vulgate romance," the Grail story is fully integrated with the legend of Arthur, the Round Table *motif* attains its "classical" form: the Round Table is made for Uther by Merlin and comes into the possession of Leodegran, king of Carmelide, who gives it to Arthur together with a company of knights when the latter marries his daughter Guinevere. The order of the Round Table is now a formal order of knighthood, admission to which is reserved for the most valiant, and the Siege Perilous is left vacant waiting for the coming of the strange figure of Galahad who will bring the marvels of Arthur's kingdom to an end. (*See* also ARTHURIAN LEGEND; GRAIL, THE HOLY.)

The existence of a round table at Winchester in the 15th century is attested by William Caxton (1485) and John Hardyng, who says in his *Chronicle* (*post* 1464) that the Round Table "began at Winchester and ended at Winchester, and there it hangs still." The tabletop 18 ft. in diameter and divided into 25 sectors which is now fixed to the wall of the great hall was, according to R. S. Loomis, perhaps constructed in the late medieval period for one of those feasts followed by a tournament and known as *tables rondes,* so common at the time. The present form of the table, with its alternate sectors of green and white (the Tudor colours), its central Tudor rose, and the names of the knights based on Malory, cannot be earlier than the reign of Henry VII.

BIBLIOGRAPHY.—A. C. L. Brown, *Harvard Studies in Philology and Literature,* vol. vii, pp. 183–285 (1900); R. S. and L. H. Loomis, *Arthurian Legends in Medieval Art,* vol. ii (1938); A. Micha, "La table ronde dans Robert de Boron," in *Les Romans du Graal, Colloques internationaux du Centre national de la Recherche scientifique,* no. iii (1956).
(F. WH.)

ROUNDWORM (NEMATODE), the name for invertebrate animals that constitute the phylum Nemata (some regard them as a class, Nematoda, of the phylum Nemathelminthes). The terms nema or nematode mean "threadlike," the reference being to the elongate threadlike body typical of the group. Free-living and plant-parasitic nematodes are often called eelworms or anguillules, terms descriptive of the body form and locomotion of some roundworms. Included among the nematodes parasitic in animals are the intestinal roundworms, pinworms, hookworms, filarial worms, trichina worms and whipworms.

Free-living and parasitic forms are mostly from $\frac{1}{32}$ to $\frac{1}{64}$ in. long, rarely larger or smaller; however, they are so thin that they are not usually seen without the aid of a microscope. Certain nematode parasites are much larger: *Ascaris,* intestinal parasites of man, may be 10 in. long and $\frac{1}{4}$ in. in diameter; mermithid parasites of insects, several inches long; kidney worms of dogs, up to 1 yd. The largest known form, *Placentonema gigantissima,* in the placenta of an arctic whale, may reach 9 yd. long. Most roundworms are spindle-shaped or filiform, but some may be sausage-shaped (insect parasites like *Howardula, Tylenchinema*); spherical, subspherical, lemon-shaped, pear-shaped (females of sedentary plant parasites, such as *Heterodera, Meloidogyne*); kidney-shaped (*Rotylenchulus,* ectoparasites on roots) or pouch-shaped (female of *Tetrameres,* a parasite in the proventriculus of the chicken).

In colour, roundworms are usually whitish to yellowish brown, exceptionally red (female kidney worm of dogs), black (*Siphonolaimus,* marine; *Dorylaimus atratus* from hot springs) or rarely other colours. Many species are transparent, others opaque.

Nematodes differ from other nemathelminthes in having a body wall that is a cuticular-hypodermal-muscular tube with longitudinal hypodermal ridges (chords) separating the bands of body muscles; a complete absence of cilia; a ring-shaped, circumesophageal nerve centre, with six radially (one each lateral and submedial) arranged nerves extending toward the head end and a usually unpaired main ventral nerve extending toward the tail; lateral chemoreceptors (amphids, or lateral organs) on or near the head; radially arranged circumoral tactile head sense organs; an absence of nephridial flame cells; and a cloaca in the male.

OCCURRENCE AND SIGNIFICANCE

Occurrence.—About 10,000 species of nematodes have been described (this number is thought to be only a fraction of the existing species). Nematodes occupy a great variety of habitats. Free-living species are so numerous in soils that a handful of earth often contains hundreds of individuals of several different species; they live in fresh-water streams and ponds, in brackish and salt water and have been found at all latitudes where a search for them has been made. Agricultural soils contain hundreds of millions of free-living nematodes and often large numbers of plant-parasitic species; the same is true of forest and grass lands. Man and all of his domestic animals are often parasitized by a large number of nematode species; wild animals and insects and other invertebrates also have a large variety of nematode parasites. In general, nematodes are found wherever they can find enough food to survive. They are certainly one of the most abundant

BY COURTESY OF THE ARMED FORCES INSTITUTE OF PATHOLOGY

FIG. 1.—HOOKWORMS: (LEFT) LONGITUDINAL SECTION OF A HOOKWORM SHOWING THE CLOSE ORGANIC ATTACHMENT TO THE HOST INTESTINAL LINING; (RIGHT) HOOKWORMS (NECATOR AMERICANUS) COPULATING. THE LONGER WORMS, THE FEMALES, ARE ABOUT ONE-HALF INCH LONG

groups of multicellular animals, but because of their small size and hidden habitats they are seldom seen unless a special search is made to find them.

Plant Parasites.—All the several hundred species of nematodes demonstrated to be plant parasites belong to two orders: most are in the Tylenchida; only a few species are in the Dorylaimoida (*see* classification below). The great majority feed on the underground parts of plants (roots, tubers, corms, rhizomes and bulbs); only a relatively few species feed on the stems, leaves

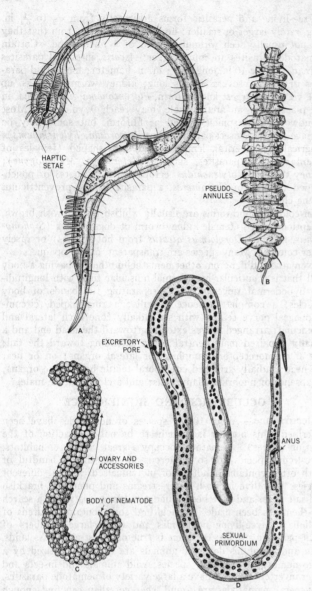

FIG. 2.—(A) DRACONEMA, A CLIMBING MARINE NEMATODE; (B) DESMO-SCOLEX, A MARINE NEMATODE WITH PSEUDOANNULES; (C) SPHAERULARIA, PARASITE OF BUMBLEBEE; (D) MICROFILARIA OF WUCHERERIA BANCROFTI, A PARASITE OF THE HUMAN LYMPHATIC SYSTEM

and flower parts of plants. Apparently all of the higher plants without exception are attacked by plant-parasitic nematodes. Nematode species are somewhat specialized so far as feeding and reproducing are concerned. For the most part they are obligate parasites, and a given species will be able to reproduce only on a more or less limited variety of plants.

Most information available relates to agricultural crops, and known host ranges of some of the species that have been extensively studied range from a few related plant species to many plant species of different families. Very often a given nematode species is able to reproduce on certain cultivated varieties of plants, known as "susceptible," but not on other cultivated varieties, known as "immune," with all degrees of resistance between the two categories.

Plant-parasitic nematodes are serious agricultural pests, responsible for an estimated billion dollars of crop damage in the United States each year. The greater part of this loss is from reduction of yields due to root damage by nematodes, often in association with bacteria and fungi, which weakens the plant. Some of the loss is due to reduction in quality of produce because of malformation (distorted potato tubers, carrots, etc.).

Some plant-parasitic nematodes cause the formation of galls. The attached tissue enlarges, root growth may stop (resulting in an abnormally reduced root system) or cells may die. Often the nematode damage is extended by bacteria or fungi that secondarily invade the attacked tissue. Nematodes also transmit several virus diseases of plants.

Plant-parasitic nematodes are controlled in agricultural soils by crop rotations, which take advantage of the specialized feeding habits of the nematodes. The parasites are starved out by planting crops on which they cannot reproduce. The same thing can be accomplished by leaving the land fallow for a time. For crops of high value it is possible and economical to use chemical control. Nematocides (or nematicides) in common use include dichloropropenes, ethylene dibromide, dibromochloropropane and methyl bromide.

Animal Parasites.—Round-worms, however, have been best known as parasites of animals, particularly as disease agents of man and domesticated animals. Practically all organs and body parts—intestine, liver, kidney, lungs, diaphragm, brain, eyes, blood, heart—have their specific nematode parasites. About 60 different species have been observed in man, about 70 in horses, 40 in pigs and similar numbers in other mammals, birds (chickens, about 60), reptiles, amphibians, fishes, insects and other arthropods, mollusks, earthworms, echinoderms, leeches, etc.

Human Disease.—Roundworms are a most significant factor in human health and the welfare of domesticated and game animals. Infections in man are of worldwide occurrence. The whipworm (*Trichuris trichiura*), relatively harmless, has been estimated to be infecting more than 335,000,000 persons. The trichina worm (*Trichinella spiralis*), often a dangerous parasite, has been stated to affect annually more than 20,000,000 persons in the United States and Canada, more than 1,000,000 in South America, almost 4,000,000 in Europe, perhaps 200,000 in Africa and 100,000 each in Asia and the Pacific (*see* TRICHINOSIS). Infestations of hookworms (*Ancylostoma duodenale, Necator americanus*), said to affect more than 500,000,000 inhabitants of the warmer regions of the earth, were mentioned in Egyptian papyrus records of earliest history (*see* HOOKWORM). Another parasite of man, *Strongyloides stercoralis*, also is an inhabitant of the tropics and subtropics; it is estimated to affect some 35,000,-000 persons, mostly in America and Southern Asia. The intestinal worms, *Ascaris*, too, have been referred to in ancient medical scripts. They are cosmopolitan and are estimated to be present in almost 650,000,000 persons, causing a variety of often serious disease symptoms, including allergies. The pinworm (*Enterobius vermicularis*), of widest distribution, occurring in certain locations in 50% to 100% of the population, also is mentioned in early medical writings. Filarial worms affect man mostly in the tropics. They are remarkable because their life cycles require an intermediate host, either a mosquito or a bloodsucking fly. The medically most important filariae are *Wuchereria ban-*

BY COURTESY OF G. STEINER

FIG. 3.—MALE HOPLOLAIMUS CORONATUS, FEEDING ON KNOT WEED ROOT

BY COURTESY OF G. STEINER

FIG. 4.—GLOBULAR FEMALES OF GOLDEN NEMATODE (HETERODERA ROSTOCHIENSIS) ON POTATO ROOT

crofti, W. malayi, Loa loa and *Onchocerca volvulus,* in all of which the larval stages (microfilariae) live in man's bloodstream. Elephantiasis, an abnormal swelling of various parts of the human body, particularly legs, arms and the scrotum, is a late development of a filarial infection (*see* FILARIASIS). The guinea worm or medinaworm (*Dracunculus medinensis*) is another remarkable roundworm, estimated to affect 50,000,000, particularly the people of the Nile and India; it too has been reported in earliest medical papers (*see* GUINEA-WORM INFECTION).

Free-Living Nematodes.—The over-all role of free-living nematodes is intimately connected with the soil and the life therein: bacteria, fungi, algae and protozoa. There are no proper planktonic nematodes nor forms that are truly aerial; nematodes occur in these environments only as parasites, commensals or passengers on other organisms. These nematodes, neither plant nor animal parasites, include forms that normally live in soil, fresh water, salt water or in such habitats as crevices in trees. Probably the best-known of the free-living nematodes, though not a typical one, is the "vinegar eel," capable of living in vinegar or other similarly acidic environments. The food of free-living nematodes is not well defined. Certainly some live on bacteria or other organisms associated with the decay of organic matter, others live on algae and some kill and feed on other small animals, including other kinds of nematodes.

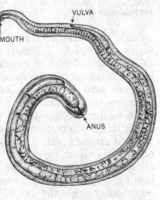

Value.—Roundworms are also useful to man. Through their parasitism, or through their ability to transfer pathogenic bacteria, they help control such noxious pests as Japanese beetles, grasshoppers and bark beetles.

In basic biological science nematodes have been favoured forms for the study of cell division, cell lineage, sexual phenomena, the problem of heat and cold resistance of living matter, and the unsolved features of dormancy and

FIG. 5.—TRICHINA WORM: (TOP) FEMALE OF TRICHINELLA SPIRALIS; (BOTTOM) YOUNG TRICHINELLA EMBEDDED IN MUSCLE OF HOST

parasitism. Research questions have been raised by the discovery of certain terrestrial nematodes withstanding temperatures as low as −271° C. and by the observation of wheat gall nematodes and some related kinds returning to life after a dormancy of many years (*Tylenchus polyhypnus* resumed life after 39 years).

STRUCTURE AND FUNCTION

Like other nemathelminths, roundworms have an unsegmented, often cylindrical body with a pseudocoel; *i.e.*, a body cavity without an epithelial wall of its own between the intestinal tract and the outer body wall.

Body Covering.—This is a resilient cuticula, richly structured, smooth or annulated; in many free-living types thick and articulated but also with numerous surface formations: membranous projections, inflations, folds, cordons, spines and warty or scale-like structures. The lateral surface is often marked by wings, grooves, areolations or striae that interrupt the body annulation. The cuticula may bear bristles or setae, papillae or outlets of hypodermal glands. Beneath the cuticula is a usually syncytial hypodermis (epidermis) that forms four longitudinal thickenings or chords (two lateral, a ventral and a dorsal) or, exceptionally, six (two additional ventrosubmedial) or eight chords (two additional dorsosubmedial). Lateral chords are the strongest and

have the largest number of nuclei, the ventral one being smaller, the dorsal and submedial ones smallest. Cuticula, hypodermis and chords form the exoskeleton.

Musculature.—Arranged between the chords are longitudinal muscles. With the exoskeleton, they constitute the tubelike outer body wall. Additional muscles are present particularly in the digestive tract and in the male copulatory system. Circular muscles are absent.

Body Cavity.—The pseudocoel between the outer wall and the intestinal tract is filled with fluid that maintains a proper turgor pressure. Strands of mesenchymatic tissue, fenestrated membranes and cells called pseudocoelomocytes may occur in the body cavity.

Digestive Tract.—Anteriorly, the terminal, or rarely subterminal, mouth leads to a variously shaped buccal cavity that may or may not have teeth and other armature, may be transformed into a stylet or may be absent. A tubular esophagus, with three radiating branches, and digestive glands connect the mouth and intestine, usually through an esophageo-intestinal valve. The intestine, with an epithelial wall, ends in a rectum, with or without rectal glands; the anus is ventral and subterminal, seldom terminal.

Nervous System.—This system consists of a circumesophageal central organ or nerve ring (a kind of brain) with various ganglia; six nerves, one each lateral and submedial, extend from the nerve ring anteriorly and innervate the radially arranged tactile labial and cephalic papillae or setae and the amphids. Posteriorly from the nerve ring there extend in each pertaining chord, a main ventral and lesser dorsal and lateral nerves. Some fresh-water and marine forms are provided with primitive eyes.

Respiration.—There is no specific respiratory-circulatory system. Respiration occurs through the cuticle, even in parasites that are embedded in host tissue. In contrast, intestinal parasites living in the digestive food mass may respire anaerobically.

Excretory Apparatus.—The excretory system is unique, consisting of either an H- or inverted U-shaped canal system located in lateral chords, with a ventral pore usually in the anterior third of the body in the region of the nerve ring; or this canal system may be combined with ventrally located glands. There may be no canal system, but only one to several ventral glands. In some cases a specific excretory apparatus is not known. The canal system is considered a remnant of a protonephridial excretory apparatus, but in no instance has the presence of flame cells been definitely established.

Additional Glandular Systems.—The esophageal glands, mainly digestive in function, are also used as poison glands to immobilize prey. In plant parasites the secretions of these glands, when injected into host tissues, induce hypertrophies and production by the plant host of assimilable food material (perioral digestion). Foot glands, commonly located in the tail of mainly aquatic free-living types, are adhesive.

REPRODUCTION AND DEVELOPMENT

Reproductive System.—The female has a single, ventrally located vulva that may open in middle region of the body, in positions farther forward (exceptionally near the head) or more frequently

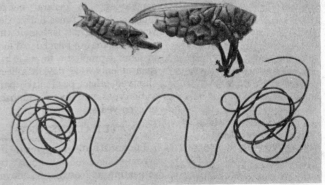

BY COURTESY OF G. STEINER

FIG. 6.—A MERMITHID ROUNDWORM DISSECTED FROM A GRASSHOPPER

farther backward, but always in front of the anus (exception: *Randonia randoni*, a fish parasite with the vulva and rectum combined into a cloaca). The vagina is commonly a short, inward-leading tube that connects with the outlets of the two ovaries, one directed forward, the other backward. The oviduct and uterus are frequently complex structures. In many nematodes the posterior, less frequently the anterior, ovary and outlets are wholly or partly obliterated. Multiple ovaries and outlets are rare.

The male organs, the testis and its outlet, extend forward but empty in the rectum, always forming a cloaca. Sclerotized, mostly curved, usually paired, seldom single spicula function as copulatory organs; of diverse form in the various groups (absent, *e.g.*, in some *Trichiuroidea*), they are inserted into the vulva and vagina of the female. Additional structures, such as sclerotized gubernacula, setae, papillae, glands, special muscles and membranes (bursal) are further aids in copulation. Males are often smaller than females and may also differ in many other respects. Although the condition of separate sexes prevails, parthenogenesis and hermaphroditism also occur; here males are rare or apparently absent. In *Trichosomoides crassicauda*, a parasite of the urinary tract of the rat, the male dwells in the vagina of the much larger female roundworm.

Development and Life Cycle.—Free-living nematodes produce small numbers of eggs, while parasitic kinds are extremely prolific (an *Ascaris* generates about 27,000,000 eggs in its lifetime; about 200,000 daily). Cleavage is determinate, and cell constancy is a remarkable feature in nematodes. After termination of the larval development, the cell number remains constant, except in the gonads; further growth is accomplished only by cell enlargement. This is associated with the absence of regenerative powers in nematodes. In general nematodes molt four times during development; at the last molt the sexual organs are formed. While in some saprophytic forms a life span of only 8–12 days has been observed, others, particularly parasitic types, may live for months or even years.

NATURAL HISTORY

Locomotion.—Movement is accomplished fundamentally by serpentine and oscillating movements in a dorsoventral plane, through alternating contraction

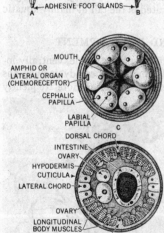

FIG. 7.—DIAGRAM OF GENERALIZED ROUNDWORM (A) FEMALE AND (B) MALE; (C) FRONT VIEW OF HEAD WITH SIX LIPS AROUND BUCCAL ENTRANCE; (D) CROSS SECTION NEAR MIDBODY OF FEMALE

Labels in figure:
MOUTH
HEAD
BUCCAL CAVITY
ESOPHAGUS
NERVE RING
EXCRETORY PORE
VALVE
INTESTINE
OVARY
OVIDUCT
VULVA
TESTIS
EGG IN OVIDUCT
OVARY
EJACULATORY DUCT
RECTAL GLANDS
SPICULUM
RECTUM
GUBERNACULUM
ANUS
SETOSE COPULATORY PAPILLAE
ADHESIVE FOOT GLANDS
OPENING OF ADHESIVE FOOT GLANDS

MOUTH
AMPHID OR LATERAL ORGAN (CHEMORECEPTOR)
CEPHALIC PAPILLA
LABIAL PAPILLA
DORSAL CHORD
INTESTINE
OVARY
HYPODERMIS
CUTICULA
LATERAL CHORD
OVARY
LONGITUDINAL BODY MUSCLES
VENTRAL CHORD

of the subventral and subdorsal bands of body muscles. A unique feature is the use in some species of one of the lateral, not the ventral, sides as a creeping surface. However, certain marine groups, *e.g.*, the *Epsilonematidae*, move like geometrid caterpillars with the ventral side of body turned toward the substratum; *Draconematidae*, climbers, also apply the ventral side against the substratum; certain *Desmoscolecidae* walk on their backs, using stiff setae and pseudoannules as locomotory structures; some *Criconematinae* (root parasites) use backward directed annules and retrograde spines, scales and rims fot locomotion by contraction and relaxation in the longitudinal axis. Swimming is performed by some by oscillating movements in the dorsoventral plane.

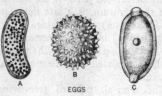

FIG. 8.—EGGS OF VARIOUS NEMATODES (GREATLY MAGNIFIED): (A) MEADOW NEMATODE (PRATYLENCHUS); (B) MONOCHUS; (C) A TRICHIUROID

Food and Feeding.—Nematodes are sucking organisms. Primitive roundworms were originally feeders on bacteria and organic matter decomposed by bacterial action; many types still retain this mode of feeding. But other kinds of microorganisms are also preyed upon: protozoans, rotifers, annelid worms, other nematodes, algae, fungi and, by parasitism, many animals and plants. Some nematodes are food specialists, requiring definite host tissue; others are quite omnivorous. Food may be ingested; absorbed through the cuticle as in many parasites; or, as in *Sphaerularia bombi* (a parasite of the bumblebee), the prolapsed uterus and ovary of the nematode may assimilate food directly from the hemolymph of the host. Parasitic nematodes in intestinal tracts and forms living in plant digestive fluids, as in leafy containers of the pitcher plant *Nepenthes*, are immune to digestive action because of protective enzymes.

Enemies and Diseases.—Amoebas, earthworms, tardigrades, predatory nematodes, mites, carnivorous insects, crustaceans and fish have been observed feeding on nematodes. Most fascinating are the nematode-trapping fungi that catch their prey with contractile loops and sticky outgrowths. Nematodes are subject to bacterial and fungus diseases. Sporozoan infections are common and usually lethal.

RELATIONSHIPS AND CLASSIFICATION

Phylogeny.—There are two main concepts of the phylogenetic relationship of nematodes: one assumes their origin from turbellarian flat worms via forms resembling gastrotrichs, tiny aquatic

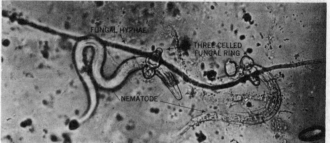

BY COURTESY OF "DISCOVERY," LONDON

FIG. 9.—NEMATODES CAPTURED BY A PREDACEOUS FUNGUS. THE RINGS ON THE FUNGAL HYPHAE CONSTRICT WHEN A NEMATODE PASSES THROUGH AND FUNGUS THEN ABSORBS BODY JUICES OF THE NEMATODE

Labels in photo: FUNGAL HYPHAE, THREE-CELLED FUNGAL RING, NEMATODE

bottom dwellers; the other traces nematode origin from annelid ancestry via forms resembling rotifers.

Classification.—Authorities disagree on the taxonomic rank of the nematodes. Some regard them as constituting an order or a class of the phylum Nemathelminthes (as treated here), while others consider them a phylum, Nemata. The classification of lower groups is likewise unsettled, particularly as to superfamilies, orders and subclasses. The classification of the animal parasites is more advanced than that of the free-living and plant parasitic forms.

The following classification, by L. H. Hyman, is one of several schemes in general use. The first seven orders are mostly free living. The remaining orders include the economically important parasitic nematodes.

Order Enoploidea, chiefly marine
" Dorylaimoidea, common in soil and fresh water
" Mermithoidea, parasitic juvenile stage in invertebrates; free-living adults
" Chromadoroidea, chiefly marine
" Araeolaimoidea, soil and fresh water
" Monhysteroidea, marine and soil
" Desmoscolecoidea, marine
" Rhabditoidea (Anguilluloidea), eelworm, plant parasites
" Rhabdiasoidea, lung nematodes of amphibians and reptiles; intestinal parasites in mammals
" Oxyuroidea, threadworm, pinworm of vertebrates
" Ascaroidea, ascaris and other intestinal worms of vertebrates
" Strongyloidea, hookworms, lung worms of mammals especially
" Spiruroidea, eye worm, gullet worm of vertebrates
" Dracunculoidea, guinea worm of vertebrates
" Filarioidea, filarial worms of vertebrates; dog heart worm
" Trichuroidea (Trichinelloidea), whipworm, trichina worm of birds and mammals especially
" Dioctophymoidea, dog kidney worm

See also references under "Roundworm" in the Index.

Bibliography.—B. G. Chitwood and others, *An Introduction to Nematology,* Section I Anatomy, rev. ed. (1950); C. L. Duddington, *The Friendly Fungi* (1957); L. H. Hyman, *The Invertebrates:* vol. iii (1951); N. R. Stoll, "This Wormy World," *Jour. Parasit.* 33:1–18 (1947); W. Yorke and P. A. Maplestone, *The Nematode Parasites of Vertebrates* (1926); J. N. Sasser and W. R. Jenkins, eds., *Nematology* (1960); J. R. Christie, *Plant Nematodes* (1959); G. Thorne, *Principles of Nematology* (1961); T. Goodey, *Soil and Freshwater Nematodes,* rev. by J. B. Goodey (1963). (Gd. S.)

ROUS, FRANCIS (1579–1659), though an Independent and a layman, was the author of a metrical version of the Psalms which was approved by the Westminster Assembly and authorized by Parliament. It became the staple form of praise in worship in the Church of Scotland, where (in a revised form) it is still in use. Rous was born at Dittisham, Devon, and educated at Broadgates Hall, Oxford, and Leiden University. From 1625 until 1657, whenever Parliament was in being, he was a member, and of the Nominated Parliament of 1653 he was speaker. In 1657 he was summoned by Cromwell to the new House of Lords. From 1644 he was also provost of Eton. He died at Acton in January 1659 and was buried in Eton College chapel. The title of his book, *The Mystical Marriage: or Experimental Discourses of the Heavenly Marriage Between a Soule and Her Saviour,* which was issued more than once in his lifetime, in both English and Latin, well expresses his piety. He turned increasingly toward a light within: "We want not the Glow-worm of demonstration." (G. F. N.)

ROUSSEAU, HENRI JULIEN FÉLIX, called Le Douanier (1844–1910), French painter famous for his "primitive" or untutored style, was born at Laval, Mayenne, May 20, 1844. A soldier in Mexico in 1862–66, he served intermittently till 1871 when he entered the customs service (hence the title Le Douanier or customs official), but retired in 1885, at the age of 41, to professionally adopt his hobby of painting. He then began to exhibit portraits, still-life paintings and views of Paris and its people, such as "Un Soir de Carnaval" (1886; L. E. Stern collection, U.S.), "Myself: Portrait-Landscape" (1890; Prague) and "The Centenary of Independence" (1892). These are deceptively simple and arranged frontally with clear contours separating fields of even, solid, often brilliant colour; but their strength lies in their wholehearted regard for the occasion they represent. Between 1886 and 1890 Rousseau exhibited 20 works at the Paris Salon des Indépendants and was attacked by critics both "advanced" and orthodox. But he was defended by Degas and Toulouse-Lautrec, and later was befriended by Picasso and the poet Alfred Jarry. After 1890 his work became less static and included jungle and animal scenes. Some landscape studies are unexpectedly tentative and atmospheric; large works such as the "Sleeping Gipsy" (1897; Museum of Modern Art, New York city) have an imaginative, remote lyricism which later recommended them to Jean Cocteau and Guillaume Apollinaire. Some of Rousseau's best work dates from 1900 on; it includes "Jungle

With a Lion" (1904–06; Museum of Modern Art) and "The Cart of Père Juniet" (1908; Mme. Paul Guillaume's collection, Paris). He died in Paris, Sept. 4, 1910.

See also Painting: *Early 20th-Century Trends.*

See D. C. Rich, *Henri Rousseau,* 2nd ed., with bibliography (1946); M. Garçon, *Le Douanier Rousseau accusé naïf* (1953). (D. C. T. T.)

ROUSSEAU, JEAN BAPTISTE (1671–1741), French poet, who enjoyed great renown in his day, was born at Paris on April 6, 1671, of humble parentage. As a young man he began to move in literary circles and received some encouragement from Boileau. Rousseau wrote a number of plays of which *Le Flatteur* (1696) was the most successful, several cantatas (an original genre in France), and many poems, some of them serious and reflective, like his ode to La Fare, others frivolous and even scandalous. The libellous character of some of these involved him more than once in trouble. In 1712, because of defamatory couplets which he denied having written, he was expelled from France. He remained in exile until his death in Brussels on March 16 or 17, 1741. He was a member of the Académie des Inscriptions.

See H. A. Grubbs, *Jean-Baptiste Rousseau* (1941). (Rt. S.)

ROUSSEAU, JEAN JACQUES (1712–1778), French-Swiss moralist whose writings are among the most influential of the 18th century in political and social theory and literature, was born at Geneva, Switz., on June 28, 1712. His ancestor, Didier Rousseau, a convert to Calvinism, had taken refuge in Geneva in the middle of the 16th century, and Jean Jacques belonged to the fifth generation of his descendants. His mother, Suzanne (*née* Bernard) died a few days after his birth. His father Isaac, a watchmaker, an affectionate but irritable and feckless man, looked after him until he was ten years old, giving him no regular schooling but encouraging a precocious taste for Plutarch and for novels. In June 1722, Isaac, after a quarrel with a fellow citizen in which he was probably the aggressor, had to take refuge at Nyon in the Pays de Vaud, leaving his two sons, Jean Jacques and his elder brother François, in the charge of their maternal uncle, Gabriel Bernard. François was apprenticed, and Jean Jacques sent to live with Pastor J. J. Lambercier at Bossey, near Geneva. He returned from Bossey to his uncle in Geneva in Sept. 1724 and was soon afterward set to work as a clerk to J. L. Masseron, a notary, with whom he stayed only a few weeks. In April 1725 he was apprenticed to Abel du Commun, an engraver, with whom he stayed until he fled from Geneva on March 14, 1728. In his *Confessions* Rousseau complains that du Commun treated him brutally, though he admits his own idleness, untruthfulness and dishonesty, which he ascribes to his master's harshness. He felt humiliated and was made rebellious by his master's punishment, but earlier Mlle Lambercier at Bossey had had to give up beating him because he had enjoyed it too much. Fierce resentment at injustice and masochism were both strong motives with him.

His Formative Years.—From Geneva Rousseau found his way to Annecy, in Savoy, to Mme de Warens (Louise Éléonore de Latour de Pil), who had left her husband and become a convert to Catholicism, receiving a pension from the king of Sardinia for helping to make other converts. Through Mme de Warens he was sent to Turin, to the Hospice of the Holy Spirit, which he entered on April 12, 1728. According to the register of the hospice, he abjured the heresies of Calvin on April 21 and was received into the Roman Catholic Church two days later, though in the *Confessions* he describes a much longer resistance to conversion and says that he finally succumbed in order to escape the pernicious moral atmosphere of the hospice. For several months he stayed in Turin working as an engraver and as a lackey. He returned to Mme de Warens in the spring of 1729 and was sent for a time to a Lazarist seminary, but he soon found that he had no vocation for the priesthood and later went to the choir school attached to the cathedral at Annecy. In 1730, while Mme de Warens was away in Paris, he returned to Switzerland and set himself up at Lausanne and then at Neuchâtel as a teacher of music (though he had no proper qualifications). After several months of vagabondage and precarious living, he was sent to Paris in the autumn of 1731 by the marquis de Bonac (Jean Louis d'Usson), the French ambassador at Soleure. This first visit to Paris led to nothing and lasted only a few days. Rousseau returned on foot to Mme de Warens, who by this time had moved to Chambéry. She offered herself to him as his mistress in 1733, saying that she thought it would be good for him, and he accepted, though he continued to feel himself more her son than her lover and knew that he would have to share her favours with her steward, Claude Anet. Except for occasional journeys to Switzerland and France, he stayed with her, either at Chambéry or in the country nearby, at a house called Les Charmettes, until 1740. It was during this time that he became a diligent but unsystematic reader and that he first began to write.

JEAN JACQUES ROUSSEAU, PASTEL PORTRAIT BY MAURICE QUENTIN DE LA TOUR, 1752

In May 1740 he went to tutor the children of M. de Mably, *prévôt des maréchaux* for the Lyonnais and elder brother of Etienne Bonnot de Condillac and of the abbé de Mably; but when his year's contract was over he was not asked to stay. He returned for a time to Mme de Warens, who received him coolly. Though she had begun to grow tired of him several years before and had acquired a new and younger lover, she had not lost all maternal solicitude for him, especially as he had been ill several times since 1737. He suffered from uremia and his condition grew worse as he grew older. In 1742 he went to Paris for the second time, taking with him a new scheme of musical notation, an opera, a comedy and a collection of poems.

Rousseau went to Paris seeking fame and fortune, but for years had no success. He was invited to read his scheme for musical notation to the Académie des Sciences but nothing came of it; he spent a year, from Sept. 1743 to Aug. 1744, in Venice as secretary to the French ambassador there, but quarrelled so violently with his master that he had to leave; he wrote a ballet, *Les Muses galantes,* which was eventually performed at the Opéra in Paris in 1747 but attracted only slight notice. On two occasions he was so deeply humiliated that he fell ill: once, when he declared his love to Mme Dupin, his protectress, who left the room and for a long time forbade him her house; and again, when an opera, with words by Voltaire and music by J. P. Rameau, whose score he had been asked to alter for a shortened version, was played at Versailles without his name being mentioned. Rousseau, at this period, devoted more of his energies to music and to the writing of comedies than to social and political matters. He lived in frequent, but not intimate or equal, contact with the rich and the famous. His best, perhaps his only true, friend was Denis Diderot, who commissioned him to write the articles on music for the *Encyclopédie.* He dined once a week at the Hôtel du Panier Fleuri with Diderot and with Condillac, and these were the happiest moments of an otherwise awkward and anxious period of his life. Early in 1745, soon after his return from Venice, he had taken up with Thérèse le Vasseur, a servant at the hotel where he was staying. He kept her for the rest of his life and had five children by her, who were all sent to a foundling hospital. In disposing of his children in this way, he was doing what was often done at that time and felt, so he says in the *Confessions,* no shame. He was poor and sickly and for years was heartlessly exploited by Thérèse's mother and some of her relatives. Later, after he had become famous as a moralist, he was morbidly sensitive about his abandoned children, and the emotional burden of a guilt that he would not admit helped in the end to put him out of his mind.

The Citizen and the Moralist (1749–62).—One day, toward the end of July 1749, Rousseau, on his way to Vincennes to visit Diderot who was in prison there, read in the *Mercure de France* that the academy of Dijon offered a prize for an essay on the

question whether the revival of the sciences and the arts had helped to corrupt or to purify morals. Rousseau tells us, in his *Confessions,* that when he read that notice "he saw another world and became another man" and that when he reached Diderot he was so excited as to be almost delirious. Diderot urged him to compete for the prize and even (so some of his friends said afterward) suggested to Rousseau that he should treat the subject in an unexpected way, arguing that science and art had corrupted morals. Whether or not it was from Diderot that Rousseau got this idea (and Diderot never said that it was), the idea itself was more congenial to Rousseau than to his friend. It released emotions pent up within him for years. The result of the competition was announced in July 1750, and Rousseau got the first prize. His essay, subsequently known under the abbreviated title of *Discours sur les sciences et les arts,* was published at the end of the year, and he found himself famous. In his *Confessions,* he gives the impression that, soon after the publication of his first *Discours,* he decided abruptly to change his way of life, to give up all hope of fortune and of worldly success and always to remain poor and independent. Though the change was more gradual and hesitant than he afterward remembered it, it is true that he never, for all his fame, was a worldly success. He never sought riches and never allowed himself to be lionized. He resented both indifference and flattery; he wanted to be emotionally independent of others and yet felt a need for their affection and respect. Self-absorbed as he was, he demanded that others should feel toward him as he, though he did not know it, was incapable of feeling toward them.

Whatever he did, whether it was liked or disliked, seemed, for the rest of his life, to add to his fame. In 1752 he composed an operatic intermezzo, *Le Devin du village,* which was first performed at Fontainebleau before the court. Next day he was to be presented to Louis XV to receive a pension, but he refused to go, partly from pride, partly from shyness and partly because of his peculiar illness. That same year his comedy, *Narcisse,* was played at the Théâtre Français. Next year, the *Lettre sur la musique française,* in which he expressed a strong preference for Italian over French music, was widely and hotly discussed. In the summer of 1754 he visited his native Geneva, was well received there, became once again a Protestant and recovered his citizen rights. Early in 1755, he published his *Discours sur l'origine de l'inégalité parmi les hommes,* greatly superior in thought and argument to his first *Discours,* though the academy of Dijon, for which it was also written, gave it no prize; in the same year appeared also his *Discours sur l'économie politique* commissioned by Diderot for the *Encyclopédie.* In April 1756 he moved out of Paris to the Hermitage, a house near Montmorency placed at his disposal by Mme d'Épinay (q.v.), where he began work on his novel *Julie, ou la nouvelle Héloïse.* It was there that he fell genuinely in love, perhaps for the first time in his life, with Mme d'Houdetot, nearly 20 years his junior and herself in love with another man. Rousseau did not expect her to return his love but believed in her friendship; and his passion for her deeply affected his novel, which is as remarkable for eloquence and for subtlety as for the artificiality and even absurdity of many of its situations and attitudes. It is the novel of a man who has dreamed of love more than he has known it. Out of this unfortunate passion there arose misunderstandings with Mme d'Épinay, which quickly, other causes supervening, led Rousseau to break with her, with her lover Baron de Grimm and (saddest of all) with Diderot. It was then that he first gave obvious signs of the persecution mania from which he suffered, intermittently but with increasing severity, for the rest of his life.

In Dec. 1757 Rousseau moved to Montlouis, another house near Montmorency, at which he stayed until June 1762. This shelter he owed to the maréchal-duc de Luxembourg (Charles François de Montmorency) and his wife, who were among the most devoted, tactful and considerate of his powerful friends. At Montlouis he spent his most productive and in some ways his happiest years. In Oct. 1758, there appeared his *Lettre à M. d'Alembert,* commonly known as the *Lettre sur les spectacles,* against the establishment of a theatre at Geneva. This letter, criticizing an article on Geneva written by d'Alembert for the *Encyclopédie*, marks his final breach with the coterie of the philosophers and contains in its preface a quotation from *Ecclesiasticus* deeply offensive to Diderot. At Montmorency he completed *La Nouvelle Héloïse*, which was published early in 1761 and was immediately and enormously popular. *Du contrat social* appeared in April 1762 and the first copies of *Émile*, a long treatise on education in the form of a novel, a month later.

Exile in Switzerland and in England (1762–67).—Both *Du contrat social* and *Émile*, which contains a long profession of faith (the "Profession de foi du vicaire savoyard") equally critical of dogmatic Christianity and of philosophical scepticism, were offensive to authority. An order was issued for Rousseau's arrest, and he was obliged to leave France, taking refuge at Môtiers-Travers in the territory of Neuchâtel, which was then subject to the king of Prussia and governed in Frederick II's name by Marshal Keith, a Jacobite in the Prussian service. Rousseau stayed at Môtiers from July 1762 to Sept. 1765 and found a good friend and protector in Marshal Keith. In 1763 he published the *Lettre à Christophe de Beaumont*, an attack on the archbishop of Paris who had condemned *Émile*. In the same year he renounced his citizenship of Geneva; and in 1764 he wrote the *Lettres écrites de la montagne* in reply to J. B. Tronchin, procurator-general of the Genevan republic, who had written in defense of the executive council of Geneva (the Petit Conseil) for having ordered the burning of *Émile* and of *Du contrat social*. In Sept. 1764 Rousseau was asked by Matteo Buttafuoco, a friend of Pasquale Paoli, to prepare a constitution for Corsica. He never completed the task, though he did make a rough draft (published in 1861 under the title *Projet de constitution pour la Corse*). On the last day of 1764 he received an anonymous pamphlet, *Le Sentiment des citoyens*, attacking him savagely as a hypocrite, a heartless father and an ungrateful friend. It was written by Voltaire, and its effect on Rousseau was terrible. When he recovered from the shock, he decided to write his autobiography, the *Confessions*.

The *Lettres écrites de la montagne* had turned the Protestant pastors, both in Geneva and in Neuchâtel, even more strongly against him, and in Sept. 1765, after some stones had been thrown at his house, he decided to leave Môtiers, though he still enjoyed Frederick II's protection. He fled to the Île Saint Pierre, on Bernese territory, but was not allowed to stay there and eventually, on the advice of Keith and other friends and with the help of David Hume, went to England, where he arrived in Jan. 1766. Well received in London, he moved in March to Wootton in Derbyshire, to a house let to him at a nominal rent by Richard Davenport, a friend of Hume. Even before his departure for Wootton, he had heard that a mocking letter to himself, supposedly from the king of Prussia but actually written by Horace Walpole, was being circulated in Paris; and he had suspected that Hume might have had a hand in it. At Wootton his suspicions grew stronger, causing him to receive equivocally an offer of a pension from George III, which he badly needed but was loath to obtain through the good offices of Hume, whom he now believed to be a false friend, won over by the "philosophers" into a conspiracy to ruin his name. This fear and Hume's excessive zeal to justify himself publicly at Rousseau's expense led to an open quarrel between them, which excited and amused all cultivated Europe. In May 1767 Rousseau, by this time more than a little mad, fled in panic from England to France, where the order for his arrest, issued in 1762, was still unrevoked.

His Last Years in France (1767–78).—Rousseau went first to stay for a few days with the marquis de Mirabeau (Victor Riqueti) and then, taking the name of M. Renou, moved to the Château de Trye, near Gisors, lent to him by the prince de Conti (Louis François de Bourbon). While he was at Trye his *Dictionnaire de musique*, which he had been working on for years, was at last published. He left Trye abruptly in June 1768, again in a panic, going first to Bourgoin near Lyon, where he married Thérèse le Vasseur, and then to Monquin, whence he moved to Paris early in the summer of 1770, to defend himself against the "conspirators." There he resumed his own name, but was left unmolested. To justify himself to the world, he read extracts from his *Confes-*

sions in various Parisian drawing rooms until, at the request of Mme d'Épinay, he was asked by the police to desist. In 1771 Count Wielhorski begged him to advise the Poles how they should reform their institutions, and he wrote the *Considérations sur le gouvernement de la Pologne*, first published in 1782. Still eager to justify himself, he wrote the *Dialogues: Rousseau juge de Jean-Jacques*. He tried in Dec. 1775 to place his work under God's protection on the high altar of Notre Dame, but was prevented from doing so by the iron grille surrounding the choir, which he had never noticed on his many previous visits to the great church. It seemed to him that God had joined his persecutors, and for a time he was in despair. During the last two years of his life, his madness weighed less heavily on him, and he wrote the most serene and the most delicate of his works, the *Rêveries du promeneur solitaire*, which contains descriptions of nature and of man's feelings for nature of a wonderful freshness and beauty. In May 1778 he moved to Ermenonville, to a pavilion on the estate of the marquis René de Girardin, where he died, about six weeks later, on July 2. He was buried on the Île des Peupliers in the lake at Ermenonville, but his remains were moved to Paris to the Panthéon during the Revolution.

The Importance of his Writings.—Rousseau was not a systematic, lucid or rigorous thinker. It has been said that he was not original, that he discovered nothing but merely gave passionate and eloquent expression to other men's ideas. This denial of his originality is probably based on a misunderstanding of the nature of political and social theory. Most of the ideas that the political and social theorist uses have a long ancestry; they do not, of course, always remain the same, for they change imperceptibly as a result of continual discussion and argument. Reputations for originality are more often made by giving names to ideas already coming into circulation than by inventing new ideas. In this way the fruits of many men's thinking are appropriated by the more lucid and articulate among them. The man with a gift for sorting out ideas is apt to be the first to see what new expressions are needed to prevent confusion between old and new ways of thinking, but his having this gift is not enough to make him original. New ideas do not usually get their distinctive names until some time after they have begun to circulate, and so their novelty is often not noticed even by the people who are influenced by them. Rousseau invented no new expressions, not even "the general will," for that phrase was used before him by Diderot. But that does not mean that he lacked originality. On the contrary, he had it in much larger measure than he appeared to have it, for he put a great deal of new wine into old bottles. To the utilitarian and to the positivist he has appeared extravagant and superficial, but the idealist has seen much more that is admirable in him.

Rousseau, when he said that man is naturally good, did not mean that the savage is better than the civilized man; he meant only to deny original sin and to suggest that, if civilized man is now feeble, anxious and unhappy, it is not because of any evil inherent in him but because his social environment is not suited to his nature. Man is born neither good nor bad, but with certain potentialities which he strives to realize; and if he is thwarted, he acquires ambitions and needs which cannot satisfy him, either because they are in themselves insatiable or because they bring him into conflict with other men. Rousseau saw a close connection between the structure of society and the moral and psychological condition of the individual. It seemed to him that society in his own day necessarily set men against one another and also frustrated and bewildered them, preventing them from acquiring the self-knowledge and self-mastery which alone bring happiness and social harmony. He believed that discord and moral confusion are the ineluctable consequences of excessive inequalities of wealth and of the size and complexity of modern society. Man cannot be happy and free, cannot be on good terms with himself and with his neighbours, except in a community simple enough to be intelligible to him and small enough to enable him to take a full and equal part in its government. In a vast community with a complex economy, there must be hierarchy and inequality, and the great majority of passive citizens are inevitably controlled and exploited by the active few. No community, he thought, can be united and strong unless its members share certain fundamental beliefs and loyalties, and men cannot be truly free unless they are emotionally secure, which they will be only in a society of equals, where each man depends, not on the caprice or protection of some person or group stronger or wealthier than himself, but on a system of laws which are the same for all men and are made by the entire community. Though his ideal of the small and simple egalitarian state could not be realized, even in his own day, his criticism of contemporary society went deep. He taught men to think about society and the individual in new ways and to put new questions; and it is here, much more than in the specific solutions which he offered, that his originality and his insight are revealed.

If the reader is not to get a distorted and misleading conception of Rousseau's social and political theory, the *Discours* on inequality, which discusses the probable origins of actual society and government, and *Émile,* which lays down a plan of education to make an ordinary child morally and intellectually self-reliant and therefore well-balanced and free, must be studied as carefully as *Du contrat social,* which only describes an ideal. This outsider, this misfit, this vagabond, who felt that evil was thrust upon him by his position in a society where he could not feel spiritually at home, was the first and the most eloquent of the great radical thinkers, of the men who protested that modern society is rotten even at its roots. That he was sometimes, indeed often, one-sided and extravagant is obvious; what is less obvious, but not less true, is that he was also many-sided and equally passionate on every side. No one insisted more than he did that a people are made what they are by their customs and prejudices, that faith is stronger than reason, that freedom is the fruit of a moral self-discipline as slowly acquired as it is easily lost. He never preached revolution, believing that victims of oppression are so much debased by servitude as to be made unfit for freedom and have therefore to be brought gradually to it, as invalids to food too strong for their stomachs. In the *Projet de constitution pour la Corse* and in the *Considérations sur le gouvernement de la Pologne,* we find a cautious Rousseau, respectful of fact and of tradition. His influence was revolutionary, not because he approved of violence or of precipitate change (for that he never did), but because he felt the evils of society passionately and denounced them so eloquently that he brought the established order into hatred and contempt. He did not attack religious obscurantism or make fun of the church as Voltaire and the "philosophers" did; on the contrary, his attitude to Christianity was equivocal, for he was as much attracted by it as a moral and spiritual force as he was critical of some of its dogmas and practices. He was more dangerous than the "philosophers" precisely because he struck at the social order rather than at the old religions and because so many of the motives and emotions to which he appealed were of Christian inspiration. Among the great writers of his century, he had most in common, in his notion of society (though not in his feelings toward the established social order), with the baron de Montesquieu and with Edmund Burke (*qq.v.*); and in his notion of freedom and what constitutes the moral dignity of man, with Kant (*q.v.*).

Rousseau was much more than a moralist and a social and political theorist; he was also one of the greatest writers of his age, and the most eloquent. By his descriptions of the beauties of nature, by his idealization of romantic love and also of chastity and of fidelity as virtues that go naturally with that love, by his acute and delicate analysis of introspective moods, by his revealing and essentially sincere (though not always accurate) autobiography, he greatly enriched European literature. There was about his writings a warmth, an intimacy and a freshness not common in his day, and to these qualities, above all others, he owed his immense contemporary reputation, which was second to none, not even to Voltaire's.

See also references under "Rousseau, Jean Jacques" in the Index.

BIBLIOGRAPHY.—Collected editions of Rousseau's works appeared in the 18th and 19th centuries: *See* those by V. D. Musset-Pathay, 22 vol. (1819–25), and by P. R. Augis, 27 vol. (1825), and the Hachette editions, 8 vol. (1856–58) and 13 vol. (1865 and later issues). For his letters *see* the *Correspondance générale,* ed. by T. Dufour and P. P. Plan, 21 vol. (1924–53). *See* further L. Ducros, *Jean-Jacques Rousseau,* 3 vol. (1908–18); H. Höffding, *Jean Jacques Rousseau and his Philosophy,* Eng. trans. (1930); P. M. Masson, *La Religion de Jean Jacques Rousseau,* 3 vol. (1916); A. Schinz, *La Pensée de Jean Jacques Rousseau* (1929) and *État présent des travaux sur Jean Jacques Rousseau* (1941); E. H. Wright, *The Meaning of Rousseau* (1929); C. W. Hendel, *Jean-Jacques Rousseau, Moralist,* 2 vol. (1934); E. Cassirer, *The Question of Jean-Jacques Rousseau,* Eng. trans. (1954); and R. Derathe, *Jean Jacques Rousseau et la science politique de son temps* and *Le Rationalisme de Jean Jacques Rousseau* (both 1950).

(J. Pz.).

ROUSSEAU, (PIERRE ÉTIENNE) THÉODORE

(1812–1867), French landscape painter, a leading member of the Barbizon School (*q.v.*), was born in Paris on April 15, 1812. The son of a tailor, he began his artistic education in 1826 under a relative, Pau de St. Martin, and then studied landscape with Charles Rémond and figure painting with Guillon Lethière. Rémond and Lethière were painters in the neoclassical tradition, but the formation of Rousseau's style was based rather on extensive study of such painters as Claude Lorrain, Jan van Goyen, Jacob van Ruisdael, and Karel Dujardin.

After a visit to the Auvergne in 1830, he first exhibited at the Salon in 1831, then again in 1833 ("Shores of Granville") and 1834 ("Edge of the Wood, Compiègne," which earned him a third class medal).

In 1836 Rousseau's big work, "Descent of Cattle," resulting from a visit to the Jura mountains, was rejected by the Salon, as were all his entries during the next seven years. He was, however, vigorously defended by Étienne Thoré and was intimate with such painters as Ary Scheffer, N. V. Diaz de La Peña, and Jules Dupré.

Rousseau first visited the Fontainebleau area in 1833 and, in the following decade, finally settled at Barbizon, where eventually he became intimate with J. F. Millet. Unlike Millet, Rousseau continued to travel widely throughout France in search of subjects. In 1848, with the changes governing the composition of the Salon jury, Rousseau was elected a member, and in the same year received a state commission. Official recognition of his work increased so that he was well represented in the International exhibition of 1855 and became president of the fine art jury for the Exposition of 1867. He died at Barbizon on Dec. 22, 1867.

Rousseau's reaction against the neoclassical landscape puts him midway between the romantics and the realists. He made studies direct from nature ("The Valley of St. Vincent," National gallery, London), but his exhibition pictures were developed over long periods in the studio ("The Marsh in the Landes," Louvre, Paris, begun in 1844 but not exhibited until 1853). A traditional procedure of preparation in grisaille, with colour added in the later stages, was used for this painting. Comparison of "Edge of the Forest at Fontainebleau; Sunset" (Louvre) with the nearly identical composition of "A Glade in the Forest of Fontainebleau" (Wallace collection, London) suggests a willful reorganization of nature in the manner of the Dutch tradition and somewhat at variance with the intense analysis of appearances to be found in such works as "Oak at Fontainebleau."

BIBLIOGRAPHY.—A. Sensier, *Souvenirs sur Th. Rousseau* (1872); E. Chesneau, *Peintres Romantiques: Th. Rousseau* (1880); D. C. Thomson, *The Barbizon School of Painters* (1892); W. Gensel, *Millet und Rousseau* (1902). (R. A. Dy.)

ROUSSEL, ALBERT (CHARLES PAUL MARIE)

(1869–1937), French composer whose music is notable for its lyrical fervour, its austerely intellectual approach, and its harmonic audacities, was born at Tourcoing on April 5, 1869. His parents died when he was a child and he was brought up by his grandfather and later by his uncle and aunt. In 1884 he studied at the Collège Stanislas in Paris, and at the age of 18 joined the French Navy. As a sailor he made several journeys to the Far East, the exotic impressions of which he was able to recall in his later orchestral and dramatic works. At 25 he resigned his commission in the Navy and devoted himself to music, becoming a pupil of Vincent d'Indy at the Schola Cantorum in Paris. After studying there for six years, he joined the teaching staff in 1902.

Among his early compositions inspired by his knowledge of the Far East are the three *Évocations,* for solo voices, chorus, and orchestra, and the opera-ballet *Padmâvatî* (composed 1914–18; produced in Paris, 1923). An earlier ballet, *Le Festin de l'araignée* (1913), long remained in the repertory of the Opéra-Comique. Other notable stage works are the one-act opera *La Naissance de la lyre* (1925) and the ballet *Bacchus et Ariane* (1931). Of his purely orchestral works the best known are the symphonic poem *Pour une fête de printemps,* four symphonies (of which the third, in G minor, is particularly striking), the Suite in F, and the Sinfonietta for strings, all of which show his bold, personal style. In spite of his early training at the Schola Cantorum, where he came under the influence of César Franck, Roussel soon broke away from the Franckist as well as from the Impressionist tradition. His distinguished chamber music includes two violin and piano sonatas, a string quartet, a piano trio, and a trio for violin, viola, and cello. His songs show a completely unsentimental approach to the problem of setting words to music. They include settings of translations from the Chinese, among them *La Réponse d'une épouse sage;* and an English poem, *A Flower Given to My Daughter,* by James Joyce. Among his large-scale choral works the finest, apart from the *Évocations,* is his setting of the English text of Psalm 80, for chorus and orchestra (1928). Unlike his contemporaries, Debussy, Fauré, and Ravel, he wrote little for piano alone. The Suite, op. 14, and the Sonatina, op. 16, for piano are both fine works for the instrument, and so is the rarely performed Piano Concerto, which would doubtless be heard more often if the solo part had been conceived as a vehicle for virtuosity rather than as an integral part of the symphonic texture.

BIBLIOGRAPHY.—N. Demuth, *Albert Roussel* (1947); A. Hoérée, *Albert Roussel* (1938); R. H. Myers, "Albert Roussel" in *The Music Masters* (1954); M. Pincherle, *Roussel* (1957). (R. H. My.)

ROUSSILLON, GIRART DE, the hero of a 12th-century *chanson de geste* (q.v.) of the same name, which tells of his conflicts with his suzerain Charles, generally referred to as Charles Martel but also as Charles the Bald. The causes of the conflicts are not always clear. According to the earlier section of the story they are romantic, in that Charles forces his vassal Girart de Roussillon to exchange fiancées, taking Élissent, the more beautiful, for himself and giving her sister, Berte, to Girart; but elsewhere it is indicated that he is jealous of Girart's territorial possessions or believes him to be guilty of murder. The ideal of Christian peace which pervades the poem is emphasized by the miracle which stops the principal battle at Vaubeton, when the standards are burned by fire from heaven. Girart is finally vanquished, loses all his lands, and is forced to flee into exile. After 22 years in the forest of Ardenne, where he works as a charcoal-burner and his wife, Berte, as a seamstress, they return to France. Girart is reconciled to the king, receives his lands again, and founds a number of abbeys, including Vézelay.

The hero has been identified with a certain historical figure, Gerardus, regent of the kingdom of Provence in the reign of Charles the Bald, with whom he came into conflict. This Gerardus founded the abbeys of Vézelay and Pothières. He also appears as Girart de Vienne, in the epic of that name, and as Girart de Fraite in *Aspremont* and other poems (see R. Louis' works cited in the bibliography). There exist also a life in Latin of Girart de Roussillon, probably dating from the 13th century, a 14th-century poem in alexandrines, and two prose versions, one in 1447 by Jean Wauquelin (d. 1453), a translator employed by the dukes of Burgundy, and the other forming part of the anonymous 15th-century *Histoire de Charles Martel.* Girart de Roussillon figures also in the *Chanson de Roland* (see ROLAND, CHANSON DE), as one of the 12 peers slain at Roncevaux, in contradiction with both historical fact and the poems. An earlier version of the legend may well have been connected with the province of Roussillon, but in the extant poems Girart's castle of Roussillon is in Burgundy. Louis identifies it with Vix, near Chatillon-sur-Seine.

Girart de Roussillon is unique among *chansons de geste* for its language, its style, and the blending of feudal, romantic, and realistic features. The main theme is the iniquity of private war, especially when waged without just cause. The language is a curious and probably artificial mixture of Provençal and French; there are indications that the extant version may have been composed in Poitou. The poem is an early example of the use of rhyme in a *chanson de geste,* and the ten-syllable line has the caesura after the sixth syllable, which is rare.

BIBLIOGRAPHY.—*Editions:* Critical edition of the *chanson de geste* by W. M. Hackett, Société des Anciens Textes Français (1953–55); French translation from the original Provençal by P. Meyer (1884); abridged version by H. Berthaut (1929). The 14th-century poem has been edited by E. B. Ham, Yale Romanic Studies (1939).
Studies: R. Louis, *De l'histoire à la légende. Girart, comte de Vienne, et ses fondations monastiques* (1946) and *Girart, comte de Vienne, dans les chansons de geste* (1947). (W. M. Ha.)

ROUSSILLON, a province of France for the last 130 years of the *ancien régime,* corresponding to the major part of the modern Pyrénées-Orientales (q.v.). It comprised the former countship of Roussillon proper (Spanish Rosellón), that is, the coastal zone, with Perpignan; the northern half of that of Besalú, from the upper Tech Valley northward to the Corbières; and the northern half of that of Cerdagne (Spanish Cerdaña), including Conflent on the upper Têt River.

Ruscino (near Perpignan) was settled by a people with markedly Iberian affinities from the 7th century B.C. to the latter part of the 3rd, when it came under the control of the Gallic Volci. Conquered by the Romans in the 2nd century B.C., the country passed to the Visigoths (see GOTHS) in A.D. 462 and remained theirs till the Arabs overran it c. 720. Pepin the Short expelled the Arabs in the 750s and annexed the country to Carolingian France. At the final separation, in 865, between Septimania (part of the future Languedoc) and the Spanish March (Frankish Catalonia), Roussillon was included in the latter. Later in the 9th century feudalism gave rise to hereditary countships in the area, the holders of which all seem to have been related to the contemporary counts of Barcelona (q.v.). The latter dynasty acquired Besalú in 1111, Cerdagne in 1117, and Roussillon proper in 1172, by which time it had also inherited Aragon. France renounced its theoretical suzerainty over the Pyrenean countships by the Treaty of Corbeil (1258), which fixed the Franco-Aragonese frontier on the Pas-de-Salces, passageway between the Corbières and the sea. Meanwhile, from the 10th century onward, there had been a great florescence of monasticism in the area, well exemplified by outstanding Romanesque architecture. The House of Barcelona-Aragon granted privileges to the towns, and commerce benefited from the integration of Roussillon with Catalonia (q.v.).

Roussillon formed the mainland core of the Kingdom of Majorca, which James I of Aragon and Majorca left in 1276 to his younger son James II (sometimes reckoned as James I; d. 1311). James II's grandson James III (II; d. 1349), who succeeded his uncle Sancho in 1324, was dispossessed by Peter IV of Aragon in 1344.

In 1461 the Catalans revolted against John II of Aragon. Louis XI of France, under the pretext of helping John (Treaty of Bayonne, 1462), sent two expeditions to overrun Roussillon and Cerdagne, which were then held for France till 1472. John then recovered Perpignan; but in 1475, while John was preoccupied with Castilian affairs, Louis XI annexed the country again. Charles VIII of France, seeking goodwill for his Neapolitan schemes, retroceded Roussillon and Cerdagne to Ferdinand II of Aragon (Treaty of Barcelona, 1493). Spanish fortification of the country in the 16th century was offset by French immigration. During the Thirty Years' War (q.v.), the Catalan revolt of 1640 led to the rapid occupation of the lands north of the Pyrenees by the French, to whom Perpignan fell in 1642. Spain finally renounced the province by the Treaty of the Pyrenees (1659).

ROUVIER, MAURICE (1842–1911), French statesman whose career well illustrates the political history of his time, was born at Aix-en-Provence on April 17, 1842. Having supported Léon Gambetta (q.v.) in his candidature at Marseilles in 1869 and founded a republican journal, *L'Égalité,* in 1870, he was elected to the National Assembly as deputy for Marseilles in July 1871. A financial expert, he repeatedly served on the budget commission and was minister for commerce and the colonies under Gambetta

(1881–82) and for commerce under Jules Ferry (1884–85).

At the end of May 1887, Rouvier took office as premier and minister of finance, with the support of the moderate republican group, but without that of the Radicals. His government withstood the agitation for Gen. Georges Boulanger (q.v.); but when Daniel Wilson, son-in-law of the president of the Republic, Jules Grévy (q.v.), was exposed for trafficking in honours, Rouvier resigned (Nov. 19, 1887) to force the resignation of Grévy.

Minister of finance again in four successive ministries (1889–92), Rouvier became implicated in the Panama Scandal (q.v.) and resigned his portfolio on Dec. 12, 1892. Claiming that the money that he had received from the Panama Company had been for the defense of the Republic, he discredited himself by arguing that he had been engaged in the country's most important affairs without his fortune having increased "abnormally." The commission of inquiry found no case against him.

Elected senator for Alpes-Maritimes in spring 1902, Rouvier became minister of finance under the Radical Émile Combes in June. He then prepared a project for introducing income tax. Premier and minister of finance again from Jan. 24, 1905, he took the ministry of foreign affairs also in June, after his personal approach to the Franco-German crisis over Morocco had provoked the resignation of Théophile Delcassé (q.v.). He fell from power on March 7, 1906, over questions arising from the government's decisive act of 1905 for the separation of church and state. Rouvier died at Neuilly on June 7, 1911.

ROUX, PIERRE PAUL ÉMILE (1853–1933), French bacteriologist noted for his work on diphtheria (q.v.), was born at Confolens, Charente, on Dec. 17, 1853. He studied medicine at the University of Paris and afterward held a faculty appointment there (1874–78). He then worked for ten years in Louis Pasteur's laboratory. Subsequently he held a post in the Pasteur Institute, and was its director from 1904 to 1918.

As Pasteur's pupil and collaborator, Roux studied hydrophobia, anthrax, and other infectious diseases. He and Alexandre Yersin were the first to demonstrate (1888) the toxic nature of filtrates from cultures of diphtheria bacilli. This discovery, together with the serological discoveries of Emil von Behring (q.v.), led directly to the development of diphtheria immunization and serum therapy—for which Roux campaigned ardently in the 1890s. He died in Paris on Nov. 3, 1933.

See *Lancet*, vol. 225, p. 1124 (1933).

ROUYN, a mining city on Lake Osisko in western Quebec, Can., is 394 mi. (634 km.) NW of Montreal. Mining (copper and gold) and smelting are the chief sources of employment. Rouyn is the urban and commercial centre for the whole mining area of western Quebec, which lies on a continuation of the mineral-bearing rocks of the Porcupine gold district and the Cobalt silver district of Ontario. The earliest homes in Rouyn date from 1922 when gold and copper ores in the area were first exploited. It was incorporated as a village in 1926, a town in 1927, and a city in 1948.

Population (1961) 18,716; with its twin city of Noranda (immediately adjoining but under separate administration) the 1961 population was 30,193. Of the total, 79% are French-Canadian; the remaining 21% are chiefly of European origin, comprising some 30 different nationalities. Rouyn is connected with Montreal, Quebec, and Toronto by rail and by a highway. (M. C. Ba.)

ROVERETO, a town in the province of Trento, region of Trentino-Alto Adige, northern Italy, lies in the Lagarina Valley on both sides of the Leno River, a left-bank tributary of the Adige, 15 mi. (23 km.) SSW of Trento on the Brenner-Verona railway. Pop. (1961) 25,911 (commune). The old quarter has narrow streets and parts of the 14th-century walls remain. The castle, once a Roman fortress and now a war museum, has a bell commemorating the fallen of World War I, during which Rovereto was heavily damaged. The newer section has broad avenues (e.g., the Corso Rosmini, named after Antonio Rosmini-Serbati [q.v.], a native of Rovereto) and numerous 18th-century houses. Rovereto is a tourist and industrial centre and produces tobacco, silk, cotton, paper, gasoline engines, and wood and metal manufactures. First mentioned in 1154, it was ruled by the Castelbarco family

from about 1300, then by Venice (1416–1509) and Austria (1509–1918). (F. Zu.)

ROVIGO, a town in the region of Veneto, northern Italy, capital of Rovigo Province and the seat of a bishopric, lies between the Adige and the Po, 27 mi. (43 km.) SSW of Padua and 45 mi. (72 km.) SW of Venice by rail. Pop. (1961) 46,502. Its oldest historical monument is the remains of a 10th-century castle. The 16th-century octagonal church of the Beata Vergine del Soccorso, called the Rotonda, by F. Zamberlano, a pupil of Palladio, has a campanile by B. Longhena and paintings of the Venetian School. The Accademia dei Concordi (founded by G. Campo [1557–1629]) contains paintings by Venetian masters, Holbein, and Dürer. The Palazzo Roncale (1555) is by M. Sanmicheli. Rovigo is on the Adigetto Canal and is a junction of the Bologna–Padua railway with eastward and westward branches. It is an important agricultural centre. As Rodigo (Neo-Latin, Rhodigium) it is mentioned in a document of 838. Ruled by the Estensi from the 12th century, it passed to Venice in 1482 and to Austria in 1797. It was annexed to Italy in 1866.

ROVIGO PROVINCE, called the Polesine (Neo-Latin, Policinium—"land emerged from the waters"), is a fertile region stretching inland from the mouths of the Adige and Po and bordered north and south by their lower reaches. Area 696 sq.mi. (1,803 sq.km.). Pop. (1961) 270,983. Grains and sugar beet are the leading crops. (M. T. A. N.)

ROVNO, a town and *oblast* centre of the Ukrainian Soviet Socialist Republic, U.S.S.R., lies on the northeastern edge of the Volyno-Podolsk upland, 110 mi. (177 km.) NE of Lvov. Pop. (1959) 56,163. At the junction of railways to Brest, Baranovichi, Berdichev, and Lvov, it has food-processing, building-materials, and light-engineering industries. There is a pedagogic institute. Rovno town was taken by the U.S.S.R. from Poland in 1939 and by Germany in 1941, and returned to the U.S.S.R. in 1945.

ROVNO OBLAST covers an area of 7,838 sq.mi. (20,300 sq.km.). Pop. (1959) 926,225. Of this figure 17% (157,702) were urban, living in 9 towns and 17 urban districts. The *oblast* falls into two distinct regions. The larger, northern part, centred on Sarny, belongs to Polesye and forms an extensive lowland of swamp and forest. It is thinly inhabited and the only significant branch of the economy is timber working. The southern part lies on the Volyno-Podolsk upland, and is hilly and much dissected by river valleys and erosion gullies. There agriculture, especially grain and sugar-beet growing, is important. (R. A. F.)

ROWE, NICHOLAS (1674–1718), the most considerable 18th-century English tragic dramatist, the first person to produce a critical edition of Shakespeare's plays, and a poet laureate, was born at Little Barford, Bedfordshire, on June 20, 1674, the son of John Rowe (d. 1692), a successful lawyer, who left him £300 a year. He was educated at Highgate Free School and at Westminster School, where he was elected a king's scholar in 1688. Admitted to the Middle Temple in 1691, he was called to the bar in 1696. An ardent Whig, he held several minor government posts, and in 1715 succeeded Nahum Tate as poet laureate. He died in London on Dec. 6, 1718.

Rowe's first two plays, *The Ambitious Stepmother* (1700) and *Tamerlane* (? 1701), were both popular. The latter—in which the monstrous villain Bajazet represents Louis XIV and the priggish hero represents William III—was habitually revived until 1750 on the anniversaries of William's birth and landing. Both plays, like the later *Royal Convert* (1707), retain much of the blustering pomp of Drydenesque heroic drama, though the self-sacrifice of Cleone in the one and the loves of Moneses and Arpasia in the other foreshadow that sentimental blank-verse drama which Rowe, following Thomas Otway (q.v.), developed in *The Fair Penitent* (1703), adapted from Massinger and Field's *Fatal Dowry*. This, the first of Rowe's "she tragedies," was the forerunner of many 18th-century bourgeois domestic dramas; and one of its characters, Lothario (apparently the prototype of Samuel Richardson's Lovelace, as Calista, its heroine, was of his Clarissa), gave a new word to the language. *Jane Shore* (1714), "written in imitation of Shakespeare's style," and *Lady Jane Gray* (1715) are in the same lachrymose strain. His only comedy, *The Biter* (1704), described by Congreve as "a foolish farce," was a failure, though the author himself, Dr. Johnson relates (*Lives of the Poets,* vol. ii), laughed "with great vehemence" at every joke.

Rowe's poetic output included occasional odes and some translations, the most important being that of Lucan's *Pharsalia* into heroic couplets (published posthumously, 1718), which was greatly admired throughout the century.

The Work of Mr. William Shakespear, Revis'd and Corrected (six volumes, 1709; nine volumes, including poems, 1714) was the first "edited" edition of Shakespeare. Rowe claimed to have compared "the several Editions," but his text mainly follows the Fourth Folio (1685) and is poor by modern standards. He was, however, the first to attempt to establish the text by reference to the original editions, and in *Hamlet, Romeo and Juliet, Henry V,* and *King Lear* he restored some passages from early texts. By abandoning the clumsy folio format (a 9 × 12 in. page size), he brought the plays within reach of the average reader; and he also gave lists of *dramatis personae,* attempted act and scene divisions, and supplied a *Life,* mainly from material collected in Warwickshire by Thomas Betterton (*q.v.*). Though mostly dubious tradition, this remained the basis of accounts of Shakespeare until the end of the century. *See also* SHAKESPEARE, WILLIAM.

BIBLIOGRAPHY.—Rowe's *Works* were last printed in 2 vol. in 1792. For a critical account and bibliography, see *Three Plays by Nicholas Rowe,* ed. by J. R. Sutherland (1929).   (Jo. C.)

ROWELL, NEWTON WESLEY (1867–1941), Canadian jurist and politician, chief justice of Ontario, 1936–38, and chairman of the Royal Commission on Dominion-Provincial Relations, 1937–38, was born Nov. 1, 1867, in Middlesex County, Ont. Called to the bar in 1891, he practised law in Toronto (king's counsel, 1902). Active in the Methodist Church, from 1904 he had a prominent part in discussions leading to the formation of the United Church of Canada in 1925. In 1911 he accepted the invitation of the Liberal opposition in the Ontario Legislature to become party leader and was elected from North Oxford in that year.

Rowell entered federal politics as a member of R. L. Borden's Unionist government, formed in October 1917 and pledged to the enforcement of military conscription. He was president of the council and vice-chairman of the war committee of the cabinet, and was elected in the constituency of Durham in the 1917 election. Rowell represented Canada in the Imperial War Cabinet and Imperial War Conference, 1918; at the Washington conference of the International Labour Organization, 1919; and at the first Assembly of the League of Nations at Geneva, 1920. He also organized and administered Canada's first federal department of health, 1919–20. A strong nationalist, he consistently advocated the extension of Canadian autonomy within the British Commonwealth.

Favouring more liberal social policies than most of his colleagues, he retired from the cabinet in 1920 and from Parliament in 1921 to return to his legal practice; he thereafter argued a number of Canadian cases before the Judicial Committee of the Privy Council, London. He was president of the Toronto General Trust Corporation, 1925–35, active in the League of Nations Society in Canada, and president of the Canadian Bar Association, 1932–34. He was appointed chief justice of Ontario in 1936 and chairman of the Royal Commission on Dominion-Provincial Relations in 1937 but illness forced his resignation from both positions in 1938. His name continued to be associated with the commission, and with the significant report it issued in 1940, popularly known as the Rowell-Sirois Report. He wrote *The British Empire and World Peace* (1922), *Canada: a Nation* (1923), and a chapter on the evolution of Canadian autonomy for *The Cambridge History of the British Empire* (1930), vol. vi. He died at Toronto on Nov. 22, 1941.   (M. E. P.)

ROWING, the propulsion of a boat by means of oars in a succession of strokes. An oar is a shaft of wood with a rounded handle at one end and a blade at the other. The blade, a thin broadened surface, is either flat or slightly curved to offer increased resistance to the water (spoon oar). The loom or middle portion rests in a notch or rowlock or between tholepins on the gunwale or outrigger of the boat.

Racing oars are provided with leather buttons to prevent the oar from slipping outward. An oar may be regarded as a lever of the first order, the weight to be moved being the water and the fulcrum being the lock or tholepin; or as a lever of the second order, the weight to be moved being the boat, and the fulcrum the water pressing against the blade. Theoretically an oar functions at one and the same time in both capacities, but practically the lock or pin is the fulcrum, and the point at which the oar is buttoned determines the leverage and is a fundamental factor in the mechanics of rowing.

Rowing a boat and paddling a canoe (*q.v.*) have in common the propulsion of a floating craft through the water by muscular power applied to a lever, oar or paddle, in a succession of strokes. But in rowing, the oarsman, seated on a thwart, faces toward the stern and pulls the oar handle toward his body with the tholepin or oarlock as a fixed fulcrum, while in paddling a canoe the canoeist, generally in a kneeling position, faces toward the bow and throws forward the weight of his body, using one arm as a moving fulcrum.

In nautical use sculling is the propulsion of a boat by a single long oar worked to and fro from a notch in the stern transom, the blade being turned under water so as to give both projection and direction and acting like the tail of a fish. "Sweeps" and "sculls" are traditional terms for long and short oars.

As rowing developed into a form of competitive sport new terms were introduced and traditional terms acquired special meanings. Technically a stroke includes all the motions of an oarsman from the time he dips his oar for the catch to the time when it is again in the same position. The recovery is the part of the stroke during which the blade is in the air. Feathering is turning the blade by a wrist motion as it is lifted from the water and carrying it toward the bow in a nearly horizontal position until it is squared or bevelled (*i.e.,* the upper edge inclined slightly to the stern) for the next stroke. If the oarsman fails to clear the water with his blade on the recovery, because he has feathered too soon or too much or too little or because the boat has lurched down on his side, he "catches a crab."

Sculling as distinguished from its nautical sense is propelling a light racing craft with an oar in each hand. Oars so used are called sculls. "Singles" and "doubles" are popular entries in all regattas, and champion scullers have won wide acclaim. Rowing in the specialized sense is the art of propelling a racing craft by two or more oarsmen, each of whom handles a single oar, called a sweep. Paddling in boat racing parlance is rowing at reduced speed and at a leisurely pace. Sweep oarsmen row in pairs, fours, sixes (obsolete) and eights. Eights are numbered from the bow, and number eight is known as stroke.

The coxswain (cock, a small boat; swain as in boatswain) not only steers but gives the necessary commands and in a race calls for spurts and in a stern chase informs the captain or the stroke of the position of the competing boats.

History.—Rowing is now confined almost entirely to small boats and racing shells, but in ancient times it was the chief means of propelling vessels of war. As the size of vessels increased, sails gradually displaced oars, in both warships and merchant ships, but large galleys (*q.v.*) continued to be rowed in the Mediterranean until the 18th century. The oarsmen, generally captives of war or criminals, were chained to the benches, whence the term "galley slaves." Ancient galleys were rated according to the number of rowing banks or tiers of oars. The first recorded Roman fleet consisted of triremes (three-bank galleys). The earliest recorded amateur oarsmen were the islanders who entertained Ulysses on his return to Ithaca. Boat races probably formed part of Panathenaic and Isthmian festivals (*see* BOAT).

Virgil, in his account of the funeral games instituted by Aeneas for his father Anchises, gives a vivid description of a boat race:

The waiting crews are crowned with poplar wreaths;
Their naked shoulders glisten, moist with oil.
Ranged in a row, their arms stretched to the oars,
All tense the starting signal they await.
Together at the trumpet's thrilling blast
Their bent arms churn the water into foam;

The sea gapes open by the oars up-torn;
With shouts and cheers of eager partisans
The woodlands ring, the sheltered beach rolls up
The sound, the hills re-echo with the din.

The earliest invasions of England were effected with the help of oars. The Britons, paddling wicker coracles, were no match for the legions that Caesar landed on their beachheads from his Roman triremes. Later the Anglo-Saxons, rowing and sailing across the North sea, and after them the Danes, entered the estuaries of the east coast. Sails are mentioned oftener than oars in Old English literature, and rowing had not yet become a sport that could be described in Shakespeare's words:

There be some sports are painful, and their labour
Delight in them sets off.

William of Malmesbury (c. 1090–c. 1143) records that Edgar the Peaceful was rowed in state on the river Dee by tributary kings, himself acting as coxswain.

Boat Racing in England.—The Thames may fairly be called the cradle of rowing as a pastime and competitive sport in modern times. The nobility and gentry who had mansions on the banks of the river relied almost entirely on their elaborately fitted barges as a means of conveyance. As early as 1454 Sir John Norman, mayor of London, "built a noble barge, and was rowed by watermen with silver oars." The lord mayor's procession by water to Westminster was an annual event until 1856. From the 15th century on, a considerable body of men lived by "the trade of rowing" as the statutes define the occupation of the watermen. In Queen Anne's time the river was still the highway of London, and there were about 10,000 licensed watermen on the tidal reaches of the Thames above London bridge. There were undoubtedly competitions between these in the 16th and 17th centuries, but the first race of which there is record is that for the "Doggett's Coat and Badge." Thomas Doggett, an Irish comedian, in 1716 offered an "Orange coloured Livery with a Badge representing Liberty, to be rowed for by six watermen from London Bridge to Chelsea, annually on the same day, August 1, forever." Except during World Wars I and II, the race was rowed regularly under the administration of the Fishmongers' company.

The first English regatta (Italian *regata*, originally a gondola race in Venice) took place on the Thames in 1775. Though there are numerous instances of professional matches at the beginning of the 19th century, the increased participation in boat racing by amateur oarsmen, after the Napoleonic wars, overshadowed professional rowing, which never had the vogue in England which it attained in the United States (*see* below). Eton had a ten-oared boat, the "Monarch," and three eight-oars as early as 1811, but there is no record of any formal racing between amateur crews until 1817, the date of the founding of the Leander club, which rapidly gained the prestige it maintained from that time, as the oldest and most distinguished rowing club, whose eights, composed mainly of Oxford and Cambridge varsity oarsmen, upheld the highest standards of English rowing and sportsmanship.

The first race between Oxford and Cambridge was rowed in 1829 over a 2-mi. course at Henley-on-Thames, but it was not renewed until 1836. In 1845 the race was rowed over a 4¼-mi. course from Putney to Mortlake, and in 1856 became an annual event except during World Wars I and II, attracting huge crowds along the banks of the river.

The Henley Royal Regatta.—The reaches of the Thames at Henley are not only the most beautiful along the river but, because of a straight stretch of more than a mile immediately below the town, offer an ideal course for racing shells.

The Henley Royal regatta, established in 1839, has brought together not only the pick of English crews but, in the open events, has attracted competitors from Europe, America and Australia. Like other comparable events, it was interrupted by World Wars I and II. The course is 1 mi. 550 yd. with its finish near the town bridge in sheltered water, with sunny meadows and the shaded lawns of country houses on each side of the river. The races are rowed in the first week of July and furnish three days of continuous excitement to the spectators that throng the towpath and the enclosures at the finish. Because of the narrowness of the river and the many entries, the races are now rowed in heats of two or more entries. The course is protected by booms on each side, behind which spectators in punts and on houseboats moored along the banks obtain an unobstructed and close view of the competing oarsmen. There have for many years been eight events, four of which are open to all amateurs; viz., the Grand Challenge cup for eight oars (the oldest, established in 1839), the Stewards' cup for fours, the Silver Goblets for pair-oars and the Diamond Challenge Sculls for single scullers. In 1939 a ninth event, the Double Sculls, was added. The Grand Challenge cup and the Diamond Challenge Sculls have long been the most coveted trophies in the rowing world.

Australia and Canada.—Rowing as a sport began in Tasmania about 1830, and by 1880 eight-oared races between crews representing the various states had become annual fixtures, held alternately in the six capital cities. Interuniversity rowing originated in 1870. In 1893 Old Blues from Oxford and Cambridge presented the magnificent Oxford and Cambridge cup, which thereafter was contested for by the six state universities and like the interstate contest is rowed in each capital city by rotation.

In Canada, the 1870s were the heyday of the professional scullers. Purses ran from $50 upward to $1,000 and in international matches from £500 to £2,000. The outstanding world champion was Edward Hanlan of Toronto, who defeated the best scullers of Canada, the U.S., England and Australia. As the distinction between professional and amateur rowing became more sharply drawn, following the lead of England, Canada developed numerous amateur rowing clubs, among them the famous Argonauts of Toronto. The Canadian national championships are contested at the Royal Canadian Henley regatta held annually on the old Welland canal at St. Catherines, Ont.

United States.—In the United States, as in England, rowing as

FINISH OF THE 4¼-MI. OXFORD-CAMBRIDGE BOAT RACE AT MORTLAKE, 1960. THE OXFORD CREW (AT LEFT) WON BY 1¼ LENGTHS

a competitive sport originated in contests between "occupational" oarsmen. In 1811 and 1823 the ferrymen of Whitehall in New York city defeated their Long Island and Staten Island rivals on the Hudson. In 1824 they outrowed a crew of Thames watermen from the visiting British frigate "Hussar," in a four-mile race finishing at the Battery. This international race aroused tremendous local interest and the betting far exceeded the original stake of $1,000 offered by the captain of the "Hussar." Light keelless racing shells soon displaced the service boats of the early contests. The cleavage between amateur and professional, following the organization of the National Association of Amateur Oarsmen (N.A.A.O.) in 1872, inaugurated the golden age of professional sculling. Among the scullers who won national and international fame were James Hamill, J. A. Ten Eyck, Wallace Ross, George Hosmer, Fred A. Plaisted, Walter Brown and Joshua Ward. The four Ward brothers had won an international race at Saratoga, N.Y., in 1871. Charles Courtney, who had begun as an amateur, turned professional and became the leading rival of the great Canadian Hanlan for championship honours and rewards. He was defeated by Hanlan in an exciting race at Lachine, Que., in 1878. A return match for a purse of $6,000 at Lake Chautauqua was never rowed because Courtney's shell was found hacked in two on the morning of the race. This fiasco and the suspicion that betting and shady "deals" influenced the results of races were responsible for the decline of professional sculling in the United States. Courtney's later reputation was based on his striking success as coach of the Cornell crews, as was Ten Eyck's as coach of the Syracuse university crews for 35 years.

Amateur Clubs.—The first organization of amateur clubs was the Castle Garden Boat Club association of New York (1834); pleasure boating rather than racing was the main interest of these early clubs, their membership being based on social rather than aquatic prestige. The Detroit Boat club, 1839, the oldest survivor of these early clubs, became one of the most important members of the N.A.A.O. and has entered crews in many regattas. In 1858 the boat clubs along the Schuylkill river, Philadelphia, Pa., were organized as the Schuylkill Navy. The boathouses of the Navy stretch for nearly a quarter-mile, known as boathouse row, along the banks of the river in Fairmount park, and until the silting up of the river, the Schuylkill course was one of the most popular and picturesque in the U.S., during the years when Philadelphia was a centre of the two great English sports of cricket and rowing. One of the most famous of these Philadelphia clubs is the Vesper Boat club, whose eight-oared crew furnished a sensation in defeating the world-champion Ratzeburg club crew of Germany to win the gold medal in the Tokyo Olympic games in 1964. The first regatta to which only amateur oarsmen were admitted followed the organization of the N.A.A.O. in 1872 and was rowed on the Schuylkill under the auspices of the Schuylkill Navy. The N.A.A.O. thereafter was the chief promoter of rowing among the amateur clubs, holding annual regattas for the championship of the United States in single, double and quadruple sculls, and pairs, fours and eights.

Intercollegiate Rowing.—The first formal intercollegiate boat race was rowed between Harvard and Yale in 1852 on Lake Winnepesaukee. With a few exceptions the race was rowed at four miles after 1876, at New London. The Yale-Harvard boat race is the oldest intercollegiate contest in the United States and antedates football by 17 years.

In the 1870s rowing became popular at a number of eastern colleges. In 1875 there was a regatta on Saratoga lake in which 13 colleges participated. When Yale and Harvard in 1878 went to New London for their dual race, Lake George became the scene of college races in fours in which Cornell or Pennsylvania generally won, Wesleyan, Bowdoin, Columbia and Princeton affording good competition. In 1887 eights took the place of fours, and, until the establishment of the Poughkeepsie regatta in 1895, these races were rowed at New London, Cayuga lake, Lake Minnetonka and one on the Delaware at Torresdale (1894). From the inauguration of the four-mile race at New London, Harvard and Yale regarded this as the culmination of their rowing season. Though the record of the Cornell crews in the 1890s, the defeats of Yale and Harvard

EWING GALLOWAY

AN EIGHT-OARED SHELL AND CREW. THE COXSWAIN SITS IN THE STERN FACING THE OARSMEN

by Cornell and Princeton crews in the decade 1911–21, and the appearance of California and Washington and the U.S. Naval academy at Poughkeepsie challenged the leadership in college rowing that formerly could fairly be claimed by Harvard and Yale, the picturesqueness of the New London course, the tradition of the race and the prestige of Yale and Harvard among U.S. universities continued to surround the Harvard-Yale boat race with an interest analogous to that surrounding the Oxford-Cambridge race in England, the one rowed on the English Thames at London and the other on the United States Thames at New London. In 1895 Cornell, Columbia, Syracuse and Pennsylvania joined in a rowing association with annual regattas open to invited crews at Poughkeepsie. The Poughkeepsie regatta continued not only to attract the foremost eastern college crews but also brought to the Hudson winning eights from the universities of California, Washington and Wisconsin and the United States Naval academy. Because of unsatisfactory water conditions, the Intercollegiate Rowing association (I.R.A.) regatta was moved to Marietta, O., for 1950 and 1951. Bad water conditions there caused its removal to Onondaga lake, Syracuse, N.Y., where a satisfactory regatta, the 50th anniversary of the I.R.A., was held in 1952 and each year thereafter.

In contrast to the dual race at New London, Poughkeepsie has had as many as 12 starters in the interuniversity race and Syracuse has had 16. From 1895 to 1915 Cornell led in number of victories. Thereafter the U.S. Naval academy, Washington, California and Cornell were the most frequent winners. Navy set a U.S. record in winning 31 successive races, including the Olympic championship in 1952 and three intercollegiate championships, from 1952 through 1955.

Rowing was established on the Pacific coast in 1899. The first race, in fours, was between Washington and California. In 1907 eights displaced fours, and the Washington-California race, alternating between Lake Washington and the estuary at Oakland, Calif., became the rowing feature in the far west, and these crews began winning laurels at Poughkeepsie and in Olympic competitions. The favourable climatic conditions of the far west, permitting rowing in the open the year round, the abundance of material in the great state universities and the program of rowing developed in the western universities all contributed to the enviable record of the western crews.

Princeton had abandoned rowing in 1884, but, as a result of Andrew Carnegie's gift of a lake formed by the damming of two streams and affording $3\frac{1}{2}$ mi. of rowing water, resumed the sport in 1910. At this time the only races that college crews trained for were the long-distance contests at New London and Poughkeepsie. Princeton's revival of rowing was responsible for the inauguration of a series of short-distance races, $1\frac{7}{8}$ to 2 mi., rowed on college waters and during term time, generally participated in by three crews and called triangular races. In 1912 the Childs cup race, next to the Yale and Harvard race the oldest intercollegiate fixture, was revived. This trophy had been given in 1879 by George W. Childs, the publisher of the *Philadelphia Ledger*, to be competed for by Columbia, Princeton and Pennsylvania, but the race had lapsed after 1884. In 1911 Princeton inaugurated intercollegiate rowing on Lake Carnegie with a triangular race between Yale, Cornell and Princeton, in which Princeton defeated Yale and came in a close second to a fast Cornell crew that later won at Poughkeepsie. The Carnegie cup offered for this race in 1921 came into annual competition. Later races between Yale, Columbia and Pennsylvania for the Blackwell cup, between the U.S. Naval academy, Pennsylvania and Harvard for the Adams cup, between Harvard, Princeton and Massachusetts Institute of Technology for the Compton cup, between Navy, Cornell and Syracuse for the Goes trophy, and between Pennsylvania and Cornell for the Madeira cup became annual fixtures. All these races are alternately rowed on college waters, on Cayuga lake, Carnegie lake, the Charles river, the Housatonic river, the Harlem river, the Schuylkill river and the Severn river at Annapolis before the close of the spring term. Rutgers, Boston university, Wisconsin, Dartmouth, Brown, Marietta, Stanford, Northeastern, U.C.L.A. and Georgetown are other participating colleges.

An annual regatta conducted by a group of smaller colleges under the name of the Dad Vail Rowing association, in honour of a former coach of Wisconsin, is participated in by Amherst college, Boston university, Brown university, Dartmouth college, Florida Southern college, La Salle college, Marietta college, Rollins college, Rutgers university, the University of Tampa, Georgetown university, Drexel Institute of Technology, Purdue university, St. Joseph's college of Philadelphia, Fordham university, George Washington university, Howard university, Trinity college, Notre Dame, University of Massachusetts, Villanova university, Wesleyan university, Temple university, College of the Holy Cross, Wayne State, Marist college, Stony Brook, American university, Clark, East Carolina college, St. John's (Brooklyn), C. W. Post college and Canisius college.

The increased interest in rowing at the colleges led to the organization of lightweight crews averaging 150 lb. per man. Some of these crews made up in skill and speed for lack of weight, and in competing at the Royal Henley for the Thames Challenge cup defeated some of the best English college crews.

Rowing became a popular sport among both public and private schools, particularly at Kent school, Kent, Conn. U.S. schoolboy crews have won the Thames cup at Henley. There are various regattas especially for school crews and attracting numerous entries.

In 1902 the American Rowing association was formed to increase intercollegiate competition by means of short-distance races in the early season, concluding with an annual regatta at the Henley distance of 1 mi. 550 yd. Thus this regatta became popularly known as the American Henley. This association, with the introduction of short-distance races, did a great deal to stimulate college rowing. It likewise had events at its annual regatta open for club crews who thereby matched their skill against college crews.

U.S. College Crews in Europe.—In 1869 Harvard challenged Oxford and Cambridge to a four-oared race on the Thames from Putney to Mortlake; Oxford accepted and won.

In the only other interuniversity race between English and Americans, Cambridge in 1906 defeated Harvard by about two lengths. There have been many U.S. entries at Henley. In 1878 a four from Columbia university won the Visitors' cup. In 1881 a Cornell four was defeated for the Stewards' cup, and in 1895 a Cornell eight lost to Trinity hall, Cambridge. In 1896 Leander beat a Yale crew coached by Bob Cook. In 1901 a University of Pennsylvania eight lost by a few seconds to Leander in the finals for the Grand Challenge cup. In 1914 the survivors in the finals for the Grand Challenge cup were Harvard and the Union Boat club of Boston, composed of former Harvard oarsmen; Harvard won, bringing the cup to the United States for the first time. Princeton in 1934 was defeated by Leander in the finals of the Grand Challenge; both crews broke the Henley record established in 1891.

In 1939 and 1950 Harvard again brought the Grand Challenge cup to the U.S., and in 1955 it was won by the University of Pennsylvania's champion sprint eight. In 1957 Cornell defeated Yale in an All-American final, breaking the course record. Harvard won the cup in 1959. Princeton in 1930 and 1934 and Yale and Harvard in 1938 entered 150-lb. crews for the Thames cup, which was won by Kent school in 1933, 1938, 1947 and 1950, by Tabor academy in 1936, 1937 and 1939 (both schoolboy crews), and by the University of Pennsylvania in 1951 and 1952, by M.I.T. in 1954 and 1955, by Princeton in 1956 and 1957, by Harvard in 1958, 1959, 1960, and 1966, by Eliot House of Harvard in 1964 and by Cornell in 1967.

Strokes, Styles and Coaches.—Sweep rowing was early differentiated from sculling in England. The so-called "English stroke" was developed by Oxford and Cambridge oarsmen. As exemplified by the best Leander crews and described by Edmond Warre, provost of Eton (*A Grammar of Rowing*, 1909), and R. C. Lehman of Cambridge (*The Complete Oarsman*, 1924), this stroke was based on early fixed-seat rowing, when body swing was the main source of power and the arms were used chiefly as connecting rods to transfer the weight of the body to the oar. When the sliding seat was introduced in the 1870s, the leg drive was added but the main stress was still on the body swing with shoulders carried well beyond the perpendicular at the finish. This required muscles which only years of practice could develop. The first challenge to this "orthodox" stroke came from a Cambridge student, Stephen Fairbairn, who had entered Jesus college from Australia in 1881 and as a member and coach of his college crews upset tradition by winning races in a style taboo to the "rigidly righteous" of the old school. Fairbairn (*Rowing Notes; Chats on Rowing*, 1934) emphasized leg drive and arm pull and considered smooth bladework more important than what he called the "showy style" of body work. If the proponents of the traditional stroke sometimes laid more emphasis on form than on speed, Fairbairn's stroke sacrificed form for speed.

The success of his and foreign crews was responsible for the adoption of several innovations, such as the lengthened slide, the use of the swivel oarlock in place of tholepins and the seating of crews amidships in straight alignment instead of in the staggered order formerly used to increase leverage.

The British have devoted much time to the technical and theoretic aspects of rowing. A good exposition of the British system is G. C. Bourne's *A Text-Book of Oarsmanship*. R. C. Lehman, a leading exponent of the British system, was in 1896 invited to coach the Harvard crews. To Yale in 1914 went Guy Nickalls as head coach, and to Pennsylvania his brother Vivian. Though all these men had brilliant records as oarsmen and coaches in England and stimulated interest in rowing at the universities they visited, the English system did not permanently strike root in the U.S. Many English university dons assisted in coaching their college crews. Sir Leslie Stephen was an enthusiastic coach in his Oxford days. At Henley may frequently be seen on the towpath coaches who are equally at home among books and boats and who combine reading as a vocation with rowing as an avocation.

In the United States as in England the colleges first popularized rowing as a competitive amateur sport. The first college coaches were former professional scullers. Charles Courtney at Cornell, Ellis Ward at Pennsylvania, James Ten Eyck at Syracuse, Richard Glendon at Annapolis and William Haines at Harvard and M.I.T. were types of "professionals" who instilled into their charges principles of sportsmanship besides rowing technique and strict conformity to training rules.

The stroke they taught was essentially a sculling stroke adapted to sweep rowing. The first attempt to introduce a stroke differentiated from sculling and based on the scientific principles of the English stroke was made by Robert Cook of Yale, who, as an undergraduate in 1873, when captain of his crew, went to England and studied the system prevailing at Oxford and Cambridge. The Yale crews of the next 20 years coached by him were noted both for speed and form. The "Bob Cook" stroke was characterized by a hard catch with squared shoulders, straight back, straight arms, quick hand shoot and slow slide on the recovery, length in the water and lower beat than the prevailing sculling strokes. After the Cornell experience at Henley in 1895, Courtney, always ready to experiment and improve both rigging and rowing, modified the short sculling stroke his crew had previously rowed, and in the Poughkeepsie regatta of 1896, in which both Yale and Harvard participated, it was difficult to distinguish Cornell from Yale.

In later years Courtney modified the hard catch, shortened the swing at the finish and developed the slow slide and run between strokes that enabled Cornell to defeat crews rowing a much higher stroke. The advocates of the lower stroke say, "If men were machines, the crew rowing the highest stroke would always win, but men are not machines and a lower stroke and smooth form conserve power." Richard Glendon at the U.S. Naval academy taught a stroke with exaggerated swing of the body at the finish. The fine physique of the midshipmen, combined with their finished watermanship, brought victories to this stroke at Poughkeepsie and in the Olympics. The nearest approach to what may be called an "American stroke" was made by Hiram Conibear and his pupils at the University of Washington. Conibear, himself not an oarsman, when appointed rowing coach at Washington in 1907, studied Yale, Cornell and Syracuse methods, and on his return became an expert technician. He developed at the University of Washington, aided by the Pocock brothers, expert builders and riggers of racing shells, a system that by the 1940s dominated college rowing east and west. Edward Leader at Yale, Thomas Bolles and Harvey Love at Harvard, Fred Spuhn and Delos Schoch at Princeton, Russell Callow at Pennsylvania and Navy, Harrison Sanford at Cornell, Walter Raney at Columbia, Gosta Eriksen and Loren Schoel at Syracuse, Norman Sonju at Wisconsin, Alvin Ulbrickson, Fil Leanderson and Richard Erickson at Washington, Carroll Ebright at California, Robert Mock and James McMillin at M.I.T., Victor Michalson at Brown, Charles Logg at Rutgers, Louis Gellerman at Navy and John Bisset at U.C.L.A. were all products of the University of Washington and as coaches belonged to what may be called the "Washington school" of rowing. In fact there were only a few universities whose coaches were not former Washington oarsmen; viz., James Ten Eyck and William Sanford of Syracuse, Charles S. Walsh and Paul Quinn of the U.S. Naval academy, Hubert Glendon, Carl Ullrich and William Stowe of Columbia, Allen W. Walz of Wisconsin and Yale, James Rathschmidt of Yale, Harry Parker of Harvard, Joseph W. Burk of Pennsylvania, Pete Sparhawk of Princeton, Pete Gardner of Dartmouth, George James Lemmon of California, William Leavitt of Rutgers, Jack Frailey of M.I.T. and Ernest Arlett of Northeastern.

The winning Ratzeburg crew in the 1960 Olympics, recognized for several years as the world's fastest, changed the thinking of some American coaches on a tour of the United States in 1963. The faster, shorter stroke and interval training methods of the Germans, and their style of rigging and "shovel" oars, with broader blades, were taken up by a number of crews, including the Vesper Boat club Olympic champions of 1964 and the Harvard varsity eights of Harry Parker, which were invincible in college competition in 1964, 1965, 1966, 1967 and 1968. Harvard represented the U.S. in the 1968 Olympics in which Karl Adams' Ratzeburg crew, in a lighter, newly designed shell, again won the gold medal.

While in England college coaches are "invited" by the captains of crews or boat clubs, in the United States intercollegiate athletics became increasingly subject to faculty control, and coaches of major sports such as football and rowing are appointed by college authorities as part of the salaried staff of the institution.

Robert F. Herrick at Harvard, Averell Harriman and Mather Abbott at Yale, J. Duncan Spaeth and Gordon Sikes at Princeton and Father Frederick H. Sill at Kent acted as volunteer amateur coaches at their institutions; similar examples among the rowing clubs could be noted. However, the system of salaried, nonprofessional coaches became prevalent in the U.S.

Governing Bodies.—The first duty of the governing bodies for rowing in each nation is to establish an amateur role specifying the qualifications necessary for anyone to engage in amateur rowing competition. The governing body's authority and rulings must be respected by those participating in the sport, and it must have power to disqualify and suspend those who violate the amateur status or other rules prescribed for rowing competition.

It is also the responsibility of the national governing body in each nation to hold a championship regatta each year which shall be open to all classes that are eligible under the amateur rule.

The National Association of Amateur Oarsmen is the governing body for the clubs in the U.S. For college rowing the Intercollegiate Rowing association, the Eastern Association of Rowing Colleges, the Western Crew association and the Dad Vail Rowing association are the governing bodies in all regattas. In Canada it is the Canadian Association of Amateur Oarsmen, and in Great Britain it is the British Amateur Rowing association. The U.S. Olympic committee conducts tryouts every four years to select those who are to compete in the international Olympic regatta.

The National Rowing Foundation was organized in the United States in 1966 to foster national and international competition and to finance U.S. teams in regattas abroad.

For international competition, the International Rowing federation, whose exact name is the Fédération Internationale Sociétés d'Aviron (F.I.S.A.), is composed of the recognized national rowing organization in each nation. The F.I.S.A., which is recognized by the International Olympic committee, is given charge of organizing and conducting the rowing competition in the Olympic games which are held every four years. In addition to this the international federation conducts a European championship regatta every year. At this regatta entries are accepted only from the nations whose governing bodies are members of the international federation. For the Olympic regatta, entries from any nation are acceptable providing that the amateur status of the oarsman entered is in accordance with the Olympic rules.

The National Association of Amateur Oarsmen was organized in 1872 in order to make a necessary distinction between amateur and professional competition. There was much professional rowing up to that time; amateurs and professionals were competing together and it was necessary that some means be found to meet this situation.

Outstanding Oarsmen.—Records indicate that the three most outstanding English oarsmen were Guy Nickalls, Sr., who won the Diamonds five times and stroked pairs, fours and eights to victory many times at Henley; F. S. Kelly, a great sculler who won the Diamonds three times; and J. Beresford, Jr., who won the Diamonds four times and competed in five Olympic regattas, being a victor in three and second in two.

Among the oarsmen of the United States, perhaps the most outstanding were James Ten Eyck, John B. Kelly, Paul Costello, Walter M. Hoover, William G. Miller, Joseph W. Burk, Joseph Angyal, John B. Kelly, Jr., Seymour Cromwell and Don M. Spero. The elder Kelly was the most versatile. In addition to winning three Olympic championships, he stroked pairs, fours and eights to victory many times. Burk made a most outstanding record in single sculling. In four years, 1937–40 inclusive, he won a total of 46 races in single sculls. These included the United States national championship four times, the Canadian championship four times, the Diamond Challenge Sculls twice and the Philadelphia Gold Challenge cup. He was voted the most outstanding athlete in the United States in 1939 when he was awarded the James E. Sullivan trophy. Spero won the Diamond Challenge Sculls at Henley in record time in 1965 and the world championship at Bled, Yugos., in 1966.

In Canada, the dean of rowing and the most outstanding oarsman was Joseph Wright, Sr., of the Argonaut Rowing club, who won many races as stroke of pairs, fours and eights and competed at Henley five times. Other outstanding oarsmen were Lou Scholes, first Canadian to win the Diamonds, Robert Dibble, Joseph Wright, Jr., and later H. R. Pearce; the last represented Australia in his first Olympic competition in 1928 and thereby under the rules was required to represent Australia in 1932, although he had in the meantime transferred his residence to Canada.

Australia produced many good crews and scullers. An Australian crew won the Grand Challenge cup at Henley and the Diamond Challenge Sculls. In single sculling, the most outstanding were H. R. Pearce, who won the Olympic single sculls championship in 1928 and 1932; Mervyn Wood, who was world champion single sculler for nearly a decade until his defeat at the XVth Olympiad in 1952 by Y. Chukalov of the U.S.S.R.; V. Ivanov, of the U.S.S.R., Olympic champion in 1956, 1960 and 1964; and Stuart MacKenzie, who won the Diamonds from 1957 through 1961.

See SPORTING RECORD: *Rowing;* OLYMPIC GAMES.

(J. D. S.; H. P. B.; C. Gs.; A. Da.)

BIBLIOGRAPHY.—R. C. Lehman, *The Complete Oarsman,* 3rd ed. (1924); G. C. Bourne, *A Text-Book of Oarsmanship* (1925); R. A. Glendon and R. J. Glendon, *Rowing* (1923); R. F. Kelley, *American Rowing* (1932); C. V. P. Young, *Courtney and Cornell Rowing* (1923); George Pocock, "Technique and History of Shell Building," *N.A.A.O. Official Guide* (1940); Henry Penn Burke, *N.A.A.O. Year Books;* R. D. Burnell, *The Oxford & Cambridge Boat Race, 1829–1953* (1954); R. F. Herrick, comp., *Red Top; Reminiscences of Harvard Rowing* (1948); Malcolm R. Alama, *Mark of the Oarsmen* (1963); Hylton R. Cleaver, *A History of Rowing* (1957); Desmond Hill, *Instructions in Rowing* (1963). (S. J. R.)

ROWLAND, HENRY AUGUSTUS (1848–1901), U.S. physicist, a major contributor to the study of electricity, heat, and spectrum analysis, was born at Honesdale, Pa., on Nov. 27, 1848. He graduated in civil engineering at the Rensselaer Polytechnic Institute, Troy, N.Y., in 1870, where he later became instructor in physics and then assistant professor. In 1875 he was elected to the chair of physics in the newly founded Johns Hopkins University, where he remained for the rest of his life. On a visit to Europe he studied under H. L. F. von Helmholtz in Berlin, where he showed experimentally that an electrostatic charge moving at high speed has the same magnetic action as an electric current. At Johns Hopkins he redetermined the mechanical equivalent of heat in a long series of experiments with improved thermometric and calorimetric methods; and in similarly refined studies he redetermined the value of the ohm. Turning to spectrum analysis, he constructed a dividing engine capable of ruling 14,000–20,000 lines to the inch on diffraction gratings. He then studied gratings ruled on spherical concave surfaces and applied their advantages to the development of exact spectrometry. He mapped the solar spectrum and made a systematic study of the arc spectra of numerous elements.

Rowland won many honours: he was the first president of the American Physical Society (1899–1900) and was elected a foreign member of the Royal Society of London in 1899. He died in Baltimore, Md., on April 16, 1901. His collected *Physical Papers* appeared in 1902.

See S. Rezneck, "An American Physicist's Year in Europe: Henry A. Rowland (1875–1876)," *Am. J. Phys.,* vol. 30 (Dec. 1962).

(D. McK.)

ROWLANDSON, THOMAS (1756–1827), English caricaturist, was born in Old Jewry, London, in July 1756, the son of a tradesman or City merchant. On leaving school he became a student in the Royal Academy, but at the age of 16 he went to study in Paris and afterward made frequent tours on the continent. In 1775 he exhibited at the Royal Academy a drawing of "Delilah Visiting Samson in Prison." He took to drawing caricatures as a means of livelihood. His Academy drawing of Vauxhall (1784) had been engraved by Pollard, and the print was a success.

Rowlandson was largely employed by Rudolph Ackermann, the art publisher, who in 1809–11 issued in his *Poetical Magazine* "The Schoolmaster's Tour"—a series of plates with verses by William Coombe which became very popular. Again engraved by Rowlandson himself in 1812, and issued under the title of the "Tour of Dr. Syntax in Search of the Picturesque," they had reached a fifth edition by 1813 and were followed by "Dr. Syntax in Search of Consolation" (1820) and by the "Third Tour of Dr. Syntax in Search of a Wife" (1821). The same collaboration of designer, author, and publisher resulted in the English "Dance of Death" (1814–16) and the "Dance of Life" (1822). Rowlandson also illustrated Smollett, Goldsmith, and Sterne. Other designs are in *The Spirit of the Public Journals* (1825), *The English Spy* (1825), and *The Humourist* (1831). He died in London on April 22, 1827.

Rowlandson's designs were usually executed in outline with a reed pen and delicately washed with colour. They were then etched by the artist on copper and afterward aquatinted—usually by a professional engraver, the impressions being finally coloured by hand. As a designer the quality of his work suffered from haste and overproduction.

See J. Grego, *Rowlandson the Caricaturist, a Selection from His Works,* etc., 2 vol. (1880).

ROWLEY, WILLIAM (? 1585–? 1624), English dramatist and actor, who collaborated with several Jacobean dramatists, notably with Thomas Middleton (*q.v.*). It is probable he was born in London, but the dates of his birth and death are much disputed. C. J. Sisson (in *The Lost Plays of Shakespeare's Age,* 1936) produces evidence that he died in 1624: it had previously been thought that Rowley outlived Middleton, but that he probably retired from the stage after Middleton's death in 1627. Rowley became an actor before 1610, when he was with the Duke of York's Men, a company which amalgamated with Lady Elizabeth's Men to form Prince Charles's Men. When the two groups separated again (1616–17), Rowley remained with the Prince's Men, but probably joined the King's Men in 1623. He had met Middleton c. 1614, but was already writing plays for his company in 1612–13, and in 1609 had published *A Search for Money* (reprinted for the Percy Society, 1840), a pamphlet in punning, Euphuistic prose, giving a lively picture of London life.

Of some 50 plays known to have been written by Rowley alone or in collaboration, comparatively few are extant. The most important of those by Rowley alone is *All's Lost by Lust* (performed 1619; published 1633), a romantic tragedy with a strong strain of dramatic morality, written in harsh but powerful verse. His other extant plays are comedies, and include *A New Wonder, A Woman Never Vext* (c. 1610; publ. 1631), *A Match at Mid-Night* (c. 1607; publ. 1633), and *A Shoo-maker a Gentleman* (c. 1608; publ. 1638). Plays written with Middleton include *The Old Law* (performed c. 1615), in which Massinger also collaborated; *A Fair Quarrel* (c. 1616) and *The Changeling* (1622), in both of which Rowley wrote the subplot, and helped with the plan of the whole; *Wit at Several Weapons* (c. 1616), incorrectly attributed also to Fletcher (*see* BEAUMONT AND FLETCHER); and *The World Tost at Tennis* (1620).

Other plays in which he collaborated are *Fortune by Land and Sea* (c. 1609), with Thomas Heywood; *The Witch of Edmonton* (1621), with Thomas Dekker and John Ford (*qq.v.*); *The Maid in the Mill* (1623), with Fletcher; and *The Birth of Merlin, or: The Child Hath Found His Father,* the 1662 title page of which wrongly attributes part authorship to Shakespeare. Study of his own plays and those in which he collaborated reveals development of style from brutal comedy to eloquent expression of pathos, and also an evolving concept of the character of the comic clown.

SAMUEL ROWLEY (fl. 1597–c. 1624), a dramatist apparently employed by Philip Henslowe (*q.v.*), has been described as William Rowley's brother, but they seem not to have been related. After 1601 he acted with, and wrote plays for, the Admiral's Men and other companies. Several plays in which he is thought to have collaborated are lost. His *When You See Me, You Know Me, Or the famous Chronicle Historie of King Henrie the Eight . . .* (probably performed 1604; publ. 1605; ed. by F. P. Wilson, 1952) resembles Shakespeare's *Henry VIII* (which may have been influenced by it) in owing something to popular tradition. His only other extant play, *The Noble Souldier. Or, A Contract Broken, Justly Reveng'd,* a tragedy (publ. 1634; reprinted in *Tudor Facsimile Texts,* vol. 142, 1913), was probably written largely by Dekker. He has also been credited with the prose scenes in some of Shakespeare's plays.

BIBLIOGRAPHY.—For William Rowley *see* P. G. Wiggin, *An Inquiry Into the Authorship of the Middleton-Rowley Plays* (1897); *All's Lost by Lust and A Shoo-maker a Gentleman,* ed. by C. W. Stork, with introduction on Rowley's life and place in drama (1910); D. M. Robb, "The Canon of Rowley's Plays," in *Modern Language Review,* vol. 45 (1950); *see also The Changeling,* ed. by C. Leech for the "New Mermaid Series" (1964), with introduction on Rowley. For Samuel Rowley *see* H. D. Sykes, *Sidelights on Elizabethan Drama* (1925).

ROWLEY REGIS, a municipal borough (since 1933) in the Rowley Regis and Tipton parliamentary division of Staffordshire,

Eng., in a hilly district 7 mi. (11 km.) W of Birmingham. Pop. (1961) 48,146. Area 6 sq.mi. The word Regis was added to Rowley (Roughlea) in 1140. Coal instead of charcoal is said to have been first used for smelting iron in 1619 by Ironmaster Dud Dudley. The oldest and biggest industries are nailmaking (17th century) and chainmaking. By 1820 "Rowley rag," a basaltic stone, was being quarried extensively for roads and Rowley was thoroughly industrialized. Heavy engineering, enameled hollow ware, brickworks at Blackheath, and clay mines at Netherton are other industries. Haden Hill Park was given to the council in 1921 and the Elizabethan house is used as a restaurant.

ROXAS Y ACUÑA, MANUEL (1892–1948), first president of the Republic of the Philippines, was born at Capiz, Panay, P.I., on Jan. 1, 1892. He studied law at the University of the Philippines, entered politics, and in 1917 was appointed to the municipal council of Capiz (now Roxas City). He was governor of Capiz from 1919 to 1921, when he was elected to the House of Representatives in the Philippines, later becoming Speaker of the House. He was a member of the Philippine Constitutional Convention in 1934 and Secretary of Finance from 1938 to 1940.

During World War II he served as a colonel under Gen. Douglas MacArthur and later was captured by the Japanese. As a prisoner he helped to coordinate underground resistance to the invaders for three years. In 1945 he was president of the Senate when, as a Liberal candidate, he was elected president of the Philippine Commonwealth. When the country achieved its independence, July 4, 1946, Roxas became the first president of the new republic. He died at Clark Field, Pampanga, on April 15, 1948.

ROXBURGH, a border county of Scotland (area 664.9 sq.mi. [1,722 sq.km.]) which forms a rough rectangle about 18 by 35 mi. (29 by 56 km.), stretching from southwest to northeast between Northumberland (Eng.) and the Scottish counties of Berwick, Midlothian, Selkirk, and Dumfries.

Physical Features.—Much of the county comprises the basin of the Teviot (q.v.), the entire 40 mi. of its course as it flows northeastward to join the Tweed lying within Roxburgh. The Teviot is fed by numerous turbulent waters, such as the Borthwick, Ale, and Jed, all prone to flooding. The Tweed, joined on its left bank by the Leader, flows for 30 mi. near the northern edge of the county and opens into a western part of the low-lying Merse of Berwick. In the southwest, the Liddel opens the county toward the Solway Firth, and a low pass also links Liddesdale with the valley of the North Tyne. The highest land (Auchope Cairn, 2,382 ft. [726 m.]) lies in the southeast, where about 80 sq.mi. of lavas of Old Red Sandstone Age flank the great granitic intrusion of Cheviot (itself over the border); they form rolling moorland. Carboniferous rocks sweep round them from the south giving lower surfaces (Carter Fell, 1,815 ft.) planed over thick Fell sandstones, with thin shales and even coal seams (as in Liddesdale); the poor wet soils are peat-covered or heathery. A wedge of Carboniferous rocks also penetrates up the Tweed Valley, overlying basalts at the base of this series, which reach the surface in the "Kelso Traps," a V-shaped belt about 5 mi. wide which yields warm soils invaluable for early-ripening grain. The central third of the county comprises Upper Old Red Sandstone rocks molded into rolling countryside interrupted by volcanic hills like the Eildons south of Melrose and by many igneous dikes. Some rivers in this region have eroded down to the underlying Silurian rocks which form the surface rocks in the west of the county; they are the continuation of the closely folded graywackes, shales, and grits of the Southern Uplands, and share their characteristically rounded outlines, at a general level of about 1,000 ft.; dry grass moorland predominates. In the hills the rivers have cut notches into the U-shaped valleys eroded by the ice, and in the dales they have cut terraces in the gravels, boulder clay, and alluvium. There are several Forestry Commission plantations, all in the hills, the largest being Wauchope (13,495 ac.) which, with Newcastleton (7,754 ac.), is within the Border National Forest Park; the lowlands are well wooded.

Rainfall decreases from 70 in. (1,780 mm., mean annual) in the hills between Liddesdale and Teviotdale, to 27 in. (685 mm.) along the Tweed; the Cheviots have about 50 in. and the rest of

the county 30 to 40 in. Spring is cold but dry, most rain comes from October to December, and snowfalls can be severe in the east. (A. M. Le.; A. T. A. L.)

History and Antiquities.—Among the more important remains of the original inhabitants are the standing stones and circles at Plenderleith between the Kale and Oxnam; on Hownam Steeple, a few miles to the northwest; and at Midshiels on the Teviot. The stones on Ninestane Rig (943 ft.), near Hermitage Castle, and on Whisgill are supposed to commemorate the Scots of Dalriada who, under Aidan (Aedan), were defeated with great slaughter by Aethelfrith of Bernicia, king of Northumbria, at the Battle of Degsastan in 603. There are hill-forts in Liddesdale, Teviotdale, and Jedvale, but the largest example of its kind in Scotland is said to be on the most easterly of the three summits of the Eildon Hills in Tweeddale. One of the mysteries of the county is the Catrail, a linear earthwork consisting of a ditch and bank of quite modest dimensions which runs from Robert's Linn to the head of the Dean Burn—a tributary of the Borthwick Water. The Roman Dere Street crossed the border north of Brownhart Law in the Cheviots, then took a mainly northwesterly direction across the Kale, Oxnam, Jed, and Teviot to Newstead, near Melrose, where it is conjectured to have crossed the Tweed and run up Lauderdale into East Lothian. There are many sites of Roman forts, signal stations, and camps, the principal camps seeming to have been at Cappuck, southeast of Jedburgh, and near Newstead at the base of the Eildons, the site of Trimontium. After the retreat of the Romans the county was occupied by the Britons of Strathclyde in the west and the Bernicians in the east. It was then annexed to Northumbria for more than four centuries until it was ceded, along with Lothian, to Scotland in 1018. The Wheel Causeway or Causey which enters the county north of Deadwater is an ancient roadway. Between the heads of Wolfehopelee Burn and Battling Sike, and before splitting up and entering the improved lands, the road passes through a linear earthwork in two main tracks.

Roxburgh was constituted a shire by David I, its ancient town of Roxburgh (see KELSO) forming one of the Court of Four Burghs. The town was abandoned when the castle was destroyed and James II killed in 1460; the castle was partially rebuilt in 1547, but was destroyed finally in 1550. The burgh of Kelso, 14 mi. NE, superseded it. Other towns were repeatedly burned down, and the abbeys of Jedburgh, Kelso, and Melrose (qq.v.) were ultimately ruined in the expedition of the earl of Hertford in 1544–45. Of the ancient castles, that of Hermitage, though now only a shell, is the most striking. Dating from the 13th century, it was a stronghold of the Douglases from 1341 to 1492. Abbotsford (q.v.), near Melrose, was the last home of Sir Walter Scott (q.v.) and the country around Melrose is known as "the Scott country."

Population and Administration.—The population increased by about 53% in the first 60 years of the 19th century and then fell almost continuously; in 1966 it was 43,490. There were (1961) 72 persons who spoke Gaelic and English. The small burghs are Hawick (pop. [1961] 16,290), Kelso (4,320), Jedburgh (3,460), the only royal burgh and the county town, and Melrose (2,130). The four county districts have the same names. The county returns one member to Parliament with Selkirk and Peebles. The shires of Roxburgh, Berwick, and Selkirk form a sheriffdom, and a resident sheriff-substitute sits at Jedburgh and Hawick. The county offices are at Newtown St. Boswells (q.v.).

Agriculture and Industries.—Half of the total area of the county is improved land, the rest being rough grazing. Of the improved land, two-thirds is either temporary or improved grassland, sheep-rearing being the predominant farming type. South of Kelso, sheep farms average about 1,200 ac. and carry self-contained flocks of South Country Cheviot ewes. South of Hawick, Cheviot sheep still predominate but Blackface, the original breed, are also kept on some hirsels (sheep farms). West of Hawick, farming is nearly all hill sheep-farming in character, the only remaining area of hill sheep-farming (chiefly Cheviots) being north of Melrose. The arable stock farms combine sheep-breeding with cattle-breeding, which is on the increase, and cropping in oats, barley, and turnips. Typical arable stock farms carry half-bred ewes (Cheviot crossed with Border Leicester), which are crossed with Oxford Down or Suffolk Down rams to produce Down-cross lambs. The cattle are mainly pedigreed Shorthorns and the principal breed on the hill farms is the Galloway crossed with a white Shorthorn. Pig-breeding is increasing. Annually in September the largest outdoor ram sales in Scotland are held at Kelso and are attended by buyers from all parts of the country and from overseas. Great numbers of sheep are sold at the autumn sales at Hawick. Arable farming is important in the rich low-lying areas round Kelso, where wheat, barley, and some sugar beets are grown in addition to oats and roots which are the common crops on upland stock farms. In some parts of Tweedside and Jedvale several kinds of fruit are successfully grown.

The "Common Ridings," celebrated each year with much pageantry at Hawick (q.v.) and other border towns, date from the time when the community grazed their stock on common land which had to be held against encroachment.

The two basic industries in the county are agriculture and textiles. Milling, agricultural implements, wire nail making, timber, and sawmilling are Kelso's trades; also the making of fertilizers and fishing tackle—the salmon fisheries on the Tweed are of considerable value. Hawick is famous for its hosiery and knitwear. Jedburgh manufactures tweed and woolen goods, and precision tools.

BIBLIOGRAPHY.—*Royal Commission on the Ancient and Historical Monuments and Constructions of Scotland . . . Roxburghshire . . .* (1956); A. Jeffrey, *History and Antiquities of Roxburghshire* (1864); W. S. Crockett, *Berwickshire and Roxburghshire* (1926); G. Watson, *Roxburghshire Word-Book* (1923); Land Utilisation Survey of Britain, *The Land of Britain,* pt. 24–26, *Roxburgh* by A. C. O'Dell (1946). (C. W. Bl.)

ROXBURGHE, EARLS AND DUKES OF.

ROBERT KER (c. 1570–1650), 1st earl of Roxburghe, eldest son of William Ker (d. 1600) of Cessford in Roxburghshire, was a grandson of Sir Walter Ker (d. c. 1583), who had fought against Mary Stuart at Carberry Hill (1567) and Langside (1568), and a great grandson of Sir Andrew Ker (d. 1526), who had fought at Flodden (1513). James VI of Scotland appointed him privy councilor in 1599 and created him Lord Roxburghe in 1600. Robert accompanied James to London in 1603, where he became gentleman of the bedchamber (1607) and was created earl of Roxburghe (1616). Lord privy seal for Scotland (1637–49), he took no part in the Civil War except for supporting the Scottish Engagers, who invaded England in 1648 in support of Charles I. His surviving son Harry Ker (d. 1643), Lord Ker, left no male issue and on Robert's death in 1650 the estates and titles passed by special arrangement to SIR WILLIAM DRUMMOND (d. 1675), the youngest son of Robert's eldest daughter Jean and of John, 2nd earl of Perth. William took the name of Ker, became 2nd earl, and married his cousin Jean, first daughter of Harry Ker. His grandson, JOHN KER (c. 1680–1741), who succeeded his brother in 1696 as 5th earl, was created duke of Roxburghe in 1707 for his services in promoting the union between Scotland and England. This was the last creation in the Scottish peerage. A representative peer for Scotland in four parliaments, he was secretary of state for Scotland (1704–05 and 1716–25) and keeper of the privy seal for Scotland (1714–16). He fought against the Jacobite rebels at the battle of Sherrifmuir (1715).

His grandson, JOHN KER (1740–1804), the 3rd duke, who became lord of the bedchamber (1767) and groom of the stole (1796), was a famous bibliophile, whose library included a unique collection of books from Caxton's press and rare volumes of broadside ballads. To commemorate its sale in 1812, Thomas Frognall Dibdin proposed a dinner of bibliophiles, from which developed the Roxburghe Club. His cousin WILLIAM BELLENDEN (1728–1805), 7th Lord Bellenden, who succeeded as 4th duke, taking the name Bellenden-Ker, died childless in 1805. Seven years of litigation ensued, but in 1812 SIR JAMES INNES of Innes (1736–1823), 6th bart. (a descendant of Lady Margaret, 3rd daughter of Harry, Lord Ker), who had taken the name Innes-Ker in 1807, established his claim to the title and estates and became 5th duke.

His son JAMES HENRY ROBERT INNES-KER (1816–1879), the 6th duke, was created Earl Innes in the peerage of the United Kingdom in 1837. His descendant, GEORGE VICTOR ROBERT JOHN INNES-KER (1913–   ), is the 9th duke. (T. I.)

ROXBURY, since 1868 a section of Boston (q.v.), Suffolk County, Mass., and previously a town of Norfolk County situated between Boston and Dorchester. Earliest spellings included Rocksbury, Roxburie, and Rocsbury.

The town was founded in 1630 by Puritan immigrants who came with Gov. John Winthrop. The early settlers were led by William Pynchon, who in 1636 led a party from there and founded Springfield, Mass. Anne Hutchinson (q.v.) was held in custody during the winter of 1637–38 at the home of the first minister, Thomas Welde. John Eliot, the apostle to the Indians, moved to Roxbury in 1632 and died there in 1690. Roxbury was the home of Thomas Dudley (q.v.), of his son Joseph, and of his grandson Paul; of Robert Calef (d. 1719), the leader of the opposition to the witchcraft craze; of Gen. Joseph Warren (q.v.); and of William Eustis (1753–1825), U.S. secretary of war (1809–12) and governor of Massachusetts (1823–25). Theodore Parker (q.v.) was the pastor of the Unitarian Church of West Roxbury from 1837 to 1846.

The Roxbury Latin School, a boys' preparatory school, was founded in 1645 by a group of town fathers, among them John Eliot; it was first known as the Free School of Roxburie.

West Roxbury was the scene of the Brook Farm (q.v.) experiment. (J. F. Co.)

ROY, RAM MOHUN (1772–1833), the founder of Brahmo Samaj (q.v.) in India, was not only a great religious leader and social reformer but also a far-seeing statesman who indicated the lines of progress for India under British rule. Hence he is sometimes called the father of modern India. He was born in 1772 in a village in Burdwan district in Bengal. During the first 30 years of his life he seems to have traveled widely outside his province and mastered several languages—Sanskrit, Persian, Arabic, Hebrew, Greek, and English, in addition to Bengali, his mother tongue. In 1803 he secured an appointment under the East India Company, served its administration in various capacities until he retired in 1815 and settled in Calcutta. There he began his great agitation against the rite of suttee (q.v.) and vigorously kept it up until suttee was abolished by law by Lord William Bentinck in 1829.

During 1815–19 Ram Mohun published his translations of the *Upanishads* and his papers on Hindu theism. His object in these and similar writings was to wean his countrymen from what he regarded as the corruptions of medieval Hinduism and the evils of Hindu society, viz., idol worship, animal sacrifices, polygamy and the caste system, and to draw their attention to the original purity of the teachings of Vedanta (see INDIAN PHILOSOPHY: *Vedanta*). It was for achieving this object that he also later founded the Brahmo Samaj (1828).

Ram Mohun next turned his attention to the problem of education, and in a famous letter to Lord Amherst (1823) made a vigorous plea for scientific and English education for India in preference to the traditional Sanskrit education. He was as great a champion of political freedom as he was of scientific education; his memorial for the repeal of the Press ordinance of 1823 has been hailed as the *Areopagitica* of Indian history. Ram Mohun's letters show that he greatly admired the progress of freedom in Europe and hoped that India through its British connection would grow in knowledge and freedom and ultimately claim equal partnership with Britain.

In 1830 Ram Mohun went to England on behalf of the titular emperor of Delhi to plead his cause before the British government. He fell ill there and died at Bristol on Sept. 27, 1833. (D. S. Sa.)

ROYAL AIR FORCE: see GREAT BRITAIN AND NORTHERN IRELAND, UNITED KINGDOM OF: *Defense: Air Force; AIR POWER.*

ROYAL AIR FORCE COLLEGE: see MILITARY, NAVAL AND AIR ACADEMIES.

ROYAL BALLET, THE, English ballet company and school, was formed on Oct. 31, 1956, under a charter of incorporation granted by Queen Elizabeth II to the Sadler's Wells Ballet, the Sadler's Wells Theatre Ballet, and the Sadler's Wells School. The Royal Ballet promotes the art, produces ballet, and trains dancers. The queen was patron at its inception and Princess Margaret was its first president. The Royal Ballet is administered by governors and a council.

The founders of the Sadler's Wells Ballet, Lilian Baylis and Ninette de Valois (*qq.v.*), began their work together in 1928 when Miss Baylis, who had taken over the Old Vic Theatre, London, invited Miss de Valois to produce dances for plays there. When Miss Baylis took over the Sadler's Wells Theatre, London, in 1931, Miss de Valois followed to open a school of ballet. The first performance of ballet at Sadler's Wells was given on May 15, 1931; by September 1931 ballet had become a regular feature there. At the time of the outbreak of World War II the ballet company had grown in stature and repertoire and counted among its members some of the finest dancers in the world.

In 1946 Miss de Valois founded as a junior company the Sadler's Wells Theatre Ballet (the "Second Company") mainly for foreign and provincial tours. In the early 1950s it toured the U.S., South Africa, and the Continent. In 1955 it officially became the touring company with its own repertoire and in 1957 became the touring section of the Royal Ballet.

See also BALLET: *Ballet in England.*

ROYAL CANADIAN MOUNTED POLICE, Canada's federal police force, was originally called the North West Mounted Rifles. The reaction of the U.S. to the thought of having an armed force patrolling the border caused the name to be changed to the North West Mounted Police. It was instituted in 1873 to establish law and order between the Manitoba border and the Rockies. Three hundred members assembled at Dufferin, Man., in the summer of 1874, and on July 8, with freight wagons, oxcarts, cattle for food, field guns, mortars, and an assortment of farm machinery, struck out across the plains to the Oldman River, in what is now southern Alberta, where they built Ft. Macleod and took up the task of policing 300,000 sq.mi. of wilderness. As the only authority in the region the force inherited a variety of work in caring for the stream of settlers that followed in its wake. It abolished the whisky traffic that had been ruining the Indian, tracked and brought to justice murderers, horse thieves, and desperadoes, and contained the warlike Sioux who had fled to Canada to escape U.S. wrath at the annihilation of General Custer's command in 1876. Just treatment of the Indian by the force resulted in the neutrality of the powerful Blackfoot Confederacy during the Northwest Rebellion of 1885 (*see* RIEL, LOUIS). As more than 300,000 settlers poured into Canada following the turn of the century the North West Mounted Police were of considerable assistance to the many who were without experience in surviving the wilderness. Under its vigilance the western extension of the Canadian Pacific Railway was completed. Anticipating the gold rush of 1898, the North West Mounted Police preceded the vanguard of prospectors to the Yukon. In 1904 the prefix "Royal" was added to its title in recognition of its services. In 1905 the provinces of Saskatchewan and Alberta were formed and retained the services of the Royal North West Mounted Police. In 1920 the force received its present title, undertook the enforcement of federal legislation throughout Canada, and transferred its headquarters from Regina to Ottawa.

The 1930s saw the inception of the present "marine" and "air" divisions of the force, the dog section, and the first of three crime detection laboratories. RCMP patrols emphasized Canada's claim to arctic sovereignty, ranging far and wide from detachments in the northland; between 1940 and 1942 the RCMP vessel "St. Roch" became the first ship to complete the west to east journey through the Northwest Passage.

The Royal Canadian Mounted Police employs several thousand uniformed personnel, special constables, civilians, and civil servants in its 17 divisions across Canada; its operations are directed by a commissioner from headquarters at Ottawa. As well as the federal statutes throughout Canada, it is responsible for the enforcement of the provincial statutes and the criminal code in all provinces except Ontario and Quebec. It polices more than 100 municipalities. It is charged with the internal security of the country and is the only police force in the Yukon and Northwest Territories where on behalf of other government departments it performs numerous administrative duties. The facilities of the national police services of the RCMP, comprising the crime detection laboratories and the identification branch of the force, are available to all authorized police forces. The RCMP-sponsored Canadian Police College is attended by selected members of the force and outside forces. The RCMP holds membership in the International Criminal Police Organization and maintains liaison offices at London, Eng., and Washington, D.C. Contingents from the force served overseas in World Wars I and II.

Applicants for the Royal Canadian Mounted Police are required to be British subjects or Canadian citizens and if accepted must engage for an initial term of five years. Recruits are trained at Regina, Sask., and Ottawa, Ont., and upon completion of training may be posted to any point in Canada excepting the extreme northern regions where service is voluntary.

The dress of the force has several variations, but symbolic of the RCMP is the broad-brimmed hat, scarlet tunic, blue breeches with wide yellow stripe, brown top boots, spurs, and Sam Browne equipment. Horses were long ago supplanted by motorized vehicles and the last equestrian class for recruits graduated in 1966.

ROYAL GEOGRAPHICAL SOCIETY. Founded in 1830 as the Geographical Society of London and incorporated by charter as the Royal Geographical Society in 1859, the "R.G.S." originated in the Raleigh Travellers' Club, formed in 1827. Soon after its foundation it absorbed the African Association, founded in 1788. The society promoted, or supported, in the 19th century, explorations in British Guiana (Sir Robert Schomburgk), Australia, Africa (David Livingstone, Sir Richard Burton, John H. Speke, James A. Grant, and Joseph Thomson), and the Arctic (Sir John Franklin and Sir George Nares); and in the 20th century, among others, Robert F. Scott's first Antarctic expedition; Sir Ernest Shackleton's Imperial Trans-Antarctic expedition; consecutive Mt. Everest expeditions culminating in Sir John Hunt's successful ascent of 1953; the Norwegian-British-Swedish Antarctic expedition (1949–52); and Sir Vivian Fuchs's Commonwealth Trans-Antarctic expedition (1955–58). In 1954, with the Alpine Club (partner in the Everest expeditions), the society established the Mount Everest Foundation to assist financially mountain exploration and research. The R.G.S. annually supports university, particularly student, expeditions. It is also active in forwarding geography in British universities, having promoted departments of geography at Oxford (1899) and at Cambridge (1903).

Its objects are to advance geographical knowledge through lectures and publications (including original maps and its quarterly publication, *The Geographical Journal*), through its library and public map room, and through instruction in exploratory surveying and the support of exploration and research. It has arbitrated in boundary disputes; *e.g.*, between Peru and Bolivia from 1911 to 1913. The society, which receives a small amount of state aid for its public map room, is governed by an annually elected council served by a permanent staff. The British sovereign annually awards two gold medals for exploration on the council's recommendation.

See H. R. Mill, *The Record of the Royal Geographical Society, 1830–1930* (1930); G. R. Crone, *The Royal Geographical Society: a Record 1931–55* (1955). (L. P. K.)

ROYAL MARINES: *see* MARINES.

ROYAL MILITARY ACADEMY: *see* MILITARY, NAVAL AND AIR ACADEMIES.

ROYAL NAVAL COLLEGE: *see* MILITARY, NAVAL AND AIR ACADEMIES.

ROYAL NAVY: *see* GREAT BRITAIN AND NORTHERN IRELAND, UNITED KINGDOM OF: *Defense: Navy;* ADMIRALTY; FLEET, NAVAL.

ROYAL OAK, a city of Oakland County, Mich., U.S., 11 mi. N of Detroit, has backed its slogan, "city of homes," by zoning three-fifths of its area for single dwellings. The population grew rapidly from 25,087 in 1940 to 80,612 in 1960. The site of early settlement, which dates from the 1820s, was originally surrounded by marshlands. The name is credited to Gov. Lewis Cass, who rested there in 1818 under a giant oak tree which he supposedly likened to the "royal oak" in Scotland whose foliage once concealed Prince Charles from the Roundheads. Royal Oak was chartered in 1921; the commission-manager government, in effect since 1917, includes a full-time planning director and municipal court.

Cultural life (literary, historical, dramatic, and musical activities for all age groups) centres on the public library. The Detroit Zoo lies partly within Royal Oak. The Shrine of the Little Flower has become well known mainly because of the former radio activities of the church pastor, Father Charles E. Coughlin. Industry, which is of minor importance, includes tools, paint, hydraulic mechanisms, and automotive parts. (E. R. I.)

ROYAL SOCIETY, the oldest scientific society in Great Britain and one of the oldest in Europe. The Royal Society (more fully, The Royal Society of London for Improving Natural Knowledge) is usually considered to have been founded in 1660, but a nucleus had been in existence for several years before that date. As early as the year 1645 weekly meetings were held in London of "divers worthy persons, inquisitive into natural philosophy and other parts of human learning, and particularly of what hath been called the *New Philosophy* or *Experimental Philosophy*," and there can be little doubt that this gathering of philosophers is identical with the "Invisible College" of which Robert Boyle speaks in sundry letters written in 1646 and 1647.

Some of these "philosophers," resident in Oxford about 1648, formed an association there under the title of the Philosophical Society of Oxford, and used to meet, most usually in the rooms of John Wilkins, warden of Wadham College. A close intercommunication was maintained between the Oxford and London philosophers; but ultimately the activity of the society was concentrated in the London meetings, held principally at Gresham College.

On Nov. 28, 1660, the first journal book of the society was opened with a "memorandum," from which the following is an extract:

Memorandum that Novemb. 28, 1660, These persons following, according to the usuall custom of most of them, mett together at Gresham Colledge to heare Mr. Wren's lecture, viz., The Lord Brouncker, Mr. Boyle, Mr. Bruce, Sir Robert Moray, Sir Paul Neile, Dr. Wilkins, Dr. Goddard, Dr. Petty, Mr. Ball, Mr. Rooke, Mr. Wren, Mr. Hill. And after the lecture was ended, they did, according to the usuall manner, withdrawe for mutuall converse. Where amongst other matters that were discoursed of, something was offered about a designe of founding a Colledge for the promoting of Physico-Mathematicall Experimentall Learning.

It was agreed at this meeting that the company should continue to assemble on Wednesdays at three o'clock; an admission fee of 10s. with a subscription of 1s. a week was instituted; Wilkins was appointed chairman; and a list of 41 persons judged likely and fit to join the design was drawn up. On the following Wednesday Sir Robert Moray (or Murray) brought word that the king (Charles II) approved the design of the meetings; a form of obligation was framed and was signed by all the persons enumerated in the memorandum of Nov. 28 and by 73 others. On Dec. 12 another meeting was held at which 55 was fixed as the number of the society—persons of the degree of baron, fellows of the College of Physicians, and public professors of mathematics, physics, and natural philosophy of both universities being supernumeraries.

Gresham College was now appointed to be the regular meeting place of the society. Sir Robert Moray was chosen president (March 6, 1661) and continued from time to time to occupy the chair until the incorporation of the society, when Lord Brouncker was appointed the first president under the charter. In October 1661 the king offered to be entered one of the society, and next year the society was incorporated under its present title. The name "Royal Society" appears to have been first applied to the "philosophers" by John Evelyn, in the dedication of his translation of a book by Gabriel Naudé, published in 1661.

The charter of incorporation passed the great seal on July 15, 1662, to be modified, however, by a second charter in the following year, repeating the incorporating clauses of the first charter but conferring further privileges on the society. The second charter passed the great seal on April 22, 1663, and was followed in 1669 by a third, confirming the powers granted by the second charter, with some modifications of detail, and granting certain lands in Chelsea to the society. The council of the Royal Society met for the first time on May 13, 1663.

At this early stage of its history the "correspondence" which was actively maintained with continental philosophers formed an important part of the society's labours, and selections from this correspondence furnished the beginnings of the *Philosophical Transactions*. At first the publication of the *Transactions* was entirely "the act of the respective secretaries." The first number, consisting of 16 quarto pages, appeared on Monday, March 6, 1664/65, under the title of *Philosophical Transactions: giving some Accompt of the present undertakings, studies and labours of the Ingenious in many considerable parts of the world*, with a dedication to the Royal Society signed by Henry Oldenburg, the society's first secretary. The society also from its earliest years published, or directed the publication of, separate treatises and books on matters of philosophy, most notable among these being the *Philosophiae naturalis principia mathematica Autore Is. Newton. Imprimatur: S. Pepys, Reg. Soc. Praeses. Julii 5, 1686, 4to Londini 1687*.

In 1887 the *Philosophical Transactions* were divided into two series, labeled A and B, respectively, the former containing papers of a mathematical or physical character and the latter papers of a biological character. In 1832 appeared the first volume of *Abstracts of papers, printed in the Philosophical Transactions from the year 1800*. This publication developed in a few years into the *Proceedings of the Royal Society*.

One of the most important functions of the society at its inception was the performance of experiments before the members. In the royal warrant of 1663 ordering the mace which the king presented to the society, it is described as "The Royal Society for the improving of Natural Knowledge by experiments." The society early exercised the power granted by charter to appoint two "curators of experiments," the first holder of that office being Robert Hooke, who was afterward elected a secretary of the society.

Another matter to which the society gave attention was the formation of a museum, the nucleus being "the collection of rarities formerly belonging to Mr. Hubbard," which, by a resolution of council passed in 1666, was purchased for £100. This museum was presented to the trustees of the British Museum in 1781, upon the removal of the society to Somerset House. A certain number, however, of instruments and models of historical interest remained in the possession of the society, and some of them, more peculiarly associated with its earlier years, are still preserved at Burlington House. The remainder have been deposited in the Victoria and Albert Museum, South Kensington.

After the Great Fire of London in September 1666 the apartments of the Royal Society in Gresham College were required for the use of the city authorities, and the society was invited by Henry Howard (later duke of Norfolk) to meet in Arundel House. At the same time he presented them with the library purchased by his grandfather Thomas, earl of Arundel, and thus the foundation was laid of the important collection of scientific works, exceeding 140,000 volumes, which the society possesses. Of the Arundel manuscripts the bulk was sold to the trustees of the British Museum in 1831 for £3,559, the proceeds being devoted to the purchase of scientific books. These manuscripts are still kept in the British Museum as a separate collection. The society, however, still possesses a valuable collection of scientific correspondence, official records, and other manuscripts, including the original manuscript, with Newton's autograph corrections, from which the first edition of the *Principia* was printed.

Under date Dec. 21, 1671, the journal book records that "the lord bishop of Sarum proposed for candidate Mr. Isaac Newton, professor of the mathematicks at Cambridge." Newton was elected a fellow on Jan. 11, 1671 (old style; Jan. 21, 1672, new style), and in 1703 he was appointed president, a post which he held till his death in 1727. During his presidency the society moved to Crane Court, its first meeting in the new quarters being held on Nov. 8, 1710. In the same year its members were appointed visitors and directors of the Royal Observatory at Greenwich, a function which they continued to perform until the accession of William IV, when by the new warrant then issued the president and six fellows of the Royal Astronomical Society were added to the list of visitors.

In 1780, under the presidency of Sir Joseph Banks, the Royal Society removed from Crane Court to the apartments assigned to it by the government in the new Somerset House, where it remained until its removal to Burlington House in 1857. The policy of Sir Joseph Banks was to raise the status of the fellowship. A step in pursuance of the same policy was taken in 1847, when the number of candidates recommended for election by the council was limited to 15, and the election was made annual. This was augmented to 20 in 1938, to 25 in 1945, and 32 in 1964. Concurrent with the gradual restriction of the fellowship was the successive establishment of other scientific bodies. The founding of the Linnean Society in 1788 under the auspices of several fellows of the Royal Society was the first instance of the establishment of a distinct scientific association under royal charter; and this was followed by the formation of many more societies to promote special branches of science.

From Charles II's reign onward British governments have constantly appealed to the Royal Society for advice in connection with scientific undertakings of national or supranational importance. The following are some of the principal matters of this character upon which the society has been consulted by, or which it has successfully urged upon the attention of, the government: the improvement and equipment of the Royal Observatory, Greenwich; the change of the calendar in 1751; ventilation of prisons; protection of buildings and ships from lightning; measurement of a degree of latitude; determination of the length of a seconds pendulum; comparison of the British and French standards of length; the Geodetic survey in 1784, and the General Trigonometrical survey begun in 1791; expeditions to observe the transits of Venus in 1761, 1769 (commanded by Capt. James Cook), 1874, and 1882; the Antarctic expeditions of 1772 (under Cook, whose voyage extended to the circumnavigation of the globe), 1839 (under Sir James Clark Ross), and 1900; help with the reports of the British Antarctic expedition of 1910–13; observations for determining the density of the earth; Arctic expeditions of 1817 (in search of the Northwest Passage), of 1819 (under Lieut. William Parry), of 1827 (Parry and Ross), of 1845 (under Sir John Franklin), of 1875 (under Capt. George Nares); numerous expeditions for observing eclipses of the sun; 1822, use of coal tar in vessels of war; best manner of measuring tonnage of ships; 1823, corrosion of copper sheathing by seawater; Charles Babbage's calculating machine; lightning conductors for vessels of war; 1825, supervision of gasworks; 1832, tidal observations; 1835, instruments and tables for testing the strength of spirits; magnetic observatories in the colonies; 1862, the great Melbourne telegraph; 1865, pendulum observations in India; 1866, reorganization of the meteorological department; 1868, deep-sea research; 1872, "Challenger" expedition; 1879, prevention of accidents in mines; 1881, pendulum observations; cruise of the "Triton" in Faeroe Channel; 1883, borings in delta of the Nile; 1884, Bureau des Poids et Mesures; international conference on a prime meridian; 1888, inquiry into lighthouse illuminants; 1890, the investigation of colour blindness; 1895, examination of the structure of a coral reef by boring; 1896, inquiry into cylinders for compressed gases; the establishment of an International Geodetic Bureau; 1897, determination of the relations between the metric and imperial units of weights and measures; an inquiry into the volcanic eruptions in the West Indies; international seismological investigation; international exploration of the upper atmosphere; measurement of an arc of the meridian across Africa. During 1913–17 the society completed a magnetic survey of the British Isles. In 1919 it sent two expeditions to observe the total solar eclipse of May 29, and to note any deflection of rays of light by the sun's gravitational field, as required by Albert Einstein's general theory of relativity. In later years also the society, acting at the request of the government, has taken the leading part in fruitful investigations into various tropical diseases, beginning with the tsetse-fly disease of cattle in Africa, followed by investigations into malaria, Mediterranean fever, and sleeping sickness. In 1924 it received a bequest of £10,000 for medical research on tropical diseases, etc., and sent an expedition to study

BY COURTESY OF THE ROYAL SOCIETY, LONDON

MEETING OF THE ROYAL SOCIETY IN SOMERSET HOUSE, LONDON, WHERE IT OCCUPIED APARTMENTS FROM 1780 TO 1857

kala azar in northern China. The society has also shown an active interest in problems of respiration and circulation in high altitudes (Peru expedition, 1921), and in investigations into glassworkers' cataract. It did much to promote the *International Catalogue of Scientific Literature* and the International Association of Academies.

In addition the Royal Society exercises a variety of important public functions of a more permanent nature. It still provides seven of the board of visitors of the Royal Observatory, has 11 representatives on the Joint Permanent Eclipse committee and has a Solar Research committee of its own. From 1877 until the reconstitution of the Meteorological Office in 1906 the society nominated the Meteorological council, which had the control of that office. The Gassiot and other committees of the society continued to cooperate with the Meteorological Office. Since 1919, when the Meteorological Office was attached to the Air ministry, the society has two representatives on the Meteorological committee. The society has the custody of standard copies of the imperial standard yard and pound. The president and council have the scientific control of the National Physical Laboratory, an institution established in 1900 as a result of representations from the Royal Society (financial control was transferred to the Department of Scientific and Industrial Research in 1918). It also appoints British delegates to meetings of the International Research council.

One of the most important duties which the Royal Society performs on behalf of the government is the administration of an annual grant for the promotion of scientific research and the assistance of scientific publications. This grant originated in a proposal by Lord John Russell in 1849 that at the close of the year the president and council should point out to the first lord of the treasury a limited number of persons to whom the grant of a reward or of a sum to defray the cost of experiments might be of essential service. The majority of these grants are utilized to provide apparatus, and they are made with the advice of eight scientific boards of eight experts each and a publications board.

A proposal for bursaries to assist investigators of proved ability to work in other parts of the Commonwealth of Nations for short periods when this would augment their capacity to advance knowledge was put forward by Sir Edward Salisbury in 1953. This was implemented as the Royal Society and Nuffield Foundation Bursaries scheme, and is mainly financed by the Nuffield Foundation and contributions from various countries of the Commonwealth. In 1962 five Royal Society research professorships were established by means of a special government grant; three more were added in 1964.

A statement of the trust funds administered by the Royal Society will be found in the *Year Book of the Royal Society* (published annually), and the origin and history of these funds in the *Record of the Royal Society*.

Five medals (the Copley Medal, two Royal, the Davy, and the Hughes) are awarded by the society every year, the Rumford and the Darwin medals biennially, the Sylvester triennially, and the Buchanan quinquennially. The first of these originated in a bequest by Sir Godfrey Copley (1709) and is awarded "to the living author of such philosophical research, either published or communicated to the society, as may appear to the council to be deserving of that honour"; the author may be an Englishman or a foreigner. The Rumford Medal originated in a gift from Count von Rumford (Sir Benjamin Thompson) in 1796 for the most important discoveries in heat or light made during the preceding two years. The Royal medals were instituted by George IV and are awarded annually for the two most important contributions to science published in the British dominions not more than ten years nor less than one year before the date of the award. The Davy Medal was founded by the will of John Davy, F.R.S., the brother of Sir Humphry Davy, and is given annually for the most important discovery in chemistry made in Europe or Anglo-America. An enumeration of the awards of each of the medals and the conditions of the awards are published in the *Year Book*.

Six special lectures endowed by the benefactors named are delivered to the society, namely the Croonian (William Croone, 1684), the Bakerian (Henry Baker, 1775), and the Ferrier (Sir David Ferrier, 1928), to be delivered triennially, on the advances in knowledge of the structure and function of the brain; the Wilkins (J. D. Griffith Davis, 1947) on the history of science; the Leeuwenhoek (George Gabb, 1948) on some microbiological subject; and, in 1952, lectures in memory of Lord Rutherford.

Under the existing statutes of the Royal Society every candidate for election into the society must be recommended by a certificate in writing signed by six or more fellows, of whom three at least must sign from personal knowledge. From the candidates so recommended the council annually selects 32, and the names so selected are submitted to the society for election by ballot. Princes of the blood, however, and not more than 2 persons selected by the council on special grounds once in two years, may be elected by a more summary procedure. Foreign members, not exceeding 50, may be selected by the council from among men of the greatest scientific eminence abroad, and proposed to the society for election.

The anniversary meeting for the election of the council and officers is held on St. Andrew's Day. The council for the ensuing year, which includes the president, treasurer, two scientific secretaries (one for the biological and one for the physical sciences), and a foreign secretary, must consist of 11 members of the existing council and 10 fellows who are not members of the existing council. These are nominated by the president and council previous to the anniversary meeting. The president and foreign secretary normally hold office for five years, the two scientific secretaries and the treasurer for ten years. There is also a permanent executive secretary who is not usually a fellow. The session of the society is from November to June; the ordinary meetings are held on Thursdays during the session at 4:30 P.M. The selection for publication from the papers read before the society is made by the Committee of Papers, which consists of the members of the council for the time being aided by committees appointed for the purpose. The papers so selected are published in the society's *Philosophical Transactions* (quarto) or *Proceedings* (octavo).

BIBLIOGRAPHY.—T. Sprat, *The History of the Royal-Society of London* (1667; 4th ed., 1734); T. Thomson, *History of the Royal Society* (1812); A. B. Granville, *The Royal Society in the 19th Century* (1836); C. R. Weld, *A History of the Royal Society*, 2 vol. (1848); H. B. Wheatley, *The Early History of the Royal Society* (1905); Sir W. Huggins, *The Royal Society* (1906); A. H. Church, *The Royal Society: Some Account of the Classified Papers in the Archives* (1907, etc.); T. G. Bonney, *Annals of the Philosophical Club of the Royal Society* (1919); D. Stimson, *Scientists and Amateurs* (1949); E. N. da C. Andrade, *A Brief History of the Royal Society* (1960). *See also Notes and Records of the Royal Society* (1938–   ); *The Record of the Royal Society of London*, 4th ed. (1940); *Signatures in the First Journal-book and the Charter-book of the Royal Society*, 3rd ed. (1950); and *Year Book of the Royal Society* (annual); *Biographical Memoirs of Fellows of the Royal Society* (annual; 1955–   ).

(R. W. F. H.; A. Wo.; E. J. S.)

ROYALTY, the payment made to the owners of certain types of rights by those who are permitted by the owners to exercise the rights. The rights concerned are literary, musical, and artistic copyright, rights in inventions and designs, and rights in mineral deposits, including oil and natural gas. The term originated from the fact that in Great Britain for centuries gold and silver mines were the property of the crown; such "royal" metals could be mined only if a payment ("royalty") were made to the crown. (*See also* COPYRIGHT; PATENT; PUBLISHING.)

It is uncommon for the author of a book to be in a position to exploit it fully himself: he requires the resources of a publishing organization. Similarly, a playwright needs the services of a theatrical management and actors to perform his play and a publisher to produce and sell copies. A musical composer must arrange for the performance of his work, for the sale of copies, and for the making of recordings. An artist, if he wants to make any profit from a picture beyond the price he obtains for it, must arrange for reproductions to be published in books and as prints. An individual inventor without capital or plant must license others to manufacture his invention. When owners of rights make arrangements for such exploitation by others the remuneration they receive in exchange is often in the form of a royalty, usually based on the actual extent of the exploitation.

Mineral deposits have nothing in common with the fruits of intellectual and artistic endeavour, the subject of the other rights mentioned above, except that they are often exploited by persons other than the owners upon payment of royalties.

Literary and Musical Works.—*Books.*—Payment in the form of royalties based on a percentage of the published price of the work is the customary method of sharing receipts between author and publisher. Generally the royalty is 10% of the published price, rising to 15 or $17\frac{1}{2}$% according to the number of copies sold. This method is much fairer to both parties than the older system of outright payment by the publisher for all rights in the books he agreed to publish. The rate of royalties depends upon the cost of production and advertising and the estimated sales and also on the respective bargaining powers of author and publisher. It is usual for the publisher to agree to pay an advance of royalties either upon the signing of the agreement, upon delivery of the manuscript, or upon publication date. Authors whose previous books have sold well command proportionately large advances. In addition to providing for the periodic rendering of accounts by the publisher and for inspection of account books by the author, agreements normally deal expressly with the responsibilities of the parties regarding all matters affecting the efficient production of the book. Sometimes the publisher is given an option to acquire rights in subsequent books by the author.

Agreements for the publication of fictional works in the United States and Great Britain almost invariably give the publisher control of anthology, digest, and paperback rights and provide for the sharing of the proceedings of exploitation of these rights. Translation rights, film rights, dramatization rights, and broadcasting rights are usually retained by the author and disposed of separately. For some of these rights lump sum payments are more appropriate than royalties.

Plays.—Agreements between playwrights and theatre managements for professional productions normally provide for the payment of royalties on the box-office receipts after certain deductions. Translation rights, performing rights in other countries, and film and broadcasting (radio and television) rights may or may not be dealt with in the initial agreement, the terms of which depend greatly upon the standing and bargaining power of the playwright. If reading and acting editions of the play are published the publishers will pay royalties to the playwright. The publisher of the acting edition usually controls the amateur performing rights and sometimes other rights, such as repertory rights, as well. Royalties for amateur performances may be on a sliding scale but are usually a fixed sum for each performance, possibly with a reduction for second and subsequent performances. The exploitation of rights in plays is normally timed so that a film is not produced while the first stage production is still running.

Music.—The full exploitation of the copyright in a musical work is a complex matter and ordinarily depends on both the nature of the work and the position and reputation of the composer. At one time, unless a work had been commissioned, the first step was to secure the interest of a music publisher who would publish the sheet music, in those days often the most fruitful source of revenue. Now, the first step may well be to arrange for a public performance or a broadcast, and it is likely that recordings will be made very soon afterward, probably with the performers who give the first public performance. The popularity of performing groups in the field of popular music often waxes and wanes rapidly and exploitation of music which is associated with particular groups is usually intensive. The pace is slower for serious works. Once a work of any kind has become popular with the public the composer, acting alone, could have no expectation of collecting the performing royalties due to him in respect of the performances of his work in innumerable places all over the world. To deal with this situation collecting societies have been formed in most countries. The oldest such society in Great Britain is the Performing Right Society. In the United States the American Society of Composers, Authors and Publishers (ASCAP) was formed in 1914 and Broadcast Music, Inc., in the early 1940s after dissension between radio broadcasters and ASCAP. The two organizations compete. National collecting societies have reciprocal arrangements for collection of royalties in respect of performances in other countries. In Great Britain most composers, authors, and publishers of musical works assign their performing rights to the Performing Right Society, which has a staff of inspectors, collects fees, and restrains unauthorized performances. After deduction of the costs of administration the fees collected are divided between the members. Licensees submit returns of performances and the division of the fees depends upon the number of times a particular work has been performed and upon the nature of the work, a weighting system being in operation to give serious but less popular music a larger share than would otherwise be the case. Other national societies operate similarly.

Composers also receive royalties from recording companies. In Great Britain, once a licence to record has been given, others may record the work concerned on payment of a prescribed royalty to the copyright owner. Public performance of records is controlled by another collecting society, Phonographic Performance Ltd., which issues licences and collects fees. Licences are not usually granted for performances at functions at which bands have previously been or would normally be engaged.

Two other British collecting societies, the Mechanical Copyright Protection Society and the Sound Film Music Bureau, are associations of owners of musical copyright concerned with the exercise of recording rights in connection with the making of gramophone records and film sound tracks. (J. N. B. P.)

Historical Background.—The royalty system came into general use only in the 19th century, although before that authors were occasionally paid a stipulated sum for the first printing of a book, and a further sum if another printing was called for. Samuel Simmonds paid Milton £5 for *Paradise Lost* and agreed to pay a further £5 at the end of the sale of each of the first three printings. Richard Baxter, the noted 17th-century English Puritan minister, records that when he arranged with Thomas Underhill and Francis Tyton to publish his *Saints' Everlasting Rest,* a quarto of nearly 1,000 pages, the publishers agreed to pay him £10 for the first printing and £20 for every subsequent printing up to the year 1665.

The Shakespearean scholar Sidney Lee records that the highest price known to be paid before 1599 to an author for a play by the manager of an acting company was £11. "A small additional gratuity, rarely exceeding 10s., was bestowed on a dramatist whose piece on its first production was especially well received, and the author was customarily awarded, by way of benefit, a certain proportion of the receipts of the theatre on the production of a play for the second time. The 19 plays which may be set to Shakespeare's credit between 1591 and 1599 combined with such revising work as fell to his lot during those nine years cannot consequently have brought him less than £200 or some £20 a year. Between 1599 and 1611 his remuneration as both actor and dramatist was on the upward grade. The fees paid dramatists rose rapidly. The

exceptional popularity of Shakespeare's work after 1599 gave him the full advantage of the higher rates of pecuniary reward in all directions. The 17 plays that were produced by him between that time and the close of his professional career could not have brought him less on an average than £25 each, or some £400 in all." Later prices improved and Fielding, for example, received £1,000 from Andrew Millar for *Amelia*, while Gibbon received two-thirds of the proceeds on his history.

Edward Chapman, of Chapman and Hall, in a letter to John Forster, the biographer of Charles Dickens, said: "There was no agreement about *Pickwick* except a verbal one. Each number was to consist of a sheet and a half, for which we were to pay 15 guineas, and we paid him for the first two numbers at once, as he required the money to go and get married with. We were also to pay more according to the sale, and I think *Pickwick* cost us altogether £3,000." Forster adds: "I had always pressed so strongly the importance to him of some share in the copyright that this at last was conceded in the deed above mentioned (though five years were to elapse before the rights should accrue) and it was only yielded as part consideration for a further agreement entered into on the same date (Nov. 19, 1837) whereby Dickens engaged to write a new work (*Nickleby*) the first number of which was to be delivered on the 15th of the following March and each of the numbers on the same day of each of the successive 19 months, which was also to be the date of the payment to him by Chapman and Hall, and 20 several sums of £150 each for five years' use of the copyright, the entire ownership in which was then to revert to Dickens."

On July 2, 1840, Dickens wrote to Chapman and Hall: "Your purchase of *Barnaby Rudge* is made upon the following terms: It is to consist of matter sufficient for ten monthly numbers of the size of *Pickwick* and *Nickleby*, which you are, however, at liberty to divide and publish in 15 smaller numbers if you think fit. The terms for the purchase of this edition in numbers and for the copyright of the whole book for six months after the publication of the last number are £3,000. At the expiration of six months, the whole copyright reverts to me." (C. Bn.; X.)

Inventions.—As to inventions, a royalty may be said to be a compensation paid under a licence granted by the owner of a patent ("the licensor") to another person ("the licensee") who wishes to make use of the invention, the subject of the patent. The patent remains the property of the licensor. A licence may be exclusive, in which case the patent owner precludes himself from granting licences to third parties, or nonexclusive, in which case the patent owner may grant licences to as many persons as he wishes. The granting of licences and the payment of royalties thereunder are purely a matter of contract between licensor and licensee. It is essential that all relevant matters be provided for in the contract, especially the amount of royalties, and the precise method of computing them. A licence may be limited or not, according to the intentions of the parties. It may be limited to certain purposes or to geographical areas or in any other way permissible under the national laws having jurisdiction over the transaction. It will normally be for the full term of the patent.

A royalty may be a single payment covering the whole use of the patent for the whole term, but the more usual practice is to make periodic payments and to relate the amounts of those payments to the actual use of the patent by the licensee. It is common to charge royalties on the basis of a percentage of the price for which the licensee sells the articles or on the basis of the number of the articles made under the patent. Although the amount of royalties is generally a matter of free bargaining between licensor and licensee, in some countries governments preclude their nationals from paying royalties to foreign patent owners in excess of a certain maximum fixed by the government. Some governments also reserve the right to approve the entire licence contract concluded between their nationals and aliens.

Royalty payments may be in exchange for something in addition to the mere use of the invention. The most common example is that wherein the licensor not only grants the right to use the invention but also undertakes to supply the licensee with technical "know-how," that is to say, information from his own experience on the most economical and efficient way of working the patent. It is estimated that more than 50% of licence contracts include "know-how" provisions.

Designs.—When applied to industrial designs, the meaning of the word royalty is roughly the same as in the case of patented inventions. Designs, depending on their nature or the various national laws, may be protected by patents, copyright, or registration. The form of legal protection, however, does little to change the system of royalty payment as described in regard to patents.

(R. Wo.)

Mining and Mineral Operations.—Mineral royalty is payment to the mineral owner partly as consideration for the right of exploitation, partly as compensation for the exhaustion of an irreplaceable asset, and tends therefore to be proportionate to the net value of the product. Though the word "minerals" includes petroleum and natural gas, their peculiar modes of occurrence and of exploitation warrant their separation from ores and nonmetallics for royalty purposes. Depending on the country, ownership may be vested in the state, as in Communist countries; in the surface owner, as is virtually the case in the United States; or in a dual system, as in Great Britain, where mineral ownership is vested in the surface owner subject to ancient customs in certain areas and to state ownership of coal and petroleum. The miner's title is seldom equivalent to a fee title but is a bundle of rights and obligations, the composition of which varies greatly from country to country. Exceptionally, as in France, mineral exploitation rights are granted by government in perpetuity without payment of royalty, though a ground rent unrelated to production or profitability is paid to the surface owner to compensate him for the loss of certain statutory rights. More generally, royalties are negotiated and leased for a fixed period and are assessed in accordance with one of three principles. (1) A fixed sum per ton. (solid materials, *e.g.*, gypsum) or cubic yard (unconsolidated materials such as sand and gravel) is the simplest system and is usual for nonmetallics but is not applicable to ores because of fluctuations in grade (*i.e.*, percent content of metal). (2) A sliding scale charge based on the value of the product is the most common method for ores. Its simplest form, a fixed percentage of selling price, has a linear effect, but an exponential element may be introduced by the use of a formula or by a schedule of graduated charges. A "certain" or "dead" rent, *i.e.*, a minimum annual payment, is occasionally specified and can sometimes be deducted from the gross royalty payment. A surface rental may likewise be charged and deducted from the gross payment. (3) Royalty may be based on the profitability of the operation, more commonly in the oil industry than in mining.

Oil and gas royalties are less variable in application. Following the example set by Venezuela, a 50–50 profit-sharing basis has become the standard pattern in South American countries and in the Middle East. The United States distinguishes between "competitive" leases (on a known producing geological structure), which pay royalty of 12–25% of the value of the oil and $12\frac{1}{2}$–$16\frac{2}{3}$% of the value of the gas; and "noncompetitive" leases in virgin areas, where the royalty when production begins is $12\frac{1}{2}$%. In some other countries, natural gas bears a fixed charge per 1,000 cu.ft. Great Britain is not a significant oil producer, but for continental shelf operations in the North Sea has adopted the principle of an area rental of £25–£290 per square kilometre which is deductible from a royalty of $12\frac{1}{2}$% of the wellhead value of the product.

(G. A. Sc.)

BIBLIOGRAPHY.—Philip Wittenberg, *Protection and Marketing of Literary Property* (1937); F. E. Skone James (ed.), *Copinger and Skone James on the Law of Copyright,* 9th ed. (1958); Margaret Nicholson, *Manual of Copyright Practice for Writers, Publishers and Agents* (1956); Lawrence J. Eckstrom, *Licensing in Domestic and Foreign Operations* (1964); A. K. Berle and L. Sprague de Camp, *Inventions, Patents, and Their Management* (1959); *Terrell and Shelley on the Law of Patents,* 10th ed. (1961); Northcutt Ely, "Summary of Mining and Petroleum Laws of the World," U.S. Bureau of Mines *Information Circular 8017* (1961); F. R. H. Green, "Mining Legislation in British Commonwealth Countries Where Minerals Are Vested in the Crown," *Trans. Instn. Min. Metall.,* vol. 173 (1963–64).

ROYCE, SIR (FREDERICK) HENRY, 1ST BART. (1863–1933), British engineer, designer of Rolls-Royce cars and airplane engines, was born at Alwalton, Huntingdonshire, on March 27, 1863. At 15 he was an engineer apprentice to the Great Northern Railway company at Peterborough, and in 1882 he was chief electrical engineer for the first electric street-lighting system in Liverpool. In 1884 he started his own engineering business in Manchester, which developed into Royce Ltd., manufacturers of electrically driven cranes, dynamos and motors. In 1903 he built three experimental cars of his own design, the outstanding qualities of which came to the attention of motor dealer C. S. Rolls (*q.v.*), who soon agreed to take his whole output. Their firms were combined in 1906 as Rolls-Royce, Ltd.; the motor section of the business was moved to Derby in 1908. Royce was made a baronet in 1930. He died at West Wittering, Sussex, on April 22, 1933.

See Sir Max Pemberton, *The Life of Sir Henry Royce* (1934).

(ST. J. C. N.)

ROYCE, JOSIAH (1855–1916), U.S. philosopher and teacher, was born at Grass Valley, a California mining town, on Nov. 20, 1855. At 16 he entered the newly opened University of California, inclined to the study of engineering. But the teachings of the geologist Joseph LeConte and of the poet Edward Rowland Sill roused his extraordinary speculative power; and on receiving his baccalaureate degree in 1875, he gave himself to the study of philosophy, first in Leipzig and Göttingen, Ger. (under R. H. Lotze) and then, as one of the first fellows of Johns Hopkins university, with William James and Charles Peirce. There, he received the degree of Ph.D. in 1878. After teaching English for four years at the University of California, he was called to Harvard university as lecturer in philosophy, becoming assistant professor in 1885, professor in 1892 and succeeding George Herbert Palmer as Alford professor in 1914. He received various honorary degrees and in 1916 was made honorary fellow of the British Academy. He died at Cambridge, Mass., Sept. 14, 1916.

Royce's effect as teacher and writer was profound: no previous U.S. thinker had so united moral energy with wide historical learning, command of scientific method and intense interest in logical technique. His versatile mind concerned itself effectively with a wide range of subjects; he contributed to mathematical logic, psychology, social ethics, literary criticism and history, as well as to metaphysics. His thought was massive and intimately human; yet it was sustained with a dialectical skill of such evident virtuosity as, on the one hand, to excite the critical opposition first of pragmatic and then of realistic schools, and, on the other hand, to set a new standard in the systematic treatment of philosophy. In this latter respect, Royce did for U.S. philosophy what his older contemporary F. H. Bradley (*q.v.*) did for British philosophy: in many ways the views of these thinkers are akin. Like Bradley, Royce teaches a monistic idealism. Scientific laws he describes—anticipating certain developments of later physics—as statistical formulas of average behaviour. His absolute idealism is supplemented, not corrected, by the ethical and social teachings of his later years and, in particular, by the conception of the world of human selves as the Great Community, the literally personal object of moral loyalty (*see also* IDEALISM).

Among Royce's more important publications (selected from a far greater number) are: *The Religious Aspect of Philosophy* (1885); *The Spirit of Modern Philosophy* (1892); *The Conception of God,* with supplementary essay (1897); *Studies of Good and Evil* (1898); *The World and the Individual* (Gifford Lectures), volumes I and II (1900–01); *The Conception of Immortality* (1900); *Outlines of Psychology* (1903); "The Relations of the Principles of Logic to the Foundations of Geometry," in *Transactions of the American Mathematical Society,* volume VI, 3 (1905); *The Philosophy of Loyalty* (1908); *The Sources of Religious Insight* (1912); *The Problem of Christianity* (lectures delivered at Lowell institute, Boston, Mass., and at Manchester college, Oxford Eng.), volumes I and II (1913); "The Mechanical, the Historical and the Statistical," *Science,* New Series XXXIX (1914); *Lectures on Modern Idealism* (1919) For a bibliography (exclusive of posthumous publications) *see* B. Rand, *Philosophical Review,* volume XXV (1916) and *Royce's Logical Essays,* edited by D. S. Robinson (1951).

BIBLIOGRAPHY.—J. H. Muirhead, *The Platonic Tradition in Anglo-*

Saxon Philosophy (1931); J. E. Smith, *Royce's Social Infinite* (1950); J. H. Cotton, *Royce on the Human Self* (1954); *see* special Royce issue of the *Journal of Philosophy* (1956). (M. W. C.; W. E. H.)

ROYER-COLLARD, PIERRE PAUL (1763–1845), French statesman and philosopher, a moderate partisan of the Revolution who became a liberal Legitimist and the exponent of a realist psychology sometimes described as "spiritualism." He was born on June 21, 1763, at Sompuis in Champagne, the son of a small proprietor. Brought up in a strongly Jansenist atmosphere, he went to schools of the Brothers of the Christian Doctrine. In 1787 he began practice as a lawyer in Paris. During the French Revolution he was elected to the Paris commune by the Île Saint-Louis in 1790 and was its secretary till the insurrection of Aug. 10, 1792. After the overthrow of the Girondins (summer 1793) his life might have been in danger, and he retired to Sompuis, where he was not molested. In 1797 he was elected by the Marne *département* to the Council of Five Hundred, in which he made a great speech demanding justice, that is, freedom, for the Catholic clergy; but after the *coup d'état* of 18 Fructidor (Sept. 4) his election was annulled. Invited to send clandestine reports on French internal affairs to the exile Louis XVIII, he became a member of the "secret royal council" constituted on Feb. 23, 1800. Though this soon dissolved itself, he seems to have continued sending his reports till 1803.

For the next ten years Royer-Collard was mainly devoted to philosophy. While his education had familiarized him with the great 17th-century thinkers (Descartes, the Cartesians, Antoine Arnauld, and Leibniz), he was immediately concerned to refute the sensationism of Condillac (*q.v.*). For this purpose he developed a "philosophy of perception" which owed much to Thomas Reid (*q.v.*). The existence of the external world, duration, and causality, he argued, are realities known to us through "consciousness" and memory, not through the senses, which reveal only extension and solidity. The "false philosophy" of skepticism had to be combated both for the sake of society as a whole and for that of individual happiness. In 1811 he was appointed professor of the history of philosophy at the Imperial University (the Sorbonne).

Under the First Restoration (1814), Louis XVIII made Royer-Collard director of the book trade (supervisor of the press) and a counselor of state, with particular responsibility for public education. Under the Second Restoration (1815) Royer-Collard retained these posts and was elected by his old *département* to the Chamber of Deputies. At first a supporter of royal authority as the basis of all order, he soon developed a theory of liberal monarchy or Legitimist democracy which made him a critical opponent of the more reactionary ministers. These views, together with his philosophical program, made him the moving spirit of the Doctrinaires (*q.v.*). He resigned his control of education in 1819 and was dismissed from the council of state in 1820.

Constantly reelected deputy, Royer-Collard became president of the Chamber in 1828. As such he presented the protest of the 221 deputies (March 18, 1830) against Charles X's arbitrary appointment of Prince Jules de Polignac as prime minister. After the July Revolution of 1830 he remained a deputy till 1842, but as a Legitimist he could not sympathize with the new regime. He died at Châteauvieux (Loir-et-Cher) on Sept. 4, 1845. Philosophically his most important disciple was the Frenchman Victor Cousin (*q.v.*).

ROZANOV, VASILI VASILIEVICH (1856–1919), Russian critic, essayist, and mystic, whose works are highly original in thought and style, was born at Vetluga, Kastroma province, in 1856. He studied at Moscow University and became a teacher of history and geography in provincial secondary schools. He attracted attention in 1890 with a critical analysis of the "Legend of the Grand Inquisitor" chapter in *The Brothers Karamazov*, the first of many depth studies of Dostoevski. In such works as *V mire neyasnago i nereshennago* ("In the Realm of Riddle and Mystery," 1901), *Russkaya Tserkov* ("The Russian Church," 1906), and *Ludi lunnago sveta* ("Moonlight Men," 1913), he attacked Christianity as an essentially ascetic religion and developed his own theories of a naturalistic religion of sex and procreation. During the 1905 revolution, he was attracted by the revolutionary movement, which he praised in *Kogda nachalstvo ushlo* ("When the Authorities Were Away," 1910). His *Vedinennoe, pochti na pravakh* ("Solitary Thoughts, Printed Almost Privately"; translated as *Solitaria*, 1927), written in 1912, is generally considered his most important book: its original style—which reflects the freedom, variety, and rhythms of speech—is equaled by originality of thought. *Opavshie listya* (1913, 2nd series, 1915; English translation, *Fallen Leaves*, 1929) is in the same form.

After 1917, Rozanov lived at the Troitski monastery near Moscow. He there wrote *Apokalipsis nashego vremeni* ("Apocalypse of Our Time," 1918–19), and before his death, on Feb. 5, 1919, was reconciled to the Orthodox Church.

BIBLIOGRAPHY.—A. Rezimov, *Kukkha* (Rozanov's letters, etc., 1922); M. G. Kurdyumov, *O Rozanov* (1929); M. Spasovski, *Rozanov v poslednie gody svoivei zhizni* (1935). (D. Mk.)

ROZAS, JUAN MARTINEZ DE (1759–1813), the earliest leader in the Chilean struggle for independence, was born at Mendoza in 1759. In early life he was a professor of law, and of theology and philosophy at Santiago.

He was acting governor of Concepción at one time, and was also colonel in a militia regiment. In 1808 he became secretary to the last Spanish governor, Francisco Antonio Carrasco, and used his position to prepare the nationalist movement that began in 1809. After resigning as secretary, Rozas was mainly responsible for the resignation of the Spanish governor, and the formation of a national junta on Sept. 18, 1810, of which he was the real leader. Under his influence many reforms were initiated, freedom of trade was established, an army was organized, and a National Congress was called in July 1811.

Rozas died at Mendoza, March 3, 1813.

RUANDA: *see* RWANDA.

RUANDA-URUNDI was until 1962 a United Nations trust territory in eastern equatorial Africa administered by Belgium. In that year its two parts achieved independence, the northern part as the republic of Rwanda (*see* RWANDA) and the southern part as the kingdom of Burundi (*q.v.*). This article deals with the history of the territory up to the time of independence.

BY COURTESY OF SABENA BELGIAN WORLD AIRLINES

AT LEFT, TUTSI TRIBESMAN; RIGHT, A PYGMY OF THE TWA CLASS

The kingdoms of Ruanda and Urundi were founded by Tutsi people from Ethiopia who subdued the Hutu. Ruanda seems to have been a powerful state in the 14th century, and the history of its kings, or *bami* (singular *mwami*), is known from traditions describing their wars and tribal struggles. Ruanda-Urundi came within the German sphere of influence in 1890 as part of German East Africa. Although a military post was established at Usumbura on Lake Tanganyika, German control was slight and there was no occupation.

During World War I Ruanda-Urundi fell into Belgian hands, and in 1924 Belgium formally accepted the administration under a mandate of the League of Nations, which was replaced by a United Nations trusteeship in 1946. While retaining its identity and a separate budget, the territory was in 1925 linked to the Belgian Congo by an administrative union. But within Ruanda-Urundi, the Belgians held more to the principles of indirect rule.

Each native kingdom remained separate, with its own sovereign, justice, administration, and taxation. The feudal structure and the dominant position of the Tutsi remained, although the Belgians progressively eliminated the more medieval features of the regime and latterly sought to establish a more democratic atmosphere, which implied the political emancipation of the Hutu.

In 1959 tribal war in Ruanda caused the expulsion or departure of many of the Tutsi, and the *mwami* Kigeri V later went into exile. In the same year Belgian reforms were introduced to prepare the territory for independence, and in 1960 provisional governments were set up. Hutu parties won the 1960 communal elections in both kingdoms. As a result of an internal *coup d'état* in January 1961, Ruanda declared itself a republic and deposed Kigeri; in Urundi the provisional government agreed to exercise power jointly with the *mwami* Mwambutsa IV. Elections held the following September under United Nations supervision again were won by the Hutu in Ruanda but by a predominantly Tutsi party in Urundi. The two states rejected a United Nations proposal to federate.

Both countries attained complete independence on July 1, 1962, as Rwanda and Burundi.   (JE. S.)

BIBLIOGRAPHY.—P. Gourou, *La Densité de la population au Ruanda-Urundi* (1953); N. de Cleene, *Introduction à l'ethnographie du Congo Belge et du Ruanda-Urundi,* 2nd ed. (1957); A. Michiels and N. Laude, *Le Congo Belge et le Ruanda-Urundi,* 18th ed. (1958); Ministère des Affaires Africaines, *La Situation économique du Congo Belge et du Ruanda-Urundi en 1959* (1960).

RUBBER is the substance caoutchouc (*q.v.*), a milklike fluid that is obtained from certain tropical shrubs or trees and then subjected to various processes of manufacture; or it may be a product of chemical synthesis. Beginning in the 19th century with the crudest manufacturing methods and equipment, the rubber industry has undergone continuous and dramatic change to become one of the most complex industries of modern times and an indispensable part of all mechanical civilization. Especially dramatic has been the manner in which rubber was first obtained from the relatively inaccessible forests of the Amazon valley, then from the plantations of the east and, since World War I, increasingly by syntheses.

This article is arranged as follows:

I. HISTORICAL DEVELOPMENT

1. Earliest References.—India rubber, or caoutchouc, has been known in Europe since the discovery of the new world. The first European to describe the elastic gum was Pietro Martyre d'Anghiera (1457–1526), chaplain to the court of Ferdinand of Aragon, Castile and Léon and his wife Isabella, who, in his *De Orbo Novo* (1530 edition), describes an Aztec game played with balls "made of the juice of a certain herbe . . . [which] being stricken upon the ground but softly [rebounded] incredibly into the ayer." Other early references are contained in the work of Antonio de Herrera y Tordesillas, historian to Philip II of Spain (1556–98), who told how Columbus on his second voyage to the new world in 1493–96 saw balls "made of the gum of a tree" being used by the Indians of Haiti (*General History of the Vast Continent and Islands of America,* trans. by J. Stevens, 1725). The first mention of rubber being used for purposes other than sport was made by F. Juan de Torquemada in *De la Monarquia Indiana* (1615). He related how the Indians, having gathered the milk from incisions made in the various trees, brushed it onto their cloaks; and they obtained crude footwear and bottles by coating earthen molds and allowing them to dry. He also made reference to the use of a medicinal oil obtained by distillation.

In the 18th century rubber from the East Indies began to be used in Europe to rub out lead pencil marks—hence "india rubber."

2. First Scientific Descriptions.—The first serious accounts of rubber production and the primitive native system of manufacture were given in the 18th century by two Frenchmen, Charles Marie de la Condamine and François Fresneau. De la Condamine, a member of a French geographical expedition sent to South America in 1735, described caoutchouc, in a report to the French academy in 1736, as the condensed juice of the *Hevea* tree. The results of Fresneau's more comprehensive researches were presented to the academy as a memoir by de la Condamine in 1751. The first accurate account of the botanical characteristics of the *Hevea* species was given by the agricultural chemist J. C. Fusée-Aublet in 1775.

3. Origins of the Industry in Europe.—At the outset, not chemical knowledge but the ability to devise a suitable method of rubber manipulation was of paramount importance to the development of the rubber industry. It was two other Frenchmen, L. A. P. Herissant, a physician, and Pierre Joseph Macquer, a chemist, who first attempted to employ caoutchouc in Europe. Their efforts in the 1760s to discover a cheap and effective solvent for the crude mass of rubber brought from South America— usually in cakes and balls—were not entirely successful, although they are to be credited with introducing the use of turpentine and pure ether as solvents; by this imperfect means some of the earliest rubber surgical instruments were made.

The greatest progress in the easy manipulation of rubber came at the beginning of the 19th century from the experiments of a Scottish chemist, Charles Macintosh (1766–1843), and an English inventor, Thomas Hancock (1786–1865). The solvents they used, normally turpentine or camphene, were expensive and imperfect and the dissolved rubber was applied without the aid of machinery in a manner almost as primitive as that used by the natives themselves. Macintosh's contribution was the rediscovery, about 1820, of the use of coal-tar naphtha as a cheap and effective solvent. His experiments proving a success, Macintosh placed the resulting solution of rubber and naphtha between two fabrics and in so doing avoided the sticky or brittle surfaces that had been common in earlier single-texture garments treated with rubber. Manufacture of these double-textured waterproofed cloaks, henceforth to be known in English under the misspelling "mackintoshes," began in the Glasgow area and was later removed to Manchester. The work of Hancock, who became Macintosh's colleague and partner, is of even greater importance. Convinced that "something must eventually be done with so singular a substance," he first attempted to dissolve the rubber with turpentine, but his hand-coated fabrics were unsatisfactory in surface and smell. He then turned to the production of elastic thread. Strips of rubber were cut from the imported lumps and applied in their crude state to clothing and footwear. On April 29, 1820, he obtained an English patent (No. 4451) for this process. In the same year, in an effort to find use for his waste cuttings, he introduced his famous masticator, which became the model for the much larger rubber masticators that followed. Constructed of a hollow wooden cylinder equipped with teeth in which a hand-driven spiked roller was turned, this tiny machine, originally taking a charge of two ounces of rubber, fulfilled Hancock's greatest hopes. Instead of the masticator's tearing the rubber to shreds, as he thought it might do, the heat of friction welded together the scraps of rubber, which could then be applied in further manufacture. This was only the first of many important successes; in 1820–47 Hancock took out 16 patents.

Although the efforts of Macintosh and Hancock had resolved the initial problem of manipulating the raw material, there could be no rapid extension of the use of india rubber until one further obstacle had been overcome—the effect of temperature on natural rubber, which softens with heat and hardens with cold. The solution of this problem was bound up with the progress of manufacturing methods in the United States (see *Charles Goodyear and the Discovery of Vulcanization,* below).

4. Origins of the Industry in the United States.—The establishment of the rubber manufacturing industry took place toward the end of the commercial and industrial expansion of 1819–37. Formerly rubber had been largely a curiosity (the estimated net imports into the U.S. in 1830 being 160 long tons), although attempts had been made to imitate the crude native-manufactured shoes imported from South America. With the quickening of the economy in the 1830s numerous factories came into operation along the waterfalls of the eastern seaboard. Later, in the prosperity following the gold discoveries of 1848, efforts were made to extend the use of rubber from footwear to clothing and machinery.

Pioneer Machinery.—U.S. attempts to reduce rubber to a plastic state with the aid of machinery followed along lines other than those followed in Britain. Instead of the rubber's being mixed inside a chamber, as with Hancock's masticator, it was compressed by passing it between wooden or iron cylinders. The earliest U.S. patent (April 10, 1820) for rubber machinery was that secured by John J. Howe for a grinding, or mixing, mill consisting of two heavy iron rolls. In 1836 Edwin M. Chaffee took out a patent for a much more important mill and a spreading machine. Chaffee's invention, foreshadowed in Howe's patent and owing a good deal to the earlier efforts of the U.S. rubber pioneers Nathaniel and Martin Hayward, represented the culmination of a series of experiments extending over many years. His two-roll mill, one roll being 6 ft. long and 27 in. in diameter, the other the same length but only 18 in. in diameter, compressed the rubber and aided the compounding process. In this respect it followed the pattern of earlier inventions. Unlike them, however, Chaffee's rolls were steam heated to about 200° F. and they ground and mixed the rubber either without the addition of solvents or by using only a limited amount. The calender, or coating machine, included in this patent set the pattern for calenders beyond the mid-20th century. Built in 1837 at a cost of $30,000 and weighing 30 tons, Chaffee's invention was called the "Monster" because of its great size. With four 6-ft.-long steam-heated rolls of varying diameter, built one above another, it was the biggest machine operating in the rubber industry at that time. After the rubber had been ground and mixed in the mill, it was fed into this machine together with the cloth to be proofed. The revolving cylinders possessed such tremendous power that they forced a thin film of rubber into the fabric. Apart from the economies in labour costs and the speeding-up of the whole process of manufacture, the calender, which before vulcanization could be regarded as the final machine employed in the manufacturing process, meant in certain instances the almost total elimination of the use of solvents.

Charles Goodyear and the Discovery of Vulcanization.—Al-though the industry had received a fillip from the mechanical progress made in rubber technology, this did not stave off a recession when the inherent faults of the early manufactured rubber became apparent. It softened with heat and hardened with cold (particularly in the more extreme climate of the United States); it was tacky, odorous and perished easily. These fundamental weaknesses were removed by the discovery of the vulcanization process in 1839 by the U.S. inventor Charles Goodyear (*q.v.;* 1800–60).

Becoming interested in the manufacture of rubber while still a young man, Goodyear—unaided at the outset by any chemical knowledge—continued these experiments until his death. His innumerable experiments with india rubber are described in his book *Gum-Elastic* (vol. i, 1855; vol. ii, 1853). His invaluable compound of rubber, lead and sulfur was at first called "heated" or "fireproof" gum, but afterward "vulcanized" rubber. The effect of the invention was to impart to rubber a durable quality that it had not hitherto possessed. Previously the backbone of the rubber industry had been the proofing of fabric (largely British) and the making of overshoes (largely U.S.) but now, while the use of rubber in the unvulcanized state continued on a by-no-means insignificant scale, Goodyear's discovery made possible the future rise of the mechanical trade (the use of rubber with machinery) and of the bicycle and automobile tire industry. In an attempt to raise capital to carry forward his other experiments, he sent the first samples of the "improved rubber" to England. These samples came to the notice of Thomas Hancock, who was able to appreciate what had been achieved and who worked unceasingly for more than a year to discover their secret. Eight weeks before Goodyear, dogged by ill health and in sore financial straits, belatedly applied for his English patent on Jan. 30, 1844, Hancock entered his specification for an improvement in rubber manufacture at the British Patent office. Whereas Goodyear had included compounds of lead, which accelerated the change and enabled it to occur at lower temperatures, Hancock considered that only sulfur and a certain degree of heat were required for vulcanization.

Competing claims for the honour of originating the vulcanization process have been made by the supporters of Goodyear and Hancock. Claims have also been made on behalf of the German F. W. Lüdersdorff, the Swede Peter Jonas Bergius and the Dutchman Jan van Geuns. As far as Goodyear and Hancock are concerned, there can be no doubt that priority rests with Goodyear—though the contributions of both men were vital to the industry's development. From Goodyear came an inspired dedication to remove from rubber its fundamental weakness and to seek out new means of employing this material. From Hancock, a more practical man, came outstanding contributions in the mechanical manipulation of rubber.

5. Development of the Industry, 1850–1960.—Important branches of the industry had been established in Austria in 1821; France, 1828; Germany, 1829; and Russia, 1830; and in its expansion in Europe, U.S. assistance was considerable. The widespread adoption and improvement of vulcanization since 1850, coupled with the growing demand for mechanical rubber devices (created by the extension of steam and electrical power and the needs of the ever widening railway networks), resulted in the expansion of the rubber industry both in Europe and in North America. The increase of population and the rising standards of living created vast new markets for rubber footwear and clothing. The rediscovery of the pneumatic tire by John B. Dunlop (*q.v.*) in 1887, followed by the cycling craze of the 1890s, was felt on both sides of the Atlantic. Yet by the end of the 19th century, with the exception of the discovery of "cold vulcanization" in 1846 by the Englishman Alexander Parkes (1813–90) and the introduction by another Englishman, H. H. Waddington, of a dry heat process of vulcanization (1887), the industrial process remained much as it had been in the 1850s. The only major developments in the period 1850–1900 were the discovery of the acid and alkali processes of reclaiming rubber by the Americans H. L. Hall in 1856 and A. H. Marks in 1899. Progress, where it came, resulted from continuous improvements made by the practical man, rather than from new scientific methods. The stimulus given to the science of rubber chemistry by German developments in the last quarter of the century did little to alter the empirical nature of the industry before the automobile age.

There are, in fact, no fundamental differences between the basic manufacturing processes of natural rubber used in 1900 and those of the 1960s. All the separate stages—preparing, cleansing, cutting, masticating, compounding, milling, vulcanizing, hardening, molding and finishing—are still essentially what they were in 1900, although the machinery has been continuously refined and improved. Even in the tire (q.v.) industry, apart from weftless cord, only one important innovation was made: the introduction in the 1920s of the flat-drum process of tire building. Of the other changes mention must be made of the introduction of several additional vulcanization and reclaiming processes, and of the growing direct use of latex, which opened up new industries in latex thread, foam rubber and many other products. Compounding formulas are much more complicated and varied than they were. One must also record the introduction in 1904 of the use of carbon black, the all-important reinforcing agent in modern rubber manufacture, and the discovery in 1905 by George Oenslager of the U.S. of organic accelerators, which speeded up the vulcanization process.

The greatest change in the industry in the 20th century has been the development of synthetic rubber, which in the mid-1960s was rapidly replacing the natural product.

6. Development of Natural Rubber Supply.—The traditional source of rubber, the wild trees of Central and South America, yielded a material that was of varying quality and uncertain supply. This fact ruled out the establishment of a futures market, making the rubber trade an attractive field for the speculator and a hazardous one for the manufacturer. So efforts were made to add to the supply of rubber by reclaiming scrap. While progress in this field was made on both sides of the Atlantic, it was the Americans who undertook its earliest production on a commercial scale and by the end of the 19th century U.S. consumption of reclaimed rubber equaled that of the natural product. The British sought to combat short supplies and fluctuating prices by increasing imports of wild rubber from Africa and by transplanting rubber seeds from the Amazon valley to British colonies in the east.

The Plantation Industry.—The origins of plantation rubber lie in the early 19th century—both Charles Goodyear and Thomas Hancock made reference to it—but the establishment of the industry in southeast Asia did not take place until the last quarter of the 19th century, when the growing demand had accentuated the need to widen the sources of supply.; its founding was due to a group of British botanists. Among them were Sir Clements R. Markham, botanist and senior official of the India office; Sir Joseph Dalton Hooker, director of Kew gardens; and Henry N. Ridley, director of Singapore Botanical gardens from 1888 to 1911. Markham had already transplanted the quinine-yielding cinchona tree from South America to India and in 1870, working closely with Hooker, he turned to the cultivation of rubber. James Collins, formerly curator of the museum of the Pharmaceutical Society of Great Britain, was commissioned by the India office to make preliminary investigations. Collins recommended the establishment of plantations of the indigenous *Ficus elastica* tree in Assam and the introduction into India of the South American species. Effect was given to the former recommendation in 1873. Markham next turned to the problem of cultivating the *Hevea* and *Castilloa* plants. In 1875 and 1876 the botanist Robert Cross was sent to Central and South America to collect specimens and report on their requirements regarding climate and soil. The plants and seeds that he brought back with him, along with the very much larger number delivered later by Sir Henry Wickham (who has been undeservedly credited with starting the plantation industry), were soon distributed through the Botanical gardens at Kew to the tropical colonies of Ceylon, India and Malaya, and from there throughout the east.

Hevea brasiliensis proved to be much the most successful rubber plant, soon ousting other varieties. *Ficus elastica* grew well in Java and Burma but its great disadvantages were the long period that must elapse before tapping can begin and the irregular production. *Manihot* varieties, such as *M. glaziovii* (Ceara or Manicoba rubber), were cultivated in Malaya and Ceylon but later abandoned when it was proved that *Hevea* had a much higher yield; and *Castilloa elastica*, planted in India, Ceylon and Malaya, did not prove to have as regular a yield as *Hevea*.

The development of the plantation industry in southeast Asia, once the *Hevea* tree had been successfully transplanted, was rapid and considerable quantities of plantation rubber were on the market by 1910. Many factors facilitated this: labour was plentiful, soil and climate were favourable, and, in contrast with the supplies of wild rubber, plantation rubber was accessible and could be shipped easily to the industrial centres of Europe and North America. With the growth in world demand in the 20th century, the area of land planted to rubber trees in this region increased enormously. Whereas up to the end of 1910 world demand could be met by wild rubber, most of which was supplied by Brazil and other South and Central American countries, wild rubber supplies have since dwindled into insignificance—apart from the brief resurgence of American rubber in 1942–45 when southeast Asia was overrun by the Japanese. By the 1960s Brazil produced less than 2% of the world total.

Another important source of supply in the late 19th and early 20th century, the giant vines of the *Landolphia* and *Clitandra* species growing in widely separated areas of tropical Africa, gradually fell into disuse after 1914. Because of the critical shortages of World War II, interest shifted at that time to temperate-zone plants that contain latex. The most important proved to be the guayule (q.v.), a shrub native to north-central Mexico and southern Texas. The second most important source, as far as yield and low-cost production are concerned, is the wild dandelion plant Kok-saghyz. Discovered by the Russian L. E. Rodin in the Tien Shan mountains in Kazakhstan in 1931, it was first developed by the Russians in the 1930s, and production spread to the United States during the war years. Another rubber-yielding plant, which received considerable attention during World War II, is the "Mexican" rubber vine (*Cryptostegia*), a plant indigenous to Madagascar, which was cultivated in India and the middle east before being introduced into Mexico and other parts of the American continent. After 1945 developments in plantation and synthetic rubber completely overshadowed these attempts to find alternative supplies of rubber latex. By 1950 world output of natural rubber was about double the prewar figure, the vast majority of it coming from Malaya, Indonesia, Ceylon and Indochina. The growth of world demand after 1945 and the fact that natural rubber continued to be preferred for about 30% of the rubber industry's products enabled the plantation industry to withstand the competition of synthetic rubber. Because of the technical factors that determine the use of natural and synthetic rubbers, competition between the two varieties was confined to about 40% of total consumption. Producers of synthetic rubber have two advantages over producers of the natural product: prices are relatively stable and production can be increased fairly quickly.

7. Development of Synthetic Rubber.—The synthetic rubber industry developed rapidly from 1914 onward, owing partly to the search by many peoples for national self-sufficiency and partly to the growing world demand for rubber, but its origins can be traced back to the first half of the 19th century. A synthesis of rubber could not be provided until more was known about the natural product itself and in this connection the pioneering work of the English scientist Michael Faraday (1791–1867) is important. It was Faraday who, in 1826, made one of the earliest chemical analyses of natural rubber and gave it the formula $C_{10}H_{16}$, later superseded by $(C_5H_8)_n$. Since that time many analyses have been made in the search for a cheap and easily produced synthetic rubber. In 1838 the German F. C. Himly obtained a volatile distillate from natural rubber, and in 1860 the Englishman C. G. Williams broke down rubber by distillation into three parts: oil, tar and "spirit" (the more volatile fraction and the main constituent), which he named isoprene. Thereafter the task was to explore the chemical nature of isoprene and if possible to reconvert it to rubber. The Frenchman Georges Bouchardat took the first step in 1875, when with the aid of hydrogen chloride gas and prolonged distillation he converted isoprene to a rubberlike substance.

In 1882 another Englishman, W. A. Tilden, produced isoprene by the destructive distillation of turpentine. He gave isoprene the formula $CH_2=C(CH_3)\cdot CH=CH_2$ and also reported that specimens of isoprene (even those obtained from nonrubber sources), either spontaneously on storage or under the influence of chemical agents, changed into a product resembling rubber. This "polymerization"—the process of causing simple molecules to join together and form long chains—was eventually represented by the equation $nC_5H_8 \rightarrow (C_5H_8)_n$; the n indicates the number is unknown. With the growing knowledge of the molecular structure of rubber the way was opened to many other experiments. After 1910, as a result of the progress made in England by F. E. Matthews, metallic sodium became the general polymerizing agent in converting isoprene to rubber. C. D. Harries made the same discovery almost simultaneously in Germany. From Russia came several significant contributions. In 1901 I. Kondakov discovered that dimethyl butadiene when heated with potash produced a rubberlike substance. In 1910 S. V. Lebedev polymerized butadiene (*q.v.*) to produce an elastic material and also achieved a considerable measure of success in obtaining butadiene from ethyl alcohol. Another Russian scientist, I. Ostromislensky, in 1913 published a book on his researches describing a number of procedures for the preparation of isoprene, as well as providing rubber chemists everywhere with much valuable data on the sources of butadiene.

The greatest stimulus to these efforts came, however, with the blockade of Germany during World War I. Faced by the greatest need, the Germans succeeded in manufacturing a synthetic rubbery material. Because of the shortage of essential raw materials this was based not on the more satisfactory isoprene or butadiene but on Kondakov's process for dimethyl butadiene. Two chief kinds of synthetic rubber resulted: Methyl "H" for use in hard rubbers and methyl "W" for use in soft rubber goods. Only about 2,500 tons were produced and with the cessation of hostilities the Germans resumed using the less costly and more satisfactory natural product. Research and experiments continued, however, throughout the western world and in 1926 the German G. Ebert succeeded in producing a sodium-polymerized rubber from butadiene.

The U.S.S.R. began to produce synthetic rubber in the early 1930s employing B. V. Byzov's process (SKA) from petroleum and Lebedev's alcohol process (SKB) using potatoes and limestone as raw materials. In Germany developments in the 1930s lay in improving three "buna" rubbers (so called from the initial syllables of the two materials used to make it, butadiene and natrium [sodium]): Buna 85, 115 and 120, the numbers referring to the length of the carbon chain in the polymerized molecule. From another series of experiments came the discovery of buna-S, referred to by the British as SBR (styrene-butadiene rubber) and by the Americans as GR-S (government rubber-styrene). Vulcanized synthetic rubbers, first produced on a commercial scale from buna rubbers in the late 1930s, were superior in mechanical properties to the earlier synthetic rubbers and often to the vulcanized natural product. In 1937 buna-N (or nitrile), developed in Germany, was introduced into the United States and proved to be of remarkable value because of its oil-resistant qualities.

As World War II approached, both Germany and the U.S.S.R. made tremendous efforts to achieve self-sufficiency; by Aug. 1939 the first large synthetic rubber plant had been opened in Germany with an annual capacity of 25,000 tons, and the two countries together accounted for almost the entire world output of synthetic rubber. The only other country then in the field was the United States, where the quantities produced experimentally were negligible for military purposes. However, the spur of wartime needs quickly brought about a transformation, and the U.S. mastered what became the five chief types of synthetic rubber—buna-S, buna-N, butyl, neoprene and Thiokol. By 1945 a total of 820,000 tons was available.

U.S. experiments before 1939 resulted in the discovery of new types of synthetic rubbers, notably neoprene, Thiokol and butyl.

The first of these, neoprene (first called Duprene), arose out of the work of Father J. A. Nieuwland, professor of chemistry at the University of Notre Dame; it was developed with the assistance of W. H. Carothers and Elmer K. Bolton of the E. I. du Pont de Nemours and Co. and was first manufactured and marketed by that company in 1931. The second, Thiokol, developed simultaneously by J. C. Patrick in the United States and J. Baer in Switzerland in 1926, is not sufficiently resilient to qualify as a true synthetic rubber but has proved useful because of its oil-resistant qualities. Butyl rubber was discovered in 1937 by two Americans, R. M. Thomas and W. J. Sparks, and was developed by the Standard Oil Company (New Jersey). This discovery and subsequent developments owed much to the stimulus provided by the Germans and to the existence of an arrangement for the exchange of scientific information between the I. G. Farbenindustrie A.G. and the Standard Oil company.

Although very large quantities of synthetic rubbers continued to be manufactured after World War II, none of the polymers possessed the precise molecular order of natural rubber. The lack of order in the molecular chain accounted for deficiencies in important properties, such as low resilience with corresponding increased heat buildup, compared with natural rubber. In 1953 two chemists, Karl Ziegler and Giulio Natta, discovered a family of stereospecific catalysts that were capable of introducing an exact and regular order to the structure of the polymers of various materials. The use of the Ziegler-type catalyst triethyl aluminium, combined with titanium tetrachloride, could be used to polymerize isoprene so that each molecule in the long-chain polymer was in a regular position and was virtually identical with the molecular structure of natural rubber. Commercial production of cis-1,4-polyisoprene was undertaken by firms in the U.S. and the Netherlands.

The same type of catalyst with butadiene as the monomer has been used to manufacture cis-1,4-polybutadiene rubber, which has been found to possess excellent abrasion resistance, especially in tires subjected to severe service conditions.

The introduction of catalysts that affect stereospecific polymerization opened up wide avenues for the development of new polymers such as ethylene-propylene rubber, which shows useful properties (*e.g.*, excellent weathering resistance). It is probably too early to assess the future of these new polymers, but they show promise of great potential. In 1956 H. J. Teas and R. S. Banduski announced the test tube synthesis of small amounts of natural rubber from acetate by the activity of enzymes that had been separated by centrifugation from freshly tapped *Hevea* latex. Whereas the synthesis of rubber began with the search for a substitute for caoutchouc, the development of the petrochemical industry after 1945 produced so many new "rubbery" materials that it became impossible to distinguish between synthetic rubber and plastics.

Because of British interest in natural rubber, research into synthetic rubber was not pursued during 1918–39 with the same intensity as in the U.S.S.R., Germany and the U.S. With the fall of Malaya (1942) British deficiencies in this field became apparent, and for the rest of World War II Britain was dependent upon the U.S. for supplies of synthetic rubber. In the period of 1945–50, in contrast to the course taken by the United States and the U.S.S.R., British manufacturers returned to an almost total dependence upon the natural product. After 1950, however, there developed in the United Kingdom a synthetic rubber industry whose output almost equaled the amount of natural rubber consumed by British industry.

For the chemistry of synthetic rubber and further details about world production see *Raw Materials, Synthetic Rubber,* below.

8. Production of Reclaimed Rubber and Rubber Latex.— The improvements in reclaimed rubber manufacture in the 20th century were so great that, in the 1960s, reclaimed rubber was no longer looked upon as a poor substitute for the natural product but was regarded as a compounding ingredient that is valuable because of its own physical and chemical properties.

Reclaimed rubber costs about 50% less than new rubber and is widely used in footwear and other branches of the industry. Consumption varies from country to country and in the 1960s amounted to about 15%–20% of new rubber consumption.

More recent has been the expansion of the trade in latex, which is now used directly, making the earlier expensive methods of preparing rubber solutions unnecessary. It is employed in the production of cellular or sponge rubber, footwear, for impregnating and proofing textile materials, and for making dipped goods of all kinds. All this has become possible since P. Schidrowitz's discovery (1921) that latex can be vulcanized and since the development of satisfactory methods of preserving, concentrating and shipping natural latex to manufacturing countries. German experiments with the polymerization and copolymerization of monomers in aqueous emulsions, which began before World War I, led the way to the modern production of synthetic latices of buna-S, buna-N and neoprene.

Until World War II the chief suppliers of latex were Malaya (now Malaysia) and the Dutch East Indies (now Indonesia). During the war increased quantities were obtained from the U.S. plantations in Liberia, but in the 1960s Malaya recovered its position as the principal source. (*See also Raw Materials, Natural Rubber Latex,* below.)

9. Distribution of the Industry.—In the 20th century the industry extended gradually from the older centres of manufacture in Europe and the United States to newer and less industrialized parts of the world. Increasingly, after the early 1930s, the British and especially the Americans established branch factories in many parts of the non-Communist world, including Japan, Australia, Argentina, Brazil and the Republic of South Africa. By doing so they were able to manufacture more economically for their foreign markets, to combat rising tariffs and, to a certain extent, to assuage the political and national susceptibilities of other nations.

II. RAW MATERIALS OF THE INDUSTRY
A. NATURAL RUBBER

1. Physical and Chemical Properties.—The uniqueness of rubber lies in its physical properties of extensibility and toughness. In its natural state, it is greatly affected by temperature, becoming harder when cooled (at 0°–10° C. it is opaque) and softer when heated (above 50° C. it becomes tackier and less elastic, decomposing into liquid form at 190°–200° C.). When vulcanized (*i.e.,* heated with sulfur at 120°–160° C.) it loses its thermoplasticity and becomes stronger and more elastic. The range of its plasticity, depending on the degree of vulcanization, can vary from extreme softness to the hardness of ebonite (hard rubber). Soft vulcanized rubber can be stretched repeatedly from 7–10 times its original length and immediately regain its approximate original dimensions. Natural rubber exhibits a tensile strength of 275–350 kg. per square centimetre and a modulus of elasticity of 11–24 kg. per square centimetre at 300% elongation (when compounded with 25% carbon black the modulus can increase to 50–90 kg. per square centimetre). Rubber is impermeable to water and to a large degree to gases. Because of its electrical resistivity soft rubber is used as an insulant and ebonite is employed as a high-grade dielectric.

Chemically, rubber is a polymer of isoprene (C_5H_8). Thousands (perhaps 40,000–50,000) of isoprene molecules are linked together by primary valence bonds

$$\begin{array}{ccccc} H & CH_3 & H & H \\ | & | & | & | \\ C & = & C & - & C & = & C \\ | & & & & | \\ H & & & & H \end{array}$$

Isoprene

(2-methyl-1, 3-butadiene)

into chains of enormous length. Because of the enormous size of its molecule, rubber has a molecular weight of about 300,000. The structure of rubber may be represented by the following diagram, which indicates the middle isoprene unit is repeated for an unknown number of times; the exact nature of the end groups also is not known:

$$\left[\begin{array}{cccc} H & CH_3 & H & H \\ | & | & | & | \\ C & - & C & = & C & - & C \\ | & & & & | \\ H & & & & H \end{array} \left(\begin{array}{cccc} H & CH_3 & H & H \\ | & | & | & | \\ C & - & C & = & C & - & C \\ | & & & & | \\ H & & & & H \end{array} \right)_n \begin{array}{cccc} H & CH_3 & H & H \\ | & | & | & | \\ C & - & C & = & C & - & C \\ | & & & & | \\ H & & & & H \end{array} \right]$$

Isoprene belongs to the class of organic compounds called terpenes (*q.v.*) and is related to turpentine in its chemical composition. Rubber is soluble in a number of solvents such as benzene, chloroform, carbon tetrachloride or ether, and, when treated with these solvents, can be changed into a viscous mass. In this plastic state it is workable and can be molded and compressed under pressure into any shape, which it will later retain permanently. A comparative table of the physical and chemical properties of natural and the most commonly used synthetic rubbers is given in *Manufacturing Processes,* below.

2. Botany.—Rubber, or caoutchouc (literally, "weeping wood"), is produced by a wide variety of plants. Commercially it has nearly always been obtained from the white, milky liquid known as latex (not to be confused with sap) that is found in small tubes or veins of the inner bark of rubber-yielding trees of the tropical and semitropical regions. The function of the latex juice in the life of the tree is not clear. It is easily obtained by cutting, or "tapping," the bark of the tree and catching the latex so released.

The chief source of crude rubber has been the *Hevea brasiliensis* (family Euphorbiaceae), a tall tree of soft wood with high branching limbs and a large area of bark. In its wild state it has been known to grow more than 125 ft. in height with a trunk girth of more than 18 ft. On the eastern plantations the average tree is usually 60–80 ft. high. The leaves are pointed trifoliate, smooth and dark green, about 8 in. in length. They are shed once a year while new leaves are forming. The small yellowish-green blossoms grow in clusters, each tree bearing both male and female flowers. The fruit capsules contain three speckled brown seeds, about an inch in length, which are exploded out of the seed pods when ripe. The structure of the bark is as follows: on the outside is a layer of cork, next to which lies a stone cell layer and then the soft latex-bearing cortex containing the latex tubes. Between the cortex and the heartwood lies the cambium, a paper-thin layer of tissues that propagates the growth of the bark cells on one side and of the heartwood on the other. When the tree is tapped the latex flows from the portion of the tree below the cut, not above it.

Another Brazilian tree, which spread throughout the tropics but was soon ousted by the *Hevea*, was the ceara, or manicoba, one of the well-known *Manihot* varieties. Earlier known and the most productive wild tree in Central America was the *Castilloa elastica* (family Moraceae). In the east, both the *Ficus elastica* tree (also of the Moraceae family and one of many rubber-producing *Ficus* species distributed throughout southeast Asia and the Pacific Islands) and the *Urceola elastica* (family Apocynaceae), a vinelike plant of the East Indies, yielded considerable quantities of wild rubber. The sources of African wild rubber were various. *Funtumia elastica* trees (family Apocynaceae) are widely distributed in tropical regions. Unlike the American and Asiatic supplies, however, most African rubber was produced by the giant vines of the *Landolphia* and *Clitandra* species (family Apocynaceae). The plants gutta-percha (family Sapotaceae) and balata (of the genus *Mimusops*) also provide a rubberlike material. Gutta-percha is obtained from a species of trees mainly indigenous to Malaya. Introduced to Europe in the middle of the 17th century, it came to be used in many ways, including the insulation of underwater cables. Trees that yield balata latex are native to the northwestern parts of South America. After World War II gutta-percha and balata were replaced by synthetic plastics based on polyethylene. (*See also* GUTTA-PERCHA.)

Many other plants contain rubber latex. The two best-known are members of the Compositae—guayule (*Parthenium argentatum*), a low-growing shrub of many varieties indigenous to America, and the Russian dandelion *Taraxacum kok-saghyz*. Unlike the trees and vines mentioned above, the rubber in the guayule plant is contained in the bark, roots, leaves and stems; the latex of the Russian dandelion is contained largely in the roots. The guayule bush, in its wild state, usually requires four to five years before it can be harvested; Kok-saghyz appears to be a perennial plant but under cultivation it is treated as an annual or biennial. Besides the Kok-saghyz two other wild dandelion plants have come to be regarded as secondary rubber-yielding plants: *Scorzonera tau-saghyz* and *krym-saghyz*. Other plants introduced into the U.S. are *Cryptostegia grandiflora* and *C. madagascarensis* (hybrid: *C. florida*). These are shrublike vines whose rubber is uniformly high in quality; they give their maximum yield within a year of seeding and flourish in a wide variety of soils and climates. Like that of the guayule bush the rubber of *Cryptostegia* is contained in the leaves, bark, seed pods and stems. (*See also* DANDELION; EUPHORBIACEAE; FIG; GUAYULE.)

BY COURTESY OF U.S. RUBBER CO.

TRUNK OF A RUBBER TREE (HEVEA BRASILIENSIS) SHOWING LATEX FLOWING FROM TAPPING CUT INTO CUP. DIAGONAL LINES ABOVE TAP ARE SCARS OF PREVIOUS CUTTINGS

3. Wild Rubber.—*Tapping.* —The methods employed in harvesting wild rubber have been, and still are, numerous and usually primitive. The aim has been to obtain the maximum amount of latex and this has been done either by stripping the bark and tapping the laticiferous system or, on occasions, by felling and draining the tree.

Coagulation.—The processes used are varied and largely primitive. Most wild rubber is coagulated by revolving a latex-covered stick above a smoke fire until several layers of dried latex form themselves into a "ball," or "biscuit," of hard rubber. By this means the rubber is freed of the water and proteid matter that encourage putrefaction and reduce elasticity. The latex of some trees, such as the *Castilloa,* does not respond readily to smoking and has to be coagulated by mixing with the juice of certain vines.

Marketing.—Wild rubber has usually reached the market in the same condition as prepared by the native. The weight of the consignments, described as "balls," "knuckles," "lumps," "flakes," "tongues," etc., varied from 80 to 300 lb.

4. Plantation Rubber.—*Climate and Soil.*—The *Hevea brasiliensis* plantations of southeast Asia are mainly in the tropical and subtropical regions of Malaya, Indonesia, Ceylon, India, Burma, Thailand, Indo-China and Borneo, the first two being the most important. These regions provide the necessary conditions of rainfall, humidity, equable temperature and altitude. An example of favourable climatic conditions is Malaya, where the maximum day temperature in planting districts is 85°–87° F., the night temperatures about 10° lower, the annual rainfall 80–120 in., and the humidity 80%–90%, accompanied by heavy night dews.

Although certain species of rubber trees can be grown at higher elevations, 1,500 ft. is thought to be the highest altitude for *Hevea* plantings. A well-drained, light to medium sandy loam is most suitable. Considerable variations exist: in Java most soils used for rubber planting are of volcanic origin; in Sumatra and in Malaya rubber grows on either light, sandy or heavier alluvial soils. Land planted to rubber trees has usually had to be cleared of virgin jungle and the extent to which the ground is cleared and kept clear can only be determined by local conditions. Much depends on whether the weeds surrounding the trees have a deep root system, which might interfere with rubber growing. A protective covering of indigenous plants (except for the harmful lalang grass) is desirable to avoid soil erosion, to provide humus and to help combat the attacks of insects and microorganisms. In young plantations the protective interplanting of cover crops such as coffee and cacao is sometimes practised.

Planting Methods.—Seeds are selected from clones that have shown high yields, good bark characteristics and resistance to disease. The seedlings, which have been raised in a nursery, are planted in even rows. Density varies from 100 to 300 trees per acre and the trees are gradually thinned out over seven or eight years. Generally speaking, the more widely spaced trees are sturdier and have a larger girth and thicker bark. Another method of propagation is bud grafting; in this method, a dormant bud selected from a high-yielding tree is grafted onto the seedling, usually after the first or second year of growth. Depending upon the climatic conditions, grafting is carried out either in the nursery or in the plantation. After ten days the seedling is pruned just above the grafted bud, which later grows to form the new tree. The advantage of bud grafting, as of artificial pollination, is that it is more likely to reproduce high-quality yielding trees. Careful seed selection and bud grafting have raised the average annual yield from the 1920 level of about 300 lb. of dry sheet rubber per acre to over 1,000 lb. per acre and, in some individual cases, to even higher yields. However, these high yields apply only to the most carefully managed and scientifically directed estate plantations. Extensive propagation techniques still have to be applied to most plantations and to small native holdings.

Diseases.—Despite the hardiness of the *Hevea* tree it is not free from attack by diseases and insect pests. Damage can be done by termites, caterpillars and scale insects. Various types of fungus and mildew also affect roots, branches and leaves. Of the root and branch diseases *Ustulina zonata* is the most common. The leaf-fall disease, of greatest significance in the eastern plantations, is due to *Oidium,* a parasitic mildew. This parasite attacks young leaves and buds after refoliation. Unscientific tapping can cause various rots and diseases of the tapping panel, thus preventing the healthy growth of the renewing bark and, in the case of the brown bast disease, causing the bark to crack and the latex to coagulate and stop flowing altogether.

Tapping.—The tapping is generally begun 3–4 ft. from the ground. A thin shaving of bark is removed with a diagonal cut extending a third or half the distance around the tree at an angle of 30°. Some estates employ a V-shaped cut. Depending upon the thickness of the shaving and the frequency of tapping, the incisions continue to be made until they reach the ground or another tapping panel is begun on another part of the tree. If the tree is not injured in tapping, the renewed bark and latex vessels, which take several years to recover, may be tapped again. As latex flows more freely around dawn, tapping is begun at sunrise. Tapping methods and systems vary from year to year and from estate to estate. The best system can only be decided upon after several years of experiment and observation, and different techniques are necessary with the different species. The *Castilloa elastica,* for instance, gives its best yield with two to six tappings per year, whereas the *Hevea* responds best to tappings every day or every alternate day. To avoid exhausting the tree, and to encourage growth and yield, some estates rest the trees over a period of several months.

On *Hevea* plantations it is usual to begin tapping when the tree has reached five or six years of age. Normally output continues to increase (although there is an astonishing inconsistency of yield) for 10 to 15 years and, with care, the economical life of a plantation tree may extend over 25 to 30 years.

Collection of Latex.—The latex runs into cups attached to the trees. It is then emptied into pails and taken to the nearest collecting station, where it is weighed for payment. From there it goes in larger tanks to the nearest rubber factory and is prepared for shipment abroad. As the quality of the rubber is materially affected by the standard of cleanliness in handling the latex, on the large estates every precaution is taken to ensure that the latex reaches the rubber factory uncontaminated. However, standards of cleanliness vary. In the case of guayule shrubs rubber is obtained by chopping and grinding the entire plant. The latex of Kok-saghyz is extracted from the roots.

Coagulation and Preparation for Market.—The latex juice as it comes from the tree consists largely of water with small quantities of sugars, inorganic salts and proteins in solution. Moving hither and thither in this liquid (Brownian movement) are the

BY COURTESY OF B. F. GOODRICH CO.

SLABS OF RUBBER RISING TO THE SURFACE OF A COAGULATING TANK

Year	U.S.	U.K.	France	Federal Republic of Germany	Canada	World Total*
1951 . . .	46,750	16,445	3,833	1,489	2,185	83,500
1955 . . .	86,478	31,600	8,139	12,437	3,756	166,750
1957 . . .	75,009	27,000	10,474	12,000	3,037	164,000
1959 . . .	71,745	30,500	13,047	13,850	3,337	183,000
1961 . . .	43,795	24,300	12,748	13,500	1,487	158,750
1962 . . .	41,936	23,000	12,859	16,600	1,306	166,000

*Including estimates for Communist countries.
Note: The world totals include estimated consumption of countries other than those mentioned.

globules of rubber, about $\frac{1}{16,000}$ in. in diameter, that account for 30%–40% by weight of the latex juice. When acids or certain salts are added to the latex the particles of rubber unite to form a clot of solid rubber, a process known as coagulation.

On modern eastern plantations the latex is first strained to remove dirt and foreign matter. It is then poured into tanks where it is diluted with an approximately equal amount of water, and a solution of acetic or formic acid or sodium silicofluoride is added to cause coagulation. This must be done within 24 hr. after collection, otherwise the latex will turn sour and decompose. The tanks are equipped with a series of aluminum partitions that can be lowered into the liquid so that, as the rubber rises to the surface, it is held between them and coagulates in the form of slabs. These slabs of soft doughy mass (coagulum) are then washed and pressed between several pairs of metal cylinders, by which means most of the liquid and impurities are removed. When "smoked sheet" is made the last pair of rollers is ribbed and sheets emerge about 0.125 in. thick. They are cut into convenient lengths and hung in a smokehouse for about a week. "Smoked sheet" makes up most of the produce of the average estate. "Pale crepe" is obtained by passing the slabs of coagulum between heavy corrugated iron rollers revolving at irregular speeds. They are further processed and air-dried in large sheds or drying rooms. A small quantity of sodium bisulfite mixed with acetic acid produces the pale yellow colour. The care taken with these processes determines the grade the rubber will obtain in the market.

Much rubber is still coagulated and processed by primitive methods. The native with a few trees, who cannot get his produce to a central rubber station, coagulates his latex by pouring it into pans and permitting the moisture to evaporate gradually. Sometimes sulfuric acid or alum, which later adversely affect the manufacturing process, are used. Most of this produce is milled to crepe in one of the plantation factories and sold as an inferior grade. After being graded and packed, the slabs are shipped to their destination, usually in squat 200-lb. bales.

Natural Rubber Latex.—After about 1920 a considerable trade in *Hevea* latex grew up as improved methods of concentrating, preserving and transporting the latex were developed. The major problem was to secure a steady supply of the uncoagulated liquid. Ammonia was adopted as the standard preservative and later formaldehyde and potassium hydroxide were used for special purposes. From 1934 onward the latex was transported in special ships in bulk, instead of in steel drums as formerly. Gradually, through a system of centrifugation and creaming (patented in 1923 by W. L. Utermark) and the later electrodecantation process, it be-

came possible to obtain concentrated latices with dry rubber content of 60%, or even higher; an evaporation process developed in the east yielded a concentration of 75%. By the 1930s the bulk of the world's dipped goods were made with latex rather than the older-style rubber solutions. Table I shows world consumption of natural latex in representative years beginning with 1951.

Marketing.—Few commodities have experienced greater fluctuations in price levels than rubber. In the 19th century, when the supply was principally wild rubber, prices fluctuated between 50 cents and $1 a pound. From a high in 1910 of $2.88 a pound for plantation rubber, the price fell in 1915 to a low of $58\frac{1}{2}$ cents a pound. By the early 1920s the price was lower still and in 1922 the British government's Stevenson restriction plan came into force to control average prices. The refusal of the Dutch producers to enter the plan, along with other causes, led to its abandonment in 1928. Price fluctuations continued and in June 1932 the monthly average spot price of plantation ribbed smoked sheets on the New York market was at a record low level of less than three cents a pound. With the introduction of the International Rubber Regulation agreement in June 1934 the British and the Dutch governments tried to control supplies. Until the agreement was discontinued in 1943 prices varied from 9 cents to 25 cents per pound. From 1942 to 1947 the price of plantation rubber was controlled by the British and U.S. governments. There was a subsequent upsurge in 1950 when the price rose to $64\frac{1}{2}$ cents a pound. In the mid-1960s it was approximately 31 cents, prices having dropped because of a rapid increase in the consumption of synthetics and also because of changes in demand conditions. The development of synthetic rubber tended to stabilize prices.

The most striking change in the distribution of plantation supplies has been the extent to which Britain lost its 19th-century lead as the chief distributor of all types of rubber. Another important change has been the extent to which the chief fault of wild rubber, its variability, has given way to the more uniform standards of plantation produce.

Geographical Distribution of Plantation Industry.—The total area of plantations in the east amounted in 1900 to 5,000 ac.; in 1910 to 1,000,000; and in 1920 to 4,000,000. After the end of World War II the total area exceeded 9,000,000 ac. (including small native holdings as well as large plantations) and in the mid-1960s it was in the region of 11,500,000 ac. In the 1960s, even allowing for the African plantations and the cultivation of Kok-saghyz in the U.S.S.R., all but 2% or 3% of the world's supply of natural rubber still came from the *Hevea* trees in the eastern plantations.

Most of the plantation acreage in the mid-1960s was in Malaya and Indonesia, each country accounting for about 3,400,-000 ac. Slightly more than half of the acres in Malaya were in estates, whereas in Indonesia about three-fourths of the acreage was in small holdings. The third largest number of plantation acres was the 715,000 in Africa. Smaller acreages were in Ceylon, Indochina, India, Sarawak and Latin America.

B. SYNTHETIC RUBBER

The term synthetic rubber is used to describe an ever growing number of elastic materials, some of which closely resemble natural rubber while others have completely different physical properties. Since World War II, precise terminology has not kept pace with the rapid developments in the synthetic and plastics industries. Hence, the following description of the production of certain synthetic rubbers can serve only as an introduction to the developments whose scope now extends far beyond the early efforts of rubber chemists to reproduce the properties of natural rubber.

Synthetic rubber is produced by chemically rearranging the molecular structures of certain unsaturated hydrocarbons and their derivatives. By polymerization, great numbers of hydrocarbon molecules are made to link up in long chains, the repeating units being known as monomers and the resulting macromolecule as a polymer. The size and structure of the macromolecule confers on rubber its resilience and extensibility. (*See* also NATURAL PRODUCTS, TOTAL SYNTHESIS OF.)

The production of synthetic rubber proceeds in two stages, the first being the preparation of the monomers, the second the polymerization process. Petroleum has so far been the most suitable and most important raw material, but other substances, such as potatoes and grains (which produce alcohol), coke, limestone, salt and sulfur all play an important part.

1. SBR (GR-S, or Buna-S).—This synthetic rubber is a copolymer of butadiene (CH_2=CH—CH=CH_2) and styrene (C_6H_5—CH=CH_2). Butadiene can be produced from petroleum or alcohol by several methods: (a) the pyrolysis or "cracking" of petroleum; (b) the treatment of butane found in natural gas and petroleum; (c) the passing of alcohol over a heated mixture of oxides of aluminum and zinc; (d) the fermentation of carbohydrates to produce butylene glycol.

Styrene is usually prepared by the distillation of a mixture of benzene (extracted from coal tar) and ethylene (produced either from alcohol or petroleum) in the presence of catalyst, usually aluminum chloride.

The copolymerization of the butadiene and the styrene takes place in an emulsion in the presence of an active initiator, such as cumene hydroperoxide and *p*-menthane hydroperoxide, which allows the conversion to occur at a low temperature (5° C.). SBR is usually prepared with 75% butadiene and 25% styrene; the proportion will, however, vary according to the desired degree of elasticity. Its molecular structure after polymerization may be represented as:

SBR type rubber can then be subjected to the same manufacturing processes as natural rubber. Its essential differences from natural rubber are its poorer resilience, lack of building tack and greater heat build-up, making it unsuitable for use in heavy-duty truck tires; its advantages are better resistance to oxygen and weathering and greater uniformity of curing rate and plasticity.

2. Nitrile (Buna-N).—This second synthetic rubber is a copolymer of butadiene and acrylonitrile, CH_2=$CHCN$. The butadiene is produced by the same methods as for buna-S. Acrylonitrile can be obtained (1) through a reaction process of ethylene chlorohydrin and sodium cyanide that gives hydracrylic nitrile, from which acrylonitrile is obtained through a dehydration process; (2) by the addition of hydrocyanic acid to acetylene in presence of a catalyst.

The polymerization process takes place in the presence of an emulsifier and a catalyst at a temperature of about 13° C. Varying combinations of butadiene and acrylonitrile produce different rubbers that are valued chiefly for their resistance to petroleum, aromatic oils, abrasion and high temperatures. The molecular structure of nitrile after polymerization may be shown as:

3. Butyl.—Butyl is a copolymer of isobutylene (also known as isobutene),

and 2%–3% of isoprene or small amounts of other unsaturated hydrocarbons. Isobutylene and isoprene are obtained from cracked refinery gas. The four-carbon fraction usually contains 10%–35% isobutylene, which is extracted by absorption in sulfuric acid, neutralized and distilled to yield pure isobutylene. Isoprene is obtained from the five-carbon fraction through an extractive distillation process.

The polymerization of butyl rubber is a low-temperature ionic process, initiated at temperatures of about −94° C. (−140° F.) in the presence of an initiator of the Friedel-Crafts type (*see* also FRIEDEL-CRAFTS REACTION). Boron fluoride is passed through the isobutylene to ensure induction, while pentane or ethylene are added to absorb the heat of reaction. The molecular structure of the polymer is as follows:

The major advantages of butyl over natural rubber are its greater resistance to oxidative aging, ozone and acids.

4. Neoprene.—Neoprene is a polymer of chloroprene (2-chloro-1,3-butadiene), C_4H_5Cl, which is produced by a process that uses acetylene as the starting material. In synthetic rubber factories acetylene is usually made by cracking hydrocarbons from petroleum or natural gas with a high-temperature electric arc. The acetylene yields vinylacetylene through catalytic diminution, and hydrochloric acid is then combined with the vinylacetylene in the presence of a catalyst to produce chloroprene.

Chloroprene will polymerize spontaneously to form a rubbery substance. Commercially the polymerization process is achieved in an emulsion, sulfur being used as a modifier. The latex is allowed to age in a solution of tetramethylthiuram disulfide, which restores the plasticity of the polymer, or it can be milled dry. Its molecular structure can be represented as follows:

Neoprene rubbers show high tensile strength in the absence of carbon black and resist oxidative degeneration, weathering and ozone and are only slightly inferior to nitrile in oil resistance.

5. Thiokols.—The Thiokols, or polysulfide rubbers, are compounds of an ethylene dihalide and an alkali polysulfide. Thiokol A is a compound of ethylene dichloride and sodium polysulfide. Ethylene dichloride, CH_2Cl—CH_2Cl, is a direct compound of ethylene and chlorine. Sodium polysulfide (Na_2S_n, where $n = 2$ to 5) can be prepared by dissolving sulfur in a solution of sodium sulfide or by heating it with aqueous caustic soda.

The polymerization process is carried out at a temperature of approximately 70° C. The ethylene dichloride is added to an aqueous solution of sulfur in sodium hydroxide. Only two or three hours are necessary for the formation of the synthetic latex, which can be represented as follows:

There are a number of Thiokol rubbers, their qualities varying according to the ingredients used. Thiokol B is obtained from dichloroethyl ether and a sodium polysulfide; its structure may be represented thus:

$$\left[\begin{array}{cccccc} H & H & & H & H & S & S \\ | & | & & | & | & \| & \| \\ -C & -C & -O & -C & -C & -S & -S- \\ | & | & & | & | & & \\ H & H & & H & H & & \end{array} \right]_n$$

The advantages of Thiokol rubbers are their oil and solvent resistance and their impermeability to gases.

6. Stereospecific Rubbers.—Although polybutadiene and polyisoprene had been manufactured by emulsion polymerization processes similar to that used for SBR, the resultant polymers were of poor quality because of the lack of regularity in the configuration of the molecular chain.

The discovery of stereospecific catalysts by Karl Ziegler led to the announcement in Dec. 1954 by the B. F. Goodrich Co. of the synthesis of natural rubber. This cis-1,4-polyisoprene possessed a very high degree of regularity in long-chain molecules; its properties and characteristics closely resembled natural rubber. By the early 1960s polyisoprene rubber had been substituted for natural rubber to only a very limited extent and only in fields where its cheaper cost made it economically attractive, *e.g.*, in shoe soles, and where technical requirements were minimal. Polyisoprene rubber was, in the early 1960s, seriously inferior to natural rubber in many properties, particularly processability and versatility. In April 1956 Phillips Petroleum revealed that it had produced cis-1,4-polybutadiene, which has proved to have excellent wearing qualities and much better low-temperature performance than natural rubber.

These newer stereospecific polymers were produced in a solution process. The monomers are dissolved in a solvent and the catalyst is added, the ingredients being carefully dried to remove any water. The polymer produced in this solution process dissolves in the solvent as it is formed and when the polymerization has proceeded to the desired degree the reaction is terminated by destroying the catalyst. The spent catalyst is then removed, and the solvent and rubber are recovered.

All stereoregular rubbers are produced through polymerization in the presence of an ionic type catalyst (metallic lithium or a Ziegler-type initiator). The Firestone process calls for 0.1 part of lithium per 100 parts of isoprene, which are heated at 30°–40° C. in the polymerization process.

Natural rubber continued in the mid-1960s to be superior to synthetics for many purposes because of its oxygen-containing substances and peroxide linkages, which give natural rubber better milling characteristics.

7. World Production of Synthetic Rubber.—The world output of synthetic rubber in 1935 was estimated at 10,000 tons; by 1939 it had increased to 72,000 tons, of which Germany and the U.S.S.R. together produced all but a small fraction that was made in the U.S. on an experimental scale. (World production of synthetic rubber in 1962 was estimated at 2,242,500 tons, compared with 2,105,000 tons of natural rubber.) A Russian report states that in 1938 the U.S.S.R. produced 53,000 tons; by 1943 Germany had an annual production of about 116,000 tons. The output of synthetic rubber in the U.S. was enlarged from approximately 8,000 long tons in 1941 to 235,000 by 1943 and 820,000 in 1945. In 1939 the U.S. consumed 54% of world rubber supplies, but only 0.3% of this was synthetic. In 1950 the U.S. proportion of world consumption of crude rubber was still more than half (55%), but 43% of American needs were met by the synthetic rubber industry. By 1960 the U.S. proportion of total world consumption was 41.3%, 68.6% being synthetic. A comparison of world consumption figures of natural and synthetic rubber shows that in 1940 the percentage of synthetic rubber was about 4% but by 1960 this had risen to 47.3%. Approximate prices of synthetic supplies in the mid-1960s were as follows: nitrile 49 cents; SBR 23 cents; neoprene 41 cents; butyl 23 cents; and Thiokol 50 cents per pound. Table II gives information on the production of synthetic rubber since the end of World War II. The material was obtainable after the war only from the United States, the U.S.S.R., Canada and the Federal Republic of Germany, and the problem of dollar exchange made its purchase from North America problematic for many European countries. In the immediate postwar years there was a natural tendency in the case of Britain, France and the Netherlands to concentrate on the natural produce of their overseas territories. However, the importance of the new U.K. synthetic rubber producing industry (56,990 tons in 1959; 90,015 tons in 1960) should not be overlooked.

TABLE II.—*Production of Synthetic Rubber in Selected Countries* (in long tons)

	United States				Canada Total	Federal Republic of Germany Total	Total
Year	SBR	Neo-prene	Butyl	Nitrile			
1945 . . .	719,404	45,651	47,426	7,871	45,717	——	866,069*
1950 . . .	358,248	50,067	55,832	12,037	58,440	——	534,624*
1955 . . .	791,197†	91,357	55,291	32,623	103,896	10,902	1,085,266
1957 . . .	907,534	110,721	66,936	32,982	132,141	11,602	1,262,666
1959 . . .	1,130,660	124,815	81,008	43,169	100,682	48,126	1,640,000
1960 . . .	1,166,151	134,442	97,950	37,899	159,673	79,792	1,887,500

*Excluding German production. †Previous to 1955, excluding oil content.

Table II shows that synthetic rubber was playing an increasingly important part in world supplies by the 1960s. In the United States the government-owned synthetic plants, built to meet war needs, were transferred to private control on May 1, 1955.

C. RECLAIMED, OR SCRAP, RUBBER

Scrap, such as is obtained from used tires and tubes, can be prepared for reuse in manufacture by a number of processes. It is first chopped and ground and then subjected either to the heater process or (especially if the scrap contains fabric) the alkali process. This reduces the reclaim to a clean, softened mixture, which after washing and drying is ready for reprocessing by the customary means (see *Manufacturing Processes*, below).

The reclaimed rubber industry has grown to important proportions in the 20th century, especially in the United States, where output tripled, for example, in the 1920s alone. The trade rose and fell with economic conditions (in the depression of 1933 reclaim was no more than one-fifth of total supplies) until under the stimulus of war shortages it rose to 261,000 long tons in 1944. After World War II about 80%–85% of all reclaimed rubber was recovered in the United States (346,000 tons consumed in 1951). The United Kingdom, the Federal Republic of Germany, the U.S.S.R., France and Japan also became leading producers: the U.K. accounted for 7%–8%; the Federal Republic of Germany increased production from 15,339 long tons in 1950 to 45,944 in 1960; France similarly increased production from 14,410 long tons in 1950 to 29,546 in 1960; and Japan's reclaiming capacity was put at about 40,000 long tons in the mid-1960s.

D. MATERIALS OTHER THAN RUBBER

1. Reinforcing and Filling Materials.—These materials are used in rubber manufacture to strengthen or cheapen, or to produce a specific physical effect, in the finished product; for example, to increase hardness, to build up resistance to abrasion, chemicals and heat, to improve electrical properties or to change specific gravity. The most common fillers (*i.e.*, cheaper materials used to bulk out the rubber) include barites (a mineral containing barium sulfate), asbestos powder, hard clays, Factice (a rubbery substance made by the action of sulfur on various vegetable oils), talc (hydrated silicate of magnesium) and limestone. Carbon black is used in the compounding of both natural and synthetic rubbers. Other common reinforcing agents, which are used according to the properties desired in the final product, are zinc oxide, magnesium carbonate, calcium silicate and silicon dioxide.

2. Colours.—Until the introduction in the 20th century of organic accelerators, the colours used in rubber were almost entirely earth colours and inorganic pigments, such as iron oxides, zinc oxide, zinc sulfide and lithopone (a mixture of barium sulfate and zinc sulfide). Some of these have been replaced by more varied and stronger organic dyestuffs (phthalocyanine colours) and the pure iron oxides. Most significant was the introduction in the 1930s of titanium dioxide, which is now regarded as the best white pigment. Many considerations influence the choice of colours, including the possible interactions between the colours employed and the other raw materials used in rubber manufacture.

3. Plasticizers and Softeners.—Since the earliest days of the industry all kinds of vegetable and mineral oils, oxidized petroleum residues (mineral rubber), fatty acids or their zinc salts, waxes, tars, pitches and resins have been used to facilitate and improve the mixing and processing of rubber compounds. For softening synthetic rubbers, resins derived from coal by distillation have been most successful.

4. Curing or Vulcanizing Agents.—These are compounding ingredients that induce vulcanization. The most common was, and still is, sulfur, used in the form of ground brimstone. Tetramethylthiuram disulfide, selenium and tellurium are also used, usually with some sulfur. Vulcanization can also result from the employment of benzoyl peroxide, aromatic (i.e., ring) compounds containing either two or three nitrogen atoms, dioximes, diisocyanates and dinitroso compounds.

5. Accelerators of Vulcanization.—These substances not only accelerate the vulcanization process but also enable it to be carried out at a much lower temperature; in addition, they improve the quality of the manufactured product. Since George Oenslager's discovery in 1905 of the accelerating value of certain organic substances, many new accelerators have appeared; they include the thiurams, dithiocarbamates, zinc alkylxanthates, nitrosodimethylaniline, diphenylguanidine and mercaptobenzothiazole. The latter is the principal accelerator used in tire and other high-grade manufacture. Accelerators usually achieve economies in time, heat and sulfur. A combination of stearic acid and zinc oxide is among the so-called "activators" often used with organic accelerators to increase their efficiency.

The traditional inorganic accelerators—litharge (lead monoxide), red and white lead, zinc oxide (the most widely used), magnesium oxide and lime—are used mainly as fillers and as activators of the organic accelerators.

6. Antioxidants and Age Resistors.—These are organic chemicals that are used to delay the perishing effect oxygen has on rubber. Certain of them also help to resist deterioration from repeated flexure, such as that suffered by automobile tires, and from heat. The most commonly used are aldol-alpha-naphthylamine, phenyl-beta-naphthylamine, di-beta-naphthyl-para-phenylenediamine, and polymerized trimethyldihydroquinoline.

7. Fabrics.—Besides rubber and chemicals, cotton, rayon and nylon are consumed by the industry in the manufacture of tires, footwear, mechanical devices of all kinds and waterproof garments.

III. MANUFACTURING PROCESSES

Mention has already been made at the beginning of this article of the principal developments in the evolution of the industry.

While natural rubber is more easily manufactured than synthetic rubber, the manufacturing processes for the two forms are roughly the same. Table III compares the salient features and properties of the most commonly used synthetic rubbers with those of natural rubber. The criterion of success of these synthetic rubbers lay not in their resemblance to the natural product but rather in their improved functional properties.

1. Washing and Drying.—Before the advent of high-grade plantation rubber and synthetic supplies, wild rubber often came on the market in adulterated form. The practice of washing rubber has almost ceased except when dealing with small quantities of wild rubber. Similarly, the practice of drying rubber after it has been washed has almost been abandoned; where it continues it is usual to dry in a vacuum dryer or by warm air.

2. Masticating.—After the rubber is cut, it is placed in a mill that first masticates and then compounds it. There are several types of such machines but the purpose of all of them is to plasticize the rubber and ensure a uniform dispersion of the chemicals added. Until the reappearance of internal mixers in the 1920s, more than 100 years after Thomas Hancock discovered the process of rubber mastication, developments followed along the lines of the machinery devised by E. M. Chaffee, the U.S. pioneer. The original design, consisting of two parallel cast-iron rolls so adjusted that the rubber could be ground and compressed between them, has remained. The important changes have been in the size of the machine and the speed of operation. Mixing mills vary from 20 to 84 in. in length and 16 to 28 in. in diameter. The rolls of 84 in., regarded as the mechanical limit, are capable of handling a batch of 300 lb. of rubber in 25 to 40 min. The rolls are water-cooled internally. The tremendous power of these two rolls, operating at different speeds (the back roll turns faster than the front one; speed ratios from 1.2:1 to 1.5:1 are customary), coupled with slight oxidation and the heat generated by the resulting friction, eventually reduces the chunks of cold rubber into a plasticized sheet that adheres to one of the cylinders.

As the demands for manufactured rubber products have grown, and the need for larger, faster and more powerful machines has been felt, there has been a tendency to return to the earlier enclosed mixing machines, along the lines of Hancock's pioneering masticator. About three-fourths of the rubber consumed worldwide in the 1960s was processed in internal mixers such as the "Banbury." These machines, working by internal pressure and rotating parts, have a capacity ranging from 600 to 1,000 lb. As against the 25 to 40 min. required to handle 150 to 300 lb. of rubber on the external mixer, the internal mixers may reduce this to 5 or 8 min. In addition to saving time these machines produce a much more uniform product than that dependent on hand operations on the external mill. On the other hand, the high power requirements and the fact that the process is essentially batch-type mixing rather than continuous flow have led to the development of mixer-extruders and to experiments with a new kind of open three-roll mill, which mixes and compounds the rubber and delivers it in a continuous sheet. Milling and mixing procedures vary according to the kind of rubber used.

3. Compounding or Mixing.—When the rubber is sufficiently masticated and softened either on an external or internal mill, it is ready to have the dry pigments added. This is one of the most

TABLE III.—*Features and Properties of the Most Commonly Used Polymers*

Common name	Natural rubber	SBR	Butyl	Poly-butadiene	Neoprene	Nitrile	Polyisoprene
Main features	High pure gum strength. Good general mechanical properties.	Resistant to moderate heat, aging and abrasion. Fairly good mechanical properties.	Outstanding air retention, good damping. Resists elevated temperature, ozone and weathering.	High resilience and abrasion resistance. Resistant to moderate heat, aging. Good low temperature properties.	Resistant to weather, ozone and elevated temperature. Moderate oil resistance. Flame resistant.	Good resistance to gasoline and oils. Good abrasion resistance.	High pure gum strength. Can be used as a direct replacement for natural rubber.
Tensile strength	Excellent	Good-excellent	Fair	Fair	Good	Good	Excellent
Elongation	Excellent	Good	Good	Fair-good	Good	Good	Excellent
Resilience	Excellent	Good	Poor	Excellent	Fair	Fair	Excellent
Hardness range (durometer)	30–100	40–100	30–100	45–80	40–95	20–90	30–90
Electrical resistivity	Excellent	Good	Excellent	Good	Fair	Poor	Excellent
Gas impermeability	Good	Good	Outstanding	Good	Good	Good	Good
Abrasion resistance	Good	Good-excellent	Fair	Outstanding	Good	Excellent	Good
Resistance to aliphatic hydrocarbons (gasoline, oils)	Poor	Poor	Poor	Poor	Fair	Good	Poor
Resistance to aromatic hydrocarbons (e.g., benzene)	Poor	Poor	Poor	Poor	Poor	Fair	Poor
Resistance to alcohol	Good	Fair	Excellent	Fair	Fair	Excellent	Good
Resistance to heat aging at 100° C.	Fair	Fair-good	Excellent	Fair-good	Good	Good	Fair
Resistance at low temperature	Good	Good	Good	Excellent	Fair	Fair-good	Good

BY COURTESY OF U.S. RUBBER CO.

CALENDER, OR COATING MACHINE, WHICH PRODUCES RUBBERIZED FABRICS AND RUBBER SHEETING

critical stages in rubber manufacture. There are a few uses of rubber, for example in adhesive tape and rubber cements, where natural and synthetic latices are used in the raw, *i.e.*, uncompounded, state. However, these rubbers are sensitive to temperature changes and cannot be employed where resilience and toughness are needed, and consequently nearly all rubbers, natural or synthetic, are treated with varying amounts of general compounding ingredients (see *Raw Materials of the Industry,* above). The same classes of ingredients—plasticizers, fillers, reinforcing materials, antioxidants, lubricants, accelerators (stabilizers), activators, colorants and curing (vulcanizing) agents—appear in most formulations but the quantities of each, and the type selected within each class, depend on the material to be treated and the physical and chemical properties desired in the finished product. There can be few industrial processes where generalizations are so misleading.

Hard rubber, or ebonite, requires among other things a high proportion of sulfur in the mixture. Articles made directly from latex do not require plasticizers and softeners. With synthetic rubbers—particularly SBR type rubbers—the proportional gain in tensile strength due to the incorporation of reinforcing agents is much greater than it is with natural rubber. Less sulfur is also required. Softeners are not so effective, and it is usual, because of the slow curing rate of synthetics, to use more or faster-acting accelerators (such as the thiazoles, thiuram disulfides or aldehyde amines). There are many differences between the compounding of the different types of synthetics. Nitrile, for instance, needs proportionately less sulfur and more accelerator than SBR. Butyl, unlike SBR, shows little improvement when treated with reinforcing agents, nor will it harden with the addition of sulfur as SBR does. In the production of neoprene the use of plasticizers and softeners is of importance and, more than that of any other synthetic, its successful use depends upon the amount of filler added. Although neoprene is different from natural rubber, its manufacture—even more so than for the other synthetics—presents no problem to standard rubber manufacturing plant procedure. The Thiokols have a great resistance to solvents and do not readily respond to softening and plasticizing ingredients. Their use is greatly increased by the fact that they are available as molding powder. Neither neoprene nor Thiokol rubbers can be vulcanized with sulfur; metallic oxides such as magnesium oxide and zinc oxide are used instead. The compounding of the new polyisoprene rubbers is expected to follow the lines employed in the manufacture of SBR.

Compounding ingredients are usually worked into the raw material on an open mill by the process of "cutting back and forth," the rubber being cut away from the roll by means of a sharp knife and fed back again between the rolls until the ingredients have been uniformly dispersed. In the case of an internal mixer the ingredients are paid in. In the manufacture of both synthetic and natural rubber the ingredients are added in a certain order, plasticizers and softeners usually preceding fillers and other pigments, with the curing agents being added last of all.

4. Calendering.—The calender, or coating, machine is equipped with adjustable hollow rollers and produces sheeted stock of predetermined size and thickness. It can also be used to coat fabric with rubber. In practice, most calenders consist of three rolls arranged vertically. But there are many four-roll calenders and some two- and six-roll machines. The rolls can be operated independently or together over a wide range of speeds. They are automatically raised or lowered according to the thickness of rubber desired, and they are heated or cooled by passing either steam or cold water through them. Sizes range from 12 in. in length and 6 in. in diameter to 92 and 36 in. respectively.

In the sheeting of rubber, the warm unvulcanized compounded rubber is fed between the two top rolls, passed round the central roller and under the lower roller, and then carried to other parts of the mill for further processing. The rolls usually operate at the same speed, or the middle and bottom rolls may turn one and a half to three times as fast as the top roll. Special rolls with embossed or engraved surfaces are used for rubber footwear and matting. Where rubber-covered cloth or canvas is required, the rubber is placed between the top and the middle rolls while the fabric is fed between the two bottom rolls. The middle roll revolves one and a half to three times faster than the others and the discrepancy in speed "frictions" a thin film of warm rubber into the fabric. When the rubber is not to be pressed into the cloth but is merely to be applied as a coat to the surface, the "skim coat" method is employed. It allows lightweight coatings of rubber to be applied without revealing the texture of the underlying fabric, and it is usually used on fabric that is already frictioned. Frictioning and coating may be repeated on the opposite side of the material. Important modern changes in calender design and operation have sprung from the needs to meet the increasing demands for plastic (especially polyvinyl chloride) as well as rubber sheeting. Some of the best rubber calenders are being used for the vinyl resins.

5. Spreading.—The spreading and proofing machine is sometimes used as an alternative to the calender. In the mid-20th century its design remains similar to the first spreaders developed more than a century ago. It consists of a hollow revolving drum, above which is a long piece of metal whose lower part tapers to an edge. This metal sheet is known as the spreading knife, or doctor. Both the roller and the knife are mounted at one end and level with the surface of a steam-heated table. The fabric to be proofed passes over the roll and underneath the knife, carrying with it—from a supply at the incoming side—a layer of dissolved rubber, which the knife distributes uniformly over the cloth. The material is then drawn over the steam-heated table to evaporate the solvent. In the case of single-texture fabric the operation is repeated until the desired thickness of rubber is obtained. With double-texture fabric, the two textures are coated and then forced together between metal rolls under high pressure, so that the coated surfaces unite permanently. Rubberized fabric has many uses other than waterproof clothing.

6. Extruding.—When the rubber is to be shaped into strips or tubes rather than sheets it is put into an extruder, a device for forcing compounded heat-softened rubber through orifices or dies. The rubber is ground in the machine and forced through a heated die by means of a screw. The extended material retains the shape of the die, which may be, for example, circular or rectangular in cross section and which has a diameter varying from 1 to 8 in. When first constructed in the 1880s, extruders were simple machines used for producing both cushion and solid tires. Modern extruders are complex, with a wide range of output. They are employed for the production of tire tubes, treads and cable covering; and they have eliminated the need to mold certain articles.

7. Vulcanizing (Curing).—*Hot Vulcanization.*—If rubber is heated with sulfur it not only changes to a relatively nonthermoplastic material, but it also increases in elasticity, strength and resilience. Vulcanization is a type of polymerization in which cross-linkages are formed between the long chainlike molecules of rubber, forming a three-dimensional structure. Although means have been developed to vulcanize rubber without either sulfur or heat, sulfur remains the chief curing agent and hot vulcanization is still the process most generally used. Even in so-called sulfurless cures, such as with tetramethylthiuram disulfide and the polysulfides, the curing agent is still sulfur, which is released by these chemicals under vulcanizing conditions. At first the "vulcanizer" was a simple steam-heated chamber fitted with a mobile rack on rails on which the rubber goods—cut into their final shapes—were subjected to heat, the sulfur having previously been added at the compounding stage. Gradually it was realized that for the production of well-formed homogeneous rubber this process was inadequate and that curing needed to be done under pressure. In the last quarter of the 19th century steam-heated hydraulic presses giving pressures of 100 to 800 lb. per square inch of platen surface were introduced. In the 1960s pressures between 4,000 and 8,000 lb. per square inch were possible.

Articles to be molded are generally both molded and vulcanized in one operation. The steam is conveyed to the molds from steam-heated platens and from there directly to the rubber. Cast-iron molds were replaced first by improved steel molds and later by aluminum molds. Some companies developed an intermittent method of press operations that amounts to almost continuous curing. Hollow articles like syringe bulbs and balls are vulcanized under inflation either by air or by nitrogen generated by the action of heat upon a mixture such as sodium nitrate and ammonium chloride in pelleted form. Special presses are used for curing long, flat belts and matting, a section of 20–36 ft. being cured at one time. Conveyor belt and sheet flooring can be continuously cured on a U.S. machine originating from developments in the linoleum trade. Tires are cured in a steam-jacketed mold, which is subjected to powerful internal steam and air pressure that forces the tread and sidewall of the tire into the design cut into the metal mold. Average passenger-car tires are vulcanized in 20 to 30 min. at a temperature of 300°–320° F. (148°–160° C.). The molds for the making and vulcanizing of inner tubes, like those used for the tire casings, are also steam-jacketed. The rubber-hose branch

POST INFLATION PROCESS IN TIRE MANUFACTURE

When tires are removed from vulcanizing molds which give them shape and tread, they are inflated to high pressures and allowed to cool. This process is designed to relieve internal stress. The tires then move by conveyor to further finishing processes

of the industry employs lead presses that make possible the continuous curing of hose up to $2\frac{1}{4}$ in. in diameter. Sometimes hot water is applied to the inside of the hose, while steam heat is applied externally. Insulated wire is cured by a continuous process: as the coated cable comes from the extruder it is passed through a special valve into a superheated steampipe where high temperatures effect a cure in about one minute.

Some items, such as rubber sheet to be cut into thread, are immersed in hot water at the bottom of the autoclave. By this means higher pressures are obtained than with steam at the same temperature, and the possibility of oxidation and discoloration is avoided. Large items are sometimes vulcanized in boiling water in open tanks.

High-Energy Radiation and Radio-Frequency Heating.—These are relatively new vulcanization processes awaiting further development. Thick rubber articles placed in an intense field of radio waves of 5 to 30 mc. can be heated and vulcanized more quickly than is possible with steam heat. In a nitrogen atmosphere high-energy radiation by high-speed electrons can vulcanize sheets of rubber 0.20 in. thick in 20 sec. No sulfur is required. As knowledge of beta and gamma ray sources has grown, vulcanization by high-energy radiation has attracted increasing attention.

Cold Vulcanization.—Sulfur chloride curing was discovered by the Englishman Alexander Parkes in 1846. This process permits the vulcanization of thin-walled rubber articles (such as thin sheeting, gloves, balloons and single-texture garments) by immersing them in sulfur monochloride dissolved in liquid carbon disulfide, or by subjecting them to a gas of the same chemicals. The Peachey cure makes use of sulfur dioxide or hydrogen sulfide. In the 1960s cold vulcanization was being employed increasingly with synthetic rubber and rubberlike materials, some of which, like Thiokol, do not require the addition of sulfur in any form. This tendency was particularly noticeable where waterproofed fabrics are concerned.

8. Direct Use of Latex.—Mention of the problems of transporting *Hevea* latex from the plantations of the east to the industrial centres of the west has been made elsewhere (see *Raw Materials,* above). The advantages of using rubber in its liquid form were evident from the beginning of the rubber industry; *e.g.,* the physical properties of products made directly from latex are superior to articles prepared from solutions of crude rubber, and their preparation is simpler and cheaper.

Dipping.—Latices are compounded along the same lines as rubber used for other purposes. Most formulations contain stabilizers, plasticizers, colours, fillers, antioxidants, accelerators and vulcanizing agents. The basic process consists of dipping a solid object ("former") into the latex and allowing the film that forms to dry, then vulcanizing it. By this method tire cords are impregnated, medical and surgical supplies and electricians' gloves made, textiles waterproofed, footwear impregnated and rubber yarns and thread obtained. The development of latex thread, which is much finer than cut thread, had a considerable impact upon the clothing industry.

Most multiple dip goods (goods that have to be dipped more than once) are made by the coagulant method, in which the former is immersed in a coagulating solution either before or after it is dipped into the latex. The "heat-sensitive" dipping process depends on the fact that latex may be coagulated by heat and that therefore a hot former picks up a heavier coating than a cold one. The addition of polyvinyl methyl ether to latex increases its sensitivity to heat and when a hot shape is immersed in a mixture of these two substances the layer of coagulum forms quickly. This process, discovered by the Germans during World War II and developed further by the British, is probably the most important technical advance made in the 1940s. Several electrical processes have been devised to assist the building-up of latex film on formers; these are especially useful for coating irregularly shaped articles. The method of electrolytic deposition employs direct electric current to deposit the latex, the form to be coated being used as the anode in an electrolytic system. A method that is employed with natural, but has little application for synthetic, latex is the use of dry porous forms made of plaster of Paris, which, when dipped

(TOP) WHIPPED LIQUID LATEX BEING POURED INTO MATTRESS MOLD; (BOTTOM) FOAM RUBBER MATTRESS BEING REMOVED FROM MOLD. EACH MATTRESS IS MOLDED AND CURED SEPARATELY

into the latex, dehydrate the film that has been deposited.

Prevulcanized latex compounds were first used by P. Schidrowitz in England about 1920. However, the tensile strength of articles made from this prevulcanized latex is usually lower than that of articles made from latices that are vulcanized after they have been dipped or molded.

Latex Foam.—One of the most interesting and important developments in the use of natural and synthetic (mostly neoprene and some SBR) latices is their application as latex foam, or sponge rubber. A new and extensive market grew up for latex-foam upholstery, automobile seating, mattresses and pillows. The manufacturing process consists of frothing up the latex, which has been compounded with the usual ingredients together with soaps and special gelling agents such as sodium silicofluoride, polyvinyl methyl ether or ammonium-zinc compounds. The foam is produced by continuous process on a foam whipping machine and contains approximately 85% air and 15% rubber. It is poured into molds and vulcanized in hermetically sealed vulcanization units. The products are then washed and dried in electrically heated drying chambers. Another process of manufacturing foam rubber mixes the latex with hydrogen peroxide and the enzyme catalase from live yeast. The oxygen released by the action of the catalase on the hydrogen peroxide blows up the foam, which is then frozen, coagulated with carbon dioxide and vulcanized in the wet state.

9. Productivity.—In the absence of comparative data from which it would be possible to assess the output of the rubber industry at different times, it is not possible to calculate the changes in productivity per worker within the industry. One estimate of the amount of rubber processed by each worker in the United Kingdom during the period 1850–1950 shows that the consumption of crude rubber in long tons per wage earner in the U.S. and Brit-

ish industries increased from approximately one ton in 1850 to about three tons for the United Kingdom and more than six tons for the United States in 1950. The gradual rise in productivity must be largely ascribed to improved methods of production. The higher consumption of the U.S. rubber worker is possibly accounted for by specialization in that industry, the greater power and capital resources of U.S. rubber firms in comparison with those of other countries, and the tendency to replace hand labour with technically superior machine processes and automation.

IV. CONSUMPTION

1. Consumption by Countries.—The most significant trend discernible in consumption is the swing from natural to synthetic supplies. The situation in the 1960s, as compared with 1940, showed that the majority of the rubber consumed was of a synthetic nature. By 1960, certain countries, such as the United States, were consuming smaller quantities of natural rubber than they did in 1941. Even the British, with their connections in the east, were rapidly reaching that position. Developments in the petrochemical industry made available at economic prices raw materials for synthetic rubber production.

2. Consumption by Products.—The market for manufactured rubber commodities has passed through three stages. First, before the advent of the vulcanization process in 1839, there were the crude attempts at rubber footwear and waterproof clothing. Of the two countries that have dominated the rubber trade, the United States and the United Kingdom, the former led in the manufacture of footwear, the latter in the manufacture of waterproof clothing. The footwear industry remained the greatest single market for rubber until the introduction of the automobile. Secondly, from the 1840s to the end of the 19th century, rubber was used increasingly for many purposes where prior to vulcanization it had proved unsuitable. In particular, the growth of industrialization since the 1850s in North America, Europe and other parts of the world, coupled with the improvement of the vulcanizing and manufacturing process, greatly accelerated the application of rubber to mechanical devices. These devices, such as hose and tubing, packing and washers, springs and rings (especially in the field of railway mechanical devices), belting, diaphragms, etc., played an important part in the development of modern transport and manufacturing processes. The manifold demands of the growing electrical industry provided a vast new market, particularly for hard rubber. The third and most expansive stage has lasted from the beginning of the 20th century to the 1960s and is bound up with the enormous demands of the pneumatic tire and the automobile industry generally.

3. Consolidation and Competition.—The industry has always been at the mercy of rapid and drastic changes both in the cost of raw rubber and the prices of finished goods. Also, since about 1920, it has been largely dependent on the automobile industry, the biggest consumer of rubber products. In consequence of these susceptibilities, small firms have often been in difficulties and the tendency has been to amalgamate. The industry has also concentrated its forces in order to finance its rapid growth and vigorous research programs.

In the 1960s the picture was a complex one. While the total number of rubber undertakings continued to grow throughout western Europe and America, control of most of the market was passing into fewer hands, especially in the tire division. Thus the United States tire establishments declined in numbers from 178 in 1921 to 57 in 1947, and the trend continued; by 1960 the Goodyear Tire and Rubber Co., the United States Rubber Co., the B. F. Goodrich Co. and the Firestone Tire and Rubber Co. together had a larger share of the gross output of the U.S. industry than they had had 20 years before. In Britain the number of rubber workers employed by the Dunlop Co. was as high as 50% of the total for the country, and the same was true of Michelin et Cie. in France, the Continental Gummiwerke A.G. in Germany, and the Società Italiana Pirelli. This concentration of economic power did not appear, however, to have lessened the competitive and progressive nature of the industry.

See also references under "Rubber" in the Index.

BIBLIOGRAPHY.—W. Bobilioff, *Anatomy and Physiology of Hevea Brasiliensis* (1923); A. Sharples, *Diseases and Pests of the Rubber Tree* (1936); C. C. Davis and J. T. Blake (eds.), *Chemistry and Technology of Rubber* (1937); C. A. Gehlsen, *World Rubber Production and Trade: Economic and Technical Aspects, 1935–1939* for the International Institute of Agriculture (1940); A. McFadyean (ed.), *The History of Rubber Regulation, 1934–1943* for the International Rubber Regulation Committee (1944); P. T. Bauer, *The Rubber Industry: a Study in Competition and Monopoly* (1948); R. Houwink (ed.), *Elastomers and Plastomers: Their Chemistry, Physics and Technology*, 3 vol. (1948–50); H. Barron, *Modern Synthetic Rubbers*, 3rd ed. (1949); R. J. Noble, *Latex in Industry*, 2nd ed. (1953); P. Schidrowitz and T. R. Dawson (eds.), *History of the Rubber Industry*, Institution of the Rubber Industry (1953); G. S. Whitby (ed.), *Synthetic Rubber* (1954); H. J. Stern, *Rubber: Natural and Synthetic* (1954); W. Woodruff, "Growth of the Rubber Industry of Great Britain and the United States," *Journal of Economic History*, vol. xv, no. 4 (1955); *Rise of the British Rubber Industry During the Nineteenth Century* (1958); C. E. Schildknecht (ed.), *Polymer Processes* (1956); F. W. Billmeyer, Jr., *Textbook of Polymer Chemistry* (1957); A. T. Edgar, *Manual of Rubber Planting* (Malaya), 2nd ed. (1958); M. Morton (ed.), *Introduction to Rubber Technology* for American Chemical Society, Division of Rubber Chemistry (1959); W. J. S. Naunton (ed.), *The Applied Science of Rubber* (1961). For current production statistics see the *Britannica Book of the Year*. (W. Wo.)

RUBBER TILE: see FLOOR COVERINGS.

RUBELLITE, a red variety of tourmaline used as a gemstone. It generally occurs crystallized on the walls of cavities in coarse granitic rocks, where it is often associated with a pink lithia mica (lepidolite). The most valued kinds are deep red, the colour being probably due to the presence of manganese. Some of the finest rubellite is found in Siberia. Other localities include the island of Elba, the Urals, Burma, and Minas Gerais, Braz. Fine rubellite is found in the United States, notably at Paris, Me., where the crystals are often red at one end and green at the other. Mt. Rubellite near Hebron and Mt. Apatite at Auburn are other localities in the same state from which fine specimens are obtained. Chesterfield, Mass., also yields red tourmaline, frequently associated with green in the same crystal. Pink tourmaline also occurs, with lepidolite and kunzite, in San Diego County, Calif. For discussion of composition, crystal forms, electrical and optical properties, etc., see TOURMALINE.

RUBENS, PETER PAUL (1577–1640), Flemish painter and diplomat, was born at Siegen, Westphalia, June 28, 1577. His father Jan Rubens, although born a Roman Catholic, had appeared on a Calvinist list as early as 1566. After the decapitation of the counts of Egmont and Horne in Brussels in 1568, Jan fled from Antwerp to Cologne with his wife Maria Pypelincx and their four children, there to become agent and adviser to Anne of Saxony, second wife of William the Silent. An unfortunate pregnancy revealed in this princess of Orange the extent of her relationship with Jan, for whom however she obtained some clemency from her husband. Jan was nevertheless under house arrest at Siegen when both Peter Paul and his elder brother Philip were born. These boys had their grounding in the classics from their exiled father, a *doctor utriusque juris*. But Jan died in 1587, after he had been allowed to go back to Cologne. Maria then thought it prudent to bring her four surviving children to Antwerp, where their father had been an alderman.

Antwerp Training.—At the age of ten, Peter Paul was sent with Philip to the Latin school of Rumoldus Verdonck, where the future painter befriended a contemporary who was to be a future patron, as head of the Plantin press, Balthasar Moretus. In 1590 shortage of money, and the need to provide a dowry for his sister Blandina, forced Maria to take Peter Paul away from school and make him a page to the countess of Lalaing. Soon tired of courtly life, he was allowed to turn to his real vocation. He was sent first to his kinsman Tobias Verhaecht, a painter of mannerist landscapes in the stale tradition of Joos de Momper. Having quickly learned the rudiments of his profession he was apprenticed for four years to an abler master, Adam van Noort, and subsequently to the most distinguished of the Antwerp Romanists, Otto van Veen. Vaenius, as he called himself, had been in Italy an active admirer of Federigo Baroccio as well as of the strictly Roman tradition in painting, and was learned in emblems. His culture and vision impressed Rubens, whose earliest independent works are known to have resembled his style.

Italian Period.—In May 1600, with two years' seniority as a master in the Antwerp Guild of St. Luke, Rubens set out with Deodati del Monte, his constant traveling companion and first pupil, for the visual and spiritual adventure of Italy. Reaching Venice in about a month, he had early the fortune to meet a gentleman in the service of Vincenzo I Gonzaga, duke of Mantua. He was offered employment in Mantua, which duchy held the largest and finest collections outside the Vatican of works from all Italian schools. Its capital, moreover, was ideally placed for sightseeing in Lombardy, Emilia and the Veneto. During the eight years that Rubens was to call Vincenzo his lord he had unmatched opportunities of fulfilling his expressed intention "to study at close quarters the works of the ancient and modern masters, and to improve himself by their example in painting." Andrea Mantegna and Giulio Romano were his admired predecessors in Gonzagan service. The abundant achievement in decoration and architecture of Giulio Romano, artistic heir of Raphael, had a lasting and highly productive effect on him.

Recommended to Cardinal Montalto in Rome, Rubens was sent (1601–02) to paint copies for the duke. There, through his Flemish connection, he obtained his first public commission, three altarpieces for the crypt chapel of St. Helena in Sta. Croce in Gerusalemme, formerly titular church of the cardinal Archduke Albert, who was by this time consort to Isabella, regent of the Spanish Netherlands. In Rome, Annibale Carracci and his school were at work in the Farnese gallery. From their bold scale in drawing and characteristic working methods Rubens formed the decisive habits of his life. Through Annibale's example he was first enabled to digest the power of Michelangelo. Raphael and Leonardo da Vinci were his other High Renaissance heroes for nobility and energy of design. He assimilated Venetian colour, light and application of paint first through the works of Tintoretto, then through those of Veronese, long before he could penetrate the inward meaning of Titian's art. His copies, and his reworking of drawings, offer the most complete conspectus of 16th-century achievement in a pungently personal revision.

In 1603 he was entrusted with his first embassy, to bring Philip III and the Spanish court costly presents from Mantua. This mission gave him a first view of the Habsburg treasures, including more than 70 works by Titian. Two paintings in the groups of copies offered to Philip's favourite, the duke of Lerma, being rainsodden beyond repair, were promptly replaced by him with a "Democritus and Heraclitus" of his own invention. His resource, and his tact with the regular Mantuan agent at Valladolid, whither the Spanish court had moved, raised him in Vincenzo's estimation and prepared him for future diplomatic voyages. His equestrian portrait of the duke of Lerma initiated his masterpieces in this genre; its pattern of presentation inspired Van Dyck. His fruitful association with the banking patriciate of Genoa began with his return voyage and his meeting with Nicolò Pallavicini, Vincenzo's banker, in order to recoup expenses.

His only major work for Mantua, a conspicuous challenge to the memory of Michelangelo, Raphael and Tintoretto, was the threefold decoration for the Jesuit church of SS. Trinità. Nothing of his but portraits of court beauties was commissioned for the Gonzaga gallery itself, although he induced Vincenzo to buy for the gallery Caravaggio's rejected "Death of the Virgin," and he negotiated the purchase of a Cristofero Roncalli for the duchess. After his work for SS. Trinità (1604–05) and for the high altar of the Jesuit church in Genoa (1605), he obtained leave to continue his studies in Rome. There he shared a house with his brother Philip, then secretary and librarian to Ascanio Cardinal Colonna. Daily contact with Philip, the most brilliant pupil of Justus Lipsius and the hope of classical studies, added zest to his personal renascence of the antique world. The combined fruits of their learning were strung into the text and illustrations of *Electorum Libri II* (1608), published by the Plantin press. Apart from a summons in 1607 to accompany the Gonzagan court on a summer progress to the seaside resort of San Pier d'Arena, where he invented splendid means to portray the Genoese aristocracy, Rubens was left largely undisturbed. But chronic arrears in payment of his salary, and ambition to establish himself as a metropolitan, not just a Man-

KERKFABRIECK VAN O. L. VROUW

"DESCENT FROM THE CROSS," CENTRAL PANEL OF ALTARPIECE BY PETER
PAUL RUBENS, 1610–11.   IN ANTWERP CATHEDRAL

tuan, painter, caused him to seek the backing of a Genoese patron,
Jacopo Serra, in obtaining the coveted commission at the Chiesa
Nuova. The protracted difficulties of this work for the Roman
oratory, during which he brought off at speed a superb altarpiece
for the Oratorians of Fermo, still occupied him when, in Oct. 1608,
his brother Philip, already back in Antwerp, summoned him to
their mother's death bed.

Return to Antwerp.—Riding from Rome in haste, Rubens was
nevertheless too late to see his mother alive. His first altarpiece
for the Chiesa Nuova, which had been offered in vain to Mantua,
became at last her monument. Although soon "bound with golden
fetters" to the service of the Habsburg regents in Flanders
(Sept. 23, 1609), then and for long after Rubens contemplated
a return beyond the Alps to re-enter the lists of the Roman
painters. As late as the 1620s he supplied cartoons to Genoa. Of
six languages which he used with ease, Italian remained his favourite for correspondence. The house which he built for himself, the
pride of Antwerp, had a model Pantheon which he enriched with
statuary, cameos, coins and jewels. *Palazzi di Genova* (1622) was
his published souvenir of civilized modern architecture. He practised the spirit of his preface in the magnificent new church of
the Antwerp Jesuits, St. Charles Borromeo, where he, assisted in
the execution of ceiling paintings by Van Dyck, was the master
decorator and, with Peter Huyssens, the chief designer of the façade, tower and all architectural detail. This building, with the
almost contemporary banqueting house designed by Inigo Jones
at Whitehall, London, where Rubens was to achieve his long-
cherished ambition to fill the huge ceiling with paintings (delivered 1634), was the architectural sensation of northwest
Europe.

He settled in Flanders, marrying Isabella, daughter of Jan
Brandt, the Antwerp lawyer and humanist (Oct. 1609), and establishing himself not only as court portraitist but, by a trilogy of

altarpieces, as the leading painter of his country. These altarpieces were: the fully baroque "Erection of the Cross" for St.
Walpurga's, Antwerp (1610), a mature criticism of his treatment
of the subject in Sta. Croce in Gerusalemme; the more classical
"Descent from the Cross" for Antwerp cathedral; and for the
cathedral of St. Bavo, Ghent, "The Miracle of St. Bavo," which,
although conceived as a triptych like the others, was much modified
to fit a single field. Relieved of the obligation to live at the Brussels court he was also exempt from guild regulations, and so free
to engage pupils or collaborators without having to have them enrolled. By 1611 he wrote that he had to refuse more than 100 applicants to join his studio. As his international reputation grew,
in part through careful organization of printmaking to advertise
his designs, numbers of large-scale works issued from his studio
which were only in certain areas, or generally retouched, by his
hand. But to almost the last year of his fabulously productive life
he painted unaided a superior class of very large works, as well
as of cabinet pieces, oak panels being favoured for their supports.
During 1606–07 he used small panels prepared with gesso for the
various categories of oil sketches required to facilitate his manifold activity: sketches to work out his pictorial ideas, to present
models to clients or to instruct engravers, sculptors, tapestry
weavers and painting assistants. They are small works in inches
only, marvellous drawings in paint, whether *en grisaille* or fully
coloured. But he never entirely abandoned the Renaissance practice of evolving compositions in chalk and ink.

Diplomatic Activity.—Archduke Albert died in 1621, the
year in which the 12 years' truce between Spain and the Netherlands ended. Rubens became adviser to the widowed archduchess,
of whom he was to write (1628): "Long experience has taught her
how to govern these people and not to be taken in by false theories
which every newcomer brings from Spain." She, like him, desired
to prolong peace. France grew suspicious. The French ambassador wrote from Brussels (1624): "Rubens is here to take the
likeness of the prince of Poland, by order of the infanta. I am
persuaded he will succeed better in this than in his negotiations
for the truce." Early in 1622 Rubens had been summoned by
Marie de Médicis, whose wedding by proxy he had attended in
Florence in 1600, for his first visit to Paris. After six weeks of discussion he returned to Antwerp to begin work on the *Histories of
Marie de Médicis* for the walls of the first of two great galleries
to be decorated by him in her new Luxembourg palace. This cycle
of 21 canvases, his most important secular commission, was completed in two years. Being again in Paris for their installation in
1625, he met the duke of Buckingham, to whose persistence in
bidding high for his famous collection of antiquities and paintings
he was eventually to accede for diplomatic reasons. Buckingham
was in Paris for the marriage by proxy of Charles I and Henrietta
Maria of France. With him was his master of the horse, painter
and agent, Sir Balthasar Gerbier. Secret correspondence between
Rubens and Gerbier was maintained even after the fresh outbreak
of war between England and Spain, which led to Buckingham's
disastrous expedition to Cádiz. Not until the assassination of the
Stuart favourite was the way reopened for Rubens to negotiate
peace on behalf of the sorely tried Spanish Netherlands. He described Antwerp to Louis XIII's librarian as "languishing like a
consumptive body, declining little by little." Unfortunately
Philip IV's minister, the count of Olivares and duke of SanLúcar,
known as the *conde-duque*, had persuaded his master to make a
close pact with France to reconquer England for Catholicism. In
1628 Rubens had therefore to travel in secret haste to Madrid.
The papal nuncio reported of his arrival: "It is considered certain
that Rubens, the Flemish painter, is the bearer of a negotiation,
for we hear that he often confers in secret with the *conde-duque*,
and in a manner very different from that which his profession
permits. They say that he left England a short time ago; and
since he is said to be a great friend of Buckingham, it is believed
that he comes with some peace treaty between the two crowns.
Others think his main object is the truce of Flanders, and that
he has received this commission as one who enjoys the confidence
of all that country."

During nine months in Madrid, besides negotiations and royal portraiture, Rubens set himself to school again before Titian's masterpieces, revisiting the Escorial with Velázquez. He overcame Philip IV's prejudice against him as a suitable negotiator, and was named secretary of the privy council of the Netherlands to conduct a special mission to England. He hastened across France, past the hostile Richelieu, to report to Archduchess Isabella. News awaiting his return to Brussels made his mission yet more urgent and difficult. England had made a treaty with France (April 24, 1629). Charles I wished to treat with Rubens as a plenipotentiary, without waiting for the exchange of regular envoys. The Dutch alliance and the restitution of the Palatinate were crucial to Anglo-Spanish relations. Rubens succeeded, however, in laying the groundwork for the peace treaty (Nov. 15, 1630). For this he was knighted by Charles I and given an honorary degree by Cambridge university. "The Blessings of Peace," (National gallery, London), featuring Gerbier's children, is his painted proclamation of success. He discussed painting with Charles I, the only prince to whom he vouchsafed a self-portrait (Windsor castle), and, in particular, projects for the Whitehall ceiling. He was struck by the beauty and peacefulness of the English scene. The "Landscape with St. George" (Buckingham palace) was his private souvenir of the Thames view from his lodgings, with the royal pair envisaged in masquerade as patron saint and rescued princess. But a general peace was far away. His letter of March 12, 1638, explains "The Horrors of War," a late masterpiece sold to the Medici in Florence. He identifies the figures of the allegory: "that grief-stricken woman clothed in black, with torn veil, robbed of all her jewels and other ornaments, is the unfortunate Europe, who for so many years now has suffered plunder, outrage, and misery."

Later Works.—On his return to Flanders in 1630 Rubens was rewarded with exemption by the archduchess from further diplomacy. "This favour I obtained with more difficulty than any other she ever granted me," he was to write. "Now, for three

years, I have found peace of mind, having given up every sort of employment outside my beloved profession."

Having been four years a widower he married (Dec. 1630) the 16-year-old Helena Fourment, whose charms recur frequently among his later figure subjects. Many of his grandest and most romantic interpretations of landscape belong to this decade of his retirement from court affairs, when he owned the Château de Steen. But his active interest in landscape had been unbroken since at least the drawings of his Roman period. Long-established interests were revived also in his co-ordination of the work of every Antwerp painter for the stagings designed and partly executed by him to welcome the Infante Ferdinand, successor to Archduchess Isabella, in 1635. Thirty-six years before, he had assisted Vaenius to convert their city into a theatre. The great commission of Rubens' last years was, however, for the infante's brother Philip IV, the provision of models for about 120 scenes from Ovid to decorate the Torre de la Parada near Madrid.

Rubens died at Antwerp on May 30, 1640, when gout, which had for months troubled his painting arm, reached his heart.

Achievement.—Rubens remains unchallenged even by the longer-lived Picasso as the most methodically assimilative, the most prodigiously and variously productive among European artists. Schooled in the congested traditions of Antwerp mannerism, he educated himself to be heir of the full range of Renaissance design to be seen both north and south of the Alps. And he saw the masterpieces of the Renaissance as yet undisturbed from their intended places. The abundant energy and warmth of his nature not only fired him to emulate the masters both of antiquity and of the 16th century in Rome, Venice and Parma, but made him responsive to the artistic revolutions being worked by living artists: to Adam Elsheimer's *plein air* study of nature and times of day in the Roman campagna; to Federigo Barocci's colour combinations and delicate appreciation of warm and cool tones vibrant on flesh; to Michelangelo da Caravaggio's emotive exploitation of strong chiaroscuro; and, most profoundly and lastingly, to Annibale Carracci's impassioned yet strenuously disciplined approach to the practice of figure composition.

Robust powers of comprehension nourished his limitless resource in invention. The larger the scale of the undertaking the more congenial it was to his spirit. The success of his public performance as master of the greatest studio organization in Europe since Raphael's in Rome has obscured for many the personal intensity of his vision as evinced in such works as his oil sketch for "All Saints" and in his deeply felt study for the head of St. John in the Antwerp "Descent from the Cross," as well as in portraits of his family and friends and in his treatment of the mood and grandeur of landscape. Not only Van Dyck, Jacob Jordaens and his immediate following in Flanders, but artists at almost every period have responded to the force of his genius. Giovanni Lorenzo Bernini, the other seminal mind of the early baroque, developed in his Roman altarpieces figurative ideas and the dramatic handling of light instituted by Rubens. And in the fulfillment of the Italian baroque Domenico Feti, Castiglione and Bernardo Strozzi are in individual ways Rubensians. Watteau, Fragonard, Delacroix and Renoir are only the four most distinguished in the long succession of French painters who were attracted after the late 17th century to some aspect of his production. Reynolds, Gainsborough, and Constable are outstanding among his English admirers. In the history of western art he is a central figure.

His own deepest love as a painter, consummated by his second visit to Spain, was for the poetry, the control of glowing colour and the sheer mastery in handling of oil paint that excelled in the art of Titian. In these qualities Rubens himself became supreme, whether with the brilliant play of fine brushes over the white reflecting surface of a small panel, or with masterful gestures often more than six feet long, sweeping a richly loaded brush across some huge canvas.

See also references under "Rubens, Peter Paul" in the Index.

BIBLIOGRAPHY.—M. Rooses, *L'Oeuvre de P. P. Rubens*, 5 vol. (1886–92), *Rubens*, 2 vol., Eng. trans. (1904); R. Oldenbourg, *P. P. Rubens des Meisters Gemälde* (1921); G. Glück, *Rubens, Van Dyck, und ihr Kreis* (1933); P. Arents, *Geschriften van en over Rubens* (1940); F.

"SIEGE OF JULIERS," ONE OF 21 PAINTINGS ILLUSTRATING THE LIFE OF MARIE DE MÉDICIS. IN THE LOUVRE

van den Wijngaert, *Inventaris der Rubeniaansche Prentkunst* (1940); H. G. Evers, *Peter Paul Rubens* (1946); J. S. Held, *Rubens in America* (1947); J. Burckardt, *Recollections of Rubens* (1950); R. S. Magurn, *Letters of Peter Paul Rubens* (1955); J. S. Held, *Rubens; Selected Drawings* (1959). *See* also exhibition catalogues, *Olieverfschetsen van Rubens, Museum Boymans* (1953) and *Tekeningen van P. P. Rubens, Rubenshuis* (1956). (ML. J.)

RUBIACEAE, the madder family, a large family of angiospermous flowering plants, dicotyledons, belonging to the sympetalous order Rubiales and containing about 450 genera with approximately 5,500 species. The Rubiaceae have a world-wide distribution with centres in the tropics of the old and new worlds. They vary in form from herbs to trees, but most of the species are inconspicuous and subordinate elements of the vegetation. Some, such as coffee and quina bark trees, have attained major economic importance. Well-known British and North American examples of Rubiaceae are species of *Galium* such as bedstraw (*q.v.*), woodruff, cleavers (*q.v.*), etc.

Rubiaceae are characterized by opposite (or whorled), entire stipulate leaves, rotate sympetalous flowers, mostly with four or five lobes to the corolla and the same number of alternate stamens. The ovaries are nearly always inferior with a single style. The Rubiaceae have probably been derived from ancestors closely allied to recent Loganiaceae (Contortae) by gradual submergence of the superior ovary.

The taxonomy of the Rubiaceae is still a matter of some debate. Six subfamilies with many tribes may be recognized: Cinchonoideae, Urophylloideae, Ophiorrhizoideae, Guettardoideae, Ixoroideae and Rubioideae. The general phylogenetic trends within the family are manifold. Their form varies from woody trees and shrubs, predominant in the tropics, to dwarf shrubs, perennial and annual herbs, mostly found in subtropic, temperate and arctic-alpine regions. The leaves are mostly large and evergreen in tropical groups, often deciduous in temperate groups and needle- or scalelike in xeromorphic groups. The stipules tend to merge to medium stipular regions which in the Rubioideae develop from one to many leaflike stipules. In primitive groups of Rubiaceae the flowers are relatively large, single and situated in leaf axils; in derived groups they are reduced in size and combined into various kinds of inflorescences. From monomorphic hermaphrodite flowers the development is to dimorphic (long- and short-styled), or unisexual and eventually dioecious flowers. Further phylogenetic trends include shortening of corolla tubes, loss of calyces, reduction in the number of carpels from five and six to two, and of

JOHN H. GERARD

BUTTONBUSH (CEPHALANTHUS OCCIDENTALIS), WIDELY DISTRIBUTED IN MARSHES OF NORTH AMERICA

the number of ovaries per ovary chamber to one. Each chamber contains, depending on species, from one to numerous ovules. The fruits vary in form from dry capsules and drupes to schizocarpous nutlets which are sometimes covered with hooked hairs and similar devices for epizoic dispersal (*e.g.*, "cleaver" species of *Galium*).

Pollination is effected by insects or birds (very rarely by the wind) or by self-pollination. Some fluctuations of the basic chromosome number and especially polyploidy (multiplication of basic chromosome number) have played an important role in the evolution of the family. Of biological interest are the tropical epiphytes (*Myrmecodia* and *Hydnophytum*), which develop swollen stems inhabited by ants. Other genera have leaves with symbiotic, nitrogen-binding bacteria.

Rubioideae species with whorled leaves and leaflike stipules are widespread in temperate regions; *e.g.*, common species in Britain are *Galium mollugo* (hedge bedstraw), *G. verum* (lady's bedstraw) and *G. aparine* (cleavers or goosegrass); in North America species of *Cephalanthus* (buttonbush), *Mitchella* (partridge berry), *Houstonia* (bluets, innocence), *Kelloggia* and *Ga-*

lium are found. Some of the Rubiaceae are of economic importance. The bark of *Cinchona* (*q.v.*) and some other tropical South American genera contain quinine (*q.v.*). Coffee is produced from the seeds of *Coffea*, particularly *C. arabica* and *C. liberica*. The ipecacuanha root (*Uragoga*) contains vomitive glucosids. Other species provide tanning and dyeing (*e.g.*, madder, *Rubia tinctorum*) substances. Some tropical trees furnish timber. Members of the genera *Ixora, Manettia, Bouvardia, Rondeletia, Gardenia, Phuopsis, Galium, Asperula* and others are of horticultural value.

(F. Eh.)

RUBICON, a small stream of ancient Italy, which flowed into the Adriatic between Ariminum (Rimini) and Caesena (Cesena) and formed the boundary between Italy and the province of Cisalpine Gaul in republican times. Hence Caesar's crossing of it in 49 B.C. meant a declaration of war against Pompey and the Senate (*see* CAESAR, GAIUS JULIUS). The historic importance of this event gave rise to the phrase "crossing the Rubicon" to describe a step which definitely commits a person to a given course of action. Augustus later made the Crustumium, modern Conca, a few miles farther south, the boundary of Cispadane Gaul and Umbria.

The modern Rubicone (formerly Fiumicino) is officially identified with the Rubicon, but the Pisciatello to the north and the Uso to the south have also been suggested.

RUBIDIUM, a rare chemical element of the alkali metal group, the most reactive of all metals except cesium (*q.v.*). The uses of rubidium and its compounds are limited but noteworthy. Its natural radioactive isotope, Rb[87] (half life, 53,000,000,000 years), has been used to determine the age of the solar system. An estimated age of 4,500,000,000 years, based upon the decay of Rb[87] to strontium (Sr[87]) in a stony meteorite, is consistent with results based upon the decay of uranium to the final end product, lead. For the opposite extreme of precision, an atomic clock whose ticks are the natural vibrations of rubidium atoms has been proposed; ammonia clocks and cesium clocks are now in use. The purpose of such devices is to establish an invariant standard for time units, quite independently of the earth's rotation, which would be accurate to 1 part in 10,000,000,000 or more.

The discovery of rubidium (and of cesium), the first of many new elements to be detected by the spectroscope, was a crucial step in the development of the science of spectroscopy (*q.v.*). R. W. Bunsen and G. R. Kirchhoff, who perfected the spectroscope, used it to study alkali metal compounds extracted from the mineral lepidolite. They obtained a chloroplatinate whose flame spectrum had two unusually prominent red lines which did not match those of any known element. In their report, made in 1861, Bunsen and Kirchhoff told how they named the new element:

> The magnificent dark red colour of these rays of the new alkali metal led us to give this element the name rubidium and the symbol Rb from *rubidus,* which, with the ancients, served to designate the deepest red.

Although ranking 17th (0.031%) in the estimated abundances of the elements in the earth's crust, rubidium is widely dispersed

Physical and Atomic Properties

Atomic number	37
Atomic weight	85.47
Outer electron configuration	$4s^2, 4p^6, 5s^1$
Density of solid at 20° C, g. per cc.	1.53
Melting point, ° C	38.89
Boiling point, ° C	688.
Ionization potential, volts	4.16
Potential for $Rb \rightleftharpoons Rb^+ + e$, volts	2.99
Specific heat at 0° C, cal. per g.	0.080
Metallic radius, Å	2.16
Ionic radius, Å	1.48

among minerals (lepidolite, carnallite, and some feldspars) and mineral waters containing other alkali metals. The highest concentration of rubidium is found in lepidolite (lithium mica), the deposits of South West Africa containing as high as 3% of Rb_2O. To extract rubidium, the finely ground calcined mineral is treated with sulfuric or hydrochloric acid. Rubidium and cesium are then separated from the solution by fractional crystallization, generally of their alums, which are less soluble than those of lithium, sodium, and potassium. The rubidium may be partially separated from cesium by precipitation as chloride from a hot

HCl solution to which is added ethyl alcohol; or by precipitation as carbonate in ethyl alcohol. Rubidium may be quantitatively separated from the other alkali metal ions and from those of other metals in a column of cation exchange resin. Metallic rubidium can be prepared by heating the carbonate, hydroxide, or chloride with a suitable reducing agent; magnesium, aluminum, calcium, barium azide, $Ba(N_3)_2$, and calcium carbide have been used.

Rubidium is a silver-white metal which inflames in air, reacts vigorously with cold water liberating hydrogen and forming the hydroxide RbOH, a very strong base. Other properties are summarized in the Table.

The salts of rubidium resemble those of potassium and cesium; they are mostly ionic and those of the common acids, chloride, sulfate, nitrate, carbonate, and phosphate, are soluble in water. The perchlorate, acid tartrate, picrate, the hexafluorosilicate, hexanitrocobaltate, hexachlorostannate, hexachloroplatinate, and the tetrachloroantimonite are relatively insoluble. Some of the rubidium salts are used in microchemical analysis.

For bibliography *see* POTASSIUM. (J. B. Ps.)

RUBINSTEIN, ANTON GRIGORIEVICH (1829–1894), Russian composer and one of the greatest pianists of the 19th century, was born at Vykhvatintsy, Podolia province, on Nov. 28 (new style; 16, old style), 1829. In 1835 his father opened a small factory in Moscow and there in the same year his brother NIKOLAI (d. Paris, 1881) was born. Both boys were taught the piano, first by their mother and then by Alexander Villoing. Anton gave his first public recital in Moscow in 1839, and the following year Villoing took him abroad for a three-year concert tour. He appeared in Paris, London, Holland, Germany, and Sweden, attracting the attention of Chopin and Liszt. From 1844 to 1846 he and his brother studied music theory in Berlin with Siegfried Dehn. Anton spent two more years abroad alone, mainly in Vienna, studying the piano and composition. On his return to Russia in 1849 he settled in St. Petersburg where, in 1852, his first opera, *Dimitri Donskoi*, was produced; *Fomka the Fool* appeared the following year, and his *The Siberian Huntsmen* at Weimar in 1854. The original form of his once popular Second Symphony, *The Ocean*, came a little later. The years 1854–58 were spent abroad. Under the patronage of the Grand Duchess Elena Pavlovna, Rubinstein in 1859 founded the Russian Music Society, and later became conductor of its orchestral concerts; in 1862 he founded and became the director of the Petersburg Conservatory, and in 1866 his brother founded the Moscow Conservatory. Rubinstein resigned the conservatory directorship in 1867, but resumed it in 1887 and continued to hold the post until 1891. From 1871 to 1872 he directed the Vienna Philharmonic concerts, and the next year toured the United States with Henryk Wieniawski. His operas include *The Demon* (St. Petersburg, 1875), *The Maccabees* (Berlin, 1875), and *The Merchant Kalashnikov* (St. Pe-

THE BETTMANN ARCHIVE
RUBINSTEIN

tersburg, 1880). He wrote six symphonies, the oratorio *The Tower of Babel* (Königsberg, 1870), five piano concertos, songs, piano pieces, and numerous chamber works.

In 1889 Rubinstein published an autobiography, translated by A. Delano as *Autobiography of Anton Rubinstein* (1890), followed by other writings. He died at Peterhof on Nov. 20 (N.S.; 8, O.S.), 1894.

BIBLIOGRAPHY.—L. Barenboim, *Anton Grigorievich Rubinstein* (1957); C. S. D. Bowen, *Free Artist: the Story of Anton and Nicholas Rubinstein* (1939); N. Findeisen, *A. G. Rubinstein* (1907); A. Hervey, *Rubinstein* (1913). (G. Ab.)

RUBLEV, ANDREI (*c.* 1370–1430), one of the greatest Russian painters, whose most famous work is the icon of the Old Testament Trinity (*see* RUSSIAN ART). Little is known of his life except that he was the assistant of another great painter called Theophanes, a Greek who came to Russia from Constantinople, and that, fairly late in life, he became a monk, first at Zagorsk and then at the Andronikov monastery in Moscow. Russian painters did not sign their works until the 17th century, so paintings can be assigned to Rublev on the basis only of written evidence or of style.

Written evidence associates with his name wall paintings at Vladimir and Moscow and the panel, or icon, of the Old Testament Trinity; and by analogy of style a number of other icons can also be attributed to him. The chief of these are panels of St. John the Baptist, St. Paul, St. Peter and the Ascension, done in 1408 for the cathedral of the Dormition of the Virgin at Vladimir, and others of the archangel Michael and the Saviour from Zvenigorod, now in the Tretyakov gallery at Moscow. Icons of St. Paul, the archangel Gabriel, the Presentation, the Washing of the Feet and the Last Supper, from the Monastery of the Trinity and St. Sergius at Zagorsk are also probably to be assigned to him, though the attribution is not accepted by all authorities. A copy of the icon Our Lady of Vladimir in the Tretyakov gallery has also been ascribed to Rublev, and he is supposed to have painted in 1408 an icon of the Ascension in association with Daniel Chorny.

Rublev was trained wholly in the Byzantine tradition, in which the spiritual essence of art was regarded as more important than naturalistic representation. The very hieratical character of the mid-Byzantine style had, with the 14th century, given way in Constantinople to a more intimate, humanistic approach, but to this Rublev was able to add an element which was truly Russian, that of a complete unworldliness, and it is this which distinguishes his work from that of his Byzantine predecessors. Nor was any later Russian painter ever quite able to equal Rublev either in his handling or in the interpretation of his subject.

BIBLIOGRAPHY.—M. V. Alpatov, *Andrei Rublev*, in Russian (1959), "Andrei Rublev e l'arte bizantina," in *L'Arte*, 23:251–278 (1958); V. Lazarev, *Andrei Rublev*, in Russian (1960); also "La Trinité d'André Roublev," in *Gazette des Beaux Arts*, 54:289–300 (1959); W. Weidle, *Les Icones byzantines et russes* (1960). (D. T. RI.)

RUBRICS, directions for the conduct of divine service, inserted in service books at the beginning and in the course of the text and properly written or printed in red to distinguish them; hence, in popular speech, the text itself. The word comes from the Latin *rubrica* (from *ruber*, "red"), which originally meant the red earth used for colouring. Subsequently *rubrica* was applied to the red titles under which the Roman jurists arranged the laws and thence to the laws themselves. The practice of the lawyers was adapted by the Christian Church. In the earlier Christian centuries, local practices were commonly transmitted orally, and early medieval service books normally contain few rubrics. In the Latin West, however, from the 9th century onward, there was a class of compilation called *ordines* (*ordinaria*, *ordinales libri*), reference books which supply information about liturgical practice at Rome as the model for other churches.

In the 15th and 16th centuries liturgical scholars, following in a tradition already established by the great liturgical treatises *De sancto altaris mysterio* of Pope Innocent III and *Rationale divinorum officiorum* (*c.* 1286–91) of Guillaume Durand, began, with papal approbation, systematically to edit the rubrics of the missal, the breviary, and the ritual. *See also* LITURGY, CHRISTIAN.

In 1485 A. P. Piccolomini and J. Burchard published their *Pontificale*, giving the ordinary and ceremonies of the pontifical mass. Burchard followed this in 1502 with his *Ordo missae*, giving the general directions of the Roman Mass. In 1539 the *Directorium divinorum officiorum* was published by Lodovico Ciconialano. Finally, the *Rituale romanum* was published by order of Paul V in 1614. As a result of this codification, standardized rubrics appeared in the service books. The institution of the Sacred Congregation of Rites in 1587 supplied the Roman Catholic Church with a central interpreting authority for liturgical matters. The convention of writing or printing rubrics in red has long been observed by the Greek Orthodox Church. The service books of the Reformed churches, in whose worship ritual plays only a small part, have few rubrics. In early editions of the

Anglican Book of Common Prayer the rubrics were printed in black italic (in roman when a black-letter type was employed) but some modern editions have them in red. The so-called "black rubric" at the end of the communion service, denying the corporal presence of Christ in the Eucharist, is a 19th-century misnomer for a doctrinal declaration, which is not technically a rubric at all.

(GD. B.)

RUBRUQUIS (or RUBROUCK), **WILLIAM OF** (*c.* 1215–1295; *fl.* 1253–55), Franciscan friar and the author of the best eyewitness account of the Mongol realm written by a medieval Christian traveler, was a contemporary of Roger Bacon who cited him frequently in his *Opus majus*. The date and place of Friar William's birth are not known, but it has been shown that he probably came from the village of Rubrouck which lies about 8 mi. NE of Saint-Omer, France. There is no justification for the identification of his name of origin with Ruysbroeck (now Ruisbroek) in Brabant.

Though Friar William went to the Mongol Empire (Tartary) under order from Louis IX (St. Louis) in 1253, on every occasion, beginning with a sermon delivered at Hagia Sophia on Palm Sunday 1253, he denied that he was on a formal mission from the French king. This was undoubtedly because Louis's earlier envoy to Tartary (*see* ANDREW of Lonjumel) had returned bearing from the Mongol regent-mother a letter couched in terms so arrogant that the king regretted having dispatched a formal embassy. Nevertheless on learning, shortly after Friar Andrew's return, that Prince Sartak, the eldest son of Batu Khan (the Mongolian ruler on the Volga River), was a baptized Christian, Louis IX was moved to communicate with him and he appears to have chosen Friar William to lead an informal mission. The first date given by the friar is that of his sermon at Constantinople (April 13, 1253) but it is generally agreed that he received his commission at Acre where Louis resided between May 1252 and June 1253. At Constantinople he received letters to some of the Tartar chiefs from Baldwin II (de Courtenay), the last emperor of the Latin dynasty.

On May 7, 1253, Friar William and his party embarked at Constantinople and reached Soldaia (Sudak) on the Crimean coast two weeks later. There they secured oxen and carts for their long trek across the steppes to the encampment or *ordu* of Batu Khan, whom they reached when he was near the northernmost point of his summer marches (*i.e.,* about Ukek or Uvyek near Saratov). They marched with him five weeks down the Volga before he ordered them to proceed to the court of the Great Khan in the vicinity of Karakorum. This order involved an outward journey of about 5,000 mi. and an even longer return journey. So enormous a distance was not easy for "a very heavy man [*ponderosus valde*]" like Friar William. The Christians began their long journey on horseback on Sept. 16, 1253. Their route lay north of the Caspian and Aral seas to the Talas River which they reached on Nov. 8. They continued to Cailac Valley (possibly Kayalik near Kapal) where they remained 12 days. Setting out again on Nov. 30 they proceeded by way of the Ebi-nor depression to the great plains of Mongolia and came upon the Great Khan's camp at a locality about ten days' journey to the south of Karakorum (Dec. 27). There they found Nestorian priests.

Friar William and his companions were received courteously by Mangu Khan and remained with him until he ordered them to return to their own country (about May 26, 1254). They left his *ordu* about July 10 and set out once more for that of Batu Khan which they reached about Sept. 16. They followed a more northerly route than on their outward journey. About Nov. 1 they proceeded to the "Iron Gate" or defile at Derbent because the Black Sea route was closed in winter. They spent Christmas Day 1254 at Nakhichevan near Mt. Ararat. The rest of the homeward journey took nearly eight months; they traveled by way of Erzincan, Sivas, Iconium (Konya), Lajazzo, Cyprus, and Antioch (Antakya). They reached Tripoli on Aug. 15, 1255, and found that King Louis had returned to France the previous year. So Friar William wrote of his Mongolian experiences to the French king. His narrative is free from legend and shows him to have been an intelligent and honest observer. Roger Bacon, a brother Franciscan, made great use of Friar William's account in the geographical section of his own *Opus majus*. Nothing is known about the later history of Friar William save that he was alive when Marco Polo returned from the East in 1295.

After Roger Bacon's copious use of it, the narrative of Friar William was neglected, though five manuscripts survive. The chief of these are: (1) Corpus Christi College, Cambridge No. 66 (folios 67 v–110 v) of about 1320; (2) Corpus Christi College, Cambridge No. 181 (folios 321–398) of about 1270–90; (3) Leiden University Library, No. 77 (folios 160 r.–190 r.) of about 1290. The narrative did not appear in the *Speculum Historiale* of Vincent de Beauvais which pays so much attention to intercourse between Western Christendom and Tartary in the ·13th century. It was first printed imperfectly by Richard Hakluyt (1598 and 1599).

See W. W. Rockhill (ed.), *The Journey of William of Rubruck to the Eastern Parts of the World, 1253–55, as Narrated by Himself. With Two Accounts of the Earlier Journey of John of Pian de Carpini,* Hakluyt Society (1900); C. R. Beazley (ed.), *The Texts and Versions of John de Plano Carpini and William de Rubruquis,* Hakluyt Society (1903).

(E. M. J. C.)

RUBTSOVSK, a town of the Altayskiy (Altai) *kray*, Russian Soviet Federated Socialist Republic, U.S.S.R., stands on the Aley River, and on the Turksib railway from Barnaul to Semipalatinsk. Pop. (1959) 111,357. It is the centre of an important region of nonferrous ore mining. The town has a large agricultural machinery industry, producing chiefly diesel tractors and electrical equipment for tractors; also flour mills and other food-processing factories. There is a branch of the Altay Institute of Agricultural Engineering. (R. A. F.)

RUBY, a valued gem stone, is a red transparent variety of corundum, or alumina (Al_2O_3). It is named from the Latin *rubeus* ("red"). It is sometimes termed oriental ruby to distinguish it from the spinel (*q.v.*) ruby, which is a stone of inferior hardness, density, and value. The blue variety of corundum is sapphire (*q.v.*).

The ruby crystallizes in the rhombohedral system (*see* CORUNDUM); the crystals have no true cleavage, but tend to break along certain gliding planes. The colour varies from deep cochineal to pale rose-red, in some cases with a tinge of purple; the most valued tint is called pigeon's-blood. The ruby is a mineral of very limited distribution. Its most famous localities are in Upper Burma, principally in the neighbourhood of Mogok (*q.v.*), about 90 mi. (45 km.) NNE of Mandalay, where it was mined for many years. It occurs in ruby-bearing earth and in bands of a crystalline limestone, associated with granitic and gneissose rocks, some of which are highly basic; the limestone also contains spinel, garnet, graphite, wollastonite, scapolite, feldspar, mica, pyrrhotite, and other minerals. It also is found in India, Cambodia, Ceylon, Thailand, Afghanistan, and Tanganyika (Tanzania). Specimens have been reported from many places in the United States including North Carolina, Georgia, and Montana. The ruby, like other kinds of corundum, suffers alteration under certain conditions, and passes by hydration into gibbsite and diaspore, which by further alteration and union with silica, etc., may yield margarite, vermiculite, chlorite, and other hydrous silicates.

Rubies and sapphires have been produced artificially with success. It was once the practice to make "reconstructed rubies" by fusing together small fragments of the natural stone; but this process gave way to the Verneuil method of forming artificial ruby from purified ammonium alum and chromium sulfate (*see* GEM: *Synthetic Gems*). The synthetic ruby possesses the physical characters of the natural stone, but may generally be distinguished from it by microscopic bubbles and striae.

See also entries under "Ruby" in the Index.

RUDAKI (ABU ABDILLAH JA'FAR IBN MOHAMMED) (*c.* 859–941), though not the first poet to write in Persian is deservedly regarded as the "father of Persian poetry," and is still admired for the skill and freshness of his verse. He was also a talented singer and instrumentalist. He was born at Rudak near Samarkand, and served as court poet to the Samanid ruler Nasr ibn Ahmad (913–943) at Bukhara. Some writers claim that he was blind from birth, but this story is belied by the vivid descriptions of nature in his poetry.

His work is marked by an optimism that contrasts with the pessimistic tendencies of most of his successors. Of the enormous literary output attributed to him, fewer than 1,000 couplets have survived, scattered through many anthologies and biographical works, while of his most important work, the first Persian translation of the Indian *Panchatantra* (fables), only 88 couplets remain.

BIBLIOGRAPHY.—All extant verses by Rudaki are in vol. 3 of Sa'id Nafisi's biography *Ahval va ash'ar . . . Rudaki* (1940); German trans. of some by H. Ethé in "Rudagi der Samanidendichter," in *Nachrichten von der Gesellschaft der Wissenschaften Göttingen* (1873). *See also* E. G. Browne, *A Literary History of Persia*, vol. i (1928); H. Massé in *Encyclopaedia of Islam*, vol. 3 (1936). (L. P. E.-S.)

RUDDER, that part of the steering apparatus of a boat or ship which is fastened outside the hull, usually at the stern. The most common form consists of a nearly flat, smooth surface of wood or metal hinged at its forward edge to the sternpost. It operates on the principle of unequal water pressures. When the rudder is turned so that one side is more exposed to the force of the water flowing past it than the other side, the stern will be thrust way and the ship will swerve from its original course. In small craft the rudder is operated manually by a handle termed a tiller or helm. In larger vessels the rudder is turned by hydraulic, steam, or electrical machinery.

The earliest type of rudder was a paddle or an oar used to pry or row the stern of the craft around. The next development was to fasten a steering oar, in a semivertical position, to the vessel's side near the stern. This arrangement was improved by increasing the width of the blade and attaching a tiller to the upper part of the handle. Ancient Greek and Roman vessels frequently used two sets of these steering paddles. Rudders fastened to the vessel's sternpost did not come into general use until after the time of William the Conqueror. In ships having two or more screw propellers, rudders are fitted sometimes directly behind each screw.

Special types of rudders use various shapes to obtain greater effectiveness in maneuvering. The balanced rudder and the semi-balanced rudder are shaped so that the force of the water flowing by the rudder will be balanced or partially balanced on either side of its turning axis, thus easing the pressure on the steering mechanism or the helmsman. The lifting rudder is designed with a curvature along its lower edge which will lift the rudder out of danger should it strike an object or the bottom. The Kitchin reversing rudder has two semicircular blades just behind the propeller which can be adjusted to positions at various angles to the screw current and thus change the direction of its thrust; the blades can also be closed together to form a cup which catches and reverses the direction of the screw current, causing the vessel to go astern. (M. H. I.)

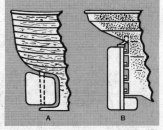

FROM FELIX RIESENBERG, "STANDARD SEAMANSHIP FOR THE MERCHANT SERVICE"; REPRODUCED BY PERMISSION OF D. VAN NOSTRAND CO.

(A) BALANCED RUDDER; (B) SEMI-BALANCED RUDDER

RUDE, FRANÇOIS (1784–1855), French romantic-realist sculptor, was born in Dijon on Jan. 4, 1784. After the death of his father, whom he had assisted in his metalworker's shop, he went to Paris determined to perfect himself in the art of sculpture. He won the Prix de Rome in 1812, but could not go to Rome because of the condition of Europe. He was an enthusiastic Bonapartist.

The attention of the public was first attracted to Rude by the Mercury attaching his winged sandals (1828; Louvre). This shows his training as a neoclassicist, but Rude was obviously uncomfortable within the restrictions of the classical canon and might be called rather a romantic-realist. In his Neapolitan fisherboy playing with a tortoise (1833; Louvre) the unusual pose and the open mouth both break with tradition. In the statue of

Marshal Ney in the Avenue de l'Observatoire in Paris, the hand with the sword raised above the head and the open mouth again violated neoclassic principles. The group of "Volunteers" (for the revolutionary campaign of 1792) on the Arc de Triomphe, although classical in detail, is romantic and impetuous in feeling. The reclining figure of Bonaparte (1847) at Fixin near Dijon (plaster cast in the Louvre), where he is represented as reclining on a rock awakening from sleep and shaking off his campaign cloak, is a famous failure. Toward the end of his life Rude returned to his early classical style. He died in Paris on Nov. 3, 1855.

See J. Calmette, *François Rude* (1920). (A. K. McC.)

RUDINI, ANTONIO STARABBA, MARCHESE DI (1839–1908), Italian statesman, twice premier of Italy, was born at Palermo, Sicily, on April 16, 1839, of an aristocratic Sicilian family that had long resented being ruled by the Neapolitan Bourbons. He was involved in the revolution which broke out against Naples in April 1860, but fled the country before Giuseppe Garibaldi (*q.v.*) arrived with his "Thousand" to support this revolt. After the Piedmontese annexation of Sicily he was for a time an attaché with the Italian Foreign Office at Turin. Then in 1864, while still only 25, he was appointed mayor of Palermo. In this position he showed great bravery during a rebellion which took place in September 1866. Considerable feeling had grown up in Sicily against the new government of Italy, and the mayor was even besieged for a week in the town hall. He was then promoted to prefect, with the task of putting down brigandage in the west of Sicily. In 1869, though not yet a deputy, he was for a month minister of the interior. On the death of Marco Minghetti in 1886 he became leader of the parliamentary right wing, and in 1891 he succeeded Francesco Crispi as premier (for one year). It was remarkable that he chose to form a coalition with Giovanni Nicotera of the left.

The crisis consequent upon the military disaster of Aduwa in Ethiopia (March 1896) brought Rudini back again to power as premier and minister of the interior. He concluded peace with Ethiopia, and to satisfy the anti-colonial party he ceded Kassala to Great Britain, thus provoking much indignation in Italy. At home his policy was not sufficiently elastic to avoid serious rioting which broke out in 1898; nor was he sufficiently forceful in putting down an incipient Socialist revolution. So he fell from power in June. He died in Rome on Aug. 7, 1908. (D. M. SH.)

RUDOLF, Holy Roman emperor: *see* RUDOLF, German kings.

RUDOLF, the name of three German kings, the first of whom was merely an antiking and the last not only king but Holy Roman emperor.

RUDOLF OF RHEINFELDEN (d. 1080), antiking from 1077, was a son of Kuno, count of Rheinfelden (on the upper Rhine east of Basel), who held lands both in the Kingdom of Burgundy and in neighbouring Swabia. The dowager empress, Agnes of Poitou, regent for her infant son Henry IV (*q.v.*), enfiefed Rudolf with the duchy of Swabia (1057) and made him administrator of the Kingdom of Burgundy. She also gave him her daughter Matilda in marriage (1059), but Matilda died in 1060. Rudolf, whose second wife, Adelaide of Turin, was sister of Henry IV's first wife, Bertha, at first supported his brother-in-law. In 1076, however, when Pope Gregory VII excommunicated Henry and proclaimed him deposed, Rudolf turned against the king. Promising to respect the elective character of the monarchy and to renounce any royal right to the investiture (*q.v.*) of prelates, he was elected king by an assembly of dissident princes at Forchheim on March 13, 1077, and crowned at Mainz on March 26. Unable to win support in Swabia, he joined forces with the Saxons and fought against Henry at Mellrichstadt in Franconia (Aug. 7, 1078) and, more successfully, at Flarchheim in Thuringia (Jan. 27, 1080). Recognized at last as king by the pope at the Lenten synod, he won a victory over Henry on the Elster River on Oct. 15, 1080, but received a wound of which he died next day. He was buried at Merseburg. (X.)

RUDOLF I (1218–1291), German king from 1273, was born at Limburg-im-Breisgau on May 1, 1218, the son of Albert IV, count of Habsburg, and Heilwic of Kyburg. At his father's death (*c.*

1239) he inherited lands in upper Alsace, the Aargau, and the Breisgau, which formed a transit point for the increasing flow of commercial traffic through the St. Gotthard pass over the Alps. A partisan of the Hohenstaufen emperor Frederick II and his son Conrad IV, he increased his territories largely at the expense of his uncle, Count Hartmann of Kyburg, and his cousin, Count Hartmann the Younger, who supported the papal cause against the Hohenstaufens; and his first marriage (c. 1245), to Gertrude of Zollern-Hohenberg-Haigerloch (d. 1281), also added to his domains.

Rudolf's election as German king, at Frankfurt on Oct. 1, 1273, was precipitated by the desire of the electors to exclude an excessively powerful rival candidate of non-German birth, Otakar II (q.v.) of Bohemia. Crowned at Aachen on Oct. 24, 1273, he was recognized by Pope Gregory X on Sept. 26, 1274, on his promise to renounce all imperial rights in Rome, in the papal territories, and in Sicily, and to lead a new crusade. The pope also persuaded Alfonso X of Castile, who had been chosen German king in 1257, to abandon his claim in 1275. Rudolf broke the Bohemian opposition on Aug. 26, 1278, at the Battle of Dürnkrut, where Otakar II was slain. By granting the duchies of Austria and Styria, former Bohemian possessions, to his sons Albert and Rudolf (Dec. 21, 1282), Rudolf I constituted the territorial nucleus of the later Habsburg power (see AUSTRIA, EMPIRE OF; HABSBURG).

Rudolf made great efforts, in concert with the territorial princes, to enforce the public peace (Landfriede) in Germany; and in 1274 he reasserted the right of the monarchy to impose taxation on the cities. But his attempt to reconstitute the duchy of Swabia came to nothing after the death, in 1290, of his younger son Rudolf, to whom he had granted it as an appanage; and his attempt, in 1290, to install his elder son Albert on the Hungarian throne was frustrated.

Rudolf combated the expansionist policy of the French kings Philip III and Philip IV on his western frontier by marrying Isabella, daughter of Hugh IV, duke of Burgundy (Feb. 5, 1284), and by compelling Otto IV, count of Burgundy, to do homage (1289). But French influence at the papal court prevented his being crowned as Holy Roman emperor by the pope in Rome. Rudolf was likewise unsuccessful in his repeated efforts, between 1287 and 1291, to secure the election of his son Albert as German king or king of the Romans, since the German electors were determined that the crown should not become a hereditary possession of the powerful house of Habsburg. Thus the electors' freedom of action remained intact when Rudolf died, at Speyer, on July 15, 1291.   (C. C. BA.)

RUDOLF II (1552–1612), Holy Roman emperor from 1576, was born in Vienna on July 18, 1552, as the eldest surviving son of the emperor Maximilian II and Maria, daughter of the emperor Charles V. He was educated in Spain from 1563 to 1571. Crowned king of Hungary on Sept. 26, 1572, and of Bohemia on Sept. 22, 1575, he was elected king of the Romans, or German king, on Oct. 25, 1575, and succeeded his father as emperor on Oct. 12, 1576. He then inherited all Maximilian's patrimonial lands; and to these he added the Tirol and other territories on the death of his uncle, the archduke Ferdinand, in 1595.

Rudolf was subject to fits of morbid depression, and soon retired to Prague, where he lived in greater and greater seclusion. He was much interested in chemistry, medicine, astronomy, astrology, and alchemy, became the patron of Tycho Brahe and Kepler and of all the arts, and himself dabbled in many sciences and arts; his collection of rare works of art was the greatest of the age. He never married, but had several illegitimate children.

During the first 20 years of Rudolf's rule, the institutions of the Reich ceased to function because of disputes between Catholics and Protestants, though Rudolf exerted considerable influence on the infrequent Reichstage (imperial Diets) by consistently supporting the Catholic viewpoint. He promoted unsuccessful negotiations between Spain and the Netherlands in 1579 and was at first on poor terms with Spain and occasionally suspicious of papal policy. In Austria he reversed Maximilian II's tolerant religious policy and sought to limit the political privileges of the Protestant Estates (the nobles and representatives of the towns).

Revolts of the Austrian peasants were suppressed (1594–97), but the Protestants and the Estates of all Rudolf's lands benefited from his financial difficulties, which were increased after 1593 by the renewal of war against the Turks.

Rudolf's mental illness grew worse after 1598, impairing his willpower and aggravating his violent and suspicious nature; he evaded political decisions and relied on the advice of his personal servants. Attacks on religious and political privileges in Rudolf's lands were intensified after 1600, and Hungary revolted in 1604 under István Bocskay, who allied himself with the Turks.

The Habsburg archdukes, long discontented with Rudolf's political incompetence and failure to provide for the succession, compelled him in 1605 to entrust the conduct of Hungarian affairs to his brother Matthias (q.v.); and in April 1606 they recognized Matthias as their head and as their candidate for Rudolf's succession. Rudolf spent the rest of his life seeking vengeance on Matthias. Disliking the treaties made by Matthias with the Hungarians and with the Turks in 1606, he prepared to renew the war,. but Matthias allied himself with the Estates of Hungary, Austria, and Moravia, and forced Rudolf to cede these lands to him in June 1608 and to promise him the succession in Bohemia. Rudolf unsuccessfully sought the assistance of the German princes and even of the Protestants, toward whom he occasionally expressed a more tolerant attitude in his last years. In July 1609 the Bohemian Estates compelled him to grant them religious freedom and political privileges in the Majestätsbrief (Letter of Majesty); and similar concessions were made in Silesia and Lusatia.

The Reichstag had collapsed in 1608, the religious parties of Germany formed rival leagues, and Rudolf's troops were expelled from Jülich (q.v.), where he had intervened in the dispute over the Cleves-Jülich-Berg inheritance. In 1611, when mutinous imperial troops under the archduke Leopold ravaged Bohemia with Rudolf's support, the Bohemian Estates sought help from Matthias, whose army virtually held Rudolf prisoner in Prague till he abdicated Bohemia to Matthias in May. Rudolf, however, prevented Matthias' election as king of the Romans, or successor designate to the Empire.

Rudolf died in Prague on Jan. 20, 1612. He had greater political acumen than Matthias, who eventually succeeded him as emperor; but illness and unpopularity weakened him in their conflict and prevented him from restraining the religious dissensions of his lands and the Empire which were to lead to the Thirty Years' War.   (H. J. Co.)

BIBLIOGRAPHY.—Rudolf I: H. Roeder, Rudolf von Habsburg als römischer König (1926); O. Brunner, Kaiser und Reich im Zeitalter der Habsburger und Luxemburger (1953).   (C. C. BA.)

  Rudolf II: A. Gindely, Rudolf II. und seine Zeit, vol. i, 2nd ed., and ii (1863–65); F. Stieve, Die Verhandlungen über die Nachfolge Kaiser Rudolfs II. (1879); M. Ritter, Deutsche Geschichte im Zeitalter der Gegenreformation und des dreissigjährigen Krieges, 1555–1648, 3 vol. (1889–1908).   (H. J. Co.)

RUDOLF (1858–1889), Austrian archduke and crown prince, concerning whose death there has been lasting speculation. He was born at Laxenburg, near Vienna, on Aug. 21, 1858, the only son of the emperor Francis Joseph (q.v.) and the empress Elizabeth. Heir to the throne, he received an extensive education and traveled widely. Politically, his anxiety to overcome the problem of the various nationalities of the Habsburg monarchy and his antipathy to Russian imperialism were combined with liberal and anticlerical views which alienated him from his father and from the prime minister, Eduard, Graf von Taaffe (q.v.). The emperor excluded him from the business of government and arranged his marriage (May 10, 1881) to Stephanie, daughter of Leopold II of the Belgians. She bore him a daughter, Elizabeth Marie, in 1883.

Rudolf in October 1881 came under the influence of a journalist, Moritz Szeps, to whose radical paper, the Neues Wiener Tagblatt, he contributed anonymous articles. He also published two books on his travels and sponsored a monumental survey of Austria-Hungary. At the same time he entertained schemes for having himself crowned king of Hungary and for resuscitating a Kingdom of Poland. Frustrated in his designs and unassuaged by transient amours, he fell into morbid despondency. The actress Mitzi

Kaspar, his mistress from 1887, declined his offer of a suicide pact in December 1888; but the baroness Mary Vetsera, an infatuated girl of 17 with whom he had begun relations only in October, accepted it. In the morning of Jan. 30, 1889, he and Mary were found shot dead in his bedroom in the hunting lodge at Mayerling. Maladroit attempts by the emperor and his advisers to disguise the facts provoked innumerable rumours; enemies of the Habsburg court added false interpretations; and romantic writers have battened on the stories. Apart from mental derangement, the most plausible explanation of Rudolf's act is that he believed that his dealings with the Hungarian opposition were about to be exposed.

BIBLIOGRAPHY.—*Das Mayerling-Original* (1955), published by the Vienna Police Directorate, gives the material of the official enquiry into the suicide. *See* further K. Lónyay, *Rudolf* (1950); R. Barkeley, *The Road to Mayerling* (1958).

RUDOLF, LAKE, is remotely situated in northern Kenya, but almost the entire northern shore lies north of the unratified boundary with Ethiopia. The physical setting of the lake comprises the low plateaus between the Kenya Highlands and the Ethiopian Highlands where Rift Valley structures give place to a downwarped surface in which faulting, though not entirely absent, is less in evidence. (*See* also KENYA: *Physical Geography*.) In the east and south the Tertiary and Quaternary volcanics give rise to rocky shores, while the lower western and northern shores, developed in Quaternary sediments, present sand dunes, sandspits, and mud flats. The three main islands, North, Central, and South, are volcanic. The lake is long and narrow (length 154 mi. [248 km.]; width varying from 10 to 20 mi.) and it has an area of 2,743 sq.mi. (7,104 sq.km.) (1958). Its surface is 1,230 ft. (375 m.) above sea level, and the greatest recorded depth is 240 ft. (73 m.), although the height of the lake and consequently its size tend to fluctuate.

At the mid-Pleistocene maximum there was an overflow northwestward to the Nile Valley; but Lake Rudolf is now situated in an inland drainage basin and its waters, though drinkable, are rendered brackish by their high soda content. The only perennial affluent is the Omo River from the Ethiopian Highlands; the Turkwel and the Kerio flow across the Turkana plains to make their intermittent contribution.

The climate of the lake and its adjacent lands is hot and, except in the extreme north, arid; and a persistent, sand-laden wind from the southeast adds to the discomfort. Sudden storms give the lake its treacherous reputation. In its waters abound huge Nile perch and various species of the carplike *tilapia*. Crocodiles are ubiquitous; the hippopotamus occurs less frequently; and migrant and local waterbirds are found on the shores. On the various delta fans a little sorghum millet is cultivated. The nomadic pastoralists of the neighbouring desert scrub, Nilo-Hamitic Turkana and Samburu on the west and south respectively, and various Hamitic-speaking groups on the east, have in the past shown little interest in the lake or in fishing.

Count Samuel Teleki and Lieut. Ludwig von Höhnel visited the lake in 1888 and named it Rudolf, after the crown prince of Austria. They approached from Lake Baringo, but the road route is now from Kitale via the administrative stations of Lodwar and Lokitaung in the Turkana district.

BIBLIOGRAPHY.—V. E. Fuchs, "The Lake Rudolf Rift Valley Expedition, 1934," in *Geogr. J.*, vol. 86 (1935), and "The Geological History of the Lake Rudolf Basin, Kenya Colony," in *Phil. Trans.*, Series B, vol. 229 (1939); F. Dixey, *Geology of Northern Kenya*, Kenya Geological Survey (1948); C. G. Richards (ed.), *Count Teleki and the Discovery of Lakes Rudolf and Stefanie* (1960). (S. J. K. B.)

RUDOLF VON EMS (c. 1200–c. 1254), probably the most prolific and versatile poet in Middle High German literature. Between about 1220 and 1254 he wrote five epic poems, totaling over 93,000 lines, still extant. Research has been unable to establish most of the facts of Rudolf's life on a basis firmer than that of conjecture, but he was probably born at Hohenems, near the Lake of Constance. Though influenced by Hartmann von Aue and Gottfried von Strassburg (*qq.v.*), his works show considerable originality. His earliest poem, *Der guote Gêrhart*, is the story of a Cologne merchant who, despite his unaristocratic calling, has all the courtly qualities of an Arthurian knight. His charity and

humility result in his being offered the crown of England, and in his rejection of the offer. The charm and realism of this poem are not equaled in Rudolf's other works, *Barlaam und Josaphat*, *Alexander*, *Willehalm von Orlens*, and the *Weltchronik*. The popularity of his writings can be gauged by the fact that there are over 80 extant manuscripts and manuscript fragments of the *Weltchronik* alone.

BIBLIOGRAPHY.—*Der guote Gêrhart*, ed. by John A. Asher (1962); *Barlaam und Josaphat*, ed. by F. Pfeiffer (1843); *Alexander*, ed. by V. Junk (1928–29); *Willehalm von Orlens*, ed. by V. Junk (1905); *Weltchronik*, ed. by G. Ehrismann (1915). *See* also F. Sengle, "Die Patrizierdichtung 'Der gute Gerhard'," *Deutsche Vierteljahrsschrift*, vol. xxiv (1950). (J. A. AR.)

RUDOLPH (RAOUL) (d. 936), duke of Burgundy, king of France from 923 to 936, was the son of Duke Richard, called le Justicier. Son-in-law of King Robert I (922–923), with whom he had rebelled (922) against the Carolingian Charles III the Simple, Rudolph was elected king by the magnates (July 13, 923) a month after Robert's death in battle. Rudolph's reign was little more than an unending series of battles, and he was at first recognized by only a few of the magnates. His troubles included attacks by the Normans (924–926), the loss of Lorraine (925) to the German king Henry I the Fowler, and a rebellion in Aquitaine (926). Meanwhile Count Herbert of Vermandois, who had captured Charles (late 923), extracted the county of Laon from Rudolph (928) by threatening to release the Carolingian. After Charles's death (929) Rudolph's position improved; his defeat of the Normans in the Limousin regained him the allegiance of Aquitaine, and by 935 he was acknowledged king throughout France. But he died on Jan. 14 or 15, 936.

See P. Lauer, *Robert Ier et Raoul de Bourgogne, rois de France* (1910), (ed.) *Les Annales de Flodoard* (1905). (J. DE.)

RUDOLSTADT, a town of East Germany in the *Bezirk* (district) of Gera, German Democratic Republic, is on the left bank of the Saale, 8 mi. (13 km.) N of Saalfeld and 23½ mi. (38 km.) SW of Jena by road. Pop. (1964) 30,087. The name of "Rudolfestat" occurs in an early 9th-century inventory of the possessions of the abbey of Hersfeld. It came into the hands of the counts of Schwarzburg-Blankenburg in 1334. From 1574 to 1918 it was the residence of the ruling house of Schwarzburg-Rudolstadt, their former seat being Schloss Heidecksburg on the wooded Hainberg above the Saale, rebuilt in Rococo style after a fire of 1735. It is now a museum. Schloss Ludwigsburg, built in 1734, their former temporary seat, is now a music school. The town is a tourist resort and has a theatre. Industries include the manufacture of porcelain, glass, chemicals, and hardware.

RUDRA, a minor god of Vedic India who doubtless personified lightning (the "red" one, probably), but also protected cattle against it. In the Rig Veda he is identified with Agni (*q.v.*), but in the later Vedas he is called an archer and his malevolence is emphasized. In the later literature also he is said to have had as spouse (or sister) Ambika, one of the names of the mother goddess Shakti. Best known as father of the storm-gods (Maruts), in the Epic period he becomes many Rudras and in modern Hinduism is identified with Shiva.

RUE, the name of a woody or bushy herb, belonging to the genus *Ruta* (family Rutaceae), especially *R. graveolens*, the common rue, a plant with bluish-green spotted leaves and greenish-yellow flowers, native to Europe and sparingly naturalized in eastern North America. It has a strong pungent smell and the leaves have a bitter taste. The plant was much used in medieval and later times as a stimulative and irritant drug. It was commonly supposed to be widely used by witches. From its association with "rue" (sorrow, repentance), the plant was also known as "herb of grace" and was taken as the symbol of repentance.

RUEDA, LOPE DE (c. 1510–1565), Spanish actor-manager and playwright, an important figure in the development of Spanish drama (*see* SPANISH LITERATURE: *The Renaissance and the Siglo de Oro: Early Drama*). Born at Seville, he became a goldbeater, and, later, an actor, and toured Spain with his own company of players. He is mentioned as an actor-manager chosen to perform before Philip II at Benavente in 1554, and in 1564 was at Seville, where his plays may have been seen by Cervantes, who praises him as a talented actor of stock comic parts, an outstanding writer of pastoral verse, and the dominant figure of early Spanish drama. He died at Córdoba in 1565.

Rueda's most important contribution to Spanish drama was his creation of the *paso*, a short one-act play or interlude, based on an incident from everyday life (*e.g.*, a quarrel between husband and wife), and written in a free, naturalistic dialogue, reflecting the tone and idiom of popular speech. He also wrote four short prose comedias (*Medora, Armelina, Eufemia, Los Engañados*) and two dramatic dialogues (*Coloquio de Camila* and *Coloquio de Tymbria*). The plots of these, chiefly on themes of accidental separation and joyful reunion, are taken from Italian comedy, and make much use of implausible vicissitudes and coincidences. They are notable, however, for their lively minor comic characters and comic scenes.

BIBLIOGRAPHY.—Rueda's plays were first published in 1567. His *Obras* were ed. by E. Cotarelo y Mori, 2 vol. (1908); and his *Teatro* (a selection), by J. Moreno Villa (1924). *See also* H. A. Rennert, *The Spanish Stage in the Time of Lope de Vega* (1909; new ed. 1964); E. Cotarelo y Mori, *Lope de Rueda y el teatro español de su tiempo* (1898); M. Bataillon, in the *Bulletin Hispanique*, xxxvii (1935); G B. Palacin, in the *Hispanic Review*, xx (1952). (L. J. Cl.)

RUEIL-MALMAISON, a town of northern France in the *arrondissement* of Saint-Germain-en-Laye, and the former *département* of Seine-et-Oise, 8½ mi. (14 km.) W of Paris. Pop. (1962) 46,515. Originally called Rotalajum, a pleasure resort of the Merovingian kings, it was given by Charles the Bald to the Abbey of Saint-Denis in 875, and later it grew by donations of land and the grant of civic rights until it was partly destroyed when Edward III devastated Normandy as far as the outskirts of Paris in 1346. In 1630 Cardinal Richelieu bought an estate there and carried out extensive building. In 1799 Josephine Bonaparte purchased the château and domain of Malmaison ("house of misfortune"). Napoleon liked the place (then called Ruel, and Rueil after 1805) and rested there between campaigns. The decree instituting the order of the Legion of Honour was signed there.

After his defeat in 1815 Napoleon spent a short while at Malmaison and said farewell to his remaining troops. The empress and her daughter, Hortense Beauharnais, are buried at Rueil in the Renaissance chapel, rebuilt by Napoleon III. The château is now a museum. (P. Fi.)

RUFF (*Philomachus pugnax*), a shore bird of the family Scolopacidae, taking its name from the frill of elongated feathers round the neck of the breeding male, to which the name is properly confined; the female, a much smaller bird, is termed the reeve. The plumage of the male is extremely variable, but the same markings

ARTHUR CHRISTIANSEN

MALE RUFFS (PHILOMACHUS PUGNAX) IN COURTSHIP DISPLAY

are reproduced after every molt in each individual bird. The ruff ranges across the whole of northern Europe and Asia and migrates south to India, Ceylon, and Africa in winter.

These birds, of no commercial or game value, are of interest because of their remarkable courtship behaviour and mating habits.

The ruffs live apart from the reeves throughout most of the year, but as breeding time nears they begin to grow their neck frills and return to ancestral courtship areas in the spring. A group of cocks display on a slightly raised patch in a field: each bird charges about in his own chosen territory, ruffling his frill and shaking his partially extended and drooping wings. When a reeve approaches, the ruffs appear entranced and shiver noticeably; she walks into the area and selects her mate by nipping him. Pairing takes place immediately. The mating behaviour varies from monogamy to polygamy and promiscuity. The female builds the nest and rears the young; the male takes no interest in nesting or in his offspring.

See also COURTSHIP, ANIMAL: *Vertebrates: Birds;* BIRD: *Breeding.*

See E. A. Armstrong, *Bird Display and Behaviour* (1947).

RUFFINI, PAOLO (1765–1822), Italian mathematician and physician whose researches on equations contained anticipations of the algebraic theory of groups, is generally regarded as the first to show that general algebraic equations of degree five or higher cannot be solved with radicals.

Born in Valentano, Viterbo, on Sept. 22, 1765, he spent almost his whole life at Modena, having moved there with his father as an infant. He taught at the University of Modena from 1787 to 1798 when he was dismissed by the Cisalpine government because he refused to take the civil oath. In 1799 he was recalled to the university as professor in clinical medicine and applied mathematics and in 1801 became professor in analysis and geometry. Ruffini remained when the university became a secondary school (1802), teaching higher mathematics there. In 1807 he left to teach applied mathematics for the military school at Modena (later the Italian Military Academy), which ceased operation in 1814 with the end of the Napoleonic reign. The ducal University of Modena having been restored, Ruffini was made rector there and again taught clinical medicine and applied mathematics.

For many years president of the Italian Society of Sciences (Society of the Forty), Ruffini was a member of the National Napoleonic Institute. He died at Modena on May 9, 1822.

Ruffini is recognized as the first (1799) to show that the general quintic (or higher) equation cannot be expressed in terms of radicals. His demonstration was criticized by his contemporaries for lack of rigour and it remained for N. H. Abel (*q.v.*) to furnish more conclusive corroboration in 1824. Ruffini's notion that a group need not include a subgroup of an order that arbitrarily divides that of the group is sometimes called Ruffini's theorem. This was fundamental to the work done later by É. Galois and A. L. Cauchy in group theory (*see* FIELDS: *Galois Theory*).

RUFINUS (FLAVIUS RUFINUS) (d. 395), a minister of the Roman emperor Arcadius, was a native of Gaul. Theodosius I, at his death on Jan. 17, 395, had left Rufinus as Arcadius' chief adviser. He at once became the rival of Stilicho (*q.v.*) and tried to strengthen his position by marrying his only daughter to Arcadius. The match was prevented, however, by the chamberlain, a eunuch called Eutropius, who eventually took Rufinus' place as the emperor's chief minister. When Stilicho landed in Greece to suppress a rising of the Visigoths, he sent some troops, commanded by Gainas, to Constantinople; they murdered Rufinus there on Nov. 27, 395. A posthumous attack on him by the poet Claudianus survives. (E. A. T.)

RUFINUS, TYRANNIUS (*c.* 345–410/411), Christian priest, writer, and translator of Origen, was born at Concordia, near Aquileia, in northern Italy. The son of Christian parents, he studied at Rome, meeting Jerome there. In his 20s he became a monk at Aquileia and was baptized; and since Jerome frequently visited his monastery the two became fast friends. About 373, drawn by his interest in Eastern theology and monasticism, Rufinus journeyed to Egypt, where after a stay with the desert fathers he became the pupil of Didymus the Blind, being fired by him with enthusiasm for Origen. He also became the friend of another devout seeker after perfection, the wealthy Roman widow Melania. In 378 he followed her to Palestine, and while she established a convent for virgins at Jerusalem he with her aid founded one for men nearby. When Jerome settled near Bethlehem in 386, the friendship between the two men was renewed. At some time during his stay in Jerusalem Rufinus was ordained priest.

Till then his life had been peaceful, but in the early 390s he, with Jerome, became involved in the acrimonious controversy about Origen's teaching, which the strictly orthodox now regarded with suspicion. In 393 both were charged with Origenist leanings, but while Jerome readily made formal abjuration of the errors alleged, Rufinus refused to do so. In 394, when Epiphanius sharply attacked Bishop John of Jerusalem, Rufinus sprang to his defense. A fierce quarrel thus broke out between Rufinus and Jerome. It had been smoothed over by 397, when Rufinus returned to Italy, but flared up with intensified bitterness when he published in Rome a whitewashing Latin translation of Origen's *De principiis* with a preface representing Jerome as an admirer of Origen's. Henceforth he was exposed to merciless abuse from Jerome, and his own orthodoxy was called in question. He even found himself obliged to address a reasoned *Apologia* to Pope Anastasius, who had summoned him to Rome. He was now deeply immersed in literary work, but in 407, shaken perhaps by the barbarian invasions menacing northern Italy, he moved south from Aquileia to Pinetum, near Terracina. Here he continued his studies, but was driven thence when Alaric's hordes invested Rome in 408. Making for Africa, he crossed over to Sicily, and he was there, busily translating Origen's homilies, when he died in 410 or 411, possibly at or near Messina.

As a writer Rufinus did valuable service by translating Greek theological works into Latin in an age when the knowledge of Greek was declining in the West. His translation of Origen's *De principiis* is the only complete text of the work surviving, and he also translated certain of Origen's Bible commentaries and a host of his homilies on Old Testament books. Rufinus' other translations include Pamphilus' *Apologia* for Origen, the *Clementine Recognitions*, eight homilies of Basil and the two versions of his rule, nine homilies by Gregory of Nazianzus, and Eusebius' ecclesiastical history. Often his renderings were loose paraphrases or even shortened adaptations, and in Origen's case he did not hesitate to modify or suppress dubious passages on the theory that they must have been altered or interpolated by unorthodox hands. His original writings include (besides his *Apologia* to Pope Anastasius) a second and more irate *Apologia* against Jerome, two books continuing Eusebius' ecclesiastical history, the *De benedictionibus patriarcharum* (allegorically expounding Gen. 49), and a commentary on the Apostles' Creed. This last is important both as a sample of intelligent contemporary catechetical teaching, and as providing the earliest continuous Latin text of the Western baptismal creed (*see* CREED).

BIBLIOGRAPHY.—Rufinus' original works are in J. P. Migne, *Patrologia Latina*, vol. 21 (1849); a critical edition of his ecclesiastical history is by T. Mommsen in E. Schwartz's edition of Eusebius' church history, vol. 2 (1908); Eng. trans. of his commentary on the Apostles' Creed by J. N. D. Kelly in the "Ancient Christian Writers Series" (1955). Rufinus' translations are in the editions of the relevant Greek authors; a critical edition of the translation of Gregory of Nazianzus' homilies is by A. Engelbrecht, *Corpus scriptorum ecclesiasticorum Latinorum*, vol. 46 (1910). *See* also F. X. Murphy, *Rufinus of Aquileia* (1945).

(J. N. D. K.)

RUFISQUE, a town and port of the Republic of Senegal, about 18 mi. (29 km.) E of the capital, Dakar. It is on the Dakar-Niger railway and is also connected by rail with Saint-Louis; roads follow the same routes. Pop. (1958) 47,000 (comm.). Formerly the Portuguese Rio Fresco, it was of considerable importance in the 14th century as a port, but declined after the development of the port of Dakar. However, its proximity to the capital has stimulated industrial development; products of the town's factories include leather, cement, edible oil, biscuits (cookies), chocolates, and cotton; titanium and zirconium are mined locally. Fishing is important and has given rise to factories for smoking, drying, and canning the catch. Rufisque has three parts: (1) The old town, parallel with the shore, retains the atmosphere of the old colonial towns. The streets, arranged in a grid pattern, are lined with buildings, with wooden balconies on the upper stories and shops below. (2) These European-type houses give way, farther from the front, to the low houses of the African traders. (3) A new modern town, associated with the industrial de-

velopment, has sprung up along the road to Dakar. The need for labour has also given rise to an increasing number of African villages lining the shore. (J. D.)

RUG AND CARPET. The term "carpet" was used until the 19th century for any cover made of a thick material, especially a table cover, but now means almost exclusively a floor covering. This article deals only with handmade carpets; in this area, and particularly with reference to Oriental carpets, the terms "carpet" and "rug" are used interchangeably. Carpets may be of felt, tapestry, a shuttle-woven material, or a pile fabric. The last is the most frequent and typical. In the ancient and primitive Orient some kind of covering was necessary, especially on beaten-earth floors. In the West the advantages of a fabric underfoot were recognized, and carpets of some kind or other have been an almost universal adjunct of civilization; in both the East and West their manufacture finally developed into a very large industry. Such floor coverings offer most interesting opportunities for ornamentation, and in the Orient, where both the craft and the art originated, carpet weaving and design attained, over a period of at least 2,500 years, a degree of excellence that warrants ranking the finest specimens with man's most notable artistic achievements.

This article is arranged as follows:

For a discussion of methods of making carpet both by hand and by machine *see* CARPET MANUFACTURE. There are also articles on the related topics TAPESTRY and TEXTILES.

I. HISTORICAL SURVEY

1. Antiquity and the Middle Ages.—Felt (*q.v.*) is almost certainly the most ancient form of carpet for it probably originated as bark felt, even as early as the Upper Paleolithic Period, about 25,000–30,000 years ago. Floor coverings of plaited rushes have also been used since very early times. Evidences of basket plaiting appear in the Upper Paleolithic Period, and archaeological finds in Iraq indicate that floor coverings of plaited rushes, such as grew in the Mesopotamian swamps, were used by the 5th or 4th millennium. These rushes made stout, durable, portable mats, and even at an early period they were probably handsomely ornamented, judging from the competence in decorative pattern shown on contemporary painted pottery and on the decorated walls of the Chalcolithic village at Persepolis. The weaving of rush mats in the Middle East had reached a high degree of artistic perfection and prestige by medieval times and has continued there to the present day.

Rug design, in western Asia at least, evolved beyond the limited possibilities of felt and plaited mats long before the 1st millennium B.C.; for example, a threshold rug, represented in a stone carving (now in the Musée du Louvre) from the Assyrian palace of Khorsabad (8th century B.C.), has an allover field pattern of quatrefoils, framed by a lotus border, completed by guard stripes. Other Assyrian carvings of the period also show rich and handsome patterns that have survived in the repertoire of

DETAIL OF THRESHOLD RUG REPRE- SENTED IN A STONE CARVING FROM THE ASSYRIAN PALACE OF KHORSA- BAD, 8TH CENTURY B.C. IN THE LOUVRE

carpets ever since.

By historic times the carpets of the Near East had attained fame and magnificence. Classi- cal authors speak with admiration of the luxurious Babylonian car- pets (see A. U. Dilley, *Oriental Rugs and Carpets*, 1931, p. 11), and, in the tomb of Cyrus, Alex- ander the Great found the gold funeral couch resting on carpets of very fine fabric. Both Athe- naeus and Xenophon indicate that some of these were thick and resilient, but we cannot be sure whether they were pile woven or made of embroidered felt, though some were evidently gold-en- riched. Certain types were re- served for court use, and were so costly that they were important items in the royal treasury. Finds from tombs dating from the 5th to the 3rd century B.C. at Pazyryk in the foothills of the western Altai include various articles of felt with appliqué patterns, and a superb carpet with a woolen pile, said to be knotted with the Ghiordes or Turkish knot. This carpet, probably of Persian origin, is about six feet (about two metres) square. The central field has a quatrefoil pattern reminiscent of the Assyrian stone carvings mentioned above. Of the two wide borders, the inner one shows a frieze of deer, the outer one a frieze of horsemen; there are guard stripes between. The carpet is now in the Hermitage Museum, Leningrad. Fragments of two more carpets of the same type were also found at Pazyryk and are now in the Hermitage.

Some embroidered carpets have been found in tombs of the 1st century B.C. to 1st century A.D. at Noin Ula in northern Mon- golia (C. Trever, *Excavations in Northern Mongolia*, 1932); these are also in the Hermitage Museum. A felt example (originally about 6 ft. 5 in. × 8 ft. 6 in.) had the field filled with a spiral meander; a broad border with animal-combat groups (alternately tiger and yak, and griffin and elk) alternating with a tree; an inner guard stripe of geometrical units; and a wide margin of Chinese lozenge-patterned silk. The pat- terns were executed with quilting (field), and couched cord on a quilted ground (main border; in- ner guard stripe solid couched cord), and the colours as re- constituted by chemical tests (V. Komonov, Moscow-Lenin- grad, 1937) were vivid; yellow quilting on a red field; a red border with blue and green fig- ures outlined with white; and green, red, yellow, and blue in varying succession in the guard stripes.

Another piece embroidered in wool on wool in stem and satin stitches was still more complex in organization: on the field, a diagonal lattice defined by scroll- ing stems, with a cross-treflé at

DETAIL FROM THE KNOTTED HAIR CARPET FROM PAZYRYK; END OF 5TH CENTURY B.C. SIZE: 6 FT. × 6 FT. 7 IN. IN THE HERMITAGE MU- SEUM, LENINGRAD

each intersection and a tortoise alternating with a fish in each unit, in blue, purple, and tans on a red ground; a diagonally hatched field margin; beyond, an inner border system, with double guard stripes on both sides; then the main wide border, filled with a concentric lozenge diaper pattern, and with an inner guard stripe; and finally an outer binding of red and brown checked flax and wool material. These pieces are datable by a lacquer bowl found with them which is inscribed with the equivalent of A.D. 3. Some of them are of great beauty; their intricate patterns are clearly

delineated and well coordinated.

The Noin Ula finds also include some fragments of pile carpets. They are woven of fine, lustrous, still elastic wool, of deep indigo blue. The pile is very thick and dense, the knots or loops having been firmly compacted, though the strands are merely wrapped round one warp thread, a simple technique that later made its way to Spain. (A. U. Pope, in Pope [ed.], *A Survey of Persian Art*, Oxford, 1938, iii, pp. 2272–73.) This same technique is also used in a number of fragments, assignable to the first three centuries A.D., found by Sir Aurel Stein in Loulan, Niya, and Tung-Huang in Chinese Turkistan (see Stein, *Serindia* [1921], Pls. 3, 7, 8; and *Innermost Asia* [1928]). The technique was continued in this region at least into the 7th or 8th century, as is proven by a frag- ment discovered by A. von Le Coq at Kizil.

By late Sasanian times (6th–7th century A.D.) carpet weaving in Persia had won international prestige, and according to the Sui annals woolen rugs were being exported to distant China (*Sui-šu*, chap. 83; Berthold Laufer, *Sino-Iranica*, 1919, p. 493). The carpets of this period were of several kinds: woolen or silk, either pile or tapestry-woven, embroidered, or even of shuttle- woven silk (*dibaj*) (Pope, *A Survey of Persian Art*, iii, 1939, p. 2273).

Carpets made for the royal palace exceeded in cost and mag- nificence anything created or imagined either before or since. Surpassing them all was the so-called Spring or Winter carpet of Khosrau, made for the vast audience hall of the palace at Ctesi- phon. It represented a formal garden with its watercourses, paths, rectangular beds filled with flowers, and blossoming shrubs and fruit trees. The body of the rug was silk, the yellow gravel was represented by gold, the blossoms, fruit, and birds were worked with pearls and every kind of jewel. The wide outer border rep- resenting a green meadow was solid with emeralds. The rug was about 84 ft. square, and when the great portal curtains were drawn back and the sun flooded the sumptuously decorated and lofty interior (121 ft. high), it must have been a spectacle of overwhelm- ing splendour.

This deployment of the national treasure, which would other- wise have been unproductively locked in dark vaults, demon- strated the power and resources of the king to the ambitious nobles, restless provincial governors, or foreign envoys who gathered in his court. In addition to its political significance and its beauty, happily alleviating the grim winter months, the carpet symbolized the divine role of the king, whose primal task was to regulate the seasons and to guarantee and compel the return of the spring, thus renewing the earth's fertility and assuring the live- lihood and prosperity of his subjects. Furthermore, the carpet had still further religious significance: it prefigured paradise (a Persian word meaning "walled park"), for, with its flowers, birds, and water, it personified deliverance from the asperities of the desert and promised eternal felicity.

The carpet was part of the fabulous booty of the Arabs, cap- tured when they defeated the Persians and took Ctesiphon (637). It was cut up into small fragments; one-fifth went to the caliph Omar, one piece to Ali, the Prophet's son-in-law, and the rest was distributed to the 60,000 victorious soldiers, who in turn sold their pieces to a jeweler's syndicate in Baghdad for an average of $3,000 each, counting the drachma as worth only 25 cents. This is on the authority of al-Tabari, one of the ablest of the Arab historians, whose account is confirmed by others and by certain internal and supplementary evidence as well. The original value of the carpet was thus certainly in excess of $200,000,000.

This most sumptuous of all fabrics made a profound impression on all, especially the Persians. It entered as a living, legendary power into history, poetry, and art; and for centuries it served to sustain Persian morale. For more than 1,000 years it furnished the model and inspiration for subsequent carpets, though even the most ambitious could no more than hint at the general design. Of the subsequent renderings of the garden scheme the oldest is a printed cotton panel to be dated between the 9th and 11th century (O. Wulff-W. F. Volbach, *Spätantike und koptische Stoffe*, Berlin, 1926, pl. 130) which shows in miniature essentially the same scheme, and this has persisted down to the present as one of the

18TH-CENTURY GARDEN CARPET FROM NORTHERN PERSIA WOVEN WITH KNOTTED WOOLEN PILE ON COTTON WARP. ITS DESIGN IS PATTERNED AFTER THAT OF THE FAMOUS SPRING OR WINTER CARPET OF KHOSRAU. SIZE: 8 FT. 8 IN. × 12 FT. 4 IN. IN THE VICTORIA AND ALBERT MUSEUM

best-defined carpet designs. The carpets for another of the royal palaces depicted the four seasons, also still a theme of carpet designing down to recent times.

The carpets of the Abbasid caliphate at Baghdad (750–1258) seem almost to have rivaled the carpet of Khosrau. Hisham (d. 743), one of the last Omayyad caliphs, had a silk, gold-enriched carpet that was approximately 150 × 300 ft. (46 × 91 m.). The history of this carpet can be traced for more than a century. It was finally inherited by the caliph al-Mutawakkil about 850. Gorgeous carpets are mentioned in all the contemporary descriptions of the period. Little is known about their actual appearance, but some had inscriptions; some actually attempted symbolic portraiture of the Sasanian kings; and in Numaniya and Hira some were decorated with all kinds of animals, showing a growing mastery of pictorial effects. Dark blue was probably the commonest colour, but the caliph al-Mahdi owned a rose-coloured carpet.

Whether these Sasanian and early Islamic carpets were pile-knotted or tapestry-woven it is impossible to say. There is no evidence to support the usual assumption that they were all done in some kind of flat stitch, but this is possible, as tapestry was by that time a much used technique as well as an old one, being well developed by 1500 B.C. Fragmentary examples, dating from the 7th to the 14th century, have been found on the rubbish heaps of Al Fustat (old Cairo), including some so stiff and heavy that they could only have been floor coverings. Many are very beautiful, with rich and harmonious colours and ingenious patterns.

Various of the Arabic geographers give valuable though meagre information about carpet weaving in the Near East from the 8th to the 14th century. Armenia was certainly one of the most productive districts. There were found good wool, clear water,

and fine dyes, especially a scarlet made from the *Coccus ilicis* called *kermes* and widely exported. Armenian rugs were famous in the 8th century, and we know that by the 10th such cities as Devin, Van, Kalikala (Erzurum), Bitlis, Vartan, Aklat, and Tiflis, all produced famous rugs. Marco Polo reported that the Armenians and Greeks in the towns of central Asia Minor (Konya, Sivas, and Caesarea Mazaca) wove the most beautiful carpets in the world, but unfortunately did not describe them.

In northwest Persia, the towns of Khvoy, Bargari, Arjig, Nachshirvan, and Mukhan are all credited with rug production. The south Caspian coast, Gilan, and Mazanderan evidently supported an immense industry. Its prayer carpets were exported widely, and in the 8th century 600 rugs were sent at one time as tribute to the caliph al-Ma'mun.

Rugs were an important part of the equipment of palaces and homes in northeast Persia and in Afghanistan. It is probable that there was local production, but we have no real knowledge of it. In the 8th and 9th centuries, Turkistan, according to contemporary literature, was famous for its carpets which were exported all over the world, particularly to China. Bukhara, Tashkent, and Darzangi are all mentioned as producing fine rugs. Darzangi was especially noted for its tapestry rugs. The designs were probably all geometrical, as in the so-called Bukhara rugs of the day. Wall paintings from the Turfan oasis, from Kizil, and fragments of Manichaean book illustration depict floor coverings with hexagonal and other simple geometric designs.

Southern Persia, Khuzistan, and Fars were also noted for carpet weaving. Basinna and Shushtar were active centres of production. Gundigan, Fasa, Darab, Jahrom, all produced rugs, and the *kilims* (flat-woven carpets) are specially mentioned as of precious quality.

In the 13th, 14th, and 15th centuries Asia Minor and the Caucasus were producing rugs, rather coarse in weave, of strong colour and simple geometric design—stars, polygons, entrelacs, often with border patterns of stylized Kufic writing, and a special group of rugs with simple, highly conventionalized animal forms. The most important of these are a group of three somewhat fragmentary carpets of strong, repeating, geometric patterns in rather harsh colours, red, yellow, and blue, which were found in the mosque of Ala-ud-Din in Konya and are now treasured in the Turk ve Islam Eserleri Muzesi, Istanbul. Local tradition assigns them, reasonably enough, to the period of the Seljuks of Rum, cousins of the Persian Seljuks, who maintained their authority in Asia Minor through the 13th century. In the Staatliche Museen, East Berlin, and in the National Museum at Stockholm are a pair of rugs of very primitive design, the former a highly conventionalized dragon-and-phoenix combat, the latter stylized birds in a tree; both are now generally regarded as Anatolian of the early 15th century, although the patterns were later richly developed in the Caucasus.

A little later there began to appear in Europe, coming from the same as yet unspecified region, a considerable number of rugs of finer weave, more delicate patterns, and richer colours. These also are almost wholly geometrical in pattern. They were depicted by the Flemish painters, such as Hans Memling, Jan Van Eyck, and Petrus Christus, with such skill and loving care that the separate knots are sometimes visible, and the considerable artistic character of the rugs is adequately presented. The designs of many of these rugs have been quite faithfully repeated in the later weavings from the Bergama district in Asia Minor and from the southern Caucasus almost to the present day—an impressive evidence of the conservatism of rug design which so complicates the problem of dating.

2. Persia: 13th–17th Century.—Little is known of carpet weaving of the 13th and 14th centuries in Persia, but by the 15th the art was rapidly moving toward an artistic climax. The horrors and devastation of the Mongol invasion certainly depressed the artistic life of most of the 13th century, which was only partly restored by the magnificence of the architecture and miniature painting of the Il-khan renaissance (1290–1335). The bloody conquests of Tamerlane (Timur) were disastrous to Persia, but he spared and favoured artisans, who were removed in large numbers to work on his great palaces in Turkistan, particularly at Samar-

DETAIL OF A 16TH-CENTURY ANIMAL-MEDALLION CARPET FROM PERSIA. THE BORDER IS DECORATED WITH DRAGONS, PHOENIXES, CLOUD BANDS, AND SCROLLS. THE FIELD IS A PATTERN OF MEDALLIONS, TREES, AND VARIOUS ANIMALS. SIZE: 9 FT. 8 IN. × 17 FT. 8 IN. IN THE VICTORIA AND ALBERT MUSEUM

kand and Bukhara, where they were chiefly responsible for a new school of painting and decorative design.

Under the enlightened and cultivated rule of Tamerlane's successors, particularly Shahrukh (1377–1447), literature and art in all its branches flourished, and among the supreme achievements of the following century were its magnificent carpets. These, like most of the finest art of the time, were produced in the palace ateliers or on court-subsidized looms, which made for unity of style. A sensitive and exacting clientele and the lavish royal support guaranteed supreme technical proficiency, the most perfect materials, and the highest skill. Moreover, the materials, both dyes and wool, were of the finest that the unlimited power and wealth of the shah could command. Sheep were specially bred and tended; dye plantations were cultivated like flower gardens; and aspiring designers and weavers could, by submitting cartoons or finished work, win a court appointment which conferred prestige and greatly prized privileges. These conditions, created under the Timurids in the 15th century, remained under the Safavids (1501–1736).

In the 15th century the art of the book, which had long been considered the supreme artistic accomplishment and which already had behind it centuries of superb achievement, reached a degree of elegance and sophistication that it has never known either before or since. The bindings, frontispieces, chapter headings, and, in the miniatures themselves, the canopies, panels, brocades, and carpets which furnished the spaces, all received the richest and most elegant patterning. The great calligraphers and illuminators ranked higher than weaver, architect, or even poet, and generally supervised all artistic enterprises at court. The beautiful designs they conceived were appropriated in various degrees by the other arts and the domination of outstanding artists accounts in no small measure for the special character of the court carpets of the period, the variety of colour, the ingenuity and imaginative range of pattern schemes, and the superlative draftsmanship which is both lucid and expressive.

Because of the difficulty of classification it has been customary to name the great court carpets of the 16th century in accordance with their presumed themes, and we read of "Hunting carpets," "Garden carpets," "Medallion carpets," "Compartment carpets," "Vase carpets," "Animal carpets." This classification is hardly more than a temporary convenience, and really evades the problem. These various themes were embodied in the carpets of many different regions and over long periods. A more serious classification attempts to connect a given carpet style with some dominant cultural unit: the court of a great monarch; the locality in which the patterns were developed; the actual place where the carpet was fabricated, including the sources of design elements. This method is difficult because of the dearth of contemporary documents, and because in a court-supervised art, material was often gathered in one place and shipped to some court-subsidized loom, while court-approved cartoons also were apparently supplied to the various weaving centres, and the provinces also copied the cosmopolitan styles in vogue at the capital. On the other hand, we know from an actual document of Shah Abbas that even at his time (early 17th century) when the imperial dominion was formally established in all matters cultural as well as political and economic, the local weaving centres were respected and the officers of the crown were charged to see that their integrity was preserved. The majority of the more important carpets of the 16th century, in colour, pattern, materials, and technique fall into groups of such marked individuality that we can refer to them as belonging to distinct schools. The complex designs are thought out with perfect lucidity controlled by a rigorous decorative logic. They are in the proper sense a monumental art. Their very size is impressive: the more important of them may be 20–40 ft. long, and in the 17th century, more than 50 ft., though such a size somewhat exceeds the power of unified comprehension. The finest of them are almost all now in museum collections.

The rugs of this period can with a certain confidence be divided into six well-defined groups.

DETAIL OF THE PARADISE PARK SECTION OF THE ANIMAL AND MEDALLION CARPET FROM TABRIZ; 16TH CENTURY. IN THE MUSÉE DES ARTS DÉCORATIFS, PARIS

The stately Medallion carpets of northwest Persia, judging by the colouring, the materials, and the subsequent history of the type, seem to have been done in the vicinity of Karabakh in northern Azerbaijan. At the same time a special court atelier, possibly located at Sultaniyeh, as an elusive contemporary document hints, translated into carpets the most gorgeous and varied creations that the illuminators could devise. A dozen or more pieces of this group have survived and they include the world's most famous carpets. Each one is a masterpiece of outstanding artistic quality, superb design, majestic size, purity and depth of colour, and perfection of detail. They all use a fine, crisp, very white wool, probably from Ahar in the extreme northwest, which takes dyes beautifully and which today furnishes the most brilliant wool found in Iran.

The two carpets from the mosque at Ardabil, dated 1539, are the best-known carpets of the period. The greater of the two, skilfully restored, is now in the Victoria and Albert Museum, London. The other, which is reduced in size, is owned by the Los Angeles County Museum. The ornamentation consists of an extremely rich and intricate system of stems and blossoms on a velvety glowing indigo field, which in turn is dominated by a complex golden star medallion.

The Ardabil weaving has a near rival in the Anhalt carpet, named after a previous owner, the duke of Anhalt, and now in the Metropolitan Museum of Art, New York. An intricate star medallion dominates a brilliant yellow field covered with an ingenious system of scrolling arabesques and fluttering cloud bands, framed by a scarlet border. Another pair of carpets from the same region has a scarlet medallion on a white field, which is interspersed with lively animal forms and framed by a dark blue arabesque border. One, unhappily severely damaged during World War II, belongs to the Staatliche Museen, East Berlin, and the other to J. Paul Getty, the American industrialist and collector. An impressive pair, one in the Musée Historique des Tissus at Lyons, and the other in the Metropolitan Museum (the Lyons piece sadly wrecked, and the New York piece mutilated by reduction), is composed entirely of cartouche patterns enclosing in their irregular spaces brilliant little arabesque compositions. The effect is somewhat incoherent but the pair rises to greatness by virtue of the superb finesse of detail and the magnificent colour.

One of the most beautiful of these carpets from northwest Persia is the Animal carpet, half of which is in the cathedral of Cracow and half in the Musée des Arts Décoratifs in Paris, by the same designers and weavers as the Anhalt carpet. It has the same glowing scarlet and gold, but with more subtle halftones (buff on yellow, gray on taupe) and a more pictorial presentation of the paradise park. One of the most striking of the series is the great Tree carpet, also somewhat reduced, which belongs to the estate of C. F. Williams, now in the Philadelphia Museum. Like the Cracow-Paris carpet it is a garden scene, with cypresses and flowering trees of glowing vernal splendour. Historically more important, and in beauty a rival of any, is the great Hunting carpet in the Poldi-Pezzoli Museum in Milan, which carries the inscription: "It is by the efforts of Giyath-ud-Din 'Jami that this renowned carpet was brought to such perfection in the year 1522–23." Again a rich scarlet and gold medallion dominates a field of deep blue, covered with an angular network of blossoming stems, across which in every direction hunters dash after their prey.

The carpets described above, in the opinion of many, represent the supreme achievement in the whole field of carpet designing. None the less, other ateliers under royal direction were also producing many beautiful specimens. One type, also under the domination of the court and possibly done at Tabriz (possibly also at a little town near Hamadan, called Derguzin, in western Persia) reflects even more precisely the art of the illuminator. Some of these are small in size, and all have medallions dominating a field which is covered with very intricate systems of beautifully coordinated two-toned arabesques, with inscription cartouches in the border. The total effect resembles a page from a 16th-century manuscript. More than a score of these have survived. The largest and best-known single example is a beautiful multiple-medallion carpet in the Victoria and Albert Museum (London) which

W. von Bode, German authority on art, was inclined to ascribe to the end of the 15th century and to rank as the finest carpet extant.

In Kashan, in the second half of the 16th century, superlative silk Animal rugs were woven, of which three large specimens survive. The finest is the silk-, gold-, and silver-enriched Hunting carpet which is one of the principal treasures in the Österreichisches Museum für angewandte Kunst, Vienna. It is a *tour de force* of both designing and weave. The cartoon was obviously the work of a master painter. Another large piece from the same looms is owned by the king of Sweden and a similar one belongs to the government of Poland. About a dozen smaller pieces of the type are known, each worth many times its weight in gold. The famous so-called Isfahan carpets, which were not from Isfahan at all, were made in east Persia in the vicinity of Herat and Sabzevar. They are the most abundant and most familiar of the so-called classical carpets. The typical field is a very rich claret or dark *rose du Barry,* covered with a pattern of tendrils and graceful lanceolate leaves, framed by a broad border either in deep emerald green or dark blue, carrying magnificently constructed palmettes alternating with lotus or peony blossoms.

The beautiful and distinctive Vase carpets were probably manufactured in Joshaghan, north of Isfahan. The pattern structure is generally a series of ogival latticelike systems which carry a profusion of blossoms interspersed with foliage. The glowing blue of the background and the very finely divided clear colours are scarcely to be caught on a colour plate. Only a scant 20 of these carpets have survived intact, among which the example now in the Victoria and Albert Museum, London, is outstanding. These rugs were apparently not exported from Persia but used almost exclusively for court and mosque. They are woven on a solid double warp, which gives

DETAIL OF A 16TH-CENTURY VASE CARPET. PROBABLY FROM JOSHAGHAN. IN THE STAATLICHE MUSEEN ZU BERLIN

them a boardlike stiffness that holds them flat to the floor—a desirable feature for a carpet. They are still called in Iran "Shah Abbas carpets." The style (which was indigenous, very ancient, and characteristically Persian), reinforced by the prestige of the court, exercised a wide influence, and derivatives appear in Kurdistan, the Caucasus, and even in the embroideries of Bukhara, as well as in the court carpets of India.

There are other beautiful carpets of the 16th and early 17th centuries for which the provenance is still doubtful. Magnificent rugs were, we know, woven in Kerman, Yazd, and Fars, and perhaps Khuzistan, but just what they were like we can only guess, as we have no extant example that can with any surety be assigned to any of these places.

From time immemorial, the rugs of Persia had been enriched by gold and silver thread, a device that was discreetly used in some of the 16th-century carpets from east Persia, but by the time of the mighty monarch Shah Abbas I (1571–1629) many sumptuous carpets were woven from silk interspersed with silver and gold. The most gorgeous of these is the so-called "Coronation carpet," still preserved in its pristine splendour in Rosenborg Castle in Copenhagen. The gold background gleams as brightly as the day it was woven and the velvetlike pile, with its accurately drawn arabesques, is no less perfect.

All these carpets were made specially for the court or for great nobles, who could afford to concentrate on perfection and disregard the often considerable expense; indeed, a carpet like the Ardabil or the Austrian Hunting carpet cost as much as a small palace. They were cared for by special custodians, brought out only as

DETAIL FROM THE DANISH "CORONATION CARPET," 17TH CENTURY, SHOW-ING THE PATTERN OF CLOUD BANDS AND FLOWERING SCROLLS. SIZE: 12 FT. 2 IN. × 17 FT. 1 IN. IN ROSENBORG CASTLE, COPENHAGEN

actually needed, often for state occasions only, and even when the king sat on them they were generally partly covered with a lighter fabric for complete protection. The mosque carpets had severer and more continuous use. Carpets that reached Europe were for the most part treasured with equal solicitude. They were precious items in royal treasuries like the Austrian Hunting carpet, which Peter the Great gave to the emperor of Austria, the Danish Coronation carpet, or the Anhalt carpet, which are all almost as fresh and perfect as the day they were taken off the loom.

As the 17th century wore on, both the demand for more luxury and the increasing wealth that sustained it multiplied the manu-facture of gold- and silver-threaded carpets until they were not only available for purchase to ordinary civilians in the bazaars, but were exported in great numbers to Europe, where more than 200 of them have been found. They are closer to the European Renais-sance and Baroque idiom, with their high-keyed fresh colours and obvious opulence, and the finest of them are indeed beautiful. A large number of them were ex-ported to Poland, for Poland had very close relations with Persia in the 17th century and Polish royalty and nobility ordered gold-threaded rugs of this type from the looms in Kashan. There had been a rug weaving industry in Poland in the 18th century and also a silk weaving industry which used gold thread. So when these Polish rugs were first exhibited at the Paris exposition in 1878 it was natural to think that they were really Polish, for nothing quite like them had at the time been found in Persia. They were accordingly labeled *Tapis polo-nais*, and the name has stuck to the type ever since. Actually, they were primarily a product of the looms of Kashan but were probably also woven in the royal shops in Isfahan. The style de-generated rather rapidly. By the second half of the 17th century materials were cheapened, weav-

"TAPIS POLONAIS," WOVEN SILK RUG FROM PERSIA, DATED EARLY 17TH CENTURY. THE ARMS OF SIG-ISMUND III, KING OF POLAND, ARE SET IN THE RECTANGULAR PENDANT MEDALLION. IN THE RESIDENZ-MUSEUM, MUNICH

ing became coarser and more careless, the designs clumsy and confused.

Similarly the east Persian Herat carpets which came into the European market by way of India and the gulf export trade, partly in Portuguese, partly in English control, became known in Europe as the typical Persian carpet. Many of the European artists of the period owned them, and Van Dyck and "Velvet" Brueghel (Jan the Elder), particularly, rendered them with com-plete fidelity in datable paintings. The Indian princes also were enamoured of them and acquired them by plunder and purchase alike. Their popularity resulted in mass production with all its attendant deleterious effects. Designers were no longer employed, cartoons were wearily repeated *ad infinitum*, the weavers had little interest or pride in their work, the desire for speed and for econ-omy debased every process, and the style finally expired in a re-pulsive mediocrity, a painful example of how a great art can be brought to ruin.

Throughout Persia as a whole during the 17th century there was an increasing emphasis on refinement and luxury coupled with a steadily slackening inspiration. The set of silk carpets woven to surround the sarcophagus of Shah Abbas II (d. 1666) in the shrine at Qom is the last really high achievement in Persian rug weaving. The rugs are of such finesse that even orientalists have mistaken them for velvet, and the drawing is beautiful, the colour varied, clear, brilliant, and harmonious. The set is dated and signed by a master artist, Nimat'ulla of Joshaghan.

3. The Low School Rugs of Persia.—By the end of the 17th century the impoverishment of the court and the general slackening of cultural energy throughout the Near East are clearly reflected in the steady decline of court art. Nonetheless, throughout most of western Asia wandering nomads and settled town dwellers alike continued to design and weave carpets, using dye methods that had been developed and tested through centuries. Each group re-tained its characteristic pattern, content to maintain its artistic tradition with little embellishment. These humbler rugs, the so-called "Low School" types, were not made for an impatient western market and are frequently of a very high artistic character, beauti-ful in colour and design, and of fine material and excellent tech-nique. Their provenance is not always certain. Names are at-tached to rugs in the international markets at Istanbul, Smyrna, and Tabriz, and frequently do not correspond to the actualities. Different and contrasting rugs are often woven in closely related districts, such as Bijar and Sehna, while similar rugs may be woven in districts far apart. The nomadic wanderings, the forcible trans-fer of populations in the 18th century, tribal intermarriages, and many other factors have tended to confuse the type and conceal their true origins. Perhaps as many as 50–100 types were woven in the 18th and 19th centuries. A few of the better-known types may be briefly designated.

Kashan, noted for its fine textiles as early as the 12th century, was producing sumptuous velvets and even more sumptuous silks by the 16th, and by the 17th the silver- and gold-threaded rugs called *Polonaise* carpets (see *Persia*, above). The skill and tradi-tion survived and Kashan has produced the finest woven, most elaborately designed, and most richly coloured rugs of recent times. Their high cost restricted the output and the best of them were finally crowded out of the market.

The principal weaving centres in the 19th century were Tabriz in the northwest, Joshaghan in central Persia, Kerman and Ravar in the southeast, and Meshed (Mashhad) in the northeast. These centres have all woven large carpets, Meshed, Kerman, and Tabriz utilizing the medallion schemes of early classical time, Joshaghan and some Kerman carpets repeating various interpretations of the garden motive. The most characteristic Joshaghans were distin-guished by flower sprays, very precisely drawn, on a field of soft red.

The Kerman rugs were made of brilliant wool, finely and skil-fully woven, and, beginning about 1870, they became the most popular of all the Persian weavings. They are light in tone, thanks to the discreet use of light ivory and pale rose, and were particu-larly in demand for western drawing rooms.

The province of Azerbaijan in the extreme northwest of Iran

is ideally fitted for rug weaving, excellent wool, water, and dye plants being readily available. Among the more important are those from Qareh Dagh (or Karadja), where the weavers remained faithful to the highest ideals until they went out of production. The region around Ardabil produced many handsome nomadic rugs difficult to identify. South of Ardabil the principal types have been the so-called Heriz, Gorevan, and Serapi carpets that make liberal use of tan and blue in bold and simple patterns.

The Kurdish region in northwest Persia produced many fine medium-sized rugs in thick lustrous wool of fine colours, repeating the designs of other parts of Persia. From the immediate vicinity of the town of Sehna (now Sanandaj), in the heart of the Kurdish district, have come finely woven carpets and kilims. The patterns are exquisitely rendered medallions or *bouté* (the so-called pear or palm leaf motive), with imbrications.

A great rug industry was developed in western Persia in the Soltanabad district. From individual towns come beautifully woven rugs like the Sarouks, with their ancient medallion pattern; the Sarabands, with their repeating *bouté* patterns on a ground of silvery rose; and the Feraghan, with their so-called Herati pattern —an allover, rather dense design with a light green border on a mordant dye that leaves the pattern in relief. The earlier Feraghans (two are known, dated at the end of the 18th century) are on fields of dark lustrous blue with a delicately drawn open pattern. Later, toward the end of the 19th century, Feraghans degenerated in colour and material and the pattern became clumsy and crowded.

From the province of Fars come many small rugs and a few sizable carpets, reflecting ancient models. The Bahtiari region west of Isfahan turned out a few large, double-warp, stoutly woven carpets and a few smaller rugs that occasionally attained very great merit. Northeastern Persia from Meshed down to Birjand and Ghayian produced large carpets predominantly violet or purplish in tone with wide multiple borders and very soft and not too durable wools.

The "Low School" rugs maintained their standards down to the latter half of the 19th century when their near ruin as art was completed by western commercialism with its insatiable demand for quantity, cheapness, and speed. Western taste also intruded destructively, and European importers began to supply designs with confused or meaningless patterns, and to order shapes and colours that were in conflict with the Oriental tradition. Competition was intensified and the weaver reduced to an animated machine. Aniline dyes, harsh and fugitive, displaced the older, far more costly dyeing processes. Poor wool was cheaper than good, and various processes of chemical washing temporarily concealed the deficiencies and imparted an enticing sheen to the carpet which

BY COURTESY OF THE HOUSE OF PEREZ (LONDON), LTD.

KERMAN RUG, 19TH CENTURY, WITH FIELD AND BORDER PATTERNS OF TREES AND FLOWERS. SIZE: 9 FT. 9 IN. × 13 FT. 2 IN.

the unsophisticated thought charming. However, the more intelligent European importers were aware of the destructiveness of such practices and endeavoured to arrest the deterioration of the craft and to restore something of the old quality, though the factory system was by then too well established ever to be displaced. The Persian government made several sporadic attempts to contest commercialization and imposed severe penalties for the use of aniline dyes, but the commercial tide was not so easily checked. Later, however, the government made a much more systematic effort to revive the art, with considerable success. A school of design under Taherzadeh Behzad in Teheran based its work on faithfully studied 15th- and 16th-century models. Sound methods of dyeing, wool selection, and testing are taught and the school graduates go into the various rug producing districts to improve their standards. In various places the original, indigenous methods have been maintained, and, particularly in Meshed and Birjand, carpets are woven which for technical competence and in beauty of colour stand comparison with the 17th-century weavings. The art of designing great carpets, however, is not so quickly recovered. The tendency to overelaboration needs to be curbed by a more sympathetic study of the early models with their aristocratic restraint and the fundamental strength of their designs.

4. India.—Very little is known of early and indigenous carpet weaving in India where it was apparently a late development. As an art it was brought from Persia by the Mughal princes in the 16th

BY COURTESY OF THE HOUSE OF PEREZ (LONDON), LTD.

RUGS FROM THREE 19TH-CENTURY WEAVING CENTRES IN PERSIA

(Left) Sarouk carpet with medallion pattern; size: 4 ft. 6 in. × 6 ft. 11 in. (Top right) Detail from Saraband carpet showing repeated *bouté* pattern; size: 3 ft. 8 in. × 17 ft. 2 in. (Bottom right) Detail from Feraghan carpet with Herati pattern; size: 4 ft. 3 in. × 6 ft. 10 in.

and 17th centuries. The emperor Akbar set up royal looms that were thought to surpass Persia's finest, although, as his biographer Abu'l-Fazl tells us, rugs were still imported from various centres in Persia. The Herat carpet-weaving establishments that made the so-called Isfahans, being the nearest centre of manufacture to India, furnished models. Apparently weavers were brought from there to continue the style in India, where it was rapidly crystallized, with the elements reduced and formalized, the drawing rigid and meagre. Colours and wool also deteriorated while there were few compensating additions from Indian sources.

The carpets made for the courts of the Grand Mughals, however, were of extravagant and luxurious beauty. The cost of fine weaving was quite ignored and a series of carpets turned out with 800 to 1,200 knots to an inch, which provided a luscious velvety texture. Special carpets were of even finer weave and a fragment of prayer rug has survived (Altman Collection, Metropolitan Museum, New York) which has the incredible fineness of nearly 2,400 knots to an inch. Master draftsmen, designers, and dyers were employed and no aspect was neglected. Shah Jahan (fl. 1627–58), for example, had a set of rugs made for his palace at Amber which were manufactured from the most precious wool, imported from Kashmir and from remote Himalayan valleys.

But the art was young and its sources were in imitation, not in the life roots of the people. The standards of taste were imposed from outside and were assimilated only by a few so that, despite the magnificent models they were worked from, despite the limitless subsidies which they could command, these wonderful fabrics never reached the artistic height that characterized many periods of Persian weaving. The patterns are often too disorganized and the aim was too pictorial; the stately palmettes and curving leaves of Persian carpets, which were in themselves noble and significant compositions, are reduced in Indian carpets to a meticulous botany,

DETAIL FROM A "LOTTO" RUG, IDENTIFIED BY PATTERN OF YELLOW ARABESQUES ON RED GROUND: TURKISH. SIZE: 3 FT. 2 IN. × 3 FT. 10 IN. IN THE VICTORIA AND ALBERT MUSEUM

faultless in detail but too photographic to sustain any poetic fancy.

The rug industry, once established, continued down to the present. It became a jail industry, particularly in the Punjab. The designs were increasingly meagre and the art could no longer sustain comparison with the Persian weaving.

The later Indian carpets are mostly very inferior, largely on account of the difficulty of obtaining good wool. Many still have the designs of Persia and of other countries but purely Indian patterns are also common. From time to time better carpets have been made in the factories and during the 19th century the government established a fairly successful manufacture in the jails, but it is rarely that in both design and quality they rival the better products of Persia. The best come from Agra and Warangal, the latter producing some good silk rugs. Carpets from Masulipatnam, Mirzapur, and Thanjavur (Tanjore) are very cheap and very substantial but the wool is harsh and the colours so dull and gray that they are quite unattractive. Cotton rugs are made in Multan, and tapestry-woven ones, called *daris,* in many places. During the 20th century carpets of good quality, with any desired pattern, are being made in Kashmir, where some handsome reproductions of famous classical carpets have been made.

5. Turkey.—Turkish rugs, after the 16th century, were of two markedly contrasting types, those following Persian designs and possibly the work of imported Persian and Egyptian weavers, and those with indigenous designs. The former were made on court looms and display exquisite cloud bands, feathery lanceolate leaves in white on grounds of pale rose relieved by blue and a deep emerald green. The more indigenous Turkish patterns are embodied in large and handsome carpets made for mosques and the residences of noblemen. Characteristic are their rich, harmonious colours and their broad, rather static, pattern. These latter contrast quite markedly with the lively and intricate movement of Persian designs, where primary, secondary, and tertiary patterns are often played against one another in subtle dissonances and resolutions.

Turkish styles are best illustrated in the Usak carpets, ornamented complex star medallions in gold and yellow and dark blue centring on a field of rich red. The "Holbein" carpets, which are somewhat similar to the Caucasian carpets, have polygons on a ground of deep red, often with green borders and a conventionalized interlacing Kufic. Such a carpet is shown in Holbein's famous portrait of Georg Gisze and accounts for their name. Similarly, a handsome carpet of interlacing yellow arabesques on a ground of deep red appears so often in the paintings of Lorenzo Lotto that the rugs are now designated as "Lotto" rugs. From some unidentified region, perhaps Bergama, come rugs with a muffled, deep red ground of wonderful depth and intensity, patterned with small medallions. In the 17th century this type developed into that known as Transylvanian, because so many of them, particularly prayer rugs, have been found in the churches of Transylvania. However, they are purely Turkish in feeling and have the Turkish merits of rich, quiet colour and sturdy designs, which, aside from prayer panels, vases, and conventionalized foliage, are ultimately

DETAIL FROM A CARPET OF TURKISH STAR USAK DESIGN, 17TH CENTURY. THE FIELD CONSISTS OF LARGE OCTAGONAL STARS ALTERNATING WITH LOZENGE-SHAPED STARS ON A GROUND OF FLOWERING BRANCHES. SIZE: 6 FT. 1 IN. × 10 FT. IN THE KÖLNISCHES STADTMUSEUM

of Persian derivation. The majority are dominated by a fine red but a few are now faded to the colour of old parchment.

The 17th century saw the development of another characteristic type, erroneously called a Bird rug because the highly conventionalized floral pattern of arabesques does suggest a bird. The few rugs that have survived are serenely beautiful; the field is of soft ivory white and all the colours discreet.

The Low School rugs of 18th- and 19th-century Asia Minor continued to show the earlier qualities of quiet and sober patterns and luxurious colour. Some of the 18th-century weavings still faithfully follow the simple geometrical patterns of the 15th century. But the chief output of the Turkish weavers were prayer rugs, with which the Turks were more lavishly supplied than any other of the faithful. Handsome carpets were woven in Melas, Konya, Ladik, Kirsehir, and Sivas, those of Ladik being the most brilliant, both in pattern and colour. The most famous prayer rugs came from the towns of Ghiordes and Kula, mostly in the 18th and 19th centuries, and in the United States became the first passion of the collector. Regions like that of Smyrna (Izmir) produced a great many utility carpets for the western world.

6. The Caucasus.—Fine rugs were woven in the Caucasus from earliest times. Later Persia became the dominant political and cultural power in the region, a position it held for many centuries, and the magnificent carpets produced at the Persian court furnished models for the more ambitious Caucasian carpets such as those woven for the local nobles, or khans. However, the Caucasus has its own individual character and while it took motives from other sources, such as the dragon and phoenix fighting (so common in Persian illuminations), sun-burst medallions, latticelike field divisions derived from the Vase carpets and other sources, or repeating lotus forms often in huge scale, all these contributory elements were completely transformed by a furious vigour of design which is without equal in the textile world.

One of the most famous weavings, the Dragon design, seems to have come from the great weaving town of Kuba. Perhaps because of questions of expense (for the little Caucasus kingdoms could never compete in luxury with sultans or shahs) Caucasian rugs were of coarse weave, the Kuba Dragon carpets being not infrequently less than 80 knots to the square inch. The designs therefore were much simplified but are nonetheless remarkable for their powerful originality.

The Low School rugs are among the most individual and satisfactory. Their patterns are practically all geometrical, densely juxtaposed, generally without organic connection, and without implied movement, but they are clear, ingenious, and entirely suitable for floor decoration. The more recent examples seem a little dry in colour but many of them, like the rugs woven by the Kazakhs, Sarouks, and other nomads, are sometimes of flaming brilliance, and the older rugs from Dagestan, Kuba, and Shirvan

DETAIL FROM A 16TH–17TH-CENTURY CAUCASIAN CARPET. FIELD OF LARGE DIAMOND-SHAPED COMPARTMENTS AND STYLIZED FLORAL FORMS ENCLOSING SIMPLIFIED DRAGONS. IN THE VICTORIA AND ALBERT MUSEUM

are done in beautifully clear, discreet, and well-balanced tones.

Kilim or tapestry rugs were woven all over the Near East, but the most artistic come from the Caucasus. The Shirvan kilims, with their broad horizontal stripes, have bold motives assembled in harmonious colours.

A more important type of flat-stitch carpet, embroidered and with a mass of loose threads at the back, which comes from the region of the ancient fortified city of Shemakha, has been improperly called cashmere because of its superficial resemblance to cashmere shawls. The design is most often composed of large, beautifully articulated mosaic tile patterns in rich and sober colour, the descendant of the carpets that so delighted Memling and Jan Van Eyck.   (A. U. P.; X.)

7. Central Asia.—The carpets of western Turkistan are made by nomadic Turkmen tribes and few extant examples go back more than 100 years, though it is almost certain that similar rugs have been made for centuries. Turkmen rugs are easily identified, for excepting the Beluchis, they all have a dark red colouring and geometric designs. Many of the older pieces are not really rugs at all: some were hangings for tent doorways while others are just bags used for storage in the tents or on the pack animals. Those called camel bags measure about 5 × 3 ft., and the tent or wall bags 3 × 1 or more. Saddle bags consist of two squares of about 2 ft., joined together. There are also long bands about 1 ft. wide and perhaps 60 yd. long, which are for wrapping round the large tents. The small squarish rugs and larger ones of about 10 × 7 ft. seem to be later in date and were made perhaps chiefly for sale. The Turkmen carpets (wrongly called Bukhara) have woolen warp, weft, and pile, two lines of weft, and are nearly always made with the Sehna knot. They are surprisingly well woven in view of the fact that they are made by nomads with only the most primitive appliances. After the predominant red, the chief colours are blue, white, and a natural black wool that tones to a very pleasant brown. The characteristic design is the octagon—or so-called elephant's foot—arranged in rows and columns, often with diamond-shaped figures in between. The doorway hangings—called Tekkes—have cross-shaped paneling and the smaller pieces

TWO 18TH-CENTURY PRAYER RUGS

(Left) Ladik; size: 3 ft. 10 in. × 6 ft. 1 in. (Right) Ghiordes rug with carnation design; size: 3 ft. 11 in. × 5 ft. 2 in.

often have a rectangular diaper. Woven end webs and tassels are freely used as embellishments. The best classification is on a tribal basis.

Tekke.—These are often very finely woven, sometimes with 400 knots to the square inch. The principal colour is a deep muffled red.

Yomud.—Of medium fineness, mostly with the Ghiordes knot. The chief colour is a purple red, and there is a good deal of white, especially in the border. In the pattern diamonds often displace the usual octagon. The long tent bands, which have the pattern in pile on a woven ground, belong to this group.

Sarouk.—Like the Tekkes but with an almost black-purple or very deep crimson colouring, together with some very prominent white. Not very common.

Ersar.—These are rarely large pieces. The chief colour is a brown-red; dark green and a little bright yellow are characteristic. The patterns are very varied, with a tendency to zigzags, diagonal lines, and spotted effects.

Afghan.—Mostly large rugs with long pile and a pattern of large octagons arranged in columns; akin to the Ersari.

Beshir.—A rare type apparently made near Bukhara, with rich colouring, including a lot of yellow, and patterns apparently based on the Persian. Many are prayer rugs with a characteristic pointed arch. Large carpets are more common.

Beluchi.—These differ from the other Turkmens in that they have a black weft and dark purple and red colouring, sometimes with natural camel-colour and very staring white. The patterns are almost geometrical but the prayer rugs often have tree forms. Most of them come from eastern Persia in the vicinity of Khvaf near the Afghan border.

8. Chinese Turkistan.—The earliest rugs of Chinese Turkistan date from the 17th century and mostly have a silk pile and some metal and gilded thread. The patterns are formal floral ones, based on the Persian but with unmistakable Chinese treatment of the

detail. The later carpets are loosely woven with the Sehna knot, wool or, more rarely, silk pile, and a cotton warp. The 18th-century examples have rich but dark colouring, which during the 19th century gets gradually more vivid until at last it becomes excessively crude. There are two important types of design:

Medallion.—These usually have three medallions placed down the centre of the rug, each being almost square in shape. One border almost invariably has a conventional Chinese pattern of foam-crested waves. This pattern is mostly called Samarkand in the trade, but the rugs themselves come from Kashgar and Yarkand.

Five Blossom.—These have a floral diaper with characteristic groups of five blossoms. The colouring is often richly red and orange with a little clear blue.

9. China.—The rugs of China proper are easily recognized by their characteristic Chinese ornament. They are of coarse texture and are woven with the Sehna knot on a cotton warp; the pile is thick with a very smooth surface. A peculiar feature is the clipping of the pile so as to form a furrow at the contours of the pattern. The prevailing colour is yellow, sometimes intentional but often resulting from fading of shades of red and orange. Blue and white are also freely used but there is little true red, brown, or green.

Some of the carpets have repeating scrolling plant forms. Others have scattered flowers, medallions of frets, and the countless symbols that are so familiar in Chinese art. Frets of the Greek type are very common in the border. Pillar carpets are peculiar to China. They are designed so that when wrapped round a pillar the edges will fit together and give a continuous pattern, which is usually a coiling dragon. Many small mats, seat covers, and the like are found. It is almost impossible to date Chinese rugs as patterns have varied very little with time, and internal evidence is almost nonexistent. During the 20th century numbers of large carpets have been made for export.

10. Morocco.—Large carpets, twice as long as wide, are made in Morocco. They are loosely woven with very bright but mostly faded colours. The field is often cut up into rectangular panels filled with ornaments taken directly from Turkish carpets.

11. Spain.—Carpets seem to have been made in Spain as early as the 14th century. They are made entirely of wool. The knot is tied, or rather twisted, on one warp thread instead of on two, and the weft passes several times after each row of knots. The colours are bright and few in number, little being used but yellow, blue, red, and green. The designs are based either upon Oriental models, such as the geometrical Turkish ones, or upon purely Spanish ornament. The latter frequently introduces heraldic motifs. One early type of long rug has shields of arms on a field with a honeycomb pattern introducing plant forms and birds. A common design is a succession of foliated wreaths; another is a diaper of ogee compartments containing the floral device known as the "artichoke." Few knotted pile carpets seem to have been made after the 17th century, but small rugs woven in narrow breadths with a looped pile were common until very recently. They come principally from Las Alpujarras in the Pyrenees.

12. United Kingdom and Ireland.—The art of making handwoven carpets in England soon followed their importation from Turkey, though actual specimens of the 16th and 17th centuries are so rare that only about a dozen complete rugs are known. They have a hempen warp and

DETAIL FROM "MADONNA WITH ST. CATHERINE" BY JAN VAN EYCK SHOWING RUG WITH LATTICE PATTERNING, A 15TH-CENTURY DESIGN FROM THE SOUTHERN CAUCASUS

FRONT OF BAG TRADITIONALLY HUNG INSIDE A TURKMEN TENT; WOVEN OF CAMELHAIR PILE ON FLAX WARPS. DESIGN CONSISTS OF INTERSECTING DIAGONAL BANDS FORMING DIAMOND-SHAPED COMPARTMENTS. IN THE VICTORIA AND ALBERT MUSEUM

DETAIL FROM AN AFGHAN CARPET, SHOWING THE PATTERN OF OCTAGONS ARRANGED IN COLUMNS. SIZE: 8 FT. 4 IN. × 8 FT. 6 IN.

RUG AND CARPET

PLATE I

RUGS FROM ANATOLIA

(Left) One piece of a 13th-century woolen carpet from Central Anatolia, found in the mosque of Ala-ud-Din in Konya, Turk. Size of whole carpet: 9 ft. 4 in. × 17 ft. (Centre left) Detail of piece at left showing small stylized plant patterning of field contrasted with large Kufic characters of the principal stripe. (Bottom left) Detail of field pattern from another piece of same period showing characteristic feature of repeating a geometrical motif, here an octagon. In the Türk ve Islam Eserleri Müzesi, Istanbul

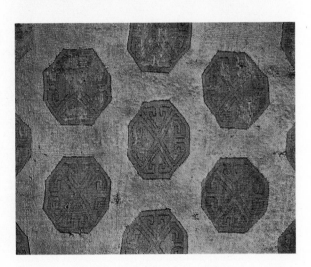

(Right) Woolen carpet with octagons containing dragon and phoenix in combat; Anatolia, early 15th century. Size: 2 ft. 11 in. × 5 ft. 8 in. In the Staatliche Museen, Berlin

PLATE II

RUG AND CARPET

Detail of about one-third of the Ardabil carpet showing the corner medallions (*see* below right), and the lamp pendant from the central medallion (*see* below left). The indigo field is ornamented with an overall pattern of scrolling stems and blossoms, the main band of the border with arabesque-filled panels. Dated 1539—40. Size of whole carpet: 17 ft. 6 in. × 37 ft. 9 in. In the Victoria and Albert Museum

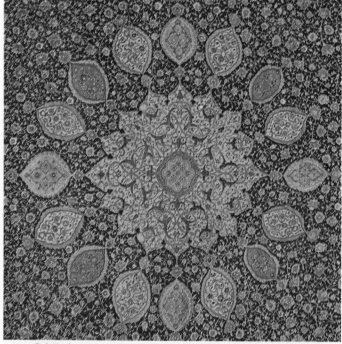

Detail of centre section showing the 16-point golden star medallion surrounded by 16 almond-shaped pendants. The medallion symbolizes the sun; at its centre are four lotus blossoms in a gray-blue pool that symbolize the source of rain in the heavens

Detail of a corner which repeats a quarter of the central medallion. The inner guard stripe is patterned with arabesques, scrolling stems and cloud bands

MEDALLION CARPET FROM THE MOSQUE OF ARDABIL; PERSIAN, 16TH CENTURY

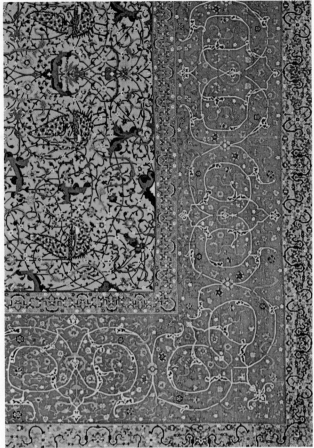

Detail of a corner showing the field and border patterns

The so-called Anhalt carpet, named after the duke of
Anhalt, a previous owner. A red medallion dominates
a yellow field covered with scrolling arabesques and
cloud bands. Size: 13 ft. 7 in. × 26 ft. 6 in. In the
Metropolitan Museum of Art, New York

Detail of the centre showing the medallion

PERSIAN COURT CARPET FROM TABRIZ; 16TH CENTURY

Plate IV

RUG AND CARPET

PERSIAN TREE CARPET

Section of a Tree carpet from northwest Persia, 17th century. Pattern consists of an overall
cartouche design in which rows of flowering trees are set. Size of whole rug: 7 ft. 2 in. × 21 ft.
4 in. In the Metropolitan Museum of Art

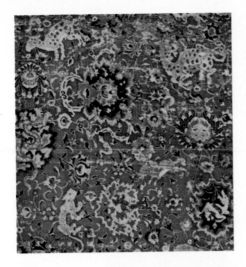

Two details of the main field showing
animals and birds set into a floral scroll
pattern

Section of the so-called Emperor's carpet from the collection of the emperors of Austria. From
Herat; period of reign of Shah Tahmasp (1524–76). Size of whole rug: 10 ft. 10 in. × 24 ft.
8 in. In the Metropolitan Museum of Art

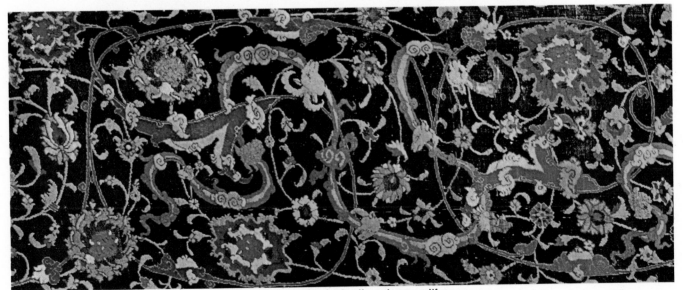

Detail of the border showing the arabesque motif, an
intricate system of scrolling tendrils

PERSIAN ANIMAL RUG; 16TH CENTURY

PLATE VI

RUG AND CARPET

PERSIAN GARDEN CARPET, EARLY 18TH CENTURY

So-called Garden carpet from northwest Persia. The pattern follows
the design of a Persian garden. In the centre are pools with four channels flowing out between beds of trees and flowers. Size: 8 ft. × 22
ft. 6 in. In the Fogg Art Museum

INDIAN LANDSCAPE RUG; MUGHAL, EARLY 17TH CENTURY

A pictorial rug with a design adapted from a wall
painting or hanging showing animals in a landscape
scene. Size: about 5 × 8 ft. In the Museum of Fine
Arts, Boston

PLATE VIII

RUG AND CARPET

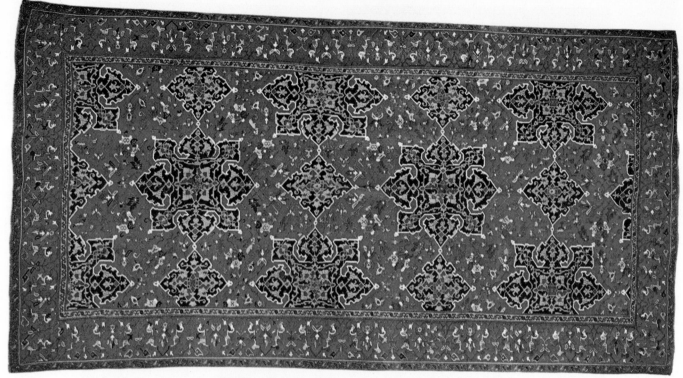

Star Usak carpet; end of 16th century. Gold and dark blue
ornamented star medallions on a red field. Size: 7 ft. 5½ in. ×
14 ft. In the Metropolitan Museum of Art

TURKISH RUGS OF THE 16TH AND 17TH CENTURIES

So-called Bird rug; about 1600. Field of soft ivory white with
a highly conventionalized floral pattern of arabesques that suggest birds. Size: 7 ft. 7 in. × 14 ft. 7 in. In the Metropolitan Museum of Art

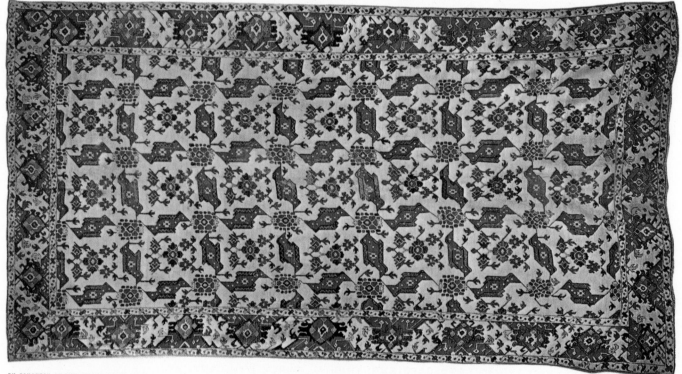

CAUCASIAN CARPET

So-called Dragon carpet from the Caucasus; early 16th century. A highly abstract, twofold lattice design including forms derived from the dragon figures common in Persian illustrations. Size: about 22 ft. 1½ in. × 7 ft. 6½ in. Partly destroyed in 1945, the rug is in the Staatliche Museen, Berlin

PLATE X   RUG AND CARPET

CAUCASIAN RUG

Section of a Kula rug from the Caucasus; 17th century. The
style is a derivative of the dragon-rug tradition but is more
floral in pattern and employs a highly abstract outline of
form. In the collection of Joseph McMullan

DETAIL OF A KHOTAN CARPET FROM CHINESE TURKISTAN SHOWING THE "FIVE BLOSSOM" PATTERN. SIZE: 2 FT. 8 IN. × 3 FT. 7 IN. IN THE VICTORIA AND ALBERT MUSEUM

weft and woolen pile of medium fineness, tied with the Ghiordes knot. The ground is usually green and there are so many shades of the other colours that the whole number of tints is greater than in Oriental carpets. The designs may be divided into two groups. In the first are found typical English patterns resembling contemporary embroidery, and often introducing heraldic devices and, fortunately, dates. The earliest known carpet of this type belongs to the earl of Verulam and is dated 1570. Large numbers of pieces of carpet knotting—called at the time "Turkey work"—were made for covering chairs and stools. As the demand for carpets increased in the 18th century small factories were started at Paddington, Fulham, Moorfields, Exeter, and Axminster, and the home production was stimulated by premiums offered by the Society of Arts in 1756. The designers continued to adopt the decoration of the time or to copy Eastern carpets. The famous Axminster factory worked on well into the 19th century and then became merged into the Wilton factory, which is still in operation. With the advent of machinery the industry dwindled and almost disappeared until, about 1880, the craft was revived by William Morris. Quite late in the century a successful factory was opened in Donegal, Ire., and during the 20th century many small rugs have been knotted by handicraft societies, though their products can scarcely compete commercially with the machine or with the Oriental rug.

13. France.—There are early records of carpet weavers in France, but nothing is known of their work until the foundation of the famous Savonnerie factory near Paris in 1627. Many large carpets were made there, mostly with flaxen warp and weft and a woolen pile tied with the Ghiordes knot. The designs accord with contemporary French decoration and few, if any, were based on Oriental carpets. In 1826 the factory was closed and the manufacture transferred to the Gobelins tapestry factory. During the 18th century and afterward many tapestry-woven carpets were made at Aubusson and in other tapestry factories.

14. North America.—Many of the Indian tribes have been making flat-woven rugs and blankets since the earliest days of their known history. Before sheep were introduced in the 16th century the principal material was cotton, together with various fibres and dog's hair; afterward wool became important. Among the most skilful tribes are the Pueblo and the Navaho (q.v.). Indian designs are traditionally abstract ones which make much use of stripes and a zig-zag, or "lightning," motif. The colours used are black, white, yellow, blue, tan, and red, the latter often being dominant.

Rugs were made by the colonists in a variety of techniques—by knitting, crocheting, or braiding thin strips of material into small squares and then sewing these together, or by embroidering on a coarse-woven foundation. Hooking began around the turn of the 18th century and became very popular. The early examples have crude floral, geometric, or animal designs and are very colourful.

No knotted carpets were manufactured among the Indians—nor among the settlers in the early days. However, in 1884 a factory established in Milwaukee (and later moved to New York City)

WOOLEN CARPET FROM THE SAVONNERIE FACTORY, FRANCE, 19TH CENTURY. DESIGN SHOWS A BASKET OF FRUIT ENCIRCLED WITH ROSES AND RESTING ON ACANTHUS LEAVES WHICH SUPPORT FLAMING TORCHES. SIZE: 8 FT. × 11 FT. 2 IN. IN THE OSTERREICHES MUSEUM FÜR ANGEWANDTE KUNST, VIENNA

began to weave carpets in traditional European designs. During the 1890s a branch of the Royal Wilton Carpet Works made Axminsters at Elizabethport, N.J., and a few beautiful, flat-woven carpets in French Baroque and Neoclassical designs were produced around the turn of the century by a tapestry factory in Williamsburg, N.Y. After this machine weaving, which had begun in the U.S. as early as the second half of the 18th century, gradually ousted hand weaving.

15. Other Countries.—A few carpets made in Poland in the 17th century are still in existence; they have floral patterns in light colouring. In Finland loosely woven rugs, often with human figures and dates, were made by peasants and seem mostly to have formed part of bridal dowries. Kilims are made in the Balkan states and in southern Russia; they resemble the Turkish pieces but have, especially the Russian, more naturalistic floral patterns. Those from Rumania generally include birds in the design.

(C. E. TA.; X.)

II. TECHNIQUE AND DESIGN

1. Knotted-Pile Technique.—From very early times weavers have produced pile fabrics, in which they have endeavoured to

CHINESE PILLAR CARPET

Dragon pattern is designed to fit together when wrapped around a pillar. Good luck symbols are represented at the top of the carpet and earth and water at the bottom. In the Victoria and Albert Museum

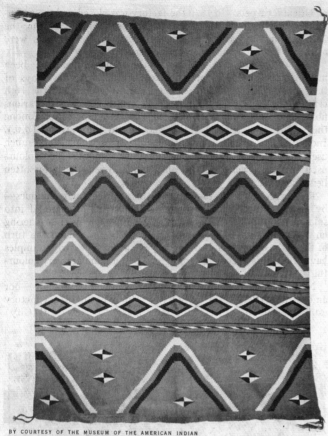

NAVAHO INDIAN WOOLEN RUG INCORPORATING THE "LIGHTNING" MOTIF
IN ITS DESIGN. SIZE: 3 FT. 4 IN. × 4 FT. 10 IN.

combine the advantages of a woven textile with those of an animal
fleece. The pile has been formed by many varieties of looping,
knotting, and weaving.

On the basis of the central Asian finds it was formerly thought
that the single-warp knot was probably the earliest type used for
carpets. By the early Middle Ages this knot had reached the east
Mediterranean, for it is found in pile carpet fragments recovered
from the Al Fustat refuse heaps. A fine example (Musée Arabe,
Cairo) bears on a dark blue ground an inscription in white Kufic
letters which makes it datable in the late 9th or early 10th century.
Not long thereafter the technique was carried into Europe and was
used in Germany, at Quedlinburg, at the end of the 12th century,
for a hanging illustrating an allegory centred on Mortian's *Marriage of Mercury and Philologia* (Ackerman, *Tapestry*, 1933, p.
33). Moreover, by the beginning of the 14th century *tapisserie
sarrazinoise* is discussed in industrial statutes, and clearly differentiated from both *tapisserie nostre* and *haute-lisse* (true tapestry).
Evidently looped-pile weaving continued in Europe (*ibid.*, pp.
312–313). The same technique was still in use in Spain in the
17th century. Meanwhile, in Egypt, and probably other east
Mediterranean centres also, two other forms of looped weaving
were being developed which made either a potential pile (uncut
pile) or actual long-ended pile surface. One of these, practised
in two variants, was a forerunner of velvet. In this a supplementary weft for the pile is carried on top of regularly spaced
foundation wefts (from the fifth to the ninth in general) and
passes under a certain number of warps to hold it firm (from three
to six overpassed warps, as a rule), then is deeply looped over
a single warp, and so repeated; or alternatively, it is deeply
looped between two warps. But the second of these loop weaves
contains the germ of the development of true rug-knotting form.
This, the supplementary weft, after passing under a certain
number of overpassed warps in the same way (*e.g.*, two), is then
floated over a certain number of them (*e.g.*, two or three), and is
carried back under the same number of warps. This leaves a cut
end at the beginning of the unit (of say seven warps in all), and

another in the middle thereof—a coarse version of the knot that
came to be known as the Persian knot. The two techniques were
used equally for garments and wall hangings but the latter was
used also for carpets as is shown by a good-sized specimen in the
Metropolitan Museum from Antinoë, datable *c.* A.D. 500–600,
with a broad conventional polychrome design (M. Dimand, in
Metropolitan Museum Studies, iv, pp. 159–161 [1932–33]).

It now transpires, however, that the earliest known carpet, that
from Pazyryk, was worked with the so-called Turkish knot, and
this knot has also been found in
some of the early specimens excavated in central Asia. It appears
again in the later Middle Ages in
the Ala-ud-Din carpets. Moreover, by the end of the 15th century it had penetrated Europe,
for a fragment of an Annunciation, probably Flemish, possibly
French, is in this technique (E. B.
Sachs in *Metropolitan Museum
Studies,* i).

In these fully evolved forms of
the technique the pile yarn, instead of being wrapped around a
single warp, is knotted around
two. These warp threads—most
often cotton, but in both Spanish
and Near Eastern nomad rugs
sometimes wool, or in some finer
qualities, silk—are stretched vertically on a loom and a length of
the pile yarn is tied on every two
threads the full width of the
loom; then two or more weft
threads likewise of any of the materials cited, or of a combination
thereof, are cloth woven (alternately over and under), back and
forth across the full width, two
or more times, and the process is
repeated. There are thus three
sets of threads involved, each
with its specific function: warp,
weft, pile. The pile is usually
wool but may be silk or cotton,
though the last is not desirable
except for very small areas where
the crisp accent of an unfadable
white is wanted. In the Turkish
pile knot the yarn is passed under
one warp, back over two, and
back again under the second so
that both ends come up together
between the two warps on the
same side of the overpass loop.
In the other type the yarn passes
under one warp, over and back
under the next, so that the two
ends stand on the surface with
one warp between them. The
pattern is obtained by changing
the colour of the pile yarn.
When a row of knots is tied it is
beaten down against the preceding rows with a heavy malletlike
comb so that, on the front, the
pile completely conceals both
warp and weft. When a certain area is woven, the pile ends are
sheared to an even height. This varies according to the character
of the rug, being short on the more aristocratic type of rug, and as
much as an inch on some shaggy nomadic rugs. (*See* further
CARPET MANUFACTURE: *Handmade Carpet.*)

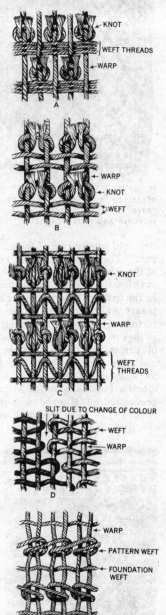

FIG. 1.—BASIC KNOTS AND WEAV-
ING PATTERNS USED IN HANDWOVEN
RUGS AND CARPETS

(A) Spanish or single-warp knot; (B)
Turkish or Ghiordes knot, and (C)
Persian or Sehna knot, the two types
used in Oriental carpets; (D) Tapestry
weaving; (E) Shemakha weaving, a
modified form of the tapestry method

The fineness of the weave depends on the number of knots to the square inch which itself varies according to the weight and spacing of the warps and also, though to a lesser extent, of the wefts, and on the thickness of the pile yarn. The range is from about 80 to the square inch, used for instance in some of the Kuba Dragon carpets of the late 16th or 17th century (see *The Caucasus,* above), to more than 2,400, found in a fragment of a Mughal prayer carpet of the 17th century, obviously an emperor's property (Altman Collection, Metropolitan Museum, New York). But the most finely woven carpets are by no means those of greatest artistic or historic importance; for example, the beautiful and famous pair of carpets from the mosque of Ardabil (dated 1539) have only

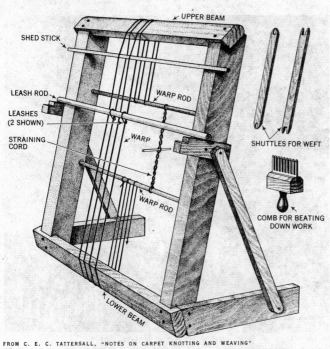

SHED STICK

UPPER BEAM

LEASH ROD

WARP ROD

LEASHES
(2 SHOWN)

STRAINING
CORD

WARP

SHUTTLES FOR WEFT

WARP ROD

COMB FOR BEATING
DOWN WORK

LOWER BEAM

FROM C. E. C. TATTERSALL, "NOTES ON CARPET KNOTTING AND WEAVING"

FIG. 2.—DIAGRAM OF A SIMPLE LOOM AND IMPLEMENTS

about 325 knots to the square inch (see *Persia,* above).

In certain types of pile rugs, both wool and silk, some areas are brocaded with gold or silver thread, usually cloth woven but with a surface float over several warps (basket weave) to obtain the maximum richness. In these the weft is carried forward over four of the warp threads and then backward behind two. This gives a kind of herringbone texture at the front and a series of ribs at the back of the fabric. Because a weft looped around the warp threads as described has much less than the usual binding effect, alternate wefts are cloth-woven, but these are concealed by compacting the loop-woven wefts, which are changed in colour according to pattern as in straight tapestry weaving.

The time required for weaving rugs has been very greatly exaggerated. They are often spoken of as having required lifetimes, but a careful check made by Heinrich Jacoby (*A Survey of Persian Art,* iii, 1939, p. 2464) shows that even the finest carpets would hardly have taken three years. Even the huge Ardabil carpet, with its 33,000,000 knots, could have been woven within four years. Great carpets like the Milan Hunting carpet probably only required a year and a half.

2. Hooked Rug.—The origin of the hooked rug is obscure. A rug of this type is made by pulling narrow strips of wool or cotton cloth or wool yarn, with a tool roughly resembling a buttonhook, up through a basic material of coarse linen or burlap. The loops, approximately $\frac{1}{2}$ in. high and the width of two, three, or four mesh openings in the basic material, are often clipped. Frames of various designs hold the basic material taut. Frequently the rug is made by pushing, instead of pulling, the loop through the basic material, the instrument used being then generally a large threaded needle.

3. Dyes.—Red is most often obtained from madder root (*Rubia tinctorum*). Thus the red of the Noin Ula carpets is madder with the usual alum mordant. The shade, which runs through the gamut of reds and pinks to reddish brown and orange, varies with the age of the plant, and also other factors, including the mordant, the density of the solution, and the duration of the immersion. Some reds, however, are obtained from the *Coccus ilicis* which breeds on oaks in the Near East, related to but not identical with, the cochineal (*q.v.; Coccus cacti*) of Mexico. Blues are made from indigo. The yellow of the Noin Ula carpet is rhamnetin, the dye obtained from unripe berries of various bushes of the genus *Rhamnus.* The famous saffron (*q.v.*) dye, made from the dried stigmas and part of the style of a crocus (*Crocus sativus*), is too expensive to use to any extent. Greens are usually blue plus yellow; violets (only rarely used), red plus blue. Black, when not the natural wool, is done with iron filings in citric acid, a corrosive dye whose destructive effect on wool especially is often conspicuous in old rugs. White is the natural wool, but occasionally, when a sharper white is desired, a little cotton is introduced.

Carpets in museums are almost all underlighted. Oriental fabrics, in particular, were all woven and used in regions where the light is very bright and their colours are at their maximum and in proper relation to one another only when the illumination is strong.

4. Design.—Rugs were not designed purely to be seen on the floor. Many of them were worked on vertical elements and the designs are traditional and derivative and not very often planned in relation to the destined environment of the carpet. The great court carpets of the 16th century, for example, were the work of illuminators who were accustomed to think of the book page and a vertical design. The designs of the great carpets, when seen on the floor from a normal eye height, are compressed and distorted. Their full effect comes only when hung where they can be viewed so that the eye is nearly equidistant from all points.

Both the pile carpet technique and the flat techniques, whether straight tapestry or the looped Shemakha weaving, permit unlimited variation within the design—in sharp contrast to all shuttle weaving which necessitates regularly recurring repeats. But while the rug designer thus theoretically has unrestricted liberty, he is constrained by habit, tradition, and his own aesthetic judgment. A division into field and border is the basis of all rug design. The border serves, like the cornice on a building or the frame on a picture, to emphasize the limits, isolate the field, and sometimes control the implied movements of the interior pattern. The value of a border had already been recognized by pottery painters in 4000 B.C. and is fully developed in rug patterns from Assyrian times onward.

The border invariably consists of a minimum of three members: the main band, which varies greatly in width according to the size of the rug and the elaborateness of the field design, and the inner and outer guard stripes, decidedly subordinate bands on either side of the main band. These latter may be the same on both sides of the band or different. Multiple border systems also are quite common, as on one of the Noin Ula carpets, very elaborate schemes having been developed in mosaic floors of the Roman period. Some of the greatest carpets, however, have the simplest border arrangements, while on certain types of commercially produced carpets of the late 19th and early 20th centuries meaninglessly multiple and complex compositions were developed. The court designers of the 16th century developed many beautiful correlations of rhythm and accent between border and field.

The field may be decorated with an allover pattern, a panel composition, or a medallion system. The allover pattern may be of identical repeats, either juxtaposed or evenly spaced, though the latter, while common on textiles, is rare on carpets; or it may be of varied motives in a unified system, *e.g.,* different plant forms of about the same size, but even this freest type of design almost invariably includes bilaterally balanced repetitions which perhaps reflect the human bilateral equilibrium. The latter type of design is found most typically in formalized representations of the parks or woods which were a feature of Persian palace grounds. Another type of allover design appears entirely free but is actually organized on systems of scrolling stems, notably on the east Persian carpets of the 16th–17th centuries.

The value of panel subdivisions for controlling patterns had been discovered in a simple rectangular version by the Upper Paleolithic Period (*c.* 25000 B.C.), and panel systems have been a basic form of design since 4000 B.C., when pottery painters were already devising varied systems. On carpets the lattice provides the simplest division of the field, often a diagonal lattice as on the embroidered carpet from Noin Ula, a scheme that also appears on Sasanian capitals and in Coptic tapestries. But a characteristic field design of the court carpets of the Shah Abbas period, the so-called Vase pattern, is constructed from the ogee, a motive that becomes prominent in Near Eastern textile design in the 14th century (see *Persia*, above). Simple rectangular paneling—really a large-scale check—is typical of one style of Spanish rugs of the 15th–16th centuries.

The most frequent medallion composition consists of a more or less elaborate medallion superimposed on the centre of a patterned field. This is also often complemented with corner pieces, which are typically quadrants of the central medallion.

But multiple-medallion systems also are developed: either a succession or a chain of medallions on the vertical axis; or two or more forms of medallions alternating in bands, a scheme typical of the Turkish ("Usak") carpets of the 16th–17th centuries; or systematically spotted medallions which may or may not be interconnected, or which may interlock so that the scheme logically becomes an elaborate lattice.

Persian carpets of the great period (15th–17th centuries) commonly have multiple-design schemes, that is, composition systems on two or more "levels." The simplest is the medallion superimposed on an allover design, but more typical are subtler inventions such as two- or three-spiral stem systems, sometimes overlarded with large-scale cloud bands, all intertwining but each carried independently to completion. The finer Vase carpets have double or triple ogival lattices set at different intervals ("staggered"), each with its own centre and tangent motives which also serve other functions in the other systems. What at first sight appears to be a great multiplicity of independent motives thus proves on careful exploration to be ingeniously contrived and firmly controlled.

Occasionally stripe systems are used, either vertical or diagonal, but this conception is more natural to shuttle-woven fabrics, and when employed in the freer techniques of rug weaving is probably an imitation of textiles.

5. Patterns.—Four main classes of motives are used: geometrical, conventional, plant, and illustrative. The geometrical repertoire is built up from variations and combinations of meanders, polygons, crosses, and stars. Meanders, chiefly for borders, range from the simple serration which was employed from earliest times (actually already much used in the Upper Paleolithic Period) to fairly complex hooked forms, characteristically the angular "running wave" or "Greek key," which is also very ancient. Such meanders typically constitute reciprocals, *i.e.*, designs which form the identical shape in the positive and negative areas, so that when they are executed in contrasted colours they can be alternatively interpreted; or differentiated reciprocals, where the negative space created by the main motive has a different but destructive form, a type of narrow border well-developed in early medieval textile design. Little trefoil reciprocals are used for guard stripes in the Caucasus, central Persia (so-called *Polonaise*), and in India. Chief among the polygons employed are the lozenge and the octagon. The Maltese cross is frequent, as is the gamma cross, or swastika. The purely geometrical stars are usually based on the cross or the octagon. Many of these motives, which are rudimentary and very ancient, may have originated in basket weaving and the related reed-mat plaiting, for they are natural to both techniques; but in rug weaving they have survived chiefly in the work of central Asia, Asia Minor, and the Caucasus, in both pile-knotted and flat-woven fabrics.

One of the principal motives in the 16th- and 17th-century Persian carpets is the so-called arabesque, an ambiguous term that generally implies an intricate scrolling-vine system. In a com-

mon Persian ornamental scheme two asymmetrical members cross at an acute angle, forming a lilylike blossom, and then describe curves in opposite directions, readily continuing into further scroll systems. This highly individual form was well begun in China in the late Chou period (*c.* 600 B.C.), notably on a few bronze mirrors, and is beautifully developed during the Han dynasty (202 B.C.–A.D. 221). Although it does not appear in Persia until the 12th century (on pottery and architectural stucco ornament), and although its intermediate history has not been traced in either country, when it does reemerge the essential forms are so close to those of early China that a hiatus and reinvention seem improbable.

Directly traceable to China, on the other hand, are the cloud

BY COURTESY OF THE PRESS OFFICE OF THE IRANIAN EMBASSY, LONDON

WOMAN WEAVING A CARPET ON A HAND LOOM. PATTERN FOR THE CARPET IS DRAWN ON THE ROLLED PAPER AT THE TOP OF THE LOOM

knot (or *'tchi*) and cloud band or ribbon—both begun by the Han period at least and with a continuous history thereafter. The cloud knot, a feature of the court carpets of the time of Shah Abbas, was continued to the end of the 18th century. The cloud band or ribbon, already skilfully used on book covers, manuscript illumination, and in architectural faience, became important on 16th-century carpets and was employed with especial elegance and skill by the Persian designers, and perhaps most beautifully in the Turkish court carpets which owed much to Persian inspiration. The combination moved from Syrian textile design into Asia Minor textile design with the Ottoman Turkish conquest in the 15th century and became typical of one group of 16th–17th-century Turkish carpets.

Palmettes, a second major class of conventional motives dominant in a considerable range of carpet designs from Asia Minor to India, are of plant derivation, and are justifiably named in that they originated in Assyrian design as stylizations of the palm, a symbol of the vitalistic power, often, if not always, in relation to the moon. Many of the almost uncountable variations that developed through the centuries continued to refer directly to the palm. Others, however, also beginning early in the 1st millennium B.C., derived from the lotus blossom, a complementary motive since it was connected primarily with the fertility symbolism of the sun. Still others involved the pomegranate, another fertility symbol, utilizing primarily the fruit, while yet another group presented the general vitalistic emblem, the vine, this last design being built on the single leaf. The forms of all these four main types of palmettes found in the rug designs are directly descended from styles current in textile designs from the 4th century onward, and are often modified by Chinese influences. These patterns in the 16th and early 17th centuries were beautifully and realistically elaborated, and blossoms like the Chinese peony sometimes compete with the more conventional lotus. The lanceolate leaf often associated with palmettes, especially in east Persian designs, is also largely conventional.

Outstanding among the more naturalistic plants are the cypresses and blossoming fruit trees, symbolizing life eternal and resurrection respectively. Willows are prominent in the Shah Abbas Vase carpet, as are jasmine flowers, and in Turkish court carpets, tulips. Many minor foliate and floral forms had no specific botanical identification though they give a realistic effect. Naturalistic red or pink roses, as on Karabakh and Kerman rugs from the 18th–19th centuries, are imitated from French patterns or English chintz and had no place in the old Persian repertoire, despite the importance of the rose in Persian poetry, life, and even economy, and its ancient symbolic importance throughout western Asia as an alternative to the lotus blossom.

In one widely distributed class of design some of the plant forms grow out of a vase, a development of an older symbolic scheme, portraying the Tree of Life, sustained by the Water of Life as implied by the "cloud jar," a design already well developed in Babylon.

The most important illustrative motifs, other than naturalistic plants, are those connected with the garden and the hunt: many small songbirds (particularly, in Persia, the nightingale), the *fêng huang* (pheasant) taken over from China and much favoured in the 16th century, and occasionally the peacock, which farther west in Asia had had considerable symbolic value; the great felines —lions and the semiconventional lion mask, sometimes used as the centre of a palmette; tigers; cheetahs; bears; foxes; deer of numerous species; goats, sometimes picturesquely prancing; or the wild ass, a fleet prey; ferocious looking Chinese dragons and the gentle *kilim*, a fantastic equine likewise imported from China. Fish sometimes swim in pools or streams, or are conventionally paired to suggest an escutcheon in the borders of the carpet. Huntsmen, usually mounted, are the major human figures though musicians also occur. Angels are occasionally present.

The underlying theme of both the conventional and illustrative vocabularies is nearly always fertility or abundance. The great carpet of Ardabil, for example, embodies a huge golden stellate medallion, developed from the multiple-pointed rosette that from time immemorial symbolized the sun. At its centre are four lotus blossoms floating on a little gray-blue pool, which represents the source of rain in the heavens. The medallion thus symbolizes the two basic vitalizing elements—sun and water. As proof of its magical potency, a complex system of tendrils and blossoms issues from it.

III. PRACTICAL CONSIDERATIONS

1. Uses of Carpets.—While many of the finest rugs were special productions for a wealthy clientele, it must be remembered that the common people also had their rugs. Throughout the Near East rugs have from the beginning been in common use and their universality was one of the reasons for their excellence. The English traveler Herbert, writing in the 17th century, said there was no house so poor but what it was furnished with carpets. From time immemorial carpets covered the floors of house and tent as well as mosque and palace, and served many other uses besides. They made handsome portieres and were sometimes hung on the wall like tapestries. They were a convenient portable and durable form of wealth, served as tribute money, and were frequently gifts of one state to another. They were used as blankets, canopies, and tomb covers. In past times they were also handy for committing and concealing murder. The last caliph of Baghdad (1258) made his tragic exit via a carpet in which he was rolled up and beaten to death, a not uncommon mode of execution, quite the reverse of Cleopatra's dramatic entrance to the presence of Julius Caesar when she stepped out of an unrolled rug. Woven with an apex that could be pointed to Mecca, they served as prayer mats for an individual or, given sufficient size and reduplicate prayer panels, they could serve simultaneously for a whole family or some religious fraternity. They made excellent saddle covers

and carryall bags as well. These modest rugs had their own merits. They were closer to the life of the people; the best of them have an air of genuineness and respect for the limits of the craft. On them were lavished loving care, and into them were woven life-protecting symbols which in early times people understood and took seriously; even now the meanings of the more obvious patterns are dimly remembered.

2. Size and Shape.—Rugs, a term understood to include all carpets for use on the floor, are mostly rectangular, though occasionally pieces are made to fit into irregular spaces, and a few round carpets are known, probably woven for tents. The rectangle may vary from a square to a strip at least six times as long as it is wide. A very usual ratio is about three to two. The strips, called runners or *kanara*, made in pairs to go along the sides of a Persian room, are very useful in corridors. A very common size for small rugs is about $6\frac{1}{2} \times 4\frac{1}{2}$ ft., while large ones may reach 25 ft. in length or occasionally more.

A very common room size for modern carpets is 10×14 ft., but not for old carpets which are much narrower in proportion to length, owing primarily to their use in combinations in the Oriental house. Some old carpets are nearly three times as long as wide; for example, the famous McCormick Vase carpet now in the Metropolitan Museum is 10×29 ft. Some of the palace carpets woven in the early 17th century (especially of the Herat type) are 50 ft. long. There are recently woven fine quality hall carpets in the ministry of foreign affairs in Teheran that are approximately 6×125 ft. (A. U. P.; X.)

3. Care of Carpets.—It is important that a carpet for use should be soundly made. Accordingly, when buying, the first thing to ascertain is that the foundation threads are sound and strong and that the pile is not unduly worn away. If a rug is held up to the light, holes and thin places are often revealed that were quite unnoticed when it lay on the floor. Holes that have been properly repaired are of little consequence. Few rugs have perfectly parallel sides but they should be of good shape and lie flat on the floor. A rug that is not flat tends to wear badly in the baggy places, but certain good rugs, such as the Shiraz, are rarely quite free from this defect. A guarantee should be asked that the rug has not been chemically treated, as is too often done with the object of effecting a supposed improvement in colour. Such treatment usually results in a hopeless deterioration of the yarns. Undesirable, though less destructive, is the process of hot-rolling, which gives to inferior wool a silky gloss that is only transitory.

Carpets will give remarkably long service if treated with proper consideration. Their two great enemies, apart from the inevitable destructive effect of wear, are moths and damp. The former is best kept at bay by frequent moving or handling and by regular exposure to light and air. If rugs must be stored, then inspection at intervals is essential. A carpet in use is rarely in danger from moths. Certain chemical applications will render the wool uneatable by moths. Damp will in time rot the threads and destroy the fabric, but it can be avoided by obvious means. If any mechanical injury is suffered, such as a cut or burn, the damage should be dealt with as soon as possible by a competent repairer, for such lesions get worse very quickly. In ordinary use, quite apart from accident, the ends and sides often tend to wear and fray out, in which case the parts should be reovercast—a very simple operation if done in time. Places in the middle of the carpet that are locally worn or damaged can have new knots inserted and even large holes can be restored so as to be almost as good as new, though such work is rather expensive. In carpets of lesser value, instead of new knotting, patches cut from a suitable rug can often be inserted at less cost, and sometimes a serviceable small rug can be made from a larger worn one by cutting away the bad parts.

From time to time, but not more often than necessary, carpets should be cleaned. If there is any doubt as to the stability of dyes, the cleaning should be entrusted to one of the many firms that specialize in this kind of work. In many cases, however, surface washing with a limited supply of hot water and carpet soap applied with a stiff brush may be done at home, though drying the fabric afterward is often a difficulty, as a clean and airy place must be available for some days. It is most important to wash out all traces of whatever cleaning agent is used. In ordinary use carpets are properly kept free from dust by brushing or by means of a vacuum cleaner, but in all cases where a brush is employed it is most important that it should not be used against the lie of the pile.

See also references under "Rug and Carpet" in the Index.

(C. E. TA.)

BIBLIOGRAPHY.—*General:* F. R. Martin, *A History of Oriental Carpets Before 1800*, 2 vol. (1908); F. Sarre, *Altorientalische Teppiche* (1908); F. Sarre and H. Trenkwald, *Altorientalische Teppiche* (1926–29), Eng. trans. *Old Oriental Carpets* by A. F. Kendrick (1926–29); A. F. Kendrick and C. E. C. Tattersall, *Hand-woven Carpets, Oriental and European*, 2 vol. (1923); A. F. Kendrick, *Guide to the Collection of Rugs and Carpets*, Victoria and Albert Museum (1931); W. G. Hasenbalg, *Der Orientteppich, seine Geschichte und seine Kultur* (1922); R. Neugebauer and S. Troll, *Handbuch der orientalischen Teppichkunde* (1930); C. B. Faraday, *European and American Carpets and Rugs* (1929); H. Jacoby, *How to Know Oriental Carpets and Rugs* (1952); M. and V. Viale, *Arazzi e tappeti antichi* (1952); C. E. C. Tattersall, *Notes on Carpet-Knotting and Weaving*, Victoria and Albert Museum (1949); K. Erdmann, *Der orientalische Knüpfteppich*, with full bibliography (1955), Eng. trans. *Oriental Carpets* by C. G. Ellis (1960); W. Bode and E. Kühnel, *Vorderasiatische Knüpfteppiche aus alter Zeit*, 4th ed. (1955), Eng. trans. *Antique Rugs from the Near East* by C. G. Ellis (1958); R. E. G. Macey, *Oriental Prayer Rugs* (1961); A. Hopf, *Oriental Carpets and Rugs* (1962); I. Schlosser, *Der schöne Teppich in Orient und Okzident* (1960), Eng. trans. *The Book of Rugs: Oriental and European* (1963).

Special works: A. U. Pope (ed.), *A Survey of Persian Art*, vol. iii and vol. vi (1939); M. S. Dimand, "An Early Cut-Pile Rug from Egypt," *Metropolitan Museum Studies*, iv (1933), *Loan Exhibition of Rugs of the So-Called Polish Type in the Metropolitan Museum* (1930), *The Ballard Collection of Oriental Rugs in the City Art Museum of St. Louis* (1935); C. J. Lamm, "The Marby Rug and Some Fragments of Carpets Found in Egypt," *Svenska Orientsällskapet Arsbok* (1937); R. M. Riefstahl, "Primitive Rugs of the 'Konya' Type in the Mosque of Beyeshehir," *Art Bulletin* (1931); A. U. Pope, "The Myth of the Armenian Dragon Carpets," in *Jahrbuch der Asiatischen Kunst*, ii (1925); K. Erdmann, "Later Caucasian Carpets," *Apollo* (1935); A. C. Edwards, *The Persian Carpet* (1953); F. Lewis, *Oriental Rugs and Textiles: The Perez Collection* (1953); A. B. Thacher, *Turkoman Rugs* (1940); T. H. Hendley, *Asian Carpets, XVIth and XVIIth Century Designs, from the Jaipur Palaces* (1905); E. Kühnel and L. Bellinger, *Catalogue of Spanish Rugs* (1953); C. E. C. Tattersall, *A History of British Carpets* (1934), and *The Carpets of Persia* (1931); K. Erdmann, *Der türkische Teppich des 15. Jahrhunderts* (1957); J. K. Mumford, *The Yerkes Collection of Oriental Rugs* (1911).

RUGBY, a municipal borough (1932) in the Rugby parliamentary division of Warwickshire, Eng., south of the Warwickshire Avon, 17 mi. (27 km.) ENE of Warwick by road. Pop. (1961) 51,698. Area 10.9 sq.mi. (28 sq.km.). Rugby was originally a hamlet of the adjoining parish of Clifton-upon-Dunsmore, and is separately treated as such in Domesday Book (where it is called Rocheberie). It became a separate parish in the reign of Henry III, who granted the town a weekly market and a yearly fair.

Oliver Cromwell was quartered there in 1645, and William III passed through on his way to Ireland. The town was not of great importance until the 19th century, its rise being mainly due to the advent of railways. It is an important railway junction with extensive engineering and electrical works, and a very large cattle market.

Rugby School for boys was founded and endowed under the will (1567) of Lawrence Sheriff of Rugby. The endowment consisted of the parsonage of Brownsover, Sheriff's mansion house in Rugby, and one-third (8 ac.) of his estate in Middlesex, which, being let in building leases, gradually increased in value. The full endowment was obtained in 1653. The school originally stood opposite the parish church, and was removed to its present site on the south side of the town between 1740 and 1750. In 1809 it was rebuilt from designs by Henry Hakewill (1771–1830); the chapel was rebuilt in 1872.

The Temple Observatory, containing an equatorial refractor by the U.S. optician Alvan Clark, was built in 1877 and the Temple reading room and the art museum were built in 1878. The Temple speech room was opened in 1909, the science schools in 1914 (enlarged in 1940), and the music schools in 1925 (enlarged in 1939). The rebuilding enabled the school to expand rapidly and become one of the largest in the country.

Tom Brown's School Days by Thomas Hughes is a chronicle of the period of the headmastership of Thomas Arnold (1828–42). Rugby football originated at the school (*see* FOOTBALL).

RUGBY FOOTBALL: *see* FOOTBALL.

RÜGEN, the largest island in Germany in the *Bezirk* (district) of Rostock, German Democratic Republic. It is situated in the Baltic Sea directly opposite Stralsund, 2 mi. (3 km.) off the northwest coast of Pomerania, from which it is separated by the narrow Strelasund, or Bodden. Its greatest length from north to south is 32 mi. (51 km.); its greatest breadth is 25 mi. (40 km.); and its area is 358 sq.mi. (927 sq.km.). The coastline is exceedingly irregular, as Rügen originally consisted of several separate islands which in geologically Recent times have been joined together by strips of land. The general name is applied locally only to the roughly triangular main trunk of the island, while the larger peninsulas, the landward extremities of which taper to narrow necks of land, are considered to be as distinct from Rügen as the various adjacent smaller islands which are also included for statistical purposes under the name. The chief peninsulas are those of Jasmund and Wittow on the north, and Mönchgut, at one time the property of the monastery of Eldena, on the southeast; and the chief neighbouring islands are Ummanz and Hiddensee, both off the west coast.

The surface of Rügen gradually rises toward the west to Rugard (299 ft. [91 m.])—the "eye of Rügen"—near Bergen, but the highest point is the Piekberg (528 ft. [161 m.]) in Jasmund. Erratic blocks are scattered throughout the island, and the roads are made with granite. The most beautiful and attractive part of the island is the east coast, with beech woods and chalk cliffs, the promontory of Stubbenkammer, where the cliffs rise to 400 ft., being the finest point. The east of Jasmund is clothed with an extensive beech wood in which lies the Borg, or Hertha Lake. Connected with Jasmund by the narrow isthmus of Schaabe to the west is the peninsula of Wittow, the most fertile part of the island. At the northeast extremity rises the height of Arkona, with a lighthouse.

Rügen is connected to the mainland by the Rügendamm, a road and rail embankment 1½ mi. long over the Strelasund between Stralsund and Altefähr. A railway with branch lines traverses the island, passing the chief town Bergen to Sassnitz on the northeast coast, the base of the deep-sea fishery and ferry station for Trelleborg, Swed. Resorts include Lohme, Binz, Sellin, Göhren, and Lauterbach-Putbus.

The morainic soil is fertile and sugar beet, oats, rye, and potatoes are grown. Cattle and sheep are reared on the drier land. The chief industry is the herring fishery and there are chalk pits in Jasmund. The tourist trade is also important. The poet and patriot Ernst Moritz Arndt (*q.v.*) was born at Schoritz. Rügen is the setting of *The Adventures of Elizabeth in Rügen* by Mary Annette Russell, the author of *Elizabeth and Her German Garden.*

Rügen is rich in prehistoric remains. The original Germanic inhabitants were dispossessed by Slavs; and there are still various relics of the long reign of paganism that ensued. In the Stubnitz and elsewhere Huns' and giants' graves are common; and near Hertha Lake are the ruins of an ancient edifice which some have sought to identify with the shrine of the heathen deity Hertha or Nerthus, referred to by Tacitus. On the promontory of Arkona in Wittow are the remains of an ancient fortress of the Wends enclosing a pagan temple which was destroyed in 1168 by the Danish king, Waldemar I, when he made himself master of the island. Rügen was ruled then by a succession of native princes under Danish supremacy until 1218. In 1325 Rügen came under Pomeranian suzerainty, being united with the duchy of Pomerania in 1478. In 1648 it passed to Sweden and in 1815 to Prussia.

BIBLIOGRAPHY.—M. Wehrmann, *Geschichte der Insel Rügen*, 2 vol., 2nd ed. (1923); W. Petzsch, *Rügens Burgwäller und die slavische Kultur der Insel* (1927); W. Petzsch, *Die Steinzeit Rügens* (1928); A. Raetz, *Die Insel Rügen, wirtschaftsgeographisch betrachtet* (1936); W. Petzsch, *Rügens Huhnengräber*, 3rd ed. (1938).

RUGGLES-BRISE, SIR EVELYN (1857–1935), prison reformer, was instrumental in the founding and development of the Borstal system (*q.v.*) of penal treatment. He was born Dec. 6, 1857, at Finchingfield, in Essex. He received his education at Eton and Oxford, from which he received an honours degree in 1880. After eight years as private secretary to home secretaries he received appointment as prison commissioner in 1895. At that time the Gladstone Committee made its report recommending significant changes in prison administration; it was Ruggles-Brise's duty as prison commissioner to apply the recommendations, and chief among his accomplishments was the establishment of what grew to be the Borstal system. The Gladstone Committee's position was that young offenders (16–21 years of age) should not be subjected to the harsh punitive treatment that was administered to older, less tractable prisoners; that they should be given education and industrial training at a "penal reformatory" under the supervision of a qualified staff; and that after release they should receive additional help.

Ruggles-Brise visited the United States in 1897 to study the state reformatory system; upon his return to England he collected together at the convict prison at Borstal, Kent, a group of young prisoners to implement the program. In 1908 at the urging of Ruggles-Brise and others, Parliament established the system that permitted magistrates to prescribe "Borstal detention" as a separate sentence for young offenders. In 1910 he became chairman of the International Prison Commission, on which he had actively served as a member for many years. He retired in 1921 and died at Peaslake, Surrey, August 18, 1935.

RUHR, a river of Germany and a major industrial region. The Ruhr River is 146 mi. (235 km.) long, an important right-bank tributary of the lower Rhine. It rises on the north side of Winterberg in the Sauerland, at a 2,376-ft. altitude. It flows north and then west in a deep, well-wooded valley past Arnsberg. Shortly after reaching Neheim it bends southwest and skirts the southern border of the coal-mining district in a tortuous course that passes Witten, Steele, Kettwig, and Mülheim, then joins the Rhine at Ruhrort. The river is navigable from Witten downward, by the aid of 11 locks. Its chief affluents are the Möhne (right) and Lenne (left).

The river has given its name to the largest single industrial area in the world. Although this area (the Ruhrgebiet or Ruhr) has no separate administrative entity it is generally accepted as comprising the district on the right bank of the Rhine as far east as Hamm between the Lippe and Ruhr rivers. Its area is about 1,280 sq.mi. (3,320 sq.km.) and its population (1961 census) 4,985,231. Five towns—Essen, Dortmund, Duisburg, Gelsenkirchen, and Bochum —each had a population of more than 350,000.

The Ruhr coalfield (which extends west as well as east of the Rhine) is one of the largest in the world. In the early 1960s its production was about 80% of the bituminous coal output of the Federal Republic of Germany. In that period the Ruhr district also supplied about 60% of West German steel production. Many kinds of chemical industries developed in the area.

Before World War I most of the iron and steel works in the German-occupied part of Lorraine were owned by or closely affiliated with concerns in the Ruhr, and some of the low-grade iron ore of Lorraine went to the blast furnaces of this region. On the other hand the coke of the Ruhr was needed for smelting Lorraine ores, while the finished iron and steel goods of Lorraine found their market in southwestern Germany.

The Interwar Period.—The return of Alsace-Lorraine to France and the retirement of Luxembourg from the German Customs Union reduced Germany's home supply of iron ore by 80% and led to the greater use of low-grade ores in north Germany. At the same time France became the greatest iron-ore producing country of Europe; moreover it acquired the well-equipped iron and steel mills in Lorraine, expropriating the German iron- and steelmasters. It also temporarily administered the Saar mines, but as the Saar coal did not coke well, special clauses in the Treaty of Versailles guaranteed to the Allies a regular supply of Ruhr coal and coke at statutory prices.

Political pressure apart, however, the German coalmasters held the winning hand. Compensation from the German government enabled them to erect new iron and steel works in the Ruhr, and to modernize and rationalize the coal-mining and coking industries. Plant facilities were adapted for the use of imported ores, chiefly the high-grade ores of Sweden. Smelting in Lorraine, on the other hand, depended on the regular supply of Ruhr coke, and the export of finished products depended mainly on German markets which were open to France without duty for five years. Thus those who controlled the Ruhr coal could influence the Lorraine iron and steel industry.

Deficiencies in German reparation deliveries of Ruhr coal and coke led in 1921 to French military occupation of Düsseldorf, Duisburg, and Ruhrort. Further deficiencies, stated by the Allied Reparation Commission to be "intentional," caused the French to occupy the entire Ruhr region in January 1923. German passive resistance paralyzed the economic life of the region and was the deciding factor in the collapse of the German currency. (*See* GERMANY: *History.*) The dispute was settled when in August 1924 the Allies' and Germany agreed to accept the Dawes Plan for reparations. The occupation of the Ruhr ended on July 31, 1925, when French troops left Essen and Mülheim, the formerly occupied districts of Düsseldorf, Duisburg, and Ruhrort being evacuated on Aug. 25.

World War II and After.—The heavy industry of the Ruhr played an important part in Germany's preparations for World War II. Plants were worked at capacity during the Hitler period, though no important new plant was built. Before the war began, annual pig-iron production was about 15,000,000 tons and that of finished steel goods about 12,000,000 tons. Coal output exceeded 110,000,000 tons, much of which was coked; and chemical industries based on coal tar were greatly expanded.

The role of the Ruhr industrialists in bringing Hitler to power and in furthering German rearmament has probably been exaggerated, but was nevertheless considerable. They themselves made far-reaching claims, probably in the hope of standing well with the Nazis. But without the industries and resources of the Ruhr, the power of Germany to wage war would have been signally reduced.

Much of the Ruhr was in ruins by the end of World War II, and more than one-third of the coal mines had discontinued operations completely or were heavily damaged. The capture in April 1945 of 325,000 German troops who were trapped in the Ruhr pocket by the U.S. 1st and 9th armies was one of the outstanding successes of the Allied campaign in Western Europe (*see* WORLD WAR II).

The Allies saw the Ruhr as a prime source of Germany's military strength and its industrialists as a leading factor in German aggression. They proposed to eradicate the danger by reducing the capacity of the Ruhr through dismantling industrial equipment deemed redundant and by breaking up the large manufacturing concerns, which were regarded as excessive concentrations of economic power. These policies were unsuccessful because, in the changed political situation after 1947, they were unrealistic. Dismantling was slowed down; then it ceased, and gave place to modernization and rebuilding. The firms created by the splintering of the older concerns were subsequently merged to form units distantly resembling those operating before the war.

The short phase of dismantling was followed by one of controlled rebuilding. The International Authority for the Ruhr was set up in April 1949, to secure an equitable distribution of the Ruhr's resources, especially coking coal. It was dissolved when, in August 1952, its functions were largely taken over by the newly created European Coal and Steel Community (ECSC).

The sovereignty of the Federal Republic of Germany was reestablished in October 1954, and this ended all Allied control over German industry. Thereafter, the only restriction on the Ruhr industries was that exercised first by the ECSC and later by the European Economic Community.

In the conditions of an expanding economy that characterized the 1950s, the industrial production of the Ruhr reached a level exceeding that achieved under the Nazis. Coal production in 1962 was 114,000,000 tons. Pig-iron production rose to 15,400,000 tons, on the basis partly of low-grade domestic ores and partly of ores imported from Sweden, Canada, Brazil, and elsewhere. Ore from Lorraine by then played a negligible role in the economy of the Ruhr, though the canalization of the Moselle offers possibilities of cheaper importation. Annual steel production increased to about 20,500,000 tons. Deprived of former markets in eastern

Europe, the Ruhr's industrialists turned increasingly to other parts of the world. By the 1960s the Ruhr firms were making a massive contribution to the expansion of plant facilities and the creation of new industries in the underdeveloped countries.

Waterborne communications depend on the Rhine and lower Ruhr rivers and the Rhine-Herne and Dortmund-Ems canals, with Ruhrort the chief port. The Ruhr has one of the densest railway networks in Europe. The Ruhrschnellweg highway (1929) between Duisburg and Dortmund was relieved of congestion by the Berlin–Cologne *Autobahn* of the 1930s, which skirts the Ruhr to the north and west. Further relief was afforded early in the 1960s by the completion of the branch *Autobahn* northeastward from Cologne. The heliport at Dortmund is used by local services; international air services use the Düsseldorf airport. *See* also references under "Ruhr" in the Index.

(M. Bo.; N. J. G. P.)

RUISDAEL (Ruysdael, Ruijsdael), **JACOB VAN** (*c.* 1629–1682), Holland's greatest landscape painter, was born at Haarlem about 1629. He was probably the pupil of his father, the frame maker Izack de Gooyer, who later styled himself Ruysdael. There is no truth in the statement that his uncle Salomon van Ruysdael (*q.v.*) influenced his artistic development, let alone was his teacher. The influence of Cornelisz Vroom, another Haarlem landscapist, is often noticeable in his early works of the 1640s; the earliest dated pictures are of 1646. Two years later he became a member of the Guild of St. Luke in Haarlem. Around 1650–52 he traveled extensively in Holland and the neighbouring parts of western Germany (several views of the castle of

"MILL AT WIJK NEAR DUURSTEDE" BY JACOB VAN RUISDAEL. IN THE RIJKSMUSEUM, AMSTERDAM

bouring parts of western Germany (several views of the castle of Bentheim). About 1655 he settled in Amsterdam, of which he became a free citizen in 1659. Meindert Hobbema must have been his pupil before 1660. Ruisdael's name was entered on the list of Amsterdam doctors in 1676, but later his name was deleted. Whether he ever practised as a doctor is not known, but his artistic work was relatively well rewarded. He died in Amsterdam but was buried in Haarlem on March 14, 1682 (the Jacob van Ruisdael who died in 1681 in the almshouse of Haarlem was another painter, the son of Salomon).

The early works of Ruisdael, mostly with motifs from the surroundings of Haarlem, are very accurately drawn and executed. Around 1650 his art developed toward a heroic-pathetic style of well-composed romantic landscapes. Unlike most of the Dutch landscape painters, he did not care for a topographical rendering of special scenes. As few of his pictures are dated after 1655, it is hard to place them in exact chronological order. It seems that the many "Waterfalls," varying a theme by A. van Everdingen (who had been in Sweden), belong to his later period, as do the

few townscapes. His main motifs are derived from forest scenery ("The Pool in the Wood," Leningrad). Beaches and stormy seas with magnificent clouds had never been painted before with such a power of expression, feeling for atmosphere and space.

The works of Ruisdael are spread over all the great galleries, the National gallery, London, possessing many good examples. His famous paintings also include: "The Jewish Burial Ground" (Dresden and Detroit), based on drawings made at Ouderkerk near Amsterdam; the "View of Haarlem" (Rijksmuseum, Amsterdam); "The Pool" (Berlin and Worcester college, Oxford); "The Wood" (Kunsthistorisches museum, Vienna); two "Views of Egmond" (Philips collection, Eindhoven, and Art gallery, Glasgow); "Wheatfields" (Metropolitan museum, New York); "Mill at Wijk Near Duurstede" (Rijksmuseum, Amsterdam); "The Winter" (Staedel, Frankfurt); "The Burst of Sunshine" ("Le Coup du Soleil," Louvre, Paris). Sometimes, but by no means always, the small figures in his pictures are added by other artists, such as A. Van de Velde, Philips Wouwerman and Nicolaes Berchem.

As can be seen from the subjects, Ruisdael's landscape vision had a wide range. His understanding for the beauty and inner life of the landscape is nowhere hampered by the fact that his poetic and romantic vision transformed the simple Dutch scenery sometimes into unnaturalistic but powerful compositions. Moreover, the rendering of the details—the trees, the water and the ground —is full of careful, sensitive observation. There are several fish markets in white, black and grayish colours, and there is a surprising church interior of the Nieuwe Kerk at Amsterdam (marquess of Bute collection; drawing in Print room, Berlin).

Bibliography.—C. Hofstede de Groot, *Catalogue of Dutch Painters* (1912); J. Rosenberg, *Jacob van Ruisdael* (1928); Wolfgang Stechow, *Dutch Landscape Painting of the Seventeenth Century* (1966).

(H. K. Gn.)

RUIZ, JUAN (*c.* 1283–*c.* 1350), Spanish poet, archpriest of Hita. He is thought to have been born at Alcalá de Henares, though the exact year is unknown. He died about 1350. One of the greatest of Spanish poets, his barefaced, jocund, and yet somewhat moralizing view of life left a profound, still traceable, mark on Castilian literature. His masterpiece, the *Libro de buen amor* (1330, expanded in 1343), was created as something of everyone for everyone, and he seems deliberately to have left it an open book, so that whoever cared to do so might add something further. Three 14th-century manuscripts of the work are extant. The general theme is the relationship between Christian and Moorish concepts as they subsist side by side. Américo Castro compares the work with the erotic poetry of Ibn Hazm, the Cordovan author of the *Tawq al-hamamaw* (1022; *see* Courtly Love). Rafael Lapesa sees it as a characteristic Mudejar work, embodying a profound understanding of Muslim life. Juan Ruiz has adapted elements from the *Ars Amatoria* of Ovid, and, even more clearly, from the 12th-century Latin comedy *Pamphilus*. The influence of the goliardic bards is also apparent, though Juan Ruiz condemns the vice of alcohol. The battle in his book between Don Carnal and Doña Cuaresma has been related to the medieval French poem *La bataille de Caresme et de Carnage,* though it is most likely that both works are based on a common and traditional theme.

The *Libro de buen amor* is rich in language and concept, highly amusing, cynical, and most substantial fare. Its realism is stark and severe and no room is allowed for abstract concepts. The use of popular refrains and figures of speech, a practice which was to yield much that is best in Castilian literature, began with the archpriest of Hita; and his character Trotaconventos is the great antecedent of La Celestina (*q.v.*).

See A. Castro, *España en su historia* (1948); R. Lapesa, "Arcipreste de Hita" in *Diccionario de literatura española* (1949). (C.-J. Ce.)

RUIZ DE ALARCÓN (Y MENDOZA), JUAN (*c.* 1581–1639), greatest Mexican writer of the colonial era and principal dramatist of early 17th-century Spain after Lope de Vega and Tirso de Molina, was born at Mexico City and educated there and, after 1600, at Salamanca, Spain. Having returned home in 1608 to practise law, he re-emigrated definitively to Spain in 1613 and began to write. A spinal deformity savagely ridiculed by his literary contemporaries isolated him from society and was thus perhaps as responsible as his colonial origin for the atypical character of his work, with its formal polish (with 20 published plays, he is the least prolific major Spanish dramatist) and ethical bias. His finest works are *La verdad sospechosa* (adapted by Corneille as *Le menteur*) and *Las paredes oyen*. He died at Madrid on Aug. 4, 1639.

BIBLIOGRAPHY.—*Teatro*, ed. by E. Abreu Gómez (1951); A. Reyes, in *Cuadernos de literatura contemporánea* (1955); O. Green, in *Bulletin of Hispanic Studies* (1956). (F. S. R.)

RULES OF ORDER, as the term is ordinarily used in the United States, embodies the generally accepted rules, precedents and practices commonly employed in the government of deliberative assemblies. Its function is to maintain decorum, ascertain the will of the majority, preserve the rights of the minority and facilitate the orderly and harmonious transaction of the business of the assembly. While it had its origin in the early British parliaments, the modern system of general parliamentary law is, in many respects, at wide variance with the current systems of procedure of both the English parliament and the U.S. congress. These legislative systems are designed for bicameral bodies, generally with paid memberships, meeting in continuous session, requiring a majority for a quorum and delegating their duties largely to committees. Their special requirements and the constantly increasing pressure of their business have produced highly complex and remarkably efficient systems peculiar to their respective bodies but which are as a whole unsuited to the needs of the ordinary assembly. (*See* CONGRESS, UNITED STATES; PARLIAMENT.) As a result there has been simultaneously developed through years of experiment and practice a simpler system of procedure adapted to the needs of deliberative assemblies generally and which, though variously interpreted in minor details by different writers, is now in the main standardized and authoritatively established.

Organization.—Assemblies convene with the implied understanding that they will be conducted and governed in accordance with these fundamental principles. The routine ordinarily followed in the preliminary organization of an assembly includes the call to order by any of those present with a request for nominations for temporary chairman. The temporary chairman having been elected and having taken the chair, a temporary secretary is chosen and those addressing the chairman are recognized to explain and discuss the purposes of the meeting. If the assembly has convened for a single session only or is in the nature of a mass meeting a presiding officer and recording officer will suffice. If permanent organization is contemplated a committee is usually appointed to draft a constitution and bylaws and on the adoption of its report, with or without amendments, the assembly proceeds to the election of the permanent officers thus authorized. In a permanent organization such officers commonly consist of a presiding officer known as the president, chairman, speaker or moderator; a vice-presiding officer; a recording officer, known as the secretary or clerk, who keeps the records, attends to the clerical work of the organization and in the absence of the presiding officers calls for the selection of a temporary president; a treasurer or bursar who receives and disburses its funds; and a sergeant at arms who preserves order and carries out the wishes of the assembly through the presiding officer.

It is the duty of the presiding officer to call the assembly to order at the appointed time, cause the journal or minutes of the preceding meeting to be read, call up the business of the assembly in the order provided by its rules and conduct its proceedings in accordance with parliamentary law. He is especially charged with the responsibility of ascertaining the presence of a quorum, the minimum number of members prescribed by the rules of the assembly as competent to transact business. In legislative assemblies a quorum is presumed to be present unless the question is raised, but where the bylaws of an ordinary assembly require a quorum it devolves upon the presiding officer to ascertain that a quorum is present before proceeding with business.

Motions.—The will of an assembly is determined and expressed by its action on proposals submitted for its consideration in the form of motions or resolutions offered by members recognized for that purpose. In order to make a motion a member must rise and address the chair and secure recognition. If the motion is in order and is seconded by another member it is "stated" by the presiding officer and is then subject to the action of the assembly. A second is not required in legislative assemblies but is requisite under general parliamentary law. Motions may be classified as main or principal motions, introducing a proposition; and secondary or ancillary motions, designed to affect the pending main motion or its consideration. A main motion is in order only when there is no other business before the assembly, and yields in precedence to all other questions. Secondary motions may be subdivided into subsidiary, incidental and privileged.

Subsidiary motions are applicable to other motions for the purpose of modifying the main question or affecting its consideration and disposition. They have precedence of the motion to which applied but yield to privileged and incidental motions. They take precedence among themselves in the following order: to lay on the table; for the previous question; to close or extend debate; to postpone to a day certain; to commit, recommit and refer; to amend; and to postpone indefinitely.

Motion to Lay on the Table.—The motion to lay on the table is in effect a motion to suspend consideration of the question and, if agreed to, also suspends consideration of all pending questions relating to the motion to which applied until such time as the assembly may determine to take it from the table for further consideration. The motion is not debatable and may not be amended, postponed, committed, divided or reconsidered.

Motion for the Previous Question.—The purpose of the motion for the previous question is to close debate peremptorily and bring the assembly to an immediate vote on the pending question. It may be ordered on a single question, a group of questions or any part of a pending question, as on an amendment. It precludes both debate and amendment and requires a two-thirds vote for passage under general parliamentary procedure. It yields to the motion to table, to the question of consideration and to privileged and incidental motions and may be reconsidered, but takes precedence of motions to postpone, amend and commit.

Motion to Close or Extend Debate.—The motion is not admitted in either house of the U.S. congress when not sitting as committee of the whole but is in order under general parliamentary law and insofar as applicable is subject to the rules governing the previous question.

Motion to Postpone to a Day Certain.—This applies to the main motion and its pending amendments and is debatable only as to the advisability of the postponement proposed, and does not open to debate the subject matter of the motion to which applied. It is subject to amendment and reconsideration, to privileged and incidental motions, to motions for the previous question and to lay on the table but has precedence of all other subsidiary motions.

Motion to Commit, Recommit and Refer.—The motions to commit, recommit and refer are practically equivalent and provide for reference of the pending proposition to a committee. While the motion to recommit ordinarily applies to the whole subject including pending amendments, it may apply to certain features only. It may be amended as by adding instructions to the committee as to time and manner of report. Debate on the motion is limited to the question of reference and instructions. It takes precedence of motions to amend and indefinitely postpone but yields to other subsidiary motions and to all incidental and privileged motions. It may be tabled or postponed with the main question but no subsidiary motions except the motions to amend and for the previous question may be applied separately. It is subject to reconsideration at any time before the committee begins consideration of the question submitted to it but after that time the subject matter may only be reclaimed by a motion to discharge the committee.

Motion to Amend.—Changes in the text or terms of the proposition require a second and must be reduced to writing if requested by the chairman. There is no limit to the number of amendments which may be proposed and new amendments may be offered as rapidly as the pending amendment is disposed of. Amendments in the second degree, that is, amendments to amendments, are admissible but amendments in the third degree, that is amendments to amendments to amendments, are not in order. Only four amendments in the first and second degrees may be pending simultaneously, as follows: (1) amendment; (2) amendment to the amendment; (3) substitute for the amendment (*i.e.,* when it is desired to replace the entire pending amendment); and (4) amendment to the substitute. The amendment must, of course, be offered first and the substitute before the amendment to the substitute, but otherwise there is no rule governing the order in which the four amendments may be presented. They must, however, be voted on in the following order: first, amendments to the amendment; second, amendments to the substitute; third, the substitute; and last, the amendment. Debate on an amendment is in order only when the main motion is debatable, and is then limited to the proposed modification. An amendment which has been rejected may not be offered the second time in identical form, and no amendment may be proposed reversing the operation of an amendment previously adopted. Motions to amend will not be entertained unless germane or relevant to the main question, and no proposition different from that under consideration will be admitted under guise of amendment. This motion yields to all privileged, incidental and subsidiary motions except indefinite postponement. It is subject to amendment, to the operation of the previous question and to reconsideration, and when laid on the table carries with it the proposition proposed to be amended. Likewise, when the main question is laid on the table, postponed or recommitted, all pending amendments accompany it. The motion to amend is not applicable to the motion to lay on the table or for the previous question, to adjourn or to suspend the rules.

Motion to Postpone Indefinitely.—The motion to postpone indefinitely provides for final adverse disposition for the session and amounts to summary rejection. It is debatable and opens to debate the question to which applied but is subject to no subsidiary motion except the motion for the previous question.

Incidental motions include questions arising incidentally in the consideration of other questions and decided before disposition of the one to which they are incident. They have no relative rank and merely take precedence of the pending question in the consideration of which they have arisen. All are undebatable with the exception of appeal. They comprise motions to suspend the rules, withdraw motions, read papers, raise the question of consideration, questions of order and appeal, reconsider, take up out of order, determine method of procedure, divide pending questions and questions relating to nominations.

The motion temporarily to suspend the rules may not be debated or reconsidered and is not subject to the application of any subsidiary motion. The vote required to pass the motion is ordinarily fixed by the rules of the assembly and in the absence of such provision is two-thirds of those present and voting.

Withdrawal or modification of a motion after it has been "stated" by the presiding officer is usually effected by unanimous consent but in event of objection by any member must be submitted to the assembly. Consent of the seconder is not required but if modified the seconder may withdraw the second. When applied to the main motion it includes all adhering motions, but when applied to amendments or adhering motions the main question is not affected. The reading of papers on which a vote is to be taken may be demanded by any member as a matter of right. Papers on which a vote is not required are usually read by unanimous consent but if objection is made the question must be submitted to the assembly.

The question of whether the assembly desires to take up a proposition regularly presented for its consideration may be tested by raising the question of consideration, which may be moved at any time before actual consideration commences and does not require a second. It is not in order after debate begins or after a subsidiary motion has been applied. When the question is properly raised the assembly may by a two-thirds adverse vote decline to take up any business it prefers not to consider.

Points of Order may be made while another has the floor, and when the question concerns the use of unparliamentary language the member so called to order must be seated pending disposition of the matter. The question must be raised at the time the proceeding giving rise to the objection occurs and will not be entertained after the assembly has passed to other business. If the point of order is overruled the member resumes the floor but if the objection is sustained he may proceed only by consent of the assembly. Debate on questions of order is for the information of the chair and may be closed by the presiding officer at any time. Any member may appeal from a decision by the chair and such appeal is debatable unless arising out of an undebatable question.

The motion to reconsider must be made by one who voted with the prevailing side but may be seconded by any member. It is only in order on the day or the next calendar day after the vote proposed to be reconsidered is taken. The motion is of the highest privilege and may be entered for record on the minutes while another has the floor, but cannot be called up for consideration until the pending question is disposed of, when it takes precedence of all new business. If applied to a debatable question it reopens the entire subject to debate. The motion may not be amended, committed or indefinitely postponed and requires a majority vote for passage. If agreed to, the motion reopens the entire question for further action as if there had been no final decision. The motion to take up out of order is merely another form of the motion to suspend the rules and requires a two-thirds vote for enactment. It is not amendable and debate is limited to the specific question presented.

A motion to divide the question is in order where the pending question includes propositions so distinct that, one being taken away, a substantive proposition will remain. Such motions are applicable to main questions and their amendments only and no subsidiary motion except the motion to amend is admitted. The rules of the U.S. house of representatives provide that any member may demand the division of a question as a matter of right, but under general parliamentary procedure the question must be submitted to the vote of the assembly.

Nominations do not require a second. Where the rules of an assembly fail to provide a method of nomination a motion for such provision is in order. The motion to close nominations is subject to none of the subsidiary motions save the motion to amend, and is decided by a two-thirds vote.

Privileged Motions relate to the needs and interests of the assembly and its members in matters of such urgent importance as to supersede temporarily pending business. They take precedence of all other motions and may be offered while other questions are pending. In this class of motions is the motion to fix the time to which to adjourn, to adjourn, to take a recess, raising questions of privilege and the call for the orders of the day, all of which are undebatable.

Other motions variously referred to as supplementary, miscellaneous and unclassified are the motions to take from the table, to discharge a committee, to accept the report of a committee, to rescind, to repeal, to annul, to expunge and to permit a member to resume the floor after having been called to order for words spoken in debate.

Rules for Debate.—In order to debate a question, a member must rise and address the chair and be recognized by the presiding officer for that purpose. The presiding officer should first recognize the mover of a proposition or the member of a committee presenting a report and should endeavour to alternate recognitions between those favouring and those opposing a question. It is also customary, though not necessarily incumbent upon the chair, to permit the proponent of a proposition to close debate. A member may speak but once on the same question at the same stage of the proceedings if others desire recognition, but is entitled to speak on the main question and on each amendment as presented. Under general parliamentary procedure a member securing the floor may speak without limit and this practice still obtains in the U.S. senate, but the house of representatives by rule limits speakers to one hour in the house and to five minutes in the committee of the whole. Most assemblies and all legislative bodies provide a limit for debate and in conventions it is customary to adopt a rule at the opening session limiting debate to a specified number of minutes. In debate a member must confine himself to the question under consideration, must avoid personalities and must not arraign motives. Members should be silent and respectful while another has the floor and in questioning the speaker should first address the chair, who will in turn inquire if the speaker desires to yield. Where the presiding officer is a member of the assembly he has the right to debate and to participate in the proceedings but should call another to the chair before taking the floor and should not resume it again until the pending question has been decided.

Voting.—Voting may be by ballot; by division, that is a rising vote; viva voce, that is by acclamation, the presiding officer deciding by the volume of voices; by show of hands; by tellers, the members passing between tellers appointed from opposite sides to count them as they pass through; and by yeas and nays, the clerk calling the roll and recording each vote as given. If there is doubt as to the result of a viva voce vote any member may request a division and the presiding officer thereupon proceeds to take a rising vote. A member may change his vote at any time prior to announcement of the result. Only members in attendance may vote and voting by proxy is never permissible unless by operation of law. A tie vote defeats an affirmative motion. The presiding officer, if a member of the assembly, may vote to break a tie or to make one.

Committees.—Much of the work of assemblies and especially of legislative bodies is transacted by committees. The committee system provides for a better division of labour and for a more detailed consideration than the assembly as a whole is ordinarily prepared to give. Committees are classified as standing committees with fixed terms of office and rendering continuous service; and special committees serving temporarily and assigned to limited service. In the absence of a rule making other provision, committees are selected by the assembly. Frequently the chair is authorized to appoint committees. Or selection may be made by ballot, by resolution or by designation in motions of reference. If no chairman is designated the member first named acts as chairman until the committee elects a chairman. As far as applicable the rules of the assembly govern its committees. The chairman of the committee submits its report to the assembly and unless it is of elementary character is required to present it in writing. Members who do not concur in the report may submit minority views over their signatures. When called up for consideration in the assembly such minority report is read in connection with the majority report unless there is objection, in which event the question of reading the minority views is submitted without debate to the vote of the assembly.

The committee of the whole consists of the entire assembly acting as a general committee. In legislative assemblies it affords greater freedom of consideration but in nonlegal bodies is rarely used.

Parliamentary Practice.—Use of motions to effect a purpose in the assembly or its committees when applicable may be summarized as follows: The body may protect itself against business which it does not wish to consider by invoking the motion to lay on the table, by raising the question of consideration or by voting to postpone indefinitely. If it is desired to suppress debate, the motion to limit debate and the demand for the previous question are available. Modification of a proposition may be secured through amendment or reference to a committee with or without instructions. Action may be deferred by postponement to a day certain, by providing a special order or by the motion to table. A question may be brought up a second time for consideration in the assembly by voting to take from the table, by reconsideration or by the motion to rescind, repeal or annul.

See H. M. Robert, *Rules of Order*, rev. ed. (1956).   (C. CA.)

RULES OF THE ROAD AT SEA are internationally agreed-upon traffic regulations for ocean waters. They apply to every type of watercraft, including seaplanes. Their purpose is to prevent collisions; this is accomplished by rules specifying the colour, arc and visibility, and arrangement of lights; the size, colour, shape, and position of daymarks; the character, duration, and frequency of sound signals; and the type of avoiding action to be taken when two craft approach each other.

Special provisions cover situations involving inability to maneuver, distress, and cases in which three craft approach each other simultaneously.

Authority is also provided for countries to have special rules for their own inland waters. In the latter case, the normal practice is for a country to limit differences to additions made necessary by the local conditions. The major exception is the United States, which has evolved complex rules for its internal waters that sometimes contradict the ocean regulations.

The history of the modern rules dates back to 1863, when nations first took into account the effect of steam on shipping. The rules have since undergone periodic revision because of advances in technology and of such new developments as seaplanes and the increase in pleasure craft. Texts of the rules normally can be obtained from the governmental agency administering shipping and/or boating in a particular country. The following is a summary of the regulations that came into force on Sept. 1, 1965, based on recommendations of the International Conference on Safety of Life at Sea, 1960.

Preliminary and Definitions.—The regulations apply to all vessels on the high seas. A "power-driven" vessel is any vessel propelled by machinery. When under sail only, a power-driven vessel is considered a sailing vessel; if under both sail and power, it is considered a power-driven vessel. The rules for seaplanes apply when the planes are waterborne, and are similar to the rules for power-driven vessels. Any vessel is under way when not at anchor, moored, or aground.

Radar.—The possession of information obtained from radar does not relieve any vessel of the obligation of conforming strictly with the regulations and, in particular, the rules applicable to restricted visibility.

Radar is considered to be an aid to navigation, which, if properly used, will assist the rules in their purpose.

Vessels Under 65 Feet.—The regulations recognize that some small vessels may not be able to comply with the basic rules regarding lights, daymarks, and sound devices. Hence, power-driven vessels of less than 65 ft. and vessels of less than 40 ft. under oars or sails are authorized where the rules so state to carry prescribed alternate items of essentially the same meaning to other vessels.

Military Vessels and Planes.—Any government may certify that a naval or other military vessel or waterborne seaplane of special construction or purpose cannot comply fully with the rules prescribing lights or shapes. In such case the vessel or plane shall be in the closest possible compliance.

Lights and Shapes.—The rules concerning lights must be complied with in all weathers from sunset to sunrise. Exhibition of these lights at other times is optional. No other lights that might be mistaken for the prescribed lights, impair their visibility, or interfere with the keeping of a proper lookout must be exhibited. Shapes of daymarks shall be not less than two feet in diameter.

Power-Driven Vessels Under Way.—(1) Masthead light: in the forepart of the vessel a white light visible for five miles over an arc of 225°, *i.e.*, from right ahead to $22\frac{1}{2}°$ abaft the beam on either side. (2) Range light: a second white light of similar character either forward or abaft the above light (not compulsory for vessels less than 150 ft. in length). These two lights must be in line with the keel, one 15 ft. higher than the other. The horizontal distance between them must be at least three times the vertical distance. The lower light shall be forward and not less than 20 ft. above the hull. (3) Sidelights: (*a*) on the starboard side a green light clearly visible for two miles over an arc of $112\frac{1}{2}°$, *i.e.*, from right ahead to $22\frac{1}{2}°$ abaft the beam; (*b*) on the port side a similar red light. These sidelights must be fitted with screens projecting three feet forward of the light. (4) Stern light: at the stern a white light visible for two miles over an arc of 135°, *i.e.*, from right astern to $67\frac{1}{2}°$ on each side.

Vessels Towing.—(1) A power-driven vessel towing or pushing another vessel shall carry in addition to her sidelights two white masthead lights vertically, not less than six feet apart; (2) if the tow exceeds 600 ft. an additional white light must be carried six feet above or below such lights; (3) if the towing vessel is 150 ft. or more in length, she shall also show her range light; (4) whether under 150 ft. or larger, a stern light or a white light must be shown abaft the funnel or aftermast for the tow to steer by; (5) in daytime, when the tow exceeds 600 ft., the towing vessel and tow shall each show a black diamond shape.

Vessels Not Under Control.—(1) A vessel not under command shall carry in lieu of masthead and range lights, where best seen, two red lights vertically, not less than six feet apart and visible all around for two miles. By day, the red lights shall be replaced by two black balls. (2) A vessel working submarine cables, navigation marks, surveying, or on underwater operations, or a vessel engaged in replenishment at sea, or in the launching or recovery of aircraft, when unable to maneuver shall carry in lieu of masthead and range lights three lights vertically six feet apart, thus— red, white, red—visible all around for two miles. By day, similarly placed, she shall carry three shapes vertically, the highest and lowest globular in shape and red in colour, the middle diamond in shape and white. (3) A vessel engaged in minesweeping operations shall carry in addition to her masthead light a green all-round light visible two miles at the foretruck and another similar green light at the end of the foreyard on the side(s) that danger exists. By day the vessel shall carry black balls in the same position as the green lights. The lights or balls indicate danger 3,000 ft. astern and 1,500 ft. to the side(s). (4) All three types shall carry sidelights and a stern light when in motion and shall turn off these lights when stopped.

Sailing Vessels Under Way.—(1) Such vessels shall carry sidelights and a stern light of the kind prescribed for power-driven vessels. (2) In addition, sailing vessels may carry an identity signal at the top of the foremast consisting of a red light over a green light. These lights shall be of the same construction as white masthead lights and shall be visible for two miles.

Vessels Towed or Pushed.—(1) Vessels towed shall each carry sidelights and a stern light or steering light. The stern light is mandatory for the last vessel of the tow. (2) A vessel pushed ahead shall carry sidelights at the forward end. If more than one vessel is pushed ahead, the group shall be lighted as one vessel. (3) In daytime, if a tow exceeds 600 ft., the tow and towing vessel shall each carry where best seen a black diamond shape.

Pilot Vessels.—(1) A power-driven pilot vessel on duty under way shall carry at the masthead a white all-round light visible three miles and eight feet below it a similar red light. In addition, the vessel shall carry sidelights and a stern light and shall exhibit one or more flare-up lights at intervals not exceeding ten minutes. (2) A sailing pilot vessel on duty under way shall not carry the above red light and shall show her sidelights at short intervals on the approach of or to other vessels. Otherwise, her lighting is the same. (3) When on duty and not under way, both types shall omit showing the sidelights and stern light and, if at anchor, shall show, in addition to remaining light(s) and flare(s), anchor lights. (4) When not on duty both types shall carry the same lights and shapes as other vessels.

Vessels at Anchor.—(1) Vessels less than 150 ft. in length shall carry forward, where best seen, a white light showing all around for two miles, and may show a second such light at the stern in the same position as larger vessels. (2) If 150 ft. or more, the above forward light must be at the stem not less than 20 ft. above the hull; and at the stern, at least 15 ft. lower than the forward light, another such light must be shown, both to be visible all around for three miles. (3) Between sunrise and sunset every vessel at anchor shall carry forward one black ball. (4) Working submarine cables, navigation marks, surveying, or on underwater operations, a vessel at anchor shall also carry the red-white-red lights and shapes previously described for such vessels.

Vessels aground shall carry by night the anchor light(s) and the two red lights prescribed for a vessel not under command; by day three black balls, vertically not less than six feet apart.

Vessels Fishing.—Only the prescribed lights and shapes must be shown, whether under way or at anchor, each visible for two miles: (1) Vessels trawling shall carry a green all-round light 4 to 12 ft. above a white all-round light, sidelights, and a stern light and, in addition, may carry a masthead-type light. The red-white lights shall be forward of and higher than the masthead-type light and, if the latter is not carried, at least twice the separating distance above the sidelights. The sidelights and stern light shall be shown only while the vessel is making way through the water. (2) Vessels fishing other than trawling shall show a red all-round light in lieu of the green all-round light and, if the gear extends over 500 ft. horizontally, shall show an all-round white light away from the vertical lights in the direction of the gear. Otherwise, the lights are the same. (3) All vessels fishing may use a flare-up light to attract attention, direct a searchlight in the direction of danger, or show working lights. (4) By day, vessels fishing shall show a black shape consisting of two cones point to point and, if the gear extends over 500 ft. horizontally shall also show a black cone, point up, in the direction of the gear. (5) Vessels trolling are not fishing for purposes of the rules.

Special Lights and Signals.—(1) Vessels may, to attract attention, show a flare-up light or use sound signals which cannot be mistaken for any signal authorized by these rules. (2) Ships of war, convoys, vessels fishing as a fleet, and seaplanes on water may operate station or signal lights duly authorized by their respective governments.

Vessels under sail and power in daytime shall display, forward, one black conical shape, point downward.

Fog Signals.—A "short blast" means one of one second; a "prolonged blast," one of four to six seconds. Signals prescribed shall be given by power-driven vessels on the whistle; sailing vessels, on the fog horn; vessels towed, on the whistle or fog horn.

In fog and restricted visibility, by day or night, the following signals shall be used (the time intervals indicated are the maximum permitted): (1) (*a*) A power-driven vessel making way must sound a prolonged blast every two minutes. (*b*) A power-driven

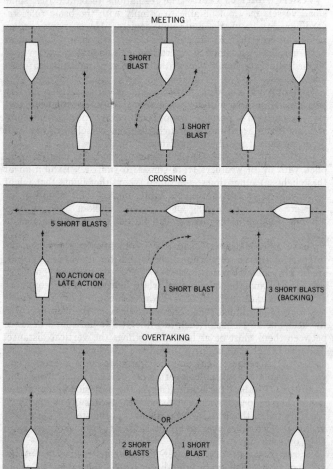

FIG. 1.—POWER-DRIVEN VESSELS PASSING EACH OTHER

vessel stopped and not making way must sound every two minutes two prolonged blasts with one second between. (2) Every minute a sailing vessel under way must sound on the starboard tack one blast; on the port tack, two blasts; and when the wind is abaft the beam, three blasts. (3) (a) A vessel anchored shall ring her bell rapidly for five seconds every minute. (b) If more than 350 ft. in length the vessel must sound the bell forward, and sound for a separate five seconds a gong or similar instrument aft. (c) Both may sound as a warning to approaching vessels, one short, one prolonged, and one short blast in succession. (4) A vessel towing or unable to maneuver must sound one prolonged and two short blasts in succession every minute. (5) The last vessel of a manned tow shall sound one prolonged and three short blasts in succession after the towing vessels signal. (6) A vessel aground shall give the bell signal and, if required, the gong signal prescribed in (3) and shall, in addition, give three separate and distinct strokes on the bell immediately before and after such rapid ringing of the bell. (7) (a) A vessel fishing, except trolling, whether under way or at anchor, shall sound at intervals of one minute the same signal as a vessel towing or unable to maneuver, i.e., one prolonged blast followed by two short blasts. (b) A vessel trolling shall give signals (1) or (2) as appropriate. (8) A power-driven pilot vessel on duty may, in addition to signals (1) and (3), sound an identity signal of four short blasts.

Speed in Fog.—(1) Every vessel shall in conditions of restricted visibility go at a moderate speed. (2) A power-driven vessel hearing, apparently forward of her beam, the fog signal of a vessel the position of which is not ascertained, shall, circumstances permitting, stop her engines and then navigate with caution until danger of collision is over. (Radar range and bearing alone do not ascertain position.) (3) A power-driven vessel detecting another forward of her beam before hearing a fog signal or sighting the vessel visually may take early substantial action to avoid close quarters, but if unable to do so shall stop her engines in proper time to avoid collision and then navigate with caution as in (2).

Steering and Sailing Rules.—In obeying these rules action taken should be positive, timely, and of good seamanship. Risk of collision may be ascertained by watching the compass bearing of another vessel; if the bearing does not appreciably change, such risk is deemed to exist. These rules apply only when vessels are in sight of one another.

Sailing vessels approaching one another with risk of collision shall take action as follows: (1) When each has the wind on a different side, the one with the wind on the port side shall keep clear of the other. (2) When both have the wind on the same side, the one to windward shall keep clear of the one to leeward.

Power-Driven Vessels.—(1) When meeting end on or nearly end on with risk of collision, each shall alter course to starboard so that they pass port to port. This applies only to cases when by day each vessel sees the masts of the other in a line or nearly so with her own and when by night each vessel is in such a position as to see both the sidelights of the other. (2) When two power-driven vessels are crossing so as to involve risk of collision, the vessel which has the other on her own starboard side shall keep out of the way of the other. (3) When one power-driven vessel is overtaking another with risk of collision, the vessel approaching from astern shall keep clear.

Power-Driven and Sailing Vessels.—When risk of collision is involved, the power-driven vessel shall keep out of the way of the sailing vessel, except when the sailing vessel is an overtaking vessel, or the power-driven vessel is fishing. In such cases the sailing vessel shall keep clear.

Additionally, no sailing vessel shall hamper, in a narrow channel, the safe passage of a power-driven vessel which can navigate only inside such channel.

General.—(1) Where by these rules one of two vessels is to keep out of the way of the other, the other shall keep her course and speed. When from any cause the latter vessel finds herself so close that collision cannot be avoided by the action of the giving-way vessel alone, she also shall take action as will best aid to

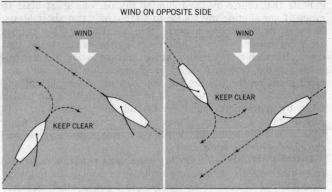

WIND ON OPPOSITE SIDE

WIND   WIND

KEEP CLEAR

KEEP CLEAR

WIND ON SAME SIDE

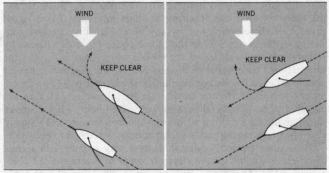

WIND   WIND

KEEP CLEAR

KEEP CLEAR

FIG. 2.—SAILING VESSELS PASSING EACH OTHER

avert collision. (2) Every vessel which is directed by these rules to keep out of the way of another vessel shall, so far as possible, take positive early action to comply with this obligation, and shall, if the circumstances of the case admit, avoid crossing ahead of the other. (3) Every power-driven vessel shall, on approaching another vessel which she is directed by these rules to keep clear of, if necessary, slacken her speed, stop, or reverse.

Vessels overtaking shall, at all times, keep out of the way of the overtaken vessel. An overtaking vessel is one coming up with another from any direction more than $22\frac{1}{2}°$ abaft her beam, i.e., a position from which by night she would be unable to see the sidelights of the vessel she is overtaking; no subsequent alteration of the bearing between them shall make the overtaking vessel a crossing vessel within the meaning of these rules or relieve her of the duty of keeping clear until she is finally past and clear. If the overtaking vessel is doubtful whether she is forward or abaft this direction from the other vessel, she shall assume that she is an overtaking vessel and keep clear.

Narrow Channels.—(1) Every power-driven vessel proceeding along the course of the channel shall, when it is safe and practicable, keep to that side of the fairway or mid-channel which lies on the starboard side of such vessel. (2) A power-driven vessel nearing a bend in a channel where another vessel approaching from the other direction cannot be seen shall give a prolonged blast when within one-half mile of the bend, which signal shall be answered by a similar blast by any approaching power-driven vessel within hearing around the bend. The bend shall be rounded with alertness and caution. (3) A power-driven vessel under 65 ft. shall not hamper the safe passage of a vessel which can navigate only inside such channel.

Vessels not engaged in fishing, except vessels not under command, mine sweeping, or at work in an occupation requiring red-white-red lights and shapes, shall keep out of the way of vessels fishing.

Navigational Dangers and Proper Precautions.—A vessel may depart from the rules to avoid immediate danger, but only to the extent necessary. Every vessel shall take the precautions required by the circumstances.

Sound Signals for Vessels in Sight of One Another.—(1) When vessels are in sight of one another, a power-driven vessel, in taking any course authorized or required by these rules, shall indicate that course by the following signals: one short blast to mean "I am altering my course to starboard"; two short blasts, "I am altering my course to port"; three short blasts, "My engines are going astern." (2) A hold-course power-driven vessel that doubts the keep-clear vessel is taking sufficient action to avert collision may indicate such doubt by giving at least five short and rapid blasts on the whistle, but this does not relieve her of any obligations under these rules or of her duty to indicate any action taken by appropriate sound signals laid down under (1). (3) Any of these whistle signals may be further indicated by a white light visible all round the horizon for five miles that is synchronized with the whistle.

Distress Signals.—Vessels in distress and requiring assistance from other vessels or the shore shall use or display the following signals either together or separately: (1) a gun or other explosive signal fired at intervals of about a minute; (2) a continuous sounding with any fog-signal apparatus; (3) rockets or shells throwing red stars fired one at a time at short intervals; (4) a signal made by radiotelegraphy or by any other signaling method consisting of the group SOS in the Morse code; (5) a signal sent by radiotelephony consisting of the spoken word "Mayday"; (6) the international code signal of distress NC; (7) a square flag having above or below it a ball or anything resembling a ball; (8) flames on the vessel (as from a burning tar barrel, etc.); (9) a rocket parachute flare or a hand flare showing a red light; (10) a smoke signal giving off a volume of orange-coloured smoke; (11) slowly and repeatedly raising and lowering arms outstretched to each side.

To secure attention, vessels in distress may actuate auto alarms of other vessels by a radiotelegraph signal of a series of 12 four-second dashes or a radiotelephone signal consisting of two tones transmitted alternately for 30 to 60 seconds.

See R. F. Farwell, *Rules of the Nautical Road*, 4th ed. prepared by A. Prunski (1968); U.S. Coast Guard Publication CG-169, *Rules of the Road, International-Inland* (1965). (A. PI.)

RUM is a spirit obtained by distillation of the fermented products of sugarcane. Although it is produced in most sugar-growing countries of the world (United States, Cuba, Australia, and South Africa) for local consumption, the world demand for rum is mainly supplied by the West Indies, where it originated. Types of rum are legion, for they depend upon the quality of the ingredients, upon methods of fermentation and distillation and upon subsequent treatment and maturation.

After Columbus discovered Cuba in 1492, the Spaniards introduced sugarcane there, whence it spread to the other West Indian islands. The manufacture of rum developed in the British West Indies in the 17th century; in Barbados, rum was certainly produced as early as 1647, possibly earlier. First known as "kill-devil," it was then referred to as "rumbullion," and by 1667 it was simply called "rum."

Rum is made out of either pure cane sugar or, more frequently, molasses. The main countries producing for export are Barbados, Trinidad, Jamaica, Guyana, Puerto Rico, and Cuba. Where the sugar industry is undeveloped, pure sugarcane juice is used rather than molasses. In the U.S. and Germany imported molasses is used.

Molasses is the commonest ingredient for fermentation; sometimes skimmings from the purer cane juice also are added. Fermentation is usually of either the Demerara or Jamaican type. In the former, sugarcane or molasses is prepared into a liquid known as the "wash" and diluted to a low specific gravity (1.060); usually a little sulfuric acid is added to assist the saccharomyces (alcohol yeasts) and sometimes a small quantity of ammonium sulfate as food for the yeast. Fermentation is completed in 48 hours. This produces a high alcohol yield but low ester content; thus the spirit is comparatively lacking in bouquet, although it is sometimes subsequently flavoured.

In the Jamaican method, the fermentation lasts for about 10 or 12 days with a wash of between 1.078 and 1.096 specific gravity. Apart from introducing into the wash some of the waste, known as dunder, from a previous distillation, no special encouragement is given to the alcohol yeasts; it is thus possible for esters to develop more easily and this is one of the origins of the distinctive

flavour possessed by Jamaican rum. Certain special Jamaican rums have such a high ester content that they are used exclusively for blending.

The flavour of a rum also is affected by the distillation method. Two methods are available: the pot still and the continuous still. In the first, a single distillation is insufficient for it produces a spirit too weak for consumption; a second distillation is necessary to bring the spirit to the required strength. In the alternative method the spirit can be brought to any strength in one "burning"; it is thus far more economical. As the separation of alcohol from water can be very quick and almost complete in the continuous still, the spirit so produced has less flavour (and is less heavy) than that produced by the pot still. A third of the stills in British Guiana and all those in Jamaica are pot stills, while the remainder of the stills in British Guiana and all those in Barbados and Trinidad are continuous.

After the rum has been distilled it is colourless, but it will pick up colour from the casks in which it is stored. It may be further coloured with caramel or burnt sugar to suit public taste.

In Cuba the distilled spirit is purified by passing through charcoal so as to obtain a flavourless alcohol, which is later flavoured independently; it has a characteristic taste, the rum flavour being weak. U.S. rum is mostly heavy bodied; it develops an excellent aroma when aged. (C. C. H. F.; X.)

RUMANIA (REPUBLICA SOCIALISTĂ ROMÂNIA), a socialist republic of southeastern Europe, lying mainly to the north of the Danube River and bordered by the Soviet Union, the Black Sea, Bulgaria, Yugoslavia, and Hungary. The Danube forms the greater part of the southern boundary. The province of Dobruja (Dobrogea) extends eastward beyond the Danube to give Rumania a frontage of about 160 mi. (258 km.) on the Black Sea. Since the creation of the Rumanian state in 1859 its extent has fluctuated greatly. It consisted until 1918 of little more than the provinces of Walachia (Valahia), Moldavia, and Dobruja; it then gained Transylvania and neighbouring territories from Hungary, Bukovina from Austria, and Bessarabia from the Soviet Union. In 1940 Bessarabia and northern Bukovina were annexed by the Soviet Union, and southern Dobruja was ceded to Bulgaria. The present area of Rumania is 91,699 sq.mi. (237,500 sq.km.) and its population, according to the 1966 census, 19,105,056. The capital is Bucharest (Bucureşti).

This article has the following sections and subsections:

RUMANIA

I. PHYSICAL GEOGRAPHY

1. Relief and Structure.—The great arc of the Carpathian Mountains and Transylvanian Alps, a branch of the Alpine system, enters northern Rumania from Czechoslovakia and southern Poland via the Ukraine, taking a curving course, first southeastward, then westward across the central part of Rumania. It then turns abruptly to the south, reaches the Danube, and is continued beyond the river in Yugoslavia and Bulgaria. It forms a major divide between the plains of Walachia, Dobruja, and Moldavia to the south, southeast, and east, and the Transylvanian Basin to the northwest of the mountain arc.

The Carpathian Mountains and the Transylvanian Alps (qq.v.).—These were folded during the Alpine mountain-building process in early Tertiary times by pressures exerted from the south and west against the resistant platforms, which now comprise southern Russia and the plains of the lower Danube Valley. The mountains, composed mainly of limestones, sandstones, and shales, have been eroded into a series of longitudinal ranges, lying parallel to the general direction of the ranges themselves. In the course of the mountain building process, the beds were intruded by igneous rocks at many places. These are especially numerous and extensive in the more westerly parts of the Transylvanian Alps, where the areas of most rugged relief are formed in granite.

After their formation, the mountains were subjected to extensive faulting and accompanying volcanic action. The northern part of the Rumanian Carpathians is dotted with the craters of former volcanoes and is covered with volcanic ash, lava, and other extrusive deposits. The average height of the Carpathian-Transylvanian chain is about 3,300 ft. (1,006 m.). The two highest mountains in Rumania are Moldoveanu, 8,343 ft. (2,543 m.), and Negoiu, 8,317 ft. (2,535 m.). Although there is abundant evidence of former glacial action in the ranges of the Munții Bucegi, Făgărașului, Parîngului, and Retezatului in the Transylvanian Alps, there are today no permanent snowfields.

The Plains of Walachia, Moldavia, and Dobruja.—The low rolling hills of this area resemble the plains of southern Russia. Walachia, lying between the Transylvanian Alps and the Danube, is a region of gentle relief which drops gradually from the mountains to the river. It is thickly covered by the Tertiary and Recent deposits, though deeply buried beneath the present surface is the stable Paleozoic massif against which the yielding beds were in part forced to build up the present mountains. Moldavia is fundamentally similar, though its altitude is somewhat greater and it has been dissected by southward flowing rivers into a maze of rounded hills. Dobruja, enclosed on west and north by the Danube and its delta, and on the east by the Black Sea, is different from the last two regions. It is part of the hidden massif which extends beneath the lower Danube and Soviet Ukraine. Its Paleozoic rocks show through at the surface, though covered in part by Cretaceous and Tertiary deposits and also by Quaternary and Recent deposits of loess and alluvium.

The Transylvanian Basin.—The segment of Rumania that is enclosed within the curve of the Carpathian Mountains is in all respects more complex. Within the arc of the mountains is the Transylvanian Basin. In late Tertiary times it constituted a lake basin in which were deposited clays, sands, and some limestones. The basin has since been drained, and with the uplift of the region rivers have cut their valleys into its surface. It is today a hilly region, in which the soft rocks yield deep and generally fertile soils, and the surrounding mountains give it some protection from the harshness of the east European climate.

The western edge of the Transylvanian Basin is formed by a series of mountains and hills which are sometimes, though erroneously, known as the Western Carpathians. They have been cut into a number of segments by the deep valleys of the rivers which drain the basin. The largest and most rugged of these are the Munții Bihorului (Bihor Mountains), a massif of hard Paleozoic and intrusive rocks, overlain in part by Cretaceous and more recent volcanic deposits. A ridge of Paleozoic rock, largely covered by Tertiary beds and cut across by the Someșul (Someș River), links this region with the mountains of the extreme north of

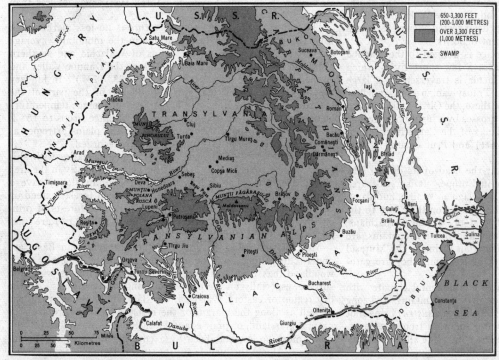

PRINCIPAL PHYSICAL FEATURES, CITIES, AND REGIONS OF RUMANIA

(LEFT) EASTFOTO; (RIGHT) CHIC DONCHIN—PIX FROM PUBLIX

(LEFT) THE OLT RIVER IN THE COZIA DEFILE BETWEEN THE COZIA AND NAURUȚU MOUNTAINS. THE VILLAS OF THE CĂLIMĂNEȘTI SPA CAN BE SEEN ON THE RIGHT BANK; (RIGHT) EASTERN ORTHODOX TYPE CHURCH IN THE CENTRE OF THE TOWN OF TIMIȘOARA

Rumania. In the opposite direction, the Mureșul (Mureș) separates the Munții Bihorului from the Munții Poiana Ruscă, as the Timișul (Timis) does the Poiana Ruscă from the Semenicului (Seminic Mountains). These latter are structurally part of the western Transylvanian Alps, from which they are separated only by recently eroded river valleys.

Extension of the Hungarian Plain.—To the west of this series of massifs lies a plain from 20 to 60 mi. (32 to 97 km.) in width, which extends along the western border of the country from the Soviet boundary in the north to that of Yugoslavia in the south. It is part of the Hungarian Plain, and, like the Walachian Plain, it is low-lying and undulating, and its deep-seated ancient rocks are thickly buried by Tertiary and Recent deposits.

Drainage.—Most of the land surface is drained to the Danube River, and only in Dobruja are there a few short rivers which flow direct to the Black Sea. Walachia is traversed by a large number of rivers which rise in the Transylvanian Alps and flow south to the Danube. The largest of these, the Olt (Oltul), rises to the north of the mountains which it crosses by a highly picturesque gorge. Moldavia and the eastern flanks of the Carpathian Mountains are drained by the Siretul (Siret) and Prut (Prutul) rivers and their tributaries.

These rivers join the Danube near the head of its delta. The Danube delta is the most extensive in Europe. It is a vast area of about 1,000 sq.mi. (2,590 sq.km.) of lagoon, swamp, and damp pasture, traversed by branches of the Danube on their way to the Black Sea. The inner or west-facing slopes of the Carpathians, together with the Transylvanian Basin and Bihor Mountains, are mainly drained westward to the Hungarian Plain, by the Mureșul and Someșul. Beyond the boundary of Rumania, they are gathered to the Tisza or the Danube.

2. Climate.—Rumania experiences a continental climate with hot summers, moderated by altitude in the mountains, and long and severe winters. The south wind of summer (*austru*) brings hot and oppressive conditions and in winter the wind from the northeast (*crivat*) imparts to the Rumanian countryside all the severity of the Russian steppe, except where mountains give some protection.

The incidence of rainfall in particular is influenced by relief. Rainfall is heaviest in the mountains, especially on the west-facing slopes of the northern Carpathians, the Bihor Mountains, and the western parts of the Transylvanian Alps. There the annual average is generally more than 31 in. (79 cm.) and rises to over 55 in. (140 cm.). In the drier eastern Carpathians it is consistently over 28 in.

By contrast, the margin of the Hungarian Plain, the Transylvanian Basin, and the plains of Walachia, Moldavia, and Dobruja are dry, with an annual average rainfall everywhere of less than 28 in.

The influence of relief on temperature is no less marked. In July, the hottest month, temperatures in the mountains average 61° F (16° C) or less, in the plains of Walachia and southern Moldavia more than 71° (22°), and along the Danube Valley and on the border of the Hungarian Plain, over 73° (23°). In January the whole country, with the exception only of the part of the Dobruja close to the Bulgarian border, has an average temperature of below freezing. In the mountains the average drops to 16° F (−9° C), and in both the mountains and the plains extremes as low as −22° F (−30° C) have been widely recorded.

3. Vegetation.—The vegetation of Rumania varies with altitude. Forest covers about 27% of the country, mostly in the area above 1,000 ft. The hills and lower mountain slopes have a plant association dominated by oak. The beech forests extend up to 4,250 ft. (about 1,300 m.) and above this are forests of principally fir and spruce. Above about 5,900 ft. (1,800 m.) are summer pastures and alpine vegetation.

Most of the plains and much of the Transylvanian Basin are under cultivation, and the original vegetation, generally open woodland, has been destroyed. Patches of deciduous woodland survive, especially on the poorer soils and steeper slopes. In the dry region of eastern Walachia, the Bărăganul (Baragan) steppe as well as along the margin of the Hungarian Plain, are areas of natural grassland, or prairie, and locally there are patches of sand dune, more or less stabilized by a covering of drought-resistant grasses. Along the valley of the lower Danube, from Turnu Severin eastward, and over the whole region of the delta are marshes, made up of shallow lakes, partially reclaimed, and sluggish streams which enclose small low islands with willows and poplars. (N. J. G. P.)

4. Animal Life.—In its fauna Walachia has far more affinity to the lands lying south of the Danube than to Transylvania, although several species of *Claudilia*, once regarded as exclusively Transylvanian, are found south of the Carpathians. Moldavia and the Bărăganul steppe resemble the Russian prairies in their variety of mollusks and the lower kinds of mammals. More than 40 species of freshwater mussels (Unionidae) have been observed in the Rumanian rivers. The lakes of the Dobruja abound in mollusks—parent forms, in many cases, of species which reappear greatly modified in the Black Sea. Salmon and trout characterize the mountain streams, and in the Danube itself carp and sturgeon are particularly important.

The mountain fauna includes the chamois and the bearded eagle; the forest fauna the bear, wolf, fox, lynx, wildcat, stag, deer, and wild boar. In the steppe region are rodents, such as the hamster and gopher.

Birds are numerous, including four varieties of crows, five of warblers, seven of woodpeckers, eight of buntings, four of falcons, and five of eagles, while among the hosts of waterfowl which inhabit the marshes of the Danube are nine varieties of ducks and four of rails. (G. W. S.; N. J. G. P.)

II. THE PEOPLE

1. Ethnic Origins.—The Rumanian people, like all national groups in Eastern Europe, are of extremely mixed ethnic origins. In the main they appear to derive from the Thracian peoples who lived in the region in late prehistoric and Roman times, but they incorporate many other elements: the Roman settlers of the 2nd century A.D., the Slav invaders of the 7th and 8th centuries, Magyar invaders of the 9th and 10th centuries, as well as Turks, Germans, gypsies, and Jews. Other groups, the Celts, Goths, and Tatars, at some time occupied some part of Rumania, and must have influenced the racial composition of its people.

This variety of ethnic origin is reflected in the physical diversity of the Rumanian people. In terms of head shape there is a marked contrast between the brachycephalic peoples of the mountains and Transylvania, and the mesocephalic peoples of the eastern and southern plains. This division ignores language and ethnic tradition. In general the Rumanians are of medium height, 5 ft. $5\frac{1}{3}$ in.–5 ft. $5\frac{3}{4}$ in. (166–167 cm.) though somewhat shorter in the northwest. Pigmentation shows greater variation; coloration is predominantly dark in the southeast, but over much of the country people are of medium to dark coloration, with a tendency for brunets to predominate. In a few areas, notably Transylvania, a blond type is numerous.

At the time when much of Rumania was conquered by the Romans, it was thinly peopled by Thracian tribes, which have come to be known as Dacians. They already possessed a complex racial history, and to this complexity the Romans contributed other elements. According to Rumanian tradition, Romans settled there in sufficient numbers to impart a veneer of Latin civilization to the region. Supposedly after the withdrawal of the Roman armies the romanized provincials maintained their Latin language and culture in the fastnesses of the mountains, and from this stock was gradually fashioned the Rumanian nation. It is more commonly held that the Rumanians are part of a wider group of romanized Dacians, known as Vlachs (*q.v.*). Their language, like Rumanian, is largely derived from Latin, and they are the descendants of the romanized inhabitants of the Balkans, as the Rumanians also claim to be. There is, however, this important difference: the ancestors of the Vlachs of the Balkan peninsula lived under Roman rule for many centuries, whereas Roman occupation of Dacia was relatively short-lived. Vlachs of the Balkans are known to have migrated northward across the Danube, and at one time were numerous in Slovakia. Some writers, especially Hungarian and Slav, doubt whether the Rumanians are the descendants of romanized Dacians and suggest that they derive from these Balkan Vlachs. The truth may perhaps lie between the two extremes, and the Rumanians of today probably derive from romanized Dacians, reinforced by Vlachs from beyond the Danube.

After the withdrawal of the Romans from Dacia, the region was invaded and probably also settled by Goths and other Germanic tribes, by invaders from the Russian steppe, and by peoples from central Europe. The cultural and linguistic pattern of many areas of Rumania was drastically changed, and undoubtedly many of these immigrant peoples were assimilated to the Rumanian people, losing their own linguistic and cultural traits in consequence. Nevertheless, the Rumanian language today has absorbed a great many Slavic and other elements. (*See* RUMANIAN LANGUAGE.)

2. Minority Groups.—Late in the 9th century the Magyar tribes invaded the Hungarian Plain from the south Russian steppe. They came by way of the Carpathian passes, and some of their number, the Szeklers (*q.v.*), were left behind in Transylvania, or were deliberately settled there after the arrival of the Magyars in the present area of Hungary, in order to protect the new state from fresh invaders from the east. The Szeklers have inhabited their present area in northern Transylvania at least since the Middle Ages. They are still a notable minority group, having retained their language, only slightly modified from the Hungarian of Hungary itself. By the terms of the present Rumanian constitution the province of Mureş (Hungarian, Maros) is a Magyar Autonomous Region.

The second most important national minority is the German, descended from settlers who came in the 13th century mainly from the Moselle Valley. They settled in the good farming country of Transylvania, and have since constituted a compact and distinctive group, perpetuating the costume, architecture, and folkways which they brought from Germany. In 1956 the number of this minority group was officially put at 384,708.

Other minority groups are relatively small. The Yugoslavs, numbering 46,517 in 1956, live mainly in the southwest, in territory annexed by Rumania in 1919 from Hungary, despite counter claims from Yugoslavia. They live in an area that is ethnically

BY COURTESY OF "CARPATI" RUMANIAN NATIONAL TOURIST OFFICE

VIEW OF ORADEA, SITUATED ON THE CRIŞUL REPEDE RIVER IN THE PANNONIAN BASIN very mixed, with German and Hungarian communities in addition to the Rumanian and Yugoslav.

Jews lived in Rumania in the 15th century, but the majority came in from Poland and Russia during the 19th. They usually lived as a class apart from the rest of the population, and in 1939, 518,754 were recorded by the census as Yiddish-speaking. The Jewish population was greatly reduced by the territorial losses of 1940. The Jewish community suffered a great deal less from wartime persecution than those of Hungary, Czechoslovakia, and Poland, and in 1947 numbered about 428,300. This was greatly reduced by emigration to Israel, and in 1956 the Jews numbered only about 146,000.

In the east Rumania includes part of the settlement area of Ukrainians, Russians, Tatars, Turks, and Bulgarians. Each of these communities is, however, quite small; the largest, the Ukrainians, Ruthenians and Hutzuls, numbered 60,479 in 1956 and the smallest, the Bulgarians, 12,040. The Ukrainians are most numerous in northern Moldavia; the Turks, Tatars, and Bulgars in Dobruja, a region which throughout its history has been of great ethnic complexity. Russians numbered 38,731; the largest groups are in Dobruja, with others in western Rumania. The rest of the population—14,996,114 out of a total in 1956 of 17,-489,450—are described as Rumanian.　　　　　(N. J. G. P.)

3. Religion.—When the Rumanian Orthodox Church (*q.v.*) joined the World Council of Churches in November 1961 it claimed a membership of 13,000,000, or more than 70% of the population, although Communism had then been in power in Rumania for about 16 years. After a break of 20 years it was thus able to resume the prominent part it played at ecumenical conferences in the years before World War II, when its relations with the Anglican Church, in particular, were close. Many Orthodox theologians, who now train students at the two Orthodox theological institutes and six seminaries in Rumania, were trained in the West in prewar years, and they contribute to the high theological and ecumenical standard of the journals published by the Rumanian Orthodox Church.

Rumania has the most active of all Orthodox churches. There are 5 metropolitanates and 12 dioceses, each with several hundred parishes, and an extensive monastic life. As in other Communist countries, however, the church has no freedom to play a part in society beyond the restricted role permitted by the state. Patriarch Justinian, appointed in 1948, did much to promote activities to conserve and strengthen Orthodoxy in Rumania, while remaining an overt supporter of state policies. His activities included the organization of regular courses for priests all over the country to equip them to carry out their pastoral duties in a Communist society in such a way as to remain loyal citizens of the state. Within a few months of his enthronement the Eastern Rite Catholics in Rumania, numbering 1,500,000, mostly in Transylvania, were reincorporated in the Orthodox Church and their five bishops were arrested. At the same time the Roman Catholic Church, with a slightly smaller membership drawn mostly from Hungarians and Swabians in Transylvania, also suffered the removal of its hierarchy through imprisonment. The smaller minority churches include the Lutheran, the Reformed or Calvinist, and the Unitarian. The Lutheran and Reformed churches are also members of the World Council of Churches.　　　　　　　　　　(X.)

4. Customs and Culture.—The Rumanians are a peasant people and have retained a strong and vigorous peasant culture. Their folkways, like their language, derive from several ethnic roots, and this, together with prolonged isolation, helps to account for both its variety and its richness. There are strongly marked regionalisms in the predominant cultural traits. Homes are built of wood in mountainous and forested regions, of mudbricks elsewhere. They are often highly decorated and, with their garden fences and entrance gates, have long been a vehicle for the expression of folk art. In the mountainous areas the churches are often of wood and highly decorated. At Bucharest is a "village museum," where examples of village houses have been gathered.

Folkways continue to show themselves in peasant dress. Men still wear the white, baggy trousers and long, white coats in many areas, and women's costumes and embroideries, conforming to

the local style and pattern, are not kept only for Sundays or for the amusement of tourists, as in more sophisticated peasant countries. Traditional peasant music, with strong gypsy overtones, is widely played, both on modern instruments and on the traditional wind and string instruments and drums. Some of this peasant music has been collected and made available by Béla Bartók and the Rumanian Georges Enesco.

The basic food is a pasta, known as *mamaligo,* prepared from corn meal. The national drink is made from plum juice, and resembles the Balkan *slivovica.* Music and costume, and even church and domestic architecture, have a gay and colourful appearance, in contrast with the tragic history and the sombre folklore—concerned above all with vampires and evil spirits—of the Rumanian people.

III. ARCHAEOLOGY

Scientific archaeological work in Rumania can be said to have begun when G. Tocilescu published his *Fouilles et recherches archéologiques en Roumanie* in 1900. Research is coordinated by the Rumanian People's Academy; annual reports with French and Russian summaries appear in *Materiale şi cercetări arheologice* and articles in foreign languages in *Dacia.*

Lower Paleolithic discoveries, especially from caves and gravels in the Dîrjov Valley, near Slatina, include early tools resembling the Oldowan of East Africa. At Mitoc and Ripiceni in Moldavia, flints akin to the Clactonian tools of England and the Levalloisian of France were found. Extensive Upper Paleolithic and Mesolithic finds were made near Ceahlău in the Moldavian Carpathians.

The Neolithic has been more widely discovered and more fully studied than the Paleolithic, and 16 distinct cultures have been identified. The earliest, the Criş culture, was closely related to the Starcevo and other cultures of the Balkan peninsula. From the Criş culture evolved a number of related cultural groups, including the Fiera-Dudeşti culture in southern Rumania and the Turdaş culture in the southwest. These were based on agricultural village settlements. At the same time cultures characterized by pottery with geometrical decoration spread from the north into Moldavia and southeastern Transylvania, and the Hamangia culture, in which southern (Aegean) elements were incorporated, evolved in the Dobruja.

The Fiera-Dudeşti culture gave rise to the Boian, characterized by terrace settlements, consisting at first of mud huts and later of fortified promontory settlements. This phase was marked by the introduction of copper axes, the extension of agriculture, and the breeding of domestic animals. The Boian culture spread northward into Transylvania and northeastward to Moldavia, assimilating the earlier cultures found there. In the core area of the Boian culture, graphite-decorated pottery, marble, gold, and terra-cotta figurines, and inhumation marked the emergence of the Gumelniţa culture.

The excavations at Cucuteni near Iaşi marked the culmination of Neolithic culture in Rumania. Three large Cucuteni-type settlements, each of from 40 to 80 dwellings, have been excavated. These were rectangular, with wattle-and-daub walls, and floored with split wooden beams. A pottery of extraordinary beauty and delicacy was made, ornamented with spirals, wavy lines, and geometrical figures, and decorated in white, red, and black.

The end of the Neolithic in Moldavia and southern Rumania was troubled. Many Neolithic settlements were destroyed by fire. Subsequent burials show a change in funerary practice, and the evidence of material culture suggests the pastoral nomads of the Russian steppe rather than the earlier Neolithic inhabitants of Rumania. There was evidently a massive westward movement of steppe dwellers, and pastoral tribes overran much of Rumania. In time new—though still primarily pastoral—cultures emerged from the ruins of the old. One of these was the Coţofeni culture, so known from its type-site in Oltenia.

The Bronze Age made its appearance in Rumania early in the 2nd millennium B.C. and bronze-working began to flourish in Transylvania and neighbouring areas, where the raw materials could be obtained. Bronze tools allowed the forest to be cleared more easily and agriculture to be extended. Lowland areas, having better soils, were brought under cultivation, and pastoralism was relegated to the hills. In three regions agricultural communities emerged with a relatively high cultural level. A large fortified settlement at Sărata-Monteoru, near Buzău, gave evidence of a well-developed culture. At Gîrla Mare, in southwestern Rumania, another culture, characterized by the practice of cremation and by elaborate ornaments and beautifully carved figurines, appeared; and at Otomani, in the Criş region, yet another developed, distinguished by its fortified settlements, beautifully decorated pottery, and bronze ax-heads. These Bronze Age cultures achieved their maximum development in the 15th century B.C., when they spread through the middle and lower Danube valleys.

In the 12th century B.C. iron appeared, first as small ornaments, then replacing bronze in tools and weapons. But Rumania never really shared the Iron Age culture that emanated from the upper Danube Valley, because invaders from the Russian steppe, this time the Scythians, again overran it. The Scythians appear to have made semipermanent settlements of their own, especially in the Dobruja, and their burials are extensively found in Transylvania and Walachia. They also greatly influenced the local societies, which now display weapons and ornaments of types commonly associated with the Scythians. Though the Scythians were ultimately assimilated by the local peoples, the prosperity of Rumania received a blow from which it never really recovered until Roman times.

Greek colonists began to settle on the coast of the Dobruja in the 7th century B.C. when the Milesians occupied the promontory of Istros (Latin Histria) in a lagoon near the Danube mouth. Excavations, begun there in 1914, recovered much of the ancient city plan. To the south, the Greeks established two other coastal cities: Callatis, a Megarian settlement at modern Mangalia, and the Milesian colony Tomis (modern Constanţa). Callatis became in classical times a port for the export of grain from its rich hinterland. Many interesting Greek and native finds have been made at Callatis and Tomis.

The contemporary native culture grew out of the fusion of Geto-Dacian peoples with Scythian and Celtic invaders; they were never hellenized as the Thracians were. Fortresses with earth defenses were widely built in Rumania. Those at Zimnicea near the Danube, at Poiana in Moldavia, and at Piscu Crîsani, Tinos, and elsewhere in Walachia, have been excavated, revealing a wide range of local artifacts and also evidence of extensive trade with the Greeks. In the Orăştie Mountains in Hunedoara are the particularly complex fortifications on a succession of hilltops leading up to the citadel of Grădiştea Muncelului; on the terraces around it were civil and religious buildings, including what appears to have been an astronomical observation platform. This is identified with the Dacian capital Sarmizegetusa (replaced by the Roman colony and modern town of the same name).

The Dacians were beginning to create an organized state but it crumbled under Roman attacks in A.D. 101–106. Traces of these campaigns are numerous, and some of the piles of Trajan's bridge across the Danube survive at Turnu Severin. One of the great walls across the Dobruja from Hinog (ancient Axiopolis) to Constanţa may also be his, but the most impressive of all the Roman monuments in Rumania is the Tropaeum Trajani at Adamclisi in the Dobruja; much of its sculptured decoration still lies around the massive concrete core. Roman towns explored in the Dobruja include Ulmetum and Capidava. Much of what is now Rumania—Banat, Transylvania, Oltenia—became the Roman province of Dacia. Roads were laid out, colonies and cities founded, and forts built along the frontiers (see LIMES). Roman inscriptions have been found almost as far north as the Ukrainian border. At Verespatak, near Cluj, there are considerable traces of Roman mining.

Probably in A.D. 271 the Roman armies of Aurelian and some of the Roman colonists withdrew from Dacia, under pressure from the Goths and other invading tribes. The Rumanians claim, on the evidence of a number of post-Roman sites excavated, that part of the romanized population lived on in humble circumstances, withdrawing to more remote and protected settlements. To the Gothic occupation belongs the famous 4th-century hoard of gold treasure found at Pietroasa. The Goths were followed by the Huns and other migrating peoples.

The civilization of Byzantium had little influence upon Rumania. Byzantine remains are not of importance until the 14th century when the church of St. Nicholas at Curtea de Argeş was built. The frescoes there rank as the finest and oldest Byzantine works of art in the country. A distinctive and beautiful architectural style later evolved, particularly in Moldavia, flourishing mostly in the 16th and early 17th centuries. The church of Trei Erarchi ("Three Saints") at Iaşi, founded in 1639, is one of the finest examples. This style owes little or nothing to Greek or Slavonic tradition in matters of decoration, though the structure is in essence Byzantine. Byzantine traditions dominated religious art down to the 18th century.   (N. J. G. P.)

IV. HISTORY

The early history of the lands which constitute modern Rumania, down to the end of the period of Roman domination, is traced in the article DACIA. Roman rule in Dacia lasted for 163 years. From the 3rd to the 12th century wave after wave of barbarian invaders from the east passed over the undefended country—first came the Germanic Goths and Gepidae, then Slavs, followed by the Avars (q.v.), and in the second half of the 7th century by the Bulgars. The Bulgarian domination, lasting for two centuries, allowed a rudimentary civic life to take shape, and it was the Bulgars who, after the conversion of their tsar Boris in 864, brought Christianity in its eastern form to the ancestors of the Rumanians, building on earlier Latin foundations (see Religion, above). At the end of the 9th century the Bulgars were overcome by the Magyars; later came a brief incursion by the now almost vanished Pechenegs and Kumans (qq.v.).

One school of historians maintains that the Daco-Roman population north of the Danube was obliterated during these invasions and that the Rumanians of today are descended from Vlach tribes south of the river who pushed northward in the early 13th century. The Rumanian view, supported by linguistic and other evidence, is that the Roman withdrawal affected only the military and official classes, while the body of the Daco-Roman inhabitants were driven by the invaders into the Carpathians, becoming the Vlachs of Transylvania. The Macedo-Romans south of the Danube, later known as Kutso-Vlachs, similarly sought shelter in the Pindus mountains. The controversy is considered in the article VLACHS.

Transylvania, regarded by Rumanians as the cradle of their nation, was conquered in the 11th century by King Stephen I of Hun-

MEDIEVAL CASTLE AT BRAN IN THE BRAŞOV REGION, BUILT IN THE 13TH CENTURY BY GERMAN SETTLERS IN TRANSYLVANIA

gary, but all records of its early inhabitants were destroyed in the Tatar-Mongol invasion of that country in 1241. The authentic history of the Vlachs does not begin until the end of the 13th century, when they are found establishing themselves south of the Carpathians in two distinct groups, one settling in the area later known as Walachia (called Muntenia by the chroniclers) and the other to the east in Moldavia. The incoming Vlachs fused with a population that already contained a Vlach element, but consisted mainly of Slavs and Tatars with an admixture of Pechenegs and Kumans.

The two regions thus colonized became the principalities of Walachia and Moldavia, whose annals remain distinct until 1774, but can thereafter be combined in one narrative, the Turkish administration being uniform. In 1859 the two principalities were formally united under the name of Rumania. The historical narrative which follows is therefore arranged under five headings, *Walachia, Moldavia, The Danubian Principalities, Rumania,* and *Greater Rumania.* The history of Transylvania is given in a separate article.

A. WALACHIA

Tradition, embodied in a local chronicle of the 16th century entitled "History of the Ruman Land Since the Arrival of the Rumans" (*Istoria tierei Românesci decându au descălicati Românii*), gives 1290 as the date of the founding of the Walachian state, asserting that in that year a voivode (prince) of Fagaraş in southern Transylvania crossed the mountains with a body of followers and established himself at Cîmpulung in the foothills, moving later to Curtea de Argeş. The name given for this first leader, Radu Negru (Ralph the Black), is probably a confusion with that of a later Walachian voivode, but the southward movement at that period of Vlach peoples from the mountains to the Danubian plain can be affirmed with certainty. Walachia itself was known to its own people as Muntenia, land of the mountains, after their former home. Historians who deny the continuity of Daco-Roman (Vlach) settlement in Transylvania have to postulate a northward migration of Vlachs from across the Danube to the Carpathians at the beginning of the 13th century to account for the indisputable southward movement at its close. The search for a new home in the south was due to the consolidation of Hungarian feudal power in Transylvania and of the feudal system, to the arrival of German settlers, and to the growing proselytizing zeal of the Hungarian kings as faithful servants of the papacy. The Vlachs, since the introduction of organized Christianity under Bulgarian influence, had belonged to the Eastern Orthodox Church, taking the Byzantine side against Rome in the schism of 1054, though later some of their leaders came under Roman influence.

The new principality remained at first under the domination of Hungary, but the prince Basarab I defeated the Hungarian king Charles I Robert in 1330 and secured independence. Vladislav (c. 1364–77), although again defeating the Hungarians, accepted a form of Hungarian suzerainty in return for investiture by Louis I the Great, Charles Robert's successor, with the banat (frontier province) of Severin and the duchy of Omlas.

The early days of the principality were conditioned by the struggle against Hungary, but with the reign of Mircea the Old (1386–1418) a new period began, that of the struggle against the Turks. The first princes of Walachia, in search of help against Hungary, had contracted matrimonial and military alliances with the two Slav states south of the Danube, Bulgaria and Serbia, but both empires were already at the point of extinction at the hands of the Turks. Tradition recounts that a Walachian contingent helped the Serbs at the Battle of Kosovo in 1389; it is a fact that the sultan followed up his victory by invading Walachia, which first appears in 1391 as a tributary of the Sublime Porte. The final overthrow of Bulgaria in 1393 left Walachia open to further Turkish advance but Mircea succeeded in holding the invaders back on the Danube marshes in 1394, and in the following year made an alliance with Hungary. The joint Christian forces, which included French and Burgundian contingents, were defeated in 1396 at the Battle of Nikopol (Nicopolis). Mircea had thrown over an earlier alliance with Poland in order to secure one with Hungary; accordingly the

Poles, taking advantage of the defeat at Nikopol, intrigued for his deposition and replaced him by his son Vlad, who accepted Polish suzerainty. Mircea later returned, reestablished, and, for a time, increased his power by exploiting the quarrels between the sons of the sultan Bayazid I. In 1417, however, Walachia was forced to capitulate to Turkey under Sultan Mohammed II, though its dynasty, territory, and Christian religion were left intact. Mircea died a year later.

1. Early Years of Turkish Rule.—After Mircea's death, Walachia, convulsed by internal struggles, could take no active part against the Turks, but they were for a time again driven back by the Hungarians under the brilliant János Hunyadi (*q.v.*), a Rumanian by race though enrolled in the Hungarian nobility. He deposed one of the weak Walachian princes and nominated Vlad IV—who in 1456 acknowledged Hungary as suzerain—a man whose unbelievable cruelties earned him the name of "the Impaler" (Tepes). Vlad (1456–62 and again in 1476) was able briefly to defy the Turks; with his death, resistance crumbled rapidly, Walachian princes succeeding one another after very short reigns.

The instability of the throne was in part due to the mixture of the hereditary and elective principles in the system of succession; the council of boyars (nobles), which came under Turkish rule to be known as the divan by analogy with the Turkish institution of that name, chose the prince from legitimate and illegitimate heirs of his dead predecessor.

The only prince of the 16th century deserving mention is Neagoe Basarab (1512–21), who founded cathedrals at Curtea de Argeş (*q.v.*) and at Tîrgovişte, which had become the Walachian capital, and endowed monasteries in Walachia, besides making noble contributions to Mount Athos. The patriarch of Constantinople honoured the dedication of the Argeş monastery with his presence.

Neagoe's son and successor was imprisoned by the Turks who proceeded to nominate Turkish governors in the towns and villages of Walachia. The Walachians resisted desperately. They elected Radu, a kinsman of Neagoe, as prince and defeated the Turkish commander Mahmud Bey with Hungarian help at Grumatz in 1522. The continuance and extension of Turkish control became inevitable, however, after the crushing defeat of Hungary in 1526 at the Battle of Mohács.

Walachia thereafter became a line of communication for Turkish expeditions against Hungary and Transylvania. The prince Alexander, who succeeded in 1591, actually farmed out his possessions to his Turkish supporters, and it seemed that Walachia must succumb to direct Ottoman rule.

2. Michael the Brave, 1593–1601.—The Turkish advance was once more to be halted, though for the last time, under a new prince, Michael (*q.v.*), son of Petraşcu, ban of Craiova. In 1593 he secured the deposition of Alexander and his own election by raising a loan at Constantinople of 400,000 ducats to make the customary presents to the Porte and was supported by Sigismund Báthory (*q.v.*), prince of Transylvania, and by the English ambassador at Constantinople, Edward Barton. Michael was to prove a thorn in the flesh to the Turks, but was much criticized for making Walachia once more subject to Hungarian princes in return for their help. In concert with the Moldavian prince Aaron, Michael organized a massacre of Turkish guards and settlers (November 1594) and with the support given by Báthory in return for the acknowledgment of his suzerainty proceeded to invade Turkish territory, taking Ruse (Ruschuk), Silistra, and other places on the right bank of the Danube. A simultaneous invasion of Walachia by a large Turkish and Tatar host was defeated in the battles of Serpăteşti and Stăneşti (1595). The sultan next sent Sinan Pasha the Renegade to invade Walachia with 100,000 men. Michael withdrew to the mountains, but with aid from Báthory and a Transylvanian contingent resumed the offensive and stormed Bucharest, pursuing the main body of Sinan's forces to the Danube. In 1597 the sultan, wearied with these defeats, reinvested Michael for life.

Walachia's subjection to Hungary was not permanent. On the abdication of Sigismund Báthory, Michael, with the support of the emperor Rudolf II, attacked and defeated his successor Andreas

Báthory in October 1599 and had himself proclaimed prince of Transylvania, being acknowledged by the emperor as his lieutenant and having his position ratified by the diet. The Vlach peasant population of Transylvania was encouraged to revolt against the Magyars by having an overlord of their own race, but Michael, whose support in Walachia rested on the boyars, helped the Magyar nobility to suppress the peasant rising. Despite this the Magyars distrusted Michael, both as a despised Vlach and as a Habsburg agent, and he found his position in Transylvania insecure while Moldavia remained as a centre for Magyar and Polish intrigue. In May 1600 he invaded that principality, deposed the prince Jeremy (Ieremia) Movilă and without waiting for the emperor's sanction had himself proclaimed "prince of Walachia, Transylvania, and of all Moldavia."

Though Rudolf confirmed Michael in his appointment he grew suspicious of his vassal's progress and determined to undermine his position. The imperial commissioner, Gen. Georgio Basta, was instructed to give support to the disaffected Magyar element in Transylvania, and Michael was driven out by a successful revolt. At the same time the Poles invaded Moldavia, and restored the unseated prince, while Walachia itself was also attacked. Michael appealed to the emperor, who restored him to favour, and in conjunction with Basta he defeated the Transylvanian forces at Goräslău in 1601. Basta, however, jealous of Michael's returning prosperity, procured his murder at Turda (Cîmpia Turzii) almost immediately after their joint victory.

Michael the Brave (Mihai Viteazul) is the leading Rumanian national hero, partly because it was he who made the last stand before the era of Turkish and Greek domination, but chiefly because for the first time since Dacian days he brought all the Rumanians, scattered in three principalities, under one rule, thus weaving the stuff of the national dream which was not to become reality until 1918.

3. The Period of Greek Penetration, 1634–1711.—After Michael's death Radu Şerban of the Basarab dynasty was appointed prince of Walachia by the emperor's wish, but was deposed by the Turks in 1611. A succession of insignificant puppet princes followed him, the Greek element becoming increasingly apparent. There was a temporary rally in the second quarter of the 17th century under Matei Basarab, who succeeded in holding the throne for 22 years—warding off repeated attacks from his rival Vasile Lupu of Moldavia—and did much for the arts and the endowment of churches. He founded a printing press at the Govora monastery which issued a compendium of canon law, *Pravila cea mică*, the first Rumanian book to be printed in the principalities (Gospels in Rumanian had been printed in the preceding century by the Protestants in Transylvania).

The successor of Matei, Constantin Serban, was the last Basarab to rule in Walachia. On his death the Turks, who in 1698 moved the capital to Bucharest—at a safer distance from the Transylvanian frontier—began to exercise a more direct influence over the ruling families, who were now frequently of Greek origin. Şerban Cantacuzino (1678–88), the first important Greek prince, was an able man; forced to assist the Turks at the siege of Vienna, he opened up secret communications with the emperor, who granted him a diploma creating him a count of the empire and recognizing his descent from the imperial house of Cantacuzino. In 1688, the year of Şerban's death, the first Rumanian Bible was printed.

Şerban's successor was his nephew Constantin Brancovan (Brîncoveanu), descended on his mother's side from the Basarabs, who pursued a policy of cautious balancing between the Porte, the emperor, Poland, and the rapidly westward-thrusting Russia. Brancovan sent congratulations to Peter I the Great on his victory at Poltava and asked for help for the Christian cause. Finally falling a victim to intrigues, Brancovan was deposed and executed at Constantinople in 1714.

4. The Phanariote Regime, 1714–1821.—At the beginning of the 18th century Turkish power was in obvious decline and the strength of Austria and Russia growing. Alarmed by the intrigues of Brancovan of Walachia and Cantemir of Moldavia with Vienna and Moscow, the Porte decided to exercise direct control over the principalities. Instead of reducing them to mere pashaliks, however, the Turks employed Greeks from the Phanar district of Constantinople as their agents. The new princes, or hospodars, insecure of tenure, had to extract the maximum from the country in the minimum of time—the average duration of a reign was only two and a half years—and thus the word Phanariote has come to stand for bribery, exaction, and corruption, though the hospodars themselves were often men of culture and intelligence.

Under this oppressive regime many peasants emigrated; in 1741 there were 147,000 peasant families in Walachia, but four years later their number was reduced by half. In the face of this, the enlightened prince Konstantinos Mavrokordatos decreed the abolition of serfdom in 1747, but after numerous rises and falls from favour he was finally imprisoned in 1763 after efforts at reform had proved abortive.

The tide of Ottoman domination was now ebbing fast under Russian pressure; after defeating the Turks at Hoţin in 1769, Russian troops occupied both principalities, the bishops and clergy taking an oath to the empress Catherine. At Focşani in 1772 Catherine demanded that the Porte recognize the independence of Walachia and Moldavia under Russian guarantee, but she was deterred by Austrian opposition, and temporarily satiated by the partition of Poland.

B. MOLDAVIA

1. From the 14th Century.—Moldavia took shape in circumstances similar to those of its sister state but somewhat later: according to chronicles, more plentiful than those dealing with Walachia, Dragoş, founder of the principality, emigrated southward with his followers from Maramureş in the northern Carpathians (the dates given vary from 1299 to 1342). An independent state first emerged about 1359 under Bogdan I. One of the early princes, Petru Muşat (1374–92), was a member of the Basarab family of Walachia and, in pursuance of the interests of his kinsman, Mircea the Old, recognized the suzerainty of the king of Poland whose sister he married. From this period date Poland's ambitions to control the new state, which had hardly emancipated itself from Hungarian tutelage. The first important prince, Alexander the Good (1400–32), acknowledged Polish overlordship and laid the foundations of organized life in the principality. Civil war reigned among Alexander's successors, but a new era in Moldavian history opened with the reign of his grandson Stephen the Great (1457–1504), who was to prove one of the greatest champions of Christendom against the Turks. Patriotic and religious, Stephen was doubly affected by the fall of Constantinople four years before his accession; the cutting of the trade route through the Bosporus was disastrous for the commerce of the principalities and the desecration of Hagia Sophia was a blow to Christian feeling. Stephen's whole reign was devoted to the attempt to rally the west against the infidel; he appealed for help to Poland, Hungary, and Venice as well as to the pope Sixtus IV, who gave him the title "athlete of Christ."

Stephen inflicted a crushing defeat on the Turks at Vaslui in 1475, and again repelled them the following year. Poland and Hungary, however, never gave him the solid support for which he had hoped; in 1484 the Turks captured his key fortresses of Chilia and Cetatea Albă (Akkerman, from 1944 Belgorod-Dnestrovski), and the following year burned the Moldavian capital Suceava. Once again Stephen rallied and defeated the Turks in 1486 at Scheia near Roman. As early as 1484, after the loss of his fortresses, he had been compelled to do public homage to King Casimir IV of Poland, but in 1499 he was able to draw up a treaty on equal terms. Poland, however, once again failed to honour its pledge to give help. On his deathbed Stephen, realizing the hopelessness of securing united action from Christendom, advised his son to submit to the Turks if they would respect the framework of church and state.

Stephen encouraged the arts, gave generous grants of monastic lands, and built more than 40 stone churches and the great monastery of Putna. Stephen's son Bogdan III, the "one-eyed" (1504–17), at feud with Poland over Pokuţia (Pokucie), which his father had annexed, and lacking support from the already shaken Hungary, was forced in 1513 to pay annual tribute to the sultan while securing guarantees for the Christian religion and Moldavian institutions. In the anarchy following the Battle of Mohács a strange figure ascended the Moldavian throne, Petru Rareş (1527–38 and 1541–46), an illegitimate son of Stephen. Allying himself with the Turks, he made war on the imperial forces in Transylvania and on Poland, attempting to recover the lost Pokuţia. Later he allied himself with the emperor against Poland and the sultan, but was defeated and deposed in 1538. In 1541 he returned to the throne with Turkish help, but concluded a secret treaty with the emperor against the Turks. His successors could no longer oppose Turkish power.

2. Turkish Penetration.—Petru's son actually accepted Islam; the sultan strengthened his hold on Moldavia by occupying a series of fortresses and increased the tribute. From the middle of the 16th century each aspirant to the Moldavian throne had to buy the consent of the Porte, and the way was thus open to adventurers. The most dramatic was Jacob Basiliscus Heraclides who seized Moldavia from the prince Alexander IV Lăpuşneanu (1552–61) with Turkish support. A Greek by birth, he had traveled over Europe and had become the friend of Philipp Melanchthon; he attempted to found an educational system in Moldavia, but his heavy taxation led to revolt and he was assassinated in 1563. Under the restored Lăpuşneanu (1563–68) and under Bogdan IV (1568–72), Moldavia relapsed into obscurity. Bogdan's successor John the Terrible (1572–74), provoked by the Porte's demand for increased tribute, rose against the oppressor, but was defeated and slain in 1574. Moldavia did not rally until the victories of Michael the Brave at the turn of the century when it was actually incorporated for a year in Michael's Great Dacian realm. After Michael's murder, the Poles again asserted supremacy, but the Porte resumed its domination in 1618. No prince of any importance occupied the throne until Vasile Lupu (1634–53), a brave soldier of Albanian origin. He might have achieved success against the Turks, but chose instead to attack his neighbour Walachia, coveting its throne. He married one of his daughters to Timothy, son of the celebrated Ukrainian hetman (general) Bohdan Chmielnicki and raided Walachia with the help of his son-in-law, but was routed by the veteran Matei Basarab. He was overthrown by a conspiracy of Moldavian boyars, and after his death Greek influence became paramount. One of the Greek princes, Dimitrie Cantemir (1710–11, q.v.), attempted to exchange Turkish for Russian sovereignty, and proving unsuccessful went into exile in St. Petersburg. He was a scholar whose *Descriptio Moldaviae* is a valuable historical source.

The Phanariote regime in Moldavia is generally reckoned from the reign of Nikolaos Mavrokordatos, Cantemir's successor; it was similar to that in Walachia, and indeed the princes were frequently shifted by the Turks from one throne to the other. Moldavia was perhaps more prosperous than Walachia at this period and had a considerable export trade in timber, salt, wine, and foodstuffs.

C. The Danubian Principalities

1. After 1774.—The Treaty of Kuchuk Kainarji which ended the Russo-Turkish War in 1774 altered the situation in both Walachia and Moldavia. Russia restored the principalities which it had occupied, to the sultan (Moldavia, however, lost its northern tip, Bukovina [q.v.], which Austria, profiting by the situation, annexed in 1775) on conditions which included provisions favourable to the territories themselves. The tribute was to be reduced, and the agents of Walachia and Moldavia at the Porte were to have diplomatic status; Russia was accorded a virtual protectorate. In view of Turkish attempts to evade fulfilment of the treaty, Russia secured a more precise definition of its rights in the convention of Ainali-Kavak (1779) and strengthened its position in 1782 by appointing a consul in Bucharest. Austria countered by dispatching an "agent" Ignazio Rajčević, whose *Osservazioni storiche intorno la Valachia* (1788) is one of the best sources for the period. In the Russo-Turkish War which broke out again in 1787 the principalities once more provided battlefields, and Prince G. A. Potemkin made his headquarters at Jassy (Iaşi). In 1791, when peace was imminent, a group of Walachian boyars, fearing the effects of renewed Ottoman rule, addressed an appeal to Austria and Russia

which, though it achieved no results, is of interest as an early sign of the awakening of national feeling. The boyars asked for the ending of Phanariote rule, the return of native princes and the creation of a national army. By the Peace of Jassy (Jan. 9 [N.S.], 1792) Russia had to evacuate the principalities, the Dniester (Nistru) being recognized as its frontier, and the privileges of the principalities accorded in earlier treaties were confirmed. In defiance of treaties the Porte continued to change the princes almost yearly, until in 1802 the Russians obtained a fresh convention under which every prince was to hold office for at least seven years and could not be dispossessed without Russian consent.

The two new princes were strongly under Russian influence. Konstantinos Ypsilantis of Walachia, encouraged by the convention, refused some Turkish requisitions, acted as intermediary between the Serbs and Russia in the Serb revolt of 1804 and tried to embroil the French and the Porte. Napoleon's envoy at Bucharest denounced both princes as traitors and influenced the Porte's decision to dethrone them in 1806 without consulting Russia. Russia occupied the principalities and the Turks declared war in December 1806; Moldavia and Walachia had become pawns in the intrigues between the emperor Alexander, the Porte, and Napoleon. The Russian occupation, which lasted six years, reduced the country to a desert; produce was carried off, the coinage debased, and labour requisitioning was enforced by the deportation of recalcitrants to Siberia. The Christian populations exchanged hope and confidence in a liberator for a profound suspicion and fear of Russia which remained rooted in Rumanian minds.

Russia's design to incorporate the principalities in its empire was frustrated by the Peace of Bucharest (1812), but it secured the cession of southeastern Moldavia, known as Bessarabia (q.v.). The two princes who were appointed after the peace in 1812, Ion Caragea in Walachia and Scarlat Callimachi in Moldavia, were masters of extortion. The former increased the taxation eightfold, partly by creating 4,000 new boyars. Both were strongly Greek in feeling, and were supported by some of the boyars, who, disappointed in Russia, dreamed of a new Greco-Rumanian Byzantium. Caragea was in secret relations with the Greek revolutionary movement, Philiki Etaireia, which was being fostered at Odessa under Russian auspices. The way was thus prepared for the adventure of Alexandros Ypsilantis, son of the Walachian prince Konstantinos and *aide-de-camp* of the tsar, who marched into Moldavia at the head of the Etairists in 1821. He received the support of the Moldavian prince Michael Suţu, but the boyars were hostile in Moldavia and still more so in Walachia where a national popular movement led by Tudor Vladimirescu (q.v.) turned not against the Turks but against the Phanariots. Turkish troops which invaded to crush Ypsilantis were not finally withdrawn until 1824. The Turks, anxious to divide the Rumanians from the Greeks, thought it wise to heed the former's demands and the Rumanians took advantage of this to secure a number of reforms in the national interest. The reforms included the promulgation of laws in Rumanian and the appointment of native princes, the first of whom were Ioan Sandu Sturdza (Sturza) in Moldavia and Grigore IV Ghica in Walachia. Ghica's family, though of Albanian extraction and settled at the Phanar, was entirely rumanized. Both princes were anti-Greek and unacceptable to the Russians; Sturdza was accused of subversive tendencies because he cherished plans for constitutional reform, including an elected assembly.

2. Kiselev and the "Règlement Organique."—Russia and Turkey resumed relations in 1825 and by the convention of Akkerman signed by them in 1826 the privileges of the principalities were once more confirmed, and Russia was again allowed a voice in elections to the two thrones. On the outbreak of hostilities between Russia and Turkey again in 1828, Russia once more occupied Walachia and Moldavia. The Peace of Adrianople in 1829 left them still tributary to the sultan, but wholly under Russian protection. The two princes were thenceforth elected for life.

Russia secured a continuation of its occupation by making evacuation conditional on the payment of an impossibly high indemnity by Turkey. The occupation, which had again been exceedingly onerous during the war, became more enlightened after the signing of the treaty, a change which was largely due to the Russian administrator, Count Pavel Kiselev. The boyars, under Kiselev's supervision, drew up a constitution known as the *Règlement organique,* promulgated in Walachia in 1831 and in Moldavia in 1832. It was wholly oligarchic in character, but was an advance insofar as legislative and administrative powers were vested in a native elected body. The economic provisions of the *Règlement,* however, deepened the cleavage between the boyars and the peasant class and were censured by Kiselev. The *Règlement* was ratified by the Porte in 1834, whereupon Russia withdrew its troops.

3. The National Movement and 1848.—The new princes, Alexandru II Ghica (1834–42) in Walachia and Mihai Sturdza in Moldavia, were, however, strongly under Russian influence. Ghica's successor Gheorghe Bibescu (1842–48) had been educated in Paris and was influenced by the new spirit of romantic nationalism. In agreement with Sturdza he removed the fiscal barriers between the principalities. Meanwhile a new generation of Rumanians was growing up, educated in Paris or looking to France for inspiration; these came rapidly to the front in the great crisis of 1848 which in the principalities took a form partly national and partly social. The national movements in Moldavia and Walachia were spurred on by the dramatic upsurge among the downtrodden Rumanian peasants of Transylvania, which culminated in the "field of liberty" demonstrations at Blaj in May 1848. Sturdza in Moldavia proved able to quell popular agitation; Bibescu, although he had some sympathy with the movement, lacked courage to lead it and fled, leaving in power a provisional government largely controlled by Ion C. Brătianu (*q.v.*), first head of the great Liberal family which for so long dominated Rumanian politics. The Turks, under Russian pressure, were forced to put down the new movement; joint Russo-Turkish military intervention restored the *Règlement organique.* The Balta-Liman convention of 1849 laid down that the princes should again be appointed for seven years only; the assemblies were replaced by so-called *diwans ad hoc.* Grigore V Ghica was appointed prince in Moldavia, and Barbu Ştirbey, brother of Gheorghe Bibescu, in Walachia.

4. Crimean War and Treaty of Paris.—Russian troops did not evacuate the principalities until 1851, and during the Crimean War they were occupied in turn by Russia and Austria. Although they suffered severely, the Austrian occupation brought material benefits and opportunities of.contact with the west. The Treaty of Paris (1856) placed the principalities with their existing privileges under the collective guarantee of the contracting powers, thus ending the Russian protectorate, though retaining the suzerainty of the Porte. The Russian frontier was withdrawn from the mouths of the Danube by the return of a strip of southern Bessarabia to Moldavia. The existing statutes were revised in 1857 by a European commission with a Turkish member meeting at Bucharest, assisted by two *diwans ad hoc* called together by the Porte.

5. Union of the Principalities.—The *diwans* voted unanimously for autonomy, union of the principalities under the name of Rumania, a foreign hereditary prince, and neutrality. The *diwans* were dissolved by the Porte in January 1858 and in August the convention of Paris accepted their decisions with modifications. There were still to be two princes and two assemblies, but a central commission at Focşani was to prepare measures of joint concern. The two assemblies, meeting at Iaşi and Bucharest respectively, then elected a single prince in the person of Alexandru Ion Cuza (*q.v.*) on Jan. 17 (N.S.), 1859. The *de facto* union of Rumania was thus accomplished.

D. Rumania

A new conference met in Paris to discuss the situation and in 1861 the election of Prince Cuza was ratified by the powers and the Porte. In February 1862 a single ministry and a single assembly replaced the *diwans* and central commission. Cuza, in May 1864, promulgated by plebiscite a new constitution providing for a senate as well as an assembly and extending the franchise to all citizens, with the reservation of a cumulative voting power for property. An important agrarian law of the same year emancipated the peasantry from forced labour. Prince Cuza's agrarian and educational

reforms were progressive, but his methods of enforcement were despotic. He alienated the boyars by abolishing forced labour, and the clergy by confiscating monastic estates (see *Religion,* above), while the agrarian reform was not radical enough to satisfy the peasantry.

In February 1866 Cuza was compelled to abdicate, and the principalities by referendum elected as prince, almost unanimously, Charles (*see* Carol I), second son of Prince Charles Antony of Hohenzollern-Sigmaringen, the candidate of Ion Brătianu, who had secured the veiled support of Napoleon III. The new prince reached Bucharest on May 22, 1866, and in July took the oath to a new constitution modeled on the Belgian Charter of 1831, which provided for upper and lower houses and gave the prince an unconditional veto on all legislation. Turkish assent was secured in October; Prince Charles was recognized as hereditary ruler and was allowed to maintain an army of 30,000 men.

1. Internal Politics, 1866–75.—Prince Charles's policy was to avoid all political adventures and to give Rumania a sound administration. The internal situation was at first unsettled; ten governments held office in five years. The dominant figure was the Liberal leader Ion Brătianu.

In 1869 Prince Charles paid a series of state visits to consolidate his position, and married Princess Elizabeth of Neuwied, the poetess later known as Carmen Sylva, who earned great popularity in her adopted country. Prince Charles was a Roman Catholic and his wife a Protestant, but he agreed to bring up his successor in the Eastern Orthodox faith.

Tension arose between the German prince and his pro-French politicians on the outbreak of the Franco-German War in 1870 and there was an abortive attempt to overthrow him in a revolutionary outbreak at Ploeşti. Anti-German feelings were increased by a scandal in the new Rumanian railways; the German contractor failed to honour the coupons of the bonds, mainly held by influential Germans, and the Prussian government attempted to coerce the Rumanian government into payment. Indignation in Rumania culminated in a mob attack on the German colony in Bucharest in March 1871, and Prince Charles contemplated abdication. A Conservative government formed under Lascăr Catargiu succeeded in restoring order, however, and retained office for five years. After another crisis threatening Prince Charles, the Liberals again took office in 1876 and Brătianu became premier; he enjoyed almost absolute power for the next 12 years.

2. The Russo-Turkish War, 1877–78, and the Treaty of Berlin.—Domestic problems were temporarily eclipsed by the reopening of the Eastern Question in 1877. Russia rejected Rumania's offer of cooperation on equal terms against Turkey and threatened occupation. On April 16, 1877, Rumania signed a secret convention allowing free passage to the Russian armies, while the tsar promised to respect Rumanian territory. The Russians crossed the Rumanian frontier in April, and on May 11 Rumania declared war on Turkey. Rumanian troops contributed materially to the joint victory at Plevna (Pleven; *q.v.*), which left the Russian forces free to march on Constantinople. Nonetheless Russia refused to admit Rumanian representatives to the peace negotiations at Adrianople and later at San Stefano. The Russians insisted on the handing back of southern Bessarabia which had been restored to Moldavia after the Crimean War, and despite bitter Rumanian protests this provision was incorporated in the Treaty of Berlin (July 13, 1878); Rumania received an alternative outlet to the mouths of the Danube in northern Dobruja, a territory with little or no Rumanian population, the possession of which later caused discord with Bulgaria.

The treaty recognized Rumanian independence and guaranteed absolute freedom of worship without loss of political rights. The latter article (XLIV) caused indignation in the country and could not be implemented without constitutional revision. Art. VII of the 1866 constitution stated that "only Christians can become citizens of Rumania," thus excluding Jews from civic rights. Jews had not been numerous in the principalities until the early 19th century, but their influx after the Treaty of Adrianople had caused the safeguard to be put into the constitution. Under pressure from the powers, Art. VII was finally repealed.

3. Independence of Rumania: the Kingdom.—The independence of Rumania was recognized by Italy in December 1879 and by Great Britain, France, and Germany in February 1880. Prince Charles, having no children, regulated the succession in 1880 in favour of his nephew Prince Ferdinand of Hohenzollern, and the idea of making Rumania a kingdom was mooted. The Liberal government, accused by the Conservatives of republican tendencies, itself took the initiative in proclaiming the kingdom. This action was hastened by the general fear of revolution consequent on the assassination of Emperor Alexander II. Charles was crowned king on May 22, 1881, and secured the immediate recognition of the powers.

4. Internal Politics, 1878–1912.—Since 1876 Brătianu had exercised almost dictatorial power. His Liberals stood for the rapid development of a strong middle class able to control the Jews, and were mainly Francophile. The Conservatives were divided into the old boyar group, which tended to look to Russia, and the so-called Young Conservatives, the Junimists, led by Petre Carp, who had studied in Germany rather than France and favoured the Central Powers. Brătianu retired after electoral defeat in 1888, and died three years later. Thereafter various Conservative and Junimist administrations held office, the Liberals under Dimitrie Sturdza returning to power in 1895.

The country was in considerable financial difficulties and there was much discontent, particularly in the countryside where the peasants, though emancipated in 1864, were forced by poverty into the hands of Jewish moneylenders. A serious peasant rising in 1907, stimulated by the Russian upheaval of 1905, attacked first the Jews and then the large landowners. The Conservative ministry had to resign and it was a Liberal government which restored order. In 1909 the Liberal leader Sturdza resigned and was succeeded by Ionel Brătianu, eldest son of the great statesman, who continued to base his policy on the expansion of the urban middle class, though some of his younger colleagues concentrated on the agrarian problem. The Conservatives under Carp came to power again in 1911, but were violently attacked by the Liberals and a group of Conservative dissidents formed after the peasant rising under Take Ionescu. Under the pressure of foreign events the cabinet was reconstituted in 1912 with Titu Maiorescu as premier and Ionescu as minister of the interior. In January 1914 Ionel Brătianu succeeded Maiorescu and formed a Liberal administration; together with the party theorist Constantine Stere, a Bessarabian boyar who had been banished to Siberia for his radical views, he worked out a program of agrarian reform.

5. Foreign Affairs, 1878–1912.—The foreign political situation remained comparatively calm between the Treaty of Berlin and the outbreak of the Balkan wars, though Rumania's relations with its neighbours could not be cordial. Bulgaria, a traditional friend, was embittered by the loss of northern Dobruja; against Russia the Rumanians were incensed by the forced retrocession of southern Bessarabia. The resentment aroused against Austria at the end of the 18th century by its seizure of Bukovina, the first home of the Moldavian principality and repository of its chief artistic and ecclesiastical treasures, had died down, but ill feeling was aroused by the commercial treaty of 1875, which Rumania considered unfair, and was intensified by Austria's insistence on having a delegate on the Danube commission, though the commission's writ only ran from Galați to Orșova and did not reach Austrian soil. The oppressed Rumanians of Transylvania had been increasingly conscious of grievance against Hungary since 1848 and their feelings were shared in Rumania. With Greece there was a constantly reviving dispute in which Bulgaria was also involved, concerning the status of the Vlach communities in Macedonia over which Rumania claimed the rights of a protector; this caused a diplomatic rupture between Rumania and Greece from 1905 to 1911.

King Charles had a natural and pronounced preference for the Central Powers, and in this he was supported by Ion Brătianu, whose fear and dislike of Russia after the Treaty of Berlin outweighed his Francophilia. It was Brătianu, with Sturdza as foreign minister, who signed the secret treaty of 1883 with Austria and Germany. The treaty, remaining a close secret, was formally renewed under a Conservative administration in 1892. It was, however, the first signatory, Sturdza, leader of the Liberals since 1893, who was most active in support of the claims of the Transylvanian Rumanians against Hungary. The Bosnian crisis of 1908 alarmed Rumania because it showed that Austria was prepared to further the fortunes of Bulgaria in order to destroy Serbia. Ionel Brătianu, however, on succeeding Sturdza in 1909, remained faithful to the secret treaty.

6. First Balkan War, 1912.—The outbreak of war between the Balkan League and Turkey in October 1912 found the Conservatives in office. Rumania's sympathies were at first uncertain; the secret Serbo-Bulgarian military convention of March 13, 1912, had provided against a possible Rumanian attack. The rapid success of the Bulgarians caused Rumania to abandon its original profession of disinterestedness and to stake a claim. Rumania intimated to Bulgaria that in the event of a partition of European Turkey it would, in the interests of the balance of power in the Balkans, require a frontier rectification in the Dobruja. Stoyan Danev, the Bulgarian foreign minister, returning through Bucharest from a visit to Vienna and Budapest, offered only minor frontier rectifications, excluding Silistra, which was the kernel of Rumania's claims. He did, however, consider the renunciation of Bulgaria's claim to northern Dobruja and the giving of a guarantee for the Vlachs of Macedonia. No agreement was reached in Bucharest or in London in January 1913. The case was finally submitted for arbitration to the Conference of St. Petersburg (May 1913) which assigned Silistra to Rumania. Bulgaria regarded the concession as excessive and Rumania no longer looked on it as a satisfactory price for neutrality.

7. Second Balkan War, 1913.—Bulgaria's attack on its allies on June 28, 1913, was used by Rumania as a pretext for intervention. The Rumanian Army, 500,000 strong and commanded by the crown prince, crossed the frontier (July 11), occupied southern Dobruja, and advanced on Sofia. Negotiations were immediately opened at Bucharest, where an armistice was signed on July 30, 1913, between Rumania, Serbia, Greece, and Bulgaria. By the Treaty of Bucharest, signed on Aug. 10, Rumania obtained southern Dobruja which it had already occupied.

Rumania's position was now precarious in view of the growing tension between Vienna and St. Petersburg. The king renewed the secret treaty with the Central Powers at the beginning of 1914 and Austria made great efforts to win Rumanian friendship, but popular sentiment ran the other way. The feeling of kinship with Transylvania grew steadily among the younger generation, while Austria's continued diplomatic support of Bulgaria aroused resentment. The growing feeling of the need for a policy covering the interests of the entire Rumanian nation, within and without the national frontiers, led to a new inclination toward Russia. Though Russia held Moldavian Bessarabia, Austria-Hungary, as arbitrator of the destinies of the much more highly developed Rumanian communities in Transylvania, was the greater obstacle to the realization of dreams of unity. The visit to St. Petersburg of Prince Ferdinand, heir to the throne, in March 1914 and of the emperor Nicholas II to Constanța in June, did not bring about a definite change of policy, however.

8. Rumania and World War I.—On the outbreak of war in 1914 Ionel Brătianu and his Liberal Party were in office. The politicians were divided in their views, not along party lines, and Rumania at first maintained armed neutrality, though tempted by the Central Powers with the promise of the return of Bessarabia and by the Allies with the offer of Transylvania. Grief at the country's failure to honour the secret alliance hastened King Charles's death in October 1914. His successor, Ferdinand, had married Marie of Edinburgh, granddaughter of Queen Victoria and of Alexander II, stronger in character than her husband and a staunch lover of Britain and Russia. Her influence, Allied promises, and alarm at the extent of German victories finally brought Rumania into the war. By a treaty of Aug. 17, 1916, Great Britain, France, Russia, and Italy guaranteed Rumania the Banat, Transylvania, the Hungarian plain up to the Tisza River, and Bukovina as far as the Prut River. Rumania declared war on Austria-Hungary on Aug. 27; its troops at once crossed the passes into

Transylvania, but were expelled by mid-November. Bucharest was occupied by the Central Powers on Dec. 6, 1916. The king and his ministers and Parliament had already retired to Iași and were followed by the Army, which reorganized in Moldavia under the shelter of the Russian forces. The Russian Revolution of February 1917 led to the collapse of the front and left the German Field Marshal August von Mackensen free to throw all his forces against the Rumanian Army, which was rendered incapable of further resistance after a prolonged stand at Mărășești (Aug. 16, 1916), Mărăști, and Oituz. After the October Revolution the Russian Army disintegrated into pillaging bands, hostilities were suspended and an armistice was concluded on Dec. 6, 1917, at Focșani.

During this period the Parliament in exile at Iași was busy with projects of agrarian and electoral reform. Brătianu had already been considering these topics in 1914, and in December 1916 he made a coalition with Take Ionescu and his dissident Conservatives, who had been concerned with the peasant question since the 1907 rising. The effects of the Russian Revolution in the Ukraine and Bessarabia, where the peasants had appropriated the land, made the question urgent. King Ferdinand was personally concerned and induced the Conservatives to agree to a project of radical expropriation, which was passed in July 1917.

9. The Treaty of Bucharest.—After Brătianu resigned on Feb. 9, 1918, Gen. Alexandru Averescu was charged with the peace negotiations at Buftea, near Bucharest. The Dobruja was ceded as far as the Danube, Bulgaria taking over the southern half which it had lost in 1913, while the Central Powers administered the northern half conjointly. Rumania was to have a trade route to the Black Sea via Constanța. The old frontier of Hungary was restored. The Central Powers secured such terms on the Danube, in the Rumanian oil fields, and over the railways as would have placed Rumania in a state of economic slavery to them for many years. Averescu's cabinet hesitated to sign and resigned on March 12 in favour of the pro-German Alexandru Marghiloman ministry, which signed the treaty at Bucharest on May 7, 1918.

Marghiloman's ministry struggled against almost unsurmountable difficulties throughout the succeeding months. The Central Powers forced the Banque Générale to issue 2,500,000,000 lei in paper money. This disorganized the finance of the kingdom, while economic ruin was ensured by the forced export of sheep and cattle, the cutting down of forests, and the dismantling of factories. The population meanwhile was starving, and the morale of the working class was being perverted by revolutionary propaganda.

On Nov. 8, 1918, when the defeat of the Central Powers was assured, the king called to power General Coandă, who repealed all laws introduced by the Marghiloman ministry and decreed universal, obligatory, and secret suffrage for all male voters over 21 years of age. War was declared again on Nov. 9. The king reentered Bucharest (Nov. 30) after the German troops had evacuated Rumania under the terms of the Armistice. Ionel Brătianu again became premier on Dec. 14.

E. Greater Rumania

The dream of greater Rumania was realized, but it was no easy task to unite provinces which had been under the domination of different alien states. Bessarabia (q.v.) was already incorporated in the old kingdom, having abandoned an earlier idea of autonomy. Its council voted for unconditional union on Dec. 9, 1918. The incorporation of Transylvania (q.v.) followed in virtue of a resolution passed by a Rumanian assembly at Alba Iulia on Dec. 1, and that of Bukovina (q.v.) on Nov. 28. The government had to carry on difficult diplomatic negotiations for the recognition by the Allies of the new frontiers. Those fixed by the agreement of August 1916 were drawn back in places to give the Hungarians a part of the hinterland of Oradea (Nagyvárad), and the Yugoslavs the western half of the Banat. A line of demarcation was fixed in Hungary, and Rumanian troops occupied the country up to this line, pending final settlement by treaty. In March 1919 a further neutral zone was established and Rumania was given the right of occupying it. Béla Kun's Communist government which then came into power in Hungary started a campaign as a result of which the Rumanians advanced to the Tisza River, where they were stopped by the Allies on May 9. On July 22 Kun started a new offensive, but the Rumanian Army defeated his troops, crossed the Tisza—despite the interdiction of the Allies—and occupied Budapest on Aug. 4. There they remained, in the face of numerous protests, until Nov. 14. The treaties of Saint-Germain and Trianon recognized as Rumanian the predominantly Rumanian territories of the old Dual Monarchy, and the Treaty of Neuilly sanctioned Rumanian possession of southern Dobruja.

1. Domestic Politics, 1919–30.—The political scene was transformed after 1918; the old Conservative Party was swept away because of its pro-German policy and the impoverishment of its chief supporters, the boyars. The Liberals became the party of the business and professional classes, while the peasants, who gained new status through the land reform, founded a party of their own in the old kingdom headed by Ion Mihalache. More radical elements came in from Transylvania, notably the National Popular Party headed by Iuliu Maniu and Alexandre Vaida-Voevod. The Socialists were not influential, as more than 80% of the population of Rumania were peasants; in the old kingdom the Socialists were mainly Marxist and supported the Russian Revolution, but in Transylvania they looked to the West.

The new parties had their chance as early as December 1919 in a coalition cabinet headed by Vaida-Voevod, the Brătianu government having resigned in protest against the minorities clause of the Treaty of Trianon (Art. LX), but their tenure of office was short. General fear of Communist propaganda and the alarm of the landowners at the proposed expropriation led to the government's resignation in March 1920 and the return of a new People's Party containing many former Conservatives, led by General Averescu, hero of two wars.

He secured the able Take Ionescu as minister of foreign affairs. The general, despite personal sympathy with the peasants, had to take strong measures to restore order. A revolutionary movement was breaking out on the Dniester and securing support among Socialists and Communists in the old kingdom, and social tension reached a climax in the general strike of October 1920. The failure of the strike split the Rumanian Socialist movement. The more moderate leaders were imprisoned, and the Communists, who had kept underground, gained the upper hand. They voted for the affiliation of the Social Democratic Party with the Comintern at a congress in May 1921, whereupon 70 leaders were arrested. The Social Democrats thereafter kept separate,

1. MOLDAVIA
2. WALACHIA } original Rumanian principalities

3. BUKOVINA: from Austria–Hungary, 1918
(a) to Russia, 1940

4. TRANSYLVANIA: from Austria–Hungary, 1918

5. DOBRUJA: from Turkey, 1878;
considerable fluctuation
in southern boundary.

6. BESSARABIA: from Russia, 1918; lost, 1940

THE GROWTH OF RUMANIA, SHOWING TERRITORIAL CHANGES IN THE 19TH AND 20TH CENTURIES

and the newly formed Communist Party was outlawed in 1924.

Meanwhile Averescu had to put through the promised land reform. The bill was introduced in the spring of 1921 by the minister of agriculture, Constantin Garoflid, himself a large land-owner. After impassioned controversy, expropriation was put through on the lines agreed in July 1917, estates being limited to 500 ha. in the old kingdom, and to much smaller areas in Bessarabia and Bukovina. The peasants were not wholly satisfied; the holdings allotted were often unduly small and there was no adequate arrangement for the granting of credits for the purchase of seed and tools. (By 1934 less than 1,500,000 peasant families had been granted land, and there were still 700,000 landless peasants.)

The Liberals came to power at the beginning of 1922, remaining in office with one short break until 1928. Brătianu dominated the scene until his death in 1927 and thus had the satisfaction of being in office for the coronation of King Ferdinand as sovereign of united Rumania at Alba Iulia on Oct. 15, 1922.

A new constitution was adopted in March 1923 based on that of 1866 but with the addition of manhood suffrage. The Jews were given citizenship rights, but their inflow in large numbers after World War I provoked violent hostility. In the financial sphere the Liberal government pushed through the difficult policy of coupling industrialization with the exclusion as far as possible of foreign capital, which bore heavily on the peasants who had to pay for it by export duties. The chief cause of Liberal unpopularity, however, was the centralization of administration. All the new provinces, even including backward Bessarabia, had hoped for a measure of autonomy, and this feeling was strongest in Transylvania where bitter hostility was aroused by the arrival of officials from the old kingdom. The minorities problem was to prove troublesome to all Rumanian administrations in the years following World War I, and none succeeded in finding a solution.

Brătianu proceeded in 1926 to push through an electoral law giving great advantages to the party in power at election time. By this law those who secured 40% or more of the votes were given half the seats in the chamber, plus a share in the remainder in proportion to the number of votes obtained. When a ministry fell as a result of an adverse vote in the chamber, the king could call on the leader of the next largest party to form a cabinet and hold elections. Until 1937 no party in charge ever failed to secure the necessary 40%. The Liberal Party's popularity was slowly waning at the end of 1925, and in the face of growing discontent King Ferdinand again called on General Averescu to form a cabinet. His party, with some peasant support, secured four-fifths of the seats in the chamber in the elections of March 1926, largely because of successful pressure at the polls. Though the Liberals only had 16 deputies it was clear that the new administration governed largely with their support. Meanwhile the opposition was greatly strengthened by the fusion, in October 1926, of Maniu's National Popular Party with Mihalache's Peasant group to form the National Peasant Party, which was to represent the majority of the Rumanian people. Averescu resigned in June 1927 and Brătianu was again returned; the newly formed National Peasant Party, despite universal popularity, polled only 22% of the votes in the obviously manipulated elections.

The political situation was complicated by the dynastic position. In December 1925 Crown Prince Carol (see CAROL II) was forced to leave Rumania, renouncing all his rights in favour of his young son Michael. In view of King Ferdinand's precarious health a council of regency was formed in January 1926 consisting of the patriarch Miron Cristea, the president of the supreme court Gheorghe Buzdugan, and the king's second son, Prince Nicholas.

King Ferdinand died on July 20, 1927, and Brătianu died in November of the same year. The Liberal Party, thus weakened, was faced with an economic crisis and peasant demonstrations. The regency council in November 1928 entrusted Maniu with forming a government and holding elections: on Dec. 12, in the first and, so far, only free elections in Rumania, his National Peasant Party was returned with a majority of 349 seats out of 387. The new government abolished censorship and martial law, mitigated the police regime, promised concessions to the minorities, and in June 1929 introduced, to the great satisfaction of the Transylvanians, an administrative reform bill aiming at extensive decentralization. The peasants were helped by the repeal of the export duties; cooperatives were encouraged and free sale of land allowed, a measure which unfortunately led to an increase of the rural proletariat rather than to a consolidation of prosperous peasant holdings as had been intended. The economic situation was greatly eased by the entry, at last allowed, of foreign capital.

2. Foreign Policy, 1920–37.—Rumania's foreign policy after Trianon was necessarily based on an endeavour to maintain the *status quo* and to protect itself against aggression. Rumania was from the first a consistent member of the League of Nations, but built up a careful system of regional pacts to buttress collective security. The first such pact was concluded with Poland in March 1921, when Take Ionescu and Prince Eustachy Sapieha signed a treaty providing for mutual assistance in the event of unprovoked attack on the eastern frontier. Both countries were threatened by the U.S.S.R., which had not recognized Rumania's right to Bessarabia and seemed little satisfied with Poland's possession of its former Ukrainian and Belorussian territories.

Take Ionescu had hoped to form a Baltic-Aegean bloc to act as a buffer between Germany and the U.S.S.R., but had to be content with joining the Little Entente (*q.v.*) system. An agreement with Czechoslovakia for mutual protection against Hungary was signed in April 1921 and with Yugoslavia for similar protection against Hungary and Bulgaria in June. He sought further to cement Balkan friendships by dynastic alliances. Marriages were concluded between Crown Prince Carol and Princess Helen of Greece (March 10, 1921), between his elder sister Princess Elizabeth and the crown prince of Greece (February 1921), and between Princess Marie and King Alexander I of Yugoslavia (June 8, 1922).

General Averescu, in his 1926–27 administration, extended Rumania's system of pacts to include its "Latin sisters." A treaty of alliance and nonaggression was signed with France in June 1926 and another in September of that year with Italy. The Italians, after long hesitation, recognized the incorporation of Bessarabia in Rumania in March 1927. Relations with the U.S.S.R. remained in a state of tension; during 1924 the Soviet Union kept up continuous agitation and threats of war, even setting up a three-day Communist republic at Tătar Bunar in southern Bessarabia. A conference held in Vienna in April 1924 between Rumanian and Soviet representatives led to no results. The situation was eased when Nicolae Titulescu became foreign minister in 1927. In 1933 both countries signed the Convention of London defining the aggressor, and with the U.S.S.R.'s entry into the League in 1934 and the exchange of letters between Titulescu and Maksim Litvinov later that year it was hoped that the Bessarabian question was settled. Rumania entered into diplomatic relations with the U.S.S.R. in 1934, but the Bessarabian question remained open and was raised again by the Russians after Titulescu had been dropped from the Rumanian cabinet in 1936.

Agreement with Bulgaria, resentful at the loss of southern Dobruja to Rumania and at the inclusion of parts of Macedonia in Yugoslavia and Greece, proved out of reach; nonetheless, the Balkan Entente, concluded on Feb. 9, 1934, between Rumania, Yugoslavia, Turkey, and Greece, was left open to Bulgaria.

3. Rumania Under King Carol.—Maniu, dissatisfied with the regency, arranged for the return of Carol from exile with the agreement of all the major parties. Carol was proclaimed king on June 9, 1930, his son Michael becoming crown prince (grand voivode). Conflict soon arose between the king and Maniu, who had exacted a promise that Carol would leave his Jewish mistress Magda Lupescu abroad if he resumed the throne and would seek reconciliation with Queen Helen. On the king's breaking this promise Maniu resigned the premiership in October 1930, though his party remained in power under Gheorghe Mironescu. King Carol was from the first determined to secure absolute power and to break up the old political parties. Maniu's resignation and the world economic crisis helped to bring down the National Peasants in 1931. After Mironescu's resignation the foreign minister Titulescu attempted to form a cabinet, and on his failure the king appointed one of his own choice headed by his former tutor Nicolae Iorga. The elections of June 1931 gave the government a majority of 291 seats out of 387, but it resigned a year later. The National Peasants had a brief return to power and it fell to Vaida-Voevod to deal with the serious Communist-inspired railway strike at Grivița in February 1933, but the party, split through King Carol's intrigues, could no longer keep itself in power. The Liberal opposition was also split; the leaders Ionel Brătianu and his brother Vințila were dead and the third brother Constantin (Dinu) had not their grip over the party, while their nephew Gheorghe was on the king's side. Nevertheless the Liberals returned to power in 1933 under an anti-Carol leader Ion Duca.

4. Rise of the Iron Guard.—The king was helped in his disruption of the older parties by the rise of a new group of fascist type which was taking shape in Moldavia, feeding on endemic Rumanian anti-Semitism and the economic crisis. The leader, a young man named Corneliu Zelea-Codreanu, first called his group the Legion of the Archangel Michael; later it had many names, the best known being the Iron Guard. Priests, officers, and students flocked to Codreanu's standard; the party had a mystical appeal and its leaders wore the trappings of romance. Its slogan was the Christian and racial renovation of Rumania: in foreign affairs it opposed cooperation with France, the U.S.S.R., or the League of Nations and sympathized with Germany and Italy and later with Francisco Franco in Spain; at home it tempted the peasants with the slogan *omul și pogonul*—"one man, one acre."

The Iron Guard gained its first five seats in Parliament in 1932; its policy of violence, which had already been demonstrated by the murder of the prefect of Iași, was carried forward by the assassination of the premier Duca, on Dec. 30, 1933, a month after he had assumed office. Unlike the neighbouring Balkan states Rumania had not in modern times been prone to political murders and the country was profoundly shocked. The new Liberal premier Gheorge Tătărescu proscribed the Iron Guard, but reappearing under another name—*Totul Pentru Țara* ("everything for the country")—it succeeded in securing Titulescu's removal from the foreign ministry in August 1936.

In the 1937 elections, presided over by Tătărescu, the government for the first time failed to secure the necessary 40% of the votes. It was highly unpopular, and the opposition was unexpectedly consolidated by the conclusion of an electoral pact between the National Peasants and the Iron Guard, which led to much criticism of Maniu. The Guard secured 16% of the votes. King Carol, alarmed at this success and not wishing to have Codreanu as a rival dictator, dropped his earlier policy of covert support and called on the elderly Transylvanian poet Octavian Goga, leader of the right wing anti-Semitic National Christian Party, to form a government. After a few weeks of violent anti-Semitic action, at which the British and French ministers protested, Goga was dismissed by King Carol, who then proclaimed a personal dictatorship. A new constitution of corporative type was published on Feb. 20, 1938, and "accepted" in a plebiscite. The patriarch Miron Cristea was made premier with Tătărescu as his deputy. In April Codreanu and other guardists were sentenced to ten years' imprisonment. The Guard replied with a renewed terror campaign, and in November King Carol, returning from a post-Munich visit to the western capitals, had Codreanu and 13 of his followers "shot while trying to escape."

On Dec. 16 the king founded a monopoly party, the National Renaissance Front, to support his government, and announced certain concessions to the minorities, who accordingly joined the front. Miron Cristea, the patriarch and premier, died in March 1939 and was succeeded by Armand Călinescu, minister of the interior in the former government. Elections on a corporative basis were held in June, the electorate under the new constitution being 2,000,000 compared with 4,500,000 in 1937. The Senate was designed to include old parliamentarians, and the leading political figures, Maniu and Mihalache of the National Peasant Party and Dinu Brătianu, head of the National Liberals who disapproved of the Tătărescu faction, automatically became members. They refused, however, to take the oath to the new constitution, and

were suspended. Women could vote and, for the first time in Rumanian history, stand as candidates, but only for the Senate. The Iron Guard continued to foment unrest during the summer of 1939 with German backing and on Sept. 21 murdered Călinescu; after the brief premiership of Gen. Gheorghe Argeșanu, who was able to secure some degree of public order, Constantin Argetoianu became premier for two months and was then succeeded by Tătărescu.

5. Foreign Policy, 1938–39.—The annexation of Austria and the sacrifice of Czechoslovakia in 1938 overthrew the whole system of Rumanian foreign policy. Relations with Italy were already embittered through Rumania's adopting sanctions at the League's bidding during the Abyssinian War, and the pact with Italy had lapsed in 1936. Rumania had been ready to fulfil its obligations under the Little Entente and to come to the aid of Czechoslovakia during the Munich crisis, even secretly agreeing to allow Soviet troops to cross its territory. The Polish alliance stood, even after Munich, but Rumania refused Poland's offer of a slice of Czechoslovak territory in Ruthenia in October 1938. Confidence in the west had been shaken by Munich, and in March 1939 a trade treaty was signed with Germany designed to put the whole of Rumania's economic life at German disposal. The new foreign minister, Grigore Gafencu, made a last attempt to seek support in the west, securing a Franco-British guarantee of Rumanian territorial integrity on April 13, 1939. Rumania's only real hope, however, lay in German-Soviet antagonism, and that was shattered by the anti-Polish Ribbentrop-Molotov agreement in August.

6. World War II.—The invasion and dismemberment of Poland in September 1939 found Rumania powerless to help its ally; Rumania declared neutrality on Sept. 4. The collapse of France in the summer of 1940 removed the last prop of Rumanian morale; nonetheless, King Carol made efforts to put the Army on a war footing and announced that the country's frontiers would be defended at any cost. Under German pressure the foreign minister, Grigore Gafencu, was forced to resign and was succeeded by the strongly pro-German Ion Gigurtu. On June 21 the king agreed to turn the National Renaissance Front into a still more totalitarian national party which included Iron Guardists, under Horia Sima, released on German orders.

The first blow fell on June 27 when in agreement with Germany the U.S.S.R. occupied not only Bessarabia but northern Bukovina, which had never been in Russian possession. Rumania was forced to accept, renounced the British guarantee on July 2 and on July 4 appointed a new pro-German cabinet with Gigurtu as premier and Horia Sima as minister of culture. On July 16 Germany was "invited" to send a military mission. Hungary now had to be conciliated. In order to prevent Hungary from going to war to win back Transylvania (thereby inviting Russia into Rumania in force), Germany and Italy imposed on Rumania the conditions that came to be known as the Vienna Award. Ribbentrop and Count Ciano, the Italian foreign minister, were sent by Hitler to meet with the foreign ministers of Hungary and Rumania. On Aug. 30, at the Belvedere Palace in Vienna, it was agreed that northern Transylvania (about 16,830 sq.mi. [43,588 sq.km.]) was to be handed over to Hungary. This was an especially bitter blow to Rumanian patriotism. (When the Allied-Rumanian armistice was negotiated in 1944, the restoration of "all or the greater part" of the territory lost in 1940 was included in the agreement.)

The people wished to fight and looked for a lead to Maniu, the grand old man of Transylvania. While he hesitated the Iron Guard, despite their pro-German attitude, led the national protest and demanded the abdication of King Carol, who was made the scapegoat. The king left on Sept. 6 with Magda Lupescu, leaving his 19-year-old son, Michael, on the throne as Mihai I. Before his departure he entrusted power to a general, Ion Antonescu, who formed a government consisting largely of Iron Guardists, with Horia Sima as vice-premier. The constitution was suspended and Antonescu given full powers. Meanwhile Bulgaria, with German support, had been agitating for the return of southern Dobruja; the agreement for its cession was signed at Craiova the day after Carol's departure. Rumania lost about 3,500,000 subjects to the

U.S.S.R., 2,400,000 to Hungary, and 360,000 to Bulgaria. Germany and Italy guaranteed rump Rumania. Rumania was declared a "national legionary state" on Sept. 15 and joined the anti-Soviet Tripartite Pact on Nov. 23.

German troops had been pouring into the country since September, but as the Germans had decided to reduce Rumania to complete subservience by playing off the Iron Guard against Antonescu, the *Wehrmacht* stood by when the guardists staged a St. Bartholomew's night on Nov. 28 in which 64 prominent members of the old regime were assassinated, including Iorga and the peasant leader Virgil Madgearu. Antonescu now secured German support in putting down the Guard, which staged a more serious rising at the end of January 1941 under the leadership of Sima, vice-premier in Antonescu's cabinet, and Ion Codreanu, father of Corneliu.

The revolt was finally suppressed with about 6,000 casualties; Sima escaped. The new administration formed at the end of January was mainly military, all guardists being excluded. About 500,000 German troops were in the country by February, and on Feb. 10 Great Britain broke off diplomatic relations. Antonescu refused to join Adolf Hitler in smashing Rumania's ally Yugoslavia in April 1941, but the country was behind him in entering the war against the U.S.S.R. as Germany's ally on June 22. Great Britain declared war on Rumania on Dec. 7 and on Dec. 12 Rumania declared war on the United States.

Rumania's recovery of Bessarabia in the summer of 1941 was highly popular in the country, but the opposition leaders underground, in particular Maniu, strongly disapproved of the Army crossing the Dniester into Soviet territory in 1942 and of the organization of a new Rumanian province beyond the river known as Transnistria. The nation, however, did not become thoroughly war weary until the disastrous casualty lists came in from Stalingrad.

7. The Communist Regime.—Although Rumania had not had a parliamentary government since 1938, the chief political parties had kept their organizations intact: the National Peasants under Maniu and the Liberals under Dinu Brătianu formed a rallying point for popular discontent with the fruits of Antonescu's pro-Axis policy and undertook secret negotiations with the Allies during 1943. These parties were supported in the desire for an armistice by the pro-Soviet left, namely the Social Democrats under Constantin Titel Petrescu and the Communists under Lucreţiu Patraşcanu. In the spring of 1944 the four parties agreed to form a National Bloc to bring Rumania out of the war.

The *coup d'état* of Aug. 23, 1944, which overthrew Antonescu and brought Rumania into the war against Germany, was largely the work of King Michael himself, supported by the National Peasants and Liberals, but the Social Democrats and Communists were given representation out of proportion to their numbers in the first postarmistice administration. The armistice was signed in Moscow on Sept. 12, Soviet troops having been in occupation of Rumania since the end of August. The peace treaty subsequently provided for their remaining until after the conclusion of the Austrian treaty, a period that would ensure their presence while Rumania was being remodeled on the Soviet pattern. The Russians had prepared during the war a division of indoctrinated Rumanian prisoners named after the hero of 1821, Tudor Vladimirescu; these marched into Rumania beside the Red Army.

Internal Affairs.—Until elections could be held, three short-lived governments of a mainly military character took office, the first two headed by Gen. Constantin Sănătescu (1885–1947) and the third by the chief of staff, Nicolae Rădescu (1874–1953), an open anti-Communist. The Soviet deputy foreign minister, Andrei Vyshinski, went in person to Bucharest to insist on Rădescu's removal and the installation as premier of Petru Groza, head of a splinter left-wing party known as the Plowmen's Front which, though not forming part of the National Bloc, had been included under Soviet pressure in the last Sănătescu administration.

The Groza government, which took office in March 1945, excluded the National Peasants and the Liberals and proved highly unpopular. In August of that year the Potsdam Conference of U.S., British, and Soviet leaders proposed the resumption of diplomatic relations with Rumania provided that the government was "recognized and democratic." The U.S.S.R. immediately resumed relations, but Great Britain and the United States refrained on the ground of the unrepresentative nature of the administration. King Michael then appealed to the three powers, which, meeting in Moscow in December 1945, advised that a government, broadened by the inclusion of a National Peasant and a Liberal member, should hold elections. (Antonescu was shot as a war criminal in 1946.)

The 1923 constitution had been restored after the armistice, but before the elections a law was passed abolishing the Senate. The government bloc announced that it had polled 71% of the votes in the elections held on Nov. 19, 1946. The Communists secured the key portfolios in the new government, excepting that of foreign affairs (which was given to Tătărescu), and split the Social Democrats, the bulk of the party remaining aloof under its leader Petrescu, who was later imprisoned. The elections were followed by a wave of arrests of former leaders and their supporters, including Maniu, Brătianu, and Petrescu. The National Peasant Party, which had the allegiance of the majority of Rumanians, was declared illegal in August 1947, and Maniu himself was tried and condemned to life imprisonment on Nov. 11; he died in prison in 1953. Evidence given at his trial was used as a pretext for removing Tătărescu from the ministry of foreign affairs, Ana Pauker, Moscow-trained, taking his place.

In December 1947 King Michael was forced to abdicate. In February 1948 the remnant of the Social Democrats under Lothar Radaceanu (d. 1955) merged with the Communists to form the Rumanian Workers' Party (Partidul Muncitoresc Român), which, together with the Plowmen's Front and the Hungarian People's Union, presented a single list as a People's Democratic Front in the ensuing elections. The front claimed 405 out of 414 seats in the Grand National Assembly elected on March 28, 1948. A constitution of Soviet type was adopted in April and the Rumanian People's Republic proclaimed, with Constantin Parhon as first president. The Communist Party purged itself by 18% during 1949; by the middle of 1950, after the admission of new members, the total membership was put at 720,000. The wartime Communist leader Lucreţiu Patraşcanu, dismissed from the ministry of justice and arrested in February 1948, was tried and executed in 1954. In May 1952 three leading Communist ministers, among them Ana Pauker, were purged. Gheorghe Gheorghiu-Dej then became premier, Groza retiring to the presidency vacated by Parhon.

A revised constitution, still closer to that of the U.S.S.R., was adopted on Sept. 24, 1952, and a new assembly elected on November 30. When Groza died in January 1958 he was succeeded by Ion Gheorghe Maurer. On Oct. 3, 1955, Gheorghiu-Dej abandoned the premiership to Chivu Stoica, himself reverting to the first secretaryship of the Rumanian Workers' Party. In March 1961 the National Assembly elected a State Council, a new organ of supreme administration to replace the former Presidium. Gheorghiu-Dej was made president of the council, while retaining his key party post. Maurer became premier in place of Stoica, who became a secretary of the Central Committee of the party. Gheorghiu-Dej died on March 19, 1965; he was succeeded as first secretary of the party by Nicolae Ceauşescu and as president of the State Council by Stoica.

A new Grand National Assembly was elected in March 1965 (only one candidate stood in each constituency). On Aug. 21 accepted a new constitution, which the congress of the Rumanian Communist (formerly Workers') Party had approved in July. In December 1967, on Ceauşescu's suggestion and with Stoica's prompt acquiescence, the assembly agreed that the presidency of the State Council should be combined with the first secretaryship of the Communist Party, in Ceauşescu's hands.

Foreign Policy.—By the peace treaty, ratified on Sept. 15, 1947, the cession of Bessarabia and northern Bukovina to the U.S.S.R. and of southern Dobruja to Bulgaria was confirmed; in exchange northern Transylvania was restored to Rumania by Hungary.

A treaty of friendship, collaboration, and mutual assistance was signed with the U.S.S.R. on Feb. 4, 1948, and Rumania later entered into the network of alliances of similar people's republics. In January 1949 Rumania became one of the members of the Council for Mutual Economic Assistance (Comecon) founded in Moscow. On May 14, 1955, in Warsaw, Rumania joined a treaty of mutual assistance concluded by the U.S.S.R. with its seven European satellite states.

Long docile to the U.S.S.R., Rumania took a more defiant line in 1963. Gheorghiu-Dej refused to follow the Soviet example in relations with Communist China or to commit Rumania to overall plans for the Comecon area. In the same spirit Ceauşescu, in May 1966, claimed that the Rumanian Communist Party was continuing the historic struggle waged by the Rumanian people for complete national independence. Symptomatic also were Rumania's friendly relations with France and, in January 1967, its opening of full diplomatic relations with the German Federal Republic.

(B. BR.; X.)

V. POPULATION, ADMINISTRATION, AND SOCIAL CONDITIONS

1. Population.—The population of Rumania has fluctuated with the changes in the extent of the state. In 1914 it was 7,600,-000. In 1939, before the losses of territory to Hungary, Bulgaria, and the Soviet Union, total population was estimated to have been 19,930,000. The 1948 census, reflecting the eventual peace settlement, with Bessarabia and northern Bukovina remaining in Soviet possession and southern Dobruja in Bulgarian, gave a total of 15,872,624. The 1956 census recorded 17,489,450 and the 1966 census total was 19,105,056. The birthrate is fairly high, 15.7 per 1,000 (1963), and the rate of population increase rapid.

Population is very unevenly distributed. The greatest densities occur in Muntenia, which includes Bucharest, and in Transylvania; the areas of sparsest population are in the mountains.

The population is predominantly rural, and the 1956 census showed only 31.3% of the total population living in urban centres. Rumania is still essentially a country of peasants. The administrative regions (*regiuni*) of Rumania, with their area and population, are given in the table.

Area and Population of Rumania

Region	Area (sq.mi.)	Population (1963 est.)	Density (per sq.mi.)
Argeş	6,100	1,189,395	195.0
Bacău	5,174	1,103,964	213.4
Banat	8,417	1,241,832	147.5
Braşov	5,826	1,062,481	182.4
Bucureşti	7,907	1,681,599	212.7
Cluj	6,494	1,217,401	187.5
Crişana	4,726	873,393	184.8
Dobruja	5,969	517,016	86.6
Galaţi	4,984	1,065,646	213.8
Hunedoara	4,247	656,452	154.6
Iaşi	4,286	1,052,378	245.5
Maramureş	4,054	782,127	192.9
Mureş (Magyar Autonomous Region)	4,730	814,632	172.2
Oltenia	7,838	1,570,574	200.4
Ploeşti	5,058	1,460,693	288.8
Suceava	5,309	1,002,883	188.9
Bucharest (city)	735	1,366,794	1,859.6
Constanţa (city)	205	153,871	750.6
Total	91,699	18,813,131	205.2

The capital and largest city is Bucharest (pop. [1963] 1,366,-794), followed by Cluj (166,428), Constanţa (153,871), Timişoara (150,257), Braşov (133,532), Ploeşti (131,379), Iaşi (126,-865), and Brăila (119,466). The urban population has increased sharply since World War II.

2. Constitution.—The 1965 constitution describes Rumania as a "socialist, sovereign, independent, and unitary state of the working people of the towns and villages." It states that in the republic "the leading political force of the whole society is the Rumanian Communist Party." It adds:

The Socialist Republic of Rumania maintains and develops relations of friendship and fraternal collaboration with the socialist countries, promotes relations of collaboration with countries having other sociopolitical systems, and acts in international organizations with a view to ensuring peace and understanding among the peoples. The foreign relations of the Socialist Republic of Rumania are based on the principles of observance of sovereignty and national independence, equal rights and mutual advantage, non-interference in internal affairs.

The constitution ensures to non-Rumanian nationalities "the free utilization of their native language as well as books, papers, magazines, theatres, and education at all levels in their own language." In districts where non-Rumanian nationalities are in the majority, "all the bodies and institutions use the language of the respective nationality in speech and in writing." "Anybody is free to share or not to share a religious belief," but "the school is separated from the church."

The Rumanian people are the "sovereign holder of power" and they exercise this power through the Grand National Assembly consisting of 465 deputies, elected in single-member constituencies, with only one official candidate, for a term of four years. All citizens who have reached the age of 18 years have the right to vote; those who have reached the age of 23 can be elected. The Grand National Assembly elects the State Council, the Council of Ministers, the Supreme Court, and the Procurator General. The State Council is "the supreme body of state power with a permanent activity." It exercises the legislative power in the interval between the cessions of the Grand National Assembly. The latter, or—in case of emergency—the State Council, declares war. According to the Art. XLIII:

War can be declared only in case of armed aggression directed against the Socialist Republic of Rumania, or against another state toward which the Socialist Republic of Rumania has mutual defense obligations arising from international treaties, if a situation has come about for which obligation to declare war has been laid down.

3. Government and the Party.—The actual government of Rumania is in two parts, the formal part described above, and that of the Rumanian Communist Party which in its organization parallels the constitution, checking and controlling its operation. The RCP is "the highest form of organization of the working class, its vanguard detachment"; it "serves the vital interests and hopes of the people"; it bases its activity "on the Marxist-Leninist teaching, applying it creatively to the specific conditions and particularities" of Rumania. The supreme body of RCP is the party congress meeting every four years and electing the Central Committee of 121 members. The Central Committee "guides the entire activity of the party in the interval between congresses"; it elects the Political Bureau, the General Secretary, and the Secretariat. "Leadership of party activity is ensured between plenary meetings by the Political Bureau," states Art. XXII of the new rules. The latter is the real policy-making body in the country.

Local Government.—For purposes of local government Rumania is divided into 16 regions (*regiuni*) and two cities, Bucharest and Constanţa, which are independent of the regions. These are subdivided into 199 counties (*raione*), which in turn are subdivided into a large number of communes. This hierarchy of local government areas is highly centralized, and provides for the downward flow of directives from the central organs of state and party to the local communities. For each administrative unit there is a People's Council with its executive officers, elected for a period of two years. The voting for the People's Councils is by adult suffrage, except that former landowners and capitalists are denied the vote. The resulting councils are made up very heavily of the top echelons of the local Communist Party members.

4. Social Conditions.—Before World War II Rumania had been a predominantly agricultural state, with about 80% of its population living in rural areas. Under such conditions it had proved difficult to organize trade unions. They were small and relatively weak, and their success in improving working conditions had not been great when World War II began. Communists infiltrated the unions to only a small degree. In 1944, the unions were reorganized. Their former Social Democratic members were excluded on account of their alleged collaboration with King Carol, and leadership within the unions quickly centred upon the Communists. Betterment of working conditions and the improvement of the lot of the working class is the policy put forward by the unions. This is now theoretically the preoccupation of the government, which claims in the fullest degree to represent the interests of the proletariat. The function of the unions has now become that of intermediary between the party and the workers; they exist to stimulate the workers and urge upon them greater efforts to implement the national plans. With the different func-

EASTFOTO

VIEW OF RUMANIAN PEOPLE'S REPUBLIC SQUARE, BUCHAREST, SHOWING PALACE HALL AT LEFT AND STATE-FINANCED HOUSING AT RIGHT

7. Defense.—The peace treaty between the Allies and Rumania (1942) permitted Rumania to maintain an army of 120,000 men, a small artillery force, an air force of 150 planes, and a navy with an overall tonnage of 15,000 tons. These limitations were soon ignored, under the protection of the Soviet Union, and the Rumanian Army in 1962 consisted of about 200,000 men, with 100,-000 more in para-military organizations such as militia and security police. The Navy, though larger than the limits permitted under the treaty, is made up of small and rather old craft, including three destroyers and ten submarines. The Black Sea naval base is Constanța. There is a Danube flotilla of small military craft, based on Brăila. The Air Force is probably more than twice the permitted size and may have 350 military aircraft; it was reorganized under Soviet supervision and reequipped largely with Soviet planes.

tion has come a change in organization. Unions are organized, not by craft or profession, but by region and area. Union members pay their union small dues, generally 1.5% of their earnings. In return it is claimed that they enjoy priorities in the social benefits, such as hospitalization, vacations, and housing, which are dispensed by the state.

Rumania is a welfare state, in that the state itself claims to furnish all social services required by the people. Doctors are employed and paid by the state, and hospitals and health services are run by the state. The people receive medical attention free of payment. All schooling is provided by the state. Public utilities are also in the hands of the state, which is extending such facilities as rural electrification, piped water supplies, and sewage.

5. Justice.—Justice is administered by the Supreme Court, by 16 regional courts and by people's courts at the *raion* level. The courts serving the larger geographical areas serve as courts of appeal from the lower and more local courts, and the Supreme Court, whose judges are chosen by the Grand National Assembly, has a general oversight of the whole judicial system. Most cases are heard by a judge and two people's assessors, but appeals to a higher court are normally heard by three judges. No use is made of a jury. The chief judicial officer of the state is the procurator-general, who is appointed by the Grand National Assembly and is a member of both the Presidium and the Council of Ministers. He combines the roles of attorney general and public prosecutor; he is described as the "defender of socialist legality," which means that it is incumbent upon him to see that every end is consistent with the policies of the state.

6. Education.—The Communists paid a great deal of attention to the problem of providing adequate elementary education for the Rumanian people. Political instruction became compulsory at each educational stage. Education was made completely secular in 1948, with the abolition of private schools, of religious instruction in school hours, and of all the religious orders.

The present educational system consists of kindergartens for children of from three to seven years, primary schools, secondary schools, and centres of technical and higher education. Primary education is both free and compulsory for eight years. At the secondary level students are divided according to their aptitudes between lyceums, normal or pedagogical schools, and technical schools. Fees are payable by students in secondary schools, but scholarships often relieve this burden in poorer families. The greatest emphasis has been placed by the government on the development of the technical schools, in order to train the technicians required by the expanding industry. Colleges of engineering have been established at Bucharest, Timișoara, Craiova, and Iași.

The higher education system is made up of four universities, at Bucharest, Iași, Cluj, and Timișoara, and a number of technical institutes and schools of music, art, and drama. An important part is also played by the Rumanian People's Republic Academy of Sciences. This is organized in departments and has branches at Iași and Cluj, a large number of institutes and research centres, observatories and experimental stations, and a network of libraries.

marines. The Black Sea naval base is Constanța. There is a Danube flotilla of small military craft, based on Brăila. The Air Force is probably more than twice the permitted size and may have 350 military aircraft; it was reorganized under Soviet supervision and reequipped largely with Soviet planes.

VI. THE ECONOMY

Rumania is one of the less-developed European countries, primarily because of its exposure to invasion and its record of unstable internal politics. The country failed during the 20th century to attract adequate investment capital, and during the 1930s came to be attached to the German economy very largely in the role of supplier of unprocessed farm products. Nevertheless, Rumania has very extensive natural resources. During World War II the oil and grain surpluses were of supreme importance to Germany. Afterward Germany's position was taken by the U.S.S.R., and Rumanian mineral production and industries were at that country's disposal. The Soviet Union took over most foreign assets in Rumania, and special Soviet-Rumanian joint-stock companies, controlled by the Soviet Union, were set up to exploit these assets. In 1954 an agreement was reached for the "sale and transfer" to Rumania of the Soviet share in 12 of these joint companies, and the others, including the petroleum company, came under exclusively Rumanian direction later.

In 1949 Rumania joined the Council of Mutual Economic Assistance. The resulting trade agreements, as well as the two five-year plans (1951–55 and 1956–60) and the overlapping six-year plan (1960–65), contributed to the more rapid expansion of the economy, which became more closely integrated with the economies of the Soviet Union and other Communist countries.

In its internal development Rumania followed the Soviet pattern. The land reform of 1945 prepared the way for the collectivization of agriculture, which started in 1949. After 1947 privately owned industry and privately operated commerce and finance, as well as western types of trade unions, were gradually destroyed. In 1948 all subsoil rights were nationalized, together with all remaining industrial, banking, insurance, mining, transport, and telecommunication undertakings. This was immediately followed by the establishment of a Supreme State Planning Commission and the reorganization of the existing industrial boards into state industrial centres charged with preparing plans for each industrial group. The work of these groups culminated in the publication of the first five-year plan for capital investment and for the increase of all branches of production. The results of this early planned development were seen in the continued scarcity of food and other consumer goods and the failure of working and living conditions to improve. The second five-year plan saw a considerable increase of industrial production and an improvement of living standards. This process continued during the six-year plan.

A. Production

1. Agriculture.—About four-fifths of the labour force of Rumania was engaged in agriculture and forestry before World War

II, and the proportion still exceeded two-thirds in the early 1960s. The farming areas fall into several natural regions: (1) the Carpathian Mountains are given over mainly to forestry, but are noted for the old-established summer pastures—the *plaiu*—above the timber line. These mountain sheep pastures are the basis of the home wool production which is adequate for the manufacture of the peasants' coarse woolen garments. The Carpathian settlements are of the characteristic line type, often strung out for five or six miles along the valleys; the houses have high-pitched roofs and thick carved beams; (2) Transylvania, an upland, hilly country with forest and a harsh climate, has mixed farming, producing oats, rye, and much cattle and other livestock; (3) the piedmont zone of Banat and Crişana are more akin to the Hungarian plains, Banat producing large quantities of feeding grain for its pigs; (4) the Carpathian foothill zone in Moldavia and Walachia is a verdant country with mixed farming, vineyards, orchards, groves of walnut trees, and market gardens; (5) the Moldavian and Walachian plains slope gradually down to the Danube, and are steppe-like and in part even semiarid. This is the region of concentrated settlement, of extensive farming, of occasional famine and outbreaks of pellagra, of large-scale wheat production, maize (corn), sunflower, rape, soybean, tobacco, cotton, and hemp. The largest areas of oilseed and industrial fibre production were lost when Bessarabia was annexed by the U.S.S.R.; (6) the Danube floodplain produces a certain amount of rice. The lower Danube, in the shallows and lagoons below Giurgiu and in the delta itself, has an important fishing industry, specializing in carp, crayfish, sturgeon, and the black caviar from sturgeon.

Of the total area devoted to agriculture, about two-thirds is arable land and the rest, apart from a relatively small acreage of vineyards and orchards, consists of meadow and pasture.

Land Reform.—By the late 19th century an acute agrarian problem had been produced by the rapid growth of the population, the survival of a feudal system of land tenure, and the failure to develop manufacturing industries. After their emancipation in 1864, the peasants were granted from time to time allotments from crown lands, but these never satisfied the general land hunger. Distribution was equally unsatisfactory in the case of Bessarabia under the Russian Empire and Transylvania under the Austro-Hungarian Empire, but the Bukovinan peasants had been more fortunate in obtaining possession of a considerable share of the land. In 1920 an expropriation law was passed for Bessarabia, which was rapidly followed by similar laws for the old kingdom (1921) and for Transylvania and Bukovina (also 1921), whereby provision was made for the total expropriation of absentee landlords, foreigners, and mortmain estates, and for partial expropriation of large landed properties. By 1927 about 16,500 estates totaling more than 14,825,000 ac. (6,000,000 ha.) had been broken up. Of this land reserve, about 8,400,000 ac. (3,400,000 ha.) had been handed to 1,370,000 poor or landless peasants, but nearly 600,000 peasants were still without land.

Under the Communist regime, two further land reform acts were passed, one in 1945 expropriating private properties in excess of 123 ac. (50 ha.) and the properties of certain categories of individuals, such as Germans and war criminals, and one in 1949 confiscating the remaining property of 15,000 larger landowners. The 1945 act was followed by the distribution of land to the landless and the poorer small landholders; but the whole aim of the Com-

munist reforms was to replace the old system not by peasant ownership but by collective farming. The liquidation of the kulak (*chiabur* in Rumanian), or larger peasant farmer, accompanied the development of collective farms. The large estates of the past and the small peasant holdings still in existence were gradually converted into large collective farms and state farms.

During the 1950s collectivization was pushed ahead rapidly. By the mid-1960s it accounted for about four-fifths of the total cropland, and in many regions agriculture was wholly collectivized. State farms, almost completely mechanized, accounted for less than one-eighth of the cropland, but it was claimed that they produced more than one-third of the wheat and about one-fifth of the meat and milk. In all, the socialist sector contributed more than nine-tenths of the wheat, rye, maize, and sunflower (a source of edible oil) and almost all the sugar-beet crop.

Crops.—Rumanian farming is dominated by grain crops—mostly maize and wheat, which between them cover about three-quarters of the cropland, but also barley, oats, rye, and rice. Vines are grown in most parts of the country, except above about 1,600 ft. (500 m.), and the area of vineyards is the ninth largest in the world. After World War II the yields of certain crops, especially sugar beet and sunflower, were greatly increased. In 1960 it was claimed that the collective farms yielded about 60% more wheat and maize per hectare than private farms, which, however, tended to be on poorer-quality land and to receive a less favourable supply of fertilizer. The use of fertilizer increased by about 30 times during the second half of the 1950s.

Another factor in the improvement of yields has been the greater use of machinery, made possible by the simultaneous development of manufacturing industry. In the mid-1960s there were about 250 machine and tractor stations supplying the collectives. In the socialist sector there were said to be about 57,500 conventional tractors, about 54,000 seeding machines (seed drills), and nearly as many cultivators. The state farms provide other sectors of agriculture with selected seed, young vines and fruit trees, and pedigree livestock.

Livestock.—After World War II improvements were effected in the number and quality of livestock. Model farms specializing in cattle breeding were set up, and between 1938 and the mid-1960s the total number of beef and dairy cattle had increased by one-fifth to about 4,700,000. In the same period the number of pigs increased from about 2,750,000 to 4,600,000. Increases were also registered in the numbers of sheep and poultry, and in the output of meat, milk, eggs, and wool.

JERRY COOKE—PHOTO RESEARCHERS, INC.

CATTLE PASSING THROUGH THE VILLAGE OF AURIG, NEAR BRAŞOV

2. Forestry.—Forestry has long been one of the most important branches of the economy, and more than one-quarter of the country, including most of the Carpathians, is forested. Lumber is traditionally floated down the mountain rivers to be marketed in the surrounding plains. Between the two world wars, however, exploitation was often not accompanied by replanting. After 1948 the government reafforested about 1,500,000 ac. (600,000 ha.) and reorganized the timber and woodworking industries. Small mills were merged into more economic undertakings, and badly sited ones were closed. New wood-using factories were built, and by the mid-1960s furniture-making capacity had increased by two-fifths and plywood capacity by nearly one-third. A far more efficient use of the timber was also achieved.

3. Mining.—Rumania has a very varied endowment in 'minerals, but reserves are large only in the case of petroleum. The oil-bearing strata are found in a crescent-shaped belt running along the edge of the Carpathian foothills in Muntenia and Moldavia. Even before oil became the leading industry this belt was one of the most populous in Rumania, and the peasants provided seasonal labour for the oil producers. The chief producing regions are Bacău and Buzău, and the Prahova and Dîmbovița valleys. Most of the refineries are situated near Ploești, from which pipelines go to Constanța and to Reni, U.S.S.R. The last-named was the former pipeline Ploești-Giurgiu, dismantled and rebuilt by the Russians after World War II.

It was not until 1854 that the extraction of petroleum began on a commercial scale. Production increased steadily, except during World War I, until a peak of 8,700,000 tons (3.5% of world production) was reached in 1936. Lack of technical skill and equipment, together with heavy wartime bomb damage, held up production after World War II. Between the end of World War II and the mid-1960s the production of crude oil increased more than threefold to about 12,000,000 metric tons annually. All the crude oil produced is now refined in Rumania.

Rumania also possesses the largest source of natural gas in Europe, with an average annual production in the mid-1960s of more than 12,000,000,000 cu.m. This methane gas, found near Mediaș, Copșa Mică, and Sărmășel in the Transylvanian Basin, as well as along the Carpathian foothills, is widely used for lighting and heating purposes, and has become an important basis for the chemical industry.

Rumania has no large resources of coal and iron. The most important coalfield, producing anthracite and lignite, centres on Petroșani and Lupeni in the upper Jiu Valley of the southern Transylvanian Alps. At Lupeni there are also plants for the processing of coal. Relatively small reserves of hard coal, some of which is suitable for coking, are found toward the western end of the Transylvanian Alps in the Anina-Reșița area of Banat. Other fields of brown coal are found in the foothills in Muntenia (Filipești), Transylvania, and Moldavia (Comănești). As a result of reopening and reequipping several old mines and sinking many new ones, brown coal production had been increased from less than 3,000,000 tons in 1938 to about 10,000,000 tons annually in the early 1960s.

There are small deposits of iron ore, mainly limonite and siderite, in the vicinity of the metallurgical centres of Reșița and Hunedoara, but large deposits were discovered in Dobruja after World War II, though they do not appear to be worked. Gold is found in the Maramureș region, where pyrites, sphalerite, and galena are also obtained. There are extensive deposits of bauxite in the Munții Apuseni (western Transylvania), and salt mines in the Carpathian foothills.

4. Power.—Before 1950 the consumption of electricity was small and large areas had no supply. A ten-year program of electrification was then introduced. New thermal power stations were built (e.g., at Doicești and Borzești) and at the same time use was made of the swift mountain streams by the construction of hydroelectric stations. By the early 1960s the installed capacity of Rumanian power stations exceeded 1,860,000 kw. and production was more than nine times that generated in 1938. The ancillary construction of transformers and cables had made great progress, and prospects were opening up for rural electrification and the introduction of district heating plants.

5. Manufacturing Industries.—The small industrial potential of Rumania was greatly diminished by World War II and its aftermath, but nationalization was followed by planned expansion. Between 1948 and 1955 more than 100 new industrial undertakings were built, and 200 more were rebuilt and expanded. Thereafter the rate of growth was even faster. Between 1948 and 1960 industrial production increased at an average annual rate of more than 16%. Overall it increased fivefold between 1938 and 1960.

In the course of this industrial growth the balance was tipped away from consumer goods, which in 1938 made up more than half of production, to capital goods, which in the mid-1960s accounted for more than three-fifths. Compared with 1938, production had increased by two or three times in the case of paper and also cotton, woolen, and silk fabrics, by four times for rolled steel goods, by six times for cement and steel, by eight times for pig iron, and tenfold for metallurgical coke. Virtually new products included: plastics and synthetic fibres; trucks, tractors, and other vehicles; electrical generators, transformers, and other equipment; fertilizers and dyes; and farm machinery.

Iron and Steel Industry.—This was the object of particular attention. The largest plant, at Hunedoara, was modernized and extended, and the number of blast furnaces increased; new steelworks, a rolling mill, and a battery of modern coke ovens were also added. Another integrated iron and steel plant was built at nearby Reșița, and a tube mill at Roman. The capacity of the smaller steel mills at Oțelu Roșu, Călan, and Cîmpia Turzii was increased, and a sheet mill built at Galați. In the early 1960s more than half the pig iron and seven-tenths of the steel was from plants erected since 1950. The new production of special and alloy steels would be greatly increased with the completion of the new Galați combine. During the 1960s as a whole it was expected that total steel production would be trebled to 4,000,000 metric tons annually.

Engineering.—Before World War II Rumania imported almost all its machines and equipment, but most domestic needs are now satisfied at home, and in some categories there is a surplus for export to other Communist countries. The engineering industry produces technically advanced kinds of oil-drilling and mining equipment, tractors, lathes, turbines, electrical apparatus, and river craft. Between 1938 and the mid-1960s the production of machinery and industrial equipment increased more than tenfold.

Chemicals.—Before World War II the chemical industry was very small. After 1948, however, fertilizer works were opened at Valea Călugăreasa, Roznov, and Făgăraș, and factories for sodium products at Govora and Borzești, and for synthetic fibres and plastics at Săvinești. Production of chemicals increased tenfold between 1938 and the mid-1960s.

Consumer Goods.—These did not keep pace with the capital goods industries. Nevertheless, by the mid-1960s the food, clothing, and light industries had in general expanded at least twofold since World War II. Ceramic and tile works and the factories making textiles, ready-made clothing, leather work, footwear, and metal consumer goods had all been extended. Two sugar refineries had been built near Cluj and Suceava, the number of food canneries increased, and a large mechanized dairy set up in Bucharest.

B. TRADE AND FINANCE

1. Foreign Trade.—Foreign commerce is completely under state control, and is carried on by bilateral agreements with other governments. In the early 1960s about two-thirds of Rumania's exports went to other Communist countries, more than two-fifths going to the Soviet Union. Imports showed a similar pattern.

Exports consist primarily of lumber and wood products, grain and other vegetable products, cement, and petroleum, but Rumania also exports an increasing volume of factory goods, including complete thermal power plants, oil refinery equipment, small ships, tractors, and a wide range of machinery. The composition of the import trade has changed from primarily finished factory goods to raw materials and semimanufactures, including iron ore, coal, and certain types of machinery.

2. Currency and Banking.

During the 1930s the financial situation was dominated by the sharp drop in world agricultural prices, and by 1935 the foreign debt had risen to four-fifths of the total national debt. A further deterioration was caused by general rearmament in the late 1930s. After 1945, and before reparations payments to the U.S.S.R. were reduced, there was serious inflation. Two currency reforms ensued, the first in August 1947 when 20,-000 old units were made exchangeable for one new leu, and the second in January 1952 when one new leu was exchanged for 37 old ones and the Rumanian currency was pegged officially to the Soviet ruble. In 1954 the exchange rates were fixed at 1.50 lei to the ruble, 6 lei to the U.S. dollar and 16.80 lei to the pound sterling, but in 1957 a highly preferential rate was introduced for tourists and business visitors.

Foreign indebtedness, estimated at more than £100,000,000 in the mid-1960s, consists mainly of obligations incurred before World War II. An agreement signed in 1960 provided for repayment in annual installments.

Most Rumanian banks were dissolved in August 1948, and shortly afterward the National Bank of Rumania (founded 1880) was transformed into the Bank of the Rumanian People's Republic. There are also a bank of investments, an agricultural bank, and a savings bank, all owned by the state.

3. National Finance.

In the 1960s the state's revenue slightly exceeded expenditure. The state's income is derived mainly from the operation of the socialized industries. In the mid-1960s, this sector provided rather more than 90% of total income, while direct taxes provided the rest. The budgetary allocation to the social services, including education, social insurance, medical care, housing, and organized vacations, has been gradually increased.

C. TRANSPORT AND COMMUNICATIONS

1. Before 1950.—Compared with those of Western Europe, transport and communication standards are low. Up to 1950 political and economic conditions prevented a great development of roads and railways. The former were few indeed, and the ox-cart and unmetaled roads were a more familiar sight than the motorcar and surfaced highway. Most railways were single-track, with the exception of certain sections of the Orient Express route, notably from Bucharest to Braşov, and parts of the Bucharest-Brăila line.

During World War II the Germans attempted to improve certain road and rail communications so that Rumanian resources would be more easily accessible, to relieve congestion at the bigger centres on the Danube by enlarging facilities at minor ports, and to aid the flow of military traffic across the Danube into Bulgaria. After 1945 similar operations were undertaken with the difference that trade was now directed mainly toward the other Communist countries. The new railways were extended into the Jiu coalfield and into the forests of the Moldavian Carpathians.

2. Modernization.—Under the two five-year plans (1951–60) steps were taken to develop the transport capacity of the country and to utilize transport equipment more efficiently. Larger-capacity freight cars, trucks, tankers, and buses were manufactured. By the mid-1960s the movement of freight within Rumania had increased threefold since 1938, while that of passengers had risen even more. The mileage of double-tracked railway lines was still only a very small fraction of the total, however.

In the mid-1960s the mileage of roads suitable for modern traffic was double that at the end of the war. Since 1948 the proportion of all freight carried by road had risen from 3 to about 25%. However, less than half the mileage of national roads was modernized.

3. Inland Waterways and Ports.—The Danube is navigable throughout its length in Rumania, but there are two distinct sectors for traffic: seagoing vessels of 2,000–3,000 tons go upstream as far as Brăila and Galaţi, and river vessels ply on the rest. Heavy-draft shipping does not enter the Danube but docks at Constanţa, as the Sulina bar needs constant dredging to maintain a depth of water of 22–23 ft. (6.7 to 7.0 m.). In the Iron Gate gorge, between Turnu Severin and Orşova, specially skilled pilots and

EASTFOTO

VIEW OF THE HARBOUR AT CONSTANŢA

smaller tows of barges are required to navigate the reefs and rapids, but below Calafat the current is slight. Ice blocks the river during three winters out of every four, the blockage lasting sometimes from mid-December to March. Occasionally late summer droughts close the Danube for a period in the autumn.

The Danube has a steep bank on the Bulgarian side but on the left bank below the Iron Gate gorge the floodplain is several miles wide. The railway bridge carrying the Bucharest-Constanţa line across the Danube at Cernavodă is $7\frac{1}{3}$ mi. (11.8 km.) in length. A new road and railway bridge, between Giurgiu and Ruse, Bulg., was inaugurated in 1954. Another project, the Danube-Black Sea Canal, first publicized in 1949, was reported to have been begun soon after but in 1953 was abandoned.

The volume of waterborne traffic remained small for a few years after World War II but increased subsequently with the development of trade between the Communist countries. The goods carried consist mainly of Soviet iron ore destined for Czechoslovakia, together with Hungarian bauxite and Rumanian timber, oil, and cement for the U.S.S.R. The ports have tended to specialize according to their hinterland and harbour facilities. Thus Constanţa is the chief oil port, Brăila is the chief grain port, and Galaţi, besides being the main port of entry and principal naval base, handles most of the timber which is floated down the Siretul or comes by rail from Bukovina and Moldavia. The chief ports, including the seaport of Constanţa and the river ports of Galaţi and Brăila, have been extended and partially reequipped.

4. Air Transport.—A modern airport has been built at Băneasa, near Bucharest, and airports in other parts of the country have been built or improved. International airlines connect Rumania with the other Communist countries, as well as with many countries of western Europe. All internal air services are operated by TAROM (Transporturi Aeriene Romîne), the state-owned airline.

5. Postal Services and Telecommunications.—These have since their establishment been under governmental control. Postal services reach into all parts of the country, and have been greatly extended, with the creation of 2,400 new post offices, since World War II. The amount of mail handled increased about seven-fold between 1948 and the 1960s. The telephone and telegraphic services have also been greatly extended. In the mid-1960s there were about 347,500 private telephones, approximately one to every 55 persons. Telephone communication has not yet penetrated the remoter areas of the country. Telephones and telegraphic services are operated by the post office.

There are 19 radio stations, all operated by the government. In the mid-1960s there were about 2,400,000 radio receivers, or about one to every eight persons. At the same time there was only one television set to each 125 persons.

See also references under "Rumania" in the Index.

(N. J. G. P.)

BIBLIOGRAPHY.—*Geography and General:* E. Pittard, *La Roumanie* (1917); F. Pax, *Pflanzengeographie von Rumänien* (1920); M. Constantinesco, *L'Evolution de la propriété rurale . . . en Roumanie* (1925); E. de Martonne, "La Roumanie," *Géographie universelle*, vol. 4, *L'Europe centrale* (1930); G. Alexiano and M. Antonesco, *Roumanie* (1933); K. Hielscher, *Rumänien* (1933); H. J. Fleure and R. A. Pelham (eds.), *Eastern Carpathian Studies: Roumania* (1936); S. Sitwell, *Roumanian Journey* (1938); C. Cormos, *Rumania* (1944); S. Fischer-Galati, *Romania* (1957); *Monografia Geografica a Republicii Populare Romîne* (Bucharest 1960).

Archaeology and History: E. Condurachi, *L'Archéologie roumaine au XXe siècle* (1963); E. de Hurmuzaki, *Documente privitoare la Istoria Românilor* (1876 et seq.); N. Iorga, *Geschichte des rumänischen Volkes*, 2 vol. (1905); N. Iorga and G. Bals, *Histoire de l'art roumain ancien* (1922); V. Pârvan, *Țara Noastra* (1934); N. Iorga, *A History of Roumania*, English trans. by J. McCabe (1925); A. D. Xenopol, *Istoria Românilor din Dacia Traiană*, 3rd ed., 14 vol. (1925–30); abridged French trans., *Histoires des Roumains*, 2 vol. (1896); G. G. Rommenhoeller, *La Grande Roumaine* (1926); V. Pârvan, *Dacia* (1928); C. U. Clark, *United Roumania* (1932); T. W. Riker, *The Making of Roumania, 1855–1866* (1931); R. W. Seton-Watson, *History of the Roumanians; from Roman Times to the Completion of Unity* (1934); J. Clark (ed.), *Politics and Political Parties in Roumania* (1936); P. Pavel, *Why Rumania Failed* (1944); R. H. Markham, *Rumania Under the Soviet Yoke* (1949); A. S. G. Lee, *Crown Against Sickle; the Story of King Michael of Rumania* (1950); H. Prost, *Destinée de la Roumanie* (1954); S. D. Spector, *Rumania at the Paris Peace Conference* (1962); G. Ionescu, *Communism in Rumania, 1944–1962* (1964).

Economy: D. Mitrany, *The Land and the Peasant in Rumania* (1930); N. Moricz, *The Fate of the Transylvania Soil* (1934); S. Mehedinți, *Le Pays et le peuple roumain* (1937); Royal Institute of International Affairs, *South-Eastern Europe: a Political and Economic Survey* (1939); N. St. Predescu, *Die Wirtschaftsstruktur Rumäniens* (1940); A. Basch, *The Danube Basin and the German Economic Sphere* (1943); H. L. Roberts, *Rumania: Political Problems of an Agrarian State* (1951); M. Pizanty, *Petroleum in Roumania* (1930); C. N. Jordan, *The Romanian Oil Industry* (1955). G. Ravaș and A. Rădoi, "Industria petrolului," and A. Rădoi, "Industria gazelor naturale," both in *Monografia a Republicii Populare Romîne*, vol. ii, part I (1960).

Current history and statistics are summarized annually in the *Britannica Book of the Year.*

RUMANIAN LANGUAGE, one of the Romance languages (*q.v.*), in the main is derived from the Latin of the province of Dacia, which roughly corresponds to modern Rumania. Four principal dialects may be distinguished: (1) Daco-Rumanian, or Rumanian par excellence, spoken by about 18,000,000 persons in modern Rumania, the Banat (Yugoslavia), and in some villages of Bulgaria and Hungary near the Rumanian border, that is, mostly on the left bank of the Danube; (2) Macedo-Rumanian, or Arumenian, spoken by some 350,000 persons scattered in various regions of the Balkan peninsula (Thessaly, Epirus, Albania, Macedonia, Bulgaria); (3) Megleno-Rumanian, or Meglenitic, spoken by a few thousand persons northwest of Salonika; (4) Istro-Rumanian, spoken by a few thousand persons on the Istrian peninsula around Monte Maggiore.

Although these dialects are sufficiently different from one another to make communication difficult if not impossible, they may all be classified together because of their similarity in structure.

Dacia was conquered by the Romans during the reign of Trajan in hard-fought campaigns of A.D. 101 and 105–107; it was named after the vanquished Dacians, of whom little is known. The inhabitants were virtually exterminated, and the province was colonized by settlers from all parts of the empire, especially Syria and Asia Minor, who romanized the land. It should be noted that in this romanization of Dacia the substratum population had a small part, if any. But only 170 years later, between 271 and 274, the old province of Dacia north of the Danube was abandoned under the emperor Aurelian, who established a new Dacia Ripuaria south of the Danube at the expense of Moesia and Thrace. Eventually the region became part of the Eastern empire and was the battleground and the gateway into the empire for successive Germanic tribes and nations moving southward and westward from the Baltic countries. From the early 7th century, this part of the Romance-speaking world has remained cut off from the remainder by intrusions of Slavonic peoples (the Slovenes to Pannonia, that is, Hungary and eastern Austria, the Serbs and Croats to the northwestern Balkans).

Linguists are faced with the paradox that in the older Dacia (abandoned by the Romans in 271) Latin speech was preserved, whereas in the newer Dacia Ripuaria south of the Danube (which remained much longer in Roman hands) Slavonic dialects are spoken. Unfortunately, the social and ethnic history of the area during the dark ages is too little known to provide a good explanation. As far as the Romance language of Rumania is concerned, linguists seeking a reason for its presence have proposed two principal theories: (a) Latin speech was continued throughout the ages in Rumania; indeed, the withdrawal of the Romans under Aurelian to regions south of the Danube was not complete, and later non-Romance-speaking invaders were absorbed, at least linguistically, by the tenacious colonists; (b) the retreat of the Romans under Aurelian was indeed total, but Romance-speaking people later recrossed the Danube when onrushing Slavs forced them out of their homes. Some of them moved into other regions, where they planted the various dispersed Rumanian dialects now lying outside of Rumania proper. Since the first report of Neo-Latin speech in Rumania dates only from the 13th century and since the first Rumanian text available stems from the early 16th century, the belief in remigration and noncontinuity of speech seems confirmed. But this is an *argumentum ex silentio* and therefore not conclusive.

The truth lies probably between these extremes: the Aurelian withdrawal was not complete, and a remigration did occur after the 6th century. Some linguists are eager to prove not only an uninterrupted continuity of Romance speech in Rumania but also an ethnic continuity which would make Rumanians the true descendants of the Romans, a notion dear to the heart of many patriots. Linguistic continuity, however, is not dependent on ethnic or local continuity. In the absence of other proofs, therefore, a Romance language in Rumania is no proof of the ethnic Roman-ness of modern Rumanians.

The historical development of the Rumanian language from Latin is quite regular, that is to say, the operation of the rules of phonemic development and substitution (the so-called sound laws) is not greatly disturbed by other factors. One of the most important such interferences is analogy, which restores paradigmatic orderliness that the strict obeisance to sound laws is apt to obliterate. Consequently, in view of the small part played by analogical leveling in Rumanian, it is from the descriptive point of view, and for the learner, a somewhat irregular language.

The following are the most important changes and features of Rumanian linguistic history. (For earliest developments from Latin *see* ROMANCE LANGUAGES.)

Phonology.—As in other Romance languages, Latin $\bar{e}$ and $\check{\imath}$ coincide as e: *credo* > *cred*, *lĭgo* > *leg*. Unlike most others, but like Sardinian, Corsican and Dalmatian, Rumanian continued the distinction between Latin $\bar{o}$ and $\check{u}$: *cōco* > *coc*, *fŭrcam* > *furcă*. The other Latin vowels have the same proto-Romance developments as they had in other Romance languages. Latin *-ct-* > *-pt-*, *-ks-(-x-)* > *-ps-*, *-gn-* > *-mn-*: *ŏcto* > *opt*, *coxam* > *coapsă*, *cognatum* > *cumnat*. A similar labialization changes *-qu-* and *-gu-* to *p* and *b*: *aquam* > *apă*, *linguam* > *limbă*; but before front vowels they become *ts* and *dz*: *quinque* > *cinci*, *sanguinem* > *sânge*. Rumanian has two high mid vowels, spelled *ă* and *â* or *î*, the first from Latin *a* in unstressed position, the second from *a* before nasal consonant: *carbonem* > *cărbune*, *aqua* > *apă*, *canto* > *cânt*. When stressed *e* or *o* is followed by a syllable containing *e* or *a* (*ă*), diphthongization occurs (through metaphony): *nigram* > *neagră* (but *nigrum* > *negru*), *mollem* > *moale*. Dental and velar consonants if followed by front vowels are palatalized: *diem* > *zi* [*dzi*]; *caelum* > *cer* [*tšer*]; *terram* > *țeară*, *țară* [*tseară*, *tsarə*]; *gelu* > *ger* [*džer*]. Intervocalic *-l-* rhotacizes: *solem* > *soare*.

Morphology and Syntax.—The noun has: (a) one singular and one plural form without article (*domn, domni* [masc.]; *soare, sori* [masc.]; *casă, case* [fem.]; *carte, cărți* [fem.]); (b) two singular and two plural forms with the article (direct case: *domnul, soarele, casa, cartea; domnii, sorii, casele, cărțile*; oblique case: *domnului, soarelui, casei, cărții; domnilor, sorilor, caselor, cărților*), where the forms of the article are derived from *illu, ille, illa, illi, illae, illui* (classical dative *illi*), *illaei* (*illi*), and *illorum*, respectively. Note that the article in Rumanian is postposited. A number of nouns have different gender in the singular and plural: *câmp* (masc.); *câmpuri* (fem.). The infinitive of the verb is shortened, *a cântà* < *cantare*, but the long form *cântare* serves as a verbal noun. The future is formed by means of *uolēre* (classical *uelle*) "to wish" followed by the infinitive: *voiu cântà* or *cântà-voiu* "I shall (*cf.* 'will') sing"; an alternative way is a form of *a avea* (< *habēre*) + să + subjunctive: *am să cânt;* in the latter case the auxiliary verb may be used in an invariable form *o: o să cânt.* (Similar formations exist also in Albanian, Bulgarian, Greek and Serbian, which induced some linguists to postulate a general Balkan linguistic area.) Characteristics of syntax are: the repetition of the personal pronoun in nonsubject case forms—*pe mine nu m'a văzut* "(me) he hasn't seen me"; the replacement (not obligatory) of the infinitive direct object by a subjunctive construction (also Albanian, Greek, Bulgarian, Serbian)—*vreau să spun* "I should like to say"; the replacement of the possessive pronoun (when the possessor is not emphasized) by the dative of the personal pronoun—*mi-ai luat cartea* "you took me the book" = "you took my book" (not uncommon in other Romance languages, especially Italian and Portuguese); the use of the preposition *pe* with the direct object if this is a person—*am văzut pe vecinul nostru,* "I have seen our neighbour" (*cf.* the use of *a* in such cases in Spanish).

Vocabulary.—Among words of Latin origin in Rumanian there are a number which do not occur in other, especially the western, Romance languages. This is, of course, due to the isolation of Rumanian. (One hundred and twenty such words, or 6% of the total Romance lexicon, have been counted—but such counts must, for a variety of reasons, be taken with reservations.) It is only natural that Rumanian should contain many loanwords from non-Latin languages, especially Slavonic, but also from Turkish, Hungarian, Albanian, depending on the geographic location of a given dialect and the cultural prestige or propagating power of the donor language at a given time. On the whole, the number of Latin words in the dictionary is smaller than that of the others all together, even smaller than that of Slavonic words alone. But in a count of frequency of occurrence the percentage of Latin would be much higher.

The Rumanian literary language is based mainly on the Daco-Rumanian dialect of Walachia. It assumed importance only at the end of the 18th and the beginning of the 19th centuries. Before that all literary output was dialectal. With the literary language came also, for a time, a purist movement favoring the exclusion of all non-Romance words; this, of course, could only have crippled the language. The change-over from Cyrillic to Latin writing and the establishment of a more etymological orthography, advocated about the same time, were successful.

BIBLIOGRAPHY.—T. Capidan, *Aromânii, dialectul aromân* (1932) and *Meglenoromânii* (1925–28); O. Densusianu, *Histoire de la langue roumaine* (1901–32); S. Pușcariu, *Etymologisches Wörterbuch der rumänischen Sprache* (1905), *Limba română* (1940; also in German trans.), and with others, *Atlasul lingvistic român* (1938 *et seq.*); M. Ruffini, *Il problema della romanità della Dacia Traiana* (1941); G. O. Seiver, *Introduction to Romanian* (1953). (E. Pm.)

RUMANIAN LITERATURE. Written Rumanian literature is paralleled by a rich folklore—lyric, epic, dramatic, and didactic—which has continued till modern times. Lyrical poetry is represented by *doine* (love songs, songs expressing an undefined longing), *bocete* (dirges), *colinde* (carols), and *cântece* (lyrics); the epic by ballads in verse (*cântece bătrânești*) and folktales in prose; and drama by mystery plays, scenes of the Nativity, new year plays (*Vicleim, Irozi*). The didactic literature is rich in proverbs, riddles, and satiric songs.

Rumania's geographical position enabled its folklore to mediate the transfer of themes from the Balkans to the Ukraine and Russia. The religious homogeneity of the region, between Byzantium and Kiev, favoured, on the other hand, the circulation all over this area of literature written or printed in the Rumanian principalities. Western influence reached the Rumanian lands through Hungary, Transylvania, and Poland when the first political organizations were founded, east and south of the Carpathians, in the 12th–14th centuries. The Reformation inspired translation of church literature from Slavonic in the 15th century. Until the 17th century Church Slavonic was the language of the church and of the chanceries. The first state paper in Rumanian was issued in Alba

Iulia, Transylvania, in 1600, by Prince Michael of Walachia. Slavonic manuscripts, of great beauty, include two "Gospel books"; one (1405) by Friar Nicodim and one, with Slavonic and Greek texts, by Gavril Urikovich, written in 1429 (now in the Bodleian Library, Oxford). In the 18th century the autochthonous ruling princes were replaced by Greek rulers from Constantinople (the Phanariotes: *see* RUMANIA: *History*) and for more than a century the culture of the principalities was mainly Greek. As, after the fall of Constantinople and the disappearance of the Slavonic states south of the Danube, the Rumanian principalities became the haven of Slavo-Byzantine culture, so in the 17th and 18th centuries they became the centre of Greek Orthodox culture. The French Revolution and the ideas of the Romantic movement shook off the domination of the Phanariotes and the national revival began under western influence.

The development of Rumanian literature may be divided into five periods: (1) from the first Rumanian texts, written in the 15th century, to the Phanariote period; this period is crowned by the translation of the Bible (1688); (2) the 18th century up to the national movement of Tudor Vladimirescu (1821); (3) the national renaissance from 1820 to World War I; (4) the period of national unity and literary integration; and (5) the period after World War II.

The Old Period.—The earliest translations from Slavonic are interlinear verses or interpolations in 15th-century religious texts. From the same period date the so-called rhotacizing texts, preserved in 16th-century copies, which were written in Maramureș, northern Transylvania, probably under the impetus of the Hussite movement. These include the Psalter of Șcheia; and the Codex of Voroneț, which contains the Acts of the Apostles and the Psalter of Voroneț. Linguistically, their characteristic feature is the change of intervocalic "n" to "r" in words of Latin origin (*e.g., bire* for *bine:* Latin, *bene*). The first secular text in Rumanian is a letter, of 1521, by the boyar Neacșu, to the judge of Brașov to inform him of a possible Turkish invasion.

The printing press was introduced in Walachia in the early 16th century from Venice, and the first printed book was a Slavonic liturgical book, published in Târgoviște in 1508. Later in the century a certain Deacon Coresi moved from Târgoviște to Brașov, where he printed a translation of the Gospels from Slavonic (1560–61). No copy has been found of a Lutheran catechism in Rumanian, printed in 1544. Assisted by local clergy, Coresi revised, completed, and printed translations of the Acts of the Apostles (1563). Other of his publications which survive are the *Tâlcul Evangheliilor și Molitvenic* ("Sermons and Book of Prayers," 1564); a Psalter (1568–70); and the *Evanghelia cu învățătură* ("Commentary on the Gospels," 1581). Coresi's publications encouraged the use of Rumanian in the churches of all three principalities. Use of Rumanian was encouraged by printing in other centres: Sas-Sebeș, where Coresi's Slavo-Rumanian Psalter was probably produced in 1577; Alba Iulia (the Gospels, 1579; *Evanghelia cu învățătură,* 1641); Orăștie, where the Old Testament was printed in 1582 for the Rumanian Calvinists. The first Rumanian book printed in Latin characters was a Calvinist hymnbook of 1570.

In this period some secular literature was also produced. Numerous translations were made from Greek and Slavonic of historical and apocryphal books—the latter mainly under the influence of the Bogomils (*q.v.*). There is a collection of such texts in the *Codex Sturdzanus.* Many Byzantine and Oriental popular books (*e.g.,* a history of Alexander the Great, *Aesop's Fables,* and the "Arabian Nights") found their way into Rumanian literature.

Didactic literature is represented by the treatise on policy and ethics compiled from the works of Greek authors and attributed to Neagoe Basarab, prince of Walachia, 1512–21. This was written in Slavonic and translated into Rumanian in *c.* 1654. It is addressed to Basarab's son, Teodosie.

The printing of biblical and religious books was continued in the 17th century, and was given new impetus in Transylvania by the controversy resulting from the Reformation. In 1648 a translation of the Gospels in which the Greek, Latin, and Slavonic texts were collated was finished by the metropolitan Simion Ștefan, and printed in Alba Iulia (*Noul Testament dela Bălgrad*).

The religious literature printed in the first half of the 17th century in Walachia and Moldavia was partly in reaction to the Reformation. The most important centres of printing in Walachia were Câmpulung (*Învățături preste toate zilele,* 1642); Govora (*Pravila,* 1640; *Evangheli învățătoare,* 1642); Mănăstirea Dealului (*Evangheli învățătoare,* 1644); Târgoviște (*Mystirio sau Sacrament,* 1651; *Îndreptarea legii,* 1652); Râmnicu Vâlcea (*Antologhion,* 1705); Bucharest (București; *Cheia Înțelesului,* 1678); Buzău (*Octoih,* 1700); and Snagov (*Carte sau lumină,* 1699). In Moldavia, where the monasteries were centres of theological scholarship, reaction against the Reformation found expression in the *Răspuns* ("Reply," 1645) of the metropolitan Varlaam (1580–1658) to the Calvinist catechism printed in Alba Iulia in 1642. In 1643 Varlaam had published in Jassy (Iași) his sermons on the Gospels (*Cartea românească de învățătură*). In 1646 the *Pravila lui Vasile Lupu* ("Laws of Vasile Lupu," prince of Moldavia) was printed in Jassy. This was later incorporated in the Walachian *Pravila lui Matei Basarab* (1652), a collection of canonical and civil laws that remained in force, with additions, until the mid-19th century.

The Moldavian metropolitan Dosoftei (1624–93), a great scholar and theologian, fled to Poland during the fighting between Poland and Turkey that began in 1671, and in 1673 published there the first Rumanian metrical Psalter (*Psaltirea a lui David*), which was also the first poetry to be written in Rumanian. Influenced by Jan Kochanowski, he adopted Polish principles of versification. He returned to Moldavia in 1675, and in 1679 translated the liturgy from the Greek. His other outstanding contribution to Rumanian literature is his *Vieața și petrecere sfintilor* ("Lives of the Saints," 4 vol., 1682–86), in which he introduced popular idioms and encouraged development of a more flexible prose style.

At this time the Orthodox see of Kiev was occupied by the Moldavian Peter Movilă (Mogila). At his request, Vasile Lupu convoked in Jassy a pan-Orthodox synod (1640) to counteract Catholic propaganda. The *Confessio Orthodoxa* which it drew up remains a doctrinal charter of the Orthodox Eastern churches (*q.v.*). A Rumanian translation, from Greek, by Radu Greceanu (*Pravoslavnica Mărturisire*) was printed in Buzău. Toward the end of the 17th century the monastery of Snagov, near Bucharest, became the centre of a pan-Orthodox literary activity, and on the initiative of the monk Antim Ivireanu, books were printed in Rumanian, Greek, Slavonic, and Arabic. A Rumanian printer, Mihai Ștefan, introduced the press into the Caucasus where he printed the first Georgian books. The humanist Udriște Năsturel translated the *Imitatio Christi* into Rumanian (Dealu, 1647) and Slavo-Russian (Moscow, 1704).

Religious literature reached its climax with the translation of the Bible (1688) from the Septuagint by a group of scholars, printed by Radu and Șerban Greceanu. This was the basis for all later translations.

Early historiography, represented by Slavonic annals and commemorative tables of the monasteries (*Letopisețul dela Bistrița, 1359–1506*), reached its climax with the humanist historiographers of 17th-century Moldavia. The Italian *Rinascimento,* through Polish humanism, finds expression in the words of Grigore Ureche (1590–1647), the father of Moldavian historiography: "We descend from Rome, and our language is made of Latin words." Miron Costin (1633–91), who studied in Poland and who wrote in Polish a chronicle of Moldavia and composed a poem on the history of his country, is the leader of this historiography. He took up the history of Moldavia where it had been left by Ureche (*Letopisețul Țării Moldovei, 1359–1594*), and continued it to 1661. Costin's son Niculae amplified the chronicle; Ion Neculce (1672–1745) carried it to 1743. He was a pioneer in folklore with a collection of historical legends (*Osamă de cuvinte*). Dimitrie Cantemir (*see* CANTEMIR), prince of Moldavia, wrote in Latin the history of the Rumanians (1698), which he translated into Rumanian in 1710 (*Hronicul vechimii Româno-Moldo-Vlahilor*). His Latin historical *Descriptio Moldaviae* (1716) was translated into German (1769), Russian (1786), Greek (1819), and Rumanian (1825).

He took his place among western historiographers as a member of the Academy of Berlin (*Societas Regia Berolmensis*) and as a knight of the Roman Empire, with his *Historia incrementorum atque decrementorum aulae Othomanicae* (1715–16), translated into French (1743), German (1745), and English (1734–35, 1756).

A special place among Moldavian historians is occupied by Nicolae Milescu (*q.v.*), who wrote theological, historical, and travel works.

The Walachian chroniclers are less original and more personal. Stoica Ludescu compiled from earlier annals a chronicle of Walachia to 1688. He was chronicler of the Cantacuzino family. Radu Popescu (1650–1729) wrote a history of the rulers of Walachia (*Cronica Țării Românești*) from the point of view of a boyar party headed by the Băleanu family. Radu Greceanu carried the history of Walachia up to 1714. The *stolnic* (steward) Constantin Cantacuzino (1650–1716), a student of the University of Padua, the political mentor and the cultural patron of his country, wrote a history of Walachia (*Istoria Țării Românești* (*c.* 1710).

The 18th Century.—Some Phanariotes patronized Christian culture in the Rumanian principalities. However, this period presents a picture of social oppression and decadence. A rich secular and apocryphal literature circulated in manuscript (*Erotocritul, Fiziologul, Istoria lui Archir, Viața lui Esop, Halimanaua*); the monastic printing presses continued to produce beautiful books; but there was no progress in comparison with that of the past. Many liturgical books were printed. In Moldavia a new cultural centre arose at Rădăuți. The achievements of the century are the *Minei* ("Lives of the Saints"; 1776–80), published in Rîmnicu Vîlcea; and the *Minei* (1807–15), published in the monastery of Neamț, each in 12 volumes. The richness and lucidity of the language put these alongside the Bible of 1688.

In 1700 a minority of Rumanians of Transylvania joined the Church of Rome to obtain protection from Vienna against the Hungarians. The disciples of the theological schools of Rome and Vienna amplified the ideas of Rumania's Latin origin, taken from the Moldavian chroniclers and from the church books in Walachia. The representatives of the Latinist school of Blaj, the cultural centre of these Uniate Rumanians, were zealous scholars and patriots. Samuil Micu-Clain (1745–1806) wrote a four-volume *Istoria . . . Românilor* (Buda, 1806) and, with Gheorghe Șincai (1754–1816), author of *Hronica Românilor* (1807), published the first Rumanian grammar, *Elementa linguae daco-romanae sive valachicae* (1780). Petru Maior (1760–1821) fought for the introduction of the Latin alphabet with his *Orthographia romana sive latino-valachica* (1819), and wrote a history of the origins of the Rumanian people (*Istoria pentru începutul Românilor in Dacia,* 1812). A collective work of this school is the *Lesicon românesc-latinesc-unguresc-nemțesc* (1825).

Lyric poetry was cultivated toward the end of the century in Anacreontic love songs (publ. 1769–99), by Alecu Văcărescu. His father Ienăchiță (1730–96?), the moralist poet, also wrote the first grammar in Rumanian: *Observații sau băgări de seamă asupra regulilor și orânduielilor gramaticii românești* (1787); his son Iancu (1792–1863), the father of Rumanian poetry, overshadowed his predecessors by his poems (first complete edition, 1830). The fourth Văcărescu poet was Nicolae (1784–1825). The lyric tradition was carried on in Walachia by B. P. Mumuleanu (*Rost de poesii,* 1820; *Caracteruri,* 1825), who was influenced by Alphonse de Lamartine, Edward Young, and neo-Greek poetry; by Eliade Rădulescu (1802–72); Vasile Cârlova (1808–31); and by Grigore Alexandrescu (1812–85). In Moldavia this early versification is represented by Costachi Conachi (1777–1849) and Enache Kogălniceanu, who versified historical events.

Epic verse was first attempted by Ion Budai-Deleanu (1760–1820), who wrote a satirical epic *Țiganiada* (1812), in which the heroes are gypsies. Vasile Aaron (1770–1822) wrote a vast epic on the Passion (*Patima și moartea Domnului Isus Christos,* 1805), an imitation of Milton's *Paradise Lost;* and also *Piram și Tisbe* (1807), inspired by the story of Pyramus and Thisbe in Ovid's *Metamorphoses.* I. Barac (1779–1848) produced the epic *Risipirea Ierusalimului* (1821) on the destruction of Jerusalem, and also translated from Homer and Ovid. Foreign plays were adapted in Greek and Rumanian: Molière, Corneille, Kotzebue, Metastasio (*Ahilefs la Schiro*, 1797), Schiller, and also Shakespeare's *Hamlet* in a translation from German by Barac.

Anton Pann (1797–1854) popularized folk literature and edited church service books with musical notations. His *Povestea vorbii* (1847–53) is a collection of proverbs in verse, connected by popular tales.

This pre-Romantic period closed with the annexation of Bukovina (1774) by Austria and of Bessarabia (1812) by Russia, which brought about translations of law codes in Russia and Austria. Law codes were also compiled in Moldavia in 1833, and in Walachia in 1780 and 1817.

The National Renaissance.—The first landmark of this period was the rising of Tudor Vladimirescu (1821) and the return of the national rulers. Romanticism carried forward the falling wave of the Latinist movement. In the second half of the 19th century a serious literary criticism, which originated in German philosophy and French culture, inaugurated modern literature.

Transylvanian Latinism crossed the Carpathians and had beneficial effects on the Hellenized culture of Walachia. Gheorghe Lazăr (1799–1823) went from Transylvania to Bucharest as a teacher and started a school, St. Sava's College, in which he humanized the teaching. One of his pupils, Eliade Rădulescu, exercised a great influence on literary development. In 1829 he founded the political newspaper, *Curierul Românesc* (the first Rumanian newspaper in Walachia), followed by a literary supplement, *Curierul de ambe sexe* (1836). He was a pioneer of Italian influence. He founded the Societatea Filarmonică (1833), which later created the national theatre in Bucharest, and was the first president of the Rumanian Academy (Societatea Academică Română, 1866). In 1828 he published his Rumanian grammar.

The Societatea Pentru Cultură (1862) in Bukovina invited the Latinist Aron Pumnul (1818–66) from Blaj to Cernăuți (Czernowitz), where he had among his pupils the greatest Rumanian poet of the 19th century, Mihail Eminescu. Pumnul published the *Lepturariu ruminesc* (4 vol., Vienna, 1862–64). The historian Simion Bărnuțiu (1808–64), who pronounced the speech of liberation on the Field of Freedom in Blaj (1848), took refuge in Jassy, where he taught in the university and created a school of lawyers and economists.

Gheorghe Asachi (1788–1869) represented the Italian influence in Moldavia; he created the historical short story, wrote verses in Rumanian and Italian, and founded the periodical *Albina Românească* (1829), with a literary supplement, *Alăuta Românească*.

A galaxy of poets enriched the romantic heritage. The Bessarabian Alexandru Donici (1806–66), with Costache Negruzzi, translated from Russian the satires and fables of Antiokh Kantemir; another Bessarabian, C. Stamate (1777–1868), wrote under the influence of the French and Russian Romantics and translated Thomas Moore and Sir Walter Scott. Andrei Mureșanu (1816–63), author of the revolutionary hymn *Deșteaptă-te, Române*, translated Young. The Macedo-Rumanian Dimitrie Bolintineanu (1819–72) versified historical legends. The outstanding literary personality among these poets is Grigore Alexandrescu (1812–85), who wrote *Poezii* (1832, 1838, 1839), *Meditații* (1863), fables and satires influenced by Boileau, Lamartine, and La Fontaine, and translated Voltaire and Byron. The learned boyar Dinicu Golescu traveled through western Europe and recorded his experiences in *Insemnare a călătoriei mele* (1826).

The national historian of this heroic period was Niculae Bălcescu (1819–52), author of *Românii sub Mihai Viteazul* (1851–52), *Puterea armată și arta militara* (1844), and other historical and literary works. He edited the periodical *Magazinul istoric pentru Dacia* (1845–47). Modern historiography was inaugurated by Mihail Kogălniceanu (*q.v.;* 1817–91), the leading statesman in the newly organized monarchy. He produced the first edition of the old chronicles (*Letopisțele Moldoviei*, 1845–52) and edited the historical review *Arhiva românească* (1840) and the literary magazine *Dacia literară* (1840), which marks the beginning of the traditionalist trend in literature. Alecu Russo (1819–59), another leader of 1848, enriched literature with his biblical prose poem, *Cântarea României* (a hymn to Rumania).

The second half of the century was dominated by Vasile Alecsandri (*q.v.;* 1819 or 1821–90) and Mihail Eminescu (*q.v.;* 1850–89). Alecsandri's rich output comprises poetry (*Doine și Lăcrimioare*, 1853; *Suvenire și Mărgăritărele*, 1856); prose (*Buchetiera din Florența; Călătorie in Africa*); and plays (*Fântâna Blanduziei; Ovidiu; Despot Vodă*). Helped by Russo, he revealed treasures of Rumanian folklore in *Balade* (1852–53) and *Poezii populare* (1866).

Eminescu, the philosophical lyric poet, created modern Rumanian poetry. He was influenced by Hindu thought and German philosophy, but he remained rooted in tradition. He raised Rumanian poetry to new heights, and was the guiding star of every aspect of cultural life. His writings include short stories and political and philosophical essays.

Free from outside influences, Ion Creangă (1837–89), a peasant by birth, from the eastern Carpathians, wrote folktales and *Amintiri din copilărie* ("Childhood Memories," 1892), which depict peasant life with unassuming artistry.

The critic under whose aegis literary creation continued to develop until the early 20th century was the statesman and eclectic philosopher Titu Maiorescu (1840–1917). He founded in Jassy (1863) the literary circle Junimea, which reacted against form without content in art and repudiated the extremism of the Latinist school. Its periodical *Convorbiri Literare* (1867) continued to appear until 1939.

Costache Negruzzi (1808–68) excelled in prose, especially with his historical short story "Alexandru Lăpușneanu," influenced by Scott. The archaeologist A. Odobescu (1834–95) also wrote historical stories (*Mihnea Vodă*, 1857; *Doamna Chiajna*, 1860), but his talent was revealed in *Pseudokinegetikos* (1874), an archaeological mosaic of high aesthetic emotion. I. Ghica (1816–97), the first Rumanian diplomatic representative in London, attempted the same genre in his *Convorbiri economice* (1867) and *Amintiri* (1890). In his short stories Ion Slavici (1848–1925) described the moral conflicts of village life. I. Popovici-Bănățeanu (1860–93) wrote about the life of the tradesmen in the Banat (*Nuvele*, 1909). Nicolae Gane (1835–1916) translated Dante's *Inferno* and wrote stories based on memories of his own early life in the countryside. Dante's *Divina Commedia* was translated by Gheorghe Coșbuc (1866–1918), the poet of rustic life (*Balade și Idile*, 1893; *Fire de Tort*, 1896; *Cântece de vitejie*, 1904). Eminescu's follower in lyrical pessimism, Alexandru Vlahuță (1858–1919), wrote a masterly description of the Rumanian landscape (*România pitoreasca*, 1903).

The greatest writer of this period was Ion Luca Caragiale (*q.v.;* 1852–1912), who created the social comedy. He also wrote a realistic drama, delightful "Moments, Sketches and Memories," and short stories. With humour and irony he presented a society in transition from orientalism to occidentalism.

Several writers stood aside from Junimea, and sometimes opposed it. Among them were the creator of the historical national drama, Barbu Stefănescu (Delavrancea) (1858–1918), with his historical trilogy *Apus de soare, Luceafărul, Viforul*, and a number of short stories; the historian-philologist B. P. Hasdeu (1836–1907); and the neoclassicist Duiliu Zamfirescu (1858–1922), whose novel-cycle, *Neamul Comăneștilor*, describes the family life of the old country gentry.

Folklore and folk literature were collected and edited by A. M. Marienescu, Urban Iarnik, and Andrei Bârseanu in Transylvania; S. F. Marian, the Czech scholar, in Bukovina; G. D. Teodorescu in Walachia; T. T. Burada in Dobruja; and G. Tocilescu. P. Ispirescu's fairy tales, *Basmele Românilor*, emulate those of Creangă. Moses Gaster (*q.v.;* 1856–1939), the pioneer in research into Rumanian folklore and folk literature, continued his activity in exile in England. I. A. Zanne published *Proverbele Românilor* (nine volumes, 1895–1901); A. Gorovei collected riddles, *Cimiliturile Românilor* (1898).

The traditionalist movement of *Dacia literară* was continued by a galaxy of writers whose organ was *Sămănătorul* (1901–10). The poets S. O. Iosif (1875–1913) and D. Anghel (1872–1914) wrote graceful verses (*Legendă funigeilor*, 1907). P. Cerna (1881–1913) attempted with success the philosophical lyric inaugurated by Eminescu. But the outstanding poet of this generation was the vigorous national bard of Transylvania, Octavian Goga (1881–1938).

Prose writers found inspiration in village life and in history. E. Gârleanu (1878–1914) described patriarchal life (*Bătrânii*); C. Hogaş (1847–1916) depicted the enchanted landscapes of his Moldavian mountains (*Amintiri d'intro călătorie; În munţii Neamţului*); C. Sandu-Aldea (d. 1927) described peasant life in the plain of the Bărăganul and the Danube delta.

A parallel movement to that of *Sămănătorul* was that of the periodical *Viaţa Românească* (Jassy, 1901). Its ideology, called *poporanism* on the pattern of the Russian "populism," had a social and political background. Russian influence is also seen in the work of the literary critic Constantin Dobrogeanu-Gherea (1855–1920), a follower of Hippolyte Taine and Karl Marx. The aesthete of the group was G. Ibrăileanu, author of the psychological novel *Adela*. The social critic was the Bessarabian, C. Stere.

Western modernism penetrated under various aspects. Symbolism found a great supporter in the learned philologist and gifted writer Ovid Densuşianu (1873–1938), who founded the periodical, *Viaţa Nouă* (1905). The poets Ion Minulescu (1881–1944), author of *Romanţe pentru mai târziu* (1908) and *De vorbă cu mine însumi* (1914), and Georghe Bacovia (1881–1947), who wrote *Plumb* (1916), compared favourably with western Symbolists. Impressionism found a devotee in E. Lovinescu, author of a history of contemporary literature (five volumes, 1926–37). Niculae Davidescu (1888–   ) in his early poems (1910) shows the influence of Baudelaire. In the epic *Cântecul omului* ("The Song of Man", 1928–37), he aimed at recreating world history. A. Macedonski (1854–1920) opposed an exotic modernism of French origin to the academic discipline of Junimea as well as to the traditionalism of *Sămănătorul;* he also wrote verses in French, as did others of his generation.

After World War I.—In the period of national unity, the novel began to compete with lyric poetry. Attempts at introducing the novel go back to 1865, when Niculae Filimon (1819–65) produced a social fresco of his period in *Ciocoii vechi şi noui* ("Old and New Upstarts," 2nd edition, 1886). Liviu Rebreanu (1885–1943?) described the peasant's thirst for soil and independence in *Ion* (1920; Eng. trans. 1965); and presented his suffering and his struggle for freedom in an epic novel, *Răscoala* (1932; *The Uprising*, 1964). In *Crăişorul Horia* (1929) he described the peasant revolt of 1784 in Transylvania. Among his psychological novels *Ciuleandra* (1927) is a fascinating clinical description, but his most powerful work, inspired by Rumanian participation in World War I, was *Pădurea spânzuraţilor* (1922; *The Forest of the Hanged*, 1930).

World War I also inspired Cezar Petrescu (1892–1961), who wrote, among other novels, *Scrisorile unui Răzeş* (1922) and *Întunecare* (1927). In *Roşu, Galben şi Albastru* (1924) the Symbolist poet Minulescu depicted life under German occupation. The lyrical novelist Ionel Teodoreanu (1897–1954) described the disappearance of patriarchal life (*La Medeleni*, 1926–27; *Turnul Mileni*, 1928). Victor Ion Popa (1897–   ) took his subjects from village life (*Velerim şi Veler, Doamne*, 1932; *Sfârleaza cu Fofează*); he also enriched the theatre with exquisite plays (*Muşcata din fereastră*). E. Bucuţa (1887–1941), in his *Fuga lui Şefki* (1926); and G. Mihăescu (1894–1935), in *Ruşoaică* (1933) and *Donna Albă* (1935), described the exotic life of the borderlands. Mircea Eliade set his novel *Maitreyi* (1933) in India. Matei Luca Caragiale, son of I. L. Caragiale, produced a refined piece of art in *Craii de Curtea Veche* (1929).

Gala Galaction (1879–1961) translated the Bible (1938), with Vasile Radu, and wrote mystical prose (*Bisericuţa din Răzoare*, 1914) and novels on biblical subjects (*Roxana*, 1930). Hortensia Papadat-Bengescu was a psychological analyst (*Concert din Muzică tui Bach*, 1927). Life in the suburbs of Bucharest found its interpreter in the novelist G. M. Zamfirescu (d. 1939). Humorous prose was written by D. D. Patraşcanu (1872–1937), who wittily described political life (*Candidat fără naroc*); by Damian Stănoiu, the caricaturist of monastic life; and by Gheorghe Brăescu, who satirized the harshness of army life.

The link with the older generation was assured by two prose writers: I. A. Brătescu-Voineşti (1868–1944), the sympathetic representative of the landed gentry, whose stories are mainly about the defeated inadaptables in life; and Mihail Sadoveanu (1880–1961) who became the leading realist writer of the early 20th century. His historical novels (*Şoimii*, 1904; *Zodia cancerului*, 1929; *Fraţii Jderi*, 1935) are epic reconstructions of the 15th and 16th centuries, and he also describes life in the small market towns of Moldavia, peasant life and its privations, and the beauties of nature. His work is of great importance in the development of Rumanian prose. In 1924 he was awarded the national prize for literature, and in 1949 won the Golden Peace Medal with his novel *Mitrea Cocor*, which describes the peasants' part in the war, and their emergence after it. His work is marked by compassion, realistic observation, a power to show man as an integral part of nature, and by the vivid, expressive language of his characters, an artistic stylization of the spoken language of Moldavia.

The Transylvanian writer I. Agârbiceanu (1892–   ) carried on Slavici's tradition, presenting in his novels and short stories the village and middle-class life of his province against a religious background (*Dela ţară*, 1906; *Arhanghelii*, 1914; *În pragul vieţii*).

Scholars and philosophers played a part in the literary life of the period as critics and writers. The classical archaeologist Vasile Pârvan (d. 1927) wrote *Parentalia*, inspired by Thucydides, to commemorate the sacrificed generation of World War I. The historian Nicolae Iorga (1871–1940) edited *Sămănătorul;* founded literary periodicals; and wrote criticism, poetry, plays, and travel descriptions. The geographer S. Mehedinţi (Soveja) edited *Convorbiri Literare* and wrote village stories (*Oameni dela munte*). The philosopher I. Rădulescu-Motru exercised great influence on intellectual life with *Personalismul energetic* (1927). Lucian Blaga (1895–1961) was a philosophic essayist (*Filosofia stilului*, 1924; *Etnografie şi artă*, 1926), as well as a poet. He began as a lyric poet (*Poemele luminii*, 1919) under the influence of western expressionism, and developed a philosophical system based on the traditional way of life interpreted as a cosmic mystery (*Trilogia cunoaşterii*, 1931–34). His poetic dramas express his philosophic thought (*Meşterul Manole*, 1927; *Cruciada copiilor*, 1930; *Avram Iancu*, 1934).

Literary criticism was represented by the aesthetician M. Dragomirescu, editor of the *Convorbiri Critice;* D. Caracostea, the analyst of Eminescu; G. Bogdan-Duică, the literary historian; Paul Zarifopol (*Pentru and literara*, 1934); A. Busuioceanu (1896–1961), the art historian, essayist, and poet of genius in Rumanian and Spanish (*Poemas patéticos*, 1948; *Innominada luz*, 1949; *Properción de vivir*, 1954).

The critic and prose writer G. Călinescu (1899–   ) wrote monographs on Eminescu and Creangă before World War II, and also a history (1944), which excelled in depicting the writers of the past and in subtle analysis of their work. After the war, he developed a view of literature and art as social phenomena and produced critical studies and monographs (on Niculae Filimon, 1953; Grigore Alexandrescu, 1954; etc.) He also wrote novels describing and analyzing the social life of Bucharest immediately after World War I, its gradual decay, and the part played by the intellectuals in the reconstruction after World War II.

National and private theatres offered great opportunities for playwrights. Alexandru Davila's historical verse drama *Vlaicu Vodă* (1902), Victor Eftimiu's *Cocoşul negru* (1913), M. Sorbul's *Letopiseţii* (1914) and *Patima roşie* (1916), Caton Theodorian's *Bujoreştii*, C. Ciprian's *Omul cu mârţoaga*, and Ion Sân-Giorgiu's *Masca* (1922) were among the best.

Lyric poetry was the most cultivated genre in modern Rumanian literature. Schools and periodicals were numerous. Nichifor Crainic (1889–   ), editor of the literary magazine *Gândirea* (1920), represented the religious traditionalist tendency (*Darurile pâmântului*, 1920); Ion Pillat was influenced by the French and German lyric, and sang the beauty of his native landscape (*Pe Argeş în sus*, 1923; *Satul meu*, 1926); V. Voiculescu was a profound mystic (*Intrezăriri*, 1940); Adrian Maniu produced the play *Meşterul* (1922) and wrote verses inspired by the rustic landscape. The poems of the mathematician I. Barbu evoke the geometric forms of the crystal (*Joc secund*, 1930). Dragoş Protopopescu, the translator of Shakespeare, was an original poet and talented essayist on English literature.

The poet who, after Eminescu, created a new lyric poetry was Tudor Arghezi (1880–   ). In his poems language acquires an unusual expressiveness and harmony. His prose essays (*Cartea cu jucării*, 1935; *Ochii Maicii Domnului*, 1935; *Cimitirul Buna Vestire*, 1936) and his verse (*Cuvinte potrivite*, 1927; *Flori de mucegai*, 1931; *Versuri de seară*, 1935) were a landmark in Rumanian letters.

Developments after World War II.—Several famous writers continued to write after World War II. Arghezi reached new lyrical heights in *1907* and a hymn to man (both 1957) praising mankind's will to live and struggle for freedom. Geo Bogza (1908–   ), who had earlier been influenced by modernist tendencies, wrote articles, essays, and poems belonging to the "social realist" movement. Sadoveanu's later work has already been mentioned. Mihail Beniuc (1907–   ), whose early verse had been a clarion call to freedom for the people, became (as he said) "the drummer of the new age," and celebrated in stirring lyrics the achievements of the postwar period. Demostene Botez (1893–   ), whose prewar poetry had described poignantly the sadness of provincial life, later revealed a vigorous optimism and confidence. Eugen Jebeleanu (1911–   ), who began as a hermetic poet, wrote poems of protest on contemporary events and themes—*Lidicze; Hiroshima*, —and praised the heroism of his countrymen (*e.g.*, Bălcescu). Among those who came to the fore during and after World War II were the poets Maria Banuş (1914–   ), who expressed the struggle for peace in poems notable for creative and forceful use of imagery; Miron Paraschivescu, a lyrical poet who took his themes from folklore; Marcel Breslaşu, a complex writer on a wide range of themes; and a number of younger poets—Dan Deşliu, Victor Tulbure, A. E. Baconski, and Andriţoiu.

Dramatists included Aurel Baranga (1913–   ), who, in a series of plays, discussed the complex problems of contemporary life; Horia Lovinescu (1917–   ), whose plays depicted changing intellectual attitudes; M. Davidoglu, author of plays set in mines and factories; and Lucia Demetrius (1910–   ), also a social dramatist.

The postwar novel also dealt with topical themes. Zaharia Stancu (1902–   ), who had acquired a reputation as a poet before the war, wrote novels evoking with dramatic power Rumanian village life in a vanished age. Eusebiu Camilar (1900–   ), in his novel *Negura* ("Mist"), gave a bitter indictment of Fascism. V. E. Galan (1921–   ) wrote notable novels on the peasants' insurrection of 1907, and in *Bărăgan* described the effects of agricultural reform; and Marin Preda's *Moromeţi* was a vast epic work depicting peasant life on the eve of World War II.

Essays and criticism were written by Călinescu (*see* above); Mihai Ralea (1896–   ), who also published travel books and philosophical and psychological works; Tudor Vianu (1897–   ), whose early works belonged to the aesthetic school, but who in his works published in the 1950s (on style, metaphor, Stendhal, etc.) revealed a materialistic and methodological approach; and D. Panaitescu-Perpessicius, whose studies of contemporary literature, and of folklore and historiography, appeared in the critical reviews. Among critics whose names were becoming known in the 1950s were Paul Georgescu; Ovid Crohmălniceanu (whose monograph on Liviu Rebreanu appeared in 1954); Silvian Iosifescu, author of a study of the Rumanian novel (1960); and Dumitru Micu, who wrote a book on the modern novel in Rumania (1959).

BIBLIOGRAPHY.—I. Bianu, N. Hodoş, and D. Simionescu, *Bibliografia Românească Veche*, 4 vol. (1903–44); N. Cartojan, *Istoria literaturii române vechi*, 3 vol. (1940–45), *Cărţile populare în literatura română*, 2 vol. (1929–38); L. Feraru, *The Development of Rumanian Poetry* (1929); P. Hanes, *Histoire de la littérature roumaine* (1934); N. Iorga, *Istoria literaturii religioase a Românilor până la 1688* (1904), *Istoria literaturii româneşti*, vol. i, 2nd ed. (1925), vol. ii (1907–09); B. Munteano, *Modern Rumanian Literature* (1939); D. Murăraşu, *Istoria literaturii române* (1940); D. Poporici, *La Littérature roumaine à l'époque des lumières* (1945); M. Niculescu, *Omul si Pământul Românesc* (1955).
(G. Ns.; X.)

RUMANIAN ORTHODOX CHURCH, an autocephalous part of the Orthodox Eastern Church, is the church to which the majority of the Rumanian people belong. Christianity first reached Dacia (which covered roughly the area of modern Rumania) under the Roman Empire at least as early as the 4th century. By the late 9th century the Rumanians appear to have accepted a Slavonic liturgy and Bulgarian ecclesiastical jurisdiction. The see of Ochrida (modern Ohrid, Yugos.) was long acknowledged and Slavonic remained the liturgical language until the 17th century, when Rumanian began to replace it. Today the Rumanian Church is almost unique among the Orthodox churches of Europe in using the modern vernacular for its liturgy. The church helped to keep alive a sense of national identity both under Turkish rule, surviving attempted hellenization, and, in Transylvania, under Hungarian rule. In the latter province it had no recognition in the post-Reformation settlement of 1571 alongside the four "received religions" (Roman Catholic, Lutheran, Calvinist, Unitarian) of the Magyar and "Saxon" peoples, and by an act of union in 1698 a large proportion of its clergy and laity accepted papal jurisdiction, becoming Eastern Rite Catholics (officially reincorporated into the Orthodox Church in 1948). The church was an important factor in the eventual emancipation of the Rumanians of Transylvania and in the integration of the greater Rumania which came into being after 1918. Outstanding was Andreiu Şaguna, first metropolitan of Transylvania, whose constitution (1868) influenced the development of the whole Rumanian Church after 1918.

Between 1917 and 1939 the Rumanian Church, as the largest of the Orthodox churches outside Russia, held a position of leadership among them. In 1935 it agreed to accept the validity of Anglican orders subject to agreement by all the rest of the Orthodox Church; this did not of course bring the two churches into communion with one another. The Rumanian patriarchate was established in 1925 and there are five metropolitan provinces: Ungro-Vlachia, Moldavia and Suceava, Ardeal (*i.e.*, Transylvania), Oltenia, and the Banat. Bukovina and Bessarabia are now incorporated into the Russian Church. In 1949 a new statute brought greater centralization and a further definition of the prerogatives of the patriarch. The church has theological institutes of university status at Bucharest and Sibiu and six seminaries for priests and chanters. A theological quarterly is published and monthly reviews by the patriarchate and each of the metropolitan sees. The Rumanian Orthodox Church became a member of the World Council of Churches in 1961.

See also ORTHODOX EASTERN CHURCH.

BIBLIOGRAPHY.—R. W. Seton-Watson, *A History of the Roumanians* (1934); M. Beza, *The Rumanian Church* (1943); G. Rosu *et al.*, "Church and State in Romania," in V. Gsovski (ed.), *Church and State Behind the Iron Curtain*, pp. 253–299 (1955); A. Johansen, *Theological Study in the Rumanian Orthodox Church Under Communist Rule* (1961); *The Rumanian Orthodox Church* (1962), official publication ed. by the Bible and Orthodox Missionary Institute, Bucharest.
(MT. P.)

RUMBA, a dance of uncertain Afro-Cuban origin, is done to music in 4/4 time, with insistent syncopation. The basic pattern is two quick side steps, a slow forward step, two more quick side steps, and a slow backward step. The foot is placed flat on the floor, the weight following as the step is taken. Delayed transference of the weight, accompanied by sinuous body movement, gives the rumba its characteristic style. In the original Cuban version, called the *son*, the dancers face each other without touching. The adaptation seen in the U.S. and Europe calls for the dancers to embrace except in "breaks," when the dancers separate to perform movements such as turning under the partner's arms.

RUMELIA, a general name formerly used by the Turks to denote their possessions in the Balkan Peninsula (Turkish *Rumeli*, the land of the Romans, *i.e.*, Byzantines). Before 1908 it comprised the vilayets of Istanbul (European part), Edirne, Salonika, Kosovo, Monastir, Scutari (Usküdar), and Ioánnina (Janina), in addition to the provinces of Eastern Rumelia (now the southern part of Bulgaria between the Balkans and the Rhodopes) and Bosnia and Hercegovina. Eastern Rumelia (capital Philippopolis or Plovdiv) became, by the Berlin Treaty of 1878, an autonomous province within the Turkish (Ottoman) Empire, but proclaimed its unity with Bulgaria on Sept. 18, 1885 (*see* BULGARIA). Turkish territory in Europe is now known as Trakya (Thrace).

(N. Tu.; S. Er.; E. Tu.)

RUMFORD, COUNT VON: *see* Thompson, Sir Benjamin.

RUMI: *see* Jalal-ud-din Rumi.

RUMINANT. A very important group of mammals, the Ruminantia constitute one of the three suborders of the artiodactyls (*q.v.*), the even-toed hoofed mammals. Hooves, cud chewing and a diet of grasses or foliage are the most obvious characteristics of this suborder, which includes not only cattle, sheep and goats but also the diverse types of antelopes, giraffes, deer and chevrotains.

Although most of these animals possess either horns or antlers, all have been derived from hornless ancestors and a few, such as the musk deer of central and eastern Asia, have never developed them.

Apart from the horns which vary strikingly in shape and construction, not only from family to family but from species to species, the ruminants are a homogeneous group; perhaps the most eccentric member is the long-necked giraffe, and even this is linked with the more normal types by the okapi, an animal belonging to the giraffe family but with a shorter neck and shorter limbs than the true giraffes. In the wild state, ruminants, like all hoofed mammals, seek safety from their carnivorous enemies in flight, using their antlers or horns as weapons of defense only if driven to bay. Swiftest of all are the deer, antelopes and gazelles, while the goats and mountain sheep have a marvelous power of rapidly scaling steep heights to which few carnivores can follow them.

It is therefore among the ruminants that there is found a more perfect adaptation to a fugitive life than among any other of the larger mammals. The skeletal and muscular systems of the ruminant together form a perfectly constructed running mechanism; their digestive system is also elaborately planned so that they may hastily snatch a meal in some favourable grazing ground and store the food temporarily in a special compartment of the stomach until they have found a refuge where they can masticate and digest it at leisure.

Limbs and Feet.—In the skeleton, the proportions of the limbs and the structure of the feet are particularly noteworthy. As in all running animals the lower leg and foot are very long compared with the upper segment of each limb; this insures a long stride and at the same time a swift one. The surfaces of the joints are grooved and keeled like pulley wheels, permitting free motion forward and backward but limiting the motion in all other directions. Joints of this type are quite strong, and are admirably adapted for swift locomotion over a smooth surface, though less efficient on rough ground.

The feet are constructed on the artiodactyl plan; in each foot no more than two of the ancestral five toes are used, the rest being either lost or reduced to vestiges. The animal steps lightly on the tip of these two remaining toes, the short terminal segments of which are encased by the hoofs. The upper segments (metapodials) of each toe, fused into a single strong bone (termed the cannon bone), are in contrast very long so that the joints corresponding to the human wrist and ankle are raised high above the ground and are consequently often regarded as elbow and knee. On account of the shortness of the upper segments of the limbs, corresponding to the human upper arm and thigh, the true elbow and knee joints of the ruminant are close against its body, enclosed within the skin of the trunk.

Dentition.—Quite as distinctive as the foot of a ruminant is its skull, and especially its dentition. It will have been noticed how a sheep, when it feeds, seems not so much to bite off the grass as to tear it off by quickly jerking its head. This is because the front teeth in the upper jaw are replaced by a horny pad, while those of the lower jaw are directed forward and simply press the grass tightly against this pad on closure of the mouth; when the head is jerked sideways the grass is cut through by the sharp edges of the lower front teeth. It is also a matter of common observation that in chewing its food a ruminant swings its lower jaw to the side: it usually swings it first a number of times

to one side and then, reversing the direction, about an equal number of times to the other side, so that the grinding teeth on both sides of the mouth are used in turn. These grinding or "cheek teeth" are admirably adapted for triturating hard grasses and coarse foliage. Viewed from the side, they appear to be made up of a number of columns, but looked at from the grinding surface they are seen to have a crown pattern of four crescents or Vs, sometimes complicated by little additional folds. Each crescent is enclosed by a border of enamel which, as it is a very hard substance, prevents the tooth from wearing down too quickly. Also, as the enamel does not wear down at the same rate as the softer substance within, the surface of the crown is alway rough and therefore all the more effective as a grinding mechanism. The great height of the crown also insures that the tooth will last out the animal's lifetime before it is quite ground away. Similar devices are characteristic of the molar teeth of all herbivorous mammals, a matter of considerable importance since most grasses contain a great deal of silica, which causes hard wear to the tooth.

In those ruminants that feed on soft leaves rather than on grasses, the cheek teeth are much shorter than in the exclusively graminivorous types and have a less complex crown pattern. However high the grinding teeth, the mandible of a ruminant is a slender bone, slung somewhat loosely onto the skull, and the joint between mandible and skull is shaped so as to permit great freedom of movement in grinding.

Digestive Processes.—The following account of the process of rumination is an abbreviation of that given by T. H. Huxley in his *Anatomy of Vertebrated Animals*. A ruminant does not masticate its food on first taking it into its mouth but swallows it hastily, well mixed with saliva. Only when its appetite is satisfied does it stop grazing and seek a place of safety where it can lie down and "chew the cud" at leisure. If we closely observe a cow which has just lain down in a field after a period of grazing, its body inclined to one side, we notice that after an interval of quiescence a sudden spasm, rather resembling a hiccough, passes over the animal's flanks; and that at the same time something is quickly forced up the gullet into the mouth. This is a bolus of grass which, rendered sodden by the fluids in the stomach, is now returned to be masticated by the grinding teeth. This process is repeated until most of the grass which was originally cropped has been reduced to pulp.

A ruminant's stomach is divided into four compartments. When the food is first hastily swallowed it passes no further than the first and second of these; on second swallowing, it passes along a groove in the roof of the second, directly into the third compartment; chemical digestion takes place in the fourth compartment, which alone has gastric glands in its walls for secretion of digestive juices.

Horns.—Four main types of horn construction are found among the ruminants.

1. The antlers of deer. These are usually found in the male deer only, but in the reindeer they are present in both sexes. They grow out from the frontal bones of the skull as solid processes which rapidly reach their full size. At first they are covered by soft and hairy skin. Then a circular ridge called the burr appears at a short distance from the base of the antler and divides the latter into pedicel on the skull side of the burr, and beam on the far side.

The circulation in the beam then gradually dwindles, and the skin dies and peels off, leaving exposed the dead bone beneath it. Absorption and sloughing take place at the extremity of the pedicel, beam and burr are shed, and the end of the pedicel scabs over. Fresh skin gradually grows up under the scab so that the pedicel becomes once more smooth and hairy. The antlers are shed and grown anew every year, usually adding additional branches each time. (*See* Deer.)

2. In the bovine ruminants the bony core formed by the frontal bone is covered by a horny sheath. The core itself is hollow, instead of solid as in the deer. The horny sheath is never shed but persists throughout life and grows with the growth of the core. This type of horn is never branched but may be curved, spirally

twisted or compressed; it is often present in both sexes. (*See* Sheep; Goat; Antelope; etc.)

3. In the giraffes (*q.v.*) the horn cores are covered with soft and hairy skin and are never shed.

4. In the North American pronghorn, *Antilocapra,* there is a permanent, unbranched horn core enclosed in a horny sheath as in the Bovidae, but this sheath is forked and furthermore is shed yearly after the rutting season since the development of a new sheath pushes the old one off. (*See* Pronghorn.)

These four types of horn are characteristic of the five families into which existing ruminants are classified: the Cervidae or deer; the Giraffidae or giraffe and okapi; the Bovidae or oxen, sheep, goats, antelopes, etc.; the Antilocapridae, solely represented by the North American pronghorn; and the Tragulidae, the chevrotains (*q.v.*), which have no horns or antlers.

Many other forms are extinct. The earliest fossil forms were small with no antlers but a pair of long slender tusks in the upper jaw like those of the musk deer. From such as these were derived not only the modern families but several families now extinct; among them the Lagomerycidae, Amphimerycidae, etc.

See also Artiodactyl and articles on the separate families and genera.

See W. H. Flower and R. Lydehker, *Introduction to the Study of Mammals, Living and Extinct* (1891); W. B. Scott, *History of Land Mammals in the Western Hemisphere* (1937).   (H. S. P.; X.)

RUMMY (Rum, Rhum, Romme), the most generally known of all card games and, with its many variants including canasta (*q.v.*) and gin rummy, the most widely played, especially in the United States. The original version, introduced early in the 20th century, was called conquian (*see* Cooncan) from the Spanish *con quién* "with whom." The English gave it its lasting name by calling it rum (queer) poker.

Though there are no official rules, the following procedure of the basic game is common to most variants.

From two to six may play, using a standard deck of 52 cards with or without jokers. Cards rank: K (high), Q, J, 10, 9 . . . . A (low). Cards are dealt face down one at a time, clockwise beginning with the player on dealer's left. For two players, ten cards are dealt to each; for three or four, seven; for five or six, six. The remainder of the deck, the stock, is placed face down; top card of the stock is faced to start the talon or discard pile.

The common goal of all rummy games is to build sets or melds such as three or four of a kind (as four 6s, three 8s) or sequences of three or more cards of the same suit (♠ J-10-9-8, etc.). A joker may represent any needed card.

Each player, at his turn, draws the top card of the stock or of the discard pile and may then face upon the table any meld or melds of three cards or more, and may also lay off any cards from his hand that match his own or another player's exposed melds. He must then discard one card face up on the discard pile (except that on the turn when he goes out, no discard is needed).

The deal is won by the first player who goes out (melds or lays off all his cards). Melding an entire hand at one turn is called going rummy and is paid double.

The winner of each deal collects from each of the other players the index value of the cards each holds unmelded (even if matched up). Face cards count 10 each; aces 1 or 11 as previously agreed; jokers, if used, count 15.

In social play, a running score is kept and the game ends when any player reaches a predetermined score (as plus 100 points) or after an agreed number of deals.

When stock is exhausted, play ends and the hand with the lowest count wins. In some games, each player is permitted an additional turn to take or refuse the top card of the talon.

500 Rum.—This version is also called pinochle rummy; variations include Michigan rum, Oklahoma, Persian rummy and canasta. From two to eight may play. With five players or more, two full packs shuffled together are used. When two play, each is dealt 13 cards; with three or more, 7 cards are dealt to each.

At his turn, each player draws the top card of the stock or any card in the discard pile provided that: (1) he melds such card at once and (2) he puts into his hand (to meld immediately or not, as he pleases) all cards lying above the one he has drawn.

Layoffs are the same as in rummy, except that each player keeps before him the cards he has melded. When the deal ends, each player receives credit for the index value of his melds, minus the index value of all cards remaining in his hand. Aces count 15 if left in hand or if melded as a group of aces; they count but 1 if melded A-2-3.

When any player has scored 500 or more the game ends. There is no bonus for winning the game.

Persian Rummy.—Four play as partners, using one pack plus four jokers which count 20 points and may be melded only in groups of jokers. Aces count 15 and may be used only as A-K-Q or as a group of aces, not as A-2-3. If all four cards of a rank are melded at once, the value of the meld is doubled. When a player has melded all his cards, the deal ends and his side scores a bonus of 25 points. After stock is exhausted, the discard pile is drawn from until no player is able to make a meld with the exposed card of the discard pile.

Two deals constitute a game. The partnership with the higher total wins the difference between the scores, plus a game bonus of 50.

Knock Rummy.—Any player, at his turn and after drawing and discarding, may knock (lay down his entire hand) and declare the total value of his unmatched cards. He does so when he believes he has the lowest total unmatched (not part of a meld). If his assumption is correct, he collects from each opponent the difference in the counts. If another hand is lower than the knocker, the low hand wins from all and collects an extra penalty of 10 points from the knocker. (Some play that the knocker must pay double.) If a player ties for low, he collects the winnings and the knocker neither pays nor collects. If two or more other players tie for low, they divide the winnings.

Gin Rummy.—First introduced in New York in 1909, this game became a nation-wide fad in the U.S. in 1941 after scoring changes were made. Two play; each is dealt ten cards face down, one at a time, beginning with nondealer. The remainder of the pack, placed face down, forms the stock. The top card of the stock is turned up beside the stock to form the first up card.

Nondealer may take the up card or refuse it; if he refuses, dealer has the same option. If both refuse, nondealer draws the top card of the stock. Thereafter, each player in turn takes either the up card or the top card of the stock, then discards one card face up on the up card pile.

Object of play is to form melds as in rummy. Cards that do not form part of a meld are called unmatched. After drawing, a player may knock (go down) if his unmatched cards (less one discard) total 10 or less. Face cards count 10, aces 1, other cards their index value. Upon knocking, a player faces his 10 cards arranged in sets and with unmatched cards to one side, then discards his 11th card. If all his cards are matched, he is gin and he receives, in addition to the index value of his opponent's unmatched cards, a bonus of 25 points.

Opponent of the knocker may lay off any of his unmatched cards upon the knocker's sets, thereby reducing his count. If the knocker has the lower count unmatched, he wins the difference. Should his opponent remain with an equal or lesser count, he may undercut the knocker and receives the difference (if any) plus a bonus of 25 points, but the knocker cannot be undercut if he has gone gin. When only two cards remain in stock and neither player has knocked, the deal is called off with no score.

First to reach 100 points wins the game and receives a 100-point bonus. Each player then adds to his score 25 points for each hand he has won, called a box. If the loser failed to score, the game is a shutout or schneider and the winner's total score is doubled.   (R. L. Fy.)

RUMYANTSEV, NIKOLAI PETROVICH, Count (1754–1826), Russian statesman, diplomat, and bibliophile, son of P. A. Rumyantsev (*q.v.*), is best remembered as a collector of books and manuscripts, and as a patron of historical research and library acquisitions; he was born on April 14 (new style; 3, old style), 1754. Educated in part at the University of Leiden, he served in Frankfurt am Main as envoy to the elector of the Rhenish

Palatinate (1781–95), and established contact with members of the French royal family who had emigrated to Germany. Appointed envoy extraordinary and minister plenipotentiary to the German diet (1799), he exerted himself to increase Russian influence on German affairs. Under Paul I he became a senator; under Alexander I he was made director of water communications (1801–09) and minister of commerce (1802–11) in which capacities he played an important role in the improvement of water communication in Russia and the development of commerce and trade with Asia. In 1808 he became foreign minister, in 1810 president of the state council. As foreign minister, Rumyantsev worked toward close relations with France. Napoleon's invasion of Russia so upset him that he suffered an apoplectic stroke and lost his hearing. In 1814, broken in health and no longer influential, he retired from government service. After his retirement, Rumyantsev personally financed a round-the-world expedition to explore the polar regions and Polynesia, as well as other voyages.

While foreign minister, Rumyantsev published diplomatic sources of the Moscow archives at his own expense and in 1813 provided the Academy of Sciences with the financial means for examining and publishing materials from the Moscow archives of the Foreign Office. He financed the publication of all available chronicles, and promoted research and the writing of history. The St. Petersburg Rumyantsev Museum, founded in 1831, after his death, with its many books, rare manuscripts, and maps, became the heart of what is now the Lenin Library, one of the world's largest collections. Rumyantsev died at St. Petersburg on Jan. 15 (N.S.; 3, O.S.), 1826.

See Anatole G. Mazour, *Modern Russian Historiography* (1958).
(G. A. Ln.)

RUMYANTSEV, PETR ALEKSANDROVICH, COUNT

(1725–1796), Russian statesman and army officer who distinguished himself in the Seven Years' War (1756–63) and in the Russo-Turkish War of 1768–74, was born in Moscow on Jan. 15 (new style; 4, old style), 1725. As a major general he won the battles of Gross-Jägersdorf (1757) and as a lieutenant general that of Kunersdorf (1759); in 1761 he took Kolberg (Kolobrzeg) by storm.

At the accession of Catherine II in 1762 Rumyantsev, who had enjoyed the favour of Peter III, expected that his career would come to an end, but in November 1764 Catherine appointed him governor-general of the Ukraine with the secret instruction to integrate the region more closely into Russia. In the Russo-Turkish War of 1768–74 Rumyantsev gained fame by his decisive victories (1770) over immensely stronger enemy forces on the Larga and Kagul rivers. Pushing on at the enemy's heels, Rumyantsev in 1771 extended the campaign to the banks of the Danube, and in 1774 not only crossed the Danube but approached the fortress of Shumla in Bulgaria. After the peace of Kuchuk-Kainarji (1774), Rumyantsev attained the rank of field marshal and received the title of Count Zadunaiski. In 1794 he was called upon by Catherine II to "pacify" the Poles, but this was achieved mainly by A. V. Suvorov (*q.v.*). Rumyantsev died at Tashan, Ukraine, on Dec. 19 (N.S.; 8, O.S.), 1796.
(Lo. L.)

RUNCORN,

a market town, river port, and urban district of Cheshire, Eng., lies on the southern shore of the Mersey, 16 mi. (26 km.) NNE of Chester by road and 15 mi. (24⅔ km.) from Liverpool. Pop. (1961) 26,035. It is on the Bridgewater Canal (1773), which descends into the Mersey by a flight of locks; it is also on the Manchester Ship Canal and is a subport of Manchester with extensive wharfage and warehouse accommodation. The town possesses shipbuilding yards, iron foundries, and large alkali and chemical works. Exports include heavy chemicals, coal, salt, and pitch; there is also a large traffic in potters' materials. Runcorn is connected with Widnes by a railway bridge and, since 1961, by an arch-type, high-level road bridge. On a rock, which then jutted into the Mersey, Aethelflaed erected a castle in 915. In 1964 it was designated a New Town under the New Towns Act of 1946, with an ultimate population of 100,000. The designated area coincides with the Runcorn urban district area of 8,036 ac.
(T. J. L.)

RUNDI

(BARUNDI, WARUNDI), an East African (Interlacus-trine Bantu) people who inhabit the Kingdom of Burundi, formerly incorporated in the Belgian trust territory of Ruanda-Urundi. Numbering about 2,500,000 in the 1960s, they very closely resemble the neighbouring Rwanda (*q.v.*) in language, traditional culture, and modern economy; legend links their kingships through common ancestry. The traditional Rundi state was more loosely organized than that of the Rwanda, among whom political and military authority was held mainly by appointees of the *mwami* (king); among the Rundi, princes of the blood ruled together as a kind of oligarchy, each having authority over a district. The overall authority of the *mwami* was frequently challenged by fellow princes and civil war was commoner than in Rwanda.

In 1962 Burundi became an independent constitutional monarchy with a bicameral legislature elected by universal adult suffrage. The aristocratic Tutsi caste, which made up about 15% of the population, remained politically dominant, though members of the commoner Hutu group played an expanding role in public affairs. See BANTU (INTERLACUSTRINE); RUANDA-URUNDI.

See E. M. Albert, "Socio-Political Organization and Receptivity to Change: Some Differences between Ruanda and Urundi," *Sthwest. J. Anthrop.*, vol. 16 (1960); H. Kitchen, *A Handbook of African Affairs* (1964).
(L. A. Fs.)

RUNDSTEDT, (KARL RUDOLF) GERD VON

(1875–1953), German army officer, leading field commander in World War II, was born at Aschersleben, near Magdeburg, on Dec. 12, 1875, of a noble Prussian family. He was chief of staff of an army corps in World War I and assisted in reorganizing the Turkish general staff. Later he was active in the secret German rearmament and on his retirement in October 1938 was the senior German field commander. Recalled to active duty before the outbreak of war in 1939, he commanded army groups in the Polish, French, and Russian campaigns and became a field marshal.

Coming into conflict with Hitler on the conduct of the Russian campaign, Rundstedt was relieved of command in 1941, but was soon restored to favour and appointed commander in chief west, with headquarters near Paris; there he prepared the defenses against the Allied invasion. He was replaced by Günther von Kluge in early July 1944, but again became commander in chief west in September and directed the Ardennes counteroffensive. He was captured by U.S. troops in May 1945 but was later released because of ill health. He died in Hanover on Feb. 24, 1953. Rundstedt regarded Hitler and his methods with contempt but never permitted conspiracy against him in his own staff.

See G. Blumentritt, *Von Rundstedt: the Soldier and the Man,* Eng. trans. (1952).
(P. N. T.)

RUNE,

a character of an alphabet used for the oldest form of Germanic writing. This form of writing was in use in the Scandinavian north in the 3rd century, and in remote districts of Sweden almost down to modern times. (*See* also ALPHABET.)

No topic has been so much disputed as runes—by scholars, patriotic (and sometimes irrational) enthusiasts, theorists, and cranks. Chronology, transcription, and translation, a regular hodgepodge of conjecture mixed both with serious scholarship and with black magic and superstition, contribute to what often descends to mere hocus-pocus. Runes have been used to trick the credulous and the superstitious. Forgeries have turned up even in North America. The Kensington Stone, which was found in Minnesota, contains writing that is 1,000 years out of style. Viking swords, found in southern Ontario and once held to support the Kensington case, are now known to have been "planted."

Runic Forms.—During the first centuries of their vogue, runes consisted of 24 letters: the so-called older or common Germanic runic staves (fig. 1). Their peculiar forms appear first in inscriptions found all over Europe from Rumania and the western

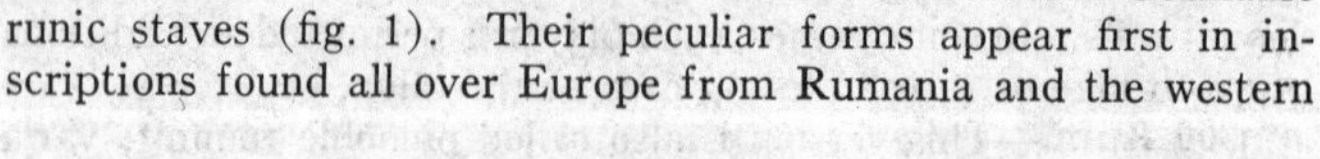

f u t h a r k g w　　h n i j e p ʀ s　　t b e m l ŋ o d

FIG. 1.—ALL-GERMANIC RUNIC STAVES

Soviet Union to the east of France and Friesland, but in greatest number in England and Scandinavia. Runes, which were derived from a subalpine script, differ from it radically in their arrangement, as may be seen from some inscriptions that use the runic staves in their entirety, the most important being the Kylver Stone on the island of Gotland, in the Baltic Sea (5th century); the Vadstena *braktea* from Östergötland, Swed. (fig. 2); the Charnay clasp from eastern France; and the Thames sword from southern England. Moreover, every rune had its special name and these names are known through the oral traditions recorded in Anglo-Saxon manuscripts. The 24 runes were divided into three groups of eight each, each group coming later to be called in Scandinavian an *ætt*, a word which probably meant "number of eight." The runic staves, at least at a later period, were called *futhark*, after their initial letters.

FIG. 2.—VADSTENA BRAKTEA

As regards sound values, it may be mentioned that *th* was pronounced approximately as in the English *thing; d* like *th* in the English *this; g* had a sound corresponding to *g* in German *sagen; b* in the same way, therefore, corresponding to *b* in the Spanish *Habana; ng* like *ng* in *England;* and *R,* when final, almost like *s* in the English *is.*

Origin.—The oldest extant decipherable runic writings whose origin is at all certain were discovered in the bogland of southwestern Denmark, at Vi-mose in Fyn, and at Thorsbjaerg in Schleswig. Most archaeologists date the former from the middle of the 3rd century, the latter from the 4th. The inscriptions are few in number and brief. Those that can be deciphered contain one or two names of men. These earliest finds of runes in Denmark were supplemented by a whole series of others from the 4th, 5th, and 6th centuries—inscriptions on single objects, arms, ornaments, and more especially gold *brakteas* (medallions, probably amulets). Archaeological research has established the fact that southwestern Denmark was really the cradle of the knowledge of runes, whence the use of runes spread to Norway and Sweden. It has been ascertained, moreover, that from Schleswig it made its way in the 5th century along the southern coast of the North Sea to England and the Continent.

If then, Schleswig and Fyn are the original home of the runes in northern and western Europe, the next question is: did the runes originate in Denmark or were they imported from elsewhere? It has been established that a number of runes that are contemporaneous with the oldest of those found in the Danish bogland have been discovered along a line of country passing through Pomorze, Brandenburg, Volhynia, and Rumania. Moreover, these discoveries include archaic objects the primary forms of which do not hail from western Europe but are found in southeastern Europe, on the northern coast of the Black Sea and along the middle and lower Danube and in Carinthia. From this fact, and also from the close agreement of the forms of the letters in these texts with those of the subalpine alphabets of northern Italy, and the agreement in date (*c.* 250 B.C.), the conclusion was drawn simultaneously by a number of scholars that the runes came to Scandinavia from central Europe and that the script itself was of subalpine origin. It is certain that runes were known and used among the Goths in the first half of the 4th century. In the 3rd and 4th centuries there is no trace of the existence of runes in the western Germanic world, *i.e.*, southwest of the line Schleswig, Berlin, Bucharest.

Ludwig Wimmer made it clear that they are derived ultimately from a Mediterranean form of alphabet that had its origins in a western Greek type. The runes have the same signs for the vowels *a, e, o,* as the Greek and Latin alphabets; the runes for *f, h,* and *r* derive from the Italic alphabets. Since a number of runes (as *a, i, b, t, m,* and *n*) may be traced typographically to the Greek and Latin alphabets and as it undoubtedly would be natural to seek the source of the runes in a single alphabet, Wim-

mer sought to trace all the runes back to Latin. In so seeking, however, he was forced into assumptions and deductions which must be regarded as improbable and irrational.

About 1928–30, three scholars saw independently that the runes derive from a subalpine Northern Etruscan alphabet which was in use in the eastern Alps among Prae-Italic tribes, and it was from these that the Germani, perhaps the Marcomanni who lived in Bohemia, developed the runes. Certain runes are more easily and naturally explained in the light of this discovery than in that of any other interpretation that has been put forward. Archaeological and chronological facts are not difficult to reconcile with this hypothesis, which is now widely accepted.

Actually its authors had been anticipated (*e.g.*, by Hempl, Skeat, C. D. Buck, and others). The resemblance between subalpine and runic scripts is great. But it is not the mere similarity that is decisive; the important facts are that the oldest known Germanic inscription is in a subalpine alphabet, and that the oldest runic texts appear at the eastern end of the Alps and beyond, not in Germany or Scandinavia.

The close relationship between the runes and cursive handwriting—the ordinary handwriting used in everyday life—indicates that the art of writing did not come to the Goths by the way of scholarship. Some individual Goths (*e.g.*, mercenaries) from the northwestern coast of the Black Sea, in the course of visits to the Roman provinces, learned Greek and Latin and the Greek and Latin forms of writing used in state edicts and in private life. In addition, they acquired an imperfect acquaintance with the lapidary and uncial style that was the basis for the ordinary cursive handwriting, wherefore some forms of the better style occasionally appear. Such a Goth, or several such Goths working together, undertook to write out the Gothic language on the basis of the knowledge of Latin and Greek writing thus acquired, and these efforts influenced the runic stave.

FIG. 3.—SPEARHEADS FOUND NEAR BREST, U.S.S.R.

Like the letters of the classic alphabets, runes soon came to be used for purposes of magic, a use which continued for a long time. But that the chief purpose of the runes was to give the spoken language a fixed form is demonstrated by the fact that at an early date both Ulfilas and those who used the Old English alphabets drew upon runes when the Greek or Latin scripts failed them. Removed from the sphere of classical culture, runic writing soon came to be used chiefly for inscriptions: it was carved or cut on wood, metal, or stone. In the process the individual letters began to undergo a certain kind of symmetrical stylization that gave them a substantially different appearance from that of their prototypes, and at the same time the runes came to be put in an order entirely different from that of the classic alphabets.

Spread and Development.—From the Danubian region, knowledge of runes spread with the migrating Goths to distant corners of the great dominion that this Germanic people established in the 3rd and 4th centuries between the Black Sea and the Baltic. Of the same period of migration is the Thorsbjaerg chape (metal mounting for scabbard) from Schleswig (fig. 4), which bears the inscription *owlthuthewaR niwajmariR;* these are probably the names of two men, *WulthuthewaR* and *NiujamariR,* both names being of the familiar old Germanic binomial compound type, but other interpretations have been advanced.

There are many signs that runic

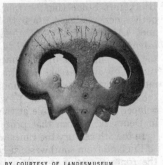

FIG. 4.—THORSBJAERG CHAPE

writing was brought to Schleswig and Fyn from the Black Sea by the Heruli (*q.v.*). Schleswig in those early days and until well into the Middle Ages was of primary importance for the intercommunication and exchange of merchandise between the Baltic regions and western and southern Europe. In particular, Schleswig had long been the traffic route from the Rhineland and England up to the Scandinavian north. A remarkable runic inscription found in Schleswig is that on a golden horn from Gallehus (fig. 5), which dates from the beginning of the 5th century. It reads: *ek hlewagastiR holtijaR horna tawido*, "I Hlewegast, Holt's son, made the horn." Altogether about a dozen inscriptions on portable objects, also inscriptions of the older type as well as about 40 runic *brakteas* dating from between the 3rd and 6th centuries, have been found in Danish soil.

FIG. 5.—GALLEHUS INSCRIPTION

At a very early period (sometime in the 3rd century) runic writing spread from Denmark into Norway. There as early as the 4th century the custom began of equipping stone monuments with runic inscriptions. One of the finest and longest inscriptions is that of the Tune Stone from southeastern Norway (*see* fig. 6). According to Helmut Arntz, the Tune Stone may be translated: "I, Wiwaz [older Wigiwaz *Geweihter* "horned"], worked the runes to my lord [literally "loaf-warden"] Woduridaz [*i.e.*, the Wild Huntsman, the name of a priest of Wodan]. Three daughters set up the stone in honour of me Woduridaz, the [kin] nearest-to-the Ases [gods] wrought the inheritance meal."

In Norway, from the period A.D. 250–800, there are extant, in addition to a number of *brakteas* with runic inscriptions, about 50 inscriptions, mostly on standing stones or stones inserted in tumuli but also on portable objects.

The runes also moved from southwestern Denmark up the Baltic. In Gotland, ancient centre for trade and intercourse in northern Europe, staves continued to be written throughout the entire period, though not to such an extent as in Norway. Runic inscriptions have been found more sparsely on the mainland of Sweden—in Uppland, Södermanland, and Östergötland. They are commoner in Västergötland. In all, about 20 runic inscriptions from the migration period have been found in Sweden, as well as a few runic *brakteas*. Of special note among them are the late (7th century) inscriptions from the westernmost parts of Blekinge which show a continuation of the development of the runic letters that had taken place in southwestern Norway, so rich in runes, during the early and middle periods of the migration era. Probably these inscriptions also came from Norwegian immigrants. The best-preserved specimen is the Björketorp Stone (fig. 7), four metres high, with inscriptions on both sides reading: *uthArAbAsbA* ("ruin-bringing prophecy") and *hAidzruno ronu fAlAhAk hAd(e)rA ginarunAR ArAgeu hAerAmAlAusR uti AR welAdAude sAR thAt bArutR*, "This is the secret meaning of the runes; I hid here magic-runes, undisturbed by evil witchcraft. In misery shall he die by means of magic art who destroys this monument." On these Blekinge stones the runic *k* has the form ᛉ which about the year 500 was developed in Norway, while at the same time the form ᛘ appeared in Denmark, a form that proceeded thence to England.

In the 5th century the runes went to the Germanic continent and to England from southwestern Denmark. On the continent, where the runic *k* retains its original form, there have been found inscriptions from the Rhine Province, Hesse, Nassau, Thuringia,

FIG. 6.—TUNE STONE

Württemberg, Bavaria, Austria, as well as in Charnay, the old Burgundian kingdom in eastern France, in what is now the *département* of Saône-et-Loire. These inscriptions are few and, like the Danish, all inscribed on portable objects, and they are quite short. They are all held to belong to the period A.D. 450–550. As an illustration may be cited the inscription on the clasp from Freilaubersheim in Rhenish Hesse: *boso wraet run-ath(i)k mafiena godd(a)*, "Boso wrote the runes—to thee, Mafiena [?], he gave [the clasp]."

England.—Knowledge and use of runes constituted merely a brief episode on the western Germanic continent, but it flourished for five centuries in England. Anglo-Saxon rune staves like continental Germanic have two cross strokes in the letter *h* and differ from it in the form of the *k;* they differ from the Scandinavian and eastern Germanic, as well as from the continental Germanic runes with their 24 letters, in that new letters were created to render the most important novelties in the rich Anglo-Frisian vowel system. Later, new consonant letters were added.

FIG. 7.—BJÖRKETORP STONE

The beginning of this development of the system of letters had already been effected on the southern portion of the coast of the North Sea in Friesland, where there are inscriptions belonging to the end of the 5th century and to the 6th century with new runic letters for *a* and *o* sounds. In England there developed a

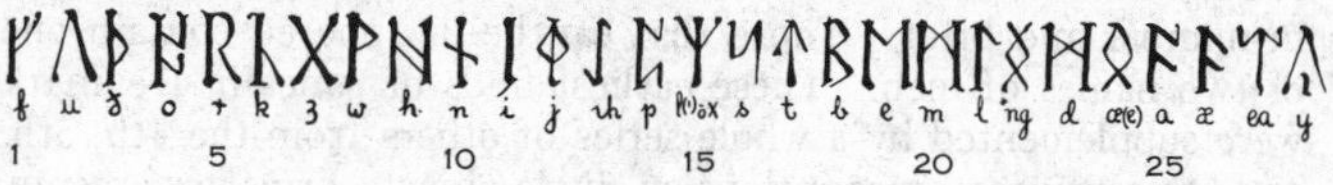

ᚠᚢᚦᚩᚱᚲᚷᚹᚻᚾᛁᛄᛇᛈᛉᛋᛏᛒᛖᛗᛚᛝᛞᛟᚪᚫᚣ

f u ð o r k g w h n i j h p x s t b e m l ŋ d œ a æ y

FIG. 8.—EARLY ANGLO-SAXON RUNES

runic stave of 28 letters (fig. 8), which in the 9th century increased to 33.

In England there are extant about 50 runic inscriptions upon portable objects and standing stones (stone crosses). Among the most remarkable and best preserved are those carved on a whalebone casket (Franks Casket, fig. 9). The inscriptions, with illustrations from biblical history and Roman and Germanic legends, cover the sides of the casket and the lid and are held to be from not later than about A.D. 700. The inscription on one side reads: *hronæs ban fisk flodu ahof on fergenberig warth gasrik grorn thær on greut giswom*, "Whalebone [is this]. The flood threw the fish on the hard rock. The monster [?] was stranded on the stone in agony [?]." Reproduced in fig. 10 is the later 33-letter Anglo-Saxon runic stave; it gives the runic names of oldest date.

In England the runes persisted for the entire Anglo-Saxon period. Remarkable monuments from later times are the two runic crosses from Bewcastle and Ruthwell on the Scottish border.

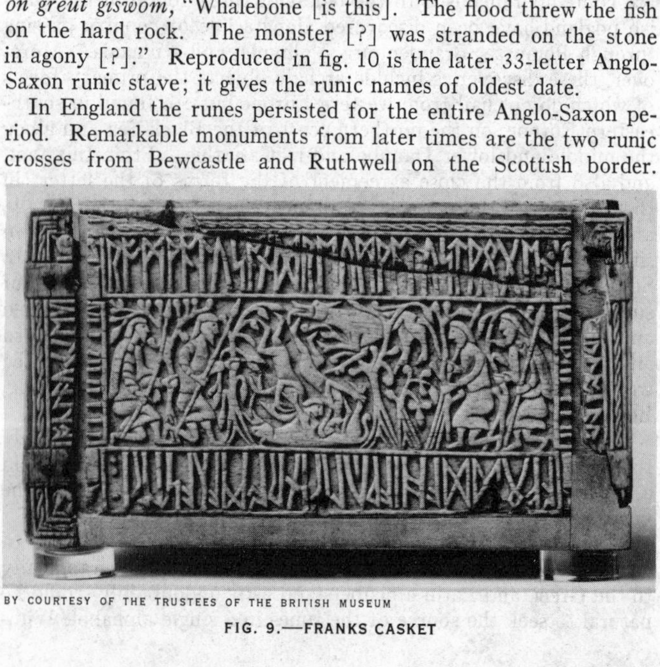

FIG. 9.—FRANKS CASKET

Names of Runic Letters

Latin equivalent	Anglo-Saxon name	Scandinavian name	Gothic name (reconstructed)
f	feh (money)	fé, fa (goods)	faihu (read fehu)
u	úr (aurochs)	úrr (aurochs)	urus
th	thorn (thorn)	thurs (giant)	thauris
a	ós (god)	óss (god)	ansus
r	rád (ride)	reið (journey)	raida
k	cán (torch)	kaun (ab oil)	kaun ?
g	geofu (gift)		giba
w	wynn (joy)		winja
h	hægl (hail)	hagl (hail)	hagl
n	nied (need)	nauð (need)	nauths
i	ís (ice)	íss (ice)	eis
j	géar (year)	aar (year, harvest)	jer
e	éoh = éow (yew tree)	ýr (small fir, bow)	eiws
þ	peorð ? (dance)		pairthra
r	eolhs (?)	elgr (elk)	algs
s	sygil (sun)	sol (sun)	sauil
t	tír (honour)	tyr (god)	teiws
b	beorc (birch)	biarkan (birch seed)	bairkan
e	eðh (horse)		aihwa
m	man (human being)	maðr (human being)	manna
l	lagu (water, sea)	legr (liquid)	lagus
—	Ing (a hero)		Iggws
o	éðel (inheritance)		othal
d	dæg (day)		dags

Because of the tradition kept alive in England from ancient times and the fact that the names borrowed by Ulfilas from the runes to render Gothic letters are indicated in a manuscript (not, indeed, in their original forms) preserved in the National Museum at Vienna, it is possible to reconstruct approximately the name that every runic letter seems to have borne from the beginning. Later traditions handed down in Scandinavia are also of value, although the later peculiarly northern runic staves contained only 16 letters and the names of 8 letters therefore have been lost. (*See* table.)

Thus the great modification of the Germanic sound system caused by vowel mutation, by breaking, and by other sound changes

FIG. 10.—LATER ANGLO-SAXON RUNES

resulted in a considerable enlargement of the runic alphabet in England.

Scandinavia.—In Scandinavia the Germanic sound shift produced a result directly opposite to that in England: the number of the runes was reduced from 24 to 16, though the Scandinavian stock of sounds reached 30 or 40 during the later migration period. The explanation of this would seem to lie in the fact that, while the original 24 runes covered adequately the old Germanic sounds, it became the habit later, as the result of the variation in the sound system, to represent different sounds by the same rune. This brought about a simpler alphabet; when a single runic letter could be used to render several sounds, many of the old letters became superfluous. Simultaneously, the formation of many of the runes are simplified. This twofold reduction of numbers and forms began in Scandinavia as far back as the 6th century, and at the beginning of the Viking era this had resulted in a special

FIG. 12.—SWEDISH-NORWEGIAN RUNES

of the 6th century, and the form of the runic *k*, as well as other details, indicates that it was through an impulse from Norway or Sweden that runes came into use again in Denmark at the close of the 8th century. There are extant over 200 inscriptions upon standing stones as well as a few upon portable objects. Most of them date from between A.D. 800 and the middle of the 11th century. Despite their laconic and often stereotyped wording, they are among the most remarkable, as regards both style and matter, that have been found in Scandinavia. They give the names of several hundred men and women who lived in Denmark during this important period, from members of the royal house down to the lower grades of society, and they provide data for visualizing the life of the people in war and peace.

The runic monuments that date from the beginning of this period are few in number. One of the oldest and most remarkable inscriptions with runes of the later period is the Helnæs stone at Fyn (fig. 13): *rhuulfR sati stain nuRa kuthi aft kuthumut bruthur sunu sin turuknathu (haliR uti) ouaiR fathi.* If it were written in a more adequate phonetic alphabet, *e.g.*, the Early Norwegian Icelandic alphabet, which includes ð, this inscription would have run: *HrólfR setti stein, NóRa goði, aft Guðmund broð urusunu sinn drunknaðu haliR uti. ÁveiR fáði;* "Rolf raised this stone, priest and chieftain of the Helnæs dwellers, in memory of his brother's son, Gudmund. The men were drowned at sea. Aveir wrote [the runes]."

From the earlier half of the 10th century the smaller of the two famous Royal stones of Jällinge in Jutland (fig. 14): *kurmR kunu(n)kR karthi ku(m)bl thusi aft thurui kunu sina tanmarkaR but,* "King Gorm made this monument in memory of his wife, Tyra: the enlarger of Denmark."

The great majority of Denmark's 200 runic stones date, however, from the end of the 10th and the beginning of the 11th centuries. It was the period when the Vikings' raids on England were renewed, resulting at last in the conquest of the country by the Danish king, Sweyn Forkbeard, who is mentioned in two of the runic inscriptions, and Canute the Great. The relations between Denmark and England are reflected in the history of the runic inscriptions inasmuch as it was probably due to influence by the Anglo-Saxon runes that the Danish alphabet then began to be enlarged by so-called pointed runes.

From Denmark the Danish runes spread about A.D. 1000 to Sweden, where runic inscriptions on standing stones became more numerous than anywhere else. Hundreds of runic inscriptions are known in Sweden, chiefly from the 11th century and the beginning of the 12th, the majority of them written in Danish runes. Half of them belong to the central region of the kingdom Uppland. These monuments make it possible to follow the upward course of the Danish runes through Sweden from Skåne and Västergötland to the southern part of Norrland; the inscriptions in the south are, on an average, of earlier date than those in

16-letter Scandinavian alphabet. The alphabet appears in two distinct forms—Danish (fig. 11) and Swedish-Norwegian (fig. 12). Danish also was used in southwestern Sweden.

In Denmark, runes seem to have been little used after the close

FIG. 11.—DANISH RUNES

FIG. 13.—HELNÆS STONE

BY COURTESY OF "DANMARKS RUNEINDSKRIFTER," DENMARK

FIG. 14.—EARLIER JÄLLINGE STONE

the north. The custom of erecting runic stones was not long-lived anywhere. Generally speaking, it was abandoned whenever a region became definitely Christianized, but it seems to have had a vigorous final revival during the missionary period.

From the beginning, runic stones were erected for the most part in village graveyards, and one principal reason for giving up the custom of erecting them must have been that with the spread of Christianity the dead had to be buried in the cemetery adjoining the parish church, often at a distance from the home. Thereby, monuments lost much of their interest for the survivors. In Uppland, more especially, the runic inscriptions were accompanied by cleverly executed ornamental designs, the patterns of which were taken from woodcuts—the art of woodcuts having been highly developed during the migration and Viking periods. Not merely the runes themselves but also these ornamental designs needed craftsmanship, and therefore many runic inscriptions were executed by expert craftsmen.

The oldest and most remarkable (c. A.D. 1025–1050) of these Uppland professional writers of runes was Asmund, probably identical with the Osmundus mentioned by the Bremen ecclesiastical historian, Adam. Osmundus was one of the Englishmen of Scandinavian origin who prepared the way in Sweden for the conquest of Christianity. Other talented masters of the art were Fot and Öpir. Asmund's stones record the names of a number of Swedes who took part in Canute the Great's conquest of England. On the Ängeby Stone (fig. 15), one of Asmund's inscriptions reads as follows: *rahnfrithr lit risa stain thina aftiR biurn sun thaiRa kitil-muntaR. kuth hialbi hans ant aukuths muthiR. hon fil a uirlanti. in osmuntr markathi*, "Ragnfrid had this stone erected in memory of Björn, her and Kättilmund's son. God and God's Mother help his soul! He fell in Estland. But Asmund engraved [the stone]" (as rendered by Otto von Friesen).

BY COURTESY OF KUNGL. VITTER-HETS HISTORIE OCH ANTIKVITETS AKADEMIEN, STOCKHOLM

FIG. 15.—ÄNGEBY STONE

When the runic alphabet was reduced from 24 letters to 16, the simplifying of the individual letters was carried furthest in the Swedish-Norwegian runes. These are to be found in Gotland, in eastern Göta-land, in Svealand, and in Norway, dating from the beginning of the Viking era, about A.D. 800. In Sweden they were displaced on monuments by Danish runes at the beginning of the 11th century, but many circumstances indicate that even after this period they were used for more private purposes. Comparatively few runic monuments have Swedish-Norwegian runes, but among these few must be mentioned the largest and most original of all, the Rök Stone (fig. 16), the top and the four sides of which are covered with runes. The

stone was erected by a father in memory of his son, and the inscriptions would seem to have in some degree a magical purpose: to wreak vengeance on the son's slayers. The beginning of the inscription reads: *aft uamuth stonta runaR thaR in uarin fathi fathiR aft faikion sunu,* "In memory of Vämod stand these runes. And Varin, the father, made them in memory of his son, overtaken by death" (Friesen).

Swedish-Norwegian runes in Sweden are characterized from the start by a great reduction in the length of the cross strokes. In order to reduce as much as possible the length of the stroke, whether written or incised, the vertical strokes were done away with as far as possible. Thus came into existence the Hälsinge runes (fig. 17), named after the

BY COURTESY OF KUNGL. VITTERHETS HISTORIE OCH ANTIKVITETS AKADEMIEN, STOCKHOLM

FIG. 16.—RÖK STONE (FRONT)

region of Hälsingland in which they have been found inscribed on a number of runic stones dating from the 11th century. They were known and used, however, in the central region of Sweden adjoining Mälaren, where they were likely invented. The Hälsinge runes are a kind of runic shorthand, and they clearly indicate that runes were used not merely on monuments but for all kinds of announcements: legal provisions, contracts, genealogies, and poems.

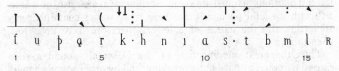

f u þ o r k h n i a s t b m l R
1   5   10   15

FIG. 17.—HÄLSINGE RUNES

In Norway there appeared in the 11th century a peculiar mixture of Swedish-Norwegian and Danish runes, which later led to an extension of the 16-letter alphabet to one better adapted to the northern sound system—the pointed runes. The Danes probably got the idea from England at the close of the 10th century. The Anglo-Saxon rune for *y* was a *u* inside which an *i* was written. This rune was used in Denmark before the year A.D. 1000, and after this model there was constructed out of the *i* a special letter for

a b c d e f g h i k l m n o p q r s t þ u R y z æ ø
1   5   10   15   20   25

FIG. 18.—COMPLETED POINTED RUNIC ALPHABET

e and out of the *k* a special letter for *g*. These new letters are used generally in the Danish runes during the 11th century, although not consistently. It would seem that toward the close of the 11th century, when the Danish and Swedish-Norwegian alphabet came to be blended in Norway, means were found to employ the wealth of letters thus produced to form a systematic representation of all the sounds in the language. The Latin alphabet, which had come into use with the introduction of Christianity, must have been of service in the construction of this radical improvement of the runes as symbols for sounds. Thus came into existence the completed pointed runic alphabet (fig. 18).

Only in Gotland was the completed runic stave used to any great extent for inscriptions on monuments though such inscriptions are found here and there in other parts of Scandinavia. Gotland, moreover, had to begin with its own pointed runic alphabet built up on the basis of the Danish runes alone. This was displaced later by the pointed runic alphabet in general use in Scandinavia.

Pointed runes were generally known and used in the whole of the Scandinavian north throughout the Middle Ages as the writing of cultured laymen, mainly used for private records. A Danish legal manuscript written in runes dates from the end of the 13th century. There is extant, too, a prayer book of later date, which is evidently intended for a layman not familiar with Latin. St. Bridget, who was a member of a Swedish family of nobles, in using the Latin alphabet spells Swedish in the way in which she learned as a child with runic letters.

There is evidence of the use of runes in Gotland as late as the 17th century. Runes were kept up longer than elsewhere in outlying parts of Sweden, where they were used for making occasional notes down to modern times.

BIBLIOGRAPHY.—For a comprehensive list, including older works: Helmut Arntz, *Bibliographie der Runenkunde* (1937); later work (after 1937): *Year's Work in Modern Language Studies* and *Jahresbericht . . . der germanischen Philologie* (both annual).

North Italic ("North Etruscan") or subalpine alphabets as the source of the runes: J. Whatmough, *Prae-Italic Dialects of Italy,* vol. ii, pp. 501–520 (1933); *Foundations of Roman Italy,* p. 188 (1937). A critical edition of runic texts; H. Arntz, with H. Zeiss, *Gesamtausgabe der älteren Runendenkmäler,* vol. i (1939) and *Die Runenschrift,* 2nd ed. (1944); Karl Schneider, *Die germanischen Runennamen* (1956); Ralph W. V. Elliott, *Runes* (1959).　　(O. v. F.; J. WH.)

RUNEBERG, JOHAN LUDVIG (1804–1877), the greatest Finnish poet, whose works expressed the patriotic spirit of his countrymen and also, because they were written in Swedish, exercised great influence on Swedish literature. The son of a sea captain, he was born at Jakobstad (Pietarsaari), on the Gulf of Bothnia, on Feb. 5, 1804, when Finland was still under Swedish rule. He studied at Åbo (Turku) university, graduating in 1827, but his academic career was interrupted by the need to earn a living, and he became a private tutor on an estate in Saarijärvi. At the university he had been inspired by romantic nationalism; in the heart of the Finnish countryside he learned to know and love Finland's landscape and people and heard at firsthand some of the stories of the heroic past which were to be the themes of his best work. He returned to the university, which had moved to Helsinki, in 1830 and became clerk to the council and (1831) lecturer in Latin language and literature. In the same year he married Fredrika Tengström, niece of the archbishop of Finland, and received a gold medal from the Swedish academy for his verse romance of Finnish life, *Grafven i Perho.* In 1837 he moved to Borgå (Porvoo), where he was lecturer in classics until 1857 and rector of the college, 1847–50. He continued to live there until his death, on May 6, 1877. For the last 13 years of his life he was partly paralyzed and unable to write.

Runeberg's first book of poems appeared in 1830 and showed the direction of his gifts in their freshness, vigour and sympathy with the Finnish peasant. His two idylls, *Elgskyttarne* ("Elk Hunters," 1832) and *Hanna* (1836), won him a place in Swedish literature second only to Esaias Tegnér. In 1844 he published *Kung Fjalar* (Eng. trans., 1904), a noble cycle of unrhymed verse romances derived from old Scandinavian legends. His *Fänrik Ståls Sägner* (2 series, 1848 and 1860; Eng. trans., *The Songs of Ensign Stal,* 1925), patriotic poems describing the war of independence (1808) as experienced by an old soldier, made a tremendous impression, and the first, "Vårt land," became the Finnish national anthem. Other works include *Nadeschda* (1841), a popular epic based on Russian folklore; a classical tragedy in verse, *Kungarne på Salamis* (1863); and two later volumes of poems, which, with the 1830 volume, made up the collected poems (1830–43).

Runeberg's work shows the influence of classical literature and of Goethe in its high-mindedness and purity of form. His originality consists in his power to combine this classicism with romantic feeling and the realism which distinguishes his understanding of peasant life and character.

Runeberg's *Samlade Arbeten* were published in eight volumes, with a study by C. G. Estlander (1899–1902). Publication of his *Samlade Skrifter,* with extensive commentary, began in 1933.

BIBLIOGRAPHY.—For his life, *see* J. E. Strömborg (Runeberg's "Boswell"), *Biografiska anteckningar om J. L. Runeberg,* 4 vol. (1880–1901; new ed., 1927–31); standard lives by W. Söderhjelm, 2 vol. (1904–06; rev., 1929); I. A. Heikel, 2 vol. (1926); L. Viljanen, 2 vol. (1944, 1948). *See also* Y. Hirn, *Runebergskulten* (1935); G. Tideström, *Runeberg som estetiker* (1941); G. Castrén, *Johan Ludvig Runeberg* (1950). For detailed criticism of the principal poems, with Eng. trans., *see* E. Gosse, *Studies in the Literature of Northern Europe* (1879). A selection of poems was trans. by E. Magnussen and E. H. Palmer, *Runeberg's Lyrical Songs, Idylls and Epigrams* (1878).　　(L. S. V.)

RUNNING. The sport of running has been popular from the earliest times, and a simple footrace run straight away from starting point to goal or once over the course of the stadium (a little over 200 yd.) formed an event in the Greek Olympic pentathlon (*q.v.*). There was also a race once over the course and return and a long race run many times (often as many as 12; *i.e.,* about 2¾ mi.) up and down the stadium. There was also a short race for warriors wearing full armour and carrying sword and shield. Except in the warriors' race, the Greek runners were naked, save occasionally for a pair of light shoes. The contests must have been severe since the ancient Olympic chronicles preserve the memory of several men who fell dead at the end of the long course. According to Virgil (*Aeneid,* v, 286 *et seq.*) running was practised in circus exhibitions in ancient Italy.

The best runners in the Middle Ages were most often found among the couriers maintained by potentates and municipalities. The Persian couriers of the Turkish sultans often ran from Constantinople to Adrianople and back, a distance of about 220 mi., in two days and nights. In districts of India and Africa not traversed by railways, runners were employed to carry the mails.

Throughout the 19th century the best runners were professionals, appearing in match races for cash stakes.

The establishment of the Cambridge University Sports in 1857, the Oxford Sports in 1860, and the British championship meetings in 1866 placed amateur athletic competition upon a formal and recognized basis in Great Britain. In the U.S. championships were sponsored by the New York Athletic Club in 1876–78, and the first National Association of Amateur Athletes of America championships were held in 1879. (*See also* TRACK AND FIELD SPORTS: *History.*)

Running at distances from the 100 m. dash to the marathon (42,195 m., or 26 mi. 385 yd.) is an integral part of the sport of track and field (athletics), the most popular event of the Olympic Games. For the history of track and field events in the Olympics and for Olympic records *see* OLYMPIC GAMES.

Modern running is divided into three classes: sprinting, middle-distance, and long-distance running.

Sprinting.—Sprinting consists of running over short distances with a full and almost continuous burst of speed, the chief distances being 100, 220, and 440 yd., and the corresponding metric distances. The course for sprint races is usually marked off in lanes for the individual runners.

All modern footraces are started by the report of a pistol or similar apparatus. Until 1884 all classes of foot runners began their races from a standing position. In that year Bobby Macdonald, a Maori resident in Scotland, demonstrated an entirely new method known as the crouch; this method of starting became universal in a short time.

Experiments made with an electrical timing apparatus of his own invention by physiologist A. V. Hill (*q.v.*) of the University of London in the 1920s brought to light many interesting points in connection with the physiological processes involved in severe muscular exercise in man. Hill's experiments indicated that from 90 to 95% of the effort made by a sprinter traveling at top speed is expended in overcoming the frictional resistance of his own muscles. The force exerted by the first-class sprinter at maximum speed is equal to from 80 to 90% of his body weight; in running 100 yd. he does sufficient work to lift himself 240 to 270 ft. into the air. He will bring into play approximately 8 hp. and attain his maximum speed at 60 or 70 yd. from the start, when he may be traveling as fast as 26 mph. Approximately one second is lost in the starting process. After the 70-yd. mark is reached the runner begins to lose speed through fatigue occasioned by the rapid appearance of lactic acid in the muscles, as much as ⅛ oz. of such acid being secreted in the muscle substance every second. In the course of a 220-yd. race the speed drops more than 10% between 70 and 190 yd.

Athletes of the United States and the British Commonwealth have dominated sprint events since the inception of the modern Olympic Games in 1896. The 100- and 220-yd. distances (and their metric equivalents, 100 and 200 m.) have been the special province of U.S. athletes, among them Bernie Wefers, Archie Hahn, Charlie Paddock, Frank Wykoff, Eddie Tolan, Jesse Owens, Mel Patton, Barney Ewell, Andy Stanfield, Bobby Morrow, Dave Sime, Frank Budd, Bob Hayes, Henry Carr, Tommie Smith, Charlie Greene, Jim Hines, and John Carlos. Though his records were later broken, Owens is still regarded as one of the finest sprinters of all time. His career was climaxed in 1936 when he won the 100 and 200 m. at the Olympic Games in Berlin. At one time Owens held alone or shared the world's records for all sprint distances recognized by the International Amateur Athletic Federation. Owens' times of 9.4 sec. for 100 yd., 10.2 sec. for 100 m., 20.3 sec. for 220 yd. and 200 m. on a straight course compare favourably with the latest record list (*see* SPORTING RECORD).

All important international races at 200 m. and 220 yd. as well as 400 m. and 440 yd. are run on an oval track, each runner being provided with his own lane, to which he must keep throughout the race. The starts are staggered so that each runner will traverse the full distance. As a result, the competitors, particularly in the 400 m. and 440 yd., have no exact knowledge of their respective positions until they have completed the final turn. Great emphasis is therefore placed on an athlete's ability to judge his speed as well as upon his speed and endurance.

First of the modern 400-m. stars was Eric Liddell of Great Britain, who lowered the world's record to 47.6 sec. at the 1924 Olympic Games. William Carr (1932 Olympic champion), Archie Williams (1936 Olympic champion), and Grover Klemmer of the U.S. took turns lowering the mark until Klemmer ran 46 sec. in 1941. Herb McKenley of Jamaica moved the 440-yd. mark to 46 sec. in 1948 and it remained there until Jim Lea of the U.S. ran 45.8 sec. in 1956. George Rhoden of Jamaica (1952 Olympic champion) did 45.8 sec. for 400 m. in 1950; this was the record until Lou Jones of the U.S. ran 45.4 sec. in 1955 and then 45.2 sec. in 1956. Glenn Davis of the U.S. lowered the 440-yd. record to 45.7 sec. in 1958. At the 1960 Rome Olympic Games Otis Davis (U.S.) and Carl Kauffmann (Germany) jointly broke the 45-sec. mark, setting a world and Olympic 400-m. record of 44.9 sec., and Adolph Plummer of the U.S. ran the same time for 440 yd. in 1963. The 1964 Olympic champion Mike Larrabee (U.S.) also ran 44.9 sec. for 400 m. at the U.S. Olympic tryouts. Smith broke both records in one 1967 race, running 44.5 for 400 m. and 44.8 for 440 yd.

Middle-Distance Running.—This comprises distances ranging from 600 yd. through 2,000 m., with the most popular races being at 880 yd. (or 800 m.) and 1 mi. (or 1,500 m.). The mile is the classic distance for all British and U.S. runners, and for years interest centred on attempts to run it in less than four minutes. This was finally achieved on May 6, 1954, by an English medical student, Roger Bannister, who did the mile in 3 min. 59.4 sec. in a dual meet at Oxford. The four-minute mark was bettered with some regularity thereafter and new records were set by John Landy (Australia), June 1954; Derek Ibbotson (Great Britain), 1957; Herb Elliott (Australia), 1958; Peter Snell (N.Z.), 1962 and 1964; Michel Jazy (France), 1965; and Jim Ryun (U.S.), 1966 and June 1967. Ryun's 1967 time was 3 min. 51.1 sec. In July 1967 Ryun lowered the 1,500-m. mark to 3 min. 33.1 sec.

In both the 880-yd. and mile distances, strategy and tactics play a far more important role than they do in the sprints. Countless theories have been advanced as to the proper way to run each race, but runners usually fall into one of two classes: pacesetters, who try to finish all opposition with an early rush, and kick runners, who try to win in the final stretch. Other things being equal, the latter usually prevail, as in the classic mile race between Landy and Bannister for the British Empire crown in 1954. Landy led for over three laps but Bannister won in 3 min. 58.8 sec.

U.S. and British Commonwealth runners have dominated in the Olympic 800-m. (880-yd.) runs, some of the great stars being Douglas Lowe, Thomas Hampson, and Sydney Wooderson of England, and John Woodruff, Mal Whitfield, Arnold Sowell, and Thomas Courtney of the U.S., and Snell. After 1939, however, the world's record often was held by Europeans, with Rudolf Harbig of Germany clocked at 1 min. 46.6 sec. in 1939 and Roger Moens of Belgium at 1 min. 45.7 sec. in 1955, until Snell ran 1 min. 44.3 sec. in 1962. In the same race, he broke Courtney's 880-yd. record, running 1 min. 45.1 sec., and in 1964 set a 1,000-m. mark with 2 min. 16.6 sec. Jim Ryun, age 19, of the U.S. was timed at 1 min. 44.9 sec. for 880 yd. in 1966; as the U.S. Track and Field Federation meet in which it was run had not been sanctioned, its ratification was delayed by the Amateur Athletic Union until June 1968.

The Mile.—Of all track-and-field events, the mile and 1,500 m. have been the most international, with Olympic champions and world's record holders coming from Great Britain, the United States, France, Italy, New Zealand, Finland, Sweden, Australia, Ireland, and even Luxembourg.

The most memorable names in mile history have been those of Walter George, Paavo Nurmi, Glenn Cunningham, Jack Lovelock, Gunder Hägg, Sydney Wooderson, Bannister, Landy, Elliott, Snell, Dyrol Burleson, Jim Beatty, Tom O'Hara, Jazy, and Ryun. (*See* table.)

George was an English professional star of the late 19th century who set a time pattern for miles that is still employed. This consists of a fast first quarter-mile, when the runner is still fresh; a slower second quarter; a still slower third quarter; and then as fast a final quarter as possible. In 1886 George ran the mile in 4 min. 12.75 sec., and no amateur broke that mark until Norman Taber of the U.S. shaded it with 4 min. 12.6 sec. in 1915.

Comparative Records of Great Mile Runners

Quarter	George (Eng.) 1886	Hägg (Swed.) 1945	Bannister (Eng.) May 1954	Landy* (Austr.) June 1954	Ryun (U.S.) June 1967
	(sec.)	(sec.)	(sec.)	(sec.)	(sec.)
1st 440 . . .	58.5	56.6	57.5	58.5†	59.2
2nd 440 . . .	63.25	61.9	60.7	60.2†	59.8
3rd 440 . . .	66.0	61.2	62.3	58.5†	58.6
4th 440 . . .	65.0	61.6	58.9	60.6†	53.5
Mile . . .	4:12.75	4:01.3	3:59.4	3:57.9	3:51.1

*Landy's race was on a 400-m. track, therefore intermediate times are only approximated.   †Calculated time.

It was Nurmi with his theory of evenly paced quarters who brought the mark down to 4 min. 10.4 sec. in 1923, and another eight years passed before Jules Ladoumègue of France broke the 4 min. 10 sec. barrier with a time of 4 min. 9.2 sec. Around this time, Cunningham began his long career in the U.S., while Lovelock came out of New Zealand to break Ladoumègue's record with 4 min. 7.6 sec. in 1933. There ensued a series of thrilling duels between Cunningham and Lovelock, climaxed by the latter's 3 min. 47.8 sec. victory in the 1,500-m. race at the 1936 Olympic Games. Meanwhile, Cunningham had reclaimed the mile record with his 4 min. 6.8 sec. race in 1934 and he later ran 4 min. 4.4 sec. in a specially paced indoor race. Wooderson then did 4 min. 6.4 sec. in 1937, and this time the record held up until the advent of Hägg.

With Sweden neutral during World War II, Hägg had an opportunity denied his contemporaries from other nations. The most picturesque miler of them all, with his fluid running style, Hägg ran the mile record down to 4 min. 1.3 sec. by 1945 in stiff competition with his countryman Arne Andersson. Both were disqualified from amateur racing while still in their prime and immediately retired.

Hägg's record remained on the books until Bannister's immortal race, but once the English star smashed the 4-min. barrier, such times became almost commonplace.

Long-Distance Running.—This includes all flat races from 3,000 m. upward, as well as steeplechasing, road, and cross-country running. Among the great distance runners have been Alfred Shrubb of England, Hannes Kolehmainen and Nurmi of Finland,

Hägg of Sweden, and Emil Zatopek of Czechoslovakia, but by 1957, most of their records had been broken by a new crop of stars headed by Sandor Iharos and Laszlo Tábori of Hungary, Gordon Pirie of England, and Vladimir Kuts of the U.S.S.R., who in turn were succeeded in the 1960s by Pyotr Bolotnikov of the U.S.S.R., Murray Halberg and Bill Baillie of New Zealand, Michel Jazy of France, Ron Clarke of Australia, Bob Schul, Beatty, and Billy Mills of the U.S., and Kipchoge Keino of Kenya. Before World War II, a premium was placed on simple endurance, an economical running style, and the ability to judge pace. Nurmi, who ran with effortless ease, exemplified this style and, in his prime, held all the world's records from 1,500 m. to the one for distance covered in one hour (11 mi. 1,648 yd.).

Kolehmainen and Nurmi initiated the Finnish domination of distance running which lasted from 1912 through 1946, or until Zatopek appeared on the scene. The rule of the "Flying Finns" ended dramatically in the 1948 Olympic Games when Zatopek won the 10,000-m. race in record time. The Czech army officer also placed second in the 5,000 m. with a running style that was the complete antithesis of Nurmi's—a driving, tortuous churning of legs and body, an alternation of fast sprints with steady running, and an apparently complete unconcern with pace. Zatopek's success at London was mild compared to his grand slam at Helsinki four years later when he won the 5,000 m., 10,000 m., and the marathon, all in record time.

The rapid improvement in distances from 1,500 m. up to the marathon after World War II could be credited to several training innovations. The first of these was *Fartlek*, or "speed play," popularized by Gosta Homer, a Swedish Olympic coach. It involved long daily workouts with intervals of fast and slow running on soft, springy surfaces like those provided by the Scandinavian pine forests. Percy Cerutty of Australia, coach of Landy and Elliott, introduced a more Spartan regime which included running up a soft sand hill to build leg strength. But the most popular form of training by the 1960s was interval running, in which a runner would repeatedly run distances of 220 to 880 yd., jogging for several minutes between workouts. By varying the speed of the workouts, this type of training could develop stamina, rhythm, speed, and a sense of pace in the runner. Most coaches preferred to complement interval training by having their runners take long, easy runs on grass surfaces several times a week.

Between the 1952 and 1956 Olympics one distance record after another fell to Iharos, Tábori, Pirie, and Kuts and, at Melbourne, it was Kuts, a Russian marine officer, who fell heir to Zatopek's crown when he won the 5,000 and the 10,000 m. Then a new Olympic 10,000-m. record was set by Bolotnikov at Rome in 1960 and another by Mills at Tokyo in 1964. Zatopek's records for the 20,000 m. and for the distance covered in one hour, set in 1951, were broken in 1963 by Baillie of New Zealand.

By 1968, Clarke had almost duplicated Nurmi's feat, holding all records from two miles to 10,000 m.

Another popular event is the marathon (26 mi. 385 yd.), which, unlike the other two, is run for the most part on the open road. This distance, adopted from that used in the 1908 Olympic Games, was internationalized in 1924. Among the most outstanding modern Olympic marathon runners has been Abebe Bikila of Ethiopia, who at Tokyo in 1964 became the first man ever to win the event twice.

Steeplechasing.—Originally only a cross-country run over a course plentifully provided with natural obstacles, the modern steeplechase takes place on the cinder track of the athletic field. This event has become standardized at 3,000 m. over 7½ laps of a 400-m. track embracing a 13 ft. 1½ in.-wide water jump with a 3-ft. rail and solid hurdle barriers making 35 obstacles all told (7 water jumps and 28 hurdling jumps).

Cross-Country Running.—This had its inception with the founding of the Crick run at Rugby School in 1837, followed by many other famous schools that also held annual cross-country races. Thirty years later in 1867 the Thames Rowing Club held cross-country runs and races as a winter sport, and in a few years many other clubs were formed throughout England. Many amateur athletes use this sport, often formerly termed paper-chasing, as a means of keeping fit and developing stamina for track athletics. English championships over the senior distance of 10 mi. were first held in 1877. The famous Midlands Club, Birchfield Harriers, won many of these events thereafter. The number of runners in this event increased from 33 in the first race to 900 in the second half of the 20th century. In England races are limited for juniors (18 to under 21 years) to 6 mi. and for youths (over 16 to under 18) to 3 mi.

The sport is also popular in the U.S. The championship distance in that country is 10,000 m.; the high school distance is 2–3 mi., and intercollegiate titles are decided at distances of 4–6 mi. The first international race was held in 1898 between England and France and an international championship was instituted in 1903 between England, Ireland, Scotland, and Wales. In 1907 France first competed, followed by Belgium in 1924; while Italy, Luxembourg, Spain, and Switzerland also competed in 1929. Other countries entered the international competition after World War II, beginning with the Netherlands in 1950 and Yugoslavia in 1953, and in 1962 the International Amateur Athletic Federation adopted rules governing championship and international cross-country running events both for men and women. The first women's international cross-country event was held at Barry, Wales, in 1967. Formerly included on the Olympic program, cross-country was dropped after the harrowingly hot 1924 games at Paris as not suitable for summer competition.

Relay Racing.—This form of competition has long been practised in the U.S. and has become popular throughout the world. Relay races are usually run by four men, each going a quarter of the distance. From 1911 to 1926 only one relay race was included in the English championships. This was really a medley race in which four men ran 880, 220, 220, and 440 yd., respectively. In the U.S. this race is known as a sprint medley relay and is included in most relay carnivals. England abandoned the event in 1927 and substituted two other relay races, a 440 yd. (4 x 110) and a mile (4 x 440).

The U.S. national championship relays, conducted by the Amateur Athletic Union, are at distances of 440 yd. (4 x 110), 1 mi. (4 x 440), and 2½ mi. (440, 880, and 1,320 yd., and 1 mi.). U.S. indoor championships are held at distances of 1 mi. (4 x 440) and 2 mi. (4 x 880), and the sprint medley (440, 100, 220, 300). The Olympic events are 400 m. (4 x 100) and 1,600 m. (4 x 400). This method of racing was started in the U.S. about 1890, on the model of the Massachusetts firemen's "bean-pot" race.

The old method was for the men running the second quarter of the course each to take over a small flag from the first man as he arrived, before departing on their own stage of the race, at the end of which they, in their turn, handed on their flags to the awaiting next runners. The flags, however, were considered cumbersome, and for a time it was sufficient for the outgoing runner to touch or be touched by his predecessor. The baton, a hollow cylinder of wood or plastic, was introduced at the 1912 Olympics. It is carried by the runner and must be exchanged between lines drawn at right angles to the side of the track 11 yd. or 10 m. on each side of the starting line for each leg of the relay. In sprint relays (440 and 880 yd.; 400 and 800 m.) a 1964 rule change permits the runner receiving the baton to start his run 11 yd. (10 m.) before the zone, but he must take the baton within the zone itself.

The growth of relay racing stems from the University of Pennsylvania, where in 1893 a relay race was included on a track program for the first time. Pennsylvania raced a team from Princeton University that year and again in 1894. In 1895 a number of eastern U.S. colleges were invited to compete in a first annual Pennsylvania Relay Carnival. By the 1960s, more than 3,000 athletes participated annually in this two-day event, and similar carnivals were held in all parts of the nation. The usual events were the 440, 880 yd. (4 x 220), 1, 2, 4 mi. (4 x 1 mi.), sprint medley (440, 220, 220, 880), and 2½ mi.

For world and Olympic records *see* SPORTING RECORD: *Track and Field Sports;* OLYMPIC GAMES; *see also* TRACK AND FIELD SPORTS.

BIBLIOGRAPHY.—J. Kenneth Doherty, *Modern Training for Running*

(1964); George T. Bresnahan *et al., Track and Field Athletics,* 6th ed. (1964); H. A. Meyer (ed.), *Track and Field Athletics* (1964); R. L. Quercetani, *A World History of Track and Field Athletics 1864–1964* (1964), (ed.), *International Athletics Annual* (Association of Track and Field Statisticians), annually (1951–); G. H. G. Dyson, *Mechanics of Athletics* (1962); Fred Wilt, *Run, Run, Run* (1965); Melvyn Watman, *The Encyclopaedia of Athletics,* 2nd ed. (1967); International Amateur Athletic Federation, *Official Handbook 1967/68* (published intermittently).   (F. A. M. W.; Sy. S.; N. D. McW.; E. J. G.)

RUNNYMEDE, the meadow celebrated as the place where King John granted the Magna Carta (*q.v.*) on June 15, 1215. It lies on the south bank of the River Thames in the urban district of Egham, Surrey, Eng., between Windsor and Staines.

The area is open to the public and is owned by the National Trust. Together with Runnymede, the slopes of Coopers Hill form the setting of a memorial commemorating Magna Carta, which was presented by the American Bar Association in 1957. The Commonwealth Air Forces Memorial, in remembrance of 20,-456 airmen from the United Kingdom and the Commonwealth who "died for freedom in raid and sortie over the British Isles and the lands and seas of northern and western Europe" in World War II and who have no known graves, was opened by Queen Elizabeth II in 1953. It crowns Coopers Hill and commands a magnificent view. Both memorials were designed by Sir Edward Maufe. At the foot of the hill, next to the Mede, is a memorial to John F. Kennedy, 35th president of the United States, which was inaugurated, also by Queen Elizabeth, in 1965. (W. W. R.)

RUPERT (called Ruprecht Klem; Lat. Clemens) (1352–1410), German king from 1400 to 1410, and, as Rupert III, elector palatine of the Rhine, a member of the house of Wittelsbach, was a son of the elector Rupert II and Beatrice, daughter of Peter II, king of Sicily. He was born at Amberg in the Palatinate on May 5, 1352, and succeeded as elector on his father's death in 1398. After the deposition of King Wenceslas at Oberlahnstein, Rupert was elected German king on Aug. 21, 1400, and was crowned at Cologne on Jan. 6, 1401. Later that year he went to Italy, seeking papal coronation. In alliance with the city of Florence, he attacked Gian Galeazzo Visconti, duke of Milan, but was defeated outside Brescia on Oct. 14, 1401, and returned to Germany in 1402. He was recognized as German king by Pope Boniface IX on Oct. 1, 1403. Henceforward his energies were absorbed in combating the partisans of Wenceslas in Germany; he did nothing to end the papal schism and his influence at the Council of Pisa (1409) was negligible. By his second wife, Elizabeth, sister of Frederick I, elector of Brandenburg, he left four sons and three daughters. He died at Landskron near Oppenheim on May 18, 1410, and was buried at Heidelberg.

See A. Winkelmann, *Der Romzug Ruprecht von der Pfalz* (1892); B. Gebhardt, *Handbuch der Deutschen Geschichte.* vol. i (1954).

RUPERT, Prince (called Rupert of the Rhine or of the Palatinate) (1619–1682), royalist cavalry commander in the English Civil War, was the third son of the elector palatine and "winter king" of Bohemia, Frederick V, and of Elizabeth, daughter of James I of England. He was born in Dec. 1619 at Prague, but within a year his father was defeated at the battle of the White Mountain and the whole family was expelled from Bohemia. They eventually found a settled home in the United Provinces and there Rupert was reared. He made a precocious start to his military career in 1633 when he attended the siege of Rheinberg in the suite of Frederick Henry, prince of Orange, and two years later he was a regular member of the prince's bodyguard. High-spirited and adventurous, Rupert soon became a general favourite when he visited the English court in 1636, and a scheme was formed to appoint him governor of a projected colony in Madagascar. Nothing came of this, but although Rupert was sent back to the Netherlands in July 1637, Charles I had formed a high opinion of his character. Rupert renewed his military career but in 1638 it was cut short by his capture (Oct. 17) at Vlotho on the bank of the Weser river, and for three years he was held by the imperialists in a relatively lenient captivity.

Rupert went to England soon after his release, and, having first escorted Queen Henrietta Maria to the Netherlands, rejoined his uncle, Charles I, just before the king raised his standard in Aug.

1642. Charles had reserved the generalship of the horse for him, independent of the earl of Lindsey, the nominal commander of the whole army. He was almost immediately involved in successful skirmishes with parliamentary detachments and began to build up a reputation as a skilful and courageous commander, taking his place as one of the most dominant figures of the war (*see* Civil War, English). His success was unbroken until the battle of Marston Moor in July 1644. The prince's contribution to royalist strategy was to instill ardour and resolution into military counsels, but his advice was not invariably followed. The plans for 1643 and 1644, both influenced by him, were drastically altered in his absence. His two brilliant and far-ranging expeditions to relieve Newark and York brought him acclaim, although the latter was followed by the defeat at Marston Moor. His influence was on the increase and in Nov. 1644 he was appointed general of the king's army. He and his party had long been opposed by factions in army and court, especially that led by Lord Digby (afterward 2nd earl of Bristol), and his appointment, although welcome to most soldiers, was distasteful to certain counselors and officers. The actions of 1645 were largely influenced by the conflict of Rupert and Digby, a cleavage made all the more apparent and disagreeable by the royalists' lack of military success. These dissensions prepared the ground for Rupert's dismissal by Charles after he had been forced to surrender Bristol to Sir Thomas Fairfax in Sept. 1645.

Rupert had brought an element of hardened professionalism to his conduct of the war and this, together with his normal hot temper, laid him open to charges of ruthlessness and even barbarity. However, Rupert was capable of generosity toward his opponents and did his best to restrain the licence of his cavalry. He even became an advocate of peace when, after the battle of Naseby (June 1645), he was convinced that the king's cause was, in a military sense, lost. This made a further point of conflict with the wildly scheming and ever optimistic Digby and a source of estrangement with the king. Royal displeasure was sudden and complete after the surrender of Bristol, and although Rupert demanded a court-martial, which gave a favourable verdict, he could be of no further use to the king.

After the capitulation of the Oxford garrison (June 1646) Rupert and his brother Maurice were hurried out of the country, but Rupert soon acquired a command of English troops in French service. He was wounded fighting against the Spanish at the siege of La Bassée in 1647. Meanwhile, he became reconciled with Charles and although the old factional jealousies survived, Rupert was given command of some royalist ships. His naval adventures were singularly unprofitable. Preying on English shipping where he could, he was chased by Robert Blake from Kinsale, Ireland (where he had been sent to assist the earl of Ormonde), to Lisbon, Cartagena and Toulon (1649–50). Driven from the Mediterranean, Rupert cruised to the Azores and to the West Indies (1651–52), losing his brother Maurice (Sept. 1652) and most of his fleet, and returning to France with one ship and a few prizes in 1653. After quarreling with Charles II, the council and his eldest brother Charles Louis, he went into retirement in Germany. The Restoration, however, tempted him to England again (Oct. 1660) and he was generously received by Charles. He was pensioned, made a privy councilor and during the Dutch wars given an active role in naval commands. He did not impress Samuel Pepys with his abilities as a naval administrator but his courage was still unquestioned. Charles rewarded him with £14,000 for his services in the second Dutch War. In times of peace Rupert sought profit in trading enterprises. He was a shareholder in the two Royal African companies (1663 and 1672) and an active member of the Hudson's Bay company (1670). He did not meddle with politics, although as a lifelong Protestant and a patriot by adoption he was disposed to sympathize with the earl of Shaftesbury's opposition to catholicizing tendencies at court. A member of the Royal society, he built himself a laboratory at Windsor castle and dabbled in scientific experiments, specializing in armaments and ballistics. But he is best known for his accomplishment as a mezzotinter.

Rupert was created duke of Cumberland and earl of Holderness in the English peerage on Jan. 24, 1644. He never married but he had a son, Dudley (d. 1686), by Frances Bard, daughter of Viscount Bellamont, and a daughter, Ruperta (d. 1740), by the actress Margaret Hughes. It is to the latter's credit that she did much to mellow Rupert's irascible nature in his last years. He died of a fever in Spring gardens, Westminster, on Nov. 29, 1682.

BIBLIOGRAPHY.—E. Warburton, *Memoirs of Prince Rupert and the Cavaliers, Including Their Private Correspondence,* 3 vol. (1849); E. Scott, *Rupert, Prince Palatine* (1899); J. Cleugh, *Prince Rupert* (1934); C. V. Wedgwood, *The Great Rebellion,* vol. ii, *The King's War, 1641–1647* (1958).   (H. G. Ro.)

RURAL ELECTRIFICATION.
In such technologically and economically advanced countries as the United States among the larger nations, and Sweden and Switzerland among the smaller, more than 90% of the farms have available a supply of electricity, while in comparatively undeveloped lands rural electrification is virtually unknown. Generally, the degree of farm electrification in any country has depended on such factors as (1) available energy sources such as coal or falling water; (2) the general development of the country and particularly the status of its electric power industry; and (3) the relative importance of agriculture in the nation's economy.

Effect on Farming Methods.—Just as the steam engine revolutionized shipping and the gasoline engine highway transportation, electric power revolutionized manufacturing and has largely revolutionized agriculture. Electric power, replacing animal and human muscle power, has greatly increased output per man-hour and the efficiency of farm operations, while offering advantages and conveniences previously available only in urban areas.

Uses in the Household.—Originally, the aim of the farmer in connecting to an electric supply line was the same as that of the city dweller—to secure electric lighting. Electricity was later used for water pumps, washing machines, electric irons, refrigerators, radios, etc. Many farmers installed electric ranges and electric water heaters, electrically controlled central heating and modern bathrooms. Home freezers rapidly came into use on U.S. farms after World War II. The cost of operating a home freezer was relatively low and it made possible the easy storage of meats, fruits and vegetables produced on the farm for use throughout the year. As television became available throughout the country, farmers quickly installed receiving sets. The popularity of home air conditioning also spread from the cities to the farms.

Dairying.—Electric lights proved particularly useful in dairy barns and milkhouses, where much of the work is done before and after daylight hours. Milking machines and milk-cooling equipment also came into wide use to reduce labour, increase production, improve the quality and promote sanitation of the milk. With the use of milking parlours and bulk milk-handling equipment, it became possible to transfer milk directly from the cow through sanitized pipes to electrically cooled, stainless steel storage tanks and then to a dairy tanker for shipment to market. During cold weather, milk production may be increased as much as 25% through the use of thermostatically controlled drinking fountains. In many dairy barns mechanical devices have been installed in the gutters behind the cows to carry the manure outside to a manure spreader or wagon.

Poultry.—Electricity is especially useful in poultry farming. Artificial illumination timed to lengthen the day to 13 or 14 hours during autumn and winter can increase egg production in these seasons as much as 20% to 30%. An automatic water supply is highly desirable and nearly always used by successful poultry farmers. In cold weather, warming the drinking water to prevent freezing is necessary for maximum egg production. Other electrical equipment used on poultry farms includes: brooders to keep young chicks warm and dry; fans to remove strong ammonia fumes and excessive moisture from the poultry house; automatic feeders; and motor-driven egg cleaners and graders.

General Farming.—Farmers have used electricity for more and more operations each year. Some of its major uses are for ventilation, crop drying, conditioning and storing, feed handling, mixing and grinding, automatic feeding and soil heating. (*See also* CROP DRYING AND PROCESSING.)

The heat lamp is extensively used by farmers as a pig brooder,

especially in the colder climates where spring pigs are raised. It has been estimated that at least one additional pig per litter can be raised with the proper use of the heat lamp.

Automatic handling of materials with electrically powered equipment has become increasingly important in such operations as livestock feeding, milk production and poultry farm operations. Environmental control of farm buildings in poultry production and in dairy operations has provided increased efficiency.

Rural Electrification in the United States.—Of the more than 3,700,000 farms in the United States in the 1960s, approximately 98% had electric service. The first steps toward rural electrification in the United States were taken only a few years after Thomas Edison's first generating plant began operation in New York city in 1882. Progress in rural areas lagged behind urban development of electric service, however, because of many technical and financial obstacles. For the first 15 years direct current, which could be transmitted only a few miles, was used and most generating plants were located in cities. In addition, the costs of constructing transmission and distribution lines to serve outlying farms were exceedingly high. Various methods were tried by the electric companies to lower costs. In some cases farmers paid for and owned line equipment and furnished the right of way to the power company in return for electric rates comparable to those in nearby towns. Some power companies bore the entire cost of stringing lines. In most cases, however, some form of "shared-cost" plan was adopted.

By 1920 the electric utility companies had built a vast network of transmission lines which provided 24-hour electric service to practically every city and village in the U.S. The steam turbine had been so perfected that the cost of manufacturing electricity had been greatly reduced, and the combined use of alternating current and transformers made possible the long-distance transmission of electric current at high voltages. These developments made it possible, for the first time, to supply rural electric lines radiating from the urban centres with adequate electric power at a price sufficiently low to fit into the farmer's economy. The foundation for farm electrification on a national scale had been built.

In 1921 the National Electric Light association (NELA) organized a rural service committee to determine what was necessary to step up the electrification of rural areas. It was discovered that a high degree of rural electrification would entail more than the mere construction of transmission lines into farming areas: new farm equipment would have to be developed and farmers would have to be informed of the advantages of increased electrical use.

To assist in solving these problems a joint committee was set up that included representatives of the American Farm Bureau federation, the National Grange, the American Society of Agricultural Engineers, the U.S. department of agriculture, electric companies and others. This organization, known as the Committee on the Relation of Electricity to Agriculture (CREA), was active from 1923 to 1939. It promoted research work at universities and among manufacturers and published and distributed publications dealing with applications of electricity to farm operations.

The aggressive efforts of CREA and scores of local electric companies resulted in a substantial increase in the number of farms connected to power lines each year. In 1928, for example, more than 113,000 farms were newly electrified, as compared with only 27,000 in 1924. The depression of the 1930s retarded this rapid expansion and between 1929 and 1935 relatively little progress was made in extending rural electrification in the United States.

REA.—As conditions resulting from the depression eased, the utility companies were once again able to step up their rural electrification programs. In addition, the federal government set up a new program to assist the farm electrification movement by instituting the Rural Electrification administration (REA) in 1935. Through the lending of funds to newly organized REA co-operatives, it became an increasingly important factor in the growth of rural electrification. The Tennessee Valley Authority (*q.v.*) was a major contributor to rural electrification, largely through REA, in that region.

In the second half of the 20th century, REA-financed co-operatives were serving about 51% of all farms receiving electric service, while electric companies served about 43% and government-owned systems supplied the remaining 6%. About 40% of all REA co-operatives' power requirements were being purchased from electric companies under wholesale contracts. The average annual use of electric power on farms east of the 100th meridian was about 5,000 kw.hr. per customer. In many areas where intensive farm development programs had been carried on, annual use averaged about 30% higher than the national figure. On farms west of the 100th meridian, where use is affected by requirements of water pumping for irrigation, average annual use totaled more than 9,000 kw.hr. In comparison, the average nonfarm residential customer in the United States used a total of about 3,600 kw.hr. (*See* also AGRICULTURAL ECONOMICS: *Agricultural Credit Systems.*) (R. F. C.)

Great Britain.—The early pattern of electricity supply in Great Britain was such that privately owned companies and municipalities electrified the urban areas first and then pushed out to the more densely populated parts of the surrounding areas. After the nationalization of the industry in 1948 rural development was rapid. In England and Wales the number of electrified farms rose from 86,500 out of a total of about 281,000 in 1948 to more than 235,000 by the early 1960s and the average annual consumption per farm from about 3,500 to more than 7,600 kw.hr. In 1953 the Central Electricity authority started a ten-year plan aimed at connecting 85% of all farms. Development of the rural load was helped by the establishment of agricultural development departments by the Central Electricity authority and Area boards, by the Electrical Development association—responsible for publicity—and by the Electrical Research association, which had a rural electrification department to investigate possible applications of electricity to agriculture and horticulture. As in the United States the most important were those for crop drying, farm grinding, water heating and sterilizing in dairies, poultry rearing and for horticulture, including soil warming, artificial illumination and the control of the environment in greenhouses.

Other Countries.—While small electric plants, driven by oil engines or windmills, could supply individual premises with power for domestic use, rural electrification depended largely on the existence of main electrical networks. In many underdeveloped countries these were very limited in extent up to the middle of the 20th century. The benefits of electricity for agricultural areas were appreciated after World War II, particularly, and a number of international conferences, *e.g.*, the World Power conferences in New Delhi (1951), Rio de Janeiro (1954) and Belgrade (1957), paid particular attention to this question.

The United Nations made studies of the energy needs, including rural electrification for Latin America, southeast Asia and Europe, and its Economic Commission for Europe published a three-volume report on rural electrification in 1954 and 1958. Substantial progress was reported, for example, for Austria, France, Hungary and Sweden. In the Netherlands rural electrification was 96% complete by 1957 with an annual increase in rural consumption of 10%. In Ireland rural electrification was not undertaken until 1947 when .5% of rural inhabitants were served and annual consumption was 300,000 kw.hr.; within five years 27% of rural inhabitants were being served and annual consumption reached 127,000,000 kw.hr. Based on abundant water power, rural electrification in Norway was widespread with the highest per capita consumption in the world.

Many farms and rural communities in the U.S.S.R. were electrified, first by small local stations, later from high-voltage networks.

Extensive rural electrification in New Zealand was done under regional power boards co-operating with groups of consumers. Canadian agriculture benefited greatly through the full rural projects of the provinces. Rural projects progressed in the coastal areas of Australia and Tasmania, where water power abounds.

In Central and South America electricity consumption was generally very low except in urban areas, but some countries, *e.g.*, Trinidad, had developed rural electrification. The per capita consumption of electrical energy was also low in most of Asia, except Japan where hydro power facilitated rural electrification. Under

the Colombo plan, development in southeast Asia progressed, especially in Ceylon, India and Malaya, though much remained to be done. In the first Indian five-year plan (1951–56) the electrified villages with populations under 5,000 increased from 2,792 to 5,300, and almost 20,000 had been electrified by 1961.

The International bank made loans in the 1950s for the Aberdeen-Laksapana hydroelectric project in Ceylon, a five-year rural development plan in Algeria, a hydroelectric station in Uruguay and the Kariba gorge hydroelectric project in the Federation of Rhodesia and Nyasaland, where a national electricity grid served most of the settled areas.

Uganda, helped by the Owen falls hydroelectric project, began to electrify rural districts. In South Africa progress was slow, because of great distances between the large farms, but plans in the intensively cultivated areas were successful. (E. W. G.)

BIBLIOGRAPHY.—Royden Stewart, "Rural Electrification in the United States," *Public Utilities Fortnightly* (May 8, May 22, June 19, 1941); J. P. Schaenzer, *Rural Electrification*, 5th ed. (1955); International Documents Service, *Rural Electrification*, vol. i and ii (March 1954, Sept. 1956, March 1957); Robert H. Brown, *Farm Electrification* (1956); Grover C. Neff, *Farm Electrification in the United States of America*, Sec. B4, Paper 3, World Power Conference (1957); "Electricity in Agriculture," *Standard Handbook for Electrical Engineers*, 9th ed., pp. 1675–84 (1957). *See* also annual and special reports of the Edison Electric Institute and issues of *Farm Electrification Magazine.* (R. F. C.)

RURIK (RYURIK, RÖRIK) (d. *c.* A.D. 879), a leader of the Scandinavian Vikings (or Varangians), the semilegendary founder of the Russian dynasty of Rurikids (Ryurikovichi). According to the Russian Primary Chronicle (compiled at the beginning of the 12th century), the people of Novgorod, tired of ceaseless strife, in A.D. 862 sent envoys to the Scandinavian Vikings, asking them to come to Novgorod and establish an orderly and just government. In response to this invitation, the Varangian prince, Rurik, came with his two brothers and with a large retinue (*druzhina*), and became ruler of the city and region of Novgorod.

Modern historians are not inclined to accept at face value this legendary story of the "calling of the Varangians." They surmise that Rurik came with his retinue from the Scandinavian peninsula (or from Jutland), seized the town of Ladoga, at the mouth of the Volkhov river on the southern shore of Lake Ladoga, and made it his stronghold (*c.* 855); then he proceeded southward and seized Novgorod. V. O. Klyuchevski suggested that Rurik could have been invited for the military protection of the Volkhov-Dnieper waterway, whereupon the hired mercenaries seized political power. Rurik's kinsman Oleg (*q.v.*) became founder of the grand principality of Kiev, and Oleg's successor Igor (*q.v.*), who was believed to be Rurik's son, became the real founder of the Russian princely house. (S. G. Pu.)

RUSE, a town and headquarters of the *okrug* (district) of that name in northeastern Bulgaria, is situated on the right bank of the Danube opposite Giurgiu, Rumania. Pop. (1961 est.) 111,983. A Roman fortress (Prista) and river port in the 2nd century A.D., Ruse later grew as the Turkish stronghold of Ruschuk, and after 1878 (when Bulgaria was liberated) developed as a trade and industrial centre. It is one of the largest industrial towns in Bulgaria and produces agricultural machinery, textiles, plastics, rubber articles, electrical materials, oil derivatives, bitumen, hides, and sugar. River vessels are built and repaired there. Ruse is the chief river port, and has regular air service to Sofia. It is linked by rail with the Stara Zagora–Plovdiv and Sofia–Varna lines, and with Rumanian routes across the Danube bridge. The town is a cultural and educational centre, modern in appearance, with no traces of its old Oriental quarters.

RUSE OKRUG (first-order administrative division) is situated within the Danubian Platform region. Its upper tableland has a fertile loess soil and grain (wheat and maize [corn]) can be grown with the aid of irrigation. The sheltered lower valleys have a higher density of population and produce a variety of crops. (AN. BE.)

RUSH, BENJAMIN (1745–1813), U.S. physician and medical educator, designated by his contemporaries as the "American Sydenham" and even as the "Hippocrates of Pennsylvania," one of the major figures in the rise of U.S. medicine, was born of a

Quaker family on a farm near Philadelphia. Having obtained his B.A. from the College of New Jersey (later Princeton university) at the age of 15, he spent six years in Philadelphia in medical apprenticeship and completed his studies with an M.D. degree from the University of Edinburgh in 1768. After a year of travel in Europe he returned to Philadelphia, where he was appointed professor of chemistry (1769) in the College of Philadelphia (later merged with the University of Pennsylvania) and subsequently professor of the institutes of medicine and clinical practices at the University of Pennsylvania (1791). He introduced clinical instruction at the Pennsylvania hospital and initiated the Philadelphia dispensary. Rush was also deeply involved in the struggle for independence. As a member of the continental congress he was among the signers of the Declaration of Independence, and he served briefly in the army as surgeon general. Involvement in political intrigues, however, led him to return to Philadelphia, where he resumed the practice and teaching of medicine until, in 1797, he accepted Pres. John Adams' appointment as treasurer of the national mint, which office he held until his death in 1813.

Rush was a prolific writer on a vast variety of subjects which also included numerous social causes. He was a fiery proponent of the abolition of slavery, the death penalty and the use of alcohol, and he fought for prison reforms, higher education for women and free public schools for the poor. He also strongly suggested the establishment of a permanent "peace office." His medical interests were equally vast, and his therapeutic opinions tended to be dogmatic.

A strong believer in bloodletting and purging, he was inclined to enfeeble his patients upon whom he expended so much devotion and clinical attention. His *Account of the Bilious Remitting Yellow Fever As It Appeared in the City of Philadelphia in the Year 1793* is outstanding for its graphic description of the disease, but his untiring efforts and courage in taking care of yellow fever patients, until he himself became a victim of the disease, were frequently offset by his insistence upon debilitating therapeutic measures.

Yet the stubbornness which misled him in certain aspects also helped him to pursue novel and important ideas. His *Medical Inquiries and Observations Upon the Diseases of the Mind* (1812) was the first systematic American book on the subject, and his improvement of the housing of mental patients at the Pennsylvania hospital represented a decisive step toward a rational treatment of mental disease. His description of cholera infantum (1773), of dengue (1780) and of the relation between rheumatism and diseases of the teeth illustrate his unusual powers of observation.

Rush died of typhus at Philadelphia on April 19, 1813.

See *Autobiography* of Benjamin Rush, ed. with introduction and notes by George W. Corner (1948); the *Letters* [of Benjamin Rush], ed. by L. H. Butterfield (1951). (I. V.)

RUSH, RICHARD (1780–1859), U.S. statesman and diplomat, who played an important part in the founding of the Smithsonian Institution, an achievement he considered the most gratifying in his long public career, was born in Philadelphia, Pa., on Aug. 29, 1780, the son of Benjamin Rush (*q.v.*). He graduated from Princeton in 1797, was admitted to the bar in Philadelphia in 1800, was appointed attorney general of Pennsylvania in February 1811, and in November 1811 became comptroller of the U.S. treasury. In February 1814 James Madison appointed him attorney general and from March to September 1817 Rush also served as acting secretary of state. During this time he completed an agreement with Charles Bagot, the British minister in Washington, for disarmament on the Great Lakes. Later in 1817 Rush was appointed minister to Great Britain where, with the U.S. minister to France, Albert Gallatin, he negotiated the convention of 1818. This drew the boundary line between Canada and the United States from the Lake of the Woods to the Rocky Mountains at the 49th parallel and provided for joint settlement of the Oregon Territory for ten years. In 1823 he negotiated with George Canning, British foreign minister, on policy toward Latin America, negotiations which led to the enunciation of the Monroe Doctrine. He returned home in 1825 to become secretary of the treasury and in 1828 was

an unsuccessful candidate for vice-president on the ticket headed by John Quincy Adams. In 1836 Rush was the U.S. government's agent to receive the James Smithson bequest in London, his first connection with what became the Smithsonian. His last public service came as minister to France from 1847 to 1849. He died in Philadelphia on July 30, 1859.

Rush was a prolific writer, the best known of his works being his account of his English mission published at various times as *Memoranda of a Residence at the Court of London*. He is remembered as a cultivated gentleman who held high office and participated in important events without shaping them.

See John H. Powell, *Richard Rush: Republican Diplomat, 1780–1859* (1942). (A. DE C.)

RUSH, WILLIAM (1756–1833), U.S. sculptor and woodcarver, considered to be "the first native American to devote himself seriously and successfully to sculpture" (Henri Marceau, *William Rush, the First Native American Sculptor*, Philadelphia Museum of Art, 1937), was born in Philadelphia, Pa., on July 4, 1756. He was trained as a maker of ornamental ship carvings and figureheads. During the Revolution he served in the American army and shortly after the close of the war he set up a shop in Philadelphia. He was one of the founders of the Pennsylvania Academy of Fine Arts (1805) and served for many years as a member of the Philadelphia city council. A number of his wood carvings are preserved in various Philadelphia institutions, among the most interesting of which are his vigorous self-portrait (Pennsylvania Academy of Fine Arts), the "Water Nymph and Bittern" (Fairmount Park), two allegorical figures, "Comedy" and "Tragedy" (Philadelphia Museum), and a statue of George Washington (Independence Hall). Few, if any, of his ship carvings and figureheads survived. Rush died at Philadelphia on Jan. 17, 1833. (A. T. G.)

RUSH, the name of any of a variety of flowering plants distinguished by cylindrical stalks or hollow, stemlike leaves. The common rushes of the genus *Juncus* in the family Juncaceae (*q.v.*) are used in many parts of the world for chair bottoms, mats, and basketwork, and the pith serves as wicks in open oil lamps and for tallow candles—hence the term rush light. The fibrous stems and leaves of the bulrush, reed mace, or cattail, *Typha angustifolia*, are used in north India for ropes, mats, and baskets. *Scirpus* and other Cyperaceae are used for chair bottoms, mats, and thatch; the rush mats of Madras are made from a species of *Cyperus*. The sweet rush, yielding essential oil, is a grass, *Cymbopogon citratus*, known also as lemongrass. Quantities of the horsetail, *Equisetum hyemale*, are used under the name of Dutch or scouring rush for scouring metal and other hard surfaces because of the silica the plant contains. Flowering rush is *Butomus umbellatus;* wood rush is the common name for *Luzula* (see JUNCACEAE). *Acorus calamus* (family Araceae), sweet flag, is also known as sweet rush.

RUTHERFORD PLATT

BULRUSH OR CATTAIL (TYPHA ANGUSTIFOLIA)

RUSHMORE, MOUNT: see MOUNT RUSHMORE NATIONAL MEMORIAL.

RUSHWORTH, JOHN (*c.* 1612–1690), English historian, whose *Historical Collections of Private Passages of State* (7 vol., 1659–1701; 8 vol., 1721), covering 1618–49, remains a valuable source of information on events leading up to and during the Civil War, was born in about 1612, of an old Northumberland family. He studied law, perhaps at Oxford (of which university he became M.A. in 1649), and in 1638 was made solicitor to the town of Berwick-upon-Tweed. He was enrolled at Lincoln's Inn in 1640 and called to the bar in 1647. Always more interested in politics than in common law, during the intermission of parliaments

(1629–40) he attended, and made shorthand notes of, all important political and judicial proceedings heard before the Star Chamber, the court of honour and the king and council. In 1640 he was appointed assistant clerk to the house of commons and he recorded events on Jan. 4, 1642, when Charles I attempted to arrest five members of parliament. He also took notes at the trials of John Hampden (1637) and Strafford (1641). After the outbreak of war he acted as a messenger between parliament and its committees at Oxford and York, and from 1644 to 1647 he was licenser of pamphlets. He himself published a number of the newssheets that preceded the establishment of regular newspapers —e.g., the daily *London Post* (1644–45; 1646–47), the *Kingdomes Weekly Post* (1643–1644)—and also the parliamentary pamphlets opposed to the royalist *Mercurius Aulicus*.

As secretary (1645–50) to Sir Thomas Fairfax, general of the New Model army, Rushworth had considerable importance. He was with Fairfax at the battle of Naseby and, for a short time in 1650, was secretary to Richard Cromwell. He was employed by the council of state and during the protectorate and, after Cromwell resigned, by the Rump. In 1657, 1659, 1660, 1679 and 1681 he represented Berwick in parliament. At the Restoration, Rushworth made peace with Charles II, and, although called to give information on the activities of the regicides, was not himself implicated. In 1667 he became secretary to the lord keeper and, later, agent to the colony of Massachusetts. Despite his many emoluments and an inherited estate, he fell into poverty and spent his last years in a lodging in the king's bench prison, Southwark, where he died on May 12, 1690.

Rushworth's *Historical Collections* was compiled from his own notes and from printed material, with the avowed intention of making it possible for a true history to be written of events which, in pamphlets and newssheets dating from the period before the control of the press, were liable to misrepresentation. It is most useful for its eye-witness accounts of Strafford's trial, the battle of Naseby and the parliamentary campaigns of 1644–45, and for its transmission of contemporary comment.

RUSKIN, JOHN (1819–1900), writer, critic and artist, who more than anyone else influenced the public taste of Victorian England and did much to inspire the opposition to a *laissez-faire* philosophy, was born in Bloomsbury, London, on Feb. 18, 1819. His grandfather was gifted, spendthrift and a little mad, and finally killed himself. His parents recognized a dangerous precocity and an unstable genius in their child and sheltered him from contact with reality. At the same time they checked and restrained him and allowed him little spontaneity of interest or action.

The father, John James Ruskin, was a successful wine merchant. He had a liking for pictures and when he toured England to solicit orders, used to see the galleries in the great houses, accompanied, in time, by his son. The Ruskins moved to Herne Hill, on the southern outskirts of London, when Ruskin was 4, and to Denmark Hill, near Dulwich, when he was 20. His natural appetite for pictures found satisfaction in the Dulwich Art gallery, and the pictures there exhibited remained the basis of his thoughts on art long after he was free to seek wider knowledge.

The Dulwich gallery, constant reading of the Bible with his mother and of the 18th-century classics with his father, and his father's encouragement of his facile talents in writing and drawing were the most valuable part of his education. His father's interest in art secured him drawing lessons from the water-colorist Copley Fielding. When he was 14 the family began a series of tours in Europe, of a most conventional kind—northern France,

JOHN RUSKIN

Flanders, the Rhine, the Black Forest and Switzerland. In the Alps he found the beauty and sublimity that he needed, and he justified his love of them (since the moral preoccupations of his parents and his own untried powers of expression made justification necessary) by amateur geologizing and botanizing.

When he was 17 Ruskin fell in love with Adèle Domecq, the daughter of his father's Spanish partner. The frustration of this affair seems to have been the effective cause of a permanent failure to attain emotional maturity which left him vulnerable and incomplete.

In 1836 Ruskin went up to Christ Church, Oxford, where his studies were desultory and his social life hampered by his mother's presence in lodgings nearby. Nonetheless he had got away from the suburbs and made friends—chief among them Henry (later Sir Henry) Acland, who became regius professor of medicine—who were permanently to enrich his life. He won the Newdigate prize for poetry in 1839 and, because of a generous allowance from his father, was able to begin to collect pictures by J. M. W. Turner.

First Visit to Italy.—Ruskin's time at Oxford was interrupted suddenly in the spring of 1840 when he suffered a hemorrhage which the doctors considered to be of phthisic origin. They advised that he should winter abroad, and the family departed for Italy. Ruskin made many sketches in the course of the long leisurely journey, but in Rome, where he made friends with the artist George Richmond, he began to have a clearer idea of the difference between amateur and professional work. They went on to Naples, where he had another attack, but on the return journey by Venice through Switzerland he regained energy and hope. He found himself able to see natural beauty in all its gamut—from great mountains to minute plants—with a new vividness, and devoted himself to describing it with artistry.

Ruskin returned to Oxford in the autumn and took the pass schools creditably in the spring of 1842. The Ruskins spent the summer at Chamonix, France. There John began to plan a book in defense of Turner, whose late style had been exemplified in his Academy pictures of that year, which had been laughed at by the critics. Returning to a new house on Denmark Hill, he began to work seriously at the National gallery and at Dulwich and to write the first draft of what was to become the first volume of *Modern Painters*. He set out to examine the "truth to Nature" of the accepted masters of landscape painting, always with the glorification of Turner in mind, and in his descriptions of landscape, in Italy and in the Alps, gave rein to his own capacity for word painting. The book appeared in May 1843, when Ruskin was just 24. It had a considerable success, though Turner himself showed nothing but embarrassment. Ruskin immediately set to work on a second volume which had no such definite scheme as the first and contained even more of the author's sensibility—a sensibility that had by then escaped from Protestant inhibitions in the study of religious painting.

Second Visit to Italy; Marriage.—In April 1845 he set out on a journey that was to mark a new stage in his development. Together with a valet and an elderly mountaineer guide, and without his parents, he set forth to explore north Italy and found in its medieval architecture and sculpture a romantic beauty he had not known before. The sketches he made were the best he ever achieved; the things he saw were forever imprinted on his memory; for once he was really happy.

When he returned to Denmark Hill it was to complete the second volume of *Modern Painters* in less congenial surroundings. It appeared in April 1846. A subsequent journey to Italy with his parents, to show them the beauties he had lately discovered, was an anticlimax and led to an attack of nervous depression. On their return he began to think of marriage, and with hesitant encouragement from his parents became engaged to Euphemia Chalmers (Effie) Gray, the pretty daughter of Scottish friends of the family, whom he married in April 1848. He was completely self-centred and very gifted; she was rather demanding, a born social climber and essentially commonplace. It is not surprising that the marriage (which was never consummated) was not a success.

After a few months in London, where Effie was determinedly social, in August they visited northern France, for Ruskin had it in mind to write a book on the essential qualities of Gothic architecture. By April *The Seven Lamps of Architecture* was finished. The book had a considerable success. It took the fruits of the labours of a generation of medievalists and gave them a generalized basis and a moral flavour; and it was extremely well-written. In the autumn of 1849, the young Ruskins went to Venice for the winter. Ruskin wished to apply the general principles of *The Seven Lamps* to Venetian architecture, and to relate its rise and fall to the working of moral and spiritual forces. He worked hard; *The Stones of Venice* duly appeared in 1851. In the course of 1851 Ruskin was induced to champion the Pre-Raphaelite brotherhood (*q.v.*), less because he admired them from the first than because he thought the critics unfair to them. He befriended Dante Gabriel Rossetti, who disliked him; established a lasting and happy friendship with Edward Burne-Jones; and he cultivated the company of John Everett Millais, with the result that the artist and Effie fell in love. As soon as Millais had been elected a member of the Royal Academy, with an assured future, Effie left Ruskin. In July 1854 she secured an annulment of her marriage on the ground of her husband's impotence, and a few months later married Millais.

Return to Denmark Hill.—Ruskin was back in the old narrow circle of Denmark Hill. His only escape was to rather futile teaching at the Working Men's college, established in 1854 by J. F. D. Maurice (*q.v.*), whom he did not like, and in sitting at the feet of Thomas Carlyle, who made him waste a good deal of time on causes irrelevant to his real interests. The third and fourth volumes of *Modern Painters* were written on an increasingly authoritarian note, and by the middle of 1855 he felt written out. His chief interest was in the construction of the Oxford University museum under the aegis of his friend Acland, according to his own principles of Gothic beauty. He offered to undertake the sorting and arrangement of the mass of drawings that Turner had left to the National gallery and from Feb. 1857 for about a year they were his chief occupation. He gave a good many lectures, less on art pure and simple than on its implications. In those on "The Political Economy of Art" (1857)—later retitled *A Joy for Ever*—he first entered the field of economics, with an able and effective disquisition on economy as "the art of managing labour."

In 1858, again alone but for a valet and the old guide, he spent six weeks in Turin, Italy, and recaptured the magic of the mature Renaissance in the paintings of Paolo Veronese. The fifth volume of *Modern Painters* (1860), written in the winter of 1858–59, is largely influenced by these interests. The volume is extremely disconnected; and indeed, Ruskin's mind was gradually declining into madness. He fell in love with a hysterical young Irish girl of good family, Rose La Touche, who, when he first knew her, was a child of ten; when she was 16 he declared himself to the parents, who were horrified. Soon after, Rose fell mentally and physically ill, and the affair dragged sadly and hectically on until her death in 1875. During these years Ruskin became a habitué of Miss Bell's girls' school at Winnington, in Cheshire, where the company of the children provided a refuge; some of his books—notably *The Ethics of the Dust* (1866)—were developed from talks he gave to her pupils. His only important work at this time was a set of essays on the nature of wealth that he wrote in 1860. His views (based to some extent on those of the reformer and socialist Robert Owen [*q.v.*]) included the theory of social justice and were utterly contrary to the *laissez-faire* Benthamite doctrines of the time. The *Cornhill* began to publish the essays, but they roused so much opposition among its readers that after the fourth essay Thackeray, as editor, discontinued them. Ruskin published them as a book under the title *Unto This Last* (1862).

He was near a breakdown, and retired for a time to Mornex near Geneva. He returned in time for his father's last illness and death in March 1864 and continued to live with his aging mother at Denmark Hill. His father left Ruskin £120,000, various properties and a fine collection of pictures; but he had neither peace of mind nor strength of purpose left. He wrote no more on art, except as a part of his social and economic theories, and when he traveled he was apt to delegate the making of sketches to artists whom he took with him.

Last Years.—In 1869 he was elected the first Slade professor of fine art at Oxford, and he had a great personal success as a lecturer, though his lectures were diffuse and on many subjects other than art. He gave a collection of prints, photographs and drawings for undergraduates to study; he set up a drawing school for them; and he encouraged them to build a road across the wet fields at Hinksey. He had a need to address himself to those of another intellectual class than himself, and wrote two series of letters to workingmen, *Time and Tide* (1867) and a much longer set, *Fors Clavigera* (1871–87). The last was the organ of the Company of St. George, which he founded in 1871 and endowed with a capital of £10,000. It was intended to carry out his economic doctrines; every "companion" was to give a tenth of his income, and for many years Ruskin did. Its activities were often ill-judged and were usually unfortunate; a museum of art at Sheffield was the most successful. Bouts of illness interrupted work at Oxford and the publication of *Fors;* after his mother's death in 1871 Ruskin sold the house at Denmark Hill and bought an ugly residence, Brantwood, beautifully situated on Coniston water in the Lake district, where he spent much of his time, with a married cousin to keep house for him. He began to be obsessed with the idea of the "Storm-Cloud and Plague-Wind" which were everywhere defiling natural beauty, and finally in 1878 suffered some months of acute mania. Early in 1879 he resigned his professorship, giving as his excuse that James Whistler (*q.v.*) had won a libel action against him for his intemperate criticism of one of the "Nocturnes."

His intellectual life was over. He showed improvement in 1880–81 and even resumed work at Oxford, with grotesque and tragic results. The years that followed were checkered by attacks of mania; yet it was in these years that he wrote the most charming of his works, the autobiography called *Praeterita* (1885–1900). It offered escape from the present and, since he had kept a diary for much of his life, he had materials to work on. It was never finished; after a sixth attack of madness in the summer of 1889 he was incapable of writing anything but his signature. He died on Jan. 20, 1900, and was buried at Coniston, Lancashire.

Ideas, Influence and Personality.—A Wordsworthian in his love of nature, and of mountain scenery in particular, Ruskin founded an aesthetic canon upon truth to nature in landscape painting, contrasting, in *Modern Painters*, the sensitive accuracy of Turner in this respect with the conventionalism of Claude Lorrain. He found the same truthfulness in union with religious feeling in Gothic architecture and in the natural forms of its decoration carved with delicate reserve by devoted craftsmen. The gesticulation of baroque and its urns, scrolls, obelisks and drums—forms not found in nature—seemed artificial and false to him and thus, in his view, constituted bad art. From his conception of good art as a permanent repository of natural truth, which was its source, and of moral feeling, which inevitably accompanied it, proceeded his ideal view of the workman, whether craftsman or manual labourer, as a dedicated individual who needed to find fulfillment through doing satisfying work with a valid purpose. Social justice required the creation of conditions which would permit all to share with the creative artist the opportunity for work of this kind, for they were not generally to be found in the heedless economic expansion of 19th-century England. Thus he was led from criticism and exposition of art to a concern with social welfare, advocating better housing, a system of national education for children and adults, old-age pensions (measures commonplace enough since, but revolutionary then); and he used his wealth in the service of these ends. Yet it is in the world of art that Ruskin is perhaps remembered best. His vision of Gothic as the norm of true art and moral value gave a new significance to its study by architectural historians and accorded so well with the feeling of the age that he was able to lend authoritative support to the carrying out of a great deal of public building in Victorian England in the neo-Gothic style.

John Ruskin was a man of true originality. His literary style, though it has echoes of the Authorized (King James) Version of the Bible and of writers such as Richard Hooker and Dr. Johnson, is nonetheless unmistakably his own; his ideas might owe something to Plato and much to the Bible, but he wrought them in his own fashion. He was a completely honest and curiously innocent man. As a rich man's son he was free to work at what he liked. He endured a measure of drudgery when he wrote the historical sections of *The Stones of Venice* and when he sorted and arranged the Turner drawings at the National gallery, but in the main he wrote easily of what interested him. This amateur quality gives a characteristic sparkle and zest to his treatment of all his themes, and they were many. His originality and his intellectual self-indulgence were inextricably mixed with his psychological weakness. He is the archetype of the manic-depressive, swinging from elation to misery, always sensitive and always expressive. The narrow religiosity of his early upbringing, his lack of systematic education and his mother's overanxious care did nothing to give him the poise and repose that might have helped him to keep a balance; and two frustrated love affairs and an unhappy marriage removed any hope of emotional maturity.

Yet, in spite of these disabilities (and sometimes because of them), he was able to perceive beauty with an infectious intensity, and to express his perception in memorable prose. He was one of the first to bring the work of art into relation with its creation and with the age in which he lived, and one of the first to preach with some effect that a respect for art must be a part of civilization. He inspired William Morris to create the Society for the Protection of Ancient Buildings, and preached the necessity for a National Art Collections fund a generation before one was founded. He included visual training in his educational schemes. He made the social condition of the workman a part of the judgment both of the work of art and of manufacture on a larger scale. It is easy and partly true to say that he lost the battle against the doctrines and practice of Manchester (*i.e.*, the political economists who followed John Bright in advocating *laissez-faire*), yet many of his words did not fall on stony ground. No one who has read any of his more important works seriously will ever be quite free from his influence; in what he wrote there was always an element of single-minded nobility. No picture of the Victorian age can be complete without him.

See also references under "Ruskin, John" in the Index.

BIBLIOGRAPHY.—*Editions and Selections:* Ruskin's *Works* were edited by E. T. Cook and A. Wedderburn, 39 vol. (1903–12). The *Diaries* were edited by Joan Evans and J. H. Whitehouse, 3 vol. (1956–59). *See* also Joan Evans (ed.), *The Lamp of Beauty* (1959), an anthology of his writings on art; Sir K. Clark (ed.), *Selections From Ruskin* (1963). *Biography and Criticism:* E. T. Cook, *Life* (1911), a classic that now seems overdiscreet; R. W. Wilenski, *John Ruskin: an Introduction to Further Study of His Life and Work* (1933); W. M. James, *The Order of Release* (1947); D. Leon, *Ruskin, the Great Victorian* (1949); P. Quennell, *John Ruskin: the Portrait of a Prophet* (1949); J. H. Whitehouse, *Vindication of Ruskin* (1950); Joan Evans, *John Ruskin* (1954); H. G. Viljoen, *Ruskin's Scottish Heritage* (1956); John D. Rosenberg, *The Darkening Glass: a Portrait of Ruskin's Genius* (1963).

(J. Ev.)

RUSSELL, the name of a famous English Whig family, the senior line of which has held the title of duke of Bedford since the late 17th century, and which first acquired prominence under the Tudor sovereigns.

The first member of the family whose existence can be proved was STEPHEN RUSSELL (d. 1438/39). Dorset records of the late 14th and early 15th centuries show him as a small merchant, often giving him the alias of Gascoigne. An alias was a common means of identification; this one possibly indicates that Russell's origin was in Aquitaine or it may merely have referred to his trading interests. He was married (*c.* 1400) to Alice de la Tour, daughter of John de la Tour of Dorset, who held some property in the county. The most important of these properties was the small manor of Berwick upon Swyre, about five miles inland and to the westward from Weymouth; but in this manor Alice brought Stephen only a reversionary interest. Stephen took his part in local affairs and may have represented Weymouth in the Parliament of 1394.

Stephen's son HENRY RUSSELL (d. 1463/64) lived much the same life as his father, but more details of his activities have survived. He also took part in local affairs and traded with France. He represented Weymouth in the Westminster parliaments of 1425, 1427 and 1441–42. His wife was Elizabeth Herring, daughter of John Herring of Chaldon-Herring in Dorset, a small landowner.

Henry prospered, and came to own four or five ships trading from Weymouth to France and Spain. He also rose in status. When he obtained a pardon for having neglected some duties as bailiff, his description was given as "Henry Russell of Weymouth otherwise called Henry Russell of Weymouth merchant, otherwise called Henry Gascoigne of Weymouth Gentilman . . . or by whatsoever name he may be styled."

A more significant development, however, was that Henry acquired a coat of arms, a fact which only again came to light two centuries later. Henry died between October 1463 and October 1464, and was buried in the church of the Holy Trinity in Dorchester, where he had a house. Early in the 17th century the church was destroyed by fire, and the reigning Russell—Francis, 4th earl—sent an emissary to Dorchester to investigate the damage. He received a report that the tomb had been destroyed, but that lying on the ground was part of a coat of arms showing "a lion rampant gules on a chief three scallop shells impaling a shield bendy argent and gules." Here, presumably, was the first representation of the Russell arms.

JOHN RUSSELL (*c.* 1432–1505), Henry's son, was married to Elizabeth Froxmere, who may have belonged to a Worcestershire family of that name. Nothing is known of his activities, but he and his wife are commemorated by a mural tablet of 1505, still existing in the church of the Holy Trinity at Swyre. This may well point to the fact that the reversion of the manor of Berwick had now fallen in, and that John lived there.

JAMES RUSSELL (d. 1505/06), John's heir but not necessarily his son, lived at Berwick with his wife, Alice Wyse, who came of a Devonshire family. They, too, are commemorated by a mural tablet in the church at Swyre, dated 1509.

Neither of the two generations succeeding Henry Russell was particularly outstanding. But the son of James and Alice, JOHN RUSSELL (*c.* 1485–1555), made his mark in history. After the accession of Henry VIII he advanced rapidly, serving the crown as soldier and diplomatic agent. Under Edward VI and Mary I he was keeper of the privy seal. After his defeat of the western rebels in August 1549 he was created earl of Bedford in January 1550. For details of his career and of those of his successors, earls and dukes of Bedford, *see* BEDFORD, EARLS AND DUKES OF. Three of the four sons of FRANCIS (*c.* 1527–1585), 2nd earl of Bedford, died before him; the third, killed in a border fray, was father of EDWARD (1572–1627), 3rd earl, who died without issue. Francis' fourth son, WILLIAM (*c.* 1558–1613), created Lord Russell of Thornhaugh in 1603, was a soldier who fought at Zutphen (1586) beside his friend Sir Philip Sidney, whom he succeeded as governor of Flushing (1587–88), and was from 1594 to 1597 lord deputy of Ireland. His only son, FRANCIS (1593–1641), succeeded his cousin as 4th earl of Bedford in 1627. WILLIAM (1616–1700), eldest surviving son of the 4th earl, succeeded as 5th earl and became 1st duke of Bedford. The youngest son of the 4th earl, Edward, was father of EDWARD RUSSELL (1653–1727), admiral of the fleet, who, having held the chief command in the victory of La Hogue (1692) against the French, was created earl of Orford in 1697.

LORD WILLIAM RUSSELL (*q.v.*), third son of the 1st duke, supported the unsuccessful attempts to exclude James, duke of York (afterward James II), from the throne. He was unwise enough to mix with conspiratorial associates and after the exposure of the alleged Rye House Plot (1683) was found guilty of attending a meeting at which treason had been talked. He was executed at Lincoln's Inn Fields on July 21, 1683.

LORD JOHN RUSSELL (1792–1878), third son of the 6th duke of Bedford, was the statesman whose name is particularly connected with projects for parliamentary reform and who was created, in 1861, Earl Russell of Kingston Russell (*see* RUSSELL, JOHN RUSSELL, 1st Earl). His nephew, Odo Russell, was ambassador at Berlin from 1871 until his death in 1884, and was created Lord Ampthill in 1881 (*see* AMPTHILL, ODO WILLIAM LEOPOLD RUSSELL, 1st Baron). Lord John's grandson, BERTRAND ARTHUR WILLIAM RUSSELL, 3rd Earl Russell (*q.v.*), is the well-known philosopher.

See G. S. Thomson, *Two Centuries of Family History* (1930), *Family Background* (1949).

(G. S. T.)

RUSSELL, BERTRAND ARTHUR WILLIAM RUSSELL, 3RD EARL (1872–), English philosopher, famous also for his eloquent championship of individual liberty, which made his position in the intellectual life of his time comparable with that of Voltaire in the 18th century or with that of J. S. Mill in the 19th, was born on May 18, 1872. His grandfathers were Lord John Russell (afterward Earl Russell) and the second Lord Stanley of Alderley. His godfather (in a purely social sense) was J. S. Mill. At the age of three he was left an orphan. His father, Lord Amberley, had wished him to be brought up as an agnostic; to avoid this he was made a ward of court and brought up by his grandmother at Pembroke lodge, in Richmond park. Instead of being sent to school he was taught by governesses and tutors and thus acquired his perfect knowledge of French and German. In Oct. 1890 he went into residence, as a shy undergraduate, at Trinity college, Cambridge. After being a high wrangler and obtaining a first class with distinction in philosophy he was elected a fellow of his college in the autumn of 1895. But he had already left Cambridge in the summer of 1894 and for some months was attaché at the British embassy in Paris.

In Dec. 1894 Russell married Alys Pearsall Smith. After spending some months in Berlin studying social democracy (*German Social Democracy*, 1896), they went to live near Haslemere, where he devoted his time to the study of philosophy and wrote *A Critical Exposition of the Philosophy of Leibniz* (1900). He published *The Principles of Mathematics* in 1903 and then, with his friend A. N. Whitehead, proceeded to develop and extend the mathematical logic of Giuseppe Peano and Gottlob Frege. The three volumes of their joint book, *Principia Mathematica*, were published in 1910, 1912 and 1913. During all this period Russell lived simply and worked hard. He was elected a fellow of the Royal society in 1908 and was appointed lecturer at his old college in 1910. In 1910 also he published *Philosophical Essays*, republished in later editions from 1918 as *Mysticism and Logic, and Other Philosophical Essays*.

After World War I broke out he took an active part in the No Conscription fellowship. He was fined £100 as the author of a leaflet criticizing a sentence of two years on a conscientious objector. His library was seized to pay the fine; it was bought in by a friend, but many valuable books were lost. His college deprived him of his lectureship. He was offered a post at Harvard university, but was refused a passport. He intended to give a course of lectures (published in the U.S. as *Political Ideals* in 1918) but was prevented by the military authorities. In 1918 he was sentenced to six months' imprisonment for a pacifist article he had written in the *Tribunal*. His excellent *Introduction to Mathematical Philosophy* (1919) was written in prison. *The Analysis of Mind* (1921) was the outcome of some lectures that he gave in London, a few friends having raised a subscription for the purpose. *The Practice and Theory of Bolshevism* (1920) was written after a short visit to Russia.

In the autumn of 1920 he went to China to lecture on philosophy at the Peking university. On his return in Sept. 1921, having been divorced by his first wife, he married Dora Black. He then earned a livelihood by lecturing, journalism and writing popular books such as *The A.B.C. of Atoms* (1923), *The A.B.C. of Relativity* (1925) and *On Education* (1926). Other publications of this period were the introduction to the second edition of *Principia Mathematica* (1925); *The Analysis of Matter* (1927); *An Outline of Philosophy* (1927); *Marriage and Morals* (1929). In 1927 he and his wife started a school for young children, which they managed until 1932. He succeeded to the earldom in 1931. Divorced by his second wife in 1935, Russell the following year married Patricia Helen Spence, with whom he published *The Amberley Papers* (1937). In 1938 he went to the United States, where he taught at many of the leading universities. When his appointment to teach philosophy at the College of the City of New York (1940) was cancelled because of his views on morality Russell accepted a five-year contract as a lecturer for the Barnes foundation, Merion, Pa., but cancellation of this was announced in Jan. 1943.

After 1944 Russell lived mostly in England, becoming well known to large audiences through his broadcasts, which included the first series of Reith lectures (*Authority and the Individual*, 1949). He received the Order of Merit in 1949 and the Nobel prize for literature in 1950. In 1952 he was divorced for the third time and married Edith Finch. A collection of five short stories appeared under the title *Satan in the Suburbs* in 1953.

Apart from those already mentioned, Russell's writings include *The Conquest of Happiness* (1930); *The Scientific Outlook* (1931); *Education and the Social Order* (1932); *Freedom and Organisation, 1814–1914* (1934); *Power: a New Social Analysis* (1938); *An Inquiry Into Meaning and Truth* (1940); *A History of Western Philosophy* (1945); *Human Knowledge, Its Scope and Limits* (1948); *Unpopular Essays* (1950); *New Hopes for a Changing World* (1951); and *Human Society in Ethics and Politics* (1954). (C. P. SA.; W. C. K.)

Philosophy.—What is fundamental in Russell's philosophy is his logic: his views on metaphysics and ethics, on the nature and relations of matter and mind, changed profoundly in the course of his life, but these changes all proceeded from successively deeper applications of his logical method. He, therefore, preferred to classify his philosophy not as a species of idealism or realism but as "logical atomism," since what distinguishes the whole of his work is his use of logical analysis as a method and his belief that by it we can arrive at ultimate "atomic facts" logically independent both of one another and of being known.

First Russell tried to free logical analysis from the domination of ordinary grammar by showing that the grammatical form of a sentence often fails to reflect the logical form of its meaning. In his *Principles of Mathematics* he insisted that relations could not be reduced to qualities of their terms and that relational facts were not of the subject-predicate forms, but he still thought that any descriptive phrase which could be made the subject of a sentence must stand for a term which had being, even if like "the round square" it were self-contradictory. In his article "On Denoting" (*Mind*, 1905) and in subsequent writings, he put forward his theory of descriptions, which is perhaps the most important and influential of his innovations in logic. According to this theory "the present king of France" is not a name for a nonexistent entity but an "incomplete symbol" which only has meaning in connection with a context. The meaning of such a statement as "the present king of France is bald" is first that there is someone who is at present both king of France and bald and secondly that there are not at present two kings of France; and when such statements are analyzed in this way the need to believe in entities such as "the present king of France" (which are said by some philosophers to have "being" but not "existence") is altogether removed. Similarly when it is said that "unicorns are not real," this does not mean that certain animals, namely unicorns, lack the characteristic of reality but that there are no horselike animals with one horn.

Russell applied similar methods to classes and to numbers and argued that each of these categories consists of what he called "logical constructions." In saying, for instance, that classes are logical constructions, he did not mean that they are entities constructed by the human mind, but that when we express facts by sentences which have for subject such a phrase as "the class of men," the true analysis of the fact does not correspond to the grammatical analysis of the sentence. When, for instance, we say "the class of men includes the class of criminals," the fact asserted by us is really about the characteristics of being a man and being a criminal and not about any such entities as classes at all. This notion of a logical construction was much employed by Russell in his work in mathematical logic, and he also used it extensively in the philosophy of matter and mind, and even adopted as a fundamental principle that constructions (in his special sense of the word) are to be substituted for inferred entities wherever possible.

By applying this method he was led to a view of the world on which the ultimate constituents of mind and matter are of the same type, the difference between minds and bodies lying in their structure and not in the elements of which they are composed. A man's mind is composed of sensations and images, which are identified by Russell with physical events in his brain, and the difference between physics and psychology lies not in the events which they study but in the kind of laws about those events which they seek to establish, physics being concerned with structure and psychology with quality. This theory was worked out in connection with physics in *The Analysis of Matter*.

In the theory of knowledge Russell's earlier rationalism was considerably modified in a pragmatist or behaviourist direction, and in *The Analysis of Mind* he rejected consciousness as a fundamental characteristic of mind and adopted a form of "neutral monism" about perception, which he combined with representationism in regard to memory and judgment.

Russell's logical atomism was the starting point for the *Tractatus logico-philosophicus* (1921) of his pupil L. Wittgenstein and so one of the sources of logical positivism. Then, after a period between World Wars I and II when it dominated the philosophy of the English-speaking world, his program was brought into doubt by the later teaching of Wittgenstein, according to which philosophical difficulties arise not from any inadequacy of ordinary language but from failure to respect the limits of normal usage. In his later writings Russell showed misgivings about logical atomism, but for different reasons. He came to think that there might be necessary connections between distinct events.

Mathematics.—Russell maintained that mathematics and formal logic are one and that the whole of pure mathematics can be rigorously deduced from a small number of logical axioms. He argued this in outline in *Principles of Mathematics* and then tried to give a detailed demonstration of his thesis in *Principia Mathematica*, written with A. N. Whitehead. In this colossal work the deduction is carried so far as to include all the essential parts of the theory of aggregates and real numbers. Besides this the great advances made by Russell in the analysis of logical concepts allowed the deductions to be carried not only much farther forward but also much farther backward toward first principles. Above all he appeared to solve the notorious paradoxes of the theory of aggregates by means of the theory of types. In this connection, however, he found it necessary to introduce an "axiom of reducibility" which has never won general acceptance, so that his work cannot be regarded as a final solution of the problem.

See MATHEMATICS, FOUNDATIONS OF; *see* also references under "Russell, Bertrand Arthur" in the Index.   (F. P. R.; W. C. K.)

RUSSELL, CHARLES TAZE (PASTOR RUSSELL) (1852–1916), founder of the International Bible Students association, forerunner of the modern Jehovah's Witnesses (*q.v.*), was born at Pittsburgh, Pa., on Feb. 16, 1852. Of Presbyterian and Congregationalist background, Russell renounced the creeds of orthodox Christian denominations and in 1872 organized an independent Bible study class in Pittsburgh. From 1877 he preached that Christ's second advent would be invisible, that the end of the Gentile times would come in 1914, followed by war between capitalism and communism or socialism, after which God's Kingdom by Christ would rule the whole earth. Russell (who, though popularly called Pastor Russell, was never ordained) dedicated his life and his considerable fortune to preaching Christ's millennial reign. In 1879 he started a Bible journal later called the *Watchtower*. His wife disputed editorship and eventually sought legal separation, which was granted; she never sought nor obtained absolute divorce. The *Washington Post* and *Chicago Mission Friend* charged marital promiscuousness, but Russell sued both papers for libel and won both cases.

Russell's religious stand opened the door for a number of controversial incidents publicized during his life. One such incident in 1911 involved a gift to Russell's organization of a quantity of "miracle wheat" (so named by its discoverer), which, at the donor's request, was sold, the proceeds (about $1,800) to be applied to charitable work. Russell in 1884 founded the Watchtower Bible and Tract society, which became a flourishing publishing business. His own books and booklets (notably six volumes of *Studies in the Scriptures*) reached a circulation of 16,000,000 copies in 35 languages, and 2,000 newspapers published his weekly sermons. Russell died on a train in Pampa, Tex., on Oct. 31, 1916, while on a speaking tour.

See M. Cole, *Jehovah's Witnesses—the New World Society* (1955).
(M. Co.)

RUSSELL, GEORGE WILLIAM (1867–1935), Irish poet and mystic, better known by his pseudonym, "Æ," was a leading figure in the Irish literary revival. He was born at Lurgan, County Armagh, on April 10, 1867, and educated at Rathmines School. He also attended the Metropolitan School of Art, Dublin, where he met W. B. Yeats. He became an accounts clerk in a drapery store but left in 1897 to organize agricultural cooperatives, becoming editor in 1906 of *The Irish Homestead* and in 1923 of *The Irish Statesman*, both cooperative organs.

In 1894 Russell published the first of many books of verse, *Homeward: Songs by the Way*. His first book of *Collected Poems* appeared in 1913, and a second in 1926. In 1935, the year of his death, he published his *Selected Poems*, containing all he wished to preserve. He was interested all his life in theosophy, the origins of religion and mystical experience, and was reputed to see frequent visions. *The Candle of Vision* (1918) is the best guide to his religious beliefs, while *Co-Operation and Nationality* (1912) and *The National Being, Thoughts on an Irish Polity* (1916) reflect his political and economic interests. He remained true to his early interest in painting, but his work lacks intensity and it was as a poet that he hoped to be remembered.

There is rather too much of the "Celtic twilight" in his verse, and it suffers also from the vagueness and imprecision of the accepted poetic diction of his youth; but in a handful of pieces, notably "Immortality," "The Twilight of Earth," "On Behalf of Some Irishmen Not Followers of Tradition," and "Companions," and especially, perhaps, in "Germinal," he memorably transcends these limitations. Russell died at Bournemouth on July 17, 1935.

BIBLIOGRAPHY.—John Eglinton (W. K. Magee), *A Memoir of Æ* (1937); Monk Gibbon, *The Living Torch* (1937); W. B. Yeats, *Autobiographies* (1926); George Moore, *Hail and Farewell* (1911–14).
(A. CR.)

RUSSELL, HENRY NORRIS (1877–1957), U.S. astronomer, the inventor (with the Danish astronomer Ejnar Hertzsprung) of the "Hertzsprung-Russell diagram," was one of the most important influences in the development of 20th-century astrophysics and stellar astronomy. He was born at Oyster Bay, N.Y., on Oct. 25, 1877, and died in Princeton, N.J., on Feb. 18, 1957. After attending Princeton university he went to Cambridge, Eng., where he was engaged in the determination of stellar parallaxes by photography—a method which at that time (1903–05) was in its infancy.

Russell returned to Princeton in 1905 to embark on a long and brilliant career in astronomy. His work included investigations in almost every field of modern astronomy, as well as in spectroscopy. He developed a method for the determination of the dimensions of double stars whose components periodically eclipse each other; in addition, he and Hertzsprung independently discovered a way to determine the distances from the solar system of double stars which are observed through the telescope to be in revolution about their common centre of gravity. The diagram known variously as the Russell diagram or Hertzsprung-Russell diagram was formulated in its modern form by Russell in 1913. The information which it gives about the stars is fundamental and its uses are varied. The diagram illustrates the relationship between the spectral types (that is to say, surface temperatures) and absolute magnitudes of the stars. (The absolute magnitude is a measure of the true brightness—as distinguished from the apparent brightness—of a star.)

The theory of stellar evolution advanced by Russell in 1913 was favoured almost universally for many years thereafter; although it is no longer supported, its importance in the development of the subject was great. Russell was one of the most active workers in the analysis of the line spectra of the elements and he utilized the new developments in studies of the characteristics of stellar atmospheres.

Among Russell's writings may be mentioned, *Modifying Our Ideas of Nature: the Einstein Theory of Relativity* (reprinted in the *Smithsonian Report for 1921*); *The Constitution and Evolution of the Stars* (reprinted in the *Smithsonian Report for 1923*); *The Composition of the Stars* (1933); *The Atmospheres of the Planets* (reprinted in the *Smithsonian Report for 1935*); and *The Solar System and Its Origin* (1935). (W. W. M.)

For a description of the spectral type-absolute magnitude diagram, *see* H. N. Russell, R. S. Dugan and J. Q. Stewart, *Astronomy,* 2 vol. (1926–27; vol. i rev., 1945; vol. ii, 2nd ed., 1938).

RUSSELL, JOHN RUSSELL, 1ST EARL (1792–1878), British statesman, prime minister from 1846 to 1852 and from October 1865 to June 1866, an indefatigable champion of liberal measures and especially of parliamentary reform, whose name is particularly connected with the Reform Bill of 1832, was born in London on Aug. 18, 1792. As the third son of the 6th duke of Bedford, he was known for most of his life as LORD JOHN RUSSELL, until himself created an earl in 1861. A frail, puny child, he attended Westminster School, the traditional school of the Russells, for one year only (1803–04). In 1809 he was sent to Edinburgh University. His contacts there with such men as the mathematician and philosopher John Playfair with whom he resided and with Dugald Stewart for whose teaching he expressed gratitude in a sonnet, and his membership of the Speculative Society of which he was president (1811–12) gave direction to his thoughts and taught him the art of debate. During vacations and after leaving Edinburgh (1812) he traveled in Spain, Portugal, and Italy.

Russell's political career began when he was returned to Parliament in 1813. The trend of his mind was clearly shown in his first notable speech, when in 1817 he opposed the suspension of the Habeas Corpus Act. To Russell, bred in the Whig tradition, the proposed suspension, one of the measures designed to repress the prevailing industrial unrest, was an infringement of civil liberty. The suspension was approved; but behind the troubles new and less illiberal ideas were slowly making headway. In presenting these, young Russell was in the van. In 1819 he began his advocacy for the reform of parliamentary representation by moving an inquiry into the corruption of one particular constituency, Grampound in Cornwall, the disfranchisement of which was secured in 1821. This was a pointer to future developments. In the meantime Russell turned his attention to the question of Catholic emancipation. On this matter, then a burning issue, the Whigs stood solid. Toleration was part of their political creed. In February 1828 Russell led the attacks on the Test and Corporation acts which since the 17th century had largely restricted public office to adherents of the Church of England. The acts were repealed and this triumph was followed by the passage of a Catholic Relief Act in 1829, under threat of rebellion in Ireland.

Office Under Grey and Melbourne (1830–41).—The Tories resigned in November 1830, and Earl Grey formed the first Whig administration since 1807. Russell was paymaster general. Grey had determined on the immediate drafting of a bill for parliamentary reform, and appointed for this purpose a committee of four, including Russell. Although not yet a member of the cabinet, he was chosen to move the first reading in the House of Commons in March 1831. When, after first a dissolution and then an attempt by the duke of Wellington to form a ministry (*see* GREY, CHARLES GREY, 2nd Earl), the bill was finally passed in the House of Lords on June 4, 1832, Russell was justly regarded as its chief architect.

Russell, who had joined the cabinet in June 1831, believed that the surplus revenues of the Church of Ireland should be diverted to secular purposes. His public pronouncement to this effect in the House of Commons (May 1834) led to the resignation of Lord Stanley (afterward 14th earl of Derby), then secretary for war and the colonies, who had until recently been chief secretary for Ireland. "Johnny Russell has upset the coach," he said. Russell was often to display this habit of calculated plain speaking, but seldom to such effect. On this question and on the renewal of the Irish "coercion" bill, the ministry was seriously divided; Viscount Melbourne succeeded Grey as premier (July) and when Lord Althorp, leader of the House of Commons, succeeded his father as Earl Spencer and went to the Lords (November), King William IV dismissed the Whigs. But they returned to power in April 1835, Russell becoming home secretary and leader of the House of Commons, a situation grudgingly accepted by the king who both disliked and distrusted him. It was a weak government, owing

much to the moderation of Sir Robert Peel as leader of the opposition. It did, however, pass the Municipal Corporations Act of 1835 (*see* BOROUGH) and various measures (1836–40) to reform the financial administration of the Church of England. Russell became secretary for war and the colonies in August 1839, a post which he retained until the Whigs left office after being defeated in the general election of 1841.

First Ministry (1846–52).—In November 1845 Russell addressed to his constituents in the City of London the "Edinburgh letter," that "blast from a trumpet" which announced his conversion to the view that the Corn Laws must be repealed. He was unaware that Peel, as prime minister, had already decided they must go. The actual repeal in 1846 was carried through by Peel, with Russell's support. The repeal of the Corn Laws split the Tories, and when Peel resigned after a tactical defeat on an Irish "coercion" bill, Lord John, "our little giant," became prime minister at the age of 53. His six years in office were not easy in either home or foreign affairs. He was not particularly successful in dealing with the Irish famine of 1846–47; continuing the imports of North American maize (corn), he also allowed outdoor relief (March 1847) on an enormous scale, but the problem of overpopulation was too serious to be solved other than by extensive emigration. But in the following year, 1848, the year of revolutions, his skilful handling of Chartism (*q.v.*) saved England from a dangerous situation. His reaction to the papal bull of 1850 creating Roman Catholic bishops in England was unfortunate; following popular prejudice, he attacked the Catholic hierarchy in an "open" letter to the bishop of Durham and in 1851 passed the Ecclesiastical Titles Act forbidding the assumption of titles already held by clergy of the established church. Abroad, the struggle for liberty in the countries of western Europe, the aftermath of 1848, commanded the sympathy and approval of Russell and no less of his foreign secretary Viscount Palmerston. But Palmerston often made trouble for the prime minister. Queen Victoria resented, not without reason, the foreign secretary's high-handed habit of acting entirely on his own responsibility, and her resentment was the deeper because her sympathies lay often with the European dynasties. The climax came in December 1851 when Palmerston, without reference to either queen or prime minister, sent a dispatch to Paris approving the *coup d'état* of Louis Napoleon (later Napoleon III). Russell dismissed Palmerston, but the latter had his revenge when in February 1852 he brought about, over the proposed Militia acts, the fall of the government. Although very weak, Russell's first ministry deserves to be remembered for its reforming legislation, and in particular for the passing of the Ten Hours Act (1847) and the Public Health Act (1848), and for the repeal (1849) of the Navigation acts. It was during his term as prime minister that Russell announced his conversion to the view that further parliamentary reform was essential.

Office Under Aberdeen, Palmerston, and Second Ministry.—In the earl of Aberdeen's coalition ministry of Whigs and Peelites, Russell was a member of the cabinet, briefly as foreign secretary (December 1852–February 1853), then without office and from June 1854 as lord president of the council. During the years 1853–54 he drafted a reform bill, but it was abandoned because it threatened to split the ministry, then faced with war with Russia. Russell subsequently made two serious political blunders. The first was his resignation in January 1855 over the inquiry into the conduct of the Crimean War, an act which appeared to the queen, and not to her only, completely selfish. The second was his unfortunate handling of the abortive peace negotiations at the Vienna Conference (March–April 1855), at which he was British representative (*see* CRIMEAN WAR). From 1855 to 1859 he was in the political wilderness.

In June 1859 he became foreign secretary, with Palmerston as prime minister, in the middle of the crisis of Italian unification. Russell, seeing the struggle in terms of the English Revolution of 1688, was strongly sympathetic to Italian liberalism and patriotism, and in this his sentiments were fully shared by his chief. But the queen and many of the cabinet were against him. He endured with ill grace the clipping of his forthright dispatches, but he was able to ensure that English policy favoured and assisted the Italian cause. This was his last great consistent effort in the cause of liberty, epitomized in his historic dispatch of Oct. 27, 1860, to the British minister at Turin, favouring the union of the Two Sicilies with the kingdom of Sardinia, on the ground that "the Italians themselves are the best judges of their own interests." He was less successful in his handling of problems arising from the American Civil War, the Polish Revolution of 1863 and the Schleswig-Holstein controversy (1863–64). On the occasion of the removal of Confederate envoys from the British ship "Trent" (November 1861), his terse dispatch to Washington might have caused a serious incident had not the prince consort suggested the addition of a conciliatory clause. The following summer he was primarily responsible for allowing a privateer, constructed in England for use by the Confederates, to sail from the River Mersey (see "ALABAMA" ARBITRATION). In Poland his continued protests against Russian policy encouraged the continuation of a hopeless insurrection. A similar lack of realism characterized his attitude to the Schleswig-Holstein question (q.v.); for while, with Palmerston, he encouraged the Danes to resist Prussian pressure, his rejection of Napoleon III's suggestion of a European congress destroyed all chance of concerted action, the only means by which Denmark might have been helped.

On the death of Palmerston in October 1865, Russell, who had received an earldom in 1861, again became prime minister, but for no more than a few troubled months. His government was defeated on a new reform bill in June 1866. He then retired from politics to spend his time writing his recollections and editing documents. He settled at Pembroke Lodge in Richmond Park, Surrey, a residence presented to him in 1847 for life by the queen, and died there on May 28, 1878.

Character and Achievements.—Russell's short stature and air of frailty proved, throughout his political life, to be in the nature of a gift to cartoonists, particularly to John Doyle, and to John Leech in *Punch*. Petty in some of his attitudes, vain of his own achievements, and nepotistic, he seemed personally cold, and sometimes petulant. Further, his style of speech and writing was so terse and direct that he gave much offense, particularly to other countries when he was foreign secretary. Many of his views were narrow. He saw churches as little more than means to the ethical education of the people, and his advocacy of religious toleration was associated with strong disapproval of Roman Catholicism and of the Oxford movement. In politics he took inordinate pride in the great Whig family tradition of aristocratic liberalism (of which he justly conceived himself to be the chief exemplar in his day), the tradition of the architects of the 1688 Revolution, of Edmund Burke before the French Revolution, of Charles James Fox and Earl Grey. He edited *The Memorials and Correspondence of Charles James Fox*, four volumes (1853–57), wrote *The Life and Times of Charles James Fox*, three volumes (1859–66), and also published the correspondence of his great-grandfather, John, 4th duke of Bedford (three volumes, 1842–46). He fancied himself as a constitutional theorist, publishing in 1821 an *Essay on the History of the English Government and Constitution*. He placed the highest value on constitutional liberty, of which he had an old-fashioned individualistic conception. He was always, as foreign secretary, recommending to other countries some formal constitutional remedy for their every ill.

Nonetheless, he had great qualities. He had a powerful intellect and was courageous in overcoming his physical disadvantages. At his best he was a great parliamentarian. As Bulwer Lytton wrote in *The New Timon*, "But see our statesman when the steam is on,/And languid Johnny glows to glorious John." In later life he was overshadowed by Palmerston, who tended to dominate his foreign policy. But his achievements before 1852, and in domestic politics, were considerable. Though not a Radical, he was, despite his antiquated cast of thought, an advanced reformer in many fields. His hand is to be seen, for example, in the extension of state provision for education after 1839. He knew something of the springs of Liberal feeling in the country, and was largely responsible for keeping Whiggery radical enough to enable it to retain the leadership of the loose coalition which from 1835 to 1866 constituted the Liberal Party, and for preparing the party for the more democratic politics of the period following the Reform Act of 1867.

Russell married first in 1835 Adelaide, daughter of Thomas Lister and widow of Thomas, 2nd Lord Ribblesdale, by whom he had two daughters; he married secondly in 1841 Frances Anna Maria Elliott, daughter of the 2nd earl of Minto, by whom he had three sons and one daughter.

BIBLIOGRAPHY.—*The Early Correspondence of Lord John Russell, 1805–40*, ed. by R. Russell, 2 vol. (1913); *The Later Correspondence of Lord John Russell, 1840–1878*, ed. by G. P. Gooch, 2 vol. (1925). See also S. Walpole, *Life of Lord John Russell*, 2 vol. (1889); S. J. Reid, *Lord John Russell* (1895); A. Wyatt Tilby, *Lord John Russell* (1930); D. Southgate, *The Passing of the Whigs, 1832–1886* (1962).
(D. E. D. B.)

RUSSELL, LILLIAN (HELEN LOUISE LEONARD) (1861–1922), U.S. singer and actress who, in a variety of light roles, charmed audiences for three decades, was born in Clinton, Ia., on Dec. 4, 1861. She made her debut as a member of the chorus in *H.M.S. Pinafore* in 1879 and achieved stardom in *The Great Mogul*, a comic opera, in 1881. Subsequently she appeared in a series of comic operas in England and America, with Weber and Fields' burlesque company, in straight comedy, and in vaudeville. She was as well known for her flamboyant personal life as for her beauty and pleasant singing voice. She made only rare stage appearances after her fourth marriage, in 1912. She died in Pittsburgh, Pa., on June 6, 1922.
(O. G. B.)

RUSSELL, LORD WILLIAM (1639–1683), English politician who was one of the first victims of the royalist reaction which followed the unsuccessful attempts to exclude James, duke of York (later James II), from the succession to the throne. Born on Sept. 29, 1639, the third son of the 5th earl (later 1st duke) of Bedford, he survived his elder brothers, to acquire, as heir, the courtesy title of Lord Russell in 1678. After being educated at Cambridge University, he traveled on the continent and returned to England in 1659. At the Restoration of Charles II in 1660, he was elected to Parliament for the family borough of Tavistock, in Devon, but for the next 12 years he did little in Parliament. But in 1669 his marriage to Rachel, second daughter of the 4th earl of Southampton, brought him responsibilities and an important political connection with Anthony Ashley Cooper (later earl of Shaftesbury), who had married a niece of Southampton. It also brought him a new home, Southampton House, in Bloomsbury which, with Stratton House, Hampshire, and Woburn Abbey, Bedfordshire, became one of his principal residences.

The Third Dutch War (1672–74) marked a turning point in Russell's political career. The incapacity of the Cabal administration, the distasteful association with France, and the evident encroachments of Roman Catholicism at court woke Russell to a sense of national danger and from this time he was associated with leading opposition speakers such as Lord Cavendish (later 4th earl of Devonshire), Henry Powle (Powell), Thomas Littleton, and Henry Capel in vehement criticism of the government. Never a fluent talker, he proved in a speech of Jan. 22, 1674, that he could be articulate and forceful in denouncing iniquities such as the attack on the Dutch Smyrna fleet (which had precipitated the war), the continuing "Stop of the Exchequer" (the king's postponement of the payment of interest on loans from the bankers), and "the ill ministers about the king." At the same time he joined in the proceedings against the 2nd duke of Buckingham and in 1675 in those against the earl of Danby (later duke of Leeds).

By 1678 hatred of the omnipotent Danby was so strong that his opponents were prepared to accept French assistance in thwarting his policies. Russell was certainly among those who joined in a temporary association with Louis XIV for this purpose, and he entered into close communication with the marquis de Ruvigny (later earl of Galway), who came to England in 1678 with funds for distribution among members of the opposition in Parliament. However, this was natural, for Ruvigny was Lady Russell's maternal cousin, and the testimony of Paul Barillon, the French ambassador, makes it clear that Russell's opportunism fell short of corruption. In March 1678 he seconded the address urging the king to declare war against France.

The revelations of the "popish plot" (see ENGLISH HISTORY)

confirmed Russell in his fears for the safety of Protestant England and he threw himself fully into the campaign to exclude James from the succession. On Nov. 4, 1678, he moved an address to the king to remove the duke of York from his person and his councils, and he began to associate himself with the group which looked to the illegitimate duke of Monmouth as a suitable heir. At the same time he encouraged Ralph Montagu (later duke of Montagu), who had married Lady Russell's stepsister, in those revelations which led to the impeachment of Danby. The dissolution of Parliament (January 1679) intervened, and in the ensuing elections Russell, who was returned for two counties, chose to sit for Bedfordshire. Danby's fall followed in April 1679 and in the same month Russell was one of the new privy council formed by Charles on the advice of Sir William Temple. Within six days, however, Russell moved for a committee to draw up a bill to secure religion and property in the event of a popish successor.

Charles had no intention of yielding influence to such a troublesome councilor and in January 1680, along with Cavendish, Capel, Powle, the earl of Essex, and Littleton, Russell tendered his resignation to the king which was received by Charles "with all my heart." On June 16 he accompanied Shaftesbury when the latter indicted James at Westminster as a popish recusant; and on Oct. 26 he took the extreme step of moving for a parliamentary decision "how to suppress popery and prevent a popish successor." He was now the leading spokesman for exclusion in the Commons, and on Nov. 2 he seconded the motion for exclusion in its most uncompromising form, carrying the bill up to the Lords on Nov. 19. He rejected the moderate scheme for imposing limitations upon James and despite the presence in England of William III of Orange (later William III, king of England), Russell resisted his influence with opposition leaders for a compromise. Instead, on Dec. 18 he proposed to refuse supplies until the king passed the Exclusion Bill, which he seconded on March 26, 1681, in Charles's last Parliament at Oxford.

With the defeat of these efforts at the dissolution (March 28), he withdrew from public life to his country seat of Stratton. Unfortunately, he was unwise enough to mix with conspiratorial associates and on one occasion in 1682 he attended a meeting at which treason, or what might be construed as treason, was talked. Monmouth, Essex, Richard Hampden, Algernon Sidney, and Lord Howard of Escrick were the principals among those who compromised themselves in this way. Thus with the exposure of the alleged Rye House Plot (June 1683), of which neither he, Essex, nor Sidney had the slightest knowledge, he was plausibly accused by informers of having promoted an insurrection and of having plotted the death of the king and the duke of York. He made no attempt to escape arrest, although given opportunity, and was sent to the Tower of London on June 26, 1683. Before a committee of the privy council on June 28, Russell acknowledged his presence at the meeting, but denied all knowledge of the proposed insurrection. At his trial (July 13), however, he was unable to disprove the allegations of two witnesses, and his betrayal by Lord Howard of Escrick, together with the suicide of the earl of Essex on the same day, were decisive in condemning him. Two prominent churchmen, Gilbert Burnet and John Tillotson, the earl of Anglesey, and the duke of Somerset were among those who testified for him. Bedford offered huge sums for his pardon, but Charles would only remit the sentence to be hung, drawn, and quartered to one of beheading. This was carried out in Lincoln's Inn Fields on July 21, 1683.

Within a year of the accession of William and Mary an act annulled the attainder and impugned the legality of the trial, but this was a partisan measure. However, the certainty that Russell's death had been sought in a spirit of revenge for such victims of the popish plot as Viscount Stafford, together with his blameless life in the company of a devout and intelligent wife, has made Russell an attractive figure in Whig martyrology.

See Lord John Russell, *The Life of William Lord Russell*, 2 vol. (1820); G. S. Thomson, *The Russells in Bloomsbury, 1669-1771* (1940). (H. G. Ro.)

RUSSELL OF KILLOWEN, CHARLES RUSSELL,

BARON (1832-1900), lord chief justice of England, was born at Newry, County Down, on Nov. 10, 1832, the son of Arthur Russell. The family was Roman Catholic. Educated first at Belfast, afterward in Newry and finally at St. Vincent's college, Castleknock, Dublin, he was articled in 1849 to a firm of solicitors in Newry. In 1854 he was admitted and began to practise his profession. In the legal proceedings arising out of Catholic and Orange disturbances young Russell distinguished himself in the cause of his co-religionists.

After practising for two years he determined to seek a wider field for his abilities. He went to London in 1856 and entered Lincoln's Inn. In 1858 he married Ellen, daughter of Joseph Mulholland of Belfast, and in 1859 he was called to the bar and joined the northern circuit. He possessed immense personality, an embodiment of energetic will that riveted attention, dominated his audience and bore down opposition. In his early years Russell's practice was mostly at the passage court at Liverpool, and he published a book on its procedure in 1862.

In 1872 Russell took silk, and his success as a queen's counsel during this period of his career was prodigious. He excelled in the conduct alike of commercial cases and of those involving, as he said, "a human interest," although undoubtedly it was the latter which more attracted him. He was seen to the least advantage in cases which involved technical or scientific detail.

In 1880 Russell was returned to parliament as an independent Liberal member for Dundalk. From that time forward until 1894 he sat in the house of commons: for Dundalk until 1885, and afterward for South Hackney. From 1880 to 1886 as a private member, and as the attorney general in Gladstone's administrations of 1886 (when he was knighted) and 1892, he worked in and out of parliament for the Liberal policy in regard to the treatment of Ireland as few men except Russell could or would work. His position throughout was clear and consistent. Before 1886 on several occasions he supported the action of the Irish Nationalist party. He opposed coercion, voted for compensation for disturbance, advocated the release of political prisoners and voted for the Maamtrasna inquiry. But he never became a member of the Irish Home Rule or of the Parnellite party; he was elected at Dundalk as an independent Liberal, and such he remained. When he warmly advocated the establishment of a subordinate parliament in Ireland, he did so because he sought the amelioration and not the destruction of Ireland's relations with the rest of the kingdom.

Russell rapidly became in London what he was already in Lancashire, a favourite leader in nisi prius actions (those held for trial on the issue of facts before a jury and single judge). More important, however, as well as more famous, than any of his successes in the ordinary courts of law during this period were his performances as an advocate in two public transactions of note in British history. The first of these was the Parnell commission of 1888-90, in which Russell appeared as leading counsel for Parnell. In April 1889, after 63 sittings of the commission, Russell, who had already destroyed the chief personal charge against Parnell by a brilliant cross-examination in which he proved it to have been based upon a forgery, made his great opening speech for the defense, lasting several days. This speech, besides its merit as a wonderful piece of advocacy, possesses permanent value as a historical survey of the Irish question during the 19th century from the point of view of an Irish Liberal. The second was the Bering sea arbitration, held in Paris in 1893. Russell, with Sir Richard Webster (afterward Lord Alverstone), was the leading counsel for Great Britain. The award was, substantially, in favour of Great Britain.

In 1894, on the death of Lord Bowen, Russell accepted the position of a lord of appeal and was raised to the peerage. A month later he was appointed lord chief justice of England in succession to Lord Coleridge. Brief as was his tenure of the office, he proved himself well worthy of it. He had dignity without pomposity, quickness without irritability, and masterfulness without tyranny. In 1896 Lord Russell presided at the trial at bar of the leaders of the Jameson raid. His conduct of this trial, in the midst of much popular excitement, was by itself sufficient to establish his reputation as a great judge. One other event at least in his career while lord chief justice deserves a record, namely, his share in the Venezuela arbitration in 1899. Lord Herschell, a British representative on the commission, died before the beginning of the proceedings, and Lord Russell took his place.

Lord Russell contributed to the reform of the law by his advocacy of improvement in the system of legal education, and in promoting measures against corruption and secret commissions, though the bills he introduced did not become law. He died on Aug. 10, 1900. Few English lawyers have ever excited the admiration abroad that Lord Russell did, both in Europe and America.

See R. B. O'Brien, *The Life of Lord Russell of Killowen* (1908).

RÜSSELSHEIM, a town of West Germany in the *Land* (state) of Hesse, Federal Republic of Germany. It is situated on the left bank of the Main, 13 km. (8 mi.) E of Mainz and 25 km. (15½ mi.) SW of Frankfurt am Main by rail. Pop. (1961) 39,507. The town hall was built in 1604, and there is a museum. The manufacture of Opel automobiles is the chief industry. Machinery and coconut matting are also made.

RUSSIA, ORTHODOX CHURCH OF, an autocephalous church within the Orthodox Eastern Church. In the 9th century, between 860 and 867 according to Byzantine sources, the Russians were converted to Christianity and accepted a bishop from Byzantium. A Christian community existed in Kiev in the first half of the 10th century, and in 957 Olga, regent of the Russian realm, was baptized in Constantinople (but *see* OLGA, SAINT). This act was followed by the acceptance of Christianity as the state religion after the baptism of Olga's grandson Vladimir, prince of Kiev, in 988 or 989. Circumstantial evidence suggests that the Russian Church established by St. Vladimir was from the outset subordinated to the patriarchate of Constantinople (*see* CONSTANTINOPLE, ECUMENICAL PATRIARCHATE OF). Under Vladimir's successors, and until 1448, the Russian Church, headed by the metropolitans of Kiev (who after 1328 resided in Moscow), was a metropolitanate of the Byzantine patriarchate.

Under Mongol rule (1237–1480) the Russian Church enjoyed a favoured position, obtaining immunity from taxation in 1270. This period saw a remarkable growth of monasticism. The Monastery of the Caves (the Pecherskaya Lavra) in Kiev, founded in the middle of the 11th century by the Russian ascetics St. Anthony and St. Theodosius, was superseded as the foremost religious centre of medieval Russia by the Monastery of the Holy Trinity (Troitse-Sergiyeva Lavra), founded in the mid-14th century by St. Sergius (*q.v.*) of Radonezh. (*See* further MONASTICISM: *Eastern Monasticism: Slav Countries*.) Sergius, as well as the metropolitans St. Peter (1308–26) and St. Alexius (1354–78), supported the rising power of the principality of Moscow. The alliance between the church and the Muscovite state became closer still after the Council of Ferrara-Florence, when, in 1448, the Russian bishops, severing in fact though not in principle their canonical dependence on the ecumenical patriarch, elected their own primate without recourse to Constantinople. The theory, advanced in clerical circles after the fall of Constantinople in 1453, that Muscovy was the third, and last, Rome gave ideological justification to the promotion of the metropolitan of Moscow to the rank of patriarch (1589), with the approval of the see of Constantinople.

The theory of "Moscow the Third Rome" provided the background to the double conflict which in the 1650s and 1660s brought the patriarch Nikon into violent collision with the tsar Alexis, on the one hand, and, on the other, with a group of conservative clergy headed by the archpriest Avvakum. Nikon, pursuing the theocratic ideal of a Russian Orthodox empire, sought to make the church dominant over, or at least independent of, the state; Avvakum, taking his stand on a more nationalistic conception of Holy Russia, resisted the patriarch's successful attempt to bring the Russian liturgical tradition into line with contemporary Greek practice. Nikon was deposed, and Avvakum, after cruel persecution, was burned at the stake. His followers, the Old Believers, formed henceforth a vigorous body of dissenters. This, the most serious crisis in the history of the Russian Church before 1917, paved the way for its partial subjugation to the state, achieved by Peter the Great. (*See* further AVVAKUM PETROVICH; NIKON; OLD BELIEVERS.)

By the second half of the 14th century the greater part of southwestern Russia had been annexed to Lithuania. This led to the creation in 1458 of a separate West Russian Orthodox Church, whose primate, the metropolitan of Kiev, owed allegiance to Constantinople. In 1596 most of the Orthodox bishops in Lithuania—now united with Poland—submitted to the authority of the pope and, in exchange for accepting Roman Catholic doctrines, were allowed to preserve their Eastern rites. This act, the Union of Brest-Litovsk, was vigorously resisted by many Orthodox laymen, who founded brotherhoods in defense of their faith. Latin theology, however, had some influence in the West Russian Orthodox Church, especially in the theological school founded in Kiev by the metropolitan Peter Mogila (*q.v.*).

In 1721 Peter the Great suppressed the patriarchate and replaced it by the Holy Governing Synod, modeled on the state-controlled synods of the Lutheran Church in Sweden and Prussia. The chief procurator of the synod, a lay official who obtained ministerial rank in the first half of the 19th century, exercised from then until 1917 effective control over church administration. This control, facilitated by the political subservience of the majority of the higher clergy, was especially marked during the procuratorship (1880–1905) of Konstantin Petrovich Pobedonostsev (*q.v.*). Yet the Russian Church in this period was not devoid of creative vitality: the revival of contemplative monasticism was exemplified in the Optina Hermitage, whose monks devoted themselves to *starchestvo* (spiritual guidance), and in the radiant spirituality of St. Seraphim (*q.v.*) of Sarov; there was a remarkable growth of independent theological thought and scholarship; and Russian missionaries in the 19th century evangelized Siberia, the Aleutian Islands, and Alaska, and founded the Orthodox Church of Japan.

In November 1917, following the breakdown of the tsarist government, a council of the Russian Church reestablished the patriarchate and elected the metropolitan Tikhon (*q.v.*) patriarch. The administrative measures taken by the Soviet government against the church in 1917–18, which included the nationalization of all ecclesiastical lands and the separation of church and state, were followed by brutal persecution, instanced in the arrest of bishops and in the trial and execution of Veniamin, metropolitan of St. Petersburg (1922). Simultaneously, in order to undermine the patriarch's authority, the government supported the schismatic, antiepiscopal, and pro-Soviet "Living Church," which enjoyed considerable vogue in 1922–23. After publicly renouncing his former opposition to the Soviet regime, Tikhon died in 1925, having done much to restore the unity of his church and to ensure its survival in a militantly atheistic state. His work was continued by the metropolitan Sergius, who, after being arrested several times, pledged his and his church's loyalty to the government (1927). Yet the church remained under constant pressure, and antireligious propaganda continued to alternate with active persecution (the latter particularly acute in 1937–38). In September 1943, partly as a result of the support it was giving to the government in World War II, the church was granted notable concessions. Sergius was elected patriarch, and in 1944 theological instruction was permitted in several ecclesiastical establishments. After Sergius' death (1944), Alexius, metropolitan of Leningrad, was elected patriarch of Moscow and all Russia (1945). Under his leadership the Russian Church, which enjoys the active or passive support of perhaps a quarter of the population of the Soviet Union, struggles to survive in the face of antireligious propaganda and growing administrative pressure. *See* also ORTHODOX EASTERN CHURCH.

BIBLIOGRAPHY.—E. Golubinsky, *Istoriya russkoy tserkvi*, 2 vol. (1900–11); A. M. Ammann, *Abriss der ostslawischen Kirchengeschichte* (1950); A. V. Kartashev, *Ocherki po istorii russkoi tserkvi*, 2 vol. (1959); Matthew Spinka, *The Church and the Russian Revolution* (1927); Nicolas Zernov, *The Russians and Their Church* (1945); John Shelton Curtiss, *The Russian Church and the Soviet State, 1917–1950* (1953); G. P. Fedotov (ed.), *A Treasury of Russian Spirituality* (1961).
(D. OB.)

RUSSIAN ARCHITECTURE. The recorded history of Russian art and architecture may be divided into four main periods: the Byzantine, from the 10th to the beginning of the 16th century; the National or Muscovite, from the 16th to the 18th century; the Petersburgian or European, from the 18th to the beginning of the 20th century; and the Soviet, from 1918 to the present. The centre of artistic and architectural activities shifted several times, generally following the political fortunes of the land—moving from Kiev, via Novgorod and Vladimir-Suzdal, to Moscow; from Moscow to St. Petersburg; and from St. Petersburg again to Moscow.

Materials and Style.—The vast forests, which for many centuries were the setting of Russian life, profoundly influenced the development of Russian architecture. For generations the entire utilitarian and artistic environment of the Russian peasant was fashioned of wood, and it was this constant, close contact with the forests that contributed so much to the arts of woodcraft and the great skill· of the Russian carpenter. Building in wood acquired a very special place in the history of Russian architecture; its distinctive and most typical forms were closely bound up, in their origin, with the characteristic virtues and limitations of wood. Because of these limitations the old palaces of the tsars, the mansions of the boyars and the churches never attained the imposing dimensions of the castles of France or England and the Rhenish cathedrals.

In the masonry architecture of Russia, which was mostly brick, the architect utilized the lay and bond of the brick, or stucco and polychrome-tile revetments, for decorative effect. The brick patterns and the coloured tiles and faïence paneling of the 17th-century Moscow region form a bright chapter in the history of Russian architecture.

Because of the geological formation of Russia's vast plains, stone was relatively scarce and, in the architecture of pre-Petrine Russia, was used mostly for decorative purposes. It was only after the 18th century, when the rich quarries of Siberia, Finland and the Ukraine became available, that stone architecture began to flourish. Variegated marble, fine-grained granite, glistening labradorites, malachites and porphyries were used with dazzling effect in the construction and interior decoration of the great cathedrals and imperial palaces.

In the formation of its architectural style Russia was subjected to many foreign influences. The Russians borrowed much from the east and the west, but always showed discrimination in selection, proving themselves to be clever adapters and thorough assimilators. The borrowed elements were consciously and unconsciously modified and transfigured, resulting in a style distinguished by a quality of monumentality, vertical continuity, picturesqueness of mass and rich decoration. The heritage from the Greco-Roman world through Byzantium was merged with the native building tradition, and this proved itself capable of diverse expression, from naked functionalism to the fantasy of the Church of St. Basil in Moscow and the multidomed churches of Kizhi and Vytegra in the north.

THE BYZANTINE PERIOD

With the Christianization of Russia in 988, Byzantine thought and art—permeated with the proselytizing spirit of its missionaries, artists and architects—soon spread throughout the Kievan, Novgorodian and Suzdalian principalities. The emphasis of the Byzantine church on the physical splendour of its edifices was a cardinal factor in determining the characteristics of ecclesiastical architecture. Everything connected with the design and decoration of the new churches in Russia followed the Byzantine pattern; and the standard scheme of the Greek church—the cross inscribed in a rectangle, and the dome supported on piers or on pendentives—became the accepted type for Orthodox churches. The design and support of the central dome or cupola, together with the number and disposition of the subsidiary cupolas, remained for a long time the principal theme of Russian architecture. (*See* Byzantine Art and Architecture.)

Kiev.—The main monuments of Kiev were the Desiatinnaia church (989–990), the Cathedral of St. Sophia (1037) and the Church of the Assumption in the Monastery of the Caves (1073–78). All of these churches were built in the Byzantine tradition, though certain influences which came from Bulgaria, Georgia and

Armenia can be discerned. The Cathedral of St. Sophia, the mother church of Russia, is the only structure of the Grand-princely period which still stands and retains, at least in the interior, something of its original form. The central part of the cathedral was in the form of a Greek cross. It had a nave and four aisles terminated in semicircular apses, and 13 cupolas (symbolizing Christ and his apostles). It was reconstructed and enlarged at the end of the 17th century when the vogue of the Ukrainian, or so-called Cossack, phase of the baroque style was at its height. It was later obscured by additional bays and stories to its lateral galleries, a new tower and many bizarre baroque cupolas. Only five apses and the central interior portion survive from the 11th century.

Novgorod and Pskov.—Novgorod was the centre of a unique and quite original Russian art that lived on long after the political death of the city; it was there that the fundamental features of Russian architecture were developed. As in Kiev, the ecclesiastical architectural history of Novgorod began with the Cathedral of St. Sophia. It was built in 1045–52, replacing a wooden 13-dome church of the same name. The new cathedral followed its Kievan namesake in plan, but the divergences from the Byzantine pattern are quite apparent; it has double aisles but only three apses. Externally the church differs even more from its southern prototype: it has only five cupolas, its walls are austere, the buttresses are flat and bare and the windows are small and narrow. There is something unmistakably Russian in the silhouette of its helmeted cupolas and in the vigour and verticality of its solid masses.

The churches of the 12th century resemble St. Sophia only in the general tendency toward simplicity and verticality; they were small, cubic in form and modest in decoration. The severe climate and heavy snowfalls of the north necessitated various modifications of the Byzantine architectural forms. In the course of time windows were narrowed and deeply splayed; roofs became steeper; and flat dome profiles assumed the bulbous form which, in different varieties, eventually became the most notable feature of Russian church architecture.

The churches of Pskov were relatively tiny and squat and usually had three low apses. The cupolas, roofs and decorative elements were similar to those of Novgorod. Because these churches were too small to contain interior columns for the support of the cupola, the Pskov builders developed the structural device of recessive rows of corbeled arches for the support of cupola drums and cupolas. This feature—the *kokoshnik*—was to become a favourite Russian structural and decorative element. The church porches, the exterior walled-in galleries and the arcaded bell towers were Pskov's other outstanding contributions to Russian architecture.

Vladimir-Suzdal.—Vladimir, as a centre of early Russian culture, was a factor in a creative fusion of Byzantine, Romanesque and Caucasian influences. The 12th- and early 13th-century structures were a further modification of the earlier Byzantine style, leading toward the innovations at Moscow in the 15th century.

Among the outstanding monuments are: the Cathedral of the Assumption (1158–89) which was to serve as a model for its namesake in the Moscow Kremlin; the Church of the Intercession on the Nerl, one of the loveliest creations of Grand-princely Russia (1165); and the Cathedral of St. Dmitri (1194–97). These churches as a group represent the continuation of the Kievo-Byzantine tradition in their ground plan, but the old scheme was given a new interpretation. From Byzantium the Suzdalians adopted the general features of the square plan with semicircular apses, and the four columns supporting a cupola with its circular drum. But instead of brick, so characteristic of Byzantine and Kievan ecclesiastical architecture, they used cut stone and instead of polychrome revetments they used carved stone embroideries. The treatment and decoration of the walls, the deeply splayed portals and windows suggest the articulation of Romanesque architecture; the character of the carved ornament is analogous to that of the Caucasus; but the organization and arrangement of the forms and patterns is definitely Russian.

THE MOSCOW PERIOD

With the fall of Constantinople (1453), Byzantine influences gradually subsided, and the hegemony in the world of Orthodoxy shifted to Muscovite Russia. Moscow, having become the new city of Constantine—the "third Rome"—and aspiring to rival the older centres of culture, launched a building program commensurate with her international importance. The Kremlin and two of its important churches were rebuilt by Italian architects between 1475 and 1510. These churches, the Cathedral of the Assumption and the Cathedral of the Archangel Michael, were largely modeled after the churches of Vladimir. The Italians were required to incorporate the basic features of Byzantine planning and design into the new cathedrals; it was only in the exterior decoration of the Archangel that they succeeded in introducing Italian decorative motifs. A third church, the modest Cathedral of the Annunciation (1484–89), with its warm beauty, was the work of Pskov architects. There the *kokoshnik* was introduced in the treatment of the roof. This element, similar in outline to the popular Russian ogee-shaped (*bochka*) roof, foreshadowed a tendency to replace the forms of the Byzantine arch by more elongated silhouettes. Ecclesiastical architecture began to lose the special features associated with the Byzantine heritage, becoming more national in character and increasingly permeated with the taste and thought of the people. The most important change in Russian church design of the 16th century was the introduction of the staged tower and tent-shaped roof developed by Russia's carpenters in her wooden age. Next was the substitution of the tent spire for the traditional Byzantine cupola. This affected the design of masonry architecture by transforming its proportions and decoration and even its structural methods. The buildings acquired a dynamic, exteriorized articulation and specifically Russian national characteristics.

The boldest departures from Byzantine architecture were the churches of the Ascension at Kolomenskoe (1532) and St. John the Baptist at Diakovo (*c.* 1532) and, above all, the Cathedral of St. Basil in Red square in Moscow (1555–60). In St. Basil the academic architectural concepts, as understood by the western world, were ignored; the structure is uniquely medieval Russian in content and form, in technique, decoration and feeling. St. Basil, like its predecessors the churches at Kolomenskoe and Diakovo, embodies the characteristic features of the wood churches of northern Russia, translated into masonry.

An effective finishing touch was given to the ensemble of the Kremlin's Cathedral square by the erection of the imposing bell tower of Ivan the Great, begun in 1505. The colossal white stone "column of fame," with its golden cupola gleaming above the Kremlin hill, was the definite expression of an era, reflecting the tastes and grandiose political ambitions of the rising Russian state.

The basic types and structural forms of the Russian multicolumned and tented churches were fully developed in the 16th century. It remained for the next century to concentrate its efforts on the refinement of those forms and on the embellishment of the façades. The tent spires degenerated into mere decoration; they were used as exterior ornamental features set loosely in numbers over gabled roofs and on top of roof vaulting (Church of the Nativity in Putinki street, 1649–52). This decorative use of the formerly functional element was combined with the liberal employment of the *kokoshnik*. The latter, in converging and ascending tiers and in diversified shapes and arrangements, was used as a decorative screen for the drumlike bases of the spires, and sometimes as parapets over the cornices. At the same time the formerly large expanses of unbroken wall surfaces (of the Novgorod-Pskov architectural traditions) were replaced by rich decorative paneling. Polychromy asserted itself: coloured and glazed tile and carved stone ornament, used in combination with brick patterns, were employed extensively. This was especially evidenced in a large group of Yaroslavl churches.

The baroque appeared on the Russian scene toward the end of the 17th century. But again the Russians imaginatively transformed its modes into a clearly expressed national style which became known as the Naryshkin baroque. A delightful example of this style is the Church of the Intercession of the Virgin at Fili (1693) on the estate of Boyarin Naryshkin, whose name had become identified with this phase of the Russian baroque. *See also* BAROQUE AND POST-BAROQUE ARCHITECTURE.

THE PETERSBURGIAN PERIOD

The founding of St. Petersburg (1703) marked the beginning of a new era in Russian art and architecture; it was at this city, later renamed Leningrad, that the spirit of western-European art broke through in a decisive manner. The heavy influx of foreign influences—Dutch, German, Italian and French—markedly affected architecture because the new capital offered a fresh field in which the wealth and adamant will of Peter the Great made it possible to obtain the best professional talent from abroad for the realization of his ambitious projects.

The western Europeans brought over the prevailing baroque art characteristics of their own countries, but the very different artistic and physical setting produced a new expression, embodying Russia's peculiar sense of form, scale, colour and choice of materials. The transformed baroque spread all over Russia and, with its vast register of variations, developed many regional idioms.

In the second half of the 18th century the baroque gave way to the rococo, and then to the rediscovered beauty of classicism, initiating a trend toward restraint and refinement. The new architectural current entered the stream of Russian art from different directions: from France, Italy and Germany. Its beginning practically coincided with the founding of the Academy of Fine Arts in 1757, and it lasted for nearly a century. It continued its existence largely through a number of foreign and foreign-trained Russian architects, who brought the classicism of the 18th century to maturity, culminating in the Russianized empire style and producing an architecture notable for its monumentality, integration of mass and space, use of colour and sculptured decoration.

The three long reigns of Peter I, Elizabeth and Catherine II denote the main successive stages of an intense architectural activity which, though principally concentrated in St. Petersburg and its vicinity, radiated from there to many parts of Russia. The impulse continued into the reign of Alexander I, especially after 1812, during the postwar years of awakened national pride. Baroque, rococo, classicism and neoclassicism all came to be represented at St. Petersburg by striking examples in close proximity to one another. Among the best are: the Cathedral of the Smolny convent (1748–64) and the Winter palace (1732), both designed in a rich Russian high-baroque style by Bartolomeo Rastrelli; the Academy of Fine Arts (1764–88) by Vallin de la Mothe and A. F. Kokorinov, a masterpiece of the so-called "Louis XV classique"; the Admiralty (1806–23), designed by Andreian Zakharov in the empire style with a strong Russian flavour; the Synod and Senate buildings (1829–34), by K. Rossi; and the new Hermitage (1840–50) by the neoclassicist Leo von Klenze.

Moscow went its own way architecturally; it yielded to St. Petersburg in range and scale of construction but outstripped St. Petersburg in picturesqueness, originality and intimacy. At a time when St. Petersburg was engaged mainly in building monumental palaces and public and government buildings, Moscow more often was building private residences and small palaces. Classicism in Moscow was less severe and more homely; the forms of the empire style was softened by giving them a freer and more colourful treatment. Outstanding examples are the old building of the Moscow university (1817–19) by D. Gilardi and the Bolshoi theatre (1821–24) by O. Beauvais.

In the 1830s classicism began to seem something foreign, or imported. Official nationalism and the growing tide of Slavophilism were instrumental in turning the Russian architect away from alien classicism toward the interrupted development of national art. Official nationalism found its expression in the projects of K. Thon, who sought to create a genuine Russian style based on old motifs derived from Russian-Byzantine architecture (the Church of Christ the Saviour, 1837, razed in the 1930s; and the Grand Kremlin palace, 1839–48). The Slavophiles' nationalism was based on the artistic activities of 16th- and 17th-century Russia and on the originality of the construction methods peculiar to that period (*e.g.*, the Historical museum in Moscow, 1875–81,

Cathedral of the Annunciation, the Kremlin, Moscow; 1484–89. Built during the early Muscovite period by architects from Pskov who introduced the *kokoshnik*, recessive rows of corbeled arches supporting cupolas

Church of the Intercession of the Virgin, at Fili, near Moscow; 1693. An example of early Russian baroque with characteristic features of the National period

Detail of the Cathedral of St. Sophia, Kiev; 1037. The 13-cupola structure was originally built in the Byzantine tradition but subsequently greatly altered by repairs and additions

Cathedral of St. Sophia, Novgorod; 1045–52. Closely related to its Kiev namesake in plan and construction, the Novgorod cathedral shows certain divergences from Byzantine practice

Bell tower of Ivan the Great, the Kremlin, Moscow; begun 1505, completed in 1600 during the reign of Boris Godunov. The National period

Cathedral of the Archangel Michael, the Kremlin, Moscow; 1505–09. Built during the early Muscovite period by the Milanese architect Aléviso Novyi, who employed Italian decorative motifs for the exterior

BYZANTINE TRADITION AND THE NATIONAL PERIOD

PLATE II

RUSSIAN ARCHITECTURE

The Winter palace, St. Petersburg (Leningrad); 1732. Designed in the style of Russian high baroque by Bartolomeo Rastrelli

Main entrance to the Admiralty, St. Petersburg; 1806–23. Designed by Andreian Zakharov in a Russian adaptation of the empire style

The Bolshoi theatre, Moscow; 1821–24. An outstanding example of Russian classicism, originally designed by O. Beauvais; reconstructed in 1856 by A. Cavos

Urals pavilion at the All-Union Agricultural exhibition, Moscow; 1939–40. An expression of nationalism in architecture with originality of form and richness of ornament

Archway; Synod and Senate bldg., St. Petersburg; 1829–34. Russian empire style by K. Rossi

Skyscraper on the Kotelnichi embankment, Moscow; 1952. An example of postwar "Stalinist" style of architecture designed by D. Chechulin and A. Rostkovskii

THE EUROPEAN AND THE SOVIET PERIODS

BY COURTESY OF (BOTTOM RIGHT) SOCIETY FOR CULTURAL RELATIONS WITH THE U.S.S.R.; PHOTOGRAPHS, (TOP LEFT, TOP RIGHT) J. ALLAN CASH, (CENTRE LEFT) GEORGE HOLTON—PHOTO RESEARCHERS, (CENTRE RIGHT) SOVFOTO, (BOTTOM LEFT) NOVOSTI PRESS AGENCY

by V. Sherwood). The tendency to revive the forms of the Russian past and to rework old traditions in the spirit of a neo-Slavonic age continued for several decades. At the beginning of the 20th century the new western-European trends—the *art nouveau*, the "Vienna secession" and the "international style"—made their appearance and Russian architecture became increasingly affected by all that was extreme and modern in western architecture.

THE SOVIET PERIOD

In 1918, after a lapse of two centuries, Moscow resumed its role as the capital of Russia and once more became the political and artistic centre of the land. The Bolshevik revolution occurred at a time when the ferment of the international style and other avant-garde architectural theories was already widespread in Russia. During the early years of militant Communism (1918–22) the left school of Soviet architecture, in its desire to embody the dynamic of the revolution in plastic forms, resorted to a symbolism supposedly inherent in the geometrical or engineering forms of architecture. Afterward it was carried away, first by Constructivism, and later by Functionalism and the theories of the German Bauhaus school. The echoes of these theories showed themselves in the works of K. Melnikov, P. Golosov, A. Gintsberg, the Vesnin brothers (Leonid, Viktor and Aleksandr) and others. Experimentation with the modern idiom continued into the 1930s, but without any conspicuous success. The chief handicap of modernism was that its strangeness and cold, functional look were distasteful to those in power and incomprehensible to the masses, whose tastes had been formed by the examples of the Russianized baroque and empire styles. A return to classicism was preferred because it was felt that the dramatization of the ideals of the new life could be best expressed by a humanized architecture based on native traditions of classical forms. The official emphasis on classicism initiated a trend toward monumentalism and florid ornamentation which affected almost every type of building. In Moscow the classic expression showed a leaning toward Palladianism (especially in the works of Ivan Zholtovsky and Zinovi Rozenfeld); in Leningrad it acquired a freer, more modernized look (as in the works of E. Levinson, I. Fomin and N. Trotsky); while in Kiev, Minsk and other cities of the various republics it was tinged with local traditions. On the whole its qualities were those of an architecture in search of forms to express the idea of socialist realism—the uniqueness of the new society.

With the growth of Russian nationalist sentiment in the late 1930s came a perceptible shift toward the expression of nationalism in architecture. The emphasis on the Russian heritage was intensified at the time of the drive against cosmopolitanism in the second half of the 1940s. Extensive use was made of national forms in some of the Moscow subway stations and especially at the All-Union Agricultural exhibition at Moscow (1939–40), where the pavilions of the Uzbek, Georgian, Armenian and Ukrainian Soviet Socialist republics were among the most attractive. The originality of form and richness of ornament reflected the architectural traditions as well as the folk arts of the various republics.

After World War II.—The mania for the monumental and for lavish decoration reached its peak in the last six or seven years of the Stalin era. It was during these years that eight skyscrapers were erected in Moscow. Since they were conceived as "prestige" buildings in the ambitious program for rebuilding and beautifying the capital, their architectural requirements were formulated by government decree; their design was to be in harmony with Moscow's historically developed architecture, and therefore modernistic tendencies were to be shunned. The buildings included the new Moscow State university, two hotels, several office buildings and apartment houses. In the general scheme of their distribution each building was to be the focal point and main theme in the composition of its immediate neighbourhood, either reflecting the architectural features of the nearby historical monuments or setting the tone for the neighbourhood to be developed around it. Rising 20 to 32 stories, they were strategically located in various districts, along the principal boulevards, squares and river embankments, so that their height and bulk would bring into greater relief the beauty of the natural terrain and affect the skyline for a distance of many miles. All of them are adorned with conventional trappings and carry tall, slender, star-topped spires. Many of the decorative motifs are strongly reminiscent of those of the Kremlin.

The massive ensemble of the Moscow State university (Lev Rudnev, chief architect), located on the summit of the Lenin hills, is the largest and tallest of the Moscow giants. It overlooks the city and the great Lenin Central stadium, with its recreation fields, and is the dominating structure in the southwestern district of Moscow. The main building, whose central tower reaches a height of 32 stories, is flanked to the right and left by two 18-story wings. The colonnade to the main entrance is almost pure classic, while the connecting wings to the right and left of the main building have an English Renaissance flàvour. The design of the entrance hall, staircases and principal auditoriums is reminiscent of the interiors of the Russian imperial palaces with their classical columns, rich marbles and mosaics, producing an impression of grandeur and opulence.

The university and the other skyscrapers can be seen for miles around and, although deceptive in scale, they are tremendously impressive. On close inspection their decorative details may seem Victorian to western eyes but, as elements in the city landscape, Moscow's skyscrapers have an undeniable dramatic impact.

The Transitional Period.—The end of the Stalin regime (1953) ushered in a period of limited liberalism in Russian artistic life. A number of rigidly Stalinist "socialist-realist" officials in the Union of Architects were replaced by less doctrinaire and more cosmopolitan leaders, who wanted to rid Soviet architecture of the classical clichés of the Stalin era and re-enter the contemporary European and international field. Moreover the vast demand for buildings of all types and the increasing tensions between the building industry's engineers and administrators on the one hand and the architects and theoretical aestheticians on the other, resulted in a widespread demand for a re-examination of the approach to style. In 1955 the government launched a program for revising the design of every type of building with a view to industrializing and standardizing the building industry. The problems posed by the need for economy, standardization and prefabrication both of components and complete buildings forced a thorough reformation in architectural practice.

Particular attention was given to the development of new building materials, especially synthetic plastics and light metals; to exploiting the full structural potential of reinforced, precast and prestressed concrete elements; and to exploring the decorative possibilities of the unconventional shapes that can be achieved with these malleable and expressive materials. Much research was devoted to the problem of reducing building weight and to saving steel and wood by replacing them with precision-engineered, prefabricated concrete and plastic elements.

In the light of their new experience Soviet architects began to reinterpret the principles of modern architecture, reconciling the old and the new. Evidence of the changing outlook is most noticeable in the planning of the satellite towns for both Moscow and Leningrad; in the fresh and imaginative approach to the design of the experimental residential blocks in the Moscow suburb of New Cheremushki; and particularly in the design of the U.S.S.R.'s hangarlike pavilion at the 1958 Brussels Universal and International exhibition, with its glass walls and trussed cantilevers. *See* also MODERN ARCHITECTURE: *20th Century*.

BIBLIOGRAPHY.—S. H. Cross, *Mediaeval Russian Churches* (1949); G. H. Hamilton, *The Art and Architecture of Russia* (1954), with bibliography and illustrations; M. I. Rzianin, *Arkhitekturnye ansambli Moskvy i Podmoskov'ia, XIV–XIX veka* (1950); S. Zabello, *Russkoe dereviannoe zodchestvo* (1942), with illustrations; V. Piliavskii, *Arkhitekturnye ansambli Leningrada* (1953), with illustrations; V. Shkvarikov (ed.), *Sovetskaia arkhitektura za XXX let* (1950), richly illustrated; A. Voyce, *The Moscow Kremlin: Its History, Architecture, and Art Treasures* (1954), with bibliography and illustrations, *Russian Architecture: Trends in Nationalism and Modernism* (1948), illustrated, "Soviet Art and Architecture" in *The Annals of the American Academy of Political and Social Science*, vol. 303, pp. 104–115 (Jan. 1956). (AR. V.)

RUSSIAN ART may be divided into four historical periods: the Byzantine, from the 10th to the early 16th century; the Moscow or National, from the 16th to the 18th century; the Petersburgian or European, from the 18th to the beginning of the 20th century; and the Soviet, from 1918 to the present.

THE BYZANTINE PERIOD (988–1530)

From the 10th century until the end of the 17th century painting in Russia was virtually confined to icon painting, an art introduced to the newly converted nation in the 10th century in the form of models sent to Kievan Russia from Byzantium. This art limited itself to the reproduction of traditional representations of the deity, the saints and scriptural events without ever using the living model.

The conversion of Russia (988) took place during the Byzantine Renaissance, and therefore the two distinct sources of Byzantine art traditions—the classical and the eastern—became the basis of early ecclesiastical art in Russia. The style and manner of Byzantium, once established at Kiev, spread from there to the northern centres and their influence persisted for several centuries.

The art of the Kievan period is revealed especially in the mosaics and frescoes of the Kiev cathedrals and in the applied arts such as filigree and enamels. Of the icons of that period few are preserved. An outstanding example that has survived is the mid-11th-century Vladimirskaia Bogomater ("Our Lady of Vladimir") brought to Russia from Constantinople in the 12th century. It played an important role in the development of the Russian iconographic type of the Virgin known as Umilenie ("Our Lady of Tenderness"), depicting the Virgin and Child as an intimate group radiating the warmth of motherly love.

The Novgorod School.—The civilization of the Kievan epoch was swept away in all of central Russia by the Mongol invasion about the middle of the 13th century. But in the northern regions of Russia—in Vladimir-Suzdal and particularly in the Novgorod district—the end of the 13th century and the whole of the 14th were marked by important developments in architecture and painting.

The city of Novgorod, free from subjugation to the Asiatic hordes, became virtually the metropolis and cultural centre of Old Russia after the fall of Kiev (1240). Together with the city of Pskov and other northwestern communities it harboured many Greek artists, most of whom were monks. They were instrumental in preserving the traditions of Byzantium. But though the latter were also zealously guarded by the Russian church, the evolution of icon painting—in Novgorod, Pskov, Suzdal and other centres—was manifesting local tendencies and characteristics. The rigid Byzantine patterns, the dark colours and the austere lines gradually became graceful, bright and less solemn. As early as the second half of the 12th century Novgorod's own style, which combined the severity of Byzantium with a folkish picturesqueness, was reflected in the frescoes of the Church of St. George in Staraya Ladoga (c. 1180) in the Church of Nereditsa (1199). The frescoes give an idea of the tendencies in the pictorial art of that period. The draftsmanship is spirited, the brush strokes are incisive and the general effect is vivid and sparkling.

The influence of Byzantine models continued to be felt more in the icons than in the frescoes. However, in the course of the 13th century Novgorod's style of icon painting gradually strengthened and took shape: the severity of faces was softened, composition was simplified, the silhouette became bold and ever more important and the palette was lightened by bright cinnabar, snow-white, emerald-green and lemon-yellow tones.

The final brilliant stage of Byzantine art—the Palaeologus Renaissance—reached its highest point in the last quarter of the 14th century and is reflected in works at Novgorod and Moscow by the highly gifted Theophanes the Greek, a Byzantine emigrant from Constantinople, who seems to have assimilated the characteristics of the country of his adoption. His paintings, though marked by a close adherence to Byzantine standards, show the features that distinguish Russian art: notably, elongated proportions, delicacy of detail and rhythmical composition. These features can be seen in his Novgorod frescoes and especially in the central part of the *deësis* range of the iconostasis in the Cathedral of the Annunciation in the Moscow Kremlin.

Among the immediate followers and collaborators of Theophanes was Andrei Rublev (c. 1370–1430)—the creator of religious types with a new spiritual expression in them. He painted the frescoes of the cathedrals of the Annunciation at Moscow (1405) and of the Assumption at Vladimir (1408). But his best-known work is the icon "The Old Testament Trinity" painted (c. 1410) for the Trinity-Sergiev monastery near Moscow. The subject—popular in Byzantine iconography—is the visit of the three angels to Abraham and Sarah. But the severe symbolism of the old Byzantine tradition is transformed into something new, more humanistic and intimate; even more important is the novel, peculiarly Russian mood of dreamy sublimation. It is one of the great creations of medieval Russian painting.

Another inspired artist of the 15th century was Dionisi (c. 1440–1508). He left an outstanding monument in the frescoes of the Ferapont monastery in the Novgorod district, and there are several icons ("The Metropolitan Aleksei," "The Crucifixion" and others) attributed to him. His art is marked by the extreme elongated stylizing of his figures combined with a subtle and glowing colour scheme. He and his predecessor Rublev succeeded in expressing the essence of the Russian icon as a reflection of a spiritual otherworldliness—the icon's highest merit.

THE MOSCOW OR NATIONAL PERIOD (1530–1700)

With the fall of Constantinople (1453) the hegemony in the world of Orthodoxy had shifted to Muscovite Russia. Profound changes began to take place in Russian icon painting, leading to the birth of a national art. This evolution first became noticeable in the gradual elimination of the Hellenistic setting of the icon—landscape and architecture. Greek basilicas with their porticoes and atria were replaced by Russian churches with their cupolas, "tents" and *kokoshniki*. Russian saints and episodes from their lives furnished subjects for the Russian artists; Muscovite types and native costumes began to appear in icon painting. The palette acquired an extraordinary brilliance and the emphasis on outline was particulary stressed. Thus the Russian icon gradually became the great national art form of medieval Russia.

Close ties between the Novgorod and the early Moscow schools were maintained for a long time, since many of the great icon and fresco painters in the 16th century worked first at Novgorod and later at Moscow; thus the features characteristic of Byzantine and Novgorodian traditions appear interwoven with the Moscow trend. The literary movement of the 16th century strongly influenced contemporary painting. New subjects appeared: some illustrated the mystical interpretation of the church dogmas or expressed the rites of the church in symbolic images; others represented parables and legends.

At the end of the 16th century the Stroganov school made its appearance introducing a particular manner of icon painting in diminutive size. Its masters became famous for the elegant attitudes of their figures, the eastern flavour of their colouring and elaborate treatment of detail. Some of them—Prokopii Chirin, Nikofor and Istoma Savin—were later to join the ranks of the icon-painting studios in the Kremlin armory in Moscow.

Moscow icon painting of the 17th century forms the last chapter in the history of Russian painting prior to the Petersburgian period. At the beginning of the century the majority of the icons still retained a strong national feeling and elements of real style. But by about 1650 little remained of what had once been so distinct in the Russian icon; not only had the original style disappeared, but also the character. By the end of the century western European influences began to spread rapidly over Russia, and Russian art entered upon a new historical period.

THE PETERSBURGIAN OR EUROPEAN PERIOD (1703–1917)

The foundation of St. Petersburg (1703) by Peter the Great marked the beginning of a significant change in Russian art—the substitution of western for Byzantine influence. The trend toward westernism was incipient before Peter was born, and went on after

"Princess Davydov and Mlle Rzhevskaya" by Dmitri Levitski, 1776. In the State Russian Museum, Leningrad

"The Last Days of Pompeii" by Karl Bryullov, 1833. In the State Russian Museum, Leningrad

Portrait of Colonel Evgraf Davydov by Orest Kiprenski, 1809. In the State Russian Museum, Leningrad

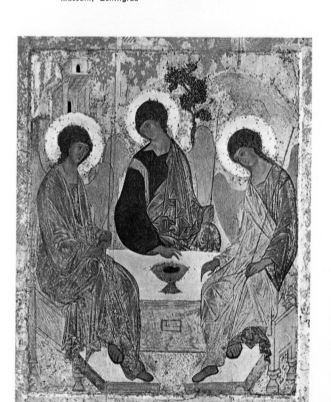

"The Old Testament Trinity" by Andrei Rublev, about 1410. In the State Tretyakov Gallery, Moscow

"Appearance of Christ to the People," by Aleksandr Ivanov, 1837–57. In the State Tretyakov Gallery, Moscow

PLATE II

RUSSIAN ART

"Boyarynya Morozova" by Vasili Surikov, 1887. In the State Tretyakov Gallery, Moscow

"Supper of the Tractor Drivers" by Arkadi Plastov, 1951. In the District Art Museum, Irkutsk

"Worker and Woman Collective Farmer," a stainless steel sculpture, by Vera Mukhina, 1937. In Moscow

"Scissors Grinder" by Kazimir Malevich, 1912. In the Yale University Art Gallery, New Haven, Conn.

"The Volga Bargemen" by Ilya Repin, 1870–73. In the State Russian Museum, Leningrad

his death, but the turning point—when the outlook and taste of the upper classes ceased to be Muscovite and became European—took place during the reign of Peter the Great. Foreign artists and architects began to come to Russia in increasing numbers, while groups of young Russians were sent to Italy, France, Holland and England to study painting and architecture. The influx of Western influences affected all spheres of Russian cultural life and determined the character of its art for more than two centuries.

The art of Peter's age shows almost no trace of Byzantine influence. Only in iconography did the old style persist for some time. Early in the 18th century religious painting began to give way to secular painting, and the church prohibition of sculpture in the round became ineffective.

The reign of Elizabeth (1741–62) ushered in an era of aristocratic culture and art. The empress had French inclinations and a taste for luxury. In her reign a great number of vast and luxurious rococo-style palaces were built; painting was primarily devoted to their interior decoration—ceilings and walls—while sculpture was employed to adorn the gardens and parks. The work was carried on mostly by Italians and Frenchmen.

In 1757 the Academy of Fine Arts was founded in St. Petersburg, and foreign artists—mostly French—were invited to direct the new school. These trained some remarkable native portraitists such as Ivan Argunov (1727–97), A. P. Losenko (1737–73) and Fedor Rokotov (1735–1808). Their works reflected the ceremonial character of Elizabeth's tastes, but showed little evidence of native Russian sensibility.

The advent of classicism in Russia is identified with Catherine the Great (1762–96), whose cultural interests were infinitely wider and more refined than those of Elizabeth. She was not only a prolific builder but a great art collector; much of the credit for the fabulous art treasures of Russia belongs to her. The number of foreign artists that she brought to Russia or encouraged—by ordering their paintings, statues and all sorts of art objects—is truly impressive; and though she mostly favoured foreign artists and architects, principally French and Italian, Russian art profited indirectly.

Russian painters extended their range during the latter half of the 18th century, adding genres of interior decoration and landscape to that of portraiture. At the same time, however, they devoted increasing attention to portraiture. Dmitri Levitski (1735–1822) painted the aristocratic ladies and gentlemen of the court and the eminent men of letters, as well as the adolescent schoolgirls of the Smolny institute. His portraits are largely of an intimate nature, concentrating on the psychological character of the model. Vladimir Borovikovski (1757–1825) also painted aristocratic society figures and members of the imperial family. His early work is permeated by a romantic melancholy mood. Later his portraits acquired a realistic quality.

Napoleon's invasion of Russia (1812) had far-reaching consequences. It marked the revival of national consciousness and the beginning of a widespread cult of Russian separateness from Europe, thus precipitating the long controversy between "westerners" and "Slavophiles" which ran through so much of Russian 19th-century literature and thought. At the same time Russia shared the European romanticism which marked the era of the Napoleonic Wars. This is reflected in the works of Orest Kiprenski (1782–1836) and Vasili Tropinin (1776–1857). The most notable contribution to the romantic spirit was made by Karl Bryullov (1799–1852) with his monumental painting "The Last Days of Pompeii" (1833). A completely different trend appears in the work of Aleksandr Ivanov (1806–58), the first Russian painter to express religious emotions in the western manner. Other outstanding artists of that period were the painters Alexei Venetsianov (1780–1847) and Paul Fedotov (1815–52), the forerunners of realist painting in Russia, and the sculptors I. Martos (1752–1835), I. Vitali (1794–1855) and F. Tolstoi (1783–1873), representatives of Russian classicism.

The second half of the 19th century marked the coming of age of realism in Russia. A popular outlook and a sympathetic attitude toward the hard life of the people is reflected in the works of most of the painters and sculptors of that time. The new trend in art had as its basis the populist revolutionary ferment prevalent toward the end of the 1850s and the beginning of the 1860s, much of it inspired by the writers Nikolai Dobrolyubov (1836–1861) and Nikolai Chernyshevski (1828–1889). Chernyshevski's dissertation *The Aesthetic Relations of Art to Reality* (published in 1855), the main thesis of which was that art must not only reflect reality but also explain and judge it, provided a starting point for the contemporary artists.

From the last third of the 19th century onward the history of Russian art is the history of a series of school struggles: the Slavophiles against the westerners; the Academy against the Peredvizhniki ("Society of Wandering [or Traveling] Exhibitions"); and later the joint effort of the last two against a new movement, born in the 1890s and directed by the art review *Mir Iskusstva* ("The World of Art").

The Peredvizhniki society was formed in 1870 by a group of realist artists who seceded from the Academy in 1863 in protest against alien dogmatic formulas and the constricting programs of the Academy's annual competitions. Most prominent among the members of the Peredvizhniki were Ivan Kramskoy (1837–87), Ilya Repin (1844–1930), Vasili Surikov (1848–1916), Vasili Perov (1833–82) and Vasili Vereshchagin (1842–1904). The society attached far more importance to the moral and literary aspects of art than to aesthetics. Its artistic creed was realism, national feeling and social consciousness. Art was to be placed at the service of humanitarian and social ideals; it was to be brought to all the people. The society therefore organized mobile (*peredvizhnye*) exhibitions, hence the name.

The outstanding paintings by the members of this society are: "The Morning of the Execution of the Streltsy" (1881) and "Boyarynya Morozova" (1887) by Surikov; "The Volga Bargemen" (1873) and "The Arrest of the Propagandist" (1878) by Repin; "After Igor's Battle with the Polovtsi" (1880) by Victor Vasnetsov (1848–1926); "The Hermit" (1889) by Mikhail Nesterov (1862–1942); and "Still Waters" (1892) and "Golden Autumn" (1895) by Isaak Levitan (1861–1900). In sculpture the best-known works are "Ivan IV" (1870), "Peter the Great" (1872) and "Mephistopheles" (1883) by Mark Antokolski (1843–1902).

The influence of the Peredvizhniki spread throughout the country and it dominated the scene for nearly 30 years. But by the end of the century (1898), when the *Mir Iskusstva* made its appearance under the editorship of Sergei Diaghilev (1872–1929), Konstantin Somov (1869–1939) and Alexandre Benois (1870–1928), the prestige of the Peredvizhniki had greatly declined. The infatuation with problem pictures and civic themes was over.

Mir Iskusstva did not proclaim any new theories, but it attacked the low artistic standards of the Peredvizhniki, as well as the deadening influence of the Academy. Individualism and artistic personality were placed first, regardless of any school. Much of the creative work of this group tended to be based on historical themes. Such artists as Benois, Somov and Léon Bakst (1866–1924) were under the spell of the 18th century and the romantic 1830s. Others like Nikolai Roerich (1874–1947), Vasnetsov and Ivan Bilibin (1876–1942) were attempting to evoke the spirit of ancient Russia. They all aspired to achieve a synthesis of new western-European trends and certain elements of traditional Russian folk art.

The important achievements of the *Mir Iskusstva* were in the fields of the artistic book (format and illustrations) and stage designing. But perhaps the greatest contribution of this group to Russian art was the revival of the sense of tradition. It is noteworthy that nearly all that Russia exported to western Europe in the way of artistic values during the early part of the 20th century (ballet, opera, stage scenery, costume and graphic arts) was the work of this group.

In the European artistic ferment of ideas of the early 1900s Russia played a significant role. A large part of ultramodernism was born and developed there during the second decade of the century. The new ideas were taken up by the group called Bubnovyi Valet ("The Jack of Diamonds"), the work of whose members—Petr Konchalovski (1876–1956), Ilya Mashkov (1881–1944), Aleksandr Kuprin (1870–1938), Aristarkh Lentulov

(1882–1943) and others—once regarded as followers of the extreme French trends, made itself felt in Soviet Russia. This group was succeeded by several "leftist" groups, consisting of Cubists, Constructivists, Suprematists and Expressionists—all of them attempting to combine the native and foreign theories under the slogan "pure form," and most of them professing to serve the Revolution with the higher forms of abstract art.

THE SOVIET PERIOD (1918–   )

The Bolshevik Revolution broke out at the time when Russia had at last caught up with western Europe in the artistic sphere. At first the Soviet regime appeared to look favourably upon avant-garde art. Extreme modernists like Wassily Kandinsky (1866–1944), Kazimir Malevich (1878–1935), Marc Chagall (1887–   ), Vladimir Tatlin (1885–   ), Naum Gabo (1890–   ) and El Lissitzki (1890–1941) were given official positions. But the teachings of these Abstractionist and Nonobjective artists—their professed indifference to subject matter and their hostility to popular ideas—soon proved to be their undoing, thus changing the direction of Soviet art.

The intellectuals who had any appreciation of modern art represented only a small minority of the population. Lenin himself had no sympathy for the extreme forms of modernism. He and a number of his latter-day disciples apparently sensed that the Suprematist paintings of Malevich or those of the Expressionist Kandinsky were addressed not to the common man but rather to a small coterie of connoisseurs and dilettanti, and that modernism, with its rarefied atmosphere of pure aesthetics, was incomprehensible to the masses. The hostility toward the abstract and nonobjective schools of art—accused of "capitalist cosmopolitanism"—was further intensified by the desire to establish a "people's" art answering, both in form and in content, the strivings of the new political and economic system.

To accomplish its objectives the Soviet regime adopted a program of measures aimed at the democratization and humanization of art. The extreme-left art groups (the "formalists," as they were labeled) were dissolved, and their conflicting aesthetics were replaced with the aesthetics of "socialist realism." Art was to be realistic enough to be comprehensible to the people without being merely a copy of external reality—an art socially useful and educational. This implied the exclusion of "subjectivism," "abstractionism" and all the other "antihumanistic" trends in art as practised by those who seemed not to care whether they were understood or not. The ban on formalism (a term that covered all nonobjective art) and the insistence on representational realism led to a frank revival of the "purpose" painting of the Peredvizhniki epoch, which soon developed into a lifeless academicism dominating every phase of art throughout the regime of Joseph Stalin.

The active role in the promulgation of socialist realism was played by the writer Maksim Gorki (1868–1936), whose views on aesthetics were based on the principles enunciated by Nikolai Chernyshevski; the doctrine was introduced by Gorki in a speech before the first congress of the Union of Soviet Writers held in 1934; shortly afterward it spread to all the other arts. According to Soviet art theoreticians, socialist realism permits of an infinite variety of stylistic methods, of the use of many expressive forms. The term "socialist" in the designation signifies that realism in Soviet art is based on the principles of philosophic materialism, appraising all phenomena of the past and present from the standpoint of that ideology. This view of the substance of art implied thematic painting and sculpture, but also implied that art is a part of the socialist dynamic. The artist therefore should not dwell on the negative, static characteristics of society, but must portray the positive, revolutionary-romantic side of socialist life by representing the inner world and the deeds of its outstanding workers and leaders: i.e., by bringing into salient relief a deliberately magnified image of the "typical."

An outstanding part in the development of Soviet art was played by Lenin's "plan for monuments," the purpose of which was to honour the memory of the great revolutionists, the men of science, art and literature by monuments, paintings and statues. Aside from portraying Soviet leaders, the artist was urged to select his subject matter from the drama of daily life and toil of the country, stressing the theme of the "new Soviet man." As a result many statues and paintings were produced depicting scientific and industrial workers and farmers—singly or in groups, at labour or at rest—in homely realism, but often tinged with imagination. Examples of socialist realism are the sculptured stainless-steel group "Worker and Woman Collective Farmer" by Vera Mukhina (1889–1954), and the paintings "Steelworker of the Hammer and Sickle Factory" by Gavriil Gorelov (1880–   ), "Farm Festival" by Sergei Gerasimov (1885–1964)· and "Supper of the Tractor Drivers" by Arkadi Plastov (1893–   ).

Another feature of this trend was the scope it gave to monumental art works in which sculptors and painters collaborated with the architect. Hundreds of artists, associated with different genres, contributed to the decoration of the new buildings—the concourses of the Moscow Subway, the halls and auditorium of Moscow university and the pavilions of the Agricultural exposition—tying in the substance of genre activities with the architecture of the structure. Some of these works are distinguished by a sense of composition, monumentalism and a sense of history; very often they display technical virtuosity and fine workmanship but they suffer from an excess of realism.

The end of the Stalin era (1953) ushered in a more liberal climate in the arts. The pressure of the tutelage system imposed from above was considerably relaxed, with the result that the artist regained a measure of freedom of expression.

See also references under "Russian Art" in the Index.

BIBLIOGRAPHY.—Byzantine and Moscow Periods: V. Lasareff and O. Demus, Early Russian Icons, in the "UNESCO World Art Series" (1956); M. Alpatov and N. Brunov, Geschichte der altrussischen Kunst (1932); N. Kondakov, The Russian Icon, trans. by E. H. Minns (1927).
Petersburgian Period: G. Hamilton, The Art and Architecture of Russia (1954); G. Lukomsky, History of Modern Russian Painting (1945); A. Benois, The Russian School of Painting (1916); L. Réau, L'Art russe de Pierre le Grand à nos jours (1922).
Soviet Period: I. Grabar (ed.), Istoriia russkogo iskusstva, vol. xi (1957); J. Chen, Soviet Art and Artists (1944); K. London, The Seven Soviet Arts (1937).   (AR. V.)

RUSSIAN HISTORY. Russia (originally RUS, later ROSSIYA) was for centuries a multinational state of eastern Europe and the northern part of Asia. At first a loose confederation of principalities it became in 1480 a sovereign tsardom (Tsarotvo Russkoe) governed centrally from Moscow and in 1721 an empire (Rossiiskaya Imperiya) that was destroyed in the Revolution of 1917.

The article that follows summarizes the history of Russia from its origins to 1917. For the history from March 1917 to the end of the civil war and foreign interventions see RUSSIAN REVOLUTION, and for the history since that time see UNION OF SOVIET SOCIALIST REPUBLICS. The latter article contains sections dealing with geography, peoples, administration, social conditions, and economy.

The main divisions of this article are as follows:

I. THE ORIGINS

The great east European plain which was united, together with Siberia, under the Russian tsars, presents in spite of its general uniformity two contrasting geographic aspects which profoundly influenced the trend of its historical development: the northern and the southern. A primitive forest extending over the northern part of Russia is reminiscent of that described by Tacitus in his *Germania*. It was indeed its continuation, connecting Russia with the western part of the European plain. It was comparatively late that this part of Europe was set free from its prehistoric ice cover. It is still full of lakes and great rivers which for long remained the only ways of communication for a scanty and scattered population. The primitive settlers added a few patches of cultivated land to their habitual means of livelihood—river fish, wild beehives, and fur-bearing animals in the forests.

Quite different is the southern Russian landscape. It is the steppe, the prehistoric seat of nomad hordes which inhabited it from time immemorial until quite recently. These lived on horseback and in tents and throve on the booty taken in regular incursions against northern sedentary tribes. In the steppe the most ancient traces of aborigines are found, of the Paleolithic stage, followed by the Neolithic, with traces of Aegean culture in its primitive form. There also we learn, by the intermediary of ancient Greek colonies on the northern Black Sea shore, the names of ancient peoples of southern Russia, whose nationality, however, cannot be identified. The most ancient of them, the Cimmerians (*q.v.*), are said to have been replaced by the Scyths and these by Sarmatians (*see* SCYTHIANS; SARMATIANS). Some patriotic Russian historians (I. E. Zabelin, D. I. Ilovaiski, D. Ya. Samokvasov) tried to prove that these populations were Slavs, but later research pointed to an Iranian origin; for instance, the modern representatives of Alans (a Sarmatian tribe) are found to be the Ossetes, who are not Slavs but a Caucasian people.

The original home of all Slavs (*q.v.*) is to be sought not in the steppe but in the forest. Lubor Niederle stated that the southern Slavs (Serbs), originating in the marshy land between the Vistula and Dnieper, descended to the Danube as early as the 1st century A.D. The first federation of eastern Slavonic tribes (Russians) appears in the 3rd–4th centuries A.D. as a powerful and numerous people called Antae, living between the Dnieper and Dniester. They were involved in the wars of the Goths and Huns and were defeated by the Avars (*q.v.*) in the 6th century. In the second half of the 6th century appears a new conquering nomad nationality in the steppe, the Khazars (*q.v.*), possessing a certain degree of civilization. They brought under their subjection some eastern Slavonic tribes whose names are given in the ancient Russian an-

nals (Severyane, Radimichi, Vyatichi, Polyane). Khazar domination lasted until the beginning of the 10th century, when other nomads of Turkic descent and wilder habits—Hungarians (middle 9th century) and Pechenegs (*q.v.;* end of 9th century)—overran the steppe and broke the connection between Slavonic settlements and the Black Sea shore.

The Russian tribes must have reached a considerable development as cultivators, especially the Polyane (or people of the plain), dwelling on both sides of the middle Dnieper, the most civilized of the eastern Slavs. The Russian tribes were organized in confederations or principalities (*knyazhenia*), when, from the first half of the 9th century, came from the north a new invader—the Rus, a Varangian tribe, in ancient annals considered as related to the Swedes, Angles, and Northmen. Both Rus and Varangians are also known to Byzantine chroniclers, first as Norse pirates, then as warriors serving in the imperial guard, and finally (10th century) as chiefs of the caravans of traders coming yearly to Constantinople by the "Great Waterway" (the Austrvegr of northern sagas) through the cataracts of the Dnieper, whose names are given by the emperor Constantine VII Porphyrogenitus (905–959) both in "Russian" (Scandinavian) and in "Slavonic" (Rossisti and Sklaviusti).

Arabian writers represent the original seat of the Rus as an island covered with woods and marshes; this brings us to the source of the waterway mentioned—Lake Ilmen, near the ancient town of Novgorod, and Lake Ladoga, where the Neva River has its origin. Excavations of 9th–10th-century tumuli confirm the presence of Norse warriors, buried (or burned) with their horses and arms, in that very tableland where four chief waterways of Russia—the Neva basin, Volga, Dnieper, and Western Dvina—converge and form outlets to the Baltic, the Caspian, and the Black seas and thus determined the direction of ancient trade routes. Numerous finds of Arabian, Byzantine, and Anglo-Saxon coins (9th–11th centuries) along all these routes testify to a flourishing trade. It corresponds exactly to the period of foundation of new states by Vikings at one end of these trade routes and to the florescence of Arabian and Persian caliphates before the Mongol invasion at the other end.

II. KIEV

Russian legend says that the Rus were first asked to come to Novgorod by the local population to put an end to their internal feuds. Rurik (Hrörekr) was the first (semilegendary) *knyaz* (*koning,* prince) of Novgorod, but his companions wished to descend the Austrvegr, nearer to Byzantium, and Oleg (Helgi) settled in Kiev. The Russian annals date the arrival of Rurik in Novgorod A.D. 862. But the first reliable datum is Oleg's commercial treaty with the Byzantines, 911. A subsequent treaty was concluded in 945 by Oleg's successor, Igor (Ingvar), together with his companions, whose signatures contain 3 Slavonic names among 50 Norse.

Constantine Porphyrogenitus gave a very picturesque description of this trade, the chief business of the Rus dynasty. During winter the princes and their *gesiths,* who distributed among themselves the towns in the basin of the Dnieper, were busy making circuits among neighbouring tribes to force them to pay annual tribute. Their booty consisted of furs, money, and slaves. As spring came they loaded their small boats "made of one single tree" (*monoxulos*) and moved their caravans down the Dnieper in convoy, ready to ward off the attacks of nomad steppe tribes. In the treaties mentioned, their rights of trading in the capital were strictly defined.

The *konings* extended their power over local tribes, and to defend the land from nomad incursions they constructed earthen walls on the frontiers of the steppe. The local aristocracy joined the ranks of their *druzhina* (*gesith,* comitatus) and the process of assimilation began. The term "Rus" was now used to designate the southern outpost of the whole system of defense; *i.e.,* Kiev with the surrounding country. The son of Igor and his wife Olga (Helga) had a Slavonic name, Svyatoslav, but he remained part northern Viking as well as part southern nomad. Svyatoslav did not yet feel at home in Kiev. He wanted to come still nearer to

Byzantium and chose Pereyaslavets on the Danube in the Bulgarian land, because, he said "there was the centre where all goods gather from all parts: gold, clothes, wine, fruits from the Greeks, silver and horses from the Czechs and Hungarians, furs, wax, honey and slaves from the Rus." Svyatoslav also defeated the Khazars and the Volga Bulgars, but he was defeated by the emperor John I Tzimisces and slain by the Pechenegs on his way back home (972). With him died the Scandinavian tradition of the Kiev dynasty.

From the reign of Svyatoslav's youngest son, Vladimir, the Norman dynasty was definitely settled in Kiev. It still preserved its connections with other parts of Europe, attempted distant military expeditions against its Slav neighbours, and ruled the large territory from the northern lakes to the steppe and from the then uncertain Polish frontier to the Volga and the Caucasus. This was the most brilliant period of southern Russian history, but its brilliance rested on an unsafe base, as the connection between the newly built state and the country inhabitants remained loose. The only link unifying the subdued tribes was the power of the grand duke of Kiev. The people paid their tribute to the prince's tax collectors, but otherwise they were left almost entirely to themselves and were able to preserve their ancient tribal organization and habits.

Another element of union of enormous importance was added by the acceptance of the Christian faith in 988–989 by St. Vladimir. He took his religion from Byzantium, but the service was in the vernacular, as the prayer books and Bible had been translated into Slavonic by the apostles of the Slavs, Cyril and Methodius, in the 9th century. From 1037 the Russian church was subject to the Constantinopolitan patriarchate, and for two centuries nearly all

metropolitans, and most bishops, were Greeks. Eventually, however, the Slavonic and Russian element prevailed. After Vladimir's death (1015), his son Svyatopolk the Damned assassinated his brothers (Boris and Gleb, canonized as saints) but was defeated by another brother, Yaroslav, elective prince of Novgorod, who reunited all territory under the grand principality of Kiev and embellished his capital with a cathedral in Byzantine style. He also founded the monastery at Pechersk (the Pecherskaya Laura) which became a famous seat of faith and learning; he collected books and had them translated. Under Yaroslav the earliest document of Russian law was revised under the name *Russkaya pravda* (*q.v.*; "Russian right"). He gave refuge to two sons of Edmund II of England who fled from Canute, to Olaf II of Norway, and also to Harald III Hardraade, who married his daughter. He

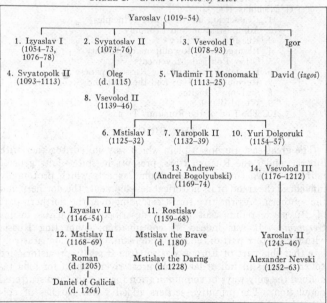

TABLE I.—*Grand Princes of Kiev**

*See text for explanation of numbers.

gave another daughter to Andrew I of Hungary and a third to Henry I of France. His sons married Polish, Greek, and German wives.

Yaroslav the Wise died in 1054. In order to prevent feuds among his descendants he introduced to the grand principality of Kiev an order of succession on the principle that all territory as a whole belonged to the family and that different parts of it were distributed among them in temporary possession according to seniority and to the profitableness of the seat of administration. The most profitable towns on the main trade route were Kiev, Pereyaslavl (on the steppe frontier), Novgorod (the first Norman residence), then Smolensk (on the upper Dnieper), and Chernigov (on its confluent, the Desna). All brothers of the first generation were considered as senior to the following generation. As soon as Kiev passed to another brother all the members of the family changed their seats and approached one step nearer to Kiev. If one died before reaching Kiev, his descendants were called *izgoi* and excluded from "mounting the scale." In Table I are numbered the successive reigns in Kiev during seven generations after Yaroslav.

The order of succession from brother to brother was kept only in the two first generations (1 to 5). Numbers 9 and 12 show preference given to nephews over uncles. And indeed, as early as 1097, at a conference held by the princes at Lyubech it was decided that the sons should keep their fathers' heritages. The direct succession from father to son prevailed in all principalities. Kiev was seen to be losing its former significance. Its great importance had been based on trade, but southern trade was destroyed by the appearance in the steppe (1054) of the Polovtsy (Kipchak [*q.v.*] or Kumans), nomads far more dangerous than the Pechenegs. It will also be seen that of all Yaroslav's sons

BORIS AND GLEB, SHOWN IN A 14TH-CENTURY ICON

Two sons of Vladimir, assassinated by their brother Svyatopolk the Damned in 1015, were later canonized as saints

only one line survived: that of Vsevolod and his brilliant son Vladimir II Monomakh. Monomakh's line was then divided into two: the elder one (6, 9, 12) remained in Kiev and in its turn it was subdivided in two—Roman and Daniel preferred to move west from the then unsafe Kiev to Halicz (Galich; *see* GALICIA), while two Mstislavs, the Brave and the Daring, as their nicknames show, remained to the end the knights errant of the chivalrous south.

The cadet branch of Vladimir Monomakh (10, 13, 14) opened a new period of Russian history. The centre of influence changed then to northern woodland, far from the steppe. It was a far poorer but safer and, in the long run, more profitable settlement. In 1169 Andrew's troops stormed Kiev. This was the end of southern brilliance, though Kiev was not definitely destroyed till 1240 by a last and most terrible invader, the Mongol Batu, Genghis Khan's grandson.

The title of grand prince of Kiev thus lost its importance and with it broke down the unity of Russia. Princely appanages became independent principalities; Russian territory was split in a dozen separate units which waged endless wars against each other. The old Kiev centre suffered the most from these internal dissensions and from incursions from the steppe. The frontier population was nearly exterminated and mixed with Turkic ethnic elements. However, the ancient tribes remained untouched to the west and north of the Dnieper. In their midst, about the 14th century, appeared new branches of Russian people, speaking their separate languages: the Ruthenians (later known as Ukrainians) and the Belorussians (the old Krivichi).

III. NOVGOROD AND MOSCOW

Eventually three distinct centres emerged from the chaos: Halicz, Novgorod, and Moscow. Each was characterized by the prevalence of one of three main features of Russian political life during the Kiev period: (1) the popular assembly (*veche*), which represented the ancient tribal organization, which met in towns and thus consisted chiefly of townsfolk; (2) the princes; (3) the boyars (*see* BOYAR) and the *druzhina* (comitatus), a landed aristocracy, partly of ancient tribal descent, partly the military companions of the prince at the conquest. This aristocracy developed especially in Halicz, where the social structure approximated to Western feudalism. On the northwestern frontier the democratic element prevailed. The chief city, Novgorod, became a republic.

SOVFOTO

KREMLIN OF NOVGOROD; PORTIONS DATE FROM THE 11TH CENTURY, THE WALLS FROM THE 14TH

"Lord Novgorod the Great" was ruled by a popular assembly (*veche*) which elected its mayor (*posadnik*) and its commandant (*tysyatski*, chiliarch) and concluded treaties with the princes who were invited only to watch over the defense. Novgorod had a well-developed trade and large dominions extending from its gates and from the mouth of the Neva over the whole Russian north up to the White Sea and the Urals. That country was rich in furs, the chief export. The higher class of citizens was formed of capitalists and rich merchants, who were to become the aristocratic element in Novgorod (*q.v.*).

Another element existed in the political structure of central

Russia: the backwoods of the Oka and Upper Volga. This country's population consisted mostly of agricultural colonists settled on princely land. Thus the prince appeared there as a proprietor and as the organizer of social life. Towns were scarce and the population scattered in clearings. The few *veches* in the chief towns had no important influence; noble landed proprietors were not so powerful as the medieval aristocracy in other European countries.

Thus, the power of the prince in central Russia was practically unlimited. Princely psychology was framed accordingly; unlike the valiant knights of the south, they formed a dynasty of great appropriators, stingy and acquisitive, ruling their principalities as private estates. They thus accumulated elements of strength which as time went on aided them in becoming masters of the whole of Russia.

After the conquest of Kiev by Andrew (Andrei Bogolyubski) the title of grand prince passed from Kiev to a northern town,

TABLE II.—*Grand Princes of Moscow*

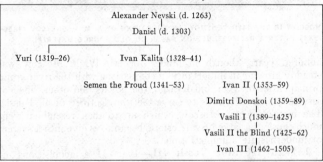

	Alexander Nevski (d. 1263)		
	Daniel (d. 1303)		
Yuri (1319–26)	Ivan Kalita (1328–41)		
Semen the Proud (1341–53)		Ivan II (1353–59)	
		Dimitri Donskoi (1359–89)	
		Vasili I (1389–1425)	
		Vasili II the Blind (1425–62)	
		Ivan III (1462–1505)	

Suzdal, and from there to Vladimir on the Klyazma. But as early as 1147 Moscow is mentioned in the annals. Its situation was exactly at the centre of Russia, between the Oka and the Upper Volga. It had long been a great centre of continental river trade, far from the southern area of Tatar devastation. The line of grand princes of Moscow starts from Alexander Nevski's younger son Daniel. Their genealogy during the domination of the Golden Horde (1240–1480) is shown in Table II.

1. The Tatar Domination.—All these princes had to ingratiate themselves with the khans of the Golden Horde (*q.v.*) to receive from them the *yarlyk* (investiture) as grand dukes. They regularly journeyed to the capital of the khans and underwent every kind of humiliation. But they returned as chief collectors of the Tatar tribute, which gave them power over neighbouring principalities. Only the principality of Tver competed with them very stubbornly.

The princes themselves involved the Tatars in their feuds and brought punitive expeditions on Russia. The khan's protection gave the Muscovite grand princes the upper hand over their enemies. They soon succeeded in increasing their possessions. Ivan I extended his domain, by purchase and by violence, over the whole province of Moscow. Dimitri (Donskoi) added to it the upper Volga region (excepting Tver and Yaroslavl), Tula, and Kasimov; Vasili I acquired the remaining part of Oka and Suzdal, Vladimir, Murom, and Nizhni-Novgorod; and Vasili II added Elets in the south and Vologda and Ustyug in the north. A religious sanction was given to Muscovite unionist tendencies by the metropolitans of the Russian church, who in the persons of Peter, Theognost, and Alexius settled in Moscow. Accordingly, the grand princes of Moscow added to their title: "of all Russia." Dimitri won a great name by his brilliant victory over the Tatars of the Golden Horde led by Mamai in a bloody battle on Kulikovo Plain (1380). He thus appeared as a leader of all the national forces (excepting the grand prince of Ryazan) against the oppressors, and he received the blessings of the church at the hand of St. Sergius (*q.v.*) of Radonezh, prior of the convent of the Holy Trinity.

Two years later, however, Moscow was sacked and burned by another conqueror, Tokhtamish, who in turn was defeated by Timur, his former protector. The Tatar yoke lasted for another

SOVFOTO

MOSCOW IN THE 14TH CENTURY, AN ENGRAVING BY A. M. VASNETSOV (1856–1933) AFTER A RECONSTRUCTION BASED ON OLD SOURCE MATERIAL

hundred years, though in milder forms. While Moscow was steadily growing in importance in comparison with the rival grand principalities of Tver and Ryazan, the boyars and other "men of service" came in crowds to serve the grand prince of all Russia. The institutions of Moscow, which up to then resembled very much those of a large private estate, began to evolve into a system of modern state administration.

2. Ivan III and Vasili III.—Ivan III's acquisitions of Novgorod and Tver (1478 and 1485) enlarged Russian territory up to the limits of settlement of the Great Russian branch of the nation and brought Russia into direct contact with other countries, Livonia, Lithuania, and the Tatar khanate of Crimea. The title of "sovereign of all Russia" became a reality, and systematic foreign relations were started. The all-Russian potentate proffered historical claims against Lithuania, which possessed the Belorussian territory. The successful wars which followed extended the western frontier to Chernigov and Novgorod Seversk, while leaving further claims for Smolensk, Kiev, "and all Russian patrimony" to Ivan's successors. Ivan also built the fortress Ivangorod close to the Gulf of Finland, thus opening the chapter of Russian pretensions on the Baltic. The Crimean khan Mengli Girei accepted his friendship and helped him to put an end to the Golden Horde. As early as 1480 Ivan refused the Tatar tribute and threw off the yoke.

The title of grand prince seemed inadequate after all these successes; more pretentious claims were based on a new theory suggested by southern Slav and Greek divines. According to this theory the Muscovite prince was a successor of the Byzantine emperors and the only representative of the Orthodox Church in the world. Indeed, the Greek Orthodox Church had accepted the "union" with the Catholics as early as 1439, at the Council of Ferrara-Florence, and Constantinople, "the second Rome," had been taken by the Turks in 1453. Obviously, the Greeks had been punished by God for their apostasy, and their succession had to pass to the third Rome, which was Moscow, and to the Russian grand prince, who remained the only faithful and really Christian prince in the world.

The realization of this new scheme began with the marriage (Nov. 12, 1472) of Ivan III with Zoë (in Russia, Sophia), the only niece of the last Byzantine emperor, Constantine Palaeologus. With her arrival new habits appeared at the Muscovite court intended to magnify the new autocrat (a title used by Ivan in foreign relations). The church that gave its sanction to that change claimed a reward: the prince had to help it against all heresies and internal dissensions. The prior of Volokolamsk convent, Joseph (*q.v.*), insisted on burning some rationalistic heretics in Novgorod. He also defended the principle that wealth gives power to the church, and he mercilessly crushed tendencies of the reformer Nil Sorski, the "abstainer from property," who opposed the persecu-

tion of heretics. Thus, the official theory on Russian church and state was formed as early as the end of the 15th century. Under Vasili III the unification of Russian territory was consummated by the acquisition of another republic, Pskov (1510); by the final annexation of Ryazan, the last independent grand principality; and by a new extension at the expense of Lithuania—the acquisition of the frontier city of Smolensk (1514). The minority of Vasili's son Ivan, who was three years old when his father died (1533), and subsequent disputes over the regency between rival factions, lasting 14 years, did not interrupt the growth of the Muscovite state. The reign of Ivan the Terrible marks the beginning of another period of Russian history. (P. M.; S. G. Pu.)

IV. THE RUSSIAN TSARDOM

A. From Ivan IV to the First Romanovs

1. Ivan IV the Terrible.—The reign (1547–84) of Ivan IV was an epoch of important development for Russia. Ivan's grandfather and father, during their rule as grand princes, had united politically all the Great Russian territories. During Ivan's reign (he was 16 when he began to rule) Russia became a vast, integrated state. Though its people were of various ethnic origins, its administrative system was centralized. Its aims in both external and internal policy were clearly defined, the tsar wielded great power, and the position and privileges of the hierarchy were sharply defined. From 1542 the metropolitan of Moscow, Makari, head of the Russian Orthodox Church and a highly educated and intelligent man, greatly influenced the young ruler, who adopted the metropolitan's ideas of the sovereign's divine right. In 1547 Ivan was crowned as first tsar (shortened from Latin *Caesar*) of Russia, and in 1549 the first *zemski sobor* (*q.v.*; "assembly of the country") was summoned. Reforms undertaken by Ivan's government during the 1550s were designed to strengthen the state, to give its subjects a better chance of justice both from the courts and the administration, and to give urban and rural dwellers some degree of local autonomy.

In the late 1540s Ivan waged a series of wars against Russia's old enemies, the Tatar khans. Kazan fell in 1552 and Astrakhan in 1556, providing Russia with an exit to the Caspian Sea but bringing a new danger, since Russia's sphere of interest now

BY COURTESY OF THE LENIN STATE LIBRARY, MOSCOW

MANUSCRIPT ILLUMINATION DEPICTING THE BATTLE OF KULIKOVO, 1380, IN WHICH DIMITRI (LEFT FOREGROUND) DEFEATED THE TATARS OF THE GOLDEN HORDE. FROM A LATE 16TH-CENTURY RUSSIAN CHRONICLE

clashed with that of the Ottoman Empire. Against the advice of his intimates, his so-called "Chosen Council," Ivan decided that Russia needed an exit to the Baltic as well. The so-called Livonian War of 1558–83 ended, after several resounding victories, in defeat for Russia, greatly undermining the state's economy. Russia's only other successful expansion was in the east, where Ermak Timofeevich entered western Siberia in the 1580s.

The internal life of the country was complicated by the fierce political struggle directed by the tsar against the princely houses and aristocracy. In 1565 Ivan divided the realm into two; his private (*oprichnina*) appanage land, which he administered personally; and the remainder (*zemschina*), which continued to be ruled in the traditional way by the council of boyars. This arbitrary division resulted in almost complete disruption of the national economy. Ivan broke the strength of the old aristocracy and that of the church. He enhanced the status of the new class of state servants, landowners who held their estates direct from the crown. In an effort to attain his military objectives he reorganized the army; formed the first regular body of troops, the fusiliers (*streltsy*); created the Russian siege train; and built several fortresses. He also ordered the compilation of the first register of taxable land, to effect a more proportionate system of taxation. He was a patron of the arts, and the first Russian printed books date from his reign.

Ivan's aims were beyond Russia's understanding. Dissatisfaction with his rule rose to such a pitch that many Russians emigrated to the borderlands, where the central government's authority was less evident. The tsar's power became absolute. Ivan said that "he was free to pardon or put to death any of his subjects at will" and illustrated the precept frequently and brutally, as in his savage destruction (1570) of the city of Novgorod and its inhabitants when they became suspect of separatist tendencies. Ivan steadfastly held to his theories of Byzantine caesaropapism, but nevertheless was one of the first Russians to work for contact with the West and in particular with England.

2. Fedor I.—The son and heir of Ivan IV, Fedor, was a weak man whom Ivan called more fit to be a bell ringer in a convent than a tsar. The *zemski sobor* confirmed his accession, but the direction of affairs fell to his brother-in-law Boris Godunov, an able man who continued Ivan's policy. The Church of Russia, already autocephalous, received its independence and equality with other Orthodox churches by the granting to its head, the metropolitan Job (Yov), of the title of patriarch at the hands of Jeremiah, patriarch of Constantinople (1589). Another important measure was intended to strengthen economically the landed gentry class created by Ivan IV as against the boyars. Peasants were forbidden temporarily to leave their estates or migrate to other landowners. All such fugitives who fled from their masters after 1592 (the time of the completion of government registers) were ordered back in 1597. The successful war with Sweden (1590–95) resulted in the return of the Russian towns of Ivangorod and Koporie, ceded by Ivan IV.

3. Boris Godunov and Vasili Shuiski.—In 1598 Fedor died; after some hesitation Boris had himself elected tsar by a *zemski sobor*. His policies remained more or less unchanged, but the stability of the realm was gravely affected by a severe famine and an outburst of plague (1601–03). Boris pursued Ivan IV's policy of weakening the boyars, but he met with opposition on their part. The only legal heir of Fedor, Dimitri, had died in Uglich, the place of his exile, in May 1591. But the boyars, with the help of the Poles, opposed to Boris a "Pseudo-Dimitri," a young and well-educated man of obscure origin. Boris died (April 1605) soon

JOHN R. FREEMAN & CO.

IVAN IV, DETAIL FROM A CONTEMPORARY ITALIAN WOODCUT

after the appearance of this pretender, who was accompanied by Polish volunteers and aided by the Cossacks. On June 30 (new style; June 20, old style), 1605, the impostor entered Moscow.[1]

On May 27 (N.S.), 1606, Pseudo-Dimitri I was killed in an outbreak caused by the boyars, led by Vasili Shuiski, who took advantage of the popular dislike of the pretender's free habits of life and the Catholic tendencies of his Polish protectors. The old dynasty was completely extinguished, and the throne of the tsar passed to Shuiski (1606–10). He gave a formal promise to the boyars not to rule without their advice and not to exterminate them by capital punishment or by exile and the confiscation of estates, without resorting to their court.

The power of the boyars, however, could not be restored; much more influential now was the rising class of small landlords. Still more dangerous for Vasili were the Cossacks and the fugitive serfs in the newly colonized south of Russia. A real social uprising was started in the south by a former serf, Ivan Ivanovich Bolotnikov. Trouble was rife in the south and the east. A second Pseudo-Dimitri appeared and in the spring of 1608 marched on Moscow, establishing his camp at Tushino. The boyars wavered between the tsar Vasili and the "Thief of Tushino"; there were many flittings. Vasili turned to Sweden for help and received aid from Charles IX. Charles's rival, Sigismund III of Poland, had entered Russia as Vasili's adversary and as pretender also to the Russian throne. In September 1609 Sigismund appeared before Smolensk. On July 3 (N.S.; June 23, O.S.), 1610, a Polish army marching toward Moscow under the hetman Stanislaw Zolkiewski defeated a Russo-Swedish army of 46,000 at Klushino, about 120 mi. W of the Russian capital. Shortly after this Vasili was dethroned and taken as prisoner to Warsaw. The throne remained empty through internal dissensions, and a real time of troubles set in which lasted for three more years (1610–13).

4. The "Time of Troubles."—The boyars preferred a Polish candidate, and together with the landed gentry they offered the Muscovite throne to Sigismund's son Wladyslaw. A delegation was sent to Smolensk, and Moscow voluntarily received Polish troops on Sept. 30 (N.S.; 20, O.S.), 1610. A treaty was concluded with Wladyslaw which secured the rights of the council of boyars and the privileges of the landed gentry. A Polish dynasty might have settled in Moscow but for Sigismund's desire to keep the throne for himself. His pretension awakened the spirit of national opposition. Pseudo-Dimitri II at once won popularity, especially among the Cossacks and the lower classes, but in December 1610 he was killed by a Tatar of his suite. The landed gentry then took action on the urging of the patriarch Hermogen. The landed gentry under Prokopi Petrovich Lyapunov and the Cossacks under Prince Dimitri Timofeevich Trubetskoi and the ataman Ivan Martynovich Zarutski blockaded Moscow; inside the town a popular uprising forced the Poles to retreat to the Kremlin. But again dissensions arose among the besiegers. Lyapunov was killed by the Cossacks, and the landed gentry returned to their homes. The south of Russia was in complete disorder; crowds of Cossacks and Polish marauders dispersed all over the north. This finally decided the gentry to make a new effort and to gather a new national army which would "exclude the Cossacks and stand firm until a new sovereign is elected by all the land." Prince Dimitri Mikhailovich Pozharski was made commander in chief of the army and Kuzma Minin, a butcher from Nizhni-Novgorod, the treasurer. All northern towns and districts sent their detachments and their representatives to the army as it advanced up the Volga. In April 1612 it stopped at Yaroslavl. As Novgorod had been taken by the Swedes, Pozharski offered the throne to Charles Philip, brother of Gustavus II (Adolphus). In August Pozharski's army moved southward to Moscow. On Dec. 7 (N.S.; Nov. 27, O.S.) the Poles capitulated in the Kremlin, and a national candidate was set free: the young Michael Romanov, whose father, the metropolitan Philaret (Fedor Nikitich Romanov), a nephew of

---

[1]After 1582 the Gregorian calendar came into general use in Europe, but it was not adopted in Russia until 1918. Consequently from 1582 to 1699 dates of the month in Russia were 10 days earlier; from 1700 to 1799, 11 days earlier; from 1800 to 1899, 12 days earlier; and from 1900 to Feb. 1, 1918, 13 days earlier. In this article new style dates peculiar to Russia are given first; the old style dates are given in parentheses.

the first wife of Ivan IV, was at that moment a prisoner in Poland. All votes were at the disposal of a national tsar, more acceptable to the gentry as he did not belong to an old princely family and was young enough (he was 17) to secure the boyars against over-bearing conduct. Michael was unanimously elected by a regular *zemski sobor* on March 3 (N.S.; Feb. 21, O.S.), 1613.

(P. M.; N. An.)

B. The Romanov Dynasty

The reign of the first three Romanovs (*see* ROMANOV) appears in retrospect to have been a period of transition between two periods of crisis: the crisis attending and following the efforts of Ivan IV to establish in Russia an absolute monarchy on the one hand, and that connected with the reforms of Peter I on the other. It was characterized by a deliberate conservative policy, a desire of those in power to stabilize the state and society and to revert to the practices that had prevailed under the previous dynasty. But powerful forces countered this effort: in varying degrees, pressures pushing toward something radically new affected the country's political system, its social structure, its foreign policy, and its cultural and religious life. In the end the reign of the first Romanovs proved more reformist than its rulers had intended. In many ways, therefore, this period marks a watershed between medieval and early modern Russia.

1. Internal Political and Social Affairs.—Conservative practices survived best in the realm of politics. The constitutional system evolved in Moscow in the preceding two centuries remained intact. The absolute tsar, advised by the boyar council (*duma*) and, on important occasions (before 1653, when they were suspended), by land assemblies (*zemskie sobory*), ruled the country through an administrative apparatus centred in bureaus known as *prikazy*. Local government was in the hands of military governors (*voevody*). Only in the armed forces, which in some ways constituted the main concern of government, could significant innovations be discerned. The traditional levy gradually gave way to a standing, professional army (some of it hired abroad), maintained by the tsar's treasury. Its growth tended to undermine Russia's social and fiscal structure and to pave the way for Peter's reforms.

Russia's social classes, during this period, were fully harnessed in the service of the state in accord with the principle of the "servitor state" evolved early in Moscow history and finally rationalized by Peter the Great. Duties, not rights, determined the status of the tsar's subjects. The landowning class had to serve in the military or civil service; the city population (legally tied to its place of residence) had to collect state taxes and was allowed to trade and to manufacture; the clergy and monks had their defined sphere of obligations; and the peasantry (almost all of which was formally tied to the land now) had to provide the other classes and the crown with the means of subsistence. Serfdom, as a legal institution, came into existence in this period. All these obligations were formally promulgated in the code (*ulozhenie*) of 1649. This period also marks the gradual decline of the ancient aristocracy, symbolized by the abolition in 1682 of *mestnichestvo,* that peculiarly Russian system of reconciling social status with office (*see* BOYAR); the gentry, on the other hand, continued to grow in power and in numbers.

2. Foreign Policy.—As far as foreign policy is concerned, the reign of the first Romanovs may be divided into two parts. In the first, extending to the early 1650s, Russia was on the defensive. Emerging from the "time of troubles," it was mainly concerned to secure recognition of the new dynasty and to gain time to rebuild. These aims were achieved by the signing of peace treaties with the country's two principal enemies, Poland (1619 and 1634) and Sweden (1617). Both required from Russia considerable territorial concessions. Commercial and industrial privileges granted to English and Dutch entrepreneurs brought the treasury badly needed subsidies and, incidentally, laid the foundations of Russian industry. After 1650, encouraged by the sudden collapse of Poland, Russia went on the offensive, from which it obtained first the areas inhabited by the Dnieper Cossacks (treaty of Pereyaslavl, 1654), and then Kiev, Smolensk, and all the lands on the eastern bank of the Dnieper (treaty of Andrusovo, 1667).

Russia now began in earnest to expand toward the Black and Baltic seas, a movement which became a constant feature of its history in the subsequent century.

3. Culture.—The profoundest changes affected Russia's cultural life. These were in large measure due to increased contact with the West brought about partly by measures sponsored by the government (influx of foreign soldiers, businessmen, artisans, and diplomats) and partly by a powerful stimulus received from the newly acquired Ukraine. By the 1660s the foreign colony in Moscow numbered over 1,000 persons, and, in addition, there were many other Westerners, mostly Protestants, engaged in trade and manufacture in the provinces, as well as serving in the army. In this period there emerged, especially in the ranks of the aristocracy, a thin layer consisting of westernized Russians who had lost much of the confidence in the superiority of Russian ways that had characterized the old elite (*e.g.,* I. A. Khvorostinin, G. K. Kotoshikhin, F. M. Rtishchev, A. L. Ordyn-Nashchokin, V. V. Golitsyn). The church, too, was subject to foreign influences emanating largely from the Ukraine and Greece. Beginning with the reign of Michael, the church authorities made efforts to rid Russian rituals and service books of accumulated errors, by carefully collating them with their Greek models—efforts which at once ran into opposition from much of the clergy and the mass of believers. Under Alexis this reform movement, given a powerful stimulus by the patriarch Nikon (*q.v.*) and backed by the tsar, engendered a dramatic crisis in the church, as a result of which it split in two: the state-supported (reformed) Orthodox Church, and the schismatic body of Old Believers (*see* also AVVAKUM PETROVICH; OLD BELIEVERS). What the church gained thereby in orthodoxy it lost in vigour and following, and it could offer no resistance when Peter I imposed on it direct bureaucratic rule.

4. Character of the Monarchy.—The early Romanovs were weak monarchs. Michael Fedorovich (1613–45), crowned at the age of 17, shared the throne during the crucial years of his reign with his father, the patriarch Philaret. Alexis Mikhailovich (1645–76) came to the throne at the age of 16; he was much under the influence first of B. I. Morozov and then of the patriarch Nikon. Fedor III Alekseevich (1676–82), a boy of 15 at the time of his accession, also yielded much power to favourites. On the other hand, all three were popular tsars, who left behind a good memory among the people and whom the Slavophils of the 19th century idealized as model Russian monarchs. Government during this period usually rested in the hands of individuals who for one reason or another exercised personal influence over the tsars, and of powerful boyar clans (often directly related to the ruling dynasty) which held in their hands the reins of administration in the council, *prikazy,* and office of the *voevoda.* Popular dissatisfaction usually turned against them, *e.g.,* during the urban uprisings (1648–50) of the reign of Alexis, and the great peasant rebellion led by Stenka Razin (*q.v.*).

In theory, the Russian monarchy was unlimited, and indeed there were no guarantees, either legal or economic, against the arbitrary power of the tsar. In practice, however, the degree of control he could exercise over the empire was effectively limited by the size of the country, the inadequacy of the administration, and a generally nonmodern conception of politics. As a consequence, the vast majority of the inhabitants rarely felt the heavy hand of the state, whose authority limited itself to the maintenance of order and the collection of taxes; some (*e.g.,* the Siberian inhabitants and the Cossacks) lived in completely autonomous communities, only nominally under the authority of the tsar.

(R. E. Pi.)

V. THE RUSSIAN EMPIRE

A. Peter I the Great

The years 1682 to 1725 cover the troubled but important regency of Sophia Alekseevna (until 1689), the joint reign of Ivan V and Peter I, and the three decades of the effective rule of Peter I (*q.v.*). In the latter period Muscovy, already established in Siberia, enters the European scene and in 1721 becomes the Russian Empire with a multinational population of about 17,500,000. Out of the 13,500,000 Russians, 5,500,000 men were liable to

PETER THE GREAT

Peter I, shown at left in 1698, traveled widely in Europe. As tsar he strove to bring European efficiency and culture to Russia. His devotion to Western culture is revealed in the design of St. Petersburg, shown above in 1725, which he founded. Repressive measures during his last years made him unpopular in some circles, as shown by the cartoon at right, "The Mice Bury the Dead Cat," satirizing his funeral in 1725

(LEFT) PAINTING BY SIR GODFREY KNELLER; REPRODUCED BY GRACIOUS PERMISSION OF HER MAJESTY QUEEN ELIZABETH II; (TOP RIGHT) ENGRAVING BY MARCELIUS IN THE STATE HISTORICAL MUSEUM, MOSCOW, SOVFOTO; (BOTTOM RIGHT) RADIO TIMES HULTON PICTURE LIBRARY

the poll tax, 3% of them being townsmen and 97% peasants. Of the peasants, 25% cultivated church lands, 19% state lands, and the remainder the estates belonging to some 100,000 families of secular landowners. Russia's territory of about 4,633,200 sq.mi. (12,000,000 sq.km.) included some recent and valuable acquisitions. By its victory over Sweden in the Northern War (*q.v.*), it regained Ingria and Finnish Karelia and acquired Estonia and Livonia, with the ports of Narva, Revel (Tallinn), and Riga. The price of success on the Baltic was failure on the Black Sea: the regions of Azov and Taganrog won from Turkey in 1696 had to be surrendered in 1711. Both parts of the adjacent area of Zaporozhye (the dominion over the left bank of the Dnieper and the protectorate over the right bank) were likewise lost to Turkey, but the *sich*, the Cossack stronghold, was razed to the ground in 1709. On the Caspian, after defeating Persia in 1722, Russia temporarily occupied Dagestan, Gilan, and Mazanderan. In eastern Siberia, in the 1720s, it annexed the Chukchi territory and the Kamchatka Peninsula. St. Petersburg, founded in 1703 among marsh and woodland, a living symbol of the new era and of its initiator, replaced Moscow as the capital of Russia in 1712. There the sea routes of the Baltic met the system of overland waterways leading to the Caspian.

1. Economy.—The peasants, in addition to bearing virtually the full weight of the fiscal burden throughout Peter's reign, were compelled to supply the state with military and civil conscripts: recruits for the army and navy; and labour for the construction of fortresses, canals, ships, and St. Petersburg. Peter's prohibition of 1723 "to sell peasants like cattle" illustrates their plight. The diminishing freedom of the rural population hindered industrial development. In addition to the lack of a free labour market, capital was in short supply and potential entrepreneurs were hard to find among the townspeople, of whom, toward the end of the period, there were only about 170,000, a bare 10% more than in 1700. The merchants proved to be the most enterprising members of this class. Anxious to stimulate industry (as well as trade),

the government took a hand in the establishment of factories but also encouraged private enterprise, especially by making up the deficiency of capital and labour. Thus state serfs were assigned to factories, and non-*dvoryane* received permission to acquire manpower through the purchase of villages. Of the 199 factories existing in 1725, 18% were textile and 31% metallurgical, and all but 13 had been established in the reign of Peter, half of them by the state. Most of the factories were located in the new industrial region of St. Petersburg, northeast of the new capital on the Svir, round Moscow and Tula, on the upper Don, and round Ekaterinburg (now Sverdlovsk) in the Urals. The factories eventually armed Peter's army and navy and nearly clothed his soldiers, thus fulfilling the purpose for which they had been created. Moreover, in 1726 Russia began to export pig iron.

2. Military, Finance, and Administration.—By 1710 Russia had a regular army recruited by conscription from among the peasantry and petty townsfolk, the first of its kind in Europe. In 1724 its effectives numbered 131,400 infantry and 38,400 cavalry, excellently trained and equipped. The Black Sea fleet had to be given up, together with Azov, in 1711. The Caspian flotilla was used against Persia in 1722. The Baltic fleet, built mostly in Russia after 1700, consisted in 1711 of 11 and in 1724 of 44 ships of the line and frigates armed with over 200 guns and manned by an establishment of about 16,000.

The cost of the army, 4,000,000 rubles annually, was the chief item in Russia's budget. After 1718, when the poll tax was first introduced, the deficit was gradually reduced until in 1724 a surplus was obtained.

Financial and administrative reform went hand in hand. The colleges (*kollegii*)—central administrative departments—established between 1718 and 1722 were severally concerned with war, the navy, foreign affairs, foreign trade, state revenue, state expenditure, audit, justice, mines, factories, spiritual affairs, the estates of the gentry, and "Little Russian" (Ukrainian) affairs. Fifty provinces (*provintsii*), each under a *voevoda*,

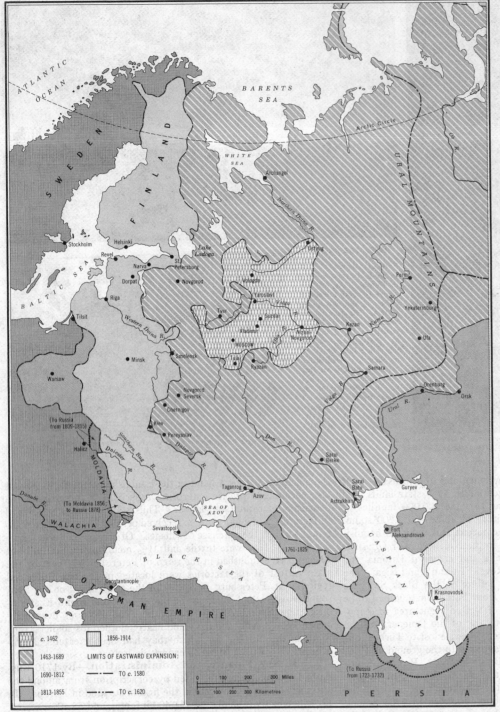

RUSSIAN TERRITORIAL ACQUISITIONS IN EUROPE AND SOUTHWESTERN ASIA BEFORE 1914

diocesan schools for the sons of clergy, in addition to maintaining the two ecclesiastical academies already in existence in Moscow and Kiev.

Lay education owed its expansion to naval and military needs. In 1701 a navigation school was established, the first of four, and in 1715 a naval academy for 300 pupils to provide in Russia the training for which hundreds of young *dvoryane* previously had been sent abroad. Knowledge of the three R's was compulsory for sons of the gentry, for whom the provincial "cipher" or elementary schools established in 1714 were primarily intended. The engineering school prepared pupils for the so-called Engineering Company created in 1719. The Moscow teaching hospital was established in 1707 and a secular academy was decreed in 1724.

4. Relations with the West. —To start the new schools and government departments, to build ships and organize workshops and train armies, foreigners were invited to Russia and Russians were sent abroad. Traffic and trade with the West increased. By 1726, via Petersburg and Archangel, Russia imported 1,500,000 rubles worth of wine, sugar, silk and woolen goods, and dyestuffs, and exported hemp, flax, sailcloth, linen, leather, tallow, and pig iron to the value of over 2,500,000 rubles. In 1724 a high protective tariff was imposed on all imports, to be levied in foreign currency. Russia's commercial relations with Holland and England were particularly close, but British exports suffered from the break in diplomatic relations between 1719 and 1730. In a number of Western ports Russia's trade interests were guarded by consuls; its Eastern trading partners were Persia and China. With permanent envoys in most European capitals, Russia was able to treat war and diplomacy as a combined operation. By 1725, having defeated and made an ally of Sweden, it had obtained supremacy in the Baltic. Its struggle with Turkey for access to the Black Sea was drawn, but the humiliating Tatar tribute had been tacitly repudiated. United by a dynastic bond to Holstein, Russia shared with Prussia a policy of keeping Poland weak; it also was drawing closer to Austria.

5. Internal Disturbances. —The new Russia, secular and westward-looking, grounded on a standing army and a tax-gathering bureaucracy, also had its internal enemies. In 1705–06 the populace of Astrakhan (one of the principal trading centres with the Middle East) overthrew the government of the province (*see* GOLITSYN, BORIS ALEKSEEVICH). In 1707–08, on the Don, runaway serfs, deserters, and conscript labourers under Kondrati Bulavin, a Cossack ataman, were up in arms against the boyars and chiefs, foreigners and tax collectors, and the official church. Be-

were subordinated in part to the colleges and in part to the senate. Established in 1711, when it replaced the council of ministers which had evolved from the boyar *duma*, the senate became a superior authority whose task it was to control and coordinate all the organs of government, including the secret police. The senate in turn was supervised by a procurator, Russia's all-powerful chief bureaucrat, from 1722 responsible to the tsar only.

3. Church and Education. —The church was subordinated to the state through the Holy Governing Synod, a ministry of ecclesiastical affairs under the direction of a lay chief procurator. The church, in 1722 the landlord of about 1,000,000 peasant families, was nationalized also in the economic sense: the income from its lands was handed on to the state. Thus the policy of control and financial exploitation applied to the church since 1696 became a fundamental law. The church was also called upon to establish

tween 1704–06 and 1720–25 hungry peasants rioted against conscription and taxation. But the secret police and punitive expeditions stamped out all opposition to Peter's government.

(L. R. Lr.)

B. From Catherine I to Paul I

1. Peter's Immediate Successors.—Peter met with opposition in his own family; his son Alexis (*q.v.*) grew up under the influence of the clergy and obviously disapproved of Peter's reform. He fled abroad from Peter's menaces, was brought back by fraud, imprisoned on suspicion of a conspiracy against his father's life, and died by torture. There remained only two daughters, Anna and Elizabeth, from the second marriage of Peter with a Lithuanian maidservant, Marfa Skavronskaya, renamed Ekaterina (Catherine) Alekseevna. In 1722 Peter reserved for the monarch the right to designate his successor. But at his death on Feb. 8 (N.S.; Jan. 28, O.S.), 1725, he failed to do so. Peter's creatures, like Aleksandr Danilovich Menshikov (*q.v.*), who had everything to fear from the survivors of old nobility, resorted to the guards and with their help proclaimed Catherine as empress. The legitimate heir, the son of Alexis, Peter, was thus put aside. The Russian throne, as Voltaire said, became "not hereditary and not elective, but *occupative*." The period from Peter's death to Catherine II's accession (1725–62) was an eclipse. Male members of the Romanov dynasty (that is to say, Peter's grandsons Peter II and Peter III, the sons of his son Alexis and of his daughter Anna of Holstein-Gottorp, respectively) were frail and feeble of mind. The women —both Peter's niece Anna (Ivan V's daughter) and his daughter Elizabeth—were stronger in mind and body. But they shared their power with favourites, and their choices were not always happy.

Court life flourished under these women's reigns, and it became very luxurious and expensive. A special school was founded by Empress Anna to teach the noble guards foreign languages, dances, and good manners. Balls, theatrical plays, musical entertainments —chiefly by foreign artists—became regular pastimes. The country was badly ruled; foreign policy was venal. Russia took part in European wars with little benefit for itself. From reign to reign the noble guards gained in influence, as they practically disposed of the throne.

Catherine I (1725–27) was followed by the rightful heir, Peter II (1727–30), thanks to a compromise between Menshikov and the representatives of the old nobility. His reign was fraught with struggle between the two. But Anna Ivanovna, the widowed duchess of Courland (daughter of Ivan V), had a claim to the throne. The aristocrats offered her the throne on the condition of limiting her power by the supreme council (created under Catherine I) in questions of her marriage, succession, war and peace, taxation, military appointments, etc. Anna signed, but, profiting by the dissensions of the gentry and nobility, tore up the signed charter and reigned as an autocrat (1730–40), aided by her favourite, Ernst Johann Biron. She tried to secure the succession in the lineage of her sister, the deceased Catherine of Mecklenburg, by designating as successor under the regency of Biron the baby Ivan VI, just born to her niece, Anna Leopoldovna, duchess of Brunswick. Anna Leopoldovna herself succeeded Biron as regent on Nov. 20 (N.S.), 1740, but on Dec. 6 (N.S.), 1741, the guards showed their hatred of the rule of the "Germans" by overthrowing her regency and enthroning Elizabeth, Peter the Great's daughter, who was expected to return to Peter's national policy. Indeed, the first fruits of Peter's reforms ripened during Elizabeth's reign (1741–62): national poetry, a theatre, and the first Russian university (Moscow, 1755), all auguring a deeper culture and knowledge for the next generation.

Elizabeth wished to secure the throne for the lineage of her sister Anna of Holstein-Gottorp, and she invited her nephew Peter, educated in the Lutheran religion and in the ideas of Prussian drill, to come to St. Petersburg to learn Orthodoxy and Russian habits. He came and was married (1745) to Princess Sophia of Anhalt-Zerbst, the future Catherine II. He was no mate for her. As fast as he lost Russian sympathy by his open aversion to everything Russian, Catherine ingratiated herself by exactly opposite behaviour. After half a year of the reign of Peter III, Catherine was

BY COURTESY OF THE STATE TRETYAKOV GALLERY, MOSCOW

CATHERINE II AS PAINTED BY D. G. LEVITSKY (1735–1822)

raised by the guards officers to the throne. The brother of her favourite Count Grigori Orlov, Aleksei, killed Peter on July 17 (N.S.; 6, O.S.), 1762.

For a representation of the succession to the throne of Peter the Great *see* the genealogical table in the article ROMANOV. Consult also the articles on the several emperors, empresses, and regents just mentioned: ANNA (Anna Ivanovna); ANNA (Anna Leopoldovna); BIRON, ERNST JOHANN; CATHERINE I; ELIZABETH (Elizaveta Petrovna); IVAN; PETER II; and PETER III.

2. Catherine II the Great.— The long reign of Catherine II was a turning point in Russian history. She received the fruit of half a century's evolution since Peter the Great's reforms. A prolific writer herself, in regular correspondence with the foremost men of her age, with Voltaire, Diderot, Jean le Rond d'Alembert, Baron Friedrich Melchior de Grimm, etc., not to speak of fellow potentates such as Frederick II, Maria Theresa, and Joseph II, she wished to make her reign brilliant and herself an ideal enlightened monarch. She began her reforms by compiling from Montesquieu and Cesare Bonesana, marchese di Beccaria, an instruction (*nakaz*) on the basis of which a new code of laws was to be composed. In order to discuss it she gathered an elective assembly of 564 deputies chosen from all classes except the clergy and the serfs, and from all parts of the empire. However, she met with opposition on the part of the gentry to her schemes to fix within definite limits their power over the serfs. Far from engaging in a struggle with the ruling class she yielded to their desires; their power was increased and a number of crown estates were distributed among the ranks of her favourites, thus turning their peasant population into serfs.

Catherine then began to search for glory in foreign politics. She conceived a bold scheme: (1) to recover from Poland the western provinces with an Orthodox Belorussian and Ukrainian population and (2) to take possession of the Black Sea shore, drive the Turks from Europe, and found in their place a series of new states in Moldavia and Walachia, in the Balkans and in Greece. She wished to take Constantinople and to place there her second grandson, Constantine, as the emperor of a new Greek empire. His very name was chosen to symbolize this project. Catherine was favoured in accomplishing at least a part of these designs by discords between two German states, Prussia (under Frederick II and Frederick William II) and Austria (under Joseph II, Leopold II, and Francis II). In her first Turkish war (1768–74) she had Prussia on her side and Austria against her; after P. A. Rumyantsev's victories she concluded a peace at Kuchuk Kainarji, the beginning of the Eastern Question (*q.v.*), as by it Russia received the right to protect Turkish Christians. Moreover, in 1772 she took part in the first partition of Poland, proposed by Frederick II in order to consolidate his territory and to compensate Russia for its war expenditure. In the second Turkish war (1787–91) Catherine had Austria on her side and Prussia against her. She had to content herself, after the victories of Aleksandr Vasilievich Suvorov, Count Rimnikski, and Prince N. V. Repnin, with the acquisition of Ochakov and the steppe between the Dniester and the Bug. But she consoled herself with new annexations from Poland (the second partition, 1793, and the third partition, 1795; *see* POLAND), while Prussia and Austria were busy fighting against the French Revolution. Catherine also annexed Courland (1795).

Catherine's numerous lovers flattered her imperial ambitions: the bold Grigori Orlov (*q.v.*) in her early years (1759–71), the ingenious Prince Grigori Potemkin (*q.v.*) in the midst of her reign (1776–91), and the young Platon Zubov, handsome but insignificant, in her declining years (1791–96).

Between her two Turkish wars Catherine returned to the legislative mania of her early years. Made wise by her experience with the commission of the code of 1767, she turned from Montesquieu to William Blackstone and profited by the administrative knowledge of J. Sievers, a skilful adviser of German Baltic origin. She then published in 1775 her statute of provinces, a good piece of organic legislation. For the first time in Russian history a local unit of administration, judiciary, and self-government was created. The statute introduced a regular system of courts of justice and separate financial and administrative offices. The system lasted until the reforms of Alexander II. The reform of 1775 was completed by two charters granted in 1785 to nobility and to burgesses. The charter of nobility introduced corporations of local gentry meeting every three years to discuss their affairs and to elect their marshals. It served to perpetuate the power of the ruling class until the liberation of the serfs in 1861, while the burgesses' charter laid the basis for real municipal self-government.

The protection extended to the gentry inevitably created a growing disaffection on the part of the serfs, who since Peter III's manifesto relieving the gentry of compulsory military service had impatiently awaited their turn for emancipation. In 1773 the Yaik (Ural) Cossacks revolted under E. I. Pugachev (q.v.), who called himself Peter III. He roused the Bashkirs and the serfs allotted to the factories in the Urals, assailed Kazan on the Volga and sacked it. Through the whole empire the peasants only awaited his coming to rise, but he did not feel equal to the task, nor could his bands stand against regular troops. He therefore suddenly returned to Cossack country, where he lost his army; he was extradited by his associates, tried, and beheaded in Moscow.

Catherine definitely turned her back on the liberal ideas of her youth after the beginning of the French Revolution. She began to persecute representatives of the advanced opinion which she herself had helped to create. A. N. Radishchev, the author of a spirited book, *A Journey from Petersburg to Moscow,* was sentenced to death as a Jacobin in 1790, but the sentence was commuted to ten years' exile in Siberia. N. I. Novikov, a Freemason who accomplished admirable educational and editorial work, was sent to Schlüsselburg prison in 1792.

3. Paul I.—Catherine's son and successor, Paul, mounted the throne on Nov. 17 (N.S.; 6, O.S.), 1796, when he was 42, barely sane, and with a bitter feeling of having been deprived by his mother of his right to succeed his assassinated father, Peter III. He hated Catherine's favourites and her policy, both internal and external. Paul stabilized the succession of the Russian throne by his imperial family statute (1797; in force until 1917). He sent Suvorov to Italy to fight against the French Revolution, and he ended his reign while preparing with Napoleon an expedition to India against England. In social questions Paul's policy was also inconsistent: he alleviated the serf's compulsory work for his landlord by reducing it to three days a week, but he gave away the peasants of the crown to noble proprietors as serfs in an even larger number than Catherine had (120,000 yearly). This did not make him popular among the nobility, however, as his exalted idea of the emperor's divine right caused him to treat them in a purely oriental way. He used to say that a person could be reputed of importance only as long as he was permitted to converse with his majesty. His ill-balanced mind and tyrannical proclivities inspired fear in his associates, and in the sixth year of his reign he was assassinated, on March 23 (N.S.; 11, O.S.), 1801, by court conspirators led by Gen. Count L. A. von Bennigsen.

C. ALEXANDER I

Paul's son and successor began his reign, as had Catherine (whom he professed to imitate), with attempts at liberal legislation, which gave place to active foreign policy and wars. There followed a new attempt at a constitutional reform, hampered by the nationalist opposition, which urged and approved the annexation of Finland and Bessarabia. The invasion of Napoleon (1812) brought the national feeling to extreme tension. The following years were devoted to the assertion of Russia's influence in Europe. The last years of the reign were marked by a reactionary policy, which provoked the first revolutionary movement in Russia.

DETAIL FROM A PORTRAIT OF ALEXANDER I PAINTED BY SIR THOMAS LAWRENCE (1769–1830)

Alexander received a careful education at the hand of his grandmother, who wished him, instead of his father, to inherit the throne. The Swiss republican F. C. de La Harpe had a strong influence on him in his early years (1784–95). But this education was interrupted by Alexander's marriage at the age of 16 and did not go beyond imparting to him some general ideas unsustained by exact knowledge. His sentimental feelings were cooled by the court intrigues, by the hidden enmity between his grandmother and father, and finally by the harsh system of Paul's reign, which Alexander was expected to approve and obliged to share in. The consequence was that he grew up a past master in dissimulation and self-restraint. His evasiveness in face of other people's strong opinions was often taken for weakness. But he knew how to promote his own views, and if impeded in his designs he was capable of violent explosions of wrath.

1. Initial Liberalism.—In the first year of his reign Alexander surrounded himself with a few friends of his youth—N. N. Novosiltsev, P. A. Stroganov, Prince Adam Jerzy Czartoryski, Prince V. P. Kochubei—a "private committee" whom he wished to help him in drafting large schemes of reforms. He at once canceled a series of reactionary measures of Paul and declared his desire to abolish arbitrariness and to inaugurate a reign of law. Public opinion received Alexander with enthusiasm. But the private committee, which met regularly from 1801 till the end of 1803, found dangerous and untimely both a formal declaration limiting the autocrat's power and the abolition of serfdom. The most important fruit of these good intentions was the introduction of ministries instead of the colleges of Peter the Great, which had been practically abolished by Catherine. A new senate statute was intended to make this institution the highest legal authority (1802).

A very cautious *ukaz* of 1803 permitted noble landowners to liberate their serfs, granting them at the same time parcels of land. Only 47,000 serfs were to be thus liberated. Somewhat larger measures limited the power of landowners over the serfs in Livonia and Estonia (1804–05). A new and important impulse was given to public education, which was considered to be a preliminary condition to all substantial reforms. Three new universities were created.

Since 1801 Alexander had feared the consequences of Napoleon's ambition, and in 1804 he joined a new coalition against France formed by England. He was involved in wars which ended in crushing defeats at Austerlitz and Friedland. He then changed his policy and concluded an accord with Napoleon directed against England, whose commerce with the continent had to be forbidden in all countries which adhered to this continental system. At his personal meeting with Napoleon at Tilsit (June 25, 1807) Alexander played a part which made Napoleon call him a "northern Talma" (a renowned actor) and a "Byzantine Greek." But he was in part genuinely under Napoleon's influence and was entangled in other wars: with Sweden, which finished with Russian annexation of Finland (1809), and with Turkey, which lasted for six full years (1806–12) and ended with Russian annexation of Bessarabia. A year after the Tilsit meeting (Oct. 12, 1808) Alexander again met Napoleon, at Erfurt, but Napoleon's intention to raise the Polish question did not please Alexander. Relations were very strained by the end of 1810.

Conservative opinion was very much incensed against Alexander's alliance with the "Corsican usurper," especially as at that very time another and more serious attempt was made to introduce in Russia a constitutional government. Mikhail Mikhailovich Speranski, a prominent statesman whose views were favoured by

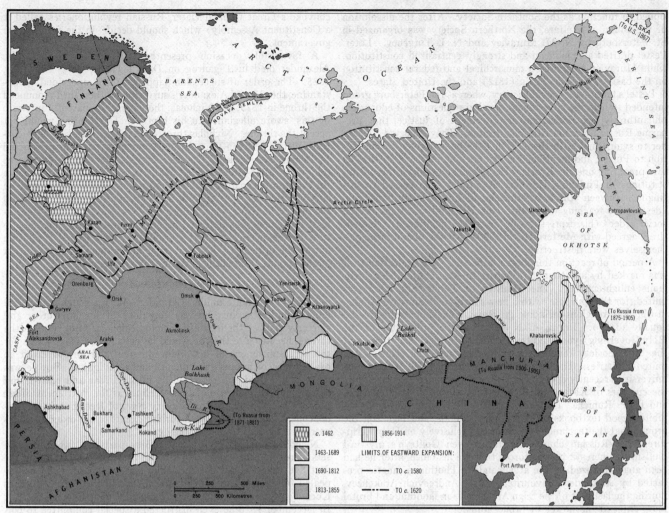

RUSSIAN TERRITORIAL ACQUISITIONS IN ASIA BEFORE 1914

the emperor at that time, prepared a moderate scheme based on the introduction of self-government in four stages, beginning with electoral assemblies (dumas) in the cantons and ending at the top with the duma of the state. Each lower duma elected deputies to the upper one: cantonal to district, district to provincial; these latter sent all their members to the state duma, a legislative assembly deprived of legislative initiative but enjoying the right to make motions concerning the interest of the state, the responsibility of functionaries, and the violation of fundamental laws. The senate retained only judicial power, while the newly reformed ministries remained organs of the executive. The council of state, composed of high dignitaries and presided over by the emperor, was to prepare drafts of laws. In fact, nothing except the council of state and the reformed ministries was realized. Conservative opinion, as represented by nobility and bureaucracy, was furious with Speranski, and the emperor did not choose to defend him. On a futile pretext Speranski was dismissed from his office of imperial secretary and sent into exile (1812). His successor was an extreme nationalist and conservative, Adm. A. S. Shishkov.

2. Nationalism and Reaction.—When the War of 1812 began, the patriotic feeling reached its pitch. It was to be a Scythian war—a war of retreat. Time and space were to be the chief allies of Russia, whose military forces were one-half or one-third the size of Napoleon's. And, indeed, the deeper Napoleon penetrated into Russia's endless plain the more equal the chances became. Alexander named M. I. Kutuzov commander in chief (in the place of M. B. Barclay de Tolly) and Count F. V. Rostopchin governor of Moscow, the capture of which was the final aim of Napoleon's strategy. After the bloody but undecided battle at Borodino (*see* BORODINO, BATTLE OF) Moscow was abandoned by its residents. For five weeks of his stay in the city Napoleon waited in vain for

a peace proposal. Moscow was burned by the inhabitants and by the marauders of the Grand Army. The latter was in process of dissolution, and winter was approaching. Then followed the famous retreat, during which the Grand Army was nearly annihilated, and the wars of liberation of 1813 and 1814, which brought Alexander and his army to Paris. (*See* further NAPOLEONIC WARS.)

All these events produced an enormous impression on the sensitive temperament of Alexander. "The fire of Moscow," he said later to the German pastor R. F. Eylert, "lit up my soul, I then got to know God and became another man." Alexander now found in the Bible the proofs of his mission and proposed to his allies to establish a Holy Alliance (*q.v.*), a monarch's league based on the precepts of the Scriptures. At the Congress of Vienna (1815) Alexander figured as a saviour of Europe, and he continued to play a leading part at Aix-la-Chapelle (1818), Troppau (Opava) and Laibach (Ljubljana, 1820–21), and Verona (1822).

3. The Revolutionary Movement.—Quite different were the impressions brought back to Russia by the younger generation of officers who took part in the Napoleonic Wars. Many of them while abroad read political newspapers and were present at the debates of representative assemblies. They learned to quote the books of J. L. Delolme, Count A. Destutt de Tracy, Benjamin Constant, Gaetano Filangieri, Baron Louis Bignon, etc. After their return to Russia they were shocked by the contrast of arbitrary rule, the abuses of bureaucracy, the venality and secrecy of the courts, the sufferings of the serfs, and the indifference to popular education. The secret Union of Salvation (later called the Society of True and Loyal Sons of the Motherland) was established in 1816 but was soon closed. The Union of Welfare, founded in 1818, was disbanded in 1821, but its Southern Board in the Ukraine, led by Pavel Ivanovich Pestel, ignored the dissolution order and con-

tinued to function as the Southern Society. After the dissolution
of the Union of Welfare, the Northern Society was organized in
St. Petersburg by N. M. Muraviev and N. I. Turgenev. Later,
Pestel drafted a republican and strongly centralized constitution,
while Muraviev composed a monarchical and federal constitution
on the basis of those of Spain (1812) and the United States.

Pestel's tactics were revolutionary, whereas the Petersburg group
intended to help the government openly in questions of education,
philanthropy, economics, and improvement of justice, thus preparing Russia for a constitutional regime. They expected Alexander to sympathize with them, as in 1815 he had given a constitution to Poland and mentioned at the opening of the *sejm* that he
was preparing one for Russia. He also acknowledged the old institutions of Finland. However, Alexander soon ceased to distinguish between "the holy principles of liberal institutions" and
"destructive teaching which threatens a calamitous attack on the
social order" (his expressions in the speech mentioned). He entirely agreed with Metternich (in 1820) that the liberal principles
themselves were destructive.

A period of reaction thus began in Russia. The transition to it
was marked by an attempt to impart to Russia Alexander's religious enlightenment. The Ministry of Public Education was
united, for that purpose, with a new Ministry of Spiritual Affairs,
in which all religions including the Russian Orthodox were treated
equally (1817). Prince A. N. Golitsyn, the procurator of the
Holy Governing Synod and the president of the Russian branch of
the Bible Society founded in 1814, was made the chief of the
united ministries. The consequence was that in 1819–21 the young
universities recently opened were entirely destroyed—especially by
the curators of Kazan and Petersburg circuits, M. L. Magnitski,
and D. P. Runich. They removed the best professors and prohibited good textbooks on natural law, morals, and logic, on the
ground that the teaching must be based exclusively on Holy Scripture. For Russian church dignitaries even Golitsyn's mystical
pietism was heresy: he was forced to leave his office, after he had
been anathematized by the archimandrite Photius, a fanatic protected by Alexander's favourite, Aleksei Andreevich Arakcheev.
During the last part of the reign Arakcheev, an ignorant and brutal
man, enjoyed the power of prime minister.

Under these conditions secret societies changed their character.
The measures of Alexander convinced them that monarchs' promises are not to be relied upon. They were also impressed by military pronunciamentos in Spain
and Naples (1820). Turgenev
recorded in his diary in 1820:
"We formerly asked, every time
we met the readers of newspapers
in the club, whether there was a
new constitution. Now we ask
whether there is a new revolution." One may judge of the
impression produced on the officers of the guard when they
learned that they had to stifle the
Neapolitan uprising, by orders of
the Laibach Congress.

The constitutionalists were losing ground; radical elements even
among them (like the poet K. F.
Ryleev) began to prevail. Proposals of regicide were heard
from P. G. Kakhovski and A. I.
Yakubovich but were rejected or
indefinitely postponed. In any
case, revolutionary tactics were
considered inevitable, but no definite scheme was in preparation.
Suggestions were made for forcing the emperor, at some favourable opportunity, to nominate a
liberal ministry under Speranski
and N. S. Mordvinov, who would

convoke a Great Council (later, Russian revolutionaries called it
a Constituent Assembly) which should decide on the form of the
government.

A favourable occasion presented itself quite unexpectedly.
Alexander died in Taganrog on Dec. 1 (N.S.; Nov. 19, O.S.),
1825. The order of succession happened to be undecided. Constantine, the elder of Alexander's surviving brothers, had renounced
the throne in 1823, but Nicholas, the younger, apparently unaware
of this, swore allegiance to his brother. Constantine would not
accept the throne. Nicholas threatened to leave Russia. The correspondence between Warsaw and Petersburg was thus protracted
for about two weeks. The Decembrists (*see* DEKABRISTS), as
they were called later, decided finally to raise the guard regiments
for Constantine against Nicholas and to force Nicholas—in case he
survived that day—to appoint a liberal ministry which would do
the rest. The rising was a failure (*see* NICHOLAS I). The Decembrist movement was defeated because its leaders did not dare to
turn to the masses, and as conspirators they lacked resolution
during the uprising; but it served as an ominous prognostication
of the coming democratic revolutionary movement.

D. NICHOLAS I

Nicholas was quite unlike Alexander. With a rough nature and
limited understanding, he was conscious of his inferiority and
sincerely disliked the idea of becoming emperor. But once on the
throne, he was sure that he would be enlightened from above for
the accomplishment of his divine mission, and he conceived an
exalted idea of his personal dignity and infallibility. But he was
no mystic. Cold and reserved, he inspired fear and hatred, and
he consciously made use of these feelings as the instrument of his
power. His aim was to freeze every germ of free thought and independent moral feeling, as disturbing agents of the order of things
entrusted by God to his personal care.

Nicholas' reign is divided into three parts by two European
sets of revolutions: those of 1830 and those of 1848. During the
first five years he did not feel quite sure of himself, and he appealed for help to advisers of Alexander's liberal period, such as
Kochubei, Speranski, and E. F. Kankrin (Count Georg Cancrin).
In December 1826 he even instructed a special committee to collect for him all useful hints about necessary reforms. While
punishing severely the Decembrists (five of them were hanged,
others sent to Siberia), he wished to make use of all their good

SOVFOTO

NICHOLAS I (MOUNTED ON WHITE HORSE AT LEFT) ORDERING CANNON TO BE FIRED ON THE DECEMBRIST REBELS,
DEC. 26, 1825. PAINTING BY K. I. KOLMAN

ideas. But he reserved for himself the control over public opinion and confided to Count A. Kh. Benckendorff (*q.v.*) the organization of a new secret police of gendarmes controlled by the "third section" of the personal and imperial chancery. Nicholas adopted Alexander's policy of protecting the kings from their peoples, but he made an exception for Christian Turkish subjects (in the first place the Greeks). He thus carried on a war against Turkey (1828–29). By the Treaty of Adrianople, Greece was liberated; the hospodars of the Danubian principalities were to be appointed for life and free from Turkish interference in internal affairs. The Straits (the Dardanelles and the Bosporus) and the Black Sea were to be open. (*See* EASTERN QUESTION.)

Nicholas especially attended to education; he wished to clear it of everything politically dangerous and confine it to the upper class. He abolished the liberal university statutes of Alexander (1804); by the new statutes of 1835 he detached the primary education intended for the lower classes from the gymnasiums and universities, where only children of gentry and of officials were to be admitted.

The expulsion of Charles X from France and the Polish insurrection of 1830–31 determined the legitimist tendency of Nicholas' foreign policy; he wished to become a real "policeman" of Europe, and at Münchengrätz (Mnichovo Hradiste), in September 1833, he renewed relations with Metternich. But his excessive interest in the "sick man" in Constantinople finished by rousing Europe against him. In 1833 Nicholas saved the sultan from the Egyptian rebel Mohammed Ali, and by the treaty of Unkiar-Skelessi (July 8, 1833) appeared to receive for that service free passage for Russian ships to the Mediterranean, while to all other powers the Dardanelles were to be closed during wartime. This concession drew the attention of the European powers, and in 1841 all the five great powers agreed that the Dardanelles should be closed to warships of all nations.

1. Slavophils and Westernizers.—In sharp contrast with Nicholas' educational policy, a new generation grew up which was bred by Russian universities, especially Moscow University, between 1830 and 1848. They were not politicians or liberals of a Franco-English type. They were idealists and students of the philosophy of Schelling, Fichte, and Hegel. In Moscow literary salons they did not discuss the form of the government, but dug deep into the very foundations of Russian history and the Russian national mind. Most of them declared that Russia was unlike Europe and that its type of civilization was potentially far higher than the European. They execrated Peter the Great's Europeanization of Russia as a fatal deviation from the genuine course of Russian history, and they wanted Russia to come back to the forsaken principles of the Eastern Church and state—to orthodoxy and autocracy. The majority of public opinion, led by A. I. Herzen, V. G. Belinski, Mikhail Bakunin, T. N. Granovski, and others, revolted against this Slavophil doctrine. They opposed to it their own doctrine of the Western origin of Russian civilization. Herzen and Bakunin emigrated from Russia on the approach of the revolutions of 1848. They became the originators of Russian socialism, and Herzen saw socialist elements in the Russian peasants' commune (mir).

Nicholas was not insensible to the chief social question in Russia —that of serfdom. How could he be when peasants' uprisings were steadily growing in frequency? They numbered about 41 in the first four years of his reign, and there were 378 between 1830 and 1849 and 137 during the last five years. Nicholas formed a series of secret committees which, after many failures, prepared the law of 1842 on voluntary accords, which abolished personal serfdom and fixed the amount of peasant lots and payments. Through P. D. Kiselev's energy, the same changes were introduced in Poland (1846) and in Russian provinces (1847).

A real persecution of intellectuals began after the revolutions of 1848. A secret committee, presided over by D. P. Buturlin, was founded to punish press offenses. S. S. Uvarov himself was found too liberal, and he resigned. His successor, Prince P. A. Shirinski-Shikhmatov, wished to "base all teaching on religious truth." The university chairs of philosophy were closed, the number of students limited; many writers were arrested, exiled, or otherwise punished. The private circle of followers of M. V. Butashevich-Petrashevski, a young socialist, was sent to forced labour in Siberia (including Fedor Dostoevski) for having read and discussed prohibited literature.

2. The Crimean War.—Nicholas also wished to dictate his will to Europe. "Submit yourselves, ye peoples, for God is with us": thus ended his manifesto published on April 8 (N.S.; March 27, O.S.), 1848. He sent a Russian army to subdue Hungary when it revolted against the Habsburgs. A few years later he inadvertently provoked a conflict with Turkey, because of a special question on the distribution of holy places in Jerusalem between Catholic and Orthodox priests, which he involved with the question of the general protectorate of Russia over Christian subjects of the sultan. European powers would not admit this protectorate, and Nicholas found against himself not only Napoleon III and England but also "thankless Austria." On Oct. 23 (N.S.), 1853, Turkish forces attacked the advanced Russian troops in the Danubian principalities; on Nov. 1, Russia declared war on Turkey. France and England declared war on Russia on March 27, 1854. The courage displayed in the defense of Sevastopol proved useless, as the whole fabric of Russian bureaucratic and autocratic government appeared incapable of competing with European technique. Corruption and lack of communication, feeble development of industry, and financial deficiency deprived the valiant soldiers of the most necessary means of defense. (*See* further CRIMEAN WAR; TURKEY.) Nicholas died in St. Petersburg on March 2 (N.S.; Feb. 18, O.S.), 1855, feeling that all his system was doomed to destruction. A wholesale change of regime was indicated to his son and successor, Alexander II. (P. M.)

E. ALEXANDER II

The emperor Alexander II (*q.v.*), a man of weak character but good-natured, possessed no steadfast views on politics. During the reign of his father he had sometimes surpassed Nicholas in reactionary intentions. But the Crimean War proved too clearly the danger of Nicholas' martinet system, and public opinion was too impetuous for Alexander to resist. He swam with the current, and this period coincides with the great reforms which made his reign a turning point in Russian history. But Alexander was always conscious of his power as unlimited monarch, and his liberalism ended as soon as his reforms brought with them a revival of political or autonomous tendencies. He then began to waver; the reforms were left unachieved or curtailed. Public opinion grew impatient, extremist tendencies won the ground, and the gap between the government and advanced opinion finally became insuperable. As a consequence, the original impulse for reform was exhausted as early as 1865. There followed a period of faltering which turned into a sheer reaction as the revolutionary movement grew.

1. Emancipation of the Serfs.—The greatest achievement of the era was the liberation of peasants. It paved the way for all other reforms and made them necessary. It also determined the line of future development of Russia. The chief motive which decided Alexander is clearly expressed in his words to the Moscow gentry: "The present position cannot last, and it is better to abolish serfdom from above than to wait till it begins to be abolished from below." Alexander knew, of course, of the mounting dissatisfaction of the peasants and of support of their grievances by the progressive intelligentsia. However, he met with passive opposition from the majority of the gentry, whose very existence as a class was menaced.

The preparatory discussion lasted from 1857 to March 1859, when the drafting commissions of the main committee were formed, composed of young officials enthusiastically devoted to the work of liberation. Ya. I. Rostovtsev, an honest but unskilled negotiator enjoying the full confidence of the emperor, was mediator. The program of emancipation was very moderate at the beginning, but was gradually extended, partly under the influence of the radical press and especially Herzen's *Kolokol* ("The Bell"). But Alexander wanted the initiative to belong to the gentry, and he exerted his personal influence to persuade reluctant landowners to open committees in all the provinces, while prom-

19TH-CENTURY CARTOON ON RELATIONS BETWEEN LANDOWNERS AND SERFS

Landed gentry are shown using serfs as stakes in a card game. From Gustave Doré, *Histoire Pittoresque . . . de la Sainte Russie* (1854)

ising to admit their delegates to discussion of the draft law in Petersburg. No fewer than 46 provincial committees comprising 1,366 representatives of noble proprietors were at work during 18 months preparing their own drafts for emancipation. But they held to the initial program, which was in contradiction with the more developed one. The delegates from the provincial committees were only permitted—each separately—to offer their opinions before the drafting committees.

By the law of March 3 (N.S.; Feb. 19, O.S.), 1861, the peasant became personally but formally free, and his landlord was obliged to grant him his plot for a fixed rent with the possibility of redeeming it at a price to be mutually agreed upon. The peasants remained "temporarily bonded" until they redeemed their allotments. The redemption price was calculated on the basis of all payments received by the landlord from his peasants before the reform. If the peasant desired to redeem his plot, the government paid at once to the landowner the whole price (in 5% bonds), which the peasant had to repay to the exchequer in 49 years. Although the government bonds fell to 77% and purchase was made voluntary, the great majority of landowners—often in debt—preferred to get the money at once and to end relations which had become insupportable. By 1880, 15% of the peasants had not made use of the redemption scheme, and in 1881 it was declared obligatory. The landowners tried, but in vain, to keep their power in local administration. The liberated peasants were organized in village communities that held comprehensive powers over their members. Nominally governed by elected elders, they were actually administered by crown administrative and police officials.

2. Administrative Reforms.—After the emancipation of the peasants, the complete reform of local government was necessary. It was accomplished by the law of Jan. 13 (N.S.; 1, O.S.), 1864, which introduced the district and provincial *zemstva* (county councils). Land proprietors had a relative majority in these assemblies. The gentry and officials were given (in all Russia) 42% of the seats, merchants and others 20%, while the peasants had 38%. The competence of *zemstva* included roads, hospitals, food, education, medical and veterinary service, and public welfare in general. Before the end of the century services in provinces with *zemstvo* (*q.v.*) government were far ahead of those in provinces without.

A third capital reform touched the law courts. The law of Dec. 2 (N.S.; Nov. 20, O.S.), 1864, put an end to secret procedure, venality, dependence on the government, etc. Russia received an independent court and trial by jury. The judges were irremovable; trials were held in public with oral procedure and trained

advocates. Appeals to the senate could take place only in case of irregularities in procedure.

A little later came the reforms of municipal self-government (1870) and of the army (1874). Gen. D. A. Milyutin (the brother of N. A. Milyutin) reduced the years of active service from 25, first to 15 and then, by the law of 1874, to 6 years, and made military service obligatory for all classes. The term of service was further shortened for holders of school diplomas. Military courts and military schools were humanized.

3. The Revolutionary Movements.—One branch of public life exempted from reform was the press, though it profited by the new spirit of Alexander's reign. While in the last ten years of Nicholas' reign only 6 newspapers and 19 (mostly specialist) monthlies were permitted, during the first ten years of Alexander's reign there were 66 newspapers and 156 monthlies. The general tendency of the press, very moderate at the beginning, soon became very radical. The leading spirits were the nihilists N. G. Chernyshevski, N. A. Dobrolyubov, and D. I. Pisarev, the last of whom preached extreme individualism. As early as 1862 temporary measures were applied against radical periodicals. Instead of a law on the liberty of the press, there appeared in 1865 new temporary rules (which remained in force for fully 40 years) compiled from Napoleon III's law of 1852. They set free from preliminary censorship books of more than ten sheets, but the censors continued to seize printed books before their issue.

A new wave of revolutionary movement set in. It proceeded from the young generation of university students, who expected an agrarian revolution directly after the liberation of the peasants. They were busy preparing workingmen, soldiers, and peasants for it through popular education. Secret circles were formed, proclamations were issued, and even a revolutionary movement was attempted in connection with the Polish uprising of 1863. Finally, an attempt was made by a student, D. V. Karakozov, to assassinate the tsar in April 1866. All these attempts were extremely naïve. A few young revolutionaries were executed or sent to Siberia, but the whole movement, though curtailed, was not destroyed.

Alexander was frightened. Gradually he dismissed his liberal advisers, and conservatives took their place. The Home Office was given (1861) to P. A. Valuev, who tried to paralyze the introduction of the emancipation law and formally prosecuted its faithful adherents. University troubles brought about the removal of the liberal minister of public instruction, A. V. Golovnin, the author of a university statute of 1863 that provided for university autonomy. His successor was a reactionary, Count Dimitri Andreevich Tolstoi. The old chief of gendarmes, Prince V. A. Dolgorukov, had to give place, after Karakozov's attack, to Count P. A. Shuvalov, who became the soul of reaction. The government-general of St. Petersburg was abolished, and the martinet Gen. F. F. Trepov was made grand master of the police. D. N. Zamyatnin, minister of justice, under whom the reform of tribunals was carried through, fell a victim to his defense of this reform against an imperial whim; he had to yield to an ignorant reactionary, Count K. I. Pahlen (1867), who nearly annihilated the reform. The same was done for the press by A. E. Timashev, who superseded Valuev as home minister in 1868. Two radical monthlies, the *Sovremennik* ("The Contemporary") and the *Russkoe Slovo* ("Russian Word"), were closed (1866). M. N. Katkov, a former European liberal who now inclined to extreme nationalism and reaction, became the most influential journalist.

Populism.—All this contributed to uphold and to increase the disaffection of educated public opinion. About 1869 a new young generation appeared which gave expression to that state of mind. Russian emigrants in Switzerland discussed at that time a new revolutionary doctrine later called populism (*see* NARODNIKI). P. L. Lavrov was giving it a "scientific" basis, but Bakunin found this too learned and plainly invited the youth to give up the study and go straight to the people (the slogan "going to the people" was coined by Herzen in 1861) with the aim of inducing disorder. He found this easy, since Russian peasants with their communes were born socialists. The youth of Russia, chiefly the young girls who went to study abroad as there were no institutes of learning for females in Russia, listened to these discussions in Zürich and, of course, most preferred Bakunin's active optimism to Lavrov's learning.

In 1873 they were all ordered back to Russia by the government, and they met, when at home, with many student circles which were busy distributing books and revolutionary pamphlets among their provincial branches and workingmen. N. V. Chaikovski, Prince P. A. Kropotkin, and Sergei Stepnyak (S. M. Kravchinski) were among the leaders of that educational and (later on) revolutionary work. They decided to go to the people—a naïve crusade by inexperienced youth, hardly out of their teens—in order both to teach the people and to learn from them their socialist wisdom. Of course they were not acknowledged by the people, in spite of their peasant attire, and were easily ferreted out by the police; 770 were arrested and 215 sent to prison.

Terrorism.—These active students then decided to change their tactics. A regular secret society was founded in 1876 under the name of Zemlya i Volya ("Land and Freedom" [or "Will"]). They still hoped to provoke a mass uprising according to the ideals of the people, but their village settlements proved useless for revolution, while in the towns they soon got engaged in a lively conflict with the police. As a result the terrorist side of their activity came to the forefront. In the autumn of 1879 the terrorist group formed a separate party, the Narodnaya Volya ("People's Freedom"), while the remaining members led by G. V. Plekhanov—under the name of Black Redistribution (*i.e.*, agrarian revolution)—remained inactive. A series of terrorist acts then followed, beginning with that of Vera Ivanovna Zasulich, who fired on Trepov for his having flogged a prisoner and was acquitted by the jury (1878). In April 1879 A. K. Soloviev fired five shots at the emperor. In February 1880, a workman, S. N. Khalturin, blew up the imperial dining room at the Winter Palace. The police seemed powerless against the famous Executive Committee which directed the blows, and the government asked the loyal elements of public opinion for support. The answer was given, in the name of the Chernigov *zemstvo*, by Ivan I. Petrunkevich: he said that no cooperation was possible with the government as long as public opinion was stifled. The Tver *zemstvo*, led by F. I. Rodichev, asked the emperor to "give us what he gave to Bulgaria" (*i.e.*, a constitution and political freedom).

Loris-Melikov.—After the Winter Palace explosion a supreme commission was appointed under the chairmanship of M. T. Loris-Melikov, who was given a sort of dictatorial power. Loris-Melikov's design was to isolate revolutionary elements by concessions to the liberals and, after exterminating the revolutionaries, to summon a sort of consultative assembly, thus renewing certain projects of aristocratic landowners in 1861–63. He submitted to the emperor, on Feb. 21 (N. S.; 9, O.S.), 1881, a proposal to appoint two drafting committees for administrative and financial reforms and to submit their drafts to a general commission, where experts chosen by the *zemstva* and municipalities should also be heard (two from each). The respective laws would be issued in the ordinary way by the Council of State, but 15 delegates should be admitted to its session. It did not at all look like a constitution, but it might have served as an introduction to it. Fate decided otherwise: on the very day when he signed Loris-Melikov's project, March 13 (N.S.; 1, O.S.), 1881, Alexander was assassinated by revolutionaries, led by Sofia Lvovna Perovskaya.

4. Foreign Policy.—Alexander II was more successful in his foreign policy. He ascended the throne at a moment of great exhaustion and humiliation for Russia. The Paris treaty (1856) substituted European control for a Russian protectorate over Turkish Christians; the Russian fleet in the Black Sea ceased to exist; the portion of Bessarabia nearest to the Black Sea was given to the Danubian principalities. However, Prince A. M. Gorchakov eluded Napoleon III's attempts to make an international question of the Polish uprising of 1863; Alexander then approached his relative William of Prussia and helped him against France in the foundation of the German empire. Russia made use of the Franco-German War to repudiate the provisions of the Paris treaty forbidding Russia to construct naval arsenals and to keep a fleet in the Black Sea (1870). In 1872 the German, Austrian, and Russian emperors met at Berlin and concluded the Three Emperors' Alliance (or Dreikaiserbund), without any formal treaty being signed. The Russo-Austrian and the Russo-German secret military conventions concluded on Oct. 22, 1873, were by-products of the Berlin meeting, but they seemingly had no effect on the subsequent course of events. In 1875 there were persistent, though unfounded, reports of an impending German attack on France. Gorchakov, much to Bismarck's annoyance, assumed the role of champion of France and European peace and claimed credit for averting the imaginary conflagration. In the same year the Eastern Question (*q.v.*) was reopened by a rising of Christian Slavs in Bosnia-Hercegovina. In May 1876 began the Bulgarian uprising.

Russia proposed cooperative action to the powers, but meeting with hidden aid to Turkey from Disraeli, Alexander decided to act alone. When Serbia and Montenegro declared war on Turkey he met Francis Joseph at Reichstadt, and on July 13 (N.S.), 1876, concluded an agreement in which the possibilities of defeat, victory, or the collapse of Turkey were anticipated. In the event of a Turkish defeat, Austria was to receive Bosnia-Hercegovina for occupation and administration; Russia was permitted to take back the lost portion of Bessarabia. A last attempt to formulate a European program of pacification of the Balkans was made by the powers at the Constantinople conference (November 1876). After its failure Count Nikolai P. Ignatiev, the Russian ambassador to Turkey, visited the European capitals to discuss the possibility of war. Austria and England put as conditions of their neutrality: no attack on Constantinople; no Russian territorial acquisitions; no thrusting Serbia into war; Bulgaria, in case of its liberation, not to be under direct Russian control. Thus, Russia was in advance deprived of possible gains in case of victory; as a matter of fact, Disraeli looked for its defeat. Nevertheless, on April 24 (N.S.), 1877, Alexander went to war (*see* RUSSO-TURKISH WARS). Close to the walls of Constantinople the Russian army was stopped by the British fleet, and the Treaty of San Stefano (March 3, 1878), favourable to the Bulgarians, was emasculated at the Congress of Berlin (*q.v.*). Russian public opinion, ignorant of the agreements concluded before the war, was much incensed against Bismarck, "the honest broker." Russia received the lost part of Bessarabia, and Kars, Ardahan, and Batum in Transcaucasia.

Far more important were the acquisitions of Alexander in Asia. From 1864 his generals were active against Kirgiz and Turkmen tribesmen who raided the unprotected frontier of Siberia. Russian soldiers marched up the Syr-Darya, subjugated Bukhara, and from there, through the desert of Khiva, reached the Caspian shore. In 1867 the territory between Issyk-Kul and the Aral Sea was constituted into a province called Turkistan, and in 1884 another province under the title of Transcaspia was formed of territories between the Amu-Darya and the Caspian Sea. Russia reached the frontiers of Afghanistan and Chinese Turkistan, while in the Far East, by the Treaty of Aigun (Ai-hun; 1858), it obtained, from China, territory running east from the Amur and Ussuri rivers to the Pacific seaboard, and the naval base of Vladivostok was founded. Japan ceded Sakhalin in 1875 in exchange for two Kuril islands. In 1867 Alaska was sold to the United States for $7,200,000.

5. Industrial Progress.—Under Alexander II Russia made further steps toward industrialization. The length of railway increased from 644 mi. (1857) to 2,260 (1867) and to 11,070 (1876).

Factory production grew from 352,000,000 rubles (1863) to 909,-000,000 (1879); the number of workingmen from 419,000 to 769,000; the export of grain from 52,800 bu. (1860–62) to 125,600 (1872–74). In 1850 and 1857 Russia (for the second time since 1819) tried the experiment of freer trade, but as it brought with it an excess of imports—a thing unusual in Russia—M. K. Reutern, the minister of finance in 1862–78, returned to the protectionist system of Kankrin (1823–44). He also favoured the organization, for the first time in Russia, of private credit institutions. The 10 land banks which were in existence at the end of the 19th century were all founded in 1871–73; there were also 28 commerical banks (founded 1864–73), 222 municipal banks (1862–73), and 71 societies of mutual credit (1877).

F. Alexander III

1. Administration and Economy.—Alexander III succeeded his father and was at first expected to continue his tradition. But the quasi-constitutional scheme of Loris-Melikov, discussed in March in the Winter Palace, met with the opposition of K. P. Pobedonostsev, the former tutor of Alexander, and his most trusted adviser. On May 11 (N.S.; April 29, O.S.), 1881, appeared a manifesto written by Pobedonostsev without the ministers' knowledge, in which the emperor described himself as "chosen to defend" autocratic power. At the same time a promise was made to continue Alexander II's reforms. Loris-Melikov, with Gen. D. A. Milyutin, at once resigned and was replaced by N. P. Ignatiev, a friend of the Slavophils, who promised to leave untouched the powers of the *zemstva* and municipalities and to alleviate the burdens of the peasants. And indeed, in June and September 1881, Ignatiev summoned the experts selected by the government among liberal *zemstvo* men. With their help he drafted a scheme for lowering the redemption prices, abolishing the poll tax, and regulating internal colonization and land rents. The new minister of finance, N. Kh. Bunge, assisted by opening a peasants' bank; he also enacted the first factory acts (1882) and appointed special factory inspectors to enforce their application. A special commission under M. S. Kakhanov (1881–84) prepared a reform of peasant self-government based on the principle of reducing the legal disabilities of the peasantry. In May 1882 Ignatiev proposed to Alexander to summon a *zemski sobor* in Moscow of about 3,000 representatives from all classes, on the day of the coronation.

Here M. N. Katkov and Pobedonostsev won their victory. Ignatiev resigned; the reactionary Count D. A. Tolstoi took his place as home minister. His tool I. D. Delyanov had enacted in his former ministry a new reactionary statute for the universities (1884). Tolstoi now became the mouthpiece of the nobility and gentry, a decaying class that tried to preserve as much as possible of its vanishing power and property. In 1885 a special Bank for the Nobility was opened with the aim of preserving the landed property of the gentry from final liquidation (for debt). Then Tolstoi proposed to A. D. Pazukhin—a sworn defender of noble privileges—to revise the *zemstvo* institution with the aim of making the nobles' influence paramount in the countryside. As a result, two important laws were published, on Aug. 3 (N.S.; July 22, O.S.), 1889, on land captains, and on June 24 (N.S.; 12, O.S.), 1890, on *zemstva*. The land captains were appointed by the home minister from the local landowners and were vested with practically unlimited powers over the peasantry, their communities, and their elected officials. The composition of district *zemstvo* assemblies was changed from the figures given above to 5,433 representatives of landed owners (57%), 1,273 municipal representatives (13%), and 2,817 representatives of village communities. However, the chief aim of the government was, rather than to favour the gentry, to incorporate both the land captains and the executive boards of the *zemstva* in its civil service by making them subordinate to the provincial governors.

An outstanding feature of Alexander III's reign was an increased persecution of everything dissimilar to the officially accepted national type. Dissenting sects, the Catholic Eastern Rite churches and the Lutherans in the western provinces, Lamaist Kalmyks and Buryats, and especially Jews, suffered a systematic persecution. The press was muzzled, revolutionary organizations were destroyed,

and revolutionary movement was stifled. Public opinion was silent until the great famine of 1891; from that year symptoms of a revival appeared. The new movement was different from the populism of the '60s and '70s. The Russian socialists became Marxists. Russia, they argued, was becoming an industrial country, and the numbers of the industrial proletariat were speedily increasing. In fact, I. A. Vyshnegradski, minister of finance since 1887, not only continued Reutern's policy in developing the railway (14,900 mi. at the beginning, 24,000 mi. at the end of Alexander's reign) and in protecting industry (prohibitive tariff, 1891) but also tried to influence the foreign market and to stabilize the rate of exchange of the Russian ruble. He also resorted to foreign capital. In 1889–94 its influx was 5,300,000 rubles, as compared with 1,500,000 during 1851–88. However, the position of the Russian consumer, who had to pay about 34% ad valorem for imported goods, instead of 13% as before the tariff of 1891, was much worsened. The peasants especially suffered, as the price of grain, their only article for sale, fell from 1.19 rubles per *pud* (1881) to 0.59 in 1894, while their allotments, which were insufficient at the moment of liberation, further diminished (1861–1900) to 54.2%. As a result, their arrears of taxes increased more than five times compared with 1871–80. Vyshnegradski tried to relieve the treasury by increasing enormously the customs and excise. In the decade 1883–92 taxation increased 29% while the population increased only 16%. Thus, elements of an agrarian crisis were increasing as the 19th century was nearing its end.

2. Foreign Policy.—Alexander III's foreign policy was peaceful. He wished to be his own foreign minister; Gorchakov gave place to a submissive Germanophile, N. K. Giers. Bismarck profited by this and, in spite of his alliance with Austria (1879), which was avowedly concluded against Russia, contrived to renew as early as 1881 the Dreikaiserbund of 1873. In 1884 it was renewed for three following years, and in 1887, as Austria seceded, Bismarck concluded his famous "reinsurance" treaty with Russia. All these treaties fettered Russia in its Balkan policy but secured the country against the opening of the Straits to England. As at the same time the Triple Alliance with Italy was concluded (1882), Bismarck's policy proved too complicated for his successor, Count Leo Caprivi, and in 1890 a Russian proposal to prolong the "reinsurance" treaty for the next six years was rejected. Thus the way was opened to a Franco-Russian *rapprochement* at a time when Germany was courting England, Russia's competitor in Asia (where Alexander in 1884 took Merv, thereby establishing Russia on the frontiers of Afghanistan). France opened to Russia its market for loans and its factories for armaments in 1889; a French squadron was enthusiastically received in Kronshtadt in 1891; and the subsequent *rapprochement* culminated in a military convention worked out in August 1892 and ratified by an exchange of letters in December 1893–January 1894.

Alexander III died at Livadia on Nov. 1 (N.S.; Oct. 20, O.S.), 1894.   (P. M.; M. T. F.)

G. Nicholas II

The death of Alexander III, like that of Nicholas I nearly 40 years earlier, aroused widespread hopes of a milder regime and of social reforms. Nicholas II (*q.v.*) had neither the imposing physical presence nor the strong will of his father. He had all the virtues of a father of a family and a country gentleman and would have had a happy and useful life as a private landowner. He had little taste for the splendours of monarchy and even less ability to handle the cumbrous, complex, and antiquated mechanism of Russian government. Unfortunately he had little aptitude for choosing good subordinates or delegating authority to them. His personal charm at first captured those who came into contact with him, but his tendency to change his mind, to agree with the last person he had been talking to, was the cause of many disappointments and won him a reputation for bad faith. His wife, Princess Alexandra (*q.v.*) of Hesse, a granddaughter of Queen Victoria, to whom he was utterly devoted, was of an imperious nature, with a much stronger will than the emperor's, and greatly influenced him.

1. Reassertion of Autocratic Principles.—Moderate liberal opinion received an early rebuff when at a reception of *zemstva* delegates on Jan. 29 (N.S.; 17, O.S.), 1895, he denounced as "senseless dreams" any suggestion of "participation of *zemstva* representatives in internal government." On the contrary, he intended to defend the principles of autocracy "as unswervingly" as his late father had. Nicholas indeed, under the influence of Pobedonostsev, believed the maintenance of autocracy to be a sacred obligation toward God himself. This view was consistently supported by the empress, who, since her official conversion to Orthodoxy before marriage to Nicholas, had become a devoted believer in the doctrines of the Russian church. When in 1904 a

CULVER PICTURES, INC.

NICHOLAS II, LAST OF THE RUSSIAN TSARS

male heir, Grand Duke Alexis, was born, the emperor felt that it was his duty to maintain the imperial heritage unimpaired—that is, with autocracy unchanged—for his son. The precarious health of the prince, who had inherited hemophilia through his mother, strengthened this conviction.

2. Administration and Economy.—During the first ten years of the reign, industrial progress continued rapidly, while agriculture lagged behind and the political system remained the same. The lack of any central direction of government, the absence of a prime minister, was more seriously felt under the weak Nicholas than under Alexander III. Uncoordinated by the emperor, the several departments of government pursued separate and even contradictory policies. The Ministry of Interior stood for paternalist principles. The improvement of agriculture and the protection of the peasants were its concern: no other authority must meddle. If the ministry was unwilling to introduce changes, nobody else must do so. The result of this mentality was that the *zemstva*, several of which had plans for valuable nonpolitical reforms that could be carried out by their own personnel locally, found themselves deprived of sufficient revenue, and their initiative obstructed, by the jealousy of the Ministry of Interior. The agricultural policy of the ministry was based on the maintenance of the village commune, which it regarded as a stronghold of peasant conservatism.

The Ministry of Finance, on the other hand, objected to the commune as a source of inefficiency, preventing the development of the initiative of the most enterprising farmers and consequent improvement of agricultural output. The Ministry of Finance in general supported individual business initiative in contrast to the Ministry of Interior's paternalism and old-fashioned collectivism. The Ministry of Finance may be said to have approximately reflected the aspirations of the rising Russian business class, the Interior those of the bureaucratic and landowning classes.

The most able minister of finance of this period was S. Yu. Witte (1892–1903). In his period of office, the metallurgical industry of the Ukraine made rapid progress. He was able to introduce the gold standard in 1897, and this proved an incentive for a substantial influx of foreign capital into Russian industry. In these years, too, the industrial working class grew rapidly. There were several big strikes in St. Petersburg in 1896 and 1897, and in the latter year Witte introduced a law imposing a maximum of 11½ hours work for all day workers and 10 hours for all engaged in night work. From 1899 to 1903 Russian industry suffered a depression, and unemployment grew. In these conditions the workers were unable to obtain further economic concessions from employers, but there were numerous short political strikes and street demonstrations, in some cases accompanied by violence.

3. Russification Policy.—The policy of russification of the non-Russian peoples of the empire, which had been a characteristic of the reign of Alexander III, continued. Nicholas II held anti-

Semitic views and favoured the continued discrimination, in economic and cultural life, against the Jews. Russification of the German schools in the Baltic provinces continued, and the old university of Dorpat (Estonian Tartu), which had been closed in 1893, was reopened as the Russian university of Yuriev. In the central provinces of European Russia, Orthodox missionaries continued their efforts to compete with Muslim Tatar missionaries for the conversion of the small, still partly pagan, Finno-Ugrian peoples of this area.

In Armenia, an imperial decree of June 25 (N.S.), 1903, transferred to Russian administration the national fund of the Armenian Church, which was formed by the individual subscriptions of Armenian Christians and had been used for the social and educational needs of the Armenian community. By this action the government turned against itself quite gratuitously the most loyal of all the non-Russian peoples, whose hatred of Turkey had long bound it devotedly to the cause of the empire. The confiscation of the fund was followed by large-scale passive resistance by the Armenians, who boycotted the Russian law courts, schools, and administrative authorities.

Similar resistance was provoked in Finland by the military conscription law of 1898 and by the imperial manifesto of February 1899, which stated that imperial decrees should have precedence in Finland over Finnish laws, and thus threatened to reduce the Finnish diet to the status of a provincial assembly. The Finnish people as a whole met these actions with passive resistance, but terrorism was also used, and in June 1904 the Russian governor-general, Gen. N. I. Bobrikov, was murdered by a Finn, Eugene Shauman.

4. Resurgence of Revolutionary Activity.—Among the Russian people political opposition revived in the late 1890s. Its most visible expressions were student demonstrations, which were especially violent in 1899 and 1900, and in some of which factory workers joined. Cossacks charged the demonstrators, many were arrested, some were conscripted into the army (where they only spread their political ideas) or merely expelled from the university. Students inclined not only to revolutionary doctrines— whether Populist socialism or Marxism—but also to terrorism. The assassins of the minister of education, N. P. Bogolepov, in February 1901, and of the minister of interior, D. S. Sipyagin, in April 1902, were both students.

In March 1898 representatives of several illegal Marxist groups met in Minsk to found the Russian Social Democratic Workers' Party (R.S.D.W.P.). Its leaders, however, were almost immediately arrested by the police, and the Social Democratic movement took political shape among Russian exiles in Western Europe. At its second congress in 1903, held partly in Brussels and partly in London, appeared the rift between the followers of V. I. Ulyanov (Lenin) and the rest. Lenin maintained that the party should be confined to full-time "professional revolutionaries," while Y. O. Tsederbaum (Martov) and others preferred as their aim a mass working-class party, without stringent conditions for membership, similar to the German or other Western European socialist parties. Lenin took for his faction the name Bolshevik (derived from *bolshinstvo*, "majority"), because it had won a majority in the election of the party's key bodies. His opponents became known as Mensheviks (*menshinstvo*, "minority"). In fact, in the following decade the factions within the movement were extremely fluid, and no single group for any length of time had clear majority support among the party membership.

The various Populist illegal groups in Russia also made efforts to unite, and at a conference held in 1902 in Switzerland they formed a Party of Socialist Revolutionaries (S.R.'s). This party's leadership, like that of the Social Democrats, came principally from the intelligentsia. Its aim was to appeal above all to the peasants, whereas the Social Democrats laid the main emphasis on the industrial working class. In practice it was hard to establish contact with peasants, because of their scattered distribution and the comparative ease with which the police could observe the entry of strangers into villages. Consequently the S.R.'s no less than the Social Democrats found their mass support in the cities. Neither party had a monopoly of proletarian support.

5. Other Political Movements.—Russian liberalism also became organized in this period. Two trends may be roughly distinguished—a cautious, limited constitutionalism favoured mainly by enlightened conservatives among the landed gentry and officers of the *zemstva*, and a radical liberalism which insisted on full parliamentary and responsible government and drew its support mainly from the urban professional classes. The second trend, forming a secret Union of Liberation, expressed its views in the weekly paper *Osvobozhdenie* ("Liberation"), published in Germany and edited by the former Marxist P. B. Struve.

Political parties also appeared among the non-Russian nationalities. Estonian, Latvian, and Lithuanian nationalist movements took form, led by middle-class professional people and supported by peasants. In Poland there were two main parties, the National Democratic Party, which stood for moderate democracy, and the Polish Socialist Party. Both wished self-government for Poland, and independence if possible. But the extremist "Social Democracy of Poland and Lithuania" bitterly opposed all Polish nationalism and aimed at a single socialist republic for the whole territory of the Russian Empire. In the Ukraine, the first political party to take the view that there was a separate Ukrainian nation, and to claim autonomy for it, was the Revolutionary Ukrainian Party, founded in 1901. It split soon into socialist, radical, and conservative nationalist sections. Both the Polish and the Ukrainian movements received help from their kinsmen in Austrian Galicia. Among Russian Jews, the main trends in these years were on the one hand various forms of socialism, on the other the new international movement of Zionism. In Armenia the Dashnak (national socialist) Party resembled, in ideas and methods, the Russian S.R.'s. In Georgia by far the strongest group was social democracy, of the Menshevik branch. Finally, among the Muslims of Russia a democratic movement was growing, in favour of secularism, modernization, emancipation of women, and political liberty. Its main centre was Kazan, its social leadership came from Tatar merchants and school teachers.

6. Foreign Policy and the Russo-Japanese War.—Russian foreign policy in the 1890s was concerned above all with the Far East. The inability of Nicholas II to decide between contradictory policies urged by different advisers was a major factor in the drift toward war with Japan. Russia refused to make a bargain with Japan, leaving it Korea in return for Russian dominance in northern Manchuria, or even in all Manchuria. By insisting on having all Manchuria and all Korea, it forced Japan first to ally itself with Britain and then to go to war with Russia. (*See* RUSSO-JAPANESE WAR.) The war brought a series of defeats to Russia, culminating in the destruction of the Baltic Fleet in the Straits of Tsushima in May 1905. It was fortunate for Russia that Japan too was exhausted by its efforts, so that peace could be concluded at Portsmouth, N.H., on fairly favourable terms. Russia abandoned all claims to Korea and surrendered Port Arthur and the South Manchurian Railway, but was able to retain its position in northern Manchuria and its control of the Chinese Eastern Railway, so essential for communication between Siberia and Vladivostok. Russia also kept the northern half of Sakhalin and did not have to pay an indemnity.

7. Revolution of 1905 and the First and Second Dumas.—Defeat by Japan brought revolution in Russia. On Sunday, Jan. 22 (N.S.; 9, O.S.), 1905, about 1,000 workers were killed when police fired on a peaceful demonstration in front of the Winter Palace in St. Petersburg. During the spring and summer the *zemstvo* constitutionalists became more outspoken in their political demands, strikes increased, and there were agrarian riots in many provinces. At the end of October a general strike, more political than economic, paralyzed the communications system of the empire. Delegates of strike committees in St. Petersburg formed a *soviet* ("council") of workers' deputies, which for a time looked as if it might develop into a revolutionary government of Russia. With extreme reluctance, Nicholas II agreed to issue a manifesto to the people on Oct. 30 (N.S.; 17, O.S.). Drafted by Witte, it promised to set up an elected legislature (*duma*) and to grant political and civil liberties. The emperor also instituted a Council of Ministers, with a president (the equivalent of a prime minister), and entrusted this office to Witte.

This was much less than the constituent assembly which the liberation movement had demanded. But the liberals, frightened by the scope of the revolution, decided to operate the new system, while the Marxists and Populists decided to boycott it. In the election to the First Duma the largest number of votes went to the Constitutional Democrats (*Kadets*), as the liberals of the Union of Liberation now called themselves. The second most numerous group in the Duma were the Labour group (*Trudoviki*), persons of Populist outlook who had stood for election though the S.R. party had officially boycotted the election. The Social Democrats had also boycotted the election except in Georgia, where they swept the board.

The left-wing majority of the First Duma naturally wished to pass a mass of radical legislation. In particular, it wished to divide up the large landed estates among the peasants (subject to compensation); to ensure equal civic rights for Jews, dissenters, members of religious sects, and minorities; and to grant a complete amnesty to all political prisoners. The emperor would not consider such things. In May, before the duma met, he dismissed Witte and appointed as minister of interior a former provincial governor who had impressed him by his firmness of character, P. A. Stolypin. In July 1906 he made Stolypin prime minister, and on July 22 (N.S.) dissolved the duma. During the summer he restored order by ruthless measures. But instead of introducing permanent dictatorial government, the emperor and Stolypin decided to hold elections for a Second Duma.

The extreme left parties—Social Democrats and Socialist Revolutionaries—now took part and won 118 seats out of 520 (*see* DUMA). The Trudoviki saw their numbers slightly reduced, from 101 in the First Duma to 98; the Kadets declined from 179 to 99; and the parties of the right increased their representation from 43 to 94. The Second Duma was thus more radical than the First. Cooperation between it and the government remained impossible. It met on March 5 (N.S.), 1907, but was dissolved on June 16. At the same time (though under the manifesto of Oct. 30 the electoral rules could be changed only with the consent of the Duma) a new electoral law was issued by decree, which greatly restricted the franchise. It was especially designed to strengthen the representation of the propertied classes in town and country and to reduce greatly the representation of the non-Russian nationalities. In the Third and Fourth Dumas, elected under this law in the autumn of 1907 and 1912, the parties of the right and the centre (the Octobrist Party of conservative constitutionalists, derived from the right wing of the former *zemstvo* liberals) predominated, and the Kadets, the socialists, and the non-Russians, together, shared only about a quarter of the seats.

8. Stolypin's Regime.—Democracy had been defeated, but the post-1907 system, usually associated with the name of Stolypin, was greatly different from the autocratic system of the years before 1905. Government was at least made more efficient with the creation of a prime minister and a Council of Ministers, though this advantage was of less importance after the murder of Stolypin in September 1911. The dumas, for all their restricted franchise and limited powers, were at least a forum in which virtually all political opinions could be expressed. Political parties and other types of associations could be legally formed. Trade unions were permitted, though strikes were still forbidden. The press was now comparatively free, and censorship of literature was virtually ended. After the grave economic losses of war and revolution, the economy recovered from 1908 onward and rapid industrial progress was made.

Agricultural Reform.—Stolypin's main interest was agricultural reform, which he hoped to achieve by a series of measures passed between 1906 and 1911, designed to encourage individual peasant ownership at the expense of the village commune. From the economic point of view, these were certainly progressive measures, for they put a premium on enterprise and removed the main factor perpetuating inefficiency. On the other hand they benefited only the enterprising minority among the peasants. As for the peasant masses, those who could not escape to employment in the growing industry were doomed to a prospect of increasing poverty, constantly accentuated by the relentless growth of rural population. Moreover, Stolypin's refusal to consider the compulsory partition of landowners' estates among the peasants ruled out policies which, though they might not have contributed to economic progress, would certainly have pleased not only the peasant masses but democratic opinion in general.

Russian Nationalism.—Perhaps the most serious fault of the policies of Stolypin was a deliberate revival of Russian nationalism and russification. In 1905 the nationalities had made certain gains, not only by representation in the first two dumas but also in the creation of cultural organizations controlled by themselves, such as the Polish Macierz Szkolna (Mother of Schools) or the Ukrainian organization Prosvita (Enlightenment). These were destroyed, or reduced to inactivity, after 1907. Special hostility was shown to all forms of Ukrainian nationalism and to the Tatar democrats and modernists, who in August 1905 had created a new party, the All-Russian Muslim League. In the Baltic provinces, however, the government treated the Germans more kindly after 1905, because it had been frightened by the violence of the Latvian peasants and workers in the revolutionary months, and now saw in the German landowners and burghers an element of stability.

Russian nationalism was in fact the official ideology of the Stolypin era, and this had its relevance to the new interest shown by the Russian government in Balkan affairs. This is, of course, not to say that Russia was more guilty than Austria-Hungary in the series of Balkan crises which led from 1908 to the outbreak of war in 1914, but only that Russia made its contribution to the tragedy.

9. World War I.—From Dec. 31 (N.S.), 1893, Russia had a defensive alliance with France. In 1904 France and Great Britain put an end to their overseas rivalries. This Entente Cordiale was followed on Sept. 13 (N.S.), 1907, by an agreement between Great Britain and Russia delimiting their mutual spheres of interest in Persia, Afghanistan, and Tibet. Thus the Triple Entente was born. By entering World War I, Russia kept the word given to its allies and partners.

Despite some reforms in the preceding decade, the Russian Army in 1914 was ill-equipped to fight a major war, and neither the political nor the military leadership was up to the standard required. Nevertheless the army fought bravely, and both soldiers and junior officers showed remarkable qualities. The Russian invasion of East Prussia in August 1914 was defeated by Paul von Hindenburg and Erich Ludendorff at Tannenberg, but it required the Germans to send reinforcements from the Western Front and so saved France from defeat and made possible the victory of the Marne. The campaigns of 1915 and 1916 brought terrible casualties to the Russian forces, which at times did not even have sufficient rifles. But as late as July 1916 the Russian Army was capable of making a successful offensive under Gen. A. A. Brusilov in Volhynia and Bukovina. (*See also* WORLD WAR I.)

The Russian people did not respond to the war with real enthusiasm. The government could not overcome its traditional distrust of any public initiative, even in the organization of medical supplies or munitions for the forces. In the Fourth Duma a majority of the centre and moderate right formed a Progressive bloc and proposed the formation of a national coalition government "possessing the confidence of the country" and a program of reforms which could be carried out even in wartime. The emperor rejected the proposal and prorogued the Duma, on Sept. 16 (N.S.), 1915. Eleven days earlier the emperor decided to assume personal command of the armies in the field. The result was that in Petrograd (as the capital had been renamed at the beginning of the war, in place of its old German-sounding name) the empress was in fact in command. She herself was under the influence of the adventurer and self-styled "holy man" G. E. Rasputin (*q.v.*), whose hold over her was due to his ability to arrest the bleeding of the hemophilic tsarevich, Alexis. Thus to the massive casualties at the front, the retreat of the armies, and the growing economic hardships was added the knowledge, widespread in the capital and among the upper classes, that the government of the country was in the hands of incompetents. Rumours of treason in high places

were widely believed, though the historical evidence does not suggest that they were true. On the night of Dec. 29–30 (N.S.), 1916, Rasputin was murdered. But the system was beyond salvation. There was in fact no hand at the helm, and the ship was drifting onto the rocks.

10. The End of the Romanov Dynasty.—The collapse came suddenly on March 8 (N.S.), 1917, planned by no one. A number of factories in Petrograd were on strike, and many of their workers were on the streets, as were the women in shopping queues and other women celebrating the international socialist anniversary of Women's Day. These crowds turned into demonstrations, and the demonstrations took over large areas of the capital. The workers came out in the streets with political slogans: "Down with Autocracy!" and "Down with War!" Two days later the emperor ordered the military governor to fire on the demonstrators, but the soldiers refused to use their rifles, and unit after unit went over to the workers. The police and gendarmes did shoot, and street fighting took place. Meanwhile the Duma, which had been prorogued, refused to disperse. A Petrograd Soviet of Workers' and Soldiers' Deputies was elected, like that of 1905. On March 14 the Duma, which had previously set up a standing committee, formed a provisional government, headed by Prince G. E. Lvov and mainly composed of leaders of the Kadet and Octobrist parties. On the next day a deputation visited the emperor at his headquarters in Pskov and accepted his abdication on behalf of himself and his son. When his brother, Grand Duke Michael, refused the throne, the Romanov dynasty came to an end. (G. H. N. S.-W.)

See also references under "Russian History" in the Index.

BIBLIOGRAPHY.—S. M. Solov'ev, *Istoriia Rossii s drevneishikh vremen,* 29 vol. (1851–79; reprinted 1959–); V. O. Klyuchevski, *A History of Russia,* Eng. trans., 5 vol. (1911–31); A. N. Rambaud, *Histoire de Russie depuis les origines* . . . (1918); K. Stählin, *Geschichte Russlands,* 4 vol. (1923–39); P. N. Milyukov, C. Seignobos, and L. Eisenman, *Histoire de Russie,* 3 vol. (1932–33); B. Pares, *History of Russia,* 5th ed. (1947); B. H. Sumner, *Survey of Russian History,* 2nd ed. (1948); G. Vernadsky and M. Karpovich, *A History of Russia,* 4 vol. (1943–59); M. T. Florinsky, *Russia: a History and an Interpretation,* 2 vol. (1953). On ancient Russia *see* B. D. Grekov, *The Culture of Kiev Rus,* Eng. trans. (1947), and *Kiev Rus,* Eng. trans. (1959); N. N. Voronin, M. K. Karger, and M. A. Tikhomirov, *Istoriia kultury drevnei Rusi,* 2 vol. (1951); H. Paszkiewicz, *Origin of Russia* (1954) and *The Making of the Russian Nation* (1963). For the modern period *see* P. N. Milyukov, *Gosudarstvennoe khozaistvo Rossii v pervoi chetverti XVIII stoletiya i reforma Petra Belikogo* (1892); M. M. Bogoslovskii, *Petr I,* 5 vol. (1940–48); B. H. Sumner, *Peter the Great and the Emergence of Russia* (1951); F. H. B. Skrine, *Expansion of Russia, 1825–1900* (1915); H. Seton-Watson, *Decline of Imperial Russia, 1855–1914* (1952).

RUSSIAN LANGUAGE. The Russian language has about 136,000,000 speakers, a majority of the population of the Soviet Union, of which it is the chief administrative language. It is sometimes called Great Russian to distinguish it from the closely related Belorussian, or White Russian, and "Little Russian" (an obsolescent term), or Ukrainian (*see* UKRAINIAN LANGUAGE), with which it makes up the eastern branch of the Slavic languages (*q.v.*).

History.—The Slavonic books translated by Saints Cyril and Methodius and their disciples (*see* CYRIL AND METHODIUS, SAINTS) and disseminated among the West and South Slavs in the 9th century must have found their way to the East Slavs quickly. Russian chronicles preserve in later copies treaties made by Kievan princes with Byzantium in 911, 944, and 971, but it was not until after the official baptism of Prince Vladimir in 988 that schools were opened and writing began to flourish. The chronicles mention intensive cultural activity under Yaroslav the Wise (1019–54), and the oldest surviving dated manuscript, the opulent Ostromir Gospel of 1056, was quickly followed by a number of other texts which testify to a high cultural level. Epigraphical materials, including graffiti and inscribed objects (whorls, bricks, jars), demonstrate a general knowledge of writing at the same epoch. In 1951 archaeologists working in the ancient north Russian city of Novgorod unearthed a hitherto unknown type of source—short texts, mostly private letters and agreements, written on birchbark. Several score *gramoty* of this type came to light, the oldest from the late 11th century; their importance for the history of language and culture is comparable with that of papyri for the classical studies.

The overwhelming majority of the writing represents Church Slavonic (Ch.Sl.) of the Russian recension; that is, a standardized written language based on a South Slavic type of speech but adapted to local conditions. This is the language of the church and the culture connected with it, and the texts are mostly translations from the Greek. The Ch.Sl., although differing in many particulars from the local speech, was probably readily comprehensible to the East Slavs in the early centuries and not difficult for them to master. Present knowledge of the everyday language comes chiefly from the scanty birchbark *gramoty* and from the occasional slips made by scribes who undertook to add notes or colophons in the Ch.Sl. manuscripts they were copying. Original compositions such as the chronicles and law codes survive in later copies in which it is not easy to distinguish older and newer linguistic habits. It seems, however, that the business language of the laws and letters used more of the East Slavic elements, particularly in vocabulary, than did annalistic and hagiographic works which had some literary pretensions. This is a common phenomenon; different genres are usually couched in different linguistic styles and it is natural that everyday matters are treated in everyday terms. The annalists made skilful stylistic use of the various linguistic elements; the contentions of Soviet critics that there were two different written languages, the foreign ecclesiastical Ch.Sl. and the vernacular secular Russian, are clearly exaggerated.

A number of the earliest texts exhibit some evidence of a difference between a northern and a southern dialect, but on the whole the language until the 13th century is best described as Old East Slavic. The conventional term Old Russian, which is too firmly established to be discarded, is to be understood as referring to the language of Rus, the whole East Slavic area, and not to the modern national group called Russians. Specifically southern dialect features warrant the identification of some texts from the late 13th century as Ukrainian, but it was not until the 16th and 17th centuries that Belorussian became clearly defined.

The use of local business languages for practical purposes in different areas long had no effect on the preeminence of Ch.Sl., which remained a unifying literary language for centuries. In the early period it had adopted consistently a number of East Slavic features, but during the 14th century it was reformed as a result of the prestige of Bulgarian and Serbian scholars who fled to Russia when the Turks overran the Balkans. This "second South Slavic influence" (which also affected literary style, art, and architecture) was decisive in establishing an archaic and partially foreign type of spelling and grammar as the only suitable vehicle for literary composition. Not until the 17th century, a time of turmoil and incipient change in all realms of Russian life, did this authority weaken. The business language of the Moscow chancelleries, which had steadily gained influence with the growth of the political power of the Muscovite state, then began to be used in more and more significant works, like the Code (*Ulozhenie*) of 1649, which was particularly important for the development of a linguistic standard because it was one of the first printed secular books. At the same time the beginnings of a style intermediate between Ch.Sl. and business usage can be discerned, and some texts in real colloquial Russian appeared (especially the autobiography of the dissident priest Avvakum Petrovich, 1673).

The radically westernizing policies of Peter I (reigned 1682–1725) and his successors made necessary new means of expression. At first the effort to catch up with Europe was manifested by a flood of translations, chiefly of practical works. Foreign words were introduced into Russian almost indiscriminately, despite the efforts of such talented writers as V. Trediakovski (d. 1769) who preferred to create new words from Russian and Slavonic materials. Persistence of the traditional view that the vernacular was not suited for literature clashed with a recognition of the fact that Ch.Sl. was too foreign a vehicle for the new culture. The problems were most clearly posed by the brilliant scientist and writer Mikhail Lomonosov (d. 1765), who distinguished three styles: a predominantly Ch.Sl. type was to serve for the most "elevated" literature (ode, tragedy), strictly colloquial Russian for the "low" genres (fable, comedy), and an intermediate type for other writings. His suggestions were largely followed, at least in principle, but there was a steady process of rejecting the most unfamiliar and archaic words and constructions of Slavonic and constant imitation of French and German models. About the beginning of the 19th century journalists and educators had elaborated a flexible intermediate style in writing about science and practical affairs; an exemplary moderate form of high style was used by N. Karamzin in his *History of the Russian State* (published 1816–29); and hitherto despised colloquial elements were made respectable by the comedies of D. I. Fonvisin (especially *The Minor*, 1782) and the fables of I. A. Krylov. But there was still an appreciable distance between the different types of language, and influential voices were still to be heard vigorously insisting on a Slavonic purism. It remained for the poet Aleksandr Pushkin (*q.v.*) to achieve a final synthesis.

Pushkin's poetry ranged from playful romance to the serious epic, from Byronic narratives to classical epigrams, from imitations of folk songs and fairy tales to poignantly personal lyrics and high tragedy. In prose he wrote history, literary criticism, travel accounts, stories, and novels. Whatever the genre, Pushkin's language remained throughout essentially the spoken Russian of an educated man, flavoured by pungent peasant proverbs or elegant allusions to French classics, by solemn Slavonic phrases or official chancellery clichés as demanded by the subject matter and tone of his approach. The brilliant success of Pushkin's works put an end to the linguistic controversy, and the history of the Russian literary language subsequently is an account of the refinement of details, of the extension of special types of vocabulary, and of the elaboration of special styles in keeping with changing literary fashions. (*See also* RUSSIAN LITERATURE.)

Dialect Forms.—In modern times three groups of Russian dialects are distinguished: the northern, which stretches from Leningrad all across Siberia; the southern, including most of central and southern Russia; and a central group occupying a relatively narrow band between the other two. There is no clear boundary between Russian and Belorussian or between the latter and Ukrainian, for the major dialect types are everywhere united by zones of transition. It is only in the east, where relatively recent settlers brought Ukrainian from the south and Russian from the north, that there is a fairly distinct linguistic frontier. Viewed historically, it seems that in the Old Russian period the chain of dialects from south to north represented closely related types, with a broad intermediate area separating the extreme north from the extreme south. The southernmost dialects soon (13th–14th centuries) became sufficiently differentiated to be identified as Ukrainian, while the central belt, first developing along the same general lines as the north, gradually split into an eastern and a western sector. The central west, though maintaining some close contacts with Ukrainian, established its identity as Belorussian (16th–17th centuries), while the central east eventually became southern Great Russian.

Great Russian dialects differ from one another in an enormous number of details, and yet they have retained an overall structural similarity which makes them on the whole mutually comprehensible. A major difference between the northern and southern (and also Belorussian) types is in vocalism; the northern (called o-dialects) have on the whole maintained all vowel distinctions regardless of position, while in the southern (called a-dialects, with *akanie*), unstressed vowels have changed quality; $o > a$, and often there are complex further changes. This *akanie* is reliably attested from the 14th century. The oldest northern texts have a confusion of the letters č and c, reflecting a typical feature of the north, where there is no functional difference between the two sounds. Ukrainian, Belorussian, and south Russian have a fricative γ (velar) or h (laryngeal) for Common Slavic and northern g; this doubtless is a prehistoric change.

The basis of standard Russian is the dialect of Moscow, the cultural centre from the 15th century. The city was originally within the northern dialect zone, but as the mutual influences between north and south created a growing central dialect type, Moscow found itself in the central zone. Thus it has on the whole the consonants of the north (though keeping separate č and c) and the vowels of the south. The word for "mountain," spelled *gorá* and so pronounced in the north, is *gará* in standard pronunciation and *γará* to the south.

Russian and Belorussian Phonology and Morphology.—

For some E.Sl. characteristics see SLAVIC LANGUAGES. In the oldest texts some common E.Sl. features already appear: *č ž* < C.Sl. **tj *dj; l < *tl *dl; u < *ǫ; a < *ę*. The extra vowel developed in words like *zóloto* "gold" < **zolto* (O.Ch.S. *zlato*) and *molokó* "milk" < **melko* (O.Ch.S. *mlěko*), initial *o-* for *je-* (R. *ózero* "lake" < **jezero*), and initial *u-* < **ju-* (OR. *ugŭ* "south" has been displaced by the Ch.Sl. form *jug*). In the early historical period the reduced vowels *ŭ ĭ* were lost in "weak position" and became *o e* in "strong position." C.S. *ě* merged with *e* in R. and BR., but became *i* in Ukr. All E.Sl. languages oppose a series of palatalized consonants to plain (or labialized) corresponding series, although the details vary from language to language. BR. has no palatalized labials before *j* or in final position (R. *s'em'* "seven," *p'ju* "I drink," BR. *s'em, pju*), no soft *r* (R. *kur'ú* "I smoke," BR. *kurú*), and soft *t'* and *d'* have become affricates *c'* and *dz'* (R. *d'ét'i* "children," BR. *dz'ec'i*).

Belorussian, spoken by about 7,000,000 persons, has two major dialect groups, northeast and southwest. Since Minsk, the capital, is on the latter's territory, the modern literary language, essentially a creation of the Soviet period, is southeastern in character.

A great many variations in phonology and morphology are still permitted, however, for usage has not yet been stabilized. BR. uses a strictly phonetic system of spelling which makes it look a great deal more different from R. than it sounds when spoken.

BIBLIOGRAPHY.—B. O. Unbegaun, *A Bibliographical Guide to the Russian Language* (1953), an excellent practical handbook for publications up to 1951. *Phonetics:* S. K. Boyanus, *Russian Pronunciation and Russian Phonetic Reader* (1955); R. I. Avanesov and S. I. Ozhegov (eds.), *Russkoe literaturnoe proiznoshenie i udarenie* (1959), an authoritative handbook; R. I. Avanesov, *Fonetika sovremennogo russkogo literaturnogo yazyka* (1956). *Grammar:* B. O. Unbegaun, *Russian Grammar* (1957); V. V. Vinogradov (ed.), *Grammatika russkogo yazyka,* 2 vol. (1952–54); V. V. Vinogradov, *Russki yazyk* (1947), amounts to a copiously annotated chrestomathy of Russian grammatical theory; L. A. Bulakhovski, *Kurs russkogo literaturnogo yazyka,* I (1935). *History:* G. O. Vinokur, *Russki yazyk: istoricheski ocherk* (1945; in French, 1947; in German, 1955); L. A. Bulakhovski, *Istoricheski kommentarii k russkomu literaturnomu yazyku,* 5th ed. (1958); R. O. Jakobson, *Remarques sur l'évolution du russe comparée à celle des autres langues slaves* (1929); V. I. Borkovski and P. S. Kuznetsov, *Istoricheskaia grammatika russkogo yazyka* (1963). *Dialects:* R. I. Avanesov, *Ocherki russkoi dialektologii,* I (1949). *Spelling:* A. B. Shapiro, *Russkoe pravopisanie* (1951); S. I. Ozhegov and A. B. Shapiro, *Orfograficheski slovar russkogo yazyka* (1956). *Dictionaries:* D. N. Ushakov (ed.), *Tolkovy slovar russkogo yazyka,* 4 vol. (1935–40); S. G. Barkhudarov (ed.), *Slovar russkogo yazyka,* 4 vol. (1957–61); *Slovar sovremennogo russkogo literaturnogo yazyka* (Soviet Academy), 17 vol. (1950–65); A. I. Smirnitsky (ed.), *Russko-angliiski slovar,* 3rd ed. (1958); *for Old Russian,* I. I. Sreznevski, *Materialy dlya slovaria drevnerusskogo yazyka,* 3 vol. (1893–1912; reprinted 1958). *Etymology:* M. Vasmer, *Russisches etymologisches Wörterbuch,* 3 vol. (1951–58). *Belorussian:* T. P. Lomtev, *Grammatika belorusskogo yazyka* (1956); P. N. Hapanovich and J. F. Mackevich, "O klassifikacii belorusskikh dialektov," in *Voprosy yazykoznania* 6, pp. 87–102 (1959); P. F. Hlebka (ed.), *Narysy pa historyi belaruskai movy* (1957); Y. Sherech, *Problems in the Formation of Belorussian* (1953); the classical history is E. F. Karski, *Belorussy,* 2 vol. (1903–12; reprint of vol. 2, 1955–56).

(H. G. L.)

RUSSIAN LITERATURE. The term Russian literature is used to describe the literature of different areas at different periods. Thus, from the beginning of written literature in the 11th century to the 16th century, it describes the literature of Kievan Russia—*i.e.,* the loose confederation of East Slav tribes ruled by the dynasty descended from Rurik (*see* RUSSIAN HISTORY: *Kiev*); from the 16th to the early 20th century, that of unified Russia, but not of other parts of the Russian Empire; and from 1917, that of the Russian Soviet Federated Soviet Republic, but not of the other republics constituting the U.S.S.R. For the literature of the Russian Empire other than Russia itself, and of other parts of the U.S.S.R., *see* ARMENIAN LITERATURE; GEORGIAN LITERATURE; LATVIAN LITERATURE; LITHUANIAN LITERATURE; UKRAINIAN LITERATURE. For the literature of Russian Jewry, *see* HEBREW LITERATURE; YIDDISH LITERATURE. *See* also DRAMA; THEATRE; NOVEL; SHORT STORY.

Division into Periods.—Russian literature is generally divided into two main periods: the Old Russian period, from the 11th to the end of the 17th century; and the modern period, which is subdivided into Pre-Revolutionary, from the end of the 17th century to 1917; and Post-Revolutionary, from 1917. The literature of the first period (which some historians date as ending in the mid-17th century) corresponds roughly to the medieval literature of Western European countries. It was dominated at first by Kievan Rus; but during the Tatar Mongol invasion in the 13th century, regional literatures gained in importance; and from the late 15th and early 16th centuries, the main literary centre was Moscow.

During the whole of this Old Russian period, literature was influenced by the connections between Russia and Byzantium, and between literature and the Orthodox Church, which began with the conversion to Eastern Christianity of St. Vladimir (*q.v.*), grand duke of Kiev, in 988. But in this period the influence of earlier East Slav oral folk poetry was also felt.

The beginnings of modern literature are marked by growing westernization, already noticeable in the 17th century, and increased by the reforms of Peter I the Great. From the beginning of the 18th to the early 20th century, Western influence was predominant, especially that of France. English influence also made itself felt, *e.g.,* in the foundation of periodicals (mid-18th century) and the rise of the sentimental school. The greatest period of Russian literature from the point of view of Western Europe, and the one which has had most influence on world literature, is the 19th century.

The Revolution of 1917 is a landmark. Post-Revolutionary literature, although developing from foundations laid in the Old Russian and Pre-Revolutionary periods, shows tendencies to some extent related to political circumstances and to the close supervision exercised by the Communist Party on all aspects of life and culture. This period is marked by a developing struggle between creative artists and the state, which, after Stalin's death in 1953, seemed to be resulting in renewed contact with Western literatures, and some degree of freedom for writers.

For the historical background to the development of Russian literature, which has always been closely connected with national and political policies, *see* RUSSIAN HISTORY. *See* also articles on many of the writers mentioned in this article.

This article is divided into the following main sections:

I. OLD RUSSIAN LITERATURE

The earliest works of Old Russian literature date from the third decade of the 11th century. Since the development of literature was connected from the first with the acceptance of Christianity by St. Vladimir in 988 and the country's Christianization, Old Russian literature was primarily religious and didactic in content and form. Didactic works were influenced by Byzantine literature in translations from the Greek, some coming to Russia from Bulgaria, and some organized and translated, as early as the reign of Yaroslav the Wise (1019–54), on Russian soil. Secular literature was influenced by oral folk poetry, which had existed among the East Slavs long before Russia had a written literature. There is no indisputable evidence of this oral poetry, since the first records of folk literature were made in the 17th century; but indirect information can be gleaned from written sources. The most valuable heritage of old Russian folklore is the epic or heroic folk song, the *bylina*. These were already being composed in the 10th century; they later ranged widely in theme and subject. They were produced in Kiev, Novgorod, and the principality of Galicia.

1. The Kievan Period.—The first phase of Old Russian literature, from the 11th to the early 13th century, is associated with Kievan Rus, and is called the Kievan period, or sometimes, because of the Tatar Mongol invasion that followed it, the pre-Mongol period.

The chief concentration of literary activity was in southern Russia, mainly in Kiev; although isolated works were written in other towns in the south (Chernigov, Turov, Galich) and in the north (Novgorod, Smolensk, Rostov). The language of both northern and southern writers was basically the same—the old literary language of the East Slavs, which had absorbed to a greater or lesser extent elements of Old Church Slavonic (*q.v.; see* also RUSSIAN LANGUAGE; BULGARIAN LANGUAGE). Consequently, the literature of the Kievan period can be regarded as being shared by Great Russians, Ukrainians, and White Russians.

The literature of the Kievan period possessed from the first many translations, mainly from Greek but some also from Latin. Among them were service books, mostly in Old Bulgarian, which included prayers and chants. The earliest surviving dated example is the Novgorod "Service Minei," a monthly service book of 1095–97 (for September, October, and November), of which there is a late 11th-century copy. At about the same time several kinds of biblical books appeared, among them "Aprakos" Gospels, in which readings from the Gospels were arranged by days of the week as part of the church service; the Gospels in the biblical arrangement; various arrangements of the Psalter; and the so-called *Pariminik*, Old Testament passages arranged to fit the church services. The earliest surviving manuscript of an "Aprakos" Gospel is the so-called *Ostromir Gospel*, copied in 1056–57 by Deacon Gregory for Ostromir, mayor of Novgorod; and the oldest known manuscript of the Four Gospels is the *Galician Gospel* (1144). Other translated works included apocryphal literature; saints' lives; the works of the Church Fathers; books about the creation of the world: *e.g.*, *Shestodnev* ("The Six Days"); such popular works as the *Physiologus* (*Fiziolog; see* BESTIARY); chronicles by John Malalas, Georgius Hamartolos, George the Syncellus, and others; part-secular, part-religious works, such as *Istoria Iudeiskoi voiny* (*De bello Judaico*, by Josephus, *q.v.*); the *Alexandria*, a translation of a version of the Alexander romance (*q.v.*); versions of the Troy legend such as the *Troyanskie deyanie;* a translation of the Byzantine romances *Devgenievo deyanie* ("The Adventures of Digenis Akritas"), the *Povest o premudrom Akire* ("The Tale of Akir the Wise"), and the *Povest o Varlaame i Iosaffe* ("The Tale of Barlaam and Josaphat"). (*See* also GREEK LITERATURE: *Byzantine*.)

One of the oldest literary genres, widely developed in Old Rus, was the chronicle. As early as the mid-11th century, compilations of chronicles were beginning to be made, and by the early 12th century a compilation of outstanding historical and literary significance was taking definite shape. This was the *Povest vremennykh let* ("The Tale of Bygone Years"; translated as *The Russian Primary Chronicle*, 1930), the first version of which was compiled *c.* 1112, probably by Nestor (*q.v.*), a monk of the Kiev-Crypt Monastery. Under the year 1096 the *Pouchenie Vladimira Monomakha* ("Testament of Vladimir Monomakh"), addressed to his children, and supplemented with an autobiography of this outstanding political figure, was inserted into a copy of the *Primary Chronicle* known as the Laurentian text (1377).

Sermons occupy an important place in the literature of the Kievan period, the best example being the *Slovo o zakone i blagodati* ("The Discourse on Law and Grace") by Hilarion, written between 1037 and 1050, before his appointment as the first Russian

FIFTEENTH-CENTURY MANUSCRIPT OF THE EARLIEST RUSSIAN CHRONICLE, "THE TALE OF BYGONE YEARS," ORIGINALLY COMPILED ABOUT 1112. ILLUMINATION SHOWS PUNISHMENT AND EXECUTION OF THE LEADERS OF AN ANTI-CHRISTIAN UPRISING. 1071

Metropolitan in 1051. Permeated with ardent patriotism, it is a work of great oratorical skill, equaling the supreme examples of Byzantine ecclesiastical rhetoric. In the 12th century, the second Russian Metropolitan, Kliment Smolyatich (Clement of Smolensk), and, in particular, Kiril (Cyril), bishop of Turov, were outstanding exponents of the art of ecclesiastical oratory in Kievan Rus. Kiril also wrote 30 prayers and 3 kanons.

Of early hagiographical works the anonymous *Skazanie* ("Legend"; late 11th or early 12th century) of the princes Boris and Gleb, the sons of St. Vladimir, merits particular attention. In form it resembles the historical legend rather than the traditional Byzantine saint's life; and it is full of lyrical laments, monologues, prayers, and meditations. It was written in support of the policies of Yaroslav the Wise.

In the first quarter of the 13th century a work was written which later (early 15th century) was called the *Kievo-Pecherski Paterik* ("The Paterikon of the Kiev-Crypt Monastery"). It is based on correspondence between Simon, bishop of Vladimir, a former monk of the Kiev-Crypt Monastery, and Polycarp, a monk at the monastery. It includes stories of the founding of the monastery (mid-11th century), and episodes from the lives of its monks. The literature of pilgrimage to the Holy Land originated in Kievan Rus. The most noteworthy work of this kind is the *Khozhdenie* ("Pilgrimage") to Palestine in 1106–08 of Daniel, prior of a southern Russian monastery. This combines topographical description with legend, and shows poetic feeling.

The most outstanding work of Kievan Russia is the *Slovo o Polku Igoreve* ("The Lay of Igor's Host," or "Tale of Igor's Expedition"; English translation from the Old Russian, by D. Ward, 1958), an account of the unsuccessful campaign in 1185 by Prince Igor of Novgorod-Seversk and the princes allied with him against the Polovtsians. It contains an appeal to the Russian princes for unity against the nomads of the steppes who were devastating the Russian land. It was written between 1185 and 1187, and preserved in a single manuscript, which was discovered in 1795 by the antiquarian, Count A. I. Musin-Pushkin, published in 1800, and lost during Napoleon's invasion of Russia in 1812. Deeply patriotic in spirit and remarkable for its literary mastery, the "Lay" ranks as an outstanding medieval epic. Its author, perhaps a member of the retinue of Prince Svyatoslav of Kiev, skilfully exploited the wealth of Russian folk poetry and contemporary written literature.

2. Development of Regional Literatures.—During its brief existence Kievan Rus created a literature distinguished for both artistry and ideas, and showing great possibility of development. However, from the mid-12th century a gradual decline of Kievan Rus set in, accentuated in the 13th century by the Tatar Mongol invasion; and there was a marked falling-off of literary activity. The traditions of the Kievan period were to some extent taken up in northeastern Russia and in the principality of Galicia-Volynia, where a lively propagandist pamphlet, *Molenie Daniila zatochnika* ("The Supplication [Epistle, Discourse] of Daniel the Exile"), was written in the first quarter of the 13th century in the region of Pereslavl near Suzdal. It is permeated with hostility toward the boyars and the monastic clergy, and calls for a strengthening of the power of the princes as a protection for the weak, and for the patronage of sages and men of letters.

The Tatar invasion was reflected as a great disaster in a number of 13th-century works. As literature, the most noteworthy is the *Povest o razorenii Batyem Ryazani* ("The Story of the Destruction of Ryazan by Batu Khan"), based on epic tales and historical songs about the devastating attacks of the Tatars on the principality of Ryazan in 1237. The eloquent, fiery sermons of Serapion, archimandrite of the Kiev-Crypt Monastery, written in the last year of his life (he died in 1275), are full of grief at the Tatar invasion. The Tatar onslaught of 1237 inspired the *Slovo o pogibeli russkoi zemli* ("Discourse on the Ruin of the Land of Rus"), which has survived only in a defective copy. It contains a vivid description of the beauty, wealth, and strength of the Russian land before the invasion. At the end of the 13th or in the early 14th century a life of Prince Aleksandr Nevski was written, probably by an ecclesiastic from the principality of Galicia, and perhaps on the basis of a secular biography which has not survived. This work is written in the traditional form of a hagiography but is closely akin to a war narrative; it is dominated by the epic figure of Aleksandr, presented both as an ideal general in war, and as a political figure, as reflected in his struggle with the Swedish and German conquerors and his diplomatic relations with the Tatars. An outstanding literary work of 13th-century southern Russia is the "Galich-Volynsk Chronicle," describing events from 1201 to 1292, which forms part of the copy of a compilation of chronicles called the Hypatian collection, written in the 1420s, and including also a copy of the *Primary Chronicle*.

The regional character of Russian literature, already fairly clearly marked in the 13th century, resulted from increased lack of communication between the territories of Russia, and was still apparent in the 14th and 15th centuries. Comparatively few literary works have survived from the 14th century because of the oppressiveness of the Tatar yoke. But by the beginning of the 15th century the literature of Moscow began to predominate, for Moscow had, from the mid-14th century, played the part of a unifying centre for Great Russian nationalism. Tendencies toward unification are particularly clear in the tales of *Mamaevo poboishche* ("The Rout of Mamay"), composed at the end of the 14th and the beginning of the 15th century about the Battle of Kulikovo (1380), at which the Tatars were defeated by a group of princes led by the Muscovite Prince Dmitri Ivanovich. Outstanding among them is the *Zadonshchina,* strongly influenced by "The Lay of Igor's Host." The conquest of Constantinople by the Turks in 1453 inspired Nestor Iskander's *Povest o Tsargrade* ("Tale of the Taking of Tsargrad," *i.e.,* Constantinople), which is mainly written in the style of the traditional war narrative. In it Russia is portrayed as the successor to Byzantium and the defender of the Orthodox faith. In the late 15th and early 16th centuries other stories were written in Moscow on the theme of Russia's political succession to the inheritance of Byzantium. Among them are stories about the Babylonian Empire, and their natural sequel, the *Skazanie o Knyazyakh Vladimirskikh* ("The Legend of the Princes of Vladimir"), which describes the descent of the Russian princes from the brother of Augustus Caesar.

Also of the 15th century is the *Khozhdenie za tri morya* ("A Journey Across Three Seas"), by Afanasi (Athanasius) Nikitin, a merchant from Tver who from 1466 to 1472 traveled chiefly in India but also in Persia. It reveals the author as a resourceful, inquisitive traveler, tolerant of foreigners and their beliefs, but loyal to his country. Specifically regional characteristics are absent; Nikitin's interests are those of the whole of Russia. The *Khozhdenie* is written in colloquial, lively Russian, with an admixture of Persian, Arabic, and Turkish words. Regional traits are also absent from the *Povest o Petre i Fevronii* ("The Tale of Peter and Fevronia"), written in the principality of Murom-Ryazan, which may be ascribed to the 15th century. It contains an abundance of themes from folklore.

Of other 15th-century regional literatures, that of Novgorod was particularly highly developed, producing a succession of literary works—*e.g.,* the *Povest o novgorodskom belom klobuke* ("The Tale of the White Cowl of Novgorod")—written in defense of Novgorod's political and ecclesiastical independence. In the literature of Tver, which vied with that of Moscow, the most outstanding work is the monk Thomas' panegyric, *Slovo Pokhvalnoe o blagovernom i velikom Knyaze Borise Aleksandroviche* ("A Eulogistic Discourse on the Orthodox Great Prince Boris Aleksandrovich"), written *c.* 1453. The most significant work of the literature of Pskov is the story *O pskovskom vzyatii* ("Of the taking of Pskov"), describing with great pathos the subjugation of Pskov by Moscow in 1510. Isolated works appeared at this period also in Rostov, Suzdal, and Smolensk.

The surge of literary activity beginning at the end of the 14th century is connected with the so-called "Second South Slavonic influence" from Bulgaria and Serbia resulting from the influx of clerics into Russia after the conquest of their countries by the Turks. Among them were the Bulgarian Kiprian (Cyprian) and the Serb Pakhomi Logofet (Pakhomius Logothetes). The latter wrote lives of numerous Russian saints. As well as retranslations from the Greek, the propagandist content and ornate style of South Slavonic literature was brought to Russia from the South Slavonic countries, largely in hagiographical works, in particular those of Epiphanius the Wise (d. 1420), author of lives of St. Stephen of Permia and St. Sergius of Radonezh.

3. Literature of Unified Russia.—The establishment of a unified Russian state, and the final subjugation of the rival principalities, dates from the reign of Ivan the Terrible. In 1480 the liberation of Russia from two and a half centuries of Tatar domination was finally achieved. The single Muscovite state under the centralized power of the autocratic lord of Moscow became a state of many nationalities under the tsar. In about the middle of the 16th century, Ivan, with the support of the rising feudal nobility, began an energetic campaign against the powerful feudal princelings, the boyars, who wished to retain their long-established independence. This struggle was reflected in literature. The most notable spokesman for the nobility was an immigrant from Lithuania, Ivan Peresvetov, whose work, dating from the late 1540s, includes several propagandist tales and two petitions to Ivan the Terrible. In these, as in his other works, he advocates autocratic tsarist power based on existing military and civil services. The boyars were represented by a publicist of exceptional literary gifts, Prince Andrei Mikhailovich Kurbski (*c.* 1528–83). Kurbski was a pupil of the widely educated ecclesiastical writer Maxim the Greek (*c.* 1480–1556), who had gone to Russia from Mt. Athos in 1518. In his four epistles to Ivan the Terrible and in his *Istoria o velikom knyaze moskovskom* ("A History of the Grand Prince of Muscovy," edited with English translation, as *History of Ivan IV,* by J. L. I. Fennell, 1965), written in the 1460s and '70s after his flight to Lithuania to escape Ivan's wrath at losing a battle in Livonia, Kurbski severely castigated Ivan for his persecution of innocent boyars, and of himself, Kurbski. It must be admitted, however, that his political views (his attempt to preserve at least part of the boyars' independence and privileges, and to acquire official recognition of their rights) were already out of date. In his answers, Ivan defends the idea that the tsar's absolute power was a divine right, and reveals, as in his satirical epistles and pamphlets, the temperament of a passionate polemicist. (See *The Correspondence Between Prince A. M. Kurbsky and Tsar Ivan IV, 1564–79,* ed., with trans. and notes, by J. L. I. Fennell, 1955.)

About the middle of the 16th century Moscow's conception of itself as the third Rome, the centre of Orthodoxy and of political authority, began to take definite shape. There began to appear a succession of vast literary undertakings aimed at exalting and strengthening the Muscovite ecclesiastical and political traditions, and demonstrating that these had come down from the very beginning of Russian statehood—from Kievan Rus. In 1552 there appeared the grandiose compilation known as the *Velikie cheti minei* ("Grand Cheti Minei"), by the metropolitan of Moscow, Makarios (Macarius; d. 1563). In 12 volumes it collected numerous works of original and translated ecclesiastical literature: saints' lives, arranged as a calendar of monthly readings. It was followed by the *Stepennaya kniga* ("Book of Degrees"; *i.e.,* generations), containing biographies of outstanding Russian princes and ecclesiastical figures, completed in 1563 by Macarius' successor Andrew (Athanasius), the imperial confessor. At this period also were collected the important Muscovite chronicle compilations, including the *Voskresenski* ("Resurrection") Chronicle and the *Nikonovski* ("Nikonian," or "Patriarchal") Chronicle. In the 1560s and '70s an enormous collection, the *Litsevoi Nikonovski svod* ("Illuminated Nikonian Compilation"), was produced. Based on the Nikonian Chronicle, it begins with the Creation and ends in the 1560s. It was enlarged and revised as the *Tsarstvennaya kniga* ("Imperial Book"). An apologia for Ivan the Terrible and the state of Muscovy is the *Kazanski letopisets* ("Kazan Chronicler"), relating the history of the empire of Kazan from its foundation to its conquest by Ivan in 1552. Works such as the *Domostroi* ("Household Management") and the *Stoglav* ("Book of a Hundred Chapters") aimed at strengthening and systematizing the moral, social, domestic, and political standards of conduct established by the mid-16th century. The introduction of printing in Moscow did much to help Russian unification. The first dated book, *Apostol* ("The Acts of the Apostles"), was printed in 1564, but the first experiments in printing in Moscow had probably been made since c. 1553.

The end of the 16th century and the beginning of the 17th were marked by stormy political events known as the *"Smuta"* ("Troubles" or "Disorders"); they were characterized by an intense anti-feudal struggle, into which were drawn both the peasants, who were impoverished by serfdom, and the boyars, who had been defeated by the feudal nobility. The situation was complicated by the intervention of the Swedes and Poles, who were only repulsed by the united efforts of the Russian people. The events of the "time of troubles" are described in a succession of tales, on the one hand echoing the social and political upheavals, and on the other commemorating the surge of patriotism against foreign intervention.

The elegance and artistry of the Muscovite literary tradition was shattered by the "time of troubles." Social groups which had earlier played only a minor part in cultural life appeared on the literary scene. New writers and readers from farther down the social scale introduced secular themes, elements of realism, and a vein of folklore into literature. Examples are the stories of the capture of the town of Azov in 1637 by the Don Cossacks, and, in particular, of its siege by the Turks in 1641, which are outstanding literary works. The international relations of the state of Muscovy, which had grown significantly stronger, helped the flow of secular literature from the West, in many cases via Ukrainian literary figures, who had established connections with Moscow, particularly after the union of the Ukraine with Russia in 1654. The secular translated story, the tale of chivalry, the humorous *novella,* replaced Byzantine religious didactic literature, or existed alongside it. Folklore began to intrude noticeably into literature: the only records of folk *byliny* date from the 17th century.

The original Russian secular story begins to appear from about the second half of the 17th century. Side by side with tales in which the conservative tradition of the Church Fathers still predominates, such as the *Povest o Gore i Zlochastii* ("The Tale of Woe-Misfortune") which tells how "Woe-Misfortune" caused a youth to turn monk; and the *Povest o Savve Grudtsyne* ("The Story of Savva Grudtsyn"), there appeared the *Povest o Frole Skobeeve* ("The Tale of Frol Skobeev"), recounting the adventures of a rogue and cheat; and the *Povest o Karpe Sutulove* ("The Story of Karp Sutulov"), a comic story about a prudent merchant's wife who tricks three admirers and so preserves her honour during her husband's absence. These last two stories are both free from accepted moral and religious principles. Satire and parody of the court, church, and legal procedure of Muscovy began to be written: *e.g.,* the *Povest o Shemyakinom sude* ("The Tale of the Trial of Shemyaka") the *Povest o Yershe* ("The Story of Ruff, son of Ruff"), the *Kalyazinskaya chelobitnaya* ("The Petition of Kalyazin Monastery"), and the *Povest o kure i lisitse* ("The Tale of the Rooster and the Fox," a satire on formal piety).

Tendencies to secularization can also be seen in the genre of hagiography. Even at the beginning of the 17th century a life of St. Juliania Lazarevskaya (d. 1604) by her son, Kalistratus Osorin, describes a saintly life lived in the world, not in a monastery. The autobiography of the head of the Old Believers, the archpriest

(LEFT) FRONTISPIECE WITH WOODCUT OF ST. LUKE FROM "APOSTOL" ("THE ACTS OF THE APOSTLES"), MOSCOW, 1564; (RIGHT) "PROLOGUE" FROM FIRST EDITION OF "THE COMEDY OF THE PARABLE OF THE PRODIGAL SON," BY SIMEON OF POLOTSK, 1685

Avvakum, written between 1672 and 1675 (translated from the 17th-century Russian as *The Life of the Archpriest Avvakum by Himself,* by J. Harrison and H. Mirrlees, with preface by D. S. Mirsky, 1924), also belongs basically to the traditional hagiographical genre, but it is full of topical material and realistic detail. Avvakum thus turns the canonical form of a typical hagiography into a polemically incisive narrative of his own life and the lives of his relatives, written, as were all his works, in the vivid, colourful, conversational speech of a literary master.

At the beginning of the 17th century, mainly under the influence of Ukrainian literature (*q.v.*), verse began to develop. At first it was clumsy and rhythmically unorganized, but later the learned Kievan monk Simeon of Polotsk (1629–80), an immigrant from White Russia, introduced syllabic verse. This was developed by his pupils, Silvestr Medvedev (1641–91) and Karion Istomin (mid-17th to early 18th century). In 1672, with the help of a German Lutheran pastor in Moscow, Johann Gottfried Gregori, a secular court theatre was created, with a basically Western European repertory. Almost at the same time in Moscow Simeon of Polotsk's first attempts at school drama appeared. His *Komedia pritchi o bludnom syne* ("The Comedy of the Parable of the Prodigal Son"; publ. 1685), in which the biblical story is adapted to treat the subject of fathers and sons in Russia before the introduction of Westernization, is particularly interesting. Thus it can be seen that Russian literature in the second half of the 17th century was transitional between the old literature and the literature of modern times, which dates from the beginning of the 18th century.

(N. K. G.)

II. MODERN PRE-REVOLUTIONARY LITERATURE

Modern Russian literature is usually said to begin in the first decade of the 18th century, when literary works, as distinct from religious, official, and educational books, began to be printed. During the century newspapers and periodicals were published—including literary magazines, which were to become so prominent a feature of the 19th-century literary scene. Classicism was the dominant movement in 18th-century literature. Toward the end of the century, however, it was displaced by the sentimental movement, though realistic tendencies can be perceived in both classical and sentimental schools.

A. THE 18TH CENTURY

The development of literature from the end of the 17th century to the beginning of the 19th can be divided roughly into five periods. The literature of the first—1690–1730—dominated by the reforms of Peter I the Great, is largely transitory, the borderline between literature and journalism being scarcely perceptible. The second—1730–50—is remarkable for the formation and consolidation of the classical movement. The third—1750–75—is notable for the growth of satire, which gradually undermined the classical movement, and the emergence of the sentimental movement. During the fourth—1775–90—the sentimental movement gained strength; and in the 1790s—the fifth period—it finally gained ascendancy, but was already giving way to the Romantic and realistic movements of the early 19th century.

1. 1690–1730.—Though some of Peter the Great's reforms (*e.g.*, reform of the alphabet, intensive development of secular printing, and the foundation of a periodical press; *see* RUSSIAN HISTORY) had no direct bearing on literature, they were to be of importance in its development. The most prominent literary figure at the beginning of the century was Feofan Prokopovich (1681–1736), archbishop of Novgorod, one of Peter's close associates. Active as publicist, poet, and dramatist, he may be described as the progenitor of two of the main themes in Russian literature: that of autocracy as a form of government and that of satire as a means of attack on, and exposure of, literary and political opponents. In his tragicomedy *Vladimir* (1705) and, particularly, in his satirical pamphlet *Ustav dukhovnia kollegii* (1721; "Rules of a Spiritual Academy"), he attacked the dissident clergy who opposed Peter's reforms; and in *Pravda voli monarshei* ("Truth of a Monarch's Will"), he maintained that the final aim of autocracy was "the well-being of the people as a whole," while "the people" (*i.e.*, the aristocracy) had no right to question the acts of the monarch, who ought to do nothing against the will of God.

The poetry of the period included solemn panegyric verse celebrating the victories of Russian arms, as well as the new genre of love lyrics and elegiac poems on the themes of death and the vanity of human wishes. This period also saw the development of Russian secular drama, mostly in translation, treating conflicts between passion and duty, feeling and reason, and the interests of the individual and of society, themes to be developed by the classical playwrights. On the whole, this period did not produce any important literary works, but merely prepared for later development.

2. 1730–1750.—During the second period the first significant names in modern Russian literature appeared. The growth of cultural institutions—the creation, for example, of the first Academy of Sciences in St. Petersburg (1725), the foundation of the first university, in Moscow (1755), and of the first theatre, in St. Petersburg (1756)—assisted literary talent to develop. The leading literary genres were the ode and tragedy, both propagating enlightened absolutism. As in Western Europe (and more particularly in France), the cult of reason lay at the foundation of neoclassicist aesthetics. Writers stressed man's rational ability to suppress passion and feeling in face of duty to the state, creating characters who were primarily servants of the state. In general, they depicted ideas rather than people.

The leading writers of the classical school were Prince Antioch Dmitrievich Cantemir (1708–44; *see* CANTEMIR), the first Russian secular poet; Vasili Kirilovich Trediakovski (1703–69), one of the most scholarly men of his time; Mikhail Vasilevich Lomonosov (1711–65), poet, grammarian, scientist, and literary critic; and Aleksandr Petrovich Sumarokov (1718–77), poet and dramatist. Cantemir, who translated Anacreon's odes and Horace's epistles, is known mainly for his love lyrics and his nine satires (written 1729–39, publ. 1762), in a colloquial style. He is regarded as the founder of Russian satire. Educated at the Sorbonne, Trediakovski began by translating Paul Tallemant's *Journey to the Isle of Love,* the first erotic work to be published in Russia. He helped to reform Russian prosody, replacing the syllabic metres inherited from Poland by tonic and accentuated measures more natural to Russian. Lomonosov was the creator of the famous "three styles" of poetic diction characteristic of Russian neoclassicism: the "high" (or grand) style for heroic poems, odes, and prose works dealing with serious subjects; the "middle" style for dramatic works de-

manding colloquial speech (except when "heroic and lofty thoughts" were to be expressed, where the "high" style was obligatory), and for "epistles, satires, eclogues and elegies, and prose descriptions of memorable deeds and noble doctrines"; and the "low" style for "comedies, epigrams, songs, letters in prose, and precise descriptions," such as his own *Pismo o polze stekla* (1752; "Epistle on the Use of Glass"). He advanced the theoretical study of the Russian language, which, he maintained in the foreword to his *Retorika* (1748; "Rhetoric"), was no whit inferior to any European language "in natural richness, beauty, and strength." In the foreword to his Russian grammar (1757) he thus defined the scope of the Russian language:

"Charles the Fifth . . . [said] that Spanish was a language fit for converse with God, French with friends, German with enemies, and Italian with women. But had he known Russian he would surely have found in it the magnificence of Spanish, the vivacity of French, the vigour of German, the tenderness of Italian and, above all, the richness and forceful succinctness of expression of Greek and Latin."

Sumarokov, who followed the rules of French classical drama and wrote the first Russian classical tragedy, *Khorev* (1747), was adept in a variety of genres, and opposed Lomonosov's "florid" style. He owed his popularity to his numerous love lyrics, elegies, eclogues, and idylls, his love lyrics in particular being noted for sincerity and spontaneity. He also wrote six tragedies, including a free adaptation of *Hamlet,* and four comedies. Four of his tragedies deal with subjects from classical history, and all but one end with the triumph of virtue over vice. His themes are the opposition between duty and feeling, reason and passion, the highest manifestation of heroism being suppression of personal desire. His tragedies, strongly influenced by Racine, are full of heroic female characters, and were intended as a school of noblemen's moral values. In his comedies he sought to improve the moral standards of the Russian aristocracy by showing up dishonest lawyers and judges, fops and pedants. In his periodical, *Trudolyubivaya pchela* ("The Industrious Bee"; 1759), he exposed corruption among officials and attacked landowners for maltreating their serfs, but defended social inequality as "natural and lawful," convinced that serfdom was necessary for "the general well-being" of the country. His satiric articles and fables laid the foundation of the satire of the next decade.

The first breach in classicism was made by Mikhail Matveevich Kheraskov (1733–1807), famous for two epic poems modeled on Voltaire's *Henriade: Rossiada* (1771–79), on the capture of Kazan by Ivan the Terrible; and *Vladimir vozrozhdenny* (1785), on St. Vladimir's introduction of Christianity to Russia. He began his literary career with a tragedy *Venetsianskaya monakhina* (1758; "The Venetian Nun"), in which he broke the classical rules. It had three, instead of five, acts, extolled the "immortal passion" of love, and introduced ordinary people. The play was an early Russian example of the middle-class drama. (*See also* DRAMA: *Modern Drama.*)

3. 1750–1775.—Influenced by the Pugachev rebellion (1773–75), the most important theme in the third period was that of serfdom and the relationship between landowner and peasant. The social influence of literature greatly increased. This led both to a widening circle of readers and to active participation in literature of people from all classes. Trediakovski and Sumarokov still contributed important works in this period. Sumarokov, in his last three tragedies, attacked the idea of a tyrannical ruler and pleaded for an "enlightened emperor," and even went so far in his most famous tragedy, *Dimitri Samozvanets* (1771; "Dimitri the Pretender"), as to justify the overthrow of a "tyrant" by the "people." In his *Telemakhida* (1766), a free rendering of Fénelon's *Télémaque,* Trediakovski declared that while "the Tsar wields power over the whole people, the laws have power over the Tsar too," a sentiment that made Catherine II pour scorn on the poem in her journal *Olla Porrida Vsyakaya vsyachina* (1769–70), modeled on the English *Spectator,* as "untalented and boring."

The two most prominent writers of the period were the playwright Denis Fonvisin (1744–92) and the writer and publisher Nikolai Novikov (1744–1818). Beginning by translating fables, Fonvisin later wrote original satirical fables, such as *Lisitsa-koz-*

РОССІЯДА
ИРОИЧЕСКАЯ ПОЕМА.

ПѢСНЬ ПЕРВАЯ.

Пою отъ варваровъ Россію свобожденну,
Попранну власть Татаръ и гордость побѣжденну,
Движенье древнихъ войскъ, труды, кроваву брань,
Россіи торжество, разрушенну Казань.
Отъ круга сихъ временъ, спокойствія начало
Какъ свѣтлая заря въ Россіи возсіяло.

FIRST PAGE FROM ORIGINAL EDITION OF THE EPIC POEM "ROSSIADA," 1779, BY MIKHAIL KHERASKOV, ON THE CAPTURE OF THE CITY OF KAZAN BY IVAN THE TERRIBLE. ENGRAVING SHOWS KAZAN UNDER SIEGE; IN THE BRITISH MUSEUM

nodei (1762; "The Fox and the Preacher"), written shortly after the death of the empress Elizabeth (Elizaveta Petrovna), in which he attacked her hypocritical courtiers, who "by their supreme powers merely sated their tyrannical passions." But it was with two prose comedies, *Brigadir* (1766–69) and *Nedorosl'* (1782), that Fonvisin triumphed as a playwright. An opponent of serfdom, Novikov, like Fonvisin, directed his satire not against serfdom itself, but against the landowners' misuse of their powers. His first periodical, *Truten* ("The Drone"; 1769–70), had the significant epigraph: "They labour and you feed upon their labour." In it he exposed the corruption of the civil servants, the ignorance of most noblemen, their hostility to learning, and their obsequious attitude to French culture. It provoked furious rejoinders from *Olla Porrida*, but its subscribers rose in three months from 600 to more than 1,200, while those to Catherine II's journal dropped from 1,500 to 500. The empress suspended *Truten* for a month in the autumn of 1769, after which Novikov moderated his satire, his journal reappearing with the epigraph: "It is dangerous to criticize where there is much brutality and madness." At the end of 1770 it had to suspend publication, and Novikov's second journal, *Pustomelya* ("The Windbag"), was suspended after only two issues. Novikov dedicated his third journal, *Zhivopisets* ("The Painter"), to "the authoress of the comedy 'Oh, Time!'" (Catherine II), begging her to imitate Molière "in looking with a dispassionate eye on our vices, our ingrained bad habits, our malpractices and all our immoral acts"—the policy he himself intended to pursue. In it he published in 1772 two of his most famous satires: *Otryvok puteshestviya v I . . . T . . .* ("A Fragment of a Journey"), and *Pismo k Falaleyu* ("Letter to Fallaley"). The first gives a shattering picture of the "poverty and slavery" of the peasants and their subjection to their masters' whims, and the second, supposedly written by a provincial landowner to his son in St. Petersburg, provides insight into the serfowners' mentality.

But, however truthful his descriptions of Russian country life, and however faithful his reproduction of the colloquial language of the cruel, greedy, and superstitious landowners (which makes the "Letter to Fallaley" one of the finest literary works of the century), the fact that he never condemned serfdom saved Novikov from Catherine's wrath but robbed his satire of efficacy as a revolutionary instrument.

By mid-century there were in circulation many translations of novels and short stories, including those by Defoe, Swift, and Fielding. In 1769 the first Russian translation of Cervantes' *Don Quixote* was published. The most important novelist of the period was Fedor Aleksandrovich Emin (?1735–70), whose best novel *Pisma Ernesta i Doravry* (1766; "Letters of Ernest and Doravra"), a free adaptation of Rousseau's *La Nouvelle Éloïse*, is interesting as the first attempt in Russian fiction at psychological analysis of the thoughts and feelings of ordinary people. It deals with the emotional experiences of two lovers prevented by circumstances from being united. "There is no greater pleasure," the hero exclaims, "than to have a sensitive soul!" But this evidence of the influence of the Western cult of sensibility is only superficially significant, for the novel adheres to classical aesthetic rules, and its hero's conception of duty triumphs over his passions. In it Emin exposes the evils of serfdom, but does not attack serfdom as an institution. His son, Nikolai Emin (1761?–1814), also a popular novelist, was less interested in the social iniquities of his time. His novels show the growing influence of the sentimental school: their heroes read Edward Young's *Night Thoughts*, and dissolve in tears. Mention should also be made of a novel by Pavel Lvov, influenced by Samuel Richardson (*q.v.*), *Rossiiskaya Pamela, ili istoria Marii, dobrodetelnoy poselyanki* (1789; "The Russian Pamela, or the Story of Maria, the Virtuous Country Girl"). "I call her the Russian Pamela," Lvov wrote, "to show that in our country too there are tender hearts and great souls among the lower classes." A popular novelist to emerge from "the lower classes," Mikhail Dimitrievich Chulkov (*c.* 1743–1792), was concerned with entertaining his readers: his novels lack the lofty moral admonitions that abound in the works of classical writers. His first fictional work, *Peresmeshnik, ili slavenskie skazki* (1768; "The Mocker, or Slavonic Fairytales"), is a collection of comic and adventurous stories narrated by the author and by a monk. His second, *Prigozhaya povarikha* (1770; "The Fair Cook," or "The Adventures of a Whore"), contains naturalistic descriptions of contemporary life and manners.

Between 1770 and 1780 the sentimental movement gained ground. Its influence first becomes noticeable in adaptations of French comic operas. These were followed by native comic operas, such as *Rosana i Lyubim* (1778), by Nikolai Petrovich Nikolev (1758–1815), the main theme of which is the superiority of moral equality over social inequality. It advances, cautiously, the idea that "The peasant too perhaps /Is as great in soul/ As the ruler of kingdoms." The anti-serfdom note can be detected in other comic operas of the period, such as *Neschastie ot karety* (1779; "An Accident with a Carriage"), by Yakov Borisovich Knyazhnin (1742–91), famous for his tragedies and translations of French classical dramas; *Kofeinitsa* ("The Coffee Fortune Teller"), by Ivan Krylov (1769–1844), author of lyric odes and epistles, the greatest Russian fabulist; and *Mel'nik, koldun, obmanshchik i svat* (1779; "The Miller, Wizard, Quack and Matchmaker"), by Aleksandr Onisimovich Ablesimov (1742–83). The American Revolution, fully reported by Novikov in his *Moskovskie Vedomosti* ("Moscow News"), raised again the problem of an autocratic ruler's duties to his subjects. Fonvisin—in his *Rassuzhdenie o nepremennykh gosudarstvennykh zakonakh* (1783; "Reflections on the Necessity of State Laws")—maintained that the tsar should be as completely subject to the laws of the land as his lowest subjects. In his satires, and, even more, in his popular fables, Ivan Ivanovich Khemnitser (1745–84) touched on the same theme, though more guardedly, while Knyazhnin, in his tragedy *Roslav* (1784), demanded that the emperor should be subject to his own laws, and in *Vadim Novgorodski* (1789; "Vadim of Novgorod") openly attacked autocracy as "responsible for all the troubles in the state" and "an enemy of the purest virtue," which made Catherine II order the destruction of all copies of the tragedy. Even Nikolev declared, in his tragedy *Sorena i Zamir* (1784), that "to destroy a tyrant is a duty not a crime," a sentiment Catherine II, whose own plays had a mildly liberal cast (it was not for nothing that she had corresponded with Voltaire), did not find dangerous since, as she remarked to a high-ranking official, "the author is merely attacking autocratic tyrants while you call Catherine your mother."

4. 1775–1790.—The first unmistakable indication of the declining power of classicism was provided by the popular narrative poems of Ippolit Fedorovich Bogdanovich (1743–1803), especially his *Dushenka* (1775), a free adaptation of La Fontaine's *Les Amours de Psyché et de Cupidon*. Bogdanovich held that poetry must "beautify" nature. He was regarded by the sentimentalist writers as their predecessor.

Gavrila Derzhavin (1743–1816), the greatest Russian poet of the 18th century, gave the most vigorous expression to the change from classicism to sentiment. His first works—odes as well as lyrics (1760)—show the influence of Lomonosov and Sumarokov. Soon, however, he took up an independent attitude toward social evils. In his famous paraphrase of Ps. 82 he tells the "rulers and judges" (as he first called the poem) that their duty is "To preserve the laws/ Not taking account of a man's station/ And from the hands of persecutors to save/ The poor, the helpless and the widows." But, he goes on, "They do not listen, villainies, robberies/ Tortures and groans of the poor/Undermine and trouble kingdoms/ And plunge the throne itself into ruin." His ode on the death of Prince Meshcherski (1779) is full of reflections on the transience of life and the inevitability of death ("On the edge of a precipice we walk/ ... we are born to die"), but ends on a characteristically Horatian note: "Life is Heaven's instant gift;/ Fashion it to your own content/ And with a soul pure and innocent/ Bless the blows of Fate." In *Bog* (1784; *Ode to the Deity*) Derzhavin upholds the classical tradition of Lomonosov, but in *Felitsa* (1785), an ode to Catherine II, he inaugurates his

TITLE-PAGE OF ORIGINAL EDITION OF "ANAKREONTICHESKIA PESNI," 1804 ("ANACREONTIC" POEMS) BY GAVRILA DERZHAVIN; IN THE BRITISH MUSEUM

own kind of humorous panegyric, extolling the virtues of the empress but satirizing the vices of her favourites. He reached his greatest heights during the next decade with odes "On the Capture of Ismail," "To the Nobleman," "To My First Neighbour," "On the Bullfinch" (on the death of Suvorov), and others, in which his attacks on "unworthy and vicious noblemen" were intensified. His finest poems—*e.g.*, the magnificent *Vodopad* (1794; "Waterfall"), and *Pavlin* ("The Peacock"), and his so-called "anacreontic" poems (collected 1804), full of the love of life and its joys, such as *Priglashenie k obedu* (1798; "Invitation to Dinner") and *Zhizn zvanskaya* (1807; "Life in Zvanka")—the poet's small estate—belong to this period. Derzhavin accepted serfdom as natural and lawful, and on the whole his poetry expresses the ideology of the ruling classes; yet his realistic representation of everyday life and his simplification of poetic diction by introducing colloquial speech tend to emphasize the democratization of poetry.

5. The 1790s.—If the literature of the mid-18th century affirmed the conception of an ideal state ruled by an enlightened monarch, and demanded subjection of individual interests to those of the state, that of the 1790s, influenced by the French Revolution, raised the themes of the rights of man and the role of the nation as a whole. Aleksandr Radishchev (1749–1802), in his ode to liberty (*Vol'nost,* written 1781–83), hailed the American Revo-

lution and attacked serfdom, but it was his denunciation of autocracy that made Catherine II describe the ode as "a rebellious poem," in which the tsar was threatened with execution. Her attitude to Radishchev's famous *Puteshestvie iz Peterburga v Moskvu* (1790; *Journey from St. Petersburg to Moscow*) is summed up in her remark: "The author does not like Tsars and ... pins his hope on the rebellion of the peasants."

Apart from violently satiric works, among them the famous comedy *Chicane* (1798), by Vasili Vasilevich Kapnist (1757–1823), and Krylov's *Pochta Dukhov* (1789; "Post of Spirits"), in which gnomes, undines, and sylphs correspond with "the Arab philosopher Malikulmuk" about the crying injustices among earth dwellers, the main literary movement was sentimentalism, led by Nikolai Karamzin (1766–1826). In Russian sentimentalism subjective perception and appraisal are combined with denial of classical abstractions and idealization of man's "natural condition." Karamzin opposed to the classical emphasis on reason a doctrine of poetry as an expression of "feeling"—of the writer's subjective experiences and attitude to life, irrespective of its objective significance. The sentimentalists, moreover, put forward the claims of "sensibility" as a precondition of aesthetic impressions, emphasizing art's emotional foundation. "A writer," Karamzin stated, "must paint the portrait of his own heart and soul." Unlike Derzhavin, Karamzin was not interested so much in reality as in the feelings and moods it arouses in the poet, whom he describes as "a cunning wizard" whose "living thought transforms, like a fairy, flowers into beautiful maidens." According to him "the first [*i.e.*, greatest] poetic creation" is "an effusion of a languorous and grieving heart." This elegiac mood, so characteristic of Karamzin's latter poetry, is expressed in his famous novel *Bednaya Liza* (1792; "Poor Liza"), in which, for the first time in Russian fiction, descriptive passages, used to emphasize the hero's feelings, are an important component. Karamzin regarded his lyric poetry as a means of creating an intimate illusory world. To him poetry was "the flower garden of sensitive souls." In his novel *Julia* (1794) he idealized country life and withdrawal into "the embraces of nature," for only there "a sensitive soul can enjoy love and tenderness to the full." His other novels—*Ostrov Borngolm* ("Island,Bornholm"), and *Sierra Morena* (both 1793)—are precursors of the Russian Romantic novel. Indeed, many of his poetic formulae—"glory is an empty sound," "friendship is a delightful gift," "the delight of careless youth," "I was the plaything of passions"—became the clichés of the 19th-century Romantics.

B. THE 19TH CENTURY

1. Poetry.—The most eminent of Karamzin's followers, Ivan Ivanovich Dmitriev (1760–1837), achieved fame with his songs, short odes, elegies, fables, and satirical narrative poems. Dmitriev's fables are written in the elegant style of the Russian upper classes, and were soon eclipsed by the masterly fables of Krylov, who combined colloquial speech with the native wisdom of the peasant, and whose fables (written 1810–20) are among the great treasures of Russian literature.

Chief among early 19th-century Romantic poets was Vasili Zhukovski (1783–1852). A follower of Karamzin, he founded with other Karamzin partisans the semi-humorous literary society, Arzámas, as a counterblast to the classicists, who had earlier founded an anti-Karamzin society, "The Conversation of Lovers of Russian Literature." Zhukovski's poetic output—Romantic poems and ballads—is not considerable: his fame rests on his translations of German and English poets. His translation of Gray's *Elegy* was published in Karamzin's journal *Vestnik Evropy* in 1802. He created a new poetic language, based on Karamzinian principles but surpassing that of Karamzin by its purity of diction and melodiousness of verse. Radishchev's political influence is shown mainly in the poetry of some of the leaders of the Decembrist insurrection, headed by Kondraty Fëdorovich Ryleev (1795–1826), who expressed abhorrence of the tyranny of the tsars in his "Meditations" (1825). Ryleev also wrote Romantic poems whose heroes gladly face death in their fight against "the oppressors of the people."

The greatest poet of the early 19th century, and the greatest

Russian poet, is Aleksandr Pushkin (1799–1837). Already his first poems, *Ruslan i Lyudmila* (1820), *Kavkazski plennik* (1822; *The Prisoner of the Caucasus*), and *Bakhchisaraiski fontan* (publ. 1824; *The Fountain of Bakhchisarai*), though Romantic (indeed, Byronic) in style, show how greatly he surpasses his contemporaries in mastery of diction and verse. It was, however, only in his great narrative poem, *Evgeny Onegin* (written 1823–31), that Pushkin achieved the clarity and compactness of his mature works. He achieved also what no other Russian poet has achieved: integration of idea and character; a warm, humane humour; ability to bring everything he touches to life; an understanding of the human heart surpassed by few of the greatest creative writers of the 19th century; and a mastery of language astonishing in its simplicity and profundity. His other narrative poems written at this time, *Count Nulin* (1828) and *Domik v Kolomne* (1830; *The Small House in Kolomna*), reveal a playful satiric vein, a blend of realism and irony with good-humoured sympathy for human foibles. *Tsygane* (publ. 1827; *The Gypsies*) and *Poltava* (publ. 1829) are masterpieces of two quite different types, the first a tragedy of frustrated passion and the second the apotheosis of a hero-king in the person of Peter the Great. During the same period Pushkin wrote his greatest lyrics and the often-quoted rhetorical *Prorok* (1826; *Prophet*). At the beginning of the 1830s he wrote his fairytales in verse, which included "The Golden Cockerel" (on which Rimski-Korsakov's opera is based), and the magnificent "King Saltan." In 1833 he wrote *Medny Vsadnik* (publ. 1837; *The Bronze Horseman*), a narrative poem in which Peter the Great personifies the elemental forces which sweep puny man, with his puny desires, out of their path. Pushkin never surpassed this poem, with its onomatopoeic undertow of horror. His poetic dramas (written in autumn, 1830) include *Boris Godunov* (publ. 1831), a full-length historical play in blank verse, and four "little tragedies."

The period's other major poet, Mikhail Lermontov (1814–41), sprang to fame in 1837 with his poem on the death of Pushkin, the last seven lines of which expressed the general feeling that Pushkin's death had been contrived by people close to the court, an accusation that resulted in his exile to the Caucasus. Lermontov's most Romantic poems, such as *Mtsyri* (1840) and the celebrated *Demon* (1839), deal with Caucasian themes. Dostoevski summed up Lermontov's significance:

> He wrote so many excellent poems for us. . . . He cursed and suffered. He revenged himself and forgave, he wrote and roared with laughter. He liked to whisper strange fairy tales to sleeping young girls, setting their virginal blood on fire. . . . He told the story of his life and his love adventures. . . . He made us feel depressed, vexed, sad and sorry, and we were filled with bitterness and spite. In the end he got tired of us. . . . We followed his fortunes for a long time, but at last he perished somewhere—aimlessly, stupidly and even ridiculously. . . .

Of minor poets of the Russian Golden Age, mention must be made of Evgeni Baratynski (1800–44), author of elegiac narrative poems; Konstantin Nikolaevich Batyushkov (1787–1855), a master of pagan and sensual poems; Prince Pëtr Andreevich Vyazemski (1792–1878), who wrote satires and epigrams; and Nikolai Mikhailovich Yazykov (1803–46), the "Bacchic" poet, whose early verse celebrates wine, women, and song. Among poets of the first half of the century must also be mentioned Fedor Ivanovich Tyutchev (1803–73), a profound and accomplished lyrical poet; and Nikolai Nekrasov (1821–78), whose narrative poems, songs, and realistic satires deal with what he described as "the sufferings of the common people."

2. Drama.—The only dramatic masterpiece of the period, *Gore ot uma* (1831; *Wit Works Woe*), is a comedy written in the French manner by Aleksandr Griboedov (1795–1829). Its hero is an intellectual rebel of great perception who, however, suffers from extraordinary lack of initiative. Its other characters are fully realized types of Moscow high society, most of whose names have passed into the Russian language.

3. Prose.—With Pushkin and Lermontov the Golden Age of poetry ended, and the great age of creative prose began. Pushkin turned increasingly to prose in the last years of his life. Lermontov's novel *Geroi nashevo vremeni* (1840; *A Hero of Our Time*) was immediately successful. Its hero, Pechorin, a man of great gifts which he dissipates in a life of debauchery, is one of the typical misfits of Lermontov's generation who, in his poem *Duma* (1839; "Meditation"), he had foretold would "pass away without leaving a trace behind, without tossing a fruitful idea to the coming generations, without the genius of work begun."

The first 19th-century novelist to achieve wide popularity was Mikhail Nikolaevich Zagoskin (1789–1852), whose *Yuri Miloslavski, or The Russians in 1612* (1829), published not long after the Napoleonic campaign of 1812, appealed to the public by its crude nationalistic spirit. The most popular Romantic novelist was Aleksandr Aleksandrovich Bestuzhev (pseudonym Marlinski; 1797–1837), who was exiled to Siberia and then to the Caucasus for his part in the Decembrist revolt, and who for a time was regarded as the foremost Russian novelist. "He left his mark on his generation," Turgenev wrote. "Heroes *à la Marlinski* were to be seen everywhere. It was about them that the word 'fatal' was invented." But the writer who was to leave his mark both on his own and on future generations was Nikolai Gogol (1809–52), who, arriving penniless in St. Petersburg, soon became one of the most discussed writers in Russia. When one considers Gogol's great influence on Russian literature and on the Russian revolutionary movement, it must be remembered that, a Ukrainian by birth, he saw the Russians as an outsider and with the irreverence of one brought up in a country where relations between big and small landowners were more patriarchal than in Russia itself. That was perhaps why, as Turgenev declared, he revealed the Russians to themselves; and why, as Dostoevski maintained, "Gogol's characters give rise in the Russian mind to the most turbulent ideas, which are impossible to solve now, if ever." Gogol became famous with five volumes of short stories (1831–35), but the revolutionary impact of his writings became evident in 1836 with the performance of his comedy *Revizor* (*The Government Inspector*). Its apparent subject was the officials of an obscure provincial town, but actually it presented a microcosm of the Russian state. What saved it from being banned was its laughter, which Gogol considered the only positive character in it. "He laughed all his life at himself and at us," Dostoevski was to write, "and we too laughed so long that in the end we began to cry with laughter." The protests aroused by the play forced Gogol to go to Italy, and he there finished the first part of his novel *Mërtvye dushi* (1842; *Dead Souls*). Gogol was a conservative, and an upholder of autocracy and serfdom, who never thought that his play and his novel were

(RIGHT) BY COURTESY OF THE STATE LITERARY MUSEUM, MOSCOW

(LEFT) NIKOLAI GOGOL, BY F. A. MOLLER, 1841; (RIGHT) THE LAST SCENE OF "REVIZOR" ("THE GOVERNMENT INSPECTOR"): LITHOGRAPH AFTER THE DESIGN OF AN UNKNOWN ARTIST, POSSIBLY GOGOL HIMSELF; IN THE STATE LITERARY MUSEUM, MOSCOW

destroying the things he stood for. When this dawned on him, he spent the rest of his life trying to undo the "harm" his writings had done.

One of Gogol's last stories, *Shinel* (1842; *The Overcoat*), led to the creation of a whole school of writers, the "natural" school, as the critic Vissarion Belinski (1811–48) called it. One of its most brilliant followers was Fëdor Dostoevski (1821–81). His literary career falls into two periods: 1844 to 1849, ending with his trial and imprisonment in Siberia; and 1860, when he returned to St. Petersburg, to 1881. The first is notable mainly for his short stories of the St. Petersburg slums and the life of the poor degraded civil servants. His first short novel, *Bednye lyudi* (1845; *Poor Folk*), brought him to Belinski's notice, but their friendship soon ended, and he joined the revolutionary circle of Mikhail Petrashevski, at whose Friday "at homes" he recited Derzhavin's paraphrase of Ps. 82, and Belinski's letter to Gogol, attacking Gogol's reactionary views as expressed in "Selected Passages from the Correspondence of My Friends" (1847), which the government had banned as seditious. This led to his exile. On his return, faced with the impending liberation of the serfs and the new relationship that would inevitably ensue between landowners and peasants, he decided to publish a magazine to help solve this problem. In *Vremya* ("Time"; 1861–63), suspended and renamed *Epokha* ("Epoch"; 1864–65), he took up an attitude midway between the Slavophils and conservatives, on the one hand, and, on the other, the westerners and revolutionaries grouped round *Sovremennik* ("The Contemporary"), the magazine owned by Nekrasov, but run by the so-called utilitarians, Nikolai Chernyshevski (1828–89) and Nikolai Aleksandrovich Dobrolyubov (1836–61), a brilliant young critic. Dostoevski's attempt to bridge the gulf between the mass of illiterate peasants and the comparatively few members of educated classes, by advocating that the latter should "return to the soil," ended in failure, but it was in *Epokha* that he published *Zapiski iz podpolya* (1864; *Letters from the Underworld*), his first psychological study of a self-centred intellectual egoist, into whose mouth he put his first violent attack on the doctrines of the "utilitarians." His four greatest novels, *Prestuplenie i nakazanie* (1866; *Crime and Punishment*), *Idiot* (1868–69; *The Idiot*), *Besy* (1871–72; *The Devils*, or *The Possessed*), and *Bratya Karamazovy* (1879–80; *The Brothers Karamazov*), show the same mixture of deep psychological study and violent attacks on hated ideas and institutions. It is his intuitive understanding of the human heart, and of the tragic aspects of life, together with his unsurpassed moments of illumination, that makes these novels immortal.

Although Ivan Turgenev (1818–83) lacked Dostoevski's moments of illumination, his stories and novels too transcended topical problems and laid bare the eternal. He won popularity with his *Zapiski okhotnika* (1852; *A Sportsman's Notebook*), in which serfs were shown to be not merely equal, but, indeed, superior, to their masters in intelligence, decency, and humanity. The book paved the way for the abolition of serfdom. With his first novels —*Rudin* (1855), *Dvoryanskoe gnezdo* (1859; *A Nobleman's Nest*), *Nakanyne* (1859; *On the Eve*)—he enhanced his reputation as a liberal-minded thinker and as one of the finest prose writers of the day. His greatest novel, *Otsy i deti* (1862; *Fathers and Sons*), set the left-wing writers of *Sovremennik* (who took Bazarov, its nihilist hero, for a caricature of themselves) against him, and he never regained popularity with the young progressives. *Dym* (1867; *Smoke*), in which he had bitter truths to say about all classes of Russian society, and *Nov* (1876; *Virgin Soil*), in which he analyzed the Russian revolutionary movement and forecast the rising power of the managerial class, deepened the enmity of the increasingly intransigent radicals. It was only on his last visit to Russia that he was again popularly acclaimed.

The third and greatest of the creative writers of the century, Count Leo Tolstoi (1828–1910), mostly stood aloof from the literary scene. His two great novels, *Voina i mir* (1863–69; *War and Peace*) and *Anna Karenina* (1873–76), raised him to a pinnacle above his contemporaries, and even his denial of his art, following his conversion to Christianity in 1876, failed to affect his supremacy. In *Kreitserova Sonata* (1889; *The Kreutzer*

Sonata), *Smert Ivana Ilyicha* (1886; *The Death of Ivan Ilyich*), *Voskresenie* (1899; *Resurrection*), and *Hajji Murad* (1901–04) his creative genius asserts itself over the philosophic and religious convictions that mar many of his last stories.

Tolstoi's distinguishing mark as a creative artist was his genius for analytical dissection of character; and a somewhat analogous gift is discernible in the novels of Ivan Goncharov (1812–91), who, in his greatest novel, *Oblomov* (1859), achieves his shattering effects by the accumulation of seemingly unimportant details. Aleksei Pisemski (1820–81) was another major novelist. He became popular with *Tysyacha dush* (1858; *A Thousand Souls*), but his popularity waned after his tendentious attacks on the radical movement in *Vzbalmuchennoe more* (1863; *Troubled Sea*). His tragedy, *Gorkaya sudbina* (1859; *A Hard Lot*), though popular, shows the dangers of too realistic a representation of life.

The most prolific professional playwright of the century, Aleksandr Ostrovski (1823–86), became famous with the banning of his first comedy *Bankrot* (1850; *The Bankrupt*), in which he exposed the low business morality of the Moscow merchants. Between 1847 and 1886 he wrote about 40 plays, including a cycle dealing with the life of the Moscow merchants. The most famous of these, the tragedy *Groza* (1860; *The Storm*), was interpreted by Dobrolyubov in his study of Ostrovski, *Tëmnoe tsarstvo* (1860; *The Realm of Darkness*), not so much as the personal tragedy of a young girl married to a weakling and in love with a man too weak to help her, but as a protest against the ignorance, brutality, and acquisitiveness of the Moscow merchant class. Ostrovski also wrote a series of historical plays; a verse fairytale *Snegurochka* (1873; "The Snow Maiden"); and a series of comedies of high life; e.g., *Na vsyakovo mudretsa dovolno prostoty* (1868; *Even a Wise Man Stumbles*), *Les* (1871; *The Forest*), and *Volki i ovtsy* (1875; *Wolves and Sheep*).

The great satirist of the century, Mikhail Saltykov (1826–89), was a pillar of the radical movement as editor of *Sovremennik* and *Otechestvennye Zapiski* ("Fatherland Annals"). Like the 18th-century satirists, he excelled as a fabulist. He wrote one of the century's most brilliant novels—*Gospoda Golovlevy* (1876; *The Golovlyov Family*). Its hero, Yudushka (Little Judas), surpasses even Gogol's most villainous characters in, as Saltykov said, "idleness, uselessness and drunkenness."

The short story was developed by Nikolai Leskov (1831–95), whose style is remarkable for richness of idiom. He became popular with his novel *Soboryane* (1872; *Cathedral Folk*), his famous picaresque story *Ocharovanny strannik* (1873; *The Enchanted Wanderer*), *Zapechatlenny angel* (1874; *The Sealed Angel*), *Levsha* (1882; *The Left-handed Craftsman*), and his anti-government satiric tale *Zayachi remiz* (1894; *The March Hare*). His starkly realistic story, *Ledi Makbet Mtsenskogo uezda* (1865; *Lady Macbeth of the Mtsensk District*), was used as the basis of an opera (1934) by Dmitri Shostakovich. Minor but original short-story writers of the last half of the century were Leonid Andreev (1871–1919), author of *Rasskaz o semi poveshennykh* (1909; *The Seven That Were Hanged*); Vsevolod Garshin (1855–88), author of *Chetyre dnya* (1877; "Four Days") and *Krasny tsvetok* (1883; "The Red Flower"); and Vladimir Korolenko (1853–1921), who was exiled to Siberia (1879–85), and whose stories with Siberian backgrounds made his reputation. It was Anton Chekhov (1860–1904), however, who became the acknowledged master of the short story, as well as a brilliant innovator in drama.

Chekhov was the first Russian writer of genius to adopt a neutral attitude to politics. Most of his short stories were written while he was a medical student and later when, as a young medical practitioner, he had to support his family in Moscow. But he never entirely gave up his practice until forced by ill health to live in Yalta. In his greatest short stories, *Step* (1888; *The Steppe*), *Skuchnaya istoria* (1889; *A Boring Story*), *Duel* (1891; *The Duel*), *Palata No. 6* (1892; *Ward 6*), *Tri Goda* (1892–95; *Three Years*), *Ionych* (1896), *Muzhiki* (1897; *The Peasants*), *Chelovek v futlyare* (1898; *A Man in a Case*), *Dushechka* (1898; *The Darling*), *V ovrage* (1900; *In the Ravine*), *Arkhierei* (1902; *The Bishop*), *Nevesta* (1903; *The Betrothed*); as well as in his

(LEFT) ANTON CHEKHOV AND MAKSIM GORKI, 1901; (CENTRE) FËDOR DOSTOEVSKI; (RIGHT) LEO TOLSTOI

four famous plays *Chaika* (1896; *The Seagull*), *Dyadya Vanya* (1897; *Uncle Vanya*), *Tri Sestry* (1900–01; *The Three Sisters*), and *Vishnevy Sad* (1903–04; *The Cherry Orchard*), his training can be seen both in the different types of medical men he introduces and in his attitude to his characters, an objectivity tempered by understanding. Maksim Gorki (1868–1936) was in this respect the opposite of Chekhov, for he was overflowing with pity and compassion, though only for the working classes. Self-educated, and bearing the brunt of the impecunious existence of the Russian worker and artisan, he early threw himself into revolutionary work. His romantic poem in prose, *Pesnya o burevestnike* (1901; *The Song of the Stormy Petrel*), with its refrain: "The Storm! The Storm is about to break!" became a powerful rallying cry of the revolutionary movement. In his first, and most popular, play, *Na dne* (1902; *Lower Depths*), Gorki introduced philosophizing down-and-outs onto the Russian stage. Apart from his early novels—*Foma Gordeev* (1899) and *Mat* (1906; *Mother*)—his most impressive work is to be found in his autobiographical trilogy: *Detstvo* (1913; *Childhood*), *V lyudyakh* (1915–16; *My Apprenticeship*), and *Moi universitety* (1923; *My Universities*).

C. EARLY 20TH CENTURY

1. Symbolism.—It was only at the end of the 19th century that the Symbolist movement brought about a revival of poetry. Among its predecessors were Semen Yakovlevich Nadson (1862–87), Aleksei Nikolaevich Apukhtin (1841–93), and the man who was perhaps more than anyone else responsible for the emergence of the Symbolist movement in Russia, the poet, philosopher, and mystic Vladimir Soloviev (1853–1900), who had apocalyptic dreams and believed in the coming of Antichrist. His poetry expressed the belief that the world is a system of symbols which express the existence of abstract metaphysical realities. Konstantin Balmont (1867–1943) and Valeri Bryusov (1873–1924) were the first considerable Russian Symbolist poets. Influenced by Baudelaire and Verlaine, Bryusov regarded the chief aim of Symbolism as being to present the world in a new light and thus to help to stimulate the imagination. He founded the Symbolist review *Vesy* ("Balance") in 1904. The greatest poet of the movement was Aleksandr Blok (1880–1921). In his first collection of poems, *Stikhi o prekrasnoi dame* (1904; "Verses About a Fair Lady"), he presents an idealized picture of a woman who is the reincarnation of Soloviev's vision of Sophia, Divine Wisdom. He later became disappointed with Soloviev's wild extrasensory fancies, and wrote a series of whimsical poems. In 1918 he wrote *Dvenadtsat* (*The Twelve*), an apocalyptic vision of the Revolution in which 12 Red Army men, personified as the apostles of the new world, are headed by Christ crowned with a wreath of white roses, all march-

ing invisibly through the raging storm. *Skify* (1918; "The Scythians") is a poetic expression of Russia's eternal love/hate for the West. Other important Symbolist poets were Vyacheslav Ivanovich Ivanov (1866–1949), Fëdor Sologub (1863–1927), and Andrei Bely (1880–1934). Ivanov was a Greek scholar who, in his *Kormchie zvezdy* (1903; "Guiding Stars"), proclaimed the identity of Christ and Dionysos. He preached ecstasy for ecstasy's sake, to be found (he claimed) in "symphonic" culture and nonacceptance of the world. Sologub published his first volume of poems in 1896. In 1905 he published his famous novel *Melki Bes* (*The Little Demon*). Bely was the outstanding theoretician of the Symbolist movement, which he conceived as a *Weltanschauung*. His *Simfonie* (1901–02; "Second, Dramatic"), were followed by First, Third, and Fourth "Symphonies." His novels include *Serebryani golub* (1910; "The Silver Dove"), a thriller written in Symbolist terms in which Gogol's influence is paramount, and *Peterburg* (1913), strongly influenced by Dostoevski's *Dvoinik* (*The Double*). Both are in rhythmic musical prose.

2. Futurism.—The most revolutionary poetic movement in Russia, Futurism, was founded in 1910 by Viktor Khlebnikov (1885–1922), an experimental poet, and author of a famous etymological poem consisting of a series of freshly coined derivatives of the Russian word *smekh* ("laughter"). The manifesto announcing the foundation of the movement, also signed by Vladimir Mayakovski (1893–1930), the future Communist "poet laureate," was issued in 1912 under the title *Poshchochina Obshchestvennomu vkusu* ("A Slap in the Face of Public Taste"). The Russian Futurists wanted to scrap the cultural tradition of the past and to wake everybody up by shock tactics. Mayakovski's Futurist poems include *Oblako v shtanakh* (1915; *A Cloud in Trousers*), *Chelovek* (1918; *Man*), and *Voina i mir* (1917; *War and Peace*). He was one of the established writers who rallied to the Soviet regime. In 1918 he wrote *Mystery Buffo*, a verse play prophesying the victory of the Revolution over capitalism. His later satirical plays, *Klop* (1929; *The Bedbug*) and *Banya* (1930; *The Bathhouse*), show signs of disillusionment with Soviet bureaucracy. In 1930 he

VLADIMIR MAYAKOVSKI SPEAKING ON "BOOK DAY"; RUSSIA, 1929

committed suicide, leaving a note in which he said: "The boat of love has crashed on the rocks of everyday life," a possible reference either to an unhappy love affair or to his political disillusionment.

Boris Pasternak (1890–1960) also began as a Futurist poet. By 1917 he had published *Poverkh Baryerov* (*Above the Barriers*) and had written most of the poems included in *Sestra moya zhizn* (1922; *My Sister Life*). (D. Mк.)

III. POST-REVOLUTIONARY LITERATURE

1. Early Years (1917–1928).—The years immediately after 1917 were a time of brilliant experimentation in the arts, in response to new forces released by the Revolution. Contending literary groups sprang up. The basic struggle was between those who clung to the literary heritage of the 19th century and those who demanded a new proletarian culture. The Futuristic poetry of Mayakovski and his followers symbolized a formal break with the past, whereas the "peasant-poet" Sergei Esenin (1895–1925) celebrated in lyrics of traditional form the joys of the countryside that would come with the Soviets. Fiction was dominated by stories of violence about the Civil War, told often in crude heroics, as in *Chapaev* (1923; Eng. trans. 1925), the account of a guerrilla leader by Dmitri Furmanov (1891–1926). More sophisticated were the realism and polished technique of the tales of Isaak Babel (1894–1941), about Budenny's Cossack army, in *Konarmia* (1926; *Red Cavalry*, 1929). The degeneration of life during the Civil War is narrated with startling naturalism by Boris Pilnyak (Boris Vogau; 1894–1937?), in *Goly God* (1922; *The Naked Year*, 1928). In contrast, *Razgrom* (1927, "The Rout"; translated as *The Nineteen*, 1929), by Aleksandr Fadeev (1901–56), is written with a realism that compels belief in its guerrilla hero. Konstantin Fedin (1892–), one of the self-styled Serapion Brothers—Trotski called them mere "fellow travelers of the Revolution"—was concerned with the struggle between old and new, especially the tragic problems of intellectuals in adapting themselves to the revolutionary present—the theme of his early novels *Goroda i gody* (1924; *Cities and Years*, 1962) and *Bratya* (1928; "The Brothers").

SOVFOTO

ISAAK BABEL

To a lesser extent these problems also concerned the fellow traveler Leonid Leonov (1899–), and there are echoes of them in his *Barsuki* (1924; *The Badgers*, 1947) and *Vor* (1927; *The Thief*, 1931). Many fellow travelers were influenced by the realism of Tolstoi, Dostoevski, and Chekhov. Yuri Olesha (1899–1960), in *Zavist* (1927; *Envy*, 1936), tackles the conflict of values created by the new society. In the absence of controls satire flourished—for example, in *Rastratchiki* (1926; *The Embezzlers*, 1929), by Valentin Kataev (1897–), an amusing tale of two crooks who exploit the foibles of Soviet life; and in sketches by Mikhail Zoschenko (1895–1958), which poke fun at Soviet stupidities. These authors were among the best in this period, which promised a glowing future for literature.

2. Five-Year-Plan Literature (1928–1934).—So bitter became the struggle between the fellow travelers, who demanded creative self-determination, and the left-wing writers, who argued for proletarian literature subservient to the Communist Party, that the Central Committee decreed, in its "Literary Manifesto" (1925), that the party would not endorse the work of any one group. However, when the first five-year plan was launched (1928), the party, determined that all cultural endeavours must support it, backed the Russian Association of Proletarian Writers (RAPP), an outgrowth of the Proletkult (a group formed soon

after the Revolution to foster specifically proletarian culture), and other left-wing groups. This enforced concentration on themes of construction and collectivization had been anticipated by Fedor Gladkov (1883–1958) in his popular novel *Tsement* (1925; *Cement*, 1929). Almost the only memorable work to emerge from this "social-command" fiction was *Podnyataya tselina* (1932–60; translated in two parts as *Virgin Soil Upturned*, 1935 [U.S. title, *Seeds of Tomorrow*], and *Harvest on the Don*, 1960), by Mikhail Sholokhov (*q.v.*; 1905–). The hero, Davidov, is believ-

SOVFOTO

MIKHAIL SHOLOKHOV, PHOTOGRAPHED IN HIS STUDY IN 1960

able because his failures in organizing a collective farm are described as convincingly as his successes. Kataev treats the theme of construction more lightly in *Vremya, vpered!* (1932; *Time, Forward!* 1933), but Pilnyak's *Volga vpadaet v Kaspiskoe more* (1930; *The Volga Falls to the Caspian Sea*, 1931) introduces a critical note on the inhuman strains involved in these vast building projects. In Leonov's *Sot* (1930; Eng. trans. *Sot*, 1931, and *Soviet River*, 1932) and *Skutarevski* (1932; Eng. trans. 1936), however, the frenzy of industrialization is sublimated in psychologically probing characters confronted with real choices in submitting to social commands. Though there was much five-year-plan poetry and drama, not even the best rose above effective propaganda.

3. Socialist Realism (1934–1941).—In 1932 a decree of the Central Committee abolished RAPP. By this time the party, under Stalin, felt able to control literature more effectively by another device. The decree suggested that all literary groups dissolve and form a single union with a dominant party faction therein. At the First All-Union Congress of Soviet Writers (1934), a national Union of Soviet Writers was organized, and the new doctrine of "socialist realism" propounded to guide creative efforts. Literature became identified with politics and the party's ideological objectives. Though the union's powers enabled it to whip recalcitrant members back into the happiness of conformity, some tolerance was permitted during this period of economic successes and "popular-front" agitation. The ablest writers took advantage of this. Melekhov, hero of Sholokhov's great epic novel, *Tikhii Don* (1928–40; translations of volumes i and ii, *And Quiet Flows the Don*, 1934; continued in *The Don Flows Home to the Sea*, 1940), remains at the end a tragic, unreconstructed "White" Cossack, and the spirit of the work is out of step with socialist realism. Kurilov, in Leonov's complicated *Doroga na okean* (1935; *Road to the Ocean*, 1944), is a humanized Communist whose dedication to the cause is saddened by memory of joyless sacrifices. Even Fedin's interesting *Pokhishchenie Evropy* (1934–35; "The Rape of Europe"), in which he attempts to identify himself with the party's aspirations, reveals distaste for its extravagantly propagandized claims. But the trilogy *Khozhdenie po mukam* (1920–41; "The Way Through Hell"; translated as *Road to Calvary*, 1946), by A. N. Tolstoi (1883–1945)—a picture

SOVFOTO

(LEFT) KONSTANTIN FEDIN; (RIGHT) LEONID LEONOV; BOTH PHOTOGRAPHED IN MOSCOW, 1962

of intellectuals during the Revolution and Civil War—betrays that the author's values have been transformed by political expediency during the period of its composition. It remained for Nikolai Ostrovski (1904–36), in *Kak zakalyalas stal* (1932–34; *How Steel Was Tempered,* 1952), to create in literature the "new Soviet man," an idealized Communist paragon. Most writers conformed to the spirit of Ostrovski's "classic"—novelists such as Kataev, Ilya Ehrenburg (1891–1967), and Fadeev; poets such as N. N. Aseev (1889–1963), N. S. Tikhonov (1896–   ), and A. T. Tvardovski (1910–   ); and dramatists such as A. N. Afinogenov (1904–41), V. M. Kirshon (1902–37), and Nikolai Pogodin (N. F. Stukalov; 1900–64). The party required "positive heroes" and optimistic themes that romanticized the heroic efforts to achieve Communism. Literary critics, who earlier had developed such brilliant schools as Formalism, now imitated one another in insistence on the party's version of socialist realism. Some authors were "liquidated" in Stalinist purges, and others, among them Anna Akhmatova (*q.v.;* 1889–1966), a major poet of exquisite skill, Pasternak (*q.v.;* 1890–1960), perhaps the most celebrated Soviet poet, Fedin, Leonov, and Sholokhov, fell virtually silent. Some escaped into historical fiction, although its vogue had begun earlier. Often these historical novels are based on careful research, but they usually stress a Marxian interpretation of history. Two of the best were *Tsushima* (1932–35; Eng. trans. 1936), by Aleksei Novikov-Priboi (1877–1944), and A. N. Tolstoi's *Pyotr I* (1929–45; *Peter I,* 1959).

SOVFOTO

ALEKSEI TOLSTOI

4. War Literature (1941–1945).—During World War II writers shared the fervent national patriotism; many were assigned to the front as correspondents. The party relaxed its controls and authors felt free to concentrate on the human fundamentals and universal emotions evoked by the tragedies of war. There was little time for lengthy fiction—among the few novels the most popular were a tale of German invaders in the Kuban, *Nepokorennye ili Semya Tarasa* (1943; *The Taras Family,* 1944), by Boris Gorbatov (1908–54); a story of the siege of Stalingrad, *Dni i nochi* (1944; *Days and Nights,* 1945), by Konstantin Simonov (1915–   ); Leonov's *Vziatie Velikoshumska* (1944, "The Taking of Velikoshumsk," trans. as *Chariot of Wrath,* 1946); and Fadeev's *Molodaia gvardia* (1945; *The Young Guard,* 1959), an account of the underground activities of members of the Young Communist League under German occupation. However, a stream of short stories and sketches on war themes appeared, as did a number of war plays. The best of the plays were Leonov's *Nashestvie* (1942; *Invasion,* 1945) and *Lyonushka* (1943), but in popularity these gave way to the sensational exposure of Red Army weaknesses in *Front* (1942; *The Front,* 1943), by Aleksandr Korneichuk (1910–   ), and Simonov's *Russkie lyudi* (1942; *The Russians,* 1944). It was in poetry that the theme of war found its most genuine expression. The finest lyrics were written by Pasternak, Olga Bergolts (1910–   ), Margarita Aliger (1915–   ), and Simonov. Perhaps the best long poems were Tvardovski's *Vasili Terkin* (1941–45), Nikolai Tikhonov's *Kirov s nami* (1941), about the siege of Leningrad, and *Pulkovo Meridian* (1942), by Vera Inber (1890–   ).

5. Zhdanovism (1945–1953).—The writers' hope that the party would continue and perhaps enlarge the creative freedom enjoyed during the war was squelched by the Central Committee's decree on literature (Aug. 14, 1946). The Politburo's literary "expert," A. A. Zhdanov, explained that all art must be politically inspired and understood. Though socialist realism would remain

the writer's credo, its principal tenet must be *partiinost* ("party spirit"). The party publicly identified itself as never before with domination of all artistic and intellectual expression. The word "Zhdanovism"—as the new policy was called—describes also this most sterile period of Soviet literature. The party expected writers to concentrate on postwar reconstruction, rehabilitation of returning soldiers, and hostility to Western Europe and the United States. Some authors took refuge in war themes, on which many novels are based, notably *Povest o nastoyashchem cheloveke* (1947; *A Story About a Real Man,* 1949), by Boris Polevoi (Boris N. Kampov; 1908–   ); Ilya Ehrenburg's *Burya* (1948; *The Storm,* 1949); Kataev's *Za vlast sovetov* (1949; "For the Power of the Soviets"); and *Belaia bereza* (1948; *The White Birch,* 1949), by Mikhail Bubonnov. Others were concerned with wartime industrial activities—*e.g.,* Vera Panova's *Kruzhilikha* (1947; *The Factory,* 1949) and Vasili Azhaev's *Daleko ot Moskvy* (1948; "Far from Moscow"). But the official demand for literature dealing with peaceful reconstruction was complied with in such novels as Pyotr Pavlenko's *Schastye* (1947; *Happiness,* 1950) and Semen Babaevski's *Kavaler zolotoi zvezdy* (1947; "Cavalier of the Golden Star"). Towering over this fiction is Fedin's trilogy, perhaps the best postwar novel. The first two parts, *Pervye radosti* (1945–46; *Early Joys,* 1948) and *Neobyknovennoe leto* (1948; *No Ordinary Summer,* 1950), which are superior to the third part, *Koster* (1962; "The Bonfire"), tell the story of the young revolutionary Kirill Izvekov during the years 1910–19. But with a few exceptions, the postwar "grey stream of colourless, mediocre literature," as Sholokov called it, has the uniformity of the dead in a cemetery.

6. The Thaw (1953 and After).—Even before Stalin's death in March 1953, articles critical of literature's stagnation had appeared, and after it they increased in number and sharpness. This protest was quickly reflected in creative writing. Leonid Zorin's play, *Gosti* (1954; "The Guests"), challenged the party's claim that the class structure had vanished. Though Leonov's *Russkii les* (1953; "Russian Forest") treats a contemporary theme in a propagandist manner, the finest things in it belong to the sections dealing with pre-Revolutionary Russia. Poets such as Vera Inber and Olga Bergolts attacked the "steam-shovel" school of verse and the writing of lyrical poems devoid of personal emotion. Pasternak, who had published no original verse since the war, brought out, in the April 1954 issue of the periodical *Znamya,* a group of ten deeply subjective poems which later appeared in the novel *Doktor Zhivago* (1957). But the work that gave a name and focus to the dissent was Ehrenburg's *Ottepel* (1954; *The Thaw,* 1955), in which he highlighted the tragedy of the artist under Stalinism. Worried party leaders called a halt, and, at the Second Writers' Congress (December 1954), offending authors and critics were reprimanded, and it was made clear that ideological orthodoxy was preferred to aesthetic merit. However, Khrushchev's "secret" speech at the 20th Party Congress (1956), in

JERRY COOKE—"LIFE," © 1953, TIME INC.

BORIS PASTERNAK, PHOTOGRAPHED IN RUSSIA IN 1953

which he exposed Stalin's crimes and the "cult of personality," revived the protest against literary controls. During 1956 and part of 1957 some of the best writing, especially by younger authors, represented an indictment not only of the abuses of Stalinism but of the abuses and hypocrisy in Soviet life. Vladimir Dudintsev's *Ne khlebom edinym* (1956; *Not by Bread Alone,* 1957), whose hero fights a lonely battle against dishonest party officials, was one of many revelatory works. This bold effort reached its height in the second volume of the anthology *Literaturnaia Moskva* (1956), in which poetry, fiction, and criticism attacked the ugly aspects of Soviet existence and questioned the omniscience

(LEFT) BLACK STAR, (RIGHT) MARC RIBOUD FROM MAGNUM

(LEFT) ILYA EHRENBURG; (RIGHT) EVGENI YEVTUSHENKO; BOTH PHOTO-GRAPHED IN 1963

of the party. What seemed like an organized attack on authority took on added significance in light of the 1956 Hungarian revolt. The party swung into action. Administrative bodies of the Writers' Union demanded recantations from authors, who were also excoriated in the party-controlled press. These efforts culminated in speeches by Khrushchev in the summer of 1957, in which he emphasized the primacy of party guidance in the arts. Publication of Pasternak's *Doktor Zhivago* in Italy (1957), and elsewhere in Western Europe in 1958, provoked another outburst of denunciation. Though Khrushchev made mollifying gestures at the Third Congress of the Union of Soviet Writers (May 1959), he again reminded them that they must "continue to be active helpers of the party and government in the task of communist education of workers. . . ." After this, writers continued to press, less overtly, for greater freedom of expression. With the rise of the so-called angry young men, of whom the much-publicized poet Evgeni Aleksandrovich Yevtushenko (1933–) is only one, a "liberal" faction began to demand that the pace of "de-Stalinization," of telling the whole truth about Russia, be speeded up.

This faction was opposed by the "conservatives," and the struggle came to a head at the Fourth Plenary Session of the Board of the Writers' Union, held in March 1963, in which leaders among the "liberal" group were forced to recant. After the fall of Khrushchev in October 1964, published statements indicated that the party under its new leadership would continued to insist on the identification of literature with party ideology, although within a framework in which more freedom would be allowed in matters of form and content. In this spirit the new liberal generation strove to achieve an individualism in literary expression alien to socialist realism. The most talented of the prose writers among them were Aleksandr Solzhenitsyn, Viktor Nekrasov, Yuri Kazakov, Vasili Aksenov, Yuri Nagibin, and Vladimir Tendryakov; the most able of the poets were Evgeni Yevtushenko, Andrei Voznesensky, Evgeni Vinokurov, and Bella Akhmadulina. But this degree of nonconformity to party dictation in literature received a setback in February 1966 when two minor writers, Andrei Sinyavski and Yuli Daniel, were sent to prison for publishing abroad (under the pseudonyms Abram Tertz and Nikolai Arzhak) works allegedly slandering the Soviet Union.

See also references under "Russian Literature" in the Index.

(E. J. Si.)

BIBLIOGRAPHY.—*General Works:* K. Waliszewski, *A History of Russian Literature* (1900); M. Baring, *Landmarks in Russian Literature* (1910) and *An Outline of Russian Literature* (1914); P. A. Kropotkin, *Russian Literature* (1905; revised as *Ideals and Realities in Russian Literature,* 1915); J. Lavrin, *Russian Literature* (1927); T. G. Masaryk, *Rusko a Evropa* (1913; trans. as *The Spirit of Russia: Studies in History, Literature and Philosophy,* 1919, reprinted with additions, 1955); P. N. Miliukov, *Outlines of Russian Culture,* ed. by M. Karpovich (1942); D. S. Mirsky, *A History of Russian Literature from the Earliest Times to the Death of Dostoevsky (1881)* (1927; new ed. 1963); H. Muchnic, *An Introduction to Russian Literature* (1947); M. Slonim, *The Epic of Russian Literature from Its Origins through Tolstoy*

(1950); *Istoria Russkoi Literatury,* ed. by A. S. Orlov and V. P. Adrianova-Perets, for the U.S.S.R. Academy of Sciences, 10 vol. (1941–48); *Istoria Russkoi Literatury v trekh tomakh* (general editor D. D. Blagoi), 3 vol. (1958).

General Anthologies and Collections in English Translation: L. Wiener (ed.), *Anthology of Russian Literature from the Earliest Period to the Present Time,* 2 vol. (1902–03); B. G. Guerney (ed.), *A Treasury of Russian Literature* (1943); C. M. Bowra (ed.), *A Book of Russian Verse* (1943), and *A Second Book of Russian Verse* (1948); A. Yarmolinsky (ed.), *A Treasury of Russian Verse* (1949); G. R. Noyes (ed.), *Masterpieces of the Russian Drama* (1933); S. Graham (ed.), *Great Russian Short Stories* (1929); J. Cournos (ed.), *A Treasury of Russian Life and Humor* (1943).   (N. K. G.; D. Mк.)

Old Russian Period: Anthologies: G. P. Fedotov (ed.), *A Treasury of Russian Spirituality* (1948); A. D. Stender-Petersen and S. Congrat-Butlar (eds.), *Anthology of Old Russian Literature* (1955); *Khudozhestvennaya proza Kievskoi Rusi,* ed. for the U.S.S.R. Academy of Sciences (1957).

Histories and Studies: Istoria Russkoi Literatury, vol. i and vol. ii (pt. 1 and 2) (1941–48); *Istoria Russkoi Literatury v trekh tomakh,* vol. i (1958); N. K. Gudzii, *History of Early Russian Literature* (Eng. trans. of 2nd Russian ed., 1949); I. F. Hapgood, *The Epic Songs of Russia* (1916); N. K. Chadwick, *Russian Heroic Poetry* (1932); G. P. Fedotov, *The Russian Religious Mind: Kievan Christianity* (1946); R. Jakobson and E. J. Simmons, *Russian Epic Studies* (1949); S. H. Cross, *The Russian Primary Chronicle* (1930), trans. with introduction and notes; J. Besharov, *Imagery of the Igor Tale in the Light of Byzantino-Slavic Poetic Theory* (1956); D. Ward, "On Translating the *Slovo o Polku Igoreve,*" in *The Slavonic and East European Review,* vol. xxxvi, no. 87 (June 1958).   (N. K. G.)

Modern Pre-Revolutionary Literature: Anthologies: Russkie povesti XV–XVI vekov (1958), and *Russkie povesti XIX veka,* 2 vol. (1952), both ed. for the U.S.S.R. Academy of Sciences; J. Lavrin (ed.), *A First Series of Representative Russian Stories; Pushkin to Gorky* (1946); E. Fen (ed.), *Modern Russian Stories* (1943); D. Magarshack (ed.), *The Storm and Other Russian Plays* (1960).

Histories and Studies: N. Jarintzov, *Russian Poets and Poems* (1917); M. J. Olgin, *A Guide to Russian Literature (1820–1917)* (1920); E. J. Simmons, *An Outline of Modern Russian Literature (1880–1940)* (1943); R. Hare, *Russian Literature from Pushkin to the Present Day* (1947), and *Maxim Gorky—Romantic Realist and Conservative Revolutionary* (1962); D. D. Blagoi, *Istoria russkoi literatury xviii veka* (1951); M. Slonim, *From Chekhov to the Revolution: Russian Literature 1900–17* (1963); A. Volkov, *Ocherki russkoi literatury kontsa XIX i nachala XX vekov* (1952); I. Spector, *The Golden Age of Russian Literature* (1943); W. L. Phelps, *Essays on Russian Novelists* (1911); E. M. de Vogüé, *The Russian Novel* (1913); S. M. Persky, *Contemporary Russian Novelists* (1913); J. Lavrin, *An Introduction to the Russian Novel* (1942); M. Gus, *Idei i obrazy F. M. Dostoevskogo* (1962); D. Magarshack, *Chekhov the Dramatist* (1952), and *Turgenev's Literary Reminiscences* (1959); M. Slonim, *Russian Theater* (1963); *Simvolizm: Stat'i i issledovania (Literanosledstovo)* (1937).

(D. Mк.)

Post-Revolutionary Literature: Anthologies: G. Reavey and M. Slonim (eds.), *Soviet Literature: an Anthology* (1933); E. Lyons (ed.), *Six Soviet Plays* (1934); I. Montagu and H. Marshall (eds.), *Soviet Short Stories* (1942); J. Kunitz (ed.), *Russian Literature Since the Revolution* (1948); B. G. Guerney (ed.), *An Anthology of Russian Literature Since the Revolution* (1952); *The Year of Protest, 1956: an Anthology of Soviet Literary Materials,* trans. and ed. by H. McLean and W. N. Vickery (1961); *Russkaya Literatura XX veka* (1962); Patricia Blake and Max Hayward, *Dissonant Voices in Soviet Literature* (1964); P. Blake and M. Hayward (eds.), *Half-way to the Moon: New Writing from Russia* (1964).

Histories: D. S. Mirsky, *Contemporary Russian Literature* (1925); G. Struve, *Soviet Russian Literature, 1917–50,* with bibliography of works in Eng. trans. to 1950 (1951); M. Slonim, *Modern Russian Literature* (1953); V. Zavalishin, *Early Soviet Writers* (1958); V. Alexandrova, *A History of Soviet Literature, 1917–64* (1964); Edward J. Brown, *Russian Literature Since the Revolution* (1963); Marc Slonim, *Soviet Russian Literature* (1964).

Criticism: L. Trotsky, *Literature and Revolution* (1925); G. Z. Patrick, *Popular Poetry in Soviet Russia* (1929); M. Eastman, *Artists in Uniform* (1934); *Problems of Soviet Literature, Reports and Speeches of the First Writers' Congress* (1934); A. Kaun, *Soviet Poets and Poetry* (1943); G. Reavey, *Soviet Literature Today* (1947); H. Borland, *Soviet Literary Theory and Practice During the First Five-Year Plan* (1950); E. J. Simmons (ed.), *Through the Glass of Soviet Literature* (1953); E. J. Brown, *The Proletarian Episode in Russian Literature, 1928–32* (1953); V. Erlich, *Russian Formalism* (1955); R. W. Mathewson, Jr., *The Positive Hero in Russian Literature* (1958); E. J. Simmons, *Russian Fiction and Soviet Ideology: Introduction to Fedin, Leonov, and Sholokhov* (1958); G. Gibian, *Interval of Freedom: Soviet Literature During the Thaw, 1954–57* (1960); H. Muchnic, *From Gorky to Pasternak* (1961); Harold Swayze, *Political Control of Literature in the USSR* (1962); Walter N. Vickery, *The Cult of Optimism: Political and Ideological Problems of Recent Soviet Literature* (1963); Max Hayward and Leopold Labedz (eds.), *Literature and Revolution in Soviet Russia, 1917–1962* (1963).   (E. J. Si.)

RUSSIAN REVOLUTION, the historical events whereby, between 1917 and 1921, control of the major part of the former Russian Empire was taken over by a Soviet Communist dictatorship. The article RUSSIAN HISTORY ends with an account of the collapse of the tsarist or imperial regime of the Romanovs, during World War I, in the March Revolution of 1917—known to Russian writers as the February Revolution because the Russian calendar observed the Old Style till Feb. 14, 1918. The present article describes how the Provisional Government, set up by the March Revolution, was overthrown eight months later in the November Revolution—or Great October Socialist Revolution—of the Bolsheviks or Communists; and how the power of the latter was consolidated, despite internal resistance and foreign intervention, in the following years.

The article is composed as follows:

1. March 1917.—In Petrograd, the Russian capital, there were in March 1917 two separate authorities, both claiming to speak for the people, but neither of them representing more than a section of it: the Provisional Government and the Soviet (council) of Workers' Deputies. The former had been chosen on March 15 (N.S.) by the members of a duma (*q.v.*) elected four years earlier on a restricted franchise. Its leaders reflected the point of view of the more conservative and patriotically minded members of the professional classes, though in A. F. Kerenski (*q.v.*), a lawyer of Trudovik (Labour) opinions, they had a representative of moderate socialism. The soviet represented primarily the working class of the capital, but could in a wider sense speak for the industrial workers of all Russia; and, as its ranks were swollen by the arrival of socialists released from prison or returned from exile, it became a sort of parliament of Russian socialism, from the Socialist-Revolutionaries (S.R.) to the Bolsheviks.

A fundamental question facing the new regime was that of legitimacy. The old legitimacy of the monarchy had been destroyed. It could be replaced only by the legitimacy of the will of the whole people of Russia, but this could be ascertained only by an elected Constituent Assembly. To hold such an election while Russia was at war with Germany, Austria-Hungary, and Turkey (*see* WORLD WAR I) seemed hardly possible, both because it would divert energies from the war effort (and the first Provisional Government was eager to win the war) and because so many citizens were away in the army. The men of the Provisional Government were high-minded democrats who would be content with nothing less than a completely free and comprehensive election and were willing to wait for the end of the war, if need be, to have one. Their perfectionism was disastrous. An election held forthwith would have caused less chaos than occurred later without it, and would have created an imperfect but substantial democratic legitimacy. As things were, there was no legitimacy. The Provisional Govern-

ment was left in the air, and found itself acting as if it were responsible to the Petrograd Soviet.

The most important problem was whether to continue the war or, if not, how to get out of the war. The foreign minister, P. N. Milyukov (*q.v.*), a convinced patriot, believed that the war was just, that it was being fought to liberate the peoples oppressed by Austria-Hungary and by Turkey, and that Russia should be rewarded by acquiring Constantinople, the Straits, and Turkish Armenia. The socialists, however, were not interested in these aims and believed that the war should be ended "without annexations and without indemnities." But there was no evidence that the German government would grant a just peace simply because the revolutionary Russians recited peaceful slogans. Until the Germans were willing to make peace the Russian fatherland had to be defended. And in any case the new Russian leaders admitted that they could not make peace without their allies' consent.

It has often been argued by historians of a later epoch that the Western Allies were foolish not to have agreed to release Russia from its obligations. But at the time it was inconceivable that the Western governments should do so. The release of the German divisions held on the Russian front might have made it possible for Gen. Erich Ludendorff finally to crush the West, and to the Western Allies defeat by Germany understandably appeared the worst disaster that could befall them.

It followed that the war must continue. And if it were accepted that a Constituent Assembly could not be elected while the war went on, it followed that various problems which could be decided only by such an assembly must remain for the time being unsolved. First among these was the redistribution of the landed estates among the peasants. Second was the claim of the non-Russian subjects of the empire for self-government (in the case of Poles and Finns perhaps for complete independence). Third were various demands which might be put forward on behalf of the industrial workers, such as "workers' control" in the factories, or even nationalization of some enterprises or some branches of industry. But as long as these problems remained unsolved, the discontent of land-hungry peasants, non-Russian nationalists, and miserably paid workers grew. Meanwhile the Provisional Government had to rely on the old imperial bureaucracy, which was ever more demoralized. The lack of legitimacy made it difficult either to give or to carry out orders. For the two years past, Russia had lacked firm leadership at the top, but now the machinery of government was breaking down on lower levels as well. It was a perfect opportunity for an uninhibited revolutionary demagogue.

2. Lenin's Arrival in Petrograd.—A revolutionary of genius appeared when on April 16 (new style; 3, old style), 1917, V. I. Lenin (*q.v.*) arrived in Petrograd from Switzerland. With a group of 200 Russian émigrés, including L. Martov and other Mensheviks, this leader of the Bolsheviks had journeyed to Russia across Germany, Sweden, and Finland. The German general staff, which reckoned that Lenin's defeatist activities in Russia would be to the Central Powers' advantage, authorized this passage. Lenin, of course, was no agent of the Germans, but there is evidence that in the following months his party received financial aid from the German authorities. This it badly needed in order to organize its propaganda.

Lenin introduced a new note into the Petrograd Soviet. He at once urged a policy of complete opposition to the Provisional Government. He said the party should demand immediate peace and immediate distribution of land to the peasants and should declare that it had no confidence in the Provisional Government. Lenin announced the slogan "All power to the soviets."

3. Marxist Doctrines of Revolution.—All Russian Marxist Socialists—Bolsheviks and Mensheviks alike—had long maintained that the next revolution in Russia would be a "bourgeois revolution," which would do for Russia what the Revolution of 1789 had done for France, and would replace the semi-autocratic tsarist regime by a "bourgeois" democratic republic. Normally it would be expected that a bourgeois revolution would be carried out by the bourgeoisie. But Lenin held that the experience of 1905 had shown that the Russian bourgeoisie was incapable of carrying out any revolution: it was too weak, too cowardly, too reactionary, and it lacked awareness of its "historical function." The "bourgeois" revolution must therefore be carried out by the working class, or rather by the "vanguard" of the working class, "its own" political party, that is, the Bolshevik Party led by Lenin. The party was to lead the workers, and the workers were to lead the peasant masses into action and to form a "revolutionary democratic dictatorship of the proletariat and peasantry."

Lenin had first expounded these views in a pamphlet, *Two Tactics for Social-Democracy in a Democratic Revolution,* in 1905. They had been rejected by the Mensheviks, who stuck to the more orthodox opinion that bourgeois revolutions were to be carried out by the bourgeoisie. Neither Lenin nor the Mensheviks expected a socialist revolution immediately. Socialist revolution, according to Marxist doctrine, was a much more advanced stage, when the proletariat would overthrow the bourgeois regime. Before this could happen, the proletariat must grow stronger, more numerous, more skilled, and politically more conscious, and the class struggle must develop freely within the framework of a democratic republic. In this connection Lenin paid great attention to the role of the poor peasants. He believed that only when the great landed estates had been divided up among the peasants, and the peasants had been freed from the last remnants of subordination to the landed nobility, would it be possible for a rural class struggle freely to develop, as rural bourgeoisie and rural proletariat became more sharply differentiated. The rural proletariat would be the ally of the urban proletariat when the time came for socialist revolution. How long would be the interval between the bourgeois and socialist revolutions, neither Lenin nor the Mensheviks could predict.

There was, however, another Russian Marxist who had a somewhat different view. L. D. Trotski (*q.v.*) agreed with Lenin that the bourgeois revolution had to be made by the party of the proletariat, but he did not agree with Lenin that once the workers had made a revolution, they could impose on themselves a self-denying ordinance and deliberately maintain things at the stage of a bourgeois republic, ruled in the interests and according to the ideas of the bourgeoisie. They would have to go on to set up a socialist regime. But in so backward an agrarian society as Russia, socialism was not possible unless socialist revolutions at once took place in at least one major industrial country in Europe. The best hope for the Russian revolution, as Trotski saw it, was that the action of the Russian workers would provide the spark to set off the European revolutionary conflagration.

Lenin, too, even before 1917, had recognized the importance of European revolutions, but he believed that, if necessary, a worker-peasant dictatorship led by his party could keep Russia at the stage of a bourgeois republic. He now regarded the March Revolution as a bourgeois-democratic one, which had gone beyond the framework of a bourgeois revolution and had led to the establishment of soviets as organs of the revolutionary and democratic dictatorship of the proletariat and peasantry. The Provisional Government, he argued, was the organ of the bourgeoisie and the bourgeois revolution, while the Petrograd Soviet and the soviets which soon sprang up in other cities were the organs of the proletariat and of the socialist revolution. The dual power would not last: either the bourgeois revolution would suppress the socialist, or the socialist revolution would triumph over the bourgeois. This theoretical change of opinion was remarkable, considering that the conditions previously thought necessary for the transition from the bourgeois to the socialist revolution had not yet been fulfilled: the working class was not much stronger or more numerous than in 1905, and the redistribution of land which Lenin had believed necessary for the development of the peasants' class struggle had not yet gone very far, as the effects of the tsarist statesman P. A. Stolypin's land policy were only beginning to be felt. On the other hand, it might be argued that after three years of war the discontent of the European working classes was such that the prospects of socialist revolution in Europe had increased in comparison with 1905.

4. Lenin and the Soviets.—Theoretical analysis was only partly responsible for Lenin's decisions. Lenin was a man of action and a natural leader, at his best in a time of crisis and chaos.

He wanted power, and he now saw a way to win it. In a bourgeois republic, with a parliamentary system of government, his prospects would not be good. Parliamentary governments would be formed by agreements between party leaders, whose ideas were already formed, and the parties' representatives in the parliament would form disciplined groups. In such conditions, the Bolsheviks would have to bargain and compromise with the other parties if they wished to take part in government coalitions, or they would be driven into ineffective opposition. They could not hope to win an absolute majority in a Russian parliament.

The soviets, on the other hand, were a very different forum. Their members were not trained politicians, but the masses from the factories and—with the addition of "soldiers' deputies" to the "workers' deputies"—from the armed forces. Through the soviets, for the first time, the masses were being brought into political life—the raw material to be molded by an audacious leader. In the soviets, votes were taken not according to fixed party allegiances but according to the momentary passions of the workers and soldiers. Socialist-Revolutionaries, Mensheviks, and Bolsheviks were represented, but they could not count on any automatic discipline. Oratory and propaganda could sway them to and fro. Here was Lenin's opportunity. The greater the authority given to the soviets, the better his chances of seizing power. Hence his slogan "All power to the soviets."

In the soviets the Bolsheviks were at first a small minority. But once Lenin had converted his party to his views (which needed some days of hard arguing), the Bolsheviks in the soviets adopted unrestrainedly demagogic slogans. They stood, they said, for peace at once, land reform at once, workers' control of the factories at once, self-determination for the non-Russian peoples at once. If the Provisional Government's spokesmen declared that these things could not be done at once and that they were the task of the future Constituent Assembly, then this, Lenin claimed, was proof that the Provisional Government intended to prevent these things from ever being done, proof that its leaders were enemies of the Russian workers and peasants and were mere agents of French and British capitalists and imperialists.

5. The April–May Crisis.—The first crisis of the Provisional Government came at the end of April 1917, on the war issue. Milyukov, the foreign minister, not only reassured the Western Allies that Russia would continue the war on their side, but, in a press interview on April 5 (N.S.), declared that Russia's war aims included annexation of the Ukrainian provinces of Austria-Hungary, and of Constantinople and the Straits. On April 9 the Petrograd Soviet issued a declaration that Russia sought no gains from the war and was ready to conclude peace on the basis of "no annexations, no indemnities." The members of the government were not in fact agreed on these problems. An attempt was made to bring about a compromise between Milyukov and the soviet by a

CULVER PICTURES, INC.

SOLDIERS DISPLAYING THE RED FLAG IN 1917

(Above) Members of a battalion of women guards at the Winter Palace, Petrograd, 1917. (Left) General Kornilov urging Russian soldiers to fight against Germany, during the summer of 1917. (Below) Bolsheviks canvassing for the Constituent Assembly, 1917

means of raising the morale and restoring the determination of their men. Many of the commissars considered it their patriotic duty to defend the revolutionary fatherland and believed that, now that Russia belonged to all its sons instead of to the tsar, they would fight with renewed vigour.

7. Kerenski and the Summer Offensive.—Kerenski, who became minister of war in the coalition of May 18, 1917, believed in fighting on for the new Russia. He hoped to make the soldiers' committees an instrument for increasing the efficiency of the Russian Army, and did his best to strengthen their efforts by speeches of fiery eloquence during his visits to the front. But the parties of the extreme left were resolved that the committees should be instruments of defeatism. Bolshevik propaganda at the front, by word of mouth and by the newspapers which they distributed in profusion, was especially active. Kerenski, however, believed the Army capable of a new offensive, for which the Western Allies were clamouring. The offensive opened on July 1 in Galicia. After small initial successes, it came to a standstill, and two weeks later the enemy counteroffensive drove the Russians back in confusion. Many units simply refused to fight.

8. The July Demonstrations.—In June 1917 the first All-Russian Congress of Soviets was held in Petrograd, with soldiers' as well as workers' deputies present. Only about one-eighth of those attending declared themselves for the Bolsheviks. But at a mass demonstration held by the moderate leaders of the Petrograd Soviet on July 1 as a sign of the unity of the "revolutionary democracy," the Bolsheviks turned out in force with banners calling for an end to the war and a cessation of offensive movements on the front. Two weeks later, on July 16–17, vast demonstrations took place in the capital, amounting to an insurrection against the government. The crowds included workers, soldiers, and a contingent of sailors from the naval base of Kronstadt (Kronshtadt). The Bolsheviks had not planned this insurrection, but assumed leadership of it once it had started. For two days the demonstrators were in control of the capital. Chernov narrowly escaped being lynched. But the crowd made no determined effort to occupy government buildings, nor did the Bolshevik leadership wish a premature rising. At the end of the second day the crowd drifted away.

The government made some effort to take action against the Bolsheviks. Lenin went into hiding in Finland. Documents (most probably forgeries) were published in the press which purported to prove that Lenin was a German agent. For a time the Bolsheviks lost ground in the soviets. On July 21 the government was reorganized, and Kerenski became prime minister.

9. The Nationalities and the Provisional Government.—Meanwhile the nationalist movements among the non-Russians were growing. The main Ukrainian nationalist organization was the Society of Ukrainian Progressives, a moderate socialist group headed by the leading Ukrainian nationalist intellectual figure, the historian Myhaylo Hrushevsky (*see* UKRAINIAN SOVIET SOCIALIST REPUBLIC). On March 17, 1917, it took the initiative in summoning a Ukrainian central council, the rada, in Kiev. The rada's aims were at first strictly cultural, but soon it put forward demands for political self-government. During the early summer

government declaration of April 22 which described Russia's aim as "the establishment of durable peace on the basis of national self-determination." The soviet insisted that the text of this declaration be officially handed to the Allied governments. Milyukov on May 1 transmitted the text, but with a covering note in which he stated that Russia remained faithful to wartime agreements and intended to pursue the war to victory. When the covering note became known to the soviet, it was naturally understood as a direct challenge.

The leaders of the soviet organized mass demonstrations against war and Milyukov. The result was that he and the minister of war, the Octobrist leader A. I. Guchkov, resigned on May 15, and a new coalition was formed, including the Socialist-Revolutionary leader V. M. Chernov and the Menshevik I. G. Tsereteli. The April–May events were important not only because the right wing of the Provisional Government was forced out of power, but because they showed that the government was being forced in effect into a position of responsibility to the soviet.

6. The Soldiers' Committees.—In the meantime the discipline of the army was collapsing. This was of course due, above all, to the losses and sufferings of three years of war, the deterioration in the quality of officers, and the continuing supply difficulties. But defeatist propaganda and interference by the revolutionary parties also played an important part. On March 15 the Petrograd Soviet had issued its Order No. 1 to the Army. This laid down that the soldiers should elect committees in their units, from which in turn deputies should be elected to the soviet. The committees should have political authority over the soldiers, while the officers' authority should be limited to strictly professional matters. The committees should have control over the arms of the units and should not give them up to officers on demand. This fantastic arrangement was not put fully into effect, but elected committees of soldiers spread to units both in the rear and at the front, and the political commissars elected by the committees were in fact a challenge to the authority of officers.

Not all committees or commissars were defeatist. Indeed in many cases the committees were welcomed by the officers, as a

congresses were held of Ukrainian peasants, soldiers, and workers, and three political parties emerged—Ukrainian Socialist-Revolutionaries, Ukrainian Social Democrats, and Socialist-Federalists—all of which stood for some form of national autonomy. The rada was enlarged to include representatives of these forces, and in May it sent a delegation to Petrograd to ask for recognition of its claims.

The Provisional Government refused to regard the rada, which had not been regularly elected by popular suffrage, as representing the people of the Ukraine, and insisted that the question of any future Ukrainian autonomy could be decided only by the All-Russian Constituent Assembly. On June 23 the rada issued a solemn proclamation, the "First Universal" (the name is taken from the proclamations issued by the hetmans of the Ukraine in the 17th century), declaring its intention to organize a system of democratic government for the Ukraine, but recognizing that this would later have to be confirmed by the Constituent Assembly. It also set up an executive authority called the General Secretariat, a rudimentary cabinet of the Ukraine. On July 12 Kerenski and two other ministers went to Kiev for further discussions. These resulted in the issuance of a "Second Universal," the text of which represented no more than a verbal agreement. However, such power as existed in the increasing chaos was in the rada's hands.

The Provisional Government in March had already repealed all legislation incompatible with the Finnish constitution, promised to extend Finland's autonomy, and ordered the Finnish Diet to be summoned. In the diet the strongest party was the Social Democrats, who desired independence and showed little patience with the Petrograd government's scruples about a Constituent Assembly. In the Baltic provinces Estonian, Latvian, and Lithuanian nationalist movements gathered strength, while the local Germans were divided between loyalty to Russia and hopes of German victory in the war. In Transcaucasia the Armenians remained loyal to Russia, and the Georgian Mensheviks, the strongest party in their country, insisted on loyalty to the Russian republic which the Constituent Assembly was expected to proclaim.

The Muslim peoples also made their feelings known. On May 14 the first All-Russian Muslim Congress was held in Moscow. There was a division of opinion between the people of the borderlands (Central Asia and Azerbaijan), who wished for territorial self-government within a Russian republic, and the Tatars of the Volga, who, being geographically more scattered, preferred to have a central administrative organ for all the Muslims of Russia and to be directly represented in the Russian government. This notion was disliked by the border peoples not only because they wished their own lands to be autonomous but also because they suspected the Tatars of aiming at a privileged status for themselves. The congress adopted the autonomists' point of view by a substantial majority. It also set up a Muslim National Council, the Shuro, in Petrograd to put Muslim views before the government. Its hopes of obtaining a ministerial post for one of its members, however, were disappointed.

10. The Moscow State Conference.—To reinforce his authority by the support of some sort of representative body, Kerenski convened in Moscow, from Aug. 25 to Aug. 28, 1917, a State Conference, composed of members of the four dumas and representatives of soviets, local government authorities, trade unions, business interests, and the professions—numbering in all nearly 2,500.

The point that most clearly emerged from this conference was the sharp division on the conduct of the war. The parties of the left at the conference continued to demand peace without annexations and without indemnities, but admitted that the country had to be defended until peace was obtained, and put their faith in further "democratization of the army" and further proliferation of committees and commissars. The Bolsheviks, who were not represented at the conference, continued to demand immediate peace and to denounce all other parties as warmongers and agents of the Western Allies.

On the other hand were the forces that believed in a restoration of old-fashioned military discipline. This new formation of the right consisted mainly of persons who a year earlier would have been considered to be on the left, persons with a radical or liberal political background. They were not reactionaries in the sense

of wishing to return to the past; they were certainly not monarchists. They believed in a democratic Russia, but they insisted that it must be defended. The difference between them and the non-Bolshevik left was that national defense seemed to them the most urgent task, the precondition for the internal social reforms, many of which they accepted as necessary, though of course they were less radical in this respect than the left.

11. Kornilov's Rebellion.—The most effective spokesman of the new right was Gen. L. G. Kornilov (*q.v.*), an officer of humble origin, son of poor Cossack parents, basically ignorant of politics but certainly no admirer of Nicholas II. Impressed by his military record and his personal qualities, Kerenski had on Aug. 1, 1917, appointed him commander in chief. For a time these two tried to cooperate, each believing that the other was necessary to the salvation of Russia. But at the Moscow State Conference the relations between them, and the profound hostility between the political groups which looked respectively to each of them as leader, became clear. On Sept. 3, 1917, the Germans occupied Riga, and Petrograd itself appeared to be in danger. This intensified the urgency of more efficient military command, and Kornilov became convinced that he must assume control of the civil government as well as of the army. Kornilov was surrounded by a number of right-wing politicians, whose clumsy efforts to obtain Kerenski's support for the proposed military *coup d'état* only brought about a complete breach between the two.

On Sept. 9 Kerenski denounced Kornilov as a traitor and relieved him of his command. Kornilov replied by sending a cavalry corps against the capital. Kerenski appealed to the soviets and the workers to defend the revolution. This provided the Bolsheviks with an excellent opportunity to put themselves at the head of the resistance. When the troops reached the outskirts of Petrograd they were met by delegates of the soviets who harangued them with revolutionary appeals. The morale of the troops was low and they had no desire to fight their own countrymen; they therefore submitted to the Provisional Government. Their commander, Gen. A. M. Krymov, committed suicide, and Kornilov himself, who had remained at his headquarters at the front, was arrested. On Sept. 14 (N.S.; 1, O.S.), Kerenski proclaimed Russia a republic.

The Kornilov rebellion was a defeat for the right, but it was no victory for Kerenski. Those who gained were the Bolsheviks, who had always argued that Kerenski and the moderates were incompetent to defend the revolution, and who themselves had played a large part in the defeat of Kornilov. Bolshevik prestige had never been so high among the working class of Petrograd and among the ranks of the military forces in the capital. By mid-September the Bolsheviks had a majority in the soviets of both Petrograd and Moscow. Lenin, still in hiding, decided that the time had come to seize power, and urgently exhorted the party, by correspondence from Finland, to prepare for insurrection. At the 6th Congress of the Bolshevik Party, held in Petrograd early in August, the intention to seize power, regardless of the formal majority in the soviets, had already been asserted. The loss of Bolshevik popularity in the soviets, as the result of the July demonstrations and the charge of serving the Germans, had not deterred Lenin from his aim. Now that the Bolsheviks were once more popular, the arguments for action were further strengthened. The party leaders were, however, divided. G. E. Zinoviev and L. B. Kamenev (*qq.v.*), two of the most eminent, were opposed to early action. On the other hand the able recruit, Trotski, who had brought his own faction into the Bolshevik ranks, strongly supported Lenin and began active preparations.

The Kornilov rebellion was a turning point of the Russian Revolution. It is essential to note that the struggle was between not two forces, but three. These were the right (conservatives, liberals, and Russian patriots), the left (moderate socialists, from the right wing of the Socialist-Revolutionaries to the left wing of the Mensheviks), and Lenin. The struggle that impressed politically minded people in Russia and observers of the Russian scene abroad was that between the first and the second. Both sides in this struggle underestimated the Bolsheviks. To Kornilov, the real enemy was socialism, personified in Kerenski. The socialists, to him and his friends, appeared a gang of cosmopolitan anarchists

(Left) General disorder ensues as Leninists besiege the duma of the Provisional Government in 1917; (above) guarding the soviet, 1917

who were ruining Russia—at best, undisciplined and dangerous utopians, at worst, traitors to their country. To Kerenski, conversely, Kornilov and his supporters represented counterrevolution, the bloody repression of the working masses by incorrigibly reactionary militarists, and the denial of all the ideals of liberty and justice for which the Revolution stood. The image which each side had of the other may have been distorted and unjust, but there could be no doubt of the profound and sincere conviction of each.

Lenin was underrated by both the contending groups. To Kerenski, Lenin was another revolutionary, misguided and fanatical and perverse perhaps, but still on his side of the barricade. The whole tradition of the revolutionary movement made it impossible for Kerenski to compare Lenin with Kornilov; and he had shown long forbearance toward Lenin's provocative action before ordering his arrest. But Lenin himself was completely free from revolutionary sentimentality. To him, Kerenski was every bit as much an enemy as was Kornilov or Nicholas II. Unshakably convinced that he and his party held a monopoly of revolutionary wisdom and that they embodied the will of the revolutionary working class, regardless of what any individual workers might or might not wish, Lenin had no doubt that it was his duty to lead his party to victory against all opposition. The defeat of Kornilov and the exhaustion of the Provisional Government gave him his chance.

12. The November Revolution.—Trotski, elected chairman of the Petrograd Soviet on Oct. 6, 1917, set up a "military revolutionary committee" of the soviet, which planned insurrection without much attempt at secrecy. Kerenski pursued his efforts to create some sort of representative assembly to give his government authority. Neither the Democratic Conference, which had opened in Petrograd on Sept. 27 and met for a week, nor the Council of the Republic (or "pre-parliament"), which met on Oct. 20, had any influence on events. But Kerenski seemed unable to take any action against the military preparations of the Bolsheviks, who were busily subverting the troops in the capital, distributing arms, and appointing reliable men as commissars in military units. In the night of Nov. 6–7 (N.S.; Oct. 24–25, O.S.) the Bolsheviks acted. They met with very little resistance, and by the following evening the capital was in their hands. In Moscow the fighting went on for several days. Kerenski escaped from Petrograd to the front, but was unable to bring sufficient forces back to threaten the Bolsheviks. No effective resistance was organized from the headquarters of the front at Mogilev, and in mid-November the

commander in chief, Gen. N. N. Dukhonin, was replaced by the Bolsheviks' nominee, Ensign N. V. Krylenko. A number of senior officers, including Kornilov, escaped to the southeast and began to plan an anti-Bolshevik force, the so-called Volunteer Army, in the region of the Don.

13. The First Soviet Government.—In the evening of Nov. 7, 1917, the second All-Russian Congress of Soviets met in Petrograd. Since the slogan of the Bolsheviks since April (with the exception of some weeks following the July demonstrations) had been "All power to the soviets," and since indeed the Bolsheviks had now seized power in the name of the soviets, it might have been expected that the new government would be a coalition of the leftist parties represented in the soviets. But the majority of the Menshevik and Socialist-Revolutionary delegates (together constituting only a minority in the congress) walked out of the opening session in protest against the Bolsheviks' insurrection, thus strengthening the Bolsheviks' claim to represent the will of the soviets. Lenin's new government, which he entitled Soviet of People's Commissars, was composed solely of Bolsheviks. But several of its members still wished to form a coalition, and on Nov. 17 five of them resigned in protest, while Kamenev, Zinoviev, and three others resigned from the party's Central Committee. Zinoviev recanted within a few days, but the others remained in opposition for a month. Their return to the fold was made easier when, at the beginning of December, the Socialist-Revolutionary Party split, and its left-wing minority decided to enter the government on Lenin's terms.

The first public acts of the Bolsheviks were decrees on peace and on the land, both of which were approved by the majority of the Congress of Soviets on Nov. 8. The peace decree invited all belligerent governments to begin immediate negotiations for a peace without annexations and without indemnities, and announced the government's willingness to consider any peace proposals made to it and its intention to publish all existing secret agreements concluded by previous Russian governments and to repudiate all such agreements as were aimed at "advantages and privileges for the Russian landlords and capitalists" or at "the retention or expansion of Great Russian annexations." The land decree abolished, without compensation, all private ownership of large landed estates, which, together with possessions of the imperial family, the church, and the monasteries, were to be taken over by the state. The land was to be made available to the peasants. The government reserved its liberty to decide the settlement of the land question by referring it to the future Constituent Assembly. The decree, however, laid down general principles which amounted to the adoption of the Socialist-Revolutionaries' ideas and the extension of the system of the village commune (*obshchina*) to the whole country. Lenin had not, of course, been converted to the Socialist-Revolutionaries' ideology: rather he realized clearly that to steal their program was the best way to win the peasants gradually away from them.

The Bolshevik approach to the organization of industry was piecemeal. On Nov. 11 the eight-hour day was made compulsory in all enterprises of whatever size. A decree of Nov. 27 conferred on factory committees, elected by the workers, far-reaching rights to supervise the activities of their enterprises, which were obliged to open all their archives and correspondence to them. In principle the committees were not to take over direct management, but in practice they often did so. In any case the real power had passed to the committees. Some individual firms were nationalized, and on Dec. 27 all banking institutions were nationalized; but a general nationalization of industry was not decreed until June 1918. In mid-December 1917, however, was set up the Supreme Economic Council, which began to concentrate in itself the direction of the economy.

14. The Bolsheviks and the Nationalities.—Lenin had long proclaimed the doctrine of self-determination for the non-Russian nationalities, "up to the point of secession." Everything would, however, depend on whom the Bolsheviks recognized as expressing in practice the will of each individual nationality. If the majority of a nationality supported a nationalist movement whose leaders were not socialists, should they be allowed to claim territorial independence and take their homeland out of the Russian Soviet Republic? If a minority supported a socialist party which wished to remain within the Russian Republic, should it be forcibly supported by the Bolsheviks, on the ground that it represented the true interests of the proletariat? Which, in fact, should come first, the whole nationality or its working class? Most of the nationalities, being overwhelmingly composed of peasants, had only a small "working class" in the sense of urban proletariat. And which

party should be recognized as representing the working class? In some cases there were numerous parties claiming the title "socialist."

In practice these questions were answered in terms not of doctrine but of force. Where the Bolsheviks were able to support kindred parties, or to impose their direct will, they did so. At the time of the November Revolution, all Poland and a large part of the Baltic provinces were in German hands. In Finland the parliament proclaimed independence from Russia on Dec. 6, 1917. The Bolshevik government recognized this act. But soon conflict broke out between left and right in Finland. On Jan. 26, 1918, the left wing of the Social Democratic Party seized control of Helsinki and proclaimed a Finnish Workers' Socialist Republic. The new government was recognized by Lenin and received some supplies from Russia, while Russian soldiers stationed in Finland gave it some armed assistance. Civil war broke out, with the Reds at first holding the south and the Whites the northwest. In March 1918 the Whites appealed to Germany, and in May the combined White Finnish and German forces defeated the forces of the left.

Lenin in principle recognized the Ukrainians' right to national self-determination. He had, however, two practical objections to their rada. One was that it was composed of non-Bolshevik parties and was based on the intelligentsia and peasantry, while the working class of the big Ukrainian cities was mainly Russian, and indeed formed a large part of the Russian proletariat in whose name the Bolsheviks ruled. The second objection was that the rada was permitting Russian officers and even small units to cross its territory to the Don area, where Kornilov and the Cossack leader, Gen. A. M. Kaledin, were organizing the Volunteer Army, but was at the same time refusing to allow forces loyal to the Bolsheviks to cross the Ukraine to attack them.

The Bolsheviks had only a minority in the All-Ukrainian Congress of Soviets held in Kiev early in December. They therefore walked out of the congress, organized their own counter-congress in Kharkov, and on Dec. 26, 1917, set up a rival government of the Ukraine. On Jan. 4, 1918, the Kharkov government denounced the rada as "enemies of the people," and Bolshevik troops invaded

THE SOVIET OF WORKERS' DEPUTIES IN SESSION, AT PETROGRAD, 1917

the Ukraine. The rada replied with a "Fourth Universal" on Jan. 22, which proclaimed the Ukraine independent. The Bolsheviks, however, had the military advantage. The rada had only very few loyal troops. Kiev fell to the Bolsheviks on Feb. 8. The rada leaders fled beyond the Dnieper. They made some attempts to enlist Allied support, but the Allied governments could neither recognize in principle the independence of the Ukraine nor find any means of giving practical assistance. The rada leaders therefore had no alternative to throwing themselves on the mercy of the Germans.

In Transcaucasia a local assembly was set up after the November Revolution, and from it was formed a regional government, the Transcaucasian Commissariat, in which the most active figures were Georgian Mensheviks. The assembly was suspicious of the Bolshevik government, but did not wish to secede from the Russian Republic. It claimed to exercise authority pending only the convocation of the All-Russian Constituent Assembly.

In the Muslim regions of European Russia the Bolsheviks at first had some hope of success. Lenin's government included a Commissariat of Nationalities, which was entrusted to a Georgian Bolshevik named J. V. Stalin (Dzhugashvili). He set up a commissariat for Muslim affairs within his commissariat and enlisted the support of several Tatar intellectuals. The Tatars, with their preference for a centralized republic, were more likely to support the Bolsheviks than the other Muslim peoples, and their more complex social structure—with a considerable intelligentsia and the beginnings of an industrial working class—made it possible to organize some Communist following among them. Even so, the predominant trend among the Tatars was hostile to Bolshevism.

In the Kazakh steppes, where the hostility of Kazakhs to Russians was due mainly to the colonization of the land by Russian peasants (there had been a large-scale Kazakh armed rising in 1916), a nationalist organization called Alash Orda came into being.

In Turkistan a Muslim Central Council had been set up in the spring of 1917, and presented some rather moderate political and cultural demands to the Russian authorities in Tashkent. The November Revolution in Petrograd had its exact parallel in Tashkent. The Tashkent soviet, representing the local Russian working class—largely railwaymen—and dominated by Bolsheviks, took power. The Muslim council therefore reopened its negotiations with the new rulers of Tashkent, but without success. The Tashkent railwaymen rejected Muslim requests for autonomy and refused to allow Muslims to become members of "the higher organs of the regional revolutionary authority." The Muslims therefore held a congress of their own in Kokand and set up a counter-government of Turkistan. For the next months they held effective power in a large part of the countryside, while those cities which had a Russian population were under Bolshevik control. Bolshevik forces captured Kokand, but their hopes of a rising in Bukhara by the left-wing Young Bukhara Party were disappointed.

15. The Constituent Assembly, Jan. 18–19, 1918.—The Bolsheviks before November had frequently demanded that a Constituent Assembly be summoned. Shortly before October the Kerenski government had fixed the election for the end of November 1917. Lenin decided to let it go ahead. The results are open to some dispute, but the most careful available study estimates them as follows: Russian and Ukrainian Socialist-Revolutionaries, 419 seats; Bolsheviks, 168; Mensheviks, 18; Constitutional Democrats (Kadets) and the right, 17; others, 81. The conditions in which the election was held certainly fell short of ideal freedom, but pressure had been used against the right, not the left.

The fact that only a quarter of the electors had voted for the Bolsheviks therefore came as a disagreeable surprise. Lenin, however, was not dismayed. He had the power, and he did not lack arguments against the assembly. First, the electoral lists had been drawn up before the Socialist-Revolutionaries split: had they been made after the split, then, Lenin claimed, more than 39 out of the 419 S.R. would have been Left S.R. Secondly, he reiterated his argument of April 1917 that the soviets, organs of proletarian revolution, are "a higher form of democratic principle" than the

assembly, which is an organ of the bourgeois stage of revolution. Thirdly, the results of the election could not really be taken seriously, because it had been held at a time when "the people could not yet know the full scope and meaning of the November socialist proletarian-peasant revolution." The true expression of the wishes of the Russian people was not the election that actually took place, but the election that would have given the Bolsheviks a majority if it had been held somewhat later, after the people had seen the light.

The Constituent Assembly was therefore condemned by "history" before it ever met. Somewhat more than half its members in fact met in Petrograd on Jan. 18, 1918. After it had rejected by 237 votes to 136 the demand of the Bolsheviks that it should recognize the soviets as superior to itself, the Bolsheviks and the Left S.R. walked out. On Jan. 19, at 5 A.M., the remaining majority of members were asked to disperse "as the guard is tired," and next day they were prevented from reassembling. Some persons demonstrating in the street in favour of the assembly were fired on, but there was no effective force willing to defend it.

16. The Treaties of Brest-Litovsk.—Meanwhile, having unsuccessfully appealed for a general peace, the Bolshevik government had decided to negotiate a separate peace with the Central Powers. An armistice was signed on Dec. 15, 1917, and negotiations began at Brest-Litovsk. The Bolsheviks believed that revolution was imminent in Germany. A series of strikes in January 1918 in Vienna and in Berlin seemed to support this view. The Bolsheviks came not so much to negotiate as to harangue their opponents with revolutionary eloquence, hoping to expedite the German revolution by subverting the German forces. They were also pleased that the Germans were prepared to accept the principle of self-determination and of a peace without annexations. When confronted, however, with Gen. Max Hoffmann and his team, they found that the Germans' interpretation of these terms was no less elastic or unscrupulous than their own. Self-determination did not apply to Poland, Lithuania, and Latvia, now under German occupation. These territories were no longer part of Russia. If their peoples should choose to unite with the German Empire, this would not be annexation. On the other hand, the demand of the Ukrainian rada for separation from Russia was a legitimate claim for self-determination.

On Feb. 9, 1918, the rada, reduced to desperation by the Bolshevik invasion of the Ukraine, signed a peace treaty with the Germans, who recognized the Ukrainian People's Republic. The price of this German support was that the Ukraine should deliver large quantities of grain, of which Germany, and still more Austria-Hungary, stood in dire need. The Bolshevik government refused to accept this, but it was also clear that it would not at present get tolerable terms from the Germans. Hopes of revolution in Germany still remained bright. The solution found by Trotski, who as commissar for foreign affairs was at this time in charge of the Bolshevik delegation at Brest-Litovsk, was to declare a condition of "no war, no peace." Russia refused, he said, to sign an annexationist peace, but at the same time refused to carry on the war. On Feb. 10 he and his delegation returned home.

On Feb. 18 the German and Austro-Hungarian armies advanced along the whole front. As early as January the Central Committee of the Bolshevik Party had been bitterly divided on the negotiations. One section, the "Left Communists," of whom the most prominent was N. I. Bukharin (q.v.), urged a "revolutionary war" against the Germans. Trotski's "no war, no peace" proved to be a verbal slogan rather than a policy. Lenin, whose indifference to the defense of Russia in the summer had been the height of utopianism, now was forced to be a realist. He saw that Russia was incapable of resistance to the Germans, its army demoralized (not least by his own propaganda). He was prepared to accept help from the Western enemies of Germany, but his conversations with Western representatives convinced him that the Western governments had neither the will nor the means to help. The choice was a crippling loss of territory or the destruction of his regime. The terms offered by the Germans—even less favourable now than before Feb. 10—at least offered some breathing space until the revolutions came in western and central Europe. Lenin therefore decided for acceptance, and obtained a bare majority in the Central Committee. Peace was signed on March 3 at Brest-Litovsk. The capital was moved from Petrograd to Moscow, to be further from the Germans. (*See* BREST-LITOVSK, TREATIES OF.)

By the Brest-Litovsk peace, Russia lost all the Baltic provinces, Lithuania, Poland, and part of Belorussia, whose fate was left to the Germans to decide. The independence of Finland and Ukraine was recognized. In Transcaucasia, the districts of Batumi, Kars, and Ardahan were ceded to Turkey. The lost lands included not only Russia's most fertile grain-producing provinces but also most of its coal-mining and metallurgical industry.

17. The Loss of Bessarabia.—Russia also lost Bessarabia to Rumania, a former ally. Annexed by Russia from the Turks in 1812, Bessarabia had a predominantly Rumanian population, though the landowning nobility had become Russian and the urban business class were Russian-speaking Jews. Before 1914 a Rumanian nationalist movement, led by intellectuals and based on the peasants, had begun to make itself felt, with encouragement and support from Rumania. In 1917 the Rumanian Army, driven back into Moldavia, continued to resist German attacks; but when the Russian Army disintegrated the position of Rumania became hopeless. In Bessarabia, Rumanian nationalists profited from the weakness of Russia to seize power, and an assembly of Bessarabian Rumanians appealed to the Rumanian Army to defend them. Thus when Rumania sued for a separate peace with Germany, it was already in possession of Bessarabia. The Germans imposed severe terms by the Treaty of Bucharest, signed on May 7, 1918, but were willing to allow Rumania the compensation of annexing Bessarabia. The annexation was, however, not recognized by the Moscow government. (*See* BESSARABIA.)

18. Ukraine and Transcaucasia, Spring–Summer 1918.—German and Austro-Hungarian forces restored the Ukrainian rada to power, but their relations with it were unsatisfactory. It was either unable or unwilling to ensure the grain deliveries which it had promised. The German officers disliked both the left-wing phrases and the administrative incompetence of the rada. On April 24, 1918, the rada government was dismissed, and a former general of the Russian Army, Pavel Skoropadski, a descendant of a 17th-century hetman, was placed in power, assuming his ancestor's title. This monarchical regime was never popular, but it did for six months ensure a minimum of public order and made some progress toward creating a system of schools in the Ukrainian language.

In Transcaucasia the Brest-Litovsk peace was received with dismay. The Turks occupied Batumi, ceded by Lenin without consulting the Georgians. The obvious inability of Russia to give any protection caused the Transcaucasian assembly on April 22, 1918, to proclaim the Transcaucasian Federal Republic. In the city of Baku, however, the Communists (Bolsheviks), supported by the Russian workers in the oil industry, set up their own government, recognizing the Moscow government but cut off from it. The Transcaucasian Republic split in three as a result of the lack of common interest between the three nations—Georgians, Armenians, and Azerbaijanis. The first two had territorial disputes of their own, while the third had more in common with the Turks than with their neighbours. At the end of May separate republics of Georgia, Armenia, and Azerbaijan were proclaimed. The Turks, however, continued to advance. They overran Armenia and enlisted some Azerbaijani support for an attack on Baku. Here the Communist regime was overthrown in July by Russian-Socialist-Revolutionaries, who, with a small British force from Persia, defended the city until mid-September, when the Turks captured it. Georgia made a treaty with Germany on May 28, obtaining tacit German protection against further Turkish claims in return for placing the country's mineral resources at the disposal of the Germans. Thus by the late summer of 1918 Georgia was a German vassal state, Azerbaijan a Turkish vassal, while Armenia had ceased to exist.

19. The Outbreak of Civil War: Intervention and Terrorism.—At their party's 7th Congress (March 6–8, 1918), which approved the signature of the Treaty of Brest-Litovsk, the Bolsheviks took the name of Russian Communist Party. The treaty was finally ratified by the 4th All-Russian Congress of Soviets (March 15); but it caused a breach between the Communists and the Left Socialist-Revolutionaries, who thereupon left the coalition. In the next months there was a marked drawing together of two main groups of Russian opponents of Lenin. These were on the one hand those of the non-Bolshevik left who had been finally alienated from Lenin by his dissolution of the Constituent Assembly, and on the other hand the right, whose main asset was the Volunteer Army in the Kuban steppes. This army, which had survived great hardships in the winter of 1917–18 and of which Gen. A. I. Denikin took command on Kornilov's death in action (April 1918), was now a fine fighting force, though small in numbers. Patriotic indignation at the "betrayal" of Russia to Germany (however inevitable) was a common factor between the right and the left in opposition to the Communist government.

At the same time the Western Allies, desperately pressed by the new German offensive in the spring of 1918, were eager to create another front in the east by reviving at least a part of the Russian Army. In March 1918 a small British force was landed

(Left) A demonstration on Red Square in Moscow, Nov. 7, 1920. (Below) Trotski and staff crossing Red Square to inspect troops

(LEFT) SOVFOTO, (BOTTOM) THE BETTMANN ARCHIVE

at Murmansk with the consent of the local soviet. On April 4 Japanese forces landed at Vladivostok, without any approval.

A further factor was the Czechoslovak Legion, composed of Czech and Slovak deserters from the Austro-Hungarian Army, whom previous Russian governments had allowed to form their own units. In March 1918 the Communist government agreed to let these units leave Russia by the Far East, but in May violent incidents took place during the evacuation, and on May 29 Trotski (now commissar for war) ordered them to surrender their arms. They refused, defeated attempts of the local soviets to disarm them, and took control of the Trans-Siberian Railway. In the vacuum created by this action, two anti-Bolshevik authorities appeared: the West Siberian Commissariat, of predominantly liberal complexion, based at Omsk; and the Committee of Members of the Constituent Assembly, composed of Socialist-Revolutionaries, based at Samara.

These events caused the Moscow government to sweep away the remnants of liberty still enjoyed by non-Bolshevik socialists. The Menshevik and Socialist-Revolutionary deputies were expelled from the central and local soviets and prevented from engaging in any organized political activity. On July 9 Left Socialist-Revolutionaries murdered Graf Wilhelm von Mirbach-Harff, the German ambassador in Moscow, and for a short time seized the headquarters of the security police, or Cheka (*Chrezvychainaya Komissia; i.e.*, "Extraordinary Commission"). Shortly afterward other S.R. groups organized unsuccessful armed risings in Yaroslavl and other cities of central Russia. On Aug. 30 an S.R. woman, Fanny Kaplan, shot and severely wounded Lenin, and the same day a leading Bolshevik, M. S. Uritski, was assassinated in Petrograd. The government replied by proclaiming a campaign of "Red terror," including shooting hostages and giving increased powers to the Cheka of summary arrest, trial, and execution of suspects.

Among the early victims of the civil war, which may be considered to have begun in earnest in June 1918, were the former imperial family. Nicholas II, his wife, and his children had been moved in August 1917 to Tobolsk and in the spring of 1918 to Ekaterinburg (Sverdlovsk). With the development of anti-Bolshevik forces in Siberia, the local soviet feared that Nicholas might be liberated. In the night of July 29–30, 1918, all the members of the family were taken to the cellar of the house in which they were living, and butchered by revolvers and bayonets.

20. The All-Russian Directory and Kolchak.—The Russian civil war fell into two main periods, divided by the defeat of Germany in the European war in November 1918. During the first period the anti-Communist forces included a variety of political opinions from right to left. In September 1918 a State Conference was held at Ufa in the Urals, attended by a number of persons who had been elected to the dissolved Constituent Assembly, mostly Socialist-Revolutionaries, with some other political figures. The conference set up an All-Russian Directory, as a provisional government to exercise authority only until the duly elected Constituent Assembly could reassemble. In the late summer the Communists' hastily reorganized armed forces, the Red Army, whose commander in chief was Trotski, the commissar for war, recovered most of eastern European Russia. At Omsk, which became the centre of the anti-Communists, a new army was hastily trained under the command of Adm. A. V. Kolchak, with the assistance of British and U.S. military missions. Meanwhile the British forces at Murmansk were at war with the Communists. In August further, British forces landed at Archangel, and the Japanese forces in the Far Eastern territories of Russia had been greatly reinforced.

In Omsk relations between the Directory and Kolchak steadily deteriorated. Kolchak and his officers disliked the left-wing views of the politicians and found it difficult to distinguish between Socialist-Revolutionaries and Communists, lumping together all "Reds" as enemies. To political hostility was added contempt for civilians as such, with a belief that all power should be in the hands of patriotic officers. The S.R. reciprocated the dislike and antagonized their partners by tactless and demagogic gestures. The conflict came to a head when, on Nov. 18, 1918, Kolchak overthrew the Directory and set up his own dictatorship. From this time onward, anti-Communist forces in the East were controlled by the extreme right, and many Russians of socialist views were driven to the conclusion that, if the struggle was now to be one between the Revolution and a restoration of the old regime, then the Communists were the lesser of the two evils. Kolchak's *coup d'état*, moreover, coincided with the end of the European war. Now that the Germans were defeated, the question whether Lenin was or was not pro-German became purely academic. Russians no longer opposed him on patriotic grounds.

21. War in Ukraine, Winter 1918–19.—The end of German power brought the collapse of Skoropadski's regime in the Ukraine. The left-wing Ukrainian nationalists set up a Directory, based on Ukrainian Socialist-Revolutionaries and Social Democrats, and in November took over a large part of the Ukraine. The Communists, however, formed a counter-government of the Ukraine in Kharkov, and at the beginning of 1919 Red Army forces invaded the Ukraine. On Feb. 6 they entered Kiev. The remnants of the forces of the Directory, headed by Simon Petlyura, retreated westward, where they joined forces with the Ukrainian nationalist forces from formerly Austrian Galicia, which had been driven eastward by the army of the new Polish Republic. For the next months the mixed Petlyurist-Galician forces held parts of the Ukraine; other areas were in the hands of anarchist bands led by Nestor Makhno; and the main cities were held by the Communists, ruling not directly from Moscow but through a puppet Ukrainian "government" in Kharkov. The defeat of Germany had also opened the Black Sea to the Allies, and in mid-December 1918 some mixed forces under French command were landed at Odessa, Sevastopol, Kherson, and Nikolayev.

22. The Allies' Dilemma.—The Allied governments now had to decide on their policy in the confused Russian situation. The original purpose of intervention, to revive an Eastern front against Germany, was now meaningless. Russian exiles argued that, since the pre-Bolshevik governments of Russia had remained loyal to the Allies, the Allies were bound to help them; and moreover the small Volunteer Army had never laid down its arms. The Communists, in the exiles' view, were now strong because they had obtained power through German aid, had betrayed Russia to Germany at Brest-Litovsk, and had used the breathing space to build up their own forces; and this unfairly obtained advantage could only be counteracted by massive Allied aid to Denikin and to Kolchak.

To these moral arguments was added the political argument that the Communist regime in Moscow was a menace to the whole of Europe, with its subversive propaganda and its determination to spread revolution. In Germany, in Hungary, and in the Balkans revolutionary movements were strong. In fact the conditions for a collapse of the state machine, such as took place in Russia in 1917, were not present at this time in central Europe, with the partial exception of Hungary. But the fear of such collapse, and of Communist machinations, was strongly felt in the upper classes and the government circles of the West.

On the other hand the prospect of keeping large armies in being to fight a major war in Russia could hardly be entertained by parliamentary politicians. The war against Germany had brought terrible sufferings to France and to Great Britain. The danger from Germany was at last removed. Frenchmen and Englishmen could not believe that their security and liberty depended on who won a civil war in distant Russia. The British and French electors wanted the boys home, and no party was going to win an election which tried to keep them in uniform. This was the main reason against large-scale Western intervention, but there was an important secondary reason in the opposition of organized labour in both countries to any action against a "workers' state." "Hands off Russia!" movements and threats of strike action impressed the governments.

At the beginning of 1919 the French and Italian governments favoured strong support (in the form of munitions and supplies rather than in men) to the Whites (as the anti-Communist forces now came to be called), while the British and U.S. governments were more cautious and even hoped to reconcile the warring Russian parties. In January the Allies, on U.S. initiative, proposed to

(Above) Training the youth of Petrograd to fight against the troops of General Yudenich, 1919. (Below left) Red Guards firing from an armoured car, Moscow, October 1917. (Below right) Distributing clothing and fabrics to the famine-stricken population of the Volga area, 1921

(TOP, BOTTOM RIGHT) NOVOSTI PRESS AGENCY, (ABOVE) RADIO TIMES HULTON PICTURE LIBRARY

all Russian belligerents to hold armistice talks on the island of Prinkipo in the Sea of Marmara. The Communists accepted, but the Whites refused. In March the U.S. diplomat William C. Bullitt went to Moscow and returned with peace proposals from the Communists, which were not accepted by the Allies. After this the Allies ceased trying to come to terms with the Communists and gave increased assistance to Kolchak and Denikin.

Direct intervention by Allied military forces was, however, on a very small scale. The French in the Ukraine were bewildered by the confused struggle between Russian Communists, Russian Whites, and Ukrainian nationalists, and they withdrew their forces during March and April 1919, having hardly fired a shot. The British in the Archangel and Murmansk areas did some fighting, but the northern front was of only minor importance to the civil war as a whole. The last British forces were withdrawn from Archangel on Sept. 27, 1919, and from Murmansk on Oct. 12. The only "interventionists" who represented a real danger were the Japanese, who established themselves systematically in the Far Eastern provinces.

23. The Defeat of the Whites, 1919–20.—In the first half of 1919 the main fighting was in the east. Kolchak advanced in the Urals and had attained his greatest success by April. In May the Red Army's counteroffensive began. Ufa fell in June, and Kolchak's armies retreated through Siberia, harassed by partisans (many of them not Communists but all with reasons to hate Kolchak's regime). By the end of summer the retreat had become a rout. Kolchak set up an administration in November at Irkutsk, but it was overthrown in December by Socialist-Revolutionaries. He himself was handed over to the Communists in January 1920 and shot on Feb. 7.

Meanwhile, in the late summer of 1919, Denikin had made a last effort in European Russia. By August most of the Ukraine was in White hands. The Communists had been driven out, and the

Ukrainian nationalists were divided in their attitude to Denikin, Petlyura being hostile to him, but the Galicians preferring him to the Poles, whom they considered their main enemy. In September the White forces moved northward from the Ukraine and from the lower Volga toward Moscow. On Oct. 13 they took Orel. At the same time General N. N. Yudenich advanced from Estonia to the outskirts of Petrograd. But both cities were saved by Red Army counterattacks. Yudenich retreated into Estonia, and Denikin, his communications greatly overextended, was driven back from Orel in an increasingly disorderly march, which ended with the evacuation of the remnants of his army, in March 1920, from Novorossisk.

In 1920 there was still an organized White force in the Crimea, under Gen. P. N. Wrangel. In June, when the Poles had invaded the Ukraine (*see* below), Wrangel struck northward at the Red Army and, for a time, occupied part of the Ukraine and Kuban. But when the Poles retreated, the Red Army had greater forces to spare and could subdue Wrangel, whose rearguards held out long enough to ensure the evacuation of 150,000 soldiers and civilians by sea from the Crimea. This ended the civil war in November 1920.

The Communist victory was at the same time a defeat for the various nationalist movements of the non-Russian peoples. The hopes of the Tatars and Bashkirs, between the Kazan area and the southern Urals, were ruined in the course of the civil war. Kolchak showed no understanding whatever for their aspirations. The Communists proclaimed the right of self-determination, but in practice imposed the dictatorship of the Russian Communist Party on them. The Alash Orda of the Kazakhs suffered a similar fate. In Turkistan, the beleaguered Communist regime in Tashkent established direct contact with the Red Army at the end of 1919. The Moscow government now tried to force the Tashkent Communists to abandon their crudely anti-Muslim policy. But the

Muslim population remained mistrustful of any Russian authorities, and for some years guerrilla bands of nationalists, known as Basmachi, harassed the Communist authorities.

24. The Russo-Polish War and the Baltic States.—In the Ukraine the collapse of Denikin had led to reconquest by the Red Army, as the Ukrainian nationalists had no military forces capable of resisting it. Moreover, after three years of terror, war, and anarchy, it was questionable how much enthusiasm the Ukrainian peasants still had left for the nationalist cause. Petlyura went into exile in Poland. In contrast to the Galicians, Petlyura preferred the Poles to any Russian regime. He made an agreement with Jozef Pilsudski on April 21, 1920: he renounced all claim to eastern Galicia as part of the Ukraine, but would support Pilsudski in his war with Russia. Both men aimed at some future federal association between Poland and the Ukraine. In fact the invading Polish Army received no significant help from the Ukrainian population.

The Russo-Polish War (*q.v.*) was primarily caused by inability to agree on the frontier. The Poles hoped to restore the frontiers of 1772, which would have given them huge areas of Ukrainian and Belorussian population. After initial successes, including the capture of Kiev (May 6, 1920), the Poles were driven back, with the Red Army in hot pursuit. The Communist leaders now hoped that they would be able to link up, through Poland, with the Communists in Germany, and bring about a new wave of revolution in Europe. In Bialystok they set up a provisional government of Polish Communists. But in August they were in turn defeated by a Polish counterattack near Warsaw, and retreated. An armistice was signed on Oct. 12, 1920, and the Treaty of Riga on March 18, 1921. The new frontier left to the Poles considerable Ukrainian and Belorussian populations, but much less than the frontier of 1772.

In 1919 the Communists had attempted to recover the Baltic provinces, and Soviet republics of Latvia and Estonia were declared. In the city of Riga there was a strong Communist movement, which held out until May 1919; but elsewhere the population was predominantly nationalist and nonsocialist. British naval power in the Baltic was also an important factor in the situation. The government of Lenin was obliged to accept these facts. In 1920 it recognized the three Baltic republics as independent states by separate treaties with Estonia (Feb. 2), Lithuania (July 12), and Latvia (Aug. 11). In the southwest, however, the annexation of Bessarabia by Rumania was still not recognized, and diplomatic relations were not established with Rumania until June 9, 1934.

25. Transcaucasia Reconquered, 1920–21.—The defeat of Turkey in World War I led to the revival of the three separate Transcaucasian republics. The Western powers gave them *de facto* recognition. The Armenian cause aroused some sympathy in the West, especially in the United States. But the governments of Armenia and Georgia quarreled with each other, and the Turks under Mustafa Kemal put an end to Armenian hopes of a large state to be carved out of eastern Anatolia. The fatal weakness of Azerbaijan was that, although the democratic nationalist Musavat party had the support of the Azerbaijani peasants, the great city of Baku, with its Russian and Armenian working-class population, was loyal to Moscow. Only Georgia had a strongly supported government, as the Mensheviks were genuinely popular with both workers and peasants. The Moscow government did not intend to respect Transcaucasian independence long. In April 1920 the Azerbaijan government surrendered to the double threat of invasion by the Red Army and rebellion in Baku. On Dec. 3, 1920, the formerly Russian portion of Armenia was incorporated into Soviet Russia, and the Moscow government recognized the rest of Armenia as part of Turkey. In February 1921 the Red Army invaded Georgia. The conquest of this state, which had been recognized by the Moscow government by formal treaty in May 1920 and which had been a rather successful social democratic republic, aroused some indignation in Western Europe, but no practical help could be given. The frontier between Soviet Russia and Turkey was a compromise between those of 1878 and 1918: Batumi returned to Russia, but Turkey kept Kars and Ardahan.

26. The Far Eastern Settlement, 1922.—For the territory around Lake Baikal, and east of it, from the spring of 1920 the fiction of a Far Eastern Republic, independent of Soviet Russia, was maintained. This government was in practice fully controlled from Moscow. The Japanese were sufficiently impressed by the appearance of a buffer state to remove their troops to the Pacific coast region. They showed no desire to evacuate this region; and that they eventually did so was mainly due to diplomatic pressure by the U.S. government, which feared the excessive aggrandizement of Japan in the Pacific. The Japanese delegates at the Washington Conference of Pacific States in the autumn of 1922 were obliged to promise the U.S. government that they would withdraw all their troops from Russian territory. This they did at the end of October. The Far Eastern Republic had now served its purpose, and its assembly in November formally voted it out of existence and united it to Soviet Russia.

27. Trotski and War Communism.—The political system which emerged victorious from the civil war bore the name Russian Soviet Federated Socialist Republic. In fact the soviets were of small importance. All power belonged to the Communist Party, members of which occupied all the posts in the Soviet of People's Commissars and the key posts at all lower levels of the machinery of government. The party itself was governed by its Central Committee, which Lenin dominated.

Second only to Lenin was Trotski, who as commissar for war not only had supreme command of the armed forces but was also largely responsible for organizing supplies and for the mobilization of manpower. The Red Army was at first a rabble of demoralized soldiers and raw recruits. Having preached defeatism for months, it was difficult for the Communists to preach patriotism and military discipline. This, however, was what Trotski did. His personal eloquence and his continuous display of courage and hard work were important factors. It was he too who decided, against opposition from within the party, that the Red Army must employ former imperial officers if it was to be efficient. A combination of threats, material inducements, and appeals to Russian patriotism enlisted thousands of officers, and on the whole they proved loyal. The rigid discipline of the Communist Party also provided a stiffening element, through the Communists serving in the army. By 1919 the Red Army had become at any rate much better than the armies of its White opponents. The victory of the Communists in the civil war is indeed mainly due to this simple fact of military superiority, reinforced by the fact that, holding the central core of European Russia throughout the war, they could plan operations and move men more easily than their enemies, whose bases were on the periphery and cut off from each other.

The relationship of the Communists to the people of Russia was rather complex. On the one hand they used ruthless terror through their Cheka, headed by the Polish Communist Feliks Dzerzhinski (Dzierżynski). This helped them by quelling opposition, but also harmed them by creating still greater hatred, by wasting many innocent lives, and by setting up an organization with a permanent vested interest in suspicion and denunciation, which remained after the war was over. On the other hand the Communists won genuine support by offering the people the vision of a new order of justice and liberty and by extending opportunities to men and women of natural ability but of humble social origins. They could thus draw on millions whom the old regime had ignored.

The early agrarian policy of the Communists, essentially copied from the Socialist-Revolutionaries, had won peasant support. But during the civil war the government had been forced ruthlessly to requisition supplies and to mobilize peasants. The resultant policy, which became known as "War Communism," was due partly to military necessity, but partly also to the belief of party doctrinaires that "socialism" could suddenly be created by decree. Lenin's earlier views about the gradual class differentiation of the peasantry were forgotten. Instead, the doctrinaires arbitrarily divided the existing peasantry into three "classes," labeled "rich" (*kulak*), "medium" (*serednyak*), and "poor" (*bednyak*); and a "class war" was to be instigated by the third, with as much support as possible from the second, against the first. Some attempt was also made to experiment with collective farms. Events did not in fact conform to any tidy theoretical plan, but there was much suffering, injustice, and resentment. In 1919 and 1920 the government made greater efforts to curb the excesses of local zealots than in 1918. A large part of the peasantry became extremely hostile to the Communists. Yet they probably disliked them less than the Whites, to whom they attributed the intention of handing the former estates back to the landowners.

The industrial workers certainly had little to hope for from the Whites, who showed a complete lack of understanding for their interests in such large cities as they temporarily occupied. The civil war brought a striking decline of all industry. Raw materials were scarce, and workers left the towns for the country in search of food. Many of the ablest skilled workers became organizers of the Communist Party, civil administrators, or army officers: the working class was thus deprived of most of its *élite*. For the minimum essential industry and construction works, men were ruthlessly mobilized. The brief period of blissful anarchy at the end of 1917, with factory committees doing whatever they wished, was replaced by one of direction of labour, in which the trade unions were used by the party as recruiting sergeants.

28. The Kronstadt Mutiny, 1921.—The sacrifices demanded of workers and peasants were tolerable in war, but when the enemy was defeated the mood changed. At the beginning of 1921 there were strikes in Petrograd affecting almost all the city's industry. The strikers demanded not only economic concessions but free elections to the soviets and the release of socialists who were in prison. At the beginning of March a revolt broke out in the nearby naval base of Kronstadt. The sailors' demands were also for political freedom, and there had been contact between the sailors and the Petrograd strikers. The program of the Kronstadt mutiny was definitely socialist and definitely accepted soviets as the form of government, but it rejected the dictatorship of the Communist Party over the soviets and over the working class. But Lenin, though willing to make far-reaching economic concessions, would not for a moment consider any compromise on the matter which for him always had first priority—political power. The Communist Party's dictatorship must at all costs be maintained. The Kronstadt mutineers were denounced as agents of the Whites and as intending to restore capitalism. Though no shred of evidence has been found to support either accusation, both were endlessly repeated by the propaganda machine. On March 7, 1921, military operations were begun against Kronstadt, and on March 18 the fortress was stormed.

29. The 10th Congress and Lenin's Dictatorship.—The Communist Party held its 10th Congress in Moscow in March 1921. Its debates were lively, for there were two opposition groups within the party, the "Workers' Opposition," which wished to transfer power to the trade unions and form something like a syndicalist state, and the "Democratic Centralism" group, which wished for greater freedom within the party and within the soviets while maintaining the ban on parties other than the Communist. Lenin was unwilling to compromise with either group, and both were defeated by large majorities. The most important consequence of the 10th Congress was its formal prohibition of "fractionalism": members of the party had the right to criticize the party's policies as individuals, but they must put their criticisms before the party as a whole, not before any smaller group within the party; an individual might make a proposal to the Central Committee, but if he first enlisted the support of even one other individual, he was thereby guilty of creating a "fraction." One clause of the resolution on "the unity of the party," which was kept secret for the next three years, provided that persons guilty of fractionalism could be expelled from the party.

Lenin went far to meet popular economic discontent by the introduction in 1921 of his "New Economic Policy," which reaffirmed the right of peasants to the ownership of their land, reduced the burden of taxation on them, and also permitted a certain amount of private business enterprise—especially in trade. But in the political field he was inflexible. No political opinions, let alone organizations, other than the Communist were to be allowed. The Communist Party itself was controlled nominally by its Central Committee, but to an increasing extent by smaller bodies

elected by it—the Political Bureau, the Organization Bureau, and the Secretariat, all set up by the 8th Congress in March 1918. At the head of the pyramid was Lenin himself, the man of genius who had swept all rivals out of his path and set up in Russia a form of government more rigidly dictatorial than that of any tsar. But in his own view and in that of all subsequent writers of works published in Soviet Russia, this was no mere seizure of power but "the great October Socialist Revolution," opening a new era in the ineluctable progress of the human race toward Communism.

For later events *see* UNION OF SOVIET SOCIALIST REPUBLICS: *History; see* also COMMUNISM; COMMUNIST PARTIES.

BIBLIOGRAPHY.—The English edition, by A. Rothstein and Clemens Dutt, of the *History of the Communist Party of the Soviet Union* (1960) gives the latest version of the official Soviet line on the history of the Revolution. Lenin's actions can be documented from his *Works*, 5th Russian ed., vol. 31–45 (1958–64), or select English ed., vol. 7–12 (1936). Trotski's version is in his *History of the Russian Revolution* (1934). For a general survey, particularly good on foreign policy, *see* E. H. Carr, *The Bolshevik Revolution*, 3 vol. (1950–53). For the Socialist-Revolutionaries, *see* O. H. Radkey, *The Agrarian Foes of Bolshevism* (1958), *The Sickle Under the Hammer* (1963). For the opposition to the Bolsheviks, *see* L. B. Schapiro, *The Origin of the Communist Autocracy* (1955). For the non-Russian nationalities *see* R. E. Pipes, *The Formation of the Soviet Union* (1954).

(G. H. N. S.-W.)

RUSSIAN SOVIET FEDERATED SOCIALIST REPUBLIC, the largest of the 15 constituent Union Republics of the U.S.S.R. Established immediately after the October Revolution (1917), it became a Union Republic on Dec. 30, 1922, when the U.S.S.R. as a federal state was created. Area, 6,592,658 sq.mi. Pop. (1959 census) 117,534,315, (1964 est.) 124,777,000. Its huge area extends from the Baltic Sea to the Pacific Ocean, across 11 time zones, and from the Arctic Ocean to the Caspian Sea, and includes the greater part of European Russia and all Siberia and

TABLE I.—*Largest Nationality Groups in the R.S.F.S.R.*

Nationality group	Population (1959 census)	Percentage of total
Russians	97,863,579	83.3
Tatars	4,074,669	3.5
Ukrainians	3,359,083	2.9
Chuvash	1,436,218	1.2
Mordvinians	1,211,105	1.0
Bashkirs	953,801	0.8
Jews	875,307	0.7
White Russians	843,985	0.7
Germans	820,016	0.7
Udmurts	615,640	0.5
Mari	498,066	0.4
Komi and Komi-Permyaks	425,810	0.36
Kazakhs	382,431	0.3
Armenians	255,978	0.2
Buryats	251,504	0.2
Ossetians	247,834	0.2
Yakuts	236,125	0.2
Kabardinians	200,634	0.2
Karelians	164,050	0.1
Poles	118,422	0.1

the far east. Generally speaking, the R.S.F.S.R. includes those parts of the Soviet Union where the Russian nationality forms the majority, although since World War II Russians have also become the majority in the Kazakh Soviet Socialist Republic. Within the R.S.F.S.R. are many non-Russian peoples and it should be remembered that the word "Russian" of its title is a translation not of Russkaya ("pertaining to the Russian nationality"), but of Rossiyskaya ("pertaining to the country Russia"). The larger nationalities have their own areas, with varying degrees of autonomy. Thus in the R.S.F.S.R. there are 16 Autonomous Soviet Socialist Republics: for the Bashkirs, Buryats, Chechen and Ingush, Chuvash, Dagestanis, Kabardinians and Balkars, Kalmyks, Karelians, Komi, Mari, Mordvinians, Ossetians, Tatars, Tuvinians, Udmurts, and Yakuts. Smaller groups have Autonomous *oblasts*, of which there are five, and the smallest have National *okrugs* (districts), of which there are 10, mostly in the extreme north and northeast. The largest nationality groups are shown in Table I.

Apart from the national areas the R.S.F.S.R. is divided administratively into 49 *oblasts* and 6 *kray* (marchlands or territories), the latter representing former areas of pioneer settlement in the North Caucasus and Siberia.

TABLE II.—*The R.S.F.S.R.; Percentage Comparison with the U.S.S.R.*
(1962)

Item	Percentage of U.S.S.R.	Item	Percentage of U.S.S.R.
Area	76	Iron ore	35
Population	55	Petroleum	82
Cropped area . . .	60	Coal	57
Agricultural production		Electricity	67
Wheat	59	Motor vehicles . . .	89
Flax	62	Combine harvesters . .	100
Sugar beet . . .	45	Tractors	45
Head of cattle . .	51	Paper	81
pigs . .	52	Cotton cloth . . .	86
sheep . .	47	Woolen cloth . . .	78
Industrial production		Preserved foodstuffs . .	44
Steel	56		

The administrative centre of the republic is the capital of the U.S.S.R., Moscow. Altogether there are 901 cities and 1,678 settlements of urban type, containing 61,611,074 people, 52% of the total population. Of the towns, three had more than 1,000,000 inhabitants in 1961: Greater Moscow (6,208,000), Leningrad (2,888,000), and Gorki (1,003,000). Since the R.S.F.S.R. represents so much of the Soviet Union, its geography and history are largely those of the larger unit, but Table II indicates its significance in the country as a whole.

See also UNION OF SOVIET SOCIALIST REPUBLICS. (R. A. F.)

RUSSKAYA PRAVDA, a codification of old Russian customary law and of those princely statutes and enactments which were considered precedents for future court decisions. *Russkaya Pravda* was compiled in Kievan Russia during the 11th–12th centuries, and is usually classified by scholars in two basic "versions": short and expanded. The short version, compiled under Yaroslav the Wise, grand prince of Kiev from 1019 to 1054, contains primarily norms of penal law, based on contemporary custom which at that time still recognized the right of blood revenge for a murdered relative. After Yaroslav's death his sons abolished blood revenge and, instead, introduced punishment by money payment ("bloodwite"), according to the law and to the decision of the princely court. In the course of the 12th century the code was considerably enlarged and revised and thus the so-called expanded version came into being. An important part of it was a statute of Prince Vladimir II Monomakh (reigned 1113–25) concerning loans and interest, designed to prohibit severe usurious practices. Many additional provisions regulated family and inheritance law, commerce, and the legal position of indentured labourers (*zakupy*), and laid down detailed rules concerning slavery.

The *Russkaya Pravda* not only gives evidence of the legal norms and court procedures of the 11th–12th centuries; it also gives an insight into the social structure of Russian society in that period. In the repeal of the old custom of blood revenge can be seen the influence of newly introduced Christianity. It is also noteworthy that the *Russkaya Pravda* did not admit capital punishment and allowed corporal punishment only for slaves.

See *Medieval Russian Laws*, Eng. trans. by G. V. Vernadsky (1947); B. D. Grekov (ed.), *Pravda Russkaya*, 2 vol. (1940–47).

(S. G. PU.)

RUSSO-FINNISH WAR: *see* WORLD WAR II; EUROPE: *History;* FINLAND: *History;* UNION OF SOVIET SOCIALIST REPUBLICS: *History.*

RUSSO-JAPANESE WAR (1904–05). By the early 17th century Russia had established its authority over all of Siberia, but its attempts to move southward were consistently blocked by China. Fully engaged in Western Europe and against Turkey during the 18th century, Russia was in no position to press its interests in the Far East. As the settlement of Siberia developed, however, it became more alive to its need for outlets to the sea and, since China continued to deny it access to the Amur region, it resorted to force toward the end of the reign of the emperor Nicholas I (1825–55).

In the 1850s Russian towns and settlements appeared along the left bank of the Amur (Hei-lung) River. The Chinese government made repeated protests, but engaged at this time in its struggle against Great Britain and France, and distracted by the T'ai P'ing Rebellion, China was unable to resist Russian pressure. Finally by the Treaty of Aigun (Aihun, or Aihui; 1858, confirmed by the Treaty of Peking, 1860) China ceded to Russia all the territory north of the Amur, together with the maritime region east of the Ussuri (Wu-su-li) River from the mouth of the Amur to the boundary of Korea, including the splendid site where Vladivostok was soon to be founded. Russian expansionist policy was now alarming other European powers, however, and in 1861 Great Britain thwarted a Russian attempt to establish a naval base on the island of Tsushima, lying between Korea and Japan. For the next 30 years Russia was content to consolidate its gains.

The reign of the emperor Alexander III (1881–94) witnessed a revival of interest in the development of the Asiatic parts of the Russian empire. In 1891 Alexander sent his son, soon to reign as Nicholas II, on a much publicized tour of the Far East, and at this time work began on the Trans-Siberian Railway. After the accession of Nicholas II in 1894 Russian expansionist policy became more active and pronounced, but in this year the Sino-Japanese War demonstrated that in Japan a new power had emerged.

The Emergence of Japan.—The transformation of Japan from a backward feudal state into a vigorous modern power, a process begun only in 1868, had been carried through with such dramatic speed that within a quarter of a century Japan was ready to assert itself against the vast, but backward, Chinese Empire. In its foreign policy Japan aimed first at extending its authority into Korea, a state over which China had long claimed suzerainty. Its struggle with China for predominance in Korea gave rise to several crises and finally, in 1894, to war. Japan with its modernized army and navy at once won a series of striking victories against the Chinese, who in the Treaty of Shimonoseki, signed on April 17, 1895, ceded to Japan the Kwantung (Liaotung) Peninsula, on which Port Arthur (Lü-shun) stands, together with Formosa (Taiwan) and the Pescadores Islands, and agreed to pay a heavy indemnity.

This display of Japanese power and its decisive victory over China threatened to close the door on Russia in the Far East, and made conflict between Russia and Japan inevitable. The Russian government was quick to react to the Treaty of Shimonoseki. On the initiative of Nicholas II, Russia, Germany, and France intervened by diplomacy and compelled Japan to give up its territorial gains in return for an increased indemnity. Guided by S. Y. Witte, his minister of communications and finance, Nicholas II at once obtained for China a loan, enabling it to pay the large indemnity to Japan, and in 1896 Russia concluded an alliance with China against Japan, guaranteeing the integrity of Chinese territory. Also under this treaty of alliance Russia obtained the right to lay the eastern section of the Trans-Siberian Railway across Manchuria by way of Harbin (Ha-erh-pin) to Vladivostok, to extend a branch line from Harbin to Mukden (Shen-yang) and Talien (Lü-ta, Dalny, or Dairen), and to administer and patrol a strip of territory on either side of the railway, using Russian troops.

European Rivalry in China.—An era of European rivalry had now begun in the Far East. The German emperor William II during a visit to Russia in 1897 secured the support of his cousin, Nicholas II, for the German annexation of Kiaochow (Chiaohsien). Subsequently Nicholas II himself decided to seize Port Arthur, in spite of his own guarantees of the integrity of Chinese territory, and in spite of the strong opposition of his minister, Witte, who nevertheless managed to win Chinese agreement to a lease of Port Arthur for 25 years (April 8 [new style]; March 27 [old style], 1898). Russia thus entered into the occupation of the Kwantung Peninsula from which only three years earlier it had excluded Japan.

The seizure of Chinese territory by Germany and Russia was followed by British demands for Wei-hai (Wei-hai-wei) and French demands on Kwangchow (Kuang-chou). A wave of xenophobic feeling in China erupted in the so-called Boxer Rebellion (1899–1900), and Japan and the European powers intervened to restore order. Russia made this rebellion the excuse to pour troops into Manchuria, whence it planned to invade Korea, the independence of which since the Treaty of Shimonoseki was "guaranteed" by Japan.

During the years of intensive preparation to assert its power in the Far East, Japan had built up an efficient army and navy. As a result of its recruiting law of 1896, by January 1904 its front-line army numbered 270,000 highly trained troops and although its reserves amounted only to some 200,000 men of older classes, it had gained a distinct preponderance over Russia in the Far East. Including all patrols on the Manchurian railways and the small garrisons at Port Arthur and Vladivostok, Russia had only some 80,000 troops. At the other end of the Trans-Siberian Railway, however, it had almost overwhelming manpower available, for the peacetime strength of the Russian Army was approximately 1,000,-000 men. The Japanese, of course, entertained no thought of attacking Russia itself, but were concerned wholly with winning an early and decisive victory which would securely establish their hegemony in the Far East. In this strategy they were counting on the Trans-Siberian Railway's proving inadequate to the task of bringing up timely reinforcements, and their miscalculation on this score might have involved them in disaster.

Russian Policy in the Far East.—The Russian government was confused and unrealistic in its policy, leading up to this war with Japan, and indeed in the conduct of the war itself. This fact, combined with the ineffective leadership of its troops, was more than any other factor responsible for its defeat. Gen. A. N. Kuropatkin, Nicholas II's minister of war, had watched with anxiety the growth of Japanese armed strength and, realizing that Japan had gained preponderance in the Far East, he had in the summer of 1903 recommended that Russia should abandon its projects in Manchuria and restore Port Arthur to China in return for concessions in the Vladivostok region. His proposals were accepted, but extremists at the imperial court and the powerful commercial interests behind the Russian expansionist movement in the Far East nullified Kuropatkin's policy. Meanwhile nothing was done to strengthen Russian forces and the Russian government simply ignored Japan's preparations and obvious intentions.

The Outbreak of War.—On the night of Feb. 8/9 (N.S.), 1904, without any declaration of war, the main Japanese fleet under the command of Adm. Togŏ Heihachirŏ took the Russian squadron by surprise at Port Arthur, inflicting serious losses and imposing a blockade on the harbour. Adm. E. I. Alekseev, a sycophantic and incompetent favourite of the emperor, who was viceroy and at first commander in chief of the Russian forces in the Far East, gave the demoralizing order that the navy was not to risk proceeding to sea. When Adm. S. O. Makarov, a brave and

TWO RUSSIAN SHIPS SUNK DURING THE SIEGE OF PORT ARTHUR

able officer, assumed command of the navy, however, he took his ships to sea daily and seriously harassed the Japanese fleet, but unfortunately lost his life on April 13 when his flagship "Petropavlovsk" struck a mine and sank. The Russian squadron was thereafter kept in harbour for months, while the Japanese fleet lay off Port Arthur unchallenged. Thus the Japanese fleet, although in strength about equal to the Russian Far Eastern Fleet, kept the enemy fleet divided and confined in Port Arthur and Vladivostok.

Without waiting to gain command of the sea, the Japanese had begun in March transporting their 1st Army (under the command of Gen. Tamemoto Kuroki) across the sea to Korea, landing them at Chemulpo (or Inch'ŏn), not far from Seoul, and at Nampo in the north. The roads were so bad, because of the thaw, that it took many days before the Japanese Army was in position before the town of Wiju (Sinŭiju) on the Yalu River. On May 1 the Japanese attacked and after bitter fighting defeated the Russian forces. Japanese losses were about 1,100 men out of a force of 40,000 while Russian losses were 2,500 out of their force of 7,000 troops engaged in this action. It was a victory of tremendous significance, for, although the outnumbered Russians had made an orderly withdrawal, it was Japan's first victorious engagement against a Western nation.

Russian Strategy.—A public outcry against Alekseev as commander in chief compelled Nicholas II to send Kuropatkin to take over the command, although Alekseev remained as viceroy. Kuropatkin had proved a competent minister of war, but was to show himself sadly irresolute and passive as a commander in action. His policy was to avoid action, wherever possible, until he had superiority in numbers. He placed his forces so that they could delay the enemy and then retire to positions prepared in the rear.

During May the Japanese 2nd Army (Gen. Yasukata Oku) landed on the Kwantung Peninsula and on May 26, outnumbering the Russians by ten to one, won the Battle of Nanshan, cutting off the Port Arthur garrison from the main forces in Manchuria. Two more divisions landed on the eastern Korean coast to form the 3rd Army (Gen. Kiten Maresuke Nogi) to operate against Port Arthur, while a further division, to form the nucleus of a 4th Army (Gen. Michitsura Nodzu), was landed on the Manchurian coast at Ku-shan.

Kuropatkin was disturbed by this enemy concentration. He ordered preparations to make Mukden a stronghold to which he could retreat, but at this time he received an order, signed by the emperor himself, impressing on him that the fate of Port Arthur was his direct responsibility. Kuropatkin therefore disposed his main forces around Liao-yang (south of Mukden). But at Wafangtien (Fu-hsien) on June 14, the Japanese with 35,000 men decisively defeated a 25,000-strong Russian army. The Japanese then advanced in three columns on Liao-yang, where the main Russian force under Kuropatkin had retired and taken up strong positions. Even an unexpected sortie of the Russian squadron at Port Arthur, which for a time paralyzed the Japanese land offensive, and then the sudden appearance of the Russian Vladivostok squadron in the straits of Tsushima, which added to the anxieties of the Japanese high command, did not embolden the Russian command to adopt more aggressive tactics. Toward the end of July Kuropatkin engaged General Kuroki in what proved an in-

JAPANESE SOLDIERS AWAITING RUSSIAN CHARGE DURING THE BATTLE OF LIAO-YANG

decisive battle, after which Kuropatkin himself fell back on Liao-yang and there remained on the defensive, although he had considerable opportunities to attack the advancing enemy columns.

On Aug. 25 (N.S.) the Battle of Liao-yang was joined, and after nine days of stubborn fighting the Japanese won a significant victory, and with inferior numbers: 130,000 against 180,000 Russians. Nevertheless their losses of some 23,000 men faced them with serious difficulties, for they had limited trained reserves, whereas the Russians had withdrawn in good order toward Mukden, where they were now receiving reinforcements via the Trans-Siberian Railway at the rate of 30,000 men a month.

Realizing that the Japanese were nearing the end of their resources, while the Russian Army was gaining in strength, Kuropatkin resolved now to take the offensive, while making careful preparations to hold Mukden, which as the capital of Manchuria had special political importance. The first battle, resulting from Kuropatkin's new offensive tactics, was fought on the Sha-ho River during Oct. 5–17 (N.S.), 1904, and a subsequent battle took place at Sandepu during Jan. 26–27, 1905; both might have been decisive victories for Russia had Kuropatkin and his senior officers shown more resolution and aggression, but in the event both battles proved indecisive.

Capture of Port Arthur.—Meantime at Port Arthur the Japanese had found the Russian garrison much stronger than they had expected. After several very costly attempts to take the fortress, they abandoned general assaults and resorted to siege tactics. The dragging on of these operations distressed the Japanese command, for it not only tied down their 3rd Army, which they needed urgently in the main theatre of war, but it also reacted badly on the morale of their troops in Manchuria.

The news of the sailing of the Russian Baltic Fleet for the Far East made the Japanese redouble their efforts to take Port Arthur. They suffered very heavy casualties in the storming tactics to which they had once again resorted. Among the officers of the Russian garrison, however, there was serious disagreement; some urged surrender while others insisted that the garrison must resist to the end. But on Jan. 2 (N.S.), 1905, Lieut. Gen. A. M. Stössel, the commander of the fortress, a man not only grossly incompetent, but also corrupt, sent out the white flag without reference to his officers, and thus surrendered Port Arthur. It was an act of treachery, for the fortress contained provisions for over three months and adequate supplies of ammunition.

The Battle of Mukden.—The final and greatest battle of the war was fought for Mukden (Feb. 19–March 10 [N.S.], 1905). Again Kuropatkin had decided to attack, but this time the Japanese forestalled him. Three Russian armies—from right to left, the 2nd (under Gen. Baron A. V. Kaulbars), the 3rd (under General Bilderling) and the 1st (under Gen. N. P. Linevich), comprising 330,000 men and 1,475 guns in all—held firm against three Japanese armies under the command of Marshal Iwao Oyama (who had 270,000 men and 1,062 guns). After long and stubborn fighting and heavy casualties, Kuropatkin decided to draw off his troops to the north, a movement carried out successfully, but it left Mukden to fall into the hands of the Japanese. Losses in this battle were exceptionally heavy, approximately 89,000 Russians and 71,000 Japanese having fallen. Japan was now exhausted and could not hope to pursue the war to a successful conclusion. But the naval victory of Tsushima, together with the increasing internal unrest throughout Russia, where the war, which had never been popular, had become a focal point for the widespread movement against the regime, brought the Russian government to agree to peace.

The Russian Baltic Fleet.—The Japanese had been unable to secure the complete command of the sea on which their campaign depended. The Russian squadrons at Port Arthur and Vladivostok had made sorties and both sides had suffered losses in engagements. Meanwhile in St. Petersburg it was decided to send the Baltic Fleet to the Far East under the command of Adm. Zinovi Petrovich Rozhestvenski, for it was clear that once the Russians had gained command of the sea, the Japanese campaign would collapse.

The Baltic Fleet, having spent the whole summer fitting out,

sailed from Liepaja on Oct. 15 (N.S.), 1904. Off the Dogger Bank on Oct. 21, several Russian ships opened fire on British trawlers in the mistaken belief that they were Japanese torpedo boats, and this incident aroused such anger in England that war was only avoided by the immediate apology and promise of full compensation made by the Russian government. At Nossi-Bé, near Madagascar, Rozhestvenski learned of the surrender of Port Arthur and proposed returning to Russia, but, expecting naval reinforcements which had been sent from the Baltic via Suez early in March, 1905, and which later joined him at Camranh Bay (Vietnam) he decided to proceed. His full fleet amounted to a formidable armada, but many of the ships were old and unserviceable. Early in May the fleet reached the China Sea and Rozhestvenski made for Vladivostok via the Tsushima Strait. Admiral Togō lay in wait for him on the south Korean coast near Pusan and on May 27, as the Russian Fleet approached, he attacked. The Japanese ships were superior in speed and armament and in the course of the two-day battle two-thirds of the Russian Fleet was sunk, six ships were captured, four reached Vladivostok, and six took refuge in neutral ports. It was a dramatic and decisive defeat; after a voyage lasting seven months and when within a few hundred miles of its destination, the Baltic Fleet was shattered and with it Russia's hope of regaining mastery of the sea was crushed.

The Treaty of Portsmouth.—The disastrous course of the war had seriously aggravated unrest inside Russia, and the surrender of Port Arthur, followed by the loss of Mukden and the devastating defeat at Tsushima made the emperor accept the proffered mediation of Pres. Theodore Roosevelt of the United States. It was, however, the Japanese government which had taken the initiative in proposing peace negotiations. Exhausted financially and fearing a long-drawn-out war of attrition far from their bases, the Japanese hoped that the acute unrest in Russia would compel the government to discuss terms, and their hopes proved justified.

Negotiations began at Portsmouth, N.H., on Aug. 9 and by the peace treaty signed on Sept. 5, 1905, Russia agreed to surrender its lease of the Kwantung Peninsula and of Port Arthur, to evacuate Manchuria, to cede the half of Sakhalin annexed in 1875, and to recognize Korea as within Japan's sphere of interest.

With this treaty ended the Far Eastern expansionist policy directed toward establishing Russian hegemony over the whole of Asia. Furthermore the humiliating defeats at the hands of an Asiatic power which had until so recently been primitive and backward, added to the national anger and disgust. Within two months a revolution had compelled Nicholas II to issue the October manifesto, which was the equivalent of a constitutional charter. This defeat also had profound repercussions throughout Asia and Europe. Russia nevertheless remained an Asiatic power, possessing as it did the railways across Siberia and northern Manchuria to Vladivostok, and being closely allied with China.

See also references under "Russo-Japanese War" in the Index.

BIBLIOGRAPHY.—Wasuke Jikemura, *The Russo-Japanese War,* 2 vol. (1904–05); Heihachiro Togo, *La Bataille de Tsouchima* (1905); E. L. H. von Tettau, *Achtzehn Monate mit Russlands Heeren in Mandschurei,* 2nd ed. (1907); *The Russo-Japanese War: Reports from British Officers,* issued by the War Office (1908); J. L. E. Bujac, *La Guerre russo-japonaise* (1909); A. N. Kuropatkin, *The Russian Army and the Japanese War* (1909); F. B. Maurice, "The Russo-Japanese War," *The Cambridge Modern History,* vol. xii, ch. xix (1910); S. Yu. Witte, *La guerre avec le Japon: Réponse à l'ouvrage du général Kouropatkine* (1911); Sir Ian Hamilton, *A Staff Officer's Scrap-book During the Russo-Japanese War,* 2nd ed. (1912). (I. Gy.)

RUSSO-POLISH WAR (1919–20). The Russo-Polish War was a result of the German defeat in the west at the end of World War I and of the Soviet determination to carry the Communist revolution to central Europe. On the day of Germany's surrender (Nov. 11, 1918), Poland's independence was proclaimed in Warsaw, but huge German armies were still in occupation of the western part of the former Russian Empire. Jozef Pilsudski (*q.v.*), provisional head of the Polish state and commander in chief of the nascent Polish Army, decided not to interfere with the retreat of the German forces from Russia, provided that they went through East Prussia. A temporary demarcation line between Polish and German forces was established to the west of the railway Kovel-

Brest(Brzesc)-Bialystok-Grajewo. Evacuation of the former Russian lands by the German forces had to be completed by the beginning of February 1919.

Because of German-Soviet collusion, every strip of land evacuated by the Germans was immediately occupied by the Red Army. German generals were hoping to bring Soviet Russia and Poland into war which would destroy the latter and enable Germany to appear as the sole defender of Europe against the revolutionary flood. On the Soviet side, Lenin's strategy was the converse: the mission of the Red Army was "to destroy the wall separating Soviet Russia from revolutionary Germany." Thus at the beginning of February 1919 the Red Army was approaching the line Grodno-Brest-Kovel.

Pilsudski decided that it was vital "to reject . . . the forces aiming at imposing a foreign form of government on Poland." The Polish counteroffensive began on Feb. 9, 1919. At the end of the year the Polish forces stood on the middle Dvina and along the Berezina, Ptich, Ubort, and upper Sluch rivers to a point east of Kamenets-Podolski near the Rumanian frontier. The Polish advance had of course been helped by the fact that the Red Army was also engaged against White Russian armies.

Pilsudski expected a second and more powerful Soviet offensive in the spring of 1920. But on Jan. 28, 1920, the Soviet government sent to the Polish government proposals for an armistice based on the existing front line and for a peace conference. Pilsudski, however, knew that the Soviet high command was concentrating big new units on the Polish front; and, moreover, he was convinced that the moment was favourable for reviving the historic idea of a Polish-Lithuanian-Ukrainian federation. On April 21, he and the Ukrainian leader Symon Petlyura (q.v.) signed a treaty of alliance. Three days later an army group of ten infantry divisions (including two Ukrainian) and four cavalry brigades was launched against two weak Soviet armies south of the Pripet River. On May 7, Kiev was occupied by a Polish army under Gen. Edward Smigly-Rydz, while between the Dnieper and Dniester rivers Polish-Ukrainian forces held the line Belaya Tserkov-Lipovets-Gaysin-Vapnyarka-Yampol.

Further advance southward was halted when Pilsudski learned that, on May 15, 1920, M. N. Tukhachevski, commander of the Soviet Western Army Group, had attacked across the Dvina. Tukhachevski reached Lake Naroch, but by June 7 was driven back on the Berezina. In the meantime, however, the Soviet supreme commander, Sergei S. Kamenev, had ordered S. M. Budenny to march northward from the Guman area with four cavalry divisions. On June 7, Budenny was at Zhitomir and Berdichev in the rear of Smigly-Rydz, who was therefore ordered to evacuate Kiev (June 12) and to retreat westward. He succeeded in doing so, but on July 5 Budenny entered Rovno.

The decisive battles started north of the Pripet marshes. On July 2, 1920, Tukhachevski issued an Order of the Day proclaiming to his armies that "the fate of the general revolution will be decided in the west" and that "the road to world conflagration leads over Poland's corpse." Two days later, on a front of about 500 km., he attacked with 21 infantry divisions and with Gai Khan's cavalry corps on his right flank (about 220,000 combatants). The Polish army group under the elderly Stanislaw Szeptycki, comprising 12 infantry divisions and one cavalry brigade (about 120,000 combatants), started a general retreat. Minsk fell to the Russians on July 11, Wilno (Vilnius) on July 14, Grodno on July 19.

Pilsudski never lost his nerve. Needing arms and ammunition, he sent his prime minister, Wladyslaw Grabski, and his chief of general staff, Tadeusz Rozwadowski, on a mission to the Supreme Allied Council, which was then in session in Belgium. The Western Powers promised help which either did not materialize (as from Great Britain) or arrived too late (as from France). But a Franco-British diplomatic and military mission, including Gen. Maxime Weygand, was sent to Warsaw. Pilsudski offered Weygand the post of chief of Polish general staff, but Weygand sensibly declined and became, instead, an adviser to Rozwadowski.

Tukhachevski was still advancing westward, with the bold plan of crossing the Vistula at Plock so as to be able to attack Warsaw's defenders from the rear. Pilsudski divined this intention and, after discussions with Rozwadowski and Weygand, wrote in the night on Aug. 5–6, 1920, his historic Order of the Day prescribing (1) that in the south the enemy should be stopped east of Lwow (Lvov); (2) that in the north the left flank of the Polish forces should be covered and the right bank of the Vistula should be held for the defense of Warsaw; and (3) that in the centre an army of five divisions should be concentrated on the Wieprz River for a strategic maneuver designed to disrupt the rear of the Soviet armies as they approached Warsaw.

On Aug. 16, 1920, Pilsudski himself took command of the Wieprz operation and started marching northward with his shock divisions. It was a crushing attack which completely surprised the enemy. Two days later, when Pilsudski was at Drohiczyn on the Bug River, Tukhachevski recognized the failure of his enterprise and ordered a general retreat. This disengagement, however, was a disastrous one: the Poles made 66,000 prisoners of war, taking 231 guns and 1,023 machine guns. Tens of thousands of Soviet soldiers fled across East Prussia and Lithuania. Tukhachevski's attempt to make a stand along the line Sejny-Grodno-Volkovysk ended in another defeat (Sept. 20–28). At the beginning of October, Polish forces reconquered the major part of the territory occupied during 1919. An armistice was signed at Riga on Oct. 12 and military operations ceased six days later.

BIBLIOGRAPHY.—Polish sources: J. Pilsudski, *Rok 1920* (1924; French trans. *L'Année 1920,* 1929); W. Sikorski, *Nad Wisłą i Wkrą* (1928; French trans. *La Campagne Polono-Russe de 1920,* 1928); A. Przybylski, *La Pologne en lutte pour ses frontières* (1929). Soviet sources: M. N. Tukhachevski, *Pokhod za Vislu* (1923; French trans. *La Marche au delà de la Vistule,* in annex to Pilsudski's book, 1929); N. E. Kakurin and V. A. Melikov, *Voina z Belopolyakami* (1925); E. N. Sergeev, *Od Dviny k Visle* (1923); Vitovt Putna, *K Visle i obratno* (1927). Other sources: H. Camon, *La Manoeuvre libératrice du Maréchal Pilsudski* (1929); Lord D'Abernon (Sir Edgar Vincent), *The Eighteenth Decisive Battle of the World* (1931); J. F. C. Fuller, *The Decisive Battles of the Western World,* vol. iii, ch. 9 (1956); M. Weygand, *Mémoires,* vol. ii, part 2 (1957). (K. Sm.)

RUSSO-TURKISH WARS.

Wars fought by Russia against the Ottoman Turkish Empire resulted in the eventual extension of the Russian frontier to the line of the Prut River in Europe and to beyond the Caucasus Range in Asia. In the 17th century Russia was faced with the problem of an ill-defended southern frontier over which little control could be exercised. The Cossacks (q.v.) of the Dnieper and the Don were unruly frontiersmen with institutions of their own, while the Tatars of the Crimea, vassals of the sultan, annually drove their herds and flocks out into the grasslands of the Ukraine and, from time to time, sent their horsemen to raid deep into Poland and Russia.

The 17th Century and Peter the Great.—The first Russo-Turkish War (1676–81) was fought in right-bank Ukraine (that is, Ukraine west of the Dnieper), without success for Russia. Having concluded a "perpetual peace" with Poland to settle disputes over the Ukraine (1686), Russia renewed the war in 1687, and V. V. Golitsyn (q.v.) tried unsuccessfully to invade the Crimea (1687 and 1689). When the tsar Peter I (q.v.) renewed the attempt to push back the Turks, he chose instead to march by the easier route down the valley of the Don to besiege the Turkish fortress of Azov. He failed in his attempt of 1695, but in the following year he succeeded in taking the fortress. Russia did not make substantial gains at the expense of Turkey, since Austria, Poland, and Venice, in league against the Turks from 1684, made their peace of Karlowitz early in 1699; but the Russo-Turkish peace of 1700 left Russia in possession of the towns of Azov and Taganrog, while the tribute, formerly paid by the tsar to the Crimean Tatars, was abolished and Russia for the first time obtained the right to appoint a resident minister to the Porte.

In November 1710, Turkey declared war on Russia just as Russia was beginning to get the upper hand in the Northern War (q.v.) against Sweden. Peter I had no wish for war with Turkey, but the strategy that he devised was original. Turning to the west, Peter planned to enter Moldavia and Walachia (see RUMANIA) in order to arouse the Christian population of European Turkey against the sultan. Unfortunately for Peter he was surrounded at Stănilești on the Prut (July 19, 1711, new style; July 8, old style) and forced to sue for peace, which was granted (July 23). Peter was compelled to surrender the fortress of Azov to the Turks and to promise to abstain from interference in the internal affairs of Poland, as well as to guarantee free passage across his territory to Charles XII of Sweden, then a refugee with the Turks (this last proviso had no effect). These were moderate terms in view of the predicament in which Peter found himself. Disputes concerning the fulfillment of the peace of the Prut led to a fresh Turkish declaration of war in November 1712, but peace was reaffirmed in 1713 at Adrianople (Edirne).

The strategy of Russo-Turkish conflict changed in the 1720s when the anarchy prevailing in Persia as a result of the Afghan invasion made it possible for Turkey to envisage establishing a base on the Caspian Sea from which to threaten Astrakhan. Peter's expeditions of 1722–23 in the Caspian regions enabled him to establish a tenuous hold on the western Caspian shores and a claim to the southern shores of the Caspian as far eastward as Astrabad (Gorgan). In 1724 Russia and Turkey recognized one another's spheres of influence in Transcaucasia, but the situation remained unsettled and Russia was unable to make a major effort in this theatre of operations.

The War of 1735–39.—With the revival of Persian power the Russian government curtailed its commitments in the Caspian area. By the Russo-Persian treaties of Resht (1732) and of Gandzha (1735), Russia withdrew by stages to the left bank of the Terek River, on condition that no third power (i.e., Turkey) should annex the ceded territories. The Turks, however, resumed their eastward pressure in spite of the agreement of 1724 with Russia. In 1734 the Crimean Tatars actually violated the Russian frontier in an expedition to the Caspian, which provided the *casus belli*. Russia began hostilities against Turkey in autumn 1735.

Russian strategy under Field Marshal B. C. Münnich was at first directed against the Crimea and the Dnieper mouth in the campaigns of 1736–38, but in 1739 Russia reverted to the strategy of 1711 and sent an army through Polish territory to attack the Turks in Moldavia. On Aug. 28 (N.S.), 1739, the Turkish army was severely defeated at Stavuchany. The Austrians, however, who had allied themselves with the Russians in 1737, suffered defeats in Serbia and in the Danube Valley, and once again made a separate peace. All that Russia obtained by the Treaty of Belgrade (Sept. 18 [N.S.], 1739) was the destruction of Azov as a fortress and the recognition of Russian sovereignty over the territories of the Zaporozhian Cossacks, which Turkey had hitherto claimed.

The War of 1768–74.—Russian preoccupation with the affairs of central Europe prevented further activity in the south until after the end of the Seven Years' War. In 1768 the crisis in Poland over the Confederation of Bar (q.v.) enabled Turkey to demand that Russia, in accordance with the terms of the treaties of 1711–13, should abstain from interference in Poland's internal affairs. Russian strategy in this war was to concentrate on Azov and Taganrog (both conquered in 1769) and the penetration of Moldavia and Walachia. In 1770 Field Marshal P. A. Rumyantsev won substantial victories on the Larga and Kagula rivers in Moldavia, while in June a Russian squadron appeared in the Aegean—a novel departure. Russia would have been willing to conclude peace in 1770, but Austria and Prussia wanted to take advantage of the situation to make annexations at the expense of Poland, which Russia controlled indirectly. On July 6, 1771, the Austrian government made an agreement with Turkey, by which it undertook to seek a restitution of the Russian conquests to the Turks. Russia was therefore compelled, on the one hand, to buy off Prussian and Austrian hostility by cessions of Polish territory and, on the other, to seek a reasonable peace with Turkey. The Turks, however, were disposed to offer resistance in the talks held at Focșani (in Moldavia) and at Bucharest and to demand the restoration of Russian conquests.

With part of her diplomatic difficulties solved by the First Partition of Poland (1772), the Russian empress Catherine II ordered Rumyantsev to cross the Danube in 1773 and to engage the main Turkish forces; but the situation was difficult in view of the formidable rebellion of E. I. Pugachev (q.v.) on the lower Volga.

In 1774, however, Rumyantsev crossed the Danube into Bulgaria and, on June 20 (N.S.), defeated the Turks decisively at Kozludzha (the modern Suvorovo). The Turks were therefore compelled to seek peace, which was concluded at Kuchuk Kainarji on July 21 (N.S.), 1774. The Russian frontier was advanced to the line of the southern Bug; the fortresses of Kerch and Yenikale at the eastern end of the Crimean Peninsula and that of Kinburn on the southern side of the Dnieper estuary were ceded to Russia; and Russia obtained the right to maintain a fleet on the Black Sea and vague rights of protection over the Christian population of European Turkey. The khanate of Crimea was declared to be independent of the Porte in all except religious matters.

The War of 1787–91.—Russia was now in a much stronger position to expand. In 1783 Catherine II, taking advantage of civil disturbances among the Tatars, annexed the Crimean peninsula and the Kuban territories of the khanate. Likewise in 1783 the policy of Peter I in the extreme south was resumed when the Georgian king of Kakhetia and Kartalinia (Kartlia), Erekle II, accepted Russian overlordship.

In 1787 disputes over fields of influence led to the delivery of a Turkish ultimatum demanding Russia's recognition of Turkish sovereignty in Georgia and the admission of Turkish consuls to the Crimea. The Turkish fleet attacked Kinburn without success in October 1787, but the war in the south brought complications in the north. Sweden declared war on Russia in July 1788, in order to obtain restitution of the territories ceded under the treaties of Nystad (1721) and Åbo (1743); and Prussian intrigues induced the Polish opposition to overthrow the pro-Russian regime in October. Austria, however, in alliance with Russia from 1786, had entered the war against Turkey.

The aim of the Russian campaign of 1788 was the capture of the fortress of Ochakov on the northern side of the Dnieper estuary, which fell to Gen. A. V. Suvorov in December. Suvorov heavily defeated the Turks at Focșani on Aug. 1 (N.S.), 1789, and again on the Rîmnic River on Sept. 22. The Russians thus came to control the lower reaches of the Dniester and of the Danube, on which their hold was confirmed by Suvorov's storming of Izmail on Dec. 22, 1790; but diplomatic circumstances complicated the military position. Sweden made peace with Russia in August 1790, but Prussia had formed an alliance with Turkey and, by the Convention of Reichenbach (July 1790), persuaded Austria to abandon the Russian side, with the result that Austria and Turkey concluded the Peace of Sistova in August 1791. Russia's greatest danger was that Great Britain, already allied with Prussia, would enter the war, which would make possible a coalition of Turkey, Great Britain, Poland, and Prussia. Pressure of British public opinion, however, compelled the younger Pitt to withdraw his ultimatum to Russia demanding the restoration of Ochakov to Turkey, while at the last moment Prussia's nerve failed.

Further Russian military successes in 1791 forced the Turks to sign the Peace of Iași (Jassy) on Jan. 9, 1792 (N.S.; Dec. 29, 1791 O.S.). By this treaty the terms of the Treaty of Kuchuk Kainarji were confirmed and the Russian frontier was advanced to the Dniester, while Russia restored Bessarabia, Moldavia, and Walachia to Turkey. Thus Russia was established on the Black Sea coast from the mouth of the Dniester to the Kerch Strait. Nevertheless, the Russian government was still embarrassed enough to cut its commitments and to agree with Prussia to further partition of Polish territory in 1792. Both in 1772 and in 1792 the Turkish campaigns had led to a contraction of Russia's invisible empire in Poland.

The War of 1806–12.—The next war was largely a product of French diplomacy in Turkey during the Napoleonic Wars (q.v.). Though Turkey's position in the Balkans was threatened by a rebellion of the Serbs (from 1804), Russia was involved in war against Persia in the Caucasus (also from 1804); and the Turks believed that, with French support, they might recover the Crimea from Russia. Turkey provoked Russia by deposing the hospodars of Moldavia and Walachia in summer 1806; the Russians invaded those principalities in November; and on Dec. 30 the Porte declared war on Russia. The Franco-Russian Treaty of Tilsit (1807) obliged Russia to evacuate the principalities and to promise that war would not be resumed before April 1808 if peace with Turkey could not be achieved. Hostilities began again in March 1809, after the Russian emperor Alexander I's meeting at Erfurt with Napoleon (autumn 1808), when Napoleon renounced his claim to mediate between Russia and Turkey.

The complicating factor was that Alexander, apart from his war against Persia, could not concentrate large forces against Turkey when his relations with France were so tenuous. In 1811, with the prospect of an imminent Franco-Russian war, it was imperative that Russia should seek a quick decision. The Russian commander in chief, Field Marshal M. I. Kutuzov, defeated the Turks at Ruschuk (Ruse) on July 4 (N.S.), 1811, and then surprisingly withdrew. The Turks resumed their offensive across the Danube, whereupon Kutuzov sent a detachment to the right bank and cut off the Turkish line of retreat. On Dec. 9 (N.S.), 1811, the Turks capitulated at Slobozia and, by the Treaty of Bucharest (May 28, [N.S.], 1812), ceded Bessarabia to Russia and granted an amnesty and local autonomy to the Serbs, with whom Russia had been in close relations from 1807. Thus Russia was free from embarrassment in the south just before Napoleon launched his attack in summer 1812; and the new frontier on the Prut held out advantages for the future.

The War of 1828–29.—Russo-Turkish relations between the Treaty of Bucharest and the Convention of Akkerman (Oct. 7 [N.S.], 1826) are described in the appropriate section of the article EASTERN QUESTION. Since Turkey refused to honour that Convention, Russia opened an offensive in the Balkan theatre of operations on May 8 (N.S.; April 26, O.S.), 1828, and occupied the Danubian principalities without difficulty. The Russian forces under Gen. P. K. Wittgenstein crossed the Danube on June 8, took the fortress of Brăila on June 19, and marched forward as far as Varna (Oct. 11), but the year was too far advanced and Russian movement too sluggish for further operations. In the Caucasian theatre Gen. I. F. Paskevich, the conqueror of Yerevan from the Persians, advanced across the frontier and took the fortress of Kars on July 5, pressing forward into the pashaliks of Akhaltsikhe and Bayazid.

In the spring of 1829 Wittgenstein was replaced by Gen. I. I. Diebitsch as Russian commander in chief in Bulgaria. Diebitsch's instructions were to cross the Balkan Mountains with a flying column and seize Burgas; if the Turks then refused peace, he was to march on to Istanbul. In April 1829 the campaign was opened with the siege of the Danubian fortress of Silistria, while the small force of 40,000 under Diebitsch pressed forward to take Adrianople on Aug. 20. On the Caucasian front the Russian forces entered Erzurum on July 9 and were prepared to press advance as far as Trebizond (Trapzun). The Turks were thus in a very difficult position and were once more obliged to sue for peace, though the Russian Army in the Balkan theatre of war had been reduced by sickness to a mere 12,000 men.

The Treaty of Adrianople (Sept. 14, 1829) gave Russia all the islands in the mouth of the Danube and all the eastern shore of the Black Sea from Kerch Strait as far as the St. Nicholas Bay in the south, together with the fortresses of Anapa, Poti, Akhaltsikhe, and Akhalkalaki. Turkey recognized that the principalities of Georgia, Imeretia, Mingrelia, and Guria, together with the khanates of Yerevan and Nakhichevan, ceded by Persia by the Treaty of Turkmanchai (Feb. 22, 1828), formed part of the Russian Empire. The results were thus more important in Transcaucasia than in Europe. Russia was now firmly based beyond the Caucasus Range, though it was several decades before the local highlanders, especially the Circassians, were reduced to obedience.

The War of 1853–56.—For this war see CRIMEAN WAR. For the Treaty of Paris (1856), whereby Russia lost the Danubian Islands won in 1829, together with the southern part of the left bank of the Prut, see EASTERN QUESTION.

The War of 1877–78.—As a result of the Turkish refusal to comply with the demands of the Powers for reform in European Turkey (see again EASTERN QUESTION), Russia opened hostilities on April 24, 1877. The campaign was the first undertaken by the Russian Army after the Crimean War, and the military reforms instituted by the minister of war, Gen. D. A. Milyutin, had not had

time to make their effect. For the Balkan theatre of operations 185,000 troops (including a few Rumanian battalions and about 7,500 Bulgarian volunteers) were made available under Grand Duke Nicholas (Nikolai) Nikolaevich, the emperor Alexander II's brother; and 144,000 of these were allotted to the striking force with 500 guns. The smallness of the force indicates that the Russian general staff intended to make a rapid penetration of European Turkey and force the Turks to make an early peace. In the Caucasian theatre only 58,000 men were allocated to the striking force under Grand Duke Michael (Mikhail) Nikolaevich.

The Turks were not as badly prepared for war as the Russians had supposed. Between 160,000 and 180,000 men were available for operations in Bulgaria, and the Turks frequently had better arms than the Russians. The Russians moreover were disturbed by internal differences in the high command; Grand Duke Nicholas was not an able commander, while native Russians were jealous of staff officers of Polish origin. The presence, moreover, of the emperor and of the tsarevitch with the army led to many recriminations.

The Russians at first achieved some successes. On the Caucasian front Bayazid fell on April 30 (N.S.) and Ardahan on May 17. On the Bulgarian front the Russians crossed the Danube in June, and a flying column under Gen. I. V. Gurko seized the Shipka Pass through the Balkan Range on July 19. At this point the Russian plans received a setback. On July 20 a Turkish force under Osman Pasha repulsed the Russians at Pleven (q.v.) and stemmed their advance. Attempts to break the resistance of Osman Pasha failed. The Russian assaults of July 30 and Sept. 11–12 were repulsed with severe losses. The Russian commander then called up Col. Count E. I. von Todleben, the engineer officer who had organized the defense of Sevastopol during the Crimean War, and Todleben pronounced in favour of a siege of Pleven. The other Turkish commanders did little to relieve the pressure on Osman Pasha, who had considerable doubts concerning the order to hold on to Pleven. In the end Osman perceived that his position was hopeless and attempted to break through the Russian cordon but was defeated and compelled to surrender (Dec. 10, 1877). In the meantime Kars had fallen on the Caucasian front on Nov. 18. The Russians could now execute the original plan of penetration deep into European Turkey: passing the Balkan Range, they took Adrianople on Jan. 20, 1878.

The British Cabinet then ordered the Mediterranean fleet to steam through the Dardanelles and anchor at Istanbul. Undeterred by the British action, the Russian Army advanced on Istanbul as far as the Chatalja (Catalca) lines. Eventually the Russians agreed to a truce, and on March 3, concluded with Turkey the Treaty of San Stefano, but the provisions of this treaty were annulled by the Congress of Berlin (q.v.).

See also references to "Russo-Turkish Wars" in the Index.

BIBLIOGRAPHY.—B. H. Sumner, *Peter the Great and the Ottoman Empire* (1949) and *Russia and the Balkans, 1870–1880* (1937); Y. R. Klokman, *Feldmarshal P. A. Rumyantsev v period russko-turetskoi voiny 1768–1774 gg.* (1951); A. V. Fadeyev, *Rossiya i vostochnyi krizis 20-kh godov xix veka* (1958); N. I. Belayev, *Russko-turetskaya voina 1877–1878 gg.* (1956); P. A. Zayonchkovski, *Voennye reformy 1860–1870 godov v Rossii* (1952); A. V. Fedorov, *Russkaya armia v 50-70 gg. xix veka* (1959). (R. F. Le.)

RUST, a term usually applied to the reddish deposit formed on iron in moist air. It has a variable composition, chiefly approximating $Fe_2O_3 \cdot H_2O$.

See also CORROSION AND OXIDATION OF METALS.

For a description of plant rusts *see* FUNGI: *Basidiomycetes (Club Fungi)*.

RUSTAVI, a town in the Georgian Soviet Socialist Republic, U.S.S.R., lies 26 km. (16 mi.) SE of Tbilisi (Tiflis) on the left bank of the Kura River. Pop. (1959) 62,395. The town developed after World War II with the establishment there of a fully integrated iron and steel works. Based on ore from Dashkesan in Azerbaijan, the plant supplies rolled steel and steel tubes to the whole Transcaucasus area. Rustavi lies on the main Tbilisi-Baku railway. The town is the centre also of an important agricultural region based on irrigation and it has several small food-processing industries. (R. A. F.)

RUSTICATION, in architecture, a form of masonry in which the stones have their edges cut back to a careful plane surface but with the central portion of the stone face either left rough or projecting markedly. Rusticated masonry is found in the platform of the tomb of Cyrus at Pasargadae in Persia (560 B.C.) and is common in certain types of Greek and Hellenistic work, such as retaining walls and the like. It was similarly used for terrace and retaining walls by the Romans, who also realized its decorative value and employed it not only for such utilitarian works as the Pont du Gard at Nîmes, France, and the aqueduct at Segovia, Spain (c. 109), but also decoratively as in the Porta Maggiore at Rome (time of Claudius), where the rustication is very rough, and the walls of the temple of Augustus at Vienne, France (c. 41), in which the rustication is carefully finished, the faces of the stone cut to a plane, and the edges very delicately sunk.

The early Renaissance architects developed this tradition still further and in the 15th-century palaces in Florence used it with magnificent effect. Thus in the Pitti palace by Brunelleschi (1458), the Mediti-Riccardi by Michelozzo di Bartolommeo (1444–52), and the Strozzi by Benedetto da Majano (1489), the carefully studied rustication forms the chief element in the design; and in the Rucellai, from designs by Alberti (1446–51), the wall surfaces between the pilasters are delicately rusticated. During the Baroque period rustication assumed great importance in garden and villa design, and fantastic surfaces were employed on the projecting portions of the stones, such as vermiculated work, in which the surface is covered with wavy and serpentine sinkages like worm-eaten wood or treated with vertical dripping forms like lime deposits from dripping water. Sometimes the stones had sides beveled and brought to a point or ridge in the centre.

The use of rustication was introduced into England by Inigo Jones, as in the gate of the Botanic Gardens at Oxford (1632), and became a dominant feature in much English Renaissance work. In American colonial work this influence is seen in the occasional shaping of outside sheathing boards to imitate rusticated masonry, as in portions of the Morris-Jumel house in New York (1765). Quoins, or corner blocks, are, in many styles, rusticated, where the face of the wall is left smooth.

RUTABAGA: see TURNIP.

RUTACEAE, a family of dicotyledonous plants, mostly shrubs and trees, comprising about 144 genera and 1,600 species, found in temperate and tropical regions, and especially abundant in Australia and southern Africa. *Ruta graveolens* is rue (q.v.). *Citrus* includes the grapefruit, orange, lemon (qq.v.), etc. *Chloroxylon swietenia* is satinwood; *Ptelea trifoliata* is shrubby trefoil or wafer ash; *Zanthoxylum americanum* is prickly ash.

RUTBAH WELLS (AR RUTBAH), a small oasis in the desert of western Iraq. It lies almost equidistant between Baghdad and Damascus in the Wadi Harwan and is the westernmost major settlement in Iraq. It long possessed a certain utility as a watering point on the ancient route, which is now followed by a modern surfaced road, but grew in importance with the establishment of new frontiers after 1918, when it became an Iraqi control post for travelers from Syria, Jordan, and Saudi Arabia. It was a pumping station on the Haifa branch of the Iraq Petroleum Company's oil pipeline (closed in 1947) from Kirkuk; the pipeline is also paralleled by a road direct from Kirkuk. (W. B. Fr.)

. **RUTEBEUF** (RUTEBUEF; RUSTEBUEF) (fl. 1248–1277?), French poet whose works, which include social, political, and religious satire, verse *contes* and *fabliaux,* laments, crusading poems, saints' lives, a miracle play, hymns to the Virgin Mary, and personal lyrics, bear the impress of a talented, complex, and original personality. Probably of *champenois* origin, he lived mainly in Paris, but his name, certainly a pseudonym, is nowhere mentioned by his contemporaries, and knowledge of him is derived from his poems, written between 1248 and 1277 or, possibly, 1285. There is evidence that much of his work—especially the narrative poems and the miracle play—influenced later writers; but his significance lies chiefly in the fact that in him is first powerfully heard, in France, the voice of popular opinion. His pungent commentaries are directed at virtually every order of society—even the highest, including Louis IX and the pope himself, do not escape criticism.

As with later pamphleteers and political columnists, it is not easy to say how far his work reflects, and how far it creates, public opinion. However, the consistency of his views over a long period argues a certain independence of mind; and the high rank of some of his patrons, among them the king's brother, Alphonse, count of Poitiers, suggests that his talents may have been recognized as a powerful means of courting public opinion, and implies that that opinion was a factor to be reckoned with.

In fact, the key to his attitude is to be found in his personal and professional loyalties, and in his innate humanity and sense of justice. Himself a penniless scholar—he foreshadows François Villon in the keen observation and humanity of his sketches of the seamier side of Paris life—Rutebeuf remains the champion of the University of Paris (q.v.) against the mendicant orders. It is significant, too, that his hatred of the mendicants appears to date from 1254, when he espoused the cause of Guillaume de St. Amour, the leader of the secular masters, against the Dominicans. Again, his enthusiasm for the Crusades is at least partly explained by his attachment to particular individuals—Geoffroi de Sergines, Eudes de Nevers, and Erard de Valéry, for example.

Rutebeuf's is a reforming, rather than a revolutionary, zeal: he attacks not institutions but the individuals who betray them. Above all, whether or not he led popular opinion in 13th-century France, his work is the most eloquent surviving expression of it.

The Poems.—Rutebeuf's surviving poems—55 written between 1248 and 1277, and one possibly in 1285—have been preserved in 12 manuscripts. The greatest number consist of satires and polemical poems on the church, the university, and the friars, and include *Le Dit des Cordeliers*, written at Troyes (1249); *La Descorde de l'Université et des Jacobins* (1264); the *Dit de Guillaume de St. Amour* and the *Complainte de Guillaume de St. Amour;* the *Dit des Règles,* on the occasion of Alexander IV's order to destroy pamphlets against the Dominicans; *Le Dit de Sainte Église,* written when the university attempted to persuade the king to recall Guillaume from exile; *Le Dit d'Hypocrisie,* on the election of Urban IV; and *La Vie du Monde* (1285?). His poems on the Crusades include a call to aid Geoffroi de Sergines at Acre (1255–56); *La Complainte de Constantinople* (1262), on its capture from the Latins by Michael Palaeologus; *La Complainte d'Outremer* (1266) and *La Nouvelle Complainte d'Outremer* (1277), in which he takes to task all grades of society for their lack of zeal for the Crusades (but in *La Disputaison du Croisé et du Décroisé,* 1267?, he represents fairly the views, both of the "crusading party," and of those who, like Jean Joinville [q.v.], felt that their duty to God and their neighbour could best be discharged in France); several *Complaintes* on the deaths of noble patrons on the Crusade; poems in support of Louis IX's second Crusade (*La Voie de Tunes,* 1267) and even of Charles of Anjou's (Charles I of Naples and Sicily, q.v.) adventure (Crusade so-called) in Sicily (*Chanson de Pouille* and *Dit de Pouille,* 1264–66). The personal poems (*La Griesche d'hiver* and *La Griesche d'Esté,* 1261; *Le Mariage Rutebeuf,* 1262?; *La Paix Rutebeuf* and *La Povreté Rutebeuf,* 1276–77?) give poignant expression, not untinged with sardonic humour, to the sufferings of Rutebeuf and others of his class. The religious poems include two saints' lives and a number of works in honour of the Virgin, to whom he seems to have been especially devoted: hymns (*l'Ave Maria Rutebeuf*) and two miracles—one, *Le Sacristain et la Femme du Chevalier,* in the form of a verse *conte,* while relating a typical story of an intervention of the Virgin in favour of a devotee, is also a light-hearted satire on the clergy; the other, *Le Miracle de Théophile,* is one of the earliest miracle plays (*see* DRAMA: *Medieval Drama*), on the traditional theme of the priest who sells his soul to the devil and is saved by the Virgin. Finally, the humorous poems include *fabliaux* (*La Dame qui fist trois tours entour le Moustier, le Pet au Vilain, Le testament de l'Âne*); *Le Dit de l'Herberie*—a parody on a charlatan's patter; and personal satires against some of his *confrères* (*Charlot le Juif et la Peau du lièvre* and *Charlot et le Barbier,* etc.).

All Rutebeuf's poems may be described as occasional poetry, although the occasions differ. His most characteristic notes are biting satire and personal involvement. His learning is wide, and many of his poems are based on Latin originals. He handles with skill a wide range of verse forms, but his outstanding gift is his power to use everyday language, vivid imagery, colloquial phraseology, and proverbial wisdom to express both his own personality and public opinion.

See *Les Oeuvres complètes de Rutebeuf,* ed. by E. Faral and J. Bastin, 2 vol. (1959). (H. H. Lu.)

RUTH, BABE (George Herman Ruth) (1895–1948), U.S. baseball player, the game's most popular figure and holder of the all-time home-run record of 60 in a 154-game season (1927), was born on Feb. 6, 1895, in Baltimore, Md., into a poverty-stricken environment. At age seven he went to live at St. Mary's Industrial school in Baltimore, where he spent much of his boyhood and where he first became interested in athletics.

The "Sultan of Swat" hit a total of 714 home runs in 22 big league seasons. He finished with a lifetime batting average of .342, but of all his records he was proudest of having pitched 29$\frac{2}{3}$ scoreless innings for the Boston Red Sox in the world series—against the Brooklyn Dodgers in 1916 and the Chicago Cubs in 1918. He was the best left-handed pitcher in the American league when he was moved to the outfield because of his slugging.

Ruth batted and threw left-handed. He stood 6 ft. 2 in. and weighed 215 lb. He began his professional career at Baltimore in 1914 and was sold later that season to the Boston Red Sox for an estimated $2,900. In Jan. 1920 Ruth was sold to the New York Yankees for $125,000. During his major-league career Ruth broke more than 50 records. He led the American league in home runs for 12 years; he hit at least 50 home runs in four separate seasons and at least 40 in each of 11 seasons. He played in ten world series—three with the Red Sox and seven with the Yankees.

In 1922 he was suspended for 30 days for an unauthorized barnstorming tour. In 1925 he was fined $5,000 by Yankee manager Miller Huggins for "misconduct off the ball field." In 1930 and 1931 Ruth received a salary of $85,000 per season, then the all-time high. He played his last season (1935) with the Boston Braves, was released June 2, 1935, and concluded his baseball career as coach of the Brooklyn Dodgers in 1938. He was one of the first five players elected to Baseball's Hall of Fame at Cooperstown, N.Y., in 1936. Ruth died on Aug. 16, 1948, in New York city. In 1961 Roger Maris of the New York Yankees hit 61 home runs, a record for the 162-game baseball season, but because Maris hit only 59 in the first 154 games of the season Ruth's record stood. (J. D. McC.; X.)

RUTH, BOOK OF, in the Old Testament, the story of Ruth, the Moabite great-grandmother of David. It belongs to the third division of the Hebrew Bible, the Writings, or Hagiographa. It is one of the five festal Rolls (Megilloth): Song of Solomon (Song of Songs), Ruth, Lamentations, Ecclesiastes, and Esther; in the Septuagint, Vulgate, and English versions, however, it follows the Book of Judges.

Contents.—The book falls into fairly well-defined sections:

1:1–5	Elimelech of Bethlehem, with his wife, Naomi (Noemi), and his two sons, Mahlon and Chilion, sojourned in Moab. After his death his sons married Moabite women, Ruth and Orpah, respectively. In about ten years the sons died also
1:6–18	Orpah returned to her own people, but Ruth elected to remain with Naomi
1:19–22	Naomi and Ruth returned to Bethlehem
2:1–23	there Ruth met Boaz (Booz), a kinsman of Elimelech, while gleaning in his field
3:1–5	Naomi, to provide for Ruth, planned that Boaz should marry her
3:6–18	Naomi sent Ruth to the threshing floor at night to claim Boaz' protection
4:1–12	after a nearer kinsman forfeited the right to marry Ruth and redeem the land of Elimelech, Boaz performed the obligation
4:13–17	to this union was born Obed
4:18–22	David's genealogy is given from Perez through Boaz, Obed, and Jesse

Purpose.—Many purposes have been assigned to the book: to entertain, to delineate the ancestry of David, to uphold levirate marriage as a means of perpetuating a family name (*see* Levirate), to commend loyalty in family relationships, to protest the

narrowness of Ezra and Nehemiah in relation to marriages with non-Jews, to inculcate kindness toward converts to Judaism, to teach that a person who becomes a worshiper of Yahweh will be blessed by him, and to illustrate the providence of God in human affairs. The book may have served all these "purposes," but the author's objective cannot be determined with certainty. His broad outlook regarding foreigners is akin to that found in Isa. 56:3–8 and Jonah.

Literary History.—This little gem has been called an idyll, a short story, literal history, and pure fiction. It is best classified as a short story based upon a solid core of fact: no one would have invented a Moabite ancestress for Israel's greatest king. The work has been variously dated in the time of David, in the later monarchy, and in the postexilic period. It cannot be earlier than David (4:17). Light from archaeology on the Hebrew language and on marriage customs suggests a preexilic date for the bulk of the story. However, the book probably reached its final form in postexilic times since the writer knew the Deuteronomic edition of Judges (1:1; Judg. 2:16, 18), and 4:7 gives the impression that the custom mentioned therein was already obsolete. Many have regarded 4:18–22 as a gloss (*cf.* I Chron. 2:4–15).

Interpretation and Use.—Literally speaking, the marriage of Boaz and Ruth (ch. 4) was not a levirate marriage (Deut. 25:5–10), because Boaz was not Ruth's *levir* (brother-in-law). It was probably a forerunner of levirate marriage (*cf.* Gen. 38; 19:30–38), though it may have been an extension of the levirate principle to more distant kinsmen. The association of levirate marriage with the redemption of property was inevitable. The spirit of the book stands in contrast to Deut. 23:3 (*cf.* Neh. 13:1–3), which prohibits a Moabite from entering the assembly of the Lord, and to the severe marriage reforms of Ezra (Ezra 9–10) and Nehemiah (Neh. 13:23–31). The story of Ruth may represent a pre-Deuteronomic point of view concerning Moabites; yet it may have been retold in such a way as to be a subtle polemic against exclusiveness in the postexilic community. In any case, it is probably significant that Ruth was already a convert to Yahwism at the time of her marriage to Boaz (1:16; 2:12). Cultic interpretations, which find the origin of the story in fertility myths and rituals, have received meagre endorsement.

The book has enjoyed a degree of popularity in Judaism, Roman Catholicism, and Protestantism. It is read in Judaism as a part of the liturgy on Pentecost. "The Lord be with you" of Boaz (2:4) is repeated eight times in the Latin Mass, and the words of Naomi (1:20) and Ruth (2:13) are used in responsories. Ruth's moving commitment to Naomi (1:16–17) is sometimes found in Protestant wedding ceremonies. *See also* Bible.

Bibliography.—A. Bentzen, *Introduction to the Old Testament,* 2nd ed. (1953); M. Haller, in *Handbuch zum Alten Testament* (1940); C. Lattey (ed.), *The Book of Ruth* (1935); W. Leonard, "Ruth," *A Catholic Commentary on Holy Scripture,* pp. 303–305 (1953); H. H. Rowley, "The Marriage of Ruth," *Harvard Theological Review,* xl, 77–99 (1949); L. P. Smith, in *The Interpreter's Bible,* vol. ii, pp. 829–852 (1953); J. J. Slotki, in *The Five Megilloth,* Soncino Books of the Bible (1946). (A. B. Rh.)

RUTHENIA: *see* Transcarpathian Oblast.

RUTHENIUM is one of the platinum metals and resembles platinum in its silver-gray colour and lustre. It is found in small percentages in a number of platinum ores. It was identified as a chemical element in 1844 by Carl Claus, in Russia, and was the last of the platinum metals to be characterized. (*See* Platinum Metals.) The name was selected in honour of Russia (Latin, Ruthenia) by G. W. Osann in 1828, when he made a premature announcement of the discovery of the element in platinum ore from the Ural Mountains. Although Osann's announcement was never confirmed, Claus retained the name.

Among the metals of the platinum group, only osmium is more infusible than ruthenium; the melting point of ruthenium is 2,250° C., and its boiling point, which can only be surmised, is estimated to be above 2,700° C. Because of the high melting point, ruthenium is not easily cast; its brittleness, even at a white heat, makes it very difficult to roll or draw into wires. Thus the industrial application of ruthenium is restricted to use as an alloy for platinum and other metals of the platinum group. It serves the same function as iridium for the hardening of platinum and, in conjunction with rhodium, is used to harden palladium. Ruthenium-hardened alloys of platinum and palladium have been found much superior to the pure metals in the manufacture of fine jewelry.

The chemical symbol of ruthenium is Ru, atomic number 44, atomic weight 101.07, specific gravity about 12.41. Ruthenium is one of the group of more than 30 elements whose radioactive isotopes are formed when uranium and plutonium atoms disintegrate by the fission process. One of these ruthenium isotopes (Ru^{106}) emits beta rays with a half-life of one year to yield a daughter, rhodium-106, which is also radioactive. Rh^{106} emits high-energy beta rays and gamma rays with the half-life of 30 seconds. This pair of isotopes contributes an important fraction of the residual radiation from uranium or plutonium fuels of fission-type atomic reactors which have "cooled" for a year following their use. The separation of ruthenium from the fissionable elements must be effected before these expensive fuels can be recovered and reprocessed to attain economically competitive atomic power. The chemical effects and hazards of intense radiation impose severe difficulties on the separation process. Similarities in the chemical behaviour of plutonium and ruthenium, in many cases, make the separation even more difficult.

Ruthenium metal is not attacked by air in the cold. Heated in air or oxygen from about 700° to 1,200° C., the powdered metal yields a dark blue dioxide, RuO_2, which decomposes at still higher temperatures. The element effectively resists attack by strong acids, even by aqua regia which readily dissolves platinum and gold. Ruthenium metal and the mineral alloys of ruthenium, osmium, and iridium are most easily brought into soluble form by fusion with an alkaline oxidizing flux. Compounds, such as K_2RuO_4 (+6 state) and $KRuO_4$ (+7 state), are formed. When these compounds dissolve in aqueous systems, they usually decompose rapidly to lower oxidation states. Like all platinum elements, ruthenium can be readily reduced from its compounds to give free metal. Separation of ruthenium from other heavy metals is conveniently achieved by forming the tetraoxide, RuO_4, which is so volatile it readily distills from aqueous solutions. Osmium is the only other element which can form so high an oxidation state. However, OsO_4 is formed more readily and can be distilled from nitric acid alone. The formation of RuO_4 requires stronger oxidizing agents, such as bromate ion in acids or chlorine in alkaline solutions. RuO_4 is the only known compound of the element with the +8 oxidation state. It must be handled cautiously, for it is extremely poisonous, and above 100° C. it may decompose explosively. Although evidence for compounds of ruthenium in every oxidation state from 0 through +8 has been claimed, the +3, +4, +6, and +8 states are the most important.

The +3 and +4 oxidation states include numerous coordination complexes in which water or ammonia molecules, chloride ions, or other groups are bonded covalently to a central ruthenium ion. Typically, six atoms bond to ruthenium, and the complexes are the inert type, in that groups are not replaced rapidly. Many of these coordination complexes possess striking colours, which facilitate chemical studies. The +3 or +4 oxidation states are readily interconvertible so that frequently in the past, errors have been made in the assignment of state to a particular compound; e.g., the compound which Claus originally thought was $K_2[RuCl_5]$, +3 state, proved to be $K_2[RuCl_5(OH)]$, +4 state. Exceptionally stable nitrosoruthenium compounds, containing NO groups bonded to the ruthenium ion, frequently form in the presence of nitric oxide, NO, or nitrate ion. Indeed, a salt which early workers believed was $K_2[RuCl_6]$ was later shown to be $K_2[RuCl_5(NO)]$. More nitroso compounds are known for ruthenium than for any other element.

Solutions of ruthenium compounds with many reducing agents, such as zinc or hydrogen sulfide, give blue solutions containing the +2 state. A compound, $K_4[Ru(CN)_6]$, is an analogue of the familiar iron (II) compound. The carbonyl, $Ru(CO)_5$, represents the zero state. The only compound in the +5 state is the fluoride, RuF_5, prepared by the reaction between the elements.

(D. S. Mn.)

RUTHERFORD, ERNEST RUTHERFORD, 1st BARON, OF NELSON AND CAMBRIDGE (1871–1937), British physicist, winner of the Nobel Prize in Chemistry for 1908, whose researches in radiation and atomic structure were basic to the later 20th-century developments in nuclear physics. Born at Nelson, N.Z., on Aug. 30, 1871, he received his secondary training at Nelson College and, on graduation in 1889, gained a scholarship at Canterbury University College, Christchurch. By 1893 he had taken his M.A. degree with a double first in mathematics and physics.

In 1895 Rutherford won an 1851 exhibition scholarship which took him to Cambridge University. At the Cavendish Laboratory

THE BETTMANN ARCHIVE INC.
BARON RUTHERFORD OF NELSON

his ability was recognized at once by J. J. Thomson. His earliest product there was a detector for electromagnetic waves, its essential feature being a small magnetizing coil containing a tiny bundle of magnetized iron wire. Rutherford's second piece of work, done jointly with Thomson, dealt with the temporary conduction in gases which results from ionization produced by X-rays.

In 1897 Rutherford worked with Thomson on topics related to the mobility of ions, but especially upon the negative ions emitted when ultraviolet light falls upon a clean metal surface. The discovery of Becquerel rays and radium had aroused his curiosity as to just what kind of ions are emitted by radium. At this juncture Rutherford accepted a call to McGill University, Montreal, Que. On reaching the Macdonald Laboratory there, in the autumn of 1898, he at once continued work begun at Cambridge on the radiation from radium, and reported in 1899 that it is quite complex, consisting first of all of easily absorbed rays—rays that are stopped by a few centimetres of air. These he called alpha rays. Besides these, he found uranium giving a far more penetrating radiation, able to pass through a sheet of aluminum several millimetres thick. These he named beta rays, and they proved to be high-speed electrons (see RADIOACTIVITY).

Rutherford's next work at Montreal was done jointly with R. B. Owens. It was a study of thorium emanation, which led to the discovery of a new noble gas, an isotope of radon, later known as thoron. After Frederick Soddy came to McGill University in 1900, he and Rutherford created a modern theory of radioactivity, excellently set forth in Rutherford's *Radioactive Substances and Their Radiations*.

In 1907 Rutherford accepted an invitation to succeed Sir Arthur Schuster in the Langworthy professorship at Manchester University. It was about this time that he and J. T. Royds showed that alpha particles consist of helium atoms. The Nobel Prize was presented to Rutherford on Dec. 11, 1908, two years before he began thinking about the scattering of alpha rays and the nature of a nucleus which could produce such scattering—his nuclear theory—the greatest of all his contributions to physics. In 1912 Niels Bohr came to work in the Manchester laboratory, and it was there that Bohr adapted the nuclear structure of Rutherford to the quantum theory of Max Planck and thus theorized an atomic structure which satisfied the experimental findings of J. R. Rydberg and other spectroscopists. About this time H. G.-J. Moseley got in touch with Rutherford and worked with him during the year 1913. Moseley bombarded the atoms of various elements with cathode rays (X rays) and showed that the inner structures of these atoms respond in groups of lines in the X-ray spectra which characterize the elements much as the natural numbers might do (see MOSELEY, HENRY GWYN-JEFFREYS).

After World War I, during which he worked on methods of submarine detection, Rutherford succeeded, by the bombardment of nitrogen with alpha particles, in transmuting the element nitrogen into an isotope of oxygen. (*See* NUCLEUS: *Description and History*.)

In 1919 Rutherford was invited to succeed Thomson in the Cavendish chair at Cambridge. Honours now came in rapid succession. Rutherford had been knighted in 1914. The Copley Medal of the Royal Society was bestowed on him in 1922; the presidency of the British Association for the Advancement of Science in 1923, to be followed, two years later, by the presidency of the Royal Society. In 1925 he was appointed to the Order of Merit. In 1931 he was created 1st Baron Rutherford of Nelson. He died at Cambridge on Oct. 19, 1937.

Rutherford, together with J. Chadwick and C. Ellis, wrote *Radiations From Radioactive Substances* (1930), a book so thoroughly documented that it serves most needs in the way of a chronological list of Rutherford's published papers.

See also references to "Rutherford, Ernest Rutherford, 1st Baron" in the Index.

See A. S. Eve, *Rutherford* (1939); J. B. Birks (ed.), *Rutherford at Manchester* (1963). (H. Cw.; X.)

RUTHERFORD, MARK (pen name of WILLIAM HALE WHITE) (1831–1913), English writer, distinguished as a novelist, critic, and religious thinker, was born at Bedford on Dec. 22, 1831, the son of William White, printer, book-seller, member of the Bunyan meeting, prominent citizen, and Whig, who later became well known as doorkeeper of the House of Commons.

The story of Hale White's inner life is of unusual interest, and is largely told in his novels and other writings; outwardly his life was uneventful. He was trained for the Congregational ministry at Cheshunt College, and later at New College, London, where he was one of three students expelled for heresy after an examination about the inspiration of Scripture. The rest of his life, after a spell of journalism, was spent in the civil service (the Admiralty). The books by which he is best remembered all appeared under the name of "Mark Rutherford," and so completely did he conceal his authorship that even his immediate circle knew nothing of it for years. *The Autobiography of Mark Rutherford* appeared in 1881; *Mark Rutherford's Deliverance* in 1885; *The Revolution in Tanner's Lane* in 1887. These were followed by *Miriam's Schooling and Other Papers* (1890), *Catherine Furze* (1893), and *Clara Hopgood* (1896).

Hale White has been called "a minor George Eliot": "minor" because of his slender output and meagre inventiveness as a novelist, but a "George Eliot" in the truth and insight with which he renders the life and religion of mid-Victorian provincial society. What George Eliot did for rural and small-town Anglicanism, he did for Bedford nonconformity. Both were refugees from provincial ignorance and religious decadence; both sought the larger, freer life of nature, books, and educated companionship; yet both found in their early memories the richest source of literary material. Both, in maturity, brought a deep and sympathetic understanding to the portrayal of the life and worship they had transcended. Hale White lacks George Eliot's copiousness and breadth, but the quiet intensity of everything he wrote gives him a place among the best stylists of his time. "His art," said André Gide, "is made of the renunciation of all false riches"; it was the utterance of a man acquainted with grief and doubt, yet habituated by Puritanism to self-control and veracity. Hale White was representative of the many "escaped Puritans" of the 19th century who, though deeply religious to the last, had ceased to be orthodox. All his books deal with spiritual problems, with ordeals of the heart, the intellect, or the conscience; and nearly all present, against a provincial background sketched with restrained irony and humour, some "superior" person at war with circumstance, yet no less at war with his or her own spiritual pride and seeking for repentance and reconciliation. Hale White died at Groombridge, Sussex, on March 14, 1913, after a short second marriage which brought him unlooked-for happiness at the close of a life predominantly sad.

BIBLIOGRAPHY.—*Works:* A translation of Spinoza's *Ethics* (1883), *John Bunyan* (1904), and *The Early Life of Mark Rutherford* (1913) appeared under his own name. Selections from his private journals (described as "by Mark Rutherford") were: *Pages from a Journal* (1900); *More Pages*, etc. (1910); and *Last Pages*, etc., ed. by his widow, Mrs. D. V. White (1915). *See also Letters to Three Friends* (1924) and *The Groombridge Diary* (1924), both ed. by Mrs. White. *Criticism and Biography:* W. H. Stone, *Religion and Art of William Hale White* (1954); C. M. Maclean, *Mark Rutherford* (1955); Irvin Stock, *William Hale White (Mark Rutherford)* (1956); Basil Willey, *More 19th-Century Studies* (1956). (B. WY.)

RUTHERGLEN (locally pronounced *Rŭglen*), a royal and large burgh of Lanarkshire, Scot., 3 mi. SE of Glasgow, on the left bank of the Clyde. Pop. (1961) 25,067. Area 1.6 sq.mi. It is connected with the east of Glasgow by two bridges. The parish church stands near the spire of the ancient church where, according to tradition, the treaty was made in 1297 with Edward I, by which Sir John Menteith undertook to betray William Wallace to the English. Rutherglen was erected into a royal burgh by David I in 1126 and claims to be the oldest in Scotland. It then included a portion of Glasgow, but in 1226 the boundaries were rectified so as to exclude the city, and Rutherglen continued to resist incorporation with Glasgow. In early times it had a castle, which after the Battle of Langside (1568) was burned by order of the regent Moray. In 1679 the Covenanters published their "Declaration and Testimony" at Rutherglen. The collieries in the area were worked out; the principal industries now include chemical works, paper mills, laundries, and oatcake bakeries, and the making of fireplaces, chairs, and textiles, and light and structural engineering.

RUTHIN (RHUTHUN), a market town and municipal borough (1282) of Denbighshire, Wales, lies 8 mi. SE of Denbigh. Pop. (1961) 3,502. It stands on a hill above the Clwyd River and is the administrative centre for Denbighshire. Though the borough was incorporated under a charter of Edward I, the natives were excluded from its privileges until Henry VII, who was himself of Welsh descent, confirmed the charter and made the borough "free." The castle was founded in 1281; it was unsuccessfully besieged by Owen Glendower in 1400, and in 1646 it was demolished by order of Parliament. The ruins stand in the grounds of a hospital built in 1826–52. St. Peter's Church, made collegiate in 1310 by Lord Grey of Ruthin, has a roof of black oak divided into about 500 small panels; the incumbent is known as the warden. The old buildings of the grammar school, founded in 1574, are known as the Ellinor Roberts Memorial Buildings. Nantclwyd House, with its fine medieval hall, has been used as judges' lodgings from *c.* 1400. Ruthin has a mineral water (soft drink) industry.

RUTHVEN, the name of a Scottish noble family allegedly tracing descent from a certain Thor who flourished during the reign of David I (1124–53). In 1488 one of its members, SIR WILLIAM RUTHVEN (d. 1528), was created a lord of Parliament as Lord Ruthven.

PATRICK (*c.* 1520–66), 3rd Lord Ruthven, and his second son WILLIAM (*c.* 1543–84), the 4th lord, were prominent in the political intrigues of their time. Both belonged to the Protestant Party and neither was averse to using violence to accomplish his political ends. Having been one of the leaders of the reforming opposition to the regent Mary of Lorraine, the 3rd lord was prominent in arranging the marriage (1565) between Mary Stuart and Lord Darnley. In 1566 he rose from a sickbed to lead the murderers of the queen's secretary, David Rizzio, after which he fled to England where he died in the same year. His *Relation of the Death of David Rizzi* is preserved in the British Museum (MS. Cotton, Cal., B, ix) and was first printed in 1699. His son, the 4th lord, created earl of Gowrie (1581), was also concerned in the Rizzio murder. For a time he had charge of Queen Mary at Lochleven, and he was the last known custodian of the famous "casket letters" (*q.v.*). In 1582 he was the principal actor in the raid of Ruthven which took the young king James VI out of the hands of the favourites Lennox and Arran and two years later a further abortive plot led to his trial and execution. His second son was JOHN RUTHVEN, 3rd earl of Gowrie (*q.v.*), whose death and forfeiture involved the ruin of the family.

PATRICK RUTHVEN (*c.* 1573–1651), descendant of the 1st Lord Ruthven in a collateral line, distinguished himself in the service of Sweden (c. 1606–38). He was then employed by Charles I in Scotland where in 1640 he for a time defended Edinburgh Castle against the Covenanters. On the outbreak of the Civil War he joined the king at Shrewsbury and after the Battle of Edgehill (October 1642) was appointed general-in-chief of the royalist army. He compelled the earl of Essex to surrender at Lostwithiel (September 1644) and was wounded at both battles of Newbury (1643 and 1644). In November 1644 he was superseded in his command by Prince Rupert but continued to play an active part in royalist affairs until his death at Dundee in 1651. For his services he was created Lord Ruthven of Ettrick in 1639, earl of Forth in 1642, and earl of Brentford in 1644.

In 1651 Sir Thomas Ruthven (d. 1671), a collateral descendant of the 2nd lord Ruthven (d. 1552), was created Lord Ruthven of Freeland. The present earls of Gowrie are descended from this branch through the female line.   (J. K. Ba.)

RUTILE is the most abundant of the three native forms of titanium dioxide, the others being anatase and brookite (q.v.). Ordinary rutile is red or brown (hence the name from the Latin *rutilus*, "red").

Rutile, with the composition TiO_2, is a commercially important titanium mineral (See Titanium: *Occurrence; Compounds*), although commercial TiO_2 is produced largely from ilmenite (q.v.), or titanic iron ore. Rutile has minor uses as a colouring agent in porcelain and glass, and in certain steels and copper alloys. Synthetic rutile, superior to natural crystals as a gem, is produced by the flame fusion (Verneuil) process. The boule as it comes from the furnace is black and is deficient in oxygen. Subsequent heating in an electric furnace in an atmosphere of oxygen produces a clear material. However, because of the high absorption of light in the violet end of the spectrum, the material has a yellow tinge. It has a very high index of refraction and high dispersion, hence shows "fire" and brilliance like the diamond, but is of inferior hardness. Synthetic gems can be produced in various colours by adding appropriate metal oxides to the original titanium dioxide. (*See also* Gem: *Synthetic Gems.*)

Like anatase, rutile crystallizes in the tetragonal system, but with different angles. It is isomorphous with cassiterite, SnO_2, the common ore of tin, which it resembles in crystal form, twinning, colour and streak, which is pale brown to yellow. The specific gravity is lower, being 4.2 in contrast to 7.0 for cassiterite. The hardness is 6 to 6.5. It is opaque, with a brilliant metallic to adamantine lustre. Some varieties contain significant amounts of iron, niobium, or tantalum and are black, with a specific gravity as high as 5.5. Oriented microscopic crystals of rutile produce asterism in phlogopite, ruby, and sapphire. The term sagenite is applied to needlelike crystals twinned to form reticulated, or netlike, skeletal plates. Rutilated quartz is rock crystal containing long delicate translucent needles of rutile. Venus's-hairstone (Pliny's *Veneris crinis*) refers to similar needles in smoky quartz.

Rutile is an accessory mineral in igneous rocks, but is more common in schists and gneisses. It is found in some pegmatites and in crystalline limestones. It occurs in apatite veins in Norway, where it is mined. Microscopic needles of rutile are of wide distribution in clays and shales and also in slates. It is common in detrital deposits, as in Florida sand deposits. Australia is the chief producing country.   (L. S. Rl.)

RUTILIUS CLAUDIUS NAMATIANUS (fl. A.D. 417), Roman poet, author of an elegiac poem *De reditu suo* describing a journey from Rome to his native Gaul in the autumn of A.D. 417. The poem is chiefly interesting for the light it throws on the ideology of the pagan landowning aristocracy of the rapidly disintegrating western Roman Empire.

Rutilius was a native of southern Gaul (Poitiers, Toulouse, and Narbonne have all been suggested as his birthplace) and a member of one of the wealthy landowning families who almost monopolized high government office in the late empire. His father, Lachanius, had held provincial governorships, high financial and legal offices, and the prefecture of Rome. The poet himself was master of offices and later, in 414, prefect of Rome. Among friends whom he mentions, several are known to have held high office, and at least

one was a close friend of Symmachus, leader of the pagan group in the Senate and patron of letters. Rutilius was clearly, like Symmachus, a pagan, out of sympathy with the government of Theodosius and Honorius, hostile to Stilicho's policy of rapprochement with the Goths, ready to support any usurper who looked like winning, and preoccupied with an idealized picture of the strength and justice of Rome which had little to do with the hard realities of the 5th century A.D.

The occasion of his journey was his return to his Gaulish estates, which had been ravished by Franks, Burgundians, and Visigoths in 412–414. Leaving Portus Romae (Porto, near Ostia) on Oct. 31, 417, he sailed up the Italian coast by short stages (the land route was unsafe since the Gothic invasion of 410), reached Faleriae (the medieval Porto Falese, now silted up) on Nov. 3, and Luna (on the Gulf of La Spezia) a few days later. Here the poem breaks off; only 68 lines of book ii are preserved.

The narrative is smooth and relaxed, full of personal observations, and giving the impression of a diary. Much of the poem is taken up by digressions occasioned by places or events of the journey, and it is in these that the attitudes and values of the poet and his circle find their clearest expression. Noteworthy is the stirring farewell to Rome (i, 47–164) in which Rutilius proclaims his faith in the perpetuity of the Roman Empire: "by permitting those whom you conquer to participate in your own right," he says, "you have made one city of what was a whole world" (*Dumque offers victis proprii consortia iuris, Urbem fecisti quod prius orbis erat*). These motifs have a long ancestry in Latin and Greek literature, and Rutilius draws upon many predecessors. Yet there can be no doubt of the sincerity of the faith which he proclaims so fervently. Other digressions deal with the harm done to Rome by the family of the Lepidi (i, 295–312)—a rather frigid piece of antiquarianism in the taste of the time; on the Jews (ii, 381–398); on the ruins of Populonia (i, 401–414); on monks (i, 439–448), whom Rutilius passionately hates; on his Gaulish friends Victorinus, a refugee from Toulouse (i, 491–510), and Protadius (i, 541–558); on the career of his father Lachanius (i, 575–596); on the shape of Italy (ii, 17–40); on the treachery of Stilicho and his responsibility for the capture of Rome by Alaric in 410 (ii, 41–60).

Rutilius writes Latin of unusual purity for his age, and his elegant and correct elegiac couplets bear witness to his close familiarity with the Augustan elegiac poets, particularly Ovid. A curious metrical feature is the unusually high frequency of spondees as first feet, especially in the pentameter. Rutilius is an accomplished and pleasing poet and, had more of his work survived, he might have vied with his contemporary Claudian for the title of last of the Roman poets.

Bibliography.—Editions by E. Baehrens, *Poetae Latini minores*, vol. 5 (1883); by J. Vessereau (1904) with copious critical and historical appendixes; by C. H. Keene with Eng. verse trans. by G. F. Savage-Armstrong and commentary (1907); by J. Vessereau and F. Préchac with good introduction, French trans., and historical notes (1933); by R. Helm with excellent notes on language and style (1933); by J. W. and A. M. Duff with Eng. trans., *Minor Latin Poets*, 2nd ed. (1935) in the Loeb series; by E. Merone with rich collection of literary parallels (1955). On the manuscript tradition *see* M. Schuster, *Wiener Studien*, 51:109–140 (1933), 57:147–164 (1939). On the date of the poem *see* J. Carcopino, *Revue des études latines* 6:180–200 (1928). Good studies of Rutilius' world view and its sources are J. Cirino, *L'idea di Roma negli scrittori latini e particolarmente in Rutilio Namaziano* (1934); G. Boano in *Rivista di filologia classica* 76:54–87 (1948); L. Alfonsi in *Studi romani* 3:125–139 (1955).   (R. Bg.)

RUTLAND, EARLS AND DUKES OF. The English title earl of Rutland, held by members of the Manners family since the 16th century, was first granted in 1390 to Edward Plantagenet, 2nd duke of York (q.v.), a grandson of Edward III. By the terms of the grant, however, he was to hold the title only until his father's death (1402). The next acknowledged earl of Rutland was his great-nephew Edmund (1443–1460), son of Richard, duke of York. Edmund was killed with his father at the battle of Wakefield in December 1460.

Thomas Manners (c. 1492–1543), 12th Baron Ros (or Roos), a great-nephew of Edmund, was created earl of Rutland in 1525 by Henry VIII who also gave him various estates and properties, including Belvoir Castle which became the chief family seat.

HENRY (1526–1563), 2nd Manners earl of Rutland, his son by his second wife Eleanor Paston, held various military offices and in 1547, as lieutenant of the king's army in Scotland, captured and sacked Haddington. He died of plague and was succeeded by his son EDWARD (1549–1587), who fought against the rebel northern earls in 1569 and took part in the trial (1586) of Mary Stuart. As he left no son, the barony of Ros devolved on his daughter but he was succeeded in the earldom of Rutland by his brother JOHN (c. 1552–1588). John's son ROGER (1576–1612), 5th earl, took part in the Islands voyage (1597) led by Sir Walter Ralegh and Robert Devereux, 2nd earl of Essex, and was with Essex in Ireland (1599–1600). Implicated in the Essex plot of February 1601, he spent six months in the Tower. His wife was Elizabeth, daughter of Sir Philip Sidney. They had no children and Roger was succeeded by his brother FRANCIS (1578–1632). Francis succeeded his cousin as Baron Ros in 1618, but both his sons died young (allegedly by witchcraft) and while the barony passed to his only daughter, he was succeeded in the earldom by a third brother, GEORGE (c. 1580–1641).

George had no children and the next earl of Rutland was his second cousin JOHN MANNERS (1604–1679), a descendant of the 1st Manners earl. His son JOHN (1638–1711) supported the Revolution of 1688, and received Princess Anne at Belvoir Castle when she fled from London. When she became queen she created him marquess of Granby (Nottinghamshire) and duke of Rutland in 1703. His son JOHN (1676–1721), the 2nd duke, was a commissioner (1706) for the Union between England and Scotland. The 3rd duke, JOHN (1696–1779), son of the 2nd duke, was a lord of the bedchamber (1721–27) to George I and in 1745 raised a regiment of foot against the Jacobites. His son John (see GRANBY, JOHN MANNERS, Marquess of), who had a distinguished military career, predeceased him, and he was succeeded by his grandson CHARLES (1754–1787). Charles was lord steward of the household (February–April 1783), with a seat in the earl of Shelburne's cabinet; he was lord privy seal from December 1783 to February 1784 and lord lieutenant of Ireland from then until his death. His son JOHN HENRY (1778–1857), 5th duke, and his grandson CHARLES CECIL JOHN (1815–1888), 6th duke, both supported the Tory party, the latter leading the Protectionists after 1848. The 7th duke of Rutland, JOHN JAMES ROBERT MANNERS (see below), brother of the 6th duke, was a notable supporter of Disraeli and a leader of the "Young England" movement. His son HENRY JOHN BRINSLEY (1852–1925), 8th duke, was for a time principal private secretary to the marquess of Salisbury. His son was JOHN HENRY MONTAGU (1886–1940), 9th duke, and his grandson CHARLES JOHN ROBERT MANNERS (1919–   ) became the 10th duke.

RUTLAND, JOHN JAMES ROBERT MANNERS,

7TH DUKE OF (1818–1906), Conservative politician, exponent and last survivor of the "Young England" movement of the 1840s, was born at Belvoir Castle on Dec. 13, 1818, younger son of the 5th duke of Rutland. Educated at Eton and at Trinity College, Cambridge, he entered Parliament as Gladstone's colleague for Newark in 1841. Manners, together with George Smythe (later 7th Viscount Strangford), his closest friend, became a disciple of Disraeli who immortalized them as Lord Henry Sidney and Coningsby respectively in his famous novel Coningsby: or, The New Generation. The "Young England" group, as they came to be called, stood for a romantic Toryism, hostile alike to Manchester Radicalism, orthodox Whiggery, and Sir Robert Peel's Conservatism. The political counterpart of the Oxford movement, it looked back to an imaginary golden age in which aristocracy treated with benevolent paternalism a prosperous and grateful peasantry. Manners and Smythe opposed the middle class bourgeoisie and sought to ameliorate the condition of the working class in the industrial towns. Manners, together with Disraeli, supported a proposed ten hours' bill in 1844 (it became law in 1847) and opposed the repeal of the Corn Laws in 1846. He did not contest Newark in 1847, but sat for Colchester from 1850 to 1857, North Leicestershire from 1857 to 1885, and East Leicestershire from 1885 to 1888 when he succeeded his brother as duke. During the earl of Derby's ministries of 1852, 1858–59, and 1866–68 he was first commissioner of works. From 1874 to 1880 he was postmaster general in

Disraeli's second administration and again in the marquess of Salisbury's first government (1885–86). He was chancellor of the duchy of Lancaster in Salisbury's second government (1886–92). He died at Belvoir Castle on Aug. 4, 1906. His only child by his first wife, Catherine Marlay, succeeded him as 8th duke of Rutland. By his second wife, Janetta Hughan, he had five sons and three daughters.

Lord John Manners has often been ridiculed for the couplet in his poem "England's Trust":

> Let wealth and commerce, laws and learning die,
> But leave us still our old nobility,

This is unfair. He was no believer in a caste system or class privilege. He believed on the contrary that the aristocracy should only survive if it remembered its duties as well as its rights, and he was a keen supporter of social reform, intensely loyal to Disraeli whose greatness he never ceased to admire.

See C. Whibley, Lord John Manners and His Friends, 2 vol. (1925).

(R. N. W. B.)

RUTLAND, the smallest county in England with an area of 152 sq.mi., lies in the east Midlands bordered by Leicestershire on the north and the west, by Lincolnshire on the northeast and east, and by Northamptonshire on the south.

Physical Features.—Generally, the surface is varied with gentle elevations and depressions running in an east-west direction as rolling upland rather than hill and dale. Most of the county is between 300 and 500 ft. above sea level, the highest land being on the western boundary with Leicestershire where heights of 600 ft. are to be found. From there the land slopes gradually eastward except where it is interrupted by the Vale of Catmose in the west and by outcropping escarpments of limestone in the east.

Topographically, Rutland can be divided into three natural areas: the Vale of Catmose, the eastern plateau, and the ridge and vale region of the south. The Vale of Catmose, which stretches northward from the west centre of the county, is bounded by the Leicestershire Hills in the west and by the oolite escarpment in the east. It is between 300 and 400 ft. above sea level and is Rutland's flattest area. The eastern plateau slopes gradually down from the east of the Vale of Catmose to the Welland Valley. From heights of 500 ft. in places it falls on the eastern side of the county to about 200 to 300 ft. above sea level. The ridge and vale region of the south is due to the alternating beds of hard and soft rocks, limestone on the ridges, and clays in the vales. The limestone ridges are spurs from the eastern plateau and have been carved by streams and rains into the present formation.

The drainage falls into three catchment areas. The small rivers, the Gwash and the Chater, rise in the Leicestershire Hills to the west and flow into the Welland which forms the southern boundary of the county with Northamptonshire. A small area in the north is drained by streams into the River Trent while the Witham takes a small stream flowing out of the county to the east.

The height above sea level, coupled with the fact that there is no natural barrier between Rutland and the North Sea, ensures a bracing climate with moderate rainfall and a reasonably good record of sunshine. The absence of heavy industry makes for clear, pure air.

The soil is of a rich red colour producing an exciting variation of flora which provide rare hunting grounds for the botanist. Because of the presence of minerals in the soil one of the major industries is the working of ironstone. The rural character of the whole of the county is of considerable landscape value, but two areas are of exceptional interest: the Eye Brook Reservoir on the southwest boundary where a number of rare birds are to be found, and Clipsham District in the northeast where there are well-wooded limestone lands. Clipsham Hall has a remarkably fine avenue of trimmed yew trees. There is a wealth of historic buildings, and the building stones of Clipsham, Ketton, and Northampton sandstone have provided materials not only for the churches and mansions and the greater part of the cottages in the villages of Rutland but also for Buckingham Palace, the rebuilt House of Commons in London, many of the Oxford and some of the Cambridge colleges.

History.—In the pre-Norman period the royal forest of Leighfield stretched from Oakham to Uppingham, and some believe that it is from the magnificent oak trees to be found there that the name of Oakham is derived. In various parts of Rutland worked flints from arable fields have been discovered, suggesting a culture of primitive hunters. Later they may have been joined by fugitives from the Saxon invaders. The Roman road, Ermine Street, crosses the county and may have had a very great influence on its early development, for excavations have revealed an important Roman settlement at Great Casterton. Finds in the Cottesmore and Market Overton districts and at North Luffenham indicate important Saxon settlements in the 5th and 6th centuries.

Rutland was given by Edward the Confessor to his queen, Edith, and the village of Edith Weston is believed to have derived its name from this gift. Though not mentioned as such at the time of the Domesday survey, Rutland was mentioned as a distinct county with a separate sheriff about the middle of the 12th century. At Oakham Castle there is one of the finest examples of late Norman domestic architecture. It is the banqueting hall of what was probably a fortified manor house and is believed to have been built in the 12th century by Walkelin de Ferrers. Many Rutland men supported the barons in their conflict with John, and a minor battle of the Wars of the Roses was fought at Empingham in 1470, resulting in a decisive royalist victory. Jeffrey Hudson, a dwarf who was served in a pie to Charles I and Queen Henrietta in the early 17th century and was subsequently knighted, and Titus Oates, who is said to have originated the Popish Plot, were both born in Oakham, while Sir Everard Digby, one of the conspirators in the Gunpowder Plot, lived at Stoke Dry.

Population and Administration.—The administrative area is 152 sq.mi. and the population (1961) 23,504. Local government is administered by the county council, one urban district council, and three rural district councils. The urban district and county town is Oakham (*q.v.*). Uppingham (*q.v.*) with nearly 1,900 and Ketton with about 1,000 population are next in size. A regular pattern of more than 50 small villages at about two-mile intervals covers the county. There is a court of assize and quarter session at Oakham, and there is one petty sessional division for the county. Rutland is joined with part of the Kesteven division of Lincolnshire for parliamentary purposes.

The Economy.—Agriculture and forestry still remain the predominant industries, though mining and quarrying are becoming basic industries due to the presence of rich deposits of iron ore extending over two-thirds of the county. Engineering is to be found at Oakham and Essendine, plastics at Oakham and Uppingham, a cement works at Ketton, and clothing factories at Oakham. Two large Royal Air Force stations and an open prison also provide employment. There are boys' public schools at Uppingham and Oakham.

The Great North Road crosses Rutland, and the Birmingham to Great Yarmouth Trunk Road traverses it from east to west.

BIBLIOGRAPHY.—C. G. Smith, *Domesday Book: Lincolnshire and Rutlandshire* (1870); G. Phillips (ed.), *The Rutland Magazine and County Historical Record*, 5 vol. (1903–12); Philip Corder (ed.), *The Roman Town and Villa at Great Casterton, Rutland* (1951); *The Victoria County History of the Counties of England—Rutland*, 2 vol. and index (1908–36); Thomas Blore, *The History and Antiquities of the County of Rutland*, vol. i, pt. 2 (1811); A. R. Horwood and the 3rd Earl of Gainsborough, *The Flora of Leicestershire and Rutland* (1933); James Wright, *The History and Antiquities of the County of Rutland* (1684); *Land Utilisation Survey of Britain, The Land of Britain*, pt. 53, *Rutland* by M. E. Broughton (1937); J. and A. E. Stokes, *Just Rutland* (1953); W. G. Hoskins, *Rutland*, a shell guide (1963).   (A. BD.)

RUTLAND, a city of Vermont, U.S., is located 95 mi. NE of Albany, N.Y.; the seat of Rutland County. In 1759 the site was an outpost on Gen. Jeffrey Amherst's military road across Vermont, connecting forts on Lake Champlain with the Connecticut Valley. Chartered in 1761 Rutland was settled by New England Yankees in 1770 and became one of the capitals of Vermont.

After 1847 railroad construction and marble quarrying attracted many Irish, French Canadian, and Italian settlers; around 1880 Rutland was Vermont's largest municipality. In 1886 three marble-producing areas (Proctor, Rutland Town, and West Rut-

land) seceded; since then Rutland has been second in size to Burlington.

Rutland arrivals since 1900 include Scots, Swedes, and Poles, who found work in factories making scales, castings, dresses, gloves, plywood, machinery, and airplane parts. Other economic opportunities came with Rutland's new highways, ski areas, golf courses, hospitals, hydroelectric plants, and tourist accommodations; the city is also the business centre for west-central Vermont. Modern schools, public and parochial, are augmented by a public library. For comparative population figures *see* table in VERMONT: *Population*.   (J. C. HU.)

RUTLEDGE, JOHN (1739–1800), U.S. jurist and statesman who was a member of the Constitutional Convention of 1787, was born in Charleston, S.C., in September 1739. After studying law in England he returned to Charleston, where he began to practise in 1761. He was a delegate to the Stamp Act Congress in 1765 and to the Continental Congress in 1774–77 and 1782–83. He served as chairman of the committee that framed the South Carolina constitution of 1776 and as the first president or governor of the state from 1776 to 1778 and again from 1779 to 1782. In 1787 he was sent to the Constitutional Convention in Philadelphia as one of South Carolina's representatives. There he championed the cause of slavery, urged the assumption of state debts by the national government, and argued in favour of dividing society into classes as a basis for representation and requiring high property qualifications for officeholding. Having secured safeguards for slavery in the Constitution, he took a strong nationalistic position, recommending as chairman of the Committee of Detail the granting to the national government of indefinite powers of legislation for the purpose of promoting the general welfare. He was associate justice of the U.S. Supreme Court in 1789–91, and chief justice of the Supreme Court of South Carolina in 1791–95. Nominated chief justice of the U.S. Supreme Court in 1795, he failed to win confirmation by the Senate. He died in Charleston on July 18, 1800.   (JN. C. M.)

His brother, EDWARD RUTLEDGE (1749–1800), a signer of the Declaration of Independence, was born in Charleston on Nov. 23, 1749. He studied law in his brother's office, and in London in 1769–73, and practised in Charleston. He served in the Continental Congress in 1774–77 and was sent with John Adams and Benjamin Franklin to confer on terms of peace with Lord Howe on Staten Island in September 1776. As captain of artillery and as lieutenant colonel he served against the British in South Carolina. He was a member of the state legislature from 1782 to 1798, and in 1791 drafted the act that abolished primogeniture in South Carolina. From 1798 until his death on Jan. 23, 1800, he was governor of South Carolina.

RUTULI, a people of ancient Italy inhabiting Ardea (*q.v.*) and the district round it on the coast of Latium, near Aricia (*q.v.*), and just west of the territory of the Volsci. They are comparable in the form of their name with the Siculi and Appuli (Apuli), and also with the Itali, whose real Italic name would probably have been Vituli. Names with this ending are thought to belong to a fairly early stratum of the Indo-European population of Italy.

RUVO DI PUGLIA, a town and episcopal see in Bari Province, region of Apulia (Puglia), southeastern Italy, stands on the eastern slopes of the Murge, 853 ft. above sea level and 36 km. (22 mi.) W of Bari by road. Pop. (1961) 22,990 (commune). It consists of a central group of medieval buildings surrounded by a belt of modern dwellings. The 13th-century Romanesque cathedral has a richly carved main portal and a beautiful rose window; the free-standing campanile was reconstructed in the 18th century. Ruvo, then known as Rubi, was a centre of the Peucettii, an ancient Apulian tribe, and then a flourishing Greek town. At the end of the 5th century B.C. potteries there began to produce imitations of imported Corinthian and Attic black- and red-figure ware, which developed a marked local character in the 4th century. The Palazzo Jatta contains a collection of these wares.   (M. T. A. N.)

RUVUMA (ROVUMA), a river rising in the Matagoro Mountains in southern Tanzania, flows eastward into the Indian Ocean, about 20 mi. (32 km.) N of Cape Delgado. It forms the boundary for 400 mi. (644 km.) between Tanzania and Mozambique (Portuguese East Africa); total length is about 475 mi.

The basin can be divided into four major structural areas from west to east: (1) the Basement granites, gneisses, and schists; (2) a zone of Karroo sediments about 50 mi. (80 km.) wide; (3) a second zone of Basement rocks (the inselberg corridor) extending to about 39° E; (4) the Mesozoic and Tertiary sandstones and limestones of the Makonde Plateau (84 mi. [135 km.] wide). These areas allow the river course to be divided into three main tracts. In the upper, from the source to the confluence with the Messinge tributary, the river is a strong, perennial stream. The middle continues eastward to the west-facing scarp of the Makonde Plateau, and contains several cataracts of which the largest are the Bandara, the Sunda (with the Lisenge Narrows), and the Upinde rapids, respectively about 286, 190, and 124 mi. (460, 306, and 200 km.) from the mouth. In the lower, the Makonde Plateau, the valley is 5 to 6 mi. (8 to 10 km.) wide, bounded by prominent sandstone scarps, and the river is divided into many channels by sand islands. The mouth is an estuary without permanent bar.

The chief tributaries include the great southern affluent, the Lujenda from Lake Chiuta, on the borders of Mozambique and Malawi (Nyasaland), which Livingstone thought should be called the main stream. From the Tanzania side come the Mgunguti, Likonde, Mahesi, and Lumesule. The river has not been systematically gauged. It is perennial, but navigable for small craft only up to the Upinde Rapids. The limit of tidal flow is about 9 or 10 mi. (14 or 16 km.) from the mouth.   (J. H. WN.)

RUVUMA REGION, in Tanzania, established in May 1963 following a reorganization of administrative units in what was then Tanganyika, comprises Songea, Mbinga, and Tunduru districts, which belonged to the former Southern Region. It is bounded northwest and north by Iringa and Morogoro regions respectively, north and east by Mtwara Region, south by Mozambique, and west by Malawi. Area approximately 23,650 sq.mi. (61,253 sq.km.). Pop. (1963 est.) 288,000. The western boundary of the region lies along the eastern shore of Lake Nyasa in the Great Rift Valley, near which the Matengo Highlands rise to more than 7,000 ft. (2,134 m.). Originating close to Lake Nyasa, the headwaters of the Ruvuma River flow into a deep gorge along the territorial boundary in the south of Iringa Region. The Luwegu and the Mbarangano (which forms part of the northeastern boundary) are major tributaries of the Rufiji. Mean annual rainfall varies from about 35 in. in the northeast to more than 65 in. on the lake shore, where hot, humid conditions contrast with the cooler climate of the highlands. Regional headquarters is at Songea (pop. [1957] 1,401), and the population is concentrated around there, in the western highlands, and around Tunduru. The main tribal groups are the Nyasa, Matengo, Ngoni (of Zulu descent), Yao, and Makua. Cash crops include sesame, tobacco, cotton, sunflower and castor seed, cashew nuts, and some peanuts, rice, and beans. Beeswax is an important product. Large areas are infested by tsetse fly and sleeping sickness is endemic.   (J. M. KE.)

RUWENZORI RANGE, thought to be the "Mountains of the Moon" of the geographer Ptolemy. Its name probably means "the rain maker." Standing on the border of the Democratic Republic of the Congo and Uganda, this mountain range, 60 mi. (97 km.) long and with a maximum breadth of 30 mi. (48 km.), lies slightly north of the equator between Lakes Edward and Albert. It falls steeply westward to the western branch of the East African Rift Valley which is traversed by the Semliki, the western headstream of the Nile, while on the east the fall is somewhat more gradual toward the uplands of western Uganda. The range can be divided into six groups of summits on which snow lies permanently, and several lower eminences which are periodically snow-covered. There are ten peaks rising over 16,000 ft. (4,877 m.), all but one being found on Mount Stanley, which claims the highest point, Margherita Peak (16,763 ft.). The six largest mountains are separated by passes, the average elevation of which is 14,000 ft. (4,267 m.), and deeply cut river valleys with fast-flowing rivers. The entire drainage finds its way into the Semliki, either directly or via Lakes George and Edward. Many small lakes occur in the upper valleys.

The range is a gigantic uplifted horst and its origin is connected with the complex tectonics of the Rift Valley. Although the greatest upheaval appears to have taken place since Tertiary times some of the faults are Archaean in age. Unlike the other snow peaks of East Africa the range is not of volcanic origin, although a number of Pleistocene explosion craters occur on surrounding lowlands. Composed in its outer parts of Archaean gneisses and mica schists offering no great resistance to denudation, in its centre the range consists of amphibolites, diorites, diabases, and granites, to which fact, coupled with steep dips and vertical fractures, the existence and separation of the higher summits are due.

The permanent snow line on the Uganda side stands at about 14,900 ft., but it is 1,000 ft. higher on the Congo slopes. More than 30 small glaciers have been recorded, several of which have disappeared since they were first seen in 1906. The lowest ice descends to slightly below 14,000 ft., although there is evidence of earlier glaciation down to 7,000 ft. on the eastern slopes.

The range is influenced periodically by convergent moist air streams from the Atlantic and Indian oceans, so that the precipitation received is considerable. Nearly 100 in. of rainfall have been recorded at 10,000 ft. (3,048 m.) on the Uganda slopes, although there is a marked decrease with elevation above this height. The climate is excessively humid and thick cloud is characteristic.

The vegetation displays well-marked zones, varying with the altitude, and the following approximate upper limits of each were defined by R. B. Woosnam (1907) for the eastern slopes: grassland (6,500 ft.), forest (8,500 ft.), bamboos (10,000 ft.), tree-heaths (12,500 ft.), and lobelias and senecios (14,500 ft.), above which is the summit region of helichrysum, moss, lichen, bare rock, and snow. A characteristic of the 10,000–13,000 ft. zone is the occurrence of valley bogs, many of which are impounded by recessional moraines. The larger mammals (elephant, buffalo, etc.) ascend only to the lower fringes of the forest zone, but small buck, hyrax, serval cats, and leopards have been recorded at all heights up to the snow line. Among the birds, kites, buzzards, ravens, sunbirds, and various warblers are the most common.

The Ba'amba and Bakonjo tribes, who dwell on the Uganda slopes below 6,700 ft., are mainly cultivators of beans, sweet potatoes, and bananas, although some find employment as porters for climbing parties, as hunters of small game, and, more recently, as miners and artisans at the Kilembe copper mine in the eastern foothills. Power for Kilembe is obtained from a hydroelectric plant on the Mobuku, the largest river of the Ruwenzori.

In modern times the existence of this snow-capped mountain range was first made known by Sir Henry Stanley during the Emin Pasha relief expedition of 1887–89, and it was Stanley who named it Ruwenzori. Partial ascents were made by Lieut. W. Stairs, F. Stuhlmann, J. David, Sir Harry Johnston, and G. F. Scott-Elliot, J. E. S. Moore, D. Freshfield, and R. Grauer, before the British Museum expedition of 1906 when A. Wollaston and R. B. Woosnam also reached the snows. But it was the large-scale expedition led by the duke of the Abruzzi later in 1906 which conquered almost all the highest summits and produced the first adequate map of the Ruwenzori. This well-equipped expedition was responsible not only for the first detailed knowledge of the geology, topography, and glaciology but it also named the major peaks, passes, and glaciers after European royal personages and eminent explorers of central Africa. Since 1906 nearly all the remaining high peaks have been climbed and most of the valleys explored, first by N. Humphreys, and later by geologists and surveyors from Uganda and the former Belgian Congo. Scientific expeditions have included the Belgian Scientific Mission of De Grunne (1930), the British Ruwenzori Expedition (1952), and a series of glaciological expeditions from Makerere University College, Uganda (1957–60), as part of the International Geophysical Year.

BIBLIOGRAPHY.—Sir H. M. Stanley, *In Darkest Africa* (1890); J. E. S. Moore, *To the Mountains of the Moon* (1901); R. M. Bere and P. H. Hicks, "Ruwenzori," *Uganda J.* 10:84–96 (1946); D. Busk, "The Southern Glaciers of the Stanley Group of the Ruwenzori," *Geogr. J.*, 120: 137–145 (1954); E. Bergström, "The British Ruwenzori Expedition, 1952: Glaciological Observations—Preliminary Report," *J. Glaciol.*, 2:468–476 (1955); R. B. McConnell, "Outline of the Geology of the Ruwenzori Mountains: a Preliminary Account of the Results of the

British Ruwenzori Expedition, 1951–52," *Overseas Geology and Mineral Resources,* 7:245–268 (1959); J. B. Whittow, "The Glaciers of Mount Baker, Ruwenzori," *Geogr. J.* 125:370–379 (1959); "Some Observations on the Snowfall of Ruwenzori," *J. Glaciol.,* 3:765–772 (1960); J. B. Whittow *et al.,* "Observations on the Glaciers of the Ruwenzori," *J. Glaciol.,* 4:581–616 (1963).   (J. B. Wh.)

RUYSBROECK (Ruusbroec), **JAN VAN** (1293–1381), Dutch mystic of considerable influence in the 14th century, was born at Ruisbroek near Brussels in 1293. After holding the chaplaincy of Ste. Gudule, Brussels (1317–43), he became the founder of the Augustinian abbey at Groenendaal, where he wrote all his works except the first, *Vanden Rike der Ghelieven.* Ruysbroeck developed the Trinitarian system of this work in his masterpiece, *Die Chierheit der gheesteliker Brulocht,* and his other books, including *Vanden Kersten ghelove; Het Boec vanden gheesteleken Tabernacule,* an allegorical treatise on the ark or tabernacle as the meeting point of the divine and human in the world; *De Spieghel der ewigher salicheit,* which summarizes his systematic theology; and *Het Boec vanden Twaelf Beghinen.* (*Vanden Twaelf Dogheden,* sometimes ascribed to Ruysbroeck, is almost certainly not his.) Though his considerable writings were produced for his contemporary Augustinians, in their criticism of abuse in the church they anticipate the *devotio moderna* (*see* Brethren of the Common Life; Groote, Gerhard) and had a widespread influence on the clergy and laity throughout the Netherlands and in France, Germany (Johann Tauler and Heinrich Suso), Italy, and Spain as late as the 16th century. With deep conviction and devotion, Ruysbroeck builds his powerful and fine prose on the mystical ethos of Hadewych (*q.v.*), developing a compendious system of teaching and belief. Although he had friends among the German mystics, Eckhart seems to have had little or no influence on him. He died at Groenendaal on Dec. 2, 1381. Ruysbroeck was beatified in 1908; his feast is celebrated on the anniversary of his death.

See complete works ed. by J. B. Poukens *et al.,* 4 vol. (1932–34); 2nd ed. (1944). English translations are as follows: *Vanden Rike der Ghelieven,* as *The Kingdom of the Lovers of God,* by T. Arnold Hyde (1919); *Die Chierheit der gheesteliker Brulocht,* as *The Spiritual Espousals,* by E. Colledge (1952); *Vanden Kersten ghelove,* as *The Book of the Sparkling Stone,* in *Mediaeval Netherlands Religious Literature* by E. Colledge (1965); *De Spieghel der ewigher salicheit,* as *The Book of Supreme Truth,* by Dom (1916); *Het Boec vanden Twaelf Beghinen,* as *The Book of the Twelve Béguines,* by J. Francis (1913). *See* also V. Scully, *A Mediaeval Mystic* (1910).   (P. K. K.)

RUYSDAEL (Ruisdael, Ruijsdael), **SALOMON VAN** (*c.* 1602–1670), Dutch painter, best known for his landscapes, was born in Naarden. He originally had the name of De Gooyer, as did his brother Izack, the father of Jacob van Ruisdael (*q.v.*). Salomon entered the Haarlem Guild of St. Luke in 1628. His first dated pictures are from 1627. He spent his whole life in Haarlem, where he was head of the guild in 1648. He belonged to the Mennonites. He died as a well-to-do person in 1670.

Salomon's early works—winter scenes—continue the tradition of Esaias van de Velde, and his early landscapes are based on the colour scheme and composition of Pieter de Molyn. In the diagonal composition of the dunes and river scenes of the 1630s he is the equal of Jan van Goyen. The colours tend to a green. Around 1645 the composition becomes more powerful, with framing motifs of great trees on one side and a distant view on the other. The colours become warmer and more transparent. In later years the light effects are more outspoken, and the decorative elements become stronger. It is probable that this change was partly caused by the influence of painters returning from Italy; *e.g.,* J. Both. In the 1660s a blue colour prevails, especially in the river scenes, which the artist loved to paint. Another favourite subject was the village inn at the roadside with cattle and herdsmen.

Salomon van Ruysdael was a clever figure painter; all the small figures, which add much to the pleasant effects of his landscapes, are by his own hand. Unlike Jacob, he preferred to render actual scenery of Dutch towns, like Alkmaar, Arnhem, Dordrecht and Utrecht, but sometimes he combined motifs from different places in one picture. In later years he also painted large winter scenes, with skating on frozen rivers, of great decorative beauty.

See C. Hofstede de Groot, *Catalogue of Dutch Painters* (1912); W. Stechow, *Salomon van Ruysdael* (1938).   (H. K. Gn.)

RUYTER, MICHIEL ADRIAANSZOON DE (1607–1676), Dutch seaman reckoned as his country's greatest admiral, was born at Flushing on March 24, 1607. Going to sea as a boatswain's boy in 1618, he worked his way up during the next 20 years to become an independent merchant captain. In 1641 he was appointed rear admiral of a fleet sent to assist Portugal against Spain and distinguished himself in a battle off Cape St. Vincent. He resumed his activities as a merchant captain in 1642, but on the outbreak of war with England in 1652 was persuaded to accept a command in the navy. Under Adm. M. H. Tromp, he showed outstanding skill in the First Dutch War (*see* Dutch Wars).

Appointed vice-admiral of Holland in 1653, he subsequently served against French privateers and Barbary pirates in the Mediterranean. In 1659 he supported the Danes against the Swedes in the Baltic, but from 1661–64 he was again employed in the Mediterranean. In 1664–65, on secret orders from Holland, he took successful reprisals against the English on the Guinea coast, where they had seized some Dutch trading settlements, but his campaign in the West Indies, where he went immediately afterward, was a failure. On his return to the Netherlands he became lieutenant admiral of Holland and collaborated closely with the grand pensionary, Johan de Witt, in strengthening the navy. His greatest successes in the Second Dutch War were the Four Days' Battle (June 1666) and the raid on the Medway (June 1667), when he burned some of the finest English ships and carried off the flagship to Holland as a prize. Perhaps his greatest services, however, were in the Third Dutch War, when his saving of the Dutch fleet in the Battle of Solebay (Southwold Bay) in 1672 and his victories over superior forces in the battles of Schooneveld and the Texel in 1673 prevented an Anglo-French invasion of Holland by sea. In 1675 and 1676 he was fighting against the French in the Mediterranean. Wounded off Sicily on April 22, 1676, he died on April 29, at Syracuse.   (E. H. K.)

RWANDA (Banyaruanda, Wanyaruanda, Ruanda), an East African people belonging to the Interlacustrine Bantu. Their homelands are in the Republic of Rwanda, the northern portion of the former United Nations Trust Territory of Ruanda-Urundi. In the mid-1960s about 3,300,000 Rwanda occupied an area of roughly 10,000 sq.mi. (26,000 sq.km.), yielding one of the highest overall population densities in Africa. Severe food shortages have resulted in large-scale migrations to neighbouring territories.

The people are divided into two main socioracial groups: the Hutu (Bahutu), the shorter, darker-skinned group, a subordinate majority of cultivators of plantains, millet, and sweet potatoes; and the Tutsi (Batutsi), an aristocratic minority of taller, lighter-skinned pastoralists. A third group, the pygmy Twa (Batwa), are hunters and potters. In former times, intermarriage among these groups was forbidden. The ruler, the *mwami,* administered the kingdom through a hierarchy of Tutsi chiefs and military captains bound to him by clientship. These, in turn, ruled and drew tribute from local communities of Hutu agriculturalists. Although the Rwanda shared a common language and formed a single polity under the *mwami,* the occurrence of Hutu revolts, both before and after the establishment of colonial rule in 1907, shows that the superiority of the Tutsi was not always accepted by the Hutu.

Traditionally, the Rwanda believed in a supreme creator-god, Imana, and in a first ancestor, Kazikamuntu, whose three children, Gatutsi, Gahutu, and Gatwa, were the ancestors of the three castes. Communication with these, as well as with ancestors and other spirit beings, takes place through spirit-possession by mediums.

See also Rwanda; Rundi; Bantu (Interlacustrine); Africa: *Ethnography (Anthropology): East Africa.*

Bibliography.—J. J. Maquet, "The Kingdom of Ruanda," *African Worlds,* ed. by C. D. Forde (1954), *Le système des relations sociales dans le Ruanda ancien* (1954), *The Premise of Inequality in Ruanda* (1961); J. Nicaise, "Applied Anthropology in the Congo and Ruanda-Urundi," *Human Organization,* vol. xix (1960); H. Kitchen, *A Handbook of African Affairs* (1964).   (L. A. Fs.)

RWANDA, a republic of eastern equatorial Africa bounded north by Uganda, east by Tanzania (the Kagera River forms the frontier), south by Burundi, and west and northwest by the Democratic Republic of the Congo (the frontier crosses Lake Kivu and follows the Ruzizi River). Roughly rectangular in shape, Rwanda has an area of 10,169 sq.mi. (26,338 sq.km.). The capital is Kigali.

Physical Features.—The country lies at an altitude of more than 5,000 ft. (1,500 m.) except on the shores of Lake Kivu and along the Kagera on the Tanzanian border, where the altitude is somewhat less. The western part of Rwanda is very hilly. The Congo-Nile Divide (whose crest is covered with forests) falls steeply to Lake Kivu in the west and crosses a volcanic range in the north. The highest points of the divide exceed 9,500 ft. (2,900 m.). The rest of the country is a high plateau inclined generally eastward and entirely composed of Precambrian rocks, including granite massifs and quartzite ridges. North of Lake Kivu are lava fields dominated by the Virunga Mountains; the highest point is Volcan Karisimbi, at 14,787 ft. (4,507 m.). The barrier formed by these volcanoes blocked the flow of the rivers toward the north and led to the formation of Lake Kivu, and also of Lakes Ruhondo and Burera. Other lakes are scattered about the eastern part of the country. The most remote of the sources of the Nile lies in Rwanda.

Rwanda has a tropical climate softened by altitude. The average annual temperature at Kigali is 20° C (68° F). The shores of Lake Kivu are well known for the mildness of their climate. Rain, plentiful in the west at 47 to 51 in. (1,200 to 1,300 mm.) annually, declines toward the east to less than 40 in. (1,000 mm.) in the Kagera plain. The dry season lasts from two to three months (June, July, August). Within Rwanda are Kagera National Park and a part of Albert National Park.

People.—The population is composed of three elements: the Hutu, the Tutsi, and the Twa. The last named are very small in numbers (0.5% of the total population) and occupy the lowest rung of the social ladder, being relegated to the functions of hunters, artisans, and entertainers. The Tutsi (16.5%), very often of tall stature, formerly constituted the aristocratic class and possessed both power and wealth, notably in cattle. The Hutu (83%), Bantu agriculturalists, were bound to the Tutsi as vassals and clients; they had the task of safeguarding the herds and providing agricultural produce. There was little intermarriage between the two groups. Tutsi and Hutu speak Kirwanda (or Kinyarwanda), a Bantu language. About 50% of the Rwandans practise traditional religious beliefs; the rest are Christians, the vast majority being Roman Catholics.

The population of Rwanda in 1965 was estimated at 2,903,071 (including fewer than 5,000 Europeans and Asians). The country is the most densely populated in Africa, with more than 300 persons to the square mile. Certain western parts of the country are very heavily populated (more than 1,000 per square mile). The urban population is insignificant—about 15,000, or 0.5% of the total population. Kigali, the capital, has a population of about 5,000. The annual rate of increase in the population in the mid-1960s was 3.2%.

History.—Until its achievement of independence in July 1962 Rwanda (then known as Ruanda) had formed part of the Belgian trust territory of Ruanda-Urundi (*q.v.* for previous history). Bloody conflicts broke out in November 1961 between the Tutsi and the Hutu and continued after independence. Many Tutsi took refuge in the Congo, Burundi, and Uganda, and subsequently launched a number of raids from neighbouring countries into Rwanda. An incursion from Burundi in December 1963 was followed in early 1964 by severe reprisals (involving large-scale massacres) against Tutsi still living in Rwanda. Many Tutsi were later resettled in Uganda and Tanzania.

Administration and Social Conditions.—*Government.*—Rwanda is a republic with a president who is both head of state and head of government, assisted by a Council of Ministers. The National Assembly, elected by universal suffrage, has 47 members. Most of the seats in the assembly are held by the Parmehutu Party, which campaigned for the emancipation of the Hutu from the Tutsi. For administrative purposes Rwanda is divided into ten prefectures, which are themselves subdivided into communes.

Justice.—There is a tribunal of first instance in each prefecture, cantonal tribunals, a Court of Appeal, and a Supreme Court (comprising various sections including a Supreme Court of Appeal and a Constitutional Court).

Education and Health.—In the 1960s about 320,000 children were receiving primary education and about 3,000 secondary education. A university, still incomplete, was established at Butare in 1963; its courses include medicine, the social sciences, and teacher training. Butare also has institutions providing training in husbandry, medicine, and veterinary medicine. More than one-fifth of the national budget is devoted to education.

Malaria is endemic in certain parts of the country, and pulmonary diseases are common. There is a shortage of doctors (1 to 55,000 inhabitants).

The Economy.—The economy of Rwanda is essentially subsistence agriculture, the main crops being sorghum, beans, peas, sweet potatoes, corn (maize), cassava, and bananas. The main cash crop is coffee, of which 8,000 tons were exported in 1964. Some tea and pyrethrum are also exported. Rwanda has considerable stock of cattle (about 500,000 head in the 1960s) whose social value is greater than their value as a source of food. There were also about 250,000 sheep, 1,000,000 goats, and 60,000 pigs.

Mineral production accounts for just under 40% of exports by value: cassiterite, wolfram, beryllium, columbium-tantalite, amblygonite, and some gold. Lake Kivu has a little methane, exploitation of which has begun near Gisenyi. The only industry consists of small factories for the processing of agricultural products (a brewery, soap works, etc.). Industrial expansion is hindered by the country's remoteness from the sea. Rwanda has three hydroelectric stations, including one on the Ruzizi River. Installed capacity is 21,440 kw., but only one-third is being used. In the mid-1960s the annual value of exports amounted to about 580,000,000 Rwanda francs (officially at par with the Belgian franc) and imports to 600,000,000 RFr. There are no railways, but Rwanda has a fairly dense network of dirt roads, which link it with the Congo, Burundi, and Uganda (the chief route for the export of agricultural products). There is a weekly air service between Kigali airport and Brussels. Small airfields serve the interior of the country. Kigali Radio broadcasts in French and Kirwanda, and also in English and Swahili.

BIBLIOGRAPHY.—H. Scaetta, *Le Climat écologique de la dorsale Congo-Nil* (1934); P. Gourou, *La Densité de la population au Ruanda-Urundi* (1953); Ministère des Affaires Etrangères, *Investissez au Rwanda* (1965); European Economic Community, Direction Générale du Développement de l'Outre-Mer, *Renseignements de base sur les états africains et malgache associés*, vol. 1, *Données statistiques* (1965).
(HE. NI.)

RYAZAN, PRINCES OF. Ryazan, with its capital city the old Ryazan on the Oka River about 150 mi. (241 km.) SE of Moscow, became an independent principality early in the 12th century under Yaroslav, son of Grand Prince Svyatoslav Yaroslavich of Kiev. The history of the principality and its princes for 100 years was one of internecine strife and conflict with the princes of Vladimir. But by 1237, when the Mongol-Tatar army under Batu Khan attacked and sacked the capital, stability had been restored and the territory of the principality had been enlarged under Grand Prince Yuri Igorevich. After the sack of old Ryazan economic and political life centred around Pereyaslavl-Ryazanski (modern Ryazan is about 30 mi. [48 km.] upstream from old Ryazan) and Pronsk, and for a century the princes frittered away their strength in the struggle for supremacy between the two centres. In the reign of Ivan I Kalita, grand prince of Vladimir and Moscow from 1331 to 1341, Ryazan was relatively weak; but under Oleg Ivanovich (1351–1402), who dared to resist Moscow, the fortunes of Ryazan revived, and, with the support of the Golden Horde, the principality acquired a measure of independence and even temporarily extended its frontiers.

The struggle with Moscow continued, to Ryazan's detriment. Fedor Olgovich (reigned 1402–27) was too weak to resist and was obliged to recognize his dependence on Moscow. Ivan Fedorovich (1427–56) acknowledged the suzerainty of Vytautas of Lithuania in 1427, but after Vytautas' death (1430) he only recognized whoever held the throne of Moscow. By the treaty of 1447 with Vasili II he agreed to hold the grand prince of Moscow as his "elder brother" and renounce all independent foreign relations. At his death his eight-year-old son Vasili Ivanovich (1456–83) was entrusted to the care of Vasili II, who sent his governors to rule Ryazan. Vasili Ivanovich, however, having married Grand Prince Ivan III's sister, was allowed to rule Ryazan from 1464, though in complete subordination to Moscow. His son Ivan (1483–1500) was equally submissive. In 1521, when Ivan Ivanovich, last of the princes of Ryazan, having entered into secret negotiations with the Tatars, was arrested by Grand Prince Vasili III, Ryazan was formally annexed by Moscow.

See D. I. Ilovaiski, *Istoria Ryazanskogo Knyazhestva* (1858).

(J. L. I. F.)

RYAZAN, an *oblast* of the Russian Soviet Federated Socialist Republic, U.S.S.R., was established in 1937. Area 15,290 sq.mi. (39,601 sq.km.). Pop. (1959) 1,444,755. The larger, northern part lies in the middle Oka basin. That part of the *oblast* north of the Oka forms an extensive swampy depression, known as Meshchera, thinly populated and largely forested, where some reclamation has been carried out from the late 19th century on. The broad plain of the Oka right bank is drained by its tributaries, the Pronya and Para. In the south the *oblast* falls within the basin of the upper Don. The rolling hills of the central Russian upland, greatly cut up by both river valleys and erosion gullies, occupy the southwest, dropping to the plain of the Oka-Don lowland in the southeast. All the Oka basin lies in the mixed forest zone, with a natural cover of oak, spruce, pine, and birch forest. A high proportion of the forest (except in Meshchera) has been cleared for agriculture. In the south the *oblast* passes into the forest-steppe zone with patches of open grassland, also largely plowed, on gray forest soils or degraded chernozems. The Meshchera swamps are mostly reed or grass marsh, although peat bogs are occasionally found.

A small proportion (30%) of the 1959 population was urban. Of these, almost half lived in the one sizable town, Ryazan (*q.v.*). The other 8 towns and 26 urban districts are small, local centres, chiefly concerned with processing agricultural products and timber working. Near Skopin a little lignite is mined. Agriculture is mainly concerned with rye, oats, and spring wheat. Vegetables are important along the Oka, while the main industrial crops are flax and hemp in the north and sugar beets and tobacco in the south. (R. A. F.)

RYAZAN, a town and *oblast* centre of the Russian Soviet Federated Socialist Republic, U.S.S.R., stands on the right bank of the Oka River, 196 km. (122 mi.) SE of Moscow. Pop. (1959) 214,130. Present-day Ryazan stands on the site of the ancient Russian town of Pereyaslavl-Ryazanski, but the original Ryazan, now known as Staraya (Old) Ryazan, lay farther downstream at the Pronya confluence. Staraya Ryazan, first recorded in 1096, was the seat of the early princedom, with a kremlin (citadel) and two 12th-century cathedrals. Its princes waged a constant and bitter struggle with those of Vladimir. The town was the first to meet the Tatar invasion and was utterly destroyed in 1237. Although it was later reestablished Ryazan lost all importance and today only the ruins of the ramparts remain.

Pereyaslavl-Ryazanski is believed to have been founded in 1095 by Yaroslav Svyatoslavich, although some sources give a later date. It was unimportant until the later 13th century when the Ryazan bishopric was moved there. It was sacked by the Muscovites in 1371 and by the Tatars in 1372 and 1378, when it was completely laid waste. In the 15th century it became the centre of the Ryazan princedom, but in 1521 Ryazan passed under the rule of Moscow. Thereafter it served as a key fortress on the approaches to Moscow and the eastern anchor of the Tula defensive line. In 1778 its name was changed to Ryazan. The 18th and 19th centuries brought considerable importance to the town as a focus of the grain trade to Moscow. Modern Ryazan has large engineering industries, making agricultural machinery, electric lamps, radios, calculating machines, and machine tools. Oil refining is fast developing. It is still a major route centre; the Oka is navigable and there are railways to Moscow, Vladimir, Kuibyshev, and Voronezh. (R. A. F.)

RYBINSK (formerly SHCHERBAKOV), a town in Yaroslavl *oblast* of the Russian Soviet Federated Socialist Republic,

U.S.S.R., stands on the Volga near its most northerly point, 50 mi. (80 km.) NW of Yaroslavl. Pop. (1959) 181,685. The place developed in the 14th–15th centuries as Rybnaya Sloboda ("the fishing settlement") and became the town of Rybinsk in the 1770s. After the Revolution it was renamed Shcherbakov, until 1957. Its trade grew with the opening of the Mariinsk Waterway from the Volga to Leningrad (St. Petersburg) and it is now an important river port. There is a large engineering industry, producing printing machinery, cranes, road-making machinery, river tugs, dredgers, and timber-working equipment. Other products are roofing and insulating materials, ropes, matches, leather goods and foodstuffs. Rybinsk is linked by rail with Yaroslavl and Bologoye (on the Moscow–Leningrad line) and by road with Vologda, Uglich, and Yaroslavl (and thence with Moscow).

In 1941 a large barrage and hydroelectric station was completed on the Volga, immediately above Rybinsk, to form the Rybinsk Reservoir. It created what was then the largest man-made lake in the world, covering about 1,757 sq.mi. (4,550 sq.km.). This area makes it the fourth largest lake in Europe. The power station has a capacity of 330,000 kw. (R. A. F.)

RYBNIK, a town in southern Poland in the Katowice *wojewodztwo* (province). Pop. (1960) 34,099. It lies in the sub-Carpathian Valley, on the Nacyna River (a secondary tributary of the Oder), and near extensive woods. In 1282 it became the capital of the Racibórz principality under a member of the Polish Piast dynasty. In 1327 it was given in pledge to Bohemia. Like Bohemia itself Rybnik passed into the hands of the Habsburgs in the 16th century. It became part of Prussia when Frederick the Great conquered Silesia in 1742. When Upper Silesia was partitioned in 1921 between Poland and Germany, the town and district returned to Poland.

Exploitation of the mineral resources of the district started in the Middle Ages (iron foundries, rolling mills), and from the 19th century, coal mining made the town a major industrial area of the province. It also produces metal tools. (K. M. WI.)

RYDBERG, (ABRAHAM) VIKTOR (1828–1895), Swedish author, whose wide range of activities enabled him to exercise great influence on Swedish cultural life, was born at Jönköping on Dec. 18, 1828. His mother died in a cholera epidemic, his father became a dipsomaniac, and he grew up among strangers, with no home of his own. He matriculated at Lund but had to break off his studies for lack of money. In 1855 he found employment with the liberal newspaper *Göteborgs handelstidning*, in which *Den siste atenaren*, the novel which made his name, appeared serially in 1859. Its description of the clash between paganism and Christianity in ancient Athens, showing a bias against clerical intolerance and orthodoxy, had a direct bearing on conditions in Sweden. He had previously published *Singoalla* (1857; revised 1865), a romantic lyrical tale of the middle ages in Sweden. His *Bibelns lära om Kristus* (1862), in which he maintained that, according to the Bible, Christ was not God, did much to further a liberal outlook in theology and the church.

In the 1870s Rydberg engaged in many new activities. He entered the *riksdag* for a short time. He advocated linguistic reform, being particularly anxious to reduce the number of words borrowed from the German. In 1874 he visited Rome and on his return wrote *Romerska dagar* (1877), in which his interest in classical antiquity finds its most mature expression. In 1876 he completed his translation of part i of Goethe's *Faust*, which had occupied him for many years. During these years also he revealed outstanding talent as a poet: his collection *Dikter* (1882) established him as the foremost lyrical poet since Esaias Tegnér and Erik Stagnelius. He gradually gained official recognition and was given an honorary doctorate by Uppsala university in 1877, elected to the Swedish Academy in 1878 and in 1884 called to the chair of cultural history at the Stockholm *högskola*, this professorship being subsequently changed to one in the theory and history of art. In the 1880s he was chiefly concerned with research into mythology, the results of which were published in the learned and imaginative *Undersökningar i germanisk mytologi*, 2 vol. (1886–89). In 1891 he published two late flowerings of his literary genius: *Vapensmeden*, a novel describing life at the time of the

Reformation in Sweden, and a new collection of poems, one of which, "Den nya Grottesången," is a remarkable indictment of existing social conditions.

Rydberg was an idealist, faithful to the romantic tradition in poetry and thought but with a mind receptive to the ideas of a new age. He achieved an unequaled position of authority in Swedish culture. He died at Djursholm on Sept. 21, 1895. His *Samlade Skrifter* were edited by K. Warburg, 14 vol. (1896–99).

(AT. WN.)

RYDE, a municipal borough and seaside resort in the Isle of Wight, Eng., 4½ mi. SW of Portsmouth across the Solent. Area 12.3 sq.mi. (31.9 sq.km.). Pop. (1961) 19,845. On rising ground on the northeast coast, overlooking Spithead, Ryde has woods reaching to the water's edge, and miles of golden sands. It is built on the site of a village called La Rye or La Riche, which was destroyed by the French in the reign of Edward II. At the close of the 18th century it was a small fishing hamlet, but it rapidly grew as a holiday place, and catering for tourists became its chief industry, with agriculture second in importance. The ancient Ryde Carnival is held annually in September. The town was incorporated in 1868. Ryde is connected by boat with Portsmouth. The principal buildings are All Saints Church, the market house and town hall, the Royal Victoria Yacht Club, the pavilion, the Royal Isle of Wight Infirmary, and the Commodore Theatre.

RYDER, ALBERT PINKHAM (1847–1917), U.S. painter, noted for his lunar landscapes and allegorical scenes, was born at New Bedford, Mass., March 19, 1847. About 1868 the family settled in New York City, where Ryder briefly studied painting. He first exhibited at the National Academy of Design in 1873, but most of his exhibited work was shown at the Society of American Artists, of which he was a founding member. In 1882 he traveled in Europe, but paintings in the art galleries interested him little. He was an imaginative, solitary painter; his lifework of about 150 pictures was produced slowly.

By 1900 his powers were impaired, and he injured some earlier paintings with misjudged reworkings; thus he unconsciously prepared the way for the many forged examples that appeared. After a critical illness, friends took him to their home in Elmhurst, Long Island, N.Y., where he died March 28, 1917. Major works include "Siegfried," "The Race Track," and "Toilers of the Sea." Extraordinary colourfulness triumphs over technical imperfections, and his themes range from an idyllic pastoralism through intensifying romanticism to an epic splendour. Many of Ryder's paintings have suffered rapid deterioration.

See Frederic Fairchild Sherman, *Albert Pinkham Ryder* (1920); L. Goodrich, *Albert Pinkham Ryder* (1947). (VL. B.; X.)

RYE, a municipal borough and market town in the Rye parliamentary division of East Sussex, Eng., 11 mi. N.E. from Hastings by road. Pop. (1961) 4,438. Area 1.2 sq.mi. (3.1 sq.km.). Rye is a picturesque market town, built up a hill by the Rother river, with cobbled streets and timber-framed and Georgian houses. Ypres tower (12th century), which stands on the cliff, was its only defense until Edward III walled the town, but Landgate (1329), one of the three original entrance gates, is all that remains of the 14th century fortifications. The Norman to Perpendicular church of St. Mary has a notable quarter-boy 16th-century clock, and in the churchyard is a Georgian reservoir. Other interesting buildings are the old grammar school (1636), the town hall (1742), the old hospital, the Mermaid inn (*c.* 1420) and the Flushing inn, which contains a mural dated 1547.

As part of the manor of Rameslie, Rye was granted by Edward the Confessor to the monks of Fécamp, by whom it was retained until resumed by Henry III in 1247. The town became a full member of the Cinque Ports *c.* 1350 when, with Winchelsea, the other ancient town, it was added to the confederation. It was then a flourishing port but declined in the late 14th century, partly recovered its prosperity with the decay of Winchelsea in the 15th and 16th centuries and then sank again when the sedimentation and consequent receding of the sea, which had been going on slowly since the 14th century, made the use of the harbour impracticable. By the mid-20th century the Rother's mouth was 2 mi. from the town. Rye was twice burned down by the French,

in 1377 and 1448. The town was incorporated in 1289 and was granted a three days' fair. Twice-weekly markets had been held before 1405 when the Friday market was changed to Saturday. The market now serves a wide agricultural area. Industries include light engineering, dry cleaning and the tourist trade.

RYE. A cereal grass, rye is grown for use in making rye bread and rye whisky and for livestock feed. The cultivated types of rye, known botanically as *Secale cereale,* are grown extensively in Europe, Asia and North America. As one of the less important of the cereal crops, rye generally is grown for grain only where the environmental conditions are relatively unfavourable for other

J. HORACE MCFARLAND CO.

RYE (SECALE CEREALE)

cereals. Rye probably originated in southwestern Asia, like several other important cereals, such as wheat, oats and barley, with westward migration across the Balkan peninsula and over Europe (*see* AGRICULTURE). No trace of cultivated rye has been found in early Egyptian monuments; likewise no reference to this crop is found in ancient writings. However, the name occurs in northern European languages, suggesting early cultivation in this area.

Only one species of cultivated rye is recognized, *Secale cereale,* although several other species have been found growing wild; there are annual and perennial species and many varieties of weedy plants are closely related to the cultivated species. Rye has 14 somatic chromosomes, and there is no evidence of a polyploid series except for artificially produced tetraploids with 28 chromosomes. Most rye is grown as a fall-sown annual, though a little is spring sown with spring instead of winter varieties.

The greatest production of rye occurs in the temperate and cool regions of the world; it grows also where altitudes are high. It has the greatest winter hardiness of all small grains, and its culture extends to the more northerly parts of North America and as far north as the Arctic circle of Europe and Asia. The type of soil has an important influence on geographic distribution. Rye is frequently grown where other crops fail because of low fertility. Most production is from the poorer soils of Europe and the U.S.S.R. and the sandier and poorer soils of North America where it is too cool for winter wheat. Soil requirements are modest—even more so than for oats. Rye will produce well on fertile soil, such as the chernozem (black earth) of eastern Europe, but this type of soil is reserved for growing other crops.

Cultivation and Uses.—Rye is grown much the same as other cereal crops. Usually it is planted with a grain drill at a rate of five to six pecks per acre, depending upon the size of seed. It is not used generally as a companion crop in establishing forages as is common with wheat and oats. Usually it is rotated with other crops, taking the place of winter wheat. Where it is used for pasture, it serves largely as an emergency crop. Seedings are made in the fall, and the crop matures somewhat earlier than the other small grain crops such as wheat, oats and barley. Harvesting in the northern areas comes in late June and early July.

The principal uses of rye are as flour for bread, as feed for livestock and as a pasture plant. Of the cereals, only wheat and rye have the qualities necessary for making a loaf of bread from the flour. The rye flour, however, is very inferior to wheat for baking, lacking the elasticity so essential to a good loaf and being heavy and dark in colour. In Eurasia a loaf made from pure rye flour commonly is referred to as black bread because of its colour. Relatively little rye flour is used for breadmaking in the United States; when so used, it is commonly blended in varying proportions with wheat flour.

Livestock feed is one of the main uses of the rye crop. For most classes of livestock it is usually fed in a mixture. It has less fats than has wheat, about the same protein content and compares favourably with wheat and corn for carbohydrates. Vitamin B₁ content is slightly lower than in barley and wheat and much lower than in oats. Rye is used also in the making of alcoholic beverages (*see* WHISKY).

Rye straw is fibrous and tough and used less for feed than for litter or bedding. It is used for mattresses and thatching in certain areas of the world, and in the manufacture of hats and paper.

Rye has considerable use for fall and spring cattle grazing. As a spring pasture it is available before permanent pastures have made sufficient growth for livestock use. The leaves are high in vitamin A content. In warmer areas the grain is used for fall grazing and cover cropping. It is also used as a green manure crop, being plowed under in the spring and followed by a crop of greater economic value.

Diseases.—Ergot is a disease condition that follows when the young kernel is penetrated by the fungus *Claviceps purpurea.* This results in purplish-black ergot bodies called sclerotia, which contain several alkaloid drugs (*see* ERGOT).

Although other diseases, including snow mold, attack rye, most of them cause only minor yield reduction. There are several leaf and stem diseases, such as leaf and stem rust, stalk and head smut, scald and blotch, and some root rots. On the whole, if ergot is discounted, disease losses in rye are less than in other small grains.

Botanical Characteristics.—The spike of the rye plant resembles wheat in having alternately ranked spikelets attached to a zigzag axis or rachis, forming a fairly dense head or ear. Spikelets are composed of two thin, narrow, chaffy scales or glumes that subtend two or more florets, which, in turn, are enclosed by a lemma and palea (*see* GRASSES: *Structure*). The lemmas taper into slender bristles or awns that are about two to four centimetres long. Each floret contains three stamens and a pistil, which, after pollination, develop into a one-seeded fruit that is partly exposed. The threshed seed or fruit is known as a caryopsis, a term applied generally to the fruits of cereal crops. Grain colour varies, but grayish-green and light brown predominate, while some are almost white. The thin shell or pericarp sometimes ruptures over the germ. Sterile florets occur to the extent of 25% to 30%, thereby reducing production. Cross-pollination occurs almost completely because the flowers are largely self-sterile. The first foliage leaf is reddish or purplish tinged. Other leaves are long, narrow and thin with a short ligule and a moderate-sized auricle at the juncture of the blade and sheath. The leaf sheaths have a bluish-green bloom. The height and number of the jointed stems or culms depend upon growth conditions.

Rye has the tallest and strongest straw of all of the small grain crops. The straw may attain a height of seven to eight feet on fertile soils but is usually five feet or less. Improved varieties generally have straw of a length more suitable for the use of harvesting equipment. There are numerous fibrous roots, and they penetrate more deeply than do those of other small grains.

Breeding and Hybridization.—Improvement of the rye plant by breeding is difficult because of the high degree of self-sterility. Most improvement has been accomplished by mass selection rather than by the pure line method of breeding. Varieties are genetically impure because of cross-pollination. Moderately self-fertile inbred lines can be perpetuated without difficulty. Hybrid vigour with greater productivity than open-pollinated varieties results when selected inbred lines are properly mated. No method has been found to utilize this biologic principle commercially. Since rye is thrifty and winter hardy it has been hybridized with wheat, resulting in winter-hardy selections with the appearance and quality of wheat. However, commercial production of varieties from wheat-rye hybrid origin is rather small. Hybrids with other genera have been made.

During the 1940s tetraploids (28 somatic chromosomes) in rye were produced by several scientists. One tetraploid called Tetra Petkus gained some prominence in the early 1950s; it is stiff strawed, leafy and late in maturity. Kernels are large, weighing 1½ to 2 times as much as common rye. Tests indicate Tetra Petkus flour will bake satisfactorily. Reduced yield may result if the tetraploids are sown close to the common varieties, because

cross-pollinated flowers do not produce seed.

In North America the following varieties of common rye are used commercially: Adams, Caribou, Dakold, Elk, Pierre, Abruzzi, Balbo, Elbon and Weser. The Balbo variety is especially valuable as a pasture crop. Tetra Petkus has proved excellent for pasture in some sections. Most of these varieties have come from stocks of European and Russian origin.

In other countries some important varieties are: Petkus, Kings II, Steel, Ensi, Toivo, Borris, Pearl, Vjatka and Kolarovka.

Production and Trade.—The estimated world production of rye in the late 1960s was near 1,270,000,000 bu. a year. Of this total approximately 43% was produced in the U.S.S.R. The leading rye-producing countries in order of importance were the U.S.S.R., Poland, West Germany, East Germany, Czechoslovakia, Turkey and the U.S. The U.S. and Canada produced approximately 3.4% of the world total. The average acre yield in Switzerland was about 50 bu. per ac.; in the U.S. near 20 bu.; and in the U.S.S.R. about 13.5. The leading rye-producing states are North Dakota, South Dakota, Nebraska, Kansas and Minnesota.

Trade in rye has been more limited than that in other grains. Seasonal production influences trade between countries. The U.S.S.R., Canada, Turkey and Argentina usually export rye, while West Germany, mainland China, Finland, the Netherlands, Austria and Norway import more than they export. The United States trade has fluctuated with exports averaging more than imports.

See also CEREALS; FOOD SUPPLY OF THE WORLD: *Cereals;* GRAIN PRODUCTION AND TRADE; and references under "Rye" in the Index.

(H. L. Ss.; H. K. W.)

BIBLIOGRAPHY.—For further reading and comprehensive treatment of rye *see* G. B. Deodikar, *Rye (Secale cereale Linn.),* Indian Council of Agricultural Research, New Delhi, Cereal Crop Series no. iii:1–152 (1963), which contains discussions on *Secale* (rye) taxonomy, genetics, improvement, mutations, nutrition and the position of rye in world agriculture. For a shorter and more popular review, *see* "Rye" by H. L. Shands in S. A. Matz (ed.), *Chemistry and Technology of Cereals as Food and Feed* (1959). (H. L. Ss.)

RYKOV, ALEKSEI IVANOVICH (1881–1938), Russian Communist leader who at different times opposed both Lenin and Stalin, was born at Saratov on Feb. 25 (new style; 13, old style), 1881, the son of a peasant. At 18 he joined the Russian Social-Democratic Workers' Party (RSDWP), visited Lenin in Geneva in 1902, and returned to Russia to work as a revolutionary. He was many times arrested and deported, but each time escaped. In 1904, after Lenin's break with the predominantly Bolshevik official party leadership, Rykov assisted him in forming the subfaction of "stone-hard" Bolsheviks and was a member of its bureau. He attended the third party congress of the RSDWP (London, 1905) and was elected to its central committee. He took part in the 1905 revolution, and was again in London, as a delegate to the fifth congress, in 1907. After 1907 Rykov took up a conciliatory attitude toward non-Leninist factions in the party, and in 1910 became one of the "party-minded Bolsheviks" (a group consisting of such conciliators). He lived in Paris during 1910–11, returned to Russia, and in 1913 was banished to Siberia; he escaped in 1915 but was recaptured and remained in banishment until the revolution of March 1917. He opposed Lenin's idea of a unilateral seizure of power by the Bolsheviks and advocated a coalition government of all Socialist parties.

Rykov took an active part in the November revolution, and became people's commissar of the interior in the first Bolshevik government headed by Lenin. He was chairman (1918–21) of the Supreme Council of National Economy, and deputy chairman (1921–24) of the Council of Labour and Defense and of the Council of People's Commissars, succeeding Lenin as chairman of the latter in 1924. A member of the Politburo from 1923, Rykov sided with Stalin against Trotski, but during 1928–29 was a leader of the "Right Opposition" against Stalin. The defeat of the "Right Opposition" led to Rykov being replaced (1930) by V. M. Molotov as chairman of the Council of People's Commissars. He became people's commissar for communications in 1931 but was dismissed in 1936 and expelled from the Communist Party for his alleged "treacherous anti-party activity" in 1937. In 1938 he was, together with N. I. Bukharin, principal defendant in a great show "trial." Sentenced to death on March 13, he was shot next day.

(L. B. Sc.)

RYMER, THOMAS (1643?–1713), English critic who introduced to England the principles of French formalist, neo-classical criticism and who also, as historiographer royal, compiled a famous collection of treaties (the *Foedera*), was born, probably in 1643, at Yafforth Hall, near Northallerton, Yorkshire. He was the younger son of Ralph Rymer, a zealous Roundhead who in 1656 became lord of the manor of Brafferton, Yorkshire, and who was executed in 1664 for complicity in the abortive insurrection at Farnley Wood, near Leeds (October 1663), which aimed to restore the Long Parliament. Thomas, however, was educated at Northallerton Free School, under Thomas Smelt, a noted Royalist. He was admitted to Sidney Sussex College, Cambridge, in 1659, but left without taking a degree, and, having become a member of Gray's Inn in 1666, was called to the bar in 1673. He then turned his attention to literature, and in 1674 produced a translation of René Rapin's recent *Réflexions sur la poétique d'Aristote*, which made known to English readers the rational, neo-classical critical principles then current in France. This was followed in 1677 by *The Tragedies of the Last Age*, an epistle in which he "consider'd and examin'd" (and severely criticized) plays by Beaumont and Fletcher, and Milton's *Paradise Lost*, in the light of classical practice and rational principle. In the same year he wrote *Edgar, or the English Monarch*, a "heroick tragedy" in appalling verse, never performed, but published in 1678, of which Sir Sidney Lee, in his article on Rymer for the *Dictionary of National Biography*, rightly said that "the only service [it] rendered to art was to show how a play might faithfully observe all the classical laws without betraying any dramatic quality." His rendering into English of the "Life of Nicias" was included in the collection of translations of Plutarch's *Lives* (1683–86), for which Dryden wrote a life of Plutarch, and in 1693 he published *A Short View of Tragedy*, which contains his notorious attack upon Shakespeare's *Othello* ("a Bloody farce, without salt or savour").

Rymer's critical principles were inherited from the French formalist critics, especially from Jules de la Mesnardière's *Poétique* (1640), from the abbé d'Aubignac's *La Pratique du théâtre* (1657), and from Rapin. Invoking "the practice of the Ancients" and "the Common Sense of all Ages" as his criteria, he insists that dramatic action should be probable and reasonable, that it should instruct by moral precept and example (it was he who coined the term "poetical justice") and that characters should behave either as idealized types or as average representatives of their class. In the *Short View*, in which his neo-classicism is at its narrowest, he rejects all modern drama and recommends a return to Aeschylus. This work provoked many indignant replies, notably from John Dennis (*q.v.*), and from the essayist and critic Charles Gildon who, however, later himself became quite as rigid a formalist as Rymer. That Rymer's criticism stimulated Dryden, the greatest critic of the century, to reformulate his own theories about drama, is clear from Dryden's notes on *The Tragedies of the Last Age*, first published in Jacob Tonson's 1711 edition of Beaumont and Fletcher.

Pope called Rymer "a learned and strict critic," and although he was ridiculed in the 19th century—Macaulay thought him "the worst critic that ever lived"—he did realize, as did few of his contemporaries, that admiration for Elizabethan and Jacobean drama was incompatible with reverence for the classical "rules," and he was, moreover, the first critic to examine a Shakespeare play (*Othello*) systematically. His chief faults were lack of taste and inability to appreciate purely imaginative writing.

Rymer's interest in history, as well as his adherence to the Whigs, is attested by his *General Draught and Prospect of Government in Europe* (1681), a tract which argues, partly from medieval chronicles, the rights of parliaments against royal prerogative. In 1692 he succeeded Thomas Shadwell as historiographer royal, at a salary of £200 a year, and in 1693, when William III's government, probably at the suggestion of Lord Somers and Charles Montague (later earl of Halifax), decided to publish for the first time copies of all past treaties entered into by England, Rymer was appointed editor and granted access to all necessary documents. He worked with great determination, taking as his model Leibniz' *Codex juris gentium diplomaticus* (1693), and corresponding with Leibniz, who influenced him considerably, from 1694 onward. He made use, also, of an Elizabethan manuscript catalogue of treaties compiled between 1570 and 1610 by Arthur Agarde. Unfortunately, he exposed himself to the shafts of Scottish antiquaries, when he ordered, perhaps unwittingly, an ancient forgery from the Chapter House collection, which purported to be a charter of King Malcolm, acknowledging Edward the Confessor's overlordship, to be engraved in facsimile. Rymer later denied that he ever intended to publish this copy. In the ten years he spent collecting materials, he received no remuneration from the treasury for his editorial work, and was forced to cover all expenses from his own resources. By 1698, he had expended £1,253 on the project, engravers and amanuenses alone costing him £240 a year. Many petitions were needed, supported by Montague's influence, before the government would set aside money for printing the work. Eventually the first volume of the *Foedera conventiones literae et cujuscunque generis acta publica, inter reges Angliae, et alios quosvis imperatores, reges, etc.*, which covered the years 1101–1273, was published in 1704. One or more volumes appeared annually until 1713, the year of Rymer's death, when the 15th volume, containing documents dated from 1543 to 1586, was produced. Robert Sanderson, who had been appointed Rymer's assistant in 1707, succeeded him as editor, and published the 16th volume, compiled from Rymer's papers, in 1715, and the 17th, in which the last treaty is dated 1625, in 1717. Sanderson also published three supplemental volumes in 1726, 1732, and 1735, bringing the total to 20. In spite of numerous omissions, occasional errors of dating, inaccurate transcriptions, and the inclusion of many items, without acknowledgment, from printed, not manuscript, sources, and of many not properly either *foedera* or *acta publica*, Rymer's work remains of considerable value to the student of medieval and 16th-century history.

Rymer died in London, on Dec. 14, 1713.

BIBLIOGRAPHY.—The *Syllabus* of the *Foedera*, ed. by Sir T. D. Hardy, 3 vol. (1869–85), provides a good account of Rymer's life and historical work in the prefaces to vol. i and ii. This is corrected and implemented in the introduction to C. A. Zimansky's edition of *The Critical Works of Thomas Rymer* (1956), which includes a full bibliography. For an estimate of Rymer's achievement as editor of the *Foedera*, see D. Douglas, *English Scholars*, 2nd rev. ed. (1951). *See* also G. B. Dutton, "The French Aristotelian Formalists and Thomas Rymer," in *Publications of the Modern Language Association of America*, vol. xxix, pp. 152–188 (1914).

(Jo. C.)

RYSBRACK, JOHN MICHAEL (1694–1770), one of the principal sculptors and designers in England in the 18th century, was born at Antwerp in 1694 and studied there, probably in the workshop of Michael van de Voort. He was also influenced by the sculpture of F. Duquesnoy. He worked in Copenhagen, Paris, and Rome and in 1720 established himself in London, where, except for another journey to France and Italy, he lived until his death on Jan. 8, 1770.

Rysbrack worked in a classical, sometimes eclectic manner, avoiding emphatic gestures, exaggerated asymmetry, and extremes of illusionism. His work includes 16 monuments in Westminster Abbey, the splendid equestrian statue of William III at Bristol, tombs in parish churches all over England and innumerable portrait busts. In some respects Rysbrack outshone L. F. Roubillac, his only rival for preeminence in England at that time. Pyramidal composition and judicious choice of material are characteristic features of Rysbrack's funeral sculpture.

See M. Batten, *Michael Rysbrack, Sculptor* (1954). (J. A. Dr.)

RYSWICK: *see* RIJSWIJK.

RYUKYU ISLANDS (NANSEI-SHOTŌ), a chain of islands and islets extending almost 400 mi. (644 km.) NE-SW from southern Japan to the northern tip of Formosa. The land area of the chain is 848 sq.mi. (2,196 sq.km.), and the population in 1960 was 883,122. The largest and by far the most populous of the islands is Okinawa, which became well known as the site of a fierce battle between U.S. and Japanese forces during World War II. The capital and the largest city is Naha on Okinawa with a population in 1960 of 223,047.

The Ryukyus consist of three major groups: the Amami-guntō

in the north, the Okinawa islands in the central area, and the Sakishima islands to the south. The larger islands are generally volcanic in origin and have mountainous terrain; most of the smaller islands were formed by coral and are relatively flat. The climate is semitropical with a mean annual temperature of 70° F (21.1° C). About 12 to 45 typhoons occur annually, affecting all aspects of life. Major types of plant life include Japanese cedars and pines on the northern islands, and camphor, banyan, and banana trees in the south. Snakes, wild boars, deer, and black rabbits are found on some of the Ryukyus. (X.)

The people of the islands seem to be a result of prehistoric southward migrations from Japan mixed with northward migrations from southeast Asia. They most closely resemble the Japanese in physical type. Similarly, the Ryukyuan language (with its various dialects) is classified with Japanese, although there is no mutual intelligibility. This suggests that the peoples of the islands may be linked historically with those of Japan despite the absence of political unity in the past.

Culturally, the Ryukyuans are subjected to influences emanating from both Japan and China. The islands are primarily rural, with the local farming village providing a basic pattern of life. As in China and Japan, social emphasis lies in kinship, the Ryukyuans having developed the common descent group with its stress on ancestral relationships and consanguinity. This, in turn, may cut across settlement or village lines. Religion relates to kinship, revolving around an ancestral cult with elaborated mortuary observances and tombs. The Ryukyuan family system is somewhat more extended than the Japanese. This and the funerary rituals, indicate south Chinese influence, but the association of Buddhism with an ancestral cult suggests Japanese practice. (R. F. Sr.)

In ancient times the Ryukyus formed an independent kingdom. How early China exerted influence is not known, but a major invasion occurred in the 7th century A.D. Chinese supremacy was established by the late 1300s and for the next five centuries the Ryukyuans paid tribute to China. Contacts with Japan probably began in the 8th century A.D. Japan invaded the Ryukyus in 1607 and joined China in exacting tribute from the islanders. In 1872 the Ryukyuan king became one of Japan's feudal lords, establishing complete Japanese supremacy. With the abolition of feudalism in 1879, the Ryukyus became Okinawa Prefecture.

After the defeat of Japan in World War II, the U.S. took control of the islands. Okinawa was occupied by U.S. military forces and became an important American base. The military government was replaced in 1951 by a U.S. civil administration, headed by a high commissioner. In 1953 the Amami-guntō group was returned to Japan. The islands are locally governed under the auspices of the U.S. administration. The government consists of an executive, a legislative, and a judicial branch. Until 1966 the chief executive was appointed by the U.S. high commissioner after consultation with the 29-member elected legislature. In that year, however, a higher measure of self-government was instituted, and the chief executive was elected by the legislature.

Agriculture is the dominant occupation of the islands, with sweet potatoes and rice the staple foods. Black sugar and canned pineapples are among the leading exports. Traditional industries include lacquer and pottery, while newer enterprises manufacture whale products, industrial compounds, and refined sulfur. U.S. armed forces provide considerable revenue on Okinawa.

Because of high birth rates and declining death rates, a large proportion of the population attends school, and generally about one-third of the annual budget is applied to education. The University of the Ryukyus, established in 1950, annually enrolls more than 2,000 students. (R. B. H.; X.)

RZESZOW, a town in southeastern Poland and capital of the *wojewodztwo* (province) of the same name. Pop. (1960) 62,526. A settlement developed along the Wislok, a tributary of the San River, between two different types of landscape, the Carpathians and the Sandomierz plain, at the place where the route to Hungary branched from the east-west route through the sub-Carpathian region. Both routes are now used by railway lines. Rzeszow is on the main Cracow–Lvov, U.S.S.R., road and railway. Town rights were probably acquired in the mid-14th century. Rzeszow's development ceased in the 17th century during a period of prolonged wars. After the first partition of Poland in 1772 it was seized by Austria and was not returned to Poland until 1918. The metal industry was greatly built up there after World War II; it includes some of the largest plants in Poland producing rolling stock. Cotton and clothing are also manufactured, and there is an expanding food industry. The town has a museum.

RZESZOW WOJEWODZTWO borders on the U.S.S.R. and Czechoslovakia. Area 7,203 sq.mi. (18,656 sq.km.). Pop. (1960) 1,586,157. It consists of two regions: the northern (Sandomierz) plain and the mountainous southern region (the Carpathians); the economy of the province varies accordingly. The submontane portion, with its good loess soils, is a populous agricultural area whereas the southeastern corner is sparsely populated. The most important raw materials are sulfur, of which rich deposits were discovered near Tarnobrzeg and industrially exploited in the 1960s; petroleum in the Carpathians; and natural gas. The principal manufacturing activity is the iron-smelting and metallurgical industry at Stalowa Wola and Mielec. Forests occupy about 30% of the area and are important to the economy; and (after Cracow) it is the second most important province in Poland for cattle breeding. Rymanow and Iwonicz are popular tourist resorts. The economic development of the province is impeded by a deficiency of railways and roads. Besides Rzeszow, the principal towns are Przemysl (pop. [1960] 47,400), Jaroslaw (25,500), Stalowa Wola (22,900), Mielec (22,000), Krosno (25,900), Sanok (17,100) and Debica (16,500). (T. K. W.)

RZHEV, a town in Kalinin *oblast* of the Russian Soviet Federated Socialist Republic, U.S.S.R., stands on both banks of the upper Volga, at the crossing of the trunk railways Moscow–Riga and Leningrad–Bryansk. Pop. (1959) 48,971. First mentioned in 1216, when it was an independent princedom, Rzhev has always been a route centre on the western approaches to Moscow and its history has been stormy. At various times under the princes of Tver or Smolensk, and taken by Lithuania in 1356 for two years, Rzhev passed to Moscow in 1390. In 1610, during the Time of Troubles, it was captured by the Poles. In World War II bitter fighting took place there. The modern town has brick and other building-materials industries, butter and meat processing, timber working and flax retting. (R. A. F.)

17 68

S THIS letter corresponds to the Semitic W (*sin* "tooth"). The Greek treatment of the sibilants that occur in the Semitic alphabet is somewhat complicated. Semitic ≢ (*samech*) appears in Greek as Ξ (*ksi*) with the value in early times of *ss*, later and more generally of *x* or *ks*. The name *samech*, however, which through its Aramaean form became in Greek *sigma*, was applied to the letter Ϟ which corresponded to Semitic W (*sin*) and stood for *s*. In certain Greek alphabets the letter was called by the name *san*. Semitic *ssade* appears in the early alphabets of Thera and Corinth in the form M representing *s*. These alphabets have no *sigma*, while those that have *sigma* do not have M.

Greek forms of the letter were Ϟ, Ɛ, ≺, ʃ, Ϟ. A rounded form appeared in the Chalcidian alphabet and from this it was

NAME OF FORM	APPROXIMATE DATE	FORM OF LETTER
PHOENICIAN	1200 B.C.	W
CRETAN	600	ʔ ʒ
THERAEAN	700-600	ʔ ʃ
ARCHAIC LATIN	700-500	≲
ATTIC	600	ʃ ʒ
CORINTHIAN	600	ʔ ʃ
CHALCIDIAN	600	≲
IONIC	403	ʃ ʒ
ROMAN COLONIAL		ʃ ϛ ʃ S
URBAN ROMAN	PRECLASSICAL	S
FALISCAN	AND	≳ S
OSCAN	CLASSICAL TIMES	≳ ≵
UMBRIAN		⁊
CLASSICAL LATIN AND ONWARD		S

DEVELOPMENT OF THE LETTER "S" FROM THE PHOENICIAN THROUGH CLAS-SICAL LATIN TO THE PRESENT FORM

taken into Latin. Etruscan had no rounded form, but it appears in Umbrian and Faliscan. In Latin cursive writing of the 6th century the form was Ɣ, and from this descended the Irish and Saxon forms Γ. The Carolingian form on the other hand was extended above the line instead of below, *e.g.*, ſ. In England in the 17th century the form was ſ and this is occasionally still seen in handwriting when followed by another *s*. The form ẞ also occurs, the left-hand oblique stroke being really part of a ligature with a preceding letter. There was a Greek minuscule form Ϲ or ϲ of the 9th century A.D., which may be the source both of the Cyrillic ϲ and of the lunate *sigma* ϲ used in some fonts of Greek type at the present time. (*See* also ALPHABET.)

The letter represents an unvoiced sibilant. This has become voiced in English when intervocalic (e.g., *houses, nose*). In most other positions it remains unvoiced (e.g., *sing, save, stamp, speak, aspect*). When doubled the letter represents the unvoiced sound in all positions (e.g., *grasses, miss, assess*). In *vision* and other words ending in *sion* the *s*, provided it is not doubled, has the voiced sound *ž*, and similarly in *pleasure, leisure*.

(B. F. C. A.; J. W. P.)

SAADIA BEN JOSEPH (SAID AL-FAYYUMI) (882–942), the greatest figure in the literary and political history of medieval Judaism, was born at Dilaz in Al Fayyum, Egypt. Nothing certain is known of his father or of his early life. Saadia's literary work appears at a time when learning seemed to be dead in both east and west. Since the completion of the Talmud very little of any literary importance, except for a few midrashim, had been produced among the orthodox (rabbanite) Jews, although the Babylonian schools at Sura and Pumbeditha continued to enjoy a somewhat intermittent prosperity. On the other hand, learning was cultivated among the Karaites. In Saadia, however, the rabbanites found a powerful champion. Almost his first work was an attack on the teaching of 'Anan ben David, the founder of Karaism (*q.v.*). This, like most of Saadia's polemical writings, is no longer extant, but something of its contents may be inferred from references in the author's other works and from the statements of his opponents. The controversy turned largely on the calendar, which of course involved the dates of festivals, and, since the rabbanite calendar had come down from ancient times, opened up the whole question of oral tradition and the authority of the Talmud. The conflict raged for many years, the chief representative of the other side being Solomon ben Yeruham, a virulent if not successful opponent. In 922 Ben Meir, a person of importance in Palestine, attempted to make alterations in the calendar, against the authority of the Babylonian schools. Saadia, who was then at Baghdad, warned him of his errors, refuted him in a work called "The Book of the Festivals," and finally procured his excommunication by David ben Zakkai, the exilarch or head of the Jewish community in Babylonia. The exilarch appointed Saadia as gaon (*q.v.*) of Sura, but within two years the exilarch, influenced by rival scholars, dismissed Saadia, while Saadia retorted by declaring the exilarch deposed (930). After three years of contention David ben Zakkai succeeded in sufficiently bribing the new and needy caliph, who definitely forbade Saadia to act as gaon.

The next four years, spent in retirement at Baghdad, were devoted to literary labours. Eventually a reconciliation was effected with David ben Zakkai, favoured probably by the new caliph al-Radi, and Saadia was reinstated as gaon of Sura in 938. Under his brief rule the school attained the highest reputation among the Jewish communities of east and west. His health was broken, however, and he died in 942.

Works.—Saadia's works were for the most part written in

Arabic, the vernacular of the Jews in the east, so that after the breakup of the Babylonian schools in the middle of the 11th century they would be studied only in Spain, the new centre of Jewish learning, and in Egypt. After the expulsion of the Jews from Spain, Arabic practically ceased to be used by them for literary purposes, and in the rest of Europe (except perhaps in southern Italy) it was never understood. Even some Hebrew works, of great modern interest, must have been regarded at the time as of purely temporary value. The anti-Karaite works against 'Anan, Ibn Sakawaihi and Ben Zuta, the *Kitab at-tamyiz*, *Kitab al-Shara'i*, *Kitab al-'Ibbur* (calendar) and a book on anthropomorphisms, all in Arabic, are lost and only known from quotations. So also are the refutation of the skeptic Hivi of Balkh, and the *Sefer 'Orayoth* (on prohibited marriage, against Karaites). Of the *Sefer ha-Mo'adim* and *Sefer ha-Galui* (against David ben Zakkai), both in Hebrew, some fragments have been recovered.

Closely allied to Saadia's polemical writings are his exegetical works. He translated most of the Bible into Arabic and commented on at least some of the books; the memorial edition of his complete works, edited by J. Derenbourg (1893), contains part of this work. The translation of the five Megilloth (Song of Solomon, Ruth, Lamentations, Ecclesiastes and Esther) and of Daniel (with commentary), usually ascribed to Saadia, are not really by him, but a genuine translation of Daniel, with commentary, exists in manuscript. There is also ascribed to him a midrashic work on the Decalogue. These all, no doubt, exhibit the defects necessary to the time in which their author lived. But it must be remembered that Saadia was a pioneer. Hayyuj, the father of Hebrew grammar, was not yet born, nor had the scientific and comparative study of the language begun. In this respect Saadia contributed little to the subject. But both translations and commentaries are remarkable for their great learning, sound sense and an honest endeavour to arrive at the true meaning of the original. They were thus admirably suited for their purpose, which was, like the earlier Targums and the later work of Moses Mendelssohn (*q.v.*), to render the sacred text more intelligible to the faithful generally and to check the growth of error.

The grammatical work called *Agron*, a sort of dictionary, is lost, as are also the *Kutub al-Lughah* and perhaps other treatises on Hebrew grammar. The explanation of the 70 (really 90) *hapax legomena* in the Bible (these are words or terms used only once and of uncertain meaning) and a poem on the number of letters in the Bible are extant.

On talmudic subjects again little is preserved beyond the *Kitab al-Mawarith* and a short treatise in Hebrew on the 13 *Middoth* or canons of exegesis of R. Ishmael and some *responsa* mostly in Hebrew. The translation of the Mishna, the introduction to the Talmud and other works of the kind are known only by repute.

Of the *Siddur* or arrangement of the liturgy by Saadia, a large part exists in a single manuscript at Oxford, and several additional fragments were recovered from the Geniza (archive) of the old synagogue at Cairo. Numerous other liturgical poems, or parts of them, were obtained from the same source, and several were subsequently published in periodicals. His *Azharoth*, a poetical enumeration of the 613 precepts, in Hebrew, is included in the complete works.

Saadia's philosophical works are (1) a commentary on the *Sefer Yezira*, a mystical treatise ascribed to the patriarch Abraham, which, as a foundation of the Cabala, had great influence on Jewish thought, and was the subject of numerous commentaries; (2) the *Kitab al-Amanat w'al-I'tiqadat* ("Book of Beliefs and Convictions"), written in 933. Its system is based on reason in conjunction with revelation, the two being not opposed but mutually complementary. It is thus concerned, as the title implies, with the rational foundation of the faith and deals with creation, the nature of God, revelation, free will, the soul, the future life and the doctrine of the Messiah. It shows a thorough knowledge of Aristotle, on whom much of the argument is based, and incidentally refutes the views of Christians, Muslims, Brahmans and skeptics such as Hivi. From its nature, however, the work, although of great interest and value, never had the same

wide influence as that of Ibn Gabirol (*q.v.*). The Arabic text was published by S. Landauer (1880), the Hebrew version at Constantinople in 1562 and frequently thereafter. *See also* HEBREW LITERATURE; JEWISH PHILOSOPHY.

BIBLIOGRAPHY.—H. H. Graetz, *History of the Jews* (1926); Steinschneider, *Arab. Literatur der Juden* (1902); W. Bacher, "Saadia ben Joseph" in the *Jewish Encyclopedia*; M. Friedländer in the *Jewish Quarterly Review*, 5:177; S. Poznański in the *Jewish Quarterly Review*, 10:238; J. Guttmann, *Die Religionsphilosophie des Saadias* (1882); S. Schechter, *Saadyana* (1903) (texts from the Cairo Geniza, reprinted from the *Jewish Quarterly Review*). (A. Cy.)

SAALE, a river of Germany and tributary to the Elbe, is 265 mi. (426 km.) long and drains about 10,000 sq.mi. (25,900 sq.km.). It rises in the Fichtelgebirge, and from there flows north and northeast to join the Elbe just above Barby. It crosses Thuringia, first through forested plateau and then through fertile lowland. Its main tributaries are the Ilm and Unstrut (left bank) and Weisse Elster (right bank). Ancient towns along its course include Jena, Naumburg, and Halle. The river has a rapid upper course and an irregular regime. Its upper course has two very large storage dams with lakes: Bleiloch and Hohenwarte. The Saale is navigable by 200-ton barges as far as Naumburg and by those of 1,000 tons to Halle.   (R. E. DI.)

SAALFELD, a town of East Germany, the headquarters of the Saalfeld *Landkreis* (rural district) in the Gera *Bezirk* (district) of the German Democratic Republic. Pop. (1964) 31,048. The town lies 42 mi. (67 km.) SW of Gera by road on the northern edge of the Thuringian Forest. The Saale River flows through the town, which is a railway junction. To the southwest the "fairy grottoes" and the Hubertushöhle are coloured stalactite caves containing mineral springs; they were formerly mines. Nearby to the east of Saalfeld are the state-owned Unterwellenborn iron and steel works. Other industries include the production of electrical machinery, chocolate, and cardboard boxes in Saalfeld; and forestry, slate mining, the manufacture of glass, ceramics, and paper in the rural district.

Saalfeld was first mentioned, in documents dated 899, as a royal palace. A Benedictine monastery was established there in 1074, when the town received its market charter. The present town dates from about 1200 and contains some interesting medieval buildings.

SAAR (French SARRE), a right-bank tributary of the Moselle (Mosel) River, 153 mi. (246 km.) long and draining an area of about 2,800 sq.mi. (7,300 sq.km.). It rises at the foot of the Donon summit in the northern Vosges and flows generally northward to its confluence with the Moselle at Konz, 6 mi. (9 km.) SW of Trier. Within Germany the Saar flows in meanders (which north of Merzig are deeply entrenched and include a remarkable hairpin bend above Mettlach) through the Saar coalfield and the wooded southern outliers of the Hunsrück. Its chief tributaries are the left-bank Nied and the right-bank Blies and Prims. The northern part of the valley is a wine-growing district; the middle stretch between Saarbrücken and Dillingen is a centre of heavy industry. The Saar is canalized upstream of Völklinger and is navigable from its mouth to its junction near Sarralbe (Saaralben) with the 39-mi. Houillères Canal, which joins the Rhine-Marne Canal.   (R. E. DI.)

SAARBRÜCKEN, a city in West Germany and capital of the *Land* (state) of Saarland, Federal Republic of Germany, lies on both banks of the Saar River, 100 mi. (161 km.) SW of Frankfurt. Saarbrücken, which was formed in 1909 from the union of the former Saarbrücken with Malstatt-Burbach and St. Johann, is the centre of the Saar's industrial, commercial, and cultural life. Pop. (1961) 130,705. It is finely situated among wooded hills and has been called the city of parks and Baroque architecture. Among buildings of historic interest are the old town hall and the Baroque Ludwigskirche (both of the 18th century), and the 13th-century Stiftskirche, a Gothic church in the St. Arnual district of the town. The 18th-century castle, formerly belonging to the princes of Nassau-Saarbrücken, stands on the site of the earlier royal castle of Sarabrucca; the castle church is of the 15th century. There is a university, an advanced college for electrical engineering and machine construction, and colleges for adult education, arts and crafts, music, local government, and other specialized studies. The town is the seat of the Saar parliament and government and of the government's administrative offices. The district and higher courts meet there.

Situated in one of the world's great coal-mining regions, Saarbrücken is principally an industrial city. Its chief importance lies in its iron and steel industries, but manufactures, which are many and various, include optical instruments, lime and cement, soap, sugar, and foodstuffs. There are breweries, potteries, and printing works. The international Saar fair is held there annually.

Saarbrücken is a frontier town lying at the intersection of Germany's chief arteries of road and rail communication with France, the Netherlands, Belgium, Luxembourg, Switzerland, and Italy, as well as with the rest of Germany. There is an airport to the east of the city in the district of Ensheim.

History.—The town's history has been traced back to Celtic times from the discoveries of coins, jewels, and other artifacts. During the 1st and 3rd centuries there were Roman settlements where Saarbrücken now stands, but an entirely German settlement was later established by the Franks. The present town grew up around the royal castle of Sarabrucca, built by the Frankish kings and first mentioned in A.D. 999. Its early rulers were the bishops of Metz and the counts of Saarbrücken. The city received its charter in 1321. It belonged to the counts of Nassau-Saarbrücken from 1381 to 1793, when it was occupied by the French. In 1815 it passed to Prussia. Saarbrücken became the capital of the Saarland in 1919. As a vital centre of coal production, industry, and communications, it was subjected to heavy bombing during World War II. By the late 1950s, however, extensive rebuilding had restored it to its former status.

(Fr. Sc.)

SAAREMAA (formerly ÖSEL), an island in the Estonian Soviet Socialist Republic, U.S.S.R., lies to the westward of the mainland of Estonia, from which it is separated by the Suur Väin (Sur-Vyain) Strait. To the north and west is the Baltic, to the south the Gulf of Riga. The greatest length of the island is from southwest to northeast, 106 km. (65 mi.), and its area is 1,050 sq.mi. There is a link by causeway with the smaller island of Muhu (Mukhu) to the northeast. The island is low-lying, the highest point being no more than 165 ft. above sea level. Saaremaa consists of Silurian rocks, including limestones, with a covering in places of glacial materials. In parts the surface is stony, soils are poor, and vegetation scanty. Elsewhere the surface is marshy, forest-covered (mainly with coniferous species), or suitable for arable farming or grazing, cattle breeding being the principal farming activity. Fishing is a supplementary occupation. Economic minerals include only various building materials. The largest town on the island is the resort of Kuressaare (Kingisepp) on the south coast, renowned for its mud baths.

(J. P. Co.)

SAARINEN, the name of two architects, father and son, both major figures in the development of modern architecture.

(GOTTLIEB) ELIEL SAARINEN (1873–1950) was born Aug. 20, 1873, in Rantasalmi, Fin., and became the foremost architect of his generation in Finland before he moved to the United States in 1923. By 1914 he was widely known in Europe for his Helsinki railroad station (1905–14) and urban planning projects for Reval, Estonia, and Canberra, Austr. In 1922 he won second prize in the Chicago Tribune Tower competition. His design, with its bold approach to massing, had a far more profound influence on skyscraper design in the United States than did the winning design.

From 1932 to 1948 Saarinen was president of the Cranbrook Academy of Art at Bloomfield Hills, near Detroit, Mich., and thereafter, until his death, head of the graduate department of architecture and city planning. He designed a group of buildings in Bloomfield Hills, including the Cranbrook School for boys (1927), the Kingswood School for girls (1931), the Science Museum (1933), and the Art Academy (1934). In 1947 he and his son Eero won the American Institute of Architects' highest award for their design for an addition to the Smithsonian Institution, Washington, D.C. Notable are his two churches: Tabernacle Church of Christ in Columbus, Ind. (1942), and Christ Lutheran

Church in Minneapolis, Minn. (1950)—his last and perhaps his finest building. His writings include: *The City: Its Growth, Its Decay, Its Future* (1943) and *Search for Form* (1948). Eliel Saarinen died at Bloomfield Hills on July 1, 1950.

His son, EERO SAARINEN (1910–1961), was born Aug. 20, 1910, at Kirkkonummi, Fin., and began his career in his father's office. They collaborated from 1937 till the elder Saarinen's death in 1950. Eero Saarinen first received independent notice in 1948 for his stainless steel arch that won first prize in the St. Louis Jefferson National Expansion Memorial competition. The General Motors Technical Center in Warren, Mich., built from his design (1948–56), won him national acclaim. Among his other notable works are: chapel and auditorium at the Massachusetts Institute of Technology, Cambridge (1956); U.S. embassy, London (1956); Trans World Airlines terminal at Kennedy (formerly Idlewild) Airport, New York (1962); Dulles Airport, near Washington, D.C. (1962); the Beaumont Theater, Lincoln Center, New York (1963); and the North Christian Church, Columbus, Ind. (1964). Eero Saarinen died at Ann Arbor, Mich., on Sept. 1, 1961.

(H. Mn.)

SAARLAND, since 1957 one of the *Länder* (states) of the Federal Republic of Germany, bounded west by Luxembourg and south by France. Area 991 sq.mi. (2,567 sq.km.). Its capital is Saarbrücken. The heart of the Saarland is an area of woodland and meadows in hilly country crossed by the valley of the Saar. This is underlain by the coal measures, and the mines and homes of the miners are dispersed in the wooded countryside. Along the valley, from Saarbrücken to Völklingen, are concentrated blast furnaces and steelworks. This lowland is framed northward by the edge of the Hunsrück highland and southward by the scarps of Lorraine. About half the total area is cultivated and nearly one-third is forest.

(R. E. Di.)

History.—From 1381 to 1793 the city of Saarbrücken on the Saar River was ruled by the counts of Nassau-Saarbrücken, the territory around it, although inhabited by a German-speaking population, being latterly much influenced by, and partially ruled, by France in the 150 years which followed the treaties of Westphalia (1648). After the defeat of Napoleon the Saar Valley was included in the new Prussian province on the Rhine except for a small portion which was given to Bavaria. After World War I the Saar mines were ceded to the French state "as compensation for the damage to the north of France and as part payment toward the total reparation," and in January 1920 the Saar was placed under a governing commission of the League of Nations for 15 years, at the end of which time a plebiscite was to be held enabling the inhabitants to choose between Germany, France, or a continuation of the authority of the League.

The first president of the governing commission was a French chauvinist, Victor Rault. His attitude, and above all the French occupation of the Ruhr in 1923, aroused much anti-French feeling in the Saar, causing the first large-scale miners' strike there which lasted for 100 days. After this the Saar prospered under League of Nations rule, but when the full force of the Nazi propaganda machine was brought to bear upon the Saarlanders in 1933 it was easy enough to arouse antiforeign feelings together with chauvinistic exaltation and personal fear. When it came to the plebiscite on Jan. 13, 1935, the attempts made by the League to ensure a free and secret vote failed to carry much conviction, and more than 90% of the votes went to Germany with 8.8% for the status quo and only 0.4% for France. The Saar territory was therefore handed over to Germany, which bought back the coal mines as the Treaty of Versailles had stipulated.

In 1945 the Saar was occupied by the French. Two years later, having slightly extended its frontiers, the French military governor, Gilbert Grandval, arranged for the election of a representative assembly. The new Diet consisted mainly of representatives of the Christian People's Party led by a Catholic, Johannes Hoffmann, who had opposed the Nazis in 1935, and of Social Democrats; it agreed to the political autonomy of the Saar within a diplomatic, tariff, and financial union with France. By a Franco-Saar convention (1950), the Saar mines were leased to France for 50 years.

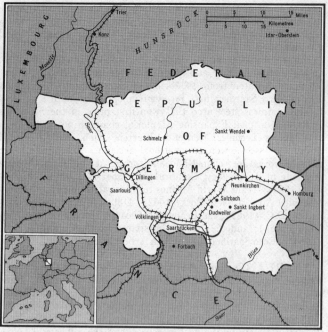

SAARLAND REGION OF THE FEDERAL REPUBLIC OF GERMANY

Hoffmann was elected prime minister of the autonomous Saar in 1947. He was attacked by German patriots as the tool of France, but his second success in the elections of November 1952 showed that he was not unpopular. On this occasion his party alone, apart from his Socialist allies, polled 54.8% of the valid votes, while only 24.4% of the voters spoiled their papers to indicate their support of the suppressed pro-German parties. Indeed, because of its autonomy, the Saar recovered economically faster than the rest of Germany, and enjoyed more generous social services. It was only in 1954 that Hoffmann and autonomy lost ground, partly because of the failure of the European Defense Community project with which he linked his policy, and partly because West German prosperity by then magnetically attracted the sympathies of the Saarlanders.

In October 1954 the French and German governments agreed to a statute for the Saar according to which French control should be replaced by that of the Western European Union; the Saarlanders were to give consent to this plan by referendum, the prohibited parties which favoured reunion with Germany being permitted three months before the vote. The referendum was fixed for Oct. 23, 1955, and the pro-German parties therefore began their activities in July, and immediately announced that to reject the statute would be to vote for Germany. Their campaign, dominated by the lawyer, Heinrich Schneider, was passionate, and culminated in rejecting the "Europeanization" of the Saar by 423,434 votes to 201,973. Hoffmann immediately resigned and the pro-German parties formed a government led by Hubert Ney. A new Diet was elected in December 1955, leaving the party position unchanged with the Hoffmann party still holding 13 of the 40 seats. The French agreed in principle to the return of the Saar to Germany and negotiations began early in 1956. In June agreement was reached. The Saar became the tenth *Land* of the Federal Republic of Germany on Jan. 1, 1957. France was allowed to continue to exploit the Warndt coalfield on the Franco-Saar border and to canalize the Moselle between Coblenz and Thionville; concessions were made by France about the projected Alsace Canal and the damming of the Rhine.   (E. WI.)

Population and Economy.—The population of Saarland was 1,072,600 in 1961. In the early 1960s the working population exceeded 410,000, of whom 56% were employed in industry and building (including 47,000 in coal mining and 44,000 in iron and steel production), 19% in commerce and transport, 20% in public and private service, and 5% in agriculture.

The principal towns are Saarbrücken, Neunkirchen (*qq.v.*), Völklingen, Saarlouis (*q.v.*), Sankt Ingbert (*q.v.*), Sulzbach, Hom-

burg, and Dillingen. The population is predominantly Roman Catholic (73%), with 25% Protestants. The common and official language is German, but at the University of the Saarland at Saarbrücken, French and German are on an equal footing.

In July 1959 the economy of Saarland was completely integrated with that of the Federal Republic. Its annual production of about 16,000,000 tons of coal, 3,500,000 tons of pig iron, and 4,000,000 tons of crude steel is the base of French interest in the territory, whose traditional associations are with Germany. The coal is used in the Lorraine iron and steel works, following technical improvements enabling some Saar coal to be made into coke. The Saarland iron and steel works, with more than 25 blast furnaces, draw their ores from the Lorraine ore field.

The industrialized belt lies along the Saar Valley and contains most of the population. Chemical, glass, and ceramic industries are pursued, in addition to coal, iron, and steel, giving the area a balanced economy. The economic future of Saarland, despite its integration in the Federal Republic of Germany, remains closely linked with Lorraine. The region is an important focus of the European Coal and Steel Community (*see* EUROPEAN UNITY).

The main centre of communication is Saarbrücken, which is an important rail junction and from which a motorway leads eastward to join the Cologne–Basel motorway near Mannheim.

(R. E. DI.)

BIBLIOGRAPHY.—R. Capot-Rey, *La Région industrielle Sarroise* (1934); H. Overbeck and G. W. Sante, *Saaratlas* (1934); R. Reinhard and K. Voppel, *Land und Volk an der Saar* (1934); S. Wambaugh, *The Saar Plebiscite* (1940); H. Hirsch, *The Saar Territory* (1946); *Materialen zur Saarfrage*, 5 vol. (1949); R. E. Dickinson, *Germany: a General and Regional Geography* (1953); F. Hellwig, *Saar zwischen Ost und West* (1954); Statistical Office of the Saar, *Statistisches Handbuch für das Saarland* (annually from 1955); J. Freymond, *Saar Conflict, 1945–1955* (1960); J. Hoffmann, *Das Ziel war Europa: der Weg der Saar 1945–1955* (1964).

SAARLOUIS, a town of Germany in the Saarland, which in 1957 was included in the Federal Republic of Germany, lies on both banks of the Saar River, 41 mi. (66 km.) S of Trier by road. Pop. (1961) 36,807. Situated on the fringe of the Saar coalfield, Saarlouis has industrial surroundings, especially iron and steel works. It was founded by Louis XIV of France as a fortress, built in 1680–85 by Sebastien Vauban. In 1815 the town was ceded to Prussia, which razed the fortress after 1889. The parade ground and remnants of the fortifications still exist. The town centre, largely destroyed in 1944–45, was rebuilt. From 1936 to 1945 the town was called Saarlautern.

SAAVEDRA FAJARDO, DIEGO DE (1584–1648), Spanish diplomatist and man of letters, born at Algezares (Murcia) on May 6, 1584, is best known for his anti-Machiavellian emblem book, the *Idea de un Príncipe político-cristiano* (1640; English translation by Sir James Astry, 1700), which urged a return to traditional virtues as the remedy for national decadence; the extent of Saavedra's erudition and his personal knowledge of the Europe of his day are evident. His principal other works are the *República literaria* (1655), of interest as representing Baroque critical attitudes to earlier and contemporary literature, and the *Corona gótica* (1646), a history of Spain under the Goths. He died at Madrid on Aug. 24, 1648.

See *Obras*, ed. by A. G. Palencia (1946).   (F. S. R.)

SAAVEDRA LAMAS, CARLOS (1878–1959), Argentine lawyer, professor, diplomat, and Nobel Peace Prize winner, was born on Nov. 1, 1878, in Buenos Aires. He received the degree of doctor of law *summa cum laude* from the University of Buenos Aires (1903). He held numerous political posts, appointive and elective, in the municipal and national governments of Argentina, including those of minister of justice and public education (1915), and minister of foreign affairs (1932–38). He was Argentine delegate to conferences on world peace and international law, and became a member of learned societies and academies the world over. For his untiring work for world peace he received the Nobel Prize (1936) and numerous decorations and honours from Latin-American and European governments. He held various professorial chairs in the social sciences at the University of Buenos Aires and was rector of that university from 1941 to 1943. He wrote treatises on economics, education, and Argentine and international law, some of which have been translated into French and English. His most noteworthy work is *Por la Paz de las Américas* (1937). He died in Buenos Aires on May 5, 1959. (C. S. Sn.)

SABA (Sabas), **SAINT** (439–532), founder and first abbot of the monastery of Mar Saba, was born at Moutalaske near Caesarea in Cappadocia (modern Kayseri, Turk.). As a child he joined a local monastery, where he spent ten years before moving to a monastery in Palestine (457). In 469 he became a hermit for five days of the week and in 474 left the monastery to live alone in the western desert. In 478, in obedience to a vision, he moved to a cave by the Kidron, about halfway between Jerusalem and the northern end of the Dead Sea, where in 484 he began to be joined by other solitaries living in cells nearby. He was ordained in 491 and made abbot of his community, the Great Laura of Mar Saba, which is still in existence. Saba was a defender of the faith against the Monophysites, and founded other monasteries and religious houses in Palestine. He died at Mar Saba in 532, on Dec. 5, which is kept as his feast day. *See also* Monasticism: *Eastern Monasticism.*

See H. Leclercq in F. Cabrol (ed.), *Dictionnaire d'archéologie chrétienne et de liturgie,* vol. xv, col. 189–211 (1950).

SABAEANS, a people occupying the kingdom of Saba in pre-Islamic southwest Arabia. Mention of them, and of the kingdom under the name Sheba, is made several times in the Bible, notably in the legend of King Solomon and the queen of Sheba. The Assyrian annals mention two occasions when tribute was sent to the king of Assyria by kings of the Sabai; first, *c.* 715 B.C. by Itiamra, and again about 30 years later by Karibailu. The Greek geographer Eratosthenes (3rd century B.C.) describes the Sabaeans, with a capital at Mariaba (the modern Ma'rib), along with three other folk, the Minaeans, Qatabanians, and Hadhramautites, as constituting the main elements in the population of southwest Arabia. (*See* Arabia: *History: The South Arabian Kingdoms.*) In 24 B.C. a Roman expedition under Marcus Aelius Gallus, prefect of Egypt, had to beat a disastrous retreat after getting as far as Ma'rib. The *Periplus of the Erythraean Sea* (an account of the Red Sea and Indian Ocean, written in Greek and usually dated to the mid-1st century A.D.) speaks of a joint kingdom of Sabaeans and Homerites (Himyar), the royal residence being at Zafar in the southern Yemeni Highlands. A little later Pliny referred to the Sabaeans as a wealthy folk, at the same time describing the Homerites as "most numerous"; but in the Greek authorities of the 4th century onward the names of all these older people fade out, except for the Homerites, a term which they apply indiscriminately to the inhabitants of the whole of southwest Arabia.

These meagre details are capable of being considerably amplified from the vast mass of inscriptions left by the Sabaeans themselves. Unfortunately, these texts are often very difficult to interpret, and many points remain obscure and the subject of sharp dispute among specialists. But paleographic and linguistic criteria indicate pretty clearly that a broad division of the Sabaean inscriptions can be made into three periods, of which, however, only the last can be dated with certainty, namely from the last quarter of the 4th century A.D. to the third quarter of the 6th century.

The kernel of the Sabaeans' land was divided into two parts: a highland area, coinciding with the mountain massif of central Yemen, around present-day San'a'; and a lowland area lying to the east and southeast of the highland area and consisting principally of the extensive drainage basin of the Wadi Adhana. The latter, in its lower course, breaks through a rocky barrier, the Jabal Balaq, and soon afterward loses itself in the Ramlat Sab'atein, a western outlier of the great sand desert of the Rub' al Khali. Just below this opening in the Jabal Balaq is situated Ma'rib, the Sabaean capital. A little to the west, on one of the tributary valleys draining into the Wadi Adhana, is Sirwah, a site second only to Ma'rib in importance. Ma'rib owes its situation and its prosperity to the opening in the Jabal Balaq where it was possible, by the construction of a dam, to control substantial amounts of water for the irrigation of the valley immediately below it. The great dam of Ma'rib figures prominently in Islamic legend, which attributes the downfall of the pre-Islamic civilization of south Arabia to the bursting of the dam. This account probably puts the effect before the cause: it is known from the inscriptions that the dam was extensively repaired in the 5th and 6th centuries A.D., and the likelihood is that it was political weakness that led to inability to continue repairing it, rather than the other way round.

The culture of the Sabaeans, and of the other ancient peoples in the area, is Semitic, having numerous and marked affinities with the culture of the Semitic peoples to the north of them. Unless, therefore, south Arabia is to be envisaged as the original home of the Semites, it must be concluded that in prehistoric times one or more waves of Semitic immigrants entered south Arabia from the north, bringing with them their Semitic culture which they imposed on a pre-Semitic population substratum. An ethnic mingling of this kind is perhaps hinted at by the biblical "genealogies" (fictional, of course, as genealogies in the strict sense, but representing faithfully Hebrew ideas of the geography and ethnology of the world known to the writers): for in Gen. 10:28, Sheba is numbered among the descendants of Shem (*i.e.,* as Semites), whereas in Gen. 10:7, Sheba is also listed as descended from Ham, along with the Egyptians and the peoples of east Africa.

In the early Sabaean period, besides "kings of Saba," individuals are found styling themselves *"mkrb* of Saba." It was for long thought that the latter constituted a dynasty of priest-rulers antedating the institution of the kingship, but more recent research indicates that kings and *mkrbs* were contemporaneous. The modern tendency is to regard the title of *mkrb* as indicating some political function exercised parallel with the kingly function. The early period is characterized above all by a tremendous outburst of building activity, principally at Ma'rib and Sirwah, and most of the great temples and monuments, including the Ma'rib Dam, date back to this period. Further, there was an ever-shifting pattern of alliances and wars between Saba and other peoples of southwest Arabia—not only the important kingdoms of Qataban (Gr. Kattabanoi) and Hadhramaut (Gr. Chatramotitai) but also a number of lesser but still independent kingdoms and city-states.

The date to be assigned to the earliest Sabaean inscriptions is a matter of controversy. Some date them back to the 8th century B.C. This view was founded mainly on the identification of the two "kings of Saba" who sent tribute to Assyria around 700 B.C. with two *mkrbs* of Saba, Yithi'amar and his son Karibail. Unfortunately, both kings and *mkrbs* of the early period used altogether only some half dozen names, which constantly recur in connection with different individuals; hence it is extremely hazardous to attempt to identify an individual by name alone. Another school of thought gives the 5th century B.C. as the beginning of the early Sabaean period, as known inscriptionally. In either case, several centuries of development certainly preceded the appearance of the inscriptional material, for the bulk of the early Sabaean texts already attest a fully evolved civilization. Early Sabaean texts from the highland area are comparatively few, and it is apparent that political and cultural emphasis in this period was centred in the lowlands.

The chronological boundary between the early and middle Sabaean periods is uncertain but may be tentatively regarded as somewhere around the 1st century B.C. In the middle Sabaean period there is no longer any mention of a *mkrb.* The names of the kings were no longer chosen from the restricted list used in the early period. While some kings still contented themselves with the title "king of Saba," the majority had the extended title "king of Saba and the Raydan territory." It is uncertain exactly where the latter was, for Raydan is a geographical name occurring in several places. Some think that Jabal Raydan close to Zafar is meant, which has the advantage of fitting in with the *Periplus* reference to a dual monarchy with the royal residence at Zafar. Otherwise "Raydan" might refer to the peak of that name which is the most conspicuous feature in the landscape of Wadi Bayhan; this would imply that Saba had absorbed the former Qatabanian dominions, which were centred on the Wadi Bayhan.

A number of the middle Sabaean kings had affiliations with the tribe of Hamdan, located in the highland massif; in addition, there is a notable increase in the frequency of texts from this area. Evidently the political emphasis by the middle period had shifted from lowland to highland Saba. There were still wars and alliances with other peoples of southwest Arabia, but the smaller independent city-states had then disappeared and the tribe of Himyar (the Greek Homerites) made its first appearance on the Sabaean scene. Mention is also made for the first time in the inscriptions of "Arabs," *i.e.*, nomad Bedouin.

Toward the end of the 3rd century A.D., a powerful king named Shamir Yuhar'ish (who seems incidentally to be the first really historical personage whose fame has survived in the Islamic traditions) assumed the title "king of Saba and the Raydan territory and of Hadhramaut and Yamanat." By this time, therefore, the political independence of Hadhramaut had succumbed to Saba, which had thus become the controlling power in all southwest Arabia. In the mid-4th century A.D. it underwent a temporary eclipse, for the title of "king of Saba and the Raydan territory" was then claimed by the king of Aksum on the east African coast (*see* ETHIOPIA: *History: Kingdom of Aksum*). At the end of the 4th century, south Arabia was again independent under the rule of a "king of Saba and the Raydan territory and Hadhramaut and Yamanat." For the events of the 6th century *see* ARABIA: *History*.

Religion.—The religion of the Sabaeans down to the 3rd century A.D., like that of the other peoples of south Arabia, was a polytheism having strong similarities with the cults of the northern Semitic world. Of particular importance in the pantheon was a triad of deities: 'Athtar the Venus-star (masculine in south Arabia, although Sidonian Astarte, Canaanite Ashtoreth, and Mesopotamian Ishtar, all varieties of the same name, are feminine), a moon-god, and a sun-goddess. The moon-god was adored in Saba under the name Ilmuqah, and the function of this deity seems to have been in the early Sabaean period principally that of a national god, whose cult served as a unifying factor, binding together a variety of communities having local cults and loyalties covering smaller areas than the Sabaean state as a whole. "The children of Ilmuqah" appears to be a term roughly equivalent to "Sabaean citizens."

In the middle Sabaean period, on the other hand, the Hamdanid kings and their vassals in the highland area adhered to the cult of a deity named Ta'lab, whose shrine, Riyam, was situated in the Wadi Kharid, which runs northeast from San'a'. At the same time, a detached area of the Ilmuqah cult lay at and around 'Umran in the southwest corner of the highland area.

The ancient polytheism disappeared after the episode of Aksumite domination in the 4th century A.D. There followed a monotheistic cult of Rahman "the merciful" (sometimes also qualified as "the lord of heaven"); and finally in the 6th century explicit Jewish and Christian formulas. In the Christian formulas the name Rahman is applied to the first person of the Trinity, followed by "and Christ Victorious and the Holy Spirit," or "and His Messiah and the Holy Spirit."

BIBLIOGRAPHY.—J. Ryckmans, *L'Institution monarchique en Arabie méridionale avant l'islam* (1951), to be used with caution, since the author subsequently abandoned some of the hypotheses here put forward specially in matter of chronology; G. Ryckmans, *Les Religions arabes préislamiques,* 2nd ed. (1951); J. Pirenne, *La Grèce et Saba* (1955).
(A. F. L. B.)

SABAH, a state of the federation of Malaysia (*q.v.*) forming the northern tip of Borneo. It was formerly a British colony. Pop. (1965 est.) 518,000; cap. Jesselton (pop. [1964 est.] 32,-000). Area 29,490 sq.mi. (76,380 sq.km.). Sabah is bounded on the north by the South China and Sulu seas; on the southwest by Sarawak; and on the south by Indonesian Borneo (Kalimantan).

SABANG, a port of Indonesia situated on We Island, about 20 mi. N of Kutaradja, the capital of Atjeh (Achin) Province in northern Sumatra, 308 mi. (496 km.) from Penang, Malaysia (from which it lies due west) and 1,100 mi. (1,770 km.) from Jakarta. Pop. (1960 est.) 10,000.

Sabang, a free port, is the first port of call in the Malay archipelago for vessels coming from the west, being the westernmost point of Indonesia at the entrance to the Straits of Malacca. The harbour, built in 1887, principally as a coaling station, is sheltered by hills and high stretches of coastline from the heavy swell of the Indian Ocean and its strong winds.

SABARAGAMUWA, a province consisting of generally hilly country stretching in an arc along the southwestern flank of the main central highlands of Ceylon. Area 1,893 sq.mi. (4,903 sq.km.). Pop. (1960 est.) 1,080,000. The dominant rocks are the altered sediments of the Khondalites, whose inclinations are apparent in the series of parallel ridges and valleys that are so characteristic of the Ratnapura District, though they are less well developed in the northern part of the province. The ridges of this series increase in height southward till they culminate in the Rakwana Hills (more than 4,000 ft. [1,200 m.]) overlooking the Walawe Ganga, which forms the eastern boundary of the province. On its inland side the province terminates along the line of the great vertical escarpment of the central highlands, which rises to 7,360 ft. (2,243 m.) in Adams Peak.

The major part of the province lies in the wet zone of Ceylon, with rain at most seasons of the year. The annual total approaches 200 in. (5,100 mm.) near Ratnapura but is somewhat less to the north, south, and west. The extreme eastern part of the province, in the Walawe watershed, lies in the dry zone and suffers drought in the southwest monsoon (*see* CEYLON: *Physical Geography*). Much of the province is now under cultivation, and the vegetation of considerable areas has degraded into *kekilla* (fern land).

It is known that Sabaragamuwa was peopled in prehistoric times, and it is thought that it derives its name from the Habaras (Veddas) who once inhabited it. Sabaragamuwa played relatively little part in the ancient civilization of Ceylon, though Adams Peak was very early a place of worship and, from the Polonnaruwa period, of pilgrimage. Later Sabaragamuwa became of greater importance: it was a province under the Portuguese and grew cinnamon for the Dutch. However, much of the province remained uncultivated till the planting of rubber in the 20th century.

Kandyan Sinhalese formed the majority of the population at the 1953 census, but there were also 141,539 Indians (mainly estate workers). The chief towns are Ratnapura (*q.v.*; pop. [1963] 21,582) and Kegalla, both district capitals.

The northern part of the province, around Kegalla, has villages of the wet-zone type, with rice fields and groves of coconut, areca nut, and other trees. Such villages thin out in the central part of Sabaragamuwa and become of dry-zone type on the Walawe watershed. The chief product of a wide area of the province is rubber, which covers about 225,000 ac. Some tea is also grown. The main railway to Kandy runs across the northern tip of Sabaragamuwa, and the Ratnapura area is served by a narrow-gauge line. (B. H. F.)

SABARKANTHA, a district in the northeast of Gujarat State, India. Area 2,843 sq.mi.; pop. (1961) 918,587. The district, which formed part of Bombay State until 1960, includes some areas of the former Sabarkantha Agency. The agency occupied a large tract in northwestern Gujarat and five detached areas to the southeast; it merged with Bombay State in 1948. The capital is Himatnagar (pop. [1961] 15,287). To the south and west most of the land is cultivated. Chief crops are wheat, rice, millet, cotton, the herb sesamum, and sugarcane. Weaving and the dyeing of silk and cotton yarn are the main industries. (M. R. P.)

SABATIER, (LOUIS) AUGUSTE (1839–1901), French Protestant theologian, who applied to New Testament studies the methods of historical criticism and, particularly through his symbolic interpretation of Christian dogma, exerted influence on the Modernist movement (*see* LIBERALISM, THEOLOGICAL), was born at Vallon, Ardèche, in the Cévennes, on Oct. 22, 1839. He was educated at the Protestant Theological Faculty of Montauban and the universities of Tübingen and Heidelberg. After four years' work as a pastor he became professor of reformed dogmatics at Strasbourg (1867–73) and then (1877) at the newly established Protestant Theological Faculty at Paris. He died April 12, 1901.

Among Sabatier's works were *The Apostle Paul* (1870; English translation 1891); *Outlines of a Philosophy of Religion* (1897; English translation 1897); and his posthumous *Religions of Authority and the Religion of the Spirit* (1903; English translation 1904).

See E. Ménégoz, "The Theology of Auguste Sabatier of Paris," *Expository Times,* 15:30–34 (1903–04).

SABATIER, PAUL (1854–1941), French organic chemist, shared the Nobel Prize for Chemistry in 1912 with Victor Grignard for researches in catalytic organic synthesis, and particularly for discovering the use of nickel in hydrogenation (the addition of hydrogen to molecules of carbon compounds). Born at Carcassonne, Nov. 5, 1854, Sabatier studied at the École Normale Supérieure and under P. E. Marcellin Berthelot at the Collège de France, taking his doctor's degree in 1880. After a year at Bordeaux, he moved to the University of Toulouse in 1882, where he became professor (1884) and dean (1905).

Sabatier's discoveries formed the bases of the margarine, oil hydrogenation, and synthetic methanol industries, as well as of numerous laboratory syntheses. He explored nearly the whole field of catalytic syntheses in organic chemistry, personally investigating several hundred hydrogenation and dehydrogenation reactions, showing that several other metals besides nickel possess catalytic activity, though in smaller degree. He also studied catalytic hydration and dehydration, examining carefully both the feasibility of specific reactions and the general activity of the various catalysts.

Sabatier's great discovery was made in 1897 when he and his pupil J. B. Senderens passed ethylene over hot nickel, in an effort to prepare a nickel compound of ethylene. They believed that since carbon monoxide, which has unsaturated valences, combines with nickel to form a carbonyl, then ethylene, too, which is also an unsaturated compound, might form an analogous compound with nickel. Actually, they obtained much carbon, indicating decomposition of the ethylene, and some ethane. Concluding that the ethane could have come only from undecomposed ethylene which had been reduced by hydrogen formed from the ethylene which had decomposed, they tried passing a mixture of hydrogen and ethylene over the nickel, and immediately obtained a smooth reduction. (*See also* HYDROGENATION.)

Sabatier was invited to succeed Henri Moissan at the University of Paris, but he remained at the University of Toulouse until his retirement in 1930. He died Aug. 14, 1941.

See H. S. Taylor, *J. Amer. Chem. Soc.*, 66:1615 (1944); H. Vincent, *C. R. Acad. Clerm.-Ferrand*, 213:281 (1941).   (P. O.)

SABATIER, PAUL (1858–1928), French historian who is chiefly remembered as a biographer of St. Francis of Assisi, was born at Saint-Michel-de-Chabrillanoux (Ardèche) on Aug. 3, 1858. A Calvinist from birth, he began his studies at the Protestant faculty of theology in Paris in 1880 and became pastor of St. Nicholas, Strasbourg, in 1885. He was expelled from Alsace in 1889 because he refused to become a German subject, and although he was given a parish in the Cévennes, ill health forced him to retire and he devoted himself to historical research. He was professor of Protestant theology at Strasbourg from 1919 until his death there on March 4, 1928.

Sabatier's *Vie de St. François d'Assise* (1893; Eng. trans. 1894) enjoyed an immediate and spectacular success, running through more than 40 editions during its author's lifetime. The work, however, has many defects, not the least of which is Sabatier's disregard for the ideal of historical objectivity. He viewed St. Francis as an earlier counterpart of the 19th-century Protestant liberal, whose obedience to the church was mere conformity and who was in reality the leader of the laity in the 12th century in rebellion against ecclesiastical authority.

SABAZIUS, in Greek mythology, a Phrygian or Thracian deity frequently identified with Dionysus and sometimes with Zeus. His worship, which was connected with that of Cybele and Attis, reached Greece in the 5th century B.C. By the late 2nd century B.C. Jews in Asia Minor identified Zeus Sabazius with their God of Sabaoth (God of Hosts). The etymology of the name Sabazius is uncertain. The commonest representation of him is in the form of a votive hand with the fingers in the gesture of benediction, adorned with various emblems whose significance is obscure.

See K. Prümm, *Religionsgeschichtliches Handbuch für den Raum der altchristlichen Umwelt*, 2nd ed., p. 650 (1954); C. Blinkenberg, *Archaeologische Studien*, pp. 66–128 (1904).   (H. W. PA.)

SABBATAI ZEBI (ZEVI or SEBI) (1626–1676), Jewish Cabalist and pseudo-Messiah, was born in Smyrna (modern Izmir, Turk.) of Spanish descent. As a boy he was attracted by the mysticism of Isaac Luria (*q.v.*), which led him to adopt the ascetic life. He passed his days and nights in a condition of ecstasy, and attracted a steadily increasing number of followers. Sabbatai began to dream of the fulfillment of messianiac hopes, being supported in his vision by the outbreak of English millenarianism (*see* MILLENNIUM). Christian visionaries had fixed the year 1666 for the millennium, and since Sabbatai's father, Mordecai, was the Smyrna agent for an English firm, Sabbatai often heard of the expectations of the English Fifth Monarchy men (*q.v.*). In 1648 (the year the cabalists had calculated as the year of salvation), Sabbatai proclaimed himself Messiah. He left Smyrna in 1651 and went first to Salonika, an old cabalist centre, and then to Constantinople, where he encountered a man who pretended that he had been warned by a prophetic voice that Sabbatai was indeed the long-awaited redeemer. He journeyed to Palestine and then to Cairo, where he secured the support of Raphael Halebi, a philanthropist and treasurer of the Turkish governor. With a retinue of believers and considerable funds, Sabbatai returned in triumph to the Holy Land, transferring the centre of his growing movement to Jerusalem. Nathan of Gaza assumed the role of Elijah, the Messiah's forerunner, proclaimed the coming restoration of Israel and the salvation of the world through the bloodless victory of Sabbatai, "riding on a lion with a seven-headed dragon in his jaws." Again 1666 was given as the apocalyptic year.

Threatened with excommunication by the rabbis of Jerusalem, Sabbatai returned in the autumn of 1665 to Smyrna, where he was received with wild enthusiasm. From the Levant the Sabbatian movement spread to Venice, Amsterdam (hailed particularly by the numerous marranos who had fled there from Portugal), Hamburg, London, and other centres of Europe and north Africa. Day by day Sabbatai was hailed by all the world as king of the Jews.

At the beginning of the fateful year 1666 he went (or was summoned) to Constantinople. He was placed under arrest, but the reports of miracles continued, and many of the Turks were inclined to become converts. Soon he was transferred to Abydos, where, in prison, he lived like a king, holding court and even receiving foreign delegates. In September Sabbatai was brought before the sultan, and he had not the courage to refuse to accept Islam. He became a Muslim and was appointed doorkeeper to the sultan. The messianic imposture thus ended in the apostasy of Sabbatai. He died in obscurity in Albania in 1676.

A sect of Muslim Sabbatians—the Donmeh of Salonika—survived him, and within the Jewish faith the controversy for and against his Messiahship continued up to the modern period, erupting into the Frankist movement in southern Poland and Czechoslovakia in the 18th century (*see* FRANK, JAKOB).

BIBLIOGRAPHY.—H. H. Graetz, *History of the Jews*, vol. v (1926). Israel Zangwill has a brilliant sketch of Sabbatai's career in his *Dreamers of the Ghetto* (1898). *See* also Gershon Scholem, *Major Trends in Jewish Mysticism* (1941); Josef Kastein, *The Messiah of Ismir, Sabbatai Zevi* (1931); H. C. Schnur, *Mystic Rebels* (1949); S. Schechter, *Studies in Judaism* (1958).

SABBATARIANISM, the doctrine of those Christians who regard the first day of the week as a sabbath (*q.v.*), asserting the perpetual obligation of the Fourth Commandment (Ex. 20:8–11; Deut. 5:12–15), which forbids work on the sabbath because it is a holy day. The transference of the name sabbath to Sunday was first made by Alcuin (8th century), and in 1647 the Westminster Assembly gave the classic statement of this position: "From the beginning of the world to the resurrection of Christ, God appointed the seventh day of the week to be the weekly Sabbath; and the first day of the week, ever since, to continue to the end of the world, which is the Christian Sabbath" (*Shorter Catechism*, question 59). Over against this there were those who contended that the Fourth Commandment, being part of the ceremonial, not the moral, law, was completely abolished by Christ, and that a totally new and different kind of day began with his resurrection, toward the observance of which the only guides were the nature of the gospel and Christ's own relation to the sabbath. Glad worship was the keynote of the new, as respite from servile toil had been of the old (*see* SUNDAY).

In Christianity today there are many shades of opinion, which combine, in varying proportions, these two positions. The name Sabbatarian is given to those trends which appear to give too much weight to continuity, and, in consequence, to be concerned mainly with the things that may not be done on that day. Sabbatarianism in this sense of excessive strictness in observance of Sunday, and legislation on the subject, is as old as the time of Constantine, who decreed regulations against Sunday labour in 321, but in its most stringent form it was a creation of the Scottish and English Reformers, especially John Knox. With the Puritans and the Scottish Presbyterians it came to the United States, where possibly the most rigorous "blue laws" were enacted (see BLUE LAWS). Though much reduced in number, and still more in effect, Sunday observance laws are still successfully promoted in England by the Lord's Day Observance Society, and in the United States there are many effective state or local laws barring certain business activities (e.g., selling of liquor, automobiles, or real estate) and sporting events on Sunday.

A few Christian communities hold that the whole church went astray in changing, without express divine command, the weekly holy day from the seventh day to the first; the largest of these bodies is the Seventh-day Adventists, whose central theological principle is loyalty to the Ten Commandments, with special emphasis on the Fourth. But these groups of "seventh dayers" are not those to whom the name Sabbatarian is commonly given.

(H. WA.)

SABBATH, the seventh day of the week as a day of rest and sanctification according to the Jewish religion.

In the Pentateuch the institution of Sabbath is connected with various ideas. (1) It is associated with the doctrine of creation: the creation of the world was completed in six days; and God rested on the seventh day (Gen. ii, 1–2; Ex. xx, 11). (2) Sabbath has a social aspect: it is a day of rest for all men, servants and strangers (Ex. xx, 10; Deut. v, 12–15; Ex. xxiii, 12), and thus stands for the idea of equality of man. On that day there is neither master nor slave; in rest all men are alike. (3) Sabbath also is associated with the idea of holiness: "You shall be holy . . . and you shall keep my sabbaths" (Lev. xix, 1–3). (4) Sabbath is a covenant between God and Israel: "Wherefore the people of Israel shall keep the sabbath, observing the sabbath throughout their generations, as a perpetual covenant. It is a sign for ever between me and the people of Israel" (Ex. xxxi, 16–17). All these ideas must have arisen in different times; their historical sequence, however, is difficult to establish.

Observances.—In the prophetic writings the people are continuously admonished to keep the Sabbath holy. Few commandments received the same emphasis. Deutero-Isaiah connects it with doing justice and righteousness: "Keep justice and do righteousness . . . Blessed is the man who does this . . . who keeps the sabbath, not profaning it, and keeps his hand from doing any evil" (Isaiah lvi, 1–2). The attainment of the highest blessings is made dependent on the keeping of the Sabbath (Isaiah lviii, 13–14). Jeremiah warns the people of the impending destruction of the Temple as a punishment for their desecration of the Sabbath: "But if you do not listen to me, to keep the sabbath day holy . . . then I will kindle a fire in its gates" (Jer. xvii, 27). Ezekiel singles out the sin of desecration of the Sabbath along with that of idolatry, as the only reasons for the wrath of God (Ex. xx, 13–24).

The strict observance of the laws of Sabbath since ancient times may be seen from the book of I Maccabees (ch. ii). When the soldiers of Antiochus Epiphanes were arrayed against the Jews on the Sabbath, the Jews "answered them not, neither cast they a stone at them . . . And they rose up against them in battle on the Sabbath and they died, they and their wives and their children." Realizing that this policy could lead to the annihilation of the people, the Maccabees took counsel and decided, "Whosoever shall come against us to battle on the Sabbath day we shall fight against him and we shall in no wise all die." It was later established as a rule by the authorities that in war the laws of Sabbath are suspended (Babylonian Talmud, Sabbath 19a). The Essenes went to the extreme of not leaving their houses on that day (Josephus, Wars of the Jews), and the Jewish sect of Karaites followed this practice, assigning literal meaning to Ex. xvi, 29: "let no man go out of his place on the seventh day." Since the Sabbath begins Friday at sunset, they also insisted on remaining in darkness on Friday night, basing their action on their interpretation of Ex. xxxv, 3. On the other hand, rabbinic law ordained the kindling of lights before the beginning of Sabbath, and upon the lady of the house imposed the duty of inaugurating the Sabbath with a benediction on the kindling of lights.

In the Pentateuch there is no general definition of the kinds of work prohibited. There are, however, specific references to interdicted labours, such as plowing and harvesting (Ex. xxxiv, 21), the kindling of fire (Ex. xxxv, 3), gathering of wood (Num. xv, 32–36) and baking and cooking (Ex. xvi, 23). The types of work prohibited on Sabbath were established by the rabbinic authorities as consisting of 39 main categories of work and are enumerated in the tractate Sabbath of the Talmud. The basis for the derivation of these prohibited categories was the consideration of the kinds of work the Jews must have performed while in the wilderness in connection with the building of the Tabernacle. From each of the main categories of work cognate types were derived.

The positive duties of Sabbath observance are to wear one's best clothes, to rejoice (derived from Isaiah lviii, 13) and to eat at least three meals during the day. Before the evening meal a special blessing of sanctification, Kiddush, is read. An abbreviated Kiddush is recited before the meal following the morning service (see KIDDUSH AND HABDALAH). The service in the synagogue includes psalms extolling the majesty of God's work and of the Sabbath day. The entire Pentateuch is divided into sections (Sidroth), designed to be read on the 52 Sabbaths of the year. A prophetic selection (Haftarah; q.v.) is chanted after the reading of the Torah.

At the conclusion of the Sabbath a special blessing (Habdalah) is recited, emphasizing the idea of separation or distinction—separation between Sabbath and weekdays, between the holy and the profane, between light and darkness, etc. In the evening service at the end of the day a reference to the idea of separation is included in the prayer for wisdom and understanding. The concept of separation and discrimination is as indispensable to understanding as is the act of identification.

The precepts prohibiting all kinds of work on the Sabbath are suspended in case of danger to life. A very ancient rabbinic text reads: "It is written: 'You shall keep the Sabbath, because it is holy for you' [Ex. xxxi, 14], the Sabbath is given to you, you are not given to the Sabbath" (Talmud, Yoma 85b). The laws of Sabbath are thus not ends in themselves but are subordinated to a higher principle, the enhancement of human life. The statutes of the law were given that man might live by them (Lev. xviii, 5; Yoma 85b). The Sabbath laws are suspended even when the danger to health is doubtful. Where human life or health is jeopardized, "It is better to profane one Sabbath for the sake of making possible the observance of many Sabbaths" (Yoma 85b). All affairs of business, even when they do not involve physical exertion, are prohibited on the Sabbath. But the law allows the exercise of offices of humanity, such as caring for the poor, and attending to communal matters, as well as the hiring of a teacher, even for the purpose of teaching one's child a trade (Talmud, Sabbath 150a).

Some of the pagan Greek and Latin authors attacked the institution of Sabbath on the ground of its wastefulness; to be idle every seventh day is to lose a seventh part of one's life. Because of the Sabbath, the Roman emperors exempted Jews from military service. In modern times the austerity of the Sabbath laws has been criticized, but in fact, in the great age of faith, the Sabbath was pre-eminently a day of spiritual delight, not of either idleness or austerity. Complete abstention from the profane tasks of everyday life made possible the cultivation of intellectual and spiritual interests; worship in the synagogue, study of religious literature, and discourses on religious subjects occupied the better part of the day. It was a day of happiness and spiritual joy that guarded the Jew against the strains and stresses of a hostile world in the long history of his wanderings. "More than the Jew kept the Sabbath, the Sabbath kept the Jew." The close relationship between the observance of the Sabbath and the preservation of Israel was expressed in a poem by Abraham ibn Ezra (12th century): "I keep the Sabbath, God keeps me; it is a sign between Him and me."

Origin.—The question concerning the origin of the Sabbath and the part it played in the life of the Israelites before the Exile is still shrouded in mystery, despite the attempts that have been made to shed light upon it. Friedrich Delitzsch (*Babel und Bibel*) was the first to propound the theory of the Babylonian origin of the Jewish Sabbath. From Babylonian sources it is known that certain days of the month, the 7th, 14th, 21st and 28th, were days in which the king might not perform certain acts, such as eating roast flesh, changing his dress, offering sacrifice, mounting his chariot or pronouncing judgment; neither might the *magus* prophesy, nor the physician minister to the sick. Thus Delitzsch found the original home of the biblical Sabbath in Babylonia. This theory remains unconvincing for the following reasons: The Babylonian days were "evil days," not propitious for certain actions. Furthermore, those actions were prohibited only to particular persons, such as the king, the *magus* and the physician. In addition to the days mentioned, the 19th day of the month also was an "evil day," on which those actions were prohibited. Those days in the Babylonian calendar must have had their origin in some magical concept. This has nothing in common with the biblical Sabbath as a day of rest for all men, slave and stranger included—an institution that is bound up with the ethical and monotheistic concept of God as Creator. To be sure, the name Sabbath seems to have its origin in Babylonia. It may be a loan word from the Babylonian *Šappattu,* or *Šabbattu,* the 15th day of the month; it is, however, equally possible that both *Šappattu* and Sabbath are derived from a common ground in a prehistoric Semitic tradition. In any case there is a long step from days of taboo to a day of spiritual delight.

There is no evidence of Sabbath observance in the patriarchal period. The references in the historical and prophetic books of the Bible seem to indicate that a close connection existed between the Sabbath and the new-moon festival, and much has been made of the passages implying such a connection. When the Shunammite proposed to visit the prophet, her husband asks: "Why will you go to him today? It is neither new moon nor sabbath" (II Kings, iv, 23). Hosea warned the people in the name of the Lord: "And I will put an end to all her mirth, her feasts, her new moons, her sabbaths, and all her appointed feasts" (Hosea ii, 11). Amos denounced the dishonest traders who say: "When will the new moon be over, that we may sell grain? And the sabbath that we may offer wheat for sale?" (Amos viii, 5). In excoriating the offensive manner of the religious observances, Isaiah says: "Incense is an abomination to me. New moon and sabbath and the calling of assemblies" (Isaiah i, 13). New moon and Sabbath thus are commonly linked together. Hosea implies that Sabbath and new moon were days of festal joy, and from Amos it follows that on those days ordinary business activity was suspended. That carrying any burden on the Sabbath was not allowed can be seen from Jer. xvii, 21–27. That it was customary to visit the Temple on Sabbath days is clear from Isaiah lxvi, 23: "From new moon to new moon, and from sabbath to sabbath, all flesh shall come to worship before me." The linking together of Sabbath and the new moon led I. Meinhold to suggest that the Sabbath must have been originally the day of the full moon, since the counterpart of "new moon" is "full moon" and not the seventh day of the week. It is further noted that among the Phoenicians the new moon and the full moon were the chief days of sacrifice.

Various theories have been suggested as to when the day of the full moon became the Sabbath. Meinhold attributes the change to Ezekiel. S. Mowinckel suggests a time shortly before the Exile. Max Weber rejects the exilic origin of the Sabbath, citing Neh. xiii, 15 as clear demonstration that those who remained in Palestine knew of the Sabbath as a weekly day. These theories, however, are little more than stabs in the dark, since the transition from a moon-oriented day to the unvarying observance of a seventh day is left unexplained. The law of *Shmita* (*i.e.,* the sabbatical year) is associated with the Sabbath day. Both require cessation of work, the former prohibiting work in general on the seventh day and the latter forbidding agricultural labour in the seventh year. The law demanding the release of slaves in the seventh year (Ex. xxi, 2) again suggests the Sabbath as occurring on the seventh day. (*See* JUBILEE, YEAR OF.)

Max Weber accepted the theory that the Sabbath is related to the Babylonian *Šappattu,* but only as a matter of common heritage and not as a borrowing from Babylonia. Weber argued on the basis of Neh. xiii, 15 that the seventh day was originally a day of rest and joy, on which the farmers came to the town markets to sell their produce and perhaps also to amuse themselves. He compared this day with the Roman *nundinae,* the first day of the eight-day week, which had the same social function in Roman life. Likewise, Eduard Meyer compared the Sabbath with the Roman *nundinae,* stressing the economic-social origin of the holiday. He repudiated the connection of the week-day Sabbath with the moon and considers its association with the Babylonian *Šappattu* improbable. He left the name Sabbath unexplained, however. The analogy of the Roman *nundinae* with the Sabbath, as it appears to Meyer and Weber from Nehemiah, is a sociological hypothesis, thus repudiating the speculations of an astrological origin of the Sabbath.

The nature of the Sabbath, however, can hardly be deduced from references to the practice of the people at a certain historical period. This practice was more likely a deviation from a previously existing law or tradition. In denouncing the people for their conduct on the Sabbath and characterizing it as a profanation, Nehemiah clearly implied the prior existence of a different tradition. " 'What is this evil thing which you are doing, profaning the sabbath day? Did not your fathers act in this way, and did not our God bring all this evil on us and on this city? Yet you bring more wrath upon Israel by profaning the sabbath' " (Neh. xiii, 17–18). Not the practice of the people, but rather Nehemiah's reaction to their practice should serve as a basis for the understanding of the original nature of the Sabbath as a Jewish institution. Nehemiah is here not instituting something new but referring to a hallowed tradition concerning a day of rest, the profanation of which has in the past brought down upon Israel the wrath of God.

The various attempts to explain the origin of the Sabbath do not take into account the probability of a core of Mosaic or prophetic legislation with which the Sabbath law was closely connected. Admitting that biblical legislation in the form in which it came down to us is of a later date, its essential elements, such as the contents of the Decalogue, were known as a Mosaic tradition, as can be seen from the prophetic references to the "law of Moses." The laws relating to Sabbath as a rest day for all men, to the sabbatical year and to the release of slaves in the seventh year of servitude, imposing restrictions on ownership and on the power of the individual, were revolutionary and idealistic in character; apparently they were grounded in a concept of property and labour closely connected with the prophetic philosophy of God and man. Just as the prophetic concept of ethical monotheism was a new, indeed a unique idea, neither to be derived from, nor to be reduced to the various conceptions of God prevalent in the ancient world, so was the biblical institution of the Sabbath. The new concept of God transformed the sociological and astrological raw material into a new institution; with the result that the analogies to the Sabbath that can be found in the ancient world serve only to accentuate its uniqueness.

Modern Period.—Conservative and Reform Judaism have been confronted by the problem of Sabbath observance in the modern age. Conservative Judaism has not developed a unified point of view with regard to the laws of Sabbath observance. The traditionalists of that movement deny that there is any difference between conservative and orthodox Judaism as to observance of the law. The spokesmen of the liberal wing of the movement plead for certain changes, taking into consideration the conditions of modern life, such as allowing travel to the synagogue. Such modifications, however, have not received the unanimous approval of the official authoritative bodies.

The Reform movement also has wrestled with the problem of

preserving the Sabbath under modern conditions. It realizes the serious obstacles standing in the way of full observance of the Sabbath laws. The consensus, however, is that Sunday could never become the Jewish Sabbath. The institution of public services on Sunday aims merely at reaching those who are prevented from observing the Sabbath. The distinctive character of the Sabbath as a day of sanctification is necessarily bound up with the Sabbath as hallowed by tradition. A day of rest could be shifted to another day. But Sabbath is the symbol of the covenant of Israel with God and of creation; it is therefore indispensable for the Jew as a sign of his religion. If it is difficult to observe the day in accordance with traditional prescription, it is necessary to strive to observe it to the best of our ability. The humanitarian idea of the Sabbath has a universal message, which constitutes an essential element of the Jewish religion. Recognizing the distinctive and the positive idea of the day, Reform Judaism has striven to preserve it. Such an authoritative body as the Central Conference of American Rabbis recommended conscientious abstention from all those activities that would obscure the difference between Sabbath and the weekdays. By emphasizing in practice the line of cleavage between Sabbath and the weekdays, the idea of the Sabbath will be preserved and intensified. Reform Judaism instituted late Friday evening services and the reading of the Torah portion at that hour. This, of course, is in addition to the regular Sabbath morning Torah service. Reform liturgy provides also for a service in the home (Kiddush). These provisions aim at preserving the Sabbath in its essential elements.

Christianity.—The position Jesus took—that "the sabbath was made for man, not man for the sabbath" (Mark ii, 27)—was essentially in keeping with the rabbinic saying cited above. It appears, however, that Jesus or his followers went far beyond the rabbis in the application of this. The early Christians taught that the principle of the love of God superseded the law of Moses. Jesus thus justified the conduct of the disciples in plucking ears of corn on the Sabbath, though this act violated the rule prohibiting harvesting. He himself, in healing the sick, broke the rule that one should not administer aid to a sick man when it involves a transgression of the precepts of Sabbath, except when life is threatened. For Jesus and for his followers, the love of God was a surer guide of conduct than mere obedience to the law of Moses.

The Jewish Christians of the early church continued to observe the Sabbath. According to Eusebius, the Ebionites kept both the Sabbath, as a memorial of the creation, and the Lord's day (Sunday), the weekly celebration of the Resurrection; and this was the general practice of the early Christians, as recommended by the Apostolic Constitutions (see CONSTITUTIONS, APOSTOLIC). The Eastern Church in recognizing the festive character of the Sabbath and prohibiting fasting on that day is in accordance with Jewish law. The spread of Christianity to the gentile world brought about a change in the Christian attitude. Paul began by insisting that the Jewish Sabbath was not binding on Christians. He ended by asserting that the principle of love was in contradiction of the law of Moses, and bitterly condemned the Christians who abided by the laws of Sabbath (Col. ii, 16 and Gal. iv, 9–11).

Chiefly because of the fact that the Resurrection took place on Sunday (q.v.), that day eventually replaced the Sabbath in Christian religion. A few post-Reformation bodies (as the Seventh-day Adventists) observe the Sabbath rather than Sunday.

BIBLIOGRAPHY.—I. Meinhold, "Die Entstehung des Sabbath," *Zeitschrift für die alttestamentliche Wissenschaft*, vol. ii, p. 108 (1916), and "Zur Sabbathfrage," *ibid.*, vol. ii, p. 121 (1930); Benziger, *Hebräische Archäologie* (1927); Max Weber, *Aufsätze zur Religionssoziologie* (1921); E. G. Kraeling, "The Present Status of the Sabbath Question," *AJSL*, 49:218–228 (1932–33); *Yearbook of the Central Conference of American Rabbis,* 20:62 (1910) and 23:210 (1913). (S. At.)

SABELLIANISM, a Christian heresy, a more developed and less naïve form of modalistic monarchianism, propounded by Sabellius (fl. *c.* 215–*c.* 220), possibly a presbyter, who worked in Rome toward the end of the pontificate of Zephyrinus (*c.* 199–217) and during that of Calixtus I (217/218–222). Little is known of Sabellius' life, the most detailed information extant deriving from the prejudiced reports of the contemporary antimonarchian

Roman theologian Hippolytus (*Refutatio* ix). The scene of his theological activity was Rome, where the struggle was in full swing between those who affirmed permanent distinctions ("persons" in the language of later theology) within the Godhead, and the monarchians or modalists, who in their concern for the divine "monarchy" (*i.e.*, the absolute unity and indivisibility of God) denied that such distinctions were ultimate or permanent. Sabellius, who became the acknowledged leader of the latter party, giving their teaching its fully developed form, appears to have taught that the Godhead is a monad, expressing itself in three operations: as Father, in creation; as Son, in redemption; as Holy Spirit, in sanctification. It is possible (the evidence is uncertain) that he also held that the divine monad underwent a process of "expansion" or "extension," projecting itself first as Son and then as Spirit. Sabellius thus advanced on the earlier monarchianism in finding a place in his system for the Holy Spirit, in avoiding the patripassian idea that the Father suffered, and in approximating to the Catholic doctrine of the Trinity.

Pope Calixtus was at first inclined to be sympathetic (indeed, according to Hippolytus, it was he who first corrupted Sabellius' ideas), but then condemned the teaching and excommunicated Sabellius. The heresy broke out afresh 30 years later in Libya to be opposed by Dionysius of Alexandria (*see* DIONYSIUS, SAINT). In the 4th century Arius accused his bishop of Sabellianism, and throughout the Arian controversy this charge was leveled at the supporters of Nicene orthodoxy, whose emphasis upon the unity of substance of Father and Son was interpreted to mean that they denied any personal distinctions within the Godhead. (*See* ARIANISM.)

Marcellus of Ancyra was constantly attacked on these grounds, and although perhaps not a strict Sabellian he did maintain that the monad expanded into a dyad at creation and into a triad at the outpouring of the Spirit, and that after the Last Judgment the process would be reversed. About 375 the heresy was renewed at Neocaesarea, being attacked by Basil the Great, and in Spain Priscillian seems to have enunciated a doctrine of the divine unity in Sabellian terms.

At the Reformation Sabellianism was reformulated by Michael Servetus (*q.v.*) to the effect that Christ and the Holy Spirit are merely representative forms of the one Godhead, the Father. In the 18th century this was the teaching of Emanuel Swedenborg (*q.v.*), who asserted that "by three persons I understand three proceeding divine attributes, which are creation, redemption and generation . . . before the creation of the world this Trinity did not exist"; Father, Son, and Holy Spirit are therefore "three Modes of manifestation." Sabellianism is thus perpetuated by the New Church (*q.v.*) founded by Swedenborg's disciples. *See also* MONARCHIANISM.

BIBLIOGRAPHY.—J. J. I. von Döllinger, *Hippolyt und Kallistus* (1853; Eng. trans., 1876); G. Bardy, "Monarchianisme" in A. Vacant (ed.), *Dictionnaire de théologie catholique,* vol. 10, col. 2193–2209 (1929); J. N. D. Kelly, *Early Christian Doctrines,* 2nd ed. (1960).
(J. N. D. K.; J. G. Da.)

SABELLIC (from Latin *Sabellus*, "Samnite") has often been used of a minor group of the Italic dialects (*q.v.*), the pre-Latin dialects of the Paeligni, Marrucini and Vestini (better called North Oscan), of the Volsci, and of the Marsi, Aequi, Sabini and other central Italian tribes (conveniently called Latinian); these dialects are all closely related to Oscan (*q.v.*). The same name, or sometimes Old Sabellic, is also used, but inaccurately, to describe two small but distinct groups of inscriptions from various sites near the east coast of central Italy: (1) from Novilara and Fano (near Pesaro); (2) from Belmonte Piceno, Cupra Marittima, Castignano, Bellante, Grecchio and Superequo. These may be better designated, by "East Italic."

The second group, not more recent in date than the 6th century B.C., are doubtless the oldest written documents known from Italian soil. The lines of writing run alternately left to right and right to left, the positions of the letters being both reversed and inverted in the lines written right to left. Their alphabet is clearly of the same Chalcid-Etruscan origin as that of all the other alphabets of ancient Italy (except the Greek and Phoenician), but shows some peculiarities which suggest direct Greek influence;

the language, still untranslated, will probably prove to be an Indo-European (two I.-E. stems, *pater* "father," *mater* "mother" have been identified) and ancient Illyrian dialect (*meitime* is an Illyrian name). For it is known from the elder Pliny, from the Iguvine tables (*iapuzkum* "Iapydian," *i.e.*, "belonging to the Illyrian Iapydes"), and from archaeological evidence, that there were Illyrian settlers in or near that district, the ancient Picenum, where these inscriptions were discovered.

But the documents of the Novilara group are later in date, distinct in alphabet—this is perhaps of Etruscan origin, but shows certain resemblances both to the Umbrian and to the Oscan alphabets—and probably also in dialect. The suggestion that the dialect, however, is allied to Etruscan itself, is quite unsupported by the evidence; the decorative motifs, for example the spiral, which appear on all three of the inscriptions of this group, point rather to the opposite coast of the Adriatic, where similar motifs occur, especially round Nesazio, on contemporary monuments; and there is nothing in the word forms of these documents which may not be Indo-European, while the characteristic Etruscan syncope and elision (at least in the writing) are entirely lacking.

BIBLIOGRAPHY.—R. von Planta, *Grammatik der oskisch-umbrischen Dialekte*, vol. ii, pp. 551 ff., 644 ff. (1897); G. Herbig in M. Ebert's *Real-lexikon der Vorgeschichte, s.v.v.* Novilara, Vorsabeller (1927–32; bibl.); the inscriptions have been edited anew by J. Whatmough, *Prae-Italic Dialects of Italy*, vol. ii, no. 342–355 (1933).

Texts discovered since 1933: *Historia* 7, p. 543 (1933); *Rivista Indo-Greco-Italica* 19, p. 89 (1935); *Classical Philology* 31, p. 195 (1936); *Notizie degli Scavi di Antichità*, pp. 423–25 (1936). *See also* J. Whatmough, *Foundations of Roman Italy*, ch. 10 (1937); E. Vetter, *Handbuch der italischen Dialekte I*, pp. 360–361 (1953). (J. WH.)

SABIANS, a name given by Arab chroniclers to two different religious groups whom they confused: the Mandaeans (*q.v.*) and the pagan inhabitants of Harran (*q.v.*; a city of Mesopotamia now in eastern Turkey just north of the Syrian border). Sabians (*i.e.*, Mandaeans) are mentioned three times in the Koran together with Jews and Christians. According to tradition the 9th-century moon worshipers of Harran claimed to be Sabians in order to be granted by the Muslims the same religious privileges as Jews and Christians. These "Sabians," usually called pseudo-Sabians by modern scholars, made Harran a flourishing centre of learning in the 9th–10th centuries, and the astronomer al-Battani belonged to their number. In the 13th century they were overwhelmed by the Mongols.

The Sabians should not be confused with the Sabaeans, who were pre-Islamic inhabitants of the kingdom of Saba, in southwest Arabia (*see* SABAEANS).

SABINE, SIR EDWARD (1788–1883), English astronomer and geodesist known for his work on terrestial magnetism, was born in Dublin, Ire. on Oct. 14, 1788. He served in the Royal Artillery and was appointed astronomer to the arctic expeditions of Sir John Ross (1818) and Sir William Parry (1819; *qq.v.*) in search of the northwest passage. From 1821 to 1823 Sabine conducted pendulum experiments, to determine the figure of the earth, on the coasts of Africa, America and the arctic, publishing the results in 1825. These experiments he continued on the length of the seconds pendulum in London and Paris, the results appearing in 1828, in which year he was appointed one of the three scientific advisers to the admiralty. Most of his life was devoted to researches on terrestial magnetism, and he superintended the establishment of magnetic observatories on British territory throughout the world. The results appeared in *Observations on Days of Unusual Magnetic Disturbance* (1843). In 1852 he discovered a connection between the periodic variation of sun spots and magnetic disturbances on the earth. Sabine was president of the Royal society (1861–71) and was made a knight commander of the Order of the Bath (1869). He died at East Sheen, Surrey, on June 26, 1883.

SABINE RIVER in the southwestern United States flows southeast and south for 576 mi. from Hunt county in eastern Texas to Sabine lake and on through Sabine pass into the Gulf of Mexico. The drainage basin of 10,400 sq.mi. lies entirely in Texas and in the Louisiana coastal plain. Discharge of the river varies from 372 to 61,200 cu.ft. per second. From southeast Panola county, Tex., to the gulf the Texas-Louisiana boundary

follows the river, Sabine lake and Sabine pass. The Sabine has successively served as a boundary between France and Spain, Spain and the United States, Mexico and the United States, and Texas and Louisiana; it has been in dispute many times.

The Sabine-Neches waterway, a portion of the Gulf Intracoastal waterway, provides 52 mi. of deep waterway through Sabine pass, along western Sabine lake and the lower Neches river to Beaumont, Tex., and 44 mi. of deep waterway to Orange, Tex., located 10 mi. N. of the Sabine river mouth. The Neches river, originating near Tyler, Tex., flows 280 mi. S.E. to Sabine lake.

Commodities transported on the waterway are mostly crude petroleum and petroleum products. Navigation of the river above Orange, Tex., is not important. Port Arthur, Tex., is another important city on the Sabine-Neches waterway. (M. W. M.)

SABINI, an ancient Italic tribe which had very close relations with early Rome. Its people lived in the mountainous country east of the Tiber, and north of the Latins and Aequi, with the Umbrians on the northwest and the Picenes on the northeast. Many probably lived in hilltop villages; their chief towns were Reate (Rieti), Amiternum (San Vittorino, near L'Aquila), and Nursia (Norcia), and in early times Cures, Nomentum, and Fidenae (all near the Tiber). They were well known for their religious practices and beliefs, and many Roman institutions (*e.g.*, the worship of Jupiter, Mars, and the Sabine Quirinus, and the form of marriage called *confarreatio*) were said to have derived from them. The story of the rape (seizing) of the Sabine women by Romulus' men is legendary; thereafter the Sabine king Titus Tatius is said to have captured the Capitol at Rome through the treachery of Tarpeia, daughter of the Capitol's commander, and then to have ruled jointly with Romulus. But their successor at Rome, the Sabine Numa Pompilius (*q.v.*), has greater claim to historicity. The view is widely accepted that the people settled on the Quirinal and Esquiline hills (practising burial by inhumation) who joined with another people on the Palatine Hill (practising cremation) to form Rome were Sabines. In 505 B.C. the Sabine Attius Clausus (= Appius Claudius Sabinus; *see* CLAUDIUS) settled in Rome with his followers. Thus there was a considerable Sabine infiltration into Rome. Nonetheless, the view that the Sabines conquered Rome in the first half of the 5th century is improbable; rather, the Romans had to fight many skirmishes with the Sabines before their final victory in 449. For a century and a half thereafter relations may have been friendly, but nothing is known until in 290 the Sabines were conquered by Curius Dentatus and were granted *civitas sine suffragio;* in 268 they received full Roman citizenship and ceased to be a separate people. They were quickly romanized. Their towns were administered by annual boards of *octoviri*.

The Sabines probably spoke Oscan. Of their language as distinct from that of the Latins no memorial has survived, but there are a large number of single words attributed to them by Latin writers— *e.g.*, *fircus* (Lat. *hircus*, "he-goat"), *ausum* (*aurum*, "gold"), Pompilius (the Latin name Quinctilius)—which indicate clearly certain peculiarities in Sabine phonology, among them the change of Indo-European q^u to p. The tradition that the Sabines were the parent stock of the Samnites (*q.v.*) is confirmed by the name which the Samnites apparently used for themselves, which, with a latinized ending, would be Safini. By the time of the Roman scholar Varro (mid-1st century B.C.), who never refers to the language of the Sabines as a living speech, their speech had become latinized, although Varro does imply that the dialect used in their district differed somewhat from urban Latin. *See also* ITALIC DIALECTS; OSCAN.

BIBLIOGRAPHY.—R. S. Conway in *Cambridge Ancient History*, vol. iv, ch. 13 (1926); H. Last *et al., ibid.*, vol. vii, esp. ch. 15 and 18 (1928); J. Whatmough, *The Foundations of Roman Italy*, ch. 12 (1937); E. C. Evans, "The Cults of the Sabine Territory," *Papers of the American Academy in Rome*, xi, pp. 1 ff. (1939). *Language:* R. S. Conway, *The Italic Dialects*, pp. 351 ff. (1897). (H. H. SD.)

SABINIAN (d. 606), pope from 604 to 606, was of Tuscan origin. Little is known of his life and pontificate. Under Pope Gregory the Great he served in the important post of papal apocrisiary (legate) at Constantinople. As Gregory's successor, elected in 604, he seems to have been markedly more conservative than his predecessor. This, together with his cautious administration of the papal granaries during a winter famine, probably explains the later untrustworthy legend of his stinginess, which is moreover refuted by the praise of his generosity in his epitaph. It is uncertain modern conjecture that because of his unpopularity disorders threatened to erupt at his funeral in 606.   (Jn. Sr.)

SABLE, one of the weasel family, *Martes zibellina,* highly valued for its fine fur. The common name is sometimes also applied to related European and Asian species and the American marten. The sable is native to the forests of northern Asia, from the Ural Mountains eastward and south to about latitude 45° N. It ranges from about 14 to 20 in. long, including the 5- to 7-in. tail. The body colour varies from brown to almost black, with a throat patch from dusky to salmon.

The sable is solitary and arboreal in habits, feeding on squirrels and other rodents, birds, eggs, insects, and other small animals. Mating occurs from June to August; gestation lasts from 249 to 299 days (implantation of the early embryo being delayed as in certain other weasels). The litter numbers from 1 to 4 kits.   (J. N. L.)

SABLE ANTELOPE, a large and handsome South African antelope (*Hippotragus niger*), exhibiting the rare feature of blackness or dark colour in both sexes. The sable and the roan antelope (*H. equinus*) belong to a genus nearly related to the oryxes (*q.v.*), but distinguished by the stout, thickly ringed horns (present in both sexes) rising vertically from a ridge over the eyes and then sweeping backward in a bold curve. Sable antelopes are endowed with great speed and staying power. They are commonly met with in herds including from 10 to 20 individuals. Forest-clad highlands are their favourite resorts. *See also* ANTELOPE.

SABLE ISLAND, an island of Nova Scotia, Canada, 110 mi. SE of Cape Canso. Composed of shifting sand, it is the exposed portion of a 50 mi. long, gently curved bar. The island itself is about 20 mi. long and 1 mi. wide, and the sand hills shaped by the wind rise to elevations up to 100 ft. It is reported to be moving slowly eastward, owing to the encroachment of the sea on the western end and the continual sand accumulation at the eastern end. The smooth coast line is without a harbour. Vegetation consists of grasses and other plants but no trees. It has long been known as "the graveyard of the Atlantic"; over 200 known wrecks have been catalogued. During the frequent fogs and storms this slender ribbon of land is virtually indistinguishable until close at hand. The danger of shipwreck has been minimized, however, by the Canadian government's maintenance of several lighthouses and lifesaving stations.   (C. N. F.)

SABOTAGE, originally a designation for labour protest that took the form of action to impair the profitable operation of the employer's business; it acquired a broadened meaning during the first half of the 20th century when the tactics of social revolution and of conventional military conflict became closely intertwined. The modern conception of sabotage traces from the French railway strike of 1910 when workers cut wooden "shoes" (*sabots*) that held the rails in place. From 1912 to 1918 the U.S. branch of the Industrial Workers of the World (IWW) officially approved sabotage, the slowing down of work so that output would be deceptively yet effectively diminished in quantity and quality. The IWW's sanction of sabotage as a means of protest reflected the casual migratory worker's tenuous position which made difficult the use of formally organized strikes and the application of conventional economic pressure. The anti-war stand taken in 1914 by the American IWW and world syndicalists generally gave "sabotage" a mingled social and military meaning. In the Spanish Civil War of the late 1930s, social and military aspects of sabotage took on organized form as the concept of "the fifth column" emerged when Gen. Francisco Franco's supporters used sabotage among other means of damaging the government's Loyalist forces; at the same time, trained cadres of infiltrators into Franco's ranks and territories held by him harassed his troops. By the advent of World War II the stage had been set for the militarily disciplined use of sabotage in planned support of regular armed forces.

Sabotage was attempted by the Axis powers no less than by the Allies. The Allies, however, had a stronger foundation for their efforts in the resistance movements of the occupied nations. The airdrop of liaison officers and demolition supplies, combined with long-distance radio communication, enabled the Allies to provide effective assistance to the liberation fighters. Sabotage was generally carried out by experts with professional skill. Though the emotionally or romantically dedicated partisan sporadically engaged in sabotage, and persons having property to lose practised sabotage cautiously, it was the trained and disciplined resistance member who had the major effect.

BIBLIOGRAPHY.—É. Pouget, *Le Sabotage,* Eng. tr. (1913); E. F. Dowell, *A History of Criminal Syndicalism Legislation in the United States* (1939); Dorothy L. Tompkins, *Sabotage and Its Prevention During Wartime* (1951); 86th Congress, 2nd Session, U. S. Senate Document No. 126, *Internal Security Manual* (1961); Thorstein Veblen, *The Engineers and the Price System* (1921); American Academy of Political and Social Science, *Unconventional Warfare,* ed. by J. K. Zawodny (1962).   (G. W. Z.)

SABRATHA (SABRATA), the westernmost of the three cities of ancient Tripolis, near the site of which lies the modern town of Sabratha (Arab. Sabratah), some 48 mi. W of Tripoli, in Libya. Founded by the Carthaginians as a seasonal trading post, it was first permanently settled in the 4th century B.C. Lying along an inhospitable coastline, it possessed a modest natural harbour, later improved by the Romans, and together with Oea (Tripoli) it served as an outlet for the trans-Saharan caravan route through Ghadames (Ghudamis). After a period of quasi-independence following the fall of Carthage in 146 B.C., it passed under Roman rule, enjoying a considerable prosperity, which reached its peak in the late 2nd century A.D. Rebuilt after a disastrous sack by the Austuriani *c.* A.D. 365, it declined rapidly in the 5th century under Vandal misrule. The revival that followed the Byzantine reconquest (534) was on a greatly reduced scale, and soon after the Arab conquest (643) the city ceased to exist.

Excavation has uncovered more than half the area of the ancient city, including the forum area, many of the harbourside installations, and a large 2nd-century residential quarter adjoining the theatre, the stage building of which has been restored to the full height of its three classical orders. The forum occupies the site of an open space within the late Punic city, and its buildings, which include the civil basilica, the capitolium and four other temples, and the meeting place of the local senate (*curia*), had a long and complex evolution. Other Roman buildings include baths, temples (of Hercules, Isis, and Sarapis), fountains, and private buildings; there are many mosaics. Christian remains include a catacomb and four churches, one of them with a magnificent Justinianic mosaic, and the Byzantine walls. Flavia Domitilla, wife of Vespasian, came from Sabratha, and it was there that Lucius Apuleius (*q.v.*) stood trial for witchcraft.

See D. E. L. Haynes, *The Antiquities of Tripolitania* (1955); J. M. Reynolds and J. B. Ward-Perkins (eds.), *Inscriptions of Roman Tripolitania* (1952).   (J. B. W.-P.)

SABRE FENCING: *see* FENCING.

SABRE-TOOTHED TIGER, an extinct subfamily, Machairodontinae, of the cat family, Felidae. The most characteristic feature, the basis of the name, is the pair of elongated, blade-like canine teeth in the upper jaw. The subfamily ranges in age from the Oligocene epoch, 30,000,000 to 35,000,000 years ago, to the Pleistocene, with final extinction not more than a few thousand years in the past. Well known as this subfamily is, there remain unresolved differences of opinion about its relationships to other felids and indeed differences as to the placement of some Oligocene and Miocene genera as sabretooths, false sabretooths (nimravines), or true cats (felines). In this article only the animals that can be placed without serious question among true sabre-toothed tigers (Machairodontinae) are considered.

The best-known genus of the subfamily is *Smilodon* of the Pleistocene of North and South America. This was a large, massive, short-limbed carnivore with immense canine teeth. These teeth appear to have been used for stabbing and slashing attacks upon the large, thick-skinned herbivores that formed the chief prey of the sabretooths. The skull was notably modified in adaptation to this type of feeding. The occipital region was high and the ventral mastoid processes long, in accommodation of strong neck muscles. The lower jaw was formed in such a way that it could be widely opened, thus freeing the daggerlike canines for action. Molar teeth were shearing blades, with no vestiges of grinding surfaces. Among living cats, only the lion approaches *Smilodon* in massiveness, and even the largest lions do not reach the proportions of the largest sabretooths.

The basic sabretooth characters were present, but less fully developed, in *Hoplophoneus*, a moderate sized Oligocene ancestor of *Smilodon*. Other early members of the family Felidae, such as *Dinictis* of the Oligocene, also had fairly well-developed sabre-like teeth but for the most part lacked the other specializations seen in the true sabretooths. Such forms have been variously classified as true cats or as false sabretooths.

BY COURTESY OF CHICAGO NATURAL HISTORY MUSEUM, FROM A MURAL BY CHARLES R. KNIGHT

RESTORATION DRAWING OF EXTINCT SABRE-TOOTHED TIGER

Throughout the Miocene and Pliocene epochs of the Tertiary, machairodonts were present in North America and Europe, although, as for most carnivores, their remains are relatively rare. By Pliocene times they had spread to Asia and Africa, and in the Pleistocene were present in South America. The pattern of extinction of the sabre-toothed cats follows closely the pattern of extinction of the mastodons, which appear to have been one of their principal sources of food. As these large, elephantlike animals became reduced and extinct in the late Pliocene of the old world, the sabre-toothed cats died out and are not found in the Pleistocene. In North and South America, where mastodons persisted through the Pleistocene, sabre-toothed tigers continued successfully to the end of that epoch. The best-known occurrence of *Smilodon* is in the tar pits of Rancho La Brea, in Los Angeles, Calif., where many individuals were trapped in the tar, apparently as they preyed upon large herbivores that also had become bogged. The tar deposits have preserved a wealth of bones virtually unaltered since the deaths of the animals. (E. C. O.)

SÁ-CARNEIRO, MÁRIO DE (1890–1916), Portuguese poet and novelist of the so-called modernist generation and one of the most original and complex figures in Portuguese literature in the first half of the 20th century, was born in Lisbon on May 19, 1890. After leaving the secondary school there, he went to Paris where he studied for a year (1912–13) in the law faculty at the Sorbonne. Before leaving Lisbon he had made the acquaintance of Fernando Pessoa, the greatest literary figure of the generation, and maintained a regular correspondence with him while he was in France. Sá-Carneiro's first literary production was the play *Amizade* written in collaboration with a fellow-pupil while he was still at school. In 1912 he published *Princípio*, a collection of prose tales. His first poems were written in Paris in 1914 and were published in the same year under the title *Dispersão*. In 1914 also he published the novel *A Confissão de Lúcio* and, back in Portugal, he launched the review *Orpheu* in 1915 in collaboration with Fernando Pessoa and other young men of the modernist group. The same year saw also the appearance of his collection of short stories, *Céu em Fogo*. Having returned to Paris, he suffered a moral and financial crisis, abandoned his studies, quarreled with his father, and gave himself up to the life of a literary Bohemian. The crisis came to a head in 1916 when the poet, the victim of a sensibility which left him facing life disarmed—"without support" as he himself put it—committed suicide in the Hotel de Nice in Paris on April 26. Before his death he had sent his unpublished poems to Pessoa, and these appeared in 1937 under the title *Indícios de Oiro*. His *Poesias* were edited, with a preface, by J. Gaspar Simões in 1946.

See A. Casais Monteiro, "Mário de Sá-Carneiro," in *Considerações Pessoais* (1933); J. Gaspar Simões, *Historia da Poesia Portuguesa do Seculo xx* (1959). (J. G. Ss.)

SACASA, JUAN BAUTISTA (1874–1946), president of Nicaragua from 1932 through 1936, was largely overshadowed by two of his nominal subordinates, César Augusto Sandino and Anastasio Somoza. Born in León, Nic., on Dec. 21, 1874, Sacasa studied in the United States from 1889 to 1901, earning an M.D. from Columbia University. As leader of the Liberal Party he was elected vice-president in 1924 on a coalition ticket with Carlos Solórzano of the Conservative Party. However, Sacasa was forced into exile the following year by a *coup d'état* which installed Gen. Emiliano Chamorro Vargas as president. When Chamorro was replaced by Adolfo Díaz, Sacasa returned to Nicaragua and asserted his claim to the presidency. The resulting unrest caused the U.S. government to send Marines to Nicaragua to maintain order, and with their arrival Sacasa (in April 1927) reluctantly accepted a compromise imposed by U.S. Special Commissioner Henry L. Stimson. Elected president in 1932, Sacasa was ousted on June 6, 1936, by his nephew and military commander, Gen. Anastasio Somoza, who coveted the presidency for himself. Sacasa died in Los Angeles, Calif., on April 17, 1946. (R. M. Sc.)

SACATEPÉQUEZ, a department in the highlands of central Guatemala, just west of Guatemala City. Area 179 sq.mi. Pop. (1964) 80,479. Its capital is Antigua, pop. (1964) 21,984, former capital of Guatemala. The department is a part of the chief coffee-producing area of the country. Other crops include corn (maize), beans, and hay. Much land is used for the grazing of beef cattle. The department is served by the Inter-American Highway and by several all-weather feeder roads. Antigua was abandoned as the national capital because of frequent earthquakes. (P. E. J.)

SACCHARIN is a name applied to several organic substances used as sweetening agents. The saccharin of commerce is derived from toluene. Commercial saccharin is marketed as insoluble saccharin (I—the imide of ortho-sulfobenzoic acid) and as soluble saccharin (II—the sodium salt of the former substance).

For consumer use, pharmaceutical manufacturers prepare tiny pellets containing $\frac{1}{4}$, $\frac{1}{2}$, or 1 gr. of pure saccharin. The pellets may contain the saccharin in the form of the soluble sodium salt or in the acid form combined with sodium bicarbonate which converts

$$\text{I} \qquad \text{II}$$

the acid to the sodium salt upon dissolving. The sweetening power of the commercial powder is estimated at 425 times the sweetening power of ordinary sugar; the commercial crystals, which contain some water of crystallization, are estimated to have a sweetening power 375 times that of sugar. A one-quarter grain pellet has roughly the same sweetening power as a level teaspoon of sugar. Saccharin has no food value at all. It is used in the diets of diabetics and other persons who must avoid excessive sugar intake and also in the preparation of dietetic foods, dentifrices, mouthwashes, and cosmetics, and for sweetening tobacco and medicinal preparations, particularly where the presence of sugar might lead to spoilage by fermentation or mold growth. Saccharin is not metabolized; it is excreted unchanged from the body in the urine.

Saccharin was discovered by Ira Remsen and C. Fahlberg in 1879 in the course of investigations at the Johns Hopkins University on the oxidation *o*-toluene-sulfonamide. Fahlberg noticed an unaccountable sweet taste to his food and found that this sweetness was present on his hands and arms, despite his having washed thoroughly after leaving the laboratory. Checking over his laboratory apparatus by taste tests, Fahlberg was led to the discovery of the source of this sweetness—saccharin.

Saccharin is made by treating toluene with chlorosulfonic acid. The reaction produces ortho- and para-toluene sulfonylchlorides. The two products are separated and the ortho-toluene sulfonylchloride is treated with ammonia to form the amide. The amide is then oxidized to saccharin.

See T. E. Thorpe, *Dictionary of Applied Chemistry*, 4th ed., vol. x (1950). (F. D. Sh.; X.)

SACCHETTI, FRANCO (c. 1330–1400), Italian poet and novelist whose work is typical of late 14th-century Florentine literature, was born in Ragusa of a noble Florentine family. Both as merchant and as *podestà* he traveled widely, thus acquiring an experience of life which compensated for his lack of a regular education. In his letters, in some of his verses and in the *Sposizioni di Vangeli* he expressed his political and moral views. Although poetry was not his main interest, some of his poems, written to be set to music, are among the best of 14th-century minor poetry. As a novelist he wrote 300 stories of which only 223 are known: they consist mainly of anecdotes and jokes derived from oral tradition and the author's direct observation of life. Their artistic value is to be found in the colourful and vivid description of people and places, and their best passages depict scenes from everyday life. Sacchetti does not convey the substance of human life, but only its external appearance.

BIBLIOGRAPHY.—The best modern editions of Sacchetti's works are *Il libro delle Rime* (1936) and *Battaglia, Lettere, Sposizioni* (1938), both ed. by A. Chiari; *Il Trecentonovelle*, ed. by V. Pernicone (1946). *See also* E. Li Gotti, *F. Sacchetti* (1940); L. Caretti, *Saggio sul Sacchetti* (1951).   (G. A.)

SACCHI, ANDREA (1599–1661), Italian painter, was the chief representative of the classical current in Roman mid-17th-century painting (Nicolas Poussin, being a Frenchman, belonging in a sense apart) and as such he stood in opposition to the full baroque. He was born at Nettuno, 30 mi. S. of Rome, but trained under Francesco Albani at Bologna. After returning to Rome in 1621 he worked there till his death (June 21, 1661), except for short visits to north Italy after 1635 and to Paris in 1640.

His Bolognese training gave him an initial bias toward classicism and a taste for colour. But the direct influence of Raphael is already added to these qualities in the "Miracle of St. Gregory" of 1625–27 (chapter house, St. Peter's). This work brought Sacchi to the notice of the Sacchetti family, who employed him, with Pietro da Cortona, in the decoration of their villa at Castel Fusano in 1627–29. Both artists were next taken on by Antonio Cardinal Barberini to decorate the Barberini palace in Rome, and it was then that the classical and baroque currents became separated. Sacchi's ceiling fresco, "The Allegory of Divine Wisdom" (1629–33), is a grave, static work, markedly Raphaelesque in conception and containing relatively few figures, in contrast with Pietro da Cortona's full baroque "Triumph of Divine Providence" in an adjoining room. Sacchi's two altarpieces in Sta. Maria della Concezione, Rome (1631–38), are likewise distinguished by their classicism from the other pictures in the church.

His most important work after the "Divine Wisdom" is the series of eight canvases illustrating the life of St. John the Baptist in the cupola of S. Giovanni in Fonte, Rome (1639–45). He painted a few portraits but concentrated mainly on religious works.   (M. W. L. K.)

SACCO-VANZETTI CASE, a murder trial in Massachusetts, extending over seven years, 1920–27, and resulting in the execution of the defendants, Nicola Sacco and Bartolomeo Vanzetti. The trial resulted from the murders in South Braintree, Mass., on April 15, 1920, of F. A. Parmenter, paymaster of a shoe factory, and Alessandro Berardelli, the guard accompanying him, in order to secure the payroll they were carrying. On May 5 Sacco and Vanzetti, two Italians who had immigrated to the United States in 1908, one a shoe worker and the other a fish peddler, were arrested for the crime. On May 31, 1921, they were brought to trial before Judge Webster Thayer of the Massachusetts Superior Court, and on July 14 both were found guilty by verdict of the jury. Socialists and radicals protested the men's innocence. Many people felt that there was less than a fair trial and that the defendants were convicted for their radical, anarchist beliefs rather than for the crime for which they were tried. All attempts for retrial on the ground of false identification failed. On Nov. 18, 1925, one Celestino Madeiros, then under a sentence for murder, confessed that he had participated in the crime with the Joe Morelli gang. The state supreme court refused to upset the verdict, since at that time the trial judge had the final power to reopen on the ground of additional evidence. The two men were sentenced to death on April 9, 1927.

A storm of protest arose with mass meetings throughout the world. Gov. A. T. Fuller appointed an independent investigatory committee of Pres. A. Lawrence Lowell of Harvard University, Pres. Samuel W. Stratton of the Massachusetts Institute of Technology, and Robert Grant, a former judge. On Aug. 3, 1927, the governor refused to exercise his power of clemency; his advisory committee agreed with this stand. Demonstrations proceeded in many cities throughout the world and bombs were set off in New York and Philadelphia. The men, maintaining their innocence, were executed Aug. 23, 1927. Sacco-Vanzetti agitation continued and as late as April 1959, a legislative committee sat in Boston giving a full day for hearing on a proposal by Rep. Alexander J. Cella to the legislature to recommend to the present governor a retroactive pardon. The committee and the legislature declined to take such a step. Evidence was offered at the hearings, however, by correspondence and otherwise pointing to the guilt of Morelli and his gang. The entire record of the case has been preserved in printed form with a foreword written by a group of the leading attorneys of the nation.

BIBLIOGRAPHY.—N. D. Baker *et al.* (eds.), *The Sacco-Vanzetti Case: a Transcript of the Record of the Trial* (1928); F. Frankfurter, *The Case of Sacco and Vanzetti* (1927), 2nd ed. (1954); Herbert B. Ehrmann, one of the attorneys for the defendants, *The Untried Case: the Sacco-Vanzetti Case and the Morelli Gang* (1933); R. P. Weeks (ed.), *Commonwealth v. Sacco and Vanzetti* (1958).   (M. L. E.)

SACHEVERELL, HENRY (1674–1724), English political preacher, impeached by the Whig junto for his inflammatory sermons in the high church Tory interest, was a son of Joshua Sacheverell, rector of St. Peter's, Marlborough, Wiltshire. He entered Magdalen College, Oxford, in 1689. Sacheverell took his degrees in arts and divinity, and became bursar in 1709. From the beginning (1702) of Anne's reign he obtained great notoriety as a high church scourge of Whigs, Dissenters, and Latitudinarians, and was known as the author of a violent pamphlet entitled *The Character of a Low Churchman* (1701) in which he denounced any political or doctrinal concessions to Nonconformists. In December 1705 he preached before the University of Oxford a sermon on the perils among false brethren, in which he attacked Whigs, Dissenters, and moderate Tories. This sermon passed without public notice, but he reproduced the substance at St. Paul's before the lord mayor on Nov. 5, 1709, assailing the Whig ministers as "wily Volpones," using the current nickname (taken from Ben Jonson's comedy *Volpone, or the Fox*) of the earl of Godolphin, lord treasurer. Godolphin, who had long been smarting under clerical attacks, demanded satisfaction; the extremer members of the Whig junto wanted to end Tory sniping from the pulpit before the election due in 1710, and Sacheverell was impeached. The result was calamitous for the government. There was a deluge of pamphlets. The London mob rioted wildly in sympathy with Sacheverell. Dissenting meetinghouses were wrecked and troops were called out. The trial was a public spectacle. The preacher was condemned by only 69 votes to 52, and was sentenced merely to three years suspension from preaching. This was as good as a Tory victory. Sacheverell's journeys to and fro were like royal progresses, and the enthusiasm encouraged Anne to dismiss Godolphin and the Whigs before the next election.

Sacheverell was despised even by those who took advantage of his notoriety, but when his sentence expired, he was presented (1713) by the queen to the valuable living of St. Andrew's, Holborn, in London. In 1716 he married a rich widow. He quarreled on various occasions with his parishioners. He died at Highgate on June 5, 1724, and was buried in St. Andrew's, Holborn. In 1747 the sexton of that church was imprisoned for stealing his lead coffin.

See A. T. Scudi, *The Sacheverell Affair* (1939); Falconer Madan, *A Bibliography of Dr. Henry Sacheverell* (1884).   (W. R. WD.)

SACHEVERELL, WILLIAM (1638–1691), English Whig politician, orator, and prominent opponent of the succession to the throne of James, duke of York (later James II), came from an ancient and prosperous landed family. Elected to Parliament for Derbyshire in 1670, he at once embarked on an intensely political career. His efforts were directed mainly against French and Roman Catholic influence at the court of Charles II. In 1673 he helped to inspire the first Test Act, whereby holders of office had to take Anglican Communion, and in 1678 pressed the investigation of the "Popish Plot" (see OATES, TITUS) and moved the first bill to exclude the duke of York from the succession. Although he never compromised over the succession, he withdrew from national politics at the height of the exclusion crisis in 1681.

He played no direct part in the Revolution of 1688, but sat for Heytesbury in Wiltshire in the Convention Parliament, which welcomed William III in 1689. His lifelong interest in the Navy was then rewarded with a place as a lord of the Admiralty, but he still proved troublesome to the court. In the drafting of a corporation bill he was responsible for a clause (which bears his name) designed to prevent the Tories from controlling the elections, which was so repugnant to William that he dissolved Parliament (February 1690). Sacheverell was returned for Nottinghamshire for the new Parliament, but died at his seat at Barton, Nottinghamshire, on Oct. 9, 1691. He was one of the most notable orators of his time, and about 400 of his speeches are recorded in A. Grey, *Debates of the House of Commons from . . . 1667 to . . . 1694,* ten volumes (1769). (H. G. Ro.)

SACHS, HANS (1494–1576), the most prolific German poet and dramatist in the 16th century, born in Nürnberg, Nov. 5, 1494, son of a tailor, was educated at the Latin school and apprenticed in 1509 to a shoemaker. Lienhard Nunnenbeck, a weaver, taught him the art of the Meistersinger (q.v.). As a journeyman (1511–16) he visited most of south and central Germany, making contact everywhere with Meistersinger guilds. In 1517 he became a master in the Nürnberg *Singschule* and in 1519, when he married, a master shoemaker. *Die Wittembergisch Nachtigall* (1523), a verse allegory supporting Luther, made him famous. Other Protestant writings followed, until in 1527 the Nürnberg council forbade further publications. Thereafter his life was devoted to his trade and especially his poetry. He died in Nürnberg, Jan. 19, 1576.

Besides 13 *Meisterlied* tunes and seven prose dialogues, Sachs wrote more than 6,000 poems, including some 200 dramas. His subject matter comes from the Bible, Greek, Latin and Italian literature (in translation), Germanic legend, courtly romances and collections of anecdotes, historical events and daily life. But everything is reduced to a common level of thought and language; his characters are essentially contemporary Nürnberg citizens. Subjects are used with little concern for their appropriateness to a particular genre; indeed Sachs's guiding principles are moral and didactic rather than aesthetic.

Sachs is regarded—especially since Wagner's *Meistersinger von Nürnberg*—as the greatest of the Meistersingers. His compositions (over 4,000 *Meisterlieder*) certainly contributed to Nürnberg's pre-eminence in Meistergesang; but his popularity rests on other foundations, for Meistergesang was not a popular art. Again, his tragedies and comedies, long-winded and formless, are simple stories in dialogue form, divided arbitrarily into acts in imitation of the humanists; they have only historical interest. His best and most popular works are his short, humorous narrative poems—*Sankt Peter mit der Geiss* (1555), *Das Kälberbrüten* (1557), *Der Müller mit dem Studenten* (1559)—and his *Fastnachtsspiele,* some of which are still performed—*Der farend Schüler im Paradeis* (1550), *Der bös Rauch* (1557), *Das heiss Eisen* (1551) and *Der Rossdieb zu Fünsing* (1553). His work, though it has been overpraised, reflects a common-sense, realistic attitude to life, a strong moral sense, a deep—but tolerant—attachment to Protestant Christianity, and a sometimes uproarious but always kindly humour.

BIBLIOGRAPHY.—*Werke* (without *Meisterlieder,* but with full bibliography), ed. by A. von Keller and E. Goetze, 26 vol. (1870–1908); *Sämtliche Fastnachtsspiele,* ed. by E. Goetze, 7 vol. (1880–87); *Sämtliche Fabeln und Schwänke,* ed. by E. Goetze and K. Drescher, 6 vol. (1893–1913), vol. 1, 2nd ed. (1953). Selections (in modern spelling) by P. Merker and R. Buchwald, 2 vol., 2nd ed. (1923–24). *See also* E. Goetze, *H. Sachs* (1890); R. Genée, *H. Sachs und seine Zeit,* 2nd ed. (1902); H. Cattanès, *Les "Fastnachtsspiele" de H. Sachs* (1923); W. Stammler, *Von der Mystik zum Barock,* 2nd ed. (1950); E. Geiger, *Der Meistergesang des H. Sachs* (1956). (J. R. WE.)

SACHS, JULIUS VON (1832–1897), German botanist and outstanding plant physiologist, was born at Breslau (Wroclaw) on Oct. 2, 1832. On leaving school in 1851 he became assistant to the physiologist J. E. Purkinje at Prague. In 1856 he graduated

as doctor of philosophy, and established himself as *Privatdozent* (official but unpaid lecturer) for plant physiology in the University of Prague. In 1859 he was appointed physiological assistant to the Agricultural academy of Tharandt in Saxony, and in 1861 he went to the Agricultural academy at Poppelsdorf, near Bonn. He remained there until 1867, when he was nominated professor of botany in the University of Freiburg im Breisgau. In 1868 he accepted the chair of botany in the University of Würzburg, which he continued to occupy until his death on May 29, 1897.

Sachs was especially associated with the development of plant physiology which marked the latter half of the 19th century, though he contributed to every branch of botany. His earlier papers, in botanical journals and publications of learned societies, are of interest. Prominent among them is the series of "Keimungsgeschichten," which laid the foundation of knowledge of microchemical methods and the morphological and physiological details of germination. There is also his resuscitation of the method of water culture first used by J. Woodward in 1699, and its application to problems of nutrition; and, further, his discovery that the starch grains to be found in chloroplasts are the first visible product of their assimilatory activity. Sachs's later papers were published in the three volumes of the *Arbeiten des botanischen Instituts in Würzburg* (1871–88). Among these are his investigation of the periodicity of growth in length; his researches on heliotropism and geotropism, in which he introduced the "clinostat"; his work on the structure and arrangement of cells in growing points; the evidence upon which he based his imbibition theory of the transpiration current; and his studies of the assimilatory activity of the green leaf. Sachs was a great teacher, and botanists from all over the world worked in his laboratory. He had a great influence on British and American botany at the time when there was a swing over from purely systematic studies, an influence to which the English translations of his textbooks contributed.

Sachs's works are: *Handbuch der Experimentalphysiologie der Pflanzen* (1865; French ed., 1868); *Lehrbuch der Botanik* (1868; Eng. ed., 1875 and 1882), a comprehensive work, giving a summary of the botanical science of the period, including the results of original investigations; *Vorlesungen über Pflanzenphysiologie* (1882; 2nd ed., 1887; Eng. ed., 1887); *Geschichte der Botanik* (1875; Eng. ed., 1890).

See E. G. Pringsheim, *Julius Sachs* (1932).

SACHS, NELLY (LEONIE) (1891–   ), German-born Jewish poet and dramatist, shared the 1966 Nobel Prize for Literature, awarded for her "lyrical and dramatic writing, which interprets Israel's destiny with touching strength." Born in Berlin on Dec. 10, 1891, only child of a cultured liberal Jewish industrialist, she wanted to be a dancer, then became interested in puppetry and mime, for which she later wrote many plays, and at 17 began to write poetry. Her *Legenden und Erzählungen* (1921), dedicated to the Swedish novelist Selma Lagerlöf, made little stir. Though Stefan Zweig praised the "ecstatic quality" of her lyrics, they were cast in conventional Romantic, rather than in current Expressionist patterns; they appeared in newspapers from the late 1920s and in the Jewish *Der Morgen* (1936–38).

Nazi policy however was effective, and she was destined for a concentration camp, but her appeal, carried clandestinely to Selma Lagerlöf, persuaded the Swedish royal family personally to intercede with Hitler and thus secured the transfer of Nelly Sachs and her mother to Sweden early in 1940. To her grief Selma Lagerlöf died in March; Nelly became a Swedish citizen and learned Swedish well enough to translate most of the modern Swedish poets into German (*Von Welle und Granit . . .*, 1947). Meanwhile, before its extent was known, she became the "poet of the holocaust," each of her poems, in the words of a German critic, being "a flower planted on the grave of another victim." Her work appeared in both East and West Germany and in the Netherlands: *In den Wohnungen des Todes* ("In the Abodes of Death," 1947), *Sternverdunkelung* ("Eclipse of the Stars," 1949), *Und Niemand weiss weiter* ("And No One Knows Where to Turn," 1955), *Flucht und Verwandlung* ("Flight and Transformation," 1959), *Fahrt ins Staublose* ("Journey into Dustlessness," 1961, her collected poems to 1960), *Glühende Rätsel* ("Burning Enigmas," 1964); *Späte Gedichte* ("Late Poems," 1965); and *Das Buch der Nelly Sachs* (ed. by B. Holmquist, collected poems with bibl., 1968).

German cities and associations bestowed many honours on her, to be crowned, (as she said) "as in a fairy-tale," by King Gustav's presentation of the Nobel Prize on her 75th birthday. A sensitive molder of the German language, revered for poetry of forgiveness and reconciliation drawn from blackest sources of tragedy, she writes with subtle imagery derived from both Hebrew Hasidist mysticism and German tradition. Her best-known play, *Eli: Ein Mysterienspiel von Leiden Israels* (written 1943; publ. 1951; performed 1962; Eng. trans. in *O the Chimneys* with selected poems, 1967) is popular throughout Europe.

BIBLIOGRAPHY.—14 plays collected in *Zeichen im Sand* (1962); *Nelly Sachs zu Ehren: ein Festschrift* (1961); W. Berendsohn (ed.), *Nelly Sachs* (1963); Eng. trans. in *Jewish Quarterly* (winter, 1965–66), and in *Adam International Review*, vol. xxxi, no. 307 (1966).

(M. GR.)

SACKVILLE, GEORGE SACKVILLE (afterward **GERMAIN**), 1ST VISCOUNT (1716–1785), English soldier, dismissed from the service for failing to obey orders at the Battle of Minden, and the politician partly responsible for the British surrender at Saratoga, was the third son of the 1st duke of Dorset. Born in London on Jan. 26, 1716, he was educated at Westminster School (1723–31) and at Trinity College, Dublin (1731–34, his father being then chief governor of Ireland). Commissioned in 1737, he distinguished himself in the War of the Austrian Succession, particularly at the Battle of Fontenoy (May 1745) where he led his regiment, the 28th Foot, so deep into the French ranks that he was taken prisoner and his wounds were treated in Louis XV's own tent. Later, as colonel of the 20th Foot, he served in Scotland and Ireland and was highly esteemed by all his officers, including James Wolfe. Sackville then transferred to the cavalry as colonel, first of the 12th and then of the 6th Dragoon Guards. Promoted major-general (1755), he was a member of the committee of enquiry which condemned the conduct of the Rochefort expedition of 1757. The attack on Saint-Malo in 1758, in which Sackville himself held high command, was equally mismanaged and unsuccessful. A British contingent, commanded after October 1758 by Sackville, was then sent to Germany as part of the allied army under Prince Ferdinand of Brunswick (*see* SEVEN YEARS' WAR). At the Battle of Minden (August 1759), after the British infantry had shattered the cavalry forming the French centre, he inexplicably failed to obey repeated orders from the prince to exploit the success, and the enemy retreated unpursued. A court martial declared him "unfit to serve his majesty in any military capacity whatsoever," and his name was struck off the rolls of the privy council (1760), to which, however, it was restored in 1765.

In 1770, under the terms of a will by which he inherited the estate of Drayton, Northamptonshire, he assumed the name of Germain. As colonial secretary (1775) under Lord North, he was the minister responsible for the general conduct of the war against the American colonists, and as such was largely but not solely to blame for the failure to coordinate operations from Canada and New York against New England which led to the surrender of Gen. John Burgoyne's army at Saratoga (1777). Created Viscount Sackville of Drayton (February 1782), he retired from politics when North resigned (March 1782) and died at Stoneland Lodge (now Buckhurst Park), Withyham, Sussex, on Aug. 26, 1785. His elder son, Charles Sackville-Germain, succeeded his cousin as 5th duke of Dorset.

See F. E. Whitton, *Service Trials and Tragedies* (1930).

(E. W. SH.)

SACKVILLE, THOMAS, 1ST EARL OF DORSET (1536?–1608), English statesman, poet, and dramatist, remembered largely for his share in two achievements of significance in the development of Elizabethan poetry and drama: the collection *A Mirror for Magistrates*, and the tragedy *Gorboduc*. He was born, probably at Buckhurst, Withyham, Sussex, almost certainly in 1536, the only son of Sir Richard Sackville, Anne Boleyn's cousin, who became under-treasurer of the exchequer and chancellor of the court of augmentations, and who established his family's fortunes by acquiring money and lands. Although Thomas Sackville is de-

scribed as a member of Hart Hall, Oxford, and of St. John's College, Cambridge, he probably never studied at either university, though he received honorary degrees at Cambridge in 1571 and Oxford in 1591. In 1553 he settled in London, and in 1555 was admitted to the Inner Temple, becoming a barrister in 1558. He was elected to Parliament for Westmorland (1558), for East Grinstead, Sussex (1559), and for Aylesbury, Buckinghamshire (1563). In *c.* 1563 he went to Italy, returning on his father's death (April 21, 1566); he was invested with a knighthood and the title of baron of Buckhurst in June 1567.

On a mission to France in 1571, Sackville opened negotiations for a marriage between Elizabeth I and the duke of Anjou and in 1572 he was one of the peers who tried Thomas Howard, duke of Norfolk. He became a privy councilor in 1585, and in 1586 conveyed the sentence of death to Mary, queen of Scots. In March 1587 he went to The Hague to report on the situation after the earl of Leicester's expedition (1585–86) and to tell the states-general that the queen could no longer aid them in the war with Spain, but was recalled in disgrace in June when the queen decided to continue the war. On Leicester's death (September 1588), he was restored to favour, and in 1589 and 1598 was again sent to The Hague. He became chancellor of the University of Oxford in 1591, and in 1599 succeeded Lord Burghley as lord high treasurer, an appointment confirmed for life by James I in 1603. In March 1604 he was created earl of Dorset. Among estates he acquired in Kent and Sussex was Knole House, Sevenoaks, Kent, still occupied by his descendants: he rebuilt part of it during 1603–05. He died suddenly at the council table on April 19, 1608.

By his marriage (1555) to Cecily, daughter of Sir John Baker of Sissinghurst, Kent, he had three sons. Robert, the 2nd earl (1561–1609), was a member of Parliament (1585–1608) and a man of considerable learning; William (*c.* 1568–1591) was killed in the service of Henry IV of France; and Thomas (1571–1646) was also a soldier.

The works by which Sackville is chiefly remembered were written in the 1550s. It is likely that he began the *Complaint of Henry, Duke of Buckingham*, included in T. Marsh's 1563 edition of *A Mirror for Magistrates*, in 1554, although it did not appear in W. Baldwin's editions of 1555 (suppressed) and 1559. His *Induction*, also included in the 1563 edition, and, in the enlarged edition of 1610, transposed to the beginning of the work (thus making Sackville appear responsible for the whole collection), was also begun much earlier. *A Mirror for Magistrates*, published in 1563 as an addition to *The Fall of Princes* by John Lydgate (*q.v.*), takes the form of tragic lamentations by the ghosts of great men, contributed by various writers, and indicates the development of style and taste in the early Elizabethan age. Its material, according to the 1555 title page, had been "diligently collected out of the Chronicles," and it thus has a place in the fusion of poetry and history which later found expression in the work of Drayton, Daniel, Spenser, and Shakespeare. It includes pieces written soon after the death of James IV of Scotland (1513), metrical experiments similar to those in *Tottel's Miscellany* (1557), and early examples of the conceits and poetic passion characteristic of the later part of the Elizabethan period.

Of Sackville's contributions, the most notable is the *Induction*. Written in rime royal (*q.v.*), this describes the poet's visit to the infernal regions, led by Sorrow, who promises that he will see there the wretchedness of those ruined by ambition, and will recognize the transience of earthly pleasure. At hell's approaches, he encounters figures representing remorse, dread, revenge, misery, care, sleep, old age, malady, famine, death, and war. After crossing Acheron, he is surrounded by shades, and Sorrow indicates those "that whilom sat on top of Fortune's wheel," of whom Buckingham advances first; thus introducing the *Complaint*. Sackville has little feeling for drama, but the *Induction* allows him to develop his gift for allegorical description, in which he shows an energy and a stateliness of tone which directly anticipate Spenser. The stanzas describing "Heavy sleep, the cousin of death" are deservedly famous.

Sackville's other important literary work, written with Thomas

Norton (*q.v.*), was *The Tragedy of Gorboduc,* the earliest English drama in blank verse (*q.v.*). The unauthorized first edition (1565) credits Sackville with the last two acts. *Gorboduc* is broadly Senecan in character, the action being related by messengers, and the dialogue consisting almost entirely of long addresses with little dramatic quality. A dumb show precedes each of the five acts, and four "ancient and sage men of Britain" act as chorus. The plot, taken from the *Historia regum Britanniae* of Geoffrey of Monmouth (*q.v.*), concerns a legendary king of Britain, Gorboduc, whose sons, Ferrex and Porrex, quarrel when their aged father divides the kingdom between them. Ferrex is killed by his younger brother, and the queen, Widen, takes revenge by murdering Porrex. When Fergus, duke of Albany, tries to seize the kingdom, civil war breaks out and the play ends with a warning against the evil consequences of rebellion. As this suggests, *Gorboduc* is a moral *exemplum* rather than a piece of entertainment, offering no concessions of comic or romantic relief. After presentation at the Inner Temple at the 1560 Christmas revels, it was performed before the queen at Whitehall on Jan. 18, 1562. The 1565 edition was followed by an undated edition, *c.* 1571. (*See also* DRAMA: *Modern Drama: Neoclassic Imitation;* ENGLISH LITERATURE: *Elizabethan and Jacobean Drama.*)

In the address to his translation of Seneca's *Thyestes* (1560), Jasper Heywood mentions "Sackvylde's Sonnets, sweetly sauste." Of these only the poem prefixed to Hoby's translation (1561) of Castiglione's *Il Cortegiano* is known.

According to Sackville's funeral sermon (Westminster Abbey, May 26, 1608), by his chaplain, George Abbot, later archbishop of Canterbury, Elizabeth I shared the general high opinion of Sackville's merits as a writer.

BIBLIOGRAPHY.—*Works,* including letters, ed. by R. W. Sackville-West (1859). The best edition of *A Mirror for Magistrates* is by Lily B. Campbell (1938); *see also* her *Parts Added to the Mirror for Magistrates* (1946). *Gorboduc* is included in *Early English Classical Tragedies,* ed. by J. W. Cunliffe (1912). *See also* J. Swart, *Thomas Sackville: a Study in 16th-Century Poetry* (1949); W. Clemen, *English Tragedy Before Shakespeare* (1961); V. Sackville-West, *Knole and the Sackvilles,* 2nd ed. (1947). (JA. WI.)

SACRAMENT, in Christian theology, has been defined as "the visible form of an invisible grace" (Augustine). This definition underlies most Western definitions, both Roman Catholic and Protestant, including those of the Council of Trent, the Book of Common Prayer, the Lutheran Book of Concord, and many of the Reformed confessions; it would also be acceptable to Eastern Orthodox theologians.

Despite efforts to find a general "sacramental principle" in the Christian doctrines of creation and incarnation, the meaning of "sacrament" must be worked out *a posteriori*. According to the New Testament, Jesus instituted and commanded various practices, among them baptism, a common meal, the washing of feet, anointing, and the casting out of demons. Some of these were continued by Christians; some were dropped; still others were adopted and attributed to the institution of Christ. Consideration of all these rites and ordinances led to the development of the concept "sacrament," but both the definition and the exact number remained fluid well beyond the end of the 1st millennium of church history. As finally set forth by Peter Lombard, codified by Thomas Aquinas, and promulgated by the Council of Trent, the sacraments were said to be seven in number (baptism, confirmation, Eucharist, penance, anointing or extreme unction, holy orders or ordination, and matrimony) and to be efficacious signs of the grace of God instituted by Christ for permanent observance by the church. The Reformation questioned both the definition and the number of sacraments in scholastic theology, as well as the use of the sacraments in medieval piety, liturgy, and churchmanship.

Specific information about the theological, biblical, historical, and liturgical aspects of each of the "sacraments" is presented in the several articles dealing with them. Nevertheless, the importance of the general concept in Christian language requires that attention be given here to at least two issues in the sacramental theology of the various Christian traditions and denominations.

Sacraments as Signs.—Everyone would agree that a sacrament involves the use of external means or signs, which scholastic theology calls the "matter" of the sacrament: a physical element and the action of using that element. Theologians in the Platonic tradition, for all of whom the entire external world of things is a "sign" or "symbol" of the spiritual world and for some of whom it is nothing more than that, have very little difficulty regarding baptism, Eucharist, etc., as signs of the efficacious presence of God; they have more difficulty extricating these signs from the welter of symbols all about them. For quite different reasons, radical Protestants, who object to traditional ideas of the sacraments as a means of grace, also face the issue of finding a qualitative distinction between the sacraments and other signs, as, for example, the cross. The Council of Trent proclaimed that "the sacraments of the New Testament contain the grace that they signify" and are not "merely outward signs . . . and some sort of marks of the Christian profession"; this seems to underemphasize the role of the sacraments as signs of the personal reality of the presence of grace in the recipient.

Nevertheless, the vigorous efforts of the proponents of each of these traditions to meet the objections mentioned are themselves worthy of note. Augustine transcended his Neoplatonic propensities to develop a theory of signs and sacraments; even very radical Protestants treat baptism and the Eucharist with utmost seriousness; much of the history of Roman Catholic sacramental theology since Trent has been marked by the combination of the traditional stress upon the sacraments as means of grace with a further clarification of the difference between this stress and any "magical" interpretation of the effect of the sacraments. The differences among Christians on this issue remain profound and in many ways basic; no less significant, however, is the *rapprochement* between the Protestants who seek to avoid the rationalism of a theory of "mere symbols" and the Roman Catholics who seek to avoid the superstition of a theory of "efficacy apart from the disposition of the recipient."

Sacraments as Institutions of Christ.—Part of almost every definition of a sacrament is the requirement that it have been, in some sense, "instituted by Christ." Of the seven sacraments accepted by Eastern Orthodoxy and Roman Catholicism, such institution can be incontrovertibly documented from the New Testament for only two, baptism and the Eucharist. In fact, the very concept of "institution" appears to have entered sacramental theology from consideration of the Eucharist, for every reference to baptism in the sayings of Jesus seems to presuppose its prior existence and there are no "words of institution" for baptism to correspond to the four versions of such words that the New Testament presents for the Eucharist.

During the debates of the 16th and 17th centuries, the language of the New Testament was strained by both sides in an effort to prove that the historical Jesus really did, or really could not have, instituted marriage, ordination, etc., as sacraments. Protestant biblical scholarship eventually came to recognize that even the accounts of the institution of the Eucharist by Christ are, in their present form at least, products of the recollection of the primitive Christian community rather than verbatim transcripts of the sayings of the historical Jesus. Roman Catholic theology likewise surrendered the effort to find explicit historical support for each of the seven sacraments in such sayings and concentrated instead on the implicit significance of the very establishment of the church: Christ instituted the sacraments in a theological sense, even though there is no way of proving that the historical Jesus instituted them in a historical sense.

Discussion of both these forms of theological revision thus replaced earlier controversy "about the number and the use of the sacraments." Baptism and the Eucharist are unquestionably primary for all Christians. Is confirmation, for example, derived from baptism as a necessary adjustment to the development of infant baptism? Is a sacramental view of penance the answer of the church, in harmony with the ordinance of Christ, to the unforeseen question of sin after baptism? Such questions as these made conventional debates obsolete, while at the same time putting the concerns of an earlier generation into a new and more favourable light.

Christianity is not, of course, the only world religion that has "sacraments"; the use of worship rituals as means of effecting the right relation between God and man is one of the most nearly universal phenomena in religion. Thus the clarification of what Christianity means by its sacraments is both an examination of its uniqueness and an affirmation of its link—as correction and fulfillment, if not as continuity—with other pictures of the relation between God and man.

See also RELIGION; RELIGION, PRIMITIVE; and references under "Sacrament" in the Index.

BIBLIOGRAPHY.—In addition to the works listed in the bibliographies of the several articles on the sacraments, the following deserve consideration: O. C. Quick, *The Christian Sacraments* (1927); Bernard Leeming, S.J., *Principles of Sacramental Theology* (1956); A. M. Landgraf, *Dogmengeschichte der Frühscholastik,* iii–1 and iii–2 (1954–55); P. T. Forsyth, *The Nature and Function of the Sacraments* (1917).

(J. J. PN.)

SACRAMENTALS, in the Roman Catholic Church, originally denoted the ceremonies, outside the essentials, used in the administration of the sacraments to elevate the mind to the contemplation of the divine mysteries; *e.g.,* genuflections during Mass, the anointing of the priest's hands during ordination, the triple pouring at baptism. In a larger sense, they are all the other external signs employed by the church to obtain spiritual effects. These signs can be actions (exorcisms, making the sign of the cross, saying of grace at meals, blessings, etc.) or things (holy water, blessed candles, vestments, palms and ashes, crucifixes, rosaries, etc.).

The sacramentals are like sacraments in that they are sensible signs and symbols. They differ from the sacraments in that they do not give grace of themselves; rather, their special spiritual effects, *e.g.,* an increase of charity, derive from the power of the church's prayer and are conditioned by the dispositions of the user.

See also LITURGY, CHRISTIAN.

See J. Sullivan, *The Externals of the Catholic Church* (1959); *The Documents of Vatican II,* ch. 3 (1966). (E. J. A.)

SACRAMENTO, the capital city of California, U.S., and seat of Sacramento County, is located about 75 mi. NE of San Francisco at the confluence of the American and Sacramento rivers, midway between the Sierra Nevada Range and the Pacific Ocean. Because of climatic factors favourable to growing camellias, the city became known as "the camellia capital."

History.—In August 1839, John Augustus Sutter (*q.v.*), a Mexican citizen, established a colony, known as New Helvetia, on the site of the future city. He had received a land grant of 11 square leagues (about 73 sq.mi.) from the Mexican governor Juan Alvarado and between 1839 and 1844 he used Indian labour to build an adobe fortress known as Fort Sutter. Situated as it was on the main line of travel, Fort Sutter soon became one of the greatest trading posts in California. Sutter extended unbounded hospitality to American immigrants between 1843 and 1848. James W. Marshall, an employee of Sutter, was supervising the construction of a sawmill on the American River near Coloma, 35 mi. NE of the fort, when, on Jan. 24, 1848, he found a gold nugget in the millrace. The discovery of gold on his land was, ironically, the cause of Sutter's ruin, for his men deserted him, gold seekers pillaged his property, and he died a poor man.

Sutter's son, who had been deeded the family property near the Embarcadero along the river, laid out a town there named after the Sacramento River. The federal census reported a population of 6,820 as early as 1850, the year that Sacramento was incorporated. Strategically located at the entrance to the gold areas, the city became a typical mining boomtown of about 10,000 within a few months.

When state government was established in 1849, Sacramento campaigned to be named the capital and offered $1,000,000 for the honour; in 1854 it was chosen the permanent seat of government. Three times between 1849 and 1853, and again in 1861, the city suffered from devastating floods, and in 1852 two-thirds of it was destroyed by fire.

Sacramento was a major depot on the overland mail routes between the Missouri frontier and the Pacific during the 1850s.

When the pony express was established in 1860, the city became the western terminal. As early as 1856 the Sacramento Valley Railroad was completed to Folsom, 24 mi. NE, and was the first railway in the state to tap the freighting business between the gold camps by providing faster service than the freight wagons on the roads and trails. Theodore Dehone Judah, the chief engineer of the railroad, planned to extend the line across the Sierra Nevada. He found four merchants in Sacramento, Leland Stanford, Mark Hopkins, Charles Crocker, and Collis P. Huntington, willing to help finance and promote his transcontinental project. These men became the founders of the Republican Party in California and gained generous government support for their Central Pacific Railroad, constructed 1863–69. With the advent of rail transportation into the area, the future of Sacramento was assured.

Population.—The population of Sacramento city in 1960 was 191,667, an increase of 54,095 since the 1950 census representing a 39.3% growth. The standard metropolitan statistical area (SMSA) of Sacramento comprising Sacramento County had a population of 502,778 in 1960 and included North Sacramento, Arden, Folsom, Natomas, Del Paso Heights, Town and Country area, Carmichael, Fair Oaks, North Highlands, Citrus Heights, and Orangeville, all on the east side of the Sacramento River, with populations ranging from 5,000 to 45,000. The rapid growth of suburban communities in the Sacramento vicinity has caused the population growth of the county (81.4% between 1950 and 1960) to exceed that of the state. In 1963 Placer and Yolo counties were added to the SMSA, resulting in a new area of 3,441 sq.mi. and an adjusted 1960 census figure of 625,503. (For comparative population figures *see* table in CALIFORNIA: *Population.*)

Administration.—Sacramento adopted a council-manager form of government in 1921. The nine members of the city council are elected for a two-year term. Sacramento County government is based upon a state charter providing for the election of five supervisors for four-year terms from defined geographic districts. A city-planning board was established in 1926 and zoning ordinances are in effect.

Transportation, Commerce, and Industry.—Sacramento is on the main line of two transcontinental railroads and there is a connection with a third. Two major east-west transcontinental highways and the principal north-south Central Valley route come together at Sacramento, making it a hub of highway transportation. Sacramento County has 14 airports: one is municipally controlled, one is administered by the county, two are United States Air Force installations, and the remainder are privately owned. Barge service along the Sacramento River connects the city with the port of San Francisco and is used extensively in transporting agricultural and petroleum products.

Sacramento is the centre of an extensive wholesale and retail trade. Because of the surrounding region's high agricultural productivity, canning and food processing is the principal manufac-

BY COURTESY OF SACRAMENTO CITY-COUNTY CHAMBER OF COMMERCE

THE STATE CAPITOL, CONSTRUCTED 1869–74, IN THE HEART OF DOWNTOWN SACRAMENTO

turing activity with more than 100 plants. Associated with this agricultural processing are flour millers, bean and rice cleaners and polishers, olive-packing plants, and one of the world's largest almond-shelling plants. Among other large industrial establishments are manufacturers of jet-propellants, soaps and detergents, furniture, machine engine parts, boxes, brick and clay pipe, and mining equipment. There are also large railroad shops and three military installations that maintain and repair aircraft. Natural gas fields in the vicinity and water power from the Sacramento River system provide the area with ample power facilities.

Education and Cultural Activities.—Public education is available from kindergarten through college. A public junior college, Sacramento City College, was established in 1916. American River Junior College, opened in 1955, was relocated on a new campus in 1958. Sacramento State College (1947) emphasizes teacher education. The University of California Davis campus is 15 mi. W.

The state library has an outstanding collection on the history of California, a fine law library, and is an extensive depository of government documents. The E. B. Crocker Art Gallery houses one of the largest and most valuable collections west of the Mississippi River. The municipal auditorium, completed in 1927, seats 5,000 and is a centre of cultural entertainment.

Parks and Recreation.—The state capitol, located in the heart of downtown Sacramento, is surrounded by a 40-ac. park, with numerous varieties of native American and foreign trees and shrubs, comprising one of the most diversified horticultural collections to be found within an area of similar size. The capitol, constructed 1869–74, is four stories high, surmounted by a large dome, and is Roman Corinthian in design. In 1951 a large annex, the east wing, was added to the building. One mile east of the capitol is old Fort Sutter, maintained by the state as a historic museum, surrounded by a public garden.

A vast network of waterways in the Sacramento area provides about 1,500 mi. of picturesque routes for boating enthusiasts. Folsom Lake, 14 mi. long and covering 11,500 ac., provides for water skiing and other aquatic sports.　　　　(W. T. J.)

SACRAMENTO RIVER, the largest and most important stream in northern California, U.S., rises in the Klamath Mountains near Mt. Shasta and empties into San Francisco Bay. The river is slightly less than 400 mi. long, but close to 600 if measured from the source of its longest tributary, the Pit. Flowing southward for most of its length, it turns westward just below the city of Sacramento, unites with the northward-flowing San Joaquin near Pittsburg, and passes through Suisun and San Pablo bays and San Pablo Strait into San Francisco Bay. Its navigability varies with water level and dredging operations, with Red Bluff, about 250 mi. upstream, being accessible to small craft at high water. The Sacramento and its tributaries, especially the American and Feather rivers, were the scene of the famous California Gold Rush of 1849. Together with the San Joaquin, the Sacramento forms the great Central Valley of California, one of the richest agricultural areas in the world.

The Sacramento (northern) portion of the valley has only one-third of the arable land but it has two-thirds of the water resources (an average annual runoff of about 22,000,000 ac-ft.). In order to control floods and shift surplus water to the more arid San Joaquin region, the Central Valley Project was launched by the Federal Bureau of Reclamation in the 1930s. The project includes various dams, such as Shasta near Redding, reservoirs, power plants, and canals. The state-financed multipurpose Feather River Project, rated as the largest single water project in history and including the immense Oroville Dam, was undertaken in the 1960s.　　　　(D. E. F.)

SACRED HEART. Devotion to the Sacred Heart of Jesus is a cult peculiar to the modern Roman Catholic Church. The principal object of this devotion is the Saviour himself. Though it had its origins in the Middle Ages, when it was confined to a few mystics, was later fostered by the Carthusians and the Jesuits, and was further promoted by St. Francis of Sales and the Visitandines, it was the Visitandine nun St. Margaret Mary Alacoque (*q.v.*), assisted by Claude de la Colombière, who gave shape to and spread the devotion. It was strongly opposed by the

Jansenists, who claimed that the heart of Christ was being adored as separate from the rest of his being. The Jansenist Synod of Pistoia (*q.v.*), which formulated this objection, was condemned by Pius VI in the bull *auctorem fidei*, Aug. 28, 1794. In 1856 Pius IX introduced the feast into the general calendar of the Roman Catholic Church, fixing the Friday after the Octave of Corpus Christi for its celebration.

BIBLIOGRAPHY.—*Catholic Encyclopedia*, vol. vii, pp. 163–167; *Dictionnaire de théologie catholique*, tome iii, col. 271–351 (1908); *Enciclopedia Cattolica*, vol. iv, col. 1059–64 (1950).

SACRED HEART, BROTHERS OF THE (SOCIETAS FRATRUM SACRIS CORDIS; S.C.), a Roman Catholic religious order founded in 1821 in Lyons, France, by André Coindre, a missionary priest, is primarily a teaching order, specializing in high school and elementary school education in both parochial and private schools. The brothers arrived in the United States in 1847, from where they spread rapidly into Canada; there are seven Canadian provinces and three U.S. provinces. The brothers are also a missionary society with missions all over the world. The motherhouse is in Rome. *See* ORDERS AND CONGREGATIONS, RELIGIOUS.　　(A. Ro.)

SACRED HEART, MISSIONARIES OF THE (in full, SOCIETY OF THE MISSIONARIES OF THE SACRED HEART OF JESUS; SOCIETAS MISSIONARIORUM SACRATISSIMI CORDIS JESU; M.S.C.), is a Roman Catholic congregation of men founded at Issoudun, France, Dec. 8, 1854, by Jules Chevalier, a secular priest, for restoring the faith in the rural sections of France. Pius IX directed the congregation to foreign-mission work. The M.S.C. have provinces in Europe, the Americas (two in the U.S.), and Australia, and do foreign-mission work on all the continents and in the Pacific islands. The general motherhouse is in Rome. In 1968 the society had more than 3,200 members. *See* ORDERS AND CONGREGATIONS, RELIGIOUS.　　　　(L. F. P.)

SACRED HEART, PRIESTS OF THE (in full, CONGREGATION OF THE PRIESTS OF THE SACRED HEART OF JESUS; CONGREGATIO SACERDOTUM A SACRO CORDE JESU; S.C.J.), a congregation of priests and brothers founded in Saint-Quentin, France, in 1878, by P. Dehon. Its aim is to spread the apostolate of the Sacred Heart and to undertake all forms of the priestly ministry: teaching, missions, retreats, home and foreign missions. The congregation has spread to five continents and to several states in the U.S. Generalate headquarters are located in Rome. *See* ORDERS AND CONGREGATIONS, RELIGIOUS.　　　　(J. T. O'C.)

SACRED SCRIPTURES. Most religions, primitive and advanced, have either what may be truly designated as sacred scriptures or what fulfills in some degree the function of sacred scriptures. In the case of preliterate peoples, the material, handed down orally from generation to generation, though it may lack the precise form and content of written scriptures, is usually a fairly well-defined body of material, considered authoritative and even sacred.

Sacred scriptures may be said to provide the fundamental basis of beliefs concerning the God or gods and man's relationship to them, as well as the practices that flow from that relationship, whether ritual, social, or what may be regarded as moral. In short, they form the authoritative basis for the religious and usually also for the ethical beliefs and practices of a people or faith. They may contain much more—*e.g.*, the storied origins of the world and of the people as well as their early history, though ordinarily that is merely the detailed account of the God or gods and their dealings with man. They may include also the best of the ancient poetry of a people, but this is likely to be chiefly the expression of man's sentiments as he seeks to relate himself to the divine, in praise of, in thanksgiving, or in devotion to deity. They may also contain a great deal of what might appear to be secular law, or binding custom, but this too is usually but the logical extension of the divine rule over man's behaviour.

Most of the world's great religions have written scriptures, definitely limited as to what they include—that is, with a fixed canon, to which nothing can be added and from which nothing may be taken away. There may be sectarian differences within a religion as to the exact content of a canon (as, for example, between the Roman Catholic and Protestant churches within

Christianity), but within a given group it is usually invariable. Some of the older religions, now no longer current—as those of Greece, Rome, Egypt, and Babylonia—had all the materials of scripture but never a specifically limited canon. Most scriptures are considered to be of divine origin, divinely inspired or revealed in some way to man.

Some religions, as Islam, fundamentalist Christianity, and others, hold to a strict verbal inspiration that extends to every word of the sacred text. The Hindus have one group of writings, *shruti*, which is regarded as the *ipsissima verba*, the very, very word of God, and another group that, while still sacred, was inspired in a more general way. In some religions, such as Buddhism and Jainism, there is no claim of divine inspiration, but long tradition has given the scriptures almost the same authority as the divinely inspired writings.

As a corollary to this belief in the revealed or authoritative nature of the scriptures, they are practically inviolable. They may even become an object of cult as seems to be the case of the Sikh Bible, the Granth. They are not to be treated as other writings. The first beginnings of scientific critical study of sacred scriptures usually provoke violent resistance.

Because of their great influence on their respective cultures the sacred scriptures have frequently been (and still are, where education has not become secular) the major basis of the education of children and often also the basis of civil and even criminal law.

The best-known scriptures are: (1) Judaeo-Christian faith, the Bible (*q.v.*); this for Jews means the Old Testament only. (2) Islam, the Koran (*q.v.*). (3) Zoroastrianism (*q.v.*), the Avesta. (4) Sikhism, the Granth (*q.v.*). (5) Buddhism, in the south, the Theravadin or Pali canon; although there was a Sanskrit canon upon which Mahayana or northern Buddhism was largely based, Mahayana has no fixed canon (*see* BUDDHISM; TRIPITAKA). (6) Confucianism, the five canonical books and the four classics. (7) Taoism (*q.v.*), the *Tao-te ching* (*see* LAO-TZU) and the writings of Chuang-Tzu. (8) Hinduism has no single name to cover all the scriptures, but the Vedas, which term usually is taken to include also the Brahmanas (*q.v.*) and the Upanishads, constitute the major part of the *shruti* writings. (9) Shinto has no concept of scripture as discussed here, but the *Kojiki* (*q.v.*) and *Nihongi* (*q.v.*) are quasi-scriptural writings. (10) Jainism has a sacred hterature comprising several works (*see* JAINISM).

See also references under "Sacred Scriptures" in the Index.

BIBLIOGRAPHY.—Selections from most of the scriptures may be found in Robert O. Ballou (ed.), *The Bible of the World* (1939); Lewis Browne, *The World's Great Scriptures* (1946). A general introduction to all the sacred scriptures is Charles S. Braden, *The Scriptures of Mankind* (1952), with ample bibliographies, including the better translations into English, for each faith.　　　　　　　　(C. S. B.)

SACRIFICE. The Latin *sacrificare* (*sacer*, "holy"; *facere*, "to make") referred to the act of offering objects to a god (or other supernatural being), thereby making them the property of the god and thus holy. In a sense, what is always offered in sacrifice is, in one form or another, life itself. Sacrifice is a celebration of life, a recognition of its divine and imperishable nature. In the sacrifice the consecrated life of an oblation is liberated as a sacred potency which establishes a bond between the sacrificer and the Sacred. Through sacrifice life is returned to its divine source, regenerating the power (*i.e.*, life) of that source; life is fed by life. Hence the word of the Roman sacrificer to his god: "Be thou increased [*machte*] by this offering." It is, however, an increase of sacred power which is ultimately beneficial to the sacrificer. In a sense, sacrifice is the impetus and guarantee of the reciprocal flow of the divine life force between its source and its manifestations.

Often the act of sacrifice involves the destruction of the oblation, but this destruction—whether by burning, slaughter, or whatever means—is not in itself the sacrifice, the "making holy." The killing of an animal is the means by which its consecrated life is "liberated" and thus made available to the deity, and the destruction of a food offering in an altar's fire is the means by which the deity receives (by olfaction, rather than ingestion) the offering. Sacrifice as such, however, is the total act of offering and not merely the mode in which it is performed.

Sacrificial rites are known throughout the history of religions, and although they have assumed a multitude of forms and intentions, the fundamental meaning is that of effecting a necessary and efficacious relationship with sacred power and of establishing man and his world in the sacred order.

As a manifestation of man's experience of sacred reality, sacrifice is rooted in the religious consciousness. Hence any consideration of its possible origins, like that of the origins of religion itself, is more a matter of conjecture and speculation than of verifiable historical or phenomenological investigation. Attempts have been made (notably by E. B. Tylor, W. Robertson Smith, and J. G. Frazer) to discover the genesis of sacrifice, but these attempts, though helpful for a greater understanding of sacrifice, have not been conclusive.

Sacrifices may be broadly classified according to the material of the oblation, the mode in which the oblation is offered, the frequency of performance, and the specific intention of the rite. These categories, of course, often overlap.

Material of the Oblation.—Any form under which life manifests itself in the world may be a sacrificial oblation. The variety of sacrificial offerings can conveniently be discussed as (1) blood offerings (animal and human) and (2) bloodless offerings (libations and vegetation).

Blood Offerings.—Basic to both animal and human sacrifice is the recognition of blood as the sacred life force in man and beast. Thus its great potency has been utilized through sacrifice for a number of purposes—*e.g.*, earth fertility, purification, and expiation. However, as will be discussed below, the letting of blood was neither the only end nor the only mode of human and animal sacrifice.

A wide variety of animals have served as sacrificial offerings. In ancient Greece and India, for example, oblations included a number of important domestic animals such as the goat, ram, bull, ox, and horse. Moreover, in Greek religion all edible birds, wild animals of the hunt, and fish were used. In ancient Judaism the kind and number of animals for the various sacrifices was carefully stipulated so that the offering might be acceptable and thus fully effective. This sort of regulation is generally found in sacrificial cults: the offering must be appropriate either to the deity to whom, or to the intention for which, it is to be presented. Very often the sacrificial species (animal or vegetable) was closely associated with the deity to whom it was offered as the deity's symbolic representation or even its incarnation. Thus in the Vedic ritual the goddesses of Night and Morning received the milk of a black cow having a white calf; while the "bull of heaven," Indra, was offered a bull, and Surya, the sun-god, a white, male goat. Likewise the ancient Greeks sacrificed black animals to the deities of the dark underworld; swift horses to the sun-god, Helios; pregnant sows to the earth mother, Demeter; and the dog, guardian of the dead, to Hecate, goddess of darkness. The Syrians sacrificed fish, regarded as the lord of the sea and guardian of the realm of the dead, to the goddess Atargatis, and ate the consecrated offering in a communion meal with the deity, sharing in the divine power. An especially prominent sacrificial animal was the bull (or its counterparts, the boar and the ram), which, as the representation and embodiment of the cosmic powers of fertility, was sacrificed to numerous fertility gods (*e.g.*, the Norse god Freyr; the Greek "bull of the earth," Zeus Cthonios; and the Indian "bull of heaven," Indra). It is because the divine nature of these animals is recognized that they are sacrificed. Through the sacrifice—through the return of the sacred life revealed in these species—the god lives, and therefore man and nature live.

The occurrence of human sacrifice appears to have been universal and its intentions various, ranging from communion with a god and participation in his divine life to expiation and the promotion of the earth's fertility. Of all the worldly manifestations of the life force, the human undoubtedly impressed men as the most valuable and thus the most potent and efficacious as an oblation. In many societies human victims gave place to animal substitutes or to effigies made of dough, wood, or other materials. Thus in India with the advent of British rule human sacrifices to the Dravidian village goddesses (*gramadevata*) were replaced by animal. In Tibet, under the influence of Buddhism, which prohibits all blood sacrifice, human sacrifice to the pre-Buddhist Bön deities was replaced by the offering of dough images or reduced to pantomime. Moreover, in some cults both human and animal oblations could be "ransomed"—*i.e.*, replaced by offerings of money or other inanimate valuables. (*See* also HUMAN SACRIFICE.)

Bloodless Offerings.—Among the many life-giving substances which have been used as libations are milk, honey, vegetable and animal oils, beer, wine, and water. Of these the last two have been especially prominent. Wine is the "blood of the grape" and thus the "blood of the earth," a spiritual beverage which invigorates gods and men. Water is always the sacred "water of life," the primordial source of existence (thus the symbolism of the waters of creation, the placental waters), and the bearer of the life of plants, animals, human beings, and even the gods. Because of its great potency water, like blood, has been widely used in purificatory and expiatory rites to wash away defilements and restore spiritual life. It has also, along with wine, been an important offering to the dead as a revivifying force.

Vegetable offerings have included not only the edible herbaceous plants but also grains, fruits, and flowers. In both Hinduism and Jainism, flowers, fruits, and grains (cooked and uncooked) are included in the daily temple offerings. In some agricultural societies (*e.g.*, those of West Africa) yams and other tuber plants have been important in planting and harvest sacrifices and in other rites concerned with the fertility and fecundity of the earth. These plants have been regarded as especially embodying the life force of the deified earth and are frequently buried or plowed into the soil to replenish and reactivate its energies.

Mode of Sacrifice.—Along with libation and the sacrificial effusion of blood, one of the commonest means of making an oblation available to sacred beings is to burn it. In both ancient Judaism and Greek religion the major offering was the burnt or fire offering. Through the medium of the fire the oblation was conveyed to the divine receiver as a "sweet smelling savour." In ancient Greece the generic term for sacrifice (*thusia*), as well as that for altar (*thuein*), was derived from a root meaning "to burn" or "to smoke." In Judaism the important sacrifices ('*olah* and *zevach*) involved the ritual burning, either entirely or in part, of the oblation, be it animal or vegetation, and according to the Levitical code a sacred fire was to be kept burning in the Temple as the only fire for ritual use. For the Babylonians, also, fire was essential to sacrifice, and all oblations were conveyed to the gods by the fire-god, Girru-Nusku, whose presence as intermediary between the gods and men was indispensable. Likewise in the Vedic cult of ancient India the god of fire, Agni, received the offerings of men and brought them into the presence of the gods.

As burning is the appropriate mode for sacrifice to celestial divinities, so burial is the appropriate mode for sacrifice to earth divinities. Hence, in Greece, for example, sacrifices to the chthonic powers were often buried rather than burned or, if burned, burned near the ground or even in a trench. In Vedic India the blood and entrails of animals sacrificed on the fire altar to the sky-gods were put upon the ground for the earth divinities, including the ghosts and malevolent spirits. In West Africa yams and fowls sacrificed to promote the fertility of the earth are planted in the soil.

In sacrifice by burning and by burial, as also in the effusion of blood, the prior death of the human or animal victim, even if ritually performed, is in a sense incidental to the sacrificial action. There are, however, sacrifices (including, of course, live burial and burning) in which the ritual killing is itself the means by which the offering is effected. Illustrative of this mode was the practice in ancient Greek and Indian cults of making sacrifices to aquatic spirits by drowning the oblations in sacred lakes or rivers. Similarly the Norse cast human and animal victims over cliffs and into wells and waterfalls as offerings to the divinities dwelling therein. The Norse also sacrificed by hanging animal or human offerings by the neck from poles or trees in sacred groves. In the Aztec sacrifice of human beings to the god Xipe, the victim was lashed to a scaffold and shot to death with bow and arrow.

There are, finally, sacrifices that do not involve the death or destruction of the oblation. Such were the sacrifices in ancient Greece of fruits and vegetables at the so-called "pure" (*katharos*) altar of Apollo at Delos, at the shrine of Athena at Lindos, and at the altar of Zeus "Most High" in Athens. These "fireless oblations" (*apura hiera*) were especially appropriate for the deities of vegetation and fertility; *e.g.*, Demeter and Dionysus. In Egypt bloodless offerings of food and drink were simply laid before the god on mats or a table in a daily ceremony called "performing the presentation of the divine oblations." In both Greek and Egyptian cults such offerings were never to be eaten by the worshipers, but they were probably surreptitiously consumed by the priests or temple attendants. In ancient Israel, on the other hand, the food offerings of the "table of the shewbread" (the "bread of the presence") were regarded as available to the priests and could be given by them to the laity. Likewise in Hinduism the daily offering of cooked rice and vegetable, after its consecration, is distributed by the priests to the worshipers as the deity's "grace" (*prasada*). In some cases the sacrificial gifts are put out to be eaten by an animal representative of the deity. Offerings of cakes to the Vedic god Rudra were left at a mole's hole to be consumed by an animal sacred to the deity. In Dahomey wandering dogs consume, on behalf of the trickster deity Legba-Eshu, the consecrated food oblations presented to the god each morning at his shrines.

Frequency of Sacrifice.—In many cults sacrifices are distinguished by frequency of performance into two types, regular and special. Regular sacrifices may be daily, weekly, or monthly, or seasonal (as at planting, harvest, and New Year). Also often included are sacrifices made at specific times in each man's life—birth, puberty, marriage, and death. Offerings made on special occasions and for special intentions include, for example, sacrifices in times of danger, sickness, or crop failure, and those performed at the construction of a building, for success in battle, or in thanksgiving for a divine favour.

In the Vedic cult of India the regular sacrifices were daily, monthly, and seasonal. The daily rites included fire offerings to the gods and libations and food offerings to the ancestors and the earth divinities and spirits. The monthly sacrifices, conducted at the times of new and full moons, were of cakes or cooked oblations to sundry deities, especially the storm-god Indra. Some daily and monthly sacrifices could be celebrated in the home by a householder, but only the official priesthood could perform the complex seasonal sacrifices, offered three times a year for the purpose of expiation and of abundance at the beginning of spring, of the rainy season, and of the cool weather. Of the occasional sacrifices, which could be celebrated at any time, especially important were those associated with kingship, such as the royal consecration and the great "horse sacrifice" performed for the increase of the king's power and domain.

In ancient Judaism the regular or periodic sacrifices included the twice daily burnt offerings, the weekly sabbath sacrifices, the monthly offering at the new moon, and annual celebrations such as Passover, Purification (Yom Kippur), first fruits, and the Feast of Booths (Sukkoth). Special sacrifices were usually of a personal nature, such as thank and votive offerings and "guilt offerings."

Intentions.—Sacrifices have been offered for a multiplicity of intentions, and it is possible here to list only some of the most prominent. In any one sacrificial rite a number of intentions may be expressed, and the ultimate goal of all sacrifice is to establish a beneficial relationship with the Sacred, to make the sacred power present and efficacious.

Propitiation and Expiation.—Serious illness, drought, pestilence, epidemic, famine, and other misfortune and calamity have universally been regarded as the workings of supernatural forces. Often they have been understood as the effects of offenses against the sacred order committed by individuals or communities, deliberately or unintentionally. Such offenses break the relationship with the Sacred, or impede the flow of divine life, in either case bringing woe to man. Thus it has been considered necessary in times of crisis, individual or communal, to offer sacrifices to propitiate sacred powers and to wipe out offenses (or at least neutralize their effects) and restore the relationship.

Among the Yoruba of West Africa, blood sacrifice must be made to the gods, especially the earth divinities, who, as elsewhere in Africa, are regarded as the divine punishers of sin. For the individual the oblation may be a fowl or a goat; for an entire community it may be hundreds of animals (in former days the principal oblation was human). Once consecrated and ritually slain the oblations are buried, burnt, or left exposed, but never shared by the sacrificer.

Similar to the Yoruba rite was the ancient Greek *sphagia*, a propitiatory sacrifice made to the chthonic deities and forces (including the winds and the spirits of the dead). Contrary to the practice in the joyful sacrifices to the celestial gods, there was no sharing of the oblation by the worshipers in the *sphagia*. The victim (a human being or animal substitute) was hacked to pieces and burned, buried, or cast into a river.

In ancient Judaism the *chattah* or so-called "sin offering" was an important ritual for the expiation of certain, especially unwittingly committed, defilements. The guilty (a priest, king, commoner, or entire community) laid their hands upon the head of the sacrificial animal (an unblemished bullock or goat), thereby identifying themselves with the victim, making it their representative (but not their substitute, for their sins were not transferred to the victim). After the priest had killed the beast, blood was sprinkled upon the altar and elsewhere in the sacred precincts. The point of the ritual was to purify the guilty and to reestablish the holy bond (covenant) with God through the blood of the consecrated victim. It was as such an expiatory sacrifice that early Christianity regarded the life and death of Christ. By the shedding of his blood, the sin of mankind was wiped out and a new relationship of life—eternal life—was effected between God and man. Like the innocent and "spotless" victim of the *chattah*, Christ died for men—*i.e.*, on behalf of, not in place of them. Also like the *chattah*, the point of his death was not the appeasement of divine wrath but the shedding of his blood for the wiping out of sin. The major difference between the sacrifice of Christ and that of the *chattah* animal is that his was regarded as a voluntary and effective sacrifice for *all* men, and as the perfect sacrifice, made once in time and space but perpetuated in eternity by the risen Lord.

There are sacrifices, however, in which the victim does serve as a substitute for the guilty. In some West African cults a person believed to be under death penalty by the gods offers an animal substitute to which he transfers his sins. The animal, ritually killed, is buried with full funeral rites as though it were the human person.

Finally, some propitiatory sacrifices are clearly prophylactic, intended to avert possible misfortune and calamity, and as such they are really bribes offered to the gods. Thus in Dahomey libations and animal and food offerings are frequently made to a variety of earth spirits to ensure their good favour.

Gift Sacrifices.—Although all sacrifice involves the giving of something, there are some sacrificial rites in which the oblation is regarded as a gift made to a deity either in expectation of a return gift or as the result of a promise upon the fulfillment of a requested divine favour.

The exchange of gifts is expressed in the Roman sacrificial formula *do ut des:* "I give that thou mayest give." In India a similar view of sacrifice was expressed in the *suktavata* formula near the end of the Vedic ritual, where upon the declaration that the god has accepted and been strengthened by the offering, the sacrificer states his hope that he may prosper by the god as the god has by him. Usually the expected or desired return gift is made known to the god, and it is understood that by accepting the gift the god has obligated himself to the sacrificer. There is, however, no sense of bribe or coercion here, for the worshiper knows that the deity is all-powerful and will finally do what he wishes, gift or no gift. Moreover the giver always gives something of himself in his gift so that by the reciprocal act of giving and receiving man and god are bound together and "participate" in one another.

Of the second sort of gift sacrifice, the votive offering, numerous instances are recorded. In ancient Greece, sacrifices were vowed to Athena, Zeus, Artemis, and other gods in return for victory in battle. The solemnity and irrevocability of the votive offering is seen in the Old Testament account of Jephthah's sacrifice of his only child in fulfillment of a vow to Yahweh (Judg. 11:30–40).

Thank Offerings.—One form of thank offering is the offering of the first fruits in agricultural societies. Until the first fruits of the harvest have been presented with homage and thanks (and often with animal sacrifices) to the deity of the harvest (sometimes regarded as embodied in the crop) the whole crop is considered sacred and thus taboo and may not be used as food. The first-fruits sacrifice has the effect of "desacralizing" the crops and making them available for profane consumption. It is a recognition of the divine source and ownership of the harvest and the means by which man is reconciled with the vegetational, chthonic powers from whom he takes it.

Fertility.—Another distinctive feature of the first-fruits offering is that it serves to replenish the sacred potencies of the earth depleted by the harvest and to ensure thereby the continued regeneration of the crop. Thus it is one of many sacrificial rites which have as their intention the seasonal renewal and reactivation of the fertility of the earth. Fertility rites usually involve some form of blood sacrifice—in former days especially human sacrifice (*e.g.*, India, Egypt, Africa, America). In some human sacrifices the victim represented a deity who "in the beginning" allowed himself to be killed so that from his body edible vegetation might grow. The ritual slaying of the human victim amounted to a repetition of the primordial act of creation and thus a renewal of vegetational life. In other human sacrifices the victim was regarded as representing a vegetation spirit that annually died at harvest time so that it might be reborn in a new crop. In still other sacrifices at planting time or in time of famine the blood of the victim—animal or human—was let upon the ground and its flesh buried in the soil, to fertilize the earth and recharge its potencies.

Building Sacrifices.—Numerous instances are known of animal and human sacrifices made in the course of the construction of houses, shrines, and other buildings, and in the laying out of villages and towns. Their purpose has been to consecrate the ground by establishing the beneficent presence of the Sacred and by expelling or rendering harmless the demonical powers of the place. In some West African cults, for example, before the central pole of a shrine or a house is installed, an animal is ritually slain, its blood being poured around the foundations and its body being put into the post hole. On the one hand this sacrifice is made to the earth deities and the supernatural powers of the place—the real owners—so that the human owner may take possession and be ensured against malevolent interference with the construction of the building, its later occupation and use. On the other hand, the sacrifice is presented to the cult deity in order to establish its benevolent presence in the building.

Mortuary Sacrifice.—Throughout the history of man's religions the dead have been the recipients of offerings from the living. In ancient Greece an entire group of offerings (*enagismata*) was consecrated to the dead; these were libations of milk, honey, water, wine, and oil poured onto the grave. In India water and balls of cooked rice were sacrificed to the spirits of the departed. In West Africa offerings of cooked grain, yams, and animals are made to the ancestors residing in the earth. The point of such offerings is not (as popularly regarded) that the dead get hungry and thirsty, nor are they merely propitiatory offerings. Their fundamental intention seems to be that of increasing the power (*i.e.*, the life) of the departed. The dead partake of the life of the gods (usually the chthonic deities), and sacrifices to the dead are in effect sacrifices to the gods who bestow never-ending life. In Hittite funeral rites, for example, sacrifices were made to the sun-god and the other celestial deities—transcendent sources of life—as well as to the divinities of earth.

Communion Sacrifices.—Communion in the sense of a bond between the worshiper and the Sacred is, of course, fundamental to all sacrifice. Certain sacrifices, however, promote this communion by means of a sacramental meal. The meal may be one in which the sacrificial oblation is simply shared by the deity and the worshipers. Of this sort were the Greek *thusia* and the Jewish *zevach* sacrifices in which one portion of the oblation was burned upon the altar and the remainder eaten by the worshipers. Among the African Yoruba special meals are offered the deity; if the deity accepts the oblation (as divination will disclose) a portion of the food is placed before his shrine while the remainder is joyfully eaten as a sacred communion by the worshipers.

The communion sacrifice may be one in which the deity somehow indwells the oblation so that the worshipers actually consume the divine. The Aztecs, for example, twice yearly made dough images of the sun-god Huitzilopochtli which were consecrated to the god and thereby transubstantiated into his flesh to be eaten with fear and reverence by the worshipers. (For the Christian Holy Communion as sacrifice, *see* EUCHARIST.)

The Ritual of Sacrifice.—The sacrificial ritual, of course, varies widely according to the specific nature and intention of the sacrifice. Frequently special acts must be performed by the sacrificer before and sometimes also after the sacrifice. In the Vedic cult the sacrificer and his wife were required to undergo an initiation (*diksha*) involving ritual bathing, seclusion, fasting, and prayer, the purpose of which was to remove them from the profane world and to purify them for contact with the Sacred. At the termination of the sacrifice came a rite of "desacralization" (*avabhritha*) in which they, along with the priests, bathed in order to remove any sacred potencies which might have attached themselves during the sacrifice.

Another feature of many sacrifices is an "apology" addressed to the animal or human victim before its killing. In the Vedic rites the sacrificial animal was assured by the priests before its strangulation, "Thou dost not die; no harm is done thee; thou goest to the gods by pleasant paths."

A distinction is frequently made between the person offering the sacrifice and the person by whom the sacrifice is ritually performed. Sometimes this is one and the same person, as in Judaism when the male head of the family celebrates the liturgy of Passover on behalf of himself and his family, or in Hinduism when the householder performs the daily sacrifices of the domestic ritual. More often, however, the sacrifices are performed by a recognized priesthood (*q.v.*) which alone is regarded as possessing (by virtue of initiation or ordination) the knowledge or supernatural power to execute an acceptable and effective offering. Thus in ancient Judaism all Temple sacrifices had to be performed by the priesthood. In India sacrificial rituals often required three or four priests and on occasion as many as sixteen.

The common place of sacrifice in most cults is an altar (*q.v.*). However, the table type of altar is uncommon; more often it is only a pillar, a mound of earth, a stone, or a pile of stones. Among the Hebrews (in early times) and other Semitic peoples the altar of the god was frequently an upright stone (*mazzebah*) established at a place in which the deity had manifested itself (*see* HIGH PLACE). It was *beth-el*, the "House of God."

Frequently the altar is regarded as the centre or the image of the universe. For the ancient Greeks the grave marker (a mound of earth or a stone) was the earth altar upon which sacrifices to the dead were made and, like other earth altars, it was called the *ompholos*, "the navel of the earth"—*i.e.*, the central point from which terrestrial life originated. In Vedic India the altar was regarded as a microcosm, its parts representing the various parts of the universe and its construction being interpreted as a repetition of the creation of the cosmos.

See also references under "Sacrifice" in the Index.

BIBLIOGRAPHY.—For general discussions of sacrifice *see* J. G. Frazer, *The Golden Bough*, vol. iv–ix; E. O. James, *Sacrifice and Sacrament* (1962); W. B. Kristensen, *The Meaning of Religion* (1960); A. Loisy, *Essai historique sur le sacrifice* (1920); W. R. Smith, *Lectures on the Religion of the Semites*, 3rd ed. (1927); E. B. Tylor, *Primitive Culture*, esp. Part ii; G. van der Leeuw, *Religion in Essence and Manifestation* (1938). For discussions of sacrifice in various religions *see* (on India) A. Barth, *Religions of India* (1882); P. E. Dumont, *L'Agnihotra: description de l'agnihotra dans le rituel védique* (1939); H. D. W. Griswold, *The Religion of the Rigveda* (1924); A. Keith, *Religion and Philosophy of the Veda and Upanishads*, vol. i–ii (1926); A. Hillebrandt, *Ritual-litteratur, vedische opfer und zauber* (1897); M. Stevenson, *The Heart of Jainism* (1915); L. A. Waddell, *The Buddhism of Tibet*, 2nd ed. (1958); (on Egypt) J. H. Breasted, *Development of Religion and Thought in Ancient Egypt* (1912); J. Campbell, *The Masks of God: Occidental Mythology* (1964); (on ancient Judaism and Christianity) R. Dussaud, *Les Origines Cananéennes du sacrifice Israélite* (1942); S. C. Gayford, *Sacrifice and Priesthood* (1924); G. B. Gray, *Sacrifice in the Old Testament* (1925); A. Médebielle, *L'Expiation dans l'ancien et le nouveau testament* (1923); O. Schmidt, *Das Opfer in der Jahve-religion und in Polytheismus* (1920); R. K. Yerkes, *Sacrifice in Greek and Roman Religions and Early Judaism* (1952); (on Greece and Rome) J. E. Harrison, *Prolegomena to the Study of Greek Religion* (1903); M. P. Nilsson, *Greek Popular Religion* (1940); H. J. Rose, *Religion in Greece and Rome* (1959); also Yerkes above; (on prehistoric and primitive) M. Herskovitz, *Dahomey*, vol. i–ii (1950); A. E. Jensen, *Myth and Cult Among Primitive Peoples* (1963); J. Maringer, *The Gods of Prehistoric Man* (1960); E. Meyerowitz, *The Divine Kingship in Ghana and Ancient Egypt* (1960); E. B. Idowu, *Olódùmarè: God in Yoruba Belief* (1962); A. Schoch, *Rituelle Menschen-tötungen in Polynesien* (1954); L. Spence, *The Gods of Mexico* (1923); E. O. G. Turville-Petre, *Myth and Religion of the North* (1964); G. C. Vaillant, *The Aztecs of Mexico* (1941).

(H. P. S.)

SACRILEGE, the violation or profanation of sacred things, a crime of varying scope in different religions. The word comes from the Latin *sacrilegium* (from *sacer*, "sacred"; *legere*, "to purloin"), which originally meant merely the theft of sacred things, although as early as Cicero's time it had grown to include in popular speech any insult or injury to them.

The primitive defense against sacrilege lay in the nature of sacred things, which held a curse for any violation or profanation (*see* TABU). As the concept of the sacred became less associated with magic, legal punishments for sacrilege came into being. The levitical code of ancient Israel exacted of the offender reparation for the damage with the addition of one-fifth of the amount and an expiatory sacrifice (Lev. 5:15–16). The story of the stoning of Achan, who stole some of the spoils of Jericho which Joshua had consecrated to the treasury of Yahweh, is one of the most graphic details of Old Testament history (Josh. 7:20–25). No religion was more prodigal in rules to safeguard that which was holy or consecrated than the Hebrew, especially in its Temple laws, violation of which often led to mob violence as well as divine chastisement. The Temple rules do not apply to synagogues, however, and unseemly conduct in the synagogue is liable only to civil action.

In Greece, sacrilege was closely connected with treason: a temple was regarded as the home of a protector of the state, hence thievery of temple property was a crime against the state. In addition to sacrilege, the Greeks held the concept of "impiety," a lesser crime and more widely applicable. The mutilation of the hermae of Athens just before the Athenian expedition to Sicily in 415 B.C. thus ranked as an impiety (*see* HERM).

While the Roman cults were amply protected by tabus, there was no comprehensive term in Roman law for religious violations and profanations in general. According to Ulpian the punishment for *sacrilegium*, narrowly construed as the theft of sacred things from a sacred place, varied according to the position and standing of the culprit and the circumstances under which the crime was committed.

During classical times the law kept to the narrow meaning of *sacrilegium*, but in popular usage it had grown to mean about the same as the English word. Traces of this usage are frequent in Augustan writers. The early Church Fathers use the word most frequently in the restricted sense (though an effort has been made to read the wider meaning in Tertullian). But by the middle of the 4th century the narrower meaning had disappeared. In Ambrose, Augustine, and Pope Leo I, *sacrilegium* means sacrilege. The wider meaning had invaded the Roman law as well, due partly to the influence of Christianity, which sought to include as objects of sacrilege all forms of church property rather than merely those things consecrated in pagan cults, partly to the efforts of the later emperors to surround themselves and everything emanating from them with highest sanctions. In the Theodosian Code (effective Jan. 1, 439) the various crimes which are accounted sacrilege include apostasy (from Christianity), heresy, schism, Judaism, paganism, and attempts against the immunity of churches and clergy or privileges of church courts, the desecration of sacraments, etc., and even of Sunday. There is no formal definition of sacrilege in the Code of Justinian (529), but the conception remains as wide.

The penitentials, early collections of disciplinary canons, gave much attention to sacrilege. The Frankish synods of the Middle Ages emphasize the crime of seizing church property of every kind, including the vast estates so envied by the lay nobility. The worst sacrilege of all, defiling the Host, is mentioned frequently, and generally brought the death penalty accompanied by torture. The period of the Reformation naturally increased the commonness of the crime of sacrilege. Under the emperor Charles V the penalty for stealing the Host was the stake; that for other crimes was graded accordingly. In France, in 1561, it was forbidden under penalty of death to demolish crosses and images and to commit other acts of scandal and impious sedition. In the declaration of 1682, Louis XIV decreed the same penalty for sacrilege joined to superstition and impiety. A sacrilege trial made famous by Voltaire's vain protests against its decision was that of J. F. Lefebvre de La Barre at Abbeville in 1766. Convicted of wearing his hat while a religious procession was passing, of blasphemy, and of having mutilated a crucifix standing on the town bridge, he was sentenced to have his tongue cut out, to be beheaded and the body to be burned; the sentence was confirmed by the *parlement* of Paris and Louis XV, and carried out. In the midst of the French Revolution respect for civic festivals was sternly enacted, but sacrilege was an almost daily matter of state policy. In 1825 the reactionary *parlement* once more brought back the Middle Ages by decreeing the death penalty for public profanation. "Theft sacrilege" was treated in a separate series of clauses. This legislation was expressly and summarily abrogated in 1830.

In the contemporary Christian Church sacrilege is held to be either personal (*e.g.*, ill treatment of, or sins against chastity by, clerics or religious); real (*e.g.*, abuse or theft of, or irreverence toward, the sacraments or other sacred things, including simony [*q.v.*], or administering or receiving a sacrament while in a state of mortal sin); or local (*e.g.*, murder committed in a church). The Roman Catholic Code of Canon Law deals with it. Protestants, who generally deny the inherent sacredness of objects, give it little emphasis.

SACY, ANTOINE ISAAC SILVESTRE DE, BARON

(1758–1838), French scholar, was the leading orientalist of his age, specializing in Arabic and Islamic studies. His interest in these was aroused early by a monk in an abbey opposite his home in Paris, where he was born on Sept. 22, 1758. He learned, privately, Arabic, Hebrew, Persian, and Turkish, and his studies ranged over Oriental history, geography, religion, and numismatics, as well as grammar and philology. He obtained an official appointment at the Cour des Monnaies in 1781, but resigned in 1792. As a fervent Catholic and monarchist, he was out of sympathy with the Revolution. Nevertheless, in 1795, despite his refusal to take an oath against monarchism, he was given the chair of Arabic in the newly founded École des Langues Orientales Vivantes. During the Napoleonic regime he was appointed professor of Persian in the Collège de France (1806) and made a baron (1813). At the Restoration (1815) he became rector of the University of Paris; and from 1815 he was active in the Commission of Public Instruction. He was also official orientalist in the Ministry of Foreign Affairs (1805–29), making Arabic translations of state documents. He was created a peer of France by King Louis Philippe in 1832.

Despite his distinction as an orientalist, Sacy only once traveled outside France, and then no further than Genoa. He died in Paris, Feb. 21, 1838.

Sacy's skill as a teacher is attested by the long list of his pupils —especially French and German—who achieved fame. His works include editions of the *Kalila wa Dimna* of Ibn al-Muqaffa' (1816), and of al-Hariri's *Maqamat* (1821–22), and the incomplete *Exposé de la religion des Druzes*, 2 vol. (1838), the result of over 30 years' study. Of immense influence were his textbooks: his *Grammaire arabe*, 2 vol. (1810) set a new standard for such works, and his *Chrestomathie arabe*, 3 vol. (1806), and *Anthologie grammaticale arabe* (1829) were also important.

BIBLIOGRAPHY.—Henri Dehérain, *Silvestre de Sacy—ses contemporains et ses disciples* (1938); G. Salmon *et al.*, *Silvestre de Sacy*, 2 vol.

(1905–13); J. Fück, *Die arabischen Studien in Europa* (1955).
(J. A. HD.)

SADDLE: *see* HARNESS AND SADDLERY.

SADDUCEES, the name of a party in Judaism which was opposed to the Pharisees down to the destruction of Jerusalem in A.D. 70. The basic difference between the two parties lay in their respective attitudes toward the Torah, the Sadducees representing the extreme conservative view. *See* JEWISH SECTS DURING THE SECOND COMMONWEALTH: *Pharisees* and *Sadducees;* JUDAISM.

SADE, DONATIEN ALPHONSE FRANÇOIS, COMTE

DE (usually called the MARQUIS DE SADE) (1740–1814), French author, whose erotic and licentious writings have given his name to sadism. He was born in Paris on June 2, 1740, a descendant of one of the best Provençal families. In 1754 he began a military career, abandoning it in 1763, at the end of the Seven Years' War. He married in 1763 the elder daughter of the president of the Cour des Aides in Paris. He had two sons by her.

As governor-general of Bresse and Bugey, as lord of Saumane, La Coste, and other places, he led the life of a libertine. He was early convicted of debauchery and acts of violence; the police kept a watchful eye on him, and several times he was committed to prison. After an incident at Marseilles, involving four girls, in 1772 Sade was sentenced to death, in his absence, at Aix-en-Provence for "crimes of poisoning and sodomy." Though he was reprieved, he was recaptured and imprisoned at Miolans; he escaped and rejoined his wife at the château of La Coste, where he again attracted attention by new scandals. He fled to Italy in 1775 with his sister-in-law. On return to Paris in 1777, he was arrested, imprisoned at Vincennes, and again tried at Aix. He escaped, but was soon rearrested; after six years at Vincennes (1778–84), he was incarcerated at the Bastille, and finally, in 1789, at Charenton.

On his release in 1790, he offered several plays to the Comédie Française. In 1792 he became secretary of the Section des Piques, was one of four delegates appointed to visit the hospitals of Paris, and wrote several patriotic addresses. Because his name was mistakenly included on the list of *émigrés*, he was detained during the Terror but released a year later. He then lived in a state of near poverty with Mme Quesnet, an actress. In 1801 he was arrested as the author of *Justine*. He was moved from prison to prison, and in 1803 ended up at the Charenton lunatic asylum, near Paris, where he caused new scandals and where he died on Dec. 2, 1814.

Most of Sade's works were written in prison, where he spent more than 27 years of his life. His prose fiction includes *Justine* (1791), *Juliette* (1792), *Les 120 Journées de Sodome* (written in 1785; the manuscript was discovered in Germany and published in 1904), *Aline et Valcour* (1795), *La Philosophie dans le boudoir* (1795), and *Les Crimes de l'amour* (1800). Most of these works are still considered obscene; nearly all editions are unofficial. They were, however, esteemed by Sainte-Beuve, Baudelaire, and Swinburne; their influence on Lamartine, Barbey d'Aurevilly, Lautréamont, Dostoevski, and Kafka is well known. Guillaume Apollinaire and the Surrealists in general did much to rehabilitate them. Some French writers and critics (including Maurice Heine, Jean Paulhan, Maurice Blanchot, Maurice Nadeau, and Simone de Beauvoir) have undertaken the study of Sade's peculiar personality and have demonstrated the "infernale grandeur" of his writings. For many he has become more than the inventor of a sexual perversion: the type of the eternal rebel, the example of man seeking, in unbounded fury, to surpass the limits of the human condition.

BIBLIOGRAPHY.—There is no complete edition of Sade's works, but good selections have been edited by M. Heine (1933), M. Nadeau (1947), and G. Lély (1948). *See also Correspondance*, ed. by P. Bourdin (1929). *See also* E. Dühren (Iwan Bloch), *Der Marquis de Sade und seine Zeit* (1900); W. Stekel, *Sadismus und Masochismus* (1925; first Eng. trans. 1935); C. R. Dawes, *The Marquis de Sade: His Life and Works* (1927); M. Blanchot, *Lautréamont et Sade* (1949); M. Praz, *The Romantic Agony*, 2nd Eng. ed. (1951); S. de Beauvoir, *Faut-il brûler Sade?* (1951–52; Eng. trans. in S. de Beauvoir, *The Marquis de Sade*, 1962, with selections from Sade); G. Lély, *Vie du Marquis de Sade*, 2 vol. (1952, 1957; Eng. trans. 1961). (MA. N.)

SADEDDIN, HOCA (1536–1599), Turkish historian, was

the author of the renowned *Tac üt-tevarih* ("Crown of Histories"). The son of Hasan Can, court chamberlain to Selim I, he was tutor to Prince Murad, governor of Manisa, and followed him to Istanbul when he became sultan as Murad III. He was influential in the palace and later accompanied Murad's son, Sultan Mohammed III, on his campaign in Hungary, playing an important part in the victory at Erlau (1596) by the moral support he gave at a critical hour. He was made shaikh ul-Islam in 1598.

The *Tac üt-tevarih*, which covers the period from the origins of the Ottoman empire to the end of the reign of Selim I (1520), is based on earlier works. Its reputation can be attributed partly to its rhetorical and ornate style, popular in the 16th century, and to the fact that the author's family were influential in the palace for nearly a century. (F. I.)

SÁ DE MIRANDA, FRANCISCO DE (1481–1558), the first of the Portuguese Renaissance poets, was probably born on Aug. 28, 1481, the illegitimate son of a canon of Coimbra, Gonçalo Mendes de Sá, and Dona Inês de Melo. He was made legitimate in 1490. He studied at the university, which was then in Lisbon, and seems to have lived mainly in the capital until 1521, frequenting the royal court and taking part in the poetical improvisations there and, possibly, teaching at the university. The years from 1521 to 1526 he spent in Italy, visiting Milan, Venice, Florence, Rome, Naples and Sicily. He made the acquaintance of Giovanni Ruccellai, Lattanzio Tolomei and Jacopo Sannazzaro; he met the illustrious Vittoria Colonna, a distant connection of his family, and in her house he probably talked with Cardinal Pietro Bembo and Ariosto, and perhaps met Machiavelli and Francesco Guicciardini. By the time he returned home in 1526 he had become familiar with Italian verse forms and metres: the sonnet and *canzone* of Petrarch, the tercet of Dante, the ottava rima of Ariosto, the eclogue in the manner of Sannazzaro, and Italian hendecasyllabic verse. He did not, however, abandon the short national metre, which he carried to perfection in his *Cartas* or epistles in verse.

His play *Os Estrangeiros*, written *c.* 1527, was the first Portuguese prose comedy in the classical manner, and he wrote another, *Os Vilhalpandos, c.* 1538 (published 1560). His *Cleópatra* (written *c.* 1550), of which only a dozen lines are extant, was probably the first Portuguese classical tragedy. About 1528 Sá de Miranda made his first attempt to introduce the new Renaissance forms of verse by writing in Spanish a *canzone* entitled *Fábula do Mondego*, and this was followed a year or two later by the eclogue *Alexo*.

About 1530, in which year he married, he left Lisbon finally and settled on his country estate in the Minho. It is in this later period that he produced his best work: the eclogue *Basto*, the *Cartas* and the satires, in which he shows himself a stern critic of contemporary society. Some of the sonnets of this period are admirable, combining a grave tenderness of feeling and refinement of thought with simplicity of expression. He died on his estate at Tapada probably in May 1558.

Sá de Miranda was the leader of a revolution in Portuguese literature, and especially in poetry, which under his influence became higher in aim, purer in tone and broader in sympathy. As well as introducing the poetic and dramatic forms and spirit of the Renaissance into Portugal, he made an austere stand against the growing materialism of his time. *Poesias de F. de Sá de Miranda* was edited, with life, notes and glossary, by C. Michaëlis de Vasconcelos (1885); *Obras completas de F. de Sá de Miranda* was edited by M. Rodrigues Lapa, 2 vol. (1937).

BIBLIOGRAPHY.—T. Braga, *Sá de Miranda e a Escola Italiana* (1896); C. Michaëlis de Vasconcelos, "Novos Estudos sobre Sá de Miranda" in the proceedings of the Lisbon *Academia das Ciências, Boletim da Segunda Classe*, vol. v (1912); Mendes dos Remédios, "As Comédias de Sá de Miranda" in *Miscelânea de estudos em honra de C. Michaëlis de Vasconcelos* (1933). (N. J. L.)

SA'DI (MUSHARIFF-UD-DIN) (*c.* 1184–*c.* 1291), Persian poet and prose writer, the author of two works, the *Bustan* ("Orchard") and *Gulistan* ("Rose Garden"), which came to be regarded as classics of Persian literature. He lost his father Muslih ud-din in early childhood; later he was sent to study in Baghdad at the renowned Nizamiya college where he acquired the traditional learning of Islam.

The unsettled conditions following the Mongol invasion of Persia, when, in the words of Sa'di, the world resembled "the curly hair of a Negro," led the poet to wander in many countries. He refers to his adventures in north Africa, central Asia and India; in Syria he was captured by the Franks and put to work in the trenches of the fortress of Tripoli. When he reappeared in his native Shiraz he was an elderly man. He dedicated the *Bustan* (1257) and the *Gulistan* (1258) to the local ruler (atabeg) Abu-Bakr ibn Sa'd. (His pen-name Sa'di was derived from the name Sa'd borne both by the father and the son of Abu-Bakr.) He seems to have spent the rest of his life in Shiraz, for his poems were dedicated to the later atabegs and governors, both heathen and Muslim, whom the Mongol *ilkhans*, established in Tabriz, sent to the province of Fars. References to contemporary events in Sa'di's works stop at about 1270.

That Sa'di produced his two greatest works so late in life and in such quick succession is not surprising. The material for them must have been collected and many of the poems written long before an opportunity for their publication occurred. The *Bustan* is entirely in verse (in the metre used in epic) and consists of stories aptly illustrating the standard virtues recommended to Muslims (justice, liberality, modesty, contentment), as well as of reflections on the behaviour of dervishes and their ecstatic practices.

The *Gulistan* is mainly in prose, and contains stories and personal recollections. The text is interspersed with a variety of charming little poems containing aphorisms, advice and humorous reflections. The morals preached in the *Gulistan* border on expediency; *e.g.*, a salutary lie is admitted to be preferable to a blunt truth. The fate of those who depend on the changeable moods of kings is contrasted with the freedom of the dervishes:

I am neither riding a camel, nor carrying a load like a camel; I am neither a lord of subjects, nor the slave of a potentate; grief for what there is or distress for what there is not do not trouble me; I draw my breath freely and thus spend my life.

For western students the *Bustan* and *Gulistan* have a special attraction, but Sa'di is also remembered as a great poet, the author of a number of masterly general odes portraying human experience and also of particular odes (such as the lament on the destruction of the caliphate by the Mongols in 1258), which have a great appeal for Persian readers. A special section of his complete works is in Arabic, but Arabs find some of his methods of expression strange.

The peculiar blend of human kindness, resignation and humour displayed in Sa'di's works, together with a tendency to avoid the hard dilemma, make him, to many, the most typical and lovable writer in the world of Iranian culture.

BIBLIOGRAPHY.—Best editions of the *Bustan* and *Gulistan* are by M. A. Furughi (1938). The first competent trans. of the *Gulistan* is by F. Gladwin (1806, reprinted 1928), followed by that of E. B. Eastwick (1852, reprinted 1880); partial trans. are by Sir Edwin Arnold (1899), Sir R. Burton (1928) and A. J. Arberry (1945). A good French trans. of the *Bustan* is by Barbier de Meynard (1880). Sir L. W. King trans. two series of the odes, the *Tayyibāt* (1919–21) and the *Badāyi'* (1925). A comprehensive bibliography is in H. Massé, *Biographie de Saadi* (1919). For a general appreciation *see* E. G. Browne, *A Literary History of Persia*, vol. ii (1928); A. J. Arberry, *Classical Persian Literature* (1958). Critical ed. of the *Gulistan* with Russian trans. by R. Aliyev (1960). (V. F. M.)

SADLER, MICHAEL THOMAS (1780–1835), English social reformer, politician, and a leader of the movement for factory reform, was born at Snelston, Derbyshire, on Jan. 3, 1780. While still young he became a Wesleyan Methodist and his religion turned him into a philanthropist. He started business in Leeds in 1800, importing Irish linens, and soon afterward turned to politics. A critic of Catholic emancipation, in 1828 he published a book *Ireland: its Evils and Their Remedies*. He was Tory M.P. for Newark-on-Trent (1829–30) and for Aldborough (1831–32). He contested the new Leeds seat in December 1832, after the passing of the Reform Bill, but was defeated by Thomas Babington (later Lord) Macaulay, who had already criticized his *Law of Population* (1830), a massive treatise attacking the theories of Thomas Malthus. In the Leeds election Sadler received a large amount of working class support, because, along with Richard

Oastler, he had become an advocate of factory reform and of government intervention to regulate the hours of child labour and factory conditions in general.

As parliamentary representative of the newly founded "short-time committees" in the north of England, which were agitating for shorter working hours, he had introduced a factory-reform bill in the House of Commons in 1831 and had subsequently acted as chairman of the select committee to which it was referred. While in Parliament he had also moved unsuccessfully for the establishment of a poor law system for Ireland (1830) and for legislation to better the condition of the agricultural poor in England (1831).

Sadler died in Belfast on July 29, 1835.

Sadler's Toryism had a strongly radical tinge, which was shared by other Tories in the north of England: it remained a powerful force among the factory operatives until the growth of Chartism (q.v.).   (A. Bri.)

SADO, Japanese island of Niigata prefecture, 32 mi. W. of Niigata, the prefectural capital. Area 248 sq.mi., pop. (1960) 84,404. Sado, long known as an island of romance, is the home of *okesa* (folk-dancing songs, ballads). Camellia trees grow in abundance. The climate is mild all the year.

Sado was famous as a place of exile and among many statesmen and scholars banished two of the most exalted were the emperor Juntoku (1197–1242) and the Buddhist priest Nichiren (1222–1282). Sado is known for its gold and silver mines, continuously operated from 1601. Rice is the first product, followed by fishing. Tourism provides an important source of income. Ryōtsu, on the east shore, is the only city. It is the centre of the island's administration, and of its fishing industry. Serving as an outer port of Niigata, it is the principal port on the island. Aikawa is the largest town on the west coast.   (R. B. H.)

SÁENZ, MANUELA (1797–1856), known throughout Latin America as "La Sáenz," mistress of the liberator Simón Bolívar, was born in Quito, Ecuador, on Dec. 27, 1797. At the time of her birth her mother was unwed, and the stain of illegitimacy left its mark. For years she shrouded her origins in mystery. In 1817 she married a British merchant, James Thorne, who took her to Lima, Peru; there Manuela first came into contact with the movement for independence which was then challenging Spanish rule throughout Latin America. On her return to Quito in 1822 she met Simón Bolívar, who had just completed the liberation of Ecuador. Manuela became the great passion of his life; she threw caution to the winds and united her life with his—and with the cause for which he was fighting.

The exigencies of war separated the couple for long periods, and there were occasions of neglect which Manuela bitterly resented. In return for her unflinching devotion she demanded an exclusiveness to which Bolívar was unaccustomed. When the war took Bolívar to Peru Manuela did not hesitate to follow him.

As she had shared the zenith of Bolívar's life, she also became engulfed in his decline. Her efforts to keep the Peruvians on his side were in vain. She was exiled from Lima and joined Bolívar in Bogotá, Colombia, where on Sept. 25, 1828, she saved him from conspirators.

In the spring of 1830, when Bolívar resigned his office to go into exile, Manuela was left behind. His papers remained in her care and she refused to hand them over to his enemies. When she learned of his death (Dec. 17, 1830) she unsuccessfully attempted to take her own life.

In 1834, Manuela was exiled from Bogotá and went to the small Peruvian port of Paita, where she made a living as a vendor of sweets and tobacco. She died at Paita on Nov. 23, 1856.

Bibliography.—Daniel Florencio O'Leary, *Memories*, vol. 3, appendix (1879–88); Alfonso Rumazo Gonzales, *Manuela Sáenz* (1944); Gerhard Masur, *Simón Bolívar* (1948); Victor von Hagen, *The Four Seasons of Manuela* (1952).   (G. S. M.)

SÁENZ PEÑA, ROQUE (1851–1914), Argentine president and diplomat. Although a wealthy leader of the landed aristocracy, he was responsible during his presidency for a broad suffrage law, which placed Argentina in the vanguard of Latin-American democracy.

Sáenz Peña was born in Buenos Aires on March 19, 1851, the descendant of a famous family. He was educated in Argentina, traveled in Europe and entered politics in the 1870s, when Argentina's population and economy were rapidly expanding. Among the many posts he held were those of minister of foreign affairs, delegate to the first International Conference of American States (Washington, D.C., 1889–90) and ambassador to Spain and to Italy (1901–10). He was elected president in 1910 in a conservative-controlled election, but he had the vision to respond to the mounting demands of the popular majority, represented by Hipólito Irigoyen's Radical party, and forced a series of electoral reforms through the oligarchy-dominated congress. These laws, which have since borne his name and have been the basis of Argentine democracy, gave every Argentine male at the age of 18 the right to vote on a secret ballot.

Sáenz Peña died in office on Aug. 9, 1914, as Argentina was entering an era of change marked by World War I and the election to the presidency in 1916 of his former opponent, Irigoyen.   (T. F. McG.)

SAFAD (Safed), a town of Israel in the hills (2,600 ft. [800 m.]) of northern Galilee, lies 15 mi. (24 km.) NW of Lake Tiberias and 30 mi. ENE of Haifa. The population (8,252 at the 1961 census) is mainly Jewish. Safad is considered to be one of the four Jewish holy cities and has been identified with the "city set on a hill" (Matt. 5:14). It became the chief centre of Jewish learning after the expulsion of Jews from Spain (1492). The corpus of Jewish law was composed there (1542) and a modern school of the Cabala (mystic lore) flourished until the town was destroyed by earthquake in 1837. The first printing press in Palestine was set up in Safad (1563). The town was a stronghold of the crusaders during the Latin Kingdom and then of the Mamelukes.

Before the earthquake in the 19th century Safad was a considerable commercial centre. It is now a thriving tourist and pilgrimage centre; it has four historic synagogues. Main roads link it with Acre, Metulla, and Tiberias.   (No. B.)

ŠAFAŘÍK, PAVEL JOSEF (1795–1861), one of the leading figures of the Czech national revival and a pioneer of Slavonic philology and archaeology. Born at Kobeliarov, Slovakia, May 13, 1795, of a Protestant family, he studied at Jena and was director of the Serbian Orthodox grammar school at Novi Sad before settling in Prague in 1833. In 1841 he refused an invitation to occupy the chair of Slavonic philology at Berlin, preferring to remain as a private scholar in his own country. He died at Prague, June 26, 1861.

Erudition and scholarly integrity characterize a series of influential works on the history and languages of the Slavs: *Geschichte der slavischen Sprache und Literatur nach allen Mundarten* (1826); *Slovanské starožitnosti* (1837), better known in the German translation *Slawische Altertümer* (1843); *Über den Ursprung und die Heimat des Glagolitismus* (1858); *Geschichte der südslawischen Literatur* (1864).

Although his work on the origins and migrations of the Slavs has been superseded, it was of great value in its time. His philological works can still be read with profit: in his belief in the priority of the Glagolitic alphabet over the Cyrillic he was far ahead of his time.   (R. Ay.)

SAFAVIDS (Safawids), the ruling dynasty of Iran from 1501 to 1736. The dynasty, founded by Shah Ismail I, was named after his ancestor, the saintly Sheikh Safi al-Din of Ardabil. After reaching its peak under Shah Abbas I the dynasty declined and was brought to an end by Nadir Shah in 1736. *See* Persian History.

SAFED KOH, a remarkable range of mountains on the northwest frontier of West Pakistan, extending like a 14,000-ft. wall, straight and rigid, towering above all surrounding hills. It separates the Kabul basin from the Kurram and Afridi Tirah and thus forms a natural boundary between Afghanistan and Pakistan. The highest peak, Sikaram, is 15,600 ft. above sea level. Geographically the Safed Koh is not an isolated range, for there is no break in the continuity of water divide which connects it with the great Shandur offshoot of the Hindu Kush except the narrow trough of the Kabul River, which cuts a deep waterway where it makes its way from Dakka into the Peshawar plain. The northern spurs are extremely barren but the intervening valleys support agriculture and gardens abounding in mulberries, pomegranates, etc. The main range and the upper portions of the spurs are wooded with pine and deodar.

The same name is often used for the mountain range north of the Hari Rud River in its upper course.

SAFES, STRONG ROOMS, AND VAULTS. From earliest times various devices have been used to protect valued objects from fire and flood, as well as from the common menace of thieves. Safekeeping measures—which range from burying treasure to installing electronic safety devices—provide a fascinating story in man's attempt to protect his possessions.

Historical Background.—In ancient Egypt, Greece, and Rome the function of the modern safe was served by massive chests (*see* CABINET FURNITURE). Homer tells of wooden coffers that were used for storing valuable clothes as well as gold and silver. In the 7th century B.C., one of the boasted possessions of Cypselus, tyrant of Corinth, was a cedar treasure chest inlaid with gold and ivory.

The Roman treasure chest (*arca*) was a large coffer made of iron or of wood reinforced with iron or bronze bands and equipped with a padlock. A proscribed citizen is said to have hidden for several days in an *arca* belonging to one of his freedmen. The *arca* usually stood in the atrium of the house, in care of the porter or a servant, called *arcarius,* who was assigned to make disbursements. Some Roman houses were also equipped with vaulted underground storage rooms.

Greek and Roman temple treasures were stored in strong rooms which were sometimes used also as repositories for the state's tax money or for private treasures. The public treasury of Rome was maintained for centuries, under both the republic and the empire, in a cavity in the great mass of concrete that underlay the floor of the Temple of Saturn and Ops. In some Greek temples, including the Parthenon, a special chamber was divided from the main storeroom as a repository for temple treasures and for citizens' property left there for safekeeping.

In medieval times the treasures of bankers and feudal lords were usually stored in chests in underground rooms, sometimes further protected by armed guards. In Renaissance Europe, huge, often beautifully decorated, iron chests, fitted with cumbersome and elaborate locks, were widely used. These were succeeded by the drab iron boxes that were characteristic of commercial life in the era of the Industrial Revolution.

Various attempts at fireproofing chests, none very effective, were made early in the 19th century. In 1801 Richard Scott was granted a British patent for a fireproof chest, but this does not appear to have been manufactured. About 1820 a French manufacturer produced a portable metal box with double walls, the space between which was filled with heat-resistant material. In 1826 a supposedly fireproof safe, patented by J. Delano, was produced in New England. It was composed of oaken planks saturated with brine or an alkali and covered with thin sheets of iron reinforced by riveted iron bands. Many of these were destroyed in the disastrous New York fire of 1835. In 1830 Thomas Milner began producing tinplate and sheet-iron boxes in Liverpool, Eng., and as his business grew he became a manufacturer of prototypes of the modern safe. A British patent for a chest lined with nonconducting material was issued to William Marr in 1834. A safe utilizing plaster of paris as the nonconductor was produced by Daniel Fitzgerald of New York City in 1843. The improvement in fire resistance thus effected was offset by the corrosive action of the filler, which destroyed the protective value of the iron plates within a few years.

In mid-19th century, thousands of merchants in Britain and the U.S. were keeping their cash in iron safes. Many of these contained an inner shell slightly smaller than the outer one, with the intervening space stuffed with such insulating materials as ferromanganese, marble dust, or burned clay. Later, a cement and water mixture came into general use for insulation, the water creating a protective blanket of steam between the heat of a fire and the objects in the safe.

These key-lock chests offered slight protection against burglary, since the keys could be duplicated and the locks jimmied. A combination lock, introduced in the U.S. in 1862 by Linus Yale, Jr., represented a temporary improvement, but skilful burglars learned to manipulate the combinations, and it was not until 1947 that a method of preventing this was developed (*see* also LOCK). The problem of burglary caused the introduction of high-carbon steel, heavier plating, and stronger combination spindles.

The prototype of the modern safe-deposit vault was installed in 1865 in New York City. In 1874 a time lock was installed in a vault in Morrison, Ill., and time locks gradually came into general use in banks.

Many safes and their contents survived the Chicago fire of 1871, even after falling from considerable heights through fire-ravaged buildings. However, in many cases, in this and other fires, the metal shells of safes and their supporting bands warped, allowing heat to enter; manufacturers learned to be cautious about using the term "fireproof." In 1917 tests measuring the degree of protection against fire afforded by safes uncovered a number of basic weaknesses that were later corrected. For example, the water on which the manufacturers had relied for the protective action of steam might have evaporated before it was needed. It was found also that the sudden heat changes of a fire could cause explosion. In the half-century of evolution after the first tests, new construction methods brought great improvements. For example, the moisture needed for insulation was stored in the form of crystals that yielded water, then steam, when exposed to great heat. Two basic methods of construction were developed to provide effective insulation—the safe was cast as a single oven-dried unit, with the metal shell built around it, or the metal shell was formed first and the insulation mixture poured into it. In either case, the fittings in the door and jamb that had tended to communicate heat were eliminated.

Modern Safes.—One of the methods used by burglars to force safes was to knock off the combination lock and drive out the spindle. A device to combat this is a relocking mechanism that operates automatically when the lock is jarred by cutting tools or explosives, throwing an emergency bolt—in some cases two or three bolts—into action.

A new alloy, containing solid hardened particles introduced into the metal in its molten state, is used to cover the door and front of a safe, offering protection against pressure-applied carbide cutting tools, which could penetrate the case-hardened steel of earlier models. The alternation of soft and hard layers in this protective coat causes sufficient stress to chip or shatter a drill. A device to defeat the acetylene torch is a front layer of copper supplemented by an inner ring of copper surrounding the inside of the door opening. The high thermal conductivity of copper tends to dissipate the heat before the entire plate can be heated to the fusing point, and its ductility makes it resistant to the impact of explosives. As a further protection for some models, the body of the safe is encased in a steel-clad cement block.

In the U.S. a manual of the National Stationery and Office Equipment Association divides safes into three categories. The type commonly referred to merely as a safe is designed primarily for protection against fire. The type built for protection against experienced burglars is called a money chest. The third type, insulated against heat and containing a built-in money chest, is termed a combination safe and money chest. Models in each category provide varying degrees of tested protection. For example, a two-hour safe is one that has been exposed in a furnace to temperatures up to 1,850° F (1,010° C) for two hours without damage to the papers stored in it, has survived without rupture for one-half hour in a test furnace preheated to 2,000°, and has survived intact a 30-ft. fall within two minutes after the fire was extinguished. Specifications of this type carry the certification of the Safe Manufacturers National Association and of the Underwriters' Laboratories.

Modern Vaults, Strong Rooms, and File Rooms.—The term vault, which once signified a room with a vaulted ceiling, generally denotes a below ground room that has been reinforced for the safekeeping of valuables. Other rooms built for this purpose are usually designated as strong rooms. However, "vault" is sometimes used in the sense of any room designed for the protection of valuables.

Various types of bank vaults and strong rooms are designed to protect records, cash, securities, or other valuable items against fire, water, burglary, and mob violence. Money vaults usually have concrete walls, floors, and ceilings, with inner coverings of steel plates. The concrete itself is sometimes reinforced with vertical and horizontal steel rods. The concrete and steel may be three feet thick.

Specifications for the construction of vaults and strong rooms are usually drawn up by architects and engineers. Doors have been standardized to fit most ordinary requirements, however, and the rooms are sometimes constructed according to specifications provided by manufacturers. A vault door designed to meet typical needs is $3\frac{1}{2}$ in. thick, constructed of layers of high-carbon steel, copper, and hardened drill-resistant steel.

Vault doors are classified by the Underwriters' Laboratories according to their fire resistance. To determine this, the door is installed in the opening of a chamber facing a test furnace and subjected to the heat of the furnace for a specified time. A stream of water is then played on the door for one minute, and the exposure to the furnace is repeated. The tests are made in accordance with a time-temperature curve based on fire reports, which indicates that the typical fire reaches a temperature of 1,700° F (927° C) after one hour and 2,150° (1177°) after six hours. On the basis of satisfactory performance in the tests, the doors are given two-, four-, or six-hour fire classification labels.

The fact that a building is itself fireproof offers no guarantee that its contents will not be destroyed by fire; insurance companies report that documents in ordinary metal files can be counted on to survive typical office fires for only three to five minutes. Accordingly, insulated doors have been designed to retard the spreading of fire to rooms used for storage of files and records. Fire-insulated file-room doors have ratings of one-half hour and one hour. For additional protection, file rooms are equipped with heat-resistant filing cabinets.

Among burglar-alarm systems for the protection of vaults and strong rooms is a device that works on the principle of radar—a sound-wave transmitter that is set after business hours to send out waves of ultrasonic frequency. Any movement by an intruder distorts the wave reaching the ultrasonic receiver and triggers an alarm that may be audible on the premises or only to the police. Another system utilizes a network of wires embedded in the walls and so arranged that any chipping of the wall sets off an alarm. Another device sets off jets of live steam if an intruder reaches the interior of the room.

Burglars have been known to kidnap bank officials and force them to work the combination of a bank safe at the time for which its lock had been set. To combat this, the combination locks of safes and vault doors can be fitted with a device by which a simple manipulation of the dial touches off an alarm that is heard only at police headquarters. Another protective device enables a person locked inside a vault to open the door.

After the atomic attack on Hiroshima, Jap., U.S. manufacturers who had installed vaults in bank buildings there learned that the vaults had survived with their contents intact. In one case, that of the Teikoku Bank, the centre of the bomb's destruction was located about 300 yds. away, demolishing all of the building except the front walls. The vault door, which was only superficially damaged, was six inches thick—a fraction of the thickness of some vault doors. No vault, however, would be impervious to destruction by explosion of a hydrogen bomb without additional shielding.

At Hudson, N.Y., 125 mi. from New York City, is a vault hewn from iron-bearing rock on several levels of a mountainside, with 1,500 ft. of flanking passageways. Great quantities of microfilmed business records have been stored in it, as well as motion-picture film, valuable works of art, etc. The vault is air conditioned, humidity controlled, and equipped with emergency supplies of food and water. Another such installation is located on an estate 42 mi. from Boston, Mass., designed to protect the records of the member and associate banks of the Boston Clearing House Association.

SAFETY is concerned with the taking of precautions against bodily injury caused by accident, either by preventing the occurrence or by mitigating its effect. Safety operates in two broad categories, occupational safety and public safety. The former covers hazards of employment, e.g., in factories, offices, and shops and on farms and building sites; the latter deals with exposure to risk at all other times, as at home, during recreation, or while traveling.

In ancient times a fatalistic view of accidents prevailed, and the preventive measures occasionally advocated by medical men and humanitarians were largely ignored. The awakening of the public conscience to the need for protecting human life from accidental injury sprang from the inhumane conditions of employment in the early stages of the Industrial Revolution. Therefore, in all industrialized countries, the early 19th century saw the start of legislation for the protection of workers. Legislation of this kind has been expanded continuously either to deal with new industrial processes or to increase coverage for ever wider ranges of employees.

However, it is not only in the factory that modern man has created hazards for himself. The farm tractor, the labour-saving appliances in the home, the boats and guns for sport, and countless other inventions—above all, the motor vehicle—all take their toll of life and limb. The problem of the 20th century is to keep safety provisions in pace with the swiftness of technological advance and the resultant stresses on mind and body—as is particularly clear in motoring. Each year there is improvement in car performance, with ever higher cruising speeds and parallel improvement in roadholding and braking. The drivers, however, have no better capabilities; they are assumed to be able to condition themselves to the higher speeds at their disposal. Investigation shows that nearly all accidents are caused by human failure involving at least one (usually more than one) act of commission or omission by an individual. Most accidents could have been avoided had any of the persons concerned acted differently.

Accident Statistics.—Road accidents account for one-third or more of fatalities in a country with a highly developed motor transportation system. Home fatalities are comparably numerous. In the United States, recreational pursuits account for over 6,000 deaths yearly; and in the United Kingdom, accidental drownings alone number around 1,000 a year. The number of occupational fatalities varies greatly from country to country owing to the differing nature and size of their industries. For example, average annual fatalities at work in the United States total 14,000, of which no fewer than 3,000 occur in farm work; whereas the United Kingdom's yearly total of 1,300 killed at work includes only 130 in its proportionately smaller agricultural industry.

Care must be taken to avoid making unfair comparisons between the safety records of various countries. Absolute figures mean little without relation to the number of persons at risk and the duration of their exposure to risk. Road-death rates are usually compiled in relation either to number of vehicles licensed or to number of population; although, clearly, rates per million vehicle-miles would be more useful and rates per million vehicle-occupant-miles better still. Even then, in order to arrive at a fair comparison of safety records, it would still be necessary to know the densities of traffic in the respective countries and the relative incidence of accidents on urban and rural roads. For example, in the U.S. there are about seven fatalities on rural roads for every three on urban roads; whereas in Great Britain the ratio is about three on urban roads to two on rural roads. This difficulty in drawing conclusions from international fatality figures is even greater in the case of injury statistics. Injuries can range from a minor bruise to a permanent total disability; which makes simple categorization by severity difficult between separate fields of activity, e.g., roads and industry, even within one country. Accident statistics, therefore, are usable only in comparing changes in safety performance within a unit (such as a factory, an accident-prevention organization, or a nation) which maintains its records on a clearly defined basis.

It may be assumed from U.S. and British experience that the number of persons injured seriously enough to require admission to hospital is approximately ten times the number of those killed; and that accidents are the greatest single killers in the age group 1–34 years. Humanitarian considerations apart, the drain on the economic life of every nation is obvious.

Measures of Prevention make use of three approaches known to safety workers as the three "E's"—Engineering, Enforcement, and Education.

Engineering embraces matters of design, layout, and construction that have a bearing on the creation of a safe environment. In the factory, it covers the production process itself; *e.g.,* working conditions can be improved by substituting nontoxic for toxic substances within the process. The most opportune time to ensure a safe environment, however, is at the preliminary stage of designing the building, machinery, and production routines. Engineering's part in road safety is obvious, as witness the rising importance of traffic engineering on the one hand and of safe vehicle and accessory design on the other. In the home, engineering ideally covers the safe design of the house itself (with particular regard to the frailties of the very young and the very old), and also that of all the tools of housekeeping, from electrical appliances to can openers.

Enforcement refers not merely to enforcement of safety laws by the police but to the legislation itself, including factory safety rules as a condition of employment.

Education, in its safety connotation, covers methods of teaching the public to avoid accidents. It includes instruction in schools and colleges and on-the-job training courses (*e.g.,* for car and truck drivers, managers, supervisors, operators and apprentices), conferences, and safety campaigns that use mass publicity media.

Application of Safety Methods.—The effectiveness of each of the three approaches varies according to the accident-producing situation. Thus, voluntary safety organizations, whose role is primarily that of education, are affected by engineering and enforcement work, since these two methods provide the background against which they operate.

Industrial Safety.—In modern industry it is accepted that management must provide a safe workplace and working system. The tendency in western Europe and Great Britain is to enforce this by comprehensive legislation; in the U.S. there is more reliance on education of personnel. However, the end result has been much the same, since enlightened firms have always gone beyond current legislation, which tends to lag behind the most up-to-date industrial techniques, and, in any case, cannot make enactments against human failure. Unguarded machinery has long ceased to be the major cause of factory accidents. There is, however, still a wide gap between the safety performances of the enlightened and of the laggard firms in each industry.

In most countries, employees have effective rights under common law or workmen's compensation laws in case of accident, even should the blame be partly theirs. The resultant increase in compensation awards is rapidly reflected in the rising insurance contributions for employer's liability which firms have to pay. More and more firms, therefore, are operating safety programs, employing trained safety staffs to act as advisers to line management. Such firms, should an accident occur, regard the subsequent investigation not as a means of apportioning blame but as a means of preventing further accidents. The chain of causation will be examined, considering first the possibility of failure of design, then that of failure of supervision, and only lastly personal failure on the part of the operative.

Agricultural Safety.—Farming has its special problems. The isolation, in many countries, of the agricultural community and of farmers at their work, and the difficulty of adequately guarding farm machinery, weaken the enforcement weapon and hinder educational efforts. Nevertheless, since World War II safety regulations have been widely introduced.

Road Safety.—Controversy over road safety stems from the lack of comprehensive research into the causes of road accidents and from the ease with which road-accident statistics can be interpreted to suit the case of a particular theorist. There is agreement, however, on the safety value of the modern high-speed limited-access road (expressway or throughway) and of the ordinary dual highway. But in towns, and in small countries where land is scarce, the engineering solution tends to be too long-term for such a pressing problem. So recourse is had everywhere to enforcement as an immediate remedy. The trouble, however, is that most accidents are caused not by a criminally selfish minority against whom law is the only sanction, but by the unskilled and unimaginative, who comprise the majority of motorists: hence the vital need for driver education.

The pedestrian and the cyclist also contribute sizably to the accident situation. The best remedy, that of complete segregation of these categories of road user from motor vehicle traffic, is being pursued in the design of new towns. Meanwhile, many countries have regulations for the control of pedestrians in certain areas, requiring them to use specially marked crossing places and to observe traffic signals.

Public Transport Passenger Safety.—Owing to stringent regulations, accidents to passengers in air, rail, and sea transportation form only a very small fraction of the total accidents in any country. Buses are more vulnerable than aircraft, trains, and ships, since they face all the risks of the road.

Home Safety.—Although direct enforcement can hardly be applied to the occupants of the home, legislation regarding the engineering of a house and its fittings is important. Most countries have laws providing measures of safety for the consumer; *e.g.,* laws covering the labeling of flammable liquids, sale of poisons, design of appliances, and standards of electric wiring. However, home hazards are so numerous and varied that the role of education is as vital here as on the roads. Recreational safety, although in a sense an aspect of home safety, is increasingly considered in its own right; here education assumes the form of training in the taking of considered risks.

Organization of Safety Work.—In many countries national voluntary bodies exist for education in safety work. The majority confine themselves either to occupational safety or to road safety; only a few are concerned with safety in general. This is because (1) in those countries with little industry the most immediate requirement has been a road safety organization; (2) finance is a difficulty, particularly where government aid is involved. Hence, overall safety bodies have usually resulted from a merger of separate entities. Admittedly, with specialist bodies all effort can be concentrated on one objective. On the other hand, comprehensive organizations can obtain wider and more influential support; their scope for public relations is greater; and their overheads can be spread and they can support activities, such as home and recreational safety, which might otherwise be neglected completely through lack of money.

Whatever the pros and cons of organizing safety on an all-embracing basis at the national level, at the local level there is everything to be said for specialist groups and safety workers. Of this sort are police and motoring organizations with their concern for road safety; and medical officers of health, health visitors, and firemen, who have a special interest in home safety.

Safety organizations carry out their work by securing the cooperation and support of the public. Members of safety committees both advise and promulgate decisions, either through their organizations or directly. The effectiveness of a safety association lies in the degree of its cooperation with the public, more particularly road-user groups, employers' federations, trade unions, educators, the armed services, central and local government representatives, and the first aid, lifesaving, and medical authorities. There is liaison with the professional safety institutions, such as the American Society of Safety Engineers in the U.S. and the Institution of Industrial Safety Officers in the U.K., and also with the bodies which lay down national safety standards of design.

National Organizations.—The National Safety Council (United States) is the world's largest safety organization. Formed in 1913 as the National Council for Industrial Safety in the United States, in 1914 it enlarged its scope to include traffic safety and adopted its present title, subsequently extending its activities to all safety fields. Each field is served by a department under the direction of a permanent committee; a board of directors exercises general control. The council is financed primarily by subscriptions and by sales of its publications; it also accepts donations through its trustees.

Throughout the U.S., state and local safety councils have been established which, although autonomous, are accredited by the National Safety Council provided they meet its standards of performance. Over 60% of the population is served by such accredited councils. The national council's staff of field service officers helps to achieve uniformity of performance.

In Great Britain, the Royal Society for the Prevention of Accidents (RoSPA), with headquarters in London, is a comprehensive safety organization somewhat like the National Safety Council. It began in 1916 as the London "Safety First" Council. In 1923 it became the National "Safety First" Association by merging with the British Industrial "Safety First" Association of 1918. In 1941 it received its current title under the patronage of King George VI. Its funds are derived from sources similar to those of the National Safety Council, but the cost of its 12 regional road safety offices and their staff is met by the government, which also gives some support to the society's home and agricultural safety activities.

Throughout the U.K., road, home, industrial, and agricultural safety are separately organized by local committees, the first two by local government authorities in the towns and rural areas and the last two by the communities concerned. RoSPA coordinates their work through regional bodies. Internationally known is the society's road safety training centre and exhibition in London, largely financed by local authorities in and around London, and attended by some 50,000 people every year, ranging from schoolchildren to commercial drivers.

All national safety organizations perform a similar educational role within their countries. The facilities at the disposal of the organizations, however, vary according to the funds available. In some countries where there is a government-controlled workmen's compensation fund, the industrial safety organization receives a percentage of the income of this fund to cover its operations. Likewise, in some countries where road-accident insurance is centralized, the road safety organization receives direct financial support.

International Organizations.—National safety associations cooperate through international safety organizations and conferences. Since 1955, world congresses on the prevention of occupational accidents and diseases have been held at three-year intervals. Participation is organized locally by the appropriate national safety body, with the help of the International Social Security Association (ISSA) and the International Labour Organization (ILO). The Permanent International Association of Road Congresses, supported by the ministries of transport of constituent countries and by organizations connected with road construction, holds congresses every four years on subjects which include engineering aspects of safety.

An international road safety congress, held every other year by the World Touring and Automobile Organization (OTA), is organized in collaboration with the International Federation of Senior Police Officers and the Prévention Routière Internationale. This last is an international road safety body based on the Prévention Routière Française in Paris; its membership includes the road safety organizations of Austria, Belgium, Chile, France, Ireland, West Germany, Greece, Israel, Italy, Morocco, Luxembourg, the Netherlands, the province of Quebec (Canada), Switzerland, and the United Kingdom.

In addition to these regular international conferences (and those called at longer intervals, *e.g.*, the International Conference on Alcohol and Road Traffic) there are the annual safety conferences of the major national bodies, which foreign visitors attend.

The International Occupational Safety and Health Information Centre was founded in 1957 in Geneva by the ILO in collaboration with the ISSA, with the support of the European Coal and Steel Community, the European Economic Community, and the World Health Organization. Specialized national institutions in 25 countries also participated. The centre provides information on accident prevention and health protection by means of abstracts from a wide range of safety literature.

The International Organization for Standardization, constituted in 1946 in Geneva, has 50 member countries; France, the U.K., the U.S., and the U.S.S.R. are permanently represented in its council. In addition to representatives of national standards organizations, nominees of safety organizations serve on those of its committees that recommend safety standards. Topics considered include safety codes, safety in the nuclear energy field, and personal equipment and clothing.

See also Dangerous Occupations; Drowning and Life-saving; Health and Safety Laws; Industrial Accidents; Industrial Medicine; Workmen's Compensation; and references under "Accident Prevention," "Accidents," and "Health and Safety Laws" in the Index. For information on safety in the air and at sea, *see* Air Law; Rules of the Road at Sea.

See American Public Health Association, Inc., *Accident Prevention: the Role of Physicians and Public Health Workers,* ed. by Maxwell N. Halsey (1961, 1962); Royal College of Surgeons (London), *Accident Prevention and Life Saving* (papers presented at Convention on Accident Prevention and Life Saving, 1963).   (R. F. E. S.)

SAFETY GLASS: *see* Glass Manufacture: *Safety Glass.*

SAFETY LAMP. Toward the end of the 18th century coal mine explosions became increasingly common as the seams were dug to deeper levels where firedamp (methane gas) was more prevalent, and efforts were made to devise means of lighting which would be safe in the presence of the gas. The explosive nature of a cloud of fine coal dust was not then recognized, and explosions were attributed wholly to gas. The explosions usually originated at the flame of a tallow candle.

Davy Lamp.—W. Reid Clanny invented a form of lamp in 1813 in which the external air was blown by bellows through a small cistern of water and the products of combustion forced through a similar water seal. George Stephenson, who was experimenting with lamps for underground use in 1815, concluded that "if a lamp could be made to contain the burnt air above the flame, and permit the firedamp to come in below in small quantity to be burnt as it came in, the burnt air would prevent the passing of the explosion upwards and the velocity of the current from below would also prevent its passing downwards." Though neither type of lamp was satisfactory, some of the ideas of Clanny and Stephenson were incorporated in the Davy lamp as the latter was developed and improved. In Aug. 1815 the Sunderland Society of the Prevention of Accidents in Mines interested Sir Humphry Davy in the problem of mine explosion, and by the end of that year the first Davy lamp was ready for testing.

Although many others worked along the same lines, his name is more generally known as the inventor of a relatively safe oil-burning lamp. He demonstrated the fact that a metal gauze having 28 openings to the linear inch would cool the products of combustion so that the heat of the flame would not ignite inflammable gas on the other side of the gauze. In order to avoid danger resulting from failure of a single gauze cylinder surrounding the flame, he found it necessary to use two concentric cylinders, one slightly smaller than the other. The lower edges fit snugly to the bowl containing the fuel; the upper ends of the cylinders were, of course, covered by disks of similar gauze. In the hands of a careful person, the Davy lamp could be used safely, but it could not be used in a strong air current because of the danger of passage of the flame through the gauze.

Electric Lamps.—Portable electric hand lamps and cap lamps were introduced in coal mines in the early 1900s, but their weight and cost retarded their widespread adoption until after World War I. By mid-20th century, however, portable electric cap lamps were used almost exclusively by miners in both coal and metal mines. The headpiece on the cap, attached by flexible rubber-insulated cable to the battery on the belt of the wearer, furnishes the miner with a powerful beam of light directed at the work in hand. Batteries use either an alkaline or acid solution and are recharged between working shifts to maintain almost constant illumination for eight hours or more. In the headpiece, there is a safety device that shuts off the electric current if the bulb or bulbs are broken. A single bulb may be fitted with two filaments. If one burns out, a switch may be turned to bring the other into use with no loss of time.

While the electric cap lamp gives excellent illumination, it is completely independent of the surrounding air. Therefore, it gives no warning of noxious gases or lack of oxygen. Consequently, a flame safety lamp must be kept burning within easy reach of the workers or frequent inspections must be made by an official, using a flame safety lamp or other form of detector. When the flame safety lamp is placed in an atmosphere containing firedamp the flame elongates, and if the gas is present in considerable quantity the lamp is filled with blue flame. For testing the presence of gas the flame of the lamp is lowered until the yellow part is at a minimum, when the gas will be discernible as a small blue cap to the flame. U.S. usage, based on federal and state laws, recommends that a minimum of two flame safety lamps in good operating condition be available at all mines for testing the presence of methane or oxygen deficiency. Specifications require that each lamp be equipped with double steel or brass gauzes constructed of wire between 29 and 27 American wire gauge (0.0113 to 0.014 in. in diameter), with mesh openings from 28 to 30 per lineal inch. There should be a shield or bonnet so constructed as to prevent injury to the gauzes and shield the gauzes from strong air currents. Lamp locks should be of the magnetic type and the relighting device simple and safe to use in the presence of flammable gas.

The statutory regulations governing the manufacture and use of safety lamps vary slightly from country to country but are alike in substance. In addition to portable safety lamps, electric lighting from power mains may be allowed underground provided adequate safety features are incorporated in the design of the lighting fixtures, and care is exercised in their installation. *See also* COAL AND COAL MINING: *Hazards of Mining.* (M. D. CR.)

SAFETY RAZOR: see RAZOR.

SAFETY VALVE is a valve which lifts at a predetermined pressure and "lets off steam," thus preventing the accumulation of a dangerous pressure in a steam boiler or hydraulic system. The resistance to pressure is provided by a weight or by springs, the use of the latter being obligatory if the boiler is not a stationary one. The lever valve (*see* diagram) is loaded with a weight at the end, to keep the valve shut. A casing with lock may be fitted over the device to prevent tampering by an unauthorized person. Many boilers carry two safety valves as a precaution, one being locked up. Marine boiler valves are of the direct spring-loaded type, the spring encircling the valve spindle. The pop valve blows off sharply with a pop, and is used for yacht and launch boilers. The valve closes again quickly when the pressure has been slightly reduced.

SCHEMATIC DIAGRAM OF SAFETY VALVE ON STEAM BOILER

VALVE LEVER
FLANGE CONNECTED TO BOILER
WEIGHT

SAFFARIDS, a Persian dynasty of the 9th century, founded *c.* A.D. 866 by Yaqub ibn al-Layth al-Saffar ("the Coppersmith"), who gained command of a body of local troops and took control of his native province of Seistan. He soon added the Kabul Valley, Sind, Makran, Kerman, Fars, and Bactria to his possessions. In 873 he seized Khurasan, Tabaristan, and neighbouring territories. Finally in 876 he was defeated by the caliph's army when marching on Baghdad. He died in 879 and was succeeded by his brother Amr, who was declared by the caliph viceroy of Khurasan, Isfahan, Fars, Seistan, and Sind. In 900 he was defeated near Balkh by Ismail, the Samanid. Thereafter few of the later Saffarids had any wide authority, though they maintained their position in Seistan intermittently for more than two centuries.

See V. V. Barthold, *Turkestan Down to the Mongol Invasion,* 2nd ed. (1959).

SAFFLOWER, the common name for *Carthamus tinctorius,* a flowering annual plant of the composite family (Compositae), and native to a large area from central India through the Middle East to the upper reaches of the Nile River into Ethiopia. It grows from one to four feet high and has flowers that may be red, orange, yellow, or white.

It was important at one time as a source of a red textile dye called carthamin, obtained from the dried flowers. Carthamin was replaced by synthetic aniline dyes, except in local areas of Southwest Asia. Occasionally it has been an adulterant of saffron (*q.v.*). Safflower is grown now primarily for the oil obtained from the seed. Because the oil does not yellow with age, it has been useful in the preparation of surface coatings such as varnish and paint. Most of the oil, however, has been used for edible purposes, in soft margarines, as a cooking oil, and as a salad oil.

Although safflower oil has been promoted commercially as a regulator of blood cholesterol levels, the medical results have been inconclusive. The meal or cake residue is used as a protein supplement for dairy cows, beef cattle, and sheep.

The plant is grown chiefly in India. It has been introduced as an oil crop to the United States, Australia, Israel, Turkey, and Canada. It requires a growing season of 120 days or more and dry atmospheres after the appearance of the buds.

See P. F. Knowles, "Safflower: Production, Processing and Utilization" in *Economic Botany,* vol. 9 (1955). (P. F. K.; X.)

SAFFRON, the orange powdered product manufactured from the dried stigmas and part of the style of the saffron crocus (*Crocus sativus*). The purple flower, which blooms late in the autumn, is very similar to that of the common spring crocus. The conspicuous protruding stigmas are of a characteristic orange colour; the fruit is rarely formed. The Egyptians, though acquainted with the bastard safflower (*Carthamus tinctorius;* often used to adulterate saffron), do not seem to have possessed the true saffron, but it is named in Songs of Solomon 4:14 among other sweet-smelling herbs. It is also mentioned by Homer and Hippocrates.

The saffron crocus has long been cultivated in Iran and Kashmir, and is supposed to have been introduced into China by the Mongol invasion. It is mentioned in the Chinese materia medica (*Pun tsaou,* 1552–78). The chief seat of cultivation in early times, however, was in Cilicia, in Asia Minor. It was cultivated by the Arabs in Spain about 961, and is mentioned in an English leech-book of the 10th century, but seems to have disappeared from Western Europe until reintroduced by the crusaders. According to Hakluyt, it was taken to England from Tripoli by a pilgrim, who hid a stolen corm in the hollow of his staff. It was especially cultivated near Histon in Cambridgeshire and in Essex at Saffron Walden (*q.v.*), its cultivators being called "crokers."

As a perfume, saffron was strewn in Greek halls, courts, and theatres, and in the Roman baths. The streets of Rome were sprinkled with saffron when Nero made his entry into the city. It was a royal colour in early Greek times, though afterward, perhaps from its abundant use in the baths and as a scented salve, it was especially appropriated by the hetaerae, professional female entertainers of the time.

ROCHE
SAFFRON CROCUS (CROCUS SATIVUS)

Saffron was used as an ingredient in many of the complicated medicines of early times. That it was much used in cookery and as a dye is evidenced by many writers. It is no longer used as a fabric dye, since it is water soluble, but is used for colouring foods, to which it imparts a characteristic subtle flavour.

Saffron is chiefly cultivated in Spain, France, Sicily, on the lower spurs of the Apennines, and in Iran and Kashmir. It occurs in the form of cake saffron, which consists of the stigmas and part of the style, which have been "sweated" and pressed together into a cake, and also as hay saffron, which consists of the dried stigmas alone.

SAFFRON WALDEN, a market town and municipal borough in the Saffron Walden parliamentary division of Essex, Eng., 27 mi. NNW of Chelmsford by road. Pop. (1961) 7,817. Area

11.7 sq.mi. Of the old castle, dating probably from the 12th century, the keep and a few other portions still remain. Near it is a series of curious circular excavations in the chalk, called the Maze, of unknown date or purpose. The earthworks west and south of the town are of great extent; a large Saxon burial ground was there. The large church of St. Mary the Virgin contains the tomb of Lord Audley, chancellor to Henry VIII. The town has a museum with good archaeological and natural history collections. In the neighbourhood is the fine mansion of Audley End, built by Thomas, 1st earl of Suffolk, in 1603 on the ruins of the abbey, converted in 1190 from a Benedictine priory founded by Geoffrey de Mandeville in 1136.

The town corporation grew out of the Guild of the Holy Trinity, which was incorporated under Henry VIII, the lord of the town, in 1513. It was dissolved under Edward VI, and a charter was obtained appointing a treasurer and chamberlain and 24 assistants, who, with the commonalty, formed the corporation. In 1694 William and Mary made Walden a free borough. The culture of saffron was the most characteristic industry at Walden from the reign of Edward III until its gradual extinction about 1768; market gardening is now the main industry.

SAFI (Asfi), a port on the west coast of Morocco south of Cape Cantin about 105 mi. (170 km.) NW of Marrakesh City by road. It is the chief town of the Abda-Ahmar region. Pop. (1960) 81,072. In the 13th century, it was a *ribat* (fortress of the holy war). The Portuguese occupied it from 1508 till 1541, and built a citadel (kechla), which included a castle at the edge of the sea, and repaired the ancient kasbah. These fortifications still exist. Safi was formerly headquarters of a province of 270,000 inhabitants, but following an administrative reorganization after Morocco's independence it became part of Marrakesh Province (*q.v.*). On Nov. 8, 1942, Safi was one of the points at which the American forces landed.

The port is connected by rail to the phosphates centre of Youssoufia (formerly Louis-Gentil) of which it exports the entire output. It is also the chief sardine port of Morocco and the site of an important canning industry. (A. Am.)

SAFID RUD, the longest river of northern Iran, flows into the Caspian Sea. With its main tributary, the Qezel Owzan (Qizil Uzun), the Safid Rud has an approximate length of 487 mi. (785 km.) and a total drainage area of 21,700 sq.mi. (56,200 sq.km.). It is formed by the union of its tributaries Qezel Owzan and Shahrud near Manjil at an elevation of 920 ft. (280 m.); it at once breaks through the Elburz Mountains, in an impressive gorge 23 mi. (37 km.) long, to emerge on the plain of Gilan (*q.v.*), where it forms a delta. Heavy floods and frequent changes of course—six major changes between the mid-19th and mid-20th centuries—have wrought havoc upon the dense population of the delta. A dam completed in 1962 at Manjil at the upper end of the gorge was designed to prevent floods, improve and extend irrigation, and provide electric power. The average discharge of the Safid Rud at the town of Rudbar was calculated in the mid-1950s as 22,900 cu.ft. (651 cu.m.) per sec., with an average daily maximum of 32,666 (925) in April–May, but only 1,328 (37.6) in August–September. (H. Bo.)

SAFIYE SULTAN (fl. *c.* A.D. 1600), the favourite consort of the Ottoman sultan Murad III (reigned 1574–95) and the mother of his son Mohammed III (1595–1603), who exercised a strong influence on Ottoman affairs during the reigns of both sultans. Her name Safiye signifies "the pure one." She has often been confused with Nur Banu, the wife of Sultan Selim II (1566–74) and mother of Murad III, who descended from the Venetian house of Venier-Baffo. Safiye Sultan is said, in the *Ottomanno* of the well-informed Venetian L. Soranzo, whose book appeared at Ferrara in 1599, to have been a native of Rezi, a mountain town in Albania. Until the death, in 1583, of Nur Banu, the *valide sultan* (mother of the sultan on the throne), her influence over the conduct of affairs was circumscribed. Thereafter, as *khasseki sultan, i.e.*, mother of the heir to the throne, Mohammed, and, after 1595, as *valide sultan* during the reign of her son, she wielded great influence at the Ottoman court. Of those who enjoyed her favour, mention can be made here of Ibrahim Pasha (d.

1601), three times grand vizier in the reign of Mohammed III. Safiye Sultan is said to have shown herself favourable, during the years of her greatest influence, to the interests of Venice at the Ottoman Porte. Sent into retirement on the death of her son Mohammed III in 1603, Safiye Sultan died in 1605 according to some authorities and according to others not until 1619. A mosque at Cairo, the Malika Safiye, bears her name. She also began in 1597–98 (or 1614, according to some authorities) the construction at Istanbul of a mosque which, at first left unfinished, was later completed in the reign of Sultan Mohammed IV (1648–87) to become the Yeni Valide Camii. (V. J. P.)

SAGA, a prefecture (*ken*) in northern Kyushu, Japan, and also the name of the capital of the prefecture. The *ken* has an area of 927.76 sq.mi. (2,403 sq.km.) and a population (1965) of 871,885. Within it is the Tsukushi plain, dissected by a network of creeks used for irrigation and drainage. Advanced agricultural techniques have been developed and mechanization is extensive. Saga Prefecture is believed to be the point at which the earliest contact between Japan and the continent of Asia was made. In late Edo time (1603–1867), it was influenced by European culture via the city of Nagasaki. The town of Arita (pop. [1960] 15,706) is noted for its china and pottery. Arita ware (Arita-yaki), developed by Ri Sampei, a Korean potter, in the 16th and 17th centuries, is made in approximately 300 small factories, with an annual output valued at about $2,000,000.

Saga, the capital of the prefecture, was the castle town of the lord Nabeshima. Pop. (1960) 129,888. Traces of feudal days still remain in the thatched roofs and the lotus-covered castle moats. Saga is noted for cotton textiles and ceramic wares. (R. B. H.)

SAGA: *see* Icelandic Literature.

SAGAING, a district of the Union of Burma lying to the west of Mandalay on both sides of the Irrawaddy River and in the heart of the Dry Belt. The district has an area of 968 sq.mi. (2,507 sq.km.) and a population (1962 est.) of 379,392. Chief crops are the grain sesamum, millet, rice, peas, wheat, and cotton. Rainfall ranges from about 25 to 35 in. (635 to 890 mm.). In the hot season the maximum shade temperature rises to a little more than 100° F (38° C). The lowest readings in the cold season average about 56° F (13° C).

Sagaing, the headquarters town, picturesquely situated at the southern end of a north-south ridge conspicuously dotted with white pagodas, is opposite Ava (*q.v.*), 10 mi. SW of Mandalay; pop. (1953) 15,439. It was formerly a capital of Burma (18th century). The Ava Bridge (3,940 ft., completed in 1934 and destroyed during the Japanese invasion but rebuilt later), with its western end at Sagaing, carries the Mandalay-Myitkyina railway and also road traffic. Sagaing is also a river port served by steamers of the Inland Water Transport Board.

Sagaing also gives its name to a division which comprises the districts of Upper and Lower Chindwin, Katha, Shwebo, and Sagaing. (L. D. S.)

SAGAR (Saugor), so named after its fine lake (Hindi *sagar*, "lake"), a town and district in the Jabalpur division of Madhya Pradesh, India. The town, headquarters of the district, is picturesquely situated around a lake amidst the spurs of the Vindhya Mountains, 90 mi. (145 km.) NW of Jabalpur. Pop. (1961) 85,491. There is an old Maratha fort now used as a police training college. Saugar University, founded in 1946, has a central campus on one of the spurs (2,000 ft.) overlooking the town. There are some oil and flour mills and a flourishing *bidi* (local cigarette) industry. The town is on the Katni-Bina section of the Central Railway.

Sagar District (area 3,961 sq.mi. [10,295 sq.km.]; pop. [1961] 796,547) is an extensive plain, broken in places by low hills of basalt and sandstone covered with teak forests. The southern and central parts have lava soil, while the northern and eastern have reddish brown soil, formed mostly over granites. The principal crops are wheat, gram, jowar, linseed, and sesamum. The chief landholding classes are Brahmans, Dangis, Lodhis, and Bundela Rajputs. About 42% of the total area is arable and 29% is under forests. Thermal electricity produced at Sagar is transmitted to the adjoining Damoh district also. Sagar district has a number of factories and iron ore and limestone deposits occur in the Shahgarh tract. The Rahatgarh waterfall, the old Rahatgarh fort, and the archaeological site at Eran (to the west) are of tourist interest. The chief towns are Bina-Etawah, Khurai, Bamora, Garhakota, and Deori. (S. M. A.)

SAGE, the common name applied to plants of the genus *Salvia* of the mint family, especially to *S. officinalis,* the leaves of which are used for seasoning. *See* SALVIA.

SAGEBRUSH, the name given to various shrubby species of *Artemisia* native to plains and mountain slopes of western North America. The common sagebrush (*A. tridentata*) is a much-branched shrub, usually 3 ft. to 6 ft., but sometimes 12 ft. high, with silvery gray, bitter-aromatic foliage, the small, wedge-shaped leaves mostly with three teeth at the outer end. This shrub is very abundant on semiarid plains, mainly between 1,500 ft. and 6,000 ft. altitude, where it is often a conspicuous and characteristic feature of the vegetation. It occurs from Montana and western Nebraska to British Columbia and California.

SAGINAW, a city of Michigan, U.S., and seat of Saginaw county, is located 10 mi. S. of Bay City and 92 mi. N.W. of Detroit, on both banks of the Saginaw river 15 mi. from its entrance into Saginaw bay (Lake Huron). It is a centre of farming and manufacturing and a port of entry. Nearby communities include Chesaning, Carrollton and Frankenmuth.

Saginaw means "land of the Sauks" in the language of the Chippewa Indians who once dominated the valley after driving out the Sauks in the 16th century. A post was established in 1816 by the American Fur company and Fort Saginaw was constructed on the west bank of the river in 1822. Although the fort was abandoned the following year, a settlement known as Saginaw City grew up around the fur-trading post and received its charter in 1870. East Saginaw, established in 1849 and chartered 1859, joined with Saginaw City in 1889 to form Saginaw. In 1936 the city adopted a council-manager form of government.

Saginaw was a major lumbering centre from 1834 when a steam sawmill began operations until about 1890, by which time the pine forests were depleted. Salt deposits, coal and oil are productive mineral resources of the area and their development helped to offset the decline in lumber trade. Served by major railroads, highways and an airport, Saginaw became a wholesale and trading centre for northeastern Michigan. It manufactures automotive parts, particularly steering gears, malleable and gray iron, graphite, baking machinery, mobile homes, truck trailers and paper products. The county contains approximately 4,500 farms averaging 45 ac. in size and producing sugar beets, beans and wheat. One of the world's largest bean elevators is in Saginaw. Parks include the Ezra Rust and Hoyt parks and Ojibway Island. The Schuch hotel contains a museum of Indian artifacts.

Population of the city in 1960 was 98,265 and the Saginaw standard metropolitan statistical area comprising Saginaw county had a population of 190,752. For comparative population figures *see* table in MICHIGAN: *Population*. (MA. R.)

SAGITTARIUS (the "Archer"), in astronomy, a constellation and sign of the zodiac. In mythology, Sagittarius was pictured as a centaur preparing to shoot an arrow. The southernmost zodiacal constellation, it appears rather low in the south in the early evenings of the late summer for observers in middle northern latitudes. Six of its stars outline the inverted Milk Dipper, which has its handle thrust into the Milky Way. Near the western border of Sagittarius is the winter solstice, the southernmost point of the sun's apparent annual course around the heavens. Also in this region is the direction of the centre of our spiral galaxy, some 30,000 light-years distant from Earth. This area is accordingly one of exceptional complexity and interest as viewed with the naked eye and with the optical and radio telescope. The great star cloud in the central region of Sagittarius is one of the brightest features of the Milky Way. *See* CONSTELLATION.

(R. H. BR.)

SAGO, a food starch prepared from a deposit in the trunk of several palms, the principal source being the sago palms (*Metroxylon rumphii* and *M. sagu*), native to the Indonesian archipelago, the sago forests being especially extensive in the island of Ceram. The trees flourish only in low marshy situations, seldom attaining a height of 30 ft., with a thickset trunk. They attain maturity and produce an inflorescence (flower spike) at the age of 15 years, when the enormous pith of the stem is gorged with starch. If the fruit is allowed to form and ripen, the whole of this starchy core material passes into the developing fruits, leaving the stem a mere hollow shell; and the tree after ripening its fruit dies. Accordingly the palms are cut down as soon as the inflorescence appears, the stems are divided into sections and split up and the starchy pith extracted and grated to a powder. The powder is then kneaded with water over a strainer, through which the starch passes, leaving the woody fibre behind. The starch settles in the bottom of a trough, in which it is floated, and after one or two washings is fit for use by the natives for cakes and soups. That intended for exportation is mixed into a paste with water and rubbed through sieves into small grains, whence it is known according to size as pearl sago, bullet sago, etc.

A large proportion of the sago imported into Europe comes from Borneo, and the increasing demand has led to a large extension of sago-palm planting. Sago is also obtained from various other Indonesian palms such as the Gomuti palm (*Arenga pinnata*), the Kittul palm (*Caryota urens*), the cabbage palm (*Corypha umbraculifera*), besides *Corypha utan, Raphia flabelliformis* and *Phoenix pusilla,* also from *Mauritia flexuosa* and *Guilielma gasipaes,* two South American species. It is also obtained from the pith of species of *Cycas.*

SAGUARO (*Cereus giganteus* or *Carnegiea gigantea*), a remarkable tree cactus, rising to 50 ft. in height, called also giant cactus and monument cactus, native to arid districts in southern Arizona, southeastern California and Sonora, Mex. It has a stout, woody, vertically ribbed stem, one to two feet in diameter, sometimes rising unbranched, like a green, fluted column, whence the name monument cactus; more frequently it bears a few large, stout, widely diverging candelabralike branches, but occasionally it bears numerous branches which rise vertically from near the base like a group of organ pipes. Close to the top of the stem or branches it bears white flowers which are followed by crimson edible fruits. In Arizona, of which it is the floral emblem or state flower, a desert tract containing numerous fine living specimens of the tree was set apart and is now known as Saguaro National monument. *See also* CACTUS.

RUTHERFORD PLATT

SAGUARO (CEREUS GIGANTEUS)

SAGUENAY, a river of Quebec, Can., which drains the waters of Lake St. John into the St. Lawrence River about 120 mi. northeast of Quebec City. Flowing ESE, the Saguenay, in the first third of its 105-mi. length (475 mi. long from the head of the Peribonca River), descends about 300 ft. in a turbulent stream. Thereafter, the valley is virtually a fjord through which the river, without shoals (average depth, about 800 ft.) or obstructions, continues between precipitous cliffs which culminate in the majestic capes Trinity and Eternity, more than 1,600 ft. high. The upper river is an important source of hydroelectric power, used primarily for aluminum production at Arvida. The river is navigable from its mouth at Tadoussac, the oldest European trading post in Canada, to Chicoutimi, above which the rapids begin. Ha Ha Bay, about 20 mi. downstream from Chicoutimi, is a fjordlike arm of the Saguenay into which the Ha Ha River and the Rivière Mars empty near Port Alfred at the head of the bay. (J. D. I.)

SAGUIA EL HAMRA: *see* SPANISH SAHARA.

SAGUNTO (formerly MURVIEDRO), a town of eastern Spain

about 15½ mi. (25 km:) NNE of Valencia on the Valencia–Barcelona coast railway, and a junction for the railway to Aragon. Pop. (1960) 40,293 (mun.). The town has light industries, and its port (2½ mi.) exports minerals and fruit. Sagunto is the ancient Saguntum, a town thought to have been founded by colonists from Zacynthus (Zanti; whence its name). About 225 B.C. the Romans, disquieted by the growth of Carthaginian power in Spain, concluded an alliance with Hasdrubal which guaranteed the independence of Saguntum and required the Carthaginians not to cross the Ebro. In 219, however, Hannibal attacked Saguntum. The town resisted for eight months, at the end of which it was taken by storm. Rome complained to Carthage, requiring the surrender of Hannibal; the council refused, and the Second Punic War began. Afterward the Romans restored the ancient importance of Saguntum, whose inhabitants received Roman citizenship, and enriched the town with the monuments of which the remains may be seen today. The Roman theatre built under Septimius Severus and Caracalla is the most notable building. There are also remains of different periods: the acropolis, the temple of Diana, the temple of Venus, and the aqueduct (constructed from rough Iberian stones through the Roman period to the Moorish). (R. A. DE.)

SAHA, MEGHNAD N. (1893–1956), Indian physicist noted for his development of the thermal ionization equation (which, in the perfected form due to E. A. Milne, has remained fundamental in all work on stellar atmospheres and other plasmas) and for his application of it to the interpretation of stellar spectra. Born on Oct. 6, 1893, in Bengal, Saha received his first training in Calcutta, and carried out postgraduate work at Imperial College, London, and in Berlin. After returning to India, he became professor of physics at Allahabad (1923–38) and at Calcutta (1938–55). He was elected a fellow of the Royal Society in 1927 and was president of the United Provinces Academy of Sciences and of other Indian scientific bodies. He was mainly instrumental in the foundation of the Calcutta Institute of Nuclear Physics, of which he became honorary director.

In his later years, while not neglecting research, Saha increasingly turned his attention to the social relations of science; he founded the outspoken journal *Science and Culture* in 1935. In 1951 he was elected to the Indian parliament as an independent. He continued publishing papers on nuclear physics and astrophysics until his death in New Delhi on Feb. 16, 1956.

Among his works are: *A Treatise on Heat,* with B. N. Srivastava, 3rd ed. (1950), and *A Treatise on Modern Physics,* vol. i, with N. K. Saha (1934). An important paper is "Ionization in the Solar Chromosphere," *Phil. Mag.,* vol. 40, p. 472 (1920).

See S. N. Sen (ed.), *Professor Meghnad Saha: His Life, Work and Philosophy* (1954). (B. E. J. P.)

SAHAPTIN, a large American Indian linguistic stock, spoken in what is now southeastern Washington, west-central Idaho, part of eastern Oregon, and north-central California. The four major divisions, all mutually unintelligible, were: northern Sahaptin, spoken by the Yakima, Klikitat, Palus, Wanapam, Tenino, Umatilla, and Wallawalla tribes; Nez Percé; Cayuse-Molala; and Klamath-Modoc. Cayuse-Molala was formerly called Waiilatpuan and considered a separate stock. Similarly, Klamath-Modoc was separated under the name Lutuamian. Further studies have shown these to be divergent branches of Sahaptin.

Earlier the spelling Shahaptian was sometimes used; also, the name occasionally was employed as a designation for the Nez Percé tribe (see INDIAN, NORTH AMERICAN; PENUTIAN).

See M. Jacobs, *Northwest Sahaptin Texts* (1929), *A Sketch of Northern Sahaptin Grammar* (1931); T. Stern, "Klamath Myth Abstracts," *Journal of American Folklore,* vol. 76 (Jan. 1963).

SAHARA, from the Arabic word *sahrá* ("wilderness"), is the great desert of North Africa, the largest desert in the world. It stretches across Africa from the Atlantic coast through Egypt to the Red Sea, beyond which desert conditions continue into Arabia and Iran. Around its edges are transitional areas where rainfall is greater and true desert conditions gradually disappear, so that nowhere has it precise boundaries. Its greatest west-east extension exceeds 3,000 mi., and it is seldom less than 1,000 mi. wide. Its total area, perhaps 3,500,000 sq.mi. (9,100,000 sq.km.),

occupies between one-quarter and one-third of the African continent. Despite the physical unity of the whole area, it includes many political divisions. Much of the Sahara consists of a plateau of an average elevation of 1,000 ft., but it is far from uniform in character. There are, for example, considerable areas that are 600 ft. or less above sea level (the chotts or salt lakes near Biskra being actually below sea level), while some of the highest points in the Ahaggar Massif reach nearly 10,000 ft., and parts of Tibesti exceed 11,000 ft.

Geology, Structure, and Physiographical Evolution.— The main features of geology and structure are now reasonably well understood, although much detailed work remains to be done. The area as a whole is quite distinct from the Atlas Mountains, which belong, tectonically, to Europe. The oldest rocks, of Archean and Precambrian Age, were folded and denuded to form the Saharan platform, upon which later deposits have been laid. There have been numerous dislocations, the more marked of which have been accompanied by volcanic activity; several of the highest peaks in the central Sahara, such as Mt. Tousside (10,712 ft. [3,265 m.]) in Tibesti, are the remains of extinct volcanoes of Tertiary and Quaternary Age. Elsewhere, uplift has caused the renewal of erosion leading to the cutting of deep valleys and gorges, such as those of the Tasili N'Ajjer. During Cretaceous and later times much of the Sahara was submerged; in consequence extensive areas are covered by sandstones, such as the Nubian sandstone, of Cretaceous Age, and limestones, which were laid down on the floor of the sea. There are also large basins occupied by sediments of continental origin deposited by wind or in shallow fresh or saline waters. The horizontally bedded Cretaceous and other rocks form plains, plateaus, and escarpments that are dissected by former river valleys (wadis) and are in striking contrast to the volcanic topography of other areas.

At one time the vast quantities of sand in the Sahara were believed to have a marine origin, but the sand is now known to be of Quaternary (probably Pleistocene) Age, and there is no evidence of any marine transgression since pre-Tertiary times. During the Quaternary Ice Age in Europe, the Sahara's climate was much wetter; erosion occurred as it does in moist temperate or subtropical regions today, and there was an extensive system of rivers. Much of the Sahara was probably covered by grass with some trees. With the retreat of the ice sheets from Europe, this vegetation disappeared and arid conditions were established; the soil dried out and became liable to large-scale wind erosion. Some authorities claim that there is considerable evidence to suggest that desert conditions are extending, at the present time, into many of the semidesert and savanna regions surrounding the Sahara. The alarmist reports of certain writers about the advance of the desert have been fairly conclusively proved to be exaggerated; moreover, the explanation of any extension of desertlike conditions may be unrelated to climatic conditions. The whole question of climatic change in historic times, in the Sahara and elsewhere in the world, is highly controversial and is under constant review by experts in many fields, notably those associated with the work of UNESCO's Arid Zone Research Group. (See *Bibliography.*)

Physical Characteristics.—Three main types of surface and scenery are commonly recognized in the Sahara today: the erg, the reg (or areg), and the hammada. The erg is the desert of shifting sand dunes, which lie in the bottoms of the great basins where former rivers piled up most alluvium. In some areas there is still movement among the dunes; elsewhere movement has ceased and the sand dunes appear "fossilized." The Great Western and Eastern Ergs, between Beni Abbès and Ghudamis (Ghadames), are the most difficult of all Saharan areas and are avoided, as far as possible, by modern trans-Saharan routes. The Libyan Desert is another extensive area of unmitigated sandy waste. The reg desert consists of wind-scoured plains strewn with pebbles, boulders, and gravels. The hammada are rocky plateaus with bare rock outcrops, often much dissected by deeply eroded valleys and gorges; they are common around the Ahaggar and Tibesti and, at lower altitudes, in the Western Sahara.

The high central ridge crossing the Sahara from west to east is dominated by the Ahaggar Massif of Archean and Paleozoic

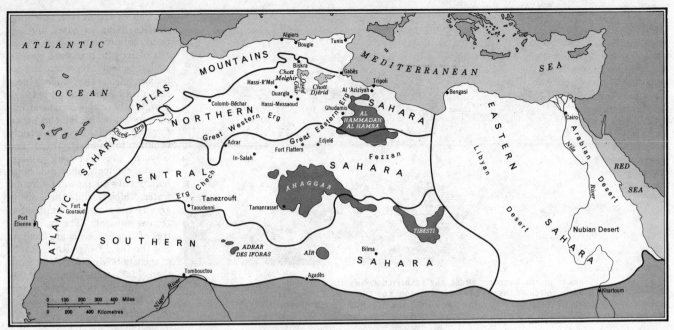

THE EXTENT OF THE SAHARA DESERT, AFRICA

rocks. Its highest peak, Tahat (9,842 ft. [3,000 m.]), is sometimes snowcapped. Associated with the massif are the plateaus of Ahenet, Mouydir, and Tasili N'Ajjer. Westward is the harsh and sterile Tanezrouft and the Erg Chech, eastward the Fezzan.

Around the central ridge the Sahara extends in all directions. The Western, or Atlantic, Sahara in Spanish Sahara (Río de Oro) and Mauritania is relatively low-lying (1,500 ft. at most and often below 600 ft.) and of monotonous relief. The Southern Sahara, reaching almost to the Niger Valley, includes the high massifs of the Adrar des Iforas, Aïr (Azbine). Tibesti (Emi Koussi, 11,204 ft. above sea level), and Ennedi. The Eastern Sahara extends eastward to the Red Sea between the latitudes of Khartoum and the Mediterranean Sea. The Libyan Desert (and its continuation in Egypt known as the Western Desert) consists of uniform low relief with almost level dunes and sandy wastes crossed by very few routes. Beyond the Nile is the Arabian (or Eastern) Desert in Egypt and the Nubian Desert in northeastern Sudan, where Jebel Oda reaches 7,412 ft. near the Red Sea. The Northern Sahara consists of the Great Western (Saoura) Erg, the Great Eastern (Igharghar) Erg, and the Hammada el Homra (Al Hammadah al Hamra), with the relatively small oasis areas of Gourara, Touat, and Tidikelt. A depression along the southern side of the Saharan Atlas is marked in the west by the Oued Dra, draining to the Atlantic, and in the east by a line of chotts, of which the Chott Melghir (Melrhir) south of Biskra is below sea level and the Chott Djérid in southern Tunisia is the largest. The Gulf of Gabès (Qābis) was part of this same depression but is now submerged and forms an arm of the Mediterranean Sea.

Climate.—*Rainfall.*—Lack of rainfall is the distinguishing feature of the Sahara as of all the world's great deserts. Rainfall averages less than 10 in. (254 mm.) a year in the north (south of the Atlas Mountains) and 15 in. (380 mm.) in the south, where evaporation is greater, in the latitude of Tombouctou (Timbuktu) and Agadès. The true desert, with 5 in. or less in a year, occupies a more restricted area, and absolute desert is most common in the extensive flat areas of the Tanezrouft, or "land of thirst," to the west of the Ahaggar. Every-

where the general lack of rainfall is marked by great variations from year to year and by the liability for such rain as falls to occur in sudden and violent storms at very irregular intervals. At Adrar 3.7 in. have been recorded in a few hours, but at In-Salah only 0.4 in. was recorded in four years. El Goléa experienced only one fall of rain in seven years, and Tidikelt only one in ten years.

Systematic meteorological observations have been made at an increasing number of stations on the edge of the desert. The table illustrates rainfall and other climatic conditions at the Jules Carde Observatory at Tamanrasset (Fort Laperrine) in the Ahaggar Mountains at 4,429 ft. above sea level, where regular records are available from 1932.

Temperature.—The Sahara is one of the hottest regions of the world. Tamanrasset (*see* table) shows some of the special aspects of the temperature conditions of Saharan stations. Mean annual temperatures of more than 80° F (27° C) and even 85° (29°) are widely recorded, with particularly high monthly figures for June, July, and August when the highest-known shade temperatures on the earth's surface are recorded. Al 'Aziziyah in Tripolitania has recorded 136.4° F (58° C). Diurnal range of temperature is great; because of cloudless skies and the clarity of the atmosphere, with relative humidity sometimes less than 10%, there is often rapid loss of heat from the ground after sunset so that the nights are commonly cool and refreshing, with temperatures that may be as much as 60° F (33° C) below those of midday.

The prevalent winds nearly everywhere are the northeast trades, though in the Western Sahara westerly winds are also common. Along the southern edge of the desert, especially in West Africa,

Climatic Conditions Recorded at Tamanrasset, Sahara

Month	Mean rainfall (in.)	Mean number of rainy days	Relative humidity (%)	Mean temperature		Mean daily temperature				Absolute temperature			
						Maximum		Minimum		Maximum		Minimum	
				°F	°C	°F	°C	°F	°C	°F	°C	°F	°C
January . .	0.3	1	31	54	12	67	19	40	4	79	26	20	−7
February . .	0.0	0.4	25	58	14	72	22	43	6	82	28	25	−4
March . .	0.0	0.4	23	64	18	79	26	49	9	90	32	32	0
April . .	0.2	0.7	20	72	22	86	30	58	14	96	36	42	6
May . .	0.5	2	24	78	26	92	33	64	18	98	37	45	7
June . .	0.2	3	21	83	28	95	35	70	21	101	38	59	15
July . .	0.1	2	23	84	29	96	36	72	22	99	37	62	17
August . .	0.4	3	25	83	28	95	35	71	22	100	38	62	17
September . .	0.1	3	24	79	26	91	33	67	19	97	36	56	13
October . .	0.1	0.5	26	74	23	86	30	60	16	91	33	47	8
November . .	0.0	0.6	28	65	18	79	26	51	11	86	30	36	2
December . .	0.0	0.5	31	58	14	71	22	44	7	81	27	27	−3
Year (total or mean) . .	1.9	17	25	71	22	84	29	57	14	101	38	20	−7

NEBKAS IN THE DESERT. THESE ARE PETRIFIED FORMATIONS OF VEGETAL ORIGIN WHICH FORMERLY CLUNG TO THE ROOTS OF TREES, NOW DEAD. TIME AND WEATHER HAVE MOULDED THEM INTO THE STRANGE SHAPES SHOWN IN THE PICTURE

the Sahara are, in fact, sedentary peoples living in oases and depending upon irrigation. Methods of irrigation include springs, wells, shadoofs, *foggaras*, and artesian wells. The shadoof consists of a beam, pivoted between uprights, bearing a weight at one end and a bucket at the other. *Foggaras*, which are especially common in Tidikelt, Touat, and Gourara, are man-made subterranean channels, dug not quite horizontally to tap underground water, which is led to the oasis by gravity and supplies a limited but regular amount. The main centres of artesian wells are Ouargla and the Oued Ghir (Rhir), south of the Chott Melghir, where more than 1,000 wells supply 69,000 gal. a minute to irrigate nearly 2,000,000 palms. Unfortunately the withdrawal of these large quantities of water has caused a drop in the water table, but countermeasures have been taken with some success.

southwesterly winds are drawn in from the Guinea coast toward the central Sahara, particularly in July, and bring limited amounts of rainfall. Their degree of penetration, and the quantity of rainfall, vary from year to year: they reach the Adrar des Iforas regularly and sometimes affect the Ahaggar Massif. In the northern Sahara frontal activity from the Mediterranean occasionally brings north and northwest winds, with moist air and storms, during the winter months. Hot, dry, desiccating winds originating in the central Sahara also blow outward to affect areas adjacent to, and beyond, the desert; these include the northeasterly harmattan, which regularly affects many parts of western Africa from November to March and occasionally reaches right to the Guinea coast, and the northerly blowing winds that bring very dry conditions to parts of the Mediterranean seaboard and are variously known as sirocco, khamsin, *guebli, chehili,* and simoom.

Vegetation and Animal Life.—Areas from which all plant life is absent, such as the Tanezrouft and the Hammadat Tinghert (Hammada of Tinrhert) south of Ghudamis, form a relatively small part of the Sahara. Mobile sand dunes are generally devoid of plants, but the sandy parts of the basins of the great rivers of Quaternary times often have a moderate vegetation cover which draws on the water reserves available underground. Nevertheless plant life is usually poorly developed. It consists of two very distinct types: the permanent, such as betoum (Atlantic turpentine tree) and acacia trees and thorny shrubs such as tamarisk and jujube; and the ephemeral, widely known by the desert peoples as *acheb* (*ashab*)—delicate herbs whose seeds germinate immediately after rain, grow rapidly, flower for a brief period, set fruits and seeds, and then die. The natural vegetation of the oases was probably the oleander with tamarisk. Of the introduced plants, the date palm is of outstanding importance. Its fruits provide food for local consumption as well as for trade, and the crushed seeds are fed to camels.

As with the vegetation, the Sahara has a highly specialized wild fauna. Gazelles, desert antelopes, and wild goats are common on the northern and southern edges of the desert; jackal, fox, and badger also occur. Bustards are found on the south side of the Saharan Atlas; ostriches are now scarce. Horned vipers, scorpions, lizards, locusts, flies, and ticks are common. The Egyptian monitor, which looks like a small crocodile, survives in certain areas such as the tributaries of the Igharghar (Irharhar). Domesticated animals, especially camels, sheep, and goats, have been introduced to all the oases.

Economic Development.—When water can be made available to soils that are often fertile, in a region with temperatures that are conducive to rapid vegetative growth, the desert may be made to "blossom as the rose." Two-thirds of the total population of

In all Saharan oases the date palm is the chief tree and the main source of food, while in its shade are grown citrus fruits, figs, peaches, apricots, vegetables, and cereals such as wheat, barley, and millets.

In marked contrast to the agriculturalists are the nomadic pastoralists of the desert border and of the fringes of the central mountain areas; the difference in the way of life is indeed far more significant than racial or linguistic differences. In general the poorer or drier the desert, the more scattered the population. Camels play an important part in the lives of the nomads, though numerically sheep and goats dominate. The availability of fodder and drinking water determines the extent of the grazing of livestock and the migrations of their owners. The Regibat of Spanish Sahara sometimes travel 400 mi. eastward to the Erg Chech to find water for their camels. The razzias or raids by nomads upon oasis cultivators are much less common than they were, the result of the pacification of all but the most remote areas.

Apart from some modern developments connected with mineral exploitation (*see* below), Saharan commerce still largely follows the traditional pattern: the supplying of the desert peoples with cereals, wool, and manufactured goods in exchange for dates, and the maintenance of the trans-Saharan trade, always the monopoly of the nomads. Salt and ivory in particular have been carried across the desert for centuries. Even today salt remains an important product, especially at Taoudénni and Bilma, and thousands of tons of salt are transported on camels in huge caravans (*azalais*), especially on the great salt route from Taoudénni to Tombouctou (Timbuktu).

Important deposits of iron ore occur at Fort Gouraud in Mauritania, from which a 400-mi.-long railway has been built to the coast near Port Étienne. Intensive prospecting for oil in many parts of the Sahara since 1952 has proved the existence of a North African oil province. In Algeria there are large resources at Hassi-Messaoud (60 mi. ESE of Ouargla), and 300 mi. farther southeastward at Edjelé (Edjeleh) and Zarzaitine on the Libyan boundary. Pipelines have been built from Hassi-Messaoud to the port of Bougie and from Edjelé to the Tunisian oil port of La Skhirra (Cekhira) north of Gabès. Additional pipelines were under construction in the 1960s to other ports on the Mediterranean coast. In Libya the principal resources so far discovered are at Zelten (Zaltan) and Dahra, both south of the Gulf of Sidra, to which pipelines have been built to new port terminals at Marsa el Brega (Marsa al Burayqah) and Sidra (Surt). Exports started in 1961.

Considerable supplies of natural gas are available at Hassi-R'Mel (40 mi. NW of Ghardaia), at Hassi-Messaoud, and at In-

Salah (600 mi. S of Algiers). From Hassi-R'Mel a pipeline takes gas to Algiers, Arzew, and Oran, whence it is taken to Europe by methane tankers.

Improved communications have made possible such economic developments, but despite the introduction of new methods of transport, some caravan routes remain important and Biskra, Ghardaia, and Agadès are still large caravan centres. Roads are replacing tracks on the Colomb-Béchar–Reggane, the Laghouat–El Goléa–In-Salah, and the Biskra–Touggourt–Fort Flatters routes. Railways, despite many proposals for trans-Saharan routes, do not penetrate farther into the desert than the line that stops 60 mi. south of Colomb-Béchar on its intended route across the Tanezrouft to Gao in Mali. Numerous air routes linking Europe with tropical and southern Africa cross the desert using airports on the fringes such as Kano and Tripoli.

Peoples.—In prehistoric times the Sahara was undoubtedly wetter and had a better vegetation cover than it does today, and there is evidence of Neolithic and Paleolithic culture, including rock drawings of animals no longer found in the desert. Archaeological studies of flora and fauna, as well as of cave paintings, have indeed revealed flourishing prehistoric periods that preceded the desiccation of historic times. This desiccation is suggested by the abandonment of Roman military establishments in North Africa, although contributory and even decisive reasons may have been the neglect of the water supply and of irrigation works.

The earliest inhabitants, probably Negroes, retreated before the Berbers who came with their swift-moving camels (*see* BERBER). They in turn were pushed back, especially into the uplands of the central Sahara, by the Arabs who also used camels and were spurred on by their zeal for Islam. The Arabs also introduced the Arabic language and instituted slavery which remained a lucrative trade until well into the 20th century.

From the mixture of Berber and Arab there emerged the three great ethnic groups of today: in the central Sahara the Tuareg (*q.v.*), the "people of the veil," who are camel nomads; in the east the Tebu (*q.v.*), who closely resemble the Tuareg though there has been considerable admixture with negroid peoples; and in the Western Sahara the Moors (*q.v.*) or *beidan* ("whites") as they are often called to distinguish them from the black peoples of the Sudan, a cultured group who, unlike the Tuareg, have been completely islamized. Of the smaller communities, the Mozabites of the Mzab are of special interest since their commercial wisdom has given them an importance out of all proportion to their numbers. In the oases the Negroes are still numerically dominant and are divided into three distinct classes: the free men, who are the proprietors; the Haratin, the tradesmen; and the slaves.

History and Exploration.—Despite some Egyptian, Carthaginian, and Roman penetration, European contacts with the Sahara proper were never well developed, and European influence was wholly eliminated after the Muslim conquest of North Africa. During medieval times Jewish and Genoese merchants acquired considerable knowledge of the desert, but the real opening up of the Sahara came with the 19th century through the observations of travelers like Dixon Denham (*q.v.*), Hugh Clapperton (*q.v.*), Walter Oudney, and R. A. Caillié (*q.v.*), and the scientific observations of expeditions such as those of Heinrich Barth (*q.v.*).

The French have played a leading part in the exploration and pacification of the desert. Following their occupation of Algiers in 1830, they advanced slowly southward, occupying the northern oases of Laghouat and Ghardaia in 1852 and Touggourt and Ouargla in 1854. Plans for a vast French African empire were formulated; surveys for trans-Saharan railways were made; and official missions such as that of F. Foureau and F. J. A. Lamy (1898–1900) were undertaken to establish French claims in the Sahara. During the period 1890–1910 three Anglo-French agreements fixed various boundaries and much of the desert was conquered by the French in a series of campaigns under the command of Gen. M. J. F. H. Laperrine, Capt. Charlet, Col. J. Tilho, and others. French and other travelers and scientists added greatly to the modern knowledge of the Sahara, though extensive areas remained to be surveyed and scientifically investigated.

By 1964 the only part of the Sahara remaining directly under European control was Spanish Sahara (Río de Oro). Of former French areas with important Saharan interests, Morocco and Tunisia gained independence in 1956, Mauritania, Mali, Niger, and Chad in 1960, and Algeria in 1962. Libya, originally an Italian colony and then a trust territory of the United Nations, was recognized as independent in 1951. The Republic of the Sudan replaced the Anglo-Egyptian condominium in 1956.

See AFRICA; *see* also references under "Sahara" in the Index.

BIBLIOGRAPHY.—B. Verlet, *Le Sahara* (1958); J. Gottmann, "New Facts and Some Reflections on the Sahara," *Geogr. Rev.*, vol. 32 (1942); R. Perret, "Le Climat du Sahara," *Ann. Geogr.*, vol. 44 (1935); J. Dubief, *Essai sur l'hydrologie superficielle au Sahara* (1953); T. F. Chipp, "The Vegetation of the Central Sahara," *Geogr. J.*, vol. 76 (1930); E. P. Stebbing, "The Encroaching Sahara: the Threat to the West African Colonies," *Geogr. J.*, vol. 85 (1935); B. Jones, "Desiccation and the West African Colonies," *ibid.*, vol. 91 (1938); UNESCO Arid Zone Research Series, no. 20, *Changes of Climate* (1963); R. Furon, *Le Sahara: géologie, ressources minérales, mise en valeur* (1957); A. Bernard, *Afrique septentrionale et occidentale*, in *Géogr. Univ.*, vol. 11, part 2 (1939); N. Barbour, *A Survey of North West Africa* (1959); International Bank for Reconstruction and Development, *The Economic Development of Libya* (1960); J. I. Clarke, "Oil in Libya: Some Implications," *Econ. Geogr.*, vol. 39 (1963), and "Economic and Political Changes in the Sahara," *Geography*, vol. 46 (1961); S. G. Willimott and J. I. Clarke (eds.), *Field Studies in Libya* (1960); B. Blaudin de Thé, *Essai de bibliographie du Sahara français et des régions avoisinantes* (1959); H. P. Eydoux, *L'Exploration du Sahara* (1938); T. Monod, "Travels in the Western Sahara, 1934–35," *Geogr. J.*, vol. 87 (1936), and "New Journey to the Western Sahara, 1935–36," *ibid.*, vol. 89 (1937); E. W. Bovill, *Caravans of the Old Sahara* (1933) and *The Golden Trade of the Moors* (1958); B. E. Thomas, *Trade Routes of Algeria and the Sahara* (1957); L. C. Briggs, *Tribes of the Sahara* (1960); F. R. Rodd, *People of the Veil* (1926); J. Despois, "Types of Native Life in Tripolitania," *Geogr. Rev.*, vol. 35 (1945).

(R. W. SL.)

SAHARANPUR, a town and district in the Meerut division of Uttar Pradesh, India. The town lies on the Damaula Nadi (stream) about 95 mi. (155 km.) NNE of Delhi and is an important railway junction. Pop. (1961) 185,213. It has a sugar and a paper mill, a wood-carving industry, railway workshops, and is the site of the Government Botanical Gardens. Two colleges are affiliated to Agra University. Saharanpur was founded about 1340 and derives its name from a Muslim saint, Shah Haran Chisti.

SAHARANPUR DISTRICT (area 2,132 sq.mi. [5,522 sq.km.]; pop. [1961] 1,615,478) forms the uppermost part of the Ganges-Jumna doab (interfluve), its eastern boundary being marked by the Ganges and the western by the Jumna. The area rises gently to the north where elevations of about 3,000 ft. above sea level are reached in the foothills of the outer Siwalik Range. The submontane belt, extending over one-sixth of the district, has slopes covered with forests and is intersected by numerous seasonal torrents that are lost in the *bhabar* (detrital piedmont) belt skirting the Siwalik Hills on the south. Wheat, gram, rice, and sugarcane are the main crops. The area under sugarcane nearly doubled in the two decades after World War II, and sugar manufacture is important. More than half of the district's working population is engaged in occupations other than cultivation. The chief towns include Hardwar (pop., 58,513), Roorkee (33,651), Deoband (29,980), Gangoh (18,886), and Manglaur (15,206). (S. S. BH.)

SAHARSA, a district in the Bhagalpur division, Bihar, India, stretches southward from Nepal to a line about 10 mi. N of the Ganges River. Area 2,093 sq.mi. (5,421 sq.km.). Pop. (1961) 1,723,566. It is traversed by the oscillating Kosi River and its distributaries which have ravaged the district. Large areas of fertile paddy lands have become sandy areas or grass-covered marshes and wastes. Rice, maize (corn), oilseeds, and jute are the principal crops. The flood embankment and irrigation canals of the Kosi project were constructed to protect and enrich the district. The district headquarters are at Saharsa on the Mansi-Supaul branch of the North Eastern Railway. (E. AH.)

SAHIWAL (formerly MONTGOMERY), a town and district in Multan division, West Pakistan. The town, headquarters of the district, lies 95 mi. SW of Lahore. Pop. (1961) 75,180. In 1865 Sahiwal village, which lay on the newly opened railway from Lahore, was chosen as the district headquarters and named Montgomery after Sir Robert Montgomery, lieutenant governor (1859–65) of the Punjab (Panjab). It was then in a desolate sandy area and singularly comfortless until reached by irrigation from the Lower Bari doab canal in 1913. The town (renamed Sahiwal) is well planned and is an important cotton centre. There are two colleges affiliated with the University of the Panjab.

SAHIWAL DISTRICT lies in the Bari doab, or tract between the Sutlej and Ravi rivers, extending also northwestward across the latter. Pop. (1961) 2,134,072; area, 4,224 sq.mi. The climate is arid and hot, the average annual rainfall at Sahiwal town being 10 in. The principal crops are wheat, cotton, pulses, and oilseeds; manufactures include cotton goods and lacquered woodwork, and there is cotton ginning and pressing. Okara (pop. 68,299 [mun.]) has a factory for cotton spinning and weaving.

The important archaeological site of Harappa (see INDUS CIVILIZATION) in the southwest indicates a very early connection between the northwestern part of the subcontinent and Sumerian culture. Ruins at Kamalia, Akbar, Satghara, and Bavanni mark the sites of forgotten towns. (K. S. AD.)

SAHO-AFAR, two closely related Cushitic peoples (q.v.) inhabiting the arid coastal regions of French Somaliland and Ethiopia. The Afar, who are known to the Arabs as Danakil, in the 1960s numbered about 100,000, and the Saho about 50,000. They are chiefly pastoral nomads with considerable numbers of camels, sheep, goats, and cattle, but the Saho also cultivate. Both are Sunni Muslims (see ISLAM) although Christianity has found some adherents among the Saho. They are warlike, especially the Afar, and each community is divided into a large number of patrilineal segments ruled by chiefs and lineage assemblies, there being several Muslim sultanates of considerable antiquity among the Afar. The Afar have a pervasive class division between the Asaimara ("Red") nobles and the Adoimara ("White") tributary commoners; the former are thought to descend from immigrant peoples from the Ethiopian highlands.

See also ETHIOPIA: *The People;* SOMALILAND, FRENCH.

See I. M. Lewis, *Peoples of the Horn of Africa: Somali, Afar and Saho* (1955); G. A. Lipsky *et al., Ethiopia* (1962). (I. M. L.)

SAHRA' AL GHARBIYAH, AS (WESTERN DESERT), a *muhafaza* (governorate) of Egypt (United Arab Republic), comprising the whole of Egypt west of the Nile valley and delta and north of latitude 26°20′ N. It is administered from Matruh on the Mediterranean coast. Pop. (1960) 103,453. The greater part is a massive plateau averaging 700–800 ft. (215–245 m.) above sea level and nowhere surpassing 1,500 ft. It comprises great thicknesses of sedimentary rocks little disturbed but dipping gently to the north. Successively younger rocks outcrop from south to north with Cretaceous and Eocene limestones in the southern and central parts and marly limestone and calcareous sandstones of Miocene Age in the north. The surface is little dissected; its nature results more from wind than water action and it thus offers direct contrast with the heavily dissected Arabian (Eastern) Desert. Stone covered wastes and in places sandy plains prevail. Longitudinal belts of parallel sand dunes occur in the centre and west, some up to 200 ft. high in the Great Sand Sea which extends south from Siwah oasis. The greater part of the desert is extremely arid; only along the coast is there a light rainfall, of 4–6 in. (100–150 mm.) in winter. Notable, however, are the depressions in the plateau surface that permit shallow wells to reach underground water and thus to support life and create oases (Al Bahriyah, Al Farafirah, and Siwah). At both Qattarah and Siwah (q.v.) the depressions are below sea level. The Qattarah depression reaches 435 ft. below sea level and occupies nearly 7,000 sq.mi. (18,100 sq.km.). Its floor is largely covered with salt marsh and lagoons of brackish water. Its northeastern edge is only 35 mi. from the coast at Al 'Alamayn (El Alamein), a neck held by the British against Field Marshal Rommel's final advance (1942) during World War II. Small oil strikes were made near the depression in the 1960s.

Al Bahriyah and Al Farafirah oases are linked only by desert tracks with the Nile valley. The principal settlements within these oases are Al Bawiti (Al Bahriyah) and Qasr Farafirah. Most of the population resides in the line of small towns along the narrow coastal plain where ruins of dwellings, cisterns, and abandoned wells indicate a far heavier population in the period of Roman occupation. A railway from Alexandria reaches Matruh (the termi-

nus of the road from Siwah oasis) and was extended to As Sallum (Sollum) by the Allied forces; both these settlements are small ports. *See also* EGYPT: *Physical Geography.* (A. B. M.)

SAHRA' AL JANUBIYAH, AS (SOUTHERN DESERT), a *muhafaza* (governorate) of Egypt (United Arab Republic), comprising the whole of southern Egypt west of the Nile and south of latitude 26°20′ N from Dakhilah oasis to the frontier with the Republic of the Sudan, excluding Al Kharijah (Kharga) oasis (administered under Asyut *muhafaza; see* KHARIJAH, AL WAHAT AL) and the Nile valley. As Sahra' al Janubiyah is administered from Al Kharijah. Pop. (1960) 33,932. It is virtually a rainless region of the eastern Sahara, and forms the east-central sector of the Libyan Desert. It is mainly composed of Nubian sandstone, which has weathered to undulating plains, in places extensively covered with sand desert. In the extreme north and east, limestone escarpments diversify the landscape. In the west, the rocky Hadabat al Jilf al Kabir (plateau), rising on the north side from sand desert, attains 3,116 ft. (950 m.). A series of depressions, superficially resembling one continuous depression, begins near the Sudan frontier and continues north into the Western Desert (As Sahra' al Gharbiyah). These depressions permit shallow wells to reach underground water in aquifers in the Nubian sandstone, and a number of oases (including Al Kharijah and Dakhilah) occur within As Sahra' al Janubiyah. Projects to expand irrigation and settlement in this area, now termed the New Valley, are in progress. There is evidence of large pastoral populations in this area in ancient times when aquifers may have outcropped and discharged at the surface because of heavy erosion and a higher water table than now exists.

Dakhilah oasis lies about 80 mi. W of Al Kharijah and contains two principal settlements, Balat and Mut. It lies in the depression at only 118 ft. above sea level. The people are a mixture of Berber and Bedouin stock, relying for subsistence mainly upon their gardens and date palms. Wheat, and bersim for fodder, are the principal crops. Dakhilah is practically isolated except for a motorable desert track extending from Al Kharijah through Balat to Mut. *See also* EGYPT: *Physical Geography.* (A. B. M.)

SAICHO (767–822), eminent Japanese Buddhist monk who established the Tendai sect in Japan. He is also known as Dengyō Daishi, his posthumous name and title. His zeal for reform and the location of his monastery on Mt. Hiei (788), northeast of the new imperial capital Heian-kyō (Kyōto), established in 794, strengthened his affiliation with the court. Sent to China in 804, he returned the next year and introduced the highly eclectic Tendai (Chinese *T'ien-t'ai*) teachings. His cooperation with the court brought generous patronage and his monastery soon became the most powerful, a centre of Buddhist learning and discipline from which emerged most of the new sects during the next five centuries. He foreshadowed later Japanese Buddhist trends by his reverence for the native Shintō deities and emphasis on the patriotic mission of Buddhism to serve and protect the state. Although frequently engaged in polemics, his contribution was more significant as an effective leader and organizer than as a religious thinker. (D. H. SH.)

SAIDA (as ancient SIDON one of the two principal cities of Phoenicia), the administrative centre of the *muhafaza* (province) of Southern Lebanon, Lebanon, lies on the Mediterranean, 25 mi. (40 km.) SSW of Beirut. Pop. (1961 est.) 32,200. The town is the terminal of the Trans-Arabian Pipe Line (Tapline) from the oil centre of Abqaiq in the Hasa (q.v.) province of Saudi Arabia, and has huge storage tanks. It is also a trade and market centre for the agricultural products of the surrounding area. *See* SIDON.

SAID HALIM PASHA (1863–1921), Turkish statesman who served as grand vizier from 1913 to 1916, was born in Cairo in 1863. He was a grandson of the khedive of Egypt, Mohammed Ali Pasha. Educated in Turkey and afterward in Switzerland, he returned to live in Istanbul and in 1888 was appointed a member of the state judicial council. In 1911 he was president of that council in Mahmud Shevket's cabinet and became foreign minister later in the year. After the murder of Mahmud Shevket in 1913 he became grand vizier. Although he signed the treaty of alliance with Germany in 1914, he was known to be opposed to Turkey's entry into World War I. He wished to resign when war became a *fait accompli* but remained at his post on the insistence of the Union and Progress Party. In 1916, however, he did resign and became a member of the Senate. After the armistice of Mudros in 1918 he was banished to Malta by the British authorities. He was later released and went to Rome where he was assassinated by an Armenian on Dec. 6, 1921.

Said Halim was also a prolific essayist: his subjects included constitutional monarchy, bigotry, the social, political and intellectual crises of Turkey, and the fall of Islam.   (M. P. P.)

SA'ID IBN SULTAN (c. 1791–1856), the Saiyid (ruler) and sultan of Muscat and Oman and Zanzibar from 1806 to 1856, the most powerful and enlightened ruler of the Al Bu Sa'id dynasty, was born near Muscat, about 1791. He was the only sultan of Muscat to establish effective control over Zanzibar, Mombasa, and 660 mi. of coastal East Africa, as well as over the coast of Baluchistan. He was never elected, nor claimed the religious title of, Imam; but he upheld the austere Ibadi sect of Islam as temporal ruler of the sect. Saiyid Sa'id succeeded, with British naval help, in keeping Muscat and Oman independent of the Wahhabi Arabs of Najd (*see* WAHHABI) though he thrice paid them tribute (1833, 1845, and 1853). Family feuds shadowed his life; he was acclaimed Saiyid only after assassinating a traitorous relative. In 1824 he made a triumphant pilgrimage to Mecca.

After establishing permanent residence in Zanzibar in 1837–40, Saiyid Sa'id beautified the island with palaces and expanded Arabian-African trade; he developed clove plantations and experimented with sugar and indigo. He signed a treaty of amity and commerce with the United States (1833) and a commercial treaty with France (1844). His relations with England were close: he signed a treaty of commerce (1839) and two anti-slave trade treaties (1822, 1845) and cooperated with the British in suppressing African-European slave trading (to his own detriment). He also ceded the guano-covered Kuria Muria Islands to Britain (1854). Saiyid Sa'id died at sea on Oct. 19, 1856. *See also* MUSCAT AND OMAN; TANZANIA, UNITED REPUBLIC OF.

BIBLIOGRAPHY.—R. Said-Ruete, *Said bin Sultan (1791–1856) Ruler of Oman and Zanzibar* (1929); C. U. Aitchison, *Treaties, Engagements, and Sanads* ... (1892); B. Thomas, *Arab Rule Under the Al Bu Sa'id Dynasty of Oman, 1741–1937* (1938).   (C. P. H.)

SAID PASHA (MOHAMMED SA'ID PASHA) (1822–1863), Ottoman viceroy of Egypt from 1854 to 1863, fourth son of Mohammed Ali Pasha, was born in Cairo on March 17, 1822. Educated privately and in Paris, he succeeded the viceroy Abbas I on July 13, 1854. Ferdinand de Lesseps (*q.v.*), a friend of his youth, then immediately hurried to Egypt and persuaded him to grant a concession empowering De Lesseps to form a company for the construction of the Suez Canal with Egyptian labour. (*See* SUEZ CANAL.) Said continued Abbas' efforts in the Crimean War and in 1854 strongly reinforced the Egyptian contingent with the Ottoman Army. In 1855 he fortified the Nile barrage near Cairo. In the winter of 1856–57 he visited the Sudan where his over-hasty reorganization brought administrative confusion. Self-indulgent, credulous, and generous to a fault, he enjoyed without discrimination the company of European adventurers whose activities were to ruin his successor, Ismail. He borrowed extravagantly in Europe in 1858, 1861, and 1862, and died at Alexandria on Jan. 18, 1863, leaving a foreign debt of over £3,000,000 and personal debts of about £6,000,000. *See also* EGYPT: *History: Modern Period: Abbas I and Said (1848–63)*.

See A. Sammarco, *Les Règnes d'Abbas, de Said et d'Ismail (1848–1879)* in *Précis de l'histoire d'Égypte,* vol. iv (1935).   (R. L. HL.)

SAIGON, the capital and river port of South Vietnam (Republic of Vietnam) and formerly of French Indochina (*q.v.*), lies about 60 mi. (97 km.) from the South China Sea on the Saigon River, the delta of which merges with that of the Mekong. It forms the easternmost part of an urban district which includes Cholon (*q.v.*) and the northern suburb of Gia Dinh. The population in 1964 was estimated at 1,332,900, including Cholon. The average annual rainfall is 81 in. (2,060 mm.) and Saigon suffers a dusty drought from January to March.

The city is laid out in the French style with boulevards, offices, grand public buildings, fine residences, theatres, shops, and banks, justifying its fame as "the Little Paris of the East." There are many squares and public parks. Among notable buildings are the Romanesque-style cathedral and the Vietnamese museum in the botanical garden. The university was founded in 1917 as the Université Indochinoise and became the University of Saigon in 1955. There are faculties of letters, science, law, medicine, pharmacy, education, and architecture. In addition, there are advanced schools for teaching, arts and crafts, fine arts, and architecture.

Saigon is readily accessible to vessels of up to 30 ft. draft. Quays stretch about three miles along the riverside with bulk-handling facilities for rice, which is the basis of Saigon's trade. Local junks and shallow-draft craft from the Mekong delta bring great tonnages of rice cheaply from the interior for export to China, Japan, the Philippines, and Malaya. Overland communications were constructed during the French administration; these included arterial roads to Hanoi and Hue, to the Laotian Mekong, and to Phnom Penh, Cambodia; and railways to Hanoi and Phnom Penh which still exist. However, the new boundaries which resulted from the partition of Indochina into the separate states greatly reduced the rice export from Saigon, and although the influx of refugees, after the Indochinese War (1947–54), increased the population of the town, its importance as a port diminished. Saigon, however, retains its international air services to Hong Kong, Bangkok, Manila, Singapore, Tokyo, and Calcutta.

Relations with France began in the 18th century when French missionaries were sent to Saigon. In 1859 the town was captured by the French and in 1862 it came under French administration as part of the French colony of Cochin China. In 1932 Saigon and Cholon were merged for administrative purposes to form the prefecture of Saigon-Cholon, which was retitled the prefecture of Saigon in 1956. Saigon became the capital of South Vietnam in July 1954, following the Convention of Geneva, which divided Vietnam *de facto* into two republics. World attention focused on the city as South Vietnam suffered both internal and external strife. The United States maintained headquarters in Saigon for its staffs of military and economic advisers supporting the war effort against North Vietnam. *See also* VIETNAM.   (E. H. G. D.)

SAIGŌ TAKAMORI (1827–1877), Japanese rebel, a member of the warrior class and one of the best known of the leaders of the movement that overthrew the Tokugawa shogunate and restored power to the emperor, was born at Kagoshima in Kyushu on Dec. 7, 1827.

On the Meiji restoration in 1868, Saigō immediately assumed an important position in the new government. He left it in 1873, ostensibly over differences within the government on matters of foreign policy—though some historians regard his departure mainly as part of a factional struggle for power under the emperor—and retired to Kagoshima, where he founded a school and gathered around him a group of young men sympathetic to his personality and views on government.

In 1877 Saigō led an uprising, known as the Satsuma Rebellion, intending to replace the existing incumbent government with one headed by himself. His forces were crushed and, rather than fall into enemy hands, he ordered one of his subordinates to put him to death with his sword, Sept. 14, 1877.

Saigō became a national hero despite the rebellion, personifying to the Japanese the loyal subject who risks all to serve the emperor as he sees best.   (T. C. SH.)

SAIGYŌ (1118–1190), Japanese Buddhist priest-poet, one of the greatest masters of the 5-line, 31-syllable tanka, whose life and works became the subject matter of many narratives, plays, and puppet dramas, was born SATŌ NORIKIYO in a samurai family in 1118. The son of an officer in the Imperial Gate Guards, he himself originally followed a military career. Like others of his day, Saigyō was oppressed by the sense of disaster which overwhelmed Japan as the brilliant court life of the Heian era passed into a period of civil wars in the latter half of the 12th century. In his early 20s he chose the way of a priest, leaving behind a life which "try as he might he could not regret." Initially trained in the quietism of the Tendai sect, he passed to Jōdo, with its emphasis on faith, and to the mysteries of Shingon. (*See* BUDDHISM:

Regional Variations in Buddhism: Japan.) His life was spent in travel throughout Japan, punctuated by periodic returns to the capital at Kyōto to participate in imperial ceremonies. He died at Kōsenji Temple in what is now Ōsaka in 1190.

Informing Saigyō's poetry are the love of nature and devotion to Buddhism. The flowers and the moon recur as constant objects of praise. "Would that I might die in the spring, under the cherry blossoms, at the time of the full moon in the month of May!" His poems, though deceptive because there is a sense of flatness about them, are, technically, the work of a master: often a caesural stop comes at the end of the first line of a poem; imperative forms are used, as are questions; the fourth and fifth lines are often parallel in construction, and the vocabulary is unusually complex.

Saigyō left many works, of which the most famous is the anthology entitled *Sankashū,* which contained 1,571 poems when first compiled. His *Mimosusogawa utaawase* ("Poetry Contest at Mimosuso River") is a tour de force in which he pitted his own poems against each other. Attracted to Saigyō's poems were such priest-poets of later times as Ton'a, Sōgi, Bashō, and Jiun.

BIBLIOGRAPHY.—Translations of Saigyō's poetry into English are found in D. Keene (ed.), *Anthology of Japanese Literature,* pp. 195–196 (1955), and in A. Miyamori, *Masterpieces of Japanese Poetry, Ancient and Modern,* pp. 375–392 (1936).   (J. K. Y.)

SAIKAKU: *see* IHARA SAIKAKU.

SAILFISH, a large, powerful fish of the open seas, in which the bones of the upper jaw are consolidated and prolonged to form a rounded spear and the dorsal fin is greatly enlarged to form a saillike superstructure. Sailfishes (*Istiophorus* species), closely related to the marlins are classified with them in the family Istiophoridae. Like their relatives, sailfishes are strong and far-ranging swimmers, whose streamlined bodies cut the water at considerable speeds (perhaps 60 m.p.h. for short distances). The upper part of the torpedo-shaped body is a rich blue, the remainder a bright silver; the sides are often marked with vertical lines of lavender dots. The sail, deep purple at the base, blends into dark blue and is more or less spotted with dark dots. The fish folds the sail into a groove on the back when swimming rapidly and unfurls it when sunning itself, when breaking the

CHARLES MEYER—PHOTO RESEARCHERS, INC.
PACIFIC SAILFISH. (ISTIOPHORUS GREYI)

surface or when fighting a sportsman's line. The spear is perhaps used to stun prey, such as mackerel, sierra, sauries and squid.

Sailfishes are widely distributed in the warm waters of all oceans and seasonally visit temperate regions as far south as the Cape of Good Hope and as far north as Massachusetts. There is much uncertainty regarding the number of species.

Two well-known species are the Atlantic sailfish (*Istiophorus albicans*), averaging less than 50 lb. in weight, and the Pacific form (*I. greyi*), averaging about 100 lb. Large specimens on record, caught with rod and reel, are an Atlantic sailfish 10 ft., 4 in. long and weighing 123 lb.; and a Pacific form 10 ft., 9 in. and 221 lb. Even though sailfishes are only fair quality as food, they are among the most highly prized of big game fish.
          (L. A. WD.)

SAILING: *see* BOATING; RIGGING; YACHTING.

SAILS. The origin of sailcloth is obscure, although it can be assumed that primitive man first used the skins of animals as sails for his raft or canoe. The next probable step was to use woven mats of reeds stretched on poles. Sailcloth is mentioned by Homer in the *Odyssey,* in which he states that Calypso brought Odysseus "a web of cloth to make him sails."

Sailcloth was woven from flax fibre during the period when Eng-

land, France and Spain were striving for supremacy. Fibre flax, grown chiefly in the U.S.S.R. and European countries, is still used for sails, although cotton has replaced it for better quality canvas. Cotton sails became popular in Europe after the U.S. racing yacht "America," using cotton sails, decisively defeated a fleet of British yachts in 1851.

Cotton sailcloth has the advantage over flax, hemp, ramie, jute and combinations of these materials as a fabric in that it can be woven more closely, and therefore will not stretch out of shape as easily nor lose as much wind through the pores of the material. Sails made of cotton, however, are very stiff, which makes them difficult to handle, and many a fingernail has been torn to the quick in furling cotton duck.

The best cotton fibre is grown in the United Arab Republic (Egypt), and sails made of this material are used chiefly aboard the larger sailing yachts. Egyptian cotton is superior to U.S. cotton because the fibres are longer and stronger, and their greater degree of natural twist is conducive to producing a tightly woven fabric.

The chief modern users of quality sailcloth are yachtsmen, who generally prefer dacron (or Terylene, its British equivalent). These synthetic fabrics were first introduced in 1950, and they proved much superior to any type of cotton or other synthetic materials, such as nylon, dynel, Fortisan and Orlon.

Sails made of dacron maintain just the correct amount of stretch and so require no "breaking in" period. The greater strength of the fabric permits the use of lighter weight sails, which maintain their original shape for years. Dacron sails will not mildew except when in contact with mildew on some other object. Because this fabric is heat-treated by pressing it between hot rollers of metal, the fibres are flattened and interlock. This "stabilizing" process gives the fabric a smooth, almost frictionless surface and very little porosity. A slight drawback resulting from this closely woven, smooth surface is that the stitches do not mesh with the fabric but protrude above the surface of the sail, causing the sail twine to become abraded more rapidly than with other sailcloth. Nevertheless, sailmakers seemed convinced that dacron

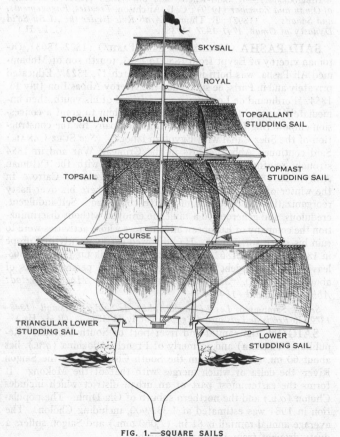

FIG. 1.—SQUARE SAILS
Studding sails are shown with their rigging, seen astern

Labels in figure: SKYSAIL, ROYAL, TOPGALLANT, TOPGALLANT STUDDING SAIL, TOPSAIL, TOPMAST STUDDING SAIL, COURSE, TRIANGULAR LOWER STUDDING SAIL, LOWER STUDDING SAIL

(or Terylene) is a nearly perfect material for racing sails. A possible future development in sail material is a plastic that can be glued together.

Sailmaking.—The basic steps in manufacturing a sail may be outlined as follows: (1) The sailmaker studies the sail plan or measures the vessel's rig. (2) He calculates the stretch and the amount of draft, *i.e.*, the curvature of the surface. (3) The actual plan of the sail is chalked out to full scale on the floor of the sail loft. (4) The cloths are laid down over this plan and their actual length and shape are marked on each individual cloth. (5) The cloths are numbered and then cut to the dimensions outlined by the markings. (6) The cloths are sewn together. If the sail is hand sewn, a flat stitch is used on a double flat seam in which the edge of one cloth overlaps the cloth next to it from ½ to 1½ in., depending on the material. A special sail twine is used as thread, and after the needle is threaded the twine is waxed so it will hold the right-hand twist then given to it. This twist helps the thread to mesh with the fabric. The sailmaker sews from right to left,

using a leather palm having a solid thimble attached near the heel of the thumb and a special three-sided sail needle. The cloths are prevented from slipping off the sailmaker's lap by a bench hook attached to the right side of his bench. The size of the sail needle depends on the weight of the material and the type of sewing. For the usual flat stitch, 10 to 12 stitches are taken within the distance corresponding to the length of the needle. (7) After all the cloths are sewn together, patches are attached to the corners and tabling (hems on the edges) is sewn on the luff (forward edge) and the foot—the places where the greatest strain develops. (8) The finishing touches are applied. The luff rope is sewn inside the leading edge of the sail to prevent the sail from being stretched out of shape. Strong ropes (boltropes) are sewn to the luff and foot, and various fittings, such as metal slides, grommets, reef points, cringles, etc., are attached to the sail.

Some Types of Sails.—The two major categories of sails are square sails and fore-and-aft sails. The first type is generally set in a position across the longitudinal axis of the ship; the second

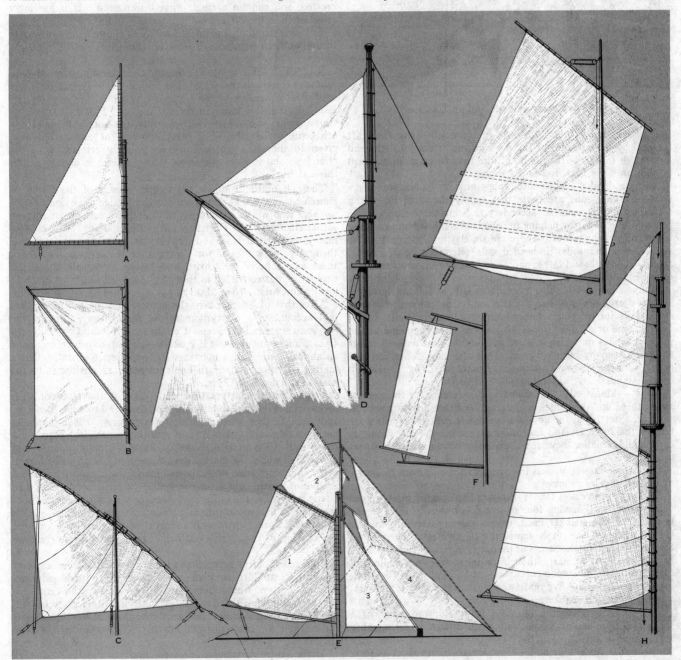

FIG. 2.—FORE-AND-AFT SAILS

(A) Sliding gunter; (B) spritsail; (C) lateen; (D) gaff topsail; (E) rig as used on cutter with (1) mainsail, (2) club-headed gaff topsail, (3) staysail, (4) jib, and (5) jib topsail; (F) ringtail; (G) standing lugsail; (H) loose-footed spanker and jib-headed topsail

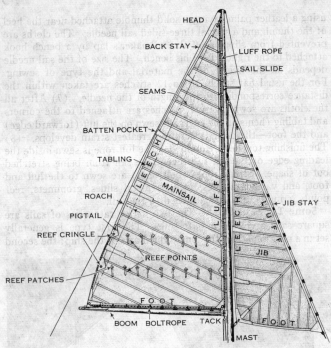

FIG. 3.—PARTS OF MAINSAIL AND WORKING JIB

type of sails are set along this axis. Square sails drive the craft forward by the pressure of the wind on the afterside of the sail only; with fore-and-aft sails both sides may be used for forward propulsion. (*See* Figs. 1, 2 and 3.)

Sails are divided further into groups of primary and secondary sails. Primary sails are those that supply the chief propelling force in ordinary weather; secondary sails are those that aid the primary sails either by helping to balance the ship or by providing additional driving power. There are six classes of primary sails: square sails, gaff sails, jib-headed sails (Bermuda or Marconi), spritsails, lugsails and lateen sails. Secondary sails are variations of these basic types.

Many sailing vessels also group their sails as follows: cruising sails for ordinary weather, summer sails for tropical weather, storm sails for extremely heavy weather and racing sails.

The name of a sail is frequently derived from the name of the piece of rigging on which it is set, or from its location with reference to a near-by piece of gear. Thus the main topgallant sail hangs from the topgallant yard of the main mast (fig. 1), the jib topsail stands above the other jibs and so on.

Masts.—Many sails are named with reference to the nearest mast; therefore, the names of the masts and their location are important. Starting at the bow in a two-masted vessel the masts are termed the foremast and the mainmast; when the after mast is considerably smaller they are named the mainmast and the mizzenmast.

In all three-masted vessels the names of the masts are foremast, mainmast and mizzenmast.

Square-rigged vessels (those that have two or more masts rigged with square sails) having four or five masts usually refer to the last mast as the spanker mast, unless it is considerably smaller than the others, when it is named the jigger mast. There is no fixed rule regarding the names of the masts of square-rigged vessels having five or more masts, though the terms foreward mainmast, after mainmast and middlemast are used. With sails fore-and-aft on vessels having five masts the mast names are: fore, main, mizzen, jigger and spanker.

One authority gives the following names for the masts of a six-masted, fore-and-aft vessel: fore, main, mizzen, jigger, spanker and pusher or driver. For the "Thomas W. Lawson"—the only seven-masted vessel ever built—the mast names are given as fore, main, mizzen, jigger, spanker, pusher and driver. Other authorities state that the seven masts were named for the days in the week, but that this method was later abandoned in favour of num-

bering them from one to seven. The names and locations of the working sails of a full-rigged ship are illustrated in the article on RIGGING.

See SHIP; *see* also references under "Sails" in the Index.

BIBLIOGRAPHY.—Ernest A. Ratsey and W. H. De Fontaine, *Yacht Sails, Their Care and Handling*, rev. ed. (1957); R. M. Bowker and S. A. Budd, *Make Your Own Sails*, 2nd ed. (1961); Felix Riesenberg, *Standard Seamanship for the Merchant Service* (1922).   (M. H. I.)

SAINFOIN (*Onobrychis viciaefolia*) is a low-growing perennial plant of the pea family (Leguminosae), with a woody rootstock, whence proceed the stems, which are covered with fine hairs and bear numerous long pinnate leaves, the segments of which are elliptic.

The flowers are borne in close pyramidal or cylindrical clusters on the end of long stalks. Each flower is about half an inch in length with lanceolate calyx teeth shorter than the corolla, which is pink, with darker stripes of the same colour. The pods or legumes are flattened, wrinkled, somewhat sickle shaped and crested, and contain a single olive-brown seed. It is sparingly naturalized in the eastern United States.

In Great Britain the plant is a native of the calcareous districts of the southern counties. It is native through central Europe and Siberia.

SAINT, a term applied in the Old Testament to any Israelite as one of the chosen people of God. In the New Testament it was used of any member of the Christian churches; for example, St. Paul addresses his letter to the Philippians "To all the saints in Christ Jesus who are at Philippi." It was not until about the 6th century that the word became a title of honour specially given to the dead whose cult was publicly celebrated in the churches; and it is in this sense that the term is understood in this article.

The cult of the saints in the public worship of the Christian church began with the primitive church practice of paying honour to those who willingly endured death at the hands of persecutors rather than deny the Christian faith; *i.e.*, martyrs. The title of martyr at first was bestowed generally on those who distinguished themselves as witnesses for Christ, then the term was given to those who suffered for Christ, and, in the latter half of the 3rd century, it was restricted to those witnesses who endured death in loyalty to Christ. (*See* MARTYR.)

After that of St. Stephen, the earliest and most complete extant account of a martyrdom is the *Martyrium Polycarpi*, the Smyrna congregation's account of the martyrdom of St. Polycarp (*q.v.*), important because it contains the first-known reference to an annual festival of a martyr. In the letter it is stated that a martyr's passion and death are considered as analogous to the passion and death of Christ.

Veneration of martyrs took place first at the place of their torments and burial; from thence it often spread to other localities, and even farther abroad as the church grew. The power of deciding true martyrdom and of granting consequent permission to worship in any particular case belonged originally to the bishop of the area where the martyr gave witness to Christ. The bishop made an investigation of a reported martyrdom, inquiring into the motive of death; and after concluding that the person had died a true martyr for the faith, the bishop permitted his cult and sent the name of the person with an account of the martyrdom to other churches, in order that, with approval of the respective bishops, the worship of the martyr might be carried on in those churches also.

This geographical restriction of cult is evident from exploration of ancient Christian cemeteries in which are found paintings only of martyrs who suffered in the region near the cemetery. At the same time, the practice of notifying other churches explains the rapid and almost universal veneration of certain martyrs, for example St. Lawrence (d. 258) or St. Cyprian of Carthage (d. 258).

At the centre of veneration of the martyrs was the Eucharist, celebrated in an atmosphere of triumph. Often it took place over the tomb of the martyr. Hence, there arose the practice of constructing altars like graves and of providing them with relics.

The first churches were dedicated to the martyrs. The word *martyrium,* designating first a church built over the grave of a martyr, later was used for churches in general, even for those churches not dedicated to martyr saints. Even today the relics of the saints that are sealed into every altar stone or antimension (in the Eastern Church, a silk or linen cloth used as a portable altar or as covering for the true altar) must include relics of at least one martyr. The martyr's body was guarded with great care in the beginning, but translation of the remains and severing of the body for relics later came into practice as Greek innovations.

Taking the name of a martyr, as an act of reverence, was another custom that arose and soon became established. St. Dionysius of Alexander (d. 265) relates, for example, that two favourite names in his time were Peter and Paul.

Veneration paid to the martyrs was not given to others—not even to the Blessed Virgin Mary—until later. Thus, veneration of the confessor saints, as they are called (*see* CONFESSOR), is not so ancient as cult of the martyrs. The term confessor was given originally to those who confessed Christ when questioned in the presence of enemies of the faith, thus exposing themselves to danger and suffering, but did not endure martyrdom. After the early Christian period the word took on another meaning, being applied to anyone who had led a life of heroic virtue and had died a holy death in peace. This is the meaning of confessor as understood here; and, according to common opinion, confessors so understood first received public ecclesiastical honour some time in the 4th century. In the east, for example, Hilarius and Ephraem Syrus, and in the west St. Martin of Tours and St. Hilary of Poitiers, were venerated in the 4th century. The first persons to be considered confessors were the ascetics, perhaps due to the fact that they were seen to resemble the martyrs by their acts of self-denial and their lives of heroic virtue.

Worship of confessor saints grew and expanded according to time and place. Nevertheless, cult of neither martyr saints nor confessor saints was ever lawful unless carried on with ecclesiastical permission, despite the fact that in both cases it was dependent primarily on the consciousness of the faithful as a whole.

Roman Catholic Church.—Throughout the 1st millennium of the Christian era bishops on their own authority could allow public veneration of martyrs or confessors for determined localities. (In certain areas, however, it was a prerogative of the primates and patriarchs.) This was carried on even beyond the 12th century, as is evidenced by the fact that in 1215 Peter of Trevi was canonized by the bishop of Anagni. According to the present discipline in the Roman Catholic Church, however, canonization is beyond the power of a bishop, and it is a procedure distinct from that of beatification, a stage prior to canonization. Canonization, as taught today, is a solemn declaration by the pope that a person has attained the beatific vision and that veneration of the person as a saint is imposed on the entire church. In this judgment, according to the common doctrine, the Roman pontiff is infallible.

Beatification—the declaration that a person is blessed—on the other hand, is not an infallible judgment, and it grants only restricted authorization to venerate. Beatification, thus, implies a permission, while canonization connotes a precept that is universal. The medieval centuries had no such distinct procedures. The titles *beatus* and *sanctus,* technically different in meaning and application in the Roman Catholic Church today, were used with no distinction in the middle ages.

The history of the development of law concerning canonization and beatification, and the procedures laid down in the Code of Canon Law, are described in the article CANONIZATION.

Dogmatically the veneration of saints in the Roman Catholic Church can be understood only in the light of the dogma of the unique mediatorship of Jesus Christ (I Tim. 2:5). Jesus Christ alone, according to Roman Catholic teaching, redeemed men by his death on the cross; no divine gift can come to man except through man's Redeemer. Hence, all the prayers of those on earth and of the saints in heaven are efficacious only through Christ.

The saints, who are specially pleasing to God, join their prayers to the prayers of those who invoke them, and their aid to men is through the merits of Christ, man's Redeemer and one Mediator. The Council of Trent states it thus:

The saints, reigning together with Christ, pray to God for men. It is a good and useful thing to invoke the saints humbly and to have recourse to their prayers and to their efficacious help to obtain favors from God through His Son Jesus Christ, Our Lord, who alone is our Redeemer and Savior.

Intercession of the saints was unanimously taught by the early Fathers. For example, St. Cyril of Jerusalem, in his *Catecheses,* says:

We then commemorate those who have fallen asleep before us, patriarchs, prophets, Apostles, and martyrs, in order that God, by their prayers and intercessions, may receive our petitions.

St. Jerome, in his work against Vigilantius, writes:

If apostles and martyrs, while still in the flesh and still needing to care for themselves, can pray for others, how much more will they pray for others after they have won their crowns, their victories, their triumphs.

And against the Manichaean Faustus, St. Augustine of Hippo states:

Faustus blames us for honoring the memory of the martyrs, as if this were idolatry. The accusation is not worthy of a reply. Christians celebrate the memory of the martyrs with religious ceremony in order to arouse emulation and in order that they may be associated with their merits and helped by their prayers.

From the second Council of Nicaea (787) came the theological terms *dulia* and *latria* to indicate a distinction between the worship paid the saints and that paid to God. The two terms correspond, more or less, with the English words veneration and adoration. *Latria* is the worship reserved to God alone and *dulia* is worship given to the saints.

Another term, *hyperdulia,* was composed in the middle ages as a technical theological word to designate the special worship paid to the Blessed Virgin Mary because of her special gifts and holiness bestowed on her by God.

Closely connected with veneration of the saints in the Roman Catholic Church is the cult that is paid to the relics and images of saints, a worship that is referred to the holy person whom the image represents or to whom the relic belonged by contact. St. Thomas Aquinas, in the *Summa Theologica,* states briefly the principle underlying this veneration of relics and images:

It is manifest that we should show honor to the saints of God as being members of Christ, the children and friends of God and our intercessors. Wherefore in memory of them we ought to honor every relic of theirs in a fitting manner: principally their bodies which were temples and organs of the Holy Ghost dwelling and operating in them, and as destined to be likened to the body of Christ by the glory of the Resurrection. Hence God himself fittingly honors such relics by working miracles at their presence.

(For liturgical veneration of saints, *see* LITURGY, CHRISTIAN.)

Orthodox Eastern Church.—Veneration of the saints is also a practice in the Orthodox Eastern Church, the liturgy of which takes account of the feasts of the saints throughout the year and establishes the manner of celebrating the feasts. Moreover, the Orthodox venerate images of the saints, called icons, and they show reverence to the relics of saints; the latter are placed in the antimension, as in the Roman Catholic Church they are placed in the altar stone.

The teaching of the Eastern Church concerning the state of those who have passed out of this world is different from that of the Roman Catholic Church. Though the Orthodox pray for their dead and offer prayers to the saints, the church teaches that all the dead are asleep, awaiting the coming of the Day of Judgment, when the good will receive their reward of heaven and the wicked will be judged deserving of hell. The saints too appear to be in this middle state, although they are invoked. In fact, prayers to the saints play as large a part in Orthodox as in Roman Catholic devotions, and stories of miraculous apparitions of the Blessed Virgin Mary and of the saints are equally numerous.

The process of canonization in the Orthodox Eastern Church is less juridical than that in the Roman Catholic Church (*see* CANONIZATION).

The Menaion, a liturgical work of 12 volumes (one for each month) contains the proper of the immovable feasts of Christ and the saints, corresponding to the *Proprium Sanctorum* of the Roman Catholic breviary. For each day, it includes a *synaxarion,* a short narrative of the life of a saint or exposition of a feast, taken from the menology (a liturgical book containing the lives of the saints, arranged by months) and read after the sixth ode of the canon for the day.

The Eastern Church also celebrates the Feast of All Saints, on the Sunday after Pentecost. In the churches representations of the saints are found on the iconostasis (the screen separating the sanctuary from the nave); in private homes icons are used.

The saint that occupies the first place of honour among the Orthodox, after the Blessed Virgin, is St. John the Baptist, venerated as the precursor of Our Lord. Greatly beloved, and particularly so in the Russian Church, is St. Nicholas, the saint who helps those in need. The protector of trade, virginity and the family is St. Paraskeva. Among the modern saints is the Russian St. Seraphim of Sarov (canonized in 1903), who is held in special honour.

Anglican Communion.—Teaching in regard to worship and invocation of saints is one of the distinguishing differences between the Roman Catholic Church and the churches of the Reformation. According to Protestant doctrine, worship of the saints tends to detract from the position of Christ himself. Though the churches of the Reformation do not teach the nonexistence of saints, they maintain that to pray to the saints and to ask their intercession is to contradict the commands of our Lord when he taught us how to pray directly to the Father. The saints should be considered ideal examples of the faith, but men ought not to invoke their intercession by name.

The Anglican Church, like other churches of the Reformation, rejects doctrinally the worship and invocation of the saints. Its teaching and faith are contained in the Thirty-Nine Articles drawn up under Queen Elizabeth I in 1562 and amplified by the Book of Common Prayer. Article xxii states:

The Romish doctrine concerning purgatory, pardons, worshipping and adoration, as well of images as of relics, and also invocation of saints, is a fond thing, vainly invented, and grounded upon no warranty of Scripture, but rather repugnant to the Word of God.

Nevertheless, Anglican doctrine allows the *veneration* of the saints provided veneration does not become worship or invocation. On the one hand, there is no solid reason for stating that the departed saints cannot hear our prayers, if no solid reason for stating that they can; hence a private practice of addressing them cannot be condemned. It cannot be known whether or not they know individual men on earth, for there is no revelation or other knowledge on this matter. Thus, honour can be given to the saints, and Anglicans pray that they may "follow the blessed saints in all virtuous and godly living."

Under the influence of the Oxford movement, veneration of saints was revived in the Church of England. Nor are the Thirty-Nine Articles considered representative of the ritual and doctrinal position of the Protestant Episcopal Church in America, despite the fact that they are included in the American Book of Common Prayer.

In the Episcopal Church some teach that the saints do intercede for men; moreover, the saints bear witness to man's efforts to serve God on earth, and they aid men by their prayers.

Patron Saints.—During the middle ages the practice arose of bestowing on a saint honour for possessing definite attributes and then of considering the saint as an intercessor with special power regarding particular human needs. Thus, the saints became, in time, special patrons even of countries, cities and vocational groups. The practice of patron saints has continued, although changes in the liturgical calendar that were made by the Vatican in 1969 involved the feast days of many of these saints, including St. Christopher, patron saint of travelers, and St. Barbara.

A group of 14 saints, the auxiliary saints or holy helpers, are venerated for the efficacy of their prayers on behalf of human necessities. They are: St. George (April 23); St. Blaise (Feb. 3); St. Erasmus (June 2); St. Pantaleon (July 27); St. Vitus (June 15); St. Christopher (July 25); St. Denis (Oct. 9); St. Cyriacus

(Aug. 8); St. Acacius (May 8); St. Eustace (Sept. 20); St. Giles (Sept. 1); St. Margaret (July 20); St. Barbara (Dec. 4); and St. Catherine of Alexandria (Nov. 25).

In addition to the auxiliary saints, there are many others who are invoked for special needs, among them St. Peregrinus Laziosi (May 1), cancer patients; St. Dympna (May 15), the mentally ill; St. Anne (July 26), women in labour; St. Ottilia (Dec. 13), the blind; St. Roch (Aug. 16), invalids.

Patron saints exist also for various occupations: St. George (April 23), farmers; St. Florian (May 4), firemen; St. Andrew (Nov. 30), fishermen; St. Apollonia (Feb. 9), dentists; St. Ferdinand III (May 30), engineers; St. Francis de Sales (Jan. 29), journalists; St. Thomas More (July 9), lawyers; St. Albert (Nov. 15), scientists; St. Barbara (Dec. 4), miners; St. Luke (Oct. 18), physicians; St. Michael (Sept. 29), policemen; St. John Baptist de la Salle (May 15), teachers.

Most nations also have one or more patron saints, examples being: the Immaculate Conception (Dec. 8), United States; St. George (April 23), England; St. Andrew (Nov. 30), Scotland; St. David (March 1), Wales; St. Patrick (March 17), Ireland; St. Denis (Oct. 9), France; St. Boniface (June 5), Germany; St. James (July 25), Chile; Our Lady of Lujan (May 3), Argentina; St. Francis of Assisi (Oct. 4), Italy; St. Joseph (March 19), Canada; St. Lawrence (Aug. 10), Ceylon; St. James (Santiago de Compostela; July 25), Spain; Our Lady of Guadalupe (Dec. 12), Mexico. St. Benedict of Nursia (March 21; July 11) was proclaimed patron saint of all Europe in 1964.

BIBLIOGRAPHY.—H. Thurston, "Saints and Martyrs (Christian)" in Hastings, *Encyclopaedia of Religion and Ethics,* vol. xi, p. 51 ff.; C. Beccari, "Beatification and Canonization" in *The Catholic Encyclopedia,* vol. ii, p. 364 ff.; L. Duchesne, *Christian Worship: Its Origin And Evolution,* Eng. trans. of 4th French ed. (1912); A. Fortescue, *The Orthodox Eastern Church* (1920); L. Hertling and E. Kirschbaum, *The Roman Catacombs and Their Martyrs* (1956); J. A. Pike and W. Pittenger, *The Faith of the Church* (1951); F. Gavin, *Some Aspects of Contemporary Greek Orthodox Thought* (1923); R. French, *The Eastern Orthodox Church* (1951); P. More and F. Cross, *Anglicanism* (1957); G. De Mille, *The Episcopal Church Since 1900* (1955); H. Delehaye, *Sanctus* (Subsidia Hagiographica, vol. xvii), and *Les Origines du culte des martyrs* (Subsidia Hagiographica, vol. xx, 1933).

(W. J. EL.)

SAINT ALBANS, HENRY JERMYN, EARL OF (*c.* 1604–1684), English courtier and favourite of Henrietta Maria, queen of Charles I, was the son of Sir Thomas Jermyn of Rushbrooke, Suffolk. He became M.P. for Bodmin in 1625 and for Liverpool in 1628, in which year he entered Henrietta Maria's household as vice-chamberlain. He became her master of horse in 1639. A member of the Short Parliament for Corfe Castle, Dorset, in 1640, he was implicated in the army plot of 1641, by which certain royalists planned to intimidate Parliament by a show of force, and early in the Civil War he was engaged in several military exploits for the king. He was created Baron Jermyn in September 1643. After accompanying the queen to France in 1644 he was made governor of Jersey (January 1645) but rarely visited the island. He later proposed the sale of the Channel Islands to France in exchange for military assistance for Charles I. Lord chamberlain to Henrietta Maria in 1645, his influence with the queen (sufficient for rumour later to credit him with being her husband) secured his creation as earl of St. Albans by Charles II in April 1660. Although he held several English court appointments after the Restoration (May 1660), St. Albans spent much time in France, where as ambassador extraordinary in 1669 he helped to arrange the secret Treaty of Dover (1670) between Charles II and Louis XIV. In 1665 he obtained the freehold of land near St. James's Palace, Westminster (where Jermyn Street and St. Albans Street now preserve his name) and developed the area between St. James's Street and the Haymarket which included St. James's Square and Market. St. Albans was well known as a gambler and a glutton, and Andrew Marvell's satirical portrait of him in his poem "Last Instructions to a Painter" (lines 29–48, *Poems and Letters,* edited by H. M. Margoliouth, volume 1, 1952) includes a description of him as "full of soup and gold."

St. Albans, aged 80, died in London on Jan. 2, 1684.

(H. G. RO.)

SAINT ALBANS, a cathedral city, market town and municipal borough in the St. Albans parliamentary division of Hertfordshire, Eng., 19 mi. N.N.W. of Marble arch, London, by road, centred on the junction of Watling street with the road from London via Barnet to the midlands. Pop. (1961) 50,293. Area 8.0 sq.mi. The diocese of St. Albans covers Hertfordshire and Bedfordshire.

The city is named after the first English martyr, St. Alban, and the Abbey church (cathedral) stands on the hill which is the traditional site of the martyrdom, c. A.D. 303. The present church, built after the Conquest by Paul de Caen (1077) of Roman bricks from the ruins of nearby Verulamium (q.v.), succeeded the Saxon church of the monastery founded by Offa of Mercia, about 793, on the site of a still earlier church. The most famous Saxon abbot was Ulsinus who, in 948, founded three churches, St. Stephen's, St. Michael's and St. Peter's, planned and laid out the town, and founded the market which is still held. The school (not a monastic school) was already flourishing by 1100, and an early headmaster was Alexander Neckam, foster brother of Richard I. Nicholas Breakspear, afterward Pope Adrian IV, was the son of an abbey tenant. The church was reconsecrated in 1116. Of this church, the tower, the transepts and the east end of the nave remain. The west front and part of the nave were pulled down for rebuilding by John de Cella (1195–1214), but his money was exhausted and the work was completed by his successor, William de Trumpington, in Early English style. During the second half of the 13th century, the Lady chapel and the sanctuary were built, but in 1323, five Norman pillars on the south side of the nave, the roof of the south aisle and part of the cloisters collapsed. This part of the abbey was repaired in Decorated style. The high altar screen was completed in 1484 by William Wallingford, though it was probably commenced by John Wheathampstead or Bostock, friend of Humphrey, duke of Gloucester, who is buried in the abbey. After the Dissolution, the school was housed in the Lady chapel, and remained there until a jail was built in St. Albans, and the prisoners transferred from the Great gateway, which had been used as the town jail. The school took over this building in 1871 and it still remains part of the premises. By the 19th century, the abbey was in urgent need of restoration, and this was carried out, first by Sir George Gilbert Scott, and then a more extensive reconstruction was financed by Lord Grimthorpe. His alterations have been much criticized, but they made the structure safe. The extreme length of the abbey is 550 ft., while the nave, 292 ft., is the longest Gothic nave in Christendom.

The abbey played a large part in English history. As their power grew, the abbots obtained the right to destroy the Saxon royal borough of Kingsbury, on a neighbouring hilltop, and it finally disappeared in the reign of Stephen. The constant visits of kings and nobles, English and foreign, led to the development of a famous school of history, in charge, first, of Roger of Wendover, and later, of Matthew Paris. In 1213, the first draft of Magna Carta was read to an assembly of clergy and nobles in the abbey by Archbishop Stephen Langton. Later the town was occupied by troops of the dauphin. After the battle of Poitiers, the captured King John of France was held in the abbey as a prisoner until his ransom was paid. In the time of the Peasants' revolt, 1381, the Great gate of the monastery was stormed by the townsfolk, and Abbot Thomas de la Mare was forced to grant a charter, which was later revoked when the revolt collapsed. John Ball, the famous preacher, was executed at St. Albans. The clock tower, a town belfry almost unique in England, was built between 1402 and 1411, but the bell is older. During the Wars of the Roses, two battles were fought at St. Albans (see ROSES, WARS OF THE). In 1455 Richard, duke of York, defeated the Lancastrians there. In 1461 Henry VI's queen, Margaret of Anjou, routed Richard Neville, earl of Warwick (who was then fighting for the Yorkists) and allowed her troops to sack the town.

Like other abbeys, St. Albans declined in wealth and importance during the late 15th and early 16th centuries. Cardinal Thomas Wolsey was for a time abbot but never visited the abbey. It was dissolved in 1539 and St. Albans became a borough, its first charter being dated 1553. The Gorhambury lands of the abbey came eventually into the possession of Sir Nicholas Bacon, lord keeper

to Elizabeth I, who visited him there several times. His son, Sir Francis Bacon, Baron Verulam, is commemorated by a statue in St. Michael's church, which is within the site of Verulam and contains much ancient work. During the Civil War, the town was the headquarters of the army of the earl of Essex.

Sarah Jennings, later duchess of Marlborough, was baptized in the abbey and spent many years, both as a girl and with her husband, John Churchill, at her family home in St. Albans, founding some still existing almshouses. In the 18th century the town became notorious for bribery and corruption at parliamentary elections, and in 1852 the separate borough representation was abolished. The diocese was formed in 1877 and St. Albans became a cathedral city.

Many old buildings are to be seen in the streets, though many others have been pulled down or altered in the 20th century. The most important industry is printing. One of the earliest printing presses was set up in the town by the "Scolemaster Printer," and operated from about 1479 to 1486. One of his books, *The Book of St. Albans*, contains the first example of colour printing in England.

Other local trades are horticulture, musical instruments, clothing, electrical apparatus, chronometer making and a large variety of other light industries.

BIBLIOGRAPHY.—*Victoria County History of Hertfordshire,* vol. ii (London, 1908); L. F. R. Williams, *History of the Abbey of St. Albans* (London, 1917); A. E. Gibbs, *Corporation Records of St. Albans* (London, 1890); H. T. Riley (ed.), *Gesta Abbatum Monasterii Sancti Albani a Thoma Walsingham,* "Rolls Series" (London, 1867–69); Royal Commission on Historical Monuments, *Guide to St. Albans Abbey* (London, 1952); *St. Albans: the Story of the City and Its People* (St. Albans, 1949; rev. 1956); N. Pevsner, *Hertfordshire* (Harmondsworth, 1953); E. Toms, *Story of St. Albans* (1962, rev. 1966).

(E. Ts.)

SAINT ALDWYN, MICHAEL EDWARD HICKS BEACH, 1ST EARL (1837–1916), English statesman, chancellor of the exchequer from 1885 to 1886 and from 1895 to 1902, was born in London on Oct. 23, 1837, the son of Sir Michael Hicks Beach, 8th bart., and was educated at Eton and Christ Church, Oxford. Succeeding as 9th bart. in 1854, Hicks Beach became Conservative M.P. for East Gloucestershire in 1864, retaining the seat until 1885; thereafter he represented West Bristol until 1906. He held minor office under Benjamin Disraeli (later earl of Beaconsfield) in 1868, and was appointed chief secretary for Ireland in 1874, joining the Cabinet two years later. In 1878 Beaconsfield promoted him to the Colonial Office, where he remained until the government's resignation in 1880.

During the Conservative dissensions between the supporters of Lord Randolph Churchill and the marquess of Salisbury after 1880, Hicks Beach emerged as an influential figure, and became chairman of the party organization in the reconciliation of 1884. Chancellor of the exchequer and leader of the Commons in Salisbury's caretaker government of 1885, he surrendered both positions to Churchill when Salisbury's second ministry was formed in July 1886, becoming instead chief secretary for Ireland. Resigning in 1887, largely for reasons of health, he returned to the Cabinet to serve as president of the Board of Trade (1888–92). From 1895 until 1902, when he retired with Salisbury, he proved an efficient and authoritative chancellor of the exchequer, who insisted upon increased taxation to help finance the South African War (1899–1902). Though an orthodox free trader, he revived certain duties for revenue purposes. The controversy over his corn tax of 1902 was the occasion in the following year for the start of Joseph Chamberlain's tariff reform campaign, against which Hicks Beach fought bitterly. Created Viscount St. Aldwyn in 1906, he played little further part in politics. His earldom was conferred in 1915, and he died in London on April 30, 1916.

Hicks Beach was a highly respected member of his party, regarded as stern and austere, especially during his last years at the treasury. However, his nickname, "Black Michael," referred to his appearance rather than his character. He was considered an "old Tory" on most questions except Ireland, but he was nevertheless an arbitrator much in demand in industrial disputes.

See V. A. Hicks Beach, *Life of Sir Michael Hicks Beach,* 2 vol. (1932).

(A. F. T.)

SAINT-AMANT, MARC ANTOINE DE GÉRARD,
SIEUR DE (originally ANTOINE GIRARD) (1594–1661), French poet, and one of the original members of the Académie Française, was born at Rouen *c.* Sept. 30, 1594, the son of a merchant. Of Huguenot stock, he was converted to Catholicism. By his own account he traveled to America and Africa; and visits to Italy and England inspired the fierce satires *La Rome ridicule* (1643) and *L'Albion* (1644). He died in Paris on Dec. 23, 1661.

Saint-Amant is remembered for poems in praise of eating and drinking (*e.g., Le Fromage, La Vigne, Le Melon*); these are Rabelaisian in their wealth and crudity of vocabulary, and show a sense of the beauty of material objects. His best works, however, are those combining natural description (often of the sea), mythology, and supernatural horrors—*La Solitude, Le Contemplateur,* and, especially, the four sonnets on the seasons, in which his imaginative qualities are revealed with peculiar intensity. The epic *Moïse sauvé* (1653), on the life of Moses, shows the same qualities, but his vivid grasp of detail found its best expression in smaller compass.

BIBLIOGRAPHY.—*Oeuvres complètes,* ed. by C. L. Livet, 2 vol. (1855); *Oeuvres choisies,* ed. by R. de Gourmont (1907); P. Durand-Lapie, *Saint-Amant: son temps, sa vie, ses poésies* (1898); J. Lagny, *Le Poète Saint-Amant (1594–1661): essai sur sa vie et ses oeuvres* (1964).

                                        (R. A. SA.)

SAINT ANDREWS, a city, royal burgh, university town and seaport of Fife, Scot. Pop. (1966) 10,520. It is on a bay of the North Sea, 13 mi. SE of Dundee by road and ferry. It occupies a plateau of sandstone rock about 50 ft. high, breaking off on the north in precipitous cliffs. The Eden enters St. Andrews Bay northwest of the golf links, which rank among the finest in the world.

St. Andrews originated in a Celtic ecclesiastical settlement that may have been first formed by St. Kenneth in the 6th century. In the 8th century a new church was built by Angus MacFergus, king of the Picts, and dedicated to St. Andrew, who was adopted as the patron saint of the Pictish and thereafter of the Scottish nation. Relics of the saint were brought there and acquired such celebrity that the place, first called Mucross ("the headland of the wild boar") and then Kilrymont ("the cell of the king's mount"), came to be known as St. Andrews. About 908 the bishop of the Scots transferred his seat there from Dunkeld. In the early 12th century the bishopric of St. Andrews was regarded as the most important in the kingdom and was in due course raised to the dignity of an archbishopric in 1472 when its holder was recognized as primate of Scotland.

The medieval cathedral and priory of St. Andrews began with a foundation of Augustinian canons established between 1127 and 1144 by Bishop Robert in association with the so-called church of St. Regulus that still survives. In 1160 a larger cathedral and priory church was begun by Bishop Arnold and eventually consecrated in 1318. Built partly in the Norman and partly in the early Gothic style it was considerably the largest church in Scotland with an internal length of 357 ft. The cathedral and priory were enclosed by an elaborate precinct wall. In addition to the Augustinians, St. Andrews in the Middle Ages contained communities of Dominicans (*c.* 1275) and Observantine Franciscans (*c.* 1450). The bishops and archbishops resided in a formidable castle founded on a rocky headland to the northwest of the cathedral in about 1200 by Bishop Roger. An organized municipality or burgh was founded by Bishop Robert about 1140.

St. Andrews was granted most of the privileges of a royal burgh by King Malcolm IV about 1160 and grew into one of the largest towns in medieval Scotland. The parish church of the Holy Trinity was rebuilt to a commensurate scale on a central site in 1410 by Bishop Henry Wardlaw.

As the ecclesiastical capital of the country, St. Andrews was the centre of many of the most critical episodes in the Scottish Reformation. After the triumph of the Reformers in 1560 the cathedral and priory were abandoned and fell into ruins but the town remained a place of considerable importance until the close of the 17th century. In the 18th century it underwent a serious decline from which it was rescued mainly through the activity of Sir Lyon Playfair, provost from 1840 to 1861. Already well-known as a golfing centre, especially since the foundation of the

W. SUSCHITZKY

CHURCHYARD AND RUINS OF ST. ANDREWS CATHEDRAL

Royal and Ancient Club in 1754, St. Andrews acquired the favourable reputation as a holiday resort which it still retains. During the 20th century it consolidated its position as an educational centre and as the commercial and administrative focus of the adjoining region of Fife. St. Andrews is the seat of a presbytery of the Church of Scotland and gives its name to a bishopric of the Scottish Episcopal Church (but combined with Dunkeld and Dunblane and with its seat at Perth) and to an archbishopric of the Roman Catholic Church (but combined with Edinburgh and with its seat in the latter city).

Of the buildings of the medieval city comparatively little remains. The cathedral largely vanished apart from the east and west gables and part of the south wall, but the priory precinct wall was preserved throughout practically its entire length. Also to be seen are the north transept (1525) of the Dominican Church and a great part of the castle. Holy Trinity Church, after undergoing considerable alteration in 1799, was well restored in 1907–09 and is one of the most impressive churches in Scotland. The town is notable for its wide and handsome streets and retains many interesting domestic buildings of the 16th and 17th centuries and the fine gateway of the West Port (1589).

The University of St. Andrews, the oldest in Scotland, owed its origin to a society of scholars formed in 1410. A charter of incorporation was issued in 1412 by Bishop Wardlaw and in 1413 the full privileges of a university were conferred by the antipope Benedict XIII. The first buildings consisted of a "College and Chapel of St. John" appropriated to the use of the university in 1419 and in 1430 associated with a "Pedagogy" on an adjacent site. In 1450 St. Salvator's College was founded and richly endowed by Bishop Kennedy. In 1512 St. Leonard's College was established and between 1537 and 1554 the early Pedagogy was erected into St. Mary's College. Following the Reformation, in 1579, St. Mary's College was assigned to the study of theology and in 1747 the other two colleges were combined as the United College of St. Salvator and St. Leonard. University College, Dundee, founded in 1881, was in 1897 affiliated to the University of St. Andrews and in 1954 (following the act of 1953) joined with the University Advanced Medical School (1898) and Dental

School (1914) as a constituent college of the university entitled Queen's College.

In 1892 women were admitted to all courses of instruction in the university.

The buildings of the university include the splendid tower and church of St. Salvator's College, the church of St. Leonard's College, and the courtyard of St. Mary's College, all of which date from the Middle Ages. The University Library, which was refounded by King James VI in 1612, is partly housed in the original building, within which the Scottish Parliament met in 1645. The library contains over 400,000 printed books, some of great rarity, and important collections of manuscripts. The university expanded greatly during the 20th century and by the early 1960s included some 3,000 students, of whom approximately half pursued their studies in St. Andrews itself and the remainder in Dundee.

SAINT-ARNAUD, ARMAND JACQUES LEROY DE (1798–1854), French army officer and later marshal of France, who distinguished himself in Algeria, was minister of war under Louis Napoleon, and commander in chief of the French forces in the Crimean War. He was born in Paris on Aug. 20, 1798, the son of a prefect named Leroy. His full name is self-styled.

In March 1833 he became aide-de-camp to Gen. Bugeaud de la Piconnerie, whose protection thenceforth made his career easier. On obtaining an appointment to the Foreign Legion, he went to Algiers in January 1837.

Rising rapidly in rank, he served for a time at Metz before returning to Algeria in 1841 when Bugeaud became governor-general. He was on leave in Paris when the revolution of February 1848 broke out, and tried in vain to save the monarchy. Having returned to Algeria in 1851 as major general, he was appointed commander of the province of Constantine. In the autumn of 1851 he was made minister of war. He thus played a decisive part in the *coup d'état* of December 1851, and Napoleon III rewarded him by creating him a senator and a marshal of France. In 1854 he relinquished his ministerial post, and, although seriously ill, he took command of the French forces in the Crimea, planning the landing at Evpatoria (Sept. 14). With the assistance of the British forces under Lord Raglan, he won the Battle of the Alma (Sept. 20). Returning to France, he died at sea on Sept. 29, 1854.

BIBLIOGRAPHY.—J. F. H. B. Cabrol, *Le Maréchal de Saint-Arnaud en Crimée* (1895); M. Quatrelles L'Épine, *Le Maréchal de Saint-Arnaud* (1928); J. Dinfreville, *L'effervescent Maréchal de Saint-Arnaud* (1960). See also *Lettres du Maréchal de Saint-Arnaud,* 2 vol., ed. by his brother, A. L. de Saint-Arnaud (1855; 2nd ed., with memoir by Sainte-Beuve, 1858). (L. G.)

SAINT ASAPH, a cathedral village-city of Flintshire, north Wales, on the Chester-Holyhead trunk road, and 15 mi. W of Flint by road. Pop. (1961) 9,479. Its Welsh name, Llanelwy, is derived from the Elwy, between which river and the Clwyd it stands. Asaph, to whom the cathedral (the smallest in Great Britain, excluding converted parish churches) is dedicated, was bishop there in the 6th century. The small, irregularly built town also has a parish church, remains of a Perpendicular chapel near Ffynnon Fair (St. Mary's Well) and almshouses founded in 1678 by Bishop Isaac Barrow. The hill on which St. Asaph stands is Bryn Paulin, with early associations. The early cathedral, of wood, was burned by the English in 1247 and 1282, and that built by Bishop Anian in the 13th century (Decorated) was mostly destroyed during the raids of Owen Glendower (c. 1402). Bishop Richard Redman's building (c. 1480) was completed by the erection of the choir about 1770. Further restoration took place in the 19th century. The church is plain, cruciform, chiefly Decorated but partly Early English, with a square tower; it has a library of nearly 2,000 volumes, some of which are rare and which include the Welsh translation of the Bible by Bishop William Morgan, who is buried in the cathedral. In 1920 the bishop of St. Asaph was enthroned in his cathedral as the first archbishop of the disestablished Church in Wales.

SAINT AUGUSTINE, a city of Florida, U.S., the oldest city in the U.S., and the seat of St. Johns County, is in the northeastern part of the state 75 mi. S of the Georgia border, on the Intracoastal Waterway. It is connected with Anastasia Island on

EWING GALLOWAY

CASTILLO DE SAN MARCOS (c. 1672), THE OLDEST FORT STANDING IN THE UNITED STATES

the Atlantic Ocean by the Bridge of Lions across Matanzas River and is served by the Florida East Coast Railway, which also has its headquarters and shops there.

In 1564 France established Fort Caroline near the mouth of the St. Johns River. A year later, in order to defend and maintain Spanish sovereignty over Florida, Adm. Pedro Menéndez de Avilés destroyed the French colony and founded St. Augustine. Throughout the following 256 years it was the northernmost outpost of the Spanish colonial empire except for 20 years, 1763–83, when Florida belonged to England.

Since 1821 it has been a part of the United States. A plaza, narrow streets, stucco houses, balconies, patios, and gates from the wall that once protected the town are evidences of its heritage. A symbol of Spanish power is the grim and massive Castillo de San Marcos, a rectangular bastioned fortress with walls 30 ft. high and from 9 to 12 ft. thick, surrounded by a moat 40 ft. wide.

St. Augustine was plundered by Sir Francis Drake and besieged by James Oglethorpe; it became a refuge for Loyalists during the American Revolution and during the Indian wars provided a prison for captured Seminoles, including Osceola. The Federals occupied it the last three years of the American Civil War.

In the 1880s Henry M. Flagler (q.v.) became interested in developing the east coast of Florida as a resort area. Among the structures he erected in St. Augustine were the luxury hotel Ponce de Leon, and the Memorial Presbyterian Church, both designed by the architects John M. Carrère and Thomas Hastings.

St. Augustine is the site of a Roman Catholic cathedral and of the oldest Episcopal church in the state. The city has had a council-manager form of government in effect since 1915. There are numerous shrines and museums. The economy is based on tourism, commercial fishing, and some industry.

For comparative population figures *see* table in FLORIDA: *Population.*

SAINT AUSTELL, a market town and urban district in the Truro parliamentary division of Cornwall, Eng., 11½ mi. SSW of Bodmin by road. Pop. (1961) 25,074. Area 28.7 sq.mi. To the north, the high ground on which St. Austell stands culminates in Hensbarrow Beacon (1,027 ft.). The town is the centre of the china clay (kaolin) district, and many people are employed in the industry, exports being made to the Potteries and Lancashire and abroad; huge white spoil heaps abound.

Nearby is Menacuddle Well, a good example of an Early English baptistery. The harbours of Mevagissey, Par, and Charlestown are in the district.

SAINT BARTHOLOMEW'S DAY, MASSACRE OF,

the massacre of Huguenots which began in Paris on St. Bartholomew's Day, Aug. 24, 1572. It was ordered by King Charles IX, probably at the instigation of his mother, Catherine (q.v.) de Médicis. Various theories have been suggested as to how the idea of the massacre originated. Some Protestants at the time believed that Catherine had planned the crime during her meeting with the duque de Alba (q.v.) at Bayonne in 1565, notwithstanding the conciliatory policy toward the Huguenots which she pursued during the seven years that followed. A more likely theory is that Catherine grew jealous of the influence Huguenot leader Admiral de Coligny (q.v.) was exercising over Charles IX from 1571, and feared the possible consequences of his policy of French military intervention against Spain in the Low Countries. She accordingly gave her approval to a plot which the Catholic House of Guise (q.v.) had been hatching to assassinate Coligny, whom it held responsible for the murder of François de Guise in 1563.

On Aug. 18, 1572, Catherine's daughter, Margaret of France (Marguerite de Valois), was married to the Huguenot Henry of Navarre (the future Henry IV of France), and a large part of the Huguenot nobility came to Paris for the wedding. But the attempt on the admiral's life (Aug. 22) misfired: he was only wounded. The government thus had to placate the angry Huguenots by setting up a commission of inquiry. It seems that it was only when Catherine realized that the admiral would survive and that her part in the conspiracy might come to light that she decided to have all the Huguenot leaders exterminated. The massacre was planned at a meeting in the Tuileries Palace, attended by Catherine, the duc d'Anjou (later Henry III of France), the marshal de Tavannes (Gaspard de Saulx), the duc de Nevers (Ludovico Gonzaga), the baron de Retz (Albert de Gondi, later duc de Retz), and the keeper of the seals, René de Birague. Charles IX was persuaded to approve of the scheme, and the night of Aug. 23, members of the Paris municipality were called to the Louvre and given their orders.

Shortly before dawn on Aug. 24 the bell of Saint-Germain-l'Auxerrois began to toll and the massacre began. One of the first victims was Coligny, who was killed under the supervision of Henry de Guise himself. Even within the Louvre, Navarre's attendants were slaughtered, though Navarre himself and the prince de Condé (Henry I de Bourbon) were taken into protective custody. The homes and shops of Huguenots were pillaged, and their occupants brutally murdered, many of their bodies being thrown into the Seine. On Aug. 25 the government ordered the killings to stop, but the bloodthirsty mob would not listen.

As order was gradually restored, the crown had to explain the massacre: after blaming the Guises, Charles IX assumed responsibility for the deed himself, claiming that it had been necessitated by the discovery of a Huguenot plot to exterminate the royal family and seize power. The papacy was jubilant and had a medal struck to celebrate the event. Spain, too, welcomed the news. Protestant countries were horrified, and only the efforts of Catherine's ambassadors prevented the collapse of her policy of remaining on good terms with them.

Meanwhile the massacre spread to the provinces of France in a sporadic and haphazard way, continuing till the first week of October. Some towns, notably Rouen, Lyons, Bourges, Orléans, Bordeaux, and Toulouse, were scenes of carnage. Often the Huguenots were killed in cold blood in prisons where they had been detained for their own safety. Elsewhere, notably in Brittany, Normandy apart from Rouen, Picardy, Dauphiné, Provence, and most of Languedoc, the local governors ensured the peace.

No precise assessment can be given of the number of victims for the whole of France. Estimates vary considerably: the Huguenot duc de Sully, a contemporary, put the number as high as 70,000, but the 18th-century Catholic apologist Jean Novi de Caveirac calculated that only 2,000 were killed. The effect of the massacre disappointed Catherine's hopes: henceforth the Huguenots abandoned Calvin's principle of obedience to the civil magistrate, that is, to the royal authority, and adopted the view that rebellion and tyrannicide were justifiable under certain circumstances. *See* also references under "Saint Bartholomew's Day, Massacre of" in the Index.

BIBLIOGRAPHY.—S. L. England, *The Massacre of Saint Bartholomew* (1938); P. Erlanger, *St. Bartholomew's Night*, Eng. trans. (1962); N. Sutherland, *Catherine de Medici and the Ancien Régime* (1966).
(R. J. K.)

SAINT-BENOÎT-SUR-LOIRE,

a village of northern central France, in the *département* of Loiret, on the right bank of the Loire 25 mi. (40 km.) ESE of Orléans by road. Pop. (1962) 553. The splendid 11th-century Romanesque basilica is the only survival of the Benedictine abbey of Fleury, founded *c.* 651. The abbey acquired renown when the relics of St. Benedict were brought there from Monte Cassino in Italy in 672, and Fleury then became known by its present name. The basilica is entered through a two-storied narthex surmounted by a square belfry, with pillars crowned by Romanesque, Corinthian, and symbolically carved capitals. The choir, with a double colonnade in the manner of Roman basilicas, contains the tomb of Philip I (d. 1108). The carved northern portal (early 13th century) has a lintel representing the translation of St. Benedict's relics from Monte Cassino to Fleury. The relics are contained within the massive axial pillar of the crypt (1067), below the choir. In ancient times Fleury was a centre of druidism. The abbey, famous in the Middle Ages for its school and manuscripts, was pillaged by the Huguenots in 1562. It was restored by Richelieu, but was destroyed in 1760–1800. In 1944 the construction of a new monastery was begun by Benedictine monks from La Pierre-qui-Vire.

SAINT BERNARD PASSES,

two passes across the Pennine Alps, both followed by motor roads. The Great St. Bernard (8,100 ft. [2,469 m.]), one of the highest of the frontier passes, leads (53 mi.) from Martigny (Roman Octodurus) in the Rhône valley (Switzerland) to Aosta (Roman Augusta Praetoria) in Italy. It was used in Roman times. The hospice on the pass was founded (or refounded) by St. Bernard of Menthon (d. *c.* 1081), and since the 12th or early 13th century has been in charge of a community of Augustinian (Austin) canons, the mother house being at Martigny. In former days the servants of the canons and the famous St. Bernard dogs saved many lives, especially of Italian workmen, but rescue by helicopter has largely reduced their work. In May 1800 Napoleon led his army over the pass, which was then traversed only by a bridle road. The Little St. Bernard (7,178 ft. [2,188 m.]) was also known in Roman times; the hospice was refounded by St. Bernard, though later it was in charge of the military and religious order of SS. Maurice and Lazarus. The pass leads (39 mi.) from Bourg-Saint-Maurice in the Isère valley (Savoie) to Aosta.

There is no certain mention of the road over the pass of the

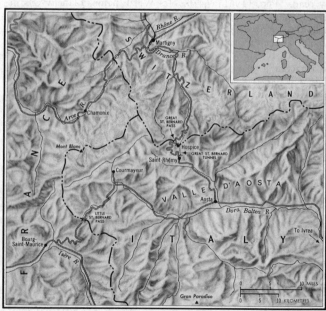

SAINT BERNARD PASSES, THE ALPS

Great St. Bernard (Alpis Poenina, Poeninus Mons) before 57 B.C., when Julius Caesar sent Servius Galba over it. Even in Strabo's time it was impassable for wheeled traffic. Augusta Praetoria originally had but two gates, one opening toward the Little St. Bernard (Alpis Graia), the other toward Eporedia (Ivrea), but none toward the Alpis Poenina. The military arrangement of the province of Germania rendered the construction of the road necessary, and it is mentioned as existing in A.D. 69. Remains of it, about 12 ft. in width, still exist cut in the rock near the lake at the summit of the pass. The temple of Jupiter Poeninus (Penninus) is found at the summit. As a modern route the pass, open for only about five months of the year, has been partly superseded for motor traffic by the Great St. Bernard highway tunnel (first used in 1964), which is open all the year. The tunnel (5,880 m. or 3.6 mi. long) runs from Cantine de Proz to Saint-Rhémy.

The Little St. Bernard was known to the Romans as Alpis Graia. Its name, interpreted to mean "Greek" pass, was associated with the legend that Hercules, returning from Spain with the oxen of Geryon, crossed the Alps by this route, though the legend better suits the route through the Maritime Alps. According to some scholars Hannibal passed this way over the Alps, but the route via the Durance valley and the Col de la Traversette or via the Mont Cenis are more favoured. Alpis Graia was the principal pass over the Alps into Gallia Comata until the pass of the Alpis Cottia (Mont Genèvre) was opened by Pompeius (Pompey) in 77 B.C., and became the principal route, though the road was completed only under Augustus by Cottius in 3 B.C.

See W. W. Hyde, *Roman Alpine Routes* (1935); H. Merrick, *The Great Motor Highways of the Alps* (1958). (A. F. A. M.)

SAINT BONIFACE, a city in Manitoba, Can., situated at the confluence of the Seine and Red rivers opposite Winnipeg, and part of the Winnipeg metropolitan area. Pop. (1966) 43,214.

The city was founded in 1818 by French missionaries upon the site of an earlier, unsuccessful settlement by Swiss mercenaries, who gave the place its present name in honour of the patron saint of Germany.

As a Roman Catholic religious centre it attracted French-speaking colonists from the east as well as local métis (Indian mixed bloods). It was incorporated as a town in 1883 and as a city in 1908. Railways and roads converged there to bridge the Red River for Winnipeg, creating conditions favourable to industrial development. There are meat-packing plants, flour mills, paint and soap works, and oil refineries. Large numbers of livestock move daily into its famous stockyards.

St. Boniface is the centre of French-Canadian culture in the west; it has a French-language radio station and a French-language college affiliated with the University of Manitoba. Principal among its buildings are the Roman Catholic basilica and large hospitals overlooking the Red River. The basilica is the oldest church in western Canada. Besides the French-speaking community, there are large British, Ukrainian, German, and Polish groups. The city suffered severely from a disastrous flood in 1950. (W. H. Pr.)

SAINT-BRIEUC, chief town of the *département* of Côtes-du-Nord, northwestern France, and the seat of a bishopric, lies on the right bank of the Gouët River about 2 mi. (3 km.) from its mouth in the English Channel and 62 mi. (100 km.) NW of Rennes by road. Pop. (1962) 42,211. Extending across a promontory formed by the junction of the ravines of the Gouët and its tributary, the Gouëdic, which are spanned by viaducts, Saint-Brieuc is a busy centre of administration, commerce, and tourism. Chief among its few remaining buildings of historic interest is the 13th-century fortress-cathedral of Saint-Étienne. The town has pleasant parks and gardens; points of vantage on the boulevards bordering the ravines overlook its commercial and fishing port, Le Légué, in the Gouët estuary, the ruined 14th-century tower of Cesson dominating the estuary mouth, and the Bay of Saint-Brieuc. The *hôtel-de-ville* houses a museum and art gallery. A railway junction on the main Paris-Brest line, Saint-Brieuc also has an airport, with services to Jersey in the Channel Islands.

Saint-Brieuc is named after a Welsh monk who established an oratory there in the 5th century. In 1375 the town was defended

against the duke of Brittany by Olivier de Clisson, who in 1394 attacked it himself, the cathedral suffering greatly in both sieges. In 1592 it was pillaged by the Spaniards and in 1601 ravaged by the plague. During 1602–1768 the states of Brittany met several times at Saint-Brieuc.

SAINT CATHARINES, seat of Lincoln County, Ont., Can., on the old Welland Ship Canal 2 mi. S of Lake Ontario. The first settlement was about 1790 and by 1797 part of the present site was known as Shipman's Corner. St. Catharines became a town in 1845 and a city in 1876. Known as the garden city, St. Catharines adjoins the towns of Thorold and Merritton in a continuously built-up area extending along the old canal where it climbs the Niagara escarpment. In the late 19th century St. Catharines was famed for its mineral springs but in modern times it became a manufacturing centre and the warehousing and distribution centre for the Niagara fruit belt in which it is located. Its larger industries produce automobile parts, heavy electrical apparatus, structural engineering goods and service, light and heavy hardware, and hosiery.

Pop. (1966) 97,101. (G. Fn.)

SAINT CHARLES, a suburb of St. Louis, Mo. See SAINT LOUIS (Mo.).

SAINT CHRISTOPHER: see SAINT KITTS-NEVIS.

SAINT CLAIR, LAKE, is an expansive shallow basin in the St. Clair–Detroit River waterway which connects Lakes Huron and Erie and forms the boundary between the state of Michigan and the province of Ontario. The nearly circular lake is 26 mi. long, north to south, and 24 mi. wide, and has a surface area of 490 sq.mi. The area of its drainage basin, exclusive of lake surface (and exclusive of the upper Great Lakes) is 7,430 sq.mi. The principal irregularity of the shoreline is the large delta of the St. Clair River, with seven channels. The lake has low and marshy shores and a gently sloping bottom with a maximum natural depth of about 21 ft. Ship channel improvements provide a minimum depth of 27 ft. across the lake from the mouth of the St. Clair River south channel to the head of the Detroit River. The mean surface altitude of the lake is 573 ft.—6 ft. below the level of Lake Huron and 2½ ft. above that of Lake Erie. As in the connecting rivers, the monthly mean level of water surface has fluctuated through a range of about 3 ft. during the navigation seasons.

There are no port cities of importance on Lake St. Clair, but Detroit, Mich., and Windsor, Ont., have dock facilities on the Detroit River a few miles downstream from the lake.

For a discussion of the regional relationships of Lake St. Clair see GREAT LAKES, THE. See also SAINT CLAIR RIVER; SAINT LAWRENCE SEAWAY. (J. L. Hh.)

SAINT CLAIR RIVER, the outlet for Lake Huron, which in turn receives the waters from Lakes Superior and Michigan, forms part of the boundary between the state of Michigan, U.S., and the province of Ontario, Can. Flowing in a southerly direction into Lake St. Clair with a fall of about 5.8 ft. in 40 mi., the river discharges through seven mouths, the one known as the south channel being used for deep-draft vessels, while several of the other channels are used for small craft. The south channel was improved by the dredging of separate channels to provide a minimum depth of 27 ft. for St. Lawrence Seaway traffic. The river has a velocity near its upper end of more than 5 mph through the rapids section, and a velocity of about 2 mph through the channels entering Lake St. Clair.

The river level fluctuates with the levels of the lakes above and below. From the year 1910 on, the difference between the highest and lowest monthly mean levels during the navigation season (generally from March to December) has been about 3 ft.

Near the head of the river are the cities of Port Huron, Mich., and Sarnia, Ont., both of which handle some water-borne commerce, but the great bulk of the traffic moves through the river without intermediate stop. This traffic is composed principally of iron ore, grain and limestone downbound and coal upbound.

There are several small towns and industrial plants along the shores of the river.

For a discussion of the regional relationships of the St. Clair

River *see* GREAT LAKES, THE. *See* also SAINT CLAIR, LAKE; SAINT LAWRENCE SEAWAY.   (J. L. HH.)

SAINT CLAIR SHORES, a city of Michigan, U.S., in Macomb County, 10 mi. NE of Detroit, is located on the western shore of Lake St. Clair. Settled in the 18th century by the French, who laid out farms along the Detroit River and Lake St. Clair, it remained a farming area until after 1920. By mid-20th century it developed as a suburban residential community. Its excellent boat harbours support its claim as the boating capital of Michigan. Many of its subdivisions along the lake provide canals from the lake terminating in boat-wells at the rear of residences. Private beaches for residents are available. It was incorporated as a village in 1925, as a city in 1950, and adopted a council-manager form of government in 1951. The population rapidly increased from 10,405 in 1940 to 76,657 in 1960.   (P. P. M.)

SAINT-CLOUD, a town of northern France, in the *département* of Seine-et-Oise, lies on the left bank of the Seine, 7½ mi. (12 km.) W of Notre Dame, Paris, by road. Pop. (1962) 26,433. The town is named after Clodoald or Cloud (grandson of Clovis), whose tomb was discovered in a crypt near the present church. He had granted the domain to the bishops of Paris, who possessed it as a fief till the 18th century. Henry III and the king of Navarre (Henry IV) established their camp at Saint-Cloud during the league for the siege of Paris, and the former was assassinated there. The castle, at that time a plain country house belonging to Pierre de Gondi, archbishop of Paris, was acquired in 1658 by the duke of Orléans, who built a palace which was destroyed in 1870. It was at Saint-Cloud that Napoleon carried out the *coup d'état* of 18 Brumaire (1799); after he became emperor the palace was his favourite residence, and he celebrated his marriage there to Marie Louise. In 1815 it was the scene of the signing of the capitulation of Paris. Seized by the Prussians at the beginning of the investment of Paris in 1870, Saint-Cloud was sacked during the siege. In World War II it was in German hands from June 14, 1940, to Aug. 24, 1944. Built on a hillslope overlooking the river, the Bois de Boulogne, and Paris, the town is one of the favourite resorts of Parisians. Every September, at the time of the pilgrimage of St. Cloud, a fair is held in its beautiful park. Within the area of the park is the national Sèvres porcelain factory.

SAINT CLOUD, a city and seat of Stearns County in the central part of Minnesota, U.S., is located at the junction of the Mississippi and Sauk rivers, 65 mi. NW of Minneapolis. The fertile surrounding country produces dairy products and grain in particular. Extensive ledges of high quality granite have given St. Cloud the nickname of the "granite city," and its chief industries are granite quarrying and granite products. It also has smaller printing, metal and optical supplies industries, and extensive railroad shops are maintained there. Pop. (1960) 33,815.

It is the seat of St. Cloud State College (established 1869), and of the state reformatory (1887), a U.S. veterans hospital (with 350 ac. of ground), a Roman Catholic cathedral, and several schools and charitable institutions under religious auspices. Nearby are located two Roman Catholic colleges—St. John's University (1857) at Collegeville, for men; and the College of St. Benedict (1913) at St. Joseph, for women. The population is predominantly of German descent, and Roman Catholicism is the main religion of the community.

St. Cloud was settled in 1851, platted in 1854, by John L. Wilson of Maine and named for the French city, incorporated as a village in 1868, and chartered as a city in 1889. Since 1912 it has had a commission form of government. Before the coming of the railroad it was the terminus of the Hudson's Bay Company for unloading furs brought down from the Red River Valley in wooden oxcarts. During the Sioux uprising of 1862 in the Minnesota River Valley, the men of St. Cloud hastily erected fortifications, and the settlement served as a refuge for thousands of homesteaders who fled from the Sioux attack.

For comparative population figures *see* table in MINNESOTA: *Population*.   (R. W. F.)

SAINT CROIX (SANTA CRUZ), the largest (80 sq.mi.) of the Virgin Islands (*q.v.*), purchased by the United States from Denmark in 1917. The island was discovered Nov. 14, 1493,

by Columbus who called it Santa Cruz, a name still sometimes used. After the fierce aboriginal Carib Indians were exterminated, it was occupied and partly settled in turn by small numbers of Spanish, Dutch, English and French. It was held by the Knights of Malta (1651–65). The island was virtually deserted (1695–1733) when the Danish West India and Guinea company purchased it. By 1742 there were 1,900 slaves.

Denmark acquired the island in 1754 and, after an insurrection of the slaves, emancipated them in 1848. About 90% of the 14,973 inhabitants (1960) are of Negro and Negro-white descent. The literacy rate is high.

The island is served by a network of asphalt roads. There is air service to all parts of the Caribbean from the Alexander Hamilton airport. Frederiksted is a west coast port and Christiansted, the chief town (sometimes called Bassin), is located on the northeast coast. Hills rise abruptly from the northern shore (highest point Mt. Eagle 1,165 ft.) and give way to fertile rolling lands, lagoons and beaches to the south. The climate is healthful with a mean annual temperature of 74° F. and an average rainfall of 45.7 in.

The tourist trade, rum, sugar cane and cattle raising constitute the island's basic economy. Despite appropriations by the United States, housing, potable water, sewage, road construction and maintenance and a higher standard of living remain continuing problems. After the fall of Batista in Cuba, Jan. 1, 1959, and the subsequent unrest under Castro the number of tourists increased.   (R. W. LN.)

SAINT CROIX RIVER, 129 mi. long, forms the international boundary between Maine in the U.S. and New Brunswick in Canada. It arises as the outlet of the Chiputneticook lakes, which are also the boundary, and discharges into Passamaquoddy bay. From the mouth upstream for approximately 10 mi. it is a tidal estuary, navigable to Calais, Me., where power dams block the channel.

SAINT CROIX RIVER of Wisconsin flows 164 mi. southwestward across the state emptying into the Mississippi at Prescott, Wis., about 20 mi. south of St. Paul. For 130 mi. upstream from its mouth it forms the boundary between Wisconsin and Minnesota.   (C. M. DA.)

SAINT CYR-L'ÉCOLE: *see* MILITARY, NAVAL, AND AIR ACADEMIES: *France*.

SAINT DAVID'S (TYDDEWI), cathedral village of Pembrokeshire, Wales, situated near the sea, southeast of St. David's head, the most westerly promontory of south Wales. Pop. (1961) 1,690. St. David's is 16 mi. N.W. of Haverfordwest and 16 mi. S.W. of Fishguard by road. The little town, locally known as "the city," stands in a lofty position near the cathedral close, and consists of four streets focusing on the square, called Cross square, the ancient market place still possessing its market cross (restored 1873). The origin of the fine cathedral and its village "city" in an area so remote under modern conditions is of special interest. Northwestern Pembrokeshire, like most western promontories of Britain, France and Spain, is remarkably rich in old stone monuments (menhirs, dolmens and stone circles), a fact pointing in all probability to its being on the coastwise and transpeninsular route frequented by prehistoric traders from the Mediterranean to Ireland. (*See* PEMBROKESHIRE.) The little boats of old were driven hither and thither at the mercy of wind and tide, and so the coast in these parts became dotted with alternate landing places, *e.g.,* Porth y Rhaw, St. Non's Bay, Porth Clais, Porth Stinian, Whitesand Bay, which seem to have made the neighbourhood important in pre-Christian times, as one may judge from folk tradition, monuments on the headland, etc.

The pre-Christian tradition was continued by the Celtic saints moving between Ireland and Wales. In early medieval days the same route grew important, as pilgrims moved to and from the shrine of Santiago de Compostela in northwestern Spain. (*See* Hartwell Jones, "Celtic Britain and the Pilgrim Movement," *Y Cymmrodor*, 1912.) The little landing places on the shore had Christian chapels, where prayers were possibly said for safe voyages. The most important ruins at present are those of St. Justinian and St. Non. At a focal point behind a group of these small ports, in the quiet sheltered, well-watered valley of the Alun, the fine cathedral (from Norman times with the double dedication to St. David and St. Andrew) was built, and on the high plateau around, as if sheltering it still further, the "village-city" grew. Throughout the middle ages the cathedral was the centre of pilgrimage and the medieval roads (often marked by sacred wells) may be traced across Pembrokeshire focusing on St. David's. Two pilgrimages to St. David's were popularly thought to equal one to Rome, and three pilgrimages to St. David's one to Jerusalem. The early holders of the see ventured, while the central government was weak, to exercise metropolitan rights over much of south Wales, but the increasing power of the Norman penetration reached St. David's, and Anselm's forcible appointment of Bernard—a Norman monk—to be bishop in 1115 made St. David's a suffragan see of Canterbury. A conciliatory step, it would appear, was the canonization of David about 1120. Gerald de Barri (Giraldus Cambrensis) strove vainly to regain the ancient power of St. David's from 1199–1203.

The Cathedral.—The cathedral church is partly built of a beautiful purple-hued sandstone, quarried locally. Its central tower, rebuilt after the original had fallen in 1220, was restored by Sir George Gilbert Scott who also designed the west front and did an extensive restoration of the cathedral. The earliest and main portion of the existing fabric, the fourth on the site, was erected

KENNETH SCOWEN

ST. DAVID'S CATHEDRAL, BUILT MAINLY IN THE 12TH CENTURY IN TRANSITIONAL NORMAN-ENGLISH STYLE

under Bishop Peter de Leia (1176–98) in the transitional Norman-English style. Bishop David Martin (1296–1328) built the Lady chapel; Bishop Henry de Gower (1328–47) made many additions in the Decorated style, including the stone rood screen and southern porch; and Bishop Edward Vaughan (1509–22) roofed over the space between the choir and Lady chapel now known as the Trinity chapel. The cathedral suffered severely during the changes brought about by the Reformation and at the hands of Bishop William Barlow (1536–48) and again during the civil wars of the 17th century. Subsequent restorations took place. The interior of the nave, separated by six wide bays from the aisles, is imposing with its triforium and clerestory. It has an elaborate roof of Irish oak, the gift of Treasurer Owen Pole (c. 1500). The nave is divided from the choir by Bishop Gower's fine stone screen, while the choir contains the richly carved stalls erected by Bishop Tully (1460–81), the episcopal throne and an oaken screen separating choir and presbytery. Bishop Vaughan's chapel contains fine Tudor fan-vaulting, and the Lady chapel decorated sedilia.

To the north of the cathedral is the ruined shell of the beautiful chapel, with an adjoining tower, that formed part of the college of St. Mary, founded by John of Gaunt and Bishop Adam Houghton in 1377. On the west bank of the Alun stand the ruins of the episcopal palace erected by Bishop Gower (c. 1342). The palace was built for residential purposes rather than for defense and occupies three sides of a quadrangle 120 ft. square, and, though

roofless and deserted for nearly three centuries, retains most of its principal features. The great hall possesses a traceried wheel window, the chief portal is still imposing, and the chapel retains its curious bell turret, while the peculiar but graceful arcaded parapet of the roof extends intact throughout the whole length of the building. Partially dismantled by Bishop Barlow (c. 1540), the palace was occasionally occupied by succeeding bishops prior to the civil wars. The close contains the deanery and other residences of the cathedral clergy, mostly on the sites of ancient buildings. It was formerly surrounded by a wall, traces of which survive; there were four gateways but the Tower gate alone remains.

SAINT DENIS, RUTH (RUTH DENNIS) (1877–1968), whose active dance career spanned half a century, was one of the most important pioneers of 20th-century American dance. Her personal influence was enormous, and through the pupils she shared with her husband, Ted Shawn (q.v.), it extended into almost every phase of the dance art in the United States.

Born in Newark, N.J., Ruth St. Denis was a comparatively successful vaudeville and musical-comedy dancer and also an actress before she became a serious dance artist and innovator. A cigarette poster accidentally seen in 1904, while she was touring in David Belasco's production of *Du Barry*, turned her attention to Egypt and the Orient. Careful study of Hindu philosophy and art led to the production of her ballet, *Radha*, in 1906. Its success brought her a triumphant three-year tour of Europe.

Returning to the United States, she produced *Egypta* and a Japanese dance drama, *O-Mika*. In 1914 she met and married the young dancer Ted Shawn, who shared her serious, idealistic approach to the dance. Together they founded the Denishawn School, which fostered many figures of importance in American dance, including Martha Graham, Doris Humphrey, and Charles Weidman.

The Denishawn Company toured widely in the United States, and visited the Orient in 1925–26. Never divorced, she and her husband separated in 1931. After brief semiretirement, she soon resumed performing her famous solos. Deeply concerned with the spiritual aspects of her art, Miss St. Denis devoted herself intensively to the furtherance of dance in religion. She died in Los Angeles on July 21, 1968.

See her autobiography, *Unfinished Life* (1939); Walter Terry, "Ruth St. Denis," ch. 6 in *The Dance in America* (1956). (LN. ME.)

SAINT-DENIS, capital town of the French overseas *département* of Réunion in the Indian Ocean, lies in a basin at the mouth of the St. Denis River on the north coast of the island. Pop. (1962) 37,047, including most of the metropolitan French in Réunion. The town is built to a grid plan, with a suburb occupied by the *élite* on the southern bluff, Le Brûlé. There are some notable colonial buildings. Saint-Denis is connected with the other main centres of population by a railway along the island's northern and western coast. Commerce is largely in the hands of an Arab minority. (HA. C. BD.)

SAINT-DENIS, an industrial suburb of Paris on the Seine River in the *département* of Seine-Saint-Denis, formerly in the *département* of Seine. It is 6 mi. (9½ km.) N of Notre-Dame. Pop. (1962) 93,783. The town is centred on the abbey church of Saint-Denis and associated monastic buildings; the latter, designed by Robert de Cotte in the 18th century, were transformed by Napoleon I into a school for the daughters of members of the Legion of Honour. Opposite is the municipal Museum of History and Art, founded in 1902 to house Merovingian, Romanesque, and Gothic remains excavated nearby. It has also a collection of documents relating to the abbey and its history, works of the Impressionist painters, and a reconstruction of the study of the poet Paul Éluard (q.v.), a native of Saint-Denis. The abbey was founded in the 7th century by Dagobert I. The foundations of the 7th-century abbey church were uncovered in 1957.

A reconstructed church, of traditional Roman basilical plan, was dedicated by Charlemagne in 775, and traces of it are to be found in the narthex of the present church, begun under Abbot Suger (q.v.) about 1135. Suger's church was to transform western architecture; it marks the transition from Romanesque to Gothic. This is best seen in the chancel, and the ambulatory with its great stained-glass windows. In the chapels radiating from the ambulatory are altar screens of the 12th and 13th centuries and a Romanesque altar front with sculptures of the Apostles. The west facade (1137–40) is uneven and was much restored with other parts of the church during the 19th century by E. E. Viollet-le-Duc (*q.v.*), who also built Saint-Denis de l'Estrée in Gothic style. The choir, apse, and nave were rebuilt under Louis IX. The church was the burial place of the French kings and their families; the most remarkable tombs are those that date from the 16th century, including that of Louis XII and Anne of Brittany; that of Francis I and Claude of France, made under the direction of Philibert Delorme; that of Henry II and Catherine de Médicis, the masterpiece of Germain Pilon; that of the dukes of Orléans and of the poet Charles d'Orléans. There is also a curious medieval work, the tomb of Dagobert I. The crypt dates partly from the 10th and 11th cen-

GIRAUDON

NAVE OF THE ABBEY CHURCH OF SAINT-DENIS

turies, and contains some interesting Romanesque capitals, but it has been heavily restored. Formerly, the coffin of the dead king lay there until, on the death of his successor, it was removed to its tomb in the nave. The remains of Louis XVI, Marie Antoinette, and Louis XVIII were walled off from public view in 1957.

Known in Roman times as Catulliacum, Saint-Denis was of little importance until the foundation of its abbey, built over the tomb of St. Denis. In the 12th century, Abbot Suger developed the Foire du Lendit, which has now been revived and is held in June. Under Suger the town became a great artistic and intellectual centre. From the 12th to the 15th centuries, French kings carried the oriflamme (banner) of Saint-Denis into battle. The *Grandes Chroniques de France* were produced in the abbey, and Peter Abelard (*q.v.*) was a monk there for a time. The town suffered in the Hundred Years' War, and in 1567 was the scene of a battle between Huguenots and Catholics. During the Revolution many

of the tombs of the French kings were destroyed, and part of the treasure melted down.

Saint-Denis is on the main railway north from Paris, and is a point of convergence of main roads from the north. It is also linked to Paris by *métro* and bus, and lies near Le Bourget airport. The Canal Saint-Denis crosses the town from northwest to southeast and leads to the Canal de l'Ourcq in Paris. A modern residential area extends to the north and northeast of the town and industrial quarters to the south. Saint-Denis has important industries manufacturing diesel engines, tractors, printing machines, chemicals, plastics, glues, inks, penicillin, leather (an industry with its roots in the Middle Ages), fireworks, and printed materials.

See E. Panofsky (ed.), *Abbot Suger on the Abbey Church of St-Denis and Its Art Treasures* (1946); S. McK. Crosby, *L'abbaye royale de Saint-Denis* (1953). (OL. F.)

SAINTE ANNE DE BEAUPRÉ, a village of Montmorency County, Quebec, Can., is about 20 mi. NE of Quebec City at the junction of the Ste. Anne and St. Lawrence rivers. Laid out along the St. Lawrence, the village is located on a narrow agricultural plain with hills in the background. Pop. (1966) 1,523. The shrine of Ste. Anne de Beaupré is a notable Roman Catholic place of pilgrimage where numerous miraculous cures have been recorded. Settled about 1650, the first chapel was built in 1658, according to tradition, by French sailors who, having been shipwrecked in the St. Lawrence, promised, if saved, to build a small chapel where they would reach land.

The first reported miracle, the curing of a local resident's rheumatism, occurred that same year. The Huron Indians, in 1670, were the first pilgrims to visit the chapel. In the 20th century the shrine was visited by pilgrims from all over Canada and the United States. The basilica of Ste. Anne de Beaupré, of 12th-century Roman Gothic style, is 375 ft. long, 200 ft. wide, and 100 ft. high. It has five naves, 10 small chapels, and can accommodate approximately 9,000 worshipers. Begun in 1923, it was completed in 1963.

Sainte Anne de Beaupré is the headquarters of the French Canadian Redemptorists and the seat of their college. An attraction of the village is a huge cyclorama depicting the day of the Crucifixion. (P. CA.)

SAINTE-BEUVE, CHARLES AUGUSTIN (1804–1869), French author and literary critic, regarded as the "father of modern French criticism," was born at Boulogne on Dec. 23, 1804. His father died two months before he was born, and his mother, daughter of an Englishwoman and of a Boulogne sea captain, was 40. The milieu in which he spent his childhood profoundly affected him; his mother and his father's sister, both of slender means, brought him up, and from them he derived those qualities of shrewdness, prudence, moderation, and lucidity found in his work. A studious and meditative child, he had no distractions except the reading of Latin authors and the French classics.

At 13 he had finished his studies at Boulogne and wished to complete them at Paris, where he hoped to learn Greek. In 1818 he became a boarder at the Pension Landry in Paris and followed courses first at the Collège Charlemagne, then at the Collège Bourbon. His masters allowed him to take the evening courses in science and philosophy at the Athénée, where he heard the "Idéologues" Destutt de Tracy and Georges Cabanis, whose theories of psychology and physiology influenced his development. He then turned to medicine, which he studied at the École de Médecine from 1823 to 1827. Nobody ever thought that the young man could earn a living by writing; but when his former master of rhetoric, Paul Dubois, founded the literary review *Le Globe* in 1824, Sainte-Beuve was eager to join in the new adventure and started contributing his first articles.

His review of Hugo's *Odes et ballades*, published early in 1827, marked the beginning of his friendship with Hugo and his sympathetic articles on the Romantic poets. By this time Sainte-Beuve devoted himself entirely to literature, having given up his medical pursuits. His allegiance to the Romantic movement is reflected in his first big study, *Tableau historique et critique de la Poésie française du XVIe siècle* (1828), which equates, for example, the great Ronsard with Hugo and compares the Pléiade and the

Cénacle. After a visit to England in 1828, he published a series of literary portraits (of Boileau, Corneille, etc.) in the new *Revue de Paris* (1829). At the same time he was working on two volumes of poetry: *Vie, Poésies et pensées de Joseph Delorme* (1829; published anonymously) and *Consolations* (1830). From 1831 onward, he contributed to another new periodical, the *Revue des deux Mondes*. The success of his articles in the two reviews prompted him to collect them as *Critiques et Portraits littéraires* (1832; volumes ii, iii, 1836; volumes iv, v, 1839).

The friendship with Hugo, which had already begun to cool in 1830, was almost extinguished by the anonymous publication of Sainte-Beuve's autobiographical novel, *Volupté* (July 1834). The hero Amaury's hopeless love, which ends only with the death of the saintly and unapproachable Mme de Couaën, reflects the author's passion for Mme Hugo. This same passion is given poetic expression in the secret *Livre d'Amour* (written 1831–32; published 1843) and, to a lesser extent, in the *Pensées d'août* (1837), which mark the end of Sainte-Beuve's career as a poet.

In October 1837 he left Paris for Switzerland, where a Swiss friend had arranged for him to lecture on Port Royal at the University of Lausanne. The 81 lectures (November 1837 to May 1838) covered the religious and literary history of half the 17th century. When *Port-Royal* appeared in three volumes (1840–48), it was a masterly piece of scholarship, and it remains an important historical document of the period.

Sainte-Beuve, by now an established scholar and critic, presented himself unsuccessfully for election to the Académie Française in 1843. He was elected in 1844 and received in February 1845. In August 1840 Victor Cousin, then minister of public instruction, had appointed him as a *conservateur* at the Bibliothèque Mazarine, with an annual salary of Fr. 4,000 and a lodging at the *Institut*. This gave him leisure to perfect his Greek. He published articles on Homer, Theocritus, Apollonius of Rhodes, and Meleager in the *Journal des débats* and the *Revue des deux Mondes;* these and others were collected in the series *Portraits littéraires* (1844), *Portraits de Femmes* (1844), and *Portraits contemporains* (1846). These portraits are typical of his method of re-creative criticism. He pursued his researches on Jansenism and on Pascal, to complete the third volume of *Port-Royal;* the Revolution of 1848 delayed publication until September. When, in March 1848, he was wrongly accused of having taken from the secret funds the sum of Fr. 100 (an expense incurred probably by a repair to his chimney), he resigned his position. He asked for a post in Belgium and was appointed to the University of Liège. There he gave 21 lectures (October 1848 to June 1849) on *Chateaubriand et son groupe littéraire* (published 1860).

Soon after his return to Paris in the summer of 1849, he was asked by Louis Véron, editor of the newspaper *Le Constitutionnel,* to write a weekly article, to appear every Monday, on current literary topics. This was the start of his famous *Lundis,* the critical and biographical essays which appeared in *Le Constitutionnel* (October 1849 to November 1852; September 1861 to January 1867), *Le Moniteur* (December 1852 to August 1861; September 1867 to November 1868), and *Le Temps* (1869). The success of his articles was such that he began collecting them as *Causeries du Lundi,* 3 volumes (1851); the third edition, augmented by notes, formed altogether 15 volumes (1857–62). A new series, the articles of 1861–69, was published as *Nouveaux Lundis,* 13 volumes (1863–70).

On his mother's death in 1850, Sainte-Beuve established himself at 11 rue de Montparnasse. In 1854 he was appointed to teach Latin poetry at the Collège de France. He gave his first lecture on March 9, 1855; but, because of interruptions and hostile manifestations by his former liberal friends, whom he had alienated by his support of Louis Napoleon (Napoleon III) and the Second Empire, he resigned after the second lecture (March 14). The intended course of lectures was published as *Étude sur Virgile* (1857). As a result of a general reform of the École Normale, he was chosen for the chair of French literature in October 1857. He lectured there twice a week from April 1858 to July 1861. Sainte-Beuve did not publish any collected volumes of these lectures, but his edited notes, transcripts, exordiums, and conclusions

GIRAUDON

SAINTE-BEUVE, PORTRAIT BY F. J. HEIM, 1856. IN THE LOUVRE

form seven folio volumes of the Collection Lovenjoul.

On April 28, 1865, he was made a senator by imperial decree. His addresses to the Senate were unpopular with his colleagues because of his liberal views, but two were epoch making: that on public libraries and liberty of thought (June 25, 1867), and that on liberty of education (May 19, 1868). Meanwhile he had written four outstanding articles on *Proudhon étudié dans ses correspondances intimes* for the *Revue Contemporaine* (October–December 1865). In December 1868 *Le Moniteur,* which had been independent, was reorganized and became *Le Journal officiel de l'Empire français.* An article (*"Sur la poésie," de Paul Albert*) which Sainte-Beuve wished to publish caused difficulties; for the first time he was asked to correct and to cut a sentence. He withdrew the article and offered it to *Le Temps,* for which he remained a contributor until his death, on Oct. 13, 1869, in Paris. He was buried at the cemetery of Montparnasse.

Assessment.—It was with Sainte-Beuve that French criticism first became fully independent and freed itself from prejudice and partisan passions. That he was able to revolutionize critical methods was partly a result of the rise of the newspaper and the critical review, which gave prestige and wide circulation to criticism and guaranteed its independence. When Sainte-Beuve began to write, the French attitude to the great literary heritage of the past, studded with illustrious names, was one of undiscriminating admiration and respect.

His critical works, published over a period of about 45 years, constitute a unique collection of literary portraits. He ranged widely, covering every genre of literature and reinstating writers whose works had been forgotten or misunderstood. An enemy of all kinds of bias, he wished above all to see clearly; by his definition, a critic was one who knew how to read and who could teach others how to read. His delicate discrimination, itself a proof of sincerity, is equaled only by his love of the truth. All his life he was faithful to the words he wrote to Victor Duruy (Dec. 9, 1865): "Si j'avais une devise ce serait le vrai, le vrai seul" ("If I had a motto, it would be 'Truth, truth alone'")—words inscribed on the pedestal of his bust in the Jardin du Luxembourg, Paris.

To use his own phrase, Sainte-Beuve was primarily a creator of likenesses (*imagier des grands hommes*). Every one of the articles he wrote was based on wide reading and extensive research. He devoted at least four days to preparing his Monday articles and to verifying references; he corrected the proofs himself with great care. He wished, as he said, to understand fully those about whom he wrote, not to be hasty in judgment, but to live alongside them, to allow them to explain themselves, to develop day by day, and to portray themselves to us. He sought to re-create the past, not as it was, but as it is for us today. His conception of criticism was that of a moralist, but, preferring insight to regimentation, his chosen instrument was an eyeglass (*lorgnon*) not a cane (*férule*). He was able to achieve his enormous output, which constitutes an encyclopaedia of thought, only by relentless labour and an unequaled tenacity of purpose, linked with unusually subtle intellectual power. The supplementary footnotes added to each successive edition of his works show his scrupulous and continuous attention to detail. This scholarly concern is seen already in 1836, when he wrote, "the devil of exactitude and of literary detail is as tormenting as any other kind of devil. . . . I would go to the end of the world for a minute detail, like a mad geologist after a pebble."

The field of criticism has widened since the time of Sainte-

Beuve, and as a result he has come to be reproached for his omissions and injustices. As one who prepared the way for modern poetry, he is disappointing when writing on Baudelaire; he was unfair, it is said, to Flaubert, Stendhal, and especially to Balzac. But this is only partially true. His article on Balzac in vol. ii of the *Causeries* is, despite the few reservations made in it, sound in judgment. As for Stendhal, who, except Balzac, did justice to him while he was still alive? The publication of Marcel Proust's *Contre Sainte-Beuve* in 1954 revived some of the earlier objections but in itself contributed little. That Sainte-Beuve has gained a place in the "Bibliothèque de la Pléiade" (see *Bibliography*) is, perhaps, sufficient proof that he is still read and reread.

As a poet, Sainte-Beuve was admired by Baudelaire and Verlaine; as a novelist, he remains an important innovator (Amaury and Mme de Couaën were to have descendants in later novels throughout the 19th century). But as a critic, he is unrivaled. A fitting summary of his life and work was given by Barbey d'Aurevilly in his words, "Sainte-Beuve, abeille des livres . . . faisant miel de tout pour le compte de la littérature" ("Sainte-Beuve, like a bee among books . . . distilling honey from everything of literary value").

BIBLIOGRAPHY.—There is no edition of Sainte-Beuve's complete works, but good selective editions are M. Wilmotte, *La Littérature française des origines à 1870*, 10 vol. (1926); M. Allem, *Les Grands Écrivains français par Sainte-Beuve*, 23 vol. (1926–32); and M. Leroy, *Sainte-Beuve*, "Bibliothèque de la Pléiade," 5 vol. (1949–55). English translations include *Causeries du Lundi*, selected and ed. by G. Saintsbury (1885); *Essays by Sainte-Beuve*, trans., with an introduction, by E. Lee (1910); *Selections from Sainte-Beuve*, ed. by A. Tilley (1918); and *Sainte-Beuve: Selected Essays*, ed. by F. Steegmuller and N. Guterman (1963). See also J. Bonnerot, *Bibliographie de l'oeuvre de Sainte-Beuve*, 3 vol. (1937–52), *Un Demi-siècle d'études sur Sainte-Beuve, 1904–54* (1957); *Correspondance générale de Sainte-Beuve* (1935–), ed. by J. Bonnerot and from 1965, by A. Bonnerot: 15 volumes had appeared by 1965.

Biography and criticism: G. Michaut, *Sainte-Beuve* (1921); M. Leroy, *La Pensée de Sainte-Beuve* (1940), *La Politique de Sainte-Beuve* (1941), *Vie de Sainte-Beuve* (1947); R. G. Mahieu, *Sainte-Beuve aux États-Unis* (1945); A. Billy, *Sainte-Beuve, sa vie et son temps* (1952); M. Allem, *Portrait de Sainte-Beuve* (1954); M. Regard, *Sainte-Beuve* (1960); H. Nicolson, *Sainte-Beuve* (1957); A. G. Lehmann, *Sainte-Beuve: a Portrait of the Critic, 1804–42* (1962). (J. Bt.)

SAINTE-CLAIRE DEVILLE, HENRI ÉTIENNE

(1818–1881), French chemist whose most important work was in inorganic and thermal chemistry, was born on March 11, 1818, on the island of St. Thomas, West Indies, where his father was French consul. In 1844, having graduated in Paris as doctor of medicine, he was appointed to organize the new faculty of science at Besançon, where he acted as dean and professor of chemistry from 1845 to 1851. He succeeded A. J. Balard at the École Normale, Paris, in 1851, and in 1853 became professor at the Sorbonne in place of J. B. A. Dumas. He died at Boulogne-sur-Seine on July 1, 1881.

He began his experimental work in 1841 with investigations of oil of turpentine and tolu balsam, in the course of which he discovered toluene. In 1849 he discovered dinitrogen pentoxide, the first of the so-called anhydrides of the monobasic acids to be isolated. In 1854 he devised a method by which aluminum (*q.v.*) could be prepared on a large scale by the aid of sodium, the manufacture of which he also developed. He contributed notably to the chemistry of magnesium and silicon (*qq.v.*), and did important work on the phenomena of reversible reactions.

SAINT ELMO'S FIRE,

the glow accompanying the brushlike discharges of atmospheric electricity which usually appears as a tip of light on the extremities of pointed objects such as church towers or the masts of ships during stormy weather. It is commonly accompanied by a crackling or fizzing noise.

St. Elmo's fire, or corona discharge, is commonly observed on the periphery of propellers, along the wing tips, windshield and nose of aircraft flying in dry snow, ice crystals, or in the vicinity of thunderstorms. Various flight procedures, in addition to mechanical and electrical devices designed to reduce the charge accumulation, are utilized as safeguards in preventing or minimizing discharges. (*See also* LIGHTNING: *Effects of Lightning.*)

The name St. Elmo is an Italian corruption, through *Sant' Ermo*, of St. Erasmus, the patron saint of Mediterranean sailors, who regard St. Elmo's fire as the visible sign of his guardianship over them. (E. J. Mr.)

SAINTE-PALAYE, JEAN BAPTISTE LA CURNE DE

(1697–1781), French medievalist and lexicographer, was born at Auxerre on June 6, 1697, the son of a gentleman of the household of the duc d'Orléans. Elected to the Académie des Inscriptions in 1724, he devoted himself at first to historical studies. He worked on a number of medieval chronicles for the series edited by Dom Bouquet (1738 *et seq.*) and went twice to Italy (1739 and 1749) to pursue his researches. He became director of the Académie des Inscriptions in 1754. In 1756, however, he produced an ambitious plan for a glossary of Old French. For this he was elected to the Académie Française in 1758. The first volume of the work was ready for the press in 1780, but publication was halted by Sainte-Palaye's death (in Paris on March 1, 1781) and then by the Revolution of 1789. The whole work finally appeared as *Dictionnaire historique de l'ancien langage françois, ou Glossaire de la langue françoise depuis son origine jusqu'au siècle de Louis XIV*, ten volumes, edited by L. Favre and M. Pajot (1875–82), with a life of Sainte-Palaye in volume ten.

SAINTES,

a market town of western France and subprefecture in the *département* of Charente-Maritime, is situated on the left bank of the Charente River 47 mi. (76 km.) SE of La Rochelle. Pop. (1962) 23,594. The Roman town (Mediolanum) was established in the tribal area of the Santones and the town became the chief centre of the district later known as Saintonge. The most noteworthy Roman remains are the ruins of an amphitheatre of the end of 1st century A.D., and an arch that has been transferred from the Roman bridge. Saintes was the seat of a bishopric until the Revolution. Its old cathedral of St. Peter, dating from the 15th and 16th centuries, was badly damaged by the Huguenots in 1568. Remnants of an older Romanesque church are incorporated in its structure, and there is pure Romanesque work in the church of St. Eutropius, which contains the tomb of Eutropius, first bishop of Saintes. Saintes is now a typical French provincial town, the market centre for the surrounding district, which is noted for its production of cognac. It has the regional museum of Saintonge, and there are iron foundries and pottery and tile-making industries. Small craft can use the Charente, but Saintes is no longer important as a river port. (Ar. E. S.)

SAINTES-MARIES-DE-LA-MER, LES,

a fishing village of the Camargue (*q.v.*), southern France, in the *département* of Bouches-du-Rhône, lies on the Mediterranean coast near the Étang de Vaccarès (lagoon), 24 mi. (38 km.) SSW of Arles by road. Pop. (1962) 871. The name has its origin in the ancient Provençal tradition that Mary, sister of the Virgin, and Mary, mother of James and John, together with their black servant Sara, Lazarus, Martha, Mary Magdalen, and St. Maximin fled there to escape persecution in Judaea. Relics of the first two Marys and of Sara are preserved in the 12th-century Romanesque fortress-church, which is the object of pilgrimages twice a year, on May 24–25 and on the Saturday and Sunday following Oct. 22. A feature of the May pilgrimage is the large number of gypsies who take part to do honour to their patroness Sara. In addition to the religious ceremonies there are bullfights, cattle branding, and other attractions. Saintes-Maries has a Camargue museum, and nearby, at Pont de Gau, is a zoological park with flamingos and other birds which breed in the Camargue nature reserve.

SAINT-ÉTIENNE,

an industrial town of east-central France and *préfecture* of the *département* of Loire, lies 310 mi. (499 km.) SSE of Paris and 36 mi. (58 km.) SW of Lyons.

From its old nucleus, huddled round the church from which the town takes its name, it experienced considerable industrial growth from the 16th century. The manufacture of firearms for the state dates from the time of Francis I, and the silk industry was also introduced into the area in the 16th century. Metalworking first depended upon local iron ore, smelted with charcoal. The local coal is excellent for coking and some of the earliest coke-smelting furnaces were established in the district. Although small, the local coalfield has been worked along the outcrops since the Middle Ages, and the high quality of its coal encouraged mining development early in the 19th century to serve the needs of local industries and of railways. The earliest railway in France connected Saint-Étienne with Andrézieux, 10 mi. away on the Loire, in 1828, and with Lyons in 1832.

As a major textile manufacturing centre, Saint-Étienne is especially concerned with ribbons, elastic fabrics, and mixtures of cotton and silk or rayon. There is a large dyeing industry. Coal mining has declined, and there is no longer any iron smelting at Saint-Étienne, but the manufacture of alloy steels is important, especially for armaments. The town has a huge state armaments factory, and great quantities of small arms are made by private firms as well as by independent gunsmiths in small workshops. Manufactures of hardware, cycles, aircraft engines, textile machinery, and chemicals are other leading industries.

Saint-Étienne's industrial growth from a town of 17,000 inhabitants in 1800 to 200,528 in 1962 greatly extended the built-up area, especially along the axial road from the Rhône valley to Roanne. An important focus of roads and railways, Saint-Étienne is not only the administrative centre of the *département* and of the coextensive diocese but is a regional capital and the shopping centre for the coalfield area, which includes a total population of about 300,000. (Ar. E. S.)

SAINT EUSTATIUS (Sint Eustatius), a Caribbean island in the Bovendewinds (Windward) group of the Netherlands Antilles, lies 9 mi. (14 km.) NW of St. Kitts. Pop. (1960) 1,014. With Saba (pop. 980) 7 mi. NW, it forms the northwestern termination of the inner volcanic arc of the Lesser Antilles. The annual rainfall of the two islands (about 42 in. [1,067 mm.] for St. Eustatius and 47 in. for Saba) exceeds that of the other Netherlands Antilles, and falls mainly between May and November, occasionally associated with hurricanes. St. Eustatius (area 12 sq.mi. [31 sq.km.]) is dominated by the Quill, an extinct volcano (1,968 ft. [600 m.]) in the south with a large forested crater. A flat central plain separates it from low hills in the north.

St. Eustatius, first colonized by the French and English in 1625, was taken by the Dutch in 1632. It became the main centre of slave trade in the eastern Caribbean and by 1780 had a prosperous population of 2,500. In 1781 the capital, Oranjestad, was sacked by the British and the island never regained its trade. In the 17th and 18th centuries most of the land was under sugar cultivation, but it is now used only for subsistence crops and rough grazing. Many men emigrate to work in the oil refineries of Curaçao and Aruba.

Saba (area 5 sq.mi. [13 sq.km.]) consists of the peak of an extinct volcano, The Mountain (2,821 ft. [860 m.]), surrounded by sea cliffs. The villages of Bottom and Windwardside are located on the only flat land and are approached up a steep road from a rocky landing place on the south coast. Saba was settled by the Dutch in 1632 but, because of its inaccessibility and ruggedness, never achieved any economic importance and often functioned as a buccaneers' stronghold. Its population, mainly white, is engaged chiefly in raising livestock and the cultivation of vegetables, particularly potatoes, which are exported to neighbouring islands. English is the principal language. (D. R. H.)

SAINT-ÉVREMOND, CHARLES DE MARGUETEL DE SAINT-DENIS, Seigneur de (1614–1703), French man of letters who earned a reputation as a free thinker by his writings on religious and moral questions, which represent an important stage in the origins of the French Enlightenment. He was the first French critic to judge English comedy for its intrinsic merits rather than by the canons of French "classical" taste, and his comments on the Quarrel of the Ancients and Moderns are models of sound judgment.

Saint-Évremond was born at Saint-Denis-le-Gast in Normandy on or just before Jan. 5, 1614, and was educated in Paris by the Jesuits. Though he had a distinguished military career and reached the rank of *maréchal de camp,* his political sympathies which he expressed more than once in an uncompromisingly satirical style, made him appear a hostile and potentially dangerous critic of the absolute system of government which Mazarin and Louis XIV were trying to establish. His accidental implication in the fall of Fouquet, in September 1661, provided a pretext for his disgrace, and he fled to England where, apart from a stay of five years (1665–70) in Holland, he spent the rest of his life. He died in

London on Sept. 29, 1703, and was buried in Westminster Abbey, where he is commemorated in Poets' Corner.

Saint-Évremond devoted himself seriously to writing after his exile, in order to compensate for the failure of his ambitions as a man of action. In France, he had already had conversations with Pierre Gassendi, the French Epicurean philosopher; in England, he knew Hobbes, and in Holland, Spinoza. He was greatly stimulated by the cosmopolitan society which met in the house of Hortense Mancini, the Duchess Mazarin, who settled in London in 1675. His best works are the witty *Conversation du maréchal d'Hocquincourt avec le Père Canaye (c. 1668)*, which is a satire on religious fideism, and the *Discours* written in 1671, in the final chapter of which he advocates the subordination of religious dogma to ethics and calls for toleration in the interests of Christian reunion, although the tendencies of his thought are deistic rather than Christian.

In the original text, Saint-Évremond's work circulated in manuscript among his friends, the author refusing to take any part in their publication; many, however, were printed in France and Holland (and translated into English) without his consent, often in heavily censored versions. Shortly before his death, he was persuaded by Des Maizeaux, his Huguenot friend and biographer, to revise what he could of his writings, and it was on the basis of this not entirely adequate revision that they were posthumously published in London (two volumes, 1705) in what became the standard text. A critical edition by R. Ternois of the *Oeuvres en prose* (four volumes) and *Correspondance* (two volumes) began to appear in 1962, based on manuscripts not known to Des Maizeaux and on printed versions which he had unjustifiably neglected. There is a good selection of the literary criticism by M. Wilmotte (1921) and an English translation of his *Letters*, excellently annotated, by John Hayward (1930). The best critical account is in A. Adam's *Histoire de la littérature française au XVIIᵉ siècle*, volume v (1957). *See also* Fronde. (D. C. P.)

SAINT-EXUPÉRY, ANTOINE MARIE ROGER DE (1900–1944), French aviator and writer, outstanding for his lyrical evocations of the pioneer years of transcontinental flying. He was born at Lyons on June 29, 1900, of an impoverished aristocratic family; received his early education at Jesuit and Marist schools (1909–17); then studied in Paris at the École Bossuet and the Lycée Saint-Louis, hoping to enter the École Navale. Having failed his entrance examination in 1919, he studied architecture for 15 months at the École des Beaux-Arts, and in 1921 was conscripted into the Air Force. He became a qualified pilot in 1922, worked for three years in industry, joined the Compagnie Latécoère in 1926, and helped to open up airmail routes over northwest Africa, the South Atlantic, and South America. In the 1930s he worked as a test pilot, a publicity attaché for Air France, and a reporter for *Paris-Soir*. In 1939, despite permanent disabilities resulting from several serious flying accidents, he became a military reconnaissance pilot; he took part in the Battle of France (1940), and after the fall of France escaped via North Africa to the U.S. In 1943 he rejoined the air force in North Africa, and was shot down over the Mediterranean while on a reconnaissance mission on July 31, 1944.

Saint-Exupéry's writings were all directly inspired by his flying experiences. The novels, *Courrier sud* (1929; English translation *Southern Mail*, 1933) and *Vol de nuit* (1931; Eng. trans. *Night Flight*, 1932), the authentic reminiscences of his civil flying adventures in *Terre des hommes* (1939; Eng. trans. *Wind, Sand and Stars*) and of a reconnaissance sortie in May 1940 in *Pilote de guerre* (1942; Eng. trans. *Flight to Arras*), all extol the virtues of comradeship and devotion to duty, while portraying pilots pitting themselves against desperate odds; the books are a unique blend of graphic narrative, rich in imagery, and of poetic meditation on human values.

Saint-Exupéry's other works include *Le Petit Prince* (1943; Eng. trans. *The Little Prince*), a child's fable for adults, illustrated by himself; *Lettre à un otage* (1943; Eng. trans. *Letter to a Hostage*, 1950); a large unfinished volume of reflections, *Citadelle* (1948; Eng. trans. *The Wisdom of the Sands,* 1952); and several posthumously published volumes of letters, diary extracts, and collected newspaper articles. These all show Saint-Exupéry characteristically preoccupied with the spiritual dangers threatening modern civilization.

See L. Estang, *Saint-Exupéry par lui-même* (1956); R. Rumbold and Lady M. Stewart, *The Winged Life: a Portrait of Antoine de Saint-Exupéry, Poet and Airman* (1953); J. Roy, *Passion et mort de Saint-Exupéry* (1961). (R. D. D. G.)

SAINT FRANCIS RIVER, a tributary of the Mississippi River, U.S., rises in the rugged St. Francois Mountains of southeastern Missouri, flows south to the abrupt edge of the Ozark Plateau at Wappapello, Mo., and thence across the Mississippi alluvial plain to its mouth near Helena in northeastern Arkansas. The topographic contrast between the Ozarks and the alluvial plain is repeated in land use and in stream hydrology. In the plateau lead is mined, much land is forested and beef and dairy cattle are raised, whereas downstream land is almost entirely under crops—cotton, corn, and wheat being most important. Heavy rainfalls in the Ozarks, which make up 70% of the basin, run off rapidly and despite the building of Wappapello Dam in 1941 still cause floods in the lower basin where a shallow gradient, meandering course, and small channel capacity make the river seriously flood-prone. In the 1960s work was partially completed on a Corps of Engineers project to construct levees and ditches and realign channels for practically every mile between Wappapello and the mouth. The lower basin is also flooded by the Mississippi. The river is 425 mi. long, drains 8,400 sq.mi., and crests from January to May. (D. S. St.)

SAINT-GALL: *see* SANKT GALLEN.

SAINT-GAUDENS, AUGUSTUS (1848–1907), U.S. sculptor, well known for his large public monuments, was born in Dublin, Ire., on March 1, 1848. His father was French, his mother Irish. He was taken to New York City in infancy and at 13 was apprenticed to a cameo cutter. By this craft he earned his living, while studying at night at Cooper Union (1861–65) and the National Academy of Design (1865–66) in New York. In 1867 he went to Paris and was admitted to the École des Beaux-Arts. Late in 1870 he set out for Rome, where, still supporting himself by cameo cutting, he worked two years, copying famous antique statues on commission and starting his first imaginative composition, "Hiawatha." Back in New York during the winter of 1872–73 he made several clay portrait studies, including the bust of William M. Evarts, which were carved in Rome between 1873 and 1875.

Saint-Gaudens, now a mature and recognized sculptor, returned to New York early in 1875 and began to play an increasingly active role in U.S. artistic life. With an unusual capacity for friendship, he became acquainted with a group of men who formed a nucleus for an American artistic renascence. The group included Henry Hobson Richardson, Stanford White, Charles McKim, and John La Farge (qq.v.). In 1877 Saint-Gaudens went again to Paris, where he carried out, on drawings made in collaboration with La Farge, a reredos for St. Thomas' Church, New York (later burned). He also executed the "Admiral Farragut Monument," Madison Square, New York, the base of which was designed with White.

During his middle period (1880–97) Saint-Gaudens executed most of the well-known works that gained him great reputation and many honours. Again working with La Farge, in 1881 he did two caryatids for a fireplace (now in the Metropolitan Museum, New York) in Cornelius Vanderbilt's residence. In 1887 came the "Amor Caritas," which, with variations, long preoccupied him, and also the standing Abraham Lincoln in Lincoln Park, Chicago. The memorial to Mrs. Henry Adams (1891) in Rock Creek Cemetery, Washington, D.C., is frequently considered Saint-Gaudens' greatest work. The mysterious figure with shadowed face is often called "Grief," but the sculptor had no such intention; "Peace" or "Nirvana" better conveys the meaning. In Boston a monument to Robert G. Shaw, colonel of a Negro regiment in the Civil War, was completed in 1897 and is remarkable for its expression of movement.

Saint-Gaudens also did many medallions, undertaken originally as diversion from more serious tasks, which show the influence of

LEET BROTHERS

ADAMS MEMORIAL BY AUGUSTUS SAINT-GAUDENS, 1891. IN ROCK CREEK CEMETERY, WASHINGTON, D.C.

Renaissance medals and his early cameo cutting. Among these are designs for U.S. coins (the $20 gold piece of 1907 and the head on the $10 gold piece) and a considerable number of portraits, including heads on small bronze plaques ("McKim," 1878), half-length figures on larger plaques ("Bastien-Lepage," 1880), and three-quarter or full-length figures, some in bronze ("Robert Louis Stevenson," 1888), some in marble ("Mrs. Stanford White," 1889). *See* further SCULPTURE: *Late 19th- and Early 20th-Century Conservative Sculpture.*

BIBLIOGRAPHY.—Royal Cortissoz, *Augustus Saint-Gaudens* (1907); C. Lewis Hind, *Augustus Saint-Gaudens* (1908); Homer Saint-Gaudens, *The Reminiscences of Augustus Saint-Gaudens* (1913); Lorado Taft, *History of American Sculpture* (1903). (M. I. B.)

SAINT-GERMAIN-EN-LAYE, a town of France in the *département* of Yvelines, and a western suburb of Paris, lies 12 mi. (19 km.) from the city centre by road. Pop. (1962) 32,-916. Because of its situation (on a plateau about 200 ft. [61 m.] above the left bank of the Seine and protected to the north by the forest of St. Germain), its pure air, the absence of factories, its historical associations, and its proximity to other towns of the Île-de-France (Versailles, Pontoise, Marly-le-Roi, and Mantes), it is a residential and tourist centre. The château, built by Louis VI (1125), burned by the prince of Wales (1346), and reconstructed by Charles V, was finally restored by Francis I. It was the home of many French kings. Mary Stuart lived there, as well as James II of England, who died in exile there and whose tomb is in the parish church. The château now houses the Museum of National Antiquities. Another château, begun in the 16th century, was pulled down two centuries later; all that survives of it is the pavilion, named after Henry IV, in which Louis XIV is reputed to have been born. Near the château is the famous ter-

race of Le Nôtre, 1½ mi. long, opening on an immense panorama of the valley of the Seine, Paris, and the surrounding countryside.
(ME. P.)

SAINT GOTTHARD PASS, Switzerland, is an important motor and railway route between central Europe and Italy. It is generally accepted that the pass-route was known to the Romans as far as Hospental, but the pass (6,916 ft. [2,108 m.]) was not generally used as a through Alpine route until the early 13th century. The name St. Gotthard Pass, first mentioned in the early 14th century, is believed to have derived from a hospice built at the summit by the dukes of Bavaria in honour of St. Godehard or Gotthard (d. 1038), bishop of Hildesheim, Ger. First mentioned in 1331, the hospice was from 1683 in the charge of two Capuchin friars. In 1775 the buildings near it were damaged by an avalanche, and in 1799–1800 all buildings were destroyed by French troops. Rebuilt in 1834, the hospice was burned in 1905. A modern hotel now stands at the summit. A mule path across the pass served for many centuries. A carriage road (1820–30) has been replaced by a motorway. Beneath the pass is the St. Gotthard Tunnel (constructed in 1872–80, 9⅓ mi. [15 km.] in length, attaining a maximum height of 3,786 ft. [1,154 m.]), through which runs the railway (opened in 1882) from Lucerne to Milan. This route includes several spiral tunnels in the Reuss and Ticino valleys. A special service enables cars to board trains through the St. Gotthard Tunnel, thus avoiding the long, devious route over the pass, which is often crowded in summer.

See W. W. Hyde, *Roman Alpine Routes* (1935); J. E. Tyler, *The Alpine Passes in the Middle Ages* (1930). (A. F. A. M.)

SAINT HELENA, an island and British colony in the South Atlantic situated 1,150 mi. (1,850 km.) from the west coast of Africa, in latitude 16° S and longitude 5° 45′ W. Area 47 sq.mi. (122 sq.km.); extreme length, southwest to northeast, 10½ mi. (17 km.), extreme breadth 6½ mi. (10½ km.).

Physical Features.—The island is of volcanic origin, activity being long extinct, while subaerial denudation has greatly modified the landscape and marine erosion has formed perpendicular cliffs 450 to 2,000 ft. high on the east, north, and west. Its principal feature, a semicircular ridge of mountains, with the twin culminating summits of Mt. Actaeon (2,685 ft. [818 m.]) and Diana Peak (2,800 ft. [853 m.]), forms the northern rim of the great amphitheatre of Sandy Bay. South of the ridge water-cut gorges stretch in all directions, widening as they approach the sea into valleys, some 1,000 ft. deep, containing small streams. Springs of pure water are numerous. The lavas are basalts, andesites, trachytes, and phonolites; there is much volcanic ash, tuff, scoriae, etc., and conspicuous features are formed by rocks representing a late period of activity. Such features are The Asses Ears, Lot and

EMIL BRUNNER—PIX FROM PUBLIX

JAMESTOWN, THE CAPITAL OF ST. HELENA, AND JAMES BAY

Lot's Wife, and The Chimney. The only practicable landing place is on the leeward side at James Bay. From the head of the bay a narrow valley extends for 1½ mi. The greatest extent of level ground is in the northeast of the island where the Deadwood and Longwood plains lie at an altitude of more than 1,600 ft.

Although the island is within the tropics, its climate is healthy and temperate because of the southeast trade wind and the effect of the cold waters of the South Atlantic Current. The temperature varies at sea level from 20°–32° C (68°–90° F) in summer and 14°–29° C (57°–84° F) in winter. The higher regions are 5°–6° C cooler. The rainfall varies greatly with altitude, from 8 in. at sea level to more than 30 in. in the centre of the island.

Vegetation.—St. Helena has three vegetation zones: (1) the coast zone, extending inland for 1 to 1½ mi., now "dry, barren, soilless, lichen-coated, and rocky," with little except prickly pears, wire grass, and *Mesembryanthemum;* (2) the middle zone (1,400–1,800 ft.), extending ¼ to 1 mi. farther inland, with shallower valleys and grassier slopes with English broom and gorse, brambles, willows, poplars, and Scotch pines; and (3) the central zone, about 3 mi. long and 2 mi. wide, the home, for the most part, of the indigenous vegetation. Many of the indigenous species have become extinct, but by the early 1960s all the surviving ones were protected. The indigenous vegetation shows affinities with that of Africa, and the many exotics give the island almost the aspect of a botanical garden; the oak, thoroughly naturalized, grows next to the bamboo and banana. Common trees include the indigenous cabbage tree (*Senecio*), the cedar, and the eucalyptus. The New Zealand flax (*Phormium tenax*) was introduced from that country, its commercial success varying with market conditions.

Animal Life.—Besides domestic animals the only land mammals are rabbits, rats, and mice, the rats being especially abundant. The only native land bird is a small plover called the wirebird, *Charadrius sanctaehelenae.* Introduced birds now common on the island include the Indian mynah, avadavat, Java sparrow, cardinal, ground dove, partridge (the Indian chukar), and ring-necked pheasant. Among sea birds are the sooty, white, and noddy terns. There are no freshwater fish but of 65 species of sea fish caught 17 are peculiar to St. Helena; economically the more important kinds are gurnard, eel, cod, mackerel, tunny, bullseye, cavally, flounder, hogfish, mullet, and sculpin.

(G. A. J.; J. D. HA.; Ro. E. A.)

History.—The island was discovered on May 21, 1502, the anniversary of St. Helena, mother of the emperor Constantine, by the Portuguese João da Nova Castella, on his voyage home from India. Its first known permanent resident was Fernando Lopez, a Portuguese in India who had turned traitor and had been mutilated by order of Affonso de Albuquerque. Rather than return to Portugal, he was voluntarily marooned on the island in 1516 and died there in 1545. The first Englishman known to have visited St. Helena was Thomas Cavendish, who touched there in June 1588 during his voyage around the world. Another English seaman, Capt. G. Kendall, visited St. Helena in 1591, and Sir James Lancaster stopped at the island on his way home from the east in 1593 and again in 1603. The Portuguese had by this time given up calling at the island, which may have been occupied by the Dutch from about 1645 to 1651. The English East India Company dispatched a small force of troops and others under John Dutton to form a settlement there in 1659. The company, which was confirmed in possession by a clause in their charter of 1661, built a fort and named it after the duke of York (afterward James II).

On New Year's Day, 1673, the Dutch succeeded in capturing St. Helena, but they were ejected the following May by Sir Richard Munden. By a new charter granted in December 1673 the East India Company was declared "the true and absolute lords and proprietors of the island." Thereafter St. Helena was in the undisturbed possession of Great Britain. In 1673 nearly half the inhabitants were slaves imported from the East Indies or Madagascar. In 1810 the company began to bring in Chinese from their factory at Canton. During the company's rule the island prospered; vessels bound for England, numbering hundreds in a year, anchored in the roadstead and stayed for considerable periods, refitting and revictualing. Large sums of money were thus expended in the island, where wealthy merchants and officials had their residence. The slaves who worked the plantations were subjected to barbarous laws until 1792, when a new code of regulations ensured their humane treatment and prohibited the importation of any new slaves. Later it was enacted that all children of slaves born on or after Christmas Day, 1818, should be free, and between 1826 and 1836 all slaves were set at liberty.

Among the governors appointed by the company to rule at St. Helena was one of the Huguenot refugees, Capt. Stephen Poirier (1697–1707). A later governor (1740–42) was Robert Jenkins of "Jenkins' Ear" fame (see JENKINS, ROBERT). The astronomer Edmund Halley resided in the island in 1676–78 and his observatory was on Halley's Mount.

In 1815 the British government selected St. Helena as Napoleon's place of detention. The former emperor was taken to the island in October of that year and lodged at Longwood, where he died in May 1821. During this period the island was strongly garrisoned by regular troops, and the governor, Sir Hudson Lowe, was nominated by the crown. After Napoleon's death the East India Company resumed full control of St. Helena until April 22, 1834, on which date, by virtue of an act passed in 1833, it was vested in the crown. As a port of call the island continued to enjoy a fair measure of prosperity until about 1870.

Afterward the great decrease in the number of vessels visiting Jamestown deprived the islanders of their principal means of subsistence. When steamers began to be substituted for sailing vessels and when the Suez Canal was opened (1869), fewer ships passed the island and fewer still found it necessary to call. The withdrawal in 1906 of the small garrison hitherto maintained by the imperial government was another cause of depression, but during World War I the island was again garrisoned. During the South African War (1899–1902) nearly 6,000 prisoners were detained at St. Helena. In 1922 Ascension Island, up to that time under the care of the British Admiralty, was made a dependency of St. Helena. Similarly, Tristan da Cunha and its associated islands became dependencies of St. Helena in 1938.

The island was of strategic importance in the naval operations of World War II. After the war, it returned to its quiet and uneventful life. The rapid development, from 1960 onward, of both St. Helena and Ascension (q.v.) as important telecommunication centres restored St. Helena to a modest state of prosperity.

(G. A. J.; J. D. HA.; J. O. F.)

Population.—The majority of the population are of mixed European (mostly British), Asian, and African descent. After the original settlement by John Dutton, more soldiers and settlers were sent from England and their numbers were augmented by members of the crews of ships returning to Europe from the east. For a considerable period from 1840 onward there was an influx of freed slaves of west African origin. The population of the colony in 1964 was 4,613, of whom about one-third lived in Jamestown, the port and capital. Longwood is 3½ mi. SE of Jamestown. Most of the population is Anglican by religion. St. Helena is the seat of an Anglican bishopric (now within the province of South Africa) established in 1859. Ascension Island (q.v.) is also in the diocese. English is the only language spoken.

Administration.—St. Helena is administered by a governor. The St. Helena Royal Instructions provide for an executive council consisting of the government secretary and the colonial treasurer ex officio, two other official members, and from one to three unofficial members appointed by the governor from among the members of the advisory council, of whom at least one must be an elected member; and for an advisory council consisting of four officials, four unofficial members appointed by the governor, and eight elected members. The governor makes ordinances, after consulting the advisory council, but power is reserved to the sovereign in council to legislate by order.

The Supreme Court exercises jurisdiction over St. Helena and Ascension Island (q.v.); the chief justice, who is normally the governor, is the only judge. There are also a magistrate's court and a court for adjudicating small debts.

There is a single general hospital, in Jamestown, and in the country districts six health clinics. The health service is wholly operated by government medical and sanitary staffs.

Education is compulsory and is provided free for all children between the ages of 5 and 15 years. There are 11 senior and junior primary and infants' schools and one secondary school; the total number of pupils is about 1,400.

No defense forces are stationed or based on the island, the defense of which is a United Kingdom responsibility.

Economy.—Less than a third of the area of the island is suitable for farming or forestry. The principal crops are *Phormium* flax, potatoes, and green vegetables. Cattle, sheep, pigs, and goats are raised for local consumption. Lace and drawn-thread work of excellent quality are sold to passengers from the few ships which now call. Lack of frequent communications with the island operates against the development of a tourist industry on a residential basis. The principal exports are *Phormium* fibre, tow, rope and twine, and small quantities of wool. Attempts to exploit the commercial possibilities of the fisheries on an export basis have more than once proved unsuccessful. Electricity was becoming available in the early 1960s throughout the island. Funds provided under the series of Colonial Development and Welfare acts have enabled the government to undertake extensive reafforestation and pasture reclamation; dilapidated institutions and school buildings have been replaced; the road system is in excellent condition; and attention has been paid to water supplies and housing. The colony's expenditure runs at more than £200,000 ($560,000); local revenue is about one-third of this, the balance being made up from U.K. funds. The only banking institution is the government savings bank. Bank of England notes and the coinage of the United Kingdom are legal tender. There is a mail shipping service to England and to South Africa, but no air service. There are direct cable communications with Cape Town and Porthcurno, Eng. (for London). (J. D. HA.; RO. E. A.)

BIBLIOGRAPHY.—*A St. Helena Bibliography* (1937); N. Young, *Napoleon in Exile: St. Helena, 1815–1821*, 2 vol. (1915); Sir A. Kitson et al., *Geological Notes on St. Helena* (1931); O. Aubry, *St. Helena* (1936); P. Gosse, *St. Helena, 1502–1938* (1938); *Colonial Report on St. Helena* (HMSO, two-yearly). (G. A. J.; J. D. HA.)

SAINT HELENS, a municipal, county, and parliamentary borough, Lancashire, England, 12 mi. (19 km.) ENE of Liverpool by road. Pop. (1961) 108,674. Area 12.4 sq.mi. (32 sq.km.). The town's modern development began with the opening of coal mines in the 17th century and was furthered when glass works were started in 1773. It is one of the world's biggest glass-making centres. The industry is based on field sand found in southwest Lancashire. Other important manufactures include patent medicines, iron and brass foundries, pottery, and textiles. There is a trading estate at Parr. St. Mary's Church occupies the site of "Sainct Elyn's Chapell" after which the town is named. The Gamble Institute houses a technical school and a public library. The town was incorporated in 1868, became a parliamentary borough in 1885 and a county borough in 1888.

SAINT HELIER, the chief town in Jersey (q.v.), Channel Islands, takes its name from a Frankish saint who came to the island in the 6th century. Pop. (1961) 26,594. Its nucleus is built on marshy ground by the southeastern shore of St. Aubin's Bay, opposite a tidal island known as l'Islet. There was no harbour until the 18th century, the chief landing-place throughout the Middle Ages and later being at St. Aubin's across the bay; and the principal medieval castle was at Gorey a few miles away on the east coast. There was at that time no settlement in Jersey that could be called a town, for the island, lying off the shipping lanes, had no share in general mercantile activity such as Guernsey enjoyed.

The saint's memory is preserved in a small oratory (c. 12th century) perched on a rock off l'Islet, in the dedication of the parish church (the earliest mention of which in surviving documents is of the mid-11th century), and in the Abbey (later priory) of St. Helier founded on l'Islet in the mid-12th century by Robert Fitz Hamon, earl of Gloucester. A fishing village must have grown up beside the parish church; from the 13th century onward the king's courts usually met there, and a market was held there. The virtual abandonment of Mont Orgueil Castle at Gorey during the 16th century and its replacement by Elizabeth Castle on l'Islet (begun 1550; more serious work from 1594 when Paul Ivy was engineer), and the building of a courthouse made St. Helier the centre of island government. Harbour works were begun in 1700 and the modern harbour in 1841. In 1736 the historian Philippe Falle (who recorded the number of houses in St. Helier as 400 in 1734) left his books to the island and these formed the nucleus of a fine public library. The market place (now Royal Square) is still the natural centre of the town and its chief claim to architectural distinction. About half the population of Jersey lives in St. Helier, which is now the focus of transport and commerce as well as of government and cultural activity.

See E. T. Nicolle, *The Town of St. Helier* (1931); N. V. L. Rybot, *The Islet of St. Helier and Elizabeth Castle, Jersey* (1934). (Le P.)

SAINT HUBERT, a town of Belgium in the province of Luxembourg, on the Ardennes Plateau, 48 mi. (77 km.) SE of Namur by road. Pop. (1961) 3,108. The 16th–17th century abbey church contains relics of St. Hubert, patron of huntsmen, whose vision of a stag with a crucifix between its antlers is said to have occurred in the nearby Forest of Freyr in 683. An abbey founded in 687 by Plectrude, wife of Pepin of Herstal, preceded the Benedictine abbey of 817, which was occupied until 1789. The last abbot, Nicolas Spirlet, established steel forges and gun foundries nearby. The present buildings (1729) were used as a penitentiary until 1954. Pierre Joseph Redouté (1759–1840), the celebrated flower painter, was born at St. Hubert. (R. M. An.)

SAINT-HYACINTHE, a city in Quebec, Can., the seat of Saint-Hyacinthe County, is 50 mi. (80 km.) ENE of Montreal on the Yamaska River and the Canadian National Railway. Pop. (1961) 22,354 of whom 98% are French-Canadian. It is the seat of a Roman Catholic bishopric and contains a classical college, a technical school, a dairy school, monasteries, and other educational institutions. It is the commercial, cultural, and administrative centre for the surrounding agricultural area. Manufactures are important and include organs, woolen and other textiles, garments, marine engines, cutlery, hairpins, leather and rubber goods, cigars, and precision instruments. Its name is derived from Hyacinthe de Lorme who bought the territory in 1753. (W. F. Ss.)

SAINT IVES, a municipal borough and fishing port in the St. Ives parliamentary division of Cornwall, Eng., 20 mi. (32 km.) NE of Land's End and 8 mi. (13 km.) N by E of Penzance by road. Pop. (1961) 9,346. Area 6.7 sq.mi. (17 sq.km.). It lies on the north coast, its small harbour sheltered from the Atlantic by The Island, a strip of land running out to a granite knoll. The picturesque old town, with its winding streets and colour-washed stone cottages housing fishermen and artists, with their boats, clusters along this strip and round the harbour; the ground rises steeply behind, and to the southeast a modern residential quarter extends around the sandy bay for about 2½ mi. to Carbis Bay. Fishing and tin-mining were important until the late 19th century when pilchards ceased to visit the waters and many miners emigrated. The beautiful sandy beaches and the mild climate inspired the inhabitants to make St. Ives a holiday centre, and this trade has superseded the others.

The name St. Ives commemorates St. Eia, a 5th-century woman missionary who, according to tradition, floated over from Ireland on a leaf (coracle) and was later martyred. The present church of St. Ia is of the 15th century with a noble tower. Perkin Warbeck was proclaimed King Richard IV when he anchored in St. Ives Bay in 1497. In 1639 a charter of incorporation was granted with provision for four fairs annually, two weekly markets, and a grammar school, but as the town declared for Parliament in the Civil War its charter was withdrawn by Charles II. The present charter was granted in 1690. The guildhall was completed in 1940.

SAINT IVES, a market town and municipal borough in Huntingdon and Peterborough, Eng., mainly on the left bank of the Ouse, 6 mi. (10 km.) E of Huntingdon. Pop. (1961) 4,082. The river is crossed by a 15th-century bridge with a chapel over the centre pier that was restored in 1689. The Church of All Saints is Perpendicular. Oliver Cromwell lived in Old Slepe Hall (demolished 1848) for five years, and his statue stands in the market place, the centre of the town. St. Ives was noted for its eight-day

fair beginning on Monday in Easter week, granted to the abbot of Ramsey by Henry I. In the reign of Henry III merchants from Flanders came to the fair, which had become so important that the king granted it to be continued beyond the eight days if the abbot agreed to pay a fee of £50 yearly for the extra days. The fair, with a market on Monday granted to the abbot in 1286, survives and was purchased by the town in 1874, the year of incorporation, from the duke of Manchester. The markets, extremely important to St. Ives as an agricultural centre, were substantially altered to give greater facilities for auction sales. The Norris Library and Museum, opened in 1933, is mainly devoted to books and collections relating to the county.

SAINT JAMES, a city adjacent to Winnipeg in Manitoba, Can., was incorporated in 1956. Pop. (1964) 34,459. The district was named in 1853 when a parish was established and a church begun to accommodate Church of England settlers along the Assiniboine River. From 1880 to 1920, when St. James municipality was organized, the parish was part of the rural municipality of Assiniboia. Almost completely residential until after World War II, the city experienced considerable growth in apartment and home building, and attracted many commercial firms and light industries, most of which came from the older commercial district of downtown Winnipeg. Within the city limits are the airport for Greater Winnipeg which serves a number of domestic and international airlines; a permanent RCAF base; and Deer Lodge Military Hospital, established after World War I to provide hospital and medical care for veterans from Manitoba and northwestern Ontario. (H. W. L. B.)

SAINT-JEAN (St. Johns), the county seat of Saint-Jean County, Que., Can., 20 mi. SE of Montreal and on the west bank of the Richelieu River. Pop. (1961) 26,988, of which over 88% was French-speaking. Fort St. John was established on the site in 1748. Later the city was important as a trading centre on the canal system which connected Sorel, on the St. Lawrence below Montreal, to Lake Champlain, and thence to the Hudson River in New York State, and as the terminus of the first railway in Canada from Montreal. Its excellent location in respect to rail, road, and canal routes, markets, and available labour force helped to maintain it as an important commercial and industrial centre. Manufacturing is important, the principal products being sewing machines, ribbons, wooden articles, bricks, textiles, and metallurgical products. (W. F. Ss.)

SAINT-JEAN-DE-LUZ, a coastal town of the extreme southwest of France, in the *département* of Basses-Pyrénées, lies on the Bay of Biscay, 13 mi. (21 km.) SW of Bayonne by road. Pop. (1962) 9,056. The town is situated on the right bank of the Nivelle River at its mouth. A fine esplanade occupies the curving sandspit that obstructs the river as it enters the sea, and the channel is protected by moles. Across the river, Ciboure, as its name signifies, is a bridgehead settlement, and most of the fishermen now live there. The composer Maurice Ravel was born at Ciboure. The 13th-century church at Saint-Jean-de-Luz is the finest of the distinctive Basque churches, with wooden galleries in the nave reserved for men, according to Basque custom. From the 14th to the 17th century Saint-Jean-de-Luz was a prosperous fishing port, whose sailors were the first to fish the waters off Newfoundland early in the 16th century. In 1660 the marriage of Louis XIV and Maria Theresa took place at Saint-Jean-de-Luz. At this time its population numbered about 15,000. The cession of Newfoundland to England in 1713 and the loss of Canada contributed, along with the silting of the harbour and a disastrous storm of 1749, to bring about the decline of the port and decay of the town. It has revived in modern times as a tourist resort, active in winter as well as in summer. Sardine fishing was formerly important, but fishing is now chiefly concerned with tunny, for which Saint-Jean-de-Luz leads among French ports. Since 1953 the Basque Yacht Club has organized a tunny fishing championship there for amateurs. (Ar. E. S.)

SAINT-JÉRÔME, a city and the seat of Terrebonne County, Que., Can., is on the North River 38 mi. (61 km.) N of Montreal. Pop. (1961) 24,546. Known as "Queen of the North," it is the gateway to the Laurentians, the basis of its profitable tourist industry. The first settlers arrived in 1818, and the parish was established in 1834. First called Dumontville, in honour of Seigneur Dumont of Saint-Eustache, the name was changed on incorporation as a village in 1856. Saint-Jérôme enjoyed a period of rapid expansion after the arrival in 1868 of Curé Antoine Labelle, a physical giant who served for some years as Deputy Minister of Colonization, and whose zeal and energy helped make Saint-Jérôme an important distribution centre for new colonization districts, the tourist industry, and forest exploitation. Other important industries include a rubber footwear company, knitting and textile mills, and foundries.   (J. P. Le.)

SAINT JOHN, OLIVER (c. 1598–1673), English parliamentarian, a prominent Independent during the Civil War and an intimate of Cromwell, was chief justice of the Court of Common Pleas during the Commonwealth. He was the son of Oliver St. John of Cayshoe, Bedfordshire, and great-grandson of the 1st Baron St. John of Bletso. Educated at Queens' College, Cambridge, he was called to the bar at Lincoln's Inn in 1626. He was brought before the Star Chamber in 1630, together with the earl of Bedford who employed him as his lawyer, charged with the publication of a seditious libel, but the case was dismissed. He was a member of the company formed to colonize Providence Island (now Providencia) in the Caribbean Sea in 1630. In 1638 his marriage to his second wife, Elizabeth Cromwell, a cousin of Oliver Cromwell, led to an intimate friendship with Cromwell. M.P. for Totnes, Devon, in both the Short and the Long parliaments, St. John was closely allied with Bedford, John Pym, and Hampden and led the attack on ship money (q.v.). In an attempt to win his support, Charles I appointed him solicitor general in January 1641. St. John's political views, however, remained unchanged and in the same year he took an active and savage part in promoting the impeachment and attainder of Thomas Wentworth, earl of Strafford, and helped in preparing other bills, such as the Militia Bill, for the opposition.

During the Civil War St. John became a recognized leader of the Independents and supported the Army in its quarrel with Parliament in 1647. He was appointed chief justice of the Court of Common Pleas in October 1648. Although he retained his seat for Totnes, his legal office debarred him from sitting in the Commons and he took no part in the debates and refused to act as a commissioner at the king's trial (1649). In 1652 he was one of the commissioners responsible for bringing about the union between England and Scotland, and he was among those who pressed Cromwell to take the title of king in 1657. After the Restoration of Charles II, he published in 1660 a defense of his past conduct, *The Case of Oliver St. John,* and his only punishment was exclusion from holding public office. He retired to Northamptonshire until 1662 when he went to the continent. He died on Dec. 31, 1673. The place of his death is not known.   (G. H. J.)

SAINT JOHN, the capital of St. John County and the largest city in New Brunswick, Can. Pop. (1966) city 89,764, metropolitan area 101,192. On Jan. 1, 1967, the city of Lancaster, the parish of Lancaster, and a portion of the parish of Simonds were incorporated into it. On a rocky peninsula at the mouth of the St. John River, the city has enjoyed importance as a port and as the gateway to the vast timber resources of the St. John River Valley. The sheltered harbour has a depth of 32 ft. at low tide and 58 to 60 ft. at high tide, and is ice-free throughout the year. The river enters the harbour through a narrow rock gorge, making a 17-ft. descent to the ocean at low tide. At slack tide ships may pass through the gorge. With the rising tide ocean waters force themselves upstream, giving rise to the phenomena called the "reversing falls." (*See also* FUNDY, BAY OF.)

The site was visited in 1604 by Sieur de Monts and Samuel de Champlain, but it was not until 1635 that Charles de la Tour established a trading post called Fort St. Jean, a fortification which was subsequently renamed, abandoned, and rebuilt several times. In 1713 Acadia was ceded to England and in 1758 Col. Robert Monckton refortified the site, calling it Fort Frederick. In 1783 a large body of United Empire Loyalists landed at Saint John, establishing Parr Town on the peninsula and Carleton across the harbour. By royal charter in 1785 the two areas became the city of Saint John,

the oldest incorporated city in present-day Canada. Council-manager government was adopted in 1962.

Under protective British tariffs the city flourished during the early and middle 1800s. Wooden shipbuilding was a major industry and the lumber and fish trades boomed. Railway connections with Moncton were completed in 1860, and in 1890 with Montreal via the Canadian Pacific Railway's "short line" through the state of Maine. The city's growth was checked by a disastrous fire in 1877 and by the decline of the lumber trade and wooden ships in the late 1800s.

The city is an important distributing centre and a major Canadian winter port. A pulp and paper plant, an oil refinery, a large brush factory, a large dry dock, and a variety of light manufacturing industries are located in the area. The municipal airport gives connections with Halifax and Montreal, and there is regular boat service across the Bay of Fundy to Digby, Nova Scotia.

     (W. S. MacN.)

SAINT JOHN ISLAND, the smallest (20 sq.mi.) of the Virgin Islands (q.v.) purchased by the United States from Denmark in 1917. It was discovered by Columbus, Nov. 17, 1493. The fierce aboriginal Carib Indians were exterminated, but the island was not settled until 1717 by planters from Saint Thomas Island (q.v.), 4 mi. E. In 1733 the population consisted of 208 whites and 1,087 slaves. The latter launched a formidable insurrection on Nov. 13, 1733, that was not crushed until July 1734. Denmark emancipated the slaves in 1848. The predominantly Negro population (928 in 1960) is concentrated in the two settlements: Cruz Bay and Coral Bay (the best harbour refuge in the West Indies) at the western and southeastern ends of the island.

Some cattle are raised and bay leaves (for bay rum) gathered from the forest around Bordeaux Mountain (1,277 ft.).

The Caneel Bay Tourist Development and the preservation of a large part of the island by the U.S. National Park Service serve to attract an increasing number of tourists.   (R. W. Ln.)

SAINT JOHN OF JERUSALEM, ORDER OF THE HOSPITAL OF, a religious and military order of hospitallers founded at Jerusalem in the Middle Ages, which continues its humanitarian tasks in most parts of the modern world under several slightly different names and jurisdictions. It was known as the Order of the Knights of Rhodes while it ruled that island (1309–1522) and as the Sovereign and Military Order of the Knights of Malta during its tenure of Malta (1530–1798). From 1834 it has been called the Sovereign and Military Order of the Knights Hospitaller of St. John of Jerusalem, with headquarters in Rome. The English grand priory, suppressed by Henry VIII, was revived in 1831 and received a royal charter in 1888 as a British order of chivalry. The German branch of the order, which became Protestant at the Reformation, kept its old name of Johanniterorden, and there are associations and independent orders in other northern European countries and associations in the United States.

In Palestine.—The origin of the Hospitallers was an 11th-century hospital in Jerusalem, close to the church of St. John the Baptist, founded by Italian merchants from Amalfi to care for sick pilgrims. After the crusaders' conquest of Jerusalem in 1099, the hospital's superior, a monk named Gerard, intensified his work in Jerusalem and founded hostels in Provençal and Italian cities on the route to the Holy Land. On Feb. 15, 1113, the hospital was taken under papal protection, a status confirmed by later popes. Raymond de Puy, who succeeded Gerard in 1120, substituted the Augustinian rule for the Benedictine and took the title of master of the Hospital of St. John of Jerusalem. Under Raymond the hospital was soon involved in responsibilities entirely transcending its original eleemosynary character. Grateful crusader knights healed of their wounds in the hospital bestowed on it portions of their estates, while others remained in the Holy Land as members of the hospital, which thus developed into a wealthy and powerful body, dedicated to combining the task of tending the sick and poor with waging war on Islam in the Levant.

The Hospitallers and the Templars (q.v.), another military order of contemporary foundation, became, although often acting in opposition to one another, the most formidable instruments of war of the Latin kingdom. Ultimately the two orders weakened the secular monarchies by usurping, through their greater resources, the place of the sovereigns' direct feudal lieges, while their spiritual independence of the bishops rendered them obnoxious to the secular clergy. But the Hospitallers never ceased to be honoured for their hospital, where the sick were tenderly cared for no matter what their religion or country of origin.

Until the defeat of the crusaders at Hattin in 1187, the Hospitallers, based on the two great castles of Margat (Marqat), and Krak des Chevaliers (Qalat al Hosn), played a vigorous part in holding the Muslims at bay. When the latter recaptured Jerusalem in 1187, the Hospitallers removed their headquarters first to Margat and then in 1197 to Acre, where they established their hospital. During the Third Crusade, which failed to recapture Jerusalem, they supported Richard I of England in his victory at Arsuf. In later Crusades they held Krak until 1271 and Margat until 1285.

Cyprus and Rhodes.—When the crusader principalities came to an end after the fall of Acre in 1291, the Hospitallers moved to Limassol in Cyprus. At a chapter-general held in their commandery at Kolossi nearby, they decided to continue their work for the pilgrims and the sick and to remain close to the Holy Land in the hope of its reconquest. A hospital was built and the grand master Guillaume de Villaret carried out internal reforms through a new body of statutes. In 1309 the Hospitallers acquired Rhodes, where almost at once they began to build a hospital, which was later enlarged and improved. They ruled the island as an independent state, with the right of coinage and other attributes of sovereignty, and for more than two centuries they were the scourge of Muslim shipping on the eastern Mediterranean (see Rhodes).

By the 15th century the Turks had succeeded the Arabs and Kurds as the protagonists of militant Islam. The sultan Mohammed the Conqueror decided that this Christian spearhead must be broken, but his siege was repelled by the knights under their grand master Pierre d'Aubusson in 1480. Suleiman the Magnificent renewed the siege in 1522 when the knights' spectacular resistance was hamstrung by lack of support from other Christian powers. After six months the grand master Philip Villiers de l'Isle Adam capitulated, to save the civil population from massacre, and on Jan. 1, 1523, the knights sailed out of Rhodes with as many of the citizens as chose to follow them.

Organization.—Under the order's rule, the master (grand master from c. 1430) was elected for life and ruled a celibate brotherhood of knights, chaplains, and serving brothers. His election was subject to papal confirmation. Only the knights had a voice in the government of the order, through its legislative body, the chapter-general, convoked by the grand master. Always an international body, the order of St. John while at Rhodes evolved its characteristic form by grouping the knights into Langues (i.e., "tongues"). Originally seven (Provence, Auvergne, France, Italy, Spain, England, and Germany), they became eight when the Spanish Langue split into those of Castile-Portugal and Aragon. (In 1782 during the order's last days in Malta, the two Langues of England and Germany were unexpectedly brought together through the creation of an Anglo-Bavarian Langue by the grand master Emmanuel de Rohan and the elector of Bavaria, with the consent in 1783 of King George III of England.) To each Langue was entrusted, in Rhodes as later in Malta, the defense of one sector of the fortifications.

In Rhodes, as in Malta, each Langue had its headquarters in its own *auberge* ("inn" or hostel) where its members messed and lodged. The head of the Langue, known as the "pillar," presided over his *auberge* and was *ex officio* a bailiff of the order, a member of the chapter-general, and one of the great officers of the convent. There grew up in Rhodes and was maintained in Malta the practice of permanently allocating the various great offices to the pillar of a particular Langue. The pillar of France was the grand Hospitaller, the senior dignitary after the grand master; the pillar of Castile was the grand chancellor, the pillar of Italy the grand admiral, and the pillar of Provence the grand commander, with charge of the treasury. The pillar of England held the important command of the coastal defenses and bore the title of Turcopolier,

derived from the native mounted bowmen known as Turcopoles whom the order recruited in Palestine during the Crusades. The chaplains were subordinate to the prior of St. John.

The considerable estates of the order belonged to the Langue of the country in which they were situated and were graded, according to size and importance, into commanderies, priories, and bailiwicks, under commanders, priors, and bailiffs, respectively. National or territorial groups of priories and other units were termed grand priories, and the grand priors were members of the chapter-general. Each unit contributed at least one-third of its revenues to the upkeep of the armed forces, hospital, and other activities of the order at its centre. The badge of the order is the white eight-pointed cross of Amalfi.

In Malta.—After their expulsion from Rhodes, the knights were without a base for seven years, while their grand master De l'Isle Adam made the rounds of the courts of western Europe in a vain quest of aid toward its reconquest. In 1530 the emperor Charles V gave them the Maltese archipelago in return for the annual presentation of a falcon to his viceroy of Sicily and the obligation of securing Tripoli in Libya against the Muslims. Their failure to hold Tripoli in 1551 led to Suleiman the Magnificent's attempt to dislodge them from Malta in 1565. The superb leadership of the grand master Jean Parisot de La Valette, the sustained heroism of the members of the order, and the endurance of the Maltese population prevented one of the most famous sieges of history from ending in disaster (see Malta: *History*). What was left of the Turkish Navy as a striking force was permanently crippled in 1571 at the Battle of Lepanto by the combined fleets of Philip II, the Knights of St. John, Venice, Genoa, Savoy, and the pope.

After the victory, the knights proceeded with the building of their new capital, which they named after La Valette, the hero of the siege (see Valletta), and with their work on the defenses of both sides of the grand harbour. The hospital, with its ward 502 ft. in length, attracted many patients from outside Malta. These were well cared for, with no more than one to a bed, their food was well planned, and the mentally sick were treated humanely. Surgical and medical cases were kept separate, infectious diseases were isolated, and ophthalmology was a specialty. In 1674 the grand master founded a school of anatomy and medicine for the order's physicians. Anatomy was studied with the bodies of deceased knights and patients, at a time when dissection elsewhere tended to be forbidden.

As the 17th century advanced, the Turkish menace receded. For a brief period the order possessed the nucleus of a colonial dominion in the New World: the West Indian Islands of St. Martin, St. Croix, and St. Bartholomew, and part of St. Christopher (St. Kitts), bought from King Louis XIV of France in 1653 but relinquished by the order, as an unnecessary encumbrance, to the French West India Company at a handsome profit in 1665. By the 18th century the order as a territorial sovereign state committed to wage war on Islam had become an anachronism, but its hospital continued to be in the forefront of medical care. After the outbreak of the French Revolution the rich properties of the three French Langues were confiscated in 1792, and in 1798 Malta was occupied by Napoleon on his way to Egypt, the grand master Ferdinand von Hompesch offering no resistance. The order's return to Malta was provided for in the Treaty of Amiens (1802) but eliminated by the Treaty of Paris (1814), which assigned Malta to Great Britain.

In Russia.—On the final partition of Poland in 1797, the grand priory of Poland, which had formed a part of the Anglo-Bavarian Langue, became known as the grand priory of Russia and was taken under the protection of the emperor Paul I, who, though Orthodox, became grand master of the order (1798), in the face of strong papal disapproval. Paul's successor, Alexander I, declined to be grand master and discontinued the Russian grand priory in 1817.

The Sovereign Military Order from 1801.—G. B. Tommasi, who became grand master in 1803, died in 1805, disappointed in his hope to lead the knights back to Malta from his temporary headquarters in Sicily, at Messina. Thenceforth the Sovereign and Military Order of the Knights Hospitaller of St. John of

Jerusalem, permanently established in Rome in 1834, confined its activities to its original humanitarian tasks. From 1805 it was ruled by lieutenants until Pope Leo XIII revived the grand mastership in 1879. Toward the end of the life of the grand master (1931–51) Ludovico Chigi della Rovere Albani differences with the Holy See delayed until 1962 the election of a successor. A new constitutional charter was drawn up in 1957.

Although the order no longer exercises territorial rule it issues passports and its sovereign status is recognized by the Holy See and those other Roman Catholic states to which it accredits ministers plenipotentiary or delegates with diplomatic status. Of its original regional units there survive five grand priories: of Rome, Lombardy-Venice, Naples-Sicily, Austria, and Bohemia-Moravia (the last only in name). Elsewhere the members are grouped under national associations, as for instance that in the United States.

Membership is confined to Roman Catholics and is divided into three categories, each with subdivisions. The first consists of the "professed" knights of justice and chaplains who can prove the nobility of their four grandparents for two centuries and have taken either "simple" or "solemn" religious vows including that of celibacy; the second, of knights and Donats (men of knightly but not sufficiently noble birth) of honour and devotion, who must prove the same nobility but are not "professed"; the third, of seven grades differing in nobiliary and other qualifications. While the order remains essentially an aristocratic body, the requisite "quarters" for the third category vary with grade and country (particularly in the New World); in the case of knights of magistral grace appointed "by merit" they may be dispensed with altogether. Women are admitted to the second and third categories.

The Most Venerable Order.—With the sequestration of the English grand priory's properties by Henry VIII in 1540 the English Langue virtually became dormant for three centuries except for a brief revival by Mary I (whose letters patent restoring it were not revoked) and the appointment by the grand masters of titular nonresident grand priors of England, the last of whom held his nominal office from 1806 until 1815. In 1831 the grand priory was resuscitated on a basis mainly Anglican on the initiative of a group of knights of the French Langues known as the "Capitular Commission." The Sovereign Military Order in Rome first accepted this step, then repudiated it in 1858. In 1963, however, the Sovereign Military Order and the Most Venerable Order signed a formal declaration defining their mutual relationship.

By royal charter of 1888 the revived grand priory of England was converted by Queen Victoria into a British order of chivalry, bearing the prefix "most venerable." The reigning monarch is its sovereign head, and the grand priors appointed since 1888 have been members of the British royal house. A later royal charter of 1926 authorized the creation of priories and commanderies in the Commonwealth overseas. For day-to-day purposes the grand prior acts through his deputy, the lord prior of St. John. All Christians are eligible, and women are admitted to all grades of the order except the last (bailiffs and dames grand cross; knights and dames of justice or of grace; commanders; officers; serving brothers and sisters; esquires) but not to membership of the chapter-general, which under the sovereign head and the grand prior is the governing body. The executive officers are the heads of the order's departments. Appointments to and promotions in the order are made by the sovereign head on the recommendation of the chapter-general as approved by the grand prior. This direct access to the throne is a relic of the independent status of the original order. The "establishments" of the order are the priories of Scotland, Wales, Canada, Australia, New Zealand, and South Africa. There are commanderies in Western Australia, Northern Ireland, and Central Africa, and St. John organizations in most of the colonies and dependencies. An American Society of the Most Venerable Order of the Hospital of St. John of Jerusalem was set up in the United States in 1960.

The order performs its humanitarian work through its three "foundations": the St. John Ophthalmic Hospital in Jerusalem (founded 1882), among whose essential functions is research on trachoma; the St. John Ambulance Association (founded 1878), the teaching body of the order, which compiles first-aid manuals,

conducts courses of instruction, and issues first-aid certificates; the St. John Ambulance Brigade (founded 1888), whose unpaid members of both sexes give voluntary service throughout the Commonwealth at public gatherings and which works in wartime with the British Red Cross Society. The St. John Cadet Divisions, composed of younger persons, have become a leading British youth organization.

The order's headquarters (including its library and museum) are at St. John's Gate, Clerkenwell, London, in the surviving buildings of the original English grand priory. The order has a small share in the ancient commandery of Kolossi in Cyprus. It accredits liaison officers to the Sovereign Military Order in Rome and to other orders of St. John.

In Northern Europe.—The core of the ancient Langue of Germany was the bailiwick of Brandenburg. At the Reformation the bailiwick became Lutheran without, however, severing all relations with the grand master in Malta. Well endowed, it was active in philanthropic work until the Napoleonic Wars, when its property was confiscated by Prussia. In 1852 it was reestablished with its old name, Johanniterorden, by Frederick William IV of Prussia, who entrusted to it the task of maintaining existing hospitals and creating new ones in Prussia, with funds to be found by the knights themselves. Its head, called the *Herrenmeister*, is elected by the chapter and has generally been a member of the Prussian royal house. Membership is confined to Protestants and to noblemen, although the rule regarding nobility was slightly relaxed after World War II. After World War I the Johanniterorden lost the greater part of its funds through successive inflations and deflations, and then suffered further from the active hostility of the Hitler regime. After World War II it lost its headquarters and most of its hospitals, which lay in East Germany and Poland. Its headquarters were transferred to Rolandseck in the Rhineland, and it has rebuilt its hospital work in the German Federal Republic.

Three national associations (*Genossenschaften*) have remained under the jurisdiction of the *Herrenmeister*: those of Hungary, France, and Finland. The Swedish and Dutch commanderies separated themselves from the Johanniterorden in 1920 and 1945, respectively, to become independent orders. In 1958 a series of conferences between the British, German, Dutch, and Swedish orders and the three associations on matters of common interest was inaugurated in the castle of Bubikon, near Zürich, an important Swiss commandery of the order in the Middle Ages, resulting in a formal alliance concluded in 1961.

BIBLIOGRAPHY.—Chief source is the archives in the Royal Malta Library, Valletta. Other collections of manuscripts are in the Vatican Library; the Palazzo Malta, Rome; and the library of the order at Clerkenwell, London. Chief published sources are ed. by J. Delaville le Roulx, *Cartulaire général des Hospitaliers de Saint-Jean de Jérusalem, 1100–1310*, 4 vol. (1894–1906); *see also* his *Les Hospitaliers en terre sainte et à Chypre, 1100–1310* (1904); E. J. King, *The Rule, Statutes and Customs of the Hospitallers, 1099–1310* (1934), *The Knights Hospitallers in the Holy Land* (1931), with H. Luke, *The Knights of St. John in the British Realm* (1967); E. W. Schermerhorn, *Malta of the Knights* (1929); E. E. Hume, "A Proposed Alliance Between the Order of Malta and the United States, 1794," *William and Mary College Quarterly Historical Magazine*, 2nd series, vol. 16, pp. 223–233 (1936), *Medical Work of the Knights Hospitallers of St. John of Jerusalem* (1940); J. Riley-Smith, *The Knights of St. John in Jerusalem and Cyprus, c. 1050–1310*, vol. 1 (1967).   (H. L.)

SAINT JOHN PERSE: see PERSE, SAINT JOHN.

SAINT JOHN RIVER, the largest river in New Brunswick, Can., discovered by De Monts and Champlain in 1604 and named after St. John the Baptist. It is 418 mi. long and drains a basin of 21,600 sq.mi., of which 14,000 are in the provinces of New Brunswick and Quebec, and the remainder in the state of Maine. The river rises in northwestern Maine and flows northeasterly to the New Brunswick border, whence it gradually turns southeastward and for 80 mi. forms the international boundary. Just above Grand Falls the river enters Canada and flows through New Brunswick into the Bay of Fundy at Saint John. The lower 81 mi. are tidal and navigable for large steamers as far as Fredericton. There are hydroelectric power developments at Grand Falls, Beechwood and Mactaquac on the St. John, as well as on its tributaries, the Tobique, Aroostook, and Madawaska rivers.   (C. W. RD.)

SAINT JOHN'S, the provincial capital of Newfoundland, Can., lies on the east coast of the island and is the most easterly city of the North American continent. The city's population in 1961 was 63,633 and that of the metropolitan area was 90,838. The people of St. John's are almost entirely of Irish and English origin. Nearly half are adherents of the Roman Catholic Church and the remainder belong to several Protestant churches, chiefly the Anglican and the United Church of Canada.

The city stands on the steep, western slope of its excellent land-locked harbour which opens suddenly in the lofty coast. The entrance, known as The Narrows, guarded by Signal hill (500 ft.) and South Side hills (620 ft.), is about 1,400 ft. wide, narrowing to 600 ft. between Pancake and Chain rocks.

At an early date the harbour of St. John's was recognized as one of the most outstanding in this part of North America and was used as a haven for fishing vessels. The earliest allusion to the name St. John's (from St. John the Baptist) was in a letter written in 1527 by an English ship captain who mentioned that he had stopped at the harbour and found Norman, Breton, and Portuguese ships anchored there. In early years settlement was discouraged by the English government in order to protect the fishery for the exploitation of the home fishermen (*see* NEWFOUNDLAND: *History*) and permanent settlement was not established until the beginning of the 17th century. In spite of this delay, St. John's is one of the oldest cities in North America. During its history frequent conflagrations swept through the town, destroying extensive areas.

St. John's occupies a most important position in the economic and cultural life of the province. Within the economic structure of Newfoundland the city is outstanding in retail and wholesale trade and is important also in service trade and performs a prominent role in transportation. Its substantial and varied commodity exchanges in the shipping trade are especially noteworthy. It is the major terminal point for rail, highway, and air transportation systems. (C. N. F.)

SAINT-JOHN'S-WORT, any low, shrubby plant of the genus *Hypericum* of the St.-John's-wort family (Hypericaceae), having usually yellow flowers, and opposite, often stalkless leaves that are dotted with transparent glands. Of over 300 species, widely distributed in temperate and tropical regions, more than 40 are found in the United States, chiefly in the eastern part. Among them are some cultivated for their showy flowers: *H. frondosum* (*aureum*), *H. densiflorum*, and *H. prolificum*, all from the eastern and southeastern states.

Over 50 species, mostly of Eurasian origin, are cultivated in British gardens, especially *H. perforatum* and the tutsan (*H. androsaemum*), both once widely used in medicine. Aaron's-beard, the rose of Sharon (*H. calycinum*) from the Mediterranean region, is naturalized in Great Britain and has evergreen leaves and very showy yellow flowers. Mostly perennials, all are easily grown from seed in any ordinary garden soil, preferably in a shady situation; in the U.S. many species are hardy north to New York and New England. (N. TR.)

SAINT JOSEPH, a city of southwestern Michigan, U.S., and seat of Berrien County, is situated on Lake Michigan at the mouth of the St. Joseph River about 60 mi. across the lake northeast of Chicago. In the 1670s both Father Jacques Marquette and René Robert Cavelier, Sieur de La Salle, visited the region; later the river's mouth became the site of a French military and trading post because of its strategic location. In the early 19th century the soil and climatic conditions of the area attracted settlers from New England and New York who early turned to fruit and grape cultivation. St. Joseph was incorporated as a village in 1834; its eastern portion gained incorporation as Benton Harbor (*q.v.*) in 1869; and in 1891 both communities received separate city charters. The two cities, connected by a wide thoroughfare and a ship canal, are integrated economically and culturally and are virtually a unit. In the mid-19th century St. Joseph's importance as a port city was curtailed by expanding midwestern railroad facilities. From that time it has continued to serve as a regional marketing centre for fruit growers, a resort with beaches and mineral springs, and an industrial centre specializing in canning and in manufacturing automotive parts, castings, and rubber goods. For comparative population figures *see* table in MICHIGAN: *Population*. (E. O. E.)

SAINT JOSEPH, a city of northwestern Missouri, U.S., on the east bank of the Missouri River, 55 mi. NW of Kansas City; the seat of Buchanan County. Rich in historical tradition, St. Joseph is known as the city "where Southern hospitality meets Western democracy." A post was established there in 1826 by Joseph Robidoux, a French-Canadian trapper from St. Louis. The site was regarded as a sacred area by local Indians, who called the river "road to paradise" and the high bluffs above "Blacksnake Hills." In 1836, by the Platte Purchase, the Sac, Fox, and Iowa tribes surrendered their lands and six counties were added to northwestern Missouri; subsequently there was an influx of white settlers. Robidoux laid out the town in 1843 and named it after his patron saint; it was made the county seat in 1846 and was chartered as a city in 1851. With the coming of the railroad era, complementing the already thriving steamboat traffic, St. Joseph appeared destined to become the metropolis of the trans-Mississippi West. In 1859 the Hannibal-St. Joseph, a landgrant railroad, was completed and in April 1860, it delivered the first mail pouch to the rider who launched the brief but spectacular history of the Pony Express (*q.v.*).

St. Joseph boomed as a major outfitting centre for emigrants headed for the gold fields of California and other points on the Pacific coast. Before and during the American Civil War the frontier town was on the fringe of the bloody guerrilla warfare in Kansas and Missouri and was visited by such border outlaws as W. C. Quantrill and Jesse James, who was killed in his home there in 1882. Between 1860 and 1900 St. Joseph enjoyed its greatest period of expansion but was eclipsed by Omaha, Neb., and Kansas City when transcontinental railroads passed it by. In the mid-20th century the city again grew fairly rapidly, partly by annexation (for comparative population figures *see* table in MISSOURI: *Population*). The population of the city in 1960 was 79,673 and of the standard metropolitan statistical area (Buchanan County) 90,581. Corn, tobacco, blue grass, small grains, livestock, and fruit are produced and marketed there. Major industries include meat-packing, milling, cereal and dairy products, clothing, foundry, machine-shop and electrical products, and wholesale distribution. The state mental hospital is in St. Joseph. (Jo. L. H.)

SAINT JOSEPH RIVER, the name of two rivers in the United States, both of which rise in south-central Michigan. The larger of the two flows generally westward for 210 mi. to empty into Lake Michigan at a point between Benton Harbor and St. Joseph, Mich. Midway in its course it swings southward into northern Indiana past the cities of Elkhart and South Bend. At Elkhart the average flow is 3,350 cu.ft. per sec. The maximum rate of flow, an average of 9,380 cu.ft. per sec., comes in February; the minimum flow, 620 cu.ft. per sec., in September. The St. Joseph has been dammed at Union City, Mich., for waterpower development. The river is also an important source of urban and industrial water supply.

The other St. Joseph River flows southward over 100 mi. through Michigan, Ohio, and Indiana to join the St. Marys River. The two form the Maumee River at Fort Wayne, Ind.; the Maumee in turn flows northeastward to empty into Lake Erie at Toledo. Except for Fort Wayne, there are no large cities in the St. Joseph basin. (R. R. D.)

SAINT JOSSE-TEN-NOODE (Flemish SINT-JOOST-TEN-NODE), a northeastern commune of Brussels (*q.v.*), Belg. Pop. (1961) 24,463. In the mid-19th century it changed from a rural area to a residential and commercial suburb of Brussels. The Botanical Gardens date from 1826 and the Charlier Museum was a patrician residence, bequeathed with its contents to the commune. The dukes of Burgundy had a castle there and royal processions entered the capital through the village. Charles Rogier (*q.v.*) lived there for 50 years and Charles de Bériot from 1841–68. It is a centre of the Belgian film industry. (Y. E. D. J.)

SAINT-JUST, LOUIS ANTOINE LÉON (1767–1794), French revolutionary, famous for his inflammatory speeches in the National Convention and for his rallying of the French Army by his missions, was born at Decize in the Nivernais on Aug. 25, 1767, the son of a cavalry captain. He studied at the College of the Oratorians at Soissons and later became a clerk to the public prosecutor of Soissons, completing his legal studies at the University of Reims in 1788. In May 1789 he published anonymously his romantic epic poem *Organt,* in which he satirized the *ancien régime.*

He was in Paris at the fall of the Bastille (*see* FRANCE: *History;* FRENCH REVOLUTION) and then was prominent in the politics of his home town, Blérancourt, near Soissons, becoming secretary to the municipality. Lieutenant colonel of the local national guard, he represented it at the Fête de la Fédération in Paris on July 14, 1790. He first expressed his admiration for Maximilien Robespierre (*q.v.*), with whom he was later closely associated, in a letter to Robespierre in August 1790.

Although elected, he was too young to sit in the Legislative Assembly, but on Sept. 5, 1792, he was elected as deputy for the Aisne to the National Convention; his maiden speech on Nov. 13 began his meteoric career. His speeches at the trial of Louis XVI (December 1792–January 1793) helped to defeat the demand for a plebiscite on the death sentence and for the postponement of the execution. In March he went to the Aisne and to the Ardennes to supervise recruiting for the war. On his return he opposed in the Convention and in the Jacobin Club the draft constitution proposed by the Girondins (*q.v.*) and advocated a legislature elected by universal suffrage and with absolute power over the executive. After the Girondin leaders had been arrested in the Convention on June 2, 1793, Saint-Just made a violent attack on them in his report of July 8, as spokesman for the Committee of Public Safety, which he had joined on May 30.

On Oct. 10 he gave his report stating that the government would remain revolutionary until peace was made. He was sent on Oct. 22 to the Army of the Rhine with Philippe Lebas, whose sister Henriette was Saint-Just's fiancée for a time, and he restored the morale of the troops and provided them with food and clothing. He imposed a forced loan on the rich of Strasbourg and Nancy, distributed relief to the poor, replaced the civic authorities, and brought to justice the extremists, including Johann (Euloge) Schneider, the public prosecutor of the Strasbourg revolutionary tribunal. These rigorous measures won him the support of the *sans-culottes* and contributed to the successes of the Army: the relief of Bitche and Landau (December) made the eastern frontier secure.

On 3 Pluviôse, year II (Jan. 22, 1794), he went on a mission to the Army of the North and on 1 Ventôse (Feb. 19) was elected president of the Convention. In his report of 8 Ventôse he justified the revolutionary government and the Terror, and the Convention adopted his proposals for the confiscation of suspects' property and for its distribution to the poor. During March 1794 Saint-Just supported Robespierre's attack on Jacques Hébert (*q.v.*) and took the leading role in the conviction of Georges Danton (*q.v.*). The decree of 27 Germinal (April 16), by which all those accused of conspiring against the republic were to be brought to the revolutionary tribunal at Paris, was also his work.

Again sent to the Army of the North, he led the attack at the victory of Fleurus. He was thought to have wanted to end the Terror, but as he was in Paris when the law of 22 Prairial (June 10) was drawn up, streamlining the revolutionary tribunal, he almost certainly approved of it and he gave continuous support to Robespierre during the crisis of Thermidor. The Convention decreed his arrest on 9 Thermidor (July 27, 1794), when he was prevented from making his prepared speech; after escaping he was captured in the Hôtel de Ville the next day and was guillotined on the Place de la Révolution (now the Place de la Concorde). His complete works, edited by C. Vellay, were published in two volumes in 1908, and his *Discours et rapports,* edited by A. Soboul, in 1957.

(MA. Bo.)

SAINT KILDA, the collective name for a group of seven islands and stacks lying 45 mi. W of Griminish Point, North Uist, Outer Hebrides, Inverness County, Scot. The largest island, Hirta, is 3 mi. by 2 mi. rising to 1,397 ft. (426 m.). The precipitous cliffs rise from deep water except at the southeast landing place. The group escaped glaciation and constitutes the most spectacular cliff scenery in Britain. Soay reaches 1,225 ft.; Boreray, 1,245 ft.; Dun, 576 ft.; Stac an Armin, 627 ft.; Stac Lee, 544 ft.; and Levenish, 185 ft. It is the premier seabird station of Britain with the largest gannetry in the world. Subspecies of wren and long-tailed field mouse have evolved on St. Kilda, and the Soay sheep is of Mouflon type. Once a possession of the Macleods of Dunvegan, St. Kilda was bought by the Marquis of Bute after evacuation of the Gaelic-speaking population (36) in 1930. The group now belongs to the National Trust for Scotland and is kept as a National Nature Reserve.

(F. F. DG.)

SAINT KITTS-NEVIS-ANGUILLA (SAINT CHRISTOPHER-NEVIS-ANGUILLA), a former British colony consisting of the three Caribbean islands St. Kitts (or St. Christopher), Nevis, and Anguilla, which changed its colonial status in February 1967 to one of free association with Great Britain, the islands as a group being granted full internal self-government, while Britain retained responsibility for defense and foreign affairs. Area 138 sq.mi. (357 sq.km.) including the islet of Sombrero. Pop. (1966 est.): St. Kitts 37,150; Nevis 15,072; Anguilla 5,395; total 57,617. The population is almost entirely Negro. The capital is Basseterre on St. Kitts.

St. Kitts is a long, narrow island with an area of 68 sq.mi. (176 sq.km.). It is well watered, fertile, and has a cool, healthful climate, drier than most West Indian islands. Temperatures vary from 62° to 92° F (16.6° to 33.3° C); annual rainfall is 55 in. (1,397 mm.). The island has a mountainous backbone of volcanic origin (Mt. Misery, 3,711 ft. [1,131 m.]). The narrow coastal plain, the skirts of the mountains, and the Basseterre Valley are devoted to the cultivation of sugarcane and cotton. Basseterre (pop. 15,579) on the southwest coast is the only port; Golden Rock Airport nearby provides services to other Caribbean islands and New York City. Most of the working population is employed on the sugar estates or in the sugar refinery at Basseterre.

To the southeast Nevis, also volcanic, separated from St. Kitts by a narrow channel, is almost circular and has a conical appearance (Nevis Peak, 3,596 ft. [1,096 m.]). Its area is 36 sq.mi. (93 sq.km.) and its population includes many small farmers. The chief crop is cotton, but some sugarcane is also grown. Charlestown, on the southwest coast, is the chief town and port, and an airfield provides services to other islands.

Anguilla, about 60 mi. (95 km.) NNW of St. Kitts, is a bare, flat island, with an area of 35 sq.mi. (91 sq.km.). Most of the farmers own their land. Stock raising, salt production, and fishing are the main industries, and Anguilla-built sloops are highly esteemed. There are two villages and an airstrip.

After the islands had attained the position of an associated state Anguilla complained of domination by the St. Kitts administration. In May 1967 the Anguillans ejected the St. Kitts police and set up their own council: in July they proclaimed their independence. A senior civil servant was sent to negotiate a political solution. Early in 1969 British troops and police occupied the island to put down a rebellion.

There are about 43 primary and 5 secondary schools, mostly government-operated, on the islands. Health facilities include 4 general hospitals and about 21 health centres. The principal exports are sugar, molasses, and cotton.

The islands were discovered and named by Christopher Columbus in 1493, and were colonized by the English in the 17th century. Sir Thomas Warner made the first English settlement in the West Indies on St. Kitts in 1623, and the indigenous Caribs were driven out in 1629. Divided for a time between the French and the English, the island was finally ceded to Britain in 1783. The great fortress on Brimstone Hill is an impressive example of British military architecture.

(R. To.; MI. W.)

SAINT LAURENT, LOUIS STEPHEN (1882–   ), Canadian statesman and Liberal prime minister (1948–57), was born on Feb. 1, 1882, at Compton, Que. He studied at St. Charles College, Sherbrooke, and at Laval University, Quebec. He was called to the bar at Quebec in 1905 and became one of Canada's leading lawyers, serving two terms as president of the Canadian Bar Association. On Dec. 10, 1941, he entered federal politics as minister of justice, succeeding Ernest Lapointe, leading representative of French-speaking Canadians in the Mackenzie King administration.

In the face of widespread opposition in French-speaking Canada, St. Laurent defended the government's limited use of military conscription in 1944. By his forthright attitude, he maintained Quebec's place in the wartime government and thereby avoided a serious split within the Canadian population. In the election of June 1945, his position was overwhelmingly endorsed by the electorate of his province. He took a leading part at the San Francisco conference (1945) that created the United Nations, and in 1946 became Canada's secretary of state for external affairs.

Despite a personal preference to return to his law practice, St. Laurent was persuaded to accept the leadership of the Liberal Party in August 1948, and succeeded Mackenzie King as prime minister on Nov. 15, 1948. He was one of the main architects of the North Atlantic Treaty Organization (q.v.). His government gave instant and substantial military support to the United Nations intervention in Korea in 1950. The St. Laurent government declined to support the British and French intervention at Suez in 1956, but took a leading part in establishing the United Nations emergency force to restore peace and order there. A firm believer in the Commonwealth of Nations, St. Laurent's influence contributed greatly to keeping India and Pakistan within that voluntary association of free nations. His bold initiative removed the obstacles to the joint construction of the St. Lawrence Seaway by Canada and the United States.

By the union of Newfoundland with Canada in 1949, the St. Laurent government completed the grand design of the fathers of confederation. His government was responsible for giving final jurisdiction to the Supreme Court of Canada, thereby ending appeals to the judicial committee of the United Kingdom Privy Council. He strengthened the unity and fostered the development of the Canadian nation by instituting measures for the equalization of provincial revenues, enlarged social security, grants to universities, and the establishment of the Canada council for the promotion of arts and letters.

After winning overwhelming victories in the 1949 and 1953 elections, the St. Laurent government was defeated by a narrow majority on June 10, 1957. He served as leader of the opposition until a national Liberal convention chose Lester B. Pearson to succeed him as Liberal leader in January 1958. He then retired from public life and resumed his law practice in the city of Quebec.

(D. C. T.)

SAINT-LAURENT, a suburban city of Quebec, Can., on the northwest side of Montreal Island; part of the Montreal metropolitan area. Industries include the manufacture of aircraft, railway cars, foundry products, chemicals, and textiles. Pop. (1961) 49,805. Founded in 1845 on the site of a mission which dated back to 1720, the village of Saint-Laurent became a town in 1893 and was incorporated as a city in 1955. In 1952, in an exchange with Montreal, Saint-Laurent ceded part of its eastern section to the larger city.

In 1954, after residential developments had nearly filled the available land, Saint-Laurent city annexed Saint-Laurent parish, thus quadrupling its area. (M. C. BA.)

SAINT LAWRENCE RIVER, the greatest North American river draining to the Atlantic coast. At its head is the Great Lakes basin which has a land and water area of about 291,900 sq.mi. (756,000 sq.km.) and discharges into the St. Lawrence an average yearly volume of 239,500 cu.ft. per sec. The tremendous storage capacity of the Great Lakes stabilizes the supply of water contributed to the river to an unusual extent; the maximum and minimum mean monthly outflow of the lakes since 1860 has ranged from 315,000 cu.ft. per sec. (May 1870) down to 154,000 cu.ft. per sec. (February 1936). This maximum-minimum ratio of about 2 to 1 makes the St. Lawrence one of the world's most dependable rivers.

While the St. Lawrence drainage area extends as far as the headwaters of the St. Louis River, a stream which flows into Lake Superior at its western extremity (Duluth, Minn.), the St. Lawrence River has its head at the eastern end of Lake Ontario. The river thus becomes the connecting link between the Great Lakes

basin and the Atlantic Ocean. It has, however, a number of major rivers which are direct tributaries—the Ottawa, Saint-Maurice, Saguenay, and Richelieu (draining Lake Champlain). The drainage area in Canada, excluding the Great Lakes section, is estimated by official sources as 198,000 sq.mi. (513,000 sq.km.).

In determining the length of the St. Lawrence River the figure arrived at depends upon the locality taken as the mouth. On many official maps and in the U.S. Navy's *Sailing Directions for the Gulf and River St. Lawrence*, it is extended as far seaward as the eastern part of the Gaspé Peninsula, where the west end of Anticosti Island serves as the transition point between the river and Gulf of St. Lawrence. From northern to southern shore is about 70 mi., and the distance to Lake Ontario at Kingston, Ont., is 725 statute miles. A more restrictive definition, one which is preferred in geographical terms, places the mouth between Pointe des Monts and Cap Chat on the northern and southern shores, respectively. This locality is about 595 mi. downstream from Lake Ontario. There the river is 25 mi. wide; seaward from this point the width increases rapidly as the left shore turns abruptly northward.

The St. Lawrence was discovered in 1535 when Jacques Cartier, a French explorer, entered what is now known as the Gulf of St. Lawrence via the Strait of Belle Isle. On Aug. 10, feast day of St. Lawrence (a Christian martyr who died Aug. 10, 258), Cartier discovered a bay on the mainland north of Anticosti Island, which he named for the saint. Noting the current in the strait which now bears his name, Cartier continued westward up the river until he reached the present site of Montreal. He referred to the river as the River of Canada but through usage it gradually became the St. Lawrence. No settlement was established along the river until 1599, when Pierre Chauvin settled Tadoussac at the mouth of the Saguenay. In 1608 Samuel de Champlain laid the foundation for Quebec, the first permanent settlement.

The St. Lawrence is one of the principal routes through the highlands of eastern North America and its course is the focal centre of one of Canada's most important economic and culture areas—the St. Lawrence lowlands. This area lies between the Laurentian Upland or Canadian Shield to the north and Appalachian Highlands and Adirondack Mountains on the south. It extends from Quebec city westward to the vicinity of the Thousand Islands near the head of the river. These islands mark the zone where the Precambrian rocks of the Canadian Shield extend south of the St. Lawrence and form the Adirondacks in New York State. About midway on the long axis of the lowland is Montreal; here the width of the lowland is about 70 mi. The area is underlain by sedimentary rocks—limestone, shale, and sandstone—in contrast to the older, harder rocks of the adjacent highlands. Following the retreat of the continental ice sheet of the Pleistocene period, the sea invaded the lowland and formed the Champlain Sea. Marine sediments deposited during this period of inundation produced deep, fertile soils over the lower levels of the lowland. The soil materials in the higher sections are of glacial origin including fluvioglacial outwash.

For purposes of analysis the St. Lawrence and its borderlands divide conveniently into three segments: the upper river (above Montreal), the middle river (Montreal to Quebec), and the lower river (the estuary).

The Upper River.—This section extends 182 mi. (293 km.) from Kingston, at the outlet of Lake Ontario, to Montreal. From its head to a point where it crosses the 45° parallel N, a distance of 114 mi., the St. Lawrence forms the boundary between the United States and Canada (New York State and the province of Ontario). The remainder of its course to the sea lies wholly in Canada. A former system of 14-ft. navigation canals and the present 27-ft. seaway, constructed to avoid the series of rapids in the river, are located entirely within this upper segment of the St. Lawrence. At Lake Ontario the surface elevation of the river is about 245 ft. (75 m.) above sea level and at Montreal it is about 20 ft. The international power dam and two control dams constructed in connection with the seaway development have eliminated some of the upper rapids, including the well-known Long Sault Rapids, and in their place is a broad man-made water body of about 100 sq.mi. (260 sq.km.) named Lake St. Lawrence. In the construction of this lake about 38,000 ac. (15,000 ha.) of land were inundated, and it was necessary to relocate several river-front communities. Flooding of the area began on July 1, 1958, and the new level was achieved within several days.

Downstream from Lake St. Lawrence and above Montreal the river broadens in two areas to form Lake St. Francis, about 28 mi. (45 km.) long, and Lake St. Louis, about 15 mi. long. To utilize the hydroelectric power potential resulting from a difference of about 82 ft. (25 m.) in the water level of these two lakes, a power canal 15 mi. long was completed in 1932. It later became part of the St. Lawrence Seaway (q.v.).

At the head of Lake St. Louis is the confluence of the Ottawa River, a stream which served as an outlet to the sea for the postglacial upper Great Lakes before rise of land to the north diverted their discharge to Lake Erie and to the present upper course of the St. Lawrence. Part of the Ottawa's flow discharges into the St. Lawrence below Montreal and thus forms an island on which the city of Montreal is located. In the St. Lawrence River at Montreal, about 500 ac. (200 ha.) of additional island area was created to provide space for the city's 1967 world's fair.

The Middle River.—Montreal developed at the head of navigation on the St. Lawrence—the point where further progress upstream was blocked by the Lachine Rapids. Completion of the St. Lawrence canals in the 1800s and the seaway in 1959 permitted small and medium-sized ocean vessels to continue past Montreal but the port remains the terminal point for the larger merchant ships of the world. A ship channel 35 ft. (11 m.) in depth extends from Montreal to a point 40 mi. below Quebec city. Of the 200 mi. (320 km.) of the middle river, about 113 mi. is dredged canal. Montreal is one of the great seaports of the world and is accessible for ocean vessels for about 8½ months of the year; overseas ships reinforced for ice navigation initiated winter service in January 1964.

From Montreal to Quebec, a distance of 160 mi. (256 km.), the St. Lawrence has a low gradient and a mean width of more than a mile. In the harbour of Montreal the elevation is 20 ft. (6 m.); about midway to Quebec, at Trois-Rivières (Three Rivers), mean sea level is reached. Trois-Rivières hence becomes the upstream limit of tidal conditions. About 45 mi. downstream from Montreal is the port of Sorel, at the mouth of the Richelieu River and at the head of Lake St. Peter. The Richelieu-Lake Champlain route provides a shallow-draft waterway which connects with the Hudson River. In the large impounded section of the St. Lawrence called Lake St. Peter the river widens to more than 8 mi. (13 km.) but has a natural depth of only about 11 ft. (3 m.). At the head of the lake, near Sorel, is a delta with many islands formed from river deposits.

Trois-Rivières, about 77 mi. (124 km.) above Quebec, is at the mouth of the Saint-Maurice River. This river valley is Canada's leading pulp- and paper-producing region, and Trois-Rivières is the capital of this industry. By the 1950s this ocean port handled more traffic than Quebec. Below Trois-Rivières the St. Lawrence follows an irregular course and narrows to less than ¾ mi. at Quebec bridge, about 7 mi. upstream from the city, and between Quebec and Levis. Because of the narrowness of the river, the ebb current has a velocity up to 5.8 knots and the flood current 4.7 knots.

The Lower River.—At the head of the estuary section of the St. Lawrence stands the city of Quebec. In the language of the Algonkian Indians its name means "where the river narrows." The city, which is the capital of Canada's largest province, is divided into an Upper Town and Lower Town by steep cliffs, and commanding a site 340 ft. (104 m.) high is the famous old fortress named the Citadel.

Tidal action is increased in the long funnel-shaped estuary, with the result that spring tides in Quebec Harbour rise from 16 ft. to 19 ft. (5 m. to 6 m.) and neap tides about 13 ft. The regular navigation season of eight to nine months has been supplemented since 1959 by all-winter ocean vessel service. The length of the estuary to Pointe des Monts is 253 statute mi. (407 km.); to Anticosti Island is an additional 130 mi. St. Paul Island in Cabot Strait is 620 statute (538 nautical) mi. from Quebec.

Below Quebec the St. Lawrence has a littoral lowland which is more extensive on the south shore, with a resulting greater population and agricultural development than on the narrow, discontinuous lowland on the opposite shore. The Island of Orleans, near the head of the estuary, narrows the river into two channels, the main one lying to the south of the island. Waters of the St. Lawrence are considered fresh to the lower end of this island. At Les Escoumins, on the north shore and about 150 mi. (241 km.) below Quebec, is the pilotage station for the St. Lawrence River. Pilotage is optional but payment of the fee is compulsory.

Along the north shore of the lower estuary several significant commercial ports have been developed. Baie Comeau, a producer of paper and aluminum, has become an important transshipping point for U.S. and Canadian export grains since operation of a huge elevator started in 1961. To the northeast, on Sept-Iles Bay, the first of three ports for shipping iron ore from the vast Quebec-Labrador deposits opened in 1954. This was Sept-Iles (Seven Islands), the terminus of a railroad extending 360 mi. (579 km.) northward. Port Cartier, another iron ore port about 40 mi. to the west, opened in 1961. The third ore port was Pointe Noire, on the west shore of Sept-Iles Bay, which began operations in 1965. The St. Lawrence Seaway has played a vital role in enhancing the competitive position of Canadian ores for steel plants in the Great Lakes area.

The fisheries of the St. Lawrence are of relatively minor importance compared with those of the Maritime Provinces and Newfoundland. Nevertheless, the river and estuary remain well known for several saltwater species which frequent these waters at certain periods of the year. Sea sturgeon abound in the estuary; there is intensive commercial fishing from the Island of Orleans to Rivière du Loup. Atlantic salmon spawn in the many tributaries of the St. Lawrence seaward of Île aux Coudres. The American eel (*Anguilla rostrata*) is among the most important species caught in the fresh or brackish waters of the river. Other prominent species in the lower river and estuary are catfish, cod, herring, and smelt.

The St. Lawrence has two major hydroelectric power developments in its upper course. The Beauharnois Dam has an installed capacity of 2,145,000 hp. The international power dam, constructed jointly by the state of New York and province of Ontario concurrently with the seaway development, has an installed capacity of 2,472,000 hp.

See also GREAT LAKES, THE; SAINT LAWRENCE SEAWAY; and references under "Saint Lawrence River" in the Index.

BIBLIOGRAPHY.—*Sailing Directions for the Gulf and River St. Lawrence,* U.S. Navy Hydrographic Office (1951); A. W. Currie, *Economic Geography of Canada* (1945); D. F. Putnam (ed.), *Canadian Regions* (1952); P. Camu, E. P. Weeks, and Z. W. Sametz, *Economic Geography of Canada* (1964); Henry Beston, *The St. Lawrence* (1942); W. Toye, *The St. Lawrence* (1959); *Canada Year Book* (annual); *Fishes of Quebec,* "Album Series," Quebec Department of Fisheries.

(A. G. BT.)

SAINT LAWRENCE SEAWAY, a major improvement of the St. Lawrence Waterway which made a highly important interior section of North America accessible for the first time to deep-draft, oceangoing vessels, and also permitted the large Great Lakes freighters to extend their range of operations to the ports on the lower St. Lawrence. The waterway was completed for the opening of the navigation season on the St. Lawrence River and Great Lakes in April 1959 and was dedicated June 26, 1959.

The project which brought about this development was a joint undertaking of the governments of the United States and Canada to provide 27-ft. (8-m.) navigation channels between Montreal and Lake Erie. A related United States project, which required widening and deepening of the connecting channels of the Great Lakes (the Detroit, St. Clair, and St. Marys rivers) to make them commensurate in depth with those of the seaway, was essentially completed in 1964.

Strictly speaking, the seaway is the St. Lawrence River portion of the waterway, but the Welland Ship Canal was officially incorporated into the project through legislation, and improvements were made in it as a part of the total seaway undertaking. However, the broader concept of the "seaway," and one which is in general usage, includes the entire system of lakes, locks, canals, and rivers which have converted over 6,600 mi. (10,621 km.) of mainland Great Lakes shore line of the United States and Canada into another seacoast.

History of Navigation on the St. Lawrence. Since 1535, when the explorer Jacques Cartier was turned back from his quest for the Northwest Passage by the Lachine Rapids of the St. Lawrence, men have made plans and built works to provide a through waterway from the Atlantic to the "inland seas."

Segments of the pre-seaway canal system were begun in the early 1700s. After union of the provinces of Upper and Lower Canada in 1841, work was undertaken to deepen all of the canals along the St. Lawrence route to 9 ft. (3 m.) and the project was completed in 1848. Following the Acts of Confederation in 1867 the Canadian government decided upon a program for the improvement of the canal system to a depth of 14 ft., with locks to be 270 ft. by 45 ft. The enlargement and deepening was carried out in stages, and the canal system was opened for traffic in 1901, although some work was not completed until 1913. Improvement of the Welland Canal, a 27-mi. (43-km.) waterway built to overcome the 326-ft. (99-m.) difference in the levels of Lakes Erie and Ontario, was carried out concurrently with work on the St. Lawrence canals and a 14-ft. (4-m.) channel was completed in 1887. The Welland Ship Canal (q.v.), completed in 1932, was built with a controlling depth of 25 ft. (8 m.); it included eight locks which had dimensions equal to those subsequently built as a part of the seaway project.

The 14-ft. St. Lawrence canals system as it existed for over a half century prior to the seaway was entirely a Canadian facility. To overcome the obstacles to navigation in the 112-mi. (180-km.) section of the river between Montreal and the head of the Galops Rapids, a series of six canals was built along the north shore to bypass eight rapids. The canal segments totaled 47 mi. (76 km.) in length, and 21 locks accounted for a total lift of 209 ft. (64 m.) of the 225-ft. (69-m.) difference in river levels between Montreal and Lake Ontario. The maximum lift of any single lock was 23.5 ft. Lock dimensions varied slightly, the smallest, and hence the controlling lock for ship dimensions, being 43 ft. 8 in. wide and 270 ft. long, with a depth over the lock sills restricting the draft to

14 ft. The maximum overall length for a vessel using this lock was 259 ft. The maximum cargo which could be carried through this canal system was about 1,600 tons for ocean vessels and about 2,800 tons for "canallers," vessels especially designed for transporting bulk cargo through the canals. Ocean vessels of the size using this waterway could load to their maximum drafts of about 20–21 ft. from Montreal eastward, since the St. Lawrence Ship Channel, with a depth of 35 ft., extended up the river to this port.

International negotiations toward establishing a deep waterway from the sea to the Great Lakes date back at least to 1905 when an International Waterways Commission was created. After lack of U.S. congressional approval prevented international agreements in 1932 and again in 1941, the governments of Canada and of the province of Ontario began to plan for a joint seaway and power project. In 1951 the (Canadian) St. Lawrence Seaway Authority was established. Negotiations followed which resulted in agreement for the joint development of power in the International Rapids section by Ontario and New York State power agencies. Legal obstacles followed, but in June 1954 the U.S. Supreme Court upheld the action of the Federal Power Commission in granting a license to the Power Authority of the State of New York.

Meanwhile, bills were introduced in 1953 in Congress to provide for United States participation in construction of the seaway. Enactment of the Wiley-Dondero Bill in May 1954 created the Saint Lawrence Seaway Development Corporation to construct part of the seaway in United States territory and authorized the agency to issue revenue bonds up to $105,000,000 to finance its activities. In 1957 the amount was increased to $140,000,000. The two public power entities began their joint project in August 1954, and soon thereafter the work of the two seaway authorities was started.

The total cost for construction of the dual-purpose undertaking, which was over $1,000,000,000, marked it as the greatest peacetime task that two nations had ever jointly attempted.

The Present Seaway.—The seaway project in the St. Lawrence River consisted of constructing seven locks, dredging long sections of channel, constructing protective dikes, digging canals, and raising and building bridges. The related power project re-

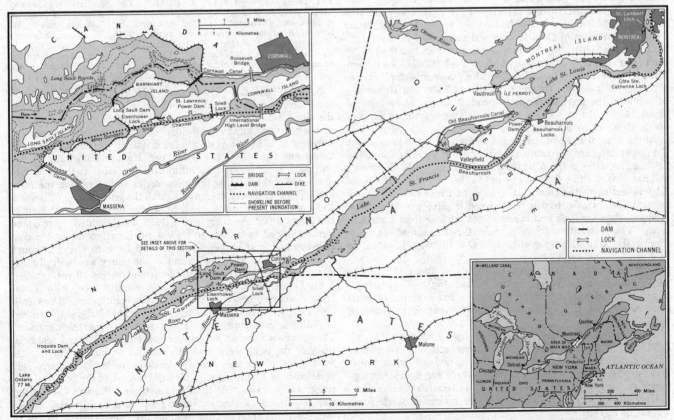

THE ST. LAWRENCE SEAWAY, SHOWING NAVIGATION CHANNEL, LOCKS, AND POWER PROJECTS OF ST. LAWRENCE RIVER PORTION

quired construction of a power dam and two control dams, and the relocation of several towns, railroads, and highways as a result of flooding areas bordering part of the river course.

Limitations on the maximum size of ships operating through the seaway are imposed by channel depth, lock dimensions, and overhead clearances. The 27-ft. (8 m.) depth restricts vessel drafts to 25.5 ft. for minimum safe clearance. All locks are 800 ft. long and 80 ft. wide and have a 30-ft. depth over the sills. Because of these dimensions, traffic is limited to ships 730 ft. (223 m.) in length with a beam of 75 ft. (23 m.). Minimum clearance for fixed bridges is 120 ft. above water level. The seaway dimensions permit oceangoing vessels with cargo capacities up to 8,000 or 9,000 short tons to enter the Great Lakes and allow the transit of bulk-cargo "lakers" with capacities of 27,000–28,000 tons.

The seaway route from Montreal to the head of Lake St. Francis (76 mi. [122 km.]) is wholly in Canada, and all works were carried out by the Canadian seaway agency. A canal about 16 mi. long leads from Montreal Harbour to Lake St. Louis, and two locks—St. Lambert and Côte Sainte-Catherine—overcome a drop of about 45 ft. (14 m.) in water levels between these two areas. At the head of Lake St. Louis the seaway bypasses the Beauharnois power dam to enter a 16-mi. power canal. Two locks—the Upper and Lower Beauharnois—each have a lift of approximately 40 ft. The power canal, which extends to Lake St. Francis, was completed in 1932 with a navigable depth of 27 ft. in anticipation of the seaway.

The international boundary extends along the St. Lawrence River from the head of Lake St. Francis to Lake Ontario. At the lower end of this section, the seaway route is constructed through United States territory in order to bypass the power dam, a structure divided evenly by the international boundary. The United States navigation works consist of the 10-mi. Wiley-Dondero Ship Channel and two locks—Bertrand H. Snell (lower, 45-ft. [14-m.]) lift and Dwight D. Eisenhower (upper, 40-ft.) lift. These facilities were opened July 4, 1958. The upper end of the ship channel terminates in Lake St. Lawrence. This head pond was created by flooding about 38,000 ac. (15,000 ha.) of land above the power dam.

The major structure in the $600,000,000 power project is a dam with 32 generators (16 belonging to each power entity), which have a total installed turbine capacity of 2,472,000 hp. (generator capacity 1,824,000 kw.). The half owned by the Hydro-Electric Power Commission of Ontario is named the Robert H. Saunders-St. Lawrence Generating Station, and the portion constructed by the Power Authority of the State of New York is called the Robert Moses Power Dam. In addition to the power structure, it was necessary to build two control dams—Long Sault and Iroquois—to maintain the level of the head pond at an operating level of about 242 ft. (74 m.) above sea level. This provides a drop of about 81–85 ft. to the level below the dam.

At the head of Lake St. Lawrence, about 25 mi. (40 km.) above the power dam, are the Iroquois Dam and the Iroquois Canal and Lock. The latter is the fifth Canadian lock on the St. Lawrence and has a lift of 1 to 6 ft. (.3 to 1.8 m.) to the level of the Thousand Islands section of the river. It was the first seaway lock opened to commercial traffic, having been placed in service in May 1958. Iroquois Dam controls and regulates the outflow from Lake Ontario. The International Joint Commission has agreed on maintaining this lake at an elevation of 242.8 to 246.8 ft. (74.0 to 75.2 m.).

From the Iroquois facilities to Lake Ontario, about 77 mi. (124 km.), is the Thousand Islands section of the seaway. The improvements required were channel enlargement and lowering of scattered rock shoals. Both the power and seaway entities participated in this work.

The Welland Ship Canal entrance on Lake Ontario is 157 mi. (253 km.) W of the head of the St. Lawrence River. Deepening of the canal channel to 27 ft. (8 m.) was carried out by the Canadian seaway agency. The eight locks—three are double for upbound and downbound traffic—required no alteration to serve deepdraft vessels. A project for twinning the remaining single locks was begun in 1964.

Tolls for use of the seaway are used to liquidate the cost of the project within a 50-year period as required by legislation. The toll rates established were based on an estimated total cost of $471,-000,000 (U.S., $131,000,000; Canada, $340,000,000) at the time the project was completed. The composite toll system is based partly on the gross registered tonnage of the ship and partly on the actual cargo tonnage. The division of the toll revenues for transit between Montreal and Lake Ontario is 71% to Canada and 29% to the United States. All tolls derived from transit of the Welland Ship Canal accrue to Canada. Pleasure craft and passenger vessels also are assessed for transit of any segment.

The seaway's primary economic benefit is to the shipping industry; upon its completion the size of general-cargo and bulk-cargo vessels which could utilize the upper St. Lawrence River route was increased greatly, and this brought about a marked gain in annual cargo tonnage. From a pre-seaway peak of 13,500,000 tons, reached in 1956, the traffic volume of the new facility advanced steadily during the first five years of operation, rising from 20,600,000 (1959) to 39,300,000 tons (1964).

Bulk commodities account for about 90% of the cargo tonnage of the St. Lawrence River section of the seaway, the leading products being iron ore moving westward and grains eastbound. Much of the grain shipped to eastern Canadian ports in lake freighters ultimately is transshipped overseas. Direct commerce between the Great Lakes ports and overseas areas accounts for about one-quarter of the seaway's cargo tonnage.

From some Great Lakes ports the seaway route to western Europe is shorter than the transatlantic routes from the U.S. East Coast, and all of the lake ports are hundreds of miles nearer Europe than are the Gulf Coast ports. Ice conditions limit the navigation season on the seaway to about 240–250 days, from early April to early December.

See also GREAT LAKES, THE; SAINT LAWRENCE RIVER; and references under "Saint Lawrence Seaway" in the Index.

BIBLIOGRAPHY.—The Seaway Handbook, The St. Lawrence Seaway Authority and the Saint Lawrence Seaway Development Corporation (1964); Traffic Report of the St. Lawrence Seaway, The St. Lawrence Seaway Authority and the Saint Lawrence Seaway Development Corporation (annual); Canal Statistics, Dominion Bureau of Statistics (annual); F. J. Bullock, Ships and the Seaway (1959); Carleton Mabee, The Seaway Story (1961); T. L. Hills, The St. Lawrence Seaway (1959); W. R. Willoughby, The St. Lawrence Waterway: a Study in Politics and Diplomacy (1961); P. Camu, E. P. Weeks, and Z. W. Sametz, Economic Geography of Canada (1964); St. Lawrence Seaway Manual, Senate Document No. 165, 83rd Congress, 2nd Session (1955); Annual Report, Saint Lawrence Seaway Development Corporation (annual); Changing Shipping Patterns on the St. Lawrence Seaway, U.S. Department of Agriculture (September 1963).   (A. G. Br.)

SAINT LEGER (SENTLEGER), **SIR ANTHONY** (c. 1496–1559), English lord deputy (1540–48, 1553–56) of Ireland, was the eldest son of Ralph St. Leger, of Ulcombe, Kent. Educated on the continent and at Cambridge, he was a member of a commission sent in 1535 to investigate the condition of Calais. After the defeat and execution (1537) of Lord Thomas Fitzgerald, he was sent as a commissioner to intimidate the Irish Parliament into passing bills confiscating the monasteries and increasing the revenue. The commission also investigated the general state of Ireland. Returning to England in 1538, St. Leger became a gentleman of the king's privy chamber, and in 1539 was knighted. Appointed lord deputy of Ireland in July 1540, St. Leger continued the conciliatory policy of his predecessor, Lord Leonard Grey; although Grey had been recalled and executed, the policy was basically that advised by Henry VIII to Lord Lieutenant Surrey 20 years earlier.

St. Leger, probably the most able English viceroy in Tudor Ireland, secured peace for the succeeding eight years. The Geraldine League broke up after the young Gerald Fitzgerald, 11th earl of Kildare, was smuggled (1540) to safety on the continent. Thenceforward, public submissions to Henry VIII and renunciations of the pope were made by various prominent chiefs. On St. Leger's advice they were given titles to lands formerly held in defiance of English law. This has been called the policy of surrender and re-grant. At the Parliament in Ireland in 1542 Henry was recognized as king of Ireland and not, as hitherto, merely lord (by papal grant) as had been his predecessors since Henry II. St. Leger, however, like Grey, was the subject of Dublin intrigues, but accusations against him in 1544 proved unsuccessful.

Early in Edward VI's reign St. Leger was recalled, his moderate policy being abandoned for one of aggression. But this rough policy's shortsightedness became evident and he was again restored for the last years of the reign of Edward VI and the first of Mary I. His moderating influence was successful but Mary then appointed as deputy Thomas Radcliffe, Viscount Fitzwalter (later earl of Sussex), with orders to reconcile Ireland with Rome, drive the Scots from Ulster, and plant military colonies in Leix and Offaly. St. Leger probably had little sympathy with the old faith or the new policy. After his recall he was accused of being accessory to alleged financial defalcations by the former vice-treasurer, Sir William Brabazon, but he died at Ulcombe on March 16, 1559, before the investigations were completed. (R. D. Es.)

SAINT LEONARDS, EDWARD BURTENSHAW SUGDEN, 1st Baron (1781–1875), lord chancellor of Great Britain, was born on Feb. 12, 1781, the son of a hairdresser of Duke Street, Westminster. After practising for some years as a conveyancer, he was called to the bar by Lincoln's Inn in 1807, having already published his well-known *Practical Treatise of the Law of Vendors and Purchasers of Estates* (14th edition, 1862). His parliamentary career was notable for his opposition to the Reform Bill of 1832. He was appointed solicitor general in 1829, and was lord chancellor of Ireland in 1835 and again from 1841 to 1846. Under Lord Derby's first administration in 1852 he became lord chancellor as Lord St. Leonards. He devoted himself with energy and vigour to the reform of the law; in 1855 he was offered the great seal again, but had to refuse. He was learned and lucid, though inclined to be waspish and overbearing. He died at Thames Ditton on Jan. 20, 1875. He was the author of various important legal publications, many of which passed through several editions.

See J. B. Atlay, *Lives of the Victorian Chancellors,* vol. ii (1906); E. Manson, *The Builders of Our Law, etc.,* 2nd ed. (1904).

SAINT-LÔ, capital town of the *département* of Manche, northwestern France, stands on the right bank of the Vire 48.5 mi. (78 km.) SSE of Cherbourg by road. Pop. (1962) 14,884. The town was almost completely destroyed in heavy fighting after the Allied landings in June 1944, being taken by U.S. forces on July 18. Its reconstruction, begun in 1948, included restoration of medieval ramparts (revealed by the bombardment) overlooking the Vire Valley. The Gothic Cathedral of Notre-Dame (14th–17th centuries) has also been restored. The 450-bed France–United States Memorial Hospital, designed by the U.S. architect Paul Nelson, was inaugurated in 1956. Saint-Lô is an administrative centre, the seat of a *préfecture,* and a market town. Light industry, chiefly the processing of local agricultural produce, has been developed. There is a large horse breeding farm.

Called Briovera in Gallo-Roman times, Saint-Lô owes its present name to Laudus, bishop of Coutances (d. 565). In the Middle Ages it was an important fortress and a centre of the weaving industry. In 1574, having embraced Calvinism, it was stormed by the Catholics. In 1796 it replaced Coutances as capital of its *département.* (Y. Nc.)

SAINT-LOUIS, a town in the Republic of Senegal and former administrative capital of the French West African territories of Senegal and Mauritania. Pop. (1960) 48,840, including about 1,140 Europeans. Saint-Louis is 163 mi. (262 km.) NNE of Dakar by rail and lies on a narrow island near the right (west) bank, and 13 mi. (21 km.) from the mouth, of the Senegal River, which is there separated from the sea by the Langue de Barbarie sandspit. The island is linked to the mainland by the Faidherbe road bridge, which has an opening span at the western end, and with the suburbs on the Langue by two other bridges. The seaport, now in decline, is along the eastern shore of the island, the river port on the western. Around the square in the town centre are the Roman Catholic church, the buildings of the former administration of Senegal, and European shops. The town has spread to both banks of the river. The part on the Langue facing the island has wider streets, where the houses of the European community, around the buildings of the former administration of Mauritania, contrast with the thatched huts forming the fishing

villages of N'Dar Toute and Guet N'Dar. Sor on the mainland has a European quarter along the river and African villages extending toward the marshes; it is the terminus of the railway from Dakar. From the airfield 2½ mi. NE scheduled services connect with Dakar and with Nouackchott, Mauritania. Saint-Louis has lost the importance it had as a capital, and as a seaport has been eclipsed by Dakar, but it remains an important trade centre whose development grows with the agricultural expansion in the Senegal valley. Founded in 1659, it was the first French settlement in West Africa. (J. D.)

SAINT LOUIS, the chief city of Missouri, U.S., 200 years old in 1964, is a mid-continental focal point of transport and manufacture. The incorporated area extends almost 20 mi. on the west bank of the Mississippi River, within 3½ mi. of the mouth of the Missouri River on the north. St. Louis is the central city of a standard metropolitan statistical area (SMSA) of 4,119 sq.mi., comprising, in addition to the city itself, the separately established St. Louis County, with 98 incorporated communities, and St. Charles, Franklin, and Jefferson counties in Missouri as well as Madison and St. Clair counties in Illinois. Among the separately incorporated Missouri municipalities in the metropolitan area are Florissant, University City, Kirkwood, Clayton, St. Charles, and Webster Groves. For further information on these, and on Illinois cities in the metropolitan area, see *Government,* below.

Migration from the inner city is reflected in the population, which declined from 856,796 in 1950 (when it was eighth in population among U.S. cities) to 750,026 in 1960 (ranking it tenth); in 1967 (est.) it had declined further, to 699,000. The population of the metropolitan area in 1960 was 2,060,103; after the area was considerably expanded in 1963, the population of the metropolitan area rose to 2,345,000 (1967 est.). *See also Population Characteristics,* below.

History.—*French Period.*—The original site of St. Louis was a shelf of riverfront under a bluff, bordered by a wide prairie to which the community later spread. The location was chosen by Pierre Laclède Liguest, junior partner in a fur-trading company, organized in New Orleans, which had obtained the exclusive right to trade with the Missouri River Indians and with those west of the Mississippi above the Missouri. The monopoly was granted by the French director-general of Louisiana, who had not yet been informed that the territory had been ceded to Spain in 1762; it was withdrawn by the Spanish government in 1765 but by that time Laclède was already well established and he and his successors long remained important in the fur trade. The site for the community was well chosen for trade: downstream over 1,000 mi. was New Orleans, La., already a thriving commercial centre and a major fur market; the Great Lakes, Detroit, Mich., and Montreal, Que., were accessible by the Illinois River, entered 38 mi. upstream; the Ohio, joining the Mississippi 180 mi. to the south, was to become important later as a route for settlers from the east.

The village was named by Laclède for Louis IX, the crusader king of France. Clearing of the site began Feb. 15, 1764, under the direction of Auguste Chouteau, destined to become a leading citizen, though then only in his 14th year. Settlers in addition to the original party began arriving almost immediately; the treaty of 1763, ending the French and Indian War, had given Great Britain all the territory east of the Mississippi and many of the French residents of Cahokia and other Illinois villages began to cross the river to the new outpost rather than live under British rule. On the invitation of Laclède, Capt. Louis St. Ange de Bellerive, the French-Canadian commandant of the surrendered Fort de Chartres, brought over his garrison of 20 men and assumed administrative duties that Spain did not take over until 1770, when the first Spanish lieutenant governor of Upper Louisiana arrived.

Spanish Period.—The change in administrations did not significantly alter the course of the city's history or make any particular impress upon its culture, which remained predominantly French until large numbers of Americans arrived in the 19th century. Laclède died in 1778 and most of his functions fell upon Auguste Chouteau and his younger brother, Pierre Chouteau. The fur trade was a profitable business, with furs, acquired in exchange for supplies and showy articles of trifling value, bringing as much as 500% profit overseas. Spain's sympathy with the American Revolution drew an attack on St. Louis in 1780 by a Sioux war party under British auspices. This was driven off by a garrison of 29 Spanish soldiers and 281 residents, who had been warned in time to prepare for the attack. Except for such isolated incidents the community had a peaceful life; close and generally friendly relations were maintained with the Indians, and visiting chiefs often pitched their tepees in the gardens of their business hosts. In 1788 the Mississippi was cleared of pirates. The increased trade made St. Louis the centre of wealth and culture in the upper valley, in spite of its isolation; although by 1800 its population was still somewhat less than 1,000, some of its homes had good libraries and furniture, glass and china brought from France.

American Period.—Under the Louisiana Purchase (*q.v.*), St. Louis passed from France to the U.S. (the territory having previously been retroceded to France in 1800). On March 10, 1804, Capt. Amos Stoddard of the U.S. Army officially took possession of Upper Louisiana for the U.S. In 1804 Congress created the district of Louisiana, with St. Louis as district headquarters; in 1805 the territory of Louisiana was created, with St. Louis again the seat of government; and in 1812 the territory of Missouri was created, with St. Louis still the territorial capital. It was incorporated as a town in 1809. Population growth was slow; by 1815 it probably did not exceed 2,600, and in 1821, when Missouri was admitted to the union, there were 621 buildings and a population of 5,600. In 1822 St. Louis was incorporated as a city by the state legislature. As a result of urban-rural friction St. Louis ceased to be the capital upon the coming of statehood.

After the Louisiana Purchase, St. Louis became the crossroad of westward expansion of the U.S. and was also the starting point for exploring parties, one of the best known being that of Meriwether Lewis and William Clark in 1804–06. Jefferson Barracks on the Mississippi became an important military post; among the officers stationed there were U. S. Grant, Robert E. Lee and Jefferson Davis. Early in the 19th century fur trading, which had been carried on mostly by individual traders, began to be done by companies. In 1809 the Missouri Fur Company was organized by William Clark, Manuel Lisa, Pierre and Auguste Chouteau, Sylvestre Labadie and others, and a branch of John Jacob Astor's American Fur Company was established in the city in 1822.

In the War of 1812 the settlement raised 500 mounted rangers to patrol a cordon of 22 stations or family blockhouses along a 75-mi. line from Fort Bellefontaine to Kaskaskia, thus confining Indian forays to petty pilfering and raids on isolated homesteads. In the Mexican War of 1846 young St. Louisans volunteered enthusiastically, interest being heightened by a well-developed trade in mules and silver with the southwest. Cholera struck the city in 1832 and a recurrence in 1849 cost more than 4,000 lives. Fire spreading from burning steamboats made 1849 a year of disaster along the waterfront as well, hundreds of buildings being destroyed; this area, however, was rebuilt more substantially, with wider and better streets. In spite of these reverses, the census of 1850 showed a population of 77,860.

The American Civil War and Afterward.—In a border state where slavery was legalized, St. Louis was bitterly divided throughout the Civil War and was kept under martial law. Although early settlers had come mainly from Virginia, the Carolinas, Tennessee and Kentucky, they were followed by New Englanders and other northerners who, with the vigorous support of German-born residents, swung the balance to the Union side. A state-wide delegate convention held in St. Louis early in 1861 voted against secession and called for peaceful adjustment, impossible after the firing on Fort Sumter. Gov. Claiborne F. Jackson, having rejected President Lincoln's call for troops from Missouri, set up Camp Jackson in the neighbourhood of Olive and Grand avenues and assembled 800 militiamen. Meantime, discovery of Confederate arms shipments labeled "ale" and "marble" raised fear of an attack on the large Federal arsenal. Suspecting disaffection among regular army officers, Capt. Nathaniel Lyon supplemented a small Federal force by home guards made up largely of German voters who had been organized in political marching clubs during Lincoln's presidential campaign. Camp Jackson surrendered without bloodshed until pistol shots from a crowd of spectators drew fire from the raw recruits, leaving about 15 dead, including some of the captive militiamen, and 5 more mortally injured. Sympathy was further alienated from the Union cause the following day, May 11, when more newly enlisted "Wide Awakes," excited by a pistol shot killing one of their marchers, wheeled and fired down a city street, killing four of their own number and two civilians. Only the return of Gen. W. S. Harney, who marched four regiments of regulars into the heart of the city, restored order and stemmed a rush to leave the community.

War orders for clothing and supplies gave impetus to the city's commercial growth, already accelerated by the building of railroads in the 1850s. An earlier stimulus to the economy had been steamboat traffic, beginning in 1817 and declining by 1870. The city also developed as an outfitting point for trade with the southwest and the 1849 California gold rush. In the ten years up to 1870 population almost doubled, reaching 310,864. Eads Bridge across the Mississippi, completed in 1874, gave access to the city for trains from Cincinnati; previously passengers from the east had been ferried. A world's fair, the Louisiana Purchase Exposition, was held in St. Louis in 1904. The city grew steadily in the late 19th and early 20th centuries, with both commerce and industry becoming increasingly important. World Wars I and II stimulated industrial development of the area. Other modern developments are discussed in *Government*, below.

Historic Sites.—A permanent Jefferson National Expansion Memorial, administered by the National Park Service since 1935, was begun with the clearing of derelict buildings from 40 blocks along the riverfront. It includes, on the old levee, the 630-ft. stainless-steel arch designed by Eero Saarinen and symbolizing the gateway to the west. The observation chamber, 8 ft. wide and 65 ft. long, overlooks the city and the riverfront's tourist, recreational, residential and business development, including Busch Memorial Sports Stadium and a Spanish pavilion from the 1964–65 New York World's Fair. The Old Cathedral of St. Louis of France dates from 1831–34. The Old Courthouse of 1839, now a historical museum with dioramas of early events, contains the courtroom of the Dred Scott case, and around the high dome are frescoes by Carl Wimar, a frontier artist.

Population Characteristics.—From the beginning St. Louis has been a cosmopolitan community, indicating the varieties of its heritages by wildly acclaiming the marquis de La Fayette on his visit in 1825, welcoming the Hungarian patriot Lajos Kossuth in 1852, and firing a 100-gun salute on the 100th anniversary of the birth of the German poet Schiller in 1859. The earliest settlers were French Creoles from New Orleans, French Canadians and a handful of Spaniards; after 1804 Americans began settling in the area and soon outnumbered the French. In the 19th century Germans became most numerous among the foreign born, their influx starting in the 1830s in response to glowing reports sent home by Gottfried Duden, a pioneering Prussian. Most numerous after the Germans were the Irish, and after them the British. In the population shift in the middle years of the 20th century a part of the outward movement from the city was compensated for by an influx from rural areas, including a large number of Negroes from the south. The nonwhite proportion of the population increased from 13.4% in 1940 to 36% by 1965, including 242,000 in the city and only 29,000 in St. Louis County, about 3%.

Government.—By a charter of 1876, the city of St. Louis was established as a unit completely independent of the county and free from control of the state legislature except for general laws. A new charter in 1914, while retaining this feature, introduced several changes: the number of elective offices was reduced, the appointive powers of the mayor were increased, the city council was made a unicameral body, the budget system was introduced, the right to municipal ownership of utilities was granted, and provisions were made for the use of the initiative, referendum and recall.

City boundaries as established in 1876 (and subsequently unchanged) prevented city services from following families moving out to less expensive or more satisfactory housing in suburban surroundings. The rapid, and largely planless, spread of the metro-

PIAGET

UNION STATION, 1896, WITH THE CARL MILLES FOUNTAIN "THE MEETING OF THE WATERS" IN FOREGROUND. THE FOUNTAIN, COMPOSED OF 14 BRONZE FIGURES, WAS COMPLETED IN 1940

Jennings, Richmond Heights, Maplewood, and Overland.

The municipality of St. Charles, across the Missouri River, dates from Spanish days, about 1679. It has a considerable industry. In Jefferson County are the twin towns of Festus and Crystal City. (For comparative population figures for the city of St. Louis and these suburbs *see* table in MISSOURI: *Population.*)

Illinois communities in this metropolitan complex had an early advantage in heavy industry because of high railroad rates for freight crossing the river; however, many of their residents now commute to daily employment in the central city. The largest of the Illinois suburbs is East St. Louis; ranking next is its neighbour, Granite City; followed by Belleville, Alton (*qq.v.*), Wood River and Edwardsville. (For comparative population figures for these municipalities *see* table in ILLINOIS: *Population.*)

The Economy.—Industry in the St. Louis area profits from adequate supplies of labour, raw materials and water, plus transportation service by radiating air, truck, rail and river-barge lines. Natural gas for industry is supplemented by coal from nearby Illinois mines. A greatly diversified manufacture includes automotive assembly plants of three major concerns, two in the county. Many business facilities are in suburban locations, and much retail trade is at one-stop shopping centres scattered about the county. Two large shoe manufacturers with headquarters in St. Louis have factories in outlying rural communities. Other important categories: beer and other beverages, petroleum refining, electrical industrial apparatus, meat products, organic chemicals, drugs and medicines, iron and steel foundries, paints and allied products, miscellaneous foods, structural and ornamental fabricated metalwork, service and household machines, bakery products, soap and related items, and women's outerwear.

Education and Cultural Activities.—Four urban universities and numerous colleges, seminaries and trade schools draw thousands of students to the area. Newest are the University of Missouri at St. Louis with its campus in suburban Normandy (1960), and the 2,600-ac. campus of Southern Illinois University at Edwardsville, including its extensive Elijah P. Lovejoy Memorial Library, named for the martyred abolitionist editor, and with undergraduate centres at Alton and East St. Louis. Washington University, chartered in 1853, was founded by William Greenleaf Eliot, grandfather of the poet T. S. Eliot. Its adult education division, the School of Continuing Education, enrolls nearly half of the student body. Among outstanding projects in teaching, research and community service are the Center for the Biology of Natural Systems, Laboratory for Space Physics, Biomedical Computer Center, Institute for Urban and Regional Studies, and Social Science Institute. St. Louis University, a Roman Catholic school founded in 1818, has branches in Florissant and East St. Louis. Its Pius XII library, built to preserve microfilms of Vatican library treasures, is on the midtown campus.

Webster College (1915), transferred by the Sisters of Loretto to a lay board in 1967, is noted for its Loretto-Hilton Center for the Performing Arts, with a repertory theatre, and for its experimental educational programs. Maryville College of the Sacred Heart (1872) and Fontbonne College (1917) are Roman Catholic schools for women. The Principia, for children of Christian Scientists, has two campuses, elementary and secondary in St. Louis

politan area in the 20th century deprived the city of needed tax income; well-to-do and middle-class out-migrants were usually replaced by in-migrants of lesser means, who came largely from rural areas where the demand for labour was reduced. At the same time problems of traffic, parking and transportation were multiplied in the central city. The complexity of local government is indicated by the fact that there were 200 municipalities in the standard metropolitan statistical area, and as late as 1968 St. Louis County alone had 26 school districts.

A privately financed metropolitan survey in 1958 recommended a functional but not political consolidation of city and county for joint handling of such common services as traffic and health. Three high-speed trafficways from beyond the city limits were built to bring more traffic into the downtown business district, suffering from the competition of one-stop shopping centres and places of amusement in outlying areas. New residential apartments for middle-income families were made possible in the vicinity of the business centre by urban renewal and slum clearance projects. Smoke elimination through regulation of the use of highly volatile coal was carried out successfully in the 1940s by an engineer, Raymond R. Tucker, who was later elected mayor.

A housing-rehabilitation program was allotted $4,000,000 from a $110,639,000 bond issue voted in 1955 for public improvements. Included was $10,000,000 for slum clearance. Neighbourhood pilot projects demonstrated that it cost less to rehabilitate some blighted areas than to clear slums and rebuild. In other areas public housing replaced substandard dwellings. These buildings were in many instances 8 to 11 stories high and in one 28-block section doubled the density of population, with consequent traffic, school, and other complications. Extensive urban renewal was undertaken in large sections of the core city, which is in the Model Cities program, and in adjacent University City.

Though the suburbs are not without their fringe of shacks, in the main the old amenities have persisted. University City, second largest residential suburb in the county, was incorporated in 1906 and adopted a council-manager plan of government in 1947. Other nearby communities having a city manager are Webster Groves, Clayton, Berkeley, Olivette, and Ferguson. Kirkwood dates from 1853, when 40 families moved there after railroad service was opened. Other county communities are Normandy, Pine Lawn,

BY COURTESY OF SANTA FE RAILWAY

**WASHINGTON UNIVERSITY ADMINIS-
TRATION BUILDING**

County, and the college at Elsah, Ill. Lindenwood, established as a women's college in 1827 at St. Charles under Presbyterian auspices, has admitted a limited number of young men students in special classes. Monticello, a private junior college for women, was founded in 1835 at Alton. A junior college district maintains three schools, and a special-school district opened a vocational-technical high school in Sunset Hills (1917), with a second at Florissant (1968). Harris Teachers College (1857), under the St. Louis Board of Education, prepares new staff for city schools.

The St. Louis public-school system was integrated racially in 1955, without difficulty. The first public high school west of the Mississippi was established in St. Louis in 1856, followed in 1873 by the nation's first public kindergarten, installed by Susan Blow. William T. Harris (q.v.), then superintendent, introduced a phonetic system for reading and added natural sciences to the curriculum. He also founded and edited the *Journal of Speculative Philosophy* (1867–93), the first periodical of the sort in English.

Works of early artists such as George C. Bingham, Chester Harding, and Carl Wimar, together with a large collection of historical writings, are part of the privately endowed Mercantile Library (1846). The public library, with many neighbourhood branches, dates from 1865; the symphony orchestra from 1881; the Academy of Science from 1856. The Missouri Botanical Garden (1858) includes the headquarters of the National Council of State Garden Clubs. Relics of the past include the birthplace of Eugene Field (q.v.); the Campbell house (1851), an antebellum mansion open to the public, with a display of Victorian furnishings and clothing; and the log cabin in which U. S. Grant lived as a farmer for five years. A famous example of the original skyscraper architecture is the Wainwright Building (1891), designed by Louis Sullivan. Other landmarks are Sappington house (1808), the Gen. Daniel Bissell house (1812), Taille de Noyer (1790), and the Chatillon deMenil mansion (1848–63).

In the latter part of the 20th century the city had two large daily newspapers, the *Post-Dispatch* and the *Globe-Democrat*, many local and neighbourhood journals, several television stations and a number of radio stations.

Parks and Recreation.—Forest Park (1,380 ac.) contains a tax-supported zoo and the City Art Museum, the latter designed by Cass Gilbert for the 1904 world's fair which was held at that location. At one entrance is the Jefferson Memorial, housing the Missouri Historical Society with extensive exhibits of pioneer life, the Lewis and Clark expedition, and the collected souvenirs of Charles A. Lindbergh's flight across the Atlantic in 1927. In the park also is the 12,000-seat outdoor Municipal Opera Theatre (1919), the municipal planetarium (1963), golf courses and other facilities including a large ice-skating and roller rink, boating, and notable flower displays in the Jewel Box. Elsewhere is a Museum of Science and Natural History, a National Museum of Transport and the Jefferson Barracks Historical Park. Alton Lake, on the Mississippi, harbours small pleasure craft. Cahokia Mounds Park, between East St. Louis and Collinsville, preserves handiwork of a prehistoric race of Mound Builders.

The city is the home of the Cardinal baseball team and the Cardinal football team, and many athletic and other events are staged in Kiel Auditorium, part of the civic centre. On the adjoining Aloe Memorial Plaza, facing Union Station, is the Carl Milles fountain "The Meeting of the Waters." An annual event since 1878 is the Veiled Prophet parade and ball.

See also references under "Saint Louis, Mo." in the Index.

BIBLIOGRAPHY.—John Thomas Scharf, *History of St. Louis City and County* (1883); Richard Edwards and M. Hopewell, *The Great West and Her Commercial Metropolis* (1860); Frederick L. Billon, *Annals of St. Louis in Its Early Days Under the French and Spanish Dominations* (1886); Metropolitan St. Louis Survey, *Path of Progress for Metropolitan St. Louis* (1957); Hiram M. Chittenden, *The American Fur Trade of the Far West* (1902); E. M. Coyle, *St. Louis* (1966); E. Kirschten, *Catfish and Crystal* (1967).   (Pl. G.)

SAINT LOUIS PARK, a city of Hennepin County, Minn., U.S., on the southwestern edge of Minneapolis (q.v.) and a part of the Minneapolis-St. Paul metropolitan area. After World War II it experienced great population growth.

The first settlers in St. Louis Park were William Laycock and his wife, who built a log cabin on their claim in 1854. Sometime before 1886, the first depot was built by the Minneapolis and St. Louis railway. The village, first called Elmwood, was renamed after that railroad.

Farming was the main industry in the early days but gradually disappeared with the advent of suburban growth. Plans for the development of the city as a manufacturing suburb began as early as 1886. The panic of 1893 bankrupted several flourishing factories. Then new industries moved in and between 1900 and 1913 another cycle of decline and boom was experienced. From 1914 to 1920 industry was on a reduced scale with the exception of important dairying and truck farming. Chief industries in the second half of the 20th century were metal and wood products.

St. Louis Park was incorporated in 1886 and its residents adopted a home-rule charter in 1954; a council-manager form of government went into effect in 1955. For comparative population figures *see* table in MINNESOTA: *Population.*   (R. W. F.)

SAINT LUCIA, a British colony, an island of the Lesser Antilles in the Caribbean Sea, forming part of the Windward Islands group, lies about 20 mi. (32 km.) S of Martinique, and about 25 mi. (40 km.) NE of St. Vincent. St. Lucia is 27 mi. (43.5 km.) long, has a maximum width of 14 mi. (22.5 km.) and an area of 238 sq.mi. (616 sq.km.).

Physical Features and Climate.—The island is of volcanic origin, and is bisected from north to south by a central ridge of wooded mountains, the highest point being Mt. Gimie (3,145 ft. [958.6 m.]) in the south. Many streams flow from the mountains through fertile valleys. In the southwest are the Pitons (2,619 ft. [798.3 m.] and 2,461 ft. [750.1 m.]), two immense pyramids of rock rising sharply from the sea and enclosing a small bay. Near Petit Piton is Soufrière, a low-lying volcanic crater. The boiling sulfur springs from which the town of Soufrière takes its name are at Ventine, 2½ mi. SE of the town. St. Lucia lies in the path of the northeastern trade winds and has a tropical maritime climate. Rainfall and temperature vary with altitude. Average annual rainfall ranges from 51 in. (1,295 mm.) on the coast to 117 in. (2,972 mm.) in the interior, the wettest months being from May to August. The temperature averages between 25.8° C (78.5° F) on the coast and 20.8° C (69.5° F) in the interior.

Population, Education, and Administration.—At the 1960 census the population of St. Lucia was 86,108. The original Carib race is extinct, the majority of the inhabitants of the island being Negroes and mulattoes; the remainder are whites or of East Indian extraction. The chief town is Castries, built on a fine landlocked harbour, with a population (1960) of 4,353; other towns are Soufrière (2,692) and Vieux Fort (3,228). A French patois is spoken by most of the inhabitants, but is being gradually supplanted by English. Primary education is compulsory and the government subsidizes education through grants-in-aid to the island's denominational primary schools (about 50, principally Roman Catholic) and two Roman Catholic secondary schools.

St. Lucia's system of government is ministerial. The executive council consists of four elected members (including the chief minister and three other ministers), one nominated member, and one official member. The council is presided over by an administrator, who is appointed by the U.K. government. The legislative council, which has an elected majority, is presided over by a speaker elected by the council.

The Economy.—The island's economy is based on agriculture. Sugarcane was the chief crop until the mid-1950s, but by the early

1960s bananas had become by far the most important crop, comprising about two-thirds of the total value of exports. Other crops are coconuts, cocoa, cassava, fruit, vegetables, rice, spices, and cotton. The chief imports are flour, milk, cotton piece goods, cement, hardware, vehicles, machinery, chemical fertilizers, and boots and shoes. The unit of currency is the West Indian dollar with a par value of WI$1.714 to the U.S. dollar. The annual value of imports in the mid-1960s was about WI$14,000,000, and of exports about WI$7,000,000.

About one-fifth of the island is forested. There is a flourishing charcoal trade with Barbados. Fishing is carried on extensively for the local market. The island's few industries process sugar, rum, citrus produce, and edible oils; cigarettes and mineral waters are also manufactured. In the mid-1960s government revenues (including grants from colonial development and welfare funds) and expenditures balanced out at about WI$8,000,000.

There are two airports in St. Lucia—Beane Field and Vigie, which has an extended runway. Air services are provided by British West Indian Airways, and charter flights by KLM and British Guiana Airways. Steamers of the Harrison Line and Geest Industries Co. call at St. Lucia, and there are numerous small interisland craft.

History.—The exact date of the discovery of St. Lucia is not known, but it is thought to have been about 1500. It is quite possible that it was named by Columbus, although there is no record of this. The first attempts at colonization were made by the English in 1605 and 1638, but they were frustrated by sickness and the hostility of the native Caribs. A successful settlement was achieved in 1650 by the French from Martinique who made a treaty with the Caribs in 1660. Shortly afterward England regained the island, but it was restored to France by the Peace of Breda in 1667.

Another British settlement under a grant made in 1722 by George I to the duke of Montague was frustrated by France, and the island was declared neutral. In 1743 the French resumed possession, retaining the island until 1748 when the two countries again agreed to regard St. Lucia as neutral. In 1762 it was captured by Adm. George Rodney and Gen. Robert Monckton, only to be given up once more by the Treaty of Paris (1763). In 1778 it again surrendered to the British, who used its harbours as a naval base. Between 1782 and 1803 the possession of St. Lucia passed several times between Britain and France, the British having to suppress a vigorous revolutionary party, which was aided by insurgent slaves, before gaining possession in 1803. St. Lucia was finally ceded to Britain in 1814, when it became a crown colony. During 1838–85, together with the other islands of the Windward group, it was placed under the governor of Barbados.

French influence on the development of St. Lucia is illustrated by the preponderance of the Roman Catholic Church and the survival of a French patois. In the years following 1763 French planters came from St. Vincent and Grenada and established cotton and sugar plantations. In 1834, when the slaves were emancipated, there were in St. Lucia more than 13,000 Negro slaves, 2,600 free Negroes, and 2,300 whites. Prosperity was greatly retarded by frequent wars, epidemics of cholera and smallpox, and by the decline of the sugarcane industry. Improvement came with the increase of banana and cocoa cultivation and the revival of sugarcane.

Representative government was obtained by the constitution of 1924, which introduced an elective element into the legislative council; the constitution of 1936 provided for an unofficial majority in the council.

In 1958 St. Lucia joined the Federation of The West Indies. Under the 1960 constitution the post of governor of the Windward Islands was abolished and St. Lucia became an autonomous unit within the Federation, also achieving a greater degree of internal self-government. The Federation was dissolved on May 31, 1962. In November 1964 agreement on the establishment of a new West Indies Federation was reached by the regional council of ministers of the "little seven"—Barbados, Antigua, Dominica, Montserrat, St. Kitts-Nevis, St. Lucia, and St. Vincent. *See also* WEST INDIES; WEST INDIES (FEDERATION), THE.   (R. To.)

SAINT-MALO, a seaport of Brittany, France, lying on the right bank of the Rance River at its mouth. It is the chief town of an *arrondissement* in the *département* of Ille-et-Vilaine. Pop. (1962) 16,981. The old walled city stands on a granite isle which is joined to the mainland by an old causeway, *Le Sillon* ("furrow"), and the modern boulevard Louis-Martin. Largely destroyed in 1944, the town and its suburbs were rebuilt and its historic buildings were restored or reconstructed. The cathedral (Saint-Vincent's Church since the bishopric was lost in 1790), shipowners' mansions, law courts, and the 14th–15th-century castle with four towers (one of which, the great keep, houses a history museum) are still to be seen. The ramparts surrounding the town include portions dating from the 12th century but were mainly rebuilt at the end of the 17th and the beginning of the 18th century and restored in the 19th. An important tourist resort, the town has sandy beaches, a casino, sports stadium, race course, swimming pool, yacht club, tennis courts, and fishing facilities.

The town is connected by road and rail with Rennes, and British steamer services link it with both Southampton and Jersey. The nearest airport is at Pleurtuit near Dinard. The harbour is contiguous with that of Saint-Servan. Apples, potatoes, and cauliflowers are principal exports; imports include coal, timber, and wine. Trade is mainly with Britain and Scandinavia. A substantial fleet of trawlers visits the cod fisheries of Newfoundland and Greenland. Saint-Malo probably derives its name from the Welsh monk Maclow (Maclou or Malo) who fled there in the 6th century and later became bishop of Aleth (Saint-Servan). In the 12th century the see of Aleth was transferred to Saint-Malo, when the bishop Jean de Châtillon took refuge there from the Normans. He built the cathedral, manor houses, and ramparts. The city thereafter became a great seaport and the dukes of Brittany and the kings of France granted it many privileges. For four years in the 16th century it was an independent republic. In the 17th and 18th centuries Saint-Malo flourished, both as a centre for privateering and as a participant in many colonial ventures. Shipbuilding, deep-sea fishing, slave trading, and foreign trade were then the main occupations. Among the famous men born at Saint-Malo are J. O. de Lamettrie, F. R. de Chateaubriand, Hugues F. R. de Lamennais, F. J. Broussais and the mariners J. Cartier and R. Duguay-Trouin (*qq.v.*).

Saint-Servan, one mile south of Saint-Malo and formerly a suburb, was made a separate commune in 1789. Pop. (1962) 13,479. Its origins go back to the Gallo-Roman city of Aleth. The 14th-century tower of Solidor was built by John IV, duke of Brittany, as a lookout over the Rance estuary, and was later used as a prison. Saint-Servan was also formerly involved in Corsair activities, ships being built in the small harbours of Port Saint-Père and Port Solidor. The old site of Aleth was made into a powerful German stronghold in World War II.

In the 1960s a dam crossing the Rance estuary and carrying an 800-yd. road was under construction. The project was expected to include the first tidal power station in the world.   (D. La.)

SAINT-MARTIN, LOUIS CLAUDE DE (1743–1803), French illuminist who signed his works "LE PHILOSOPHE INCONNU," was born at Amboise on Jan. 18, 1743. He studied law and practised for six months at Tours, but joined the army in 1765. Stationed at Bordeaux, he came under the influence of the Jewish visionary, Martinez Pasqualis. Saint-Martin left the army in 1771 and began to propagate mysticism, first in Paris under Martinez Pasqualis and later in Lyons, where he was active in masonic lodges. His first book, *Des Erreurs et de la vérité* (1775), in which Gnostic theories were used to refute Condillac's materialism, won him the favour of certain literary groups among the nobility. On his return to France in 1788 after visiting England and Italy he settled in Strasbourg, where he met Charlotte de Boecklin and Rudolphe Salzmann. These two introduced him to the writings of Jakob Boehme, under whose influence he gradually broke loose from that of Martinez Pasqualis. In 1794 he was exiled from Paris and retired to Amboise.

During the French Revolution he was arrested as an aristocrat and was about to appear before the revolutionary tribunal when the overthrow of Robespierre in July 1794 freed him. Two years later he published his *Considérations sur la révolution française,* in which he proposed theocracy as the ideal form of society. Later he came under the influence of Swedenborg. He died at Aulnay, near Paris, on Oct. 13, 1803. His works include *L'Homme de désir* (1790); *Le Nouvel Homme* (1792); *Éclair sur l'association humaine* (1797); *Le Crocodile* (1798), an allegorical poem; *De l'Esprit des choses* (1800); and *Le Ministère de l'homme-esprit* (1802; Eng. trans., *The Ministry of Man and Spirit,* 1864). Other treatises appeared in his *Oeuvres posthumes* (1807).

See A. E. Waite, *The Life of Louis Claude de Saint-Martin* (1901); R. Amadou, *Louis Claude de Saint-Martin et le Martinisme* (1946).

SAINT MARYS, a city of western Auglaize County, O., U.S., on the eastern shore of Grand Lake (Lake Saint Marys), 95 mi. N of Cincinnati. On an important portage between rivers connecting the Great Lakes and the Ohio River, it was the site of Girty's Town, the trading post of an American renegade named James Girty, in the 1780s; Ft. Saint Marys, supply post in the Indian wars of the 1790s; Ft. Barbee in the War of 1812; and the negotiation of an important Indian treaty in 1818. Platted in 1823, it became a city in 1903. German and Irish ancestry predominate in the population. Industrial output includes blankets, rubber products, heavy machinery, and processed foodstuffs. Grand Lake, constructed (1837–1845) as a reservoir to feed the Miami and Erie Canal, is now used for recreation and contains a large warmwater fish hatchery. For comparative population figures *see* table in OHIO: *Population.* (D. L. S.)

SAINT MARYS RIVER, a stream, about 63 mi. long, connecting Lake Superior with Lake Huron and forming part of the international boundary between northeastern Michigan, U.S., and Canada. The upper third of the river is at the Lake Superior level, but at Sault Ste. Marie (*q.v.*) it drops about 20 ft. in a distance of about one mile through the Sault Ste. Marie Rapids to the level of Lake Huron. The rapids, impassable for navigation, are bypassed by the American and Canadian ship canals which contain a total of five locks. The lower river is divided into a series of lakes and channels by large islands. The river is the narrowest part of the Great Lakes system and a natural crossing site which was used by the Indians and visited by early French explorers.
(C. M. DA.)

SAINT-MAUR-DES-FOSSÉS, a town in the *département* of Val-de-Marne, France, and a southeastern suburb of Paris, lies on the right bank of the Marne, within a loop of the river, about 6 mi. (10 km.) from the city centre. Pop. (1962) 70,295. Saint-Maur developed as a residential district after the apportionment of the Condé domains in 1831, and in spite of increasing urbanization has retained the character of a garden suburb. Horticulture flourishes and the few industries include the production of chemicals, corks, and felt. There is an observatory (founded 1880) and a waterworks which supplies Paris from the Marne.

In the Middle Ages the land belonged to an abbey founded in the 7th century. This was secularized in the 16th century, and on the site of the abbot's quarters Philibert Delorme built a château (1541–47) for the bishop of Paris, Cardinal Jean du Bellay, which later passed to Catherine de Médicis and then to the house of Condé. Rabelais stayed there. The other abbey buildings were demolished in the 18th century. (H. DE S.-R.)

SAINT MICHAEL'S MOUNT, a lofty pyramidal island of granite, rising about 400 yd. (365 m.) from the shore of Mount's Bay, and included in the West Penwith rural district of Cornwall, Eng. Pop. (1961) 47. It is united with Marazion by a natural causeway passable only at low tide. The Mount, topped by a very ancient building, can be seen from any part of the coast between Mousehole and Cudden Point. It was given by Edward the Confessor to Mont-Saint-Michel in Normandy, of which abbey it continued to be a priory until the dissolution of the alien houses by Henry V, when it was given to the abbess and convent of Syon in Middlesex. It came into the possession of the crown after the Reformation and governors were appointed by the monarch.

It was a resort of pilgrims, encouraged by Pope Gregory, in the 11th century and in the 12th century the monastery was rebuilt by Bernard, the abbot of Mont-Saint-Michel. The Mount was captured by Henry Pomeroy in the reign of Richard I, and John de Vere, earl of Oxford, seized it and held it against the king's troops in 1473. Perkin Warbeck occupied it in 1497. Humphry Arundell, governor of St. Michael's Mount, led the rebellion of 1549. During the reign of Elizabeth I it was given to Robert, earl of Salisbury, by whose son it was sold to Sir Francis Basset, whose brother, Sir Arthur Basset, held it against the parliament until July 1646. It was sold in 1659 to Col. John St. Aubyn, and his descendant, Lord St. Levan, has a residence in the castle. In 1954 an arrangement was made between the St. Aubyn family and the National Trust, whereby the latter have taken over the Mount, subject to certain rights in favour of the present Lord St. Levan and his heirs. Of the original monastic buildings, the refectory (Chevy Chase room) is the chief survival. The chapel of St. Michael, which is extra-diocesan, is a beautiful 15th-century building with an embattled tower.

The harbour, widened in 1823–24 to allow vessels of 500 tons to enter, has a pier dating from the 15th century.

SAINT-MIHIEL, a small town (5,203 inhabitants in 1962) of northeastern France, in the *département* of Meuse, is situated on the right bank of the Meuse River, where its valley is entrenched in the Corallian limestone plateau of western Lorraine, 22 mi. (35 km.) S of Verdun by rail. Its nucleus was the Benedictine abbey established in 709. The abbey buildings, which are now occupied by municipal offices, date from the end of the 17th century and the beginning of the 18th. Both the abbey church and that of Saint-Étienne contain famous work by Ligier Richier (1506–67). Though less important than the great fortress of Verdun (*q.v.*), Saint-Mihiel was one of the fortified towns guarding the strategic line of the Meuse on the approach to the heart of the Paris Basin from the east. Captured by the Germans in September 1914 at the beginning of World War I, the town was not retaken by the Allies until September 1918 in an offensive in which the American troops under General Pershing played the major role. This was the first occasion on which the American Army in France had mounted an offensive as a unit. The rapid and successful outcome of their attack was a heavy blow to the morale of the German Army. (AR. E. S.)

SAINT MORITZ, a spa, winter sports, and summer resort in the Upper Engadine and the southeastern Swiss canton of Graubünden (Grisons), 6,089 ft. (1,856 m.) above sea level. The area is part of the great watershed from which the glacier waters feed the Rhine, Po, and Danube. The commune comprises the Dorf (village), Bad (spa), Suvretta, and Champfèr. There were (1960) 3,751 inhabitants, and 10,000 visitors can be accommodated. The chief buildings are the curative baths, the Engadine Museum, the museum named after the landscape painter Giovanni Segantini (1858–99), the 12th-century (restored) leaning tower (part of the former church of St. Maurice), and the Druidenstein, the remains of a druid stone system. There are many miles of promenade, three funiculars, and several cableways and ski lifts. The resort is on an international highway and has local coach services; it is linked by rail with international lines, and the airport of Samedán is about 4 mi. (6 km.) NE. The life of St. Moritz depends on tourism and the hotel industry, which, with its sports facilities, are well developed.

SAINT-NAZAIRE, a west-coast port of France and outport for Nantes. Chief town of an *arrondissement* in the *département* of Loire-Atlantique, it lies at the mouth of the Loire on the right bank 37 mi. (60 km.) WNW of Nantes by rail and 28 mi. (45 km.) by river. Pop. (1962) 49,331. The town was almost completely destroyed during World War II. During its rebuilding it was given wide streets, such as the central shopping district, Avenue de la République. The shipbuilding yards are among the largest in Europe, and the liners "Normandie" and "France" and the battleship "Jean Bart" were built there. There is also a fishing port; the catch consists of sardines, tunny, and shellfish. The town has aircraft works, canning plants, steelworks, and a chemical factory for processing phosphates.

Saint-Nazaire is believed to be the site of Corbilo, which Strabo mentions among the most important coastal towns of Gaul. Toward the end of the 4th century it was occupied by Saxons, and they were converted to Christianity in the 6th century by St. Felix, bishop of Nantes (d. 582), when the town took its present name. It was a small fishing village until the mid-19th century, when work began on the port. The first dock was opened in 1856 and shipbuilding yards were installed in 1861–62. During World War II the town was occupied by the Germans, who used the port as a major Atlantic submarine base. The ships "Tirpitz" and "Bismarck" harboured there. In 1942 the docks were blown up by the British and were not restored for service till 1946.

The seat of the *sous-préfecture* was transferred from Savernay to Saint-Nazaire in 1868; in 1879 a chamber of commerce was established and later a tribunal of commerce.   (M. Mt.)

SAINT NICOLAS, Belgium: see SINT-NIKLAAS.

SAINT-OMER, chief town of an *arrondissement* in the *département* of Pas-de-Calais, northern France, is situated near the plain of Flanders on the Aa River at its junction with the Neuffossé Canal. Pop. (1962) 18,180. Saint-Omer was the seat of a bishopric and the church of Notre Dame was a cathedral from 1563 to 1801. The 13th–15th-century church contains the 8th-century tomb of St. Erkembode and the 13th-century tomb of St. Omer. There are two museums, the Henri Dupuis Museum of Natural History and Folklore, and the Fine Arts Museum, housed in the 18th-century hôtel Sandelin, and a municipal library with illuminated manuscripts of the 8th–16th centuries.

St. Omer, bishop of Thérouanne, founded a monastery there in the 7th century, and built a small church, Notre Dame, on a hill above the Aa; St. Bertin gave his name to the abbey on the river, and a village known as Saint-Omer grew up between the two churches during the 8th century. St. Bertin's abbey fell into ruin at the Revolution, and its tower finally collapsed in 1947. In the 9th century the counts of Flanders erected a fortress and the settlement was enclosed by walls. In the 10th century, under Abbot Odbert, the abbey became a cultural centre producing fine illuminated manuscripts in the style of Winchester. In the 11th and 12th centuries the town had important commercial relations with England and Scotland, which provided much of the wool necessary for its cloth trade. In 1154 Henry II gave privileges to the merchants of Saint-Omer to trade in London, privileges which remained in force until Edward III banned the export of English wool. The cloth industry never recovered from this blow or the subsequent wars, famine, and plague, though some cloth was exported to France, Spain, Italy, and even Russia. In the early 17th century tobacco processing was introduced, and this new industry continued until the tobacco monopoly was set up in 1810. Saint-Omer now produces paper, glass, cement, and linen goods. The surrounding marshes have been drained since the late 18th century and produce fruit and vegetables which are exported to other parts of France.   (Ge. C.)

SAINT-OUEN, an industrial suburb of greater Paris in the *département* of Seine-Saint-Denis, lies on the right bank of the Seine River, 8 km. (5 mi.) N of Notre Dame Cathedral. Pop. (1962) 51,471. Formerly a village, formed around a sanctuary in the Carolingian period (8th–10th centuries), where the kings of France had a residence in the Middle Ages, Saint-Ouen developed into an industrial centre in the 19th century. Docks, factories, and workshops were built around the 12th-century church and the château (1822) in a disorderly fashion to the detriment of the residential quarters. Metallurgical industry and automobile manufacturing are the principal activities and there are some light industries. To the east stretches a large cemetery; a picturesque and lively "flea market" is held three times a week and attracts Parisians in search of bargains in furniture, curios, and antiques.   (H. de S.-R.)

SAINT PAUL, capital city of Minnesota, U.S., seat of Ramsey county and a port of entry, is located adjacent to Minneapolis at the head of navigation on the Mississippi river; it is about 350 mi. N.W. of Chicago. It has 16 mi. of river frontage along a deep S-shaped bend of the Mississippi which flows south to its confluence with the wider Minnesota river, northeast past the business district, and then sharply south again in its broadening valley. The heart of the city, built upon a series of terraces which rise from the river (altitude, 703 ft.) to the sur-

rounding glacial plains (altitude, 900 ft.), presents a striking skyline from the southern and eastern approaches, and various points along the heights within the city afford sweeping views across the river valley. The downtown area, surrounded by hills, grew up with an irregular street pattern which is reminiscent of older eastern cities. St. Paul and Minneapolis (q.v.), to the west and north, are contiguous and, though very different in character and development, are often called the Twin cities.

History.—In 1680 Father Louis Hennepin passed the site of St. Paul, and in 1766 Jonathan Carver, searching for the northwest passage, explored a cave near the area. In 1805 Lieut. Zebulon Montgomery Pike, leader of a U.S. expedition, camped beneath the bluffs of the Minnesota and Mississippi rivers on what is known as Pike Island where he made an unofficial treaty with the Sioux for possession of the region, including the commanding site above him on which Fort Snelling was later built. The first claim in what is now St. Paul was made in 1838 by Pierre "Pig's Eye" Parrant. The landing was known as Pig's Eye until 1841 when Father Lucian Galtier built a log chapel dedicated to St. Paul. In 1849 St. Paul became the capital of the newly formed Minnesota territory. Settlers, mainly from the eastern states, poured into the river town which was incorporated in 1854, its population by 1860 exceeding 10,000.

Industrial and Commercial Growth.—St. Paul's historic importance in the development of the upper midwest was as a commercial centre located near the head of navigation on the Mississippi river. Furs were its first products for the outside market, with groceries and dry goods assuming early importance. The first private bank in the territory was established in St. Paul in 1852, and the First National Bank of St. Paul was organized in 1863. In 1862 the first train left the city on the 10-mi. track of the St. Paul and Pacific railroad. In 1883 a great celebration marked the completion of the Northern Pacific railroad to the west coast, and 11 years later the Great Northern railroad, under the leadership of James J. Hill (q.v.), was completed. Banking in St. Paul has continued its close affiliation with the railroads whose development gave it the name, "gateway to the great northwest."

St. Paul's manufacturing developed slowly in a diversified pattern based upon the resources and needs of the surrounding country. Boots and shoes ranked first among the industries in the 1870s. In 1882 the Union Stock Yards company was established by the railroads. By mid-20th century the livestock market, now in suburban South St. Paul, was one of the world's largest public livestock markets in salable receipts. There are numerous printing and publishing houses including an important law publishing firm. Among the largest employers are manufacturers of automobiles, electronic communications equipment, abrasives and magnetic tape, refrigerators, construction equipment, advertising specialties and beer. Two large oil refineries, a steel mill and three chemical plants were brought to the St. Paul area by the development of industrial sites along the river to the south of the city.

Population and Administration.—St. Paul is in the Minneapolis-St. Paul standard metropolitan statistical area comprising the counties of Anoka, Dakota, Hennepin, Ramsey and Washington, which according to the federal census of 1960 had a population of 1,482,030. The population of St. Paul proper was 311,349 in 1950 and 313,411 in 1960 (for comparative population figures *see* table in MINNESOTA: *Population*). Its period of greatest growth was between 1880 and 1895 when the population increased from approximately 40,000 to 140,000. During this period also the proportion of foreign born reached its peak, with Germans and Irish leading in numbers. This phase of immigration underlies the character of the modern city, though by 1930 when the population was 271,606 the foreign born included a high percentage of Scandinavians and also east Europeans, Italians and Mexicans. St. Paul is the seat of a Roman Catholic archdiocese which was built up by Archbishop John Ireland (q.v.), who greatly influenced the development of the city. Roman Catholics in the early 1960s numbered about two-fifths of the population, though Protestant, Jewish and Orthodox faiths were well represented.

Under the commission plan of government, adopted by the voters in 1912, city officials are elected for two-year terms. The legislative council consists of the mayor and six commissioners who serve as administrators of the various city departments. Judges of the municipal court are also elected officials, as are the seven members of the board of education, who serve without pay.

Transportation.—St. Paul is served by nine first-class railroads which own and operate a terminal switching line in the city. By mid-20th century it had become one of the largest trucking centres in the nation. The rafting industry, carrying logs and lumber down the river, was important to St. Paul until about 1900. The last raft left in 1914, but river traffic attained a new significance in the late 1950s and 1960s with 25 barge lines carrying about 2,000,000 tons of bulk commodities such as coal, grain, oil and fertilizers between the Port of St. Paul and Mississippi river markets and Gulf ports. St. Paul and Minneapolis are jointly served by the Wold-Chamberlain International airport, and St. Paul is also served by its Downtown airport, which accommodates business jets.

Education, Culture and Recreation.—Liberal arts colleges in St. Paul include the College of St. Thomas, for men (Roman Catholic, 1885); the College of St. Catherine, for women (Roman Catholic, 1905); Macalester college (Presbyterian, 1885); Concordia college (Lutheran, 1905); Hamline university (Methodist, 1854); and Bethel College and Seminary (originally established in 1871 as Scandinavian Department of Baptist Union Theological Seminary of the University of Chicago), since 1947, a four-year college. The University of Minnesota Institute of Agriculture has a large campus in the northeast corner of the city. Luther Theological seminary and St. Paul seminary (Roman Catholic) are in St. Paul, and the William Mitchell College of Law gives a full degree through evening courses. Parochial and private schools are well represented, and a recognized program for pupils of all levels of ability was instituted in the city's public schools.

An Italian Renaissance building, built in 1916, houses both the public library and the James Jerome Hill reference library, a private corporation with especially extensive collections in economics, science and technology. The Minnesota Historical society, founded in 1849, has an outstanding collection of manuscripts and printed materials and also a museum relating to the region. One of the major arts councils in the U.S., the Council of Arts and Sciences, operates an Arts and Sciences centre, built in 1964, to house the exhibits and educational activities of the Science museum and the Art centre. Other Council members include the Schubert club, the St. Paul Philharmonic society and the Civic opera. More than 1,000,000 people attend the annual state fair, held in the grounds near the Institute of Agriculture, and since 1886, when the first ice palace was built, the St. Paul Winter carnival has been a colourful annual event. Perhaps the most distinctive of the city's entertainment events is the biennial Festival of Nations, first sponsored in 1932 by the International institute and featuring dances, handicrafts and foods of many nations. A distinctive social service in the city is the Wilder Charities, established in 1910 under a trust fund by Amherst H. Wilder "for the benefit of the poor of the city." The Municipal auditorium, built in 1907, and enlarged in 1932, seats 15,000, and the Municipal stadium, built in 1957, holds 10,000.

Buildings and Parks.—A city of quiet, tree-shaded streets and middle-class homes, St. Paul is crowned by Summit avenue which, progressing westward from the bluffs overlooking the business district, reveals along its 4½-mi. length the changing styles of residential and church architecture, beginning with the impressively located baroque Cathedral of St. Paul which overlooks the city and the mansion of James J. Hill, built in 1887, passing the bold and symbolic structure of Mount Zion temple, completed in 1954, and ending with the homes of the mid-20th century. Among the landmarks is the home of Gov. Alexander Ramsey, a fine example of the dignified domestic architecture of the 1880s. The Federal Courts building (1900) is a delightfully bizarre example of French Renaissance architecture. In the concourse of the 19-story functional City hall and Ramsey County courthouse, erected in 1931, stands the huge rotating onyx figure of the Indian God of Peace by the Swedish sculptor Carl Milles. The Woman's City

club overlooks the river. The First National bank has, since 1931, with the Cathedral of St. Paul and the capitol (designed by Cass Gilbert and inspired by Italian High Renaissance) both on the bluffs behind it, dominated the sky line. Urban renewal has resulted in the construction of a number of new high-rise office buildings, both private and governmental. Extensive clearing, begun in 1956, has beautified the capitol approach which gives, from its height, a spectacular vista of the city and the valley beyond.

St. Paul has 11 major parks, the most interesting of which are Como park, begun in 1872, with its lake, greenhouse and zoo, and Indian Mounds park, where Indian burial mounds dot the margin of the bluff. (Ma. C. B.; J. A. Eg.)

SAINT PAUL ROCKS, also known as Rochedos São Paulo and as St. Peter and St. Paul, a number of islets in the Atlantic, nearly 1° N. of the equator and 540 mi. from South America, in 29° 15′ W. The whole space occupied does not exceed 1,400 ft. in length by about half as much in breadth. Besides seafowl the only land creatures are insects and spiders. Fish are abundant, seven species being collected by the "Challenger" expedition (q.v.). The islets contain rock that geologists estimate may be 4,500,000,-000 years old, about 1,000,000,000 years older than any other terrestrial rock that has been studied. (J. L. Tr.)

SAINT PETER PORT, the chief urban agglomeration and centre of government of Guernsey (q.v.), Channel Islands, is situated on the east coast of the island where a narrow valley reaches the sea between moderately high cliffs and where there was a good landing beach protected from prevailing winds and also an excellent roadstead for ships riding at anchor. Early in the 13th century this roadstead was protected by the building of Castle Cornet on a tidal islet less than half a mile offshore, reinforced later with La Tour Beauregard on the mainland of Guernsey. The Anglo-Gascon wine trade was then beginning to develop and the existence of this well-protected roadstead, together with Guernsey's position so near the natural route of medieval shipping up and down the English Channel, meant that St. Peter Port was used increasingly as a refuge and port of call (in 1329 by more than 500 ships). A small town naturally grew up there. Pop. (1961) 15,706.

Late in the 13th century a quay was built, and in 1309 the chief market of the island was moved to St. Peter Port, then described as "a kind of borough" (quasi-burgum). In 1350 the king ordered that it should be surrounded with a wall, though there is no clear evidence that this order was carried out.

From the middle of the 14th century the fortunes of the town and port have followed those of the island. The quay was extended in the 16th century, a second arm built in the 18th, and the present fine harbour constructed between 1853 and 1874. Until the 19th century the built-up area of the town hardly extended beyond the original valley and a northern extension along what is now High Street and the Pollet, but now almost the whole island has become an urban area. The earliest surviving reference to the church of St. Peter (ecclesia Sancti Petri de Portu) occurs in a charter of c. 1048. This ancient church preserves work of almost every century from the 13th (the walls of the nave may be older) and has some claim to architectural distinction. Other buildings of note are the Royal Court House (1799), the Markets (1822), Elizabeth College (1826; founded 1563), the Constables' Office, and several fine houses. Hauteville House, former residence of Victor Hugo (1856–70), is now the property of the city of Paris.

See J. H. Le Patourel, "The Early History of St. Peter Port," *Transactions of La Société Guernesiaise*, xii, 171–208 (1934); E. F. Carey, "The Growth of St. Peter Port in the Early 19th Century," *ibid.*, 153–170. (Le P.)

SAINT PETERSBURG: see Leningrad.

SAINT PETERSBURG, a resort city, is located on the west coast of Florida, U.S., in Pinellas county. Occupying the tip of Pinellas peninsula in Tampa bay, it is connected by the 7-mi. Gandy bridge with the mainland toward Tampa, 20 mi. N.E., and by the 15-mi. Sunshine skyway, consisting of five bridges and six causeways, with the mainland south-southwest toward Bradenton and Sarasota. Bridges and causeways to the west provide access across Boca Ciega bay to island beaches along the Gulf of Mexico.

Pop. (1960) 181,298; Tampa-St. Petersburg standard metropolitan statistical area (Hillsborough and Pinellas counties), 772,453. (For comparative population figures *see* table in FLORIDA: *Population; see* also TAMPA.)

Known as the "Sunshine city," St. Petersburg was named for the birthplace in Russia of Peter A. Demens who with John C. Williams of Detroit founded the Florida city. In 1888 Demens completed a railway connecting it with the St. Johns river, then the main artery of traffic to interior Florida. Settlers and tourists were attracted by development projects of the Hamilton Disston corporations which owned much of the surrounding area. The city was incorporated in 1892 and adopted a council-manager form of government in 1931. There are several hundred small, diversified industries and branch shops and plants of national corporations. A large number of retired persons live in the city.

A one-half mile municipal pier has fishing balconies, a museum, a solarium and pools. Bays, harbours and marinas about the city accommodate a large fleet of pleasure craft which frequently participate in races and regattas. Other recreational and entertainment attractions are band concerts, major-league baseball teams in spring training, fishing, golf and other out-of-door sports.

The public-school system is headed by the St. Petersburg junior college, founded in 1927. Among other educational institutions are the Admiral Farragut Naval academy (preparatory) and the Law College of Stetson university.

SAINT-PIERRE, CHARLES IRÉNÉE CASTEL, ABBÉ DE (1658–1743), French publicist and theoretical reformer who was one of the first authors of modern times to propose the establishment of an international organization for the maintenance of peace. He was born at Saint-Pierre-Église, near Cherbourg, on Feb. 13, 1658, the son of a Norman aristocrat. After wide-ranging studies at Rouen and Caen, he went to Paris in 1680, where he frequented the *salons* of Mme de la Fayette and of the marquise de Lambert. In 1693 he gained a footing at court as almoner to Madame (the duchesse d'Orléans), who presented him to the abbacy of Tiron, a comfortable benefice. He entered the Académie Française in 1695. From 1712 to 1714 he acted as secretary to Melchior de Polignac, the French plenipotentiary at the Congress of Utrecht. Because of the political offense given by his *Discours sur la polysynodie,* he was expelled from the Académie in 1718. He died in Paris on April 29, 1743.

Saint-Pierre's works are almost entirely occupied with an acute criticism of politics, law, and social institutions. They had considerable influence on Montesquieu and on Rousseau, who edited and redressed several of them and reproduced many of their ideas in his own work. Saint-Pierre's chief work, *Le Projet de paix perpétuelle* (1713; several later modified editions; *see* bibliography), was translated into English as early as 1714, and, as a scheme for securing universal peace, it has exercised continual influence up to the 20th century.

BIBLIOGRAPHY.—*Ouvrages de morale et de politique,* 16 vol. (1729–41); *Annales politiques* (1757; ed. by J. Drouet, 1912); *A Project of Perpetual Peace* (1927), Rousseau's modified edition and essay (both written in 1756), trans. by E. M. Nuttall, and printed in French and English, with an introduction by G. Lowes Dickinson; J. Drouet, *L'Abbé de Saint-Pierre: l'homme et l'oeuvre* (1912); M. L. Perkins, *The Moral and Political Philosophy of the Abbé de Saint-Pierre* (1959). *See* also F. H. Hinsley, *Power and the Pursuit of Peace,* ch. 2 (1963).

SAINT PIERRE AND MIQUELON, an archipelago off the south coast of Newfoundland, Canada, is the only remaining overseas territory of France in North America. The area of the main islands is 93 sq.mi. (241 sq.km.), 83 sq.mi. (215 sq.km.) of which are in the Miquelons (Miquelon and Langlade, sometimes known as Great and Little Miquelon, connected by the slim, sandy Isthmus of Langlade); but St. Pierre, only 10 sq.mi. (26 sq.km.), has almost seven-eighths of the population and is the administrative and commercial centre.

The landscape is stark and hilly with a rugged shoreline. Bedrock protrudes widely from the thin glacial soils. The forest cover was long ago removed for fuel, and the existing vegetation is scrubby heath, with some stunted trees on Langlade. Vegetable gardens and hayfields adjoin settlements and there is some rough grazing. The climate is humid with an annual precipitation of

about 60 in. (1,500 mm.), of which about 12% occurs as snow in winter. The local fogs increase the dampness, but the winters are milder than in the Newfoundland interior, and sunshine is plentiful in winter and midsummer. Average temperatures are between 15° and 16° C (60° F) in July and −4° C (25° F) in January; the extreme minimum is about −18° C (0° F).

The islands were first settled by France during the early 17th century; they subsequently changed hands with the British several times, but were restored to France in 1816 under the Treaty of Paris. The people are descended from inhabitants of the Atlantic coast of France. The language is French, and French customs and traditions are sustained by exchanges with the mother country, although modern communications have introduced North American influences. Most of the people live in the capital city, St. Pierre (pop. [1962] 4,287), and only 628 inhabit the island of Miquelon. There are Roman Catholic churches in St. Pierre and in Miquelon. Primary education is free and parochial; state and private primary and secondary schools have a total enrollment of about 1,400.

The inhabitants are French citizens and enjoy universal suffrage. The territory is represented in the French National Assembly and Senate by one deputy in each. The governor is assisted by a privy council and an elected general council. St. Pierre is the seat of the law courts and of the Apostolic Prefecture. The importance attached to this last foothold in North America has led France to subsidize the islanders, since the meagre local resources cannot support the population. Fishing is the chief occupation based on local resources and it was fishing that first attracted settlement. Those not so engaged work in trade, commerce, or government service. About 2,500 tons of codfish products are exported annually to France and the United States, frozen fillets processed in St. Pierre far outweighing the traditional dried and salted cod. Pelts exported from fox and mink farms are of

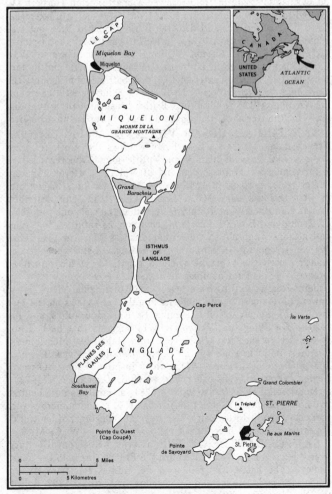

ST. PIERRE AND MIQUELON

minor importance, but with the improved transport within Newfoundland the tourist trade has become substantial.

Supply ships from France and from the Canadian mainland serve the islands. Regular services connect with Sydney and Halifax, Nova Scotia, and scheduled air services with Sydney and with St. John's, Nfd. There are telegraph and telephone communications with Europe and North America.

BIBLIOGRAPHY.—E. de Curton, *Saint-Pierre et Miquelon* (1944); E. Aubert de la Rüe, *Saint-Pierre et Miquelon* (1963); *Annuaire des Îles de St. Pierre et Miquelon* (annually). (W. F. Ss.)

SAINT-QUENTIN (ancient AUGUSTA VIROMANDUORUM), an industrial town of northern France, capital of an *arrondissement* in the *département* of Aisne, 32 mi. (51 km.) NNW of Laon by rail. Pop. (1962) 60,633. The town stands on the right bank of the Somme, at its junction with the Saint-Quentin and Crozat canals.

The collegiate church of Saint-Quentin (12th–15th centuries) contains the tombs of Gaius Quintinus (the town's namesake), Victoricus, and Gentianus, all of whom were 3rd-century martyrs. The *hôtel de ville* is a Gothic building of the 14th–16th centuries, adorned with curious sculptures. The Musée Lécuyer houses pastels by Quentin de la Tour, born in the town in 1704. The Musée d'Entomologie is one of the most remarkable in Europe.

Saint-Quentin is the seat of a subprefect, of a tribunal of commerce, of a board of trade arbitrators, and a chamber of commerce. The town, centre of a district which manufactures cotton and woolen fabrics, expanded rapidly after 1947. Iron goods, machinery, and chemicals are also produced.

The date of the founding of the bishopric is uncertain, but *c.* 530 it was transferred to Noyon. St. Eloi (Eligius; d. 660), bishop of Noyon, established a collegiate chapter at St. Quentin's tomb, which became a famous place of pilgrimage. Its cloth manufacture also made the town important during the Middle Ages. In the 9th century it became the headquarters of the comtes de Vermandois, and in 1080 received a charter from Herbert IV. United to the royal domain in 1191, Saint-Quentin, with other districts of Picardy, was ceded to the Burgundians in 1435 but was reunited to the crown in 1477. In 1557 it was the site of a Spanish victory against the French. During the Franco-German War, Saint-Quentin was attacked by the Germans in 1870; and in January 1871 it was the centre of the great battle fought against the Germans. In World War I the Battle of Saint-Quentin (September–October 1918) resulted in a British breakthrough, a final disaster for the Germans which caused them to propose an armistice.

SAINT-RÉAL, CÉSAR VICHARD, ABBÉ DE (d. 1692), French man of letters whose lively writings did much to bring about a new view of history and entitle him to be regarded as a forerunner of Montesquieu and of Voltaire. Born in Savoy (after 1638; perhaps in 1643 or 1644), the son of a magistrate, he went to Paris about 1663. Gabriel Guéret, in 1669, described him as an authority on literary taste and as the constant counselor of Racine and Boileau. In 1674, however, he returned to Savoy and attached himself to the errant duchess Mazarin (Hortense Mancini), whom in 1676 he followed to England and whose reconciliation with the court he tried to negotiate on his return to France. He died in Chambéry in September 1692.

Saint-Réal is said to have been a man of original views, great powers of persuasion, and doubtful morals. His views on the real motives of human activity resemble La Rochefoucauld's, and his treatise *De l'usage de l'histoire* (1671) suggests that he had absorbed a reverence for Machiavelli from Italian historiographers. His most popular work was *La Conjuration des Espagnols contre la république de Venise* (1674), which inspired Thomas Otway's *Venice Preserved*. His other works include *Dom Carlos* (1672); a remarkable *Vie de Jésus-Christ* (1678); a translation of the first two books of Cicero's letters to Atticus (1691); and numerous further essays on historical subjects. Several collections of his works appeared in the 18th century. (W. G. ME.)

SAINTS, BATTLE OF THE, a major British naval victory over the French in 1782 that ended the French threat to the West Indies. The battle was fought in the Saintes Passage between the islands of Dominica and Guadeloupe on April 12, 1782, during the American Revolution. A French fleet of 34 ships under the

comte de Grasse, having sailed from Martinique on April 8 to attack Jamaica, was intercepted by a British fleet of 36 ships under Adm. Sir George Rodney (*q.v.*). On April 9 the British van under Rear Adm. Sir Samuel Hood, having caught up with the French rear, was threatened by De Grasse until the arrival of Rodney with the rest of the fleet relieved it. The French withdrew and on the night of the 10th two of their ships were damaged in a collision. To prevent them from falling into the hands of the British, De Grasse altered course so that a general action occurred on the 12th.

The two fleets approached on opposite courses and might have passed each other with the customary ineffective cannonade had not the wind shifted, so that two French ships were taken aback. This accident created two gaps in the French line of battle, into which Rodney, in the "Formidable," steered with the centre division, and Capt. E. Affleck, in the "Bedford," with the rear. A line of battle was thus broken for the first time in nearly a century of naval warfare. The French fleet was scattered, with the result that De Grasse surrendered his flagship, the "Ville de Paris," and many other ships; only comte Louis de Bougainville with the van escaped. The credit for originating this then unorthodox maneuver has been claimed by others, but the completeness of Rodney's victory (although Hood criticized him for not exploiting the pursuit) created a revolution in tactics of which Nelson later made good use.

The victory had an important effect upon the peace negotiations then in progress, which culminated in the Treaty of Versailles (1783): Britain regained most of its islands in the West Indies and kept Canada and India, though the American colonies were lost.

BIBLIOGRAPHY.—J. K. Laughton (ed.), *Letters and Papers of Charles, Lord Barham*, vol. 1 (1907); J. Clerk, *An Essay on Naval Tactics*, 2nd ed. (1804); Sir H. Douglas, *Naval Evolutions* (1832); D. MacIntyre, *Admiral Rodney* (1962); P. Mackesy, *The War for America* (1964). (C. C. L.)

SAINT-SAËNS, CHARLES CAMILLE (1835–1921), French composer, pianist, and organist known for his symphonic poems and his opera, *Samson et Dalila*. Born on Oct. 9, 1835, in Paris, he studied the piano with C. M. Stamaty and gave his first recital as a child prodigy in 1846. At the Paris Conservatoire he studied the organ under F. Benoist and composition under J. F. Halévy. His First Symphony was performed in 1853. He was appointed organist at the church of Saint-Merry in Paris, in the same year, and at the Madeleine in 1857. About this time he met Liszt who described him as "the finest organist in the world." From 1861 to 1865 he was professor of piano at the École Niedermeyer where his pupils were Gabriel Fauré and André Messager. In 1865 he played his First Piano Concerto at Leipzig, and in 1871, after the Franco-German War, he founded, with the singer, Romain Bussine, the Société Nationale de Musique, with the motto, *Ars Gallica*, which promoted performances of the main French orchestral works of the following generation. In the same

RADIO TIMES HULTON PICTURE LIBRARY

CHARLES CAMILLE SAINT-SAËNS

year he produced his first symphonic poem, *Le Rouet d'Omphale;* other later symphonic poems were *Phaëton, Danse Macabre,* and *La Jeunesse d'Hercule.* Following the production of his first operas, *La Princesse jaune* (1872) and *Le Timbre d'argent* (1877), his biblical opera, *Samson et Dalila,* rejected in Paris on account of its subject, was given in German at Weimar on Dec. 2, 1877, on the recommendation of Liszt. Despite its success, the prejudice in France and elsewhere against the portrayal of biblical characters on the stage persisted, and early performances in London, New York, and Brussels had to be given in concert form. It was first given in Paris on the stage on Oct. 31, 1890, at the Théâtre Eden, and subsequently became Saint-Saëns' most popular dramatic work.

In 1878 Saint-Saëns lost his elder son, who fell to his death from a window, and six weeks later his younger son died in infancy. It is possible that he imputed these tragedies to his wife's negligence: certainly he separated from her three years later, and undertook over the following years extensive tours throughout Europe, the United States, South America, the Near East and the Far East. On these tours he played the piano in the performances of his five concertos and other works and conducted his symphonic works. As a pianist he was admired by Wagner for his brilliant technique and was the subject of a study by Marcel Proust. From about 1880 until the end of his life his large number of works covered all fields of dramatic and instrumental music. Between 1879 and 1911 he wrote ten operas, including *Henry VIII, Les Barbares,* and *Déjanire,* and between 1915 and 1921 a series of works for wind instruments and piano. His Third Symphony (1886), dedicated to the memory of Liszt, shows a romantic tendency. The *Carnaval des Animaux* for small orchestra, written in 1886 but not publicly performed in his lifetime, is a humorous work with realistic effects, conceived as "a zoological fantasy." *Africa,* for piano and orchestra (1891), and the *Caprice Arabe,* for two pianos (1894), show an Oriental influence. Among the best of his later works are the Fifth Piano Concerto (1896) and the Second Cello Concerto (1902). He died in Algiers, on Dec. 16, 1921.

Under the influence of Liszt, Saint-Saëns developed the symphonic poem and wrote for the piano in an elegant, virtuoso style. The clarity of his orchestration long remained a model. Though he lived through the period of the Wagnerian influence he remained unaffected by it, adhered to the Classical models, and upheld a conservative ideal in French music, admired for its polished craftsmanship and sense of form. In his essays and memoirs he described the contemporary musical scene in a shrewd and often an ironic manner.

BIBLIOGRAPHY.—C. Saint-Saëns, *Musical Memories,* Eng. trans. by E. G. Rich (1919); W. Lyle, *Saint-Saëns: His Life and Art* (1923); A. Dandelot, *La Vie et l'Oeuvre de Saint-Saëns* (1930). (E. LR.)

SAINTSBURY, GEORGE EDWARD BATEMAN

(1845–1933), the most influential English literary historian and critic of the early 20th century, was born at Southampton on Oct. 23, 1845. Disappointed of a fellowship at Merton College, Oxford, where he studied *literae humaniores* (1863–66), he became a schoolmaster, and, while at Elizabeth College, Guernsey, read widely in French literature and began to write for reviews. In 1876 he settled in London, combining political journalism with a vast output, first on French, then on English, literature. Notable were the 35 biographies and article on French literature for the 9th edition of the *Encyclopædia Britannica* (1875–89), and *The History of Elizabethan Literature* (1887)—the first to begin with Wyatt and Surrey. Lively style and wide knowledge made his work popular and authoritative; and his reputation was assured by the ambitious surveys written while professor of rhetoric and English literature at Edinburgh (1895–1915): *The Flourishing of Romance and the Rise of Allegory* (1897), still a valuable pioneer work, histories of criticism and literary taste in Europe (3 vol., 1900–04), of English prosody (2 vol., 1906; abridged, 1910), and prose rhythm (1912), and of the French novel (2 vol., 1917–19). In retirement (at Bath, where he died on Jan. 28, 1933), he gained new readers with *Collected Essays and Papers 1875–1920* (4 vol., 1923–24), containing some of his most enjoyable work. His standard edition of *Minor Poets of the Caroline Period* (3 vol., 1921; new ed. 1968) helped to revive interest in 17th-century poetry.

Saintsbury, deliberately, formulated no philosophy of criticism and preferred criteria of "universal reading" and personal response. He looked to poetry for the "poetic moment," and to the novel for criticism of life. Though a stricter approach has replaced his copious, wide-ranging writing, he yet opened the way to a broad view of Western literature; and, by his enthusiasm, emphasized enjoyment as literature's primary aim.

BIBLIOGRAPHY.—A. B. Webster, *G. Saintsbury* (1934); A. Muir *et al.* (eds.), *G. Saintsbury: the Memorial Volume* (1945; U.S., *A Saints-*bury Miscellany, 1947); R. Wellek, *A History of Modern Criticism,* vol. iv: *The Later 19th Century* (1965), with bibliography.

SAINT-SIMON, CLAUDE HENRI DE ROUVROY,

COMTE DE (1760–1825), French social reformer and one of the founders of Socialism (*q.v.*). Grandnephew of the memorialist the duc de Saint-Simon (*q.v.*), he was born in Paris on Oct. 17, 1760. He fought in the American War of Independence, was imprisoned in the Palais de Luxembourg during the Terror, and, after his release, amassed a small

HENRI DE SAINT-SIMON, 19TH-CENTURY LITHOGRAPH BY L. DEYMARU

fortune by land speculation. He was also the originator of schemes to unite the Atlantic and Pacific by a canal, and to construct a waterway from Madrid to the sea. He continued his experiments throughout his life with the result that he was completely impoverished. In 1823 he attempted suicide. He died two years later, on May 19, in Paris. Despite being prolific, his work attracted little attention during his lifetime, and it was only after his death that his influence became considerable.

As a thinker Saint-Simon was deficient in system, clearness, and coherence; but his influence on modern thought is undeniable. He suggested, for example, much of what was afterward elaborated into Comtism (*see* COMTE, AUGUSTE). Apart from the details of his socialistic teaching, his main ideas are simple and are a reaction against both the French Revolution and the militarism of Napoleon. So far was he from advocating fresh social revolt that he appealed to Louis XVIII to inaugurate the new order of things. In opposition, however, to the feudal and military system, he advocated an arrangement by which the industrial chiefs should control society. The spiritual direction of society should fall to the men of science, who would thus take the place occupied by the church in the Middle Ages. What Saint-Simon desired, therefore, was an industrialist state directed by modern science in which universal association should suppress war, and society should be organized for productive labour by the most capable men. The aim of society should be to produce things useful to life.

Although the contrast between labour and capital is not emphasized by Saint-Simon, the cause of the poor is discussed, and in his greatest work, *Nouveau Christianisme* (1825), it takes the form of a religion. It was this development of his teaching that occasioned his final quarrel with Comte. Before the publication of *Nouveau Christianisme,* Saint-Simon had not concerned himself with theology; but here, beginning with a belief in God, he endeavours to resolve Christianity into its essential elements, and finally propounds this precept—"The whole of society ought to strive toward the amelioration of the moral and physical existence of the poorest class; society ought to organize itself in the way best adapted for attaining this end." This became the watchword of the entire school of Saint-Simon.

Saint-Simonians.—Of the disciples who propagated his doctrines the most important were Olinde Rodrigues (1794–1851) and Prosper Enfantin (*q.v.;* 1796–1864), who had received Saint-Simon's last instructions. Their first step was to establish in 1825 a journal, *Le Producteur,* but it was discontinued in 1826. The sect, however, had begun to grow, and, before the end of 1828, had meetings not only in Paris but in many provincial towns. An important departure was made in 1828 by Saint-Amand Bazard (1791–1832), who gave a "complete exposition of the Saint-Simonian faith" in a long course of public lectures in Paris (1828–30), which were well attended and won more adherents. The revolution of July 1830 brought a new freedom to the socialist reformers. A proclamation was issued demanding the community of goods, the abolition of the right of inheritance, and the enfranchisement of women. Early next year the school obtained possession of *Le Globe* through Pierre Leroux (*q.v.; 1797–1871*), who had joined the school, which by this time included some of the ablest and most promising young men of France.

The Saint-Simonians formed themselves into an association arranged in three grades, and constituting a society or family, which lived out of a common purse in the Rue Monsigny. Before long, however, the sect was split by dissensions between Bazard, a man of logical and solid temperament, and Enfantin, who wished to establish a fantastic sacerdotalism with lax notions about the relationships between the sexes. After a time Bazard seceded, with many of the strongest supporters of the school. A series of extravagant entertainments given by the society during the winter of 1832 reduced its financial resources and discredited it. The Saint-Simonians finally removed to Ménilmontant, to a property of Enfantin, where they lived in a communistic society, distinguished by a peculiar dress. Shortly after, the chiefs were tried and condemned for proceedings offending against the social order; and the sect was broken up (1832). Many of its members became famous as engineers, economists, and men of business.

Saint-Simonism.—In the doctrine of Saint-Simon's followers there is a great advance on the confused views of Saint-Simon himself. In the philosophy of history they recognize epochs of two kinds, the critical or negative, and the organic or constructive. The former, in which philosophy is the dominating force, is characterized by war, egotism, and anarchy; the latter, which is controlled by religion, is marked by the spirit of obedience, devotion, and association. The two spirits of antagonism and association are the social principles whose prevalence determines the character of an epoch. The spirit of association, tending more and more to prevail over that of antagonism, is to be the keynote of the social development of the future. Under the prevailing system the industrial chief exploits the proletariat, the members of which, though nominally free, must accept his terms or starve. The only remedy for this is the abolition of the law of inheritance, and the union of all the instruments of labour in a social fund, which shall be exploited by association. Society thus becomes sole proprietor, entrusting to social groups and social functionaries the management of the various properties, and the right of succession is transferred from the family to the state.

The school of Saint-Simon insists strongly on the claims of merit; they advocate a social hierarchy in which each man shall be placed according to his capacity and rewarded according to his works. This is, indeed, a special and pronounced feature of Saint-Simonian socialism. Its theory of government is a kind of spiritual or scientific autocracy, degenerating into the excessive sacerdotalism of Enfantin, the "pope" of Saint-Simonism. With regard to the family and the relation of the sexes the school of Saint-Simon advocates the complete emancipation of woman and her entire equality with man. The "social individual" is man-and-woman, associated in the exercise of the triple function of religion, the state, and the family. In its official declarations the school maintained the sanctity of the Christian law of marriage. Connected with these doctrines was their famous theory of the "rehabilitation of the flesh," deduced from the philosophic theory of the school, which was a species of Pantheism, though they repudiated the name. On this theory they rejected the dualism so greatly emphasized by the Catholic Church in its system of penances and mortifications, and held that the body should be given its due place of honour.

BIBLIOGRAPHY.—*Works and Editions:* Important works are *Lettres d'un habitant de Genève à ses contemporains* (1803), *De la Réorganisation de la société européenne* (1814), *Du Système industriel* (1820–21), *Catéchisme des industriels* (1823–24), and *Nouveau Christianisme* (1825). The standard and most complete edition is *Oeuvres de Saint-Simon et d'Enfantin,* 47 vol. (1865–78). Useful selections are those edited by C. Bouglé (1925), J. Dautry (1951), and, in English, by F. M. H. Markham (1952).

Biography and Criticism: N. G. Hubbard, *Saint-Simon, sa vie et ses travaux* (1857); A. J. Booth, *Saint-Simon and Saint-Simonism* (1871); G. Weill, *Un Précurseur du socialisme: Saint-Simon et son oeuvre* (1894), and *L'École Saint-Simonienne* (1896); S. Charléty, *Histoire du Saint-Simonisme, 1825–1864* (1896; rev. ed. 1931); M. Leroy, *La Vie véritable du Comte Henri de Saint-Simon* (1925); E. M. Butler, *The Saint-Simonian Religion in Germany* (1926); H. R. d'Allemagne, *Les Saint-Simoniens, 1827–1837* (1930); M. Dondo, *The French Faust: Henri de Saint-Simon* (1955); F. E. Manuel, *The New World of Henri Saint-Simon* (1956). See also the relevant chapters in E. Durkheim, *Le Socialisme* (1928; Eng. trans., *Socialism and Saint-Simon* 1959); A. Gray, *The Socialist Tradition* (1946; rev. ed. 1963); M. Leroy, *Histoire des idées sociales en France,* 3 vol. (1946–54); G. D. H. Cole, *A History of Socialist Thought,* vol. i (1953); D. G. Charlton, *Secular Religions in France, 1815–1870* (1963). (T. Kɪ.; J. T. S.; X.)

SAINT-SIMON, LOUIS DE ROUVROY, Duc de (1675–1755), French soldier and diplomatist, remembered for his outstanding memoirs, was born in Paris on Jan. 15, 1675, the only son of an aged noble raised to the peerage by Louis XIII. Physically unattractive, he had a violent, vindictive temper and a bitter tongue, along with great charm, a lively intelligence, independence of judgment, and unassailable moral principles, supported by deep religious convictions.

His immense pride of birth and rank was in part responsible for the disappointments of his career. This opened auspiciously in 1691 with honourable service in the army, but Saint-Simon quickly jeopardized his future by plain speaking and tactless opposition to Louis XIV on a point of precedence; he was against "the bastards' " (*i.e.*, the illegitimate sons of Louis XIV) having precedence of the peers. For several years the king refused to employ him, and only ambition and his wife's success at court prevented him from retiring in disgust to his large but financially embarrassed estates. His position improved momentarily through his connection with Louis, duc de Bourgogne, who became heir to the throne in 1711 and the centre of a liberal, aristocratic reform group, including Fénelon. Unhappily, the Dauphin died suddenly a year later, and Saint-Simon then attached himself to the future regent, Philippe, duc d'Orléans, whose dissolute private life had not impaired their long friendship. After Louis XIV's death in 1715, Saint-Simon might have played the decisive political role to which he aspired, but the regent found him unrealistically obsessed with the social and political prerogatives of the peerage and increasingly ignored his advice. He nevertheless appointed him to the council of regency and in 1721 sent him as ambassador to Spain to negotiate a marriage between Louis XV and the Infanta. Saint-Simon realized that his influence was waning, and with the death of Orléans on Dec. 2, 1723, he retired into private life. Until he died in Paris on March 2, 1755, he immersed himself in the study of history and the composition of his *Mémoires* (first published in a reliable, complete text in 1829–30).

The idea of leaving some such record of his life and times had been in Saint-Simon's mind since 1694, and after keeping a fragmentary diary he had collected miscellaneous material concerning current events. In 1729 there came into his hands a manuscript copy of the *Journal* of the marquis de Dangeau (Philippe de Courcillon), which he was prompted to annotate and which provided him with a chronological framework when, some ten years later, he began, instead, to compose his own memoirs.

The last part of the work, dealing with the period 1723–43, has been lost. The text that has survived covers the years 1691–1723. It is a composite narrative for which Saint-Simon draws on his own memories and papers, on oral and written information supplied by participants and witnesses of all ranks, and on printed and manuscript sources of varying reliability, ranging from the marquis de Torcy's diplomatic papers and standard historical works to Courtilz de Sandras' historical romances. Saint-Simon set himself standards of historical accuracy and impartiality which he did not always observe. He defined his purpose in writing his memoirs as the evocation from within of the living contemporary scene, made intelligible for the edification of posterity. This accounts for his narrative and descriptive detail, his myopic perspective, and his failure to disentangle fundamental causes and events and to establish the true pattern of contemporary history. Living at court in the complex tangle of personal and family relationships which complicated the struggle for preference and power, Saint-Simon almost inevitably overemphasized matters involving personalities and petty intrigue. Convinced that the disorders of Louis XIV's reign were caused by the development of royal absolutism and in particular by the whittling away of the political power of the peerage, it was almost equally inevitable that he should be preoccupied with the niceties of ceremonial, etiquette, and precedence which in his day constituted the essential outward symbols of the realities of power. Nor must impartiality be expected from Saint-Simon, whose estimate of persons and events was often distorted by vanity, disappointment, and personal and political prejudice.

Despite these shortcomings, Saint-Simon's work is the stuff of which history is made. It unfolds before the enthralled spectator an unforgettable fresco of the later years of Louis XIV's reign and of the regency. The wealth of information is staggering; the vividness with which Saint-Simon conjures up the past has few parallels. He analyzes with the pitiless accuracy and penetration of a Racine the traits and motives of his fellow actors; with no less virtuosity and deadly concision he can etch in the physical characteristics that mirror a man's soul. Dislike produces savage, animated caricatures worthy of a Dickens or a Balzac. His style is an admirable instrument for his purpose. It aims not at classical purity but at complete, graphic expression. It is at times incorrect and obscure, but it is normally vigorous and picturesque. Saint-Simon does not recoil before the familiar or the archaic word or expression, nor does he hesitate to adopt a neologism or to coin a phrase. His *Mémoires* are probably the greatest of those for which France is justly renowned.

BIBLIOGRAPHY.—The definitive edition of the *Mémoires* is by A. de Boislisle, 43 vol. (1879–1928) ; a convenient edition is that by G. Truc, in the "Pléiade Series," 7 vol. (1947–64). *See also Memoirs of the Duc de Saint-Simon,* selections ed. by W. H. Lewis (1964).
Biography and Criticism: G. Boissier, *Saint-Simon* (1892) ; A. Le Breton, *La "Comédie Humaine" de Saint-Simon* (1914) ; J. de La Varende, *M. le duc de Saint-Simon et sa comédie humaine* (1955) ; J. Roujon, *Le Duc de Saint-Simon* (1958) ; E. d'Astier, *Sur Saint-Simon* (1962). (O. R. T.)

SAINT THOMAS, a city and port of entry of Ontario, Can., the seat of Elgin County, is on Kettle Creek, midway between Windsor and Niagara Falls. Pop. (1961) 22,469. It was founded about 1810 under the name of Stirling and renamed after Col. Thomas Talbot who made it the capital of the extensive settlement he had founded in 1803. It is a railway division point. Manufactures include roller and powdered metal bearings, heavy-duty tractors, electric motors, truck-mounted concrete mixers, auto and airplane accessories, gaskets, vitrified tile, and metal signs. Educational facilities include Alma College (established 1878), a junior college for women, affiliated with the University of Western Ontario at London. A large publicly owned arena offers year-round ice skating and hockey-training schools. (T. KE.)

SAINT THOMAS ISLAND (ILHA DE SÃO TOMÉ) : *see* SÃO TOMÉ E PRÍNCIPE.

SAINT THOMAS ISLAND, the most important, commercially, of the Virgin Islands purchased by the United States from Denmark in 1917. Pop. (1960) 16,201.

Saint Thomas lies 40 mi. (64 km.) east of Puerto Rico, 1,442 mi. SE of New York City and 1,020 mi. from the Panama Canal. It is 14 mi. (23 km.) long, has a width of 2 mi. (3 km.), and has an area of 32 sq.mi. (83 sq.km.). It is of volcanic origin. The main ridge, peaks of a submerged range, extends east and west the length of the island. Its hills are steep and rocky and sparsely covered with vegetation, the original timber having been cut away for lumber and charcoal. Two summits, Crown Mountain and Signal Hill, rise above 1,500 ft. Many of the spurs of the ridge slope down to the shore and form protected bays where the buccaneers of the 17th and 18th centuries found refuge.

The climate of the island is salubrious, particularly during the first quarter of the year when the trade winds blow. The mean temperature is 78° F (25.6° C), the thermometer rarely falling below 64° (17.8°) and rarely rising above 91° (32.8°). The average rainfall is 38.23 in. (971.04 mm.); the driest weather is in March and the rainy season in October and November. Drinking water is stored in cisterns because of the dearth of wells.

After the abolition of slavery in 1848, agriculture became decadent. Destruction of the once profitable rum export trade as a result of prohibition of liquor in the United States contributed heavily to economic decline. From 1926 to 1933 the annual fed-

eral government contribution to the municipal treasury of the U.S. Virgin Islands averaged around $100,000; however, gradual improvement was made after 1931. By the early 1960s federal contributions to grant-in-aid programs had increased to more than $650,000.

Improved hotels and a stimulation of the tourist trade, along with governmental encouragement of small landholdings, were important among the economic developments. There is an agricultural experimental station at Estate Dorothea. Most of the island's agricultural and dairy produce is for local consumption and ship supplies. Native handicraft work and rum distilleries provide the chief direct exports.

St. Thomas Island was discovered and named by Christopher Columbus on his second voyage in 1493. The first colony was planted in 1657 by the Dutch who soon after abandoned it and migrated to New Amsterdam (New York). The Danes arrived and took formal possession in 1666, but their first colony also failed. The Danish West India company dispatched an expedition under Gov. Jorgen Iversen which landed in St. Thomas harbour on May 25, 1672, and effected a permanent settlement. Later Huguenot refugees from St. Kitts were granted asylum.

In 1755 the king of Denmark acquired the company's rights and made the harbour a free port. The island was temporarily seized by England in 1801–02, and again held in 1807–15, but was restored to and held by Denmark until 1917, when it was sold to the United States.

The chief value of the island is the harbour of Charlotte Amalie, one of the best in the Antilles, important as a United States naval base. It is perfectly landlocked, with a bottlenecked entrance, and has a deserved reputation for refuge. It commands the gateway to the Caribbean through the Virgin passage and is a port of call for passenger steamers from New York and European ports bound for the Panama canal and Central America via the Lesser Antilles. There are ample coaling facilities, oil reservoirs, shipyards and machine shops, floating docks and wharves with electric cranes.

Charlotte Amalie, pop. (1960) 12,880 (known as St. Thomas city from 1917 to 1932), the seat of government of the Virgin Islands, lies on three low spurs of the island ridge; the spurs are dubbed Foretop, Maintop and Mizzentop. A single level street parallel to the water front forms a common base for three cone-shaped clusters of white dwellings on the green background of the ridges. Government hill is one of the attractive residential sections, the location affording constant enjoyment of the breezes and panorama. The population is predominantly Negro, but there is a considerable minority group of French-Norman origin who have lived there for many generations. English is the prevailing language, but Danish, Dutch, French and Spanish are also common. Air services connect with all parts of the Caribbean. (M. F. DE C.)

For general government, *see* VIRGIN ISLANDS.

SAINT VINCENT, JOHN JERVIS, EARL OF (1735–1823), British admiral who won fame as a commander at the battle of St. Vincent (1797) (*q.v.*), was born at Meaford, Staffordshire, on Jan. 9, 1735. He entered the navy on Jan. 4, 1749, and became lieutenant on Feb. 19, 1755; he served in that rank till 1759, taking part in the conquest of Quebec. He was made commander of the "Scorpion" sloop in 1759, and post captain in 1760. During the peace he commanded the "Alarm" (32 guns) in the Mediterranean, and when he was put on half pay he traveled in Europe, taking professional notes everywhere. While the American Revolutionary War lasted, he commanded the "Foudroyant" (80) in the English channel, taking part in the battle of Ushant (1778) and in the various reliefs of Gibraltar. His most signal service was the capture (April 19, 1782) of the French "Pégase" (74) after a long chase.

In 1783 he entered parliament as member for Launceston, and in the general election of 1784 as member for Yarmouth. In politics he was a strong Whig. On Sept. 24, 1787, he attained flag rank, and was promoted vice-admiral in 1793. From 1793 to 1795 he was in the West Indies co-operating with the army in the conquest of the French islands. On his return he was promoted admiral. In Nov. 1795 he took command in the Mediterranean, where he maintained the blockade of Toulon, and aided the allies of Great Britain in Italy.

But in 1796 the occupation of Italy by the French armies closed all the ports to his ships, and Malta was not yet in the possession of Great Britain. Then the addition of the Spanish fleet to the French altered the balance of strength in the Mediterranean. The Spaniards were very inefficient and Jervis would have held his ground if one of his subordinates had not taken the extraordinary course of returning to England because he thought that the dangerous state of the country required that all its forces should be concentrated at home. He was therefore obliged to act on the instructions sent to him and to retire to the Atlantic, withdrawing the garrisons from Corsica and other places. His headquarters were now on the coast of Portugal, and his chief duty was to watch the Spanish fleet at Cadiz. On Feb. 14, 1797, he gained a complete victory against heavy odds. (See SAINT VINCENT, BATTLE OF.) For this victory, which came at a critical time, he was made an earl and was granted a pension of £3,000.

St. Vincent's qualities as a disciplinarian were soon to be put to a severe test. In 1797 the grievances of the sailors, which were of old standing, and had led to many mutinies of single ships, came to a head in the great general mutinies at Spithead and the Nore. Similar movements took place on the coast of Ireland and at the Cape of Good Hope. The spirit spread to the fleet under St. Vincent, and there was a danger that some outbreak would take place in his command. The peril was averted, however, by enforcement of the strictest discipline. St. Vincent had always taken great care of the health of his men, and was as strict with the officers as with sailors. He carried his strictness with his officers to an extent which aroused the actual hatred of many among them, and exasperated Sir John Orde (1751–1824) into challenging him to fight a duel. Yet he has been credited with having raised the discipline of the navy to a high level. His health broke down and in June 1799 he resigned his command.

When St. Vincent's health was restored in the following year he took the command of the channel fleet, into which he introduced his own rigid system of discipline to the bitter anger of the captains. But he was able to maintain the blockade of Brest for 121 days with his fleet. In 1801 he became first lord and held the office till William Pitt returned to power in 1803. His administration is famous in the history of the navy, for he now applied himself to the task of reforming the corruptions of the dockyards. He was fiercely attacked in and out of parliament, and he gave an opening to his critics by devoting himself so wholly to the reform of the dockyards that he neglected the preparation of the fleet for war. He would not recognize the possibility that the peace of Amiens would not last. Pitt made himself the mouthpiece of St. Vincent's enemies, mainly because he considered him as a dangerous member of the party which was weakening the position of England in the face of Napoleon. When Pitt's second ministry was formed in 1803, St. Vincent refused to take the command of the channel fleet at his request. After Pitt's death he resumed the duty with the temporary rank of admiral of the fleet in 1806, but held it only until the following year. After 1810 he retired to his house at Rochetts in Essex.

The rank of admiral of the fleet was conferred on him in 1821 on the coronation of George IV, and he died on March 14, 1823.

(D. H.; X.)

SAINT VINCENT, a British colony, an island of the Lesser Antilles in the Caribbean Sea, forming part of the Windward Islands group, lies about 25 mi. (40 km.) SW of St. Lucia and about 100 mi. (160 km.) W of Barbados. St. Vincent is 18 mi. (29 km.) long, has a maximum width of 11 mi. (18 km.) and an area of 133 sq.mi. (344.5 sq.km.). For administrative purposes most of the Grenadine Islands (q.v.) are included in St. Vincent, giving the territory a total area of 150 sq.mi. (388.5 sq.km.).

Running from north to south, thickly wooded volcanic mountains, from which flow many short swift streams, form the backbone of the island. The highest peak is the volcano Soufrière (4,018 ft. [1,224.7 m.]) in the north, which erupted disastrously in 1821 and 1902. St. Vincent lies in the path of the northeasterly trade winds and has a tropical maritime climate. Rainfall and tempera-

ture vary with altitude. Average annual rainfall ranges from 50 in. (1,270 mm.) on the coast to 150 in. (3,810 mm.) in the central mountains. The temperature averages between 19.4° C (67° F) and 31.7° C (89° F). Hurricanes usually pass north of St. Vincent, but the island suffered severely in 1780 and 1898.

At the 1960 census the population of St. Vincent was 79,948. About 75% of the inhabitants are Negroes, 2½% are whites, and the rest are of mixed or of East Indian extraction; only a few are of pure Carib Indian stock. The capital and chief port is Kingstown, on the southwest coast, with a population (1960) of 4,556. In the mid-1960s there were more than 50 primary schools, 5 secondary schools, and 4 teacher-training establishments. Primary education is free but not compulsory.

St. Vincent's system of government is ministerial. The executive council consists of four elected members (including the chief minister and three other ministers), one nominated member, and one official member. The council is presided over by an administrator, who is appointed by the U.K. government. The legislative council, which has an elected majority, is presided over by a speaker elected by the council.

St. Vincent's economy is agricultural. Traditional crops are arrowroot (of which the colony is the chief world exporter) and sugarcane, but in the late 1950s bananas became the leading export and by the early 1960s comprised about 50% of the total value of exports. Other crops include coconuts, cotton, cassava, groundnuts (peanuts), and sweet potatoes. The chief imports are food, clothing, cement, timber, and gasoline (petrol). The unit of currency is the West Indian dollar with a par value of WI$1.714 to the U.S. dollar. The annual value of imports in the mid-1960s was about WI$12,600,000, and of exports about WI$5,600,000. Nearly half the island is forested, the woodland being used for charcoal burning. Arrowroot and sugar are processed, and soap and edible oils are produced. A limited air service operates from an airfield at Arnos Vale. Two ships, which run between Jamaica and Trinidad, provide a weekly cargo and passenger service.

The date of the discovery of St. Vincent is not known; it is thought that the island may have been given its name by Columbus. Its Carib inhabitants were left almost undisturbed until the 18th century. French, Dutch, and British settlements were attempted, with the French dominant until the Seven Years' War, when British Gen. Robert Monckton occupied it (1762). The Treaty of Paris (1763) confirmed British possession, and settlement proceeded in spite of Carib refusal to accept British sovereignty. In 1779 the island was seized by the French, but it was restored to Britain in 1783. In 1795 the Caribs rose in revolt, assisted by the French from Martinique, but were finally subdued the following year. Most of them were then deported to the Islas de la Bahía (Bay Islands) off Honduras. The emancipation of Negro slaves in 1834 disrupted the island's economy by decreasing the labour supply, and Portuguese and East Indian labourers were introduced later in the century.

In 1958 St. Vincent joined the Federation of The West Indies. In 1960 it received a new constitution. When the Federation was dissolved in 1962, the colony planned to join the other Windward Islands and the Leeward Islands in a smaller federation. In November 1964 agreement on the establishment of a new West Indies federation was reached by the regional council of ministers of the "little seven"—Barbados, Antigua, Dominica, Montserrat, Saint Kitts-Nevis, Saint-Lucia, and Saint-Vincent. See also WEST INDIES; WEST INDIES (FEDERATION), THE. (R. To.)

SAINT VINCENT, BATTLE OF, a famous British naval victory fought off Cape St. Vincent, Portugal, on Feb. 14, 1797, between an English fleet under Admiral Sir John Jervis and a superior Spanish fleet. At that time Spain, which was allied to Revolutionary France, had a force of 27 ships at sea under Don José de Córdoba. Jervis, whose fleet was based on the Tagus River, kept continuous watch for the Spaniards off Cadiz, for which port they were making. When sighted off Cape St. Vincent the Spaniards were in two divisions. Although Jervis had with him only 15 ships of the line, he did not hesitate to give battle. He formed single line ahead and steered to pass between the two groups. He then intended to turn and destroy the larger group. He left the signal late, but Nelson, who was flying a commodore's pennant in the "Captain," which was third from the rear of the British line, anticipated his commander in chief's orders, made a sweep to the rear, and attacked a number of Spanish ships which he saw might otherwise escape. He was supported by Capt. Cuthbert Collingwood in the "Excellent," Capt. Thomas L. Frederick in the "Blenheim," Capt. Thomas Troubridge in the "Culloden," and by other ships. As a result of this initiative, four fine prizes were taken: the "San Josef" and the "Salvador del Mundo," which were larger than most British "first-rate" ships, the "San Nicolas," and the "San Ysidro." The huge "Santissima Trinidada" was thought to have struck her flag, but she managed to escape. Jervis lost no ships, and suffered only about 300 casualties. There were more than 600 casualties in the prize ships, and the Spaniards admitted to 200 more in the "Santissima Trinidada" alone.

The victory heartened Great Britain at a time when she had no effective allies. Jervis was created an earl and took his title from the scene of the action. Nelson was created a Knight of the Bath and gained wide renown for his personal exploits in boarding the "San Nicolas" and the "San Josef." The battle showed the ineptitude of the Spanish leaders and their shortage of skilled manpower; all their ships were short of complement and the guns were manned by soldiers. It prepared the way for Britain's reentry into the Mediterranean, from which her fleet had temporarily been driven by French successes in Italy.

Several previous battles had been fought in the 18th century at Cape St. Vincent, including one in 1780 won by Adm. George Rodney (*q.v.*).

BIBLIOGRAPHY.—*A Narrative of the Proceedings of the British Fleet,* an eye-witness account by Col. Drinkwater Bethune, was published anonymously in 1797; *Dispatches and Letters of Nelson,* with notes by Sir N. H. Nicolas, vol. ii (1845); C. C. Lloyd, *St. Vincent and Camperdown* (1963). (O. M. W. W.)

SAINT VINCENT, CAPE (CABO DE SÃO VICENTE), forms with Sagres Point a promontory in the extreme southwest portion of Portugal. It was referred to by Strabo as the "most westerly point not only of Europe, but of all the inhabited world." To the Greeks and Romans it was known as the Sacred Promontory owing to the presence there of a shrine. Near Sagres was the town Vila do Infante where (*c.* 1420) Henry the Navigator formed a naval observatory and a school for navigators. Nearby were won the naval victories of Sir John Jervis, with Horatio Nelson, in 1797 (*see* SAINT VINCENT, BATTLE OF), and of Sir Charles Napier (*q.v.*) in 1833.

The promontory consists of differentially eroded hard Liassic and Malm dolomites, separated by soft marls. The coastal formation has also been influenced by faults; the cliffs rise 160–230 ft. (50–70 m.) from sea level to a plateau planed by marine abrasion. The climate is humid, subtropical, and windy. Vegetation consists of an extensive cover of gum cistus and other shrubs. Pastoralism and fishing are the mainstay of this desolate district; Sagres is the main settlement. (J. M. Ho.)

SAINT VITUS' DANCE: *see* CHOREA.

SAIONJI KIMMOCHI, PRINCE (1849–1940), Japanese statesman who tried to moderate the nation's then increasing militarism, was born in October 1849 in Kyōto. The son of an imperial noble, Tokudaiji, he was adopted as heir of the Saionji family in 1852. After nominal participation in the movement that led to the restoration of imperial rule in the 1860s, he studied in France until 1881. Holding thereafter many high governmental posts at home and abroad, he was prime minister in 1901–02, 1906–08, and from 1911 until 1912, when he removed himself from public party politics and government office, though he headed Japan's delegation to the Conference of Paris in 1919.

For the last 25 years of his life, Saionji's power stemmed from his position as genro, or elder statesman, an honour reserved for a small group of political leaders who had both participated in the imperial restoration of 1868 and had also been prime minister. As such, he was a close and trusted advisor of the emperors. Consulted on matters of highest state policy, he was particularly influential in recommending the imperial appointments of prime minister. He was considered a liberal during his entire career and often exercised a moderating influence upon ultranationalistic and militaristic trends. After the occupation of Manchuria in 1931–32 fanatic extremists frequently sought to assassinate him. He died, "the last genro," on Nov. 24, 1940. (HN. KN.)

SAIS, the Greek form of the name of the ancient Egyptian city Sai, in the delta on the Canopic or Rosetta branch of the Nile. From prehistoric times it was the location of the chief shrine of the warrior goddess Neith, who was also worshiped as the creatrix who wove the world on her loom. The city became politically important late in its history. Tefnakhte of Sais was defeated by the Napatan Piankhi, but Tefnakhte's son Bocchoris, whom Manetho accounts the only ruler of the 24th dynasty, regained control of lower Egypt for six years till slain by Shabaka. When Assyria defeated the Napatans, Saite princes, as Assyrian vassals, gained control of the delta once more and after expelling his masters, Psamtik I (663–610 B.C.) won for himself all Egypt. Under this pharaoh and his successors of the 26th dynasty, Sais was the capital. (*See* also EGYPT: *History: Ancient Period.*) Enriched by Mediterranean and African trade, the Saite kings lavished their wealth on temples and palaces and built near them their tombs. In Herodotus' day Sais was still one of the finest cities in Egypt. Like many Greek visitors, he stayed there, and the priests of the Temple of Neith were his informants.

Known in modern times as Sa al Hajar (Sa el-Hagar), the extensive and imposing mound has been little explored, though very much denuded since it was first described by J. F. Champollion in 1818. Inscribed stones found on the site and in nearby villages are all that remains of this once-great city.

See Herodotus, Book ii, 62, 163, 169–171, 175–176; L. Habachi, "Sais and Its Monuments," in *Annales du service des antiquités de l'Égypte,* vol. xlii, pp. 369–416 (1943). (M. S. DR.)

SAISSET, BERNARD (*c.* 1232–*c.* 1311), the first bishop of Pamiers (southern France), was an aggressive and outspoken prelate whose activities exacerbated the disputes between Pope Boniface VIII and Philip IV of France. Of a noble Toulousain family, Saisset became an Augustinian canon and in 1267 was elected abbot of Saint-Antonin at Pamiers.

Saisset was involved in two major incidents. The first was a dispute over control of the town of Pamiers, originally shared between the abbey and the counts of Foix (*q.v.*). The count's authority had recently been exercised by the crown, but Philip IV restored it to Count Roger Bernard III (February 1295). At this point Saisset was made bishop of Pamiers (July 1295), the pope carving for him a diocese from the territory of that of Toulouse. Eventually a compromise was negotiated between count and bishop (December 1297) and they were formally reconciled (June 1300).

Soon afterward, Saisset was denounced to the king as a traitor, probably by the bishop of Toulouse. Two royal officials took evidence (May 1301) from more than 20 people, including Roger Bernard. In July Saisset was summoned to appear before the king, his goods were sequestrated, and some of his servants imprisoned. At Senlis (October 1301) he was charged with treasonable utterances, plotting with Aragon and England against Philip, and with simony, heresy, and blasphemy. Philip communicated the charges to the pope; but the latter also heard of the violence done in this case to the persons and property of churchmen, and ordered Saisset's release. For the subsequent quarrel between king and pope, *see* PHILIP IV. Expelled from Philip's kingdom (February 1302), Saisset went to Rome but was apparently back in Pamiers late in 1305. He died probably in December 1311.

See J. M. Vidal, *Histoire des évêques de Pamiers,* vol. i (1926); G. Digard, *Philippe le Bel et le saint siège,* 2 vol. (1936).

SAITAMA, a Japanese prefecture (*Ken*) north of Tokyo, with an area of 1,468 sq.mi. and a population (1960) of 2,430,871. Its level land areas are extensive and the ratio of cultivated area (38%) is the highest among the prefectures. Horticultural produce for consumption in Tokyo is the characteristic feature of agriculture. The Sayama area produces a choice green tea. The western section is devoted to sericulture. The chief products of manufacturing are textile goods and machinery. Cities in the south, including Urawa, the prefectural capital, have become suburban residential centres for Tokyo commuters.

(R. B. H.)

SAIT FAIK ABASIYANIK (1907–1954), Turkish author, who introduced a new form of short-story writing into Turkish literature. Born at Adapazari and educated in Istanbul and Bursa, he spent four years in France (1931–35), mainly in Grenoble, and on his return began to publish his short stories in *Varlik*, the leading avant-garde periodical. These were in a style new to Turkish literature: shapeless, without definite plot, but gripping, and conveying in a single episode a wide range of human experience.

In 1936 he published his first volume of short stories, *Semaver*. A dozen others followed, including *Lüzumsuz Adam* (1948), *Kumpanya* (1951), *Havuzbashi* (1952), and *Alem Daginda var bir Yilan* (1953). He also experimented with a novel, *Bir Takim Insanlar* (1952), and published a volume of verse. The subjects of his powerful sketches and stories are taken from the life of simple people in humble occupations; his style, though realistic, has an element of poetry. He died in Istanbul, May 11, 1954.   (F. I.)

SAKA (SHAKA), a Scythian tribe identified with the Sacae of classical literature and the Sai (Sok) of the Chinese annals, who are often mentioned along with the Yavanas and Pahlavas (Parthians) in Indian literature, originated near the upper reaches of the Ili River, south of Lake Balkhash, but were forced by the Yue-chi (Yüeh-chih; *q.v.*) to move southward *c.* 160 B.C. Passing through Kashgar and crossing the Pamirs, they reached Gilgit and, in course of time, occupied the Swat Valley and Gandhara (Northwest Frontier area), after having overthrown the Indo-Greeks.

Coins and inscriptions show that the earliest king bearing a Saka name in Gandhara was Maues (Mauakes, Moga). He ruled, probably from *c.* 95 to 75 B.C., over Gandhara and contiguous areas. His coins, which consist of more than 20 types of silver and copper, with inscriptions in Greek and Kharosthi, are found in considerable numbers and portray Greek deities; *e.g.*, Zeus, Apollo, Herakles, Poseidon, Artemis, and Nike. Inscriptions dating from Maues' reign have been found in Shahdara, Mansehra, Fatehjang, and Taxila (all in West Pakistan). Soon after Maues' death the Sakas were driven eastward by the Pahlavas. Mathura (in modern Uttar Pradesh) became their new headquarters, and there the Saka kings best known from coins and inscriptions were Rajuvala and Sodasa. Some of the Rajuvala coins found in excavations at Taxila may date from a period when Rajuvala had still some control over that city. Some of the coin inscriptions again are in Greek and Kharosthi, others are in Brahmi only. Similarly, the Indian goddess Lakshmi is depicted on Rajuvala's money in addition to the Greek Pallas Athene and Herakles.

It was in Malwa, however, that the Sakas became firmly established. These Sakas often referred to as the Western Kshatrapas (*i.e.*, satraps), with their capital city at Ujjain, ruled Malwa and parts of Rajputana and Maharashtra for more than 300 years. Theirs is the only coinage series in ancient India which always gives the year of issue and the name of the father of the reigning king and his status. The founder of this house of Saka kings was Cashtana, with whose reign the Saka era, starting from A.D. 78, may be associated (but *see* CHRONOLOGY: *Hindu*). He is generally identified with Tiastenes mentioned in Ptolemy's *Guide to Geography*. The most powerful king of this dynasty was Rudradaman, whose famous Junagadh inscription, dated A.D. 150, noted for its fine Sanskrit prose, describes his military exploits and the steps taken by him to reconstruct the Sudarshana Lake, an irrigation work built by order of Chandragupta Maurya. After Rudradaman the dynasty suffered reverses, but it continued to rule until the end of the 4th century A.D. when Rudrasimha III was overthrown, probably by Chandra Gupta II Vikramaditya.

BIBLIOGRAPHY.—J. E. van Lohuizen-de Leeuw, *The Scythian Period* (1949); H. C. Raychaudhuri, *Political History of Ancient India*, 6th ed. (1953); P. B. Whitehead, *Catalogue of Coins in the Punjab Museum*, Lahore, vol. i (1914); E. J. Rapson, *Catalogue of Indian Coins in the British Museum, Andhras, Western Ksatrapas*, etc. (1908); John Allan, *Catalogue of Indian Coins in the British Museum: Ancient India* (1936); Sten Konow (ed.), *Corpus Inscriptionum Indicarum*, vol. ii, pt. i (1929).   (A. K. N.)

SAKAI, a city in Ōsaka urban prefecture, Japan. Pop. (1960) 339,863. Many large earthen tomb mounds around the city attest its antiquity; Emperor Nintoku's tomb (1,574 ft. long, 105 ft. high) is the largest in Japan. Sakai was celebrated in the 16th century as the leading eastern inland seaport and was noted for its rich merchants. A shift in the course of the Yamato River silted its harbour, and the city sank in obscurity with the rise of neighbouring Ōsaka to commercial and industrial greatness. Sakai has revived as an Ōsaka industrial satellite since the opening of rail service between the two cities. Machinery, bicycle and automotive parts, fertilizer, *tabi* (cotton socks), dyestuffs, and chemicals are among its chief products. The main industrial belt is located along the coast on reclaimed land, while residential areas spread inland on elevated sites. The port handles an active traffic in small native craft.   (J. D. EE.)

SAKE, the national beverage of Japan, is a rice beer, often mistakenly called a wine because of its high alcoholic content, usually 17 to 18%. Brewing of sake dates back many centuries.

Production of sake begins with steamed rice or *koji*, which is mixed with *Aspergillus oryzae*, a specially cultured mold that converts the rice starch into fermentable sugars. Preparation of the *koji* takes place in warm, draft-free cellars. The next step is the mixing together of 36 litres of *koji*, 90 l. of fresh steamed rice, and 108 l. of water. The resulting mass is worked and kneaded by hand for two hours until a smooth, lump-free paste of even consistency is obtained. It is allowed to rest for 24 hours, after which it is put into a large vat containing more steamed rice and water. A wooden or enameled iron bucket 18 in. deep, with a diameter of 12 in. at the top and 8 in. at the bottom, filled with boiling water, is suspended and immersed in the mash, being moved about periodically to heat the mash evenly. A slow, free fermentation occurs over a period of four weeks, the result of which is *moto*, with an alcoholic content of $10\frac{1}{2}$ to 11%. Additional quantities of *koji*, steamed rice, and water are added to the *moto* in the fermenting vat and a new fermentation takes place, lasting seven days. In order to facilitate fermentation a culture of the yeast *Saccharomyces sake* is sometimes added to the fermentation mixture. Lactic acid also may be added, to prevent bacterial contamination. The fresh sake is rested for another week, after which it is filtered and bottled.

The drinking of sake is a delicate, even poetic ceremony. It is always served warm, in tiny porcelain bowls that hold little more than an ounce. It is sipped.

Though each drink of sake is small, consumption in Japan is an important economic factor. The average annual consumption of alcoholic beverages in Japan after World War II was about 350,000,000 U.S. gal., of which sake represented 40%.

(H. J. GN.)

SAKHALIN, an island of the U.S.S.R. lying off the far eastern coast between the Tatar Strait and the Sea of Okhotsk. Area 29,300 sq.mi. (76,000 sq.km.) Together with the Kuril Islands (*q.v.*) it forms Sakhalin *oblast* of the Russian Soviet Federated Socialist Republic. Area of *oblast*, 33,600 sq.mi. (87,100 sq.km.). Pop. (1959) 649,405.

Physical Features.—The island is long and narrow, orientated north–south for 589 mi. (948 km.) while the average width is 62 mi. (100 km.). At the nearest point, in the Nevelskogo Strait, the island is only 4 mi. (6.4 km.) from the mainland. The greater part of Sakhalin is mountainous. The main chain is that of the Western Sakhalin Mountains, which extend from the extreme southern tip, Cape Krilon, to approximately 51° 30′ N, although isolated hills continue to Mt. Vagis. This range rises to 4,347 ft. (1,325 m.) in Mt. Zhuravleva. To the east of the range is a tectonic trough, occupied by the south-flowing Poronay and north-flowing Tym. East of the trough is a much shorter, nearly parallel range, the Eastern Sakhalin Mountains, which rise to 5,279 ft. (1,609 m.) in Mt. Lopatin, the highest peak of the island. The northern third of Sakhalin is a hilly lowland, with an isolated group of higher hills on the Shmidta Peninsula at the northern end. The great extent of latitude (over 8°) covered by the island means there is a considerable range of climate, soil, and vegetation. The overall climatic regime is of the cold monsoon type, with onshore summer winds bringing a rainfall of 20–30 in. (510–760 mm.) a year and cool conditions (July average temperatures 15° C [59° F] in the north and 17° C [63° F] in the south). The winter offshore monsoon brings exceptionally bitter weather for the latitude, ranging from −23° C (−9° to −10° F) January average in the north to −8° C (17° F) in the south. Snowfall is high. The maritime location causes high cloudiness all the year round and a high frequency of fogs in summer. These fogs are encouraged by the meeting of the cold Okhotsk current from the north, which also contributes to severe conditions in northern Sakhalin, and the warm Tsushima current, which modifies the climatic regime of the south. This severe and unpleasant climate brings forest-tundra conditions in the north with stunted forest of birch and willow and much peat bog. The mountains are mostly in taiga of Yeddo spruce and Sakhalin fir. In the south is mixed forest, with a rich variety of eastern deciduous species, such as Manchurian oak and elm and Korean willow. On the west coast wild bamboo is found. Soils are mostly podzolic.

History.—Sakhalin was first settled by Japanese fishermen along the southern coasts. In 1853 the first Russians entered the northern part. In 1855 an agreement with Japan shared control of the island, but in 1875 Russia acquired all Sakhalin in exchange for the Kurils. As a result of the Russo-Japanese War Japan in 1905 (Treaty of Portsmouth) gained Sakhalin south of the 50th parallel and gave this part the Japanese name of Karafuto. In 1918, after the Revolution, the Japanese occupied all Sakhalin, but they withdrew in 1924 and in the following year White Russian forces were driven out of the north by Soviet troops. The Soviet Union regained the southern half in 1945, at the end of World War II, together with the Kurils, and the entire Japanese population was repatriated. In 1932 an *oblast* subordinate to Khabarovsk *krai* had been established in the north; in 1947 the whole island was made a fully independent *oblast*.

Population.—Of the 1959 population, the exceptionally high proportion of 75% was urban, living in 19 towns and 33 urban districts. The large number of urban districts indicates a youthful stage in the development of the island's economy. The largest town is the administrative centre of Yuzhno-Sakhalinsk (formerly Toyohara) with 85,510 people. Other towns are small, the most important being the old administrative centre of Aleksandrovsk-Sakhalinskiy on the west coast, the coal-mining towns of Uglegorsk and Poronaysk, and the oil town of Okha. The overwhelming bulk of the population is formed by Russian settlers, with some Ukrainians and Belorussians. In the north are a few hundred of the indigenous tribes, the Gilyaks (Nivkhi), Evenki, and Oroke.

The Economy.—First place in the economy of Sakhalin belongs to fishing, which is carried on from all the coastal settlements. Crab, herring, cod, and salmon are caught and canned in the larger centres. The annual output exceeds 33,000,000 cans. Second in importance is timber working and many of the southern towns manufacture pulp and paper, notably Yuzhno-Sakhalinsk, Uglegorsk, and Kholmsk. In all there are eight paper mills. Third place is taken by mineral extraction. Deposits of coal are found all along the flanks of the Western Sakhalin Mountains. The main mining centres are Uglegorsk, Shakhtersk, Aleksandrovsk-Sakhalinskiy, and Poronaysk. Although the deposits are small, they form an important source of supply for the Soviet far east. In the extreme north, around Okha, petroleum is obtained and sent by pipeline under the Tatar Strait to the refineries of Komsomolsk-on-Amur and Khabarovsk. As with the coal, the deposits have an importance out of proportion to their small size, because they are the only source of petroleum in the Soviet far east. Small-scale shipbuilding and repair are carried on at Korsakov, in the far south, and Aleksandrovsk-Sakhalinskiy. The severe climate and mountainous relief have caused agriculture to be weakly developed, as the low rural population indicates. Only in the south and in the Tym Valley are limited areas of arable found. By far the greater part is under potatoes; other vegetables, oats, and fodder-maize are the only other significant crops. Pigs and cattle are kept and there are nearly 14,000 head of reindeer. Fur-bearing animals include bears, foxes, otters, and sables; rodents are numerous. Communications are few. In the south railways flank the Western Sakhalin Mountains, extending on the east side as far north as Pobedino. In the north a short line crosses the island through Okha and then runs south along the east coast to Katangli.

A motor road runs from north to south through the central trough. There are airfields at Yuzhno-Sakhalinsk and Okha.   (R. A. F.)

SAKJEGOZU, a village in a piedmont valley of the Anti-Taurus near Zincirli Huyuk in the Gaziantep *il* of southern Turkey. Sakjegozu first attracted the attention of archaeologists as the source of a Late Hittite slab relief depicting a royal lion hunt, which had been taken from the walls of the village chief's house and placed in the Berlin Museum. There it was noticed by the British archaeologist J. Garstang, who traced its original source to a small mound called Jobba Huyuk, adjacent to the village. Excavations undertaken on this mound between 1907 and 1911 revealed a Late Hittite palace of moderate dimensions at its summit, fortified with a practically rectangular enclosure measuring 400 × 300 ft. The gateway of the enclosure was on the lower side of the mound, while the palace occupied the opposite higher section of the walled precinct. The walls, which were nearly 12 ft. thick and rested on massive foundations, were strengthened by projecting external buttresses and, at the corners, by turrets.

The palace itself was approached through a portico containing an outstanding series of sculptures. Notable among these are the two life-size gate lions flanking the entrance to the palace and forming its cornerstones. The representations comprise sphinxes and other fabulous creatures in the Assyrian manner; likenesses of human beings and symbolic scenes, such as the "fertilizing of the sacred tree," reflect equally thoroughgoing Assyrian influence.

Since no inscriptional material was found at Sakjegozu, neither the ancient name nor the precise date of the palace settlement could be determined. To provide a stratigraphic substitute for more immediate chronological evidence, a deep sounding was made underneath the palace foundations down to virgin soil. The whole mound was found to be made up of the stratified debris of successive habitation layers, reaching back to Neolithic times; *i.e.*, the 5th and early 4th millennia B.C. Flint and obsidian implements and burnished monochrome pottery (mostly rather simple black, gray or brown bowls) characterize the early Neolithic phase. During the latter half of the period a new style of pottery using coloured paint makes its appearance.

See J. Garstang, *The Hittite Empire,* pp. 262–278 (1929); S. Lloyd, *Early Anatolia* (1956).   (J. Pl.)

SAKKARA: *see* Saqqarah.

SALADIN (Arabian Salah al-Din, "Honour of the Faith") (1138–1193), a successful leader of Muslim armies against the crusaders and founder of the Ayyubid dynasty (*see* Ayyubids) in Egypt, was born in Tikrit (Iraq). He belonged to a Kurdish family which had emigrated from Armenia in 1130. His father, Ayyub, and his uncle, Shirquh, rose to prominence in Syria, in the service of the famous anti-crusader champion Nureddin (*q.v.*). The climate of holy war (*jihad*) as well as the religious and cultural atmosphere animating the Muslim elite in Syria must have decisively influenced the young Saladin.

The struggle against the Latin-Christian states established by the First Crusade (whose European ruling caste is usually referred to as the "Franks") constituted the most important issue in the political and economic life of Syria and Egypt. Egypt's position had become vulnerable as a result of the decadence of the heterodox (Isma'ili) regime of its Fatimid caliphs. Internal struggles for power between various political and military Muslim factions had created favourable conditions for foreign intervention, and the Franks, covetous of the economic resources of Egypt, decided to turn to their own advantage the military impotence of the country. On the other hand, Nureddin was determined to prevent Egypt from falling into the hands of the Franks and to win it himself by military intervention. In the ensuing "battle of Egypt" (1164–68) Syrian troops commanded by Shirquh defeated the Franks and established their rule in the country. In the three expeditions of Shirquh's army, Saladin had played a major part. After the death of Shirquh (1169) Saladin was appointed as vizier of the Fatimid caliphate and as commander of the Syrian troops in Egypt. Fully conscious of Egypt's critical position, Saladin proceeded with various drastic measures intended to restore its former strength. In 1171, at the strong insistence of Nureddin, Saladin abolished the Fatimid caliphate and officially proclaimed the return of Egypt to the traditional Sunni form of Islam. (*See* also FATIMIDS.)

Although nominally subject to the authority of Nureddin, Saladin was determined to conduct his own policy. Thus he was reluctant to commit his troops in the campaigns of Nureddin against the Franks. This clash of interests was brought to an end by the death of Nureddin in 1174. With his independence decisively secured, Saladin could devote his attention to the economic and military buildup of Egypt. Having organized strong land and naval forces, he carried out the internal pacification of the country and restored a zone of security around the southern and western approaches to Egypt, so essential for the normal operation of the Egyptian transit trade. A number of buildings, including colleges, a citadel, and an aqueduct, erected in Cairo during his rule, clearly indicated an improvement in the Egyptian economy.

Relying on the economic and military resources of Egypt, Saladin could proceed with an effective policy against the Franks. To strengthen the power of the Muslim front he planned to control Syria, the unity of which was shattered after the death of Nureddin. Between 1174 and 1186 Saladin, by diplomatic and military measures, succeeded in asserting his authority over many important Syrian cities, such as Damascus and Aleppo, and over Mosul and Irbil in Iraq. With strong armies under his command, he was then ready for war against the Franks. His task was facilitated by the popularity of the *jihad* against the Franks, for which he made frequent appeals. After the violation of peace by the Franks Saladin engaged his army on July 4, 1187, at Hittin (Hattin) near Tiberias in northern Palestine and after a bloody battle won a decisive victory. He then overran Palestine and, after offering generous terms to the Christian inhabitants of Jerusalem, entered the holy city on Oct. 2. Thus Jerusalem was restored to Islam after having been for 88 years in the hands of the Franks.

During his otherwise successful campaign in Palestine Saladin failed to conquer Tyre, where the remnants of the Frankish forces held him off. Ultimately they resumed the initiative by laying siege to Acre, and from June 1189 Acre became the concentration point for the land and naval forces of the crusaders arriving from Europe to reestablish their domination in the Holy Land. The European counteroffensive, known as the Third Crusade, directed all its power against Acre, whose heroic garrison, assisted from the outside by Saladin, sustained a siege of more than two years. It was only a tight naval blockade and the arrival of fresh English troops under the leadership of Richard I Coeur de Lion that forced Acre to capitulate (July 12, 1191). Yet, despite this setback, despite the superior forces of the Christians, despite heavy losses in men and armament resulting from the loss of Acre, and despite the destruction of his fleet and the straining to the utmost of the Egyptian economy, Saladin's stubborn determination in resisting the invasion of the crusaders turned the scales of victory at least partly in his favour. Most of the European contingents, worn out by the prolonged siege operations, returned home after the capitulation of Acre. Even the brilliant military exploits of Richard during his campaigns of 1191–92 did not change the overall results of that major showdown between the crusaders and the Muslims. The terms of the armistice concluded on Sept. 2, 1192, between Saladin and Richard, confirmed the ascendance of the Muslim forces. While the crusaders were given a coastal strip in Syria, Saladin remained in possession of the rest of the formerly contested territory, including Jerusalem. Thus his achievements definitely crippled the holdings of the crusaders in the Near East.

After the conclusion of the armistice Saladin returned to Damascus, where, on March 4, 1193, after a few days' illness, he died. He was buried in Damascus, his tomb becoming an object of great reverence. The regime of the Ayyubid family over Egypt and Syria, founded by Saladin, was continued by his brothers and their immediate descendants.

The character of Saladin and of his work is singularly vivid. In many ways he was a typical Muslim leader of the period of the Crusades. He was fiercely hostile toward the unbelievers who had established the crusader kingdoms, merciless toward the perjurers guilty of armistice violations, and yet tolerant of his own Christian subjects. His piety and strict observance of the rites of Islam did not affect his political judgment. To further the cause of Shirquh, Saladin did not shrink from the assassination of Shawar, the Egyptian vizier, in 1169. To protect his own independence he obstructed the operations of Nureddin against the Franks. To strengthen the position of Egypt he did not hesitate to conclude a treaty with the Christian empire of the Byzantines. He was certainly a great personality, inspiring awe in Christendom and attracting the admiration of the Muslim world. His achievements profoundly affected the history of Egypt, as well as the destiny of the Near East. *See* also CRUSADES; EGYPT: *History;* and references under "Saladin" in the Index.

BIBLIOGRAPHY.—H. A. R. Gibb, "The Arabic Sources for the Life of Saladin," *Speculum,* vol. 25, i (1950), and "The Achievement of Saladin," *Bulletin of the John Rylands Library,* vol. 35, no. 1 (1952). A more general study on Saladin, also contributed by H. A. R. Gibb, can be found in K. M. Setton (ed.), *A History of the Crusades,* vol. i, pp. 563–589 (1955).   (A. S. EH.)

SALADS: *see* FOOD PREPARATION.

SALAJAR (SALAYAR), the largest of a group of islands, including Bahuluang, Pulasi, and Tambulongan, lying south of Celebes (Sulawesi), Indonesia. It is more than 50 mi. (80 km.) long and 8 mi. (13 km.) at its widest point; area 259 sq.mi. (671 sq.km.). The population of the group (regency) was 87,278 in 1961, mainly a mixture of Makasars and Bugis. This is one of the most thickly populated parts of Celebes and is administered from Makasar. The islands are mountainous, but Salajar has fertile lowlands. Trepang, tortoise shell, copra, coconut oil, and salt are exported.   (J. O. M. B.)

SALAMANCA, a city of west-central Spain and the capital of Salamanca Province. The adjoining provinces are Zamora and Valladolid to the north, Ávila to the east, and Cáceres to the south. Portugal lies to the west, and the northern part of the frontier is marked by the Duero River (Port., Douro). Pop. (1960) 90,498 (mun.).

The city rises to 2,631 ft. (802 m.) above sea level on the right (north) bank of the Tormes River, a tributary of the Duero. Its towers can be seen from some distance to the south. The Old Cathedral (Catedral Vieja, begun *c.* 1140) is a fine example of Romanesque, its domed clock tower rising above two circular tiers of windows and a vaulted roof. In 1512 it was described as a "very small, dark, low building"; fortunately it was not destroyed, and the New Cathedral (Catedral Nueva) was built round it on three sides, though not completed till the 18th century. The main building of the university faces the New Cathedral. It was built by 1494 and a stone medallion over the western doorway portrays Ferdinand and Isabella. The adjoining buildings include the former residence of Salamanca's most famous rector, Miguel de Unamuno (*q.v.*), with his library and personal relics.

To the south of the New Cathedral, a broad flight of steps leads up to the Neoclassical façade of the Colegio de Anaya (1760–68), designed by José Hermosilla and containing the faculties of science and of philosophy and letters. During the French occupation Gen. André Masséna made it his palace. The faculty of law adjoins the university, but the new faculty of medicine is in the valley to the west. Next to it stands the only remaining old residential college, the Colegio de Fonseca, generally known as the Colegio de los Irlandeses because it was ceded after the Peninsular War to the Irish as a seminary and so used until World War II. The property has reverted to the university but is not in use. It was built between 1527 and 1578 from funds provided by Archbishop Alonso de Fonseca. Its Renaissance quadrangle is the finest in Salamanca. Fonseca was also responsible for the Casa de las Muertes (so called from the death's heads formerly over the doorway), intended also for a university college, and for the Diputación Provincial (county hall). The former Jesuit seminary, built between 1617 and 1755 from plans by Juan Gómez de Mora, is now the Pontifical University, most of whose students are priests or seminarians. The Jesuits still officiate in its church of La Clerecía.

The Church of the Convent of the Augustinian Nuns was built

between 1636 and 1687, by order of Count Gaspar de Acevedo y Zúñiga, viceroy of Naples, for a natural daughter who became mother superior of the convent; the style is clearly Italian. It contains a famous painting of the Immaculate Conception by Jusepe de Ribera (*q.v.*, known as "Lo Spagnoletto"). The Dominican Convent, San Estéban, was mostly rebuilt under Juan de Álava from 1524 onward; older remaining portions include the cloister where Christopher Columbus was reputedly examined by the Council of Theologians in 1486. The Church of St. Thomas of Canterbury was originally built in 1175, two years after Thomas Becket's canonization, apparently under the direction of two English brothers and priests, named Richard and Randolph, who were lecturers at the university. Only the south wall of the original Romanesque building remains, the rest dating from the 15th century.

The Torre del Clavero (*c.* 1480) is almost all that remains of the town walls. The legendary Cave of Salamanca is the ruined crypt of the former Church of St. Cyprian; there, reputedly, the writer Enrique de Villena (*q.v.*) practised black magic. The walls of the 16th-century Casa de las Conchas are covered with carvings of scallop shells, the symbol of the military Order of Santiago of which its first owner, Talavera Maldonado, was chancellor. Gen. Viscount Wellington (later the duke of Wellington) in 1812 lodged in the 16th-century Palacio de San Boal, which suffered in later renovations.

The town centres round its fine arcaded Plaza Mayor, built (1729–33) by Andrés García de Quiñones, with the town hall on its west side by Alberto Churriguera. The square was originally intended to serve on occasion as a bull ring. The surrounding arcade is ornamented on two sides with medallions of the kings of Spain and Gen. Francisco Franco. During the French invasion, Masséna had his medallion put up, but it was afterward removed.

Three residential colleges for university students were built in the 1950s. North of the Plaza Mayor an avenue named the Gran Vía was still under construction in the 1960s; the arcades at the bottoms of some of the buildings recall those of the main square.

Fifteen of the 26 arches of the Roman bridge date from Roman times; a headless bull of Iberian date stands in the square at the end of it. Other bridges carry motor traffic and the railway. Rail services run direct to Madrid, Zamora, Plasencia, and Oporto, Port.; Salamanca is also on the direct line from the Spanish frontier at Irún to Lisbon. A military airfield at Matacán lies 12 mi. (19 km.) E. The town is an agricultural centre with few factories.

Hannibal ravaged the town in 220 B.C. A Roman town grew up because Salamanca (Salmantica) and its bridge were on the "Silver Road" from Astorga to Seville. It became a bishopric after the 3rd Council of Toledo in the 7th century, though during the Moorish occupation the bishop lived in Oviedo. From the 8th to the 11th centuries, the town was in the warring area between Christians and Moors. The Christian repopulation took place from 1087 to 1102. In 1178, Ferdinand II of León held his *Cortes* there and granted a special *fuero* (charter) to the city, by then the second in importance in his kingdom. The university came into existence under Alfonso IX of León in 1218, but the year of its real foundation was 1253 under Alfonso X (the Wise) of Castile and León. It was a leading centre of learning in Europe till the end of the 16th century. Francisco de Vitoria (*q.v.*) laid down the first principles of international law there in about 1526. St. Theresa or Teresa (*q.v.*) of Ávila founded a Carmelite convent in the town in 1570 and sought for other buildings there. Luis Ponce de León lectured in the university from 1561 until his death in 1591, except for the years 1572–76 when he was in an inquisition prison on a charge of unorthodoxy; a room in the university, still furnished with benches and other furniture of his day, is known as his *aula* (lecture hall). The French occupied Salamanca in 1808 until dislodged by Wellington in 1812; before leaving, they destroyed a quarter containing many university buildings. The university continued ecclesiastical until 1835, after which it was forcibly secularized. In the Civil War from 1936 to 1939 Gen. Franco took up residence in Salamanca in what is normally the episcopal palace.

SALAMANCA PROVINCE. Pop. (1960) 405,729. Area 4,763 sq.mi. (12,337 sq.km.), more than half of which is covered by typical *meseta* country. The Sierra de la Peña de Francia rises in the south, its highest point being Peña de Francia (5,653 ft. [1,723 m.]), crowned by a monastery and hostel. This part of the province is richly forested. The Sierra de Gata lies along the boundary with Cáceres Province. In spite of its dryness and relatively few trees, Salamanca is rich in vegetables, including sugar beet, and holm oaks, fruit trees, and cereals, especially wheat (Unamuno described it as "bread-bearing country"). Livestock and fighting bulls are plentiful, though Andalusian bulls are supposed to show more spirit. The town of Béjar has numerous cloth factories. Wellington won victories at the frontier village of Fuentes de Oñoro in 1811, and in 1812 at Salamanca and at the ancient walled town of Ciudad Rodrigo; for the last battle he was given the Spanish title of duke of Ciudad Rodrigo. Teresa of Ávila died in the Carmelite Convent of Alba de Tormes. (C. D. L.)

SALAMANDER, generally, any of the tailed amphibians, order Caudata, or Urodela, a group that includes eight very diverse families, most of which are exclusively North American. In a restricted sense, however, the name is applied to the European fire salamander, *Salamandra salamandra*, and its close relative *S. atra*. The family includes the cosmopolitan newts (*q.v.*) and several allied Eurasian genera. The fire salamander, with many differently coloured geographic races, ranges from Asia Minor through most of southern Europe to northwestern Africa. *S. atra* is confined to the Alps and the western Balkan Mountains.

The fire salamander, black with irregular yellow blotches, may reach a total length of 11 in. Contrary to the ancient belief that it can withstand the heat of a fire, it is ordinarily active only in the cool of the night, when it hunts insects, worms, slugs, and similar food. It winters beneath leaf litter and logs, more rarely under stones. Although it is normally solitary, aggregations are found in late autumn at favoured hibernating places. The salamander is tolerant of cold, however, and occasionally is seen on the surface on mild winter days.

The striking coloration of the fire salamander may serve more for concealment (due to the disruptive patterns) than for chromatic warning to predators. Most predators that attack a salamander are apt to leave it in distaste because of the salamander's poisonous skin glands. The glands' secretion is irritating to mucous membranes and if taken internally may be lethal, because of its adverse effect on the nervous system. The European water snake or ringed snake (*Natrix natrix*) is relatively immune to the secretion and preys frequently on *Salamandra*.

The fire salamander becomes sexually mature at four years of age. Courtship takes place in summer and fall. The breeding male noses under a receptive female and after moving about with her on his back, deposits a spermatophore that is picked up by the female's cloacal lips. Sperm overwinter in the female's reproductive tract and fertilize eggs internally the following spring. The embryos, generally about 30 in number, develop into gilled larvae by autumn but are usually not deposited until the next spring. The larvae are about one inch long when the female backs into a stream to release them. They double in size before transforming into adults and leaving the water permanently three to four months later. In *S. atra*, two young, half the length of the mother, are born fully metamorphosed. There are numerous eggs, as in *S. salamandra*, but normally only one survives in each oviduct. While growing, the embryo uses material from the other eggs, and late in development the gills effect a nutritive exchange with the oviductal walls resembling that of the mammalian placenta.

See also AMPHIBIA; and references under "Salamander" in the Index. (G. B. R.)

SALAMIS, a rocky island lying off the coasts of Megaris and Attica, Greece. Pop. (1961) 20,645; area 37 sq.mi. (95 sq.km.). Salamis encloses the wide Bay of Eleusis, which is entered from the Saronic Gulf by two narrow straits on the west and east. Neolithic and Bronze Age remains have been found, and the Late Mycenaean period is represented by many chamber tombs. The capital then lay at the narrow waist of the island and faced west to the Saronic Gulf, which was dominated by Aegina, and the Homeric poems associated Salamis and Aegina in the persons of the Salaminian princes Ajax and Teucer, sons of Telamon, who came from Aegina.

Some time after the Dorian occupation of Megaris (c. 1050 B.C.), Megara acquired Salamis and planted Megarian settlers (cleruchs) on the best land. Megara and Athens fought for the island at the turn of the 7th century, and Sparta, acting as arbitrator, awarded it to the Athenians, who allocated the best land to Athenian cleruchs, built a new capital on the east side at Kamatero facing Attica, and held the native Salaminians in a position of inferior status. The importance of Salamis grew with Athenian commercial expansion, since it lay close to the Piraeus and offered alternative anchorage. An Athenian magistrate was appointed annually to supervise the island.

In September 480 the Greek fleet, having withdrawn from Artemisium (see GRECO-PERSIAN WARS), stationed itself off Kamatero in narrow waters, while the much larger Persian fleet lay at Phaleron east of Piraeus. The Persians sent a squadron to close the narrow western strait, landed troops at night on Psyttaleia, an island in the eastern strait (probably Ayios Yeoryios), and advanced at dawn up the eastern strait. The Greeks made a withdrawal up the channel, formed their battle order, sailed out to engage the Persian fleet south of the bend in the channel (i.e., off Kamatero), and proceeded to ram the Persian ships, which fell into disorder in the narrow space with reinforcements pressing up from behind. The Greek victory was decisive at sea, for the Persian navy never tried to reverse the verdict of Salamis.

The Athenians retained the island until the Macedonian period, when Cassander placed a garrison there in 318. The Athenians recovered it in 229 and planted cleruchs once more. Today there is a Greek naval base on Salamis at Arapis north of Kamatero, and a ferry service runs regularly to Attica.

BIBLIOGRAPHY.—Strabo, Geography, pp. 393–395; Pausanias, book i, 35–36; M. N. Tod (ed.), Selection of Greek Historical Inscriptions, 2nd ed., vol. i, no. 11 (1946), for cleruchs in Salamis; N. G. L. Hammond, "The Battle of Salamis," Journal of Hellenic Studies, 76:32 ff. (1956); W. K. Pritchett, "Toward a Restudy of the Battle of Salamis," American Journal of Archaeology, 63:251–262 (July 1959). (N. G. L. H.)

SALAMIS, the principal city of ancient Cyprus, situated on the east coast, north of the Pedias River and about 6 mi. (10 km.) N of Famagusta. It had a good harbour, well situated for commerce with Phoenicia, Egypt, and Cilicia, which was replaced in medieval times by Famagusta (q.v.) and is now wholly silted. Its trade was mainly in grain, wine, and oil from the midland plain and in salt from the neighbouring lagoons.

Traditionally, Salamis was founded after the Trojan War by Teucer, from the island of Salamis off Attica. There was certainly a Mycenaean colony at the neighbouring town of Enkomi. A king Kisu of Sillua is mentioned in a list of tributaries of Esarhaddon of Assyria in 672 B.C., and Sillua is usually identified with Salamis. Salamis seems to have been the principal Greek power in the island. The revolts against Persia c. 498 B.C., 386–380 B.C., and 351 B.C. were led by its kings Onesilos, Evagoras (q.v.), and Pnytagoras, respectively. In 306 B.C. Demetrius Poliorcetes won a great naval victory there over Ptolemy I of Egypt. Under Ptolemaic and Roman administration, Salamis flourished greatly, though the seat of the governors was at Paphos (q.v.). Roman remains include a gymnasium, a theatre, and an amphitheatre. Salamis was sacked in the Jewish revolt of A.D. 115–117; suffered repeatedly from earthquakes; and was wholly rebuilt by the emperor Constantius II (reigned 337–361) under the name Constantia. There was a large Jewish colony, and a Christian community was founded by Paul and Barnabas. Barnabas was himself a Cypriot, and his reputed tomb, discovered in 488, is still shown near the monastery of St. Barnabas. St. Epiphanius was bishop from 367 to 403. Salamis was the metropolitan see of Cyprus until the Latin conquest. The Greek city was destroyed by the Arabs under Mu'awiya c. 648; Christian survivors migrated to the neighbouring Ammochostos (Famagusta). See also CYPRUS: History.

BIBLIOGRAPHY.—J. A. R. Munro and H. A. Tubbs, "Excavations in Cyprus, 1890," Journal of Hellenic Studies, xii, pp. 59 ff. (1891); E. Oberhummer in Pauly-Wissowa, Real-Encyclopädie der classischen Altertumswissenschaft, 2nd series, i, 1832–44 (1920). Enkomi: A. S. Murray in British Museum, Excavations in Cyprus, pp. 1 ff. (1900); E. Sjöqvist in The Swedish Cyprus Expedition, vol. i, pp. 467 ff. (1934); C. F. A. Schaeffer, Enkomi-Alasia (1952).

SAL AMMONIAC (AMMONIUM CHLORIDE): see AMMONIA.

SALANDRA, ANTONIO (1853–1931), premier of Italy at the start of World War I, was born of a wealthy family at Troia, Puglia, on Aug. 13, 1853. He became a barrister, taught public administration at Rome University and was a conservative in politics. He became minister of agriculture in 1899 and was finance minister on two occasions, in 1906 and in 1909–10. When, in March 1914, Premier Giolitti resigned, Salandra was called upon to form the new cabinet.

Salandra was premier on the outbreak of World War I, and it was his cabinet that took the momentous decision of proclaiming Italy's neutrality, in spite of the existence of the Triple Alliance (Germany, Austria-Hungary, and Italy) because Austria-Hungary had declared war on Serbia without a previous agreement with Italy. After bargaining with both sides, in May 1915 Salandra assumed the still greater responsibility of bringing Italy into the war on the side of the Allies. This highhanded decision was taken during a parliamentary recess. Subsequently he had to resign office in June 1916, in consequence of the successful Austrian offensive in the Trentino. (See ITALY: History.)

During the disturbed period from 1919 to 1922 Salandra upheld the principles of authoritarian conservatism. He succeeded T. Tittoni as Italian delegate on the League of Nations council and in its assembly, and represented Italy in the Italo-Greek conflict of August–September 1923 (see CORFU). He supported the Fascist movement from the first but did not join the Fascist Party; and when he felt that Fascism was incompatible with the old Liberal tradition, especially after Mussolini's speech of Jan. 3, 1925, he modified his support. In 1928 on the proposal of Mussolini he was created a senator. He died on Dec. 9, 1931.

Salandra's war policy is covered in his two books La Neutralità italiana, 1914: ricordi e pensieri, published in 1928, and L'Intervento, 1915 (1930). (D. M. SH.)

SALAZAR, ANTÓNIO DE OLIVEIRA (1889–   ), the foremost Portuguese statesman of the 20th century, premier from 1932 to 1968, was born to a peasant family at Vimieiro, near Santa Comba Dão, in Beira Alta Province, on April 28, 1889. After eight years at the seminary at Viseu, he decided against the priesthood and in 1910 entered the law school of Coimbra University, from which he graduated with high honours in 1914. He returned to Coimbra as a lecturer in economics in 1917 and was appointed to the chair of economics in 1918.

Salazar soon made a name for himself through his writings and speeches on political economy. After two previous attempts, he entered practical politics at the Army revolt of May 28, 1926, when the liberal and anticlerical parliamentary regime, which he despised, was replaced by a military dictatorship. He became finance minister on May 30 but held the post for only a few days. When the generals would not give him a free hand, he returned to Coimbra. On April 27, 1928, Salazar rejoined the cabinet under Pres. António Óscar de Fragoso Carmona (q.v.) in the same capacity but with control over income and expenditure.

Named premier by Carmona on July 5, 1932, Salazar became the strong man of Portugal and, with the widest power at his command, undertook to transform the Army revolt into a national revolution. The 1933 constitution of his Estado Novo ("New State"), which provided for an authoritarian state based on principles of social justice, incorporated ideas expounded by him since his student days. He was strongly influenced by the writings of Frédéric Le Play, Pope Leo XIII, and Charles Maurras (qq.v.), and of the Portuguese poet and historian António Sardinha, but his subsequent organization of the state also owed much to Fascist examples. During his period in office he also held the posts of minister of colonies (1930), minister of finance (1928–40), minister of war (1936–44), and minister of foreign affairs (1936–47).

Speaking at Braga on May 28, 1966, on the 40th anniversary of the Army revolt, Salazar claimed that the greatest achievement of his national revolution was the rehabilitation of the public finances. He had also modernized the railways, expanded the merchant marine, and carried out numerous public works projects. He increased the nation's international prestige by strengthening Portugal's ties with Brazil, Spain, Great Britain, and the United States, and a concordat in 1940 established a new modus vivendi with the Vatican. He was less successful in solving Portugal's other problems. The rate of progress in education continued to be inadequate; the slow rise in the standard of living had little effect on the widespread poverty of the people; his government regulated political life to the exclusion of any effective opposition; and censorship of the press was never abolished. (*See* PORTUGAL: *History: The Republic, from 1910*.)

Salazar had lived a life of frugal simplicity; a bachelor, he shared a small apartment with two adopted daughters, shunned publicity, rarely granted interviews or made personal appearances or speeches. In September 1968 brain damage from a fall left him in a coma following surgery, and he was replaced as prime minister by Marcello Cætano.

Salazar's collected *Discursos e notas políticas* began to appear in 1935; a selection in English of some of his speeches, *Doctrine and Action*, appeared in 1939.

BIBLIOGRAPHY.—A. Ferro, *Salazar: Portugal and Her Leader*, Eng. trans. (1939); C. Garnier, *Salazar: an Intimate Portrait* (1954); L. Mégeban, *Le Vrai Salazar* (1958); J. Ploncard d'Assac (ed.), *Dictionnaire politique de Salazar* (1964).   (M. Ca.)

SALCEDO, a province in northern Dominican Republic, is the smallest province in area (191 sq.mi. [493 sq.km.]) and has the greatest density of population (1960 average, 415.5 per sq.mi. [160.4 per sq.km.]). Its many small farms produce a great quantity of cacao, coffee, corn, and some tobacco. The province is crossed by the eastern section of the low Cordillera Septentrional, which divides the drainage northward to the Atlantic from the streams that flow southward to the fertile Vega Real.

Salcedo was created in 1952 from Espaillat province. The population of Salcedo province was 79,140 in 1960.

The capital is Salcedo (pop. [1960] 6,810).   (D. R. D.)

SALDANHA, JOÃO CARLOS DE SALDANHA OLIVEIRA E DAUN, DUQUE DE (1790–1876), Portuguese general and statesman whose turbulent career made him prominent for more than 50 years, was born at Azinhaga on Nov. 17, 1790, the son of the conde de Rio Maior and Maria, daughter of the marquês de Pombal. He joined the army in 1805 and fought throughout the Peninsular War (1808–14). With the rank of colonel he went to Brazil in 1815 and until 1821 fought in the Portuguese campaigns against the rebel José Artigas, attaining the rank of general. He returned to Portugal in 1823 and was appointed military governor of Oporto in 1825. After the accession in 1826 of Pedro IV (Pedro I of Brazil), Saldanha was responsible for the proclamation (July 1826) in Portugal of Pedro's constitutional charter (*see* PORTUGAL: *History*). Created a count in 1827, he emigrated to London with other liberals in October 1827, when Pedro's brother Dom Miguel became regent. After he was proclaimed King Miguel I (1828), Saldanha commanded two unsuccessful expeditions against him; to Portugal in 1828 and to the Azores in 1829.

He went to France, returning to Portugal in 1833 to fight for Pedro in the war against Miguel, which ended in the latter's abdication (May 1834). Saldanha was then created marquês. Following the accession of Maria II (September 1834), he headed the government from May to November 1835. He opposed the revolution of September 1836, and took part in the unsuccessful revolution of the marshals in 1837. Created duque in 1847 he was again head of the government in the disturbed political periods of 1847–49 and 1851–56. Ambassador to Rome (1862–65 and 1866–69) and envoy to Paris (1869), he returned to Portugal in 1865 to oppose the government; and in May 1870, in Lisbon, he made a military *pronunciamento* taking over the government. He later became ambassador in London, where he died on Nov. 21, 1876.

See the Conde da Carnota, *Memoirs of ... the Duke of Saldanha*, 2 vol. (1880).   (DA. A. P.)

SALE, a municipal borough of Cheshire, Eng., lies 5 mi. (8 km.) SW of Manchester by road. Pop. (1961) 51,336. In 1930 the urban districts of Sale and Ashton-upon-Mersey were amalgamated. Sale was incorporated in 1935, and has since grown considerably. It is mainly residential in character but there are a few light industries. The Mersey River separates Sale from Manchester, Stretford and Urmston, and the Cheshire-Lancashire county boundary which follows the line of the Mersey also forms part of the borough boundary. The borough is situated astride the trunk road A. 56 (the Chester–Manchester road known as Watling Street), and the Bridgewater Canal (constructed 1770 by the Duke of Bridgewater) passes through the town. St. Martin's Church, founded in 1304, was rebuilt in 1714.   (I. Hu.)

SALÉ (Arabic SLA), an old walled town and former seaport on the Atlantic coast of Morocco, at the mouth of the Bou Regreg opposite Rabat (*q.v.*). The right bank of the river has silted up and Salé port is no longer in use. Pop. (1960) 75,799. Essentially a Muslim town, it has many mosques and tombs of saints and a *medersa* (Muslim school) built in 1333 during the Beni Marin dynasty. In the Middle Ages it was the most important merchant port and entrepôt of western Morocco. In the 17th century it became, with Rabat, a corsair republic. Several unsuccessful attempts were made by the French and British to overthrow it. Piracy organized by the "Sallee rovers" continued until 1829.
     (A. Am.)

SALEM, a town and district of Madras (Tamilnad), India. The town, headquarters of the district, lies in the picturesque valley of the Tirumanimuttar between the Shevaroy Hills in the north and the Jaruguwalai Hills in the south, 206 mi. (332 km.) SW of Madras by rail. Pop. (1961) 249,145. It is well known for its handloom products, and manufactures cotton and silk dhoties (loincloths). A government college is affiliated with Madras University. The town is on the main road from Madurai to Bangalore.

SALEM DISTRICT (area 7,028 sq.mi. [18,203 sq.km.]; pop. [1961] 3,804,108) comprises three distinct plateaus: the first in the extreme north on the Mysore tableland (3,000 ft. [914 m.]); the second, or intermediate zone, comprising mostly the Eastern Ghats between 1,200 and 2,000 ft. (366 to 610 m.); the third in the south below the Eastern Ghats, descending from 1,200 to 300 ft. (91 m.). The northern and central parts have inferior soils, the prevailing types being red sand. About 1,500 sq.mi. (3,885 sq.km.) are under forests. The district is well known for mangoes, but the chief commercial crop is peanuts. In the Shevaroy Hills oranges, pears, and bananas are cultivated, and at Krishnagiri (north) grapes are grown. The Mettur Dam on the Cauvery, with a hydroelectric plant, lies 25 mi. (40 km.) NW of Salem. Since its completion in 1934 industrial development has been rapid, and there are chemical and textile industries at Mettur, Salem, and several other centres outside the district.

The district is sparsely dotted with thin bedded schistose gneisses which include crystalline marbles and iron ores. The iron ore deposits in the Kanjamalai and Thirthamalai hills alone are estimated to be more than 300,000,000 tons. Besides iron ore, the district has an abundance of bauxite reserves in the Shevaroy Hills. Emery powder is manufactured. With the Mettur power, the average annual output of aluminum was expected to be greatly expanded.
     (G. Kn.)

SALEM, one of New England's most historic cities, is an old seaport in Essex county, Mass., U.S., about 15 mi. NE of Boston. Its diversified industry includes a large parlor-game plant; electronic devices and leather goods are also important products. Its principal modern interest, however, is linked with its distinguished past, particularly its remarkable early maritime achievements, its witchcraft trials and executions, and its associations with Nathaniel Hawthorne (*q.v.*).

Salem was founded in 1626 by Roger Conant, six years after the settlement of the "Old Colony" at Plymouth. In 1628 Gov. John Endecott brought a band of settlers there as an advance guard of the Massachusetts Bay colony, which was established in force at Boston in 1630. In 1629 the first Congregational church in America was organized at Salem by the Rev. Francis Higginson; Roger Williams was one of its early pastors. Several 17th-century homes are still standing, including the Pickering house (1660); the John Turner house (1668), immortalized by Hawthorne as "the house of the seven gables"; and the John Ward house (1684), preserved with 17th-century furnishings by the Essex institute. There is also the "witch house," where Judge Jonathan Corwin held some of the preliminary examinations during the witchcraft hysteria of 1692, in which about 30 persons, chiefly women, were condemned and 19 were hanged for supposedly practising the occult arts.

Salem's chief distinction to historical fame comes from its achievements at sea during the 50 years following the outbreak of the American Revolution. It had a very mediocre harbour and a meagre hinterland but during the "golden age" of the American merchant marine its ships and mariners voyaged with great success to distant seas, particularly beyond the Cape of Good Hope. The boom came from privateering during the American Revolution, when Salem vessels made about 445 captures. With trade routes open in 1783 after British colonial regulations were removed, some of the larger Salem privateers, especially those of Elias Haskett Derby, opened up new contacts with the Baltic, the Mediterranean, India and what Samuel E. Morison in his *Maritime History of Massachusetts* has called the Salem East Indies, with pepper from Sumatra as a specialty. Particularly high profits were made by the Derbys, the Crowninshields and others by neutral traffic during the Anglo-French wars from 1793 until the end of 1807, when the Embargo act ended virtually all commerce with foreign nations. Salem still contains much atmosphere from the heyday of that trade, particularly in the high, square brick houses, with beautiful carved woodwork, designed by Samuel McIntire (q.v.). Of these, the Pingree house (1804), beautifully furnished, is opened to the public by the adjacent Essex institute. The atmosphere of the great age of Salem shipping has been ably preserved by the national park service's 9-ac. Salem Maritime National historic site, established in 1938. It includes the great Derby wharf, commenced around 1760, and the adjacent, shorter Central wharf; the Derby house (1762); the McIntire-designed Hawes house (1801); and the Salem Custom house (1819), where Hawthorne, as surveyor of the port from 1846 to 1849, wrote part of *The Scarlet Letter*. Salem's commerce never regained its former volume, although after the embargo was lifted there developed a lively trade with Zanzibar and a factory was started to produce cloth for that market. Eventually, as ships became larger, the harbour could not accommodate them and Salem controlled and manned vessels operated out of Boston or New York.

Important custodians of the Salem tradition are the Essex institute, with its rich library and its quarterly *Historical Collections,* and the Peabody museum, housed in the old granite building of the East India Marine society and possessing maritime and ethnographic collections. In addition to Hawthorne, other distinguished Salem natives were Nathaniel Bowditch, pioneer in navigation; Timothy Pickering, early postmaster general and secretary of state; and William Hickling Prescott, the historian. Alexander Graham Bell did much of his significant telephone research while a resident of Salem.

For comparative population figures *see* table in MASSACHUSETTS: *Population.*   (R. G. A.)

SALEM, a city of New Jersey, U.S., 38 mi. S.W. of Philadelphia, Pa., is the oldest permanent English settlement in the Delaware valley and many of its houses, as well as its Quaker meeting house, have been preserved from colonial times. It was established in 1675 on Salem creek, 2 mi. from the Delaware, by John Fenwick, an English Quaker. Fenwick took the name Salem, meaning "land of peace," from the Old Testament. In 1682 Salem received royal permission to become a port of entry. In the decade before the American Revolution, however, the collector of customs reported that smuggling, especially of rum, sugar and molasses, was prevalent. During the American Revolution, the British occupied Salem in 1778, following Anthony Wayne's foraging expedition into the area for supplies for Washington's army at Valley Forge. It was during these years that the massacre of American militia at the William Hancock house, 4 mi. from Salem, occurred. The house is now a state museum.

The railroad reached the edge of Salem in 1863 but did not come into the town itself until 1882, when a bridge was built over Salem creek. The decade of the 1860s also witnessed the establishment of a glass works and an "oil cloth" factory to make floor coverings. By the second half of the 20th century these two industries, along with canned foods, were the major sources of employment. Many inhabitants, however, commuted to work in nearby industries.

A point of historical interest is the Alexander Grant house (1721), home of the county historical society museum. The an-

cient oak tree under which Fenwick bartered with the Indians continues to attract visitors.

For comparative population figures *see* table in NEW JERSEY: *Population.*   (H. F. WI.)

SALEM, the capital of Oregon, U.S., and the seat of Marion County, is situated in the centre of the rich Willamette Valley, about 40 mi. from the Pacific coast and 50 mi. S of Portland. The government buildings, built along an open mall and dominated by a modern neoclassical capitol completed in 1939, are in the heart of the city. Volcanic peaks of the Cascade Mountains can be seen to the east and the forested Coast Range to the west.

In 1834 a group of Methodist missionaries came to Oregon under the leadership of Jason Lee, a native of the Canadian border, of New England parentage and education. The first site chosen for the mission, 10 mi. N of the present city of Salem, proved unhealthful, and in 1840 the mission was moved to a site known as Chemeketa, an Indian name which meant "place of peace." This they translated to the biblical name of Salem and there they erected a grist and sawmill and an Indian school.

In 1842 the missionaries decided to found a second school, for white children, called the Oregon Institute, which they hoped would become a university; the first instruction was given in 1844. To provide funds for the institute, the missionaries decided in 1846 to lay out a town and sell lots. The Willamette Valley was the focal point of the first migrations over the Oregon trail and as the population grew the mission townsite prospered. By a charter granted in 1853 the Oregon Institute became Willamette University, the oldest institution of higher learning in the western United States. It is still related to the Methodist Church and offers liberal arts training and graduate work in law, music and education.

Salem became territorial capital of Oregon in 1851 and was confirmed as state capital by popular vote in 1864. The city was chartered in 1857. As the state grew, city and government grew, the city spreading from the flood plain by the river to surrounding hills. The city has had a council-manager form of government since 1947.

An eight-month growing season, an annual rainfall of 40 in. and a variety of soils produces a diversity of more than 100 crops in the area and Salem's canneries and frozen-food plants make it an important processing centre. Strawberries, beans, blackberries, sweet corn, onions, cherries, and broccoli had the largest pack in the 1960s. As highways widened the market area, the city became a major retail centre. Wood, paper products, and metal fabrications are long standing and growing industries. The community used the Willamette River for transportation until 1933. It is served by north–south rail lines, an interstate highway and airlines.

The Salem Art Museum in the Asahel Bush house (1878) is a city cultural centre. In the city or nearby are state schools for the blind and deaf, state hospitals, Fairview Home for the Mentally Retarded, and penal institutions.

The population of Salem in 1960 was 49,142. In 1964 the U.S. Bureau of the Budget designated Marion and Polk counties as the Salem standard metropolitan statistical area. In 1960 this area had a combined population of 147,411. For comparative population figures *see* table in OREGON: *Population.*

BIBLIOGRAPHY.—Robert C. Clark, *History of the Willamette Valley, Oregon* (1927); Robert M. Gatke, *Chronicles of Willamette* (1943); Salem Chamber of Commerce, *Salem, Oregon* (1957); Marion County Historical Society, *Marion County History,* vol. i–vi (1955–60).
                                      (D. C. D.)

SALE OF GOODS. The law of sale may be regarded as a branch of the law of contract, because sale is effected by contract. Thus the French jurist R. J. Pothier entitles his classical treatise on the subject *Traité du contrat de vente.* A completed contract of sale is a contract plus a transfer of property. If there be no agreement for a price, express or implied, the transaction is of the nature of a gift. If a transaction called a sale is, in fact, intended to secure the repayment of a debt, and not to transfer the absolute property in the thing sold, the law at once annexes to the transaction the complex consequences which attach to a mortgage. So, too, it is not always easy to distinguish a contract for the sale of an article from a contract for the supply of work and materials.

If a man orders a dental plate from a dentist, the contract is one of sale; but if he employs a dentist to fill one of his teeth with gold, the contract is for the supply of work and materials. The distinction is of practical importance because different rules of law apply to the two classes of contract. The property which may be the subject of sale may be either movable or immovable, tangible or intangible. The present article relates only to the sale of goods—that is to say, tangible movable property.

GREAT BRITAIN

Codification in Britain: The Sale of Goods Act, 1893.—In 1847, when W. W. Story wrote his work on the sale of personal property, the law of sale was still in process of development. Many rules were still unsettled, especially the rules relating to implied conditions and warranties. But for several years the main principles had been well settled. In 1891 the subject seemed ripe for codification in Britain, and Lord Herschell introduced a bill which two years later passed into law as the Sale of Goods Act, 1893.

Sale is a consensual contract. The parties to the contract may supplement it with many stipulations or conditions they may see fit to agree to. The code of 1893 does not seek to fetter this discretion. The main object of the act is to provide clear rules for those cases in which the parties have either formed no intention or have failed to express it. When parties enter into a contract they contemplate its smooth performance, and they seldom provide for contingencies which may interrupt that performance, such as the insolvency of the buyer or the destruction of the thing sold before it is delivered. It is the province of the code to provide for these contingencies, leaving the parties free to modify by express stipulation the provisions imparted by law.

When the code was in contemplation the case of Scotland gave rise to difficulty. To speak broadly, the Scottish law of sale differs from the English by adhering to the rules of Roman law, while the English common law has worked out rules of its own. The codifying bill of 1891 applied only to England, but on the advice of Lord Watson it was extended to Scotland. As the English and Irish laws of sale were the same, the case of Ireland gave rise to no difficulty, and the act applies to the whole of Great Britain. As regards England and Ireland, very little change in the law has been effected. As regards Scotland, the process of assimilation has been carried further but has not been completed. In a few cases the Scottish rule has been saved or reenacted, in a few other cases it has been modified, while on other points, where the laws were dissimilar, the English rules have been adopted.

Definition.—The act is divided into six parts, the first dealing with the formation of the contract. The first part, which may be regarded as the keystone of the act, is in the following terms:

A contract of sale of goods is a contract whereby the seller transfers or agrees to transfer the property in goods to the buyer for a money consideration called the price. A contract of sale may be absolute or conditional. When under a contract of sale the property in the goods is transferred from the seller to the buyer the contract is called a "sale," but when the transfer of the property in the goods is to take place at a future time or subject to some condition thereafter to be fulfilled the contract is called an "agreement to sell." An agreement to sell becomes a sale when the time elapses or the conditions are fulfilled subject to which the property in the goods is to be transferred.

This section clearly enunciates the consensual nature of the contract, and this is confirmed by sec. 55, which provides that "where any right, duty or liability would arise under a contract of sale by implication of law," it may be negatived or varied by express agreement, or by the course of dealing between the parties, or by usage, if the usage be such as to bind both parties to the contract.

The next question is who can sell and buy. The act is framed on the plan that if the law of contract were codified, this act would form a chapter in the code. The question of capacity is therefore referred to the general law, but a special provision is inserted (sec. 2) relating to the supply of necessaries to infants and other persons who are incompetent to contract. Though an infant cannot contract, he must live, and he can only get goods by paying for them. The law, therefore, provides that he is liable to pay a reasonable price for necessaries supplied to him, and it defines necessaries as "goods suitable to the condition in life of such minor or other person, and to his actual requirements at the time of the sale and delivery."

Prevention of Fraud.—The fourth part of the act reproduced the famous 17th section of the Statute of Frauds, which was an act "for the prevention of frauds and perjuries." The object of that statute was to prevent people from setting up bogus contracts of sale by requiring material evidence of the contract, such as a written and signed agreement. It was long a much-disputed question whether this enactment brought about good or harm. It defeated many an honest claim, though it may have prevented many a dishonest one from being put forward. In 1954, in response to recommendations of the Law Revision Commission, this requirement of a writing to evidence the sale of goods was repealed (Law Reform [Enforcement of Contracts] Act, 1956, sec. 2).

As noted above, the obligation to pay a price is an essential element in a contract of sale, as distinguished from a gift. The price may be either fixed by the contract itself, or left to be determined in some manner thereby agreed upon; e.g., by the award of a third party. But there are many cases in which the parties intend to effect a sale and yet say nothing about the price. Suppose that a man goes into a hotel and orders dinner without asking the price. How is it to be fixed? The law steps in and says that, in the absence of any agreement, a reasonable price must be paid (sec. 8). This prevents extortion on the part of the seller and unreasonableness or fraud on the part of the buyer.

Warranty.—The next question dealt with is the difficult one of conditions and warranties (sec. 10 and 11). The parties may insert what stipulations they like in a contract of sale, but the law has to interpret them. The term "warranty" has acquired a peculiar and technical meaning in the English law of sale. It denotes a stipulation which the law regards as collateral to the main purpose of the contract. A breach, therefore, does not entitle the buyer to reject the goods but only to claim damages. Suppose that a man buys a particular horse, which is warranted quiet to ride. If the horse turns out to be vicious, the buyer's only remedy is to claim damages, unless he has expressly reserved a right to return it. But if, instead of buying a particular horse, a man applies to a dealer to supply him with a quiet horse, and the dealer supplies him with a vicious one, the stipulation is a condition. The buyer can either return the horse, or keep it and claim damages. Of course the right of rejection must be exercised within a reasonable time.

In Scotland no distinction has been drawn between conditions and warranties, and the act preserves the Scottish rule by providing that, in Scotland, "failure by the seller to perform any material part of a contract of sale" entitles the buyer either to reject the goods within a reasonable time after delivery, or to retain them and claim compensation (sec. II [2]). In England it is a very common trick for the buyer to keep the goods, and then set up in reduction of the price that they are of inferior quality to what was ordered. To discourage this practice in Scotland the act provides that, in that country, the court may require the buyer who alleges a breach of contract to bring the agreed price into court pending a decision of the case (sec. 59).

In early English law there developed the principle that the buyer had only his carelessness to blame if the goods proved to be defective. This view, often called *caveat emptor* (let the purchaser beware), was well suited to primitive times. Men either bought their goods in the open marketplace, or from their neighbours, and buyer and seller contracted on a footing of equality. The complexity of modern commerce, the division of labour, and the increase of technical skill have altogether altered this state of affairs. The buyer is more and more driven to rely on the honesty, skill, and judgment of the seller or manufacturer. Modern law has recognized this and protects the buyer by implying various obligations in contracts of sale. The most important are imposed upon manufacturers or sellers who deal in particular classes of goods. They naturally have better means of judging their merchandise than the outside public, and the buyer is entitled within limits to rely on their skill or judgment. A tea merchant knows more about tea than his customers can, and so does a gunsmith about guns. In such cases, if the buyer makes known to the seller the particular purpose for which the goods are required, there is an implied condition that the goods are reasonably fit for it, and if no particular purpose be indicated there is an implied condition that the goods supplied are of merchantable quality (sec. 14).

Effects of Contract.—The main object of sale is the transfer of ownership from seller to buyer, and it is often both difficult and important to determine the precise moment at which the change of ownership is effected. According to Roman law, which is still the foundation of most European systems, the property in a thing sold did not pass until delivery to the buyer. English law has adopted the principle that the property passes at such time as the parties intend it to pass. Express stipulations as to the time when the property is to pass are very rare. The intention of the parties has to be gathered from their conduct. A long train of judicial decisions has worked out a series of rules for determining the presumed intention of the parties, and these rules are embodied in sec. 16 to 20 of the act.

The first rule is negative. In the case of unascertained goods, *i.e.*, goods defined by description only, and not specifically identified, "no property in the goods is transferred to the buyer unless and until the goods are ascertained." If a man orders ten tons of scrap iron from a dealer, it is obvious that the dealer can fulfill his contract by delivering any ten tons of scrap that he may select, and that until the ten tons have been set apart, no question of change of ownership can arise. But when a specific article is bought, or when goods ordered by description are appropriated to the contract, the passing of the property is a question of intention. Delivery to the buyer is strong evidence of intention to change the ownership, but it is not conclusive. Goods may be delivered to the buyer on approval, or for sale or return. Delivery to a carrier for the buyer operates in the main as a delivery to the buyer, but the seller may deliver to the carrier and yet reserve to himself a right of disposal. On the other hand, when there is a sale of a specific article, which is in a fit state for delivery, the property in the article *prima facie* passes at once, even though delivery be delayed. When the contract is for the sale of unascertained goods, which are ordered by description, the property in the goods passes to the buyer, when, with the express or implied consent of the parties, goods of the required description are "unconditionally appropriated to the contract." It is perhaps to be regretted that the codifying act did not adopt the test of delivery, but it was thought better to adhere to the familiar phraseology of the cases.

Sec. 20 deals with the transfer of risk from seller to buyer and lays down the *prima facie* rule that "the goods remain at the seller's risk until the property therein is transferred to the buyer, but when the property therein is transferred to the buyer, the goods are at the buyer's risk whether delivery has been made or not." *Res perit domino* is therefore the maxim of English, as well as of Roman law.

Conflicting Claims to Goods.—In the vast majority of cases people sell only what they have a right to sell, but the law has to make provision for cases where a man sells goods which he is not entitled to sell. An agent may misconceive or exceed his authority. Stolen goods may be passed from buyer to buyer. Then comes the question, which of two innocent parties is to suffer? Is the original owner to be permanently deprived of his property, or is the loss to fall on the innocent purchaser? Roman law threw the loss on the buyer. French law, in deference to modern commerce, protects the innocent purchaser and throws the loss on the original owner. English law is a compromise between these opposing theories. It adopts the Roman rule as its guiding principle, but qualifies it with certain exceptions, which cover perhaps the majority of the actual cases which occur (sec. 21 to 26).

In the first place, the provisions of the Factor's Act, 1889 (extended to Scotland by 53 and 54 Vict. c. 40), are preserved. That act validates sales and other dispositions of goods by mercantile agents acting within the apparent scope of their authority, and also protects innocent purchasers who obtain goods from sellers left in possession, or from intending buyers who have got possession of the goods while negotiations are pending. In most cases a contract induced by fraud is voidable only, and not void, and

the act, accordingly, protects an innocent purchaser from a seller who obtained the goods by fraud.

The ancient privilege of market overt (*i.e.*, "open market"), under which rights may be obtained even in stolen goods, is preserved virtually intact (sec. 22). The operation of this rule is fitful and capricious. For example, every shop in the City of London is within the custom, but the custom does not extend to the Greater London outside. If then a man buys a stolen watch in Fleet Street, he may get a good title to it, but he cannot do so if he buys it a few doors off in the Strand. There is, however, a qualification of the rights acquired by purchase even in market overt. When goods have been stolen and the thief is prosecuted to conviction, the property in the goods thereupon revests in the original owner, and he is entitled to get them back either by a summary order of the convicting court or by action. This rule dates back to the statute 21 Hen. VIII. c. II. It was probably intended rather to encourage prosecutions in the interests of public justice than to protect people whose goods were stolen.

Seller's and Buyer's Rights and Duties.—Having dealt with the effects of sale, first, as between seller and buyer, and, second, as between the buyer and third parties, the act proceeds to determine what, in the absence of convention, are the reciprocal rights and duties of the parties in the performance of their contract (sec. 27 to 37). "It is the duty of the seller to deliver the goods and of the buyer to accept and pay for them in accordance with the terms of the contract of sale" (sec. 27). In ordinary cases the seller's duty to deliver the goods is satisfied if he puts them at the disposal of the buyer at the place of sale. The normal contract of sale is represented by a cash sale in a shop. The buyer pays the price and takes away the goods. "Unless otherwise agreed, delivery of the goods and payment of the price are concurrent conditions" (sec. 27). But agreement, express or implied, may create infinite variations on the normal contract. It is to be noted that when goods are sent to the buyer which he is entitled to reject, and does reject, he is not bound to send them back to the seller. It is sufficient if he intimates to the seller his refusal to accept them (sec. 36).

Remedies of Buyer and Seller.—The ultimate sanction of a contract is the legal remedy for its breach. Seller and buyer each have their appropriate remedies. If the property in the goods has passed to the buyer, or if, under the contract, "the price is payable on a day certain irrespective of delivery," the seller's remedy for breach of the contract is an action for the price (sec. 49). In other cases his remedy is an action for damages for nonacceptance. In the case of ordinary goods of commerce the measure of damages is the difference between the contract price and the market or current price at the time when the goods ought to have been accepted. The convenient market-price rule is subordinate to the general principle that "the measure of damages is the estimated loss directly and naturally resulting in the ordinary course of events from the buyer's breach of contract" (sec. 56). Similar considerations apply to the buyer's right of action for nondelivery of the goods (sec. 51). In exceptional circumstances the remedy of specific performance is available to the buyer (sec. 52). Thus the court might order the specific delivery of an autograph letter of an otherwise unrecorded signatory of the Declaration of Independence. The seller's rights are further protected by the rules as to lien and stoppage *in transitu* (sec. 38 to 48).

The Sale of Goods Act has been adopted in substance by many countries of the Commonwealth of Nations and was followed in the main by the Uniform Sales Act in the United States (*see* below). (M. D. C.; J. O. Ho.)

UNITED STATES

The English law, as stated above, gives in general outline a picture of the United States law as it developed in early case law and as it was codified in the Uniform Sales Act. Samuel Williston, in drafting the Uniform Sales Act for the Commissioners on Uniform State Laws, closely followed the British Sale of Goods Act both in structure and language, though making significant changes at a few points. The Uniform Sales Act, completed in 1906, was adopted in over 30 states. But in 1953 the states began to adopt the thorough revision of sales law contained in the Uniform Commercial Code.

Uniform Sales Act.—*Warranty.*—The chief divergence of American sales law, as reflected in the Uniform Sales Act, from the English law described above has to do with warranties; *i.e.*, the nature of the seller's obligation with reference to the kind and quality of goods sold. The facts which will place some obligation on the seller with reference to quality are substantially the same in both countries. But in the United States, if the seller has undertaken any obligation in this respect, the buyer, in the majority of states, will be entitled not only to damages (the English "warranty") but also (at his election) to return the goods and recover the price (the English "condition").

The long controversy over the buyer's power to return defective goods indicates the extent to which the law of warranty has been a creature of mercantile law, designated to settle disputes about goods between merchants. The law of warranty, however, has been put to another striking social use: that of allocating the risks incident, in a highly industrialized society, to the use of goods manufactured by persons with whom the user has no direct contact, who may be located in a distant place, whose methods the user has neither skill nor opportunity to know, but whose efficiency he is forced by the nature of the market to rely upon. Injury in those cases results, *e.g.*, from a tack or a piece of glass concealed in a cake or a can of beans, from the explosion of an automatic water heater, or from the breaking of an automobile wheel. In such cases return of the goods is not in question, but only the allocation of the damage suffered. The device of an action for negligence (*q.v.*) has been extended for this purpose; but recovery on this ground may fail if the injured party cannot prove carelessness in manufacture, or if the jury is persuaded by the defendant's evidence of sound manufacturing methods.

On the other hand, wherever remedy in warranty is available, it requires no proof of negligence at all: the seller is held to guarantee against dangerous defects in the article. Traditionally, recovery for warranty depends on a sales transaction between the parties involved. This rule has freed manufacturers from direct liability to the injured party, who nearly always buys from a retail store or other intermediary and not directly from the manufacturer. But a very different judicial approach has developed based in part upon the need to protect consumers, especially from dangerous food—and later other commodities; this trend has been strengthened by the view that through mass advertising manufacturers establish direct contact with consumers and should be responsible directly to consumers for defective goods. The courts have moved far toward satisfying a definite social need, which the traditional legal devices based on proof of negligence can satisfy only with delay and distortion.

Documents of Title.—One feature of American law in which wide changes have been worked requires mention. The old rule that no man might convey goods which he did not own imposes on buyers either a noticeable risk (of having any goods which have been improperly sold to them recovered by their true owners) or a degree of investigation incompatible with rapid turnover. Especially dangerous and impracticable is this in the case of bankers advancing money on the security of goods in warehouse or in transit; a banker's margin of profit is too low to make losses readily compensable, and inquiry into title is in general outside his competence. A practice therefore grew up, in the case of goods in warehouse, of accepting the warehouseman's receipt for the goods, if fair on its face, as full evidence of title to the goods, and of dealing with the receipt as with the goods themselves. The same practice developed, even earlier, with reference to bills of lading; *i.e.*, carriers' receipts for goods entrusted to their care.

This mercantile custom has received full warrant at law in the United States, not only in the states which adopted the Uniform Sales Act (beginning in 1906) but also, as to bills of lading, in the more than 30 states which adopted the Uniform Bills of Lading Act (from 1909). In addition, the federal version of the latter act covers bills of lading arising from interstate shipments, and all states adopted the Uniform Warehouse Receipts Act (be-

ginning in 1906). The Uniform Sales Act, the Uniform Bills of Lading Act, and the Uniform Warehouse Receipts Act are superseded in states adopting the Uniform Commercial Code (*see* below). All these laws distinguish sharply between straight or *nonnegotiable* documents of title and *order* or negotiable documents. The former can transfer only such rights as the transferor possesses, and, in case of fraud, the true owner can regain the property from a purchaser of the documents; on the other hand, negotiable documents carry a promise to deliver to the order of a named person, and in general give a bona fide purchaser (or pledgee) all the rights apparent on their face, even though the transferor may have lacked such rights. The English law is to the same effect, and even expressly extends the same rules to policies of marine insurance drawn in proper form. (K.N.L.; J.O.Ho.)

Uniform Commercial Code.—In 1940 the Commissioners on Uniform State Laws, later joined by the American Law Institute, undertook the revision of several fields of law relating to commercial activity, including the sale of goods. More than a decade later this project culminated in the Uniform Commercial Code, the chief reporter of which was Karl N. Llewellyn. The code was first adopted in Pennsylvania in 1953 and within a few years by a substantial majority of the states.

One of the divisions of the code, art. 2, revises the law for the sale of goods, supplanting the rules embodied in the Uniform Sales Act and, in addition, establishing statutory rules for sales of goods which had been left to traditional case law; these include rules governing offer and acceptance in the making of contracts, assignment of contracts, and the effect of "unconscionable" contract provisions.

The sales article of the code does not closely follow either the language or the approach of the Uniform Sales Act. The fewest innovations are in the field of seller's responsibility for the quality of the goods (seller's "warranties," discussed above), but even in this several difficulties in the older law are removed, such as the rule limiting seller's responsibility for goods purchased under a patent or trade name.

The most striking feature of the code is its statement of separate rules for a number of sales problems instead of referring them to the concept of "property" or "title." Under the Uniform Sales Act a wide variety of legal problems are referable to the question of who has "property" in the goods. Deciding whether property in the goods has passed may determine whether the seller may recover the full price or only damages from a buyer who has wrongfully refused to accept delivery of the goods. The same test may determine whether the buyer may replevy goods from a seller who wrongfully refuses to deliver them. The buyer may bear the risk of fire or other loss before he receives the goods if "property" has passed. In measuring the buyer's damages the point at which property passed has been employed instead of the market in which the buyer purchases substitute goods.

The code provides separate rules for these different problems. The goal of its drafters was to state the rules in terms of objective facts which could be seen and ascertained more readily than could a legal concept such as "property" or "title." Thus, the code makes risk of loss turn on events such as delivery to the carrier or, if shipment is not involved, on receipt of the goods by buyer. The seller's right to recover the full price rather than damages turns on events such as whether the buyer has accepted the goods. A buyer's right to replevy goods turns on whether they have been "identified" and on whether the buyer has been able to procure substitute goods. The code does set forth rules for the passage of "property" in goods, but since they apply only to problems for which no specific rule is provided, their impact is slight. In this manner the code has developed rules which, while more detailed, are more clearly suited to the separate practical problems at hand than the general concepts of property or title.

INTERNATIONAL UNIFICATION

Various measures have been attempted to cope with the legal problems arising from sales transactions that cross international boundaries and thus often involve legal systems with different traditions and understandings. The differences may be so great that the obligations and understandings in the country at one end of the transaction may be unintelligible to traders and their attorneys in the other.

The most fruitful approach to unification has been a uniform contract for voluntary adoption by the traders involved. Trade organizations in the United States have formulated the Revised American Foreign Trade Definitions giving the implications of important terms, such as "c.i.f.," "f.a.s.," and "f.o.b." (*see* F.O.B.); the International Chamber of Commerce has promulgated a similar set of definitions entitled *Incoterms*. The Economic Commission for Europe has formulated detailed standard contracts designed to prevent misunderstanding in international trade in several commodities such as lumber, citrus fruit, machinery, and grain. The International Institute for the Unification of Private Law, an organization of 40 nations (including the United States), with headquarters in Rome, has sponsored the drafting of a Uniform Law for the International Sale of Goods. In 1964 a diplomatic conference at The Hague attended by 28 nations, including the United States, redrafted this Uniform Law and offered a convention implementing it to the states of the world for ratification. The conference also completed work on a Uniform Law on the Formation of Contracts for the International Sale of Goods. Each law would go into effect when ratified by five states.

See also references under "Sale of Goods" in the Index.

(J. O. Ho.)

BIBLIOGRAPHY.—C. Blackburn, *A Treatise on the Effect of Contract of Sale* (1845; 3rd ed. by W. R. Norman and L. C. Thomas, 1910); J. Hamel, *Contrats Civils* in Planiol and Ripert, *Traité pratique de droit civil français,* vol. x, 2nd ed. (1956); J. P. Benjamin, *Treatise on the Law of Sale of Personal Property* (1868; 8th ed. 1951); W. W. Story, *A Treatise on the Sale of Personal Property,* 4th ed. by E. H. Bennett (1871); J. B. Moyle, *Contract of Sale in the Civil Law* (1892); Sir M. D. E. S. Chalmers, *Sale of Goods Act, 1893* (1894; 13th ed., 1957); S. Williston, *Law Governing Sales of Goods at Common Law and Under the Uniform Sales Act,* rev. ed. (1948).

SALERNO, a Tyrrhenian seaport of Campania, Italy, capital of Salerno Province and an archiepiscopal see, lies west of the mouth of the Irno River in the Gulf of Salerno, 34 mi. (54 km.) SE of Naples by rail. Pop. (1961) 123,391 (commune). The modern town, bordered seaward by a fine promenade with public gardens, skirts a hill on whose summit (the site of a Roman fortress) are the ruins of the castle of Arechi, duke of Benevento and Lombard prince. The Porta Rateprandi, or Arco di Arechi, and the remains of a palace also date from the Lombard period. The town's principal monument is the Cathedral of S. Matteo, founded in 845 and rebuilt in 1076–85 by Robert Guiscard. In the crypt beneath the apse is the sepulchre of St. Matthew, whose body, according to legend, was brought to Salerno in the 10th century. In the Chapel of the Crusades, founded by Giovanni da Procida (1210–98), hero of the Sicilian Vespers and a native of Salerno, is the tomb of Pope Gregory VII, who died at Salerno in 1085. The cathedral also contains the tomb of Margaret of Durazzo (d. 1412), wife of Charles III, king of Naples. The town has grown considerably since World War II, when it was damaged by bombardment.

Salerno is on the Naples-Paola Railway and is traversed by the main road to Calabria. The Naples-Salerno extension of the Autostrada del Sole from Milan was completed in 1962. The main industrial products and exports are foodstuffs, cement and construction materials, textiles, machinery (steam boilers), ceramics, and wrought ironwork.

The Roman colony of Salernum was founded in 197 B.C. on the site of an earlier town, possibly Etruscan, called Irnthi. From A.D. 646 it was part of the duchy of Benevento and from 839 capital of an independent Lombard principality. In 1076 it was conquered by Robert Guiscard, whose splendid capital it became. Sacked by the Swabians in 1194, it revived under Giovanni da Procida, who enlarged the port and started a great annual fair. In 1419 it passed to the Colonna and later to the Orsini and the Sanseverino. In 1799 it adhered to the Parthenopaean Republic, following the fortunes of Naples.

Much of Salerno's historic interest derives from the medical school—the earliest in Europe—which flourished there in the 11th century and to which flocked students from Europe, Asia, and Africa to qualify as doctors of medicine. (*See* also MEDICINE AND SURGERY, HISTORY OF: *Arabian Teaching and the School of Salerno.*)

Battle of Salerno.—On Sept. 9, 1943, the Allies landed on the Salerno coast and became engaged in a hard-fought battle with the Germans. Air and naval support enabled them to hold off strong counterattacks until the arrival from Calabria on Sept. 18 of the advance guard of the British 8th Army, after which the Germans were forced to withdraw.

SALERNO PROVINCE forms the southern part of Campania, bordering the Tyrrhenian Sea and the provinces of Naples (northwest), Avellino (north), and Potenza (east). Area 1,901 sq.mi. (4,923 sq.km.). Pop. (1961) 887,857. Apart from the fertile alluvial plain of the Sele and lesser coastal areas, the province is mountainous or hilly.. The highest points are Mt. Cervati (6,230 ft. [1,899 m.]) in the Cilento group and Mt. Polveracchio (5,873 ft. [1,790 m.]) in the Picentini chain. The main crops are grain, grapes, citrus fruits, olives, chestnuts, and tobacco. There are canning factories at Nocera Inferiore, Pontecagnano, and Battipaglia, and the last-named has the largest tobacco factory in southern Italy. The coastal road along the Sorrento Peninsula through Amalfi to Salerno is a noted tourist attraction. (M. T. A. N.)

SALESBURY (SALISBURY), **WILLIAM** (c. 1520–c. 1584), the greatest Welsh scholar of his time, first translator of the New Testament into Welsh, was a native of Denbighshire. He was educated at Oxford, where he accepted the Protestant faith, but he passed most of his life at Llanrwst, working at his literary undertakings. Salesbury was acquainted with nine languages, including Latin, Greek, and Hebrew, and was learned in philology and botany. About 1546 he edited a collection of Welsh proverbs (*Oll synwyr pen kembero*), probably the first book printed in Welsh, and in 1547 his *Dictionary in Englyshe and Welshe* was published (facsimile edition, 1877). In 1563 the English Parliament ordered the Welsh bishops to arrange for the translation of the Scriptures and the Book of Common Prayer into Welsh. The New Testament was assigned to Salesbury, who had previously translated parts of it. He received assistance from Richard Davies, bishop of St. David's, and also from Thomas Huet, or Hewett (d. 1591), but he himself did the greater part of the work, basing it on the Greek version. In October 1567 the New Testament was published in Welsh for the first time. This translation, never popular, served as the basis for the new one made by Bishop William Morgan (c. 1547–1604).

Salesbury and Davies continued to work together, translating various writings into Welsh, until about 1576 when the literary partnership was broken. After this, Salesbury produced nothing of importance.

SALESIANS (SOCIETY OF ST. FRANCIS DE SALES OR SALESIANS OF DON BOSCO; SOCIETAS S. FRANCISCI SALESII; S.D.B.), a Roman Catholic religious congregation of men founded at Turin, northern Italy, in 1859, by St. John Bosco. It was the spirit of meekness and charity of St. Francis de Sales that the founder sought to incorporate into his religious society, which he created for the purpose of educating poor boys (especially for the priesthood) and combating the irreligion widespread in Italy at that time. His congregation was approved in 1874. The Salesians continue to be dedicated to the Christian education of youth, using the practical educational method of St. John Bosco, which they call the "preventive system," a method based on reason, religion, and kindness. The Salesian Sisters (Daughters of Our Lady of Help of Christians) was founded in 1872 by Don Bosco and St. Mary Mazzarello (1837–81), the first mother general, to do for girls what the Salesians do for boys. The Salesian Cooperators, a third order consisting of lay people, was also started by Don Bosco, in 1875.

The Salesians' growth has been extraordinary; among Catholic orders it is exceeded in membership only by the Jesuits and the Franciscans. Its works of charity for the social, economic, and professional welfare of youth include recreational centres in large cities, youth clubs, trade and agricultural schools, academic schools, parishes, summer camps, seminaries, foreign missions, etc. Though not a missionary organization, it also ranks third among all Catholic foreign missionary societies. The motherhouse is at Rome.

See also Bosco, Saint John; Orders and Congregations, Religious.

Bibliography.—Henry Hughes, *St. John Bosco* (1934); A. Auffray, *St. John Bosco* (1959); Lancelot Sheppard, *Don Bosco* (1957); Paul P. Avallone, *Don Bosco and His Preventive Technique in Education* (1957); E. Ceria, *Annali della Società Salesiana,* 4 vol. (1941–51).

(F. J. Pe.)

SALFORD, a city and a municipal, county and parliamentary borough, Lancashire, Eng., 2 mi. W of Manchester. Pop. (1961) 155,090. Area 8.1 sq.mi. The parliamentary borough returns two members, for Salford East and Salford West. Salford is a quarter sessions borough.

The borough, composed of three townships identical with the ancient manors of Salford, Pendleton and Broughton, is for the most part separated from Manchester by the River Irwell. The main railway station is Exchange station which is connected with Victoria station, Manchester, by one of the longest railway platforms in the world. Salford town hall was built in 1825 and Pendleton town hall in 1866. St. John's Roman Catholic cathedral was opened in 1848. Peel Park, formerly Lark Hill but renamed after Sir Robert Peel, contains the art gallery and museum and the Royal Technical College (1896). In Buile Hill Park is the natural history museum.

The only old building remaining in Salford is Ordsall Hall, the ancient seat of the Radcliffe family, which dates from 1350. Kersal Cell, the site of a 12th-century Cluniac monastery, was the birthplace of John Byrom (1692–1763). James Joule (1818–89), the physicist, was born in Salford.

The Flemish weavers settled first in Salford in about 1360, and from that date it has been one of the foremost cotton towns. To the opening of the Manchester Ship Canal (*q.v.*) in 1894 is due its great commercial importance, for it contains the largest docks on this canal. Raw cotton is imported and among many exports are manufactured cotton and woolen goods, machinery and locomotives. Salford is an important centre for importing timber and also a great distributing centre. It has more than 1,000 factories which include cotton spinning, bleaching and dyeing, brewing, the making of rubber goods and waterproofed fabrics, paper mills, and engineering.

Neolithic implements, British urns and Roman coins have been found within the borough. Domesday Book mentions the Great Hundred of Salford (of which Manchester formed a part) as held by Edward the Confessor and covering some 400 sq.mi. At the Conquest it was part of the domain granted to Roger le Poitevin. In 1228 Henry III granted the town an annual fair and market and a weekly market; in 1825 George IV granted two annual fairs and a weekly market. When the corporation bought the market rights they built a new market, on the site of the old cattle market, which was opened in 1939.

In 1230 Ranulf de Blundeville, earl of Chester, granted a charter constituting Salford a free borough and it was administered according to this charter until 1791. In 1267 Salford was granted by Henry III, with all the crown demesne, to his son Edmund, earl of Lancaster.

When the house of Lancaster succeeded to the throne its Lancashire possessions were kept separate and Salford remained part of the duchy of Lancaster thereafter. The borough was incorporated as a municipal borough in 1844; Broughton and Pendleton were amalgamated with it in 1853; in 1888 it became a county borough. It was raised to the status of a city in 1926.

SALICACEAE, the willow family of woody plants, consists of two genera, *Populus* (poplars) and *Salix* (willows). The members are typically catkin bearing, with simple deciduous leaves. Male and female flowers are borne on different individuals, are subtended by bracts, and are each provided with a nectar gland; the seeds are circled by tufts of hairs. Salicaceae are indigenous in most parts of the world, especially in the temperate and subarctic zone of the Northern Hemisphere. Hybridization occurs freely. The main economic importance lies in their fast growth and easy propagation by cuttings. Many species of *Salix* have flexible twigs used for making baskets. *See* Willow; Poplar; Osier.

(K. H. R.)

SALICETO (Guglielmo Saliceti) (*c.* 1210–1277), Italian physician who did much to initiate the early renaissance of surgery, was born in the village of Saliceto, in Piacenza, a province of Lombardy. He had a university education and extensive military and hospital experience. He taught surgery at the University of Bologna (*c.* 1268) and later became city physician of Verona. Saliceto wrote books on both medicine and surgery, and insisted (against the practice of his time) on the close relationship of these arts. His most important work, the *Cyrurgia* (first printed in 1476), is the earliest complete treatise on surgery. The book contains many acute clinical observations but is most remarkable for its section on anatomy for the surgeon, and for the author's insistence that surgical practice be based on careful case histories, of which he provides examples. His most influential pupil was Lanfranchi of Milan, who taught in Paris; from there the doctrines of Saliceto spread to England and the Low Countries.

See P. Pifteau, *Chirurgie de Guillaume de Salicet* (1898); F. H. Garrison, *An Introduction to the History of Medicine,* 4th ed. (1929).

(L. M. Z.)

SALIC LAW, the code of laws of the Salian Franks (*see* Franks) who conquered Gaul in the 5th century A.D., is the most important, although not the oldest, of all the early Teutonic laws (*leges Germanorum*). The code was issued late (*c.* 507–511) in the reign of Clovis, the founder of Merovingian power in Western Europe. It was twice reissued and enlarged under the descendants of Clovis, and under the Carolingians it was repeatedly altered and systematized and was translated into Old High German.

In its original form the code is structurally of the pre-Christian era, the only one of the kind that exists. The laws of the Visigoths and the Burgundians, which are earlier in date than the Salic Law (*see* Germanic Laws, Early), as well as the laws of the Lombards and the Anglo-Saxons, which are later, all show appreciable Christian influence; the Scandinavian codes, although archaic in other respects, all begin with a section on ecclesiastical law. Despite the fact that it was first written down in Latin, the Salic Law was very little influenced by Roman law. The Frankish legal terms used in it are sometimes latinized, but remained in Frankish in the so-called Malberg glosses surviving in some manuscripts. These are not glosses in the normal sense, but Frankish words and sentences which remained in the text and which were probably those in common use in the Frankish *mallus* or *mallobergus,* the court of law. The Salic Law is preeminently a penal code, giving a long list of fines (*compositio*) for various offenses and crimes. But it also contains some civil-law enactments. Among these is the chapter *de alode* which declares that daughters cannot inherit land. Under the later Valois, lawyers incorrectly attributed to this chapter the existing assumption that women should not succeed to the crown, though it had not been invoked to exclude the daughters of Louis X, Philip V, and Charles IV (*see* Salic Law of Succession).

In addition to the Salic Law, a few other Frankish laws are known. The *Lex Ribuaria* was the law of the Ripuarian Franks, whose centre was Cologne. Surviving manuscripts all date from Carolingian times, but historians are agreed that there must have been two previous codifications. The first was begun under the Merovingian king Clotaire II after his acquisition of Austrasia (613), so that the duchy of the Ripuarians, part of the Austrasian kingdom, might be assimilated in law to the remainder of his possessions; it was finally promulgated by Clotaire's son Dagobert I, probably *c.* 623–625. The second codification was made when the powerful Grimoald was mayor of the palace (*see* Mayor of the Palace) in Austrasia (643–662); it borrowed extensively from the Salic Law and was intended to expand the *Lex Ribuaria* into a general code of laws for all Austrasian Franks.

Finally, there is a judicial text in 48 titles, headed *Notitia vel commemoratio de illa ewa* [law] *quae se ad Amorem habet* and also called *Lex Francorum Chamavorum.* The duchy within whose frontiers it was followed comprised probably the whole Frankish part of the diocese of Utrecht, between the Rhine and IJssel rivers. As the law was written down by a royal *missus* (an official regularly used by the Carolingians to supervise provincial administration), this must have been done in the Carolingian period, probably in 802–803.

BIBLIOGRAPHY.—K. A. Eckhardt, *Pactus legis Salicae*, 2 vol. (1954–56), and *Lex Salica* (1953), quarto edition in progress, 2 vol. (1962–), in the series *Monumenta Germaniae historica*. F. Beyerle and R. Buchner (eds.), *The Lex Ribuaria* (1954), and R. Sohm (ed.), *Lex Francorum Chamavorum* (1883), are also in the *Monumenta Germaniae historica*. (K. A. ECK.)

SALIC LAW OF SUCCESSION, the rule by which in certain sovereign dynasties women and also males whose descent from a former sovereign is traced only through a woman are excluded from succession to the throne. Gradually formulated in France, the rule takes its name, somewhat misleadingly, from the *lex Salica* or law of the Salian Franks (*see* SALIC LAW).

From Hugh Capet, who died in 996, to Philip IV, who died in 1314, Capetian kings of the direct line were not faced with any problem about the succession to the throne of France because each one had a son who could take his place (*see* FRANCE: *History*). Even so, it was the custom down to Louis VII's reign for the king during his own lifetime to associate his son with him in the exercise of power—partly out of loyalty to Carolingian tradition, partly from a vague sentiment of the elective character of the monarchy. From the reign of Philip II Augustus onward, however, it came to be regularly accepted that the eldest son should succeed to the crown of his own right on his father's death, even though no document was ever produced to sanction this tradition. At the same time there was likewise no document prescribing how the succession should be settled if a king were to die without leaving any male descendants. When Louis X died, on June 5, 1316, his queen, Clémence of Hungary, was pregnant; but his posthumous son, John I, died on Nov. 19, only five days old.

It was between 1316 and 1328 that the principle whereby women were excluded from succession to the French throne was established; and between 1328, when Philip of Valois became king as Philip VI, and 1437, when Charles VII made his royal entry into Paris, the corollary principle came to be accepted, namely that descent from the daughters of French kings could not be admitted as constituting a claim to the royal succession. It is important meanwhile to note that on Louis X's death the Salic law was never invoked as a ground for excluding Joan, his daughter by an earlier marriage, from the succession; and that his brother, the future Philip V, promptly convened an assembly of barons and prelates which invested him with the government of the kingdom and simply proclaimed, without adducing any proof, that women did not succeed in France: *Hoc tamen probari non poterat evidenter* ("this nevertheless could not be proved evidently"), as Jean de Saint-Victor wrote at the time. Consecrated as king on Jan. 9, 1317, Philip immediately convened a new assembly of prelates, barons and Parisian bourgeois, as it were an "assembly of notables," which ratified his accession without any contradictory discussion; and a year later, on March 27, 1318, Eudes, duke of Burgundy, Joan's uncle and guardian, renounced in her name all rights that she might have to the kingdoms of France and Navarre.

Neither Philip V, who died in 1322, nor his younger brother and successor, Charles IV, who died in 1328, left any sons; and in each case their daughters were tacitly excluded from the succession, no protest being made on their behalf. Charles IV, however, was the last male of the direct line of the Capetians; and on his death the question of the succession appeared in an entirely new light, since it had now to be determined whether the son of a French king's daughter who had herself been excluded from the succession by virtue of her sex could advance any claim to it on his own account. The claims of Edward III of England, grandson of Philip IV of France through the latter's daughter Isabella, and those of Charles II of Navarre, son of Louis X's daughter Joan, can be seen from the genealogical table in the article HUNDRED YEARS' WAR. What is certain is that there was still no reference to the Salic law when a new assembly of prelates, barons, and bourgeois designated Philip of Valois, representative of a junior line of the Capetians, to be king in succession to Charles IV. Two points, however, should be borne in mind as symptomatic of the confused state of the issue at that time: on the one hand, the *Grandes Chroniques de France* make it clear that the assembly's preference for Philip over Edward was founded on its abhorrence at the idea of France's passing under the rule of an English king,

and that there was also an objection on the ground of feudal law, since the king of England was the French king's vassal for the duchy of Guienne and one could not be lord and vassal for a fief at one and the same time; on the other hand, the fact that Philip VI's accession had been determined by an assembly does not seem to have been used by any contemporary as an argument for calling in question the hereditary character of the French monarchy, which the Capetians had taken so long to promote.

Attempts to provide juridical grounds for the exclusion of women from the royal succession in France were made under Charles V—notably by the anonymous author of the *Somnium viridarii*—and in the last years of Charles VI's reign, when Jean de Terre-Vermeille began writing; but these writers derive their arguments in the first place from custom, in the second place from Roman law and from the priestly character of the kingship. It is noteworthy that when the first mention of the Salic law in connection with the exclusion of women occurs, namely in the memorandum submitted by the chronicler Jean Lescot to King John II and to his son the regent Charles in 1358, the writer declares that the legal experts whom he had consulted did not seem to know anything in it relevant to the question; and though the Salic law is again mentioned in Jean de Montreuil's polemical *Traité contre les Anglois* (1416), in an anonymous treatise of 1422, and by Jean Jouvenel des Ursins (1435), nevertheless the writers in each case resort finally to custom as the justification for excluding women.

At last, as late as 1464, there appeared an anonymous work entitled *La Loy salicque, premiere loy des François faicte par le roy Pharamon par laquelle est démonstré comme les femmes ne peuvent estre héritières de la couronne de France* ("The Salick Law, first law of the Franks, made by King Pharamond, whereby is shown how women cannot be heiresses to the crown of France"). First printed in 1488, this work was republished many times in the first six decades of the 16th century, notably as an appendix to editions of Claude de Seyssel's famous treatise *La Grant Monarchie de France* in 1541 and 1558. Yet here the anonymous writer, though he mentions the chapter "De alode" ("On Allodial Property") in the law of the Salian Franks, which declares that women could not inherit Salian land, nevertheless spends very little time on that chapter and is more concerned with the law of the Salians in general: his main purpose is to show how the *lex Salica*, as promulgated by Pharamond, was the first expression of the royal will, and how Charlemagne, who gave it its definitive form, conferred on it his own unrivaled prestige, and made it binding on succeeding French kings no less than on the kingdom of France as a whole. The author notes that since Pharamond's time no woman had succeeded to the throne of France, but the reasons which he adduces for this are in fact quite external to the text of the *lex Salica*: he gives more weight to the argument (already advanced by Jean de Terre-Vermeille) about the priestly character of the king, anointed as he was with the oil from the Sainte Ampoule on the day of his consecration (*see* CORONATION), and to the king's duty, which a woman could not perform, of defending the Oriflamme or sacred banner by force of arms.

The text of the Salic law, however, was taken up by statesmen and by expositors of the theory of the royal power in the 16th century and advanced as a fundamental law of the kingdom, with the exclusion of women from succession to the throne as one of its provisions. Thus when Francis I, on his return from captivity in 1526, declared that he was not obliged to execute the terms of the Treaty of Madrid, he was fully upheld by the Paris *parlement*, whose premier president, Jean de Selve, maintained that "by the Salic law, the rights of the crown are inalienable." In the same year Jacques Bonnaud de Sauset, in his edition of Jean de Terre-Vermeille's works, presented the Salic law as the basis of absolute monarchy and, in particular, of the absolute power of the kings of France. The same idea was later taken up by Guillaume Postel in his commentaries on the Salic law in *La Loy salique, livret de la première humaine vérité* (1552), in which he went so far as to assert that the word "Salic" must be the result of a misreading and that one ought really to speak of "the Gallic law." At the estates-general of the League, convened by the duc de Mayenne in Paris in June 1593, the authority of the Salic law was expressly invoked to set aside the candidature of the infanta Isabella, granddaughter of Henry II of France by his daughter Elizabeth's marriage to Philip II of Spain, for the French throne—despite the strongly pro-Spanish attitude of the dominant faction in Paris at the time. Thenceforward the Salic law was invariably accepted as a fundamental law of the kingdom.

Yet the Salic law was not invariably cited, even in France, as the ground for excluding women from succession to the crown. Jean Bodin, in his *Methodus ad facilem historiarum cognitionem* (1566), remarks that, while the law might be supposed to be the most ancient constitutional law of the kingdom, the interpretation of it with regard to the succession was due to an error of the jurist Baldus de Ubaldis and others "who have confused the law of succession with sovereignty"; and Jean du Tillet, in his *Recueil des roys de France* (1580) insists that, if women are excluded from the succession in France, it is not because of any provision of the Salic law, which was written "for subjects only" or, in other words, was a code of private, not of public or constitutional law. This latter argument, however, overlooks the fact that in Merovingian times there was not yet any distinction between public and private law and that the rules for succession to the kingdom were not different from those for succession to private property. Moreover, for the Merovingians all male heirs had equal rights, whereas the later interpretation of the Salic law with regard to the royal succession was bound up with primogeniture.

The commentators on the Salic law insist on its being a law peculiar to the kingdom of France. However, the French allegation of the Salic law to justify the exclusion of women led to the loose but convenient use of the term Salic law to designate rules excluding women in other dynasties' systems of succession. In Germany, where the kingship was elective, there could in theory be no question of regulating a hereditary succession to the royal crown; and in theory too the Holy Roman emperor's monarchy was not hereditary. In other German principalities, however, the hereditary principle came to be established. Insofar as these principalities were based mainly on fiefs of the empire, the general rule under feudal law (*Lehnrecht*) excluded women at least in the so-called "masculine" fiefs, though in a few cases there were "feminine" fiefs to which a woman could succeed; but for allodial property the local law of the land (*Landrecht*) might allow female succession. Moreover, when a masculine fief fell vacant, the king would usually invest the husband of the heiress rather than anyone else with it. With the decline of feudalism and the consolidation of the sovereign status of the princes, family laws or *Hausgesetze* fixed the system of succession to the German principalities. These *Hausgesetze* generally either excluded women altogether or only allowed them to succeed if the entire male line of the dynasty should become extinct. For the Hohenzollerns of Brandenburg-Prussia, for instance, the succession was expressly confined to the male line: what should happen if the male line died out was uncertain. For the Habsburgs, female succession if the male line should have died out was carefully arranged under Charles VI's Pragmatic Sanction. It is this overriding preference for the male line that is meant by Salic law in German connections. When Victoria of Great Britain was excluded from the succession to the kingdom of Hanover on her uncle William IV's death, the "Salic law" involved was the *Hausgesetze* that preferred any male of the whole house of Brunswick-Lüneburg to any female for the Hanoverian succession, but would have allowed female succession if all such males had been extinct.

In England, in Scandinavia, and in Angevin Naples there was no principle against succession by daughters in default of sons. In Spain likewise there was no such principle until Philip V, the first Spanish king of the French Bourbon dynasty, introduced the Salic law by his *Auto acordado* of 1713. It was Ferdinand VII's final revocation of the *Auto acordado* by a codicil to his will of 1832 that provoked the Carlist Wars, as it set aside the claims of his brother Don Carlos by reverting to the old principle whereby his daughter Isabella could succeed. For the kingdom of Italy under the House of Savoy the Salic principle was accepted.

BIBLIOGRAPHY.—P. Viollet, "Comment les femmes ont été exclues, en France, de la succession à la couronne," *Mémoires de l'Académie des Inscriptions et Belles-Lettres* (1893); A. Lemaire, *Les Lois fondamentales de la monarchie française d'après les théoriciens de l'ancien régime* (1907); J. Milton Potter, "The Development and Significance of the Salic Law of the French," *English Historical Review* (1907); W. Church, *Constitutional Thought in Sixteenth-Century France* (1941); R. Villers, "Aspect politique et aspect juridique de la loi de Catholicité (1589–1593)," *Revue historique de droit français et étranger* (1959). (MI. F.)

SALICYLIC ACID, a white, crystalline solid, is used, with its derivatives, in medicines and flavouring agents and in the manufacture of dyes. The largest single use is in the preparation of aspirin (*q.v.*).

Salicylic acid occurs naturally in small amounts in the roots, leaves, blossoms and fruits of many plants, particularly in the oils from various species of *Spiraea*. The methyl ester is widely distributed in nature in the roots, bark and leaves of plants and is the principal constituent of oil of wintergreen from the wintergreen shrub, *Gaultheria procumbens*.

Chemically, salicylic acid is orthohydroxybenzoic acid, $C_6H_4(OH)(COOH)$. It crystallizes from hot water in the form of white needles which melt at 159° C, and sublimes without decomposition at temperatures up to 155° C. It is very soluble in alcohol and ether, but soluble in water to the extent of only 1.8 g. per litre at 20° C and 20.5 g. per litre at 80° C. Salicylic acid decomposes at about 200° C into phenol and carbon dioxide. It develops a violet colour in aqueous solution with ferric chloride. In its chemical behaviour it undergoes the typical reactions of an aromatic carboxylic acid as well as a phenol. Salts, esters, ethers and acyl derivatives are readily prepared.

Preparation.—Salicylic acid was first prepared by R. Piria in 1838 by treating salicylaldehyde with potassium hydroxide. Until 1874 the only commercial source was the hydrolysis of the methyl salicylate obtained from the bark of sweet birch (*Betula lenta*) or the leaves of the wintergreen shrub. Large-scale manufacture was made possible by a synthesis discovered in 1859 by H. Kolbe in which phenol was treated with carbon dioxide in the presence of metallic sodium. In 1874 the method was modified to the treatment of dry sodium phenate with carbon dioxide at elevated temperature and pressure.

Commercial Preparation.—Phenol and a hot concentrated solution of sodium hydroxide in water are mixed in an autoclave and the solution heated to about 130° C. The resulting sodium phenate is dried by heating and stirring in the autoclave, initially at atmospheric pressure and then under reduced pressure. The dry pulverized sodium phenate is cooled to about 100° C, and continuously stirred while carbon dioxide is admitted to the autoclave under a pressure of approximately 100 lbs. per square inch. After the desired amount of carbon dioxide has been absorbed, the autoclave is heated at about 150° C for several hours and then cooled. The resulting sodium salicylate is dissolved in water and the solution acidified with mineral acid to precipitate crude salicylic acid, which is recovered by centrifuging and drying. The crude acid thus obtained is purified by recrystallization and sublimation.

Uses of Salicylic Acid and Derivatives.—Salicylic acid finds some use as a preservative in nonfood products, but its use in food is objectionable and is unlawful in many countries. Lotions, ointments and powders containing from 2% to 10% of the acid are used in the treatment of skin diseases.

Salicylic acid applied to unbroken skin causes a softening of the horny layer of the epidermis and hence is used as a wart, corn and callus remover.

Large quantities of crude salicylic acid are used in the manufacture of dyes such as monoazo mordant dyes, direct diazo and triazo dyes and mordant-type dyes of the triphenylmethane series.

The sodium salt of salicylic acid, sodium salicylate, is used medicinally as an antipyretic (an agent that relieves fever) and as an analgesic (an agent that alleviates pain), particularly in the treatment of rheumatic fever.

The largest use of salicylic acid is in the preparation of its acetyl derivative, aspirin, which is made by treating the acid with acetic anhydride. Aspirin is widely used both as an analgesic in the treatment of headache, neuralgia, etc., and as an antipyretic in the treatment of colds, flu, etc. The annual world-wide production of acetylsalicylic acid is in the many millions of pounds.

The second largest use of salicylic acid is in the preparation of its methyl ester (synthetic oil of wintergreen). It is made by esterifying the acid with methyl alcohol, sulfuric acid being used as a catalyst. Methyl salicylate is widely used as a flavouring agent in confectionery, beverages, dentifrices, etc. Medicinally it is used externally as a counterirritant in ointments and lotions.

Phenyl salicylate, since it absorbs ultraviolet light, has been used in antisunburn creams. It is also used for enteric-coated (protected from absorption until reaching the intestine) pills. Salicylanilide is a fungicide and finds use as a mildewproofing agent for cotton articles.

BIBLIOGRAPHY.—*For preparation, chemical properties and uses:* T. E. Thorpe, *Dictionary of Applied Chemistry,* 12 vol., 4th ed. (1937–56); R. E. Kirk and D. F. Othmer, *Encyclopedia of Chemical Technology,* 15 vol. (1948–57); F. Ullmann, *Enzyklopädie der technischen Chemie,* 10 vol., 2nd ed. (1928–36); L. S. Goodman and A. Gilman, *The Pharmacological Basis of Therapeutics,* 2nd ed. (1955). *For application in medicine and therapeutics:* W. Martindale, *Extra Pharmacopoeia,* 23rd ed., 2 vol. (1952–55).
(D. W. J.)

SALIENTIA, the scientific term for the amphibian superorder that includes living frogs and toads (order Anura), and ancestral types (order Proanura). Some zoologists relegate Salientia to the rank of order, placing all forms in this group. In such a scheme Salientia becomes practically synonymous with Anura. *See* AMPHIBIA.

SALIERI, ANTONIO (1750–1825), Italian composer whose gifts are apparent both in his operas and in his sacred music, but whose memory has suffered at the hands of posterity, was born at Legnano on Aug. 18, 1750. In 1766 he was taken to Vienna by F. L. Gassmann, the imperial court composer and music director, who introduced him to the emperor Joseph II. His first opera, *Le donne letterate,* was produced at the Burgtheater in 1770. This was followed by a succession of operas, among them *Armida* (1771) which was enthusiastically received. On Gassmann's death in 1774 Salieri became *Kapellmeister,* and on G. Bonno's death in 1788 he was appointed *Hofkapellmeister.* He held court office for 50 years, during which time he made frequent visits to Italy and France and composed music for many European theatres, one such work being *Les Danaïdes* (Paris, 1784), commissioned by the Académie de Musique on Gluck's recommendation. His most important work was the opera *Tarare* (1787), later called *Axur, re d'Ormus,* which the Viennese public preferred to Mozart's *Don Giovanni.* Salieri's last opera was *Die Negersclaven.* After its production in 1804 he devoted himself to the composition of sacred music. In 1824 he retired from court office on full salary, and died in Vienna on May 7, 1825.

Throughout his life he remained on friendly terms with Haydn and with Beethoven, whom he had given lessons in counterpoint and who dedicated the three violin sonatas, Op. 12, to him. Salieri was distrusted by Mozart; there is, however, no foundation for Mozart's belief that Salieri had tried to poison him—a legend that formed the basis of Rimski-Korsakov's opera *Mozart and Salieri* and of Cedric Glover's novel, *The Mysterious Barricades* (1964).

See G. Magnani, *Antonio Salieri* (1934).   (Cs. CH.)

SALII ("the dancers"), an age-old priesthood found in classical antiquity in a group of central Italian towns (Alba, Anagnia, Aricia, Lavinium, Tibur, Tusculum) and at Rome. They are normally associated with the worship of Mars, the god of war, though at Tibur they celebrated Hercules, the dominant deity. At Rome the Salii consisted of two groups of 12, with separate sodality houses, the Palatini, who worshiped Mars, and the Collini (or Agonenses), who originally worshiped Quirinus. They had to be of patrician birth, with both father and mother living. They were normally young men, and resignation from the priesthood was common on assuming high political office, which might conflict with the punctilious discharge of priestly duties. Vacancies were filled by co-option. The priests wore a distinctive costume, including a short military cloak of vivid red with bronze breastplate beneath a conical helmet, and carried the ancile (a shield in the shape of a figure-of-eight) and the old-fashioned long spear. This is the archaic Roman war dress, and there is little doubt that the Salii represented a section of the early Roman army.

The priesthood was most active in March (Mars's month and the beginning of the campaigning season) and in October (when summer campaigns were wound up). Their chief festivals were the Quinquatrus on March 19 and the Armilustrium on Oct. 19. The Salii moved in procession through the city along a traditional route, stopping for the night at appointed stations, where they stored their arms and feasted, the luxury of their banquets becoming proverbial. At specified points they paused to perform ritual dances in triple time under their leader (*praesul*), beating their shields with their spears and singing their traditional song transmitted from an antiquity so remote that its formulas and languages were largely unintelligible in classical times. There still survive a few fragments of their *Carmen Saliare,* a primitive war chant meant to enlist Mars's support and ensure victory.

In later times the character of these ceremonies changed. The ancilia came to be regarded as magical relics and the *Carmen Saliare* as a community prayer on behalf of the Roman state, so that the names of members of the imperial house could be inserted. Existence of Salii is attested in several towns of Cisalpine Gaul and at Saguntum, where they were almost certainly instituted in imitation of the Roman priesthood.

See also MARS.

See Pauly-Wissowa, *Real-Encyclopädie der classischen Altertumswissenschaft,* 2nd series, vol. i, col. 1874–94 (1920).   (D. E. W. W.)

SALINA, a city of central Kansas, U.S., 75 mi. NW of Wichita, is located on the Smoky Hill River near its confluence with the Saline; the seat of Saline County. Salina is a distribution and trade centre for the great central Kansas wheat-growing area; grain milling is the chief industry and there are extensive facilities for the storage and processing of wheat. The city was founded in 1858 by Col. William A. Phillips; much of its early trade was with Indians and settlers and with soldiers from nearby Ft. Riley. By 1862, however, only about 12 families lived there; the first real growth of the community came with the arrival of the Kansas Pacific (part of the Union Pacific) railway in 1867. The city was chartered in 1870. It has a council-manager form of government, in effect since 1921. Kansas Wesleyan University (Methodist, established 1885), Marymount College (Roman Catholic, 1922), and St. John's Military School (Episcopal, 1887, a private preparatory school for boys) are among the educational institutions in Salina. Schilling Air Force Base (formerly Smoky Hill Air Base) is near the city. For comparative population figures *see* table in KANSAS: *Population.*   (D. P. G.)

SALINAS (Y SERRANO), PEDRO (1891–1951), Spanish poet, scholar, playwright, and essayist, one of the outstanding writers of a famous generation, was born in Madrid on Nov. 27, 1891. After studying and lecturing in Paris, in 1918 he became professor of Spanish at Seville. He there became known both as poet and scholar, publishing two volumes of poetry, *Presagios* (1923) and *Seguro azar* (1929); a critical edition of Juan Meléndez Valdés (1925); and a modern rendering of the *Poema del Cid* (1925). The appearance of *La voz a ti debida* (1934), perhaps the greatest modern Spanish love poem, established him as one of the leading poets in Spanish of the first half of the 20th century. Meanwhile, he had become professor at Madrid (1930), and received various honours from the government. In 1936, on the outbreak of the Spanish Civil War, he went to the United States, where he lectured at Wellesley College, Mass., and, after 1940, at the Johns Hopkins University, Maryland. He died at Boston, Mass., on Dec. 4, 1951. The works published in America reveal his many-sided talents. In the poems in *El Contemplado* (1946; Eng. trans. *Sea of San Juan: a Contemplation,* 1950) and *Todo más claro* (1949), he primarily expresses the exile's longing for his native country; and in *El Defensor* (1948), a volume of essays, and in his literary studies, *Jorge Manrique o tradición y originalidad* (1947) and *La poesía de Rubén Darío* (1948), he shows a profound human concern and personal anguish at the experiences of a tragic age.

BIBLIOGRAPHY.—*Poesías completas* (1955), and *Teatro completo* (1957), ed. by Juan Marichal. *See also* A. del Rio, *Pedro Salinas* (1942); Juan Marichal, in *La voluntad de estilo* (1957). Translations include *Lost Angel and Other Poems* (1938), *Truth of Two* (1940), and *Zero* (1947).
(JU. MA.)

SALINAS, a city in western California, U.S., the seat of Monterey County, is situated near the Pacific Ocean, about 10 mi. from Monterey Bay and less than 100 mi. S of San Francisco. The city lies on a broad plain which is just above sea level and which extends southward for 50 mi. along the Salinas River, so named because of the salt pools along its lower course. This area is protected by the Coast range and the Gabilans on the east and the Santa Lucias on the west. The original site of Salinas and its growth were determined by the route of the Southern Pacific Railroad. Settlement on El Camino Real, now a U.S. highway, began in the 1850s and the town was incorporated in 1874. It adopted the city-manager form of government in 1936. The economy is mostly agricultural, the valley being under irrigation except for the foothills which are used for grazing and dry-land farming. Salinas is the shipping centre for vegetables, including beets, lettuce, celery, broccoli, cauliflower, spinach, artichokes, peas, and onions. Some fruits are grown, especially strawberries. The production of sugar beets, once the primary crop, centres around the largest sugar beet factory in the United States. Many beets are still grown in the valley and tons are also shipped in from adjacent and remote valleys, thereby keeping the factory at high-level production for several months each year. Salinas is the centre of a bulb and seed industry, with experimentation and production possible all year because of the excellent climate and fertility of the soil. It is the home of Hartnell College (1920), a public junior college. Salinas is widely known as the home of the annual California rodeo. For comparative population figures *see* table in CALIFORNIA: *Population.*   (B. L. B.)

SALINGER, JEROME DAVID (1919–   ), U.S. writer, whose novel *The Catcher in the Rye* was a major influence on the post-World War II generation and its novelists, was born in New York City on Jan. 1, 1919. After brief periods at New York and Columbia universities, he devoted himself entirely to writing, except for service in the U.S. Army (1942–44). His popular, somewhat sentimental stories began to appear in periodicals in 1940; those written after the war frequently exploited his army experiences. "For Esmé—with Love and Squalor" (1950), set in England, tells the poignant tale of an encounter of an American soldier and two British children; "A Perfect Day for Bananafish" (1948) describes the suicide of the sensitive, despairing veteran, Seymour Glass. But Salinger's major work was *The Catcher in the Rye* (1951), in which the central character, Holden Caulfield, relates in an authentic, teen-age idiom his flight from the hypocrisies of the adult world, his search for innocence and truth, and his final collapse on a psychiatrist's couch. The novel's language and humour placed it in the native tradition of Mark Twain's *Huckleberry Finn.* From the beginning it attracted devoted admirers and serious critics. *Nine Stories* (1953), a selection of Salinger's best work, added to his reputation. After 1953 his work declined in quality and quantity. *Franny and Zooey* (1961) reprinted two *New Yorker* stories of 1955 and 1957; both deal with the Glass family, as do the two stories in *Raise High the Roof Beam, Carpenters; and, Seymour: an Introduction* (1963). Salinger appears at his best in his dramatization of children; all of his work seems haunted with the lost innocence of childhood.   (J. E. MR.)

SALISBURY, JAMES EDWARD HUBERT GASCOYNE-CECIL, 4TH MARQUESS OF (1861–1947), British statesman and extreme right-wing Conservative politician, was born in London on Oct. 23, 1861, the eldest son of Lord Robert Cecil. Styled Viscount Cranborne from 1868 when his father became the 3rd marquess of Salisbury, he was educated at Eton and at University College, Oxford. As a member of the House of Commons (1885–92 and 1893–1903), he won a reputation as a zealous defender of the Established Church. He served with distinction in the South African War (1899–1902), but was recalled in 1900 to become undersecretary for foreign affairs. Succeeding as the 4th marquess of Salisbury in August 1903, he entered A. J. Balfour's cabinet in October as lord privy seal, and became president of the board of trade in March 1905. Deeply conservative, he was a natural "diehard" in the crisis over the budget of 1909 and the Parliament Bill of 1911 (*see* ENGLISH HISTORY), voting against both to the end. During World War I he did not join either

of the coalition governments and remained critical of both.

After 1918 he gradually assumed the informal leadership of the Conservative opposition, first in the House of Lords and afterward in the party generally. In a speech on Oct. 17, 1922, he demanded that the Conservative party free itself from supporting the coalition government. Two days later his policy was accepted at the Carlton Club meeting. In the cabinet of Andrew Bonar Law, which replaced the coalition in November 1922, Salisbury was lord president of the council and chancellor of the duchy of Lancaster. He was appointed in March 1923 chairman of a subcommittee to consider the coordination of home and imperial defense, and his valuable recommendations became the basis of the British military organization until after World War II.

In Stanley Baldwin's second cabinet (1924–29) he was lord privy seal and from 1925 to 1929 was leader of the House of Lords. Gradually alienated, however, by Baldwin's "liberalism," he resigned his leadership of the Conservative peers in June 1931, stayed out of the National government formed in August, and devoted his energies to vain endeavours to reform (*i.e.,* strengthen) the House of Lords and to oppose self-government for India. He was more successful in his efforts, in company with Winston Churchill, to organize British defenses against Hitler. From 1942 to 1945 he was president of the National Union of Conservative and Unionist Associations. Salisbury died in London on April 4, 1947.

(H. G. N.)

SALISBURY, ROBERT ARTHUR TALBOT GASCOYNE-CECIL, 3RD MARQUESS OF (1830–1903), British statesman and prime minister (1885–86, 1886–92, 1895–1902), who also acted as foreign secretary at a time when the British Empire was rapidly expanding, was born at Hatfield House, Hertfordshire, on Feb. 3, 1830, the third son of James, 2nd marquess, by his first wife,

THE 3RD MARQUESS OF SALISBURY

Frances Mary Gascoyne. Lord Robert Cecil, as he was then styled, was educated at Eton and Christ Church, Oxford. His scholastic career was cut short by ill health and in July 1851 he was sent on a journey round the world. He returned to England in May 1853 and in August was elected unopposed to Parliament for Stamford, in Lincolnshire. In his early years, however, he was more active as a writer than as a politician, and he contributed to the *Quarterly Review* a total of 32 unsigned articles, the most notable of which dealt with foreign affairs or were biographical sketches. In 1864 Cecil began to take an active part in parliamentary life, as an uncompromising Conservative. In the next year his elder brother James died and he took the courtesy title of Viscount Cranborne as heir to his father. In July 1866 he was appointed secretary of state for India, but in the following year he quarreled with the prime minister, Lord Derby, and with Disraeli over the second Reform Bill, and resigned in March 1867.

His father died in 1868 and he succeeded as the 3rd marquess of Salisbury; all but the first 15 years of his political career were therefore spent in the House of Lords, where until 1874 he was in opposition during Gladstone's first ministry. When Disraeli became prime minister (1874) his first care was to secure the services of Salisbury, who was reluctant to work under a man whom he distrusted; but he was persuaded to resume his post of secretary of state for India. He took drastic measures to fight a serious famine in that country. Two years later a crisis arose in southeast Europe, and Salisbury began the close association with foreign policy which was to last for the rest of his life.

The Eastern Question.—The Bulgars rebelled in 1876 against the suzerainty of Turkey and the rising was suppressed with great cruelty. Gladstone advocated the expulsion of the Turks from Europe "bag and baggage," and Russian volunteers poured into the Balkans to help the insurgents. After Turkey had rejected (January 1877) proposals made at a conference of the great powers of Constantinople (at which Salisbury was the British representative), Russia declared war and invaded Turkey (see EASTERN QUESTION). By the Treaty of San Stefano (March 3, 1878) the Russians forced the Turks to place their Balkan territories under Russian suzerainty. The British cabinet refused to admit the treaty's validity. The army reserves in England were called out and Indian troops were ordered to proceed to Malta. The 15th earl of Derby disapproved of these measures and resigned the foreign office. Disraeli (now earl of Beaconsfield) thereupon appointed Salisbury to take his place, and the very next day (April 1, 1878), before he had been formally gazetted as foreign secretary, he telegraphed to all the great powers a dispatch, which came to be known as the Salisbury Circular, and which insisted that the position of Turkey in Europe was a matter of concern to all the powers and could not be determined by Russia alone. Despite the Turkish atrocities Salisbury held that the independence of Turkey must be maintained. His Liberal rival, the earl of Rosebery, called the dispatch "one of the historic state papers of the English language." It rallied the major powers to the British view that the future of the Balkans could only be decided at a European congress. The German chancellor, Prince von Bismarck, thereupon proposed that the congress should be held in Berlin. It met there on June 13 with Bismarck presiding. Prince A. M. Gorchakov represented Russia, and Beaconsfield and Salisbury attended for Britain (see BERLIN, CONGRESS OF).

Salisbury had carefully prepared the ground by negotiating secret treaties first with Russia (May) and then with Turkey (June), Turkey agreeing to lease Cyprus to Britain as a base for military or naval action in its own support. Most of the points made in Salisbury's Circular note were approved at the congress, and on their return to London after the signing of the Treaty of Berlin (July 13, 1878), the two British delegates were greeted with enthusiasm and Beaconsfield's claim that they had brought back "peace with honour" was heartily accepted. Two unhappy minor wars, however, in Afghanistan (1878–80) and Zululand (1879) now dimmed the earlier successes of the government, and at the general election in 1880 Gladstone gained a substantial majority.

First Ministry (1885–86).—The Liberal success had been furthered by Gladstone's brilliant Midlothian campaign (1879–80) denouncing the Turkish atrocities in Bulgaria. Gladstone's domestic measures proved popular, but his foreign policy lost Britain her friends abroad and his colonial policy was disastrous, culminating in the loss of the Anglo-Egyptian Sudan and the murder of Gen. C. G. Gordon at Khartoum (Jan. 26, 1885). In a snap division on the budget in June 1885 Gladstone was defeated, and Queen Victoria summoned Salisbury. He accepted the premiership unwillingly, knowing that he would be dependent for a majority on the supporters of Home Rule for Ireland (see PARNELL, CHARLES STEWART). He kept the foreign office in his own hands, and again won success for his country. The two states, Bulgaria and Eastern Rumelia, into which the old Bulgaria had been divided by the Treaty of Berlin, united in September 1885 to call Prince Alexander of Battenberg, the head of the new, reduced Bulgaria, to be ruler of a united Bulgaria. While Russia and the other signatories of the treaty wished to re-enforce the arrangement made at Berlin, Salisbury accepted the Bulgars' desire for unification and persuaded the other powers to do the same. But his government was defeated in Parliament on Jan. 26, 1886, Gladstone having secured the Irish vote by his promise of Home Rule. In Gladstone's third ministry (February–July 1886) his Home Rule bill was rejected on June 8 when 93 of his Liberal followers announced themselves to be Unionists and voted with the Conservatives. Parliament was dissolved, and the general election gave Salisbury a majority dependent upon the Liberal Unionists. Salisbury first suggested to their leader, the marquess of Hartington (later 8th duke of Devonshire), that he should take the premiership; on his refusal, Salisbury himself took office on July 25, 1886, and formed his second government, which was to remain in office for six years. The Liberal Unionists followed Hartington in refusing to join the cabinet.

Second Ministry (1886–92).—The earlier months of Salisbury's new ministry were inauspicious. Apart from Irish obstruction of business in the House of Commons, difficulty was caused in the cabinet by the tempestuous personality of Lord Randolph Churchill, whom Salisbury had appointed chancellor of the exchequer. Churchill soon came into collision with the more sedate service ministers, William Henry Smith and Lord George Hamilton, over their departmental estimates which he wanted to reduce. The prime minister supported Smith and Hamilton, and Churchill resigned in December 1886. The loss of this brilliant leader of the House, who was popular in the country and was also the link between the Conservatives and the Liberal Unionists, seemed to shake the ministry to its foundations. Salisbury, however, was unperturbed; he appointed one of the former Liberals, George Joachim (later Viscount) Goschen, to be chancellor, and himself took over the foreign office (Jan. 14, 1887), which he had first entrusted to the earl of Iddesleigh. There his immediate care was to reestablish good personal relations with Bismarck, the outstanding statesman of Europe, an eminence to which Salisbury succeeded when the latter was arbitrarily dismissed by William II (March 1890).

Bismarck had more than once urged the British government to join the Triple Alliance (Germany, Austria-Hungary, and Italy), and his disappearance made it easier for Salisbury to maintain an independent position in European affairs, following a policy which later came to be known by the phrase "splendid isolation," although he himself never employed the term. During the whole of this second ministry foreign policy was largely dictated by colonial questions. The race among the European nations to obtain territory in Africa caused Salisbury to find himself at loggerheads sometimes with the Germans or with the Portuguese, and all the time with the French. Behind the rush of explorers, missionaries, and traders stood the governments of their respective countries. Salisbury's policy was to establish agreed and separate spheres of influence. The British part in colonization was carried out by chartered companies, directed by such pioneers as Cecil Rhodes, and usually supported by regular or irregular forces. Salisbury was at first a reluctant imperialist, but by the end of his career he had added enormous stretches of territory to the British Empire; and he was the less loath to colonize because he made it an absolute rule that the slave trade should be prohibited in any territory administered by Great Britain. Since Germany was less fastidious in this respect, negotiations were complicated and long-drawn-out; in Southwest Africa also, for different reasons, settlement was hard to reach. Finally, on July 1, 1890, Great Britain agreed to cede the island of Heligoland and some territory in Southwest Africa to Germany, in exchange for the explicit recognition of British sovereignty over territories in East Africa which gave control of the upper waters of the Nile.

Negotiations with Portugal over central Africa (1889–91) were even sharper. Salisbury endowed Cecil Rhodes's British South Africa Company with a royal charter in 1889, and when Rhodes's forces south of Lake Nyasa came into contact with those of Portugal, which sought to establish a Portuguese belt from West to East Africa, Salisbury dispatched what amounted to an ultimatum to Lisbon (January 1890), demanding the withdrawal of the Portuguese forces. Portugal yielded and a treaty signed on June 11, 1891, secured for Rhodes the territory later known as Rhodesia, with Salisbury (founded in 1890 and named after the prime minister) as its capital. Colonial rivalry with France in West Africa was less severe. In the agreements of 1889 and 1890 between Britain and France the respective boundaries of the colonial territories were regularized, leaving Gambia, Sierra Leone, and the Gold Coast to Britain, and a vast area covering part of the Congo basin and the western Sahara to France.

As usual when Salisbury was prime minister the output of domestic legislation was small, and during the whole of his second premiership parliamentary business was impeded by the obstructive tactics of the Irish members, who were goaded by the repressive measures taken by the government against the frequent Fenian outrages in Ireland. Time was found, however, for the important Local Government Act (1888), which established county councils throughout England and Wales (including notably the London County Council), and also for a Free Education Act (1891), Salisbury considering that since the previous Liberal government had made education compulsory it was for the government to take over from the parents the payment of the fees. His outlook on the "working man" had been succinctly expressed in the general election of 1885. "The Conservative," he said, "points the working man forward to obtain wealth which is as yet uncreated: the Radical, on the contrary, does not tell him to create new sources of wealth, but says that the wealth which has already been obtained is badly divided." Nevertheless he drew large audiences when he spoke in industrial centres like Manchester or Glasgow, and became noted for his unexpected homeliness of speech. When Salisbury's second ministry had almost run its course, the general election of 1892 gave the Liberals a working majority, with first Gladstone and then the earl of Rosebery as prime minister. But Gladstone's bill for the disestablishment of the Welsh Church and his second Home Rule bill (1893) were not popular and were rejected by the House of Lords. After Rosebery resigned (June 1895), Salisbury was returned to power in the election that immediately followed.

Third Ministry (1895–1902).—The Liberal Unionists now abandoned their independent position and the new cabinet was strengthened by the inclusion of the duke of Devonshire as lord president of the council and of Joseph Chamberlain as colonial secretary. Combining once more the foreign office with the premiership, Salisbury was able to give almost undivided attention to foreign affairs. He was faced at once with a violent outbreak of Turkish cruelty in Armenia and was now hampered by the pro-Turkish policy of Germany under William II, who was scheming for German expansion in the Persian Gulf. Salisbury, however, persuaded the great powers in 1896 that reforms should be enforced on Turkey (though no action was in fact taken); and he recreated the idea of the "Concert of Europe," the cooperation of the great powers to maintain peace.

Although the powers did intervene in 1897 in a quarrel over Crete, claimed by Greece from Turkey, the existence of the "Concert" was short-lived. The competition for predominance in Egypt still separated England and France; and in the winter of 1897–98 Russia seized two Chinese ports, Port Arthur (Lü-shun) and Talien (Dairen). Salisbury, however, refused to become embroiled in the Far East, for along with his other commitments there had arisen since 1895 a sharp and unexpected quarrel with the United States over a frontier dispute between Venezuela and British Guiana, the only British colony on the South American mainland. Pres. Grover Cleveland claimed the right of the United States to apply the Monroe Doctrine (q.v.). Salisbury, when it suited him, was a master of "do-nothing" diplomacy and in spite of angry speeches and press articles on both sides of the Atlantic he remained inactive in public while closely studying the details of the disputed boundary. He composed at leisure a long dispatch which he sent in November 1895 to the American secretary of state, Richard Olney, maintaining that the Monroe Doctrine was not applicable in this case. President Cleveland responded in a fierce speech to Congress (Dec. 17). The prince of Wales (later Edward VII) wrote an appeasing letter to Joseph Pulitzer, owner of the *New York World*, whom he knew; Chamberlain, with his American wife, Mary, paid a "private" visit to the United States; Pulitzer described the Cleveland policy as "jingo bugaboo," and American public opinion came round to Salisbury's view when he suggested a joint Anglo-American commission with a neutral chairman (February 1897). The committee finally presented its report in October 1899 and the chosen frontier differed little from that proposed by Salisbury.

In the meantime Salisbury had to deal with the hostility of European opinion after the buccaneering raid of L. S. Jameson (q.v.) in South Africa (December 1895), which was followed by the South African War (1899–1902); and he had come to the verge of war with France owing to the collision of the two countries' interests on the upper waters of the Nile. A French secret expedition under Comdt. J. B. Marchand had set out from West Africa to march eastward and establish French hegemony on the upper Nile (1896–98). Britain had agreed with the khedive of Egypt, Abbas II, to redeem the Sudan from the chaos and misgovernment it had suffered after the death of General Gordon, and to link the fate of the Sudan with that of Egypt. The aims of the two European governments were incompatible. Gen. Sir Herbert (later Earl) Kitchener was sirdar (commander in chief) of the Egyptian army, and with an Anglo-Egyptian force he marched up the Nile, defeated the dervish Khalifa 'Abdullahi at Omdurman (Sept. 2, 1898), and on the secret instruction of Salisbury then proceeded up the White Nile as far as Fashoda (now Kodok), where he met Marchand. After a cold, polite exchange of words it was agreed to leave negotiations to London and Paris. It was the age of jingoism in both capitals. But the French foreign minister, Théophile Delcassé, was as determined as Salisbury that there should be no war. It was agreed to regard Marchand only as an explorer and in November he was given facilities to retire from the Sudan via Abyssinia. An Anglo-Egyptian condominium was established over the Sudan in January 1899.

The sum of home legislation was again small during Salisbury's third ministry. A Merchant Shipping Act (1897), which fixed the loading line for ships, was its chief item. But it is noticeable that a private member's women's suffrage bill received a second reading in the House of Commons, and Salisbury, considered old-fashioned in his outlook, was by no means unfavourable to its proposals. In 1898 the Local Government Act for Ireland found its way to the statute book, as well as one or two minor measures.

During this last period of office Salisbury was, as usual, more concerned with foreign than with home affairs. In 1898 he had serious trouble with his own followers, A. J. Balfour and Chamberlain. He was in the habit of taking two holidays abroad every year, and on this occasion he left Balfour in charge of the foreign office. Chamberlain, however, was the dominant member of the cabinet, and persuaded Balfour to make an agreement and to sign a secret treaty (August 1898) with Germany according to which, if Portugal could not maintain the integrity of her colonies, these were to pass to Britain and Germany in exchange for financial support. Hearing of this proposition on his return from the south of France, Salisbury was very angry. He summoned the Portuguese ambassador, the popular marquês de Soveral, and denounced the pact concluded by his subordinates. In the so-called Windsor Treaty (Oct. 14, 1899), he re-engaged Britain to defend and protect all colonies and conquests belonging to the crown of Portugal against all its enemies. In appeasement of Germany he agreed (December 1899) to cede Britain's rights in the Samoa Islands in part to Germany and in part to the United States, the two countries with which Britain had shared a virtual protectorate over the islands since 1889. In return, British rights in Tonga and the Solomon Islands were specifically recognized. He also agreed not to impede Germany in her project of constructing a railway across Asia Minor from Constantinople to Baghdad. But he would not allow Russia to have a "sphere of influence" there; and he concluded with the sheikh of Kuwait, who ruled at the head of the Persian Gulf, a secret agreement (1899) by which the sheikh agreed not to cede any part of his territory. In the following year, after the murder of the German minister in Peking, Salisbury added a British contingent to the European force under the command of a German field marshal, Graf Waldersee, which marched to Peking to avenge the outrage and to crush the so-called Boxers who had risen against the European settlers in China.

On Oct. 11, 1899, the South African War broke out between Great Britain and the two Boer republics, the Transvaal and the Orange Free State. For the first few months the meagre British forces were defeated in one engagement after another; Britain's unpopularity on the continent of Europe was manifested by the united hostility of its governments and press. The two leading British generals, Frederick S. (later Earl) Roberts and Kitchener, were sent to South Africa in December 1899 to direct the campaign with the help of reinforcements, and thereafter it became only a matter of time before the Boers were defeated (see SOUTH AFRICAN WAR).

Salisbury's government was returned to power in the "khaki

election" (October 1900), and in November, aged 70, Salisbury handed over the foreign office to the marquess of Lansdowne. The latter, convinced that the days of "isolation" were past, was at first inclined to further Chamberlain's policy of alliance with Germany, but was dissuaded by a long and forcible state paper from Salisbury (May 29, 1901). Salisbury, however, warmly supported Lansdowne when the latter proposed a treaty of alliance with Japan, which was signed in January 1902; he was willing to oppose Russia in the Far East and the Middle East, but was all his life unwilling to sign a treaty which might involve him in a European war. These were his last decisions. After a peace treaty had been signed with the Boers (May 1902), by which the two republics were incorporated into the British Empire, he resigned on July 11, 1902, and surrendered the premiership to his nephew, A. J. Balfour. Worn out, he retired to Hatfield, where he died on Aug. 22, 1903. He was buried in Hatfield churchyard.

Character.—Salisbury was the last British statesman to govern Britain from the House of Lords, and the last (except for J. Ramsay MacDonald during a brief period) to combine the foreign office with the premiership. His death marked, politically, the end of the Victorian Age (though Queen Victoria had predeceased him, in January 1901). He stood for a paternal form of government which had become outmoded; and at the next general election (1905), the Liberals gained an overwhelming majority. Salisbury was a singular compound of hard common sense and idiosyncrasy. He suffered miserably at Eton, which he left prematurely and only once visited in later life. Nor was he much happier at Oxford, where his ill health, brought about by a nervous disorder, was a constant worry. All this changed in 1857 when he married Georgina, the eldest daughter of Sir Edward Alderson, a baron of the exchequer, and his ultimate success must largely be credited to his wife's understanding and loving care. She first encouraged him to make politics his career and was an immense help to him both as a counselor and as the dispenser of hospitality at Hatfield, to which most of the distinguished men of the day went for a weekend or garden party at one time or another. Much of Salisbury's spare time was spent with his family at Hatfield, where he also did a great deal of his official work, enjoying the isolation from public affairs. He was a big man, 6 ft. 4 in. in height, and felt the need for regular exercise; he often played tennis in the hard court at Hatfield and took long walks in the grounds. In later life his favourite exercise was tricycling, for which purpose he tarred most of the paths near the house.

Deeply interested in science, he spent many hours in the laboratory he built in the basement of Hatfield. There he carried out his experiments and indulged in his hobby of photography. He also experimented with electricity and through his enterprise Hatfield could claim to be the first private house in Great Britain to be equipped with electric lighting. His laboratory work was regarded seriously by eminent scientists of the day, and a well-earned tribute to his scholarship, and one which he valued above all others, was his appointment as chancellor of Oxford University in 1869. He combined his love of science with a devout religious belief, and his humility forbade him to take any credit for the successes he achieved in the course of his career. In diplomacy he could be very subtle, or very direct, as circumstance demanded. In both home and colonial affairs his statesmanship had a negative character. He did not originate. He was the pilot of the ship of state and not its engine; yet while he was in charge some 6,000,000 sq.mi. (15,540,000 sq.km.) were added to the British Empire and its population increased by approximately 100,000,000. Queen Elizabeth I had called his ancestor, the great Lord Burghley, her "spirit"; Salisbury might equally be called the "spirit" of the Victorian Age.

Salisbury had three daughters, Beatrix Maud (whose husband was the 2nd earl of Selborne), Gwendolen and Fanny Georgina (who died in infancy), and five sons, all of whom gained distinction in public life: James Edward Hubert Gascoyne-Cecil, 4th marquess of Salisbury, Edgar Algernon Robert Cecil, 1st Viscount Cecil of Chelwood (qq.v.), Hugh Richard Heathcote Gascoyne-Cecil, Baron Quickswood, Edward Herbert Gascoyne-Cecil, who served in the governments of Egypt and the Sudan, and William

Rupert Ernest Gascoyne-Cecil, bishop of Exeter. Salisbury's *Speeches,* edited by H. W. Lucy, were published in 1885 and his *Essays,* reprinted from the *Quarterly Review,* in two volumes in 1905.

BIBLIOGRAPHY.—F. S. Pulling, *The Life and Speeches of the Marquis of Salisbury* (1885); S. H. Jeyes, *Life and Times of the . . . Marquis of Salisbury,* 4 vol. (1895–96); Lady G. Cecil, *Life of Robert, Marquis of Salisbury,* 4 vol. (1921–32), covers the period 1830–1892; A. L. Kennedy, *Salisbury, 1830–1903: Portrait of a Statesman* (1953).

(A. L. KE.)

SALISBURY, ROBERT CECIL, 1ST EARL OF (1563–1612), English statesman, secretary of state from 1596 to 1612 and lord high treasurer from 1608 to 1612, was born in London on June 1, 1563, the second surviving son of William Cecil, Baron Burghley. His mother was Burghley's second wife, Mildred, daughter of Sir Anthony Cooke, tutor to Edward VI, and sister to Ann, Sir Francis Bacon's mother. Robert Cecil was educated at home and at St. John's College, Cambridge, for an unknown period around 1581. He was given his M.A. degree in 1605, although he had been steward of the university from 1591 and was chancellor from 1601 until his death. He was admitted to Gray's Inn in 1580. He went to the Spanish Netherlands in 1588 with the 4th earl of Derby's mission which tried to negotiate a peace with the duke of Parma. He was married on Aug. 31, 1589, to Elizabeth Brooke, daughter of William, Lord Cobham. After Sir Francis Walsingham's death in 1590, Cecil gradually took over the work of the secretaryship of state, although not formally appointed to that office until July 5, 1596. He had been knighted and sworn of the privy council in 1591. He was elected to Parliament for Westminster in 1584 and 1586, and for Hertfordshire in 1588, 1592, 1597, and 1601, and was the official exponent of government policy in the House of Commons from 1593 until 1603, when he was created Baron Cecil of Essendine, in Rutland, and then in the House of Lords. Early in 1598 he headed a mission to Henry IV of France to try to prevent the inclusion of anything prejudicial to the English or Dutch in the Treaty of Vervins (May) between France and Spain. After his father's death in 1598 he became and remained the chief minister of the crown until his own death.

His chief rival for the favour of Elizabeth I was Robert Devereux, 2nd earl of Essex. He had already had a tussle with the earl over the appointment of the attorney general in 1594 when his candidate, Sir Edward Coke, was preferred to Bacon, whom Essex supported. When Essex was on trial for rebellion in 1601 he alleged that Cecil had once said that only the Spanish infanta had any claim to succeed Elizabeth. Cecil's denial was supported by the witness Essex named. The incident had an important bearing upon his future because he could now disprove the false rumours which had reached James VI of Scotland that the secretary was hostile to his claims to the English throne. In 1601 Cecil began a secret correspondence with the king and gave him the excellent advice not to plague Elizabeth formally to recognize him as her successor, but to be careful to cultivate her good will. James succeeded Elizabeth unopposed as James I of Great Britain and Ireland in March 1603 and retained Cecil as his chief minister.

Sir Walter Ralegh was accused of a conspiracy, on behalf of Arabella Stuart, a cousin of James and next to him in the line of succession, on whose behalf Spanish assistance was being sought, and was tried (November 1603) and condemned to death, but his sentence was commuted to imprisonment in the Tower. Cecil was held responsible for Ralegh's prolonged incarceration, but as it continued for four years after his death he was probably not blameworthy. He was one of the chief examiners of the conspirators in the Gunpowder Plot (November 1605) to blow up the two houses of Parliament, but the suggestion that he fabricated it to enhance his position has been decisively refuted. He was a persecutor of those Catholics who upheld the papal claims to depose heretical monarchs and release subjects from their allegiance. The test of loyalty for Catholics in the oath of allegiance of 1606 was willingness or refusal to denounce those claims. His tract, entitled *An Answere to Certaine Scandalous Papers* (1606), denied that he intended to exterminate all English Catholics. A Calvinist in doctrine but not in church organization, he felt that the "turbulent humours" of the Puritans necessitated their coercion. He was not, like the king, an enthusiastic advocate of the union of England and Scotland, but he supported the plantation of Ulster and accepted the barony of Clogher in Tyrone, Ireland, of 12,500 ac.

Cecil was created Viscount Cranborne in 1604 and the next year earl of Salisbury. In 1608 he became lord high treasurer, and found that the king was £1,400,000 in debt. By new impositions on merchandise and other measures he reduced the debt to £300,000 but could not balance expenditures and revenue. He failed, however, to persuade the king to accept the Great Contract of 1610 by which the Commons were willing to grant £200,000 a year in return for the abolition of feudal dues worth £115,000. He was equally unsuccessful in curbing James's extravagances. In foreign affairs he negotiated peace with Spain in 1604, but sympathized with the Dutch in their war of independence. When the 12-year truce between Spain and the United Provinces was arranged in 1609, England joined France in guaranteeing the Dutch against any infringement of it by Spain. One of his last services was the betrothal of James's daughter Elizabeth to the Protestant Frederick V, elector palatine.

Salisbury died at Marlborough, Wiltshire, on May 24, 1612, worn out by his labours, and was buried in Hatfield Church, Hertfordshire. James gave him the nickname of "little beagle" because of his diminutive body. It is uncertain whether he ever occupied the new house he built at Hatfield, an estate he acquired by exchange with James for Theobalds, Hertfordshire. He was a good administrator but not a great statesman because of his lack of originality. He saw that the crown revenue was inadequate and that Parliament should supply the deficit, but failed to see that frequent applications to Parliament must change its relations to the monarchy. He tried to prolong the Elizabethan system after it had outgrown its usefulness but cannot be held responsible for James's attempts to magnify the royal prerogative.

BIBLIOGRAPHY.—The Salisbury papers at Hatfield have been calendared from 1306 to 1606, parts i–xviii (1883–1940), later material in progress, by the Historical Manuscripts Commission. Other letters are in *Correspondence of King James VI of Scotland with Sir Robert Cecil*, ed. by J. Bruce (1861); *The Secret Correspondence of Sir Robert Cecil with James VI*, ed. by Sir D. Dalrymple, Lord Hailes (1766); *Illustrations of British History*, 2nd ed. by E. Lodge, 3 vol. (1838); R. Winwood, *Memorials of Affairs of State*, ed. by E. Sawyer, 3 vol. (1725). A small tract, *The State and Dignitie of a Secretarie of Estates Place* (1642), reprinted in the *Harleian Miscellany*, vol. ii (1808) is ascribed to Salisbury. *See also* A. Cecil, *A Life of Robert Cecil, First Earl of Salisbury* (1915); P. M. Handover, *The Second Cecil: the Rise to Power, 1563–1604* (1959). (G. Ds.; X.)

SALISBURY, ROLLIN D. (1858–1922), U.S. geologist,
was born at Spring Prairie, Wis., Aug. 17, 1858, graduated from Beloit College in 1881, and later spent a year in graduate study at the University of Heidelberg, Ger. He taught successively at Beloit College, at the University of Wisconsin, and, from 1892, at the new University of Chicago. From 1899 until his death Aug. 15, 1922, he was dean of Chicago's Ogden Graduate School of Science. Salisbury's chief researches were in glacial geology. His early studies made famous the "driftless area" of the upper Mississippi Valley. In 1895, as a member of the Peary Relief Expedition, he studied glaciers in Greenland. His most systematic field work was on the Pleistocene formations of New Jersey. In 1904–06 appeared the three volumes of *Geology*, written jointly with T. C. Chamberlin. (R. T. Cn.)

SALISBURY, THOMAS DE MONTAGU, 4TH EARL OF
(1388–1428), was son of John, the third Montagu earl, who was beheaded and attainted of treason (1400) for revolt against Henry IV. Summoned to Parliament as earl of Salisbury in 1409, Thomas was not formally restored to his father's dignities until 1421. He continued his family's distinguished record in the war against France. His first expedition was in 1412, and from the Agincourt campaign in 1415 until his death, he was in France almost continuously. He took part in the naval engagement off Harfleur (1416), and in 1417 sailed again to France with Henry V, distinguishing himself in the attack on Rouen (1418) and in other sieges in Normandy. In 1419 he was rewarded by the grant of the *comté* of Perche, and he was appointed lieutenant general of Normandy. In 1421 he accompanied Thomas, duke of Clarence, into Maine, but did not reach Baugé with the infantry in time to

assist the duke, who had prematurely engaged the enemy there and was defeated and killed (March 22, 1421). Salisbury then led a successful raid into Anjou.

When Henry V died (1422) the earl became an active lieutenant of John, duke of Bedford, the regent of France. He daringly led an Anglo-Burgundian force from Burgundy across the River Yonne to defeat a French army besieging Cravant (July 30, 1423), and his "judgement and valour" were vital to Bedford's victory at Verneuil (Aug. 17, 1424). Appointed governor of Champagne in 1423, Salisbury gradually gained control of that province. Operations in Champagne and Maine and the defense of the Norman border engaged him until he left for England late in 1426. He returned to France with reinforcements in July 1428. It is likely that he began his last campaign with instructions to attack Angers, but instead he chose to besiege Orléans. On Oct. 27 he was wounded by a cannonball which struck the window in Tourelles, a nearby fortification, from which he was surveying the city; he died at Meung-sur-Loire on Nov. 3, 1428. By his first wife, Eleanor Holand, daughter of Thomas, earl of Kent, Salisbury had an only daughter, Alice, through whom the earldom of Salisbury passed to her husband, Richard Neville (*see* NEVILLE; MONTAGU). His second wife, Alice, daughter of Thomas Chaucer and granddaughter of the poet, subsequently married William de la Pole, earl (later duke) of Suffolk.

See J. H. Ramsay, *Lancaster and York* (1892); A. H. Burne, *The Agincourt War* (1956). (J. W. Se.)

SALISBURY, WILLIAM LONGSWORD (LONGESPÉE),
3RD EARL OF (d. 1226), an illegitimate son of Henry II of England, and a prominent baron, soldier, and administrator under John and Henry III. He acquired his lands and title from Richard I who in 1196 gave him the hand of the heiress Ela, or Isabel, daughter of William, earl of Salisbury. He held numerous official positions in England under John.

He was sent on missions to France (1202) and to Germany (1209). In 1213–14 he organized John's Flemish allies, taking part in the destruction (1213) of the French fleet at Damme, then the port of Bruges, and leading the right wing of the allied army at Bouvines (July 27, 1214), where he was captured. He was exchanged and was back in England by May 1215, when he was employed by John in inspecting the defenses of royal castles and fighting the rebels in the southwest. He is among the loyal barons listed in the preamble of Magna Carta, but his presence at Runnymede is not certain.

During John's war against the barons Salisbury deserted the king after the landing of Louis of France (May 1216), but returned to royal allegiance by March 1217, fought at Lincoln (May) and Sandwich (August), and attested the Treaty of Kingston (September 1217). He held various posts during the minority of Henry III and served against the Welsh in 1223 and in Gascony in 1225. He died at Salisbury on March 7, 1226. He and his wife were benefactors of Salisbury Cathedral and laid foundation stones of the new cathedral in 1220. William was buried there and his effigy, a splendid early example, still survives.

See S. Painter, *The Reign of King John* (1949); F. M. Powicke, *King Henry III and the Lord Edward*, 2 vol. (1947). (J. C. Ho.)

SALISBURY,
a city and municipal borough of Wiltshire, Eng., is situated in the southeast of the county at the junction of the Avon and Wylye rivers, 24 mi. (38.6 km.) W of Winchester by road. It is officially known as the City of New Sarum and is an Anglican bishopric and a parliamentary constituency. Historically it is the principal town of Wiltshire, although Trowbridge is the centre of local government. Pop. (1961) 35,492.

The centre of the city remains much as it was in the Middle Ages, divided into square blocks of houses by streets at right angles to each other. Through most of these streets watercourses ran until 1852. The architecture is small-scale and friendly, most of the houses having warm tiled roofs. A large number of timber-framed buildings survive, some of them behind Georgian fronts, but serious inroads have been made into this pattern by undiscriminating development.

The cathedral stands in the spacious walled Close, containing medieval canonical and other houses, on the south side of the town. The Close is entered on the north from the High Street, the principal shopping street, and there are three other ancient gates. The graceful cathedral was built between 1220 and 1258 in the Early English style throughout; the tower and spire (404 ft. [123 m.], the highest church spire in England), both in the Decorated style, were added in the 14th century. The architect James Wyatt, under Bishop Shute Barrington, carried out extensive interior alterations at the end of the 18th century.

A general market is held in the Market Square. The October Fair also held there is probably the fair granted on St. Remigius' Day (Oct. 1) by a charter of 1269. In the Guildhall, a severely classical building of 1795 in the southeastern corner of the square, the assize courts and magistrates' courts are held. The Council House on Bourne Hill is on the site of the 13th-century College of St. Edmund for secular canons. The Salisbury, South Wilts and Blackmore Museum (1860) in St. Ann Street holds important archaeological and historical collections of south Wiltshire material. Two merchants' halls survive, that of John Halle (c. 1470) in the New Canal, and that of the Webb family in Crane Street, now a part of the Church House. Surviving guildhalls include the Joiners' Hall and the Cordwainers' Hall. There are two ancient hospitals, Trinity Hospital and St. Nicholas's, now old people's homes. The 15th-century Poultry Cross has been greatly restored. The medieval parish churches are St. Thomas's, St. Martin's (both mainly 15th century), and St. Edmund's. There are several Roman Catholic and Nonconformist places of worship. The road approaches to Salisbury have been considerably disfigured by unsightly commercial building, but the ancient entity of the central part, bounded on the south and west by the Avon and formerly by an earth rampart on the other two sides, has not been lost.

Salisbury is a shopping and a tourist centre, being within easy reach of Stonehenge (q.v.), Old Sarum (see below), and many fine country houses. The main occupations are cattle and poultry marketing, engineering, brewing, leatherwork, typesetting and printing, the manufacture of visual colour-measuring instruments (tintometers) and fireworks, and the production of farm seeds. Schools include the Godolphin School and the South Wilts Grammar School, for girls, Bishop Wordsworth's School for boys, and the cathedral choristers' school. There are teachers' training and theological colleges and colleges of art and further education.

History.—The origins of Salisbury lie in Old Sarum, 1½ mi. (2.4 km.) to the north of the present town. This was an Early Iron Age hill fort which was taken over by the Romans. Under the Saxons it became an important town, and by the 11th century it possessed a mint. The Normans built a castle on the mound and Old Sarum became a bishopric when the see was transferred from Sherborne in 1075.

The first cathedral, a small basilica, was completed by St. Osmund (the second bishop) in 1092 and was immediately wrecked in a storm. Osmund began the introduction of new customs and ceremonies which later became widely known as the Sarum Use. The cathedral was rebuilt by Bishop Roger (1107–39), but friction increased between the castellan of the castle and the bishop and Pope Honorius III gave permission for the removal of the see. In 1220 the present cathedral was founded in the valley and the new city quickly grew up round it, receiving a charter from Henry III in 1227.

The bishop, as lord of the manor of Milford, was overlord of the city which was within the manor, and the history of Salisbury is largely the struggle of the citizens to be free of the bishop's control. The charter of James I (1612) put an end to the temporal authority of the bishop.

In 1244 Bishop Bingham built Ayleswade Bridge over the Avon at Harnham, thus deflecting trade from the older town of Wilton. The first mayor was appointed in 1261, and in the same year Bishop Bridport founded the College of St. Nicholas de Vaux, the first university college in England, which was attended by students from Oxford. Two friaries, Black and Grey, were founded in the 13th century. In 1302 the citizens refused to pay tallage to the bishop but capitulated in order to secure a new charter in 1306. An earthen rampart was built round the city in 1310, and soon afterward gates were added to the rampart.

At this time the wool and cloth trades flourished and wealthy merchants such as John Halle and William Swayne enriched the city and its churches. Another industry, that of cutlery, became prominent and Nell Gwyn paid 100 guineas for a pair of Salisbury scissors. In post-Reformation times tobacco pipes and pins were made and in modern times automobiles and motorcycles.

John of Salisbury, bishop of Chartres, the 12th-century scholar, was a native of Old Sarum. John Jewel and Gilbert Burnet are among the bishops of Salisbury who have enriched English literature. George Herbert, Henry Fielding, and Anthony Trollope had close associations with the city, and Rowlandson, Constable, and Turner found in Salisbury inspiration for their painting.

(H. DE S. S.)

SALISBURY, the capital of Rhodesia, lies in the northeastern part of the country, at an altitude of 4,865 ft. (1,483 m.) above sea level. Rhodesia (the British colony of Southern Rhodesia) assumed independence on Nov. 11, 1965.

The climate is temperate, the average mean annual temperature being 65° F (18° C), and the average annual rainfall 31.92 in. (811 mm.). Greater Salisbury comprises the city and numerous adjoining satellite towns. The non-African population in 1961 was 94,550. African population, enumerated in 1962, was 215,810.

Salisbury was founded on Sept. 12, 1890, and named after the British prime minister, Lord Salisbury. Chartered in 1935, it is well laid out, with tree-lined avenues and, in the business and governmental centre, many multistoried buildings. The main streets run from north to south and from east to west.

There are several notable buildings including the Anglican and Roman Catholic cathedrals, the Dutch Reformed Church, the Queen Victoria Memorial Library, the Queen Victoria Museum, and the town house. Adequate educational, medical, recreational, and cultural facilities have been established. The National Archives; the University of Rhodesia, opened in 1957; and the National Art Galleries are in the city. The Salisbury Gardens and Cecil Square are the chief parks. Salisbury is on the main rail, road and air routes of Africa. The international airport is situated at Kentucky, close to the city. The city is the centre for the agricultural industry of Rhodesia, of which Virginia tobacco is one of the main crops. A gold-mining area also surrounds it. Secondary industries range from clothing factories to steel foundries.

(B. J. N.)

SALISBURY, a city of North Carolina, U.S., the seat of Rowan County, is located 120 mi. WSW of Raleigh in the rolling countryside of the industrial piedmont section midway between Charlotte and Greensboro. The town's tree-lined streets dotted with ante-bellum homes are reminiscent of colonial times when Salisbury was one of the six largest boroughs in the colony. Settled by Scotch-Irish and Germans in the mid-18th century and named for Salisbury, Eng., it was laid out in 1753 as the county seat. It was incorporated in 1755 and chartered in 1770. It has had a council-manager government since 1927.

Daniel Boone lived with his parents nearby from 1755 until 1767, and Andrew Jackson received his licence to practise law there in 1787 after studying for a year under Judge Spruce Macay. The British general Cornwallis pursued Gen. Nathanael Greene through Salisbury in February 1781, just prior to the Battle of Guilford Courthouse, and a small action occurred at Trading Ford 6 mi. E. During the American Civil War a large Confederate prison was established in an old cotton mill which housed, in the latter months of the war, 10,000 Federal prisoners of which about 6,000 died of starvation and disease. A national cemetery now marks the place where these unknown soldiers were buried in long trenches.

Salisbury has been sustained historically by the textile industry and, during the first half of the 20th century, by major repair shops of the Southern Railway, since abandoned. There has been marked diversification in small industries, and remarkable growth of livestock, small grain farming, and dairying activity in the immediate area. A 1,000-bed veterans hospital was completed there in 1953. Catawba College (1851) and Livingstone College (founded as Zion Wesley Institute in 1879) bulwark the town's cultural life. For comparative population figures see table in NORTH CAROLINA: *Population.*

(JA. S. B.)

SALISHAN, the linguistic stock of a large number of North American Indian tribes of southern British Columbia, western and northern Washington State, northern Idaho, and northwestern Montana. Distribution was continuous except for the west coast of Vancouver Island (Nootka [*q.v.*] tribe, Wakashan stock) and three tribal areas just south of Juan de Fuca Strait (Makah tribe, Wakashan; Quileute and Chemakum tribes, Chimakuan stock). One Salishan tribe, the Bella Coola (*q.v.*), resided north of the area and another south (Tillamook). Grammatical and lexical differences of a major order characterized the two principal divisions of the stock, coastal and interior, on the two sides of the Cascade-Coast Range. The many dialects of each often were mutually unintelligible. Tribes of the coastal division were of Northwest Coast culture; the interior division, Plateau culture. *See* also CENTRAL AND NORTH AMERICAN LANGUAGES; FLATHEAD; INDIANS, NORTHWEST COAST.

See W. W. Elmendorf, "Lexical Relation Models as a Possible Check on Lexicostatic Inferences," *Amer. Anthrop.,* vol. 64 (August 1962).
(V. F. R.)

SALIS-SEEWIS, JOHANN GAUDENZ VON (1762–1834), Swiss poet whose work, influenced by Salomon Gessner, Klopstock, and L. H. C. Hölty, as well as by Rousseau's ideas, is tender and sometimes elegiac, celebrating friendship, humanity, and the serenity of nature. Some of his poems, such as "Lied eines Landmanns in der Fremde," became anthology pieces. He was born on Dec. 26, 1762, in Schloss Bothmar, near Malans in the Grisons, a member of an ancient Grison family. In 1779 he became an officer in the Swiss guards in Paris but he supported the ideas of the French Revolution and voluntarily remained in Paris until 1793. In 1799 he became chief of staff of the Swiss militia, taking part in the Battle of Zürich, and later filled several public offices. He died at Malans on Jan. 29, 1834.

BIBLIOGRAPHY.—His *Gedichte* were first edited by F. Matthisson (1793); *Gesammelte Gedichte,* ed. by C. Erni (1964); *Werke,* ed. by E. Korrodi (1937). *See* also Emil Jenal, *J. G. von Salis-Seewis* (1934); A. Rufer, *Salis-Seewis als bündnerischer Patriot und helvetischer Generalstabschef* (1938).
(M. WE.)

SÁLIVA, a tribe of South American Indians who lived near the Orinoco River in eastern Colombia (*q.v.*). Manioc was the major crop, supplemented with fish and game. Villages of one or more large communal houses were sometimes palisaded, giving evidence of warlike neighbours. The Sáliva had such tropical-forest traits as hammocks, dugout canoes, and signal drums; each village seems to have had a men's house. An ancestor cult is suggested by the exhumation and burning of bones of the dead, the ashes being drunk commemoratively in manioc beer. Religious leaders undertook curing and divination under the influence of a narcotic snuff. In the 1960s the Sáliva were largely acculturated to Colombian society.

See G. H. de Alba, "The Achagua and Their Neighbors," in *Handbook of South American Indians,* ed. by J. H. Steward, vol. 4 (1948).
(SE. L.)

SALIVARY GLANDS are certain glands, located in the mouth, that secrete saliva, a substance whose chief functions are to moisten and soften food and to keep the mouth moist. Saliva also contains a digestive enzyme and thus takes part in the chemical as well as the mechanical digestion of food. Numerous glands in the walls of the oral cavity pour their secretions into the mouth (*q.v.*); they are lodged in the submucosal tissue of the lips, cheeks, gums, tongue and palate. They are numerous in the lips, less so in the cheeks; the lingual glands are richly distributed at the base and lateral margin of the tongue and on the undersurface on each side of the frenulum. The glands of the roof of the mouth make up a large portion of the palatal mucosa and submucosa.

In addition to the above-described glands, which are intrinsic to the mouth cavity, there are three larger pairs: the salivary glands proper. They are the parotid, the submaxillary and the sublingual.

Anatomy.—*Parotid.*—The parotid gland is the largest of the salivary glands and is situated between the ear and the ascending branch of the lower jaw. In cross section it is roughly triangular. The parotid is molded into the shape of a prism or wedge by the structures that bound the pit in which it is lodged. In front, the

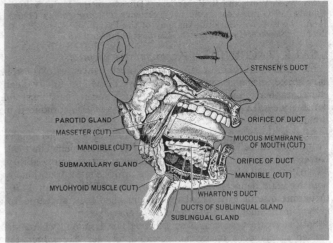

ADAPTED FROM A. BIRMINGHAM, IN "CUNNINGHAM'S TEXTBOOK OF ANATOMY" (OXFORD MEDICAL PUBLICATIONS)

THE SALIVARY GLANDS AND THEIR DUCTS, WITH THE GREATER PORTION OF THE BODY OF THE MANDIBLE REMOVED TO SHOW THE SUBLINGUAL GLAND

gland embraces the ascending branch of the lower jaw; behind, it is delimited by the external opening of the ear, the styloid process of the temporal bone and the sternocleidomastoid muscle; on the deep (internal) aspect it approaches the wall of the pharynx; on the superficial (external) aspect it is covered by fascia prolonged upward from the platysma muscle of the neck. The gland is disposed in two partly overlapping leaves that are continuous behind at a so-called isthmus. The branches of the facial nerves course forward between these leaves, as do also branches of the external maxillary artery and tributaries of the external jugular vein. Accessory glandular masses are fairly common. They are likely to be situated above the parotid duct, sometimes partly overlapping it. The parotid duct terminates in a minute orifice, opposite the second molar tooth of the upper jaw. The parotid duct (Stensen's duct) crosses the upper part of the masseter muscle and then pierces the buccinator muscle on its way to the mouth; it is about two inches long.

Submaxillary.—The submaxillary gland lies deep to the posterior half of the body of the lower jaw; it is about the size of a walnut. The facial artery is embedded in the upper part of the gland. The submaxillary duct (Wharton's duct) runs forward to the sublingual papilla.

Sublingual.—The sublingual gland is placed farther forward than the submaxillary; it is like an almond in shape though larger; its outer flattened surface rests against the lower jaw; its ducts are small and numerous. Certain of the sublingual ducts unite to form Bartholin's duct, which empties into the submaxillary duct.

Embryology.—The submaxillary and sublingual salivary glands develop embryologically as solid outgrowths of the buccal epithelium that are canalized later, while the parotid appears first as a groove. The parotid is ectodermal in origin, all the others entodermal.

Diseases.—Tumours constitute the most common ailment of the salivary glands. The parotid gland is most frequently involved, and about 15% of its tumorous lesions are cancerous. These glands are often the site of infection, both bacterial and viral. Epidemic viral infection of the parotid gland (mumps) is sometimes associated with severe nerve deafness of one ear. Bacterial infections are most common in the submaxillary glands, where a stone (sialolithiasis) is frequently the cause. Disturbances of salivation may occur. Undersecretion may be the result of the generalized drying-out of lining tissues associated with the aging process, but are more frequently the result of specific diseases (Sjögren's syndrome, fatty or fibrous atrophy, and others) or drugs (anti-histamines, certain tranquilizers, and belladonna alkaloids).

Oversecretion (sialorrhea) is rare but when it does occur is most frequently caused by hormonal shifts during pregnancy, or from the use of certain drugs.

See W. P. Work and B. F. McCabe, "Diseases of the Major Salivary Glands," in G. M. Coates and H. P. Schenck, *Otolaryngology* (1964); R. A. Davis *et al.*, "Surgical Anatomy of the Facial Nerve and Parotid Gland," *Surgery Gynec. Obstet.*, 102:384–412 (April 1956).

(W. S. L.-B.; B. J. A.)

SALK VACCINE: see POLIOMYELITIS: *Control.*

SALLÉ, MARIE (1707–1756), French dancer of extraordinary grace, elegance and dramatic power, was the first woman choreographer. She was also first to unify music, costumes and dance style with the theme of a ballet (*Pygmalion,* produced in London, 1734).

After childhood appearances in England, Sallé studied under Françoise Prévost, who sponsored her Paris opera debut in 1721. Never a virtuosa, Sallé was noted for her sensitive acting ability. As early as 1729, she had her partner discard the mask traditionally used by male dancers (and only formally abolished about 1770) to permit interplay of facial expression when they appeared together in the duet *Les Caractères de la Danse.*

Sallé's greatest success was achieved in London, where she danced in Handel's operas and created, besides *Pygmalion,* the brilliant solo *Les Caractères de l'Amour* and a ballet, *Bacchus and Ariadne,* which revealed her power as a tragic actress.

Returning to Paris, she danced the rose in J. P. Rameau's *Les Indes Galantes,* and attained great distinction as Hébé in *Castor et Pollux.* In 1740 Sallé retired from the opera, but continued to appear at French court performances until 1752. She was painted by Nicolas Lancret.

See Émile Dacier, *Mlle. Sallé* (1909).   (LN. ME.)

SALLUST (GAIUS SALLUSTIUS CRISPUS) (86–*c.* 34 B.C.), Roman historian and one of the great Roman literary stylists. He came of a plebeian family from the Sabine town of Amiternum. After a gay youth in Roman society he took up public life to obtain the quaestorship and enter the senate. His intellectual energy and personal ambition brought him into conflict with Pompey and the nobles. As tribune of the people (52) he was among those who bitterly attacked Cicero during the trial of the political agitator Milo. A freedman of Pompey, Lenaeus, satirized him for his criticism of the great man. It was doubtless for political reasons as well as on grounds of vice that in 50 he was removed from the senate. Caesar made him quaestor again in 49 so that he regained senatorial standing. In the Civil War he commanded a legion in 48, without distinction, and failed to control mutinous troops in Campania in 47, but as praetor in 46 he rendered Caesar valuable service in Africa and fought at Thapsus. For this he was rewarded with the proconsular governorship of Africa Nova. His administration of the province laid him under prosecution for extortion. Although he escaped conviction, he had become wealthy enough to build a magnificent mansion and gardens in Rome—the *horti Sallustiani*—and to retire from public life and devote himself to history.

The *Catilinae Coniuratio* (or *Bellum Catilinae*), a study of Catiline's attempt at revolution (63), appeared in 44, and was followed by the *Bellum Iugurthinum,* which treated the war with Jugurtha in 111–106; both monographs survive complete. Then the *Historiae* in five books took up the events of 78–67, as a sequel to the work of L. Cornelius Sisenna; but only fragments (including speeches) remain. Sallust conceived the history of his age in terms of political degeneracy, which set in after the destruction of Carthage in 146. The war with Jugurtha, in his view, revealed the corruptness of the nobles, successfully challenged by popular leadership under Marius, despite his faults; Sulla intensified the troubles of the state, and after him both the nobles and Pompey proved unworthy to govern; the subsequent moral chaos threw up Catiline. His judgment involved an ideal of public morality, which declined through ambition, avarice and luxury, and this he expounds in his prefaces. Some critics have considered him a mere party propagandist who chose to write about Catiline in order to create an opportunity to exonerate Caesar from charges of complicity in the plot and who chose his ground in the other works so as to attack the senatorial regime; but his real scope is wider, and he castigates not only the nobles but their rivals. His prefaces are not merely platitudinous; they provide the key to his selection of material. His conception, in fact,

represents the political issue between the nobles, who regarded birth as the qualification for leadership, and the popular leaders, who—as Marius states in the *Jugurtha*—held that ability established the right to rule. He applies this test of "Roman virtue" against the nobles, stressing it by his very praise of Cato, but equally against their unscrupulous rivals, apart from Q. Sertorius and Caesar. His analysis is too penetrating to be merely partisan —whatever secondary motives he had—but it is historically rigid. Rome was more unsettled before 146, less venal in 111, than he admits. His setting of Catiline's conspiracy may exaggerate its significance, just as it reduces the part of Cicero. His pattern of generalization led to chronological errors in detail.

As a stylist and in his generalizations about events Sallust shows the influence of Thucydides—with a Roman interest in typical personalities. What he grasps politically, he depicts dramatically, with an eye for a historical scene. In applying traditional standards he had recourse to the elder Cato, whose robust archaic style he consciously imitated. But he has a mordant, aggressive power of expression, which is his own. His style is an artificial creation —he took professional advice over it—and he fuses archaism with rhetoric, common speech with conventional vocabulary, under the pressure of a syntactical technique that used asymmetry and antithesis to point his distinctive analysis. The form of his language represents the character of his thought, as he conceived his theme. Occasional obscurity is the price for a powerful severity: his reward was to inspire Tacitus.

Doubtful Attributions.—Certain anonymous pieces in Sallust's historical style, which appear alongside his work in the manuscripts, have been dubiously attributed to him. An attack on Cicero (*Invectiva in Ciceronem*) in terms of the year 54 seems certainly spurious. Of two letters addressed to Caesar (*Epistulae ad Caesarem senem de re publica*) the first reflects conditions in 46, the second those in 49 (if not in 51 or 50). Both appear well-informed, but standard histories could have provided the material; and the second letter contains anachronisms that mark it as a later work. Stylistic comparisons may be deceptive, because Sallust was a likely object for imitation. In an age of literary conventions he would hardly have composed an "open letter" in his archaic historical style. In any event he had probably not evolved it before 45, and so even the first letter falls under suspicion.

BIBLIOGRAPHY.—The best editions of the historical works are those in the "Teubner Series": *Catilinae Coniuratio* (1911) and *Bellum Jugurthinum* (1915) by A. W. Ahlberg; rev. by A. Kurfess (1954); *Invectiva* and *Epistulae* by A. Kurfess in *Appendix Sallustiana* (1950). Full text, with French trans. by A. Ernout, "Budé Series" (1947); with Eng. trans. by J. C. Rolfe, "Loeb Series," 2nd ed. (1931). On Sallust as a historian *see* E. Schwartz, "Catilinische Verschwörung," in *Hermes,* 32 (1897); W. A. Baehrens, *Sallust als Historiker, Politiker und Tendenzschriftsteller* (1927); W. Schur, *Sallust als Historiker* (1934); L. O. Sangiacomo, *Sallustio* (1953); W. Steidle, "Sallusts historische Monographien," *Historia,* Einzelschriften 3 (1958); D. C. Earl, *The Political Thought of Sallust* (1961); R. Syme, *Sallust* (1964). On his literary composition *see* K. Latte, *Sallust* (1935). On his style *see* W. Kroll, "Die Sprache des Sallust," in *Glotta,* 15 (1927); P. Perrochat, *Les modèles grecs de Salluste* (1949). On the *Epistulae see* H. Last, *Classical Quarterly,* vol. 17 (1923); vol. 18 (1924); K. Latte, *Journal of Roman Studies,* 27 (1937). *See also* A. D. Leeman, *A Systematical Bibliography of Sallust, 1879–1950* (1952).

(A. H. McD.)

SALMAN AL-FARISI, a Companion of the Prophet Mohammed, a popular figure in Muslim legend, and the national hero of Muslim Persia, was, as the name indicates, a Persian ("Solomon the Persian"). While still a boy he became a Christian, left his father's house, and embarked on a long religious quest. Salman first contacted Mohammed about the time of the Prophet's hegira (emigration) to Medina (A.D. 622). Legend recounts that Salman, living in Syria, had heard of the new Arabian prophet and set out to find him. Bedouin guides hired for the journey betrayed him, however, and sold him into slavery. Eventually Salman reached Medina, became a Muslim, and with the miraculous help of Mohammed purchased his freedom.

The most important event connected with Salman is the "Battle of the Ditch." In the year A.H. 5 (A.D. 627) the Meccans mounted a massive attack upon Mohammed's stronghold in Medina. Mohammed's vigorous harassment of Meccan caravans had necessitated a decisive blow if the commercial life of Mecca were to survive. To protect Medina against cavalry charges, Mohammed caused a ditch or trench to be dug across the approaches to the town. This device had never been seen in Arabian warfare previously, and it so baffled the Meccans that they withdrew without pressing their attack. (*See also* MOHAMMED.) Salman is traditionally credited with suggesting the ditch, though some modern scholars question the role thus assigned to him.

Salman has also been important in Muslim religious thought. The moderate Shi'ah give him a special respect because of his nearness to the family of Mohammed, and the extreme Shi'ah count him one of the divine emanations recognized by their theology. Several Muslim mystical orders make him an important link in their chains of spiritual authority. (C. J. A.)

SALMASIUS, CLAUDIUS (CLAUDE DE SAUMAISE) (1588–1653), French classical scholar, best remembered for his least worthy work (a defense of Charles I), who, by his scholarship and judgment, acquired great contemporary influence. Born at Semur-en-Auxois, Burgundy, on April 15, 1588, he studied at Paris (1604–06), where he turned Calvinist, and at Heidelberg (1606–09), where he discovered the Palatine manuscript of the Greek Anthology (*see* ANTHOLOGY). In 1610 he became *avocat* of the Dijon *parlement*, but in 1629, as a Protestant, was not allowed to succeed his father as *conseiller*. In this year, his monumental commentary on Solinus' *Polyhistor* appeared. His erudition, especially in philology—he knew Hebrew, Arabic, Syriac, Persian, and Coptic, as well as Greek and Latin—led to invitations from several universities, and in 1631 he became professor at Leiden. There, despite jealousy, ill-health aggravated by the climate, and numerous incitements to return to France, he remained, except for a year (1650–51) at the Swedish court, until his death at Spa, on Sept. 3, 1653. His independence is also shown by his refusal, between 1640, when his *De primatu papae* (with an edition of two 14th-century antipapal tracts) was announced, and 1645, when it was published, of several offers in exchange for a promise to withdraw it.

During the English Civil War, Salmasius was regarded as an ally by Presbyterians and parliamentarians, and at the time of Charles I's execution he was preparing, at the Scots' request, an attack on the Independent sects. At whose instigation he wrote a *Defensio regia pro Carolo I* (published anonymously November 1649) is not clear, but it seems certain that Charles II paid for the printing. It contains an attack on Independency, and, in contradiction of Salmasius' earlier views, a defense of prelacy as well as of the absolute monarchy. It provoked a *Defensio pro populo anglicano* (1651) from John Milton (*q.v.*). Also controversial were Salmasius' defenses of usury, *De usuris liber* (1638) and *De modo usurarum* (1639), which persuaded the Dutch church to admit moneylenders to the sacrament.

BIBLIOGRAPHY.—Salmasius' *Epistolae* were edited by A. Clément (1656), with biography; a manuscript life by Philibert de la Mare was used by P. Papillon, in his *Bibliothèque des auteurs de Bourgogne*, vol. 2 (1747), with list of works. *See also* G. Cohen, *Écrivains français en Hollande* (1920); R. Pintard, *Le Libertinage érudit* (1943). (F. E. SU.)

SALMON, in the broadest sense, the common name of the fish family Salmonidae, which includes salmons proper, trouts, and chars. Commonly, the term is used for the Atlantic salmon (*Salmo salar*) and the six species of Pacific salmons (*Oncorhyn-*

JUVENILE LANDLOCKED ATLANTIC SALMON

chus). These latter are *O. masu*, the "cherry" salmon found off Japan; *O. gorbuscha*, the pink or humpback salmon, ranging from the Arctic to Japan and the Klamath River; *O. nerka*, the sockeye or red salmon, ranging from northern Bering Sea to Japan and the Columbia River; *O. kisutch*, the coho or silver salmon, ranging from the Bering Sea to Japan and the Salinas River of Monterey Bay; *O. keta*, the chum or dog salmon, ranging from the Mackenzie and Lena rivers in the Arctic south to Japan and the Rogue River; and *O. tshawytscha*, the king, spring, or chinook salmon (earlier called also quinnat and tyee), ranging from the Yukon River to China and the Sacramento River. The Atlantic salmon ranges from the European Arctic to northern Portugal, Iceland, Greenland, the Ungava Peninsula of Quebec, and formerly south to Connecticut. Lake populations of Atlantic salmon are called ouananiche, landlocked salmon, or sebago salmon.

The adult Atlantic salmon averages about 10 lb. King salmon

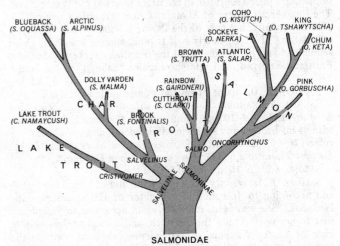

RELATIONSHIPS OF THE PRINCIPAL AMERICAN SPECIES OF SALMONIDAE. FROM LEFT TO RIGHT THE GROUPS ARE PROGRESSIVELY MORE ANADROMOUS

average about 23 lb., but individuals of 50 to 80 lb. are not uncommon. Chum salmon average about 10–12 lb.; coho salmon, 7–10 lb.; sockeye, 4–7 lb.; and pink salmon 3–6 lb.

Pacific salmon are anadromous; *i.e.*, they live most of their life in the ocean, but as adults they return to the stream where they hatched in order to spawn. To spawn, the female digs a pit in the stream gravel into which she and a male spawn simultaneously; she then covers the eggs with gravel. Adult Pacific salmon die soon after spawning, but many Atlantic salmon return to the sea and after one or two years in open waters may spawn again, some up to three or four times. Most spawning takes place in late summer or fall, when temperatures are dropping, and the eggs usually hatch in late winter. Incubation rates depend on temperature, taking about 60 up to 200 days. After hatching, the fry consume the yolk in the attached sac before wriggling up through the gravel to seek food. Young pink salmon descend immediately to the sea, other anadromous young remain longer. Chum salmon leave in a few weeks; coho salmon remain a whole year in the streams. Young of king salmon and Atlantic salmon may remain feeding in streams from one to three or more years. Young sockeye salmon dwell one to five years in lakes before migrating seaward. A race of sockeyes that matures in lakes and spawns in tributary streams is called kokanee.

Spawning grounds may be close to the sea, but the king and the chum salmons swim more than 2,000 mi. up the Yukon to spawn in its headwaters. Sockeye ascend the Fraser River for more than 700 mi. to spawn east of the Alaska panhandle. The migrating hordes of salmon, compelled by instinct, fight rapids and leap high falls until they reach their natal stream. Many pink salmon spawn on tidal flats where the water becomes salty on every tide.

Atlantic salmon, although fished commercially in certain areas such as Iceland, Newfoundland, and the Gulf of St. Lawrence, are valued chiefly as a sport fish. Fishing rights are leased for large sums along rivers in Europe and Canada. The king and coho

BY COURTESY OF THE FISHERIES RESEARCH INSTITUTE, UNIVERSITY OF WASHINGTON, SEATTLE

SOCKEYE SALMON IN DENSE SCHOOL ASCENDING THE KVICHAK RIVER, ALASKA

salmons are prized sport fish in the larger rivers of the Pacific coast. The commercial fishery of Atlantic salmon nets only a few million pounds annually, but that of the Pacific salmon is close to 2,000,-000,000 lb., of which nearly half is pink salmon, one-third chum salmon, and all but about 5% of the remainder sockeye. *See* also Fish and Fishing; and references under "Salmon" in the Index.

(G. A. Rl.)

SALOME, the name of several women in Jewish history.

Salome Alexandra (d. 67 B.C.), wife of the Maccabean king Aristobulus I (104–103 B.C.) and possibly the same Salome as the wife of his brother and successor Alexander Jannaeus, who as sole ruler (76–67) favoured the Pharisees. (*See* Maccabees; Jews: *Earliest Times to* A.D. *135: Greek and Roman Conquests.*)

Salome (d. A.D. 10), sister of Herod the Great.

Salome (fl. 1st century A.D.), granddaughter of Herod the Great, and according to Josephus the daughter of Herod Antipas and Herodias. She was twice married (again according to Josephus), first to her uncle Philip the Tetrarch, and second to Aristobulus, king of Lesser Armenia. This Salome has been traditionally identified with the young daughter of Herodias (presumably by her first husband, Philip, Herod Antipas' brother) who according to the Gospels of Mark (6:14–29) and Matthew (14:1–12), where she is unnamed, was the immediate cause of the death of John the Baptist. Herod Antipas had imprisoned John for condemning his marriage with his deceased brother's wife, but was afraid to execute him. However, when Herodias' daughter danced before him and his guests at a festival, he promised to give her whatever she asked. Prompted by her mother, Herodias, the girl demanded the head of John the Baptist on a platter, and the unwilling Herod was forced by his oath to have John beheaded.

This story, which is quite likely true, proved popular in Christian art from an early period. Oscar Wilde's *Salome* (1893) was translated by Hedwig Lachmann as the libretto for Richard Strauss's opera of the same name (1905).

Salome (1st century A.D.), wife of Zebedee and mother of the apostles James and John; she should perhaps be identified with the sister of Mary the mother of Jesus (John 19:25).

Bibliography.—*Daughter of Herodias:* H. von Daffner, *Salome: Ihre Gestalt in Geschichte und Kunst* (1912); E. Stauffer, *Jerusalem und Rom* (1957); A. H. M. Jones, *The Herods of Judaea* (1938).
Mother of James and John: T. Zahn, *Forschungen zur Geschichte des neutestamentlichen Kanons,* vol. 6, pp. 227–363 (1900).　(E. Bl.)

SALOMON, ALICE (1872–1948), German social worker and founder of one of the earliest schools of social work, was born April 19, 1872, in Berlin. She was one of the first women granted a Ph.D. from the University of Berlin (1906), where her doctoral thesis concerned the inequality of pay between men and women doing equivalent work.

Convinced of the need for special training for social workers, in 1899 Miss Salomon organized regular training courses which soon evolved into the first German social work school, of which she was president until 1928 and which was named the Alice Salomon School in her honour in 1932. As president also of the federation of German schools of social work, her ideas and influence spread throughout that nation and to other countries. Miss Salomon was active in international feminist work and wrote on problems of public health and on the position of women and children in in-

dustry. In 1937, exiled from Nazi Germany, Miss Salomon went to the United States where she continued her work as a lecturer on social work administration. She died Aug. 30, 1948, in New York City.

(M. C. E.)

SALOMON, HAYM (1740–1785), early American financier and patriot, was born in Lissa, Pol., in 1740. He moved to America following revolutionary activities in defense of Polish liberty.

When he arrived in New York, he established himself as a commission merchant, and his personality and keen discernment soon made him a successful financier. During the American Revolution, Salomon was with the patriotic party known as Sons of Liberty. Within a short time he was made financial agent of the French government, for which services he accepted no commission. His ability and patriotic activities brought him to the attention of Robert Morris, the financier of the Revolution, who assigned him to the office of the superintendent of finance, where he handled bills of exchange.

Among his many contributions to the colonies, Salomon subscribed heavily to government loans, endorsed notes, gave generously to soldiers and statesmen, and equipped several military units with his own money. He was made interpreter during the war, and was permitted to go into the British lines, but on two occasions was thrown into prison. He escaped, but suffered ill-health from exposure, which later led to his death.

While living in Philadelphia (1778–85), Salomon, an Ashkenazic Jew, initiated a measure in behalf of Jews in the state of Pennsylvania that later resulted in more liberal conditions of employment for them. At that time, persons seeking to qualify for civic employment in Pennsylvania were required to take an oath affirming their belief in the New as well as the Old Testament. Salomon presented a petition to the Council of Censors on Dec. 23, 1783, in which he requested the removal of this condition, so that public service might not be closed to orthodox Jews. Later, the constitution of the state was so amended.

Salomon died in Philadelphia, Pa., on Jan. 6, 1785.

Bibliography.—Patriotic Foundation of Chicago, *The Story of the George Washington-Robert Morris-Haym Salomon Monument* (1942); Charles Edward Russell, *Haym Salomon and the Revolution* (1930); Howard Fast, *Haym Salomon, Son of Liberty* (1941).

SALONIKA (Salonica; ancient Greek Thessalonike, Latin Thessalonica, modern Thessaloniki), the capital and seat of the governor-general of northern Greece, of the region of Macedonia, and of the department (*nomos*) of Salonika, is one of the principal seaports of southeastern Europe. It lies on the west side of the Chalcidic peninsula, at the head of the Gulf of Salonika (ancient Thermaic Gulf), on a fine bay whose southern edge is formed by the Kalamaria heights, while on its northern and western sides is the broad alluvial plain produced by the Vardar and Aliakmon rivers. The city is built on the foothills and slopes of Mt. Khortiatis overlooking the bay. Its centre, largely destroyed by a disastrous fire in August 1917, was rebuilt in European style, and much reconstruction was done after World War II; but the older parts retain something of their Turkish character. Salonika is the seat of a metropolitan bishop of the Greek Orthodox Church. It has a university, founded in 1926, with over 7,000 students, and a large number of Greek and foreign schools, including the American college, the German school, and the French *lycée*. It is a divisional headquarters of the Greek army and has a military and a civil airport. At the census of 1961 the department had a population of 544,394, the city 250,920; the city population included the remnants (about 1,300 in 1961) of a large colony of Jews, numbering about 50,000 before the German occupation of 1941–44, whose ancestors fled to Salonika from Germany, Italy, Spain, and Portugal in the 15th and 16th centuries.

History.—Thessalonica was built near the site of the older Greek city of Therme, so called from the hot springs of the neighbourhood. It was founded in 315 B.C. by Cassander, who gave it the name of his wife, a sister of Alexander the Great. It became the capital of the Roman province of Macedonia after 148 B.C. and was Pompey's base of operations during the Civil War. As a military and commercial station on the Via Egnatia, which ran from the Adriatic to Byzantium, it grew to great importance in the

Roman Empire. It became famous in connection with the early history of Christianity through the two epistles addressed by St. Paul to the community he founded there (see THESSALONIANS, EPISTLES TO THE); and its first bishop, Gaius, was one of Paul's companions (Acts 19:29). Under Constantine, who repaired the port and enriched the city, it became capital of the prefecture of Illyricum. In A.D. 390, 7,000 citizens accused of insurrection were massacred in the hippodrome by command of the emperor Theodosius I. In the Byzantine Empire Thessalonica was a most prosperous centre of trade, famous for its annual Fair of St. Demetrius, its patron saint, who was martyred in the reign of Maximian. Confident of the protection and guidance of their saint, the inhabitants beat off repeated attacks of Goths in the 3rd and 5th centuries and of Avars and Slavs in the 6th and 7th. In 732 the emperor Leo III detached the city from the jurisdiction of the papacy and made it, with Illyricum, dependent on the patriarch of Constantinople. During the iconoclastic regime (see ICONOCLASTIC CONTROVERSY) of the same emperor and his successors it stood on the defensive and succeeded in saving some of the artistic treasures of its churches, although its bishop, Joseph (807–832), a brother of St. Theodore Studites, suffered exile for his defense of image worship.

Thessalonica was made into a special theme or military district of the empire in the 9th century; and an attempt to transfer the whole Bulgarian trade to Thessalonica in the close of that century caused the invasion of the empire by Simeon of Bulgaria. In 904 the Arabs from Crete took the city by storm, and 22,000 inhabitants were sold into slavery. It was attacked by Samuel of Bulgaria in 985. In 1185 the Normans of Sicily took the city after ten days' siege and perpetrated endless barbarities, of which Eustathius, then bishop of the see, has left an account.

After the Fourth Crusade in 1204, Baldwin, conqueror of Constantinople, conferred the kingdom of Thessalonica on Boniface, marquis of Montferrat; but Theodore Angelus Comnenus Ducas, the Greek ruler of Epirus, captured the city in 1224, and had himself crowned emperor there by the archbishop of Ochrida in Macedonia. Demetrius of Montferrat, supported by Pope Honorius III, tried without success to recover his father's throne; and when he died the empty title of king of Thessalonica was adopted by several claimants, including Frederick II of Sicily, the house of Burgundy, and Philip of Tarentum.

In 1246 the independent Greek empire of Thessalonica ceased to exist; the city was incorporated into the rival empire of Nicaea and thence passed into the revived Byzantine Empire after 1261. It was unsuccessfully attacked by the Catalans or Almogávares (q.v.) in 1308, and soon after became deeply involved in the civil war between John V Palaeologus and John VI Cantacuzenus, and in the controversy over hesychasm (q.v.). The great hesychast apologist, Gregory Palamas, became bishop of Thessalonica in 1350. From 1342 to 1350 the city governed itself as an independent commune under the rule of a popular party calling themselves the zealots. In the latter part of the 14th century it fell twice (1387 and 1391) into the hands of the Ottoman Turks, only to be recovered by the emperor Manuel II in 1403. But when the Turks finally closed in, Manuel's son, Andronicus, in desperation ceded the city to the Venetians in 1423. It was still in Venetian hands when the sultan Murad II appeared and, on March 29, 1430, after a short siege, took it by assault. The Turkish conquerors devastated the city, massacred thousands of its inhabitants, and converted many of the churches into mosques. Salonika became a vilayet of the Ottoman Empire.

In the late 17th century the influence of Sabbatai Zebi (q.v.) led to the foundation of the Donmeh sect of Jews professing Islam but preserving many Jewish customs and regarding Sabbatai as the Messiah. In 1876 the French and German consuls in the city were murdered by the Turkish populace. In September 1890 much of the southeastern quarter was destroyed by fire. It was the birthplace of Mustafa Kemal (Atatürk), and during the early years of the 20th century it was the headquarters of the Committee of Union and Progress, the central organization of the Young Turk movement, which carried out the constitutional revolution of 1908. Before this event the weakness of Turkey had encouraged

the belief that Salonika would ultimately pass under the control of Austria-Hungary or one of the Balkan states, and this gave rise to many political intrigues which helped to delay the solution of the Macedonian question.

When the First Balkan War broke out in 1912, Salonika surrendered to the Greeks on Nov. 8, after 482 years of Turkish occupation. King George I visited what was now the second largest city of his kingdom and was assassinated there on March 18, 1913. The Treaty of London in the same year assigned Salonika to Greece, and the Battle of Kilkis in the Second Balkan War in 1913 prevented the Bulgarians from approaching it. Salonika was becoming more and more hellenized when World War I brought it into prominence as the base of Allied operations in the Near East in 1915–18 (see WORLD WAR I). In 1916 a revolution against King Constantine by supporters of Eleutherios Venizelos (q.v.) broke out there, with the formation of the League of National Defense; in October Venizelos arrived and formed a provisional government, which the Allies recognized, and which declared war against Bulgaria and Germany.

After the war an arrangement, not finally ratified until 1929, was made by which Yugoslavia should have a free zone in the harbour; similar but less extensive facilities were offered to Bulgaria in 1939. After the proclamation of the Greek republic in 1924, Salonika often had a decisive voice in politics, and the large immigration of Greek refugees from Asia Minor further hellenized the country round it.

Salonika again figured prominently in World War II. It was bombed by Italian aircraft in 1940. German forces driving southward from Bulgaria and from Yugoslavia drove back the Greek and British armies and captured the city on April 9, 1941, thus cutting off all Thrace from the rest of Greece and splitting Macedonia in two. During the civil war following the German occupation Salonika was crowded with refugees from the towns and villages of Macedonia. Since the restoration of the Greek monarchy it has increasingly taken its place as the second capital of Greece.

Antiquities.—Numerous remains of the earliest or Hellenistic period of the city have been excavated. The Via Egnatia of the Romans, once spanned by two Roman arches, traverses it from east to west, between the Vardar Gate and the Kalamaria Gate. The arch near the Vardar Gate, a massive stone structure probably erected toward the end of the 1st century A.D., was destroyed in 1867. The other arch, built of brick and partly faced with sculptured marble, dates from the reign of Galerius (A.D. 305–311), who extended the city walls to the southeast to include a palace and hippodrome. Remains of a large octagonal building of the same period have been found a little to the south of the arch. The walls of Salonika and of the upper citadel, which forms a separate fortress, date originally from the time of Theodosius I (379–395), though rebuilt and restored on many occasions, with towers and gates added by the Palaeologi and by the Turks. The sea walls were demolished in 1866 to accommodate the quay, though the Levkos Pirgos ("White Tower") still stands on the quay. The *Heptapyrgion,* the keep of the citadel, is now a prison.

Once the second city of the Byzantine Empire after Constantinople, Salonika is remarkable for its many fine Byzantine churches. The domed Basilica of Hagia Sophia, probably erected early in the 8th century, was converted into a mosque in 1589 and damaged by fire in 1890 and by bombing in 1940. The nave, forming a Greek cross, is surmounted by a hemispherical dome covered with a rich mosaic, probably of the 9th century, representing the Ascension. The Church of St. Demetrius, originally of the early 5th century, was destroyed by the fire of 1917 but has been lavishly reconstructed. It is a five-naved basilica with an atrium and narthex and a transept at the east end; it still contains mosaics dating from the 7th century, and frescoes of 1303 adorn the chapel on the right of the sanctuary. The Church of St. George, a rotunda with eight niches in the walls, was originally a Roman construction (possibly a mausoleum), converted to Christian use in the 5th century with the addition of a circular gallery (now destroyed) and the enlargement of the eastern niche to make a sanctuary and apse. The dome is decorated with 5th-century mosaics, of which the lower zone survives, showing martyr-saints against a background of architectural compositions. The three-naved Basilica of the Panagia Acheiropoietos (formerly St. Paraskevi; Turkish Eski Djouma) also dates from the 5th century and contains mosaics of that period. The little Church of Hosios David has a fine 5th-century mosaic of the Vision of Ezekiel; and the domed churches of St. Catherine and of the Holy Apostles with their mosaics date from the 13th and 14th centuries respectively.

Railways, Harbour, and Commerce.—Salonika is the principal Aegean seaport of the Balkan Peninsula, the centre of the import trade of all Macedonia, and the natural port of shipment for the products of an even larger area. It is the terminus of four railways: one goes north to Skopje and Nis in Yugoslavia, where it meets the main Paris-Vienna-Istanbul line; another runs westward from Salonika to Bitola (Yugoslavia); a third runs via Serrai and Drama to join the main line at Kuleli Burgas (Pithion, Gr.); a fourth extends south to Larissa and Athens. The present harbour, opened to navigation in December 1901, allows the direct loading and unloading of all merchandise. The harbour works consist of a breakwater 1,835 ft. (559 m.) long and 492 ft. (150 m.) wide, with 28 ft. (8½ m.) of water on its landward side. Opposite is a quay 1,475 ft. (450 m.) long, which was widened in 1903–07 to 306 ft. (93 m.); at each end of the quay a 656-ft. (200-m.) pier projects into the sea. Between the extremities of these two piers and those of the breakwater are the two entrances to the harbour. Salonika exports grain, flour, bran, silk cocoons, chrome, manganese, hides and skins, cattle and sheep, wool, eggs, and tobacco. Other industries are cotton spinning, brewing, tanning, and the production of bricks, tiles, carpets, textiles, soap, flour, ice, wines, and spirits.

MACEDONIA REGION, of which Salonika is the capital, is rich in minerals, including chrome, manganese, zinc, iron, lead, and lignite, but some of these are unworked. The chief agricultural products are grain, rice, beans, cotton, fennel, and red pepper; there is also some trade in timber, livestock, furs, wool, and silk cocoons. The tobacco industry is one of the largest, but wine, liqueurs, sesame oil, macaroni, and soap are also manufactured. The principal towns, besides Salonika, are Edessa, Kavalla (qq.v.), and Serrai. Drama is one of the centres of tobacco cultivation; and the towns of Veroia, Kozani, Naousa, Florina, and Katerini all have populations over 10,000. The total population of the region was 1,890,-654 in 1961.

See also references under "Salonika" in the Index.

BIBLIOGRAPHY.—T. L. F. Tafel, De Thessalonica eiusque agro dissertatio geographica (1839); O. Tafrali, Thessalonique au XIVe siècle (1913), Thessalonique des origines au XIVe siècle (1919); P. Risal, La Ville convoitée, Salonique (1914); M. Sarrail, Mon Commandement en Orient, 1916–18 (1920); C. Diehl, M. le Tourneau, and H. Saladin, Les Monuments chrétiens de Salonique (1918); C. Diehl, Salonique (1920); M. Laskaris, Salonique à la fin du XVIIIe siècle (1939); A. Xyngopoulos (Xungopoulos), The Basilica of St. Demetrius of Thessalonike, in Greek (1946); A. E. Vakalopoulos (Bakalopoulos), History of Thessalonike, 315 B.C.–1912, Eng. trans. (1962); G. Ostrogorsky, History of the Byzantine State, Eng. trans. (1956); E. S. Forster, A Short History of Modern Greece, 1821–1956, rev. ed. by D. Dakin (1958); R. F. Hoddinott, Early Byzantine Churches in Macedonia and Southern Serbia (1963).   (D. M. N.)

SALSETTE (a corruption of the Marathi SASHTI), a large island north of Bombay city in India. Area 246 sq.mi. (637 sq.km.). Pop. (1961) 186,449. The island was taken from the Portuguese by the Marathas in 1739 and from them by the British in 1774; it was formally annexed by the East India Company in 1782. In 1950 it was divided administratively between Greater Bombay and Thana district (within which the whole island formerly lay). In various parts of the island are ruins of Portuguese churches, convents, and villas, and at Kanheri are more than 100 Buddhist cave shrines dating from the end of the 2nd century to the 6th century A.D. Salsette is crossed by the Central and Western railways and is encircled by a motor road. It is connected with Bombay Island and also with the mainland by bridge and causeway.
                                              (F. R. A.)

SALSIFY, sometimes called oyster plant or vegetable oyster because of its taste, is a hardy biennial with long, cylindrical, fleshy, edible roots resembling small parsnips. Botanically it is Tragopogon porrifolius, of the family Compositae. When properly cooked, the roots are extremely delicate and wholesome. Native to the Mediterranean region, salsify has escaped from cultivation and become a troublesome weed in many temperate regions, as in Great Britain and North America.

Salsify succeeds best in a free, rich, deep soil. Since the plant requires a long season to develop usable roots, the first seed should be sown an inch deep in early spring (more, a month later) in rows a foot apart; when three inches tall, the plants should be thinned to four to eight inches apart. The first season's growth produces a rosette of grasslike leaves up to one foot long. In late autumn some of the whitish roots may be taken up and stored in sand or in a moist cellar for immediate use; others may be dug as desired during intervals of mild weather. The roots may be left in the garden until spring, but should be dug up before growth starts. The second season's growth produces an erect branching stem two to four feet tall and handsome purple flower heads followed by elongate, plumed seeds.

Other related root vegetables, also native to the Old World and used as is salsify, are black salsify (Scorzonera hispanica), having a white-fleshed but black-skinned root, and Spanish salsify or golden thistle (Scolymus hispanicus), longer-rooted than salsify and milder-flavoured, with prickly leaves.

In the U.S. salsify is occasionally grown in home gardens but is of little importance as a market vegetable. Black salsify and Spanish salsify are little known in the U.S.

SALT (AS SALT), the chief town of the liwa' (district) of Balqa, Jordan, lies about 18 mi. (29 km.) WNW of Amman on the old Jerusalem road. Pop. (1961) 16,176. The town is picturesquely built on steep hillsides. It contains fine examples of old Turkish houses, for under Turkish rule (16th century) it was the chief town of Transjordan. It is noted for its grapes and raisins. The name Salt may derive from the Latin Saltus (meaning a narrow pass or mountain valley), for under this name it was the seat of a bishopric in Byzantine times.   (G. W. L. H.)

SALT, a mineral substance of great importance to man, is chiefly sodium chloride, NaCl. It is sometimes called common salt to distinguish it from chemical compounds of the same kind, called salts (see ACIDS AND BASES). This article is concerned with common salt only.

Properties.—Pure sodium chloride may be made by passing dry hydrogen chloride gas into a saturated solution of common salt, whereupon the purified salt is deposited as a colourless crystalline powder. It crystallizes in the cubic system, usually as cubes; the mineral form is known as halite (see below, Rock Salt). The melting point is 800° C, which is a bright red heat. Vaporization begins near this temperature. It dissolves easily in cold water and a little more readily in hot water; 100 parts by weight of water dissolve 35.8 parts of salt at 20° C, 39.2 parts at 100° C and 39.6 parts at 108.7° C, the boiling point of the saturated solution. If a saturated solution in water is cooled below 0° C a crystalline hydrate, $NaCl.2H_2O$, separates.

Common salt (and other salts such as calcium chloride), when mixed with snow or ice, lowers the melting point of the latter. Hence salt is frequently used to rid walks and roads of accumulated snow and ice.

Uses.—Table salt, used universally as a condiment, is fine-grained common salt of high purity. To ensure that it will remain free-flowing when exposed to the atmosphere, small quantities of sodium carbonate or trisodium phosphate are added to combine with such moisture-absorbing impurities as calcium and magnesium chlorides. Usually potassium iodide is added in small quantity to overcome any possible iodine deficiency of the consumer.

Salt is essential to man's health (see BLOOD: Plasma: Salts; NUTRITION: Components of Nutrition: Inorganic Materials); it is fed to livestock for the same reason.

Common salt used for various manufacturing purposes may be coarser in grain than table salt. It is employed as a preservative or seasoning, or both, in meat packing, fish curing, and the food-processing industries; for curing hides, and as a brine for refrigeration. It is indispensable to the manufacture of sodium carbonate (washing soda), sodium bicarbonate (baking soda), sodium hydroxide (caustic soda), hydrochloric acid, bleaching powder, chlorine and many other heavy and fine chemicals. The glass and soap industries are dependent upon it, and it is used also in the glaze and enamel trades. As a flux, it enters into metallurgical processes and has been used in the manufacture of cement to aid in the recovery of potash as a by-product. Salt also is used to melt snow and ice from streets and highways (*see above, Properties*).

The production of salt is one of the world's most widely distributed mineral industries. Outputs of salt vary with the population and industrial activity of the country in question. Heavily populated countries like India and China require the major part of their production for food uses only; the United States on the other hand requires several times as much salt for industrial purposes as is consumed in food. Many countries contribute to the total world production of salt; leading producers include the United States, United Kingdom, U.S.S.R., China, India, France, West Germany and Italy, with a total annual production of about 50,000,000 tons. In the 1960s U.S. consumption of salt was about 25,000,000 tons a year; about three-fourths of the amount was used in manufacturing.

Historical Background.—Salt must have been quite unattainable to primitive man in many parts of the world. Thus the *Odyssey* speaks of inlanders who did not know the sea and used no salt with their food. In some parts of America, and even of India (among the Todas), salt was first introduced by Europeans; and there are still parts of central Africa where its use is a luxury confined to the rich. Indeed, where men live mainly on milk and flesh, consuming the latter raw or roasted, so that its salts are not lost, it is not necessary to add sodium chloride, and thus it can be understood how the Numidian nomads in the time of Sallust and the Bedouins of Hadhramaut at the present day never eat salt with their food. On the other hand, a cereal or vegetable diet calls for a supplement of salt, and so does boiled meat.

The habitual use of salt is intimately connected with the advance from nomadic to agricultural life; *i.e.*, with precisely that step in civilization which had most influence on the cults of almost all ancient nations. The gods were worshiped as the givers of the kindly fruits of the earth, and, as all over the world "bread and salt" go together in common use and common phrase, salt was habitually associated with offerings, at least with all offerings which consisted in whole or in part of cereal elements. This practice was prevalent among the Greeks and Romans and among the Semitic peoples (Lev. ii, 13).

As covenants were ordinarily made over a sacrificial meal, in which salt was a necessary element, the expression "a covenant of salt" (Num. xviii, 19) is easily understood; it is probable, moreover, that the preservative qualities of salt made it a peculiarly fitting symbol of an enduring compact, and influenced the choice of this particular element of the covenant meal as that which sealed an obligation to fidelity. Hence the Greek saying "Trespass not against the salt and the board," the Arab avowal "There is salt between us," the expression "to eat the salt of the palace" (Ezra iv, 14), and the modern Persian phrase *namak haram*, "untrue to salt" (*i.e.*, disloyal or ungrateful). In English the metaphor "salt of the earth" describes a person held in high esteem.

Salt and incense were economic and religious necessities of the ancient world and contribute greatly to knowledge of the ancient highways of commerce. Thus one of the oldest roads in Italy is the Via Salaria, by which the produce of the salt pans of Ostia was carried into the Sabine country. Herodotus' account of the caravan route uniting the salt oases of the Libyan desert makes it plain that this was mainly a salt road, and to the present day the caravan trade of the Sahara is largely in salt. The salt of Palmyra was an important element in the trade between the Syrian ports and the Persian gulf. In like manner the ancient trade between the Aegean and the coasts of southern Russia was largely dependent on the salt pans at the mouth of the Dnieper and on the salt fish brought from this district. The vast salt mines of northern India were worked before the time of Alexander. The economic importance of salt is further indicated by the prevalence down to the present day of salt taxes or of government monopolies. In oriental systems of taxation high imposts on salt are seldom lacking and are often carried out oppressively with the result that the arti-

cle is apt to reach the consumer in an impure state largely mixed with earth. "The salt which has lost its savour" (Matt. v, 13) is simply the earthy residuum of such an impure salt after the sodium chloride has been washed out.

Cakes of salt have been used as money; *e.g.*, in Abyssinia and elsewhere in Africa, and in Tibet and adjoining parts. In the Roman army an allowance of salt was made to officers and men; in imperial times this *salarium* was converted into an allowance of money for salt.

Salt in 'Sea Water.—Many substances make up the salt in sea water, but sodium chloride is by far the dominant compound. Assuming that each gallon of sea water contains 0.2547 lb. of salt, and allowing an average density of 2.24 for rock salt (the natural form of salt occurring in the earth), it has been computed that if dried up the oceans of the world would yield no less than 4,500,000 cubic miles of rock salt, or about 14½ times the bulk of the entire continent of Europe above high-water mark.

Sea water contains on the average about 3.33% salt, but the concentration varies from about 2.9% in the polar seas to 3.55% and upward at the equator. Enclosed seas such as the Mediterranean and Red seas contain a higher proportion of salt than the open ocean at the same latitude. The salt obtained by evaporation of sea water has, however, the following composition irrespective of the source of the sea water: sodium chloride 77.82%, magnesium chloride 9.44%, magnesium sulfate 6.57%, calcium sulfate 3.44%, potassium chloride 2.11%, magnesium bromide 0.22% and some calcium carbonate. (*See also* OCEAN AND OCEANOGRAPHY: *Chemistry of Sea Water: Elements in the Sea Salts.*)

Natural Brines.—Brine is water containing a high concentration of salt. Natural brines of commercial importance are found in Austria; France; Germany; Kharaghoda and Kuda, India; Michigan, New York state, Ohio, Pennsylvania, West Virginia and the salt lakes of Utah in the United States; and in the Dead sea. In Great Britain there are salt brines in Cheshire, Worcestershire, Lancaster and Yorkshire and in deep wells in Derbyshire, Staffordshire and Midlothian. Salt in brines is nearly always accompanied by chlorides and sulfates of potassium, calcium and magnesium; in many cases carbonates and the element bromine are present.

The Dead sea, which covers an area of 394 sq.mi., contains approximately 11,600,000,000 tons of salt, and the river Jordan, which contains only 35 parts of salt per 100,000 of water, adds each year 850,000 tons of salt to this total. The composition of Dead sea water is given in Table I (although the salts exist as ions in solution and are so analyzed; it is customary to express the analyses in terms of compounds):

TABLE I.—*Composition of Dead Sea Water*

Item	Surface water	Deep water (250 ft.)
Specific gravity	1.1651	1.2356
Sodium chloride	6.11%	7.20%
Potassium chloride	0.85%	1.25%
Magnesium bromide	0.38%	0.61%
Magnesium chloride	9.46%	13.73%
Calcium chloride	2.63%	3.82%
Calcium sulfate	0.11%	0.05%
Total solids	19.54%	26.66%

The concentration of salts in the Dead sea increases to a depth of about 250 ft., after which it remains practically constant. At this depth and below it is a concentrated solution, which, indeed, is supersaturated when pumped up, for a slight deposition of salt takes place owing to diminished pressure. Noteworthy features of Dead sea water are its relative freedom from sulfates and the high proportions of potassium and bromine. These facts, coupled with the circumstance that atmospheric conditions in Palestine are favourable to solar evaporation for about eight months of the year, indicate that the production of salt, potassium and even bromine is feasible in the Dead sea area, the process as regards salt and potash being similar to that described below under *Manufacture*. The brines at Kharaghoda resemble sea water in the character of their dissolved salts, but are much more concentrated and in some cases practically saturated.

TABLE II.—*Composition of Some Concentrated Natural Brines*

Item	Droitwich	Winsford	Syracuse, N.Y.	St. Charles, Mich.	Artern, Saxony	Friedrichshall, Württemberg
	%	%	%	%	%	%
Sodium chloride	24.97	25.46	21.71	22.84	25.27	25.49
Sodium sulfate	0.26	..	..	..	..	..
Potassium chloride	..	..	..	..	0.12	..
Potassium sulfate	..	..	..	..	0.29	..
Magnesium bromide	..	..	..	0.26	..	..
Magnesium chloride	0.05	0.21	0.14	4.03	0.42	0.01
Calcium sulfate	0.37	0.45	0.50	0.20	0.40	0.44
Calcium chloride	..	..	0.19	0.77	..	..
Total solids	25.65	26.12	22.54	28.10	26.50	25.94

Table II gives the composition of some concentrated natural brines used for the production of salt in various countries.

Certain natural brines occurring in England and the United States are of interest, not only from the economic point of view, but also because they contain salts not usually found in brines, such as the chlorides of barium and strontium; when salt is produced from such brines special methods of manufacture are adopted.

In Great Britain these brines were found at great depth in boreholes in Derbyshire, Staffordshire and Midlothian during the search for petroleum. In the U.S. they occur in deep wells in West Virginia, Ohio, Texas, and other places.

TABLE III.—*Natural Brines Containing Unusual Salts*

Item	Renishaw, Derbyshire	West Calder, Scotland	Pomeroy, Ohio	Malden, W. Virginia
Depth (feet)	3,198	3,910	..	..
Specific gravity	1.127	1.063	1.075	1.063
Sodium chloride	10.28%	6.26%	7.92%	6.01%
Potassium chloride	0.03%	0.04%	0.04%	0.06%
Magnesium bromide	0.11%	0.07%	..	..
Magnesium chloride	0.84%	0.55%	0.57%	0.50%
Calcium chloride	4.23%	1.34%	1.36%	1.49%
Strontium chloride	0.12%	0.16%	0.03%	0.02%
Barium chloride	0.14%	0.07%	0.04%	0.07%
Total solids	15.75%	8.49%	9.96%	8.15%

It has been suggested that those brines which are characterized by the absence of carbonates and sulfates have been produced by a natural process akin to the ion exchange (*q.v.*) process for softening water. (J. J. F.; A. G. F.; R. H. RN.; X.)

Rock Salt.—Rock salt is crystalline sodium chloride, called halite by mineralogists. It occurs in the form of rock masses and beds. It has a wide geographic distribution and occurs abundantly in rocks of all ages. Because of its great solubility in water it occurs under extremely thick cover in humid regions, but lies close to the surface in arid regions.

All important rock-salt deposits originated from the evaporation of sea water at some time during the geologic past. Some 77% of the mineral matter in normal sea water is sodium chloride. Upon evaporation of about nine-tenths of the volume of sea water, rock salt is precipitated. The precipitation of rock salt overlaps the precipitation of calcium sulfate (gypsum and anhydrite) on the one hand and potassium and magnesium salts on the other. Thus these compounds commonly occur with rock salt. Deposits are found in beds from a few feet to many hundreds of feet thick. In age these beds are distributed through much of geologic time from the Cambrian through the Mesozoic.

Since it is necessary to evaporate a large quantity of sea water to deposit a small amount of salt, it is thought that many extremely thick rock-salt beds were deposited in partly enclosed arms of the seas in which evaporation was greater than inflow of fresher water. The supply of water was continually renewed by inflowing currents while a barrier on the sea floor at the entrance to the basin prevented the outflow of the concentrated saline water so that the salts were deposited in thick beds on the basin floor.

Such bedded salt deposits occur in the Lower Cambrian of the Punjab Salt range in Pakistan and in Iran, but are little exploited. The Silurian and Devonian rocks of the northeastern United States and Ontario in Canada contain important rock-salt deposits which are extensively worked for industrial and domestic use. The Carboniferous of Nova Scotia contains extensive rock-salt deposits which are utilized in eastern Canada and northeastern United States. The Pennsylvanian (Carboniferous) of Colorado and Utah contains large amounts of rock salt.

The rocks of Permian age contain some of the largest rock-salt deposits in the world. The most important are the Zechstein deposits of Germany, long exploited not only for their common salt but for their potassium content. The salt deposits of the sub-Carpathian region extending from Poland through Hungary and Rumania may be of this age. In the Donetz basin and the Volga region of European U.S.S.R. are extremely important deposits of Permian rock salt. In the United States enormous thicknesses of rock salt underlie much of the Permian basin extending from Kansas to western Texas.

The Triassic of England contains important rock-salt deposits which have been worked for many years. In the Tirol the Triassic strata also contain important salt deposits. In the province of Szechwan, China, rock salt occurs in beds of Triassic Age and has been exploited through salt wells for more than 2,000 years.

Another type of rock-salt deposit which is economically important is the salt dome. This deposit has been forced up by earth pressure from great depths in the form of plugs of roughly circular shape a few yards to a mile across. The domes appear to be a development of folding, in which the salt is forced up through other rocks, because of its great plasticity under high pressure, from depths as great as 20,000 ft. Such salt domes are abundant along the Gulf coast of southern United States and extend into the east Texas basin and northern Louisiana. Many domes occur at shallow depths and are extensively mined to supply the southern United States. Similar domes in the sub-Carpathian region of Europe have been worked since ancient times. The north German plain has many domes, extensively worked, which are thought to have originated below 6,000 feet. (*See* SALT DOME.)

Rock salt may be exploited by usual mining methods. Another method of exploitation is by drilling wells into the salt strata, pumping water down them to dissolve the salt and treating the returning brine in a manner similar to the treatment of natural brines. It is difficult to arrive at any estimate of the relative importance of rock-salt production as compared with production of other types of salt since most available statistics make no distinction between natural and artificial brines. The United States and Europe are leaders in exploitation of rock-salt deposits. However, South American countries are developing their deposits rapidly with Brazil the largest producer. (J. M. Hs.; R. H. RN.)

Manufacture.—At one time almost all of the salt used in commerce was produced from the evaporation of sea water, and sea salt still is a staple commodity in many maritime countries, especially where the climate is dry and the summer of long duration. Commercial salt is manufactured (1) from rock salt and (2) from sea water and other natural and artificial brines. Most of the artificial brines are obtained by pumping water into wells drilled into underground salt beds and pumping up the solution which results when this water dissolves salt from the deposit. In addition to the ordinary uses of crystalline salts, much is used directly in the form of brine in industrial countries.

Manufacture From Rock Salt.—The beds of rock salt are mined or quarried by the usual excavation methods, depending upon the depths and thicknesses of the deposits and upon local conditions. In some cases the mined rock salt is dissolved and salt manufactured by treatment of the brine as described below. This treatment affords opportunities for purification of the salt. Where the rock salt is of high degree of purity, as in the United States and in Galicia, the salt is ground, sieved and marketed with no further treatment. The mined salt in large lumps is first crushed, then more finely ground and screened to separate the various size grades; the oversize material going back to the mill and the acceptable sizes being packed for market, usually by bagging. A disadvantage of such salt is the tendency to revert to hard masses in storage. In Germany rock salt is treated in similar fashion, except that the larger fragments of impurities such as anhydrite and gypsum are hand picked from the coarsely crushed rock salt.

Less pure German rock salt is purified by fusion, either alone or with sodium carbonate and silica or with chalk and saltpetre (sodium nitrate). In some cases, the fused mass is "blown" with air to burn away carbonaceous material, leaving a clear melt which crystallizes on cooling. After separation from the slag by concussion, the salt is ground and sieved. Alternately, an impure salt is leached with a saturated solution of pure salt in dilute hydrochloric acid whereby impurities such as gypsum, magnesium salts and iron oxide are dissolved. The treated salt is filtered, washed with a saturated solution of pure salt, dried, ground and graded for market.

Manufacture From Sea Water and Brines.—When an aqueous solution of several salts is evaporated, the salts separate, each as it reaches its point of saturation in the solution. The solubilities of the salts in the complex solution will, in general, be similar to but not the same as the solubilities for the same salts in water. In the case of sea water and many brines the order of deposition is calcium carbonate, calcium sulfate, sodium chloride, magnesium sulfate, carnallite (potassium magnesium chloride) and magnesium chloride. These salts are not, however, deposited within sharply defined limits of concentration. As each salt reaches its own point of saturation it deposits along with all the other salts which have reached their own saturation points. Therefore each salt deposited is contaminated by some of the other salts and by the residual brine. Further, the relative solubilities are altered by temperature and hence in solar evaporation the difference in temperature between day and night and also the seasonal temperature changes affect the character of the salt deposited. The art of the saltmaker is to produce grades of salt suitable for the particular use to which it is to be put.

Salt is produced by solar evaporation from sea water in France, Portugal, Spain, Italy, India, the U.S.S.R. and the United States—in fact, in nearly all maritime countries. The processes generally adopted are similar in principle, although details of evaporating pans and of manufacturing plants vary with local conditions. A preliminary concentration is usually carried out by allowing the brine to flow through a series of channels to concentration ponds constructed of wood, puddled clay or concrete. The areas of the ponds vary from 280 sq. ft. to 50 ac. in different countries. The solution is concentrated first to a specific gravity of about 1.21. At this stage, suspended impurities (sand and clay) and the less soluble salts (calcium carbonate or chalk and calcium sulfate) are removed. The clear concentrated brine is then run successively into a series of crystallizing pans, usually three, where the salt is deposited. The total area of the crystallizing pans is approximately one-tenth of that of the evaporating pans. In the first crystallizing pan the brine is concentrated to a specific gravity of 1.25 and here the best grade of salt is produced. The specific gravity of the mother liquor increases slowly during crystallization of the salt because of the increasing concentration of the other salts. The mother liquor reaches a specific gravity of 1.26 in the second pan where a second grade of salt is obtained. In the third pan a specific gravity of 1.275 is obtained and here the lowest grade of salt is deposited. The final mother liquor, termed bitterns, is used in some countries (*e.g.*, France, India and the United States) for the manufacture of potash, bromine, Epsom salts (magnesium sulfate) and magnesium chloride.

The salt in each crystallizing pan is raked into rows and allowed to drain for several days, is then collected into heaps, drained again, lifted from the pans and finally dried. As a tax is levied on salt (by weight) in most European countries, it is obviously an advantage to trade in the dried material. The salt from the first pan is frequently used locally as table salt, that from the second pan may go into the chemical industry and that from the third pan is used for pickling fish, refrigeration and other purposes. Typical compositions of the salts thus produced are given in Table IV.

In Palestine, solar evaporation of the Dead sea water is aided by dye added to the water. The dye permits complete absorption of sunlight in thinner layers of water so that shallow ponds may be used and absorption of brine by the ground is reduced.

In England, Germany, most of the eastern part of the United States and other places where it is impractical to manufacture salt by means of solar heat, the brines are concentrated and evaporated by artificial heat. Formerly the brine was concentrated in open pans over fire. More recently steam-jacketed vessels were used, but now the largest part of the salt produced in the colder countries is manufactured in multiple-effect vacuum evaporators and an important quantity is made in open crystallizers or grainers which produce a type of crystal preferred for use in some of the food industries. The brine, natural or artificial, is first pumped into settling tanks, where calcium and magnesium compounds may be removed by chemical treatment, usually lime and sodium hydroxide are used. After settling and filtration, the brine is delivered to the grainer, which is a long open trough with steam coils. The brine is fed into the grainer at approximately the same rate as that at which evaporation is taking place and at a temperature only slightly below that of the brine in the grainer. The residue of brine or bitterns, may be removed daily or less often or may be withdrawn continuously. The evaporation occurs at the surface of the liquid and the crystals originate there. They remain at the surface, held up by the surface tension of the brine. The crystal grows at the top edges, becoming a small inverted hollow pyramid or hopper. Eventually the hopper sinks and ceases to grow. When the crystals are recovered the salt is largely in the form of flakes, whence the name "flake salt." When multiple-effect evaporators are used, the vacuum in each vessel is adjusted so that the vapour from the first vessel is sufficiently hot to boil the brine in the second; the vapour from the second supplying the heat to operate the third vessel or effect. The brine is usually sent through the stages or effects in succession, although in the case of salt manufacture, fresh brine may be fed to each stage if desired. In a triple-effect system, vacuums of 15 in., 25 in. and 27 in. of mercury have been found efficient. With open pans, one ton of coal will produce about two to two and one-half tons of salt whereas it will yield five to six tons of salt with an efficient triple-effect plant.

After crystallization, with either closed or open equipment, the brine is separated from the salt by draining or by centrifugal separation. The moist salt is then dried by a current of hot air, usually in rotary driers; however, a "fluid bed" type of drier may be used.

During the 1960s the proportions of salt produced in the United States by various processes were approximately: open-pan evaporation 2%, vacuum evaporation 10%, solar evaporation 5%, rock salt 20%, used in brine 59%.

See also references under "Salt" in the Index.

BIBLIOGRAPHY.—W. C. Phalen, "Technology of Salt Making in the United States," U.S. Bureau of Mines Bulletin no. 146 (1917), and "Salt Resources of the United States," U.S. Geological Survey Bulletin no. 669 (1919); R. L. Sherlock, *Rock-Salt and Brine*, vol. xviii of the *Memoirs of the Geological Survey of the U.K.* (1921); D. K. Tressler *et al.*, *Marine Products of Commerce* (1923); U.S. Bureau of Mines, *Information Circular 7062* (1939); U.S. Bureau of Mines, *Minerals Yearbook* (1954); C. D. Looker, "Salt as a Chemical Raw Material," *Chem. Ind.*, vol. 49 (1941); U.S. Bureau of Standards, *Simplified Practice Recommendation R70–42* (1942); F. Kutnewsky, "Salt of the Earth," *Compr. Air (Mag.)*, vol. 47 (1942); W. T. Read, *Industrial Chemistry*, 3rd ed. (1944); E. R. Riegel, *Industrial Chemistry*, 5th ed. (1949); "Manufacture of Sodium Chloride," *Industr. Engng. Chem.*, vol. 49, no. 11, p. 59A (Nov. 1957). (R. H. Rn.)

SALTA, a city of Argentina and capital of Salta Province, lies in the picturesque and historic Andean valley of Lerma, 1,007 mi. (1,621 km.) NNW of Buenos Aires by rail. Population (1960) 121,491. The city was founded in 1582 as San Felipe de Lerma by Hernando de Lerma, governor of Tucumán. In 1813, during the War of Independence, the Spanish royalist forces, following their decisive defeat at Salta, capitulated to Gen. Manuel Belgrano.

TABLE IV.—*Typical Compositions of Salts from Evaporation Pans*

Item	Grade I	Grade II	Grade III
	%	%	%
Sodium chloride	96.0	95.0	91.0
Calcium sulfate	1.0	0.9	0.4
Magnesium sulfate . . .	0.2	0.5	1.0
Magnesium chloride. . . .	0.2	0.5	1.2
Insoluble matter . . .	..	trace	0.2
Water (moisture)	2.6	3.1	6.2
	100.0	100.0	100.0

Situated 3,895 ft. (1,187 m.) above sea level, the city is an important industrial and trading centre. Its commercial prominence dates from colonial times when it was the scene of the largest pastoral fairs of northwest Argentina.

Despite earthquakes the city has preserved many of its colonial buildings, including the cathedral, and colonial styles are imitated in many modern buildings. It is a tourist centre with thermal springs nearby. At an annual fiesta in September a revered 16th-century image of Christ is honoured in commemoration of the city's deliverance from a severe earthquake in 1692.

SALTA PROVINCE in northwestern Argentina has, since the breakup of the territory of Los Andes in 1943, included the departments of San Antonio de los Cobres and Pastos Grandes. Pop. (1960) 408,987. Area 59,759 sq.mi. (154,776 sq.km.). Bounded on the west by Chile, the Andean half of the province, with its high *sierras* and *valles,* forms part of the Puna de Atacama, the highest region of Argentina, some mountains exceeding 19,000 ft. (5,790 m.). It is a bleak, arid, and cold plateau with desert-like inland drainage basins (*salares*). The eastern half, bounded on the north by Bolivia and Paraguay, is the highest part of the Gran Chaco plain. Drained to the southeast by several rivers, of which the Bermejo is the chief, this part of Salta has forested valleys which deteriorate in the drier west into scrub-covered mountain slopes. The western *puna,* or high plateau, is the home of Coya Indian tribes, but the eastern valleys contain many settlements peopled by mestizo Argentines.

The railway links the province with Bolivia via Yacuiba and Villazón, and since 1948 with the Chilean port of Antofagasta. There are rail and road connections with all parts of Argentina. The province has been important since colonial times for its pastoral activities, especially the raising of mules and cattle for north Chilean markets. Its trade throughout the colonial period was predominantly with Bolivia and Chile, and it had little intercourse with Buenos Aires. Lumbering, sheep raising, and the growing of sugarcane, tobacco, grapes, and maize (corn) are other occupations; the mining of soda and borax from the *salares* is also important. The upper Bermejo valley contains an important oil field, the chief centres being Orán and Tartagal, with a refinery at Embarcación. Lead, silver, iron, and copper are mined. Most of the factories in the province are concerned with processing agricultural products; predominant among them are sugar and vegetable oil refineries, tobacco curing works, flour mills, tanneries, and plants for meat packing and wine making. (G. J. B.)

SALTASH, a municipal borough in the Bodmin parliamentary division of Cornwall, Eng., 4 mi. W.N.W. of Plymouth by road and ferry. Pop. (1961) 7,425. Area 8.3 sq.mi. It is on the wooded west shore of the Tamar estuary, on the opposite side of which lies Plymouth. Communications are maintained by two floating ferry bridges. At Saltash the Royal Albert bridge (1848-59), built by I. K. Brunel, carries the railway across the estuary. The church of St. Nicholas and St. Faith has an early Norman tower and that of St. Stephen retains its ornate Norman font. Saltash (*Aysh,* 1284; *Saltesh,* 1337), the oldest borough in Cornwall, belonged to the manor of Trematon, and at the Domesday survey was held by Reginald de Valletort. A charter was granted sometime at the end of the 12th century. Roger de Valletort gave the borough to the earl of Cornwall, and thenceforth the earls and, subsequently, the dukes of Cornwall were lords of Saltash. The privilege of parliamentary representation was conferred by Edward VI.

In 1584 Elizabeth I granted the town a charter of incorporation which was superseded by another in 1683, and the modern charter was adopted in 1886. In 1832 Saltash was deprived of its two members of parliament. Saltash is in part a fishing town. One mi. S.W. is Trematon castle, associated with the Black Prince.

SALT DOME. Geologic structures in which salt is a controlling factor may be steep folds in which salt flowage modifies the geologic deformation or structures in which the flow and uplift of the salt itself is the primary geologic movement. It is this latter type of geologic phenomenon which is commonly meant by salt dome. Such structures commonly are roughly circular in plan although some may be greatly elongated. Usually the vertical

dimensions are of the same order or greater than the horizontal dimensions. A typical dome may consist of a more or less cylindrical vertical salt column about two miles across and with a vertical dimension of three to six miles. However, the size of individual domes in the same area may vary greatly.

Salt domes always occur in areas underlain by thick layers of salt, or halite, which is primarily sodium chloride (NaCl). Domes are not found in all areas of thick salt deposits but only where such deposits have been buried to great depth by subsequent deposition. It appears that a minimum overburden of the order of 10,000 ft. is required for salt domes to form and domes are known where the depth to the salt is estimated to be as great as 30,000 to 40,000 ft.

Origin and Mode of Formation.—There has been considerable controversy and speculation in geological literature on the mechanics of the formation of domes. European geologists, from studies of the German and Rumanian salt structures, recognized that the domes were formed from bedded salt which had flowed under pressure. In some areas the salt flowage resulted from recognized tectonic forces. In other cases, however, such as in the Gulf coast of the United States, there is no recognized tectonic pattern. The intrusive uplift of the domes now is generally attributed to buoyancy resulting from the fact that the density of the salt is less than that of the surrounding sedimentary rocks. The existence of a density difference is shown by the negative gravity anomalies of practically all of the simple, round intrusive salt domes of the Gulf coast and many other areas, as determined by geophysical prospecting (*q.v.*) methods.

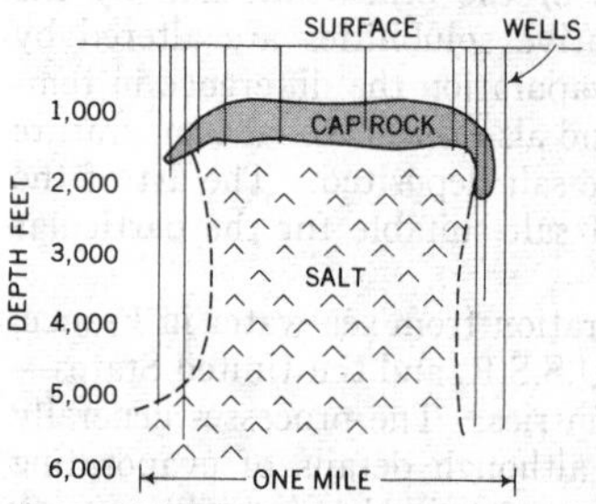

This theory, which appears to account for many of the major features of salt domes, may be likened to the flow of fluids. One can compare the layer of low density salt under heavier sediments with a low density fluid under a heavier one, and models based on this principle produce forms which are rather strikingly similar to the forms which salt domes have in nature. Figure 1 shows a cross section of a salt dome and fig. 2 a fluid model consisting of a layer of asphalt with a density of 1.0 beneath heavy sirup with a density of 1.4. After the flow is localized by an initial disturbance, the asphalt rises up through the sirup because of its lower density and takes a form very similar to that which many of the Gulf coast domes are known to have from drilling and from analysis of geophysical surveys. Moreover, the ratios between the mechanical properties of the model and those of its prototype in nature are such that the dimensional relations are approximately correct for dynamic similitude. Thus, it appears quite clear that a major factor in the uplift of intrusive salt domes is simple isostatic flowage of the salt because it is of lower density than the sediments.

Cap Rock.—Many of the salt domes, especially in the Gulf coast of the United States and in Germany, have a so-called cap rock. In the Gulf coast, this usually consists of an upper layer of limestone (calcium carbonate) and a lower layer of anhydrite (an-

FIG. 1.—CROSS SECTION OF A GULF COAST SALT DOME, ALLEN DOME, BRAZORIA COUNTY, TEX.

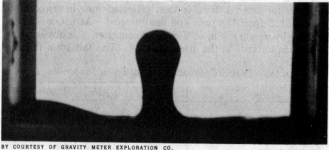

FIG. 2.—FLUID MODEL TO SIMULATE SALT DOME FORMATION. BLACK PART IS LOWER DENSITY ASPHALT FLOWING UPWARD IN HIGHER DENSITY SIRUP. ONE-FOURTH NATURAL SIZE

hydrous calcium sulfate). In some shallow domes, the limestone may be missing and part or all of the anhydrite changed to gypsum (hydrous calcium sulfate), apparently by contact with surface waters. When present, the cap rock usually covers the top of the dome completely and may extend down the flanks forming a cap or thimble over the salt. It may vary in thickness from a few feet to over 1,000 ft.

The mechanism and chemistry of the formation of cap rock is not clearly understood. It has been suggested that the cap rock is a disk of overlying evaporite deposit which was punched out and pushed up by the intrusive salt, but this theory has been largely discarded.

The more generally accepted theory is that the cap rock is formed from minerals originally disseminated through the salt which become concentrated as the salt is dissolved away by circulating waters near the surface.

Distribution of Domes.—The simple piercement salt domes resulting from isostatic flowage so that the salt plug has pierced overlying strata, are best known in the southeastern United States because of the intensive drilling around them on account of their economic importance. The Gulf coast belt of domes extends 50 to 100 mi. northward from the coast and reaches from the Mississippi river westward across Louisiana and Texas to midway between Houston and Corpus Christi. The same belt extends offshore for many miles, as shown by geophysical surveys and drilling in the waters of the continental shelf. There are now some 150 proven domes in this belt. A separate small group of five domes lies between Corpus Christi and Laredo, in southern Texas. The "interior" domes include about 20 in the Tyler basin of northeast Texas and about 70 in a belt extending southeastward from Shreveport, La., across northern Louisiana and southern Mississippi to southwestern Alabama.

In addition to these domes proved by drilling into salt, there are a great many probable and deeper domes indicated by geophysical work.

Outside of the southeastern states, the only salt structures known in North America are in the Paradox basin of western Colorado and eastern Utah, but these structures are long folds controlled by tectonic movement and not simple piercement domes. Salt occurrences, possibly in domes, are found in Nova Scotia.

Domes controlled primarily from flowage of salt, but in some cases with modification by tectonic forces, occur in northern Germany, Denmark, Poland, Rumania, northern Spain, the Isthmus of Tehuantepec in Mexico, in small areas in Colombia, Peru, and Argentina, in southern Iran along the northeasterly shore of the Persian gulf and in the Persian gulf itself, in western U.S.S.R. with the largest area being north of the Caspian sea, and on the west coast of equatorial Africa.

Economic Importance.—Salt domes are of great economic importance because of oil, sulfur, and the salt itself.

In areas where the salt domes have intruded or uplifted petroleum-bearing sedimentary rocks, the deformation which localizes oil accumulation is commonly over or around a dome (*see* PETROLEUM).

A very large fraction of the oil production of the Gulf coast of Texas and Louisiana is taken from salt dome structures. Since the discovery of the first salt dome oil field in the Gulf coast in 1901 some 350 proved or probable salt domes have been located (a large number by geophysical surveys) and many have oil fields over them or around their flanks.

The most productive salt dome area is the Texas-Louisiana coastal belt, where oil production averages about 300,000,000 barrels per year. Oil is also found in salt dome structures in Germany, Rumania, the U.S.S.R. and in West Africa.

A relatively small number of the shallow domes with thick cap rock are very prolific sources of sulfur, which occurs in the porous limestone in the upper part of the cap rock. It is mined by the Frasch process in which the sulfur is melted by superheated water and pumped, by compressed air, as a liquid. Approximately one-fourth of the domes in Texas, Louisiana, and Mississippi are shallow and have thick cap rock but of these only relatively few, in the coastal belt, have sulfur in sufficient quantity and purity to be

mined economically. Sulfur is also mined from a small number of domes in the Isthmus of Tehuantepec in Mexico.

In a small number of domes, the salt itself is mined, either by shafts into the dome and normal mining operations or by solution of the salt by circulating water. *See also* SALT.

BIBLIOGRAPHY.—American Association of Petroleum Geologists, *Geology of Salt Dome Oil Fields* (1926); D. C. Barton and G. Sawtelle, *Gulf Coast Oil Fields* (1936); Society of Exploration Geophysicists, *Geophysical Case Histories*, vol. i (1948), vol. ii (1956).   (L. L. N.)

SALTILLO, capital city of the Mexican state of Coahuila, 668 mi. (1,075 km.) N of Mexico City. Pop. (1960) 98,839. Altitude 5,244 ft. Served by the National Railways of Mexico, Saltillo is also linked by highway to Eagle Pass, Tex. (280 mi.), as well as to Torreón (180 mi.) and Monterrey (55 mi.).

Saltillo lies at the northern edge of the great central plateau of Mexico. Its cool, dry, healthful climate has made it a summer resort with facilities for golfing, hunting, and swimming. Founded in 1575, Saltillo retains but few of its colonial buildings, the main exception being an impressive cathedral. The city is chiefly significant as an active commercial and communications centre, and for the manufacture of woolen fabrics, knitted goods, and flour. Its blankets, or serapes, have for centuries been considered among Mexico's finest, and many are collector's items. Gold, silver, lead, zinc, copper, iron, and coal are mined in the vicinity. During the U.S.-Mexican War Saltillo was captured by U.S. forces under Maj. Gen. Zachary Taylor on Nov. 17, 1846. Nearby is the site of the Battle of Buena Vista (Feb. 22–23, 1847), a decisive victory by Taylor over the Mexican forces under Gen. Antonio de Santa Anna.   (R. B. McCk.)

SALT LAKE CITY, the capital of Utah, U.S., and seat of Salt Lake county, is the largest city between Denver and the Pacific coast. World capital of the Latter-day Saints (Mormons), it is also the seat of Roman Catholic and Episcopal dioceses and a regional metropolis influencing the economic, social, cultural, educational and political life of people in an area of about 185,000 sq.mi., embracing not only Utah but southern Idaho, eastern Nevada and southwestern Wyoming.

Salt Lake valley, in which the city is situated, is the southernmost of the numerous valleys which together compose the valley of the Great Salt Lake and is almost central in the longer chain of fertile irrigable valleys lying at the west base of the Wasatch mountains. Salt Lake City lies at an approximate elevation of 4,200 ft. under magnificent peaks that rise in places more than 7,000 ft. above the valley floor; its wide, generally rectangular, tree-lined streets are laid out on a series of terraces lifting gently east and north from the Jordan river. This river, which connects Utah lake with the Great Salt lake (*q.v.*), flows nearly north through the valley, bordered on the west by poorly drained, alkaline and generally infertile plains. The principal incorporated area of Salt Lake City occupies the northern part of Salt Lake valley, east of the Jordan; in the central and southern reaches are various suburban communities, including South Salt Lake, Murray, Midvale, Sandy City and Draper.

On its founding, the centre of Salt Lake City was placed close under the northern benchlands, so the city developed asymmetrically to the east, south and southeast. Major expansion westward came only during and after World War II. That same period made the whole of Salt Lake valley a residential appendage of the city, as also Davis county to the north; this growth was directly related to the development of an adequate metropolitan water supply in the late 1930s and early 1940s. The metropolitan area of Salt Lake City reaches toward that of Ogden (*q.v.*), 35 mi. N., with which it has a twin-city relationship, but because of historical priority, general economic dominance and Salt Lake City's status as a federal and state government centre, the influence of the capital city is overriding.

History.—Salt Lake City (until 1868 Great Salt Lake City) was founded in 1847 as the central city of Mormon settlement in the west, and its history since has been inextricable from that of the church (*see* LATTER-DAY SAINTS, CHURCH OF JESUS CHRIST OF) and of the state (*see* UTAH: *History*). A planned community from the outset, Salt Lake City was laid out by Brigham Young (*q.v.*) in accordance with a plat for the city of Zion drawn by Joseph Smith in 1833. Streets 8 rods wide were made to run with the cardinal directions and to cross at right angles, dividing the land into square blocks of 10 ac. each, originally divided into 1¼ ac. lots, with provision for public squares, of which one was set aside as the Temple block. Streets were numbered outward from the central Temple block, those on the south being named South Temple, 1st South, 2nd South, etc., those on the west, West Temple, 1st West, and so on. However, East Temple eventually was renamed Main street, and 1st East became State street. Later, as the city grew, "courts" and "places" were cut into many of the large central blocks, and new subdivisions were cut up into smaller areas, especially on the steep North Bench and south of 9th South street. The old rectangular street pattern continued dominant until World War II, and curving streets are found chiefly in modern subdivisions, west of the Jordan or high on the eastern benchlands.

Those who wintered in Salt Lake valley in 1847–48, numbering about 1,700, lived in a log and adobe fort centring upon the present Pioneer park. Permanent allocation of the land began when Young made his final return from the Missouri river in Sept. 1848, and most of the settlers began building on their lots the following spring. At that time the city was divided into 19 ecclesiastical wards of nine square blocks each, the bishop of each ward acting as magistrate.

Previously, reflecting the theocratic character of Mormon society, the city had been ruled by a high council, administering an ecclesiastical jurisdiction called a stake of Zion, coextensive with the city. It was the high council that enacted the first municipal ordinances, ratified in public meeting Jan. 1, 1848. Out of this original localized theocratic government evolved the broader State of Deseret, organized by the Mormons in 1849 to embrace a vast area between the Sierra Nevada and the Rocky mountains. By that time, the treaty of Guadalupe Hidalgo having been ratified, the site of Salt Lake City with the rest of Utah had passed from Mexican to U.S. sovereignty. The provisional State of Deseret was not recognized by congress, which instead created the Territory of Utah in Sept. 1850, but before its dissolution, the Deseret legislature in Jan. 1851, incorporated Great Salt Lake City. The city charter almost exactly duplicated that once granted the Mormon city of Nauvoo by the Illinois legislature, which made the city virtually an autonomous political unit, empowered to pass any law not in conflict with the state or federal constitutions and to maintain its own militia and city court. Until its repeal the Nauvoo charter was a storm centre of Illinois politics; in a different environment, the Salt Lake City charter occasioned no trouble.

Organized Mormon immigration, gathering the faithful initially from the midwest and later from the eastern states and Europe, quickly made Salt Lake City famous as "the New Jerusalem," "the City of the Saints." The unexpected discovery of gold in California in 1848 contributed greatly to its early growth, as a flood of gold seekers en route to California poured in upon the city in 1849, trading clothing, tools and manufactured goods for fresh livestock and crops. Overland migration continued as a stimulus through the 1850s, not without friction between Mormon settlers and non-Mormon travelers. The city continued as a staging point for arriving Mormon converts, who were sent from Salt Lake to open or strengthen new communities down the entire length of Utah. This planned system of colonization thus tended to drain off population that might otherwise have stimulated the early growth of the church headquarters city, but at the same time gave it deep roots in the entire mountain-desert west. Public works projects, instituted by the church in the early 1850s to furnish employment for the needy, contributed to the building up of the city, including a wall erected around the Temple block and a never-completed wall around the city itself, supposedly to protect it from the Indians but chiefly useful as an object-lesson to smaller and more exposed Mormon towns.

In 1858, during the so-called Utah war of 1857–58, when anti-Mormon agitation led to the federal government's declaring "a state of substantial rebellion" in Utah, Gen. Albert Sidney Johnston's army marched through the city en route to establish a military post, Camp Floyd, west of Utah lake. There followed a considerable influx of non-Mormons, giving Salt Lake City a rowdier character but also renewing economic vitality. These federal troops were withdrawn from Utah after the American Civil War broke out, but were replaced in 1862 by a regiment of California-Nevada volunteers commanded by Patrick Edward Connor, who established Camp (later Fort) Douglas on the benchland above the city, the better to keep the doubtfully regarded Mormons under military scrutiny. Prospecting by these soldiers soon opened up Utah's mining economy and gave non-Mormon merchants a better foothold in Salt Lake City, but their position continued precarious until the completion in 1869 of the Union Pacific railroad (which by-passed the city itself) put the mining industry on a sound basis.

The Mormon-built Utah Central railroad, completed Jan. 1, 1870, connected Salt Lake City with the Union Pacific at Ogden, and during the next decade other roads were built from Salt Lake City in all directions to now-booming mining regions. Violent political strife came for the first time with this new order of things, the non-Mormon Liberal party contending with the Mormon People's party for local supremacy, while the federal government intervened massively with legislation, ostensibly directed against the Mormon practice of polygamy but basically designed to force a separation of church and state. In 1890 the Mormon church surrendered on the polygamy issue, and though intermittent conflicts between Mormon and non-Mormon elements continued as late as 1905–07, when the American party captured the city government, the old social antagonisms gradually disappeared. Since World War I the history of the city has been primarily economic and cultural, as in the case of most other large U.S. cities.

Except between 1851 and 1856, when Fillmore was the legal capital, Salt Lake City since its founding has been capital of Utah in name as well as fact. The graceful capitol building at the head of State street overlooking the city was erected in 1912–15. Other familiar landmarks include Temple square, with the many-spired gray granite temple and the turtle-domed tabernacle; and on the adjacent block to the east, two of Brigham Young's residences, the Beehive house and the gabled Lion house. On what was once Emigration square the City and County building with its lofty sandstone clock tower was built in 1897. High office buildings and hotels along Main street were principally completed between 1909 and 1924. Along the East Bench sprawls the broad campus of the University of Utah, and above it old Ft. Douglas, established in 1862. Farther south, near the mouth of Emigration canyon, is a state park centred upon the This is the Place Monument, which commemorates the Mormon entrance into Utah in 1847.

Population.—By the 1960 census Salt Lake City's population was 189,454. The population of the standard metropolitan statistical area (Salt Lake and Davis counties) in 1960 was 447,795, an increase of 62.9% over 1950. The nonwhite percentage was less than 2% of the total and consisted principally of Japanese, Negroes, Chinese and Filipinos. Many of the early settlers came from Europe, particularly England and the Scandinavian countries, as the result of Mormon missionary work. After the Civil War the number of non-Mormons in the city steadily increased and by 1960 comprised an estimated 40% of the population. (For comparative population figures *see* table in UTAH: *Population*.)

Government.—Salt Lake City is governed by a mayor and board of five commissioners, elected in nonpartisan elections. Revenue comes mostly from taxation of real property but also from franchise and other taxes, from fees and licences, and from the municipally owned waterworks and airport.

Commerce, Industry and Transportation.—Principal industries include food processing, printing and publishing, oil refining, coking, copper refining, smelting of silver, lead and copper, manufacture of iron, steel and clay products and of radio equipment, electronics and textiles. The copper mines at Bingham and a Geneva steel plant in Utah valley have greatly contributed to the growth of metal fabricating industries since the early 1900s. The city serves a major wholesaling function in its region, aided by transportation facilities which include service by several railroads, highways and airlines. The city is the seat of a branch of the Federal Reserve Bank of San Francisco.

Education and Cultural Activities.—Public education is administered by a board made up of two members elected from each of the six municipal wards and by a superintendent appointed for a minimum term of two years. Institutions of higher learning in the city include the University of Utah (*see* UTAH: *Education*) and Westminster college (interdenominational, established in 1875). Hospitals are operated by religious denominations and a fraternal organization as well as by Salt Lake county and the Veterans administration. The Utah Symphony orchestra, Salt Lake opera, Tabernacle choir and organ recitals and University of Utah music festival are among the best known of the state's musical activities. Art collections are displayed in the state capitol, the State Historical society mansion, the University museum and the Art Barn. Besides many specialized museums at the university and displays at the capitol, pioneer collections are shown in museums of the Mormon church at Temple square and the Daughters of Utah Pioneers, and in the Pioneer Village of the Sons of Utah Pioneers. Principal libraries are those at the university, Salt Lake City Free Public library, Utah State library, and Utah State Historical society, as well as the private Historian's Office of the Mormon church.

Parks and Recreation.—The 80-ac. landscaped Liberty park, once the Brigham Young farm, is the principal municipal park. Memory grove, below the capitol, is a war memorial. Other parks and playgrounds are scattered about the city, and some are maintained in nearby canyons, a contrast to beach resorts and a yacht harbour on Great Salt lake, west of the city. Golf courses, a zoo, tennis courts and other recreational facilities are easily accessible. (D. L. M.)

SALTO, a rich department in northwest Uruguay, on the Uruguay River. Area 4,866 sq.mi. Pop. (1962 est.) 128,444. The rolling rocky soil is well suited for pasture and there are considerable numbers of both cattle and sheep on the ranches of Salto. Orange and tangerine production is also important; citrus groves stretch for about 20 mi. around the departmental capital, Salto (*q.v.*). The department's vineyards are considered the best in Uruguay. Salto also grows corn, cereals, sunflower seeds, flax, forage crops, tomatoes, and strawberries. (M. I. V.)

SALTO, capital of the department of Salto in Uruguay, a river port on the Uruguay River, rivals Paysandú, farther south, for position as Uruguay's second city. Pop. (1962 est.) 55,313. North of Salto the Uruguay River is too shallow even for river boats so the port supplies northwest Uruguay and parts of the Brazilian state of Rio Grande do Sul. Salto has air and road connections with Montevideo and other points. Wine production and orange-drink bottling, both from locally grown fruits, are outstanding among Salto's industries. Pueblo Nuevo, a new suburb north of the city, has important shipyards. Salto probably was founded as a depot where hides could be assembled for shipment downriver, either in 1756 or 1817. (M. I. V.)

SALTPETRE: see NITRIC ACID AND NITRATES.

SALT RANGE, a hill system in West Pakistan, derives its name from extensive deposits of rock salt, one of the richest salt fields in the world. The main chain begins in the Jhelum district, in Chel (Chail) hill (3,701 ft. [1,128 m.]) on the right bank of the Jhelum River. The range runs westward in two parallel ridges till it culminates in the Sakesar hills (4,992 ft. [1,522 m.]). Its average height is 2,200 ft. above sea level. Between the two lines of hills lies an elevated, fertile plateau, intersected by ravines and peaks with several passes, and containing the beautiful salt lake Kallar Kahar. From Sakesar the range swings in a north-northwest direction to Mari Indus, where it is broken through by the Indus River; then swinging south, from Kalabagh on the west of the Indus, continues into the Khattak-Maidani hills. The range contains the great salt mines of Khewra, Warcha, and Kalabagh in the Cis-Indus, the main manufacturing areas, and the good-quality but smaller mines of Jatta, Bahadur Khel, and Kharak in the Trans-Indus section. Coal is also found at Dandot, Pidh (Pidth), and Makarwal Kheji (Makerwal). High-quality gypsum occurs from Jalalpur to Kalabagh, mixed with varying quantities of anhydrite, particularly in the Khewra-Dandot and Daud Khel areas.

The range displays one of the most complete geological columns in the world, from Cambrian to Pleistocene, with the only major gap occurring in the Middle and Upper Paleozoic. Much unresolved controversy has arisen about the age of the saline series of the Cis-Indus section of the range. Supporters of the Tertiary view base their conclusion chiefly on the normal position of the series in the Trans-Indus section of the range and consider its abnormal position in the Cis-Indus section to be due to an overthrust. Another school of thought holds that Cambrian or Precambrian is the correct age, because of the consistent conformable position of the saline series for 152 mi. (245 km.) of the Cis-Indus. (K. S. AD.)

SALTYKOV, MIKHAIL EVGRAFOVICH (pseudonym, N. SHCHEDRIN) (1826–1889), Russian satirist and novelist of radical sympathies, best remembered for his novel, *Gospoda Golovlëvy*, which traces the falling fortunes of a family of landed gentry, was born on Jan. 27 (new style; old style, 15), 1826, in the village of Spas-Ugol in the province of Tver. A sensitive boy, he was deeply shocked by his mother's cruel treatment of the peasants, which he later described in one of his most important works *Poshekhonskaya starina* ("Old Times in Poshekhona," 1887–89). In 1836 he entered the Moscow Noblemen's Institute and in 1838 he was sent to the famous Imperial *lycée* at Tsarskoye Selo, Russia's training-ground for high officers of state. Reacting violently against its bureaucratic regime, he soon joined the revolutionary circles in St. Petersburg, and met the great critic Vissarion Belinski (*q.v.*). In 1847 he began his literary career as a reviewer in the radical periodicals *Sovremennik* and *Otechestvennye zapiski*. In 1848 he wrote the story *Zaputannoe delo* ("A Complicated Affair"), which expressed sympathy for the then popular French utopian socialists, and as a result, was exiled to Vyatka, where he spent eight years in a minor position in the provincial governor's office. In 1855 he returned to St. Petersburg, and, a year later, published his first successful book, *Gubernskie ocherki* (1856–57; selections in English translation, *Tchinovnicks. Sketches from Provincial Life*, 1861), in which he satirized different types of Vyatka officials. In 1857 he wrote his only comedy, *Smert Pazukhina* (performed 1893; Eng. trans. *The Death of Pazukhin*, 1924), dealing with malpractices common among Russian merchants, and between 1857 and 1863, he wrote two series of stories, *Nevinnye rasskazy* ("Innocent Stories") and *Satiry v proze* ("Satires in Prose"), both published as collections in 1863. In 1858 he was appointed vice-governor of the province of Ryazan, and in 1860 vice-governor of Tver.

After his return to St. Petersburg (1864) he was appointed president of the local taxation boards at Penza, Tula, and Ryazan successively. He retired from the civil service in 1868, and thereafter devoted himself to literature. He joined the radical poet Nikolai Nekrasov (*q.v.*) as co-editor of *Otechestvennye zapiski*, becoming editor after Nekrasov's death (1878). His major works include *Istoriya odnogo goroda* ("The History of a Town"), written in 1869–70, and *Pompadury i pompadurshi* ("The Pompadours and Their Ladies"), written between 1863 and 1874, two biting satires on the highest Russian officials; and his famous novel *Gospoda Golovlëvy* (1876; Eng. trans. *The Golovlyov Family*, 1955). Saltykov died in St. Petersburg on May 10 (N.S.; O.S., April 28), 1889. (D. MK.)

SALUS, an ancient Roman goddess of safety and welfare, later identified with the Greek Hygieia (*q.v.*) who was exclusively a personification of health. Although essentially a deified abstraction, Salus was nevertheless worshiped quite early both at Rome and throughout Italy. Her temple on the Quirinal was dedicated in 302 B.C. and was the scene of an annual sacrifice on Aug. 5. Its walls were decorated with frescoes painted by C. Fabius, consul in 269 B.C. As a result he was called Pictor, "the Painter," a name which he handed down to his descendants—among them Fabius Pictor the annalist.

The *augurium salutis*, not involving a personification and possibly antedating the deification of Salus, was an annual performance; it was an inquiring to ascertain whether it was acceptable to the gods to hear prayers for the public *salus*. Since it had to be performed on a day of peace, the constant warfare of the late republic caused its interruption, but it was revived by Augustus. In the empire the goddess appears both as Salus Publica and Salus Augusti.

In 180 B.C. on the occasion of a severe pestilence a *supplicatio* was held in honour of Apollo, Aesculapius, and Salus, revealing that the identification with Hygieia was made this early and Salus was regarded as a deity of public health. Indeed, on coins she appears regularly as Hygieia, with patera and sacred snake, although at times with ears of grain, symbolic of general prosperity.

BIBLIOGRAPHY.—G. Wissowa, *Religion und Kultus,* 2nd ed., pp. 131 ff., 306 ff. (1912) ; A. S. Pease on Cicero, *De divinatione,* I, 105 (1920) ; Platner-Ashby, *Topographical Dictionary, s.v.* (R. B. LD.)

SALUTATIONS (GREETINGS), the customary forms of kindly or respectful address, especially on meeting or parting or on occasions of ceremonious approach. Etymologically salutation (Lat. *salutatio,* "wishing health") refers only to words spoken.

Embraces.—Forms of salutation frequent in preliterate societies may persist almost unchanged in civilized custom. The habit of affectionate clasping or embracing is seen at the meetings of the Andaman islanders and Australian aborigines, or where the Fuegians in friendly salute hug "like the grip of a bear." This natural gesture appears in old Semitic and Aryan custom.

Rubbing Noses.—The salute by smelling or sniffing (often called by travelers "rubbing noses") belongs to Polynesians, Malays, Burmese and other Indochinese, Mongols, and extending thence eastward to the Eskimo and westward to Lapland.

Kissing.—The kiss, the salute by tasting, appears constantly in Semitic and Aryan antiquity. Herodotus describes the Persians of his time as kissing one another—if equals on the mouth, if one was somewhat inferior on the cheek. In Greece, in the classic period, it became customary to kiss the hand, breast, or knee of a superior. In Rome the kisses of inferiors became a burdensome civility. The early Christians made it the sign of fellowship: "greet all the brethren with an holy kiss." Of more ceremonial form is the kiss of peace given to the newly baptized and in the celebration of the Eucharist, which is retained by the Greek Church. After a time, by ecclesiastical regulations, men were only allowed to kiss men, and women women, and eventually in the Roman Catholic Church the ceremonial kiss at the communion was only exchanged by the ministers, a relic or cross called an *osculatorium* or *pax* being carried to the people to be kissed. While the kiss has thus been adopted as a religious rite, its original social use has continued. Among men, however, it has become less effusive. Court ceremonial keeps up the kiss on the cheek between sovereigns and the kissing of the hand by subjects. When these osculations cease to be performed they are still talked to by way of politeness: Austrians say, *Küss d' Hand!* and Spaniards, *Beso a Vd. las manos!* ("I kiss your hand!"). Strokings, pattings, and other caresses have been turned to use as salutations.

Weeping.—Weeping for joy is sometimes affected as a salutation. Highly ceremonious weeping is performed by several primitive peoples when, meeting after absence, they renew the lamentations over friends who have died in the meantime. Among the Australian aborigines, the male nearest of kin presses his breast to the newcomer's, and the nearest female relative, with piteous lamentations, embraces his knees with one arm, while with the other she scratches her face till the blood drops. Obviously this is mourning. So, too, the New Zealand *tangi* is performed at the reception of a distinguished visitor, whether he has really dead friends to mourn or not. Weeping, as A. R. Radcliffe-Brown has shown, is for the Andamanese a rite for the revival of sentiments that have lain dormant, the renewal of interrupted social relations, and for the recognition of a change in personal relations.

Cowering.—Cowering or crouching is a natural gesture of fear or inability to resist. Its extreme form is lying prostrate, face to the ground. In barbaric society, as soon as distinctions are marked between master and slave, chief and commoner, these tokens of submission become salutations. The sculptures of Egypt and Assyria show the lowly prostrations of the ancient East,

while in Dahomey or Thailand subjects crawl before the king. A later stage is to suggest, but not actually perform, the prostration, as the Arab bends his hand to the ground and puts it to his lips or forehead, or the Tongan would touch the sole of a chief's foot, thus symbolically placing himself under his feet.

Kneeling.—Kneeling prevailed in the middle stages of culture, as in the ceremonial of China; Hebrew custom set it rather apart as an act of homage to a deity; medieval Europe distinguished between kneeling in worship on both knees and on one knee only in homage.

Bowing.—Bowing, as a salute of reverence, appeared in its extreme in Oriental custom, as among the ancient Israelites: "bowed himself to the ground seven times." The Chinese according to the degree of respect implied bowed kneeling or standing. The bowing salutation, varying in Europe from something less than the eastern salaam down to the slightest inclination of the head, is given mutually. Uncovering is a common mode of salutation, originally a sign of disarming or defenselessness or destitution in the presence of a superior. Taking off the hat by men has for ages been the accepted mode in the Western world. Some Eastern nations are apt to see disrespect in baring the head, but insist on the feet being uncovered. Europeans have been called on to conform to custom by taking off their shoes to enter the royal presence. In Burma it is respectful to squat in the presence of a superior; elsewhere the inferior should stand.

Handshaking.—Grasping hands appears in antiquity as a legal act symbolic of the parties joining in compact, peace, or friendship. In marriage, the hand grasp was part of the ancient Hindu ceremony, as was the *dextrarum junctio* (joining of right hands) in Rome, which passed on into the Christian rite and became a mere salutation. (*See also* SUPERSTITION: *Survivals.*)

Words of Greeting.—As to words of salutation, even among primitive peoples certain ordinary phrases have passed into formal greetings. Many formulas express difference of rank and consequent respect, as where the Suto (*q.v.*) salute their chiefs with *Tama sevata!* (*i.e.,* "Greeting, wild beast!"). Congo Negroes returning from a journey salute their wives with an affectionate *Okowe!* but they, meekly kneeling round him, may not repeat the word, but must say *Ka! ka!* Among civilized peoples salutations are apt to be expressions of peace and good will. There are numerous biblical examples; *e.g.,* "Peace be to you and peace be to your house" (I Sam. 25:6). Such formulas run on from age to age and may be traced on to the Muslim greeting *Salam 'alaikum!* ("The peace be on you"), to which the reply is *Wa-'alaikum assalam!* ("And on you be the peace [of God]!"). This greeting is a password among fellow believers, for it may not be used by or to an infidel. The Babylonian form, "O king, live for ever!" (Dan. 3:9), represents a series of phrases which continue still in the *Vivat rex!* ("Long live the king!"). The Greeks said, "Be joyful!" both at meeting and at parting. The Romans applied *Salve!* ("Be in health!") especially at meeting, and *Vale!* ("Be well!") at parting. In the modern civilized world, everywhere, the old inquiry after health appears, the "How do you do?" becoming so formal as often to be said on both sides, without either waiting for an answer. Hardly less wide in range is the set of phrases "Good day!" "Good night!" etc., varying according to the hour and translated into every European language. Among other European phrases, some correspond to the English "Welcome!" and "Good-bye" ("God be with you!") and French *Adieu!* ("To God!"). Such half meaningless forms of salutation serve the purpose of keeping up social relations.

See also ADDRESS, FORMS OF; SIGN LANGUAGE.

See H. Measures, *Styles of Address,* rev. ed. (1962). (E. B. T.; X.)

SALUTE, a friendly greeting or gesture of respect. Although the salute has existed in one form or another, both civilian and military, for many centuries, the modern connotation of the word is primarily military and naval. In this sense salutes are usually performed by prescribed movements of the hand, flag, rifle, sword or sabre, or by firing guns or playing music. Cheering and manning the yards of naval ships are forms of saluting that have become obsolete. It is not possible to determine the exact origin of the various forms of salute practised today, but they all have in common the symbolism of showing defenselessness or obeisance in the presence of a superior or friend. It is assumed that the hand salute, for example, originated in prehistoric times as a means of showing one's weapon hand raised and empty. Uncovering one's head—removing or simply tipping the hat—later became a universal form of salute or obeisance. During the age of chivalry an armoured knight removed his helmet or raised the visor to reveal his identity and also to indicate defenselessness in the presence of superiors or friends. Bowing and kneeling had the same connotation.

When the wearing of uniforms became common in military forces around the mid-17th century, soldiers saluted, as did civilians of the period, by removing the hat. It was soon noted, however, that this practice soiled the hat and shortened its life. A regimental order of the Coldstream Guards in 1745 recorded: "The men ordered not to pull off their hats when they pass an officer. . . . but only to clap up their hands to their hats, and bow as they pass by." But this custom was not generally adopted by other units until the advent of more cumbersome headgear such as the busby and bearskin made doffing the hat impracticable. At one time it was proper to salute with either the left or right hand, the rule being that one used the hand opposite the person being saluted.

Raising the right hand to the cap visor is now a universal military and naval salute. The junior initiates a hand salute when approaching or leaving a superior, when addressing or being addressed by a superior except when in ranks and on other prescribed occasions. The salute is a gesture of mutual recognition and respect among fighting men and the superior normally returns it or at least acknowledges it.

In the U.S. army, navy and air force the hand salute is executed with the palm down. The British navy salutes the same way, but the British army and Royal Air Force salute with the palm turned forward. In several other European countries there are slightly different variations of the hand salute within the armed forces.

The rifle salute has various forms. When troops are in formation it consists of the movement in unison of "present arms." At this command, soldiers move their weapons to a vertical position with triggers forward. This ceremony has been traced to the restoration of Charles II in 1660. Monck's regiment (now the Coldstream Guards), wishing to come over to the king's service, was formed for his inspection in a field. On the king's approach they were given the command "Present your weapons for service under His Majesty." On this order each man held his musket or pike forward. With an eye for the dramatic, Charles prescribed that this ceremony be standardized for the entire army. When not in formation a soldier renders the rifle salute by touching his weapon in a variation of the normal hand salute.

The sword or sabre salute is executed by raising the hilt opposite the chin and then lowering the point of the weapon to one side. The first motion is believed to go back to the crusaders' custom of kissing the cross (symbolized by the hilt) before battle; the second motion symbolizes lowering one's guard. Some old military prints show the sword salute being rendered with one hand and the hand salute with the other.

Gun or cannon salutes, now used to honour distinguished persons or to mark special occasions, originate from the practice of firing all guns of a battery, fort or ship as a token of disarming them, for early guns could not be speedily reloaded. Modern gun salutes are fired with blank cartridges or charges. The number of shots is prescribed by international custom and agreement, and is determined by the rank of the person being honoured. A 21-gun salute, for example, is fired for chiefs of state, heads of government, members of a reigning royal family and others of comparable rank; it is commonly referred to as a royal salute. Nineteen guns are fired for ambassadors, cabinet members, state governors (in the U.S.) and officers above the rank of admiral or general; salutes of 17, 15, 13, 11, 7 and 5 guns are fired for persons of lesser ranks. In some cases it is prescribed that guns be fired on the person's departure as well as on arrival. The convention of firing an odd number of shots is believed to stem from an ancient

naval superstition that an even number of shots is unlucky.

In the United States the national salute of 21 guns is fired on Feb. 22 (Washington's birthday) and May 30 (Memorial day); the salute to the union, fired July 4 (Independence day), is one gun for each state.

(For saluting the flag of the United States, *see* FLAG: *Flags of the United States*.)

Musical honours consist of a prescribed number of drum ruffles and bugle or trumpet flourishes followed by a march or by the national anthem of the person honoured. They are rendered in conjunction with gun salutes to an individual.

Saluting with the colours (flags carried by troops) consists of dipping them to the ground. Although it is a fundamental rule that the U.S. national flag is never dipped, an exception is made in the interest of international courtesy: U.S. vessels dip the national ensign in return for such a compliment from a passing ship of a country formally recognized by the U.S. In this case, dipping consists of lowering the flag a short distance and then running it back to the top of the mast. The U.S. navy dips the national ensign only in return for such a compliment, and answers dip for dip. The origin of the flag salute has been traced by some authorities to the naval custom of lowering sails as a token of respect.

BIBLIOGRAPHY.—Mark M. Boatner III, *Military Customs and Traditions* (1956); U.S. Department of Defense, *The Armed Forces Officer* (1950); Leland P. Lovette, *Naval Customs, Traditions and Usage*, 4th ed. (1959). (M. M. Bo.)

SALUZZO, a town and episcopal see of Piedmont, Italy, in the province of Cuneo, 1,145 ft. (350 m.) above sea level and 37 mi. (60 km.) SSW of Turin by rail. Pop. (1961) 17,099 (commune). In the old, upper town is the 13th-century castle of the marquesses of Saluzzo, whose line ran from 1142 to 1548. Other noteworthy buildings are the 15th-century Casa Cavassa Museum, a richly furnished Renaissance mansion; the late Gothic cathedral (1480–1511); and the Church of S. Giovanni (13th–15th centuries). Saluzzo of the early 14th century is the background of Chaucer's *The Clerk's Tale*. The printer and typographer G. Bodoni (1740–1813), examples of whose work are in the public library, and the dramatist Silvio Pellico (1788–1854) were born there. There are rail connections with Cuneo, Savigliano (Turin–Cuneo), and Airasca (Turin–Pinerolo). Saluzzo is a centre for the restoration of antique furniture. From 1548 until 1601 it was under French domination. (M. Bs.)

SALVADOR, known as SÃO SALVADOR and BAHIA, one of the oldest cities and the first capital of Brazil, now the major port and capital of the state of Bahia. Pop. (1960) 630,878. Salvador is located at the southern tip of a picturesque and bluff-formed peninsula that separates All Saints bay (Bahia de Todos os Santos), a deep natural harbour 28 mi. wide and 22 mi. long, from the Atlantic. The mean temperature is 78° F. and the annual rainfall is 52 in. The terrain on which the city is built is sharply broken by a series of short, narrow valleys and steep hills that range in elevation from slightly above sea level to about 250 ft. Residences and public buildings mostly are situated on the slopes (*ladeiras*) and ridges. The valleys and open places in the city are characterized by lush tropical vegetation.

A distinctive feature of Salvador is its division into two separate sections, the lower city (*cidade baixa*) and the upper city (*cidade alta*). The port, commercial district and adjoining residential zones are located at the foot of a cliff on a low shelf of land facing west onto the bay only a few feet above the water level. The principal shopping districts, state and municipal government offices and the leading residential areas are on the upper level. This section extends northward for several miles and eastward to the Atlantic shore. The two sections of the city are connected by a few graded, winding roads, a funicular railway and several elevators. Of these, the Lacerda elevator, the outstanding landmark of Salvador, is the chief link joining the separate streetcar systems that operate on the upper and lower levels of the city.

Salvador was a major centre of the African slave trade in the colonial period and still has one of the largest concentrations of

Negro and mulatto population in Brazil. These two racial groups, which constitute the great bulk of the inhabitants of the city, have contributed many of the folkways, costumes and distinctive foods for which Salvador is noted. After 1940 the city experienced continuous and rapid population growth, increasing at the rate of about 40% per decade. During this growth the racial composition of the population remained fairly constant.

Significant economic expansion accompanied the population growth. It was reflected in extensive public works and private construction—notably in the form of new residential suburbs in the upper city and improvements in port facilities and the erection of numerous modern office buildings in the lower city. The port of Salvador is one of the finest and more important of Brazil. It is protected by two long breakwaters and is dredged to permit ocean-going vessels to tie up at the docks. There are many large warehouses, and mechanical energy has largely replaced physical labour in handling cargo. Imports consist chiefly of manufactured goods, while exports include cacao, tobacco, sugar, hides, castor beans, diamonds, hardwoods and petroleum from the nearby Candeias oil field. The number of industrial plants in Salvador rose at a slow and steady rate during the middle part of the 20th century. Food and tobacco processing, textile manufacturing, metallurgy, wood- and leatherworking and shipbuilding and repair are the chief industries. The Brazilian government maintains a naval base and dockyard in the port area. Abundant electric power is available from the Paulo Afonso hydroelectric project on the São Francisco river 250 mi. N. of the city.

In the second part of the 20th century Salvador was becoming a fairly important tourist attraction. It is served by domestic and foreign steamship lines and by domestic airlines. There are regular rail and bus connections with central and southern Brazil. Salvador is famed throughout Brazil for the number and beauty of its baroque colonial churches, the most striking of which is the church of the convent of the Third Order of St. Francis. Among other leading attractions of Salvador are examples of colonial lay architecture, the Barra lighthouse at the Atlantic tip of the peninsula and the numerous 17th-century fortresses which dot the bay shore and harbour. The city's educational facilities include a university with schools of medicine, law and engineering; normal, commercial and trade schools; and schools of fine arts and arts and crafts.

Salvador was founded in 1549 by Tomé de Sousa, first governor general of Brazil, as capital of the Portuguese colony. It was named, and is still known officially as, São Salvador da Bahia de Todos os Santos. As the seat of the colonial government and entrepôt of the thriving sugar trade that developed in the Recôncavo area along the shores of All Saints bay, Salvador soon became a tempting prize for pirates and enemies of Portugal. Chief of these were the Dutch, who attempted to wrest northeastern Brazil from Portuguese control between 1624 and 1654. Salvador was captured by Dutch forces in 1624 but was retaken the following year. It remained under the control of Portugal until 1823, when the last Portuguese troops were expelled in the war for Brazilian independence. With the transfer of the capital to Rio de Janeiro in 1763, Salvador lost political pre-eminence in Brazil and entered a long period of economic decline from which it did not emerge until after 1900.   (R. E. P.)

SALVADOR, EL, the smallest and most densely populated republic of Central America and probably the most intensively cultivated country in all of Latin America. Its capital city is San Salvador. The country is bounded on the north and east by Honduras, on the south by the Pacific Ocean, and on the west and northwest by Guatemala. It is the only republic of Central America that has no Caribbean coastline. El Salvador is 140 mi. (225 km.) long from east to west and 60 mi. (96 km.) wide and has a total land area of 8,164 sq.mi. (21,146 sq.km.).

Physical Geography.—*Geology.*—The three principal physiographic-geologic features of El Salvador are: (1) mountain ranges in the north and south; (2) broad plateaulike areas between the mountain ranges cut by the upper Lempa and San Miguel rivers; and (3) the coastal and lower Lempa and San Miguel plains bordering the Pacific. The northern mountain range consists of

lavas, andesitic rocks, and ashes of the Tertiary Period, except for small areas of older Cretaceous sandstones, shales, and conglomerates in the west. Older rocks in the southern mountain range are covered deeply with Pliocene and Pleistocene eruptives—basaltic and andesitic lavas, pumice, and ashes—forming more than 20 volcanoes. These volcanoes are clustered in five groups that stretch across the country. The westernmost are Izalco (active since 1770, 6,183 ft. [1,885 m.]), San Marcelino, Santa Ana (highest mountain in the country, 7,724 ft. [2,355 m.]), Naranjos, Aguila, San Juan de Dios, Apaneca, Tamajaso, and La Laguneta. Next in order come San Salvador (6,399 ft. [1,950 m.]) and Cojutepeque; San Vicente and Siguatepeque; Tecapa, Taburete, Buenapa, Usulután, Chinameca, and San Miguel (6,957 ft. [2,120 m.]); and, farthest east, Conchagua (4,101 ft. [1,250 m.]) and smaller ones nearby. Several of these volcanoes are still active. The coastal plain, 5 to 15 mi. (8 to 24 km.) wide, consists mostly of Pleistocene marine sediments and recent alluvium.

Relief and Drainage.—The northern and southern mountain ranges are high and rugged. Plateaulike areas between them, deeply carved by the upper Lempa and San Miguel rivers and tributaries, consist mostly of rolling to rough land between 700 and 3,500 ft. (200 and 1,000 m.) altitude. The Lempa River rises in Guatemala, crosses a corner of Honduras, cuts across the northern range, flows eastward for more than 80 mi. (128 km.), and then flows south for 65 mi. (104 km.) across the southern range to the Pacific. The San Miguel system drains eastern El Salvador. The sloping coastal plain is mostly well drained by these two rivers and many other short ones.

Climate.—The temperature of various regions varies according to their altitude. The Pacific lowlands and low areas in the middle Lempa valley have mean monthly temperatures between 78° and 85° F (25° and 29° C). At San Salvador (2,156 ft. [657 m.]) the maximum monthly mean temperature is 95° F (35° C) in March and the lowest monthly mean is 58° F (14° C) in January. At 4,800 ft. (1,400 m.) mean monthly temperatures vary between 63° and 72° F (17° and 22° C). El Salvador has two seasons, the wet or summer season from May to November and the dry or winter season from November to May. Annual precipitation on the Pacific lowlands averages about 68 in. (1,727 mm.); on the southern (volcanic) and northern mountain ranges between 2,000 and 3,500 ft. (600 and 1,000 m.) between 70 and 97 in. (1,778 and 2,464 mm.); the higher mountains receive a little more. Annual precipitation in the deep valleys and plateaulike areas is between 45 and 60 in. (1,143 and 1,524 mm.).

Vegetation.—The northern mountains have temperate grasslands and remnants of deciduous oak and pine forests. The southern volcanic mountains have temperate grasses, and below these are remnants of pine and deciduous broadleaf forests, including oak and many other species. Between these two mountain ranges the natural vegetation of the plateaulike areas and deep valleys, with 45 to 60 in. (1,143 to 1,524 mm.) of rainfall annually concentrated during six rainy months, consists of small deciduous trees, or bushes, and of subtropical grasslands. On the Pacific plains and lower southern mountain slopes are savannas and deciduous broadleaf forests. Among the many species is balsam, the trunk of which yields excellent lumber and resin, the latter used in antiseptics and medicinal gums. There are many varieties of tropical fruit and many medicinal plants.

Animal Life.—The fauna of El Salvador is less varied than that of other Central American countries because of the scanty rainfall and forest cover. However, it includes many species of land birds and waterfowl, rodents, reptiles, insects (butterflies, beetles, bees, wasps, spiders, ants, flies, and mosquitoes), and freshwater and saltwater fish. Although many fish inhabit streams and lakes, most of the catch of nearly 750,000 lb. comes from offshore waters and coastal lagoons, and consists chiefly of mullets, grunts, snappers, jacks, groupers, sharks, and anchovies.

Geographical Regions.—El Salvador may be divided into four major geographical regions: (1) northern mountains; (2) southern volcanic mountains; (3) between these two mountain ranges, the plateaus and deep valleys region; and (4) Pacific lowlands and coastal hills.

The northern mountains, comprising about 15% of El Salvador, are high and rugged. They have 6% of the national population, widely dispersed in many deep valleys; the region has no large towns. Although these mountain dwellers are engaged chiefly in subsistence farming and grazing, the region has several small coffee and lumbering districts, for the high rainy areas still have considerable stands of oak and pine forests.

As noted above, the southern volcanic mountains consist of about 20 steep cone-shaped volcanoes between 4,000 and 7,800 ft. (1,200 and 2,300 m.) and areas of gently sloping land between 1,000 and 4,000 ft. (300 and 1,200 m.) altitude. This region comprises 30% of El Salvador. It has 63% of the country's population, including most areas of dense rural settlement and most of the cities with more than 10,000 people. Its soils, derived from lava and volcanic ashes, are the country's most productive. Its temperatures range from tropical to temperate. Three-fourths of its precipitation (between 70 and nearly 100 in. [1,770 and 2,540 mm.]) falls during the period from May to November. This region produces 90% of El Salvador's coffee, tobacco, and manufactured goods; two-thirds of its corn, beans, fruits, vegetables, and sugar; and half the nation's cotton, rice, and animal and forest products.

The region of plateaus and deep valleys comprises 45% of El Salvador's area and has 25% of its population. The people live in rural areas and in many towns of less than 10,000 population. Lying between 700 and 3,500 ft. (210 and 1,060 m.) altitude, its temperatures are tropical to subtropical. With only 45 to 60 in. (1,140 to 1,520 mm.) of precipitation during the rainy months from May to November, it is the driest region of El Salvador. Its soils are generally shallow and stony. The region has much more pastureland than cropland. It is significant in supplying animal products, corn, beans, vegetables, henequen, and simple manufactures.

The Pacific lowlands and coastal hills comprise 10% of El Salvador's area and have 6% of its population. This region is hot all year round and rainy for six months. It has much more land in either pasture or forest than in crops. It is significant in the production of beef, forest products, cotton, sesame, rice, sugar, corn, and fish.

(C. F. J.)

The People.—More than four-fifths of the people of El Salvador are of mixed Spanish-Indian descent (mestizo). The remainder are pure Indians, whites, and a few Negroes. When the Spaniards arrived the land was inhabited mainly by the Pipil Indians, whose civilization resembled that of the Aztecs in Mexico. The majority of the tribes were farmers; the others were potters, carpenters, masons, weavers, etc. The Indians were great builders, left numerous ruins, and had advanced to the stage of developing hieroglyphic writing. Of the several large towns which they established, two which have continued to remain in existence are the present cities of Sonsonate and Ahuachapán.

Few Spanish settlers arrived to colonize the area but intermarriage of these few Spaniards and the Pipil Indians resulted in a racially homogeneous people. Only a few pure Indians remain today, notably the Izalco Indians, and the Panchos from the village of Panchimalco near the capital. Their bright costumes and traditional ceremonies lend much colour to the land. The language of El Salvador is Spanish, although a few of the Indians still speak their native tongue. The majority of the people are of Roman Catholic religion.

The Salvadoreans are sports loving and have been hosts to numerous national and international sports events. Many festivals are held throughout the country, such as the day of *El Salvador del Mundo* ("the Saviour of the World"), held from July 24 to Aug. 6, and the *Día del Indio* ("Day of the Indian") held on Dec. 12.

(P. H. Ar.)

History.—El Salvador was in early times the home of Indian groups who were advanced in civilization but whose identities are unknown. The Pipil, most significant of the three groups who inhabited the land in the 15th century, had their capital at Cuscatlán, a name still sometimes used as that of the country. The first Europeans to enter El Salvador were Spaniards commanded by Pedro de Alvarado (*q.v.*), who came from Guatemala in 1524. Though Cuscatlán was briefly occupied at that time, and nearby San Salvador founded in 1525, it was not until 1527 that the Pipil were subdued by Alvarado's lieutenants. San Salvador was a part of the province of Guatemala, as was San Miguel, founded east of the Lempa River in 1530 to discourage the territorial ambitions of Pedro Arias de Ávila (*q.v.*) in Nicaragua. The port of Acajutla was used by Alvarado in preparation for his illegal expedition to Ecuador in 1534. Western El Salvador became valuable to the Spaniards economically when Acajutla became the funnel through which passed a lively export trade in cacao. Nearby Sonsonate was founded in 1552 to handle this trade.

Sonsonate and San Salvador developed as separate provinces, ruled by *alcaldes mayores*, each subject to the jurisdiction of the Spanish *Audiencia de Guatemala*. Sonsonate was the smaller of the two but remained the wealthier for about a century until the cacao trade declined under competition from Ecuador. San Salvador grew more slowly, with dependence upon stock raising, general agriculture, and the manufacture of indigo, but eventually

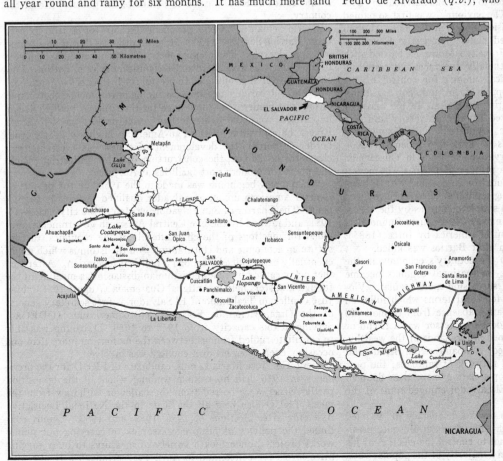

PHYSICAL FEATURES AND PRINCIPAL TOWNS, HIGHWAYS, AND RAILROADS OF EL SALVADOR

became more important. The city of San Miguel was included in its territory. The Spanish town of San Vicente, founded in 1635 to remove Spaniards, Negroes, and persons of mixed blood from nearby Indian villages, was also included in this province as was Cihuatehuacán (Santa Ana), an Indian centre which grew second in size to the city of San Salvador but went unrecognized as a Spanish town until 1812. The province of San Salvador was raised in 1786 to the rank of an intendancy, along with León (Nicaragua), Comayagua (Honduras), and Ciudad Real (Chiapas, Mexico), each continuing to be subordinate to the government in Guatemala. Both Sonsonate and San Salvador had by this time a large mestizo population, with some mixture of Negro blood as well. Most of the important "Indian" villages, including Ahuachapán, Chalchuapa, Zacatecoluca, Cojutepeque, Suchitoto, and Usulután, were becoming progressively non-Indian in their customs.

Independence Movement.—In the rapid evolution of Central American affairs from 1811 to 1840, San Salvador played a most active role. The first Central American defiance of Spain occurred there in November 1811, inspired by the deeds of Miguel Hidalgo y Costilla (*q.v.*) in Mexico, and led by another priest, José Matías Delgado (who aspired to become San Salvador's first bishop) and his nephew, Manuel José Arce. Both this attempt and another in 1814 failed. When the government in Guatemala declared independence from Spain, Sept. 15, 1821, subject to the approval of a Central American congress, the authorities in San Salvador went one step further (Sept. 22) and declared absolute independence. Battles were fought in 1822 and 1823 to resist annexation to the Mexican empire. Arce even traveled to Washington, D.C., to seek the protection of the United States. Delgado and Arce played prominent roles in the provisional government of the United Provinces of Central America (1823–25), and Arce was chosen first president of this federation (1825–29). Although San Salvador, which became a state in the union, tried unsuccessfully to secede in 1832 and 1833, the federal capital was transferred there in 1834. The union ended in 1839; Francisco Morazán, its second and last president, was forced to leave San Salvador in 1840.

The republic of El Salvador ("The Saviour") was first so named on Jan. 30, 1841, but only provisionally so until 1856. It then underwent 45 years of checkered history, in which Conservatives (heirs of the opposition to Francisco Morazán) battled with Liberals (the Morazán party, generally the more interested in a renewal of the Central American union) for control of the country. Both groups found support from and lent assistance to similar parties in the neighbouring countries. In the midst of the turmoil, El Salvador organized its first university and was finally established as a bishopric. Agitation quieted somewhat during the longer administrations of Francisco Dueñas (1863–71), who was backed by Conservative elements in Guatemala, and Rafael Zaldívar (1876–85), a protégé of Dueñas who nevertheless maintained friendly relations for some time with Liberal administrations in all the bordering republics. Coffee, introduced as a crop in 1840, was exported in sizable quantities by the 1870s. Zaldívar successfully opposed the move of Pres. Justo Rufino Barrios of Guatemala to reunify Central America by force (1885), but was pushed out of office soon after Barrios was killed.

Coffee became all-important to the country's economy in the period from 1885 to 1931, while international conflicts became less frequent and the presidential succession more regular. Violence upset only one of the eight four-year terms which followed each other starting in 1899. Relative absence from turmoil did not bring democracy. Each president's successor was a friend or close relative and all power remained in the hands of the wealthy. But the coffee plantations flourished; companies from Britain and the United States built a national network of railroads; the port of La Unión was developed; the population more than doubled (passing the million mark); and El Salvador enjoyed some of the blessings of peace.

Military Dictatorships.—A step toward democracy in 1931 led to a military dictatorship instead. Pío Romero Bosque, president from 1927 to 1931, decided not to control the election of his successor. When no candidate won a majority of the popular vote, Arturo Araujo was chosen by congress, but he was overthrown by force before the year was out. Gen. Maximiliano Hernández Martínez then came to power but was not recognized by the other Central American states or by the United States because he had been involved in the *coup d'état*. Hernández Martínez retained power only by a ruthless policy which involved mass executions.

Hernández Martínez maintained his authoritarian rule from 1931 to 1944. Reelected to the presidency in 1935, he was chosen to continue in 1939 by an assembly which he had picked to write a new constitution. Recognition of his government by neighbouring republics came in 1934. Energetic measures of the early years of this regime included the establishment of a new coinage system, the organization of a national bank, the completion of the Pan-American Highway across the country, and the extension of state control over the coffee industry. Hernández Martínez gained international attention by early recognition of the Japanese puppet regime in Manchukuo (1934) and of the regime of Francisco Franco in Spain (1936). He was generally accounted to have warm relations with Nazi Germany and Fascist Italy, and German business interests had considerable holdings in El Salvador in the late 1930s. Nevertheless, El Salvador after Pearl Harbor quickly joined the side of the United States against the Axis, and Hernández Martínez received the same material benefits from cooperation with Washington through the war as did his isthmian neighbours.

Post-World War II Era.—The end of the Hernández Martínez regime was not the end of government by military officers. Hernández Martínez' resignation came after a fierce revolt (which brought bombings and fire to the capital) and a general strike, prompted by a decision of the assembly to extend his term five more years. Gen. Andrés Menéndez, vice-president, held office from May to October 1944, when a new coup brought in Col. Osmín Aguirre y Salinas. Salvador Castaneda Castro, who took office March 1, 1945, after elections, lasted until Dec. 14, 1948 when a military junta took control. Maj. Oscar Osorio, important in this junta, was the popular choice in new elections of March 1950. His political group, the new Partido Revolucionario de Unificación Democrática (PRUD), came to dominate the political life of the country.

Osorio remained in the presidential chair for a full six-year term, starting Sept. 14, 1950. Material progress during this period was considerable. To coffee exports, which continued as valuable to the country as ever, were added significant sales of cotton. Low standards of living continued to prevail for the masses of underpaid workers, but various measures, including government construction of low-cost homes, held some hope for their future. Of particular importance were the hydroelectric power project on the Lempa River, the asphalting of the Pan-American Highway nearly from border to border, the development of a new east-west highway closer to the Pacific, the construction of a few industrial plants, and plans for modern port facilities at Acajutla.

When a new beginning was made in the 1950s on the project of Central American union, El Salvador qualified as a ready participant. The Charter of San Salvador, written in the city Oct. 8–14, 1951, and ratified by the five Central American governments, provided for meetings of the chief officials of the republics, to constitute an economic and cultural unity on the isthmus which might eventually express itself through a political federation. After further delay caused by renewed isthmian dissension, a meeting of the foreign ministers held in Antigua, Guatemala (August 1955) chose José Guillermo Trabanino of El Salvador as first secretary general of the Organización de Estados Centroamericanos (ODECA). Serving in this capacity from 1955 to 1959, Trabanino was able to conciliate ruffled feelings between the nations on more than one occasion, even when his own country was involved.

Lieut. Col. José María Lemus, candidate of PRUD for the presidency in 1956, had no trouble winning when all the opposition parties either were barred from the ballot or withdrew from the race. PRUD also held all the seats in the National Legislative Assembly after elections of 1956, 1958, and 1960. Lemus continued the policies of his predecessor as to carrying out public works projects, undertook a variety of measures to buoy sagging price levels for coffee, and in April 1957 arranged a treaty with Guatemala for mutual hydroelectric developments utilizing the waters of international Lake Güija. Continued one-party rule in the face of mass discontent with low standards of living, however, led to the ousting of the government by force on Oct. 26, 1960.

Plans for a democratic election were sponsored by the six-man junta which ruled El Salvador for the following three months. Another junta, which seized control on Jan. 25, 1961, however, first canceled the participation of parties of leftist orientation and then arranged the election of a constitutional convention all of whose seats were held by the new Partido de Conciliación Nacional (PCN). Col. Julio Adalberto Rivera, running as candidate of that party, was elected without opposition as president for a five-year term beginning July 1, 1962. Despite these arbitrary beginnings, Rivera helped to set the nation on a new course. An income tax reform in 1963 and a minimum wage for agricultural labour in 1965 showed some recognition of the imbalance in the distribution of the country's wealth. Fairer elections for municipal posts and the National Assembly in 1964 and 1966 indicated an understanding of the people's dissatisfaction with one-party rule. Business prospered, in part because of El Salvador's participation in the Central American Common Market, although an earthquake in the capital in 1965 provided a national shock.

Minority parties which gained much attention during the Rivera tenure in office were the Christian Democrats, of the democratic left, and the Partido Acción Renovadora (PAR), which dropped a conservative leadership and took on a strong Marxist flavour. When both were permitted to run candidates for the presidency in 1967, both chose civilians: lawyer Abraham Rodríguez for the Christian Democrats and university rector Fabio Castillo for the PAR. Col. Fidel Sánchez Hernández of the PCN won by a 54% majority. Before Sánchez took office on July 1, a 30,000-worker general strike made a deep impression on the nation and strengthened the hands of the labour unions. A minor border dispute with Honduras in May 1967, concerning which Sánchez took a moderate stand, enabled his opposition to play on Salvadoran nationalist feelings. In 1968, the municipal and legislative elections showed a distinct Christian Democratic gain, PCN retaining only a one-vote majority in the National Assembly.   (F. D. P.)

Population.—One of the most pressing problems of El Salvador is overpopulation. The smallest country in size in Central America, it is the most densely populated with about 389 persons per square mile in mid-1968. The annual growth rate in 1961 was 2.9% but in the late 1960s it was estimated to be 3.8%. Three-fourths of the people are concentrated in the area around the department of San Salvador, which has a population density four times the national average. In mid-1968 the population of El Salvador was estimated to be 3,210,356.

Population and Area of El Salvador by Department

Departments		Area (sq.mi.)	Population*	Capital		Population*
Ahuachapán	. .	472	130,710	Ahuachapán	. .	40,359
Cabañas	. :	423	94,590	Sensuntepeque	.	27,360
Chalatenango	. :	817	129,897	Chalatenango	.	15,137
Cuscatlán	. :	283	113,042	Cojutepeque.	.	18,347
La Libertad	. .	642	203,480	Nueva San Salvador (Santa Tecla)	.	40,817
La Paz	. .	464	130,659	Zacatecoluca	.	40,424
La Unión	. .	770	148,108	La Unión	.	21,556
Morazán	. .	666	119,381	San Francisco Gotera.	.	7,528
San Miguel	. .	837	231,821	San Miguel	.	82,491
San Salvador	. .	336	463,228	San Salvador	.	255,744
Santa Ana	. .	768	259,155	Santa Ana	.	121,095
San Vicente	. .	466	112,920	San Vicente	.	34,723
Sonsonate	. .	459	166,932	Sonsonate	.	35,531
Usulután	. .	762	207,061	Usulután	.	30,465
Total	.	8,165†	2,510,984			

*Third national census of population, 1961. †Land area only. Total area is 8,260 sq.mi.
Source: *Tercer Censo Nacional de Población, 1961,* Dirección General de Estadística y Censos, República de El Salvador, C.A.

Administration and Social Conditions.—The constitution adopted in 1962 provides for a representative form of government with three branches—legislative, executive, and judicial. All Salvadoreans, male and female, who have attained the age of 18 are permitted to vote. Executive power is exercised by the president, his cabinet ministers, and undersecretaries of state. The president is elected by direct, popular vote for a term of five years and is ineligible to succeed himself. Legislative power is vested in a unicameral National Legislative Assembly (*Asamblea Na-*

cional Legislativa), which meets in regular session on the first of June and the first of December of each year. The number of deputies is determined by apportionment. They are elected by popular vote for two-year terms and can be reelected. The judicial branch is composed of a Supreme Court of Justice, whose members are selected by the National Assembly, and of other tribunals as established by statute. The Supreme Court consists of ten magistrates, one of whom serves as president.

The territory of El Salvador is divided into 14 departments (see *Population,* above). Each department has a governor and a substitute governor, appointed by the executive power. For purposes of local government the departments are divided into municipalities, which are governed by popularly elected municipal councils (*consejos municipales*), consisting of a mayor (*alcalde*), a syndic (*síndico*), and two or more aldermen (*regidores*), the number of whom are in proportion to the population. Independent in their local functions, the municipalities are limited to economic and administrative activities.

The standard of living of the artisan class in El Salvador is high, but that of the agricultural labourer remains low. The government is taking active steps to ensure a more equitable distribution of income by emphasizing workers' education, sponsoring projects in literacy, and training workers for union activity and community life. The average per capita income in 1966 was about $276. Union organization was given government support in 1950 and soon more than 50 unions were in existence. In 1950 the Urban Housing and Rural Colonization institutes were created to help overcome the lack of low-cost housing and to ensure adequate housing facilities for future population increases. The Social Security Institute was inaugurated in 1949 as an autonomous organization to provide health, accident, unemployment, old age, and life insurance. Its benefits are financed by contributions from workers, employers, and the government.

All public and private institutions of learning are under the jurisdiction of the Ministry of Education. The school system is composed of preschool, primary, secondary, and university categories. Primary education is free and compulsory but the illiteracy rate is high. There are four institutions of higher education: the University of El Salvador, the Higher Normal School, the School of Social Service, and the new Catholic University. The National University has faculties of law and social sciences, engineering and architecture, economics, humanities, chemistry, medicine, and dentistry. There are also an Institute of Fine Arts, and a National Agricultural Institute, and there are schools of public administration, social service, and nursing, and various other vocational schools.

Military service for at least one year is compulsory for all Salvadorean males from 18 to 30 years of age. The strength of the Army is fixed annually by the National Assembly; in no case can it be less than 3,000 men.

Economy.—The foundation of El Salvador's economy continued to be agriculture, although industrial expansion was developing at a rapid pace in the 1960s. About 75% of the land area is used for agriculture, principally for growing coffee, cotton, and sugar, the chief foreign exchange earners. Coffee alone accounts for one-third of the value of the total agricultural production, and one-half of the value of exports. In the 1960s there was a steadily increasing investment in industry and other fields, stimulated by the creation of the Central American Common Market. Industrial plants rose throughout the country and existing facilities were expanded, helped by government incentives, an advanced banking system, as well as by development credits from abroad. The most important industries are those engaged in processing food and cotton, manufacturing textiles and textile products, leather, chemicals, petroleum products, and machinery. The principal source of power is hydroelectric, produced chiefly by the Comisión Hidroelectrica del Rio Lempa, a government agency. As the wooded area of the country is small (5 to 11% of the total land area), forestry is limited to the logging of balsam, indigenous to El Salvador and used in the manufacture of a valuable resin, "balsam of Peru," as well as for furniture and agricultural tools. Commercial fishing, regulated by the government, experienced rapid growth in the 1960s and became one of the largest export earners.

The monetary unit of El Salvador is the colón, which is divided into 100 centavos. The colón has been stabilized in world market quotations at $2\frac{1}{2}$ to the U.S. dollar. Central banking functions are performed by the Central Reserve Bank of El Salvador, created in 1934.

El Salvador's excellent highway system has been an important factor in the country's development. Two main routes of the Pan-American Highway traverse the country from border to border, forming the framework of a network of roads reaching almost all parts of the country. The total highway mileage in El Salvador in 1966 was 5,312 mi. (8,549 km.), of which 730 mi. (1,175 km.) were paved, 937 mi. (1,508 km.) were all weather, and 3,644 mi. (5,864 km.) were dry weather.

Two railroad companies, the International Railways of Central America and the Salvador Railway, cover a distance of 383 mi. (616 km.).

See also references under "Salvador, El" and separate articles on Salvadorean departments and the more important towns in the Index.

Bibliography.—Pan American Union, *America en Cifras* (1967), *El Salvador,* in the "American Republics Series" (1960); *Anuario Estadístico, 1966,* vol. i and ii, Dirección General de Estadística y Censos, Ministerio de Economía (1967); Committee of Nine, Alliance for Progress, *Report on the Central American National Development Plans and the Process of Integration* (1966); U.S. Department of Commerce, *Basic Data on the Economy of El Salvador* (1967). (P. H. Ar.)

SALVAGE, a term used in maritime law to designate either the act of rescuing life or certain kinds of property defined by salvage law from peril on water or the reward to which the rescuers, known as salvors, are entitled. In common English usage the term is used generally to describe rescue operations of various sorts (in commercial and banking circles, for example, the refloating of a corporation that has run on financial reefs is often referred to as a salvage operation), but it has no legal significance outside the field of maritime law. The present article is devoted exclusively to the legal aspects; for salvage engineering *see* Salvage Operations.

Rescue Efforts and the Law.—In Anglo-American law (apart from the law of the sea) there is neither a duty to go to the aid of another person when he or his property is in peril nor a right to a reward if aid is furnished and life or property preserved. At sea, however, there is both a duty to give aid and assistance and, where property is saved, a right to a reward, which is not looked on merely as a compensation for services rendered but is, it has often been said, to be generously computed in order to furnish an inducement to mariners and shipowners to risk their lives and property. The generosity with which salvage awards are computed may also serve, as one judge has realistically reminded us, "to withdraw from the salvors as far as possible every motive to depredate upon the property of the unfortunate owner" (Justice Clifford, in *The Clara* and *The Clarita,* 90 U.S. [23 Wall.] 1, 17 [1874]).

The salvage rules are a branch of property law rather than of moral law; this proposition may be illustrated by the fact that under general maritime law salvors of life at sea had no right to a reward. Life salvage was made the subject of reward, as such, in the United Kingdom in the 19th century, and this is still the law under the Merchant Shipping act, 1894. The provisions of the act extend to British ships everywhere and to foreign ships in British waters. Life salvage was formally recognized in the Salvage convention of 1910, which was adopted by many of the principal maritime countries of the world.

The U.S. version of the life salvage provision is that: "Salvors of human life, who have taken part in the services rendered on the occasion of the accident giving rise to salvage, are entitled to a fair share of the remuneration awarded to the salvors of the vessel, her cargo and accessories." It will be noted that this provision does not purport to reward "pure" life salvage. If only life is saved, the situation remains as it was before the convention. If both life and property are saved on the same "occasion," the life salvors get a "fair share" of the award to the property salvors, and there is nothing in the quoted language to suggest that the total amount of the award is to be increased over what it would have been if only property had been saved. Neither does one whose life is saved in such an operation become liable to the salvors for any fraction of the award, which is assessed exclusively against the property.

As will be seen, the courts in computing salvage awards have traditionally, and without regard to the life salvage provision of the Salvage convention, taken into account the moral aspects of the salvors' behaviour. Daring rescues of survivors inure to the benefit of good salvors when the award is computed, and the greedy salvors who let the survivors drown while they save the property find themselves appropriately punished. The only situation in which the Salvage convention appears to justify an award that would not otherwise be made is one in which, following the same accident, two sets of salvors appear and, acting independently of each other, one set saves only life and the other set saves only property. There have been a few such cases (*e.g., The Shreveport,* 42 F. 2d 524 [E.D.S.C. 1930]), and the judges have taken the life salvage provision to mean that a portion, typically a small portion, of the award made for saving the property should be taken from the property salvors and given to the life salvors.

The position under British law is that there is no life salvage reward where life alone and no property at all is saved by anyone, although the government has statutory powers to make *ex gratia* payments in such circumstances. Those who save life from a British vessel anywhere or from a foreign vessel in British waters are entitled by statute to life salvage, provided some property has been saved, although they themselves have saved none. Apart from these statutory provisions, the admiralty court in London and inferior admiralty courts usually give, and have traditionally given, higher rewards to salvors of property who also saved lives than they would have done if only property had been saved, and this is so regardless of where the services are performed. Awards for salvage of property, too, are increased where life has been in danger on board a salved vessel. All these principles also apply to aircraft (Civil Aviation act, 1949; Aircraft [Wreck and Salvage] order, 1938). Claims for life salvage as such have always been very rare and are now virtually unknown.

Salvage Defined.—The classical statement of the components of an act of salvage is: the rescue of maritime property (a ship or her cargo) on navigable waters within the jurisdiction of the admiralty from a peril which, except for the salvor's assistance, would have led to the loss or destruction of the property. Under British law aircraft may also be salved. Except for salvage performed under contract, a salvor must act voluntarily without being under any legal duty to do so, apart from the general duty, which has been reinforced by statute, to give assistance to those in peril at sea or to stand by after a collision. Since the salvage award is related to the value of the property saved, it is evident that only successful salvage attempts will be rewarded. So long as the owner or his agent remains on the ship, unwanted offers of salvage may be refused. A derelict (*q.v.*) is fair game for anyone who comes across it. It was not merely romantic heroism that in Dec. 1951 prompted Capt. H. K. Carlsen to remain aboard the "Flying Enterprise" until the contract salvors arrived but a commendable desire to protect his owners from a judicially computed salvage award.

There appears to be a fairly widespread belief that a salvor becomes the owner of the property that he rescues, at least if the property had been abandoned by the owner or was derelict. There is no foundation for this belief. The owner may always reclaim his property from the salvor on paying salvage money. The salvor has a maritime lien on the salved property. As lienor, the salvor need not return the property to the owner until his claim is satisfied or until a security to meet an award is given, and he may institute legal proceedings in rem against the property, in which case the admiralty court will take possession of the property unless the owner provides security to obtain its release. An owner may elect not to reclaim his property but to abandon it; if he does so, he cannot be made liable for a salvage award, although the admiralty court will sell the ship, reward the salvors out of the proceedings of sale and hold the residue for the owner or for other claimants.

The only basis for the popular belief about the salvage of derelict property is that awards for salvage of such property may run somewhat higher than for other property because salvage under such circumstances will usually be a more dangerous operation, the degree of danger being one of the most important factors in fixing the proper reward, than when the ship in peril is still manned by her own crew, and because derelict property is usually in grave peril.

Derelict is narrowly defined by British salvage law: a thing, such as a ship or cargo, abandoned and deserted at sea by those who were in charge of it, without hope on their part of recovering it and without intention of returning to it. For the purposes of the Merchant Shipping acts "derelict," together with flotsam, jetsam and lagan, is classed as "wreck," which is practical but historically confusing. Unclaimed derelict and other forms of "wreck" are droits of admiralty.

Any act that contributes to the preservation of property in peril may rank as a salvage service. At the bottom of the scale is the situation in which one ship merely tows another into port, without danger to the towing vessel, difficulty or delay. The owner of the towed ship, now safe in port, will naturally take the position that the towage was convenient but not necessary, that his ship could have made port under her own power, and will offer to pay for the service at the customary towage rates. The owner (and crew) of the towing ship will claim salvage on the ground that, except for the assistance rendered, the other ship would have been unable to make port and might have come ultimately into serious peril although no immediate disaster threatened. If the court finds that the danger was real, it will decree salvage and make an award that will be substantially in excess of the towage rates.

Typical acts of salvage include releasing ships that have run aground or on reefs, raising sunken ships (or their cargo), putting out fires and so on. In centuries more colourful than the 20th, one of the liberally rewarded acts of salvage was the recapture of a ship taken by pirates or taken as prize in time of war. Following the Russian Revolution of 1917 an English court made such an award to an impromptu crew of Allied soldiers who sailed a ship out of Murmansk harbour under gunfire after collapse of the Allied intervention (*The Lomonosoff*, [1921] P. 97). The salvage act need not be some kind of physical assistance directly rendered to the ships in peril. Standing by ready to give aid if necessary, summoning assistance that is given by others and even giving information as to the channel to follow in dangerous waters have all been regarded as salvage acts. Salvage by, as well as to, aircraft may be rewarded (*The American Farmer*, [1947] 80 Lloyd's Rep. 672).

Objects of Salvage.—It is often said that the only objects of salvage (known as subjects in British law) are a ship, her accessories and her cargo, and that the rescue of other types of property, looked on as nonmaritime, from peril at sea will go unrewarded. The position regarding aircraft under British law has already been explained. The U.S. author G. H. Robinson has suggested, in a hypothetical example, that there would, under this theory, be no right to salvage for raising a freight car that had fallen into the sea from a railroad trestle, and this would be so under British law. The strict "maritime property" theory is principally based on two 19th-century cases, one U.S., one English. In *Cope* v. *Vallette Dry Dock Co.*, 119 U.S. 625 (1887), the U.S. supreme court decided that no salvage could be claimed with respect to a dry dock that, having been moored in a fixed position for 20 years, had broken loose from its moorings. A few years later the house of lords came to the same conclusion in *Wells* v. *Owners of Gas Float Whitton No. 2*, [1897] A.C. 337, with respect to a navigation beacon. There seems to have been neither much reason nor much authority behind these decisions of the two highest courts. A leading U.S. admiralty judge of the period had commented, in awarding salvage on rafts of timber found floating in Boston harbour, that it would be no defense to a salvage claim "that the goods had been washed out to sea from the shore by a gale or a flood, or had been dropped from a balloon" (Lowell, Justice in *50,000 Feet*

of Timber, 9 Fed. Cas. 47 [D. Mass. 1871]). In the 20th century the invention of the airplane raised in a novel context the problem of whether "nonmaritime property" found in peril at sea is a proper object of salvage. After some initial hesitation while the courts wrestled with the distinguished authorities, the answer has been given, in England by statute, as stated above, and in the United States by the course of judicial decision, that salvage can be claimed for aircraft rescue on navigable waters. Recent U.S. cases in particular have shown a tendency to award salvage with respect to any kind of property found afloat—even money recovered from a dead body in New York harbour (*Broere* v. *$2,133*, 72 F. Supp. 115 [E.D.N.Y. 1947]). Since the supreme court has not reversed itself and since the house of lords is said not to be able to reverse itself, the *Cope* case and *The Gas Float Whitton* are still technically good law but, it may be, only as to dry docks and navigation beacons, respectively.

Legal Duty as a Bar to Claims.—There are several classes of salvage claimants against whom the legal duty rule is regularly employed to defeat the claim. One class consists of public officials and employees; municipal firemen and licensed pilots may be taken as examples. Special provisions in British law apply to claims by members of the armed forces, but the crown may claim salvage in respect of their efforts when crown property has been used. The rule is also applied to salvage claims by the crew of the salved ship. Since the crew is under a duty to save the ship at all costs, no feats of heroism, however extraordinary, will be rewarded as salvage. When the ship was recaptured from pirates or enemies, the traditional rules did allow for a liberal award to the crew; the modern formulation of such cases is that salvage can be claimed by crew members who voluntarily return to the ship after their contracts have ended, *e.g.*, by abandonment on master's orders.

The rule against crew salvage has been extended to passengers, although extraordinary contributions by passengers have occasionally been rewarded. The reason for the rule in British law is that the passenger should receive no reward for what he does solely in the interest of self-preservation. The legal duty rule applies similarly in cases where a tug claims salvage against a vessel she is towing under contract. Under the contract of towage the tug is said to be under a duty to come to the tow's assistance, and the salvage claim is denied unless, under British law at least, the tug does more than the contract of towage bound her to do. Salvage is frequently awarded in such circumstances. In most of the cases mentioned, with the possible exception of that of the crew when the master has not abandoned ship, the rule appears not to be an absolute bar. Rescue efforts that are above and beyond the call of duty may be rewarded as salvage.

In 19th-century salvage law the rule seems to have led to the conclusion that there could be no salvage claims when both the salving and the salved ship were in common ownership. Obviously the owner of the two ships had no interest in claiming salvage from himself; the effect of the rule in U.S. law was to deny salvage to the crew of the salving ship, presumably on the ground that the crew was under a duty to preserve the owner's property. Under British law, common ownership is a bar to the owner of the two vessels except, in certain circumstances, against cargo in the salved vessel; the crew of the salving ship may claim against a salved vessel and her cargo regardless of ownership. The Salvage convention of 1910 provided that common ownership of salving and salved vessels should not affect salvage claims, and in the United States a statute was passed to implement the rule of the convention. In the British case *The Kafiristan*, [1938] A.C. 136, it was decided that where a vessel is wrongfully damaged by another vessel and is salved by a third vessel (in common ownership with the second vessel), a claim for salvage by the owners of the third vessel is not barred. The salvage award will be an item in the damage claim against the owners of the wrong-doing second vessel, according to the degree to which that other vessel is to blame.

There appears to be no reason why a government should not claim salvage for rescue operations performed by its naval or merchant fleets. In several cases decided during and after World War II, both the British and the United States governments made salvage claims, sometimes apparently for the benefit of the government, sometimes for the benefit of the crew of the salving ship. The Crown Proceedings act, 1947, s. 8, provides that salvage law shall apply to crown ships or cargo (except that there is no right in rem) as if belonging to a private person. The crown as salvor has the same rights and remedies in respect of salvage services as any other salvor. Naval personnel in the U.S. would presumably be unable to bring forward such a claim without governmental sponsorship, and under British law government permission is essential in cases of claims by officers and crew of H.M. ships. Crews of government-owned merchant ships have been allowed to claim salvage as freely as the crews of privately owned ships.

Computation of Awards.—The judicial computation of salvage awards is not an exact science. A classical statement of a method of computing awards was formulated by Justice Nathan Clifford in *The Blackwall*, 77 U.S. (10 Wall.) 1 (1869), in the following often quoted language:

Courts of admiralty usually consider the following circumstances as the main ingredients in determining the amount of the award to be decreed for a salvage service:

(1) The labour expended by the salvors in rendering the salvage service.

(2) The promptitude, skill and energy displayed in rendering the service and saving the property.

(3) The value of the property employed by the salvors in rendering the service, and the danger to which such property was exposed.

(4) The risk incurred by the salvors in securing the property from the impending peril.

(5) The value of the property saved.

(6) The degree of danger from which the property was rescued.

It was noted earlier that salvage is a doctrine of property law and not of morals, but it is clear from Justice Clifford's list that in the United States the moral element intrudes to the extent of making it impossible for anyone successfully to contest the trial judge's computation. His decision depends on so many questions of judgment, such as "danger," that it will be almost impossible to say that any award he may choose to make is "wrong." Consequently, each salvage case is a law unto itself, and precedents are valueless except to indicate in a general way the maximum and minimum amounts which judges have, at various periods, in fact awarded.

In the United Kingdom appeals are infrequent but not unknown. The classic statement of principle on the topic is that of Lord Esher in *The Star of Persia,* (1887) 6 Asp. 220; "If [the court of appeal] cannot say that the learned judge has misapprehended the facts, or cannot say that he has acted contrary to any principle, then, if the amount does not seem to this court to be unreasonable, it cannot interfere." Unreasonable means greatly in excess of or greatly below the sum which the court of appeal considers should have been awarded.

The converse of the rule that good behaviour—extraordinary skill, daring, heroism or ingenuity—increases the award is that bad behaviour—negligence or incompetence or vandalism or theft—decreases the award or, in extreme cases, forfeits it entirely. In the United States it is regarded as a natural and obvious stratagem for owners to put forward such allegations, and a reading of the defense testimony in a random sample of salvage cases will leave the impression that the typical salvor is a blackhearted villain lineally descended from Captain Kidd. The admiralty courts, which sit without juries, are inclined to treat such testimony with deserved skepticism. Self-serving allegations of negligence or worse brought by owners against salvors will therefore be disregarded unless the proof is compelling. In the United Kingdom the defense is usually content to pour cold water on the statement of claim, although positive allegations of negligence or misconduct are made where the circumstances demand them. In both countries the salvor may forfeit his award, in whole or in part, for bad behaviour and is also liable to the owner for any unnecessary damage that an incompetently performed salvage service may have caused to the property.

An extension of the fault principle is that the owners and crew of a ship that has been solely or jointly at fault in a collision cannot claim salvage for services thereafter rendered to the other ship. This point is confidently stated in the leading British treatise on salvage as well as by most U.S. commentators.

The rule as to the amount of an award of salvage seems to be that though the value of the property salved is an important consideration, it must not be allowed to raise the amount of the award altogether out of proportion to the services actually rendered. (It is also customary, as the quotation from *The Blackwall* indicates, to value the salvor's property in order to determine how much he had put at risk. The valuation of the salvor's property, however, appears to have no direct relationship to the amount of the award. There is disagreement between British and U.S. commentators on whether cargo carried in the salving ship may be added to the value of the ship and her freight to increase the total value of the property at risk and thus, hopefully, the amount of the award.) The importance of the valuation of the salved property is that in U.S. law the award will be in all cases calculated as a fraction of that value; in any case of salvage that involves a large ship, this phase of the proceedings will typically be protracted, bitter and hard fought. Under British law the value of the salved property is merely one of the factors taken into consideration in assessing the award.

In arriving at the valuation the items taken into account are the value of the ship, the value of the cargo and the amount of freight that would, except for the salvage, have been lost. In valuing the ship, the customary method is to take its sound value before the salvage less the cost of repairs for damage suffered in the peril from which the ship was rescued. The owner is not, of course, entitled to deduct from sound value the cost of repairs that would put his ship in a better state than it was in before the accident or the cost of repairs not directly occasioned by the accident. The value of cargo will customarily be determined by the price for which it can be sold in the port where it is unloaded.

Another element not mentioned by Justice Clifford in *The Blackwall* that is taken into account is expenses incurred (and, less frequently, profits lost) by the salvor in the course of or as a result of a salvage service. Since the value of the salved property in any event ultimately determines the amount of the award, the salvor does not necessarily recover all that he may have lost; if he has spent, or lost, $1,000 in saving property worth $100, the loss is for his account and not for that of the owner. Items of reimbursement for expenses or for lost profits are often stated separately from the general award for the salvage. It is unclear whether such items represent an addition to the award that the judge would otherwise have made or whether all that is involved is a method of allocation. Since the expenses are incurred or the profits lost by the owner of the salving ship, such items are entirely for the owner's account and are not shared by him with the crew.

The amount of salvage awards, expressed in percentages of the value of the salved property, seems to have steadily decreased since the middle of the 19th century. This trend is obviously related to the tremendous increase in ship values that took place when steam replaced sail and that continues with 20th-century giant liners and supertankers, to say nothing of atomic-powered ships. It was once said that the general rule was a "moiety"—half the value—of the salved property; awards on that basis for the salvage of a multimillion-dollar ship would result in fortunes for the lucky salvors and, needless to say, such awards are not made. In *The Esso Greensboro,* 122 F. Supp. 133 (S.D. Tex. 1954), where the value of the salved ship was stipulated to be $1,000,000, awards of over $200,000 were made to the officers and crew of the salving ship, whose owner made no claim for his own account. The salvors of the "Greensboro" came across her in mid-ocean, burning and derelict; they boarded the burning hulk, searched for survivors, put out the fires, made necessary repairs and towed her to port, the whole affair taking eight days. At the other end of the scale, where the salvage barely rises above the level of simple towage, a customary award in the United States is double the usual towage rates.

Distribution of Awards.—A salvage award is divided between the owner of a salving ship and her officers and crew. Awards to absentee owners appear in U.S. cases as early as the end of the 18th century. In the course of the 19th century awards to owners, as owners and not as participants, came to be regularly made. The usual explanation for this development is the continuing increase in ship values, which meant that increasingly valuable property was being put at risk when used (typically in emergency situations, without the owner's prior consent) in dangerous salvage attempts. It is also true that the increased values were insured against an even wider range of risks. Thus the risk for which the owner is said to be compensated by being given a share of the salvage award is to a degree illusory, although it cannot, on the other hand, be gainsaid that a ship in being is, in most situations, more useful than a claim on an insurance policy. The increasingly important part played by the power of salving vessels after steamships were invented is another major factor. Early 19th-century cases seem to have allocated a quarter or a third of the award to the owner, while 20th-century U.S. cases reveal that two-thirds of the award is customary and the leading British authority suggests that three-fourths of the award should go to the owner.

When the salving ship is operated under charter, a term in the charter party will usually provide for a division of salvage money between owner and charterer. In the absence of such a provision salvage goes to the owner except in the case of a so-called demise or bareboat charter (one under which the charterer is responsible for manning, supplying and navigating the ship).

Among the officers and crew basic awards are normally made according to rank or monthly pay. Additional awards are often made to individuals whose participation contributed to the success of the venture or who in situations of danger displayed unusual bravery. The officers' and crew's right to salvage cannot be defeated by agreement between the owners of the salving ship and the salved property or by arbitration proceedings to which they have not consented.

Cargo that may be carried in the salving ship is said not to have a right to share in the award. At first glance, it would appear that the absentee cargo interest should have a right to a share as the absentee shipowner has, since the cargo, like the ship, may be damaged in the course of the salvage. Furthermore, under most bills of lading and charter parties it will be provided that the ship is not liable to cargo for damage suffered in an attempt to save life or property at sea (although cargo, of course, carries its own insurance against such risks). There appear to be almost no modern cases in which cargo owners have demanded a share of the salvage award, and none under British law.

Payment of Awards.—The owners of the salved property are liable to the salvors for the award in the ratio that the value of their property (*i.e.*, such of it as is saved, valued in its condition after the salvage) bears to the aggregate value of all property saved. The usual contributing values are cargo, the ship and pending freight. For example, if the salved ship, including freight, is worth $1,000,000 and the salved cargo is also worth $1,000,000, being owned in equal shares by ten people, then the shipowner is liable for 50% of the award and each of the ten cargo owners for 5%; in Britain, however, if the dangers to the cargo differ from the dangers to the ship as, for example, where the cargo is perishable and the main danger to it is delay, the proportions may be varied (*The Velox* [1906] P. 263). Since the salvors have a maritime lien against the salved property, they can proceed directly against the property by proceedings in rem or (unless the owner abandons his property) they can proceed against the owners in personam. It has been said that any person who has a direct pecuniary interest in the salved property may be held liable for salvage (Justice Augustus Hand, in *The G. L. 40*, 66 F. 2d 764 [2d Cir. 1933]; Sir James Hannen, in *Five Steel Barges*, [1890] 15 P.D. 142). There are, however, almost no cases in which salvors have attempted to proceed against such more or less remote interests as insurers, mortgagees or buyers of salved property, and it may be doubted whether the attempt, if made, would be successful.

It is customary for the owner of a salved ship to pay the salvors in full and then to seek reimbursement from the owners of other salved property for the shares of the award for which they are liable. The shipowner has a lien against cargo for salvage money paid out on cargo's behalf and may refuse to deliver the cargo until his lien is satisfied. In any situation where large values are involved, the liability of ship and cargo for salvage will be worked out in a general average settlement. (*See* AVERAGE.)

Contract Salvage.—Much salvage work is also carried out under contract by professional salvors. The amount of compensation to which a contract salvor is entitled depends on the terms of his contract, which frequently provide for arbitration as to amount, almost invariably under Lloyds Standard Form of Salvage agreement ("no cure–no pay") rather than for a finally fixed sum. Salvors get nothing unless the salvage is to some degree successful. This reflects one of the basic principles in the law of volunteer salvage, that there can be no award unless property is actually saved. A contract under which a salvor would be paid for his labours, whether or not they were successful, would of course be quite as valid as the "no cure–no pay" contract, though this would not be true salvage.

See also MARITIME LAW.

BIBLIOGRAPHY.—The leading treatise is Sir W. R. Kennedy, *Civil Salvage*, 4th ed. by K. C. McGuffie (1958). This British text is usually considered authoritative by U.S. as well as by British courts. M. J. Norris, *The Law of Salvage* (1959); G. H. Robinson, *Handbook of Admiralty Law in the United States*, ch. 15 (1939), Grant Gilmore and C. L. Black, *The Law of Admiralty*, ch. 8 (1957); *Halsbury's Laws of England*, vol. 1, "Admiralty," 3rd ed. (1952) and vol. 5, "Shipping and Navigation," 3rd ed. (1961). (G. GI.; K. C. McG.)

SALVAGE OPERATIONS are those required to refloat a ship or other vessel that has sunk or run aground or to assist her when she is in other kinds of danger; *e.g.*, when she has lost her propeller at sea and requires a salvage tow. There are many kinds of salvage operations, varying from those of utmost simplicity to those involving complicated technical studies and procedures which require special equipment, machinery and tools. One of the most important types of operation consists of services to ships which have lost their motive power; *e.g.*, by breakdown of engines, shortage of fuel, etc. The usual salvage service is by towing, sometimes for several thousand miles.

Ordinary Grounding.—The commonest salvage problem is ordinary grounding in which all or part of the grounded ship is above water. It can be simple, difficult or impossible. It is a simple problem if the ship or vessel has run only slightly aground on a mudbank or sand bar except in certain especially dangerous localities, such as the Goodwin sands, where, if the tide is falling, the ship may break her back. It is a difficult problem if grounding occurs on a rock-bound seacoast where wind and tide cause a pounding action which may spring plates or seams, thus opening the ship's interior to serious flooding from the sea. It is often impossible if the grounded vessel is "high and dry," having been lightly loaded when pushed up on the shore by heavy seas at high tide.

The first step in salvaging a ship that has run aground is to obtain the use of tugs. These powerful little vessels may be able to tow the grounded ship back into deep water. Another step is to place the ship's regular anchors, or special salvage anchors known as beach gear or ground tackle, in deep water so that the endangered vessel can hold to them and thus prevent heavy seas from forcing her farther up on the shore. A third method is to keep a strain on a towline while awaiting high tide in the hope that the grounded vessel will come afloat and can be towed away. This simple remedy of "tug and tide" is frequently successful, but when a vessel is hard aground it is usually not possible to move her by the few tons of pull exerted by a towline.

If the tug-and-tide method fails, the next step is usually to lighten ship. This consists of the removal of weight from the vessel to the extent computed to be necessary. The quickest and easiest items to remove are liquids such as water and oil that can be pumped overboard into lighters. If further lightening is required, the cargo may be removed along with, in extreme cases, boats, booms, furniture and anything else that is portable. These items may be transferred to barges alongside by the ship's own cargo-handling equipment or by onshore or floating equipment. Such removal of weight, however, should never be begun until the ship is sufficiently secured to prevent her, in her lightened condition, from being pushed farther ashore by storm and tide. This is a rule that is often violated, with the result that the ship suffers greater damage or may be lost completely.

If the ship has remained generally watertight, the steps outlined above should prove successful. If, however, the vessel has been opened to the sea it is necessary to make temporary repairs of the fractured plates or to isolate the compartments into which sea water is flowing. If the ship is high and dry at low tide the diagnosis and treatment of ailing parts are easy. Temporary repairs, both inside and outside, are made as necessary. For submerged areas, trained divers may estimate damage, do underwater cutting and welding of steel and fit and secure steel or wooden patches. The securing of these patches is usually quite simple because water pressure tends to hold them in place and make them reasonably watertight. At times wooden patches are of the caisson (q.v.) type and are attached to the ship's hull by oakum packing or underwater concrete.

Water is removed from flooded spaces by the use of suction pumps or "push" pumps placed on the deck of the stricken vessel. The suction type of pump is not the best for a large ship because the maximum height to which water can be lifted under perfect operating conditions is only about 30 ft. The push-type pump is not so limited (see PUMP; VACUUM). One push type is the submerged electric pump; another is the deep-well type which has a centrifugal pump at the bottom of a steel pipe and is driven by a steel shaft rotated by an electric motor or gas engine. When enough pumps are operating, the water can be removed from the ship faster than it flows in; and, as the inflow is gradually lessened by repair work, the ship eventually comes afloat.

The use of compressed air to empty a vessel of water is a method which has proven very effective but requires that the structure to be emptied of water be made capable of withstanding the necessary air pressure. To lower the level of water in a compartment submerged 10 ft., for example, would require a pressure of about 5 lb. per square inch (p.s.i.); for 30 ft., it would require about 15 p.s.i., which may cause bursting unless the structure is strengthened. The air compressors required are usually on the salvage tug or the ship's deck or on barges alongside, and are operated by electricity or gas.

With all of the above operations completed a ship may come afloat at high tide. If it does not float, more of the same efforts may bring success. If the ship is aground on a sloping shore, a few additional steps are called for. When a ship is hard aground, or high and dry, it is customary to attempt removing some of the rocks and rough bottom to facilitate sliding the vessel toward deep water. This cutting of a channel is normally done by dredge or, at low tide, by bulldozer.

As noted above, beach gear or ground tackle is often employed to provide means for a strong and steady pull toward deep water. This gear consists of a number of heavy anchors strategically laid out toward deep water, to which chains or wire rope are attached. By using winches on the deck of the ship and tackle with high mechanical advantage, a tremendous pull can be exerted. Then, as the tide comes in, the bow or stern or both are skewed back and forth to break the suction between the ship and the ground and to start the ship moving. If calculations are correct, or the tide is especially favourable, the ship will come afloat.

Sunken and Submerged Ships.—As a result of collisions, explosions or other maritime disasters, vessels are sometimes sunk in deep water. Whether such vessels are salvable depends on the current, sea conditions, depth of water, equipment available, estimated cost and other considerations. Small vessels are salvable in depths up to about 300 ft., but salvage of large vessels in such deep water is rarely practicable. The lift required to bring a sunken vessel to the surface is furnished by such devices as compressed air, floating cranes or pontoons. Trained divers (see DIVING, DEEP-SEA) must do the underwater work on a sunken ship. This may consist of connecting air lines to the ship's fittings, securing lifting chains or wire rope hawsers and girdling the sunken vessel's hull with lifting hawsers. Examples of such salvage operations are some of the vessels raised to clear the Suez canal in 1957 and raising of sunken submarines from time to time. The amount of lift that can be applied by pumping compressed air

into a ship or by lifting hawsers limits the size of the vessel that can be salvaged by these methods.

For salvaging larger ships, lift pontoons are attached directly to the hull or to cables that girdle the hull. The pontoons are large steel cylinders, usually sheathed with wood, and are equipped with heavy shackles and air connections. Usually they are filled with water, sunk and secured alongside the submerged ship. When their water is expelled by compressed air they become buoyant and exert lift. In raising sunken submarines pontoons are arranged in pairs connected by hawsers under the hull. Four or five pairs are usually employed to provide a combined lift of about 700 or 800 tons. A simpler type of pontoon, one not designed for use of compressed air, can be used on the surface where the rise and fall of tide is great enough to permit the wreck to be gradually moved to shallower water during succeeding high tides.

Capsized Ships.—Ordinarily, a ship lying on her side on the bottom must first be brought to an upright position. This is done by pumping air into selected compartments. Another method is to fasten pontoons to the ship, or to wire rope or chain hawsers which pass under the ship, and to exert lift on such hawsers by floating cranes, derricks or winches and tackle on the beach or pier. Raising the giant liner "Normandie," which caught fire and capsized alongside a pier in New York city in 1941, was a good example of this type of operation.

The decision as to which operations apply to a specific salvage problem depends upon study, calculations and experience. The old practice of "cut and try" is usually the rule. Ingenuity is indispensable on a complicated job. Oftentimes it is advisable to concentrate effort toward raising one end of a sunken vessel and then to proceed progressively. This is often requisite when equipment and facilities are limited.

Salvage companies and navies have in readiness well-equipped salvage tugs with crews trained to perform many operations without procuring much of the special equipment referred to above. They also have naval architects who can determine whether a ship will be stable after it is refloated.   (H. N. W.)

SALVARSAN or "606," the trade name of arsphenamine, a remedy for syphilis, was discovered by Paul Ehrlich (q.v.) in 1909. It is a yellow powder, $C_{12}H_{14}As_2Cl_2N_2O_2 \cdot 2H_2O$—the 606th organic arsenical compound tested by Ehrlich and his assistants in their search for an effective drug. Salvarsan was prepared for injection into a vein by a rather complicated process. Later, Ehrlich introduced a modification, "914" or Neosalvarsan, that was much easier to use. Salvarsan was the first successful drug developed out of Ehrlich's concept of chemotherapy (q.v.). It rapidly rendered syphilitic patients noninfectious but did not always bring a complete cure, even after several years' treatment. In some patients the drug had toxic effects on the nervous system, kidneys, or skin. Salvarsan and related arsenicals were replaced in the late 1940s by the antibiotics.   (V. E.; X.)

SALVATION ARMY, THE, a Christian international religious and charitable movement, organized and operated on a military pattern. While the Army has a dual function of church and social agency, its first purpose is the salvation of man "by the power of the Holy Spirit combined with the influence of human ingenuity and love." International headquarters of the organization are located in London, Eng.; national headquarters for the United States are in New York City. Worldwide in scope, the Army is established in nearly 70 countries and colonies, preaching the gospel in about 160 languages in 17,000 evangelical centres, and operating more than 3,000 social welfare institutions, hospitals, schools, and agencies.

HISTORY

Origins.—William Booth, founder of the Salvation Army, an ordained minister in the Methodist New Connexion body in England, left the pulpit of that church in 1861 so that he might be free to become an evangelistic preacher. This step led him, in 1865, to the worst slum areas in the East End of London, where he began his ministry among the poverty-stricken, unchurched masses in Mile End Waste. Booth's first plan was to make his work supplementary to that of the churches, but this proved impractical because many converts did not want to go where they were sent and often were not accepted when they did go; furthermore, Booth soon found that he needed his converts to help handle the great crowds that came to his meetings. Consolidating his activities in Mile End Waste, Booth began to organize the work under the name of the Christian Mission, so that his followers would have a place to worship and an opportunity to become established in their newfound faith. Aware also that needy souls could not be cared for if the body were hungry or in distress, Booth soon inaugurated his social scheme to feed and house even the most depraved so that they might then be spiritually uplifted.

Booth's mission stations soon spread beyond London, and in 1878 the name was changed to the Salvation Army. Designated general, Booth gradually set up his organization on a military pattern which provided a direct line of authority and a system of training personnel. The system of government was autocratic, and unquestioning obedience was required throughout the ranks. A deed poll filed in the court of chancery in August 1878 invested the oversight, direction, and control of the Christian Mission in one person, the general superintendent. This secured William Booth in that office for life and gave him power to appoint his successor as well as complete control of all the property and money of the Army.

In spite of strong opposition from some quarters to the type of evangelism employed by the Salvation Army, the work spread quickly over England, Scotland, and Wales. Booth then committed the Army to a policy of expansion overseas, and pioneering parties were soon sent in different directions, the first reaching the United States in 1880. Steady overseas expansion has continued.

In the adaptation of the work to overseas countries, some modifications were necessary in the Army's system of government; but the general's ultimate control was practically autocratic. This did not go uncriticized, but during the generalship of the founder there was no organized opposition to it. Under the deed poll of 1878, each general was to name his successor under seal, the name of the successor not to be divulged until the death of the incumbent. At an international staff council in 1904, a supplementary deed poll was adopted, the principal object of which was to set up machinery for removing from the position any general proved unfit to carry on his work because of health or other stated reasons; it also provided for the selection of a general by a High Council of the Salvation Army which could be called into being for these purposes should necessity arise.

On the founder's death in August 1912 his eldest son, William Bramwell Booth, formerly the founder's chief of staff, became general with the virtually unanimous approval of the Army. During the 17 years of his generalship, Bramwell Booth gave to the Army a great missionary impulse. He also laid the basic foundations from which sprang the Army's great emphasis on youth programs and activities. In January 1929 the High Council decided to relieve Bramwell Booth on the ground of incapacity. The matter went to the law courts, which confirmed the judgment of the High Council. Edward J. Higgins, chief of staff to Bramwell, was elected to succeed him. This crisis in the history of the Army was the beginning of certain constitutional reforms that led to a more vigorous and democratic international organization. Among these was provision for the regular election of the general (from 1931) by the High Council, consisting of commissioners and other leading officers. Higgins' successors were Evangeline Booth (daughter of William), George Carpenter, Albert Orsborn, Wilfred Kitching, and Frederick Coutts.

A further development in Salvation Army government came in 1947 when an Advisory Council to the General was constituted, at international headquarters, London. The council consists of senior officers in regular session and makes reports, etc., on matters that call for the general's decision. After 1947, conferences of the commissioners responsible for the work in all parts of the world were convened periodically in London, and international congresses brought together officers and soldiers to consider various aspects of Army activity and to devise new methods and means of extending the movement's influence. Rapid travel by sea and air enabling the general to maintain close personal contact with the Army's leaders and work, and a college for officers established in 1950 and attended by future leaders from all countries, still further strengthened the internationalism of the movement. Symbolic of the spirit of unity which withstood the disruption and shock of World War II and which gives the Army a unique place in the world is the International Headquarters building in London, opened in 1963, to which every Salvation Army territory in the world contributed.

United States.—The Army's life in the United States may be divided into three periods of development: 1880 to 1904, the formative era of struggle, hardship, and rapid growth; 1904 to 1934, a period of further expansion and gradual, then mass, acceptance following World War I; 1934 and after, a period of broader integration of the Salvation Army with other national fund-raising agencies, along with wider recognition and acceptance of Army personnel and program among religious and social welfare organizations.

The Army was introduced into America in 1879, when a family of English Salvationists emigrated to Philadelphia and began to conduct evangelical services. They appealed to William Booth for officers, and Commissioner George Scott Railton, with a group of pioneer officers, was sent to officially open Army work in March 1880. The first headquarters were established in Philadelphia, and in spite of opposition—sometimes from city authorities and some Christians who opposed the Army's street meetings and unorthodox methods of spreading the gospel, and sometimes from rowdies and roughs objecting to the invasion of saloons and public houses—the work advanced rapidly. As the Army gradually became established, opposition subsided and passive acceptance of the work became general.

During these early years two schisms shook the international unity of the Army. In October 1884 Maj. T. E. Moore, in violation of orders, sought to establish the incorporation of the Salvation Army in the United States independent of General Booth. Removed from office, Moore established the American Salvation Army, which, deprived of the leadership of Booth and the Army's international kinship, gradually declined and was disbanded in 1889. In January 1896 Ballington Booth, son of the general and national commander in the United States, was appointed to another post, and when, in spite of public protest and Army appeal, the order was not rescinded, he resigned from the Army and set up a similar organization called the Volunteers of America (q.v.).

Evangeline Booth was national leader in the United States from 1904 until her election as general in 1934, and under her leadership the Army gave attention to internal study and development as well as to the improvement of personnel and program within the organization. In World Wars I and II the Salvation Army enlarged its services and personnel to serve the armed forces; Salvation Army officers also served as chaplains.

The work of the Salvation Army in the United States includes treatment centres aiding 56,000 men annually; maternity homes and hospitals, annually providing service for 18,000 hospital patients and 10,000 unmarried mothers; camps, providing camping experience for 16,000 children each year; boys' and girls' clubs and community recreation centres; Salvation Army–United Service Organizations (USO) and Red Shield clubs for servicemen; mobile canteens; hotels and lodges for men and women; nurseries and settlements; missing persons' bureaus; care for alcoholics; correctional service bureaus working with prisoners and their families; community centres for persons of all ages; and other allied services. All services are given without respect to race, colour, creed, or condition; the work is financed through voluntary subscriptions, participation in federated funds or like groups, and annual maintenance appeals.

The Salvation Army participates in national and international conferences in the social welfare field and is also one of the nongovernmental organizations with consultative status to the Economic and Social Council of the United Nations.

Later History.—International activities of the Army throughout the world are still directed from London, the birthplace of the movement. Its ability to react speedily to local need is largely due to the effective coordination of administration at the international headquarters, and this has enabled the Army to make a major contribution to solving the problems of displaced persons, famine, and rehabilitation which followed World War II and subsequent national upheavals.

While pursuing its primary aim of preaching the Christian gospel, the Army has placed a new emphasis on educational and medical services in the less-developed countries. In Africa and India hundreds of Salvation Army schools are making provision for thousands of students who, with the spiritual guidance of Salvationists, are preparing themselves for future responsibility. At the same time doctors at an increasing number of Army hospitals and dispensaries are breaking through local prejudice to bring modern medicine and surgery to the relief of suffering and disease. In a world which is advancing to a deeper appreciation of social responsibility, the Army in Australia, New Zealand, Canada, and the United States is following the pattern laid down in Great Britain in making extensive provision for the aged, the homeless, and children in need of care and attention. The Army's internationalism binds together men and women of all classes and colours in a Christian, nonpolitical, worldwide community.

POLITY, WORSHIP AND DOCTRINE

Polity.—Administratively, the Salvation Army is under the command of a general, with appointed leaders in charge of 50 territorial and departmental commands of which about half encompass work in missionary lands and subsidized areas. The unit of the Army is the corps, commanded by an officer—with rank ranging from lieutenant to brigadier—who is responsible to a divisional headquarters. The work of the 45 divisions in the United States is under the supervision of divisional commanders. Divisions are grouped into four territories (regions)—Eastern, Central, Southern, and Western—with headquarters respectively in New York City, Chicago, Atlanta, and San Francisco. This same plan of organization is followed throughout the international Army, and in each territory (except in the U.S.; usually a separate country) a territorial commander is in charge with department leaders appointed to facilitate supervision and direction of all phases of the work.

Internationally, the general is the official representative and spokesman for the Army. In determining the organization's stand on matters of controversy, the general is assisted by the Advisory Council, which meets at stated intervals, as well as by the Conference of Commissioners, which is called periodically. Within the U.S., the national commander is the chief representative and administrative officer, official spokesman, and president of the Salvation Army Corporation established under the laws of New York, as well as of local corporations in a number of other states. Property and revenues are in the custody of a board of trustees or directors, and citizens' advisory boards, recruited by the Army, assist in promoting the Army's work and in public relations.

Within the structure of the Army, converts who desire to become soldiers (members) are required to sign Articles of War (pledge of membership), after which, as members, they give volunteer service to Army work. The function of officers is similar to that of ministers of other Protestant churches, and officers are commissioned to full-time service. Basic training for each officer, regardless of his work within the Army—evangelical or social welfare—is a two-year in-residence course at one of the schools for officers' training. Chief source of officer-candidates is the Salvation Army corps. After graduation from training school, each officer must continue, under supervision of qualified personnel, a five-year plan of advanced studies.

Although the Salvation Army corps performs the same basic function as the parish church does, the corps is essentially the local unit of an army whose demands—including abstention from alcohol and tobacco and rendering active Christian service—are still among the most stringent imposed upon any Christian. The parallels between Army and church terminology indicate the meaning of terms used throughout the former: the general corresponds to the head of the church; commanding officer to minister and priest; commissioning to ordination; Orders and Regulations to codes of discipline; and doctrines correspond to orders of faith.

Worship.—The simple structure of Salvation Army worship services has evolved from the determination of early officers to conduct services that would attract and hold converts largely from among poor, ignorant, unchurched, working-class people, whose greatest need was to understand clearly the power of God in their lives. William Booth was of the conviction that the sacraments were not in any way necessary to the salvation of the soul and in many instances would be a hindrance to his converts rather than a help. Church formality frightened the early converts, and Booth therefore sought to bring into his worship services an informal atmosphere that would put them at ease. Joyous singing, instrumental music, clapping of hands, personal testimony, free prayer, and an open invitation to repentance characterized the worship services. Modern services are perhaps more moderate in outward characteristics, but the same pattern is followed and the same lively spirit demonstrated. Ceremonies for enrollment of soldiers and dedication of children are comparable to acceptance into church membership and child baptism. The Lord's Supper is not observed.

Doctrine.—The motivating force of the Salvation Army in all its work is the religious faith of its officers and soldiers, and the fundamental doctrines of the organizations are stated in its Foundation Deed of 1878 in 11 cardinal affirmations. These doctrines affirm the Army recognition of the Bible as the only rule of Christian faith and practice; of God, who is the Creator and Father of all mankind; of the Trinity of Father, Son, and Holy Ghost; of Jesus Christ as the Son of God and Son of man; of sin as the great destroyer of man's soul and society; of salvation as God's remedy for man's sin and man's ultimate and eternal hope made available through Christ; of sanctification as the individual's present and maturing experience of a life set apart for the holy purposes of the Kingdom of God; and of an eternal destiny that may triumph over sin and death. As affirmations of Christian truth, these doctrines are the creed of the Salvation Army, and to those who accept them they are self-evident.

Undoubtedly William Booth's early training in the Wesleyan Methodist Church influenced the doctrinal position of the Army, but in actuality the statement of faith included the basic principles common to most Protestant evangelical denominations and ignored the controversial issues that might cause factionalism and interdenominational strife.

Distinctive Aspects.—That which preeminently sets the Salvation Army apart from other denominations is its methods and practices in the realistic presentation of religion and its use of various constraining means to bring people to salvation. Not content with reaching only those who attend indoor services, the Army regularly proclaims the gospel on the streets. Salvation Army music is also distinctive. From its primitive musical aggregations, the Army has evolved networks of music camps, institutes, and bandmasters' training courses and its many well-trained bands not only enhance Army worship services but also carry a spiritual message through the ministry of music to churches, hospitals, schools, and civic gatherings.

In maintaining its original character as a body of spiritual witnesses and aggressive evangelism, the Army continues to stress the need for conversion, preceded by penitence and followed by growth in holiness. In the series of Orders and Regulations for officers, local officers (laymen), and soldiers, definite guidance is given in all areas of everyday conduct.

Salvation Army marriages are solemnized "under the flag" and children are dedicated to become soldiers or officers in the "war." The distinctive uniform of the Salvationist, both officer and soldier, is worn "as an outward and visible sign of an inward and spiritual grace." Another of the great principles of the Army, firmly adhered to, is that women have absolute parity of privilege, position, and dignity with men.

In its worldwide activities, the Salvation Army publishes nearly 140 periodicals with 2,000,000 copies per issue. The weekly *War Cry* is the official organ, and reports and statistics of the spiritual and social operations of the Army internationally are published annually in *The Salvation Army Year Book*.

BIBLIOGRAPHY.—*Salvationist writers:* William Booth, *Orders and*

Regulations for Field Officers, rev. ed. (1925), *Orders and Regulations for Soldiers,* rev. ed. (1943), *In Darkest England and the Way Out* (1890); Charles Péan, *The Conquest of Devil's Island* (1953); Robert Sandall, *The History of The Salvation Army,* 3 vol. (1955); Albert Orsborn, *House of My Pilgrimage* (1958); Bernard Watson, *A Hundred Years' War* (1965); *The Salvation Army Year Book* (published yearly since 1905 by Salvationist Publishing and Supplies).

Non-Salvationist writers: H. Begbie, *Life of General William Booth,* 2 vol. (1920); Clarence W. Hall, *Samuel Logan Brengle: Portrait of a Prophet* (1933); St. John Ervine, *God's Soldier: General William Booth,* 2 vol. (1934); P. W. Wilson, *General Evangeline Booth* (1948); Harold C. Steele, *I Was a Stranger: the Faith of William Booth* (1954); Herbert A. Wisbey, Jr., *Soldiers Without Swords: a History of The Salvation Army in the United States* (1955); R. Collier, *The General Next to God* (1965). (J. Gr.)

SALVI, NICCOLÒ (Nicola) (1697–1751), Italian sculptor, whose masterpiece is the Trevi Fountain in Rome, was born in 1697 at Rome. He began in the studio of the painter Niccolò Ricciolini and subsequently studied architecture under Antonio Canevari. In 1732 he competed unsuccessfully for the facade of S. Giovanni in Laterano, Rome, but in the same year his project for the Trevi Fountain was chosen in preference to those of a great number of competitors. Most of his energy was absorbed by the work; he was responsible not only for the overall design but also for the details of the decoration and the program of the statuary. After Salvi's death Giuseppe Pannini finished the fountain in 1762, somewhat altering the original scheme. The idea of combining palace front and fountain was derived from a project by Pietro de Cortona, but the grand pageantry of the central triumphal arch with its mythological and allegorical figures, of the natural rock formations, and of the gushing water was Salvi's. This queen of fountains is the swan song of the Roman Baroque era. Salvi also executed minor works in churches and has the doubtful merit (with Luigi Vanvitelli) of having enlarged G. L. Bernini's Palazzo Odescalchi. He died in 1751. (Rf. W.)

SALVIA, a large genus belonging to the mint family, and containing about 550 species in the temperate and warmer regions of both hemispheres. The name is derived from the Latin *salvo,* from the healing properties of the garden sage, *S. officinalis,* which has been known for at least three centuries and which has been cultivated in kitchen gardens for the grayish-green wrinkled leaves that are commonly used in flavouring meats.

Many native species of *Salvia* occur in western North America, especially in California, where 15 species are found. Among these are *S. carduacea* (thistle sage), cultivated for its thistlelike, white woolly foliage and blue flowers; *S. columbariae* and related, mostly Mexican, species are the source of chia. *S. verbenaca* is found in Great Britain in dry pastures and waste places, as is also *S. pratensis.*

Some California sages are important bee plants, among them the black sage (*S. mellifera*) and the bigflower sage (*S. grandiflora*). Some of the salvias are among the most showy of softwooded plants, the blossoms being of a bright glowing scarlet. A useful species is *S. splendens,* a Brazilian shrub, commonly called scarlet sage. Treated as a tender annual, it is one of the most popular bedding plants in American gardens. There are other very ornamental species of easy growth, increased by cuttings in spring, and succeeding well in ordinary rich loamy soil.

SALWEEN (Chinese Nu Chiang or Lu Chiang; Thai Mae Nam Khong), a river of Asia which rises in the Tibetan Plateau and flows east and then south through the Chinese province of Yünnan, entering Burma just south of latitude 24° N. In its lower course the river forms the frontier between Burma and Thailand for about 80 mi., but a longer stretch of this border follows the Thaungyin River, a minor tributary. The Salween is 1,500 mi. (2,414 km.) long. In its upper course it has a very narrow watershed, and for nearly 600 mi. until it leaves Yünnan it parallels the Mekong, in places at a distance of as little as 20 mi. In this narrow section between high ranges (over 15,000 ft. [4,572 m.]) the valley, lying more than 6,000 ft. (1,829 m.) above sea level, is little settled, but the population is more numerous in the comparatively open, though still exceedingly rugged, plateau lands of southwest Yünnan, which continues into the Shan states of Burma. Even there, however, settlement keeps to the more healthful higher basins and spurs, avoiding the river's deep, narrow gorge. Where the Salween enters Burma it is 2,000 ft. above sea level and the crest of the ridges forming its watershed frequently rises above 6,000 ft. and in places reaches more than 9,000 ft. Every few miles there are ferries but the valley itself is remarkably devoid of settlement except where larger tributaries make transverse communication easier, as at Kunlong at the confluence of the Salween and the Nam Ting.

The Salween occupies an almost continuous gorge to within 70 mi. of the sea, with many rapids and shoals. Consequently the river is practically useless for navigation by power craft except in those last 70 mi., though it is used by native boats in many sections and is of some value for floating down teak and bamboo from the Shan states to Moulmein. In the lower, navigable course there are many islands and the river crosses obliquely a number of open valleys trending northwest-southeast where settlement is fairly dense. Among several large villages and townships that stand on the riverbank are Kamamaung, Shwegun (a steamer terminus), and Pa-an. At Moulmein the Salween cuts through the last hill ridge to enter the Gulf of Martaban of the Andaman Sea by two estuaries encumbered with sand and mud banks. Bilugyun Island at the mouth of the river separates the bifurcating estuary and has as its core an outlying hill ridge. The southern estuary is the more important and is used by ocean-going shipping calling at Moulmein. The river is tidal for about 50 mi. from the sea, to a point between Pa-an and Shwegun.

The weather pattern of the Salween region is monsoonal, and there is sometimes a 90-ft. (27 m.) range between low water and flood in narrow gorges. High water in the Salween causes flooding in the lowlands behind Moulmein, as the main stream holds back the waters of the Gyaing and the other left-bank tributaries. Hydroelectric power has been developed on the Nam Pilu, a right-bank tributary of the Salween (via the Nam Pawn). A potentially promising site for a multi-purpose scheme involving development of power, irrigation, and navigation is at Salween rapids, immediately before the river leaves its gorge. If the rapids in this part of the river were flooded by a dam, power boats might penetrate a long way upstream, perhaps as far as Kunlong.

(B. L. C. J.)

SALZBURG, a *Bundesland* (federal state) of the Republic of Austria (*q.v.*). Area 2,762 sq.mi. (7,155 sq.km.). Pop. (1961) 347,292.

Physical Geography.—The *Land,* stretching from the headwaters of the Mur River south of the main crest of the Alps northward into the Northern Alpine foreland, shares in two of Austria's main physical regions: the Alps and, to a lesser extent, the Alpine foreland. Nine-tenths of Salzburg belongs to the Alps. The area south of the trough followed by the upper Salzach and upper Enns rivers is part of the Central Alps. North of the trough are moderately high mountains, part of the Kitzbühler Alpen. Farther north are the Salzburg Limestone Alps with karst features including caves, notably the Tennengebirge ice caves. The Flysch Mountains north and east of Salzburg City are in the Salzkammergut (*q.v.*). The Alpine foreland consists of the Salzburg Basin, divided into glacial tongue basins with small lakes or bogs and moraine hills.

The climate varies greatly, proximity to the mountains producing high rainfall in the Alpine foreland (more than 39 in. [1,000 mm.]). On the mountains rainfall exceeds 59 in. annually. The Lungau (basin of the Mur headwaters) suffers in the winter from temperature inversions and has the lowest rainfall (below 28 in.). On the Sonnblick (10,187 ft. [3,105 m.]) is a meteorological observatory.

History.—Numerous rich finds from the Neolithic Period onward have been made. Because of mineral resources there were prehistoric settlements in the mountains as well as in the foreland. Copper mining (near Bischofshofen) in the Bronze Age and salt mining (Dürrnberg near Hallein) in the Iron Age were important for the whole of central Europe. The area was settled by Celts in the later Iron Age and in 15 B.C. came under the Romans. Juvavum (Salzburg City) was made a *municipium* about A.D. 50, and the country was crossed by a major road. In the 5th century the area was invaded by the Teutons and then settled by the

Baivarii, except for the Lungau where the Celto-Romans were succeeded by subsequently Germanized Slavs.

The growth of Salzburg politically was initiated by grants of land in the 8th century by the duke of Bavaria to the bishop, its elevation to an archbishopric in 797, and subsequent acquisition of territory in the 13th century. At this time Salzburg was a buffer state between Bavaria and Austria. In 1278 Rudolph I acknowledged the archbishop as a territorial ruler. The prince-archbishopric reached its greatest extent about 1400, stretching not only into present-day Bavaria, Tirol, and Carinthia (Kärnten), but including also enclaves in what is now Yugoslavia. Many of the inhabitants became Protestants, and in 1731–32 Archbishop Firmian forced about 20,000 of them to emigrate, most going to East Prussia. Salzburg lost some of its possessions, but when it was secularized in 1803 its territory was still larger than the present *Land*. From the 17th century the archbishop has had the honorary title Primus Germania, and since 1184 he has been entitled to wear a cardinal's purple. Until 1951 he retained the status and title of prince. After 1803 Salzburg was an independent electorate and then changed hands between Austria, France, and Bavaria until in 1816 it became permanently part of Austria but lost some territory. It was an administrative district of Oberösterreich until 1850 when it became a duchy and Habsburg crownland. In 1918 it became a *Bundesland* and during the *Anschluss* (1938–45) it was a *Reichsgau* of Greater Germany. It again became a *Bundesland* in 1945.

Population.—Although the *Land* has shown a large increase in population since World War II, its population density per square mile is, except for Tirol, the lowest in Austria. Ethnically Salzburg is German, the dialect spoken belonging to the Bavarian group. Nearly 90% of the inhabitants are Roman Catholic, and Protestants form nearly 9%. The ecclesiastical province includes also Vorarlberg, Tirol, Carinthia, and Steiermark.

The principal towns (pop. 1961) are: Salzburg, the capital (*q.v.*; 108,114), Hallein (13,329), Saalfelden (8,901), Bischofshofen (8,287), Zell am See (6,455), St. Johann im Pongau (5,777), and Badgastein (5,742). Radstadt is a medieval town still enclosed by walls. Apart from some large villages in the lower areas, rural settlement consists mainly of hamlets and isolated farms. About three-quarters of the farms are larger than 12 ac. (5 ha.) but are mainly classified as mountain farms because of their inaccessibility.

Administration and Social Conditions.—Matters not reserved by the constitution for the federal government are dealt with by the *Bundesland* government, consisting of the governor and six ministers elected by and responsible to the provincial legislature (*Landtag*), which has 32 members elected for five years by popular vote. The *Landtag* is a legislative body, but its acts must be approved by the federal government. In the *Bundesrat* (upper house of the federal legislature) Salzburg has three votes. It is divided into six administrative districts (*Bezirke*). Local government is in the hands of burgomasters and town and commune councils elected by popular vote.

The Economy.—Half the land surface is used for farming and one-third for forestry, the most important arable areas being in the northern, low-lying parts, with rye and wheat as the leading crops. This is the only fruit-growing area. Elsewhere farming is almost entirely devoted to cattle rearing and dairy farming on meadows and summer pasture. There is horse breeding (of a heavy-type horse) in the Pinzgau. The forests of the Alpine foreland are 52% Austrian state-owned and 5% Bavarian, nine-tenths consisting of conifers. The annual timber yield exceeds 35,300,000 cu.ft. of which about two-thirds is used in industry. Timber, timber products, and paper form 70% of Salzburg's total exports.

Hunting for game (hares, roe and red deer, chamois) and fishing are strictly controlled, the licences providing much revenue.

Salt and copper are still the most important mineral resources. Brine from Dürrnberg is used in chemical plants as well as in the evaporation plant at Hallein. Copper is mined at Mitterberg near Bischofshofen (the smelting is done at Brixlegg in Tirol). The aluminum plant at Lend (based on imported raw material) is the

second largest in Austria. Magnesite is mined at Leogang. Large reservoirs in the Tauern valleys are used for electric power stations, including the large one at Kaprun. The *Land* produces 10% of Austria's electricity. The heaviest industrial concentration is in the Salzburg Basin and apart from large breweries consists of medium-size enterprises (food processing, light manufacturing, textiles, clothing, leather, organ building). The tourist trade (including winter sports) is a major industry, the main centres being Salzburg City, Badgastein, and Zell am See.

Trade and Communications.—The area has been commercially important since copper was traded in the Bronze Age and salt in the Early Iron Age. The Roman Juvavum was the focal point of three major roads, one of which crossed the Radstädter Tauern Pass. Other crossings were used for trade with Italy. The salt trade was revived in the Middle Ages when the Salzach was an important waterway. Salzburg was again favoured by the coming of the railways, Austria's major line linking at Salzburg City with the line from the Hook of Holland which continues via the Tauern Tunnel to Villach and Belgrade. The Grossglockner Hochalpenstrasse mainly serves tourist traffic, but the *Autobahn* from Munich to Vienna, which runs north of Salzburg City, is of great commercial importance.

BIBLIOGRAPHY.—W. Del-Negro, *Geologie von Salzburg* (1950); E. Lendl (ed.), *Salzburg Atlas* (1955); E. Seefeldner, *Salzburg und seine Landschaften* (1961); H. Widmann, *Geschichte Salzburgs*, 3 vol. (1907–14); F. Martin, *Kleine Landesgeschichte von Salzburg* (1949); *Mitteilungen der Gesellschaft für Salzburger Landeskunde* (1861–); H. Jahn, *Salzburg and the Salzkammergut* (1958). (K. A. S.)

SALZBURG, a city, archbishopric, and capital of the *Bundesland* of Salzburg, Aus. It lies on the Salzach River in the northern foothills of the Alps at 1,391 ft. (424 m.) and is 192 mi. (309 km.) WSW of Vienna and 75 mi. (121 km.) SE of Munich, Ger., by road. Pop. (1961) 108,114. The celebrated traveler and geographer Humboldt described Salzburg as one of the three most beautiful towns in the world, a description due, perhaps, to its unique combination of scenic and architectural beauty. Little remains of the medieval period because of the later building activities of the prince-archbishops (*see* SALZBURG *Bundesland* above). The city's chief glories are the episcopal buildings and burghers' houses, Italian influence on the architecture leading to Salzburg's designation as the "German Rome."

The Salzach separates the older town on the left bank, overlooked by the Mönchsberg, from the newer quarters on the right bank, above which rises the Kapuzinerberg. The Untersberg (6,473 ft.) dominates the basin to the southwest, and the Gaisberg (4,226 ft.) to the east. In the centre of the older town is the spacious Residenzplatz with the Residenz (1595–1619) in the style of a Renaissance Roman palace. The facade was altered in 1710, and the northwest wing added in 1788–92. The Baroque state apartments have frescoes by Johann Michael Rottmayr and M. Altomonte. Opposite is the Neugebäude (1592–1602, enlarged about 1670) with a carillon (1702) in its tower. The cathedral on the south side of the square was built (1614–28) by Santino Solari at the instigation of Archbishop Wolf Dietrich, on the site of an earlier basilica. It was the first church in the Italian style to be built on German soil. The facade is of white and rose Untersberg marble, and the interior holds 10,500 people. Following bomb damage in World War II, new bronze doors were added in 1958.

Southwest of the cathedral is the Benedictine Abbey of St. Peter, founded by St. Rupert about 696 and the nucleus of the city. The 12th-century abbey church was remodeled in the rococo style in the 18th century. Within are a Romanesque portal (1240) and the tomb of St. Rupert. The adjoining cemetery is surrounded by arcades containing vaults built into the Mönchsberg. North of the abbey is the Franciscan church with a dark Romanesque nave, a 15th-century Gothic choir with delicate fan vaulting, and a Baroque high altar (1709). Also built into the cliff of the Mönchsberg are the various buildings forming the Festspielhaus (*see* below). In the Universitätsplatz, west of the Residenz, is the university, originally founded in 1623 and reestablished in 1964. East of the square, where a street market is held, is the Kollegien-Kirche, a masterpiece of J. B. Fischer von Erlach, built

1694–1707, with altar paintings by Rottmayr. Narrow passages lead from the Universitätsplatz north to the Getreidegasse, where Mozart was born in house no. 9, now a museum.

The great fortress of Hohensalzburg, crowning the southeast summit of the Mönchsberg, was founded in 1077 and altered to its present form about 1500. St. Georgs-Kirche (1501), in the main courtyard, has Gothic reliefs of the twelve apostles in red marble. The Mönchsberg (1,667 ft.) is a partly wooded ridge with shady paths and scenic views. To the east of the fortress is the Nonnberg, a Benedictine nunnery founded by St. Rupert and probably the oldest nunnery in existence. The church is late Gothic but has remains of an earlier building and Romanesque frescoes (1150).

The quarters on the right bank of the Salzach are reached by the Staatsbrücke, which leads to the Linzer Gasse, on the left of which is the St. Sebastianskirche, built in 1505–12 and remodeled in the 18th century. In the churchyard are the Gabriels-Kapelle, built in 1597–1603 as a mausoleum for Wolf Dietrich, the tomb of Paracelsus, and the graves of Mozart's wife Constanze and of Leopold Mozart. The Landestheater (1892) is in Makartplatz opposite the Dreifaltigkeitskirche (1694–1702), a beautifully proportioned building by J. B. Fischer von Erlach. Nearby is the Mozarteum (1910–14) comprising a music academy, concert halls, and the Mozart archives. Schloss Mirabell was originally built by Wolf Dietrich in 1606 for his mistress Salome Alt and remodeled in the high Baroque style in 1721–27. The splendid marble staircase is by Georg Raphael Donner. It has a fine Baroque landscape garden and a park. To the northeast of the city rises the wooded Kapuzinerberg (2,093 ft.) with a Capuchin friary (1599–1602).

South of the Mönchsberg is Schloss Leopoldskron (1736), with an outstanding rococo interior, once the home of Max Reinhardt and now the seat of the Salzburg Seminar in American Studies. Schloss Hellbrunn, to the south of the city, was built as a pleasure palace and garden by Santino Solari for the Prince-Archbishop Markus Sitticus in 1613–15. The Baroque garden, the oldest of its kind north of the Alps, contains an open-air theatre, statues, fountains, grottoes, and mechanical devices that spray the unsuspecting onlooker.

The Abbey of St. Peter and the Nonnberg were founded about 696 on the site of the Roman commercial centre of Juvavum. In 739 Salzburg was made a bishopric by St. Boniface and in 798 it was raised to an archbishopric. From this time the history of Salzburg (first mentioned under this name in 755) is the history of its archbishops, later prince-archbishops. The most notable of these princes were Leonhard von Keutschach (1495–1519), Wolf Dietrich von Raitenau (1587–1612), Markus Sitticus (1612–19), Paris Lodron (1619–53), Johann Ernest, Count Thun (1687–1709), and Leopold Anton von Firmian (1727–44).

Salzburg has been for many centuries a music centre. The monks of St. Peter's Abbey were famous for their church music long before Mozart was born in Salzburg in 1756, and the Salzburg Antiphony dates from the 11th century. The first Italian opera produced north of the Alps was given in the Steinernes Theater at Hellbrunn in 1619. The International Mozarteum Foundation was established in 1880. There were music festivals at irregular intervals throughout the 19th century, and in 1917 Hugo von Hofmannsthal, Richard Strauss, and Max Reinhardt formed the Festspielhausgemeinde. Hofmannsthal's *Jedermann*, based on the English morality play *Everyman*, was performed in the Domplatz on the cathedral steps in 1920, and two years later the first opera was presented. The annual festival comprises recitals, concerts of orchestral and chamber music, church music, opera, and drama as well as the presentation of *Jedermann*. The Festspielhaus, converted from the court stables, consists of the Felsenreitschule (1693) for open-air performances, two large indoor opera houses (1926, 1960), and the Winter Riding School, with a ceiling painting by Rottmayr (1690), used as a reception hall.

Salzburg is the northwestern gateway to Austria and an important road and rail junction. It is on the Munich–Vienna, Paris–Vienna, and Munich–Klagenfurt railways. The *Autobahn*

from Munich to Vienna skirts the town. There is an international airport at Maxglan. Salzburg is one of the chief tourist resorts of Austria. Its convention building (1956) attracts international conferences. Manufactures include musical instruments and hardware. The town was the headquarters of the U.S. forces in Austria from 1945 to 1956.

BIBLIOGRAPHY.—F. Fuhrmann, *Salzburger Kunstblätter* (1956); F. Martin, *Salzburg* (1954); W. Schneditz, *Salzburger Festspielbuch* (1958). (H. H. RE.)

SALZGITTER, a city of West Germany in the *Land* (state) of Lower Saxony, Federal Republic of Germany, lies 19 mi. (30 km.) SSW of Brunswick by road. Pop. (1961) 110,276. The municipality covers 82 sq.mi., being the result of the administrative merging and development of the old town of Salzgitter (now Salzgitter-Bad) and 28 adjoining villages.

Salzgitter is situated in the foothills of the Harz Mountains, rising in a ridge in the southwest to about 800 ft. (244 m.) above sea level. About 60% of the land in the municipal area is agricultural (wheat, sugar beet, grazing), 14% woodland, and 10% industrial. The area covers the largest deposit of iron ore in Germany, and iron has been smelted in the vicinity since about the time of Christ. The old town of Salzgitter was an important market for salt and produce in the Middle Ages and, together with the surrounding villages, was first mentioned in documents in about 1000, although there is evidence of settlement in antiquity.

As a result of the German policy of autarchy before World War II, the Hermann Göring Reich Company for Ore Mining and Iron Smelting was established in 1937. To bring these activities into a single administrative district, the existing municipality was created in 1942 and was until 1951 known as Watenstedt-Salzgitter. Watenstedt was chosen as the centre for the preparation of the ore and for the metallurgical works, and from the adjacent northeastern district of Hallendorf a branch canal 11 mi. long was made to the Mittelland Canal for the transport of Ruhr coal. In 1938–40 and after World War II the districts of Lebenstedt, Salzgitter-Bad, Thiede, Gebhardshagen, and Hallendorf were built up as modern residential estates. The iron ore is mined around the Salzgitter ridge and Salzgitter-Bad. The iron content of the ore is comparatively low. In addition to coking plants, blast furnaces, steel furnaces, and rolling mills, the industries include the production of railway coaches and wagons, trucks, radio and television sets, and beet sugar, canned food, textiles, and pharmaceuticals. Salzgitter-Bad is a recognized spa with an invigorating brine spring. The district of Lebenstedt in the north has the largest population and is the seat of the municipal administration. Salzgitter is linked by railway with Brunswick, Goslar, Hildesheim, and other centres and is skirted westward by the Hamburg-Frankfurt am Main motorway. (E. H. FR.)

SALZKAMMERGUT, a region comprising parts of the Austrian *Länder* Upper Austria (Oberösterreich), Styria (Steiermark), and Salzburg. It consists mainly of the Traun River Basin, and is renowned for its varied and beautiful mountain and lake scenery, often called the Austrian "Lake District." There are about 30 lakes; among them are the Atter, Traun, Mond, Aber (Wolfgang), and Hallstätter lakes. The highest mountains are the Dachstein massif in the south, rising to 9,826 ft. (2,995 m.). Together with the Totes Gebirge (Dead Mountains; 8,268 ft. [2,520 m.]) and the Warscheneck, they are formed of Triassic limestone.

The district owes its name (literally "salt exchequer property") to the salt deposits at Hallstatt, Bad Ischl, and Bad Aussee, which have been mined since the Iron Age (*see* HALLSTATT). Evaporation plants are worked at the three original centres and at Ebensee and Gmunden. The region produces half the total salt of Austria. Forestry is important; timber is used both for constructional purposes and as raw material for factories (paper, man-made fibres). There is also cattle breeding and dairy farming, production of hydroelectricity (Lake Gosau), and manufacture of cement and ceramics (Gmunden), but the most important source of income is the tourist trade. The main health and holiday resorts are Gmunden (pop. [1961] 12,518), Bad Ischl, Bad Aussee, and

Sankt Wolfgang. The region is served by a branch of the West-bahn railway, and the Salzburg-Vienna motorway, touching the Mond and Atter lakes, gives easy access by road.   (K. A. S.)

SAM'AL; see ZINCIRLI HUYUK.

SAMANÁ, a province in northeastern Dominican Republic. Area 382 sq.mi., pop. (1960) 44,592. It occupies the mountain-ous (to 1,673 ft.) Samaná Peninsula, the delta region of the Yuna River, and a large part of the northeastern coastal plain. It is a rich coconut region, a leading rice producer from reclaimed marshlands, and a significant producer of cacao, corn, and tropical hardwood. The province was created in 1908 from El Seibo Prov-ince. The capital, Santa Bárbara de Samaná (pop. [1960] 3,309), was founded in 1756 by Spaniards from the Canary Islands, and in 1825 there was a notable influx of Negro immigrants from the U.S. Sánchez is a railroad terminus and port.

SAMANÁ BAY, which is bounded on the north by the Samaná Peninsula is approximately 40 mi. long and 15 mi. wide, with deep water and well-protected anchorages, and is one of the finest nat-ural harbours in the West Indies. Apart from its importance as a fishing and tourist site, it is used relatively little for commerce. However, the bay's location, on the Mona Passage between the Atlantic and the Caribbean, makes it potentially important strate-gically. Two treaties, one leasing the bay to the United States and the other providing for the annexation of the Dominican Republic were signed in 1869, but both agreements were de-feated by opposition in the U.S. Senate when it was learned that U.S. speculators were promoting the annexation in the hope of profiting by concessions in the Samaná region.

(D. G. Mo.; D. R. D.)

SAMANIDS, the first great native dynasty which arose in Persia after the Arab conquest. In the 8th century Saman Khudat, a Persian noble of Balkh, who was a close friend of the Arab governor of Khurasan, Asad ibn 'Abdullah, was converted from Zoroastrianism to Islam. His son Asad, named after Asad ibn 'Abdullah, had four sons who rendered distinguished service to the caliph al-Ma'mun. In return they all received provinces: Nuh obtained Samarkand; Ahmad, Fergana; Yahya, Shash; and Ilyas, Herat. In 875 Ahmad's son Nasr was recognized by the caliph al-Mu'tamid as governor of Transoxiana. He was succeeded in 892 by his brother Ismail, who overthrew the Saf-farids (q.v.) in Khurasan and the Zaidites of Tabaristan (Ma-zanderan) and thus, though remaining nominally a provincial governor under the caliph of Baghdad, established an almost in-dependent rule over Transoxiana and eastern Persia, with Bukhara as his capital.

The descendants and successors of Ismail, almost all renowned for the impulse that they gave both to the patriotic feelings and the national poetry of modern Persia (see PERSIAN LITERATURE), were Ahmad ibn Ismail (907–913); Nasr II, ibn Ahmad (913–943), the patron and friend of the great poet Rudaki; Nuh I, ibn Nasr (943–954); 'Abd ul-Malik I, ibn Nuh (954–961); Man-sur I, ibn Nuh (961–976), whose vizier Bal'ami translated Tabari's universal history into Persian; Nuh II, ibn Mansur (976–997), whose court poet Daqiqi began the Shah-nama; Mansur II, ibn Nuh (997–999); and 'Abd ul-Malik II, ibn Nuh (999).

Under their government, which was organized on a loosely cen-tralized feudal system, the provinces of Transoxiana and Khurasan attained a high degree of prosperity. The expansion of their in-dustry and commerce is attested by the use of Samanid silver coins as currency all over the north of Asia. The later interrup-tion of the northern trade routes was a factor in weakening the dynasty; and it succumbed eventually to the internal feuds and rivalries of the nobles and to the pressure of the rising Turkish powers in central Asia and Afghanistan.

Under Mansur I a Turkish slave, Alptigin, formerly commander of 'Abd ul-Malik's guard at Bukhara, had to flee for refuge to the mountainous regions of Ghazni, where he established a semi-independent rule, to which, after his death c. 963, his son-in-law Subuktigin, likewise a former Turkish slave, succeeded. Nuh II, in order to retain at least a nominal sway over those Afghan ter-ritories, confirmed him in his position and invested Subuktigin's son Mahmud with the governorship of Khurasan, in reward for

the help they had given him in his struggles with a confederation of disaffected nobles under the leadership of Fa'ik. During this conflict, the greater part of Transoxiana was occupied by the Turkish Qara-khanids, whose chief, Boghra Khan, occupied Bukhara for a short time in 992. Subuktigin died in the same year as Nuh II (997); and Mahmud (see MAHMUD of Ghazni), confronted with an internal contest against his own brother Ismail, had to withdraw for a short time from Khurasan. This interval sufficed for Fa'ik, supported by a Qara-khanid force under the Ilek khan Nasr I, to concentrate power in his own hands and to involve Mansur II in a conflict with Mahmud. After the dep-osition of Mansur, who was suspected of intending to come to an agreement with Mahmud, the latter took possession of Khura-san. A few months later, the Ilek khan Nasr marched on Bukhara and carried 'Abd ul-Malik and his relatives into captivity. The last prince of the Samanid house, Muntasir, a bold warrior and a poet of no mean talent, carried on guerrilla warfare for some years against both Mahmud and the Qara-khanids, till he was assassi-nated in 1005. See also CALIPHATE; PERSIAN HISTORY.

See V. V. Barthold, *Turkestan Down to the Mongol Invasion*, 2nd ed. (1959); S. Lane-Poole, *Mohammadan Dynasties* (1894).

SAMAR, an island in the east central part of the Philippine archipelago, which with several dozen surrounding islets consti-tutes a province. Area 5,050 sq.mi.; pop. (1961) 867,994. Samar is the third largest island in the Philippines (after Luzon and Mindanao). It lacks the high mountains which characterize many of the islands in the group but is exceedingly hilly, with extensive level land found only in the coastal areas. The highest point is Mt. Capotoan (2,789 ft.), in the north central section. Annual rainfall varies from 100 to 170 in. and is evenly distributed throughout the year except on the east coast where there is a marked winter maximum. Samar receives considerable wind and flood damage from frequent typhoons.

Rice is the main food crop followed by root crops such as sweet potatoes and cassava. Coconuts and bananas are raised for cash along the coastal lowlands. Iron ore in small quantities is mined in the southeastern part of the island and is shipped from the port of General MacArthur. There are deposits of coal and phosphate rock near the west coast.

The provincial capital and important trading town is Catbalogan, pop. (1960) 34,873, on the west coast; Calbayog, a chartered city, is also a trading centre located on the northwest coast.

(R. E. HE.)

SAMARA: see KUIBYSHEV.

SAMARAN (SAMAR-LEYTE, SAMAREÑO or WARAY-WARAY), a member of the sixth largest Filipino cultural-linguistic group, occupying Samar and part of eastern Leyte. Most Samarans inhabit Samar, the third largest Philippine island; those who settled in nearby Leyte are concentrated from Calubian in the north down the island's eastern coast southward to Abuyog. Latest available estimates in the mid-1960s gave the Samaran population as 1,226,000.

Mountainous, thinly populated Samar is one of the eastern Bisayas (Visayan) Islands; most of the people are farmers, living in small villages near the sea, a river, or road (see BISAYAN). The island is largely isolated from main interisland shipping lanes; the major port is also the capital, Catbalogan. Daily buses from Leyte are ferried to western Samar across the narrow San Juanico strait. Among the island's main products are copra, abacá (Manila hemp), rice, and fish (see SAMAR).

Archaeological evidence suggests Late Paleolithic and Neolithic settlements in Samar. Samaran, as do all other Philippine lan-guages, belongs to the Malayo-Polynesian (Austronesian) lin-guistic family; closest affiliation is with the languages of Indonesia (see MALAYO-POLYNESIAN LANGUAGES). It has been suggested that Samaran is most closely interrelated with other Bisayan lan-guages and also those of central and southern Luzon (Tagalog, or Pilipino, and Bikolan). The majority of Samarans are Roman Catholics; Protestant communities, however, are found in the island.

Although the kinship system and family structure is almost identical with other Christian Filipino groups, Samarans are regarded by many Filipinos as less culturally advanced, particularly in their addiction to many pre-Hispanic beliefs related to magic and witchcraft. One of the earliest historical accounts of this region is Jesuit F. I. Alzina's *History of the Islands and Indios of the Bisayas* (Spanish, 1668). This source indicates extensive retention of older supernatural beliefs, folklore, and other cultural practices by present-day Samarans. *See also* PHILIPPINES, REPUBLIC OF THE. (D. V. H.)

SAMARIA, the central region of ancient Palestine, extending about 40 mi. from north to south and 35 mi. from east to west. It was bounded on the west by the Mediterranean sea; sea travel and commerce were discouraged by the marshy nature of the coastal Plain of Sharon and by the lack of any safe natural harbour along the coast, although Herod the Great (40–4 B.C.) built an artificial harbour at Caesarea Palestinae and that Hellenistic city became a political centre of Palestine for the next several decades. The northern boundary of Samaria was formed by the Plain of Esdraelon, part at least of which was considered to belong to Samaria. This plain made a clear separation between Galilee and Samaria. The eastern boundary was the Jordan river, easily accessible by valleys running down from Samaria and easily crossed by fords which made Samarian contacts easy with the region east of Jordan. On the south, Samaria had no natural boundary to separate it sharply from Judaea; the mountainous range of southern Samaria continued south into Judaea with no clearly marked division.

In general, the landscape in Samaria was more open than that found in Judaea, and it possessed more broad valleys that provided fertile farming land. This was particularly true of the northern half of Samaria. In the southern half, extending from the central region around Mt. Ebal (Jabal 'Aybal) and Mt. Gerizim (Jabal at Tur) to the border of Judaea, Samaria presented a continuous mountainous region, with higher altitudes and less farming land. In the northern half, marked by wide valleys and fertile plains (among which the Plain of Dothan was famous) the land supported a more prosperous civilization than Judaea could achieve.

In the centre of Samaria lay the central crossroads of the region. Mt. Gerizim rises to a height of 2,890 ft. and Mt. Ebal to a height of 3,085 ft. In the narrow valley between them lay ancient Shechem, from which roads ran west to the coastal region and east to the Jordan; from this same central area roads ran north and south to the various parts of Samaria and to regions beyond. It was thus natural that the political centre of Samaria was always near this focal point where the roads of the region met and crossed. Shechem (which excavations have shown to be at the modern Balatah in western Jordan) was the outstanding Canaanite city of this area. Later, under Israelite control, the former Canaanite city Tirzah, which may be the modern Tall al-Far'ah, 7 mi. N.E. of Shechem, became the capital until the time of Omri (876–869, or *c.* 884–*c.* 872, B.C.). He built a new and strong capital city on the hilltop which he named Samaria; it was located about 7 mi. N.W. of Shechem, and it remained the capital until its destruction in 722/721 B.C. In New Testament times Samaria was rebuilt by Herod the Great with a notable temple to Augustus and with many features of Hellenistic cities; he renamed it Sebaste, in honour of the Roman emperor Augustus (Greek Sebastus); the name is preserved in Sabastiyah, the name of the modern village at the foot of the hill on which the city of Samaria was built.

Other prominent cities of Samaria were: (1) Jezreel (*q.v.;* Zer'in), a royal city of the kings of Israel, on the northwest spur of Mt. Gilboa. (2) Beth-Shan (called Scythopolis in New Testament times; the modern Tall al Husn), on the border between Galilee and Samaria, with a strategic location which controlled the valley that sloped down from the Plain of Esdraelon to the Jordan river (*see* BEISAN); Midianite and other invaders from east of the Jordan came up this valley (Judg. vi, 33). (3) Ibleam (Tall Bel'ameh), Taanach (Tall Ta'annak), Megiddo (*q.v.;* Tall al Mutesellim) and Dor (Al Burj, near the modern Israeli settlement Nasholim, on the coast), a line of Canaanite cities which in early times cut Galilee off from Samaria; Megiddo, which commanded the strategic pass from the southern coastal plain to the Plain of Esdraelon, was of particular importance throughout the

ancient history of Palestine. (4) Shiloh (*q.v.;* Khirbat Saylun), site of the ancient sanctuary of the invading Israelites in the days of Joshua (Josh. xviii, 1) and in the days of the judges (Judg. xxi, 19; I Sam. iii, 21). (5) Bethel (*q.v.;* Beitin), a centre of worship in the days of the patriarchs, the judges, the kings Saul and David and the kingdom of Israel after its separation from Judah; during this latter period Bethel, located on the southern border of Samaria, was given importance by the kings of Israel to keep Israelites from going south to Jerusalem to worship.

Before the conquest of Palestine by the tribes of Israel, the strategic sites of the region of Samaria were in the hands of the Canaanites. When the people of Israel invaded the region, they won footholds in the hill country, but key Canaanite strongholds in the neighbouring plains or valleys successfully resisted them, in some cases until the days of David. As Josh. xvi–xvii shows, the region of Samaria was assigned to the house of Joseph, that is, to the tribes of Ephraim (south of Mt. Gerizim and Mt. Ebal) and Manasseh (north of those mountains; half of the tribe of Manasseh, as Josh. xxii, 7, recalls, occupied the Trans-Jordan area east of northern Samaria). While David and Solomon united all the tribes of Israel under one ruler, with Jerusalem as the capital, the northern tribes separated from the Jerusalem-centred kingdom after the death of Solomon, and this separate kingdom of Israel had its capital, as has been said, first in Tirzah and then, from the time of Omri, in the city of Samaria. The biblical narrative might lead the reader to think that the greater strength lay in the kingdom of Judah, but in fact the northern kingdom of Israel was often the stronger and it enjoyed the greater economic development, with the corresponding evils which the prophets, including Elijah, Elisha, Amos and Hosea, roundly denounced. Its greater wealth and its political intrigue, however, failed to give it stability and permanence, and in 722/721 B.C. the kingdom of Israel was crushed by Assyria and the cream of its population was carried into captivity to break its capacity to revolt or plot against the Assyrians, who brought settlers from other parts of their empire into Samaria to mingle with the remaining Samarians (II Kings xvii, 6, 24). During the period after the exiles from Judah had been permitted to return to their homeland by the Persians, Sanballat, the governor of Samaria, and his friends harassed the Jews settled in and near Jerusalem and hindered for a time their rebuilding of the city walls (Neh. iv–vi).

In New Testament times, under Roman control, Samaria was ruled as was the remainder of Palestine by Herod the Great and by his grandson Herod Agrippa I (A.D. 41–44); Herod the Great's son Herod Archelaus governed Samaria, Judaea and Idumaea (4 B.C.–A.D. 6), as did Romans appointed during A.D. 6–41 (Pilate's term ran from A.D. 26–36) and A.D. 44–66, when the Jewish revolt broke out. During this period Samaria was to some extent a centre of Hellenistic life. Jesus had little to do with the Samaritans (Luke xvii, 11–19; John iv), but in the apostolic age Greek-speaking Christians preached to them (Acts viii), and this preaching marked a transition stage in the outreach of the church into the gentile world. The Samaritan sect, which traces its origin back to the northern Israelite form of the Mosaic religion, still exists in small numbers at Nablus (close to the site of Shechem) and accepts the Pentateuch as Scripture (*see* SAMARITANS).

See also GALILEE; JUDAEA; ISRAEL (state); PALESTINE.

BIBLIOGRAPHY.—G. A. Smith, *Historical Geography of the Holy Land,* 4th ed. (1896); J. A. Montgomery, *The Samaritans* (1907); M. Gaster, *The Samaritans* (1925); F.-M. Abel, *Géographie de la Palestine,* 2nd ed., vol. i (1933), vol. ii (1938); N. Glueck, *The River Jordan* (1946); G. Dalman, *Sacred Sites and Ways,* Eng. tr. (1935); G. E. Wright and F. V. Filson (eds.), *Westminster Historical Atlas to the Bible,* rev. ed. (1956); E. G. Kraeling, *Rand McNally Bible Atlas* (1956); L. H. Grollenberg, *Atlas of the Bible,* Eng. trans. (1956); D. Baly, *Geography of the Bible* (1957); G. E. Wright, *Biblical Archaeology,* rev. ed. (1962). (F. V. F.)

SAMARITANS, the name given to a religious community formerly widespread throughout Samaria in Palestine (and familiar because of the parable of the Good Samaritan; Luke 10:25–37) and now represented by a few families at Nablus (in modern Jordan). The Samaritans claim to be descendants of the Ten Tribes, denying that the latter were ever deported en masse to Assyria, as related in the Old Testament (II Kings 17:23).

Their religion, they assert, represents the true, unalloyed teaching of Moses, since they accept the Pentateuch alone as holy scripture; hence they call themselves *Shamerim*, "observant," rather than *Shomeronim*, "inhabitants of Samaria." They transmit the Pentateuch in an archaic script resembling ancient Phoenician characters and in a text which differs slightly (sometimes only through dogmatic manipulation) from that of the Jews. They identify the "chosen place" of God not, as do the Jews, with Zion, but with Mt. Gerizim, overlooking Shechem (*see* GERIZIM, MOUNT). In their version of Deuteronomy 27:4 the altar of God is enjoined to be erected on that mountain, not on Mt. Ebal, as in the Jewish recension, and a similar injunction is appended to the Ten Commandments, after Ex. 20:17 and Deut. 5:21. The Temple at Jerusalem and the earlier shrine at Shiloh are regarded as apostatic.

History.—The origin of the sect is obscure because the Samaritan and the Jewish accounts (in Josephus, *Jewish Antiquities*, xi, 7, 2; c, 8) are alike tendentious, the former deliberately apologetic and the latter deliberately defamatory. Most probably, the inhabitants of Samaria first organized themselves as a schismatic community when the Jews, regarding them as mongrel stock, refused their aid in the building of the Second Temple (Ezra 4:1–3). The schism, however, seems not to have crystallized till about 200 years later, when a rival temple was established, about 332 B.C., on Mt. Gerizim.

In spite of the differences which separated the two communities, their external histories at first ran parallel. Samaritans as well as Jews were deported to Egypt by Ptolemy I Soter (4th century B.C.), the two parties subsequently continuing their rivalry in Alexandria; while under Antiochus IV Epiphanes (reigned 175–163 B.C.) they too were compelled to devote their sanctuary to the worship of a heathen god (II Macc. 6:2). Open hostility would appear to have developed especially when the Hasmonaean state of the Jews embarked upon a policy of expansion, and this reached its climax with the destruction of the Samaritan temple by John Hyrcanus I in 129 B.C. Thereupon the Samaritans found themselves caught between the Jews on the one hand and the Romans on the other.

When the Jews were subjugated by Pompey in 63 B.C., Samaria was liberated from Jewish domination and entered briefly upon a new lease of life. The capital city was restored by the Roman governor Aulus Gabinius and enjoyed the special favour of Herod the Great, who there celebrated his marriage with Mariamme. On the other hand, the Samaritans supported the Jews in their uprising of A.D. 66 and paid dearly in a retributive massacre. Like the Jews they were grievously oppressed by Hadrian, who burned their traditional writings. They seem also to have shared in the Jewish dispersion, for in later times Samaritans and their synagogues are heard of in Egypt, in Rome, and in other parts of the empire. During the 4th century, however, they enjoyed a brief renascence on their native soil under the leadership of a certain Baba Rabba, who built many synagogues (some of which have been excavated) in the villages around Shechem. Eventually, hostility to the Christians brought about their final eclipse. In 529 a rigorous edict against them was promulgated by Justinian, and although he subsequently softened its terms, renewed hostility on their part resulted, in 572, in a definitive withdrawal of all their rights and privileges by Justin II.

Under Arab and, later, Turkish rule, the history of the Samaritans is generally one of constant oppression and subjection, relieved only by occasional bright intervals. Although they are mentioned in later times by such Arab writers as al-Masudi (943) and Sharastani (d. 1153), by Jewish travelers such as Benjamin of Tudela (1163) and Obadiah Bertinoro (1488 in Egypt), by Jehan de Mandeville (Sir John Mandeville; 1322), William of Baldensel (1336), and others, little was known of them in Europe until Joseph Scaliger opened communications with them in 1583. In consequence of the interest thus aroused, the traveler Pietro della Valle visited them in 1616 and obtained from them a copy of their Pentateuch, of their ancient Aramaic translation (Targum) of it, and of various other writings. At that time they had already quit their colony in Damascus and were beginning

FRANK HORVAT COURTESY "LIFE," © TIME, INC.

SAMARITAN HIGH PRIEST ON MT. GERIZIM, IN JORDAN, RAISING THE SCROLL OF THE LAW AT PASSOVER

also to abandon their other settlements and to concentrate themselves in Nablus. By mid-20th century they lived mainly in a special quarter of that city, about 190 in number, though a few families had migrated to Tel Aviv-Jaffa. Their economic and cultural level is extremely low, and their principal problem is how to perpetuate themselves without infringing the forbidden degrees of kinship in marriage.

Religion.—Briefly summarized, the creed of the Samaritans is as follows: (1) God is one, incorporeal and without associate; (2) Moses is the only prophet, a preordained creature *sui generis*, the vessel of the divine "light" and "image" and the intercessor for man on the final Day of Judgment; (3) the Law of Moses, coeval with the world, is the only divine revelation and is immutable; (4) Mt. Gerizim is the chosen place of God, the only centre of worship and the "navel of the earth"; (5) there will be a Day of Requital and Reward, when the dead will emerge from their graves, the righteous to enter paradise, the guilty to roast in eternal fire. The Samaritans divide their history into a period of Divine Pleasure (*Rahuta*), when their temple was standing, and one of Divine Displeasure (*Fanuta*), which has continued ever since it was destroyed. Eventually, 6,000 years after creation, a Restorer (*Taheb*) will arise to ameliorate their fortunes. He will live 110 years.

In religious practice, the Samaritans observe only those laws and institutions that are prescribed in the Pentateuch. They interpret them, however, in a manner divergent from normative Jewish tradition, often agreeing with the Sadducees against the Pharisees and with sectarian Jewish usages later revived by the Karaites (*see* KARAISM). Passover, for example, begins on the 14th day of that lunar month the beginning of which falls in April (Abib; *cf.* Deut. 16:1); Pentecost falls always on a Sunday, since the law (Lev. 23:15) which dates it seven weeks "from the morrow after the sabbath" is taken to refer to the sabbath in the paschal week. They do not wear prayer shawls or phylacteries, interpreting the laws of Num. 15:37–39 and Deut. 6:6–8 symbolically. The law of levirate marriage (Deut. 25:5) is taken to enjoin the marriage of a widow to any near kinsman of her deceased husband, not specifically to his blood brother. The paschal sacrifice is still offered on Mt. Gerizim, and pilgrimages are made thither on each of the seasonal festivals.

The religious direction of the community is vested in a high priest. Formerly he traced his ancestry to Aaron, but in 1623 the Aaronid line died out, and ever since he has been known as the "priest levite," claiming descent from Aaron's uncle Uzziel (Ex. 6:18).

In Jewish tradition, the Samaritans are styled Cuthaeans, the implication being that they are not genuine Israelites but simply descendants of the foreign colonists from Cuthah allegedly imported into Samaria by the Assyrian conqueror when the kingdom of Israel fell in 722 B.C. (II Kings 17:24). Various restrictions are imposed on intercourse with them, and intermarriage is forbidden.

Language and Literature.—The Samaritan language is a dialect of Western Aramaic (*see* SEMITIC LANGUAGES: *Aramaic*). After the Muslim conquest in 632, however, it was superseded by Arabic for all but liturgical purposes.

During the Hellenistic period, the Samaritans appear to have composed several works, including a translation of their Pentateuch into Greek, but all of these have perished except for a few fragments. Of extant writings there is none which can be dated before the 4th century A.D. The Targum or Samaritan-Aramaic version of the Pentateuch was most probably redacted about that time, though it was clearly based on a much older tradition and must have undergone various recensions. It bears a strange similarity in many points to the contemporary Jewish Targum of Onkelos (see TARGUM). To the same period belong the liturgical compositions of Amram Darah and Marqah, as well as the latter's midrashic commentary (called "The Book of Wonders") on parts of the Pentateuch, all in Aramaic. The last named is especially valuable not only from the linguistic viewpoint but also because it exemplifies a tradition of exegesis divergent from that of the Jews and because it anticipates several concepts and even idioms found later in the Koran.

With the possible exception of one or two hymns there is nothing further until the 11th century, when there appears an Arabic version of the Pentateuch probably composed by Abul-hasan of Tyre and later revised by Abu Said and Abul-barakat. Of the same date (1053) is an anonymous commentary on Genesis, interesting because it quotes from books of the Bible other than the Pentateuch and from the Mishna. Other medieval writings of note are: (1) the *Kafi*, or "Ritual Compendium," by Joseph ben Solomon of Askar, a village near Shechem (1042); (2) the *Masa'il al-Khilaf*, a disquisition on differences between the Samaritans and the Jews, by Munajja ben Sadaqah (c. 1150); and (3) the *Tabakh*, or "Potpourri," a collection of ritualistic and doctrinal discussions by Abul-hasan of Tyre. All these works are in Arabic. To the same period probably belongs also an Aramaic book of biblical legends known as "The Stories [*Asatir*] of Moses," though this would appear to draw upon far older sources. Of Samaritan chronicles, mention may be made especially of the *Taulida*, begun in 1149 by Eleazar ben Amram and continued in 1334 by Jacob ben Ishmael in Damascus, as well as of the so-called Samaritan Book of Joshua, a record of events from the death of Moses until the 4th century A.D. This work appears to have been compiled from traditional material at some time in the 13th century. An Arabic chronicle by Abul-fath, written in Egypt in 1355, has survived. There are also several minor theological treatises and a more ambitious work entitled "Way of the Heart" (*Sirr al-Qalb*) by Abraham Qabazi of Damascus (1532), as well as a poetic book of praises in honour of Moses (*Molad Mosheh*) by Qabazi's pupil Ismail ar-Rumaihi (1537). In the 19th century, translations of these works were made from Arabic into Samaritan by the priests Pinehas ben Isaac and Jacob ben Aaron, and such activity was continued later by Abisha ben Pinehas and Ab Hasda (Abul-hasan) ben Jacob.

The principal collections of Samaritan manuscripts are in the British Museum and the Vatican Library. Most of the literature remains unedited and untranslated.

BIBLIOGRAPHY.—J. A. Montgomery, *The Samaritans* (1907); M. Gaster, *The Samaritans* (1925), *The Asatir of Moses* (1927), and *Samaritan Eschatology* (1932). The Pentateuch was edited with critical apparatus by A. von Gall (1914–18). A convenient edition of the Targum is that by Adolf Brüll (1874–75). For the liturgy, see A. Cowley (ed.), *The Samaritan Liturgy* (1909). The best grammar of the Samaritan language is that of J. H. Petermann in the "Porta Linguarum Orientalium Series" (1873). See also "Samaritans" in *The Interpreter's Dictionary of the Bible*, vol. iv, pp. 190–197 (1962).   (T. H. G.)

SAMARIUM is a silver-white metal of the rare-earth group. It was discovered and an impure oxide isolated in 1879 by L. de Boisbaudran; pure compounds were prepared by E. Demarçay in 1901. The element was named for the mineral samarskite, which in turn was named for a Russian engineer, Col. M. Samarski. Samarium occurs in many rare-earth minerals but is almost exclusively obtained from monazite (*q.v.*); it is also found in the products of atomic fission. Separation and purification of samarium by means of reduction to amalgams with sodium amalgam was accomplished by J. K. Marsh in 1942. Ion-exchange techniques are used for commercial production.

Because of its high absorption cross section for thermal neutrons, samarium has been suggested for limited application in nuclear reactor control rods and for neutron shielding. Other uses are in special luminescent and infrared absorbing glasses, inorganic and organic catalysis, and in the electronics and ceramics industries. Samarium is a minor constituent of Misch metal (a mixture of cerium and other rare-earth metals, used in ferrous and nonferrous alloys).

The symbol for samarium is Sm, atomic number 62, atomic weight 150.35. There are seven naturally occurring isotopes, of which three, Sm^{147}, Sm^{148}, and Sm^{149}, are radioactive alpha-emitters with very long half-lives. The most abundant of the isotopes, Sm^{154}, is stable. The metal is conveniently prepared by the thermoreduction of its oxide, Sm_2O_3, by lanthanum metal followed by distillation of the samarium metal, which is one of the three most volatile of the rare earths (the other two are europium and ytterbium). It has also been prepared by reduction of its halides by an alkaline-earth metal. The metal melts at 1,072° C. Its density for the rhombohedral structure is 7.536 g. per cc.; other forms are known.

Samarium is one of the three rare earths which have an oxidation state of plus two (the other two are europium and ytterbium); the Sm^{+2} ion is such a violent reducing agent that it reacts with water. The pure metal is not appreciably oxidized in air at room temperature, and at higher temperatures oxidation proceeds at a very slow rate.

Divalent (samarous) salts are prepared by hydrogen reduction of an anhydrous trivalent (samaric) halide at high temperatures. The reduction of the samaric ion in solution may be effected either by electrolytic methods, using a mercury pool cathode, or by alkali metal amalgams. The plus-two oxidation state is frequently stabilized by precipitation of the Sm^{+2} ion as the sulfate, $SmSO_4$, which is extremely insoluble. Other divalent salts are $SmCO_3$, $SmCl_2$, $SmBr_2$, and $Sm(OH)_2$; they are reddish brown in colour.

In its more stable trivalent oxidation state, samarium behaves as a typical rare-earth element: it forms a series of yellow salts and solutions. Solutions show discrete absorption peaks in the ultraviolet and visible regions of the spectrum which may be used for quantitative analysis. Due to the presence of unpaired electrons the trivalent ion, Sm^{+3}, is paramagnetic.

See also RARE EARTHS.   (LD. B. A.; J. B. Ps.)

SAMARKAND, a town and *oblast* centre in the Uzbek Soviet Socialist Republic, U.S.S.R. It lies at an altitude of about 2,330 ft. (710 m.) in the valley of the Zeravshan River, 168 mi. (270 km.) SW of Tashkent by rail and about 155 mi. (249 km.) N of the Afghanistan frontier. Pop. (1959) 196,484.

The old city of Samarkand, as opposed to the "new town" built after the Russian conquest of 1868, took shape in the Middle Ages. Its plan consisted of streets converging toward the centre from six gates in the 11th-century 5-mi.-long walls. The walls and gates were destroyed after the capture of the town by the Russians, but the plan of the medieval period is still preserved. Here are to be found monuments of Central Asian architecture in which the developments of six centuries can be observed. The earliest of these are the five small 14th-century edifices (in the collection of mausoleums known as the Shah-i-Zindeh) and the Ruhabad mausoleum dating from the middle of the 14th century. In the time of Timur (Tamerlane), whose capital Samarkand became, the congregational mosque of Bibi Khanum (his Chinese wife) and the mausoleum of Timur himself, known as the Gur-Amir, were built. To the second half of the 15th century belongs the Ak Saray tomb with the superb fresco of the interior. A fine example of the town planning culture of Central Asia is Registan Square with its group of monumental buildings: the *medresehs* (Muslim schools) of Ulugh Beg (1417–20), Shirdar (1619–1635/36), and Tilakari (mid-17th century), which border the square on three sides. In the environs of Samarkand are the tomb of Abd-i-Darun (15th century), the mausoleum of Chupan-Ata (mid-15th century), the mausoleum of Ishrat Khan, the ruins of the 16th-century aqueduct leading to the Zeravshan River, the mosque of Namazgah (17th century), the *medreseh* at the tomb of Khoja Ahrar (built 1630–36 by the Samarkand architect Dost Muhammad), and the Khanigah (cloister) at the tomb of Abd-i-Birun (1633–34). The main features of the 15th- to 17th-century monuments are the splendid portals, the vast coloured domes, and the remarkable exterior decoration in majolica, mosaic, marble, and gold. The new town, construction of which began in 1871, has expanded considerably during the Soviet period, and public buildings, dwelling houses, and parks have been built. There are Uzbek and Russian theatres, a university (established 1933), and higher educational institutions for agriculture, medicine, and trade.

Samarkand is on the Krasnovodsk–Tashkent railway and on the highway from Tashkent to Termez on the Afghanistan frontier. It has an airport. The town's commercial importance, which in ancient and medieval times derived from its location at the junction of trade routes from China (the "silk road") and India, declined during the 17th and 18th centuries, but greatly increased with the coming of the railway in 1896. Samarkand then became an important centre for the export of wine, dried and fresh fruits, cotton, rice, silk, and leather. Under the Soviet regime industry has been expanded and, although mainly based on agriculture (e.g., cotton ginning, silk spinning and weaving, fruit canning, production of wine, clothing, leather and footwear, and tobacco), includes the manufacture of tractor and automobile parts, and cinema apparatus.

History.—Samarkand is one of the oldest cities of Central Asia. In the 4th century B.C., then known as Maracanda, it was the capital of Sogdiana (q.v.) and was captured (329) by Alexander the Great. In the 6th century A.D. it was part of the Turkish Khaqanate. At the beginning of the 8th century it was conquered by the Arabs and in the 9th and 10th centuries it was ruled by the Samanids. In the 11th century it was conquered by the Karakhanids and later by the Seljuks, in the 12th century by the Kara Kitais, and in the 13th century it came under the domination of Khorezm. In 1220 it was captured and destroyed by Genghis Khan. In 1365 the city revolted against the Mongol amirs and at the end of the 14th and the beginning of the 15th centuries it was the capital of the empire of Timur. At this period Samarkand was the most important economic and cultural centre of Central Asia. In 1500 it was conquered by the Uzbeks and came under the dominion of the Shaibanids, who in the middle of the 16th century transferred their capital to Bukhara. Samarkand later became part of the khanate of Bukhara. During the 17th and 18th centuries, as a result of attacks by nomad tribes and by the Persian Empire, Samarkand underwent a serious economic crisis, and from the 1720s until the 1770s it was uninhabited. In 1868 it was occupied by Russian troops and became a part of the Russian empire as capital of the Zeravshan district, which in 1887 became the Samarkand province. When the Uzbek S.S.R. was constituted in 1924, Samarkand became its capital but was replaced by Tashkent in 1930.

SAMARKANDSKAYA (Samarkand) OBLAST', formed in 1938, is divided into 17 *rayons*. Area 12,008 sq.mi. (31,101 sq.km.). Pop. (1959) 1,148,281, mainly Uzbek, but including Tadzhiks, Russians, and Ukrainians. More than one-quarter of the population lives in the three towns of Samarkand, Katta-Kurgan, and Dzhizak. The *oblast* is drained by the Zeravshan River and includes the Nuratau and Ak-Tau mountain ranges in the north. In the southwest is the Karnabchul' Steppe. The geological structure includes marble, granite, limestone, gypsum, and other valuable building materials and minerals. The climate is continental and is noted for the amount of sunshine and the absence of cloud; there is no frost during 200 days in the year. The economy is mainly agricultural and includes cotton and fruit growing and sericulture in the Zeravshan Valley; elsewhere there is dry farming of wheat. Karakul sheep and goats are bred. Extensive irrigation systems have been developed. The *oblast* is traversed by the Krasnovodsk–Tashkent railway to an extent of 200 mi. (about 320 km.) and there are about 5,000 mi. (8,000 km.) of motor roads. (G. E. WR.)

SAMARRA, a town of Iraq, in Baghdad *liwa'* (province), lies on the east bank of the Tigris River about 70 mi. (113 km.) NNW of Baghdad. Pop. (1957) 16,398. Samarra is the site of a prehistoric settlement, and has given its name to a type of Neolithic painted pottery of the 5th millennium B.C. In A.D. 836 the caliph al-Mu'tasim, forced by the indiscipline of his Turkish bodyguard to leave Baghdad, founded a new capital at Samarra, which he renamed Surra-man-ra'a ("he who sees it, rejoices"); the earlier form, however, persisted in common use. Al-Mu'tasim laid out gardens on the Tigris bank, and his vast palace on

the cliff above included a quatrefoil racecourse, a polo ground, and an amphitheatre. Other palaces, barracks, and private houses were erected by al-Mu'tasim and his successors on a spacious, regular plan, extending more than 20 mi. along the river. Al-Mutawakkil (847–861) built the Great Mosque, said to be the largest mosque in Islam, with a spiral minaret probably inspired by the Babylonian ziggurat, and later added a northern suburb to the city, including a new palace and a second mosque, Abu Dulaf, with a similar minaret. In 892 the caliph al-Mu'tamid returned to Baghdad and Samarra rapidly declined; by 1300 it was largely in ruins. The town contains important Shi'ite shrines which include the tombs of the 10th and 11th imams, and the cave into which the 12th imam disappeared and from which the Imami sect of the Shi'ites expect him to reemerge as the leader of Islam (al-Mahdi). *See also* ISLAMIC ARCHITECTURE.

See E. Herzfeld, *Geschichte der Stadt Samarra* (1948); K. A. C. Creswell, *Early Muslim Architecture* (1932–41). (E. E. D. M. O.)

SAMAWAH (As SAMAWAH), a town of Iraq in Diwaniyah *liwa'* (province) at the junction of the Hindiyah and Hillah branches of the Euphrates. Pop. (1957) 26,838. The town is on the Baghdad–Basra railway and there is a clear stretch of river as far as Nasiriyah, 71 mi. downstream (upstream the river is practically impassable). It also lies on the caravan routes to Hillah, Najaf, and Basra, in a fertile area, and is a centre of trade in local agricultural products, including vegetables, rice, wheat, and barley. Like most of the Euphrates towns it is a market for such imported goods as sugar, indigo, and coffee, as well as textiles. Wool is raised locally and woolen carpets are manufactured.
(W. B. FR.)

SAMBA, a dance of Brazilian origin, is characterized by tilting, rocking motions of the body. The music, in 4/4 time, has an uneven rhythm based on the sequence of a dotted quarter note, an eighth note, and a half note. The basic pattern corresponding to these notes is a step forward or backward, a quicker step forward or backward, and a transfer of body weight to the other foot. Forward steps are taken with the knees bent and the body tilted back; backward steps, with the knees straight and the body tilted forward. The samba is performed by embracing couples, who may dance in place or across the floor; occasionally the partners may separate and perform variant steps such as the "shuffle."

SAMBALPUR, a town and district of Orissa, India. The town, headquarters of the district, lies on the left bank of the Mahanadi River, 140 mi. (225 km.) WNW of Cuttack. Pop. (1961) 38,915. It has a ruined fort and old temples, and there are three colleges, including a teacher-training college, affiliated to Utkal University. The town is connected to the South-Eastern Railway on the north and to the Raipur-Vishakhapatnam Railway on the southwest.

SAMBALPUR DISTRICT (area 6,763 sq.mi.; pop. [1961] 1,508,-686) is mostly an undulating plain with rugged hills, the largest of which, Bara Pahar, covers an area of 300 sq.mi. (777 sq.km.). The Mahanadi affords means of water communication for 90 mi. (145 km.). A dam (15,748 ft. [4,799 m.] long) was completed in 1957 across the Mahanadi at Hirakud, 8 mi. upstream from Sambalpur, for irrigation, flood control, and power production. Rice is the chief crop. The district yields graphite, bauxite, coal, and various forest products. There are a paper mill at Brajarajnagar, an aluminum factory near Hirakud, a match factory, a large number of sawmills, rice and flour mills, and ice plants. Silk and bell metal industries are widespread though on a small scale. A fishing industry has been developed in the artificial lake (400 sq.mi. [1,036 sq.km.]) at Hirakud. Burla, near Hirakud, has an engineering and a medical college affiliated to Utkal University. Jharsuguda, 27 mi. N of Sambalpur, is a rail junction. (MA. M.; N. K. S.)

SAMBATION (SANBATION; from SABATION or SABBATION, "Sabbath River"), a legendary river beyond which the Ten Lost Tribes of Israel were exiled by Shalmaneser, king of Assyria (II Kings 17–18). According to the rabbis (e.g., the *Targum* of pseudo-Jonathan on Ex. 34:10) and the Roman geographer Pliny the Elder (*Natural History*, xxxi, 17), the river flows six days a week and rests on Saturdays. According to Josephus (*Wars of the Jews,* vii, 5, 1) it rests on weekdays and flows on the sabbath. Josephus and the rabbis differ also as to the location of the river, Josephus maintaining that it is situated in Syria, whereas the rabbis assume that it is somewhere in a country far from Palestine. Pliny locates it in Judaea. Nahmanides (13th century) identifies it with the River Gozan of the Bible (II Kings 17:6).

Reports about the Ten Lost Tribes and an independent Jewish kingdom in the East stirred the imagination of the Jews through the ages and intrigued the Christian world as well. From the 12th century to the 19th, Jewish travelers left European countries for the East to search for the Sambation and the Ten Lost Tribes. The resulting legends gave rise to a vast literature concerning the miracles of the Sambation. According to the narrative of the 9th-century adventurer Eldad ha-Dani (*q.v.*), the Sambation surrounds the land inhabited by the children of Moses (*Bene Moshe*), who maintain there a powerful kingdom. It is waterless but full of sand and stones which heave with a great noise during weekdays. On the sabbath it rests, shrouded with clouds, making it impassable. (Manasseh ben Israel in the 17th century maintained that the sand, if kept in a bottle, moves restlessly during the week but rests on the sabbath.) The story of Eldad was widely repeated later, with accretions by other travelers. From Jewish sources, the legends about the Sambation penetrated into Christian and Arabic writings, among them the Alexander Romance. (*See also* TWELVE TRIBES OF ISRAEL.)

In the vernacular of Eastern European Jews an unruly child was often referred to as a "Sambation."

BIBLIOGRAPHY.—*The Jewish Encyclopedia,* vol. x, pp. 681–683; *The Universal Jewish Encyclopedia,* vol. ix, p. 339; Louis Ginzberg, *The Legends of the Jews,* vol. iv, pp. 316–317 (1909–26), and vol. vi, pp. 407–409 (1928); A. Epstein, *Eldad ha-Dani* (1891). (J. M. RL.)

SAMBHAL, a town of Moradabad district in the Rohilkhand division of Uttar Pradesh, India, lies 23 mi. (37 km.) SW of Moradabad town by road. Pop. (1961) 68,940. It is an ancient town that became an important seat of power during the Muslim rule and was for a time the imperial capital in the reign of Sikandar Lodi (1489–1517). There are several mounds and *sarais* (rest houses). The chief monuments include the Kot, once occupied by a Hindu temple and now by an old mosque (1526); the fort of Nawab Amin ud-Daula; and the tomb of Fateh Ullah Shah (a Muslim saint) in Sarai Tarin (1559), a locality named after the Tarin Pathans. Several important Hindu and Muslim fairs are held there annually. The chief industries are sugar refining, handloom weaving, and calico printing. (B. Si.)

SAMMARTINI (SAN MARTINI). The brothers of this name, Italian composers and instrumentalists of the 18th century, were sons of the French oboist Alexis Saint-Martin. They were born in Milan, and both were for a time oboists in the orchestra of the ducal theatre there.

GIUSEPPE SAMMARTINI (*c.* 1693–1751), often called "St. Martini of London" to differentiate him from his more famous brother, first appeared as oboist of the Milan opera in the early 1720s. He composed an oratorio, *La calunnia delusa,* which was performed in Milan in 1724. In 1729 he went to London where he remained for the rest of his life. He was much esteemed by the English public, first as an oboist at the opera and later as a composer and concert performer. After leaving the opera he entered the service of Frederick Louis, prince of Wales, for whom he wrote a setting of William Congreve's *The Judgment of Paris.* He died in London before June 24, 1751. His works, written in the late Baroque style, include some fine trio sonatas and *concerti grossi.* He published many of his own works, not always profitably. After his death they were a source of profit to certain music sellers, who reissued them, using the composer's plates.

GIOVANNI BATTISTA SAMMARTINI (*c.* 1698–1775), unlike his elder brother, spent most of his life in Milan. He was first known as a church organist and composer of sacred music. As early as 1734 he had composed a four-movement symphony; as his orchestral and chamber music began to be known outside Italy it attracted pupils to Milan, among them Gluck, who studied

with him from 1737 to 1741. He died in Milan on Jan. 15, 1775.

Sammartini was a prolific composer—of 2,000 works, by some estimates—and was one of the formative influences on the development of the preclassical symphony, and thus on the classical style itself. It is impossible, however, to decide whether certain works are his, or by his brother, or even by Giovanni Battista Martini (1706–1784), or by one of the numerous forgers who profited from the popularity of his genuine works.

See C. Sartori, "Sammartini postmortem," in *Hans Albrecht in memoriam* (1962). (Cs. CH.)

SAMNITES, the name given by the Romans to the warlike tribes inhabiting the mountainous centre of the southern half of Italy. The word Samnites was apparently not the name used by the Samnites themselves, which would seem rather to have been the Oscan form of the word which appears in Latin as "Sabini"; the ending of Samnites seems to be connected with the name by which they were known to the Greeks of the Campanian coast. Both from tradition and from surviving inscriptions it is clear that they spoke Oscan, and tradition records that the Samnites were an offshoot of the Sabines. On two inscriptions the form Safinim appears, which would be in Latin Sabinium (nominative or accusative singular, agreeing with some substantive understood). The abundance of the group names ending in the suffix *-no-* in all the Samnite districts classes them unmistakably with the great Safine stock (*see* SABINI; ITALIC DIALECTS; OSCAN).

Four cantons formed a Samnite confederation: the Hirpini, (*q.v.*), Caudini, Caraceni, and Pentri (the Frentani and other Sabelli were often loosely called Samnites but were not members of the confederation). Many lived in villages. Their chief towns, which were administered by a *meddix* or two *meddices,* were: of the Hirpini, Beneventum (modern Benevento), Aeclanum, and Abellinum (Avellino); of the Caudini, Caudium and Saticula; of the Caraceni, Bovianum Vetus (Pietrabbondante) and Aufidena (Alfedena); of the Pentri, Bovianum (Boiano), Aesernia (Isernia), and Saepinum. The league probably had no federal assembly, but a war leader could be chosen to lead their united forces for a campaign. Lack of a central administration and eagerness to scatter quickly for booty, however, made it difficult for these virile highlanders to sustain long wars. Common fear of the Gauls drove the Samnites and Romans into an alliance in 354 B.C. Soon the Samnites are said to have been involved in their first war against Rome (343–341), when the Sidicini had appealed to Rome for help against a Samnite attack. Details of the war are confused, and some historians doubt its historicity. At any rate in 341 Rome renewed the alliance with the Samnites. The Second Samnite War (326–304), with a lull after Rome's crushing defeat by the Samnites under Gavius Pontius at the Caudine Forks in 321, prevented Samnite expansion into Lucania and Apulia, and the Samnites found themselves being surrounded by Latin colonies. A third war (298–290), despite Samnite co-operation with Gauls and Umbrians against the Romans at Sentinum in 295, ended in defeat and the establishment of a Latin colony at Venusia (Venosa; 291) on the southern borders of Samnium. Thus the Samnites were reduced and depopulated, but they later gave Pyrrhus and Hannibal some help against Rome. They fought doggedly from 90 B.C. in the Social War (the war of the allies or *socii*) and in the subsequent civil war against L. Cornelius Sulla (*q.v.*), who defeated them at the Battle of the Colline Gate (82).

The longest and most important monument of the Oscan language as it was spoken by the Samnites (in, probably, the 3rd century B.C.) is the small bronze tablet, engraved on both sides, known as the *Tabula Agnonensis,* found in 1848 at Agnone, not very far from Bovianum. This inscription, preserved in the British Museum, is carefully engraved in full Oscan alphabet. It contains a list of deities to whom statues were erected in the precinct sacred to Ceres, or some allied divinity, and on the back a list of deities to whom altars were erected.

BIBLIOGRAPHY.—F. E. Adcock in *Cambridge Ancient History,* vol. vii, ch. 18 with bibliography (1928); R. S. Conway, *The Italic Dialects,* vol. i, pp. 180 ff. (1897); C. D. Buck, *A Grammar of Oscan and*

Umbrian, 2nd ed. (1928); S. Weinstock, "Zur oskischen Magistratur," *Klio,* xxiv, pp. 235–246 (1931); E. Vetter, *Handbuch der italischen Dialekte,* vol. i (1953). (H. H. Sɒ.)

SAMOA ISLANDS, a group of islands about 1,600 mi. N.E. of the northern tip of New Zealand, 2,700 mi. E. of Australia and 2,200 mi. S.W. of the Hawaiian Islands. The archipelago, which extends from latitudes 13° 26′ to 14° 22′ S. and from longitudes 168° 10′ to 172° 48′ W., is divided administratively into two parts: the six islands east of longitude 171° W. constitute American Samoa, a dependency of the U.S., and the nine islands west of the 171° meridian constitute Western Samoa, a self-governing nation which, until 1962, was a United Nations trust territory administered by New Zealand. American Samoa consists of the inhabited islands of Tutuila, Tau, Olosega, Ofu and Aunuu and the uninhabited coral atoll Rose Island. Swains Island, 210 mi. N.W. of Tutuila and considered to be outside the Samoan archipelago, was made a part of American Samoa in 1925. Western Samoa consists of the inhabited islands of Upolu, Savai'i, Manono and Apolima and the uninhabited islands of Fanuatapu, Namua, Nuutele, Nuulua and Nuusafee.

The total area of American Samoa is 76 sq.mi. Tutuila, the largest island of American Samoa, has an area of 53 sq.mi. and is about 18 mi. long and about 3 mi. across in the widest part.

Western Samoa has a total area of 1,097 sq.mi. Savai'i, the largest island, has an area of 602 sq.mi. and is 60 mi. long. Upolu has an area of 435 sq.mi. and is 58 mi. long. The other seven islands of Western Samoa are quite small.

All the Samoan islands, except Nuusafee, are rocky and of volcanic origin. Upolu, Savai'i and Tutuila have high inland ridges rising to peaks of 6,095 ft. in Savai'i, 3,608 ft. in Upolu and 2,141 ft. in Tutuila. These islands have little level land except along the coast and in the case of Tutuila there is a broad fertile plain in the southwestern part of the island. The soil is alluvial and quite fertile in the valleys. Because of the heavy rainfall, the soil on hillsides is thin and there is no subsoil.

The climate of the islands is tropical but equable for a good portion of the year. From May to November strong southeast winds blow and the islands have experienced many severe hurricanes. June and July are the coolest and most pleasant months. The average temperature is 26.3° C. (79.3° F.) with a mean range from 23.2° to 29.3° C. (73.8° to 84.7° F.). Rainfall is generally heavy; the central ridges receive over 200 in. annually.

History.—The archipelago was probably discovered by Jacob Roggeveen, a Dutchman, in 1722. The islands were subsequently visited by Louis Antoine de Bougainville in 1768, Jean François de Galaup de La Pérouse in 1787 and Otto von Kotzebue in 1824. The first missionaries to go to Samoa were two members of the London Missionary society who established a mission in 1830. Charles Wilkes, a U.S. explorer, surveyed the islands in 1839. Great Britain, the U.S. and Germany appointed representatives on the islands in 1847, 1853 and 1861, respectively.

In Jan. 1878 the U.S. signed a treaty with the then independent Samoan kingdom which gave the U.S. the right to establish a naval station in the harbour of Pago Pago, best in the archipelago. A trading agreement was also concluded. Germany and Great Britain received similar privileges the following year, but the interests of the three countries were often in conflict. A conference of the three powers, held in Berlin in 1889, concluded a general act providing for the neutrality of the islands and establishing in effect a tripartite protectorate over the islands.

This arrangement did not operate so successfully as planned, and on Dec. 2, 1899, a convention was signed by Great Britain, Germany and the U.S. by which the paramount interests of the United States in those Samoan islands east of longitude 171° W. were recognized and Germany's interests in the other Samoan islands were similarly recognized. Great Britain withdrew from Samoa altogether in consideration of rights in Tonga and the Solomon Islands. The high chiefs of the islands of Tutuila and Aunuu ceded those islands to the U.S. on April 17, 1900, and the chiefs of Tau, Olosega and Ofu islands ceded their islands to the U.S. on July 16, 1904. The U.S. congress accepted the islands under a joint resolution approved Feb. 20, 1929. American Samoa under navy administration (1900–51) became a strategic U.S. naval base in the Pacific.

Germany controlled Western Samoa until World War I. New Zealand troops occupied the islands on Aug. 30, 1914, and the League of Nations granted New Zealand a mandate over them in 1920. Western Samoa was made a trust territory by the United Nations with New Zealand as the administering authority on Jan. 25, 1947.

Population.—The population of American Samoa totaled 20,051 in 1960 with about four-fifths of the population on the main island of Tutuila, the site of Pago Pago, the capital (pop. [1960] 1,251), and Fagatogo (1,344). The population of Western Samoa was 114,427 in 1961 with about three-fourths on Upolu. Apia, the capital, on Upolu, had a population (1961) of 22,237. The Samoans are Polynesian and closely akin to the people of Hawaii and the Maoris of New Zealand.

The Samoan language is believed to be the oldest form of Polynesian speech in existence. It is closely related to the Maori, Tahitian, Hawaiian and Tongan languages.

Despite the increasing contacts with the western world, Samoan culture is still the dominant influence in the lives of the people. The basic unit of Samoan society is the *aiga,* an extended family system headed by the *matai.* Kinship ties are important in Samoan social and economic life and all who are related by birth or adoption are recognized as belonging to one *aiga.*

Samoa differs from most large Polynesian communities in its system of chieftainships. The basis of this system is an intricate hierarchy of graded titles. Essentially, those titles are of two kinds —*ali'i* and *tulafale.* The former may be called titular chiefs and the latter orator chiefs. All chiefs are referred to by the generic title *matai.* Succession to a title is elective within a family and while heredity is a contributory qualification, general ability, popularity and the capacity to make a good speech are governing qualifications.

Most of the population have become converts to Christianity. In Western Samoa, one-half of the population is affiliated with the London Missionary society. Other major religious affiliations in Samoa are Roman Catholic, Methodist, Mormon and Seventh-Day Adventist.

Government.—*American Samoa.*—American Samoa is a possession of the U.S. with a governor appointed by the secretary of the interior of the United States. The islands were under the jurisdiction of the navy department between 1900 and July 1, 1951, when administration was transferred to the department of the interior.

American Samoa is divided into 14 counties grouped into three administrative districts; the counties and districts correspond to the old Samoan political units. Each district has a governor who is appointed by the governor of American Samoa from the ranks of county chiefs. In each village of the district a chief is appointed by the district governor.

The first constitution of American Samoa became effective on Oct. 17, 1960, as the basic law of the territory. Under the constitution there is a bicameral legislature with certain defined legislative powers as compared with the advisory powers enjoyed by the legislature in existence prior to the constitution. The senate has 15 members, 1 elected by each of the 14 counties, who serve for four years and 1 additional senator, who serves for two years, elected on rotation from 4 of the 14 counties. The house of representatives has 17 members, popularly elected, plus 1 delegate from Swains Island who has all the privileges of a member of the house except the right to vote.

The constitution established the judicial branch independent of the executive and legislative branches. There is a high court and five district courts. The seat of the government is at Pago Pago on Tutuila.

Western Samoa.—New Zealand's trusteeship over Western Samoa was terminated on Jan. 1, 1962, when the islands achieved self-governing status. A new constitution and independence were approved by the Western Samoans at a UN-supervised referendum based on universal suffrage on May 9, 1961. The vote was 26,766 to 4,666. The first prime minister was Fiame Mata'afa

Faumuina Mulinu'u II. Western Samoa has had a legislative assembly since 1948. Village and local affairs are controlled by native village officials nominated by the villages. The seat of government is at Apìa on Upolu.

Education.—Education in American Samoa is compulsory for all children from 7 to 15 years of age, inclusive. By the 1960s only about 1% of the total population 10 years of age and over were illiterate. There were 6,500 pupils enrolled in about 60 public and 10 missionary schools with about 300 teachers in the public schools and 50 teachers in the missionary schools. About 80% of the pupils were enrolled in public schools.

Education in Western Samoa is dependent to a large extent on the activities of various missions. Education has not been compulsory and there has not been an age limit on attendance. As a result, the rate of illiteracy has been greater than in American Samoa. In the 1960s there were about 20,000 pupils enrolled in 150 government schools and 10,000 pupils in 250 private schools with about 500 government-school and 270 private-school teachers.

Economy.—The natural resources of Samoa are of little economic consequence. There are no minerals and no timber of sufficient quantity to warrant industrial development for export. The U.S. naval station at Pago Pago has been a major source of employment as well as trade. A cannery was established at Pago Pago in 1953 to process and export tuna caught by Japanese fishing vessels under contract and canned tuna has become the main product of American Samoa.

Other important products are copra and native handicraft consisting principally of mats and rugs woven from local grasses. Western Samoa's main products are copra, cocoa beans, desiccated coconut and bananas.

Agriculture is the basis of the Samoan economy. Crops cultivated are corn, beans, peas, watermelons, cucumbers, squash, eggplant, tomatoes, lettuce, radishes, sweet potatoes, breadfruit, papayas, bananas, taro and pineapples. There are also some cattle and in American Samoa there is a small dairy industry.

Fish, mostly processed tuna, account for more than 95% of American Samoa's total exports, with copra and handicraft products accounting for about 2% each. Most trade is with the U.S., New Zealand, Australia, Japan and Western Samoa. Western Samoa exports copra, cocoa and bananas to New Zealand, Australia and the United Kingdom. Chief imports, from New Zealand, Australia, the United Kingdom, the United States, Japan and Fiji, are meat, sugar, cotton goods and motor vehicles and accessories.

See PACIFIC ISLANDS; *see* also references under "Samoa Islands" in the Index.

BIBLIOGRAPHY.—Ernest Beaglehole, *Trusteeship and New Zealand's Pacific Dependencies*, in W. T. G. Hirey, *New Zealand and the Pacific* (1947); F. J. H. Grattan, *An Introduction to Samoan Culture* (1948); Margaret Mead, *Coming of Age in Samoa* (1961); Rupert Emerson *et al., America's Pacific Dependencies* (1949); V. D. Stace, *Western Samoa: an Economic Survey* (1956); U.S. Department of the Interior, *American Samoa: Information on American Samoa Transmitted by the United States to the Secretary-General of the United Nations* (annual), *Annual Report of the Governor of American Samoa to the Secretary of the Interior* (annual).

Current statistics, together with the current history, are summarized annually in the *Britannica Book of the Year,* American edition.

(S. Nr.; J. W. Mw.)

SAMORY (SAMORI TOURÉ) (c. 1830–1900), a Mandingo Negro, was a prominent figure in French colonial history in the late 19th century. Born near Sanankoro (north of Beyla, Guinea) he became a professional soldier. In 1868 he declared himself an *almami* (religious chief) and, having created a corps of warriors (the *sofa*), he occupied Wassoulou, a country east of the upper Niger River.

From 1883 he fought against the French who had recently occupied Bamako. In 1886 he accepted the Niger as his frontier, and French protection. He then turned east against the king of Sikasso, but was repulsed (1887–88). In 1891 war broke out again between him and the French. Driven out by them from the Sudan he established himself in the upper Ivory Coast colony. Having seized and pillaged Kong (1897) and Bondoukou (1898) he was pursued by French columns under the command of Capt. Henri Gouraud. He was captured on the upper reaches of the

Cavally River, on Sept. 29, 1898, and died in exile in Gabon on June 2, 1900.

Samory was a remarkable organizer but his large army lived by plundering conquered peoples. His restless, warlike temperament, coupled with the French conquests, prevented him from creating a lasting empire. (Hu. De.)

SAMOS, a Greek island in the Aegean Sea, separated from the mainland of Turkey by a strait about a mile wide. It is about 27 mi. (43 km.) in length by 14 mi. (23 km.) at its greatest breadth and is largely mountainous, the highest peak, Mt. Samos, near its western end, being 4,705 ft. (1,434 m.) high. The mountains of Samos are a continuation of Mt. Mycale (Samsun Dagi) on the mainland. Pop. (1961) 41,124. With Ikaria and the Fournoi Islands, the island forms the *nomos* (department) of Samos (pop. [1961] 52,022) and the Greek Orthodox bishopric of Samos and Ikaria. The capital of the *nomos* is at Samos (formerly called Limin Vatheos) in a deep bay on the north coast of the island, a modern town connected by road with villages round both sides of the bay and with Pithagorion (formerly Tiganion) on the south coast, the site of the ancient city. A third port, Karlovasi, farther west on the northern coast, serves a separate lowland district. The island is remarkably fertile, and a great portion of it is covered with vineyards. Oil, resins, silk, cotton, and tobacco are also grown, and barges and sailing vessels are built at Pithagorion, almost wholly from local timber. Cigarette making employs many women and girls, the tobacco coming chiefly from Thrace.

History.—The island was occupied in the Early Bronze Age and by Mycenaean Greeks. Later it received an Ionian population, reputedly from Epidaurus in Argolis. By the 7th century B.C. it had become one of the leading commercial centres of Greece because of its offshore position near the trade routes from inner Asia Minor that ran through the valleys of the Maeander and Cayster rivers. The Samians also traded with the Black Sea and with Egypt, and claimed to be the first Greeks to reach the Strait of Gibraltar. Their commerce brought them into close relations with Cyrene, Corinth, and Chalcis but made them bitter rivals of their mainland neighbour, Miletus. The feud involved both cities in the Lelantine War (8th century B.C.), when Corinth built ships for the Samians. The result favoured Miletus, but in the 6th century the insular position of Samos preserved it from the mainland aggressions to which Miletus was exposed.

About 535 B.C., when its oligarchy was overturned by the tyrant Polycrates (*q.v.*), Samos reached the height of its prosperity. Its navy "ruled the waves" from its new deep-sea harbour and blockaded the mainland subjects of Persia; the tunneled aqueduct (still open) insured a plenteous water supply, and the great Temple of Hera was built, replacing a succession of earlier temples. Polycrates first intrigued and then quarreled with the Persian governor of Lydia, and after his death by treachery (c. 522) Darius conquered Samos and partly depopulated it.

The island had regained much when, probably in 499, it joined the general revolt of the Ionians against Persia; but part of its contingent deserted at the decisive Battle of Lade (c. 495). In 479, however, following Xerxes' defeats in Greece, the Samians serving in the Persian fleet assisted the Greeks at Mycale. In the Delian League (*q.v.*) the Samians held special privileges, and they remained loyal to Athens until 440, when a dispute with Miletus which the Athenians had decided against them provoked them to secede. With a fleet of 60 ships they held their own for some time against a large Athenian fleet led by Pericles himself, but after a siege they capitulated and were degraded to a tributary rank. Throughout the Peloponnesian War Samos was one of the most loyal dependencies of Athens and a temporary home of the Athenian democracy during the revolution of the Four Hundred at Athens (411 B.C.); in the last stage of the war, it was rewarded with the Athenian franchise. After the defeat of Athens by Sparta (404), Samos was besieged by the Spartan admiral Lysander and placed under an oligarchy. In 394, when the Spartan navy withdrew, the island declared its independence and reestablished a democracy, but by the Peace of Antalcidas (386) it fell under Persian dominion. Recovered by the Athenians in 365 after a siege, Samos received a body of military settlers.

After 322, when Athens was again deprived of Samos, its fate is obscure. For some time (about 275–270 B.C.) it served as a base for the Egyptian fleet, at other periods it recognized the Seleucid kings of Syria. In 189 B.C. it was transferred by the Romans to the kings of Pergamum. Included from 133 in the Roman province of Asia, it revolted and joined Aristonicus of Pergamum (132) and Mithradates of Pontus (88) against Rome and forfeited its autonomy. Between the reigns of Augustus and Vespasian it recovered its autonomy and remained prosperous.

Under Byzantine rule Samos became the head of the Aegean *theme* (military district). After the 13th century it passed through much the same changes as Chios and became the property of the Genoese company of Giustiniani (1346–*c*. 1550; *see* CHIOS). At the Turkish conquest it was severely depopulated and provided with new settlers, partly Albanians.

The Samians declared themselves independent of Turkey in 1821 and took a great part in the ensuing war, being saved from Turkish invasion in 1824 by the naval victories of A. V. Miaoulis. On the conclusion of peace (1832), however, the island was handed back to the Turks, but it held an exceptionally advantageous position, being in fact self-governed, though paying tribute, and ruled by a Greek governor (nominated by the sultan) who had the title "prince of Samos" and was supported and controlled by a Greek council and assembly. The island prospered but was eventually annexed to Greece in 1912.

The ancient capital was on the south coast of the island, at the modern Pithagorion, directly opposite the promontory of Mycale. There a natural cove, dominated by a low hill, has been converted by ancient and modern breakwaters into a safe port for small vessels. Behind the modern town rises a steep enclosing ridge, Astipalaia, crowned by Polycrates' wall and pierced by his aqueduct. From this city a road led about 4 mi. W to the Temple of Hera, whose site, close to the shore, is still marked by a single column which has given to the neighbouring headland the name of Kolonna. German excavators have revealed its foundations, and several others of the sanctuary buildings, as well as rich finds of sculpture and minor objects.

The modern capital was at Khora, about 2 mi. from Pithagorion, until 1832, when it was moved to Vathi on the north coast (now part of the town of Samos).

Samos was the birthplace of the philosopher Pythagoras and also produced a school of sculptors, beginning with Rhoecus and Theodorus, who are said to have invented the art of casting statues in bronze and were the architects of the Temple of Hera. Another famous Samian sculptor was Pythagoras, who migrated to Rhegium. Some fine 6th-century vases can be attributed to the island. The name "Samian ware," often given to red pottery found in Roman settlements, has little scientific meaning.

See also references under "Samos," in the Index.

BIBLIOGRAPHY.—L. Bürchner in Pauly-Wissowa, *Real-Encyclopädie der classischen Altertumswissenschaft*, 2nd series, vol. i, 2162–2218 (1920). *Excavations:* Reports by E. Buschor *et al.* in *Mitteilungen des Deutschen Archäologischen Instituts: athenische Abteilung*, liv onward (1929 *et seq.*); O. Reuther, *Der Heratempel von Samos* (1957); German Archaeological Institute, *Samos*, i– (1961– ; in progress). (J. Bo.)

SAMOSATA (modern SAMSAT), a ruined city on the right bank of the upper Euphrates, the site of which is now occupied by the small village of Samsat in Adiyaman *il* (province), Turkey. The village lies about 30 mi. NNW of Edessa (modern Urfa) and has a population (1960) of 991. In ancient times Samosata was an important crossing point of the river. It formed one of the series of border forts, of which Edessa (*q.v.*) was the most important, for the frontier defense of Upper Mesopotamia. Although it is uncertain whether it was ever on the Persian royal road, there was a bridge at this point in Strabo's time, and caravan routes diverged to Diyarbakir in the north and downstream to Edessa.

Samosata appears originally to have been a Hittite city, incorporated in the Assyrian Empire in 708 B.C. It later became the capital of the Hellenistic kingdom of Commagene, and part of the

Roman province of Syria in A.D. 72. It lost its status as capital city of a district under Constantine, and in the 10th century was temporarily an administrative military district of the Byzantine Empire. (N. Tu.; S. Er.; E. Tu.)

SAMOTHRACE (modern Greek SAMOTHRAKI), an island in the north of the Aegean Sea, nearly opposite the mouth of the Hebros (Maritsa) River and 15 mi. NNW of Imbros (Imroz), included in the modern Greek *nomos* (department) of Evros. Area 69 sq.mi. (178 sq.km.). Pop. (1961) 3,830. The island rises to 5,577 ft. (1,700 m.) at Mt. Fengari, the highest peak in the northern Aegean; Homer (*Iliad*, xiii, 12) pictures Poseidon using its summit to watch the fighting round Troy. Agriculture and sponge fishing are carried on, and the hot sulfur springs on the north coast attract visitors.

Samothrace's mountainous character and lack of harbours precluded political importance, but it was famous for the cult of the Cabeiri (*q.v.*), attributed by Herodotus (ii, 51) and others to pre-Greek Pelasgians. Under the Romans it was a free state. It was captured by the Turks from the Genoese Gattilusi in 1456 and remained almost continuously Turkish until taken by the Greek fleet in 1912. During World War II it was under Bulgarian occupation (1941–44).

The ancient city was situated at Palaiopolis on the north side of the island near the sea, below the modern village of Samothraki. In the 19th century there were French and Austrian excavations on the site, renewed by the French in 1923–25, and taken up again by archaeologists from New York University in 1938. The Sanctuary of the Great Gods lay on a long terrace below the town walls. Most of the buildings are Hellenistic, notably the Rotunda dedicated by Queen Arsinoe II of Egypt in the 280s; Ptolemy II's Propylon; the Nike Fountain, over which stood the "Victory" (probably set up by the Rhodians *c*. 190 B.C. to commemorate a sea battle, discovered in 1863 and now in the Louvre, Paris; *see* GREEK ART); and the great Hieron, or sanctuary. There are traces, however, of earlier buildings of the 6th century, and of the Anaktoron, or hall of initiation, built about 500. The finds give evidence for the worship not only of the Cabeiri but also of the Anatolian Great Mother (Cybele). The earliest are of the 7th century and reflect well the interaction of the Greek and native cultures.

BIBLIOGRAPHY.—A. Conze *et al.*, *Archaeologische Untersuchungen auf Samothrake*, 2 vol. (1875–80); *Inscriptiones Graecae*, vol. xii, fasc. 8, no. 150–260 (1909; inscriptions); K. Lehmann (ed.), *Samothrace*, i (1959–), *Samothrace: a Guide to the Excavations and the Museum*, 2nd ed. (1960). (J. Bo.)

SAMOYED, a division of the Uralic linguistic stock found in the northern U.S.S.R. and comprising two language groups, Northern and Southern Samoyedic (*see* URAL-ALTAIC LANGUAGES). The former includes the Yurak or Nenets (about 25,000 in the 1960s, probably including a small number of Yenets, *see* below), reindeer pastoralists, sea-mammal hunters, and fishermen occupying tundras from Kanin Peninsula on the White Sea 900 mi. eastward to the Yenisei River in Siberia as well as the forested basin of the Pur; the Yenets (800 in 1926), sedentary fishermen on the lower Yenisei; and the Tavgi or Nganasany (about 700 in the 1960s), wild-reindeer hunters of the Taimyr Peninsula in the far north. In the 20th century the Selkup (about 4,000 in the 1960s) alone represent Southern Samoyedic. They include fishermen and trappers of the Taz River basin; fishermen, cattle and horse breeders, and trappers on the Tym and Ket (southeast branches of the Ob or Obi River), roughly half of them speaking only Russian. In the Sayan ranges, the Samoyedic dialects (Kamasin, Karagas, Mator or Koybal, and Taigi) have been totally replaced by the Turkic languages and Russian. The Nenets were (1960s) increasing at about one percent per year, while the smaller groups seemed to be barely holding even against assimilation.

Early in the Christian era, proto-Samoyedic peoples lived in southwest Siberia, probably occupying the Ob–Irtysh (Irtish) basin. They traded with archaic Turkic folk, borrowing from them terms for horses, sable and ermine, bells, and money; early contacts with Kettic peoples are also evident (*see* KET). Proto-Samoyedic culture included reindeer domestication (with castration); the casting of bronze and forging of iron; tailored arctic clothing (parka is an indirect Samoyedic loan to English); the conical tent and the cache raised off the ground; and, in religion, shamans, enchantment by singing accompanied by a drum, wooden idols, and the idea of luck. Furthermore, the archaeology of early Samoyedic sites (and, in part, Selkup ethnology) reveals villages with semisubterranean houses fortified by earthen walls and moats; subsistence from domesticated horses, cattle and sheep as well as fishing and hunting; pit-and-comb marked pottery; birch-bark manufactures; bone as well as metal tools and weapons; helmets and armour; cemeteries and votive hoards, with cast images of men, beasts, and fantastic creatures, with imported wares and money.

Ostyak (q.v.) pressures from the west, beginning about 700 A.D., displaced the Samoyeds. The Mator were identified east of the Irtysh River in the 10th century; other Samoyeds reached north Russia before 1100. Cultural change accompanied migration. Pottery disappeared. In the tundra, the Samoyeds adopted arctic aboriginal elements, such as sea-mammal hunting, reindeer hunting with decoys and enclosures, and sacrificial mounds of reindeer antlers. They transmitted reindeer domestication and many religious beliefs to the Ostyaks, the Zyrians, and the Yukaghir; they had less influence on the Lapps.

Despite variant subsistence patterns, recent Samoyedic cultures have retained similar forms of social organization and religion. All have patrilineal, named clans owning definite territories, with sanctuaries, cemeteries, and exclusive economic rights. Marriage is strictly exogamic (outside the clan) and residence is usually patrilocal; widows normally marry a younger clansman of the deceased. Older sons receive allotments, leaving to form new lineages; the youngest inherits the residual. Shamans are clan officials, curing, divining luck and ill-doing (see SHAMANISM). The cosmogony includes a high god; a universe tree upholding seven heavens; an underworld; sun, moon, forest, water, and ancestral spirits. Shamanistic magic "flights," animal sacrifices and dedications, and the "feeding" of household idols are prominent rituals.

See also KARAGAS.

BIBLIOGRAPHY.—K. Donner, "On the Oldest Relations Between Samoyeds and Turks," *J. Soc. Finno-Ougr.*, 40, no. 1, p. 42 (1924), "On the Age of Ostyak and Vogul Reindeer Domestication," *Fin.-Ugr. Forsch.*, 18:115–144 (1927), *Among the Samoyed in Siberia* (1915; Eng. trans., 1954); V. Islavin, *Samoyedy* (1847); A. A. Popov, *Tavgitsy*, Trud. Inst. Ant. i. Etno. i, no. 5, (1936); Y. D. Prokofyeva, "On Selkup Social Organization," Trud. Inst. Etnog. xviii (1952); P. Hajdú, *The Samoyed Peoples and Languages* (1963). (D. B. SH.)

SAMPAN: see BOAT.

SAMPLER, a small rectangular piece of embroidery worked as a "sample" of a beginner's skill and as a means of teaching the stitches. During the 17th–19th centuries every little girl worked her "sampler," and samplers have become of interest to collectors. They usually contained the alphabet, the worker's name, the date, Bible texts, verses, and mottoes, the whole surrounded with some conventional design.

SAMPSON, WILLIAM THOMAS (1840–1902), commander of the U.S. North Atlantic squadron during the Spanish-American War (q.v.). He was born at Palmyra, N.Y., on Feb. 9, 1840, and graduated at the head of his class from the U.S. Naval Academy, Annapolis, Md., in 1861. He served in a wide variety of assignments and rose to the rank of captain by 1890. He was chief of the Bureau of Ordnance in 1893–97; about 95% of the guns employed in the Spanish-American War were made under his superintendence. His influence was felt decisively in the distribution of guns and armour, and in the training of the personnel of the Navy. In February 1898 he was president of the board of inquiry that investigated the destruction of the battleship "Maine."

At the outbreak of the war with Spain, Sampson was placed in charge of the North Atlantic squadron, and conducted the blockade of Cuba. The ships under his command destroyed the Spanish vessels when they issued from the harbour of Santiago and attempted to escape. Sampson himself was not actually present at the battle, having started for Siboney just before it began in order to confer with General Shafter, commanding the land

forces, but the engagement was fought in accordance with his instructions. He was promoted to commodore in 1898, to rear admiral on March 3, 1899, and was made commandant of the Boston (Charlestown) Navy Yard in October of the same year. He died in Washington, D.C., on May 6, 1902.

SAMSON, a member of the tribe of Dan, was an early Israelite folk hero whose exploits against the Philistines are recorded in Judg. 14–16. The narratives, similar in essence to other stories in Judges and Samuel, fall into seven episodes in which individual anecdotes relate the circumstances of his birth and his various escapades with the Philistines. Samson, though listed among the judges, was neither a liberator nor a counselor of Israel as were other judges before him. His personal exploits serve not merely as a preview of the impending struggle between Israel and her most dangerous and toughest enemy; they also reflect the early Israelite customs and provide some information about the Philistine civilization. (*See* PHILISTINES.)

Although the narratives throw little light on the existing Israelite religion, they do show a religious motivation. The circumstances of Samson's birth (Judg. 13) have a strong resemblance to the birth stories of other Israelite heroes whose mothers conceived through supernatural intervention (cf. Gen. 17–18; 25:21; 29:31). Moreover, Samson, before his conception, was dedicated to God as a lifelong Nazirite (cf. Jer. 1:5). As such, he was to abstain from (1) wine and all other products of the grape, (2) cutting his hair, and (3) contact with the dead (Num. 6). He is described as a charismatic figure who is periodically seized by the Spirit of the Lord. (*See* NAZIRITE.) Thus, all his acts, even those without apparent religious significance, are presented as divinely guided. Some of this may be due to later editorial revisions, but undoubtedly much of it was an organic part of the original text.

Points of resemblance between Samson and various Babylonian and Greek mythological characters have often been noted. While these cannot be denied, Samson is much more human than his counterparts in the pagan myths and legends. On the other hand, to regard him as a solar cult hero is assuming too much. This theory is based on the facts that his home was near the shrine of the sun, Beth-Shemesh; and his power lay in his hair, which might be equated with the sun's rays, giving agricultural life, and cut off by night (the name "Delilah" could be a pun on the Hebrew word for "night"). Further, his name could conceivably be derived from the Hebrew word "sun" (shemesh). But Samson is in fact a good Canaanite personal name, derived probably from shamshiyanu, which later became shimshon, a personal name whose equivalent has been found in the 14th- or 15th-century B.C. Ugaritic texts; it is also found as the name of a Syrian town in a 12th-century Egyptian list.

Although the narratives in their present state show legendary accretions and contain some later theological ideas, Samson was a historical character. His individual exploits against the Philistines, which may have provoked their later aggression against Israel, must have so impressed the popular imagination that the people credited him with superhuman strength. The anecdotes about his marvelous deeds were probably related by storytellers with a great deal of gusto, yet the tragic end of the blind hero, crushed under the collapsed temple of Dagon at Gaza when with a surge of strength he pushed apart its supporting pillars, must have had a sobering effect on the listeners.

Samson narratives—especially the episode (Judg. 16:4–21) in which Delilah, bribed by the Philistines, wheedled from him the secret of his strength and betrayed him into their hands, and that of Samson's death—have been a source for many artistic creations. Rembrandt, Rubens, and Van Dyck used them as subjects for paintings, Dürer for woodcuts, Saint-Saëns for his opera *Samson et Dalila*, and Handel for his oratorio *Samson*. Milton made Samson's death the subject of his *Samson Agonistes*.

See also JUDGES, BOOK OF.

BIBLIOGRAPHY.—C. F. Burney, *Judges*, 2nd ed., pp. 335–408 (1930); J. M. Myers, "Judges" in *The Interpreter's Bible*, vol. ii, pp. 775–798 (1953); H. W. Hertzberg, *Die Bücher Joshua, Richter, Ruth*, pp. 223–235 (1953); A. Smythe Palmer, *The Samson-Saga and Its Place in Comparative Religion* (1913). (J. L. MI.)

SAMSUN (ancient AMISUS), the chief town of Samsun *il* (province) of Turkey, lies on the south coast of the Black Sea between the deltas of the Kizil Irmak and Yesil Irmak, 200 mi. (322 km.) NE of Ankara. Pop. (1960) 87,688. A broad street with government offices, hotels, and shops traverses the town from east to west along the coast. An annual Black Sea Fair is held there in July. Samsun is a thriving town and the outlet for the trade of the interior regions and of the middle Black Sea coast. Its port is well protected and is the principal northern shipping point for Turkish tobacco, cereals, and wool. The chief industries are the manufacture of cigarettes and textiles. The town is connected by rail and road with Sivas and Ankara, and by sea with Istanbul.

Ancient Amisus, which stood on a promontory about 1½ mi. NW of Samsun, was, next to Sinop (*q.v.*), the most flourishing of the Greek settlements on the Euxine Sea, and under the kings of Pontus it was a rich trading town. By the 1st century A.D. it had displaced Sinop as the north port of the great trade route from Central Asia, and later it was one of the chief towns of the Comneni of Trabzon.

SAMSUN IL (pop. [1960] 654,602) is agricultural and densely populated. It is one of the principal sources of Turkish tobacco, one variety of which is known as "Samsun."

(N. TU.; E. TU.; S. ER.)

SAMUDRA GUPTA (reigned *c.* A.D. 335–375), Indian emperor, son of Chandra Gupta I and the Licchavi princess Kumaradevi. Most of the information about his reign is derived from the long inscription engraved on the Asokan pillar at Allahabad. According to this record, Samudra was appointed emperor by his father in preference to other claimants, and he seems to have had to repress revolts in the earlier part of his reign. On the pacification of the kingdom, which probably then reached from Allahabad to the borders of Bengal, he began a series of wars which much increased its extent. One of these led him to southern India where, after defeating a number of minor rulers, he penetrated to the Pallava kingdom of Kancheepuram (Kanchipuram), defeating a king called Vishnugopa. In this southern campaign he restored the defeated kings to their thrones on the payment of tribute, but several kings of northern India were "violently uprooted" and their territories added to that of the Gupta Empire. At the height of his power nearly the whole of the valley of the Ganges was directly administered and he received homage and tribute from rulers of parts of east Bengal, Assam, Nepal, the eastern part of the Punjab, and various independent tribes of Rajasthan.

Samudra Gupta issued gold *dinaras* of many types, all of high gold content and excellent workmanship. He performed the ancient Vedic horse sacrifice, which is commemorated by a special coin. According to the Allahabad inscription he was a skilled musician and poet, and on one of his coins he is shown playing the harp.

BIBLIOGRAPHY.—A. S. Altekar, *Corpus of Indian Coins*, vol. iv, *The Coinage of the Gupta Empire* (1957); R. C. Majumdar (ed.), *History and Culture of the Indian People*, vol. iii, *The Classical Age* (1954); R. K. Mookerji, *The Gupta Empire* (1948). (A. L. BA.)

SAMUEL, the most outstanding character in Israel's history between Moses and David, is represented in I Samuel in every role of leadership open to a man of his day—seer, Nazirite, priest, judge, and military leader. The traditions concerning him have been much edited and embellished with legend, so that it is not easy to form a clear historical picture of him. One episode must be dismissed as fabrication: the story of his miraculous and conclusive defeat of the Philistines (7) is contradicted by the subsequent military exploits of Saul and David and is best ascribed to a late editor who wished to belittle the achievement of Saul. The story of Samuel's childhood (1–3) contains elements of folklore, but there is no reason to doubt that he grew up as a Nazirite associated with the priesthood at Shiloh, or that he had prophetic clairvoyance. As a Nazirite, dedicated to the defense of the religion of Yahweh against syncretism with the fertility cults of the Canaanite Baals, he had some affinity with the prophetic guilds of wandering ecstatics who made their first appearance at this time; but his visions, in his role of seer, owed nothing to their collective and contagious ecstasy, so that he resembled more closely the great prophets of later times than those who bore the name of prophet in his own day. As priest his chief function was the giving of authoritative decisions from God, including perhaps the dispensation of justice; and here too his gifts as seer differentiated him from ordinary priests who derived their decisions from the sacred lot (14:36–42; 23:6–12; 30:7–8).

Samuel's greatest claim to fame was the establishment of monarchy in Israel. The biblical account of this is a conflation of two apparently irreconcilable sources. According to the earlier one (9; 10:1–16; 11:1–11, 15), written probably in the reign of Solomon, Samuel, prompted by God, took the initiative in anointing Saul as king, to give unity to the divided tribes of Israel, and to lead them to freedom from Philistine domination. According to the later source (8; 10:17–24), written when the monarchy had fallen into disrepute, Samuel, already the theocratic ruler of a united Israel, resisted the popular demand for a king, because it involved a repudiation of the sovereignty of Yahweh. The early source is the more trustworthy, and it is possible to regard the later one as evidence only for the antimonarchical feeling of the prophetic school that produced it. On the other hand, it is unlikely that these prophetic writers would have depicted Samuel as the critic of monarchy if he had in fact been its wholehearted advocate. It may be, then, that the two sources preserve the two sides of an early and long-continued debate, and that Samuel the kingmaker was a big enough man to see both the advantages and the dangers of his innovation. *See also* SAMUEL, BOOKS OF; SAUL.

(G. B. CA.)

SAMUEL OF NEHARDEA, usually called MAR SAMUEL OR YARHINAI (*c.* 165– *c.* 257), Babylonian rabbi, master of the traditional Law and famed for his scientific attainments, was born and died in Nehardea in Babylonia. He was one of the first to compile a calendar of the Jewish year, thus preparing the way for the fixation of the festivals by means of scientific calculations. But Samuel's fame rests on the service he rendered in adapting the life of the Jews of the diaspora to the law of the land: "The law of the state is binding law" was the principle he enunciated. When the shah of Persia, Shapur, captured Caesarea Mazaca, the Cappadocian capital (modern Kayseri, Turk.), Samuel refused to mourn for the 12,000 Jews who lost their lives in its defense.

See H. Graetz, *History of the Jews,* Eng. trans., vol. ii, ch. xix (1893). (I. A.)

SAMUEL, HERBERT LOUIS SAMUEL, 1ST VISCOUNT (1870–1963), English statesman and philosopher whose career as a social legislator, administrator, and Liberal leader was distinguished by adherence to principle and a gift for persuading others to compromise. He was born at Liverpool on Nov. 6, 1870. After working in the Whitechapel slums of London he resolved to enter Parliament and press for social legislation. Twice defeated in South Oxfordshire (1895 and 1900), he was elected (1902) Liberal M.P. for the Cleveland Division of Yorkshire. As parliamentary undersecretary to the Home Office (1905) in the new Liberal government he was responsible for the Children Act (1908) which established, among other things, juvenile courts, the probation system, and the detention centres which Samuel called "Borstals." Appointed chancellor of the Duchy of Lancaster (May 1909), he became the first member of the Jewish community to attain cabinet rank. As postmaster general (1910–14; 1915–16) he recognized the postal trades unions and nationalized the telephone services. In January 1916 he became home secretary, but resigned when Lloyd George formed his coalition government. He was chairman of the select committee on national expenditure (1917–18) and special commissioner to Belgium (1919).

Defeated in the general election (1918), in 1920 Samuel was appointed first high commissioner for Palestine, an office of especial delicacy and difficulty which he discharged with great distinction, improving Palestine's economy and fostering harmony among the different religious communities. On his return (1925) he presided over the royal commission on the coal industry; its report (1926) revealed his acute power of analysis and balanced judgment. Subsequently his skill as a mediator was a vital factor in negotiations which secured the settlement of the general strike.

As Liberal Party chairman (1927–29) he held the balance between Lloyd George and Asquith. Returned to Parliament for Darwen, Lancashire (1929), in 1931 he became home secretary in the national government; but his free trade principles led him to resign with other Liberal ministers in September 1932, in opposition to the Ottawa Agreements. In 1935 he was defeated at Darwen but in 1937 entered the House of Lords as Viscount Samuel of Mount Carmel, and of Toxteth in the City of Liverpool. In the Lords as Liberal representative, and leader (1944–55), he spoke with authority, lucidity, and wit. A visit to Palestine (1940) and the chairmanship of several committees showed his continued interest in the Jewish national home.

Empiricism marked Lord Samuel's career as both politician and philosopher. As president (1931–59) of the British (later Royal) Institute of Philosophy, he interpreted philosophy to the public in such books as *Practical Ethics* (1935) and *Belief and Action; an Everyday Philosophy* (1937; new edition 1953). The breadth of his liberal humanity was revealed in his *Memoirs* (1945), in *A Book of Quotations* (1947; 2nd edition 1954), and in broadcasts which made widely known the warmth and idealism underlying his intellectual brilliance. He died in London on Feb. 5, 1963.

See J. Bowle, *Viscount Samuel* (1957). (W. R. Da.)

SAMUEL, BOOKS OF, two books of the Hebrew Old Testament covering the stories of the prophet Samuel and of Saul and David, the first two kings of Israel. The Jews rank these books among the Former Prophets (Joshua to Kings) in distinction from the Latter Prophets (Isaiah to Malachi). They were originally one book and are so written in Hebrew manuscripts and so printed in the earliest printed Hebrew Bibles. The first complete Bible to divide the book into two parts was the sixth, known as the first great rabbinic Bible (printed by Daniel Bomberg, Venice, 1517). The division into two books first appears in the Septuagint, the Greek translation of the Old Testament made in the 3rd and 2nd centuries B.C. Here the two parts are called "I and II Kingdoms." This division is continued in the Vulgate, Jerome's Latin translation, but with the title "Kings," and so also in the Douai version. The Authorized or King James version, however (and other English versions derived from it), uses the Hebrew title. Thus I and II Samuel in the original Hebrew and in the King James version are I and II Kingdoms in the Septuagint and I and II Kings in the Vulgate and its translations, while I and II Kings in the Hebrew and in the King James version are III and IV Kingdoms in the Septuagint and III and IV Kings in the Vulgate.

The Books of Samuel form a link in the history of Israel and Judah between the settlement in Canaan under Joshua, and the early sporadic and local struggles with the original inhabitants described in the Book of Judges, on the one hand; and the story of the kingdoms of Judah and Israel, with unified control and central organization, that form the subject of the Books of Kings. The two books of Samuel give the history of "the making of the realm": they tell the story of the change from tribal chiefs to a country and a king.

Contents.—The Books of Samuel fall naturally into four parts:

I Sam. 1–15	stories of Samuel, of the fall of the house of Eli, and of Saul until his rejection
I Sam. 16–II Sam. 5	story of Saul and David
II Sam. 6–20:22	story of David the king
II Sam. 20:23–24:25	miscellaneous appendix

Stories of Samuel.—The book opens with a picture that is clearly contemporary of the ark-shrine of Shiloh at the annual festival. Elkanah and his wives come for the annual sacrifice and festal meal. His hitherto childless wife Hannah prays for a son and promises to dedicate him to God's service. Samuel (*q.v.*) is born, brought to Shiloh after weaning, and is left there to grow up in the holy service. The boy Samuel hears the voice of God in the night, and through him God warns Eli of the doom of his house. The ark is lost to the Philistines, who cannot hold it. After many wanderings it comes to rest in Israelite territory at Kiriath-jearim, the modern Israeli "forest of the martyrs." After 20 years, Samuel, now grown in prestige and wisdom, obtains some

relief from the Philistine domination, but the clouds gather once more until Saul (*q.v.*) rallies Israel and obtains some respite. Saul, anointed by Samuel as first king of Israel, seeks to build up a small standing army and gathers around him all the strong fighting men he can find. Among them is David, whose friendship with Saul's son Jonathan is comparable with that of Orestes and Pylades in Greek story and that of Aeneas and "faithful" Achates in Roman story. David's lament for Saul and Jonathan is one of the treasures of Israel's literature.

Saul and David.—The second part of the two books tells of the rift between Saul and David. Saul ultimately becomes jealous of David's popularity and seeks to kill him. Partly because of his jealousy and partly because of increasing pressure from the Philistines, the king becomes afflicted with bouts of melancholia and ungovernable rage, until at last David flees for his life to the fastnesses of the Negev. For Saul, all grows dark. God has deserted him, Samuel turns against him, the witch of Endor can give him no hope, his resources become more and more limited as more and more of his toughest warriors join David's band of freebooters in the far south, and at last Saul and his three strong sons die with the flower of Israel in the last fight against the Philistines on the slopes of Mt. Gilboa.

David the King.—The third section of the books tells of David's rise to power. At the news of Saul's death, he sets up a rival kingdom in the south, and at the death of Saul's son Ish-baal (Ishbosheth) seven and a half years later he gains control of the whole country. David was "a man of war" and he "conquered all his enemies round about" from the border of Egypt to away beyond Hermon, and from the Mediterranean to beyond Damascus. He established a dynasty in Judah which lasted for over 400 years, until there ceased to be a king in Judah. He was a man to whom both men and women could be loyal, and this was especially notable in his cousin Joab, his general in the field. He was a great fighter, a great lover, a foolishly indulgent father, a great singer, and a great sinner. He came to be the type of a God-fearing man, the type of the true king and the "father" of the coming Messiah and king. But was David really the generous hero and Saul the ill-tempered villain? Or was Saul the honest rugged ruler called to a task beyond the wit and power of man, and David the handsome villain? And was Samuel like Warwick, the kingmaker of English history, who made one king, could not control him, and therefore made another? This third part of the two books is continued in I Kings 1:1–2:11, the account of David's abdication which was broken off in order to be used to introduce the story of Solomon. (*See* also DAVID.)

Appendix.—The fourth section contains some early material, but it appears to have been added after the rest of the book had been compiled. After a fragmentary list of David's officers (II Sam. 20:23–26), there are six short sections: (*a*) 21:1–14, famine and reparation, and (*f*) 24:1–25, pestilence and penitence; (*b*) 21:15–22 and (*e*) 23:8–23, tales of prowess, with another list of heroes (23:24–39) added; (*c*) and (*d*) 22 and 23:1–7, psalms, the first of which is equivalent to Ps. 18 and the second a very ancient psalm. Apparently (*af*) was the first addition to the book, then (*be*) was inserted into (*af*), and finally (*cd*) was inserted into (*ab*)–(*ef*).

Composition and Date.—Scholars are for the most part agreed that there are two main strands in the two books of Samuel. The first, designated *A*, is the earlier history, in which Samuel is a local obscure seer and the prime mover in anointing Saul to be king, the man who set out to seek lost asses and found a kingdom. The second strand, designated *B*, is the later account, where Samuel is a national figure, judge of all Israel, and the last of the judges. After a preliminary doubt, he comes out strongly against the idea of a king, and finally, unwillingly and with dreadful warnings, agrees to the popular demand and makes Saul king.

Evidence of the existence of these two strands is to be seen not only in the two accounts of the founding of the monarchy (*A:* I Sam. 9:1–10:16 and 11:1–11; *B:* 8, 10:17–25a, 12) but also in the two accounts of David's coming to Saul's notice. In *A* (I Sam. 16:14–23) David is brought to court to play on his harp and thereby to soothe Saul's troubled mind. In *B* (I Sam. 17:12–58) the boy David comes with supplies to visit his brothers who are serving in the Israelite army, pleads to stay and see the fight, accepts the challenge of the giant Goliath, and kills him with his slingstone and the giant's own sword. There are two accounts of the origin of the saying "Is Saul also among the prophets?" (*A:* I Sam. 10:10–12; and *B:* I Sam. 19:18–24); two accounts, so interwoven as to make a confused story, of David's flight from Saul (I Sam. 20); two accounts of the treachery to David of the Ziphites (I Sam. 23:19–28; and I Sam. 26:1–3), and two accounts (which, however, may genuinely refer to two occasions) of how David spares Saul's life (I Sam. 24:1–22; and I Sam. 26:4–25a). Some verses, scattered throughout the two books, have unmistakable associations with the Deuteronomic writings, and there are the miscellaneous additions of II Sam. 20:23–24:25. O. Eissfeldt maintains that there are three main sources, and there are certainly many passages which do not fit into the two main sources, *A* and *B*.

It has been suggested that the opening chapters are from a lost history of the ark. It is clear that II Sam. 9–20 is drawn from the court history of David and thus forms the oldest piece of continuous prose in the Old Testament. It bears every evidence of being contemporary with the events it describes, and whoever wrote this story (Ahimaaz? Zadok?) was the true father of history rather than the Greek Herodotus who flourished some 500 years later. The *A* strand is earlier than 800 B.C., the *B* strand is from the end of the 8th century; and the two books probably achieved finality (apart possibly from the appendix) in the great revision under Deuteronomic influence about 550 B.C. This was the revision which produced the long history which stretches from Deuteronomy through Joshua, Judges, and Samuel to the end of Kings.

Influence.—The influence of the Books of Samuel is general rather than particular, though there are three passages of great influence. The books take their place in the general pattern of God's providential care for his people of Israel and of his mighty acts of salvation on their behalf. The first of the three particular passages is the song of Hannah (I Sam. 2:1–10). This passage is part of the original reading from the prophets for the Jewish New Year's Day festival, already established before the time of Christ. The reading from the Law was Gen. 21, and both passages deal with a distressed and barren woman who at long last bore a son (*cf.* I Sam. 2:5, "the barren has borne seven"). The song is also the basis of the Magnificat (Luke 1:46–55), with its emphasis, so strong in both testaments, on God's particular care for and intervention on behalf of all that are distressed, the poor, the widow, the fatherless, and the stranger. The second important passage describes Samuel's sacrifice and prayer in I Sam. 7:9, which is mentioned in Ecclus. 46:16. Samuel and Moses in Hebrew tradition are the two great intercessors for Israel, the two men who were "mighty in prayer." The third passage, the most important of the three, is God's prophecy to David in II Sam. 7. Just as the song of Moses after crossing the Red Sea (Ex. 15) is the seedbed for all subsequent growth of the idea of the Kingdom of God, so this chapter is the seedbed for ideas of the Davidic Messiah. For both Christian and Jewish exegeses there is no element more fundamental. *See also* BIBLE.

BIBLIOGRAPHY.—Eng. trans. with commentary by A. R. S. Kennedy (1905) in *Century Bible* and by G. B. Caird, J. C. Schroeder, and G. Little in G. A. Buttrick (ed.), *Interpreter's Bible*, vol. ii (1953); commentary by L. H. Brockington in *Peake's Commentary* (1962); commentary on the Hebrew text by H. P. Smith (1899) in *International Critical Commentary*. German trans. with commentary by H. W. Hertzberg (1956) in *Das Alte Testament Deutsch;* French trans. with commentary, 2nd ed. (1961), in *La Sainte Bible. See also* S. R. Driver, *Notes on the Hebrew Text and the Topography of the Books of Samuel,* 2nd ed. (1913); O. Eissfeldt, *Die Komposition der Samuelisbücher* (1931); A. C. Welch, *Kings and Prophets of Israel* (1952).
(N. H. S.)

SAMUEL HA-NAGID (in full, ABU IBRAHIM SAMUEL BEN YOSEF HALEVI IBN NAGRELA) (993–1056), Jewish statesman, warrior, talmudic scholar, grammarian, philologist, poet, and polemicist, a man of remarkable talents who served simultaneously as vizier of the Sinhaja Berber kingdom of Granada and as the *nagid* ("chief") of Granadan Jewry, was born in Córdoba, Spain.

The son of wealthy parents, he was accorded a thoroughgoing education in all branches of Jewish and Islamic learning. When Córdoba was sacked in 1013, he fled to Málaga, where he opened a small shop. His skill in Arabic calligraphy and literature caught the attention of the vizier of King Habbus of Granada, and Samuel was employed to serve as the vizier's secretary and adviser on affairs of state. On the death of his patron, Samuel succeeded in attaining the office of vizier, and on the death of the king soon after succeeded also in having King Habbus' younger son Badis elevated to the throne. From that moment until his death, Samuel was the power behind the throne. In this capacity, he steered Granada through years of continuous warfare, and he himself actively participated in all the major campaigns. His influence was so great that he was even able to have his son Joseph succeed him as vizier.

Samuel ruled not only Muslims but the Jews as well. As *nagid* of the Jewish community, he appointed all the judges and took strong measures against the schismatic Karaites. As head of the talmudic academy, he exercised control over the training of legal experts. He was a gifted poet whose songs of friendship, love, and war reveal an individual asserting his individuality with superb intensity. As a philologist and grammarian, he not only wrote a concordance to the Bible but was an active participant in the wars of the Jewish grammarians. As a student of Jewish Law, he is reputed to be the author of a long-lived introduction to the Talmud (*Mebo ha-Talmud*) and a treatise on the Law. He was even so audacious as to write a polemic exposing the contradictions in the Koran.

BIBLIOGRAPHY.—Samuel's works were written in either Hebrew or Arabic and are not available in English. For his life and works, *see* in English, Jefem Schirman, "Samuel Hannagid, the Man, the Soldier, the Politician," *Jewish Social Studies,* vol. xiii, pp. 99–126 (1951); Heinrich Graetz, *History of the Jews,* Eng. trans., vol. iii, pp. 254–261 (1927).
(Es. R.)

SAMURAI, the Japanese warrior caste. In Japan in the 11th century, the power of the imperial government to maintain order in the provinces waned. It was then that the samurai emerged as a distinct social group. Held together by personal loyalty to powerful chiefs, warrior groups brought ever more territory under their control, fighting wars for local and, eventually, national supremacy. From the end of the 11th century until 1868, government was exclusively in the hands of the samurai class. In the early years of almost continual warfare, when manpower was short and physical courage and prowess were at a premium, entry into the group was relatively open. But after 1600, when, under the strict rule of the Tokugawa shogun, the country was at peace for 250 years, warriors became a closed caste.

The establishment of warrior dominance at the end of the 12th century marked a break with the classical culture of the court. New forms of literature, religion, and drama emerged, forms congenial to the samurai, which helped mold samurai taste. But samurai political dominance lasted longer than samurai cultural dominance, which was surpassed around 1700 by the lusty plebeian culture of Japan's growing cities.

The samurai virtues of pride and loyalty are illustrated in the story of the Forty-Seven Ronin (*q.v.*). *See also* JAPAN: *History: Minamoto Yoritomo.*
(T. C. SH.)

SAN'A', capital of Yemen, lies at an altitude of about 7,700 ft. at the foot of Jabal Nuqum, and 160 mi. (257 km.) NE of Al Hudaydah by road. In 1964 the population was in excess of 80,000. The city, walled and shaped like the figure eight, is divided into three parts: San'a' itself, the old city; Bir al 'Azab, the garden city enclosed in Turkish times; and Qa' al-Yahud, the Jewish quarter. The old city, forming the eastern half of the eight, is dominated by the Qasr, the citadel, on a spur of Jabal Nuqum. It is traversed from north to south by a broad *wadi* (watercourse), dry except in times of flood, east of which are fine houses of several stories lining narrow streets. A broad street of shops, the Harat an Nahrein, extends from the western wall to the *wadi,* and the *suqs* (markets), each devoted to one craft or trade, are centrally situated to the east of the *wadi.* These include streets of sandal makers, dagger-sheath makers, silversmiths, tailors and embroiderers, locksmiths, jewel polishers, workers in brass, alabaster workers, blacksmiths, pawnshops, carpet sellers, and booksellers. San'a' is probably the only town in south Arabia with flower shops.

The imam's seven-storied palace, the Mutawakkil, stands in the neck of the eight. It was badly damaged in the revolution of September 1962. The other half of the eight contains the Bir al 'Azab and, at the western end, the Qa' al-Yahud. The Bir al 'Azab is residential, with large houses in walled gardens, mostly Turkish. In the Jewish quarter houses are two-storied; almost all the Jews have migrated to Israel. San'a' has eight gates, the most imposing of which the Bab ("gate") al Yemen, leading south, is of Turkish origin. Bab ar Rum, the Constantinople gate, leads north from the Bir al 'Azab. All except six of the 44 mosques are in the old city. The Great Mosque, built on the site of the Christian church (see below), is peculiar in having a Ka'ba (q.v.) similar to that at Mecca. Al Bakiliya mosque, with a large cupola and a fine minaret, belongs to the early Turkish period. Many mosques have minarets richly ornamented in Zaidi (Zeidi) style. There are numerous wells, caravansaries, public baths, and good markets.

Outside the city walls to the south are the old Turkish barracks, now used by the Yemeni forces, and an airfield. San'a' is linked with Al Hudaydah (the chief port of Yemen) by a modern road built with Chinese aid, and with Aden (288 mi. [463 km.] SSE) via Yarim, Ibb, and Ta'izz. Rawdah, a suburb well-known for its vineyards, lies six miles (10 km.) to the north.

San'a' is an ancient city, its foundation being legendarily attributed to Shem or the giant Ad. It was well known for its fortress, Ghumdan (1st century A.D.), of which some rubble remains. At first known as Uwal or Azal, identified with Uzal of Gen. 10:27, it became the capital of the Himyarites and later of the Abyssinian Abraha (A.D. 525), who built the Christian church which was destroyed two centuries later. The later history of San'a' has been a record of desert raids interspersed with periods of prosperity. After the withdrawal of the Turks (1918), San'a' became the capital of the imam of Yemen proper, and from 1962 it was the capital of the Yemeni Arab Republic. See also ARABIA: *Exploration;* YEMEN. (W. H. Is.)

SANA'I (ABU'L-MAJD MAJDUD) (c. 1070–c. 1140), Persian poet and mystic, author of the first great mystical epic in Persian. He was born in Ghazni, where as a young man he served as a panegyrist at the court of the Ghaznavid sultans. He later traveled to Balkh and other cities of Khorasan, and as a result of his association with mystics and philosophers, abandoned the life of the court, and devoted himself to the pursuit of the mystical life. Late in life he returned to Ghazni, where he lived in retirement, resisting the blandishments of the Ghaznavid ruler Bahramshah, and completed the composition of his most important work, the philosophical poem *Hadiqat al-Haqiqa* ("Garden of Truth"; Eng. trans. of book i by J. Stephenson, 1911).

Sana'i's poetical writings show clearly the spiritual change that divided his life; his early court panegyrics, though skilful, lack originality, whereas his mystical and philosophical poetry is full of deep feeling and sensibility. Sana'i wrote five or six other *mathnavi* (rhymed couplet) poems in addition to the *Hadiqa,* and also a number of fine *ghazals* (lyrics). He was the first major Persian poet to use verse for the expression of the mystical, philosophical, and ethical ideas of Sufism (q.v.) and so influenced the whole trend of Persian poetry. In particular he paved the way for both Farid ud-din 'Attar and Jalal-ud-din Rumi (qq.v.).

For discussions of Sana'i's life and work *see* E. G. Browne, *A Literary History of Persia,* vol. ii (1928); T. W. Haig in *Encyclopaedia of Islam,* vol. iv (1934). (L. P. E.-S.)

SAN ANDRÉS Y PROVIDENCIA, an *intendencia* of Colombia, consisting of San Andrés Island, Providencia Island, and three small keys in the Caribbean Sea, 250 mi. SW of Jamaica and 100 mi. E of Nicaragua. Area 21 sq.mi. Pop. (1964) 11,620. The islands were settled in 1629 by English Puritans and later by planters, woodcutters, and Negro slaves from Jamaica. They were awarded to Spain in 1786 and became part of Colombia in 1821. The population remains English-speaking and Protestant but decreased after 1938 by emigration. San Andrés produces coconuts, copra, and oranges; Providencia relies on subsistence agriculture. (G. J. B.)

SAN ANGELO, a city of southwestern Texas, U.S., is located 90 mi. SW of Abilene; the seat of Tom Green County. It was founded in 1867 near Ft. Concho at the confluence of the North Concho and Middle Concho rivers; the fort, abandoned as an army installation in 1889, is now a public museum. The mild climate (mean temperature 65° F.) and diversified recreational facilities attract tourists and sportsmen. San Angelo is also the educational, cultural, medical, and trade centre for an area larger than New England; its public-school system includes a municipal junior college. The region produces oil, gas, sheep, wool, a major portion of the nation's Angora goats and mohair, and diversified farm crops; San Angelo is a major wool market. Oil and Goodfellow Air Force Base, converted in 1958 from flight to security-service training, have been important in the growth of the city. Manufactures include boots, saddles, western-style jewelry, meat and dairy products, shoes and moccasins, cottonseed products, tile, trailers, printing and binding, and metal products. The multipurpose Twin Buttes dam, completed in 1961, provides the municipal water supply. The city has a large coliseum in which a ram show, fat-stock show, and rodeo are presented annually. San Angelo has a council-manager form of government, in effect since 1916. The population of the city in 1960 was 58,815, an increase of 12.9% from 1950; that of the standard metropolitan statistical area (Tom Green county) was 64,630, an increase of 9.7%. For comparative population figures *see* table in TEXAS: *Population.*

(J. S. Sp.)

SAN ANTONIO, a city of Texas, U.S., is located 80 mi. S.S.W. of Austin on the headwaters of the San Antonio river; the seat of Bexar county. San Antonio is exceptional among the larger cities of the U.S. in that its modern American character is blended with a considerable amount of foreign influence. This effect is due less to the fact that it was for 118 years a Spanish-Mexican outpost than to the close cultural ties which the city now has with Mexico. Situated on the plains of south-central Texas (see LLANO ESTACADO) at the foot of the Edwards plateau to the northwest, San Antonio is only 150 mi. from the Mexican border at Laredo and is on the most traveled route between the U.S. and Mexico by air, rail or highway. Spanish is spoken in most downtown retail establishments. The Latin section of the city, south and west of the business district, resembles an indigenous Mexican city, with its own shops, theatres, cafés, clubs, a weekly newspaper (*La Prensa*) and a Spanish-language television station. The population of the city in 1960 was 587,718, an increase of 43.9% over 1950; that part of the population which is of Spanish-Indian origin (estimated at 40%) has increased by a steady flow of immigration as well as by birth. The population of the standard metropolitan statistical area (Bexar and Guadalupe counties) was 716,168 in 1960. (For comparative population figures *see* table in TEXAS: *Population.*)

History.—San Antonio was founded on May 1, 1718, by a Spanish military expedition from Monclova, then capital of Coahuila, in northern Mexico, on the trail through the Texas wilderness to the recently opened trading posts of the French in Louisiana. The site was chosen for the springs welling up within what is now the city to form the San Antonio river, which flows southeastward into the Gulf of Mexico. Before the Spaniards came the site had been occupied by a Coahuiltecan Indian village, Yanaguana.

On the west side of the river the soldiers built a small fort which they called the presidio of Béjar; on the other side arose a Franciscan mission, San Antonio de Valero. In 1731 a party of 55 indigent settlers arrived, after an arduous journey from the Canary Islands (a Spanish possession), to colonize the lonely frontier post. Given land, they laid out a town near the fort and named it San Fernando. In time the three settlements grew together into a pueblo which was called San Antonio de Béjar. Eventually the presidio gave its name to Bexar county, of which modern San Antonio is the major part. For reasons which are now obscure, Mission San Antonio de Valero came to be known as the Alamo, from the Spanish word for "cottonwood tree."

Between 1720 and 1731 four more Franciscan missions were established at intervals for a distance of eight miles down the San Antonio river. When the missions were secularized in 1794 their cultivated lands were distributed among the Indians under their tutelage and the buildings were abandoned. The Alamo was then used as a garrison by the soldiers defending San Antonio, replacing the old presidio.

With the Mexican revolution of 1821 San Antonio passed out of the hands of Spain and became a part of Mexico. It was still one of only three established communities in Texas, the others being Goliad, on the San Antonio river toward the Gulf, and Nacogdoches, near the Louisiana border. In August of that year, however, Stephen F. Austin arrived in San Antonio, where he arranged with the Mexican government to admit 300 families into Texas from the U.S. By 1836, when Texas in turn declared its independence, the Anglo-American settlers around the Gulf coast had grown to at least 35,000.

The high moment in San Antonio's history was the battle of the Alamo during the war between Texas and Mexico (see TEXAS: *Revolution and Republic*). At that time San Antonio had 2,500 inhabitants and was still the foremost city of Texas. Within 14 years, while it continued to grow, it had lost first place to Galveston, the Gulf port through which immigrants were pouring into Texas, and was being challenged by the new city of Houston.

During the last decades of the 19th century San Antonio was a major cattle centre, where herds were assembled for the long drives overland to the railroads in Kansas. The famous Chisholm trail, with its various offshoots, began in San Antonio; and it was usually to this city that cattlemen and cowhands repaired for relaxation after the drives. They brought a resurgence of prosperity to San Antonio. From 1900, when a hurricane virtually destroyed Galveston, until 1930, when both Houston and Dallas overtook San Antonio, it was again the first city of Texas.

The Economy.—Lacking the oil and chemical deposits around Houston and the rich trade area around Dallas, San Antonio after World War I gradually fell behind as a business and industrial capital. On the other hand, Ft. Sam Houston, on a tract of 3,365 ac. inside the present city, is the headquarters of the 4th U.S. army, an administrative district covering the five states of Texas, Louisiana, Arkansas, Oklahoma and New Mexico. Also at Ft. Sam

Houston is Brooke army medical centre, which includes a large hospital, research laboratories and the army's basic school for medical officers, nurses and technicians.

Surrounding the city are four important U.S. air force bases. Kelly, the oldest, was established in 1917. Until 1943 it was the advanced flight training centre of the air force. Then it was converted into an aircraft maintenance and supply base. By the end of World War II Kelly had grown into a vast industrial complex, with 24,000 civilian employees, acres of shops and warehouses, 8 mi. of concrete runways and 28 mi. of railway spurs and sidings.

An offshoot of Kelly, and adjacent to it, is Lackland air force base, the principal air force training school for recruits and officer candidates. Randolph air force base, 17 mi. N.E. of the city, is the headquarters of the Air Training command.

Brooks air force base, near Kelly and Lackland, is the site of the new Aerospace medical centre occupied in 1959 by the former school of aviation medicine. There the air force gives postgraduate training to flight surgeons and conducts advanced research on problems of atmospheric and space flight. The model air force hospital at Lackland is a unit of the centre.

These military operations largely account for the phenomenal growth of San Antonio after 1940, the city being without private industry of any great significance. They also explain its attraction for retired members of the armed forces, who permeate its social, business and professional life.

Education and Cultural Activities.—Among the many educational institutions in San Antonio are St. Mary's university (Roman Catholic; established 1852) and Trinity university (Presbyterian; established 1869); and two Roman Catholic colleges for women, Incarnate Word (chartered 1881) and Our Lady of the Lake (founded 1896). The Protestant Episcopal bishop of west Texas has his diocesan centre in San Antonio. Cultural exhibits are found in the Witte Memorial museum and in the Marion Koogler McNay Art institute, which contains a notable collection of modern French paintings.

Historic Sites.—Among places of interest to visitors in San Antonio, the most notable is the Alamo (*q.v.*). A small section of the Spanish colonial town near the Alamo has been restored with later additions; it is known as La Villita and is used as a civic centre. San Fernando cathedral, built by the Canary Islanders, is the seat of a Roman Catholic archbishop. For a discussion of the missions and the governor's palace, all of great architectural and historic interest, see TEXAS: *State and National Parks*. San Antonio river, formally channeled and landscaped, winds unobtrusively below the level of the downtown streets.

BIBLIOGRAPHY.—Samuel M. Buck, *Yanaguana's Successors* (1949); William Corner, *San Antonio de Bexar* (1890); George Sessions Perry, *Cities of America*, pp. 135–146 (1947); Green Peyton, *San Antonio— City in the Sun* (1946).   (G. PE.)

SANATRUCES (SINATRUCES; Parthian *Sntrwk*), Parthian king in Persia (*c.* 77–70 B.C.). In the troublous times after the death of Mithradates II (*c.* 87 B.C.) he was made king by the Sacaraucae, a Scythian tribe which had invaded Persia *c.* 77 B.C. He was 80 years old and reigned seven years. See PERSIAN HISTORY.

See Lucian, *Makrobioi*, 15; Appian, *Mithridateios*, 104.

SAN BERNARDINO, central city of the San Bernardino-Riverside-Ontario standard metropolitan area in southern California, is the seat of San Bernardino County (area 20,160 sq.mi., constituting 12% of the area of California). The city lies 60 mi. E of Los Angeles at an elevation of 1,054 ft. at the southern base of the San Bernardino Mountains (maximum altitude 11,502 ft.). Pop. (1960) of city 91,922; of standard metropolitan statistical area (San Bernardino and Riverside counties), 809,782. (For comparative population figures see table in CALIFORNIA: *Population*.)

Spanish military commandant Pedro Fages first explored the area in 1772. On May 20, 1810, Franciscan Father Francisco Dumetz from the San Gabriel mission named the valley for St. Bernardino of Siena. About 1820 the mission fathers started an irrigation ditch and a chapel. Diego Sepulveda established a great cattle ranch in the valley in 1839. The Rancho San Bernardino

PARK SETTING OF THE FORMALLY CHANNELED AND LANDSCAPED SAN ANTONIO RIVER IN DOWNTOWN SAN ANTONIO

was sold to Mormon immigrants who came by wagon train from Salt Lake City in 1851. In that year the leaders of this group, Charles C. Rich and Amasa Lyman, founded the city of San Bernardino. The county was created in 1853. The city was incorporated in 1854, and its present charter dates from 1904.

San Bernardino city, surrounded by orange groves and vineyards, is the centre of a rich, irrigated agricultural region. Adjoining is Norton Air Force Base, headquarters of the San Bernardino air matériel area. Numerous other large military installations are located in the vicinity. Seven miles west of the city is the largest integrated steel operation in the western U.S. The Santa Fe railroad maintains extensive shops; other important industries are foundries, aircraft and rocket factories, plumbing material, cement, and colour printing plants. San Bernardino is the centre of a large trade area with numerous wholesale distributors.

The city has fine churches and schools. In the metropolitan area are the University of Redlands (1907), the University of California Riverside campus (1905) with its Citrus Experiment station, Loma Linda University (1905), and Chaffey College (established in 1883 as Chaffey College of Agriculture). The state, county, and municipal buildings are grouped in a civic centre. The National Orange Show, held annually since 1915, has permanent exposition buildings.

Immediately to the north of the city the San Bernardino Mountains and National Forest provide a resort area with fishing, boating, and swimming in summer and skiing in winter. Beyond the mountains, on the way to Las Vegas and Palm Springs, are the numerous playgrounds of the Mojave Desert (*q.v.*).

(E. L. S.)

SAN BRUNO, a city of California, U.S., in San Mateo county, is located 14 mi. S. of San Francisco near the west shore of San Francisco bay. Tanforan race track, established in 1899, attracted early settlements, and the town was incorporated in 1914. Favoured by a cool, sunny climate and easy access to the metropolis, the city grew slowly as a commuter's suburb until the 1940s. Sharing in the bay area's rapid population growth, its size tripled between 1940 and 1960. Many of its residents work in San Francisco but a number are employed locally in printing, aircraft operation and maintenance (San Francisco International airport) and electronics. A U.S. naval personnel depot and the U.S. marine corps reserve 7th infantry battalion were stationed in San Bruno after World War II. For comparative population figures *see* table in CALIFORNIA: *Population.* (J. H. ST.)

SAN BUENAVENTURA: see VENTURA.

SAN CARLOS, a city in California, U.S., in San Mateo County on the San Francisco Peninsula, is located 26 mi. SE of San Francisco on historic El Camino Real, now a federal highway. Local tradition seems to have suggested the city's name, for it is believed that it was on the feast day (Nov. 4) of St. Charles Borromeo, in 1769, that the expedition of Gaspar de Portolá first sighted San Francisco Bay from the nearby hills. The original townsite was plotted in 1888 for the Southern Pacific Railway on sections of an old Spanish land grant, but the city was not incorporated until 1925. The city-manager form of government was adopted in 1949. San Carlos shared in California's spectacular growth after World War II; its population increased about 80% from 1940 to 1960. Although predominantly a suburban residential community, it includes within its limits some light industry, mainly electronics. For comparative population figures *see* table in CALIFORNIA: *Population.* (S. B. KN.)

SÁNCHEZ COELLO, ALONSO (1531/32–1588), Spanish painter who was one of the pioneers of the great tradition of Spanish portrait painting, was born at Benifayó, near Valencia. By 1540 he had moved with his family to Portugal, and before 1550 visited the Netherlands where he received his decisive training under Antonio Moro. Returning to Portugal *c.* 1550, where he worked for the court, he transferred in 1557 to the Spanish court, which he served until his death on Aug. 8, 1588, in Madrid. Philip II's favourite portrait painter, he introduced into Spain a style of portrait painting of specific Spanish character which was to continue to the time that Velázquez moved to the court in the 1620s. The basis of his style was Moro's painting, but, influenced

also by the Venetians, and especially by Titian, Alonso's portraits show a lesser insistence on detail, a greater ease of pose and of execution, and a warmer colouring; *e.g.*, portraits of Philip II (*c.* 1575) and the Infanta Isabel Clara Eugenia (1579), both in the Prado. The many religious paintings he produced, especially for the Escorial, are comparatively conventional works. (P. O. T.)

SÁNCHEZ COTÁN, JUAN (1561–1627), Spanish artist, a great still-life painter, was born near Toledo, Spain, where he studied with Blas del Prado. Toledo was the spiritual and ecclesiastic capital of Spain, and at the time leading minds there, among them El Greco, were interested in ecstatic mysticism as well as sober rational thought. In 1603 Sánchez Cotán became a Carthusian lay brother, near Segovia, and in 1612 at Granada; there he died in 1627, venerated almost as a saint.

Sánchez Cotán's mysticism is expressed in both his still lifes and his figure paintings. His work is characterized by lovingly careful realism and dramatic depth; the sensations of harmony and ascetic withdrawal they induce were inspired by his own mystic spirituality. His best work, "Quince, Cabbage, Melon and Cucumber" (1602), was exhibited in 1823 in Philadelphia, where it influenced Raphaelle Peale. It is now in the Fine Arts Gallery of San Diego, Calif. With Alonzo Vázquez (*c.* 1564–1608), the earliest Baroque painter at Seville, Sánchez Cotán influenced Francisco de Zurbarán and other painters at Seville and Madrid.

See George Kubler and Martin Soria, *Art and Architecture in Spain and Portugal and Their American Dominions 1500–1800* (1959).

(M. S. S.)

SÁNCHEZ DE BUSTAMANTE Y SIRVÉN, ANTONIO (1865–1951), Cuban lawyer, statesman, and publicist who drew up the Bustamante Code dealing with international private law. He was born on April 13, 1865, in Havana, Cuba, where his father was professor and dean of the Faculty of Medicine in the university. He received most of his education in his native city, and obtained his law degree there. In 1884, before he was 20, he won the chair of international law at the university in public competitive examinations. In 1902, when the republic of Cuba was constituted, he was elected senator for the province of Pinar del Río; in 1909 he was reelected to represent Havana. In 1895 he was made a member of the Institute of International Law, the first Cuban to gain that honour, and in 1907 he was selected as delegate plenipotentiary of Cuba to the Second Peace Conference at The Hague. In 1908 he was made a member of the Permanent Court of Arbitration at The Hague.

Bustamante's codification of international private law was adopted by the sixth Pan-American Congress, which also elected him president in 1928. It was ratified by 15 Latin-American countries, 6 of them without reservations.

Bustamante also served as dean of Havana University; dean of the Havana bar; Cuban delegate to the League of Nations; and judge of the Permanent Court of International Justice. Among his numerous works, many of them pertaining to international law, are: *El orden público* (1893); *Tratado de derecho internacional privado* (1896); *Discursos,* five volumes (1915–23); *El Tribunal Permanente de Justicia Internacional* (1925); *Derecho internacional público,* five volumes (1933–38); *Derecho internacional aéreo* (1945). He died on Aug. 24, 1951, in Havana.

SÁNCHEZ RAMÍREZ, a province in central Dominican Republic. It occupies 453 sq.mi. (1,173 sq.km.) on the northern slope of the Cordillera Central (to 2,265 ft. [690 m.]) and in the eastern section of the fertile Vega Real, south of the Camu River. Cocoa accounts for nearly one-half of the area under cultivation. Other significant crops are bananas, corn, rice, and coffee. Silver, gold, and copper were mined during the colonial period, and a rich deposit of iron ore was mined near Hatillo after 1952. Sánchez Ramírez was created in 1952 from Duarte Province. Its 1960 population was 90,280. The capital, Cotuí (pop. [1960] 4,540), was founded in 1505. (D. R. D.)

SANCHI, a village in Madhya Pradesh state, India, the site of probably the oldest surviving buildings in the Indian subcontinent, apart from the Indus Valley remains of the Harappan civilization (*see* INDIA-PAKISTAN, SUBCONTINENT OF: *Archaeology*) which belong to an earlier and different archaeological period.

Pop. (1961) 796. The main structures of interest are the Buddhist stupas on Sanchi Hill, a 300-ft. sandstone feature on the left bank of the Betwa River. Although the remains include an Asokan pillar, a fact which points to the importance of Sanchi in the early growth of the Buddhist religion, it has not proved possible to identify Sanchi in the textual geography of early Buddhism. The evolved style at Sanchi seems to form part of an artistic sequence from the Bhaja Cave, near Poona, through the material from Bharhut and Gaya, to the Great Stupa which is Sanchi's chief glory. The stupa consists of a base bearing a hemispherical dome (*anda*) representing the dome of heaven enclosing the earth, which is surmounted by a square railed unit (*harmika*), the world mountain, from which rises a mast (*yashti*) to symbolize the cosmic axis. The mast bears umbrellas (*chatravalis*) which represent, by their tiered arrangement, the various heavens of the gods (*devaloka*). Provision is made for a railed circumambulatory (*pradaksinapatha*) about 16 ft. above the base of the dome, and the whole is surrounded by a flagged path with an enclosing railing and ceremonial gateways (*torana*) at the cardinal points. The Great Stupa in its present form—the basal diameter of the dome is about 115 ft., rising to a height of about 50 ft. at the *harmika* platform, which has a diameter of some 40 ft.—is the result of additions to an original, probably Asokan foundation of much less imposing proportions and ornamentation.

Other features of interest in Sanchi include a *chaitya* or assembly hall, apparently forming part of a complex, Asokan pillar-stupa-*chaitya;* monastic buildings, perhaps to be assigned to the Theravadin sect; and a small early Gupta temple (No. 17; early 5th century A.D.). *See* also INDIAN ARCHITECTURE.

BIBLIOGRAPHY.—Sir J. Marshall and A. Foucher, *Monuments of Sanchi* (1940). Studies in: A. K. Coomaraswamy, *History of Indian and Indonesian Art* (1927); Sir L. Ashton (ed.), *The Art of India and Pakistan* (1950); B. Rowland, *The Art and Architecture of India* (1953); S. Kramrisch, *The Art of India* (1954). (A. H. CE.; X.)

SANCHO, the name of four kings of León and Castile.

SANCHO I (d. 965), king of León from 956 to 965 a younger son of Ramiro II, succeeded his brother Ordoño III, but was overthrown by a revolt of his nobles and replaced by a usurper, his cousin, Ordoño IV. Sancho went to Córdoba to seek help from Abd-al-Rahman III and was restored (960) by an army sent by the caliph.

SANCHO II (*c.* 1038–1072), king of Castile from 1065 to 1072, was the eldest son of Ferdinand I. He was allocated the kingdom of Castile in his father's will, León and Galicia being given to his brothers. He refused to accept this division and dispossessed García of Galicia by force (1071). Alfonso VI of León, defeated at Golpejera on the Carrión River in January 1072, had to seek refuge with the Moorish king of Toledo. Sancho's triumph was short-lived, for he was killed on Oct. 7, 1072, while besieging the rebel fortress-city of Zamora, held by his sister Urraca in Alfonso's name.

SANCHO III (*c.* 1134–1158), king of Castile from 1157 until his death in 1158, was the eldest son of the emperor Alfonso VII.

SANCHO IV (1258–1295), king of Castile and León from 1284 to 1295, second son of Alfonso X, was born on May 12, 1258. Though ambitious, ruthless, and violent-tempered, he was also an able politician and a cultivated man. In 1275 his elder brother, Fernando de La Cerda, was killed, leaving a son, Alfonso de La Cerda, heir to Alfonso X. Sancho, supported by the nobles and the military orders, sought recognition as heir instead of his nephew and took up arms against the king. After some years of strife he succeeded in making good his usurpation on his father's death (April 1284). Support for Alfonso de La Cerda came from factions at home and from France and Aragon. Sancho finally removed this threat by arranging a marriage (1291) between his eldest daughter Isabel and James II of Aragon. Despite these political troubles he succeeded in defeating an invasion of Andalusia by the king of Fez (1290). Sancho owed much to his ablest supporter, López Díaz de Haro, whom he—characteristically—killed in anger during an argument at Alfaro (1288). He also depended greatly on the courage and wisdom of his warrior-queen, María de Molina, who on his death (April 25, 1295) became regent for his son Ferdinand IV. (P. E. R.)

SANCHO, the name of seven kings of Pamplona (Navarre) and Aragon.

SANCHO I GARCÉS (d. 925), king of Pamplona from 905 to 925, expanded his kingdom south of the Ebro and maintained its independence despite the sack of his capital (924) by Abd-al-Rahman III, amir and caliph of Córdoba.

SANCHO II GARCÉS (Sancho Abarca) (d. *c.* 994), king of Pamplona from 970 to *c.* 994, count of Aragon, the son of García II, was defeated by the Moors in 973 and 981 when allied with Castilians and Leonese. He then submitted to the caliphate, one of his daughters marrying the dictator Almanzor and becoming a Muslim. Sancho visited Córdoba in 992 to pay homage to Almanzor.

SANCHO III GARCÉS (*c.* 992–1035), called "the Great," king of Pamplona from 1005 to 1035, the son of García III, established Navarrese hegemony over all the Christian states of Spain. A skilled politician, he pursued his aims more by subversion than by force of arms. Sancho was uninterested in the crusade against the Moors or the Visigothicizing traditions of the Leonese monarchy. The expansion of the kingdom of Pamplona began by the seizure of the ancient Frankish counties of Sobrarbe and Ribagorza (1016–19). Next Sancho persuaded the count of Barcelona, Berenguer Ramón I, to accept him as overlord. Gascony did likewise, giving him direct sovereignty over Labourd. As a consequence of his marriage (1010) to Munia, daughter of count Sancho García (d. 1017) of Castile, he secured his own acceptance as count when Sancho García's son, the child count García, was assassinated (1029). He then took up Castilian irredentist claims in eastern León and occupied the Leonese capital, where he was crowned (1034)—taking the imperial title. Sancho, who introduced some feudal practices into his new dominions, also encouraged the Cluniac reformers and established much closer contacts generally between Christian Spain and trans-Pyrenean Europe. In his will, however, he deliberately destroyed the empire he had created: he divided it into four kingdoms and left these to his four sons, thus making inevitable the fratricidal wars which followed his death (Oct. 18, 1035). Sancho created the kingdom of Aragon and was responsible for the elevation of Castile from county to kingdom, though he transferred some Castilian territory to Pamplona, which he left to his eldest son, García IV.

SANCHO IV (*c.* 1039–1076), king of Pamplona from 1054 to 1076, son of García IV, had to contend with Castilian irredentism and Aragonese ambition. He persuaded the Moorish king of Saragossa to become his vassal. This offended Alfonso VI of Castile who invaded Navarre (1074), conspiring with Sancho's brothers and magnates to assassinate him at Peñalén. The kingdom of Pamplona was then occupied by Sancho Ramírez of Aragon, with Navarrese approval.

SANCHO V RAMÍREZ (1043–1094), king of Aragon from 1063 to 1094 and of Pamplona from 1076 to 1094, was the son of Ramiro I of Aragon. After the murder of Sancho IV (*see* above) he, with Navarrese consent, became king of Pamplona, forestalling the ambition of Alfonso VI to annex that kingdom. Sancho's main historical importance, however, was as king of Aragon. After his father's death (1063) fighting the Moors at Graus, the papacy organized three international crusades against Spanish Islam (1063, 1073, and 1087). These all failed, but Sancho himself reconquered many places from his own resources, notably in the regions of Huesca and Monzón; at the end of his reign Aragon began to edge toward the Mediterranean coast. Sancho placed his kingdoms under the feudal protection of the Holy See in 1089—an act fraught with political consequences for Aragon. He died of wounds during the siege of Huesca (1094).

SANCHO VI (d. 1194), called "the Wise," king of Navarre from 1150 to 1194, son of García V the Restorer, was the first monarch to be known as king of Navarre rather than of Pamplona. At the beginning of his reign Castile and Aragon signed at Tudillén (1151) a treaty for the partition of Navarre. By skilled diplomacy Sancho escaped destruction, accepting the emperor Alfonso VII of Castile as his suzerain and marrying the emperor's daughter (1157). He himself intervened in Castilian affairs during the minority (1158–70) of Alfonso VIII. In 1176 both countries submitted their longstanding territorial disputes to Henry II of England as arbiter. Henry assigned Rioja to Castile. Sancho accepted this decision. He was a legislator of importance, conceding many municipal fueros (charters) and protecting Jews and immigrants (*francos*) from the north. He died on June 27, 1194.

SANCHO VII (d. 1234), called "the Strong," king of Navarre from 1194 to 1234, the son of Sancho VI, was a swashbuckling but enigmatic personality who offended the Holy See by his friendship with the Saracens; he was in Africa in the service of the Almohads (1198–c. 1200). His absence cost Navarre the provinces of Álava and Guipúzcoa, seized by Castile (1200). In 1212, however, Sancho fought with the allied army which crushed the Almohads at Las Navas de Tolosa. Like his predecessor, Sancho granted many municipal fueros. He received (1196) the feudal homage of the viscount of Tartas (Gascony), took the burgesses of Bayonne under his protection (1204), and became lord of Ostabat (near Mauléon) in 1228. He died at Tudela on April 7, 1234, and was buried in the collegiate church at Roncesvalles, which he had built. Sancho was the last Spanish-descended king of Navarre for 200 years. (P. E. R.)

SANCHO, the name of two kings of Portugal.

SANCHO I (1154–1211), king from 1185 to 1211, was the son of Afonso I. His reign was marked by a resettlement of the depopulated areas of his country, by the establishment of new towns, and by the rebuilding of frontier strongholds and castles. The king encouraged foreign settlers, and enlisted bishops, religious orders, and nobles in his colonization projects, granting vast territories to the military orders (the Hospitallers, the Templars, the Orders of Calatrava and Santiago). After an invasion by the Almohad prince Abu Yusuf Yaqub al-Mansur, he used the help of a passing Crusader fleet to capture Silves from the Moors (1189), but lost it (1191) and other lands south of the Tagus when al-Mansur again attacked. Sancho was involved in various disputes with his bishops and quarreled with Rome over the payment of tribute. He died on March 26, 1211.

SANCHO II (c. 1209–48), king from 1223 to 1245, was the son of Afonso II and of Urraca, daughter of Alfonso VIII of Castile. Factions were so fostered during his minority that his later government was never anything more than a series of vain attempts to achieve political stability in the kingdom. Renewing the struggle against the Moors, he took Tavira and Cacela (1238–39), thereby extending Portuguese sovereignty over a large part of the Algarve. But from 1240 onward internal disorders increased, and Pope Innocent IV's recognition of the king's political incapacity to govern led to Sancho's deposition (1245) and the entrusting of the administration to his brother Afonso (later Afonso III). Sancho's supporters were defeated and he retired to Toledo (1247), where he died on Jan. 4, 1248. (V. R. R.)

SANCHUNIATHON, a Phoenician writer who probably flourished before Trojan times. All information concerning him derives from the works of Philo of Byblos (fl. A.D. 100), who claimed to have translated Sanchuniathon's *Phoenicica* from the original text. The authenticity of this has been questioned, but excavations at Ras Shamra (ancient Ugarit) in 1929 revealed Phoenician documents supporting much of Sanchuniathon's information concerning Phoenician mythology and religious beliefs. According to Philo, Sanchuniathon derived the sacred lore from mystic inscriptions on the *Ammouneis* (i.e., images or pillars of Baal Amon), which stood in Phoenician temples. *See also* PHOENICIA: *Religion.*

SAN CRISTÓBAL, a province in southern Dominican Republic (area 1,445 sq.mi. [3,742 sq.km.]; pop. [1960] 252,280), is mostly mountainous, occupying a section of the Cordillera Central (to 4,265 ft. [1,300 m.]) in the northern part, and an outlying range in the southwestern part. It is a significant producer of rice, sugar, cacao, and coffee. The province was established in 1935 when the coastal plain around the national capital, Santo Domingo, was set aside and designated as the federal district of Santo Domingo.

The provincial capital, San Cristóbal (pop. [1960] 16,580), was founded in 1575. The name of the province was Trujillo until 1961. (D. R. D.)

SAN CRISTÓBAL, capital of Táchira State, most populous of the Andean states of Venezuela, enjoys the climate of the *tierra templada* because of its location at an elevation of 2,700 ft. (820 m.) in an intermontane basin. In an isolated region on three sloping alluvial terraces on the Torbes River, where there is not much room for expansion, San Cristóbal nonetheless became the sixth largest city in the country, the centre of a thriving coffee trade, the largest of three cities in the so-called Andean Region, and an outstanding transportation and communication centre with highways extending from it in all directions. San Cristóbal is on the trans-Andean highway, 410 mi. (660 km.) SW of Caracas. Founded in 1561 by Spanish conquistadores, the city, pop. (1961) 97,977, is geared to local and regional requirements. It was heavily damaged by an earthquake in 1875. San Cristóbal in the 1960s had textile mills, tanneries, a shoe factory, cigarette factories, and a cement plant. The surrounding area produced corn, cassava, pineapple, sugarcane, coffee, and a little cacao and cotton. Most of the coffee, destined for export, was sent to the Maracaibo basin for shipment. (L. WE.)

SANCROFT, WILLIAM (1617–1693), English archbishop of Canterbury, leader of the seven bishops who opposed James II's Declaration of Indulgence and later leader of the nonjurors (*q.v.*), was born at Fressingfield, Suffolk, on Jan. 30, 1617. Educated at Emmanuel College, Cambridge, he became a fellow (1642), but was ejected (1651) because of his refusal from 1649 to take an oath of loyalty to the existing government. On the restoration (1660) of Charles II, he was appointed chaplain to John Cosin, bishop of Durham. He was master of Emmanuel College (1662–65) and dean of St. Paul's in London (1664–77), doing much to speed the rebuilding of the cathedral after the Great Fire (1666). He was consecrated archbishop of Canterbury in January 1678.

The accession of James II (1685) brought Sancroft fresh difficulties. He refused to serve on the king's Court of Ecclesiastical Commission and James ignored his advice on appointments. With six other bishops he petitioned against James's second Declaration of Indulgence (April 1688), was imprisoned in the Tower (June 8–15) and tried for seditious libel (June 29–30). Finding James intractable, Sancroft accepted the arrival of William of Orange, but gave William no support as soon as it became clear that William meant to obtain the crown. Suspended in August 1689, Sancroft was deprived in February 1690, having failed to take the oath of allegiance to William III. In 1691 he retired to Fressingfield. He died Nov. 24, 1693. As well as sermons, he wrote *Modern Policies* (1652), an indictment of the Commonwealth.

SANCTION AND GUARANTEE in international law are methods of enforcing rules of international law through the collective action of states. Sanctions may range from votes of censure in international organizations, through economic boycott, to the use of military force.

Following World War I, statesmen, led by Pres. Woodrow Wilson, sought to find a new security system to replace the older one of flexible alliances which had characterized the 19th-century "balance of power" political system (*see* ALLIANCE). Wilson believed a new security system could be built around a League of Nations in which states would unite to guarantee each other's security through employing collective sanctions against any state which forcibly transgressed the established legal rights of another state. Sanctions and guarantees were to replace alliances as the cornerstone of peace, a concept embodied in the Covenant of the League of Nations, the key provision of which was article 16.

The League of Nations.—Article 16 of the Covenant obligated League members to adopt common coercive measures, including the severance of all trade and financial relations, against any state which, in violation of the Covenant, resorted to war. In addition, armed force could be used against such an offender if the League Council so recommended. Unfortunately, art. 16 contained ambiguities which seriously diminished the confidence of governments in its efficacy, and efforts to supplement League sanction by regional guarantees were therefore undertaken. To avoid being stigmatized as old-fashioned "alliances," these were explicitly subordinated to League sanctions. The most important were the

Locarno treaties of 1925, which guaranteed French and Belgian borders with Germany; England and Italy signed as guarantors.

The failure of the League system of sanctions lay in its tendency to fragment opposition to an aggressor nation by placing emphasis on collective sanctions when particular states might have preferred to let others act for them and to remain inactive themselves. Italy was not deterred from conquest of Ethiopia by economic sanctions brought into play by the League, nor were the Japanese prevented from conquering Manchuria. Germany reentered the Rhineland and later absorbed Austria and the Sudetenland.

The United Nations.—Despite the failure of the League, the concept of collective security guaranteed by collective sanctions reappeared in 1945 in the United Nations Organization. Recognizing that the military capabilities of the world would be in the hands of the great powers, the United Nations provided machinery through which states represented in the Security Council could cooperate to enforce peace. The Charter contains an absolute prohibition of the use of force by a state against the territorial integrity or political independence of another state, qualified only by the right of individual and collective self-defense against armed attack provided in art. 51.

Sanctions available to the organization are detailed in Ch. VI and VII, which call upon the Security Council to take necessary action whenever a dispute or situation threatening international peace or security occurs. Chapter VI permits the Security Council to invoke a variety of sanctions, including the use of force, to enforce its decisions. Decisions are binding upon all members. Chapter VII, also available to the General Assembly, provides for "recommendations" of peaceful settlement. Charter provisions contemplating United Nations forces (art. 43–47) have not been implemented because of the inability of the great powers to agree on their composition, but the council can call upon individual states to supply military forces on an *ad hoc* basis. This procedure was followed in 1950 when the Security Council, acting during the absence of the Soviet Union, authorized UN military action in Korea.

The possibility that the veto in the Security Council could prevent the United Nations from applying effective sanctions has led to two alternative means of ensuring collective security. First, the creation of regional organizations, permitted by art. 52 of the Charter: these are multilateral defensive alliances against aggression, the most important of which are the North Atlantic Treaty Organization (*q.v.*), the Southeast Asia Treaty Organization (*q.v.*), the Organization of American States (*see* PAN-AMERICAN CONFERENCES), the Central Treaty Organization (*see* BAGHDAD PACT), and the Warsaw Treaty Organization (*q.v.*), which includes the Soviet Union and its satellites. These treaties provide that an armed attack against any member will be regarded as an armed attack against all other members, and each member will assist the party attacked by taking forthwith such action as it deems necessary. Second, there have been efforts since Korea to transfer to the General Assembly as many powers of the Security Council as possible under the Charter if the council, because of the veto, cannot act. This is the purport of the "Uniting for Peace Resolution" of 1950. The United Nations invoked forcible sanctions in Korea in 1950 but has not in other instances attempted to do so. In the case of the aggression of the Soviet Union in Hungary it was prevented from taking action by the veto. In other instances, *e.g.*, Arab-Israeli conflicts and the Anglo-French-Israeli attack on Egypt during the dispute over the Suez Canal in 1956, it has been successful in maintaining peace without the need to employ sanctions.

See also PEACE, INTERNATIONAL: *Collective Security.*

BIBLIOGRAPHY.—P. S. Wild, *Sanctions and Treaty Enforcement* (1934); L. M. Goodrich and E. I. Hambro, *The Charter of the United Nations,* 2nd ed. (1949); J. Stone, *Legal Controls of International Conflict,* rev. ed. (1959).   (N. DEB. K.)

SANCTI SPÍRITUS, a city in Las Villas Province in east-central Cuba, about 45 mi. (72 km.) SE of Santa Clara. It is situated in a hilly region on the Central Highway about 20 mi. (32 km.) N of its port, Tunas de Zaza. Pop. (1964 est.) 55,400. The city serves as a commercial centre of a fertile agricultural region producing sugar cane, tobacco, and dairy products.

Sancti Spíritus was founded in 1516 on the Tuinicú River but was moved to the banks of the Yayabo River in 1524. It is the oldest interior city of Cuba, and the narrow, crooked streets, old churches, and plazas preserve its colonial atmosphere.

(D. R. D.)

SANCTORIUS (SANTORIO SANTORIO) (1561–1636), Italian physician who introduced quantitative experimentation and exact measurement into the field of medicine, was born at Capodistria (now Koper, Yugos.) on March 29, 1561. He studied at Venice and Padua and received his medical degree in 1582. From 1587 to 1599, he lived and traveled in Cracow (Pol.), Hungary, and Croatia. In 1611 he was named professor of medical theory at Padua. He died in Venice on Feb. 22, 1636.

Sanctorius was an exponent of the iatrophysical school of medicine, which took a mechanistic view of the body and its processes. Inspired by the inventions of his friend Galileo, he devised a clinical thermometer, a pulse clock, and a hygroscope. His major interest was the investigation of "insensible perspiration"; *i.e.*, metabolism. He constructed a large scale, on which he ate, worked, and slept, so that he might study the fluctuations of his body weight in relation to his solid and liquid excretions. After 30 years of continuous experimentation he published his findings in *De statica medicina* (1614). The book was widely read and hastened the acceptance of measurement and instrumentation in medicine. *See* also DIAGNOSIS: *Instruments of Precision.*

See A. Castiglioni, "La vita e l'opera di Santorio Santorio," *Medical Life,* vol. 38, pp. 727–786 (1920).   (I. V.)

SANCTUARY, a sacred or consecrated place, and particularly one that affords refuge, protection, or right of asylum. The word is also applied to the privilege itself, the right of safe refuge. It refers even to places of refuge for animals, such as a "bird sanctuary." (In a Christian church the word sanctuary usually refers to the area within the altar rails, though in Orthodox churches it is the space enclosed by the iconostasis, the icon-decorated partition between the holiest part of the edifice and that occupied by the laity.) Sanctuaries or "asylums" existed among many peoples at different stages of civilization: among primitive tribes as well as among the Phoenicians, Syrians, Egyptians, and Greeks. Sanctuary provisions may be found in Hebrew, Roman, Germanic, Irish, canon, common, and civil law.

Sanctuary has been granted to many types of beneficiaries—to enemies, to all criminals, to perpetrators of certain crimes only, to accidental killers (Deut. 4:41, 42), to killers in the heat of passion, and to animals—and has emanated from many different places, things, and persons. Thus at various times and in various places sacred trees, altars, temples, "cities of refuge," eagles of the Roman legions, statues and pictures of Roman emperors, tombs, and churches have represented sanctuary. Sometimes the quality of sanctuary adhered to a person rather than a place: to priests or priestesses (for example, the Vestal Virgins in Rome), or even, in some cultures, to all women, owing to belief in their magical qualities. Often the sanctuary was merely a place in which blood might not be shed, hence it was permissible to remove the fugitive and kill him elsewhere; in other cases, he could carry the immunity conferred by the place beyond its limits.

Various explanations of the institution of sanctuary have been suggested. The belief that it was rooted in a deterministic philosophy is supported by the biblical grant of refuge to the "accidental" as contrasted with the intentional killer, on the ground that God let the victim "fall into his hand" (Ex. 21:13), without knowledge on his part (Josh. 20:5). The Greek practice probably was referable to the role generally attributed by the Greeks to fate as a factor in crime (best evidenced by Orestes' tragic destiny and the sanctuary accorded to him).

According to another view, the right of sanctuary is based on the inviolability of sacred things and is derived from the primitive and universal belief in the contagion of holiness. Edward Westermarck questioned this explanation; in his view, in addition to the fear of shedding blood in a holy place, the dominant motive in protecting the fugitive who took shelter in such a place was fear of the evil magic force that would emanate from his curse, dangerous to gods as well as to men. Such fear is reflected in the protective measures taken both by certain primitive peoples and by the Romans; they gagged a condemned man to avoid exposing the king to contact with him or to his curse. It may have been one reason for the Hebrew practice, reported in the Talmud, whereby the mother of the high priest took care of fugitives to prevent them from praying for his death, which, by law, would set them free.

It is possible that all these reasons may have been combined in the institution of sanctuary. The Freudian view of the connection of opposites in primitive thought and in the unconscious makes it possible to interpret belief in the holiness of sanctuary and fear of the evil curse as related to one another rather than mutually exclusive. Both can be reconciled with belief in blood magic and the doctrine of fate.

Christian sanctuaries, first recognized by Roman law toward the end of the 4th century, developed through recognition of the office of bishop as intercessor. Definitely recognized in 399, sanctuary privileges were extended to wider areas of and around churches in 419 and 431. Justinian, in a statute of 535, limited the privilege to persons not guilty of the grosser crimes. In the Germanic kingdoms, while violent desecration of the right of sanctuary was forbidden, the fugitive was given up after an oath had been taken not to put him to death. This practice was copied by the church in a decree of the Council of Orléans in 511.

Canon law afforded sanctuary for a limited time to persons guilty of crimes of violence, in order that compensation might be paid to the victim or his kinsmen and to check blood vengeance.

In English common law a person accused of a felony might take refuge in a sanctuary; once there, he had a choice between submitting to trial or confessing the crime to the coroner and swearing to quit the kingdom (abjuration of the realm) and not return without the king's leave. Upon confession, he was deemed convicted; his lands passed to the Crown, his chattels were forfeited, he suffered attainder of blood (*i.e.*, could neither inherit nor transmit land), and his wife was regarded as a widow; if he returned without leave, his fate was that of an outlaw. If the fugitive would neither submit to trial nor abjure the realm, after 40 days he was to be starved into submission. Besides the general sanctuary which belonged to every church and which afforded temporary protection, there developed on obscure grounds a number of sanctuaries based upon royal charters. In at least 22 places throughout England the king's process did not run, the coroner could not enter, and the fugitive could remain there for life. The local lords regulated the activities of, and exacted oaths of fealty from, the fugitives.

The Reformation curtailed sanctuaries. Henry VIII abolished many and substituted, after the biblical pattern, seven "cities of refuge": Wells, Westminster, Northampton, Manchester (afterward transferred to Chester), York, Derby, and Launceston. An act of James I (1623) abolished sanctuary in cases of crime, but the privilege lingered on for civil processes in certain districts which had formerly been sanctuaries and which became the haunts of criminals who there resisted arrest. A notable example was the district known as Whitefriars in London, between Fleet Street and the Thames, east of the Temple. In this locality, nicknamed Alsatia, criminals were able to a large extent to defy the law, arrests being possible only under writs of the lord chief justice. So flagrant became the abuses that all such privileges were finally abolished in 1697, by the "Escape from Prison Act." A further amending act of 1723 completed the work of extinction of sanctuaries.

In Scotland, all religious sanctuaries were abolished at the time of the Reformation, but certain debtors were accorded sanctuary in and around Holyroodhouse, Edinburgh, until late in the 17th century. In continental Europe, the right of sanctuary (called asylum), though much restricted in the 16th century, survived until the French Revolution.

Whatever its origin and historically varying meaning, the institution of sanctuary seems to have performed an eminently useful social function. Although often abused, it prevented excessive use of capital punishment and safeguarded against uncontrolled blood vengeance and execution without trial. The sanctuary was also the root from which grew parliamentary immunities and the custom of diplomatic asylum in embassies; for these, *see* IMMUNITY; ASYLUM, RIGHT OF; DIPLOMACY: *Diplomatic Immunities.*

BIBLIOGRAPHY.—E. A. Westermarck, "Asylum," in J. Hastings (ed.), *Encyclopædia of Religion and Ethics* (1928); Sir William Blackstone, *Commentaries on the Laws of England*, book 4, ch. 26, Jones ed. (1916); André Réville, *"L'Abjuratio regni," histoire d'une institution anglaise* (1892); J. C. Cox, *The Sanctuaries and Sanctuary Seekers of Medieval England* (1911); Theodore F. T. Plucknett, *A Concise History of the Common Law*, p. 431, 5th ed. (1956). (HN. S.)

SAND, GEORGE (real name AMANDINE AURORE LUCILE DUDEVANT, *née* DUPIN) (1804–1876), French Romantic novelist who is also famous for her numerous love affairs. She was born in Paris on July 1, 1804, the daughter of a curiously ill-assorted couple: her mother, Sophie Victoire Delaborde, was the lowborn daughter of a Paris bird-fancier, while her father, Maurice Dupin, was the young officer son of Marie Aurore Dupin de Francueil, the natural daughter of the maréchal de Saxe and the granddaughter of Augustus II of Poland. Maurice Dupin and Sophie Delaborde married barely a month before their daughter was born, and Maurice died in a riding accident when the child was only four.

George Sand's plebeian mother and aristocratic grandmother, who had never liked each other, disagreed violently about the education of little Aurore until Mme Dupin de Francueil bribed Sophie with an allowance to go to Paris, leaving Aurore to be brought up

BY COURTESY OF THE VICTORIA AND ALBERT MUSEUM. PHOTOGRAPH C. H. CANNINGS

GEORGE SAND

at Nohant, near La Châtre in Berry, her grandmother's country home. Although the girl remained stubbornly loyal to her mother, she inevitably imbibed something of her grandmother's proud, skeptical, 18th-century view of life, as well as the profound love and understanding of the countryside which was to inform most of her works. In 1817 she was sent to the convent of the English Augustinians in Paris, where she was deeply attracted by the religious life, acquiring a mystical fervour which, though it soon abated, left its mark on her for the rest of her life. Returning to Nohant in 1820, she spent nearly two years of unrestricted freedom there, going shooting with her old tutor Deschatres, riding in masculine dress, talking with the peasants, reading widely if unsystematically in French and English, and consorting—innocently as yet—with the young men of the neighbourhood.

Her grandmother died in December 1821, and a year later Aurore married a young Berrichon squire called Casimir Dudevant, to whom she bore a son, Maurice, in 1823. The first years of the marriage were happy enough, but soon Aurore tired of her well-intentioned but somewhat insensitive husband and sought consolation first in a platonic friendship with a young magistrate, Aurélien de Sèze, and then in a passionate liaison with Stéphane de Grandsagne, a free-thinking, free-living neighbour. Grandsagne did more than anyone else to turn Aurore Dudevant into George Sand, for it was he who broke down her moral inhibitions, shook her religious faith, and widened the breach between her and her husband until it was an unbridgeable gap; he was probably also the father of her second child, Solange, who was born in September 1828. For his part, Dudevant took to heavy drinking and making love to the maidservants. Finally, in January 1831, under the terms of an amicable agreement with her husband, Aurore left Nohant for Paris, in order to take part in the Romantic movement and also to join her latest lover, the young Jules Sandeau (*q.v.*).

In Paris, she found a good friend in Henri de Latouche, a native of Berry like herself and the director of *Le Figaro,* who taught her the trade of journalism and accepted some of the articles which she wrote with Sandeau under the pseudonym of "Jules Sand." In 1832, however, she adopted a new pseudonym, "George

Sand," for a novel in which Sandeau had had no part. This novel, *Indiana*, which brought George Sand immediate fame, is a transcript of its author's emotional experience in her married life. But it is also a passionate protest against the social conventions which bind a wife to her husband against her will, and an apologia for a heroine who "sets up against the interests of society, raised to the level of principles, the straightforward ideas and simple laws of common sense and humanity." On this point George Sand's opinion never changed. Toward the end of her life, though she might then preach the virtues of monogamy, she would still insist in a letter to Flaubert that "a union in which there is neither liberty nor reciprocity is an offence against the sanctity of nature."

In *Valentine* (1832) and *Lélia* (1833) this ideal of free association is extended to the wider sphere of social and class relationships. *Valentine* is the story of a country squire's wife who falls in love with a young peasant, and it is the first of many Sand novels in which the hero is a peasant or a workman and the setting is the Berry countryside.

Meanwhile George Sand had discarded Sandeau and was seeking satisfaction with a succession of other men. The list of her lovers is a long one, including Mérimée (for one unsatisfactory, much-publicized encounter), Musset (in the stormy liaison which gave rise to his *Confession d'un enfant du siècle* [1836] and her *Elle et lui* [1859]), Michel de Bourges (the advocate who, in 1836, secured her legal separation from Dudevant), Chopin (in an affair that lasted from 1838 to 1847), and Alexandre Manceau (an engraver, 13 years her junior, who was her favourite from 1850 until his death in 1865). (*See* MUSSET, [LOUIS CHARLES] ALFRED DE; CHOPIN, FRÉDÉRIC FRANÇOIS.) Yet it would be a mistake to accept the popular impression of George Sand as a nymphomaniac who betrayed Musset, destroyed Chopin, and changed her philosophy and politics to suit the views of each successive lover. Although reputed to be the most promiscuous of women, she longed for the stability of a single faithful love, and she once declared, in a letter which may raise a smile but which was nonetheless sincere:

I have always believed above all else in fidelity, I have preached it, I have practised it, I have demanded it. Others have failed to live up to it and I too. And yet I have never felt remorse, because in my infidelities I have suffered a sort of fatality, an instinctive idealism which impelled me to abandon the imperfect for what seemed to me to be closer to perfection.

The proof of her sincerity is that when she thought she had found something approaching perfection in a man, she lived with him for years, caring for him with a love which was more that of a mother than a mistress: she stayed 8 years with Chopin for example, until he left her after a quarrel, and 15 years with Manceau, until his death from tuberculosis. It is patently untrue that she changed her religion and politics with every lover: she remained impervious to Musset's skeptical views and Chopin's aristocratic prejudices, while the man whose opinions she adopted wholeheartedly and preached for some 30 years, the philosopher Pierre Leroux, was never her lover.

The fact remains that most of her early works show the influence of one or other of the men with whom she consorted as friend, disciple, or mistress. Thus *Lélia* is full of pessimistic utterances which bear the mark of Gustave Planche, the dogmatic young literary critic; *Mauprat* (1837) reflects the vague longing for social betterment which George Sand had derived from her association with Michel de Bourges and Lamennais; *Spiridion* (1839) and *Les Sept Cordes de la lyre* (1840) echo the philosophic ideas of Pierre Leroux; while *Le Compagnon du tour de France* (1841) propounds the theories of Agricol Perdiguier on the union of the classes and the liberation of the manual worker from the shackles of overwork and exploitation.

After an ambitious *Entwicklungsroman*, a novel of development of character, entitled *Consuelo* (1842–43), which harked back to *Spiridion* and the idea of perpetual reincarnation, and some more novels in the socialist tradition, *Le Meunier d'Angibault* (1845) and *Le Péché de Monsieur Antoine* (1847), she eventually found her true form in her so-called rustic novels, which, though they owed something to the theories of Bourges, Leroux, and Perdiguier, drew their chief inspiration from her lifelong love of the countryside and sympathy for the poor. In *La Mare au diable* (1846), *François le Champi* (1848) and *La Petite Fadette* (1849), the old familiar theme of George Sand's work—love transcending the obstacles of convention and class—in the old familiar setting of the Berry countryside, regained pride of place. These rustic tales are probably her finest works; certainly she wrote no novels to surpass them between 1849 and her death.

In the revolution of February 1848, she played a self-important but courageous part, writing a whole series of appeals to the people. Later, however, the romantic and the revolutionary died in George Sand, and she produced a series of novels and plays of impeccable morality and conservatism, exalting marriage in *Constance Verrier* (1860) and condemning romantic passion in *Valvèdre* (1861). Probably the only works of the later George Sand, "la bonne dame de Nohant," which are likely to endure are her *Histoire de ma vie* (published 1854–55), which contains some brilliant character sketches, and *Contes d'une grand'mère* (1873), stories which she wrote for her grandchildren.

After a peaceful old age spent entertaining and corresponding with friends such as Flaubert and Dumas, organizing amateur theatricals and puppet shows, and educating her grandchildren, George Sand died at Nohant on June 8, 1876. She was mourned as a great writer, one of the greatest of her time; but, with a few exceptions, her works soon fell into neglect.

Two explanations are usually advanced for this neglect. It is said that she wrote too much and too quickly, and her detractors are fond of telling how one night, working as usual from midnight until four o'clock, she finished a novel at one o'clock and promptly started writing another. She certainly wrote with astonishing ease and fluency, and her collected works fill more than 100 volumes. But fluency does not necessarily imply facility; when a scene called for careful documentation, George Sand could provide it, and when an important problem of style presented itself, she grappled with it. One of the most remarkable features of her novels of country life is the speech of the peasants, which is neither literary French nor provincial patois but a cunningly devised halfway tongue which succeeds in being both intelligible and credible.

The other charge leveled at George Sand as a writer is that she was an idealist, that in her memoirs she shut her eyes to the unpleasant aspects of reality while in her novels she created characters of unbelievable innocence and charm. But in the opening pages of *Histoire de ma vie* she states explicitly that she has no intention of creating any scandals or settling any scores. She was well aware that the characters in most of her novels were idealized, and quite honest about it. "The novel," she declared, "need not necessarily be the representation of reality." And in a report of a conversation with Balzac, she quoted herself as saying to the elder novelist: "You aim at painting and do paint man as he is, but I am inclined to paint him as I wish he were, as I believe he ought to be." As she explained to Flaubert:

Life is not composed *entirely* of criminals and scoundrels. That rogues should be exhibited and condemned is right, is even moral, but we should be shown the other side of the medal as well, otherwise the simple-minded reader—who is the common-or-garden reader—will react against such books, and will grow depressed and fearful.

This was no doubt her sincere conviction, but the real reason for her idealism was more instinctive than theoretical. She was a born storyteller, and with her childlike optimism and ingenuous faith in life, it was natural that her stories should be fairy tales, her peasants good and kind, her endings happy. And as long as there are readers with a similar view of life, George Sand's memoirs and rustic novels—the Bucolics of France as they have been called —seem destined to survive.

BIBLIOGRAPHY.—*Editions, etc.:* the fullest edition is that of Calmann-Lévy, 105 vol. (1862–1926); later annotated editions of single works include *La Mare au diable* (1956), *La Petite Fadette* (1958), *Les Maîtres sonneurs* (1958), *Consuelo* (1959), *La Comtesse de Rudolstadt* (1959), *Lélia* (1960), and *Indiana* (1961), all in the Classiques Garnier series. *See also* S. de Lovenjoul, *George Sand: Étude bibliographique sur ses oeuvres* (1914); M. Cordroc'h, "Répertoire des lettres publiées de George Sand," *Revue d'histoire littéraire de la France*, vol. 60 ff. (1959–60).
   Biography and Criticism: W. Karénine, *George Sand, sa vie et ses oeuvres*, 4 vol. (1899–1926); M. L. Pailleron, *George Sand*, 3 vol.

(1938–53); A. Maurois, *Lélia ou la vie de George Sand* (1952; Eng. trans. by G. Hopkins, 1953); P. Salomon, *George Sand* (1953); T. Marix-Spire, *Les Romantiques et la musique: le cas George Sand* (1954); E. Thomas, *George Sand* (1959).   (R. BA.)

SAND. The products of rocks and minerals broken down by natural or artificial agencies are gravels, sands, silts, and clays. In the U.S. the term sand is applied to particles $\frac{1}{16}$ to 2 mm. diameter, and in Europe to those from .02 to 2 mm. diameter. Although most of the rock-making minerals occurring on the earth's crust are found in sands, only a limited number are met with at all frequently.

For several reasons quartz is by far the commonest; it is abundant in rocks, is comparatively hard, and has practically no cleavage so that it is not readily worn down to a fine state. Moreover, it is nearly insoluble in water and does not decompose. In certain localities feldspar, calcareous material, iron ores, and volcanic glass, among other substances, have been found to be dominant constituents of sand. Most quartzose sands contain a small quantity of feldspar. Small plates of white mica, which, though soft and very fissile, decompose slowly, are often present. In addition, all sands contain small quantities of "heavy" rock-forming minerals among which may be garnet, tourmaline, zircon, rutile, topaz, pyroxenes, amphiboles, iron ores, etc.

In certain shore and river sands these heavier constituents become concentrated as a result of current action and the removal of the lighter constituents. Economically valuable deposits may then be yielded. Such are the sands worked for diamonds and other gem stones, gold, platinum, tin, monazite, and other ores. The greensands, widely distributed over the floor of the ocean and found in ancient strata on the continents, owe their colour to the presence of glauconite, a potash-bearing mineral. These sands are used for water softening and for land dressing, and attempts have been made to extract potash from them.

In the pottery, glassmaking, and silicate (water glass) industries very pure quartzose sands are used in large quantities as a source of silica. Similar sands are required for lining the hearths of acid-steel furnaces. Molding sands, that is, the sands utilized in foundries for making the molds in which metal is cast, usually have a clayey bond uniting the grains of quartz. Because of the hardness and poor cleavage of quartz, sands are used extensively as abrasives. Garnet sands, although of more restricted occurrence, are similarly used. Ordinary sands find a multitude of other uses, among which may be mentioned the preparation of mortar, cement, and concrete. In underground formations, sand strata are frequently sources of water supply.

See also references under "Sand" in the Index.

(P. G. H. B.; X.)

SANDAGE, ALLAN REX (1926–   ), U.S. astronomer, made some crucial discoveries in stellar evolution and observational cosmology. He was born in Iowa City, Ia., on June 18, 1926; he graduated from the University of Illinois and received the Ph.D. from the California Institute of Technology; he became a member of the staff of the Mount Wilson and Palomar observatories in 1952 and carried out most of his investigations there.

Following theoretical work on the evolution of stars by several astronomers in the early 1950s, H. L. Johnson, with Sandage, demonstrated that the observed characteristics of the light and colour of the brightest stars in various clusters indicate that the latter can be arranged in a smooth order in terms of evolution, or age. This result, in the form of a diagram, proved to be a rich source of furthering knowledge in stellar evolution and galactic structure.

Later, Sandage became a leader in the discovery and study of quasi-stellar radio sources (*q.v.*), the starlike objects which are strong radiators of radio waves; their identification is carried out by comparing accurate positions of radio sources with photographic sky maps such as that obtained with the 48-in. Schmidt telescope of the Palomar Observatory. Sandage and T. A. Matthews identified the first of these objects in 1961; and many others have been identified since by Sandage and others. (*See* SPACE-TIME: *Recent Developments.*)

Later, Sandage discovered a class of remote, starlike objects with similar characteristics—except that they are not radio sources.

The discovery of these classes of objects stirred up tremendous interest among astronomers and physicists because of their possible bearing on the origin and present large-scale characteristics of the universe. Work by Maarten Schmidt (*q.v.*) indicated that the quasi-stellar sources may be the most distant objects observable with instruments of the late 1960s. If this is so, then the energy they radiate is enormous. Some astronomers do not accept such interpretations. A number of the quasi-stellar sources have been found (by Sandage and others) to vary irregularly and rapidly in light.

See also NEBULA: *The Galaxies (Extragalactic Nebulae): Statistical Properties.*   (W. W. M.; X.)

SANDALWOOD, a hardwood, rich in fragrant oil, obtained from various oriental trees, and principally from *Santalum album,* a native of India. The use of sandalwood dates at least as far back as the 5th century B.C. It is still extensively used in India and China, wherever Buddhism prevails, being employed in funeral rites and religious ceremonies. In India it is used in the manufacture of boxes, fans, and other ornamental articles of inlaid work.

Sandalwood oil, obtained by distilling the wood in chips, is used as a perfume, few native Indian attars or essential oils being free from admixture with it. As a powder or paste, the wood is employed in the pigments used by the Brahmans for their distinguishing caste marks. As a substitute for copaiba (*q.v.*), which is used as a diuretic and stimulant, sandalwood oil, distilled from the wood of *Santalum album,* is pleasanter to take, but it is less efficient and more expensive.

Red sandalwood is the product of a small leguminous tree, *Pterocarpus santalinus,* native to southern India, Ceylon, and the Philippine Islands. The freshly cut surface of the wood has a rich deep red colour which on exposure assumes a dark brownish tint; this pigment is used in wool dyeing. Several other species of *Pterocarpus,* notably *P. indicus,* contain the same dyeing principle and can be used as substitutes for red sandalwood. The barwood and camwood of the Guinea coast of Africa, from *Baphia nitida* or an allied species, called *santal rouge d'Afrique* by the French, are also allied to the red sandalwood of the Orient.

SANDAWE, a tribe of about 25,000 persons in the 1960s living near Kondoa, Tanzania (*q.v.*), between the Bubu and Mponde rivers. The Sandawe have been known to anthropological and linguistic science since 1894.

Many aspects of their culture show the influence of their Bantu neighbours. Their isolated wooden houses with roofs of clay are built in the lee of the wind. The staple food is millet, supplemented with fat, milk, and butter, meat being rarely eaten; culinary utensils are largely wooden. Their traditional clothes were of *hika*-grass, feathers, and hides, and the dominant cosmetic practices include shaving of the hair, earlobe piercing, and face tattooing. Circumcision, general for both sexes, seems a recently acquired practice. Their weapons are bows and iron-tipped arrows; they also trap animals but regard hunting with a net as an occupation of the poor. Their hunting weapons, as well as the conservative beehive huts which are occasionally seen, resemble those of the Hadzapi (*see* AFRICA: *Ethnography [Anthropology]: East Africa*).

The Sandawe cultivate the soil with a mattock, fertilize with manure, and keep cattle, sheep, and goats. The men clear the land, tend the animals, and hunt, while the women do the cultivation and food gathering. They drink beer and mead, but the term for the latter is borrowed from Bantu.

Their legal practices, which have an indigenous terminology, relate to such subjects as inheritance and indemnity for adultery; the latter is not so serious a transgression as it is among the Bantu.

Households, each comprising a nuclear family, are organized into patrilineal exogamous clans that form the basis for autonomous local communities. Marriage, which is monogamous (as with the nearby Mbugwe) and requires bridewealth (*q.v.*), is forbidden with parallel cousins and preferred with the maternal uncle's daughter. Residence is patrilocal, often after an initial period near the wife's parents.

Language.—Sandawe shares certain syntactic features with Bushman-Hottentot: inflection is accomplished by suffixes, and not by prefixes as in Bantu languages; the modifying noun precedes the modified ("cow's head"; not "head-of-cow" as in Bantu); and the basic sentence order is subject—object—verb (*see* BUSHMAN LANGUAGES; KHOISAN).

Pronominal reference is expressed either by independent words or by suffixes to verbs and nouns; it distinguishes subject function from other relationships, including possession. Pronouns and many nouns distinguish two grammatical genders, feminine and "indifferent," and indifferent forms also show plural (feminine rarely so). Nouns are inflected in a limited way for case, such as instrumental and locative. Suffixes serve, too, to mark commands and interrogations. Certain of the most common verbs are anomalous in having totally unrelated shapes in the singular and plural.

The most striking feature is the presence, in addition to a rich set of about 26 conventional consonants, of three types of clicks (*q.v.*): alveolar, lateral, and palatal. In acoustic effect, these match the corresponding clicks of Hottentot and Hadzapi (which each have a fourth type) and of Bushman (Southern Bushman has five varieties). Like Bushman-Hottentot, Sandawe has tones, but no accurate description of them has been made.

Sandawe, Bushman-Hottentot and Hadzapi are genetically related not only by lexical agreements but also by specific suffixal grammatical correspondences: noun plural *-ko* = Hottentot masculine plural *-ku*, and /kham Southern Bushman personal plural *gu;* feminine singular *-su* = Hottentot *-s*, Naron Bushman and Hadzapi *-sa;* feminine plural *-tsi*, *-si* = Hottentot and Central Bushman **dzi* and Hadzapi *-ti*, Naron *-si*, and perhaps Southern Bushman *si;* predicative indifferent *-we* = Hottentot masculine singular *-p*, Naron *-ba*, Hadzapi *-wa;* interrogative *-ne* = Hie Bushman *na-*. Among pronominal correspondences there are first singular *ts-*, *s-* = Hottentot and Central Bushman *ti-;* first singular subject form *tsa* = Hadzapi and Hottentot first singular *-ta;* first plural *so*, *su* = ≠hũa Southern Bushman *si*. The vocalism of Bushman *ha* "that" and *he* "this" exactly matches that of Sandawe *ha* "that," *he* "this," and *na* "there," *ne* "here." Thus in perfect accord are Sandawe *ha-we*, Hadzapi *ha-wa*, Naron *xa-ba* "he"; and the Central Bushman and Hottentot equivalent *e-b-* is precisely parallel formed on the base for "this."

Despite their geographic proximity, the relationship of Sandawe seems no closer to Hadzapi than to Bushman-Hottentot. If anything, it seems most akin to Central Bushman-Hottentot.

BIBLIOGRAPHY.—O. Dempwolff, *Die Sandawe* (1916); M. van de Kimmenade, "Les Sandawe," *Anthropos*, 31:395–416 (1936); J. H. Greenberg, *The Languages of Africa*, ch. iv (1963); E. O. J. Westphal, "The Non-Bantu Languages of Southern Africa," in A. N. Tucker and M. A. Bryan, *The Non-Bantu Languages of Northeastern Africa* (1956); O. Köhler, "Observations on the Central Khoisan Language Group," *Journal of African Languages*, 2:227–234 (1963). (E. P. H.)

SANDAY, WILLIAM (1843–1920), English New Testament scholar, one of the pioneers in introducing to English students the mass of work done by continent scholars in biblical criticism, was born at Holme Pierrepont, Notts., Aug. 1, 1843. Educated at Repton and Balliol College, Oxford, he became a scholar of Corpus Christi in 1863. He was a fellow and lecturer at Trinity in 1866, and was ordained in 1867. In 1876 he was appointed principal of Hatfield Hall, Durham. In 1882 he was appointed Ireland professor of exegesis at Oxford, and in 1895 Lady Margaret professor of divinity and canon of Christ Church, positions he held until 1919. He died at Oxford on Sept. 16, 1920.

See obituary by W. Lock in *Journal of Theological Studies*, 22:97–104, also pp. 193–204 of the same issue list a bibliography of his published works by A. Souter.

SANDBLASTING: *see* BLAST CLEANING AND SHOT PEENING.

SANDBURG, CARL (1878–1967), U.S. poet, historian, novelist, and folklorist, one of the group of writers responsible for the pre-World War I "Chicago Renaissance" in letters, was born Jan. 6, 1878, at Galesburg, Ill. The son of a Swedish immigrant, he began earning his keep at the age of 11. He worked in a barbershop, drove a milk wagon, and turned hobo for a time in the Kansas wheat fields. When the Spanish-American War broke out, he enlisted in the 6th Illinois infantry. These early years Sandburg later described in his autobiography *Always the Young Strangers* (1953).

After attending Lombard College in Galesburg, he acted as an organizer for the Social Democratic Party and secretary to the mayor of Milwaukee (1910–12). Moving to Chicago in 1913, he was an editor of *System* and then joined the staff of the *Daily News*.

CARL SANDBURG

In 1914 he made his appearance in Harriet Monroe's *Poetry* magazine with a group of his *Chicago Poems*, which were issued in book form in 1916. Sandburg's poetry made an instant and favourable impression. In this and succeeding volumes—*Cornhuskers* (1918), *Smoke and Steel* (1920), and *Slabs of the Sunburnt West* (1922)—he was recognized as a genuine poet of the people. In *Good Morning, America* (1928) Sandburg seemed to have lost some of his faith in democracy, but from the depths of the depression he wrote a poetic testament, unique in form, to the power of the people to go forward, *The People, Yes* (1936).

Few Americans have known the lore of their country as Sandburg did. Some of its folk say is in *The People, Yes*. The folk songs that he sang before delighted audiences were issued in two collections, *The American Songbag* (1927) and *Carl Sandburg's New American Songbag* (1950). In 1923 his publishers suggested that he write a life of Lincoln for young people. The project grew into one of the most deservedly popular of biographies, *Abraham Lincoln: the Prairie Years* (2 vol., 1926) and *Abraham Lincoln: the War Years* (4 vol., 1939; Pulitzer Prize, history, 1940). In 1948 Sandburg published a long novel, *Remembrance Rock*, which recapitulates the American experience from Plymouth Rock to World War II. *Complete Poems* (1950) won the Pulitzer Prize for poetry in 1951. *The Sandburg Range* (1957) contains selections from his work. It is abundantly illustrated with photographs taken at various stages in his career. He died on July 22, 1967, at Flat Rock, N.C.

BIBLIOGRAPHY.—Karl W. Detzer, *Carl Sandburg: a Study in Personality and Background* (1941); Bruce Weirick, *From Whitman to Sandburg in American Poetry* (1924); Horace Gregory and Marya Zaturenska, *A History of American Poetry, 1900–1940* (1946); R. Crowder, *Carl Sandburg* (1964). (W. T.)

SAND DOLLAR, a common name for small, disk-shaped marine animals, the most specialized members of the Clypeastroidea, a group of sea urchins (*q.v.*). Throughout the temperate and tropical zones, they live molelike in sand at moderate depths. The sand dollar has a flattened body, from less than ½ in. to about 4 in. in diameter, with the plates of the test (or shell) firmly united and rather thick; the inside of the test is reinforced by pillars. The spines on the upper side are short and crowded, forming a dense fur which holds the sand out, while those on the underside are longer and assist in pushing the animal through the sand. The colour varies but is usually a dark shade—olive, purplish, brown, or black.

A bilateral symmetry is superimposed upon the original five-rayed symmetry, and these forms can only move forward, not in all directions as can the ordinary five-rayed sea urchins. When it meets an obstacle, the sand dollar stops and, with the aid of ventral spines, pivots around the axis which runs vertical through the mouth, and then continues in the new direction. The anus lies on the underside. In these forms the tube feet spread out from the radial canals over large parts of the underside, whereas those on the central part of the upper side are modified for respiration and form flattened leaves. On the dead tests, after the spines have dropped off, the characteristic star-shaped pattern of the gill pores is revealed. The centrally placed mouth has five ciliated grooves radiating out from it, along which food particles are carried in, sifted, and subdivided by the teeth.

Sand dollars live more or less concealed in the sand, at a depth of a few feet—sometimes placed at a sharp angle with the anterior edge downward. They have been extremely successful in utilizing a niche in nature which few other forms have invaded, and they occur usually in very large numbers, as evidenced by the thousands of shells washed up after a heavy storm.

BIBLIOGRAPHY.—Libbie H. Hyman, *The Invertebrates*, vol. 4 (1955); T. Mortensen, *Monograph of the Echinoidea* (1928–53); J. Wyatt Durham, "Classification of Clypeasteroid Echinoids," University of California, *Geol. Sci.* 31 (1955). (EL. D.)

SANDEAU, LÉONARD SILVAIN JULIEN, known as JULES SANDEAU (1811–1883), French writer, is remembered chiefly for his collaboration with other authors. Born at Aubusson on Feb. 19, 1811, he began his literary life in the company of George Sand (*q.v.*), whose lover he became in 1830 when he was a young law student in Paris. Under the pseudonym "Jules Sand," they published a novel, *Rose et Blanche* (1831), and some *nouvelles*. At the end of 1832 she broke off the affair, but retained her pen name, which had become George Sand.

In the following years Sandeau often met Balzac. He had a brief liaison with Marie Dorval, the actress. In 1842 he married, reverting to a regular, bourgeois life. Although in his writing he aims at simplicity, he is unable to escape romantic idealism. He expresses himself in a mannered style, full of false finery. His best novels are *Marianna* (1839), in which he portrays George Sand, *Mlle de la Seiglière* (1848), *La Roche aux mouettes* (1871), and *Jean de Thommeray* (1873). In collaboration with Émile Augier (*q.v.*) he wrote several plays: *Le Gendre de M. Poirier* (1854) was a particularly lasting success. Under the Second Empire Sandeau was a favourite at court. In 1858 he was elected to the Académie Française. He died in Paris on April 24, 1883.

See M. Silver, *Jules Sandeau, l'homme et la vie* (1936). (P. SA.)

SANDERS (SANDER), **NICHOLAS** (*c.* 1530–1581), English Roman Catholic scholar, controversialist, and historian of the English Reformation, was born in Surrey about 1530 and educated at Winchester and New College, Oxford, at which university he became a lecturer in canon law. He left England shortly after the accession of Elizabeth I in order to be free to practise Roman Catholicism, and by 1561 had been ordained priest at Rome. Stanislaus Cardinal Hosius, prince-bishop of Ermeland, having been appointed one of the five papal legates at the renewed sessions of the Council of Trent, took Sanders with him as one of his theologians. Sanders' immense reputation among the English Catholic exiles in the Low Countries, however, caused the cardinal to allow him to go to Louvain, where Sanders became professor of theology and was soon busy controverting the claims of Episcopalian divines, especially Bishop John Jewel.

Of Sanders' many books the best known was a history of the English Reformation written in Latin, left unfinished at his death, and published with additions by a fellow exile, Father Edward Rishton, at Cologne in 1585. Many editions and translations followed rapidly; eventually it was put into English by David Lewis, entitled *The Rise and Growth of the Anglican Schism* (1877). Bitterly attacked at first by English Protestant writers as malicious and erroneous, it has come more and more to be appreciated as an outstanding piece of historical writing for its time.

The later part of Sanders' life was occupied in promoting a military invasion of England for the restoration of Catholicism. Lengthy and unsatisfactory negotiations for this purpose in both Rome and Madrid culminated in his landing in Ireland in 1579 as a papal agent to promote rebellion and his failure and death there in 1581.

BIBLIOGRAPHY.—Thomas McNevin Veech, *Dr. Nicholas Sanders and the English Reformation, 1530–1581*, with bibliography (1935); "Dr. Nicholas Sanders' Report to Cardinal Moroni on the Change of Religion in 1558–9 (1561)," *Publications of the Catholic Record Society*, vol. i (1905); John B. Wainewright (ed.), "Some Letters and Papers of Nicolas Sander, 1562–1580," *Publications of the Catholic Record Society*, vol. xiii (1926). (E. McD.)

SANDERSON, FREDERICK WILLIAM (1857–1922), distinguished English schoolmaster whose maxim that "Education must be fitted to the boy, not the boy to education," has had considerable influence on the curriculum and methods of secondary education, was born at Brancepeth, County Durham, on May 13, 1857. He was educated at the local school, at Durham University, and at Christ's College, Cambridge. In 1889 he became senior physics master at Dulwich College, where he formed a successful "engineering side." His appointment as headmaster of Oundle School, near Peterborough, Northamptonshire, in 1892, came at a critical period in the fortunes of the school. In spite of initial opposition he transformed the school and completed an ambitious building program which included laboratories, workshops, a foundry, an observatory, an experimental farm, and a spacious library.

A scientist and a practical teacher, he understood boys and their interests. During his 30-year headship Oundle developed from a school of less than 100 pupils to one which accommodated five times that number. Though not mentioning him by name, the Hadow report on the *Education of the Adolescent* (1926) was strongly influenced by his ideas.

Sanderson died in London on June 15, 1922.

See Sanderson of Oundle (1923), an account of his work compiled by his colleagues; H. G. Wells, *The Story of a Great Schoolmaster* (1924). (S. J. C.)

SAND FLY, any of several small bloodsucking flies, particularly of the family Psychodidae, but the name is also applied loosely to certain species of the Ceratopogonidae and Simuliidae. The name comes from the fact that the aquatic larvae of some species live in the intertidal zone of coastal beaches, or in saturated sand elsewhere; however, most species pass their immature stages in water, mud, or wet, decomposing organic debris.

Sand flies are of considerable medical importance, in addition to being extremely annoying to man when present in large numbers. Species of *Phlebotomus* (family Psychodidae) transmit through their bite the virus of Pappataci fever (*q.v.*), in the Mediterranean area and southern Asia, and the protozoan parasites causing kala azar, Oriental sore, and espundia (*see* LEISHMANIASIS), in parts of South America, Africa, and Asia. Five species of *Simulium* (family Simuliidae), locally known as sand flies but more often as black flies (*q.v.*), have been found to infect man with the parasitic worm causing onchocerciasis, which may result in blindness.

Far more pestiferous than these medically important species, but not known to transmit any pathogen to man, are the tiny biting midges, species of *Culicoides, Leptoconops,* and related genera (family Ceratopogonidae), sometimes called punkies or "no-see-ums." While individual bites are not painful, these flies often attack man in great numbers, causing extreme discomfort. *See also* FLY. (G. W. Bs.)

SANDHURST, a large village of Berkshire, Eng., 9 mi. (14 km.) N of Aldershot, Hampshire, is the site of the Royal Military Academy (RMA), which stands in wooded grounds, with a lake and playing fields, between the village and the town of Camberley, Surrey. At the academy most of the potential regular officers for the British Army undergo training as officer cadets. *See* MILITARY, NAVAL AND AIR ACADEMIES.

SAN DIEGO, a Pacific coast city of California, U.S., an important naval base and seat of San Diego county, is situated 16 mi. N. of the Mexican border and about 110 mi. S.S.E. of Los Angeles. Between 1950 and 1960, the population, stimulated by industrial growth, naval and military activities, and a mild climate, increased from 334,387 to 573,224, one of the highest percentage increases for any major U.S. city. The population of the San Diego standard metropolitan statistical area, comprising San Diego county, was 556,808 in 1950 and 1,033,011 in 1960. (For comparative population figures *see* table in CALIFORNIA: *Population*.)

History.—Juan Rodríguez Cabrillo, a Portuguese explorer in the service of Spain, discovered the bay on Sept. 28, 1542, and named it San Miguel. Sebastián Vizcaíno, who was sent in 1602 to reconnoitre California preparatory to the establishment of a Spanish colony, renamed the bay for San Diego de Alcalá de Henares, a Spanish monk whose name Vizcaíno's flagship bore.

In 1769 the harbour was chosen as the base for the exploration and settlement of California because of its excellence and its relative proximity to Mexico. The sacred expedition of that year, led by the first governor, Gaspar de Portolá, founded the San Diego presidio as the initial settlement in the new colony. On the same day, July 16, 1769, Father Junípero Serra dedicated San Diego mission, the first of the California missions. The settlement was slow to spread beyond the presidio walls because of the menace of Indian and foreign attack. In 1774 the missionaries removed to the site of an Indian village, but the new mission buildings were soon destroyed by Indians and a brief return to the protection of the ramparts was necessary. Not until 50 years had passed did the town itself expand outside the presidio, which was strategically located on a hill. Then, with the overthrow of Spanish control by Mexico, and the pacification of savage tribes, inhabitants were able to go below the walls onto flat lands to build what has become known as Old Town, which was organized a pueblo in 1834.

American conquest in 1846 brought few immediate changes. The Old Town was incorporated in 1850 but did not grow and lost its charter two years later. San Diego then remained a Mexican adobe village until Alonzo E. Horton arrived in 1867 with the intention of founding a new town. He purchased a tract by the bay, 3 mi. S. of Old Town, for 26 cents an acre. In a few years his promotion became the largest California community south of Los Angeles, and has remained so ever since. The new city was incorporated in 1872. In 1931 the council-manager form of government was adopted.

Favourable year-round climate proved the great attraction to early settlement. Rainfall averages only 10 in. a year, which comes mostly in the mild winters. Growth tended to be extremely influenced by California land booms. The Santa Fe railway arrived in 1884, at the time of a general boom, and population and real estate values multiplied. Most of the towns in the county were founded at that time. Except for hard times that followed and lasted through the early 1890s, the city's growth thereafter was rapid.

Commerce and Industry.—San Diego is the headquarters of the 11th naval district and the extensive development of installations including army, marine and coast guard establishments added a great government payroll to the income of the area. The pleasant living conditions attract retired persons, especially naval personnel.

Equable climate and recreational facilities have encouraged a considerable tourist trade. Before World War II, climatic factors attracted San Diego's principal industry, aircraft construction, and later stimulated an increase of management personnel and the establishment of important new industries, such as electronics and rocketry. San Diego is one of the leading agricultural counties in the U.S. in the value of production. Citrus, avocado, truck garden crops and livestock are the major products.

The roomy (22 sq.mi.), landlocked bay, one of the great natural harbours of the world, is a first port of call for coastwise and foreign shipping, operating through the Panama canal. As an outlet for growing amounts of Imperial valley cotton, its export tonnage is increasing yearly. Shipbuilding developed as an industry in the mid-1950s. San Diego was once the country's leading tuna-packing area, but after World War II there was a decline, as Japan became a major source.

Recreation and Culture.—Deep-sea fishing is a popular recreation. Opportunities for other aquatic sports, swimming, motorboat racing, water skiing and sailing, were expanded by the development of Mission bay, a shallow harbour just north of San Diego bay, as a large aquatic park area. There are many well-situated golf courses about the metropolitan area.

Cultural establishments are centred in Balboa park. An annual Shakespeare festival, which offers scholarships to promising actors, is centred around a replica of London's Old Globe theatre. The art gallery, the Museum of Man, the Natural History museum, an open-air amphitheatre and one of the world's largest outdoor organs are all set amid the park's landscaped area. Light opera productions are given outdoors in summer. Also in Balboa park is the San Diego zoo, housing one of the largest collections of animals in the world.

The southern city limit is also the Mexican border. The international gate is the busiest crossing on the southern frontier of the United States. Principal attractions in Mexico are bullfights, horse and dog racing, jai alai and Mexican and foreign merchandise.

Educational facilities include San Diego State college (1897), San Diego College for Women (Roman Catholic; 1949), University of San Diego (Roman Catholic; 1949), California Western university (Methodist; chartered in 1924 as Balboa university and rechartered in 1952) and San Diego Junior colleges (1914), including City college, Evening college and Mesa college. A rapidly developing branch of the University of California is at La Jolla, which is also the site of the Scripps Institution of Oceanography.

(A. P. N.)

SANDINO, CÉSAR AUGUSTO (1893–1934), Nicaraguan guerrilla leader, was one of the most controversial figures of recent Central American history. Although he was considered a bandit by the United States government, many Latin Americans viewed him as a patriot and fighter against "Yankee imperialism."

The son of a small farmer, Sandino first gained national recognition in 1926 when he took up arms in support of Vice-Pres. Juan Bautista Sacasa's claim to the presidency. After the United States intervened in 1927 to impose peace, Sandino refused to lay down his arms and with several hundred men withdrew to the mountains of northern Nicaragua. His success in eluding capture by the U.S. Marine Corps and the Nicaraguan National Guard attracted widespread sympathy for him throughout the hemisphere. The resulting anti-United States feeling helped bring about a change in U.S. foreign policy toward Latin America, which culminated in Pres. Franklin D. Roosevelt's "Good Neighbor Policy." Following the withdrawal of the Marines in January 1933 and the inauguration of Sacasa as president, Sandino finally laid down his arms. On Feb. 21, 1934, upon leaving a dinner with the president, Sandino and several aides were assassinated by members of the National Guard who resented the lenient treatment accorded him by the government.

(R. M. Sc.)

SANDOMIERZ, a town in Kielce *województwo* (province), southeastern Poland, and seat of a Roman Catholic diocese. Pop. (1960) 12,300. It stands on the high left bank of the Vistula above its confluence with the San. The town early gained importance from its geographical and defensive position between the fertile Little Polish Highlands and the once wooded Sandomierz Plain, on a wide navigable river and on the old trade routes between the Baltic and Black seas and Ruthenia; it was one of the oldest Little Polish fortresses, mentioned in 11th-century sources. It was the capital of the independent principality of Sandomierz when Poland was divided into smaller states, and acquired town rights in 1286. After the third partition of Poland it was occupied by Austria. During 1807–15 it belonged to the Duchy of Warsaw and became part of the Polish kingdom (dependent on Russia) in 1815. It was returned to Poland in 1918.

One of the largest Polish towns in the 16th century, Sandomierz is now a small township. Its old buildings, in their picturesque setting, give the town much charm. Among the finest are the Romanesque Church of St. Jakub (James), with its door and murals of glazed brick, the Gothic cathedral with Byzantine murals, the town hall (Renaissance façade), and the Gothic Opatowska Gate, part of the old fortifications. The town's food industry has developed; a large glassworks began operating in the mid-1960s; and a new industrial centre, based on local sulfur deposits, has grown up near the confluence of the rivers. (K. M. Wɪ.)

SANDOWAY, a town and the southernmost of the three districts in the Arakan division of the Union of Burma. The town (pop. [1962 est.] 69,924), 150 mi. (241 km.) SE of Akyab, is ancient and is said to have once been the capital of Arakan (*q.v.*). It was formerly accessible from the remainder of Burma only by sea but the institution of air service from Rangoon made possible such developments as a delightful bathing beach at Ngapali near Sandoway.

The district has an area of 4,149 sq.mi. (10,746 sq.km.) and a population (1962 est.) of 164,670. The country is mountainous, with peaks of 4,000 ft. and more in the north. Only small areas are available for cultivation, and almost the only crop is rice. The chief pass is the Taungup, crossed by a cart track converted to a motor road in 1959–60, leading from Taungup village to Prome on the Irrawaddy River. (L. D. S.)

SANDOWN-SHANKLIN, a holiday resort and urban district in the Isle of Wight, Hampshire, Eng. Sandown is 6 mi. and Shanklin 8 mi. S of Ryde by road. Pop. (1961) 14,386. Area 5.5 sq.mi. Sandown rises from the wide sandy shore of Sandown Bay, on the southeast of the island, and is bordered to the north by the white Culver cliff. Shanklin stands on the cliffs at the southerly end of the bay, with the esplanade below, and the winding chasm of Shanklin chine (ridge) lies to the south. The district is noted for its floral beauty and long hours of sunshine.

SANDPAPER, an abrasive material prepared by coating heavy paper with glue and sifting fine sand over its surface before the glue sets. It is used for smoothing the surface of wood, for rubbing down paint, and similar purposes.

See ABRASIVE.

SANDPIPER, an indefinite group name used for certain of the smaller shore birds of the family Scolopacidae, which also includes snipe, curlew, godwit, woodcock, etc. In North America, when these birds were shot in numbers, gunners had many alternative names for some of them, including "peeps" and "oxeyes." In Europe the name "stint" is used for species that in America would be called sandpipers.

In general, sandpipers are sparrow- to thrush-sized birds with moderately long bills and legs, long narrow wings, and fairly short tails, and often with a complicated "dead-grass" pattern of browns, buffs, and black on the upperparts. Sandpipers usually nest on the ground in the open, in a scantily lined little hollow; they lay four spotted eggs, from which hatch active downy young. Many sandpipers nest in the Arctic and sub-Arctic regions and pass through the North Temperate Zone in great flocks. They feed on beaches and mud flats of oceans and inland waters, running along near the water, picking up their food of insects, crustaceans, and worms. In flight the flocks show remarkable correlation of movement, all the birds turning and wheeling in unison.

ERIC HOSKING

COMMON SANDPIPER (ACTITIS HYPO-LEUCOS)

Some sandpipers undergo long migrations, like the white-rumped sandpiper (*Erolia fuscicollis*) of the American Arctic, which winters in southern South America; and the rufous-necked sandpiper (*Erolia ruficollis*) of Siberia, which winters to New Zealand and Tasmania. Others, like the least sandpiper (*Erolia minutilla*) of the American Arctic and sub-Arctic, winter from the United States to Peru, while the purple sandpiper (*E. maritima*) winters as far north as the rocky coasts of southern Greenland. The common sandpiper (*Actitis*—formerly *Tringa*—*hypoleucos*) of Eurasia and the closely related spotted sandpiper (*A. macularia*) of America, gray-brown above, are notable for frequenting gravelly borders of streams and lakes and having a nervous mannerism of wagging the tail. The green sandpiper (*Tringa ochropus*) of Europe and the solitary sandpiper (*T. solitaria*) of America are unusual in nesting not on the ground but in old tree nests of songbirds such as thrushes and in looking more like the tall slender yellowlegs (*Totanus* species). (A. L. RD.)

SANDRINGHAM, a village in the Freebridge Lynn rural district of Norfolk, Eng., is 9 mi. (14 km.) NNE of King's Lynn by road. Sandringham House, a country seat of the sovereign, was acquired for the prince of Wales, later Edward VII, in 1861. The Sandringham estate of 19,500 ac. (7,890 ha.), including a park of 200 ac. (80 ha.), has appealed to successive sovereigns for its bracing air and excellent shooting. Since World War II its farming has been organized on business lines to make a substantial contribution to the royal economy. The church of St. Mary Magdalene contains memorials of the royal family. George VI was born at York cottage in the grounds on Dec. 14, 1895, and died at Sandringham House on Feb. 6, 1952. (R. R. C.)

SANDSTONE is a consolidated rock built up dominantly of grains of sand (*q.v.*) held together by a cementing substance. Sandstones are composed mainly of quartz, but may vary in composition in the same manner as sands. By increase in the size of their constituents they pass into conglomerates (*q.v.*) and by decrease into arenaceous shales and clay rocks. When the grains of sand are angular, the rock is termed a grit.

The minerals of sandstones are the same as those of sands. Quartz is the commonest; with it often occurs a certain amount of feldspar (as in the rock arkose) and frequently white mica. The flakes of mica may often be seen lying on the bedding planes and may give the sandstone a cleavable character (*e.g.*, paving stone) of much value in quarrying. The cementing material is often fine chalcedonic silica, or it may be secondary quartz, producing a quartzitelike rock. Calcareous material (calcite), glauconite, iron oxides, carbonaceous matter, and other substances also act as cements and give the sandstones characteristic colours. Glauconitic sandstones are greenish; ferruginous sandstones, red, brown, and yellow or gray. When the cementing substance is clay, the rock is often of white or gray colour and firmly compacted.

Pure sandstones may contain as much as 99% of silica. If relatively soft they are crushed to sand for commercial purposes. If firmly cemented they are utilized, on account of the resistance of silica to heat, for the manufacture of silica bricks, furnace linings, hearths, etc. Of this character is the well-known rock "ganister" worked in the districts of Sheffield, South Wales, etc. Less pure, but firmly cemented siliceous sandstones are used to make grindstones and millstones. Similar rocks, as well as calcareous, dolomitic (*see* DOLOMITES), and ferruginous sandstones, are extensively worked as building stones, mostly by quarries but sometimes by mines. As sandstones are porous, they do not take a good polish, and are not used as ornamental stones, but this property makes sandstone formations valuable storage basins and sources of water.

See also references under "Sandstone" in the Index.

(P. G. H. B.)

SANDUSKY, a city of northern Ohio, U.S., a port of entry and the seat of Erie County, is situated on Sandusky Bay off Lake Erie, 56 mi. SW of Cleveland. It was platted in 1818 and incorporated in 1824; the name is Indian, referring to "clear water." Both French and British traders established posts in the area and the English fort built in 1761 was burned during Pontiac's conspiracy in 1763. During the War of 1812 Sandusky was a supply depot; Perry's naval victory of Sept. 10, 1813, occurred about 25 mi. NW, near Put-in-Bay. (*See* WAR OF 1812.)

This terminated Indian and British aggressions in the area and it was then settled by Connecticut residents; the townsite was in that portion of the Connecticut Western Reserve set aside for persons who had suffered losses from British raids in Connecticut during the American Revolution. A large number of Germans came in 1840–60. Bypassed as a terminus of a lake to Ohio River canal, Sandusky obtained the first Ohio Railroad charter, and service began in 1838. Johnson's Island in Sandusky Bay was a prison for Confederate officers from 1862 to 1865. Sandusky's early trade was in lumber, fish, and wood and agricultural products. Principal trade items in modern times include crayons, school paints, ball bearings, automotive and small steel castings, corrugated paper products, pleasure boats, rubber toys, radios, paper and textile machine rolls, quarry products, and lake shipment of coal. The city is located in a boating, fishing, and sand beach vacationing area and has many municipal parks. Sandusky has a commission-manager form of government, in effect since 1916. For comparative population figures *see* table in OHIO: *Population*. (C. E. F.)

SANDWICH, EDWARD MONTAGU (MOUNTAGU), 1ST EARL OF (1625–1672), English admiral who brought Charles II to England at the Restoration in 1660 and who subsequently fought in the Second and Third Dutch Wars, was born at Barnwell, Northamptonshire, on July 27, 1625, the son of Sir Sydney Montagu. Following the outbreak of the Civil War, he raised a regiment for the Parliament in 1643 and fought at the battles of Marston Moor (July 2, 1644), Naseby (June 14, 1645), and at the siege of Bristol (September 1645). Although one of Oliver Cromwell's intimate friends and M.P. for Huntingdonshire from

1645 to 1648, he took little part in public affairs until 1653, when he was appointed a member of the council of state. In January 1656 he was made a general at sea, an office he held jointly with Robert Blake. He was sent by Richard Cromwell to Denmark with a fleet in April 1659 to arrange a peace between Denmark and Sweden, but after Richard's fall (May) he returned to England and in September resigned his command. Reappointed general at sea in February 1660, he secured the fleet for Charles II, then in Holland, and was entrusted with the duty of bringing the king to England. He was created earl of Sandwich in July 1660 and was the patron of Samuel Pepys at the Admiralty for some years.

In the Second Dutch War (1665–67) Sandwich commanded a squadron under the duke of York (later James II) and distinguished himself in the battle off Lowestoft on June 13, 1665 (new style; June 3, old style). When the duke retired in July, Sandwich became commander in chief, but after he had allowed the distribution of valuable cargoes from some captured Dutch ships without obtaining the king's permission he was dismissed from his command (November). Sent as ambassador extraordinary to Madrid in 1666, he arranged a commercial treaty with Spain (May 1667) and acted as a mediator between Spain and Portugal in the Treaty of Lisbon (February 1668). In 1670 he was appointed president of the council for trade and plantations. On the outbreak of the Third Dutch War in 1672, Sandwich again commanded a squadron under the duke of York and during the fight in Solebay (Southwold Bay) on June 7, 1672 (N.S., May 28, O.S.), his ship the "Royal James," which had taken a conspicuous part in the action, was destroyed by fire. Sandwich's body was found at sea some days later and was buried in Westminster Abbey. His *Journal* for the years 1659 to 1665, edited by R. C. Anderson, was published in 1929.

See F. R. Harris, *The Life of Edward Mountagu,* 2 vol. (1912).
(C. C. L.)

SANDWICH, JOHN MONTAGU, 4TH EARL OF (1718–1792), English statesman and first lord of the admiralty during the American Revolution, was born on Nov. 3, 1718. He succeeded to the earldom in 1729, and after traveling abroad took his seat in the House of Lords in 1739, joining the Whig group led by John Russell, 4th duke of Bedford. He served on the board of admiralty (1744–49) and was first lord (1749–51 and 1763). As secretary of state for the northern department (September 1763–July 1765), he took a leading part in November 1763 in the prosecution of John Wilkes, whose friend he had been, thereby earning the nickname of "Jemmy Twitcher," after a treacherous character in John Gay's *The Beggar's Opera.* He was postmaster general (1768–70) and secretary of state for the northern department (December 1770–January 1771). As first lord of the admiralty from 1771 to 1782, he was the most important member of Lord North's ministry, but it was his misfortune to be the principal enemy of the Whigs and to be ruined by the failures in the American Revolutionary War. Throughout his life he was keenly interested in naval affairs, the administration and patronage of the Navy, and the promotion of exploration. In 1778 Capt. James Cook named the Sandwich Islands (*see* HAWAII) after him. Sandwich has been frequently attacked for corruption, and in private life he was a profligate gambler and rake; but recently his administrative gifts have been recognized. He died in London on April 30, 1792. His *Voyage . . . Round the Mediterranean in the Years 1738 and 1739* was published in 1799. The "sandwich" was named after him in 1762 when he spent 24 hours at the gaming table without other food.

See G. R. Barnes and J. H. Owen (eds.), *The Private Papers of John, Earl of Sandwich, 1771–1782,* 4 vol. (1932–38); G. Martelli, *Jemmy Twitcher* (1962).
(C. C. L.)

SANDWICH, a market town and municipal borough in the Dover parliamentary division of Kent, Eng., 12 mi. E of Canterbury on the Stour River. Pop. (1961) 4,264. Area 3.3 sq.mi. One of the original Cinque Ports, and second in precedence to Hastings, it is now 2 mi. from the sea. In the line of the old defensive ramparts, now marked by a public walk, the Fisher Gate (dating from 1384, restored 1954) is the only gateway remaining, the other three —Newgate, Sandown, and Canterbury gates—having been pulled

down in the 18th century; the Barbican was built in 1539 as one of a chain of blockhouses along the coast. In the twisting streets of Sandwich are timber-framed houses, and others built by the Flemings; e.g., White Friars on the site of a 13th-century Carmelite priory; three ancient hospitals—St. Bartholomew's (probably founded 1217), just outside the town, with a fine Early English chapel, St. Thomas' dating from 1392 and rebuilt in 1864, and St. John's; three old churches—St. Clement's (the parish church since 1948) which dates from the 12th century and has a beautiful Norman tower, St. Mary the Virgin which stands on the site of a 7th-century monastery, but is not now in regular use, and St. Peter's, of various dates from the 12th century, where the curfew is still rung at 8 P.M. on the tenor bell and which is now the chapel of Sir Roger Manwood's Grammar School (1563). The school's present buildings were put up in 1895 and the old house, Manwood Court (1564), is now a private house. The guildhall, a 16th-century building, is still in use.

Rutupiae (Richborough, q.v.), 1¼ mi. N of Sandwich, was established as a Roman town in A.D. 43 and was the centre of administration and one of the main entries from the continent. Sandwich was called Lundenvic by the Saxons and later became Sandwic; it was a borough by prescription before 1226, when the record of mayors begins. The governing charter until 1835 was that granted by Charles II in 1684. For many centuries the naval headquarters, the port for the wool trade, and chief port of embarkation for the European continent, Sandwich lost its importance in the 16th century when the harbour became silted up. The town flourished again when the Flemish refugees were given permission by Elizabeth I to live there; during the Napoleonic Wars; during World War I; and in World War II when it was extensively used for the construction of Mulberry Harbour. The chief industries are agriculture, and the manufacture of antibiotics, rubber products, shuttlecocks, textiles, and welding equipment. It is also a holiday town with fine golf links and sands at Sandwich Bay.

SANDYS, SIR EDWIN (1561–1629), English parliamentarian and a founder of the colony of Virginia, was born in Worcestershire on Dec. 9, 1561, the second son of Edwin Sandys, archbishop of York. He was an elder brother of George Sandys (*q.v.*). After 12 years at Corpus Christi College, Oxford, he entered the Middle Temple in 1590, where he maintained a close friendship with Richard Hooker (*q.v.*). From 1596 to 1599 he traveled abroad, and wrote his *A Relation of the State of Religion . . .* (1605), a remarkably tolerant analysis of contemporary creeds. Knighted in 1603, Sandys was returned to Parliament in 1604 and emerged unexpectedly as a leader of opposition to the crown, rapidly achieving great influence by a combination of shrewd oratory, legal experience, and mastery of procedure. He also led the gentry's agitation to open to nonmerchants, through joint-stock companies, the profits of England's expansion overseas. He joined the Virginia Company in 1607, the East India Company by 1611, the Somers Islands Company in 1615, and became a director of all three. In 1619 he gained control of the Virginia Company, but his management was a failure despite the fact that the year saw a rush of colonists, the first meeting of a representative assembly in Virginia, and the arrangement that enabled the Pilgrim fathers to sail to America in 1620. Plagued by constant setbacks, the company was dissolved in 1624. After Sir Edward Coke became leader of the parliamentary opposition in 1621, Sandys became its elder statesman. He died in October 1629. His work paved the way for a new generation of opposition leaders who eventually took Parliament into open revolt against the crown.
(T. K. RA.)

SANDYS, GEORGE (1578–1644), English traveler, poet, colonist, and early foreign service career officer, whose life exemplifies the interests and accomplishments of his age and who played an important part in the development of English verse, especially of the heroic couplet. He is of particular interest, also, for his connection with the founding of the colony of Virginia. The seventh and youngest son of Edwin Sandys, archbishop of York, and brother of Edwin Sandys (*q.v.*), he was born near York, on March 2, 1578. He studied at St. Mary's Hall, Oxford, and Corpus Christi College and in 1596 was admitted to the Middle

Temple. Probably about two years later he married Elizabeth Norton, his father's ward. By 1606 the marriage had ended in permanent separation.

In May 1610 Sandys set out on the travels described in *A Relation of a Journey begun An:Dom:1610. Four Books containing a description of the Turkish Empire, of Egypt, the Holy Land, of the Remote Parts of Italy, and Islands adjoyning* (1615), which went through nine editions during the 17th century and was used as source material by Sir Francis Bacon, Sir Thomas Browne, Milton, and other writers. In the dedication Sandys explains that his aim is "to draw a right image of the frailty of man. . . ; and assurance that as there is nothing unchangeable saving God, so nothing stable but his grace and protection." His account shows his keen interest in the customs and beliefs of other peoples, his knowledge of classical myth and literature, and a lively curiosity about the history, topography, and animal life of the places visited. His prose style, though weighted with references to a wide range of authorities, is balanced and condensed and has an easy yet dignified rhythm. The book has an important place in the development of Elizabethan travel literature.

Sandys had returned home by March 1612. After he had prepared his book for publication, he was active in the companies established for colonization in America. His brother, Sir Edwin Sandys, had been instrumental in drawing up the Virginia Company's charter (1609), and George had been a member of the company since 1607. In July 1621 he accompanied his nephew-in-law, the governor, Sir Francis Wyatt, to Virginia as its first resident treasurer and director of industry and agriculture, continuing in these duties when the crown took over government of the colony in 1624. For about 15 years after his return to England (1625) he was a member of various committees administering the colonies and, finally (1640), agent for the Virginia colony.

Sandys had published a translation of the first five books of Ovid's *Metamorphoses* in 1621. During the hours he could snatch from "night and repose" on his voyage to, and while in, the New World, he completed the 15 books, publishing the whole in 1626. In 1632 he brought out a revised illustrated edition, including philosophical commentaries collected out of "sundrie Authors"—Plato, Apollodorus, Strabo, Plutarch, Lucian, Cicero, Pliny, Macrobius, Eusebius, St. Augustine, Fulgentius, Geraldus, Pontanus, Scaliger, and many others—and also a translation of Book I of Virgil's *Aeneid*. On this work, composed in remarkably compressed heroic couplets, his poetic fame largely rests; the 1632 edition has been described as the greatest repository of allegorized myth in English. Dryden (who called him "the ingenious and learned Sandys, the best versifier of the former age," and who commended his ability to give his verse the same turn as the original) and many later poet-critics have attested its value. In his compression, latinization of syntax, and balanced antithesis, he prepared the way for the heroic couplet of Dryden and Pope (who praised him as "one of the chief refiners of our language"), and his versions of, and commentary upon, classical myth were to be a valuable source for Keats.

On returning from Virginia, Sandys was made a gentleman of the king's privy chamber, and became one of the group of courtier-scholars and poets who gathered round Lord Falkland (*q.v.*), with whom he shared an interest in theological debate. His later works, less well known than the *Metamorphoses,* include *A Paraphrase upon the Psalmes of David* (1636), which includes Sandys' own finest original poem, a hymn to the Redeemer recounting with dignity and sincerity his own experiences of God's mercy and grace; *A Paraphrase upon the Divine Poems* (1638) in a variety of metres, which adds passages from Job, Ecclesiastes, and Lamentations to the psalms (here set to "new tunes for private devotion" by Henry Lawes, *q.v.*) and "hymns dispersed through the Old and New Testaments" of the 1636 edition; a translation of Grotius' *Christus Patiens* as *Christ's Passion* (1640); and *A Paraphrase upon the Song of Solomon* (1641), which contains some of Sandys' most sensuous and lyrical verse. Sandys' last years were spent in London, in Oxfordshire with the Falkland circle at Great Tew, and in Kent with Sir Francis Wyatt at Boxley Abbey, where he died in March 1644, being buried at Boxley Church on March 7.

BIBLIOGRAPHY.—*The Poetical Works of George Sandys,* ed. by R. Hooper, 2 vol. (1872), which does not include the *Metamorphoses.* See also Fredson Bowers and R. B. Davis, *George Sandys: a Bibliographical Catalogue* (1950); R. B. Davis, *George Sandys, Poet-Adventurer* (1955). (RI. B. D.)

SAN FERNANDO, a naval station of southern Spain in the province of Cádiz, on a rocky island among the salt marshes which line the southern shore of Cádiz Bay. It is linked with Cádiz by road (9 mi. [14 km.]) and by rail. Pop. (1960) 52,389. To the east is a Roman bridge, rebuilt in the 15th century after partial demolition by the Moors. To the northeast is the arsenal or dockyard of La Carraca, founded in 1790. The town has establishments of the naval department, and an observatory dating from the 18th century. In the neighbourhood salt is produced and stone is quarried, and there are some light industries. (M. B. F.)

SAN FERNANDO, a town and port of Trinidad, lies at the western end of the central range of hills on the flat, shallow coast of the Gulf of Paria, 32 mi. by rail and 35 mi. by road from Port-of-Spain. Pop. (1960) 39,830. San Fernando is Trinidad's second largest town and its chief function is that of an administrative and trading centre for the southern half of the island. The original area of the town was in a 1786 land grant.

In 1818 the town was destroyed by fire and the rebuilding caused such an expansion that in 1846 San Fernando acquired a town council as well as its present boundaries. It became a borough in 1853. (D. L. N.)

SAN FERNANDO (SAN FERNANDO DE APURE), capital of Apure State in central Venezuela, occupies a site on the south bank of the Apure River, 185 mi. (300 km.) S of Caracas. Pop. (1961) 24,470. The city was in the 1960s one of three major river ports of the llanos, a port of call for steamers on both the Orinoco and the Apure. A good highway from Maracay penetrates deep into the llanos, reaching the Apure River opposite San Fernando. Construction of highways is difficult and costly because of floods which inundate much of the llanos during the rainy season. San Fernando is particularly vulnerable, despite its great distance from the sea, since it lies only 200 ft. above sea level.

Live cattle, beef, alligator and cattle hides, and egret feathers are the city's leading products. San Fernando is not reached by railway, but is an important air traffic centre; much beef is flown into the heavily populated area near the coast, particularly during the season of floods. (L. WE.)

SAN FRANCISCO, a city and port of California, U.S., co-extensive with San Francisco County, is centrally located on the California coast about 350 mi. (563 km.) NW of Los Angeles. It is the cultural, maritime, financial, and trading centre of a densely populated metropolitan area.

PHYSICAL CHARACTERISTICS

Covering the tip of the southernmost of two peninsulas which guard the Golden Gate (*q.v.*) between the Pacific Ocean and San Francisco Bay, the city commands one of the world's finest land-locked harbours. Around the bay is a band of contiguous metropolitan subcentres. Inland lie the rich valleys and metropolitan zones which are linked geographically and economically to the bay area. Heavily traveled sea and air lanes make San Francisco a major U.S. Pacific Coast port and the gateway to the Orient.

From the ocean to the midline of the bay, the city controls 129.4 sq.mi. (335 sq.km.), 46.6 on land. It is hilly, with Telegraph, Nob, Russian, and other hills rising almost from the water's edge; Twin Peaks, Mt. Davidson, and Mt. Sutro stand more than 900 ft. (274 m.) high. San Bruno Mountain (1,314 ft. [401 m.]) is just south of the city line. Encircling the bay, ridges of the Coast Range rise from about 1,200 ft. (366 m.) to such peaks as Mt. Tamalpais (2,604 ft. [794 m.]), on the northern Marin Peninsula; Mt. Diablo (3,849 ft. [1,173 m.]), east; and Mt. Hamilton (4,223 ft. [1,287 m.]), well south. The foothill vegetation varies from rich groves of redwood to oak, chaparral, and grass. In some places, large stands of eucalyptus were planted in modern times.

San Francisco Bay.—Geologically, the bay is a drowned valley which drains the great central basin of California. The Golden Gate, the outlet carved by an ancient river before the valley was

ANSEL ADAMS

VIEW OF SAN FRANCISCO AND THE EAST BAY AREA FROM TWIN PEAKS: (CENTRE)
CIVIC CENTRE AND MARKET STREET; (UPPER RIGHT) SAN FRANCISCO-OAKLAND BRIDGE

minimum of 50.9° F (10.5° C) and a daily mean maximum of 62.8° F (16.7° C). The average daily temperature range is only 12° F (6.7° C). The ocean's proximity produces not only equable temperatures but bracing breezes and a cooling fog. The annual mean wind velocity is only 9.1 mph, and the city enjoys sun during 66% of the possible sunlight hours. Precipitation consists entirely of rain, the mean annual fall being 20.78 in. (528 mm.), mostly from November through March. The average annual relative humidity is 78%, ranging monthly from 74% (November) to 85% (August). Greater climatic variation occurs in the surrounding metropolitan region. Some valley points are notably warmer and drier, while on the slopes of the ridges greater precipitation and wider temperature ranges are encountered. Variability in rainfall characterizes the entire area, changes as high as 100% from year to year being not infrequent.

HISTORY

Inhabited by the Penutian linguistic family of Indians, the San Francisco area was unknown to Europeans until the late 18th century. From the 16th century onward the Spanish, who claimed California, had sailed along the coast without discovering the bay's entrance, although they had charted the Farallon Islands offshore. Sir Francis Drake, in 1579, had also sailed past the Golden Gate, anchoring briefly in a cove (Drake's Bay) a few miles north. Rumours of Russian overseas expansion, however, stirred the Spanish into an effort to establish permanent control over Upper California. To that end Gaspar de Portolá (q.v.) led a party northward from San Diego during the summer of 1769. The expedition passed Monterey Bay, its intended destination, without recognizing it, and continued northward until a scouting party under José Francisco de Ortega sighted San Francisco Bay from the hills of the southern peninsula. Four years later, another party explored the region more thoroughly, and in 1775 the vessel "San Carlos," commanded by Juan Manuel de Ayala, sailed into the bay.

Early the following year, Capt. Juan Bautista de Anza selected a site for a permanent colony on the bay. Lieut. José Joaquín Moraga and Father Francisco Palóu, leading a band of settlers and soldiers from Monterey, then established a presidio (Sept. 17, 1776) and the Mission San Francisco de Asís (Oct. 9, 1776). The mission was soon more familiarly called for the stream near which it was situated, Mission Dolores. Beside a shallow cove inside the Golden Gate, the colonists settled in the pueblo of Yerba Buena (named for the "good herb," an aromatic vine growing on the sand dunes). In 1777 Father Junípero Serra (q.v.), founder of the Upper California missions, visited the new colony. Within a few years a group of six missions was located in the region which, 150 years later, comprised the modern San Francisco metropolitan area.

For a half-century, the small outpost led an isolated existence. Beginning in 1806, however, Russia spread its fur-trading activities into the area, unsuccessfully at San Francisco and with moderate success after 1812 at Fort Ross, about 75 mi. N. The Russian venture, which ended in 1841, was the forerunner of increasingly frequent visits from traders in hides and tallow, whalers and, by 1840, explorers, fur hunters, and merchants. Meanwhile, Upper California became a province of Mexico (1825), and San Francisco

inundated, is 1 to 1.7 mi. wide and about 3 mi. long. The bay varies from 5 to 13 mi. in width and stretches its two arms northeast about 40 mi. through San Pablo Bay, the Carquinez Strait, and Suisun Bay; and south about 35 mi. The total surface area is approximately 400 sq.mi. Although the bay is 382 ft. deep in the Golden Gate Channel, and from 40 to 150 ft. deep in the centre, about 70% of it is no more than 18 ft. in depth. At its northeastern extremity, the confluence of the Sacramento and the San Joaquin rivers passes through Carquinez Strait, and numerous small streams descend from the surrounding hills.

Seven highway and two railroad bridges span the bay. Across the southern arm, a railroad bridge and two highway bridges were built in 1927 and 1929. The double-tiered bridge with two main spans of 2,310 ft. each across the central bay between San Francisco and Oakland, and the spectacular suspension bridge with a span of 4,200 ft. across the Golden Gate were completed in 1936 and 1937, at costs of more than $77,000,000 and $35,000,000, respectively. A bridge across San Pablo Bay was built in 1956, and a matching span to an older bridge at Carquinez Strait was completed in 1958. With its completion, ferry service on the bay ended after a century of operation. A bridge between Benicia and Martinez opened in 1963. Suisun Bay is crossed by a railway bridge.

Several islands are within the bay. On Alcatraz, 12 ac. of rock just inside the Golden Gate, are a 214-ft. lighthouse and the buildings that were used (1934-63) for a federal prison. Farther inside the Gate, Angel Island, the largest in the bay, rises 771 ft. above sea level; on it is old Ft. McDowell. Yerba Buena (formerly Goat Island) and adjacent Treasure Island (built by fill for the 1939 Golden Gate International Exposition) are about in the bay's centre. The first anchors the San Francisco–Oakland Bridge midway in its course; the second is the site of a naval training centre. Extending to the bay are two main valleys, the Santa Clara from the south and the Sonoma from the north. East of the ridges, more extensive valley systems open upon the delta and sedimentary lands of the central valley of California.

Climate.—San Francisco's climate is mild, cool, and even. The annual mean temperature is 56.8° F (13.5° C), with a daily mean

Bay was made a Mexican port of entry (1835). In the same year, the United States attempted to buy the bay from Mexico, after traders and whalers had reported the commercial possibilities of the area.

With the outbreak of war between Mexico and the United States on May 13, 1846, a new era began. North of the bay at Sonoma, the insurgents of Capt. John Charles Frémont (q.v.) raised the "Bear Flag" of an independent California, and on July 9, 1846, Capt. John B. Montgomery in the sloop of war "Portsmouth" entered the bay, hoisted the Stars and Stripes in the plaza, now known as Portsmouth Plaza, and claimed the territory for the United States. On Jan. 30, 1847, the pueblo was renamed San Francisco. It was incorporated in 1850. Even without the political stir which this turn of history produced, the moment was propitious for change. By the mid-1840s, immigrant parties were struggling across the Rockies, bound for Oregon and California. However, the discovery of gold on the American River at Coloma in January 1848 produced social and economic results overnight which no mere shift of political fortune could have produced in decades.

Gold and Growth.—Within three months, San Francisco was almost deserted, its residents off to the mother-lode country. Then, in February 1849, fortune hunters from all over the world crowded into the town. Abandoned ships choked the bay. Shacks and tents, mire and dust, fantastic prices, and a spate of gambling, drinking, and vice appeared ashore. While gold fever was acute, many people in the city were transients. An increasing number, however, stayed to provide equipment, supplies, and capital to the prospectors. Maritime enterprises, of course, flourished from the start. Merchants extended wharves out toward deep water. More improvements followed the transfer of harbour management from the city to a state board of harbour commissioners in 1863. Between 1877 and 1914, a great stone wall was built well outside the early waterfront; the bay was filled in behind it; and out from it finger piers were projected. Sardine fishing began in the 1850s, followed soon by shrimp fishing and, on the Sacramento River, salmon fishing. Whalers based their operations at San Francisco more and more, and the bay was one of the world's most important whaling bases between 1885–1905. Oyster beds were planted in the bay after 1870.

Inland shippers swarmed on the bay and built up river ports at Sacramento and Stockton. Shipbuilding and repair works rose at numerous points. The first dry dock was built in 1851; in 1885 the Union Iron Works launched the first steel ship built on the Pacific Coast. Overseas trade thrived. Exports of $8,500,000 in 1860 had increased sixfold by 1890, a period which saw the fast grain clippers give way to the more prosaic freighter fleets plying with monthly regularity to the Orient (after 1867), Hawaii (after 1878), Australia (after 1885), and Europe (after 1899).

As a trading centre, the city increased its range significantly after the first transcontinental railroad was completed in 1869. By then, its commerce and local industries were firmly founded upon the rich resources of central and northern California. Food processing, meat packing, flour milling, lumber milling, woolen textile, tanning, iron foundries, and implement manufacturing establishments appeared in the 1850s. Sugar refining, smelting and refining of minerals, and a wide variety of fabricating industries developed in the 1860s. By 1870 the value of manufactured goods exceeded $22,000,000, and 20 years later manufacturing products had multiplied in value to $120,000,000.

In contrast to this steady development, the city's financial growth was spectacularly unstable. Connected to the risks of gold mining in the 1850s and heavily capitalized silver mining in the 1860s, as well as to vast railroad construction projects and speculative land development, San Francisco capital not only sustained long-term growth in the entire West, but provided some of the most acute fluctuations in banking and stock exchange in U.S. history.

Periodic panics wiped out fortunes; new waves of optimism and economic growth built them up again repeatedly. The city remained the centre of regional finance, however, and, with the more stable fiscal practices enjoined by national and state legislation in the 20th century, it increased its preeminence and security in this economic domain.

Political and social turbulence matched economic growth. Vicious gangs nearly overwhelmed the early city until they were forcibly suppressed by citizen vigilance committees on two occasions in the 1850s. Demagoguery often swept the city in the 1860s and 1870s, sometimes mixed with demands on behalf of the working class or based on hostility toward Chinese labourers who, having been brought to work on the railroads, drifted into San Francisco. Reform programs in government intermittently succeeded careless or corrupt administration. A notable outburst of public indignation early in the 20th century gave rise to a series of trials of public officials and ushered in the more businesslike governments of the modern period.

Rapid introduction of technological improvements enhanced the open physical structure of the ambitious city. Steam and horse-drawn street railroads appeared in the 1860s; they were replaced by electric streetcars in 1900 (partially discontinued in 1963). On the hills, cable-drawn cars introduced by Andrew S. Hallidie in 1873 continued in use in the 20th century. After the turn of the century, rail transportation to outlying districts and nearby villages provided means for daily commuting. The telegraph was introduced in 1853, the telephone in 1877, gas lighting in 1854, and electric lighting and power after 1876.

Cultural growth accompanied the improvement of economic and physical resources. Numerous educational institutions arose in the latter half of the 19th century. The city had welcomed the theatre and opera as early as 1849 and enthusiastically supported them thereafter. Symphony performances became annual occurrences after 1874, receiving public funds in 1911. In the sciences and arts, appropriate associations appeared in 1853 and 1871, respectively. In journalism, the *Alta California* (est. 1849) outlived

EARTHQUAKE AND FIRE OF 1906, PHOTOGRAPHED BY ARNOLD GENTHE. (TOP) RUINS OF MANSIONS ON NOB HILL; (BOTTOM) HOMELESS RESIDENTS EATING AT IMPROVISED TABLES SET UP AT EMERGENCY RELIEF CENTRE

many fugitive papers until its own demise in 1891, while the 20th-century *San Francisco Examiner* and the *San Francisco Chronicle* dated from the mid-1860s.

Earthquake and Reconstruction.—If the results of a city's early growth are measured not only by absolute achievement but by recuperative vitality, San Francisco met and passed the most severe of tests in 1906. The city had experienced earthquake disturbances in 1864, 1898, and 1900, but on April 18, 1906, a violent earthquake, followed by fire, demolished most of its central business and residential districts. (*See* EARTHQUAKE: *Great Earthquakes: California* [1906].) Hundreds were killed or injured. Homeless residents camped in thousands on the dunes west of the city, while others fled to outlying towns (incidentally giving impetus for 20th-century suburban growth). The loss in buildings was estimated to be more than $100,000,000, while the total property loss was believed to be well over three times as much. Within a short time, relief shipments of food and clothing reached the city, and some $10,000,000 in financial aid came from Europe and America. Although insurance payments in the neighbourhood of $300,000,000 were forthcoming, the long task of reconstruction was sustained by local courage and persistence. Much of the city was rebuilt to be earthquake and fire resistant, and new plans for civic development made headway as the debris of the old city vanished. With pardonable pride, in 1915 San Francisco invited the world to see the results of its efforts at the Panama-Pacific International Exposition.

Change and Challenge.—The opening of the Panama Canal, celebrated by the aforementioned exposition, maintained San Francisco's traditional eminence as gateway to the Orient. It was the natural choice 30 years later for the historic conference, April–June 1945, at which the United Nations Charter was promulgated; and the Peace Treaty with Japan was signed there in 1951. But other 20th-century developments increasingly changed the character and role of the city. Westward migrations of the American population, drawn by the rich agricultural and new industrial opportunities in California; war industry and shipping during World Wars I and II; and diversified growth in the 1920s and 1950s ushered in a new epoch of metropolitan history—the development of a regional urban complex of which San Francisco was the heart, but not the whole.

Nineteenth-century San Francisco had been the unrivaled urban centre of a vast agricultural region. In the 20th century it became a city of international rank. It retained authority in many social, economic, and cultural activities. But the remarkable growth of population, economic institutions, and cultural centres throughout the metropolitan bay area (as well as in Southern California and, to a lesser extent, the central valley of the state) became the most prominent change and the most urgent source of challenge.

Internally, San Francisco confronted local forms of nationwide needs for technological, political, economic, and social reformation of urban processes. Externally, it faced a social environment no longer embodied in dependent suburban villages; modest, isolated towns; or great rural regions for which San Francisco was the only possible window to the world. Rather, it was in an environment of contiguous urban communities, themselves suffering the strain of rapid, ill-planned growth. From the mid-20th century onward, San Francisco would depend more on the quality of its leadership than on the mere weight of its activity and resources if the city were to retain its distinction as the pacesetter and lodestone of the West.

POPULATION

San Francisco, with a population of 740,316 in 1960, is the principal city in the San Francisco-Oakland standard metropolitan statistical area of five counties (Alameda, Contra Costa, Marin, San Francisco, and San Mateo), 2,486 sq.mi. (6,439 sq.km.), and 2,648,762 inhabitants. Population trends were indicated by the slight decline in San Francisco's size after 1950 and the relatively rapid growth of population elsewhere in the area to an estimated total of 3,056,000 by 1966. With its nearby counties of Marin and San Mateo, San Francisco and the West Bay urban zone had somewhat more than half the metropolitan area population in 1960,

but somewhat less than half in 1966. By the mid-1960s nearly 60% of the area's inhabitants lived in cities of 75,000 or more. It was expected that by the end of the century predominantly urban conditions would form a megalopolis extending outward from the bay area to the inland cities of San Jose, 45 mi. S; Sacramento, 80 mi. NE on the Sacramento River; Stockton, 50 mi. E on the San Joaquin River; and northward throughout much of the Marin Peninsula.

San Francisco's population, like that of the entire area, was predominantly white in 1960. Foreign-born and Oriental peoples were relatively much more numerous in San Francisco, however, than elsewhere in the metropolitan complex. Added to the indigenous inhabitants of foreign descent, they gave the city a pronounced cosmopolitan atmosphere. The Italian and Chinese subcommunities were particularly conspicuous. The Negro population of San Francisco and of the area approximated the national proportion of 11%. Within it were large numbers of men and women new to San Francisco and new to urban life, generally. As in other cities throughout the United States, the depressed economic, educational, legal, and domestic status of nonwhite residents, despite improvements over earlier conditions, constituted a severe hazard to urban peace, decency, and vitality. During the 1960s, therefore, Negro and other minority group efforts at self-assistance, ranging from sporadic violence to demands for more effective national, state, and community programs in favour of the depressed and disadvantaged, evoked continuous public anxiety and received increasing financial support.

Both in the city and the area, women were slightly more numerous than men. The median age of San Franciscans, 37.3, was higher than that of the area's population, due to the city's relatively smaller number in young age groups and its higher proportion of aged persons. Correlatively, San Francisco's unmarried population was proportionately greater (44%) than that of the total area (34%). Economically, San Francisco's residents were more frequently in upper income brackets, and the "poverty pockets" of the city, though painful to contemplate, costly to ignore, and difficult to eradicate, imperiled somewhat fewer people (relatively) than did certain other distressed points in the metropolitan zone.

Compared with averages throughout the area, the city population was much more dense and more mobile. Reflecting these traits, San Francisco was the site of urban renewal programs to replace slums by modern apartments and commercial establishments, as well as programs to construct automobile freeways, parking centres, a new rapid transit system, and new office and public buildings. Conversely, home owners were more numerous in the metropolitan area at large than in the central city. Ribbons of new houses encircled the hills and filled the valleys throughout the area, and workers thronged the highways each day as they commuted to and from San Francisco and other major cities of the metropolitan zone.

Finally—whether because of the traditional sophistication of its wealthy elite, the vivacity and iconoclasm of its artists and young social critics, or the sensitivity to international and national dynamics derived from its long-standing responsibilities in Western history—the character ascribed to San Francisco's residents by observers and natives alike emphasized the traits of diversity and animation. Perhaps such an image lacked a conclusive foundation in the gross statistics of its social structure and composition. Nonetheless, it significantly entered into the patterns of thought and action whereby the city related itself to other parts of the metropolitan area and sought to control its own urban processes.

GOVERNMENT

San Francisco's five charters were granted respectively in 1850, 1856, 1861, 1898, and 1932. Initiative and referendum clauses were first included in the 1898 charter. Under its 1932 charter, San Francisco has a consolidated city and county government in which the mayor, certain executives, the judiciary, and the 11-member Board of Supervisors are elected. The mayor appoints the city's chief administrative officer and a variety of administrative boards, including police, utilities, civil service, and planning. Water supply, based on the Hetch-Hetchy system of dams and reservoirs, and a surface public transportation system are municipally owned; gas and electricity are supplied through private enterprise.

Peculiar to the mid-20th century were complex intergovernmental relationships involving the city with many overlapping county and community agencies, as well as with state and national institutions. Within the nine-county San Francisco Bay region there were almost a thousand local governmental units, including more than 100 city governments, more than 200 school districts with elected boards, and approximately 600 special districts. Of these special districts, about half were headed by elected commissions or boards, while the remainder were governed by the supervisors of the various counties. There was also a scattering of local authorities established for housing or urban redevelopment and renewal purposes.

In addition to these local units, a number of quasi-political boards with metropolitan area scope were developed, in order to coordinate local attacks on regional problems such as transportation, air pollution, waste disposal, and economic resource development. In the majority of cases, these authorities were creatures of the state legislature in Sacramento. Some of them, such as the San Francisco Port Authority and the San Francisco-Oakland Toll Bridge Authority, possessed operational and administrative powers. Others, such as the Bay Area Transportation Study and the San Francisco Bay Conservation and Development commissions, were mainly investigating and planning agencies, although the latter had authority to approve or disapprove proposals which would modify the shorelines of the bay. The Association of Bay Area Governments offered opportunities for regional planning but had no actual authority over the various towns and cities represented in it.

This fragmentation of governmental responsibility and the separation of active authority from the planning function, not unusual in large metropolitan areas of the United States, served to inhibit efforts to deal with the area's problems in a coordinated manner. Furthermore, although San Francisco exercised leadership in a number of metropolitan area enterprises, it no longer had independent control over many problems of vital concern to it.

Foreign consulates and branches of national and state political agencies are located in the city. Both the Navy and the Army maintain important headquarters.

ECONOMY

The economic prosperity of San Francisco was founded on its maritime trade and its proximity to diversified resources. It is a great cosmopolitan seaport, the commercial and distributing centre for inland California, and the financial hub of the western United States.

Finance.—As the financial and insurance centre of the West, San Francisco's position grew far more rapidly than its population in the middle decades of the 20th century. In the Federal Reserve System (12th district headquarters), the city's banks ranked high in the nation in volume of transactions, debits, and clearings. There are 16 banks (several with branches), including the headquarters of one of the world's largest, and 15 savings and loan associations. More than half the insurance companies authorized to transact business in California have their headquarters in San Francisco. The San Francisco transactions of the stock exchange, which became part of the Pacific Coast Exchange in 1957, amount to several billion dollars a year, and the San Francisco Mining Exchange trades in millions of shares annually.

Commerce.—In the 1960s, San Francisco Bay was eighth in importance as a U.S. port. In volumes of general waterborne cargo transactions, San Francisco's own port led all others on the Pacific Coast. The waterfront (the Embarcadero) is state-owned and operated and has 1,912 ac. (774 ha.) of harbour facilities, but port developments at Oakland, Richmond, and Mare Island reduced its earlier relative eminence in the bay. However, its U.S. customs receipts annually account for more than 30% of Pacific Coast export and import tariffs. A World Trade Centre opened in 1956. Coastal and other domestic traffic accounted for almost two-thirds of the port activity. In foreign trade, commerce with Asia and the Pacific area took the lead; second, in imports, was trade with eastern South America (especially Brazil), and, in exports, Europe.

The totals of both had increased by more than 50% since 1950. In the 1960s, foodstuffs, machinery, and raw materials were the chief export items of value; foodstuffs (especially coffee and sugar), machinery, and manufactured goods were the major import items.

As a wholesale centre, San Francisco's activity comprised over half of that in the bay area, with annual sales above $5,000,000,-000. The principal items handled were machinery and equipment, foodstuffs, apparel, and electrical products. For the metropolitan area, petroleum products distributed from the East Bay refineries were far more important than for San Francisco, as were automotive products and construction materials. By the mid-1960s San Francisco's retail establishments sold approximately $2,000,000,000 of goods annually. As an increasingly selective and specialized commercial centre, San Francisco's chief retail sales were in eating and drinking establishments, general and specialized merchandise, automobiles, apparel, and foods. For the metropolitan area, however, the figures stood almost in reverse order: foods, automobiles, general merchandise, eating and drinking establishments, and apparel. The services sector of the metropolitan economy had become prominent and rapid growth continued in the 1960s. Medical, business, professional, and hotel services were preeminent in San Francisco; the receipts of the city's service establishments (over $600,000,000) exceeded half of those for the entire area.

Industry and Labour.—By the 1960s, although San Francisco retained its historical lead in industry, compared with other bay cities, its industrial and labour strength had declined to one-third that of the metropolitan area. By the mid-1960s, after the impetus given industrial growth by World War II, the area had become the second largest manufacturing complex in the western United States. In value added by manufacture, food industries far outdistanced the other important industries of metal fabrication, petroleum refining, printing and publishing, chemicals, electrical machinery, and transportation equipment. In these fields, as well as in shipbuilding and repairing, the area was the major centre of the state.

San Francisco's labour force in 1966–67 equaled two-thirds of its population (many workers actually residing, however, in other bay area cities). It was highly organized, relatively well educated, and highly trained. Compared to the labour force of the metropolitan area, San Francisco's employees included one-quarter of the area's workers and earned one-third of the area's wages. Women employees were relatively more numerous in the city than in the area as a whole. In both city and area, 60% of the labour force was employed in service, trade, and government. The proportion working in manufacturing was larger in the area than in the city itself.

Transportation and Communication.—Serving the bay area and terminating in San Francisco are: 4 class-1 railroads connecting to 7 transcontinental routes; more than 150 truck lines; 2 transcontinental bus lines; and, at the International Airport (opened 1954) south of the city, overseas, national, regional, and freight airlines. About 250 air and marine shippers have San Francisco offices. The great bridge system and the automobile freeways built in the 1940s and 1950s—and still expanding—were key forces in both the growth and the internal shifts in activity within the metropolitan area. Vast increases in automobile and truck movements precipitated serious problems of city parking and traffic flow, as well as safety and air pollution.

In the early 1950s study was begun on the possibility of constructing an integrated high-speed rapid transit system for the San Francisco Bay area. The aim of the planners was to provide an attractive alternative to commutation by private automobile, thereby relieving the overburdened freeways. Scheduled for completion in 1971, the Bay Area Rapid Transit (BART) system was to consist of approximately 75 mi. of elevated and subway lines linking San Francisco, Alameda, and Contra Costa counties. The system would use lightweight electric trains, computer-operated and capable of traveling up to 80 mph. Construction began in 1967.

In air and maritime traffic, city and area growth was reflected by gains of more than 100% between 1950 and 1960. The fact that rail freight movements in and out of the city remained about level in the same period reflected changes in the economic relation of San Francisco to the rest of the metropolitan area, as well as technological changes in transportation.

San Francisco is the leading communications centre of northern and central California. It is the trans-Pacific headquarters of five radio systems and western headquarters for all telephone and telegraph networks. Military, naval, and aeronautical headquarters and communications grids are in the city. There are 10 standard and 13 frequency modulation radio stations and four television stations in the city.

EDUCATION AND CULTURAL ACTIVITIES

From its early days, San Francisco's concern with education was vigorous and area wide. It passed its first public school law in 1851. A century later there were 120,000 students enrolled in the public schools of the city. An additional 30,000 pupils were in Catholic and Protestant schools. About 40,000 more were students in the colleges and universities in or near San Francisco. Nearly 40,000 men and women were participants in various forms of adult education.

In higher education, St. Ignatius' College (Roman Catholic) was chartered in 1855 and rechartered in 1930 as the University of San Francisco, St. Mary's College (Roman Catholic, later moved to Oakland and, finally, to St. Mary's College) in 1863. Mills College (founded 1852) for women moved from Benicia to Oakland in 1871. The site of the University of California, a land-grant

BY COURTESY OF THE UNION PACIFIC RAILROAD

A CORNER OF CHINATOWN, WITH CALIFORNIA STREET CABLE CAR CROSSING GRANT AVENUE

institution, was selected in Berkeley in 1867; and in 1885, at Palo Alto, Leland Stanford, California's Civil War governor and one of the "Big Four" in railroad development, executed the founding grant for the university he named as a memorial to his deceased son, Leland Stanford, Jr. Within the city, in addition to the University of San Francisco, are San Francisco State College (1899), San Francisco College for Women (Roman Catholic, 1930, formerly College of the Sacred Heart at Menlo Park, 1898), City College of San Francisco (1935, a two-year public junior college), and the San Francisco Art Institute College (established as School of Design, 1874). Important branches of the University of California, including the medical centre, and Hastings College (law) are also located in the city. Extension programs of the colleges and universities and public adult education programs engaged an increasingly large number of residents.

The city's 19th-century cultural history was distinguished in literature. Among its writers in the 1860s and 1870s were Samuel L. Clemens (Mark Twain), Bret Harte, Joaquin (Cincinnatus Heine) Miller, and Henry George; followed by George Sterling, Gelett Burgess, Ambrose G. Bierce, Edwin Markham, Hubert H. Bancroft, the historian, and the turn-of-the-century naturalistic novelists Jack London and Frank Norris.

Early San Francisco theatres and concert halls were important centres of Western American culture. They continued to flourish in the 20th century and, in the 1960s, to occupy a preeminent, although not exclusive, role in the artistic life of the metropolitan bay area. The San Francisco opera, symphony, and ballet companies were of national stature. There were excellent repertory companies, New York and European casts on tour, and numerous semiprofessional and amateur dramatic groups. The De Young Memorial Museum and the San Francisco Museum of Arts maintained continuous exhibits from their own fine holdings and works on tour; private galleries were numerous, as well. Visiting and local musicians and ensembles offered a year-round succession of concerts and recitals. Composers, painters, sculptors, novelists, poets, critics, and literary scholars of first rank congregated in San Francisco and such nearby artistic and educational centres as Berkeley, Sausalito, and Stanford. Not a few were noteworthy for their avant-garde and experimental work. In the later 1960s San Francisco was probably next to New York as a centre for creative exploration in mixed media, electronic and acoustical musical effects, and "underground" cinema.

BUILDINGS, STREETS, AND PARKS

In its public and domestic buildings, San Francisco reflects all the prominent architectural styles of the later 19th century and modern periods. A distinguished group of 20th-century Renaissance classic buildings in the civic centre includes the city hall, public library, auditorium, and state building. Elsewhere, a notable example of the mid-19th-century Greek Revival is found in the building formerly housing the U.S. branch mint. The California Palace of the Legion of Honor, overlooking the Golden Gate, is a replica of the Palace of the Legion of Honour in Paris. Reflecting Victorian and early 20th-century eclecticism are numerous homes originally designed for wealthy 19th-century business and financial leaders; the Palace of Fine Arts near the Presidio (a U.S. military reservation of 1,542 ac., which includes Ft. Winfield Scott and Letterman General Hospital); the post office and old Hall of Justice; the Ferry Building, built by the state in 1896, 659 ft. long and 156 ft. wide; and the older churches of the city. Notable examples of contemporary design include the V. C. Morris store (Frank Lloyd Wright); the Maimonides Health Centre (Eric Mendelsohn); the Crown Zellerbach office building (Skidmore, Owings and Merrill); the Golden Gateway redevelopment buildings (Wurster, Bernardi and Emmons).

Important San Francisco churches include the historic Mission Dolores, built in 1782. Grace Cathedral (Episcopal), of modified Gothic design, was begun in 1910 and dedicated in 1966, the third largest cathedral in the United States. Old St. Mary's Church and St. Patrick's Church represent Gothic Revival styles; the former dates from 1853, and the latter, built in 1906, replaced a predecessor erected in 1854. St. Mary's Cathedral, seat of the

Roman Catholic diocese, was destroyed by fire in 1962; plans for a replacement of modern design were approved in 1967. The SS. Peter and Paul Church (1924), serving the Italian community, is of Romanesque design. Temples Emanu-el and Sherith Israel are the San Francisco centres of Reform Judaism. The unique Kong Chow and Tin How temples are monuments to the pioneer Chinese.

San Francisco is the home of national professional athletic teams in football, baseball, ice hockey, soccer, and basketball. General recreational facilities are provided by more than 50 parks. The parks and several government reservations account for an aggregate of about one-ninth of the city's area. Golden Gate Park, in the midst of residential districts, comprises 1.017 ac. and is about 3 mi. long and ½ mi. wide. In the park are the De Young Memorial Museum, Academy of Sciences, Steinhart Aquarium, the Morrison Planetarium, and other facilities. At the western end of the park is to be seen the sloop "Gjöa," the first vessel to navigate the Northwest Passage; it was given to San Francisco by its owner, Capt. Roald Amundsen.

San Francisco's first street grid was established in 1835 in the area now constituting the financial district. In 1847, a new sur-

FISHERMAN'S WHARF WITH TELEGRAPH HILL IN THE BACKGROUND

vey by Jasper O'Farrell laid out a second grid adjacent to but diagonally related to the first. The two systems were interlocked at Market Street, which then became the principal thoroughfare of the city. Added to them by the necessities of mid-20th century automobile transportation are the major multi-laned freeways planned to provide an uninterrupted loop around the entire bay.

Notable are the city's sharply defined "quarters," the most famous being Chinatown. The largest Chinese settlement outside the Orient, Chinatown is hedged in by financial, hotel, and commercial districts. Near it is the "North Beach," once the riotous "Barbary Coast" of vice, crime, and indulgence, and still a lively after-dark entertainment district. The Latin Quarter, where many artists and colonies of Italians, French, Spanish, and Portuguese reside, centres on Telegraph and Russian hills. Fisherman's Wharf is the picturesque home of the fishing fleet and is renowned for its seafood restaurants. Elsewhere, beaches, peninsular camping and picnic grounds, and other recreational facilities are within easy motoring distance.

See also references under "San Francisco (Calif.)" in the Index.

(J. H. St.)

SAN GABRIEL, a city of California, U.S., 9 mi. E. of Los Angeles and a part of the Los Angeles standard metropolitan statistical area, is famous as the site of the fourth Franciscan mission

in the settlement of the region. Founded in 1771, the well-preserved mission (dating from 1775) owes its massive style of architecture to Father Antonio Gruzado, who modeled the church after a fortress of his native Andalusia. The first settlement was composed of Indians and their mission guardians who engaged in agriculture until 1834 when the Mexican government took over the lands. After years of confusion, during which California became part of the United States, the mission lands passed almost completely into private ownership. This second community was made up of wheat farms, cattle ranches, vineyards and citrus groves. Modern San Gabriel, incorporated in 1913, is a residential town whose inhabitants work mostly in neighbouring Alhambra and Los Angeles. It has a council-manager form of government, in effect since 1943. For comparative population figures *see* table in CALIFORNIA: *Population.*   (J. A. Sz.)

SANGALLO, the name of a family of Italian Renaissance architects and military engineers active in Florence and Rome.

GIULIANO DA SANGALLO (1445?–1516), who worked for the Medici in Florence and built their villa at Poggio a Caiano in 1485. His masterpiece is a church of Greek cross plan, the Madonna delle Carceri in Prato (1485–91). Strongly influenced by Filippo Brunelleschi, it is the purest, most classic expression of that style of 15th-century architecture. In Rome Giuliano was overshadowed by Bramante. He designed influential facade projects for S. Lorenzo, Florence, in 1515–16.

ANTONIO DA SANGALLO, THE ELDER (1455?–1534), who often worked with his brother Giuliano but, under the influence of Bramante, became a more powerful designer. In S. Biagio, Montepulciano (1518–29), he created an ideal central church of the High Renaissance.

ANTONIO PICCONI DA SANGALLO, THE YOUNGER (1483–1546), nephew of the two preceding, was trained in Rome under Bramante and became the most influential architect of his time. In 1520 he succeeded Raphael as architect of St. Peter's and held the position until the end of his life. His design, an elaboration of Bramante's, survives in a wooden model. He designed buildings for the Farnese family, including a palace-fortress at Caprarola; his most important work is the Farnese Palace in Rome, begun in 1541. Antonio the younger was an important military engineer and city planner as well as a keen student of ancient architectural remains.

See G. Clausse, *Les San Gallo* (1900–02); G. Giovannoni, *Antonio da Sangallo il giovane* (1959).   (H. H.)

SANGER, FREDERICK (1918–   ), British biochemist awarded the Nobel Prize for Chemistry in 1958 in recognition of his outstanding achievement in determining the structure of the insulin molecule, was born on Aug. 13, 1918. Educated at Bryanston School and at St. John's College, Cambridge, he worked continuously from 1939 on biochemical research at Cambridge. He was a Beit memorial fellow from 1944 to 1951, and thereafter worked under the auspices of the Medical Research Council. In 1951 he was awarded the Corday-Morgan medal and prize of the Chemical Society, and in 1954 was elected a fellow of the Royal Society and a fellow of King's College, Cambridge. At the time of the completion in 1955 of Sanger's ten years' research on the insulin molecule, this was the largest protein molecule to have its chemical structure elucidated. Sanger's discovery opened the road to the determination of protein structure in general, and it was an essential preliminary to the chemical synthesis of insulin by P. G. Katsoyannis and associates in 1964.   (W. J. Bp.)

SANGER, MARGARET (1883–1966), founder of the birth control movement in the United States and an international leader in the field, was born in Corning, N.Y., on Sept. 14, 1883, the sixth of 11 children of Michael H. and Annie (Purcell) Higgins. She took nurse's training at the White Plains (N.Y.) Hospital and in 1900 she married William Sanger. Following a divorce she married J. Noah H. Slee in 1922; Slee died in 1948.

As a nurse in the Lower East Side of New York City, Mrs. Sanger saw the coexistence of poverty, uncontrolled fertility, and high rates of infant and maternal mortality. A feminist who believed strongly in every woman's right to plan the size of her family, she devoted herself to the task of removing the legal barriers to the dissemination of information about contraception. In 1914 she was indicted for sending in the mail copies of *Woman Rebel*, a periodical advocating the practice of birth control. The case was dismissed in 1916. Later that year she opened in Brooklyn the first birth control clinic in the United States. She was arrested for "maintaining a public nuisance" and in 1917 served 30 days in the workhouse. In 1929 the Sanger Clinic was raided and the files were confiscated. Doctors, social workers, and others came to her defense and the case was dismissed. These episodes helped to crystallize public opinion in favour of the birth control movement and in November 1936 the application of the federal Comstock "Obscenity" Act of 1873, which classified contraceptive literature and devices as obscene materials, was modified when the United States Circuit Court of Appeals affirmed the right of physicians to prescribe contraceptives ". . . for the purpose of saving life or promoting the well-being of patients."

In 1921 Mrs. Sanger founded the American Birth Control League and served as its president until 1928. In 1929 she organized the National Committee on Federal Legislation for Birth Control. In 1939 the League and the Education Department of Birth Control Clinical Research Bureau united to form the Birth Control Federation of America, which in 1942 became the Planned Parenthood Federation of America. Mrs. Sanger was first president of the International Planned Parenthood Federation (organized in 1953) and devoted much energy to the cause of birth control in the countries of the Far East, especially India and Japan.

Margaret Sanger wrote many books, some of the best known of which were: *What Every Girl Should Know* (1916); *What Every Mother Should Know* (1917); *Women, Morality, and Birth Control* (1922); *Happiness in Marriage* (1926); *Motherhood in Bondage* (1928); *My Fight for Birth Control* (1931); and *Margaret Sanger: an Autobiography* (1938). She died in Tucson, Ariz., on Sept. 6, 1966.

See also BIRTH CONTROL. (C. V. K.)

SAN GERMÁN, a town in the southwestern part of Puerto Rico, is one of the two original settlements established by the Spaniards on the island. Pop. (1960) town 7,790, municipal district 27,667. Founded in 1508 by order of Diego Colón, a son of Columbus, San Germán was repeatedly destroyed by attacks of Indians and French pirates and was moved inland from the exposed seacoast in 1573. The modern town was the seat of government for the western district during several centuries. Along one of the town's plazas stands the Porta Coeli Convent, more than 400 years old and one of the oldest buildings in the West Indies. It is now a museum. San Germán is the home of Inter-American University, a private and fully accredited institution whose campus is built on a series of hills near the town.

Modern highways connect San Germán with Ponce on the south coast and Mayagüez on the west coast. The rural area surrounding San Germán produces sugar and coffee. To the south on the Caribbean coast near the fishing village of La Parguera is a famous phosphorescent bay where the College of Agriculture and Mechanical Arts of the University of Puerto Rico maintains an institute of marine biology and a zoological park. (T. G. Ms.)

SANGIHE AND TALAUD ISLANDS, a group of islands off the northeast coast of Celebes (Sulawesi), Indonesia. Area 712 sq.mi. The population of the islands in 1961 was 194,-253, three-fourths of whom lived in the Sangihe group.

The Sangihe Islands continue the northeastern extension of Celebes toward Mindanao, in the Philippines, and are set upon a long, narrow ridge along a volcanic band, with very deep water on either side. Although fringed with recent coral formation, they are distinctly volcanic, Mount Awu (6,050 ft.) on Sangihe Island having experienced recent severe eruptions. Earthquakes also have occurred. Sangihe, Siau, and Tahulandang are the chief islands; Talise and Bangka lie off the north point of Celebes.

Bangka gives its name to Bangka Strait, the channel from the Celebes Sea to the Molucca Passage. Sangihe is 27 mi. long and from 9 to 17 mi. in width; it is mountainous in the north, its elevation decreasing considerably in the south, and has a coast that is generally steep. The average annual rainfall is 195 in. and, with Siau, it has an exceptionally fertile volcanic soil with extensive cultivation of nutmegs, coconuts, and manila hemp. Tahuna (Taruna), on the west coast, is the capital of the Sangihe Islands. Tahuna and Peta (or Enemawira), on the east coast, are regular ports of call; so are Ulu (Hulu), the capital and port of Siau, and Tahulandang and Talise on the islands of those names. Tahulandang Island has two mountains of 2,500 ft., and Ruang, a small island southwest of Tahulandang, has an active volcano.

The people of Sangihe and Siau are closely related to the people of Minahasa (the northern peninsula of Celebes) and of portions of the Philippine Islands, with fair complexion, high nose, and stiff, short, black hair. They were formerly terrorized by the pirates of Sulu (*q.v.*); but later, under Dutch rule, the Sangihe and Siau islanders advanced culturally and became mostly Christians. Society is based on the matriarchal system, and the people, who speak a language of their own, live by agriculture, fishing, and trading in wood, copra, and nutmegs. Manila hemp is grown for domestic consumption, and its weaving is the most important industry.

The Talaud Islands consist of a group lying northeast of Sangihe, the chief of which is Karakelong, 39 mi. long and 15 mi. wide, in the north. Heights of 2,300 ft. are said to exist in the southern part. The coast is steep, except on the south shore, which is fringed by a wide reef. Some tiny islands known as the Nenusa Islands lie northeast of Karakelong; vessels run regularly to these, to Beo, the capital of the Talaud group, and to Lirung, the port of a long island lying close to and southwest of Karakelong.

The Islands were incorporated under the Dutch governor of Ternate as early as 1677; later they were attached to the residency of Manado. During World War II they passed under Japanese military control, and in 1949 they became part of Indonesia, forming two districts of the province of Sulawesi Utara-Tengah (North and Central Celebes). (E. E. L.; J. O. M. B.)

SAN GIMIGNANO, a town of Tuscany, Italy, in the province of Siena, 18 mi. (30 km.) NW of Siena by road. Pop. (1961)

BY COURTESY OF THE ITALIAN STATE TOURIST OFFICE

MEDIEVAL TOWERS OF SAN GIMIGNANO

4,085 town; 10,099 commune. Originally called "City of Silva," it later took its name from the bishop of Modena (d. 397) who liberated the city from a barbarian invasion. Parts of the ancient fortifications are still intact including the city walls and gates, and 14 of the towers, which numbered 72 in 1350. With its predominantly Gothic architecture San Gimignano is one of the best-preserved Italian medieval towns. The Palazzo del Podestà was built in 1288. In the Sala di Dante is the *Maestà* (1317) by Lippo Memmi, a pupil of Simone Martini. In 1467 Benozzo Gozzoli added two figures of saints to the work. The Palazzo del Podestà also houses the museum which contains works by Gozzoli, Filippino Lippi, Pinturicchio (Bernardino di Betto), and many other Florentine and Sienese masters. The Collegiata (the former cathedral) was consecrated in 1148. The interior walls are decorated with numerous frescoes including Old Testament scenes (1356) by Bartolo di Fredi, New Testament scenes (1380) by Barna da Siena, and the "Martyrdom of St. Sebastian" (1465) by Gozzoli; the Chapel of Sta. Fina (a local saint who died at the age of 15 in 1253) has a marble altar carved by Benedetto da Maiano (1475), and frescoes depicting the death and funeral rites of Fina by Domenico Ghirlandaio. Close to the city gate of San Matteo is the Church of S. Agostino (1280–98) containing frescoes (1463–67) by Gozzoli, with scenes from the life of St. Augustine.

An independent republic in the Middle Ages, San Gimignano was dominated by two powerful, continually warring families, the Ardinghelli (Guelph) and the Salvucci (Ghibelline). In May 1300 Dante Alighieri, as ambassador of Florence, spoke in favour of the Guelph League (in the Sala di Dante). In 1352, its finances exhausted, the city placed itself under Florence. The present city, an important tourist centre, is noted for its wines.   (A. M.)

SANGLI, a town and district in the Poona division of Maharashtra, India. The town, formerly the capital of the princely state of Sangli and now the district headquarters, lies 11 mi. NW of Miraj junction on the Southern Railway and 185 mi. SSE of Bombay. Pop. (1961) 73,838. It is well laid out with broad streets and several parks. There are five colleges, including those of commerce, education, and engineering, affiliated to Shivaji University at Kolhapur. The old Ganpati temple is known for its architecture and was the seat of the family deity of the former princely rulers. The town is a trade centre for tobacco, turmeric, chilies, peanuts, and ghee (clarified butter). It has textile and oil mills and manufactures of brass and copper vessels. *Bidi* (local cigarette) making is a large-scale industry.

SANGLI DISTRICT, originally constituted as South Satara District on Aug. 1, 1949, comprises the former princely states of Sangli, Miraj, and Jath, and a number of *taluks* of the former Satara District. Area 3,299 sq.mi. Pop. (1961) 1,230,716. The district is fertile, its principal crops being jowar, bajra, peanuts, tobacco, chilies, turmeric, wheat, and sugarcane; other crops include cotton, rice, and oilseeds. Handloom weaving, flour milling, oil crushing, and engineering are the chief industries. Miraj is the only important town besides Sangli. It has a weaving mill, an oil mill, a mission hospital, a sanatorium, and a leprosarium. A medical college is affiliated with Shivaji University.   (M. R. P.)

SANGRE DE CRISTO, a complexly folded and faulted range of the Rocky Mountains, consists of a narrow, elongated anticlinal uplift extending for about 250 mi. (402 km.) from Salida, Colo., southward to Santa Fe, N.M., U.S. The range was supposedly named by the Spanish explorer Antonio Valverde y Cosío in 1719 while breaking camp in the Purgatoire Valley in Colorado. He was so impressed by the red-tinted, snowy peaks at sunrise that he uttered a fervent "Sangre de Cristo" ("blood of Christ"). These colourfully named alpine mountains have many spectacularly glaciated peaks including the highest elevation, Blanca Peak, 14,317 ft. (4,364 m.). Located near the western and eastern foothills, respectively, are two outstanding landforms, Great Sand Dunes National Monument and the granitic Spanish Peaks (13,623 ft. [4,152 m.]).   (A. W. Sm.)

SANGRUR, a municipal town and district in the Patiala division of Punjab State, India. The town, headquarters of the district, lies 48 mi. (77 km.) S of Ludhiana. Pop. (1961) 28,344. It was founded about the mid-17th century and was remodeled by Raja Raghubir Singh on the lines of Jaipur City. Raja Sangat Singh made it the capital of Jind State in 1827, and it remained so until 1949 when the Punjab princely states were merged into the Patiala and East Punjab States Union. A college is affiliated to Panjab University, and there are two hospitals and several parks. The town is on the Jakhal-Ludhiana railway line and is also linked by road with the rest of Punjab.

SANGRUR DISTRICT is a flat plain dotted with sand dunes. Area (before 1966) 3,031 sq.mi.; pop. (1961) 1,424,688. In 1966 the district was divided between Punjab and the new state of Hariana. It is predominantly agricultural and a considerable area is irrigated. Wheat, gram, bajra (pearl millet), and cotton are the chief crops of the district. The principal towns include Barnala (pop. [1961] 21,354); Malerkotla (39,543); and Sunam (21,408), a trade centre.   (O. P. B.)

SANHEDRIN (sometimes incorrectly written SYNEDRIUM or SANHEDRIM), the supreme rabbinic court in Jerusalem during the Second Commonwealth era. The term is a hebraization of the Greek *synedrion,* meaning "assembly"; the term also is used for the Areopagus in Athens.

Rabbinic sources speak of a Great Sanhedrin of 71 members and of smaller Sanhedrins, trial courts of 23, judging criminal cases or violations of Jewish law. The Great Sanhedrin as a permanent institution is to be distinguished from the temporary Great Assembly of that era. Meetings of the Great Sanhedrin were held on the Temple Mount in Lishkat Hagazit (Chamber of Hewn Stone [or Decision]). Talmudic tradition pictures the Great Sanhedrin as the highest legislative and judicial court of Halakha (rabbinic law), headed by a duumvirate known as *nasi* (head) and *ab bet din* (father of the court), whereas nonrabbinic sources describe the institution as a political-executive and judicial body headed by the high priest. Though some scholars have sought to regard the rabbinic picture as an academic reconstruction, descriptive of the patriarchal court of the 2nd century C.E., the discrepancy of sources is easily explained in recognizing the existence of two contemporary bodies, one strictly religious, the other wholly secular or the civil authority.

The Mishnaic Sanhedrin consisted of scribes (*soferim*) who interpreted the Halakha, whereas the Synedrion, described in Josephus and the Gospels, was composed of the aristocracy of the state, including Pharisees and Sadducees, and served only as the secular state council of the high priest. The trials of Jesus and the Apostles as portrayed in the New Testament were before the priestly state Synedrion, sanctioned by Pontius Pilate. Jesus was crucified by the Romans and not by the Great Sanhedrin as "king of the Jews." Though the Jews were allowed to administer capital punishment, this right was restricted to religious law.

In biblical days justice was administered by the kings (such as David or Solomon) or by the chieftains (*shofetim*). In early postexilic days (4th and 3rd centuries B.C.E.) the priests with their *gerousia* (council of elders) served as the judges. However, in 141 B.C.E., with the Hasmonaean victory over the Syrian Greeks, a new commonwealth was established. The Great Sanhedrin was then instituted as a specialized body of Halakha to interpret Jewish law. Ritual matters of the Temple were left to the council of priests, and the government administration belonged to the monarchs and city officials in their executive *boule* (council).

Among the functions of the Great Sanhedrin were the enactment of decrees for religious observances, judging violations thereof, serving as the court of higher appeal, supervising smaller courts and controlling the priestly ceremonials in the Temple. Particularly did the body uphold the sanctity of the traditional law and its oral interpretations as based upon the written law of the Torah. The functions and procedure of the Great Sanhedrin are discussed in the talmudic tractate Sanhedrin.

The first heads of the Sanhedrin were known as *zugot* (pairs). They were not merely president and vice-president of the body, but majority and minority leaders, representing the conflicting opinions current in the institution. The Sanhedrin was dissolved in 66 C.E., four years before the destruction of Jerusalem by the Romans in 70 C.E.

Among the leaders of the Great Sanhedrin were such men as

Simon ben Shetah, who enacted laws for universal education, for rights of women, and for the administration of trial courts and acceptance of testimony; he was a contemporary of Alexander Jannaeus (c. 100 B.C.). Another head was Hillel (q.v.), whose dictum, "That which is hateful to you, do not do unto your neighbour," is considered as the basis for the similar maxim found in the Sermon on the Mount. Hillel's leniency in halakhic interpretation illustrates the mode of Jewish harmonization of law and life. His descendants established the patriarchate in Palestine.

In the course of Jewish history many rabbinic institutions sought to exercise the power of this traditional Sanhedrin. Such were the patriarchate in Palestine (100–415 C.E.) and the gaonate (see GAON) of Babylonia (660–1040 C.E.), where various academies of learning thrived. A bold attempt to reinstitute the body was made by Rabbi Jacob Birab and Rabbi Joseph Qaro in the early 16th century, after the expulsion of the Jews from Spain, with the direct purpose of receiving the marranos back to Judaism. Napoleon Bonaparte also, in 1806, sought to organize a Sanhedrin to decide the conduct of laws for the French Jews. The Paris Sanhedrin met in February 1807 and agreed that the principles of a liberal, secular state were compatible with the laws of the Jewish religion. With the establishment of the state of Israel in 1948, hopes rose among some Orthodox Jews for the revival of the Great Sanhedrin. Many groups within Orthodoxy and outside its ranks oppose any such effort.

BIBLIOGRAPHY.—S. B. Hoenig, *The Great Sanhedrin* (1953); S. Zeitlin, *Who Crucified Jesus?*, 2nd ed. (1947); J. Newman, *Semikhah (Ordination)* (1951). (S. B. Ho.)

SAN ILDEFONSO (LA GRANJA), a town and summer resort in the province of Segovia, Spain, seat of the former summer palace of the kings of Spain, lies at the foot of Pico de Peñalara surrounded by a dense forest of pines, firs, and birches, 7 mi. (11 km.) SE of Segovia city. The original *granja* ("grange" or "farm") was purchased in 1720 from Hieronymite monks by Philip V, the first Bourbon king of Spain, as the site for a summer palace to rival those of Versailles and Parma. The original design by Teodoro Ardemáns was Herreran in its simplicity, but it was modified by French and Italian artists, notably F. Juvarra and G. B. Sacchetti. The palace chapel, with a fine dome and two towers, has frescoes by F. Bayeu y Subías and contains the tomb of Philip V and his wife, Isabella Farnese. The gardens, laid out by E. Boutelou, have 26 fountains, mostly by R. Frémin and J. Thierri. The royal apartments contain a splendid collection of tapestries, some Flemish and some from cartoons by Goya. La Granja was the scene of many important events in Spanish history including Philip V's abdication (1724), the signing of various treaties (notably in 1796 whereby Spain was tied to the French republic), and the revocation of the Pragmatic Sanction (1830) by Ferdinand VII. The palace was damaged by fire in 1918. (M. Fu.)

SANITATION: *see* HYGIENE; PREVENTIVE MEDICINE; PUBLIC HEALTH; and such specific related articles as PLUMBING; SEWAGE DISPOSAL; etc.

SANJAR (1086 or 1084–1157), Seljuk prince of Khurasan from 1096 to 1157, was born on Nov. 5, 1086, or, according to some authorities, on Nov. 27, 1084. In the Persian historical tradition his fame almost eclipses that of the "great Seljuks" because of the length of his reign, his power and victories in its first half, his disasters in the second, and the fact that he was the last real Seljuk sultan in Iran, after whom came only chaos and misery.

Appointed governor of Khurasan in 1096 by his half brother Barkiyarok, who succeeded Malik Shah (q.v.) as sultan, Sanjar in fact acted as an independent prince throughout his reign and after the death of his full brother Mohammed in 1018 was regarded as the head of the Seljuk house. His longevity saved Khurasan from the internecine struggles which destroyed the other Seljuk lines and enabled him to maintain the authority of an organized government (of which valuable documents have survived) in spite of the growing dangers which gathered round him.

In the first part of his reign Sanjar established his suzerainty over the Turkish Qarakhanid princes of Transoxiana and even over the Ghaznavids of the Indian borderland. He entered Ghazni itself in 1117 and there installed his own nominee on the throne.

Later, however, he was faced with problems he could neither solve nor escape. First, there was the insubordination of his viceroy Atsiz in Khorezmia (modern Khiva). In 1138 Sanjar defeated Atsiz and occupied Khorezmia, but Atsiz returned and renewed his rebellion. Second, a new and dangerous enemy appeared in Transoxiana: this was the recently founded confederacy of Central Asian tribes under the Khara-Khitai, with whom the Turkish Karluks of Transoxiana made common cause. Sanjar suffered a terrible defeat near Samarkand in 1141; Transoxiana was lost and the Khara-Khitai established a distant suzerainty over Khorezmia. Sanjar maintained his hold over Khurasan in spite of Atsiz, but he had suffered a great loss of prestige and power; the fame of his defeat even reached Europe, where it took the form of the legend of Prester John (q.v.), the Christian priest-king who was to destroy Islam (there were Nestorian Christians among the Khara-Khitai). Finally there was a general uprising of the Oghuz (Ghuzz) tribes in Sanjar's realm. Although these tribes had originally been the instrument of the Seljukid conquests they had never become reconciled to a centralized administration. In 1153 they captured the old sultan and, although bestowing on him every kind of respect, kept him prisoner for two years. He escaped but died on May 8, 1157, without having restored order in Khurasan. *See also* SELJUKS.

See V. V. Bartold, *Turkestan Down to the Mongol Invasion* (1958); Ann Lambton, "The Administration of Sanjar's Empire," *Bulletin of the School of Oriental and African Studies*, vol. xx (1957).

(H. A. R. G.; CL. CA.)

SANJŌ SANETOMI (1837–1891) was one of the court noble statesmen in the Japanese imperial government established in 1868. Sanjō's service in high office helped emphasize the importance of the throne and the imperial court, whose power the feudal lords had usurped for so long. He held the post of first minister of the Council of State during most of the period from 1871 to 1885. His most important function was to serve as spokesman for the bureaucracy which ruled in the name of the emperor Meiji. For example, it was Sanjō who promulgated the imperial rescript of Oct. 12, 1881, promising a parliament and constitution. The most important and dramatic moment in his career occurred in 1873, when the faction which advocated war with Korea pressed him to secure imperial approval. Unable to bear the pressure of decision, he turned his post over to his colleague, Iwakura Tomomi, who was able to defeat the plans of the war party. Finally, in 1885, when the modern cabinet system was instituted in preparation for constitutional government, Sanjō was elevated to the post of lord keeper of the privy seal. (GE. M. B.)

SAN JOSÉ, a department in southern Uruguay. Pop. (1963) 77,284. Area 2,688 sq.mi. A major steel railroad bridge permits easy communication with Montevideo, about 60 mi. away. There are also road, sea, and air routes to the national capital. As elsewhere in southern Uruguay, closeness to Montevideo's markets encourages dairying and agriculture. Poultry and swine are increasingly important. San José is a ranching region and its breeding establishments service a wide area; both cattle and sheep are raised. The departmental capital is San José (pop. [1963] 17,706). (M. I. V.)

SAN JOSÉ (SAN JOSÉ DE COSTA RICA), the capital of the Republic of Costa Rica, on the Meseta Central, 3,805 ft. (1,160 m.) above sea level, is an important point on the Inter-American Highway and the junction of the Northern Railway from Limón and the Pacific Railway from Puntarenas. Pop. (1963) 101,162. The year-round climate is moderate, divided into a wet and a dry season. Called Villa Nueva when settlement began in 1736, San José developed very slowly in the Spanish colonial era. Its early source of wealth was the tobacco trade. Following independence in 1821, San José citizens briefly fought those of Cartago and in 1823 the capital of the Republic of Costa Rica was moved from Cartago to San José.

In the 1840s San José emerged as the centre of coffee production, chief source of Costa Rican wealth throughout the 19th century. The political, social, and economic centre of Costa Rica and an episcopal see, San José grew rapidly in the 20th century, especially in its suburbs. After 1950 the number of industrial establishments more than doubled. Commerce is carried on mainly by a large number of small operations. Costa Rica's substantial import trade is centred in San José.

The city has electrically lighted paved streets, a large central market, and excellent hospitals, schools, and parks. The University of Costa Rica is in San José as are the 19th-century cathedral and the imposing national theatre. The city is the capital of San José province (2,008 sq.mi. [5,200 sq.km.]), a fertile coffee- and livestock-raising area. The population of the province increased nearly 100% between 1927 and 1968. Serving the province is the international airport, El Coco, about 12 mi. from San José. Just outside the city is the beautiful plain known as La Sabana, lined with lovely homes. The National Stadium occupies one section of the Sabana. The city is popular with tourists.

(T. L. K.)

SAN JOSE, known as the "Garden city," in west central California, U.S., is the principal city and county seat of Santa Clara county. Located on the level floor of the Santa Clara valley between the Diablo range and the Santa Cruz mountains, it is 50 mi. S. of San Francisco and 30 mi. N.E. of Monterey bay. Pop. (1960) city 204,196; standard metropolitan statistical area (Santa Clara county) 642,315. Included within the metropolitan area are the cities of Palo Alto, Santa Clara and Sunnyvale (qq.v.). For comparative population figures see the table in CALIFORNIA: *Population.*

Founded on Nov. 29, 1777, as El Pueblo de San José de Guadalupe by José Joaquin Moraga under orders from Felipe de Neve, Spanish governor of Alta California (Upper California), and named for St. Joseph, California's patron saint, it was California's first civil community. During the Spanish and Mexican periods it supplied wheat, vegetables and cattle to the garrisons of the presidios in Monterey and San Francisco. Located 3 mi. from Mission Santa Clara (founded 1777) and 16 mi. from Mission San José (founded 1797), San Jose also became the centre for ecclesiastical activities in the area. Some of this rich heritage is retained in the colourful Spanish place names for streets and districts.

REFLECTING POOL, SCULPTURE, AND LANDSCAPED GARDEN PROVIDE THE SETTING FOR AN INDUSTRIAL EDUCATION, RESEARCH, ENGINEERING, AND MANUFACTURING COMPLEX IN SAN JOSE

The U.S. flag was raised above San Jose during the Mexican War on July 14, 1846, and it remained a U.S. city. It became California's first state capital, and the first state legislature ("the legislature of 1,000 drinks") convened there on Dec. 15, 1849. It was also the home of Peter H. Burnett, the state's first elected governor. However, San Jose was not destined to be the seat of government for long; in Jan. 1852 the capital was removed to Vallejo. One of California's first cities, San Jose was incorporated in March 1850, and by this date had changed from a drowsy little Spanish pueblo to a bustling trading centre and quicksilver depot for the gold fields. Most of California's quicksilver, used in the amalgamation process of extracting gold from ores, came from New Almaden, 13 mi. S.

In 1864 the coming of the railroad from San Francisco gave San Jose improved trade connections and new industries began to vie with the agriculture of the valley. The area soon developed into a fruit-producing region with French prunes (introduced by Louis Pellier, 1856) and apricots predominating. San Jose was long the centre of the world's dried-fruit and canning industry and until 1940 most of its industry was concerned with food processing or preserving and with manufacturing orchard supplies and food machinery. After World War II, however, there was a meteoric rise in the manufacture of durable goods such as electrical machinery, ordnance, aircraft parts and automobiles. During this period the population of San Jose quadrupled and thousands of single-story, single-family homes began to replace the orchards and farms. Displaying the better features of suburbia and without the worst features of a metropolis, San Jose's newer districts contain dispersed shopping facilities in several subcentres like Willow Glen, Valley Fair and East San Jose, each a complete community for family living within the confines of the city. With a moderate climate and only one hour's drive from San Francisco, San Jose also became an attractive suburban settlement for many workers in the bay area.

The council-manager type of government came into effect in 1916. The city's public-school system includes a large modern junior college, established in 1921. San Jose State college (founded 1857) is the oldest and the largest California state college. Two universities, Santa Clara (Roman Catholic) and Stanford (private), are nearby. The civic auditorium, city symphony, Alum Rock park, the municipal rose garden, the Egyptian museum and numerous parks and playgrounds are other noteworthy community assets of San Jose.

(D. T. M.)

SAN JUAN, a city of Argentina and capital of San Juan Province, lies on the San Juan River, 97 mi. (156 km.) N of Mendoza and 650 mi. (1,046 km.) WNW of Buenos Aires. Pop. (1960) 106,564. The original settlement was founded in 1562, 4 mi. (6.4 km.) N of the present city, but was abandoned in 1593 because of its liability to floods. The existing location, 2,165 ft. (660 m.) above sea level, is defended from inundation by an embankment. A devastating earthquake on Jan. 15, 1944, killed thousands in the city and destroyed 90% of its buildings. San Juan was the birthplace of the educator and statesman Domingo Sarmiento. It is an important administrative, ecclesiastical, commercial, and industrial city, processing the products of the province.

SAN JUAN PROVINCE, one of the Andean provinces, is bounded on the north and east by La Rioja, on the south by Mendoza, and on the west by Chile, from which it is separated by the Andean Cordillera. The mountains on the frontier exceed 10,000 ft. (3,000 m.) and several peaks rise above 20,000 ft. (6,100 m.). Pop. (1960) 352,387. Area 33,257 sq.mi. (86,137 sq.km.). It is one of the three parts of the old Argentinian province of Cuyo (San Luis and Mendoza are the others), an Araucanian word meaning "land of sand," indicating the aridity of large stretches of the province.

Most of the terrain is mountainous, snow-fed rivers from the Andes dissecting its western margins. The largest of these rivers are the Bermejo, Zanjón, and San Juan, all of which are used for irrigation. In the southeast of the province they discharge into swamps and lagoons which ultimately drain by the Desaguadero into the Salado River. The climate is hot and dry in summer, but the winters are mild with a light rainfall, which rarely exceeds 5 in. (127 mm.) annually. Stock raising is of some importance, and the irrigated valleys produce excellent grapes and other fruits. Wheat, maize (corn), olives, and alfalfa are also grown, the latter for feeding cattle supplied to Chilean markets. The province contains much mineral wealth, including gold, silver, lead, copper, iron, coal, mica, asbestos, and lime, but their exploitation is limited. Industrial activity in the urban centres is concentrated on the processing of food products.

Four roads across the Andes link San Juan with the Chilean provinces of Coquimbo and Atacama, and much of San Juan's trade is carried on via these routes. Rail and road communications southward to Mendoza and to the trans-Andean line and eastward to Córdoba unite the province to the rest of Argentina. Jachal on the Zanjón River, 90 mi. (145 km.) N of San Juan, is an important agricultural and coal-mining centre. The province suffered severely in 1944 from the earthquake that destroyed San Juan city.   (G. J. B.)

SAN JUAN, the capital of the island of Puerto Rico, is the oldest city under the U.S. flag. Pop. (1960) 451,658. In 1508 Ponce de León founded the original settlement, called Villa de Caparra, near the shore of a perfectly protected harbour opposite the present site of San Juan. The unhealthful conditions forced the Spaniards to move in 1521 to the present location on a very small island protecting the entrance to the harbour (*see* PUERTO RICO: *History*). Since the city was subject to frequent foreign attacks the Spanish constructed several large fortifications and a massive wall, two parts of which still stand, with moats, gates and bridges. On a high bluff guarding the entrance to the harbour is the formidable El Morro fortress; and to the east overlooking the Atlantic is the great fortress of San Cristóbal.

Other buildings of historical interest include La Fortaleza, the home and office of the governors, the construction of which was

BY COURTESY OF PUERTO RICO NEWS SERVICE

EL MORRO FORTRESS LOCATED AT THE ENTRANCE TO SAN JUAN HARBOUR

started in 1533; the Casa Blanca, built for the descendants of Ponce de León (1523); the cathedral, originally constructed in 1512 but rebuilt in 1549; and the city hall, built on the principal plaza in 1602. The government of Puerto Rico, through the Institute of Puerto Rican Culture, has undertaken in every way possible the restoration of the historical aspect of old San Juan, with its narrow cobblestone streets, overhanging balconies, cool porticoes and 19th-century lights.

In the 20th century the city expanded rapidly beyond its walled confines, incorporating such suburban areas as Miramar, Santurce and El Condado along the coast and Río Piedras and Hato Rey inland. In 1960 the standard metropolitan area of San Juan, with a population of 588,805, included the urban areas of Bayamón, Cataño, Guaynabo and San Juan. In these newer areas are found beautiful modern buildings, such as the Lawyers' Association building in Santurce, the Roman Catholic church of Cataño and in Río Piedras the library of the University of Puerto Rico with its famous mural by the Mexican painter Rufino Tamayo.

Politically, culturally, socially and commercially the metropolitan area is the centre of Puerto Rico. The governor's home and office are still in the Fortaleza in old San Juan. A marble capitol of the classic type houses the bicameral legislature and nearby, in the same area of Puerto de Tierra, is the modern building of the supreme court of the island. In an effort to decentralize the metropolitan area many government offices and agencies have been moved back across the bay to a location not too distant from the original site of Caparra.

The Institute of Puerto Rican Culture, Carnegie library, the Atheneum and the School of Tropical Medicine are centrally located near old San Juan. In addition to the University of

Puerto Rico an excellent bicultural education is offered by such schools as the College of the Sacred Heart and Robinson school. The Casa de España, the Puerto Rico casino, the Yacht club and a number of private country clubs offer social activity for their members. Entertainment facilities include horse racing at a large modern hippodrome between Río Piedras and Carolina and night baseball during the winter season with big league players.

San Juan has one of the largest and best protected harbours in the West Indies. Fully equipped with modern docking facilities and a dry-dock service, the harbour receives freight and passengers from the Atlantic, Gulf and Pacific ports of the U.S., from South and Central America, the countries of Europe and the other West Indian islands. Most of the people coming to the island arrive by air at the San Juan International airport. The airlines of three continents and the West Indies make San Juan a regular stop. Most of those arriving for the first time, whether by plane or boat, are tourists staying for short periods at the ultramodern tourist hotels located for the most part along the Atlantic coast between old San Juan and the airport to the east. In the commercial centres of San Juan, Santurce and the other suburban areas many U.S. chain stores, banks and important corporations have local offices and distributing centres.   (T. G. Ms.)

SAN JUAN DEL NORTE (also called GREYTOWN), at one time the chief port of Nicaragua on the Caribbean Sea, is situated at the mouth of the northern channel in the delta of the San Juan River. Pop. (1963) 599. During the large movement of people from the eastern United States to California between 1850 and 1870, when the Nicaragua route was a relatively comfortable line of travel, San Juan del Norte was a terminus for Atlantic steamers and the starting point for the small boats that went up the San Juan River and across Lake Nicaragua, whence travelers took a stage for 12 mi. to the Pacific port of San Juan del Sur. San Juan del Norte lost its importance as a port because coastal currents moved sand into the northern delta entrance. In 1850 the San Juan del Norte channel was 25 ft. deep but by 1875 it was only 5 ft., eliminating it as an ocean port.   (C. F. J.)

SAN JUAN (HARO) **ISLANDS,** an archipelago of 172 habitable islands and several hundred tide-washed rocks in upper Puget Sound south of Georgia Strait and east of the Strait of Juan de Fuca; politically it is a part of the State of Washington. The islands are geologically part of a submerged mountain chain whose summits appear in the ocean-filled trough where British Columbia and Washington meet. They were first explored and named during the expedition of Francisco Eliza in 1790–92. They were also visited by Capt. George Vancouver in 1792 and Charles Wilkes of the U.S. Navy in 1841. They were occupied for a time by the Hudson's Bay Company, then subjected to a dispute between Great Britain and the United States over their ownership. In 1859 troops of both nations landed on San Juan Island. For a few weeks there was imminent danger of war but trouble was averted when both nations agreed to arbitration. In 1872 the emperor of Germany assigned them to the United States.

The islands are used extensively for summer homes and camps. The highest point in the group is Mt. Constitution on Orcas Island, at 2,408 ft. The rainfall of the islands is light, averaging less than 30 in. a year. Most of the islands have been grouped together as San Juan County, which has an area of 172 sq.mi.; the population of the county declined from 3,245 in 1950 to 2,872 in 1960. The three largest islands are San Juan (71 sq.mi.), Orcas (83 sq.mi.), and Lopez (55 sq.mi.).

See David Lavender, *Land of Giants* (1958); Dorothy O. Johansen and Charles M. Gates, *Empire of the Columbia* (1957).   (K. A. M.)

SAN JUAN RIVER, in the southwestern United States, the second most important tributary of the Colorado River system, rises in the San Juan Mountains of southwestern Colorado on the west side of the continental divide in Mineral County. The river flows west and is 360 mi. long; it empties into the Colorado 80 mi. upstream from Lee Ferry, Ariz. Important tributaries of the San Juan in northwestern New Mexico are the Animas, Los Pinos, Piedra, La Plata, and Mancos rivers. In this area the river valley widens and some irrigation agriculture is practised. At "Four Corners," where the boundaries of New Mexico, Utah, Arizona, and Colorado meet, the San Juan enters the Colorado plateau into which it has carved numerous S-shaped canyons over 1,000 ft. deep. This section of the river is known as the Goosenecks. From the Goosenecks the San Juan flows through wild, rugged, desert country in a relatively straight, deep canyon to the Colorado. The San Juan is one of the important rivers in the multiple-purpose development of the upper Colorado River, discharging almost 2,000,000 ac-ft. of water annually into the Colorado. The Navajo Dam is an irrigation and flood-control project on the San Juan in northwest New Mexico. (M. J. L.)

SANKA, a pariah group in Japan, one of a series of so-called tribes or ethnic enclaves against whom the Japanese developed a marked sense of prejudice and discrimination. These groups, commonly designated as the *senmin,* a term referring to their low social status, became in effect outcastes, living at the very bottom of the rigidly structured social system of feudal Japan. The Sanka are sometimes called the Japanese gypsies, being small bands of wandering people traditionally limited to the mountainous regions of Honshu. Their descendants are generally located in the mountains behind Niigata and in the area of Mt. Chausu. Although such people are mentioned in Japanese chronicles from the 11th century A.D., much of the information about them is vague, being dependent in some measure on Japanese folklore. There seems no reason to equate the Sanka with the aboriginal Japanese Ainu; indeed, they are not distinguishable in either physical type or language from the Japanese proper. In general, the Sanka may be appraised along with such other outcaste elements in Japan as the Hinin and Eta. The fact that they were landless people, living isolated lives, may have served to establish their unfortunate reputation (*see* ETA; AINU).

When it is remembered that traditional Japanese society viewed the nonagriculturalist with contempt, the position of the Sanka may become clearer. Little is known of Sanka organization. Like other depressed castes in Japan, they had chiefs through whom they dealt with feudal authority and who were responsible for the conduct of the group. Socially they were forced into endogamy. There is no evidence to support the common Japanese claim that the Sanka were a wild people who lacked houses and lived in caves. In their mountain habitat they seem to have been wood gatherers and charcoal burners as well as hunters. Although the Japanese in 1869 legislated against social discrimination, the feelings of contempt still applied to the descendants of the Sanka in the 1960s as they did to the Eta. (R. F. SR.)

SANKARAN NAIR, SIR CHETTUR (1857–1934), Indian jurist, rose to high positions in the government rarely open to Indians of his time and was noted for his robust independence and frank expression of views. Born in Malabar on July 11, 1857, he was educated at the Madras Presidency College. A member of the Madras legislature and a prominent delegate to the Indian National Congress for a number of years, he was a keen social reformer; he presided at the Amrovati session of the Congress (1897) and at the Indian Social Reform Conference, Madras. He became advocate general of Madras in 1907 and judge of the Madras High Court in 1908. As a judge he expressed himself fearlessly even against the government, and in a famous judgment upheld conversion to Hinduism and decided that such converts were not outcastes. In 1915 he became a member of the viceroy's council, and as such had many conferences with the secretary of state for India in connection with constitutional reforms. Holding that martial law was continued too long in the Punjab, he resigned; however, for his sympathies with the Montague-Chelmsford reforms he was appointed in 1920 to the council of the secretary of state for India in London. He resigned in 1921 to take office in Indore. In his book *Gandhi and Anarchy* (1922) he attacked both the noncooperation movement and the government actions under martial law; a costly libel action brought by Sir Michael O'Dwyer, then governor of the Punjab, followed. In 1925 he was elected to the Council of State, and in 1928 was appointed chairman of the All-India Committee to sit with the Simon Commission to report on constitutional progress. He was founder and editor of the *Madras Review* and the *Madras Law Journal.* He was knighted in 1912. He died at Madras on April 24, 1934. (L. R. S.)

SANKEY, JOHN SANKEY, 1ST VISCOUNT (1866–1948), British lord chancellor, was born at Moreton, Gloucestershire, on Oct. 26, 1866. Educated at Lancing College and at Jesus College, Oxford, he was called to the bar at the Middle Temple in 1892. He took silk in 1909 and from that time advanced rapidly in his profession. He became a judge in the King's Bench Division in 1914 and a lord justice of appeal in 1928. He was chairman of the Royal Commission on the coal industry in 1919. In 1929 he was raised to the peerage and appointed lord chancellor in the second Labour government, retaining the appointment in the national government formed in 1931. He was created a viscount in 1932 and retired in 1935. He died in London on Feb. 6, 1948.

SANKHYA (SAMKHYA), the oldest system of Indian philosophy, its founder, Kapila, having been born probably a century before Buddha's birth. *See* INDIAN PHILOSOPHY: *Sankhya.*

SANKT GALLEN (SAINT-GALL), a canton in northeast Switzerland and the name of its capital town. The name derives from that of the Celtic missionary St. Gall (*c.* 550–645), who with St. Columban left Bangor, Ire., as a missionary and in 612 made a hermitage in the valley of the Steinach River on the site of Sankt Gallen. Disciples joined him and about 720 the foundation became a Benedictine abbey under Abbot Otmar. Until the 11th century the abbey school, to which laymen were admitted, was the most important educational institution north of the Alps, and in its scriptorium were laid the foundations of the world-famed library.

Sankt Gallen town (pop. [1960 est.] 76,279) stands 7½ mi. (12 km.) S of the Lake of Constance at an elevation of 2,198 ft., the Steinach Valley there extending east-west between hills. To the south of the town centre the abbey church and former monastic buildings form an imposing block. The church (1755–67) is one of the finest Baroque structures in Switzerland and is now the Roman Catholic cathedral. The library (1758–67) with its unique rococo hall, contains about 2,000 precious manuscripts, many showing Celtic influence and with elaborate illumination, as well as numerous incunabula and books, including psalters, gospels, and antiphonals dating from the Carolingian and Ottonian empires.

THE 18TH-CENTURY BAROQUE ABBEY CHURCH AT SANKT GALLEN. THE TWIN-TOWERED EAST FRONT WAS DESIGNED BY JOHANN MICHAEL BEER

Other notable features of the town include the old quarter with bay windows in Gothic Renaissance and later styles, the Baroque and modern churches, the botanic gardens, and the Peter and Paul wildlife reserve. The Commercial University is a degree-granting institution, and other cultural establishments include schools of textiles, embroidery, and fashion as well as museums, a theatre, and concert hall. Sankt Gallen had a long association with linen and cotton textiles and early in the 20th century was a leading world centre of embroidery. The industry still flourishes but has been balanced by the introduction of factories for ready-made clothing, textiles, glass, and metalworking. Most of these factories lie outside the town.

The extensive network of communications includes rail and road bridges west of the town of which the highest in Europe spans the Sitter River 325 ft. above the water. Important local events include the biennial children's summer festival, the biennial international horse show, and the Swiss National Fair for agriculture and dairying.

BY COURTESY OF THE SWISS NATIONAL TOURIST OFFICE

THE ROCOCO HALL OF THE ABBEY LIBRARY, DESIGNED BY PETER THUM; CEILING PAINTINGS ARE BY JOSEF WANNENMACHER

The town of Sankt Gallen evolved from the settlement associated with the abbey. The abbots, who after 1206 were princes of the Holy Roman Empire, governed the town and its environs, and in 1454 abbey and town were affiliated to the eight cantons of the Swiss confederation.

Clerical rule ended with the introduction by Mayor Vadian of the Reformation in the 16th century. The abbey was disendowed when the canton of Sankt Gallen was established in 1803. The town then became a municipality and the capital of the canton. Its outlying parishes were incorporated in 1918, when a communal constitution was adopted.

SANKT GALLEN CANTON, with an area of 778 sq.mi., is bounded north by the Lake of Constance; east by the Rhine Valley, separating it from the Austrian *Bundesland* (federal province) of Vorarlberg and from Liechtenstein; south by the cantons of Graubünden, Glarus, and Schwyz; west by the canton of Zürich; and northwest by that of Thurgau. The canton of Appenzell forms an enclave in northern Sankt Gallen.

Topographically the canton exhibits great variety. The Fürstenland in the northwest is rolling country, and in the east the Rhine Valley forms an extensive plain between Rorschach and Bad Ragaz. At Sargans the valley of the Seez branches westward to the Walensee (Lake of Walenstadt) from that of the Rhine, with the Churfirsten Range to the north and Alpine peaks to the south. Beyond the Walensee the Seez flows through the Linth plain (*see* LINTH) to enter the Lake of Zürich. The valley of the Thur is known as the Toggenburg; its upper part, noted as a holiday and winter-sports region, lies between the Churfirsten and Alpstein ranges and it then curves northward toward Wil.

Much of the hilly region in the canton is covered by glacial debris deposited in the Ice Age by the glaciers of the Rhine, Linth, and Säntis. These shaped the existing river valleys and the Lake of Constance, and the upland owes its fertility to their debris. More than one-fifth of the area is afforested and most of the rest is meadowland and alpine pastures. North and west of the Alpstein Range the climate is similar to that of the prealpine Swiss plateau, but foehn winds (especially in spring) create warmer conditions in the Rhine Valley.

The canton has a population of 339,489 (1960), three-quarters of whom are Roman Catholics, and all are German-speaking. The chief towns besides Sankt Gallen are Rorschach, Altstätten, Buchs, Sargans, Bad Ragaz, Rapperswil, Wattwil, Wil, and Gossau. The predominant farming activity is dairying, with stock raising in the uplands, but there is also a substantial production of orchard fruit and of wine in the Rhine and Seez valleys, with some mixed farming.

Iron ore and manganese are mined near Sargans. The principal industry, textiles and embroidery, is widely distributed, and includes cotton and silk weaving, the production of artificial silk (Widnau, Rorschach), and textile machinery (Sankt Gallen, Wattwil). Many peasant families engage in home weaving or embroidery.

Other industries in the canton include the production of chemicals, pharmaceuticals, chocolate, foodstuffs, pyrotechnics and matches, optical goods, felt, and paper. Numerous holiday resorts in the canton include those in the Toggenburg, the Flumserberge and Pizol district with winter-sports facilities and the national ski schools, the thermal spa of Bad Ragaz, and many other health resorts and sanatoriums.

Important rail connections are the lines Zürich–Sankt Gallen–Munich, Zürich–Sargans–Buchs–Vienna, and Basel–Zürich–Sargans–Chur. The motorway past the Lake of Walenstadt from Zürich joins at Sargans the route linking St. Margrethen through Sargans, Chur, and the San Bernardino Tunnel with Ticino and Milan. Within the canton rail and road networks are adequate. Rorschach on the Lake of Constance is the cantonal port.

The canton, which was formed in 1803, is divided into 14 administrative districts. The cantonal legislature of 193 members and its executive of 7 members are popularly elected quadrennially; the *Landammann* presides over the executive. The constitution prescribes which financial decisions of the legislature are obligatory and which are facultative, that is, requiring a referendum to the people. Any petition for revision of the constitution requires 8,000 signatures. The Protestant, Roman Catholic, and Jewish confessions are recognized officially and form public corporations. The canton administers two agricultural colleges, a teachers' training college, a commercial university, the cantonal school at Sankt Gallen with secondary, trade, and technical departments and a branch at Sargans, and the training school for postal, railway, and public administration. (A. Mr.)

SANKT INGBERT, a town of West Germany in the Saarland, Federal Republic of Germany. It lies 8 mi. (13 km.) NE of Saarbrücken by road. Pop. (1961) 28,352, mostly Roman Catholic. Situated amid hilly woodland country on the Rohrbach, an affluent of the Saar, the town is the district headquarters and is important industrially, with coal mining and brewing, and the production of iron, steel, machinery, glass, and foodstuffs. The art gallery contains paintings by the Sankt Ingbert artist Albert Weisgerber (1878–1915), who was then a leader of the Munich school. Sankt Ingbert, first mentioned in documents in 888, became a municipality in 1829. (M. U.)

SANKT PÖLTEN, a town of Lower Austria, lies on the Traisen River between the foothills of the Alps and the Danube, 37 mi. (60 km.) W of Vienna. Pop. (1961) 40,112. Notable buildings include the cathedral and the town hall, both of medieval origin but restored in the 18th century; and the convent of the Institute of the Blessed Virgin Mary and the Prandtauer Church, both by the Sankt Pölten architect Jacob Prandtauer (1660–1726). Other institutions include a seminary and a teachers' training college. The old town is surrounded by blocks of flats and factories. Paper, machinery, twine, and furniture are produced, and the town is an important rail junction.

The Roman settlement of Aelium Cetium occupied the site of the town, which grew around an abbey dedicated to St. Hippolytus, whose name in corrupted form became Sankt Pölten. The town's charter dates from 1159 and it became an episcopal see in 1785. (K. Gu.)

SAN LEANDRO, a city of Alameda County, Calif., U.S., bordered by Oakland on the north and Hayward on the south, a part of the San Francisco-Oakland standard metropolitan statistical area. The city lies on a coastal plain 47 ft. above sea level, adjacent to San Francisco Bay. It forms part of the East Bay metropolitan strip characterized by suburban developments, commercial trading centres, and waterfront industries. Manufacturing includes tractors, calculating machines, electrical appliances, paper products, hosiery, and processed foods. The area also has a large cut-flower business.

José Joaquin Estudillo established the first residence in 1837 and named the site after St. Leander, a former bishop and patron saint of Seville, Spain. From 1855 to 1871 the town was the county seat of Alameda County. It was incorporated in 1872. It has a council-manager form of government, in effect from 1928. Pop. (1960) 65,962. (R. M. W.)

SANLÚCAR DE BARRAMEDA, a fortified seaport of southern Spain in the province of Cádiz, lies 27 mi. (43 km.) by sea from Cádiz, on the left bank of the Guadalquivir estuary, and on the Puerto de Santa Maria–Sanlúcar and Jerez de la Frontera-Bonanza railways. Pop. (1960) 40,335 (mun.). Sanlúcar or *sant lugar* was the "holy place" of the Tartessian temple dedicated to the morning star, Venus. *Barrameda* is an Arabic word signifying "sandy gateway," and alludes to the sandbank which obstructed the passage of boats up the Guadalquivir as far as Seville, of which Sanlúcar was the anteport in the days of Seville's monopoly of trade with the Spanish American colonies. The first lord and the builder of a castle was Guzman the Good. Later the town was the court of the dukes of Medina Sidonia. From this port Columbus sailed across the Atlantic in 1498 (his third voyage), and Magellan started in 1519 to circumnavigate the world. The 14th-century church and the palace of the dukes of Medina Sidonia contain many valuable pictures. The hospital of St. George was established by Henry VIII of England. The town produces the famous aromatic white wine of Andalusia known as manzanilla. On the other bank of the Guadalquivir lies Coto de Doñana, held by the German archaeologist Adolf Schulten to be the site of Tartessus. (M. B. F.)

SAN LUIS, a central Argentine province and the name of its capital town. Area 29,632 sq.mi. (76,747 sq.km.). Pop. (1960) 174,251 (province). The province is bounded on the west by the Desaguadero (Salado) River, and is mostly less than 2,000 ft. (600 m.) above sea level, but some mountain ridges exceed 6,000 ft. (1,800 m.), the Sierra de San Luis dominating the relief of the north. The climate is warm and dry, San Luis city having 22 in. (559 mm.) of rain annually. The moister areas support quebracho forests and there is some lumbering and charcoal burning, but cattle, sheep, and goat raising on the extensive plateau country is more important. In the Conlara and Quinto river basins irrigation permits crops of grapes, maize (corn), alfalfa, wheat, and fruit. The processing of these products, including meat packing, tanning, and woodworking, provides most of the industrial employment in the towns of San Luis and Mercedes.

The province's mineral resources are extensive, the Sierra de San Luis containing rich deposits of silver, lead, and zinc, with tin at Quines on its northern flank, gold at San Francisco, Cañada Honda, and Las Carolinas on its western margins, and copper, sulfur, mica, and nickel at Trapiche in the southeast. Tungsten is produced from ore mined in the northeastern sierras of El Morro and Comechingones, particularly at the Los Cóndores mine in Concarán; and gypsum is quarried in the Sierra del Alto Pencoso, a spur of the Sierra de Córdoba. Granite and onyx deposits are worked at Cuatro de Junio, and salt at El Balde.

The capital, San Luis (pop. [1960] 28,024), was founded in 1596 by Martín de Loyola, governor of the captaincy-general of Chile; until 1776 the province (together with San Juan and Mendoza) was administered by Chile. Although an old colonial town, San Luis has modern industries based on hydroelectric power and is an important point on the Pan-American Highway from Mendoza to Buenos Aires, and on the Trans-Andean rail link with Santiago de Chile. (G. J. B.)

SAN LUIS POTOSÍ, a central state of Mexico, bounded north by Coahuila, east by Nuevo León, Tamaulipas, and Veracruz, south by Hidalgo, Querétaro, and Guanajuato, and west by Zacatecas. Area 24,266 sq.mi. Pop. (1960) 1,048,297. The state comprises the high plateau region with the exception of a small area in the southeast angle, where the tableland breaks down into the tropical valley of the Pánuco. The surface is comparatively level, with some low mountainous wooded ridges. The mean elevation is about 6,000 ft., ensuring a temperate climate. The rainfall is light and uncertain and the state is poorly provided with rivers. The soil is fertile and in favourable seasons large crops of wheat, maize, beans, and cotton are grown on the uplands. In the low tropical valleys, sugar, coffee, tobacco, peppers, and fruit are staple products. Stock raising is an important industry and hides, tallow, and wool are exported. Fine cabinet and construction woods are also exported to a limited extent.

San Luis Potosí ranks among the leading mining states of Mexico. The Catorce District, which includes Matehuala and the once-important mining station of Real de Catorce, has some of the richest silver mines in the country. Other well-known silver-mining districts are Peñón Blanco, Ramos, and Guadalcázar. The development of Guadalcázar dates from 1620 and its ores yield gold, copper, zinc, and bismuth as well as silver. In the Ramos District, Cocinera lode is said to have had a total yield of more than $60,000,000. The state has good air, rail, and highway connections. Río Verde, an agricultural centre with a national agricultural experiment station in its vicinity, is 65 mi. ESE of the state capital, San Luis Potosí. (J. A. Cw.)

SAN LUIS POTOSÍ, a city of Mexico and capital of the state of the same name, 215 air miles (327 mi. via rail; 409 mi. via paved highway) NW of Mexico City. Pop. (1960) 159,980. Its altitude, 6,168 ft. above sea level, ensures a temperate climate.

San Luis Potosí is the hub of a rich silver-mining and agricultural region and a leading manufacturing centre. The city produces a variety of products including rope, brushes, shoes, cotton and woolen textiles and clothing. There are several large plants for the smelting and refining of various ores and crude metals brought from adjacent states. It has a large arsenic plant. The state-supported Instituto Científico offers courses in law, medicine and science. Notable buildings include the cathedral, conspicuous for its typical Churrigueresque style; the state capitol, noted for its façade of rose-coloured stone; the churches of Nuestra Señora del Carmen, San Francisco and Guadalupe; and the mint.

The city dates from the founding of the Franciscan mission of San Luis Rey by Diego de la Magdalena in 1583, and takes its name from the Cerro de Potosí, a nearby hill of silver, said to resemble the famous Potosí mines of upper Peru (Bolivia). It was the centre of the region's colonial administration and played an important part in the political disorders following Mexican independence. For a brief time in 1863 it was the seat of the government of Benito Juárez. Imprisoned there by Porfirio Díaz in June 1910, Francisco I. Madero drew up his famous "Plan of San Luis Potosí" (Oct. 7) which contained the political and social goals for the Mexican revolution launched Nov. 20, 1910.

                            (R. B. McCк.)

SAN MARCOS, the department in western Guatemala that borders Mexico. Area 1,464 sq.mi. Pop. (1964) 332,303. Its capital is San Marcos (pop. [1964] 10,557). In the highlands the Maya Indian farmers raise maize, beans, and wheat. On the south-facing slopes there are plantations of coffee. On the coastal lowland there are bananas, sugarcane, and rice. A branch of the Inter-American highway passes through San Marcos to the Mexican border. Ayutla is the railroad terminus opposite the end of the Mexican railroad. Ocós is the port.   (P. E. J.)

SAN MARINO, an independent republic in northern Italy, bounded to the north and east by the Emilia-Romagna region and to the south and west by the Marches. Area 24 sq.mi. (61 sq.km.); pop. (1963 est.) 17,000. San Marino occupies the slopes of Mt. Titano, 2,421 ft. (738 m.), in the northern Apennines; the three peaks of Mt. Titano, each surmounted by a castle, are represented on the coat of arms of the republic. San Marino consists of nine parishes and ten districts (*castelli*). The largest town is San Marino. To the east Serravalle, given to San Marino in 1463 by Pope Pius II as a reward for the republic's help in the war against Sigismondo Malatesta, is the only other major centre. San Marino is connected by road with the Italian city of Rimini, about 14 mi. (22.5 km.) distant on the Adriatic shore, and there are secondary roads leading to the surrounding Italian villages.

According to tradition, the republic was founded by Marinus, a Dalmatian stonecutter and a native of the island of Arbe (Rab),

ROCCA GUAITA, ONE OF THREE FORTRESSES OVERLOOKING THE COUNTRY-SIDE FROM THE TOWN OF SAN MARINO

probably about the middle of the 4th century. He was a Christian, and was said to have fled there from Rimini, where he was working, to escape religious persecution. The *Castellum Sancti Marini* is mentioned in 755; the oldest document in the republican archives mentions the abbot of San Marino in 885. The republic, as a rule, avoided the factional fights of the Middle Ages but joined the Ghibellines and was interdicted by the pope in 1247–49. After this it was protected by the Montefeltro family (later dukes of Urbino) and the papacy and successfully resisted the attempts of Sigismondo Malatesta against its liberty. It fell into the hands of Cesare Borgia in 1503 but soon regained its freedom. Other attacks failed, but civil discords increased. Its independence was recognized in 1631 by the papacy. In 1739 Cardinal Alberoni attempted to deprive it of its independence, but this was restored in 1740 and was respected by Napoleon. In 1849, San Marino gave asylum to Garibaldi. It put itself under the protection of the kingdom of Italy in 1862. In World War II San Marino remained neutral but suffered a severe bombing raid and other infringements of its neutrality. It had a Communist government from 1945 to 1957.

The Grand and General Council of 60 members is elected by popular vote every five years. Its functions are deliberative and legislative. The executive functions of the government are exercised through the Congress of State, which comprises ten departments and two *capitani reggenti* (captains regent) who are appointed every six months (April 1 and Oct. 1). The peaceful revolution of March 25, 1906, restored the original system of election to the council (which had become a close corporation, renewed by co-option) by the *Arengo,* or assembly of heads of families, one-third of the council being thereafter renewable every three years. In 1909 the household suffrage was replaced by universal male suffrage. Women received the vote in 1960. Residence in the republic is not necessary for voting.

The available armed forces of the republic include about 1,200 men, all citizens able to bear arms being technically obliged to do so from 16 to 55 years. The language spoken is Italian and the inhabitants are Roman Catholics. Italian and Vatican City currencies are used, but the republic also issues its own coins. A considerable part of the revenue is drawn from the Italian government in exchange for an acknowledgment of the Italian state monopolies in tobacco, playing cards, etc. Only in 1922 did San Marino introduce an income tax. A fruitful source of revenue is found in the frequent change of postage stamps (first issued in 1877); other chief exports are building stone from Mt. Titano, wine, textiles, tiles, and ceramics. The main occupation is agriculture.

There are traces of three different circles of walls surrounding the three peaks of Mt. Titano and dating from the 14th, 15th, and 16th centuries. The town of San Marino is on the most northerly peak. The old church, first mentioned in 951, was rebuilt as a Franciscan church in the 14th century. The principal church (Pieve), in classical style, dates from 1826 to 1838 and contains the body of St. Marinus. The museum contains among other curiosities the banner of Garibaldi's "Italic Legion" which sought refuge at San Marino in 1849. The archives were rearranged and described by C. Malagola.

BIBLIOGRAPHY.—M. Delfico, *Memorie storiche della Repubblica di S. Marino,* 4th ed. (1865); J. T. Bent, *A Freak of Freedom: or, the Republic of San Marino* (1879); C. Malagola, *L'Archivio governativo della Repubblica di San Marino* (1888–90); C. Ricci, *La Repubblica di San Marino* (1903); *Verbale dell'Arringo Generale dei Capi-Famiglia tenutosi il giorno di Domenica, 25 Marzo, 1906* (1906); M. Fattori, *Ricordi storici della Repubblica di S. Marino,* 6th ed. (1912); *Verbale del Consiglio Grande e Generale della Seduta, 18 Settembre, 1920* (1920); W. Miller, "Democracy at San Marino," *History,* vol. vii (1922); F. Balsimelli, *Guida storico-artistica della Repubblica di San Marino* (1932); Ente Nazionale Industrie Turistiche, *La Repubblica di San Marino* (1933); E. Armstrong, *Italian Studies* (1934).   (G. Kн.)

SAN MARTÍN, JOSÉ DE (1778–1850), South American soldier and statesman, whose heroic efforts together with those of Simón Bolívar (*q.v.*) helped to make South American independence a reality, was born on Feb. 25, 1778, in Yapeyú, a Jesuit village at the northern frontier of Argentina. He was the son of an aristocratic Spanish family which, when he was seven, returned to Spain. His upbringing therefore was European. His biographer, Ricardo

Rojas, divides San Martín's life into three periods: 1778–1817, the years of initiation; 1817–22, the years of achievement; 1822–50, the years of renunciation.

San Martín served 22 years in the Spanish army, attaining the rank of lieutenant colonel. When in 1812 he learned that a movement for the independence of his native Argentina had flared up in Buenos Aires, he offered his services to the revolutionary government. On his return to Argentina he found his homeland in chaos. No stable government had emerged, nor had the ties with Spain been severed by a formal declaration of independence. San Martín did not aspire to political power. He was a soldier first and foremost, though he expressed a preference for constitutional monarchy. His primary purpose was to defeat the Spanish forces and establish the independence of the Americas. He was convinced that the Spanish hold on America would not be broken until Peru should be liberated: "The war," he said, "will not end until we are in Lima." His plan therefore was to train a small, disciplined army in western Argentina, then go to Chile and clear out the Spaniards, establish a friendly and stable government there, and finally lead his army across the sea to Peru.

THE BETTMANN ARCHIVE INC.

JOSÉ DE SAN MARTÍN, PORTRAIT REPRODUCED FROM A PAINTING PRESENTED BY THE ARGENTINE GOVERNMENT TO THE UNITED STATES MILITARY ACADEMY

Argentina proclaimed its independence in 1816, while San Martín patiently bided his time. For three years he organized and drilled his army and then, at the beginning of 1817, crossed the Andes at two points, Los Patos and Uspallata, catching the Spanish off guard. He defeated them at Chacabuco and entered Santiago de Chile on Feb. 15, 1817. Naming his friend and collaborator Bernardo O'Higgins as political director of Chile, he braced himself for the next step. A second victory over the Spaniards at Maipú sealed the independence of Chile.

The conquest of Peru, however, was another matter. San Martín spent nearly two years in assembling a fleet for the transportation of his army. At last, in August 1820, he set sail for Lima, and entering the city on July 9, 1821, he proclaimed the independence of Peru. But the Spanish forces retreated into the Peruvian Highlands, and San Martín was unable to cope with them. It was natural that his mind should turn toward Bolívar, who was then moving southward in his campaign to liberate Ecuador. The two men met in Guayaquil in July 1822. The content of their conversation is one of the most debated issues in Hispano-American history. One thing is certain: no agreement was reached on a plan to liberate Peru or to design a political future for Latin America that would be pleasing to both. Disappointed, San Martín left Guayaquil, confessing that Bolívar was "not the man we imagined him to be." In September 1822 he presented his resignation to the Peruvian Congress. Whether he took this action to give Bolívar a free field or because of his own blighted hopes will never be completely clear. His farewell to America was a silent one. He wrote to O'Higgins: "I am tired of being called a tyrant . . . of having the people say that I want to be king, emperor, or even the devil." His life in exile was spent first in Belgium, later in Paris and finally in Boulogne-sur-Mer. He died at Boulogne on Aug. 17, 1850.

San Martín's influence on the South American independence movement is not so great as Bolívar's, nor have his political ideas found acceptance. He favoured a centralized constitutional monarchy, which most Latin-American nations believed unsatisfactory. As soldier and human being, he reaches a place among South America's great men. For San Martín one precept was essential:

"Be what you must be or you will be nothing." By this principle he lived, in action as well as in exile, taciturn, proud, stoic, selfless. The victories of Chacabuco and Maipú are landmarks in the independence of Argentina, Chile, and Peru, but even so, the final triumph over the Spanish forces was obtained only after San Martín had retired from the struggle.

BIBLIOGRAPHY.—B. Mitre, *Historia de San Martín y de la emancipación sudamericana,* 4 vol. (1890; Eng. trans., *The Emancipation of South America,* 1893); J. de San Martín, *Correspondencia* (1925); R. Rojas, *San Martín, Knight of the Andes* (1945); J. C. Metford, *San Martín, the Liberator* (1950).   (G. S. M.)

SAN MARTÍN, a department in northeastern Peru, bounded on the north by Amazonas and Loreto, on the east by Loreto, on the south by Huánuco and on the west by Libertad and Amazonas. Area 20,488 sq.mi. Pop. (1961) 162,602. The department was created from a part of Loreto in 1906. The chief centre of settlement is around the capital, Moyobamba (pop. [1961] 8,308). Most of the inhabitants are farmers, whose products include sugarcane, cacao, coca, rice, maize, coffee, tobacco, cassava, and fruit. San Martín is known to contain mineral resources such as gold, salt, gypsum, lignite, lime, and petroleum, but these resources are little developed. The warm, rainy climate supports dense forests in which there are sources of rubber, balata, vanilla, and cabinet woods. At Moyobamba straw hats are woven and *aguardiente* or sugar brandy is distilled.   (P. E. J.)

SAN MATEO, in San Mateo County, a city on the shore of San Francisco Bay, 18 mi. S of San Francisco, Calif., U.S., and a part of the San Francisco-Oakland standard metropolitan statistical area; it is served by the San Francisco International Airport. Sheltered by hills from ocean wind and fog, San Mateo enjoys a mild marine climate.

A Spanish exploring party (1776) named the creek at this place after St. Matthew. Later a mission outpost was established there, and in the 1850s an American village appeared, surrounded by farms. After a railroad was built (1863), men with gold-rush fortunes bought up farms to establish their country "estates," surrounding the village and preventing its expansion but supplying much of its economic sustenance.

The village was incorporated in 1894 and by 1900 had a population of 1,832. Some estates were then being subdivided and the number of "commuters" to San Francisco was growing, a trend that continued until about 1950. Thereafter the proportion of commuters in the city's population declined because of employment opportunities presented by the increasing number of administrative offices, mercantile businesses, and light industries there.

Cultural and recreational facilities include a public library with neighbourhood branches, a two-year public junior college, two museums, a little theatre, a city park system, a county-owned beach and yacht harbour, and a municipal golf course. The city has a council-manager form of government, in effect from 1923.

Pop. (1960) 69,870. For comparative population figures *see* table in CALIFORNIA: *Population.*   (F. M. St.)

SANMICHELI, MICHELE (1484–1559), architect of the Italian Renaissance, noted for his original treatment of military fortifications, was born in San Michele near Verona. He was a pupil of his father, Giovanni, and his uncle Bartolommeo, both architects at Verona, and went at an early age to Rome to study Classical sculpture and architecture. Among his first works are the *duomo* of Montefiascone, the church of S. Domenico at Orvieto, several palaces, and a fine tomb in S. Domenico. He was also employed by the *signoria* of Venice as a military architect and designed elaborate fortresses for Venice, Cyprus, and Crete. One of his most graceful designs is the Cappella Pellegrini in the church of S. Bernardino at Verona. He built a number of fine palaces at Verona, including those of Canossa, Bevilacqua, and Pompei, as well as the graceful Ponte Nuovo. In 1527 Sanmicheli began to transform the fortifications of Verona according to the newer system of corner bastions which he did much to advance. His last work (1559) was the round church of the Madonna di Campagna, 1½ mi. from Verona. He also wrote a work on Classical architecture, *I cinque ordini dell' architettura,* printed in 1735.

SAN MIGUEL, a department in east central El Salvador and its capital city. Pop. of department (1961) 231,821. Extending from the Pacific Ocean to the Honduran border, the department has some large lowlands along the Río Grande de San Miguel, the second river in the country, and also some of the country's highest mountains, including San Miguel Volcano, 6,957 ft. Important agriculturally, the department produces sesame, cattle, poultry, cheese, corn, tobacco, cotton, and swine.

San Miguel City (pop. [1961] 82,974) was founded in 1530 by Spanish settlers near the right bank of the Río Grande. Near it are the ruins of an ancient Indian town. It is 80 mi. SE of San Salvador (q.v.) on the Inter-American Highway and the International Railways of Central America, and 29 mi. by road from La Unión (q.v.), its port. Because of these transportation facilities it is an important commercial centre for eastern El Salvador. It possesses handsome municipal buildings, several churches, law courts, well-equipped hospitals, and schools. It has cotton-textile, vegetable-oil, meat-processing, grain-milling, clothing, clay-product, leather, cordage, and tobacco factories. (C. F. J.)

SANNAZZARO, JACOPO (1456–1530), Italian poet whose *Arcadia* was, until the rise of the Romantic movement, one of the most influential and popular works of Italian literature, was born at Naples on July 28, 1456. He spent his early years in San Cipriano Picentino. Returning to Naples at the age of 20, he became court poet of the kings of the House of Aragon, whom he served devotedly. In 1501 when Frederic, last king of the dynasty, lost his throne, Sannazzaro accompanied him into exile in France. During this period he brought to light several lost Latin works, including Ovid's *Halieutica* and Nemesianus' *Cynegetica*. After Frederic's death in 1504 Sannazzaro returned to Naples, where he spent the rest of his life and died on April 24, 1530.

Sannazzaro wrote both in Italian and in Latin. His Italian works include a *canzoniere* in Petrarchan style, but he is remembered chiefly for *Arcadia* (1504; critical edition, 1926), a pastoral romance, partly autobiographical, partly allegorical, consisting of eclogues linked by prose narrative. Its hero, Sincero, wishing to forget his unrequited love, decides to leave Naples and retire into Arcadia. There he shares the simple life of the shepherds, joining in their poetical contests and pagan festivals. To this central part of the work, written between 1480 and 1485, was subsequently added a second part, more erudite and elaborate, describing how Sincero, unable to find in Arcadia the peace he desires, returns through underground caves, guided by a nymph, to Naples. The success of *Arcadia* is due not so much to Sannazzaro's use of many formal artifices as to his delicate and introspective analyses of the impulses of the human mind and to his fanciful creation of a dream world which introduced a new type of poetic sensibility. Less important were his works in Latin, including the *Eclogae piscatoriae* (1526; Eng. trans., 1726; critical edition, 1914) in which he revived the Classical bucolics, substituting the world of fishermen for that of shepherds, and the *De partu virginis* (1526; critical edition, 1948), a poem in hexameters in which Sannazzaro, a sincere Christian, celebrates in a Classical and sometimes pagan form the birth of the Redeemer. His best achievement in Latin was, however, the *Elegiae* and *Epigrammata*, in which he expressed his upright and tender personality.

See F. Torraca, "Jacopo Sannazzaro" in *Scritti critici* (1907); E. Percopo, "Vita di Jacopo Sannazzaro" in *Archivio Storico per le Provincie Napoletane*, vol. 56 (1931); E. Carrara, *La poesia pastorale* (1908); A. Momigliano, *Studi di poesia* (1938). (G. P. G.)

SAN NICOLÁS, a town and river port of Argentina, in the province of Buenos Aires, on the west bank of the Paraná, 150 mi. NW of the city of Buenos Aires by rail. Pop. (1956 est.) 30,179. It is a flourishing commercial town and a port of call for both river and oceangoing steamers of medium tonnage. It is a rail station on the main line from Buenos Aires to Rosario and the north, and also the terminus of a branch line running from Pergamino. It exports wheat, flour, wool, and meat. During the Perón regime San Nicolás was chosen as the site for a large thermoelectric station (which now provides electric power to Buenos Aires and the province of Santa Fe) and for the construction of a completely integrated steel plant. These have greatly increased the town's importance. It was founded in 1748 as San Nicolás de Bari y de los Arroyos. (Ge. P.)

SAN PABLO, a chartered city in Laguna Province, Philippines, 45 mi. SSE of Manila. The city was created May 7, 1940. Its 52.6 sq.mi. constitute a single municipality divided into 43 barrios (villages) and a *población* (administrative centre). Pop. (1960) 70,680, about 43% of which was in the *población*. The main line of the Manila Railroad traverses the city, while four important highways radiate from the *población*. The city lies in a fertile pocket of volcanic soil and is almost surrounded by quiescent cones. Within the city are seven small crater lakes. The *población* is an important copra-processing and shipping centre as well as the trading centre for a well-populated hinterland. (R. E. He.)

SAN PEDRO, a department of central Paraguay, drains toward the Paraguay River which forms its 100-mi.-long western boundary. Area 7,723 sq.mi. A well-watered lowland of savanna and forest, it is one of the principal maté (Paraguayan tea) producing areas. Lumbering, cattle raising, and a little agriculture (oranges and petitgrain) provide for the department's 90,991 population (1962). There are several small river ports and centres processing the region's products; San Pedro is the largest town and the departmental capital. There are no railways or all-weather roads.

Limestone is quarried for cement in the south and there are also iron-ore deposits. (G. J. B.)

SAN PEDRO DE MACORÍS, a province and its capital city in southeastern Dominican Republic. Area 450 sq.mi. The province occupies a wide strip of the southern coastal plain and a part of the rolling interior (to 950 ft. elevation) that slopes gently southward from the centre of the country. It is a region given over chiefly to sugarcane cultivation. The province is the nation's leading sugar producer, accounting for one-fourth of the national output. Cattle raising is important in the drier parts. Lumbering of tropical hardwoods is also significant. The province was established in 1908. Pop. (1960) 68,953.

The capital city is situated at the mouth of the wide estuary of the Higuamo River, 38 mi. E of Santo Domingo. As the chief city of the southeastern region of the sugar industry, the most vital economic activity in the country, it serves actively as a commercial and industrial centre. The port has been developed along modern lines and handles about one-fifth of the nation's exports, including sugar, molasses, cattle, and timber. Its industries include corn milling, manufacture of clothing, and soap and alcohol distilling. Its international airport signifies its importance as a transport centre. Pop. (1960) 22,935. (D. R. D.)

SAN PEDRO SULA, capital of the department of Cortés, Honduras. Pop. (1961) 58,632. San Pedro Sula, the second city of Honduras, is the centre of an important agricultural area, producing bananas for export, and sugar, rice, plantains, bananas, corn, sweet potatoes, yuca, cattle, swine, and poultry for domestic consumption.

Located 48 mi. by railway from Puerto Cortés (the leading port of the country), 182 mi. by the Inter-Ocean Highway from Tegucigalpa and with other railway and road connections, San Pedro Sula is a financial and distributing point for northern and western Honduras. It manufactures foodstuffs, clothing, hats, beer, soap, candles, cigarettes, shoes, brick and other clay products, and furniture, and it has fine public buildings and some beautiful private residences. (C. F. J.)

SANQUHAR, a royal and small burgh of Dumfries County, Scot., lies on the Nith, 57 mi. SW of Edinburgh by road. Pop. (1961) 2,182. Sanquhar Castle, on a hill overlooking the Nith, is now in ruins. The town has a tollbooth, built in 1735. Sanquhar was reerected a burgh of barony in 1484 and was created a royal burgh by James VI in 1598. The first "declaration of Sanquhar" was affixed to the market cross (now replaced by a granite monument) in 1680 by the Covenanter Richard Cameron, the second in 1685 by James Renwick (qq.v.). The town is a summer resort and the principal coal mart in the county. Industries include coal mining and iron- and brickworks. The Riding of the Marches (the confirmation of the town boundaries) is celebrated each year in August.

SAN RAFAEL: see Estrelleta.

SAN REMO, a seaport and resort in Imperia province, Liguria, Italy, on the Riviera di Ponente, 10 mi. (16 km.) E of Ventimiglia and 91 mi. (146 km.) SW of Genoa by road. Pop. (1961) 56,945 (mun.). The town lies in an amphitheatre on the slopes of the Maritime Alps, which protect it on the north. Its mild climate has made it popular as both a summer and a winter resort. The old town on the hillside contains narrow, steep streets with tall houses connected by arches, the Cathedral of S. Siro (12th–14th centuries), and the Church of the Madonna della Costa (17th–18th centuries). In contrast is the new town on the coast, with the casino, theatre, villas, hotels, gardens, and fine promenades. The small harbour is sheltered by a 4,000-ft. mole. The Raccolta Rambaldi art gallery is in the neighbouring village of Coldirodi. San Remo became a popular resort after the visit of Frederick III of Germany in 1887–88. The town's cut-flower market, the most important in Italy, provides a major part of cut-flower exports to continental Europe. Olives and lemons are also cultivated. San Remo is connected by road and rail to Ventimiglia and to Genoa.

SAN REMO, CONFERENCE OF, one of the international meetings in the period of peacemaking after World War I. It was held at San Remo, on the Italian Riviera, from April 19 to 26, 1920. This conference was preceded by a meeting of the Supreme Allied Council in London (Feb. 12–23, 1920), where the main lines of the future treaty with Turkey were laid down and where the draft treaty with Hungary and the question of Fiume (see RIJEKA) were also discussed.

At San Remo, Great Britain was represented by David Lloyd George, France by Alexandre Millerand, Italy by Francesco Saverio Nitti (all three were prime ministers), and Japan by K. Matsui, ambassador in Paris. They were joined by Eleutherios Venizelos, the Greek prime minister, in connection with the Turkish treaty, and by Paul Hymans, the Belgian foreign minister, because certain aspects of the German problem were also on the agenda of the conference.

The Turkish treaty was the principal business, and its framework was finally approved. At the same time the conference decided that Syria (with Lebanon) and Iraq should become independent but subject to a mandatory power till they were able to stand alone; and that the mandates for Iraq and for Palestine should be assigned to Great Britain and for Syria to France.

An Anglo-French oil agreement was signed on April 24–25, covering not only the Middle East but also Rumania, as well as the British and French non-self-governing colonies.

The most controversial matter was the strength of the German armed forces. Because of disorders the German government had sent troops into the Ruhr Valley in excess of the maximum permitted there by the Treaty of Versailles, whereupon the French had reacted by occupying Frankfurt, Darmstadt, and Homburg (April 6–7); and Germany now asked the conference to permit the increase of the total strength of the *Reichswehr* to 200,000 (double that permitted by the treaty). This request was refused, and Germany was charged with default in respect both of reparations and of disarmament. As soon, however, as the German troops in the Ruhr Valley were reduced to the permitted strength, the French withdrew from the newly occupied towns (May 17, 1920). (K. SM.)

SAN SALVADOR, a department near the centre of El Salvador, extending from near the Pacific ocean on the south to the deep Lempa valley on the north. Pop. (1961) 463,228, of which about 75% was urban. Population is concentrated in the highland portion of the department, the southern lowlands and the slopes to the Lempa valley having few people. In the western part of the department rises the massive volcano San Salvador, 6,399 ft. high. The department produces tobacco, sugar, fruits and cotton and also has considerable manufacturing. (C. F. J.)

SAN SALVADOR, the capital of the republic of El Salvador, is situated in Las Hamacas Valley, a tributary of the Río Acelhaute, at an altitude of 2,115 ft. Pop. (1961) 255,744, about one-fourth of the urban population of the country. It is connected by modern highways with all principal cities of the country and with the ports of La Libertad (24 mi.), Acajutla (53 mi.), and La Unión (116 mi.), and is served by International Railways of Central America, which connects it with Guatemala and La Unión, and by the older El Salvador Railway to Acajutla.

San Salvador was founded in 1524 at a spot near the present site, to which it was transferred in 1528. It served as capital of the colonial province of Cuscatlán and of San Salvador Province of the United Provinces of Central America, and except for the period 1854–59 it has been capital of El Salvador since 1841. It was temporarily ruined by earthquakes in 1854 and 1873.

San Salvador has sturdy government buildings, a modest cathedral, a handsome national university, an academy of science and literature, several theatres, a national astronomical observatory, a national library, several modern hospitals and charitable institutions, a country club, excellent botanical gardens, several beautiful parks and plazas, and a modern water system. Among its several rapidly growing residential suburbs are Mejicanos and Villa Delgado in the hills to the northeast and Soyapango to the east. Six miles to the east is beautiful Lake Ilopango, the largest lake in the country, in an ancient volcanic crater. With shores dotted with private homes, resort hotels, and older fishing villages, the lake is San Salvador's playground.

San Salvador is the leading financial, commercial, and industrial centre of the country. It manufactures cotton and silk textiles, clothing, hosiery, hats, foodstuffs, leather goods, wood products, liquors, clay products, cement, soap, matches, cordage, cigarettes, and cigars. (C. F. J.)

SAN SEBASTIÁN, a port and seaside resort of northern Spain, capital town of the Basque province of Guipúzcoa, and the seat of a bishopric, lies at the mouth of the Urumea River in the Bay of Biscay, 10½ mi. (17 km.) W of Irún on the French frontier by rail. Pop. (1960) 135,149 (mun.). The old town and harbour occupy the isthmus between the mainland and Mt. Urgull (425 ft. [129.5 m.]), on whose summit stands the 16th-century Castillo de la Mota. A broad avenue, the Alameda, has replaced the landward defenses (demolished 1863), and beyond it the well-planned modern town extends on both banks of the Urumea. A coastal promenade encircles Mt. Urgull, and another borders the broad sandy beaches of La Concha Bay to the west. In the old town are the Gothic Church of San Vicente (1507), the Baroque Church of Santa María (1743–64), and the former convent of San Telmo (1531–51), now a museum with a Basque ethnographic section. In the Gros district on the right bank of the Urumea are the Kursaal and the Plaza de Toros (bullring). The principal industries are fishing and the manufacture of cement, chemical and metallurgical products, beer, chocolate, and phonograph records.

San Sebastián, first mentioned in a document of 1014, was granted privileges by Sancho the Wise of Navarre about 1160–90. In 1813 it was devastated when Anglo-Portuguese troops set fire to it after taking it from the French. It was formerly the summer residence of the Spanish court.

SAN SEVERO, a city and episcopal see of Apulia, Italy, in the province of Foggia. It lies 17 mi. (27 km.) N of Foggia in the north of the Tavoliere Plain between Monte Gargano on the east and the main Apennine chain on the west. Pop. (1961) 47,756. It is a commercial and industrial centre (mainly agricultural produce) for the surrounding region. San Severo was a flourishing market town in the 12th century. Frederick II ceded it to the Templars but it was restored to the secular rulers when the order was suppressed; it passed to several succeeding owners and finally to the Sangro family until the end of feudalism. Of the medieval city, parts of the walls and two gates remain. In 1627 the town was badly damaged by an earthquake. (M. T. A. N.)

SANSEVIERIA, a genus of herbaceous perennials of the lily family, commonly known as bowstring hemp or snake plant. The genus is important in the production of a strong fibre. Sansevierias, native to Africa, are commonly grown as porch and house plants in colder climates and out-of-doors in warmer regions, requiring little direct sun and doing best in a rather heavy soil. Propagation is by division or by leaf cuttings, about three inches long, set in sand. The plant is frequently called old-woman's tongue or mother-in-law's tongue, though the latter name is applied also to *Dieffenbachia*, or dumb cane.

See also HOUSE PLANTS. (J. M. BL.)

SANSKRIT LANGUAGE, the classical language of the Hindu inhabitants of India. Its records begin in the 2nd millennium B.C. (probably not before 1500 B.C.), and it is still written in the present day. When Sanskrit ceased to be spoken as a mother or home tongue is a matter on which the evidence is not exact. The earliest records—the Vedas, the Brāhmaṇas, and their allied texts—undoubtedly were representatives of a spoken language, at least during their earliest period; no fixed chronology can be given. Toward the end of the Vedic record the language of the texts began to approximate that which was later described and standardized in Pāṇini's grammar of the 5th century B.C. However, it is known that the Buddha, who may be placed about a century before Pāṇini, required that his doctrines be preached in popular vernaculars and not in "Vedic." This implies that Sanskrit was no longer a mother tongue but was already the language of the learned schools, taught there and used in religious and other discussions. Pāṇini's grammar would have been the final codification of this school language.

Even at this early period, in everyday life Middle Indo-Aryan dialects would have been spoken, such as those found in Aśoka's inscriptions (3rd century B.C.), in the Buddhist scriptures in Pali and other Middle Indo-Aryan languages, in the Prakrit languages of the Jain scriptures, and in the Prakrits of the later dramas and grammarians. That Middle Indo-Aryan tendencies are much older than the period of the Buddha is clear from certain grammatical forms already found in the Ṛgveda (Rigveda), the earliest of the Vedic texts. During the latter part of the millennium or more during which the Vedic literature was composed, the Vedic dialect and the Sanskrit which superseded it were already school languages into which vernacular forms could intrude. No date at all can be suggested for the time when Sanskrit can be said to have ceased being a home vernacular.

History.—The Vedic language and classical Sanskrit are two closely related dialects of Old Indo-Aryan (see INDO-ARYAN LANGUAGES), belonging to the Indo-European family of languages, most of whose members are European (Greek, Latin, Germanic, Slavic, etc.). The nearest relative of Indo-Aryan is Iranian (Persian, Avestan, etc.; see IRANIAN LANGUAGES); the two together are Aryan or Indo-Iranian. The assumed history is that of a migration of the Indo-Aryan branch of Indo-Iranian speakers into northwestern India at some time during (probably) the first half of the 2nd millennium B.C. Several dialects may have been represented in the migrations; or, on the other hand, dialect divergences may have resulted chiefly from changes that took place as time passed and migrations went eastward within India. The early Vedic dialect is placed in northwestern India and the Punjab; by the end of the Vedic period the Ganges Valley and some areas south of it were already aryanized in speech and there is evidence of much dialect variation. From this diversity arose the great diversity of the Middle Indo-Aryan languages and of the Modern Indo-Aryan languages derived from them—Hindī, Bengali, Marathi, etc., in India; Sinhalese in Ceylon; and the Gypsy languages of western Asia, Europe, and the rest of the world (see INDIAN LANGUAGES; ROMANY LANGUAGE).

After the standardization of Sanskrit by Pāṇini the language in the classical form described by him was that used by learned Hindus in all their writings. Much of their literature has not survived, and in fact there is a long gap between Pāṇini and the earliest texts of the classical Hindu literature surviving and even approximately datable, viz., the poems and plays of Kālidāsa (perhaps 4th–5th centuries A.D.). The gap is partly bridged by the grammarians Kātyāyana and Patañjali and by the Buddhist author Aśvaghoṣa, whose poems are in the same stylistic tradition as those of Kālidāsa and who probably belongs around the 1st century A.D.; the ascription of Bhāsa's plays to a period earlier than Kālidāsa is disputed. Other classes of writing that survive may preserve material from the period between Pāṇini and Kālidāsa, but scarcely any is identifiable as so early; that the work on statecraft called the *Kauṭilīya Artha Śāstra* is genuinely a work of the minister to Chandragupta Maurya (end of 4th century B.C.) has been much discussed, and the question is still uncertain.

For secular purposes such as official inscriptions, Prakrit was used commonly for centuries, until it was finally generally superseded by Sanskrit in these uses in about the 4th century A.D.; the earliest inscription known in Sanskrit dates from about A.D. 150. The two epics, the Mahābhārata and the Rāmāyaṇa, in the forms of text which can be reached by the methods of textual criticism, belong probably to the first centuries after Christ. Their language is essentially that of Pāṇini; differences from his norms probably result from the fact that these works spring from a tradition of oral poetry which was practised in schools and lines of transmission somewhat apart from those represented by the Pāṇinean and classical tradition.

The Sanskrit of Pāṇini was carried outside India by colonial expansion, especially into Indonesia and southeastern Asia (Champa, Cambodia, Siam), in the 1st millennium A.D. The Sanskrit used by some Buddhist doctrinal schools was carried into central and eastern Asia. The Buddhists, however, in their expansion from India more commonly used Middle Indo-Aryan languages, Pali especially in Ceylon and southeastern Asia, Buddhist Hybrid Sanskrit in central and eastern Asia. The political expansion of the Kushan empire into central Asia carried a Prakrit there as official language.

The Grammar of Pāṇini.—This grammar, called the *Aṣṭādhyāyī*, "the work in eight chapters," was the culmination of a long tradition of work in phonetics and morphological analysis. It has been judged by far the best grammar ever written. The analysis of Sanskrit that it presented was never thereafter challenged or reexamined seriously in India; most later Indian grammatical work merely attempted to rearrange its statements so that they should not be so concisely and intricately ordered. Pāṇini himself does not give a phonetic description of the language, relying for this on earlier works (the Prātiśākhyas of the Vedas). He deals with a set of phonemes. With these he states morphemes in basic forms and from these morphemes derives their various allomorphs by means of morphophonemic statements. On the basis of the allomorphs he states the forms of the language up to the sentence. The morphology is stated in great detail, the syntax is less completely stated. This type of description is labeled in modern linguistics "item and process" statement. For a language so complex in its morphology it yields very transparent, though still complex, statements. All modern grammars of Sanskrit are essentially based on translation and adaptation of Pāṇini's grammar, with paradigms added to ease the student's task.

It was the discovery of Sanskrit as taught traditionally in India by the old methods that gave the impetus to modern linguistic studies in the Western world. Sir William Jones in 1786 was led by his study of Sanskrit in India to a recognition of the Indo-European family of languages. From this developed Indo-European comparative grammar in the 19th century. The phonetic part of Hindu grammar led to the exact observations of Western phoneticians. The method and style of grammatical analysis seen in Pāṇini was assimilated in the West by such scholars as Otto von Böhtlingk, William Dwight Whitney, and Leonard Bloomfield, and finally led to modern descriptive methods in linguistics. (*See* also SANSKRIT LITERATURE: *Scientific and Technical Literature: Grammar* [*Vyākaraṇa*].)

Writing.—It is unknown when writing was first reintroduced into India after the loss of the writing system of the pre-Indo-Aryan Indus Valley culture; guesses have ranged from the 8th to the 5th century B.C. The Vedic period was without writing, as were the early grammarians. Pāṇini knew of writing but seems not to have used it. Two forms of Semitic writing were introduced into India, one at least through intercourse with the Persian empire of the Achaemenids. One of these, Kharoṣṭhī, remained in use down to the 5th century A.D. in northwestern India. The other, Brāhmī, was the source of all later Indian alphabets, including the Devanāgarī illustrated in the table, in which Sanskrit is usually written and printed at the present time.

Originally, it seems, writing was used chiefly for affairs of business and administration. Only rather late, perhaps in the last few centuries B.C., did it come to be used for literary purposes. In spite of this, the earliest known writing surviving in India, that of Aśoka's inscriptions, already shows that the borrowings from

SANSKRIT ALPHABET (DEVANĀGARĪ SCRIPT)

VOWELS

SIGN (INITIAL)	SIGN (MEDIAL)	EQUIVALENT
अ	—	a
आ	ा	ā
इ ई	ि	i
ई	ी	ī
उ	ु	u
ऊ	ू	ū
ऋ	ृ	ṛ
ॠ	ॄ	ṝ
ऌ	ॢ	ḷ

DIPHTHONGS

SIGN (INITIAL)	SIGN (MEDIAL)	EQUIVALENT
ए	े	ē
ऐ	ै	āi
ओ	ो	ō
औ	ौ	āu

CONSONANTS

VELARS

SIGN	EQUIVALENT
क	k
ख	kh
ग	g
घ	gh
ङ	ṅ

PALATALS

SIGN	EQUIVALENT
च	c
छ	ch
ज	j
झ	jh
ञ	ñ

RETROFLEXES

SIGN	EQUIVALENT
ट	ṭ
ठ	ṭh
ड	ḍ
ढ	ḍh
ण	ṇ
ळ	ḷ

DENTALS

SIGN	EQUIVALENT
त	t
थ	th
द	d
ध	dh
न	n

LABIALS

SIGN	EQUIVALENT
प	p
फ	ph
ब	b
भ	bh
म	m

SEMIVOWELS

SIGN	EQUIVALENT
य	y
र	r
ल	l
व	v

SIBILANTS

SIGN	EQUIVALENT
श	ś
ष	ṣ
स	s

ASPIRATES

SIGN	EQUIVALENT
ह	h
ः	ḥ

NASALIZED VOWEL

SIGN	EQUIVALENT
ं	ṃ (or ṁ)

FROM A. A. MACDONELL, "SANSKRIT GRAMMAR FOR STUDENTS," CLARENDON PRESS

SANSKRIT ALPHABET (DEVANĀGARĪ SCRIPT)

Semitic sources had been thoroughly worked over by grammarians and adapted to the phonemic system found in the grammars of Sanskrit. This is a notable advance over Semitic writing systems in general, but a trace of Semitic origin is still seen in Devanāgarī. Semitic alphabets did not usually write vowels. Devanāgarī writes them, but only as appendages to the consonants, and the commonest vowel, short *a*, is not written but is understood as inhering in the consonantal characters. The system is in fact syllabic rather than strictly alphabetic. It is, however, strictly representative of the phonemes, and in this respect probably surpasses every other writing system known.

Phonemes.—*Vowels.*—Vowels are *a, ā, i, ī, u, ū, ṛ, ṝ, ḷ*; diphthongs are *ē, ō, āi, āu*. The *ṛ, ṝ*, and *ḷ* are syllabic trills (short and long) and syllabic liquid. The alphabet gives also a long syllabic liquid (*ḹ*), but this is only the result of striving for symmetry. The "short" diphthongs *ē* and *ō* are phonetically pronounced as long vowels but are morphophonemically equal to *ai (ay)* and *au (av)*, just as the "long" diphthongs are *āi (āy)* and *āu (āv)*.

Consonants.—There are five series of stops and nasals: velar (*k, kh, g, gh, ṅ*); palatal (*c, ch, j, jh, ñ*); retroflex, otherwise called cerebral, domal, or lingual (*ṭ, ṭh, ḍ, ḍh, ṇ, ḷ*); dental (*t, th, d, dh, n*); and labial (*p, ph, b, bh, m*). The combinations written with *h* are voiceless aspirated stops (*e.g., kh*) and voiced aspirated stops (*e.g., gh*), respectively. Semivowels are *y, r, l, v*. Sibilants are palatal *ś* (in old style transcribed *ç*), retroflex *ṣ*, and dental *s*. Aspirates are voiced *h*, voiceless *ḥ* (called *visarga*). Nasalization of vowel (or optionally nasal in the position of the following conso-nant when it is a stop) is *ṃ* (called *anusvāra;* also transcribed *ṁ*).

Accent.—In some of the Vedic texts an accent is marked, and Pāṇini's grammar gives rules for the accent. This was a pitch or tone accent, in which some syllables in the sentence had a higher pitch than the others. This accent was phonemic, in that its place in the word was not mechanically predictable. The rules for its position are partly stated in the morphology, partly in the lexicon. In the classical period of the writing of Sanskrit the pitch accent was ignored and replaced in pronunciation by a mechanically fixed stress accent. Sanskrit poetry at all periods depended on lengths of syllables or on syllable counting or on a combination of the two principles; the accent, whether pitch or stress, was entirely ignored in verse construction.

Distribution of Phonemes and Morphophonemics.—The palatal nasal *ñ* appears only before and after palatal stops and should not properly have been treated as a phoneme. The velar nasal *ṅ* is almost restricted to position before velar stops but is a phoneme since it appears also at the ends of words after morphophonemic loss of a following velar stop in that position.

The distribution of consonant phonemes in general shows many restrictions. Long consonant clusters occur between vowels, with up to five or six consonants. Initially in a word there are shorter clusters. In final position in a sentence a word can end only in one consonant, which can be only *k, ṅ, ṭ, ṇ, t, n, p, m*, or *ḥ*; within the sentence a word can end in a larger range of consonants or even in a cluster of two consonants, but there are still many restrictions. One of the important restrictions found in the makeup of consonant clusters is that adjoining stops must be either both voiced or both voiceless. Another is that a cluster of stops may contain an aspirated stop only last in the cluster. Another restriction is that (with a few exceptions) only one aspirated stop may occur in a syllable and that only one of two successive syllables may begin with an aspirated stop; for the statement of this restriction, *h* is classed with the aspirated stops. The palatal stops and sibilant are very much restricted in occurrence, never occurring final in a word or followed by a stop.

Since morphemes are stated in basic forms—*i.e.*, one allomorph of a morpheme is given as basic—much complicated morphophonemic statement is necessary to achieve the analysis of forms which show these restrictions in the occurrence of phonemes. In fact, many morphemes have numerous allomorphs, all of which are related to the basic morphemes by morphophonemic statements which in effect relate an almost unlimited distribution of consonant phonemes in the basic morphemes to a more severely limited distribution in the actual form as uttered. For example, *vac-* "to say" has other allomorphs *vak-, vag-;* there occur such forms as *vacmi* "I say," *vakti* "he says," *vakṣyati* "he will say," *vagdhi* "say!" The grammarians recognized also morphophonemic relationships of similar kinds between vowels or between vowels and various combinations of semivowels and vowels. These are exemplified by further allomorphs of *vac-*, such as *uc-, uk-, vāc-, vāk-;* for example, *uvāca* "he said," *ūcuḥ* "they said" (which is analyzed as containing *uc-* with a prefixed reduplicating vowel *u; u-uc-* is represented by *ūc-*), *ucyatē* "it is said," *uktam* "that which was said," *vācyam* "that which must be said," *vāk* or *vākyam* "speech." These examples do not by any means show the most complicated types of morphophonemics in the description.

The vowel relationships are perhaps the most interesting of the morphophonemic statements worked out by the grammarians. They go a long way toward the *ablaut* relationships (systematic variations, as in English "sing," "sang," "sung," "song") discovered in Indo-European comparative grammar, as far in fact as one could go within Sanskrit itself without knowledge of the related languages. A sample of the statements is that *a, i, u*, and *ṛ* are related in the way called *guṇa* to *a, ē (= ay)* or *ya, ō (= av)* or *va, ar* or *ra* respectively, and in the way called *vṛddhi* to *ā, āi (= āy)* or *yā, āu (= āv)* or *vā, ār* or *rā* respectively. The relationships *u, va, vā* are seen in the allomorphs of *vac-* given above. Whether a morpheme shows *ō* or *va* (*ē* or *ya*, etc.) must be stated for each morpheme; the Hindu grammarians stated it in a practical way that is slightly different from that implied here.

This section of the morphophonemics about vowels is used very extensively in the description of the morphology. An example (with some simplification) is the description of one of the types of future in the verb: it is described as having *guṇa* of the basic morpheme and a suffix -*sya*-, *e.g.*,

i- "to go": *ē-ṣya-ti* "he will go" (*ṣ* is related to *s* in the basic form of the future suffix by a morphophonemic statement);

duh- "to milk": *dhōk-ṣya-ti* "he will milk" (*dhōk*- is related to *duh*- by a complicated set of morphophonemic statements, one of which is the *guṇa* relationship *u*: *ō*; another involves the restrictions on the occurrence of aspirated stops to only one in a syllable);

nud- "to push": *nōt-sya-ti* "he will push."

In one of the types of present tense of the verb there is found a suffix -*nu*- which has *guṇa*, *i.e.*, has the allomorph -*nō*-, in the singular of the active voice of the indicative mode; *e.g.*, *āpnōti* "he obtains," *āpnuvanti* "they obtain." Certain noun derivatives of the basic verb morphemes have *guṇa* and the suffix -*a*-; *e.g.*,

vid- "to know": *vēda*- "knowledge";
plu- "to float": *plava*- "raft, boat."

Some nouns and adjectives are derived from other nouns with *vṛddhi* and the suffix -*ya*- which replaces a final *a* or *i* of the basic noun; *e.g.*,

dēva- "god": *dāivya*- "divine";
kavi- "poet": *kāvya*- "poetry."

Morphology.—Sanskrit grammar is of the type of the older Indo-European languages (*e.g.*, Latin, Greek). Words fall into two major classes—substantives, including nouns, adjectives, and pronouns, and verbs—and several minor classes—adverbs, conjunctions, interjections. The substantive and verb classes are distinguished by two different types of inflection, called respectively declension and conjugation.

Nouns and Adjectives.—The declension of these subclasses shows large paradigms in which the forms are classifiable by three categories: number, case, and gender. Much complication is introduced by the fact that nouns, and adjectives parallel to them, fall into a fairly large number of subclasses which have little or nothing to do with these categories but are strictly formal; these are referred to as declensions. There are three numbers—singular, dual, and plural. With very few exceptions forms in these three numbers express natural number; a few words are found only in the plural; *e.g.*, *dārās* "wife," *āpas* "water." Eight cases are found—nominative, accusative, instrumental, dative, ablative, genitive, locative, vocative. It is only in the singular of the commonest declension that all eight cases have different forms. In the other declensions and in the other numbers various of the cases coincide in form; *e.g.*, in the dual there are only three different forms.

Nouns fall into three gender classes, called masculine, feminine, and neuter. The gender class of a noun is on the whole better distinguished through the form of an adjective accompanying it than through its own form. Most adjectives have three sets of number and case forms, one set for each of the genders, and the form of the adjective and the gender class of the noun are in agreement. Gender corresponds with sex only for those nouns that denote persons and animals. Nouns denoting males belong to the masculine class, those denoting females to the feminine class; there are very few exceptions such as *mitram* "friend," which is neuter. All other nouns are divided among the three gender classes (as in the Latin or the German system).

The Vedic dialect differs from classical Sanskrit in numerous details of form; the system is the same.

Some forms from a paradigm are: singular nominative *dēvás* "god," accusative *dēvám*, genitive *dēvásya*; dual nominative-accusative *dēváu*, Vedic *dēvā́*; plural nominative *dēvās*, Vedic *dēvā́s*, accusative *dēvān*.

Compounds of noun and adjective stems are found in Sanskrit as in other Indo-European languages. In the Vedic period they seldom have more than two members, but in the epic longer ones occur and later in the classical literature they often attain inordinate length.

Pronouns.—As in other Indo-European languages, the first and second personal pronouns have many unique forms based on a complicated stem allomorphy; *e.g.*, first personal singular nominative *ahám*, accusative *mām*, or *mā*, dual nominative-accusative *āvám*, plural nominative *vayám*, accusative *asmān* or *nas*. No gender distinctions are found in these pronouns. There are numerous third personal demonstrative pronouns with declension somewhat similar to that of nouns but showing numerous differences; these pronouns, as well as the relative and the interrogative, have gender.

Verbs.—The categories indicated in the conjugation of verbs are tense, mode, voice, and number and person of the subject. The numbers are the three found in substantives, the persons are the three of the pronouns. A finite verb form contains these two categories or agrees in them with its substantive subject.

The basic allomorph given for a verb is called the root. The tense systems include a present system, with two tenses, present and imperfect. There are numerous types of present system, derivable from the root by specific present suffixes or other affixes. The aorist tense has several subsystems, in general derivable from the root more simply than the present systems; aorists often contain an *s*-suffix. A perfect tense is derivable from the root by initial reduplication. A future occurs of the type given above in the paragraphs on morphophonemics. In classical Sanskrit aorist and perfect are rare in comparison with imperfects; all three have merely past meaning. In the older Vedic texts there are distinctions of meaning: the aorist often means a past that occurred shortly before the speaker spoke; the imperfect often denotes a past event not known to the speaker from his own knowledge (*e.g.*, a mythical past); the perfect often means present result of past action.

In the present system there are three modes: indicative, imperative, and optative ("he might, would do"). The Vedic dialect in addition had a subjunctive. It also had numerous modal forms besides the indicative in the aorist and perfect.

For each of the combinations of tense and mode there are two voices, active and middle. When a verb is conjugated in both voices, there is sometimes a middle meaning, "action done for oneself." In general, however, there is no distinction, and many verbs are prevailingly conjugated in only one or the other voice. In the Vedic dialect many middle forms have passive meaning. There is also at all periods a special present system with middle voice and passive meaning.

The person and number inflectional endings show a complicated allomorphy. There is a special set of endings for the perfect, another for the imperfect and aorist (combined with a prefix *a*-), another for the imperative, and a fourth found especially in the present and future tenses.

Besides these types of conjugation there are also intensive, desiderative, and causative stems, which occur usually in forms of the present system.

Adjective forms, *i.e.*, participles, are found in the present, perfect, and future systems, and also in the aorist in the Vedic dialect. There are also past participles, active for intransitive verbs and passive for transitive verbs, and future passive participles, the meaning of which usually includes necessity, "which must be done."

Nonfinite forms are an infinitive, usually denoting purpose, "in order to do," and a gerund (also called absolutive, indeclinable participle, etc.), which means "having done."

In general, the Vedic dialect has a much more complex and richer verb morphology than classical Sanskrit.

Verb roots are very frequently compounded with adverbial prefixes. The meaning is sometimes a simple combination of the elements; more often it is much specialized (*cf*. English "understand," which in meaning is not a simple combination of "under" and "stand").

Syntax.—Much of the syntax is concerned with the construction of noun cases with verbs and other nouns. Word order is somewhat free, but statements can be made, *e.g.*, that there is a normal order of subject + oblique cases + direct object (accusative) + verb; or that the demonstrative with *sa*-/*ta*- tends to occur as first word in the sentence, no matter what its case. Along with simple predications, there occur also subordinate predications which contain subordinating conjunctions or relative pronouns; such complex predications do not attain the complexities familiar in Latin.

Relations Within Indo-European.—The Indo-European (IE) vowel system underwent considerable simplification in Sanskrit. The sounds *a, *e, *o coalesced as *a*, and *ā, *ē, *ō as *ā*. This resulted in the obscuring of the qualitative section of the IE morphophonemic system called *ablaut;* the sets *e, *o, *ē, *ō*, zero and *a, *o, *ā, *ō*, zero resulted in Sanskrit *a, ā*, zero. The IE consonant phonemes were in part better preserved, in that Sanskrit *t, d, dh* (and similar sets) represent three IE phonemes (a contrast preserved also in Greek and partly in Latin and Germanic). On the other hand, IE labiovelars and velars coalesced and, when followed by the IE palatal vowels, were palatalized at a period before *e became Sanskrit *a*. The IE voiceless palatal stop remained separate from the velar and labiovelar in some contexts (IE *k̂: Skt. *ś*).

In general, Sanskrit has been considered to preserve the IE morphological system somewhat better than the other languages, and to this extent it deserves its old reputation as an archaic IE language.

See also INDO-EUROPEAN.

BIBLIOGRAPHY.—T. Burrow, *The Sanskrit Language* (1955). *Elementary Grammar:* E. D. Perry, *Sanskrit Primer* (1957); C. R. Lanman, *Sanskrit Reader* (1884); A. A. Macdonell, *Sanskrit Grammar for Students* (1927), *Vedic Grammar for Students* (1916), *Vedic Reader* (1917). *Advanced Grammar:* W. D. Whitney, *Sanskrit Grammar* (1889); A. A. Macdonell, *Vedic Grammar* (1910). *Dictionaries:* M. Monier-Williams, *Sanskrit-English Dictionary* (1899); smaller dictionaries by C. Cappeller (1887), A. A. Macdonell (1954), V. S. Apte (1936). (M. B. E.)

SANSKRIT LITERATURE.

Literature in Sanskrit (*see* SANSKRIT LANGUAGE) was produced by the Aryan peoples who entered India from the northwest, probably during the 2nd millennium B.C. (*see* INDIA-PAKISTAN, SUBCONTINENT OF: *History*), and developed as the vehicle of expression for the brahmanical society which gradually established itself as the main cultural force throughout India in the period before the Muslim conquest. Beginning *c.* 1500 B.C., with the era of the Vedic hymns, the Classical period of Sanskrit literature drew to a close *c.* A.D. 1000. Throughout this period of two and a half millennia the dating of most literary works (as, indeed, of most historical events), even to the nearest century, is problematical; the difficulty is aggravated by such factors as the tendency traditionally to ascribe authorship to famous or legendary names. Two main periods in the development of the literature are discernible: the Vedic period, approximately 1500–200 B.C.; and, somewhat overlapping it, the Classical period, approximately 500 B.C.–A.D. 1000.

THE VEDIC PERIOD
GENERAL OUTLINE

The following outline of the literature of the Vedic period leads to a more detailed study, below, of some of the main texts.

Vedas.—The peoples who entered India from the northwest in 2000–1500 B.C., and who gradually spread over the Gangetic plain, brought with them a religion which had close affinities with that of the Iranian Avesta (*see* ZOROASTRIANISM). Their earliest literary products are the *Vedas,* sacred hymns extolling the Aryan deities and forming a liturgical corpus which grew up around the Vedic sacrifices (*see* VEDIC RELIGION). The foremost collection, or *saṃhitā,* of such hymns, from which the *hotar* (chief priest) drew the material for his recitations, is the *Rigveda.* Sacred formulas known as *mantras* (some probably more ancient in origin than the hymns; *see* MANTRA) were recited by the *adhvaryu,* the priest responsible for the sacrificial fire and the offering of oblations; these *mantras* and verses in time were collected into *saṃhitās* known as *Yajurveda.* The *hotar* and his group spoke aloud or intoned their utterances, while the *adhvaryu* for the most part moved about his tasks, helped by assistants, uttering prayers in a low voice. A third group of priests, headed by the *udgātar* ("chanter"), performed melodic recitations linked to verses which, although drawn almost entirely from the *Rigveda,* came to be arranged as a separate *saṃhitā,* the *Sāmaveda* ("Veda of the Chants"). To these three *Vedas*—Rig-, Yajur-, and Sāma-, known as the *trayī vidyā* ("threefold knowledge")—is added a fourth, the *Atharvaveda,* a collection of hymns, magic spells, and incantations which represents a more domestic level of religion and remains outside the Vedic sacrifice.

Fundamental to the performance of all these religious ceremonies was the belief that if they were performed correctly in every detail the sacrificer would gain control over the gods, who must reward him with religious merit and success in worldly endeavour.

The sacrifices themselves grew so complex that manuals (*paddhatis* or *prayogas*) relating to particular sacrifices were devised to help the priests remember their tasks. These manuals, together with the role of the fourth main priestly office, that of the *brahman,* grew in importance as the sacrificial tradition weakened. The performance of certain of these ceremonies still continues, the oral tradition being particularly strong in certain parts of southern India (Madras, Godavari district, and Kerala), while elsewhere a greater reliance on the *prayogas* and the assistance of the *brahman* is apparent.

Brāhmaṇas.—Attached to the *saṃhitās* are prose works, called *brāhmaṇas,* written to explain the significance of the *Vedas* as used in the sacrifices, as well as the symbolical import of the actions performed by the priests. (*See also* BRAHMANAS.)

Āraṇyakas and Upaniṣads.—These are connected with the *brāhmaṇas,* often forming part of them. The *āraṇyakas* ("forest treatises") represent philosophical speculations suitable only for the initiated (ascetics who lived as hermits in the forest) and therefore not taught openly in the village. The more mystical *upaniṣads* (Upanishads; *q.v.*) treat of the metaphysical questions already vaguely formulated in the later hymns of the *Rigveda.* Although more than 200 *upaniṣads* are extant, probably not many more than a dozen are intimately connected with the *Veda.* These are conjecturally dated between 800 and 200 B.C.

Evolution of Different Schools.—On the basis of locality, differences of tradition arose within each *Veda,* and in time these differences gave rise to schools, or *śākhās* ("branches"), at one time numerous. The works were transmitted orally from teacher to pupil, a tradition still widely continued despite the existence of manuscripts and printed books.

Vedāṅgas.—Since it was the sacred duty of a Brahman to hand down the texts faithfully, considerable discussion arose on linguistic problems, the beginnings of which may already be observed in the *brāhmaṇas.* As a result of these and other inquiries there developed a sixfold group of texts known as *vedāṅgas* ("members [or limbs] of the [body of the] *Veda*"). In contrast with the other texts of the *Veda,* called *śruti* ("divine revelation"), these *vedāṅgas,* representing in some cases a link between the literatures of the Vedic and Classical periods, are regarded as of human origin and are termed *smṛti* (smriti; "tradition"). Their more scientific content is also indicated in their style, some being composed in abbreviated language or aphorisms known as *sūtras* ("threads"), so that they would be easier to remember. The *vedāṅgas* fall into six groups:

Śikṣā ("*Instruction* [*in Recitation*]").—To ensure faithful transmission, *padapāṭhas* ("word recitations") were instituted at an early date and taught orally with the *saṃhitās.* In the *padapāṭhas* the words of the *saṃhitās* are recited one by one, each being followed by a short pause, so that the phonetic combinations that occur between words in continuous utterance (the normal method of recitation) are separated. A further safeguard against error in transmission existed in the *kramapāṭhas,* in which words are recited in pairs (*ab, bc, cd,* etc.). These exercises, with other still more elaborate combinations, are still practised. The *prātiśākhyas* (instruction "according to the *śākhā*") were composed in conjunction with these *pāṭhas.* Their primary aim was to discuss the phonetic relationship between the *padapāṭha* and the *saṃhitā* ("continuous utterance") and to give rules for the conversion of the *padapāṭha* into the *saṃhitā.* In addition, there are numerous smaller texts, the *śikṣās,* designed to aid the young pupil, or to deal with particular difficulties of pronunciation encountered in different regions.

Kalpa ("*Ritual*").—*Kalpa sūtra* is a general term denoting the manuals on religious practice which emerged within the different Vedic schools. The *śrauta sūtras,* based on *śruti,* were devised to guide the priest, each according to his own school, in his function at the sacrifice (which was so complex that as many as 17 priests might be involved, thus giving rise to many points of difference). The *gṛhya sūtras*, based on *smṛti*, were related to the householder's domestic rites—e.g., birth ceremonies, name giving, investiture with the sacred cord, and marriage, as well as the five daily sacrifices (*mahāyajña*) and certain offerings (*pākayajña*).

Chandas ("*Metre*").—The Vedic metres, as distinct from those of Classical Sanskrit, are dealt with in the last three chapters of the *Ṛk Prātiśākhya*, and those of the *Sāmaveda* are also discussed in the *Nidāna Sūtra*. A *vedāṅga* by tradition is the *Chandaḥ Sūtra* of Piṅgala (which exists in two recensions, ascribed to the *Rig-* and *Yajurvedas*); but this is, in fact, a late work and treats other metres as well as Vedic.

Vyākaraṇa ("*Grammar*").—The *sūtras* of Pāṇini, who lived *c.* 5th century B.C. (*see also Grammar*, below), are known as the *Aṣṭādhyāyī* ("Eight Chapters") and are considered the foremost *vedāṅga*. While recording fully many features of Vedic, the *Aṣṭādhyāyī* is devoted chiefly to the post-Vedic language, testifying to a long grammatical tradition outside the Vedic schools.

Nirukta ("*Etymology*").—Yāska's *Nirukta*, of the same era as Pāṇini's work and the only extant etymological *vedāṅga*, reveals the existence of word lists, *nighaṇṭus*, traditionally threefold, consisting of synonyms, obscure words, and names of gods. Possibly owing to a broken exegetical tradition, since reciters of the *Vedas* were not *ipso facto* scholars, even at that period these words were not clearly understood. Yāska comments on one such list, quoting 16 forerunners and giving many illustrations, chiefly from the *Rigveda*.

Jyotiṣā ("*Astronomy*").—Two recensions of a brief, and possibly post-Vedic, metrical work survive, attached to the *Rig-* and *Yajurvedas*. They deal with the positions of the sun and moon at the solstices, and with that of the new and full moon with regard to the constellations.

THE FOUR VEDAS AND THE UPANIṢADS

Rigveda.—The *Rigveda* (properly *Ṛgveda*) *Saṃhitā*, which has come down in the recension of the Śākala school, consists of 1,028 hymns, including 11 so-called *Vālakhilyas*, probably of later date. The hymns, composed in a great variety of metres, consist, on an average, of rather more than ten verses each; there are about 10,600 verses altogether. This body of sacred lyrics was subdivided by ancient authorities in two ways: either artificially into eight *aṣṭakas* of about equal length; or, more naturally, according to the origin of the hymns, into ten books, or *maṇḍalas*, of unequal length. The latter is the method adopted by European scholars. Tradition has handed down the names of the reputed authors, or, rather, the inspired "seers" (*ṛṣis*), of most of the hymns. These indications have enabled scholars to form some idea as to the probable way in which the *Rigveda* originated, though much remains to be clarified.

Maṇḍalas ii–vii are each ascribed to a different family of *ṛṣis*, whence they are usually called the six "family books": ii, the *Gṛtsamadas*; iii, the *Viśvāmitras* or *Kuśikas*; iv, the *Vāmadevyas*; v, the *Atris*; vi, the *Bharadvājas*; and vii, the *Vasiṣṭhas*. These books all follow a similar plan, each beginning with hymns addressed to Agni, the god of fire, followed by hymns to Indra and to minor deities—the Viśve Devās ("all-gods"), the Maruts (storm-gods), etc. Again, the hymns addressed to each deity are arranged in descending order, according to number of verses.

Maṇḍala i, the longest in the whole *saṃhitā*, contains 191 hymns ascribed, with a few isolated exceptions, to 16 poets of different families. They consist of one large collection (of 50 hymns) and nine shorter collections. The hymns of each author are arranged on the same principle as that used for the "family books."

Maṇḍalas viii and ix have a special character. They contribute a much larger proportion of verses to the *Sāmaveda* than do any of the other *maṇḍalas*. The hymns of the eighth book are ascribed to a number of different *ṛṣis*, mostly belonging to the Kāṇva family. The chief peculiarity of this *maṇḍala*, however, consists in the strophic character of its composition and in the numerous repetitions throughout. It is closely connected with the first half of the first *maṇḍala*; these two books were evidently added as

beginning and end to the collected ii–vii. The ninth *maṇḍala* consists entirely of hymns (114) addressed to Soma (*q.v.*) and ascribed to poets of different families. They are called *pāvamānī* ("purificatory") because they were to be recited by the *hotar* while the juice pressed from the soma plant was clarifying. These hymns and those of *maṇḍalas* ii–vii were composed by poets of the same families, and it is evident that when the collection was made the soma hymns were taken out and put into a single group. There are also a few soma hymns in some of the later books (i, viii, and x).

Maṇḍala x contains the same number of hymns (191) as the first *maṇḍala*, which it nearly equals in actual length. In the second half of the book the hymns are clearly arranged according to the number of verses, in decreasing order; occasional exceptions to this rule can easily be adjusted by removing a few apparently added verses. There is evidence that this *maṇḍala* came into existence after the other nine were in their present form. It shows considerable uniformity, and all of it is older than the latest insertions in the other books.

It is usual to call the *Rigveda* (and also the *Atharvaveda*) a historical collection, as compared with the other two *saṃhitās*, which were compiled for purely ritualistic purposes. The *Rigveda* contains additional material, some of it secular, which the collectors must have thought worth preserving despite its lack of liturgical purpose.

Brāhmaṇas of the Rigveda.—Of the *brāhmaṇas* that were handed down in the schools of the Bahvṛcas ("possessed of many verses"), as the followers of the *Rigveda* are called, two have been preserved: that of the Aitareyins and that of the Kauṣītakins. The *Aitareya Brāhmaṇa* and the *Kauṣītaki* (or *Śāṅkhāyana*) *Brāhmaṇa* evidently have for their basis the same stock of traditional exegetic matter; they differ considerably in arrangement, however. The *Kauṣītaki* is, on the whole, far more concise in style and systematic in arrangement—features that suggest that it is probably the later of the two works. Sāyaṇa, in the introduction to his commentary on the *Aitareya*, ascribes it to the sage Mahidāsa Aitareya, and it seems likely that he arranged the *brāhmaṇa* and founded the school of the Aitareyins. About the authorship of the *Kauṣītaki* there is no definite statement. Probably it is what one manuscript calls it—the *brāhmaṇa* of Śāṅkhāyana, composed in accordance with the views of Kauṣītaki.

Āraṇyakas.—Each of these two *brāhmaṇas* is supplemented by an *āraṇyaka*. The *Aitareya Āraṇyaka* consists of five books (*adhyāya*), the first and last two of which are liturgical, treating the ceremony called *mahāvrata* ("great vow"). The last, composed in *sūtra* form, is, however, probably of later origin. The second and third books are purely speculative. The last four chapters of the second book are usually distinguished as the *Aitareya Upaniṣad*, ascribed, like its *brāhmaṇa* (and the first book), to Mahidāsa Aitareya; and the third book is also referred to as the *Saṃhitā Upaniṣad*.

The *Kauṣītaki Āraṇyaka* consists of 15 *adhyāyas*. The first two (treating the *mahāvrata* ceremony) and the seventh and eighth correspond to the first, fifth, and third books of the *Aitareya Āraṇyaka* respectively, while the four *adhyāyas* usually inserted between them constitute the interesting *Kauṣītaki Upaniṣad*, of which two different recensions exist. The remaining portions (9–15) of the *āraṇyaka* discuss the vital airs, the internal *agnihotra*, and end with the *vaṃśa* ("succession of teachers").

Of *kalpa sūtras* (manuals of sacrificial ceremonial), composed for the use of the *hotar* priest, two different sets are extant: the *Āśvalāyana* and the *Śāṅkhāyana Sūtra*. The former follows the *Aitareya*, the latter the *Kauṣītaki*, and both consist of a *śrauta* and a *gṛhya sūtra* (see *Vedāṅgas: Kalpa*, above).

Sāmaveda.—The term *sāman*, of uncertain derivation, denotes a solemn tune or melody to be sung or chanted to a *ṛc* ("verse text"). The set chants (*stotra*) of the soma sacrifice are generally performed in triplets, consisting either of three different verses or of two verses which, by repetition of certain parts, are made to form three. The three verses are usually chanted to the same tune; but, in certain cases, two verses sung to the same tune are separated by a different *sāman*. One and the same *sāman* may thus be sung to many different verse texts; but, as in teaching and practising the tunes, the same text was invariably used for a particular tune, the term *sāman,* as well as the special technical names of *sāmans,* are sometimes applied to the verse texts with which they were generally connected.

In accordance with the distinction between *ṛc* ("text") and *sāman* ("tune"), the *sāman* hymnal consists of two parts: the *Sāmaveda Saṃhitā*—or collection of *ṛc* used for making up *sāman* hymns—and the *Gāna* ("tune books," "song books"). The textual matter of the *saṃhitā* consists of rather fewer than 1,600 different verses, all selected from the *Rigveda* except for about 75 verses, some of which have been taken from *Khila* hymns while others (some of which also occur in the *Atharva-* or the *Yajurveda*) may have formed part of some other recension of the *Rigveda.* The *Sāmaveda Saṃhitā* is divided into two main parts: the *Pūrva* ("first") and the *Uttara* ("second") *Ārcika.* The second part contains the texts of the *sāman* hymns, arranged in the order in which they are actually required for the chants of the various soma sacrifices. The first part contains the body of "tune verses" (verses used for practising the several *sāmans*), the tunes themselves being given in the *Grāma-geyagāna* (*i.e.,* songs to be sung in the village), the tune book specially belonging to the *Pūrva Ārcika.*

The title *brāhmaṇa* is given by the Chandogas, or followers of the *Sāmaveda,* to a considerable number of treatises. The majority of the *brāhmaṇas* of the *Sāmaveda* present, however, none of the characteristic features of other *brāhmaṇas;* they are rather of the nature of *sūtras* and kindred treatises and probably belong to the same period.

Yajurveda.—This, the sacrificial *Veda* of the *adhvaryu* priests, exists in an earlier and a later form, usually called the Black (*Kṛṣṇa*) and the White (*Śukla*) *Yajurvedas.*

The Black Yajurveda.—There are three recensions of the earlier form: the *Kāṭhaka,* the *Maitrāyaṇīya,* and the *Taittirīya Saṃhitā.* The *Kāṭhaka* and *Maitrāyaṇīya* are mentioned together, and from them various schools seem to have branched off fairly early, each with its own recension of the text. The *Taittirīya Saṃhitā,* too, in time gave rise to a number of different schools, the text handed down being that of the *Āpastamba* school.

The four extant collections of the early *Yajurveda* texts, while differing fairly considerably in arrangement and verbal points, have most of their textual matter in common. This consists both of sacrificial prayers (*yajus*), in verse and prose, and of exegetic or illustrative prose portions (*brāhmaṇa*). A prominent feature of these early texts, as compared with the other *Vedas,* is the constant intermixture of the textual and exegetic portions. Thus Carakas and Taittirīyas do not recognize the distinction between *saṃhitā* and *brāhmaṇa,* in the sense of two separate collections of texts: they have only a *saṃhitā* ("collection") which includes the exegetic (or *brāhmaṇa*) portions. The Taittirīyas seem to have been impressed eventually with their lack of a separate *brāhmaṇa* and to have supplied the deficiency rather awkwardly. Instead of separating the textual and exegetic portions of their *saṃhitā,* they merely added to the latter a supplement (in three books), which is also a mixture, and called it the *Taittirīya Brāhmaṇa.*

The White Yajurveda.—The defective arrangement of the *Yajurveda* texts was finally remedied by a different school of *adhvaryus,* the Vājasaneyins. The reputed originator of this school and its text recension is Yājñavalkya Vājasaneya (*i.e.,* son of Vājasani). The result of the rearrangement of the texts was a collection of sacrificial *mantras,* the *Vājasaneyi Saṃhitā,* and a *brāhmaṇa,* the *Śatapatha.* Because of the greater clarity of this arrangement, the Vājasaneyins called their texts the White (or clear) *Yajurveda*—the name of Black (or obscure) *Yajurveda* being applied by them to the Caraka texts. Both the *saṃhitā* and the *brāhmaṇa* of the Vājasaneyins have been preserved in two different recensions, those of the Mādhyaṃdina and Kāṇva schools. In several points of difference the Kāṇva recension agrees with the practice of the *Rigveda,* and there probably was some connection between the Yajus school of Kāṇvas and the famous family of *ṛṣis* of that name to which the eighth *maṇḍala* of the *Rigveda* is attributed.

The *Vājasaneyi Saṃhitā* consists of 40 *adhyāyas.* The first contains the formulas of the ordinary sacrifices. The last 15 (or even 22) *adhyāyas* are probably a later addition. The last *adhyāya* is commonly known as the *Īśā Upaniṣad.*

Atharvaveda.—The *Atharvaveda* was the last of the Vedic collections to be recognized as part of the sacred canon. That it is also the latest is proved by its language, which in vocabulary and grammar marks an intermediate stage between the main body of the *Rigveda* and the *brāhmaṇa* period. In the nature of its contents and the spirit pervading it, this collection occupies a position apart. While the older *Vedas* seem to reflect the recognized religious notions and practices of the upper classes of the Aryan tribes, jealously watched over by a priesthood deeply interested in maintaining the traditional observances, the fourth *Veda* deals mainly with superstitious practices. The character of the old gods, too, has changed; they are required merely to promote the votary's cabalistic practices and to avert the malicious designs of his mortal enemies and of the demoniac influences to which he ascribes his fears and failures as well as his bodily ailments. The fourth *Veda* may thus be said to supplement in a remarkable way the picture of the domestic life of the Vedic Aryan presented in the *gṛhya sūtras* ("house rules"). While the latter deal only with the daily duties and periodic observances in the life of the respectable householder, the *Atharvaveda* provides insight into "the obscurer relations and emotions of human life"; and it may be said that "the literary diligence of the Hindus has in this instance preserved a document of priceless value for the institutional history of early India as well as for the ethnological history of the human race" (M. Bloomfield; see *Bibliography*). The *Atharvaveda* is practically unknown in southern India.

This body of spells and hymns is traditionally associated with two ancient and mythical priestly families, the Atharvans and the Aṅgiras. Their names, in the plural, are used, either singly or combined (*Atharvāṅgirasas*), as the oldest name of the collection. Both families, or classes, of priests are by tradition connected with the service of the sacred fire; but while the Atharvans seem to have devoted themselves to the auspicious aspects of the fire cult and the performance of propitiatory rites, the Aṅgiras were mainly engaged in sorcery and exorcism. The current text of the *Atharvaveda Saṃhitā*—apparently the recension of the Śaunaka school—consists of some 750 different pieces, about five-sixths of which are in various metres, the rest being in prose. The whole is divided into 20 books. The principle of distribution is for the most part merely formal. In books i–xiii pieces of the same, or about the same, number of verses are placed together in the same book. Of the next five books (xiv–xviii), each has its own subject: xiv treats of marriage and sexual union; xv, in prose, of the *vrātya* ("religious vagrant"); xvi consists chiefly of prose formulas of conjuration; xvii is a lengthy mystic hymn; and xviii contains all that relates to death and funeral rites. Of the last two books no account is taken in the *Atharva Prātiśākhya* (a linguistic treatise —*śikṣa*—relating to the *Atharvaveda,* and treating books i–xviii), and they are clearly supplements to the original collection. The 19th book is evidently a later anthology; and the 20th, consisting almost entirely of hymns to Indra taken from the *Rigveda,* is merely a liturgical manual of recitations and chants required at the soma sacrifice. Its only original portion is the ten so-called *kuntāpa* hymns (127–136), consisting partly of riddles and didactic material. The *saṃhitā* of the Paippalāda school, previously known only from a corrupt Kashmiri manuscript, in the late 1950s was found current in the Singhbhum district (southeastern Bihar), but the manuscripts had not been edited in the mid-1960s.

The only *brāhmaṇa* of the Atharvan, the *Gopatha Brāhmaṇa,* is one of the latest and least important of its class. The *kalpa sūtras* comprise both a manual of *śrauta* rites, the *Vaitāna Sūtra,* and a manual of domestic rites, the *Kauśika Sūtra.* The teacher Kauśika is repeatedly referred to in this on points of ceremonial doctrine. The last *sūtra* work to be mentioned in connection with the *Atharvaveda* is the *Śaunakīya Caturādhyāyikā* ("four lectures"— *catur-adhyāya*), which is a *prātiśākhya* of the *Atharva Saṃhitā.*

Upaniṣads.—Another class of writings traditionally connected with the *Atharvaveda* are the numerous *upaniṣads* which do not specially attach themselves to one or other of the *saṃhitās* or *brāhmaṇas* of the other *Vedas*. The *Ātharvaṇa Upaniṣads*, mainly composed in *ślokas* ("epic couplets"), may be roughly divided into two classes: those of a purely speculative or general pantheistic character, treating chiefly of the nature of the Supreme Spirit, and the means of attaining union with it; and those of a sectarian tendency. Of the former, a limited number—such as the *Praśna, Muṇḍaka,* and *Māṇḍūkya Upaniṣads*—must probably be assigned to the later period of Vedic literature; while the others presuppose more or less distinctly the existence of some fully developed system of philosophy, especially the Vedanta or the Yoga. The sectarian *upaniṣads*, on the other hand—identifying the Supreme Spirit either with one of the forms of Viṣṇu (Vishnu; *e.g.,* the *Nārāyaṇa, Nṛsiṃha Tāpanīya, Rāma Tāpanīya, Gopāla Tāpanīya Upaniṣads*), or with Śiva (Shiva; *e.g.,* the *Rudra Upaniṣad*), or with some other deity—belong to post-Vedic times. *See also* VISHNUISM; SHIVAISM.

THE CLASSICAL PERIOD

The Classical literature of India is almost entirely of artificial growth, in the sense that it is written not in the language of the people but in that of a small educated class. It would scarcely be possible to fix, even approximately, the date when the literary language ceased to be understood by the people (*see* SANSKRIT LANGUAGE). It is only known that in the 3rd century B.C. there existed several dialects in different parts of northern India which differed considerably from Sanskrit. But there is no reason why, even with the development of local dialects, the literary language should not have kept in touch with the people in India, as elsewhere, except that, from a certain period, this language remained stationary, allowing the vernacular dialects increasingly to diverge from it. Although linguistic research had been successfully carried on in India for centuries, the actual grammatical fixation of Sanskrit seems to have taken place at about the same time as the first spread of Buddhism; and that popular religious movement undoubtedly exercised a powerful influence on the linguistic development of India.

POETRY

The Hindus possess two great national epics, the *Mahābhārata* and the *Rāmāyaṇa* (*qq.v.*).

The Mahābhārata.—The *Mahābhārata* (*i.e.,* "the great [poem or tale] of the Bharatas") is not so much a unified epic poem as a great collection of poetry, consisting of a mass of legendary and didactic matter, worked into and around a central heroic narrative. The authorship of this work is aptly attributed to Vyāsa ("the arranger"), the personification of Indian recension. Only a bare outline of the leading story can be given.

The Story.—At Hastināpura (near modern Delhi) in the Bharata country, Dhṛtarāṣṭra, the elder of two princes, because he was blind, was passed over for his brother Pāṇḍu on their father's death. On Pāṇḍu's death, however, Dhṛtarāṣṭra assumed the government, assisted by his uncle Bhīṣma. Pāṇḍu had five sons, Yudhiṣṭhira, Bhīma, and Arjuna, by his chief wife, Kuntī; and the twins Nakula and Sahadeva by his wife Mādrī. From their great-grandfather, Kuru, both families are called Kauravas; but for distinction that name is more usually applied to the sons of Dhṛtarāṣṭra, while their cousins, as the younger line, are named Pāṇḍavas after their father. The Pāṇḍavas were brought up at their uncle's court like his own sons. The rivalry and varying fortunes of these two houses form the main plot of the epic. The Pāṇḍu princes soon proved themselves greatly superior to their cousins; and Yudhiṣṭhira, the eldest, was to be appointed heir apparent. But they were forced to leave the country to escape the plots of their jealous cousins. In their exile Draupadī, daughter of King Drupada of Panchāla, won by Arjuna in open contest, became the wife of the five brothers. At the contest they met their cousin, the famous Yādava prince Kṛṣṇa (Krishna; *q.v.*) of Dvārakā (Dwarka), who ever after remained their faithful friend and confidential adviser.

Dhṛtarāṣṭra divided the kingdom between the two houses; whereupon the Pāṇḍavas built themselves the city of Indraprastha (on the site of modern Delhi). After a time of great prosperity,

Yudhiṣṭhira, in a game of dice, lost everything to Duryodhana (the eldest son of Dhṛtarāṣṭra), and it was settled that the Pāṇḍavas should retire to the forest for 12 years and should be restored to their kingdom if they succeeded in passing an additional year in disguise. During their forest life they met with many adventures, among which may be mentioned their encounter with King Jayadratha of Cedi, who had carried off Draupadī from their hermitage. After the end of the 12th year they left the forest, and, assuming various disguises, took service at the court of King Virāṭa of Matsya. There they lived at peace until the queen's brother, Kīcaka, a great warrior and commander of the royal forces, fell in love with Draupadī and was slain by Bhīma. The Kauravas, profiting by Kīcaka's death, thereupon invaded the Matsyan kingdom. The Pāṇḍavas sided with King Virāṭa, and there ensued, on the field of Kurutṣetra, a series of fierce battles which lasted for 18 days and ended in the annihilation of the Kauravas. Only the Pāṇḍavas and Kṛṣṇa survived on the victorious side. At last Yudhiṣṭhira became *yuva-rāja* ("heir apparent"), and, eventually, king—Dhṛtarāṣṭra having resigned and retired with his wife and Kuntī to the forest, where they soon perished in a fire. Learning of the death of Kṛṣṇa (who had withdrawn to the forest, where he was accidentally shot by a hunter), Yudhiṣṭhira tired of life and resigned his crown; and the five princes, with their faithful wife and a dog that had joined them, set out for Mt. Meru to seek admission to Indra's heaven. On the way one by one fell away, until Yudhiṣṭhira alone, with the dog, reached the gate of heaven; but, the dog being refused admittance, the king declined to enter without it. The dog then turned out to be no other than the god of justice himself, who had assumed the form to test Yudhiṣṭhira's constancy. But, finding neither his wife nor his brothers in heaven, and being told that they had been sent to the nether world to expiate their sins, the king insisted on sharing their fate. This, too, proved to be a test, and at last they were all reunited to enjoy perpetual bliss.

The complete work consists of more than 100,000 couplets, its length thus being nearly eight times that of the *Iliad* and *Odyssey* combined. It is divided into 18 books, with a supplement, entitled *Harivaṃśa* ("genealogy of the god Hari"; *i.e.,* Kṛṣṇa-Viṣṇu). The part relating to the feud of the rival houses constitutes somewhere between a fourth and a fifth of the work; and it is by no means improbable that this portion once formed a separate poem, the *Bhārata*. While some of the episodes are so loosely connected with the story as to be readily separated from it, others are so closely interwoven with it that their removal would seriously injure its texture. This, however, only shows that the original poem must have undergone some kind of revision, or perhaps repeated revisions, by Brahmans, for sectarian and caste purposes.

The Date.—In time, the *Mahābhārata* became a great treatise on duty (*dharma*), inculcating the divine origin of Brahman institutions, the caste system, and the superiority of the priestly caste not only over the people but over kings. From inscriptions it is known that by the end of the 5th century A.D. the *Mahābhārata* was appealed to as an authority on matters of law, and that its extent was practically what it now is, including its supplement, the *Harivaṃśa*. Indeed, everything points to the probability of the work's having been complete by *c.* A.D. 200. But while Bharata and Kuru heroic lays probably go back to a much earlier age, it seems hardly possible that the Pāṇḍava epic in its present form can have been written before the Greek invasion of India (*c.* 300 B.C.). Moreover, it is possible that the epic narrative was originally composed—like some other parts of the work—either in continuous prose or in prose mixed with snatches of verse. The leading position occupied in the existing epic by Kṛṣṇa (as a result of which it is actually called the *Kārṣṇaveda,* "the *Veda* of Kṛṣṇa"), and the Vaiṣṇava spirit pervading it, make it probable that it assumed its final form under the influence of the Bhāgavata sect with whom Vāsudeva (Kṛṣṇa), originally apparently a venerated local hero, came to be regarded as a god and the incarnation of Viṣṇu. This sectarian feature attains its culminating point in the *Bhagavad Gītā* (*q.v.;* "Song of the Holy One"), the famous theosophic episode of the *Mahābhārata,* in which Kṛṣṇa, in lofty and poetic language, expounds the doctrine of devotion (*bhakti*) and claims adoration as the incarnation of the Supreme Spirit. Of the purely legendary material incorporated with the poem's main narrative, much is probably at least as old as this story itself. Some of these legendary episodes—especially the story of Nala and Damayantī, and the touching legend of Sāvitrī—themselves form epic poems of great literary merit.

The Rāmāyaṇa.—The other great epic, the *Rāmāyaṇa* (poem "relating to Rāma"), is ascribed to the poet Vālmīki; and, allowing for some later additions, it presents the appearance of being the work of an individual genius. In its present form it consists of some 24,000 *ślokas*, i.e., 48,000 lines, each of 16 syllables, and is divided into seven books.

The first book tells how King Daśaratha of Kośala, reigning at Ayodhyā (Oudh), has four sons born to him by three wives: Rāma (q.v.), Bharata, and the twins Lakṣmaṇa and Śatrughna. Rāma wins for his wife Sītā, daughter of Janaka, king of Videha. The second book describes how, on his return to Ayodhyā, Rāma is to be appointed heir apparent; but Bharata's mother persuades the king to grant her a long-promised boon, and insists on his banishing Rāma for 14 years and appointing Bharata heir apparent instead. Separation from his favourite son soon breaks the king's heart, whereupon the ministers call on Bharata to assume the government. He refuses and, going himself to Rāma's retreat on the Chitrakūta Mountain (in Bundelkhand), he implores him to return. Unable to shake Rāma's resolve to complete his exile, Bharata agrees to take charge of the kingdom until the 14 years are over.

In the third book, after Rāma and Sītā have lived happily in the forest for 14 years, together with Lakṣmaṇa, who always stays by his brother's side, Rāvaṇa, the *rākṣasa* ("demon-king"), of Ceylon, carries off Sītā to his capital, Laṅkā, while her two protectors are away in pursuit of a golden deer sent to mislead them. While she resolutely rejects Rāvaṇa's addresses, Rāma and his brother set out to rescue her. In the fourth book, after numerous adventures, they enter into alliance with Sugrīva, king of the monkeys; and, with the assistance of the monkey-general, Hanumān, and Rāvaṇa's own brother, Vibhīṣaṇa, they prepare to attack Laṅkā. The fifth book tells how the monkeys, tearing up rocks and trees, construct a passage across the straits—the so-called Adam's Bridge (q.v.), still called Rāma's Bridge in India. In book vi, Rāma crosses this bridge with his allies, slays the demon-king, and captures the stronghold. Sītā, by undergoing an ordeal by fire, clears herself of the suspicion of infidelity; and together they return to Ayodhyā, where, after a triumphal entry, Rāma is installed. In book vii, Rāma, seeing that the people are not yet satisfied of Sītā's chastity, decides to send her away. Then in the forest, she meets the sage Vālmīki himself (the reputed author of the *Rāmāyaṇa*), and, at his hermitage, gives birth to two sons. While growing up there, they are taught by Vālmīki the use of the bow, as well as the *Vedas*, and the *Rāmāyaṇa* as far as the capture of Laṅkā and the entry into Ayodhyā. Ultimately Rāma discovers and recognizes them by their wonderful deeds and their likeness to himself, and takes his wife and sons back.

The first and last books are later additions by which the poem has been turned to the glory of Viṣṇu. In these, Rāma has become deified and identified with the god Viṣṇu, although in the main part of the poem he is merely a perfect man and model hero. The background of the epic is purely mythological. Rāma represents the god Indra, and Sītā (in accordance with the meaning of the name), the personified "Furrow," as which she is already invoked in the *Rigveda*. She is thus a tutelary spirit of the tilled earth, wedded to Indra. Rāvaṇa thus corresponds to the demon Vṛtra of the *Rigveda*.

One version of the story, with, however, many important variations of detail, forms an episode of the *Mahābhārata*, the *Rāmopākhyāna*. The relation of this to Vālmīki's work is uncertain. In both versification and diction the *Rāmāyaṇa* is of a more refined character than the *Mahābhārata*; and, indeed, Vālmīki already cultivates some of that artistic poetic style which was carried to excess in the later artificial poems (the *kāvyas; see* below). For this reason the title of *ādikavi* ("first poet") is generally applied to him. The *Rāmāyaṇa* itself contains a prophecy that it will always live on the lips of men, and this has been fulfilled. No story in India has attained such popularity. It has been translated into many vernaculars, and through the version of Tulsi Das (q.v.) has exerted a great influence on spiritual life.

Purāṇas and Tantras.—The term *purāṇa* means "ancient," and by tradition a *purāṇa* treats five subjects: the creation of the world, its destruction and renewal, the genealogy of gods and seers, the great ages of mankind, and the history of the dynasties. The *purāṇas* are popular encyclopaedias of useful knowledge, mostly with a Vaiṣṇava tendency. They are connected in subject with the *Mahābhārata* and have some relationship to the law books (*see* below), going back to a common source. They are almost entirely written in epic couplets and are in much the same easy, flowing style as the epic poems, to which, however, they are generally greatly inferior poetically. (*See* also PURĀṆAS.)

According to the traditional classification, there are 18 *mahā* ("great") *purāṇas* and 18 *upa* ("subordinate") *purāṇas*. The former are divided by some authorities into three groups of six, according to which of the three primary qualities of external existence—goodness, darkness (ignorance), and passion—is supposed to prevail in them. These are: (1) the *Viṣṇu, Nāradīya, Bhāgavata, Garuḍa, Padma,* and *Varāha;* (2) the *Matsya, Kūrma, Liṅga, Śiva, Skanda,* and *Agni;* and (3) the *Brahmāṇḍa, Brahmavaivarta, Mārkaṇḍeya, Bhaviṣya, Vāmana,* and *Brahma Purāṇas.* The 18 principal *purāṇas* are said to consist of altogether 400,000 couplets. In northern India the Vaiṣṇava *purāṇas*, especially the *Bhāgavata* and the *Viṣṇu*, are much the most popular. The *Bhāgavata* is held in the highest esteem and, especially through the vernacular versions of its tenth book, treating the story of Kṛṣṇa, has powerfully influenced the religious beliefs of India. From the little known about the *upa purāṇas*, their character does not seem to differ very greatly from that of the main sectarian *purāṇas*.

Besides these two main classes, there is a large number of so-called *sthala purāṇas*, chronicles recounting the history and merits of some holy place, or shrine, at which their recitation usually forms an important part of the daily service.

The *tantras* must be considered as partly a collateral and partly a later development of the sectarian *Purāṇas*, although, unlike the *purāṇas*, they have little intrinsic poetic value. The Śaktas—worshipers of the female energy (*see* SHAKTISM)—look upon them as their sacred writings. This worship of a female representation of the divine power appears already in some of the *purāṇas;* but in the *tantras* it assumes an unusual character, being much intermixed with magic performances and mystic rites.

Artificial Epics and Romances.—At about the beginning of the Christian era, a new class of epic poems began to appear, differing greatly from those that had preceded it. These later poems are very artificial in character and must have been beyond the understanding of any but the most highly educated. They are, on the whole, lacking in incident and invention, their subject matter being almost entirely derived from the older epics. Nevertheless, they are not without interest, and a number of them show considerable descriptive powers and genuine poetic sentiment. In them, the simple epic couplet has been largely discarded for various more elaborate metres; and, as a result, the diction has become gradually more complicated.

The generic name for these epic works is *kāvya*, a term which, with the meaning "poem," or "the work of an individual poet (*kavi*)," had already been applied to the *Rāmāyaṇa*. Six poems of this kind are singled out by Indian rhetoricians as standard works, under the title *mahākāvya* ("great poems"). Two are ascribed to the famous dramatist Kālidāsa (q.v.), the most outstanding figure of this period of Indian literature and a master of the art of poetry. Of the main *kāvya* poets whose works have been preserved, he seems to be one of the earliest; but he was probably preceded in this, as in other kinds of poetic composition, by many lesser poets who have been eclipsed by his fame and forgotten. Thus, the *Buddhacarita*—a Sanskrit poem on the life of the Buddha, which was translated into Chinese c. A.D. 420 and of which the author, Aśvaghoṣa, is placed by Buddhist tradition as early as the time of Kaniṣka (whose reign began in A.D. 78)—describes itself as a *mahākāvya;* and the panegyrics (in both verse and ornate prose) contained in some of the inscriptions of the 4th century A.D. also show many of the characteristic features of the *kāvya* style.

Of the six generally recognized *mahākāvya,* the two first and finest are those attributed to Kālidāsa. The first, the *Raghu-vaṃśa* ("Race of Raghu"), celebrates the ancestry and deeds of Rāma. Consisting of 19 cantos, it is clearly incomplete; but no copy has been discovered of the six additional cantos which are supposed to have completed it. The second, the *Kumāra-sambhava* ("The Birth of [the war-god] Kumāra" [called Skanda or Karttikeya; *q.v.*], the son of Śiva and Pārvatī), consists of 17 cantos, the last 10 of which are regarded as spurious by some scholars, mainly because of their erotic character. There is no doubt that the eighth canto is by Kālidāsa, but he cannot have written much of the other nine.

The third *mahākāvya,* the *Kirātārjunīya,* describing the combat between the Pāṇḍava prince Arjuna and the god Śiva, in the guise of a Kirāta ("wild mountaineer"), is a poem in 18 cantos, by Bhāravi, who is mentioned, with Kālidāsa, in an inscription dated A.D. 634. The fourth, *Śiśupāla-vadha* ("Slaying of Śiśupāla"), who, being a prince of Cedi, reviled Kṛṣṇa, who had carried off his intended wife, and was killed by him at the inauguration sacrifice of Yudhiṣṭhira, consists of 20 cantos, and is attributed to Māgha (9th century A.D.), for which reason it is also called the *Māgha Kāvya.* The fifth, Bhatti's *Rāvaṇavadha* ("Slaying of Rāvaṇa"), more commonly called *Bhaṭṭi Kāvya* (7th century A.D.), was written for the practical purpose of illustrating the less common grammatical forms and the figures of rhetoric and poetry.

The sixth, the *Naiṣadhīya,* or *Naiṣadha-carita* (the life of Nala, king of Niṣadha), is ascribed to Śrī-Harṣa (son of Hīra), who is supposed to have lived in the latter part of the 12th century.

In addition to these there are further self-styled *mahākāvyas.* The *Nalodaya* (the seventh) deals with the story of Nala; its author's main aim is to show his skill in stylistic and metrical devices. The eighth, the *Jānakī-haraṇa* of Kumāradāsa (8th century), takes its subject (the rape of Sītā) from the *Rāmāyaṇa,* and, although strongly imitative of Kālidāsa, is clearly the work of a poet of considerable ability. The stanzas of the *Rāghavapāṇḍavīya* (the ninth *mahākāvya*) are so ambiguously worded that the poem may be interpreted as relating to the main narrative of either the *Rāmāyaṇa* or the *Mahābhārata.* Less ambitious in composition, though styling itself a *mahākāvya,* is the *Vikramānka-devacarita,* a panegyric written *c.* A.D. 1085 by the Kashmir poet Bilhaṇa in honour of his patron the Calukya (Chalukya) king Vikramāditya of Kalyāṇa. It contains valuable information about the history of the dynasty.

There may also be mentioned here, as being composed in accordance with the Hindu poetic canon, Kalhaṇa's *Rāja-taraṅginī* ("River of Kings"; *c.* A.D. 1150), a chronicle of the kings of Kashmir, and the only important historical work in Sanskrit, although even in this considerable allowance must be made for poetic licence and fancy.

Under the general term *kāvya* Indian critics include, as well as compositions in verse, certain kinds of prose works written in highly rhetorical language. Worthy of mention among them are Daṇḍin's *Daśa-kumāra-carita* ("The Adventures of the Ten Princes"; *c.* 6th century A.D.); the *Vāsavadattā* of Subandhu (early 7th century); and, especially, the *Kādambarī* and *Harṣa-carita* of Bāṇa, of about the same time, or slightly later.

The feature generally regarded by writers on poetics as the chief mark of excellence in this ornate prose style is the frequency and length of its compound words; but in metrical compositions, use of long compounds is discouraged by some schools of rhetoric.

Drama.—Sanskrit writers regard drama as *kāvya:* it may therefore be considered under the heading of poetry.

The Hindus ascribe the origin of dramatic representation to the sage Bharata (a word meaning also "actor" in Sanskrit). It is known that treatises on the dramatic art existed at the time of Pāṇini (see *Grammar,* below), as he mentions two authors of *naṭa sūtras* ("rules for actors"), Śilālin and Kṛśāva. The words *naṭa* and *nāṭya* (as well as *nāṭaka,* the usual term for "drama") are derived from the root *naṭ* (*nṛt*), "to dance," and this seems to suggest a pantomimic or choral origin of the dramatic art. (*See* also DANCE: *The Orient;* THEATRE: *The East.*) However, Patañjali (see *Grammar,* below) in his "Great Commentary" speaks of the actor as singing and of people going "to hear the actor." He even mentions two subjects, taken from the cycle of Viṣṇu legends, the slaying of Kaṃsa (by Kṛṣṇa) and the binding of Bali (by Viṣṇu), which were represented on the stage both by mimic action and declamation. Judging from these allusions, theatrical entertainments in this period (the centuries B.C.) seem to have been much like the more spectacular European mystery plays (*see* DRAMA: *Medieval*).

The long-disputed possibility of Greek influence on Sanskrit drama is not now maintained, although there are some superficial resemblances. The Hindu dramatist has little regard for the three classical unities of space, time, and action, though he is rarely extravagantly disregardful of them. It is an invariable rule of Indian dramaturgy that every play, however much of the tragic element it may contain, must have a happy ending. A death never takes place on the stage, nor is anything indecorous allowed. The dialogue is in prose, interspersed with neatly turned lyrical stanzas typically Indian in their depiction of some aspect of nature, or of some temporary physical or mental condition. The outstanding feature of the Hindu play, however, is the mixed nature of its language. While the hero and leading male characters speak Sanskrit, women and inferior male characters use various Prakrit dialects, which at the time when they were first used in this way were probably local vernacular dialects. In time, however, these became permanently fixed for special dramatic purposes, just as Sanskrit, long before, had become fixed for general literary purposes. Thus it happened that these Prakrit dialects, having once become stationary, were soon left behind by the spoken vernaculars, until the difference between them was as great as that between the Sanskrit and the Prakrits (*see* also PRAKRIT LANGUAGES).

Sanskrit drama proper begins with Bhāsa, author of several plays, of which the most noted are *Svapnavāsavadattā, Pratijñā-yaugandharāyaṇa,* and *Pratimānāṭaka,* the last named deriving its theme from the *Rāmāyaṇa.* Bhāsa's date is uncertain, but he lived probably a century before Kālidāsa (for whom the generally accepted date is A.D. 400). Bhāsa shows a firm mastery of dramatic technique, but it is in Kālidāsa's three plays, *Śakuntalā, Vikramor-vaśīya,* and *Mālavikāgnimitra,* that the dramatic *kāvya* reaches its height. *Śakuntalā,* relating the story of the love of King Duṣyanta for a hermit girl of high birth, was the earliest Sanskrit drama to become known in Europe and is superior, in some respects, to the *Vikramorvaśīya.* The latter treats the theme, old as the *Veda,* of Purūravas' passion for the celestial maiden Urvaśī. The *Māla-vikāgnimitra,* a tale of courtly intrigue, is of less importance.

Of Kālidāsa's successors, the most important are Bhavabhūti (*q.v.*), author of three plays, two drawing their themes from the *Rāmāyaṇa;* and Harṣadeva (*see* HARSHA), to whom have been ascribed the *Ratnāvalī,* the *Nāgānanda,* and the *Priyadarśikā.* Though Bhavabhūti's verses are sometimes marred by prolixity, he has the best claim to rank with Kālidāsa, and by Indian critics has been credited with deeper insight into human nature. Apart from the plays ascribed to King Harṣa, the other outstanding Sanskrit dramatic works are the *Mṛcchakaṭikā,* the *Veṇīsaṃhāra,* the *Mudrārākṣasa,* and the *Prabodhacandrodaya.* The date of the first is uncertain, but in describing the love of a noble Brahman for the courtesan Vasantasenā it recreates the plot of one of Bhāsa's dramas. The *Veṇīsaṃhāra* and the *Mudrārākṣasa* were written in the 9th century, or possibly somewhat earlier. The former takes its plot from an incident in the *Mahābhārata,* and the latter is an extremely able exposition of a political intrigue. Whether *Prabodhacandrodaya,* an allegorical drama written by Kṛṣṇamiśra *c.* A.D. 1100, represents the final flowering of a tradition of mystery plays is uncertain, for the only other evidence of it consists in the few fragments of an allegorical drama by Aśvaghoṣa surviving from the 1st century.

Lyrical, Descriptive, and Didactic Poetry.—The medieval Indian poets had a marked predilection for depicting in a single stanza some particular physical or mental situation. Secular lyrical poetry consists chiefly of these little poetic pictures, which form a prominent feature also of dramatic compositions (see *Drama,* above). Numerous poets, both men and women, are known only through such detached stanzas, preserved in native anthologies and manuals of rhetoric and enshrining a vast quantity of descriptive and contemplative poetry. An excellent specimen of a longer poem of a partly descriptive, partly erotic character is Kālidāsa's *Megha-dūta* ("Cloud Messenger"), in which a banished *yakṣa* ("demigod") sends a love message across India to his wife in the Himalayas. This poem describes, in verse pictures written in the stately *mandākrāntā* ("slow-stepping") metre, the places over which the "cloud messenger" will sail. More directly in this tradition are the collections composed by Bhartṛhari on the themes of love, detachment, and wise conduct—the *Śṛṅgāra, Vairāgya,* and *Nīti Śatakas.*

Religious lyrics inspired by sectarian fervour include the large collection of hymns and detached stanzas extolling some special deity that could be made from the *purāṇas* and other works. Of independent productions of this kind only a few of the more important can be mentioned here. Śaṅkara Ācārya (see SHANKARA), the great Vedāntist, is credited with several devotional poems, notably the *Ānanda-laharī* ("Wave of Joy"), a hymn of 103 stanzas in praise of the goddess Pārvatī. The *Sūrya Śataka* ("Century of [Stanzas in Praise of] Sūrya," the Sun) is ascribed to Mayūra, the contemporary (and, according to a tradition, the father-in-law) of Bāṇa (early 7th century).

The particular branch of didactic poetry in which India is especially rich, however, is that of moral maxims, or *subhāṣitas,* in single stanzas or couplets, and forming the chief means of expression of *Nīti Śāstra* ("ethic science").

Fables and Narratives.—For popular instruction, ethical stanzas were early added to existing prose fables and popular stories. A collection of this kind, "A Mirror for Princes," was translated into Pahlavī (Middle Persian) in the reign of the Persian King Khosrau I Anushirvan (A.D. 531–579), but neither this translation nor the original is extant. A Syriac translation exists, however, made from the Pahlavī in the same century. The Sanskrit original, which probably consisted of 14 chapters, was later recast, the result being the *Pañcatantra* ("Five Chapters [or Headings of Wisdom]"), of which several recensions exist. A popular but late summary of this in four books, the *Hitopadeśa* ("Good Counsel"), has been shown to have been composed by one Nārāyaṇa (see also PERSIAN LITERATURE; BIDPAI, FABLES OF; FABLE). Other popular collections of stories and fairy tales, interspersed with sententious verses, are the *Śuka-saptati* ("Seventy [stories related] by the Parrot"), the author and date of which are unknown; and the *Vetālapañcaviṃśati* ("Twenty-Five [stories] of the Vetāla"), which must be earlier than the 11th century since it was used by two 11th-century authors: Somadeva, who composed the *Kathā-sarit-sāgara* ("Ocean of Streams of Story"), a collection of tales in some 22,000 couplets; and Kṣemendra, author of a smaller compilation of tales, the *Bṛhat-kathā-mañjarī.*

SCIENTIFIC AND TECHNICAL LITERATURE

Law (Dharma).—Among the technical treatises of the later Vedic period, certain portions of the *kalpa sūtras* (the manuals of ceremonial; *see* above) peculiar to particular schools are the earliest attempts at a systematic treatment of law subjects. These are the *dharma sūtras* ("rules of [religious] law"), which consist chiefly of strings of terse rules containing the essentials of the science of law and intended to be committed to memory and expounded orally by the teacher—thus forming, as it were, epitomes of class lectures. These rules are interspersed with *gāthās* ("stanzas") in various metres, either composed by the author himself or quoted from elsewhere, each generally giving the substance of the rules immediately preceding it. It can be easily understood why such couplets should have become increasingly popular and should ultimately have led to the appearance of works entirely in verse. Such metrical lawbooks did spring up in large numbers, not all at once but over a long period. These are the metrical *dharma śāstras,* or as they are usually called, the *smṛti* ("recollection, tradition"), a term which, as has been seen, belongs to the whole body of *sūtras* (as opposed to the *śruti,* "revelation") but which has become the almost exclusive title of the versified institutes of law (and of the few *dharma sūtras* still extant). About 40 metrical *smṛtis* are known to exist, but their total number probably amounted to at least 80. The *Mānava Dharma Śāstra,* the most widely known, consists of 12 books, the first and last of which, treating the processes of creation, transmigration, and final beatitude, are, however, generally regarded as later additions. In them the legendary sage Bhṛgu (described as a Mānava) is introduced as a disciple of Manu (*q.v.*), through whom the great teacher's work is promulgated. Except in these two books, this work as a whole shows no special relation to Manu, for, though he is occasionally referred to in it, he is mentioned also in other *smṛtis.*

The oldest existing commentary on the *Mānava Dharma Śāstra* is that by Medhātithi, who is usually supposed to have lived in the 10th century. The most highly esteemed is that by Kullūka Bhaṭṭa, written at Benares (Varanāsī) in the 15th century.

Of importance also is the *Yājñavalkya Dharma Śāstra.* Based on the *Manu Smṛti,* it represents a more advanced stage of legal theory and definition. Yājñavalkya is regarded as the founder of the Vājasaneyins, or White Yajus (*see* above), and as the author of the *Śatapatha Brāhmaṇa.* The work bearing his name bears some resemblance to the *Pāraskara Gṛhya Sūtra* of the White *Yajurveda,* but a connection between it and the *Mānava Gṛhya Sūtra* seems also evident. As in the *Manu Smṛti, ślokas* are quoted in various works from a *Bṛhat* and a *Vṛddha Yājñavalkya.* The *Yājñavalkya Smṛti* consists of three books, corresponding to the three great divisions of the Indian theory of law: *ācāra,* the rule of conduct (social and caste duties); *vyavahāra,* the civil and criminal law; and *prāyaścitta,* penance or expiation. (*See* also CASTE [INDIAN].)

Whether any of the *dharma śāstras* were ever used in India as actual codes of law for the practical administration of justice is doubtful. No doubt they were regarded as being of the highest authority as laying down the principles of religious and civil duty; but it was not so much any single text as the whole body of the *smṛti* that was regarded as the embodiment of the divine law. Hence, the moment the actual work of law codification began, in the 11th century, jurists were engaged in showing practically how the *smṛtis* confirm and supplement one another and in reconciling seeming contradictions between them. This new phase of Indian jurisprudence begins with Vijñāneśvara's *Mitākṣarā,* which, although primarily a commentary on Yājñavalkya, is so rich in original matter and in illustrations from other *smṛtis* that it is far better adapted to serve as a code of law than is the work it professes to explain. This treatise is greatly esteemed all over India, except by the Bengal or Gauriya school of law, which recognizes as its chief authority the digest of its founder, Jīmūtavāhana, especially the chapter on succession, called the *Dāyabhāga.* (*See* also INDIAN LAW.)

Philosophy.—The contemplative Indian mind shows at all times a strong disposition toward metaphysical speculation. This may be seen in the earliest religious lyrics. As well as in the abstract nature of some of even the earliest Vedic deities, this tendency is shown in a certain mystic symbolism, which inclines to refine and spiritualize the originally purely physical character and activity of some of the more important gods and to impart a deep and subtle significance to the rites of the sacrifice. The primitive worship of more or less isolated elemental forces and phenomena had evidently early ceased to satisfy the religious wants of more thoughtful minds. Various syncretist tendencies show the drift of religious thought toward some kind of unity of the divine powers, whether in the direction of pantheism, organized polytheism, or even monotheism. In the latter age of the Vedic hymns the pantheistic idea rapidly gained ground, and found expression in various cosmogonic speculations; and by the *brāhmaṇa* period it was fully developed. The fundamental conception of this doctrine is expressed in the two synonymous terms *brahman* (neuter), probably originally meaning "mystic effusion, devotional utterance," and later "holy impulse"; and *ātman* (masculine), meaning "breath, self, soul."

The recognition of the essential sameness of individual souls, all equally emanating (whether actually or imaginarily) from the ultimate spiritual essence (*parama-brāhman*) "as sparks issue from the fire," and destined to return thither, involves important problems. Considering the infinite diversity of individual souls of the animal and vegetable world, exhibiting various degrees of perfection, is it conceivable that each of them is the immediate efflux of the Supreme Being, the All-Perfect, and that each, from the lowest to the highest, could reunite directly with this Being at the end of its existence on earth? The difficulty implied in this question was at first met by the assumption of an intermediate stage of expiation and purification, a kind of purgatory; but the whole problem found at last a more comprehensive solution in the doctrine of transmigration (*saṃsāra; see* METEMPSYCHOSIS). This doctrine, not found in the *Rigveda*, was probably aboriginal and adopted by the Aryan invaders. The idea of *saṃsāra* has become an axiom, a universally conceded principle of Indian philosophy. Thus this philosophy has never risen to the heights of pure thought; its object is indeed *jijñāsā*, the search for saving knowledge; but it is an inquiry (*mīmāṃsā*) into the nature of things, undertaken not only for the attainment of the truth but with a view to a specific object—the discontinuance of *saṃsāra*, the cessation of mundane existence after the present life. The task of the philosopher is to discover the means of attaining *mokṣa* ("release") from the bondage of material existence, and union with the Supreme Self—in fact, salvation. Desire results from ignorance or from incorrect understanding of the true nature of things, and is the cause of transmigration.

The purpose of each philosophical school is to attain true and saving knowledge. As intense self-contemplation was the only way of attaining this all-important knowledge, this doctrine left little or no room for those mediatorial offices of the priest which are so indispensable to ceremonial worship. Indeed the *Upaniṣads* speak of Brahman sages resorting to Kṣatriya (warrior caste) princes to hear them expound the true doctrine of salvation. But in spite of their antihierarchical tendency, these speculations continued to gain ground; and in the end the body of treatises propounding the pantheistic doctrine, the *upaniṣads*, were admitted into the sacred canon, as appendages to the ceremonial writings, the *brāhmaṇas*. The *upaniṣads* thus form literally "the end of the *Veda*," the *Vedānta;* but their adherents claim this title for their doctrines in a metaphorical rather than in a material sense, as "the ultimate aim and consummation of the *Veda.*"

Later—*i.e.,* very roughly, between the *upaniṣadic* period (*c.* 800–200 B.C.) and the first extant writings of the philosophers in about the 5th or 6th century A.D.—the radical distinction between these speculative appendages and the bulk of the Vedic writings was strongly accentuated in a new classification of the sacred scriptures. According to this scheme they were supposed to consist of two great divisions—the *karma kāṇḍa* ("the work section"), or practical ceremonial (exoteric) part, consisting of the *saṃhitās* and *brāhmaṇas* (including the ritual portions of the *āraṇyakas*), and the *jñāna kāṇḍa* ("the knowledge section"), or speculative (esoteric) part. These two divisions are also called respectively the *pūrva* ("former") and the *uttara* ("latter," or higher) *kāṇḍa;* and when the speculative tenets of the *upaniṣads* came to be formulated into a regular system it was thought desirable that there should also be a special system corresponding to the older, and larger, part of the Vedic writings. Thus there arose the two systems: the *Pūrva* (or *Karma*) *Mīmāṃsā* ("prior [practical] speculation"), and the *Uttara* (or *Brāhma*) *Mīmāṃsā* ("higher inquiry" into the nature of the godhead), usually called the Vedānta philosophy. (For the further development of Indian philosophy, *see* INDIAN PHILOSOPHY: *Six Systems.*)

Grammar (Vyākarana).—*Pāṇini.*—Linguistic inquiry, phonetic as well as grammatical, was early resorted to, both to elucidate the meaning of the *Veda* and to settle its textual form. The work that came ultimately to be looked upon as the "*vedāṅga*" representative of grammatical science, and that has remained the standard authority on Sanskrit grammar in India, is Pāṇini's *Aṣṭādhyāyī* (5th century B.C.), so-called from its consisting of eight lectures (*adhyāya*), each of four *padas.* For a comprehen-sive grasp of linguistic facts and a penetrating insight into the structure of the vernacular language, this work is probably unrivaled in the literature of any nation—though few other languages afford such facilities as Sanskrit for scientific analysis. Pāṇini's system of arrangement differs entirely from that usually adopted in Western grammars, that is, arrangement according to the parts of speech. As the work is written in aphorisms intended to be learned by heart, economy of memory matter was the author's chief consideration. This is attained mainly by grouping together all cases showing the same phonetic or formative feature, whether or not they belong to the same part of speech. For the same reason he also makes use of a highly artificial and ingenious system of algebraic symbols, consisting of technical letters (*anubandha*), used chiefly with suffixes, and indicative of the changes which the roots or stems have to undergo in word formation. (*See also* SANSKRIT LANGUAGE: *The Grammar of Pāṇini.*)

Perhaps the most important of Pāṇini's predecessors was Śākaṭāyana, also mentioned by Yāska—the author of the *Nirukta* (see *Vedāṅgas,* above), who is also supposed to have preceded Pāṇini—as the only grammarian (*vaiyākaraṇa*) who held with the etymologists (*nairukta*) that all nouns are derived from verbal roots.

Kātyāyana.—The earliest of Pāṇini's successors whose work has been preserved (though perhaps not in a separate form) is Kātyāyana, author of a large collection of concise critical notes, called *vārttika,* intended to supplement and correct the *sūtras* or to give them greater precision.

Patañjali.—Kātyāyana was followed by Patañjali (*q.v.*), author of the (*Vyākarana*) *Mahā Bhāshya* ("Great Commentary"), who lived *c.* 150 B.C. For the great variety of information it incidentally supplies about the literature and manners of the period, his is, from a historical and antiquarian point of view, one of the most important works of Classical Sanskrit literature. The *Mahā Bhāshya* is not a continuous commentary on Pāṇini's grammar but a recollection of the critical comments (*kārikās*) on 1,713 of Pāṇini's 4,000 rules.

Other Grammarians.—The successors of Pāṇini and Patañjali continued to flourish with random distinction until as late as the 17th century, but for originality of approach to the subject of Sanskrit grammar, mention must be made of Bhartṛhari (7th century), whose *Vākyapadīya* made a notable contribution to philosophical inquiry into the nature of language.

Lexicography.—Sanskrit dictionaries (*kośa*), always in verse, are either homonymous or synonymous, or partly one and partly the other. There are occasional attempts at alphabetical order in the homonymous dictionaries, but not in the synonymous. Many, intended for use by poets, are collections of rare words and synonyms rather than lexicons of the language. The great dictionary is the *Amara-kośa* ("Immortal Treasury") by Amarasiṃha, who probably lived early in the 6th century. This consists of a synonymous part and a short homonymous part. In the first part the words are arranged in sections according to subjects, such as heaven and the gods, time and the seasons, etc.; in the second part, they are arranged according to their final letter, without regard to the number of syllables.

Prosody (Chandas).—The earliest treatises on prosody are referred to above in the account of the technical branches of later Vedic literature. Among later treatises the most important is the *Mṛta-sañjīvanī,* a commentary on Piṅgala's *Sūtra,* by Halāyudha. Sanskrit prosody, which is probably unsurpassed in variety of metre and harmoniousness of rhythm, recognizes two classes of metres: those consisting of a certain number of syllables of fixed quantity; and those regulated by groups of breves, or metrical instants, this second class being also of two kinds, according to whether or not it is bound by a fixed order of feet.

Music (Saṅgīta).—The art of music has been practised in India from early times. The extant theoretic treatises on music are, however, quite modern productions. The two most highly esteemed works are the *Saṅgīta-ratnākara* ("Jewel Mine of Music"), by Śārṅgadeva; and the *Saṅgīta-darpaṇa* ("Mirror of Music"), by Dāmodara. Each consists of seven chapters, treating: (1) sound and musical notes (*svara*); (2) melodies (*rāga*);

(3) music in connection with the human voice (*prakīrnaka*); (4) musical compositions (*prabandha*); (5) time and measure (*tāla*); (6) musical instruments and instrumental music (*vādya*); (7) dancing and acting (*nrtta* or *nrtya*). (*See also* Indian Music; Music in Ancient Civilizations.)

Rhetoric (Alamkāra Śāstra).—There are numerous treatises on the theory of literary composition. Indeed, a subject of this kind—involving fine distinctions as regards the various kinds of poetic composition, the particular subjects and characters adapted to each, and the different sentiments or mental conditions capable of being both depicted and called forth by them—is naturally congenial to the Indian mind. The *Nātyaśāstra* of Bharata is possibly as early as the 4th century. Not much later is the *Kāvyadarśa* ("Mirror of Poetry") by Dandin, author of the novel *Daśa-kumāra-carita* (*see* above). The *Kāvyadarśa* consists of three chapters: (1) on the two different local styles (*rīti*) of poetry, the Gaudī, or eastern, and the Vaidarbhī, or southern (to which later critics add four others, the Pāñcālī, Māgadhī, Lātī, and Āvantikā); (2) on the graces and ornaments of style, as, for example, tropes, figures, and similes; (3) on alliteration, literary puzzles, and 12 kinds of faults to be avoided in composing poems. Other important works are the *Kāvyamīmāmsā*, by Rājaśekhara, and the *Kāvyalankāra*, by the Kashmiri Rudrata (9th century); the *Daśarūpa* ("Ten Kinds of Drama"), by Dhanamjaya (10th century); the *Sarasvatīkanthābharana* ("Neck Ornament of Sarasvati," the goddess of eloquence), a treatise in five chapters on poetics generally (11th century); the *Kāvyaprakāśa* ("Lustre of Poetry"; 12th century), by Mammata, a Kashmiri; and the late but important *Sāhityadarpana* (*c.* 1450).

Medicine (Āyurveda, Vaidya Śāstra).—Though early knowledge of medicine is attested by frequent allusions in the Vedic writings, it was probably not till much later that medical practice advanced beyond a certain degree of empirical skill and pharmaceutical routine. From the mention of the "three humours" (wind, bile, phlegm) in a *vārttika* to Pānini, some kind of humoral pathology seems, however, to have been prevalent among Indian physicians several centuries before the Christian era. The oldest existing medical work is thought to be the *Caraka Samhitā*, a bulky encyclopaedia in *ślokas* mixed with prose sections. It consists of eight chapters and was probably written for the most part in the early centuries of the Christian era. Of equal authority, but somewhat later, is the *Suśruta* (*Samhitā*), which Suśruta is said to have received from Dhanvantari, the Indian Asclepius. (*See also* Science, History of: *Indian Science: Medicine*.)

Astronomy and Mathematics.—Early Indian astronomical knowledge is summed up in the *Jyotisa Vedānga*. A more scientific approach is marked by the appearance of the five original *siddhāntas* (partly extant in revised redactions and in quotations), even the names of two of which suggest Western influence. These are the *Paitāmaha*, *Vasistha*, *Romaka* (*i.e.*, Roman) and *Paulīśa Siddhāntas*. Based on these are the works of the most distinguished Indian astronomers: Āryabhata (probably b. 476); Varāha-mihira (probably 505–587); Brahmagupta, who completed his *Brāhma-sphuta Siddhānta* in 628; Bhatta Utpala (10th century), distinguished as the commentator of Varāha-mihira; and Bhāskara Ācārya (b. 1114) who finished his course of astronomy, the *Siddhānta Śiromani*, in 1150. In the works of several of these writers, from Āryabhata onward, special attention is paid to mathematical (especially arithmetical and algebraic) computations.

For the development of vernacular Indian literatures and their connection with Sanskrit literature, *see* Indian Literature and articles there cited: Hindī Literature; Urdu Literature; Tamil Literature; Bengali Literature; etc. *See* also articles on some Indian languages, where literature may be treated: *e.g.*, Gujarati Language; Marathi Language; etc.

Bibliography.—*Translations*: R. H. T. Griffith, *Translation of the Rigveda*, 2 vol. (1896–97); K. F. Geldner, *Der Rigveda*, German trans. with notes, 4 vol. (1951); M. Bloomfield, *Hymns of the Atharvaveda* (1897), vol. 42 of the *Sacred Books of the East;* W. D. Whitney, *Atharvaveda Samhitā*, 2 vol. (1905); P. Deussen, *Sechzig Upanishaden* (German trans.), 1897); R. E. Hume, *The 13 Principal Upanishads* (1934); H. Oldenberg, *The Grihyasūtras* (1886), vol. 29 and 30 of the *Sacred Books of the East;* W. Caland, *Das Vaitānasūtra des Atharvaveda* (German trans., 1910); P. C. Roy, *The Mahābhārata* (selections), vol. 1 (1956–   ); M. N. Dutt, *Translation of the Rāmāyana* (1896); F. Edgerton, *Pañcatantra* (1965); A. W. Ryder, *Kālidāsa: Translations of Śakuntalā and Other Works* (1920), *The Ten Princes* (1927); H. H. Wilson, *Specimens of the Theatre of the Hindus*, 2 vol. (1871); C. M. Ridding, *Bāna's Kādambarī* (1896); E. B. Cowell and F. W. Thomas, *Bāna's Harsacarita* (1907); C. H. Tawney, *Ocean of Story*, with notes by N. M. Penzer, 10 vol. (1924–28).

General Histories: A. A. Macdonell, *Sanskrit Literature* (1909), *India's Past* (1927); L. D. Barnett, *Antiquities of India* (1913); A. B. Keith, *History of Sanskrit Literature* (1928); M. Winternitz, *History of Indian Literature*, vol. 1 (1927); S. N. Dasgupta and S. K. De, *History of Sanskrit Literature* (1947).

Works on Special Subjects: A. A. Macdonell and A. B. Keith, *Vedic Index*, 2 vol. (1896–97); A. B. Keith, *Religion and Philosophy of the Veda and Upanisads*, 2 vol. (1925); H. Oldenberg, *Die Religion des Vedas* (1896); P. Deussen, *Philosophie des Vedas* (1896), *Philosophie der Upanishaden* (1899; Eng. trans. 1906); W. Caland, *Altindisches Zauber Ritual* (1900); W. Hopkins, *The Great Epic of India* (1902); H. Jacobi, *Das Rāmāyana* (1893); G. Buhler, *Die indischen Inschriften und das Alter der indischen Kunstpoesie* (1890); A. B. Keith, *The Sanskrit Drama* (1926); S. Levi, *Le Théâtre Indien* (1890); S. K. De, *History of Sanskrit Poetics*, 2nd rev. ed., 2 vol. (1960).

(H. J. E.; J. Al.; J. E. B. G.)

SANSOVINO, ANDREA (*c.* 1467–1529), Florentine architect and sculptor, the outstanding sculptor of the transition from early to high Renaissance, was born at Monte San Savino, probably between 1467 and 1470. His earliest great work was the marble altar of the Sacrament in S. Spirito, Florence, executed for the Corbinelli family between 1485 and 1490, where the fineness of detail, high emotional pitch, and lively narrative quality are typical of his early style. After several years, said by Vasari to have been spent in Portugal, Sansovino was again in Florence in 1502, when he began the marble group of the "Baptism of Christ," now above the central door of the baptistery. The calm and dignified poses, the strong but suppressed emotion, and the generalized beauty of the bodies mark this as one of the first works in the style of the high Renaissance.

In 1505 Sansovino went to Rome and was commissioned by Pope Julius II to execute the almost identical tombs of cardinals Ascanio Sforza and Girolamo Basso della Rovere in S. Maria del Popolo. These tombs, completed by 1509, were the most influential of all Sansovino's innovations with their adaptation of the triumphal arch form and the novel sleeping attitude of the deceased cardinals. Sansovino's last great charge was to supervise (1514–27) both the decoration of the Santa Casa (Holy House of the Virgin) and the construction of several buildings at Loreto. His marble relief of the "Annunciation" on the shrine there is a composition of great richness which still has some of the narrative charm of his very early work. He died at Monte San Savino in 1529.

The influence of Sansovino's suave and graceful style acted as a counterbalance to Michelangelo's titanic and muscular sculpture throughout the 16th century. His most important follower was Jacopo Tatti, called Sansovino after his master.

See J. Pope-Hennessy, *Italian High Renaissance and Baroque Sculpture* (1963), for critical bibliography. (G. H. Hy.)

SANSOVINO, JACOPO (1486–1570), Italian sculptor and architect, whose palaces and churches determined the Renaissance character of Venice, was born in Florence on July 2, 1486. In 1502 he entered the Florence workshop of the sculptor Andrea Sansovino, and soon thereafter, as a sign of admiration, he adopted his master's name in exchange for his own family name of Tatti. In 1505 he accompanied Giuliano da Sangallo to Rome, studying there ancient architecture and sculpture while employed by Pope Julius II in the restoration of ancient statues. Back in Florence he carved, from 1511 to 1518, the statue of St. James the Elder as the first of 12 statues of the apostles for the piers under the dome of the cathedral; these had been commissioned originally in 1503 to Michelangelo, who only began one of them, the St. Matthew. It is the influence of this St. Matthew as well as that of Andrea Sansovino which inspired the "St. James." The "Bacchus" in the Museo Nazionale, Florence, created during the same period, was entirely un-Michelangelesque, full of the uncomplicated movement and gaiety of Hellenistic bronzes. From 1518 Jacopo worked in Rome, first on the Madonna and Child in S. Agostino and, probably slightly later, on the St. James (Sta. Maria di Monserrato), building at the same time the churches of S. Marcello in Corso and S. Giovanni dei Fiorentini.

In 1527, after the sack of Rome by the troops of Emperor Charles V, he fled to Venice, where he remained the rest of his life. Appointed chief architect of the city, he built, on the Grand Canal, the Palazzo Corner (1532), still very austerely Tuscan with two stories of doubled half columns over a rustic base; in 1536 he began the library of S. Marco, with an open loggia on the ground floor and that free and festive decoration which the spirit of Venice demanded; at the same time he built the adjoining mint, with sombre rusticated half columns. The Loggetta, an open porch at the foot of the campanile of S. Marco, was built in 1540 and decorated with four bronze statues of Apollo, Mercury, Minerva, and Peace, symbols of the city's power in war and in the peaceful pursuit of trade and the arts. These figures, elegant, sprightly, strongly moved within themselves, continued an older Venetian tradition that took its inspiration from Titian. The solemn portrait style of the mature Titian is found in a late work, the bronze portrait of the physician Tommaso Rangone over the entrance door to the church of S. Giuliano (1554), which Jacopo also built. The colossal statues of Mars and Neptune in the court of the ducal palace show the severe style of Jacopo's old age (1554–56), as does the monument to the doge Francesco Venier in S. Salvatore (1556–61). Among earlier works are the bronze statuettes of the four evangelists and the bronze door of the sacristy in S. Marco (1540s). The marble statue of the youthful St. John the Baptist (1554) in Sta. Maria de' Frari shows the transition from this style to that of Jacopo's old age. He died in Venice on Nov. 27, 1570.

MANSELL—ALINARI

APOLLO, ONE OF THE FOUR BRONZE STATUES BY JACOPO SANSOVINO (1540–45) ADORNING THE LOGGETTA AT THE FOOT OF THE CAMPANILE OF S. MARCO, VENICE

BIBLIOGRAPHY.—Giorgio Vasari, *Lives*; T. Temanza, *Vita di J. Sansovino* (1752); L. Pittoni, *J. Sansovino* (1909); L. Planiscig, *Venetianische Bildhauer* (1921); H. R. Weihrauch, *Studien zum bildnerischen Werke des Jacopo Sansovino* (1935).　　　(M. Wr.)

SANTA ANA, in area the largest department in El Salvador, bordering Guatemala. Area 768 sq.mi. Pop. (1961) 259,155, about half rural and concentrated in the southern third of the department. Most of the department is rough land; in the southern third there are several volcanoes, including Volcán de Santa Ana (altitude 7,724 ft.), the highest mountain in the country. The northern part has many deep valleys, tributaries of Lempa valley. Santa Ana produces a substantial portion of El Salvador's coffee, mostly on fertile soils on slopes of volcanoes at altitudes between 1,800 and 4,000 ft. It also produces beans, livestock, vegetables, corn, fruits, and cheese. The city of Santa Ana (*q.v.*) is the departmental capital.　　　(C. F. J.)

SANTA ANA, capital of the department of Santa Ana, El Salvador, 44 mi. by Inter-American highway and 50 mi. by railway NW of San Salvador. Pop. (1961) 121,095. It is situated at 2,120 ft. altitude in a rich agricultural area and a few miles north of several high volcanoes and Lake Coatepeque, famous for its beauty, mineral waters, bathing, fishing, and sailing. Santa Ana has modern schools, hospitals, theatres and public buildings, and a colonial cathedral of fine Spanish Gothic architecture. It is important in commerce and industry. Textiles, clothing, foodstuffs, leather goods, liquors, cigars, pottery, and wood products are manufactured. Nine miles west of Santa Ana is the city of Chalchuapa, in the midst of extensive archaeological remains.　　　(C. F. J.)

SANTA ANA, a city in the coastal region of southern California, U.S., 35 mi. SE of Los Angeles (*q.v.*), 10 mi. inland from the ocean shore line, and approximately 40 mi. from the mountain ranges to the north and east; the county seat of Orange County, which comprises the Anaheim-Santa Ana-Garden Grove standard metropolitan statistical area. Santa Ana is on the Los Angeles-San Diego freeway that bears its name; it is also served by the Orange County Airport and the Los Angeles International Airport. The city is within driving range of beach, mountain, and desert resorts. The mixing of cool breezes from the ocean and drier winds from the desert over the coastal plains gives it an ideal climate. The public school system includes facilities through junior college, with special provision for the training of exceptional children. The rich Santa Ana Valley is noted for its oranges, avocados, dairy products, beans, and cattle. The city also possesses some industry. Santa Ana was laid out in 1869 on land procured from Rancho Santiago de Santa Ana, an old Spanish land grant, and was incorporated in 1886. It has a council-manager form of government, in effect from 1952.

Pop. (1960) 100,350. For comparative population figures *see* table in CALIFORNIA: *Population.*　　　(Wm. H. K.)

SANTA ANNA, ANTONIO LÓPEZ DE (1794–1876), Mexican army officer and political figure, the storm centre of Mexican history for half a century, was born the son of a petty colonial official in Jalapa, Veracruz, on Feb. 21, 1794. He became a cadet in the Spanish colonial army in 1810 and for several years served on the northern frontier against Indians and border ruffians. In 1821 he supported the Plan de Iguala, from which emerged independent Mexico (*see* MEXICO: *Colonial Period*). Rebuffed for preferment under the new emperor Agustín de Iturbide—he was already considered a dangerous man—Santa Anna pronounced for the republic which overthrew the empire. After more frontier service he commanded the abortive effort to effect a revolution in Cuba from Yucatán. After helping to overthrow the president he continued his military service in 1829 by defeating an invading Spanish force at Tampico. Following a short retirement he seized power and began the first of five personal administrations, three times as representative of one party and twice as spokesman of the opposition. In 20 years he veered from liberal to ultra-conservative.

He led Mexican troops to suppress the Texan revolt but was captured at San Jacinto in east Texas in 1836. He returned to retirement in Mexico through Washington, D.C., but emerged to fight the French occupation forces at Veracruz. Wounded, he lost a leg; a hero, he again became president until he was exiled to Cuba for incompetence and extravagance. In the Mexican War, after a secret agreement with U.S. Pres. James K. Polk, he assumed the Mexican presidency, but as commander he prematurely rushed his troops to the north, where desert campaigning, complicated by a drawn battle with Gen. Zachary Taylor, cost him an army. Back in Mexico City he re-formed the demoralized government, then engaged Gen. Winfield Scott, who was advancing from Veracruz. He was defeated, his capital was lost, and he returned to exile in Jamaica and New Granada. In 1853 governmental chaos again recalled him to become president, but age had exaggerated his shortcomings and he was again banished in 1855. Ten years later he sought United States support with which to oust Maximilian, whom French forces had placed on the Mexican throne; at the same time he had offered his services to Maximilian. Santa Anna had prostituted his

THE BETTMANN ARCHIVE INC.

ANTONIO LÓPEZ DE SANTA ANNA, PORTRAIT PAINTED BY PAUL L'OUVRIER ABOUT 1858 talents too often; both proposals were refused. A decade later still, a blind and broken old man, he was permitted to return to Mexico City, where he died in poverty on June 21, 1876.

Santa Anna possessed a magnetic personality and real qualities of leadership, but his lack of principles, his pride, love of military glory and extravagance, coupled with disregard for and incompetence in civil affairs, led his country into a series of disasters and himself into obloquy and tragedy.

See also references under "Santa Anna, Antonio López de" in the Index. (W. H. Cт.)

SANTA BÁRBARA, a department in northwestern Honduras, bordering Guatemala, and its capital city. Pop. (1961), department, 146,909; city, 4,915. Area (department) 1,975 sq.mi. The population is chiefly in the Ulúa and tributary mountain valleys in the southern third of the department and in the Chamelecón lowland across the north central part; the mountainous areas in the northern and central portions are sparsely settled. Modern highways connect some settled areas with railways and with the Inter-Ocean highway near San Pedro Sula. About 50% of the area of the department is in farms. Products include coffee and corn, tobacco, sugar, beans, poultry and rice. (C. F. J.)

SANTA BARBARA, a seaside resort and residential city of California, U.S., 97 mi. N.W. of Los Angeles; the county seat of Santa Barbara county. While the city lies on a coastal shelf, it spreads like a fan from curving beaches to the mesas, slopes and oak-covered canyons of the Santa Ynez mountains. Protected by the Channel Islands and the mountains, Santa Barbara has a mild climate throughout the year.

The city's Museum of Natural History has artifacts recording the area's early Indian cultures, and the Santa Barbara Historical society's holdings describe the beginnings of the Spanish presidio in 1782 and the story of the construction of the neoclassical "Queen of the Missions," which was founded in 1786. The mission is now the Franciscan headquarters for the Pacific coast. John Charles Frémont (*q.v.*) raised the U.S. flag at the presidio in 1846, claiming the area for the U.S. (*see* CALIFORNIA: *History*). In 1850 Santa Barbara was incorporated as a city and in 1887 the railroad reached it. Descendants of original Spanish, Mexican and Yankee settlers participate in the annual Old Spanish Days *fiesta*, recalling Santa Barbara's early history. The city is the centre of a rich orchid, citrus, walnut and cattle-raising area with oil fields and light manufacturing.

Nearby are the Vandenberg air force base and many research industries; a campus of the University of California and the Center for the Study of Democratic Institutions, directed by Robert M. Hutchins under the auspices of the Fund for the Republic, are located there. Attractions include an art museum, a music academy, botanical gardens and theatre arts, with multiple opportunities for outdoor recreation and sports. Pop. (1960) 58,-768; standard metropolitan statistical area (Santa Barbara county), 168,962. For comparative population figures *see* table in CALIFORNIA: *Population*.

See *Santa Barbara, a Guide to the Channel City and Its Environs* in the "American Guide Series" (1953). (W. R. J.)

SANTA BÁRBARA ISLANDS, a chain of four islands lying parallel to the southern coast line of California, at an average distance of 20 mi. from the mainland. The term Channel Islands is sometimes used to designate these islands and four others, including Santa Catalina (*q.v.*). All are part of the state of California.

Santa Cruz is the largest of the Santa Barbara Islands, covering nearly 98 sq.mi. The terrain varies from sea-level valleys to sharp-sloped wooded peaks which exceed 2,400 ft. Two ranches and a small military installation have constituted its maximum population. Sheep and cattle raising are the primary enterprises; the island abounds with wild and semiwild sheep which are descendants of former domestic flocks. Prior to the advent of prohibition in 1920 the island was also noted for its fine wines.

Anacapa, the smallest of the group, is a razorbacked volcanic ridge which stretches 4½ mi. but averages less than ½ mi. in width. It is broken into three segments, one of which supports a coast guard station and lighthouse.

Santa Rosa, a cattle ranch, shows a marked change in topography. Its 84 sq.mi. are mostly open grasslands, intersected by numerous spring-fed canyons.

San Miguel is a rapidly eroding uninhabited island made up of 15 sq.mi. of weather-cut ravines and shifting sands. It was once valuable for raising livestock, but heavy overgrazing in the mid-1800s surrendered its soil to the ever-present winds. There are large sea elephant and sea lion colonies on the westernmost tip.

The island chain has plant and animal life not found on the mainland, and there are often differences in characteristics of a plant or animal on one island as compared with the same type on another island.

Juan Rodríguez Cabrillo, who explored the coast of California in 1542–43, is believed to have been buried on one of these islands. He found them populated with the now extinct Canaliño Indians. Two of the eight islands termed Channel Islands, Santa Barbara and Anacapa, were included in the Channel Islands National monument established in 1938. (EA. W.)

SANTA CATALINA, an island near the coast of California, 24 mi. S.S.W. of Los Angeles harbour. The most highly developed of the eight Channel Islands off the coast of southern California, it is 20 mi. long, 8 mi. wide at its greatest width, and has an area of 74 sq.mi. Structurally, Santa Catalina is a small mountain range rising from the continental shelf to a maximum elevation of 2,125 ft. above sea level at Mt. Orizaba. Mountain spurs and canyons transverse to the main range form many interesting headlands and protected coves at the shore line. The climate is of Mediterranean type with warm, dry summers, mild winters and light winter rains. It is generally cooler in summer and milder in winter than the adjacent mainland.

Santa Catalina has been a tourist centre for decades, drawing tens of thousands of visitors annually to its gentle climate, beaches, boating and scenery. Notable attractions are the famous undersea "gardens" near Avalon bay, where luxuriant marine life may be viewed from glass-bottomed boats, and Catalina Bird park. The island's waters, visited throughout the year by thousands of boating enthusiasts and sportfishermen from nearby mainland ports, are noted fishing grounds. Avalon, near the southeastern end of the island, is the only city (population about 1,500) and is the centre of the tourist industry. It has frequent boat and air service from both Long Beach and Los Angeles.

Santa Catalina was discovered in 1542 by Juan Rodríguez Cabrillo, Portuguese navigator in the service of Spain. Sebastián Vizcaíno, also sailing under the flag of Spain, rediscovered the island in 1602 on the eve of the feast of St. Catherine and named it Santa Catalina in honour of the saint. A part of the republic of Mexico after 1822, it became part of California with the signing of the Treaty of Guadalupe Hidalgo ending the Mexican War in 1848. Its development as a tourist centre dates from 1919, when it was purchased by William Wrigley. (R. A. K.)

SANTA CATARINA, a southern state of Brazil, bounded on the north by Paraná, on the east by the Atlantic ocean, on the south by Rio Grande do Sul and on the west by the Argentine territory of Misiones. Area 37,060 sq.mi. Pop. (1960) 2,146,909.

Immediately behind the coast the Great Escarpment rises like a mountain wall, and the state contains very little level land. Only along the lower Itajaí river and around Joinvile and São Francisco are there narrow bits of wet lowland. Santa Catarina Island, on which the state capital, Florianópolis (*q.v.*), is situated, is a ridge of steep hills. The Great Escarpment in the state is broken into a series of steps, deeply dissected by the Itajaí-Açu and its tributaries. Above the scarp, the surface of the Paraná plateau slopes gently westward, drained by the Uruguai river. The coastal zone is hot and rainy, but on the plateau frosts are sometimes experienced in the winter. The southernmost extension of the tropical rain forest occurs along the coast, but in the frost zone at higher altitudes the forest comprises a mixture of broadleaf deciduous trees and taller *Araucaria* pines. Among the latter are grassy openings, originally covered with tall prairie grasses.

The first settlements by the Portuguese from São Paulo were on the prairies of the highlands and on Santa Catarina Island off the shore. The dense coastal forests were left empty until the arrival of German colonists after 1850. Blumenau, in the valley of the Itajaí, was one of the first German towns, and Brazilians of German origin have now spread out from Blumenau throughout the coastal zone and in the valleys of the plateau. Colonies of Italians and Poles also settled in this state.

The economy of the area is varied. The farmers grow maize, to be fed to hogs, and also wheat, potatoes, tobacco, rice and a variety of fruits and vegetables. The chief industries include meat processing, vegetable and fruit canning, textile milling, maté processing (from the leaves of the yerba maté tree), sawmilling and brewing. A paper factory is in operation at Blumenau. The best coal in Brazil is mined 69 mi. N.W. of Tubarão along the southern coast.

(P. E. J.)

SANTA CLARA (locally Villa Clara), capital of Las Villas province, Cuba, about 160 mi. ESE of Havana. It is situated near the geographic centre of the island on the Central Highway and is the junction point of the main railroads of Cuba. Initially dependent on the livestock industry, it flourished on sugar and tobacco in the 20th century. Pop. (1953) 77,398.

The city was founded in 1689 by 18 families from Remedios, escaping constant dangers of pirates. It occupies the site of the ancient Indian Cubanacán, which according to some authorities Columbus mistakenly took to be the headquarters of Kublai Khan.

(D. R. D.)

SANTA CLARA, a city of Santa Clara County in west-central California, U.S., 48 mi. S of San Francisco and immediately adjacent to the city of San Jose (q.v.) on the southeast; a part of the San Jose standard metropolitan statistical area. Santa Clara has a mean temperature of 57° F (about 14° C) and an annual rainfall of 15.19 in. Founded in 1777 as the eighth of the Spanish Franciscan missions in California—hence its title "the Mission city"—it was incorporated as a city in 1852 and adopted the council-manager form of government in 1952. The Spanish influence is evident in place names, architecture and the restored mission. The city's economy historically rested upon the processing of prunes, apricots, and other fruits and vegetables of the rich Santa Clara Valley. In 1941, however, manufacturing for the first time surpassed agriculture in importance and World War II accelerated the industrial trend; after 1950 the population increased considerably. Leading classes of products from the manufacturing plants include glass fibre, millwork, electrical machinery, chemicals, fabricated metals, processed foods, and paper products. The University of Santa Clara, the oldest institution of higher learning in the west, was founded by the Jesuits in 1851 as a college and became a university in 1885.

Pop. (1960) 58,880. For comparative population figures *see* table in California: *Population*.

(J. J. Ha.)

SANTA CRUZ, ÁLVARO DE BAZÁN, Marqués de (1526–1588), the most famous and successful Spanish admiral of his time, who was responsible for the preparation of the Spanish Armada (q.v.), was born at Granada on Dec. 12, 1526. From an early age he fought against the Turks in the Mediterranean. He was given the command of the galleys of Naples in 1568 and was created marqués de Santa Cruz in 1569. In the Lepanto campaign (1571) against the Turks he was Don John of Austria's principal Spanish adviser, and in the Battle of Lepanto (q.v.; Oct. 7, 1571) he commanded the reserve and intervened decisively when the Turks threatened to outflank the Christian fleet. In 1580 he commanded the fleet which supported the duque de Alba's successful conquest of Portugal for Philip II of Spain. Meanwhile Antonio, the Prior of Crato, the pretender to the Portuguese throne, still held the Azores with the help of warships sent unofficially from France. Santa Cruz defeated the superior French squadron at Terceira (1583) and thus captured the Azores for Philip II. Despite the protests of his own soldiers he executed all his prisoners "for the service of God, of the king our master and of the king of France," as he reported to Spain. His excuse for this action was that France and Spain were not officially at war. Philip II accepted the argument and made him captain-general of the ocean.

From 1583 Santa Cruz urged on Philip II the invasion of England and, in 1586, he presented a memorandum for a fleet of 556 ships and 94,000 soldiers and sailors. From then until his death,

on Feb. 9, 1588, he was in Lisbon, fitting out the Armada and battling against shortages of money and materials and with the king's contradictory orders. It is unlikely that even his leadership would have made the Armada campaign (summer 1588) a success, but he had done much to develop the Spanish navy and had designed the great galleons which traded between Spain and the New World.

Bibliography.—C. Fernández Duro, *La Armada Invencible*, 2 vol. (1884–85); A. Altolaguirre y Duvale, *Don Álvaro de Bazán* (1888); G. Mattingly, *The Defeat of the Spanish Armada* (1959).

(H. G. Ko.)

SANTA CRUZ, a very sparsely inhabited province of southern Argentina, composing a large part of the area generally known as Patagonia (q.v.). The province, which was created by a decree of the federal government in 1956 (with effect from Jan. 1, 1957), is bounded north and south by the 46th and 52nd parallels. It stretches from the Atlantic Ocean to the Chilean frontier in the cordillera of the Andes. Pop. (1960) 52,853. Area 94,186 sq.mi. Santa Cruz is a region of constant winds and dust storms which sweep over its dry table lands and its arid, precipitous coast. Rainfall is slight. In spite of the latitude, however, the climate is relatively mild, the temperature being moderated by the proximity of the ocean. The western rim of the province includes forested Andean foothills and a number of beautiful lakes, notably Lake Argentino, which can be reached by traveling up the Santa Cruz River from the port of Santa Cruz. Huge glaciers descend from the cordillera into this lake.

There are sheep ranches in the sheltered canyons that cross the desert, but little agriculture. The province's principal line of communication is the shipping service which links its Atlantic ports, where the produce of the interior (mainly wool and sheepskins) is collected for dispatch to Buenos Aires. The southernmost port is Río Gallegos, the provincial capital, which is a centre for the sheep trade and has a meat-packing plant and a tallow-making industry. It is also the outlet for Argentina's chief coalfield at Río Turbio (160 mi. inland), with which it is connected by railway. The other principal ports are Santa Cruz (about 135 mi. N of Gallegos) and Puerto Deseado (about 185 mi. N of Santa Cruz). A railway runs inland from Deseado to Colonia las Heras. Across the northern border, in the province of Chubut, are the military zone and the oil fields of Comodoro Rivadavia.

(Ge. P.)

SANTA CRUZ, a department in the lowland region of eastern Bolivia, bounded north by Beni, east by Brazil, south by Paraguay and Chuquisaca, and west by Chuquisaca and Cochabamba. It is a frontier area of extraordinary economic potential lying between the Andes and the Mato Grosso Plateau. Pop. (1961 est.) 314,-000. Area 143,097 sq.mi. The topography is generally level, with a few gently rising elevations, notably the Chiquitos Highlands. Average annual rainfall, coming largely from October through March, ranges from 100 in. in the north to 50 in. in Santa Cruz city and less farther south. The department is drained by two river systems, flowing north, which converge in the northeastern corner of Beni. The first comprises the Rio Grande, Piray, Yapacani, and Maraco, upper tributaries of the Mamoré; the second comprises the San Miguel, Blanco, Baures, and Paraguá, tributaries of the Iténez (Guaporé). A few smaller streams flow eastward into the Paraguay. About 40% of the department is prairie and the remainder is woodland. Except for the northern part, which is flooded during the rainy season, the region is quite healthful and has an agreeable climate. The prairie affords good pasturage, and the cleared forest land is unusually fertile. Rice, sugarcane, coffee, cotton, manioc, corn, citrus fruits, vegetables, and tobacco are the most commonly produced items, but agriculture in the 1960s was still in an infant stage of development owing to the historic isolation of the area. The region supports 500,000 cattle and large numbers of horses. The population is about one-third of Spanish colonial descent and two-thirds mestizos and Indians.

Post-World War II developments included the completion of three important transportation facilities: a highway 312 mi. in length connecting the department with Cochabamba and the Altiplano; the Corumbá (Braz.)-Santa Cruz Railway, providing an outlet to the Atlantic ports of Brazil; and another railway extending from the Argentine frontier to Santa Cruz. Oil exploration and production in the Camiri area were significantly advanced by several foreign companies together with the Bolivian government corporation (Yacimientos Petrolíferos Fiscales Bolivianos). Pipelines extend to Sucre and Cochabamba. Petroleum deposits are found throughout much of the sub-Andean zone of Bolivia. Agriculture was enhanced by the introduction of immigrants, chiefly Okinawans and Japanese, and by land reform laws.

The city of Santa Cruz (pop. [1961 est.] 69,560), founded by the Spanish explorer Nuflo de Chávez in 1560, is the capital and only town of consequence in the department. It is situated on the Piray at 1,575 ft. elevation. Local industries comprise sugar mills, distilleries, sawmills, tanneries, furniture and leather goods factories, and food-processing plants. The railways converge on Santa Cruz; it is the terminus of the Cochabamba Highway, and air service facilities are available.   (J. L. Tr.)

SANTA CRUZ, a city of California, U.S., 80 mi. S of San Francisco on the northern promontory of Monterey Bay; the county seat of Santa Cruz County. The scenic beauty of the area and its mild climate are its foremost attractions. The area is enhanced by clumps of redwoods which increase to forest proportions in the Santa Cruz Mountains just north of the city. The state of California has incorporated much of this area into a state park.

The city was founded by the Franciscans in 1791 and became one of the mission links whereby Spanish civilization was extended all the way from San Diego to San Francisco. The U.S. flag was raised over the town in 1846 and the town was chartered as a city in 1876. The city's growth has been steady with a marked increase after 1950 resulting from the increasing industrialization of the area. In agriculture, Santa Cruz has made marked progress, especially in horticulture. Strawberries are grown almost the year around, and loganberries thrive, having originated in the region (*see* Loganberry). Artichokes are produced in abundance, as are cherries, apples, and grapes. The area also excels in the production of bulbs.

One of the features of Santa Cruz attractive to thousands of tourists is its magnificent sweep of beach. To accommodate these crowds the city has built several facilities, including a long wharf which extends a half mile into the bay. The bay also affords a considerable income from fishing. Santa Cruz has a council-manager form of government, in effect from 1948, and a public junior college called Cabrillo. For comparative population figures *see* table in California: *Population.*   (B. L. B.)

SANTA CRUZ DE TENERIFE, chief seaport and capital of Tenerife, one of the Canary Islands (*q.v.*), on the northeast coast. Pop. (1960) 133,100. The town occupies a small plain, mainly between two usually waterless ravines. Except where irrigated, the neighbourhood is arid and abounds in cacti and euphorbias. Santa Cruz was founded in 1494 but had only 16,689 inhabitants by 1877. Then the banana and tomato trade and, later, harbour improvements and the tourist trade caused rapid growth. The many notable public buildings include the fine parish church of the Concepción, two museums, a theatre, and a bullring. The water supply comes by aqueduct from the interior mountains. The well-planned seafront adjoins a harbour sheltered by two moles with, in parts, up to 40 ft. depth alongside. Santa Cruz is an important oil-bunkering port with an oil refinery. It is linked with the rest of the island by various roads and there is a railway service to La Laguna. The airport of Los Rodeos is 5½ mi. (9 km.) NW of the town.

A treasure fleet in Santa Cruz was largely destroyed by a British fleet under Robert Blake in 1657. Horatio Nelson lost his right arm there during an unsuccessful assault in 1797, and two British flags captured then hang in the parish church. Gen. Francisco Franco, then captain general of the Canaries, organized in .Santa Cruz the national rising that led to the Spanish Civil War in 1936.   (R. P. Be.)

SANTA ELENA PENINSULA, in southwestern Guayas Province, Ecuador. On the peninsula is Ecuador's one important oil field. Libertad has a small refinery. Also on the peninsula are salt-extracting works and a popular seaside resort. Ores of sulfur,

platinum, and gold are said to exist but in the early 1960s had not been developed. The peninsula offers fine recreational facilities at Salinas, 75 mi. W of Guayaquil, which has ocean beaches and an arid climate. It is the northernmost extension of the west-coast desert of South America, only 2°12′ S of the Equator.
    (P. E. J.)

SANTA FE, a province of central Argentina, between the Chaco in the north and the province of Buenos Aires in the south. Pop. (1960) 1,865,537. Area 51,354 sq.mi. The two chief cities are the provincial capital, Santa Fe, and Rosario (*qq.v.*), which is the second largest city in the republic. The province lies almost entirely within the great humid pampas region and has no wooded land in the south except along the river courses. In the north there are extensive forests of commercially valuable woods, interspersed with grassy fields. The surface is a level alluvial plain and the soil is among the most productive in the country. The climate is healthy and moderate, with mean annual temperatures ranging from 63° F in the south to 68° in the north. Annual rainfall varies from 28 to 35 in. and is more abundant in the river littoral region than in the interior.

The leading crops are alfalfa (lucerne), maize, wheat, and flax (the order of importance changes according to world prices and government subsidies), together with oats, rye, and barley. In the northern part of the province peanuts, tobacco, sugarcane, and cotton are grown. Although agriculture is the chief source of wealth, the livestock industry is well developed. The ratio of agriculture to cattle raising varies with alterations in prices and subsidies, as both are competing for the same land. In addition to beef and dairy cattle, large numbers of pigs are raised. The principal industries are based on dairy and forest products, and there are large sugar refineries, flour mills, breweries, and distilleries.

The provincial capital has exceptionally good communications with the surrounding country. It is served by the Mitre and Belgrano railways (300 mi. to Buenos Aires) and is the centre of a highway network which includes roads southward to Rosario (100 mi.) and northward to Formosa (500 mi.). The capital has an airport. But the traditional line of communication is by the Paraná River. Oceangoing steamers can reach the town of Santa Fe, which has adequate docks to receive them, and the province's long littoral has many small ports where the farmers of the interior can load their products onto the steamers that ply up and down the Paraná. The ports are linked by regular river services with Buenos Aires (downstream) and Corrientes and Paraguay (upstream).   (Ge. P.)

SANTA FE, Argentine city and capital of the province of the same name, located on a channel of the Paraná River approximately 300 mi. NW of Buenos Aires. Pop. (1960) 208,350. It was founded in 1573 by a group of settlers under Juan de Garay as Santa Fe de Vera Cruz, several years before the final establishment of Buenos Aires, as a supporting port for the Spanish settlement at Asunción, Parag. During the colonial period it served as a centre for Jesuit missionary activity; the Jesuit college and church date from 1660. Until mid-19th century the city marked the northern limit of provincial expansion and served as a strategic outpost against the Indians of the Chaco region. During the national period the city was one of the centres which attempted to counteract the growing dominance of Buenos Aires. The Argentine constitution was adopted by an assembly at Santa Fe in 1853. In the mid-1850s the first agricultural colonies of European immigrants in Argentina were established north and west of the city. The national University of the Littoral is a 20th-century addition to the culture of Santa Fe. Modernization of the port facilities in 1911 made it possible for oceangoing vessels to reach the city, and considerable river trade is carried on with Paraná, capital of Entre Ríos, across the Paraná River from Santa Fe. Railroads and highways link the city with the Chaco frontier and the provinces of Santiago del Estero and Córdoba. There is an airport at Sauce Viejo just outside the city. Although Rosario remains the major port of the province, Santa Fe serves as an outlet for the cotton, flax, and grain from the northern area.   (Js. R. S.)

SANTA FE, capital of New Mexico, U.S., and seat of Santa Fe county, is located in the north central part of the state on the Santa Fe river, a tributary of the Rio Grande, about 60 mi. N.E. of Albuquerque. Lying about 7,000 ft. above sea level at the foot of the southern extremity of the Sangre de Cristo mountains, the city has a dry, invigorating climate which makes it a popular summer resort, while skiing in the nearby mountains attracts winter visitors.

About half of the city's permanent residents are Spanish-speaking. (For comparative population figures *see* table in NEW MEXICO: *Population*.) In 1955 Santa Fe adopted a council-manager form of government.

The oldest continuously used seat of government and one of the earliest European settlements in North America, Santa Fe was founded about 1610 by Don Pedro de Peralta, governor of the "Kingdom of New Mexico," to serve as his capital. Officially named Villa Real de la Santa Fé de San Francisco de Asis ("Royal City of the Holy Faith of St. Francis of Assisi"), Santa Fe developed around a central plaza and along the still-extant irrigation ditches leading from the Santa Fe river, becoming a centre of Spanish exploration and Franciscan missionary work in New Mexico. In 1680 the Pueblo Indians revolted, and laid siege to Santa Fe, which was eventually evacuated. It remained in Indian hands until in 1692 Diego de Vargas reconquered New Mexico and secured the fresh submission of the Pueblos. The re-entry of the Spanish into the city is marked by an annual fiesta.

During the 18th century Santa Fe developed a trade in sheep, wool and pelts, chiefly with Chihuahua, Mex., and the Plains Indians. It was also administrative, military and ecclesiastical headquarters of a vast, sparsely populated Spanish frontier province. United States interest in Santa Fe was aroused by the report of Lieut. Zebulon M. Pike (*q.v.*) who was imprisoned there during his exploration of the southwest in 1806. After Mexican independence (1821) a brisk wagon-train commerce developed with the U.S. over the Santa Fe trail (*q.v.*) to Missouri. In Aug. 1846, during the Mexican War, the city was occupied without resistance by U.S. forces under Gen. Stephen Watts Kearny. The city's first English-language newspaper was established in 1847.

Bishop John B. Lamy, important in the cultural life of New Mexico and inspiration for "Bishop Latour" in Willa Cather's novel *Death Comes for the Archbishop*, was appointed first bishop of the diocese (archdiocese from 1875) of Santa Fe in 1851. Through his efforts schools were founded and a hospital built. In 1862 the city was occupied for two weeks by Confederate forces under Gen. H. H. Sibley. The railroad arrived in 1880 but the main line passed through Lamy, 18 mi. S. of Santa Fe, and in 1894 the last garrison troops were withdrawn. Brief mining booms in the nearby mountains toward the end of the 19th century did not materially enlarge Santa Fe, which remained a trading centre for ranchers, farmers and Indians.

The 20th century has seen much literary and artistic activity in Santa Fe, much of it with a regional character, as well as archaeological and anthropological research in the surrounding Indian country. By 1940 tourism had become the city's second largest source of income, exceeded only by government payrolls. Construction in the early 1940s of the Los Alamos Scientific laboratories for atomic research, 35 mi. N.W. of Santa Fe, brought new economic vitality to the area.

Santa Fe's charm resides chiefly in its narrow, irregular streets, the unexpected intrusion of greenery and its domestic architecture. Aside from the plaza, the main points of interest in the heart of Santa Fe are the Governor's palace (built by Peralta in 1610 and restored as a museum in 1914), continuously occupied by Spanish, Mexican and U.S. governors from 1610 to 1909; the chapel of San Miguel (mid-17th century, rebuilt in 1710, restored in 1955); the "Oldest House," believed to be partly of pre-Spanish Indian construction; the Prince patio, now devoted to shops; the Cathedral of St. Francis (1869), built by Bishop Lamy on the site of two earlier churches; and numerous private houses in the older section. Built of adobe brick, the traditional low, flat-roofed Spanish-American dwelling with its walled garden adds much to the foreign appearance of the city.

In the 20th century the native architectural idiom, often com-

bined with Pueblo-Indian elements, has been adapted to larger buildings, including the Laboratory of Anthropology (1933), the regional headquarters of the national park service (1942) and the Church of Cristo Rey (1939), probably the largest adobe edifice in the U.S. With the traditional architectural character of Santa Fe threatened by a growing population, public action resulted in the passage of a historical zoning ordinance (1958) designed to protect the harmonious atmosphere of the older section of the city.

The absence of any important industry, the large Spanish-American population, the influence of numerous writers, artists, musicians and craftsmen, and the dignity associated with a state capital and an archdiocesan cathedral combine to give Santa Fe a diversified and sophisticated cultural life. The Museum of New Mexico occupies five buildings: the Governor's palace (archaeological and historical exhibits and historical library), the Hall of Ethnology, the Laboratory of Anthropology, the Museum of International Folk Art and the Art gallery. The privately endowed Museum of Navaho Ceremonial Art, the State School for the Deaf and an Indian school under the U.S. department of the interior are also located there. (J. B. JA.)

SANTA FE TRAIL, the famed wagon trail from Independence, Mo., to Santa Fe, N.M., and an important commercial route for 59 years, from 1821 to 1880, when the last section of the railroad was completed. It is possible that in 1541 the Spaniard Francisco Vázquez de Coronado traveled portions of what became the trail, and it is known that in 1806 Zebulon Montgomery Pike, the U.S. government explorer, passed over sections of it. A commercial venture was attempted by William Morrison, an Illinois merchant, who sent Jean Baptiste LaLande with trading goods to Santa Fe in 1804. Neglecting to account to Morrison, LaLande settled in Santa Fe, where Captain Pike saw him in 1807. That the Spaniards were hostile to foreign traders is shown by the reception given Robert McKnight's trading expedition of 1812. Arriving after a revolt against the Spaniards had been suppressed, McKnight and members of his party were imprisoned in Spanish jails until after Mexico won independence from Spain in 1821.

The earliest successful commercial expedition was that of William Becknell, who in 1821 made a profitable journey with $300 worth of goods on pack animals and returned the next year to open the trail with wagons. Although Becknell has been called father of the trail, a number of other traders, John McKnight, Hugh Glenn, Jacob Fowler and Stephen Cooper, followed close on his heels.

The Missouri river terminus was first Franklin, Mo., then Independence, and later Westport, now Kansas City, Mo. When the early traders set out in May of each year they at first used horses, but these were replaced in subsequent years by teams of mules or oxen, sometimes five or six pairs to a wagon. Though Santa Fe had gold and silver, together with furs, skins and a plentiful supply of wool, the simplest manufactured goods were

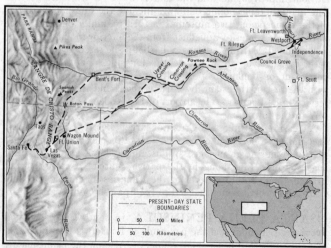

THE ROUTE OF THE SANTA FE TRAIL BETWEEN INDEPENDENCE, MO., AND SANTA FE, N.M.

in great demand. On the westward route the huge wagons were crammed almost to overflowing with hardware and assorted dry goods. After arriving in July and reaching an understanding with Mexican customs officials, most traders sold their cargoes and departed in August with a net profit that ranged from 20% to 40%, though there were some who sold for a loss.

A significant portion of the goods carried to Santa Fe was shipped on to interior parts of northern Mexico and to California. Before 1843 there were no yearly shipments of goods worth more than $450,000, according to Josiah Gregg. Yet it is safe to assume, from other records, that the trade increased.

From its terminus in Missouri the main trail followed almost a straight line for nearly 800 mi. The first of four sections of the journey was from Independence over grasslands to the green meadows and woods of Council Grove in what is now Kansas. Here the freighters organized their train for protection against marauding Indians and made any necessary repairs, aided by a resident blacksmith. From Council Grove to the river crossing west of the Big Bend on the Arkansas was a second division. The traders then moved from the ford on the Arkansas across the arid, desolate Cimarron desert, and finally, in the fourth section of the trip, to the more hospitable grasses and cedars east of Santa Fe.

An alternative route, to avoid the hot, dry Indian country of the Cimarron, was to follow the Arkansas river westward to an adobe stockade near modern La Junta, Colo., called Bent's Fort (see BENT, CHARLES), the leading trading post of the American southwest. Thence the mountain route turned southward through the Raton pass to meet the main trail. This route, though mountainous, had the advantages of better water supply, opportunities for trading at Bent's Fort and less danger from Indians. Yet there were few Indian attacks on any portion of the trail. Josiah Gregg reported that only 11 men were killed by Indians in the period before 1843. Traveling in parallel columns, the wagons could easily form a circle to protect livestock and repel attacking warriors.

The Santa Fe trail was not the one-way wilderness highway of the pioneer settler and his family. Rather it was the two-way route of international trade. Contemporaries have described in their journals the variety of merchants and frontiersmen who sought adventure and profit on the road to Santa Fe. These men opened and maintained a prairie thoroughfare that brought bullion into the United States (especially needed in the years following the panic of 1837), gave Missouri its celebrated mules and helped dispel the notion that the southwest was the great American desert. The traders came to know the varied routes of the southwest and reported weaknesses of the Mexican military forces. Indirectly they hastened United States expansion and prepared the way for assent to U.S. control which came in 1846, when Col. Stephen W. Kearny entered Santa Fe without opposition at the beginning of the Mexican War. Under U.S. rule the Santa Fe trade continued to flourish, especially after U.S. mail by stagecoach was instituted in 1849. In the period after the Civil War the yearly freight expeditions persisted until the tracks of the Santa Fe railroad in 1880 ended the wagon caravans.

See Josiah Gregg, *Commerce of the Prairies*, 2 vol. (1844 and numerous later editions), the classical account of the trail; R. L. Duffus, *The Santa Fe Trail* (1930), a readable and entertaining account.

(W. R. J.)

SANTAL, a tribal people of eastern India; in the 1960s the latest population figure available (from the 1951 census) was about 2,811,000. Areas of greatest concentration are: Bihar (districts of Santal Parganas, Hazaribagh, Manbhum, Singhbhum); Bengal (Midnapur, Burdwan, Bankura); Orissa (Mayurbhanj). Their language is Santali, a dialect of Kherwari, a Munda language. In physical type they belong to the proto-Australoid group, characterized by short stature, dark skin, wavy to curly hair, and broad flat nose. (*See* MUNDA LANGUAGES; MUNDA PEOPLES.)

Many Santal are employed seasonally or permanently in the coal mines near Asansol or the steel factories in Jamshedpur, while others work during part of the year as paid agricultural labourers. In the villages, where tribal life continues, the most important economic activity is the cultivation of rice. Each village has a hereditary headman who, assisted by a council of elders, administers the affairs of the village; he also has some religious and ceremonial functions. A special headman is charged with the supervision of morals. Two priests perform the duties of sacrificing on behalf of the villagers. Groups of villages are linked together in a larger territorial unit termed a pargana, which also has a hereditary headman. Traditionally men of the pargana met together annually to hunt and to settle disputes involving the members, and the custom persists where game may be found.

The Santal have a patrilineal exogamous clan organization. The clans, 12 in number, are each divided into a number of subdivisions, also based on descent. Membership in the clan and subclan carries certain injunctions and prohibitions with regard to style of ornaments, food, house type, and religious ritual. Marriage, endogamous with respect to the tribe as a whole, is normally arranged by the parents; payment of bridewealth (*q.v.*) and the marking of the bride's head with vermilion are essential features of the ceremony. Marriage is generally monogamous; polygyny, though permitted, is rare.

Religion centres around the worship of spirits by means of periodic public sacrifices to avert disease and ensure rainfall. The ancestral spirits of the headmen are objects of an important cult.

See also SANTAL PARGANAS.

BIBLIOGRAPHY.—L. O. Skefsrud, *The Traditions and Institutions of the Santals*, trans. by P. O. Bodding (1942); W. J. Culshaw, *Tribal Heritage: a Study of the Santals* (1949); N. Datta-Majumdar, "The Santal, a Study in Culture Change," Government of India Department of Anthropology, *Memoir No. 2, 1955* (1956); J. Gausdal, *The Santal Khuts* (1960); N. K. Das Gupta, *Problems of Tribal Education and the Santals* (1963). (D. M. SP.)

SANTALACEAE, the sandalwood family of dicotyledonous, semiparasitic shrubs, trees, and herbs of tropical and temperate regions. There are about 30 genera and about 400 species. *Santalum album* is the true sandalwood (*q.v.*). The bastard toadflax, a North American species of *Commandra*, is sometimes parasitic. Another North American species is oil nut or buffalo nut (*Pyrularia pubera*) of the Appalachian region. *Thesium humifusum*, also called bastard toadflax, is native to Great Britain and is a herbaceous root parasite.

SANTAL PARGANAS, a district of the Bhagalpur division of Bihar, India. Area 5,470 sq.mi. Pop. (1961) 2,675,203. It consists of three regions: a strip of alluvial country along the Ganges; a north-south, basaltic, forested, hilly tract (Rajmahal Hills) in the east-central part; and a rolling gneissic peneplain in the west and south. The Rajmahal Hills mark the eastern limit of the hot winds that sweep the Gangetic plain during the hot season. The administrative headquarters of the district are at Dumka (pop. [1961] 18,720). The main crops are rice, maize (corn), and oilseeds. Coal is mined in the small Jainti field. Pakur is the chief centre of the shellac industry.

The Santals (*see* SANTAL), numbering 829,029 in 1941, had begun to migrate from Chota Nagpur and adjoining districts in the late 18th century. The oppression of landlords, the exactions of moneylenders, and the consequent loss of land caused a rebellion (the Santal War) in 1855–56. This led to the setting up of a form of administration acceptable to the immigrants. The Daman-i-Koh ("the skirts of the hills"), a government estate of more than 1,000 sq.mi., was established as a reserve for them and other tribal peoples, such as the Paharias. (E. AH.)

SANTA MARIA, the southeasternmost island of the Portuguese Azores Archipelago in the North Atlantic Ocean. Area 37 sq.mi. Pop. (1960) 13,164. Administratively it is part of Ponta Delgada District. Its capital, Vila do Pôrto (pop. 5,373), founded in the 1430s, is the oldest town in the Azores. Columbus, returning from his first voyage to America (1493), called at Anjos on its northern coast. Limestone found on Santa Maria is mixed with volcanic material and used for building. The people are engaged in whaling and cattle raising and grow cereals and vines. On the western plateau is an important international airport (originally constructed as a U.S. air base in 1944) for transatlantic flights. *See also* AZORES. (J. AO.)

SANTA MARIA, a town in Rio Grande do Sul state, Braz., located near the head of the Jacuí Valley, 150 mi. W of Pôrto Alegre. Pop. (1960) 78,682. It is an important railroad centre at the crossing of the main line running from São Paulo to the Uruguay border and the main line running from Pôrto Alegre to the Argentine border. It is also served by an airfield and is the junction of several major highways. Industries include railroad shops, breweries, tanneries and meat-processing plants. Santa Maria carries on a large trade in livestock, alfalfa, rice, wine, fruit, maté, coal and timber. The town was once called Santa Maria da Bocca do Monte (St. Mary of the Mountain's Mouth) because of its position at the foot of the Serra Geral. (P. E. J.)

SANTA MARTA, a Caribbean port city of Colombia, capital of the department of Magdalena, on a small bay 40 mi. ENE of the mouth of the Magdalena River. Pop. (1964) 89,161; metropolitan area, 104,471. Santa Marta was founded by Rodrigo de Bastidas in 1525 and is the oldest city of Colombia. From there Gonzalo Jiménez de Quesada led the celebrated expedition inland to found Santa Fe de Bogotá (*see* BOGOTÁ). Connected by swampy channels and lakes with the river, Santa Marta became a port for colonial New Granada. Like its more famous neighbour, Cartagena (*q.v.*), it was occasionally attacked and sacked by foreign corsairs. Simón Bolívar, hero of the independence wars, died at an estate on the edge of the town in 1830. Santa Marta's commerce overtook that of Cartagena in the mid-19th century but then experienced a decline, chiefly because the channels to the Magdalena were inadequate for steamboats. In the 1880s Santa Marta began shipping bananas grown in the hinterland to the south; the United Fruit Company dominated the industry after 1899. Its success was especially striking after the completion of the Santa Marta–Fundación railroad. This industry was almost killed by a plant disease in the early 1940s but later revived. The Atlantic Railroad, completed in 1961, was the city's first rail connection with Bogotá, the national capital. In the late 1960s the beaches and hotels attracted many tourists. The city is a bishopric seat and has a cathedral. (T. E. N.)

SANTA MONICA, an oceanside resort and residential city in northwestern Los Angeles county, Calif., U.S., and a part of the Los Angeles standard metropolitan statistical area. It is known for its excellent beaches and its suburban homes.

Santa Monica was given its name by Spanish soldiers, who applied it to a spring near the modern city. From 1828 to 1872 it was part of a large ranch owned by Don Francisco Sepulveda. In 1872 the area was acquired by Col. R. S. Baker as a sheep farm.

The city appeared three years later, in 1875, as a result of the railroad craze of the 1870s. Santa Monica was selected as the Pacific coast terminus of the Los Angeles to Independence railroad, built to compete with the dominant Southern Pacific. The railroad advertised the advantages of the location as a resort area, an auction of land was held and the settlement of Santa Monica began. Although the only rails laid connected Santa Monica and Los Angeles, population continued to flow in. As early as Nov. 20, 1885, Santa Monica was incorporated as a sixth-class California city. It became a freeholder city through a charter ratified and approved in 1906. A council-manager form of government was established by freehold charter granted March 25, 1947. Industrial development has been limited, but the aircraft industry and various light industries were established.

Pop. (1960) 83,249. For comparative population figures *see* table in CALIFORNIA: *Population.* (J. M. Wo.)

SANTANDER, FRANCISCO DE PAULA (1792–1840), Colombian political figure, an able soldier and administrator with most of the gifts of a statesman, was born April 2, 1792, at Rosario de Cúcuta, near the Venezuelan frontier. At the inception of independence in 1810, Santander left law school to join the patriot army. Promoted rapidly, he escaped the Spanish reconquest of 1816 by fleeing to the eastern lowlands, and returned as brigadier general in the invading force of Simón Bolívar (*q.v.*). Santander was vice-president of Nueva Granada in the republic of Colombia from 1819 to 1821, at which time the constituent congress named him vice-president of Colombia. Re-elected in 1826, Santander continued to be the acting president of Colombia until Sept. 10, 1827. He shaped the government, and found the men, money and supplies for President Bolívar's campaigns in Colombia, Peru and Bolivia. His measures to hold Colombia to-

gether after the fighting had ended, however, were undercut by Bolívar, who returned from Peru late in 1826 to end the Venezuelan rebellion. Bolívar retained Venezuela in Colombia only on the basis of obedience to his person, a demand that ended relations between Santander and Bolívar. Santander was exiled in 1828 after the attempt to assassinate Bolívar, but evidence shows only that he knew of the plot, tried to dissuade the conspirators and gave no warning. After dissolution of Gran Colombia in 1830, Santander returned as president (1832–36) of the state of Nueva Granada and then served as senator until his death.

Proud, sensitive, exact in his accounting, Santander typified the best tradition of the colonial official. Legalistic yet flexible, regalistic and centralist, he helped form the tradition of nonmilitaristic governments in Colombia. Colombians justly call him the "man of laws." He was equally important as a defender and focus of Granadian nationalism, especially during 1816–19 and 1827–32. In his last years he restrained the liberal elements of Granadian society who viewed the electoral victory of centrists and conservatives in 1836 as the return of colonial evils. His death, on May 6, 1840, was followed promptly by outbreak of the major civil conflict of 1840–42. *See also* COLOMBIA: *History.*

(R. L. GE.)

SANTANDER (SANTANDER DEL SUR), an interior department of the republic of Colombia. Pop. (1961 est.) 860,550. Area 11,706 sq.mi. The topography is extremely rugged; the Eastern cordillera of the Andes traverses the department from north to south. Toward the west it includes an extensive area of rainy tropical lowlands, extending to the Magdalena River, that did not become subject to colonization till about mid-20th century. Santander is the principal petroleum-producing department of Colombia, with production centring around Barrancabermeja. Among the agricultural crops tobacco is outstanding, and the manufacture of cigars and cigarettes is an important industry. Coffee is grown on the temperate midslopes of the Andes. A railroad connects the capital city, Bucaramanga (pop. [1961 est., mun.] 208,-640), with the Magdalena at Puerto Wilches. San Gil, Socorro, Málaga, and Vélez are other principal cities, all lying between 3,000 and 7,000 ft. above sea level. (Js. J. P.)

SANTANDER, a town on the north coast of Spain and the capital of Santander Province, is an episcopal see and one of the chief Spanish seaports. It is 316 mi. (509 km.) N of Madrid by rail. Pop. (1960) 118,435. The town lies on the southern shore of Cabo Mayor, a rocky peninsula extending eastward to shelter the Bay of Santander, which is an inlet of the Bay of Biscay.

The centre of the lower town (except for the 12th-century crypt of the cathedral) has been rebuilt since it was destroyed by a fire spread by a windstorm in 1941. The Magdalena Palace, with its park, stands near the extremity of Cabo Mayor; it was presented by the town to King Alfonso XIII. A special building houses the library of the writer Marcelino Menéndez y Pelayo (*q.v.*) and the provincial museum with important prehistoric collections from caves in the neighbourhood. The summer university, which meets yearly, is also named for Menéndez. Santander is linked by rail with Madrid, Bilbao, and Oviedo and by scheduled air services with Barcelona, San Sebastián, and Santiago de Compostela.

SANTANDER PROVINCE (area 2,042 sq.mi. [5,289 sq.km.]; pop. [1960] 432,132) is popularly known as La Montaña, being covered with hills and mountains increasing in height toward the south, where they lead up to the *meseta* province of Palencia. The Asturian border to the southwest is marked by the Picos de Europa ("peaks of Europe"), of which Peña Vieja (8,573 ft. [2,613 m.]) is the most noted; a few bears survive there. Rain is frequent throughout the province all the year round.

The prehistoric paintings and engravings of animals in the Altamira cave (*q.v.*) show unusual skill. Nearby, Santillana, with its Romanesque collegiate church containing the shrine of Santa Juliana, has streets of houses mostly of the 16th century with escutcheons over the doors, long abandoned by the families of their original owners. The province is noted for the family pride and indigence of its minor nobility.

The principal towns are Santander; Torrelavega, an industrial and mining centre (zinc, iron, lead); Reinosa, where steel is produced for the Spanish Society of Naval Construction; Castro Urdiales with its Templars' castle; Camargo; and Laredo. Much of the land in the province is divided into very small peasant holdings. There are some good fishing ports (Santoña, Laredo, San Vicente de la Barquera, Castro Urdiales).   (C. D. L.)

SANTARÉM, a city of Brazil in Pará state, on the right bank of the Tapajós near its entrance into the Amazon. Pop. (1960) 24,924. It is the most important town on the Amazon between Belém and Manaus and is a port of call for all river steamers. Santarém is 434 mi. from Belém by air. The red tile roofs of the whitewashed buildings of the business district give the town an attractive appearance from the river. Most valuable exports of the region are rosewood oil, rubber, lumber and jute. Santarém is a noted distributing centre for native handicraft articles. A few miles south of the city the escarpment of the Santarém plateau rises to an elevation of 400 ft. This plateau, which is crossed by a motor road to Belterra, is one of the most active areas of agricultural colonization in the Amazon valley. Rice, corn, beans, mandioca and malva are the principal crops. The shallow strips of fertile black soils on this high surface also contain large numbers of aboriginal baked clay artifacts.

The Tapajós is navigable for steamers to the rapids 170 mi. above Santarém and for small boats nearly to Diamantino (Mato Grosso). A considerable trade comes from Mato Grosso state and the settlements along the river banks.

Santarém was founded in 1661 as the site of a Jesuit mission to a Tapajó Indian settlement (*aldeia*) and was formed around a fort built by Pedro Teixeira. It became a city in 1848. A group of Confederate exiles settled in Santarém after the U.S. Civil War; some of their descendants still live in the area, but most of the original settlers returned disillusioned to the United States.
(Js. J. P.)

SANTARÉM, a city and river port on the right bank of the Tagus River, in the Ribatejo Province, Portugal, 51 mi. NE of Lisbon by rail. Pop. (1960) 17,276. The Portas do Sol are the ruins of Alcáçova Castle, a royal residence in the Middle Ages. Notable buildings are the former Jesuit seminary (1676), the late Gothic church of the convent of Graça (with the tomb of the navigator Pedro Álvares Cabral, *q.v.*), the early Gothic basilica of São João de Alporão (now housing the municipal museum), and the churches of Milagre (early Renaissance) and São Francisco (1240). Santarém, the Roman Scallabis (renamed Praesidium Iulium by Julius Caesar), was an important fortress in the wars between the Moors and Christians; it was recovered from the Moors in 1147.

The rich agricultural district of Santarém (area 2,583 sq.mi.; pop. [1960] 462,121) provides the city with produce for its processing industries. Santarém is also a tourist centre and its bullfights with parades of *campinos* (shepherds mounted and traditionally dressed) are well known.

SANTA RITA DURÃO, JOSÉ DE: see DURÃO, JOSÉ DE SANTA RITA.

SANTA ROSA, a department in southern Guatemala. Area 1,141 sq.mi. Pop. (1964) 155,488. Its capital is Cuilapa (pop. [1964, mun.] 12,621). In the highlands there are plantations of coffee, and the farmers raise maize (corn) and beans. In the Pacific lowlands the products include sugarcane, rice, and sesame. Large herds of beef cattle are fed on hay. In the northeast corner of the department is the beautiful Lake Ayarza. The capital is served by the Inter-American highway, and a branch descends to the coastal lowlands.   (P. E. J.)

SANTA TECLA, officially NUEVA SAN SALVADOR, capital of the department of La Libertad, El Salvador. Pop. (1961) 40,-817. It was founded in 1854 at the southern base of Volcán de San Salvador, at an altitude of 2,953 ft., to replace the national capital, San Salvador, devastated by an earthquake. It enjoyed that distinction only briefly, however, for in 1859 the government was moved back to a rebuilt San Salvador. Santa Tecla, 7½ mi. by Inter-American highway from San Salvador, is in the most densely settled part of the department and in an important coffee, livestock, corn, vegetable, and fruit producing area.   (C. F. J.)

SANTAYANA, GEORGE (1863–1952), U.S. philosopher, poet, novelist and literary critic, combined the wisdom of the old world and the new and created his own many-sided world of the mind. He was born in Madrid of Spanish parents on Dec. 16, 1863, and went to the U.S. in 1872. He received his B.A. degree from Harvard university in 1886 and taught philosophy continuously at Harvard from 1889 until 1912, with the exception of a year spent as an advanced student at Cambridge university. In 1912 he resigned his Harvard professorship and returned to Europe, where for many years he traveled extensively. Having settled at a convent in Rome early in World War II, he remained there till his death, which took place on Sept. 26, 1952.

GEORGE SANTAYANA, PHOTOGRAPHED DURING HIS PROFESSORSHIP AT HARVARD UNIVERSITY

Santayana's reputation rests chiefly on the richness and perceptiveness of his account of human experience in its ethical, social, religious and artistic aspects; on the skill with which he wove such diverse philosophical themes as naturalism, Platonic realism and idealism into the texture of his system; and on the exquisite, poetic quality of his prose style. His system, however, lacks speculative originality and the unity conferred by a single great speculative insight.

The several themes of his philosophy are incongruous or perhaps even conflict with one another; his basic naturalism is difficult to reconcile both with his realism of essences (or universals) and with his idealistic interpretation of mind or spirit. Yet despite these weaknesses of structure his philosophy is comprehensive, penetrating and to a degree systematic. His greatness resides in the catholicity of his interests; in his sensitivity to values in diverserealms of human experience; and in the freedom of his imaginative powers.

Santayana's first published essay in philosophy was *The Sense of Beauty* (1896). It is a major contribution to aesthetics—perhaps the most important American work in this field. The essay is concerned with "the nature and elements of our aesthetic judgments"; "it is" he adds, "a theoretical inquiry and has no directly hortatory quality." The main thesis of the essay is that aesthetic judgments are the expression of artistic taste and that "to make a judgment is virtually to establish an ideal." Santayana's emphasis on the ideal or formal aspects of aesthetic judgment is combined with an appreciation of the importance of its material or sensuous aspect.

The Life of Reason (1905–06) is a major work consisting of five volumes: *Reason in Common Sense, Reason in Society, Reason in Religion, Reason in Art* and *Reason in Science.* "The life of reason," which Santayana describes as "a presumptive biography of the human intellect," is an interpretation of the role of reason in the manifold activities of the human spirit. The first suggestion for such a work occurred to Santayana in his student days as a result of reading Hegel's *Phenomenology of Spirit;* and, indeed, *The Life of Reason* resembles the *Phenomenology* of Hegel in its conception, though not in its execution. The life of reason, for Santayana as for Hegel, is not restricted to the rational in the sense of the purely intellectual activities of man (though it includes them). The recurrent theme of the five volumes comprising *The Life of Reason* is that reason in all its manifestations is a union of instinct and ideation; it is instinct become reflective and enlightened.

Scepticism and Animal Faith (1923) marks an important departure from his earlier philosophy and serves as "a critical introduction" to his new system developed in *The Realms of Being,* a four-volume work composed of *The Realm of Essence* (1927/28), *The Realm of Matter* (1930), *The Realm of Truth* (1937) and *The Realm of Spirit* (1940). Santayana displayed in these later works the penetrating insight, the breadth of philosophical vision and the stylistic elegance characteristic of his earlier writings and, at the same time, enhanced his stature as a philosopher by achieving greater theoretical precision, clarity and coherence. *Scepticism and Animal Faith* conveys better than any other single volume of his works the essential import of his philosophy and can be commended as an introduction to and *résumé* of his later system. This essay formulates his skepticism and his theory of immediately apprehended essences and describes the role played by "animal faith" in various forms of knowledge.

"The realm of essence" is the domain of the mind's certain and indubitable knowledge. Essences are universals which possess being or reality but do not exist. The realm of essence comprises colours, tastes, odours and other data of sense as well as the ideal objects of thought and imagination. "The realm of matter" is the world of natural objects; belief in matter rests—as does all belief concerning existence—on animal faith. Naturalism, the dominant theme of his entire philosophy, appears in his later work in his insistence that the realm of matter is prior to the other realms of being.

Santayana's other writings include *Lucifer: a Theological Tragedy* (1924); *Interpretations of Poetry and Religion* (1900); *Three Philosophical Poets: Lucretius, Dante, and Goethe* (1910); *Winds of Doctrine* (1926); *Egotism in German Philosophy* (1940); *Philosophical Opinion in America* (1918); *Character and Opinion in the United States* (1920); *Soliloquies in England* (1922); *Poems* (1923); *The Unknowable* (1923); *Dialogues in Limbo* (1925); *Platonism and the Spiritual Life* (1927); *Some Turns of Thought in Modern Philosophy* (1933); *The Last Puritan*, a novel (1936); *Obiter Scripta* (1936); *Persons and Places*, 2 vol. (1944–45); *The Idea of Christ in the Gospels* (1946); *Dominations and Powers* (1951).

BIBLIOGRAPHY.—P. A. Schilpp (ed.), *The Philosophy of George Santayana* (1940); F. Thilly and L. Wood, *A History of Philosophy*, 3rd ed., pp. 618–623 (1957); Irwin Edman, *The Philosophy of Santayana*, new and enlarged edition (1953).   (LR. W.)

SANTEE-WATEREE-CATAWBA RIVER SYSTEM,

a 538-mi.-long inland waterway in the southeastern U.S., begins in North Carolina in the Blue Ridge mountains as the Catawba river. The headwaters of the Catawba originate near Mt. Mitchell (6,684 ft.), highest point in the United States east of the Mississippi river. The Catawba flows into South Carolina to Great Falls, a distance of 220 mi., where it becomes the Wateree river. Lakes or reservoirs formed by dams on the Catawba are Rhodhiss lake (15 mi. long); Hickory lake (10 mi.); Lake James (10 mi.); Lookout Shoals lake (10 mi.); Mountain Island lake (11 mi.); and Catawba lake (20 mi.). The Santee river is formed 30 mi. S.E. of Columbia, S.C., where the Wateree joins the Congaree river. The Congaree, in turn, is formed at Columbia by the junction of the Saluda and Broad rivers, both of which originate in the eastern segments of the southern Blue Ridge. The stream is known as the Wateree river between Great Falls and its junction with the Congaree river, a distance of 75 mi. The Wateree is navigable for 58 mi. below Camden, S.C. Eight miles northwest of Camden a hydroelectric dam forms Wateree pond (sometimes called Wateree reservoir; 15 mi. long). Near Stateburg, S.C., is Wateree swamp, a densely wooded area which abounds in mink, raccoon, otter, squirrel, opossum, deer, fox, quail and wild turkey.

The Santee, the most important river in South Carolina, flows 143 mi. S.E. into the Atlantic by two mouths, the North Santee and the South Santee, about 15 mi. S. of Georgetown. It flows through comparatively high hills which aid in the erection of dams and has been subjected to extensive navigational and hydroelectric development. Two large dams are Santee dam (48 ft. high, 7.5 mi. long), which forms Lake Marion or Santee reservoir (40 mi. long); and Pinopolis dam (140 ft. high, 2.2 mi. long), on the Cooper river, which forms Lake Moultrie, the latter receiving water diverted from Lake Marion. Lower sections of the Santee river, near its mouth, are lined by old rice plantations now devoted to cattle, vegetable, pulpwood and hunting activities.

(M. C. P.)

SANTIAGO, a province in north central Chile. Although one of eight provinces formed in 1826, Santiago has been subjected to several alterations in outline and administrative subdivisions. Area 6,727 sq.mi. Pop. (1960) 2,437,425, of whom 646,731 live in Santiago (*q.v.*), the provincial and national capital. The province embraces Andean cordillera, longitudinal valley and coastal range and valley terrain. Winter season rains and snow melt in the Maipo watershed supply the water used for power development and farm and urban needs. River canyons provide summer recreation areas and access to winter resorts (Farellones, Lagunillas and Refugio Alemán). Santiago is a major industrial and agricultural province; in the 1950s its factories employed more than half of Chile's industrial personnel and produced more than half the value of manufactured goods. The bulk of industrial and commercial activity is concentrated in the capital, but there are important farm supply, marketing and product-processing activities at San Bernardo, location of major railroad shops; Puente Alto, a paper and gypsum-processing centre; and Melipilla, Talagante and Buin. In agriculture, dairy and beef production are important, and the main crops (by acreage) are wheat, alfalfa, clover, barley, maize, grapes, potatoes and beans.

Marketing is facilitated by the proximity of urban centres and by the best-developed road system in Chile. Road and rail carriers make almost every point in the province accessible; service to other provinces is good.

San Antonio, the chief port and fishing centre, has a flourishing traffic in copper from O'Higgins province (*q.v.*) and such regional products as malting barley, wine and legumes. Nearby are such fashionable beach resorts as Santo Domingo, Cartagena and Algarrobo (Valparaíso province). Mining is conducted at Las Condes-Naltagua (copper), El Volcán (gypsum) and Polpaico (limestone for cement). Chacabuco and Maipú are famed battlefields of the war for independence.   (J. T.)

SANTIAGO (SANTIAGO DE LOS CABALLEROS), a province and its capital city in northern Dominican Republic. A relatively large province (1,201 sq.mi.), it is bounded on the north by the Cordillera Septentrional (to 3,993 ft.) and on the south by the Cordillera Central (to 10,417 ft.). The heart is a wide, east-west plain, known as the Cibao region, which is intersected by the Río Yaque del Norte. This fertile and populous region makes the province a leading rice and corn producer and the centre of the nation's tobacco industry. Coffee and lumbering are important. The province was established in 1845. Pop. (1960) 292,130.

The city of Santiago is situated at about 500 ft. elevation on the banks of the Río Yaque. Pop. (1960) 85,640. It was founded about 1500 by Bartholomew Columbus and was inhabited by 30 knights of the Order of St. James (Santiago). It was rebuilt near the original site after the 1564 earthquake. Its location near the centre of the Cibao, the most productive region of the nation, has made it a vital hub of communications and trade. Its factories manufacture cigars and cigarettes, coffee, pharmaceuticals, furniture, and other products.   (D. R. D.)

SANTIAGO (SANTIAGO DE CHILE), capital of the republic of Chile and of the province of Santiago (*q.v.*), is the centre of the nation's political, economic, cultural and ecclesiastical life. The city's preponderance of power and prestige is suggested by the fact that its population (1968 est. 2,447,741 for the greater city area) is 26% of Chile's total.

The city was founded by Pedro de Valdivia on Feb. 12, 1541. Its nucleus occupied a defensively advantageous position to the west of Cerro Santa Lucía and between the Mapocho river (north) and a periodic channel of the Mapocho (south), now the Avenida Bernardo O'Higgins, called the Alameda. The westward-sloping alluvial land over which the city has spread ranges in elevation from about 1,600 to 2,100 ft. Dominating the central city is Cerro San Cristóbal (2,779 ft. [847 m.]), which lies to the northeast of Cerro Santa Lucía and north of the Mapocho. A few miles to the west are the coastal ranges, remote and modest ridges compared to the 8,000-ft. (2,400-m.) cordilleran buttress which looms above the city on the east. The higher summits of the Andes form a massive backdrop.

Santiago, originally Santiago del Nuevo Estremo, was elevated

EWING GALLOWAY

ENTRANCE TO CERRO SANTA LUCÍA, ONCE THE CITADEL OF PEDRO DE VALDIVIA, WHO FOUNDED SANTIAGO IN 1541

to city status and given a coat of arms in 1552. In 1609 the royal *audiencia* was transferred to the community, and in 1651 an episcopal see was created. Few traces of early architecture have survived earthquakes and the pressures of city modernization. The 16th-century churches and convents were shattered in the earthquakes of 1647 and 1730. The cathedral, also damaged in the disasters, burned down in 1769. Only San Francisco among existing churches preserves part of the original colonial structure. The Valparaíso road was finished and the Mapocho bridged by mid-18th century. Efforts to control the river were nullified by the floods of 1609, 1684, 1779 and 1783.

The cathedral, completed in 1619, was reconstructed several times; the Moneda (since 1848 the executive residence), Aduana and Cabildo were finished between 1775 and 1807, and the Alameda was transformed from river bed to principal thoroughfare soon after independence. Nevertheless, major changes in the city's appearance did not occur until after mid-19th century, when wealthy miners and landowners began to build monumental houses. The municipal theatre was constructed in 1857 (reconstructed 1873). It and much of the contemporary architecture were French-inspired.

Broad-scale municipal improvements were notable in the 1870s. Streets were paved and lined with trees, streetcars were introduced, the water system was improved, and the central market was constructed. Numerous plazas were created, but the transformation of rocky Cerro Santa Lucía into a park was the finest gift to posterity. In the 1890s the Mapocho was effectively canalized and the splendid riverside Parque Forestal planted. Later urban improvements are notable in the middle- and upper-class residential districts, which spread upslope from the city nucleus, chiefly after 1930. Industrial development has been greatest in the western part of the city, where low-cost housing projects and spontaneous housing developments are commonly found. In this area city expansion has been greatest toward San Bernardo. In the nuclear part of Santiago, the *Centro,* modern structures of 8–12 stories are clustered. These buildings tend to combine several functions: shops, restaurants and theatres open to the street and to street-level galleries; offices, hotels and apartments occupy higher floors. The Plaza de Armas, with its bandstand, statuary and fountains, the flanking cathedral and old public buildings, is a link with the past. Nearby are the congress and supreme court buildings. To the southwest, in the civic centre, the Moneda is surrounded by tall ministry and commercial buildings. Groups of multistoried structures, chiefly residential, lie farther west; other clusters arise east of Cerro Santa Lucía and along major avenues. The pattern of public transportation is adequate, but peak period congestion is serious. Among the public services common to great cities Santiago's spirited volunteer fire department is unique.

City parks include San Cristóbal, which contains gardens, the

zoological park, a funicular and the shrine to the Virgin of the Immaculate Conception. The once fashionable Cousiño park remains so only for the independence day military review (Sept. 18). The Quinta Normal de Agricultura contains a boating lagoon, exhibition and rodeo grounds and the museum of natural history. In the Parque Forestal is the Palace of Fine Arts. The museum of contemporary art is located on Cerro Santa Lucía; nearby is the national library building, where archives and historical and archaeological collections are housed.

The University of Chile (founded 1843), the Catholic university (founded 1888) and the military academy are the best-known educational institutions. There are good civilian and military technical schools.

Santiago is Chile's major and most diversified manufacturing centre. Textiles, food products, shoes and clothing and beverages represent about 60% of manufactures in value. Although the city is the chief market, rail and highway carriers reach most of the country. Passenger rail and bus service with other cities is good. There are two modern international airports.

Summers (October to March) are warm; winter temperatures are not excessively low, but the combination with the atmosphere's high relative humidity produces a penetrating cold. The warm month (January) mean temperature is 69° F (20° C); cold month (July) mean temperature is 46.4° F (7.7° C). Fog is common in winter, and atmospheric pollution (smog) is noticeable most of the year. Precipitation, chiefly a winter phenomenon, averages 15.3 in. (390 mm.) per year. Snow, uncommon in the lowlands, forms a mantle upon the cordillera in the winter.

See also references to "Santiago (Santiago de Chile)" in the Index. (J. T.)

SANTIAGO (SANTIAGO DE COMPOSTELA), a city, place of pilgrimage, and archiepiscopal see in the province of La Coruña, northwestern Spain, situated near the confluence of the Sar and Sarela rivers, 32 mi. (51 km.) SW of the city of La Coruña by road, and at the terminus of a railway from Madrid. Pop. (1960) 57,165 (municipal). "Santiago" is the Spanish for St. James, whose shrine the city possesses. In the first half of the 9th century a tomb discovered at Padrón was said to have been supernaturally revealed to be that of the apostle St. James the Great, martyred at Jerusalem some years after the crucifixion (Acts 12:2). According to legend his body was taken to Spain where he had formerly evangelized, according to a tradition not known before the 7th century. (This St. James was sometimes confusedly thought to be the same person as St. James the Less, the "brother of Jesus.")

The discovery of the relics provided a rallying point for Christian Spain, then confined to a narrow strip at the north of the Muslim-occupied majority of the peninsula. Alfonso II (791–842) of Asturias built over the tomb an earthen church which Alfonso III (866–910) replaced by a stone one, and the town that grew up around it became the most important place of pilgrimage after Jerusalem and Rome during the Middle Ages. The whole town, except the tomb itself, was destroyed in 997 by al-Mansur (Almanzor), military commander of the Caliphate of Córdoba, and it was not until 1078 that the present church was begun under Alfonso VI of León and Castile, whose introduction of Cluniac reforms to Spain through his marriage to the duke of Burgundy's daughter increased the flow of pilgrims by uniting his country more closely to the rest of Western Europe. This fine Romanesque building (consecrated 1128, completed 1211), at the east of the Plaza Mayor, has a Baroque west facade, the *Obradoiro,* above a flight of steps, built by Fernando de Casas y Novoa in 1738–47. An outstanding feature of the interior is the Pórtico de la Gloria (behind the facade), showing a Last Judgment, Romanesque but tinged with Gothic features, by Maestro Mateo. At the north of the Plaza Mayor is the Hospicio de los Reyes Católicos, built in 1501–11 by Enrique de Egas to receive the pilgrims. Other noteworthy secular buildings are the colleges of San Jerónimo (founded 1501), Fonseca (founded 1530), and San Clemente (founded 1601), and the university (founded 1532, though the building dates from 1750). The monastery of San Martín Pinario, now a seminary, was founded in the 10th century and rebuilt in the

17th. The church of Santa María Salomé and the collegiate church of Santa María La Real de Sar in the suburbs both date from the 12th century, with later facades.

Santiago's chief economic activities, apart from agriculture and the artistic industries of silverwork, jetwork, and wood engraving, include brewing and the distillation of spirits, foundries, and the manufacture of linen, paper, furniture, soap, and matches.

BIBLIOGRAPHY.—Américo Castro, *The Structure of Spanish History*, ch. 6 (1954); T. D. Kendrick, *St. James in Spain* (1960); A. López Ferreiro, *Historia de la iglesia de Santiago de Compostela*, 10 vol. (1898–1908). (M. Fu.)

SANTIAGO DE CUBA, Cuban city and seaport which is second to Havana among the nation's cities. Pop. (1962 est.) 215,616. Santiago lies in a valley or basin of the same name located near the southeastern end of the island. The valley, which measures about 8 mi. from north to south and 19 mi. from east to west, is pierced by the great bay on which Santiago is situated and which gives the city much of its commercial importance. The bay, a safe and commodious anchorage approximately 6 mi. long and 2 mi. wide, is of the pouch shape characteristic of the Cuban coast. The overall width of the entrance channel is only 300 yd., and it is only 60 yd. between the 5-fathom marks; the entrance is nearly invisible from a distance offshore, cutting as it does into the high bluffs which rise from the sea. The chief bluff, about 200 ft. high, is the Morro, crowned by a colonial fortress, Morro Castle. The channel entrance depth is 32 ft. and anchorage depths within the harbour are 26 ft., although there is considerably less water (about 14 ft.) alongside some of the piers. There are seven principal wharves, some with railroad sidings; the Malecón, or concrete quay, is also used for handling cargoes and fuel oil.

Santiago, capital of the province of Oriente, is the hottest city of the island, the annual mean temperature in winter being 28° C (82° F) and in summer 31° C (88° F). This condition is caused in part by the fact that the city is cupped in by outlying ranges of the Sierra Maestra Mountains, which rise around the basin to heights of 3,000 ft. Because of the hilliness of the city it affords interesting panoramas of mountains and ocean. Its relative isolation until the 20th century has resulted in an air of colonial antiquity, provided by the red-tiled roofs of the low houses which line the narrow streets of the older sections. The city has suffered occasional severe earthquakes, the most recent in 1932.

In the mountains of the region are substantial mineral deposits—iron, manganese, and copper—which have stimulated shipping activity at the port; near or within the city there are also distilleries, textile mills and other types of factories, and an oil refinery. In addition to ores, sugar (of which Santiago in recent years has exported approximately 5% of Cuba's total exports), rum, tobacco, and cocoa beans are the principal exports. There are good rail, road, and air connections with other parts of the island, including Havana, 540 mi. WNW, and there is also ship service to foreign countries.

Santiago was founded in 1514 by Diego Velázquez, first governor of Cuba; it was moved a few miles to the present site in 1522. Commanding as it did a strategic location upon the northern Caribbean in the early colonial period, the city was until 1589 the capital of Cuba. In that year, with the shift of settlement toward the western end of the island, Santiago lost its leading position to Havana and sank to a secondary role. Cortés was the first alcalde, or mayor, of Santiago, and it was from there that he set out in 1518 on the expedition which culminated in the conquest of Mexico. The growth of the city was slow in the colonial period (when pirates harassed the port) and in the 19th century, and the principal additions to the population and progress of the municipality came as a result of the settlement in the city in the mid-17th century of Spaniards driven out of Jamaica when that island was captured by the British, and again by the settlement in the first decade of the 19th century of several thousand French refugees from nearby and newly independent Haiti.

Santiago was a focal point of the Spanish-American War, and many historic reminders of that conflict are found in the area. Near the city, on the hills of El Viso (at the village of El Caney)

and San Juan, decisive engagements were fought; the harbour of the city was partially blocked by the scuttled collier, *Merrimac;* and the principal naval action of the war was fought along the coast near the port.

On July 26, 1953, Fidel Castro led an attack of 165 young revolutionists against the Moncada army barracks in the city. The attack was defeated by the government troops of the dictator, Fulgencio Batista. Castro and his remaining followers were tried in Santiago and sentenced to prison. But a name—the 26th of July Movement—had been given to Castro's cause and in 1956, after his release from prison, he led a handful of men back into the Sierra Maestra Mountains west of Santiago. This group of rebels gradually isolated the city from the rest of the island, although it remained in the hands of Batista forces until Castro's victory on Jan. 1, 1959. (T. F. McG.)

SANTIAGO DEL ESTERO, a province in northern Argentina, separated from Tucumán in 1820. It is bounded by the provinces of Salta and Chaco in the north and Córdoba in the south. Pop. (1960) 477,156. Area 52,222 sq.mi. Santiago del Estero lies within the Argentine section of the Gran Chaco (*q.v.*) and has the general characteristics of that region. Almost the entire surface is a lowland plain, a large part of which is covered with scrub forest. Some of the trees, notably the quebracho, are of considerable commercial value. There are extensive saline areas in the southwest. The climate is extremely hot in summer, the temperature rising to 118° F. Frosts occur occasionally in winter. Rainfall is slight (about 20 in. a year) and quickly evaporates. Therefore agriculture is possible only where the land can be irrigated from the rivers Salado and Dulce, or where seasonal flooding by the rivers takes place. The existence of large swamps (*esteros*) bordering the Dulce in the vicinity of the provincial capital, Santiago del Estero, explains the name of town and province. The main crops in the irrigated districts are maize, wheat, linseed, and cotton. Cattle are raised on the rough Chaco pastures.

The province is crossed by several railways which connect it with many parts of Argentina and with Bolivia and Chile. The railway via Salta to the Chilean port of Antofagasta on the Pacific coast was designed to facilitate exchange of the products of the Chaco for the minerals of Chile's northern desert (copper and nitrate). (GE. P.)

SANTIAGO DEL ESTERO, Argentine city, capital of the province of the same name, located 700 mi. NW of Buenos Aires. Pop. (1960) 103,115. Although the climate is extremely hot and dry, the surrounding plains produce considerable wheat, cotton, flax, corn, and alfalfa. Founded in 1553 by Spaniards arriving from Peru and moved to its present location on the Dulce River three years later, it is the oldest continuous settlement in Argentine territory. Highways and excellent rail connections link the city with Córdoba, Tucumán, and the Argentine northwest and with the ports of Santa Fe and Rosario. (Js. R. S.)

SANTIAGO MOUNTAINS, a narrow range in the southwestern U.S., extending southeastward across central Brewster County in the Big Bend section of Texas. Formerly the entire 90-mi. chain from near Alpine to the Boquillas Canyon of the Rio Grande was mapped as Santiago Mountains, but increasing usage restricts the name to the 35-mi. range between Del Norte Gap and the Del Norte Mountains to the northwest and Dog Canyon and the Dead Horse Mountains to the southeast, with the portion continuing from Dog Canyon across the Boquillas into Mexico frequently known as the Sierra del Carmen. Santiago Peak (6,521 ft.), a truncated butte of intrusive rocks, rises about 1,500 ft. above the mountain crest of vertical and overturned Cretaceous limestone strata, which averages about 1,500 ft. above the Marathon Basin on the east. Annual precipitation, ranging from 5 to 15 in., supports an open arid scrub on the lower slopes and a piñon-juniper association higher up. The drainage system of Maravillas Creek practically surrounds the range. Intermittent arroyos and a few springs help support sheep and cattle.

A U.S. highway from Marathon crosses the range at Persimmon Gap (through which went the Comanche Trail) to enter the Big Bend National Park. (D. D. B.)

SANTIAGO RODRÍGUEZ, a province in northwestern Dominican Republic. Area 394 sq.mi. Pop. (1960) 40,730. It occupies the northern slope and foothills of the Cordillera Central and is drained by several tributaries of the Río Yaque del Norte, the nation's largest river. Because of semiarid conditions in much of the region, livestock raising rather than cultivation is a principal activity. Crops include cassava, plantains, peanuts, coffee and tobacco. Some lumbering is done in the mountains. The province was created in 1951 from Montecristi province.

The capital, Santiago Rodríguez (pop. [1960] 3,620), was called Sabaneta until 1936.
(D. R. D.)

SANTILLANA, ÍÑIGO LÓPEZ DE MENDOZA, MARQUÉS DE (1398–1458), Spanish poet and one of the great figures of his time in both politics and literature, was born at Carrión de los Condes, Palencia, Aug. 19, 1398, and died at Guadalajara, March 25, 1458. As lord of the vast Mendoza estates, he took a leading part in opposing John II and led expeditions against the Moslems. He found time, however, to manage his lands benevolently, patronize the arts, build up an important library and write poetry of high quality. In part his poetry is typical of the 15th century, didactic and stoical in outlook, Latinized in style, often allegorical. He showed originality in collecting proverbs and in writing 42 sonnets, the first in Spanish; these, although angular and uncertain, have an occasional fine line and great historical importance. He is chiefly read for his ten *serranillas,* charming light lyrics in the traditional manner, describing encounters between the knight and the shepherdess; and for his *Proemio,* or preface to his collected works, the first document of literary history and poetic principle in Spanish.

See R. Lapesa, *La obra literaria del Marqués de Santillana* (1957).
(C. C. Sh.)

SANTINIKETAN (Hindi "abode of peace"), a university town in Birbhum district, West Bengal, India, lies about a mile from Bolpur and 96 mi. (154 km.) NW of Calcutta by rail. It has grown out of Santiniketan Asrama, a place for meditation in peaceful seclusion, founded and endowed in 1863 by Maharshi Devendranath, the father of the poet Rabindranath Tagore (*q.v.*). The latter, in turn, set up a school called the Brahma Vidyalaya, with the object of imparting sound education in a religious atmosphere. In 1901 Tagore started another experimental school at Santiniketan to provide for children an education which would not be divorced from nature, where the pupils could feel themselves to be members of a large community, and where they could acquire knowledge and grow up in an atmosphere of joy, freedom, and mutual trust. Since 1921 Santiniketan has been the seat of the Visva-Bharati University (also founded by Tagore), which seeks to develop a basis on which the cultures of east and west may meet in common fellowship. The university draws students and teachers from all over India, and also from other countries. It is a residential university (incorporated by an act of 1951) with hostels and extensive grounds. The teaching departments include a college of fine arts and crafts, a college of music and the dance, an institute for Sino-Indian studies and research, a teachers' training college, and colleges of technology and of postgraduate studies and research. At the nearby settlement of Sriniketan an institute of rural reconstruction was started in 1922 by Tagore with the help of L. K. Elmhirst.
(S. P. C.)

SANTO DOMINGO, a geographic name of several usages in the island of Hispaniola, West Indies. This was the original name of the capital of the Dominican Republic, the oldest European city in the western hemisphere. Christopher Columbus established the first European settlement in the new world on the northern coast of Hispaniola on his second voyage in 1493. After he returned to Spain, his brother Bartolomé founded the city of Santo Domingo on the southern coast in 1496. This name, officially changed in 1936 to Ciudad Trujillo, was restored in 1961 after the assassination of Rafael Trujillo Molina.

Santo Domingo is also the name sometimes given to the entire island of Hispaniola. During the colonial period it was the name given to the Spanish portion, and when the French occupied the western third of the island they called their colony St. Domingue. Also during the colonial period both Spanish and French names

were applied to the whole island. The name was frequently corrupted incorrectly to San Domingo in English-speaking countries. The former Spanish colony, officially the Dominican Republic since 1844, is still frequently referred to as Santo Domingo. The former French colony became the Republic of Haiti in 1804.

Santo Domingo is the official name of the federal district of the Dominican Republic, comprising the wide coastal plain and hilly interior region surrounding the capital city of the same name. This district was set up in 1935 out of the former Santo Domingo province and corresponds to the old commune of Santo Domingo. Its 570 sq.mi. area consists of sugarcane plantations and cattle estates, as well as the capital city, and its population (1960) was 464,970. Boca Chica beach resort is located about 20 mi. E. of the capital. *See also* DOMINICAN REPUBLIC; HAITI; HISPANIOLA.
(D. R. D.)

SANTO DOMINGO, capital of the Dominican Republic, on the southeast coast of the island of Hispaniola. Pop. (1960) 369,980. It was founded in 1496 when Bartolomé Columbus moved the first Spanish settlement in Hispaniola to the Ozama river on the south coast. It was called Santo Domingo until 1936, when the name was changed to Ciudad Trujillo in honour of Rafael Leonidas Trujillo Molina; its original name was restored in 1961 after Trujillo was assassinated and his regime was overthrown. It is the oldest permanent city founded by Europeans in the new world and the seat of the oldest archbishopric; it claims the oldest university (St. Thomas Aquinas, now Santo Domingo university) in the western hemisphere. Until the conquest of Mexico and Peru, Santo Domingo was the centre from which the Spanish possessions in the Americas were governed, but by the end of the colonial period it was a relatively unimportant provincial town. In 1655 its inhabitants defeated a force which was sent by the British government to seize the colony and which later conquered Jamaica.

It has retained in part many of the aspects of a Spanish colonial town, with straight, narrow streets intersecting at right angles and low houses abutting on the sidewalk. The cathedral, in Spanish Renaissance style, dates from 1514 and contains the reputed tomb of Christopher Columbus. There are remains of the city walls, with their fortified gates, and of the palace of Diego Columbus. (*See* COLUMBUS, CHRISTOPHER.)

Santo Domingo has grown rapidly since World War II, and there was much reconstruction after the devastating hurricane of 1930. There are fine public buildings and parks and luxurious tourist hotels. It is the chief seaport of the Dominican Republic; and the harbour, at the mouth of the Ozama river, has been improved so that large vessels can tie up at the dock. It also has modern airports and is connected by air services with the United States and other foreign countries.

See also DOMINICAN REPUBLIC; HISPANIOLA. (D. G. Mo.)

SANTORIN: *see* THERA.

SANTOS, a city and seaport of Brazil, in the state of São Paulo, 210 mi. S.W. of Rio de Janeiro and 49 mi. by rail S.E. of São Paulo city. Pop. (1960) 262,048; (1950) 198,405. Santos covers an alluvial plain on the inner side of an island (São Vicente) formed by a tidal channel called the Santos channel or Guarujá river. The commercial district is several miles from the mouth of the channel, but the residential sections extend across the plain and line the beach facing the sea.

Santos is only a few feet above sea level, and its swampy island is drained by deep cement conduits. The channel is free from obstructions, and in front of the city it widens into a bay deep enough for the largest vessels. The water front, once beds of mud and slime and source of many fever epidemics, is faced by a wall of stone and cement. The docks are 4 mi. long and can accommodate about 50 steamers at one time; belt conveyors load several thousand bags of coffee per hour. The British-built but Brazilian-government-owned railway to São Paulo transports the bulk of the state's coffee to Santos. The trains of this profitable railway are hauled up and down the steep coastal range (the Serra do Mar) by cables. A paved highway, including the magnificent Via Anchieta, links Santos with São Paulo.

Santos, the world's leading coffee port, is dominated by its leading export, the aroma of which permeates the city. Its chief public building houses the Coffee exchange, a stock company in which the state government is liable for a part of its liquidating commitments. Santos exceeds Rio de Janeiro in annual tonnage of shipping. Other exports include cotton, sugar, bananas, castor oil, beef, oranges, hides and some manufactures.

An annual rainfall of about 77 in. and a mean temperature of 69° F. once created unhealthful conditions, but drainage canals, the paving of streets, better housing, sanitation and port improvements made Santos a healthful city. A suburban seaside resort, Guarujá, attracts many visitors from inland Brazil.

The first settlement on the São Paulo coast was made in 1532 at São Vicente, about 6 mi. S. of Santos on the island. Other settlements followed, including Santos (1543), and later a small fort was built at the harbour entrance. The name of the city was taken from the Hospital dos Santos, established by the city's founder, Brás Cubas, and named after a hospital in Lisbon, Port. São Paulo succeeded as the capital (1681) and Santos became the seaport of the colony. Santos was sacked by the English privateer Thomas Cavendish in 1591. (R. M. M.)

SANTOS-DUMONT, ALBERTO (1873–1932), Brazilian aviation pioneer, was born in the state of Minas Gerais, Braz., on July 20, 1873. Educated in France, he spent most of his life in that country. Becoming interested in aerial flight, he made a balloon ascent in 1897 and then began to construct dirigible airships. After many failures he built one which in 1901 won the Deutsch Prize and a prize from the Brazilian government for the first flight in a given time from Saint-Cloud to the Eiffel Tower and return. In 1903 he erected at Neuilly the first airship station, where he kept his fleet of dirigibles. Shortly after the successful flight by the Wright brothers in 1903, Santos-Dumont turned his attention to heavier-than-air machines. After experimenting with a vertical-propeller model, he built in 1906 a machine on the principle of the box kite. With it he won the Deutsch-Archdeacon Prize in October, and in November he flew 220 m. in 21 sec. In 1909 he produced his famous "demoiselle" or "grasshopper" monoplane, the forerunner of the modern light plane. In 1928, after many years of residence in France, he returned to Brazil. He died July 24, 1932.

SANTO TOMÉ DE GUAYANA (renamed CIUDAD GUAYANA) is a planned city built in an area of Venezuela that was remote from all major economic development until the end of World War II. There, in a frontier area of the wild, lonely Guiana highlands, occurred planned regional growth on a metropolitan scale. The impressive economy is rooted in basic natural resources. The Venezuelan government donated land for the city and consulted with foreign planning experts.

The city is situated south of the Orinoco River at its confluence with the Caroní River, one of its major tributaries. It lies some 300 mi. SE of Caracas, 67 mi. E of Ciudad Bolívar, and 215 mi. up the Orinoco River and delta from the Atlantic Ocean. Actually, it incorporates Matanzas and Puerto Ordaz on the west bank of the Caroní, and Palúa, San Felix, and Castillito on the east bank at the confluence of the two rivers. The two sectors are connected by a bridge over the Caroní. Ciudad Guayana did not develop in a haphazard manner. It was carefully planned from the beginning, with residential, commercial, recreational, and industrial sectors set apart from one another. Rectangular blocks are divided by broad avenues with median strips planted with trees and shrubbery. The homes were designed for the tropics and benefit from the cooling effects of the steady northeast trade winds.

The structure of the city is keyed to a major vehicular artery, Avenida Guayana, as the main axis connecting key functional centres. The site is such that the city enjoys a commanding physical position. (L. We.)

SANUDO, MARINO (1466–1536), Venetian historian whose *Diarii* are an invaluable source for the history of his period, was born at Venice on June 22, 1466. In his enthusiasm for historical and classical learning, he collected a notable library of manuscripts, rare books, maps, and ethnographical drawings. He began his *Vite dei Dogi c.* 1490 (published in *Rerum Italicarum Scriptores*, vol. xxii, 1733; *ibid.*, vol. xxii, iv, edited by G. Monticolo,

1900). It covers the period from the origins of Venice to September 1494, and includes material from his earlier writings. In his unpublished *La spedizione di Carlo VIII*, he brought the story up to 1495. On Jan. 1, 1496, he began his diaries. These are his most important work, and constitute a kind of universal history, written from the Venetian point of view. They contain many letters, original documents, and firsthand accounts, as well as detailed digressions on culture, trade, public works, and social customs. After he became a senator in 1498, Sanudo was able to continue his diaries with even greater efficiency, because he not only observed but took part in the events he was describing. In 1531 he was given a pension to continue the work, which thenceforward was semiofficial in character, and he carried it on until 1533; the result was 40,000 closely written pages published as *I Diarii*, 58 vol. (1879–1902).

Sanudo possessed a certain vigour of style but lacked the true historian's sureness of touch and sense of the relationship between particular events and general causes. He died at Venice on April 4, 1536.

See M. R. Brown, *Ragguagli sulla vita e sulle opere di M. Sanudo*, 3 vol. (1837–38); *Archivio Muratoriano*, I, pp. 153 ff. (1904). (G. Go.)

SAN VICENTE, a department in El Salvador, bordering the Pacific Ocean, and its capital city. Area 466 sq.mi. Population of the department (1961) 112,920, of which two-thirds was rural; population is concentrated in the highland valleys of the western part of the department. On the southwestern border rises San Vicente volcano, altitude 7,156 ft. The department produces rice, sugar, cotton, livestock, cheese, and vegetables. (C. F. J.)

SAO (So), an extinct African people who left traces of an important pre-Islamic civilization in Chad, northern Cameroons, and Nigeria (see CHAD, REPUBLIC OF: *History*). The name Sao cannot be attributed with certainty to any ethnic group; it includes Negroid and some non-Negroid elements from the north and east who apparently settled (starting about the 9th century A.D.) in successive waves on the banks of Lake Chad and the lower valleys of the Yobe, Shari, and Logone rivers as far as the 11th parallel. At the end of the 14th century the neighbouring kingdom of Kanem was invaded by the Bulala, and the Kanem peoples fled to Bornu in Sao territory to reestablish their empire. The northern Sao struggled against Kanem authority for two centuries until the king of Kanem-Bornu, *mai* Idris Alooma, overcame and largely exterminated them. In the south the Sao managed to hold out until the country was converted to Islam at the end of the 18th century. Local tradition has made them a people of giants, whose exploits are legendary (see BORNU: *History*; KANEM).

Archaeological data show that the Sao were hunters and farmers, later joined by fishermen; they introduced weaving and metalworking (iron and bronze) to the region. Their villages were built on semiartificial mounds originally (Sao I) protected by wooden palisades, replaced in more recent times (Sao II) by wide earthen ramparts. Urn burials with the body in fetal position, bronzes, and pottery date from Sao II. Remarkable examples of craftsmanship are jewelry and ritual objects made by the lost-wax method (see SCULPTURE TECHNIQUES: *Bronze Casting*), and clay figurines representing men and animals.

Direct descendants of the Sao are the Kotoko who keep their settlements on the ancient sites. In spite of conversion to Islam, most Sao religious beliefs (*e.g.*, a peculiar form of totemism) have been retained. The Buduma and Kuri (see CHAD, LAKE), the Mobber (see KANURI) of the banks of the Yobe, the Ngouma of the valley of the Yadseram, and the Ngizim of Bornu, although very much mixed with Kanuri elements, may all be traced to the same Sao origin. In the south, far beyond modern Kotoko country, the Guéwé, the Njei, Bata, and Holma, in the region of Benue, and the Gamergu living in the region around Mandara, also regard the Sao as their ancestors. The ancient Sao should not be confused with contemporary Saho (see SAHO-AFAR), who are also sometimes called Sao, nor with the So people living in the Congo Basin.

BIBLIOGRAPHY.—J. P. Lebeuf, "Bibliographie sao-kotoko," *Études camerounaises*, vol. 21–22 (June–Sept. 1948), *L'Archéologie tchadienne* (1962); A. M. D. Lebeuf, *Les populations du Tchad* (1959); R. Hartweg, "Les squelettes humains anciens du village de Sao," *J. Soc. Afric.*, vol. xii (1942); F. R. Wulsin, "An Archaeological Reconnaissance of the Chari Basin," *Harv. Afr. Stud.*, iii–xi (1932).   (A. M. D. L.)

SÃO FRANCISCO, a river of eastern Brazil, rises in the Serra da Canastra, southwest Minas Gerais. It flows in a general north-northeasterly direction across the great central plateau of Brazil and turns northeastward through the *sertão* (semiarid interior plains) and then southeast in a great bend, entering the Atlantic about 60 mi. N.E. of Aracajú, Sergipe state. Along its course the São Francisco forms the Pernambuco-Bahia and Alagôas-Sergipe state borders. The river has a total length of 1,988 mi. and a fall of 2,700–2,800 ft. It is navigable from Pirapora, in the state of Minas Gerais, for more than 1,000 mi. to a point downstream from Juàzeiro, Bahia, and from Piranhas, in the state of Alagôas, 172 mi. to the sea. The upper and lower sections of the river are separated by a stretch of nearly 300 mi. in which the São Francisco drops, first gradually and then abruptly, from the plateau toward the coastal plain. The upper portion of this stretch, nearly 100 mi. long above Petrolândia, comprises a series of rapids known as the Sobradinho, navigable at high water. In the lower portion are the spectacular São Francisco falls, where the river plunges through a narrow gorge—in one place only 51 ft. wide—and over three successive falls, altogether 265 ft. This obstructed part of the river is about 190 mi. long, and consists of a series of rapids above the falls and a deep canyon with whirlpools for some distance below. The Paulo Afonso falls are about 193 mi. from the river mouth. Sandbars at the mouth prevent the entry of deep-draft ocean vessels. The river is nearly 1 mi. wide at Penedo, 22 mi. from the Atlantic. Above Juàzeiro its width varies from a narrow channel during drought periods to several miles at flood stage in the rainy season (December to March). Below Pirapora the only bridge spanning the São Francisco connects Juàzeiro with Petrolina, in Pernambuco state.

The principal tributaries of the São Francisco are: to the south and east, the Paraopeba, Velhas and Verde-Grande; to the north and west, the Indayá, Abaeté, Paracatú, Urucuia, Carinhanha, Corrente and Grande. Several of these are navigable for long distances by small boats. Estimates of the aggregate navigable channels of the São Francisco river system range from about 1,000 mi. to over 4,000 mi.

The São Francisco river has been a major artery of travel between northeastern and central Brazil since colonial times. Along most of its course it flows through a sparsely settled pastoral region, frequently subject to prolonged drought. It serves to link the highway and railroad that converge at Pirapora with routes running north and east from Juàzeiro and Petrolina. However, river transport is slow and difficult because of shifting channels and great variations in depth and current speed in different seasons. During the dry season steamboats may take two weeks to run from Pirapora to Juàzeiro and over a month to return.

The Brazilian government has undertaken a series of related, long-range development programs in the São Francisco valley designed to improve navigation on the river, to reduce disease in the area, to provide flood control and irrigation to make the valley more attractive for agricultural settlement, and to harness the great hydroelectric potential of the Paulo Afonso falls. A major accomplishment was the virtual elimination of malaria, formerly endemic in the upper valley. Construction on the Paulo Afonso hydroelectric project began in 1949, and the Tres Marias dam and power station was completed in 1960. It is expected that the power available from the project will eventually be distributed throughout most of the states of northeastern Brazil.   (R. E. P.)

SÃO LEOPOLDO, a city in Rio Grande do Sul, Braz., located 20 mi. N. of Pôrto Alegre. Pop. (1960) 41,023. This was the first German colony (1824) established in southern Brazil. It is now a rail centre with factories producing pig iron, tanned leather, matches and aluminum ware. São Leopoldo is also served by river boats and is on the main all-weather highway that connects Pôrto Alegre with São Paulo. It is located in the midst of an agricultural country producing rice, hogs, cattle, maize, potatoes, beans, manioc, tobacco and a great variety of old world fruits and vegetables. There are Jesuit and Protestant seminaries in the city.   (P. E. J.)

SÃO LUÍS, chief city and capital of the state of Maranhão, Braz., is located on the west side of São Luís Island 300 mi. E.S.E. of Belém. Pop. (1960) 124,606. The island is really a long narrow peninsula between the drowned mouths of the Mearim and Itapecurú rivers (São Marcos bay on the west and São José bay on the east), and it is cut off from the mainland by a shallow side channel, the Canal do Mosquito. It was founded on this strategic site in 1612 by a French naval officer, Daniel de la Touche de La Ravardière, and named in honour of Louis XIII. It was captured by the Portuguese in 1615; from 1641 to 1644 it was held by the Dutch. Because of its position where two systems of navigable rivers converge, São Luís has long controlled the commerce of the main part of Maranhão, and it is the chief port for the products of Teresina in Piauí, with which it is connected by rail. Its exports include babaçu (babassu) oil, castor beans, balsam, hides and skins, lumber, cotton, sugar, rice and maize. In the city there are sugar refineries, a brandy distillery (*caxaça*) and plants for the processing of babaçu oil and cacao, for the preserving of fruit and for the manufacture of hammocks and margarine. Since 1679 it has been the seat of a bishopric, and its buildings preserve much of the Portuguese colonial atmosphere, especially the large 17th-century cathedral. Its Institute of History and Geography is one of the oldest in Brazil. São Luís has been the birthplace of many distinguished Brazilian writers and poets. The city was formerly called São Luiz do Maranhão or simply Maranhão.   (P. E. J.)

SAÔNE, a river of eastern France, 298 mi. (480 km.) long, rises in the Faucilles hills of Lorraine at 1,300 ft. (400 m.), 15 mi. SW of Épinal, and joins the Rhône River at Lyons. It flows south into the wide structural depression between the plateau of Langres and the Massif Central and the Jura. It receives important left-bank tributaries, the Ognon and Doubs, which drain the Gate of Burgundy (Belfort Gap). Near Allerey the Saône unites with the Doubs (left), which rivals it in volume and exceeds it in length at this point. At Chalon the Saône turns south and closely follows the margin of the Massif Central past Mâcon. The slopes to the west form the great wine district of Burgundy; to the east the fertile plain of Bresse stretches to the foot of the Jura, but it is succeeded farther south, toward the Rhône confluence, by the ill-drained moraine country of the Dombes. The Saône is canalized above Lyons for a distance of 233 mi. to Corre, where it is connected with the Canal de l'Est. It is also linked by canals with the Rhine (via the Doubs), the Marne, the Seine (Burgundy canal), and the Loire (Canal du Centre).   (Ar. E. S.)

SAÔNE-ET-LOIRE, a large *département* of east-central France, formed in 1790 of part of the ancient province of Burgundy (*q.v.*). It is bounded north by Côte-d'Or, east by Jura, south by Ain and Rhône, southwest by Loire, west by Allier and Nièvre, and includes part of the Saône plain, the floor of a Pliocene lake, with the crystalline highlands that border it to the west. Area 3,331 sq.mi. (8,627 sq.km.). Pop. (1962) 535,772.

The Saône Valley and the Plain of Bresse, which stretches to the east, crossed by the Seille, Reyssouze, and Veyle from the Jura, support rich agriculture, with wheat and maize (corn), sugar beet, tobacco, and fodder crops on the calcareous loams that cover the old lake floor. Large numbers of poultry are kept. West of the Saône the limestone foothills constitute the rich vinegrowing district of Mâconnais, where Pouilly, Fuissé, and Brouilly provide well-known vintages. The crystalline highlands of the western part of the *département* are concerned with poorer farming, mainly cattle rearing, but the flanking Jurassic sediments give richer pastures, used for fattening. There the ancient region of Charolais (*q.v.*) is the home of one of the most famous breeds of French cattle. Between the Morvan and the Beaujolais highlands, each rising to about 3,000 ft. (900 m.) in the extreme northwest and south of the *département,* a synclinal groove makes an important break. There the watershed between the Dheune tributary of the Saône and the Bourbince tributary of the Loire is low, and the easy route provided is used by the Canal du Centre, linking the

Saône at Chalon with the Loire at Digoin, and by one of the earliest of French railways. Along this valley patches of Coal Measures have been preserved in the synclinal structure, and these are worked at Blanzy and Montceau-les-Mines. The coal is of high quality, including coking type, though the amount produced is small and is now declining. The district had the first coke-fired blast furnaces in France. The famous Schneider works were established at Le Creusot in 1837. Although the old iron industry once used local ores, all the ore is now imported, and the district is mainly concerned with finishing processes and the manufacture of special steels and associated engineering. Refractory materials are also produced from the coalfield, and farther north oil shales are worked at Épinac, near Autun. To the west uranium ore is produced at Gueugnon.

Mâcon is the *préfecture* of the *département*, which is divided into five *arrondissements*, centred upon Autun, Charolles, Chalon, Louhans, and Mâcon. The *département* forms the diocese of Autun, and comes under the court of appeal and the *académie* at Dijon. At Autun there are considerable remains of the Roman wall and gates, as well as the isolated tower known as the Temple of Janus. The cathedral of St. Lazare is a magnificent example of Burgundian Romanesque architecture and is especially noteworthy for the sculpture of its main portal. Another Romanesque cathedral is at Chalon, and Cluny (*q.v.*) has the remains of an abbey that was for long the largest Christian church in the world. Solutré, near Mâcon, is famous for the extensive remains of Paleolithic man that were found in its limestone caves.   (Ar. E. S.)

SÃO PAULO, a state of Brazil, bounded north by Mato Grosso and Minas Gerais, east by Minas Gerais, Rio de Janeiro and the Atlantic, south by the Atlantic and Paraná and west by Mato Grosso. Pop. (1960) 12,974,699. Area 95,713 sq.mi. The state has a coast 373 mi. long, skirted by the well-wooded western slopes of the Serra do Mar. The narrow coastal zone is broken by lagoons, tidal channels and mountain spurs. Above is an extensive plateau with wide grassy plains, 1,500 to 3,000 ft. above sea level. Isolated ranges of low elevation break the surface in places, but in general the state may be described as an undulating tableland sloping toward the Paraná river, its western boundary. The extreme eastern part, however, has an eastward slope and belongs to the Paraíba basin. A number of large rivers flow westward to the Paraná, including the Grande (part of the state's northern boundary), Tietê (traversing the whole state), Aguapeí, Peixe and Paranapanema (part of the southern boundary). The Pardo and Turvo are important tributaries of the Grande. Much of western São Paulo is still unsettled. The coastal zone has a hot climate and a heavy rainfall. On the plateau rainfall is ample, but the air is drier and more bracing, the sun temperature being high and the nights cool.

São Paulo is the heartland both for coffee planting and for industry in Brazil; it has been called a locomotive pulling the other states like empty freight cars. Brazil's most populous state, São Paulo in the mid-20th century contained more than 17% of the nation's population, although only 3% of its area. The value of São Paulo's agricultural production was 40%, that of its industrial production 60%, of the total for Brazil. It grew more than half of the country's leading crop, coffee. It accounted for almost half of Brazil's foreign trade. Figures for income, hydroelectric power, banks, motor vehicles and daily newspapers ranged between 30% and 40% of the national total. The literacy rate was appreciably higher than the average for Brazil. The dynamic capital, São Paulo, dominates the life of the state; with a population of more than 3,000,000 it overtook Rio de Janeiro in the 1950s as Brazil's largest city.

Political importance came with São Paulo's economic growth. The nation's first three civilian presidents after the downfall of Emperor Pedro II in 1889 were Paulistas. Later, São Paulo and Minas Gerais reached a "rotation" agreement regarding the presidency. This broke down in 1930 when Wáshington Luís from São Paulo, tried to impose a Paulista successor during the severe coffee crisis that accompanied the world depression. Getúlio Vargas from Rio Grande do Sul was then swept into office with army backing. Paulistas resented his measures against their state and rose

against his regime in July 1932. Although São Paulo's industry was swiftly converted to military production, and 50,000 men were placed in the field, the revolt was put down in three months. Thereafter the state recouped only a part of its political influence.

In the mid-19th century, intensive coffee planting began near Campinas, northwest of the capital. The coffee frontier then moved steadily northward, westward and, in the 20th century, southward into Paraná. The best land occurs in the streaks of *terra roxa* (red-purple earth), a deep, porous soil containing humus. Periodic overproduction of coffee and exhaustion of the older coffee lands led to land subdivision and diversification of agriculture after the 1930s. The other leading crops include cotton, rice, corn, sugar, beans, potatoes, tomatoes, bananas, peanuts, oranges and manioc. Cereals are grown despite somewhat unfavourable climatic conditions. Cotton enjoyed a boom during the American Civil War; then, after nearly disappearing, the industry revived to meet the demand of Brazilian cotton factories. Sugar cane was planted with the first Portuguese settlement and remained the leading crop until the advent of coffee. Stock raising is important in northern and western parts of the state. After 1929 much coffee land was converted to pasturage, and the number of cattle increased fivefold within 25 years. Herds have been improved by imported stock, and horses and mules are also bred; another profitable animal industry is the breeding of swine. Truck farming and dairying have developed with urbanization. The state has excellent agricultural schools and experiment stations at Piracicaba and Campinas and a zootechnic station in the capital.

Immigration is one of the keys to São Paulo's economic progress. Coffee was first cultivated by Negro slaves. When these were emancipated in 1888, European workers were already arriving as replacement, aided by private and official subsidies. Between 1870 and 1952 over 2,500,000 immigrants entered, half of them as permanent residents. The principal foreign groups were Italians, Portuguese, Spaniards and Germans. After federal immigration restrictions were imposed in 1934, migration from other Brazilian states met São Paulo's labour needs. Many immigrants were attracted from farms to cities, especially the capital, where they furnished industrial labour. Nearly 200,000 Japanese arrived in the 20th century; they showed greater cohesion as rural settlers, as evidenced by their efficient agricultural co-operative at Cotia, near the capital.

São Paulo is the industrial centre of Brazil, with most of the state's factories located in the capital or within 75 mi. of it. Manufacturing was stimulated during World War I, and Paulistas used their political influence with the federal government to obtain a tax exemption for the port of Santos and protective tariffs. In the 1960s the state had over 52,000 industrial firms employing more than 900,000 persons; although the vast majority were small enterprises, more than 200 plants had 500 or more employees. The output of pig iron, cast iron and steel was over 600,000 tons annually. Other heavy industries included the assembly of motor vehicles and manufacture of farm machinery. Raw materials for many industries, such as textiles, ceramics, cement, furniture and food processing, are locally available. The principal source of power is hydroelectric. South America's first nuclear energy power plant was purchased for São Paulo in England in 1957. Although poor in minerals, São Paulo produces significant quantities of alumina, mineral water and dolomite.

The state has an extensive network of federal, state and private railroads of varying gauges. These converge upon the capital and upon the cable railway of the pioneer Santos-Jundiaí line which links São Paulo with its port. Santos in the 1960s was the nation's busiest port and the largest coffee-shipping port in the world. Cananéia, Iguape, São Sebastião and Ubatuba are engaged in the coasting trade only; the first two are known for the rice grown in their vicinity. In addition to 4,600 mi. of railroads, São Paulo has 63,000 mi. of highways and 46 airports.

São Paulo was settled in 1532 by the Portuguese under Martim Afonso de Sousa, who established a colony near Santos at São Vicente, now a resort town. It was originally called the *capitania* of São Vicente (organized 1534) and included the whole of Brazil south from Rio de Janeiro. After the founding in 1554 of São

Paulo city (which succeeded São Vicente as capital of the captaincy in 1681), the Paulista plateau was for a long time the main region of inland settlement in Brazil. Seventeenth-century expeditions (*bandeiras*) roaming the interior from bases on the plateau were largely responsible for the boundaries of the modern nation. From time to time parts of São Vicente were cut off to form other captaincies, from which developed the present southern states. After national independence, São Paulo was a province under the Brazilian empire (1822–89). (R. M. M.)

SÃO PAULO, the largest city of Brazil, capital of the state of the same name, largest industrial centre of the nation, and one of the five most populous cities in the Western Hemisphere, is on the Tietê River southwest of Rio de Janeiro. Pop. (1950) 2,017,-025; (1960) 3,164,804; (1968 est.) 5,733,570 (mun.). São Paulo is connected by rail and highway with Rio de Janeiro and most inland cities, and with Santos, its port, by a cable railway and a four-lane highway over the steep coastal escarpment. Its airport is one of the busiest in the world. São Paulo is surrounded by many functionally specialized satellite towns, and it dominates a vast agricultural hinterland. Part of the city occupies ridges that command broad vistas, and part is on the alluvial land along the Tietê and smaller rivers. The elevated regions provide healthful residential districts. The surrounding lands, clayey with sandy deposits, are extensively used for truck farming. Nearby hills and reservoirs and the beaches at Santos and Guarujá provide pleasant resort areas. The city is just within the tropics and has high daytime temperatures in summer, but its elevation (2,400 ft. [700 m.] above the sea) gives it a temperate climate which occasionally reaches freezing in winter.

São Paulo grew rapidly in modern times. Its population of less than 25,000 in 1872 reached 250,000 in 1901 and 1,000,000 in 1933. To create an adequate source of hydroelectric power, nearby rivers were dammed and their waters pumped over the coastal mountains to supply the Cubatão power plant. The mounting power needs of the Greater São Paulo area in the 1950s and 1960s quickly outstripped nearby sources of hydroelectric supply and necessitated adoption of a long-distance transmission system to convey power to the city from the gigantic Urubupungá complex (4,600,000 kw. eventual capacity) under construction some 400 mi. (600 km.) to the north. The initial phase of this system became operational in 1968.

Because of its great activity, the city has been called the "Chicago of South America." In the 1950s the annual number of licences issued for new buildings averaged more than 16,000, and São Paulo continues to grow at a more rapid rate than most of the world's larger cities. The historic Triangle, or city centre, contains only a portion of São Paulo's characteristic skyscrapers. Traffic is handled by viaducts and by a loop-and-spoke system of broad radial and perimetric avenues; but in general, urban growth has been swift and uncontrolled. Sustained efforts have been made, however, by city governments to stimulate more rational urban growth and to modernize the city's transportation system and traffic patterns. In 1968 plans were approved for a 40-mi. (60 km.) subway network to initially handle up to 70,000 passengers an hour. Residential districts of the well-to-do, such as Jardim Europa and Jardim América, are attractively laid out; the more recent—influenced by English town planning—contrasting sharply with the crowded poorer sections of the industrial Braz and Moóca districts. Recreation facilities include a stadium seating 80,000 spectators, the Jockey Club racecourse, and one of the world's largest autodromes.

São Paulo's long history has few visible traces in the modern metropolis. The Jesuits under Manuel da Nóbrega founded it as an Indian settlement in 1554, on the anniversary of the conversion of St. Paul, from whom the city takes its name. The site was a hill at the confluence of two streams defensible against hostile Indians. Three 16th-century paths on the hilltop formed the Triangle which permanently identified the city centre. In the 17th century São Paulo was a base for expeditions (*bandeiras*) searching the continent for Indian slaves and precious minerals. Although São Paulo succeeded São Vicente as capital of the captaincy in 1681 and was raised to the status of city in 1711, it

remained an agrarian town into the 19th century.

In 1822 Emperor Pedro I declared national independence in São Paulo at a site marked by the museum and monument of Ipiranga.

The city's modest fortunes before the mid-19th century derived from commerce, sugar growing, and diversified agriculture. The spread of coffee planting to the province opened a source of wealth that contributed to the city's sudden growth after 1880. Favoured by its climate, its strategic location in the transportation network, and the availability of a port, São Paulo became a centre for commerce, banking, and industry.

Immigrants arrived in large numbers as workers and entrepreneurs. For a time Italians outnumbered native Brazilians in the city. Other prominent groups were Portuguese, Spaniards, Germans, East Europeans, Levantines, and Japanese. Although immigration fell off after 1934, many foreign quarters kept their identity. Only about 7% of the inhabitants are Negroes, in contrast to the heavy Negro population of northeastern Brazil. Some 250,000 migrants from other parts of the country arrived annually in São Paulo in the 1960s.

Industrial development, beginning in the late 19th century, in a few decades made São Paulo with its neighbouring municipalities, notably Santo André, the foremost industrial centre of Latin America. Southern Brazil, more prosperous and densely settled than the north, furnished a market for manufactures. The territory within easy commercial reach of São Paulo contains only 20% of the area of the nation, but roughly 50% of its population, 75% of its highways and railways, and 90% of its electric power. In the 1960s São Paulo state produced nearly two-thirds of the value of Brazilian manufactures and the city alone about one-third. Some heavy industry existed—for producing steel, manufacturing plant equipment, and trucks and automobiles, for example—but was secondary to the production of light consumer goods. The industry employing the most workers was textiles, followed by mechanical and electrical appliances, building and furniture, foodstuffs, and chemical and pharmaceutical products. Except for foreign subsidiaries, industries tend to be owned by families and small groups. The 650,000 industrial workers in Greater São Paulo enjoy the highest wage level in Latin America. In 1952 Brazil's first intercity oil pipeline was opened between Santos and São Paulo, and in 1955 the Cubatão oil refinery, the nation's largest, began operation. Over 50% of U.S. investments ($1,200,000,000) and comparable proportions of other foreign investments in Brazil

DAVIS PRATT—RAPHO GUILLUMETTE

THE OPERA HOUSE, SÃO PAULO

(total: $4,000,000,000) were in the Greater São Paulo area in the 1960s.

São Paulo throughout its history exerted strong influence politically and economically at the federal government level. Local figures, who first served as mayors, governors, or local political or industrial leaders, later occupied the presidency, cabinet, and other federal positions with significant regularity in the 20th century. Throughout the 19th century São Paulo was a prominent cultural and intellectual centre, largely because of the opening in 1827 of a law academy, one of the first two in Brazil, where many of the nation's most eminent men were educated. This cultural leadership continued in the 20th century. In 1922 Modern Art Week, celebrated by a group of young writers, artists, and musicians in the Municipal Theatre, introduced modernism in the arts to Brazil. São Paulo is a leading centre for libraries (which include a skyscraper municipal library), publishing houses, theatres, and museums. It also houses a major concentration of news media services, including several of the largest and most important newspapers, television stations, and radio networks in Latin America. The Museum of Modern Art organized the first biennial exhibition in the Americas (1951). The permanent fairgrounds, erected for the fourth centennial of the city (1954), are distinguished for their modern architecture.

São Paulo has a well-developed system of primary and secondary schools, public and private, and a variety of vocational schools. The literacy rate for persons over six years of age rose from 45% in 1887 to 85% in 1946. The state-supported University of São Paulo, established in 1934, incorporated preexisting schools of law, polytechnic training, pharmacy and dentistry, agriculture, and medicine; faculties of economics, architecture, and engineering were added later. An affiliated institution is the School of Sociology and Politics, founded in 1933 by industrialists and civic leaders as the first advanced course in the social sciences in South America. Another is the Butantã Institute, a world-famous research centre for the study of snakes and the production of antitoxins and antivenins. Catholic University was created in 1946, and a third university, Mackenzie, was recognized a decade later.

Roman Catholicism is the prevailing religion, although Protestant, Jewish, and spiritist groups are of some importance.

(W. N. S.)

SÃO PAULO DE LUANDA, Angola: see LUANDA.

SÃO SALVADOR, Brazil: see SALVADOR.

SÃO TOMÉ E PRÍNCIPE, a Portuguese overseas province on the Equator in that part of the Gulf of Guinea called the Bight of Biafra, off the west coast of Africa. It consists of the islands of São Tomé (137 mi. [220 km.] WNW of Cape Lopez, Gabon) and Príncipe (93 mi. [150 km.] NNE of São Tomé). The area of the province is 372 sq.mi. (963 sq.km.), of which São Tomé occupies 330 sq.mi.

Physical Characteristics.—São Tomé, which is about 21 mi. broad and about 32 mi. from northeast to southwest, is volcanic and has many craters and old lava flows. It rises centrally to 6,640 ft. (2,024 m.) (Pico de São Tomé) and in the west-centre has ten peaks of over 3,500 ft., some of which culminate in phonolites resembling upward-pointing fingers. From these peaks the land falls sharply to the often sheer west coast, but there are a number of bays on the other coast. The southern lowlands have much volcanic ash and cinder and the off-lying Gago Coutinho islet (which is crossed by the Equator) is of basalt, with two craters. Príncipe is rectangular, measuring about 5 mi. across and 11 mi. (18 km.) from northeast to southwest. It rises to 3,110 ft. and is largely basaltic.

Climatically the islands belong to the southern hemisphere, as the drier season (*gravana*) is from June to September. Equatorial conditions are modified by the cold Benguela current, by coastal breezes, and by altitude. Four regions can be distinguished on both islands: (1) the hot and humid northeast lowlands with about 40 in. annual rainfall; (2) above 1,300 ft., where temperatures are lower, though variable, and rainfall heavier; (3) above 2,000 ft., where temperatures are yet lower, the nights cold, and mist frequent; (4) the southeast lowlands where there is no drier sea-

son. The lowlands are reputed to be malarial. The volcanic soil is extremely fertile. Rain forest is densely developed above 3,200 ft. on São Tomé but below that height the land has been largely cleared for cultivation.   (R. J. H. C.)

History.—São Tomé was probably uninhabited when it was first discovered by European sailors in the 1470s. In the late 15th century the Portuguese began to settle convicts and exiled Jews on the island and established sugar plantations. This industry used slave labour from the mainland, and for some years São Tomé became important as a slave entrepôt. In the 17th century the island was held briefly by the Dutch. Thereafter its importance declined. In the late 19th century the colony recovered its prosperity with the introduction of cocoa, but by 1909 British and German chocolate manufacturers were boycotting São Tomé cocoa on the ground that the indentured labourers used on the plantations were virtually slaves. In the 1960s São Tomé e Príncipe remained a Portuguese overseas province; it played only a minor role in the initial conflicts between African nationalism and Portuguese resistance.   (D. BI.)

Population and Administration.—The population of the province was 60,159 at the 1950 census and in 1960 was 63,485; of the total, 4,605 live on Príncipe. São Tomé has developed clusters of population in and around the provincial capital, São Tomé, in the more level northeast. In the west there are fewer people. Of the total population about 1,200 are Europeans and about 4,300 of mixed ancestry. Among the Negroes, men outnumber women because of the presence of numerous immigrant plantation labourers, recruited largely from Angola or Mozambique on long contract. In the 1950s fairly successful efforts were made to encourage fixed labour by making land grants on new roads south of São Tomé town and by improved education and housing. In Príncipe, Santo António on the east coast is the chief settlement.

With other Portuguese colonies, São Tomé e Príncipe was in 1951 given the status of an overseas province. The governor resides at São Tomé, which is also the residence of the *curador,* the legal guardian of the *serviçaes* (labourers). The province has more than 20 elementary schools, a secondary school, and a technical school.

Economy.—The earliest crop on São Tomé was sugar, but this was ruined by Brazilian competition in the late 16th century. Agriculture was not revived until coffee was introduced in 1800 and cocoa in 1822. Most agriculture is on plantations, one estate alone occupying one-tenth of São Tomé. Coconuts and oil palms grown in the coastal belts yield respectively about 20% and 5% of the exports by value. Between about 650 and 1,300 ft. elevation, especially on the northeast of both islands, cocoa is dominant, and until about 1905 the islands were the world's leading cocoa producers. Production has since declined but cocoa still makes up about two-thirds of the exports by value. Coffee, grown on higher ground, accounts for almost all remaining exports. Subsistence crops include yams. Fishing, especially for sharks, has some importance.

Communications.—A 12-mi. state-owned railway connects São Tomé with Trinidade in the interior. There are about 160 mi. of roads. São Tomé has a sheltered harbour on Ana de Chaves Bay and clears about 200 vessels with a net tonnage of 800,000 annually. Several shipping lines call regularly. São Tomé is linked by scheduled air services with Lisbon, Portuguese Guinea, Fernando Pó, and Príncipe.   (R. J. H. C.)

See R. J. Harrison Church, *West Africa,* pp. 521–526 (1963); F. Tenreiro, *A Ilha de São Tomé, Memórias da Junta de Investigações do Ultramar* (1961).

SAPIEHA (originally SOPIHA), a Polish princely family, descended from Ruthenian (Russian) boyars under Lithuanian rule.

LEW (1557–1633) was a Calvinist and a supporter of the Radziwills in his youth, but later turned Catholic and adhered to King Sigismund III of Poland. Chancellor of Lithuania from 1589 to 1623, he approved the Polish intervention in Russian affairs in 1609–11, and promoted the unfortunate expedition of 1617–18 with the aim of making the king's son Wladyslaw tsar in Moscow. His first cousin, JAN PIOTR (1569–1611), fought well against the Swedes and, in 1608, took service under the second False Dimitri (q.v.), whose hetman he became. He died in the Moscow Kremlin. Jan Piotr's son PAWEL JAN (c. 1610–1665) took part in the wars against the Muscovites, the Cossacks, and the Swedes; as hetman of Lithuania (1656), he combated King John Casimir's plans for strengthening the royal authority.

Pawel Jan's sons KAZIMIERZ JAN (1637–1720; hetman in 1682) and BENEDYKT (d. 1707; grand treasurer from 1676 to 1703) sought to make themselves predominant in Lithuania and resisted the Polish king John III Sobieski; but a confederation of nobles was formed against them, the brothers were defeated in battle at Olkienniki (1700), and Kazimierz's son MICHAL was murdered.

KAZIMIERZ NESTOR (1757–1798), descended from a brother of Lew's great-grandfather, became general of the Lithuanian artillery in 1773. He was one of the magnates in opposition to King Stanislaw II Poniatowski. Marshal of the Lithuanian Confederation during the Four Years' *Sejm* (1788–92), he joined the partisans of the Constitution of May 3 in 1791. His first cousin ALEKSANDER (1773–1812), a traveler and an ethnographer of the Slavs, was in close contact with Napoleon Bonaparte from the time of the Consulate in France and was a member of the provisional government of Lithuania in 1812, when Napoleon attacked Russia.

Aleksander's son LEON (1803–1878) forfeited his lands for participating in the anti-Russian insurrection of 1830. Settling in Galicia, he was active in political and economic life there; from 1861 to 1875 he was speaker of the Galician *Sejm*. His memoirs appeared in 1913. Leon's son ADAM (1828–1878), called "the Red Prince," was a parliamentarian and a journalist who wanted insurrection in Russian Poland and the restoration of an independent Poland with Austrian help. His youngest son, ADAM (1867–1951), from 1925 archbishop of Cracow, was created cardinal in 1946.

EUSTACHY (1881–1963), in the seventh generation from Kazimierz Jan, was Polish envoy to London (1919–20) and foreign minister (June 1920–May 1921), becoming later one of the leaders of the monarchist movement. (EM. R.)

SAPIR, EDWARD

SAPIR, EDWARD (1884–1939), U.S. linguist and anthropologist, who made important contributions in the field of American Indian languages, was born on Jan. 26, 1884, in Lauenburg, Pomerania. His parents took him to the United States in 1889 and he was educated at Columbia University (Ph.D., 1909). In 1910 he was named chief of the division of anthropology at the Canadian National Museum; in 1925 he joined the staff of the University of Chicago; and in 1927 he moved to Yale University, New Haven, Conn., where he remained as professor of anthropology and general linguistics until his death on Feb. 4, 1939.

Sapir early became interested in linguistics and, chiefly through the influence of Franz Boas (q.v.), in American Indian languages, the study of which he continued widely and intensively most of his life. His profound grasp of problems in the Indo-European languages, his quick recognition of contrasts in structure, and his ability to abstract the essential characteristics from masses of complex data enabled him to maintain a detached, synoptic view of language even while at work on minute linguistic problems in languages widely different from one another both genetically and structurally. His mind was vigorous, poetic, and searching, his style crisp and lucid; by personal contact as well as through his published words he was often productive of work in others. Sapir was a scientist of extraordinary breadth who kept the study of linguistic phenomena in proper perspective as part of the study of man. His book *Language* (1921) is one of the finest on the subject.

A collection of Sapir's essays was edited by David G. Mandelbaum as *Selected Writings in Language, Culture, and Personality* (1949). *See also* LINGUISTICS: *The History of Linguistics; Linguistics and Other Disciplines.* (MY. F.)

SAPODILLA

SAPODILLA, a tropical evergreen tree, *Achras sapota* (*zapota*), of the sapote family (Sapotaceae), and its delicious fruit. Sapodilla, the name used in southern Florida (the only part of the U.S. where this tree can be grown successfully), doubtless is an adaptation of the Spanish *zapotillo,* "small zapote." In Spanish-speaking countries the name *chicozapote* is commoner, and in certain English-speaking countries, notably India, naseberry (a corruption of *nispero,* Spanish for the medlar; q.v.) is used.

While the fruit is of no great commercial importance in any part of the world, it is much appreciated in many tropical and subtropical areas. It is spheroid to ovoid in shape, rusty brown on the surface, and two to four inches in rough diameter. The flavour, very sweet and difficult to describe, has been compared to a combination of pears and brown sugar. The seeds, two to five in number, shining black, and the size of flattened beans, are surrounded (when the fruit is ripe) by translucent, yellowish-brown, juicy flesh. When immature, the flesh contains tannin and milky latex and is quite unpalatable. The milky latex, chief source of gum chicle (q.v.), once important in the chewing-gum industry, is extracted by tapping the trunk.

Sapodilla trees occur wild in the forests of southern Mexico and northern Central America. As a cultivated species the tree is medium-sized and of slow growth. The reddish wood is very hard and durable (elaborately carved lintels a thousand years old are still to be seen in some Mayan ruins). The leaves, two to five inches long, are glossy and light green in colour, ovate to elliptic in outline; the flowers are small and inconspicuous. Propagation is usually by means of seed, but superior trees can be reproduced by grafting. (W. Po.)

SAPONINS AND SAPOGENINS

SAPONINS AND SAPOGENINS. Saponins are water-soluble plant substances characterized by special properties, namely, the ability to lower the surface tension of water and hence to cause foaming, the ability to destroy red blood corpuscles (hemolysis) and the ability to kill fish, all at relatively low concentrations. They probably are present in all plants, having been identified in more than 75 families and more than 500 species. They may be distributed throughout the plant or occur in high concentration in one part of the plant; *e.g.*, the root or bulb, leaves, bark, flowers, fruit flesh or seeds. Their function in the plant is not known. Some appear to serve as a storage form of carbohydrates (sugars and starches) in the plant, whereas others seem to be waste products of plant metabolism.

Common names for plants containing high concentrations of saponins are soaproot, soapwort, soapbark, soap plant and amole. These names are indicative of their use as cleansing agents by peoples throughout the world since ancient times. They do not form a scum in hard water, and even in comparatively modern times were preferred to soap for laundering fine fabrics, such as silk shawls. They formerly were used as foaming agents in foam-type fire extinguishers and as wetting agents in agricultural sprays, but were displaced for these purposes by the less expensive synthetic detergents and wetting agents. Saponin solutions are used in photographic emulsions to permit even spreading on the base, and in multilayered coatings to permit spreading and adhesion of successive layers.

Aboriginal peoples throughout all parts of the world have used saponins for catching fish. A quantity of a plant having a high saponin content is crushed and stirred into a pool. After a short time the fish rise to the surface and are taken easily. It is estimated that from 300 to 400 species of plants have been used for this purpose. As early as the 13th century, in order to prevent extermination of fish, laws were passed forbidding the use of fish poisons. Saponins cause death in fish probably by disabling the breathing mechanism of the gills. Although saponins are hemolytic and toxic to warm-blooded animals when injected into the blood stream, they are not absorbed from the intestines. Hence fish killed by saponins can be eaten with safety. The nontoxicity to man on ingestion is evident when one considers that the foaming properties of certain beverages, such as root beer, result from the presence of saponins.

Chemically the saponins belong to a large class of substances known as glycosides (*see* GLYCOSIDES, NATURAL). When a water solution of a saponin is heated in the presence of a strong acid, the saponin molecule is split into fragments with the addition of the elements of one molecule of water at every point at which scission takes place (hydrolysis). The products are a molecule of sapogenin and several molecules of one or more kinds of sugar. For example, in the hydrolysis of digitonin, one of three different saponins isolated from foxglove leaves, each molecule combines with five molecules of water to yield one molecule of a sapogenin, called digitogenin, one molecule of xylose and four molecules of galactose.

Because several different saponins may occur in the same plant, and because the saponins are amorphous and not readily crystallized, it has been difficult to isolate them in a pure state, and at mid-20th century relatively little work had been done on the chemistry of the saponins themselves. The sapogenins, on the other hand, are crystalline compounds that are purified readily, and a large amount of work had been expended in attempts to determine the way in which the constituent atoms are linked together.

The sapogenins thus far isolated belong to two main types. One type contains 27 carbon atoms with varying numbers of hydrogen and oxygen atoms. They have at least one alcoholic function (hydroxyl group), and contain a carbon framework like that present in the animal and plant alcohols known as sterols. Hence they are called steroid sapogenins. The saponins from foxglove leaves, sarsaparilla root, yucca and agave belong to this class. Some steroid sapogenins, such as diosgenin, prepared commercially from a Mexican yam, have become valuable raw materials for the synthesis of the female hormone, progesterone, and the adrenal cortical hormone, cortisone. (*See* also STEROIDS: *Classes of Steroids: Sapogenins.*)

The second type of sapogenin contains 30 carbon atoms, along with varying amounts of hydrogen and oxygen. They are called triterpene sapogenins because there are three times as many carbon atoms in the molecule as in a terpene molecule (*see* TERPENES). Like the steroid sapogenins, they contain at least one alcohol function (hydroxyl group), but in addition they contain an acid function (carboxyl group) and sometimes are called acid sapogenins. Saponins yielding triterpene sapogenins appear to be more widely distributed than those yielding steroid sapogenins. Moreover, the same triterpene sapogenin may occur free, as well as combined with sugars as a saponin. A further point of interest is that the triterpene alcohols, which occur in plant resins, are related closely in structure to the triterpene sapogenins. By replacing the acid function, COOH, of oleanolic acid (which occurs free in clove buds) by the group CH_3, a compound is obtained which is identical with beta-amyrin, a triterpene alcohol isolated from Manila elemi and other resins.   (C. R. N.)

SAPOTACEAE, the sapote family of tropical dicotyledonous plants, most of which are trees with leathery leaves. There are about 40 genera and about 600 species, many of which are of economic importance as sources of latex products and fruits.

Chrysophyllum cainito is the West Indian star apple. *Mimusops huberi* is the Brazilian milk tree. *Achras sapota* (*zapota*) of tropical America, cultivated in all tropical countries, yields the excellent fruit known as the sapodilla (*q.v.*) and the important chicle (*q.v.*), the basis of much chewing gum. *Lucuma nervosa* is the eggfruit or canistel of South America, now naturalized in Florida and the West Indies. The zapote, sapote, or marmalade plum is *Calocarpum mammosum* (*sapota*), one of the commonest fruit trees in Central America.

The important commercial product gutta-percha (*q.v.*) is chiefly derived from various species of *Palaquium* and *Payena* growing in the Malay Peninsula and Archipelago.

SAPPHICS, Greek lyric four-line stanza named after and presumably invented by Sappho and used by Alcaeus and, in Latin, by Catullus and Horace. The first three lines, each 11 syllables long, are each divisible into five poetic feet, all disyllabic (and commonly predominantly trochaic) except for the third foot, a (trisyllabic) dactyl; *e.g.,*

> —∪∣— ∪∣—∪ ∪∣∪ ∪∣—   —
> otium Catulle, tibi molest(um) est

The fourth line, five syllables long, consists of a dactyl followed by a spondee; *e.g.,*

> — ∪∪∣— —
> perdidit urbes

In the use of the Sapphic from Sappho to Horace it is possible to trace a growing tendency to insert a break or pause in the sense (caesura) after the fifth syllable of the 11-syllable (hendecasyllabic) line. About one-third of Sappho's hendecasyllables end a word after the fifth syllable, half of Alcaeus', and two-thirds of

Catullus'; in Horace, Odes I–III, there is almost always a caesura after the fifth syllable. *See* also PROSODY, CLASSICAL.

SAPPHIRE, a transparent to translucent variety of corundum (*q.v.*), or native aluminum oxide, has been highly prized as a gem stone since about 800 B.C. Its colour normally ranges from very pale blue to deep indigo; the most valued is a medium deep cornflower blue. The colour is due mainly to the presence of small amounts of iron and titanium. Colourless, gray, yellow, pale pink, orange, green, violet and brown varieties of gem corundum also are known as sapphire. Ruby (*q.v.*) is essentially the same mineral, but this name is restricted to corundum that is deep pink, red or purple.

Sapphire generally occurs as pyramidal, rhombohedral, tabular or barrel-shaped crystals. Repeated twinning and lamellar parting are characteristic. The lustre is vitreous to adamantine, but

BENJAMIN M. SHAUB

UNCUT SAPPHIRE

somewhat pearly on parting surfaces. Most sapphire contains abundant inclusions of microscopic size, and reflections of light from these yield a faint whitish sheen, known as "silk." Tiny, regularly arranged mineral inclusions and elongate cavities are responsible for the asterism shown by star sapphire. Such translucent, milky appearing stones, when properly cut, seem to contain a floating luminous star with six rays.

Much sapphire is unevenly coloured in bands, zones or blotches. It also is dichroic, so that in most varieties the colour changes according to the direction of view in transmitted light. Alexandrite-sapphire appears blue in daylight and reddish or violet in artificial illumination, somewhat like true alexandrite (*q.v.*), a variety of chrysoberyl.

Sapphire is a primary constituent of many igneous rocks, especially syenites, pegmatites and various basic types, and also is found in schists and metamorphosed carbonate rocks. Most commercial production has come from alluvial gravels and other placer deposits, where the sapphire commonly is associated with ruby, garnet, spinel, topaz, tourmaline, zircon and other gem minerals. The best-known occurrences, including some lode deposits, are in Ceylon, Burma, Thailand, Australia (Victoria, Queensland, New South Wales), India, Madagascar, the U.S.S.R., South Africa and the United States (Montana, North Carolina).

Most transparent sapphire is facet cut, generally in the brilliant style (*see* GEM). Such gems have considerable sparkle, but they exhibit little fire because of their modest dispersion. Skilful cutting of unevenly coloured stones yields gems with a uniform appearance derived from only small portions of relatively deep colour. Star sapphire and other nontransparent varieties are cut *en cabochon* rather than faceted.

Despite its great hardness (9), some sapphire is carved or engraved, especially in the orient. Careful heating and cooling under various conditions can induce essentially permanent colour changes in sapphire; *e.g.,* from yellow to colourless or greenish blue and from violet to pink. Other colour changes result from exposure to certain kinds of intense radiation.

Synthetic Sapphire.—Synthetic sapphire has been produced commercially since 1902. Clear, sound material of various colours is manufactured in the form of carrot-shaped boules and slender rods. Much is consumed by the jewelry trade, but most synthetic sapphire is used in place of natural sapphire and other materials for the manufacture of jewel bearings, gauges, dies, needle points, thread guides and other specialized components. Some also is used as a high-grade abrasive.

Synthetic star sapphire, with luminous stars more regular and distinct than in most natural stones, is made for gem uses. The asterism is obtained through controlled exsolution of impurities, generally rutile (titanium dioxide) in the form of tiny needles that assume preferred orientations within the host crystals of corundum. *See also* GEM: *Synthetic Gems.*   (R. H. J.)

SAPPHO (spelled PSAPPHO by herself) (fl. *c.* 610–*c.* 580 B.C.), the celebrated Greek lyric poetess, was a native of the island Lesbos, off the northwest coast of Asia Minor. Her father's name is most commonly given as Scamandronymus; her mother's name was Cleis. She had three brothers, Charaxus, Larichus, and Erigyus; she is said to have been married to Cercolas, a wealthy man from the island Andros; she had at least one child, a daughter, named Cleis. There is just sufficient evidence to prove that her family belonged to the upper class of society.

Her poetry is composed in the local Lesbian-Aeolic dialect. She had at her disposal a variety of metres (*see* SAPPHICS), some of which may well be of her own invention. Except for the epithalamiums (which seem to have formed a small and relatively insignificant part of her work) her poems are almost invariably concerned with personal themes. Cult-song and mythological narrative are seldom if at all to be found, and there are only a couple of apparent allusions to the political disturbances of the time which are so frequently reflected in the verse of her contemporary Alcaeus. The tradition that she herself was banished and went to Sicily is likely to be true, but is not confirmed by the extant fragments of her poetry. Alcaeus himself appears to be the person addressed in a stanza which rejects indelicate advances. Her brother Charaxus was the subject of several poems: Sappho prays for him a safe return home from Egypt, and release from entanglement with the notorious courtesan Doricha (whom Herodotus calls Rhodopis); in other poems, according to Herodotus, she "taunted him considerably." These, however, are exceptional examples: most of Sappho's poems are concerned with her friendships and enmities with other women.

It was the fashion in Lesbos at this period for women of good family to assemble in informal societies and spend their days in idle, graceful pleasures, especially the composition and recitation of poetry. Sappho, the leading spirit of one of these associations, attracted a number of admirers, some from distant places abroad. The principal themes of her poetry are the loves and jealousies and hates which flourished in that sultry atmosphere. Rival associations are fiercely or contemptuously attacked: Atthis deserted from Sappho to Andromeda; Archeanassa becomes the darling of a hated rival, Gorgo. For other girls, some named (Anactoria, Gongyla) but much more often nameless, Sappho expresses her feelings in terms which range from gentle affection to passionate love. Ancient writers over a period of time, having a large volume of her work in front of them, allege that Sappho was addicted to Lesbianism. It must be admitted that her poetry shows that she entertained emotions stronger than mere friendship toward other women, but in the extant remains there is not a word to connect herself or her companions with homosexual practices and only half a word—but that decisive enough—to show her awareness of their existence.

The beauty of her writing has been greatly, and justly, admired in all ages. Her vocabulary, like her dialect, is for the most part vernacular, not literary. Her phrasing is concise, direct, and picturesque, sparing of the customary poetic artifices and embellishments, owing little to that Homeric tradition which is elsewhere almost all-pervasive. Definite pains are taken to achieve an effect of simplicity and spontaneity. She has the power of standing aloof and critically judging her own ecstasies and pains; but her emotions lose nothing of their force by being recollected in comparative tranquillity. Her simple, candid, and luminous language compels the listener not only to understand but also to participate —to recognize his potential in her actual experience. It is doubtful whether any other poet in the history of Greek literature, ex-

cept Archilochus and Alcaeus, enters into so close a personal relation with the reader or listener. It is probable that, if the works of Anacreon and Ibycus were extant in much greater volume, it would be found that Sappho influenced them strongly; the only other Greek poet who owes much to her is Theocritus.

It is not known how her poems were published and circulated in her own lifetime and for the following three or four centuries. In the era of Alexandrian scholarship (especially the 3rd and 2nd centuries B.C.), what remained of her work was collected and republished in a standard edition comprising nine books of lyrical verse and one of elegiac (the latter, so far as the extant specimens permit a judgment, supposititious). The principles of book-division appear to have been purely metrical for the first eight; this is certain enough for the first four and the eighth, probable for the fifth; little or nothing is known of the sixth and seventh. The ninth book was arranged according to subject matter, comprising epithalamian poems, designed for recitation by choirs at weddings, in a variety of metres. The known lengths of books are 1,320 lines for book i, and about 130 (the last digit uncertain) for book viii.

This edition did not survive the early Middle Ages. By the 8th or 9th century A.D. Sappho was represented only by quotations in other authors, comprising one complete poem of 28 lines, the first 16 lines of another, and about 110 short one-line to four-line fragments. Since 1898 the fragments have been greatly increased by papyrus finds, though no complete and unmutilated poem has been recovered, and nothing equal in quality to the two longer pieces preserved in quotations. Fragments of 17 different papyrus copies of the Alexandrian edition have been found at Oxyrhynchus in Egypt (all of the 2nd or 3rd centuries A.D.), and valuable additions are made by an ostracon and a papyrus of Ptolemaic date and by two pieces of parchment from the 6th or 7th century A.D.

BIBLIOGRAPHY.—The first scholarly collection and edition of the remains of Sappho's poetry was that of C. F. Neue (1827), soon eclipsed by the masterly work of T. Bergk (*Poetae lyrici Graeci*, 1843; 4th ed. 1878–82). From 1898 onward the papyrus texts were edited and interpreted with incomparable skill by W. Schubart and U. von Wilamowitz-Moellendorff in Germany, and by A. S. Hunt and E. Lobel in England. In 1925 appeared *Sapphous Mele*, by E. Lobel, an edition of unprecedented acumen and accuracy, with an epoch-making introduction on the dialect. This edition was brought up to date by E. Lobel and D. L. Page in *Poetarum Lesbiorum fragmenta* (1955, 2nd ed. 1963; together with Alcaeus and complete indexes of vocabulary); the 12 more complete poems are reprinted with Eng. trans. and fully discussed by D. L. Page in *Sappho and Alcaeus* (1955; 2nd ed. 1959). These two publications supersede all other editions and essays published before 1954; of later works the most useful are the edition with German trans. by M. Treu (1954) and M. Fernández Galiano, *Safo* (1958, including the fullest extant bibliography, supplemented by the same author's *La Lirica griega*, 1958).   (D. L. P.)

SAPPORO, the capital of the prefecture of Hokkaido, Japan, situated 43°4′ N and 141°21′ E, on the Ishikari River with Otaru as its outer port. With a population of 523,839 (1960), it is the largest Japanese city north of Tokyo. The average temperature is 43° F and the snow season lasts from October to April, making Sapporo a popular centre for skiing and winter sports. Sapporo is the administrative, business, and educational centre of Hokkaido.

The city was laid out in 1871 on the American plan, with wide treelined boulevards intersecting each other at right angles. Sapporo was made the prefectural capital of Hokkaido in 1886, and owed its early development chiefly to the colonization bureau of the government. Hokkaido University pays special attention to agricultural science. The manufacture of foodstuffs (including flour, dairy products, and "Sapporo beer"), sawmills, printing, and publishing constitute the chief industries.   (R. B. H.)

SAPROPEL is an unconsolidated sedimentary deposit rich in bituminous substances. It is distinguished from peat in being rich in fatty and waxy substances and poor in cellulosic material. When consolidated into rock, sapropel becomes oil shale, bituminous shale, or boghead coal. The principal components are certain types of algae which are rich in fats and waxes. Minor constituents are mineral grains and decomposed fragments of spores, fungi, bacteria, and nonvascular plants. The organic materials accumulate in water under reducing conditions.

See also SEDIMENTARY ROCKS.   (P. D. T.)

SAPRU, SIR TEJ BAHADUR (1875–1949), Indian jurist and scholar who played a prominent role in India's constitutional progress, was born on Dec. 8, 1875. Educated at Agra College, he was a member of the United Provinces Legislative Council (1913–16) and of the Imperial Legislative Council (1916–20). A liberal in politics, he was trusted both by the British government and the Indian intelligentsia for his integrity and wisdom. He was a law member of the Viceroy's Council (1920–23), and India's delegate to the imperial conference (1923) and to all the three round-table conferences (1930–32), as well as to the joint parliamentary select committee on Indian constitutional reforms. He was chiefly responsible for bringing about the Gandhi-Irwin Pact (1931) which enabled Gandhi to attend the second round-table conference, and the Poona Pact (1932), which resulted in the modification of the communal award and ending of Gandhi's epic fast. He died on Jan. 20, 1949, at Allahabad.   (L. R. S.)

SAPSUCKER, the name applied to three aberrant forms of American woodpeckers that have acquired the habit of tapping trees for sap in the spring. They constitute the genus *Sphyrapicus*. The yellow-bellied sapsucker (*S. varius*) is black above, heavily spotted with white, and has a white rump and wing patch. Its crown and throat are bright red, bordered with black and white, forming a prominent face pattern. It drills its holes close together, usually in horizontal lines around a tree trunk, penetrating the bark to the wood, and visits them periodically to lap up the exuding sap and to eat the cambium. In trees that are visited frequently, permanent damage may result. Birch and maple are favourite trees, but about 250 species of trees and woody vines are attacked. Large quantities of sap are consumed: young captive sapsuckers have ingested eight teaspoonfuls of dilute syrup in a day. Insects, particularly ants, are also eaten. These birds hold the body away from the tree trunk on which they are feeding so that only the feet and tip of the tail touch the bark—unlike many woodpeckers which hug the trunk closely. Like some other woodpeckers, sapsuckers are expert aerial flycatchers. The call is a mewing note.

G. RONALD AUSTING FROM NATIONAL AUDUBON SOCIETY

YELLOW-BELLIED SAPSUCKER (SPHYRAPICUS VARIUS)

The yellow-bellied sapsucker breeds in northeastern North America, west to Alberta, and winters as far south as Central America. It lays four to six glossy white eggs in a gourd-shaped cavity in a tree trunk, which it excavates, generally leaving a very tight entrance hole. Williamson's sapsucker (*S. thyroideus*) is a species found in western North America; it lacks the white spotting of the back and the red on the head. The red-breasted sapsucker is a California race of *S. varius* with a completely red head and breast.   (W. J. Be.)

SAQQARAH (SAKKARA), an area containing part of the necropolis of the ancient city of Memphis (*q.v.*), 15 mi. (24 km.) SW of Cairo, Egypt; the modern Arab village of Saqqarah stands nearby. It has been suggested that the name derives from that of the hawk-headed god of the dead, Sokar (Gr. Sokaris), but not all scholars agree. The site extends along the edge of the desert plateau for about five miles from Abu Sir in the north to Dahshur in the south. The limestone rock is honeycombed with tombs of every age from the Archaic period to the Roman (for chronology, *see* EGYPT: *History;* CHRONOLOGY: *Egyptian*), and a number of royal pyramids break the horizon. Archaeologists of many nationalities have excavated at Saqqarah, and some of the finest examples of sculpture in the Museum of Egyptian Antiquities in Cairo were found there in Old Kingdom tombs.

The Royal Tombs.—The earliest remains at Saqqarah are those in the Archaic cemetery at the northernmost end of the site, where large mud-brick mastaba tombs have been found which date to the very beginning of Egyptian history. The superstructures of these tombs were ornamented with elaborate paneling; storage jars found in the magazines bore the names of kings of the 1st dynasty from Ahai onward. Similar royal tombs, somewhat smaller, were found by Sir Flinders Petrie at Abydos (*q.v.*), and it is uncertain which were the actual burials and which were cenotaphs. Sealings of officials of the kings' entourage were also found in the tombs.

South of the Archaic cemetery lies the so-called Zoser complex, in many respects the most remarkable of Saqqarah's antiquities. The second king of the 3rd dynasty, Zoser Neterikhet, and his architect Imhotep (*q.v.*) here devised a new form of burial in the shape of a pyramid in six stages, the 200-ft.-high Step Pyramid which dominates the area. (*See* PYRAMID: *Early Forms.*) At its foot, the builders of this first of pyramids constructed a huge complex of halls and courts in which prototype structures of mud brick, wood, and reed were translated into fine limestone. Shepseskaf, one of the last kings of the 4th dynasty, was buried in the large tomb known as Mastabat Fara'un in South Saqqarah some 4 mi. (6½ km.) S of the Step Pyramid. Userkaf, at the beginning of the 5th dynasty, built his pyramid near the Zoser complex, but his successors moved to Abu Sir. The later kings of this dynasty, however, returned to Saqqarah. Unas, the last king, whose pyramid is to the west of the Zoser temple, was the first of five kings to inscribe on the walls of his pyramid chambers the Pyramid Texts, designed to protect the dead king and to ensure him life and sustenance in the hereafter. A limestone corridor 700 yd. (640 m.) long leads to his valley temple. Succeeding kings of the 6th dynasty built their pyramids to the south, and the most southerly is that of a 13th-dynasty king.

The Mastabas.—Around the pyramids of their sovereigns the nobles of the Old Kingdom were buried in mastaba tombs (*see* EGYPTIAN ARCHITECTURE: *Tombs*). On the walls of the corridors, store chambers, and chapels contained within these tombs are carved innumerable scenes from the daily life of the deceased, showing him inspecting the varied activities of peasants and workmen on his estate, and with his family engaged in the pursuits of leisure, fishing and fowling, or seated at home with his wife and children. Some scenes retain a little of their original colour, and they are full of lively detail and variety.

Later Tombs.—The decline in importance of Memphis during the Middle Kingdom is reflected in the comparatively few tombs of this period found in the Saqqarah necropolis, but in the New Empire Memphis became a garrison city and naval base, and a number of New Empire tombs have been found on the edge of the plateau near the pyramid of King Teti. The tomb of Horemheb is the best known of these. In the New Empire and after, the Apis (*q.v.*) bulls were buried in large subterranean galleries, three of which were found by Auguste Mariette; the latest, known as the Serapeum, is open to visitors. In the northwest of the necropolis,

A. F. KERSTING

THE STEP PYRAMID AT SAQQARAH

beneath a field of mastabas of the 3rd and 4th dynasties, another complex of underground passages, known in part to travelers in the early 19th century, has been re-excavated from 1964 onward by the Egypt Exploration Society in collaboration with the Egyptian Antiquities Service; the hypogeum contains thousands of ibis mummies of the Ptolemaic period, packed in jars. The shafts of imposing tombs of the Saite and Persian periods were sunk near the pyramid of Unas. The monastery of Apa Jeremias nearby dates from the 5th century A.D.

BIBLIOGRAPHY.—G. Jéquier, *Le Mastabat Faraoun* (1928); W. B. Emery, *Archaic Egypt* (1961), *The Tomb of Hemaka* (1938), *Hor-aha* (1939), *Excavations at Sakkara: Great Tombs of the First Dynasty*, I–III (1949–58); Preliminary Reports on the Excavations at North Saqqara, in *Journal of Egyptian Archaeology*, vol. 51 (1965) and vol. 52 (1966); J. E. Quibell, *Excavations at Saqqara, 1905–1914*, 6 vol. (1907–23); J. P. Lauer, *Fouilles à Saqqarah: La Pyramide à degrés*, 4 vol. (1936–59); Z. Y. Saad, *Royal Excavations at Saqqara and Helwan 1941–45* (1947). (M. S. Dr.)

SARABAND, a bawdy dance of medieval Spain, probably of Arabic-Moorish origin. Suppressed during the reign of Philip II, it was later revived in purer form, playing a prominent part in religious dramas. Transplanted to the French court early in the 17th century, it became a slow, serious, processional dance in triple rhythm. The music, of simple structure, was adapted as an important part of the suite (*q.v.*), in which it generally follows the Courante. *See also* DANCE FORMS IN MUSIC. (L. Ht.)

SARACENS, a name best known for its use by Christians in the Middle Ages to identify their Muslim enemies, both Arab and Turkish. The name has survived until modern times. There are several references to Saracens (*Sarakenoi*) by late classical authors in the first three centuries A.D., the term being then applied to an Arab tribe living in the Sinai Peninsula. In the following centuries the use of the term was extended to cover Arab tribes in general, and after the establishment of the caliphate the Byzantines referred to all Muslim subjects of the caliph as Saracens. Through the Byzantines and the crusaders the name spread into western Europe where it was long in general use.

See J. H. Mordtmann, "Saracens," in *Encyclopaedia of Islam*, vol. iv (1934).

SARACOGLU, SHUKRU (1887–1953), Turkish statesman, prime minister of Turkey during 1942–46, was born at Odemish near Izmir in 1887. He was educated in Izmir, Istanbul, and in Switzerland. After his return to Turkey in 1918 he joined the nationalist movement led by Mustafa Kemal. Elected to the Grand National Assembly as deputy for Izmir in 1923, he was minister of education for a short period in 1925. Thereafter he became chairman of the Turkish delegation to the Greco-Turkish Population Exchange Commission. He was minister of finance (1927–30) in Ismet Inonu's government. In 1931 he was sent on a financial mission to the United States, and on his return he prepared a report which served as the basis for the reorganization of the Turkish cotton industry. He served as minister of justice (1933–38) and was then appointed minister of foreign affairs. In 1939 he concluded a treaty of alliance with Great Britain and France: France, as a prerequisite, ceded to Turkey, at Saracoglu's insistence, the Hatay province of Syria with the valuable port of Alexandretta (Iskenderun). His policy, nevertheless, was to maintain Turkey as a neutral power during World War II. He was appointed prime minister in 1942 on the death of Reyfik Saydam, and as prime minister he successfully continued this policy until Turkey's declaration of war on the Axis powers in February 1945.

Saracoglu was elected president of the Grand National Assembly in 1948 but lost his seat as deputy for Izmir after the Democratic electoral victory in 1950. He died at Istanbul on Dec. 27, 1953. (M. P. P.)

SARAGOSSA (ZARAGOZA), a city of northeastern Spain, capital of the province of the same name, and of the metropolitan archdiocesan see of Aragon, lies on the right bank of the Ebro River, 212 mi. (341 km.) NE of Madrid by rail. Pop. (1960) 326,316. Saragossa preserves much of the character of an old Aragonese city, especially in the area enclosed by the Calle del Coso, the curving highway which follows the line of the old fortifications and bounds the old town on the south. Between the Coso and the river is a network of narrow streets cut by two modern arteries. The easternmost, the Calle de Don Jaime I, connects the Coso with the seven-arched stone bridge, Puente de Piedra, dating from 1447, linking Saragossa with the suburb of Arrabal or Altabás. To the west is the Calle de Don Alfonso I, which runs down to the Plaza del Pilar, where stands one of the two cathedrals. The Coso runs into the Plaza de España and from there the broad Paseo de la Independencia leads to a well-planned late-19th-century residential area to the south. Newer suburbs have sprung up south and southwest of the town.

Saragossa has two cathedrals united into one by papal bull in 1675. One chapter serves both buildings. The older of the two is the Catedral de la Seo (Lat. *sedes*) or del Salvador, chiefly a Gothic building (12th–16th centuries) but showing some traces of the earlier Romanesque church built on the site of the first mosque erected in Spain, which itself had replaced an earlier church. The Catedral del Pilar, dedicated to the Virgin of the Pillar who is patron of all Spain, commemorates the traditional appearance on Jan. 2, A.D. 40, of the Virgin Mary standing on a pillar erected in honour of St. James the Great, whose shrine is at Santiago (*q.v.*). The miraculous image representing this appearance is preserved in the cathedral, which stands on the site of an earlier chapel. The cathedral was begun in 1681 to a design by Herrera el Mozo and contains some frescoes by Goya. The 14th-century Gothic churches of San Pablo and the Magdalena and the Renaissance church of Santa Engracia are also notable.

La Lonja, the exchange building, in Plateresque Gothic style, the palace of the counts of Luna, where the Court of Justice sits, and the palace of the Condes de Sástago y Argillo are notable public buildings. The Aljafería Palace, to the west of the town, contains an oratory dome and tower dating from the Islamic period, which are among Spain's most beautiful examples of Arab civil architecture. The University of Saragossa was founded in 1474, the medical school being its most famous faculty, but the buildings date from later periods.

Saragossa is an industrial centre, manufacturing agricultural machinery, railway rolling stock, textiles, glass, leather, chocolate, soap, paper, cement, and chemicals. The industries have expanded with the supply of hydroelectric power from the dams in the Aragonese Pyrenees and with oil from the pipeline from Rota (near Cádiz). It is also a trade centre for the agricultural products of Aragon, and an important railway junction, connected with Valladolid, Madrid, Valencia, the region of Catalonia, and the Basque Provinces, and France, via the Somport Tunnel.

History.—Toward the end of the 1st century B.C. the Cantabrian town of Salduba was taken by the Romans who made it a colony under Augustus with the name of Caesaraugusta (from which its Arabic name Sarakusta and its modern name Zaragoza were derived). The chief commercial and military station in the Ebro Valley, it was one of the first towns in Spain to which Christianity penetrated, and it had a bishop by the middle of the 3rd century A.D. The Latin poet Prudentius names 18 Saragossan martyrs. In 380 a church synod at Saragossa condemned the Priscillianist heresy. After falling to the Suebi and then to the Visigoths in the 6th century, Saragossa was taken by the Arabs *c.* 713. In 778 it was besieged by Charlemagne, who had to withdraw because of a Saxon rebellion. After being captured by the Almoravids in 1110 Saragossa was taken by Alfonso I of Aragon in 1118, and thereafter enjoyed three and a half centuries of prosperity as capital of Aragon. In the Peninsular War it was famed for the heroic resistance of its inhabitants under J. de Palafox y Melzi during a protracted siege (1808–09) by the French who finally took the city. Among the defenders was María Augustín, the "Maid of Saragossa," whose exploits are described in Byron's *Childe Harold*. In the Spanish Civil War (1936–39) Saragossa was on the Nationalist side.

(L. G. L.; X.)

SARAGOSSA PROVINCE, together with the provinces of Huesca and Teruel, formed the old kingdom of Aragon (*q.v.*). The province extends north and south of the middle course of the Ebro River, its most northerly extension reaching the foot of the Pyrenees. It is bounded west by the provinces of Navarre, Logroño, and Soria, south by Guadalajara and Teruel, and east and northeast by Tarragona, Lérida, and Huesca. Area, 6,639 sq.mi. (17,195 sq.km.).

Pop. (1960) 656,772. The relief is mostly gently rolling tableland drained by the Ebro and its tributaries. The climate is continental with the average temperature in January 5° C (41° F), in July 24° (76°) at Saragossa city.

The annual rainfall of less than 15–18 in. (38–46 cm.) explains the importance of irrigation. All the main settlements are in the irrigated valleys, the Ebro being the chief link. Two canals border the Ebro, the Canal Imperial de Aragón (60 mi. [97 km.] long, watering 69,000 ac. [28,000 ha.]) on the right bank and the Tauste Canal (27 mi. [43 km.] long, watering 22,000 ac. [9,000 ha.]) on the left bank. The Jalón Valley is next in importance. Cereals, especially wheat and barley, are the mainstay of the economy, followed by alfalfa, stock rearing, industrial crops such as sugar beet, and horticulture. From Daroca down the Jiloca Valley into the Jalón Valley is an important fruit growing district. Apart from a sugar refinery at Calatayud, industry is largely concentrated in the capital, Saragossa. The second town is Calatayud (pop. 17,940), followed by Tarazona de Aragón (12,059), an episcopal see, Caspe (9,507), Ejea de los Caballeros (10,998), and Tauste (6,634).   (J. M. Ho.)

SARAJEVO, capital of the Socialist Republic of Bosnia-Hercegovina, Yugos., lies in the Miljacka River Valley, 1,800 ft. above sea level at the foot of Trebevic Mountain, about 185 mi. (300 km.) SW of Belgrade (Beograd) by road. Pop. (1961) 198,-914, including Serbs and Croats and a proportion of Muslims. The town retains a strong Turkish character and is very picturesque, with its many mosques, ancient Turkish bazaar, wooden houses, and cypress groves. Sarajevo is the seat of a Roman Catholic archbishop, a Serbian Orthodox metropolitan, and the Reis ul-Ulema, the highest Muslim religious authority in Yugoslavia. The town has three ancient mosques, Begova, Careva, and Alipasina. The Begova, founded in 1465, is considered the most beautiful building in Yugoslavia surviving from the days of Ottoman rule. Other notable buildings are the Roman Catholic and Orthodox cathedrals, the hospitals, the town hall, the museum, and the university (founded in 1946). Near the bazaar is the oldest church in Bosnia, the Orthodox Church of St. Archangel, containing a 14th-century icon of the Virgin.

Sarajevo is a road centre and is linked by rail with Brod and Dubrovnik (Ragusa). Industries include a steel mill, potteries, silk and flour mills, timber works, a sugar-beet refinery, a brewery, and factories producing railway coaches, tobacco, embroidery, and carpets. Weaving on hand looms is still important.

Near Sarajevo are the remains of a Neolithic dwelling. Under the Romans the 8th Legion (Augusta) was stationed there. In 1415 Sarajevo is mentioned for the first time as Vrh-Bosna, a citadel just above the present site of the town. The Turks later founded a town below the citadel, naming it Bosna-Seraj. In 1480 Hungarian forces plundered the town. The most prosperous period of history was between 1494 and 1591 when many of the mosques were built. In the second part of the 16th century the traders of Dubrovnik built their quarter called Latinluk. Sephardi Jews came to Sarajevo in the same century and founded their quarter, Cifuthani. In 1697 Prince Eugène of Savoy burned Sarajevo, which was several times devastated by fire between the 15th and 18th centuries.

Sarajevo was chosen in 1850 as the seat of the Turkish administration of Bosnia-Hercegovina instead of Travnik. In 1878 it became the seat of the Austro-Hungarian administration and subsequently of the first Bosnian diet, the Sabor, and under Austrian rule it was largely modernized. In this period it also became the centre of the Serbian national movement. Students at Sarajevo perpetrated the murder of the Archduke Francis Ferdinand in 1914. The Austro-Hungarian government used this event as a pretext for the attack on Serbia which led to World War I. In November 1918 the diet of Sarajevo proclaimed its union with Yugoslavia. During World War II it was nominally included in the Kingdom of Croatia and suffered considerable damage from Allied bombing. In 1944 it was reincorporated into Yugoslavia.   (V. De.)

SARAN, a district in the west of Tirhut division, Bihar, India, is a wedge-shaped alluvial tract of light, well-drained loam between the Gandak River in the northeast and the Gogra (Ghaghara) and Ganges (Ganga) rivers in the south and southeast, all of which are perennially navigable. Area 2,669 sq.mi. Pop. (1961) 3,584,918. The important crops in this closely cultivated district are rice, barley, maize (corn), oilseeds, wheat, and sugarcane. Mango groves are common. Saran, with many sugar mills, is the leading district of Bihar in this industry. Notable developments since India's independence include several hundred tube wells, particularly in the west-central areas, and the remodeling of the flood protective embankment along the Gogra. The district headquarters are at Chapra (pop. 75,580), a rail and road junction. The district is served by the North Eastern Railway.   (E. Ah.)

SARANAC LAKE, a village of northeastern New York, U.S., is located on Flower Lake in the Adirondack Mountains, 8 mi. NW of Lake Placid on the boundary line between Essex and Franklin counties. Nearby are the Saranac and St. Regis chain of lakes. It is a summer and winter resort with a considerable influx of visitors during the summer season. The U.S. Eastern Amateur Ski Association was originally formed there and skiing is a major winter activity. The Mt. Van Hoevenberg bobsled run, operated by the New York State Conservation Department, is located a short distance from Saranac Lake.

Settlement dates from 1819 and the village originated as an isolated lumbering community and a centre for Adirondack guides. Situated at an altitude of 1,600 ft., Saranac Lake became a pioneer area for the open-air treatment of tuberculosis. The Trudeau Sanitarium, founded in 1884 as the Adirondack Cottage Sanatorium by Edward L. Trudeau, was the first semicharitable institution of its kind in the U.S. Other sanitariums were established in the vicinity, one of the largest being the New York State Ray Brook Institution. In 1957 the American Management Association acquired the property of the Trudeau Sanitarium, consisting of 90 ac. and about 50 buildings, and established an academy where management personnel pursue advanced training. Robert Louis Stevenson spent the winter of 1887–1888 as a patient at Saranac Lake and it was there he began *The Master of Ballantrae*. Saranac Lake was incorporated in 1880 and in 1929 adopted the village-manager plan of government. For comparative population figures *see* table in New York: *Population*.   (D. E. A.)

SARANSK, a town and the administrative centre of the Mordvinian Autonomous Soviet Socialist Republic of the Russian Soviet Federated Socialist Republic, U.S.S.R., stands on the upper Insar on the western flank of the Volga uplands. Pop. (1959) 91,034. The town was founded in 1641 as a stronghold on the Saransk defensive line, the eastern extension of the Belgorod line. It is an important focus with rail links to Ryazan and Moscow, Gorki, Kazan, Kuybyshev (Kuibyshev), and Penza. It acquired

VIEW OF SARAJEVO SHOWING THE MILJACKA RIVER AND SEVERAL OF THE MINARETS WHICH OVERLOOK THE CITY. IN THE CENTRE IS THE TOWN HALL

machinery industries during World War II, and there is also a wide range of industries producing electric lamps, rectifiers, cables, rope and cord, footwear, clothing, and penicillin. Saransk has a university, founded in 1957, and a research institute of Mordvinian culture. (R. A. F.)

SARAPION (Serapion), **SAINT** (fl. mid-4th century A.D.), bishop of Thmuis in Egypt, was a friend and correspondent of St. Athanasius and the author of an anti-Manichaean thesis and some liturgical prayers. The church historian Sozomen refers to him as "distinguished by the extraordinary holiness of his life and by the power of his eloquence," and Jerome records that the qualities of his mind earned for him the surname "scholasticus." The facts of his life are few and their dating uncertain. In his earlier life he was a monk in the desert and subsequently an abbot, becoming a close friend of St. Anthony. He had become bishop of Thmuis, a city in the Nile delta, by 339, to which year belongs the earliest of the four letters on the divinity of the Holy Spirit addressed to him by Athanasius. It has been asserted that Sarapion was present with Athanasius at the Council of Sardica (343), but evidence for this is inconclusive. In 353 he was chosen by Athanasius to lead a mission of Egyptian bishops and presbyters to the emperor Constantius II to refute the slanders of Athanasius' enemies and to conciliate the emperor. In 356, however, Athanasius and his supporters were declared to be enemies of the emperor. (*See also* ATHANASIUS, SAINT.) It seems likely that, in the violent measures taken against those Egyptian bishops who upheld the cause of Athanasius, Sarapion was banished from his see. Jerome describes him as "celebrated for his confession"; and in 359 an Arian, Ptolemaeus, claimed to be bishop of Thmuis. The manner and date of Sarapion's death are unknown. His feast day is March 21.

Jerome attributes to Sarapion the authorship of "an excellent book against Manichaeus" (Mani), which has survived; of another "on the titles of the Psalms," now lost; and of "useful letters on different subjects," of which only two have survived entire. There is the fragment of a Syriac version of another letter and one of a treatise on virginity. The name of "Sarapion bishop of Thmuis" is also connected with a collection of liturgical prayers for the Eucharist, baptism, ordinations, unction, and burial, and there is no reason to doubt its connection with Sarapion. The eucharistic prayer, entitled "Prayer of Oblation of Bishop Sarapion," is remarkable for containing a petition for the coming of the Logos (the Divine Word) upon the bread and wine to effect their consecration.

BIBLIOGRAPHY.—Letters in J. P. Migne, *Patrologia Graeca,* vol. 40, col. 924–941 (1858). Anti-Manichaean treatise ed. by R. P. Casey in *Harvard Theological Studies,* vol. 15 (1931). Liturgical prayers ed. by F. E. Brightman in *Journal of Theological Studies,* 1:88–113, 247–277 (1899–1900); Eng. trans. by J. Wordsworth (1899); *see also* B. Capelle, "L'Anaphore de Sérapion: Essai d'exégèse," *Le Muséon,* 59: 425–443 (1946). For discussion of the possible dates of Sarapion's banishment and death *see* the French trans. of Athanasius' letters to Sarapion by J. Lebon (1947) in *Sources chrétiennes,* and the Eng. trans. of the same by C. R. B. Shapland (1951). (E. C. RA.)

SARAPIS (Serapis), a Greco-Egyptian deity, first encountered at Memphis, where the dead Apis bull was worshiped underground as Osorapis, whereas the cult of Sarapis, originally a god of the underworld, was celebrated in the temple above. It was part of the religious policy inaugurated by Ptolemy I (323–285 B.C.), and continued by his successors, to mark the beginning of his dynasty by promoting the worship of a new deity, Sarapis, and by centring that worship on the new capital, Alexandria. No doubt Ptolemy felt his way at first, and the cult with its many Hellenic features took time to establish itself in the face of the deadweight of Egyptian religious conservatism. But its syncretism appealed to the Macedonians and Greeks among his subjects, and civil and military officials increasingly encouraged its spread.

The Sarapeum built to Parmeniscus' design at Alexandria was the largest and best known of the god's temples. It contained a famous cult statue by Bryaxis. Sarapis was represented as a majestic robed and bearded figure regally enthroned, a *modius* (a grain measure indicative of fruitfulness) on his head, his right hand resting on Cerberus, while his left held an upraised sceptre.

Cerberus symbolized Sarapis' chthonian aspect; initially, like Osiris, he was Lord of the Dead. Countenance and posture were meant to be reminiscent of Zeus; "there is one Zeus Sarapis" was a ritual formula. From this it was an easy step to the assimilation of Sarapis to the sun-god. His temple at Alexandria was so sited that on the anniversary of its foundation the rays of the rising sun shone through a window and kissed the lips of the statue. The sceptre recalled not only Zeus but also Asclepius; Sarapis was a god of healing whose cures could be miraculous. Finally the *modius* suggested that Sarapis was a god of fertility, and as such he was equated with Dionysus.

BY COURTESY OF THE CAPITOLINE MUSEUM, ROME

MARBLE STATUE OF SARAPIS IN THE CAPITOLINE MUSEUM, ROME. DATING FROM THE 2ND CENTURY A.D., IT IS ROMAN WORK AND DERIVED FROM THE CULT STATUE BY BRYAXIS AT ALEXANDRIA

After some initial hostility the Roman emperors, especially in the 2nd and 3rd centuries, were well disposed; temples to Sarapis were built in Rome on the Campus Martius and the Quirinal. Along with the worship of Isis and the Egyptian gods, the Sarapis cult spread widely throughout the Mediterranean, following the trade routes and being particularly prominent in the great commercial cities; hence, perhaps, the frequent identification of Sarapis with Poseidon, king of the sea. Clearly this pantheistic all-embracing deity had a wide appeal in a cosmopolitan multiracial society. Among the Gnostics Sarapis was a symbol of the universal godhead. The destruction of the Sarapeum at Alexandria, in accordance with the edict of Theodosius I, by the patriarch Theophilus and his followers in 391 A.D. signaled the final triumph of Christianity not only in Egypt but throughout the empire.

See F. Cumont, *Les Religions orientales dans le paganisme romain,* 4th ed. (1929); M. P. Nilsson, *Geschichte der griechischen Religion,* 2nd ed., vol. 2 (1961). (D. E. W. W.)

SARASIN (Sarrazin), **JEAN FRANÇOIS** (1614–1654), French author of elegant *vers de société,* best known for the mock epic *Dulot vaincu,* for the epic fragments *Rollon conquérant* and *La Guerre espagnole,* and for *La Pompe funèbre de Voiture.* The son of Roger Sarasin, the treasurer-general, he was born at Caen in December 1614. In 1648 he entered the household of the prince de Conti, in whose service he remained until his death at Pézenas on Dec. 5, 1654. As well as witty satiric poems, he wrote a *Discours de la tragédie* (1639) and historical works (*Histoire du siège de Dunkerque,* 1649; and the unfinished *La Conspiration de Walstein*).

BIBLIOGRAPHY.—The best modern edition of his *Oeuvres* (1656; *Nouvelles Oeuvres,* 2 vol., 1674) is by P. Festugière, 2 vol. (1926). *See also* A. Mennung, *J.-F. Sarasins Leben und Werke,* 2 vol. (1902–04). (R. A. SA.)

SARASOTA, a resort city on the west coast of Florida, U.S., is located 50 mi. S of Tampa on Sarasota Bay; the seat of Sarasota County. It is connected by causeways with white-sand beaches on four islands, lying between the bay and the Gulf of Mexico. Its origin is unknown; Sarasota, variously spelled, appeared on maps in the 1700s. Its development from a fishing hamlet began in 1885 when Scotch promoters, headed by Sir John Gillespie, induced 60 families from Scotland to settle there. A quarter of a century later Mrs. Potter Palmer, Chicago social leader, purchased several tracts of land, helped popularize it as a resort, and promoted the economy by establishing a model cattle ranch. The city was incorporated in 1914 and has a council-manager form of government in effect since 1946. The economy depends primarily on tourism, cattle raising, and the growing of winter vegetables.

Sarasota is the site of the Ringling museums consisting of a large gallery of Baroque art, including the most extensive collection in the Western Hemisphere of the works of Rubens; the Asolo Theatre (1790) brought from near Venice and used for dramatic and musical productions; the John Ringling home, a $1,000,000 replica of a doge's palace, containing rare Venetian art; and a museum of the circus. The first three were a bequest to the state by John Ringling; the museum of the circus was built by the state in 1948 as a memorial to him. Recreation and sports programs include fishing for tarpon and other saltwater fish, baseball, and golf. The city has a symphony orchestra and art schools.

For comparative population figures *see* table in FLORIDA: *Population.*

SARASVATI (SARASWATI), a river frequently mentioned in the Rigveda; although it was known to be located in the Punjab, its actual identity remains one of the fascinating problems of history. Its meaning, "abounding in pools," suggests that it was a large river. The ancient name still appears on maps as that of a tributary (otherwise the Sarsuti) of the Ghaggar, sweeping down in times of flood from the Siwalik Hills. (The Ghaggar loses itself in the desert sands toward Rajasthan but through dry channels may be traced to its former junction with the Indus.) Corresponding phonetically to the Iranian Haraqaiti (the modern Helmand), the name Sarasvati may have been applied to the Indus by the invading Aryans before they reached the eastern Punjab, but it soon ceased to refer to that river. It was most likely used for what is now the Ghaggar-Hakra-Indus channel, the lost river of the Indian Desert. With the Drishadvati, the Sarasvati formed the western boundary of Brahmavarta, and was the holy stream of Vedic India. It became personified as the goddess of eloquence, learning, and wisdom, and wife of Brahma. Another Sarasvati, in Gujarat, also loses itself in the sand. (L. D. S.)

SARATOGA, BATTLES OF, closely related engagements of the American Revolution (*q.v.*) that were fought in September and October 1777 and are often called the turning point of the war. The failure of the American invasion of Canada in 1775–76 had left a large body of surplus British troops on the St. Lawrence River, and under the British plan of campaign for 1777 they were to move south and join forces with Gen. William Howe's troops on the Hudson River. Gen. John Burgoyne, coming down from Canada via Lakes Champlain and George, was to meet at Albany a much smaller force under Col. Barry St. Leger advancing from Oswego along the Mohawk Valley. Burgoyne, with about 8,000 men, including seven regiments of British regulars and 3,000 Germans, reached Ticonderoga (July 1), which was evacuated by its weak garrison (July 6). He then marched his army through the woods and swamps to Ft. Edward on the upper Hudson; the fort was evacuated by the American commander, Gen. Philip Schuyler,

who retreated across the Hudson to Stillwater, 30 mi. above Albany (July 31). Burgoyne's laborious march involved the construction of 40 bridges and required a long halt at Ft. Edward.

A German detachment was sent to Bennington, Vt., to seize horses and supplies, but was surrounded and almost annihilated by a force under Gen. John Stark (Aug. 16). Burgoyne now became uneasy: he had left nearly 1,000 men to garrison Ticonderoga; he had heard from Howe of his intention to invade Pennsylvania; and St. Leger was held up before Ft. Stanwix (actually St. Leger retreated Aug. 22). But he considered himself bound by his orders to press on to Albany. Having collected 30 days' rations, he crossed the Hudson (Sept. 13) and encamped near Saratoga. Gen. Horatio Gates, an experienced and trusted officer who had replaced Schuyler in command (Aug. 19), was encamped 4 mi. away, on Bemis Heights, with 12,000 men and was daily receiving reinforcements. Burgoyne advanced to the attack (Sept. 19); but, though successful in driving back the troops sent out by Gates and in holding the field of battle at Freeman's Farm, he failed to envelop or pierce Gates's lines. Moreover, he lost over 500 men, including a large number of officers, victims of Col. Daniel Morgan's sharpshooters, while Gates's losses were less than 400. Burgoyne heard (Sept. 21) from Gen. Sir Henry Clinton, who had been left in command at New York, that he was about to make a diversion up the Hudson. He sent a dispatch to Clinton (Sept. 27) asking for orders. The answer was never received. Clinton started with a small force (Oct. 3) and captured two forts on the west bank, but he never had any intention of penetrating to Albany.

Burgoyne now had less than 5,000 "effectives" left, and his supplies were running short. He reckoned that they might last till the 20th. He led out 1,500 men on reconnaissance (Oct. 7), but the Americans made a fierce counterattack, and, inspired by Gen. Benedict Arnold, inflicted a severe defeat upon the British Army. The next day Burgoyne began his retreat, but Gates, with 20,000 men, surrounded him at Saratoga. On Oct. 17 Burgoyne surrendered his entire army under an agreement (the Convention of Saratoga) that his troops might return to Great Britain by way of Boston on condition that they would not serve again in North America during the war.

Burgoyne's surrender, by inducing the French to recognize the colonies' independence and to give the Americans open military assistance, marked the turning point of the Revolution, virtually ensuring ultimate victory for the colonies.

BIBLIOGRAPHY.—Christopher Ward and John R. Alden, *The American Revolution* (1954); Bernhard Knollenberg, *Washington and the Revolution* (1940); Hoffman Nickerson, *The Turning Point of the Revolution* (1928). (B. KN.)

SARATOGA SPRINGS, a city of Saratoga County, New York, U.S., is located in the Adirondack foothills about 30 mi. N of Albany and 12 mi. W of the Hudson River. The city is in a region of great historic interest, and is a health and pleasure resort noted since colonial days for the medicinal mineral springs which gave the community its name. Located in the city is Skidmore College for women (1911). Saratoga Lake (5 mi. long) is 3 mi. SE. The city is renowned for its thoroughbred and harness races, which attract thousands of summer visitors, and has a National Museum of Racing and a Hall of Fame containing mementos of great horses and riders of the past.

The name comes from an Indian word written in the original Saratoga patent as Ochserantongue or Sarachtogie and is believed to mean "at the beaver dam" or "the place of beavers." It has also been spelled Saraghoga and interpreted "place of swift water."

The 122 springs (heavily charged with carbonic acid gas and containing in varying proportions bicarbonates of lime, sodium, magnesium, chloride of sodium, and other minerals) are in a New York State reservation of 1,100 ac. The first iodine in the U.S. was discovered there in 1828. Sir William Johnson is said to have been the first white person who used the waters for medicinal purposes (1767). The therapeutic value of the springs had been known long before to the Indians. A log house for lodging visitors was built in 1771; in 1791 Gideon Putnam bought a large tract of land and put up the first inn; in 1793 Valentine Seaman published a book about the waters which spread the knowledge of their

BY COURTESY OF THE LIBRARY OF CONGRESS

BRITISH SURRENDER AT SARATOGA, ENGRAVED BY FRANÇOIS GODEFROY FROM A DRAWING BY LOUIS FRANÇOIS SÉBASTIEN FAUVEL, ABOUT 1784

BOB MAYETTE

THE RACE TRACK AT SARATOGA SPRINGS

curative properties. Other hotels were built early in the 19th century and by 1820 the springs had become a popular resort. The American Civil War cut off the patronage from the south and brought depression; but soon afterward, with the rebuilding of the United States Hotel and the establishment of racing (the August races of the Saratoga Association for the Improvement of the Breed of Horses, organized 1863, drew large attendances) Saratoga Springs again became popular. In the 1870s and 1880s it was one of the most fashionable watering places of North America ("the Queen of Spas"). Commercial exploitation of the springs (bottling the water and liquefying the carbonic acid gas) diminished their flow until they almost disappeared, and the resort was again depressed until the state intervened, first prohibiting pumping of the springs, later acquiring the property (1909) and placing it in charge of the conservation commission (1916).

The Saratoga country was a favourite camping ground of the Iroquois. It became a theatre of hostilities between the English and the French colonists with their Indian allies. In 1693 a French expedition was checked in a sharp conflict near Mt. McGregor by an English and colonial force. In 1745 the settlement on the Hudson directly east of the present city of Saratoga Springs (called Saratoga at first, later Old Saratoga, and now Schuylerville) was attacked by the French and Indians, who massacred many of its inhabitants. The battles of Saratoga (q.v.) in the Revolutionary War were fought at Bemis Heights, 12 mi. SE of Saratoga Springs. Most of the battlefield was acquired by the state of New York, and Congress in 1926 authorized its establishment as a national military park. Saratoga Springs was incorporated as a village in 1826 and as a city in 1915.

Industry is of minor importance and includes chemicals, wallpaper, clothing, and bait. For comparative population figures *see* table in NEW YORK: *Population.* (G. L. F.)

SARATOV, an *oblast* of the Russian Soviet Federated Socialist Republic, U.S.S.R., was formed in 1934 from the Lower Volga Krai (territory), originally as Saratov Krai; in 1936 it was converted to an *oblast.* Area 38,687 sq.mi. (100,199 sq.km.). Pop. (1959) 2,162,751. The *oblast* lies in the basin of the middle Volga, which bisects it from north to south. The greater part of the right (west)-bank area is occupied by the Volga Uplands, which reach a maximum height of 1,260 ft. (384 m.) in the Khvalynsk Hills. The uplands, which form a steep, high bank along the Volga, are greatly dissected by river valleys and their surface is cut up by a dense network of erosion gullies. Toward the west the uplands fall away to the Oka-Don Lowland, and this part is drained south to the Don by the Khoper and Medveditsa rivers. From 1954 to 1957 the extreme west formed part of Balashov Oblast, now abolished. The left bank of the Volga is a low, rolling plain drained partly by tributaries of the Volga and partly by the Bolshoi and Maly Uzen rivers, which form a basin of inland drainage. This left-bank area up to World War II formed the separate German Volga Republic (*q.v.*), dispersed for security reasons during the war.

The climate is sharply continental, with an annual range of 58° F (32° C), from a January average of 12° F (−11° C) to a July average of 70° F (21° C). Rainfall is low, about 15 in. (381 mm.) a year with a summer maximum at Saratov, and it decreases to the east. Droughts are frequent, occurring three or four years in five. Dry *sukhovei* winds, common in spring and early summer, do great damage to crops. Almost the entire *oblast* belongs to the steppe zone. Only in the extreme northwest is there forest-steppe, with rare surviving groves of oak. The right-bank steppe is almost wholly plowed up, the removal of the natural grass cover being the cause of the intensive erosion of this area. The left-bank area is dry steppe, with conditions becoming increasingly akin to semidesert to the southeast, where sage is more important in the vegetation than grass. Soils are fertile chernozems, except in the southeast, where chestnut soils are dominant and extensive areas of saline soils occur. Broad floodplain meadows fringe the left bank of the river.

In 1959, 54% (1,164,417) of the population were urban, living in 13 towns and 21 urban districts. Most of the larger towns lie along the Volga: the administrative centre, Saratov (581,071), Engels (90,724) on the opposite bank, and Volsk (61,792). The main centre of the west of the *oblast* is Balashov (64,349). In these larger towns is concentrated the heavy industry, oil refining, engineering, timber working, and manufacture of consumer goods. Other towns are chiefly concerned with processing agricultural products (flour milling, distilling, and the extraction of vegetable oil) or mineral extraction. The *oblast* contains the southwestern end of the Second Baku (*q.v.*) oilfield, and petroleum is found in relatively small quantities and natural gas in large quantities. Elshanka and Uvek near Saratov are the main centres of gas production. Oil shales are worked in the Trans-Volga. Agriculture, although affected by the recurrent droughts, is highly developed. More than three-quarters of the plowed area is under grains, chiefly spring wheat, maize (corn), and rye. Toward the east millet replaces rye. Sunflowers and mustard are important industrial crops, and melons, potatoes, and other vegetables are widely grown. The area under irrigation is constantly being extended, especially on the lower Trans-Volga, and the water supply for this is facilitated by the cascade of barrages on the Volga. Toward the drier eastern part of the *oblast* livestock husbandry becomes increasingly important and large numbers of beef and dairy cattle and sheep are kept. The *oblast* is crossed by east-west and north-south railways and Saratov town is the centre of a road network. (R. A. F.)

SARATOV, a town and *oblast* centre of the Russian Soviet Federated Socialist Republic, U.S.S.R., stands on the right bank of the middle Volga, 200 mi. (322 km.) SW of Kuibyshev. Pop. (1959) 581,071. The modern town, extending for nearly 30 mi.

STREET SCENE IN SARATOV

(48 km.) along the river, is a major river port and transshipment point. Since 1935 the railway crosses the river and runs east to Uralsk and Central Asia and south to Astrakhan, while on the west bank railways follow the Volga upstream to Syzran and downstream to Volgograd.

A large-scale and varied manufacturing industry produces ball bearings, combine harvesters, tractor parts, machine tools, mobile generating plant, precision measuring instruments, and lifting equipment. The large pre-Revolutionary industry, flour milling, is still important, and footwear, clothing, and foodstuffs are produced. Timber rafted down the Volga is processed in the sawmills and made into furniture.

Saratov lies at the southwestern extremity of the Second Baku (q.v.) oilfield and oil refining is part of its industrial activity. Natural gas deposits around the town supply power locally and are also linked with Moscow by pipeline. In the early 1960s a large barrage and hydroelectric station were under construction on the Volga immediately above Saratov. The town has a university (established in 1919), as well as several higher educational institutes, a musical conservatory, and an agricultural research institute.

After the campaign of Ivan IV "the Terrible" down the Volga in 1556 to take Astrakhan, a series of fortresses was built to protect the river. Saratov was established in 1590, halfway between the fortresses of Samara (Kuibyshev) and Tsaritsyn (later Stalingrad and then Volgograd). The original site is not exactly known, but in 1616 the fortress was moved to the left bank at the confluence of the small Saratovka stream. Destroyed in the rising of Stepan Timofeevich Razin (q.v.), the fortress was reestablished on the present site in 1674. In the 18th century its defensive function disappeared, but trade along the Volga brought great commercial importance and in 1750 Saratov became centre of a *guberniya* (province). In the 1870s a railway from Moscow was built to Saratov and the town developed rapidly.

(R. A. F.)

SARAWAK, a state of the federation of Malaysia, comprising, with Sabah, East Malaysia; it lies on the northwestern coast of the island of Borneo and was formerly a British colony. Pop. (1960) 744,529. The capital is Kuching (q.v.). With a coastline of 450 mi. (724 km.) on the South China Sea, Sarawak is bounded on the northeast by Brunei and Sabah and on the east and south by Indonesian Borneo (Kalimantan). *See* MALAYSIA.

SARCOPHAGUS, the name given by the Greeks and Romans to a stone coffin. The original term is of doubtful meaning; Pliny explains that the word denotes a coffin of limestone from the Troad (the region around Troy), which had the property of dissolving the body quickly (Gr. *sarx*, "flesh"; *phagein*, "to eat"). This explanation is doubtful; perhaps religious and folkloristic ideas are involved in calling a coffin a body eater. It came into general use as a word for a large coffin in Roman imperial times and is used in the 1960s as an archaeological term.

The earliest stone coffins in use among the 5th-dynasty Egyp-

tians were designed to represent palaces of mud-brick architecture, with an ornamental arrangement of false doors and windows. Such is the coffin of Ra'wer in the Cairo museum. In 12th-dynasty times, boxlike sarcophagi of limestone were in use in Egypt and on the Lebanese coast at Byblos. These retain knoblike projections for the attachment of the ropes used in handling these heavy objects. By the 18th dynasty mummiform anthropoid coffins had come into use, usually of wood with a carved portrait head and sometimes plated with gold like that of Tutankhamen (q.v.).

In the Aegean world, terra-cotta, cistlike coffins (*larnakes*), with elaborate painted designs, came into general use in Middle Minoan times (c. 2200–1580 B.C.), but the custom was not generally adopted by the Mycenaeans of the Greek mainland. Sometimes these cists resemble houses, sometimes bathtubs with large handles. Bathtub coffins of bronze came into use in Mesopotamia in the Assyrian period. Painted terra-cotta coffins (6th century B.C.) from Clazomenae (western Asia Minor) resemble the Cretan cists.

The Phoenicians developed a white-marble anthropoid sarcophagus of Egyptian type in the 5th century B.C. (Sidon, Sicily, Cádiz) and in Hellenistic times specialized in making leaden coffins and elaborately carved marble sarcophagi. The most elaborate of these, found at Sidon (Lebanon) are the sarcophagi of the Satrap (c. 430 B.C.) and of the Mourners (c. 370 B.C.) and the later sarcophagus of Alexander the Great with its painted, sculptured friezes. Sculptured pieces of the same period are known from Greece, where the majority of sarcophagi date from the Roman period, however.

In Italy both stone and terra-cotta sarcophagi were in use by the Etruscans from c. 600 B.C. onward. These often have figures of the deceased reclining on the couch-shaped lids. The earliest

TUFF SARCOPHAGUS FROM VULCI, ITALY, SHOWING WEDDING SCENES AND A WEDDED COUPLE ON THE LID; 4TH CENTURY B.C.

dated Roman sarcophagus is that of the consul Scipio Barbatus (298 B.C.), but after this date sculptured sarcophagi were in use throughout the empire by pagan and Christian alike.

See COFFIN; EARLY CHRISTIAN ART; ETRUSCANS; SCULPTURE, SEPULCHRAL; TERRA COTTA; *see* also references under "Sarcophagus" in the Index.   (WM. C.)

SARDANAPALUS (SARDANAPALLUS) was, according to the Greek historian Diodorus Siculus, the last of a line of 30 kings of Assyria, who exceeded all his predecessors in his sybaritic way of life. Arbaces, a Median chief, rebelled and besieged Sardanapalus in his capital. When, after three years, a flood breached the defenses, Sardanapalus made a pyre of his palace treasures and with his concubines perished in the flames. The figure of Sardanapalus apparently represents an amalgamation of two Assyrian kings: his name and status, but not his character, represent Ashurbanipal (q.v.; reigned 669–630 or 626 B.C.), while his fate recalls that of Ashurbanipal's brother, Shamash-shum-ukin, king of Babylon.   (H. W. F. S.)

SARDICA, COUNCIL OF, an ecclesiastical council held at Sardica (modern Sofia, Bulg.) in 342, or perhaps 343. Convened by the joint emperors Constantius II (Eastern, sympathetic to the Arian party) and Constans I (Western, sympathetic to the Nicene party) to attempt a settlement of the Arian controversies, the council in fact merely embittered still further the relations between the two great religious parties and those between the Western and Eastern halves of the empire. As Athanasius (*see* ATHANASIUS, SAINT), whom the East had removed from his bishopric, appeared on the scene, and the Western bishops declined to exclude him, the bishops of the East absolutely refused to take part and contented themselves with formulating a written protest addressed to numerous foreign prelates. The Western bishops, presided over by Hosius of Córdoba, confirmed the restoration of Athanasius and acquitted Marcellus of Ancyra of heresy. Canons iii–v of this council invest the Roman bishop with a prerogative which became of great historical importance, as the first legal recognition of his jurisdiction over other sees and the basis for the further development of his primacy. *See* COUNCIL: *Councils to the 9th Century: Councils Between 325 and 381.*

SARDINE is a word with two more or less distinct usages: (1) it is the common name in various parts of the world for certain species of fish of the herring family; (2) it applies to these and a number of other small herringlike fish when preserved and canned in oil, often with special sauces. The fish most generally called sardines, sometimes with the adjective "true," regardless of size and whether or not they are canned, are the European *Sardina pilchardus* (called pilchard in Britain), the Pacific genus *Sardinops*, and a number of tropical fishes of the genus *Sardinella*. The common name of *Sardinops* is "sardine" in the United States and "pilchard" in British Columbia, southern Africa, Australia, and New Zealand.

The European sardine has a peculiar arrangement of scales, in which alternate oblique rows of small scales are covered by intervening rows of larger ones. It occurs from Spanish Sahara north to southern Norway, including the Mediterranean and part of the Black Sea as well as the Canary Islands, Madeira, and the Azores.

In *Sardinops* there is a normal arrangement of scales, and the gill covering, or operculum, is striated with grooves running obliquely downward. Five species have been recognized: *S. caerulea* of the west coast of North America, *S. melanosticta* of Japan, *S. sagax* of the west coast of South America, *S. neopilchardus* of New Zealand and southern Australia, and *S. ocellata* of southern Africa. These are so similar that some authorities consider that all should be classified as one species, *S. sagax,* with *neopilchardus* having subspecific rank. *Sardinops* associate according to size in dense schools or shoals, feed on plankton, and grow to be 10 to 12 in. long. They spawn principally in the spring. The eggs are extruded into the open sea and are fertilized there. Suspended near the surface, the fertilized eggs drift passively with the currents, then hatch within a few days into larvae, which continue to drift passively until they metamorphose into free-swimming fish. *Sardinops* migrate extensively along the coasts they inhabit, those in the Northern Hemisphere moving north in summer and south in winter.

Sardinella differ from *Sardina* and *Sardinops* in having strongly developed spiny shields along the belly, and in having a poorly developed fleshy eyelid. They are tropical and subtropical coastal fishes occurring in the Atlantic, Pacific, and Indian oceans.

Sardines of any species are commercially fished for a variety of uses—for bait; for fresh fish markets; for drying, salting, or smoking; for canning; and for reduction into fish meal and oil. The most important catching apparatus is an encircling net, of which there are many modifications, and of which the best known is the purse seine. In Maine and New Brunswick, the fishery for young herring to be canned as sardines is based almost entirely on fishing with traps or weirs, which are large impoundments near the shore, made of shrubs driven into the bottom. In eastern Asia similar traps, also used to catch sardines, are made of bamboo.

Around 230,000 tons of canned product are produced in the world annually from sardines, about half of it from European sardines, around 12% from young herring in northeastern North America, and the largest part of the remainder from *Sardinops* in southern Africa, Japan, and California. Fish meal, once used as fertilizer, has become an important ingredient of feeds for poultry, pigs, and cattle, because of its high content of protein and other essential nutrients. The oil has many uses, including the manufacture of paints, varnish, and linoleum; much of it is used in Europe for the manufacture of margarine. (L. A. WD.)

SARDINIA (SARDEGNA), the second largest island in the Mediterranean and politically part of Italy. It has an area of 9,301 sq.mi. (24,089 sq.km.), including the offshore islands, the largest of which are Asinara, San Pietro, Maddalena, and Caprera. Sardinia is separated from the French island of Corsica to the north by the 7½-mi. (12-km.)-wide Strait of Bonifacio; 120 mi. (193 km.) NE lie the islands of Capraia and Elba; 115 mi. (185 km.) S is the coast of Africa. The island is divided into three administrative provinces, Sassari, Nuoro, and Cagliari, which form the region of Sardegna. The capital is Cagliari.

PHYSICAL GEOGRAPHY

Geological Structure.—Sardinia is united geologically to Corsica, both being aligned along a mountain belt rising over 13,000 ft. (3,950 m.) from the surrounding sea floor, with a continental slope deeply fretted by submarine canyons. The island is a remnant of a Hercynian block known as the Tyrrhenian continent; its rocks are mostly Paleozoic. Cambrian slates predominate in the southwest, while Carbo-Permian granites comprise over a third of the total area of the island, chiefly in the eastern highlands of Gallura, Goceano, Nuoro, and Sarrabus. In Mesozoic times, at least, the island margins were below sea level; remnants of the eroded cover now remain only in the hills overlooking the Gulf of Orosei, the Sarcidano tableland, and La Nurra Hills. Tertiary limestones and marls (chiefly Miocene) outcrop in the hills of Arborea and Trexenta and in the Sassari Plain. Before the alpine fractures that dislocated the island, vulcanism occurred, and Oligocene volcanics are represented by the trachytes and tuffs of the northwest (Logudoro and Auglona), the middle Tirso Basin, and northern Sulcis. Subsequently the Campidano trough was fractured (in Tertiary times), and the Tyrrhenian continent was reduced to an archipelago, in which the Corso-Sardinia land mass was first separated from the mainland. Plio-Pleistocene volcanics explain the great spreads of basaltic lavas that form the trap relief of Macomer and Abbasanta, with smaller cappings in Arborea and north of the Gulf of Orosei. Since the mid-Quaternary, the Campidano and the drowned coastline of La Nurra area have emerged from the sea.

Relief and Drainage.—The island is mainly mountainous, but its relief is monotonous and rolling, with no clear ranges. More than one-third consists of plateaus rising between 600 and 1,300 ft. (183–396 m.) above sea level, and only 7% rises above 2,600 ft. (792 m.). The highest mountains, the Gennargentu (6,017 ft. [1,834 m.]), form the east central dorsal descending northward into the rugged granitic plateaus of Gallura and southwestward into the dissected Tertiary hills of Arborea and Trexenta. The twin mountain masses of the southwestern region of Iglesiente (Mt. Linas 4,055 ft. [1,236 m.], Caravius 3,661 ft. [1,116 m.]) drop sharply into the Campidano Plain, the only considerable lowland in Sardinia, which runs for about 60 mi. (97 km.) between the Gulfs of Cagliari and Oristano. The Tirso River flows through the major valley of Sardinia, which, overlooked to the north by the largest fault scarp of the island, unites three types of relief: in the upper course are the dissected Hercynian plateaus of Goceano; in the middle course the river cuts through volcanic tablelands in narrow defiles and flows through Lake Omodeo; in the lower course the river crosses the marshy Plain of Oristano. The other major rivers are the Flumendosa, draining southeastward from the Gennargentu Mountains to the east coast; and the Coghinas, flowing northward through Lake Coghinas into the Gulf of Asinara. Gradients are low in the Campidano trough, which is drained by many minor streams, including the Mannu and Mogoro.

Geographical Regions.—Sardinia is rich in local district names. Its isolation, poor communications, archaic modes of life, and the formerly intensely developed tribal economy in part explain the human importance of these regional units. The core of the eastern highlands is the Gennargentu, flanked by three districts: Barbagia Ollolai, Seulo, and Bèlvi. Pastoralism dominates these highland communes, the *ogliastra,* which originally formed summer pastures for transhumant flocks. Settlements are markedly in large villages. Gallura to the north is a notable contrast, where lower granite plateaus have a dispersed settlement pattern resulting from clearances of the wasteland; ridge and valley relief is characteristic. Iglesiente and Sulcis in the southwest also have Hercynian relief, but the coastline is less indented and the climate more arid. Hamlets with patches of wheat cultivation among sheep pastures are characteristic. Above the Oristano Plain the western regions are dominated by trachyte and basalt landscapes, bare, treeless, tabular skylines, across which snake the dark stone walls surrounding *tancas* (units of grazing land); remains of ancient nuraghi settlements are common. Around Sassari there is an abrupt change, the Miocene limestone tablelands favouring olive groves and denser settlement. In the northwest La Nurra Hills are scrub covered and sparsely settled with isolated farms. The Campidano Plain and its adjoining rich region of Arborea are in marked contrast, forming the economic axis of the island, with the most intensive agriculture, especially of cereals, and densest concentration of communal village life.

Climate.—The position of Sardinia at the western Mediterranean crossroads of cyclonic tracks and trajectories of cold northerly air explains its climatic characteristic of violent winds, especially the northwesterly mistral and the hot southern sirocco. Air masses crossing the northern Mediterranean are sufficiently modified in transit to create marked fluctuations in rainfall from year to year over Sardinia, falling chiefly in autumn and winter. The summer drought usually lasts for several months. The average precipitation for the whole island is 30.5 in. (775 mm.), with over 40 in. on the high plateaus, but only 15 in. on the Cagliari Plain. The January and July mean temperatures indicate a moderate annual range: in the north Sassari (735 ft.; 224 m.) has 47° F (8° C) and 75° (24°), respectively; in the south Cagliari (246 ft.; 75 m.) has 48° and 76°. Compared with these maritime conditions, those of the interior mountains are very different: Val Lecciola (3,314 ft.; 1,010 m.) has 38° (3°) and 66° (19°). There are three main climatic regions: the subtropical and semiarid conditions of the southern Campidano and coastal Sulcis; the hot temperate climate of all western and northern Sardinia; and the subhumid climate of the eastern highlands with altitudes over 1,500 ft. (457 m.).   (J. M. Ho.)

Vegetation and Animal Life.—Sardinia belongs to the Sardo-Corsican group of the Mediterranean type of vegetation. The natural vegetation has largely been destroyed and given place to grass pastures, cereal cultivation, and fruit growing. A rich salt-loving vegetation is found along the shores and cliffs, and salty marshes extend along the coast. Inland from the littoral communities is the *garigue,* which covers a vast part of the island. The mastic tree, rockrose, myrtle, rosemary, headed thyme, scarlet oak, stoechas, and *Phillyrea* are common plants. In the regions of La Nurra and Sulcis and near Orosei, dwarf palm occurs. The *maqui,* with olive tree, mastic tree, *Phillyrea,* tree heath, and holm oak, is less widespread. In the east central part of the island are communities of junipers. In this belt, farther inland, woods of cork oak cover vast areas, chiefly in Gallura, but holm oak is the most common and attains a higher altitude. Also scattered communities of true, or bay, laurel and formations of wild olive tree are found. Oleander frequently occurs in the riverbeds. The submontane belt restricted to Mt. Gennargentu and a few other minor mountains consists of deciduous woods of oak or chestnut. The ancient Mediterranean montane vegetation is represented by small scattered areas of woods of holly or yew tree. The montane belt occurs in the highest parts and includes species of juniper, the Etna barberry, ground-cherry, and a currant, *Ribes sardoum,* endemic to Sardinia.   (R. E. G. P.-S.)

Most of the mammals are like those found in Italy (*q.v.*), although many of the Italian mammals are not found in Sardinia; there are no bears, wolves, otters, squirrels, or moles, but boar, fox, marten, hare, and rabbit abound, especially in the Gennargentu uplands. Deserving special mention are a Sardinian weasel, a native wild cat, the mouflon (wild sheep), found only in Sardinia and Corsica, and the Cape hare, which belongs more properly to Africa. The birds are much the same as in Italy except that there is less variety. There are no magpies, and the Italian sparrow is absent, but the Spanish sparrow, found in Spain, southern Italy, and the Balkans, also lives in Sardinia. The Barbary or Sardinian partridge

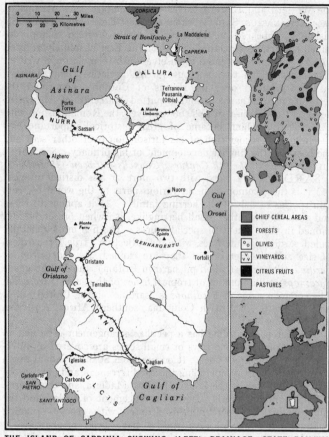

THE ISLAND OF SARDINIA SHOWING (LEFT) DRAINAGE, STATE RAILWAY SYSTEM, AND TOWNS AND (UPPER RIGHT) LAND USE

is protected in the Golfo Aranci reserve. The birds of prey include the black and bearded vultures and the white-tailed eagle. There is only one kind of lizard, one newt (found also in North Africa), and one toad, the green or changeable toad. The trout are like those of Algeria, Asia Minor, and Iran.   (MA. BU.)

ARCHAEOLOGY

The earliest evidence of human occupation in Sardinia dates from the time when metal was coming into use in the western Mediterranean. Although some stations, *e.g.,* Macomer in central Sardinia, have yielded lithic industries without metal, a pure Neolithic phase is not so far distinguishable from the Chalcolithic stage. The first habitations were perhaps cave dwellings, *e.g.,* San Bartolomeo and other grottoes near Cagliari and in western Sardinia, but the Proto-Sardinians soon began to live a farming life in hut villages. Cult places in caves (San Michele near Ozieri) and religious monuments (a square platform built of large stones at Monte d'Accoddi, northwest of Sassari) are known. The dead were buried in artificial grottoes, with an antechamber and one or more cells, generally rectangular, sometimes with pillars and roughly carved symbols or figures. These tombs are called by the Sardinians *domus de gianas* ("witches' houses") and are grouped in cemeteries, the best known of which was excavated at Anghelu Ruju near Alghero. Cist graves in stone circles were found in northern Sardinia (Arzachena), and the 40 or so small dolmens (megalithic graves) still existing in the island must go back to the same period. Menhirs (standing stones) are not infrequent and may be related to sanctuaries and burial places. A good idea of the material civilization and common life is furnished by the funerary equipment at Anghelu Ruju, which includes flint blades, stone axes, maceheads, arrowheads, copper daggers and implements, and personal ornaments. Stone "idols" are also present and may be interpreted as attendants of the dead; their schematized female forms recall similar although not identical figures from the Aegean. Pottery comprises undecorated, impressed, and incised wares, differing in shape and ornament; curvilinear and "spiral-ribbon" patterns are frequent. The typical bell beakers demonstrate a direct link with the Spanish beaker culture.

This Sardinian Copper Age was still flourishing in the first half of the 2nd millennium B.C. and was apparently influenced and very slowly transformed by the older Bronze Age civilizations of the Near East. Minoan and Mycenaean influence was not so direct as in Sicily, but commercial contacts with Crete may be proved from the beginning of the Late Minoan period, toward 1500 B.C. (copper pig ingots with Minoan linear signs were found at Serra Ilixi, though some scholars would date these *c.* 1200 B.C.). A real Bronze Age culture in Sardinia cannot be perceived till near the end of the 2nd millennium, and in spite of the Oriental influence its substantial local ancestry seems indisputable. Its peak is not to be dated earlier than the 9th to the 6th century B.C., that is to say, in the period of historical Phoenician and Greek colonization in the western Mediterranean, and it survived in more or less degenerated forms down to the Carthaginian and Roman conquest of the island.

The monuments suggest a period of cultural flowering and prosperity hardly to be found in any later phase of the history of the island. About 6,500 stone towers, the so-called nuraghi (singular, nuraghe), are still a distinctive feature of the Sardinian landscape. They belong to the Sardinian Bronze Age civilization (hence called the nuraghi culture). These towers are in the shape of a truncated cone and built of large stones laid in more or less regular courses; they contain superposed round chambers capped by tall, pointed corbeled roofs and connected with a winding staircase. Such towers form the chief element of complex buildings comprising bastions and turrets with corridors, round chambers, and cisterns; *e.g.,* those excavated at Abbasanta (the so-called Nuraghe Losa), at Torralba, and at Barumini. The nuraghi are sometimes interlinked in defensive systems; *e.g.,* Giara di Gesturi. But in many cases fortified villages of partially stone-built round huts appear in close connection with the nuraghi, which may therefore have been the residential castles of chieftains, including storerooms, foundries, and even places for religious use. Other isolated buildings are in the form of rectangular temples (Serra Orrios), monumental wells (Sardara, Serri, Ballao), and fountains (Lomarzu). The graves show a development of earlier types. The subterranean chamber tombs become bigger, imitating more closely the internal structure of civil habitations. There are also grandiose megalithic grave monuments, deriving from simpler dolmen corridors or cists, with a rectangular cell covered by a corbeled roof and with a paneled portal slab in the centre of an exedra facade—the so-called giants' tombs. Objects for everyday life and for religion, found in buildings or hoards, include bronze implements and weapons, ornaments, and decorated and coarse pottery. There are noteworthy bronze votive statuettes, portraying men, chiefly warriors, women, animals, more infrequently mythological beings, and small models of ships or buildings.

The Phoenician and Carthaginian periods are chiefly represented by cemeteries and sacred sites; some of the latter were clearly used for human sacrifice. Trade with the Sardinians and influence on their culture are evident. Civil buildings are more available from the Roman period, at, for instance, Cagliari and Nora.

HISTORY

Prehistoric and Phoenician Settlement.—The race that built the nuraghi was probably a definite ethnic unity, having its roots in the first prehistoric population of the island, but its origins and affinities are uncertain, and it left no written records. It is possible that the Sherden, who with the Philistines and other sea peoples (*q.v.*) fought in Egypt in the 13th and 12th centuries B.C., either came from or, more probably, settled in Sardinia, to which they gave their name. Archaeological evidence from the nuraghi culture suggests a strongly organized power of tribal states. The working of metal from the local mines was presumably the chief source of wealth. However, the presence of Phoenician trade settlements along the Sardinian coasts since the 9th or 8th century B.C. must have vigorously contributed to Proto-Sardinian prosperity.

BY COURTESY OF THE MUSEO ARCHEOLOGICO NAZIONALE, CAGLIARI; PHOTOGRAPHS, FRIEDRICH HEWICKER

BRONZE STATUETTES FOUND IN SARDINIAN NURAGHI

(Top left) Tribal chieftain, about 15¼ in. high, found at Uta, Monti Arcosu; (top right) warrior with horned helmet, about 5¾ in. high, found at Padria; (bottom) boat with stag figurehead, about 4 in. high, found at nuraghe Spiena, Chiaramonti. All figures in the Museo Archeologico Nazionale, Cagliari

The Phoenician shippers and traders were naturally interested in the Sardinian mines and founded trading posts, which became the important towns of Caralis (Cagliari), Nora and Bithia (both on the coast southwest of Cagliari), Sulcis (Sant' Antioco), and Tharros (Capo San Marco). Attempts at colonization by the Greeks in the early 6th century (Olbia in northeastern Sardinia) were unsuccessful because of the jealous opposition of the Phoenicians. After Carthage had attained leadership over the western Phoenicians, the struggle for supremacy in the west caused a more direct control to be exercised over the colonists on the island. After a long period of peaceful coexistence with the indigenous peoples, the Carthaginians began, about 500 B.C., the military conquest of the most productive parts of Sardinia, driving the Proto-Sardinians into the mountains.

Roman Period.—During the First Punic War the Romans tried to take Sardinia, but it was not until after the war that, in 238 B.C., they took advantage of a revolt of Carthaginian mercenaries to demand the surrender of the island. The native tribes opposed the Romans but were conquered after several bloody campaigns; the island became a province under a praetor or propraetor, to whose jurisdiction Corsica was added soon afterward (227). A rebellion in 215 B.C., fostered by the Carthaginians, was quelled by T. Manlius Torquatus. After this the island began to furnish considerable supplies of corn (grain); it was treated as a conquered country, not containing a single free city, and the inhabitants were obliged to pay a tithe in corn and a further money contribution. There were saltworks as early as about 150 B.C. There were insurrections of the mountain tribes in 181 (crushed in 177–176) and in 114 B.C., but even in the time of Strabo there was considerable brigandage.

In the division of provinces made by Augustus, Sardinia and Corsica fell to the Senate, but in A.D. 6, Augustus, because of the frequent disturbances, took them over and placed them under a *praefectus.* In A.D. 67 Nero restored Sardinia to the Senate (but not Corsica) in exchange for Achaea, and the former was then governed by a *legatus pro praetore;* but Vespasian took it over again before A.D. 78 and placed it under an imperial procurator as *praefectus.* It returned to the Senate, not before A.D. 83 but certainly before the reign of Marcus Aurelius, when it was governed by a proconsul, as it was under Commodus; the latter, or perhaps Septimius Severus, took it over again and placed it under a procurator as *praefectus* once more. Caralis was the only city with Roman civic rights in Sardinia in Pliny's time (when it received the privilege is unknown). A Roman colony had been founded at Turris Libisonis (Porto Torres), and others, later on, at Usellis and Cornus (Santa Caterina di Pitinuri). Little is heard of the island under the empire, except as a granary and as remarkable for its unhealthiness and the audacity of its brigands. It was often used as a place of exile.   (MA. P.; X.)

Vandal and Byzantine Rule.—After they had crossed over into Africa from Spain in 429, the Vandals occupied Sardinia *c.* 456. The Roman general Marcellinus reoccupied the island as a preliminary to the expedition sent against the Vandals by the emperors Leo I and Anthemius and led by Basiliscus (468), but on its failure the Vandals returned. Their rule was a period of cultural revival, largely the result of the enforced residence for about 20 years at Cagliari of 60 or even 120 North African bishops, who had been banished by King Thrasamund. Among them were St. Fulgentius and the bishop of Hippo, who had brought with him the relics of St. Augustine. From this "African" cultural renaissance in Sardinia date the remains of the monastery built by Fulgentius near the basilica of S. Saturnino, Cagliari.

In 533–534, following the defeat of the Vandals, Sardinia was recovered by the Byzantine duke Cyril. Under the Byzantine Empire it was one of the seven provinces of the praetorian prefecture of Africa. It was under a *praeses* for civil affairs and a dux for military. In 550–551 Sardinia was occupied by the Goths under Totila, but after his death in 552 it was recovered for the Byzantine Empire. Letters from Pope Gregory I written at the end of the 6th century denounce Byzantine misgovernment and mention attacks by the Lombards on the Sardinian coast. Between 663 and 668 Sardinia was heavily taxed by the Byzantine emperor Constans II; when it was finally separated from the Byzantine Empire is quite unknown.

The Arabs.—In the 720s the Lombard king Liutprand acquired St. Augustine's relics and removed them to Pavia, but the Lombards did not occupy Sardinia as they did Corsica. The first raid by the Arabs was in 711; these raids for loot and prisoners recurred throughout the 8th and 9th centuries. The Sardinians sent ambassadors in 815 to the Frankish emperor Louis I and cooperated with Leo IV and subsequent popes against the Arabs. The need for them to organize their own defense probably led to formation of the four self-governing *giudicati* (*see* below), though the history of this period is obscure.

The 10th century was comparatively peaceful, but in 1015 Mujahid al-'Amiri, ruler of Denia in Spain and the Balearic Islands, overran much of Sardinia. This, though not the last Arab attack, was the most serious, being a real attempt at conquest; in 1016, however, Mujahid was defeated at sea with the help of the fleets of Genoa and Pisa, and evacuated Sardinia.

The Giudicati and Italian Influence.—The four Sardinian *giudicati* of Cagliari, Arborea (capital Tharros, then Oristano), Torres, and Gallura (capital Olbia) appear clearly defined territorially and politically only in the 11th century. These self-governing divisions gradually became hereditary principalities under lifelong *giudici* (literally "judges"). After the defeat of Mujahid, Sardinia became a field for expansion for Pisa and Genoa, as well as for Marseilles and Gaeta, and was opened to the monastic im-

migration encouraged by the popes, who now claimed sovereignty over the island. Pisa and Genoa, through alliances with the *giudici,* secured politico-mercantile zones of influence—Genoa mostly in the north and west, Pisa in the south and east. The archbishop of Pisa was appointed apostolic legate and primate of Sardinia by Innocent II (1133). Subsequently Genoa, to counteract its rival, lent Barisone I, *giudice* of Arborea, the price of his coronation by the emperor Frederick I as king of Sardinia (1164), but he could neither subdue the other *giudicati* nor repay the loan. The peace of 1169 brought about a temporary truce between the two republics, soon broken by dissensions among the *giudici.* The *giudicati* of Cagliari and Gallura passed through marriage to Pisan families (Massa and Donoratico, and Visconti, respectively) and finally to the republic itself. The *giudicato* of Torres passed from the protection of Pisa to that of Genoa until the marriage (1238) of Adelasia, heiress of Gallura and Torres, to Enzio, natural son of the emperor Frederick II. Enzio took the title of king of Sardinia, but he was seldom there, and his rule was carried on by vicars. In the wars after Enzio's imprisonment (1249), Pisa prevailed, but after the Battle of Meloria (1284) Pisan influence was limited to the districts of Cagliari and Gallura; Genoa controlled the other districts, also through its noble families (Spinola, Malaspina, Doria). Throughout the 11th, 12th, and 13th centuries, however, Pisan influence predominated in the arts, as shown by the many churches built at this time, especially the basilica of S. Gavino, Porto Torres, and the church of Sta. Maria del Regno, Ardara.

Aragonese Domination.—In 1297 Boniface VIII invested James II of Aragon as king of Sardinia and Corsica, but Sardinia was conquered by the Aragonese under the infante Alfonso (later Alfonso IV) only in 1323–24, with the help of the *giudicato* of Arborea, which, however, kept its independence and defended itself strenuously against the same Aragonese throughout the 14th century. A war that broke out about 1350 between the *giudice* Mariano IV and King Peter IV of Aragon was won by the latter, and peace was made at a meeting of the Sardinian *stamenti,* or Estates (1355). A few years later war was started again by Mariano and carried on after his death (1376) by his son, Hugo (d. 1384), and his daughter, Eleonora of Arborea. After the death of Eleonora (1404) the *giudicato* was reduced to a fief of Aragon (1410) and, after a last revolt had been suppressed at the Battle of Macomer (1478), brought wholly under the Aragonese crown. Under Aragonese rule the administration was unified and placed under a viceroy residing at Cagliari. Subsequently the three orders or branches—military, ecclesiastical, and royal—of the Sardinian *stamenti* began to meet at regular intervals. Despite the provisions extended by Alfonso V of Aragon to the whole island for the observance of the law code promulgated by Mariano IV of Arborea and perfected by Eleonora (1392)—the *Carta de Logu* (University Library, Cagliari)—the island's economy, flourishing under the *giudici,* declined. The population, oppressed by taxation, decreased, and the island fell into a state of lethargy.

(R. Du.; X.)

Sardinia, which passed with Aragon to the unified Spanish monarchy, suffered in the 16th century from raids by the Barbary pirates. In 1527 a French fleet under Andrea Doria invaded the island and took Sassari but was driven off. Another French fleet, under the comte d'Harcourt, was also repulsed after taking Oristano in 1637.

Austria and Savoy.—During the War of the Spanish Succession (*q.v.*), Cagliari was bombarded by an English fleet and capitulated; Sardinia became Austrian (1708). Austria was confirmed in possession by the Treaty of Utrecht in 1713. Giulio Cardinal Alberoni (*q.v.*) hoped to make Sardinia a jumping-off point for the recapture of Spain's former Italian possessions, and in 1717 he dispatched a squadron from Barcelona, which recaptured the island, but in 1718 the Treaty of London compensated Victor Amadeus II of Savoy for his loss of Sicily by entitling him king of Sardinia. He took possession in 1720; from that time until 1861 he and his successors were known as kings of Sardinia, though the seat of their power was Piedmont.

The House of Savoy sought to establish its authority over the feudal nobles (of mostly Spanish descent) and over the church. In 1726 Pope Benedict XIII confirmed the king in the right of presentation to bishoprics. Under Victor Amadeus II (1720–30) and Charles Emmanuel III (1730–73), some efforts were made to improve the social and economic conditions of Sardinia. In 1793, during the French Revolutionary Wars, the French attacked Sardinia and bombarded Cagliari but were attacked by the islanders and withdrew. The *stamenti* then presented a memorandum to the king asking for a measure of local autonomy and the opening of all posts, except that of viceroy, to all citizens. Their request was rejected, but the movement that it represented found support in a popular revolt arising out of the economic discontent of the people. The revolt, however, faded out on the flight to France of the popular leader Gian Maria Angioj (1796). In 1799 Charles Emmanuel IV took refuge for a few months in Sardinia after his expulsion from Piedmont by the French. His successor, Victor Emmanuel I, lived in Cagliari from 1806 till 1814. His brother Charles Felix, both as viceroy and, from 1821, as king, embarked on various reforms affecting agriculture, taxation, public health, and the administration of justice, but it was Charles Albert (1831–49) who took real account of Sardinia's needs. In 1836 he abolished the ancient seigniorial rights, and, though in practice some continued to exist, the ensuing division of lands among private owners and communes formed the basis of the 19th- and 20th-century agrarian economy of Sardinia. The problem was not only Sardinia's backwardness but also its isolation in language and culture from the Italian mainland. In 1847, at the request of the *stamenti*, Sardinia was united to the other provinces of Piedmont with the same standing in the kingdom; this position was confirmed by the constitution of 1848, and Sardinians sat in the Piedmontese Parliament.

Italy.—From 1861 Sardinia formed a part of the kingdom of Italy, but it remained something of a forgotten province. After World War I the Sardinian Action Party was formed to press for autonomy for the island, but the advent of Fascism obliged it to cease its activities.

On the outbreak of war between Italy and the Allies in 1940 (*see* WORLD WAR II), Sardinia had a garrison of between 200,000 and 250,000, including the 9th German Armoured Division. The island's airfields were used as bases for attacks in the Mediterranean. In 1943 Allied air attacks on the island began and increased in intensity as the time for the invasion of Sicily drew near. The Germans had increased the number of air squadrons in Sardinia, but in July Allied air attacks made many airfields unusable. On Sept. 18, 1943, Italian forces expelled the last of the German troops from the island. It was occupied by a small number of Allied troops.

The movement for autonomy revived after the war, and in February 1948 Sardinia finally became a self-governing *regione* of Italy (see *Administration and Social Conditions*, below).

(X.)

POPULATION, ADMINISTRATION, AND SOCIAL CONDITIONS

Population.—According to the 1961 census, Sardinia had a population of 1,372,606, with a density of about 148 per sq.mi. (57 per sq.km.), compared with the general Italian average of 428 (167). The first census taken in 1728 showed a count of only 309,994. It appears that the population declined steadily after Roman times and only regained its estimated Roman total of 500,000 during the 18th century. Its history has been one of foreign exploitation, economic neglect, and the threat of malaria, which was encouraged by the presence of extensive coastal marshes. A campaign launched in 1946 has virtually eliminated the malaria-carrying mosquito (*Anopheles labranchiae*) since 1952.

Sardinia has the greatest concentration of villages of all Italian provinces. In 1951, 93.1% of the population lived in 544 nucleated settlements, 279 of which had over 1,000 inhabitants. Only 6.4% were located on the coast, 54.8% being on inland slopes and hills, a reflection of Sardinia's former insecurity from corsairs and its own tribal rivalries. The west central districts excluding the lower Tirso Valley and the Campidano are the traditional areas of popu-

FRITZ HENLE—PHOTO RESEARCHERS

VIEW DOWN A NARROW, BALCONY-LINED STREET IN CAGLIARI, CAPITAL OF SARDINIA

lation concentration, but 20th-century population movements have intensified concentration in and around the towns of Cagliari and Sassari (with over 400 per sq.mi.) and in the Campidano (180). In the western zone, population has moved toward the coast, while large tracts of the eastern highlands have less than 65 or even 25 per sq.mi. During the late 19th and 20th centuries there has been some rural depopulation, with a tendency for the lower lands to receive the migrants, though not on the scale that has occurred on the Italian mainland.

According to the 1961 census, 41% of the active male population was employed in agriculture and fishing (28% for Italy) and 42% in industry (39% for Italy).

Administration and Social Conditions.—Sardinia is one of five regions that obtained special forms of self-government by the Italian constitution of 1948 (see ITALY: *Administration and Social Conditions*). The isolation of Sardinia during World War II encouraged some measure of self-government after the summer of 1943, when it was occupied by the Allies. In March 1944 a high commissioner was appointed, and regional autonomy was granted in 1946. But the poverty of the island made it undesirable to leave the economic planning entirely in the hands of the Regional Assembly, first elected in May 1949. Administration of the region is carried out by the Assembly (*consiglio regionale*) and its president and Executive Committee (*giunta regionale*). The president of the Assembly, elected from its members, has not the rank of minister in the Council of Italian Ministers as in Sicily but represents the region, promulgates its laws, and has the right to speak in the council on Sardinian affairs. The Sardinian Assembly has less extensive powers than that of Sicily. It cannot legislate on educational affairs, nor can it legislate on all questions concerning agriculture, land reclamation, industry, and commerce. The Italian state retains control of communications, justice, and the armed forces, though the government may delegate to Sardinia the right to safeguard public order.

Sardinia is one of the poorest of the southern regions of Italy, and with a shortage of productive land and of occupations other than in agriculture, the island experiences problems of unemployment and emigration. Great strides have been made under the auspices of the Cassa del Mezzogiorno (Southern Italy Development Fund) to increase employment and improve living conditions. Projects embarked upon include, notably, those in the Campidano Plain and Arborea to resettle peasants on reclaimed land or amalgamated agricultural holdings. But many landless day labourers and small farmers maintain a low standard of living. The general lack of employment for women has resulted in an effort to develop light industries.

Education follows the Italian national educational pattern. Though in the early 1950s it was estimated that almost a quarter of the population was illiterate, by the 1960s illiteracy had been almost eliminated. The considerable need for adult education is being met by an increasing number of *corsi popolari*. There are universities at Sassari and Cagliari.

Social services as a whole are organized like those on the mainland. In the early 1960s there were 18 general, 13 private, and 7 specialist hospitals. *See* ITALY: *Administration and Social Conditions*.

THE ECONOMY

Agriculture.—Although Sardinia's rural economy has been modified by far-reaching development plans instituted after World War II, by the early 1960s the emphasis was still on pastoralism, which has an agelong tradition on the island. Nearly half the total area is under permanent grazing. Sardinia has about one-quarter of all Italy's sheep and goats. The chief sheep-rearing districts are in the western pastures of Planargia, in the Temo and Tirso valleys, Logudoro, and the mountains of Nuoro, Gennargentu, Iglesiente, and La Nurra. Much ewe's milk cheese of the Pecorino Romano type is exported. Sardinian lamb, in demand on the mainland, and coarse wool, chiefly marketed at Macomer, are also important products. Native breeds of cattle are well adapted to the poorer districts of Sulcis, Trexenta, the Baronie, Gallura, and La Nurra but are poor milk yielders and are used chiefly for draft purposes. Under development plans milk cows have been imported from Switzerland and the Netherlands. Altogether, stock raising provides more than two-fifths of Sardinia's revenue from land utilization.

About one-third of the cultivated land, which covers little more than a quarter of the island's total area and is continuously cropped only in the Campidano, is under cereals, of which hard varieties of wheat are the most important. With primitive methods still

SMALL FIELDS AND STONE RUINS SURROUNDING THE VILLAGE OF ORGOSOLO, LOCATED AT THE FOOT OF SOPRAMONTE MOUNTAIN IN EAST CENTRAL SARDINIA

predominating, yields are considerably lower than the average for the rest of Italy. Minor cereal crops are barley (for fodder), oats, and maize (corn). The production and yield of rice have been increased, and sugar beet, virtually a new crop since 1948, supplies regional requirements.

Tree crops represent about one-third of the agricultural produce by value. Olives cover the most extensive area, partly in specialized groves, partly in mixed land use. Vineyards, less important than in the 19th century, are chiefly around Cagliari. Citrus fruit, peaches, and almonds have local importance.

Sardinian agriculture has been greatly handicapped by the fact that land tenure is rooted in feudal practices. The prevalence of very small holdings—less than half exceed 3 ha. (7½ ac.)—and of latifundia, mostly in grazing and forest lands, is characteristic; the fragmentation of holdings is excessive, especially in the Campidano. Following legislation by the Italian government in 1950, the Ente per la Trasformazione Fondiaria Agraria per la Sardegna (ETFAS) has done much to promote land reform. Life in the villages, however, has changed little since ancient times: homespun woven on domestic looms, wheat ground by primitive mills and baked into *pillonca*, fields worked with wooden plows, and grazings maintained communally are symbolic of its traditions.

Fishing, never an occupation of the Sardinians, is largely in the hands of immigrants from the Italian mainland. It has been encouraged by subsidies for new boats and the construction of new fishing villages to replace the primitive dwellings still to be found around the coast. Tunny is the chief catch.

Industry.—Minerals, chiefly from Iglesiente, contribute about half the island's industrial revenues from natural resources, and the output of lead and zinc represents about nine-tenths and three-quarters, respectively, of Italy's total production. Silver and cadmium are by-products of lead and zinc extraction, and small quantities of antimony, copper, iron, manganese, molybdenum, nickel, cobalt, and tin are also mined. Inferior coal is mined at Sulcis and anthracite at Seui near Tortoli. The annual production of coal is about 900,000 metric tons. Sea-salt extraction is the second most important source of industrial revenue. Lesser industries are chiefly concerned with the processing of food and other regional products (leather, cork, tobacco, dwarf palm fibre, etc.). There are also plastics and cement factories.

Development.—Financial provisions for economic development are framed with regard to the island's poverty. In addition to the proceeds of local taxation, the region receives rents paid for hydroelectric concessions, while state grants are made for specific public works and land improvement projects. Since the establishment of the Cassa del Mezzogiorno in 1950, numerous irrigation and water supply schemes have been promoted, and a great area of the Nuoro is being improved. The largest single project has been undertaken by the Ente Autonomo del Flumendosa, set up in 1946 to develop the hydrographic resources of the Flumendosa Basin. This has provided irrigation of 125,000 ac. (50,000 ha.) of the Campidano, drinking water for 22 communes with a total population of almost 100,000, a further supply of 10,000,000 cu.m. of water annually to Cagliari, and 125,000,000 kw-hr. of hydroelectric power annually. The Sardinian Recovery Plan inaugurated in 1963 involved the planned investment by the government of 400,000,000,000 lire in a series of economic projects over a period of 13 years.

Communications and Ports.—The road network is not dense, as the population is mostly concentrated in large villages: the chief settlements are linked within a mesh of four main roads running east-west, and another four running north-south. The principal highway runs between Cagliari and Sassari via the eastern edge of the Campidano. Despite the difficulties of relief, Sardinia is well provided for in its railway system. There are 257 mi. (414 km.) of the Italian State system (standard-gauge lines), connecting Cagliari-Iglesias, Oristano-Sassari-Porto Torres, and Olbia-Golfo Aranci. Another 591 mi. (951 km.) of privately owned narrow-gauge lines run chiefly southwest-northeast. The Iglesiente is served by 80 mi. (129 km.) of private mineral lines. Significantly, neither the railways nor the main roads follow the coast.

Cagliari, Olbia, and Porto Torres are the chief ports. Cagliari's harbour is artificial, consisting of an old inner harbour and a new one protected by moles. It owes much of its importance to the export of lead, zinc, and salt. It is also a secondary naval base and a fishing and, especially, a passenger port. There are weekly services to Naples, Genoa-Palermo, and Genoa-Tunis. Olbia, the principal passenger port, is linked with Civitavecchia; Porto Torres acts as outpost for Sassari and the iron mines of La Nurra District. Trade has been vastly improved by the introduction of new ferry services (*navitraghetto*), especially between Olbia and Civitavecchia, which allow faster transport of goods. La Maddalena in the northeast is a naval base on Maddalena Island. The annual increase in the number of tourists has led to improved communications with the mainland. Olbia's function as the gateway to Sardinia is declining with the increase in air transport. Air services link Cagliari and Rome direct. The airport at Alghero has direct connection with London during the summer months.

See also references under "Sardinia" in the Index.

BIBLIOGRAPHY.—*Geography and General: Atti del XVII Congresso geografico italiano* (1957); M. Le Lannou, *Pâtres et Paysans de la Sardaigne* (1941); Le Play Society, *Sardinian Studies,* ed. by W. G. Walker (1938); F. Milone, *L'Italia nell' economia delle sue regioni* (1955); J. Pelletier, *Le Relief de la Sardaigne* (1960); M. Pinna and L. Corda, *La distribuzione della popolazione e i centri abitati della Sardegna* (1956–57); Societa Elettrica Sarda, *Atti del Congresso per la rinascita della Sardegna* (1950); C. L. Dozier, "Establishing a Framework for Development in Sardinia: the Campidano," *Geogr. Rev.* vol. 47 (1957); J. M. Houston, *The Western Mediterranean World*, pp. 623–634 (1964). (J. M. Ho.)

Archaeology and Prehistory: M. Pallottino, *La Sardegna nuragica* (1950); C. Zervos, *La Civilisation de la Sardaigne du début de l'énéolithique à la fin de la période nouragique,* especially for pictures (1954); G. Pesce, *Sardegna punica* (1961); M. Guido, *Sardinia,* in the "Ancient Peoples and Places" Series, with bibliography (1963).

History: C. Bellieni, *La Sardegna e i Sardi nella civiltà del mondo antico,* 2 vol. (1928–31); E. Pais, *Storia della Sardegna e della Corsica durante il dominio romano,* 2 vol. (1923); P. Meloni, *L'amministrazione della Sardegna da Augusto all'invasione vandalica* (1958); E. Besta, *La Sardegna medioevale,* 2 vol. (1908–09); R. Delogu, *L'Architettura del medioevo in Sardegna* (1953); R. Carta Raspi, *Breve storia di Sardegna* (1950).

SARDIS (SARDES), a ruined city lying about 45 mi. (72 km.) E of Izmir in the Manisa *il* of Turkey, was the capital of the ancient kingdom of Lydia (*q.v.*), the western terminus of the Persian royal road from Susa described by Herodotus, the seat of a *conventus* (a centre for the administration of justice) under the Roman Empire, and the metropolis of the province of Lydia in later Roman and Byzantine times. It was situated in the middle Hermus (Gediz) Valley, at the foot of Mt. Tmolus (Boz Dag), a steep and lofty spur of which formed the citadel. It was about 2½ mi. S of the Hermus. The area was settled in the 3rd millennium B.C., but the earliest reference to Sardis is in Alcman (*c.* 650 B.C.). An older name for Sardis seems to have been Hyde, a name given in the *Iliad* to the city of the Maeonian chiefs. Sardis was the capital of the powerful Lydian kingdom under Gyges (*c.* 687–645 B.C.). It was captured by the Cimmerians in the 7th century, by the Persians in the 6th, by the Athenians in 499 (or 498) B.C., and by Antiochus the Great at the end of the 3rd century. In 133 B.C. the city was bequeathed to Rome with the kingdom of Pergamum by Attalus III Philometor Euergetes. Under the emperor Tiberius, in A.D. 17, it was destroyed by an earthquake, but it was one of the great cities of Asia Minor till the later Byzantine period. As one of the seven churches of Asia, it was addressed by the author of the Book of Revelation. Its importance was due, first to its military strength, secondly to its situation on an important highway leading from the interior to the Aegean coast, and thirdly to its commanding the wide and fertile plain of the Hermus.

In Roman times Sardis lost some of its importance but became the seat of the metropolitan bishop of the province of Lydia formed *c.* A.D. 295. In the 10th century Constantine VII Porphyrogenitus (in his work *De Thematibus*) enumerates it as third, after Ephesus and Smyrna, in the list of cities of the Thracesian *thema*. The Hermus Valley began to suffer from the inroads of the Seljuk Turks about the end of the 11th century; but the successes of the Greek general Eustathius Philocales in 1110 relieved the district of Turkish pressure for the time. The fort on the citadel of Sardis was handed over by treaty to Turkish invaders from the east in 1306. Finally, about 1390, with the termination of the independent Turkish amirates, Sardis was merged in the Ottoman Empire. The latest reference to the city relates its capture by Timur in 1402.

The ruins of Sardis, so far as they are now visible, are Lydian, Roman, and early Byzantine. The great Ionic temple of Artemis on the east bank of the Pactolus River is Hellenistic. The temple and 1,000 Lydian graves were excavated by H. C. Butler and T. L. Shear (1910–14, 1922). A Harvard-Cornell expedition resumed study of the site in 1958. Remains of habitations indicate that the city of Lydian kings extended along the modern highway and into the side valley of the Pactolus.

BIBLIOGRAPHY.—Reports by G. M. A. Hanfmann in *Bulletin of the American Schools of Oriental Research* (1959 *et seq.*). For excavations during 1910–14 *see* H. C. Butler, *Sardis,* publications of the American Society for the Excavation of Sardis, vol. i (1922) and vol. ii (1925); for the Lydian inscriptions *see* W. H. Buckler, *Sardis,* vol. vi, pt. 2 (1924). *See* also Alfred Heubeck, *Lydiaka* (1959); R. Gusmani, *Lydisches Wörterbuch* (1964). For the city's history in early Christian times *see* W. M. Ramsay, *Letters to the Seven Churches of Asia* (1906); V. Schultze, *Altchristliche Städte,* vol. ii, 2, pp. 145 ff. (1926).

(G. M. A. H.)

SARDOU, VICTORIEN (1831–1908), French playwright who, with E. Augier and Dumas, dominated the French stage in the late 19th century. He was born in Paris, Sept. 5, 1831. His *Les Pattes de mouche* (1860; English translation *A Scrap of Paper,* 1861) is a model of the well-made play. He relied on theatrical devices to create an illusion of life and this explains his rapid eclipse, but *Madame Sans-Gêne* (1893), his last success, is still performed although his other successful historical plays—*Patrie!* (1869; Eng. trans. 1915), *Théodora* (1884; Eng. trans. 1885), *Thermidor* (1891; Eng. trans. 1891) and *L'Affaire des poisons* (1907)—and those in which he satirized his contemporaries—*Nos intimes* (1861; Eng. trans. 1862), *Les Ganaches* (1862; Eng. trans. 1893), *Les Vieux Garçons* (1865)—are never played. His initial successes he owed to the actress Virginie Déjazet, and several of his 70 works were written for her; others were written for Sarah Bernhardt. In 1877 he was elected to the Académie Française. He died in Paris, Nov. 8, 1908.

See J. A. Hart, *Sardou and the Sardou Plays* (1913); G. Mouly, *La Vie prodigieuse de V. Sardou* (1931). (D. Ks.)

SARGASSO SEA, a relatively still tract in the central North Atlantic ocean strewn with floating seaweed of the genus *Sargassum* (originally named *Sargaço* by the Portuguese). This tract, bounded approximately by 20° and 35° N. and 30° and 70° W., is roughly elliptical and lies inside of a clockwise setting current system of which the Gulf stream forms part of the western rim. The precipitation is low, evaporation is high and winds are light. Its waters are remarkably clear, warm and saline. *Sargassum,* or gulfweed, belongs to the brown algae and bears small but prominent berrylike bladders (*see* ALGAE: *Survey and Classification: Brown Algae*). The pelagic weed drifts with wind and current but apparently maintains itself vegetatively with possibly minor replenishment by coastal plants drifting in from the southwest. The weed supports specialized animals of a type more characteristic of the littoral zone than the open ocean, some of which are found nowhere else. The Sargasso sea was first reported by Columbus who crossed it on his initial "West Indies" voyage; however, Columbus implies in the journal of his first voyage that he had evidence of earlier voyagers through the area and the seaweeds therein, and it is possible that the Carthaginians reached the Sargasso sea as early as 530 B.C. The widely credited story of ships becoming helplessly embedded in the weed has been disproved. The "Michael Sars" oceanographic expedition in 1910 helped delimit the weed area and provided new evidence that the Sargasso sea was the spawning ground of the common eel.

(C. A. Bs.)

SARGENT, JOHN SINGER (1856–1925), U.S. painter and portraitist, was born in Florence, It., on Jan. 12, 1856, and brought up in an expatriate environment. He first saw America in 1876 when his mother took him and his sister Emily to the Philadelphia Centennial Exhibition. On that visit he established U.S.

citizenship which he never relinquished. Serious and reserved, he possessed a passion for European art and literature, and a talent for drawing, which his mother was careful to encourage. It was Mrs. Sargent, frustrated by the American way of life, who had persuaded her husband to exchange his secure medical practice in Philadelphia for a rootless and migratory existence in Europe. What seems in retrospect a depressing existence introduced Sargent to European culture from his earliest years, and fostered in him a passion for art. In 1874 his parents reluctantly agreed that he should go to Paris to study painting and in the autumn of that year he entered the studio of Carolus-Duran. A fashionable society portraitist, Carolus-Duran was small and dynamic, teaching his pupils to paint what they saw with precision and tonal refinement. His god was Velázquez, but he was also a leader of the new French school, and a friend of Édouard Manet. Hard-working and receptive, Sargent was soon displaying remarkable assurance in his oil studies from life. His early portraits of "Fanny Watts" (1877) and "Carolus-Duran" (1879; Clark Institute, Williamstown, Mass.) are elegantly posed and realistic; Sargent's use of low-toned harmonies and sparkling highlights reveals his debt to Carolus-Duran. His informal sketches, with their direct handling and atmospheric colour, are strongly impressionist (Sargent knew and admired Monet)—sunlight filtering through leaves in his "Two Wine Glasses" (1875), or the "Pasdeloup Orchestra at the Cirque d'Hiver" (1878; Museum of Fine Arts, Boston) seen in a blur of movement from above. Sargent's larger subject pictures, such as the "Oyster Gatherers of Cancale" (1878; Corcoran Gallery, Washington, D.C.), were still part of a figurative and narrative tradition, and tend to be more theatrical and self-conscious.

Sargent mixed freely in artistic and social circles in Paris. One of his earliest patrons was Édouard Pailleron, the novelist and playwright, and Sargent's portrait of "Madame Pailleron" (1879; Corcoran Gallery), dressed in black satin against a sunlit Savoyard meadow, and the intently gazing "Pailleron Children" (1881) are among his most original early works. More ambitious in design was his portrait of the "Boit Children" (c. 1882; Museum of Fine Arts, Boston), "four corners and a void," where the distilled light and delicately adjusted forms recall the work of Velázquez. In 1879 Sargent had gone specially to Madrid to study the Spanish master's work, and this journey, together with his visit to Haarlem to see the paintings of Frans Hals in 1880, constituted the final process in his artistic education.

In spite of his growing reputation, Sargent did not find it easy to attract fashionable sitters to his studio. His portraits of friends, like the brilliantly alive sketch of Vernon Lee (1881; Tate Gallery), were not remunerative, and presentation portraits of fashionable hostesses, like "Madame Escudier" (1882; Clark Institute, Williamstown, Mass.), did not lead to commissions. In 1883 Sargent began work on a portrait of the celebrated beauty Madame Gautreau ("Madame X"; Metropolitan Museum of Art, New York), which he intended to be a masterpiece. In a décolleté black dress, with her extraordinary head in profile and her right arm twisted sinuously outward, Madame Gautreau is shown in a tautly linear and provocative pose. Brilliantly characterized, it is Sargent's most original and exciting work, but it caused a scandal at the Paris Salon of 1884, where it was stigmatized as eccentric and erotic. Sargent's studio became emptier than ever, and after a successful visit to England in the summer of 1884 he decided to move to London permanently. The following year he took the house at 13 Tite Street, Chelsea, which Whistler was just vacating. It remained his home for 40 years.

Sargent's work was probably too continental and avant-garde to appeal immediately to English taste; his portrait of "The Misses Vickers" (1884), with its unusual perspective and grouping, was voted the worst picture of the year by the *Pall Mall Gazette* when it was exhibited at the Royal Academy in 1886. In 1888 he was sketching with Monet at Giverny (a picture "Monet Painting by the Edge of a Wood" is in the Tate Gallery), and the following year he executed several full-length studies of Javanese dancing girls at the Universal Exhibition in Paris. These paintings temporarily mark the end of his subject work, as he became increasingly involved with portraiture. His work at Broadway,

Worcestershire, had resulted in one large picture, "Carnation, Lily, Lily, Rose" (1885–86; Tate Gallery), a study of two little girls lighting Japanese lanterns in a garden at dusk, which went straight to the hearts of the British public when it was exhibited in 1887. In the same year Sargent went again to the United States, and was overwhelmed with commissions. His popularity was now assured, and from the 1890s onward his portraits were to create an enduring image of the Edwardian age.

His portraits are conceived in a formal tradition. Always elegant and decisive, they are neither intimate nor psychologically profound. His sitters are dignified but remote. It is the painterly quality of Sargent's style which is so impressive. His broad, slashing brush-strokes and brilliant palette evoke the accidents of a particular moment, the play of light and shadow across features caught forever in a momentary impression. He painted what he saw before him with incredible accuracy, and in a style that is, for all its surface scintillation, brilliantly economical. He was surprisingly unrepetitive, responding to each sitter differently, rather than relying on any set formula. "Lady Meyer and her Children" (1896), resplendent in silks and satins, or the rococo "Lady Faudel-Phillips" (1898) proclaim the opulence and luxury of the pre-Edwardian world. The austere design and subdued grays of "Graham Robertson" (1894; Tate Gallery) are entirely appropriate for this refined and elongated aesthete. "Lord Ribblesdale" (1902; Tate Gallery) is the epitome of aristocratic hauteur and vanity. The list of Sargent's sitters includes the wealthy and aristocratic on both sides of the Atlantic; they came to his studio to be immortalized.

Sargent grew increasingly bored with portraiture and the limits it imposed on him, and around 1910 he refused to paint any more; the portraits "Henry James" (1913; National Portrait Gallery) and "President Wilson" (1917; Dublin) are rare exceptions. This was a remarkable decision for an artist who was regarded as the greatest portraitist of the age, the "Van Dyck of our times" as Rodin called him, and who could command any price he liked. Immune to social and monetary pressures, Sargent had decided to devote the rest of his life to his decorative work, his watercolours, and his landscape oils.

Sargent was not a great imaginative artist. The large mural decorations which he executed in the upper corridor of the Boston

"CARNATION, LILY, LILY, ROSE," 1885–86. IN THE TATE GALLERY, LONDON

Public Library illustrating the development of religious thought are eclectic, and coherent, but they do not reveal any considerable powers of design or formal inventiveness. Unusual in their intermingling of painting and molded bas-relief, they blend well with the neo-Renaissance architecture of the building. Commissioned in 1890, they took Sargent over 20 years to complete. His later decorative scheme for the Boston Museum of Fine Arts is lighter in tone and more classical in subject, but, for all its technical virtuosity, it seems a misuse of his powers.

From 1900 Sargent spent almost all his summers abroad, usually dividing his time between Italy and the Alps. Watercolour became his favourite medium, and he executed endless studies of buildings, canals, meadows, streams, rocks, marble quarries, olive groves, or whatever attracted his attention. Scintillating in colour and technique, combining soft luminous washes with slashing, quill-shaped brush strokes, they capture his immediate response to the play of light and shadow, the warm and enveloping atmosphere of the Mediterranean world. His later oil paintings are similar in subject to his watercolours. The most successful of them have a breathtaking freedom where the thick impasto takes on a life of its own. During World War I, Sargent was an official war artist, and painted two huge works, "Gassed" (1918) and "General Officers of the Great War" (1918–22; National Portrait Gallery).

Sargent was a shy and reserved man who lived entirely for his painting. He never married. A member of the Royal Academy, his work was denigrated by the supporters of the modern movement, who used him as a butt for their attacks on the establishment. He remained popular, however, and at his death on April 15, 1925, there were large retrospective exhibitions in London, Boston, and New York. Then his reputation slumped, and he was remembered as a glossy and superficial society portraitist. His work was shown in Birmingham, Eng., and Washington, D.C., in 1964.

BIBLIOGRAPHY.—W. H. Downes, *John S. Sargent* (1925); E. Charteris, *John Sargent* (1927); C. M. Mount, *John Singer Sargent* (1955); D. McKibbin, *Sargent's Boston* (1956); *The Private World of John Singer Sargent,* Corcoran Gallery (1964); *Exhibition of Works by John Singer Sargent,* City Museum and Art Gallery, Birmingham (1964).
(R. L. O.)

SARGODHA, a town, district, and division of West Pakistan. The town, headquarters of the district and of the division, lies in the Chaj, or Jech, doab, 125 mi. (201 km.) WNW of Lahore. Pop. (1961) 83,141. Notable buildings in Sargodha include Jinnah Hall (with its library), a sports stadium, and the mosques. Among the town's educational and cultural institutions are De Montmorency College (affiliated to the University of the Punjab), the municipal college for girls, the Pakistan Air Force public school, and the Sargodha Academy. The town lies on the main road between Lahore and Mianwali, and is also a railway junction. Sargodha is a grain and cash-crop market and an important industrial centre, with textile and hosiery manufacture, cotton ginning, flour and oilseed milling, and chemical and soap factories. Immigrants from Jagadhri (Ambala District, India) established the metal industry in the town after 1947. The town derives its name from the words *sar,* meaning "pond," and Godha, the name of a mendicant who lived by the pond and who was considered sacred by the Hindus. Sargodha was founded in 1903 and developed as the headquarters of the Lower Jhelum Canal colony. It became a municipality in 1914, when the courts and offices of Shahpur district were moved to Sargodha from Shahpur town. However, the district continued to be known officially as Shahpur until 1960. With the location of divisional headquarters, the city grew considerably.

Sargodha District (area 4,775 sq.mi.; pop. [1961] 1,467,621) is bordered by the Salt Range in the north, the Jhelum flows through the centre, and the eastern part is irrigated by the Lower Jhelum Canal. West of the Jhelum are undulating sand hills which form part of the Thal Desert. Wheat, grain, cotton, and bajra are the principal crops. Besides Sargodha other important towns are Shahpur (pop. [1961] 6,330) and Bhera (pop. [1961] 17,992).

Sargodha Division was formed in December 1960 and consists of the districts of Sargodha, Mianwali, Lyallpur, and Jhang. Area 17,095 sq.mi. (44,276 sq.km.). Pop. (1961) 5,976,939.
(K. S. Ad.)

SARGON (Akkadian Sharru-ken or Sharrum-kin) was the name borne by three notable rulers in the ancient Near East:

Sargon of Agade (reigned *c.* 2350–2300 B.C.), a former vizier of a king of Kish, founded the city of Agade (not certainly identified) in north Babylonia and, wresting the hegemony of the city-states from the Sumerian Lugalzaggesi of Erech (Uruk), established the first Semitic dynasty. This implied no racial conquest but merely a climax in the process of Semitic infiltration from the desert. The dynasty of Agade, though it endured for little more than a century, left a permanent imprint on Mesopotamian society, notably in connection with land tenure, for private ownership of land, rare in the Sumerian city-state, from this period became much more common.

Sargon himself gained possession not only of Sumer and Akkad (south and north Babylonia) but claimed control of regions as far distant as the Lebanon and the Amanus range (Alma Dag), while later literary tradition accords him an empire extending to Asia Minor; cylinder seals of the Agade period have been found in Cyprus. International trade flourished, and Sargon boasted that at the quay of his capital city might be found ships from Tilmun (Bahrain), Magan (probably Oman), and Meluhha (either Aden, the Somali coast, or India).

Sargon I of Assyria (fl. *c.* 1850 B.C.) was a ruler of the Old Assyrian period. Little is known in detail of Assyria in his time, but clearly the Assyrian trading colony in Cappadocia, known from the tablets discovered at Kultepe, was then in its heyday. This implies the ability of Sargon I to maintain the security of the trade routes, and the argument has been advanced that the colony in Cappadocia was actually within an area constituting an Assyrian province, a suggestion which derives some support from the existence of a tablet in Cappadocia bearing Sargon's seal.

Sargon II of Assyria (reigned 722–705 B.C.), an able king, was the founder of the last Assyrian dynasty. His greatest achievement lay in holding the pressure of tribal movements north and east of Assyria. As one measure to counter the threat to Assyrian east-west trade routes, he founded a new fortress-capital, Dur Sharrukin (modern Khorsabad), north of the traditional Assyrian capitals. The importance of an event shortly after his accession, the fall of Samaria, has been exaggerated by modern biblical historians.

In 721 B.C., Sargon had to deal with an anti-Assyrian coalition in Syria, organized by the king of Hamath, while in Babylonia Merodach-baladan, paramount chief of the Chaldean tribes in the south, took advantage of the change of ruler to claim the kingship, allying himself with Elam. Assyrian military action failed to displace Merodach-baladan, who remained in control of Babylonia until 710 B.C.

The following years were spent mainly in campaigns to counter Urartian intrigues among the tribes north and northeast of Assyria, and to consolidate Assyrian influence in Manna, south of Lake Urmia. In 714 B.C. Sargon invaded Urartu from the east, compelling Rusa (Rusas, Ursa) I to leave his capital, Tushpa. On its return a flying column from the victorious Assyrian army captured the wealthy mountain city of Musasir.

In the northwest the resurgent power of Mushku (Phrygia), which had already supported a rebellion by Carchemish in 717 B.C., was planning a coalition of neighbouring states, in alliance with Urartu. Prompt action by Sargon in 713 and 712 B.C. drove a wedge between Urartu and Mushku, and the foreign policy of the latter, now isolated and probably already under pressure from Cimmerian hordes, changed in favour of Assyria, so that by 709 B.C. the two powers were in alliance. Further south, there arose in 713 B.C. an anti-Assyrian coalition headed by Ashdod and encouraged by Egypt; this was crushed by prompt Assyrian military action.

Thus by 710 B.C. Sargon was free to turn his attention to Babylonia, where he was able to clear the Babylonian cities of the forces of Merodach-baladan, though the latter remained as paramount chief in the tribal territories of the south.

A new danger arose in the northwest in 707 B.C. with the breakthrough of the Cimmerians, who had already overrun Urartu. Sargon opposed them in Tabal (around Kayseri in Turkey) and deflected them westward. His death in 705 B.C. has generally been assumed, on the basis of an enigmatic letter, to have taken place in action on the northwest frontier, but this view has been disputed. *See also* BABYLONIA AND ASSYRIA: *History.*

BIBLIOGRAPHY.—For Sargon of Agade *see* H. Schmökel, *Geschichte des alten Vorderasiens,* pp. 39–42, 47–51 (1957). For Sargon II of Assyria *see* H. W. F. Saggs, *The Greatness that Was Babylon,* pp. 111–118 (1962); "The Nimrud Letters, 1952—Part II: Relations with the West," *Iraq,* vol. xvii (1955), and "The Nimrud Letters, 1952—Part IV: The Urartian Frontier," *Iraq,* vol. xx (1958).   (H. W. F. S.)

SARK (French SERCQ), one of the smaller Channel Islands (*q.v.*), lying 7 mi. (11 km.) E of Guernsey, is 3 mi. long and 1½ mi. in extreme breadth; area (including Brecqhou) 2.1 sq.mi. (5 sq.km.). Pop. (1961) 560. Brecqhou (privately owned and with 10 inhabitants in 1951) is separated from Great Sark by a narrow channel of the sea; Great Sark on the north and Little Sark on the south are connected by La Coupée, a 100-yd. (91-m.) isthmus only 6 ft. (2 m.) wide at the top, flanked by precipitous cliffs. Sark forms a plateau about 300 ft. (91 m.) high, rising to 375 ft.; the coast is wholly encircled by cliffs and scenically attractive. Creux Harbour on the east communicates with the interior by two tunnels, dating from 1588 and 1868; a second harbour was opened in 1949 at La Masseline. Sark and Brecqhou are cut in granite, schist, and gneiss. Mineral veins include silver ore (no longer worked) and amethyst, known as Sark stone.   (G. H. D.)

History.—Apart from the legends of St. Magloire (6th century), Sark first appears as part of a gift by William the Conqueror to Mont-Saint-Michel, *c.* 1040. A century later it was in the hands of the De Vernon family, lords of Néhou, who endowed the priory of St. Magloire as a dependency of the abbey of Montebourg. Sark reverted to the king in 1203 by Richard de Vernon's forfeiture. For part of the 13th century an attempt seems to have been made to administer Sark and Alderney together; later Sark was governed by a royal *prévôt* (provost) who presided over a court of six *jurats.* The island suffered severely from the wars of the 14th century and may have been uninhabited for much of the 15th and early 16th centuries. It was captured by the French in 1549, seized by a Flemish corsair and held momentarily in the name of the emperor Charles V, retaken by the French, and was in English hands again by 1558. To prevent it from becoming a nest of pirates, it was colonized by Hélier de Carteret, seigneur of St. Ouen in Jersey, under a patent of Elizabeth I dated Aug. 6, 1565. The colonists, mostly Jerseymen, were settled on a number of farms, subsequently fixed at 40. At first the court was modeled on that of Jersey, with bailiff and *jurats,* but this was changed in 1675 to one composed of seneschal, *prévôt,* greffier, tenants, seigneur, constable, and vingtenier. In 1922 12 deputies were added; but in 1951 the members were reduced to seigneur, seneschal, tenants, and 12 deputies. The De Carterets were seigneurs until 1720 since when the seigneury has changed hands several times.   (LE P.)

Government.—The seigneur appoints the seneschal who presides over the Chief Pleas, a body consisting of 40 tenants and 12 deputies, which regulates local affairs by ordinance. The seigneur can, by temporary veto, delay the enactment of ordinances, which can also be annulled by the Royal Court of Guernsey, subject to appeal to the sovereign in Council. Sark is part of the bailiwick of Guernsey. Justice is administered by the court of the seneschal, with rights of appeal to the Royal Court of Guernsey. Police, if required in Sark, are supplied from Guernsey on repayment.

Automobiles are forbidden on the roads of Sark. The canine population is controlled and none but the seigneur (in the 1960s the dame) may keep a female dog.

The Economy.—The island is subdivided into tenements with fixed boundaries, and settlement is scattered. Dairying is practised, but the farmland (about a third of the island) includes substantial tillage. There is a little market gardening. External trade is directed through Guernsey. Sark offers accommodation to visitors, but its capacity is limited and most people come on day trips from Guernsey or on cruises.   (G. H. D.)

BIBLIOGRAPHY.—J. H. Le Patourel, "The Medieval Administration of Sark," *Trans. Soc. Guernesiaise,* XII, 310–336 (1935), "The Capture of Sark by a Flemish Corsair in 1553," *ibid.,* XIV, 358–360 (1949); L. Selosse, *L'Ile de Sark* (1928); A. B. de Carteret, *The Story of Sark* (1956); Dame Sibyl Hathaway, *Dame of Sark* (1961).

SARMATIANS, a people who, during the 4th century B.C.–4th century A.D., occupied much of southern European Russia and penetrated into the eastern Balkans and beyond.

Sarmatian studies were in their infancy in the 1920s; but numerous excavations in the U.S.S.R. in recent decades have provided much information. There was good reason to accept the views of Herodotus and other ancient Greek historians that the Sarmatians, or Sauromatians, were an association of tribes. As with the Scythians and the Cimmerians (*qq.v.*) before them, the most vital element in their political group came from central Asia. Its members were of Iranian stock and language; their tongue closely resembled that of the Scythians (Herodotus, book iv, 117). Like the Scythians they were nomadic, excelling in horsemanship and displaying the same skill in warfare. They also had a keen political sense and administrative ability, and followed their conquest of the western Eurasian plain by obtaining full political control over what is now southern European Russia. In consequence their name acquired generic significance; it quickly came to represent a large group of kindred and allied tribes that remained thenceforth attached to the smaller Sarmatian core. The Alani (*q.v.*) and Roxolani were the most important of these secondary tribes (*see* also IAZYGES), yet even when acting independently, all retained their place in the Sarmatian community. All of them accepted the culture and artistic style favoured by the Sarmatians, practising and disseminating them with such vigour that Sarmatian taste was felt even in the Greek cities on the shores of the Black Sea.

History.—It is evident now that the Sarmatians advanced from central Asia to invade and conquer the Scythians and did not, as stated by Diodorus Siculus (book ii, 43), rise against them from within their own territory. It has become possible to divide Sarmatian history into four periods. The first extends from the 6th to the 4th century B.C. and deals with the Sarmatian migration from Asia and penetration to the western foothills of the Urals. Toward the end of this period the Roxolani pushed on toward the Volga River and the Alani settled in the Kuban Valley. For the most part they remained till they were dislodged in the period of the great migration, when some of the latter infiltrated into Ossetia (*q.v.*), surviving there till about the 9th century A.D.

The Sarmatians followed closely in the steps of these tribes and by Herodotus' day they had already made themselves masters of the plain between the Urals and the Don River. This encouraged them to intensify their pressure on the Scythians, and in the 4th century B.C. they crossed the Don and entered Scythia proper. This rapid advance may well have coincided with a decline in Scythian might, resulting from the death of their aged king Ateas in battle against Philip II of Macedonia in 339 B.C.; if so, this would help to account for its speed. The incursion serves to herald the second (Early Sarmatian) period in Sarmatian history, often called the Prokhorov Period after the important burials of that name with which it is associated. This phase stretched from the 4th to the 2nd century B.C., during which time the Sarmatians partially overcame the Scythians and gradually succeeded them as rulers over most of what later became southern European Russia. The Roxolani had begun by joining with the Sarmatians in attacking the Scythians, advancing upon them from the south. Toward the end of this period, when the Sarmatians had strengthened their hold over the territory of the Royal Scyths, the Roxolani changed their allegiance, joining forces with the Scythians to attack the Greek Black Sea cities.

In the third (Mid-Sarmatian) period, between the 1st century B.C. and the 1st century A.D., the Sarmatians conquered all but the Crimean Scythians, bringing the assaults on the Greek cities to an end. Having consolidated their hold over the captured areas the Sarmatians did not attempt to annex any of these cities; instead, early in Nero's reign they invaded the Roman province of Lower Moesia (Bulgaria). Although the Roman general Plautius Silvanus Aelianus ejected them in A.D. 62–63, the Sarmatians and some Germanic tribes they had joined were thenceforth a menace to the Romans in the west, as were the Alani in the Caucasian area. Vespasian, Trajan, and Marcus Aurelius were forced to adopt such defensive measures as to attempt to transform the vassal Bosporan kingdom into a buffer state (*see* BOSPORUS, KINGDOM OF THE). Hadrian had to build a network of fortresses manned with Roman troops along the borders of Lower Moesia and Cappadocia.

In the last phase of their history, spanning the 2nd to 4th centuries A.D., the Sarmatians and their Germanic allies entered Dacia (Rumania) and began raiding the lower reaches of the Danube, but in the 3rd century the Gothic invasion set a term to their independence. Nevertheless, many Sarmatians retained their position and influence under the Goths; others joined them to sweep into western Europe, fighting at their sides. However, soon after A.D. 370 waves of migrating Huns (*q.v.*) effectively ended the very existence of Sarmatia; the majority of the Sarmatians who remained in southern Russia perished at the hands of these Asian invaders. Some of the survivors were assimilated by their new masters and others by the Slavs of the lower Dnieper, but most fled westward to join their neighbours in harassing the Huns and the remaining Goths. Their descendants continued to do so until the 6th century when they finally disappeared from history.

Social Structure and Way of Life.—Very little was known till the 1960s about the social structure or way of life developed by the Sarmatians. Basically both at first followed closely those rendered familiar by the Scythians, largely as the result of a common central-Asian origin and heritage. Nevertheless, several fundamental differences serve to distinguish the two peoples. Scythians venerated nature deities, while the Sarmatians were fire worshipers who sacrificed horses to their god. Scythian women were relegated to a life of semiseclusion; the Sarmatians treated theirs as equals, during their earlier history expecting them to fight in time of war, and forbidding them to marry till they had killed an enemy in battle. However, after marriage, women were obliged to abandon warfare and to devote themselves to their homes and families. Greek tales about Amazons may have been based on exploits of early Sarmatian women, many of whom were buried with their weapons (*see* AMAZON).

When the Sarmatians penetrated into southeastern Europe they were already accomplished horsemen. They followed a nomadic way of life, devoting themselves to hunting and to pastoral occupations; most of them adhered to this form of existence to the end. There is evidence that some of them practised an elementary form of husbandry, but few settlements of Sarmatian origin have been discovered. In the earlier periods their customs, clothes, and many other possessions resembled those of the Scythians, but their society was matriarchal in character. Gradually, as a prosperous class began to form, the tribe entered a transitional phase during which tribal chieftains tended to replace women as rulers; eventually, kings seem to have predominated.

This may have been stimulated by the formation of a male corps of heavy cavalry, facilitated by the probably Sarmatian invention of a metal stirrup, soon followed by that of the spur. The methods of warfare thus made possible were largely responsible for Sarmatia's military supremacy. The Romans noted and gradually adopted these inventions. During the 3rd century they went so far as to incorporate in some Roman regiments Sarmatian units equipped with their traditional weapons and encouraged to fight in their own manner. From early times onward Sarmatian military accoutrements included conically shaped helmets worn with scale, ring, or plate armour of iron that often protected horses as well as riders. Unlike the Scythians, the Sarmatians did not excel at archery; they relied on long lances or spears and long, sharply pointed swords, all of distinctive shape.

The Sarmatians were excellent craftsmen. Perhaps artistically less inventive than the Scythians, they were nevertheless equally proficient metalworkers, better potters, and no less adept at curing hides; they were thus able to maintain the important trade in furs, grain (levied from local settlers), honey, fish, and metal that the Scythians had established with the Greek cities on the northern shores of the Black Sea. They also developed commercial contact with the Syr-Darya region, the borderlands of China, and the kingdom of Khorezm (Chorasmia).

Until disrupted by the Huns, Sarmatian culture presented a uniform and all-embracing character, even though it altered with each period in its history. Its evolution is reflected in burials

that distinguish each of the four periods. Thus no large mounds are associated with the earliest phase when objects were seldom included in the graves, though the occasional presence of articles points to the beginnings of a class society. Burials of the second period often display considerable wealth; those of the third phase also reflect the growth of a more complex way of life, stemming in part from the Sarmatian subjugation of alien tribes, and assimilation of many of their customs. It also was a result of the flourishing trade the Sarmatians had established. During these periods the truly typical Sarmatian culture evolved and was imposed on the entire region. In the last phase Germanic influence led to the introduction of fibulae (brooches or clasps like safety pins), with resulting changes in costume.

Tombs and Their Contents.—The richest Sarmatian burials have been found in the Kuban area, and on the edges of the great riverbeds of the southern Russian S.F.S.R. and the Ukraine, where many have been subjected to regular seasonal flooding. Hundreds of other graves are to be found throughout the area the Sarmatians once occupied. Many of these were excavated in the second half of the 19th and in the first half of the 20th centuries and sufficient material has become available to permit an overall picture to be outlined.

Except in the Kuban, where they are generally oval in shape, the mounds the Sarmatians constructed are very similar to those of the Scythians; but the tombs beneath them are very different from the elaborate Scythian mortuary chambers. For the most part Sarmatian graves consist of simple square, circular, or oval holes (sometimes pocketed trenches); very occasionally, tombs are found lined with rushes. No coffins were used; the body was usually wrapped in a leather or fur rug and laid on the bare earth, though sometimes on a rush mat. In the vicinity of Kerch (*q.v.*) paintings survive on the walls of some graves of late date, some showing Sarmatians wearing cloaks held in place by fibulae; some contain traces of what may be the beginnings of an alphabet.

Diagonal and crouched burials and cremations occur side by side; thus although Sarmatian culture prevailed, local habits evi-

MANSELL—ALINARI

SARMATIAN CAVALRY BEING ATTACKED BY ROMAN SOLDIERS; DETAIL OF A RELIEF ON TRAJAN'S COLUMN, ROME

dently persisted. In the last phase the influence of the Huns is reflected in the practice of cranial deformation. In the graves of earlier periods Scythian influence is often apparent throughout; horses are associated with most burials, their trappings being generally placed in the graves. In richer burials, such as those of Starobelsk and Yanchokarski, their hooves and skulls were often included, but not, as was customary in Scythian times, the rest of their bodies. Most of the tombs also contained cauldrons of the Scythian type as well as outfits for inhaling hemp, bronze vessels, and mirrors of oriental form in silver alloy. Tiny gold

Goldwork from the burial at Novocherkassk, U.S.S.R., 2nd century B.C. (Left) Covered bottle with representations of elks, lions, and monsters; (above) bottle in the form of an animal and ornament with embossed pattern; (below) crown decorated with stylized animals

plaques designed as trimmings for clothes are also common but, in contrast to similar gold plaques of Scythian date (which were generally decorated with an animal design), these are usually geometric in character. Among articles of personal adornment fibulae make their first appearance in graves of Sarmatian date; little gold bottles set with jewels are especially characteristic of the period; and various types of glass are numerous. The locally made pottery is of a higher quality than that typical of the Scythian age.

Sarmatian horse trappings differ from those used by the Scythians, as do some of their arms. The iron Sarmatian bits had rings to hold the leather and had fewer animal terminals and decorations than those of Scythian date; hard saddles with a high frontal arch were also new to the Black Sea region. The saddles were often covered with gold leaf studded with bosses and adorned with coloured glass or precious stones; trappings tended to be less ornate than those of the Scythians, although often of silver or silver gilt. The long swords peculiar to the Sarmatians were set into wooden hilts surmounted by a knob of precious stone (e.g., agate or onyx) or in wood laced with gold; the handguards were generally cut from a single large stone. Spears were longer and sharper than the Scythian, but the variety of knives and daggers was equally great.

Metalwork and the Polychrome Style.—Whereas the Scythian was an animal art the Sarmatian, though it retained many animal forms, was primarily geometric and was largely in polychrome (many colours). The Sarmatians apparently delighted in glass inlay, gold-wire granulations, and embossed effects achieved by repoussé (see METALWORK, DECORATIVE) or inset stones and jewels; the taste was basically Asian, the designs primarily geometric and floral, though frequently also of an animal character. Jewelers produced diadems, torques, bracelets, rings, fibulae, gold plaques, buckles, buttons, and mounts of various sorts. Hoards that have been found and objects acquired from the more important tombs constitute an important collection of jewelry and fine metalwork. The Pashkov group of burials in the Kuban, excavated during 1929–37 and 1946–49, were among the earliest known in the 1960s. They are associated with a Meteo-Sarmatian tribe and date in the main from the 5th to the 3rd century B.C., though one mound contained jewelry and vessels assigned to the 3rd century A.D. In the earlier instances the men were buried with spears, swords, and arrows; the women were adorned with beads and with bronze bracelets of local manufacture. The Prokhorov burials lie near Sharlyk in Orenburg *oblast,* Russian S.F.S.R., and were excavated by the Russian archaeologist S. I. Rudenko in 1916.

The largest belonged to a chieftain who had been buried in an iron chain-mail coat with gold torque and bronze bracelets; a sword and gold-handled knives were placed within easy reach of his hands, and two magnificent silver vessels of Persian workmanship stood close to him. One of these was inscribed in Aramaic with the words "the cup of Atromitra." The richest burial known in the 1960s belonged to the Novocherkassk group and is to be dated to the 2nd century B.C. Discovered in 1864, it produced objects of such value that it seems probable the tomb was for a queen. In addition to a magnificent crown the woman wore a gold necklace and gold bracelets. A small agate bottle mounted in gold and adorned with animal designs, and several gold cups and silver vessels lay beside her. All these were of Sarmatian workmanship, but placed with them was a terra-cotta statuette of Eros, of Greek origin, and two Greek-inscribed silver dishes; these testify to the links which the Sarmatians maintained with their Greek neighbours. Another burial in the same region produced a gold vessel, dating from between the 2nd century B.C. and the 1st century A.D., signed in Greek letters with the name of its Sarmatian maker, Tarulla.

BIBLIOGRAPHY.—M. I. Rostovtsev, *Iranians and Greeks in South Russia* (1922); B. N. Grakov, "Perezhytki matriarkhata u Sarmatov," in *Vestnik Drevnei Istorii,* no. 3 (1947); K. F. Smirnov, *Sarmatskie plemena Severnogo Prikaspiya* (1950), "Voprosy izuchenya Sarmatskikh plemen," in *Voprosy Skifo-Sarmatskoi Arkheologii* (1952); T. Sulimirski, "The Forgotten Sarmatians," in E. Bacon (ed.), *Vanished Civilizations* (1963). (T. T. R.)

SARMIENTO, DOMINGO FAUSTINO

SARMIENTO, DOMINGO FAUSTINO (1811–1888), Argentine educator, writer, and statesman, the "schoolmaster president," representative of liberal and anticlerical elements receptive to ideas from abroad, was born in the interior province of San Juan on Feb. 14, 1811. Sarmiento liked to compare his career as a self-made man with that of Abraham Lincoln, whom he greatly admired. Throughout his long public career as provincial legislator, cabinet minister, and governor, diplomatic representative, president, and national senator, Sarmiento's motto was "to govern is to educate." That motto emphasized the role he believed public education must play in creating a nation of industrious and responsible citizens. In his efforts to build a new Argentina, Sarmiento's principal model was the United States, but he used ideas from other countries also, adapting them to his country's needs.

Exiled to Chile for political activities (1840–52), Sarmiento became an important figure in Chilean journalism and politics as a newspaper editor and as an intimate friend and supporter of Manuel Montt (q.v.). In 1842, under Montt's sponsorship, Sarmiento became the founding director of the first normal school in South America, the second such school in the Western Hemisphere. In 1845 the Chilean government sent Sarmiento abroad to study educational methods in Europe and the United States. He returned in early 1848 a fervent admirer of Horace Mann's educational ideas and convinced that the United States was the nation Latin America should emulate. Subsequently, Sarmiento participated in Gen. J. J. de Urquiza's overthrow of the dictator Juan Manuel de Rosas (q.v.) at Caseros on Feb. 3, 1852, and during the next decade enhanced his reputation as a publicist and educator while also playing an active role in Argentine politics.

For three years (1865–68) Sarmiento represented Argentina in Washington. He spent little time there, however, preferring instead to travel extensively through the United States studying everything that might be useful to his country. In 1868 Sarmiento was elected to the presidency, although he did not return to Argentina until after the election was over. Despite a war with

SARMIENTO

Paraguay, Sarmiento's administration (1868–74) laid the foundations for later national progress by fostering public education, immigration, commerce, agriculture, and the construction of transportation and communication facilities. After 1874, though he continued active in public affairs, education remained his primary interest until his death on Sept. 11, 1888, in Asunción, Parag.

Many pages of the 52 volumes of Sarmiento's published works are devoted to educational themes. His *Facundo* (1845), a sociological interpretation of Argentine dictatorship, has been translated into several languages as one of the masterpieces of Latin-American literature. The celebration of the 50th anniversary of Sarmiento's death (1938) occurred when reactionary indigenous Fascists were launching bitter attacks on Argentine civil liberties and democratic principles. Defenders of those institutions have fostered public interest in Sarmiento's career by publicizing his efforts in support of those institutions and his opposition to dictatorial regimes.

BIBLIOGRAPHY.—A. W. Bunkley, *The Life of Sarmiento* (1952); R. Rojas, *El Profeta de la Pampa* (1945); A. Palcos, *Sarmiento—la vida—la obra—las ideas—el genio,* 3rd ed. (1938); E. Martínez Estrada, *Sarmiento* (1946); L. Lugones, *Historia de Sarmiento,* 3rd ed. (1945).   (J. R. BA.)

SARNEN, capital town of Obwalden demicanton, Switz., lies at the northern end of the Lake of Sarnen, 13 mi. (21 km.) S of Lucerne by rail. Pop. (1960) 6,554. In its town hall (1729–32) the ancient White Book contains the oldest chronicle of the fight against Habsburg tyranny; the book is also the prime source of the William Tell legend. On the Landenberg, once the site of the Habsburg Castle, open-air elections with voting by show of hands are held annually on the fourth Sunday in April, the ceremony being called the *Landsgemeinde.* Interesting buildings include the Witches Tower (13th century), the Schützenhaus (1752), the Baroque parish Church of St. Peter built in 1739–42 (with a remarkable carved ceiling in the nearby cemetery chapel), the Benedictine monastery (founded 1022), Capuchin monastery (1644), a fine modern hospital (1956), and a college of national repute. Sarnen is an important station on the Lucerne–Brünig electric railway.

SARNIA, county seat of Lambton County, Ontario, Can., on the St. Clair River and Lake Huron. Sarnia is well served by highways and railroads and has transriver communication with Port Huron, Mich., via the St. Clair Railway tunnel, the Bluewater Bridge, and ferry service. The site was visited by French explorers as early as 1627. The first French settlers arrived in 1807, but Malcolm Cameron was the real founder of an English-speaking settlement in 1833. In 1836 it was named (Port) Sarnia, the Roman name for the island of Guernsey, upon the suggestion of Sir John Colborne, lieutenant governor of Upper Canada and formerly lieutenant governor of Guernsey. Oil was discovered in Lambton County in 1858; by 1899 there was a refinery at Sarnia and the city became a petroleum centre. Sarnia has extensive harbour facilities, oil refineries (crude oil is supplied by pipeline from western Canada), extensive petrochemical industries, a salt industry, a grain elevator, and a diversity of small manufacturing industries. Oil products are transmitted to central Ontario by two pipelines. The publicly owned Polymer Corporation, built in 1942, pioneered the manufacture of synthetic rubber in Canada. Pop. (1966) 54,552.   (G. FN.)

SARNO, a town of Campania in the province of Salerno, Italy. Pop. (1961) 29,538 (commune). It lies at the foot of Mt. Saretto to the east of the Sarno (ancient Sarnus) River, 14 mi. (23 km.) N of Salerno by rail. Near Sarno in A.D. 552 Teias, leader of the Goths, was killed and his men defeated by Narses, the Byzantine general. Malaria retarded the growth of the town for centuries. In 1460 the battle between the Angevins and Aragonese for the possession of southern Italy took place nearby; the Aragonese were defeated and Ferdinand I fled to Naples. The ruined medieval castle in Sarno belonged to Count Francesco Coppola, who took part in the barons' conspiracy against Ferdinand of Aragon in 1485. Walter of Brienne is buried in the 13th-century church of Sta. Marie della Foce (rebuilt in 1701). There are hot springs near the town and industries include manufacture of preserves, and hemp and cotton mills.   (M. T. A. N.)

SARPEDON, in Greek legend, son of Zeus and Laodameia, Lycian prince, and hero of the Trojan War. He fought on the side of the Trojans, and after greatly distinguishing himself by his bravery, was slain by Patroclus. A terrible struggle took place for the possession of his body, until Apollo rescued it from the Greeks, and by the command of Zeus washed and cleansed it, anointed it with ambrosia, and handed it over to Sleep and Death (Hypnos and Thanatos), by whom it was conveyed for burial to Lycia, where a sanctuary (Sarpedoneum) was erected in honour of the fallen hero. Virgil's *Aeneid* says nothing of the removal of the body to Lycia.

In later tradition Sarpedon was the son of Zeus and Europa and the brother of Minos. Having been expelled from Crete by Minos, he and his comrades sailed for Asia, where he finally became king of Lycia. Euripides confuses the two Sarpedons.

SARPI, PAOLO (baptized PIETRO) (1552–1623), Venetian state theologian, who led an effective resistance by the Venetian republic against what it regarded as papal encroachment on temporal sovereignty, was born in Venice on Aug. 14, 1552. After the premature death of his father, he came into the care of an uncle and a Servite friar, under whose influence he entered the Servite Order in his 15th year. Sarpi's talents were outstanding and his intellectual curiosity unlimited. In the field of physics and even of anatomy he is credited with important discoveries, but his writings on scientific subjects are lost. In 1570, at Mantua, he caused a sensation by a brilliant defense of more than 100 theses, upon which Duke Gonzaga secured his transfer from Venice to Mantua where the friar often exhibited his skill in debate by defending the most daring propositions. In 1579 he became provincial of his order, and in 1588 its procurator general in Rome. Three attempts to get him a bishopric proved unsuccessful, in spite of Venice's backing, because his relations with leading Protestants were well known in Rome. Sir Henry Wotton, the English envoy, described him as "a true Protestant in a monk's habit." These disappointments further exacerbated his long-standing antipapal feelings.

In 1606 Sarpi became official theologian to the Venetian republic. In the conflict between Venice and Pope Paul V over papal jurisdiction and ecclesiastical immunity within the republic, Sarpi encouraged resistance. The censures threatened by Rome, he urged, must be ignored; they were invalid, for the pope was exceeding his powers. Fear of Venice's breaking with Rome and the risk of civil war in Italy induced the neighbouring states to intervene, and a compromise was reached on April 21, 1607, chiefly through France's mediation. On Oct. 5, 1607, Sarpi was the object of a murderous attack; there is no evidence of the crime's having been engineered in Rome, and Paul V reprobated it energetically. Though excommunicated in the same year, Sarpi retained his official position and continued to carry on his functions as priest. He died on Jan. 16, 1623, unreconciled, it seems, with the church.

Sarpi's literary remains consist largely of pamphlets written by himself or under his inspiration during the conflict between Venice and Paul V. He is now chiefly remembered for his exceedingly biased *Istoria del concilio tridentino* ("History of the Council of Trent"), published, in English, in London in 1619, under the pseudonym of Pietro Soave Polano, by Marcantonio de Dominis, archbishop of Spalato, a fugitive from the Inquisition. The book created a sensation: it was the first detailed account of a council which Sarpi described as "a large-scale, highly successful deception maneuver" of the papal curia. But the work is important, for its author seems to have had access to documents that were later lost.

BIBLIOGRAPHY.—*Opere,* 6 vol. (1761–65). Best modern edition of the history is by G. Gamborin, 3 vol. (1935). A selection of his letters written 1608–16 was ed. by K. Beurath (1909); his letters to the Protestants were ed. by M. D. Busnelli (1931). *See also* A. Vacant (ed.), *Dictionnaire de théologie catholique,* vol. xiv, col. 1115–21 (1939); H. Jedin, *History of the Council of Trent,* Eng. trans., vol ii (1960); L. Pastor, *History of the Popes,* Eng. trans., vol. xxv–xxvii (1937–38).   (ER. G.)

SARRAUT, ALBERT PIERRE (1872–1962), French Radical statesman, distinguished as a governor general of Indochina and twice premier of France, was born in Bordeaux on July 28, 1872, a member of the important Radical family that owned the newspaper *Dépêche de Toulouse*. Educated at the *lycée* of Carcassonne and the law faculty of Toulouse, he became a barrister and served as a member of the chamber of deputies from 1902 to 1924. He was undersecretary of state under Georges Clemenceau and Aristide Briand (1906–10); and he was minister of education under René Viviani (1914–15) between his two terms as governor general of Indochina (1911–14 and 1916–19). As governor general he applied liberal policies, increasing the proportion of native Indochinese in the civil service, recognizing the use of the local languages and local law and continuing the public works policy of his predecessor, Paul Doumer. He was minister for the colonies from 1920 to 1924. A senator from 1926 to 1940, Sarraut was minister of the interior (1926–28), for the navy (1930–31) and for the colonies again (1932–33). He was premier for the first time from Oct. 26 to Nov. 24, 1933. Having been minister of the interior again in 1934, he was premier again from Jan. 24 to June 4, 1936; his government secured the approval of the chamber of deputies for the Franco-Soviet mutual assistance treaty but failed to deal effectively with the German reoccupation of the Rhineland. From June 1937 to June 1940 he was continuously in office, mostly as minister of the interior.

Sarraut played little part in politics during World War II. He became editor of the *Dépêche de Toulouse* in 1943, after his brother Maurice had been murdered by a pro-Nazi gang. He was arrested by the Gestapo in 1944 and released by the Allies in 1945. Unable to gain a seat in parliament, he became in 1947 a member of the advisory assembly of the French union, of which he was president from 1949 to 1958.

Sarraut died in Paris on Nov. 26, 1962. He had published *La Mise en valeur des colonies françaises* (1923) and *Grandeur et servitude coloniales* (1931).   (P. W. C.)

SARSAPARILLA, an aromatic flavouring agent prepared from the roots of several tropical species of *Smilax*, a genus of the lily family (Liliaceae). The origin of the name is Spanish, *zarza* meaning "bramble" and *parrilla*, "little vine." The plants are native from the southern and western coasts of Mexico to Peru. Chiefly, three species provide the sarsaparillas of commerce: *Smilax aristolochiifolia*, *S. regeli*, and *S. febrifuga*, known respectively, as Mexican, Honduras, and Ecuadorian sarsaparillas. Other varieties, known commercially as Ecuadorian (or Guayaquil) and Central American (Jamaica or Guatemala), are derived from other species of *Smilax*.

The introduction of sarsaparilla into European medicine dates from the middle of the 16th century. Monardes, a physician of Seville, records that it was brought to that city from New Spain about 1536–45. Sarsaparilla must have come into extensive use soon afterward, for John Gerard, about the close of the century, states that it was imported into England from Peru in great abundance.

The plants are large, perennial, climbing or trailing vines. Short, thick, underground stems give rise to numerous semiwoody, prickly, angular aboveground stems, which bear large alternate stalked leaves. The tendrils that provide support for the plants spring from the bases of the leaves.

The roots are dried in the sun, then gathered loosely into bundles or bound tightly into cylinders, depending on the place of origin, and exported. Several sterols and a crystalline glycoside, sarsaponin, which yields sarsapogenin on hydrolysis, have been isolated from the root. Sarsapogenin is related to steroids such as progesterone and is used in their synthesis. Sarsaparilla was formerly regarded popularly as a tonic, but in fact is inert and useless; it is now used merely to mask the unpleasant taste of medicines. A liquid extract in which it is combined with wintergreen and other flavouring agents is an ingredient of such carbonated drinks as root beer.

In North America the strongly aromatic roots of the wild sarsaparilla (*Aralia nudicaulis*) and false or bristly sarsaparilla (*A. hispida*) are sometimes used as a substitute for true sarsaparilla.   (V. E.; X.)

SARSFIELD, PATRICK (d. 1693), titular earl of Lucan, Irish patriot and Jacobite soldier, who took part in the Irish resistance (1689–91) to William III, belonged to an Anglo-Norman family long settled in Ireland. His mother Anne was a daughter of Rory O'More, a leader of the Irish rising in 1641. Sarsfield, a Roman Catholic, began his military career as an ensign in George Hamilton's regiment, which was raised in Ireland in 1671 for service under Louis XIV. He continued in the French service in the duke of Monmouth's regiment until 1678.

After the accession of James II in February 1685, Sarsfield was commissioned as a captain in the English Army and fought against Monmouth at Sedgemoor (July 6), where he was wounded. Rapid promotion followed, and in 1686 he was a colonel in the Royal Horse Guards. King James had adopted the policy of remodeling the Irish Army so as to turn it from a Protestant to a Roman Catholic force, and Sarsfield was selected to assist in this reorganization. He went to Ireland with Richard Talbot, afterward earl of Tyrconnel (*q.v.*), who was appointed commander in chief by the king. In 1688 the death of his elder brother put him in possession of the family estate. When the king brought over a few Irish soldiers to coerce the English, Sarsfield came in command of them. As the king was deserted by his army there was no serious fighting, but Sarsfield had a brush with some of the Scottish soldiers at Wincanton. After the Revolution of 1688 he followed James to France, and in March 1689 accompanied him to Ireland. During the early part of the Jacobite War (*see* IRELAND: *History*) he distinguished himself as a cavalry commander, and was promoted brigadier and then major general. After the Battle of the Boyne (July 1, 1690) he played the chief part in rallying the Irish Army, organized the defense of Limerick, and in August made a spectacular attack on William III's artillery train at Ballyneety, on the road from Cashel to Limerick. In January 1691 he was created earl of Lucan by James. However, as an opponent of the earl (titular duke) of Tyrconnel, James's lord lieutenant in Ireland, Sarsfield was relegated to the background and at the Battle of Aughrim (July 12, 1691) was given command only of the reserve.

After Tyrconnel's death in August, Sarsfield came to the fore again at the second siege of Limerick, where he negotiated the treaty (Oct. 3, 1691) which ended the war. With most of the Irish Army, Sarsfield went to France in December 1691 to fight for Louis XIV and distinguished himself at Steenkirk (1692). He was mortally wounded at Neerwinden, near Landen, on July 19 (old style; July 29, new style), 1693, and died at Huy, a nearby village, a few days later. Sarsfield remains a favourite hero of Irish national tradition, and his name is widely commemorated in Ireland.

See J. Todhunter, *Life of Patrick Sarsfield* (1895).   (J. G. SI.)

SART, a central Asian name of Indian origin, was first used by Turkic tribesmen to mean "merchant." Later, the Mongols who ruled the area in the 13th and 14th centuries applied it to Muslims in general but particularly to the Iranian-speaking people of Turkistan (*q.v.*). These had been the chief town dwellers and merchants when the Turkic and Mongol pastoral nomads began to flow into the area. Through the centuries many tribes settled and adopted the way of life of the Iranian-speaking oasis dwellers, while many of the latter took over Turkic speech. Under the Uzbek (*see* UZBEK SOVIET SOCIALIST REPUBLIC: *History*), a confederation of Turko-Mongol tribes who became overlords of Turkistan in the 15th century, the name Sart acquired still another usage. It was applied to Turkic-speaking town dwellers of the oases to distinguish them from the Tadzhik (*q.v.*) who spoke Iranian dialects. In the 19th century Russians took over this usage, as did travelers during the czarist period.   (EL. B.)

Thus, the term was once applied only to people of Iranian origin, then to those of Turkic or Iranian origin, and finally only to Turkic peoples. Russian ethnographers gave the term tribal and linguistic significance. After the Russian Revolution it became derogatory and is now obsolete.   (G. E. WR.)

See V. V. Barthold, "A Short History of Turkestan," in *Four Studies on the History of Central Asia,* vol. i (1956).

SARTHE, a *département* of northwestern France, formed in 1790 out of the eastern part of Maine (*q.v.*) and neighbouring parts of Anjou (*q.v.*). Area 2,398 sq.mi. Pop. (1962) 443,019. It is bounded north by Orne, east by Eure-et-Loir and Loir-et-Cher, south by Indre-et-Loire and Maine-et-Loire, and west by Mayenne. It includes most of the basin of the Sarthe River draining with its tributary the Huisne from the Collines de Normandie southwestward to the Loire. The Loir River flows west through the southernmost part of the *département* toward its confluence with the Sarthe above Angers.

Most of the *département* is floored by Cretaceous rocks and is undulating lowland, but in the west the old rocks of the Armorican massif form a hilly margin in the Bocage Manceau. The soil is mainly of poor or moderate quality and there is much fragmentary woodland, but the *département* is predominantly agricultural, concerned with a variety of crops and livestock, among which cattle and poultry are especially important. The vine appears only in the Loir valley in the south, but cider apple orchards are widespread. Mineral resources are quite unimportant and there is little manufacturing, except at Le Mans, the only large town (128,814 in 1962), which under national plans for decentralizing industry has received an important accession of industry in the form of motor-engineering works (Renault). Agricultural tractors, trucks, and other vehicles are made. Near Le Mans is a famous motor-racing circuit.

The *département* is divided into three *arrondissements*, centred upon Le Mans, La Flèche in the valley of the Loir, and Mamers, but apart from Le Mans the towns are merely small market centres. Le Mans, the ancient capital of Maine, is the *préfecture* and centre of the diocese, but the *département* comes under the court of appeal at Angers and under the *académie* at Caen. Le Mans retains many old buildings of great charm, besides its fine Romanesque and Gothic cathedral (11th–13th centuries), and in its townscape epitomizes the historic development of a French provincial city from a Roman foundation. Solesmes (*q.v.*) is noteworthy for its priory (founded 1010), which became a Benedictine monastery in 1830 and later an abbey, and La Ferté-Bernard has an interesting Renaissance church.   (Ar. E. S.)

SARTHE RIVER, a river of northwestern France, about 177 mi. (285 km.) long, converges with the Loir and Mayenne rivers near Angers to form the Maine tributary of the Loire River. The Sarthe, flowing south, and its tributary, the Huisne, flowing southwest, from the Collines du Perche, join at Le Mans in the centre of the *département* of Sarthe. The river then flows in a winding trench across the Cretaceous rocks on the western margin of the Paris Basin in the ancient province of Maine. Its basin is almost entirely agricultural, and Le Mans is the only considerable town. The river is used for navigation only on a very small scale below Le Mans.   (Ar. E. S.)

SARTI, GIUSEPPE (1729–1802), Italian opera composer whose career included a long and influential sojourn in Russia, was baptized Dec. 1, 1729, at Faenza. After studying under F. A. Vallotti in Padua and G. Martini in Bologna he became organist at the cathedral of Faenza (1748–50). His first two operas were successfully produced in Faenza and Venice in 1752 and 1753. At the end of 1753 he went as conductor of an Italian opera company to Copenhagen where, in 1755, Frederick V appointed him director of court music and later of the opera. In Copenhagen, where he remained intermittently until 1775, he wrote many instrumental works and operas, including a Danish opera, *Gram og Signe* (1754). He then went to Venice where he became director of the Ospedaletto Conservatory. In 1779 he was appointed *maestro di cappella* at Milan Cathedral, but continued writing operas in both the serious and the comic styles, among them *Giulio Sabino* (Venice, 1781) and *Fra i due litiganti* (Milan, 1782). Among his pupils was Cherubini, who became his assistant.

In 1784 he was invited by Catherine II to St. Petersburg to succeed G. Paisiello as director of court music there. On his way he stopped at Vienna where he met Mozart, who used an aria of Sarti's both as a theme for a set of variations (K. 460) and as a tune played by the band on the stage in *Don Giovanni*. Sarti greatly improved the standard of Italian opera in St. Petersburg and wrote both sacred and operatic works. Of his sacred compositions perhaps the most notable is a *Te Deum* which was composed to commemorate the victory of G. A. Potemkin at Ochakov; in it he introduced fireworks and the firing of real cannon for their dramatic effects. Sarti's operas include a Russian opera, *Nakalnoy upravlenye Olega* ("The Early Reign of Oleg"), a work composed in collaboration with V. Pashkeyevitch and C. Cannobio; the libretto was written by Catherine. Sarti was out of the court's favour due to the intrigues of Luiza Todi, a Portuguese singer who exercised a considerable influence with the empress. During the time of Sarti's exile he depended upon the patronage of Potemkin, and with his help founded a school of singing in the Ukraine. He returned to St. Petersburg in 1793, at which time he was restored to his position as court composer and became director of the conservatory at St. Petersburg, established on the model of the Italian schools. After the death of Catherine and the murder of her successor, Paul I, Sarti left Russia (1802) and returned to Berlin, where he died in July 1802.

Although the melodic and harmonic aspects of Sarti's serious operas are not always distinguished, his accompanied recitatives have much character, and his comic operas are remarkable for their ensembles.

See C. Rivalta, *Giuseppe Sarti* (1928).   (Cs. Ch.)

SARTO, ANDREA DEL (1486–1530), one of the most popular Florentine painters of the early 16th century, was born in Florence on July 14, 1486. His father, Agnolo di Francesco, was a tailor (*sarto*), and from this fact the painter derived his name. In 1508 Andrea was enrolled in the guild of the Medici e Speziali. According to G. Vasari, he was trained initially by a goldsmith, was later apprenticed for three years to a painter, Gian Barile, and subsequently worked with Piero di Cosimo, traces of whose influence are found in his earliest authenticated works— five frescoes of scenes from the life of St. Philip Benizzi, executed in the entrance court of the Annunziata in Florence in 1509–10. A sixth of the "Adoration of the Magi" dates from 1511 and a seventh of the "Birth of the Virgin" from 1514. Whereas the earlier of these frescoes are dry and somewhat academic in style, in the latest the scale of the figures is increased and the execution reveals the boldness and beauty of colouring of Andrea's mature work. At this time Andrea was closely associated with the painter Franciabigio, as well as with the sculptor Jacopo Sansovino, who exercised a deep influence on his figurative style. His relation to both artists can be traced in a celebrated cycle of grisaille frescoes of scenes from the life of St. John the Baptist in the Chiostro

ALINARI

"MADONNA OF THE HARPIES" BY ANDREA DEL SARTO. IN THE UFFIZI GALLERY, FLORENCE dello Scalzo, Florence. The Scalzo frescoes were interrupted in 1518 by a visit to France, where Andrea entered the employment of Francis I. The single relic of his activity in France is a painting of "Charity" dated 1518 in the Louvre, Paris. Returning to Florence in 1519, he resumed work in the Scalzo between 1522 and 1526. To this period belong his most ambitious frescoes, the "Tribute to Caesar" at Poggia a Cajano (1521), the great "Last Supper" at S. Salvi (about 1526) and the "Madonna del Sacco" in the cloister of the Annunziata (dated 1525). This last fresco, with its bold pyramidal design and delicate handling, is perhaps Andrea's finest work.

With a few exceptions, Andrea's most notable panel paintings are in the Uffizi and Pitti galleries in Florence. They include his best-known work, the "Madonna of the Harpies" (1517), the "Dispute about the Trinity" (1517–18), a magnificent "Lamentation over the Dead Christ" (1524) and three large altarpieces of the Assumption. In these he combines the compositional procedure of the Tuscan High Renaissance with a splendour of colour reminiscent of Venetian painting.

Andrea was also a distinguished portrait painter. His best work in this genre is the introspective "Portrait of a Sculptor" in the National gallery, London. A self-portrait is in the Uffizi gallery. As a draftsman, Andrea favoured the medium of red chalk, which he employed with exceptional directness and accomplishment. A large collection of his drawings is in the Uffizi gallery. Endowed with a less original talent than his great contemporaries Raphael and Leonardo da Vinci, and a more equable temperament than his disciples Rosso and Jacopo da Pontormo, Andrea del Sarto remains a central figure in Florentine High Renaissance art, whose work is marked by monumentality, sincerity and sensibility and by its disregard of external effect. The romantic story of his marriage to Lucrezia del Fede (probably 1517) is recounted by Vasari. Andrea del Sarto died of the plague at Florence on Sept. 29, 1530.

(J. W. P.-H.)

SARTON, GEORGE ALFRED LEON (1884–1956), historian of science, who was instrumental in making his field an independent discipline, was born in Ghent, Belg., on Aug. 31, 1884. As a student at the University of Ghent he abandoned traditional philosophy to study chemistry, celestial mechanics, and mathematics, earning a gold medal in chemistry in 1907. He obtained his doctorate in mathematics in 1911, marrying Eleanor Mabel Elwes of London in the same year. At the invasion of Belgium in 1914 Sarton went to England, and, the following year, to the U.S.; he became a U.S. citizen in 1922. He took with him the scholarly journal *Isis,* which he had founded in 1912 and which he continued to edit for 40 years; in 1936 he founded *Osiris,* a second journal that published lengthier papers on the history and philosophy of science. He was an associate of the Carnegie Institution, Washington, D.C. (1918–48), and professor of the history of science at Harvard University (1940–51). His best-known work is *Introduction to the History of Science,* 3 vol. (1927–47). Other works include *Life of Science* (1960) and *Sarton on the History of Science,* ed. by D. Stimson (1962). He died in Cambridge, Mass., on March 22, 1956.

His daughter, MAY SARTON (1912–   ), became a distinguished poet and novelist.

See the George Sarton memorial issue of *Isis,* vol. 48 (Sept. 1957), ed. I. B. Cohen, centenary appreciations, a short biography, and bibliography. (I. B. C.; X.)

SARTRE, JEAN PAUL (1905–   ), French philosopher, playwright, and novelist, a world-famous figure in contemporary intellectual life who in 1964 was awarded, but refused, the Nobel Prize for Literature. Born in Paris on June 21, 1905, and orphaned in infancy, he was brought up by his grandfather, Charles Schweitzer, an uncle of Albert Schweitzer. A graduate (1929) of the École Normale Supérieure, where he reacted strongly against Cartesian rationalism, Sartre worked before World War II as a schoolmaster in the provinces. In 1933–34 he spent a year's leave at the Institut Français in Berlin, studying the work of German philosophers, notably Husserl and Heidegger.

He first achieved fame by his early fictional works—*e.g.,* the short stories of *Le Mur* (1939; *The Wall,* 1948)—and by helping to introduce into France from Germany the theories of phenomenology and Existentialism (*qq.v.*). In three early philosophical works, *L'Imagination* (1936; *Imagination,* 1962), *Esquisse d'une théorie des émotions* (1939; *Sketch for a Theory of the Emotions,* 1962), and *L'Imaginaire* (1940; *The Psychology of Imagination,* 1950), Sartre proved his ability to deploy the phenomenological technique with success and originality in the treatment of particular problems. *L'Être et le néant* (1943; *Being and Nothingness,* 1956), his massive attempt to construct a full-scale Existentialist theory of Being, earned him his place among the leading philosophers of the first half of the 20th century. By the time it appeared Sartre had already a considerable reputation in France as a novelist. From the Existentialist standpoint, fiction or drama was as much a form of philosophical literature as the conventional essay, and in some ways a medium even better able to communicate the experience and meaning of existence.

JEAN PAUL SARTRE

His first novel—and in the opinion of many critics his best—was *La Nausée* (1938; *Nausea,* 1949), cast in the form of the diary of a writer, Antoine Roquentin, who is disturbed by the sickening, chaotic, viscous quality of the external world, and yearns in vain for a universe which is certain, hard, predictable, and masculine, like the universe of Newtonian physics. Finally he finds salvation in art, in creating imaginary worlds which have the formal perfection that the real world lacks. Sartre evidently shared his hero's sense of alienation from a "viscous" world, but soon lost his faith in the possibility of salvation through art. Instead he moved increasingly closer to the Marxist doctrine of salvation through action. This idea is adumbrated elliptically in his wartime plays *Les Mouches* (1943; *The Flies,* 1946) and *Huis-clos* (1944; *In Camera;* U.S. title, *No Exit,* 1946), and more directly in his postwar plays, notably *Les Mains sales* (1948, *Crime Passionnel;* U.S., *Dirty Hands;* acting version, *Red Gloves,* 1949), *Le Diable et le Bon Dieu* (1951; *Lucifer and the Lord,* 1953), *Nekrassov* (1956; Eng. trans. 1956), and *Les Séquestrés d'Altona* (1960, *Loser Wins;* U.S., *The Condemned of Altona,* 1960). The recurrent theme of these political dramas is that the man who wants to do good in the world must be willing to "soil his hands."

After *La Nausée,* Sartre wrote only one novel, a work in four volumes, collectively entitled *Les Chemins de la liberté* ("Paths of Freedom"). This is a sort of tapestry, intended to give a synoptic picture of different peoples' "paths to freedom"; but it is woven in a variety of styles, and was eventually abandoned unfinished. The first volume, *L'Âge de raison* (1945; *The Age of Reason,* 1947), can nevertheless stand as a novel on its own. It has a hero, Mathieu, whose concentrated experiences over a few days lead him from one set of illusions about freedom to another, equally unreal. The second volume, *Le Sursis* (1945; *The Reprieve,* 1947), is based on the "realist" or "documentary" U.S. novel, and is an attempt to convey the inner story of the week of the Munich crisis (September 1938) in France by a montage of different characters' reactions. In volume three, *La Mort dans l'âme* (1949, *Iron in the Soul;* U.S., *Troubled Sleep,* 1950), Sartre returned to the particular case history of Mathieu, the hero of his first volume, and followed his adventures up to the fall of France in 1940. Having been hitherto an ineffectual character—something of an "antihero"—Mathieu is transformed under the stress of battle into a military hero. Sartre left the fourth volume unfinished, but the two chapters of it which he did complete he published in 1949 in his review *Les Temps modernes* with the title *Drôle d'amitié* ("Strange Friendship"); this incident dates from the period of Nazi-Soviet friendship, and describes how a renegade Communist is betrayed by the party hacks. The whole tone of the novel is heavily pessimistic.

L'Être et le néant also contains a notable element of pessimism, and even nihilism, and this earned for its author a notoriety that hindered appreciation of his theories. However, these theories are not always consistent. In *L'Être et le néant* Sartre argues that there is no moral law, that "man is a useless passion," that no one can really respect the freedom of others, and that the basis of all relations between human beings is conflict. On the other hand, in *L'Existentialisme est un humanisme* (1946; *Existentialism and Humanism*, 1948), an exposition and discussion of his moral theory, he puts forward the view that the pursuit of one's own freedom requires one to promote the freedom of others, and that each man is responsible to all for the values affirmed by his way of life. These "humanistic" notions are elaborated in greater detail in *Question de Méthode* (1960; *The Problem of Method*, 1964) and in a longer work, *Critique de la raison dialectique* (1960), in which he tries to formulate a revitalized Marxist sociology; that is, one which incorporates Existentialism, and which is purged of such "19th-century anachronisms" as determinism. In the latter Sartre also argues that conflict between men is simply the result of economic scarcity and of the shortsighted measures their ancestors have taken to deal with scarcity. Conflict is thus seen as being in principle curable. In all his work Sartre puts the strongest emphasis on his belief in indeterminism, or "human freedom." He sees freedom as a heavy burden on mankind, since it brings with it responsibility, guilt, remorse, punishment; but he sees it also as the unique source of human nobility, since it is his freedom alone which "makes man like a God."

After the liberation, Sartre took an active interest in French political movements. In 1945 he founded a monthly periodical, *Les Temps modernes*, as a platform for independent left-wing thought. Several of his works were first published in this review, especially his critical essays—*e.g.*, *Qu'est-ce que la littérature?* (1947; *What Is Literature?*, 1949)—many of which have reappeared in the seven volumes of *Situations* (1947–65). Other more extensive essays on philosophy and the arts include *Baudelaire* (1947; trans. 1949) and *Saint Genet, comédien et martyr* (1952; *Saint Genet, Actor and Martyr*, 1963), the latter being a remarkable psychological study of the poet Jean Genet (*q.v.*), a homosexual with a police record.

In 1949 Sartre helped to found a political party, the Republican Democratic Rally; after its collapse in 1952, he moved closer to the Communists. In 1954 he visited the U.S.S.R.; and he traveled widely in the Soviet Union, Scandinavia, Africa, the United States, and Cuba, where he became a champion of the Castro regime. In 1967 he acted as chairman of Bertrand Russell's "Vietnam War Crimes Tribunal" in Stockholm; he advocated Soviet intervention in Vietnam on behalf of the North, even at the risk of a third World War.

Sartre resisted what he called "bourgeois marriage," but while still a student he formed with Simone de Beauvoir (*q.v.*) a union which has remained a settled partnership in life. Simone de Beauvoir's memoirs, notably the second volume, *La Force de l'âge* (1960; *The Prime of Life*, 1962), provide an intimate account of Sartre's life from student years until his middle 50s. He himself published in 1964 (1963 in *Les Temps modernes*) an autobiography of his childhood, *Les Mots* (*The Words*, 1964). This short book is of outstanding literary distinction, and marks a return, after the diffuse, teutonic, jargon-ridden style of *Critique de la raison dialectique*, to the Cartesian clarity of his early writing. A popular book, it earned for Sartre the 1964 Nobel Prize for Literature, which, with characteristic intransigence, he refused to accept.

In *Les Mots*, Sartre analyzed the formation of his mind and temperament as an intellectual. He looked on the early death of his father as in some ways advantageous, since it had given him "undisputed possession" of his mother; on the other hand, his loneliness, and the fact that he was an exceedingly ugly child, had driven him into a fantasy world. This world was in the first place inhabited by imaginary beings that he read about; and then by imaginary beings that he wrote about—for Sartre became an author as soon as he learned how to write at all. He attributed his later

obsession with metaphysics to this early experience of fantasy; and he claimed that he owed his deliverance from this metaphysical obsession to Marxism, when it came into his life in middle age.

BIBLIOGRAPHY.—R. Campbell, *J.-P. Sartre ou une littérature philosophique* (1945); M. Beigbeder, *L'Homme Sartre* (1947); F. Jeanson, *Le Problème moral et la pensée de Sartre* (1947) and *Sartre par lui-même* (1955); I. Murdoch, *Sartre* (1953); W. Desan, *The Tragic Finale: an Essay on the Philosophy of Jean-Paul Sartre* (1954); R.-M. Albérès, *Sartre* (1957); P. Thody, *Jean-Paul Sartre* (1960); F. Jameson, *Sartre: the Origins of a Style* (1961); E. Kern (ed.), *Sartre: a Collection of Critical Essays* (1962); M. Cranston, *Sartre* (1962); R. D. Laing and D. G. Cooper, *Reason and Violence: a Decade of Sartre's Philosophy, 1950–1960* (1964); M. Warnock, *The Philosophy of Sartre* (1965).

(M. Cn.)

SARUGAKU ("monkey music") was a primitive form of Japanese popular entertainment that consisted of comic mimicry and acrobatic stunts. During the Kamakura period (1185–1333) this plebeian stage art began to be performed at shrine and temple festivals, attracting the attention of the upper classes. It gradually developed into a more controlled dramatic form, *sarugaku-nō*. At the same time another popular art form, *dengaku* ("rustic music"), underwent similar development. *Dengaku* consisted of dancing and posturing, in costumes of legendary figures, by farmers at rice plantings. In the 15th century, Kan-ami Kiyotsugu and his son Zeami Motokiyo (*q.v.*) combined the two art forms, originating what is now the nō drama (*q.v.*).

See also JAPANESE MUSIC.

SARZANA, a town and episcopal see of Liguria, Italy, in La Spezia province. Pop. (1961) 16,869 (commune). It lies on the fertile plain of the Magra River, 11 mi. (18 km.) SE of La Spezia by road. Sarzana is mentioned as being a fortress in 963 and as being a town in 1084; it is believed to have been founded by the survivors of the abandoned town of Luni near the site of the Etruscan Luna. The Gothic style cathedral (1355–1474) contains a monument to the mother of Pope Nicholas V (born at Sarzana). In the church of S. Francesco are paintings by the Sarzana-born painter D. Fiasella. The old citadel, built by the Pisans in 1263 and destroyed in 1486, was rebuilt in 1488 by Lorenzo de' Medici; the castle of Sarzanello was built by Castruccio Castracani (d. 1328). The present town is especially important as a centre for early market-garden produce and is on the main Rome-Genoa road and rail routes. (P. Ra.)

SASARAM, a town in Shahabad district, Bihar, India, near the edge of the Kaimur Plateau, lies on the Grand Trunk Road and on the Grand Chord line of the Eastern Railway about 90 mi. (145 km.) SW of Patna. Pop. (1961) 37,782. A notable feature of the town and one of the finest examples of Pathan architecture in India is the mausoleum of the emperor Sher Shah (1540–45), which stands in the middle of an artificial lake 1,000 ft. (300 m.) square. The central dome, with a span of 72 ft. (22 m.), is 101 ft. (31 m.) high. Sasaram also contains the mausoleum of Sher Shah's father and the unfinished tomb of his son. On the outskirts of the town are the ruined tomb of Alawal Khan, the reputed builder of Sher Shah's and his father's mausoleums, and an edict of Asoka inscribed on a rock on the Chandan Pir Shahid Hill. (E. Ah.)

SASEBO, a port town in Nagasaki prefecture, Kyushu, Jap. Pop. (1965) 247,000. Provided with a good natural harbour near the mouth of Ōmura Bay, Sasebo was a naval base from 1896 until the end of World War II. It was a small village until the restoration (1868), but expanded rapidly after the wars with China and Russia. The town was partially destroyed in World War II, but because of facilities which years of experience had perfected, Sasebo revived as a commercial and fishing port. (R. B. H.)

SASKATCHEWAN, a prairie province of Canada lying between Manitoba to the east and Alberta to the west and containing part of one of the great grain-producing regions of the world. It has an area of 251,700 sq.mi. (651,900 sq.km.), of which 31,518 sq.mi., mainly in the north, are covered by water. The capital is Regina (*q.v.*).

Physical Geography.—*Geology and Physiography.*—Saskatchewan has purely artificial boundaries cutting across the major geologic and geographic zones of west central Canada (*see*

CANADA: *Physical Geography; Geographical Regions*). The northern one-third is a part of the Canadian shield. Precambrian rock is exposed at the surface or underlies shallow glacial drift and sedimentary sands in a terrain which is rugged but not mountainous. Muskegs (swamps), many lakes, and small streams are indicative of two immature drainage systems which carry the brackish water to Hudson Bay via the Churchill or to the Arctic Ocean via the Athabasca and Mackenzie. The southern two-thirds of the province forms part of the great interior continental plains. In Saskatchewan these comprise two distinct levels or prairie steppes. The westernmost, at about 2,500 ft. (762 m.) above sea level, extends to the Missouri *coteau* (cuesta or scarp), a dominant feature which approximately defines the eastern edge of the remnant Tertiary formations. The Cypress Hills and Wood Mountains rise to 1,000 ft. (305 km.) above this level and comprise the youngest Tertiary beds. The second prairie steppe, at about 1,500 ft., terminates in the Manitoba escarpment, the eastern edge of Cretaceous formations on the prairies. Various series of hills between the two escarpments, including the Moose and Duck mountains and the Porcupine and Pasqua hills, are outriders of the older Tertiary beds. The province was almost entirely glaciated in Pleistocene times and the present surface soils of the plains originated from glacial depositions.

The Saskatchewan River (*q.v.*) drains a large part of the southern plains. Its two branches, entering the province from Alberta nearly 200 mi. (322 km.) apart, meet east of Prince Albert and flow toward Lake Winnipeg in Manitoba. A southwestern area drains southward to the Missouri River, and the southeastern cor-

ner of the province is drained by the Souris and Qu'Appelle rivers to Lake Winnipeg via the Assiniboine and Red rivers of Manitoba. Most southern Saskatchewan rivers flow through deep, U-shaped valleys which were eroded by glacial melt water in unconsolidated sedimentary beds as the last continental ice sheet retreated.

Climate, Soils, and Vegetation.—Saskatchewan has a continental climate with relatively little marine influence, prevailing westerly winds and wide seasonal and daily ranges of temperature. Average monthly temperatures decrease northward, particularly in winter. The average January temperature in the south is 0° F (−18° C) while in the extreme northeast it is −20° F (−29° C). The isotherm of 65° F (18° C) in July runs along the southern border and that of 60° F (16° C) through the middle of the province. The low annual precipitation is concentrated fortunately in the growing season. Average precipitation varies from 11 in. (270 mm.) in the southwest to 18 in. (441 mm.) in the northeast part of the agricultural region, with wide local and seasonal fluctuations. Repeated low annual averages of precipitation led to the disastrous prairie drought of the 1930s which was accompanied by dust storms and insect infestations.

As a result of their glacial origin the clay and loam soils of the great plains in Saskatchewan are rich in mineral content. Modification in well-defined zones of vegetative cover, each in turn a characteristic of a particular set of climatic factors, has produced brown soils in the arid southwest, black soils in the prairies (grasslands) proper, degraded black soils in the parklands, and gray wooded soils in the northern extremes of the plains area. The grasslands are primary producers of wheat, but the higher levels, particularly the Cypress Hills, are wooded and break the monotony of the landscape. Scattered clumps of quaking aspen in the wide belt of parklands eventually thicken and merge into the mixed wood forest at a northwest-southeast line across the province between Prince Albert and Saskatoon. Northward a further transition takes place to dominantly coniferous species. It is the northern part of this mixed wood belt which contains the best of the province's merchantable timber. Still farther northward a wide expanse of potential pulpwood (chiefly black spruce and jack pine) deteriorates into a zone of little commercial value. There poor soil and low temperatures reduce the quality of the tree cover.

Wildlife.—Saskatchewan is rich in wildlife resources. The vast prairies, once the home of great herds of bison, continue to provide an almost unlimited habitat for deer and antelope, upland birds such as grouse, partridge, and pheasant, and waterfowl—ducks, geese, cranes, and swans. Deer, elk, moose, and bear inhabit the parklands and forests, with caribou in the far north. Of the fur bearers, muskrat, beaver, mink, squirrel, otter, and fisher are common. Nearly all Saskatchewan lakes and streams contain fish, many in sufficient abundance to be fished commercially.

History.—Saskatchewan takes its name from the Indian name for the great river of the plains, which is in full Sis-Sis-Katchewan-Sepie, the "Big Angry Water" or "Rapid River." The territory, then unexplored, was granted by Charles II in 1670 to the Hudson's Bay Company for the exploitation of its fur. The first knowledge of this part of the territory came from an expedition of Henry Kelsey of the company (1690–92). Subsequent exploration was accomplished by the La Vérendrye brothers about 1750, and thereafter by Anthony Henday and Samuel Hearne. In 1774 Hearne established the first white habitation to remain a permanent community, at Cumberland House on the lower Saskatchewan River.

Until their merger in 1821 the Hudson's Bay Company and the North West Company were rivals in the fur trade, particularly in the forested regions of the territory. They set up numerous temporary forts and trading posts, often in direct competition at one location. The consolidated Hudson's Bay Company established additional permanent posts, such as Carlton House and Ft. Pitt, by the 1840s. All other settlement was confined to the vicinity of these posts.

The transfer of the territory to Canada in 1869 and railway connection from Winnipeg to St. Paul, Minn., in 1878 prompted immigration and homestead settlement. The dispossession of the resident half-breed population without proper recognition of their rights led to two uprisings, the Riel rebellions, in the Red River

PRINCIPAL PHYSICAL FEATURES AND MAJOR CITIES OF SASKATCHEWAN

BY COURTESY OF THE SASKATCHEWAN GOVERNMENT

LEGISLATIVE BUILDING AT REGINA, SASKATCHEWAN

Valley in Manitoba (1869–70) and in Saskatchewan (1885). The North West Mounted Police were established in 1873 (*see* ROYAL CANADIAN MOUNTED POLICE). Organized government of the Northwest Territories south of latitude 60° came in 1875, with Ft. Livingstone the first government seat and Ft. Battleford taking over in 1877. In 1882 Pile O'Bones was renamed Regina and made the territorial seat of government. Completion of the Canadian Pacific Railway in 1885 aided farm settlement and a surge of immigrants after 1901 led to the creation of the province of Saskatchewan in 1905, with Regina (*q.v.*) selected to be the capital city.

Rapid growth continued until World War I, the population increasing from 91,279 in 1901 to 492,432 in 1911, and municipalities, towns, and cities were established. The University of Saskatchewan at Saskatoon was founded in 1907. There was wide diversity among settlers in nationality, culture, and religion. Immigration slackened and practically stopped between World Wars I and II, and the desperate depression years of the 1930s saw some emigration from Saskatchewan and some relocation within the province. Settlers from the "dust bowl" moved northward into the forested regions to resume agricultural and other activities there. The return of wetter seasons and improved crops in the 1940s encouraged reconsolidation and diversification of the provincial economy.

In 1955, the jubilee year for Saskatchewan, a recognition program was undertaken to mark many historic sites throughout the province. The 1950s and 1960s saw greatly increased development of the province's natural resources—oil, gas, potash, uranium, pulpwood, water, and hydroelectric resources.

Politically, through Saskatchewan's first 25 years as a province, the Liberal Party remained in control, to be replaced for one five-year term through the worst of the drought and depression years by a Conservative administration. The Liberal Party then returned, but the growing unrest and organization of farmer groups and their dissatisfaction with the control over the prairie economy exerted by eastern interests contributed to the election in 1944 of a social democratic (socialist) party entitled the Cooperative Commonwealth Federation (C.C.F.), headed provincially by the premier, T. C. Douglas. Reelected in 1948, 1952, 1956, and 1960, Douglas became head of the New Democratic Party (formed by C.C.F., organized labour, and farmers) and resigned in 1961 to run for the commons. Douglas was succeeded as premier by W. S. Lloyd (C.C.F.). In 1964 the Liberals under W. Ross Thatcher won, obtaining 31 of the 59 assembly seats; in 1967 the Liberals won 35 seats.

Population.—Saskatchewan's population, 955,344 in 1966, is concentrated in the southern half of the province. Less than 2% live north of the agricultural region. Settlement took place fairly rapidly in the grasslands and parklands, more slowly in the forest fringe. The main rail line of the Canadian National Railway passing through Saskatoon and the park belt, where the risk of drought is less than on the prairies proper, enabled this zone to reach and retain the greatest nonurban density of population in

the province. A gradual shift of urban-rural ratios continued after World War II, from 6% urban in 1901 to 21% in 1941 to 74% in 1966, in centres of 1,000 population and over. About 40% of Saskatchewan people were of British origin, 6% French, 17% German, 7% Scandinavian, and 9% Ukrainian, with a scattering of over 16 other national groups. About 31,000 Indians lived in Saskatchewan under federal care. The largest religious groups were United Church of Canada (30%) and Roman Catholic (26%), followed by Anglicans (10%) and Lutherans (10%). Over 24 other creeds were represented.

Saskatchewan: Places of 5,000 or More Population*

| Place | Population | | | | |
	1966	1961	1951	1941	1921
Total province	955,344	925,181	831,728	895,992	757,510
Estevan	9,062	7,728	3,935	2,774	2,290
Flin Flon†	10,201	11,104	9,899	—	—
Lloydminster‡	7,071	5,667	3,938	1,624	755
Melville	5,690	5,191	4,458	4,011	2,808
Moose Jaw	33,417	33,206	24,355	20,753	19,285
North Battleford	12,262	11,230	7,473	4,745	2,923
Prince Albert	26,269	24,168	17,149	12,508	7,352
Regina	131,127	112,141	71,319	58,245	34,432
Saskatoon	115,892	95,526	53,268	43,027	25,739
Swift Current	14,485	12,186	7,458	5,594	3,518
Weyburn	9,000	9,101	7,148	6,179	3,193
Yorkton	12,645	9,995	7,074	5,577	5,151

*Populations are reported as constituted at date of each census. †Flin Flon is shared with Manitoba. ‡Lloydminster is shared with Alberta.

Government and Public Finance.—The lieutenant governor, appointed by the federal government, is the titular head in the province; he acts on the advice of the executive council, headed by the premier and comprised of selected members of the provincial legislature. The legislative assembly has 59 members, elected for five years unless the assembly is dissolved sooner. There is a nonpolitical civil service. The province is represented at Ottawa by six senators (after 1915) and by members of the House of Commons according to population; the 1952 Representation Act gave Saskatchewan 17 members.

Twelve crown corporations and subsidiaries perform such administrative services as government finance, and business functions ranging from fur marketing to electric power.

By 1960 there was elective municipal government in 11 cities, 106 towns, 372 incorporated villages, and 296 rural municipalities. There are no counties.

Public revenue in Saskatchewan as in other provinces is drawn from retail sales and income taxes, licences, royalties, and crown corporation profits; under a dominion-provincial tax rental agreement the dominion compensates Saskatchewan for income and corporation taxes, formerly levied by the province. Provincial revenue increased from under $12,000,000 in 1921 to over $200,000,000 in the second half of the 20th century. After the economic crisis of the 1930s, stringent provincial controls were imposed on municipal borrowing.

Education.—Throughout Canada the control of education is vested in the provinces. Elementary education in Saskatchewan is public, undenominational, compulsory, and free of charge. Private denominational schools are permitted if they conform to the general standard. Both types of schools are supported by public funds. Enrollment in public day schools totals about 200,000, in private schools about 3,000. The University of Saskatchewan at Saskatoon, with a branch at Regina, offers a wide variety of advanced academic training and extension services, particularly in agriculture.

Health and Welfare.—Universal compulsory prepaid medical insurance established under the Medical Care Insurance Act of 1961 went into effect July 1, 1962. Strenuously opposed by the College of Physicians and Surgeons, the act was amended to provide safeguards for professional freedom and opportunity both for doctors to practise outside the plan and for voluntary insurance schemes to continue to operate; the principles of universal coverage and administration through a public agency responsible to the government were preserved. The government-sponsored hospital services plan covers more than 95% of the total population. Welfare programs include old-age security supplementary allowances, blind persons' allowances, mothers' allowances, and social aid.

(LEFT) GEORGE HUNTER—FROM PUBLIX; (TOP RIGHT) NATIONAL FILM BOARD OF CANADA; (BOTTOM RIGHT) SASKATCHEWAN GOVERNMENT

GRAIN, LIVESTOCK, AND LUMBER ARE IMPORTANT ECONOMIC PRODUCTS OF SASKATCHEWAN: (LEFT) WHEAT FIELDS ON THE GREAT REGINA PLAIN; (TOP RIGHT) CATTLE ROUNDUP NEAR ABBEY ON THE EDGE OF THE GREAT SAND HILLS; (BOTTOM RIGHT) MOBILE SAWMILL OPERATING IN A FOREST IN THE PORCUPINE HILLS

with large volumes ready for cutting. The remote location in relation to major markets retarded postwar development of forest industries, particularly pulp and paper, and the annual market value of production in the 1960s averaged less than $10,000,000, with white spruce the most used species, followed by jack pine and black spruce. Saskatchewan's first pulp mill was built in 1966, with the province as a 30% participant. After World War II the provincial government implemented conservation and development policies in forest management.

Fish and Fur.—The most important commercially fished lakes are in the north. They include Athabasca, Reindeer, Wollaston, La Ronge, and six others which all support fish-processing and freezing plants serving many lesser lakes as well. These allow better utilization, particularly in summer operations, and a more stable industry. Air transport of produce is necessary in some instances. Major commercial fish species are whitefish, lake trout, and pickerel. The provincial catch averages over 10,000,000 lb. annually, with an average market value of $1,600,000. The expanding northern mink-rearing industry consumes 5,600,000 lb.

The wild fur industry remains important to a small section of the province's people as a supplementary source of income, with an annual market value of more than $2,000,000. A provincial government marketing service established after World War II did much to stabilize the industry.

Minerals.—The metals and petroleum industries made great progress after World War II. The value of output grew from only $2,000,000 in 1931 to $36,000,000 in 1949 and to more than $300,000,000 in the 1960s. Base-metal operations started early in the 1930s at Flin Flon on the province's eastern boundary and contributed over $30,000,000 of the total mineral output. From a slow start based on the heavy crude oils of the Lloydminster area, the petroleum industry expanded rapidly through the 1950s. By the mid-1960s production had surpassed 80,000,000 bbl. annually, with a value exceeding $150,000,000.

A series of spectacular potash discoveries began in 1954. Production commenced in 1958. By 1967 ten mines were operating or under development, with projected investment of over $650,-000,000; annual production had exceeded 2,500,000 tons, worth more than $80,000,000.

The uranium industry started production in 1954 and by 1958 reached a milling capacity of 4,500 tons of ore daily, with seven mines operating, all in the Uranium-Beaverlodge area. Production was reduced with the drop in demand after 1959 for uranium for military purposes. Other leading minerals are zinc, coal, sodium sulfate, gold, and salt.

Exploration in the south for petroleum and potash was still very active. Reserves of industrial minerals, potash, and lignite coal appeared to be very substantial. A northern development road-construction program was undertaken to facilitate prospecting and exploration.

Power.—The major developed source of electric power in Saskatchewan in the early 1960s was the surface lignite coal deposits of the Souris Valley, which provided relatively cheap fuel for thermal generation. By the mid-1960s electrical energy production had reached 3,300,000 kw-hr. annually. In 1967 Gardiner

Production.—Until well after World War II, Saskatchewan's economy was primarily agricultural. During the war years the output of nonfarm industry represented just 20% of the value of total commodity production. The growth of the petroleum, mining, manufacturing, and construction industries was rapid in the postwar years and by the 1960s nonagricultural industries accounted for more than 60% of gross commodity production.

Agriculture.—Agriculture accounted for 66% of the net value of all production over the ten-year period to 1958 but for less than 40% in the 1960s. Grain crops lead production; the average wheat crop during the 1960s was about 500,000,000 bu. Long-term average yields for wheat, oats, and barley are 15, 29, and 22 bu. per acre, respectively. Other major field crops are flax, rye, and forage. Livestock production expanded during the 1950s and 1960s to add stability to the agricultural economy. By the mid-1960s, farm cash receipts, excluding government assistance, were approaching $900,000,000 annually.

The climate limits production of many orchard and specialty crops, but research, experimentation, and assistance programs of provincial and federal departments of agriculture and the provincial university have assisted greatly in improving this and the entire agricultural situation.

Minimum economic farm-unit size varies from several sections per family (a section is 640 ac.) in the arid southwest to between one-half and one section in regions with good soil and moisture conditions. Nearly 38% of Saskatchewan's farms are fully owned by operators. Investment in farm mechanization is exceptionally high. Over 40,000,000 ac. are under cultivation and very little suitable arable land remains uncultivated. Irrigation projects, such as that on the South Saskatchewan River, were planned to provide water for land already in agricultural use. Completion of the gigantic Gardiner Dam on the South Saskatchewan in 1967 opened a wide area to more diversified agriculture. The last free homestead land was taken up in 1930.

Forestry.—The accessible commercial forest zone in Saskatchewan covers 38,000 sq.mi. Despite heavy exploitation early in the 20th century and during World Wars I and II, inventories carried out in the 1950s indicated a very large increment in both saw timber and pulpwood species, totaling 232,000,000 cu.ft. per year,

Dam was completed on the South Saskatchewan River, creating a lake 140 mi. long. It will eventually provide an additional 475,-000,000 kw-hr. per year. Most of Saskatchewan (urban and rural) receives electricity services under a provincial government plan implemented by the Saskatchewan Power Corporation.

The hydroelectric potentials of the northern rivers, chiefly the Churchill and the Fond du Lac, had not been completely determined. One Churchill River site of 100,000 hp. was developed in the early 1930s to serve the Flin Flon mining operations.

Manufacturing.—Resources development in Saskatchewan stimulated a growth of secondary industries, and manufacturing made steady advances after World War II. Manufacturing production climbed from $298,000,000 in 1956 to $404,000,000 in 1964. In the 1960s the province had about 1,200 manufacturing operations employing over 15,000 persons.

Postwar development brought the province new industries producing cement, wire and cable, paper products, steel pipe, clay products, building board, transformers, mobile trailer homes, and a variety of operations which serve the oil and gas industries. Total capacity of the nine oil refineries in the province was 71,000 bbl. per day, with the two largest in Regina. The province's first steel mill went into production in 1960.

Recreation.—Prior to World War II little attention was paid to the province's recreation resources. After the war, however, major development took place, prompted by local and tourist demands resulting from easier transportation and greater leisure and prosperity. Resident and nonresident angling and hunting licence sales increased from 61,000 to 215,000 in a ten-year period. Many new businesses were established, particularly in the north, to serve the sportsmen's needs. Provincial resources authorities intensified research and improved management techniques in an effort to ensure sustained yields.

The lake and forest scenery of the northern Precambrian landscape and the many lakes still inaccessible to sportsmen other than by float aircraft in the 1960s appeared to ensure broad expansion in the province's tourist industry as northern access improved.

Use of the northerly Prince Albert National Park increased greatly for summer family recreation in the 1950s and 1960s. A comparable increase was evident in the use of the developed provincial parks in the Cypress Hills, at Moose Mountain in the southwest, and Duck Mountain near Kamsack.

Communications.—The southern populated area is well netted with railways. Main trans-Canada lines serve Regina and Saskatoon east and west, as well as Moose Jaw, Swift Current, North Battleford, and Yorkton, with good connections to Minneapolis and Chicago. Although northern Saskatchewan is trackless, the province had over 8,700 of Canada's almost 60,000 mi. of track in the 1960s. In 1960 improved municipal road mileage totaled 95,000, provincial highway mileage about 6,500 with graveled surface and about 1,500 with hard-top surface. The Trans-Canada Highway passing through Regina, Moose Jaw, and Swift Current was completed in Saskatchewan in 1957. Major oil fields are connected with the interprovincial pipeline and pipelines supply oil and gas to many urban centres.

Air Canada services Regina and Saskatoon regularly east and west. Regular north-south and intercity aircraft routes cover most of the province, including the extreme north. Saskatchewan Government Telephones Corporation services all cities and towns and much of rural Saskatchewan. Government-operated two-way radio services all northern points from Prince Albert.

Saskatchewan has no seaports and the rivers are generally not navigable. Lake Athabasca, however, allows lake transport from the railhead in northern Alberta to penetrate to the centre line of northern Saskatchewan.

BIBLIOGRAPHY.—*Canadian Annual Review; Canada Year Book* (annually); N. F. Black, *History of Saskatchewan* (1913); John Hawkes, *Story of Saskatchewan* (1924); G. F. G. Stanley, *The Birth of Western Canada*, 2nd ed. (1961); S. M. Lipset, *Agrarian Socialism* (1950); M. W. Campbell, *Saskatchewan* (1950); Robert Moon, *This Is Saskatchewan* (1953); Erik Munsterhjelm, *The Wind and the Caribou* (1953); J. F. C. Wright, *Saskatchewan: the History of a Province* (1955); *Report of the Royal Commission on Agriculture and Rural Life* (1956–57); S. F. Olson, *The Lonely Land* (1961). (J. E. CL.)

SASKATCHEWAN RIVER (RAPID RIVER), a river system of Alberta and Saskatchewan provinces, Can. Two large streams, the North and South Saskatchewan, which have their headwaters in the Rocky mountains in Alberta, cross the Saskatchewan boundary 200 mi. apart, unite east of Prince Albert and continue flowing eastward to empty into Lake Winnipeg. Through much of their courses both streams are well contained in deep immature valleys gouged out by escaping glacial melt water. Major tributaries are the Battle, joining the north branch, the Bow, Belly and Red Deer, joining the south branch, and the Carrot and Sturgeon Weir joining the main Saskatchewan. The length of the united Saskatchewan is 369 mi. and the total length to the head of the Bow is 1,205 mi. The Saskatchewan is believed to have been first explored by Henry Kelsey in 1690.

In the fur-trade days the river system served as an important transportation route and numerous forts and trading posts, such as Cumberland House, Carlton House, Ft. Pitt and Ft. Battleford, were located along its banks during the 18th and 19th centuries. It was later plied by steam-driven river boats in the early days of settlement, and in the forested area in Saskatchewan it served for log and lumber transport. It is now navigated only in its lower reaches.

Hydroelectric development on the river began in the late 1950s; *see* SASKATCHEWAN: *Power*. (C. S. BR.)

SASKATOON, a city in the province of Saskatchewan, Can., was founded in 1883 as the proposed capital of a temperance colony and named after a local edible berry (Cree *Missaskatoomina*). Pop. (1966) 115,892. It is situated on the banks of the South Saskatchewan River 150 mi. NW of Regina, almost at the centre of the settled area of the province. Both major Canadian railway systems serve the city and major provincial highways converge on it. It is served by Air Canada and TransAir and has regular air service with other Saskatchewan cities and the far north. One radio station is French speaking to serve French communities to the north.

Its central position gives Saskatoon wide freight-control and distribution advantages in the province's famous wheat lands. It is a major centre for grain storage and flour milling, and also for livestock marketing and meat packing. It contains an oil refinery and iron foundries. Saskatoon is the centre of a booming potash mining and refining industry. It is the metropolitan area nearest the huge Gardiner Dam. (*See* SASKATCHEWAN.)

It is the seat of the University of Saskatchewan, founded 1907, and several affiliated colleges, a university hospital, schools of medicine and veterinary medicine, a teacher's college and school for the deaf, a National Research Council laboratory, and the Saskatchewan Research Council headquarters. The university school of agriculture and associated experimental farm have made major contributions to provincial agriculture and rural life. (J. E. CL.)

SASSAFRAS (*Sassafras albidum*), a North American tree of the laurel family (Lauraceae), called also ague tree, with aromatic bark and foliage. It is native to sandy soils from Maine to Ontario and Iowa and south to Florida and Texas. While usually a small tree, it sometimes attains a height of 80 ft. or more. It has furrowed bark, bright green twigs and entire, mitten-shaped or three-lobed leaves, the three forms often on the same twig. Yellow flowers, in small clusters, are followed by dark blue berries. The root, especially its bark, is used in household medicine and root beer; it yields oil of sassafras, used in perfume.

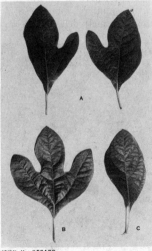

JOHN H. GERARD

SASSAFRAS (S. ALBIDUM) LEAVES. THE THREE FORMS, (A) MITTEN-SHAPED, (B) THREE-LOBED AND (C) ENTIRE, ARE OFTEN ON THE SAME TWIG

SASSANIDS (SASANIANS; sometimes SASSANIANS), the rul-
ing dynasty of the neo-Persian Empire founded by Ardashir I *c.*
A.D. 224 and destroyed by the Arabs during the years 637–651.
The dynasty is named after Sasan, an ancestor of Ardashir I.
See PERSIAN HISTORY: *Sasanian Empire.*

SASSARI, a town and archiepiscopal see in northwestern
Sardinia, Italy, and capital of Sassari province. Pop. (1961) 90,-
477. It stands about 6 mi. (10 km.) from the sea on the edge
of the limestone hills above the plain of the Mannu River. The
town is mainly modern, but has an old quarter with narrow, winding streets which was once surrounded by walls. Notable monuments are the cathedral, with a baroque facade; the Romanesque
churches Sta. Maria of Bethlehem and Sta. Donata; and the
Rosello Fountain (1606), ornamented with statues representing
the four seasons. The Sanna National Museum houses archaeological finds from all parts of the island belonging to the prehistoric, Phoenician, and Roman periods, and paintings by local 17th-
century artists. The University of Sassari was founded in 1565.
The town's industries are mainly concerned with agricultural produce. Rail and road connections link Sassari with Porto Torres,
Olbia, and Cagliari. The traditional festival, the Processione dei
Candelieri (Aug. 14), is held in honour of Our Lady in fulfillment
of a vow made during the plague (1600).

Sassari, then called Tathari, grew in the 12th century as the
coastal peoples retreated inland from the raiding barbarians. It
was a free town under Pisan rule, but was ceded to Genoa after
1284. It passed under Aragon, but rebelled in 1325. In 1718 it
passed with the rest of Sardinia to the House of Savoy. It suffered heavy Allied bombing in World War II.

SASSARI PROVINCE covers all of northern Sardinia, including the
islands of Asinara, Maddalena, and Caprera. Area 2,903 sq.mi.
(7,519 sq.km.). Pop. (1961) 373,367. It is divided into 75 communes. Agricultural activities include olive and fruit cultivation,
collection of cork-bark, stock breeding, and fishing; small quantities of lead and zinc are mined. Other towns in the province include Porto Torres, Olbia, Alghero, and Tempio Pausania.
(M. T. A. N.)

SASSETTA (STEFANO DI GIOVANNI) (d. 1450) was the
greatest Sienese painter of the first half of the 15th century.
The date and place of his birth are uncertain, but he seems to
have been trained in Siena, and the force of the Sienese tradition
is evident in the surviving panels of his first commissioned work,
an altarpiece for the Arte della Lana in Siena (1423–26). Thereafter he came in contact with the work of the first generation of
Florentine Renaissance painters; this is reflected in the monumental altarpiece of the Madonna of the Snow, painted for Siena
Cathedral in 1430–32 (Contini-Bonacossi collection, Florence),
and in a Crucifix executed for S. Martino at Siena in 1433 (Chigi-
Saraceni collection, Siena). From this point on, under Gothic
influence, Sassetta's style assumes an increasingly decorative char-

acter, manifest initially in a polyptych in S. Domenico at Cortona
(probably 1437) and reaching its climax in a cycle of scenes from
the legend of St. Anthony the Abbot (Yale University Art Gallery,
National Gallery of Art, Washington, and elsewhere). His best-
known and most ambitious work was carried out for S. Francesco
at Borgo San Sepolcro (1437–44), and was originally a double-
sided altarpiece with a Virgin and Child and four Saints (Louvre,
Paris, and Berenson collection, Settignano) on the front, and a
celebrated panel of St. Francis in Ecstacy (Berenson collection)
and eight scenes from the life of the Saint (National Gallery,
London, and Musée Condé, Chantilly) on the back. These are
perhaps the most eloquent interpretations of the Franciscan legend
produced in the 15th century, and mark the peak of Sassetta's
career as a narrative artist. Sassetta died in 1450 while engaged
on a fresco of the Coronation of the Virgin on the Porta Romana
at Siena (completed by Sano di Pietro).

See J. Pope-Hennessy, *Sassetta* (1939); E. Carli, *Sassetta e il Maestro
dell'Osservanza* (1957).   (J. W. P.-H.)

SASTRI, SRINIVASA (VALANGIMAN SANKARANA-RAYANA
SRINIVASA SASTRI) (1869–1946), liberal Indian statesman, founder
of the Indian Liberal Federation, who served his country well
in many important posts at home and abroad, was born of poor
Brahman parents at Valangiman, near Kumbakonam, Madras,
on Sept. 22, 1869. He became a schoolmaster, but his powers of
oratory and his interest in public causes soon brought him national fame. In 1907 he joined the Servants of India Society
and succeeded G. K. Gokhale (*q.v.*) as its president in 1915.
Already a member of the Madras Legislative Council, he was
elected to the central legislature in the following year. He welcomed the Montagu-Chelmsford reforms of the Indian constitution, served on Lord Southborough's franchise committee, and
was elected to the new council of state. Finding himself increasingly out of sympathy with the dominant group in the Congress
Party, which declined to cooperate in the reforms and preferred
methods of civil disobedience, he left the party and founded the
Indian Liberal Federation, of which he was president in 1922.

Abroad, he represented India in 1921 at the Imperial Conference in London, at the League of Nations Assembly at Geneva,
and at the Washington Conference on the reduction of naval armaments. In 1922 the government of India sent him to Australia,
New Zealand, and Canada to help make arrangements to improve
the position of Indians domiciled in those countries. In 1926 he
went to South Africa for a similar purpose, and in the following
year was appointed the first agent general of the government of
India in that country. In 1929 he was appointed a member of
the Royal Commission on Labour in India. The Indian government also appointed him to report on the conditions of Indian
labour in Malaya. During 1930–31 he took an active part in the
Round Table Constitutional Conference in London. Finally, his
concern for education was given scope with his appointment as
vice-chancellor of the Annamalai University (1935–40). He died
on April 17, 1946, in the Madras presidency.   (KE. A. B.)

SATAN is the English transliteration of a Hebrew word for
"adversary" in the Old Testament. With the definite article the
Hebrew word denotes "the adversary" par excellence, mainly in
the Book of Job where the adversary comes to the heavenly court
with the "sons of God" (Job i, 6). His task is to roam (the
Hebrew word here has a play on sounds with the word "satan")
through the earth (like a contemporaneous Persian official) seeking
out acts or persons to be reported adversely (to the king); his
function thus is the opposite of that of the "eyes of the Lord,"
which roam through the earth strengthening all that is good (II
Chron. xvi, 9). Satan is cynical about disinterested human goodness and is permitted to test it under God's authority and control
and within the limits God sets. (As G. Papini points out, the relations in Job between God and Satan are far closer than is usually
imagined; Satan, too, belongs to the spiritual and supernatural
world.) (*See* JOB.)

In the New Testament the Greek transliteration Satanas is used
and this usually appears as "Satan" in English translations. He
is spoken of as the prince of evil spirits, the inveterate enemy of
God and of Christ, with his throne among men (Rev. ii, 13), and

THE "JOURNEY OF THE MAGI," BY SASSETTA. IN THE METROPOLITAN MU-
SEUM OF ART

takes the guise of an angel of light (II Cor. xi, 14). He can enter a man and act through him (John xiii, 27), almost as the Spirit of God in Old Testament thought could clothe itself in Gideon and rush on Samson; hence a man can be called Satan because of his acts or attitude (Matt. xvi, 23). By his subordinate demons Satan can take possession of men's bodies, afflicting them (II Cor. xii, 7) or making them diseased (Matt. xii, 26; Luke xi, 18). To him sinners are delivered for the destruction of the flesh that the spirit may be saved (I Cor. v, 5). After the preaching of the 70 disciples, during which devils were subjected to them, Jesus saw Satan fall like lightning from heaven (Luke x, 18). According to the visions in the Book of Revelation, when the risen Christ returns from heaven to reign on earth, Satan will be bound with a great chain for a thousand years, then released, but almost immediately face final defeat and be cast into eternal punishment (Rev. xx, 2, 7–10). He is identified with the ancient serpent (Rev. xii, 9, xx, 2; cf. Gen. iii). His name, Beelzebul, used in the Gospels mainly in reference to demoniac possession, comes from the name of the god of Ekron, Baalzebub (II Kings i). (See BEELZEBUL.) He is also identified with the devil (diabolos), and this term occurs more frequently in the New Testament than "Satan." In the Koran the proper name Shaitan, "Satan," is used.

In Hebrew thought in the Old Testament there is no suggestion of any dualism, whether temporal, spatial or ethical. God himself forms light and creates darkness, makes weal and creates woe (Isa. xlv, 7). The evil spirit that terrifies men and leads them to murderous action is from the Lord (I Sam. xvi, 14). Hostile heathen powers could be spoken of as fighting against God and his people Israel, but they were the "rod of his anger" (Isa. x, 5), although there is an interesting interchange of God and Satan between two Old Testament writers (II Sam. xxiv, 1; I Chron. xxi, 1). There was thought to be a constant fight between light and darkness, chaos and law, life and death. Myths of which fragments survive in the Old Testament spoke of God's fight against the dragon of chaos, called Rahab or Leviathan (e.g., Job ix, 13; Isa. xxvii, 1) and this fight, which took place at creation, continues constantly. Any philosophy of evil culled from the Bible must find room for evil within the concept of God and within his purpose: his sun and rain, poured out on the good and the evil, make both weeds and wheat grow.

In later Judaism, under Persian influence, a form of dualism developed, finding expression in cosmic speculation and in the idea of successive millenniums; traces can be seen in the Book of Daniel and in Revelation. Two ages or aeons of world history were spoken of as "this age" and "the age to come." In the former, the cosmic power of evil prevails, known variously in apocalyptic writings as Satan, Beliar, Mastema or Azazel, and identified with death and the evil impulse in man; this evil power will be overthrown by the messianic kingdom foretold in the Old Testament, and God will reign on a re-created earth, in paradise or in heaven. The devil and all his hosts were thought of as fallen angels who, like the heathen powers hostile to God, had lapsed through pride and envy into sin and abused their power as God's deputies. But Jewish thought did not depict the fallen angels as the strong energetic element in life, in contrast to the anemic, reasonable forces of good, as Blake accuses Milton of doing.

Persian dualism conceived of the conflict of good and evil as existent from the beginning, outside man, who could take sides and assist one or the other (see DUALISM). Later Jewish dualism thought man himself and all nature and creation were affected by sin and the fall of man, and needed a new creation to remove the taint of evil. This was to be achieved not, as in the Old Testament, by a new heart and spirit in man (Jer. xxxi, 33 ff.; Ezek. xviii, 31) but by a dramatic divine intervention to overthrow Satan, whether in human form as the Anti-Christ (q.v.) or the beast or false prophet, or as a supernatural being.

Biblical ideas, mediated through the speculation of postbiblical Judaism, were transmitted to the theology of early Christian writers, in which the figure of Satan played a large part in the discussion of the nature of evil, the meaning of salvation and the purpose and efficacy of the atoning work of Christ. Early and medieval church writers discussed at length problems raised by belief in the existence of a spiritual being such as Satan in a universe created and sustained by an all-powerful, all-wise and all-loving God. Under the influence of the 18th-century revolt against belief in the supernatural, liberal Christian theology tends to treat the biblical language about Satan as "picture thinking" not to be taken literally—as a mythological attempt to express the reality and extent of evil in the universe, existing outside and apart from man but profoundly influencing the human sphere. See also DEVIL.

BIBLIOGRAPHY.—G. F. Moore, Judaism in the First Centuries of the Christian Era, 3 vol. (1927–30); S. Mowinckel, He That Cometh (1956); G. Papini, The Devil (1954); J. Pedersen, Israel, Its Life and Culture, 2 vol. (1948); J. N. Schofield, The Religious Background of the Bible (1944). (J. N. Sc.)

SATARA, a town and district in the Poona division of Maharashtra, India. The town, which is the headquarters of the district, lies near the confluence of the Krishna and Venna rivers, 56 mi. (90 km.) S of Poona and 10 mi. (16 km.) SW of Satara Road Station on the Southern Railway, at a height of 2,320 ft. (707 m.) above sea level. Pop. (1961) 44,353. Satara (Hindi "seventeen") is named after the 17 walls, towers, and gates which the fort on the southern side of the town is supposed to have possessed. On the overthrow of the Yadava dynasty in the early 14th century, Satara passed under Muslim rule which was consolidated in the reign of the Bahmani kings. On their decline toward the end of the 15th century the Bijapur kings asserted their authority. Satara subsequently came under Maratha rule and was for a time capital of the Maratha kingdom. (See MARATHA; MAHARASHTRA.) In the mid-19th century the town and part of the surrounding area were annexed to British India and formed into Satara District, with Satara town as its headquarters.

SATARA DISTRICT. Area 4,041 sq.mi. (10,466 sq.km.). Pop. (1961) 1,430,105. After Indian independence the boundaries of Satara were enlarged by the inclusion of additional territory and the district was split into two—North Satara and South Satara. In 1960 South Satara was renamed Sangli (q.v.) and North Satara became known simply as Satara. The highest point in the district is Mahabaleshwar on the main range of the Western Ghats. The chief river is the Krishna, whose tributaries include the Kudali, Venna, and Urmodi. In some parts the average annual rainfall is more than 200 in. (5,080 mm.). The black, loamy clay soil grows millet, pulses, oilseed, and sugar cane. The main industries are sugar refining, engineering, and glassmaking. Cotton cloth, blankets, and brassware are also manufactured.

(M. R. P.)

SATELLITE, in astronomy, a small opaque body revolving around a planet, as the moon around the earth (see PLANETS and the articles on individual planets). Man-made space capsules and instrument packages that are propelled into space for scientific and exploratory purposes and which then go into orbit around the earth, another planet, or the sun are also referred to as satellites (see SPACE EXPLORATION). In the theory of cubic curves, Arthur Cayley defined the satellite of a given line to be the line joining the three points in which tangents at the intersections of the given (primary) line and curve again meet the curve.

SATIE, ERIK ALFRED LESLIE (1866–1925), French composer whose highly individual style gives him a unique place in modern music, was born at Honfleur on May 17, 1866. He studied at the Paris Conservatoire from 1879 and later worked as a café pianist. About 1890 he became associated with the Rosicrucian movement and wrote several works under its influence, notably the Messe des pauvres (1895). In his 40th year, in 1905, he went to study at the Schola Cantorum under V. d'Indy and A. Roussel.

Satie made a deliberate cult of eccentricity by giving his works grotesque titles and sprinkling their pages with comical annotations, but the genuine originality of his compositions won for him the admiration of composers greater than himself, including Debussy (who orchestrated two of the Gymnopédies for piano) and Ravel. His Sarabandes (1887) and Gymnopédies (1888) revealed him as a pioneer in harmony. In his ballets, Parade (1916) and Mercure and Relâche (both 1924), he created a new style of choreographic music. He wrote little for the voice, but his masterpiece, Socrate (1918), for four sopranos and chamber orchestra, on extracts from the *Dialogues* of Plato, showed that he was capable of writing deeply felt music.

Satie died in Paris on July 1, 1925.

See R. H. Myers, *Erik Satie* (1948); "Erik Satie, son Temps et ses Amis," special number of *La Revue musicale,* ed. by R. H. Myers (1952).   (R. H. My.)

SATIN, one of the basic weave structures, and a fabric so constructed (*see* WEAVING). The fabric has a smooth surface and usually a lustrous face and dull back; it is made in a wide variety of weights for various uses, including dresses, particularly evening wear; linings; bedspreads; and upholstery. Originally a silk fabric, it is now made of yarns of other fibres also.

SATIN SPAR, a name given to certain fibrous minerals which exhibit, especially when cut and polished, a soft satiny or silky lustre, and are therefore sometimes used as gem or ornamental stones. Such fibrous minerals occur usually in the form of veins or bands, having the fibres disposed transversely. The most common kind of satin spar is a white finely fibrous gypsum, used for beads, etc. Other kinds of satin spar consist of calcium carbonate, in the form of either aragonite or calcite (*qq.v.*).

See also GYPSUM.

SATIRE, as a literary genre, may be defined as the expression in adequate terms of the sense of amusement or disgust excited by the ridiculous or unseemly, provided that humour is a distinctly recognizable element, and that the utterance is invested with literary form. Without humour, satire is invective; without literary form, it is mere clownish jeering.

The first exercise of satire no doubt consisted in gibing at personal defects. To dignify satire by rendering it the instrument of morality or the associate of poetry was a development implying considerable advance in the literary art. In the accounts that have come down of the writings of Archilochus, the first great master of satire, we seem to trace the elevation of the instrument of private animosity to an element in public life. Simonides of Amorgos and Hipponax were, like Archilochus, distinguished for the bitterness of their attacks on individuals, with which the former combined a strong ethical feeling and the latter a bright active fancy. The loss of their writings, which would have thrown great light on the politics as well as the manners of Greece, is to be lamented. With Hipponax the direct line of Greek satire is interrupted; but two new forms of literary composition, capable of being the vehicles of satire, almost simultaneously appear. Although the original intention of fable does not seem to have been satirical its adaptability to satiric purposes was soon discovered. A far more important step was the elevation of the rude fun of rustic merrymakings to a literary status by the evolution of the drama from the Bacchic festival. The means had now been found of allying the satiric spirit with exalted poetry, and their union was consummated in the comedies of Aristophanes. (*See also* GREEK LITERATURE.)

A rude form of satire had early existed in Italy in the Fescennine verses (*q.v.*), the rough and licentious pleasantry of the vintage and harvest. As in Greece, these eventually were developed into a rude drama. Verse, "like to the Fescennine verses in point of style and manner," was added to accompany the mimetic action, and these probably improvised compositions were entitled *Saturae*, a word meaning a hodgepodge, or medley.

The Romans thus originated the name, and, insofar as the Fescennine drama consisted of raillery and ridicule, essentially possessed satire; but it had not yet assumed a literary form. The real inventor of Roman satire is Gaius Lucilius (*c.* 180–*c.* 102 or 101 B.C.). The fragments of Lucilius preserved are scanty, but the verdict of Horace, Cicero, and Quintilian demonstrates that he was a considerable poet. It is needless to dwell on compositions so well known as the *Satires* of Lucilius's successor, Horace, in whose hands this class of composition received a new development, becoming genial, playful, and persuasive. The didactic element preponderates still more in the philosophical satires of Persius (A.D. 34–62). Yet another form of satire, the rhetorical, was carried to the utmost limits of excellence by Juvenal (*c.* 60–after 128), the first example of a great tragic satirist. His slightly older contemporary Martial, improving on earlier Roman models

now lost, gave that satirical turn to the epigram (*q.v.*) which it only exceptionally possessed in Greece, but has ever since retained. At about the same time another variety of satire came into vogue, destined to become the most important of any. The Milesian tale, a form of entertainment probably of Eastern origin, grew in the hands of Petronius and Apuleius into the satirical romance, immensely widening the satirist's field and exempting him from the restraints of metre. Petronius' "Banquet of Trimalchio" is the revelation of a new vein, never fully worked till much later. As the novel arose upon the ruins of the epic, so dialogue sprang up upon the wreck of comedy. In Lucian, comedy appears adapted to suit the exigencies of an age in which a living drama had become impossible. With him classical satire expires as a distinct branch of literature. (*See also* LATIN LITERATURE: *The Genres: Satire.*)

In the Byzantine Empire, indeed, the link of continuity is unbroken, and such raillery of abuses as is possible under a despotism finds vent in pale copies of Lucian (*see also* GREEK LITERATURE: *Byzantine*). The first really important medieval satire, however, is a product of Western Europe, recurring to the primitive form of fable, upon which, nevertheless, it constitutes a decided advance. *Reynard the Fox* (*q.v.; see* also FABLE), a genuine expression of the shrewd and homely Teutonic mind, is a landmark in literature. It gave the beast-epic a development of which classical authors had not dreamed. The medieval popular instinct, perhaps deriving a hint from rabbinical literature, fashioned Morolf, the prototype of Sancho Panza, the incarnation of sublunar mother-wit contrasted with the starry wisdom of Solomon; and *Till Eulenspiegel* (*q.v.*) is a kindred Teutonic creation, but later and less significant. *Piers Plowman* (*c.* 1370 onward), by William Langland, the next great work of the class, adapts the apocalyptic machinery of monastic and anchoritic vision to the purposes of satire. The clergy were scourged with their own rod by a poet and a Puritan too earnest to be urbane.

The Renaissance, restoring the knowledge of classical models, enlarged the armoury of the satirist. Partly, perhaps, because Erasmus himself was no poet, the Lucianic dialogue was the form in the ascendant in his age. Erasmus not merely employed it against superstition and ignorance with infinite and irresistible pleasantry, but fired by his example a bolder writer, untrammelled by the dignity of an arbiter in the republic of letters. The ridicule of Ulrich von Hutten (*q.v.*) in his contributions to the *Epistolae obscurorum virorum* (1515–17) is annihilating, and the art of putting the ridicule into the mouth of the victim is perhaps the most deadly shaft in the quiver of sarcasm. It was later used with even more pointed wit though with less exuberance of humour by Pascal. Sir Thomas More cannot be accounted a satirist, but his idea of an imaginary commonwealth (*Utopia; q.v.*) embodied the germ of much subsequent satire.

In the succeeding period politics took the place of literature and religion, producing in France the *Satyre Ménippée* (*see* FRENCH LITERATURE: *The 16th Century: Prose*) and elsewhere the satirical romance as represented by the *Argenis* of John Barclay, which may be defined as the adaptation of the style of Petronius to state affairs. In Spain, where no freedom of criticism existed, the satiric spirit took refuge in the picaresque novel (*q.v.*), the prototype of Le Sage and the ancestor of Henry Fielding; Quevedo revived the medieval device of the vision as the vehicle of reproof; and Cervantes' immortal *Don Quixote* might be classed as a satire were it not so much more. Direct imitation of the Roman satirists first appears in English literature in the writings of John Donne, Joseph Hall, and John Marston. The development of the drama at this time probably absorbed talent that would otherwise have been devoted to satire proper. Most of the great dramatists of the 17th century were satirists, more or less, Molière perhaps the most consummate that ever existed; but, with an occasional exception, the range of their work is too wide to admit of their being regarded as satirists. The next great example of unadulterated satire is Samuel Butler's *Hudibras* (1663). Dignified political satire, bordering on invective, was carried to perfection in Dryden's *Absalom and Achitophel*. In France Boileau was long held to have attained the *ne plus ultra* of the Horatian style in satire and of the mock-heroic, but Alexander Pope was soon to show that further progress was possible in both. The polish, point, and concentration of Pope remain unsurpassed, as do the amenity of Joseph Addison and the daring yet severely logical imagination of Jonathan Swift; while the *History of John Bull* places their friend John Arbuthnot in the first rank of political satirists (*see* also JOHN BULL).

The 18th century was, indeed, the age of satire. Serious poetry had for the time worn itself out; the most original geniuses of the age are decidedly prosaic, and Pope, though a true poet, is less of a poet than Dryden. In process of time imaginative power revived, but meanwhile Fielding and Smollett had fitted the novel (*q.v.*) to be the vehicle of satire and much besides, and the literary stage had been almost wholly engrossed by a colossal satirist, a man who dared the universal application of Shaftesbury's maxim that ridicule is the test of truth. The world had never before seen a satirist on the scale of Voltaire, nor had satire ever played such a part as a factor in impending change. As a master of sarcastic mockery he is unsurpassed; his manner is entirely his own; and he is one of the most intensely national of writers, notwithstanding his vast obligations to English humorists, statesmen, and philosophers.

English humour also played an important part in the literary regeneration of Germany, where G. E. Lessing, imbued with Pope but not mastered by him, showed how powerful an auxiliary satire can be to criticism. Another great German writer, Christoph Wieland, owed little to the English, but adapted Lucian and Petronius to the 18th century with playful if somewhat mannered grace. Goethe and Schiller, Scott and Wordsworth, were by this time at hand, and as Romantic imagination gained ground satire declined. Byron, who in the 18th century would have been the greatest of satirists, was hurried by the spirit of his age into passion and description, bequeathing, however, a splendid proof of the possibility of allying satire with sublimity in his *Vision of Judgment.* Two great satiric figures remain—one representative of his nation, the other most difficult to class. In all the characteristics of his genius Thackeray is thoroughly English; his satire is a thoroughly British article, a little solid, a little wanting in finish, but honest, weighty, and durable. But Heine hardly belongs to any nation or country, time, or place. In him the satiric spirit, long confined to established literary forms, seems to obtain unrestrained freedom.

In no age was the spirit of satire so generally diffused as in the 19th century, but many of its eminent writers, while bordering on the domains of satire, escape the definition satirist. The term cannot be properly applied to Dickens, the keen observer of the oddities of human life; or to George Eliot, the critic of its emptiness when not inspired by a worthy purpose; or to Balzac, the painter of French society; or to Trollope, the mirror of the English middle classes. If *Sartor Resartus* could be regarded as a satire, Carlyle would rank among the first of satirists; but the satire, though obvious, rather accompanies than inspires the work.

The number of minor satirists of merit, on the other hand, is legion. James Russell Lowell's *Biglow Papers* represent perhaps the highest moral level yet attained by satire. W. H. Mallock, in his *New Republic,* made the most of personal mimicry, the lowest form of satire; in *Erewhon* (1872) Samuel Butler held an inverting mirror to the world's face with imperturbable gravity; the humour of George Bernard Shaw had always an essential character of satire—the sharpest social lash. One remarkable feature of the period was the union of caricature with literature.

In the 20th century, although pure satire was developed by Aldous Huxley and George Orwell, the prevailing mood was ironic or sardonic rather than satiric. Evelyn Waugh, who began as a pure satirist, with *Decline and Fall* (1928), later became increasingly depressed at declining standards: the title of the last volume of his war trilogy (*Unconditional Surrender,* 1961), indicates something of the resigned acceptance of moral and spiritual impoverishment that is the negation of the true satirist's art.

See also articles on writers mentioned; on PAMPHLET; COMEDY; DRAMA; LAMPOON; PARODY; on the national literatures: AMERI-CAN LITERATURE; ENGLISH LITERATURE; etc.; and references to "Satire" in the Index.

BIBLIOGRAPHY.—J. Dryden, "A Discourse Concerning the Original and Progress of Satire," in *Essays of John Dryden,* ed. by W. P. Ker (1900); H. Nettleship, "The Original Form of the Roman Satura," in *Lectures and Essays,* 2nd series (1895); S. Tucker, *Verse Satire in England Before the Renaissance* (1908); C. M. Fuess, *Lord Byron as a Satirist in Verse,* with a general chapter on satire (1912); "Satire," in the *Times Literary Supplement* (June 23, 1927); J. W. Duff, *Roman Satire* (1936); M. C. Randolph, "The Structural Design of the Formal Verse Satire," in the *Philological Quarterly* (1942); A. M. Clark, *Studies in Literary Modes* (1946); G. Highet, *The Classical Tradition* (1949), and *The Anatomy of Satire* (1962); I. Jack, *Augustan Satire* (1952); H. Smith, *Elizabethan Poetry* (1952); L. Bredvold, "A Note in Defense of Satire," and M. Mack, "The Muse of Satire," in *Studies in the Literature of the Augustan Age,* ed. by R. Boys (1952); J. Lawlor, "Radical Satire and the Realistic Novel," in *Essays and Studies,* new series, vol. 8 (1955); E. Leyburn, *Satiric Allegory* (1956); J. Peter, *Complaint and Satire in Early English Literature* (1956); J. McCormick, *Catastrophe and Imagination* (1957) with a chapter on 20th-century American and English satiric novelists; J. Sutherland, *English Satire* (1958); K. Hopkins, *Portraits in Satire* (1958); A. Kernan, *The Cankered Muse: Satire of the English Renaissance* (1959); R. C. Elliott, *The Power of Satire* (1960); L. Feinberg, *The Satirist* (1963); A. E. Dyson, *The Crazy Fabric* (1965).

(R. G.; X.)

SATNA, a town in Madhya Pradesh, India, and the headquarters of the district of the same name. Pop. (1961) 38,046. It is situated on Vindhyan outcrop at a height of 821 ft. (250 m.) above sea level on the left bank of the Tons River, a tributary of the Ganges. Satna is connected by rail with Allahabad, 104 mi. (167 km.) to the north, and Katni, 61 mi. (98 km.) to the south. Metaled roads radiate from the town toward Rewa, Katni, and Chhatarpur.

SATNA DISTRICT is mostly hilly country. Area 2,823 sq.mi. (7,312 sq.km.); pop. (1961) 694,370. In the north a conspicuous feature of the district is the Panna Hills, which are famous for their diamonds. The Tons River, with its tributary, drains the area in a northeasterly direction. Cultivation is carried on in shallow depressions covered mostly with laterite soil. The chief crops are millets, maize (corn), pulses, oilseeds, and fodder. Most of the population is engaged in agriculture, but a large number work in the stone quarries. Many of the inhabitants of the hilly areas are tribesmen, such as the Gonds. (M. N. K.)

SATPURA RANGE, a line of hills between the Narbada (Narmada) and Tapti rivers in central India. It is the western element of an upland series known collectively as the Satpura Line and including the Mahadeo Hills, Maikal Range, and Chota Nagpur Plateau. Stretching westward from about longitude 85° 5′ E almost to the shores of the Gulf of Cambay, this line is usually regarded as the northern limit of the Deccan Plateau or Peninsular India. Historically it was important as a barrier to the southern advance of the Aryan invaders, and it forms the dividing line between Aryan and Dravidian India. The range proper is about 200 mi. (320 km.) long and reaches heights of about 4,000 ft. (1,200 m.) It is mainly composed of Deccan lavas and is forested. Plateaulike in form, it is bordered by steep scarps on both north and south. The main railway from Bombay to the middle and lower Ganges crosses a low section of the range between Burhanpur and Khandwa. Farther west the main Bombay-Indore road crosses the range. (T. HER.; L. D. S.)

SATRAP, a hellenized rendering of Median *Khshathrapavan,* "protector of the kingdom," the title of provincial governors in the Persian Empire under Achaemenid rule. The division of the empire into provinces was begun by Cyrus the Great (559–530 B.C.) and completed by Darius I (522–486 B.C.), who established 20 satrapies and fixed their annual tribute. Their boundaries varied from time to time and on occasion two or more might be united under a single governor. Each satrapy was divided into districts under subordinate governors, also called satraps. The satraps, appointed by the king, normally were members of the royal family or Persian nobility. They held office indefinitely, often retaining their position through more than one reign; some were hereditary. The satrap was head of the administration of his province and was assisted by a council of Persians, to which provincials were admitted. He controlled local officials, collected the taxes, and was the supreme judicial authority. He was responsible for internal security and the safety of the roads and raised and maintained his army. He conducted wars with neighbours and engaged in diplomatic relations with foreign states, although major matters of policy were referred to the king. To guard against abuse of powers, Darius instituted a system of controls over the satrap. His secretary, chief financial official, and the commander of the garrison troops stationed in the province were directly responsible to the king, and periodical inspections were carried out by royal officials, especially "the king's eye," who traveled with their own military escort. With the weakening of central authority, however, the satraps often enjoyed practical independence, and after the mid-5th century their rebellions became frequent. The satrapal administration was retained by Alexander the Great and his successors, especially in the Seleucid Empire, but the provinces were smaller than under the Achaemenids. (J. M. M.-R.)

SATU MARE, a town and administrative centre of Satu Mare district in Maramureş *regiunea* of northwestern Rumania, lies near the border of Hungary on the right bank of the Someş River, 80 mi. (129 km.) NNW of Cluj. Pop. (1963) 63,656. Satu Mare was mentioned in the 14th century, and in 1599 Michael the Brave, of Walachia, rallied his army there to reconquer Transylvania (*q.v.*), which was then part of Hungary. In the town are an old palace, a state theatre, and several museums and libraries. It is a commercial centre and has industries that include machine building, metalworking, and the manufacture of textiles (lace, silk, and cotton fabrics). The town is an important railway junction with connections to Hungary and the Ukrainian Soviet Socialist Republic, U.S.S.R.

SATURN (SATURNUS), a Roman god whose cult was so overlaid with Greek features as to obscure his original native character. His name is commonly connected with Latin *satus*, and thus he is a god of sowing or seed. The ancients themselves regarded him as an importation and equated him with the Greek Cronus (*q.v.*), which may well be correct; there is some linguistic evidence (disregarding the connection with *satus*) that he came to Rome through Etruria. Further, he was worshiped in the Greek manner (*i.e.*, with head uncovered and not wrapped in the toga as was the Roman custom).

The remains of his temple at Rome, eight columns of the pronaos, still dominate the west end of the Forum at the foot of the *clivus Capitolinus*. The present remains are of a later rebuilding, but it was the oldest temple whose building is recorded, going back to the beginning of the republic. It served as the treasury (*aerarium Saturni*) of the Roman state. Saturn's cult partner is the obscure goddess Lua, whose name is connected with lues (plague or destruction) and to whom captive arms were sometimes burned. But he was also associated with Ops, the cult partner of Consus, through her identification with Rhea, wife of Cronus.

His great festival, the *Saturnalia,* became the most popular of Roman festivals, and its influence is still felt throughout the western world. Originally on Dec. 17, it was extended first to three and eventually to seven days. The date has been connected with the winter sowing season, which in modern Italy varies from October to January. Remarkably like the Greek Kronia (*see* CRONUS), it was the gayest festival of the year. All work and business were suspended. Slaves were given temporary freedom to say and do what they liked, and certain moral restrictions were eased. The streets were infected with a Mardi Gras madness; a mock king was chosen (*Saturnalicius princeps*); the seasonal greeting *io Saturnalia* was heard everywhere; presents were freely exchanged, principally wax candles and little clay dolls (*sigillaria*). The cult statue of Saturn himself, traditionally bound at the feet with woolen bands, was untied, presumably to come out and join the fun. The influence of the *Saturnalia* upon the celebrations of Christmas and the New Year has been direct. Concerning the gift candles, the ancients had a quaint story that an old prophecy bade the earliest inhabitants of Latium send heads to Hades and *phota* to Saturn; that they interpreted this to mean human sacrifices, but that Hercules advised using lights (*phos* means "light" or "man" according to accent) and not human "heads."

Another tradition regarding Saturn, fostered chiefly by the poets, made him an early Italian king, or perhaps Cronus in flight from Zeus, who established in Italy a new height of civilization (*Saturnia regna*) and a Golden Age (*aurea saecula; cf.* Virgil, *Aeneid*, viii, 319 ff.). Saturday of course was named for Saturn (*Saturni dies*).

BIBLIOGRAPHY.—W. W. Fowler, *Roman Festivals*, p. 268 ff. (1899); G. Wissowa, *Religion und Kultus*, 2nd ed., p. 204 ff. (1912); Roscher's *Lexikon, s.v.*; Platner-Ashby, *Topographical Dictionary, s.v.*
(R. B. Ld.)

SATURN is unique as being the only planet shown by telescopes to be encircled by a bright ring system. The Babylonians noted that Saturn moved more slowly against the background of the "fixed" stars than did the other planets visible to the naked eye; therefore, until the discovery of Uranus in 1781, it was thought to be the most remote planet, and it is in fact the sixth major planet in order of distance from the sun, the earth being the third. Saturn's mean distance from the sun is about 886,000,000 mi., and its period of revolution round the sun is nearly 29½ years. Its mean synodic period (interval between successive oppositions) is 378 days. Its least distance from the earth is about 744,000,000 mi., and its greatest about 1,028,000,000 mi. At opposition its light takes about 72 minutes to reach the earth. To the naked eye Saturn, at opposition, always appears as a star brighter than first magnitude; and at a close opposition, with its rings fully opened, it can appear three times as bright as at a distant one with its rings edgewise.

Description of the Globe.—When viewed through a telescope Saturn's globe strongly resembles Jupiter's, but is yellower in colour. It is even more flattened at the poles, its polar and equatorial diameters being respectively about 67,000 mi. and 75,000 mi.; it is less bright near the margin of its disk than at the centre; and its surface shows dusky, cloudlike belts with light zones between them; however, Saturn's belts are usually feeble and ill-defined, compared with those of Jupiter.

The volume of Saturn is about 744 times that of the earth, but its mass is only about 95 times the earth's mass. Therefore, Saturn's mean density is but 13 per cent that of the earth; *i.e.*, about 0.7 times that of water.

Rotation.—The infrequent occurrence of spots on Saturn long delayed determination of the period in which it rotates on its axis. What is observed from the earth is the gaseous envelope of the planet and not its solid core; and the rotation period of this gaseous atmosphere is not uniform but varies according to latitude. In 1794 William Herschel derived a value of 10 hr. 16 min. by noting variations of width and darkness in the planet's southern belts. The accepted period, 10 hr. 14 min., for Saturn's equatorial region is based on the value (10 hr. 14 min. 24 sec.) derived by Asaph Hall from a brilliant white spot which he discovered in 1876, and has been confirmed within about 1 min. by observations of subsequent spots, including those of the brilliant white spot discovered by Will Hay in 1933. Spectrographic observations (1936–37) by J. H. Moore at the Lick Observatory, Calif., confirmed that Saturn's rotation is slower at medium than at low latitudes, and suggested an even slower rate at high latitudes; but in 1960 a conspicuous white spot on the edge of the north polar region discovered by J. H. Botham (Johannesburg, S.Af.) gave a period of 10 hr. 39 min. for latitude +60°, almost the same period as that found in 1903 for spots at latitude +36°. A. Dollfus showed by polarimetric measures that the 1960 spot was at high altitude in Saturn's atmosphere.

Physical Conditions.—In 1923 H. Jeffreys showed on theoretical grounds that Saturn and the other outer planets, previously assumed to be hot and gaseous, are more probably cold and solid. Radiometric measures by W. W. Coblentz and C. O. Lampland verified this, indicating a surface temperature for Saturn of about −150° C (−238° F). This extremely low temperature, with the low mean density, suggested that much of Saturn's apparent globe consisted of a deep atmosphere and that a layer of frozen gases covered the solid surface.

The nature of the atmosphere was revealed in 1932–34 when R. Wildt, V. M. Slipher, and T. Dunham, Jr. proved mathematically and by laboratory experiment that the dark absorption bands (discovered by A. Secchi 70 years before) in Saturn's spectrum resulted chiefly from methane; weak absorption bands indicated the presence of ammonia. Saturn's atmosphere therefore consists mainly of methane, hydrogen, and helium, most of the ammonia being frozen out at the planet's low temperature.

In 1951–52 W. H. Ramsey showed that the low mean density of Jupiter and Saturn in proportion to their mass could only be accounted for by assuming that they are hydrogen planets, *i.e.*, having abundant hydrogen in their atmosphere and with a solid globe consisting mostly of metallic hydrogen, heavier elements being strongly concentrated in a small central core. Saturn would thus have a hydrogen content of 62–69% by mass.

The Rings.—*Discovery of the Rings.*—A strangeness in Saturn's appearance was noted at once by Galileo when he first observed the planet with his small telescope in 1610; however, his instrument was too weak to reveal the narrower parts of the ring next to the globe, and so he thought that the system was a triple planet consisting of a large body with a small attendant on each side. But the "attendants" had dwindled and disappeared by 1612 (when the rings had turned edgewise to the earth), and Galileo feared that he had been misled by an illusion. They later reappeared and continued to puzzle astronomers for nearly 50 years, for they generally looked like handles ("ansae") attached to the sides of the globe. Curious drawings by P. Gassendi, G. Riccioli, J. Hevel, and others showed how puzzled the observers were and also how near some of them came to solving the mystery.

In 1655 Christiaan Huygens, having discovered Saturn's satellite Titan with its approximately 16-day revolution around the planet, inferred a rotation of Saturn itself in less than 16 days and found the true explanation of its variable appearance. To secure priority for his theory while giving himself more time for observational tests, he published the key sentence of it as an anagram (1656). This sentence, published in 1659 in his *Systema Saturnium* with a full discussion, was: *Annulo cingitur, tenui, plano, nusquam cohaerente, ad eclipticam inclinato* ("It is girdled by a thin, flat ring, nowhere touching, inclined to the ecliptic"). It was the fixed inclination of the ring-plane (about 28° to the ecliptic and about 27° to Saturn's own orbit) that explained the striking changes in the planet's appearance so perplexing to other astronomers, though some at first rejected Huygens' theory.

At two opposite points of Saturn's orbit (near its heliocentric longitudes 172° and 352°, where Saturn is in the constellations Leo and Aquarius, respectively), the earth passes through the planet's ring-plane. When this occurs, the ring becomes exactly edgewise to the earth, and, because of its thinness, disappears from view, even (for a few hours) in powerful telescopes. These edgewise epochs occur at alternate intervals of about $13\frac{3}{4}$ and $15\frac{3}{4}$ years, and at each epoch the earth may pass once or three times through the ring (*e.g.*, 1937, once; 1950, once; 1966, three times; 1979–80, three times; 1995–96, three times). Between one edgewise epoch and the next, the ring appears to open out for some years, thereafter closing gradually again. Fullest opening, at an angle of $26\frac{1}{2}°$, occurs when Saturn is in Taurus-Gemini and in Ophiuchus-Sagittarius, the ring then covering most of one hemisphere of the globe, and, behind the other hemisphere, projecting beyond the polar limb.

Divisions of the Rings.—In 1675 G. D. Cassini made the important telescopic discovery of a black line, now known as "Cassini's division," dividing the ring into two concentric rings. A century later William Herschel proved this to be a gap dividing the ring into two parts: an outer ring (A) and an inner ring (B). Ring A is narrower and less bright than B, the outer part of which is the most brilliant part of the system.

TABLE I.—*Dimensions of Saturn's Ring System*

Ring	Exterior diameter (mi.)	Breadth of ring (mi.)
A	169,300	10,000
B	145,500	16,500
C	112,600	10,000

Source: *British Astronomical Association Handbook*, 1965.

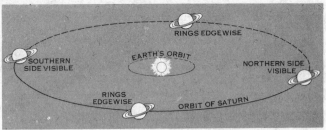

FROM "ASTRONOMY" BY R. H. BAKER (D. VAN NOSTRAND COMPANY, INC.)

PHASES OF SATURN'S RINGS

The discovery of a third, innermost ring, C, a dusky, semitransparent, continuous ring in both ansae and across the disk, was made in 1850 at Harvard College Observatory by W. C. and G. P. Bond, whose assistant C. W. Tuttle pronounced it a third ring; and independently in England by W. R. Dawes, whose friend W. Lassell named it the "crepe ring." It had probably been seen across the disk, but not in the ansae, and taken to be an atmospheric belt, by Herschel and other earlier astronomers. From the early 19th century many observations have been made in the ansae of various concentric markings rather similar to Cassini's division, but narrower and less dark. Their reality has been much debated. It seems likely that some at least are real markings, but merely ripples, light minima, or edges of shaded areas, and not gaps through the rings.

The breadth of Cassini's division is estimated at 1,750 mi. The total span of the ring system is nearly 170,000 mi. The system is very thin, being probably less than 10 mi. thick. Though casting a strong shadow on the globe, it is at least partly transparent.

When the rings are nearly edgewise to earth and sun, curious lighting and colour effects can be seen. With sun and earth both at low elevation from the ring-plane and on opposite sides of the plane, the dark face of the rings, wide and black across the disk, has appeared on each side against the sky as a faint, ghostly line with two bright condensations on each ansa due to the filtering of sunlight through the crepe ring and the Cassini division.

Nature of the Rings.—In 1785 P. S. Laplace proved that the continued existence of wide, solid rings round Saturn was a physical impossibility. But it took the discovery of the diaphanous crepe ring in 1850 to rouse mathematicians to try to find out the true nature of the rings. Success came in 1857 when J. Clerk Maxwell proved mathematically that the rings must consist of myriads of discrete particles, each orbiting Saturn in accordance with the law of gravitation—a theory suggested (without proof) by G. D. Cassini. In 1895 J. E. Keeler, by photographing the spectrum across the globe and rings and examining the shift of its lines resulting from Saturn's rotation, directly proved Maxwell's hypothesis. He found that the inner edge of ring B was rotating faster than the middle, and the middle of that ring faster than its outer edge, exactly contrary to the way in which a solid ring rotates. It was later found that the rotation period of the outer edge of ring A was more than twice as long as that of the inner edge of ring C. Direct observational proofs of the nonsolidity of the bright rings were obtained with rather small telescopes: in 1917, when M. A. Ainslie and J. Knight independently watched the passage of a seventh-magnitude star behind ring A, and in 1920, when W. Reid and others at Rondebosch, S.Af., made a similar observation of a star behind ring B.

Other studies of the rings have shown: (1) that Cassini's division is due to the attractions on the ring particles by Saturn's inner satellites (especially Mimas, *see* below), and that these attractions could theoretically cause narrower gaps or thinnings to occur at certain other places in the rings; (2) that the greater brightness of parts of the rings is due to greater crowding of the particles and not to differences in the types of particles; (3) that frequent collisions among the particles have probably reduced them to fine dust; (4) that they may be ice crystals; and (5) that they are unlikely to be spherical in shape. In 1958 A. Dollfus deduced, from the polarization of light on ring B, that its particles are probably cigar-shaped or elliptical, each with major axis parallel to its orbit.

TABLE II.—*Saturn's Satellites*

Name	Distance from Saturn's centre (000 mi.)	Synodic period of revolution				Inclination of orbit to Saturn's equatorial plane (degrees)	Eccentricity of orbit	Visual magnitude at mean opposition	Diameter (mi.)	Discoverer and year of discovery	
		days	hr.	min.	sec.						
Janus	100		17	58	30	0.0	0.000	14.0	186	A. Dollfus	1966
Mimas	115		22	37	12	1.5	0.0202	12.1	300	W. Herschel	1789
Enceladus	148	1	08	53	22	0.0	0.0045	11.8	400	W. Herschel	1789
Tethys	183	1	21	18	55	1.1	0.000	10.3	600	G. D. Cassini	1684
Dione	235	2	17	42	10	0.0	0.0022	10.4	600	G. D. Cassini	1684
Rhea	328	4	12	27	56	0.3	0.0010	9.8	800	G. D. Cassini	1672
Titan	759	15	23	15	32	0.3	0.0292	8.4	3,000	C. Huygens	1655
Hyperion	922	21	07	39	06	0.6	0.1042	14.2	300	W. and G. Bond; W. Lassell	1848
Iapetus	2,213	79	22	04	59	14.8	0.0283	10.1 to 11.9	700	G. D. Cassini	1671
Phoebe	8,050	523	13			150.6	0.1633	16.5	100	W. H. Pickering	1898

Sources: *British Astronomical Association Handbook*, 1965; A. F. O'D. Alexander, *The Planet Saturn*, 1962.

The Satellites.—Saturn has ten satellites (*see* Table II). J. Herschel chose mythological names for eight of them. By 1954 G. P. Kuiper and H. Camichel, with disk meters attached to large telescopes, had measured to within ±50 mi. the diameters of all but Hyperion and Phoebe, Kuiper using the 200-in. reflector of the Mount Palomar Observatory, Calif.

Six of the inner satellites (Mimas to Titan inclusive) have almost circular orbits nearly in the plane of Saturn's equator. Hyperion's orbit is eccentric with a small but variable inclination; that of Iapetus is highly inclined but almost circular; while Phoebe's is eccentric, very highly inclined, and retrograde.

Titan, the brightest, largest, and most massive of Saturn's satellites, is the only one in the solar system that has been proved to possess an atmosphere. In 1943–44 Kuiper photographed its spectrum, using the 82-in. reflector of McDonald Observatory, Tex., and found striking evidence of methane and a suspected ammonia band. Iapetus has the peculiarity of always appearing about two magnitudes brighter at its western elongation than at its eastern elongation from Saturn. Cassini drew attention to this in 1672, the year after he discovered Iapetus, and suggested that one-half of its surface must reflect sunlight better than the other, and that Iapetus, like the earth's moon, must present always the same face to its primary planet. A century later William Herschel, after many observations, endorsed both the peculiarity and Cassini's explanation of it.

Phoebe, extremely remote from Saturn, was the first satellite of any planet to be detected by photography and the first to be discovered from the southern hemisphere (at Arequipa, Peru). Transits of satellites across the face of Saturn (except of Titan and its shadow) are difficult to observe, and infrequent, as are eclipses of the satellites.

On Dec. 15, 1966, when the almost edgewise ring was presenting its unilluminated face, A. Dollfus discovered, by photography at the Pic du Midi Observatory, a faint inner satellite (named Janus) not far outside the ring's outer edge. He obtained further photographic positions on the next two days, and the discovery was confirmed by photographs taken at McDonald and Flagstaff observatories.

See also PLANETS.

See A. F. O'D. Alexander, *The Planet Saturn* (1962).

(A. F. O'D. A.)

SATURNIID MOTH, any of about 800 species of chiefly large, broad-winged moths of the family Saturniidae, commonly called giant silkworm moths. Although almost worldwide in distribution, most of the species are found in the tropics, especially in South America and Africa. These night flyers are often vividly coloured and remarkably patterned. Certain Asian kinds, called wild silkworms, spin a commercially valuable silk—not so fine, however, as that of the common Chinese silkworm (*Bombyx mori*) of another family (*see* SILK).

The Saturniidae includes some of the largest insects; a few tropical specimens have a wingspan of about 9 in., whereas those in North America are smaller, having wingspans up to 6 in. The larvae are large, usually green, caterpillars, most of which have colourful knobs or spines and, in many American sorts, irritant barbs. They are voracious leaf-eaters as caterpillars, but, unlike many other moths, they never feed after obtaining wings.

Some species have been used for commercial silk from time immemorial and the silkworm which Aristotle cited (his *nekydalos*) as a familiar example of metamorphosis was almost certainly *Saturnia pyri*. Saturniids are used in the modern silk industry only in southeast Asia, and only the tussah silkworm (*Antheraea pernyi*) and the eria, ailanthus or cynthia moth (*Samia cynthia*) have been used long enough to break into cultivated varieties. The North American polyphemus moth (*Antheraea polyphemus*) would be as useful in the silk industry as is the tussah, except for the cost of labour. Being large, handsome and often easy to rear, saturniids are favourites with amateur lepidopterists. They have also served as subjects in studies on hybridization and variation; more recently, the giant cecropia moth (*Hyalophora* or *Platysamia cecropia*) has been used extensively in studies on endocrine control of transformation and hibernation.

Other members of the family include the emperor moth (*Saturnia pavonia*) of temperate Europe and Asia; the yellow (male) or reddish (female) io moth (*Automeris io*), the bright grass-green luna moth (*Actias luna*) and the maroon (female) to blackish (male) promethea moth (*Callosamia promethea*), all found in North America. The genera *Rothschildia* and *Copiopteryx*, common to South America, are among the most beautiful of the saturniids.

See also INSECT; LEPIDOPTERA.

BIBLIOGRAPHY.—W. J. Holland, *Moth Book* (1940); H. Schüssler, *Lepidopterorum Catalogus*, lv, lvi, lviii (Saturniidae) (1930–35); lxv, pp. 30–144 (as Syssphingidæ) (1936); C. D. Michener, "The Saturniidae (Lepidoptera) of the Western Hemisphere," *Bull. Am. Mus. Nat. Hist.*, vol. 98, art. 5 (1952).

(W. T. M. F.)

SATURNINUS, LUCIUS APPULEIUS (d. 100 B.C.), with Gaius Servilius Glaucia, was a political opponent of the Senate at Rome from 104 to 100 B.C., at first on behalf of and with the cooperation of Gaius Marius (*q.v.*). He was quaestor in 104. As tribune in 103 he bid for the support of the proletarian in Rome by a law which reduced the price of the monthly grain ration from $6\frac{1}{3}$ *asses* to the uneconomic figure of $\frac{5}{6}$ of an *as* per measure. By another bill he assigned grants of land in Africa, amounting to a little over 60 ac. per man, to the soldiers discharged after service in the Jugurthine War. He established the first permanent court to try charges of treason (*quaestio maiestatis*); secured the exile of Gnaeus Mallius Maximus, consul of 105, for his defeat by the Cimbri at Arausio (*see* ARAUSIO, BATTLE OF); and, perhaps wishing to emphasize some resemblance between his own acts and the reforms of the Gracchi, encouraged the claim of L. Equitius to be a son of Tiberius Gracchus.

The conservative censors of 102 (Metellus Numidicus and his cousin Metellus Caprarius) tried unsuccessfully to expel Saturninus and Glaucia from the Senate. The support of the *equites* (*q.v.*) having been secured by the bill of Glaucia as tribune (probably in 101) restoring to them the exclusive right of constituting the juries in the permanent courts, Saturninus was acquitted on a capital charge resulting from his public allegation that senators had taken bribes from envoys of Mithradates VI Eupator, king of Pontus. In 100 Saturninus was tribune again, Marius consul for the sixth time, and Glaucia praetor. The crisis came with Saturninus' proposals for land allotments in Transalpine Gaul for Marius' soldiers discharged after service in the Cimbric War, and for Latin colonies in Sicily and Macedonia-Achaea. The agrarian bill was passed with a stipulation that senators should swear within five days to observe it; Metellus Numidicus refused, and went into exile.

Saturninus was elected tribune again for 99, with L. Equitius, but Marius was now alive to the danger of his extremist policy. The consular elections (for which Glaucia's candidature was disallowed) broke down in disorder, and Gaius Memmius, a candidate, was murdered. The Senate passed the last decree (*senatus consultum ultimum*), and on Dec. 10, the first day of the new tribunes' office, Saturninus and Glaucia, who, with their gangsters, had seized the capitol, were forced to surrender and were locked in the Senate house, whose roof was then torn off and they were stoned to death. (Among the executioners was Gaius Rabirius, who was tried for treason on this account and defended by Cicero 37 years later.) Saturninus' offensive legislation was rescinded after his death.

Although surviving accounts of Saturninus derive from hostile sources, it is clear that he lacked the integrity and statesmanship of Gaius Gracchus, in whose steps he followed.

BIBLIOGRAPHY.—Ancient sources (in the main, Appian and Plutarch) in A. H. J. Greenidge and A. M. Clay, *Sources for Roman History, 133–70 B.C.*, 2nd ed. (1960); H. Last in *Cambridge Ancient History*, vol. ix, ch. 4 (1932); E. Badian, *Foreign Clientelae* (1958); H. H. Scullard, *From the Gracchi to Nero* (1959). (J. P. V. D. B.)

SATYRS AND SILENI, in Greek mythology, creatures of the wild, part man, part beast, who in classical times were closely associated with Dionysus. Their Italian counterparts were the Fauns (*see* FAUNUS). Satyrs and Sileni are not mentioned in Homer, but they occur in art and literature from the archaic period, at first represented as uncouth men, each with horse's tail and ears and erect phallus. The occurrence of two different names for these creatures has been explained by two rival theories: that Silenus is the East Greek and Satyr the mainland name for the same mythical being, or that the Sileni were part horse and the Satyrs part goat. But it is difficult to make either theory fit all the examples in early art and literature. The type with goat's legs and tail appears to have been developed from the mid-5th century B.C. under the influence of Pan (*q.v.*). Also from the same period the name Silenus was applied to Dionysus' foster father, treated by the youthful Satyrs as representing the older generation. This was part of the gradual absorption of these creatures into the Dionysiac cult. In the Dionysiac festival at Athens the three tragedies were followed by a satyr play (*e.g.*, Euripides' *Cyclops*), in which the chorus was dressed to represent Satyrs (*see* DRAMA: *Greek Drama: Origins*). This play was a parody of the heroic legends, and the chorus of Satyrs was cowardly, lecherous, and wine-bibbing; but Silenus, although bibulous, also appears in legend as a dispenser of homely wisdom. In the story of Midas, Silenus when drunk strays into Midas' rose garden and is kindly treated, being finally restored to Dionysus, who in gratitude grants Midas the magic gift of producing gold at a touch.

In art the Satyrs and Sileni are depicted in company with nymphs or Maenads whom they pursue. Praxiteles represented a new artistic type in which the Satyr is young and handsome, with the smallest vestiges of animal parts but more graceful and fanciful than the classical ideal of manhood. Hellenistic art developed this concept into humorous or forceful representations of half-animal subjects as an escape from the merely human.

See M. P. Nilsson, *Geschichte der griechischen Religion*, vol. i, part 2, pp. 215–219 (1941); Pauly-Wissowa, *Real-Encyclopädie der classischen Altertumswissenschaft*, 2nd series, vol. 3, col. 35–53 (1927).

(H. W. PA.)

SAUD (SA'UD IBN 'ABD AL-'AZIZ IBN 'ABD AL-RAHMAN AL SA'UD) (1902–1969), son and successor of Ibn Saud (*q.v.*), ruled over Saudi Arabia as King Saud IV from 1953 to 1964. He was born in Kuwait early in 1902. After Ibn Saud had conquered the Hejaz (1925) he made his two eldest living sons, Saud and Faisal, his deputies in Najd and Hejaz respectively. Saud's primary responsibility was for the Bedouin. He was named crown prince in 1933, and he and Faisal led the successful campaign against Yemen in 1934. When Ibn Saud established a Council of Ministers (1953), Saud became its president. In November 1953 he became king, with the support of all his brothers.

King Saud made several journeys abroad—to Europe, the United States, and to nearby Arab countries. He also made periodic tours of Saudi Arabia. At home he expanded his father's program of modernization, with special emphasis on increased medical facilities and education. The first secular university was established at Riyadh (1957), staffed with Egyptian professors, and the first girls' schools were authorized by royal proclamation (1959).

In foreign affairs, King Saud continued his father's policies of friendship with the United States; suspicion of Communism; friendship with all Arabs; and firm opposition to Israel. The Anglo-Saudi dispute over the Buraimi oasis continued, and arbitration at Geneva failed (1955), but diplomatic relations between the two countries, severed in 1956, were resumed in 1963. In 1958, for the primary purpose of restoring the financial stability of Saudi Arabia, the king reorganized the Council of Ministers. Faisal, the crown prince and foreign minister, was given full power as president of the council. The king resumed power in December 1960. During 1963 he spent months abroad for medical treatment, and dissension developed between him and Faisal. In March 1964 all powers were transferred to Faisal as viceroy of the kingdom; and on Nov. 2 King Saud was deposed by the Supreme Council of the Religious Leaders, senior members of the royal family, and the Council of Ministers. Faisal (*q.v.*) became king, and Saud formally abdicated in January 1965. He later went abroad to live and died in Athens on Feb. 23, 1969. (C. P. H.)

SAUDI ARABIA (AL MAMLAKAH AL-'ARABIYAH AS-SA'UDIYAH), a kingdom of southwest Asia, ruled by the house of Sa'ud in the 18th century and founded in the 20th century as a modern kingdom by 'Abd al-'Aziz II ibn Sa'ud, occupies most of the Arabian Peninsula. The kingdom is bounded north by Jordan, Iraq, and Kuwait, with two areas of neutral territory west and south of Kuwait; west by the Gulf of Aqaba and the Red Sea; south by Yemen and the People's Republic of Southern Yemen; southeast by Muscat and Oman; east by Trucial Oman (Trucial States), Qatar, and the Persian Gulf. Its boundaries with Yemen in part and with its southern and eastern neighbours have never been fixed. The total area is 872,722 sq.mi.(2,260,353 sq.km.). The capital is at Riyadh.

PHYSICAL GEOGRAPHY

The ancient Arabian shield of igneous and metamorphic rocks protrudes eastward from Hejaz (Al Hijaz) into Najd (Nejd) as a bulge curving round from the Gulf of Aqaba to a point less than 125 mi. (201 km.) W of Riyadh and then receding toward the southern Red Sea. The shield contains many extinct volcanoes surrounded by lava beds. Sloping eastward are the newer sedimentary areas in which rich oil fields are found. The shield gives symmetry to the landscape, as many escarpments and sand deserts follow its contour.

Saudi Arabia's coastline on the Gulf of Aqaba and the Red Sea is more than 1,100 mi. (1,770 km.) long; its Persian Gulf coastline, though of undetermined length, is somewhat shorter. Neither side has deep natural harbours. Islands and coral reefs in the Red Sea are numerous, particularly in the Farasan Bank, which runs along the Saudi Arabian coast for over 300 mi. (480 km.). In the Persian Gulf the ownership of various islands is in dispute between Saudi Arabia, on the one hand, and Kuwait, Iran, or Abu Dhabi (one of the Trucial States), on the other. A treaty signed in 1958 established a water boundary between Saudi Arabia and Bahrain.

Saudi Arabia's highest mountains are in 'Asir (*q.v.*) where peaks rise to over 9,000 ft. (2,750 m.). The mountains of Al Tubayq dominate the undefined border between Jordan and Saudi Arabia east of Aqaba. Southeast of Jabal Shammar (*q.v.*) province escarpments parallel the bulge of the shield, the most prominent being Jabal Tuwayq, 800 mi. (1,300 km.) long from north to south. The Red Sea coast plains are narrow, whereas plains in the central and eastern regions sometimes stretch over great distances. In the north the Syrian Desert reaches down into Saudi Arabia. The largest sand deserts lie east of the shield: the Great Nafud in the north and the Rub' al Khali (the Empty Quarter) in the south, connected by the Ad Dahna sand belt.

The 'Asir mountains constitute the only area in the kingdom receiving adequate rainfall. Virtually all the rest of the country is desert, apart from scattered oases fed by underground water sources or flash floods. Winters are cool, and spring and fall days are often agreeable, but spells of good weather are interspersed with gusts or storms of swirling dust and sand. The fierce summer heat, tempered by aridity in the higher regions of the interior, is aggravated along the coasts by high humidity. *See also* ARABIA: *Regional Geography.*   (G. S. RE.)

PEOPLE AND POPULATION

In 1963 the population of Saudi Arabia was estimated at 7,000,-000. There are no verified figures of the exact population. The results of a census held in 1964 were not published. It is estimated that 50% of the population is nomadic, and it is probable that both the town estimates and the estimated proportion of nomads are higher than a census would prove. Recent estimates of the principal cities are: Riyadh (225,000); Mecca (200,000); Jidda (250,000); Medina (100,000); Al Hufuf (Hofuf) (100,-000); At Ta'if (60,000); Abha (30,000); Ad Dammam (60,000); Al Qatif (30,000); Buraydah (Buraida) (35,000); Ha'il (40,000); Al Khubar (30,000); 'Unayzah (Anaiza) (30,000); Dhahran (25,-000); Ras Tanura (20,000); Al Qunfudhah and Najran (15,000 each).

Arabs are of the Caucasian family but there are some of Negroid ancestry because of past importations of Africans. The Saudi Arabs recognize no colour line, and mixed racial strains abound in Saudi Arabia, especially in the Red Sea coastal plain called the Tihamah. But on the interior plateau of Najd, the hue of the Najdis and Bedouin in general is largely the brown Mediterranean type. The colouring of the people in towns varies from white to light brown. The Arab population are predominantly Sunni Muslims who mostly adhere to the Wahhabism (puritanical) interpretation. (*See* ISLAM.) There are no native Christians or Jews, but several thousand Christians (U.S., European, and Arab) are employed in the oil industry. Jews are barred from Saudi Arabia, and non-Muslims are forbidden to enter the sacred cities of Mecca and Medina (*qq.v.*).

The creation of industries and the enormous development of the Arabian American Oil Company (Aramco) have been responsible for the growth of population (since 1945) in the cities of Jidda, Riyadh, Dhahran, Ad Dammam (*qq.v.*), Al Khubar, and Al Qatif, where the increase has been two- to tenfold.

For anthropology, *see* ARABIA: *The People;* ARAB; BEDOUIN. For language, *see* ARABIC LANGUAGE.   (K. S. Tw.)

HISTORY

For archaeology, exploration, and early history *see* ARABIA. The history of Saudi Arabia begins properly on Sept. 18, 1932, when by royal decree of King 'Abd al-'Aziz II ibn Sa'ud the dual kingdom of Hejaz and Najd (*qq.v.*) with its dependencies, administered since 1927 as two separate units under slightly different systems, was unified under the name of "The Kingdom of Saudi Arabia." The change was far from being purely nominal, though no attempt was made to "liberalize" the supreme authority of the king as the absolute monarch of the new regime. It did, however, represent a substantial change of direction, or attitude, in the domestic and foreign policies of the realm. Until 1926, when Ibn Saud had finally extended his power over the whole of inner Arabia, the country had remained in almost total isolation from the rest of the world because of its poverty, its desert character, and its fanatical religious xenophobia. The only foreign countries with which Ibn Saud was acquainted were Turkey and Great Britain; but the conquest of Hejaz had brought him into contact with other powers, and the new circumstances compelled him to take stock of his position. It was the U.S.S.R. which took the lead in recognizing his new status. Britain and France did the same soon afterward. (*See also* IBN SAUD.)

Preliminary Period, 1926–32.—Ibn Saud, enriched since 1926 by the substantial revenues of the Meccan pilgrimage, had realized from the beginning that the progress and stability of his regime would depend largely on cooperation with the West, particularly in the technical and economic spheres. He had not hesitated to temper the puritan breezes of his native Najd to the latitudinarian exigencies of his new province, and the mildness of his attitude to the non-Muslim stranger within his gates had surprised those who had confidently predicted a sharp turn of the puritan screw on Hejaz, long accustomed to Turkish apparatus and European contacts.

At the same time it had caused some searching of heart among the divines and fanatics of his desert realm, where the Wahhabi brotherhood (known as *al-Ikhwan; see* WAHHABI), though acclimatized to the use of western firearms, tended to challenge the legality of infidel contributions to peaceful progress, such as the automobile, the airplane, the telephone, and radiotelegraphy. Ibn Saud had gradually disarmed the opposition to his projects by tactful persuasion; but there still remained a hard core of irreconcilable elements, the very elements which he himself had created and trained to carry the victorious banners of God through the length and breadth of the land he now ruled. In 1929 Faisal al-Dawish, Sultan ibn Bijad, and other leaders of the *Ikhwan,* accusing him of betraying the cause for which they had fought so stoutly, took the law into their own hands and staged an attack on Iraq, for which Britain still held the mandate from the League of Nations.

The *Ikhwan* raiders were repulsed from the Iraqi border by British forces and then turned their attention to attacking other Saudi tribes. This action rallied the remainder of the population to the king's side and enabled him to defeat the rebels. The civil war, however, dragged on into 1930, when the rebels were rounded up by the British in Kuwaiti territory and their leaders were handed over to the king.

By this means the rebellion was crushed and Ibn Saud had exorcised, though not without reluctance, the devil of his own creation. He was at last free to give his undivided attention to the development of his country and to the problems of foreign policy which beset him on all sides. Above all he was concerned to assert and maintain the complete independence of his country and in it the exclusive supremacy of Islam. Subject to their respect for these fundamental objectives, he was not only ready to cooperate with all nations but prepared to regard with sympathy some of the practices which had taken root in Hejaz and other areas as the result of foreign contacts. The Wahhabi anathema on tobacco was not pressed in Hejaz, and gradually became a dead letter elsewhere. The ban on music was progressively stifled by the radio. The amenities of air travel dispelled the myth of divine displeasure at its indulgence. And so on until the latitudinarian spirit, slowly at first but with ever-increasing momentum, dispersed the inhibitions of the puritan regime.

On the other hand Ibn Saud had rigorously set his face against any foreign intervention whatever in the internal politics of the realm. Britain and other European states had been politely warned against interference in the processes of Islamic law relating to crime, slavery, etc. Requests for permission to construct churches and other public places of worship for non-Islamic communities were courteously rejected.

Foreign Relations, 1932–1953.—From the date of its establishment in September 1932, Saudi Arabia enjoyed full international recognition as an independent state.

In 1934 Ibn Saud was involved in war with Yemen over a boundary dispute. In a six-week campaign the Saudis were generally victorious, advancing as far south as the Yemeni port Al Hudaydah. Hostilities were terminated by the Treaty of At Ta'if and the disputed frontier was demarcated, after which normal relations with Yemen were renewed.

Diplomatic relations with Egypt, severed in 1926 owing to an incident on the Meccan pilgrimage, were not renewed until after the death of King Fuad of Egypt in 1936.

Fixation of the boundaries of the country remained a problem throughout the 1930s. In tribal society, where a considerable proportion of the population is nomadic, sovereignty is traditionally expressed in the form of suzerainty over certain tribes rather than in fixed territorial boundaries. Hence Ibn Saud regarded the demarcation of land frontiers with suspicion. Nevertheless the majority of the frontiers with Iraq and Jordan had been demarcated by 1930. In the south and east no agreement was reached on the exact site of the frontiers with the Trucial sheikhdoms and with Muscat and Oman. As all these states had been in treaty relations with Britain for more than a century, their boundary disputes were destined to create friction between the Saudi Arabians and Britain.

During World War II Ibn Saud declared his neutrality, though his personal bias in favour of the Western Allies was never in doubt. In 1945, however, he declared war on Germany, a purely formal action which enabled Saudi Arabia to enter the United Nations as a founder member. Ibn Saud also, after some hesitation, joined the Arab League (q.v.), but he did not play a leading part in it. The religious and conservative element in Saudi Arabian life still acted as an obstacle to integration with those Arab states which were actively imitating modern Western life.

Internal Affairs, 1932–53.—Although oil had been discovered in the Hasa Province near the shores of the Persian Gulf before World War II, it was not exploited energetically until after the entry of the United States into the war. Thereafter a considerable number of employees of the oil companies arrived in Saudi Arabia. The resulting sudden access of wealth was no unmixed blessing. The country's moral standards were adversely affected. Saudi Arabia was itself unable to supply the oil companies with sufficient skilled workers, and as a result a flood of employees entered the country from other Arab states, materially influencing the thought and behaviour of the Saudis. The American way of life imposed itself quickly on a considerable part of the population hitherto noted for its distrust of foreigners, only apparently to increase its xenophobia.

The disturbance of traditional patterns was reflected in the government. Inexperience and the advent of fortune hunters from neighbouring countries encouraged extravagance. The poor became rich overnight, but prices soared and those who were not paid by the oil companies became poorer than ever.

Ibn Saud had virtually created Saudi Arabia. Brought up in the strict puritanical faith of the Wahhabis, he viewed this flood of wealth and the consequent decline of morality with distaste and bewilderment. He died on Nov. 9, 1953, at the age of 73.

Reign of King Saud ibn 'Abd al-'Aziz.—Ibn Saud was succeeded by his eldest surviving son, Saud, his second son, Faisal, being declared heir apparent. The two brothers were remarkably unalike. Saud was a simple man who had been brought up a strict puritan with many affiliations among the desert tribes. Faisal had lived chiefly in the cities of Hejaz and had often been abroad. Saud thus represented the *ancien régime*. Those advocating modernization supported Faisal. (*See* also FAISAL; SAUD.)

Meanwhile money continued to pour into the country. There was an enormous increase in the population of the towns, notably of Riyadh and of Jidda. The character of these urban societies was changed beyond all recognition by a large influx of bourgeoisie from neighbouring countries. The foreign ways of immigrant wives were tolerated by the population, but there was as yet no sign of official recognition of the inevitability of female emancipation. In the larger towns, roads, schools, hospitals, palaces, apartment buildings, and airports replaced the old alleyways and mud-built houses.

Ibn Saud had completely dominated the political scene until his death. Afterward, however, there was constant latent rivalry between Saud and Faisal. In March 1958, as a result of pressure, Saud issued a decree transferring all executive powers to Faisal. In December 1960, however, Faisal was obliged to resign and the king himself assumed the office of prime minister. In 1962–63 the pendulum swung back again and Faisal was once more given executive powers. Finally, on Nov. 2, 1964, King Saud was deposed and Faisal was proclaimed king.

Foreign Affairs Under Saud and Faisal.—The frontier between Saudi Arabia and Muscat and Oman had never been demarcated. In the late 1940s this problem assumed importance owing to the possibility of discovery of oil in the area. In 1952 Saudi Arabian tribal forces occupied the oasis of Al Buraymi, which Britain considered as belonging to Muscat and Oman and to Abu Dhabi, with both of which states Britain had treaty relations. Consequently in January 1953 Trucial Oman levies, commanded by British officers, occupied Al Buraymi.

In July 1954 the British and Saudi governments agreed to submit the dispute to an arbitration tribunal. This met in Geneva in September 1955, but the negotiations broke down, and British-officered forces from Muscat and Oman and Abu Dhabi reoccupied

the oasis. During the Suez crisis in 1956 Saudi Arabia broke off relations with Britain, and they were not reestablished until 1963. In September 1961, following the Iraqi claim to sovereignty over Kuwait, Saudi Arabia sent troops to that state in response to a request from its ruler.

The United States remained the most influential foreign power in Saudi Arabia, though the Americans made no attempt to interfere in the administration of the country. The second five-year pact which permitted the U.S. Air Force to lease Dhahran base on the Persian Gulf was terminated in 1962.

As a result of the rise to power of Pres. Gamal 'Abd-al-Nasser, Saudi relations with Egypt were often strained. In 1958 Nasser accused King Saud of plotting his assassination. Egyptian propaganda made frequent and sometimes venomous attacks on the Saudi royal family and on the whole system of government.

When Egyptian troops were sent to Yemen (q.v.) in 1962, tension between Saudi Arabia and Egypt became even more acute. The Saudis, accused of helping the Yemeni royalists, claimed in turn that Egyptian aircraft had bombed towns in Saudi Arabia. After an agreement had been signed at Jidda by King Faisal and President Nasser in August 1965 providing for an immediate cease-fire in Yemen, some Egyptian troops were withdrawn. The cease-fire, however, broke down and fighting was resumed. After the defeat of Egypt by Israel in June 1967 a fresh agreement was concluded between King Faisal and President Nasser, according to which the Egyptian Army was to withdraw from Yemen and Saudi Arabia was to cease to give assistance to the Yemeni royalists. The agreement was concluded between King Faisal and Nasser, no Yemeni representative being present.

In December 1965 Great Britain agreed to supply Saudi Arabia with an air-defense system. The U.S., at the same time, agreed to provide Hawk missiles.

King Faisal paid a state visit to Britain in May 1967. While he was still in London, fighting broke out in Sinai between Israel and Egypt and Jordan. Saudi Arabian troops were sent to Jordan, ostensibly to assist the Jordanian Army. They did not, however, go into action.

At the same time Saudi Arabia joined in the general Arab oil ban against the U.S. and Britain. The ban was not lifted until after the Arab conference at Khartoum (Aug. 29–Sept. 3, 1967).

(H. St. J. B. P.; J. B. Gl.)

ADMINISTRATION AND SOCIAL CONDITIONS

Government.—The government of Saudi Arabia is patriarchal rather than constitutional. The nearly absolute ruler is bound by the laws of the *shari'a* (*see* ISLAMIC LAW). The ruler is assisted by a Council of Ministers (set up by decree in 1953), drawn equally from the royal family and citizens. The government is assisted by a consultative council and by the *'ulama'*, a council of learned religious men.

The laws of Islam provide the country with civil and penal codes and also regulate religious problems. But the ruler has the power to issue a decree where the religious law is not applicable. The ruler is accessible to his subjects and hears complaints from all classes. Appeals can be made to the *shari'a* or to the Bureau of Complaints.

The organized judiciary is an independent agency in the state, and the public and personal law is derived from the Koran. The qadis (*see* QADI) usually judge according to the predominant Hanbalite version of the *shari'a* law. Punishment is similar to that in the Mosaic code; the penalty for murder is decapitation by the sword. Justice, when not in conflict with religious law, can also be governed by tribal and customary law (*'urf*).

Administratively Saudi Arabia is divided into provincial areas: Hejaz, Najd, Al Hasa (Eastern Province), Northern Frontiers District, and 'Asir. In 1963 a royal decree for the regulation of provinces was issued. This proposed to decentralize administration and increase local participation by establishing regional councils to assist the provincial governors, who in turn would be responsible to the minister of the interior.

Living Conditions, Health, and Welfare.—It is sometimes thought that Arabs live only in tents. This is true of the estimated

50% of the Saudi population who are Bedouin. But there are thousands of farmers and landholders who live in two- to five-storied buildings of mud-brick and stone, similar to the dwellings in the towns. After World War II many apartments, government offices, and fine houses of reinforced concrete were constructed.

With the oil economy came the concept of hired labour, and people are now also employed in government services, in various private enterprises, in construction, and in mining. The greatest single industry is the oil operation of Aramco, which employs more than 16,000 persons, most of whom are Saudi Arabs. In 1935 wages paid in this industry were ½ riyal and food per day (1 riyal = 22 cents U.S.). Wages by the mid-1960s had reached a minimum of 8 riyals.

The traditional welfare system based on kinship continues to function throughout the kingdom. A Ministry of Social Welfare and Labour was created in 1963, and increased provision was made for various development projects. Aramco instituted a modern welfare plan which included provision for pension plans, accident compensation, and medical and educational services.

The scarcity of water contributes to unsanitary living conditions in many parts of the country. Malnutrition, a major health problem, gives rise to rickets, scurvy, and anemia. There is a high incidence of trachoma, malaria, tuberculosis, and venereal and parasitic infections. The annual influx of pilgrims aggravates public health problems, although the government has established quarantine stations, notably at Jidda. Progress was made after the formation of a Ministry of Health in 1951, and hospitals, some with mobile units, were established in the major population centres.

A royal decree of October 1936 made the importation of slaves illegal unless the importers could prove that the slaves were recognized as such in the country of their origin. Slavery was abolished in 1962.

Education.—Elementary education is free to all Saudi Arabs. The modern school system includes elementary, secondary, commercial, and industrial schools, training institutes for teachers, and night schools. By the late 1960s there were more than 2,000 government educational institutions staffed by over 12,000 instructors and attended by more than 150,000 students. There are many anti-illiteracy centres throughout the kingdom, and in 1959 a royal decree authorized the establishment of government schools for girls. Riyadh University (established in 1957) has colleges of arts and sciences, commerce, pharmacy, agriculture, and medicine. The Islamic University was founded at Medina in 1960 and it was proposed to establish King 'Abd al-'Aziz University at Jidda. There is a technological institute at Riyadh and a petroleum university at Ad Dammam. The estimated number of girls attending schools fostered by the government was 60,000 in the late 1960s. Boys attending elementary schools numbered over 190,000 and secondary or intermediate schools 44,000. In the colleges and universities, including Riyadh University, there were approximately 1,000 students. In the United States about 1,000 Saudi Arabs were attending 150 colleges and universities in most of the states; about 150 were working for M.A. and Ph.D. degrees.

Defense.—The armed forces of Saudi Arabia consist of the regular army (estimated at 15,000) and the national guard, known as the White Army (a conglomeration of tribal levies). King 'Abd al-'Aziz Military Academy at Riyadh provides training for officers. The U.S. government conducts training of Saudi Arabs at Dhahran Air Base and maintains a military training mission of the air force.   (K. S. Tw.; X.)

THE ECONOMY

The kingdom of Saudi Arabia inherited the simple, tribal economy of Arabia. Many of the people are nomads, engaged in raising camels, sheep, and goats. Agricultural production is localized and poor, but it is being steadily improved and much progress has been made in controlling the periodic locust invasions. Scarcity of rain and water is a perpetual problem; the oases provide a few staple crops; in places dams have been built to trap the seasonal valley floods, and some irrigation is practised. A notable experiment is the royal farm, covering about 4,000 ac., at Al

Kharj south of Riyadh. Agricultural development programs in the mid-1960s provided for the construction of several dams (including Wadi Qizan and Abha in the 'Asir province), for drinking water projects, and for the establishment of agricultural centres for technical assistance to farmers. Fishing methods in the Persian Gulf and Red Sea have also been modernized. But it has always been difficult for the country to be self-sustaining in essential foodstuffs, and many necessities of life (such as rice, flour, sugar, tea, and piece goods) must still be imported. Traditional exports, which before the discovery of oil paid for these imports, include skins, hides, wool, dates, horses, camels, and pearls, but the demand for these has decreased. (*See also* ARABIA: *Vegetation, Animal Life,* and *Natural Resources.*)

The Oil Economy.—The discovery of oil changed the entire economic situation of Saudi Arabia. As early as 1923 Ibn Saud granted an oil prospecting concession to a British company, but this concession was never exploited.

In 1933 a large oil concession, to terminate in 1999, was secured by Standard Oil Company of California, which eventually shared ownership of the operating concern, the Arabian American Oil Company (Aramco), with Texaco, Standard Oil (New Jersey), and Mobil Oil on a 30-30-30-10 basis. Although oil was discovered in 1938, World War II curtailed activities until near its end. Rapid expansion began with the completion in 1945 of the Ras Tanura refinery, the rated capacity of which was later increased to 189,000 bbl. a day. Abqaiq (Buqayq) and Ghawar took their place among the world's largest producing fields, and in the mid-1960s production of crude oil reached a daily average of nearly 2,400,000 bbl. In 1950 Aramco's owners put into operation the Trans-Arabian Pipe Line (Tapline), which runs 753 mi. (1,212 km.) from Qaysumah (300 mi. [480 km.] NW of Dhahran) in Saudi Arabia across Jordan and Syria to its Mediterranean terminal at Sidon, Lebanon. The capacity of the line was later increased to 470,000 bbl. a day. Crude oil not refined at Ras Tanura or pumped through Tapline is shipped from Ras Tanura port or piped to Bahrain for refining.

In 1951 Aramco discovered the first offshore field in the Near East at Safaniyah just south of the Saudi Arabia–Kuwait neutral zone. Intensive exploration of the Rub' al Khali began in 1950. Operations in this forbidding desert have led to the development of new techniques, particularly in transportation. Water has been found in a number of deep wells drilled in the heart of the sands. Aramco's second offshore field at Munifah (Manifa) was brought into production in 1964. Other offshore fields are being developed at Al Qatif, Barri (Berri), and Abu Sa'fah.

In 1950 Saudi Arabia and Aramco made a new agreement for sharing profits on the basis of the so-called 50/50 principle, this being the first application of this principle in the Near East, where it was later widely adopted. The agreement gave Saudi Arabia a substantially larger return from the venture.

In 1949 Saudi Arabia granted a concession to the Pacific Western Oil Corporation (later the Getty Oil Company) for its interest in the Saudi Arabia–Kuwait neutral zone. Oil was discovered in the zone in 1953, and Saudi Arabia's share of the production reached about 90,000 bbl. a day. Another concession was secured in 1958 by the Arabian Oil Company Ltd. of Tokyo for Saudi Arabia's interest in the neutral zone offshore, with the provision that Saudi Arabia should receive 56% of this company's profits. The first well drilled in the neutral zone offshore in 1960 proved a successful strike.

Since 1966 Saudi Arabia has been surpassed in crude oil production only by the United States, Venezuela, and the Soviet Union. Saudi Arabia's proved reserves were estimated at about 75,000,-000,000 bbl., approximately 15% of the world total.

The oil fields also contain enormous quantities of natural gas: proved reserves in Saudi Arabia were estimated at more than 25,-000,000,000,000 cu.ft. Aramco has developed the capacity to reinject about 400,000,000 cu.ft. a day to conserve gas for future use and to reinforce the underground pressure needed for oil production. Some gas is liquefied for use locally and for sale abroad.

Mining.—In 1934 the Saudi Arabian Mining Syndicate obtained a concession. After examination of 55 ancient mining sites,

(Left) Worshipers at the Great Mosque in Medina; (top) Bedouin tent; (centre) veiled women in the marketplace at Hofuf; (right) date harvester in a palm grove near Medina

BY COURTESY OF (TOP, RIGHT) ARABIAN AMERICAN OIL CO.; PHOTOS, (LEFT) V. K. ANTHONY FROM PHOTO RESEARCHERS; (CENTRE) ARIZONA PHOTOGRAPHIC ASSOCIATES, INC.

work began at one, Mahd adh Dhahab in the Hejaz mountains. Gold and silver worth over $30,000,000 were extracted before the concession was relinquished in 1954 as no longer profitable. In that year the Saudi Arabian government, the United States Geological Survey, and Aramco undertook jointly an elaborate mapping program employing aerial photography to provide the basis for a more systematic survey of mineral resources. Large deposits of iron ore occur in northern Hejaz and Najd, and copper, phosphate, and a silver belt have been found. 'Asir has rock salt; salt and gypsum are exploited commercially and cement is manufactured.

Trade and Finance.—Under the oil economy, trade in the few wares which the country had to offer, other than oil and gas, declined. In 1958 the government formed an Economic Development Committee, and trade agreements were negotiated with various countries. Many imports, such as machinery, motor vehicles, and grain, became increasingly important as the economy grew more complex. The United States, West Germany, and Japan are now the main suppliers. In 1958 a severe check was placed on the import of luxuries in order to strengthen the national currency. In 1961 a Supreme Planning Board replaced the Economic Development Committee, and this board in turn gave way in 1965 to a new body named the Central Planning Organization.

The discovery of oil caused a drastic change in Saudi Arabia's finances. Freed from the old dependence on the pilgrim traffic to Mecca and Medina (formerly a main source of income), customs duties, and taxes on crops and livestock, which together provided a maximum of about 60,000,000 Saudi riyals annually, the government's income by the mid-1960s had risen to over 5,000,000,-000 riyals, most of which came directly or indirectly from the oil industry. Oil revenues permitted a favourable balance of trade.

In 1958 the government introduced its first realistic budget, and as a result of the improvement in the financial situation the riyal was stabilized in 1960 at 4.5 riyals to the U.S. dollar and established as the only legal tender. New riyal notes were issued to replace the "pilgrim receipts" then in circulation; the Saudi gold sovereign was withdrawn and exchanged at a fixed rate of riyals.

Transport and Communications.—Difficulties of terrain kept the various regions largely isolated, with the camel as the chief means of transportation, until mechanical transport was introduced in the 20th century. The Hejaz Railway, completed from Syria to Medina in 1908, was damaged during World War I and abandoned in 1924; the rebuilding of this was undertaken in the mid-1960s. After the unification of the kingdom, all areas were linked together by radio. Penetration of the interior by airplane became common after World War II; the principal cities were equipped with airports, and airlines brought the country closer to the rest of the world. In 1951 a railroad, 350 mi. long, was completed to Riyadh from the new port of Ad Dammam on the Persian Gulf just south of the oil-shipping port of Ras Tanura. The government also built a modern port on the Red Sea at Jidda, the gateway to Mecca. Asphalt roads run from Jidda to Mecca (45 mi.) and Medina (280 mi.), and other roads were being built for a network of first-class arteries, including a trans-peninsular highway. Even where asphalt is not laid, passable motor roads traverse the desert wherever necessary. A road paralleling Tapline leads to the neighbouring states of Jordan and Syria. *See also* references under "Saudi Arabia" in the Index.

(G. S. RE.; X.)

BIBLIOGRAPHY.—H. R. P. Dickson, *The Arab of the Desert* (1949); C. M. Doughty, *Travels in Arabia Deserta,* 2 vol. (1936); G. de Gaury, *Arabia Phoenix* (1946), *Arabian Journey* (1950); Carlo Guarmani, *Northern Najd* (1938); H. Ingrams, *Arabia and the Isles,* 3rd ed. (1966); Freya Stark, *The Southern Gates of Arabia* (1936), *A Winter in Arabia* (1940); W. Bertrand, *Les Wahhabites* (1926); Henrietta M. Holm, *The Agricultural Resources of the Arabian Peninsula,* U.S. Department of Agriculture (April 1955); George Kheirallah, *Arabia Reborn* (1952); N. A. Lateef, *Characteristics and Problems of Agriculture in Saudi Arabia,* FAO (October 1956); Roy Lebkicher, George Rentz, and Max Steineke, *The Arabia of Ibn Saud* (1952); Eric Macro, *Bibliography of the Arabian Peninsula* (1958); Alois Musil, *The Manners and Customs of the Rwala Bedouins* (1928); Roderic Owen, *The Golden Bubble: Arabian Gulf Documentary* (1957); Eldon Rutter, *The Holy Cities of Arabia,* 2 vol. (1928); Richard H. Sanger, *The Arabian Peninsula* (1954); H. St. J. B. Philby, *Sa'udi Arabia* (1955); K. S. Twitchell, *Saudi Arabia,* 3rd ed. (1958); S. H. Longrigg, *Oil in the Middle East,* 2nd ed. (1961); P. K. Hitti, *History of the Arabs,* 6th ed. (1956); articles "Djazirat al-'Arab" and "al-Buraymi" in *Encyclopaedia of Islam,* vol. i, 2nd ed. (1960); D. van der Meulen, *Wells of Ibn Sa'ud* (1957); George A. Lipsky, *Saudi Arabia* (1959); G. C. Butler, *Kings and Camels* (1960); G. Lenczowski, *Oil and State in the Middle East* (1960); *Aramco Handbook* (1960); J. B. Glubb, *War in the Desert* (1960); David Howarth, *The Desert King* (1964). Current history and statistics are summarized annually in *Britannica Book of the Year.*

SAUERKRAUT, a food product of characteristic flavour, obtained by full fermentation, chiefly lactic, of properly prepared and shredded cabbage in the presence of not less than 2% nor more than 3% salt. It contains, upon the completion of fermentation, not less than 1.5% and usually not more than 2% lactic acid. The characteristic flavour and the lactic acid are produced by a sequence of bacteria which find ideal conditions for growth in the presence of the added salt and the nutrients which it withdraws from the shredded cabbage. Many refer to sauerkraut simply as "kraut." The word "sauerkraut" comes from the German *sauer,* "acid" and *kraut,* "cabbage." Sauerkraut is used as a delicious relish when served raw and as a vegetable when cooked. It is rich in vitamin C (ascorbic acid) and is excellent to add bulk without corresponding fattening properties. The juice is canned and used as an appetizer.

(F. W. Fn.)

SAUK or SAC, an Algonkian-speaking Indian tribe closely related to the Fox and Kickapoo Indians, once forming with these and the Shawnee a single tribe probably living in the Ohio Valley. When first encountered by the French in 1667 they had been driven westward by the Iroquois to the region of Green Bay, Wis. Later they settled along the Mississippi River between Rock Island, Ill., and St. Louis, Mo., and formed a close alliance with the Fox. In 1804 the U.S. commander at St. Louis persuaded some of their minor chiefs to cede most of the tribal lands to the United States and although the Sauk protested that this treaty was illegal they were unable to prevent its enforcement. When a group led by Black Hawk (q.v.) refused to leave Illinois it was attacked by the state militia, overtaken while trying to escape across the Mississippi, and massacred. After the Black Hawk War the Sauk were forced to relinquish more territory; later they were moved to Kansas and eventually were settled in Oklahoma.

Sauk culture was of the Prairie type. In summer the tribe lived in bark-house villages along bluffs near river bottoms where women raised corn and other crops. After the harvest the village broke up into family groups which erected winter houses of poles covered with reed mats; in spring the tribe gathered on the Iowa prairies to hunt buffalo. Matrilocal residence was the rule in summer, when kinswomen cooperated in tending crops, but winter and spring brought a shift to patrilocal residence. The kinship system was of Omaha type, and the social organization included patrilineal clans that were crosscut by a nonhereditary dual division with important military and ritual functions. Regulating the inheritance of personal names, the clans also controlled religious ceremonies through ownership of sacred packs on which ritual was based. Some ceremonies, however, were held by secret societies. The Sauk were governed by a tribal council and hereditary chiefs; when war broke out these were temporarily replaced by war chiefs selected for their military ability. Early estimates of their population ranged from 1,500 to 3,000. In the 1960s there were about 1,000 Sauk. *See also* ALGONKIAN TRIBES; CHIEF; FOX INDIANS.

See Alanson Skinner, "Observations on the Ethnography of the Sauk Indians," *Bulletin* of the Public Museum of the City of Milwaukee, v (1923–25); Charles Callender, *Central Algonkian Social Organization*, Anthropological Publications of the Public Museum of the City of Milwaukee (1961).   (CH. C.)

SAUL, son of Kish, a Benjamite, became the first king of Israel (reigned *c.* 1020–1000 B.C.) when promonarchist propaganda (*cf.* Judg. 17:6; 18:1; 19:1; 21:25) prevailed over the old theocratic ideal that Yahweh alone must be king (8:23). Samuel's acquiescence was probably forced by the demoralizing defeat of the Hebrews at Aphek (I Sam. 4), which demonstrated the ineffectiveness of the Israelite amphictyony (*i.e.,* federation or league) against the unified, better-armed Philistines. The inconsistency in Samuel's attitude toward unification under a king is to be explained in part by the method of composition of the author of the books of Samuel. He incorporated the traditions available without attempting to harmonize varying details (*see* SAMUEL, BOOKS OF). Because the interest of the sources utilized in I Sam. 9–31 is focused on Samuel and David rather than on Saul, less than due credit may have been given to the first king. Moreover, the author's interpretation of Samuel's judgment on the monarchy (8:6–18; 10:17–24) anticipates the sad experience which both the northern and the southern Hebrew states had with their kings. Once convinced that the kingship was Yahweh's will, Samuel took the initiative; he anointed Saul secretly (according to the "royalist" tradition, 9:1–10:16), before presenting him to the people at Mizpah, where the sacred lot also singled out the son of Kish (10:17–27).

Saul's prowess was soon proved. When the Transjordanian Ammonites threatened to wipe out the Israelites of Jabesh-gilead (11), "the spirit of God came mightily upon Saul," as upon the charismatic heroes of the period of Judges; he rallied the tribes and promptly crushed the enemy. Saul's kingship was, in fact, transitional between the saviour-judge who was looked upon as a special channel of divine power, and the royal office developed by David and Solomon. Excavations at Gibeah (Tell el-Ful, about 3 mi. N of Jerusalem) unearthed a 170- by 115-ft. stone structure, the simple, rough palace fortress of Saul, which attests the warrior who had to defend his people rather than the oriental poten-

tate who lived off them. Although he had a small permanent army, he did not levy taxes or introduce conscription; he depended on gifts and volunteers.

Saul's real challenge was the Philistines. By the victory of Michmash (13–14) he cleared Israelite territory of enemy garrisons. More important, he ended the Philistines' monopoly of iron (13:19–22) which had kept Israel in an inferior position. The increase in population, improvement in building techniques, and higher standard of living for which archaeology finds evidence in this period are doubtless due to the strength, cohesion, and enthusiasm which Saul gave the Hebrew nation.

His career, unfortunately, was blighted by his preoccupation with the growing influence of the politically more astute David and by his break with Samuel. The biblical authors depict this break as the result of conflict between the two powers, civil and religious, due to a sharp divergence between the king's and the prophet's conceptions of the theocratic character of the kingdom. According to 13:8 ff., Saul waited the week appointed for Samuel's arrival, and even then, it was only after his soldiers began to desert that he offered the sacrifices preliminary to battle. Was it not normal for kings to be chief priests? His failure to follow the current interpretation of the *herem* ("ban") after the defeat of the Amalekites (15) is a disobedience easier to pinpoint, even if his conduct strikes a modern reader as more sensible and humane than Samuel's, who insisted upon total destruction of captives and cattle. Possibly in retaliation for Samuel's prophetic word that Yahweh had repudiated him (13:13–14; 15:23–26), Saul reinstated the priestly family of Eli, appointing Eli's great-grandson, Ahimelech, priest at the royal sanctuary of Nob (21:1; 22:11 ff.; *cf.* 14:3, where Ahijah is probably an alternative name for Ahimelech). Fits of extreme melancholy seized the King, for "the Spirit of the Lord departed from Saul, and an evil spirit from the Lord tormented him" (16:14). Gradually he suspected everyone of plotting against him (20:30; 22:7 ff.). His brutal massacre of Ahimelech's family, suspected of being in league with David, gives an insight into his view of church-state relations that must be remembered when his conflict with Samuel is appraised.

Saul's mental derangement no doubt explains in part the military debacle that cost him his life and almost undid his earlier accomplishments. When Saul realized how desperate his situation was, he turned for help to the one man whom, more than anyone else, he might have blamed for his unhappiness. But Samuel was dead. The King must speak to him nevertheless; he insisted upon the services of a witch, or medium, at Endor, but the subsequent encounter with the ghost of Samuel—whatever be our judgment of the identity of the "ghost"—only confirmed his worst fears (28). The incident dramatically preluded the defeat at Gilboa, in which three of Saul's sons were slain, and the King himself, grievously wounded, took his own life (31). The elegy preserved from the Book of Jashar in II Sam. 1:19–27, pays eloquent tribute to his personal bravery and magnetic leadership. *See also* DAVID; SAMUEL.   (E. F. SI.)

SAULT SAINTE MARIE, a city in Ontario, Can., and a port of entry, is on the north bank of St. Marys River, the outlet from Lake Superior into Lake Huron, opposite the U.S. city of the same name. Pop. (1961) 43,088. Known to the French explorers from the time of Étienne Brulé, it was named Sault de Gaston early in the 17th century. The name was changed to Sault Ste. Marie ("Rapids of Saint Mary") in 1669 when a permanent mission was established by the French. The North West company established a trading post in 1783 and built a small lock to handle canoes and small boats for trading purposes, this being completed in 1797–98. The lock was destroyed by U.S. troops in the War of 1812 and rebuilt as a historical site late in the 19th century.

The growth of Sault Ste. Marie has been intimately associated with the rapids, and the locks and canal around them. The present Canadian lock was built for military purposes in the late 19th century after use of U.S. locks was denied to Canadian troops sent to suppress the Riel rebellion of 1870. It was later widened to its present size: 16.8 ft. deep, 59 ft. wide and 900 ft. long. The canal itself is 1.38 mi. long.

In the second half of the 20th century the locks and canal

handled about 3,000,000 tons of shipping annually, considerably less than the U.S. system paralleling it. Cheap transportation led to the development of heavy industry. In the 1960s the Algoma steel plant, for example, had an annual capacity of more than 1,000,000 tons. Of the gainfully employed inhabitants of the city, more than half were engaged in manufacturing, and of those four-fifths were in iron and steel.

In addition, the "Soo" is a retail and wholesale centre and a notable tourist headquarters.   (F. A. Ck.)

SAULT SAINTE MARIE, a city of Michigan, U.S., the seat of Chippewa County and a port of entry, is located at the northeast end of the upper peninsula of Michigan on the south shore of the St. Marys River, the connecting waterway between Lake Superior and the lower Great Lakes. A canal and four parallel locks provide a navigable channel for shipping past the rapids which mark a 20-ft. drop in elevation. It is connected with Sault Sainte Marie, Ont., by a vehicular and a railroad bridge. It is a dairy, hay, and small grain area and is the oldest settlement in Michigan. From 1917 it has had a commission-manager form of government. Its strategic location, both economically and geographically, makes the Sault, or "Soo," a centre of government activity: the St. Mary's Falls Canal (popularly called Soo Locks) is operated and maintained by the U.S. Army Corps of Engineers; the U.S. Air Force maintains the Kincheloe Air Force Base 18 mi. S of the Sault and a radar base at the city limits; customs and immigration offices are at Sault Ste. Marie; and the U.S. Coast Guard has a base from which it maintains and controls navigation in the area. From 1948 the Sault branch of Michigan College of Mining and Technology has occupied buildings formerly used by historic Fort Brady, built in 1822 shortly after the United States took possession of the area. It is the centre of a summer and winter resort area. The manufacture of carbide and wood products provide the main industry.

The flags of three nations have flown at Sault Ste. Marie since the first white man, explorer Étienne Brulé, visited the area some time between 1615 and 1622. Jesuit missionaries are credited with naming the rapids and river Ste. Marie and are said to have introduced Christianity there. The site was a favoured residence and stopping place for Ojibwa Indians because of the great catches of whitefish that could be taken from the rapids. In 1668 Father Jacques Marquette founded a mission at Sault Ste. Marie and thereby established the first permanent white settlement in Michigan. The French took official possession of the interior of North America in a ceremony at the Sault in 1671. British occupation began in 1762. By the Treaty of Paris (1783) Great Britain ceded land east of the Mississippi to the United States; however, it was not until 1820 that the U.S. flag was raised at the Sault by Lewis Cass, governor of Michigan territory. Writings by Henry Rowe Schoolcraft (q.v.), first Indian agent in Sault Ste. Marie, provided source material for Longfellow's poem *Song of Hiawatha*.

Sault Ste. Marie was incorporated as a village in 1879 and as a city in 1887. The original canal and state lock was opened in 1855.

The navigation season is limited to eight months because of severe winter conditions. Handling this lake traffic are the Poe, Davis, Sabin and MacArthur locks on the Michigan side of the St. Mary's River, and one lock on the Canadian shore. Construction of a new lock, 1,000 ft. long, on the site of the Poe Lock was begun in 1961 as a part of the St. Lawrence Seaway program of development on the Great Lakes. For comparative population figures *see* table in MICHIGAN: *Population*.   (G. A. Os.)

SAUMAREZ, JAMES SAUMAREZ, BARON DE (1757–1836), English admiral who fought in many naval battles during the French Revolutionary and Napoleonic wars, was born at St. Peter Port, Guernsey, on March 11, 1757. Entering the navy as a midshipman at the age of 13, he was promoted to lieutenant for his bravery at the attack on Charleston (June 1776) during the War of the American Revolution and commander for his services against the Dutch off the Dogger Bank (Aug. 5, 1781). In command of the "Russell" (74 guns) he contributed to Adm. George Rodney's victory over the French fleet under the comte de Grasse at the Battle of the Saints, off Dominica (April 12, 1782). Soon

after the outbreak of the war with revolutionary France, he captured (Oct. 20, 1793) "La Réunion," a large French frigate, and was knighted in November 1793. He took part in Adm. Lord Bridport's action against the French fleet near Lorient (June 22, 1795), distinguished himself in the battle off Cape St. Vincent (Feb. 14, 1797), and was present at the blockade of Cadiz (February 1797–April 1798). At the Battle of the Nile (Aug. 1, 1798) he was Nelson's second-in-command. He received the command of the "Caesar" (84 guns) in February 1799 and during the winters of 1799 and 1800 kept watch on the French fleet off Brest. On July 12, 1801, he routed a superior combined force of French and Spanish ships at Algeciras. He commanded the Baltic Fleet with great distinction from 1809 to 1814 when he was promoted to admiral. Raised to the peerage in 1831, he died in Guernsey on Oct. 9, 1836.

See Sir John Ross, *Memoirs . . . of . . . Saumarez*, 2 vol. (1838); O. Warner, *The Sea and the Sword* (1965).   (O. M. W. W.)

SAUMUR, a town of western France, and centre of an *arrondissement* in the *département* of Maine-et-Loire, lies on the Loire River, 41 mi. (66 km.) WSW of Tours by road or rail. Pop. (1962) 20,466. Situated between the Loire and its left-bank tributary, the Thouet, above their confluence, the town stands on rising ground dominated by the château of the dukes of Anjou. It also occupies the Île Millochau in the Loire, to whose right bank (site of the railway station) it has more recently spread. The main Rouen-Bordeaux road crosses it in a straight line on the axis of the two bridges on the Loire and the bridge on the Thouet. The château was reconstructed in the late 14th century by Louis I, duke of Anjou, on the site of earlier strongholds. The surrounding ramparts were built in the late 16th century by the governor Philippe de Mornay (q.v.), who made Saumur the centre of French Protestantism and founded there a Protestant academy (closed at the revocation of the Edict of Nantes in 1685). The château now houses a rich museum of decorative arts, and the probably unique Musée du Cheval (horse museum). Other prominent buildings on the left bank of the Loire are the 19th-century theatre, the 16th-century town hall, the 12th-century Church of Saint-Pierre (17th-century facade), and the 17th-century Church of Notre-Dame des Ardilliers, adjacent to which is the almshouse (formerly the convent of the 17th-century Oratory), partly built into the rock. The Romanesque and Gothic Church of Notre-Dame de Nantilly contains a notable collection of 15th–17th century tapestries. The horticultural gardens, on the site of a former monastery, include a museum of viticulture. The Cavalry School, built in 1768, has become the practical training school for the armoured forces, but French equestrian traditions are maintained by its famous "Black Cadre." On the island the 15th-century "House of the Queen of Sicily" holds memories of Yolande of Aragon, mother of King René.

Saumur is on the roads from Orléans to Nantes and from Le Mans to Niort, and is connected by rail via Montreuil-Bellay with Poitiers and Niort. It is famous for its dry white, red, and rosé wines, as well as its sparkling wines made by the Champagne method. Since the 17th century it has produced religious articles (medallions and rosaries); carnival masks and metal closures for wine and liqueur bottles are also made, and locally produced spring fruit and vegetables are preserved. Mushrooms are cultivated in old tufa workings.

There are prehistoric caves along the Loire and the Thouet near Saumur, and at Bagneux, a southwestern suburb, is one of the largest known dolmens. In the 9th century Saumur's stronghold was a refuge for the surrounding district (whence perhaps its name, from *Salvus Murus*). Taken by Fulk Nerra, count of Anjou, in 1025, it finally passed to the French crown on the death of René (1480). After the revocation of the Edict of Nantes its population was halved. In 1793 it was occupied by the Vendéans. During World War II it was heavily damaged when the Cavalry School cadets withstood the German advance for three days in June 1940.   (M. Ja.)

SAUROPTERYGIAN, any of the extinct reptiles of the order Sauropterygia, remarkably well-adapted to an aquatic life, and including the nothosaurs, plesiosaurs, and often placodonts.

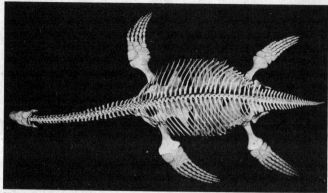

BY COURTESY OF THE AMERICAN MUSEUM OF NATURAL HISTORY

SKELETON OF A PLESIOSAUR, VIEWED FROM ABOVE

The largest of these Mesozoic creatures were certain plesiosaurs that attained a length of 40 ft. The characteristics of the Sauropterygia are associated with a mode of swimming accomplished by "rowing" motions of powerful limbs, contrasting with the more fishlike mode of progression in ichthyosaurs and mosasaurs.

Most primitive of sauropterygians are the Triassic nothosaurs. In these small reptiles the body was long and slender; the limbs were basically comparable to those in normal terrestrial reptiles, suggesting some degree of ability to progress on land. Best known from the marine Middle Triassic of Europe, nothosaurs are structurally antecedent to plesiosaurs.

Plesiosaurs appear at the end of the Triassic, and remain prominent until the Late Cretaceous; specimens are most common in the Jurassic strata of England and Germany and the Upper Cretaceous of the United States. The tail was short; the trunk broad and stoutly built, with the ventral parts of shoulder and pelvic girdles greatly expanded for the attachment of powerful limb muscles. The limbs were transformed into compactly built oarlike paddles; the number of toe-joints was greatly increased. The long jaws were armed with pointed teeth appropriate for seizing fish.

Two main trends are discernible in plesiosaur evolution. In one line, of which *Pliosaurus* of the Jurassic is typical, the neck was short but the skull large and long; a giant of the group was *Kronosaurus* of the Lower Cretaceous of Australia, with a skull some nine feet long. In a second line of plesiosaurs the head was small but the neck greatly elongated; in *Elasmosaurus* of the Upper Cretaceous the neck had as many as 76 vertebrae and constituted nearly two-thirds of the animal's entire length.

Often considered as a suborder of the Sauropterygia are the placodonts of the Middle Triassic. The body was structurally similar to that of nothosaurs but more compactly built. In *Placodus* and other typical forms there were broad flat tooth plates for crushing the mollusks on which they fed. Many placodonts developed dermal armour; *Henodus* had a shell comparable to that of a turtle. *See* also PALEONTOLOGY.   (A. S. RR.)

SAUSAGE AND READY-PREPARED MEATS.

Sausages and ready-prepared meats are many and various and are usually associated in their production. Their chief ingredient is comminuted (very finely chopped) or minced meat. With the exception of fresh sausages, they undergo some form of curing or preserving; hence a principal feature is their keeping quality, although this is variable. Fresh sausages should be eaten within a few days.

SAUSAGE

Sausage (Lat. *salsus*, "salted," hence preserved) is one of the oldest forms of processed food. Meat or mixtures of various meats, blood, offal, and other ingredients stuffed into gut or other suitable materials were known in remote antiquity. They are alluded to in Homer's *Odyssey* and in later Greek literature. The ancient Romans prepared one type from fresh pork and white pine nuts, chopped finely with cumin seed, bay leaves, and black pepper.

In the Middle Ages sausage-making became a local culinary art,

and many types of sausage derive their names from the places where they were made; *e.g.*, frankfurter (Frankfurt am Main, Ger.), bologna (Bologna, It.), romano (Rome), genoa salami (Genoa, It.), berliner (Berlin), goteborg (Göteborg, Swed.), lyons (Lyons, Fr.), d'arles (Arles, Fr.), cracow (Cracow, Pol.).

Sausage basically is very finely chopped meat, although somewhat similar preparations have been produced from fish and even vegetables. Preparation consists of the mincing, cutting, or pulverizing of lean meat, fat, and in certain cases edible offal, of the admixture of spices, curing salts, or other ingredients, and then of the filling of the mixture into a casing. In some countries, Great Britain for example, appreciable quantities of cereal binder (such as bread, rusk, ground rice, cornflour [cornstarch], and farina) may be incorporated with the comminuted meat, while in other countries the inclusion of such binders is prohibited (see *Commercial Production* below).

Casings may be natural or synthetic. Natural casings are pig, sheep, or ox gut, the bladder, and the lining of the esophagus (weasand); and a development is a casing prepared from reconstituted collagen, which can be produced to a standard dimension. In the United States the use of synthetic casings far exceeds that of natural casings. In some districts sausages are filled into fabric bags treated with paraffin wax to restrict the loss of moisture.

After filling, sausages may be smoked, cooked, or air-dried, or treated with a combination of these processes, to make them keep.

Types of Sausage.—Fresh sausages are made from fresh meat, chiefly pork and beef, sometimes with the addition of veal or mutton. The stock seasoning used includes salt, white pepper, nutmeg, mustard, mace, ginger, cayenne, cloves, pimento, and coriander. The sausages are fried, grilled, or in some cases heated in water, before consumption. The following are representative examples of sausage: beef; pork; chipolata (a small sausage, beef or pork); skinless (beef or pork); Bockwurst (German, veal and pork); Bratwurst (German, pork and veal); tomato pork; Swedish flask korv (pork and potato); thuringer (pork, veal, and sometimes beef).

Cooked sausages may consist of fresh uncured meat or cured meats and the various seasonings. A frankfurter, for example, may consist of pork, bull meat, ox cheek, veal, cooked tripe, cereal, and ice water, with white pepper, ginger, coriander, and mace as seasoning. They are cooked after being filled into casings, and some types may be smoked. Prepared ready for consumption, they usually need no further cooking, although in a few cases they may be heated before consumption. Such sausages include bologna; frankfurter and Vienna ("hot dogs"); polonies; blood sausage; tongue and blood; liver; pork luncheon; beef luncheon; hog puddings; ham and tongue; saveloys; Scotch white puddings; haggis. (Haggis has been included as a cooked sausage since it is filled into a casing. It is a pudding made from the heart, lungs, and liver of a sheep or other animal, finely minced with suet and oatmeal, seasoned with salt, pepper, onion, etc., and boiled in the animal's everted stomach. Though regarded since the mid-18th century as a distinctively Scottish dish, it was long popular in England. Formerly considered a rustic dish, it is today served with some ceremony on Scottish national anniversaries.)

Dry sausages are made by comminuting fresh meat and other ingredients, including a curing agent (basically salt and saltpetre with, in some cases, sugar) and allowing the meat to cure for a short period before being filled into casings. With some types the curing may take place in the casings. The sausage may then be smoked or cooked in the smokehouse at a high temperature before drying in air (cooked salami, cervelat, kosher salami), or may be dried without smoking. The unsmoked dried sausages include Italian, Hungarian, and German salamis and a variety of the lesser-known sausages of European origin. Garlic is sometimes an ingredient of dry sausages. The following are representative examples of these types of sausage: cappicola (though considered a sausage it consists of seasoned pork meat, unchopped, stuffed into beef bungs); cervelat; chorizos; d'arles; goteborg; holsteiner; landjaeger; lyons; mortadella (filled into beef bladders); pepperoni; and many varieties of salami.

Commercial Production.—In developed countries sausages

are now produced by factories distributing branded goods rather than by the local butcher. This has resulted in much standardization and the disappearance of some regional varieties of sausage.

A development in the United States and to a lesser degree in Great Britain has been the production of "skinless" sausages; in the U.S. their consumption soon exceeded that of the traditional cased forms. The ingredients are first filled into cellulose casings, which are tied off automatically into links. Then the sausages are immersed in hot and afterward iced water, so that a small amount of soluble protein forms a thin film immediately below the cellulose casing. On removal of the casing this layer surrounding each individual prevents the sausages from sticking together when subsequently wrapped in a transparent film in packs of standard weight. The light heating also provides a relatively firm outer layer, which obviates damage during packing.

Legal standards for sausage vary in different countries. Thus it is prohibited in Germany to use any binding material of a cereal or other nature. In the United States, the addition of up to 3.5% of cereal, starch, or dried milk is permitted if declared. The use of soya flour is prohibited, owing to the difficulty of differentiating between protein of meat origin and that from soya. In Britain sausages may contain considerable amounts of cereal binder, and during World War II the statutory minimum quantities were 65% meat in fresh pork sausages and 50% meat in fresh beef sausages. Although wartime regulations were rescinded in 1953, many courts tend to uphold prosecutions for adulteration on the basis of these figures. Regulations differ confusingly between countries concerning the use of artificial colouring agents, added preservatives, and chemical emulsifying substances, such as the extensively used phosphate derivatives. In Great Britain, certain colours from a permitted list may be used; sulfur dioxide may be added as a preservative in quantities not exceeding 450 parts per 1,000,000, subject to appropriate labeling; and the use of phosphates is not legally restricted.

Sausage Consumption.—In the United States, the main demand is for frankfurters and Vienna-type sausages (sold in huge quantities as "hot dogs"), followed by the bologna type of sausage.

Of the European countries, Italy probably produces the greatest bulk of sausages; the largest producing area is that surrounding Bologna, though many varieties are produced in and around Florence. Germany makes the greatest variety and production is widespread, notably in Frankfurt and Hamburg. In Spain greatest production is in Catalonia, Vich making sausages prepared exclusively from lean pork and a small quantity of bacon. Large quantities of sausage are prepared and consumed in Poland and Hungary, and Switzerland and the Scandinavian countries have their distinctive types. The warmer countries bordering the Mediterranean tend to use a heavier cure and more spices for their dry sausages than those of northern Europe, where preservation is less difficult.

In Great Britain fresh pork and fresh beef sausages form the vast majority of the trade, although there are local preferences. In Scotland beef sausages tend to predominate in terms of volume, but not so in England. Cumberland and Lincoln prefer a coarse-cut fresh sausage, while in the midlands and the south the demand is for a fine texture. Interest in the continental type of dry sausage has been increasing.

READY-PREPARED MEATS

Ham.—Canned ham forms a major item among ready-prepared meats. Before about 1930, practically all the U.S. processers precooked cured hams before canning, while in Europe the only cooking that the ham received was during heat-processing within the sealed can. The latter procedure has been adopted universally. To retain juiciness and palatability, the processing temperature is relatively low, the internal temperature seldom exceeding 160° F (71° C). As this does not protect the canned ham against all conditions of storage, it should be stored under refrigeration. For export to tropical countries higher processing temperatures are employed.

Luncheon Meat.—This is a popular canned product, usually consisting of chopped pork, sometimes with the addition of small amounts of chopped beef. The chopped meat is mixed with salt, nitrate, nitrite, and sugar, and a small quantity of water is added to facilitate distribution of the cure and mixing. The spicing employed is generally light, as the cured pork flavour should predominate. In those countries where regulations permit, small quantities of cereal, dried milk, or protein additives may be included. The mixing of the chopped meats is usually carried out under vacuum in order to exclude air, which might otherwise be trapped in the product. The smaller-sized domestic cans, which are subjected to shelf display at atmospheric temperatures, are heated to achieve a commercial sterility. The larger cans (3 to 6 lb., 1.36 to 2.72 kg.) are not heat-processed to the same degree and should therefore be stored under refrigeration.

Corned Beef.—The production of corned beef is a specialized operation, generally restricted to the larger meat plants and frequently prepared in combination with the manufacture of meat extracts. Corned-beef hash is popular in the United States and consists of chopped corned beef, diced potatoes, onions, and flavouring materials. The ingredients are heated in a cooking kettle prior to filling, hot, into the cans. Thermal exhaust of the air usually precedes the sealing of the can (see CANNING, COMMERCIAL). Most meat products lend themselves to canning and the more popular include ox, pig, and sheep's tongues, stews, sausages, particularly frankfurters, pork and beans, and even meat pies. Chile Con Carne consists of a meat mold prepared from coarsely cut beef and a high percentage of beef suet; the essential flavouring includes chili pepper, garlic, and onion. Gravy is mixed with cereal, soya bean flour, or milk to obtain the correct texture.

Jellied products contain parts of the carcass possessing a high proportion of connective tissues (collagen), such as the rind and head of hogs and calves' feet. Lean meat and fat may be added, a typical example being English brawn, which was traditionally prepared from a brawner. The U.S. souse and headcheese are somewhat similar products, one variety of the latter using blood, in which the meat is cooked, and consequently termed blood headcheese. Scrapple, of which there are many forms, incorporates about 10% of cereal, usually corn meal and possibly rye flour or soya flour.

Hamburger.—As its name implies, this product originated in Hamburg, but it now enjoys a huge market in the United States and elsewhere; almost one-third of the total beef consumption in Australia is sold in this form. Traditionally, hamburger should be prepared from beef, with or without added fat, chopped to a medium-coarse consistency, no moisture, spices, or cereal being added. In many countries the inclusion of moisture, cereals, flavouring, and in some cases onion, is common practice. In the United States hamburger has been popularized as an all-beef product, and pork has been considered an inappropriate ingredient partly because, as hamburger may be given only a superficial heating prior to consumption, it is potentially dangerous mixed with pork.

Meat loaves consist basically of finely comminuted meats with the addition of cereal or milk powder, a small quantity of water, and spices. The chopped meat is packed into pans and baked in a moderate oven, although some types may be cooked in water. The galantine, German *rouladen*, and continental mosaics are also cooked in water or water vapour, the mosaics being prepared to exhibit elaborate patterns on cutting.

Pâtés.—In Europe various types of pâté are produced, generally of pigs' or calves' liver and pig meat containing a high proportion of fat, reduced to a smooth paste and suitably seasoned. In France, Belgium, Switzerland, and the Netherlands, veal is often used to provide a more subtle flavour. Probably the most famous type is *pâté de foie gras* consisting of goose liver. The geese are specially fed for a period of six weeks on a diet of maize and poppy oil which induces fatty infiltration of the liver. On killing at the end of this period the liver may weigh 2 lb. (.9 kg.), instead of the normal weight of about 4 oz. (113.4 g.). Strasbourg, Fr., is a noted area for the production of this type of pâté.

Meat and Paste Products.—Meat pies consist of a meat or in some cases a meat and vegetable filling enclosed in a paste casing, usually with a paste top. They may vary in size from about 3 oz. to the large 6-lb. (2.72-kg.) oblong pie, often containing a layer of hard-boiled eggs. Their food value lies in the presence of protein, fat, and carbohydrate. Meat pie production lends itself to mechanization, the baking being carried out in automatically controlled, traveling-type ovens, and mass production has largely replaced the traditional "hand-raised" pie.

Similar products are sausage rolls and Cornish pasties, the latter consisting of meat, potatoes, and other vegetables enfolded in a layer of paste before cooking; stuffed boar's head; the Italian deboned and stuffed pigs' feet; bath chaps (the lower jaw of the pig, cured, smoked, and cooked); and haslet (chopped pork meat, covered with the caul—omentum fat—of the pig, and then baked).

BIBLIOGRAPHY.—Frank Gerrard, *Sausage and Small Goods Production,* 4th ed. (1959); A. R. Miller, *Meat Hygiene,* 2nd ed. (1958); "Sausage and Meat Specialities," part 3 of *The Packers Encyclopaedia* (1938); *Sausage and Ready-to-Serve Meats,* Committee on Recording, Institute of American Meat Packers (1938); *Sausage Manual and Textbook,* Oppenheimer Casing Co. (1934); *Hellers Secrets of Meat Curing and Sausage Making,* 8th ed. (1929).   (F. GE.)

SAUSSURE, FERDINAND DE (1857–1913), Swiss linguist, one of the most influential of modern times, who attained his eminent position not through published works but through the school of linguistics he founded and the excellence of his disciples, was born on Nov. 26, 1857, at Geneva, the scion of a family of scientists and writers. He studied at the universities of Geneva, Leipzig, and Berlin, and obtained a doctorate at Leipzig in 1880. From 1881 to 1891 he was instructor at the École des Hautes Études in Paris; from 1901 to 1913 he was professor of Indo-European linguistics and Sanskrit and from 1907 to 1913 also professor of general linguistics at the University of Geneva.

The only book from Saussure's pen was written when he was 21 years old: *Mémoire sur le système primitif des voyelles dans les langues indo-européennes* (1878). But his most important work, *Cours de linguistique générale* (2nd ed., 1922), is a collection of lectures published posthumously by his students. Saussure's principal tenet was that language is, and must be dealt with as, a social phenomenon, a structured system of signs that can be viewed descriptively (synchronically) and historically (diachronically). The systematic structure (*langue*) is realized and becomes manifest in actual speech events (*parole*)—a dichotomy that has proved extremely useful and fruitful. His own Geneva school, the French and the Prague schools of linguistics, and particularly the structuralists everywhere, owe much to Saussure. He died on Feb. 22, 1913, at Geneva.

See also LINGUISTICS: *The History of Linguistics: The Age of Structuralism.*   (E. PM.)

SAUSSURE, HORACE BÉNÉDICT DE (1740–1799), Swiss physicist, early Alpine explorer, first-known experimental petrologist, and developer of what was probably the first electrometer, was born at Geneva on Feb. 17, 1740. From 1762 to 1786 he taught at the Academy of Geneva. His early devotion to botanical studies led him to undertake numerous journeys in the Alps, and from 1773 onward he devoted much of his time to the study of that area. An interest in meteorology led him to develop the hair hygrometer, an instrument for measuring atmospheric humidity. Descriptions of seven of his Alpine journeys were published in *Voyages dans les Alpes* (1779–96). De Saussure was elected a fellow of the Royal Society and in 1772 founded at Geneva the Society for the Advancement of the Arts. He died in Geneva on Jan. 22, 1799.

See also ELECTRICITY, ATMOSPHERIC: *History.*

See W. Noyce, *Scholar Mountaineers* (1950).

SAUVEUR, ALBERT (1863–1939), U.S. metallurgist and teacher, who prior to 1900 developed methods of improving the quality of steel through studies of the crystal structure of metals. He pioneered the technique of photomicrographs in the late 1800s to further his studies of metal microstructures. Sauveur's work in the heat treatment of metal is still a scientific landmark. Born in Louvain, Belg., June 21, 1863, of French parentage, Sauveur received his early education in Europe, and graduated from the Massachusetts Institute of Technology, Cambridge, in 1889. After a period of work as a chemist and metallurgist, he left

industry in 1899 for Harvard university as an instructor. In 1905 he became a professor of metallurgy, and in 1924 he was appointed the Gordon McKay professor of mining and metallurgy at the university. From 1898 to 1903 Sauveur was editor of *Metallographist,* and in the period 1903–06 he served as editor of *Iron and Steel Magazine.* He received many medals and honorary degrees from U.S. and European societies and universities. The Legion of Honour of France and the French Academy both elected him an officer. A national award established in 1934 by the American Society for Metals bears his name. Sauveur served the French and U.S. governments in World War I as a metals consultant, and in 1925 he was a U.S. delegate to the Pan-American Scientific Congress in Lima, Peru. He died in Boston, Mass., Jan. 26, 1939.   (R. T. B.)

SAVA (SABAS), **SAINT** (c. 1174–1236), first archbishop of the independent Serbian Church, was the third and youngest son of Stephen Nemanya, the Grand Zhupan of Serbia. According to biographers, Rastko (his name in the world) left his father's court at the age of 18 and went secretly to Mt. Athos, where, resisting all Stephen's importunities, he became the monk Sava. In 1196 his father abdicated and himself embraced the religious life as the monk Simeon, joining his son two years later on Mt. Athos. Father and son together founded the monastery of Chilandari (Khilandar), where Sava lived while he remained on the holy mountain and which became the great centre of Serbian theological learning. In 1208 at the request of his brother Stephen the First Crowned, Sava brought the remains of their father back to Serbia, where they were interred at Studenitsa, of which Sava then became archimandrite.

As a statesman Sava had to cope with the quarrels of his elder brothers, with the Bogomil heresy (*see* BOGOMILS), and with the low level of culture in Serbia at that time. He did much to strengthen political and ecclesiastical unity. He visited the emperor and the patriarch of Constantinople who, after the Fourth Crusade (1204), were in exile at Nicaea, and by their appointment returned to Serbia in 1219 as the first archbishop of an independent Serbian church (*see* SERBIAN ORTHODOX CHURCH). His policy ensured the permanent adherence of the Serbian Church to Constantinople instead of Rome. He established eight bishoprics which he filled with men whom he had trained at Chilandari. He worked for the spread of education, and his account of his father's last years was the first original (not translated) piece of Serbian literature. Before his second pilgrimage to Palestine (1233) he retired from the Serbian archbishopric, nominating Arsenius as his successor. On the way back he died at Trnovo (Turnovo, in modern Bulgaria) in 1236. His feast day is Jan. 14.

See E. E. Golubinsky, *Kratkiy ocherk istorii pravoslavnykh tserkvey bolgarskoy, serbskoy i rumynskoy* (1871); J. Matl, "Der heilige Sava als Begründer der serbischen Nationalkirche," *Kyrios,* 2: 23–37 (1937).   (RE. M. F.)

SAVA (SAVE), a river of Yugoslavia and an affluent of the Danube. It rises in the Triglav group of the Julian Alps from two sources, the Sava Bohinjka and the Sava Dolinka, which join at Radovljica, at a height of 1,350 ft. (411 m.) above sea level. It then flows eastward through Slovenia, just south of Ljubljana, through Croatia touching Zagreb and, passing through part of Bosnia, joins the Danube at Belgrade. The most important tributaries of the Sava are the Kupa, Una, Vrbas, Bosna, Drina, and Kolubara. The longest river entirely in Yugoslavia, the Sava has a length of 584 mi. (940 km.), the area of its basin being 37,000 sq.mi. (95,800 sq.km.). It is navigable for small river steamers from Sisak to its mouth, a distance of 362 mi.   (V. DE.)

SAVAGE, RICHARD (c. 1697–1743), English poet and satirist, and the subject of one of the best short biographies in English, Dr. Johnson's *Life,* was by his own account in the preface to *Miscellaneous Poems* (1728) the illegitimate son of Anne, countess of Macclesfield, and Richard Savage, 4th Earl Rivers. His exact date of birth is uncertain (in Johnson's *Life,* and in the anonymous *Life of Mr Richard Savage,* 1727, it is given as Jan. 10, 1698), unless Savage is to be certainly identified with the illegitimate son by Earl Rivers born to the countess on Jan. 16, 1697, at Fox Court, Holborn, who on Jan. 18 was christened Richard

Smith, and six months later vanished from all authentic record. The supposition that Savage was born in 1697 is perhaps supported by other evidence (*see* C. Tracy's biography in *Bibliography,* below). The countess of Macclesfield was divorced in 1698 and became Mrs. Brett by a second marriage in 1700. In Nov. 1715 a young man taken into custody for treasonable, *i.e.,* Jacobite, doggerel identified himself as "Mr. Savage, natural son to the late Earl Rivers," and continued so to describe himself for the rest of his life. Mrs. Brett at no time countenanced his pretensions, and in the absence of proof most modern students have followed her example.

In addition to his claim to be the son of a nobleman Savage pressed another, to be a man of letters. In 1717 he published *The Convocation,* a poem about the religious dispute known as the Bangorian Controversy; and in 1718 had *Love in a Veil* (publ. 1719), a comedy taken from the Spanish of Calderón, produced at Drury Lane, where in 1723 a neoclassical tragedy, *Sir Thomas Overbury* (publ. 1724), was also produced. *Miscellaneous Poems* appeared in 1726 and again in 1728, this time with the preface against Mrs. Brett which Savage had originally suppressed, probably under pressure from her friends. In 1727 Savage had been tried for the murder of one James Sinclair in a tavern scuffle, but was saved from execution mainly by the intervention of Mrs. Brett's nephew John Brownlow, Viscount Tyrconnel. He marked his escape with the publication of *The Bastard* (1728), a stinging attack in verse on Mrs. Brett, and it was probably to safeguard the family's good name that Tyrconnel in 1728 took Savage into his own home and paid him a pension of £200 a year.

The poet's acquaintance included people prominent in society as well as men of letters such as James Thomson, Edward Young, and Pope. His most considerable poem, *The Wanderer,* a discursive work with passages of natural description revealing the influence of Thomson's *The Seasons,* appeared in 1729, as did his prose satire on Grub Street, *An Author to be Let;* and by 1732 he had engaged the charitable attention of Queen Caroline. But he was unstable, his charm alternated with arrogance, and he was an inveterate sponger. In 1735 he quarreled finally with Tyrconnel, failed to find patron or sinecure, and after the queen's death, in 1737, found himself destitute. In 1737–38 he met Samuel Johnson (*q.v.*), then newly arrived in London, and to Johnson's perceptive and compassionate *Account of the Life of Mr Richard Savage* (1744), rather than to his own writings, he owes his continuing fame. His friends, Pope prominent among them, eventually provided money to convey him out of London, and after a year spent in Wales he died miserably in a debtor's prison in Bristol on Aug. 1, 1743.

BIBLIOGRAPHY.—The best edition of the *Poetical Works* is by C. Tracy (1962). Of several contemporary accounts of Savage, the best-known is the anonymous *Life of Mr Richard Savage* (1727). The first effective research into his claims was that by W. Moy Thomas in *Notes and Queries,* Second Series, vol. VI (1858). S. V. Makower's *Richard Savage: a Mystery in Biography* (1909) has been superseded by C. Tracy, *The Artificial Bastard* (1953). (G. Jo.)

SAVANNAH, the leading seaport in Georgia, U.S., is situated at the mouth of the Savannah river on an elevation of 42 ft. (13 m.), 18 mi. (28 km.) W. of the Atlantic coast; it is 260 mi. (420 km.) S.E. of Atlanta and 140 mi. (225 km.) S. of Columbia, S.C. The city was laid out by James Oglethorpe according to plans drawn in England, with rectilinear streets crossing at right angles, the plat being symmetrical with numerous squares reserved for public parks. These parks, studded with semitropical trees and flowers and surrounded with Georgian colonial and Greek revival buildings, give the city an atmosphere of tranquility and grace. It exceeds all Georgia cities in historical interest and it is a leading tourist and recreation centre. It is also a city of commercial and industrial importance. Pop. (1960) city 149,245; standard metropolitan statistical area (Chatham county) 188,299. (For comparative population figures for the city *see* table in GEORGIA: *Population.*)

History.—The original Georgia settlement in 1733, Savannah was the seat of colonial government and remained the capital of the commonwealth until 1786, although sharing this distinction with Augusta after 1778 (*see also* GEORGIA: *History*). Among the early residents were the brothers John and Charles Wesley, who came in 1736, John as a representative of the Society for the Propagation of the Gospel, Charles as secretary to Oglethorpe. Charles Wesley stayed only a few months; John Wesley remained until 1738. The evangelist George Whitefield visited the settlement for the first time in 1738 and several times thereafter; he founded in Savannah the Bethesda orphanage.

As early as 1744 there was established at Savannah an exporting and importing firm engaging in coastwise traffic and by 1750 the port was clearing vessels directly to Europe. Lumber products, sago powder, rice, indigo, beef, pork, animal skins, tar and turpentine were its early exports. In 1769 Savannah merchants condemned the British acts of trade and adopted nonimportation agreements but its revolutionary sentiment was comparatively moderate. During the American Revolution the town remained only briefly in rebel hands, being occupied by loyalist forces from 1778 to near the end of the conflict. After the war Gen. Nathanael Greene, who is buried in the city, settled on an estate, 14 mi. N. of Savannah, granted him by the state of Georgia. It was while visiting the Greene family there in 1793 that Eli Whitney invented the cotton gin. There was a devastating fire in the city in 1796, and in 1820 another fire coupled with a yellow-fever epidemic destroyed considerable life and property. Cholera swept the city in 1834 and hit the slave population severely.

In the meantime the importance of the port was increasing, partly as a result of improved transportation in the hinterland. The town's early means of contact with other communities was provided by rivers and coastal waters, but by the end of the 18th century a network of roads connected it with points in the back country. The "Savannah," the first steamboat to cross the Atlantic, sailed from Savannah for Liverpool in 1819. Commercial rivalry with Charleston and Augusta caused Savannah citizens to promote a railroad, known as the Central of Georgia, which was completed to Macon in 1843. By 1860 the Atlantic and Gulf railroad connected Savannah with points in southern Georgia. The city's commerce suffered during the Civil War as a result of the Union blockade but the city was not captured until late in 1864, when it became the objective of Gen. W. T. Sherman's march to the sea. The city was occupied by Federal troops on Dec. 21, 1864.

After the Civil War Savannah recovered fairly rapidly in spite of a yellow-fever epidemic in 1876. It remained the largest urban centre in Georgia until it was surpassed by Atlanta in 1880. Savannah's history in the 20th century is largely its increasing industrialization and its increasing importance as a maritime centre. It has a council-manager form of government, in effect since 1954.

Population Characteristics.—Both the city of Savannah and its metropolitan area increased in population during the middle part of the 20th century, the rate of increase between 1950 and 1960 being 24.7% in the city and 24.3% in the metropolitan area. The population of the city in 1960 was 62.9% native-born white, 1.4% foreign-born white and 35.7% nonwhite. Although the percentage of foreign-born residents is low, in the past it has been the highest in Georgia. In 1870, for example, the foreign-born comprised 24.2% of the white population. Among the foreign-born the Irish have predominated.

Commerce, Industry and Transportation.—In the latter part of the 20th century manufacturing was the leading occupation but wholesale and retail trade ranked a close second, with public utilities, including transportation and communication, being third. Professional and related services ranked next. Less than 1% of the people of the county were engaged in farming.

The city is served by railroads and state and federal highway systems, with bridges spanning the Savannah river and other water barriers in the vicinity. It has two airports and about 1,500 vessels enter the port of Savannah annually. Piers, docks, wharves and storage warehouses are located along the west side of the Savannah river. Savannah is the leading manufacturing port city between Baltimore and New Orleans, its industry including over 250 manufacturing firms, the principal operations being pulp and paper, sugar refining, packaging, shipbuilding and repair, building materials (including felt, asphalt and roofing), fertilizers, castings and chemicals. The Hunter air force base, a permanent installation of the strategic air command, is located near the city, and within 40 mi. are two other military installations, the marine corps recruit depot at Parris Island, S.C., and Ft. Stewart, a U.S. army armour and artillery firing centre.

Education and Cultural Activities.—Savannah was the earliest centre of artistic and cultural interest in Georgia. In 1801 a library society was established there, followed shortly by a theatre which brought to the community the outstanding productions of the times. The Telfair Academy of Arts and Sciences, a museum of permanent collections of all phases of art, was founded in the city in 1875. The community has several public libraries, a symphony orchestra, a little theatre, an annual camellia show and other similar attractions. Located in the heart of the city are Armstrong Junior college and the Savannah State college, both units of the university system of Georgia (*see* GEORGIA: *Education*). A Savannah woman, Juliette Gordon Low (1860–1927), is considered the founder of the Girl Scout movement in the U.S.; a number of places of interest in this connection are marked in the city.   (Js. C. B.)

SAVANNAH RIVER, rising in northwest South Carolina, U.S., is formed 8 mi. NW of Hartwell, Ga., by the confluence of the Tugaloo and Seneca rivers and serves as a natural boundary between Georgia and South Carolina. Its course is southeastward past Augusta and Savannah, Ga., to the Atlantic, a distance of 314 mi. (505 km.). North of Augusta the Savannah is fed by the Broad and Little rivers and south of Augusta by Brier Creek. It is navigable for barge traffic from its mouth on the Atlantic to Augusta, 212 mi. (341 km.) upstream. The river is used extensively for hydroelectric power. The Hartwell dam and reservoir near Augusta provides upstream impoundment of the Savannah for hydroelectric, flood control and navigation purposes. There are three other dams near Augusta; the largest of these, Clark Hill dam, is 200 ft. (61 m.) high and 5,660 ft. (1,725 m.) long. The U.S. Atomic Energy Commission's Savannah River plant is in Aiken and Barnwell counties in South Carolina, across the river from Augusta. Clark Hill provides power for the Atomic Energy plant and the river serves as a coolant for plant processes. Savannah, 17 mi. (27 km.) upstream from the mouth of the river, was the centre for James Edward Oglethorpe's initial Georgia colony. Deepdraft navigation by ocean vessels extends 5 mi. upstream beyond the city. At Savannah are one of the world's largest naval stores markets, large state-owned docks operated by the Georgia ports authority and a large refinery for processing sugar imported from the Caribbean. Near Savannah is a large pulp-paper plant with a capacity of 1,900 tons of paper products daily. Many of the former rice and cotton plantations along the lower Savannah are large producers of pulp wood. (M. C. P.)

SAVARA (SORA, SAWARA, SAORA), a Munda-speaking tribe of eastern India, are distributed mainly in Orissa, Madhya Pradesh, Andhra Pradesh, and Bihar, with a total population of about 400,-000 in the 1960s. Of these more than 325,000 were in Orissa, especially in the Ganjam (*q.v.*) and Koraput districts.

Most Savara, living in the plains areas, have become Hinduized and generally speak Oriya (*see* ORIYA LANGUAGE). Their traditional form of Munda dialect is preserved in the hilly tracts of Koraput, Ganjam, and Vizagapatam (*see* MUNDA LANGUAGES; MUNDA PEOPLES.).

They practise shifting cultivation and settled, terraced plow agriculture. Paddy rice is the main crop; they also grow millet in the slash-and-burn fields. The Savara sell jungle products to itinerant Hindu traders or at weekly markets where they buy or barter for tobacco, yarn, and pots. Cash is used principally to purchase sacrificial animals for magico-religious ceremonies. The Savara have many specialists of both sexes for their elaborate rituals.

Those Savara who live in the hill country are divided into sub-tribes mainly on the basis of occupation: the Jati Savara, the main cultivator group (*see* JAT); the Arsi, weavers of tribal cloth; the Muli, workers in iron; the Kindal, basket makers; and the

Kumbi, potters. The Savara social unit is the exogamous extended family, including both males and females descended from a common male ancestor. There is a tendency to distinguish an aristocracy of chiefs and priests.

BIBLIOGRAPHY.—V. Elwin, *The Religion of an Indian Tribe* (1955); A. C. M. Munro and G. V. Sitapati, "The Soras of the Parlakimidi Agency," *Census of India, 1931*, vol. 1, pt. III B (1935); G. V. Ramamurti, *A Manual of the Sora (or Savara) Language* (1931); K. C. Tripathy, "Middle-phalangeal Hair Among the Saoras of Puri, Orissa," *Eastern Anthropologist*, vol. 16 (May, 1963).   (S. C. SI.)

SAVARY, ANNE JEAN MARIE RENÉ, DUC DE ROVIGO (1774–1833), French general and administrator who rose in Napoleon's service, was born at Marcq (Ardennes) on April 26, 1774. He joined the army in 1790, fought in the Rhine campaigns, and went to Egypt (1798) as aide-de-camp to Gen. Louis Desaix de Veygoux. After Desaix's death (June 1800) he became aide-de-camp to Bonaparte and was appointed chief of the First Consul's *gendarmerie d'élite* (1801), general of brigade (1803), and general of division (1805). In 1804 he threw all his energies into the investigation of the Cadoudal-Pichegru royalist conspiracy and commanded the troops at Vincennes when the duc d'Enghien was executed (*see* NAPOLEON I: *The Consulate*).

Both before and after the Battle of Austerlitz (December 1805) Savary was sent by Napoleon to discuss an armistice with Alexander I of Russia. He took a notable part in the rout of the Prussians after Jena (1806) and while in temporary command of the 5th Corps defeated the Russians at Ostroleka in Poland (February 1807). After the Treaty of Tilsit (July 1807) Savary spent five months as ambassador at St. Petersburg. In 1808 he was sent to Spain, where he skilfully exploited the differences between Charles IV and his son Ferdinand VII, in whose favour Charles had recently abdicated. He persuaded both to submit to Napoleon's arbitration and by false promises induced Ferdinand to meet Napoleon at Bayonne, a step which cost him his crown and his freedom for six years (*see* SPAIN: *History*). Created duc de Rovigo in May 1808, Savary replaced Fouché in June 1810 as minister of police, an office in which he showed more zeal than ability. Among the last to abandon Napoleon in April 1814, Savary was also one of the first to welcome his return in March 1815. He was then created a peer of France and first inspector general of constabulary. After the Battle of Waterloo (June 1815) he accompanied Napoleon to Rochefort and Plymouth but was not allowed to go with him to St. Helena. Imprisoned for seven months in Malta, he escaped (April 1816) and lived first at Smyrna (Izmir), and then at Graz in Austria. He returned to France in 1819, and a sentence of death passed on him in December 1816 was reversed and he regained his civil rights. After the Revolution of July 1830 he was commander of the army in Algeria in 1832, but illness forced him to give up his command (March 1833). He died in Paris on June 2, 1833. His *Mémoires* (eight volumes) were published in 1828 in both French and English; a French edition by D. Lacroix appeared in 1901.

See B. Melchior-Bonnet, *Savary, duc de Rovigo* (1962).
(C. E. DU.)

SAVATE, literally, "old shoe," the old French sport of fighting by kicking, whose chief practitioners were from among the lower orders of Parisians. *Savate* had died out by about 1850, its more skilful gambits being married with those of English bare-knuckle pugilism to produce *la boxe française*. The name *savate* continued to be used to describe any form of fighting in which the use of the feet was permitted. Two classic blows were a back heel aimed at the stomach and a double mule kick in the face delivered from a handstand position.

The pioneer of *la boxe française*, or modern *savate*, was Charles Lecour, who opened a school in Paris. The sport had a considerable vogue and public exhibitions were staged. The authorities frowned on these and the police intervened. The sport declined in the 20th century and tended to be thought of as confined to the wealthy. In 1927, demonstrations of it were staged at the Ring, Blackfriars, in London; but they excited more curiosity than admiration, especially since one of the exponents was a woman.

In Thailand, boxing with the feet is more popular than boxing with the fists. The sport is taught to local boys at monasteries, and competitions are held regularly. (N. D. McW.)

SAVERNAKE FOREST, a large beech wood covering 4,500 ac. (1,820 ha.) on the chalk downs just south of the market town of Marlborough, in Wiltshire, Eng. A Saxon charter dated 934 calls it Safernoc, and from the Conquest until 1550 it was a royal hunting ground extending over 20 sq.mi. (52 sq.km.). In 1083 the hereditary office of warden was granted to the family of Esturmy, and their lineal descendant, the marquess of Ailesbury, now holds the freehold.

In 1939 the woods were leased to the Forestry Commission, and during World War II they sheltered American forces before the Normandy invasion. Large fellings were made for timber at that time, but the clearings have since been replanted with beech.

The finest scenic feature is the Grand Beech Avenue which runs for 3 mi. SE from the London-Bath Road to Tottenham House.

(H. L. En.)

SAVIGNY, FRIEDRICH KARL VON (1779–1861), German legal scholar, one of the originators of the influential historical school of jurisprudence, was born in Frankfurt am Main on Feb. 21, 1779. In Savigny's classic words, law "is first developed by custom and popular faith, next by judicial decisions—everywhere, therefore, by internal silently operating powers, not by the arbitrary will of a law-giver." Savigny became a doctor of law at the University of Marburg in 1800 and was one of the first members of the German nobility to teach in a university. He subsequently taught criminal law, Roman law and its history and property and contract law at Marburg and Landshut but spent most of his academic career (1810–42) at the University of Berlin. In 1803 his book on possession, *Das Recht des Besitzes,* was published. Soon thereafter he turned to the historical and jurisprudential interests that dominated the remainder of his career.

The immediate occasion that led him in that direction was the publication of a book, *Civilistische Abhandlungen,* in 1814, by Anton Thibaut, a professor at Heidelberg, who demanded immediate codification of German law. Thibaut's book reflected the rise of German nationalism after the Napoleonic wars and a reaction against Roman and other foreign law. Savigny vigorously opposed codification in a monograph, *Vom Beruf unserer Zeit für Gesetzgebung und Rechtswissenschaft* (1814), which gave much impetus to the emerging historical theory of law. Historical jurisprudence viewed law as a slow, almost imperceptible growth, like language.

This jurisprudential perspective was a phase of the romantic movement, which had begun in the latter part of the 18th century, and it took the form in Germany of a movement back to the simplest tribal origins of the German people, to their folk songs and tales and to their distinctive ethos, their *Volksgeist* ("national spirit"). The movement found expression in the philosophy of Johann Gottfried von Herder, the fairy tales of the Grimm brothers and Barthold Niebuhr's Roman history. The national spirit was the ultimate datum to be explored in its various manifestations. From this point of view law is not something that can be made but originates in the unique spirit of the people and is expressed spontaneously in custom and, much later, in the formal decisions of the judges. Accordingly, legislation and codes can, at most, give only verbal expression to existing law the actuality and meaning of which can be discovered by careful historical investigations. Thus, historical jurisprudence opposed not only codification but also natural-law philosophy as illusory and fictitious. Instead of assuming that familiar law was "universal," as Savigny charged was done in natural-law philosophy, historical jurisprudence insisted on thorough research into legal origins and transformations.

While the philosophy of historical jurisprudence was in the 20th century perverted by the Nazis in their glorification of the German *Volk,* it is certain that Savigny would have thoroughly disapproved of racist interpretations. He was a pioneering legal scientist who made lasting contributions to jurisprudence, especially in revealing the continuity of present legal institutions with past ones; in laying the foundations of legal sociology; and in articulating the methods of historical research. These contributions greatly influenced all the social disciplines. (*See also* JURISPRUDENCE.)

In 1815, shortly after the appearance of his epochal book, Savigny, Karl Friedrich Eichhorn and Johann Friedrich Ludwig Göschen founded the *Zeitschrift für geschichtliche Rechtswissenschaft* as the organ of the new historical school. In 1815 also, the first volume of his six-volume treatise on medieval Roman law, *Geschichte des römischen Rechts im Mittelalter,* appeared, the last of which was published in 1831.

Savigny then devoted himself to an elaborate treatise on modern Roman law, *System des heutigen römischen Rechts* (8 vol., 1840–49), which contains his theory of private international law and his further study on possession and error. In March 1842 he was appointed high chancellor of Prussia by Frederick William IV and, after carrying out several important reforms especially in regard to bills of exchange and divorce, he resigned in 1848. In 1850 appeared his collected minor works, *Vermischte Schriften,* in 5 volumes, and in 1851–53 he published a book in 2 volumes on contracts (*Das Obligationenrecht*), a supplement to his work on modern Roman law.

Savigny died in Berlin on Oct. 25, 1861.

BIBLIOGRAPHY.—Jerome Hall, *Readings in Jurisprudence,* pp. 87–111 (1958); Julius Stone, *The Province and Function of Law,* pp. 421–448 (1950); S. Schultzenstein, *Savigny* (1930); I. F. Zurlgmeyer, *Die Rechtslehre Savignys* (1929). (J. Hl.)

SAVIGNY, ABBEY OF, in Normandy, was for a time the head of one of the reformed Benedictine orders of the early 12th century. It owed its foundation to Vitalis, a secular clerk who spent about 17 years as a hermit in the wild regions of Craon and the forest of Savigny. With the aid of a grant of land from Raoul of Fougères he founded a monastery in 1112 for the group of disciples who had joined him there. Savigny from the first had much in common with Cîteaux (*q.v.*), including an emphasis on agricultural work and the admission of lay brethren; annual general chapters for the daughter houses were added by Geoffrey, the second abbot. In 1147 Abbot Serlo, an admirer of St. Bernard, secured the fusion of Savigny and more than 30 French and English dependencies with the order of Cîteaux. The abbey was secularized in 1790, and only fragmentary ruins remain.

C. Auvry, *Histoire de la Congrégation de Savigny,* 3 vol. (1896–98). (M. M. Ch.)

SAVILE, SIR HENRY (1549–1622), English classical scholar, mathematician, and patron of learning, was born at Bradley, near Halifax, on Nov. 30, 1549, of a prosperous Yorkshire family. He matriculated at Brasenose (1561) and was elected a fellow of Merton College, Oxford (1565). He lectured on Ptolemy's *Almagest* and after a continental tour collecting manuscripts became Queen Elizabeth I's tutor and, in 1585, warden of Merton. Gifted, handsome, and on good terms with the earl of Essex, he persuaded the queen in 1596 to appoint him provost of Eton although he was a layman. Both his colleges benefited from his autocratic rule, for it was coupled with a determination to have genuinely learned men as fellows and scholars. His friendship with the rebellious Essex earned him a brief imprisonment in 1601 and a knighthood in 1604 when James I had come to the throne. He helped to prepare the Authorized (King James) Version of the Bible, the Acts, Revelation, and a part of the Gospels falling to his share. He died on Feb. 19, 1622, at Eton with his reputation undimmed. Savile was a pioneer in many branches of scholarship. His translations from Tacitus' histories (1591) were accompanied by one of the earliest English treatises on Roman antiquities. His eight-volume Chrysostom (1610–13) remains the best edition of Chrysostom's works. He published some neglected medieval historians, as well as the 14th-century philosopher, Thomas Bradwardine (1618), whose thought his mathematical interests helped him to appreciate. But his greatest service to learning was probably the foundation in 1619 of the two Savilian professorships of mathematics and of astronomy at Oxford, for they had the effect of bringing at a critical moment the official study of these subjects into line with the latest advances in knowledge.

See J. E. Sandys, *History of Classical Scholarship,* vol. 2 (1908); M. H. Curtis, *Oxford and Cambridge in Transition 1558–1642* (1959). (R. R. Bo.)

SAVING, NATIONAL. Saving means the setting aside for future use of part of current income—the excess over the amount currently consumed or paid in taxes. Saving may thus be performed by anybody having an income—by an individual, a family, or by a business firm. Because of disagreement as to the sense in which a government body has an income, there is some difference of opinion among economists as to whether or not it is appropriate to say that governments (as distinct from the citizens and businesses under their jurisdiction) carry on saving. But whether or not the government is said to save, the nation may be said to save the sum of the amounts saved by the individuals and business firms (plus government bodies if they are considered to have savings) which it includes. Since there are always some individuals and businesses whose current expenses and taxes outrun their incomes, and whose savings are therefore negative, national saving must be thought of as a net total with negative savings subtracted.

Forms of Saving.—Saving is often spoken of loosely as if it were synonymous with the piling up of idle cash. This interpretation is misleading. While it is true by definition that savings are not spent on the consumption of the saver, it does not follow that they are not spent at all. They may be spent directly by the saver or indirectly by business firms he helps to finance; they may be spent on the purchase of new items added to the community's stock of wealth, such as new houses or machinery. They may be spent indirectly on the consumption of some other person who borrows or sells property to finance his negative savings. They may help to finance a government deficit, thus supporting whatever spending the government is carrying on, whether for armaments, highways, food to feed the hungry, or routine government expenses.

Part of current saving—sometimes a small part, sometimes a large part—appears in the form of increase in savings deposits and other cash assets held by the individuals or business firms doing the saving. The remainder is represented in their accounts by additions to their holdings of physical property, acquisition of government or private securities, or reduction of the debts they owe to others.

Saving and Investment.—Under the generally accepted use of terms, it will always be found at the end of any accounting period that if the revenues and expenditures of government are equal (the budget balanced) and if all government expenditures are on current account, national saving for the period amounts to just as much as investment in new buildings, equipment, etc. This is a matter of definition. Saving means the excess of national income over consumption and taxes. Investment is taken to mean the excess of net national product (which is the same thing as national income) over the parts of the product made up of consumption goods and services and items bought by government expenditures.

Since economic progress depends largely on the increase of wealth through investment, it follows also that economic progress is linked with the achievement of national saving. Some increase in production might be possible without any net national saving, through increasing the labour force, finding new ways to use existing equipment and labour, and replacing old equipment and buildings as they wear out (*see* DEPRECIATION) with more modern types. But to make full use both of the growing labour force and of new methods of production requires a net increase of plant and equipment; besides this there is always a backlog of opportunities to increase production, with preexisting methods and labour force, for which more equipment would have been required.

The need of investment and saving to increase production is of course most acute in countries where modern technology has not yet been put into operation and in devastated areas where houses, workshops, and transportation equipment have been destroyed.

The meaning of the much-misunderstood doctrine of "abstinence" may be stated as follows: if there is to be an increase of productive wealth, somewhere in the economic system somebody must abstain from consuming his entire income. It does not necessarily follow that those who abstain from consuming are suffering. On the contrary, insofar as saving is left to individuals, it is per-

formed chiefly by persons with high incomes who both save heavily and consume considerably more than the average. But for the community as a whole it is impossible both to consume the whole of current income and to build up productive wealth.

It should be observed that these propositions do not prove that economic progress either will or will not be served by an increased inclination to thrift on the part of individuals and business firms. Progress depends on the achievement of substantial investment and therefore of substantial saving. But as John Maynard Keynes pointed out, decisions to save and decisions to invest are taken by different persons operating under different incentives. A decision by one individual to save more, unaccompanied by a decision by him or anybody else to invest more, cannot be guaranteed to increase the volume of saving and investment actually realized; in fact, many economists argue that the effect would be to decrease that volume. This point will be examined further below.

Effect of Government on Saving-Investment Relation.— If the government's revenues and expenditures are unequal, the relation of saving to investment just described is modified. In a period of depression, for example, the tax base shrinks and revenue declines, while the addition of relief programs to government responsibility increases expenditure. Government is therefore obliged to finance its expenditures in part either by borrowing, by paying out cash on hand, or by issuing money. Some savers, consequently, either use their savings to buy government securities, or hold more cash, or have larger balances with banks and other credit institutions while the latter have more cash and government securities. The same is true when a government deficit is incurred for war purposes.

In these circumstances it is no longer true that the net total saved by individuals and businesses is equal to the net total invested by individuals and businesses in new productive wealth. Private savings exceed private investment by the amount of the deficit. Whether national saving is said to exceed national investment is a matter of language. The part of government expenditure used to pay for productive wealth such as hydroelectric dams, roads, needed buildings, and recreation facilities can reasonably be described as investment. Any excess of the deficit over such government investment can be described as negative saving by government, reducing the net total of national saving. This way of using language has the advantage of stressing the fact that when government saving is positive (*i.e.*, when government has an excess of revenue over current expenses, the excess serving to reduce government's net debt and to finance government investment) there can be an increase of the nation's productive wealth in the absence of private saving. It has the drawback, however, of inviting dispute as to the scope and measurement of government activity to be classified as investment (particularly in time of war) and leaving statistical measurements of national saving with a much wider range of possible error than measurements of private saving.

Ways of Estimating Saving.—For an individual there are two ways to measure his saving for a given accounting period. One is to estimate his income and subtract his current expenditure, the difference being his saving. The alternative is to examine his balance sheet (his property and his debts) at the beginning and end of the period and measure the increase in net worth, which reflects his saving. While different figures are taken out of the individual's accounts under these two procedures, the two methods are logically equivalent. In either case it is necessary to make sure that we do not include in income (or in the increase of net worth) any items which reflect merely changes in price levels at which pieces of property are valued, or items reflecting events not regarded as linked with income—broadly speaking, to exclude capital gains and losses (whether realized or "paper") from income. For example, losses due to property destruction by enemy action in wartime, or gains due to a rise of prices on the stock market, would be excluded in income determination. If income is measured by the rules generally adopted by national income statisticians, the result is to exclude not merely the effects of price changes but some actual physical changes—chiefly losses—in wealth. The net total of saving estimated in this way tends to exceed the value of additions to the nation's stock of wealth to the extent that war damage, uninsured fire losses and similar events fail to appear in the income account. On the other hand, it tends to fall short to the extent that new wealth is found (for example through mineral discoveries) or that wealth becomes more useful through new techniques (for example, through the development of dry farming techniques which made previously worthless land take on value).

In standard national accounting practice, the economy's saving is generally estimated by subtracting an estimated flow of consumption outlays from an estimated flow of income. But even when both income and outlay are both well estimated this method is vulnerable to minor errors in the two figures used in the subtraction: an error of 1% in estimated income, for example, can yield an error of 10% in the residual figure of estimated saving. Hence these figures must be controlled by other methods. In the United States, estimates of assets and liabilities for individuals, corporations, and government bodies are made currently by the Securities Exchange Commission and are used to frame alternative estimates of saving, which agree fairly well with those obtained from estimates of income and consumption. In his monumental *Study of Savings in the United States* (1955–56), Raymond W. Goldsmith relied primarily on estimates of assets and liabilities, with corrections for changes in price levels.

War Saving.—Savings under war conditions follow different patterns than in peace. Individuals and businesses set aside a larger proportion of their incomes, so that net private savings grow enormously. On the other hand, private investment is restricted because war needs divert labour and materials from making buildings and equipment for private use. Public construction and acquisition of equipment by government expands, but most of the resulting facilities are either used up in the war or are inconvertible to civilian uses thereafter. The consequence is a great growth in the paper wealth of individuals and business firms (corresponding to the growth of the government's debt) with little or no growth in actual productive wealth.

Not much precise information is available about saving during World War I. Interwar studies reveal that individuals and business firms saved in 1919 a much larger proportion of income than in any year in the 1920s, and that saving in 1920, though declining, was still high. For World War II, comparatively reliable studies made at the time show that the proportion of income saved rose well above peacetime levels during 1941 and continued to rise thereafter. At the peak of war activity, individuals were saving nearly one-third of their disposable incomes (*i.e.*, income payments less personal taxes), and corporations well over one-half of theirs.

The total wartime accumulation by individuals amounted to far more than the income of any single year of the interwar period, and the great bulk took the form of additional currency, bank deposits, government securities, and claims upon life insurance companies.

It is probable that the saving of the richer groups of the population made up a much smaller proportion of the war saving than of peacetime saving, but the difference must not be exaggerated. About half of the wartime accumulation of individuals and corporations was accounted for by the growth in their holdings of government bonds—more than two-thirds in denominations of $500 and upward—which were not to any great extent small savings. The proportion of the growth in bank deposits, currency and insurance claims representing large savers was probably still higher.

Motives for Saving.—Saving is a very complex phenomenon. Different savers save for different reasons, and a given saver for a mixture of reasons. At any given moment, furthermore, many individuals find themselves spending less or more than their incomes simply because their incomes are more or less than was expected when commitments to spend were made. This is true especially for farmers and self-employed business and professional men whose incomes are subject to unexpected fluctuations.

Insofar as saving goes back to decisions to save, the main motives seem to be the following: (1) provision for a future period when income is expected to be less or the need for expenditure greater than at present—for example, provision for retirement, education or vacations; (2) provision against unpredictable decline in income or growth in need—for example, against sickness in the family or loss of earning power by the breadwinner; (3) acquisition of higher income, either by improving the equipment, etc., of a business, or by being housed better or at less expense, or by obtaining interest, dividends, rent or other property income; (4) gain in social status through acquiring property; or (5) direct subjective satisfaction from accumulation ("miser's" instinct). Pulling against these motives, of course, is the desirability of current consumption, and the desirability of having more leisure at the expense of potential income.

This hypothesis about the motives for saving explains the U.S. record fairly well. High-income individuals have greater incentives to save than low-income individuals, for example, because the former: (1) are a group many of whose members are enjoying temporary increase of income and must expect a drop later on; (2) have better opportunities to place savings where they will yield income; (3) are more able to gain power and social approbation by saving; and (4) are less hard-pressed to maintain what they regard as necessary standards of consumption and of leisure. Rural people are more inclined to save than urban people of like income because: (1) their incomes are more uncertain; (2) their opportunities to gain income from saving are better and the fruits of their savings, in buildings, livestock, equipment, etc., are more visible and thus more conducive to improved social standing and direct enjoyment; and (3) their standards of consumption and of leisure are less exacting. War saving is higher than peacetime saving because: (1) incomes are regarded as abnormally high and are above previous levels; (2) ordinary outlets for negative saving (retirement of elderly people, education, prolonged vacations and medical treatments) are reduced; (3) incomes are less secure; (4) social pressures to save are intensified; and (5) normal standards of consumption and leisure are suspended. The fact that the rising trend of real per capita income has not brought a rising trend in the proportion saved is explained by: (1) progressive urbanization; (2) rising standards of consumption and leisure; (3) the trend away from private houses and away from direct ownership by individuals of tangible business property (which reduces both opportunities to gain income and opportunities to gain social status and direct satisfaction by increase of property); (4) the downward drift in interest rates; and (5) increased importance of some sources of negative savings (in particular the increased stress upon higher education and the increased proportion in the population of elderly people who tend to live on past saving).

See also CAPITAL AND INTEREST; CONSUMPTION; DEBT, PUBLIC; NATIONAL INCOME ACCOUNTING; SOCIAL SECURITY.

(A. G. HT.; X.)

SAVINGS AND LOAN ASSOCIATION, a cooperative savings institution of the type originally established to make loans to members for the purchase of homes. Such associations are also known in the United States as building and loan associations, co-operative banks, homestead societies, building societies and savings associations. The identifying labels that promise to become most common are savings and loan associations in the United States and building societies in Great Britain.

UNITED STATES

The modern savings and loan association in the United States resembles a bank, but is differently constituted. The savers purchase shares of stock and are thus owners of the association, not depositors. They receive dividends on their shares in proportion to the profits of the organization. The association is pledged to repurchase the shares bought by savers, after reasonable notice; it invests most of its funds in long-term mortgages. These features have characterized U.S. associations since their origin and have made them highly successful in home mortgage financing. By the middle 1960s savings and loan associations held 44% of the mortgage debt on nonfarm homes in the United States.

Origins and Development.—Savings and credit institutions for noncommercial groups developed in the United States in the first half of the 19th century. The savings and loan associations were, at first, informally organized groups of neighbours or of men in the same industry who pooled their savings to purchase homes. Though there were many plans for saving and borrowing, a common pattern was followed. Each member was committed to make regular payments to a fund. A member could borrow from the fund to purchase a home. His share and his home were the collateral for the loan. The borrowing member would continue his regular payments to the fund and also make interest payments. Both savers and borrowers were penalized by fines and forfeitures if they did not maintain regular payments. The association was not a permanent institution but was created for the period necessary to enable each of the members in turn to purchase homes. By the end of the 19th century these small neighbourly associations were replaced by permanent institutions which had members who were not saving to purchase homes and borrowers who were not members of the association before making their loans.

Savers and Owners.—Associations in the United States may be chartered by the federal or state governments. All federally chartered associations are mutually owned; every saving member is an owner and can vote for the selection of the management. State chartered associations may be mutual or stock associations. If they are stock associations, the savers receive investment certificates which do not carry the right to vote or to claim the residual profits of the association. In all cases the savers are not depositors; as noted above, they do not stand in the same relation to the association as does a saver in a bank. The depositor in the bank is a creditor of the bank; the saver in an association has an ownership right or investment. In practice, since the associations must offer convenient service in order to compete for savings with other institutions, withdrawal requests are usually honoured promptly.

The formal difference of ownership shares as against deposits is of importance. The associations can be less liquid than banks; *i.e.,* more of the assets of the associations can go into long-term investments since they are not required to meet every unexpected demand by depositors for their funds. Therefore associations allocate a larger percentage of their assets to mortgages. Compared to other institutions the associations write mortgages for longer periods and their loans are for a larger percentage of the appraised value of the property. Since mortgages of this type are more risky, the associations' interest rate is usually higher than that charged by banks.

There are many patterns of savings in use. Originally the associations were characterized by forced savings schemes. Individuals were expected to make regular payments to accumulate sufficient funds for the ownership of a stated number of shares. If they did not maintain the payments for the shares the savers might be forced to pay a fine, lose part of their dividends or lose a bonus dividend. Forced savings are no longer popular and the usual form of savings is as flexible as that offered by a savings bank.

Amortized Loans.—The loan repayment provisions of the early associations were the prototype of the amortization plans used in repayment of mortgages in the 20th century. It was the pioneering work of the savings and loan associations that provided the experience for the federal government's policies in the 1930s for the reform of mortgage financing. The association plan, referred to as the direct reduction loan plan, required the home buyer to make a fixed payment each month; part of this payment was applied to the principal and part to interest, the former increasing each month as the latter decreased.

The associations generally prefer conventional mortgages to those insured by the Federal Housing Administration (FHA) or guaranteed by the Veterans Administration (VA) because these mortgages earn a higher interest rate. A higher interest rate gives the associations a higher profit and enables them to pay a higher dividend rate to savers. A higher interest rate is necessary in order to compensate savers for the slightly greater risk of investment in an association.

Local Nature.—The early associations in the United States were small and local, and most of them still are. The federally chartered associations must make most of their loans on property within a 50-mi. radius of the home office. More frequently the associations restrict themselves to a city or a neighbourhood within a city, though they may solicit savings from investors in a much wider area. Area restrictions serve to limit the size of the associations but their growth since 1950 has been rapid. The more than 6,200 associations in existence in 1960 represented only a 17% increase over the total number in existence in the year 1900, but during this 60-year period the assets of the associations had increased 100-fold. The assets of the average association increased from approximately $100,000 in 1900 to more than $10,000,000 in 1960. Some associations in the early 1960s had assets exceeding $100,000,000. These associations were no longer small groups of neighbours or fellow workers joined together to provide homes for themselves but had become big business enterprises that extended credit to nonmembers and sought funds from investors over a wide area. Their size and diffusion of ownership meant that government controls were necessary to avoid abuses.

Public Policies.—Most state regulations are based on a detailed regulatory code adopted by the legislature which severely restrains the associations' freedom of action. In addition all associations which are members of the Federal Home Loan Bank System are subject to examination according to the detailed regulatory code adopted by the Federal Home Loan Bank Board. The major purposes of the regulations are to make certain that an association is complying with its governing charter and that its investments are sound. By 1960 the great majority of all associations were members of the Federal Home Loan Bank System. Members of the system may receive loans from the Federal Home Loan Bank Board.

The Federal Savings and Loan Insurance Corporation was established in 1934 to insure savings up to $5,000. In 1952 the ceiling was extended to $10,000. (*See also* HOUSING: *Housing in the United States.*) Savings and loan associations are represented nationally by the U.S. Savings and Loan League with headquarters in Chicago, Ill.   (J. Ms.)

GREAT BRITAIN

Building societies in Great Britain perform essentially the same functions as savings and loan associations in the United States. They accept money from the public, pay interest on it, allow it to be withdrawn and, in brief, provide a convenient investment service. They also lend money on the security of a mortgage of freehold or leasehold property. Although the earliest building societies undertook the construction of houses, this function was abandoned about the middle of the 19th century and consequently the name building society has become a misnomer. The term is, however, compulsory by law and although various alternatives have been suggested, none has met with universal acceptance.

History and Development.—In the latter half of the 18th century in Great Britain the artisans of the new machine age were emerging as a social group and, in order to give themselves some measure of self-protection against the misfortunes of life, many of them made regular contributions to sick and burial clubs and friendly societies. It was a similar motive—security—which led to the formation of building societies, and according to S. J. Price, who undertook extensive research on this subject, the earliest society of which any record has been found was established in Birmingham in or before 1775.

The early societies were all "terminating"; that is to say, they were intended to have a limited life. Each member agreed to pay a fixed sum at regular intervals from the establishment of the society until it was disbanded. From this steady income the society bought a piece of land and built houses one after another until each of the subscribers had been housed. When the cost of the land and all the houses had been met, the society was dissolved.

As time went on societies began to borrow money from people who did not themselves want to buy a house and this accretion of funds enabled the borrowing members to purchase a house with less delay. As a result of this development there was no longer any need to bring each society to an end when all its original members had received an advance, so that gradually the "terminating" societies were replaced by "permanent" societies.

Building societies were first certified under the Friendly Societies Acts of 1829 and 1834. Their rapid rise led, in 1836, to a special act which extended the friendly society regulations to them in so far as they were applicable, binding all members of a society by the rules, which were certified by specially appointed officers who gave security. Provision was made for control by a committee of management. The society's property was vested in trustees empowered to bring and defend actions and to settle disputes by arbitration. Exemptions were given from stamp duty and the usury laws. By 1850 over 2,000 societies were registered in the United Kingdom.

In 1870 a royal commission was appointed to inquire into the working of friendly societies and building societies. As a result, an act was passed in 1874 and this remained the basis of later practice. Under this act the societies became corporate bodies possessing full legal powers corresponding to those of a limited company. The liability of an investing member was limited to the amount actually paid or in arrears on his shares and that of a borrowing member to the amount still payable under the terms of his mortgage.

The assets of the movement in 1890 have been estimated at £51,000,000 and from then until 1918 there was a steady but unspectacular growth to £68,000,000. Between 1919 and 1939 and again after 1945 there was an immense expansion of activity so that by the middle 1960s the total assets were approximately £4,000,000,000.

Organization and Control.—Apart from statutory control, building societies are governed by their own rules. Management is vested in a small body, usually consisting of between 5 and 12 persons and termed the board of directors. The directors are elected by the members in general meeting. The chief official is usually called either the general manager or the secretary.

The rules deal with such matters as the rights of members, the duties and powers of directors and officers, the holding of meetings of members and the method of voting. They also regulate the society's borrowing powers, the way in which shares are to be issued, how withdrawals are to be paid and upon what conditions advances may be granted and repaid.

Building societies are under the supervision of the chief registrar of friendly societies, who is, by virtue of office, also registrar of building societies. This official has a number of powers and duties derived from the Building Societies Acts. He registers new societies, approves their names, examines their rules and receives from each society an annual report which is open for inspection by the public. The report consists of a list of names of the directors and officers, together with the society's accounts in great detail. A new society may not advertise for funds until the registrar gives it permission to do so. If the registrar considers it expedient he may, with the consent of the Treasury, control and prohibit advertising and even prevent a society from accepting new investments from the public. Each year the registrar prepares a report on building societies which is submitted to Parliament. The movement is nationally represented by the Building Societies Association (founded in 1869).

Investment.—Building societies issue shares although they do not have a fixed share capital and do not offer shares for sale or purchase on the stock exchange. In a leading building society case, Lord Dunedin referred to the "so-called shares" of a building society and added that, though the word was the same, there was nothing more than a faint analogy between them and the shares of a joint-stock company. Building society shares are commonly called "paid-up shares" and the denominations vary from one society to another.

Some societies operate savings accounts under which the saver undertakes to pay a weekly or monthly amount over a period of time until he has accumulated the amount of a fully paid share, and societies often offer a higher rate of interest to encourage this type of regular saving.

There is no legal limit to the total amount of shares that a society may issue or to the number of shares that can be held by one person. In practice, however, nearly all societies impose a limit of £5,000 on the holding of any one member—husband and wife being regarded as one for this purpose. This limitation is due to special income tax arrangements with the Board of Inland Revenue by which the income tax due on interest received from a building society is paid by the society. The arrangements do not cover surtax, which is paid by the investor on the gross equivalent (at the standard rate) and not on the amount of interest actually received. The tax paid by a society on behalf of investors who are individuals is computed at a special "composite" rate. This rate is fixed by reference to the proportionate amounts invested in building societies by (1) persons liable to tax at the standard rate; (2) persons liable at a reduced rate; and (3) persons not liable to pay any income tax. In general, interest on shares held by a limited company or other corporate body is liable to tax at the standard rate, as is interest on a holding of more than £5,000 by a private person.

Interest on shares is paid every half year or year either by warrant or by addition to the shareholder's account with the society. Some societies calculate interest by the day and some by the month. The length of notice required and the conditions on which withdrawals are to be paid are governed by the rules of the society. In practice most societies pay withdrawals at a month's notice, waiving even that period if the amount is small or the money is urgently required.

The Building Societies Acts enable a society to include in its rules the power to borrow money either from an individual or from a corporate body. Such loans are known as deposits. The depositor is a creditor of the society and therefore entitled to priority of repayment over all the shareholders and his rate of interest is normally lower. The income tax arrangements for deposits are the same as for shares. A depositor is not a member and therefore has no voting rights. The Act of 1874 limits the amount a society may take on deposit to two-thirds of the amount due on mortgages. By law, deposits cannot be accepted on terms of less than one month's notice for withdrawal, although in practice if the depositor requires his money urgently such notice is often waived by the society. In general, the larger the amount of the deposit, the longer is the notice required.

Mortgages.—Building societies can lend money only on the security of a first mortgage of freehold or leasehold property. In consideration of the advance which the society makes, the borrower charges his property to the society as security until the loan has been repaid. This is effected by means of a mortgage deed, on which stamp duty is payable according to the amount of the loan. The borrower becomes a member of the society and subject to its rules. In general, societies lend their funds mainly on the security of private dwelling houses purchased for owner occupation. Some societies occasionally make loans on blocks of flats, commercial or industrial premises and farms, but the total value of such loans in any year is strictly regulated by the Building Societies Act, 1960. Many societies make loans on shops which have living accommodation.

Within the framework of the society's general lending policy the amount of the loan will be related to the value of the property, its suitability as security, the standing and reliability of the borrower and the value of any authorized additional security. The deeds of the property are retained by the society until the mortgage has been repaid.

The rate of interest charged on a mortgage loan is determined by various factors, which include the general level of interest rates, the rates paid by the society to investors, the composite rate of income tax and the level of management expenses. Interest is paid to the society without the deduction of tax, but a borrower obtains an allowance against his liability to income tax in respect of the interest paid.

The bulk of repayments are monthly, by a fixed sum from which the interest for the month is appropriated and the balance applied in reduction of the outstanding principal. Most societies calculate interest on an annual basis.

If a borrower should default in his repayments, the society can sue him on his personal covenant either for the principal debt outstanding or for the amount of subscriptions in arrears. Alternatively, the society can proceed against the property by taking possession, by appointing a receiver of the rents or by selling it.

When the mortgage debt has been fully repaid, the society will endorse the mortgage deed with a statutory vacating receipt. This receipt, which is sealed by the society, acknowledges payment of all money due under the deed. The mortgage deed together with the title deeds are then returned to the mortgagor.

Under the House Purchase and Housing Act, 1959, the registrar of building societies was empowered to "designate" certain societies, meaning that investments with them are trustee investments.

Economic and Social Aspects.—The building society movement in the range of its membership and the magnitude of its financial resources touches the life of the country at many points. From 1919 onward building societies in Great Britain attracted large sums, mainly from the smaller investors, because they offered security, a reasonable rate of interest, prompt withdrawal facilities and freedom from income tax deduction. Despite the unemployment of the interwar years, wage earners in general were better off than in 1914. Many workers had a margin of income which gave them an opportunity to save and the "small savings" institutions, including building societies, benefited. During the years of full employment and comprehensive social insurance which succeeded World War II, the margin for saving increased even further, as did the share of that saving which went to building societies.

The other major function of building societies is the promotion of home ownership. After World War I the nation became aware of an acute housing shortage and the government gave direct encouragement to building. Between 1919 and March 1940 some 4,000,000 houses were built in England and Wales and of these about 2,500,000 were built by private enterprise without subsidy of any kind. The existence of the building societies' mortgage service made this private enterprise building possible.

Home ownership also expanded after World War II, although under the Labour government, which came into power in 1945, greater encouragement was given to building by local authorities of houses to rent than to private enterprise building. It was not until 1951 when the Conservatives took office that legislation was introduced to increase the proportion of private building allowed and to permit council houses to be sold. This gave a great impetus to building societies, and the number of borrowers increased from 1,579,000 in 1951 to nearly 2,425,000 ten years later. The steady growth in the number of investors and borrowers was accompanied by a gradual reduction in the number of societies, due mainly to the difficulty of the smaller societies in attracting sufficient funds from the public and in maintaining the necessary administrative machinery.

Development Abroad.—The building society idea has spread far and wide. There are societies in many countries of the Commonwealth, most of them closely following British practice. They are also to be found in most countries of Europe and in parts of Central and South America.

BIBLIOGRAPHY.—*United States: Savings and Loan Fact Book* (annually since 1953); Leon T. Kendall, *Savings and Loan Business* (1962).
Great Britain: Sir Harold Bellman, *Bricks and Mortals* (1949); J. Mills (ed.), *Wurtzburg's Law Relating to Building Societies,* 12th ed. (1961); S. J. Price, *Building Societies: Their Origins and History* (1958); "Building Societies," *Annual Report of the Chief Registrar of Friendly Societies,* pt. v; *The Building Societies Year Book.*

(C. G. Hn.)

SAVINGS BANK. A savings bank is one of the many institutional arrangements that society makes to bring together lenders and borrowers of funds. Although it is customarily looked upon as an agency utilized by individuals who wish to accumulate funds for future spending, the savings bank is also a lending institution and could not exist in its present form were it not. It performs an important economic function in its dual capacity of borrower from individuals who wish to consume less than their income and of lender to others who wish to spend more. It serves to direct the flow of money income so that some of the economic resources of a society are turned from the production of goods for current consumption to add to its total stock of capital, or its wealth.

There are also other institutions that perform a similar economic function. The most important are the savings departments of commercial banks; building and loan, or savings and loan, associations; insurance companies; investment trusts; and a number of minor (in terms of magnitude of deposits) savings institutions, such as credit unions and similar cooperative credit organizations, industrial savings plans, and school savings programs. *See* BANKING; CREDIT UNION; DEPOSIT INSURANCE; SAVINGS AND LOAN ASSOCIATION.

HISTORICAL BACKGROUND

Savings banking is the product of two historical forces, one of which operated uniquely to create it alone and the other to create all savings institutions. The development of a liberal economic order, based upon specialization and exchange, presupposed an effective supply of money, in the creation of which all credit institutions participated. Such an order (dating from about 1550) carried with it certain ethical presuppositions concerning the nature of man, among which was the notion that he was capable of looking after himself amid the uncertainties of a market system. Savings banking, then, in addition to being one of the many credit institutions that an exchange economy finds indispensable is also a product of the effort to secure the individual against the caprices of capitalism. Not long in coming was recognition of the fact that if individuals were to be considered self-reliant they must have institutions enabling them to provide for such uncertainties as they might encounter.

In 1610, a Frenchman, Hugues de Lestre, published a treatise in which he urged the establishment of savings institutions for the poor so that their lot might be bettered and the rich might escape the necessity of almsgiving. Seventy-seven years after, the irrepressible Daniel Defoe, finding himself in a debtor's prison, wrote a tract on the wonders that could be wrought by the practice of thrift. To this end, he proposed that the government establish a pension office. If each person in the realm—rich and poor, of all ages—were to pay each year four shillings into a common fund managed by the state, they could "forever banish beggary and poverty out of the kingdom." Such a happy state could be purchased for the price of "two pots of beer a month." While the French and English continued to write about savings banks, elsewhere in Europe banks were developing out of the municipal pawnshops, the most famous of which was the Monte de Pietà that for centuries operated in the Italian city states as a savings and loan agency. The eventual product of this development was the municipal savings bank. Almost concurrent was the development of private savings banks in Germany, the first of which began in Hamburg in 1778.

The first savings bank in Britain was founded in 1810 by the Rev. Henry Duncan, pastor of an impoverished flock in Dumfriesshire, Scot. Duncan, who had been a student of the classical economist, Dugald Stewart, established the Savings and Friendly Society, the members of which were divided into three classes: ordinary members, who made regular deposits; extraordinary members, who contributed to a surplus fund out of which premiums were paid to encourage frequent deposits; and honorary members. The bank was not operated for profit, and its officers devoted their time to it as a philanthropic service. Penalties were imposed upon those who did not deposit regularly, and ordinary members who wished to withdraw their savings had first to obtain the permission of the court of directors of the society. Duncan's bank was the forerunner of the trustee savings banks in the United Kingdom and of the mutual savings banks in the United States. Its success was soon indisputable, and by 1827 the plan had spread over Scotland, England, and Ireland. They soon became subject to governmental regulation, and in 1863 the Trustee Savings Bank Act was passed. In 1861 the Post Office Savings Bank System was inaugurated, and the trustee banks declined in relative importance.

The origin of savings banking in the United States was quite similar to that in Britain, for the first banks were nonprofit institutions founded for charitable purposes. The original bank was the Provident Institution for Savings, of Boston, which received its charter in December 1816. One month earlier, the Philadelphia Saving Fund Society began business but was not incorporated until 1819. The Bank for Savings of New York was incorporated in 1819 by the Society for the Prevention of Pauperism. The founders' roll of American savings banks includes a number of men of some historical importance, such as Condy Raguet, Thomas Eddy, James Savage, and Clement and Alexander Biddle. Out of these early organizations developed the mutual savings banks of America, which are still largely confined to their place of origin in the North and Middle Atlantic states. Their growth was slow until the decade preceding the Civil War when the number of banks increased from 108 to 300, the number of depositors from 250,000 to 700,000, and total balances from $50,000,000 to $150,000,000. By 1875 this latter figure had risen to $900,000,000 and by 1913 to almost $5,000,000,000—even though the period between the close of the Civil War and the turn of the century was one of falling prices.

The success of mutual banks resulted in the creation of additional savings institutions, but the mutual structure was not copied by the new banks, which began in the middle and far western states. These were organizations operated for profit and managed in the interest of the shareholders. Stock savings banks were established, and commercial banks began to accept savings deposits toward the end of the 19th century. Prior to 1913, however, the national banks (see BANKING) did not distinguish between savings, or time, deposits and demand deposits, because there was no legal basis for such a distinction in the National Bank Act under which they operated. Their acceptance of savings deposits brought them into competition with the mutual, stock, and state banks.

When the Federal Reserve System was established in 1913, a distinction was made between kinds of deposits, and a lower reserve requirement was fixed for time deposits—those which could be withdrawn only after prior notice has been given.

The proliferation of savings plans late in the 19th century brought demands for a savings system under the control and operation of the post office, and in 1911 the Postal Savings System was started. It was discontinued by Congress in 1966.

In the entire history of savings banks, the period after World War I was the most eventful. Like other banks they reeled under two near-fatal blows. The first of these was the monetary disorder that fell upon almost every nation in the 1920s. The effect was to shake the confidence of the people in the value of money and to evoke a flight from currency to the hoarding of goods. In such circumstances, it is suicidal for an individual to abstain from current consumption in order to accumulate claims against future income, for the claims which the bank hands over to him may be worthless. That this was well realized in Germany—where inflation drove the mark down to $\frac{1}{1,000,000,000}$ of its original value —is evident in the decline of savings bank deposits from 19,700,000,000 gold marks in 1913 to 4,600,000,000 gold marks in 1927. Inflation or the fear of inflation—whichever verges upon the probable in a world of budgetary disorder—will produce a flight from the currency and the disorganization of banking.

The second catastrophe was the great depression of 1929. Depression, or deflation, produces a movement away from the holding of stocks of goods to the hoarding of money, and as the movement gains momentum these hoards are withdrawn from the banks and held privately. Concurrent with the heavy withdrawal of deposits after 1929 was a substantial decline in the value of bank assets, making it impossible for many banks to meet their obligations to depositors. The failure of thousands of banks created suspicions about the soundness of others until they, too, failed. The crisis reached its climax in the United States when all banks were closed by presidential decree in the spring of 1933 and later reopened under new conditions. The effect of the depression,

particularly in the United States, was to disturb profoundly the confidence of the people in the banking system and to disclose the inadequacy of conventional standards of bank management. It demonstrated that even the most scrupulous practices in maintaining required reserves and holding only prescribed investments did not render a bank capable of meeting all of its obligations when all depositors demanded payment and when earning assets were shrinking in value.

In the course of about 130 years both the purpose and practice of savings banking have changed drastically, and in these changes are reflected the changing character of individual saving habits. The banks are no longer benevolent institutions created by the wealthier members of the community for the succor of their less fortunate fellow citizens. They are avowed profit-making enterprises, as in the case of commercial banks engaging in the savings deposit business, or cooperative agencies, or public institutions operated by local or national governments. In the eastern United States, where mutual savings banks still flourish, their early overtones of philanthropy and paternalism have passed away. Savings bank practices have also changed. Originally the funds received from depositors were invested in government securities, which were long in maturing, comparatively safe, and bore a low rate of interest. Today savings deposits are invested as well in the securities of private enterprises, and, in the case of commercial banks in the Federal Reserve and of most state banks, they may be loaned out for short periods to businessmen.

Since the beginning of the 20th century savings banks have encountered mounting competition from other outlets for individual savings, such as insurance companies, postal savings banks, investment trusts, cooperative agencies, and, greatest of all, from governments seeking to borrow from individuals. It should also be noted that changes in the savings habits of individuals have lessened the permanence of their deposits. Studies made of the decade from 1930 to 1940 disclose that in the United States the majority of deposits were made, not as security against misfortune and old age, but for future spending anticipated with a considerable degree of certainty, with the consequence that the rate of turnover of deposits is antithetical to what were once conceived to be proper savings practices. In one important American bank—believed to be representative—three-fourths of all savings deposits were withdrawn before they were five years old.

All of these changes are symptomatic of the changing character of individual savings. The causes that once compelled an individual to lay aside funds for a rainy day have either disappeared or have found a different expression. The uncertainty that once haunted members of Western industrial society has become less terrible as governments have assumed the responsibility of looking after the jobless, the aged, and the infirm—a development that is signalized by social security legislation and the socializing of charity. Moreover, those individuals who are able to invest against misfortune have alternative methods of doing it, such as purchasing insurance policies or the securities of enterprises or governments. Savings deposits are still useful for accumulating funds for large expenditures—as for education and travel—but even for this purpose they are not as essential as they once were. The development of mass credit institutions—installment selling, small loan agencies, and the like—has diminished the necessity of saving to spend. Finally, the very notion of thrift has lost much of its enticement, because the contemporary man discounts the future at an inordinately high rate. He is a victim of what Adam Smith called "the passion for present enjoyment," and is refractory to the very instinct which Smith believed would redeem him—the desire to save which "comes with us from the womb, and never leaves us till we go into the grave." Not only does thrift no longer keep its high place among the cardinal virtues but is often looked upon as a pernicious practice by many of those very people who were once among its archadvocates: the economists.

SAVINGS INSTITUTIONS IN THE UNITED STATES

Savings institutions in the United States are of three principal kinds: commercial banks in their savings deposit departments;

mutual savings banks; and the postal savings system. In addition, savings and loan associations and credit unions receive the savings of the public in savings accounts.

Savings Accounts Trends.—During the 1920s, total savings accounts rose from $17,300,000,000 to $34,600,000,000, an increase of over $1,700,000,000 per year. About two-thirds of this increase was in time deposits at commercial banks and savings deposits in mutual savings banks. During the 1930s, because of sharp declines during the depression years, total accumulations in savings accounts fell off $2,700,000,000. The sharpest drop relatively was in savings capital of savings and loan associations, followed by the decline in time deposits at commercial banks. Time deposits in mutual savings banks showed a steady rise during these years except in 1932 and 1933, and postal savings rose sharply during the depression years. During the 1940s, total holdings of savings accounts much more than doubled, reaching $73,100,000,000 in 1950. Particularly large savings were accumulated during the World War II period and the first three postwar years. The average annual increase in total savings accounts in this decade was $4,100,000,000 per year. In the five years 1951 through 1955 there was a further marked increase in total holdings of savings accounts to an aggregate at the end of 1955 of $110,800,000,000. The average accumulation of funds in savings accounts during these five years was $7,500,000,000 per year.

In the early 1950s, time deposits in commercial banks and time deposits in mutual savings banks lagged behind savings accounts in savings and loan associations in terms of rate of increase. In dollars, the increase in savings capital at all savings and loan associations from 1950 to 1955 almost equaled the increase in savings accounts at the other four sets of institutions. In percentage terms, time deposits in commercial banks rose almost 33%, and time deposits at all mutual savings banks rose over 40%. During the same span of time total savings accounts at all savings and loan associations rose about 130%. Thus, during this period savings balances in savings and loan associations showed phenomenal gains, while the increases in savings deposits in commercial banks and mutual savings banks were more moderate.

Commercial Banks.—Time deposits in commercial banks, most of which are savings deposits, comprise a significant portion of the total deposits of these institutions. During World War II, time deposits declined from about one-fourth of total deposits in all commercial banks to about one-fifth. In the postwar period, however, they rose faster than other deposits and soon returned to their pre-World War II relationship to total deposits. By 1965, time deposits, other than interbank deposits, in all commercial banks amounted to more than $137,000,000,000. Wide differences exist among individual commercial banks in the relative importance of time and savings deposits in their deposit structure.

No member bank of the Federal Reserve System or insured nonmember bank may pay interest on any deposit that is payable on demand. Furthermore, the legal minimum and maximum reserve requirements for member banks against time deposits are between 3% and 6%, much less than the ranges of reserve requirements for member banks against demand deposits. Accordingly, in regulations of the board of governors of the Federal Reserve System, the terms "time deposits" and "savings deposits" are strictly defined. Savings deposits are evidenced by a passbook, and may be accepted only from individuals or nonprofit organizations, with the legal possibility of requiring notice of withdrawal. Furthermore, the Board of Governors of the Federal Reserve System, under provisions of the Federal Reserve Act, establishes maximum rates that may be paid by member banks on time deposits. The rate payable by a member bank may not in any event exceed the maximum rate payable by state banks and trust companies on like deposits under the laws of the states in which the member bank is located. The same maximum rates of payment were established for insured nonmember banks by the Federal Deposit Insurance Corporation (FDIC), effective Feb. 1, 1936.

Mutual Savings Banks.—Mutual savings banks concentrate on savings deposits and generally accept no commercial or checking accounts. Such banks have no capital stock and are purely mutual organizations. With no shareholders, the mutual savings banks are governed by boards of trustees, most of them self-perpetuating bodies, made up of outstanding business and professional men. Mutual savings banks operate exclusively under state law and state charter and are supervised and examined by the state banking departments in their respective states. Most mutual savings banks are quite old institutions, and many have celebrated their 100th anniversaries.

All the net income of these financial institutions, after operating expenses, is paid to the depositors as dividends or is allocated to reserves for future losses. Mutual savings banks pay "dividends" or "interest-dividends" to their depositors, but these payments have come to be viewed simply as interest. By 1965 total deposits in mutual savings banks amounted to more than $50,000,000,000. The average size of accounts was $2,108 and the number of accounts was 22,120,000.

Several states place a limit on the maximum amount that any one person or organization may have on deposit in any one savings bank. The laws pertaining to mutual savings banks provide that depositors may be required to give notice (typically 60 or 90 days) as stated in the savings account passbook before withdrawals are paid. In fact, however, savings banks ordinarily meet withdrawals without requiring notice.

The mutual savings banks have a long history of conservative operation, with emphasis placed on safety and availability of savings entrusted to them, rather than on earning a high rate of dividend. In particular, the savings banks went into the great depression with substantial reserves and strong liquidity positions. "Runs" on mutual savings banks by their depositors were not as drastic as those in commercial banks. As a result, in spite of losses on some investments and mortgages, the savings banks went through the depression without a single failure or liquidation. No mutual savings bank had to go "on notice" or delay the meeting of withdrawal requests, except when all banks were closed during the bank holiday.

Mutual savings banks are in operation under state charters in all of the New England states and in New York, New Jersey, Maryland, Delaware, Pennsylvania, Ohio, Indiana, Wisconsin, Minnesota, Washington, Oregon, and Alaska. They also operate in the Virgin Islands.

The investment powers of mutual savings banks are closely prescribed by state laws and by rules and regulations of state supervisory authorities. Investments in securities, for instance, are usually confined to a "legal list" of authorized securities from which the savings banks determine their bond portfolio. Some states limit real estate mortgage investments to 60% to 75% of savings bank deposits.

After World War II the legal investment provisions of various states were changed to enable the mutual savings banks to broaden their investments and so to increase earnings. Particularly important in this respect was the enactment of legislation which permitted mutual savings banks to purchase Federal Housing Authority (FHA)-insured and Veterans Administration (VA)-guaranteed mortgages without reference to the location of the residential property against which such loans had been made. New York passed such legislation for FHA-insured mortgages in 1948 and for VA-guaranteed mortgages in 1951. These laws provided substantially enlarged outlets for investment in mortgages, particularly by the large metropolitan savings banks, and gave rise to much greater marketability of FHA-insured and VA-guaranteed mortgage loans over the nation. In 1953 a New York law also permitted a savings bank to borrow funds for purposes other than paying depositors up to 5% of its assets. This measure was adopted to help savings banks meet varying mortgage commitments without having to sell securities. During the postwar period, the majority of mutual savings banks states legalized the purchase of some type of equity securities having an adequate earnings and dividend record and within certain restrictions in relation to surplus and assets. In certain states mutual savings banks were permitted to invest in large-scale housing developments.

Postal Savings System.—The postal savings system was authorized by Congress in 1910. It was established partly as an aftermath to the panic of 1907 and partly to attract deposits from those who lacked confidence in usual banking institutions and from the many immigrants in those times who frequently sent their savings to institutions in Europe. Over the years, both before and after its founding, the postal savings system met opposition from banking circles as an unwarranted duplication of private facilities.

The U.S. government is solemnly pledged to the payment of postal savings deposits. Accounts may be opened and deposits made by any competent person over 10 years of age. Deposits with the postal savings system are evidenced by certificates issued in denominations from $1 through $500. No depositor may have to his credit more than $2,500, exclusive of accumulated interest. The depositor may at any time withdraw all or any part of his deposits, with any interest payable thereon, from the post office where the deposits were made.

Postal savings deposits earn interest at the rate of 2% a year, a rate that has been in effect ever since the establishment of the postal savings system. Until recent years, only simple interest was paid. Interest has been compounded annually, however, on deposits represented by postal savings certificates issued on or after Sept. 1, 1954. The assets of the postal savings system are invested mainly in U.S. government obligations, although funds may also be redeposited in local banks at a required rate of $2\frac{1}{2}\%$.

Until 1930, growth of the postal savings system was limited, partly because the banks paid much higher rates than 2%, and total postal savings due depositors amounted to only $169,000,000 at the end of 1929. With the bank failures during the early 1930s, however, people withdrew savings from commercial banks and put them in postal savings deposits. By the end of 1933 the postal savings system had grown to $1,229,000,000, eight times its size before the great depression.

Then followed several years of little change in postal savings, and amounts due depositors totalled $1,315,000,000 at the end of 1939. During World War II, as a part of the general upsurge in savings at that time, and continuing in the early postwar period, the postal savings system experienced another period of rapid growth, reaching a high point of $3,523,000,000 late in 1947. Postal savings then declined, in part under the impact of vigorous competition from savings and loan associations and banks. The total amount due depositors by the postal savings system in 1965 was only $400,000,000.

Economic Significance.—The gathering together of savings of the public and the investment of these funds by the savings banks and savings institutions is a service to the U.S. economy of the greatest importance. In the capital markets the annual increase in savings accounts is the largest single component of the supply of funds. Likewise, home mortgages, in which much of "over-the-counter" savings are invested, comprise the largest single component, by far, of the demand for funds. Such savings and investment are essential to the progress and growth of the nation.

Accordingly, in the two decades after World War II there was renewed attention to the economic importance of savings, and particularly to savings deposits and savings accounts. There was also intensified competition among financial institutions for the favour of the public and the opportunity to be entrusted with savings. Nowhere was competition stiffer than among commercial banks, mutual savings banks, and savings and loan associations. Competition took several forms. Fundamental, of course, is the seeking of what is deemed fair treatment of net earnings under the federal income tax law. Rivalry was keen in new and attractive office quarters, in range of services offered, in advertising, and public relations. Competition was sharp in rate of interest or dividend. At the same time, "over-the-counter" savings were under pressure from alternative forms of saving, such as social security and pension funds and the attractiveness of common stocks. Attitudes toward savings were challenged by inflation, by less cyclical instability in the economy after World War II, and by government welfare programs. (J. K. L.)

SAVINGS BANKS IN EUROPE

United Kingdom.—After the first savings bank in Britain was established at Ruthwell, Dumfriesshire, Scot., in 1810, the movement soon spread throughout Scotland and England, with the result that in 1817 the first law governing these institutions was passed, the first act of its type ever to be adopted by any country. By 1859 there were 635 savings banks holding deposits amounting to £39,000,000. In the mid-1960s there were 79 separate savings banks with more than 1,350 offices, 9,000,000 depositors, and funds amounting to £2,100,000,000.

These banks, known as trustee savings banks, are not conducted for private profit; their sole concern is to offer the most convenient and remunerative method of saving compatible with sound administration and security. They combine the security offered by close connection with the state with the freedom that comes from independent management. The banks are under the direction of bodies of trustees and managers who do not receive any payment for their services. The banks are subject to government supervision and are also inspected on behalf of the Trustee Savings Banks Inspection Committee. The funds of the ordinary departments of the banks are invested with the National Debt Commissioners, and the funds of the special investment departments (where a higher rate of interest is paid) are, with the commissioners' approval, invested in government securities and with the municipal authorities.

The British Post Office Savings Bank, founded by W. E. Gladstone in 1861 as a department of the General Post Office, has been a model for similar banks in other countries; it works under government guarantee. (*See* POSTAL SERVICES.) The rate of interest in the Post Office Savings Bank is similar to that paid in the ordinary departments of the trustee savings banks, and in both institutions the limit of deposit is £5,000. In the special investment departments of trustee savings banks the limit of deposit is £3,000.

The post office and the trustee savings banks, together with the National Savings Committee of England and Wales (formed as the War Savings Committee in 1916 to help finance World War I by the sale of savings certificates) and its counterparts in Scotland and Northern Ireland, form the National Savings Movement, which promotes the sale of national savings certificates, national development bonds, and premium savings bonds, and encourages deposits in savings banks. In addition to the sale of national savings securities, the savings banks purchase government stocks and bonds for their depositors. The total amount of national savings in the mid-1960s was about £8,250,000,000.

Scotland has a few savings banks free of government supervision; England has only the Birmingham Municipal Bank, controlled by the city council under the Birmingham Corporation Act, 1919. The joint stock banks also accept savings deposits; other large savings institutions are the building and cooperative societies.

Interest up to £15 on deposits in the post office savings banks and in the ordinary departments of trustee savings banks is free of income tax for each individual.

France.—The first French savings bank was that of Paris, the Caisse d'Épargne de Paris, instituted in 1818. Soon thereafter other savings banks were established at Bordeaux, Metz, Marseilles, and Nantes, and by the mid-1960s there were 580 savings banks with more than 4,000 offices, 16,500,000 depositors and funds amounting to Fr. 26,400,000,000.

The French savings banks, like the British trustee savings banks, are controlled by a board of management. The funds of the banks are deposited with the Caisse des Dépôts et Consignations, a government institution, which invests them in government securities or in securities guaranteed by the government, in debentures issued by chambers of commerce, with the Crédit Foncier de France, or in French and foreign securities authorized by the minister of finance.

In addition to the savings banks there is the Caisse Nationale d'Épargne Postale, which is well established throughout France and is the equivalent of the Post Office Savings Bank in Britain, with deposits in the mid-1960s exceeding Fr. 16,800,000,000.

Federal Republic of Germany.—The first German savings banks (*Sparkassen*) were founded in Hamburg in 1778, in Oldenburg in 1786, and in Kiel in 1796. The latter two banks still exist.

The German savings banks are mostly municipal savings banks. They are common welfare institutions juridically independent, incorporated under the provisions of public law and enjoying the guarantee of the municipalities. The legal regulations concerning savings banks are voted separately by each *Land*. One of the characteristics of the German savings banks is that normal savings activities, the short-term current account and transfer deposits (*Giro*) are handled simultaneously.

In 1947, after World War II, the German savings banks founded the General League of the Savings Banks and Clearing House Association to promote the interests of its members, of member regional associations, and of clearing houses through advice, assistance, and the exchange of experience.

In the mid-1960s there were about 870 separate savings banks in the federal republic, with 11,000 branches and agencies.and a total of 51,800,000,000 DM. of savings deposited.

U.S.S.R.—The new savings banks in the U.S.S.R. began early in 1923. The principal aim of these banks, which are state organizations, is to collect the people's available resources by means of deposits or of subscriptions to state loans and to direct these resources to funds necessary for the national economy. The general management of the savings banks and of state credit, which is a section of the ministry of finance, invests the funds of the savings banks, controls their functioning, and issues instructions relating to the technique of their operations.

The foundation capital of the savings banks, supplied by the government, was 10,000,000 rubles. The reserve funds are made up from sums deducted from profits; another part of the net profit goes to the treasury and the remainder to the fund for the improvement of the material condition of the personnel.

In the early 1960s the total deposits in these savings banks exceeded 100,000,000,000 rubles; the interest paid amounted to 3% on deposits withdrawable at six months' notice and 2% on other deposits.

Other avenues through which Soviet families may invest their money include state loans, collective deposits with the cooperative banks (*Vsekobanki*), municipal banks (*Tsekombanki*), and rural banks (*Selkhozbanki*), and payments to mutual-help associations and to social insurance.

Italy.—The first Italian savings banks were established in Padua, Rovigo, Udine, and Venice in 1822, in Milan in 1823, in Verona in 1826, and in Turin in 1827. In the early 1960s there were 80 savings banks and 10 pawn banks that accepted savings deposits and deposits on current account. The funds were mainly invested in government securities, loans to local authorities, mortgage loans, overdrafts, and other short-term credits and discounts. There were about 2,500 branches, and deposits (mainly savings deposits) totaled 3,000,000,000,000 lire. The Italian Savings Banks Association was founded in 1912; there is also a central bank, whose shares are owned by the savings banks.

The Italian Post Office Savings Bank was founded in 1876. In addition to the savings and postal check business, this bank arranges the purchase of government bonds on behalf of the depositors. In the mid-1960s total savings deposits (including postal savings certificates) amounted to about 2,200,000,000,000 lire.

Netherlands.—The earliest local savings banks in the Netherlands were established through the initiative of a philanthropic society, the Society for the Promotion of Common Welfare, founded in 1783. The first bank was opened in the small town of Workum, Friesland, in 1817. In the mid-1960s there were about 260 local savings banks with 400 branches, each bank being administered by a board of trustees. The local savings banks owed their 3,700,000 depositors 4,120,000,000 guldens.

The Netherlands Savings Bank Association, established in 1907, protects the common interests of all local savings banks and endeavours to expand the services offered to depositors. There is a central auditing department, a central publicity office, and a cooperative investment fund, founded in 1958. The fund accepts deposits from the affiliated savings banks at one week's and three months' notice, investing them in easily realizable assets such as call money, treasury bonds, and short term municipal loans.

The Post Office Savings Bank was inaugurated in 1881. Its funds are mainly invested in government stock, treasury bonds, and loans to local authorities. In the mid-1960s deposits with the Post Office Savings Bank amounted to about 2,900,000,000 guldens.

(R. T. H. S.)

BIBLIOGRAPHY.—*United States:* Raymond W. Goldsmith, *A Study of Saving in the United States,* vol. 1, pt. ii, "Tables of Annual Estimates of Saving" and vol. 11, ch. vi, "Cash Savings" (1955); Report of Consultant Committee on Savings Statistics, Board of Governors of the Federal Reserve System, *Statistics of Saving* (1955); Board of Governors of the Federal Reserve System, *Flow of Funds in the United States 1939–1953* (1955); John Lintner, *Mutual Savings Banks in the Savings and Mortgage Markets* (1948); Weldon Welfling, *Savings Banking in New York State* (1939); National Association of Mutual Savings Banks, *Mutual Savings Banking: Basic Characteristics and Role in the National Economy* (1962).
Europe: H. O. Horne, *History of Savings Banks* (1947).

SAVINKOV, BORIS VIKTOROVICH (1879–1925), Russian revolutionary, a redoubtable enemy of both the imperial and the Soviet regimes, was born in Kharkov. He joined the Socialist-Revolutionary Party in 1903, and as a leading member of its "fighting organization" he participated in several terroristic acts, including the assassination in 1904 of V. K. Plehve (*q.v.*). When World War I broke out he took a patriotic stand; he enlisted in the French Army and, after returning to Russia in 1917, became a military commissar and subsequently deputy minister of war. He sought to combat defeatism and to strengthen the provisional government by concentrating power in a triumvirate consisting of the prime minister A. F. Kerenski, Gen. L. G. Kornilov and himself. But his partners fell out, and he was obliged to resign.

After the Bolshevik Revolution, Savinkov established a clandestine military organization which in July 1918 brought about abortive risings in several Russian towns. Subsequently he moved to Paris and solicited Allied intervention against Soviet Russia. In January 1920 he was invited to Warsaw by Jozef Pilsudski. There he organized a Russian volunteer corps to fight with the Polish Army. After the signature of the Polish-Soviet Peace Treaty of Riga (1921), however, he returned to Paris disillusioned. Soviet agents penetrated his organization and, it appears, tricked him into returning to the U.S.S.R. Arrested in Minsk on Aug. 18, 1924, he was tried a week later. His death sentence (Aug. 29, 1924) was commuted to imprisonment, but in May 1925 he was stated to have committed suicide at the Lubianka prison in Moscow.

See R. Gul, *Boris Savinkov,* 2 vol. (1930).   (J. L. H. K.)

SAVOIE, a *département* of southeastern France, formed in 1860 from the southern parts of the former duchy of Savoy, namely Haute-Savoie, Tarentaise, and Maurienne, which were ceded to the emperor Napoleon III by the kingdom of Sardinia. It lies along the Italian frontier between the *départements* of Haute-Savoie to the north and Hautes-Alpes to the south, and is bounded west by the *départements* of Isère and Ain. Area 2,389 sq.mi. (6,187.5 sq.km.). Pop. (1962) 266,678.

The *département* extends across the longitudinal belts of the northern French Alps. In the west are the limestone ranges of the Préalpes in the Bauges and Grande Chartreuse massifs on either side of the Chambéry-Lac du Bourget Gap. There follows the Combe de Savoie, the great longitudinal valley that separates the Préalpes from the crystalline core of the Alps. East of the latter the *département* includes the high intra-Alpine valleys of the upper basins of the Isère and the Arc, extending to the frontier, which follows the main watershed. The mountains everywhere show the strong imprint of the Quaternary glaciation, and the high valleys are a succession of basins and gorges, where the rivers cross rocky constrictions. Surrounding the Tarentaise (the upper valley of the Isère) and the Maurienne (the upper valley of the Arc) the highest peaks exceed 12,000 ft. (3,700 m.) and include the Grande Casse, Mont Pourri, Pointe de Charbonel, and Aiguille de la Grande Sassière. The Tarentaise leads to the Petit Saint-Bernard Pass into Italy, the Maurienne to the Mont Cenis Pass and tunnels. Near the valley heads the Col de l'Iseran (9,085 ft. [2,769 m.]) provides an interconnection, followed by a motor road. The north-south route of the high French Alps is continued south from the Maurienne by the road that climbs past Valloire toward the Col du Galibier.

The wet Préalpes are heavily clothed with forests. The sheltered intra-Alpine valleys are relatively dry and, although the period of snow cover is long, farming and settlement extend to high altitudes, especially on sun-facing slopes (*adrets*). Above, fine forests cover the mountain slopes up to a tree line that reaches as high as 7,000 ft. (2,000 m.), with extensive meadows still higher. The forests are an important resource, and in the rural buildings there is prodigal use of timber, great overhanging eaves and balconies being characteristic features. Below the forest, the farmland is devoted to hay and other fodder crops. The isolation that imposed a self-sufficient economy has been broken down by the development of modern communications; hence the cultivation of cereals and fruit crops, including the vine, has contracted, and these crops are mainly confined to the low-lying areas of the Combe de Savoie and the Chambéry Gap. The high Alpine valleys are concerned almost exclusively with pastoral farming, the elaborately staged cultivation and grazing zones having given way to specialized cattle farming, providing dairy products and young animals for export to the lowlands. Cheese production is well organized, and big herds on the summer pastures are looked after by only a few specialized workers.

Some anthracite is worked in the Maurienne and in the Tarentaise, where there is also a silver-lead mine at La Plagne. The abundant waterpower resources have been vigorously developed, and there are numerous electricity-generating stations. Most of the power is transmitted for use outside the Alps, but there are some local electrometallurgical and electrochemical works, notably at Ugines and along the railway approaching Modane. The chief concentration of industry is in the Chambéry Gap. Besides silk manufacture and engineering, the timber and limestone of the Préalpes provide the bases of important paper and cement industries. Lacking the benefits of manufacturing industry, the Alpine valleys that remain rural suffered severe depopulation from the mid-19th to the mid-20th century. The tourist industry has become important and widespread but has not counteracted depopulation, except in a few localities. Aix-les-Bains, on Lac du Bourget, is an important spa resort.

Chambéry (*q.v.*) is the largest town and the *préfecture* of the *département*, which comes under its court of appeal, archiepiscopal jurisdiction, and, for administration of education, its *académie*; but the diocese of Chambéry is only one of three that share the *département*. The upper basins of the Isère and the Arc constitute the separate bishoprics of Moûtiers-Tarentaise and Saint-Jean-de-Maurienne respectively. The *département* consists of three *arrondissements*, centred upon Chambéry, Albertville, and Saint-Jean-de-Maurienne. For the history of the district *see* SAVOY, HOUSE OF. (AR. E. S.)

SAVONA, a city, seaport, and episcopal see of Liguria, northwestern Italy, and capital of Savona Province, lies 27 mi. (43 km.) WSW of Genoa by rail. Pop. (1961) 72,956 (comm.). Most of the town is modern, with rectilinear streets laid out in the late-19th-century style. In the old quarter are examples of medieval, Renaissance, and Baroque architecture. The late Renaissance cathedral (1589–1602) has a 12th-century font and choir stalls, and a pulpit of the 15th century. The Sistine Chapel was built by Pope Sixtus IV; the Della Rovere Palace, built by Cardinal Giuliano Della Rovere (Pope Julius II), now houses public offices. The Chiabrera Theatre was built in 1853 in honour of the poet Gabriello Chiabrera (born in Savona 1552).

Savona is a major Italian port and an outlet for the Piedmont region and part of central Europe. Coal and fuels are the main imports; coal is distributed to the industrial centres of Bormida Valley by an extensive telpherage system. An oil pipeline runs to Trecate and Novara. Savona is one of the main centres of the Italian iron industry; it also has shipbuilding, mechanical and electrical engineering, sulfur and glass works, tanneries, and food processing. Linked by rail with Turin, it is also on the main rail and road route from Genoa to the French border.

Savona is recorded as allied with Carthage against Rome in 205 B.C. It reappears in A.D. 568–569, when the Ligurians were fighting the barbarians. Rothari, king of Lombardy, destroyed it in 641. It was capital of Marca Aleramica (950–1191) and later, as an autonomous commune, formed an alliance with Genoa, but

rivalry between the cities arose and in 1528 the Genoese destroyed Savona's port and built a fortress there in 1542–43. In 1805 Savona was annexed to the Napoleonic Empire; it was joined to the Kingdom of Sardinia in 1815, and entered the Kingdom of Italy in 1861. The city was heavily bombed in World War II.

SAVONA PROVINCE, created in 1927, stretches along the western coast of Liguria from Cogoleto to Cervo. Area 596 sq.mi. (1,544 sq.km.). Pop. (1961) 270,544. Much of the mountain zone, over 4,000 ft. (1,200 m.) in places, is wooded, especially with chestnut. Most of the coastal area is under cultivation. Early market-garden produce is exported to northern and central Europe. Industrial and commercial centres besides Savona include Vado Ligure, Cairo Montenotte, Cengio, Ferrania, Albisola Marina, Varazze, Pietra Ligure, and Finale Ligure. The coastal fringe forms part of the popular Riviera di Ponente; resorts include Alassio, Albisola Marina, Celle Ligure, and Finale Ligure. There is an airport at Villanova d'Albenga. (G. B. N. B.)

SAVONAROLA, GIROLAMO (1452–1498), Italian reformer and martyr, was born at Ferrara on Sept. 21, 1452, the son of Niccolò Savonarola and of Elena Bonaccorsi. He was educated by his paternal grandfather, Michele, a celebrated doctor and a man of rigid moral and religious principles. From this elderly scholar, whose own education was of the 14th century, Savonarola may perhaps have received certain medieval influences. In his

early poetry and other adolescent writings the main characteristics of the future reformer are seen. Even at that early date, as he wrote in a letter to his father, he "could not suffer the blind wickedness of the peoples of Italy." He found unbearable the humanistic paganism which corrupted manners, art, poetry and religion itself. He saw as the cause of this spreading corruption a clergy vicious even in the highest levels of the church hierarchy.

On April 24, 1475, he left his father's house and his medical studies, which he had embarked on after taking a degree in the liberal arts, to enter the Dominican order at Bologna. Returning to Ferrara four years later he taught scripture in the Convento degli Angeli. Scripture together with the works of Thomas

MANSELL—ALINARI

POSTHUMOUS PORTRAIT OF GIROLAMO SAVONAROLA, BY HIS DISCIPLE FRA BARTOLOMMEO (1472–1517)

Aquinas had always been his great passion. In 1482 Savonarola was sent to Florence to take up the post of lecturer in the convent of San Marco, where he gained a great reputation for his learning and asceticism. As a preacher he was unsuccessful until a sudden revelation inspired him to begin his prophetic sermons. At San Gimignano in Lent 1485 and 1486 he put forward his famous propositions: the church needed reforming: it would be scourged and then renewed.

The following year (1487) he left Florence to become master of studies in the *studium generale* of Bologna. Then, after the year of his appointment was up, he was sent to preach in various cities until Lorenzo de' Medici used his influence to have him sent back to Florence, thus opening the doors to the bitterest enemy of Medici rule. Having returned to the city of his destiny (1490), Savonarola preached boldly against the tyrannical abuses of the government. Too late Lorenzo tried to dam the dangerous eloquence with threats and flattery, but his own life was drawing to a close, while popular enthusiasm for Savonarola's preaching constantly increased. Soon afterward Savonarola gave his blessing to the dying Lorenzo. The legend that he refused Lorenzo absolution is disproved by documentary evidence.

Medici rule did not long survive Lorenzo and was overthrown by the invasion of Charles VIII (1494). Two years before, Savonarola had predicted his coming and his easy victory. These authenticated prophecies, the part he had played in negotiations with the king and in moderating the hatred of the factions after the change of government, enormously increased his authority. Once the Medici had been driven out, Florence had no other master than Savonarola's terrible voice. He introduced a democratic government, the best the city ever had. He has been accused, but unjustly, of interfering in politics. He was not ambitious or an intriguer. He wanted to found his city of God in Florence, heart of Italy, as a well-organized Christian republic which might initiate the reform of Italy and of the church. This was the object of all his actions. The results he obtained were amazing: the splendid but corrupt Renaissance capital thus miraculously transformed seemed to a contemporary a foretaste of paradise.

Savonarola's triumph was too great and too sudden not to give rise to jealousy and suspicion. A Florentine party was formed in opposition to him called the *Arrabbiati*. These internal enemies formed an alliance with powerful foreign forces, foremost of which were the duke of Milan and the pope, who had joined in the Holy League against the king of France and saw in Savonarola the main obstacle to Florence's joining them. It was then, after a firm rejection of the League by Florence, that the pope sent to Savonarola the brief of July 21, 1495, in which he praised the miraculous fruits of Savonarola's work and called him to Rome to pronounce his prophecies from his own lips. As that pope was the corrupt Alexander VI the trap was too obvious. Savonarola asked to be allowed to put off his journey, offering illness as his excuse.

The pope appeared to be satisfied, but on Sept. 8, under pressure from his political friends and Savonarola's enemies, he sent him a second brief in which praises now turned into vituperation. He ordered him to go to Bologna under pain of excommunication. Savonarola replied to this strange document with respectful firmness pointing out no fewer than 18 mistakes in it. The brief was replaced by another of Oct. 16, in which he was forbidden to preach. As the pope himself frankly confessed, it was the League which insisted. After a few months, as Lent 1496 drew near, Alexander VI, while refusing the Florentine ambassadors a formal revocation of the ban, conceded this verbally. Thus Savonarola was able to give his sermons on Amos, which are among his finest and most forceful, and in which he attacked the Roman court with renewed vigour. He also appeared to refer to the pope's scandalous private life, and the latter took offense at this. A college of theologians found nothing to criticize in what the friar had said, so that after Lent he was able to begin, without further remonstrances from Rome, the sermons on Micah.

At that time, as Savonarola's authority grew, the pope tried to win him over by offering him a cardinal's hat. He replied: "A red hat? I want a hat of blood." Then Alexander VI, pressed by the League and *Arrabbiati*, mounted a fresh attack. In a brief of Nov. 7, 1496, he incorporated the Congregation of San Marco, of which Savonarola was vicar, with another in which he would have lost all his authority. If he obeyed, his reforms would be lost. If he disobeyed, he would be excommunicated. Savonarola, however, while protesting vigorously, did not disobey, because no one came forward to put the brief into force. He therefore went on unperturbed in Advent 1496 and Lent 1497 with his series of sermons on Ezekiel. During the carnival season that year his authority received a symbolic tribute in the "burning of the vanities," when personal ornaments, lewd pictures, cards and gaming tables were burned. Destruction of books and works of art was negligible. Events in Italy now turned against Savonarola, however, and even in Florence his power was lessened by unfavourable political and economic developments. A government of *Arrabbiati* forced him to stop preaching and incited sacrilegious riots against him on Ascension day. The *Arrabbiati* obtained from the Roman court, against payment, the desired bull of excommunication against their enemy. In effect the excommunication, besides being surreptitious, was full of such obvious errors of form and substance as to render it null and void, and the pope himself had to disown it. However, the Florentine government sought in vain to obtain its formal withdrawal: wider political issues were involved. Absorbed in study and prayer, Savonarola was silent. Only when Rome proposed an unworthy deal, which made withdrawal of the censure dependent on Florence's entry into the League, did he again go into the pulpit (Lent 1498) to give those sermons on Exodus which marked his own departure from the pulpit and from life. He was soon silenced by the interdict with which the city was threatened. He had no other way out but an appeal to a church council, and he began a move in this direction but then burned the letters to the princes which he had already written, in order not to cause dissension within the church. Once this road was closed the only remaining one led to martyrdom.

The imprudence of the most impassioned of his followers, Fra Domenico da Pescia, brought events to a head. Fra Domenico took at his word a Franciscan who had challenged to ordeal by fire anyone who maintained the invalidity of Savonarola's excommunication. The *signoria* and the whole population of the most civilized city in Italy greedily encouraged that barbarous experiment, as it alone seemed to promise a solution of an insuperable problem. Only Savonarola was dissatisfied. The decree, which assigned to the ordeal Fra Domenico himself and a Franciscan, declared the loser whichever might withdraw or even vacillate. In fact the Franciscan failed to appear and so the ordeal did not take place. Savonarola, victorious by the terms of the decree, was blamed for not having achieved a miracle.

The following day the rabble led by the *Arrabbiati* rioted, marched to San Marco and overcame the defenders. Savonarola was taken like a common criminal together with Fra Domenico and another follower. After examination by a commission of his worst enemies and after savage torture, it was yet necessary to falsify the record of the inquiry if he were to be charged with any crimes. But his fate was settled. The papal commissioners came from Rome "with the verdict in their bosom," as one of them said. After the ecclesiastical trial, which was even more perfunctory, he was handed over to the secular arm, with his two companions, to be hanged and burned. The account of his last hours is like a page from the lives of the Church Fathers. Before mounting the scaffold he piously received the pope's absolution and plenary indulgence.

In fact Savonarola's quarrel was with the corruption of the clergy of whom Alexander VI was merely the most scandalous example, not with the Roman pontiff for whom he always professed obedience and respect. He was a reformer, but Catholic and Thomist to the marrow; his faith is borne out in his many works, the greatest of which is the *Triumphus crucis,* a clear exposition of Christian apologetics. His *Compendium revelationum,* an account of visions and prophecies that came true, went through many editions in several countries. Of his sermons, some exist in a version taken down verbatim.

After Savonarola's death a cult was dedicated to him which had a long history. Saints canonized by the church, such as Philip Neri and Catherine dei Ricci, venerated him as a saint; an office was said for him, and miracles he had performed were recorded. He was portrayed in paintings and medals with the title of *Beatus*. In the *Acta sanctorum* he was included among the *praetermissi*. When the 500th anniversary of his birth came round in 1952, there was again talk of his canonization.

BIBLIOGRAPHY.—Ten vol. of the Italian national edition (1953–) of Savonarola's works had appeared by 1964. Partial editions were published by P. Villari, *Scelta di prediche e scritti* (1898), and by R. Palmarocchi, *Prediche italiane ai Fiorentini,* 3 vol. (1930–35). His letters were edited and published by R. Ridolfi in 1933. *See also* R. Ridolfi (ed.), *Cronologia e bibliografia delle prediche* (1933); L. Giovannozzi, *Contributo alla bibliografia di G. Savonarola* (1953); M. Ferrara, *Bibliografia savonaroliana* (1958).

Biographies: P. Villari, *La storia di fra Girolamo Savonarola,* 2 vol. (1887), new ed. (1927), Eng. trans. (1889); J. Schnitzer, *Savonarola,* 2 vol. (1931), original German ed. (1924); R. Ridolfi, *Vita di G. Savonarola,* 2 vol. (1952), Eng. trans. (1959). (R. Ri.)

SAVOY, HOUSE OF, one of the great historic dynasties of Europe. From its medieval seat astride the western Alps, where the modern map shows France, Italy, and Switzerland converging, it spread its dominion, gradually and through numerous vicissitudes, farther and farther over Piedmont; in the 15th century it was raised from comital to ducal rank, as a principality of the Holy Roman Empire; in the 18th century it attained royal status, first with the Kingdom of Sicily, then with that of Sardinia;

and in the 19th century it merged Sardinia-Piedmont into the new Kingdom of Italy, which it retained till the establishment of the Italian Republic in 1946.

Origin.—The earliest recorded form of the name Savoy is Sapaudia or Sabaudia, which in the 4th century A.D. may have meant all the territory from Lake Neuchâtel to the middle Isère River. By the 9th century, however, the form Saboia appears, designating the so-called Savoy proper; *i.e.*, the country round Chambéry, in the modern French *département* of Savoie (*q.v.*). From this restricted connotation the name Savoy (French Savoie, Italian Savoia) was loosely extended to include adjacent areas—not only the Maurienne and Tarentaise regions now belonging to the same *département*, but also the Genevois, Faucigny, and Chablais regions, which together constitute the *département* of Haute-Savoie (*q.v.*).

Savoy in the 10th century was part of the last Kingdom of Burgundy (*q.v.*), which lay between France on the one hand and the German and Italian kingdoms on the other, the two latter kingdoms being united under the Holy Roman emperors from 962. This Burgundy was claimed in 1032 by the German king Conrad II, and one of its magnates who supported this claim was Humbert the Whitehanded (d. probably 1047 or 1048, perhaps *c.* 1050), founder of the House of Savoy. Humbert's provenance has been the subject of much speculation: a 15th-century theory named a Saxon called Berold as his ancestor, a 16th-century one the Saxon hero Widukind; some later scholars tried to connect him with the Burgundian kings, other with the Italian king Berengar of Ivrea, others again with a supposed son of the emperor Louis III the Blind. In the 1890s, however, G. de Manteyer advanced a far more likely theory, based on the location of the first certain possessions of the family: it seems that Humbert's ancestors came from Champagne or from French Burgundy in the 10th century and first established themselves in Viennois, the northern part of the future Dauphiné (*q.v.*). By Humbert's time, in any case, the family held the countship of Savoy proper (in their hands before 976); that of Belley, in Bugey, north of the Rhône, between Savoy and Bresse; that of Sermorens, in Grésivaudan, south of Viennois; and that of Aosta, on the Italian side of the Alps. Chambéry, however, the chief place in Savoy proper, was held by a separate line of viscounts.

The Counts, to 1391.—Humbert added the countship of Maurienne to his possessions; and his fourth son Odo, whose elder brothers (Amadeus I and two churchmen, Aimon and Burchard) predeceased him, gathered the whole Humbertine inheritance into his hands. Moreover, Odo's marriage to the heiress Adelaide, daughter of the margrave Olderico Manfredi, led to his investiture with the March or Mark of Turin by the emperor Henry III. By the end of the 11th century his successors had acquired Chablais (then including part of what is now Swiss Valais), Tarentaise (linking the Valle d'Aosta with Savoy and Maurienne), and the Valle di Susa (continuing southward from Maurienne). The Mont Cenis, Little St. Bernard, and Great St. Bernard passes were controlled by them.

From Odo's death (*c.* 1059), Adelaide of Turin held the mass of territory together for her sons Peter I (d. 1078) and Amadeus II (d. 1080); but both she and Peter's daughter Agnes, whose husband, Frederick of Montbéliard, had been invested with Turin, died in 1091. From the time of Amadeus II's son Humbert II (d. 1103) the Savoyard power in Italy underwent a setback, as the emperors proceeded to break up the March of Turin. Humbert II's son Amadeus III (d. on crusade 1148) was finally unsuccessful in his attempts to recover Turin; but he reduced the viscounts of Chambéry to vassalage and arranged some important marriages for his family on the French side of the Alps, including that of his sister Adelaide to King Louis VI. His son Humbert III (d. 1189), after being alternatively threatened and caressed by the emperor Frederick I (*q.v.*), finally took the side of Milan (see LOMBARD LEAGUE) and of Pope Alexander III against Frederick, who put him under the ban of the empire but could not break his resistance in his mountain strongholds. Humbert's son and successor Thomas I (d. 1233) was soon reconciled with the empire.

Amadeus IV (d. 1253), Thomas I's eldest son, succeeded to the countship of Savoy; but while two of his brothers were making their fortunes in England (Peter as lord of Richmond, Boniface as archbishop of Canterbury), another of them, Thomas II (d. 1259), built up a position for himself in Piedmont. By a pact of 1235 the dynastic lands north of the Alps, with the passes, the Valle d'Aosta, and the Valle di Susa, were reserved to Amadeus, while the rest of the Italian domains, from Avigliana southward, were assigned to Thomas. To these Thomas added not only Rivoli and other places but also Turin itself, which in 1251 accepted incorporation with his territories in order to offset the commercial rivalry of Asti. Asti, Alessandria, and Montferrat (*q.v.*) opposed this new consolidation in Piedmont; and the defeat of Thomas II's forces by those of Asti in 1255 prompted the people of Turin to revolt against him. Taken prisoner, forced to renounce his rights, and handed over to Asti, Thomas regained his freedom only a short time before his death. His son Thomas III (d. 1282), however, captured William VII of Montferrat in 1280 and then obtained recognition of his own claims and the surrender of Turin.

In Savoy, meanwhile, Amadeus IV's son Boniface (d. 1263) had been succeeded by his uncles Peter (the lord of Richmond, now Peter II of Savoy; d. 1268), and Philip I (d. 1285). Peter brought Vaud, the county north of Chablais, under his control and married the heiress of Faucigny, the country between Chablais and Tarentaise, so that his domains extended from the Alps to Lake Neuchâtel in a solid bloc dented only by Genevois, west of Faucigny, which remained under the counts of Geneva. On Peter's death, however, Faucigny was inherited by his only daughter, Beatrix, who was married to Guigues VII, dauphin of Viennois (see DAUPHINÉ). Savoy and Dauphiné thereupon embarked on a long contest for Faucigny.

The dynasty's collective inheritance was partitioned again when Philip I died childless (1285). Thomas III's brother, Amadeus V the Great (d. 1323), became count of Savoy, with the lands which Amadeus IV had had; his brother Louis (d. 1302) received Vaud; and Thomas III's son Philip (d. 1334) kept the Piedmontese lands, from Rivoli southward, but acknowledged Amadeus V as his feudal overlord. This Philip assumed the nominal style of prince of Achaea (Italian Acaia) by right of his marriage (1301) to Isabella of Villehardouin, heiress of that Frankish principality in Greece; but neither he nor his descendants, who continued to bear the title, could make it effective.

Amadeus V, who had received Bresse, west of Bugey, as the dowry of his first wife, Sibylle de Bâgé, obtained complete possession of Chambéry in 1288 and made it the capital of his dominions. He also fought a war against Genevois to defend his appointment (1285) as lay representative of the bishop of Geneva; and three wars against Dauphiné, as Faucigny was still in dispute. To preclude any more partitions, he introduced the Salic law of succession and the law of primogeniture. He also kept a close watch on Piedmont, insisting on his feudal suzerainty. Moreover, he and Philip of Achaea, in 1306 and again in 1313, agreed to hold jointly any new acquisitions that might be made by exploiting the rivalries of the three states that bordered Philip's territory, east, south, and southwest, namely Montferrat, the countship of Cuneo (held from 1259 by the Capetian House of Anjou), and the marquisate of Saluzzo; and this agreement took effect when Ivrea was annexed 1313. The emperor Henry VII recognized Amadeus as a prince of the Holy Roman Empire (1313), as well as enfiefing him, ineffectively, with Asti; but the disorders of the emperor Louis IV's reign induced Amadeus latterly to co-ordinate his external policy with that of France.

Amadeus V's sons Edward (d. 1329) and Aimon (d. 1343) and the regents for Aimon's son Amadeus VI conducted themselves practically as vassals of France; but when Amadeus VI (1334–83) came of age in 1348, the relationship soon changed. Known as the Green Count (because of the colour which he first wore at a tournament in 1353 and then adopted for his general use), Amadeus VI was strong-willed and clear-sighted alike in domestic and in foreign affairs. In 1350, seeing that he could not oppose the power of the Visconti (*q.v.*) in Milan, he married his sister Blanche to Galeazzo Visconti; in 1355 he obtained the long-desired Faucigny by ceding the ancient Savoyard rights in Dauphiné to the French; and in

1359 he bought Vaud back from the last heiress of his great-uncle Louis, whose male line had died out in 1339. Ruthlessly exploiting the quarrels and mistakes of the princes of Achaea, he brought their Piedmontese lands practically under his control. Abroad, he won prestige through his successful expedition of 1366–67, during which he took Gallipoli from the Turks and rescued the Byzantine emperor John V Palaeologus (his first cousin) from the Bulgars; and in 1381 he mediated the Peace of Turin between Venice and Genoa, at the end of the War of Chioggia. Finally, he obtained the cession of all Angevin rights in Piedmont (including Cuneo) by allying himself with Louis I of Anjou-Provence, claimant to the Neapolitan crown, against Charles III of Naples; but he died during the consequent campaign.

Amadeus VII (1360–91), the Red Count, succeeding his father in 1383, won a Mediterranean port for Savoy by annexing Nice and its hinterland in 1388, with the connivance of the local House of Grimaldi, which severed that territory's dependence on the countship of Provence. His premature death gave rise to a miasma of suspicion which persisted throughout the minority of his son.

The Dukes of Savoy, to 1675.—Amadeus VIII (1383–1451), was proclaimed of age to rule in 1393 and began to do so in 1400. Since the male line of counts of Geneva had died out, he purchased all rights to Genevois from their legatees and from the bishopric of Geneva (1401–05), thus acquiring Annecy. Insisting on Savoy's dependence on the empire, in order to counteract the designs of France and of Ducal Burgundy alike, he obtained the title of duke from the German king Sigismund in 1416. With regard to Italy, he reduced Thomas III of Saluzzo to vassalage (1413); incorporated all the lands of the Achaea line when its male line died out (1418); and pursued a course of opportunism toward Montferrat and toward the Visconti, obtaining Vercelli from the latter (1427). He created new institutions to transform his widespread dominions into a centralized state and tried to unify the legal system by his Statutes of 1430.

In 1434 Amadeus VIII withdrew to a hermitage at Ripaille, near Thonon, retaining his ducal title and his supreme authority but entrusting the detail of government to his son Louis. In 1439, however, the Council of Basel (*q.v.*) rather paradoxically elected Amadeus to the papacy, and he was its pope, as Felix V, till his resignation in 1449. Though he formally abdicated his duchy to Louis in 1440, he still concerned himself with its foreign affairs, as Louis proved incompetent. When the bishopric of Geneva fell vacant (1444), he retained it for himself.

On Amadeus VIII's death (1451) a period of decline began. Duke Louis (d. 1465) had a frivolous wife and corrupt ministers; and both he and his eldest son, Amadeus IX (1435–72), as well as the latter's young son Philibert I (1465–82), had to face disorders from which the malcontent Philip the Landless (1443–97) a younger son of Louis, sought to promote his own interests. After a brief recovery under Charles I (1468–90; Philibert's brother) there was more trouble during the regency for his infant successor Charles John Amadeus (1489–96; sometimes reckoned as Charles II), which saw the invasion of Italy by Charles VIII of France. Philip the Landless became duke himself at last, as Philip II, in 1496, but died next year; and the successive reigns of his sons, the half brothers Philibert II (1480–1504) and Charles III (1486–1553; Charles II if Charles John Amadeus is not so reckoned), were overshadowed by the Italian campaigns of the French kings Louis XII and Francis I. In the developing struggle between France and the Habsburg Empire, Savoy inclined to the latter's side: Philibert II had married an aunt of the emperor Charles V (*see* MARGARET of Austria); and Charles III in 1521 married the emperor's niece, Beatrice of Portugal. On the other hand Philibert II's sister Louise was the mother of Francis I of France; and a younger brother of Charles III received a French duchy in 1528 and became the ancestor of a line of ducs de Nemours (*q.v.*). The emperor granted Asti and Ceva to Beatrice of Portugal, so that they passed to the House of Savoy on her death (1538); but he disappointed Charles III by assigning vacant Montferrat, not to him, but to the Mantuan House of Gonzaga (1536).

Charles III sustained serious losses on his northeastern frontier.

From the time of Amadeus V and, more intensively, from that of Amadeus VIII, the House of Savoy had been tightening its hold over the bishopric of Geneva, which from the middle of the 14th century was virtually a Savoyard monopoly. In 1526, however, the citizens of Geneva, in reaction against these encroachments, allied themselves with the Swiss city-states of Bern and Fribourg; and in the early 1530s their rebellion against the bishop, Pierre de La Baume, which was followed by revolt against Catholicism in the name of the Reformed Church, led to the complete elimination of Savoyard influence. The bishop took refuge in Annecy, but Charles was unable to prevent the Swiss from overrunning Vaud and Chablais.

At war with Charles V, Francis I of France sent troops to occupy both Chambéry and Turin in 1536. When Charles III died, in 1553, at Vercelli, his lands north of the Alps had been lost, and Piedmont was little more than a battleground between the Spanish Habsburgs of Milan and the French invaders. To his son and successor Emmanuel Philibert (*q.v.*; 1528–80) fell the task of reconstruction. The Franco-Spanish Peace of Cateau-Cambrésis (1559) restored the duchy, but only when the peacemakers' hesitations had been overcome by the duke's marrying a French princess on the one hand and by his concluding a secret pact with Spain on the other; and he had to submit to the occupation of Asti and Vercelli by the Spaniards, and of Turin, Chieri, Pinerolo, Chivasso, and Villanova d'Asti by the French. This occupation was not wholly terminated till 1575, but Turin was restored to the duke in 1563, whereupon he made it the capital of his duchy. To conciliate the Swiss, he left the question of Geneva open and renounced his claims to Vaud; but he recovered the greater part of Chablais. He sheltered refugees from Guglielmo Gonzaga's despotism in Montferrat; he acquired the countship of Tenda in the 1570s, thus facilitating communications between Cuneo and Nice; and he purchased Oneglia from the Genoese House of Doria (1576). As the French rejected his offer of Bresse in exchange for Saluzzo (which they had taken in 1548), he took advantage of local rivalries in Saluzzo and was on the point of dominating the situation there when he died (1580). Meanwhile he had enforced honest administration within his duchy, organized a peasant militia, built a small fleet (which took part in the Battle of Lepanto), and withstood ecclesiastical attempts to interfere excessively in public affairs.

After years of warfare against the French, the ambitious Charles Emmanuel I (*q.v.*; 1562–1630), duke in succession to his father from 1580, obtained the formal cession of Saluzzo by the Treaty of Lyons (1601), in exchange for Bresse, Bugey, and Valromey. His efforts to subdue Geneva, however, came to nothing with the failure of his surprise attack in 1602. Thenceforward he concentrated his intentions on Italy. The Treaty of Bruzolo (or Brosolo; 1610), whereby Henry IV of France was to abet the duke's conquest of Lombardy from the Spaniards, was made abortive when Henry was murdered; but Charles Emmanuel tenaciously pursued his designs on Montferrat (*q.v.*), fighting a single-handed war against Spain for it from 1613 to 1618 and resuming the struggle, with Spanish support, on the outbreak of the War of the Mantuan Succession (1628). The French were again occupying Savoy when he died. His son Victor Amadeus I (1587–1637), duke from 1630, recovered Savoy and obtained one-third of Montferrat under the Treaty of Cherasco (1631), but had to yield the Piedmontese fortress of Pinerolo to the French, who were to hold a threat of domination over Savoy for the next 65 years.

When Victor Amadeus I died, open hostilities between France and Spain had already broken out (*see* THIRTY YEARS' WAR). His widow Christine de France, known as Madame Royale, a sister of the French king Louis XIII, became regent, first for the short-lived Francis Hyacinth (d. 1638), then for her other son, Charles Emmanuel II (1634–75); but the latter's uncles, the princes Maurice (1593–1657; a cardinal from 1607 till 1642) and Thomas of Carignano (1596–1656), challenged her authority, and civil war ensued between Madamisti and Principisti from 1639 to 1642. Charles Emmanuel in fact let Christine govern long after he came of age, and French pressure on the duchy was relaxed only after the Franco-Spanish Peace of the Pyrenees (1659). A war against

Genoa (1672–73) ended in humiliation for Savoy. In France a line of comtes de Soissons (*q.v.*), to which the famous Prince Eugene (*q.v.*) belonged, was descended from the youngest son of Prince Thomas of Carignano.

Victor Amadeus II.—Charles Emmanuel II's widow, Marie Jeanne Baptiste de Savoie-Nemours (*see* NEMOURS, DUCS DE), regent from 1675 to 1684, was wholly subservient to Louis XIV of France; but her son Victor Amadeus II (*q.v.*; 1666–1732) reversed this policy in 1690, when France wanted to occupy Turin (*see* GRAND ALLIANCE, WAR OF THE). Defeated in battles against the French, he triumphed in diplomacy, obtaining not only the dismantling of Casale (1695; *see* MONTFERRAT), but also the retrocession of Pinerolo (Treaty of Vigevano, 1696). The Treaty of Rijswijk (1697) confirmed his success. In the War of the Spanish Succession (*q.v.*), his opportunism won even greater prizes. The Peace of Utrecht, in 1713, added Montferrat, Valenza, Alessandria, Lomellina, Valsesia, and some smaller areas in Italy to Piedmont; fixed the Franco-Piedmontese frontier north of Nice by making it run along the watershed of the Alps; and furthermore assigned the Kingdom of Sicily to Victor Amadeus. By the Treaty of London, however, in 1718, it was decided that he should cede Sicily to the Austrian Habsburgs in exchange for the Kingdom of Sardinia, which Austria effectively got for him from Spain in 1720. Well-advised by excellent ministers, he carried out a thoroughgoing reform of the internal administration of his dominions before abdicating in 1730.

The Kings of Sardinia.—While the royal dignity of the House of Savoy was founded on Sardinia, that remote island was in itself not a very valuable asset; and while the kings of Sardinia continued to be numbered in the same series as the dukes of Savoy, their lands north of the Alps had long ceased to offer those prospects of aggrandizement which they had held out in the Middle Ages, when France had been in a state of feudal disruption and the Swiss Confederation had not come into being. Piedmont was the real seat of power, the nucleus from which further expansion, eastward and southward into divided Italy, seemed ever possible.

To break Austria's predominance in Italy, Charles Emmanuel III (1701–73), who succeeded his father in 1730, joined the Bourbon powers, France and Spain, in the War of the Polish Succession (*q.v.*), and his victory at Guastalla (1734) made him master of Austrian Lombardy. Though the Treaty of Vienna (1738) deprived him of much of his conquest, he retained Novara and Tortona, with their dependencies extended eastward to the Ticino River. In the War of the Austrian Succession (*q.v.*), on the other hand, he took Austria's side; and after his victory at L'Assietta (1747) the Treaty of Aix-la-Chapelle, in 1748, gave him Vigevano (so that his eastern frontier ran from Lake Maggiore down the Ticino River to the Po), the Alto Novarese (adjacent to Lake Maggiore), and also the former dependencies of Pavia on the right bank of the Po (including Voghera and a tongue of land stretching to the Trebbia).

The French Revolutionary and the Napoleonic Wars (*qq.v.*) were catastrophic for the House of Savoy. Victor Amadeus III (1726–96), king of Sardinia from 1773 in succession to his father, had some successes against the French in 1792, 1794, and 1795; but Napoleon Bonaparte's campaign of 1796 forced him to accept the Armistice of Cherasco and the Treaty of Paris, whereby he ceded Savoy and Nice and granted free passage across Piedmont to the French. His timid and ascetic son, Charles Emmanuel IV (1751–1819), king from 1796 to 1802, accepted a French garrison in Turin but was soon pressed to abdicate (1798). Retiring to Sardinia, he revoked his abdication (1799), but later again renounced everything but his royal title (1802). He died a Jesuit in Rome.

Victor Emmanuel I (1759–1824) made some unavailing claims to his brother's full succession before having to settle in Sardinia in 1806. On Napoleon's first downfall he returned to the Italian mainland. Piedmont, Nice, and the greater part of Savoy were restored to his kingdom by the Congress of Vienna in 1814, with the former territory of the Genoese Republic in addition; and the rest of Savoy, which had been left to France, was assigned to him in 1815, after Napoleon's Hundred Days.

Victor Emmanuel I abdicated in 1821, when a revolutionary *coup* in Turin confronted him with the aspirations of his subjects for constitutional freedom in the spirit of the Italian national Risorgimento (*see* ITALY: *History*). His brother Charles Felix (1765–1831), who succeeded him, died childless; and the crown then passed to a distant cousin, Charles Albert (*q.v.*), of the sixth generation from Prince Thomas of Carignano (the brother of Victor Amadeus I). Charles Albert, who had been rather sympathetic to the revolution of 1821, identified Sardinia-Piedmont with the anti-Austrian cause in the war of 1848–49 (*see* ITALIAN INDEPENDENCE, WARS OF) and had to abdicate in consequence.

The Kings of Italy.—Though Charles Albert had failed, his son and successor Victor Emmanuel II (*q.v.*), the only Italian sovereign to maintain constitutionalism during the absolutist reaction, still stood as the main practical hope of Italian patriots. While the solution of the Italian problem on the European level was mainly the achievement of the statesman Cavour (*q.v.*), Victor Emmanuel's personal action was of great importance in matters of extreme delicacy, such as his government's relationship with the radical revolutionaries Mazzini and Garibaldi. In the event, at the cost of two wars and the surrender to France of ancestral Savoy and of Nice, Victor Emmanuel II was proclaimed king of Italy in March 1861; and before his death (1878), the new kingdom was enlarged through two more wars (1866 and 1870). During the lifetime of Victor Emmanuel II his second son, the duke of Aosta, was king of Spain, as Amadeo I (*q.v.*), from 1870 to 1873.

On Victor Emmanuel's death the Italian kingdom passed to his eldest son, Humbert I (*q.v.*), who left it in turn to his son Victor Emmanuel III (*q.v.*). After World War I the frontiers of the latter's kingdom were further expanded. Moreover, the Fascist regime augmented his titles with that of emperor of Ethiopia in 1936 and with that of king of Albania in 1939. The same regime, in 1941 during World War II, set up the duke of Spoleto, Aimone (1900–48; a grandson of Amadeo of Spain), as king of Croatia under the name of Tomislav II. By the end of World War II, however, Ethiopia, Albania, and Croatia were lost; and Victor Emmanuel's abdication of his Italian crown in 1946 failed to save the monarchy for his son Humbert II (Umberto), as Italy became a republic.

Humbert II had a son Victor Emmanuel, prince of Naples, born in 1937, to continue representation of the direct royal line of Italy. The male line of Aosta branch, of which the explorer Luigi Amedeo, duke of Abruzzi (1873–1933) had been a distinguished member, was continued by Aimone's son Amedeo (Amadeus), born in 1943. There survived also the extensive Genoa branch, descended from a younger brother of Victor Emmanuel II (titular dukes of Genoa, of Pistoia, of Bergamo, and of Ancona).

SAWAI MADHOPUR, a town in Rajasthan, India, and the administrative headquarters of the district of the same name, lies about 75 mi. (120 km.) SE of Jaipur city on the Western Railway. Pop. (1961) 20,952. Sawai Madhopur, which is walled, takes its name from Madho Singh, maharaja of Jaipur from 1751 to 1768, who laid out the town somewhat on the plan of Jaipur city. The town is famous for its copper and brass vessels, and there is also a brisk trade in lacquered wooden articles, round playing cards, and the scent extracted from *khas* grass.

SAWAI MADHOPUR DISTRICT has a total area of 4,070 sq.mi. (10,541 sq.km.) and a population (1961) of 943,574. The annual rainfall is about 25 in. (635 mm.). More than 1,000,000 ac. (400,-000 ha.) are under cultivation, and the chief crops include wheat, maize (corn), rice, barley, gram, and sugarcane. (S. M. T. R.)

SAWFLY, not a true fly but a wasp relative in which the lower or anterior blades of the ovipositor are toothed and sawlike. Sawflies belong to several families of the suborder Symphyta (Chalastogastra). They are characterized by the broad base to the abdomen, where it joins the thorax, and by the wing veins being less reduced than in other members of the order. Their larvae are usually caterpillars and in most cases may be distinguished from those of moths and butterflies by having six or more pairs of abdominal feet and only a single pair of simple eyes or ocelli. When disturbed, they roll themselves in a spiral

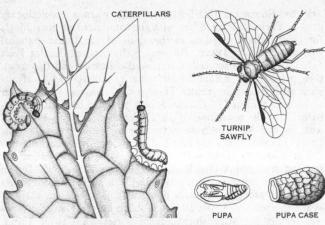

LIFE CYCLE OF TURNIP SAWFLY (ATHALIA SPINARUM)

fashion and some species discharge a thin fluid from glands above the spiracles. The females lay their eggs in incisions in plants, cut by the sawlike blades of the ovipositor. The larvae are vegetable feeders. Species of several genera, notably *Pontania,* form galls on willows. The cause of the gall is stated to be a secretion injected along with the egg, and it has been suggested that it contains an enzyme that acts upon the plant so as to induce gall formation.

Reproduction in sawflies is of considerable interest: in many species males are unknown and parthenogenesis (*q.v.*) is the rule. In the gooseberry sawfly the unfertilized eggs give rise only to males, whereas the fertilized eggs produce individuals of both sexes, females predominating.

The true sawflies belong to the large family Tenthredinidae, the larvae of many of which are injurious to plants. Among these are the currant worm, or gooseberry sawfly (*Nematus ribesii*), and the pear slug (*Caliroa limacina*). These two species and also the larch sawfly (*Lygaeonematus erichsonii*) were accidentally imported from Europe into North America, where they likewise became destructive. Other harmful species in Europe are the turnip sawfly (*Athalia spinarum*) and the pine sawfly (*Diprion pini*).

The small families Cephidae and Siricidae have larvae that are borers. The Cephidae, or stem sawflies, make burrows, usually in stems; the best-known species is *Cephus pygmaeus,* which attacks wheat. It is destructive in North America, where *Janus integer,* the stem girdler of the currant, is also troublesome. The Siricidae, which bore into solid timber, are known as wood wasps or horntails. *Sirex gigas* is the most familiar European wood wasp and is not uncommon in Great Britain.   (A. D. I.; X.)

SAWHAJ (SOHAG), a town and *muhafaza* (governorate) of Upper Egypt (United Arab Republic). The town, capital of the governorate, stands on the west bank of a large loop of the Nile 190 mi. (306 km.) NNW of Aswan on the main Cairo railway. Pop. (1962 est.) 65,000. Nearby are two important Christian monuments, the White and Red monasteries. There is cotton ginning and textile weaving, and limestone is quarried across the river at Al 'Isawiyah Sharq ('Isawiya).

SAWHAJ *muhafaza,* formerly Jirja (Girga) Province, comprises the stretch of the fertile Nile Valley between the *muhafazat* of Asyut in the north and Qina in the south. Pop. (1960) 1,578,858. Area 595 sq.mi. (1,540 sq.km.). The Nile there flows in a flat-bottomed trough, 12–14 mi. wide, called the Nile Ravine and cut in almost horizontally bedded limestone. The valley is hemmed in by precipitous limestone walls rising to nearly 1,000 ft. (305 m.). Throughout the area the Nile flows close to the eastern side of the valley; nearly all the arable land lies west of the river. There are two notable sites of antiquities, that of Abydos (*q.v.*), the pilgrim centre of the Osirian creed near Jirja town, and Bayt Khallaf, the site of a mastaba probably of King Zoser (3rd dynasty), near Sawhaj.

Sawhaj is one of Egypt's most densely peopled *muhafazat* (2,654 persons per square mile). Agriculture is the principal activity, employing 75% of the occupied population (the heaviest propor-

tion in all Egypt), but more than half of the farmland is under basin irrigation whereby only one crop can be grown annually, and there is much poverty. The principal crops are cotton (on land with perennial irrigation), millet, wheat, sugarcane, onions, peanuts, and melons. The perennially irrigated land is watered from the Jirjawiyah and Sawhajiyah canals, fed from the Naj' Hammadi Barrage to the south. The basin lands are inundated by Nile floodwater in August, drained after about 50 days, and seeds are then sown. There are stone quarries at Jabal al Haridi and Al 'Isawiyah Sharq, east of Akhmim. Industries are restricted to the processing of agricultural produce: milling, cotton ginning, and the weaving of cotton, wool, and silk, especially at Akhmim. The principal towns are Sawhaj, Tahta, Akhmim, and Jirja.

                           (A. B. M.)

SAWMILL, a mill in which logs are cut into rough-squared sections or into planks and boards for sale or further treatment. The word is often applied to a mill equipped with planing, molding, tenoning, and other machines for finishing processes. The biggest mills are usually situated where timber can be brought by river or rail, and the design of the mill is in some degree affected by the mode of transportation. More space is necessary for storage in the rail-borne system. Waterborne logs float into the mill and are dragged out in turn by a winch. An overhead crane serves the stock yard in the rail system, and carries the logs to the machines.

The cutting is performed on various kinds of big machines, a preliminary operation often being that of crosscutting to obtain convenient lengths. Cutting up into the various thicknesses is done by either reciprocating saws or band saws (known also as circular saws), the log being held on a table which feeds it past the saw. The log frame is a machine with a set of vertically reciprocating blades, suitably spaced apart; it divides a log into boards at one pass of the table. The number of blades may be few, not exceeding four in some cases for cutting thick pieces, or as many as fifty for thin boards. Resawing machines are those for further dealing with material partly broken up, such as flitches and deals. The great quantity of sawdust and chips from the machines is neatly disposed of by pneumatic ducts ending in the boiler house. *See also* LUMBERING: *Sawmill Operations;* WOODWORKING MACHINERY.

SAWS AND SAWING MACHINES: *see* HAND TOOLS, HISTORY OF; MACHINE TOOLS; WOODWORKING MACHINERY.

SAX, ANTOINE JOSEPH, known as ADOLPHE (1814–1894), maker of musical instruments and inventor of the saxophone (*q.v.*), was born at Dinant, Belgium, on Nov. 6, 1814. He was the son of CHARLES JOSEPH SAX (1791–1865), a maker of wind instruments, especially brass instruments, who also made pianos, harps, and guitars. Adolphe Sax studied the flute and clarinet at the Brussels Conservatoire and in 1842 went to Paris. There he exhibited the saxophone, a single-reed instrument made of metal, with a conical bore, overblowing at the octave, which was the result of his efforts to improve the tone of the bass clarinet. It was patented in 1846. With his father he evolved the saxhorn (*q.v.;* patented in 1845), an improvement on the bugle horn; the saxo-tromba, producing a tone between that of the bugle and the trumpet; and the saxtuba. Sax discovered that it is the proportions given to a column of air vibrating in a sonorous tube, and these alone, that determine the character of the timbre produced. In 1857 Sax was appointed instructor of the saxophone at the Paris Conservatoire. In the latter part of his life Sax improved several instruments and invented others without, however, establishing a basis for their commercial exploitation. In his 80th year he was living in abject poverty; Chabrier, Massenet, and Saint-Saëns were obliged to petition the minister of fine arts to come to his aid. He died in Paris on Feb. 7, 1894.

BIBLIOGRAPHY.—O. Comettant, *Histoire d'un inventeur au 19ᵉ siècle* (1860); Paul Gilson, *Les Géniales Inventions d'Adolphe Sax* (1939); A. Remy, *La Vie tourmentée d'Adolphe Sax* (1939); L. Kochnitzky, *Adolphe Sax and his Saxophone* (1949).

SAXE, (HERMANN) MAURICE, COMTE DE (1696–1750), one of the most brilliant commanders in the history of the French Army. He was born on Oct. 28, 1696, at Goslar in central Germany, the natural son of the elector Frederick Augustus I of Saxony (later also king of Poland as Augustus II) and Maria Aurora von Königsmark (*q.v.*). His father sent him to serve in Flanders under Prince Eugene of Savoy in 1709–10, granted him the title of count of Saxony (Graf von Sachsen; Fr., comte de Saxe) in 1711, and arranged his marriage (later annulled) to the heiress Johanna Victoria von Löben in 1714. In 1719 his father bought for him a German regiment in the French service, and with it Saxe first attracted attention by his new methods of training, especially in musketry.

In December 1725 Saxe arrived in Warsaw on a visit to his father. The future of Courland (*q.v.*) was then under discussion, and in May 1726 Saxe rode off to Mitau (Jelgava) where he quickly endeared himself to the dowager duchess, Anna Ivanovna (later empress of Russia), and was elected duke of Courland. He might have married Anna, but neither Poland nor Russia would consent to his enterprise; and in 1727 he was expelled by the Russians.

Back in France, Saxe in 1732 wrote *Mes Rêveries* (not published until 1756–57), a remarkable treatise on almost every aspect of war and military life, with many original ideas. When the War of the Polish Succession broke out, he took part in Marshal Berwick's campaign on the Rhine. Marshal de Noailles (Adrien Maurice) procured for him the rank of lieutenant general in 1734.

In the War of the Austrian Succession (*q.v.*) Saxe won fame by suggesting and personally executing the capture of Prague (Nov. 26, 1741). In July 1743 Noailles, left in control by the failure of the other marshals, gave him command of an army in Alsace; but after protests by other generals the French king, Louis XV, transferred Saxe to Dunkerque in January 1744, to command an expedition against England on behalf of the Young Pretender, Charles Edward. When Saxe embarked a storm shattered his squadron and the project was dropped.

On March 26, 1744, Saxe was made a marshal of France. He was given command of a corps in Flanders to cover Louis XV's own army in the usual sieges; but when Louis and Noailles removed part of the army to the German front, Saxe was outnumbered in Flanders by the Allied forces (British, Austrian, and Dutch). Yet he established his camp near Courtrai so skilfully that the Allies could attempt nothing.

When Louis XV and Noailles joined Saxe in 1745 for the siege of Tournai and a battle was expected, they insisted that he alone should give the orders. The result was the Battle of Fontenoy (May 11, 1745), in which the French, by hard and costly fighting, with some element of chance, won a great victory over the Allies under William Augustus, duke of Cumberland. The consequent surprise of Gand (Ghent) (July 11) and, still more, the capture of Brussels (Feb. 20, 1746), which also secured Antwerp, were operations of high skill. Saxe then marched south, took Mons and Namur, and, on Oct. 11, 1746, defeated Prince Charles of Lorraine at Raucoux (properly Rocourt, near Liège), in a long struggle of infantry.

On Jan. 10, 1747, Saxe was appointed marshal-general of France, a dignity held only by Turenne and Villars before him. All France's military effort was centred on him, and he wielded almost sovereign power over the Netherlands from his headquarters in Brussels. Many Frenchmen believed that he and his Danish protégé, Ulrich Löwendal, were prolonging the war for their own profit. Saxe's last great battle was that of Lauffeld (July 2, 1747), in which the Allies, defending the approaches to Maastricht, lost 10,000 men. Maastricht itself, however, did not fall to the French till May 1748.

After the Peace of Aix-la-Chapelle, Saxe lived mostly at his château of Chambord, with his Negro bodyguard and his German regiment encamped in the park. When he died there on Nov. 30, 1750, it was rumoured that the prince de Conti (Louis François de Bourbon) had killed him in a duel. Saxe had been insatiably promiscuous in his amours. The most devoted of his mistresses was the actress Adrienne Lecouvreur (*q.v.*). By Marie Rinteau he had a daughter from whom George Sand (*q.v.*) was descended.

See J. L. A. Colin, *Les Campagnes du comte Maurice de Saxe*, 3 vol. (1901–06); J. M. White, *Marshal of France* (1962). (I. D. E.; X.)

SAXHORN, a family of brass wind instruments patented by Adolphe Sax in Paris in 1845, provided military bands with a homogeneous series of valved brass in place of the miscellany of valved instruments, largely of German invention, that had come into use since 1825. Saxhorns, from sopranino to contrabass, had a wide bugle-like bore, while the saxo-trombas, a parallel but short-lived family, were rather narrower in bore. The deeper saxhorns became and remain regular brass-band instruments in France, the U.S., and Britain, where they are known not as saxhorns but simply as: alto in E♭ (in Britain "tenor horn"); tenor in B♭ ("baritone"); the wider-bore baritone in B♭ ("euphonium," *q.v.*); and bass in E♭ and contrabass in BB♭. *See also* Tuba. (A. C. Ba.)

SAXIFRAGACEAE, the saxifrage family of the order Rosales, embraces about 80 genera and 1,200 species of dicotyledonous plants of cosmopolitan distribution with concentration in the north temperate zone and subarctic regions. There are more than 40 genera in the western hemisphere, found from Alaska to Cape Horn. The plants are annual or perennial herbs, shrubs, or small trees. The leaves are simple or compound, alternate or opposite, without stipules, often in basal rosettes. Flowers are arranged in clusters, bisexual, rarely unisexual, with regular or bilateral symmetry. The calyx is made up of four to five sepals, usually united and prolonged to a floral tube with a glandular disc; corolla, of four to five separate petals, is common; there may be five to ten or many stamens, and one pistil, mostly two carpellate, with parietal or axile placentation; styles and stigmas are mostly separate; fruit is a many-seeded capsule or a juicy berry.

Saxifraga, or rock-breaker (garden saxifrage), is the largest genus, comprising more than 300 species, of which about 15 are British. They are crevice-loving herbs, of arctic and alpine habitats, usually with tufted leaves from crowns of rhizomes anchored by roots in mossy fissures or wet meadows. Many are prized ornamentals in rock gardens, including *S. umbrosa* (London pride),

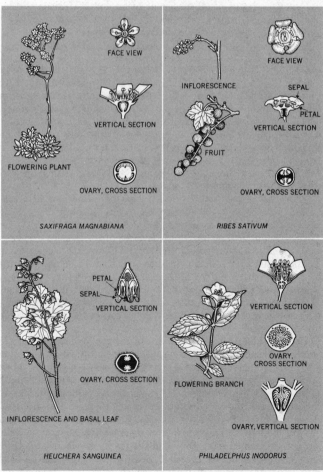

SAXIFRAGA MAGNABIANA

RIBES SATIVUM

HEUCHERA SANGUINEA

PHILADELPHUS INODORUS

FROM LIBERTY H. BAILEY, "MANUAL OF CULTIVATED PLANTS"; REPRODUCED BY PERMISSION OF THE MACMILLAN CO.

SOME SPECIAL CHARACTERISTICS OF THE FAMILY SAXIFRAGACEAE

with crimson-dotted petals, and *S. rosacea* (rose saxifrage), with scarlet petals. *S. sarmentosa* (strawberry geranium) is a popular house plant, with attractive panicles of irregular flowers, propagating by a profusion of runners with terminal rosettes of leaves.

Chrysosplenium (golden saxifrage), including 85 species of delicate creeping herbs found in springheads and creek beds, has four-parted flowers, the eight golden anthers compensating for the lack of petals.

Parnassia (grass-of-Parnassus) includes 40–45 species with circumpolar distribution; *P. palustris,* of shores and wet meadows, has showy white flowers.

Heuchera (alumroot), with 30 species, is exclusively a North American genus. The plants are characterized by a naked flowering stem with rosette leaves from thick rhizomes which contain astringent principle. *H. sanguinea* (coral-bells) is a rock garden favourite because of its graceful panicle of showy flowers. Any species, indeed, is suitable for rock gardens.

Astilbe, a genus of about 20 Asian and 2 American species, are ornamental herbs with twice or thrice compound leaves, small numerous flowers in terminal clusters, and fruits often follicular from distinct carpels. *A. japonica* is preferred in gardens.

The genus *Ribes* (currant and gooseberry, *qq.v.*) includes 140 species of smooth or prickly shrubs, widely distributed. *R. sativum* (garden currant) and *R. grossularia* (or *Grossularia reclinata;* the English gooseberry) bear edible berries. Among ornamentals are *R. odoratum* (clove currant) and *R. sanguineum* (cherry currant). All species of *Ribes* are valuable shrubs in providing shelter and food for wild life, but they also are the alternate host for the fungus that causes blister rust in white pine.

Philadelphus (or mock orange) is a genus consisting of about 70 species, several Asian, 1 European and the remainder American. *P. coronarius* and its many forms are widely cultivated for their attractive clusters of showy-white fragrant flowers.

Deutzia, a genus of 70 species of Asian and 2 Mexican shrubs, has profusely flowering ornamentals. Among choice species for borders is *D. gracilis,* with slender arching branches.

BIBLIOGRAPHY.—L. H. Bailey, *Manual of Cultivated Plants* (1949); J. K. Small, *North American Flora,* vol. xxii (2) (1905); A. Engler, *Die Natürlichen Pflanzenfamilien,* 2nd ed. (1930).   (O. LA.)

SAXO GRAMMATICUS (mid-12th century–early 13th century), Danish historian whose *Gesta Danorum* is the first important work on the history of Denmark and the first Danish contribution to world literature. Little is known except that he was a Sealander belonging to a family of warriors, and that he was probably a clerk in the service of Absalon (archbishop of Lund from 1178 to 1201). Saxo is first mentioned in Svend Aggesen's *Historia Regum Danicæ compendiosa* (1185) as writing the history of Svend Estridsen (d. 1076).

The *Gesta Danorum* was written at the suggestion of Archbishop Absalon: its 16 volumes begin with the legendary King Dan and end with the conquest of Pomerania by Canute VI in 1185. The original manuscript is lost except for four leaves which were found in a French book in 1863. The preface, dedicated to Absalon's successor, Anders Sunesen, and King Valdemar II, must have been written before 1222. Like the rest of the work, it is written in a brilliant, ornate Latin, clearly influenced by the style of Valerius Maximus, Curtius and Justin. It was his Latin eloquence which early in the 14th century caused Saxo to be called "Grammaticus."

The first nine books of the *Gesta Danorum* give an account of about 60 legendary Danish kings. For this part Saxo depended on ancient lays, romantic sagas and the accounts of Icelanders. Most famous are his tales about Uffe (Anglo-Saxon, Offa), Amleth (Hamlet [*q.v.*]), Hading, Rolf Krake, the giant Starkad, Harald Hildetand and Ragnar Lodbrok. Saxo incorporated also myths of national gods such as Balder and Hother whom tradition claimed as Danish kings, and myths of foreign heroes, including the Gothic Jarmunrik (Ermanaric; *q.v.*) and the Germans Hedin and Hild. Three heroic poems are especially noteworthy, translated by Saxo into Latin hexameters, a medium which must have been incongruously alien to the concentrated, pithy style of the originals, the oldest known Danish poetry. They are *Bjarkemaalet,* a battle

hymn designed to arouse warlike feelings; *Ingjaldskvadet,* a poem stressing the corruptive danger of luxury upon the old Viking spirit; and *Hagbard and Signe,* a tragedy of love and family feuds.

The last seven books comprise Saxo's account of the historical period, but he only achieves independent authority when writing of events close to his own time (from book 14 onward). Archbishop Absalon and his family, and oral accounts by Danish warriors, seem to have been Saxo's main sources for this period. His work is noteworthy for its sense of patriotic purpose based on a belief in the unifying influence of the monarchy. By presenting a 2,000-year-long panorama of Danish history, he aimed to show his country's antiquity and traditions. Saxo's work became a source of inspiration to many of the 19th-century Danish romantic poets.

BIBLIOGRAPHY.—Saxo's *Gesta Danorum* was first published by Christiern Pedersen (Paris, 1514), modern ed. by J. Olrik and H. Ræder (1931). Since 1575 it has been translated into Danish five times; Eng. trans. by Oliver Elton, *The First Nine Books of the Danish History of Saxo Grammaticus* (1894). See also A. Olrik, *Kilderne til Saxos oldhistorie,* i–ii (1892–94) and *Danske oldkvad i Saxos historie* (1898); C. Weibull, *Saxo* (1915); K. Malone, *The Literary History of Hamlet* (1923); S. Larsen, *Saxo Grammaticus, hans Værk og Person* (1925); Ellen Jørgensen, *Historieforskning og Historieskrivning i Danmark indtil Aar 1800* (1933).   (E. L. BF.)

SAXON DUCHIES, ERNESTINE, a collective name for the various states, in the Thuringian area of central Germany, which were ruled by members of the Ernestine line of the House of Wettin between 1485 and 1918. From 1826 there were four of them: (1) the GRAND DUCHY OF SAXE-WEIMAR-EISENACH, in all 1,394 sq.mi. (3,610 sq.km.), comprising three major blocks of territory, northern (around Weimar), southeastern (around Neustadt an der Orla), and western (around Eisenach), with ten smaller exclaves; (2) the DUCHY OF SAXE-MEININGEN-HILDBURGHAUSEN, 953 sq.mi. (2,468 sq.km.), a crescent of territory extending from Salzungen in the west, southeastward to Meiningen and Hildburghausen, and then northeastward to Saalfeld, with nine exclaves; (3) the DUCHY OF SAXE-ALTENBURG, 511 sq.mi. (1,324 sq.km.), two major blocks of territory, one (round Altenburg) in the east on the Pleisse River, the other (including Eisenberg, Roda, and Kahla) between the Weimar and Neustadt parts of the Grand Duchy, with one small exclave; and (4) the DUCHY OF SAXE-COBURG-GOTHA, 763 sq.mi. (1,977 sq.km.), two major blocks, one (Coburg) in the extreme south of the area, the other (Gotha) east of the Eisenach part of the Grand Duchy, with six exclaves. The discontinuity of the Ernestine lands was further enhanced by the existence of quite distinct territories in the same area: an exclave of Hesse-Kassel (part of Prussian Hesse-Nassau from 1866), an extension and numerous exclaves of Prussian Saxony, exclaves of Schwarzburg-Sondershausen, and the main territory of Schwarzburg-Rudolstadt in the central zone; the Unterland of Reuss (*q.v.*) between the two parts of Saxe-Altenburg; and the Oberland of Reuss in the southeast.

The House of Wettin (*q.v.*) accumulated possessions in Thuringia from the middle decades of the 13th century onward. It received the Pleissnerland, round Altenburg, from the Holy Roman emperor Frederick II in 1243; won the landgraviate of Thuringia, with control over the Eisenach and Gotha areas, in 1264, after the war of 1256–63; obtained Neustadt by marriage to the heiress of Arnshaugk in 1300; acquired Coburg and Hildburghausen from the House of Henneberg, and Weimar from that of Orlamünde, between 1347 and 1374; and purchased Saalfeld from Schwarzburg in 1389 and Weida from the House of the *Vögte* (imperial advocates) in 1410–27. The accession of the Wettins to the electorate of Saxony (*q.v.*) in 1423 gave rise to the use of the prefix Saxe- (Ger. Sachsen-) for their dynastic ramifications in Thuringia.

In 1485, at the partition of the Wettin lands under the Treaty of Leipzig between the sons of the elector Frederick II of Saxony, the elder son, Ernest (1441–86), received the Saxon electorate, Altenburg, and most of the Thuringian lands, while the younger son, Albert, received Meissen, Dresden, Leipzig, and a strip of lands in northern Thuringia. In 1547 Ernest's grandson John Frederick I (*q.v.*), taken prisoner at the Battle of Mühlberg, had to renounce not only electoral Saxony but also a great part of his Thuringian territory to his Albertine cousin Maurice. The Ernestines, however, kept Weimar (with Jena, where John Frederick I founded the university), Gotha, Eisenach, Saalfeld, Weida, and Coburg (the last held as a separate duchy by John Frederick I's half brother John Ernest from 1541 to 1553, when it reverted to John Frederick's sons); and in 1554, by the Treaty of Naumburg, they recovered Altenburg, Eisenberg, and other places from the Albertines. From 1567 Weida, Neustadt, and some other places were ceded to the Albertines as a consequence of the defeat of John Frederick II and his protégé Wilhelm von Grumbach (qq.v.); but the extinction of the House of Henneberg in 1583 eventually brought Meiningen to the Ernestines, though the final division of the Henneberg inheritance between Ernestines and Albertines was not agreed till 1660.

The Ernestines continually distributed their lands between themselves. Saxe-Weimar-Gotha and Saxe-Coburg, with respective dependencies, were separated in 1566, but realigned as Saxe-Coburg-Gotha and Saxe-Weimar in 1572. Then Saxe-Coburg-Gotha was split between Coburg and the first Eisenach branch from 1596 to 1633; and Saxe-Weimar was split between Weimar and Altenburg branches from 1603. The first Eisenach branch inherited the Coburg lands in 1633, but died out in 1638, whereupon its succession was divided between Weimar and Altenburg. In 1640 the Weimar branch was yet again split, between Weimar, Eisenach, and Gotha branches. Weimar and Gotha partitioned the Eisenach branch's lands when it died out in 1644 and the Altenburg branch's when it too died out in 1672.

Saxe-Weimar proceeded to a final division in 1672, between Weimar, Eisenach, and Jena branches, but Saxe-Jena died out in 1690 and Saxe-Eisenach in 1741. As the Weimar branch had at last adopted the rule of primogeniture in 1724, the integrity of Saxe-Weimar-Eisenach was thereafter maintained. For its most notable ruler see CHARLES AUGUSTUS (Karl August).

Meanwhile Saxe-Gotha had been split between seven branches in 1680–81. Of these, Saxe-Coburg died out in 1699, Saxe-Eisenberg in 1707, Saxe-Römhild (named after a part of the Henneberg inheritance) in 1710. There remained Saxe-Meiningen (called Saxe-Coburg-Meiningen from 1699), Saxe-Hildburghausen, Saxe-Gotha-Altenburg, and Saxe-Saalfeld (called Saxe-Coburg-Saalfeld from 1735). The extinction of the Gotha-Altenburg branch in 1825 led to a definitive redistribution of territory in 1826: Frederick of Saxe-Hildburghausen ceded his original territory to Bernard of Saxe-Meiningen and became duke of Saxe-Altenburg instead; and Ernest of Saxe-Coburg-Saalfeld ceded Saalfeld to Saxe-Meiningen likewise and became duke of Saxe-Coburg-Gotha.

The Ernestine duchies had entered the Confederation of the Rhine in 1807 and the German Confederation, as sovereign states, in 1815. The Congress of Vienna moreover raised Saxe-Weimar-Eisenach to the rank of a grand duchy, restored Weida and Neustadt to it, and also awarded it some new territory. Constitutions were granted to the Grand Duchy in 1816, to Saxe-Coburg-Saalfeld in 1821, to Saxe-Meiningen-Hildburghausen in 1829, to Saxe-Altenburg in 1831. Saxe-Altenburg underwent violent disturbances at the revolution of 1848. Saxe-Coburg-Gotha during the first half of Duke Ernest II's reign (1844–93) was a centre of liberal German nationalism (see also WETTIN for the accession of members of the House of Saxe-Coburg-Gotha to four kingdoms). During the Seven Weeks' War (1866) Saxe-Meiningen-Hildburghausen took the Austrian side, the other Ernestine states the Prussian. All four states subsequently joined the North German Confederation (1866) and the German Empire (1871). At the German revolution of 1918 all the Ernestine rulers abdicated, and in 1920 their former lands were merged in the new Thuringia (q.v.), with the exception of Coburg, which joined Bavaria.

SAXONS, a Germanic people said by Ptolemy (Guide to Geography, c. A.D. 150) to have lived on the "neck of the Cimbric Peninsula," i.e., in Schleswig, and to have extended thence along the Baltic coast. They also occupied three islands north of the Elbe estuary. The period of decay of the Roman power in the West was marked by vigorous piracy in the North Sea by the Saxons, and they made settlements on the French coast, but these seem not to have been permanent. Because of their infestation, the coasts of Britain and Gaul adjacent to the English Channel

were known as litora Saxonica at the beginning of the 5th century. Great expansion over land was taking place at the same time, and the Saxons reached the Rhine, absorbing many ancient tribes on the way. Their last conquest was that of the Boructuari shortly before 700. This expansion was, however, inland in North Germany. The coastal stretch from the Elbe to the Scheldt rivers was held by the Frisians, on whom, archaeological evidence indicates, the Saxons had great influence.

The expansion of the Saxons brought collision with the Franks. Saxons and Franks together destroyed Thuringia in 531, but the two nations had frequent clashes. In 772 Charlemagne decided on a campaign of conquest and conversion. With interruptions, the Saxon wars lasted 32 years, and ended with the incorporation of the Saxons into the Frankish empire. Although they had not developed a strongly centralized government, their national resistance was concentrated round the Westphalian chief Widukind.

Bede (Historia ecclesiastica) describes the Germanic invaders of Britain as Angles, Saxons, and Jutes. He says that the East, West, and South Saxons are descended from the Saxons, the East Angles, Middle Angles, Mercians, and Northumbrians from the Angles, the people of Kent, Wight, and parts of Hampshire from the Jutes. Bede is supported by (1) many of the names of the Old English nations, (2) the dialects of Old English, which, while their phonological differences mostly developed in England, yet show that Saxon and Anglian have a marked distinction in vocabulary, and (3) the peculiar social structure of Kent (see JUTES). Yet the memory of the Jutes quickly died out, and Bede himself is not always careful to distinguish Angles and Saxons (see ANGLES). Furthermore, all the invaders of Britain were closely related, and spoke dialects similar to each other and to the Frisian language. The dialects of the continental Saxons, on the other hand, underwent considerable approximation to High German, and their affinity to those of the English and the Frisians is only to be traced in sporadic spellings in texts now extant, of which none are older than the 9th century. When Procopius (Gothic Wars, c. 550) alleges that the inhabitants of Britain are Britons, Angles, and Frisians, he is no doubt confusing Frisians and Saxons, owing to their close relationship and to the extensive Saxon settlements among the Frisians.

For details of the Saxon conquest of southern England see ENGLISH HISTORY; see also references under "Saxons" in the Index.

BIBLIOGRAPHY.—"Rappaport" (S. Anski), "Saxones" in Pauly-Wissowa, Real-Encyclopädie der classischen Altertumswissenschaft, 2nd series, vol. iii (1921); R. Much, "Sachsen," in J. Hoops, Reallexikon der germanischen Altertumskunde, vol. iv (1918–19); E. Schwarz, Goten, Nordgermanen, Angelsachsen (1951); A. Campbell, "West Germanic Problems in the Light of Modern Dialects," Transactions of the Philological Society (1947). (AL. C.)

SAXONY (Ger. SACHSEN), the name of important territories in German history. It has been applied successively: (1) before A.D. 1180, to an extensive region including Holstein but lying mainly west and southwest of the estuary and lower course of the Elbe River; (2) between 1180 and 1423, to two much smaller and widely separated areas, one on the right bank of the lower Elbe southeast of Holstein, the other on the middle Elbe; and (3) between 1423 and 1952, to a large area with its principal axis even farther up the Elbe and including, in the widest sense, all the country from Thuringia to Lusatia. The name of the first Saxony was officially recalled, in 1946, for the German Land Lower Saxony (q.v.), or Niedersachsen, that is, Saxony lower down the Elbe; but the new Land was not coextensive with the old territory of the Saxons.

The French form of the name, SAXE, is used in English as the normal form for a prefix to designate subdivisions of Saxony or of the ruling dynasty's lands: thus Saxe-Lauenburg and Saxe-Wittenberg for the two Saxonies of the period 1180–1423; and Saxe-Weimar, Saxe-Coburg, etc., for the subdivisions of Saxon, or rather Wettin, Thuringia (see SAXON DUCHIES, ERNESTINE).

THE STEMLAND

The Ancient Saxons.—The Saxons (q.v.), a Germanic people, are mentioned by the Greek geographer Ptolemy, of the 2nd cen-

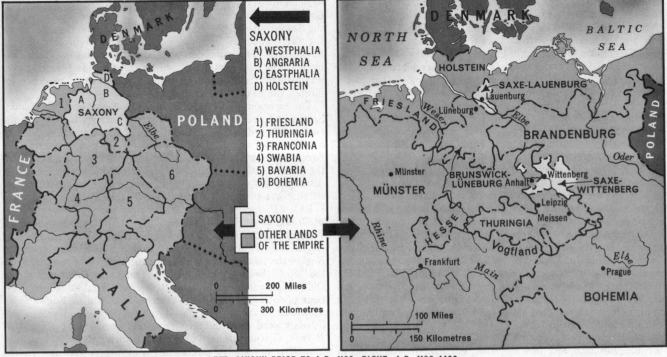

LEFT, SAXONY PRIOR TO A.D. 1180, RIGHT, A.D. 1180–1423

tury A.D., as inhabiting the neck of land between the Elbe estuary and the Baltic Sea; *i.e.*, the later Schleswig-Holstein. In the following centuries they spread westward and southwestward. While the westward migration, by sea to Britain, is irrelevant to this article, the southwestward movement is fundamental to it.

In the 1st–2nd centuries A.D. the country between the lower Rhine and the lower Elbe was occupied by various Germanic peoples. Between *c.* 200 and *c.* 700, as a product of the Germanic Völkerwanderung or Great Migration (*see* EUROPE: *History*) a great tribal union under the name of the Saxons was gradually imposed, by conquests or by confederations, on all this country except the coastal zone. In the coastal zone the Frisians (*q.v.*) withstood Saxon pressure and even, from *c.* 600, began slowly to supplant the Saxons in country taken over by the latter.

The tribal union of the Saxons was the origin of the so-called stem land or stem duchy of Saxony (Ger. *Stamm,* "people" or "nation"). It was distinct, moreover, from other products of the Völkerwanderung insofar as it was built, ethnically, on purely Germanic stock. The people adhered tenaciously to their ancient customs and, in particular, to their paganism. The central object of cult was an Irminsul or "Pillar of the World," a tall wooden column erected on a mountain and supposed to support the universe (there were several such columns). The country was divided into three great provinces: Angria or Angraria (Ger. *Engern*) in the centre along the Weser, with Marklo (probably near the modern Lohe, north of Nienburg) as the yearly meeting place of the national assembly; Eastphalia (Ger. *Ostfalen*) to the east, apparently including Nordalbingia (Holstein); and Westphalia (*q.v.*) to the west.

The Frankish Conquest.—In the 530s the Saxons had co-operated with the Franks (*q.v.*) against the Thuringians on their southeastern border, where the Saxon frontier was pushed forward to the Saale River. Subsequently, however, Franks and Saxons collided. The Frankish campaigns against the Frisians threatened Westphalia; and the Franks sponsored the unwelcome enterprises of Christian missionaries. Hostilities were intensified on the rise of the Carolingians (*q.v.*) to power in France. Finally Charlemagne (*q.v.*) embarked on a long series of wars against the Saxons. His first campaign (772) culminated in the capture of Eresburg (the modern Obermarsberg), where he destroyed a great Irminsul. The Saxon leader Widukind was the hero of the resistance in the next phase of warfare, from 775, but he submitted to Charlemagne and was baptized in 785. Even so, Charlemagne's subjec-

tion of Saxony was not completed till 804.

The incorporation of Saxony into Charlemagne's empire was accompanied by the foundation of numerous bishoprics: Bremen and Verden in the north; Osnabrück and Minden in the central area; Paderborn in the south; Halberstadt in the extreme southeast; and Münster in the west. To these the emperor Louis I added Hildesheim and Hamburg, as well as the great abbey of Corvey.

Charlemagne's eastern frontier was not altogether secured by the annexation of Saxony. By the middle of the 7th century the Slavs (*q.v.*), who for 200 years had been displacing the Germans in central Europe, were moving into Saxony. Against them, therefore, the Frankish emperors set up lines of fortification: the Limes Saxonicus from the Elbe in the vicinity of Lauenburg to the Baltic near Kiel, to protect Nordalbingia; and the Limes Sorabicus from Bardowiek in Eastphalia southward across Thuringia.

The Duchy of the Liudolfings.—The emperor Louis I's sons partitioned the Frankish Empire (843). Saxony was included in the East Frankish Kingdom, under Louis the German (*see* GERMANY: *History*). During this king's reign Liudolf, one of his local officers or counts, won recognition as duke or military leader of the East Saxons, largely because of his success in defending Nordalbingia. On Liudolf's death (866), his son Bruno maintained his position in Saxony till he was killed in battle against the Danes (880), whereupon his brother Otto took his place. By this time the decline of the Carolingian dynasty was giving rise to consolidated duchies throughout Germany—not only Saxony, but also Franconia, Swabia, and Bavaria. By defense of the frontier against the Hungarians, Duke Otto had extended his influence over Thuringia before the accession of the German king Conrad I (911), the first non-Carolingian sovereign. Thenceforward the hereditary ducal rank of the Liudolfings was incontestable. It should here be emphasized that, while in the past century feudalism (*q.v.*) had been developing steadily in the German kingdom, so that many lands were held as fiefs dependent on a higher suzerain (king, duke, or bishop), in Saxony allodial land, that is, land held in absolute ownership, remained comparatively widespread.

Otto died in 912. His son Henry I (*q.v.*), elected German king in 919, began that penetration of Slav lands to which the Saxons were to devote their maximum of effort for generations to come, thus earning most of the credit for the Germanization of Europe east of the Elbe. This work was continued by Henry's successors, the Holy Roman emperors Otto I, Otto II, and Otto

III (*qq.v.*), who with Henry constitute the direct line of German kings of the Saxon or Liudolfing dynasty. In Otto I's reign Gero conquered a vast area between the Elbe-Saale line and the Oder. On this area the Saxon Nordmark (Northern March) and the Saxon Ostmark (Eastern March to the south of the Northern), as well as the four smaller marches of Aschersleben (*see* Ascanian Dynasties), Merseburg, Zeitz, and Meissen (*q.v.*) were constituted after Gero's death in 965. The archbishopric of Magdeburg was founded in 968 for the evangelization of the Slavs.

The Billung Dukes and the Revolt against Henry IV.— The emperor Otto I in 961 transferred his Saxon ducal title to Hermann Billung, a member of the indigenous Saxon nobility (*see* Billung), to whom he had already delegated much of his local authority. Whereas the Saxon dynasty of German kings came to an end in 1024 with Otto III's second cousin, Henry II (*q.v.*), the Saxon duchy remained in the hands of the Billungs for four generations after Hermann (d. 973). These dukes energetically continued the struggle against the Slavs. Hermann's son Bernard I (d. 1011) obtained guarantees of the special privileges and customs of the Saxons from Henry II on the latter's accession in 1002, and Bernard II (d. 1059) obtained similar guarantees from Conrad II, the first German king of the Salian dynasty, in 1024. Both Bernard II and his son Ordulf (d. 1072) resisted the aggrandizement of Archbishop Adalbert (*q.v.*) of Bremen under Conrad's successors Henry III and Henry IV.

King Henry III established his principal seat for the government of Germany in the ancient royal palace at Goslar, in Eastphalia. Alarm grew when Henry IV tried on the one hand to bring the Saxon customs into line with the law for the rest of Germany and on the other to reassert control over those parts of the royal domain in Saxony which had come irregularly into other hands during his minority. He began to build a chain of castles, including the great Harzburg near Goslar, across eastern Saxony, with Swabian *ministeriales* (*q.v.;* that is, unfree officers entirely dependent on the king) in command of them.

Besides the Billungs, one of the greatest of the landowning nobles in Saxony was Otto (*q.v.*) of Nordheim. In 1070 this Otto was charged with treason, and his Saxon lands were declared forfeit; but the Saxon duke Ordulf's son, Magnus, and other nobles took his side and rebelled against Henry IV. Both Otto and Magnus, however, were captured in 1071. Though Otto was soon released, Magnus was still detained in the Harzburg when he succeeded to the Saxon dukedom on Ordulf's death (1072). Henry was clearly resolved to break the power of the Billungs.

Henry's arrival at Goslar in summer 1073, to muster forces for an expedition against the Poles, at a time when he was in dispute with the papacy, gave an opportunity for a coup by the malcontents of eastern Saxony. A widespread revolt was organized, in which the Billungs and the margraves of the frontier zones, with Otto of Nordheim again, were joined by the bishops of Magdeburg, Halberstadt, and Merseburg, and also by the Thuringians. Henry was driven from Saxony, the royal castles were attacked, and Magnus was set free. In February 1074, at Gerstungen on the Werra River, the king had to consent to the demolition of the castles and to reaffirm the autonomy of the Saxons.

The other German princes envied the Saxon success and began to rally to Henry after his first reconciliation with the papacy a few weeks later. When the Saxon peasants, demolishing the Harzburg, razed its church as well as its fortifications, their sacrilege became a pretext for concerted measures by king and *Reich* against Saxony. On June 9, 1075, at the head of a massive army of mounted knights, Henry won a great victory over the Saxon infantry under Otto of Nordheim at Homburg an der Unstrut (near Langensalza). In the following autumn he reduced all Saxony to submission. The Saxon leaders were taken into custody.

Subsequent events destroyed the effect of Henry's victory. After his excommunication by Pope Gregory VII (1076), the captive Saxons were released to make common cause with the Swabian rebels against the king. But whereas the affairs of 1070–75 had been essentially concerned with Saxony, the Saxon participation in the later troubles is best considered as an aspect of the general upheaval throughout Germany (*see* Germany: *History*).

Lothair and the Welfs.— Magnus Billung died in 1106, leaving no son. His elder daughter, Wulfhild (d. 1126) was married to the Welf duke of Bavaria, Henry IX the Black; and her sister Eilika (d. 1142) was married to Otto of Ballenstedt, ancestor of the Ascanians (*q.v.*). Welfs and Ascanians therefore shared the allodial inheritance of the Billungs, but neither succeeded to the dukedom of Saxony, which the German king Henry V bestowed instead on Lothair of Supplinburg (*see* Lothair II or III, German king). This Lothair, whose patrimonial lands lay around Helmstedt, had married Richenza (d. 1141), who was to be the

SAXONY AT MID-17TH CENTURY

ALBERTINE } SAXONY
ERNESTINE }

OTHER LANDS OF THE EMPIRE

ENLARGEMENT OF AREA FROM MAIN MAP

ultimate heiress not only of the Brunonian family's land (around Brunswick) but also of the possessions of her paternal grandfather, the great Otto of Nordheim. Lothair soon turned against Henry V, whose forces he defeated in battle at Welfesholz in 1115. In 1125, he was himself elected king in succession to Henry.

On King Lothair's death (1137) his son-in-law, Henry (q.v.) the Proud, who was moreover the son of the Billung Wulfhild, could claim the succession to the Supplinburg, Nordheim, and Brunonian lands. Henry, however, was also already duke of Bavaria; and the German king Conrad III, of the House of Hohenstaufen, refused to invest him with Saxony, on the ground that no one could hold two duchies at once. Conrad in 1138 therefore assigned the Saxon duchy to the Ascanian Albert the Bear, son of the other Billung heiress Eilika (see ALBERT I, margrave of Brandenburg). Contesting this decision, Henry the Proud lost Bavaria but prevailed over Albert in Saxony; and his son Henry (q.v.) the Lion succeeded to his claims there in 1139. Finally, in 1142, peace was made at Frankfurt, Henry being recognized as duke of Saxony.

Henry the Lion in 1154 induced Conrad III's nephew and successor the German king Frederick I Barbarossa, to invest him with Bavaria as well. There followed two decades of cooperation between Welf and Hohenstaufen, during which Henry advanced the Saxon frontiers northward and eastward. His excessive power exasperated the neighbouring German princes and eventually led to a breach between him and Frederick, who in 1180 outlawed him. Henry was ultimately allowed to keep much of his allodial land, which became the nucleus of the duchy of Brunswick, but his fiefs within the ancient duchy were redistributed: the southwest, as the duchy of Westphalia, was allotted to the archbishopric of Cologne; and other local magnates, bishops or counts, partitioned the remainder. The Ascanian Bernard of Anhalt, a younger son of Albert the Bear, received the title duke of Saxony.

For the later history of secular states in Saxon country outside the Ascanian sphere see BRUNSWICK; HANOVER; HOLSTEIN; LIPPE; OLDENBURG; WESTPHALIA. For the 20th century see LOWER SAXONY.

THE ASCANIAN DUCHIES AND THE ELECTORATE

The principal territory assigned with the ducal title to Bernard of Anhalt was on the lower Elbe northeast of Lüneburg. There he built a stronghold at Lauenburg (q.v.). At the same time he received the Hadeln land, between the Elbe and Weser estuaries. Bernard however had also considerable possessions in Anhalt (q.v.) on the lower Saale and on the right bank of the middle Elbe, namely Wittenberg and its hinterland, which tapered northward to the borders of the Brandenburg Mark beyond Belzig. When Lauenburg fell to the Danes (1203) Wittenberg was left as Bernard's major possession, and the name Saxony came to be applied to it.

After Bernard's death (1212), Anhalt passed to his elder son Henry, the duchy of Saxony to his younger son Albert I. Albert recovered Lauenburg; and before the end of his reign the duke of Saxony was in 1257 recognized as having an inalienable right to participate in the election of a German king (see ELECTORS). On Albert's death (1260), however, his sons partitioned the ducal lands: the elder, John I (d. 1285) took Lauenburg and Hadeln; the younger, Albert II (d. 1298) took Wittenberg. As both retained the ducal title, the Saxon electorate was disputed between Saxe-Lauenburg and Saxe-Wittenberg.

Saxe-Lauenburg and Saxe-Wittenberg.—Though Saxe-Lauenburg was the senior line, its possessions were scattered about the lower Elbe and hemmed in by more powerful principalities. Furthermore John I's descendants frequently subjected their inheritance to joint rule by brothers or cousins, or to division. Consequently Saxe-Lauenburg's claims to the electorate were overruled in favour of Saxe-Wittenberg, to which the countship of Brehna, extending some distance eastward and westward from Torgau, was attached from the 1290s. Albert II's son Rudolf I of Saxe-Wittenberg (d. 1356) consistently exercised the electoral right; and by the Golden Bull of the emperor Charles IV in 1356 the electorate was definitively attached to Saxe-Wittenberg.

Rudolf I's son Rudolf II (d. 1370) was succeeded by his half brother Wenceslas (d. 1388), the latter by his elder son Rudolf III (d. 1419).

Rudolf III's brother Albert III died in 1422, the last of the Ascanians of Saxe-Wittenberg. The vacant duchy and the electorate were thereupon claimed by Eric V of Saxe-Lauenburg, whose father Eric IV (d. 1412) had reunited the possessions of his greatgrandfather John I. At the same time the Hohenzollern margrave of Brandenburg put forward counterclaims. The German king Sigismund ignored both pretensions and, in 1423, gave the electoral duchy to Frederick the Warlike, margrave of Meissen.

Sigismund's act constitutes another epoch in Saxon history. Before describing its effects, Saxe-Lauenburg must be dismissed from the narrative. The Ascanians of Saxe-Lauenburg continued to claim the electorate till the time of Magnus I (d. 1543), whose pretension was overruled by the Holy Roman emperor Charles V in 1530. Magnus tried to exploit the Reformation in order to annex episcopal principalities; but both he and his successors were quite unable to prevail against stronger competitors. When the line died out with Julius Francis in 1689, a dispute over the succession ensued, till the land was finally secured by Brunswick-Lüneburg. See further LAUENBURG.

THE WETTIN ELECTORATE

The House of Wettin (q.v.), to which Frederick the Warlike belonged, had held the margraviate of Meissen (q.v.) from the 12th century and had extended its rule not only eastward into Lusatia (q.v.), which was mainly in the hands of the Bohemian crown, but also westward, over the Osterland (that is, the country round Leipzig), far into Thuringia (q.v.). The southeastern border of the Wettin territories ran along the minerally rich mountain range of the Erzgebirge, by which they were separated from Bohemia; and the Wettins were also disputing control of the Vogtland (between the Erzgebirge and Thuringia) with the Bohemians. When the margrave became elector of Saxony as Frederick I (q.v.) in 1423, his ancestral possessions were united with those of Saxe-Wittenberg. Just as the name Saxony had traveled with the duchy from the Elbe estuary upstream to Wittenberg after 1180, so after 1423 did it travel with the electorate still farther upstream, to cover the whole power block of the Wettin dynasty. Thus Meissen and Dresden on the Elbe, together with Leipzig nearer to the centre of the Wettin dominions, came to be regarded as constituting the axis of Saxony; and it is with Saxony in this sense, which obtained till the middle of the 20th century, that the rest of this article is concerned.

After Frederick I's death (1428) his successor, Frederick II, had to face invasions of Saxony by the Hussites (q.v.) of Bohemia. Of more ominous significance for Saxony, however, was the quarrel between Frederick II and his younger brother William over the partition of the Wettin inheritance, which resulted in William's detaching the landgraviate of Thuringia for himself (1445). If the Wettins had earlier established a firm rule of primogeniture, Saxony might have assumed the role which Brandenburg-Prussia was later to play in eastern Germany. Instead, they long continued to sap their strength by dividing their possessions. Constitutionally the most positive development of the reign was the meeting, at Leipzig in 1438, of the first collective Diet of the Estates (see ESTATES-GENERAL) of all Saxony, at which counts, knights, and towns were represented, but not the clergy.

On Frederick II's death (1464), his sons Ernest (1441–86) and Albert the Courageous (1443–1500) succeeded jointly to his lands. They acquired Plauen, the key point in the Vogtland, and also the distant Silesian principality of Sagan in Silesia. In 1482, however, when their uncle William died childless, so that Thuringia reverted to them, Albert demanded a partition of the collective inheritance. This was effected, in 1485, by the Treaty of Leipzig: Ernest retained Electoral Saxony (Saxe-Wittenberg) and numerous lands in Thuringia, the two units being linked by a corridor between Meissen and the Osterland; Albert, with the title of duke, took the margraviate of Meissen (with Dresden as his capital), the Osterland, and a northern slice of Thuringia. Certain rights, notably in Lusatia and in Silesia, as well as protectorates over various ecclesiastical lands, were still held in common between the brothers. The intricacy of the partition may have been designed to conserve a prospect of dynastic reunion, but the separation between Ernestine and Albertine lines persisted into the 20th century, with unfortunate consequences.

The Ernestines and the Reformation.—Frederick III (*q.v.*) the Wise, elector in succession to his father from 1486 to 1525, made Wittenberg a centre of humanism and, in 1502, founded the great university there. His later role as the foremost protector of Martin Luther (*q.v.; and see* GERMANY: *History*), made Saxony the cradle of the Reformation, and he himself accepted Lutheranism in 1524. By that time the revolt of the German peasants had spread across the Albertine lands into the Ernestine.

Frederick III's brother, John (*q.v.*) the Steadfast, adopted a more active policy for Lutheranism. He established the Saxon Church, under the control of the elector. His alliance of 1526 with Philip (*q.v.*) of Hesse and his signature of the Protest of 1529 were followed by the formation of the League of Schmalkalden (*q.v.*) for the defense of the Protestant princes in Germany against the threat of aggression by the emperor Charles V. As the emperor's dynasty, the House of Habsburg (*q.v.*), had acquired the crown of Bohemia and its dependencies (1526), relations with the Habsburgs were to be of crucial importance to Saxony.

John Frederick I (*q.v.*) succeeded John in 1532. His reign saw the downfall of the Ernestine electorate. In 1542 he took unilateral action in an ecclesiastical matter which should have been decided in consultation with the Albertine duke Maurice (*q.v.*), thus provoking the latter into threats of war. A reconciliation was patched up; but in 1546, when the emperor finally launched his campaign against the League of Schmalkalden, the ambitious and versatile Maurice seized the occasion of aggrandizing himself at the Ernestines' expense and took up arms against John Frederick. The latter, defeated and captured by the emperor, had to sign the Capitulation of Wittenberg (May 1547), renouncing the electorate, the electoral territory, the Ernestine tract between Meissen and the Osterland, and some of his Thuringian land. All this went to Maurice.

The Capitulation left some Ernestine lands in Thuringia to John Frederick's children, while he himself was kept a prisoner. Released in 1552, when Maurice was in rebellion against the emperor (*see* below), John Frederick I tried to recover the electorate. A few days before his death, however, in 1554, he concluded the Treaty of Naumburg with Maurice's successor Augustus I, whom he recognized as elector in return for the retrocession of Altenburg and some adjacent places. Though his son John Frederick II (*q.v.*) later made some disastrous attempts to win the electorate back, the complex history of the Ernestine territories is henceforward best considered apart from that of the electorate (*see* SAXON DUCHIES, ERNESTINE).

The Albertine Dukes.—Duke Albert the Courageous, instigator of the partition of 1485, left a will prescribing the rule of primogeniture for his descendants. He was therefore succeeded, in 1500, by his eldest son, George the Rich or the Bearded (1471–1539). Whereas Albert had been much occupied abroad (in the service of the Habsburg dynasty), George devoted himself to his own lands: he divided them administratively into "circles" (*Kreise*), reorganized the judicial system, laid the foundation of a central government and developed the economy—to the great advantage of the ducal treasury—by exploiting his mineral resources (tin, silver, and coal). Contrary to his Ernestine cousin, moreover, he adopted a strongly anti-Lutheran attitude from 1519 onward. To his chagrin, his sons predeceased him, so that he was succeeded by his Lutheran brother Henry (d. 1541), who had already made his court at Freiberg a centre for the new doctrine.

Henry's son Maurice began his reign as duke of Saxony with important reforms. The church was taken over by the state, and the ancient ecclesiastical lands were confiscated (1543). Much of the revenue from the confiscation was applied to educational purposes: the University of Leipzig was completely reorganized; and the three so-called *Fürstenschulen,* or Princes' Schools, were founded at Meissen, at Pforta, and at Merseburg (this one was later transplanted to Grimma) to give six-year courses, free of charge, to pupils nominated by the municipalities, by the nobles, or by the ruler.

The First Albertine Electors, to 1694.—On the acquisition of the electorate and of the greater part of the Ernestine lands in 1547 (*see* above), Maurice reorganized the system of "circles," which he made dependent on his own central council, so as to enhance his authority over the Estates. Though he had to cede the Vogtland to a local dynast under Habsburg protection (1547) and distant Sagan to Habsburg Bohemia (1549), and also to allow the restoration of Catholicism in the bishoprics of Meissen, Merseburg, and Naumburg, he had built up a great state stretching from the Werra Valley in the west over the Saale and Elbe basins to the Lusatian frontiers in the east. But he owed this to the emperor Charles V, and he could not be sure that the emperor's benevolence to a Protestant would continue. Consequently, though his conduct in 1547 had gravely compromised his relationship with the militant Protestants, he sought a *rapprochement* with them, joined their conspiracy with the French in 1551, and rebelled against Charles in 1552. (*See* again MAURICE; GERMANY: *History*.)

Under Maurice's brother Augustus I (*q.v.*), elector from 1553 to 1586, Saxony reached new levels of prosperity. The religious Peace of Augsburg (*q.v.*), in 1555, inaugurated an era in which Albertine Saxony, the leading Lutheran state, could cooperate with the Catholic Habsburgs for the maintenance of order in Germany, as Protestant militancy passed to the Calvinists. The concessions made to the Ernestines at Naumburg (*see* above) were soon offset by the absorption of ecclesiastical lands (Meissen, Merseburg, and Naumburg), by the acquisition of Weida and the Neustadt area of southeastern Thuringia in 1567, by the recovery of the Vogtland in 1569, and by a large share of the countship of Henneberg, enclaved within the Ernestine zone, in 1583. Internally the elector contrived to weaken the Estates, sponsored a major codification of the laws (1572), and made himself a pioneer of cameralism, which in practice meant the direction of the national economy by an absolute ruler for the benefit of all classes in the light of Christian thought. The development of Leipzig as a great centre of the arts was a feature of the reign, and lace making was promoted as an industry.

Augustus I's son Christian I, elector from 1586 to 1591, tried to unite Lutherans and Calvinists in a common front against the Habsburgs, but his League of Torgau fell to pieces on his death. His son Christian II reverted to cooperation with Austria.

The long reign of John George I (*q.v.*), from 1611 to 1656, saw the diminution of Saxony's prestige, notwithstanding territorial expansion, during the Thirty Years' War (*q.v.*). For the first decade of the war the elector supported the emperor Ferdinand II, on the understanding that he would receive Lusatia as his reward; but Ferdinand's Edict of Restitution (1629), which demanded the surrender of church property secularized since 1552, together with a particular quarrel over the administration of the bishopric of Magdeburg, which the Saxon electors had long coveted, drove John George, after long prevarication, into alliance with the Swedish king Gustavus II Adolphus (1631). Swedes and Saxons won a great victory at Breitenfeld; but in 1632 Gustavus was killed at Lützen, and in 1635 the elector deserted his Swedish alliance to conclude the Peace of Prague with Ferdinand. The treaty secured Lusatia for Saxony and confirmed one of the elector's younger sons, Augustus, as administrator of Magdeburg, but was followed by a Saxon declaration of war against the Swedes, against whose subsequent ravages the country could scarcely defend itself. At the general Peace of Westphalia, in 1648, John George was recognized as head of the Corpus Evangelicorum, that is, the body which was to represent Protestant interests in the *Reich;* but he had to agree that on the death of his son Augustus the administration of Magdeburg should pass to the Hohenzollerns of Brandenburg (*q.v.*). This precluded any further expansion of Albertine Saxony northward down the Elbe and marked the beginning of Brandenburg's extrusion of Saxony from leadership in eastern Germany. Finally, John George saw fit to create separate duchies for three of his younger sons: Saxe-Weissenfels for Augustus (line extinct 1746), Saxe-Merseburg for Christian (line extinct 1738), Saxe-Zeitz for Maurice (line extinct 1718).

John George I's eldest son, John George II (d. 1680) concluded alliances with Louis XIV of France, the great opponent of the Habsburgs. His son John George III (d. 1691), on the other hand, raised a considerable army to support the Habsburgs against the Turks in 1683 and against the French in the War of the Grand Alliance. John George IV, elector from 1691, died in 1694, leaving Saxony to his brother Frederick Augustus I.

The 18th Century: Saxony and Poland.—Frederick Augustus I inaugurated the expensive and ultimately fruitless connection of Saxony with Poland, of which he was elected king, as Augustus II (*q.v.*) in 1697. To win election, he had to become a Catholic, renouncing the Lutheranism to which his Saxon subjects were firmly attached and, with it, the headship of the Corpus Evangelicorum, which was passed to the Saxon Privy Council (*geheime Rat*); and to raise money for his Polish ambitions he had to pawn Saxon rights over numerous outlying territories. In 1700, in coalition with Denmark and Russia, he began, for the sake of Poland's interests, the great Northern War (*q.v.*) against Sweden. The first phase of the war culminated in a Swedish invasion of Saxony, whereupon the elector signed the Peace of Altranstädt (1706), renouncing Poland and allowing the Swedes to winter in his country; but on the collapse of the Swedish invasion of Russia (1709) he reentered the war, and finally Poland was won back. Despite opposition from the Estates (for which rules of procedure were formulated in 1728), he ruled the electorate firmly; and his institution of a Privy Cabinet (*geheime Kabinett*) enabled him to conduct policy over the head of the Privy Council. He also founded the porcelain industry of Meissen (1710).

Frederick Augustus II succeeded to Saxony in 1733 and was elected king of Poland, as Augustus III (*q.v.*) later in the year. The ensuing War of the Polish Succession (*q.v.*) ended in his favour. Saxony and Poland, however, remained without any territorial link, since Silesia, then a Habsburg possession, lay between them. Desire to obtain such a link was a principal motive in the policy of Frederick Augustus II's minister Heinrich Brühl (*q.v.*), but he was not successful. When Frederick II the Great of Prussia invaded Silesia at the start of the War of the Austrian Succession (*q.v.*), Saxony took no immediate action, but in 1741 the elector entered the war against Austria. Frederick the Great's Treaty of Breslau with Austria (1742), which gave Silesia to Prussia, ignored Saxony's interests; and Saxony's conversion to alliance with Austria for the remainder of the war proved fruitless.

The Seven Years' War (*q.v.*) opened with a Prussian invasion of Saxony to forestall an Austrian attempt to recover Silesia. Dresden was occupied without resistance; the Saxon Army, capitulating at Pirna, was absorbed into the Prussian forces; and for the duration of the war Saxony was devastated by foreigners. The Peace of Hubertusburg restored the elector in 1763, but within a few months he, his son and momentary successor Frederick Christian, and the energetic Brühl were all dead.

Frederick Christian's son was only a boy when he became elector, as Frederick Augustus III, in 1763 (*see* FREDERICK AUGUSTUS I, king of Saxony). He came of age to rule in 1768. Free from involvement with Poland, he pursued the economic rehabilitation of Saxony, whose trade began to compete keenly and successfully with Prussia's. In foreign affairs, however, he took Prussia's side against Austria in the militarily cheap War of the Bavarian Succession (*q.v.*); and the monetary compensation awarded to Saxony under the Peace of Teschen was largely devoted to redeeming rights pawned since Frederick Augustus I's time. He also joined the Fürstenbund or League of Princes organized by Prussia in 1785 to deter Austria from renewed designs on Bavaria.

On the outbreak of the French Revolutionary Wars (*q.v.*) in 1792, the elector joined the Austro-Prussian coalition. Even after Prussia's defection (1795), he fought on against the French till 1796. Ten years later, he rejoined Prussia in war against Napoleonic France (*see* NAPOLEONIC WARS). Defeat led to a momentous change of policy: after the Franco-Saxon Peace of Posen (Dec. 11, 1806), Saxony was to be one of Napoleon's most loyal allies.

THE KINGDOM OF SAXONY

On the Peace of Posen the elector of Saxony took the title of king, as Frederick Augustus I; and in 1807 the kingdom was admitted to the Confederation of the Rhine (*see* GERMANY: *History*). While some western areas had to be ceded to the Kingdom of Westphalia, Saxony got Cottbus, hitherto a Prussian enclave in Lusatia. Moreover the Duchy of Warsaw, carved out of Prussian Poland, was assigned to Frederick Augustus, who in 1809 also received Austrian Poland, though Prussia retained Silesia.

Saxony's good fortune lasted only so long as Napoleon's. The retreat of the French from Russia in the winter of 1812–13 (*see* again NAPOLEONIC WARS) was followed by a Russo-Prussian invasion of Saxony. Having tried to conciliate Austria, Frederick Augustus brought Saxony back to the French side after Napoleon's victory at Lützen (May 1813); and the defeat of Napoleon at Leipzig in October, during which much of the Saxon Army went over to his enemies, was followed by a Russian occupation of Saxony.

The fate of Saxony was one of the major issues before the Congress of Vienna (*q.v.*). Prussia wanted to annex Saxony; and Russia, to get Prussian support on the question of Poland, in September 1814 transferred to Prussia the task of occupying Saxony. Austria, however, insisted that if Prussia was to have Saxony, then Poland must be independent; and when Russia and Prussia persisted in their Polish program, Austria, Great Britain, and France made a secret alliance to withstand their arbitrary domination of central Europe. The final result was that Frederick Augustus was restored to a grievously diminished Kingdom of Saxony (May 1815): he had to cede the old Electoral Circle (Wittenberg), Torgau, northern Thuringia (with all his former possessions farther north), and most of Lusatia to Prussia, which divided the Lusatian areas between the provinces of Brandenburg and Silesia and merged the rest with older Hohenzollern possessions on the Elbe to form a new Province of Saxony (*Provinz Sachsen*); and the Weida-Neustadt area was transferred to the Ernestine Grand Duchy of Saxe-Weimar. The Kingdom of Saxony was thus reduced to less than half the size of the Albertine state before the Revolutionary Wars. It became a member state of the new German Confederation.

For the rest of his reign King Frederick Augustus I adhered to the conservative policy of the Restoration as laid down for Germany by Austria. On his death in 1827, he was succeeded by his aged brother Antony (Anton; 1755–1836), who had to face the wave of revolution that swept over Germany in 1830. When riots started in Dresden and in Leipzig (September 1830), the king was forced to accept Frederick Augustus, son of his brother Maximilian, as co-ruler; and on Sept. 4, 1831, a constitution was promulgated. This established a bicameral diet: the First, or Upper, Chamber, consisted of the ancient aristocracy of the Estates, with the difference that counts, knights, and municipal delegates sat no longer separately, but together; the Second, or Lower Chamber, comprised 20 representatives of the knights (over and above their majority in the First Chamber), 25 of the urban bourgeoisie, 25 members elected by the peasantry, and 5 members elected by workers in commerce or industry. While this attempt to compromise between conservatism and the liberal aspirations of the middle classes satisfied neither element, a responsible ministry took the place of the Privy Cabinet, and the peasant serfs were emancipated. In 1834 Saxony joined the Prussian-dominated *Zollverein* or German Customs Union.

On Antony's death his co-ruler became king as Frederick Augustus II (1836). Industrial and commercial prosperity, founded on mining and on the various manufactures of Leipzig, Dresden, Meissen, Chemnitz, Zwickau, and Bautzen, was exemplified by the opening of the Dresden-Leipzig railway (1839), but political discontent was exacerbated by Liberal demands for the publicity of judicial proceedings and for a free press. The government's intolerant attitude toward the rationalistic movement of the "German Catholics" (*Deutschkatholiker*), who held their ecclesiastical council in Leipzig in 1845, provoked further criticism.

The revolutionary events of 1848 (*see* GERMANY: *History*) precipitated a crisis. A Liberal ministry took office in March, the First Chamber was opened to representatives elected by the higher taxpayers, and suffrage for the Second Chamber was made universal, while freedom of the press, publicity of judicial proceedings, and, for some cases, trial by jury were introduced. Elections returned a majority of leftwing progressives to the Saxon Diet, which promptly demanded the king's acceptance of the German constitution proposed by the National Assembly at Frankfurt. The king, having formed a ministry in February 1849, withheld acceptance and dissolved the Diet; and insurrection broke out in Dresden (May). The king fled to Königstein, and the insurgents set up a provisional government, under the inspiration of the Russian extremist M. A. Bakunin (*q.v.*). A week later, Prussian troops, despite fierce resistance, restored Frederick Augustus.

With Prussia and Hanover, Saxony concluded the *Dreikönigsbündnis*, or Three Kings' League (May 1849), for the elaboration of a German federation under Prussian leadership. Saxony and Hanover, however, withdrew from Prussia's "Erfurt Union" when the other two German kingdoms, Bavaria and Württemberg, declined to join it. After forming the *Vierkönigsbündnis* with Hanover, Bavaria and Württemberg, Frederick Augustus finally supported Austria's policy for reviving the old German Confederation, which meant the collapse of Prussia's schemes (1850). When the First Chamber opposed him and refused to consider an urgent loan, he dissolved the Diet and restored the constitution of 1831.

F. F. von Beust (*q.v.*) had been the chief sponsor of Saxony's reorientation toward Austria. He remained in office when Frederick Augustus II's brother John (1801–73) succeeded to the throne in 1854. He allowed some liberalization, including an extension of the franchise (1861). As the Austro-Prussian conflict grew more acute the "Trias" policy of consolidating the lesser German states into a third block came to nothing; and in the Seven Weeks' War (*q.v.*) of 1866 Saxony took Austria's side. After Prussia's victory Beust resigned.

Saxony had to pay a war indemnity to Prussia and to enter the North German Confederation (*see* GERMANY: *History*). The Army became part of the Confederation's forces, under Prussian control. A law of 1868 removed the constitutional distinction of the Estates and extended the franchise still farther.

After the Franco-German War of 1870, in which the crown prince Albert (*q.v.*; 1828–1902) played a distinguished role, the Kingdom of Saxony in 1871 became a member state of Prussia's new German Empire. Albert succeeded his father as king in 1873. Economically the country prospered, but the most sensational feature of the new reign was the progress of the Social Democrats. Having won 5 seats in the Second Chamber in 1885, they won 14 in 1895, whereupon the older parties, in consternation, in 1896, revised the law, to introduce indirect suffrage, the voters being divided among three classes according to the amounts paid in direct taxation (*Dreiklassenwahlrecht*). This system grossly favoured the rural as against the urban or industrial population and eliminated the Social Democrats from the Saxon diet of 1901; but in 1903, during the short reign of Albert's brother George (1832–1904; king from 1902) the Social Democrats won 22 of Saxony's 23 seats in the *Reichstag* or Diet of the German Empire, for which universal suffrage obtained. Within "the Red Kingdom," as Saxony was now called, some reform of the franchise was evidently required; and under George's son Frederick Augustus III (1865–1932; king from 1904 to 1918) a complex system with plural voting was introduced. At the polls of 1909, the Social Democrats won 25 seats.

THE FREE STATE AND THE LAND

Saxon industries and manpower made a heavy contribution to Germany's effort in World War I. Defeat precipitated revolution, which broke out on Nov. 2, 1918. The king abdicated, and a government of Social Democrats took office. Communist guerrilla activity, led by Max Hölz, largely in reaction to right-wing coups elsewhere in Germany, had to be suppressed by the armed forces of the *Reich*. On Nov. 1, 1920, Saxony adopted a republican constitution as a Free State of the *Reich* under the Weimar regime.

Erich Zeigner, Social Democratic prime minister of Saxony, in 1923, formed a coalition government with the Communists, whose intention of promoting a proletarian revolution throughout Germany was made clear by the inflammatory speeches of his finance minister, Paul Böttcher, and by the organization of paramilitary "hundreds." Conflict ensued between the Saxon government and the *Reich* government's forces in Saxony; and finally, on Oct. 29, the German chancellor Gustav Stresemann sent more forces into Saxony to depose Zeigner. Moderate Social Democrats then governed the country, usually in coalition with other democratic parties, till 1929. In 1933 the Nazis came to power.

After World War II Saxony fell to the Soviet-occupied zone of Germany (1945) and so was organized as a *Land* of the German Democratic Republic. In 1952, when the *Länder* were dissolved, Saxony was divided between the *Bezirke* or districts of Leipzig, Karl-Marx-Stadt (the former Chemnitz), Dresden, and Cottbus.

The formerly Prussian Province of Saxony was merged with Anhalt in 1945 to form a *Land* Saxony-Anhalt (Sachsen-Anhalt), which in turn was dissolved in 1952 between the *Bezirke* of Magdeburg, Halle, Leipzig, and Cottbus.

See R. Kötzschke and H. Kretzschmar, *Sächsische Geschichte*, 2 vol. (1935).

SAXOPHONE, a family of reed wind instruments patented by Adolphe Sax in Paris in 1846. A saxophone has a conical brass tube with about 24 openings controlled by padded key-mechanisms. A single-reed mouthpiece akin to that of the clarinet is placed over the narrow end. The instrument overblows at the octave, by means of two octave-key vents operated by a thumb key. The normal compass is written from B♭ below the treble stave to F three lines above the stave—sounding, however, differently with each member of the family. The B♭ soprano saxophone, sounding a tone lower than written pitch, is built straight like a clarinet. The other members of the family have the lower end upturned and the upper end made as a detachable "crook." They are the E♭ alto, sounding a sixth lower than written; the B♭ tenor, with undulating crook, sounding a ninth lower; the E♭ baritone, with looped crook, an octave below the alto; and the rarer B♭ bass, similar in shape to the baritone but larger, an octave below the tenor. Little-used sizes include the "C melody" saxophone, a tenor in C for playing from vocal music without transposition. Originally the whole family of saxophones was pitched in C and F alternately.

CONTEMPORARY ALTO SAXOPHONE

Sax left no historical account of his invention, which was intended for military bands and which he may have discovered through experiments with reed mouthpieces on brass instruments such as ophicleides. He quickly procured its official adoption by the French Army, and saxophones from alto to baritone are regularly included in bands constituted on French models. In the U.S. they have been used in bands from P. S. Gilmore's time. In British military bands, only an alto and a tenor are obligatory. The saxophone was a popular solo instrument in the U.S. about the time of World War I and was then adopted by dance bands, in which the standard team remains two altos and a tenor. Larger bands use more than four saxophones and include the baritone.

The use of saxophones in dance bands brought mechanical improvements, as well as changes in mouthpiece design to produce brighter, more penetrating sounds.

As a serious concert instrument the saxophone was cultivated by virtuosi, notably Sigurd Rascher in the U.S., and Marcel Mule, founder both of the Paris Saxophone Quartet (soprano, alto, tenor, baritone) and of the class at the Paris Conservatoire. Debussy, Glazunov, and Ibert are among earlier composers who wrote solo works for saxophone, all for the alto instrument. From Bizet's *L'Arlésienne* (1872) until the 1920s orchestral works using the saxophone were few. Later it was occasionally used by numerous composers. Webern and others sparingly used it in small combinations. The saxophone is infrequently used not because of prejudice against a popular, nonclassical instrument but because of the scarcity of players acquainted with the concert style.

(A. C. Ba.)

SAY, JEAN BAPTISTE (1767–1832), French economist best known for his law of markets, which remained a central tenet of orthodox economics until the great depression of the 1930s, was born at Lyons on Jan. 5, 1767.

Say's law postulates that supply creates its own demand; hence there can be no general deficiency of effective demand to cause economic depression and unemployment. Actual depression Say attributed to temporarily misdirected production, which must automatically right itself because the overproducers of particular products will suffer losses; they must either redirect their production to conform with consumers' preferences or be forced out of business by continuing losses. An obvious implication of Say's law is that the capitalist system is self-adjusting and there is therefore no need for government intervention in economic affairs.

Say was perhaps the first important economist to distinguish clearly between entrepreneur and capitalist and to assign to the former the creative role of combining the other factors of production—labour, land, and capital. His career as a businessman as well as a professor of economics contributed to his insight into entrepreneurial activity. He died in Paris on Nov. 15, 1832.

Say's principal work is *Traité d'économie politique* (1st ed., 1803; 6th ed., 1846).

See E. Teilhac, *L'Oeuvre économique de Jean Baptiste Say* (1927); Leo Rogin, *The Meaning and Validity of Economic Theory*, ch. 6 (1956).   (D. Dd.)

SAY, THOMAS (1787–1834), U.S. Quaker naturalist, often termed "the father of descriptive entomology in America," was born at Philadelphia, Pa., on June 27, 1787. He was an original member of the Philadelphia Academy of Natural Sciences, founded in 1812; and after various activities, including two expeditions to the Rocky Mountains, he became curator of the American Philosophical Society in 1821 and was professor of natural history at the University of Pennsylvania from 1822 to 1828. During this period he took part in other expeditions, and joined the experimental ideal community at the village of New Harmony, Ind., where he spent the remainder of his life, dying there on Oct. 10, 1834.

His work was almost entirely taxonomic and his writings for the most part purely descriptive. His entomological papers in various journals were collected by J. L. Le Conte and published in two volumes: *The Complete Writings of Thomas Say on the Entomology of North America* (1859). His works on conchology were collected by W. G. Binney and published in 1858 as *The Complete Writings of Thomas Say on the Conchology of the United States*, with 75 plates, many of them drawn by his wife. His paleontological writings were reprinted in 1896 by G. D. Harris in *Bulletin of American Paleontology*, vol. 1, no. v.

(Ed. He.)

SAYAN MOUNTAINS (Sayany) in southern Siberia, U.S.S.R., consist of a number of ranges from 90 to 120 mi. (145 to 193 km.) wide. Peaks vary from 1,700 ft. (518 m.) in the north and 3,000 ft. (914 m.) in the south to 8,000–10,000 ft. (2,400–3,000 m.) in the centre; the elevation does not fall below 1,700 ft. (518 m.) except in the Minusinsk and other river basins. Two systems are distinguished: the Western Sayan (Sayanski Khrebet) and the Eastern Sayan. The Western Sayan in Krasnoyarsk *kray*

and Tuva Autonomous Soviet Socialist Republic stretch from the Maly (Little) Abakan River for more than 400 mi. (644 km.) to the northeast to the headwaters of the Kazyr and Uda. The highest peak is Karagosh (9,613 ft. [2,930 m.]). The Eastern Sayan in the Irkutsk *oblast* stretch from the western bank of the Yenisei River, southwest of Krasnoyarsk, for more than 620 mi. (998 km.) in a southeasterly direction to the Tunkin depression, which separates them from the Transbaikal (Zabaikalye) ranges. The mountains as far east as the Zun-Murin Valley are sometimes included in this system. Small glaciers are found in the highest parts; Munku-Sardyk (11,457 ft.) is the highest peak.

The north-flowing Yenisei and its numerous tributaries intersect both systems. The rocks are a complex of Precambrian and Caledonian Age. In the Western Sayan gold, iron quartzites, asbestos, magnetites, and copper are found and coal is mined in the Minusinsk and Tuva basins; in the Eastern Sayan are iron quartzites, asbestos, graphite, nephrite, and mica. Vegetation consists of forests of pine and larch, with some birch, aspen, and alder, giving way to cedar and fir on the higher slopes, where lichens and mosses clothe many of the scattered boulders.

(R. E. F. S.)

SAYAT-NOVA (pseudonym of Aruthin Sayadian) (1712–1795), Armenian troubadour, famous for his love songs, was born at Tiflis. He worked first as a weaver and later (1750–65) became the court minstrel of Irakli II of Georgia. In 1770 he entered a monastery in Haghbat, and he was martyred in 1795 by the Persian invaders of Georgia.

Most of his extant songs are in Azeri Turkish, the rest in Armenian and Georgian.   (C. J. F. D.)

SAYCE, ARCHIBALD HENRY (1845–1933), British philologist, whose services to Babylonian and Assyrian scholarship cannot be overestimated, was born at Shirehampton on Sept. 25, 1845. He was educated at Bath, and at Queen's College, Oxford, becoming a fellow in 1869. In 1870 he was ordained. From 1891 to 1919 he was professor of Assyriology at Oxford. He was a member of the Old Testament Revision Company (1874–84); deputy professor of comparative philology in Oxford (1876–90); Hibbert lecturer (1887); Gifford lecturer (1900–02). Sayce died on Feb. 4, 1933, at Bath.

Among his more important works are: *Assyrian Grammar* (1872); *Principles of Comparative Philology* (1874); *Introduction to the Science of Language* (1879); *Early History of the Hebrews* (1897); *Israel and the Surrounding Nations* (1898); *Babylonians and Assyrians* (1900); and *Archaeology of the Cuneiform Inscriptions* (1907). He also contributed important articles to *Encyclopædia Britannica* and published his *Reminiscences* in 1923.

SAYE AND SELE, WILLIAM FIENNES, 1st Viscount (1582–1662), a leading opponent of James I and Charles I in the House of Lords and a supporter of Parliament in the English Civil War, was born at Broughton Castle, near Banbury, Oxfordshire, on May 28, 1582, the only son of Richard Fiennes, 7th baron Saye and Sele. Educated at New College, Oxford, he succeeded as 8th baron in 1613. He opposed the policy of James I in Parliament and in 1622 was imprisoned for six months for objecting to the imposition of a benevolence by the king. Created a viscount in 1624 through the friendship of George Villiers, 1st duke of Buckingham, he nevertheless continued his opposition to the crown in the early parliaments of Charles I. From 1630 Saye became actively engaged in colonization schemes. He was a member of the company formed to colonize Providence Island (now Providencia) in the Caribbean Sea, and in 1635 was responsible with Robert Greville, Baron Brooke, for the establishment of a settlement on the Connecticut River which was named Saybrook after them. A thorough aristocrat, his ideas for the government of colonies in New England included the establishment of a hereditary aristocracy.

Saye reluctantly accompanied Charles I against the Scots in the first Bishops' War in 1639 but together with Brooke he refused to take the oath binding peers to fight for the king. In 1642 Parliament appointed him a member of the committee of safety and lord lieutenant of Oxfordshire, Cheshire, and Gloucestershire, and after the outbreak of the Civil War in August, Saye raised a regiment for the parliamentary forces. He was mainly responsible for the passage through the House of Lords of the Self-Denying Ordinance (April 1645) which discharged members of Parliament from holding civil or military commands. A supporter of the army in its struggle with Parliament in 1647, he soon became anxious for Parliament to reach an agreement with the king and was one of the parliamentary commissioners who negotiated with Charles at Newport, Isle of Wight (April–November 1648). After the king's execution (Jan. 30, 1649) Saye retired from public life. He took his seat in the Convention Parliament in April 1660, and in June, after the restoration of Charles II, was appointed a privy councilor. He died at Broughton Castle on April 14, 1662.

SAYERS, TOM (1826–1865), English middleweight boxing champion, was born on May 25, 1826, at Brighton. In 1849 he left bricklaying to become a fighter. Despite his size (height 5 ft. 8½ in.; weight 155 lb.), the "Little Wonder" often fought much bigger opponents, yet he lost only one bout during the ten years he fought —that to Nat Langham on Oct. 18, 1853, in 61 rounds.

In 1860, in the first international heavyweight title match in boxing history, he fought America's great champion John C. Heenan. Although he was outweighed by 40 lb. and was nine years older, Sayers was made the 2 to 1 betting favourite over Heenan. The fight lasted 2 hr. 20 min. (42 rounds) and was declared a draw after Sayers injured his right arm (see BOXING). Sayers then retired from the ring, and the British raised £3,000 (about $15,000) by public subscription for him. He died on Nov. 8, 1865. (J. D. McC.)

SAYYID AHMAD KHAN, SIR (1817–1898), distinguished Indian Muslim scholar and educator, founder of Aligarh Muslim University, was born in Delhi on Oct. 17, 1817. After his father's death in 1836, against the wishes of his family, he entered the civil service. During the Indian Mutiny (1857–58) he was instrumental in saving the lives of many Europeans by sending them, at great risk to himself, into safety at Meerut. The government awarded him a pension and he was appointed a companion of the Star of India (being made knight commander in 1888). In 1869 he founded a college at Ghazipur in which western methods of instruction were adopted and the teaching was carried on in English. In spite of the opposition of the more conservative Muslims, he was so successful that in 1875 he opened the Muslim Anglo-Oriental College at Aligarh, which developed into Aligarh Muslim University, chartered 1920 (see ALIGARH). Although he retired from public life in the following year, he accepted membership of the legislative council of India (1878–82). Until his death at Aligarh on March 2, 1898, the rest of Sir Sayyid's life was occupied by literary research and the advancement of his college.

See G. F. I. Graham, *The Life and Work of Sir Syed Ahmed Khan* (1909); J. M. S. Baljon, Jr., *The Reforms and Religious Ideas of Sir Sayyid Ahmad Khan* (1949). (S. J. C.)

SAZONOV, SERGEI DMITRIEVICH (1861–1927), Russian diplomat and statesman, foreign minister during the four years that preceded World War I as well as during the first two years of that war, was born in the province of Ryazan on Aug. 10 (new style; July 29, old style), 1861, the son of a large landowner. He began his career in the foreign ministry in 1883 and served subsequently in London, Washington, and the Vatican. In May 1909 he became deputy foreign minister under A. P. Izvolski (q.v.), whom he replaced on Oct. 11 (N.S.; Sept. 28, O.S.), 1910.

Sazonov's career was marked by few major diplomatic successes. Handicapped by the internal condition of Russia, which demanded a period of peace and tranquillity for political reform, Sazonov concentrated principally on the protection of Russian interests in the Balkans, the Turkish Straits, and northern Persia. The policy of cooperation with France and Great Britain, based on the Franco-Russian alliance of 1893 and the Russo-British treaty of 1907, was continued. Sazonov worked in complete subordination to the emperor, Nicholas II.

Sazonov's first steps as foreign minister were directed toward easing relations with Germany. In a meeting at Potsdam on Nov. 4–5, 1910, Nicholas and the German emperor William II reached a tentative agreement on Russia's aims in Persia and on Germany's ambitions in connection with the Baghdad Railway (q.v.). Russia's relations with Great Britain deteriorated sharply when Russian troops entered northern Persia in November 1911 to suppress a liberal movement.

In the Near East, Sazonov continued to seek a revision of the Straits agreements (see STRAITS QUESTION), but the major Russian effort in this area was the sponsorship of the Balkan League, composed of Serbia, Bulgaria, Greece, and Montenegro. Although Russia wished the alliance to function chiefly as a bulwark against Austro-Hungarian penetration of the peninsula, the Balkan states soon freed themselves of Russian control and, in October 1912, went to war against Turkey (see BALKAN WARS). A second Balkan war began on June 29, 1913. This war, in which Serbia, Greece, Rumania, and Turkey fought Bulgaria, resulted in the shattering of the Balkan League, and the alliance of Bulgaria with the Central Powers in World War I. Continued Russian concern with the Straits question was shown in 1913 in the strong opposition offered to the Turkish appointment of the German general Otto Liman von Sanders. As a result of Russian protests, which were supported by Great Britain and France, the general was forced to give up the command of the Turkish troops in Constantinople.

After the assassination of the Austrian archduke Francis Ferdinand at Sarajevo on June 28, 1914, the Russian government made it clear that it would not allow Serbia to be annihilated. When the Austrian ultimatum to Serbia was delivered on July 23, almost a month later, Sazonov played a direct and major role in the events which led to the entry of Russia into the war. Urged on by Russian military leaders, who believed that a partial mobilization against Austria-Hungary alone would be a military disaster, and with the promise of French aid, Sazonov pressed the emperor to agree to complete mobilization. This was ordered on July 30. On Aug. 1 Germany declared war on Russia.

After the outbreak of war Sazonov's main preoccupation as foreign minister was with the definition and defense of Russian war aims. With the entry of Turkey into the war in November 1914, the problem of the Straits assumed immediate urgency. In March 1915 Sazonov demanded Russian annexation of Constantinople and the Straits area, and was able to secure recognition of these claims by Great Britain and France. When the Polish question arose during the war (see POLAND: *History*), he took the position that an autonomous Poland in free union with Russia should be created on the restoration of peace. This proposal was so unpopular in Russian official circles that it brought about his dismissal (Aug. 5 [N.S.; July 23, O.S.], 1916). He was succeeded by Boris Stürmer, a friend of Rasputin (q.v.).

Shortly before the March 1917 revolution Sazonov was appointed ambassador to London. Dismissed from this post in May, he moved to Paris where he acted as foreign minister for the counterrevolutionary government of Adm. A. V. Kolchak. His *Vospominaniya* was published in 1927 (Eng. trans. *Fateful Years*, 1928). He died in Nice on Dec. 23, 1927. (B. J.)

SBEITLA, a village 19 mi. ENE of Kasserine, Tunisia, the site of the ancient Roman city of Sufetula. Sufetula probably originated as a fort during the campaigns against the rebel Tacfarinas (A.D. 17–24) and was a centre of Roman influence as the nomads became sedentary. It perhaps became a *municipium* under Vespasian (69–79) and was made a *colonia* by Marcus Aurelius (161–180) or Commodus (180–192). There, as elsewhere in the interior of Tunisia, Roman engineering skill applied to the conservation and use of the limited water supplies produced an agricultural prosperity, based primarily on olivegrowing, not reached again until modern times. There are impressive Roman remains, especially those surrounding the forum. There is a triumphal arch of Antoninus Pius opposite to which, and forming one side of the forum, are three temples. Slighter remains survive of a theatre, amphitheatre, and Christian churches. Sufetula was destroyed by the Arabs c. A.D. 646 after their victory over the Byzantines. (B. H. WA.)

SCABIES: see SKIN, DISEASES OF.

SCABIOSA, a genus of about 80 species of Eurasian annual or perennial herbs belonging to the teasel family (Dipsacaceae), and commonly grown in gardens for ornament under the names of scabious, mourning bride, or pincushion flower. In medieval times preparations of the plant were used medicinally, primarily to allay itching, hence the derivation of the generic name from the Latin *scabiosus,* meaning itchy, mangy, or scabby.

The annual sweet scabious (*S. atropurpurea*) and its variants and the perennial pincushion flower (*S. caucasica*) are the commonest sorts, available in blue, purple, brown, pink, cream, etc. Other perennial species frequently grown are *S. graminifolia* with grasslike silvery leaves and lavender-blue flowers; *S. ochroleuca* with yellowish-white flowers; *S. columbaria* with lilac flowers; and *S. fischeri* with bluish-purple flowers. Most scabiosas grow to heights of $1\frac{1}{2}$ to 3 ft., have toothed or lobed leaves, and produce almost globular to conical showy flower heads, usually 1 to 3 in. across. They are excellent as cut flowers.

Scabiosas are easily grown in ordinary garden soil in a sunny location. Seed may be planted in midspring; if pinched back when small the resulting bushy plants will produce blooms all summer if old flower heads are removed. The perennials, after two or three years' growth, may be increased by root division in early spring.

The garden plant known as shepherd's- or sheep's-bit scabious is *Jasione perennis,* a member of the bellflower family.

(G. H. M. L.)

SCAEVOLA, the name of a famous family of ancient Rome, the most important members of which are described below.

GAIUS MUCIUS SCAEVOLA, a legendary hero, who volunteered to assassinate the Etruscan king Lars Porsena when he was besieging Rome. He reached Porsena's tent but killed his attendant by mistake. Before the royal tribunal Mucius declared that he was one of 300 noble youths who had sworn to take the king's life. Threatened with death or torture, Mucius thrust his right hand into the fire blazing on an altar and held it there until it was consumed. Porsena, deeply impressed and dreading a further attempt upon his life, ordered Mucius to be freed, made peace with the Romans, and withdrew his forces. Mucius was rewarded with a grant of land beyond the Tiber, known thereafter as the *Mucia Prata,* and received the name of Scaevola ("lefthanded"). The story is presumably an attempt to explain the name Scaevola. Alternatively the word may mean an amulet worn by children. The Mucius of the legend is described as a patrician; the following were undoubtedly plebeians.

PUBLIUS MUCIUS SCAEVOLA (d. before 115 B.C.), Roman orator and jurist, was consul in 133 during the time of the Gracchan disturbances. He was not opposed to moderate reforms, advised Tiberius Gracchus on his land law, and refused to use violence against him. After the murder of Gracchus, however, he expressed his approval of the act. He was an opponent of Scipio Aemilianus, for which he was attacked by the satirist Lucilius. In 130 he succeeded his brother Crassus Mucianus as *pontifex maximus.* During his tenure of office he published a digest in 80 books of the official annals kept by the *pontifex maximus* since early times; the publication of these *annales maximi* was a landmark in Roman historiography (*see* ANNALISTS). Cicero frequently mentions him as a lawyer of repute, and he is cited several times in the collection of Roman legal extracts called the *Digest* (A.D. 533). He was also a famous player at ball and the game called *duodecim scripta.*

QUINTUS MUCIUS SCAEVOLA (d. 82 B.C.), son of the above, usually called PONTIFEX to distinguish him from his cousin (below), was consul in 95 with L. Licinius Crassus the orator. He and his colleague brought forward the *Lex Licinia Mucia* which removed from the citizen-roll Latin and Italian allies who had been illegally acting as citizens, and thus hastened the Social War ("war of the allies"). After his consulship Scaevola was governor of the province of Asia, and dealt severely with the tax farmers. His provincial edict became a model for later governors, and the Greeks of Asia established an annual festival in his honour, called the Mucia. He was subsequently (*c.* 89) appointed *pontifex maximus,* and in accordance with custom dispensed free legal advice, which was extensively sought. He regulated the priestly colleges and insisted on observance of the traditional ritual, though he himself believed that religion was only for the uneducated. He escaped

attempted murder in 86 and stayed in Rome under Cinna's government, but was killed in 82.

Scaevola was the founder of the scientific study of Roman law and the author of a systematic treatise on *ius civile,* in 18 books, frequently quoted and followed by subsequent writers. It was a compilation of legislative enactments, judicial precedents, and authorities, from older collections, partly also from oral tradition. A small handbook called *Horoi* (*Definitions*) is the oldest work from which any excerpts are made in the *Digest,* and the first example of a special kind of judicial literature (*libri definitionum* or *regularum*). It consisted of short rules of law and explanations of legal terms and phrases. A number of speeches by Scaevola, praised by Cicero for their elegance of diction, were in existence in ancient times.

QUINTUS MUCIUS SCAEVOLA (d. 88 B.C.), cousin of the above, from whom he is distinguished by the appellation of AUGUR. He was instructed in law by his father and in philosophy by the Stoic Panaetius of Rhodes. He married the daughter of Gaius Laelius and became the father-in-law of L. Crassus (consul 95 B.C.). In 120 he was governor of Asia. Accused of extortion on his return, he defended himself successfully. In 117 he was consul. He was a great authority on law, and at an advanced age he gave instruction to Cicero and Atticus. He had a high appreciation of Marius (*see* MARIUS, GAIUS) and refused to vote for Sulla's motion declaring him a public enemy. Scaevola is one of the interlocutors in Cicero's *De oratore, De amicitia,* and *De republica.*

See articles by F. Münzer and B. Kübler in Pauly-Wissowa, *Real-Encyclopädie der classischen Altertumswissenschaft,* xvi, 416–424 (no. 10), 425–428 (no. 17), 437–446 (no. 22) and 430–436 (no. 21) (1933). For the legendary Scaevola, *see* R. M. Ogilvie, *A Commentary on Livy, Books 1–5,* pp. 262 ff. (1965). For Scaevola Pontifex, *see* also E. Badian, *Studies in Greek and Roman History* (1964); F. Schulz, *History of Roman Legal Science,* pp. 94 ff. (1946).   (H. H. SD.)

SCAFELL (pronounced and sometimes written SCAWFELL), a mountain of Cumberland, Eng., in the Lake district (*q.v.*). The name is specially applied to the southern point (3,162 ft. in height) of a certain range or mass, but Scafell pike, separated from Scafell by the steep narrow ridge of Mickledore, is the highest point in England (3,210 ft.). The ridge continues northeast to Great End (2,984 ft.), which falls abruptly to a flat terrace on which lies Sprinkling tarn. The range thus defined may be termed the Scafell mass. Northwest from the pike the lesser height of Lingmell (2,649 ft.) is thrown out, and the steep flank of the range sweeps down to the head of Wastdale. On the east an even steeper wall, with splendid crags, falls to Eskdale. Above Mickledore ridge Scafell rises nearly sheer, with bold clefts.

SCAFFOLD, an elevated platform of temporary nature used to support materials and workmen in the construction or repair of a structure or machine. The term also denotes a platform used for the execution of criminals. The surface of the scaffold consists of one or more planks of convenient size and length. The method of support is varied to suit the immediate need and its form determines the type of scaffolding. Temporary built-up

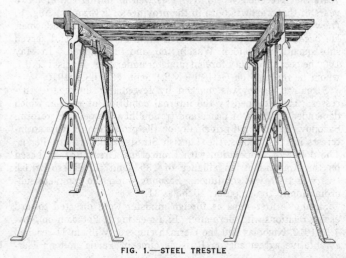

FIG. 1.—STEEL TRESTLE

seats for an athletic contest are sometimes referred to as scaffolds but should be called temporary bleachers.

Timber Scaffolding.—In this type of scaffold the support for

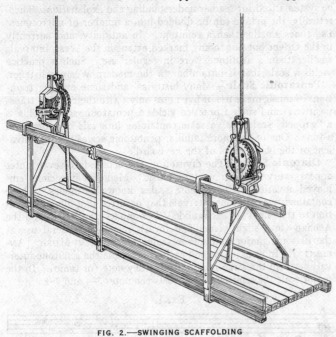

the planks is provided by a timber frame fabricated and erected at the site. The frame may consist of vertical posts, horizontal longitudinal members called ledgers, transverse members supported by the ledgers, and longitudinal and transverse cross bracing. The planks rest on the transverse members.

The posts are generally arranged in pairs with one post close to the wall and the other about 4 or 5 ft. out from the wall. Pairs of posts are placed along the wall at intervals of from 8 to 12 ft. The pairs are fastened together by ledgers running parallel to the wall and by braces. Transverse members may be cantilevered across the ledgers or may be supported by a ledger and the wall. The posts are 2×4s for light loads and short spans or 4×4s where heavier frames are needed. The posts are usually supported on a sill resting on the ground.

As with all scaffolding, the timber must be thoroughly braced and should also be tied to the wall by suitable lashings. If a scaffold is carried up on the inside of the wall as well as on the outside, the two should be tied together through window openings to provide greater stability. The vertical spacing of the ledgers is determined by the size of lift or working space desired. The members are fastened together by nails or lashings as custom dictates.

Trestle Supports.—This type is used to carry the staging where little or no adjustment of height needs to be made for each use and where the scaffolding needs to be spread over a large area, as when plastering the ceiling of a house. The trestles may be of special design or may simply be wooden sawhorses of the type used by carpenters. Some specially designed trestles may be adjusted to provide for working heights of from 7 to 18 ft. One type of adjustable trestle is shown in fig. 1.

Putlog Trestles.—This type consists of one A-frame and adjustable vertical support similar to a single-end support of the trestle shown in fig. 1. A horizontal member, the putlog, is supported at one end by the A-frame and at the other end by the wall. Planks span across the putlogs.

Common Trestle.—This type consists of two ladders so hinged that they form an inverted V when opened; they fold together for ease in transporting or storing. Two such units provide the end supports for simple or extension planks. The rungs in the ladders are spaced so that adjustments of plank heights may be made about every ten inches. The side rails of one leg of the inverted V may vary in length from 6 to 10 ft.

Extension Trestles.—The basic support unit for this type comprises two ladders similar to those of the common trestle and a third section of ladder in a vertical position and supported by the two inclined ladders forming an inverted Y. These support units may be procured in different heights and each height is adjustable. Two of the inverted Y's may support a plank for the working area or that plank may support one end of several planks to provide a wider working platform.

Scaffold Brackets.—Scaffolding is supported in frame (lumber) construction by brackets attached to the wall. A horizontal member 3 to $3\frac{1}{2}$ ft. long has one end fastened to the wall by nails and the outer end supported by a V-frame at about 45° and nailed to the timber frame. In some cases the horizontal member is so formed that it may be hooked around one of the wall studs (the vertical members in standard frame construction). The horizontal member may be manufactured with a screw end which is placed through a hole in the sheathing and fastened by a wing nut.

The diagonal support is similar in the three types. Special corner brackets are provided to turn the scaffold planks around a corner. The wall brackets fold for handling and storage.

Adjustable Roofing Brackets.—These generally consist of a rectangular frame with one member extending beyond the rectangle so it may be held by one or more nails. Attached to the frame are two members which provide an essentially horizontal

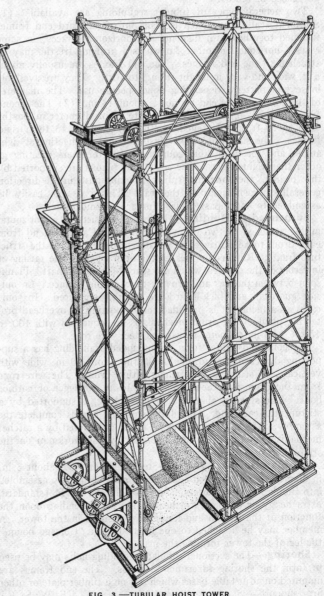

support for the plank; this triangular frame may be adjusted to provide the horizontal support on a roof of any pitch. Another type of roof bracket provides support for 2 × 4 staging so the 4-in. dimension is normal to the roof surface. This serves as footing for shinglers.

Ladder Jacks.—A ladder jack is a Y-shaped frame with an adjustable bracket which may be placed on the rungs of a ladder to provide support for staging. Two ladders, each with a jack, are used to support one span of plank. The arms of the Y hook over a rung of the ladder and the stem generally extends to the second rung below and may be clipped to it. The bracket may be adjusted to provide horizontal support for staging for different inclinations of the ladder. The jacks may be attached above the ladder or hung underneath. An alternate type hooks around the rails of the ladder instead of around the rungs. Scaffolding provided in this manner is frequently used in painting houses.

Tubular Scaffolding.—Because of its convenience and economy, steel or aluminum tubular scaffolding has very largely replaced timber scaffolding except for installations in remote areas. Tubular scaffolding can easily be erected in any shape, length or height. Furthermore, sections of the tubular scaffolding may be mounted on casters to provide a highly mobile staging. The walkway or working platform generally consists of 2 × 10 or 2 × 12 wooden planks. The scaffolding may be enclosed with canvas for protection against the weather. Tubular scaffolding may be purchased or rented.

Two general types of tubular scaffolding are available: (1) Sectional scaffolding which is made up of standard end frames fastened together with diagonal and horizontal braces; in some cases a horizontal member, known as a bridging trestle, may be attached to the end frames. The end frames are usually about 5 ft. wide and vary in height from 3 to 10 ft. They are available in several patterns depending upon specific use. The diameter of the tubing in the end frames is about $1\frac{5}{8}$ in. (2) The second type comprises pipes or tubing of 2- to $2\frac{1}{2}$-in. diameter in lengths of 6 to 20 ft. and fastened together by couplers to form rigid frames. The standard coupler fastens members meeting at right angles and the adjustable coupler fastens members meeting at other than right angles. The scaffolding planks are supported by the "bearer," the horizontal tube connecting posts in the direction generally perpendicular to the wall. This type can easily be assembled to encompass a blast furnace or smokestack.

Suspended Scaffolding.—This type consists of a horizontal putlog attached to two drum mechanisms. Cables extend from each drum to an outrigger beam attached overhead to the structure frame. Ratchet devices on the drums permit the raising or lowering of the putlogs, which are spaced 6 to 9 ft. apart. Planks span between putlogs and provide the working surface. An outside guardrail and kick board are generally required. In some cases an attachment is provided for supporting an overhead protecting plank. The drum mechanisms are equipped with 100 to 150 ft. of $\frac{1}{2}$-in. diameter galvanized steel wire rope.

A second and lighter form of suspended scaffolding has a supporting device in the form of a stirrup about 30 in. wide with vertical legs attached to a single lifting drum. The wire rope from the drum is attached overhead to an outrigger or cornice hook. The staging, about 10 to 12 ft. long, is supported by a stirrup near each end. Guardrails and kick boards complete the assembly. The scaffolding may be raised or lowered by a ratchet mechanism on the drum and operated by the workman on the scaffolding.

Tubular Hoisting Tower.—Steel tubes or pipes about 3 in. in diameter with standard connections may be quickly assembled into tubular hoisting towers. Pipe of different weight (standard, extra heavy or double extra heavy) is used depending upon the function of the section and its vertical position in the tower. A member may be attached to one leg to form a "Chicago boom," the leg of the tower forming the mast.

Shoring.—The sectional tubular scaffolding units may be used to form the shoring for concrete forms. The end frames are mounted on adjustable bases which rest on a timber plate or other firm support.   (F. W. St.)

SCALE, in music, signifies any selected sequence of notes or intervals dividing the octave. This is a theoretical conception by which the material of an existing or a historical practice can be systematized for readier understanding and explanation. Theoretically, the octave can be divided into a number of microtones; *i.e.*, tones smaller than a semitone. In antiquity, and currently in the Orient but not to any marked extent in the West, intervals smaller than a semitone were in regular use. Such a practice yields a scale that is unfamiliar to the modern Western listener.

Pentatonic Scale.—Many historical and some existing traditions of music make use of five notes only (with their octave transpositions) and such a practice yields a pentatonic scale. This is a "gapped" scale; *i.e.*, a scale containing intervals of more than a tone. One of the more familiar pentatonic scales is the equivalent of the black notes of the keyboard.

Diatonic Scale.—The division of the octave into seven notes appears very early in western music. Medieval musicians employed a variety of seven-note scales, known as modes. These contained two semitone intervals that occurred in a different relation to the "final" in each mode. Two modes, the Ionian and the Aeolian (in a slightly modified form), remain in general use as the diatonic major and minor scales (*see* GREEK MUSIC [ANCIENT]). In each major and each minor scale the semitone intervals occur in the same relation to the key note (or tonic). In the major scale the semitones occur between notes 3–4 and 7–8.

Ex. 1.

The minor scale has two forms, the "melodic minor" and the "harmonic minor." In the melodic minor the semitones occur between notes 2–3 and 7–8 ascending and between notes 6–5 and 3–2 descending.

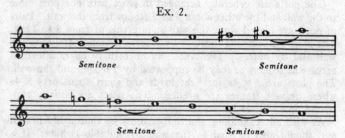

Ex. 2.

In the harmonic minor the semitones occur between 2–3, 5–6 and 7–8, with the interval of an augmented second (a tone plus a semitone) between notes 6–7.

Ex. 3.

In all forms of the diatonic scale the names given to the degrees of the ascending scale are: 1. tonic; 2. supertonic; 3. mediant; 4. subdominant; 5. dominant; 6. submediant; 7. leading note.

The Chromatic Scale, which comprises all the 12 semitones in the octave, can be considered as a "colouring" of the diatonic scale. The medieval musician regarded the notes C and C sharp, for example, not as separate notes but as two aspects of one note. This could be written as C and altered in performance "by reason of necessity or of beauty." At a later date, owing to the practice of equal temperament, diatonic scales were built on any of the 12 notes of the octave. In the late 19th century the extreme use of chromaticism (*q.v.*) brought about the partial destruction of diatonic tonality. (*See also* TEMPERAMENT, MUSICAL.)

The scale of "12-note," or dodecaphonic, music (*see* DODECAPHONY) uses the notes of the chromatic scale but does not permit the establishment of any tonal centre.

The Whole-tone Scale is often associated with Debussy, although it had been used as early as the 18th century by Mozart (in a sextet called "A Musical Joke"). As its name implies, it is a scale without semitones and therefore consists of only six notes.

Ex. 4.

Other experimental scales have been evolved by 19th- and 20th-century composers.

See also MODES, MUSICAL; MUSIC; ORIENTAL MUSIC.

SCALES: *see* WEIGHING MACHINES.

SCALIGER, from Scaligerus, the Latinized name of the Della Scala family, who ruled during the 13th and 14th centuries in Verona (*q.v.*). The name was later borne by two eminent scholars, father and son.

JULIUS CAESAR SCALIGER (1484–1558), French classical scholar of Italian descent, was born at Riva on Lake Garda on April 23, 1484. His early life is shrouded in myth. According to his own account he was descended from the Della Scala family of Verona. According to the enemies of the younger Scaliger, he was the son of Benedetto Bordone, an illuminator or schoolmaster of Verona. It is unlikely that these matters will ever be verified; the known facts about his later life are of greater importance. In 1525 he left Italy and was appointed physician to the bishop of Agen (Guienne). He settled at Agen, became a French citizen and married a young French girl, Andiettes de Roques Lobejac, by whom he had 15 children, the scholar Joseph Justus Scaliger (*see* below) being the tenth. He died at Agen on Oct. 21, 1558.

Scaliger made himself known as a scholar by two virulent orations (1531, 1536) against the *Ciceronianus* of Erasmus. The language used is the vigorous and trenchant Latin practised with so much gusto in that age of invective. But his Ciceronianism is narrow and short-sighted; Erasmus had shown greater insight when he ridiculed the stylistic excesses of contemporary Ciceronians, and Scaliger had largely misunderstood the purpose of his satire.

Scaliger's contributions to scholarship concern two widely different fields: botany and zoology, on the one hand, and grammar and literary criticism, on the other. His scholarly work (with the exception of a brief tract on Hippocrates' *De insomniis*, 1539) was published during the last few years of his life and some of it was left unfinished. It was put forward in the form of discussions of the work of standard authors. Thus his dialogue *De plantis* (1556) is a running commentary on the book on plants wrongly ascribed to Aristotle, and his *Exercitationes exotericae de subtilitate* (1557) discuss scientific and metaphysical problems raised in the *De subtilitate rerum* by one of the foremost naturalists of the 16th century, Geronimo Cardano (*q.v.*). Aristotle's *Historia animalium* and Theophrastus' *Peri phyton historia*, are the subjects of two unfinished commentaries published posthumously (1619 and 1644).

His two works on literary matters deal with grammar and poetics respectively. The *De causis linguae Latinae* (1540) is one of the most interesting attempts before the coming of comparative philology to discuss the principles of Latin grammar. His *Poetice*, published in 1561, three years after his death, came to be the most widely read of all his books. Here Greco-Roman rhetoric and poetics are used as a foundation for literary criticism. This is a most vigorous and comprehensive attempt to judge literature, made at a time when the Latin literary tradition was still unbroken. On that account alone it remains well worth reading. Scaliger's contemporaries admired his expertise in the physical sciences as much as his erudition and taste in polite letters. While being thoroughly conversant with the language and style of Latin and Greek writers, and while himself being a prolific composer of Latin verse and a competent textual critic, Scaliger aimed not so much at correcting ancient texts as at an understanding and criticism of what the ancients had written about. His teaching impressed not only such men as the younger Scaliger and Muretus (*q.v.*), who had personally learned from him, but a whole genera-

tion of savants in the great age of French classical scholarship.

JOSEPH JUSTUS SCALIGER (1540–1609), celebrated as the most eminent scholar of his time, was born at Agen on Aug. 5, 1540, the tenth child of Julius Caesar Scaliger.

The foundation of his great facility in Latin expression, both in verse and prose, was laid when (after his early education at Bordeaux), during the last three years of the elder Scaliger's life, he acted as his Latin secretary, daily taking down and copying his father's Latin verse compositions and daily writing a Latin essay on a subject of his own choosing. He had no such help with his Greek, for when he began the study of that language under A. Turnebus (Turnèbe) at the University of Paris he found the lectures too difficult. So Scaliger taught himself in a very short time, reading Homer in three weeks and thereafter other Greek poets, orators and historians, and forming a grammar on the basis of what he had read. He early acquired, too, a reading knowledge of Hebrew and Arabic. He extended his interests to ancient history (later, during 1570–72, he studied Roman law at Valence under the eminent lawyer Jacobus Cujacius). In Paris he became the tutor and friend of a young nobleman, Louis d'Abain (Louis Chastaigner de la Roche Pozay), his patron for 30 years (1563–93). With D'Abain he traveled in Italy and later visited England and Scotland. In the course of his travels Scaliger became a Protestant, and the religious upheavals of the time drove him out of France in 1572, the year of the massacre of St. Bartholomew. For the next two years he lived at Geneva as professor at the academy—the only two years of his life when he carried out the ordinary lecturing duties of a university teacher. He returned to France and resided with his patron's family for the next 20 years. During that time he produced a large part of the scholarly work for which he became famous. Unlike other great scholars of the time he remained impervious to all attempts at conversion (or reconversion) to the Roman Catholic Church. In 1590 religious partisanship, as well as his preeminence as a scholar, induced the authorities of the University of Leiden, then the foremost Protestant seat of learning in Europe, to offer him the chair of history vacated by Justus Lipsius, who had moved to the great Catholic University of Louvain. After protracted negotiations which secured him the desired freedom from academic duties, he moved to Leiden in 1593 and there remained until his death on Jan. 21, 1609.

To Scaliger's outstanding position in the scholarly world testify alike the record of his conversations in the years 1574–93 and 1603–06 (*Scaligerana*, edited most fully in 1740) and other contemporary documents. From his chair at Leiden, surrounded by a circle of able young scholars, he ruled the world of learning and determined the course literary and historical scholarship should take. Such a position spells danger: religious controversy and personal envy, sharpened by the virulence of his temper and the pungency of his sarcasm, found an easy target in the pride with which he regarded his (supposed) descent from the Scala family. There is no doubt that he firmly believed in it; whether his father did likewise is not now possible to say. Where scholarly controversy had largely failed, personal slander found its mark. The attack culminated in the publication in 1607 of *Scaliger hypobolimaeus*, "the supposititious Scaliger," by Caspar Scioppius, then a spokesman for the Jesuits. Scaliger replied with the *Confutatio fabulae Burdonum* (1608), published five months before his death. He effectually rebutted the charges of atheism and profligacy but could not establish the truth about the noble lineage by which he had set so much store, nor indeed make good the damage done to his name.

Scaliger's achievements as a scholar and man of letters are many but only two can be noticed here: the textual criticism of Latin authors and the historical criticism of ancient chronology. As a textual critic he was brilliant and imaginative though at times violent and lacking in taste. He did not care for the piecemeal publication of conjectures and sought to edit and elucidate the whole of an author's text. Among the texts of Latin authors which he published two are outstanding. One is his edition of the glosses of Festus (1565), in which he introduced the fragmentary remains of archaic Latin to the notice of his contemporaries; his investigations of the oldest Latin literature and language were not fully continued for two centuries. The second is his edition of Manilius' poem *Astronomica* (1579; 2nd ed. 1600), of which another great editor, A. E. Housman, said that "perhaps no critic has ever effected so great and permanent a change in any author's text as Scaliger in Manilius'." Scaliger's Manilius also offers a critical review of ancient astronomy from the point of view of Copernican science. Thus it forms the link with an even greater contribution to learning. In the *De emendatione temporum* (1583) he reconstructed the ancient system of chronology and brought the early history of the middle east into the purview of the west. This work was enlarged and perfected in the *Thesaurus temporum* (1606), which established Scaliger as one of the founders of modern historical scholarship.

BIBLIOGRAPHY.—J. J. Scaliger published a biography of his father, *De vetustate et splendore gentis Scaligerae et Jul. Caes. Scaligeri vita* (1594). J. J. Scaliger's own autobiography, with selections from his letters, etc., was translated with an introduction by G. W. W. Robinson (1927). There is no adequate modern biography. For earlier accounts of his life and work *see* Mark Pattison, *Essays*, vol. 1 (1889), and Jacob Bernays, *Joseph Justus Scaliger* (1855). There is a brief sketch in J. E. Sandys' *History of Classical Scholarship*, vol. ii (1908).   (C. O. BR.)

SCALLOP (ESCALLOP, FAN SHELL, or COMB SHELL) is the common name applied generally to bivalve (*q.v.*) mollusks of the family Pectenidae and particularly to species of the genus *Pecten*. Probably no group of mollusks has held a more prominent place in art, architecture, literature and religion, in addition to supplying an important item of food. The family, containing about 50 genera and subgenera and more than 400 species, is worldwide in distribution and ranges from the intertidal zone to considerable depths. Scallop shells, or valves, are fan-shaped in outline except for the straight hinge line with wings at either side of the hinge. In some species the valves are more or less equally convex while in others one valve is flat or nearly so. The shell may be smooth or sculptured with radial ribs, and the ribs may be smooth, scaly, or knobbed. They range in colour from brilliant red, purple, orange, or yellow to the white of deep-sea forms. The scallop normally lies on one valve, usually the right one; this valve is often lighter in colour and less highly sculptured than the left or upper one.

Scallops were used as food and their shells were used as utensils by primitive man in many parts of the world. During the middle ages the shell of *Pecten jacobaeus* became a religious emblem (the badge of St. James) and was worn by pilgrims visiting the shrine of St. James at Santiago, Spain, and the Holy Land. It has been used in art and architecture throughout the world since earliest times but found its greatest development in Europe, where, because of its religious significance, it was figured in church architecture and in the coats of arms of important families, indicating that some member had made a religious pilgrimage. According to mythology, Aphrodite (Venus) arose fully mature from a scallop.

Scallops are an important item of food in all areas where they occur in sufficient numbers to be dredged. The sea scallop, also known as the giant, or deep-sea, scallop (*Placopecten magellanicus*), is the species commonly dredged off New England and eastern Canada, though the bay scallop (*Aequipecten irradians*) is also fished commercially. In the British Isles *Aequipecten opercularis* is the species most commonly fished; it is used for food and for baiting the long lines in the fishing fleet. In the sea scallop fishery a wide variety of dredges are used but most are made of wire rings, about three

BY COURTESY OF THE MUSEUM OF COMPARATIVE ZOOLOGY, HARVARD COLLEGE

UPPER AND LOWER VALVES OF THE SCALLOP PECTEN JACOBAEUS

inches in diameter, linked together to form a coarse mesh bag. The dredge is usually towed from 15 to 30 minutes depending on the bed. The scallops are shucked immediately, the meats (the large adductor muscle is usually the only part eaten) are either stored in sea water or frozen on board ship. In the Bay of Fundy (between New Brunswick and Nova Scotia) the catch may average about 750,000 lb. of meats a year. There dredging is done in depths of 30 to 60 fathoms while in other areas of eastern Canada dredging is done in 4 to 10 fathoms.

The northeastern part of Georges Bank, off Massachusetts, is the most productive and most intensely fished sea scallop ground on the Atlantic coast; fishing there is done in depths of 20 to 60 fathoms. More than 15,000,000 lb. may be taken from this area in a single year.

Scallops belong to the group of bivalves having a single large adductor muscle for closing the valves, and are related to the file shells (Limidae), spiny oysters (Spondylidae), and true oysters (Ostreidae). They are usually found in areas where the bottom is composed of sand, shelly sand, or fine gravel, where the current is sufficient to prevent the deposition of fine mud and where the water is relatively clear. When the scallop is resting on the bottom the valves gape considerably but the animal itself cannot be seen because the free edges of the mantle hang down from the upper valve and extend up from the lower valve leaving only a narrow slit between the two edges.

At the edge of the mantle is a series of short tentacles and brilliant eyes. The eyes are sensitive to light and movement but they probably cannot distinguish form. The tentacles detect changes in the composition of the water and form a net through which food-bearing water is drawn into the mantle cavity. Scallops feed like most other bivalves, on microscopic plants and animals in the water, using cilia and mucus to collect the food and carry it into the mouth.

The Pectenidae are unusual among bivalves in being active, though spasmodic, swimmers. The animal swims by forcing jets of water out through two openings near the hinge. It appears to be clapping its valves as it moves through the water.

Reproduction in scallops is typical of most marine bivalves. Fertilization is external, the eggs and sperm being shed into the water. The eggs develop into normal larval bivalves with a swimming organ. After spending a short time in the plankton, they settle but may crawl for a while. The shell changes to that of a *Pecten* and the byssal gland develops. Then for a period the shell is attached to the substratum by a byssus. Some members of the family remain attached throughout life but most species break free and become spasmodic swimmers.

Starfish, the most important enemy of scallops, often plague commercial fisheries. A starfish attacks a scallop by surrounding the shell with its arms and, by the suction of its tube feet, pulls the valves apart; it then inserts its stomach between the valves and digests the scallop's soft parts.

BIBLIOGRAPHY.—Ian Cox (ed.), *The Scallop* (1957); W. J. Dakin, "Pecten," *Memoirs Liverpool Marine Biological Commission*, no. 17, pp. 1–136 (1909); Gilman A. Drew, "The Habits, Anatomy and Embryology of the Giant Scallop," *University of Maine Studies*, no. 6 (1906); J. S. MacPhail, "The Inshore Scallop Fishery of the Maritime Provinces," Fisheries Research Board of Canada, *General Series*, no. 22, pp. 1–4 (1954); J. A. Posgay, *Sea Scallop Investigations. 6th Report on Investigations of the Shell Fisheries of Massachusetts*, Commonwealth of Massachusetts, Department of Natural Resources, Division of Marine Fisheries, pp. 9–24 (1953); C. A. Fleming, "The Genus Pecten in New Zealand," *New Zealand Geological Survey, Paleontological Bulletin 26*, pp. 1–69 (1957); Gilbert Grau, "Pectinidae of the Eastern Pacific," *Allan Hancock Pacif. Exped.*, 23 (1959); L. M. Dickie, "Fluctuations in Abundance of the Giant Scallop, *Placopecten magellanicus Gmelin* in the Digby Area of the Bay of Fundy," *J. Fish. Res. Bd. Can.*, 12, pp. 797–857 (1955); Arthur S. Merrill, "Abundance and Distribution of Sea Scallops off the Middle Atlantic Coast," *Proceedings of the National Shellfisheries Association*, 51, pp. 74–80 (1962).   (R. D. T.)

SCALP, in anatomy, the skin and other tissues covering the top of the head. The skin of the scalp is thick. It contains an abundance of oil and sweat glands and about 100,000 hair follicles. (For information about loss of hair, *see* BALDNESS.) The scalp is subject to a number of ailments, such as dandruff and ringworm. (*See* SKIN, DISEASES OF.)

The arteries of the scalp are remarkable for their tortuosity, which is an adaptation to so movable a part; for their communication across the middle line with their fellows of the opposite side, an arrangement which is not usual in the body; and for the fact that, when cut, their ends are held open by the dense fibrous tissue in which they lie, so that bleeding is more free in the scalp than it is from arteries of the same size elsewhere in the body.

The veins do not follow the twists of the arteries but run a straight course; there is often a considerable distance between an artery and its companion vein. Accompanying the veins are the larger lymphatic vessels. From the forehead the lymphatics accompany the facial vein and usually reach their first gland in the submaxillary region, so that in the case of a poisoned wound of the forehead sympathetic swelling or suppuration would take place below the jaw. From the temple the lymphatics drain into a gland lying just in front of the ear, while those from the region behind the ear drain into glands lying close to the mastoid process. In the occipital region (base of the skull) a small gland (or glands) is found about a third of the distance from the external occipital protuberance to the tip of the mastoid process.

The nerve supply of the front of the scalp is from the trigeminal (5th cranial) nerve; behind the ear the scalp is served by the great auricular nerve and the smaller occipital nerve, while above and behind these, the greater occipital is distributed.

Beneath the skin and fibrous tissue lies the epicranium, formed by the two fleshy bellies of the occipitofrontalis muscle and the flattened tendon (aponeurosis) between them. The anterior belly (frontalis) is the larger, and, when it acts, throws the skin of the forehead into transverse puckers. The much smaller posterior belly (occipitalis) usually merely fixes the aponeurosis for the frontalis to act, though some people have the power of alternately contracting the two muscles and so wagging their scalps backward and forward as monkeys do.

Below the epicranium is a layer of very lax tissue constituting a lymph space and allowing great freedom of movement to the more superficial layers; it was this layer which was torn through when an American Indian scalped his foe. So lax is the tissue here that any collection of blood or pus is quickly distributed throughout its whole area, and, owing to the absence of tension as well as of nerves, very little pain accompanies any such effusion.

The deepest layer of the scalp is the pericranium (also designated the outermost layer, or external periosteum, of the skull bones). Until the sutures of the skull close in middle life, this layer is continuous with the dura mater which forms the internal periosteum, and for this reason any subpericranial effusion is localized to the area of the skull bone over which it happens to lie. Moreover, any suppurative process may extend through the sutures to the meninges of the brain. *See also* HAIR.   (F. G. P.; X.)

SCALPING, the removal of all or part of the scalp with its hair, is best known as a trait of North American Indian warfare, and the English term has entered other European languages with this meaning. European contact increased the frequency of Indian scalping greatly and the geographic spread somewhat, by the introduction of firearms (fatalities increased) and metal knives (removing the scalp became easier), and particularly by the offering of bounties for scalps of enemy Indians (and sometimes enemy whites) by the French, English, and Dutch authorities in eastern North America and Spanish authorities in northern Mexico. Many Euro-American frontiersmen and soldiers adopted the custom.

Scalps were most important among Southeastern Indians (*e.g.*, Creek, Choctaw), where obtaining them was a prime motive for warfare since they were necessary to secure status as a warrior and to placate the spirits of the dead. Most Northeastern Indians also took scalps, as proof of valour in warfare, but valued captives more highly. Among Plains Indians scalps varied in importance although all tribes took them. These groups had a graded series of war honours, of which taking a scalp was usually low on the scale since it required less daring than did touching a live enemy or stealing a horse.

Eastern and Plains Indians removed either the whole scalp (sometimes including the ears) or a circle about two to four inches in diameter centring on the hair whorl. Men of many of these tribes cut their hair short except for a long scalp lock left at the vertex as a challenge to the enemy. In the occasional cases when the victim was merely presumed to be dead, removal of a small scalp area was not necessarily fatal; numerous instances of survival are on record. The removed scalp was stretched on a small hoop, painted red, and often then carried at the end of a pole in a victory or scalp dance. Strips of scalp were used by Plains Indians to decorate their clothing, weapons, and horse gear.

Scalping was entirely absent in the Arctic and Subarctic, most of the Northwest Coast, and parts of California. In the rest of North America it was of much less importance than on the Plains or in the East, and the scalp area removed tended to be larger, often including the ears and at least some facial skin; frequently the whole head was taken as a trophy (*see* HEAD-HUNTING) from which the scalp was sometimes later removed. In California, the Southwest, and northern Mexico scalps were usually hung on a pole around which a victory dance was conducted. Among many Southwestern tribes scalps were taken but were regarded as ritually dangerous.

Scalping was absent from most of Mexico and Central and South America, but did occur in the Chaco and the Guianas. In both regions an enemy was decapitated and then the scalp removed. In the Chaco, Indian scalping survived as late as the 1920s.

There are a few references to scalping of enemies in other parts of the world: Scythians (according to Herodotus; *see* SCYTHIANS: *The Army*), some western Siberian peoples (Ostyak, Samoyed, and Vogul), and perhaps the ancient Persians.

BIBLIOGRAPHY.—G. Friederici, "Scalping in America," *Rep. Smithson. Instn. for 1906* (1907); G. Nadeau, "Indian Scalping Technique in Different Tribes," *Bull. Hist. Med.*, vol. 10 (1941); N. Knowles, "The Torture of Captives by the Indians of Eastern North America," *Proc. Amer. Phil. Soc.*, vol. 82 (1940); R. H. Lowie, *Indians of the Plains* (1954).   (W. C. ST.)

SCAMMONY (*Convolvulus scammonia*), a twining perennial plant native to the eastern Mediterranean region that yields a cathartic drug of the same name. The plant has arrowhead-shaped leaves and flowers similar to those of the bindweed or wild morning glory. The crude drug consists of the dried gum resin that exudes from incisions made in the living root. The product is brownish-black, often dusty gray externally, brittle, and has an acrid taste. Gross adulteration, high prices, and uncertainty of supply have led to true scammony being replaced almost entirely by ipomoea resin, a Mexican product known also as Mexican scammony resin, an extract of the dried, powdered root of *Ipomoea orizabensis*. Ipomoea resin and true scammony have been used as cathartics and may also be used with anthelmintics to expel intestinal worms.   (J. W. TT.)

SCAMOZZI, VINCENZO (1552–1616), Italian architect and architectural theorist of the late Renaissance, was born in Vicenza and trained under his father, a pupil of Sebastiano Serlio, and in the atmosphere of the Accademia Olimpico at Vicenza. He provided designs for Salzburg Cathedral, but worked mostly at Venice, Padua, and in the Veneto. He designed palaces, villas, and churches, as well as the permanent classical stage setting for Andrea Palladio's Teatro Olimpico at Vicenza, the ducal theatre at Sabbioneta, and the fortress town of Palmanova. He died in Venice in 1616. Through Scamozzi's writings (*L'Idea dell'architettura universale*, 1615) Palladianism (*see* PALLADIO, ANDREA) influenced English architecture from Inigo Jones onward, but Scamozzi's theories differ in certain respects from Palladio's and he may more properly be regarded as the intellectual father of neoclassicism.

The Scamozzi Ionic order is a type of column the capital of which has four identical faces with the volutes meeting at an angle at each corner. Scamozzi was once thought to have invented it, although there are Roman precedents for the design.

See F. Barbieri, *Vicenzo Scamozzi* (1952).   (F. J. B. W.; X.)

SCANDINAVIA, part of Northern Europe, is generally held to consist of the two countries of the Scandinavian Peninsula, Norway and Sweden, with the addition of Denmark. Some authorities include Finland on geological and economic grounds, and on a linguistic basis Iceland and the Faeroe Islands. (*See* SCANDINAVIAN LANGUAGES.) The language and people of Scandinavia are Nordic. The three countries are monarchies and have free democratic government. The established church is the Lutheran.

Norway and Sweden share the western and eastern sides respectively of the same mountain mass, much of which is part of the ancient Baltic Shield, and both have experienced the powerful effects of the Pleistocene glaciation, which had its main European centre in northeast Sweden and the Gulf of Bothnia. Sweden has, however, extensive slopes of fairly gentle gradient down to the Baltic Sea, while Norway's mountains reach to the actual coastline and are deeply dissected by fjords. The southern part of Sweden is mostly lowland with numerous outcrops of solid rock through the glacial deposits, and with much woodland. Denmark is considerably flatter, solid rock is scarcely to be seen, and almost the whole country is intensely cultivated. Toward the end of the glacial period southern Sweden and Denmark were joined, prior to the formation of the present Baltic Sea (q.v.).

The term "Norden" has recently come into usage in addition to the word "Scandinavia," and includes Denmark, Finland, Iceland, Norway, and Sweden, a group of countries which have affinities with one another and a distinction from the remainder of continental Europe.

See also SCANDINAVIAN ARCHAEOLOGY; SCANDINAVIAN LANGUAGES; SCANDINAVIAN LAW; DENMARK; FAEROE ISLANDS; FINLAND; ICELAND; NORWAY; DANISH LANGUAGE; DANISH LITERATURE; FINNISH LITERATURE; FINNO-UGRIC LANGUAGES; ICELANDIC LANGUAGE; ICELANDIC LITERATURE; NORWEGIAN LANGUAGE; NORWEGIAN LITERATURE; SWEDISH LANGUAGE; SWEDISH LITERATURE; VIKING.   (R. K. GR.)

SCANDINAVIAN ARCHAEOLOGY

SCANDINAVIAN ARCHAEOLOGY is treated here as the study of the traces of man in Denmark, Norway, Sweden (qq.v.), and adjacent islands from the period of earliest settlement (c. 12000 B.C.) to the time of the Vikings (c. A.D. 1050).

Paleolithic.—At the end of glacial times (see PLEISTOCENE EPOCH) the climate improved sufficiently for man to enter Scandinavia. About 12000 B.C. Denmark was inhabited by a few groups of hunters; their knives of reindeer antler suggest Hamburgian (a northern variant of Magdalenian) culture. Also, flint was made into knives, scrapers, and burins (gravers) for cutting grooves in bones or antlers. Their predominant weapon was an Aurignacian type of tanged arrowhead. The earliest known settlement at Bromme in Zealand has been dated to c. 10000 B.C. (see RADIOCARBON DATING). Climate deteriorated and tundra spread; axes came into use, made of reindeer antler on which a tine was sharpened into a cutting edge. A heavy tanged arrowhead was found in the most recent tundra layers at Lyngby in Jutland. This culture is related to that of Ahrensburg in north Germany. Two coastal cultures in Norway, Fosna (west of Trondheim) and Komsa (at North Cape, within the polar circle), may belong to the same complex.

Mesolithic.—*Continental Phase* (c. 9000–5000 B.C.).—During this phase the Baltic was a freshwater lake and, with warmer climate, southern Scandinavia was covered by dense forests, mainly of pine. Aurochs, elk, deer, and boar were stalked by the hunters and their dogs. Settlements were near water, where traces of huts with floors of birchbark strips have been found. The first proper axes of flint core or flake are from Klosterlund in Jutland, the earliest known settlement of the Maglemose culture, named from a bog site at Maglemose, Denmark. Typical bog finds in bone include barbed harpoons, leister (fishing-spear) points, and axes which sometimes have an inserted flint edge; wooden objects include bows, clubs, ladles, and paddles. Artistic work is scanty: mainly incised geometric designs and zoomorphic figures cut out of amber. A Maglemosian offshoot, the so-called Gudenaa people, lived by the lakes and streams of Jutland and made multishaped microliths (see FLINT AND OTHER STONE TOOLS). The seacoast was inhabited by another people whose (Early Coast or Early Ertebølle) culture was more akin to that of Ahrensburg. Many of their sites have been obliterated by the rising sea.

Atlantic Phase (5000–3500 B.C.).—In this phase the Baltic Sea (q.v.) was filled with salt water, the climate became warmer, and oak dominated the forests. The Ertebølle culture continued, its sites marked by huge shell mounds (kitchen middens) where the dead were also buried. Heavy tools were increasingly made of flaked flint; plump greenstone axes were made by grinding. Transverse arrowheads replaced microliths and T-shaped antler axes, and coarse pottery appeared, possibly introduced from northern Germany, from where grain cultivation and cattle breeding also may have come. The Ertebølle culture survived well into the Neolithic; similar cultures existed in southern Sweden and near Oslo Fjord in Norway.

Neolithic (2500–1500 B.C.).—In parts of Denmark and in remoter districts of Norway and Sweden the Mesolithic people long retained their primitive mode of life, during which time more advanced cultures developed to the south. Southern Sweden, as far north as Södermanland, was colonized.

Early Neolithic levels in Danish bogs bear traces of widespread fire, suggesting that farmers had cleared the forest by slash-and-burn methods. Pottery of rounded shape with little ornamentation was followed by highly decorated beakers and collared flasks. Early Neolithic settlement sites have been excavated, including a village at Barkaer in east Jutland. Pit graves, containing skeletons in flexed or contracted position, were followed by impressive megalithic graves (dolmens) set in round or oval mounds surrounded by curbstones. A long dolmen may contain as many as four burial chambers. Votive deposits in Early Neolithic burials were mostly pottery but sometimes included amber beads.

The Middle Neolithic produced larger dolmens and introduced the more elaborate passage grave with a large chamber approached by a roofed passage. Many generations were inhumed in these, along with thick-butted axes, polygonal battle-axes, transverse arrows, and amber beads. Excellent pottery shows a continuous development in shape and ornamentation. The remains indicate a highly organized society of traders in flint and amber, and of farmers living in villages. Traces of domestic animals (mainly pigs and sheep) and of cereal (wheat and barley) are found near the huts. Well into the Middle Neolithic Period, groups of the Battle-Ax (or Single Grave) culture appeared in southern Scandinavia. Excavation of low barrows in the sandy interior of Jutland revealed in each a chronological sequence of graves, all with single inhumation containing well-proportioned battle-axes, crude flint axes, amber beads, and beakers and cups shaped like flowerpots. The Battle-Ax people seem to have practised stock breeding rather than agriculture. A related culture group inhabited east Jutland and adjacent islands; and a third lived on the island of Bornholm and in Sweden. The distinct Pitted Ware culture, named after its pottery with deeply punched holes, has been found in the Scandinavian peninsula, with an offshoot on the eastern seaboard of Denmark. These were Mesolithic fishers and hunters who kept pigs and made fishhooks, long triangular arrowheads, and harpoons. The invading Battle-Ax people seem to have expelled the megalith builders, first from Jutland, later from the islands. At the end of the Middle Neolithic, however, some fusion took place.

In Late Neolithic the megaliths were still used for burials, but large stone cists became more common. Pottery was plain and coarse; flint daggers and spearheads replaced axes and elegantly shaped flint arrowheads were made to meet increasing competition from metal weapons and tools imported from the British Isles and western Europe. The extensive trade connections built up during this period shaped the background for the Scandinavian (Nordic) Bronze Age, which began late, because all metal had to be imported.

Early Bronze Age (1500–900 B.C.).—The introduction of bronze casting brought about a revolutionary change. The quality of Scandinavian workmanship and design soon became outstanding. Bronze flat axes and daggers (similar to those from Britain and central Europe, but containing very little tin) were followed by palstaves (socketed, perforated axes), spearheads with riveted sockets, and rapiers that were superseded by heavier swords with wood, bronze, or horn hilts riveted to flanged bronze tangs. Personal ornaments of bronze or gold included finger rings, bracelets, and torques (cast, hammered, or made of entwined wire); *tutuli* (ornamental buttons); belt boxes; belt discs with a central protruding spike (worn by women only); and fibulae (brooches resembling safety pins). Weapons and ornaments were decorated with incised geometric designs.

Almost all Early Bronze Age traces have come from graves; thousands of barrows in southern Scandinavia indicate dense population there. During this period the body, wrapped in oxhide and fully dressed (with weapons, ornaments, and personal belongings), was placed in a small stone cist or a hollowed oak-log coffin. Some barrows have yielded well-preserved complete outfits of twilled clothes woven from sheep's wool. Men's garments consisted of a cap, wide cloak, a short, belted, sleeveless "gown," and leather sandals. Women wore a short smock, sometimes embroidered, and a belt with tassels; a knee-length skirt of cords joined at the waist and hem was wrapped twice around the hips. A long piece of cloth belted at the waist was probably a winding sheet. Women's hair was covered by a delicate net or cap. The preserved body of a girl found at Skrydstrup in south Jutland had an elaborate coiffure arranged over a horsehair pad.

Late Bronze Age (900–400 B.C.).—Cremation, introduced at the end of the preceding period, was in use throughout the Late Bronze Age. Cremated remains were placed in stone cists and later in urns that were buried in the ground or in old barrows. Some of these urns were shaped like huts or had anthropoid features. These new customs tended to reduce the size of burial gifts, which began to include such articles as razors, tweezers, or tattooing needles; small iron objects heralded the Iron Age.

Fields and bogs have produced the richest Late Bronze Age finds, most of them women's belongings such as large ribbed neck rings, pendants and chains, hair braids, enormous belt boxes, and fibulae. These may have been offerings to a goddess represented as a tiny female bronze figure with huge golden eyes. Spearheads, swords, imported shields of bronze sheeting, and horned bronze helmets were also found. Small bronze figures have been found adorned with such horned headgear, a type also depicted in rock carvings and drawn on razor blades. The most outstanding find of the period, the lur, a type of bronze trumpet made in attuned pairs, is of Scandinavian origin and shows a very high degree of skill in metallurgy. Importation of vessels from western Europe continued and golden bowls were given handles of Scandinavian design. Most of the numerous rock carvings found throughout Scandinavia date from the Bronze Age (*see* PRIMITIVE ART: *Prehistoric Europe*).

Iron Age (400 B.C.–A.D. 400).—The Pre-Roman Iron Age may have been a period of economic decline; certainly the finds from this period are few and poor in quality; the cultural centre remained in Denmark. Cremation was at first universal, urns being deposited in large cemeteries with sparse amounts of grave goods that included pins, fibulae of the La Tène (*q.v.*) type, and belt ornaments. A boat found preserved in a bog on the island of Als in Jutland was about 58 ft. (17.7 m.) long and was propelled

by oars; little metal and no iron was used in its construction. It contained a great many shields (with no iron in them), spears, suits of chain mail, and a few iron swords; it was probably a war canoe sacrificed to the gods. Two carts found in a bog at Dejbjerg in west Jutland were overlaid with bronze mountings of Celtic design, and may have been used in Nerthus fertility rites. Several mutilated bodies, found mummified in Jutlandic bogs, may also have been sacrifices. Several imported caldrons of bronze or iron have been found, and a large silver caldron from Gundestrup in north Jutland is decorated with scenes that blend Celtic, Oriental, and classical features. Pointed ploughs found in Danish bogs have

BY COURTESY OF (TOP LEFT, TOP RIGHT, BOTTOM RIGHT) THE NATIONAL MUSEUM, DENMARK; (BOTTOM LEFT) UNIVERSITETETS OLDSAKSAMLING, OSLO

EARLY SCANDINAVIAN ARTIFACTS

(Top left) Late Bronze Age lur; (top right) Iron Age cart found in the bog at Dejbjerg, West Jutland; (bottom left) Viking ship found at Gokstad, Nor.; (bottom right) Iron Age Celtic silver caldron from Gundestrup, North Jutland

been assigned to this pre-Roman period, as have small, square or rectangular fields surrounded by low banks and associated with farmhouses.

The Roman Iron Age, beginning *c.* A.D. 1, provided rich finds from settlements, graves, and bogs. Regular trade with the Roman Empire brought silver, bronze, and glass; large numbers of Roman coins have been found, especially on the island of Gotland (*q.v.*). Roman influence is particularly noticeable in the high-quality Scandinavian pottery. Progress in agriculture is demonstrated by fully recognizable village sites surrounded by fields; and by the introduction of the wheel plow and rye. Cremation was practised but the richest graves are inhumations; the body was fully clothed, wearing ornaments and weapons. Bogs have produced great hoards including double-edged swords of Romano-Celtic design, helmets, and ornamental discs for shoulder straps, perhaps the equipment of *auxilia* (auxiliary troops) in the Roman army. Clinker-built boats from Nydam in Schleswig show great progress in shipbuilding. Many objects apparently had been deliberately damaged before deposit, probably in obedience to the custom (noted by Julius Caesar) of offering part of the spoils to the god of war. Clothes from the bogs show that men wore trousers and a long-sleeved jacket, while women wore long gowns made from beautifully woven cloth of various designs.

Migration Period (A.D. 400–800).—Scandinavian tribes may have played a part in attacks that contributed to the collapse (5th century) of the Roman Empire in the west. Evidence of contact is provided by hoards of gold coins found especially in eastern Scandinavia, to which the cultural centre had shifted. Impressive barrows and boat-shaped graves revealed princely grave furniture, visored helmets with gilded bronze decorations, coats of mail, shields, magnificent swords with golden hilts inlaid with garnets, and glass from Frankish centres on the Rhine. Graves from this period in western Norway show a distinctive Frankish influence on weapons. Apart from the island of Bornholm in the Baltic, grave and settlement finds are rare in Denmark for this period; the few graves were sparsely furnished. Nevertheless, great treasures of gold and precious stones have been found in southern Scandinavia. Most notable are two richly decorated golden horns from Jutland. Other hoards contained heavy gold neck and arm rings, square and cruciform brooches, gold coins, and bracteates (disc-shaped pendants, barbaric copies of late Roman medals). Weapons and ornaments were decorated with animal figures that were deformed to suit the shape of the object. Variations on this style provide a rough dating method.

Viking Period (A.D. 800–1050).—The extraordinary achievements of the Scandinavian sea warriors (*see* VIKING) depended primarily on their ships. It was the custom to bury the dead in ships under huge barrows; such ships were discovered in Norway, at Gokstad, Oseberg, and Tune; preserved in Oslo, they show the final stage in the evolution of the rowing boat into a craft with keel, mast, and sails. They contained special chambers for the remains, and were loaded with tents, small boats, beds, sledges and carts (many richly carved), and personal belongings. Within Scandinavia at this time there was a great variety of burial customs. Cremation was practised, gradually dying out as Christianity spread. Men were buried with weapons, riding gear, horse, and dogs; women had personal ornaments and household utensils. Stone burial chambers shaped like boats have been found throughout Scandinavia. In Denmark and Schleswig princely persons were buried in wooden chamber tombs under huge mounds.

Towns grew up rapidly in Viking times: Haitabu in Jutland, Birka in Sweden, and many others were fortified and had special areas for craftsmen. Dannevirke (Danewerk), a system of earthworks made to protect Denmark from the south (the most extensive ancient monument in Scandinavia), probably took 350 years to build. Military camps with plans that show strong Byzantine influence have been excavated in Denmark at Aggersborg, Fyrkat, Odense, and Trelleborg: in shiplike houses arranged in squares within a circular moat and wall the royal housecarls of Sweyn I and Canute (*qq.v.*) were billeted.

Among the Vikings' weapons (*e.g.*, spear, bow and arrow) the sword was most prized. Swords

HEAD OF THE TOLLUND MAN

These remains, discovered in 1948 in a peat bog at Tollund, Jutland, are the best preserved of almost 100 comparable findings dating from the Iron Age

were inlaid with gold and silver; many were of Frankish manufacture. But the typically Nordic long-handled battle-ax became the symbol of the Vikings. Defensive equipment included shields, coats of mail, and leather or iron helmets; spurs, stirrups, saddles, bridles, and collar harness were richly decorated. Men wore armlets, and women had gold and silver rings for neck and hair. For clothing there was an almost standard set of buckles (two oval and one three-lobed) usually of bronze or silver. A tapestry from Oseberg depicts Viking men in long-sleeved, thick coats and in trousers; long cloaks hang freely from their shoulders. Women wear a chemise under a sleeveless dress that reaches the ground and often has a train; a sleeveless cape is thrown back to expose the arms. Costly imported materials were used: gold brocade, Chinese silk, and Frisian worsted.

Silver hoards (deposited as offerings or concealed as treasure) contain ornaments, bars, cups, bowls, and various fragments. In the decoration a small beast with masklike face and gripping paws (as in Oseberg carvings) was constantly depicted. By the mid-9th century a fusion of styles led to that known as the Borrestyle: the animal had the elongated body typical of Migration Period art but had acquired the face and paws of the gripping beast. In the 10th century this was overshadowed by the Jelling style, of which the ribbon-shaped and tuft-headed animal betrays a strong Irish influence. The early 11th century was dominated by a style known as Ringerike, characterized by interlacing lines and conventionalized foliage borrowed from Anglo-Saxon art. The animal theme reappeared in the Urnes style, the last phase of Viking decorative art.

See also RUNE; ARCHAEOLOGY: *Neolithic and Bronze Ages in Europe; The Iron Age in Europe;* EUROPE: *Archaeology.*

BIBLIOGRAPHY.—J. Brøndsted, *Danmarks Oldtid*, 3 vol. (1957–60), *The Vikings* (1960); O. Klindt-Jensen, *Denmark Before the Vikings* (1957); E. C. G. Oxenstierna, *Die Nordgermanen* (1957).

(E. M. E. B.)

SCANDINAVIAN LANGUAGES. This term is usually limited to the Germanic languages (*q.v.*), of the Indo-European family, spoken and written in the Scandinavian countries, thus excluding Finnish and Lappish, which have most of their speakers in the same area. There are six distinct written languages in Scandinavia: the Danish language (*q.v.*), in Denmark; the Faeroese language, in the Faeroe Islands, a possession of Denmark; the Icelandic language (*q.v.*), in Iceland; the Norwegian language (*q.v.*), in Norway, split into two norms called *bokmål* and *nynorsk;* and the Swedish language (*q.v.*), in Sweden and Finland (by only 7.4% of the population of Finland). Outside Scandinavia there are small areas of Danish speech in northern Germany and of Swedish in Estonia, as well as among numerous emigrants in the United States and Canada. If these are estimated at about 1,000,000, the total number of Scandinavian speakers in the late 1960s was about 17,500,000.

In speech there is a great deal more variation than the number of written norms would indicate. Icelandic has the least dialectal differentiation, while in the Faeroes nearly every island has its own dialect.

The continental countries all show a typically European cleavage into class and regional dialects. In each country there is an upper-class urban dialect which approaches the written norm more closely than do the rest; this is often regarded as a standard, though it varies from city to city, the speech of the capital having the greatest prestige: Oslo, Stockholm, Copenhagen. Closest to it, but by contrast regarded as vulgar, is the speech of the urban working classes; more remote, and often so different as to be mutually incomprehensible, is rustic speech. The rural dialects are divided regionally, reflecting the patterns of communication in medieval and early modern times. Every parish and village may be said to have its own dialect.

It is not known when Indo-European speech entered the north; some believe it may have come with the so-called Battle-Ax people of the Neolithic (*c.* 2500 B.C.). The earliest linguistic monuments are about 150 inscriptions in the Germanic alphabet known as the older runic *futhark* (*see* RUNE). These date from *c.* A.D. 200 to 800, the earliest of which show a language close to the reconstructed Proto-Germanic branch of the Indo-European languages; it may be called either North Germanic (contrasting it with East and West Germanic) or Proto-Scandinavian. Between A.D. 500 and 700 a radical change in the word forms led to what may be called the Common Scandinavian of the Viking age (750–1050). First came a vowel assimilation known as umlaut (mutation), in which the accented vowel was coloured by the quality of the following unaccented vowel; then came a loss of unaccented vowels, which greatly shortened the length of the words; e.g., landa, "land," became land, while its plural landu became lǫnd; similarly katilaz > kætilR > ketill, "kettle." Other changes were the loss of initial j, for example, in ár, "year" (corresponding to German Jahr), and of w before u and o, as in ull, "wool," and orð, "word." Our evidence for Common Scandinavian consists of about 4,000 inscriptions in the younger runic alphabet of 16 characters, mostly memorial stones.

During this period Scandinavian was carried also to Normandy, the English Danelaw, the Orkneys, Shetlands and Hebrides, to Ireland and the Isle of Man, to Greenland and the North American continent, as well as to the Swedish kingdoms in Russia; but in these areas the Scandinavian settlers were all absorbed or died out in later centuries.

Although some of the differences within the Scandinavian area undoubtedly date back to an earlier period, they do not become evident until the use of Latin writing after the introduction of Christianity. The native languages were first written in Norway, under the influence of English missionaries, in the late 11th century. From there Anglo-Saxon influences spread to Iceland also. The earliest manuscripts from Iceland and Norway date from c. 1150, while the earliest in Denmark and Sweden are nearly a century later. These show a substantially consistent form, characteristic for each centre of writing, down to about 1350; this may be called the Old Scandinavian period, in which fall Old Icelandic, Old Norwegian, Old Swedish and Old Danish, the two former distinguishable as Old West Scandinavian (also called Old Norse), the two latter as Old East Scandinavian. In the period from 1350 to 1525 a transition took place to the essentially modern forms of the present-day languages. During this Middle Scandinavian transition the manuscripts show a gradual loss of the old case system in favour of the modern analytic structure. The political and dynastic unions of the Scandinavian countries, under the hegemony of Denmark, spread Danish norms to the other countries, gradually diluting and even supplanting those which had been developing elsewhere.

The language of the royal chancery at Copenhagen eventually supplanted completely the norms of Jutland and Skåne within the Danish realm, as well as those of Norway, which was united with Denmark. The last documents in pure Norwegian were written in the period 1450–1500, and the introduction of the Reformation in 1537 did not lead to a distinct Norwegian translation of the Bible. The authors who wrote in Norway after the Reformation used Danish in their literary composition; the notion of a separate Norwegian language did not arise again until the 18th century but acquired special force after the separation of 1814. In Iceland, on the contrary, the written tradition remained unbroken, though influenced by Danish. The same was true in Sweden, and the establishment of a separate Swedish state in 1525, with Stockholm as its capital, led to a strong and conscious reaction against Danish influences.

The modern Scandinavian era since the Reformation has led to three new norms as the result of modern nationalism: Faeroese, established by V. U. Hammershaimb in 1846, New Norwegian (landsmål, nynorsk) by Ivar Aasen in 1853, and Dano-Norwegian (riksmål, bokmål), which gradually deviated from Danish in the 19th and early 20th centuries. Icelandic is the language that has most tenaciously preserved the grammar and vocabulary of the common Scandinavian period, with Faeroese a not too close second; these languages have therefore become largely unintelligible to other Scandinavians. On the continent, Scandinavians are usually able to communicate with each other by speaking and writing their own languages. This is because of the common developments which the languages have undergone, including an extensive sim-

plification of morphology and the adoption of loanwords from common sources, especially Low German. Danish is phonetically most deviant from the rest but has a large area of vocabulary in common with Dano-Norwegian; the cleavage is therefore greatest between Danish and Swedish.

Attempts have been made to promote communication by bringing the norms closer to one another, but with little success. Instead, an active program of mutual language teaching has been instituted in the school systems, as well as cultural exchanges under the aegis of the inter-Scandinavian society Norden.

BIBLIOGRAPHY.—Gösta Bergman, A Short History of the Swedish Language, Eng. trans. by F. Magoun, Jr., and H. Kökeritz (1947); Adolf Noreen, Geschichte der nordischen Sprachen (1913); Elias Wessén, De nordiska språken (1944); Hjalmar Lindroth, De nordiska systerspråken (1942); also the bibliographies for each of the individual languages.
(E. I. H.)

SCANDINAVIAN LAW in medieval times constituted a separate and independent branch of early Germanic law (see GERMANIC LAWS, EARLY) which, originating within the territories of present-day Norway, Denmark, and Sweden, was extended between the 9th and 13th centuries to places settled or conquered by Scandinavian peoples. These were, in the west, Iceland, Greenland, and the Faeroe Islands, parts of Great Britain and Ireland with surrounding isles, Normandy, etc.; with, in the east, Finland and other territories along the Baltic shore. In modern times Scandinavian law embraces Norway, Denmark, Sweden, Iceland, Greenland, the Faeroe Islands, and Finland.

Early Times.—Before the Scandinavian states emerged as unified kingdoms in the 9th century, the several districts and provinces were virtually independent administratively and legally. Although social organization in the main was the same, and legal developments followed similar lines, there came into existence a number of separate legal systems or "laws." Originally there were no written laws; the legal system consisted of customary law which was conserved, developed, and vindicated by the people itself at the so-called things; i.e., popular meetings of all free men. Separate things were generally held in smaller localities and common things or all-things for more comprehensive regions. The meetings were conducted by one or more prominent men, conversant with the law, who made statements of law; gave directions concerning rules of law applicable in particular cases; and, with the assent of the thing, created new law when traditional law was insufficient. Consolidation of several provinces under one king did not at first effect any important change, cohesion being feeble and the central authority's influence in the legislative field restricted. However, a trend toward greater legal unity gradually asserted itself, with the formation of more comprehensive regions with common things and identical laws.

Between the 11th and 13th centuries the provincial laws were recorded in writing (invariably in the vernacular), most often as private compilations but occasionally by instructions from the king. The best-known laws of this period are the Gulathing's law (written in the 11th century, Norwegian); the law of Jutland (1241, Danish); and the laws of Uppland (1296) and Götaland (early 13th century), both Swedish. More or less complete legal unity was accomplished at different times. In Norway King Magnus V (1263–80) provided a common code of law for the rural districts as early as 1274 and for the towns two years later. A corresponding royal initiative was taken in Sweden in the 14th century (King Magnus Ericsson, c. 1350), but Denmark remained subject to three different provincial laws until the promulgation of Christian V's Danish Law (1683). Iceland, which had been organized as a free state by settlers from Norway and had developed a legal system of particular interest, came under the Norwegian crown in the 13th century (Haakon IV, 1262), and received new laws mostly borrowed from King Magnus' code.

The early laws or codes had not the character of civil codes as understood today. Besides subjects of private law (matrimony, inheritance, property, and contract), they contained constitutional and administrative law, criminal law, and law of procedure. Ecclesiastical law was usually excluded and treated separately. The codes represented chiefly codification of customary law; influences from abroad were negligible except for some traces of canon law. Whereas the provincial laws, in common with other early Germanic laws, had tolerated and regulated blood feuds (setting up detailed tariffs for manslaughter and offenses against the body), the codes are in several respects more progressive. Thus, King Magnus' code abolished private vengeance, declaring that the king's officials should initiate criminal proceedings and provide for the punishment of evildoers. Further, presumably under the influence of Christianity, legal provisions were introduced for assistance to paupers and the helpless. Rules concerning landed property (*e.g.*, the right of redemption belonging to the family) were markedly original.

Intermediate Period.—In 1380 Norway and Denmark were united under a common king (Olaf IV), but the two countries retained their separate laws. During the next 300 years, before the acquisition of absolute royal power by Frederick III (1660), supplementary laws were issued by the king in conjunction with an assembly of nobles. Finally, during the reign of Christian V, a comprehensive work of codification was accomplished and the earlier and often obsolete law replaced by Christian V's Danish Law (1683) and Norwegian Law (1687). The new codes were mainly based on the existing national laws of the two countries, and foreign influence, whether of German, Roman, or canon law, was comparatively slight. Like the early codes, they comprised public as well as private law, purporting to treat exhaustively all more or less permanent legal rules and institutions. They were excellent for their times, drafted in a plain and popular style, inspired by respect for individual rights and the idea of equality before the law. Provisions of criminal law were relatively humane as compared with other European legislation.

In Sweden a revised edition of the original code, issued by King Christopher (1442), was expressly confirmed by Charles IX (1608). The need of more modern legislation, however, made itself increasingly felt, and following the Danish-Norwegian example a royal commission was entrusted with the task of drafting a new code. The result, commonly called "the Law of 1734," was promulgated by Frederick I.

Finland, annexed by Sweden in the 13th century and made subject to Swedish law, came under the Swedish code of 1734, translated into Finnish as "Law of the Realm of Finland."

Modern Times.—These old codes have been all but completely displaced by modern parliamentary statutes. In Sweden the law of 1734 has been conserved as a formal framework. Elsewhere plans for new, all-embracing codes are no longer entertained, but an extensive codification of important parts of public and private law has taken place. Projects have been discussed for consolidation of the several codification laws into a civil code of the type found in the rest of continental Europe, and preparatory work to this end was undertaken in Norway in the mid-1950s.

An interesting feature of Scandinavian law is the organized legislative cooperation which was begun in 1872 and has steadily increased in importance. In this way the Scandinavian states, including Iceland and Finland, have to a considerable degree obtained uniform legislation, especially regarding contracts and commerce, but also in the fields of law concerned with family, the person, nationality, extradition, etc.

While conserving their national character, the Scandinavian legal systems have adopted certain conceptions of Roman or continental European (mainly German and French) origin, chiefly through the influence of the law schools; commercial law and the law of shipping and of companies, for example, conform more or less to common European patterns. Modern social welfare legislation, which has reached a high standard, also has strong international connections. Scandinavian law today is pliable and close to life, less dogmatic than other European legal systems, and little bound by formal rules and exigencies. Great attention is paid to rules and principles evolved in practice, especially by the courts. Much of the law is judge-made, and, as the principle of *stare decisis* (*i.e.*, being bound by precedent) does not obtain, the courts have been free to meet the demands of changing social conditions. Extensive participation of laymen in both civil and criminal proceedings may have contributed in some measure to the present standard of law.

See also Anglo-Saxon Law; Civil Law; Code Napoléon; Common Law; and articles on Scandinavian countries.

Bibliography.—K. Robberstad, *Rettssoga i Millomalder og Nytid* (1960); A. Taranger, *Udsigt over den norske Rets Historie*, 4 vol. (1898–1907); Poul J. Jørgensen, *Dansk Retshistorie* (1940); G. Hafström, *Land och lag* (1959); K. von Maurer, *Vorlesungen über altnordische Rechtsgeschichte*, 5 vol. (1907–10); Ó. Lárusson, *Log og saga* (1958); L. M. Larson (trans.), *The Earliest Norwegian Laws, Being the Gulathing Law and the Frostathing Law* (1935); Lester B. Orfield, *The Growth of Scandinavian Law* (1953), with comprehensive bibliography; R. Knoph, *Oversikt over Norges rett*, 3rd ed. by Sverre Grette (1949); H. V. Munch-Petersen, *Den borgerlige ret* . . . , 17th ed. (1962); *Norstedts juridiska handbok*, 6th ed. (1959). (F. Hɪ.)

SCANDINAVIAN MYTHOLOGY: see Germanic Mythology and Heroic Legends.

SCANDIUM is a metallic element of the first transition series and a member of Group III of the periodic table. Although it is usually classed with the rare-earth elements, scandium is not actually a member of that group (*see* below). The symbol for scandium is Sc. Its atomic number is 21 and its atomic weight is 44.956. There is only one stable isotope, Sc^{45}, which occurs naturally in 100% abundance.

Scandium was one of the several elements predicted in 1871 by Mendeléyev to fill gaps in the periodic classification; he called it ekaboron. The missing element was not discovered until 1879, when L. F. Nilson separated its oxide from the rare-earth minerals gadolinite and euxenite. This discovery was of great scientific interest, for the oxide, named scandia, and other compounds prepared from it had properties closely corresponding to those predicted for ekaboron.

Scandium is found in many of the heavy rare-earth ores of Scandinavia, from which its name was derived, and in many tin and tungsten ores; it also occurs in the products of atomic fission. The cosmic abundance of scandium is relatively high. It is easily separated from the rare earths with which it occurs by precipitation of the very insoluble potassium scandium sulfate or by extraction of scandium thiocyanate by diethyl ether.

The chemistry of scandium bears a superficial resemblance to that of the trivalent rare-earth elements. A series of white salts, Sc_2O_3, $Sc_2(SO_4)_3$, $ScCl_3$, $ScBr_3$, and $Sc_2(CO_3)_3$, are similar to those formed by the rare earths. The ionic radius of Sc^{+3} is 0.68 Å. The Sc^{+3} ion is a much weaker base than the corresponding ions of the rare earths and has much greater complex-forming ability. For example, the weak basic character of Sc^{+3} permits the precipitation of the hydrated oxide, $ScO(OH)$—scandium does not appear to form a definite hydroxide—at pH 4.9 whereas pH 6.3 or higher is appropriate for the precipitation of the rare-earth hydroxides. The ether extraction of scandium from chloride or thiocyanate solutions is an example of the difference in complex-ion formation. Scandium also forms soluble complex fluoride ions, a behaviour atypical of the rare earths. The Sc^{+3} ion is paramagnetic.

The metal is prepared by the thermoreduction of the halides by alkali or alkaline-earth metals. It melts at 1,539° C and its density is 2.992 g. per cc. for the hexagonal close-packed structure.

Very few uses of this unusual metal have been developed. Its low density and high melting point suggest applications as an alloying agent for devices requiring lightweight metals. Scandium might also be used as a portable source of hard radiation: when activated in an atomic pile it emits 1 Mev (million electron volts) of gamma radiation with a half-life of 85 days; hence as a "bottled X-ray" source it could compete with the artificial isotope of cobalt, Co^{60}. (Ld. B. A.; J. B. Ps.)

See also Rare Earths.

SCAPA FLOW, an extensive landlocked anchorage in the Orkney Islands, about 15 mi. (24 km.) in length from north to south and 8 mi. (13 km.) in mean breadth, bounded by Pomona on the north, by South Ronaldsay on the east and southeast, and by Hoy on the west and southwest. The principal entrance is on the south from Pentland Firth through Hoxa Sound. Hoy Sound on the west leads into the Atlantic Ocean and three intricate channels on the east lead through Holm Sound to the North Sea.

Long before 1914 Scapa Flow was frequented by the Channel and Home fleets as its spacious and well-sheltered waters provided an excellent practice ground, and the Admiralty planned that the main fleet should work from this base in wartime, to control the North Sea. However, little defensive work had been done when World War I started. The strong tides and intricate navigation of the entrances were considered sufficient defense against enemy submarines. The Grand Fleet was based there from Aug. 4, 1914, and for most of the war. On Sept. 1 as a result of an unfounded report of an enemy submarine having entered the Flow the fleet put to sea, moving to western Scotland and Northern Ireland, and returning to Scapa Flow in November. Temporary net defenses were rigged until permanent ones could be installed. In November an enemy submarine was destroyed in the outer approaches. Four years later, after the mutiny in the German fleet, one of their U-boats perished in a last desperate attempt to achieve success, but no U-boat managed to enter the Flow during World War I.

The battle cruiser force with its attendant flotillas moved to the Firth of Forth as soon as adequate antisubmarine defenses had been provided and in the latter part of the war Lord Beatty based the whole Grand Fleet there.

After the surrender of the German fleet in 1918 the Allies would not agree to Britain's definitely taking over the German vessels but, in spite of Britain's protests, the most important units of what had been the High Sea Fleet were interned in Scapa Flow with skeleton German crews on board, but not handed over. They were therefore only under distant observation by the British, and the result was that on June 21, 1919, the ships were scuttled by their German crews and the majority sank. They were later raised, broken up, and sold as scrap.

The story of Scapa Flow during 1939–40 bears a striking resemblance to that of 1914–15. Once more the main fleet was at anchor there when war broke out, and once more it had to abandon the base in the early days because of lack of defenses. In 1914 there were none, in 1939 there were only single lines of antisubmarine nets and a few antiaircraft guns. This time, however, the evacuation was due to no false alarm but to the sinking of HMS "Royal Oak" on Oct. 14, 1939, by a German submarine that had entered the Flow through the eastern entrance. This disaster (833 lives were lost) was quickly followed by the bombing of the depot ship, and once more the fleet had to move west, farther from the danger zone, which its task was to protect.

A new defense plan was immediately prepared and work proceeded with great activity. Eighty-eight heavy antiaircraft guns, together with many light ones, and more than 100 searchlights were mounted. Coast defense artillery was installed and three large controlled minefields were laid in the entrances. All antisubmarine nets were doubled and additional inner lines were laid. Airfields had to be constructed on the most unpromising sites, and there was much anxiety over the gaps continually occurring in the line of block ships closing the eastern entrance. This problem was eventually solved by joining the islands concerned with concrete emplacements. To the north the defense of Kirkwall as a large convoy assembly port also had to be organized. A most far-seeing part of the defense was the installation of the first really efficient radar system near Kirkwall by September 1939. This proved of immense value, and an efficient balloon barrage was also installed. Early in 1940 the defenses were sufficiently advanced for the fleet to return.

A successful air attack on the anchorage took place at the end of March 1940 when HMS "Norfolk" was hit by a bomb. Two further air attacks were made in April, but after this air attacks were never resumed. The efficiency of the defenses was proved by the fact that for five years the fleet's main base, although only 250 mi. (402 km.) from enemy airfields, was not again attacked.

In 1956 the base at Scapa Flow was closed, in company with many other naval shore establishments, in order to reduce the number of posts ashore held by uniformed personnel.

(R. N. Ba.)

SCAPHOPODA, a class of marine mollusks constituting the elephant's tusks, tusk shells, or tooth shells. There are four genera (of which *Dentalium* is the most familiar) and more than 350 species. Scaphopods are sedentary, and in the adult stage live on the sea bottom, into the surface layers of which they bur-

row and usually remain with part of the tubular tusklike shell, $\frac{1}{2}$ in. to 6 in. long, projecting from the surface. They are carnivorous and feed upon such small animals as foraminifers, young bivalves, etc. The majority live in fairly deep water; *Dentalium peruvianum* has been found at a depth of 2,235 fathoms. Many of the deep-sea species are cosmopolitan in distribution. The origin of the class can be traced back at least to the Ordovician Period.

External Features.—The structure of scaphopods is quite distinct from that of other mollusks. They are bilaterally symmetrical, elongate animals, in which the right and left edges of the mantle are joined in the mid-ventral line except at the anterior and posterior ends. The visceral mass is thus enclosed in a tubular sheath. The head is imperfectly developed and bears numerous long filaments. The animal is devoid of gills. The cylindrical foot is adapted for digging and burrowing into sand, in which the animals lie with the posterior extremity of the shell projecting from the surface.

The tooth shells were originally placed in the same class (Acephala) as the Lamellibranchia; but beyond the conformation of the mantle and the digging foot, there is no close resemblance to that group, whereas their possession of a radula, mandible, and buccal bulb point to affinities with the Gastropoda.

The shell of *Dentalium* is elongate, conical, and slightly curved. There are two apertures in all scaphopod shells, a larger anterior one from which the foot projects and a smaller posterior one. The smaller orifice is kept clear of the sand and admits water for respiration and allows wastes to be discharged when the animal is buried on the bottom. The mantle cavity is continuous from one end of the body to the other. The head is cylindrical and bears two lobes beset with long filaments (captacula). These are mainly sensory but also serve to capture the small organisms on which the animal feeds. The foot is capable of considerable extension and has an expansible end, of great service in digging.

Internal Anatomy.—All scaphopods have a well-developed buccal mass with mandible and radula. From the esophagus the food passes into the stomach, which is little differentiated and receives the ducts of a bilobed liver and a pyloric cecum. The intestine is provided with an anal gland. The circulation and respiratory system is extremely simple. The heart is rudimentary, and there are no proper blood vessels. The blood is oxygenated in the inner surface of the mantle. There are two kidneys in the mid-ventral region of the body, which open to the exterior, one on each side of the anus. The nervous system consists of the same pairs of ganglia, with their commissures, as in the Gastropoda. The cerebral and pleural ganglia are joined to the pedal ganglia by

RALPH BUCHSBAUM

FOUR LIVING TOOTH SHELLS

Dentalia, each about 1½ in. long, from a North Atlantic beach. Shell at left shows foot greatly extended; shell at right shows foot digging into sand

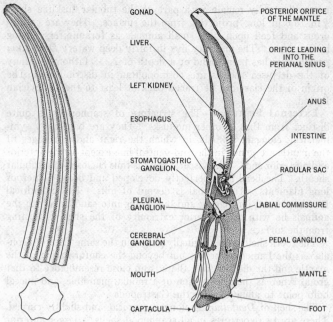

GONAD
LIVER
LEFT KIDNEY
ESOPHAGUS
STOMATOGASTRIC GANGLION
PLEURAL GANGLION
CEREBRAL GANGLION
MOUTH
CAPTACULA

POSTERIOR ORIFICE OF THE MANTLE
ORIFICE LEADING INTO THE PERIANAL SINUS
ANUS
INTESTINE
RADULAR SAC
LABIAL COMMISSURE
PEDAL GANGLION
MANTLE
FOOT

FROM (LEFT) H. A. PILSBRY, "MANUAL OF CONCHOLOGY;" (RIGHT) E. R. LANKESTER, "TREATISE ON ZOOLOGY"

DENTALIUM ELEPHANTINUM

(Left) Diagram of tusklike shell with outline of cross section below; (right) diagram of internal anatomy, shell removed

a long connective. These animals have only three kinds of sensory organs—the captacula, apparently tactile and olfactory; the subradular organ, probably an organ of taste; and the organs of balance (statocysts), situated in the foot. The sexes are separate. The ovary and the testis are unpaired and open into the right kidney, as in certain Gastropoda.

Development.—This has been studied in *Dentalium*. The eggs are laid singly, and segmentation is unequal and irregular. A gastrula arises through invagination, as in most Mollusca, and subsequently develops into a floating trochophore larva. A veliger stage succeeds, and after five or six days the velum (girdle of cilia) atrophies and the young *Dentalium* abandons its floating life and starts to creep about on the sea bottom. Interesting experiments have been done on this form. *See* EMBRYOLOGY AND DEVELOPMENT, ANIMAL: *Experimental Embryology.*

BIBLIOGRAPHY.—The most important papers up to 1906 are cited by P. Pelseneer in E. R. Lankester's *Treatise on Zoology* (part v, *Mollusca*). *See* also J. Henderson, "A Monograph of the East American Scaphopod Molluscs," *United States National Museum,* Bull. III (1920).   (G. C. R.; W. K. E.)

SCAPOLITE, a group of rock-forming minerals, which are silicates of aluminum with calcium or sodium but containing more or less chlorine, carbonate, or sulfate radicals. The name is from the Greek for "rod" and "stone" after the shape of some crystals. Scapolite also is known as wernerite.

Mineralogy.—The species of the scapolite group, ranging from marialite to meionite, must be regarded as variable isomorphous mixtures of the following five components:

$$Ma = 3NaAlSi_3O_8 \cdot NaCl\text{—chloride-marialite}$$
$$MaS = 3NaAlSi_3O_8 \cdot Na_2SO_4\text{—sulfate-marialite}$$
$$MaC = 3NaAlSi_3O_8 \cdot Na_2CO_3\text{—carbonate-marialite}$$
$$MeC = 3CaAl_2Si_2O_8 \cdot CaCO_3\text{—carbonate-meionite}$$
$$MeS = 3CaAl_2Si_2O_8 \cdot CaSO_4\text{—sulfate-meionite}$$

It seems likely that in marialite, NaCl, etc., may be replaced to a limited extent by KOH, and in meionite, $CaCO_3$, etc., may be similarly replaced by CaF_2. The close relation which this group of minerals bears to the plagioclase feldspars is apparent in the formulas indicated above (*see* FELDSPAR: *The Plagioclases*). The scapolites crystallize in the tetragonal system, the crystals being prismatic hemihedral. The hardness is 5–6, while the specific gravity varies with the composition, pure chloride marialite being 2.560 and carbonate-meionite 2.772. The colour is usually white

or gray. Between the end members, marialite and meionite, there are mixtures which have been given definite names. These include dipyre and mizzonite, and may, as in the case of the plagioclase feldspars, be arbitrarily fixed as follows:

$$\text{marialite } Ma_{100} \rightarrow Ma_{80}Me_{20}$$
$$\text{dipyre } Ma_{80}Me_{20} \rightarrow Ma_{50}Me_{50}$$
$$\text{mizzonite } Ma_{50}Me_{50} \rightarrow Ma_{20}Me_{80}$$
$$\text{meionite } Ma_{20}Me_{80} \rightarrow Me_{100}$$

The scapolites show varying resistance to acids, the meionite-rich members being most readily attacked, CO_2 being released by HCl-HF mixtures from the carbonate meionite, while marialite is only slightly attacked. They are destroyed by fusion, the lime-rich members giving plagioclase feldspar on cooling. The commonest alteration products are calcite kaolin, white mica, and zeolites. The scapolites are essentially metamorphic minerals, appearing very commonly in metamorphosed limestones.

Well-developed glassy crystals of scapolite occur in the ejected blocks of limestone of Monte Somma, Vesuvius, and large crystals occur in the apatite deposits of Bamle, southern Norway, where they arise from alteration of plagioclase feldspar in gabbro. The mode of occurrence of scapolite is referred to in detail below.

       (C. E. T.)

Scapolite Rocks.—Scapolites have three principal types of occurrence in rocks:

1. Scapolites are common in crystalline limestones and in calc-silicate hornfelses near igneous contacts. Even marialite, the variety richest in sodium, occurs in this manner as small crystals lining cavities in ejected blocks of limestone at Vesuvius and the Eifel craters in Germany. The scapolite may occur as small inconspicuous grains or as large, well-formed crystals. Minerals found with it in rocks of this sort include calcite, diopside, grossularite garnet, tremolite, wollastonite, sphene, and idocrase. In the Pyrenees, scapolite is common in limestone and calcareous shale where these rocks are in contact with diabase and peridotite.

2. Scapolite is also common in beds of marble and calc-silicate granulite associated with gneiss and mica schist. The scapolite is characteristically associated with calcite, diopside, garnet, wollastonite, or amphibole. Rocks of this sort have formed by metamorphism, on a regional scale, of impure limestones and calcareous shales. Examples are numerous in the Precambrian rocks of Canada and Fennoscandia (the Baltic shield) as well as in areas of crystalline schist formed in more recent geologic times. Some scapolite-bearing amphibolites and pyroxene-gneisses are probably metamorphosed igneous rocks. At Bolton, Mass., coarsely crystalline scapolite and scapolite-quartz rocks occur as dikelike bodies, several feet thick, cutting across dolomitic marble. These masses resemble in texture the pegmatite dikes cutting the adjacent mica schists and their origin may be similar.

3. In gabbros and related rocks, plagioclase feldspars may be wholly or partly converted to scapolite. Excellent examples occur in Norway and Sweden; in the Pyrenees; in Ontario, Can.; and in the Adirondack Mountains of New York. The pyroxenes in these rocks are altered in some occurrences to a uralitic hornblende; and the rock may have a spotted appearance with white, rounded patches of scapolite in a granular matrix of green hornblende. Chlorine-bearing apatite is commonly associated with such occurrences and it has been suggested that the scapolitization has been brought about by the action at depth of aqueous solutions rich in chlorides and phosphates, presumably from an igneous source.

       (J. B. T.)

SCARAB (Lat. *scarabaeus*, connected with Gr. *karabos*), literally a beetle, and hence an Egyptian symbol in the form of a beetle. The Egyptian hieroglyph 🪲 represents the dung beetle *Scarabaeus* (or *Ateuchus*) *sacer*, which may be seen on sunny days forming a ball of dung and rolling it over the sand to its burrow, where the morsel is consumed during the following days. The Egyptians apparently shared the widespread belief that the beetle lays its egg in this ball of dung, and saw in the life cycle of the beetle a microcosm of the cyclical processes in nature, and particularly of the daily rebirth of the sun, a parallel made even more striking by the globular shape of the pellet. The ancient sun-god Khepri was conceived of as a great scarab rolling the sun across the heavens. The scarab became as well a symbol of the enduring human soul, whence its frequent appearance, often with wings spread, in funerary art. Quantities of dead scarabs have been discovered in burials of the earliest period, apparently to ensure the continued existence of the soul; the later mummification (see MUMMY) of scarabs stems from the fact that they were sacred to Khepri at Heliopolis. Several stone scarabs of monumental size are known; one in the British Museum perhaps came from the Heliopolis temple, and another stands by the sacred lake at Karnak. The Egyptian name of the beetle was *ḫprr* (or *xprw*), a derivative from the stem *ḫpr* (or *xpr*) "become," and the hieroglyph 𓆣 was used to write these and related words (see HIEROGLYPHS).

An important class of Egyptian antiquities is in the form of scarabs of various materials, glazed steatite being most common, but other stones, faïence, and pottery also being used. Such objects usually have the bases inscribed or decorated with designs, and are simultaneously amulets and seals. They first appeared in the late Old Kingdom, when they evolved from the so-called button seals (see BABYLONIA AND ASSYRIA: *Art and Art Objects: Glyptic*). Scarabs remained rare until Middle Kingdom times, when they became abundant and replaced the earlier stamp seals and cylinders. Pierced lengthwise for stringing or mounting in ring bezels of precious metal, they were also used simply as ornaments; plain amethyst scarabs are common articles of Middle Kingdom jewelry (*q.v.*). Some scarabs are purely amuletic in purpose, as the large basalt "heart scarabs" of New Kingdom and later times. Such an amulet was placed in the mummy bandages and was inscribed with Chapter 30b of the *Book of the Dead*, a spell that identified the scarab with the heart of the deceased and conjured it not to betray him in the judgment before Osiris (*q.v.*). A winged scarab might also be placed on the breast, and later a number of amuletic scarabs were placed about the body.

The seal type of scarab is, however, the most common, and many clay sealings attesting this use have been found on sites of the Middle and New Kingdoms. Spiral motifs and names and titles of officials are characteristic of the Middle Kingdom examples, while on New Kingdom and later scarabs a wide variety of designs and inscriptions is found. Some of the inscriptions, although carefully executed, have been so corrupted by illiterate copying as to be meaningless. Various hieroglyphs expressing luck or happiness may be collected into a design. Real inscriptions are sometimes mottoes referring to places, deities and so on, or containing words of good omen or friendly wishes (*e.g.*, "Memphis [*q.v.*] is mighty forever," "Amon [*q.v.*] protecteth," "Bubastis [*q.v.*] grant a good New Year," "May thy name endure and a son be born thee").

Historically the most valuable class is that which bears royal names, ranging from the 11th dynasty to the Late period. Some great kings are commemorated on scarabs of periods long subsequent to them. Thus Cheops (see KHUFU) of the 4th dynasty appears on examples of 26th dynasty date, and Tuthmosis (Thutmose) III's name is found throughout later times. Nevertheless, distinctions of style and pattern often make it possible to recognize contemporary royal scarabs, and the names of the Hyksos dynasts have been largely recovered from collections of scarabs (see HYKSOS).

A series of exceptionally large scarabs was engraved in the reign of Amenhotep III (*c.* 1417–1379 B.C.; see AMENHOTEP), all bearing the king's titles and those of Queen Tiy. Five varieties are known; the simplest commemorates the queen's parentage and the northern and southern limits of the empire; another, dated in the king's second regnal year, a great wild-cattle hunt; the third, the arrival of Princess Gilu-Khepa of Mitanni (see MESOPOTAMIA: *Hurrians and Aryans*) in year 10; the fourth (many specimens), the number of lions slain by the king down to year 10; the last, the creation of the lake of Zarukha in year 11.

A related type of seal-amulet, called by Egyptologists the scaraboid, is similar in shape but lacks the details of the beetle's anatomy. Egyptian scarabs were carried by trade over all the eastern Mediterranean and to Mesopotamia. The Greeks, especially in their Egyptian colony of Naukratis, imitated them in soft paste. The finest Etruscan gems of the 6th and 5th centuries B.C. are in the form of scarabs, inspired by Egyptian imports.

BIBLIOGRAPHY.—P. E. Newberry, *Scarabs* (1906); H. R. Hall, *Catalogue of Egyptian Scarabs in the British Museum,* vol. 1 (1913), *Scarabs* (1929); W. M. F. Petrie, *Scarabs and Cylinders with Names* (1917), *Buttons and Design Scarabs* (1925); D. F. Brown, "Graeco-Phoenician Scarabs . . ." *American Journal of Archaeology,* vol. 40 (1936); C. Bonner, *Studies in Magical Amulets, Chiefly Graeco-Egyptian* (1950); S. H. Horn, "Scarabs from Shechem," *Journal of Near Eastern Studies,* vol. 21 (1962). (F. LL. G.; N. B. MI.)

SCARAMOUCH (English spelling) is the stage character of a comic servant created by the Italian actor Tiberio Fiorillo, leader of a company of impromptu players, who acted in Paris in 1645–47 and frequently shared the stage of the Palais-Royal with Molière from 1662 to 1673. Before going to Paris, Fiorillo had made a name for himself as a member of the Uniti company, in which he had acted the Captain's part under the name of Scaramuccia. At what point he dropped the braggart soldier and became the comic servant it is impossible to tell. As Scaramouche (the French spelling) he charmed Parisians with the finesse and suppleness of his miming. He relied very little on the spoken word, placing all the emphasis on expressive body movement. Molière learned many tricks of his trade by watching the performances of Fiorillo. In a satirical print the French actor is portrayed as aping the Italian master. (A. M. N.)

SCARBOROUGH, a municipal borough of the North Riding of Yorkshire, Eng., is 41 mi. (66 km.) NE of York by road. Pop. (1961) 43,061. Scarborough lies behind a peninsula of high land on which the ruins of the castle stand like a sentinel overlooking the North and South bays. The castle was built during the reign of King Stephen about 70 years after the town was raided by Harald Hardraade (see HARALD III) in 1066. In 1312 the earl of Pembroke captured Piers Gaveston, earl of Cornwall, after laying siege to the castle. It fell to Parliamentary forces in 1645 and 1648, and from 1665 to 1666 the Quaker George Fox was imprisoned there.

Scarborough is probably the oldest seaside resort in England, and it is now generally accepted that its name derived from a character in the Icelandic *Kormaks Saga,* which tells how two Viking brothers, Kormak and Thorgils, were the first men to set up a stronghold there (from 965 to 967). As Thorgils was nicknamed "Skarthi the harelipped," the derivation of Scarborough's medieval name Scardeburg, from Skarthiburg, seems probable. Scarborough was granted its first charter by Henry II in 1181. In the burial ground of the parish Church of St. Mary the Virgin (Early English) is the grave of Anne Brontë (d. 1849).

By 1660 the merits of the Scarborough "spaw" were becoming known throughout the country and the first spa water cistern was

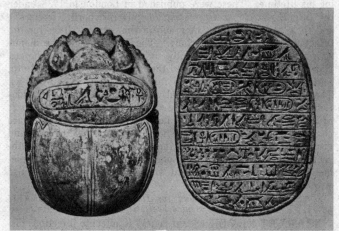

SCARAB FROM THEBES COMMEMORATING THE REIGN OF AMENHOTEP III (ABOUT 1417–1379 B.C.). THE BEETLE IS INSCRIBED TO THE KING; REVERSE (RIGHT) IS COVERED WITH HIEROGLYPHICS

built in 1698, a governor of the spa being appointed by the corporation. Many new inns catered for the "spaws"—as the visitors were known—and in the 18th century began the fashion of combining the taking of the spa waters with bathing in the sea. Thus it was that Scarborough first became famous as a sea-bathing resort. Its two bays are linked by the Marine Drive, a sea defense around the base of Castle Hill, which was opened in 1908. The modern town extends a considerable distance inland, its southern limits being dominated by Oliver's Mount (said to have been named after Oliver Cromwell) on which stands the war memorial, a gigantic obelisk.

Old houses are still to be found in Sandside and other steep winding lanes at the back of the harbour, which is enclosed by the East and West piers and divided into two basins by the Vincent Pier, at the end of which stands the lighthouse. There are two splendid beaches with boating and bathing in both bays and boating in two of the gardens and parks. On an island in the lake of Northstead Manor Gardens is the stage of the Open Air Theatre, while the auditorium, which seats 7,000 spectators, rises up the facing hillside. Wood End, formerly the home of the Sitwell family, is a museum devoted to natural history and includes a vivarium. There is also a collection of books, manuscripts, etc., connected with the Sitwells.

The stewardship of the ancient manor of Northstead, which lies under the lake in the nearby Peasholm Gardens, is given alternatively with that of the Chiltern Hundreds to members of Parliament who adopt the traditional method of retirement by taking "an office of profit under the crown."

The resort is famous for its cricket festival and tennis and golf tournaments, the latter being played on the championship course at Ganton, 9 mi. (14 km.) SW. Although mainly a residential and holiday town, Scarborough has a number of small industries. It is a quarter sessions borough and has a separate commission of the peace. (E. Go.)

SCARLATTI, (PIETRO) ALESSANDRO GASPARE

(1660–1725), Italian composer of operas and religious works, and one of the most important figures in the development of classical harmony, was born at Palermo on May 2, 1660. He was sent to Rome at about age 12; there he met Bernardo Pasquini, by whom he was greatly influenced, and Arcangelo Corelli. The first of his 115 operas, *Gli equivoci nel sembriante* (1679), written for a religious fraternity in Rome, won him the protection of Queen Christina of Sweden, for whom he wrote *L'onestà negli amori* (1680), and in whose service he remained until 1683. These works brought him commissions for operas from Naples, where, in 1684, he became *maestro di cappella* in the royal service. He remained there until 1702, writing over 40 operas and musical entertainments for the court and its circle. *Gli equivoci in amore* (1690) is a typical example of his work at that period of his life.

In 1702 Scarlatti went to Pratolino, near Florence, where, over the next two years, he wrote four operas for the theatre of Prince Ferdinando III de'Medici; the scores of these works have disappeared. In 1706 he was appointed *maestro di cappella* to Cardinal Pietro Ottoboni in Rome, and was also elected to the Arcadian Academy there. The following year he held a like post at Sta. Maria Maggiore in Rome and also wrote two operas on a larger scale, *Il trionfo della libertà* and *Mitridate Eupatore,* for production during the carnival in Venice. The latter is one of his finest works. Scarlatti traveled to Venice to supervise the performances; in 1709 he returned to his old post at Naples. There followed a period of in-

DETAIL FROM A PORTRAIT BY AN UNKNOWN ARTIST, IN THE LICEO MUSICALE, BOLOGNA; PHOTO, THE GRANGER COLLECTION

ALESSANDRO SCARLATTI

tense activity during which he wrote serenades and Masses as well as operas. *La principessa fedele* (1710), *Scipione nelle Spagne* (1714), and *Tigrane* (1715) are among his principal operatic successes of this period. The ternary aria form is developed in these works, which are also remarkable for a bolder use of the orchestral stringed instruments. In 1716 he wrote a Mass for Pope Clement XI and in the same year completed his first *opera buffa, Il trionfo dell'onore* (Naples, 1718). Between 1718 and 1721 he wrote more operas and religious works. On his return to Naples in 1723 he seems to have gone into retirement. He died there on Oct. 24, 1725.

Scarlatti uses thematic development and chromatic harmony with great mastery and in a way which anticipates the work of much later composers, among them Mozart and Schubert. Though he is chiefly remembered for his operas, in which he established the form of the "Italian overture," his chamber music is equally characteristic and shows him to have had a commanding conception of form. Over 500 chamber cantatas from all periods of his life are extant. His church music is of unequal value, though the second of his two Masses with orchestra (1720) marks a new development, anticipating the Masses of Bach and Beethoven. He wrote little orchestral music but he contributed to the development of the opera orchestra. Whereas in his youth the strings were used mainly to play introductions and *ritornelli,* Scarlatti placed more emphasis on the orchestral accompaniment to the voices. His use of wind instruments was similarly novel: trumpets, flutes, oboes, and bassoons were used for particular effects, and horns were introduced into the orchestra.

See E. J. Dent, *Alessandro Scarlatti: His Life and Works,* 2nd ed. with preface and notes by F. Walker (1960).

SCARLATTI, (GIUSEPPE) DOMENICO

(1685–1757), Italian composer whose harpsichord works represent the most fully developed style of keyboard writing in his time, was born at Naples on Oct. 26, 1685. He studied with his father, Alessandro Scarlatti, and became organist at the royal chapel in Naples in 1701. His first opera was produced in Naples in 1703. From 1705 to 1708 he studied under Francesco Gasparini in Venice. There Scarlatti met Thomas Roseingrave and also Handel, who became his lifelong friend. In 1709 in Rome, he entered the service of Maria Casimira, queen dowager of Poland, for whom, between 1710 and 1714, he wrote seven operas. Later he held posts at the Vatican and the Portuguese embassy in Rome. From 1720 to 1724 he is believed to have been both the music director of the royal chapel in Lisbon and the music teacher of Princess Maria Barbara. He was again in Naples in 1724, and in 1728 in Rome. When in 1729 the princess married the prince of Asturias, later Ferdinand VI, Scarlatti accompanied her to Spain. He spent the remainder of his life at Madrid and the royal palaces at Seville and Aranjuez. He died at Madrid on July 23, 1757.

Of his 555 published harpsichord sonatas only 30 appeared during his lifetime. These were published in London in 1738 under the title *Essercizi per Gravicembalo* ("Harpsichord Exercises") and form the first important group in this series written for the delectation of the Spanish court. The *Essercizi* and the manuscripts made for the royal family and deposited in the Biblioteca Nazionale Marciana, Venice, and the Conservatorio Arrigo Boito, Parma, are the principal sources for all but a few of the sonatas. The composition of these original works, which form the foundation of the modern keyboard style, occupied most of the latter part of Scarlatti's life. Unlike the suites of Bach and Handel, they are comparatively short pieces in binary form, written in pairs and displaying great rhythmic and harmonic subtleties. The best 20th-century edition is Alessandro Longo's (ten volumes and supplement). Besides his harpsichord works and operas Scarlatti also wrote religious works.

See S. Sitwell, *A Background for Domenico Scarlatti 1685–1757* (1935); R. Kirkpatrick, *Domenico Scarlatti* (1953).

SCARLET FEVER (SCARLATINA) is an acute infectious disease caused by certain types of hemolytic streptococcal bacteria. The first clear description of it is credited to the German physician Daniel Sennert (1619), although Michael Doering probably first observed the disease in Breslau, Pol. The English physician

Thomas Sydenham in 1676 gave a clear differentiation of scarlet fever, as follows: "The skin is marked with small, red spots, more frequent, more diffuse, and more red than in measles. These last two or three days. They then disappear, leaving the skin covered with brawny squamulae, as if powdered with meal." The disease appeared in North America about 1735 and was described by Benjamin Rush.

Practically all strains of streptococci capable of producing the disease belong to Lancefield's group A and are serologically distinguished from other groups of streptococci on the basis of a specific group antigen, the C substance, which is carbohydrate in nature. Group A is typified by *Streptococcus pyogenes*. Within group A many types of hemolytic streptococci have been identified on the basis of their M substance, which is protein in nature. Occasionally scarlet fever is caused by streptococci belonging to a group other than A. Certain types (1, 4, 18, and others) have often been associated with kidney complications.

Under suitable growth conditions the hemolytic streptococcus elaborates a number of toxic substances, some of which seem to be important factors in its disease-producing mechanism. These are erythrogenic toxin, streptolysin, fibrinolysin, leukocidin, and the so-called spreading factor, the enzyme hyaluronidase. The erythrogenic toxin causes the toxic manifestations of the disease such as the eruption, rapid pulse, fever, and delirium. Injection of a small amount of this toxin into the skin to determine susceptibility to the disease is known as the Dick test, developed by the leading U.S. investigator of scarlet fever, George Frederick Dick (*q.v.*).

Symptoms and Treatment.—The onset of the disease begins from two to seven days after exposure. The first symptoms are fever, sore throat, headache and, in children, vomiting. From two to three days later the rash appears as a reddening of the skin which begins on the neck, in the armpits and groin, and upon the chest. The face is flushed, with a ring of pallor around the lips. The throat is inflamed and red spots appear upon the palate. The tongue is coated, but the edges are deeply inflamed. After four days the coating on the tongue disappears, leaving a swollen, deeply injected surface with prominent papillae (strawberry tongue).

The eruption lasts for a week or more, and in about one-third of the cases is followed by desquamation, or peeling off of portions of the skin. The glands of the body are usually swollen; those of the neck may be tender and painful to touch. The eruption may be very faint; indeed, it may never occur in persons who have immunity to the toxin (*scarlatina sine exanthemata*). Such individuals represent important agents in the spread of the disease to others. The fever may last for a week or more.

Various clinical patterns, such as mild, moderately severe, severe, toxic, septic, and malignant scarlet fever have been described. Such classifications merely denote variations in the degree of severity and are a matter of opinion. The clinical manifestations may be regarded as primary and secondary. The primary infection usually occurs in the pharynx; the secondary features are the result of toxic and septic reactions. Toxic reactions include headache, fever, vomiting, rapid pulse, delirium, eruption, and disturbances in the heart and kidneys. The septic reactions result from invasion of the tissues by the hemolytic streptococcus and include cellulitis, swollen glands, and infections of the ear, mastoid, sinuses, blood, and brain.

Complications are frequent. The sinuses probably are always secondarily involved, frequently remain infected during convalescence and constitute an important focus in which the organism remains to cause the patient to become a carrier. Abscesses of the ear and mastoiditis occur. Infection of the glands of the neck frequently results in abscess formation. In certain instances the streptococcus enters the blood stream and is carried to various parts of the body where localized areas of infection develop. Among the late complications are nephritis (which occurs in 0.5% to 1.0% of all cases), arthritis, and rheumatic fever. The urine should be tested frequently during the course of the disease.

Diagnosis is based upon the characteristic symptoms and signs. As a general rule, a child who becomes ill with fever, sore throat, headache, and vomiting, and who develops a fine generalized rash within 24 to 72 hr. after the onset of symptoms presumably has scarlet fever until proved otherwise. The diagnosis may be confirmed by isolation of the streptococcus from the throat or from some other region of the body, which may be the focus in so-called surgical scarlet fever. When an injection of a small amount of immune serum (0.1 cc. to 0.3 cc.) is made into the skin while the rash is at its height, a blanched area results at the point of injection within 18 hr. if the rash in question is caused by scarlet fever toxin. This reaction is known as the Schultz-Charlton test. Another confirmatory test consists in the reversal of the Dick test from positive to negative during the course of the disease.

Second attacks of scarlet fever are relatively rare but the recovered patient may subsequently experience other types of streptococcal infection.

Penicillin, to which the streptococcus is highly sensitive, is the treatment of choice. Gamma globulin, prepared from human serum, is also effective. Treatment should include bed rest, adequate fluids, and a diet commensurate with the patient's appetite.

Occurrence.—Scarlet fever is extremely variable in its severity not only in different countries but in different outbreaks occurring in the same country. In the U.S. it is relatively mild, with a mortality rate of less than 1%. In the Balkans and in China severe forms of the disease exist. It is found principally in the temperate zones, rarely in the tropics. It is primarily a disease of childhood; half the cases occur between the ages of two and eight years. Most cases of scarlet fever occur during the winter and spring months, with an increase of incidence in September when schools open. Nonwhite people are less susceptible than white, and slightly more males than females develop the disease. Certain families are especially susceptible, but in general the communicability rate among susceptibles in a given family is between 5% and 15%.

The disease is spread chiefly by droplet infection but may be disseminated by contaminated dust particles and by contaminated hands, food, drinks, and fomites. Contaminated milk may give rise to an outbreak. Surgical scarlet fever may result from infected wounds and burns. Convalescent cases and persons harbouring the organism in discharges from infected ears, sinuses, and wounds may act as carriers, constituting an important factor in the spread of the disease. Control measures include isolation of the active case and the treatment of carriers, many of whom become free of streptococcus after treatment with penicillin. Because of the fact that scarlet fever is only one of several related types of infections caused by the hemolytic streptococcus (designated by some as streptococcosis), quarantine and isolation procedures alone do not prove to be adequate measures in the prevention of the disease. (W. L. Bd.)

SCARPANTO: *see* KARPATHOS.

SCARRON, PAUL (1610–1660), French writer whose burlesque poems set him among the wits of the age, whose plays show a gift of lively comedy that immediately foreshadows Molière, and whose major novel is a masterpiece of the picaresque genre. The son of a counselor in the *parlement* of Paris, he was baptized July 4, 1610. Becoming an abbé in 1629, he entered the service of Charles de Beaumanoir, bishop of Le Mans, in 1633. After a visit to Rome with him in 1635, Scarron returned to Le Mans and there, in 1638, was attacked by a disease which in 1640 became so much worse that the rest of his life was spent in pain and progressive deformity.

His life up to this point had been dissolute but he now found consolation in the chaste sympathy of Louis XIII's former favourite, Marie de Hautefort (the future maréchale de Schomberg), temporarily exiled at Le Mans. Returning to Paris, he was further troubled by lawsuits with his stepmother after his father's death (1643).

For some time Scarron enjoyed the patronage of the future cardinal de Retz (*q.v.*), and during the Fronde he eventually published a violent pamphlet against Mazarin (early in 1651). In 1652, almost entirely paralyzed, he married a beautiful but poor young girl, Françoise d'Aubigné, who later became world-famous as Madame de Maintenon (*q.v.*). He died in the night of Oct. 6–7, 1660.

Scarron's first book, *Recueil de quelques vers burlesques* (1643); supplemented by *Suite des oeuvres burlesques*, 1644) had some success, but his burlesque epic, *Typhon, ou la gigantomachie* (1644) was less well received. His play *Jodelet, ou le maître valet* (1645), named after the comedian Jodelet for whom the principal role was destined, inaugurated that tradition of developing the valet's role in comedy which Molière was to exploit so brilliantly.

The work for which Scarron was most famous in his own day, *Virgile travesty* (7 books, 1648–53), a parody of the *Aeneid*, seems rather deplorable to modern readers, but his *Roman comique* (*Le Romant comique*, 2 vol., 1651–57, unfinished; 3rd vol. by other hands, 1659) is recognized as of great merit and interest. The desultory story of a troop of strolling actors (in the style of the Spanish picaresque romances), it depicts manners and character in a singularly vivid way that makes it a landmark in the development of the French novel. Scarron's other works include eight more comedies (the most notable was *Don Japhet d'Arménie, c.* 1647) and a series of five tragicomical tales in the Spanish manner (1655–57). Of the latter, Molière drew on *La Précaution inutile* as a main source for *L'École des femmes* and on *Les Hypocrites* to a lesser extent for *Tartuffe*.

Scarron was at the centre of the literary activity of his time. He knew all the young men who were putting new life into the French drama—Jean Mairet, Tristan L'Hermite, Corneille, and Rotrou. His own plays show a gift for realistic comedy that is the nearest thing to Molière before 1650. He was moreover a most important representative of the critical strain in French literature. While his burlesque verses parody contemporary epic, the vivid scenes of the *Roman comique* seem to be meant as an antidote to idealistic and pretentious novels. The vigour and wit of his writing reveal a talent as remarkable as the personality that, in the opinion of many who knew him, triumphed over years of pain. A critical edition of Scarron's collected works began with *Le Romant comique*, edited by H. Bénac (1951).

BIBLIOGRAPHY.—G. Tallemant des Réaux, *Historiettes*, ed. by G. Mongrédien (1932); P. Morillot, *Scarron et le genre burlesque* (1888); H. Chardon, *Scarron inconnu* (1903); E. Magne, *Scarron et son milieu*, new ed. (1924) and *Bibliographie des oeuvres de Scarron* (1924).

SCAURUS, MARCUS AEMILIUS,

the name of two Roman politicians, father and son.

MARCUS AEMILIUS SCAURUS (*c.* 162–*c.* 89 B.C.) was a leader of the Optimates (or nobility). His family, though patrician, was impoverished, so he had to work his way up. Having acquired wealth, he turned from business to public life and, helped by the family of the Metelli, reached the consulship in 115 B.C., when he defeated some Alpine tribes and gained a triumph. Chosen *princeps senatus*, he held this position until his death. Sent to check the ambitions of the Numidian king Jugurtha in 112, Scaurus was alleged in 111 to have been bribed by him, but he neatly avoided trouble by getting himself selected as one of the presidents of the commission appointed to inquire into such allegations (109). In 109, as censor, he constructed a Via Aemilia through Pisa to Dertona (Tortona) and repaired the Milvian Bridge near Rome. In 104, as grain commissioner at Ostia, he replaced Saturninus, whose sedition in 100 he helped to suppress (*see* SATURNINUS, LUCIUS APPULEIUS). Accused of extortion in 92, he managed to get the trial postponed. He supported his friend the reforming tribune M. Livius Drusus (the younger) in 91, in his attempt to secure the franchise for the Italian allies, and in 90 was accused of intriguing with the allies but acquitted. He married Caecilia Metella, later Sulla's wife, and was the father of Aemilia, later Pompey's wife. He wrote three volumes of autobiography, which Sallust may have used in writing his history of the Jugurthine War. A conservative who moved with the times, Scaurus exercised great influence. Cicero (*Pro Fonteio*, 24) said that the world was almost ruled by the nod of his head; Sallust gives a less flattering portrait.

MARCUS AEMILIUS SCAURUS, son of the above, served as Pompey's quaestor and proquaestor in the Third Mithradatic War (66–61 B.C.). Sent to Judaea and Nabataea, in return for large bribes he decided the quarrel between Hyrcanus and Aristobulus (*see* HYRCANUS) in the latter's favour in 64 (Pompey later reversed this) and allowed the king Aretas to retain Nabataea (*see* NABATAEANS) in 62. The settlement with Aretas was commemorated on a coin which Scaurus, as curule aedile (*see* AEDILE), issued in 58, when he staged public games of unusual magnificence. Having been praetor (56) and propraetor in Sardinia (55), he was accused of provincial extortion in 54, was defended by Cicero and by Hortensius and was acquitted. Accused of electoral corruption, he went into exile in 52. He married Mucia, formerly Pompey's wife.

BIBLIOGRAPHY.—*Scaurus the elder:* G. Bloch, "M. Aemilius Scaurus," in *Mélanges d'histoire ancienne* (1909); E. Badian, *Studies in Greek and Roman History*, Index (1964).
Scaurus the younger: Josephus, *Antiquitates*, xiv, 2–5, and *Bellum Judaicum*, i, 6–8; Pliny, *Historia Naturalis*, xxxvi, 24, 113–115; Cicero, fragments of *Pro Scauro*, and many references in the *Epistulae*; Asconius, *In Scaurianam*; E. A. Sydenham, *The Coinage of the Roman Republic*, no. 912 (1952).   (H. H. SD.; X.)

SCAVENGER'S DAUGHTER

(corruption of Skevington's or Skeffington's daughter), an instrument of torture in use during the 16th century in England. It was invented by Sir W. Skevington, lieutenant of the Tower in the reign of Henry VIII. It consisted of a wide iron hoop which by means of screws was tightened round the victim's body until the blood was forced from the nose and ears, and sometimes from the hands and feet.

SCENERY, THEATRICAL: *see* STAGE DESIGN.

SCENTED PLANTS.

The supreme joyous notes of plant life are colour and fragrance. Colour is shared with many animal groups, among them birds, fishes and butterflies, but fragrance is the openly broadcast gift of plant life. Natural animal fragrances are rare, but it is worth noting that certain flower-visiting butterflies and moths produce a flowery fragrance composed of essential oils, the same group of substances that produces redolence in flowers.

Fragrance and colour, so welcome to the aesthetic sense, have been the practical guideposts to food, consisting of pollen and nectar, for certain insects for thousands of centuries. There are many wind-pollinated and bird-pollinated flowers, none of which possess fragrance, and of the many flowers dependent on insects for pollination, only some are fragrant.

The sweet scents of flowers are nearly always associated with the showy parts of the blossom, being released by the petals or by sepals or bracts when there are no petals, but there are a few plants with small inconspicuous flowers, such as the pussy willow and a few others, that are fragrant. In the mint family (Labiatae) the pleasant refreshing scent comes from the green parts of the flower cluster and especially from the leaves and stems.

A LEAF OF LAVENDER (LAVANDULA MULTIFIDA) ABOUT ½ ACTUAL SIZE, WITH OUTLINE OF THE EDGE OF THE SAME LEAF, ENLARGED ABOUT 50 TIMES

Globe-tipped glandular or oil-secreting hairs are present on the edge of the leaf; thousands of smaller glandular organs are on both leaf surfaces

The attractive odours of flowers and foliage are predominantly attributable to the presence of essential oils (*q.v.*). These volatile substances are found in about one plant family out of five. An essential oil is a complex secretion product, apparently a normal part of the functioning of the plant and not an isolated end in itself. The essential oils are rather powerful substances and often appear in minute quantities and perhaps never constitute more than about 2% of the floral plant material. The violet can be taken as an example, 15 tons of the flowers being needed to produce a pound of oil. The essential oils of flowers are more complicated than those of leaves—the former may consist of a dozen components while the simplest of leaf essential oils may have but one.

Both flower and leaf fragrances are much used in the manufacture of perfumes. Outstanding flowers for this purpose are rose, tuberose, hyacinth, jasmine, acacia (*Acacia farnesiana*), lily of the valley and ylang-ylang (an Asiatic tree, *Cananga odorata*); leaves (and green sepals) used in perfumery include those of geranium (*Pelargonium* species), lavender, rosemary, patchouli (*Pogostemon cablin*), clary sage and even a few species of grass (of the genus *Cymbopogon*), which produce citronella, lemon grass and palmarosa oils.

Fragrance occurs not only in flowers and leaves but also in fleshy fruits of many kinds. This odour attracts mammals which help disseminate the seeds contained within the fruit. The same scents found in fruits, or very similar ones, are found in flowers and even in leaves of unrelated species. Thus one finds apple-scented (apple mint, sweetbrier rose) among other fruit-scented leaves, and peach, lemon, raspberry and quince odours among others in flowers of plants totally unrelated to those fruits.

The particular sweetness of a flower is usually not the result of the presence of a single chemical compound, but often includes one or more unrelated compounds that closely imitate the dominating odour. The constituents of the volatile oils are esters, alcohols, aldehydes, ketones, etc. The dominating ester can be accompanied by a closely related set of esters, making for overtones, and the final fragrance results from an intricate combination and proportion of volatile substances characteristic of the species.

The oil secretion of flowers takes place in the epidermal cells of the coloured part, usually on the upper side, but occasionally on both sides, as in the rose. Additional petallike parts, interior to the normal ring of petals, which make for doubling of flowers may also secrete oils, causing many double flowers to have that much more scentedness (violets, roses). Sometimes, however, doubling results in reduction of fragrance over that in single forms of the same kind of flower (lily of the valley, poet's narcissus). In some leaves, odours originate in hairs projecting from the surface or recessed in tiny depressions.

In the mint family (lavender, thyme, basil, marjoram, sage, etc.), the short-stalked glandular hairs that secrete the oil appear among several other kinds of hairs. They have rounded heads consisting of 1 to 16 or more cells. Other families, such as citrus (Rutaceae), myrtle (Myrtaceae) and laurel (Lauraceae), produce the fragrant oils in tough sacs in the interior of the leaf. These can be readily seen with a hand lens by holding a leaf up against the light.

There has been extensive neglect in maintaining fragrance in a large number of cultivated flowers. It has been customary to think of a flower as being beautiful because of its colour, size and form, and hybridists have been concentrating on this ideal. In the course of extensive hybridization, workers have drawn parents from many sources, and when unscented flowers are crossed with scented ones, the progeny will include some without fragrance. As an example, the group of yellow rose species (of Asiatic origin) have no rose scent. When they are bred even with fragrant kinds, many of their progeny will be unscented. One large grower of sweet peas finds that after considerable hybridizing his crimson and scarlet kinds are practically devoid of fragrance. It is extremely rare for any flower to lose its scent in nature, as this factor is so fundamental in the maintenance of the species. A fragrant plant introduced into cultivation and given conditions approaching its natural habitat should retain its fragrance.

A pronounced impetus to interest in scented plants has been given by the establishment in several large cities of fragrance gardens for the blind. The first such garden was founded in Exeter, Eng., in 1939; the first in the United States at Lima, Pa., in 1949. Fragrance gardens located in large cities—*e.g.*, one (started in 1955) at the Brooklyn Botanic Garden in New York City, and another (started in 1956) at the Lighthouse for the Blind in Chicago—are, because of their locations, much visited. In these gardens the blind can "view" trees, flowers and herbs by their fragrance and texture. Braille markers are placed so that the plants can be readily identified. The gardens are so designed that the sightless can guide themselves through the paths and experience the only realities of plants that are available to them— the furry leaf, the prickly stem, the juice of crushed leaves, the

softness and fragility of the petals and, above all, the faint bouquets and the incense of the unseen blossoms.

Among plants grown for their fragrance and texture—and therefore essential in gardens for the sightless—are those with light and elusive bouquets: wallflower, cottage pink, flowering tobacco, sweet william, alyssum, heliotrope and violet; those with characteristically heavy redolence, hyacinth, rose, tuberose, jonquil, lily of the valley, lilac and mock orange. Plants with pungent piercing scent, to be tasted and bruised with the fingers, are thyme, dill, laurel, sage, lemon balm, rosemary, lavender, marigold and the astringent witch hazel and mints; and those to be touched and held in the hand, plants of interesting texture as well as unique odour, the hairy leaves of many herbs (mint, lavender, geranium), the unfolding leaves of the pungent balm of Gilead, the apple-scented foliage of sweetbrier rose and especially most needle-leaved and some broad-leaved evergreens with their aromatic resins.

BIBLIOGRAPHY.—N. Taylor, *Fragrance in the Garden* (1953); E. S. Rohde, *The Scented Garden* (1949); F. A. Hampton, *The Scent of Flowers and Leaves* (1925); D. McDonald, *Fragrant Flowers and Leaves* (1905). (G. A. KA.)

SCÈVE, MAURICE (*c.* 1501–1560/4?), French poet who was considered great in his own day, and, after long neglect, has been reinstated by 20th-century critics and poets, chiefly for his poem-cycle, *Délie.* He was born at Lyons, where his father held high municipal office, and was prominent in the affairs and literary circles of his native city. Indeed, he has often been described as the leader of the Lyonese school of writers (including Pernette du Guillet, *c.* 1520–45; and Louise Labé, *q.v.*), although there is no evidence of an organized school. Lyons, on the trade route between northern and southern Europe, was a centre of humanism, and Scève first achieved fame in 1533 by his "discovery" of the tomb of Petrarch's Laura at Avignon, and again in 1536 with his *Blason du sourcil,* adjudged the best entry in a poetic competition held at Ferrara. (A *blason* is a minute description of the qualities of an object.) This poem, with some other *blasons* of his, was later published in the anthology, *Les Blasons du Corps Féminin,* often reprinted between 1537 and 1550. His *Délie,object de plus haulte vertu* (1544) is a poetic cycle of 449 highly organized decasyllabic ten-line stanzas (*dizains*), rich in imagery, and platonic and Petrarchan in theme and style. "Délie" (an anagram of "L'Idée"), long thought to be an imaginary ideal, may have been Pernette du Guillet, whose death seems to have partly inspired Scève's *Saulsaye, églogue de la vie solitaire* (1547), written in retirement in the country. After returning to Lyons, he wrote his last poem, *Le Microcosme* (1562), an epic, praising the efforts and progress of man from Adam's fall, which sustains its ambitious conception only in occasional passages of magnificent verse. Nothing certain is known of his last years, although several conflicting hypotheses have been put forward.

BIBLIOGRAPHY.—*Oeuvres complètes,* ed. by B. Guégan (1927); *Délie,* ed. by E. Parturier (1916), and by A. M. Schmidt in *Poètes du XVIᵉ siècle* (1953); *Poésies de Maurice Scève,* with essay by J. Tortel (1961); *Le Opere Minori di M. Scève,* ed. by E. Giudici (1958); *Sixty Poems of M. Scève,* trans. by W. Fowlie (1949). See also A. Baur, *M. Scève et la Renaissance Lyonnaise* (1906); V. Larbaud, "Notes sur M. Scève," in *Ce Vice impuni, la lecture: Domaine française* (1941); V. L. Saulnier, *M. Scève,* 2 vol. (1948); P. Boutang, *Commentaire sur 49 dizains de la Délie* (1953). (K. V.)

SCHADOW, a family of German artists.

JOHANN GOTTFRIED SCHADOW (1764–1850), sculptor, was born in Berlin on May 20, 1764. He learned his craft under the court sculptor J. P. A. Tassaert and perfected it in Rome from 1785–87 in the studios of A. Trippel and A. Canova. In November 1787 he returned to Berlin, and a year later succeeded Tassaert as director of the royal school of sculpture.

His first monumental work is the tombstone for Count Alexander von der Mark (1790, Berlin); his best known is the quadriga (1793), on the Brandenburg Gate. Among his finest work is the group of the princesses Louise and Frederike of Prussia (1797, Berlin). He was also responsible for the statue of Frederick the Great at Stettin (1793) and the Luther memorial at Wittenberg (1821). From 1800 on Gottfried Schadow was increasingly surpassed by Christian Rauch. After 1807 he executed a series of busts for the Bavarian crown prince's "Valhalla." He was one of the chief representatives of classicism in Germany, but he largely replaced the idealistic by a rigorous realism. In the last three decades of his life his sight became affected; he then stood out primarily for his writings on the theory of art and for his genius as a draftsman. He died on Jan. 27, 1850, in Berlin.

See H. Mackowsky, *Die Bildwerke Gottfried Schadows* (1951).

RUDOLF SCHADOW (1786–1822), eldest son of Gottfried, also a sculptor, was born on July 9, 1786, in Rome and was first taught by his father in Berlin. In 1811 he went to Rome, where he came into contact with the J. F. Overbeck and P. von Cornelius circle. He became the pupil of B. Thorvaldsen and A. Canova and took over C. Rauch's studio in Rome. From 1812 he was a member of the S. Luca Academy. Of his youthful, versatile work must be mentioned "The Spinner" (1816, Berlin and Budapest), the "Girl Binding on her Sandals" (1817, Munich), and the model for the monumental group in Berlin "Achilles Defends the Dying Penthesilea" (1821). Rudolf Schadow died in Rome on Jan. 31, 1822.

WILHELM VON SCHADOW-GODENHAUS (1788–1862), painter, founder of the Düsseldorf school, second son of Gottfried, was born in Berlin on Sept. 6, 1788. He was the pupil of his father and later of the painters J. F. Weitsch and W. Wach. He went to Rome in 1811 with his brother Rudolf, becoming in 1813 of the "Lukasbund" founded by F. Pforr and J. F. Overbeck. From 1816 to 1817 Wilhelm, together with P. von Cornelius, Overbeck, and P. Veit, painted the frescoes in the Casa Bartholdi. From 1819 to 1826 he was professor at the Berlin Academy and then succeeded Cornelius as director of the Düsseldorf Academy. The Düsseldorf school, which he founded, soon departed completely in its special type of painting and in its anecdotal, religiously-determined realism from the artistic ideas of Overbeck and his Nazarenes. Wilhelm died in Düsseldorf on March 19, 1862. His chief works are: a portrait of Gabriele von Humboldt (1818, Berlin); "Adoration of the Shepherds" (1824, Potsdam); and the fresco of "The Wise and Foolish Virgins" (1842, Frankfurt). He educated a generation of painters, including K. F. Lessing (1808–80).

See Anton Fahne, *Die Düsseldorfer Malerschule in den Jahren 1834, 1835 und 1836,* new ed. (1937); Julius Hübner, *Schadow und seine Schule* (1869). (J. C. JE.)

SCHAFF, PHILIP (1819–1893), U.S. theologian, church historian, and pioneer in church union, was born in Chur, Switz., Jan. 1, 1819. He was educated at the *Gymnasium* of Stuttgart and at the universities of Tübingen, Halle, and Berlin. At Berlin, where he became *Privatdozent* in 1842, he was deeply influenced by the historian J. A. W. Neander. His brilliant scholarship early attracted favourable attention. In 1844 he became professor of church history and biblical literature in the Theological Seminary of the German Reformed Church at Mercersburg, Pa. His inaugural address on *The Principle of Protestantism,* published in both German and English editions, viewed the history of the Christian Church as a divinely appointed development leading to a higher form of church life in which the values of Roman Catholicism and Protestantism would be blended in an evangelical Catholicism. This address, with its prophetic interest in church union, provoked charges of heresy, from which he was exonerated. Schaff, together with the theologian John W. Nevin (1803–86), shaped the Mercersburg theology, which resisted revivalist theology and emphasized the doctrine of the church. In 1864 Schaff began a six-year term as secretary of the New York Sabbath Association, becoming a widely known Protestant leader. He became professor at Union Theological Seminary, New York City, in 1870, serving until the year of his death. An inveterate traveler, he continued active leadership in Protestant affairs, especially in the interests of church unity through the Evangelical Alliance. He won a secure place as one of America's great theological scholars, both through the quality and remarkable quantity of his work as author and editor.

Outstanding among his many productions are the seven-volume *History of the Christian Church* (1858–92) and the three-volume *Bibliotheca Symbolicae Ecclesiae Universalis: The Creeds of Christendom* (1877). He edited the translation and revision of Lange's massive *Commentary* (1864–80), the great Schaff-Herzog *Encyclopaedia of Religious Knowledge* (1884), and other biblical and historical works. He participated actively in the preparation of the Revised Version of the Bible. He founded the American Society of Church History in 1888 and served as its first president. He was an originator and general editor of the American Church History series. Schaff died in New York on Oct. 20, 1893.

See David S. Schaff, *Life of Philip Schaff* (1897). (R. T. H.)

SCHAFFHAUSEN (SCHAFFHOUSE), the name of the most northerly Swiss canton and of its capital city.

The City.—Schaffhausen stands on the right bank of the Rhine about 15 mi. (24 km.) W of Lake Constance. Pop. (1960) 30,904, of whom the majority were German speaking. Bordering one of the main squares, the Münsterplatz, is the Protestant cathedral or Münster, a Romanesque pillared basilica, once the church of the Benedictine monastery of All Saints. The early-13th-century tower is surmounted by a 17th-century spire; in the 12th-century cloisters is the bell (cast in 1486) inscribed "vivos voco, mortuos plango, fulgura frango," which is said to have inspired Schiller's famous poem *Song of the Bell.* The municipal museum is now housed in the former monastery and contains sections for archaeology and ecclesiastical works of art, and arts and crafts. Facing the Fronwagplatz are several 17th- and 18th-century houses with oriel windows. Along the Vordergasse are the late Gothic *Haus zum Ritter* with famous frescoes by Tobias Stimmer (the originals are now in the museum), and the old Rathaus (meeting place of the *Grosser Rat*) which dates from the 15th century; the new Rathaus in the Renaissance style of 1617 stands near Beekenstube. Also notable is the 16th-century Gothic Church of St. John. The massive 16th-century Munot Fort overlooks the town and the Rhine.

The site of the city was first mentioned in 1045, as "Villa Scafhusun," and in 1050 there was a ford there across the Rhine. About 1049 Count Eberhard III of Nellenburg founded the Benedictine monastery of All Saints, which henceforth became the centre of the town. Perhaps as early as 1190, certainly by 1218, it was a free imperial city, though the first seal dates from 1253. The powers of the abbot were gradually limited, and in 1277 the emperor Rudolf of Habsburg gave the town a charter of liberties. In 1454 it made an alliance with six of the Swiss confederates, by whom it was received as an ally against the Habsburgs, being finally admitted a full member of the Swiss Confederation in 1501. Schaffhausen is now an industrial city and a tourist centre; medieval architecture of the true Swabian type mingles with modern manufacturing enterprises. An important railway junction, it is on the main line from Zürich to Stuttgart and is linked by rail with Basel, Constance, and Winterthur. There are motorboat connections with Lake Constance.

The Canton.—Schaffhausen canton lies almost entirely north of the Rhine where the river flows westward on leaving Lake Constance. The Rhine forms most of the southern boundary separating Schaffhausen from the cantons of Zürich and Thurgau. The remainder of the boundary borders on Germany, penetrating portions of which divide the canton into three detached parts: a large region including the town of Schaffhausen; the small isolated district of Rüdlingen-Buchberg to the southwest; and an area extending northward from Stein (Stein am Rhein). The canton contains two small German enclaves of which the village of Büsingen is the more important. The dominant relief feature is the plateau of Randen (the summit, Hoher Randen, reaches 3,031 ft. [924 m.]) sloping gently southward to the Rhine and intersected by short glens such as Klettgau. On the Rhine just below Schaffhausen is the celebrated Rheinfall (Falls of the Rhine). Hydroelectricity produced farther west at Rheinau supplies power for the chemical industry at Rheinfelden, the aluminum plant at Neuhausen (Neuhausen am Rheinfall, an industrial suburb of Schaffhausen), and engineering works at Schaffhausen. The area of the canton is 115 sq.mi. (298 sq.km.) of which about 95% is classed as "productive." The population in 1960 was 65,981, mostly German speaking and largely Protestant. The major industries include the production of machinery and metal goods, watches, jewelry, textiles, canned food, leather goods, cement, glass, and paper; woodworking, brewing, and chemical production are also important. Vine growing is the predominant agricultural activity; forestry is a considerable source of revenue.

The canton is divided into six administrative districts, containing 34 communes. The cantonal constitution dates from 1874. The legislative assembly (*Grosser Rat*) is composed of 80 members elected every four years by the male adults. The executive council (*Regierungsrat*) of 5 members is also elected for four years by popular vote, as are the two members of the Federal Council of the States (*Ständerat*) and the two members of the Federal National Council (*Nationalrat*). Electors have the right of "initiative," both for legislative projects and for constitutional matters. Since 1895 the "obligatory referendum" for all legislative projects has prevailed. The canton, admitted into the Confederation in 1501, arose from acquisitions made at various times by the town of Schaffhausen. Of historical interest is the picturesque little town of Stein, with old painted, gabled, and turreted houses, a Benedictine monastery (1005–1526), now restored to form a museum, and the Hohenklingen Castle (12th century), overlooking the town. (W. V.)

SCHAFFNER, JAKOB (1875–1944), Swiss writer, who lived in Germany from 1913, was born at Basel on Nov. 14, 1875. He belonged to a new generation of Swiss writers who, in search of uncompromising greatness and believing in life as a boundless adventure, broke away from the saturated tradition of middle-class society. He lost his Swiss father and German mother early, and four autobiographical novels (*Johannes*, 1922; *Die Jünglingszeit des Johannes Schattenhold*, 1930; *Eine deutsche Wanderschaft*, 1931; *Kampf und Reife*, 1939) depict his experiences as a child, a charity schoolboy, a shoemaker, and a roving and autodidactic writer. Although Schaffner's colourful, spirited, imaginative style is in the realistic tradition of Gottfried Keller and of Jeremias Gotthelf, his convictions are rather those of Nietzsche and, to some extent, of Dostoevski and finally led him to follow the lure of National Socialism. Besides other novels (*Konrad Pilater*, 1910; *Der Dechant von Gottesbüren*, 1917; *Die Glücksfischer*, 1925), he wrote poems (*Bekenntnisse*, 1940) and essays (*Die Predigt der Marienburg*, 1931; *Berge, Ströme und Städte, eine schweizerische Heimatschau*, 1938). He was killed in an air raid on Strasbourg on Sept. 23, 1944.

See P. Fässler, *J. Schaffner, Leben und Werk*, with bibliography (1937); H. Bänziger, *Heimat und Fremde* (1959; on Schaffner's ambivalent attitude to Switzerland). (A. Bx.)

SCHARNHORST, GERHARD JOHANN DAVID VON (1755–1813), a general in the Prussian Army during the Napoleonic Wars and a pioneer of the general staff system (*see* STAFF, MILITARY). Born at Bordenau, Hanover, on Nov. 12, 1755, he was the son of a tenant farmer who had been a sergeant major in the Hanoverian artillery. As a young officer in the Hanoverian Army (commissioned 1778) he was brought up as a disciple of Wilhelm von Schaumburg-Lippe, who had helped to reorganize the Portuguese Army in the 1760s. He made a name for himself in Belgium during the French Revolutionary Wars, directing a successful sortie from the besieged fortress of Menin in 1794. Later he became chief of staff to Count von Wallmoden, commander in chief of the Hanoverian forces.

In 1801 he applied, in an unusual manner, to the king of Prussia for employment in the Prussian Army: then a major, he asked to be made a lieutenant colonel, to be raised to the nobility, and to be permitted to reorganize the Prussian Army in accordance with his own theories. To show his qualifications, he enclosed three military essays with the application. Somewhat surprisingly, his request was approved and all his conditions were granted: he was ennobled in 1804. On entering Prussian service he was employed at the war academy in Berlin where Karl von Clausewitz, later to become a noted military writer, was one of his pupils. While in Berlin he founded the Berlin Military Society. In 1804–05 he was chief of staff to the duke of Brunswick, and was engaged in preparing the Prussian forces for the war of 1806. In the campaign of that year he, with Gebhard von Blücher (*q.v.*), was taken prisoner at the surrender at Ratkau, near Lübeck,

following the Battle of Jena (Oct. 14). He was soon released in an exchange of prisoners, and subsequently took a prominent part in leading L'Estocq's Prussian Corps serving with the Russians. (*See* also NAPOLEONIC WARS.)

After the Peace of Tilsit (1807) Scharnhorst was made head of the Army Reform Commission, and in this capacity came into contact with August von Gneisenau (*q.v.*) and other progressively minded men. Although brought up in the military tradition of Frederick the Great, he was one of the first to realize, after the Prussian defeat at Jena, the necessity for conscripted national forces in place of small, long-service professional mercenary armies. He also realized that national service must be accompanied by political reform. His appointment to the Army Reform Commission afforded him access to the king; but Napoleon soon became suspicious of Scharnhorst's activities and forced the king to cancel many of the reforms he had proposed. When, during 1811–12, Prussia was forced into alliance with France against Russia, Scharnhorst left Berlin on indefinite leave. He returned to service with the call to arms following the retreat from Moscow, and in 1813 was made chief of staff to Blücher. He took part in the Battle of Lützen, where he received a wound from which he did not recover. He died in Prague, where he had gone to negotiate for Austria's entry into the war, on June 28, 1813.

Scharnhorst's reputation rests on his work as a military reformer rather than as a fighting general, and on his ability to impress his views on colleagues by nature and training unreceptive to new ideas. He was a founder of the general staff system: that it was not at first entirely successful was not his fault; there had been insufficient time to train officers in, and accustom them to, the new techniques. His system was later accepted and adopted by the armed forces of all the great powers. It is remarkable that, from humble origins, he rose to such heights and influence in an army of which the officers were almost entirely drawn from the hereditary nobility.

BIBLIOGRAPHY.—C. von Clausewitz, *Über das Leben und den Charakter des Generals von Scharnhorst* (1832); R. Höhn, *Scharnhorsts Vermächtnis* (1952); R. Stadelmann, *Scharnhorst: Schicksal und geistige Welt* (1952). (C. N. B.)

SCHAUDINN, FRITZ (1871–1906), German microbiologist who discovered the syphilis germ, was born at Röseningken, East Prussia, on Sept. 19, 1871. He studied zoology at the University of Berlin and took his doctorate in 1894. In 1898 he was appointed lecturer there in recognition of his work on the life histories of protozoans. His studies of fertilization in the protozoan parasite *Coccidia* provided the zoological clues which enabled Ronald Ross and Giovanni Grassi independently to work out the life cycle of the malaria parasite. Schaudinn himself made important discoveries concerning the causative organisms of human malaria and bird malaria. These researches led Robert Koch to recommend Schaudinn for a post in the German Imperial Health Office, where he carried out a series of classic studies of medically important protozoans. He was the first to differentiate between *Endamoeba histolytica*, which causes amoebic dysentery, and its harmless counterpart, *E. coli*. In 1905 he discovered the syphilis bacterium, which he named *Spirochaeta pallida* (now called *Treponema pallidum*). This discovery stimulated Paul Ehrlich to begin researches which culminated in the discovery of the antisyphilis drug arsphenamine (Salvarsan). Schaudinn died in Hamburg on June 22, 1906. (M. C. L.)

SCHAUMBURG-LIPPE, one of the smallest of the former member-states of the German Reich. With a present area of 132 sq.mi. (342 sq.km.), it lay east of the middle bend of the Weser River and was bounded on all sides by Prussian territory from 1866 to 1946. Bückeburg was its capital.

Schaumburg, or Schauenburg, northeast of Rinteln, was the ancestral seat of a line of counts recorded from the early 12th century (*see* HOLSTEIN for an important branch of the dynasty). Lutheran from 1559, this line died out in 1640. Some of its fiefs then reverted to Brunswick, and its other lands were partitioned in 1647: Hesse-Kassel took the east and the south, with Rinteln; but Philip of Lippe-Alverdissen, brother of the last countess of Schaumburg, obtained Bückeburg, Arensburg, Stadthagen, Hagenburg, and half of Sachsenhagen, as a fief of Hesse.

Schaumburg-Lippe was admitted to the Confederation of the Rhine as a sovereign principality in 1807. It joined the German Confederation in 1815, the Fiscal Union of the northwestern states in 1837, the *Zollverein* in 1854, the North German Confederation in 1866, the German Empire in 1871. The revolution of 1918 made it a "free state" with a republican and democratic constitution from 1922 (the constitution of 1868 had kept representation by Estates). In 1946 it was merged in Lower Saxony (*q.v.*).

See O. Wagenführer, *Schaumburgische Geschichte* (1908); K. Brüning, *Der Landkreis Schaumburg-Lippe* (1955).   (FH. H.)

SCHECHTER, SOLOMON (1847–1915), U.S. Jewish theologian and talmudist, president (1902–15) of the Jewish Theological Seminary of America, and for many years the leading spokesman for Conservative Judaism in the U.S. Born on Dec. 7, 1847, in Fokshan, Rum., he pursued advanced studies in Vienna and Berlin and was one of the first scholars to study the talmudic literature of Judaism in the light of modern critical research. Schechter's *Some Aspects of Rabbinic Theology,* published while he was still a lecturer in rabbinics at Cambridge University, and other writings led to a sympathetic reappraisal of the teachings of the Pharisees. In 1902 Schechter went to New York City to serve as president of the Jewish Theological Seminary of America, which he developed into a foremost institution for Jewish research and for the training of rabbis and teachers. The United Synagogue of America, which he founded in 1913, grew from an original membership of 23 Conservative congregations to about 650 congregations.

In 1896 Schechter discovered the Geniza (archive) in the old synagogue in Cairo, which contained over 90,000 manuscripts, many of them of great significance for biblical and rabbinic research. Among them was a copy of the original Hebrew text of Ecclesiasticus (*q.v.*). Schechter's identification of another manuscript as relating to an ancient Jewish sect in pre-Christian times was confirmed almost 50 years later, by the discovery among the Dead Sea Scrolls of the Manual of Discipline, which is very similar in content to what Schechter identified as a Zadokite document. He died on Nov. 19, 1915, in New York City.   (M. AT.)

SCHEELE, CARL WILHELM (1742–1786), Swedish chemist, who anticipated by several years Joseph Priestley's discovery of oxygen and made many other important investigations, was born at Stralsund, the capital of Pomerania, which then belonged to Sweden, on Dec. 9, 1742. He studied the elements of chemistry during his apprenticeship to an apothecary in Göteborg, with whom he stayed for eight years before taking similar positions in Malmö (1765) and Stockholm (1768). He read chemistry avidly and experimented constantly during his free time. In 1770 he settled at Uppsala, where he made the acquaintance of the eclectic scientist Torbern O. Bergman. A friendship sprang up between the two, and it has been said that Scheele was Bergman's greatest discovery. In 1775, the year in which he was elected to the Stockholm Academy of Sciences, he moved to Köping, a small place on Lake Mälaren, where he became proprietor of a pharmacy. Frederick the Great tried to induce him to accept a chair of chemistry at Berlin, but this flattering offer, as well as one from England, was refused.

He found time for an extraordinary amount of original research, and every year he published two or three papers, most of which contained some discovery or observation of importance. It is said that his unremitting work, especially at night, and in a poorly ventilated laboratory, together with his handling of the most toxic materials and his habit of tasting and smelling materials indiscriminately, induced illness which brought about his death in Köping at the age of 43 on May 21, 1786.

Scheele's record as a discoverer of new substances is probably unequaled, in spite of his poverty and lack of ordinary laboratory conveniences. His work touched every province of the chemistry of his time. His first paper, published in 1770 in conjunction with his friend Anders Retzius, dealt with the isolation of tartaric acid from cream of tartar. Analysis of manganese dioxide in 1774 led him to the discovery of chlorine and baryta (barium oxide) and to the description of various salts of manganese, including the

manganates and permanganates, and to the explanation of the action of manganese compounds in colouring and decolourizing glass. He showed that iron, copper, and mercury exhibit various degrees of oxidation. In 1775 he investigated arsenic acid and its reactions, discovering arsine (hydrogen arsenide) and the pigment Scheele's green (copper arsenite). Papers published in 1776 were concerned with quartz, alum, and clay and with the analysis of *calculi vesicae* (bladder stones), from which for the first time he obtained uric acid.

Scheele's only book, *Air and Fire,* was published in 1777 but was written some years before. One of the chief observations recorded in it is that the atmosphere is composed of two gases— one which supports combustion and the other which prevents it. The former, "fire-air," or oxygen, he prepared from nitric acid, saltpetre (potassium nitrate), manganese dioxide, oxide of mercury, and other substances, and there is little doubt that he obtained the gas two years before Priestley. Because of the delay in the publication of his results he is rarely given credit for this discovery. In all, he described ten methods of preparing oxygen. He showed that it played an essential part in the life processes of aquatic animals and plants, as well as those that live in air. Scheele remained in favour of the phlogiston theory (the belief that burning and rusting were caused by loss of a "substance" or "principle" called phlogiston) until his death; he apparently thought that hydrogen, which he had obtained by the action of certain acids on iron or zinc, was pure phlogiston.

In 1777 Scheele prepared hydrogen sulfide by a variety of methods and noted the chemical action of light on silver compounds and other substances. In 1778 he proposed a new method of making calomel (mercurous chloride) and powder of algaroth (antimony oxychloride), and he got molybdic acid from the mineral *molybdaena nitens* (molybdenite), which he was the first to distinguish from ordinary molybdena (graphite). In the following year he showed that graphite consists essentially of carbon, and he published a record of estimations of the proportions of oxygen in the atmosphere, which he had carried on daily during the whole of 1778—three years before Henry Cavendish made a similar experiment. In 1780 he proved that the acidity of sour milk is due to what was afterward called lactic acid, and by boiling milk sugar with nitric acid he obtained mucic acid.

His next discovery, in 1781, was in connection with the mineral scheelite (calcium tungstate), from which he obtained tungstic acid. In 1782 he published some experiments on the formation of ether and in 1783 examined the properties of glycerine, which he had discovered several years before. About the same time, in the course of some work on Prussian blue, he described the composition, properties, and compounds of prussic (hydrocyanic) acid and even ascertained its smell and taste, quite unaware of its poisonous character. In the last years of his life he returned to the vegetable acids. He isolated and investigated citric, malic, oxalic, and gallic acids.

See also references under "Scheele, Carl Wilhelm" in the Index.

BIBLIOGRAPHY.—O. F. Zekert, *C. W. Scheele: Sein Leben und seine Werken* (1931–33); E. Thorpe, *Essays in Historical Chemistry* (1923); W. Tilden, *Famous Chemists* (1921); G. Bugge (ed.), *Buch der grossen Chemiker* (1929–30); *Collected Papers of Carl Wilhelm Scheele,* trans. by L. Dobbin (1931); E. Farber (ed.), *Great Chemists* (1962).

SCHEELITE, a mineral consisting of calcium tungstate, is an important ore of tungsten. Before the development of high-speed tool steels around 1900, the ore had little commercial value. Since then, however, consumption has increased greatly as a source of tungsten for use in the manufacture of alloy steel, and in carbides and as filaments in electric lights and electronic equipment. Synthetic scheelite has the same uses. Named after C. W. Scheele, a Swedish chemist, it is the mineral in which he discovered tungstic acid. Scheelite is commonly found in heavy, compact and granular masses, but tetragonal, dipyramidal crystals occasionally occur. It is white, yellow, brown or green and has a vitreous to adamantine lustre. The hardness is 4.5 to 5 and the specific gravity 5.9 to 6.1. Most scheelite fluoresces, the colour ranging from blue-white or white to yellow, depending upon the amount of molybdenum present. The formula is $CaWO_4$. $CaO = 19.4\%$; $WO_3 = 80.6\%$. The high density, high lustre and fluorescence are distinguishing characteristics.

Scheelite is found in contact metasomatic deposits, high-temperature veins and in granite pegmatites. Associated minerals include cassiterite, fluorite, topaz, apatite, wolframite and certain sulfides. In the United States scheelite has been mined in quantity in North Carolina, California, Nevada and in smaller amounts in a number of other western states. It also occurs in Cornwall and Cumberland, Eng.; and in Bolivia, New South Wales, New Zealand and Tasmania. *See* also TUNGSTEN. (A. F. HR.)

SCHEEMAKERS, PETER (1691–1781), a sculptor who worked almost entirely in the classical tradition and may be considered one of the founders of modern sculpture in England, was born at Antwerp in 1691. He studied in the workshop of his father and worked in Rome, Copenhagen and, about 1720, in London, first with P. D. Plumier and later with F. Bird. After another stay in Rome and at Antwerp he returned to London about 1735 and worked there until about 1770. He spent the last years of his life in Antwerp, where he died in 1781.

Scheemakers is responsible for a great deal of work in England, and monuments signed by him are to be found in churches all over the country. His most famous work is the monument to Shakespeare, which was designed by William Kent and erected in Westminster abbey in 1741.

See M. Whinney, *Sculpture in Britain, 1530–1830* (1964).
(J. A. DR.)

SCHEFFEL, (JOSEPH) VIKTOR VON (1826–1886), German writer, for many years his country's most popular poet and the author of a novel *Ekkehard* of remarkable popularity, was born at Karlsruhe on Feb. 16, 1826. He studied law at Munich, Heidelberg, and Berlin (1843–47) and was appointed legal attaché at Frankfurt am Main, with a law practice at Säckingen.

His early ambition was to become a painter, but he had already written numerous poems when he suddenly achieved fame with his lyric-epic poem *Der Trompeter von Säckingen* (1854), in which his romantically idealized vision of the German past is presented with humour and charm. He left government service in 1854 and settled at Heidelberg, hoping to be appointed to the staff of the university and working on a translation of the Latin *Waltharius*, but his studies were hindered by an eye infection and he moved to Lake Constance, where he completed his novel, *Ekkehard* (1857; Eng. trans., 1872); set in the 10th century in the monastery of Sankt Gallen, it was one of the most successful German novels of the century. He returned to his beloved Heidelberg and in 1868 published a collection of student songs, *Gaudeamus, Lieder aus dem Engeren und Weiteren*, the material drawn largely from German legends and historical subjects, the tone humorous and jovial. Like his earlier successes, the book ran into many editions and some of the songs (*e.g.*, "Alt-Heidelberg, du feine!") are still sung. Eventually he returned to settle at Karlsruhe, where he died on April 9, 1886.

See Scheffel's *Gesammelte Werke*, 6 vol. (1907); W. Klinke, *Scheffel*, a biography in letters (1947). (W. D. WI.)

SCHEFFLER, JOHANNES (favourite pen name ANGELUS SILESIUS) (1624–1677), Silesian mystic, whose abiding fame derives from his poetry, was born at Breslau (now Wrocław, Pol.) and died there on July 9, 1677. Son of a Lutheran Polish nobleman, Scheffler was court physician to the duke of Oels in his native Silesia when readings in the mystics, especially Jakob Böhme (*q.v.*), and in the Church Fathers led him to the Roman Catholic Church, into which he was received in 1653. Thereafter he devoted himself almost entirely to writing. Following his ordination to the priesthood in 1661 he contributed some 55 polemical pieces to a Lutheran-Catholic controversy, notable even in that day for asperity and bad manners on both sides.

In 1657 was published his *Geistreiche Sinn- und Schlussreime* ("Epigrammatic Verses on the Spiritual Life"), a collection of couplets on various religious truths better known under the title of its second edition (1674), *Der Cherubinischer Wandersmann* ("The Pilgrim of Truth"); and *Heiligé Seelenlust* ("Holy Pleasure of the Soul"), religious songs celebrating the nuptials of the soul with God, many of which have found an honoured place in both Protestant and Catholic hymnals. The best edition of the poems is

Hans L. Held's *Angelus Silesius: Sämtliche poetische Werke*, three volumes (1949–52). *Angelus Silesius* (1909) is a selection, translated into English by P. Carus, from *Der Cherubinischer Wandersmann*.

BIBLIOGRAPHY.—The standard biography is that of G. Ellinger, *Angelus Silesius, ein Lebensbild* (1927). *See* also H. Plard, *La Mystique d'Angelus Silesius* (1942); W. Dürig, *Zur Frömmigkeit des Angelus Silesius in Amt und Sendung* (1950). (E. O'B.)

SCHEIDT, SAMUEL (1587–1654), German composer best known for his works for organ, was born in Halle in 1587. He went to Amsterdam at about 1605 and studied there with J. P. Sweelinck. In 1609 he returned to Halle where he was first appointed organist at the Moritzkirche and, about 1619, organist and later *Kapellmeister* to the margrave of Brandenburg. Scheidt remained in Halle until his death on March 30, 1654. He had a high reputation as a teacher, his most famous pupil being the composer Adam Krieger.

Scheidt's first published works contain sacred vocal music; they include *Cantiones sacrae* (1620) for eight voices, and four books of *Geistliche Concerten* (1631–40) for two to four voices and continuo. The publication of his *Tabulatura nova* (three parts, 1624) was an important event in the history of organ music. The *tabulatura* of the title is keyboard tablature in the Italian sense; *i.e.*, staff notation for a keyboard instrument, rather than the alphabetical tablature associated with early German organ music until the time of J. S. Bach. The work contains fantasias, toccatas, "echo pieces," sets of variations, and organ responses for liturgical use. Although the influence of Sweelinck is noticeable, Scheidt's work throughout displays his own technical skill and feeling for the organ, with well-developed counterpoint and carefully indicated directions for registration. By contrast, his *Tabulatur-Buch* (1650), containing harmonized accompaniments for 100 "sacred songs and psalms," is indicative of the growing practice of congregational chorale singing which was to become customary in the Lutheran Church. (C. P. CO.)

SCHELDT (French ESCAUT; Flemish SCHELDE), a river rising in northern France and flowing across Belgium to its outlet in Dutch territory. Along with the lower Rhine and the Meuse it drains one of the most populous areas in the world and as a waterway, with its navigable tributaries and numerous branch canals, it serves an area which includes the agriculturally important Flanders Plain, the Belgian textile centres, the coalfield of northern France, and the industrial complex of Lille-Roubaix-Tourcoing. Among well-known towns on its banks are Cambrai and Valenciennes in France; Tournai, Oudenaarde, Ghent, and Antwerp in Belgium. The chief tributaries are the Scarpe, Lys, Dender, and Rupel. The estuary formerly had two channels, the East and the West Scheldt, divided by the islands of Beveland and Walcheren, but in 1866 the East Scheldt was sealed off by a dike carrying the railway to Flushing. The outlet between South Beveland and Walcheren is closed by a dike and the only connection is via the South Beveland Canal. A channel in the West Scheldt, maintained at a minimum depth of 24 ft. (7.3 m.), allows vessels drawing up to 33 ft. (10 m.) to reach Antwerp at full tide. With its upper course canalized, the Scheldt is navigable for about 125 mi. (201 km.) in Belgium and 39 mi. (63 km.) in France.

The busiest section of the river lies between Antwerp and Ghent, along which are many industrial undertakings. Above Cambrai the river is unnavigable, but from this point the Saint-Quentin Canal connects it with the Somme-Seine system. The Scheldt waterway is also connected with the Sambre-Meuse system by the Mons-Condé Canal. From Ghent the Ghent-Terneuzen Ship Canal gives direct access to the West Scheldt, and the small Ghent-Ostende Canal links the Scheldt with the North Sea.

Use of the Scheldt as a shipping outlet was long a subject of bitter contention between the Flemish and the Dutch, as the latter controlled most of the estuary. Seeking to cripple the trade of Antwerp, the Dutch in 1648 secured the right to close the estuary to navigation (*see* ANTWERP: *History*). In 1863 Belgium finally bought out this right, with assistance from other maritime countries, and declared the Scheldt free, thereby giving impetus to the development of Antwerp as a great international port.

(K. C. E.)

SCHELDT QUESTION, the international problem arising from the fact that the Belgian port of Antwerp was for more than 250 years deprived of free access to the North Sea by Dutch control over both sides of the estuary of the Scheldt River.

By the middle of the 16th century, when both the northern and the southern Netherlands were under Spanish rule (*see* NETHER-LANDS, THE: *History*), Antwerp was of commercial importance. It played a considerable part in the distribution throughout western Europe of colonial produce from the Portuguese Indies and from Spanish America. It was also the seat of a notable colony of Italian merchants handling trade between the countries of the North Sea coast and the Mediterranean, while the German Hansa (*see* HANSEATIC LEAGUE) and the English Merchant Adventurers (*q.v.*) had made it the centre of commercial operations between central Europe and the Baltic countries on the one hand and England on the other. The local Antwerp firms had a leading role in international trade till 1585, when the town fell to the Spaniards. The government of the United Provinces then decided to block the estuary of the Scheldt north of Antwerp, so as to make Antwerp's sea trade impossible. This step was intended not only to thwart Spanish policy in the southern Netherlands (*i.e.*, in the future Belgium) but also to promote the trade of Amsterdam.

The Dutch, who already held the island territories of Zeeland, took possession of the left bank of the Scheldt adjacent to Flanders. In 1609 the Twelve Years' Truce between the United Provinces and Spain stipulated that the subjects of both parties could trade freely by sea and river, but in fact the Scheldt remained closed. On the expiry of the truce, war broke out again (1621), and the Dutch seized Sas van Gent in 1644 and Hulst in 1645. Furthermore, the conquest of Maastricht by Prince Frederick Henry for the Dutch in 1632 had made impossible any linking of the Scheldt with the Rhine by way of the Meuse. The Peace of Westphalia (1648), which finally recognized the Dutch conquests, laid down, in its article xiv, that the Scheldt and the seaways leading to it should be closed in favour of the United Provinces; and it even prescribed in article xv that vessels and merchandise leaving or entering the ports of Flanders should be liable to the same dues as those making use of the Scheldt and of the navigable waters specified in article xiv. Flushing, Middelburg, and, above all, Amsterdam were thus assured of keeping Antwerp's former trade, which they had diverted to themselves during the war.

These conditions were confirmed by the Barrier Treaty of Nov. 15, 1715, under which the Austrians, having succeeded to the Spanish inheritance in the southern Netherlands, had to accept from the Dutch the same treatment the Spaniards had received. But meanwhile Ostend, which was linked by a canal to Bruges and to Ghent and to the Scheldt, seemed destined to assume some of the functions of Antwerp. The Ostend Company (*q.v.*), whose capital came mainly from Antwerp, began to trade with India. The Holy Roman emperor Charles VI, however, lent an ear to the remonstrances of the Dutch, who were supported by Great Britain, France, Denmark, Prussia, and Sweden. Under the Treaty of Vienna of March 16, 1731, he suppressed the Ostend Company.

The emperor Joseph II in 1780 tried to profit from the decline of the Dutch Republic and occupied some of the forts along the canal from Bruges to Sluis. Next, at the Brussels Conference of May 1784, he demanded that the Dutch should evacuate the forts on the lower Scheldt and grant freedom of navigation; and later he declared that what he chiefly desired was the opening of the Scheldt and the reestablishment of the Indies trade, with Antwerp as a free port. He sent a small warship down the Scheldt, but when the Dutch opened fire on it he did not press the action and, finally, accepted French mediation, which, in effect, maintained the *status quo* by the Treaty of Fontainebleau (Nov. 8, 1785).

France's conquest of Belgium in the French Revolutionary Wars (*q.v.*) led to the Treaty of The Hague (May 16, 1795), whereby the Dutch ceded the left bank of the Scheldt to France

and opened not only the Scheldt but also the Rhine and the Meuse to the ships of all friendly nations. For a few years after the Peace of Amiens (1802), Antwerp enjoyed a period of prosperity; but after the inauguration of Napoleon's Continental System the Scheldt estuary was closed again by the British fleet in its retaliatory blockade of the European ports (*see* NAPOLEONIC WARS).

On the downfall of Napoleon, the Treaty of Paris of May 30, 1814, incorporated Belgium with the Kingdom of the Netherlands and once again opened the Scheldt to free navigation. Immediately the rivalry of Amsterdam made itself felt, at any rate until Dutch firms had set up branches of their own in Antwerp.

The Belgian revolution of 1830 produced fresh complications. The Treaty of 24 Articles, accepted by Belgium on Nov. 15, 1831, laid down that shipping proceeding to Antwerp should pay moderate pilotage dues, but the Dutch refused to acknowledge Belgium's independence till 1839. On April 19, 1839, the Dutch government agreed to accept a toll of 1.50 florins per ton on ships proceeding to and coming from Antwerp. The Belgian government assumed responsibility for this payment.

The rapid growth of the Antwerp traffic brought the amount of payments to a total burdensome for the Belgian treasury. Finally Auguste Lambermont was authorized to negotiate with the Dutch for the abolition of the toll; and on May 12, 1863, a convention was signed at The Hague settling the terms on which the obligations were to be redeemed. The other interested powers confirmed the convention in Brussels in July, and a sum of 32,276,566 francs was paid to the Dutch, Belgium contributing 12,000,000.

There remained some secondary issues between the Kingdom of the Netherlands and Belgium. The solution for some of them was found after World War I; others were settled after World War II. Benelux (*q.v.*) simplified the negotiations which economic development and technical progress still occasionally necessitated.

See A. Pierrard, *La Question de l'Escaut de 1648 à 1930* (1930); S. T. Bindoff, *The Scheldt Question to 1839* (1945).   (C. VE.)

SCHELER, MAX (1874–1928), German philosopher, born in Munich on Aug. 22, 1874, began teaching philosophy at Jena in 1902, when he had already come under the influence of Edmund Husserl (*q.v.*). From 1907 to 1910 he taught at Munich. Finally, after some work for the German foreign office in Geneva (1917) and at The Hague (1918), he was in 1919 appointed professor of philosophy at Cologne. He died at Frankfurt am Main on May 19, 1928.

Throughout his work Scheler's method is phenomenological, that is to say, he tries to discover what is essentially involved in mental attitudes and their objects; he differs from Husserl in his readiness to accord an independently real status to the objects of such attitudes.

In ethics Scheler's main work is *Der Formalismus in der Ethik und die materiale Wertethik* (Halle, 1913–16), in which, after severely criticizing the formalistic ethics of Kant, he pleads for a teleological ethics of value not unlike British ideal utilitarianism. Values are ranged in an objective order of higher and lower, which are presented a priori through our feelings: Scheler builds largely on Pascal's "order" or "logic of the heart." In philosophical psychology Scheler's most interesting work is *Wesen und Formen der Sympathie* (1923; Eng. trans. by P. Heath as *The Nature of Sympathy*, 1954). In the work entitled *Vom Ewigen im Menschen* (1921) Scheler gives a penetrating analysis of the religious consciousness (called by him the "religious act") and of the kind of object to which it is essentially directed; *i.e.*, an object self-sufficient, all-performing, holy, etc. The theistic flavour of this work yields to a more pantheistic attitude in the later *Die Stellung des Menschen im Kosmos* (1927, 1928). Scheler's principal contribution to philosophical sociology is *Die Wissensformen und die Gesellschaft* (1926), where he passes criticism and attempts to improve on Marxist and Comtist accounts of the relation of ideas and beliefs to social structure and development.

See the collected *Werke* (1954–   ); also the special issue of *Philosophy and Phenomenological Research*, vol. 2, no. 3 (1942), devoted to Scheler.   (J. N. F.)

SCHELLING, FRIEDRICH WILHELM JOSEPH VON (1775–1854), German philosopher who, following a departure from Fichte's ethical philosophy, formulated a system of metaphysics based on the philosophy of nature. He was born on Jan. 27, 1775, at Leonberg, a small town of Württemberg. He was educated at the cloister school of Bebenhausen, near Tübingen, where his father, an able orientalist, was chaplain and professor. In 1790 he entered the theological seminary at Tübingen. Among his (elder) contemporaries were Hegel and Hölderlin. He shared in the revolutionary sentiments common among his fellow students. In 1792 he graduated. Meanwhile he was a close student of Kant, Fichte and Spinoza, more especially of Fichte. Schelling had no sooner grasped the leading ideas of Fichte's amended form of the critical philosophy than he put together his impressions of it in his *Über die Möglichkeit einer Philosophie überhaupt* (Tübingen, 1795). The more elaborate work, *Vom Ich als Prinzip der Philosophie, oder über das Unbedingte im menschlichen Wissen* (Tübingen, 1795), while remaining within the limits of the Fichtean idealism, exhibits a tendency to give the Fichtean method a more objective application and to amalgamate with it Spinoza's more realistic view.

After two years as tutor to two youths of noble family, Schelling was called as extraordinary professor of philosophy to Jena, the centre of the poets and philosophers of the Romantic school, in midsummer 1798. He had already contributed articles and reviews to F. I. Niethammer's *Philosophisches Journal* (Neustrelitz, 1795–96; Jena, 1797–98), to which his *Philosophische Briefe über Dogmatismus und Kritizismus* (a critique of the ultimate issues of the Kantian system) and his *Neue Deduction des Naturrechts* (the composition of which, in 1795, to some extent anticipated Fichte's *Grundlage des Naturrechts*) had been sent. His studies of physical science bore rapid fruit in his *Ideen zu einer Philosophie der Natur* (Leipzig, 1797) and in the treatise *Von der Weltseele* (Hamburg, 1798); and these were followed by his *Erster Entwurf eines Systems der Naturphilosophie* (Jena and Leipzig, 1799), by the *Einleitung zu dem Entwurf eines Systems der Naturphilosophie* (Jena and Leipzig, 1799), by the *System des transzendentalen Idealismus* (Tübingen, 1800), by the *Darstellung meines Systems der Philosophie* (in the *Zeitschrift für spekulative Physik*, ii, Jena, 1801), by *Bruno, oder über das natürliche und göttliche Prinzip der Dinge* (Berlin, 1802) and by the *Vorlesungen über die Methode des akademischen Studiums* (Tübingen, 1803). The philosophical renown of Jena was at its height during Schelling's years of residence there (1798–1803). His intellectual sympathies, moreover, united him closely with some of the most active literary tendencies of the time. With Goethe he was on excellent terms, but he was repelled by Schiller's less speculative philosophy. In Schelling, essentially a self-conscious genius, eager and rash, yet with undeniable power, the Romanticists hailed a personality of the true Romantic type. With August Wilhelm von Schlegel and his wife Caroline, herself the embodiment of the Romantic spirit, Schelling's relations were close, and a marriage between Schelling and Caroline's young daughter by a previous marriage, Auguste Böhmer, was perhaps contemplated by both. Auguste's death in 1800 drew Schelling and Caroline together. Schlegel divorced his wife, and in June 1803 she married Schelling. This marriage marks the end of Schelling's life at Jena.

From 1803 to 1806 Schelling was professor at the new university of Würzburg. In 1804 he published the essay *Philosophie und Religion* (Tübingen). During this period, however, he not only broke with Fichte and with Hegel but also embroiled himself with his colleagues and with the government. In 1806, then, he moved to Munich, where he was to remain until 1841. There

DRAWING BY FRANZ KRÜGER (1797–1857); PHOTO, THE GRANGER COLLECTION

FRIEDRICH VON SCHELLING

Schelling enjoyed ease and leisure, thanks to state appointments: he was made an associate of the academy of sciences, secretary of the academy of arts and then secretary of the academy of sciences. These appointments did not prevent his lecturing for a short time at Stuttgart and annually at Erlangen (1820–26). Finally, in 1827, he became professor at Munich. Caroline's death (1809) was followed by his marriage in 1812 to one of her closest friends, Pauline Gotter, in whom he found a faithful companion.

The early years of Schelling's Munich period were marked by several publications. The aphorisms on *Naturphilosophie* in the *Jahrbücher der Medicin als Wissenschaft* (Tübingen, 1806–08) are for the most part extracts from lectures delivered at Würzburg; but the treatise *Über das Verhältniss der bildenden Künste zu der Natur* (Munich, 1807; Eng. trans. by A. Johnson, *The Philosophy of Art*, London, 1845) and the *Philosophische Untersuchungen über das Wesen der menschlichen Freiheit* (first published in *Philosophische Schriften*, Landshut, 1809; Eng. trans. by J. Gutmann, *Of Human Freedom*, Chicago, 1936) represent interesting developments in his thought. Subsequently, however, his literary activity came gradually to a standstill. The *Denkmal der Schrift von den göttlichen Dingen des Herrn F. H. Jacobi* (Tübingen, 1812) was called forth by the incident of Jacobi's book. The tract *Über die Gottheiten von Samothrake* (Stuttgart and Tübingen, 1815) was ostensibly part of a great work, *Die Weltalter*, which was frequently announced as ready for publication but which was never finished (*cf.* the fragment trans. by F. de Wolfe Bolman, *The Ages of the World*, New York, 1942).

The dominance of Hegel in the German schools appears to have silenced Schelling. It was only in 1834, after the death of Hegel, that, in a preface to a translation of a work by Cousin, he expressed in writing the antagonism in which he stood to the Hegelian and to his own earlier conceptions of philosophy. The antagonism certainly was not new: it was evidenced in his Erlangen lectures of 1822 on the history of philosophy (*Sämmtliche Werke*, x, 124–125); and Schelling had already begun the treatment of mythology and religion which in his view constituted the true positive complement to the negative of logical or speculative philosophy. The writings of D. F. Strauss, L. Feuerbach and other members of the Hegelian left having alarmed the religious element, Frederick William IV invited Schelling to Berlin in 1841 in the hope that he would lecture at the university and counteract the Hegelians. But the latter were too strongly entrenched, and in 1845 Schelling ceased to lecture. No authentic information as to the nature of the new positive philosophy was made generally available till after Schelling's death, which took place on Aug. 20, 1854, at Ragaz. His Berlin lectures were then printed in the first four volumes (1856–58) of the 2nd section of his collected works, setting forth his "philosophy of mythology" and his "philosophy of revelation."

Philosophy.—Schelling indicated the turning points of his philosophical career as follows: (1) the transition from Fichte's method to the more objective conception of nature—the advance, in other words, to *Naturphilosophie;* (2) the definite formulation, in the *Identitätsphilosophie*, of that which implicitly, as Schelling claims, was involved in the idea of *Naturphilosophie,* that is to say the thought of the identical, indifferent, absolute substratum of both nature and spirit; (3) the opposition of negative and positive philosophy, an opposition which is the theme of the Berlin lectures, though its germs may be traced back to 1804.

Schelling's philosophy of nature, though first conceived as a supplement to Fichte's mainly ethical position, soon developed into an entirely different outlook. Whereas Fichte's *Wissenschaftslehre* made the knowing and willing subject the centre of existence altogether, Schelling emphasized the self-existence of the objective world. Nature is not to be understood only from the perspective of empirical observation and scientific theory; it is rather a reality of its own which speculative or intellectual intuition has to interpret. Such an interpretation discloses that nature is a universal organism endowed with a world soul, as Plato taught. In nature as in the human ego the same original tendencies operate: the one finite and material, the other infinite and ideal.

In his system of transcendental idealism (1800) Schelling tried to unite his philosophy of nature with epistemology and ethics, the objective and the subjective aspect of speculation. He subordinated nature to mind, but he denied that morality is the zenith of subjective activity (as Kant and Fichte had assumed). Mind reaches its consummation rather in the creative act of the artist. On the one hand, the genius works as nature does, but consciously and intentionally; on the other, nature works as the genius, but unconsciously and unintentionally. This magnificent solution of the basic problem of reconciling nature and mind to one another corresponded best to the Romantic spirit of the epoch.

But impressive and fascinating as the solution was, it could not fully satisfy the thinking intellect just because it was too Romantic and not rational enough. In 1801 Hegel began his academic career in Jena, and it was probably under the influence of Hegel's more rational thinking that Schelling hastily conceived of a new scheme in which he concentrated upon the original identity of the opposites, the finite and the infinite, the objective and the subjective, the real and the ideal. This identical ground cannot be comprehended in itself, but can be known indirectly by the relative balance of the antagonistic polarity in both the objective and the subjective sphere open to our experience. This scheme was not carried out, but remained a sketch.

The objective tendency, which was dominant in Schelling, soon led him to a Platonic conception of the subjective sphere: he renewed the time-honoured doctrine of the ideas. But the ultimate unity out of which the opposites arise could not be expounded unless the realm of the ideas was understood as being the origin of the finite self and the finite world. Schelling took a new step in 1804 when he wrote his essay *Philosophie und Religion* in order to explain this most hidden relation. Like Coleridge, he longed "to know metaphysically the Spirit of God." The ideas have their absolute unity in that spirit. But since it is the nature of the ideas to be both necessary (objective) and free (subjective), they are able to fall away from their origin and centre. This defection is possible because of the absolute freedom of the ideas; but for the same reason it cannot be accounted for. Schelling here renews the doctrine of Origen. Slowly he is going back to Christian speculation. Through debasing themselves the ideas transform themselves into the phenomenal world in which we live. The original unity of ideas and God can be restored only through the return of man to his creator.

These half-religious, half-speculative conceptions were further modified under the influence of the Catholic Romantic F. X. von Baader (who in turn was inspired by Jakob Böhme) in Schelling's work on human freedom (1809). Schelling now carried the ground of the apostasy of the ideas back into the nature of God himself: in God there is an original abyss, a kind of absolute and non-rational will, which is the ultimate source of the independence and contingency of the finite world, or of its existence in contrast to its divine essence. But the final and definitive form of Schelling's speculation was gained only in the Berlin lectures.

According to these lectures, God cannot be known by any speculative effort whatsoever ("negative philosophy"): God has to be experienced. This position Schelling calls metaphysical empiricism. The experience of the absolute ground of all things is impossible apart from the self-manifestation of God. We learn his nature from the history of myth and revelation, which is at the same time God's own spiritual history ("positive philosophy"), culminating in the Incarnation and Resurrection of Christ. These lectures, which, as has been said, had no success when Schelling delivered them, were to arouse the interest of existentialists in the 20th century.

BIBLIOGRAPHY.—Collected editions are *F. W. J. von Schellings Sämmtliche Werke,* ed. by K. F. A. von Schelling, in 2 sections, 10 vol. and 4 vol. (1856–61); and the *Werke,* ed. by M. Schröter, 6 vol. (1927–28). The Munich lectures were ed. by A. Drews (1902). For selected letters *see* G. L. Plitt (ed.), *Aus Schellings Leben: in Briefen,* 3 vol. (1869–70). *See* further Kuno Fischer, *Geschichte der neueren Philosophie,* 4th ed., vol. vii (1923), particularly for biography; also K. Rosenkranz, *Schelling* (1843); L. Noack, *Schelling und die Philosophie der Romantik,* 2 vol. (1859); Constantin Frantz, *Schellings positive Philosophie,* 3 vol. (1879–80); John Watson, *Schelling's Transcendental Idealism* (1882); E. von Hartmann, *Schellings philosophisches* *System* (1897); V. Delbos, *De posteriore Schellingii philosophia quatenus Hegelianae doctrinae adversatur* (1902); G. Mehlis, *Schellings Geschichtsphilosophie in den Jahren 1799–1804* (1907); G. Schneeberger, *F. W. J. von Schelling* (1954); H. Fuhrmans, *Schellings Philosophie der Weltalter* (1954); K. Jaspers, *Schelling: Grösse und Verhängnis* (1955).   (R. KR.)

SCHENDEL, ARTHUR FRANÇOIS ÉMILE VAN (1874–1946), Dutch novelist, and one of the most important and most personal Dutch prose-writers of his time. Born on March 5, 1874, in Batavia (now Djakarta, Indonesia), he spent his youth in Haarlem, The Hague, and Amsterdam. He studied English language and literature and taught in England before becoming a writer in the Netherlands. From 1920 he lived in Italy, returning after World War II to Amsterdam, where he died on Sept. 13, 1946. He attracted attention with his first novel, *Drogon* (1896), which dealt with the period of the Crusades. His main theme in his 25 novels and many collections of short stories is the lonely but self-sufficient human being who, in his search for happiness, is constantly the victim of fate, a theme which first took shape in stories about medieval Italy: *Een Zwerver verliefd* ("A Wanderer in Love," 1904; French trans. *Le vagabond amoureux,* 1923), *Een Zwerver verdwaald* ("A Lost Wanderer," 1907), *De berg van droomen* ("The Mountain of Dreams," 1913), *Der liefde bloesems* ("The Blossoms of Love," 1921). His later works are less poetical and more realistic: the fight against fate is manfully accepted, although defeat is inevitable. The best-known are *Het Fregatschip Johanna Maria* (1930; Eng. trans. *The "Johanna Maria,"* 1935), *Een Hollandsch drama* (1935; Eng. trans. *The House in Haarlem,* 1940), *De grauwe vogels* (1937; Eng. trans. *Grey Birds,* 1939), *De wereld een dansfeest* ("The World a Dance," 1938), and *Het oude huis* ("The Old House," 1946). Van Schendel also wrote essays on Shakespeare (1910) and a biography of Paul Verlaine (1927).

See G. H.'s-Gravesande, *A. van Schendel, zijn leven en werk* (1949).
                                            (GD. W. Hs.)

SCHENECTADY, a city of New York, U.S., is located 16 mi. (25 km.) N.W. of Albany on the Mohawk River, the seat of Schenectady County. It was established in 1661 when the Mohawk Indians sold the title to the wide, flat river plain immediately above the falls of the river to Arent van Curler and his associates. The site was only 14 mi. (23 km.) by easy portage from the seaport of Albany; the place name is of Indian origin. In 1690 the little village was virtually extinguished by the Schenectady massacre, occurring when a war party of French and Indians walked by the snowmen which the overconfident citizens had erected as sentries. About 1700 there was an influx of English settlers. Schenectady was chartered as a borough in 1765 and as a city in 1798. Its location on the portage between the Hudson and Mohawk rivers assured it of a prosperous business in the transshipment of goods. In the period after the American Revolution a vast tide of New England immigrants moved into the Mohawk Valley, and Schenectady, being the transfer point, was further stimulated by new business. With the opening of the Erie Canal in 1825, however, the canal boats carried their cargoes directly into Albany, and Schenectady suffered a decline. Recovery began with the manufacture of brooms and brushes during the next decade.

New forms of transportation and industry came to Schenectady when the Mohawk and Hudson Railroad began to operate in 1831. The railroad was a forerunner of the New York Central, and the consequent demand for locomotives led to the establishment of the Schenectady Locomotive Works in 1848. This firm, which has built tanks as well as steam and diesel locomotives, became the American Locomotive Company (later Alco Products, Inc.) in 1901.

In 1886 the Edison Machine Works were moved to Schenectady and in 1892 mergers created the General Electric Company, with its main administrative offices there and, later, plants manufacturing gas turbines, motor generators, and electronic equipment, and experimental laboratories which provided research facilities for many famous scientists, including Charles Steinmetz, Willis Whitney, William David Coolidge, and Irving Langmuir. The Atomic Energy Commission's Knolls Atomic Power Laboratory, established to provide facilities for the investigation of uses of nuclear power, and its nearby establishment at West Milton, Saratoga county, are operated by the company. Other manufactures include varnish, mica products, wire and cable equipment, and athletic and sporting goods.

Union College, a private liberal arts college for men, established in 1795, is in Schenectady; the college and its affiliated professional schools in Albany form Union University.

The city has a council-manager form of government, in effect since 1936.

The population of Schenectady in 1960 was 81,682 (for comparative population figures *see* table in NEW YORK: *Population*). It is a part of the Albany-Schenectady-Troy standard metropolitan statistical area (*see* ALBANY). (H. S. PR.)

SCHERZO, the name of a musical form, means, in Italian, a jest or caprice. Humour is, however, not always a characteristic of this form. The *Scherzi musicali* (1607) of Monteverdi are canzonets which are bright rather than humorous, and in 1614 religious pieces were published in Rome under the title *Scherzi sacri*. The term acquired a new meaning in the sonatas, quartets, and symphonies of the 19th century, principally those of Beethoven. In these works the scherzo was a development of the 18-century minuet, which in fact had already acquired some of the characteristics of the scherzo. Several of the minuets of Haydn, in both his quartets and his symphonies, use reiterated or abrupt rhythms which are foreign to the stately nature of the minuet and which anticipate the gruesome humour of the Beethoven type of scherzo. In the set of six quartets, Op. 33, known as "Gli scherzi," Haydn actually uses the term scherzo in place of minuet.

The distinguishing feature of the 19th-century symphonic scherzo is that it is in rapid $\frac{3}{4}$ time, with elements of surprise in dynamics and orchestration. The solo drumbeats in the scherzo of Beethoven's Ninth Symphony form one of the most dramatic effects in this form. Frequently the playfulness of the Beethoven scherzo is designed to conceal an underlying dramatic tension. In the Fifth Symphony the theme of the jubilant scherzo is used as a bridge passage expressing a mood of terror. Other composers who developed the symphonic scherzo were Schubert and Bruckner. In sonatas and symphonies the scherzo is usually followed by a trio, a piece in a slower tempo, with a repeat of the opening scherzo according to the scheme ABA.

In the 19th century the scherzo was also an independent instrumental or orchestral movement in a vivacious, airy style. The masters of this animated type of scherzo were Weber, Berlioz, and Mendelssohn. Brilliant effects of orchestration and exhilarating, pointed rhythms in a swift tempo mark such virtuoso works of this kind as Berlioz's *Queen Mab* scherzo and Mendelssohn's scherzo from his *Midsummer Night's Dream* music. Mendelssohn's chamber works, particularly the octet, the two piano trios, and the two string quintets, contain remarkable examples of the light, swift-moving scherzo.

In the symphonies and instrumental works of Schumann the scherzos have a lyrical or a nostalgic nature, and they are frequently combined with two trios. Brahms, in his symphonies and chamber music, similarly conceived the scherzo as a movement with dark undertones. The four scherzos of Chopin are in a class by themselves. His use of the term appears to be purely arbitrary, unless it was meant to convey an element of ironic humour at the core of such highly romantic works. In later romantic music one of the most successful examples of the form is Paul Dukas' *Sorcerer's Apprentice*, described as a "scherzo based on a ballad of Goethe." The scherzo or *scherzando* movements in the symphonies of Mahler combine humour with lugubrious or even diabolic elements. In the scherzo of Mahler's Tenth Symphony these darker elements are so boldly exteriorized as to determine the essential character of the movement. The score of this scherzo bears the inscription, "The devil dances with me. Madness seizes me . . . annihilates me."

SCHEVENINGEN, a fashionable seaside resort and fishing port in South Holland province, Neth., lies on the North Sea coast, 2 mi. (3 km.) N of The Hague, of which it forms a part. Pop. (1964 est.) 38,000. Gently shelving, wide, sandy beaches stretch for miles on each side, and the country's first bathing establishments were set up there in 1818. The recreational centre, Gevers Deijnoot Square, offers many kinds of entertainment. The Holland Festival is held annually in summer, and the place is a centre for international conventions. The harbours to the south shelter most of the Dutch herring fleet; the Fish Auction Hall is the leading one in Europe and herring is widely exported. *See* also HAGUE, THE. (D. P. M.; C. A. P. P.)

SCHIAPARELLI, GIOVANNI VIRGINIO (1835–1910), Italian astronomer and senator of the kingdom of Italy who possessed exceptional powers as an observer of stars, was born March 14, 1835, at Savigliano, Piedmont. After graduating from Turin University in 1854, he went to Berlin to study astronomy under J. F. Encke. In 1859 he was appointed assistant observer at Pulkovo in Russia, a post he resigned in 1860 for a similar one at Brera, Milan. In 1862 he succeeded to the directorship at Brera, a position which he held until 1900.

Schiaparelli's first discovery was of the asteroid Hesperia in 1861. In 1866 he showed the connection between meteor streams and cometary orbits, giving, in particular, the identity of the orbits of the Perseids and Comet 1862 III, and of the Leonids and Comet 1866 I. These discoveries were amplified in his *Le Stelle cadenti* (1873) and *Norme per le osservazioni delle stelle cadenti dei bolidi* (1896). He observed double stars, and the results of his measures are published in two volumes, the first containing those made between 1875–85 and the second those between 1886–1900. He also made extensive studies of Mercury, Venus, and Mars. In 1877 he observed on Mars the peculiar markings, which he called *canali*, the nature and origin of which is still controversial. (*See* MARS.) From his observations of Mercury and Venus, Schiaparelli concluded that these planets rotated on their axes in the same amount of time as they revolved about the sun. On his retirement he studied the astronomy of the Hebrews and Babylonians, publishing in 1903 *L'Astronomia nell'Antico Testamento;* Eng. trans. *Astronomy in the Old Testament* (1905). He later published various papers on the same subject, the last being in *Scientia* (1908).

Schiaparelli died at Milan on July 4, 1910.

SCHICHAU, FERDINAND (1814–1896), German engineer and pioneer shipbuilder, was born at Elbing (now Elblag, Pol.), the son of a smith and ironworker, on Jan. 30, 1814. He established his own industrial plant at Elbing in 1837, and was soon employing 8,000 men. He began by making steam engines, hydraulic presses, and industrial machinery, then pioneered in the design and construction of dredgers (1841), and finally turned to the building of ships. His "Borussia," in 1855, was the first screw-vessel constructed in Germany. Schichau began to specialize in building torpedoboats and destroyers at an early date. From 1873 he had the cooperation of Carl H. Ziese, who married his daughter. Ziese introduced compound engines into the first vessels built by Schichau for the German Navy, the gunboats "Habicht" and "Möwe," launched in 1879, and also designed in 1881 the first triple-expansion machinery constructed on the Continent, supplying these engines to the torpedoboats built by Schichau for the German Navy in 1884. In 1889 Schichau established a floating dock and repair shops at Pillau (now Baltisk, U.S.S.R.), and soon afterward, by arrangement with the government, started a large yard at Danzig. He died at Elbing on Jan. 23, 1896.

SCHICKELE, RENÉ (1883–1940), German writer, whose personal experience of conflict between nations made his work an intense plea for peace and understanding, was born in Oberehnheim, Alsace, on Aug. 4, 1883, the son of a German father and a French mother. He was educated in Zabern and Strasbourg, and subsequently lived in Paris and Berlin, working as a journalist and editor of German *avant-garde* periodicals. He had published verse before the appearance of *Der Fremde* (1907), a novel which depicts his central preoccupation, the place of Alsace between the rival powers of France and Germany. During World War I Schickele lived in Switzerland. The play *Hans im Schnakenloch* (1916) depicts the impact of the war upon an Alsatian family. His major work is the novel-trilogy *Das Erbe am Rhein (Maria Cap-*

poni, 1925; *Blick auf die Vogesen*, 1927; *Der Wolf in der Hürde*, 1931), a saga reflecting Alsatian problems before and after World War I. Schickele's last novel, *Die Flaschenpost* (1937), is set in the south of France, where he settled in 1933, after assuming French citizenship. In his approach to the delineation of sexual relationships he found affinities with D. H. Lawrence (on whom he wrote a substantial essay). Schickele died on Jan. 31, 1940, near Nice, France.

See *R. Schickele: Werke in drei Bänden,* ed. by H. Kesten (1959).
(H. M. WA.)

SCHIEDAM, a town and river port in the province of South Holland, Neth., lies 3 mi. (5 km.) W of Rotterdam at the confluence of the Schie and Nieuwe Maas rivers. Pop. (1960) 80,299 (mun.). The buildings of interest include St. John's Church (1335), the 16th-century town hall, the municipal museum of modern art (1786), the exchange (1792), and the ruins of the Mathenesse Castle (1260). There are several recreation grounds and parks.

Schiedam is well known for its manufacture of gin and other liquors. Early in the 20th century several shipyards were established, and Schiedam also developed into an important centre of the iron industry. Manufactures include machinery, anchors and chains, metal tubes, and rivets. There are also tanker cleaning facilities. Schiedam is a rail junction and is connected by motor road with Rotterdam and The Hague. The town was chartered in 1273.
(P. TH. J. K.)

SCHIFF, MORITZ (1823–1896), German physiologist whose most notable work, on the thyroid gland, contributed greatly to the understanding of endocrine functions, was born at Frankfurt am Main on Jan. 28, 1823. He studied medicine at Heidelberg, Berlin, and Göttingen (M.D. 1844), and physiology in Paris with François Magendie and F. A. Longet. Returning to Frankfurt in 1846, he became a consultant in medicine but devoted most of his time to his duties as director of the ornithology section of the Frankfurt Zoological Museum; during this period he published memoirs on South American birds. A man of liberal views, he served as a physician to the insurgents during the Revolution of 1848; as a result, he was not granted the academic position he desired at Göttingen. He became professor of comparative anatomy at Bern in 1854. In 1863 he went to Florence as professor of physiology at the Istituto di Studi Superiori, where he remained until 1876. Opposition, led ostensibly by antivivisectionists, prompted his transfer to Geneva, where he worked and taught until his death on Oct. 6, 1896.

Schiff's work ranged over many fields of physiology: digestive functions, the role of the spleen, motor and sensory activities of nerves and brain centres, the regeneration of nerve structures, etc. Above all, he was a pioneer in the study of internal secretions, through his observations of the effects of experimental removal of the thyroid gland in dogs and the counteracting of these effects by thyroid grafts and the ingestion or injection of thyroid extract—work that foreshadowed the later development of hormonal therapy. He was esteemed by his contemporaries equally for his experimental skill, teaching abilities, and linguistic prowess. Among his many contributions to scientific literature, the most important was his four-volume *Gesammelte Beiträge zur Physiologie* (1894–96).
(R. LE.)

SCHILLER, JOHANN CHRISTOPH FRIEDRICH (1759–1805) (ennobled VON SCHILLER, 1802), one of the greatest German dramatists, poets, and literary theorists, who exemplifies in his life and work the triumph of man's spirit over adverse circumstance. In one of his last letters (April 2, 1805), he said to his friend Wilhelm von Humboldt: "After all, we are both idealists, and should be ashamed to have it said that the material world formed us, instead of being formed by us."

Schiller was born at Marbach on the River Neckar on Nov. 10, 1759, the second child of Lieut. Johann Kaspar Schiller and of his wife Dorothea (née Kodweiss). Johann Kaspar gave his only son a sound grammar school education up to the age of 13; then, in deference to what amounted to a command from his sovereign, the autocratic duke Karl Eugen of Württemberg, he reluctantly agreed to send his boy to the "military academy," an institution

founded and personally supervised by the duke. Against the wishes of the parents, who had hoped to have their son trained for the ministry, the duke decreed that young Friedrich was to prepare for the study of law; later, however, he was allowed to transfer to medicine. Having endured the irksome regimentation at the academy for eight years—during which period he was virtually cut off from his family and the outside world—Schiller left with a medical qualification to take up an appointment as an assistant medical officer (noncommissioned) to a Stuttgart regiment, a post which brought him no prestige and very little pay.

His adolescence under the rule of a petty tyrant confronted

FRIEDRICH SCHILLER, CHALK DRAWING BY FRIEDRICH GEORG WEITSCH, 1804

Schiller with the problem of power, a theme which recurs in most of his plays. His resentment found expression in some of his early poems (published in the *Anthologie auf das Jahr 1782*) and especially in his first play, *Die Räuber* (printed, at his own expense and with borrowed money, in 1781), a stirring Rousseauesque protest against stifling convention and corruption in high places. Its first performance (Jan. 13, 1782) at the National Theatre at Mannheim, in the neighbouring Palatinate, created a sensation and was a milestone in the history of the German theatre. Schiller traveled to Mannheim without leave in order to be present on the first night. When the duke heard of this and of a subsequent secret visit, he sentenced the poet to a

fortnight's detention and forbade him to write any more plays. To escape from this intolerable situation, Schiller decided to cut himself adrift. In the company of a loyal friend, the musician Andreas Streicher, he fled from Stuttgart and made for Mannheim, in the hope of receiving help from Baron von Dalberg, the director of the theatre which had launched his first play. This hope, however, proved illusory. His second play, *Fiesco*, was rejected out of hand; Dalberg kept his embarrassing protégé at arm's length, and for some weeks Schiller led the hand-to-mouth life of a refugee, until he found a temporary refuge with Henriette von Wolzogen, whose sons had been fellow students of his and who invited him to stay at her house at Bauerbach in Thuringia. There he finished his third tragedy, *Kabale und Liebe* (printed 1784), and started work on *Don Carlos.*

On second thoughts, Dalberg eventually offered Schiller an appointment as resident playwright with the Mannheim Theatre. Schiller accepted and had the satisfaction of seeing *Kabale und Liebe* score a resounding success on the stage; but his hopes of clearing his debts and gaining a measure of financial security were doomed to disappointment. When his contract lapsed after a year, it was not renewed, and once again Schiller needed the help of friends to extricate him, both from his financial predicament and from an emotional crisis precipitated by his attachment to a married woman, the charming but unstable Charlotte von Kalb. Four unknown admirers wrote to him from Leipzig and finally invited him to join them there. One of them, Christian Gottfried Körner, became his close and lifelong friend; being a man of some substance, he was able to support Schiller during his two years' stay in Saxony, toward the end of which *Don Carlos*, his first play in blank verse, was published in book form (1787). (Parts of it had previously appeared in Schiller's journal *Thalia*.)

In July 1787 Schiller went to Weimar, then the literary capital of Germany, where he met C. M. Wieland and J. G. Herder. Goethe, who was in Italy at the time, returned to Weimar in the following year. At first Goethe's studied aloofness prevented any close personal contact, but in the long run the older man could not resist the magnetism of Schiller's personality. A chance meeting in 1794 and the ensuing exchange of letters mark the beginning of their friendship, a union of opposites which forms an inspiring chapter in the history of German letters. Their fascinating correspondence is a worthy memorial to a momentous literary partnership. In spite of his initial antipathy, Goethe had recommended Schiller for appointment to a professorship of history (unsalaried) in the University of Jena, Schiller having presented the requisite credentials in his history of the revolt of the Netherlands (*Geschichte des Abfalls der vereinigten Niederlande*, 1788). His history of the Thirty Years' War (*Geschichte des dreissigjährigen Krieges*, 1791–93) further enhanced his prestige as a historian; it also provided him with the material for his greatest drama, *Wallenstein*, published in 1800, and brilliantly translated by Coleridge, who thought it "not unlike Shakespeare's historical plays—a species by itself."

Although Schiller's academic post was unremunerative, he felt sufficiently confident about his prospects to embark upon matrimony: in 1790 he married Charlotte von Lengefeld, a cultured young woman of good family, who bore him two sons and two daughters. Schiller was an affectionate husband and father, and Charlotte proved her devotion in all the trials that lay ahead. In the second year of their married life, Schiller's health gave way under the strain of perpetual overwork. For a time he lay critically ill, and although he rallied after several relapses, he never fully recovered good health. The rest of his life was a losing battle, fought with superb courage, against the inexorable advance of disease. To give him a respite from his financial worries, two Danish patrons—Prince Friedrich Christian of Holstein-Augustenburg and Count Schimmelmann—granted him a generous pension for three years. Schiller decided to devote part of this time to the study of Kant. The encounter with Kant's philosophy produced a series of essays in which Schiller sought to define the character of aesthetic activity, its function in society, and its relation to moral experience—*Über Anmut und Würde* (1793), *Briefe über die ästhetische Erziehung des Menschen* (1795), *Über das Erhabene* (1801)—as well as the essay *Über naive und sentimentalische Dichtung* (1795–96), an attempt to distinguish between two types of poetic creativity. (Like the "Letters on the Aesthetic Education of Man," this celebrated essay first appeared in *Die Horen*, an ambitious but short-lived literary periodical edited by Schiller and published by Johann Friedrich Cotta.) This period of critical stocktaking also produced some exquisite reflective poems: *Das Ideal und das Leben, Der Spaziergang, Die Macht des Gesanges.* In 1797 he wrote a group of ballads (including *Der Handschuh, Der Taucher, Die Kraniche des Ibykus*) which are among his most popular productions. In these poems, and in the famous *Lied von der Glocke*, Schiller shows how to make poetry accessible to the man in the street without debasing it. Popularity, he insists in his review of G. A. Bürger's poems, need not and should not mean pandering to vulgar taste.

In the *Wallenstein* trilogy Schiller had reached the height of his powers as a dramatist. Working against time, he produced four more plays in quick succession (apart from his adaptations of *Macbeth* and of Gozzi's *Turandot* for the German stage, and his fine translation of Racine's *Phèdre*): *Maria Stuart* (completed 1800), *Die Jungfrau von Orleans* (completed 1801), *Die Braut von Messina*, with its important preface, Schiller's last critical pronouncement (completed 1803), and *Wilhelm Tell* (completed 1804). Death overtook him at Weimar (May 9, 1805) while he was working at a new play on a Russian theme, *Demetrius*, which, to judge by the noble fragments that remain, might well have developed into a masterpiece.

At the age of 34, Schiller said in a letter to Goethe: "Now that I have begun to know and to employ my spiritual powers properly, an illness unfortunately threatens to undermine my physical ones . . . . However, I shall do what I can, and when in the end the edifice comes crashing down, I shall perhaps have salvaged what was worth preserving." He was as good as his word. "The idea of freedom," Goethe said to J. P. Eckermann, "assumed a different form as Schiller advanced in his own development and became a different man. In his youth it was physical freedom that preoccupied him and found its way into his works; in later life it was spiritual freedom." Schiller's early tragedies are attacks upon political oppression and the tyranny of social convention; his later plays are concerned with the inward freedom of the soul which enables a man to rise superior to the frailties of the flesh and to the pressure of material conditions; they show the hero torn between the claims of this world and the demands of an eternal moral order, striving to keep his integrity in the conflict. In his reflective poems and in his treatises, Schiller sets out to show how art can help man to attain this inner harmony and how, through the "aesthetic education" of the individual citizen, a happier, more humane social order may develop. His reflections on aesthetics thus link up with his political and historical thinking.

Schiller's thought has sometimes been called escapist, a retreat into an ivory tower, and yet he has also been charged with trying to press art into the service of morality or social reform. Both criticisms are unjust. Nowhere does Schiller advocate an ascetic or cowardly withdrawal from ordinary experience; on the contrary, he boldly faces the problems of modern life: the disintegration of the human personality in a highly mechanized civilization, the loss of individual freedom under forms of government which put a premium on conformity. Nor does he deny the autonomy of art: far from postulating any direct influence of art on private morals or public affairs, he insists that its effect can only be a mediate and long-term one.

One of the most striking features of Schiller's *oeuvre* is its modernity, its startling relevance to the life of the 20th century. Although for a time he fell out of favour with the German intelligentsia, the enduring value of his work is not likely to be obscured by fashions in criticism.

BIBLIOGRAPHY.—Two of the principal modern editions of Schiller's works are the centenary edition, the *Säkularausgabe*, ed. by E. von der Hellen *et al.*. 16 vol. (1904–05), and the *Horenausgabe*, ed. by C. Schüddekopf and C. Höfer, 22 vol. (1910–26), which presents Schiller's *oeuvre*, including most of his letters, in chronological order. The letters were edited by F. Jonas, 7 vol. (1892–96). Supplementary material which has since come to light is incorporated in the comprehensive *Nationalausgabe*, ed. by J. Petersen *et al.*, a major critical edition designed to consist of about 40 vol. (1943–).

Of the many critical biographies *see* Thomas Carlyle, *Life of Friedrich Schiller* (1825), the earliest monograph on Schiller of any lasting value; Jakob Minor, *Schiller*, 2 vol. (1890); Otto Harnack, *Schiller* (1898); Eugen Kühnemann, *Schiller* (1905); Karl Berger, *Schiller*, 2 vol. (1905–09); Herbert Cysarz, *Schiller* (1934); W. Witte, *Schiller* (1949); Melitta Gerhard, *Schiller* (1950); Reinhard Buchwald, *Schiller*, 2 vol., rev. ed. (1953–54); Bernhard Zeller, *Schiller, eine Bildbiographie* (1958), richly illustrated; Gerhard Storz, *Der Dichter Friedrich Schiller* (1959); B. von Wiese, *Schiller* (1959).

Various special aspects of Schiller's work and personality are treated in the following: Ludwig Bellermann, *Schillers Dramen*, 2 vol. (1888–

BY COURTESY OF THE SCHILLER-NATIONALMUSEUM, MARBACH

TITLE PAGES FROM FRIEDRICH SCHILLER'S DRAMA DIE RÄUBER: (LEFT) FIRST EDITION, 1781; (RIGHT) SECOND EDITION, 1782

91); Heinrich Düntzer, *Schillers lyrische Gedichte*, 3rd rev. ed. (1893); *Schillers Gespräche*, ed. by Julius Petersen (1911); Max Hecker, *Schillers Tod und Bestattung* (1935); E. L. Stahl, *Schiller's Drama: Theory and Practice* (1954); Thomas Mann, *Versuch über Schiller* (1955); W. F. Mainland, *Schiller and the Changing Past* (1957); W. Witte, *Schiller and Burns and Other Essays* (1959); *Schiller Bicentenary Lectures*, ed. by F. Norman (1960).

Schiller's style does not readily lend itself to translation into English; most of the existing English versions of his works do not rise above mediocrity. *Wallenstein* is the outstanding exception: *Die Piccolomini* and *Wallensteins Tod* were translated by Coleridge, at a time (December 1799–April 1800) when the poet, who had just returned from his visit to Germany, was still at the height of his powers. Among later contributions, a translation of the *Letters on the Aesthetic Education of Man* by E. M. Wilkinson and L. A. Willoughby deserves to be specially mentioned.

For detailed bibliographical information *see* Wolfgang Vulpius, *Schiller-Bibliographie 1893–1958* (1959), and "Schiller in England" in the *Publications of the English Goethe Society,* vol. xxx (1961).

(W. Wɪ.)

SCHILTBERGER, JOHANN (or Hans) (1380–1440?), Bavarian nobleman and author of the *Reisebuch*, an important record of medieval European history and topography, was born in 1380 near Lohhof, north of Munich. When King Sigismund appealed for assistance in fighting the Turks in Hungary, Schiltberger followed this call. In the Nikopol disaster of Sept. 28, 1396, he was taken prisoner and became a slave. For the next six years he served the sultan and so came to see Asia Minor and Egypt. Taking part in the battle at Ankara on July 20, 1402, when the Turks were defeated by the Tatars, he passed into the possession of the khan Timur and thus saw Samarkand, Armenia and Georgia. Having served several masters, he accompanied a Tatar prince to Siberia and the middle Volga. Later he spent some time in southeastern Russia. Near Batumi he escaped and returned via Constantinople and Kilia and then along the route north of the Carpathians to his Bavarian home which he reached in 1427. He became chamberlain to the duke of Bavaria. The place and time of his death are uncertain.

Of his *Reisebuch*, wherein he described his experiences and the countries he saw, a number of contemporary manuscripts exist. It was first printed at Augsburg *c.* 1460 and there were four other editions in the 15th and six in the 16th century. Of 19th-century editions there are two in German, one in Russian and an English edition by the Hakluyt Society in 1879.

See C. R. Beazley, *The Dawn of Modern Geography,* vol. iii, pp. 356–378, 550 (1906). (K. A. S.)

SCHIMPER, ANDREAS FRANZ WILHELM (1856–1901), German botanist best known for his work on the ecology of tropical plants, was born at Strasbourg on May 12, 1856, a member of a celebrated family of botanists. He received his doctorate at Strasbourg in 1878, and afterward studied under H. A. de Bary. From 1880 to 1881 he was a fellow at Johns Hopkins University. Upon returning to Europe he became *Privatdozent* ("official but unpaid lecturer") and professor (1886) at Bonn Botanical Institute where he remained until 1898. From 1898 to 1901 he was professor at Basel, Switz. Schimper's botanical travels took him to the West Indies (1881, 1882–83), to Brazil (1886), to Ceylon and Java (1889–90), and to the Canary Islands, Cameroons, East Africa, Seychelles, and Sumatra with the "Valdivia" deep-sea expedition (1898–99).

Schimper died on Sept. 9, 1901, at Basel.

Schimper's ecological studies included important papers on epiphytes, strand vegetation, and myrmecophilous plants. His *Pflanzengeographie auf physiologischer Grundlage* (1898; 3rd ed., 1935; English trans., *Plant-Geography upon a Physiological Basis,* 1903) ranks with Johannes Warming's *Plantesamfund* (1895) as one of the foundation works of modern plant ecology. The book is divided into three sections: the first considering factors that affect plant life; the second presenting Schimper's influential classification of world vegetation; and the third containing a systematic account of this vegetation. Schimper was instrumental in the establishment of a truly scientific and comprehensive method of ecological investigation. Apart from ecology, he made significant contributions to other branches of botany. He showed (1881) that starch grains are not formed in cytoplasm as previously maintained, and concluded (1883) that plastids do not arise through anything but the division of preexisting plastids.

See notice on Schimper, with a bibliography, in *Ber. Dtsch. Bot. Ges.,* xix, pp. 54–70 (1901). (J. W. Tt.)

SCHINKEL, KARL FRIEDRICH (1781–1841), German architect and city planner, was born near Brandenburg on March 13, 1781. He studied with Friedrich Gilly and at the Academy of Architecture, Berlin. Two years in Italy, 1803–05, completed his studies.

As state architect of Prussia, Schinkel executed many commissions for King Frederick William III and other members of the royal family. His designs were based on the revival of various historical styles of architecture, his Greek revival buildings including the Royal Theatre, Berlin, 1818–21, and the Altes Museum, Berlin, 1822–30. His design for a monument to Queen Louise, 1810, and the Werdersche Church, Berlin, 1824–30, are two of the earliest Gothic revival designs in Europe. The St. Nicholas Church, Potsdam, 1826–49, is based on Italian Renaissance prototypes. His work as city planner resulted in new boulevards and squares in Berlin. Schinkel also is remembered for his paintings of romantic landscape scenes, stage and scenery designs, and his designs for furniture, decorative ironwork, etc.

Bibliography.—Designs published in *Sammlung architektonischer Entwürfe* (1819–40, 1866), *Werke der höheren Baukunst* (1840–42, 1878). Complete bibliography in P. O. Rave, *K. F. Schinkel* (1935). *See* also "K. F. Schinkel, Das Lebenswerk" series by various authors, ed. by Rave (1942–56). (E. B. MacD.)

SCHISM, a term commonly applied to breaches of the unity of the Christian Church. In I Cor. 1:10 and 11:18 the term is used (translated "division" or "dissension") to refer simply to parties or factions within the local congregation, but it soon came to be employed more technically where groups broke communion with each other, establishing rival "churches," in particular when the division was not caused by disagreement over fundamental doctrine. Hence the formulation "heresy is sin against truth, schism sin against charity." Roman Catholic canon law defines a schismatic as a baptized person who, while continuing to call himself a Christian, refuses submission to the supreme pontiff or fellowship with the members of the church subject to him (canon 1325). Other churches have similarly defined schism juridically in terms of separation from their own communions. The underlying theological issues are difficult and controversial.

Estimates of the nature and consequences of schism necessarily vary with different conceptions of the church. Where it is held that the church's unity is not only spiritual but also visible, historical, and organizational—in the sense that there must exist according to the divine law one communion, and one only, which is the true church of Christ—a schismatic body is considered to have gone out of the church without impairing the unity and unicity of the church; Roman Catholicism and Eastern Orthodoxy maintain this view in principle. Protestant churches normally hold that schism exists (though it should not) within the visible church; denominations which are out of communion with one another may yet be within (or parts or expressions of) the one catholic church of the creed, provided that they possess the essential marks of the church. Controversy may then turn upon these marks. Again, those who, like many Anglicans, believe episcopacy in apostolic succession (*q.v.*) to be essential to the existence of the church, hold—logically, though they may not wish to draw the conclusion—that schism exists within the church between the separated episcopal churches; the nonepiscopal bodies are sects or schisms from, and outside, the one church, though they may approximate in varying degrees to it and may benefit from the Christian truths and institutions they possess.

In the early church it was usually taught (classically by the 3rd-century bishop St. Cyprian) that the visible unity of the one historic church is intrinsically unbreakable and that schismatic bodies, being by definition outside it, are deprived of all the benefits of Christianity: the Holy Spirit does not work within them, they have no ministry or sacraments and cannot mediate salvation. Cyprian believed that all schisms must quickly wither away. Gradually, and especially through the teaching of Augustine against the schismatic, puritan Donatists, there emerged a theology of schismatic ministries and sacraments outside the church, valid but still not efficacious in regard to salvation. Thus a person baptized in schism need not be rebaptized, though he cannot enjoy the spiritual benefits of baptism until he is united with the church; and so with ordination. The Augustinian theology was generally adopted in the West and it remains influential, though its inner inconsistency subsequently led to modifications in the direction of conceding efficacy as well as validity to ministries outside the church. Roman Catholicism and Orthodoxy tend to allow the efficacy of each other's sacraments. Catholicism acknowledges the efficacy of Protestant baptism when it is properly administered in good faith. Anglicans frequently recognize the efficacy, even when they deny the validity, of nonepiscopal ministries. Sometimes the concept of validity is questioned, and the acknowledgment of ministerial and sacramental efficacy is taken to involve the recognition of other bodies as true churches; or, conversely, the recognition of bodies as churches on the ground of their Christian faith and life in general is held to involve the acceptance of their ministries even if they are not in the apostolic succession as understood in the early or medieval church. Much modern discussion is therefore concerned with the relations (*e.g.*, of intercommunion) properly allowable between bodies which, though now in schism, are seeking visible unity and acknowledge one another to be churches, however imperfect, within the one catholic church.

Schisms have occurred for many secular reasons, personal, sociological, political. A frequent ecclesiastical cause has been the exercise of discipline, arising from the tension between a rigorist or puritan conception of the church, which must be kept holy by the expulsion of grave sinners, and a more comprehensive notion of it as the totality of the baptized and a school for sinners. Early examples of rigorist schisms are Novatianism and Donatism, and there are many perfectionist sects today. The "separated" Monophysite and Nestorian churches of the East originated in doctrinal controversy, but nontheological factors were also influential, as they were in the major schism between the Greek and Latin churches. The "great schism" in the West turned on rival claims to the papacy (*q.v.*) in the 14th century.

For some centuries the theological issues raised by the East-West schism were obscured, since similarity in structure and belief kept alive the hope that the breach, considered as a temporary division within the church, might soon be healed. Since the Reformation the problems, both theoretical and practical, have become more acute, particularly through the obviously splintering tendencies of Protestantism and the rapid spread of a multiform denominationalism over the world during the 19th century. In the 20th century the sinfulness of disunity, as well as the harm which it does to the mission of the church in the world, has been more deeply felt and more openly confessed. In view of the activities of the ecumenical movement (*q.v.*) and the Second Vatican Council, the older concepts of what entitles a Christian group to be considered, theologically speaking, a church within the church, and consequently the concepts of the nature and consequences of schism, must be regarded as subject to correction.

See also references under "Schism" in the Index.

BIBLIOGRAPHY.—T. A. Lacey, *Unity and Schism* (1918); A. C. Headlam, *The Doctrine of the Church and Reunion* (1920); S. L. Greenslade, *Schism in the Early Church,* 2nd ed. (1964); B. C. Butler, *The Idea of the Church* (1962); Yves Congar, *Chrétiens en Dialogue* (1964). (S. L. G.)

SCHIST, in geology, a crystalline rock that splits easily. Schists are widely distributed in all major mountain ranges. The ease of splitting is caused by a parallel arrangement of scaly, tabular or prismatic minerals. Nearly all schists are metamorphic rocks, and micas are the most common minerals composing them. Micas are a large family of minerals that have perfect cleavage, and tend to form sheetlike crystals. They are hydrous aluminum silicates with various combinations of iron, magnesium, calcium, manganese, lithium, potassium and sodium. Muscovite (white), biotite (brown to black), chlorite (green) and phlogopite (light brown) are the most common micas. (*See* also MICA.)

Where the earth's crust is being deformed, physicochemical conditions at depths of a few miles are such as to favour the growth of micas as stable minerals in any rock that has the requisite bulk composition. Elevated temperatures, intense shearing of the rock

SCHIST FROM GILPIN COUNTY, COLORADO. SPECIMEN SHOWN HAS BEEN SUBJECTED TO SEVERE FOLDING

fabric and solutions circulating through pore spaces are probably the most important factors. Siliceous ashes or lavas (rhyolite), granitic rocks or shales may be converted to schists if the deformation is intense enough. Basaltic rocks and gabbros may be converted into greenish-gray chlorite schists, or hornblende schists, composed of combinations of the minerals hornblende (a prismatic calcium-magnesium-iron-aluminum silicate), epidote, magnetite, garnet, members of the mica family and other silicates.

However, calcareous shales have a bulk composition similar to that of basalts and gabbros, and can also be converted into chlorite schists or hornblende schists. It may be impossible to determine the parent rock. Igneous rocks high in magnesia and iron but low in silica (peridotites) yield, under metamorphic conditions, aggregates of the fibrous mineral antigorite. Under intensive shear stress, these rocks develop talc and become talc schists. However, certain dolomites (magnesian limestones) may also be metamorphosed to talc or talc-tremolite schists (tremolite is a hydrous calcium-magnesium silicate).

Schists split easily even if mica is a subordinate constituent. Slightly muddy sandstone, metamorphosed and sheared, becomes a quartz-muscovite schist that flakes easily. Slightly muddy limestones turn into calcareous schists, composed of calcite, muscovite, phlogopite or other micas that induce fissility of the rocks. Tabular minerals, such as feldspar, or prismatic minerals like hornblende, tremolite and antigorite may under special conditions arrange themselves in parallel planes and give rise to a crude schistose structure of the rock.

The mineral hematite (ferric oxide) possesses a direction of good cleavage. Larger masses of this mineral, recrystallized under strong shear stress, may slip along the cleavage planes and become schistose (specular hematite, "iron mica"). Some of these rocks contain red jasper beds, and surfaces displaying these scarlet laminae intermixed with the silvery hematite flakes in intricately crumpled beds are extremely beautiful.

Metamorphic processes coarsen the grains of shaly sediments and lead to a series from shale (finest) through slate and phyllite (from the Greek *phyllon,* "leaf, sheet") to schist (coarsest). The grain size of schist averages over one millimetre. If feldspar equals or exceeds the amount of mica, the rock is called a gneiss. Other minerals commonly found in schists are quartz, garnet, tourmaline, feldspar, magnetite, staurolite, hornblende, kyanite, sillimanite, andalusite, epidote and graphite.

The origin and structure of schists discloses many interesting details of rock deformation. Nearly all larger mountain ranges of the earth have gone through a period of preparation during which a major depression in the crust received large volumes of muddy sediment. Subsequently, these large mud-filled depressions have been violently compressed, the strata folded and the folded complex uplifted to form the mountains. At depths of several miles, mud tends to recrystallize into mica aggregates. But simultaneously, the layers are being folded. Thus it can happen that these rocks, having reached their yield strength during the folding, were intimately dissected by slip planes or slip cleavage. If solutions circulate actively along them, the planes will become coated with newly grown mica flakes, extending across the truncated layers of deposition. Along the slip cleavage planes the entire mass of rocks can be further deformed, developing planes of movement unrelated to the layers of deposition. Perhaps some of the longest slip planes in the solid crust of the earth are those that connect major bodies of easily yielding schist.

Unless they contain many nonmicaceous minerals, schists weather readily, and tend to underlie smooth slopes and gentle land forms, yielding fairly good, clayey soils.

Mica crystals in schists are usually too small to be of commercial use. However, the accompanying minerals of some schists (kyanite, sillimanite, andalusite, talc, garnet, graphite and others) are important as raw materials for high-grade ceramic wares, abrasives, lubricants and other nonmetallic mineral industries.

For a more detailed discussion of the metamorphic processes and concepts referred to in this article *see* METAMORPHISM.

(R. BK.)

SCHISTOSOMIASIS (BILHARZIASIS), a group of diseases caused by parasitic microorganisms called blood flukes, produces symptoms primarily referable to the intestine and liver, with associated dysentery, or to the urinary bladder, with passage of blood in the urine.

Japonica (Eastern) schistosomiasis is endemic in Japan, much of China, the Philippines and Celebes. Manson's schistosomiasis (intestinal bilharziasis) occurs in northern Egypt and many other parts of Africa, Yemen and other places in Arabia, Puerto Rico and several islands of the Lesser Antilles, Venezuela, Dutch Guiana, and extensive areas in Brazil. Vesical schistosomiasis (bladder bilharziasis) exists throughout practically all of Africa, the southern tip of Portugal, Cyprus, and the Near East.

Causative Organisms.—These are commonly called blood flukes or schistosomes because they live in the blood vessels of their definitive host. They belong to the Trematoda, a class of flatworms (Platyhelminthes). The adult blood flukes are delicate, elongated organisms about 10 to 25 mm. long. The sexes are separate. The male holds the delicate female in his ventral sex canal during the long period of egg laying. Japonica schistosomiasis is produced by *Schistosoma japonicum*, Manson's schistosomiasis by *S. mansoni* and vesical (or urinary) schistosomiasis by *S. haematobium*. The first two types reside in the mesenteric-portal venous circulation and *S. haematobium* principally in the vesical and pelvic venous plexuses.

Life Cycle.—Eggs deposited by the female worms in the smaller venules contain rapidly maturing ciliated larvae. The larvae secrete digestive substances, aiding the eggs to escape from the blood vessels through the tissues into the lumen of the intestine or urinary bladder. When the fully embryonated eggs reach fresh water they soon hatch and the ciliated larvae (miracidia) actively swim about.

In case there are appropriate species of snails nearby (species of *Oncomelania* for *S. japonicum*, *Planorbis* for *S. mansoni* and *Bulinus* or *Physopsis* for *S. haematobium*), the miracidia attach to and penetrate the soft tissues of the mollusk and transform into simple hollow sacs (sporocysts). Each of these produces several second-generation sporocysts, which in turn give rise to numerous fork-tailed larvae, the cercariae. Broods of mature cercariae escape at frequent intervals from the snail, swim about in the water and, on contact with mammalian skin, become attached and proceed to penetrate the tissues. Man is the only natural host of *S. haematobium;* man and occasionally monkeys are natural hosts of *S. mansoni;* and almost any mammal is susceptible to infection with *S. japonicum*. Before penetrating exposed skin (or mucous membrane) the cercaria drops its tail. Upon reaching a venule it is passively carried to the pulmonary arterioles, slowly squeezes through the capillaries into the pulmonary venules and passes into the systemic circulation. It will survive only if it reaches a mesenteric artery and proceeds through the capillaries into the portal blood vessels, where it feeds on glycogen in the blood plasma and grows. On reaching adolescence the worms work their way against the venous current: *S. japonicum* migrates to the mesenteric vessels draining the small bowel, *S. mansoni* to those draining the large bowel and *S. haematobium* down the inferior mesenteric venules and through the hemorrhoidal and pudendal anastomoses into the vesical venules. In these localities the worms complete maturity and mate, and the females begin to lay eggs.

From skin exposure until egg deposition the minimum time for *S. japonicum* is about 4 weeks, for *S. mansoni* 6 to 7 weeks and for *S. haematobium* 10 to 12 weeks.

Pathogenesis and Symptoms.—There are three recognized clinical stages in schistosomiasis, namely (1) incubation period, (2) acute stage and (3) chronic stage. The incubation period be-

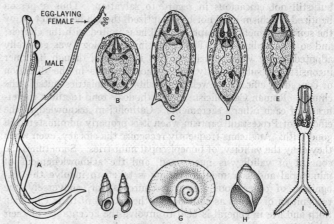

BY COURTESY OF DR. E. C. FAUST

STAGES IN THE DEVELOPMENT OF THE THREE SPECIES OF SCHISTOSOMA RESPONSIBLE FOR SCHISTOSOMIASIS

(A) Adult schistosomes in blood vessels (magnified 2.50 times). (B–D) Mature eggs (X 180): *Schistosoma japonicum, Schistosoma mansoni, Schistosoma haematobium*. (E) Miracidium hatched from egg. (F–H) Snail hosts (X 0.70): Oncomelania (*Schistosoma japonicum*), Planorbis (*Schistosoma mansoni*), Bulinus (*Schistosoma haematobium*). (I) Cercaria (X 90)

gins with the penetration of the cercariae and is terminated when egg deposition begins. During this time and continuing during the life of the worms (20 or more years if the patient survives) the by-products of the worms produce local and systemic irritation of an allergic nature. There is inflammation, increase of certain white blood cells (eosinophilia), a nonproductive cough, late afternoon fever, watery skin eruptions (giant urticaria) and swelling, pain and tenderness of the liver. In the intestinal types (*S. japonicum* and *S. mansoni*), diarrhea occurs toward the end of the incubation period. With the beginning of egg deposition the acute stage of the disease is initiated, resulting from trauma caused by eggs escaping from blood vessels through the tissues into the lumen of the intestine or the urinary bladder, typically accompanied by hemorrhages. As the chronic stage gradually develops, eggs become impacted in the walls of the organs and provoke pseudo-tubercle formation around themselves. This leads to fibrous thickening of the organs, with greatly diminished function. The intestine gradually develops the consistency of an old, nonelastic garden hose, and the bladder becomes impregnated with phosphatic deposits and possesses a gritty surface. Moreover, in the intestinal types, eggs in increasing numbers are carried in the portal current into the liver, filter out and initiate hepatic cirrhosis. This tends to block the flow of blood through the liver, produces abdominal fluid (dropsy) and indirectly causes enlargement of the spleen.

In the vesical type, eggs in the lumen of the bladder become centres for concretions ("stones"); meanwhile the fibrosis extends to the pelvic organs. In all types, eggs are frequently swept through the accessory venous circulation to the lungs where they set up centres of tissue reaction. Occasionally nests of eggs reach the brain and other organs where they produce granulomatous tumours.

Diagnosis and Prognosis.—Diagnosis is accomplished by recovery of the characteristic eggs from the stool or by rectal biopsy (*S. japonicum, S. mansoni*) and from the sediment of the urine or by bladder biopsy (*S. haematobium*).

Prognosis depends on the species of *Schistosoma* involved (*S. japonicum* is most dangerous), on the amount of exposure, on the chronicity of the disease and to a considerable degree on the patient's reactiveness to the infection. Unless exposure is overwhelming, early diagnosis and persistent effective treatment usually provide a good prognosis.

Treatment.—The only drugs consistently proved helpful in the eradication of human blood flukes are the antimony compounds. Potassium antimonyl tartrate (tartar emetic), first employed in 1917, proved on the whole satisfactory, although it must be administered intravenously and is rather poorly tolerated in concentrations higher than 0.5%. Certain synthetic antimonials, particularly stibophen and lithium antimony thiomalate, are administered intramuscularly and are better tolerated, but their cure rate is considerably lower than that of tartar emetic. Miracil D is useful in infection with *S. haematobium*.

Prevention.—There is no immunization against schistosomiasis. Theoretically, education in hygiene and public health measures to keep viable eggs from reaching fresh water constitute first-line prevention. This is impractical, however, both because of social and economic practices and, in *S. japonicum* areas, because the disease would be perpetuated by mammalian hosts. Mass chemotherapy in endemic areas likewise proved unsatisfactory. Concentrated attack on the molluskan host by naturalistic methods and by using copper sulfate in the water was moderately successful in reducing the snail population in endemic spots in Egypt, with a comparable decrease in the incidence of the disease. Molluscicides also showed considerable promise.

See also FLUKE.

BIBLIOGRAPHY.—E. C. Faust, "Schistosomiasis Japonica: Its Clinical Development and Recognition," *Ann. Internal Med.*, 25:585–600 (1946); E. C. Faust *et al.*, "Studies on Schistosomiasis Mansoni in Puerto Rico," *Puerto Rico J. Pub. Hlth and Trop. Med.*, 9:154–168, 228–282, 10:133–254 (1933–35); E. C. Faust and H. E. Meleney, *Studies on Schistosomiasis Japonica* (1924); Rameses Girges, *Schistosomiasis (Bilharziasis)* (1934); E. Koppisch, "Studies on Schistosomiasis in Puerto Rico. Morbid Anatomy of the Disease," *Puerto Rico J. Pub. Hlth and Trop. Med.*, 16:395–455 (1941); R. T. Leiper, *Report on the Results of the Bilharzia Mission in Egypt* (1918).

(E. C. F.)

SCHIZOPHRENIA is a term (replacing the older designation "dementia praecox") used by psychiatrists to indicate a group of mental disorders in which the symptoms occur in varying combinations and with varying degrees of intensity, but generally have in common disturbances of feeling, thought, and relations to the outside world. Neither dementia praecox (which means "early insanity") nor schizophrenia (literally, "splitting of the mind") is entirely satisfactory as a term to cover the various patterns of disturbances usually included in the group. During the 20th century schizophrenia has been considered, at one time or another, either as a single disease entity or a collection of somewhat similar patterns of psychological reactions to life situations.

Types and Symptoms.—Some psychiatrists hold that there are two entirely different kinds of schizophrenia: (1) "process" or "nuclear" schizophrenia, probably based on an organic causation or predisposition, with a poor prognosis, and (2) "reactive" schizophrenia, precipitated by the events of the patient's life and characterized by a relatively mild thought disorder, with a far better prognosis. Others deny the existence of these kinds and retain the traditional division of schizophrenia into four main types, differing in their specific symptomatology, as follows:

1. The "simple" type is characterized mainly by an insidious and gradual reduction in external relations and interests. Emotions are lacking in depth; ideation is simple and refers to concrete things; there is relative absence of activity, a progressive lessening in the use of inner resources, and a retreat to simpler or stereotyped forms of behaviour.

2. The "hebephrenic" type is characterized mainly by shallow and inappropriate emotional responses, foolish or bizarre behaviour, false beliefs (delusions), and false perceptions (hallucinations).

3. The "catatonic" type is characterized by striking motor behaviour. The patient may remain in a state of almost complete immobility, often assuming statuesque positions. Mutism (inability to talk), extreme compliance, and absence of almost all voluntary actions are also common. This state of inactivity is at times preceded or interrupted by episodes of excessive motor activity and excitement, generally of an impulsive, unpredictable kind.

4. The "paranoid" type, which usually arises later in life than the other types, is characterized primarily by unrealistic, illogical thinking, with delusions of persecution or of grandeur, and often by hallucinations. (*See* PARANOID REACTIONS.)

Hallucinations, although not invariably present, are a conspicuous symptom in the hebephrenic and paranoid types. The commonest are auditory: the patient hears voices and believes in their reality. Visual hallucinations are fairly common, especially in

acute episodes. Olfactory and gustatory hallucinations, and abnormal bodily perceptions, occur in a smaller number of cases. (*See also* HALLUCINATION.)

One symptom common to all types, although at times only minimally present and difficult to detect, is a disorder of thought characterized by impairment in the use of abstract concepts (*see* CONCEPT FORMATION, PSYCHOLOGY OF) and a withdrawal into a concrete frame of reference, as the neurologist Kurt Goldstein demonstrated. This disorder in the processes of thinking is neither constant nor irreversible. Especially in the initial stages it may be recognized only in the overt symptomatology or when the patient is in situations that arouse anxiety.

A special type of schizophrenia was first described by Sante de Sanctis, early in the century, under the name of dementia praecocissima; it is now usually called child schizophrenia. Margaret Mahler, who stresses the psychological aspects of this disorder, distinguishes two types of child schizophrenia: one characterized by extreme withdrawal (autistic type), the other by a symbiotic relation with the mother. Most authors, following Lauretta Bender, are inclined to believe that organic abnormalities, as yet undefined, underlie the disorder. In spite of some clinical similarities, it is by no means proved that child schizophrenia and adult schizophrenia are related.

The four adult types of schizophrenia are not mutually exclusive. Mixtures are most frequent in the early, acute phases, but may also occur in later, chronic phases. In these later phases the original symptoms sometimes disappear, and the symptom picture becomes indeterminate. In addition to the mixture of schizophrenic symptoms there may also be a mixture of schizophrenic symptoms with those of other psychoses, notably those of the manic-depressive group; patients exhibiting this combination are described as of a schizo-affective type. (For comparisons of schizophrenic symptoms with those of other mental illnesses *see* PSYCHOLOGY, ABNORMAL; PSYCHOSES.)

Incidence.—Comparable estimates for different countries and even for different parts of a single country are difficult to secure owing to variation of the criteria by which schizophrenia is diagnosed. In the U.S. schizophrenia is considered the most important of the major psychoses; it has been estimated that the number of schizophrenics is between 2.5 and 3 per 1,000 of the general population. However, the number of ambulatory patients who seek outpatient treatment is rapidly increasing, and this estimate may be too conservative. Schizophrenics constitute 20 to 25% of first admissions to U.S. public hospitals for mental disease. Because of the relative youth of patients at admittance—the maximum incidence of first admissions in men comes between the ages of 20 and 24, and in women between the ages of 35 and 39—and the relatively long stay per patient, the group makes up about 47% of the population of psychiatric hospitals. About 45% of schizophrenics who are admitted to public mental hospitals or clinics recover or improve greatly. Of those patients who are committed and improve, about 80% leave the hospital within the first year.

There seems to be some relation between the incidence of schizophrenia and the type of society. An urban society, particularly that of a large city, shows a higher incidence, and an industrial society appears to predispose to the condition more than an agricultural society. It is probable, however, that schizophrenia occurs in all cultures and all societies.

Causation.—Theories of the origin of schizophrenia vary from anatomical and biochemical to psychological and social, from genetic to environmental. The general view is that the schizophrenic types of reaction result from faulty adjustments to a variety of underlying conditions, which may be either physical or psychological, or both.

Psychological Theories.—Emil Kraepelin (1856–1926) was the first to differentiate this disorder from other psychiatric conditions. He called it dementia praecox (a term which had been used by the Belgian psychiatrist B. A. Morel in a more restricted sense) and described the essential characteristics of the disorder. Although Kraepelin considered the origin of the syndrome to be either a degenerative disease of the brain or a metabolic disturbance causing autointoxication, his description and differentiation of the psychological aspects of the disorder were an important contribution. He took a pessimistic view of the disorder and believed that all cases end in a state of permanent and complete dementia.

Eugen Bleuler (1857–1939) offered the conceptual link between Kraepelin's interpretation of schizophrenia and that of Sigmund Freud (*see* below). It was Bleuler who coined the term schizophrenia. By this term he did not mean a split, divided, or double personality, as is popularly believed, but a lack of coordination between various psychological functions. Although he did not discount the view that a toxin might be responsible for the disorder, Bleuler emphasized the importance of the impairment of association of ideas, and he considered most of the symptoms to be a direct or indirect result of this impairment. He was the first to describe the disordered thinking of the schizophrenic; he called this disorder autistic or dereistic.

Adolf Meyer (1866–1950) regarded schizophrenic reactions as disorganizations of thought and behaviour which result from a progressive maladaptation and then become habitual. The background for the progressive disturbances, he believed, might be both physiological and psychological. Meyer insisted on the psychobiological unity of the organism and refused to separate the mental from the physical.

Although Sigmund Freud (1856–1939) was not primarily interested in this psychosis, his psychoanalytic theories and investigations (*see* Psychoanalysis) have clarified many of its aspects. Many schizophrenic symptoms can readily be interpreted as symbolic manifestations; they are often similar in form, content, and motivation to the dreams of normal persons, and therefore are susceptible of psychoanalytic interpretation. The psychoanalytic view emphasizes two common features of schizophrenic behaviour. The regressive symptoms are explained as a retreat to less mature levels of the ego (the reality-testing portion of the psyche); and the restitutive symptoms are attempts to replace the existing world, from which the patient has retreated, by such phenomena as hallucinations, delusions, fantasies of world reconstruction, and peculiarities of language.

Carl Gustav Jung (1875–1961) maintained that schizophrenia is characterized by an unusual strength of the unconscious, so that an abnormal number of atavistic tendencies are not brought into adjustment with modern life. He held that the peculiar symptoms of each case result partly from the patient's past life and partly from a resurgence of the collective unconscious, *i.e.*, of the primordial images, or "archetypes," which have been deposited by the experience of primitive generations.

Harry Stack Sullivan (1892–1949) contended that schizophrenia, like most other mental disorders, is largely attributable to faulty interpersonal relations, especially poor relations between parent and child. Anxiety and lack of self-esteem, originating in these early relations, lead the patient to distort his way of living and issue in a lack of "consensual validation," *i.e.*, an unfavourable attitude on the part of others toward the patient's way of seeing the world, and finally to a schizophrenic panic.

Silvano Arieti (1914–   ) to a large extent accepts Sullivan's dynamic interpretation of schizophrenia. He emphasizes, however, the importance of the special formal mechanisms that express the patient's conflicts and way of life. These mechanisms are most conspicuous in the realm of cognition. The patient adopts a particular form of thinking called by Arieti "paleologic." Paleologic is to a large extent based on E. Von Domarus' principle: namely, whereas the normal person infers identity only on the basis of an identical subject, the schizophrenic, when he thinks in a typically schizophrenic way, infers identity on the basis of identical predicates. For instance, a patient thought she was the Virgin Mary. Asked why, she replied, "I am a virgin, I am the Virgin Mary." The common predicate "being virgin" led to the identification of the two subjects, the Virgin Mary and the patient. By resorting to this type of thinking the patient could deny her feeling of unworthiness and inadequacy and could identify herself with her ideal of feminine perfection. Paleologic thinking, in Arieti's view, is not only a regressive phenomenon but also a psychodynamic or motivational mechanism. He agrees that the schizophrenic proc-

ess may be explained psychosomatically, since intensely disturbing emotions may bring about the resurgence of obsolete functional and neural patterns.

Biological Theories.—A number of investigators, including H. Luxenburger in Germany, E. Essen-Möller in Sweden, F. J. Kallmann in the U.S., and Eliot Slater in Great Britain, have considered inheritance the most important factor in schizophrenia. The incidence of schizophrenia is higher in the families of schizophrenics than in the general population. There has been much controversy about the mode of inheritance. Kallmann believes in a single recessive gene, of limited manifestation; other investigators assume a dominant gene, and still others a multiple mode of inheritance. Recent studies of chromosomes, confirming the hereditary nature of some types of mental deficiency, have failed to indicate specific chromatin abnormality in schizophrenia.

Biochemical studies of this disorder have been stimulated by the experimental use of substances which produce conditions resembling schizophrenia. One of these substances is bulbocapnine, obtained from the ornamental herb *Corydalis cava;* in animals it produces a state similar but not identical to catatonia. Mescaline, from the peyote cactus, and lysergic acid diethylamide (LSD), from ergot, produce in human beings abnormal perceptions and thought disorders similar to those seen in schizophrenia. (*See* Neuropharmacology and Psychopharmacology.)

Great interest has been shown in the fact that a mescalinelike substance, 3,4-dimethoxyphenylethylamine, has been found in the urine of many schizophrenic patients. A dietary origin, however, has not been excluded. The same doubt could be expressed for abnormal indoles (benzopyrrole compounds) which have been found in the urine of some schizophrenics. Abnormalities of carbohydrate metabolism, occasionally found in some cases, are also believed to be the result of secondary factors. R. G. Heath and his collaborators reported the isolation of a specific protein factor from the serum of schizophrenics. This substance, named taraxein, which is believed to be related to ceruloplasmin (the alpha-globulin transporter of copper in blood plasma), is said to produce psychotic symptoms in volunteers, but this has not been adequately confirmed. Some studies have suggested that schizophrenia is related to endocrine and cardiovascular irregularities and to body build (*see* Personality: *Morphological or Physical Types*), but not all psychiatrists accept these findings.

Treatment.—Although at one time there was considerable pessimism about the outlook in schizophrenic cases, this attitude changed markedly from the 1940s onward. Freud himself was skeptical about the value of psychoanalysis in the treatment of psychoses, but this approach has since been applied with certain modifications in the technique. The modifications include the abolition of the psychoanalyst's couch, direct intervention and adoption of the symbolic language of the patient, and less reliance on free association (Freud's method of discovering the patient's unconscious processes from his spontaneous association of one thought with another).

Most patients are treated by physical methods. The most important are: (1) Shock therapy, consisting either of the artificial production of comas by administration of large doses of insulin, or electroconvulsive therapy, consisting of the production of convulsions by electrical shocks (*see* Psychiatry: *Shock Therapy*). (2) Drug therapy, consisting of the administration of large doses of ataractic drugs (so-called tranquilizers), the most important being the phenothiazines; *e.g.*, chlorpromazine (*see* Tranquilizing Drugs). (3) So-called psychosurgery—separation of certain areas of the brain—has been carried out in recalcitrant cases. The commonest operation is prefrontal lobotomy, *i.e.*, cutting the nerve fibres connecting the thalamus with the frontal lobes. Recourse to this operation became fairly frequent in the late 1940s, but eventually less drastic procedures came to be preferred even for the most difficult cases. (*See* also Psychiatry: *Psychosurgery*.)

Although mild cases may be treated outside hospitals, most patients diagnosed as schizophrenics need admission to a hospital, especially during acute episodes. Almost all psychiatric hospitals are equipped to provide the various types of physical treatment, as well as occupational therapy, mentioned above, but only a few provide psychotherapy. In most cases, what is chiefly needed is the provision of a protective environment—one in which the patient can gradually work through his periods of confusion away from the disturbing influences of his own home.

Success varies with the stage of the disease at which treatment is started. If the illness has gone on for long, success is more difficult to attain. Favourable indications are an acute or sudden onset, absence of schizophrenic history in the family, presence of an admixture of symptoms such as those found in manic-depressive states, and the presence of some fairly clear psychological conflict which precipitated the disturbance. Statistical studies of the effects of therapy indicate that shock treatment may be effective in cases with a good outlook, but it is not so successful in schizophrenia as it is in psychotic depressions.

Prevention.—Without a clear-cut understanding of the cause of the illness, specific preventive measures are not available. A number of authorities, influenced largely by psychoanalytic theories, believe that the relations with the family, particularly the mother, during early life play an important role in the development of schizophrenia. Their recommendations for prevention therefore centre largely on providing security for the child through warm, understanding relations in the family (see FAMILY: *Influence of the Family on Individual Personality*).

BIBLIOGRAPHY.—E. Bleuler, *Dementia Praecox; or, The Group of Schizophrenias*, trans. by J. Zinkin (1950); F. Fromm-Reichmann, *Principles of Intensive Psychotherapy* (1950); E. B. Brody and F. C. Redlich (eds.), *Psychotherapy with Schizophrenics* (1952); H. S. Sullivan, *The Interpersonal Theory of Psychiatry* (1953); J. N. Rosen, *Direct Analysis* (1953); F. J. Kallmann, *Heredity in Health and Mental Disorder* (1953); S. Arieti, *Interpretation of Schizophrenia* (1955) and (ed.), *American Handbook of Psychiatry* (1959); M. Sèchehaye, *A New Psychotherapy in Schizophrenia* (1956); D. Richter (ed.), *Schizophrenia: Somatic Aspects* (1957); A. P. Noyes and L. C. Kolb, *Modern Clinical Psychiatry* (1958); L. Bellak and P. K. Benedict (eds.), *Schizophrenia: a Review of the Syndrome* (1958); F. J. Fish, *Schizophrenia* (1962). (S. A.)

SCHLEGEL, AUGUST WILHELM VON (1767–1845), German translator and critic, one of the most influential disseminators of the ideas of the German Romantic movement and the originator of the standard German translation of Shakespeare. He was born on Sept. 8, 1767, in Hanover, the son of a Protestant pastor and nephew of J. E. Schlegel (q.v.). In 1787 he began his studies in Göttingen under C. G. Heyne and G. A. Bürger (qq.v.), who taught classical philology and aesthetics, respectively. In 1791 he took a post as private tutor in Amsterdam but in 1795 accepted an invitation to write for Schiller's periodical *Die Horen* and moved to Jena in 1796. When *Die Horen* ceased publication, Schlegel, together with his brother Friedrich, started a periodical, *Athenäum* (1798–1800), which became the organ of the Romantics, numbering Schleiermacher and Novalis among its contributors. He also wrote for the Jena *Allgemeine Literaturzeitung*, in which he published essays on Goethe's *Römische Elegien* and *Hermann und Dorothea*, which were forerunners in the appreciation of Goethe's mature work. In 1798 Schlegel became extraordinary professor at Jena University. In Jena he also began his long-planned poetical translation of Shakespeare (1797–1810), himself completing 17 plays; the translation was finished by Ludwig Tieck's daughter Dorothea and Graf W. H. Baudissin under Tieck's supervision (1825–33). The Schlegel Shakespeare takes a high place among German literary translations and is undoubtedly his greatest achievement. His unfortunately incomplete translation of Calderón (*Spanisches Theater*, 2 vol., 1803–09) and his other translations from the Romance literatures (*Blumensträusse italienischer, spanischer und portugiesischer Poesie*, 1804) also show his gift for catching the spirit of a foreign work and carrying it over into German.

In 1801 Schlegel went to Berlin, where he lectured on literature and art. Influenced by Herder, he gave a comprehensive survey of the nature and development of European literature and thought, scorning the implications of the concept "Enlightenment" and preaching the Middle Ages and what were for him the Romantics—Dante, Shakespeare, Calderón, and Camões. In 1807 he attracted attention with an attack on Racine's classicism, *Comparaison entre la Phèdre de Racine et celle d'Euripide*.

In 1796 Schlegel had married the brilliant Caroline Michaelis, but in 1803 she left him for the philosopher F. W. J. Schelling. After his divorce Schlegel accompanied Mme de Staël on travels in Germany, Italy, France, and Sweden, and her book *De l'Allemagne* (1813) contains many of his ideas. During his travels, in the spring of 1808, he gave a series of lectures in Vienna (*Über dramatische Kunst und Literatur*, 1809–11; Eng. trans., *Lectures on Dramatic Art and Literature*, 1815), which had a wide influence and were translated into many languages.

In 1813–14 he worked as press secretary to the Swedish crown prince Bernadotte. In 1818 he went to Bonn as professor of literature, where he concentrated largely on Oriental literature. He published the scholarly *Indische Bibliothek* (3 vol., 1820–30) and set up a Sanskrit printing press, in which he printed the Bhagavad Gita, with a Latin translation (1823), and the Ramayana (1829–46). He founded Sanskrit studies in Germany. In 1818, a year after Mme de Staël's death, Schlegel married the daughter of the Heidelberg theologian H. E. G. Paulus but was separated from her in 1819. He died in Bonn on May 12, 1845.

Schlegel's own poetry (*Gedichte*, 1800; *Ion*, a tragedy based on Euripides, 1803; *Poetische Werke*, 1811) shows a sovereign mastery of form but remains no more than cultivated verse. As a critic of poetry he was more empirical and systematic and less speculative than his brother Friedrich (q.v.). Viewing world literature as an organic whole, his literary criticism is sensitively perceptive. He contributed largely to the spread of the fundamental Romantic ideas in Europe. His view of the work of art as an organic symbol had considerable influence on Coleridge, for example. As a translator he is in the first rank.

BIBLIOGRAPHY.—*Sämtliche Werke*, ed. by E. Böcking, 12 vol. (1846–47); *Berliner Vorlesungen*, ed. by J. Minor (1884), and *Bonner Vorlesungen*, ed. by J. Körner (1913), both in *Deutsche Literaturdenkmale*, vol. 17–19 and 147; *Wiener Vorlesungen*, ed. by G. V. Amoretti, 2 vol. (1923); *Briefe von und an A. W. Schlegel*, ed. by J. Körner, 2 vol. (1930); *A. W. Schlegel's Lectures on German Literature*, notes taken in Schlegel's lectures by G. Toynbee, ed. by H. G. Fiedler (1944). See also M. Bernays, *Zur Entstehungsgeschichte des Schlegelschen Shakespeare* (1872); R. Genée, *Schlegel und Shakespeare* (1903); F. Gundolf, *Shakespeare und der deutsche Geist* (1911); J. Körner, *Die Botschaft der deutschen Romantik an Europa* (1929); P. de Pange, *A. W. Schlegel et Mme de Staël* (1938); B. von Brentano, *A. W. Schlegel* (1943); R. Wellek, *History of Modern Criticism*, vol. 2, *The Romantic Age* (1955). (Ar. H.)

SCHLEGEL, FRIEDRICH VON (1772–1829), German writer and critic, the originator of many of the philosophical ideas that inspired the early German Romantic movement (see GERMAN LITERATURE: *The Romantic Movement: First Phase*). He was born in Hanover on March 10, 1772, a younger brother of A. W. von Schlegel (q.v.). He began to study law but soon turned to philosophy, art, and the classics, which he studied at Göttingen and Leipzig. As he was later to show (*Über das Studium der griechischen Poesie*, 1797; the fragmentary *Geschichte der Poesie der Griechen und Römer*, 1798), Greek philosophy and culture were for him as for Schiller the essence of a complete and harmonious education, and he distinguished them clearly from modern psychologically "interesting" and progressive poetry.

In 1796 he joined his brother in Jena, where his criticism of the *Musenalmanach*, and personal incompatibility, soon led to a breach with Schiller. In 1798 the brothers began to publish the quarterly *Athenäum* (in which Friedrich's famous definition of Romantic poetry first appeared). It ran until 1800, and included contributions from Schleiermacher and Novalis; these four formed the group that formulated the Romantic aesthetic. Friedrich Schlegel, the deepest and most philosophical mind of the group, was at this time strongly influenced by the teaching of J. G. Fichte (q.v.), whose transcendental philosophy he transformed into a philosophy of imaginative creation. He developed his conception of the Romantic as the precondition for modern poetry in sharply pointed, paradoxical fragments (aphorisms) and in loosely woven "conversations" and "characteristics," maintaining that poetry should be at once philosophical and mythological, ironic and religious. Goethe's *Wilhelm Meister* became for him the prototype of the universal Romantic novel, and his review of it (in the *Athenäum*) was regarded as a model of critical penetration.

His imaginative work was less successful. His semiautobiographical novel fragment *Lucinde* (1799; Eng. trans. 1913–15) gives a religious significance to love as a physical and spiritual unity but disintegrates in brilliant intermezzi and arabesques. His tragedy *Alarcos* (1802) was a feeble attempt to fuse classical motifs and forms with Romantic elements from Calderón.

In 1801 Schlegel was briefly *Privatdozent* at Jena University, but a restless, difficult life followed. In 1802 he went to Paris, with Dorothea Veit, the eldest daughter of Moses Mendelssohn (*q.v.*) and former wife of Simon Veit, whom she had married in 1783, and who had divorced her in 1798. Schlegel married her in 1804. In Paris he studied Sanskrit, publishing *Über die Sprache und Weisheit der Inder* (1808)—the first attempt at comparative Indo-Germanic linguistics, and the starting point of the study of Indian languages and comparative philology.

In 1808 he and his wife became Roman Catholics, and he turned against his earlier thesis of the unconditional freedom of the individual, uniting his concept of Romanticism with ideas of medieval Christendom. He became the ideological spokesman of the anti-Napoleonic movement for German liberation, and this qualified him for a post as court secretary in the Vienna chancellery (1809). In 1809 he was at the archduke Charles's headquarters, and he helped write the appeal to the German people issued by the archduke. As an Austrian councilor of legation he took part in the Congress of Vienna. In 1820 he became editor of the right-wing Catholic paper *Concordia*, and his attack in it on the beliefs that he had himself earlier cherished led to a breach with his brother, which was never healed.

The two series of lectures that Friedrich gave in Vienna between 1810 and 1812 (*Über die neuere Geschichte*, 1811; Eng. trans. *Lectures on Modern History*, 1849, and *Geschichte der alten und neueren Literatur*, 1815; Eng. trans. *Lectures on the History of Literature*, 1818) show a new conception of history and literature; in them he developed the concept of a "new Middle Ages." During 1803–05 he was editor of *Europa*, a periodical on all the arts; and from 1812 to 1813 of a new periodical, *Deutsches Museum*. In 1828 he lectured at Dresden and died there on Jan. 12, 1829.

Although as an original writer Schlegel's importance is small, as a critic and aesthetic philosopher his achievement is considerable. Open to every new idea, he reveals a rich store of theories and projects in his provocative *Aperçus* and *Fragmente* (contributed to the *Athenäum* and other journals). His theories of creative criticism, his definitions of the Romantic, of irony, of the myth, the arabesque, and the novel, and his conception of a universal, historical, and comparative literary scholarship have had a profound influence on modern literature and criticism, although his ideas were partly communicated through the work of his brother. His wife, Dorothea (1763–1839), wrote an unfinished novel, *Florentin* (vol. i, 1801), published a collection of medieval Romantic poetry (ed. by F. Schlegel, 2 vol., 1804), and translated Mme de Staël's *Corinne* into German (1807–08).

BIBLIOGRAPHY.—*Sämtliche Werke*, 10 vol. (1822–25), augmented ed., 15 vol. (1846); *Schlegels prosaische Jugendschriften, 1794–1802*, ed. by J. Minor, 2 vol. (1882; 2nd ed., 1906); *F. Schlegels Werke*, critical ed. by E. Behler, with H. Eichner and J. J. Anstett, 22 vol. planned (1958–); *Briefe von und an F. und D. Schlegel* (1926), and *Krisenjahre der Frühromantik: Briefe aus dem Schlegelkreis*, 2 vol. (1936–37), Commentary (1958), both ed. by J. Körner; *Literary Notebooks 1797–1801*, ed. and trans. by H. Eichner (1957). *See* also I. Rouge, *F. Schlegel et la genèse du romantisme allemand* (1904); R. Haym, *Die romantische Schule*, 5th ed., with bibliography (1928); F. Gundolf, "Schlegels romantische schriften," in *Romantiker* (1930); J. J. Anstett, *La Pensée religieuse de F. Schlegel* (1942); E. R. Curtius, "F. Schlegel und Frankreich," in his *Kritische Essays* (1950); R. Wellek, *History of Modern Criticism*, vol. 2, *The Romantic Age* (1955).

(AR. H.)

SCHLEGEL, JOHANN ELIAS (1719–1749), German author and critic, uncle of August Wilhelm and Friedrich von Schlegel, was born at Meissen on Jan. 17, 1719. He attended the famous school at Pforta (Schulpforta), where F. G. Klopstock was a fellow pupil. After having studied law in Leipzig, he became private secretary to the Saxon ambassador in Copenhagen (1743) and in 1748 professor at the Sorö Academy. He died at Sorö on Aug. 13, 1749. His plays and criticism helped give the German

theatre a much-needed new impetus; at a time when Shakespeare was virtually unknown to the German public, he showed his awareness of Shakespeare's genius (*Vergleichung Shakespeares und Andreas Gryphs*, 1741); and he developed a theory of literary appreciation that anticipated later developments in the field of aesthetics. He insisted that art aims at providing pleasure rather than instruction or moral uplift. Appreciation did not mean to him, as it did to his former teacher J. C. Gottsched (*q.v.*), the mechanical application of a system of fixed rules, but a living response to variable forms. G. E. Lessing quotes Schlegel with approval in his *Hamburgische Dramaturgie* and praises his comedies *Die stumme Schönheit* (1747) and *Der Triumph der guten Frauen* (1748).

BIBLIOGRAPHY.—*Werke*, ed. by his brother J. H. Schlegel (1761–70); *Ästhetische und Dramaturgische Schriften*, ed. by J. von Antoniewicz (1887); selections ed. by F. Muncker in Kürschner's *Deutsche National-Literatur*, vol. 44 (1889). *See* also E. Wolff, *J. E. Schlegel* (1889); E. M. Wilkinson, *Johann Elias Schlegel: a German Pioneer in Aesthetics* (1945).

(W. WI.)

SCHLEICHER, AUGUST (1821–1868), German philologist, the first linguist to study an Indo-European language not from texts but directly from living speakers, was born at Meiningen, on Feb. 19, 1821. He became professor of Germanic and classical philology in Prague in 1850, and in 1857 was appointed to the chair of comparative linguistics at Jena. His *Handbook of the Lithuanian Language* (1856–57) marks an epoch in linguistic history; and his *Compendium of Comparative Grammar of Indo-European* (1861) was the first to emphasize the regularity of phonetic correspondences between the related languages, and the first to attempt reconstructions of proto-Indo-European. His work well sums up the first half century of comparative linguistics, and, methodologically, indicates the direction of much subsequent scholarship. He died on Dec. 6, 1868, at Jena.   (M. S. BR.)

SCHLEICHER, KURT VON (1882–1934), German army officer who played an important part in politics and became the last chancellor of the Weimar Republic. He was born at Brandenburg on April 7, 1882. In 1900 he joined the 3rd Foot Guards, Hindenburg's old regiment, and became a friend of Hindenburg's son, Oskar. In 1913, as captain, he joined the staff, having attracted the attention of Wilhelm Groener (*q.v.*). Groener, appointed quartermaster general in 1918, made Schleicher his personal assistant in the political division of general headquarters. In 1919 Schleicher was employed in a similar capacity in the newly created *Reichswehr*, and during the emergency of 1923–24 was aide-de-camp to Gen. Hans von Seeckt (*q.v.*), then chief of the army command, which had replaced the former general staff.

Schleicher's influence was increased when Hindenburg became president in 1925. In February 1926 Schleicher, as colonel, was appointed head of the armed forces division, immediately subordinate to the *Reichswehr* ministry, and he methodically extended the scope of this position. He welcomed Seeckt's fall (October 1926). After January 1928, when Groener became defense minister, Schleicher gained increased political influence and by 1929, as major general, was in charge of a newly created office in the *Reichswehr* ministry. His position is to be explained by the part in politics played by the *Reichswehr* at this period; Schleicher himself had helped bring this about. With Groener, the chancellor Heinrich Brüning (*q.v.*), and Hindenburg, he was one of the determining forces in the Weimar Republic between 1929 and 1933. He came into sharp conflict with Brüning and Hindenburg: his intrigues contributed to Brüning's downfall and helped bring about the appointment as chancellor of Franz von Papen (*q.v.*) in June 1932. Schleicher became defense minister and, when Papen was forced to resign (Dec. 1, 1932), also chancellor.

In the Weimar Republic's last years, Schleicher was the dominant figure in Germany who opposed the rising power of the Nazis. He was anxious, however, to avoid civil war, and he planned to save Germany by identifying the president with the *Reichswehr* and by making the *Reichswehr* the source of political power. His intrigues with Hitler were inspired by a wish to control and exploit him and his party for the good of the *Reich*. In 1932 he often offered to participate in a government of which Hitler would be chancellor, on condition that he himself should remain in charge of the *Reichswehr*. This would have enabled him to prevent Nazi violation of the law or the constitution. Hitler refused and thereafter concluded that Schleicher was his chief enemy. Meanwhile, Papen's negotiations with Hitler led to his assuring Hindenburg that a coalition government was possible. In January 1933, Hindenburg dismissed Schleicher and made Hitler chancellor. Hitler never forgave Schleicher for trying to keep the Nazi Party under control of the *Reichswehr,* and on June 30, 1934, during the so-called night of the long knives, Schleicher was murdered at his Berlin flat by the SS (*Schutzstaffel*).

BIBLIOGRAPHY.—R. Fischer, *Schleicher, Mythos und Wirchlichkeit* (1932); O. E. Schüddekopf, *Das Heer und die Republik* (1955); J. W. Wheeler-Bennett, *The Nemesis of Power: the German Army in Politics, 1918–1945* (1953; 2nd rev. ed. 1964); T. Vogelsang, *Reichswehr, Staat und NSDAP* (1962) and *Kurt von Schleicher* (1965); F. L. Carsten, *Reichswehr und Politik 1918–1933* (1964). (T. V.)

SCHLEIDEN, MATTHIAS JAKOB (1804–1881), German botanist and, with Theodor Schwann, co-founder of the cell theory, was born on April 5, 1804, in Hamburg, where he later practised law before studying medicine and botany. He became professor of botany at Jena and at Dorpat, but in his later years pursued the work of a free-lance writer and lecturer. Although his books, because of their polemics and often passionate discussions of nonbotanical problems, reflect a somewhat erratic personality, they nevertheless made their imprint on the development of biology in the 19th century. A protagonist in the fight against the speculative and vitalistic biology of his time, Schleiden recognized that the complex organization of the plant could be understood only by studying its embryonic development. Guided by this idea he came in his "Contributions to Phytogenesis" (1838) to the fundamental thesis that the different parts of the plant organism are either cells or derivatives of cells. One year after the publication of "Phytogenesis," Schwann, an anatomist who was familiar with Schleiden's discovery through personal discussions, showed by his microscopic studies that the cellular principle was as valid in animals as in plants, thus definitely establishing the cell theory (*see* CELL: *Introduction*).

Schleiden died in Frankfurt am Main on June 23, 1881.

(F. WN.)

SCHLEIERMACHER, FRIEDRICH DANIEL ERNST (1768–1834), German theologian and philosopher, one of the most influential thinkers of 19th-century Protestantism, was born in Breslau (Wroclaw) on Nov. 21, 1768, the son of a Prussian army chaplain of the Reformed confession. He was educated at schools belonging to the Moravian Church and was to have become a Moravian pastor. Under the influence of the literature of the time, however, he began to doubt Christianity in its transmitted form; and he exacted from his father permission to study at Halle university, where at the time rationalism reigned.

He early became a student of Kantian philosophy, though from the first a critical one. In 1796 he was appointed chaplain to the Charité hospital in Berlin. He then became influenced by Spinoza and still more by Plato and by Fichte. Entering the circle of the early Berlin romantics, he formed a great friendship with Friedrich von Schlegel, whom he defended in his *Vertraute Briefe über Schlegels 'Lucinde'* (1800). Schleiermacher established his fame with the *Reden über die Religion* (1799; new ed. by Rudolf Otto, 1926) in which he maintained religion to be independent of knowledge and morality. The *Monologen* (1800; new ed. by F. M. Schiele and H. Mulert, 1914) contain the first statements of his ethical system, which does not take a general moral law as its starting point but claims to establish the particularity of the individual.

From 1802 to 1804 Schleiermacher was pastor at Stolp. During these years he began his translation of Plato and published his first strictly philosophical work, the *Grundlinien einer Kritik der bisherigen Sittenlehre* (1803). In 1804 he became professor of theology at Halle; and it was there that, in 1806, he published *Die Weihnachtsfeier*, an important dialogue for his Christology. In the same year appeared the second, heavily revised edition of his *Reden,* already containing his final conception of religion.

From 1809 until his death (Feb. 12, 1834) Schleiermacher lived in Berlin, becoming professor in the newly founded university there in 1810. He took part in the national movement against Napoleon and did much to promote the union of the Lutheran and Reformed churches in the Church of Prussia (1817). His *Kurze Darstellung des theologischen Studiums* (1811; rev. ed., 1830), an encyclopaedia of theological disciplines, already presupposes the final form of his philosophical-theological system, which had built itself up by the independent use of borrowed stimuli (especially from Schelling). His chief theological work, *Der christliche Glaube nach den Grundsätzen der evangelischen Kirche,* 2 vol. (1821–22), became basic for evangelical theology in the 19th century. Schleiermacher expressed the principles of the second, heavily revised, edition of this work in two letters to his friend Friedrich Lücke (in the periodical *Theologische Studien und Kritiken,* 1829; ed. separately by H. Mulert, 1908); in these he defended his theological position in general and his book in particular. His metaphysic of knowledge, the *Dialektik,* was left incomplete at his death. His lectures on philosophical and theological ethics, as well as those on practical theology, were also printed posthumously.

Theoretical Philosophy.—In Berlin Schleiermacher was overshadowed by Hegel as a philosopher, and the significance of his fragmentary philosophical works was seldom fully appreciated in the century following his death. Although his point of departure was that of the idealist philosophy of identity, he took a critical view of the limits of our knowledge. All knowledge arises from a conflict of thoughts (hence the title *Dialektik*), as knowledge is the agreement which ends the conflict; but the content of all conflicting thoughts lies between a chaotic multiplicity of sense impressions and the general principles of reason; and only through the unity of real and ideal, that is, through the complete mutual interpenetration of these opposites, could perfect knowledge be attained. In the case of such an absolute knowledge, the one "transcendent cause" of all being, God, would be simultaneously apprehended. But the reconciliation of the opposites is never more than approximate; our perception of God is likewise confined to various approximate formulas reached by a differential method; and our knowledge remains incomplete. Nonetheless, God as transcendent cause is already presupposed in all partial knowledge. God cannot be comprehended in a definition, but is immanent to all existing beings, constituting their connection with all other existence. In immediate self-consciousness (or, as Schleiermacher calls it, feeling) God is present as the basis of the unity of the self in the transition from thinking to willing and vice versa. Although immanent in all existence, God is not identical with the world but is its origin. As such, he is not conceivable to our thought apart from the world.

Ethics.—The subject of ethics is the striving of the mind to unite physical nature with itself and to fashion that nature into its instrument and symbol. This ethical striving must presuppose that nature and reason are in principle one in the transcendent cause (in God), that nature is preordained to be the organ and symbol of the mind, just as there is an impulse in the mind working toward this same unity. This impulse is not a general moral law but expresses itself differently in each individual. It always leads the individual to participate in society, however—for example in the forms of family, state, school, and church.

Theology.—While philosophy, from perception of the world, constructs approximate formulas for the transcendent cause, theology contemplates immediate self-conciousness, or feeling, which mirrors the divine unity. Since man in his self-consciousness knows that he does not exist from himself, he feels himself absolutely dependent. This feeling is the source of all religion. All religious language is its expression, and dogmatic theology states in explicit terms what are actual religious assertions within the religious consciousness. So-called natural religion, or the religion of reason, as something distinct from positive religion, is a pure abstraction. All religion is positive because religious feeling is experienced only in conjunction with sense consciousness, and consequently every religious expression has its own particular character. The great religious communions arise through religious heroes, who awake the religious life in others by communicating their special religious experience and who found religious communities, churches, for the cultivation of this religious life. Christianity belongs to the highest, monotheistic stage of religion and is of the ethical type of religion insofar as it regards every deficiency in consciousness of God as sin and any strengthening of this consciousness as grace. The specific feature of Christianity is the relation to Christ as mediator, in whom the consciousness of God was realized prototypically and superlatively, so that one must speak of "God's being in Him." Christians are conscious of having been redeemed by their experience of Christ's religious perfection from a situation in which their religious consciousness was overpowered by their sense consciousness: they have been transplanted from this condition into one where everything is subordinated to the religious feeling. The work of Christ is now carried on in a natural way by the church; but its founder, Jesus, was a completely new and original factor in the process of religious development and was to that extent, like every new and higher stage of being, a supernatural revelation. Schleiermacher believed that this conception of Christianity overcame both the one-sidedness of rationalism and the contrary one-sidedness of supernaturalism. As he assigned to dogmatic theology the task of justifying all Christian teaching as an expression of Christian consciousness, he was compelled to exclude from that theology much that does not seem to be a necessary expression of it; e.g., all historical events, the whole of the Old Testament and also the doctrine of the Trinity. Likewise, he had to offer a considerable reinterpretation of the doctrine of sin and justification and of Christological and eschatological teaching.

BIBLIOGRAPHY.—The collected edition of Schleiermacher's works, 30 vol. (1834–64), comprises three groups of writings, (1) theology, (2) sermons and (3) philosophy and miscellanea. To these must be added the *Aesthetik*, ed. by R. Odebrecht (1931). *See* also the *Dialektik*, new ed. by R. Odebrecht (1942), in conformity with the lecture of 1822.

F. Ueberweg, *Grundriss der Geschichte der Philosophie*, iv (1923), gives a bibliography of the secondary literature. For more recent works *see* F. Flückiger, *Philosophie und Theologie bei Schleiermacher* (1947).

(W. U. P.)

SCHLEITHEIM CONFESSION, the first known Anabaptist confession, which was drawn up at a conference at Schleitheim, near Schaffhausen, Switz. (Feb. 24, 1527). It was known as the *Brüderlich Vereinigung* ("brotherly union") and, in seven articles, summarized certain tenets of the Swiss and South German Anabaptists, which were under attack from orthodox Protestantism. Baptism was held as the basis of Christian faith; the other articles concerned excommunication, the Eucharist, separation from the world, leadership by "shepherds," nonresistance (*i.e.,* refusal to carry arms), and rejection of oaths. The aim of the Anabaptists was the creation of an entirely separate church whose members were forbidden association with other churches, Catholic and Protestant alike.

The confession achieved wide recognition after the trial and execution of Michael Sattler by the civil authorities at Rottenburg (Württemberg) on May 20, 1527. His antagonists drew up nine articles refuting those of Schleitheim and demonstrating official opinion that Anabaptism was immoral and treasonable.

See relevant articles in *The Mennonite Encyclopedia*, 4 vol. (1955–59).

SCHLESINGER, FRANK (1871–1943), U.S. astronomer, "the father of modern astrometry," was born in New York City May 11, 1871, of Silesian parentage. Upon graduation from City College in 1890, Schlesinger practised surveying four years before preparing for the Ph.D. degree at Columbia (1898). After a period with the International Latitude Service in California, he became astronomer at the Yerkes Observatory (1903–05). There he demonstrated the effectiveness of long-focus telescopes for photographic measurements of distances of stars. His highly accurate method proved epoch making. As others followed his procedure, the number of stars with measured distances increased from a few dozen to over 6,000 during Schlesinger's lifetime, and the measurements became basic to knowledge of the scale of the universe beyond the solar system.

In 1905 Schlesinger accepted directorship of the Allegheny Observatory in Pittsburgh. From 1920 until his retirement in 1941 he was director of the Yale University Observatory. For

Allegheny he acquired the 30-in. Thaw refractor; for Yale the 26-in. refractor in the Southern Hemisphere. These instruments contributed a large share of the known stellar distances. He also pioneered in the use of wide-angle cameras for determining photographically positions and proper motions of stars formerly measured by laborious visual methods. Fifteen volumes of *Yale Zone Catalogues* give results for about 150,000 stars.

Schlesinger's contributions were recognized by many honours: medals, lectureships, election to the National Academy of Sciences, and the presidency of the International Astronomical union.

He died in Lyme, Conn., July 10, 1943.   (D. Br.)

SCHLESINGER, HERMANN IRVING (1882–1960), U.S. chemist and educator, was born in Minneapolis, Minn., on Oct. 11, 1882. Except for two years of study in Germany and a short stay at Johns Hopkins University, he was associated, as student and teacher, with the University of Chicago from 1900 until his death Oct. 3, 1960. In the early 1930s he and his colleagues organized the university's general course in the physical sciences and created films for classroom use in chemistry and physics. This work, together with his textbooks of chemistry and numerous articles on the place of the sciences in education, made Schlesinger an influential figure in teaching chemistry and allied fields. In research, his chief contributions were the development of practical methods of producing boron hydrides and the discovery of a new chemistry of the borohydrides and related compounds of the light elements (*see* BORON). These compounds found important uses as high-energy fuels and propellants and as agents for the industrial synthesis of certain pharmaceuticals.   (W. C. J.)

SCHLESWIG, a district headquarters town in West Germany in the *Land* (state) of Schleswig-Holstein, Federal Republic of Germany, lies 32 mi. (51 km.) NW of Kiel by road. Since World War II it has been the seat of the high courts of law and the *Land* museums (located in Gottorp Castle). Pop. (1961) 33,767. The town forms a semicircle around the head of the Schlei, a narrow inlet of the Baltic. St. Peter's Cathedral (begun before 1100, but mainly 13th-century) contains a fine oak reredos carved by Hans Brüggemann in 1514–21. The Schlei affords access to small vessels only, and fishing, tanning, sugar refining, the distillation of alcohol, and market gardening are the chief activities.

Schleswig (anc. Sliesthorp, Sliaswic) and the adjoining Haddeby (anc. Haithabu) were in the 9th–11th centuries of great importance in the trade between the Baltic and North seas. St. Ansgar (*q.v.*) built the first church there in 850; it later became the seat of a bishop. Schleswig, whose charter dates from 1200, also became the seat of the dukes of Schleswig, but its trade dwindled because of the rivalry of Lübeck, local wars, and the silting of the Schlei. From 1721 to 1848 Schleswig was the seat of the Danish governor of the duchies. *See* SCHLESWIG-HOLSTEIN QUESTION.

(W. Ku.)

SCHLESWIG-HOLSTEIN, a *Land* (state) in the northeast of the Federal Republic of Germany. Area 6,045 sq.mi. (15,658 sq.km.). Pop. (1961) 2,317,441. It extends from the lower course of the Elbe River and the *Land* of Hamburg northward to Denmark, with its eastern coast on the Baltic Sea and its western coast on the North Sea. It thus contains the southern half of the Jutland Peninsula, and on the mainland is bounded eastward by the German Democratic Republic. The *Land* includes Fehmarn Island in the Baltic; Heligoland (Helgoland) and Sylt (*qq.v.*), Föhr, Amrum, and the other German islands in the North Frisian group (*see* FRISIAN ISLANDS).

Schleswig-Holstein is part of the north German lowland. It is deeply blanketed with glacial and post-glacial deposits and the underlying chalk stratum is exposed in only a few places, such as Lägerdorf in western Holstein. The three main zones are: (1) the harbourless west coast (where the water is shallow), reclaimed marshes, mainly under grass and devoted to livestock farming; (2) a central belt of *Geest* (sandy uplands) with much peat bog, some woodland, and cultivation of rye, oats, and potatoes; (3) the eastern moraines, which are in part wooded hills and in part more fertile land under arable cultivation and dairy farming. Four-fifths of the *Land* drains to the North Sea, and only about

8% is wooded. The Baltic coast is generally steep and irregular, being pierced by *Förden,* or long narrow inlets, which afford good harbours. The climate is temperate and maritime, with mild winters, cool summers, variable weather, and plentiful rain and mist.

For the history of Schleswig-Holstein reference should be made to Holstein; Schleswig; Schleswig-Holstein Question. The people are of Lower Saxon stock and predominantly Protestant. The population density, highest on the eastern and southwestern coasts, was after World War II increased by the influx of about 1,200,000 refugees from eastern Germany, but in the 1950s decreased through resettlement of refugees in other *Länder.* By the 1960s, however, refugees still formed about one-third of the population. Low German (*Plattdeutsch*) is commonly spoken outside the towns but there is a small Danish-speaking minority in northern Schleswig. The principal towns are Kiel, which is the capital of the *Land;* Schleswig, which is the seat of the high courts; Lübeck; Flensburg; Neumünster; Rendsburg; Itzehoe; and Elmshorn.

The Prussian province of Schleswig-Holstein was in 1946 reconstituted to form the existing *Land* and in 1949 executive power passed to the *Landtag* (diet), which is elected for a four-year term. Schleswig-Holstein is divided into 4 *Stadtkreise* (urban districts) and 17 *Landkreise* (rural districts). The Christian-Albrechts University at Kiel has an attached Institute of International Commerce. There are colleges of engineering at Kiel and Lübeck, of building in Eckernförde and Lübeck, of marine engineering in Flensburg, and of textile engineering in Neumünster. Lübeck has an academy of music and Kiel an art college.

The economy is mainly agricultural, and three-quarters of the area is farmed (cattle for milk and meat, pigs, potatoes, sugar beet, wheat, and rye). At Halstenbek in the southwest is one of the largest tree nurseries in Europe. Industry employs fewer than 10% of the population (shipbuilding, foodstuffs, engineering and electrical products, and textiles) and is concentrated mainly in Kiel, Lübeck, Flensburg, and Neumünster. Petroleum obtained in western Holstein as well as that imported is refined at Heide. Extensive fisheries on both coasts support canning and curing industries. Coastal resorts, the lake district of eastern Holstein, and the islands of Heligoland and Sylt attract numerous summer tourists.

The Kiel Canal (*q.v.*) traverses Schleswig-Holstein to form an important route for shipping between the North and Baltic seas; Brunsbüttelkoog at its western end is a major oil terminal. The other leading ports are Kiel and Lübeck, the latter being linked with the inland-waterway network by the Elbe-Trave Canal. As the *Land* forms a natural bridge to Scandinavia the north-south communications are important; these were improved by the completion in 1961 of the four-lane road tunnel beneath the Kiel Canal at Rendsburg, and by the completion in 1963 of a road and rail bridge 1,053 yd. (963 m.) long between Grossenbrode and Fehmarn Island, whence a ferry service connects with Rödby Havn and Copenhagen, Den.

Bibliography.—Schleswig-Holstein Statistical Office, *Statistisches Jahrbuch Schleswig-Holsteins* (annually); R. E. Dickinson, *Germany: A General and Regional Geography* (1953); O. Brandt, *Grundriss der Geschichte Schleswig-Holsteins,* 5th ed. (1957), *Handbuch für Schleswig-Holstein,* 11th ed. (1962). (R. E. Di.)

SCHLESWIG-HOLSTEIN QUESTION, a complex of problems arising out of the relationship of Schleswig and Holstein to Denmark, to each other, and to the German Confederation. Involved in it were a disputed succession, a clash of Danish and German nationalism, a threat to the international balance of power, and a problem of minorities.

Earlier History.—The distribution of place-names shows Schleswig to have been an area of Scandinavian rather than of German settlement. At the beginning of the 12th century Southern Jutland (*i.e.,* Schleswig, with the Eider River as its southern boundary) was a distinct duchy, but dependent on the Danish crown; and early in the 13th century the duke of Schleswig, who soon afterward became king of Denmark as Valdemar II, conquered Holstein (between the Eider and the Elbe) from the Germans and Slavs. Holstein, however, was lost by Denmark in 1227; and Schleswig was held by the counts of Holstein from 1386 to

1460, sometimes without any recognition of Danish overlordship. In 1460, at Ribe, the nobility of Schleswig and Holstein elected the king of Denmark, Christian I, of the House of Oldenburg, as their duke and count and obtained a charter of privileges, which affirmed the indissoluble association of Schleswig with Holstein. Holstein, which from 1227 remained a fief of the German *Reich,* became a duchy in 1474.

The practice of dividing the inheritance in the duchies among younger brothers of the Danish king led, from 1544, to the formation of a Gottorp branch of the House of Oldenburg with claims to independent rule in the duchies. The Dano-Swedish Treaty of Frederiksborg of 1720 enabled Denmark to recover the Gottorp parts of Schleswig, but its terms were ambiguous. A second settlement in 1773, by the Treaty of Tsarskoye Selo between Denmark and Russia (after the merging of the Gottorp with the Romanov dynasty), strengthened the rights of the Danish crown in Holstein. When the German Confederation was formed in 1815, Frederick VI of Denmark was a member of it in his capacity as duke of Holstein and Lauenburg, but not in his capacity either as king of Denmark or as duke of Schleswig.

The First Crisis, 1846–52.—Frederick VI of Denmark was succeeded in 1839 by his nephew Christian VIII; but neither Christian's son, the future Frederick VII, nor Christian's brother Ferdinand had any children. In the kingdom the law of succession allowed the crown to pass through females, so that, on Frederick (VII)'s death, it might go to one of Christian VIII's sisters or her heir. In Holstein the law excluded females, so that this duchy would pass to Frederick's nearest male heir, Christian Augustus, duke of Augustenburg, a descendant of Christian III of Denmark. For Schleswig, it was uncertain whether the law was that of the kingdom or that of Holstein. A possible settlement was a royal proclamation that, since the monarchy was indivisible, the law must be reckoned the same in all three parts, and the inheritance pass intact to Frederick's female heir. But national passions rendered this difficult. The population of Schleswig was Danish in the northern countryside, German in the south, and mixed in the northern towns and the centre. The Eider-Dane (claiming the River Eider to be the national boundary) party of Schleswig and of the kingdom was the instrument of Danish nationalism, aspiring to incorporate Schleswig in Denmark, detaching it from Holstein. German nationalists conversely sought to confirm Schleswig's association with Holstein, detaching it from the kingdom. Christian VIII's *Open Letter* of July 8, 1846, proclaimed that, in Schleswig, the law of succession was that of the kingdom, and though it made

SCHLESWIG-HOLSTEIN AFTER THE PEACE OF PRAGUE, 1866

no similar assertion on the law in Holstein, reaffirmed the principle of Schleswig-Holstein solidarity.

Christian VIII sought to overcome the national conflict by drafting a constitution, which recognized the autonomy of each of the three parts, but grouped them in a single organization for common purposes. Frederick VII, who succeeded to the throne on Christian VIII's death (Jan. 20, 1848), published this constitution (Jan. 28); but German feeling was then predominant, and the Estates of each duchy answered by appealing to the German Confederation, demanding inclusion as a single state. On the outbreak of revolution in Germany, the duchies rebelled against Denmark, and on March 24 a provisional government at Kiel proclaimed their independence, offered support to German freedom and unity, and renewed the appeal to the German Confederation. Frederick VII then declared the union of the duchies dissolved and, on March 27, published a plan of a constitution linking Schleswig more closely to Denmark than to Holstein.

Danish action against the rebels was checked, in April 1848, by the military intervention of Prussia on their behalf, with the approval of the Diet of the German Confederation. Prussia's object was to induce Denmark to recognize Schleswig as part of the German system, and to enforce the principle that the duchies were indissolubly united and hereditary only in the male line. From Holstein the Prussian forces overran Schleswig and entered Jutland proper. But in June the Prussians withdrew from Jutland and, on Aug. 26, signed the seven-month truce of Malmö with Denmark. This reserved the rights of the German Confederation and of the Danish king alike. King Frederick William IV of Prussia apparently decided to withdraw at the bidding of Russia, Great Britain, France, and Sweden; but he knew that he could not prevail against the Danish fleet in the Baltic, and he disliked the antimonarchical cause in which, for the sake of an ill-thought-out German policy, he had become engaged.

The international balance of power was threatened, if Denmark were weakened either as keeper of the gate into the Baltic or as counterpoise to a possible united Germany. Lord Palmerston, the British foreign secretary, had mediated between Denmark and Prussia. In form, he acted on the British guarantee of the Treaty of Frederiksborg of 1720. France, also a guarantor, and Russia joined Great Britain in ignoring the clash of nationalities and in striving simply to maintain the Danish monarchy intact.

Negotiations for a definitive settlement after Malmö were interrupted by the renewal of war. The Danish government, in a note of Feb. 23, 1849, warned Prussia that the truce would not be renewed on its expiry (March 26) unless terms more satisfactory to Denmark had been agreed upon. The Prussian government, partly for reasons of prestige in Germany, where it had embarked on an independent attempt at reconstruction, partly to protect Prussia's Baltic trade, stood firm; fighting broke out in April; and the Prussians advanced into Jutland again. Once more, Russian threats, French pressure, and British mediation procured a six months' truce on July 10, 1849. Preliminaries of peace, signed at the same time, enunciated the principle of a separate constitution for Schleswig, which would release that duchy from Holstein but leave it united to Denmark. This was reaffirmed in the treaty of peace between Denmark and Prussia, signed at Berlin on July 2, 1850. Despite this treaty, the duchies continued to resist the Danish Army.

The Prussian government had made war for the sake of its German policy; but Austria, after the defeat of the Italian and Hungarian revolutions, had begun to react vigorously against Prussia. Consequently Frederick William got rid of the Danish war in order to concentrate on Germany. Yet failure in the Danish war had already undermined his German policy. The Schleswig-Holstein and the German question were inextricably connected; and Prussia by the Treaty of Berlin was defeated twice over. The defeat was confirmed when Prussia, by the Punctation of Olmütz (November 1850), accepted Austria's terms for the reconstitution of the German Confederation and agreed to assist Denmark to reconquer the duchies.

The Danes won a victory over the rebels at Idstedt in July 1850, but fighting continued until December and was concluded only after the intervention of an Austro-Prussian army acting in the name of the restored Confederation. Meanwhile international negotiations continued. Indeed, the Treaty of Berlin had been in part due to Palmerston's having organized a European front to maintain the territorial integrity of the Danish realm. By the London Protocol of Aug. 2, 1850, this principle was placed under the guarantee of Great Britain, Russia, France, and Sweden. Austria, after reserving the rights of the German Confederation, also signed on Aug. 23. Finally, the Treaty of London (May 8, 1852), signed by Denmark, Great Britain, France, Russia, Sweden, Austria, and Prussia, declared the integrity of the Danish realm to be a permanent element in the European balance of power and recognized Prince Christian of Glücksburg (the future Christian IX of Denmark, another descendant of Christian III, but of a branch junior to the Augustenburgs) as heir to "all the states at present united under the sceptre of His Majesty the King of Denmark." The duke of Augustenburg promised not to try to upset this arrangement, and other claimants renounced their rights.

Danish Constitutional Reforms.—Desiring a constitutional settlement adverse equally to Danish and to German nationalism, Austria had obtained a Danish undertaking, in December 1851, to reestablish the Estates in Holstein and in Schleswig and, by discussions in these assemblies and in the Danish *rigsraad,* to bring about "an organic and homogeneous union of all parts of the monarchy." The constitution of July 26, 1854, partially fulfilled this promise in a conservative sense, that of Oct. 2, 1855, in a more liberal sense; but neither had been framed in cooperation with the three assemblies. This and other grievances caused protests from the German Confederation and from Prussia; and Austria dared not lag behind. In November 1858 the constitution of 1855 was suspended for Holstein, pending the assembly of the Holstein Estates promised for 1859. One result of the crisis was thus the achievement of the Eider-Danes' ideal: Schleswig and Denmark together and Holstein left out.

The Second Crisis, 1862–66.—The meetings of the Holstein Estates in 1859 and 1861 and of those of Schleswig in 1860 failed to settle the constitutional dispute. In his so-called Gotha dispatch (Sept. 24, 1862), the British foreign secretary, Earl Russell, attempted a solution. It leaned to the German rather than to the Danish side, was neither acceptable to Denmark nor liked in Great Britain, and was soon dropped.

In autumn 1862, when Bismarck (*q.v.*) came to power in Prussia, the question was thus still open. Danish nationalism was then on top, ideas of a common Scandinavian front against Germany were being canvassed, and Eider-Denmark seemed to have been attained. Frederick VII's patent of March 30, 1863, seemed to confirm Holstein's being apart: it allowed legislation enacted for the whole monarchy to be valid for Denmark and for Schleswig and invalid for Holstein, if the Holstein Estates vetoed it.

The German Confederation summoned Denmark to withdraw the March patent, but many things encouraged Danish resistance. Prussia had apparently abandoned the patronage of German nationalism in order to develop an anti-Austrian policy and in any case was apparently immersed, from May, in an internal constitutional struggle. On July 23, 1863, Palmerston, now the British prime minister, reversing the trend of the Gotha dispatch, warned those who threatened the integrity of Denmark that it would not be Denmark alone with whom they would have to contend. In August, Prussia's antagonism to Austria was demonstrated by refusal to take part in the congress of princes which Austria had convened to consider the reconstruction of Germany. Great Britain and France were reacting against Russia's treatment of Poland, but in November the British rejected the emperor Napoleon III's proposal of a congress to settle the outstanding problems of Europe.

Danish illusions were shattered by the results of proclaiming a new Eider-Dane constitution. Announced by Frederick VII on Sept. 28, 1863, and ratified by the *rigsraad* on Nov. 13, this constitution was signed on Nov. 18 by the new king, Christian IX, three days after Frederick's death. It was similar to the constitution of 1855, except that it embodied the provisions of the March patent. Christian IX had come to the throne in accordance with the Treaty of London; but in the duchies Prince Frederick of

Augustenburg, eldest son of Christian Augustus, had been proclaimed duke (Nov. 18). Christian Augustus has been censured for passing on to his son claims which he himself was bound not to exercise. But Prince Frederick's proclamation was popular in Germany, and he was recognized by the chief German princes.

The Danes had taken too lightly the German Confederation's threats of an invasion of Holstein. They had not understood that, if Prussia would not accept Austria's views and if Austria still intended to be Prussia's equal in Germany, then Austria must accept Prussia's views on Schleswig-Holstein; or that Prussian patronage of German nationalism would be enormously strengthened by Bismarck's ruthlessness and by his new power to dominate Austria. Prussia and Austria induced the Confederation, on Nov. 21, 1863, to refuse observance of the Treaty of London, with its exclusion of Augustenburg, unless Denmark fulfilled the undertaking of December 1851; and on Dec. 7, 1863, it was resolved to begin armed enforcement of the Confederation's policy. Federal troops occupied Holstein soon afterward.

Prussia and Austria declared war upon Denmark. Their action was governed by their punctation of Jan. 16, 1864, and was followed by a fresh Danish refusal (Jan. 18) to withdraw the November constitution. The punctation provided for a joint settlement of the Schleswig-Holstein question and excluded the German Confederation. The Austro-Prussian army, therefore, ignored the federal troops in Holstein; and on Feb. 1 it invaded Schleswig. The punctation marked the separation of Prussian from federal policy. Bismarck was about to exploit the German movement so as to achieve the annexation of the duchies, with Kiel as a naval base, to Prussia.

The European situation was favourable. Napoleon III had drawn toward Prussia. Russia, unassertive after the Crimean War, was no longer inclined to support Denmark, and now backed Austro-Prussian conservatism. Though Great Britain claimed that the Treaty of London was valid whether Denmark fulfilled the undertaking of December 1851 or not, Palmerston and Russell could not win either Queen Victoria or the Cabinet for a pro-Danish policy.

In these circumstances, Bismarck signed a fresh alliance with Austria on March 6, 1864, to cover the invasion of Denmark proper. It aimed at a settlement that would discard the undertaking of December 1851, but still—to meet Austria's wishes—achieve the union of the duchies with Denmark on a personal basis. The German movement, which aimed at independence for Schleswig-Holstein under Frederick of Augustenburg, was disregarded. Austria and Prussia were still, however, faced with a European conference.

The London Conference, which met on April 25, 1864, was never master of the situation which it tried to regulate. The meeting was delayed by unavailing efforts to bring about an armistice first (the armistice eventually took effect from May 12); by the difficulty of securing the representation of the German Confederation, which was not a signatory of the Treaty of London; and by Bismarck's deliberate effort to postpone the opening until Prussia and Austria were in possession of all Denmark. Napoleon's proposal to consult the wishes of the populations was altered by Bismarck to a proposal for separating Holstein and southern Schleswig from Denmark and letting the populations decide the frontier line and the question of independence or union with Prussia—this last possibility being now first raised internationally. Though he could not publicly work for this without breaking the March alliance, Bismarck privately began to wean Austria from the principle of Danish integrity.

The London Conference tacitly abandoned the principle of Danish integrity, and the Danes rejected the proposal for personal union contained in the March alliance. This left independence for the duchies under Augustenburg as the only solution still in the field. But the conference dispersed on June 25, 1864, without achieving it: Denmark rejected independence within the frontier proposed, and Austria rejected Bismarck's stipulation that the duchies should be militarily subordinated to Prussia. A fresh spell of fighting from the end of June to July 20, 1864, enabled Bismarck to free the question from international discussion.

Fresh peace negotiations, directed toward the cession of the duchies to Austria and Prussia jointly, achieved their purpose in the Treaty of Vienna of Oct. 30, 1864.

The Austrian and the Prussian attitudes to the duchies were different and led to conflict. The Convention of Gastein (Aug. 14, 1865) therefore modified the condominium by assigning the internal administration of Holstein to Austria and that of Schleswig to Prussia. Next year, however, the wider conflict over Germany led to war between Austria and Prussia (*see* SEVEN WEEKS' WAR). The Peace of Prague (Aug. 23, 1866) ceded the duchies to Prussia.

The Question of North Schleswig.—After Prussia's formation of the German Empire (1871) the Schleswig-Holstein question was narrowed to a contest between Denmark and Germany over North Schleswig. Article v of the Peace of Prague had provided for a plebiscite to decide whether it should be German or Danish. This proviso was abrogated by an Austro-Prussian treaty of Oct. 11, 1878. The Danes of North Schleswig then adopted a policy of passive protest, and many young Danes emigrated to Denmark. The mistake of this was seen in the mid-1880s, and constructive measures were taken to strengthen the Danish minority of North Schleswig. Between 1900 and 1914 Danish organizations fought the German government for the children's allegiance through the schools and for the land through the farmers. Both sides advanced loans to their nationals so that they could buy farms.

The conscription of Danes into the German armies in World War I, when Denmark was neutral, strengthened the movement for reunion with Denmark. H. P. Hanssen, a leader of the Danish movement and deputy for a North Schleswig constituency in the German *Reichstag*, demanded the application of the Wilsonian principle of self-determination. This was accepted by the Conference of Paris, and a plebiscite was organized by the Danish government. The plebiscite took place, under the supervision of an international commission, on Feb. 10, 1920, for the northern zone of the disputed country, and on March 14 for central Schleswig. Denmark won in the first zone by 75,431 votes against 25,329, but Germany won in the second by 48,148 against 13,029. On June 15 the international commission was dissolved, and North Schleswig as far south as Tonder and the northern bank of Flensburg Fjord became part of Denmark.

The question thereafter became a contest over the claims of the German minority in Danish North Schleswig. Different groups demanded: the revision of the southern frontier; or cultural autonomy; or a self-governing farmers' state of North Schleswig (this was dropped by 1926). The advent of the Nazis strengthened the German minority, but they did not reverse the decision of 1920, because they came to aim at absorbing all Denmark in the *Reich*.

After World War II a settlement was sought by putting national allegiance on a personal instead of a territorial basis. On Denmark's side, school laws of 1946 and 1955 satisfied the Germans of North Schleswig. On Germany's side, Schleswig-Holstein was organized as a separate *Land*, with its own Parliament and ministry at Kiel by 1947; guarantees for the Danish minority in South Schleswig were embodied in the Kiel Declaration of Sept. 26, 1949; and a school law in 1950 put the Danes there on the same footing as the Germans in North Schleswig. Danish-German minority talks were held in Copenhagen in the spring of 1955, and the consequent reform of the electoral law in South Schleswig and the regulation of remaining school difficulties brought stability.

BIBLIOGRAPHY.—L. D. Steefel, *The Schleswig-Holstein Question* (1932); A. Scharff, *Die Europäischen Grossmächte und die Deutsche Revolution, 1848–1851* (1942); W. E. Mosse, *The European Powers and the German Question, 1848–71* (1958); T. Fink, *Geschichte des Schleswigschen Grenzlandes* (1958). (A. R.)

SCHLICK, MORITZ (1882–1936), German philosopher and leader of the group of neopositivists who composed the Vienna circle, was born in Berlin on April 14, 1882, the son of a manufacturer. After attending the *Realgymnasium* in Berlin, he studied physics at Heidelberg, at Lausanne and at Berlin where, as a pupil of Max Planck, he obtained his doctorate of philosophy in 1904 with a thesis on physics. In 1911 he qualified for a teaching post in Rostock with a dissertation on "The Nature of Truth According to Modern Logic." In 1921 he was appointed to a post in Kiel. In 1922 Schlick went to Vienna as professor of the philosophy of the inductive sciences. His predecessors in this chair included Ernst Mach and Ludwig Boltzmann. In Vienna he gathered around him a group of philosophers, such as Rudolf Carnap, Otto Neurath and Friedrich Waismann, and of mathematicians and scientists, such as Kurt Gödel, Philipp Frank, Karl Menger and Hans Hahn, which met regularly to discuss problems of common interest. The group, the Vienna circle, was characterized by its hostility to metaphysics, by its radical empiricism, by its faith in the techniques of modern symbolic logic and by its belief that the future of philosophy lay in its becoming the logic of science. Claiming to continue the positivist tradition of Mach and Boltzmann, it was much influenced also by Bertrand Russell and by Ludwig Wittgenstein (*qq.v.*). Its views were publicized in a series of books, *Schriften zur wissenschaftlichen Weltauffassung* (1928 ff.); and the manifesto *Wissenschaftliche Weltauffassung: der Wiener Kreis* (1929) served to organize it on a more formal basis. Making contact with philosophers of similar tendencies in other countries, it launched the international movement in philosophy which has come to be known as logical positivism. Schlick went to California in 1929 for a short period as visiting professor at Stanford university. On his return he continued to direct the activities of the Vienna circle and wrote regularly for its review *Erkenntnis*. On June 22, 1936, as he was entering the university to give his lecture, he was shot by a demented student and killed.

In his philosophical view Schlick belonged to what may be called the right wing of the Vienna circle. He did not agree with Carnap and Neurath that statements which appeared to be about mental events were all translatable into statements about physical events, nor did he accept their contention that it was metaphysical to talk of comparing statements with reality. On the contrary, he insisted always that the individual's private experience was the ultimate test of the truth of any assertion of fact. To the objection that this made it impossible to account for there being a public language, he replied that while the content of one's experience was incommunicable, its structure was not. He was thus led to the implausible conclusion that all empirical statements, insofar as they are publicly intelligible, are statements about structure. In his early days he was influenced by Kant, but he believed that the discoveries of modern physics, which he was one of the first to interpret philosophically, showed Kant's views of space and time and causality to be untenable. He also appealed to modern physics in support of the fundamental principle of the logical positivists that "the meaning of any statement turns entirely on the possibility of its empirical verification." It was from this principle that he drew the conclusion that metaphysical statements were meaningless. Metaphysics for him did not include ethics; he took a utilitarian view of ethical statements, which allowed them to be empirically verifiable. It did, however, include any attempt to characterize a transcendent reality. The philosopher, therefore, should not try to compete with the scientist. The object of philosophy was not to establish a body of philosophical propositions, but to make other propositions clear.

See also LOGICAL POSITIVISM: *Characteristic Views of the Vienna Circle.*

Schlick wrote a great many essays, of which some were collected in the posthumous *Gesammelte Aufsätze 1926–36* (1938). His most important books were *Raum und Zeit in der gegenwärtigen Physik* (1917; 2nd ed., 1919; Eng. trans., 1920); *Allgemeine Erkenntnislehre* (1918; 2nd ed., 1925); *Fragen der Ethik* (1930); and the posthumous *Grundzüge der Naturphilosophie* (1948) and *Natur und Kultur* (1952).   (AD. J. A.)

SCHLIEFFEN, ALFRED, GRAF VON (1833–1913), German army officer and author of the Schlieffen Plan that guided the German offensive in 1914, was born in Berlin on Feb. 28, 1833. Though the son of a Prussian major general, he was not entirely typical of the Prussian Junker class; he attributed his capacity for hard work and attention to detail to his descent from a line of Kolberg (Kolobrzeg) mayors and aldermen. Physically he was of aristocratic, somewhat effete, appearance. After attending a grammar school in Berlin, he studied law, but soon decided to fol-

E. BIEBER, BERLIN

GRAF VON SCHLIEFFEN

low in his father's footsteps, and in 1854 joined the 2nd Guard Uhlans as a second lieutenant. He was posted to the general staff in 1865 and shortly afterward married his cousin, Countess Anna Schlieffen. She died four years later, and thereafter he devoted his life entirely to military affairs.

Many stories are told of his obsession with military matters. Once, when one of his staff officers drew his attention to the beauty of a valley in the morning sunlight, Schlieffen replied only, "An unimportant obstacle!" He habitually presented his staff on Christmas Eve with a complicated military problem, demanding a written solution by the evening of Christmas Day. He was described by a subordinate as a proud and distant man who often offended people by his sarcasm; although admired for his efficiency and respected for his devotion to duty, he was incapable of inspiring affection in his subordinates.

Schlieffen's first experience of war was at Königgrätz (1866) as a staff officer to Prince Albrecht of Prussia. In the Franco-German War of 1870–71 he was on the staff of the grand duke of Mecklenburg-Schwerin's Corps. In 1884, as a colonel, he became head of the military history section of the great general staff, and four years later was made a general, and deputy to the chief of the general staff. He became chief of the general staff in 1891; but even before that he had begun to work out the great strategic plan that was to bear his name. For some years the likelihood of Germany's having to fight a war on two fronts—against Russia in the east and France in the west—had been apparent, and Schlieffen set about drawing up a detailed plan and making adjustments in the organization, manpower, and equipment of the army to implement it. He decided that the maximum strength must be deployed in the west to win a quick victory over France, and to discourage British intervention. Meanwhile, Russia, whose mobilization was expected to be slow, was to be contained by a weaker force, and then was to be dealt with after France had been defeated. Schlieffen, realizing that rapid success against France was impossible by frontal attack, began to study the possibilities of a flank attack, either to the south through Switzerland or to the north through the Low Countries. Because of the difficulties of terrain, the Swiss plan was rejected in favour of an outflanking movement through Belgium, or through both Belgium and Holland. This plan was thought to have much better prospect of success because of the flatness of the country and excellent rail and road communications in Belgium and Holland. Between 1893 and 1905 the plan was often revised, but all versions had the same basic principle: an overwhelmingly strong right wing was to advance rapidly through Belgium and northern France and outflank the French armies, which would eventually be encircled.

Schlieffen retired at the end of 1905, but for some years continued to interest himself in the plan of campaign that had long been his main concern. His advice was frequently sought when operations against France and Russia were under discussion. He died in Berlin on Jan. 4, 1913. It is said that his last words were: "The struggle is inevitable. Keep my right flank strong!"

As things turned out, the small forces allotted to the east succeeded in holding the Russians, but the campaign in France failed to obtain a quick victory. This failure was attributed to changes in the plan carried out by Schlieffen's successor—Graf Helmuth von Moltke (*q.v.*), the younger—on the eve of, and in the early stages of, the campaign. After the publication in 1956 of Gerhard Ritter's critical study of the Schlieffen Plan (see *Bibliography*), opinion tended to change. Many students of military history came to believe that the plan itself had inherent weaknesses, and in particular, that Schlieffen had overestimated the speed of advance possible in northwest Europe in face of artillery, machine-gun fire, and demolitions. The plan also ignored the grave political consequences of violating Belgian neutrality.

On the Schlieffen Plan, *see* also FORTIFICATION: *Permanent Fortifications: World War I*; STRATEGY: *Development of Strategy: American Civil War to World War I*; and WORLD WAR I: *Introduction: Rival Plans.*

BIBLIOGRAPHY.—Schlieffen's *Gesammelte Schriften*, 2 vol. (1913); H. von Freytag-Loringhoven, *General Feldmarschall Graf von Schlieffen* (1920); W. Groener, *Das Testament des Grafen Schlieffen*, 2nd ed. (1929); M. Paléologue, *Un Prélude à l'invasion de la Belgique: Le Plan Schlieffen* (1932); G. Ritter, *The Schlieffen Plan: Critique of a Myth* (1956; Eng. trans. 1958). (C. N. B.)

SCHLIEMANN, HEINRICH (1822–1890), German archaeologist, excavator of Troy, Mycenae, and Tiryns (*qq.v.*), is sometimes called the modern discoverer of prehistoric Greece (the Heroic or Homeric Age and the Bronze Age to as early as 3000 B.C.). Born the son of a poor pastor on Jan. 6, 1822, at Neu Buckow in Mecklenburg-Schwerin, his early fascination with antiquity was nurtured by his father. Schliemann later wrote that he resolved as a boy that he would one day excavate Troy. Family misfortunes interrupted his education, and at 14 he became apprenticed to a grocer in whose shop he first heard Homer (*q.v.*) declaimed in Greek. Poor health led him to become cabin boy on the ship "Dorothea" (soon to be wrecked) bound for Venezuela. After the wreck, while working as office boy and bookkeeper in Amsterdam, Neth., Schliemann is said to have spent half of his wages on the study of languages, eventually mastering 13.

In 1846 his employers sent him to St. Petersburg, Russia, as their agent; he established his own business there in 1847 (dealing especially in indigo) and soon became wealthy. In 1856 he learned modern and ancient Greek, steeping himself in Greek literature, especially Homer. Retiring from business at 36, he traveled extensively, including trips to Egypt, Greece, the Near and Far East, and North America. In 1866 he went to Paris to study archaeology, devoting his fortune and the next quarter-century of his life to his dream of excavating Troy.

Schliemann settled in Greece (1868) and investigated Ithaca (*q.v.*), the topography of which he felt to be in agreement with indications in the *Odyssey*. He then visited Mycenae and decided that the royal tombs mentioned by the Greek geographer Pausanias (*q.v.*) were on the citadel rather than in the lower town. Proceeding to the plain of Troy, he at once rejected the usually accepted site of Bunarbashi as that of Troy and chose instead the hill called Hisarlik (*see* Schliemann's *Ithaka, der Peloponnes und Troja*; 1869). Preliminary testing in April 1870 indicated a great depth of accumulation at

RADIO TIMES HULTON PICTURE LIBRARY
HEINRICH SCHLIEMANN

Hisarlik; late in 1871 large-scale excavations began, supervised by Schliemann and his young Greek wife, Sophia. In 1872 a large cut was gouged across the mound to the lowest levels (where he expected to find the remains of Homeric Troy), destroying much of what he was seeking. In the following year, with the discovery of fortification walls and of a "great treasure" in a "burnt city," he proclaimed he had found Priam's Troy; however, by 1890 it was known that the treasures and palatial buildings were in earlier levels, now dated about 2600–2300 B.C.

Schliemann's successful efforts in keeping the great treasure together, in the face of demands to divide it with the Ottoman government, kept him from further excavations until 1876; even then, conditions at Troy were still so adverse that he went to work at Mycenae, where initial success was so great that Troy was forgotten for the moment. A circle of royal tombs was discovered just inside the Lion Gate at Mycenae and the riches that poured from five graves dimmed the radiance of the Trojan treasures;

a sixth grave was found just after his departure. Schliemann's publication of *Mycenae* (1877) brought him full share of honours and fame, for the Mycenean treasures surpassed any known to that time. Established in the National Museum in Athens, they give glorious testimony to his vision and industry.

After a brief and unspectacular interlude at Ithaca in 1878, Schliemann resumed at Troy, continuing in 1879 with good results; he summed up the work in *Ilios* (1881), providing much new evidence to equate Hisarlik with Troy. In 1880–81 at Orchomenos (*q.v.*) he cleared the beehive tomb known as the "Treasury of Minyas," and published *Orchomenos* (1881). He returned to Troy with the young German architect-archaeologist, W. Dörpfeld, who introduced new methods of excavation; their efforts of 1882 were reported in *Troja* (1883). Excavations followed (1884) at Marathon, and at Tiryns where the ground plan of a Mycenaean palace was uncovered, to be described in *Tiryns* (1886). With less success, Schliemann tried (1886–88) to find the Caesareum at Alexandria, the Palace of Minos at Knossos (*see* CRETE), and the Temple of Aphrodite on Cythera, and to investigate "sandy Pylos." He undertook new excavations in Troy (1889–90) to answer assertions of P. A. de Lagarde that Troy was "a mere fire-necropolis" and that Schliemann's evidence had been falsified. Two delegations of archaeologists who visited Troy completely vindicated him and his colleagues. New and more extensive work at Troy was planned, but in December 1890, Schliemann fell ill at Naples and died there on Christmas Day.

See also references under "Schliemann, Heinrich" in the Index. *See* G. S. Thompson, *Heinrich Schliemann* (1964). (S. S. WE.)

SCHLÜSSELBURG: see PETROKREPOST.

SCHLÜTER, ANDREAS (1664–1714), German sculptor and architect, was the first important native master of the late Baroque style in Germany. His early life is obscure, but he is probably to be identified with the Andreas Schlüter baptized in Hamburg on May 22, 1664. He received his early training in Danzig, and was active in Warsaw (1689–1693). In 1694 he was called to Berlin as court sculptor by the elector Frederick III, and it is with Berlin and the Hohenzollern that his name is primarily associated. The bronze statue of Frederick III (1696–97), now at Kaliningrad (formerly Königsberg), and the equestrian statue of the Great Elector (completed in 1703), now in the forecourt of Schloss Charlottenburg, Berlin, are among the most important of his surviving sculptures. Both testify to Schlüter's familiarity with current trends in Rome and at the French court.

Between 1698 and 1706 Schlüter was actively engaged in Berlin in directing building operations and supplying sculptural decorations for the Arsenal, the royal palace, and the old post office. The last named was demolished in 1889, and the royal palace (his greatest achievement) was a casualty of World War II, but the sculptured keystones from the Arsenal, particularly the series of dying warriors, remain the supreme example of Schlüter's genius for synthesizing German tradition and European Baroque. The collapse of the Mint Tower, built on sandy soil adjacent to the royal palace, brought an abrupt end to Schlüter's career as supervisor of the royal buildings and saddened his last years. He was summoned by Peter the Great to St. Petersburg in 1713, but died there in 1714 without having achieved anything of note.

BIBLIOGRAPHY.—C. Gurlitt, *Andreas Schlüter* (1891); E. Benkard, *Andreas Schlüter* (1925); H. Ladendorf, *Andreas Schlüter* (1937); E. Hempel, *Baroque Art and Architecture in Central Europe* (1965).

SCHMALKALDEN, LEAGUE OF (1531–1547), a defensive organization of Protestant Estates of the Holy Roman Empire in Germany (*see* GERMANY: *History*; REFORMATION).

The final recess of the Diet of Augsburg (Nov. 19, 1530) threatened the Protestant Estates with prosecution by the Imperial Chamber (*q.v.*) and with outlawry under the ban of the Empire if they maintained their faith and retained church property which they had confiscated. In this predicament they faced the question whether an Estate of the Empire had the right to defend itself by force of arms against the emperor—in this case Charles V (*q.v.*)—if he attacked it on religious grounds. The landgrave Philip (*q.v.*) of Hesse and the jurists of Electoral Saxony convinced Martin Luther that there was such a right.

On Dec. 31, 1530, at a meeting at Schmalkalden in Thuringia, a project of defensive alliance against any aggression was concerted between John (*q.v.*) the Steadfast, elector of Saxony, Ernest, duke of Brunswick-Lüneburg, Philip of Hesse, Prince Wolfgang of Anhalt-Bernburg, Counts Gebhard and Albrecht of Mansfeld (the latter also being plenipotentiary for Philip, duke of Brunswick-Grubenhagen), and representatives of the cities of Magdeburg and Bremen. Strassburg (Strasbourg), Ulm, and some smaller South German cities accepted the project; but efforts by Philip of Hesse and by Strassburg to co-opt Zürich, Bern, and Basel failed because Saxony did not want any alliance with adherents of Zwinglianism. A treaty was signed on Feb. 27, 1531, to last for six years; but in 1535 it was renewed for ten years.

After arduous negotiations a constitution for the League was drafted in July 1533 and ratified, with some modifications, in December 1535. John Frederick I (*q.v.*) of Saxony and Philip of Hesse were to take six-monthly turns in conducting the League's affairs and were to summon diets of the League when they saw fit. Financial and military organs were set up. The army, whose strength was planned at 12,000 men, was to be mustered only in the event of war, but funds to maintain troops for two months were to be deposited in advance as a precaution against emergency. The League's defensive character remained unchanged.

The League not only helped to safeguard Protestantism in Germany but also encouraged foreign powers, especially France and England, to oppose the Habsburgs and the papacy. Menaced by the French and by the Turks, Charles V and his brother, the German king Ferdinand I, needed the support of the German Lutherans, both those of the League and those outside it. Charles more than once had to suspend the Imperial Chamber's proceedings and to grant recognition to the Lutherans' ecclesiastical systems.

The development and the decline of the League were alike due chiefly to Philip of Hesse. On the one hand it was he who, with France's backing, overthrew Habsburg rule in Württemberg and restored the long-dispossessed Duke Ulrich there in 1534. After this, Württemberg, Pomerania (Pomorze), Anhalt-Dessau, Augsburg, Frankfurt am Main, Kempten, Hamburg, and Hanover joined the League. On the other hand the outcry against Philip's bigamous marriage induced him to seek Charles V's protection: by a secret treaty (June 13, 1541) he obtained pardon for all his offenses against the Habsburgs or against the laws of the Empire in return for promising to abstain from any foreign alliance and to obstruct the entry of Charles's enemy, Duke William the Rich of Cleves, into the League. Charles's assurances to Philip, however, did not cover the case of a general war against Protestants.

With the Peace of Crépy between Charles V and France (1544), the League's position became precarious; and in summer 1546 Charles declared war on John Frederick I of Saxony and on Philip of Hesse. The League had military superiority in the first months of hostilities, but won no decisive success, and Charles's invasion of Saxony turned the scale. Defeated at Mühlberg (April 24, 1547), John Frederick was taken prisoner; and Philip gave himself up without resistance (June 20). Though individual members fought on for a time, the League disintegrated.

BIBLIOGRAPHY.—O. Winckelmann, *Der Schmalkaldische Bund 1530–1532 und der Nürnberger Religionsfriede* (1892); P. Prüser, *England und die Schmalkaldener 1535–1540* (1929); E. Fabian, *Die Entstehung des Schmalkaldischen Bundes und seiner Verfassung. . .* , 2nd ed. (1962), and his editions of the documents (1958–61).   (E. H. H.)

SCHMIDT, BERNHARD VOLDEMAR (1879–1935), Estonian optical instrument maker whose invention of the telescope named after him was an outstanding development in astronomical optics for the increase in dimension which it gave to the useful field and for its fine image definition (*see* PHOTOGRAPHY, CELESTIAL: *Photographic Telescopes*). Schmidt was born on the island of Naissaar near Reval (Tallinn), Estonia, on March 30, 1879. After little schooling, he worked until 1898 as a telegraph operator, photographer, and designer, meanwhile continuing independent studies and experiments with increasing interest in astronomy and optics. After a short period at the Chalmers Institute in Göteborg, Swed., he went in 1901 to the engineering school at Mittweida in Germany for a few terms' study, but remained until 1926, installing a small workshop and observatory there. The

parabolic mirrors which he made during this period and his 16-in. horizontal telescope of 1909 established his reputation as an optical technician, and he obtained several patents.

In 1926 Schmidt joined the staff of the Hamburg Observatory at Bergedorf in Germany. It was during the far eastern solar eclipse expedition of 1929 that he conceived the idea of a coma-free mirror system, and after initial difficulties, the first 14-in. Schmidt telescope (1:1.75) was begun at Bergedorf in 1930 and completed in 1932. *See* his "Ein lichtstarkes Komafreies Spiegelsystem," *Mitteilungen der Hamburger Sternwarte in Bergedorf,* no. 36 (1931).

Schmidt died at Bergedorf on Dec. 1, 1935. His optical system has proved its efficiency in various technical fields, including that of television projection.

See A. A. Wachmann, "From the Life of Bernhard Schmidt," *Sky and Telescope,* vol. xv, no. 1 (Nov. 1955).   (A. A. Wn.)

SCHMIDT, MAARTEN (1929–   ), Dutch astronomer who made a significant contribution to the study of the interpretation of the spectra of quasi-stellar objects. He was born at Groningen, on Dec. 28, 1929, attended the university at Groningen and received the Ph.D. degree at Leiden. He joined the group of astronomers at the California Institute of Technology and Mount Wilson and Palomar observatories in 1959. Among his early investigations was the derivation of a model of the distribution of mass (or matter) in the Milky Way galaxy. This model contributed greatly to the knowledge of the structure of the galaxy —and of its dynamical properties.

In 1963 he identified four bright lines in the spectrum of the brightest quasi-stellar radio source (*q.v.*) as four lines of hydrogen that had been shifted greatly to the red of their normal positions. This shift indicated that these starlike objects may be located at great distances; and, if so, as a class, would be the most remote objects known. In the years that followed Schmidt's discovery, the study of the quasi-stellar sources and other radio galaxies became the most active field in astronomy and certain areas of physics.

The work of Allan Sandage (*q.v.*) and his associates and Schmidt's discovery stirred certain astronomical concepts to their foundations, although some astronomers do not accept the great distances for the quasi-stellar sources.   (W. W. M.; X.)

SCHMIDT, WILHELM (1868–1954), German Roman Catholic priest and anthropologist, the leader of an influential school of ethnology, was born Feb. 16, 1868, in Hörde, Westphalia. He was educated at a seminary in the Netherlands and at the universities of Berlin and Vienna. A member of the Society of the Divine Word, Father Schmidt taught ethnology and linguistics at St. Gabriel's Seminary at Wien-Mödling, Aust., 1895–1938, and at the universities of Vienna and Fribourg (Switz.). He began his career in linguistics and soon broadened it to include ethnology, joining the culture-historical (*Kulturkreis* or "culture circle") movement founded by F. Ratzel, F. Graebner and B. Ankermann, of which he eventually became leader. Schmidt vigorously opposed the evolutionism of L. H. Morgan, E. B. Tylor and H. Spencer. Following the lead of Andrew Lang, Schmidt challenged the evolutionists' theory of the development of religion, and maintained in *Der Ursprung der Gottesidee* ("The Origin of the Idea of God," 12 vol., 1912–55), his principal work, and in *The Origin and Growth of Religion* (1931), that the most primitive peoples believed in a supreme being.

In 1906 he founded the Anthropos Institute and its journal, *Anthropos.* His philosophy of ethnology was expounded in *The Culture Historical Method of Ethnology,* translated by S. Sieber (1939). Father Schmidt died on Feb. 10, 1954, in Fribourg.

BIBLIOGRAPHY.—J. Henninger, "P. Wilhelm Schmidt, S.V.D., (1868–1954), eine biographische Skizze," *Anthropos,* vol. li, pp. 19–60 (1956); M. Gusinde "Wilhelm Schmidt, S.V.D.," *American Anthropologist,* vol. lvi, no. 5, part 1, pp. 868–870 (Oct. 1954); P. Schebesta, "Wilhelm Schmidt: 1868–1954," *Man,* vol. liv, pp. 89–90 (1954).   (LE. A. W.)

SCHMIDT-ROTTLUFF, KARL (1884–   ), German painter and graphic artist and an important figure in the Expressionist movement, was born in Rottluff near Chemnitz on Dec. 1, 1884. Originally a student of architecture, Schmidt-Rottluff turned to painting in Dresden where he became one of the founders of *die Brücke* ("the bridge")—an influential group of artists in the initial years of Expressionism. His finest work is characterized by a dynamism of brilliant colour and boldness of cubic form. His religious woodcuts, done immediately after World War I, were inspired by African sculpture. They are characterized by a power of religious statement that could not have been achieved with traditionalistic liturgical art forms. (P. H. S.)

SCHMITT, FLORENT (1870–1958), French composer, known for his orchestral works, was born at Blâmont, Meurthe-et-Moselle, Sept. 28, 1870. He studied at Nancy and in 1889 entered the Paris Conservatoire, where he was a pupil of Massenet and Fauré. In 1900 he won the Prix de Rome with his lyric scene *Sémiramis* and later traveled throughout Europe. He gained fame with the *Psaume XLVI* (1906) for chorus and orchestra, the ballet, *La Tragédie de Salomé* (1907) and a piano quintet (1908). He wrote many orchestral works, showing a bold sense of orchestral colour, and including *Antoine et Cléopâtre* (1920), *Mirages* (1924) and *Salammbô* (1927). Among his piano works, several of which he orchestrated, are the *Reflets d'Allemagne* (1905). He wrote unaccompanied choral works and chamber works, including the *Suite en rocaille* (1935), *A tour d'anches* (1947), quartets for woodwind instruments and for brass, and a sextet for clarinets. He died Aug. 17, 1958, at Neuilly-sur-Seine.

SCHMUCKER, SAMUEL SIMON (1799–1873), a leading theologian of the American Lutheran Church during the period of development of an indigenous type of liberal Lutheranism, was born at Hagerstown, Md., on Feb. 28, 1799. He was educated at first under private tutors and then at the University of Pennsylvania and at Princeton Seminary. Schmucker fostered a strongly pietistic emphasis, moving on to a prophetic ecumenical spirit. He was a pioneer in the establishment of a first united Lutheran Church of district synods in America, the General Synod (1820); he became and remained for 38 years professor in charge of Gettysburg Seminary, an institution he helped to promote (1826; now Lutheran Theological Seminary); and he founded a classical school that later became Gettysburg College (chartered 1832).

Constitutions for churches and district synods, liturgies, hymnbooks and editions of Luther's catechisms (with his own freer interpretations) were only a few of his numerous works. In 1834 appeared his *Elements of Popular Theology*, a first systematic treatment in English of Lutheran theology in America. In 1838 was published his *Appeal to the American Churches*, outlining a plan of church fraternity, a forerunner of the Federal Council of Churches which came years later. When the Evangelical Alliance was organized in 1846 he played a major role.

What has been called the crisis in American Lutheran theology centred about Schmucker's name, particularly in an anonymous pamphlet which he caused to circulate entitled *Definite Synodical Platform* in 1855. This document proposed an amended and abridged form of the Augsburg Confession as a confessional statement for the American Lutheran Churches. The incentive to its publication lay in the pressure groups of conservative Lutheran immigrants, who, in increasing numbers, began to flood the American scene, calling for a return to a stricter allegiance to the Lutheran Confessions of the 16th century. Schmucker went down to defeat, and with him the tender plant of "American Lutheranism," the term given to the liberal movement he had so strongly nurtured. He died on July 26, 1873. (V. F.)

SCHNITZLER, ARTHUR (1862–1931), Austrian writer, known for his psychological analysis of the Viennese bourgeois society at the turn of the 19th century, was most successful as a writer of short stories and *Novellen*. He was born in Vienna on May 15, 1862, the son of a well-known physician, and, following in his father's footsteps, he took a medical degree and practised medicine.

He made his name as a writer with *Anatol* (1893; trans. by H. Granville-Barker, 1911), a series of one-act plays analyzing the amorous adventures of a wealthy young Viennese man-about-town. Schnitzler's gift of characterization, power to evoke moods, skilful, entertaining dialogue, detached, though melancholic, humour, and skeptical appraisal of man are the means employed to

ARTHUR SCHNITZLER

call forth the atmosphere of illusion created by the last days of the Habsburg Empire. In most of his stories and plays he explores human psychology, portraying human egotism in love, human fear in face of death, the complexities of the erotic life, and the morbid moods induced by a weary introspection. *Reigen* (1897; *Merry-Go-Round*, 1953), a cycle of ten dialogues, amounts to an algebra of promiscuity which depicts the heartlessness of men and women in the grip of lust. Performed only in 1920, it even then gave rise to scandal (see *Der Kampf um den Reigen*, 1922), but achieved success eventually in the French film *La Ronde* (1950). As a storyteller Schnitzler experimented most successfully with the interior monologue in *Leutnant Gustl* (1901; *None but the Brave*, 1926), the first masterpiece of European literature conceived in that mode, and *Fräulein Else* (1924; trans. 1925). In the former he depicts the hollowness of the Austrian military code of honour already castigated in *Liebelei* (1896; *Playing With Love*, 1914). His most striking exploration of the darker aspects of human nature was *Flucht in die Finsternis* (1931; *Flight into Darkness*, 1931), in which incipient madness is revealed stage by stage.

His full-length plays and novels are, on the whole, disappointing; his novels *Der Weg ins Freie* (1908; *The Road to the Open*, 1923) and *Therese* (1928; *Theresa*, 1928) are of sociological rather than literary interest. In the former and in the play *Professor Bernhardi* (1912; trans. 1928) he analyzed the position of the Jews in Austria. Schnitzler died on Oct. 21, 1931.

BIBLIOGRAPHY.—Josef Körner, *A. Schnitzler, Gestalten und Probleme* (1921); R. Specht, *A. Schnitzler, der Dichter und sein Werk* (1922); S. Liptzin, *Arthur Schnitzler* (1932); R. Plaut, *A. Schnitzler als Erzähler* (1935); Bernhard Blume, *Das nihilistische Weltbild Arthur Schnitzlers* (1936); Olga Schnitzler, *Spiegelbild der Freundschaft* (1961). (H. S. R.)

SCHNORR VON CAROLSFELD, JULIUS (1794–1872), German painter, was born on March 26, 1794, at Leipzig, where he received his earliest instruction from his father, Hans Veit Schnorr (1764–1841), a draftsman, engraver, and painter. In 1818 he went to Rome, where he was associated with the German Pre-Raphaelites (the Nazarenes), a school of religious and romantic art that abjured modern styles and set itself to recover fresco painting and "monumental art." Together with Peter von Cornelius, J. F. Overbeck, and Philipp Veit, Schnorr received a commission to decorate the entrance hall of the Villa Massimi with frescoes after Ariosto. In 1825 he left Rome, settled in Munich, and served King Ludwig, transplanting to Germany the art of wall painting learned in Italy. Schnorr published a pictorial Bible, with about 200 pictures, in 1852–60; it does not bear comparison with Raphael's Bible. He also made designs, carried out in the royal factory at Munich, for windows in Glasgow cathedral and in St. Paul's cathedral, London. He died on May 24, 1872.

SCHOBER, JOHANN (1874–1932), Austrian statesman, twice chancellor, was born at Perg, Upper Austria, on Nov. 14, 1874. Entering the Imperial Austrian police service as a young man, he became the Austrian president of police in 1918, some months before the revolution at the end of World War I. On the proclamation of the Austrian Republic (Nov. 12, 1918), Schober placed his force at the disposal of the new government, and did much to ensure a peaceful change of regime. At the same time, he secured the safety of the ex-imperial family, whose departure from Vienna he supervised. During the two years of Socialist government which followed, Schober's force was reproached unjustly by the extreme left wing with being reactionary.

His administrative ability, and, above all, his honesty, gained him the confidence of moderate opinion in Austria, and especially of the inter-Allied missions and advisers. Because of this confidence it was expected that, if he were chancellor, the Allies would be willing to grant the loan necessary to restore Austria's chaotic finances, and he was selected to form, on June 20, 1921, a coalition government supported by Social Christians and by Pan-Germans. He took the first step toward establishing friendly relations between Austria and its neighbours when he concluded the Treaty of Lány with Czechoslovakia on Dec. 16, 1921. But the Pan-Germans, who formed a part of the coalition, resented any treaty with Czechoslovakia as putting difficulties in the way of ultimate union with Germany; they withdrew from the government and on May 24, 1922, Schober resigned, returning to the post of president of police.

On July 15, 1927, he suppressed a revolt of the Socialist *Schutzbund* in Vienna. He became chancellor again from Sept. 26, 1929, to Sept. 25, 1930. On Dec. 3, 1930, he was appointed vice-chancellor and minister of foreign affairs in Otto Ender's coalition of Social Christians and Pan-Germans. On March 19, 1931, he concluded an agreement with Germany which would have led to an *Anschluss* but which under French and Czechoslovak pressure had to be abandoned. Schober retired from the government on Jan. 27, 1932, and died at Baden, near Vienna, on Aug. 19.

See O. Kleinschmied, *Schober* (1930).

SCHOECK, OTHMAR (1886–1957), one of the principal composers of *Lieder* of his time, was born at Brunnen, Switz., on Sept. 1, 1886. He studied first at Zürich and in 1907 under Max Reger in Leipzig. His first songs appeared on his return the following year to Zürich where, until 1917, he conducted choral societies. From 1917 to 1944 he was conductor of the symphony concerts at Sankt Gallen. His principal song cycles, for voice and small ensemble, include *Elegie* (1915–22), on poems of N. Lenau and J. von Eichendorff; *Gaselen* (1923), on poems of G. Keller; and *Wandersprüche* (1928), on poems of Eichendorff. He also wrote eight stage works, including *Penthesilea* (1927) and *Massimilla Doni* (1937), as well as orchestral and chamber works. He died at Zürich on March 8, 1957. To further interest in his works the *Othmar Schoeck Gesellschaft* was founded in 1959.

See H. Corrodi, *Othmar Schoeck,* 3rd ed. (1956).

SCHOENBERG, ARNOLD (1874–1951), Austrian-U.S. composer whose innovations were one of the most powerful influences in 20th-century music. Born in Vienna on Sept. 13, 1874, he lived there, apart from two short periods in Berlin (1901–03 and 1911–15), until he was over 50. He learned the violin as a child and later taught himself the cello, but he was not originally destined for a musical career. He worked in a bank for several years before finally devoting himself to music (1895). As a composer he was almost entirely self-taught, though he received some help from his friend Alexander von Zemlinsky, whose sister he married in 1901. Schoenberg's first model was Brahms, but the earliest works he published, the string sextet *Verklärte Nacht* and the choral work *Gurrelieder*, are indebted to Wagner. These two influences are reconciled in the first and second string quartets (1905 and 1908) and the first chamber symphony (1906), all of which show Schoenberg's lifelong concern with structural unity and at the same time an advanced form of chromaticism that threatened to undermine the traditional major-minor tonal system.

About 1909 Schoenberg began to write music that could no longer be related to a single tonal centre; hence the term atonality, or, as he himself preferred, pantonality. Dissonances are no longer felt to need resolution, and the recapitulations and symmet-

PICTORIAL PARADE

ARNOLD SCHOENBERG

rical melodic paragraphs belonging to tonality disappear. The three piano pieces, op. 11, and the five orchestral pieces, op. 16, both of 1909, opened up unexplored fields of expression and soon became internationally famous. They were followed by two one-act operas, *Erwartung* (1909; performed 1924) and *Die glückliche Hand* (1908–13; performed 1924); *Pierrot Lunaire* (1912); and, in 1917, the oratorio *Die Jakobsleiter*, the composition of which was cut short by the second of two periods of military service.

From 1907 onward Schoenberg was also painting pictures. He became friendly with Wassily Kandinsky and in 1912 exhibited with the "Blue Rider" group. Through this association the term "expressionist" was applied to Schoenberg's music and to that of his two most gifted pupils, Anton Webern and Alban Berg. These composers were to remain his close friends, adapting his successive technical discoveries to their own needs. A by-product of his work as a teacher, which continued throughout his life, was a series of important theoretical works on music, the first of which was the *Harmonielehre* (1911; Eng. trans., *Theory of Harmony* 1947).

From 1920 Schoenberg became preoccupied with a group of works embodying a new principle of composition. Since abandoning tonality, he had confined his instrumental music to short pieces built of contrasting lyrical or dramatic elements. His longer works had been vocal, the text providing the basis for the form. Large-scale instrumental composition had formerly depended on two elements, the tonal and the thematic. Schoenberg realized that the loss of the one could be offset by strengthening the other. He gradually evolved the technique of serialism, through which a whole composition could be derived from a series of notes, usually the 12 notes of the chromatic scale (*see* DODECAPHONY), disposed in an order specially chosen for the particular work. He called it a "method of composing with twelve notes related only to one another." In the works of the 1920s, which are all serial, Schoenberg's profound sympathy with the Viennese classical tradition reasserts itself in his adaptation of his new language to symphonic forms. He wrote four important chamber works, including a third quartet, the Variations for Orchestra, a short comic opera, *Von Heute auf Morgen* (1928; produced 1930), and the first two acts of *Moses und Aron* (1930–32; produced 1957). This opera is concerned with the nature of divine revelation and the problem of its communication, and it embodies Schoenberg's deepest beliefs.

In 1923 Schoenberg's first wife died, and the following year he married Gertrud Kolisch, the sister of the violinist Rudolf Kolisch. In 1926 he went to Berlin as director of a master class in composition at the Prussian Academy of Arts but in 1933 was dismissed from this post because he was a Jew. He moved to Paris for a few months, and while there formally returned to the Jewish faith, which as a young man he had left for the Lutheran Church. In the autumn of the same year he went to Boston and spent a year teaching there and in New York. From 1936 to 1944 he taught at the University of California, Los Angeles, having become a U.S. citizen in 1940. He died at Los Angeles on July 13, 1951.

During his last months in Europe Schoenberg wrote concertos for cello and for string quartet, based on material from concertos by G. M. Monn and Handel respectively, and in 1934 a suite in G for string orchestra. After these tonal works, his first for over 20 years, Schoenberg completed two major serial works in 1936, the Violin Concerto and the fourth quartet. In the last 15 years of his life he composed less, overcome at first by the political situation in Europe and later because of failing health. Some of the works of this period are serial, among them such masterpieces as the Piano Concerto (1942), the string trio (1946), and the unfinished *Moderner Psalm* ("Modern Psalm"), on his own text (1950); others are based on tonality in one form or another. All show the composer's extraordinary mastery in developing a whole work within the terms of the opening idea. His strong personality is similarly felt through every phase of his output, for the revolutionary, who strongly influenced the course of musical history both in his break with tonality and his formulation of serialism, was also a traditionalist for whom innovation was never experiment but simply the most direct means to an end.

BIBLIOGRAPHY.—A. Schoenberg, *Style and Idea* (1950), *Briefe*, selected and edited by E. Stein (1958; Eng. trans., *Letters*, by E. Wilkins and E. Kaiser, 1964); E. Wellesz, *Arnold Schönberg* (1921; Eng. trans. by W. H. Kerridge, 1925); J. Rufer, *Die Komposition mit zwölf Tönen* (1952; Eng. trans., *Composition with Twelve Notes Related Only to One Another*, by H. Searle, 1954), *Das Werk Arnold Schoenbergs* (1959; Eng. trans. by D. Newlin, 1962); E. Stein, *Orpheus in New Guises* (1953). (O. W. N.)

SCHOENHEIMER, RUDOLF (1898–1941), German biochemist whose technique of "tagging" molecules revolutionized the study of chemical processes in the living cell, was born in Berlin on May 10, 1898. He obtained a medical degree from the University of Berlin in 1923. During his internship at the Moabit Hospital in Berlin he began a lifelong interest in the relationship of cholesterol (*q.v.*) to atherosclerosis, a form of arteriosclerosis (hardening of the arteries). He taught biochemistry in relation to pathology, at Leipzig and later at Freiburg, until 1933, when he went to the United States at the invitation of Columbia University, gratefully fleeing the rising tide of Nazism. As assistant professor of biochemistry at Columbia he was an associate of H. C. Urey, the discoverer of heavy hydrogen and investigator of many other isotopes. In collaboration with David Rittenberg, one of Urey's students, Schoenheimer developed the technique of using isotopes as labels for organic molecules of food and the like during their passage through the living cell (*see* ISOTOPE: *Uses of Isotopes*). By using this technique biochemists were able to trace the course of certain molecules and thereby demonstrate for the first time many details of the cell's metabolic processes (*see* METABOLISM). Schoenheimer, apparently despondent over the war, committed suicide in New York on Sept. 11, 1941.

(D. RG.)

SCHOLASTICISM. The word Scholasticism has been applied in many senses, but particularly to philosophy, theology, and teaching method. It is correctly used of the system of Western Christian philosophy that flourished from the 11th to the 15th century. This was not only the system of the majority of medieval thinkers but it can boast of many of the greatest names in medieval thought, *e.g.*, Anselm, Abelard, Albertus Magnus, Bonaventura, Thomas Aquinas, Duns Scotus, and William Ockham. As Neoscholasticism, it is of considerable importance in modern times.

Particularly in the 19th century, Scholastic philosophy has been regarded as being synonymous with medieval philosophy. Thus some writers defined Scholastic philosophy as being merely a teaching method, *e.g.*, philosophy as taught in the schools of the medieval period (J. B. Hauréau), or as "the child of the schools" (F. Picavet). Others would include all thinkers who lived in the medieval period among Scholastics. There is some excuse for this view because in the Middle Ages any lecturer in a recognized school was given the title of *scholasticus*, but such definitions are purely verbal and ignore fundamental points of difference. Erigena, David of Dinant, Avicenna, and Averroës, for example, are medieval philosophers who were non-Scholastic or even anti-Scholastic. The same applies to the very interesting school of Byzantine thought. Even in the West, Boëthius (*c.* 480–524) falls within the conventional chronological limits of the Middle Ages (5th to 15th centuries) but cannot be classed as a Scholastic, though, like St. Augustine and Pseudo-Dionysius, he is in some ways a precursor of Scholastic philosophy. Moreover, to view Scholasticism as medieval is to disregard its amazing resurgence in the late 19th and 20th centuries.

It has also been maintained that the chief characteristic of Scholasticism was a servile bondage to Aristotle and the dogmas of the church. This view is historically incorrect. The earlier Scholastics, *e.g.*, Anselm, were strongly influenced by Platonic and Neoplatonic ideas, which came through Augustine. The christianized Aristotelianism was mainly the work of Albertus Magnus and Aquinas, both original thinkers who were in no way subservient to the authority of Aristotle. Aquinas wrote: "The object of philosophical thought is not to know men's opinions but the truth of things," and when he found Aristotle's teaching on certain questions hesitating or inadequate, he turned to the Platonic tradition. The result of the revolution in Christian thought produced by Albertus and Aquinas was that although in theology Augustinian-

ism was still predominant, the Scholasticism of the 13th century was strongly affected by the philosophy of Aristotle.

All Scholastic philosophers accepted the truths of revelation as taught by the Scriptures and the Western Church, but their views concerning the relations between philosophy and theology varied considerably. Some few 11th-century thinkers, such as Peter Damian (*q.v.*) and Manegold of Lautenbach, were highly suspicious of all philosophy, and at best regarded it as subsidiary to theology (*ancilla fidei*). Aquinas distinguished the respective fields of theology and philosophy. He emphasized that all truth has its ultimate source in God and therefore that which is the conclusion of the right exercise of reason cannot contradict that which is derived from revelation. He admitted that some doctrines such as those concerning the Trinity and the Eucharist might be beyond the scope of human reason but were not contradictory to it. Indeed reason might be able to advance arguments in their support. Later thinkers widened the distinction between philosophy and revelation, and William Ockham completely separated them.

Method.—The Scholastic method in teaching and lecturing involved the *lectio*, the public lecture in which the master explained the text, and the *disputatio*, in which a view was expounded and objections to it proposed and answered in syllogistic form. It is often attributed to Abelard who applied dialectic to theological dogma; the idea originated in the practice of the canon lawyers during the 11th and 12th centuries. In their task of collecting and arranging the decisions of church councils and papal decrees they were faced with a mass of conflicting material, and they endeavoured to find a means of reconciling apparently conflicting statements. Anselm of Laon and Guillaume de Champeaux (*qq.v.*) adopted similar means in dealing with views expressed in the Scriptures and in the writings of the Church Fathers and Doctors. Abelard had studied under Guillaume and Anselm and developed the method in the *Sic et non*, a collection of opinions from Scripture and the Fathers for and against various propositions. This work in its turn influenced the methods of the canon lawyers, *e.g.*, in the *Decretum* or *Concordantia discordantium Canonum* (*c.* 1140) of Gratian (*q.v.*) of Bologna. Abelard's example was followed by Peter Lombard (*q.v.*; *c.* 1100–60), bishop of Paris, who was the author of the *Sentences* (*Quattuor libri sententiarum*), which became the chief textbook in the theological faculties of the medieval universities. Numerous commentaries on the *Sentences* appeared and those of the more famous masters such as Aquinas, Duns Scotus, and William Ockham are still accessible. The commentaries gave rise to more systematic and concise expositions covering the whole field of theology which became known as "Summae," *e.g.*, the *Summae* attributed to Alexander of Hales (*c.* 1170 or 1185–1245), which is probably a compilation by his disciples, and of Albertus Magnus (*c.* 1200–80), and the *Summa theologiae* of St. Thomas Aquinas (1225–74). The latter fixed the scholastic method for the next two centuries. For details of the scholastic methods that governed the *lectio* and the *disputatio*, see S. J. Curtis and M. E. A. Boultwood, *A Short History of Educational Ideas*, ch. 5, 3rd ed. (1961).

History.—This article does not attempt to deal with the teaching of individual philosophers, which appears under their respective names, but is confined to a historical outline of the development of Scholasticism (*see also* PHILOSOPHY, HISTORY OF: *Patristic and Medieval Philosophy: Western Philosophy*). The growth of medieval Scholasticism may be conveniently divided into three stages—a formative period (11th and 12th centuries), a period of consolidation (13th century), and one of criticism (14th and 15th centuries).

In the first period Scholastic thought was influenced by Platonism derived from St. Augustine, Pseudo-Dionysius (the Areopagite; 5th or early 6th century) and other writers of the Eastern and Western Churches. Aristotelian dialectic became important in the 12th century, largely through the works of Abelard, but Aristotle's philosophical works were not available in Latin translations. It was not until 1162 that John of Salisbury was able to make use of the whole of the *Organon*. This period was dominated by the controversy about the nature of universals, though it was by no means the only topic that was discussed: there was also, *e.g.*, the ontological argument of Anselm for the existence of God.

The problem of the universal is one with which philosophy is always concerned, but it has taken different forms at different periods. It is concerned with the relation between our universal conceptions and external reality. Thus it may be asked if our thought can supply a true account of the external world. Are the uniformities now known as scientific laws to be found in the objects themselves, or are they modes in which the mind is forced to think in order to explain the phenomena presented by the senses? The medievals had not reached this stage of analysis but approached the problem from the logical point of view, *e.g.*, the function of class names and the names of abstract qualities. The problem was presented to medieval thinkers through the form in which it appeared in Boëthius' *Commentary* on the *Isagoge* of Porphyry:

What does Porphyry mean by saying that he merely touches and passes over certain points which older philosophers had discussed at great length? He means this: he omits the question whether genera and species have an actual subsistence, or dwell in the mind and intellect only; whether they are corporeal or incorporeal; and whether they are separated or joined to the objects our senses perceive.

This was a challenge to the successors of Boëthius, but it was the occasion rather than the cause of the controversy. The problem is so fundamental to philosophy that sooner or later it was bound to arise. Four types of answer were possible:

(1) The first and simplest was that of extreme realism, based on Plato and developed in a modified form by Christian thinkers. This solution asserted that mental conceptions such as goodness, justice, or equality exist independently of the particular sense objects that exhibit such qualities. The latter are real insofar as they share in the independently existing ideas. Augustine had introduced an important Christian modification in making the ideas exemplars, archetypes in the mind of God. Many early medieval thinkers, influenced by Augustine and Pseudo-Dionysius, tended toward this position of extreme realism. Thus Erigena and St. Anselm, though in many ways diverse in their philosophy, fall into this group.

(2) The solution of moderate realism developed later. This was the position that was defended by Albertus Magnus and Aquinas and that had been represented in Greek philosophy by Aristotle. Moderate realists emphasized that particular things are the most real to us but universals are most real in themselves. They believed that universals exist in particular things as the common natures of them, *e.g.*, humanity exists in individual men and justice exists as realized in just men and just actions. As a result of abstraction, this common nature of the species has a secondary mode of being in the knowing mind where it exists as an idea. Thinkers of the 12th century adhered strictly to the alternatives presented by Boëthius and conducted their arguments on logical lines. In the following century, when Aquinas developed the psychology of conceptual thinking, moderate realism attained its fullest expression.

(3) The final development of Scholastic thought was conceptualism, a position adopted by William Ockham and his school. He acknowledged the existence of universal ideas as mental facts and attributed their formation to the synthetic activity of the mind.

(4) Nominalism (*i.e.*, the view that universals are mere names used for convenience's sake), the opposite of extreme realism, is an entirely modern development and was not held by any Scholastic philosopher. Earlier historians of philosophy described the thought of such men as Roscelin (*q.v.; c.* 1050–*c.* 1125), as nominalism but it was not nominalism in the modern sense of the term. Philosophers of that period had not reached the stage of psychological analysis that would have enabled them to express accurately their objections to extreme realism. Their attitude is most adequately summed up in the term antirealist and, as M. de Wulf has suggested, they were really feeling their way toward moderate realism. They restricted their discussion to the logical alternatives proposed by Boëthius; and even Abelard, who saw the

need of positing a process of abstraction, was not able to describe the formation of the concept in any detail.

The formative period also included the most important treatise on ethics that had been written since the closing of the schools of Athens, the *Ethica seu Scito te ipsum* of Abelard. This work replaced the Augustinian doctrine of original sin by one less harsh and emphasized the consent of the will as being essential in actual sin. Abelard's views were not approved by the church at that time, but they influenced the moral philosophy of Aquinas. The *Policraticus* of John of Salisbury also belongs to this period. It is a treatise on political philosophy and it was one of the most influential examples of the earlier theory of the state as an organism.

The 13th century marked the culmination and consolidation of medieval Scholastic philosophy and was dominated by such outstanding personalities as Albertus Magnus, St. Thomas Aquinas, St. Bonaventura, and Duns Scotus. Medieval mathematical and scientific speculation are represented by Robert Grosseteste (*c.* 1168–1253) and Roger Bacon (*c.* 1220–*c.* 1292) (*qq.v.*). Grosseteste's theory of light and his application of mathematics to optics and physical science in some ways anticipate modern thought. His pupil, Roger Bacon, is popularly known as the discoverer of gunpowder. From the philosophical standpoint, Bacon's emphasis on experience and the experimental method is interesting but it is probable that his admirers attribute much to him that belongs to his master.

Certain aspects of this period are extremely important. The medieval universities had originated in the latter part of the previous century but now their influence developed considerably. They were the chief agents in transmitting Scholastic theology and philosophy and their influence was bound up with two other series of events. The first was the acquisition of the Aristotelian corpus in Latin translations and commentaries. The logical works of Aristotle had been available at least since 1162, but soon translations of the philosophical works of Aristotle began to appear. These were chiefly based on versions of the Persian Avicenna and the Spanish-born Arab Averroës, and not only suffered from the influence of Arabic thought, but included treatises of Neoplatonic origin. The church was suspicious of these translations and the study of the newly acquired works of Aristotle was prohibited until more accurate translations and commentaries became available. The translations of William of Moerbeke and the commentaries of Albertus and Aquinas eventually supplied the need but meanwhile a good deal of damage had occurred. A flourishing school of Latin Averroism appeared in the universities of Paris and Oxford. This was not merely of academic importance, but because of the anti-Christian tenets of the Averroists, the Christian civilization of Europe was threatened (*see* AVERROISM, LATIN). The translations of William of Moerbeke, the commentaries of Albertus and Aquinas, and the grand syntheses of Christian belief and Aristotelian philosophy produced by these writers arrested the subversive movement.

Ernest Renan was the first to draw attention to Latin Averroism but he was unable to discover the originator of the movement. In the 20th century, P. Mandonnet ascribed it to Siger (*q.v.*) of Brabant. More recently, manuscripts have been discovered at Munich and Oxford and it is suggested that Mandonnet was mistaken and that the controversy between Siger and Aquinas was mainly an academic one concerned with the nature and aims of philosophy. The fact remains, however, that Latin Averroism was driven underground and did not appear in the open until much later in the medieval period.

The other important event was the coming of the Franciscan and Dominican orders to the universities. The Dominicans appeared in Paris about 1218 and in Oxford in 1220. Within a few years they were followed by the Franciscans. At Paris the mendicants were at first received coldly and after a short time, when they demanded chairs of theology in the university, the secular and regular clergy changed their attitude to one of open hostility. In 1229 the dispersion that followed a quarrel between "town and gown" left many professorships vacant and enabled the mendicants to press their claims successfully. The hostility continued until 1256 when St. Thomas Aquinas and St. Bonaventura were nominated as masters. At Oxford the ambitious plans of the Dominicans precipitated a dispute which came to an end only in 1320. The Franciscans profited by the unpopularity of the Dominicans and through the ability of such outstanding teachers as Grosseteste, Roger Bacon, and Duns Scotus, they gained an ascendancy in the university. On the whole, the Dominicans favoured the Christian-Aristotelian synthesis of Aquinas, while the Franciscans were more conservative and clung to the teaching of Augustine, though they made use of a good deal of Aristotelian terminology. There were, however, exceptions to this general tendency. Aquinas was regarded by some of his contemporaries as an innovator and certain of his views, such as the doctrine of the unity of substantial forms in the individual, were included in the condemnations of 1277 at Paris and Oxford.

Two important treatises in political philosophy belong to this period: the first part of the *Rule of Princes* (*De regimine principum*) by Aquinas (*c.* 1267), and the *De Monarchia* of Dante (date unknown; possibly *c.* 1313 or even earlier). The interesting Franciscan thinker Ramon Llull (*q.v.; c.* 1235–1316) was an early pioneer of symbolic logic.

The final period of medieval Scholasticism has sometimes been regarded as the beginning of the decline, but this view does less than justice to the thinkers of the 14th century and their influence on later thought. Just as the 13th century was an age of construction and synthesis, the century that followed was a period of criticism. One is reminded of the parallel of the 17th and 18th centuries. The critical attitude can be found in the works of Duns Scotus and Roger Bacon, who began to question the conclusions of previous thinkers, but it was overshadowed by their own constructive achievements. The critical spirit became more explicit in the writings of William Ockham and his followers. It is found in two predecessors of Ockham, Durandus of Saint-Pourçain (*q.v.; c.* 1270–1334) and Petrus Aureoli (*q.v.; c.* 1280–1322), who criticized the Thomist theory of knowledge. Durandus appealed to the principle of economy in thought, generally known as "Ockham's razor"; *e.g.*, relation is not to be reckoned as an extra entity: two men are similar in respect of humanity, not in respect of similarity. Petrus Aureoli was feeling his way to the conceptualism that was more fully developed by Ockham (*q.v.*). As Ockham had studied and taught at Oxford, he was influenced by the interest in natural science that was characteristic of the Franciscan masters in that university. In his moral theory he pushed to the extreme the primacy of the will over the intellect which had been taught by Duns Scotus, and he finally separated the respective fields of philosophy and theology. Ockham's teaching spread rapidly during the 14th and 15th centuries, especially at Paris. His political treatises in which he supported the secular power against the papacy provoked the antagonism of the church. His followers, Nicholas of Autrecourt (*c.* 1300–after 1350), Jean Buridan (*c.* 1295–after 1366), Albert of Saxony (1316?–1390?), and Nicole Oresme (*c.* 1320–1382), developed different aspects of Ockham's thought. Nicholas investigated the nature of relations, especially that of cause and effect, and his anticipation of modern thought led Hastings Rashdall to describe him as "the Hume of the Middle Ages." Buridan, Albert, and Oresme were interested in the mathematical and scientific tendencies of the age. Oresme can claim fame as the first to write an important philosophical work in the vernacular (in French). He also produced an economic treatise on the coinage, and his mathematical and scientific thought anticipated the work of Descartes in analytical geometry and the theories of Copernicus and Galileo.

The chief philosopher of the 15th century, Nicholas of Cusa (*q.v.;* 1401–64), is difficult to classify. M. de Wulf considered that he remained "a medieval and a Scholastic," but other writers regard him as a Renaissance philosopher. Whatever view is taken, he was an individual who combined both the old and the new in his mathematical speculations, which foreshadow the theory of relativity and non-Euclidean geometry. He also took an active interest in political affairs. In his younger days he was a supporter of the Conciliar theory, and he later brought about a temporary union between the Eastern and Western Churches.

By the close of the 15th century, medieval Scholasticism was in rapid decline, very largely because of the numerous second-rate thinkers who held themselves aloof from the great scientific discoveries of the age, and who eventually became bitterly antagonistic to the new outlook. In turn, the Renaissance thinkers despised what they termed the outworn attitude of Scholasticism. In addition, because of the theological controversies of the Reformation period, Scholasticism, at least to the inhabitants of those countries that had adopted Protestantism, appeared to be bound up with the doctrinal system of the Roman Catholic Church. The decline was not as apparent in the countries of southern Europe. Two outstanding philosophers and theologians of the 16th and 17th centuries respectively not only remained faithful to Scholasticism but show in their writings evidence of constructive thought. They were Cajetan (*q.v.;* Tommaso de Vio; 1468?–1534), in Italy, and Francisco Suárez (1548–1617), in Spain. Cajetan's development and clarification of the Thomist doctrine of analogy is accepted by many modern Thomists. Suárez was a prolific writer whose *Disputationes metaphysicae* paved the way for the numerous courses in philosophy (*Cursus philosophici*) published during the latter 17th and the 18th centuries to replace the traditional commentaries on Aristotle and later on St. Thomas Aquinas (on whom the Spanish Dominican John of St. Thomas [1589–1644] was an illuminating commentator). Suárez' *Tractatus de legibus* was an original development of Scholastic legal and political theory.

This revival was mainly the work of the Dominicans and Jesuits but was only partially successful. Though a few Scholastics were interested in mathematics and physics, the majority ignored the problems raised by the scientific discoveries of the period. Hence Scholasticism had no place in the main current of philosophical thought.

The revival of Scholasticism under the name of Neoscholasticism was one of the last of a series of changes in the attitude of the modern world to the Middle Ages, which, starting from an interest in the life and activities, the literature, art, and architecture of the medieval period, eventually reached its philosophy. A convenient starting point in the revival was the publication of Victor Cousin's *Introduction aux ouvrages inédits d'Abélard* (1836). This was followed by a series of studies by X. Rousselot, C. F. M. de Rémusat, and others, culminating in the classic *Histoire de la philosophie scolastique* of J. B. Hauréau (2 vol. [1850], revised ed., 3 vol. [1872–80]). Though defective as regards critical scholarship, it was for many years a very important contribution. The modern critical study of Scholasticism developed after 1880 and included the works of C. Baeumker, F. Ehrle, H. S. Denifle, and others. Since then most European countries and the United States have made important contributions, with the result that there is now a considerable literature on the subject of Scholasticism. Scholastic philosophers are now fully concerned with modern problems, so that Neoscholasticism is a force that commands wide recognition and respect on both sides of the Atlantic.

See also references under "Scholasticism" in the Index.

BIBLIOGRAPHY.—Articles dealing with individual philosophers should be sought under their names. The following is a selection of general studies concerned with Scholasticism:

T. N. Harper, *The Metaphysics of the School* (1879); Cardinal Mercier, *A Manual of Modern Scholastic Philosophy*, authorized trans. and 8th ed. by T. L. and S. A. Parker, 2 vol. (1916–17); R. L. Poole, *Illustrations of the History of Medieval Thought and Learning*, rev. ed. (1920); M. Grabmann, *Die Philosophie des Mittelalters* (1921), *Mittelalterliches Geistesleben*, 3 vol. (1926–56); H. O. Taylor, *The Mediaeval Mind*, 4th ed., 2 vol. (1925); F. Ueberweg, *Grundriss der Geschichte der Philosophie*, vol. ii, *Die patristische und scholastische Philosophie*, 11th rev. ed. by B. Geyer (1928); J. Maritain, *Art and Scholasticism*, Eng. trans. (1930); R. P. Phillips, *Modern Thomistic Philosophy*, 2 vol. (1934–35); M. de Wulf, *Histoire de la philosophie médiévale*, 6th ed., 3 vol. (1934–47); E. Gilson, *The Spirit of Mediaeval Philosophy*, Eng. trans. (1936), *La philosophie au moyen âge*, 3rd ed. (1947); E. C. Thomas, *History of the Schoolmen* (1941); D. J. B. Hawkins, *A Sketch of Mediaeval Philosophy* (1946); E. Bréhier, *La philosophie du moyen âge*, 2nd ed. (1949); S. J. Curtis, *A Short History of Western Philosophy in the Middle Ages* (1950); F. C. Copleston, *A History of Philosophy*, vol. ii and iii (1950–53), *Medieval Philosophy* (1952); P. Boehner, *Medieval Logic* (1952). (S. J. C.)

SCHOMBERG (Schönberg), **FRIEDRICH HERMANN,** Duke of (1615–1690), German soldier of fortune who fought in the service of various countries in the major European wars between 1634 and 1690, was born at Heidelberg on Dec. 6, 1615, the son of the Protestant court marshal of Frederick V, elector palatine, and of Anne, daughter of an English peer, the 5th Lord Dudley. He volunteered under Frederick Henry of Orange in 1633, and from 1634 to 1637 during the Thirty Years' War served in the army of Bernard of Saxe-Weimar for campaigns on the upper Rhine. In 1639 he again went to Holland for some years of service.

In 1650 Jules Cardinal Mazarin, in the crisis of the Fronde (*q.v.*), secured him and his German infantry for the French Royal Army that defeated the rebel marshal de Turenne at the Battle of Rethel (Dec. 15, 1650). Schomberg was appointed *maréchal de camp* on Oct. 28, 1652, after Turenne had changed sides, and was one of Turenne's best officers in the campaigns against the Spaniards and the prince de Condé. In the Battle of the Dunes (1658) he commanded, as lieutenant general, Turenne's second line.

In 1660 he went to Lisbon to organize a Portuguese Army against Spain. His forces recovered Évora (1663) and in 1665 defeated the Spaniards at Montes Cláros. The independence of Portugal was recognized by Spain at the Treaty of Lisbon (1668) and after placing Dom Pedro (later Pedro II) in power in a palace revolution in the same year, he returned to his position in the French Army, having become naturalized as a Frenchman.

During the Dutch War (1672–78) he went to England in 1673 on the invitation of Charles II to form an army for the proposed invasion of Holland, but soon returned to the French Army and was on Louis XIV's staff at the siege and capture of Maastricht (June 1673). Spain and the emperor Leopold I allied with the Dutch in the same year and Schomberg took command of the French in Catalonia; in 1675 he was one of eight marshals of France appointed on Turenne's death. When the marshal duc de Luxembourg was moved to the Rhine in 1676, Schomberg commanded the Netherlands front where his maneuvers gave him a reputation equal to that of Luxembourg.

The revocation of the Edict of Nantes (1685) drove Schomberg from France but he was welcomed by Frederick William of Brandenburg, "the Great Elector." In 1688 the elector lent him and a Prussian force to William of Orange (later William III of Great Britain), whom he accompanied to England. He was naturalized as English in April 1689 and in May was created duke of Schomberg. He went to Ireland as commander in chief against James II in August 1689, but could do little more than hold Ulster as there was much sickness in his small army, and he took no risks. When William joined him in 1690, Schomberg was reluctant to cross the River Boyne. He was killed by some Irish cavalry at the Battle of the Boyne on July 1, 1690, having ridden without escort to rally some troops. (I. D. E.)

SCHOMBURGK, SIR ROBERT HERMANN (1804–1865), British explorer and surveyor whose "Schomburgk line" marked the boundary of British Guiana from 1841 to 1895 (*see* Guyana), was born at Freiberg, Lower Saxony, Ger., on June 5, 1804. In 1829 he went to the United States and from there in 1831 visited Anegada, one of the British Virgin Islands. He surveyed it and noted the frequency of the wrecks, particularly of U.S. ships, which occurred upon it. In 1835 the Royal Geographical Society sent Schomburgk to explore British Guiana. On this trip he discovered the giant water lily, *Victoria regia*, and in 1840 produced his *Description of British Guiana.* In 1841 he surveyed the colony and fixed its boundary, being knighted on his return to England in 1844. He continued his geographical surveys as British consul to Santo Domingo, now the Dominican Republic (1848), and to Bangkok (1857). Schomburgk died at Berlin on March 11, 1865.

SCHÖNBEIN, CHRISTIAN FRIEDRICH (1799–1868), German-Swiss chemist, discovered and named ozone (*q.v.*) in 1840, and was the first to describe guncotton and collodion (*qq.v.;* 1846). He was born at Metzingen, Swabia, on Oct. 18, 1799. After studying at Tübingen and Erlangen, he taught chemistry

and physics, first at Keilhau, Thuringia, and then at Epsom, Eng., but most of his life was spent at Basel, where he began to lecture on chemistry and physics in 1828 and was appointed full professor in 1835. Schönbein did notable work on the passivity of iron, the properties of hydrogen peroxide, and catalysis. He was a most prolific writer, 364 papers appearing under his name in the Royal Society's *Catalogue.* He died at Sauersberg, near Baden-Baden, on Aug. 29, 1868.

Many of Schönbein's letters together with a biography will be found in G. W. A. Kahlbaum, *Monographien aus der Geschichte der Chemie,* vol. iv and vi (1899, 1901). *See also* E. Färber in G. Bugge, *Buch der grossen Chemiker* (1955).

SCHÖNEBECK, a town of East Germany in the Magdeburg *Bezirk* (district) of the German Democratic Republic, lies on the left bank of the Elbe River 9 mi. (14½ km.) SE of Magdeburg. Pop. (1964) 44,302. It is a river port and a station on the main railway between Magdeburg and Halle. Its principal industries are salt mining and the production of vehicles, cement, paints and dyes, and chemical apparatus. The town's charter dates from 1280. The brine springs in nearby Bad Salzelmen are of ancient renown.

SCHÖNEBERG, a *Bezirk* (district) of West Berlin, Germany, lies southwest of the city centre. Pop. (1961) 193,790. The 13th-century peasant settlement of Alt-Schöneberg was in 1874 merged with Neu-Schöneberg, which had been founded by Frederick the Great in 1750 to accommodate Bohemian weavers. The existing district was formed in 1920 by uniting Schöneberg with Friedenau. The Supreme Court Building on the Potsdamer Strasse became in 1945 the seat of the Allied Control Council, and the town hall on Rudolph-Wilde-Platz became in 1948 the administrative centre of West Berlin. Industries include printing, brewing, and the production of precision instruments, optical goods, and telecommunications equipment.

SCHONGAUER, MARTIN (called Martin Schön and Hipsch [Hübsch] Martin) (1445/50–1491), German engraver and painter of the early German school, was born in Colmar, Alsace, the son of the goldsmith Caspar Schongauer from Augsburg, where the family, originally from Schongau, had been prominent for two centuries. Dates of his birth proposed in German literature after 1941 range from 1425 to 1453. In 1465 he was registered at the University of Leipzig, but apparently remained there only one semester. In view of the variance of opinion on his age, it is not clear whether he was there as a student or as a visiting artist enjoying the university's protection from interference of the local painters' guild. That he was a student appears more likely because no work of his has ever been discovered which could with certainty be dated earlier than 1469 and because the wide distribution of his work did not get under way until the late 1470s, judging from the flood of copies which are dated. In 1469 his name is mentioned for the first time in the Colmar register of property. The same date appears also on three of his drawings, all obviously early works, but these dates and signatures were added by Albrecht Dürer, who may have received them from Schongauer's brothers when he arrived in Colmar the year after Martin's death. In 1488 Schongauer left Colmar and moved to Breisach, Baden. He died a bachelor in Breisach on Feb. 2, 1491, being survived by three brothers, the goldsmiths Jörg and Paulus and the painter Ludwig.

According to contemporary sources, Schongauer was a prolific painter, whose panels were sought in many countries. Few paintings by his hand survive. Among them the "Madonna in a Rose Garden" of 1473, altarpiece of the church of Saint-Martin in Colmar, ranks first in importance. This work strikingly combines monumentality with tenderness and is the only painting in which Schongauer approached the heights of the great Flemish painter Rogier van der Weyden by whom he was so profoundly influenced. Other paintings by Schongauer include two wings of the Orliac altar (Colmar museum); six small panels among which the "Nativity" (Berlin) and the "Holy Family" (Vienna) are the most mature; and finally the murals of the "Last Judgment" in the cathedral of Breisach, probably his last work (uncovered in 1932). The 24 panels depicting the "Joys of Mary" and the "Passion of

GIRAUDON, PARIS

"MADONNA IN A ROSE GARDEN," BY MARTIN SCHONGAUER (1473). THE ALTARPIECE OF THE CHURCH OF SAINT-MARTIN, COLMAR, FRANCE

Christ," painted for the church of the Dominicans (Colmar museum), appear to be mainly the work of his assistants.

As an engraver, however, Schongauer stands without rival in northern Europe in his time. His engraved work, consisting of about 115 plates, all signed with his monogram, is a final, highly refined and sensitive manifestation of the late Gothic spirit. Technically he brought the art of engraving to maturity by expanding its range of contrasts and textures, thus introducing a painter's viewpoint into an art which had been primarily the domain of the goldsmith's shop. The larger and more elaborate engravings, such as the "Temptation of St. Anthony" or the "Death of the Virgin," belong to his earlier period. In his later years, he preferred smaller plates, even for subjects as the "Passion of Christ," a set of twelve engravings. Some of his most eloquent plates are single figures, such as the "Madonna in a Courtyard" or "St. Sebastian." Within the diversity of trends in German art in this period, Schongauer represents the most idealistic and aristocratic element, devoting his art mainly to Christian subjects and shunning the gross and often bawdy humorous realism of some of his fellow engravers. The sensitive grace of his work became proverbial even in his lifetime and gave rise to such names as "Hübsch Martin" or "Schön Martin" ("Bel Martino" in Italian), whereby the adjective "Schön" became often confused with the artist's real family name. Schongauer's engravings are well represented in the print rooms of the larger museums of Europe as well as numerous U.S. museums (New York, Boston, Chicago, Cincinnati, Cleveland and Washington, D.C.).

BIBLIOGRAPHY.—Max Lehrs, *Martin Schongauer, Nachbildungen seiner Kupferstiche*, Graphische Gesellschaft (1914; facsimile reproductions of all engravings); Jakob Rosenberg, *Martin Schongauer, Handzeichnungen* (1923); Ernst Buchner, *Martin Schongauer als Maler* (1941); Julius Baum, *Martin Schongauer* (1948; reproductions of complete work; text in German); Alfred Stange, *Deutsche Malerei der Gotik*, vol. vii (1955). (H. Jm.)

SCHÖNHERR, KARL (1867–1943), Austrian writer, primarily a dramatist, whose most famous drama, *Glaube und Heimat* (1910), deals with the conflict between religion and patriotism at the time of the Counter-Reformation and aroused religious controversy, was born at Axams, Tirol, on Feb. 24, 1867. He was the son of a country schoolmaster, studied in Vienna, and became a doctor there. Following Ludwig Anzengruber and Peter Rosegger, Schönherr made the Austrian peasant the focus of his work. His first publications (1895) were dialect poems of an unassuming nature and short stories; but in 1897 he turned his attention to the stage with *Der Judas von Tirol* (remodeled 1927). Acknowledging Ibsen as his master, Schönherr stood midway between realism and symbolism. His style was vigorous and robust and his accomplished technique enabled him to write successful plays with a very limited number of characters, simple emotions and the problems and crises arising out of them being presented with inexorable consistency. He published *Der Weibsteufel* in 1915. Other important works are *Die Bildschnitzer* (1900), *Erde* (1907), *Volk in Not* (1915), *Vivat academia* (1922), *Es* (1923), and *Die Hungerblockade* (1925). His later plays, *e.g.*, *Der Armendoktor* (1927), *Passionsspiel* (1933), and *Die Fahne weht* (1938), added little to his reputation. Most of his work was first produced in the Burgtheater and in the Deutsches Volkstheater in Vienna. His stories and sketches, *Caritas* and *Aus meinem Merkbuch*, express much the same trend of thought and motif as his plays. He died in Vienna, March 15, 1943.

BIBLIOGRAPHY.—*Gesammelte Werke* (1927; new edition, 1948); M. Lederer, *Schönherr als Dramatiker* (1925); A. Bettelheim, *K. Schönherr* (1928); M. Happe, *Die Tiroler Bauernwelt in Schönherrs Dichtungen* (1940); K. Paulin, *Schönherr und seine Dichtungen* (1950). (W. I. L.)

SCHÖNLEIN, JOHANN LUKAS (1793–1864), German physician and pioneer of modern clinical medicine, was born in Bamberg on Nov. 30, 1793. He obtained his medical degree from the University of Würzburg in 1816 and was lecturer there for the next eight years. He became professor of medicine at Würzburg in 1824, at Zürich in 1833, and at Berlin in 1840. He retired in failing health to Bamberg in 1859 and died there on Jan. 23, 1864.

When Schönlein began his career German medicine was dominated by the so-called natural philosophy school, whose unscientific doctrines stemmed from the organismic theories of the philosopher Friedrich von Schelling (*q.v.*). At first a devotee of this school, Schönlein soon broke away and founded the so-called natural history school, which attempted (often with ludicrous results) to classify diseases by methods analogous to the way botanists were then classifying plants. However deficient, this scheme had the strong merit of turning medicine into a natural science. Schönlein abandoned his theory even as he concentrated more and more on the observational techniques it had relied upon—so that in time his teachings came to consist, in the words of his follower Rudolf Virchow, of "little system, many facts." He was the first to make use of the microscope, together with chemical analysis of the urine and blood, in the diagnosis of disease. He discovered the true nature of favus (a skin disease caused by a fungus) and described the minute hemorrhages of the skin in anaphylactoid (allergic) purpura (Schönlein-Henoch purpura).

Although he published little—only two very brief papers—his lectures attracted large numbers of enthusiastic students; and although his behaviour was remarkably boorish, he was consulted by patients from all over Europe, who benefited by the thoroughness of his examinations and his great therapeutic skill.

(H. D. v. W.)

SCHOOL ADMINISTRATION. School administration deals with the control, management and direction of all matters affecting the school, including organization, finances, policies, personnel, curriculum and methods, standards and related areas.

In this article school administration is treated under the following headings: types of administration; national systems; local systems; joint local and national systems; sectarian systems; political party control; and trends. For information concerning school administration in various countries, states and provinces, etc., not specifically treated here, *see* the articles on those political divisions. (*See* also EDUCATION, HISTORY OF.)

Types of Administration.—The schools of the world are organized and administered for the most part by four agencies functioning separately or in combination: the church, the state, the political party and the private group. Of these, the church and private groups have become less powerful.

Most school systems of the world are centralized; that is, they are administered by the national government. Decentralized types of administration may be classified under such headings as provincial (state), county, township, community, etc. In Communist countries much administration is determined by local or regional cultural preference, but over-all policy is governed by directives issued from party headquarters in accordance with the prevailing political philosophy.

Administration differs also with the level of education. In centralized systems of education much responsibility for the early stages of schooling is granted to local authorities, whereas secondary education tends to gravitate toward centralized control. Higher education defies generalization. Publicly controlled universities in the United States and Canada may be either local or state in nature; at the same time they are supported to a very small degree, if land-grant colleges, by the federal government. In Great Britain both private and civic universities are dependent upon public funds but remain autonomous. Governmental influences are strong in French, Spanish, Italian and Latin-American universities, while in countries similar to the Soviet Union, universities are controlled by the Communist party, trade and professional unions, and various governmental departments.

National Systems.—*France.*—The classic example of a national system of education is that of France. Its administrative structure was originated by Napoleon in 1802. The country is divided into politico-educational units decreasing in size from *académies* to *départements* to communes. Each of the 17 *académies* is headed by a university. The chief administrator of both the university and the *académie* is called a rector, who is appointed from the ranks of university professors by the president of France on recommendation of the national minister of education. He is responsible primarily for secondary and higher education within his *académie;* he nominates candidates for administrative positions in his area, appoints examination committees, supervises examination content and procedures and presides over a sort of personal cabinet called an academic council. Unlike political divisions in such countries as Australia, Canada, the United States and West Germany, the *académies* have little power or authority of their own; rather, they are administrative arms of the national ministry of education; they represent a devolution rather than a delegation of power from the central government. The 97 *départements* are likewise administrative units governed by prefects who are appointed in Paris. The prefect heads the elementary school system, acting in a manner similar to the rector. The prefect, too, has an advisory council, appointive in nature, and by no means equivalent to local boards of education in such countries as the United States and Canada. *Départements* are empowered to levy subsidiary school taxes as approved by the national government; in the early 1960s about half the cost of *département* schooling was met by local taxation. *Départements* are also permitted to provide further school services, on approval of higher authorities, including additional emoluments for teachers. There are about 38,000 communes, varying in size from the smallest community to the city of Paris. The chief officer of the commune is the mayor, who is likewise the president of the commune school board. Again, these school boards are largely advisory in nature; they also see to it that national and *département* educational procedures and policies are carried out in their particular area; they have only minor administrative responsibilities and can initiate very little school legislation and practice. In practice, the *département* prefect assumes much of the control over education in the commune, as such control is derived from higher authorities.

The French educational system is also characterized by a pyramid of bureaus which reach their apex in the ministry of national education in Paris. As in all national systems, even including Great Britain, the minister of education is a political appointee of the prime minister, and he usually falls when his government falls. Practical control is exercised by a powerful and permanent civil service, which remains relatively unaffected by political changes. The ministry of education consists of five directorates: general administration; elementary; secondary; technical; and higher education. The minister is assisted by a higher council of national education, consisting of 56 members appointed in part by the president of the republic and the minister of education and elected in part by the universities and representatives of elementary and secondary education. Although its primary function is advisory in nature, the higher council is really a sort of educational parliament, in that the minister is required to consult its members and secure their approval in nearly all major matters of educational policy and procedure. A corps of inspectors general, appointed by the ministry of education, reports on progress and needs in all areas. Although some determination of school practices is allowed local governments, especially in matters involving purely internal conduct, the responsibility for education is actually not delegated, as in such countries as the United States, Great Britain and Canada. Administration is a sort of "line and staff" arrangement ordered in such a way that directives may readily be executed by subordinate officers.

Other National Systems.—National systems of education prevail in Belgium, the Netherlands, Greece, Scandinavia and other countries where centralized controls are geographically practical and strategic; the middle east (Turkey, Iraq, Syria, Egypt, etc.); most Latin-American countries; and other political systems not federal in nature. In most national systems, however, local control over educational administration increased after World War II.

An example of a different type of centralized control is Uruguay. The highest administrative agency is the ministry of public education and social welfare, but the ministry concerns itself primarily with welfare services. Educational administration falls within the province of four national autonomous educational councils: the National Council for Primary and Teacher Education; the National Council for Secondary and Preparatory Education; the Higher University council; and the National Council for Industrial Education, which occupies itself with agricultural, vocational and industrial schools of all types, but it is divorced from the political and ideological overtones which characterize labour educational administration in such a country as Mexico. The coexistence of these four councils illustrates a form of decentralization; since the councils operate on a national basis, however, and since their functions interlock, the resulting organization might be conceived as a type of pluralistic centralized control.

Local Systems.—Included in local systems are state, provincial, county and community types of school administration. Local emphases in administration are to be found in countries where public schooling originated in grass roots or separatist movements, or where political unity was achieved out of a confederation of sovereign states. In some instances of federalization, as in Italy and to some extent Switzerland, a central ministry has been granted administrative as well as advisory power. As a rule, however, cultural and political units have jealously guarded their control over education. Characteristics of local control may be generalized thus: (1) weak central ministries or bureaus of education, which are largely advisory in character; (2) financial support for education locally derived, aid from central authorities being mostly in the form of supplementary or emergency funds accepted with a minimum amount of control; and (3) administrative power lodged in local boards of education, sometimes appointed, sometimes elected. In countries like Canada, West Germany and Australia, where the separate states are sovereign, state ministers of education are appointed and state systems of inspection prevail. In the United States the state executive officer of education becomes either a commissioner of education (if appointed) or a state superintendent of schools, each with less power than his counterpart abroad.

United States.—The United States is an outstanding example of local control on state, county and community levels. The decentralization of education characteristic of U.S. schooling is a source of bewilderment to observers from other countries who seek to understand not only the many different types of state-controlled education but yet another system in the District of Columbia, administered by the federal government.

The whole is complicated by the myriads of local county, township or community units of education, by types of schooling directly supported and controlled by the federal government, and by the great variation among the states as regards internal administration and relations with local organizations. Some states, like Delaware, tend toward centralization. Massachusetts is an example of decentralization. Even in the support of education, the amount of funds provided can vary from the practice in such a state as Nebraska, where in the 1960s, for example, about 90% of expenditures were underwritten by local authorities, to states like New Mexico where state rather than local revenues paid for most public schooling. In addition to the various state public-school systems, there exist, outside these systems, parochial schools which are administered by church groups and a large variety of privately supported schools.

Although no mention is made of education in the United States constitution, the federal government has been mindful of the need to support formal schooling, exemplified in the Land ordinance of 1785 and the Northwest ordinance of 1787, by which part of the national domain was set aside for school purposes, and in the numerous federal statutes which have supported types of education (technical, military, agricultural, etc.) necessary to national welfare. The earliest federal statutes, enacted in accordance with traditional educational practices, gave control of lands and resources to local townships; but by 1804, with the Ohio Territory act, the states had accepted custodianship and assumed control of school endowments.

Education in the United States was originally conceived as a private or local affair. If not undertaken by the family or the church, schooling became the concern of charity groups. Hence, education was considered a matter of public welfare. But the federal government did not relinquish its responsibility; acting by authority of the "general welfare clause" of the constitution (sec. 8, art. i), it required of all states joining the union that satisfactory provision for public education be stipulated in the state's constitution. By a series of supreme court decisions the federal government settled local educational disputes and in part guided the course of education in its national implications. The federal government has also supervised the educational welfare of territories, trusts and dependencies, and assumed the responsibility for educational agencies supplying the federal government with the kind of personnel and services it requires. Included in this category are the various academies and institutes which train officers and specialists for such areas as national defense, diplomacy, internal security and technology. The federal government has also supported educational relief programs, such as the National Youth administration and the Civilian Conservation corps in the 1930s, the work-study and other educational programs set up under the Economic Opportunity ("War on Poverty") act of 1964 and the school-aid bill of 1965.

The United States office of education was established by congress in 1867. In 1939 it was transferred from the department of the interior to the Federal Security agency. It became a branch of the department of health, education and welfare when that department was established in 1953. It is not an administrative agency in essence, although it has assumed control over certain projects supported by the federal government, such as certain programs of vocational education, exchange of students and teachers with other countries, certain aspects of land-grant college administration and the general promotion of educational thought and practice throughout the country. Specifically, its functions involve the collection, interpretation, publication and dissemination of factual information on education, not only in the U.S. but abroad. Its specialists may be drawn upon for counsel by any educational group in the country. Similar agencies exist in India, Canada, Australia, West Germany and other nations where federated governments and local controls determine educational administration.

Responsibility for education in the United States rests with the individual states. The states delegate this responsibility to the local communities, not simply as a devolution of power, as in France and other centralized systems, but as a matter of self-determination under fairly liberal state school codes. It is commonly claimed that the three levels of educational organization and administration in the U.S.—federal, state and local—are in matter of fact actually interdependent rather than hierarchic. Hence, a system of checks and balances is said to prevail in educational as well as other governmental matters. In practice, however, administration rests heavily on the shoulders of local communities and operates in accordance with local decisions, assuming such decisions accord with federal and state statutes.

On the state level, educational administration generally is headed by a state board of education, sometimes appointed by the governor or the state legislature, sometimes elected. As a rule, state boards of education are less powerful than state ministries of education in other countries, largely because local communities in the United States assume much more administrative responsibility.

However, the board of education of the state of New York, for example, exercises powerful control over educational standards through a system of state-wide examinations. The extensive ramifications of its operations are seen in the fact that its staff consists of over 500 full-time professionals. State boards range in size from 3 to 19 members. They are largely composed of laymen but in some instances professional educators may become members.

Again, the duties of these state boards vary from state to state, but in general they all concern themselves with the distribution of state or federal funds (allotted to the states), the enforcement of educational statutes, the determination of basic courses of study, the adoption or recommendation of textbooks, the certification of teachers, the approval of building and maintenance standards, the provision of library services and the operation of teachers' colleges. State boards likewise interest themselves in the improvement of education as a function of government, the equalization of educational opportunity, the provision of educational leadership and the improvement of local operations. The functions of state departments of education were defined by the White House Conference on Education, Nov. 1955, in which general agreement was reached on the following recommended types of services to be provided local districts: (1) establishment of minimum standards for an adequate educational program; (2) advisory or consultative services in such areas as population trends, transportation, school construction, financial planning, curriculum development and special services; (3) research and statistical studies of a nature to assist in long-term planning; (4) certification of teachers and professional staffs; (5) provision of "dynamic" leadership. Included in a minority report were the following recommended types of services: (1) provision of scholarships for qualified students in financial need; (2) establishment of a sound, equitable tax base among administrative units; (3) assumption of desirable services above or beyond the capabilities of local districts to provide.

Inspection of local schools and school systems by inspectors responsible to state boards or other authorities is found in many states but is not so highly developed as in most other countries. School and classroom supervision is provided by local systems through specialists who do not function as inspectors but rather "helping teachers." In one state they are officially so designated.

The genius, but also the weakness, of the U.S. educational system lies in its more than 30,000 school districts, each exercising an amount of freedom unequaled in any other country. Administrative authority is assumed by a local board of education, which in about 90% of cases is elected by the people. Boards of education are usually independent of other agencies of local government; in fact, school funds voted by boards of education are for the most part not subject to rejection by other bodies. In cases of dispute over budgets between boards of education and boards of finance, the courts have ruled almost exclusively in favour of the former. In most communities, school taxes have first priority; usually they are independent of other sources of revenue.

The duties of a local board of education are limited to community needs. The local board selects the superintendent of schools, who in turn recommends personnel for appointment by the board. In nearly all cases, boards of education have the power directly to appoint nonteaching employees. The local school board also determines the educational policy for the district, acting usually on professional advice, secured by way of the superintendent of schools and in accordance with the wishes of the community at large. The board assists the superintendent in the preparation of the budget, approval of which obligates the local board to see that tax funds are provided.

India.—India may be used as an example of local control strongly exercised by the various provinces under provincial or state ministries of education. Unlike the United States constitution, the Indian counterpart of 1947 states that the federal government will endeavour to provide free, compulsory education for all children till they reach the age of 14. Partly because the central government did not have sufficient funds to implement this ideal and partly because of the natural diversity of India's population, considerable responsibility for education has been delegated to the states. The functions of the Indian ministry of education approximate those of the United States office, but whereas the United States commissioner of education is appointed by the president, the Indian minister of education is elected by parliament and is directly responsible to that body. The state ministry of education has five divisions: (1) administration and cultural relations; (2) bureau of development; (3) general education; (4) technical education; and (5) scholarships. Delegation of authority by the states to the local communities is restricted to elementary education, as is the case in most countries, while secondary education is subject to state control. State ministers of education, like their federal counterparts, are both elected and appointed and are responsible to state legislative bodies. Indian state governments are responsible for educational policy, the local units being conceived largely as administrative and taxation units. Control over education is exercised through an inspection system.

Advising the Indian state minister of education is the director of public education, who is a permanent executive head of the ministry. He controls the inspectorial staff, the teachers and the government-recognized private schools, and is responsible for executing the policies of the ministry of education, principal among which is the inculcation of basic education through productive activity and local crafts to all children between the ages of 6 and 14.

There are great inequalities of educational opportunity in India, where population distribution, linguistic diversity and the heritage of the caste system aggravate an already difficult educational situation. The Indian central government has confessed its inability to assist adequately in fostering school development, not for want of desire but from sheer financial inability. It has confined its efforts to supporting higher and technical education, research in the interest of national welfare, experiments in educational methods, the production of suitable literature, the training of specialized personnel and the translation of important works into Indian languages. The administrative problem in India is therefore not one of where control ideally may be located but of securing the kind of educational organization and administration which will best serve a country which is as yet economically undeveloped, and where the many religions and sects insist upon tying public education to their own particular beliefs.

West Germany.—West Germany (the German Federal Republic) is another example of decentralization of administration. Art. 7 of the Basic law of the German Federal Republic (1949) places schools under the supervision of the respective states (*Länder*). The various states exercise fairly complete control over all schools and commit themselves to a program of close supervision in major activities. Local boards of education function

everywhere, but with less power than in the United States. Again, as in similar systems, the highest administrative agency is the state ministry of education, headed by a minister of education (*Kultusminister*), who is a political appointee. The state minister of education might be compared with the state superintendent of schools in the United States, but he also absorbs some of the duties reserved for the U.S. local superintendent of schools, exemplified by his right of control and jurisdiction over internal school practices. Co-ordination among the state school systems is achieved in part by the Conference of Educational Ministers which meets several times a year in Bonn. In 1953 a federal educational council was established to advise the Conference of Ministers. The West German local school superintendent is appointed by the state minister of education on recommendation of the *Kultusminister*. Local school boards are not elected but are chosen by local legislatures; they are responsible only for those phases of school administration not assumed by the state. External university administration, including certain financial, academic, examination and other aspects, is exercised by the division of higher education of the state ministry of education, though the universities enjoy a large amount of autonomy.

Joint Local and National Systems.—Examples of national and local systems working co-operatively, or in partnership, are to be found in England and, to some extent, Japan.

Great Britain.—Educational administration in England was fixed by the Education act of 1944, which lodged final authority in the central ministry of education but which placed immediate administrative responsibility upon local educational authorities (L.E.A.'s). (*See* EDUCATION, HISTORY OF: *Great Britain and the Commonwealth of Nations: The 1944 Act.*) The Education act sets the structure of administration and control but allows local authorities to interpret policies in accordance with local need, preference and internal school conditions. Central authority is vested in three bodies: the ministry, the central advisory councils and the civil service, representing the political, the advisory and the professional elements of education respectively. The minister of education, appointed by the prime minister, is responsible for broad educational policy and practice within the framework of existing legislation as approved by parliament. The two Central Advisory councils (for England and Wales) advise the minister on internal matters of administration. The civil service is responsible for the communication and interpretation of broad policy at the local level. The permanent education secretary guarantees continuity of policy and operations. The "eyes and ears" of the ministry are her majesty's inspectors, better known as H.M.I.'s, who are members of the civil service. The H.M.I.'s have four major duties: (1) to ensure that government appropriations are being spent wisely; (2) to see that educational legislation is being complied with; (3) to act as missionaries disseminating enlightened educational thought; and (4) to keep the ministry informed on what transpires at the grass roots of education.

The L.E.A.'s are not elected directly by popular vote but are appointed by county and borough councils, which are in turn elected directly by the people. Actual supervision is, however, delegated to education committees, which are appointed by the L.E.A.'s out of their own membership plus a minority of non-L.E.A. members who are interested in education. One of the committee's functions, like that of a local board in the United States, is to appoint a chief education officer, usually called a director of education. The director of education enjoys less power and independence of action than the U.S. superintendent of schools, his chief function being to present proposals to his committee for decision and action, to record decisions and to carry them out. On the other hand, the headmaster of an English school, especially on the secondary level, is a more powerful and influential person than his U.S. colleague; he is given wide latitude in the formulation and execution of internal policy. As the power of the headmaster increases, it is natural that the power of the director of education decreases. Nevertheless, with the aid of a corps of local inspectors and advisers, the director of education commands a post of considerable weight, which takes on added importance in view of the director's responsibility to the national ministry of education, as well as to his local education committee.

In general, it may be said that in contrast with other leading nations, England presents an educational system which not only operates co-operatively on both local and national levels but unites with private endeavour and voluntary organizations to spread the responsibility for control throughout the entire political and social structure of the nation.

Japan.—After World War II, in Japan educational administration tended to follow directives issued by the United States as the occupying power. Organization is on three levels: national; prefectural or county; and local community. The central ministry of education, though stripped of much of its power, is still, as in England, the chief administrative authority. The ministry has a secretariat and five divisions: elementary and secondary education; higher education and science; social education; research; and administration. Advice on general policy is afforded by 18 councils on education, including a central council for education. The national ministry of education is entitled to draft laws in the interest of national educational standards but its power to instruct local boards is limited by parliament. Since the ministry allots much financial aid to local systems, especially for school buildings, considerable indirect control is added to that which may be exercised directly. In consideration also of the weakness of local boards, due in part to educational tradition in Japan and in part to insufficient funds for vigorous programs at the local level, the ideal of a weak central ministry of education advocated by the United States educational mission failed to materialize. Concrete evidence is seen in such developments as the assumption by the central ministry of responsibility for the nine years of compulsory schooling and the security of teachers' salaries and emoluments. Also, the recommended transfer of university control to local authorities has failed, so that since 1954 universities have fallen within the province of the national educational administration.

Unlike England, the roots of local self-determination, especially in educational matters, are not deep in Japan, so that local controls are in a stage of growth rather difficult to delineate. Local boards of education are responsible, legally, for the establishment and maintenance of elementary and lower secondary schools; while the county (prefectural) board of education administers upper secondary and special schools, the certification of teachers, certain aspects of private schools and the choice of textbooks. Originally, too, these boards were supposed to be elected, but because educated and desirable Japanese people did not wish to run for the office (or could not afford campaign expenses), and because the Japanese themselves did not feel a strong affinity for the elective process, board members became appointive. Another difficulty with implementing the ideal of local controls in Japan has been the traditional method of collecting taxes. It has not been possible to establish a system of special school taxes, so that local boards must depend upon general local revenues, supplemented by allotments from the central ministry. Although the trend is back to a centralized administration in Japan, local authorities still exercise far more control than before the war, so that a modified type of partnership in educational administration may therefore be said to prevail in Japan, in principle if not always in practice.

Sectarian Systems.—Religious and denominational influences control school administration in Spain, Ireland, certain provinces in Canada and certain Latin-American countries. The Spanish state guarantees the teaching of the Catholic religion as a regular and compulsory subject in all educational institutions, whether state controlled or not, and no matter what their level and purpose. Publications of any type may be banned or suppressed if contrary to Catholic dogma and morals. Also, in tests for the selection of teachers, for example, examining boards are composed of five members, three of whom, including the chairman, must be church officers. In Ireland local boards of education, hence local school systems, are controlled by the prevailing local religious denomination.

Canada.—For the most part, educational administration in Canada is similar to that of the United States. Under the British

North America act (1867) jurisdiction over education is delegated to the provinces. In the provinces of Quebec and Newfoundland, administration is sectarian in nature, but the schools are otherwise "public." Education is free and compulsory but children must attend the school of their denomination, unless an "outsiders fee" is paid. Quebec developed with two distinct groups: the Protestant English and the Catholic French, each demanding the right to educate its members. There was no minister of education in Quebec until 1964 when such a ministry was established; the dual Catholic-Protestant system was retained (*see* QUEBEC: *Education*). School districts may be organized by minorities in any community, if there are a sufficient number of pupils to justify the procedure and a sufficient number of taxpayers capable of assuming the responsibility. This principle of "dissent" is guaranteed by law. Individual taxpayers may also designate the school system to which their taxes must be paid. The French-speaking school districts in Quebec are generally coterminous with the Catholic parishes; otherwise, it is obvious that political districts and school districts are not necessarily identical.

In Newfoundland, where early settlement took place along denominational lines, nearly every local community has a majority of one or another of the various denominations. This situation has produced a sectarian system of education, whereby the churches of the various groups have built and in large part control their own schools. Directors of education are nevertheless responsible to the provincial ministry of education. Increasingly the schools of Newfoundland are becoming consolidated, however, especially at the secondary level, reflecting a national trend.

Certain general observations may be made about the rest of Canada. There is neither a central ministry of education, as in England, nor an office of education, as in the United States. Instead, the dominion bureau of statistics publishes an *Annual Survey of Education in Canada;* the Canadian Education association collects and publishes research studies and disseminates information on procedures and practices in the various provinces; and a national research council assists materially in advanced research and investigation at the university level. The dominion government is not without authority, however, in educational matters. For one thing, it is empowered to overrule any act of a provincial government. It protects the educational rights of minorities; it has provided crown lands for the support of education; it is responsible for the operation of schools within the territories; it grants a limited amount of aid for vocational and higher education; it supports research and other types of educational investigation; it provides special grants to increase staff salaries in universities; it supports school broadcasts. (Pressures upon the dominion government to support education at the federal level are similar to those in the United States.)

The provincial departments of education exercise control over such matters as courses of study, teacher education, examinations, textbooks, school buildings and legislative grants. The provincial minister of education is a member of the provincial legislature and hence of the political party in power, and he is responsible to the legislature in matters involving broad educational policy. The deputy minister of education is the chief permanent officer of the provincial department of education.

The most persistent administration problem in Canada is how to find the means of providing larger and more efficient units of organization and administration, at the same time preserving local control of schooling in a sparsely settled, widely diversified, heterogeneous nation.

Political Party Control.—The Soviet Union and its satellites, Communist China and, to a limited extent, Spain, are examples of educational administration as controlled by a single political party.

U.S.S.R.—The right of all citizens to education is guaranteed by the constitution (art. 121, revised) which provides for universal, compulsory education through grade eight and for extensive development of secondary education. All forms of education, both secondary and higher, are free of charge, there is a system of state stipends for students who have distinguished themselves in higher schools, education in the schools is in the students' native language, and free technical, industrial and cultural training for the working people is organized at plants, state farms, machine tractor stations and collective farms.

The Soviet Union resembles India and China in its multiplicity of cultural, national and linguistic groups. There are nearly 200 such groups incorporated into the union; more than 100 different languages are spoken. Within the Russian Soviet Federated Socialist Republic, by far the largest union republic, are no less than 100 cultural and linguistic groups. Under such circumstances, the U.S.S.R. could not help but organize as a federal state; indeed, one secret of Soviet success may be traced to the willingness of the central government to cater in part to national and cultural differences, including instruction in vernacular languages at primary and secondary levels, with Russian the compulsory second language.

In the Soviet Union, as in other federated political systems, education is the responsibility of the individual republic. The U.S.S.R. goes one step further in providing no central ministry of education, relying instead upon ministries of education of the various republics to unify their activities in accordance with educational directives emanating from Communist party headquarters and the central government in Moscow. There is, however, a central ministry of higher educational institutions, which is part of the ministry of culture; and this agency controls all universities, most of the secondary schools (*technicums*) and most of the teachers' institutes. Another sample digression occurs in the fact that the national ministry of labour reserves is in charge of the factory schools and certain vocational institutes, even though it does not contribute materially to their support. Budgets are drawn up by local agencies and the ministries of education of the republics for approval by central authorities, who, in turn, advance direct grants for specified areas and make up deficits. Despite the apparent decentralization of administration, uniformity is guaranteed, as no decision of any consequence, certainly none contravening party directives, is made at levels lower than the republican ministry of education. Policies may originate locally, but they have to be submitted to the republican ministry for approval, or, if of sufficient importance, to the council of ministries for general agreement. The philosophy underlying all agreements and hence all policy and practice is that of the Communist party and party principles are the same for the entire nation.

Control by the Communist party is guaranteed by the central government, which administers the entire economy and the fiscal policies of the nation. In a planned economy, education becomes simply another agency of government and national life, so that all school practices must be co-ordinated with activities planned for other phases of the country's existence. Freedom is allowed only when no directives exist to the contrary. Though directives are many and detailed, the individual republics have been able to exercise a number of prerogatives which give the air of self-determination. In the Georgian Soviet Socialist Republic, for example, the compulsory study of Russian (in addition to the Georgian vernacular) was found to interfere so greatly with the time allotted to other subjects that primary schooling was extended one more year.

Because they are tied to other segments of the government, the republican ministries of education are far more complex in organization than counterparts in other nations. For one thing, the minister of education is also a member of the union republic council of ministers, so that, contrary to practice in other nations, he belongs not only to his republic but also to the central government. He therefore has a multiplicity of divided duties to perform. The following departments exist in a Soviet republican ministry of education: organization and administration (including teacher training, buildings, finance, elementary and secondary educational methods, etc.); vocational education; adult education; social and polytechnic education; literature and publications; science and art institutes; research agencies; and certain commercial trusts, such as the state publishing house, the state motionpicture enterprises and the state supply board. An inspectorial system, under control of the ministry, interests itself in the improvement of teaching and classroom management. Although inspectors must see that party policies are carried out, in practice, they interest themselves primarily in modern pedagogical methods and in supervision; they also teach demonstration classes. Inspectors co-operate closely with school principals; they do not "rate" teachers, except to recommend awards or special honours for particular tasks well done.

Local school boards are appointed by local executive committees of the local council (soviet) concerned. The local director of education is likewise appointed by the executive committee of the council. School principals are, however, named by local school boards and principals in turn select the teachers, subject to approval of the school board. The school principal is also in charge of school purchases; but he must buy all supplies from government houses. The internal duties of local school boards resemble those of most countries but they must look to higher authorities for the determination of over-all policy and practice and have no authority to levy taxes. Each school is guided by a council consisting of parents, teachers, Communist party members and others connected with school life, including clerks and janitors. These councils occupy themselves vigorously with the ongoing activities of the school, uniting with parent-teachers associations in physical (as well as ideational) projects, such as cleaning and redecorating classrooms and providing benefits and perquisites not forthcoming from governmental sources.

The Communist party not only establishes policy but also determines who may be elected to office. Education therefore has the task of preparing future leaders, for whom special party schools are established. In all schools the party exerts its influence in the organization of pupils in various types of political youth leagues, with Pioneer groups for ages between 10 and 15 and the Komsomol, or Young Communist league, for youth over 14. Members of these groups are chosen for their loyalty to party principles and their actual or potential capacity for leadership. In sum, administrative policies in the U.S.S.R. may originate in local areas but to become effective they must be approved at the top. Approved policy then sifts down through the various levels and its enactment is overseen by party members or affiliates, who penetrate every phase of public and educational life.

Communist China.—Similar practices prevail in China. In fact, following World War II Chinese schools were reorganized under the aegis of Russian counselors and modeled after the educational ideals of the Soviet Union. Art. 41 through 47 of ch. v of the Common Program contain the core of Chinese educational policy. Education, according to this program, shall be "national, scientific, and cultural." It shall promote the five "loves": fatherland, people, labour, science and public property. Education and politics become inseparable, so that educational leaders are either members of the Communist party or pledged to support its principles. The entire nation is organized under such centralized ministries as finance, trade, labour, heavy industry, fuel industry, textiles, foods, light industries, railways, communications, agriculture, conservation, forestry and land reclamation. The listing of these ministries is not merely a verbal duty; it reveals the nature of Communist China; and the school system is charged with providing trained personnel for all these ministries.

Contrary to the Soviet Union, China has a central ministry of education, which concerns itself not only with elementary and secondary education but also with the establishment and administration of institutes of higher learning. Hence, it might be said that China is an example of an educational system which is controlled not only by a political party but also by highly centralized administrative agencies. School administration is said to be democratized by the organization of educational councils, in which teachers, students and workmen enjoy equal voting status. The democratic way is also said to be practised in all kinds of meetings and discussion groups, findings of which are transferred for action to higher authorities, on the basis of "discussion by the many but decisions by the few." Heading these educational discussions, or influential in their operation, are members of the party. When one compares two such highly nationalized systems as China and France, political preference is readily discerned as perhaps the chief agent for ordering educational ends, even though the means of administration are similar.

Trends.—While trends in educational administration differ among nations, certain generalizations may be made:

(1) Nationalized or centralized systems (France, Mexico, India, etc.) are advocating the assumption of greater responsibility at the local level; conversely, local school systems (the United States, Canada, Great Britain, etc.) are looking toward centralized authorities for assistance in the support of schools. Thus, a greater co-operation among all government groups is becoming evident, influenced by two forces: more liberal sociopolitical democratic practices and the need to derive the cost of schooling from more and wider sources of revenue. (2) School-leaving ages are being raised, so that few countries remain in which children are allowed to leave school before the age of 14; only financial and material limitations prevent the fullest application of laws on compulsory education. (3) Administration is rapidly being democratized, largely in co-ordination with greater democratic practices in other phases of a culture, as evidenced in the breakdown of hierarchic controls, in less rigid forms of student selectivity, in the insistence upon basic education for all children up to school-leaving age and in provisions for secondary education for more and more young people. (4) State interest in the education of all citizens is resulting in greater provisions for scholarship help to those in economic need. (5) The single-ladder system of school organization is slowly gaining favour, though in countries like France and Germany, where entrance to secondary school has traditionally been highly selective, the idea of a single school, or "common school," system for all (*école unique; Einheitsschule*) has met considerable opposition, partly in reaction to general reforms of a socializing nature and partly because of the power of the universities over secondary school policy. Otherwise, secondary education for all, wherever physically possible, is becoming fundamental to educational progress. (6) Although more and more money is being spent on education year by year, and although more and more students are attending the world's schools, the proportion of most government budgets allotted to education is either static or actually decreasing. Teachers' salaries have not increased commensurately with the rising cost of living and with salaries paid in other professions or vocations. Problems of administration are everywhere aggravated by the lack of funds and of suitably trained, talented personnel.

See ELEMENTARY EDUCATION; SECONDARY EDUCATION.

BIBLIOGRAPHY.—*General:* J. F. Cramer and G. S. Browne, *Contemporary Education* (1956); A. B. Moehlman and J. S. Roucek (eds.), *Comparative Education* (1952); International Bureau of Education and UNESCO, *International Yearbook of Education* (annually); UNESCO, *World Handbook of Educational Organization . . .* (1955), *World Survey of Education*, vol. i (1955); vol. ii (1958); vol. iii (1961). *Canada:* Dominion Bureau of Statistics, *Organization and Administration of Public Schools in Canada* (1954), *Annual Survey of Education in Canada.* *France:* Bureau Universitaire de Statistique, *Recueil de statistiques, scolaires et professionelles* (annually). *Germany:* G. W. Prange and A. M. Lindegren, "Education in the German Federal Republic," U.S. Office of Education *Bulletin* (1954); U.S. Office of the High Commissioner for Germany, *Post-War Changes in German Education* (1951). *Great Britain:* Ministry of Education, *Pamphlets* (1945–55). *India:* UNESCO, *Compulsory Education in India* (1952). *Japan:* Education Reform Council, *Educational Reform in Japan* (1950); Ministry of Education, *Report on the Progress of Education During 1952–53* (1953). *United States:* American Association of School Administrators, *Educational Administration in a Changing Community* (1959), *Inservice Education for School Administration* (1963); F. F. Beach and R. F. Will, "The State and Education, Structure and Control of Education at the State Level," with selected references, U.S. Office of Education *Bulletin* (1955); U.S. Department of Health, Education and Welfare, *Biennial Survey of Education in the United States.* *Soviet Union:* N. De Witt, *Soviet Professional Manpower* (1955); E. N. Medynsky, *Public Education in the USSR* (1951). *See also* U.S. Department of Health, Education and Welfare, *Studies in Comparative Education* (series) and bulletins on education in various countries.   (G. F. KR.)

SCHOOL ARCHITECTURE: *see* EDUCATIONAL ARCHITECTURE.

SCHOOLCRAFT, HENRY ROWE (1793–1864), U.S. ethnologist and explorer, one of the earliest of important writers on the American Indian, was born on March 28, 1793, in Albany County, New York. He was educated at Union and Middlebury colleges, where he showed a predilection for mineralogy. His *View of the Lead Mines of Missouri* (1819) was based upon a collecting trip through the Indian country of Missouri and Arkansas and led to his appointment as topographer on the Lewis Cass expeditions to the upper Mississippi and Lake Superior copper regions, where he became increasingly interested in Indian life. In 1822 he was appointed Indian agent to the tribes of the Lake Superior region and shortly afterward married a girl of Ojibwa (*q.v.*) extraction. Her tribe became the subject of his special study. From 1836 to 1841 he was superintendent of Indian affairs for Michigan; in this capacity he supervised the treaty of March 28, 1836, by which the Ojibwa ceded much of northern Michigan to the United States. Schoolcraft's contribution to ethnology was made in his *Historical and Statistical Information Respecting the History, Condition, and Prospects of the Indian Tribes of the United States*, 6 vol. (1851–57). Repetitious and disorganized, the work nevertheless remains an invaluable source of information gathered by the author from Indians, missionaries, traders, and agents. The publication of F. Nichols' *Index to Schoolcraft's "Indian Tribes of the United States"* by the Bureau of American Ethnology (1954) greatly enhanced the value of the original volumes. An edition of Schoolcraft's *Literary Voyager* (ed. by P. Mason) appeared in 1962.

Schoolcraft continued his exploratory trips, the most important of which was in 1832, when he discovered Lake Itasca, the source of the Mississippi. Among many books was *Algic Researches* (1839; 1856 ed., *The Myth of Hiawatha*), which Longfellow used for *Hiawatha*. He died on Dec. 10, 1864, in Washington, D.C.

See also Chase S. Osborn and Stellanova Osborn, *Schoolcraft, Longfellow, Hiawatha* (1942).   (V. Kz.; X.)

SCHOONER, a sailing vessel having two or more masts and only fore-and-aft rigged sails. The masts have the same names as those of square-rigged ships and the sails forward of the foremast are similar to those of a square-rigged ship. Each mast carries a single gaff-headed sail which takes the name of the mast supporting it; gaff topsails may be carried above these sails. (*See also* RIGGING; SAILS.)

In two-masted schooners the mainmast is higher and carries more sail than the foremast. In schooners having more than two masts the masts are the same height and carry nearly equal sail areas.

Modern schooners are generally used as yachts and have but two masts. The sails on the after side of the masts of schooner yachts are triangular in shape and slide up and down the mast on metal tracks.   (M. R. D.)

SCHOPENHAUER, ARTHUR (1788–1860), German philosopher, primarily important as the exponent of a metaphysical doctrine of the will in immediate reaction against Hegelian idealism, was born at Danzig on Feb. 22, 1788, the son of a merchant, Heinrich Floris Schopenhauer, and of his wife Johanna. H. F. Schopenhauer was a liberal-minded man who disliked authoritarian and absolutist governments and moved to Hamburg in 1793 when Danzig surrendered to Prussia; he was also cultivated and cosmopolitan in his tastes and acquainted with French and English literature. Johanna shared her husband's literary interests and herself wrote novels; but otherwise they seem to have been temperamentally unsuited, and the marriage was not a happy one.

Arthur Schopenhauer's education was intermittent. After spending two years (1797–99) at Le Havre to learn French, four years in a private school at Hamburg and another two years traveling in England, France, Switzerland and Austria, he entered a merchant's office at Hamburg.

After the unexpected death of Heinrich Floris in 1805 (he fell, or threw himself, into a canal), Johanna Schopenhauer moved to Weimar. Schopenhauer eventually joined her there and studied classical literature until 1809, when he entered the University of Göttingen, reading first medicine and then philosophy. The years 1811–13 he spent at the University of Berlin, attending the lectures of J. G. Fichte, for whose philosophy he was later to express considerable contempt.

At the time of the uprising of the German states against Napoleon, Schopenhauer, who disliked all forms of militarism and was not much moved by appeals to national sentiment, retired to Rudolstadt, where he published his doctoral thesis, *Über die vierfache Wurzel des Satzes vom zureichenden Grunde* (1813; Eng. trans., *On the Fourfold Root of the Principle of Sufficient Reason*, 1889).

After his thesis had appeared Schopenhauer returned to Weimar, where in his mother's salon he met the orientalist F. Mayer, who introduced him to Indian philosophical literature. He also met Goethe. The latter having in 1810 published an essay on colours, Schopenhauer took up the same subject and sent his manuscript "On Vision and Col-

ARTHUR SCHOPENHAUER, PHOTO-GRAPHED ABOUT 1855

ours" (*Über das Sehn und die Farben*, 1816) to Goethe in 1815; it was not, however, very enthusiastically received.

Schopenhauer had meanwhile left Weimar for Dresden, having quarreled with his mother (May 1814); they were never to see one another again. At Dresden he wrote his principal work, *Die Welt als Wille und Vorstellung* (1819; Eng. trans., *The World as Will and Idea*, 3 vol., 1883). Schopenhauer expected that this would at once be recognized as a book of first-class importance; but neither was it well-received nor did it sell. More successful at this time were his efforts to save the family fortunes when the firm in Danzig in which they had been invested went bankrupt.

After the publication of his book, Schopenhauer started lecturing in the University of Berlin (1820), but this too was a failure. Philosophy in Berlin was dominated by Hegel, and Schopenhauer's disdain for Hegelian ideas met with a poor response. He went to Italy in 1822 and to Munich in 1823; there he stayed for nearly a year, sick and isolated. From 1825 to 1831 he lived in Berlin, partly in order to defend himself against a seamstress who was suing him for injuries sustained when Schopenhauer, annoyed by her chatter, had driven her downstairs from a landing outside his room. He was eventually condemned to pay her regularly a certain sum of money until her death, which took place in 1841.

In 1831 Schopenhauer settled in Frankfurt am Main. He seems to have lived very well there: he enjoyed food and wine; he was fond of the theatre and music (he himself played the flute); and he read widely in French, Italian and English literature. Happy, however, he was not. By nature misanthropic, he was also by this time profoundly embittered by lack of recognition, and his bitterness was only exacerbated by his contempt for the official Hegelian philosophy. He expressed his opinions on this score with great vigour, both in *Über den Willen in der Natur* (1836; Eng. trans., "On the Will in Nature," in *Two Essays*, 1889) and in his preface to the second edition (1844) of *Die Welt als Wille und Vorstellung*: he regarded Hegel as a charlatan who had corrupted the minds of an entire generation with bombastic sophistry and meaningless verbiage. Nor was his resentment alleviated when an essay of his, the sole entry for a competition instituted by the Danish academy of science, received no award. This essay was subsequently published in *Die beiden Grundprobleme der Ethik* (1841; Eng. trans., *The Basis of Morality*, 1903).

Schopenhauer's later writings added little that was new to what he had already written. In the second edition of his main work he added 50 supplementary chapters, including a section on sexual love in which there is only a suggestion of the misogynistic sentiment that coloured his later well-known essay "On Women."

With the publication of *Parerga und Paralipomena*, 2 vol. (1851; selective Eng. trans., *Essays From the Parerga and Paralipomena*, 1951), a collection of essays on a variety of topics, Schopenhauer at last began to acquire fame. Articles on his system appeared in English, French and Italian as well as German periodicals; in

1856 the University of Leipzig offered a prize for the best exposition and criticism of his ideas; and by 1857 his doctrines were the subject of lectures at Jena, Bonn and Breslau (Wroclaw). His reputation quickly spread beyond the confines of the academic field, and he gradually became the object of a kind of cult, with admirers in England, Russia and the U.S. He died at Frankfurt on Sept. 21, 1860.

PHILOSOPHY

The main philosophical influence upon Schopenhauer, and one that he freely acknowledged, was undoubtedly Kant. But although he never questioned Kant's greatness, *Die Welt als Wille und Vorstellung* contains a long "Criticism of the Kantian Philosophy" in which Kant's theories are subjected to a severe analysis. Other influences were Plato (particularly noticeable in Schopenhauer's references to eternal "ideas" in his account of artistic experience), Schelling, oriental philosophy and, to a lesser extent, the British empiricists: Schopenhauer speaks with respect of Locke and shared Kant's admiration for Hume.

Theory of Knowledge.—Schopenhauer accepted the Kantian distinction between the phenomenon, or the appearance that a thing presents to the perceiving mind, and the noumenon, or the thing as it is in itself. Thus in perception the mind is aware only of phenomena: what lies behind them, being beyond all possible experience, is unknowable; and the pretensions of traditional metaphysics to provide knowledge of a supra-empirical kind must accordingly be rejected. Again, Schopenhauer derived from Kant his view that the mind makes an important contribution to the general nature of our experience. The human sensibility is such that sense-data can only appear to us as spatially and temporally ordered; further, all phenomena are subject to the a priori category of cause and effect. Time, space and causality, Schopenhauer declares, are "nothing more than functions of the brain."

Schopenhauer went on to argue that we reflect upon and communicate our experience through concepts, or general terms. By means of these we are able to classify together different things in virtue of those common features which are of interest or importance to us. The function of conceptual thinking is thus essentially practical: without it what we learn from our experience could not be retained or put to use. But it is impossible to dissociate it—as some philosophers have tried to do—from the perceptual experience on which it is based: "Conceptions and abstractions which do not ultimately refer to perceptions are like paths in the wood that end without leading out of it." In saying this, Schopenhauer acknowledged his debt to the English empiricist philosophers.

Metaphysical theories that profess to be able to describe the nature of the world a priori and without reference to observed facts "move in the air without support." In the end they do no more than elicit by deductive steps the implications of the highly abstract concepts from which they start, and such a procedure can yield no more than a system of tautologies. Schopenhauer regarded Hegel's work as a prime example of such "trifling and paltry" philosophizing.

Metaphysics.—The basic tenets of Schopenhauer's theory of knowledge would seem to impugn the validity of all metaphysical speculation considered as a source of information about the world. He felt, however, a deep dissatisfaction with the purely empirical type of knowledge represented by the natural science of his time. Scientific explanation, he believed, always ultimately presupposes what is itself inexplicable in scientific terms: it may tell us how things as a matter of fact behave under certain conditions, but it cannot in the final analysis explain why things happen as they do and not otherwise; it is like "a sum which never comes out." Thus metaphysics has, after all, a genuine function, viz., to resolve certain fundamental problems which, although necessarily beyond the scope of science, seem naturally to arise. But how are these problems to be tackled in the light of what Schopenhauer, following Kant, has already said concerning the limitations of human knowledge?

The answer, for Schopenhauer, lay in the nature of our own intimate experience of ourselves. Although, from one point of view,

I am as much a "phenomenal" object as a rock or a tree, self-consciousness reveals that I am more than this. For, apart from my awareness of myself as a perceivable body, occupying space, enduring through time and causally responding to stimuli, I also know that in my overt behaviour I express my will. And just as my own activity is ultimately only explicable as the expression of my will, so it is with everything else in nature. Will is the concept in terms of which all that exists and manifests itself in the world can finally be understood. In this way Schopenhauer believed that he had arrived at a fundamental metaphysical truth by a method which escaped Kant's objections, although the reasons for his confidence are not very clear.

The picture which Schopenhauer thus drew of the inner character of the world was not—and was not intended to be—a pleasant or consoling one. For him the "real" was not, as it was for Hegel, the rational, but the irrational: the metaphysical will is "blind," an insatiable force without conscious purpose or direction. Human beings may deceive themselves into thinking that they are acting from considerations dictated by reason alone, but this is never in fact the case: the function of the intellect is only to assist the will to achieve its ends. From this the conclusion is drawn that all participation in the world is to be avoided, Schopenhauer's final remedy being not, as might be expected, suicide, but quietism.

Theory of Art.—The importance that Schopenhauer assigned to artistic experience is understandable in the light of his general theory. The scientist's attitude to the world is practical: he is concerned with phenomena only with a view to discovering the laws which govern their behaviour; and the sole value of his findings lies in the use to which they can be put in securing the objectives of the will. By contrast, the concern of art is with what Schopenhauer calls "contemplation," or "will-less" perception: the aesthetic frame of mind is characterized by a complete absence of desire or practical interest. What is perceived in artistic apprehension and what the artist strives to communicate through his works are certain archetypal "ideas," described as "the permanent essential forms of the world and all its phenomena." These "ideas" are not to be confused either with concepts or with the objects of everyday perceptual awareness to which concepts are applied: they occupy, in fact, an intermediate place in Schopenhauer's system between phenomenal appearances and the underlying noumenal reality of will. The position is further complicated by the fact that a different account is provided of music, which is regarded as directly exhibiting the inner workings of the will itself. Yet, whatever obscurities surround his theory of the ideas, the general significance of Schopenhauer's discussion of art is plain: the Romantic conception of the artist, as one who can withdraw from the material exigencies of life and reveal aspects of the world to which those dominated by considerations of practical interest are blind, could not fail to appeal to him; and the "knowledge" so achieved seemed to him to be correspondingly superior to any that could be acquired in response to the demands of the will.

Psychology and Ethics.—Schopenhauer's deterministic theory of human action and motivation is consistent with the rest of his system. Whatever a man does is necessarily an expression of his inner will, and this is fixed and unalterable. The knowledge of what we are comes to us as a result of seeing what we do: a man cannot "resolve to be this or that, nor can he become other than he is; but he *is* once and for all, and he knows in the course of his experience *what* he is." The common-sense belief in the freedom of the will is consequently an illusion: in our so-called "free" choices we merely exhibit the nature of our innermost unchangeable character. This belief did not, however, prevent Schopenhauer from distinguishing on moral grounds between different sorts of action. A wrong act is an act by which a man, in expressing his own will, "denies" or inhibits the will of another. Moreover, if justice consists in refraining from such injurious acts, goodness consists in treating the welfare of others as being as important as one's own: thus the good man acts from motives of benevolence and sympathy.

Influence and Originality.—Schopenhauer's philosophy achieved a wide popularity on the continent of Europe in the latter half of the 19th century: both Friedrich Nietzsche and Richard Wagner, for instance, were in different ways profoundly impressed by his ideas. In England, however, his influence on philosophical thinking was small: the dominant school of "absolute idealism," for example, was largely inspired by Hegel's doctrines, against which Schopenhauer had directed his most bitter attacks; and little attention was paid to his writings by British philosophers in the first half of the 20th century, when belief in the validity of metaphysical speculation was declining.

Such neglect is somewhat unjustified. Schopenhauer was not a rigorous thinker, and his theory lacks the tight, connected structure and logical ingenuity characteristic of the systems of men like Spinoza and Leibniz. Yet he compares favourably in a number of respects with other 19th-century metaphysicians—Hegel and his followers, for instance. He recognized, as they did not, the force of Kant's criticisms of metaphysics, and he had a much clearer conception of the relations holding between language and the world and, consequently, of the limitations of a priori knowledge. Moreover, he wrote with great distinction and style and with a natural clarity of expression that prevented him from camouflaging his inconsistencies beneath obscure phraseology and jargon. He showed acute psychological insight, particularly into the metaphysical urge; and his doctrine of the will foreshadowed, in metaphysical form, new categories of thought that were to emerge with advances in the nonphysical sciences—especially psychology. His avowed dissatisfaction with science can in fact be seen—partially at least—as a dissatisfaction with the mechanistic models of explanation and interpretation which theorists of the 17th and 18th centuries, fascinated by the achievements of physics, had sought to extend to all departments of human life and experience. Both here and in his rejection of the optimistic rationalism of the Enlightenment, Schopenhauer showed an originality and a prescience which it is difficult to ignore.

BIBLIOGRAPHY.—The earlier collected editions of Schopenhauer's works, by J. Frauenstädt, 6 vol. (1873–74), M. Brasch, 2 vol., 3rd ed. (1891) and E. Grisebach, 6 vol. (1892; supplemented by *Arthur Schopenhauers handschriftlicher Nachlass*, 4 vol., 1895), were superseded by A. Hübscher's rehandling of Frauenstädt's ed., 7 vol., 2nd ed. (1946–50). *See also* W. L. Hertslet, *Schopenhauer-Register* (1890); and G. F. Wagner, *Encyklopädisches Register zu Schopenhauers Werken* (1909). For selections in Eng. trans. see *The Living Thoughts of Schopenhauer, From the World as Will and Idea*, presented by Thomas Mann (1939).

For a bibliography of the earlier studies *see* F. Laban, *Die Schopenhauer-Literatur* (1880). Modern biographies are: W. Schneider, *Schopenhauer: eine Biographie* (1937); and A. Hübscher, *Schopenhauer: ein Lebensbild* (1938). For a study of his philosophy in English, *see* F. Copleston, *Arthur Schopenhauer, Philosopher of Pessimism* (1946). (P. L. G.)

SCHORL, in mineralogy the name given to coarse black varieties of tourmaline (*q.v.*). Schorl was originally a mining term applied both to black tourmaline and to hornblende.

Schorl rocks are crystalline aggregates of quartz and tourmaline and occur almost always in association with tourmaline-bearing granites or pegmatites. They originate by the action of gases and vapours on granites, porphyries and other rocks. Sometimes direct pneumatolytic derivatives of the granite itself, they are also frequent as replacement products of the country rock into which the granite is intruded (*see* also GREISEN). The altered granite known as luxullianite, from its occurrence near Luxullian, a village in Cornwall, is a tourmalinized granite in which a progressive replacement of biotite and feldspar by quartz and tourmaline can be traced. The rock still contains pink feldspars in large porphyritic feldspars set in a dark tourmaline matrix, giving polished specimens a handsome appearance. By impregnation with boron-bearing vapours, the slates and sandstones surrounding granites are locally converted into schorl rock, schorl schist or tourmaline hornfels consisting almost wholly of quartz and tourmaline. Banding, lamination or cleavage of the original slates, etc. is frequently preserved. (C. E. T.)

SCHOULER, JAMES (1839–1920), U.S. lawyer and historian, was best known as a legal writer and for his seven-volume history of the United States. Born in West Cambridge (now Arlington), Mass., on March 20, 1839, he graduated at Harvard in 1859, taught a year at St. Paul's school in Concord, N.H., studied law in Boston and was admitted to the bar in 1862. His legal practice was interrupted by service in the Union army. In 1869 he moved to Washington, where he opened an office and for several years published the *United States Jurist.* After his return to Boston, he devoted himself to office practice and to literary pursuits. He died at Intervale, N.H., on April 16, 1920. Schouler is best known as a historian, his most important work being a *History of the United States Under the Constitution* (1880–1913) covering events from 1783 to 1877.

SCHREINER, OLIVE EMILIE ALBERTINA (1855–1920), South African writer and crusader, was perhaps the most unusual personality ever to emerge from southern Africa. She had a powerful intellect, advanced and passionately held views on politics and society, and great vitality, somewhat impaired by asthma and severe depressions. Born on March 24, 1855, at Wittebergen, Cape Colony, in a remote mountainous area where her father was a Wesleyan missionary, she had no formal education, but read widely and was taught by her formidable mother. Among many unhappy childhood experiences was her revulsion from orthodox Christianity. From early childhood she led an active fantasy life. From 1874 until 1881 she earned her living as a governess; during this time she wrote two semiautobiographical novels, *Undine* (published 1928) and *The Story of an African Farm,* and began *From Man to Man* (published 1926), at which she worked intermittently for 40 years but never finished.

In 1881, having saved a little money, she sailed for England, hoping to study medicine. In 1883 *The Story of an African Farm* was published under the pseudonym "Ralph Iron"; it was an immense and immediate success in Europe and the United States. It brought her distinguished admirers, including Gladstone, and some intimate friends, among them Havelock Ellis (*q.v.*) and Eleanor Marx. The main characters are children: a sensitive and creative boy, Waldo, and a girl, Lyndall, who is beautiful, intelligent, strong-willed, and a feminist. Their lives are unhappy: ". . . a striving and a striving and an ending in nothing." The adults include a grotesque Afrikaans woman, Tant' Sannie, and a sadistic adventurer. The book has faults (as Olive was aware) but also qualities which still give it wide appeal: its originality, the assured handling of narrative and description, the exotic African background, and the vigorous expression of unconventional views on religion and marriage. In the novel there is an allegory on the search for Truth, "The Hunter." The short allegory was Olive's favourite form of expression: she wrote and published many such "Dreams," as she called them—*e.g., Dreams,* (1891); *Stories, Dreams, and Allegories* (1923). Written in rhythmic, quasi-biblical language, they have little appeal for the modern reader. Notable among her other works are a vehement attack on the activities of Cecil Rhodes (*q.v.*) and his associates (*Trooper Peter Halkett of Mashonaland,* 1897) and the widely acclaimed "bible" of the Woman's Movement, *Woman and Labour* (1911).

In 1894 she married Samuel Cronwright, who at her request added her surname to his. They had similar interests and attitudes—both were pro-Boer in the South African War—and although her ill-health and depressions frequently disrupted their lives, he was a devoted husband. His biography of her is conscientious and detailed; he also edited for publication a collection of her letters, which bear witness to her extraordinary personality.

BIBLIOGRAPHY.—*The Letters of Olive Schreiner,* ed. by S. C. Cronwright-Schreiner (1924); see also his *Life of Olive Schreiner* (1924); V. Buchanan-Gould, *Not Without Honour* (1948); M. V. Friedmann, *Olive Schreiner: a Study in Latent Meanings* (1954); Johannes Meintjes, *Olive Schreiner* (1965). (M. V. F.)

SCHRÖDER, FRIEDRICH LUDWIG (1744–1816), German actor, theatrical manager, and playwright, who was the first to bring Shakespeare to the German stage, was born in Schwerin on Nov. 3, 1744. He began his career as a child actor in the company of his stepfather, Konrad Ernst Ackermann. He learned what he could from Ackermann, who was a remarkable comedian, and from his mother, the actress Sophie Schröder. But his decisive inspiration came from Konrad Ekhof, who had joined Ackermann's company in 1764.

In 1771 Schröder became the manager of the Hamburg theatre, an office that he held for nine years. Highlights of his first Ham-

burg period were his Shakespearean productions, in which he played Hamlet's Ghost (later Hamlet), Iago, Shylock, Lear, Falstaff, and Macbeth. He established himself as the leading actor of the period, with supreme control over his body and voice. He also acquainted Hamburg audiences with the early dramas of Goethe (*Götz von Berlichingen, Clavigo, Stella*) and the plays of such other Shakespeare-inspired *Sturm und Drang* dramatists as Friedrich Maximilian von Klinger and Heinrich Leopold Wagner. From England he imported Edward Moore's *The Gamester* and George Lillo's *The London Merchant.* Schröder left Hamburg in 1780 and spent four years at the Vienna Burgtheater. From 1785 to 1798 he was again director of the Hamburg theatre, where he produced many of the plays he had written in Vienna. He died in Rellingen on Sept. 3, 1816. (A. M. N.)

SCHRÖDINGER, ERWIN (1887–1961), Austrian physicist who, with Paul A. M. Dirac (*q.v.*), was awarded the Nobel Prize for physics in 1933 for work on wave mechanics and its applications to atomic structure. His discoveries agreed with those made independently by Werner K. Heisenberg (*q.v.*).

Schrödinger was born in Vienna on Aug. 12, 1887. He was educated at the University of Vienna, Aus., and was subsequently professor of physics in Stuttgart, Ger., Breslau, Pol., and Zürich, Switz. He succeeded Max Planck as professor of physics at the University of Berlin in 1927, and in 1940 he became professor at the Institute for Advanced Studies in Dublin, Ire. He returned to Vienna in 1956 and died there on Jan. 4, 1961.

His work, which was mainly in the field of mathematical physics and especially in the physics of the atom, was an extension of the ideas of Louis de Broglie (*see* BROGLIE). N. H. D. Bohr (*q.v.*) had pictured the atom as consisting of a nucleus about which electrons rotated in fixed orbits, radiation being absorbed or emitted only when an electron changed from one orbit to another, the energy change involved being therefore discrete, and the atom regarded as being in a series of what were called "stationary states." De Broglie's theory of wave mechanics, or matter waves, had modified this by supposing that a wave, with a wavelength an exact submultiple of the length of the orbit, is associated with the electron circulating about the nucleus. Schrödinger extended these ideas further to the problem of atomic structure by supposing that such waves could be superposed on each other. The emission and absorption frequencies were thus related to the orbital frequencies and were represented by the differences of the frequencies of two standing waves. The mathematical application of these ideas was confirmed by experimental observations of spectral lines. Schrödinger wrote several works on wave mechanics and also developed a new field theory.

See QUANTUM MECHANICS: *Advent of True Quantum Mechanics.*

See W. Heitler, "Erwin Schrödinger," in *Biographical Memoirs of Fellows of the Royal Society* (1961); E. Schrödinger, *My View of the World,* trans. by C. Hastings (1964). (D. McK.)

SCHUBERT, FRANZ PETER (1797–1828), Austrian composer, one of the principal figures in romantic music of the early 19th century, was born on Jan. 31, 1797, in the Himmelpfortgrund suburb of Vienna. His father, Franz Theodor Schubert, was a schoolmaster; his mother, Elisabeth (née Vietz), was in domestic service at the time of her marriage. Schubert was their fourth surviving son. His elder brothers were Ignaz, Karl, and Ferdinand, and there was a younger sister, Maria Theresa. The elder Franz Schubert was a man of character who had established a flourishing school. The family was musical and cultivated string-quartet playing in the home, the boy Schubert playing the viola. He received the foundations of his musical education from his father and his brother Ignaz, continuing later with organ playing and musical theory under the instruction of the parish church organist, Michael Holzer. In 1808 he won a scholarship which earned him a place in the imperial court chapel choir and education at the Stadtkonvikt, the principal boarding school for commoners in Vienna, where his tutors were Wenzel Ruzicka, the imperial court organist, and later Antonio Salieri, then at the height of his fame. Schubert played the violin in the students' orchestra, was quickly promoted to leader, and in Ruzicka's absence, conducted. He also attended choir practice and, with his fellow pupils Josef von Spaun, Albert Stadler, and Anton Holzapfel, cultivated chamber music and piano playing.

From the evidence of his school friends, Schubert was inclined to be shy and was reluctant to show his first compositions. His earliest works included a long fantasia for piano duet, written in 1810, D. 1 (*i.e.*, no. 1 in O. E. Deutsch's *Schubert: Thematic Catalogue of All His Works in Chronological Order*, 1951); his first song, "Hagars Klage," D. 5 (1811); several orchestral overtures; various pieces of chamber music; and, in 1811, three string quartets. An unfinished operetta on a text by August von Kotzebue, *Der Spiegelritter*, D. 11, belongs to that year also. The interest and encouragement of his friends overcame his shyness and eventually brought his work to the notice of Salieri.

BY COURTESY OF THE HISTORISCHES MUSEUM, VIENNA

FRANZ SCHUBERT, DETAIL FROM A WATER-COLOUR BY W. A. RIEDER, 1825

In 1813 Schubert's voice broke; he left the college but continued his studies privately with Salieri for at least another three years. During this time he entered a teachers' training college in Vienna, and in the autumn of 1814 became assistant in his father's school. Rejected for military service on account of his short stature, he continued as a schoolmaster until 1818.

Years of Promise.—The numerous compositions written between 1813 and 1815 are remarkable for their variety and intrinsic worth. They are the products of young genius, still short of maturity but displaying style, originality, and imagination. Besides five string quartets, including those in E♭, D. 87, and G minor, D. 173, there were three full-scale Masses and three symphonies. The third of these symphonies, in D major, a charming example of Schubert's youthful lyricism and high spirits, was finished in 1815. His first full-length opera, *Des Teufels Lustschloss*, was finished in 1814 while he was at the training college. But at this period song composition was his chief, all-absorbing interest. On Oct. 19, 1814, he set his first poem by Goethe, "Gretchen am Spinnrade" from *Faust;* it was his 30th song and in this masterpiece he created at one stroke the German *Lied* (*q.v.*). The following year, 1815, brought the composition of over 140 songs, including many of the first order such as "Rastlose Liebe," "Meerestille," and "Erlkönig" and such exquisite specimens of his lyrical art as "Heidenröslein" and "Erster Verlust." The author of the texts of all these was Goethe, whose poems always inspired Schubert's finest songs.

The many unfinished fragments and sketches of songs left by Schubert provide some insight into the working of his creative mind. Clearly, the primary stimulus was melodic. The words of a poem engendered a tune. Harmony and modulation were then suggested by the contours of the melody. But the external details of the poet's scene—natural, domestic, or mythical—prompted such wonderfully graphic images in the accompaniments as the spinning wheel, the ripple of water, or the "shimmering robe" of Spring. These features were fully present in the songs of 1815. The years that followed deepened and enriched but did not revolutionize these novel departures in song. In 1815 also Schubert continued to be preoccupied with his ill-fated operas: between May and December he wrote *Der vierjährige Posten, Fernando, Claudine von Villa Bella,* and *Die Freunde von Salamanka.*

At this time Schubert's outward life was uneventful. Friends of his college days were faithful, particularly Spaun, who in 1814 introduced him to the poet Johann Mayrhofer. He also induced the young and brilliant Franz von Schober to visit Schubert. Late in 1815 Schober went to the schoolhouse in the Säulengasse, found Schubert in front of a class with his manuscripts piled about him,

and inflamed the young composer, a willing listener, with a desire to break free from his duties. In the spring of 1816 Schubert applied for the post of music director in a college at Laibach (now Ljubljana, Yugos.) but was unsuccessful. His friends tried to interest Goethe in the songs and in April 1816 sent a volume of 16 settings to the poet at Weimar. It produced no result. At length, in December 1816, Schober persuaded Schubert to apply for leave of absence. Despite his father's reluctance, he obtained it and spent eight months with Schober, living in the home of his friend's widowed mother and paying for his keep whenever he could.

Early in 1817 Schober brought the baritone Johann Michael Vogl to his home to meet Schubert. As a result of this meeting, Vogl's singing of Schubert's songs became the rage of the Viennese drawing rooms. His friendships with the Hüttenbrenner brothers, Anselm and Josef, and with Josef von Gahy, a pianist with whom he played duets, date from these days. But this period of freedom did not last, and in the autumn of 1817 Schubert returned to his teaching duties. He wrote to his friends of himself as a *verdorbener* ("frustrated") musician. The two earlier years had been particularly fruitful. Songs of this period include "Litanei auf das Fest aller Seelen," "An Schwager Kronos," "Ganymed" (the song which had captivated Vogl at their first meeting), "Der Wanderer," and the Harper's Songs from Goethe's novel *Wilhelm Meister*. Smaller but equally remarkable songs are "An die Musik," "Der Tod und das Mädchen," and "Die Forelle." There were two more symphonies: no. 4 in C minor, which Schubert himself named the "Tragic" (1816), and the popular no. 5 in B♭ (1816). A fourth Mass, in C major, was composed in 1816. The year 1817 is notable for the beginning of his masterly series of piano sonatas. Six were composed at Schober's home, the finest being no. 8 in E♭, D. 568, and no. 10 in B major, D. 575; both were published posthumously.

Schubert's years of uncongenial schoolmastering ended in the summer of 1818. His frustrated period in the spring had produced only one substantial work, the Sixth Symphony in C major. But in the meantime his reputation was growing, and the first public performance of one of his works, the "Italian" overture in C major, took place on March 1, 1818, in Vienna. In June he left the city to take up the post of music master to the two daughters, Marie and Karoline, of Johann, Count Esterházy, in the family's summer residence at Zseliz, Hung. Letters to his friends show him in exuberant spirits, and the summer months were marked by a fresh creative outburst. The variations for piano duet in E minor, D. 624, the piano duet sonata in B♭, D. 617, sets of dances, songs, and a German Requiem were all composed at Zseliz.

Maturity.—On his return to Vienna he shared lodgings with Mayrhofer and during the winter months composed the operetta *Die Zwillingsbrüder*. Although sponsored by Vogl the production of the work was postponed, and in June 1818 Schubert and Vogl set off for a protracted holiday in the singer's native district of Steyr, upper Austria. The composer delighted in the beauty of the countryside and was touched by the enthusiastic reception given everywhere to his music. At Steyr he composed the first of his widely known instrumental compositions, the piano sonata in A major, D. 664, and the celebrated "Trout" quintet for piano and strings, D. 667. The close of 1819 saw him engrossed in songs to poems by his friend Mayrhofer, and by Goethe, who inspired the masterly "Prometheus." A fifth Mass, in A♭, was started but laid aside. Another sacred work, begun in 1820 but left unfinished, was the cantata *Lazarus*, anticipating, by its fusion of lyrical and declamatory styles, the style of Wagner.

In June 1820 *Die Zwillingsbrüder* was performed with moderate success at the Kärntnerthor Theater, Vienna, Vogl doubling the parts of the twin brothers. It was followed by the performance of incidental music for the play *Die Zauberharfe*, given at the Theater an der Wien in August of the same year. The lovely, melodious overture became famous as the *Rosamunde* overture. Schubert was achieving renown in wider social circles than the restricted spheres of friend and patron. The Sonnleithner family was interested in his development; their son, Leopold, became a great friend and supporter. At the close of the year 1820 Schubert composed the *Quartettsatz* in C minor heralding the great string quartets of the middle 1820s, and another popular piece, the motet for female voices on the text of Psalm XXIII. In December 1820, he began the choral setting of Goethe's "Gesang der Geister über den Wassern," for male-voice octet, D. 714, completed in February 1821.

All Schubert's efforts to publish his own work were fruitless. Early in 1821, however, a few friends, including Leopold von Sonnleithner and Josef Hüttenbrenner, offered the "Erlkönig" on a subscription basis. The response was so successful that enough money was raised for the printing of "Gretchen am Spinnrade" also. "Erlkönig" appeared as Schubert's op. 1 on April 2, 1821, and "Gretchen" as op. 2 on April 30, 1821. From then on songs, part-songs, dances, and pianoforte duets were published. Eighteen months later op. 12 had been reached.

In Vienna the popularity of Schubert's songs and dance music became so great that concert parties were entirely devoted to them. These parties, called *Schubertiade*, were frequently given in the homes of wealthy merchants and civil servants. But the wider worlds of opera and public concerts still eluded him. He worked during August 1821 on a seventh symphony in E minor and major, but this too was put aside along with many other unfinished works of the period. His determination to establish himself in opera led him in September and October to spend a short holiday with Schober at St. Polten where the friends devoted their energies to the production of a 3-act opera *Alfonso und Estrella*. It was completed in February 1822 but was never performed. While spending a few days at Atzenbrugg in July 1822, with Schober and other friends, he produced the document called *Mein Traum* ("My Dream"), describing a quarrel between a music-loving youth and his father. Fanciful biographical interpretations of this document have little, if any, factual foundation. The autumn of 1822 saw the beginning of yet another unfinished composition—not, this time, destined to obscurity: the "Unfinished" Symphony no. 8 in B minor, which speaks from Schubert's very heart. Two movements were completed in October and November 1822, the abandoned work including also a half-finished scherzo. In November of the same year Schubert composed a piano fantasia in which the variations are on a theme from his song "Der Wanderer." The Mass in A♭ was also completed in this month.

At the close of 1822 Schubert contracted a venereal disease, probably syphilis, and the following year was one of illness and retirement. He continued to write almost incessantly. In February he wrote the piano sonata in A minor, D. 784, and in April he made another attempt to gain success in the Viennese theatres with the one-act operetta *Die Verschworenen* ("The Conspirators"), the title being changed later (because of political censorship) to *Der häusliche Krieg* ("War in the Home"). The famous work of the year, however, was the song-cycle *Die schöne Müllerin*, representing the epitome of Schubert's lyrical art. Other songs of this period are "Auf dem Wasser zu singen" and "Du bist die Ruh'." Schubert spent part of the summer in the hospital and probably started work while a patient on his most ambitious opera, *Fierrabras*. The work was rejected by the directorate of the Kärntnerthor Theater. The year 1823 closed with Schubert's composition of the music for the play *Rosamunde*, performed at the Theater an der Wien in December. This production failed. The text of the play is lost, and the music was subsequently heard only in the concert hall.

The early months of 1824 were again unhappy. Schubert was ill, penniless, and plagued by a sense of failure. Yet during these months he composed three masterly chamber works: the string quartet in A minor, a second string quartet in D minor containing variations on his song "Der Tod und das Mädchen," and the octet in F major for strings and wind instruments. His dejection transpires in a letter of March 31, 1824, to his friend Leopold Kupelwieser, the painter, in which he speaks of himself as "the most unfortunate, the most miserable being in the world." In desperate need of money, he returned in the summer to his teaching post with the Esterházy family and in May 1824 went again to Zseliz. Once more his health and spirits revived. The period was marked by some magnificent piano duets, the "Grand Duo"

in C major, D. 812, the variations on an original theme in A♭, D. 813, and the "Hungarian Divertissement," D. 818. The first work was published posthumously, the other two in Schubert's lifetime, in 1825 and 1826.

Although his operas remained unperformed, there were frequent public performances of his songs and part-songs in Vienna during these and the following years. Publication proceeded rapidly and his financial position, though still strained, was at any rate eased. In 1825 he spent another holiday in upper Austria, with Vogl, visiting Linz, Gmunden, and Gastein and finding a warm welcome for himself and his music wherever he went. This is the period of the "Lady of the Lake" songs (to words of Sir Walter Scott, translated by P. A. Storck), including the once popular but later neglected "Ave Maria." Instrumental compositions are the sonatas in A minor, D. 845, and in D major, D. 850, the latter composed at Gastein. He sketched a symphony during the summer holiday (in all probability the beginnings of the "Great" C-major Symphony, completed in 1828). The spring of 1825 had seen the composition of two well-known songs, "Im Abendrot" and "Die junge Nonne"; they were followed in the late summer by "Die Allmacht" and "Das Heimweh," two of his greatest songs inspired by nature. New friends, Moritz von Schwind, a young painter, and Eduard Bauernfeld, a dramatist, were almost continuously in his company during this period. Schwind left pictorial records of Schubert; Bauernfeld, reminiscences.

The resignation of Salieri as imperial *Kapellmeister* in 1824 had led to the promotion of his deputy, Josef Eybler. In 1826 Schubert applied for the vacant post of deputy *Kapellmeister*, but in spite of strong support by several influential people he was unsuccessful. From then on until his death two years later he seems to have let matters drift. Neither by application for professional posts nor submission of operatic work did he seek to establish himself. It can hardly be believed that Schubert was unaware of his exceptional powers; yet together with an awareness of genius, and the realization that it opened doors into cultivated society, went the knowledge of his humble birth and upbringing, and also of his somewhat uncouth bearing. This self-consciousness made him diffident, reserved, and hesitant. His life was almost entirely devoted to composition, and he derived his livelihood from publishers' fees and occasional teaching. The songs of 1826 include the settings of Shakespeare's "Hark! Hark! the lark!" and "Who is Silvia?" written during a brief stay in the village of Währing. Three fine instrumental works of this summer and autumn are the last string quartet in G major, the sonata in G major, D. 894, and the start of the piano trio in B♭, D. 898.

In 1827 he composed the first 12 songs of *Winterreise*, a return to the poems of Wilhelm Müller, author of *Die schöne Müllerin*. Beethoven's death in 1827 undoubtedly had a profound effect on Schubert. It is perhaps going too far to imagine that he considered himself Beethoven's heir and that henceforth he deliberately attempted to reproduce Beethoven's manner in his work. But there is no denying that a profounder, more intellectual quality appears in his last instrumental works. Some of them, especially the piano trio in E♭ (1827) and the C minor sonata (1828), suggest the authority of Beethoven, but his own strong individuality is never submerged.

In September 1827 Schubert spent a short holiday in Graz as a guest of Karl and Marie Pachler. On his return he composed the piano trio in E♭ and resumed work on Part II of the *Winterreise*; the 13th song, "Die Post," was written in October 1827. This is the period of his piano solos, the *Impromptus* and *Moments musicaux*.

A succession of masterpieces marks the last year of his life. Early in the year he composed the greatest of his piano duets, the fantasia in F minor, D. 940. The "Great" C-major Symphony was concluded in March, as was also the cantata *Miriams Siegesgesang*. In June he worked at his sixth Mass, in E♭. A return to songwriting in August produced the series published together as the *Schwanengesang*. In September and early October the succession was concluded by the last three sonatas, in C minor, A major, and B♭ (D. 958, 959, and 960), and the great string quintet in C major—the swan song of the classical era in music.

The only public concert Schubert gave took place on March 26, 1828. It was both artistically and financially a success and the impecunious composer, it is recorded, was at last able to buy himself a piano. At the end of August he moved into lodgings with his brother Ferdinand, then living in a suburb of Vienna. Schubert's health, broken by the illness of 1823, had deteriorated, and his ceaseless work had exhausted him. In October he developed typhoid fever as a result of drinking tainted water. His last days were spent in the company of his brother and several close friends. He died in Vienna on Nov. 19, 1828. On his tomb in the Währingerstrasse Cemetery was engraved the epitaph of Grillparzer: "The Art of Music has here entombed a rich treasure, but yet far fairer hopes."

Schubert's place in the history of music is equivocal: he stands between the worlds of classical and romantic music. He is, however, chiefly to be considered as the last of the classical composers. His music, subjectively emotional in the romantic manner, poetically conceived, and revolutionary in language, is nevertheless cast in the formal molds of the classical school—with the result that in the 20th century it was increasingly apparent that Schubert more truly belongs to the age of Haydn, Beethoven, and Mozart than to that of Schumann, Chopin, and Wagner.

BIBLIOGRAPHY.—K. von Hellborn, *Franz Schubert* (1865; Eng. trans. by A. D. Coleridge, 1869); A. Reissmann, *Franz Schubert: sein Leben und seine Werke* (1873); Sir G. Grove, "Schubert," *A Dictionary of Music and Musicians*, 1st ed. (1883); R. Heuberger, *Franz Schubert* (1902); O. E. Deutsch, *Franz Schubert: die Dokumente seines Lebens* (1914; Eng. trans. by E. Blom, *Schubert: a Documentary Biography*, 1947), *Thematic Catalogue* (1951); M. J. E. Brown, *Schubert: a Critical Biography* (1958); G. Nottebohm, *Thematisches Verzeichnis der Werke von Franz Schubert* (1874). (M. J. E. B.)

SCHUMAN, ROBERT (1886–1963), French statesman and an outstanding worker for European unity after World War II, was born in Luxembourg on June 29, 1886. A Catholic, he studied at several German universities, and returned to Lorraine to practise law. When Alsace-Lorraine was recovered by France, he sat in the Chamber of Deputies from November 1919, representing the Moselle *département* as a member of the Parti Démocrate Populaire (P.D.P.). A specialist on financial matters and Franco-German relations, he was appointed undersecretary of state for refugees for Alsace-Lorraine in Paul Reynaud's government (March 1940) during World War II. Under the Franco-German armistice he went back to Metz in August, but was arrested by the Germans in September 1940. Escaping in 1942, he worked with the Resistance in France till the expulsion of the Germans.

Prominent in the formation of the Mouvement Républicain Populaire (M.R.P.), which superseded the P.D.P. as the principal organ of Christian democracy, Schuman was a deputy again from 1945. Having been minister of finance (July 24–Nov. 28, 1946) and prime minister (Nov. 22, 1947–July 19, 1948), he served as foreign minister in ten successive governments, from July 1948 to December 1952, including his own second cabinet (Aug. 31–Sept. 9, 1948). In this capacity he promoted European unity and, with it, Franco-German reconciliation. The so-called Schuman Plan for the European Coal and Steel Community (*see* EUROPEAN UNITY), put forward by him in May 1950, became a reality in June 1952; but the idea of an integrated European army, launched by Schuman and by the prime minister, René Pleven, in November 1950, met with strong opposition (it was finally rejected by the Chamber of Deputies in August 1954). When the European Parliamentary Assembly, consultative body of the European Economic Community, met at Strasbourg in March 1958, it elected Schuman as its president. He resigned this post in March 1960, but remained a member of the assembly till February 1963.

Within the M.R.P., Schuman was from 1958 the chief opponent of the rightwing extremism of Georges Bidault (*q.v.*). In January 1961, he collapsed on a walk and lay all night on the ground in a freezing temperature. Never fully recovering, he died, near Metz, on Sept. 4, 1963.

SCHUMAN, WILLIAM HOWARD (1910–   ), U.S. composer of symphonies, ballets, and chamber music, one of the leading figures in 20th-century American music, was born in New York City on Aug. 4, 1910. He studied at Teachers College, Columbia University. From 1935 to 1945 he was instructor in music at Sarah Lawrence College. From 1945 to 1962 he was president of the Juilliard School of Music, New York City; in 1962 he became president of the city's Lincoln Center for the Performing Arts. Between 1935 and 1962 he wrote eight symphonies, but withdrew the first two. His third and fourth symphonies are predominantly dissonant; the fifth, scored for strings only, is more romantic in feeling, but the sixth is again contemporary in style. The seventh and eighth symphonies show his symphonic style at its best. Like his symphonies, his four string quartets, written between 1936 and 1950, show his polyphonic and rhythmic gifts. His ballets, *Undertow* (choreography by Antony Tudor), *Night Journey*, and *Judith* (choreography by Martha Graham), written between 1945 and 1950, use an expressionist technique. His *American Festival Overture* (1939) and his opera *The Mighty Casey* (1953; story from baseball legend) are conceived in a distinctively American style. In 1943 he received the first Pulitzer Prize to be awarded for a musical work to an American composer for his cantata *A Free Song* (1942), to the words of Walt Whitman.

See F. R. Schreiber and V. Persichetti, *William Schuman* (1954). (N. Sy.)

SCHUMANN, ELISABETH (1885–1952), U.S. (originally German) soprano known for her interpretation of *Lieder* and of the music of Mozart and Richard Strauss, was born at Merseburg on June 13, 1885. She made her debut at the Hamburg Opera in 1910. In 1914 she took the part of Sophie in Strauss's *Der Rosenkavalier* at the Metropolitan Opera, New York City. She sang at the Vienna Opera in 1919, and in 1921 toured the U.S. with Richard Strauss. In 1938 she settled in the U.S., taught at the Curtis Institute at Philadelphia, and in 1944 became a U.S. citizen. She was for a time married to the conductor Karl Alwin. In 1948 her work, *German Song*, was published in London. She died in New York City on April 23, 1952.

SCHUMANN, ROBERT ALEXANDER (1810–1856), German composer particularly notable for his piano music, songs, and orchestral music, was born at Zwickau, Saxony, on June 8, 1810. His father was a bookseller and publisher. After four years at a private school, the boy entered the Zwickau *Gymnasium* in 1820 and remained there for seven years. He began his musical education at the age of six and in 1822 produced his earliest known composition, a setting of Psalm 150. At the same time he began to show at least equal literary ability, embarking on plays (a comedy and two "horror dramas") and poems, including some translations of Horatian odes which have been preserved. In 1827 he came under the musical influence of Schubert and the literary influence of Jean Paul Richter, both of which proved deep and enduring; in the same year he composed some songs (two of which were published in 1933).

Early Career and Marriage.—In 1828 he left school and, under pressure from his mother and his guardian (his father having died), entered Leipzig University as a law student; but his time was devoted not to the law but to song-composition, improvisation at the piano, and attempts to write autobiographical novels in the manner of Jean Paul. For a few months he studied the piano seriously with a celebrated teacher, Friedrich Wieck, and thus got to know Wieck's nine-year-old daughter Clara, a brilliant pianist who was just then beginning a successful concert career.

In the summer of 1829 he left Leipzig for Heidelberg where one of the law professors, Justus Thibaut, was known as a writer on musical aesthetics, and under Thibaut's influence made the ac-

BY COURTESY OF THE GESELLSCHAFT DER MUSIKFREUNDE, VIENNA

ROBERT SCHUMANN, DETAIL FROM A LITHOGRAPH BY KRIEHUBER, 1839

quaintance of a great deal of early choral music, from Palestrina to Bach. He composed Schubertian waltzes, afterward used in the piano-cycle *Papillons,* and practised industriously with a view to abandoning law and becoming a virtuoso pianist—with the result that his mother agreed to allow him to return to Leipzig in October 1830 to study for a trial period with Wieck, who thought highly of his talent but doubted his stability and capacity for hard work.

Schumann's relations with Wieck were never happy, nor were they with the conductor Heinrich Dorn with whom he worked for a year at harmony and counterpoint. He always found it difficult to concentrate and he was distracted from his musical studies by the writing of yet another autobiographical novel, *Die Davidsbündler,* in which two self-projections, Florestan and Eusebius, were created. These two characters also appeared in Schumann's first published critical essay, on Chopin's *Là ci darem* variations (*Allgemeine musikalische Zeitung,* Dec. 7, 1831), and often later in critical writings, as reviewers of new music, and even as the composers of his own works. His Opus 1, also a set of variations —originally conceived, like Chopin's, for piano and orchestra— had been published just two months before the Chopin article. An accident to one of the fingers of his right hand, which put an end to his hopes of a career as a virtuoso, was perhaps not an unmitigated misfortune, since it confined him to composition. This was a period prolific in piano pieces, which were published either at once or later in revised forms. In October 1832 Schumann embarked on a symphony in G minor of which the first movement was played three times in public, the third time in Clara Wieck's concert at the Leipzig Gewandhaus, though the symphony was never quite completed.

Two important piano works of 1834 arose from a love affair with another of Wieck's pupils, Ernestine von Fricken: the cycle *Carnaval,* based on the letters A, S (Es, *i.e.,* Eb), C, H (Bﬤ in German), which spelled the town, Asch, where she lived and which were also contained in his own name; and the *Études symphoniques,* variations on a theme by her father. The affair lasted for more than a year but, long before the engagement was formally broken off (Jan. 1, 1836), Schumann had fallen in love with the now 15-year-old Clara Wieck. Clara returned his kisses but obeyed her father when he ordered her to break off the relationship. Schumann found himself abandoned for 16 months, during which he expressed his alternate despair and resignation in the great C-major *Phantasie* for piano, drank wildly, sought consolation with other girls, and even published a bitter, veiled lampoon on Clara in the *Neue Zeitschrift für Musik* (a periodical which he had helped to found in 1834 and of which he had been editor and principal proprietor since the beginning of 1835). Clara herself made the first move toward a reconciliation, and on Sept. 13, 1837 —her 18th birthday—Schumann formally asked her father's permission to marry her; the request was at first evaded rather than refused.

Schumann now entered upon one of his most fertile creative periods, producing the *Davidsbündlertänze, Novelletten, Kinderscenen, Arabeske, Blumenstück, Humoreske,* and *Faschingsschwank aus Wien,* among other well-known piano works. (Most of the *Faschingsschwank* was actually written in Vienna, during a visit in the course of which Schumann unearthed a number of Schubert manuscripts, including that of the "Great" C-major Symphony). Even this was not a time of unalloyed happiness, for Clara refused to marry without financial security and her father still withheld his consent. A formal statement by Clara on June 15, 1839, initiated legal proceedings for the setting aside of that condition. The affair dragged on for more than a year; it was taken to a court of appeal which still upheld one of Wieck's objections, that Schumann was a heavy drinker, and to a yet higher one which ruled that Wieck must produce proof of habitual drunkenness. This he failed to do and on Sept. 12, 1840, the marriage took place. Early that year Schumann returned to a field he had neglected for nearly 12 years, that of the solo song; in the space of 11 months (February–December 1840) he composed nearly all the songs on which so much of his reputation rests: the cycles *Myrthen,* the Heine and Chamisso *Liederkreis, Dichterliebe, Frauenliebe und -leben,* and many separate songs.

The Larger Works.—Clara had been pressing him to widen his scope, to launch out in other media—above all, the orchestra. He had in earlier days made at least five unsuccessful attempts at works for piano and orchestra; even the G minor Symphony was never finished. Now in January–February 1841 he composed a symphony in Bb ("No. 1"), which was at once (March 31) performed under Mendelssohn at the Leipzig Gewandhaus; an *Overture, Scherzo,* and *Finale* (April–May); a *Phantasie* for piano and orchestra (May) which was expanded into the famous Piano Concerto by the addition of two more movements in 1845; another symphony, in D minor (June–September); and the sketches for yet a third symphony, in C minor, of which only the scherzo survives as the piano piece, op. 99, no. 13. The orchestral impulse was temporarily spent. Schumann was much occupied with his *Neue Zeitschrift;* he would have liked to write an opera; and his first experience of a concert tour with Clara showed him, as every later tour was to do, that the public regarded him only as "the great pianist's husband." He returned to Leipzig alone and drowned his melancholy in "beer and champagne."

On Clara's return he essayed another new medium—new except for a youthful piano quartet in C minor (1829): chamber music. Between June 1842 and January 1843 he wrote three string quartets, the Piano Quintet, the Eb Piano Quartet, a piano trio in A minor (recast in 1850 as the *Fantasiestücke,* op. 88), and an *Andante con variazioni* for two pianos, two cellos, and horn which has become better known in a later version for pianos only. The year 1843 was marked by Schumann's most ambitious work so far, a "secular oratorio" (originally conceived as an opera), on Thomas Moore's *Paradise and the Peri.* He made his debut as a conductor—a role in which he was invariably ineffective—with its first performance (Dec. 4).

During his work on *The Peri* the Leipzig Conservatory had been opened with Mendelssohn as director and Schumann as professor of "piano playing, composition, and playing from score"; again he had embarked on activities for which he was unsuited. The period February–May 1844 was spent on a concert tour of Russia with Clara, which again depressed Schumann by the consciousness of his inferior role. On returning to Leipzig he resigned the editorship of the *Neue Zeitschrift.* In August he composed some numbers for an opera on Goethe's *Faust,* but work was interrupted by a serious nervous collapse which led to the Schumanns' leaving Leipzig. From December 1844 to September 1850 they lived in Dresden, where his health was gradually restored. He began to teach Clara counterpoint, a preoccupation which led to an outburst of contrapuntal composition: the organ fugues on BACH, and other works. Next he completed the Piano Concerto and in December 1845 he began another symphony ("No. 2"), in C major; because of aural nerve trouble nearly ten months passed before the score was finished. Other outstanding works of the Dresden period were two piano trios (op. 63 and op. 80 [1847]); an opera, *Genoveva,* based on a conflation of the dramas by Tieck and Hebbel (1847–50; produced at Leipzig, June 25, 1850); a fine overture, with incidental music, to Byron's *Manfred* (1848–49); the piano *Album für die Jugend* (1848); the *Spanisches Liederspiel* (1849; a cycle for four voices and piano); and the *Requiem für Mignon* (1849; for solo voices, chorus, and orchestra). There were also other instrumental pieces, a host of part-songs, a renewal of solo-song composition, and from time to time additions to the *Szenen aus Goethe's "Faust"* (to which the overture was written last, in 1853).

Last Years.—The insurrection of May 1849 terminated Schumann's never very close friendship with Wagner; indeed he had failed either to make close friends or to obtain any official position in Dresden. Attempts to get posts in Leipzig and Vienna had also been abortive. In the end, for want of anything better, he accepted the appointment of municipal director of music at Düsseldorf. At first things went tolerably well; in 1850–51 Schumann composed a cello concerto, the Third Symphony (the *Rhenish*); overtures to Schiller's *Die Braut von Messina* and Shakespeare's *Julius Caesar;* the cantata *Der Rose Pilgerfahrt* and other choral works; a third piano trio and two violin sonatas; and he drastically rewrote the ten-year-old D minor Symphony ultimately published as "No. 4." He also conducted eight subscription concerts, but temperamental differences soon showed themselves and Schumann's shortcomings as a conductor became obvious. There were a number of painful scenes and chaotic rehearsals; in December 1852 he was asked to resign but declined, and in October 1853 the refusal of the choir to sing Mendelssohn's *Walpurgisnacht* under him brought the final break. He conducted for the last time on Oct. 27, when the young Joseph Joachim played the *Phantasie* for violin and orchestra Schumann had just written for him. The day after the concert appeared Schumann's last contribution to the *Neue Zeitschrift,* an enthusiastic article in praise of Joachim's still younger friend Brahms. Two other works written for Joachim during October–November 1853 (but published only many years later) were the Violin Concerto and a third violin sonata.

On Feb. 10, 1854, Schumann complained of a "very strong and painful" attack of the ear malady which had troubled him before; this was followed by aural illusions such as the dictation by angels of a theme (actually a reminiscence of the Violin Concerto) on which he proceeded to write some variations for piano. On Feb. 26 he asked to be taken to a lunatic asylum, and the next day attempted suicide by drowning. (He had contemplated suicide on at least three occasions during the 1830s.) On March 4 he was removed to a private asylum at Endenich, near Bonn, where he lived for nearly two and a half years, able to correspond for a time with Clara and his friends. One or two visits by Brahms or Joachim agitated him terribly and Clara was kept from him until July 27, 1856, when it was realized that the end was near. He seemed to recognize her but was unable to speak intelligibly. On July 29, 1856, he died.

Assessment.—As a composer, Schumann was first and most naturally a miniaturist. Until after his marriage the great bulk of his work—including much of his best and that by which he is best known—consisted of short piano-pieces and songs, two genres which in his case are so closely related as to be hardly more than two facets of the same. The song "accompaniments" are often almost self-sufficient piano-pieces, and the piano-pieces often seem to have been melodically inspired by lyrical poems; indeed the slow movements of the G minor and F♯ minor piano sonatas have also survived in their original forms as songs. Even when the musical idea did not originate in literature but as a waltz or polonaise or some striking harmonic progression found at the piano by his improvising fingers, it was usually given a quasi-literary title or brought into relationship with some literary idea—which might or might not be openly revealed. All his most characteristic work is introverted, a selection of pages from a secret diary; his notebooks show how he cherished musical ideas not only for their own sake but because they recorded precise moments and their moods.

It is easy to see why the imagery of the carnival and the masked ball appealed to him so powerfully (*Papillons, Carnaval, Faschingsschwank aus Wien*), for all his early music—and much of the later—is full of enigmas, musical quotations (usually in subtle disguises), and veiled allusions. In this field of the piano-miniature and the pianistic song, Schumann is a supreme master; in the simpler kind of lyrical inspiration and in the invention of aphorisms he has seldom been surpassed.

When, however, under Clara's influence he embarked on more ambitious composition, he was often less happy. It was not only that he felt unsure in writing for the orchestra and relied too often on safe routine procedures, and that his string-writing is pianistic: his most characteristic musical ideas, which he had hitherto been content to fit together in mosaics or remold plastically by variation, were seldom suited for development on a big scale. Nor in sustained thought, in large and to some extent impersonal works directed to the great public, did he find a satisfaction comparable with that which he derived from the creations of his private dreamworld. It is astonishing that Schumann was able to overcome these natural limitations as well and as often as he did; that he was able to construct a symphony as firmly welded as the D minor or a symphonic first movement as organic as that of the E♭, and that he could conceive orchestral music of such gloomy power as the *Manfred* overture or the penultimate

movement of the E♭ Symphony, or as light-handed and imaginative as the "Witch of the Alps" scene in the incidental music to *Manfred.* Some of the large-scale works, such as the Piano Concerto and the Piano Quintet, depend overmuch on the piano for their salvation, but the piano certainly saved them. Drama was beyond him—though there are fine passages in the *Faust* music—and *Genoveva* is a failure; yet even *Genoveva* is a fascinating failure, abreast—sometimes even ahead—of the Wagner of the same period in its harmonic idiom and in its use of thematic reminiscence not only to make dramatic points but to build up a character in music.

It was long customary to detect in the works of Schumann's last years evidence of his approaching collapse. But he had been mentally unstable all his life, haunted by fears of insanity since the age of 18, and the change of style noticeable in the music of the 1850s—the increasing angularity of his themes and complication of his harmony—may be attributed to other causes, including the influence of Bach. He was rightly considered a very advanced composer in his day and his influence on later 19th-century composers as different as Brahms and Tchaikovsky, to say nothing of a host of lesser men, was very considerable. He stands in the front rank of German romantic artists. Even his critical writing, as fantastic, subjective, and lyrical as his early music, constitutes a valuable document of the trend and period.

BIBLIOGRAPHY.—G. Abraham (ed.), *Schumann: a Symposium* (1952); W. Boetticher, *Robert Schumann: Einführung in Persönlichkeit und Werk* (1941), and *Robert Schumann in seinen Schriften und Briefen* (1942); Joan Chissell, *Schumann,* 2nd ed. (1956); G. Eismann, *Robert Schumann: ein Quellenwerk über sein Leben und Schaffen* (1956); R. Schumann, *Gesammelte Schriften,* 5th ed. (1914).

(G. AB.)

SCHUMANN-HEINK, ERNESTINE (née RÖSSLER) (1861–1936), German-U.S. contralto, who was one of the principal interpreters of the operatic works of Wagner and Strauss before the outbreak of World War I. She was born at Liben, now part of Prague, on June 15, 1861, and made her debut at Dresden in 1878. She sang in Wagnerian operas at Bayreuth between 1896 and 1906 and created the role of Klytemnestra in Richard Strauss's *Elektra* at Dresden in 1909. In 1882 she married Ernst Heink, from whom she was later divorced. Her second husband was Paul Schumann, who died in 1904. In 1905 she married William Rapp, from whom she was divorced in 1914. She became a U.S. citizen in 1908. In the latter part of her life she was well-known for her radio broadcasts in the U.S. She died at Hollywood, Calif., on Nov. 17, 1936.

See M. Lawton, *Schumann-Heink* (1928).

SCHURZ, CARL (1829–1906), U.S. journalist, politician, and reformer who strove for high standards of honesty in government service, was born near Cologne, Ger., on March 2, 1829. As a student at the University of Bonn he became involved in the movement that produced the Revolution of 1848. Forced to flee from Germany, he lived for a time in Switzerland, France, and England. In 1852 he migrated to the United States, settling first in Philadelphia, then in Watertown, Wis. (1856), Detroit (1866), St. Louis (1867), and New York City (1881).

Finding in the United States the democratic system he had hoped to establish in Germany, he saw no need for revolution in his adopted land. But he did find causes to espouse and spent a half century as a political reformer. In the 1850s he opposed slavery; during Reconstruction he fought political corruption; in the 1880s he battled for civil service reform; and he concluded his public career in 1900 by opposing overseas expansion. But Schurz was no radical. He was conservative in social and economic philosophy and sought to preserve what he considered the enduring values of the republic. He viewed with distaste leaders such as Eugene Debs and Henry George, who advocated fundamental change, and he had no sympathy for agrarian inflationists like William Jennings Bryan.

Schurz came into prominence in the late 1850s when he attempted to steer German-Americans into the new Republican Party. This was difficult, for most German-Americans were Douglas Democrats who suspected the Republicans of having anti-foreign leanings. Schurz, however, made some headway with antislavery appeals and at the same time opposed nativism within Republican ranks.

In 1860 Schurz headed the Wisconsin delegation at the Republican national convention that nominated Lincoln. His reward was appointment as minister to Spain in 1861 and as brigadier general (later major general) of volunteers in 1862. Although a "political general," Schurz made a good Civil War officer, commanding troops at the second battle of Bull Run and at Chancellorsville, Gettysburg, and Chattanooga.

After the war Schurz toured the South for President Johnson. His report has interest today because of his strong advocacy of Negro rights. Johnson, however, disagreed with Schurz's views and shelved the report. In 1866 Schurz became editor of the *Detroit Post* and then editor and part owner of the *St. Louis Westliche Post*. In Missouri he won his only elective office, serving as U.S. senator from 1869 to 1875. As senator, he broke with President Grant on reconstruction policy, on the issue of political corruption, and on the proposed annexation of Santo Domingo. These conflicts led Schurz to help organize the Liberal Republican Party in 1872, but he rejoined the Republicans in 1876, supporting Hayes on the issues of hard money and good government. As

Hayes's secretary of the interior (1877–81) Schurz promoted civil service reform and an improved Indian policy.

Returning to journalism and writing, Schurz edited the *New York Evening Post* in the early 1880s and wrote biographies of Clay (1887) and of Lincoln (1889), both of whom he admired. In the 1890s he was an editorial writer for *Harper's Weekly*. Continuing his interest in honest government, Schurz headed the National Civil Service Reform League from 1892 to 1901. During this period he broke with the Republicans twice more, leading an independent Republican (Mugwump) bolt from Blaine in 1884 to back Cleveland and reluctantly abandoning McKinley in 1900 to side with Bryan on the anti-imperialist issue. He died in New York City on May 14, 1906.

Schurz was a tireless and effective speaker, a vigorous and outspoken journalist. His uncompromising manner made enemies and reduced his influence among professional politicians. Yet he was respected. Hence, while maintaining the highest standards of political morality, he managed to wield considerable influence in an era when political standards were not conspicuously high.

See his *Reminiscences* (1907–08) and Claude M. Fuess, *Carl Schurz, Reformer* (1932).

                                (F. H. Hₙ.)

17 68

PRINTED IN THE U. S. A. BY R. R. DONNELLEY & SONS CO.

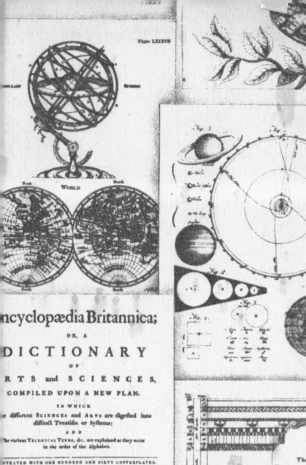

Encyclopædia Britannica;

OR, A

DICTIONARY

OF

ARTS and SCIENCES,

COMPILED UPON A NEW PLAN.

IN WHICH

the different SCIENCES and ARTS are digested into
distinct Treatises or Systems;

AND

The various TECHNICAL TERMS, &c. are explained as they occur
in the order of the Alphabet.

ILLUSTRATED WITH ONE HUNDRED AND SIXTY COPPERPLATES.

By a SOCIETY of GENTLEMEN in SCOTLAND.

IN THREE VOLUMES.

VOL. I.

EDINBURGH:

Printed for A. BELL and C. MACFARQUHAR;
and sold by COLIN MACFARQUHAR, at his Printing-office, Nicolson-street.

M.DCC.LXXI.

CONIC SECTIONS.

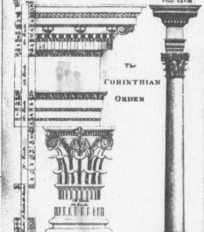

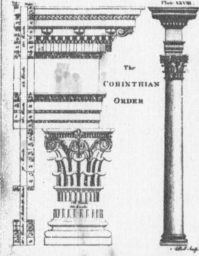

The CORINTHIAN ORDER

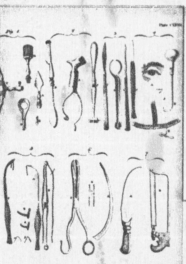

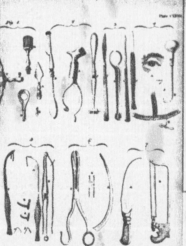

ANAS ARBOREA or Whistling Duck

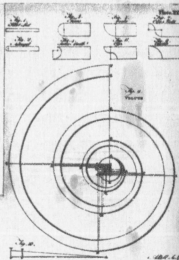

CHEMISTRY.